Lloyd's List

Ports of the World 2009

Volume 1

Published by
Informa Maritime & Professional
An Informa Business, 69-77 Paul Street,
London EC2A 4LQ, United Kingdom

Publisher
Mark Windsor
Tel: +44 (0) 20 7017 5266
Email: mark.windsor@informa.com

Editorial/Data
Paul Aldworth
Tel: +44 (0) 20 7017 5338
Email: paul.aldworth@informa.com

Advertising
Maxwell Harvey - Advertising Sales Director
Tel: +44 (0) 20 7017 5762
Email: maxwell.harvey@informa.com

Nigel Gray - Display Advertising Manager
Tel: +44 (0) 20 7017 4367
Email: nigel.gray@informa.com

Arlington Trotman - Display Sales Executive
Tel: +44 (0) 20 7017 3499
Email: arlington.trotman@informa.com

Advertising Team Fax: +44 (0) 20 7017 4098

Subscriptions
Chris Rowe
Tel: +44 (0) 20 7017 4187
Email: chris.rowe@informa.com

Production
Mark Leech - Production Manager
Tel: +44 (0) 20 7017 5229
Email: mark.leech@informa.com

Steve Legall - Production Editor
Tel: +44 (0) 20 7017 5228
Email: steve.legall@informa.com

Supported by
International Harbour Masters' Association

Contents

ISBN: 978-184311-772-8

ISSN: 1478 4696

Computer-phototypesetting, printing and binding in
Great Britain by MPG Impressions Limited,
Chessington, Surrey

Lloyd's List

Ports of the World 2009

Abbreviations Used

bbls	Barrels	bhp	Brake horsepower
bo	Boiler repairs	bu	Bushels
CALM	Catenary anchor leg mooring	cap	Capacity
CBM	Conventional buoy mooring	ch	Cargo handling equipment
co	Communication equipment repairs	d	Draught/draft
dwt	Deadweight tonnage	dd	Docking facilities
dk	Desk machinery repairs	ec	Electronic repairs
el	Electrical repairs	en	Engine repairs
ETA	Estimated time of arrival	ft	Feet
gt	Gross registered tonnage	hr	Hour
ha	Hectares	HFO	Heavy Fuel Oil
hp	Horsepower	hu	Hull repairs
IFO	Intermediate fuel oil	kg	Kilograms
kHz	Kilohertz	kl	Kilolitre
km	Kilometer	l	Litre
LASH	Lighter aboard ship	LNG	Liquefied natural gas
loa	Length overall	LPG	Liquefied petroleum gas
max	Maximum	m	Metre
MDO	Marine diesel oil	MGO	Marine Gas Oil
mHz	Megahertz	Min	Minimum
na	Navigation equipment	NIA	Nearest international airport
nt	Net registered tonnage	pr	Propeller repairs and maintenance
rb	Repair berths	SALM	Single anchor leg mooring
SBM	Single buoy mooring	sl	Slipways
SPM	Single point mooring	t	Tonne
TEU	Twenty foot equivalent units	t/h	Tonnes per hour
ULCC	Ultra large crude carrier	un	underwater repairs and equipment
VLCC	Very large crude carrier	vy	Voyage repairs

Tides

A	Astronomical	D	Datum
E	Equinoctial	H	High/higher/highest
I	Indian	L	Low/lower/lowest
M	Mean	N	Neap
O	Ordinary	R	Range/rise
S	Spring	T	Tide
W	Water		

e.g. MLWST (Mean low water spring tide), or LWONT (Low water ordinary neap tide)

KEY TO PRINCIPAL FACILITIES AVAILABLE AT EACH PORT AS INDICATED:

P	Q	Y	G	C	R	B	D	T	A	L

A	Airport (within 100km)	P	Petroleum
B	Bunkers	Q	Other liquid bulk
C	Containers	R	Ro-ro
D	Dry dock	T	Towage (where available from port)
G	General cargo	Y	Dry bulk
L	Cruise Facilities		

Lloyd's List

Ports of the World 2009

Foreword

Lloyd's List Ports of the World remains the definitive guide to the world's commercial port facilities, covering almost 2,900 ports with 28 added since the last edition. The number of shipping agents, stevedores and terminal operating companies has also been increased as the our shipping research team has worked harder than ever to ensure that the data and information that you need is here.

If you need key contact information for each port authority, details about that port's access channels, tides, cargo-handling facilities, stevedores and services, ie ships chandlers, bunker service providers, etc to handle ships once in port, then this book is for you.

The Lloyd's List Ports of the World is just one of a range of annual directories in the Lloyd's List directories portfolio, which is being expanded. With each book designed to give you the most up-to-date and accurate information to help your business, the Lloyd's Maritime Directory and Lloyd's Maritime Atlas should also find their way into your reference library.

We also publish more pocket size and desk directories for your every day needs, including the BunkerNews Directory (published May and November) and the Marine Equipment Buyers' Guide.

All of this would not be possible without the dedicated research, editorial and systems teams that work within our Marine Research department to whom I would like to express sincere thanks. I would also like to thank the International Harbour Masters' Association and the International Association of Ports & Harbors for their contribution to this edition.

Of course we always like to hear from you, the user. Your thoughts and ideas are very important to us as we strive to improve the quality of the information and the presentation of that information in the books we publish and the online services we provide.

Please e-mail your views to the editor at paul.aldworth@informa.com

Mark Windsor

Publisher

Informa Maritime & Professional

WORLD DISTANCE TABLES

Mileage extracted from BP Shipping Marine Distance Tables

Distance (nautical miles) / Voyage Time at 15 knots (days-hours)	City	AFRICA & MIDDLE EAST						ASIA							AUSTRALASIA					
		Mombasa	Algiers	Port Said	Kuwait	Lagos	Cape Town	Mumbai	Kolkata	Singapore	Hong Kong	Manila	Tokyo	Shanghai	Fremantle	Adelaide	Sydney	Hobart	Wellington	Suva
AFRICA & MIDDLE EAST	Mombasa		•4492	•2989	2828	5064	2509	2400	3701	3985	5441	5322	6885	6218	4564	5708	6505	6171	7409	8160
	Algiers	12-11		1503	•4809	3506	5502	•4549	•6194	•6517	•7973	•7854	•9417	•8750	•7804	•9002	•9799	•9465	•10703	+11088
	Port Said	8-7	4-4		•3306	5007	•5346	•3046	•4691	•5014	•6470	•6351	•7914	•7247	•6301	•7499	•8296	•7962	•9200	•9635
	Kuwait	7-21	13-9	9-14		7724	5169	1537	3522	3845	5301	5182	6745	6078	5391	6623	7420	7086	8324	8483
	Lagos	14-2	9-18	13-22	21-11		2566	7154	8044	8166	9472	9246	10918	10254	7270	8361	9158	8824	9750	10545
	Cape Town	6-23	15-7	14-20	14-9	7-3		4599	5489	5611	6917	6691	8363	7699	4715	5766	6563	6229	7467	8218
ASIA	Mumbai	6-16	12-15	8-11	4-6	19-21	12-19		2112	2435	3891	3772	5335	4668	3982	5220	6017	5683	6921	7073
	Kolkata	10-7	17-5	13-1	9-19	22-8	15-6	5-21		1650	3106	2987	4550	3883	3684	4957	5754	5420	6658	6378
	Singapore	11-2	18-2	13-22	10-16	22-16	15-14	6-18	4-14		1460	1341	2904	2237	2220	3504	4273	3967	5205	4733
	Hong Kong	15-3	22-4	17-23	14-17	26-7	19-5	10-19	8-15	4-1		632	1596	845	3504	4799	4511	5128	5266	4507
	Manila	14-19	21-20	17-15	14-9	25-16	18-14	10-13	8-7	3-17	1-18		1770	1128	2971	4266	3964	4581	4755	4033
	Tokyo	19-3	26-4	22-0	18-18	30-8	23-6	14-20	12-15	8-2	4-10	4-22		1048	4500	5299	4343	4960	5041	3957
	Shanghai	17-7	24-4	20-3	16-21	28-12	21-9	12-23	10-19	6-5	2-8	3-3	2-22		4037	5332	4632	5249	5358	4473
AUSTRALASIA	Fremantle	12-16	21-16	17-12	14-23	20-5	13-2	11-1	10-6	6-4	9-18	8-6	12-12	11-5		1343	2140	1806	3044	3795
	Adelaide	15-21	25-0	20-20	18-10	23-5	16-0	14-12	13-18	9-18	13-8	11-20	14-17	14-19	3-18		973	756	1884	2626
	Sydney	18-2	27-5	23-1	20-15	25-11	18-6	16-17	16-0	11-21	12-13	11-0	12-2	12-21	5-23	2-17		638	1236	1735
	Hobart	17-3	26-7	22-3	19-16	24-12	17-7	15-19	15-1	11-0	14-6	12-17	13-19	14-14	5-0	2-2	1-19		1293	2197
	Wellington	20-14	29-18	25-13	23-3	27-2	20-18	19-5	18-12	14-11	14-15	13-5	14-0	14-21	8-11	5-6	3-10	3-14		1476
	Suva	22-16	30-19	26-18	23-14	29-7	22-20	19-16	17-17	13-4	12-12	11-5	11-0	12-10	10-13	7-7	4-20	6-2	4-2	
SOUTH AMERICA	La Guaira	22-12	11-7	15-11	24-15	11-18	15-14	23-22	28-12	29-9	27-23	28-10	23-19	26-6	28-3	25-11	23-18	23-15	20-11	19-23
	Recife	16-2	9-20	14-0	23-4	6-20	9-5	21-22	24-9	24-17	28-8	27-17	30-7	30-12	22-5	25-6	25-2	24-14	21-17	23-22
	Buenos Aires	17-3	15-20	20-0	24-13	11-23	10-8	22-23	25-10	25-18	29-9	28-18	29-15	31-0	23-6	21-6	19-22	19-10	16-14	18-19
	Punta Arenas	18-15	18-20	23-0	26-0	14-10	11-20	24-10	26-22	26-8	26-22	25-13	25-18	27-3	20-8	17-9	16-1	15-14	12-17	14-22
	Valparaiso	22-14	20-13	24-17	30-0	18-9	15-19	28-10	31.21	27-18	28-9	26-22	25-20	28-4	21-18	18-19	17-11	16-23	14-2	16-0
	Callao	26-0	17-0	21-4	30-8	17-19	19-5	29-15	33-16	29-15	27-14	27-9	23-10	25-20	23-15	20-16	19-7	18-20	15-21	16-15
NORTH AMERICA	Montreal	22-11	9-23	14-4	23-8	14-6	19-18	22-15	27-4	28-2	32-3	31-19	30-9	32-19	31-16	32.0	30-7	30-4	27-0	26-12
	Halifax	21-4	8-16	12-20	22-1	12-13	18-1	21-8	25-21	26-19	30-20	30-12	27-21	30-7	30-9	29-13	27-19	27-17	24-13	24.1
	New York	22-13	10-1	14-5	23-10	13-13	18-21	22-16	27-6	28-4	31-3	31-14	26-23	29-9	31-7	28-15	26-22	26-19	23-15	23-3
	New Orleans	26-7	13-20	18-0	27-5	16-0	20-7	26-12	31-21	31-22	29-13	30-0	25-9	27-20	29-17	27-1	25-8	25-5	22-1	21-13
	San Francisco	31-12	22-7	26-11	31-2	23-3	26-23	27-4	25-0	20-10	16-19	17-7	12-16	15-0	23-15	20-10	17-22	19-6	16-10	13-5
	Vancouver	30-18	24-11	28-15	30-8	25-6	29-3	26-10	24-6	19-16	16-0	16-13	11-21	14-5	23-10	21-12	18-23	20-10	17-23	14-10
	Honolulu	27-9	26-7	30-6	27-0	27-3	29-12	23-2	20-22	16-8	13-10	13-6	9-11	12-17	18-2	14-20	12-7	13-17	11-10	7-18
CENTRAL AMERICA	Balboa	24-20	13-6	17-10	26-15	14-2	17-23	25-22	30-11	29-4	25-13	26-0	21-9	23-19	26-0	23-1	21-8	21-5	18-1	17-13
	Port of Spain	21-16	10-15	14-19	23-23	10-22	14-18	23-6	27-20	28-17	28-20	29-6	24-16	27-2	27-19	26-7	24-14	24-12	21-7	20-19
	Salina Cruz	28-2	16-13	20-17	29-21	17-8	21-5	29-4	30-14	26-0	22-10	22-21	18-6	20-16	25-4	21-23	19-20	20-9	16-20	15-8
	Tampico	27-3	14-15	18-19	28-0	16-17	20-20	27-6	31-20	32-18	29-18	30-4	25-14	28-0	29-22	27-6	25-12	25-10	22-6	21-18
	Kingston	24-8	12-0	16-4	25-9	13-9	17-11	24-15	29-5	30-3	27-5	27-15	23-1	25-11	27-9	24-16	22-23	22-21	19-16	19-4
EUROPE	London	17-7	4-19	9-0	18-4	11-11	17-0	17-11	22-0	22-22	26-23	26-15	30-23	29-3	26-12	29-19	32-1	31-2	31-9	30-21
	Rotterdam	17-10	4-22	9-2	18-7	11-14	17-3	17-13	22-3	23-1	27-2	26-18	31-2	29-5	26-14	29-22	32-3	31-5	31-11	30-23
	Hamburg	18-2	5-15	9-19	19-0	12-7	17-20	18-6	22-20	23-17	27-18	27-11	31-19	29-22	27-7	30-15	32-20	31-22	32-4	31-16
	Stockholm	20-2	7-15	11-19	21-0	14-7	19-20	20-6	24-20	25-17	29-18	29-11	33-19	31-22	29-7	32-15	34-20	33-22	33-14	33-2
	Marseilles	12-12	1-3	4-5	13-9	10-12	16-1	12-16	17-6	18-3	22-4	21-20	26-4	24-8	21-17	25-1	27-6	26-8	29-18	30-23
	Gibraltar	13-15	1-3	5-8	14-12	8-15	14-4	13-19	18-8	19-6	23-7	22-23	27-7	25-11	22-20	26-3	28-9	27-10	30-4	29-16
	Piraeus	9-23	2-23	1-16	10-20	12-17	16-12	10-3	14-16	15-14	19-15	19-7	23-15	21-19	19-4	22-11	24-17	23-18	27-5	28-10

WORLD DISTANCE TABLES

× Via Kiel Canal + Via Panama Canal
• Via Suez Canal

SOUTH AMERICA						NORTH AMERICA							CENTRAL AMERICA					EUROPE						
La Guaira	Recife	Buenos Aires	Punta Arenas	Valparaiso	Callao	Montreal	Halifax	New York	New Orleans	San Francisco	Vancouver	Honolulu	Balboa	Port of Spain	Salina Cruz	Tampico	Kingston	London	Rotterdam	Hamburg	Stockholm	Marseilles	Gibraltar	Piraeus
8094	5794	6168	6706	8133	9361	•8082	•7616	•8108	•9472	•11337	11063	9858	+8942	•7793	+10115	•9759	8758	•6222	•6263	•6516	•7236	•4501	•4902	•3582
4064	3540	5701	+6774	+7391	+6116	3592	3126	3618	4982	+8022	+8801	•9464	+4776	3823	+5949	5269	4325	1732	1773	2026	2746	410	412	1071
5565	5041	7202	+8275	+8892	+7617	5093	4627	5119	6483	+9523	+10302	•10887	+6277	5324	+7450	6770	5826	3233	3274	3527	4247	1512	1913	593
8871	8347	8828	9366	10793	•10923	•8399	•7933	•8425	•9789	11197	10923	9718	‡•9583	•8630	‡•10756	•10076	•9132	•6539	•6580	•6833	•7553	•4818	•5219	•3899
4230	2453	4304	5186	6613	+6412	5130	4512	4870	5754	+8318	+9097	•9760	+5072	3929	+6245	6018	4821	4130	4171	4424	5144	3784	3098	4575
5617	3318	3718	4256	5683	6911	•7115	6489	6789	7306	+9710	10489	10626	+6464	5315	+7637	7498	6279	6122	6163	6416	7136	5780	5094	5939
•8611	7884	8258	8796	10223	•10663	•8139	•7673	•8165	•9529	9787	9513	8308	‡•9323	•8370	‡•10496	•9816	•8872	•6279	•6320	•6573	•7293	•4558	•4959	•3639
•10256	8774	9148	9686	11113	12115	•9784	•9318	•9810	•11174	9002	8728	7523	‡•10968	•10015	11008	•11461	•10517	•7924	•7965	•8218	•8938	•6203	•6604	•5284
•10579	8896	9270	9482	9988	10662	•10107	•9641	•10133	•11497	7356	7082	5877	10495	•10338	9362	•11784	•10840	•8247	•8288	•8541	•9261	•6526	•6927	•5607
•10069	10202	10576	9708	10214	9929	•11563	•11097	+11207	+10638	6044	5760	4837	9196	+10375	8070	+10708	•9790	•9703	•9744	•9997	•10717	•7982	•8383	•7063
•10228	9976	10350	9202	9689	9849	•11444	•10978	•11366	•10797	6223	5950	4769	9355	•10534	8229	+10867	•9949	•9584	•9625	•9878	•10598	•7863	•8264	•6944
+8572	10911	10666	9271	9294	8424	+10928	+10036	+9710	+9141	4559	4276	3402	7699	+8878	6569	+9211	+8293	•11147	•11188	•11441	•12161	•9426	•9827	•8507
•9444	10984	11163	9768	10134	9304	+11800	+10908	+10582	+10013	5398	5114	4572	8571	9750	7443	+10083	+9165	•10480	•10521	•10774	•11494	•8759	•9160	•7840
10130	8000	8374	7321	7827	8501	+11394	+10928	+11268	+10699	8501	8428	6503	9357	+9999	9065	+10769	+9851	•9534	•9575	•9828	•10548	•7813	•8214	•6894
+9165	9091	7651	6256	6762	7436	+11521	+10629	+10303	+9734	7356	7745	5336	8292	+9471	7898	+9804	•8886	•10732	•10773	•11026	•11746	•9011	•9412	•8092
+8546	9027	7174	5779	6281	6944	+10902	+10010	+9684	+9115	6456	6822	4427	7673	+8852	7142	+9185	•8267	•11529	•11570	•11823	•12543	•9808	•10209	•8889
+8509	8848	6995	5603	6106	6780	+10865	+9973	+9647	+9078	6930	7346	4931	7636	+8815	7331	+9148	•8230	•11195	•11236	•11489	•12209	•9474	•9875	•8555
+7365	7818	5965	4570	5069	5717	+9721	+8829	+8503	+7934	5909	6459	4114	6492	+7671	6059	+8004	+7086	•11291	•11332	•11585	•12097	•10712	•10860	•9793
+7185	8617	6764	5369	5758	5980	+9541	+8649	+8323	+7754	4760	5187	2783	6312	+7491	5521	+7824	+6906	•11111	•11152	•11405	•11917	•11147	•10680	•10228
	2464	4535	+4810	+3488	+2213	2933	2058	1848	1838	+4119	+4898	+5561	+873	329	+2046	+1945	730	4193	4234	4487	5071	4342	3656	5133
6-20		2177	3248	4675	+4552	4269	3540	3670	4052	+6458	+7237	+7900	+3212	2063	+4385	4246	3027	4133	4174	4427	×4942	3818	3132	4609
12-14	6-1		1395	2822	4050	6440	5715	5845	6223	7596	8403	7765	5383	4238	5868	6419	5198	6300	6341	6594	7314	5979	5293	6770
13-9	9-1	3-21		1427	2655	7515	6786	6916	7298	6201	7008	6370	3937	5309	4473	7492	+4531	7375	7416	+7669	8389	7052	6336	7843
9-17	13-0	7-20	3-23		1299	+5844	+4952	+4626	+4057	5146	5919	5917	2615	+3794	3247	+4127	+3209	+7414	+7455	+7708	+8220	+7669	+6983	+8460
6-4	12-15	11-6	7-9	3-15		+4569	+3677	+3351	+2782	3988	4767	5157	1340	+2519	2011	+2852	+1934	+6139	+6180	+6433	+6945	+6394	+5708	+7185
8-4	11-21	17-21	20-21	16-6	12-17		958	1516	3069	+6475	+7254	+7917	+3229	2895	+4402	3354	2690	3249	3290	3412	3889	3870	3184	4661
5-17	9-20	15-21	18-20	13-18	10-5	2-16		593	2148	+5583	+6362	+7025	+2337	2055	+3510	2438	1795	2741	2782	2975	3452	3404	2718	4195
5-3	10-5	16-6	19-5	12-20	9-7	4-5	1-16		1707	+5257	+6036	+6699	2011	1932	+3184	1999	1472	3342	3303	3620	4097	3896	3210	4687
5-3	11-6	17-7	20-7	11-6	7-17	8-13	5-23	4-18		+4688	+5467	+6130	1442	2065	+2615	733	1155	4813	4854	5064	5541	5260	4574	6051
11-11	17-23	21-2	17-5	14-7	11-2	18-0	15-12	14-14	13-1		816	2095	3246	+4425	2122	+4758	+3840	+8045	+8086	+8339	+8851	+8300	+7614	+9091
13-15	20-2	23-8	19-11	16-11	13-6	20-4	17-16	16-18	15-4	2-7		2423	4025	+5204	2920	+5537	+4619	+8824	+8865	+9118	+9630	+9079	+8393	+9870
15-11	21-23	21-14	17-17	16-10	14-8	22-0	19-12	18-15	17-1	5-20	6-18		4688	+5867	3578	+6200	+5282	+9487	+9528	+9781	+10293	+9742	9056	+10533
2-10	8-22	14-23	10-22	7-6	3-17	9-6	6-12	5-14	4-0	9-0	11-4	13-1		+1179	1173	+1512	+594	+4799	+4840	5093	+5605	+5054	+4368	+5845
0-22	5-18	11-19	14-18	10-13	7-0	8-1	5-17	5-9	5-18	12-7	14-11	16-7	3-7		+2352	2220	999	4010	4051	4304	4928	4101	3415	4892
5-16	12-4	16-7	12-10	9-0	5-14	12-5	9-18	8-20	7-6	5-21	8-3	9-23	3-6	6-13		+2685	+1767	+5972	+6013	+6266	+6778	+6277	+5541	+7018
5-10	11-19	17-20	20-19	11-11	7-22	9-8	6-19	5-13	2-1	13-5	15-9	17-5	4-5	6-4	7-11		1263	5101	5142	5352	5829	5547	4861	6338
2-1	8-10	14-11	12-14	8-22	5-9	7-11	5-0	4-2	3-5	10-16	12-20	14-16	1-16	2-19	4-22	3-12		4271	4312	4565	5068	4603	3917	5394
11-16	11-12	17-12	20-12	20-14	17-1	9-1	7-15	9-7	13-9	22-8	24-12	26-8	13-8	11-3	16-14	14-4	11-21		187	428	×943	2010	1324	2801
11-18	11-14	17-15	20-14	20-17	17-4	9-3	7-17	9-10	13-12	22-11	24-15	26-11	13-11	11-6	16-17	14-7	11-23	0-12		305	×820	2051	1365	2842
12-11	12-7	18-8	21-8	21-10	17-21	9-11	8-6	10-1	14-2	23-4	25-8	27-4	14-4	11-23	17-10	14-21	12-16	1-5	0-20		×587	2304	1618	3095
14-2	13-17	20-8	23-7	22-20	19-7	10-19	9-14	11-9	15-9	24-14	26-18	28-14	15-14	13-17	18-20	16-5	14-2	2-15	2-7	1-16		3024	×2338	3815
12-1	10-15	16-15	19-14	21-7	17-18	10-18	9-11	10-20	14-15	23-1	25-5	27-1	14-1	11-9	17-10	15-10	12-19	5-14	5-17	6-10	8-10		690	1065
10-4	8-17	14-17	17-16	19-10	15-21	8-20	7-13	8-22	12-17	21-4	23-8	25-4	12-3	9-12	15-9	13-12	10-21	3-16	3-19	4-12	6-12	1-22		1481
14-6	12-19	18-19	21-19	23-12	19-23	12-23	11-16	13-0	16-19	25-6	27-10	29-6	16-6	13-14	19-12	17-15	15-0	7-19	7-21	8-14	10-14	2-23	4-3	

IHMA

International Harbour Masters' Association

The International Harbour Masters' Association (IHMA) is pleased to be associated once more with the new edition of Lloyd's Ports of the World.

The comprehensive scale of the publication's three volumes graphically illustrates the diversity of international port activity and the wide-ranging community that the IHMA now serves. With membership currently encompassing some 86 countries worldwide, the IHMA has grown to reflect the true extent of today's global port and harbour sector.

In browsing the "Officials" section of each port entry, it will soon become apparent that the term "harbour master" is not in universal usage and, consequently, today's membership of the IHMA needs to reflect the local nature of the title throughout the maritime world: for example, Port Master in Mauritius; Port Captain in Namibia; Haven Kapitein in Belgium; Commandant du Port in France; and Commander of the Port in the USA.

Whatever the specific title, the role of the harbour master has a common primary responsibility throughout the world – the safety of navigation in the waters of his/her port. But what of the countless other duties that come under the general role of the 'harbour master', and how may these duties be simplified by a common approach to the tasks and decision-making processes? These were questions that the Association sought to answer through their participation in the recent European Union Project MarNIS (Maritime Navigation and Information Services).

From the start of the study it became clear that there is not one single set of tasks that constitutes those of a 'typical' harbour master within European ports. The variation in functions, responsibilities and intervening powers led to the decision to break down the overall harbour master's functions into "roles".

Twelve potential roles were identified by a working group of European harbour masters, after discussing commonalities in roles and responsibilities and considering how information is managed and the relevant information flows. Some of these roles are executed as designated authority, based on (European) legislation or by local regulations. Other competencies are executed under an 'internal agreement' within the port organisation, thus within the framework of the port authority or port management organisation. In addition to legal duties and powers, the harbour master has a series of management responsibilities.

Under the MarNIS study, the twelve roles of the harbour master are defined as:

	Role	*Description of tasks*
1	Authority to permit ships to enter or leave the port	Permission to enter and leave the port
2	Authority for ship movement control in the port approach	For instance Traffic control, VTS, VTM
3	Authority for ship movement control in the port area	For instance Traffic control, VTS, VTM
4	Planning of port operations	Defining, co-ordinating and planning of nautical technical services (tugs, mooring, pilots, lock planning), including restrictions and information provision to nautical service providers and berth allocation; operational aspects of assigning a berth, according to vessel requirements
5	Safety Authority	Responsible for the general safety level in the port (by monitoring and enforcing; port bylaws and/or working safety and conditions ship/shore)

6	Competent Dangerous Goods Authority	Competent authority as for the IMDG code
7	Point of notification for Dangerous Goods	Competent authority or Port authority, designated by the Member states, to receive and pass on (DG) information; Title II, Annex I(3) of the Directive 2002/59/EC (Establishing a Community Vessel Traffic Monitoring and information system)
8	Point of notification Waste Directive	Authority or body, designated by the member states, to receive the "information to be notified before Entrance"; Annex II of the directive 2000/59/EC (on port reception facilities for ship-generated waste and cargo residues)
9	Controlling ships emissions	Monitoring and enforcement of future EC regulation on ballast water, exhaust gas etc. and MARPOL Annex VI
10	Calamity abatement	Co-ordinating and/or assisting in calamity abatement, based on local agreements with city, fire brigade, police etc.
11	Designated authority as by ISPS-code and EC regulations	Body (for instance PSO), appointed by the national authority or by the Competent authority for maritime security, to execute following tasks (EC Regulation No 725/2004 on enhancing ship and port facility security and EC Directive 2005/65/EC on enhancing port security); Point of notification for security information, to be notified prior to Entrance into a port; - Certification of ship and terminal security plans; - Monitoring and enforcement of certificates; - Introducing port security measures, covering whole area of port activity.
12	Administrative duties	Gathering information for administrative purposes, for instance on behalf of the statistics or fee collection authorities

These roles, and other associated matters, formed a large part of the discussion at the IHMA's biennial Congress in St Petersburg, Russia, in May 2008. Under the common theme of Ports of the Future – Meeting the Challenge, the event attracted delegates from throughout the maritime world and enjoyed contributions from both eastern and western cultures and the views of both northern and southern hemisphere perspectives. The next Congress, provisionally timed for May 2010, will be held in Perth, Western Australia, and will be hosted by seven local ports, headed by the Port of Fremantle.

On a more general basis, the IHMA continues to serve the ever-changing needs of port and harbour professionals worldwide. Members are drawn from ports large and small, publicly and privately owned, and represent a unique source of contemporary, hands-on expertise in a range of maritime operations, including: safety of navigation, vessel traffic control, port security, shipping movements, port management, protection of the marine environment, the ship/port interface, cargo handling and safe stowage, safety management and training, and the good practice of seamanship in port and harbour environs.

The IHMA has Consultative status as a Non-Governmental Organisation (NGO) at the International Maritime Organization (IMO) and regularly participates in IMO meetings and working groups. Through the participation of the European Harbour Masters' Committee (EHMA), the IHMA is also represented at the European Union and as observers at other national maritime assemblies.

Currently, IHMA Membership is available in a number of categories, including: Full Member – harbour masters as defined above; Associate Members – non-harbour masters and non-commercial members who have an interest in the workings of the Association; Commercial Members – companies and commercial organisations who wish to support the IHMA; and Regional Group Members.

The IHMA's Executive Committee has embarked on a long-term development plan to provide a number of Member services and facilities. These include the innovative bursary scheme for the Diploma for Harbour Masters by Distance Learning in association with IBC Global Academy (previously Lloyd's Maritime Academy), the popular HarbourMaster newsletter, and a range of IHMA branded marine clothing for port marine officers. Core to the Association's inter-Member communication is the IHMA website - www.harbourmaster.org - that now offers instant global access to themed discussion groups and archived reference works.

For Membership enquiries, contact: The Secretary, IHMA, PO Box 314, Fareham PO17 5XZ, United Kingdom.
Tel: +44 1329 832771; Fax: +44 1329 834975;
E-Mail: secretary.ihma@harbourmaster.org.

IAPH

International Association of Ports & Harbors

Challenges of the World's Ports

Dr. Satoshi Inoue

Secretary General, International Association of Ports & Harbors

Uniting the World's Ports

Globalization of the world society and economy has being progressing at a remarkable speed. When the International Association of Ports and Harbors (IAPH) formed in 1955, the world was nothing like the world we know today. No idea about "globalization" at all. Yet, our founding fathers thought it imperative more than 50 years ago to foster close communication and dialogue among the world's ports, separated from each other geographically, culturally and linguistically.

Since then, the IAPH has developed as the truly global organization of the world port community. Today, the IAPH has membership of some 220 ports and 140 port-related organizations from over 90 counties. The member ports combined handle about 60% of world seaborne trade and 90% of world container traffic. Leading port-related companies and academic institutes, national and regional ports associations such as the AAPA and the ESPO are also active members of the association.

The IAPH tackles a wide range of issues and challenges of common interest through technical committee activities, whose outcomes and recommendations are regarded as highly valuable guidelines and references. The IAPH also plays a proactive role in international arenas to address global issues. As the unique organization representing the world port industry, the IAPH is granted the NGO Consultative Status by six inter-governmental bodies such as the IMO, UNCTAD, ILO and WCO.

World Trade and Port Development

Over the recent decades, the world maritime trade has been expanding at an unprecedented rate. In particular, container throughputs of the world's ports have increased dramatically. In 2006, the world's ports handled a total of 430 million TEU, which is about 5 times larger than 85 million TEU in 1990 and 1.8 times larger than 230 million TEU in 2000. The annual growth rate since 2000 is as high as over 12%.

Ports around the world are therefore pressed with overwhelming demands to expand their capacity. Large-scale port expansion projects as well as innovative terminal systems are now being implemented at a number of ports. Unlike building ships, however, it often takes 5 to 10 years to develop new terminals even if we were lucky enough to find out sufficient funds and space for such development. To cope with such demands, ports are now facing serious constraints of time and space, not to mention huge investments required. Therefore, a long-term and far-sighted planning and strategic approach by port authority are more than ever indispensable to the success in this era.

Ports certainly should not become a bottleneck in the global logistics chain. To this end, ports need not only expand physical capacity for increasing cargos and bigger vessels but also speed up cargo handling productivity at terminals. Also it is vital to improve aggressively access links between port and hinterland, developing upgraded highway, railway and inland waterway systems efficiently connecting ports to their service areas.

Ports Transforming into Logistics Hubs

Moreover, not only expand facilities, but ports are also required to position themselves in a completely new environment of transportation, that is the emergence of global supply chain management. It covers an entire process from production through transportation to consumption as an integrated system rather than a set of separate and fragmented sub-systems. Ports are now drastically transforming into integrated centers of global logistics systems from traditional transferring point between ship and land as was in the long past. To this end, a number of logistics industry zones are being developed in and around ports, providing a range of value added logistics services such as warehousing, processing, assembling, distributing and etc.

As a recent World Bank survey on logistics performance concluded, while traditional elements such as port time and costs and efficient customs clearance are still important, traders put greater value on other parts of logistics performance, such as reliability and predictability. Predictable clearance of customs and timely delivery of shipments are their prime concerns, the report said. In other words, the competitiveness of ports and the countries they are located in is increasingly determined by the quality of overall logistics services.

Therefore, efforts should be addressed to not just reducing costs and delays at port terminals, but also to improving the quality of overall logistics, concentrating on elements such as the predictability and reliability of shipments and timely delivery to destination. The port industry should join forces with all logistics industries and public agencies concerned to improve overall logistics quality.

Port Security & Supply Chain Security

Since July 1, 2004, port terminals for international trade have strictly complied with requirements of the ISPS Code throughout the world. The IAPH has been helping the world's ports implement the code properly and effectively. Our worldwide surveys revealed that terminals were generally in good compliance to the code and the awareness of port security has been significantly enhanced among port personnel.

However, we should not lose momentum on port security. The Port Facility Security Plan (PFSP) adopted by each terminal can never be close to the perfect. After all, risk management of any kind is always a continuous process of improvement. Port security is no exception. Furthermore, drills and exercises should now be given a high priority. These are only a practical way to make all concerned people fully aware and familiarized with the port security plan and ensure its effective implementation. Awareness is another key to the success of security risk management.

As a weakest chain determines the security of entire logistics system, no matter how ports tighten security at their terminals, global logistics would not be sufficiently secured, unless all other players of logistics systems are fully committed to the security. The IAPH has therefore worked with the WCO to develop the "SAFE Framework of Standards", which aims at enhancing the supply chain security through the Authorized Economic Operator (AEO) system while providing AEOs with trade facilitation incentives such as fewer customs inspections and easier reporting.

The US has put in place the CT-PAT since 2002 that is a precedent to the AEO scheme, though only applied to those involved in importing goods to the US. The AEO or similar schemes are now in operation for Canada, Australia, New Zealand, Japan, Korea, China, Malaysia and Singapore. The EU has just started its AEO system since January 1st 2008. We therefore support expeditious moves to bring together these countrywide AEO schemes through bilateral or multilateral mutual-recognition, and eventually toward the formation of an international AEO scheme.

Clean Port Air and Climate Change

The IAPH has been extensively addressing a range of environmental issues over the years. It is now high on the agenda for the world's ports to improve air quality and reduce greenhouse gas emissions from port-related activity.

Adopting a significant resolution on "Clean Air Program for Ports" in Houston in May 2007, the IAPH urges ports, members and non-members alike, to take active and effective steps towards clean air programs, while recognizing that no one-size-fits-all solution exists for large variations among ports in pollution level, emission sources, geographical and meteorological conditions. As part of its efforts, the IAPH has just produced the "Tool Box for Port Clean Air Programs", a web-based guideline on air emission control planning and practical measures. (http://www.iaphworldports.org/toolbox%201/toolbox%201.htm)

In July 2008, over 50 major ports and cities discussed how to tackle the global warming and adopted the World Ports Climate Declaration in Rotterdam. The IAPH President Madam OC Phang urged the world port community to take action without delay, stressing need for a worldwide and sustained approach to abatement of the global warming. The IAPH is committed to take a lead in the world's ports endeavors to tackle this critical global issue.

Join IAPH Activity and World Ports Conference

As the world's ports are increasingly facing global issues and common concerns, I am convinced that the IAPH provides a best global forum to share experiences and learn each other to every member of the world port community. With its motto - World Peace through World Trade, World Trade through World Ports, the IAPH will continue to work for the betterment of the world port community and promote free trade across the globe, ultimately contributing to realization of the world peace.

The IAPH meets every two years at its World Ports Conference, where port executives and experts of major ports, if not all, come together from around the world. Having successfully concluded the previous one in Houston, US, 2007, we look forward to welcoming you all at the 26th IAPH World Ports Conference to be held in Genoa, Italy, from May 25th to 29th 2009.

The International Association of Ports and Harbors (IAPH)

7th Fl. South Tower, New Pier Takeshiba, 1-16-1 Kaigan, Minato-ku,

Tokyo, 105-0022, JAPAN

Tel: 81-3-5403-2770 Fax: 81-3-5403-7651

URL: http://www.iaphworldports.org

E-mail: s_inoue@iaphworldports.org

Port Statistics

Regions Ranked By Number Of Port Calls In 2007

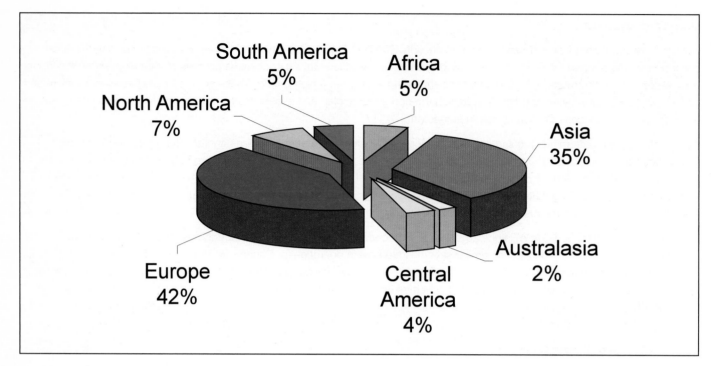

- South America 5%
- Africa 5%
- North America 7%
- Asia 35%
- Europe 42%
- Central America 4%
- Australasia 2%

© 2009 Lloyd's MIU – the only source able to provide comprehensive and immediate movement, characteristic, ownership and casualty information. For more information, please go to www.lloydsmiu.com

SERVICES:

Guaranteed berthing windows

Container Freight Station, stuffing and unstuffing of LCL containers

Consolidation of freight

Refrigerated container plugs

EDI with relevant authorities

Transhipment facilities

ADVANTAGES:

- All in one competitive tariff
- Comprehensive software suite
- Hutchinson's global relationships
- Congestion free
- Efficiency and effectiveness
- Safety and security

Port Statistics

Top 15 Ports In Each Region Ranked By Number Of Port Calls In 2007

AFRICA

Port	Calls
Alexandria (EGY)	4,965
Las Palmas	4,584
Durban	4,336
Luanda	4,049
Santa Cruz de Tenerife	3,080
Port Said	2,591
Casablanca	2,453
Dar es Salaam	2,408
Damietta	2,110
Cape Town	1,955
Abidjan	1,909
Apapa-Lagos	1,880
Algiers	1,813
Arzew	1,813
Nador	1,565
Other	48,050
Total	**89,561**

ASIA

Port	Calls
Singapore	63,593
Hong Kong	31,160
Busan	23,884
Shanghai	19,462
Kaohsiung	14,492
Yokohama	12,774
Port Klang	12,351
Qingdao	10,428
Incheon	9,609
Nagoya	9,449
Jebel Ali	8,564
Kobe	8,435
Keelung	8,029
Ulsan	7,424
Osaka	6,774
Other	357,126
Total	**603,554**

AUSTRALASIA

Port	Calls
Melbourne	3,434
Brisbane	2,606
Botany Bay	1,694
Fremantle	1,596
Newcastle (NSW)	1,499
Gladstone	1,492
Auckland	1,368
Tauranga	1,241
Papeete	1,180
Dampier	1,105
Lyttleton	1,003
Hay Point	950
Sydney	879
Port Hedland	868
Devonport (AUS)	857
Other	15,552
Total	**37,324**

EUROPE

Port	Calls
Rotterdam	30,705
Antwerp	16,337
Hamburg	14,491
Barcelona	9,283
Zeebrugge	8,756
St. Petersburg	7,785
Bremerhaven	7,574
Gothenburg	7,556
Bergen	7,399
London	7,278
Aberdeen (GBR)	7,231
Leghorn	7,018
Genoa	7,011
Valencia	6,513
Gibraltar	6,244
Other	585,765
Total	**736,946**

NORTH AMERICA

Port	Calls
Houston	7,490
New York	5,430
Port Everglades	4,459
Long Beach	3,720
New Orleans	2,906
Miami	2,775
Savannah	2,761
Los Angeles	2,643
Vancouver (CAN)	2,553
Tampa	2,484
Charleston	2,265
Jacksonville	2,151
Oakland	2,081
Honolulu	2,073
Baltimore	2,036
Other	68,281
Total	**116,108**

SOUTH AMERICA

Port	Calls
Santos	5,697
Buenaventura	3,910
Cartagena (COL)	3,276
Puerto Cabello	2,756
Buenos Aires	2,144
Rio de Janeiro	2,041
Rio Grande (BRA)	2,037
Guayaquil	2,016
Paranagua	1,986
Callao	1,819
San Lorenzo (ARG)	1,647
Turbo	1,616
Santa Marta	1,607
Valparaiso	1,577
Sepetiba	1,331
Other	47,627
Total	**83,087**

WEST INDIES/ CENTRAL AMERICA

Port	Calls
San Juan (PRI)	3,000
Freeport (BHS)	2,789
St.Thomas	2,282
Puerto Limon	2,255
Manzanillo (PAN)	1,894
Kingston (JAM)	1,707
Santo Tomas de Castilla	1,678
Rio Haina	1,582
Nassau	1,580
Puerto Quetzal	1,550
Manzanillo (MEX)	1,526
Coatzacoalcos	1,510
Veracruz	1,505
Puerto Cortes	1,497
Philipsburg	1,322
Other	33,163
Total	**60,840**

Port Statistics

Top 20 Countries Ranked By Vessel Type 2007

	CONTAINER	DRY BULK	GAS	GEN CARGO	MISC	PASS	RO RO	TANKER	TOTAL
China	52565	15192	1500	26898	2955	4296	2235	12793	118,434
Japan	34799	12499	2877	31414	1979	2113	9766	10593	106,040
United States of America	20310	14792	1217	7995	12021	13522	8829	22655	101,341
United Kingdom	8670	2883	3239	26829	15188	8466	15473	17403	98,151
Italy	10119	3678	2271	13991	1268	21333	8946	11819	73,425
South Korea	19731	5783	1888	23575	3016	2279	3442	10392	70,106
Singapore	17686	8802	1479	7337	10132	726	2254	16589	65,005
Spain	9602	4455	1639	15490	2513	15424	7578	7095	63,796
Netherlands	8163	2555	1788	17078	7045	2669	5927	10661	55,886
Norway	1922	3073	1605	21611	8885	4381	3880	6689	52,046
Indonesia	5647	4096	1295	14283	7802	3216	1950	12093	50,382
Germany	11122	1750	637	14167	1890	2090	5553	5287	42,496
Russia	3029	2959	18	20836	2488	1087	2086	8590	41,093
France	4781	1857	1581	9246	862	8121	2905	8261	37,422
Taiwan	14427	4654	1188	8451	477	444	383	5228	35,252
Malaysia	14111	1550	1078	7908	2402	371	639	6897	34,956
Turkey	4494	1845	586	17523	273	1113	2269	5061	33,164
Belgium	5759	1186	1292	7718	1684	1944	8628	4790	33,001
Brazil	9296	8185	1532	3254	350	606	1210	5834	30,267
Sweden	2095	1063	606	12933	1170	1510	4232	6388	29,997
Rest of World	103,799	67,243	13,051	149,033	38,012	41,120	45,429	97,251	554,938
Total	362,127	169,908	42,367	457,570	122,412	136,831	143,614	292,369	1,727,198

Port Statistics

Regional Number Of Port Calls Between 2000-2007

	2000	2001	2002	2003	2004	2005	2006	2007
AFRICA	79110	78696	82611	81285	82,989	85,023	87,615	89,339
ASIA	507148	486773	456358	492051	525,957	534,297	562,375	603,554
AUSTRALASIA	33945	32583	33691	35218	37,740	36,974	36,452	37,324
CENTRAL AMERICA/WEST INDIES	59429	61825	49287	56096	58,653	59,027	59,224	60,840
EUROPE	670586	678110	671994	673180	696,029	699,011	700,239	736,946
NORTH AMERICA	88979	89904	94945	102840	107,714	104,556	114,090	116,108
SOUTH AMERICA	63533	62682	62375	68882	72,146	78,987	78,454	83,087

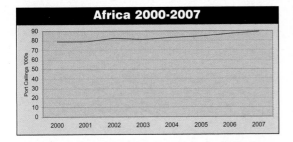

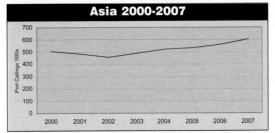

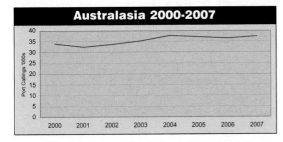

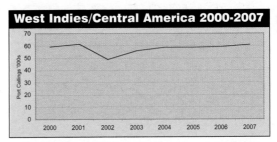

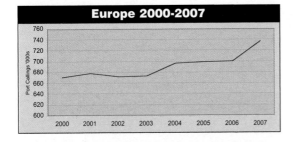

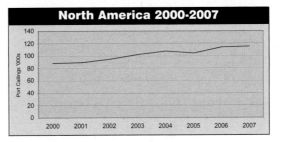

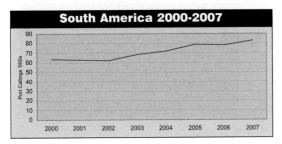

The power of innovation.

The visionary new Reachstacker from Linde.

With its outstanding agility, superb precision and smooth control the new Reachstacker from Linde embodies all the finest qualities of refined power.

Much more than just the sum of its parts, here is Man and machine in harmonious action. The fully integrated, versatile and responsive control and operating system is a visionary concept designed to make life easier. Combine this with Linde's truly global service, spares and technical back-up and you can understand why we are world leaders.

The visionary new Reachstacker from Linde: the next generation of working solutions delivering greater productivity and efficiency.

Linde Heavy Truck Division Ltd
Linde Industrial Park, Merthyr Tydfil CF48 4LA, GB
Phone +44 (0) 1443 624200, Fax +44 (0) 1443 624302
E-mail info.forklifts@linde-htd.com, www.linde-htd.com

Head Office
Linde Material Handling Division, PO Box 62, 63736 Aschaffenburg, Germany
Phone +49 6021 990, Fax +49 6021 99 1570
E-mail info.forklifts@linde-mh.com, www.linde.com/linde-forklifts

Linde Material Handling

Port Statistics

Top 50 Container Ports Ranked By TEU In 2007

RANKING 2007 (2006)	PORT	COUNTRY	2007	2006	ACTUAL VARIATION	% CHANGE 2006-2007
1 (1)	Singapore	Singapore	27,932,000	24,792,400	3,139,600	12.66%
2 (3)	Shanghai	China	26,150,000	21,710,000	4,440,000	20.45%
3 (2)	Hong Kong	China	23,998,449	23,538,580	459,869	1.95%
4 (4)	Shenzhen	China	21,099,000	18,468,900	2,630,100	14.24%
5 (5)	Busan	South Korea	13,270,000	12,030,000	1,240,000	10.31%
6 (7)	Rotterdam	Netherlands	10,790,604	9,654,508	1,136,096	11.77%
7 (8)	Dubai	UAE	10,653,026	8,923,465	1,729,561	19.38%
8 (6)	Kaohsiung	Taiwan	10,256,829	9,774,670	482,159	4.93%
9 (9)	Hamburg	Germany	9,900,000	8,861,545	1,038,455	11.72%
10 (11)	Qingdao	China	9,462,000	7,702,000	1,760,000	22.85%
11 (13)	Ningbo	China	9,360,000	7,068,000	2,292,000	32.43%
12 (15)	Guangzhou	China	9,200,000	6,600,000	2,600,000	39.39%
13 (10)	Los Angeles	USA	8,355,039	8,469,853	-114,814	-1.36%
14 (14)	Antwerp	Belgium	8,175,952	7,018,911	1,157,041	16.48%
15 (12)	Long Beach	USA	7,312,465	7,290,365	22,100	0.30%
16 (17)	Tianjin	China	7,103,000	5,950,000	1,153,000	19.38%
17 (16)	Port Klang	Malaysia	7,090,000	6,326,294	763,706	12.07%
18 (19)	Tanjung Pelepas	Malaysia	5,500,000	4,770,000	730,000	15.30%
19 (18)	New York/New Jersey	USA	5,299,105	5,092,806	206,299	4.05%
20 (20)	Bremen/Bremerhaven	Germany	4,892,239	4,428,203	464,036	10.48%
21 (21)	Laem Chabang	Thailand	4,641,914	4,123,124	518,790	12.58%
22 (22)	Xiamen	China	4,627,000	4,018,700	608,300	15.14%
23 (27)	Dalian	China	4,574,192	3,212,000	1,362,192	42.41%
24 (23)	Tokyo	Japan	4,123,920	3,969,015	154,905	3.90%
25 (25)	Jawaharlal Nehru	India	4,059,843	3,298,328	761,515	23.09%
26 (24)	Tanjung Priok	Indonesia	* 3,900,000	* 3,600,000	300,000	8.33%
27 (32)	Gioia Tauro	Italy	3,445,337	2,900,000	545,337	18.80%
28 (28)	Yokohama	Japan	3,428,112	3,199,883	228,229	7.13%
29 (26)	Algeciras	Spain	3,414,345	3,256,776	157,569	4.84%
30 (29)	Colombo	Sri Lanka	3,381,693	3,079,132	302,561	9.83%
31 (30)	Felixstowe	UK	* 3,343,000	* 3,000,000	300,000	10.00%
32 (42)	Ho Chi Minh City	Vietnam	* 3,100,000	2,327,831	772,169	33.17%
33 (31)	Jeddah	Saudi Arabia	3,067,563	2,907,723	159,840	5.50%
34 (36)	Valencia	Spain	3,042,665	2,612,049	430,616	16.49%
35 (33)	Nagoya	Japan	2,896,221	2,751,677	144,544	5.25%
36 (34)	Manila	Philippines	2,869,447	2,719,585	149,862	5.51%
37 (35)	Port Said	Egypt	2,768,900	2,640,772	128,128	4.85%
38 (43)	Barcelona	Spain	2,610,099	2,318,241	291,858	12.59%
39 (46)	Savannah	USA	2,604,312	2,160,168	444,144	20.56%
40 (40)	Salalah	Oman	2,600,000	2,390,000	210,000	8.79%
41 (48)	Le Havre	France	2,600,000	2,130,000	470,000	22.07%
42 (37)	Santos	Brazil	2,532,900	2,445,951	86,949	3.55%
43 (41)	Durban	South Africa	2,511,704	2,334,999	176,705	7.57%
44 (38)	Kobe	Japan	2,472,808	2,412,767	60,041	2.49%
45 (39)	Oakland	USA	2,387,911	2,391,598	-3,687	-0.15%
46 (44)	Osaka	Japan	2,309,820	2,231,516	78,304	3.51%
47 (45)	Vancouver BC	Canada	2,307,289	2,207,730	99,559	4.51%
48 (49)	Keelung	Taiwan	2,215,484	2,128,816	86,668	4.07%
49 (55)	Yantai	China	2,214,631	1,779,107	435,524	24.48%
50 (52)	Melbourne	Australia	2,206,567	2,031,859	174,708	8.60%
			328,014,385	**291,049,847**	**36,964,538**	**12.70%**

* Estimate

SOURCE: Containerisation International – www.ci-online.co.uk 2009

Port Statistics

Top 40 Ports Ranked By Number Of Port Calls In 2007

RANKING 2006 (2005)		PORT	CALLS
1	Singapore	(1)	
2	Hong Kong	(2)	
3	Rotterdam	(3)	20,000+
4	Busan	(4)	
5	Shanghai	(6)	
6	Antwerp	(7)	
7	Kaohsiung	(5)	10,000-20,000
8	Hamburg	(8)	
9	Yokohama	(9)	
10	Port Klang	(10)	
11	Qingdao	(19)	
12	Incheon	(12)	
13	Nagoya	(11)	
14	Barcelona	(13)	
15	Zeebrugge	(16)	
16	Jebel Ali	(22)	
17	Kobe	(15)	
18	Keelung	(14)	
19	St.Petersburg	(25)	<10,000
20	Bremerhaven	(18)	
21	Gothenburg	(21)	
22	Houston	(20)	
23	Ulsan	(30)	
24	Bergen	(23)	
25	London	(17)	
26	Aberdeen (GBR)	(24)	
27	Leghorn	(26)	
28	Genoa	(28)	
29	Osaka	(27)	
30	Tokyo	(29)	
31	Valencia	(34)	
32	Ningbo	(32)	
33	Gibraltar	(31)	
34	Taichung	(36)	
35	Jakarta	(39)	
36	Le Havre	(38)	
37	Gwangyang	(40)	
38	Santos	(37)	
39	Immingham	(33)	
40	Klaipeda	(50)	

ALBANIA

DURAZZO

alternate name, see Durres

DURRES

Lat 41° 18' N; Long 19° 27' E.

Admiralty Chart: 1590
Admiralty Pilot: 47
Time Zone: GMT +1 h
UNCTAD Locode: AL DRZ

Principal Facilities:

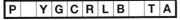

| P | | Y | G | C | R | L | B | | T | A |

Address: L.3, Sheshi STACIONI TRENIT - DURRES - ALBANIA
Tel.: +355 52 25154 - Fax +355 52 20341
E-mail: info@kad.al - http://www.kad.al

Authority: Port Authority of Durres, Lagjia Nr.1, Rruga Tregtare, Durres, Albania, *Tel:* +355 52 23427, *Fax:* +355 52 23115, *Email:* info@apdurres.com.al, *Website:* www.apdurres.com.al

Officials: General Director: Eduard Ndreu, *Email:* e.ndreu@apdurres.com.al. Marketing Director: Fatmir Lila, *Email:* flila58@yahoo.com.

Port Security: ISPS compliant

Documentation: Notice of readiness, bill of lading, cargo manifest, cargo plan, ship's stores declaration, personal effects declaration, crew list, ship's arrival notice 48 h before entering, statement of facts (after departure)
Free pratique on road

Approach: Approach channel 3.65 miles long with width of 60-195 m in depth of 8.5 m

Anchorage: Available in pos 41° 17' 07" N; 19° 28' 02" E in depth of 20 m

Pilotage: Compulsory for vessels over 500 gt. Pilot boards in pos 41° 17' 07" N; 19° 28' 02" E and is available day and night

Radio Frequency: Durres Harbour Master on VHF Channel 15. Durres Pilots on VHF Channels 10, 11, 13 and 17

Tides: Tidal range of 0.3 m to 0.4 m

Traffic: 2006, 3 423 000 t of cargo handled

Maximum Vessel Dimensions: 240 m loa, 8.5 m draught

Principal Imports and Exports: Imports: Cement, Chemical fertilisers, Coal, Construction materials, Containers, Foodstuffs, Fuels, General cargo. Exports: Chrome ore, Clinker, Containers, Ferro-chrome, General cargo, Minerals, Scrap.

Working Hours: 24 h/day (first shift 0700-1500, second shift 1500-2300, third shift 2300-0700)

Accommodation:

Name	Length (m)	Depth (m)	Remarks
Durres			See [1] below
General Cargo Berths (No's 1-4)	680	6.5–8	See [2] below
Grain Berth (No.5)	236	7.1–9.2	See [3] below
Container Berths (No's 6 & 7)	465		Yard area of 56 000 m2
Mineral Berth (No.8)	200	8.5	
Cement Berth (No.11 East Pier)	422	6.2–10.6	See [4] below

[1]*Durres:* Port area of 793 000 m2 and water area of 674 000 m2
Passenger transport is carried out in two areas of the port:
a) through the Ferry Terminal (180 m long in depth of 8.5 m)
b) through Berth No.4 (by high-speed catamarans)
Ferries to Bari, Ancona and Trieste
Liquid bulk is handled mainly on the East Quay. Tankers are handled on a jetty and a pipeline system is located on the eastern breakwater of the port. This system is connected to a tank yard which is used as a temporary storage area for fuel. Fuel is also handled at Berth No.2 (in depth of 6.5 m) directly from the vessel into trucks
Sunflower oil is also handled at the East Quay
[2]*General Cargo Berths (No's 1-4):* Four berths for vessels up to 20 000 dwt. Equipment includes electric gantry cranes with a cap of 5-7 t, forklifts, heavy forklifts and trucks
[3]*Grain Berth (No.5):* Five silo's with total cap of 1500 t. Handling is done by electric gantry cranes with cap of 10 t to trucks, grain silo's or combination operation
[4]*Cement Berth (No.11 East Pier):* A sewertell screw discharging conveyer system is used to load trucks and closed silo's are located behind the quay

Storage:

Location	Open (m²)	Covered (m²)	Grain (t)
Durres	273000	15000	1500

Mechanical Handling Equipment:

Location	Type	Capacity (t)	Qty
Durres	Floating Cranes	100	1
Durres	Mobile Cranes	16–120	4
Durres	Quay Cranes	5–45	20
Durres	Reach Stackers	40	2
Durres	Forklifts	3–32	22

Bunkering: Available

Waste Reception Facilities: Garbage disposal available
Rea sh.p.k., Durres, Albania, *Tel:* +355 52 20583, *Fax:* +355 52 64171

Towage: Compulsory. Two tugs available of 970-2200 hp

Repair & Maintenance: Durres-Kurum Shipping S.A., Port of Durres Shipyard, Durres, Albania, *Tel:* +355 52 22249, *Fax:* +355 52 22335, *Email:* durreskurum@kurum.com.tr

Shipping Agents: Dumas Shipping & Forwarding, Lagja 3 RR Tregtare, Durres, Albania, *Tel:* +355 52 24214, *Fax:* +355 52 23292, *Email:* du.ma.s@lycos.com
Managing Director: Edward Gjata
Adetare Shipping Agency Ltd, Durres Port, Durres, Albania, *Tel:* +355 52 23883, *Fax:* +355 52 23666
Albanian International Shipping Agencies, Lagja 11, Pruga A Goga 2, Durres, Albania, *Tel:* +355 52 23995/26361, *Fax:* +355 52 23995
Intermed Shipping Agency Ltd, L Nr 1, Nako Spiru Street, Durres, Albania, *Tel:* +355 52 23004, *Fax:* +355 52 23458, *Email:* intermed@epidnet.com
Kad Shipping, L4 Skenderbej Street, Durres, Albania, *Tel:* +355 52 25154, *Fax:* +355 52 20341, *Email:* info@kad.al
Pelikan Transport shpk, Rruga Lagia 3, Perballe Tatim Taksave, Pallati Alksi Kati 12, Durres, Albania, *Tel:* +355 52 24017, *Fax:* +355 52 25511, *Email:* info@pelikantransport.com, *Website:* www.pelikantransport.com
Sam Shqip Agencies Ltd, Rruga Skenderbeg 963, Durres, Albania, *Tel:* +355 52 22236, *Fax:* +355 52 25303, *Email:* samshqip@albaniaonline.net, *Website:* www.samer.com/durres

Stevedoring Companies: Liburnet, Durres, Albania, *Tel:* +355 52 24308

Medical Facilities: Health service available within Durres port 24 h/day

Airport: Rinas Airport, 22 km

Railway: 5 km length of railway in the port territory. Passenger station, 1 km and goods railway station, 4 km

Development: A new ferry terminal is under construction
Reconstruction of infrastructure at Quay 11

Lloyd's Agent: Sam Shqip Agencies Ltd, Rruga Skenderbeg 963, Durres, Albania, *Tel:* +355 52 22236, *Fax:* +355 52 25303, *Email:* samshqip@albaniaonline.net, *Website:* www.samer.com/durres

SARANDE

Lat 39° 52' N; Long 20° 0' E.

Admiralty Chart: -
Admiralty Pilot: 47
Time Zone: GMT +1 h
UNCTAD Locode: AL SAR

Principal Facilities:

| | | | G | | L | | | | |

Authority: Sarande Port Authority, Port Office, Sarande, Albania

Pilotage: Compulsory. Inward vessels must wait for pilot in pos 39° 51' 50" N; 20° 10' 10" E. Pilot available during daylight hours only

---

Key to Principal Facilities:—			
A=Airport	**C**=Containers	**G**=General Cargo	**P**=Petroleum	**R**=Ro/Ro	**Y**=Dry Bulk
B=Bunkers	**D**=Dry Dock	**L**=Cruise	**Q**=Other Liquid Bulk	**T**=Towage (where available from port)	

Accommodation:

Name	Remarks
Sarande	See [1] below

[1]*Sarande:* Open roadstead. Ocean-going vessels anchor near the middle of Sarande Bay in depths ranging from 27.4 m to 31.1 m. Good holding ground on mud and sand bottom. Loading and discharging by ships gear only

Lloyd's Agent: Sam Shqip Agencies Ltd, Rruga Skenderbeg 963, Durres, Albania, *Tel:* +355 52 22236, *Fax:* +355 52 25303, *Email:* samshqip@albaniaonline.net, *Website:* www.samer.com/durres

SHENGJIN

Lat 41° 48' N; Long 19° 35' E.

Admiralty Chart: -
Time Zone: GMT +1 h

Admiralty Pilot: 47
UNCTAD Locode: AL SHG

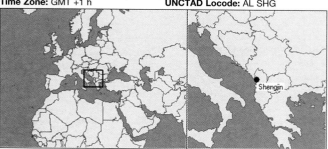

Principal Facilities:

		G					T	

Authority: Shengjin Port Authority, Port Office, Shengjin, Albania
Pilotage: Compulsory. Inward vessels must wait for pilot in pos 41° 48' N; 19° 35' E. Pilot available during daylight hours only

Accommodation:

Name	Remarks
Shengjin	See [1] below

[1]*Shengjin:* Harbour contains one pier for vessels up to max d of 5.5 m. There is also a mooring buoy in the harbour with a depth of 6.7 m. Larger vessels can be worked at anchor about 1.5 miles off the harbour in depths of 20 m to 21.9 m

Towage: One small tug is available to assist berthing
Lloyd's Agent: Sam Shqip Agencies Ltd, Rruga Skenderbeg 963, Durres, Albania, *Tel:* +355 52 22236, *Fax:* +355 52 25303, *Email:* samshqip@albaniaonline.net, *Website:* www.samer.com/durres

VALONE

alternate name, see Vlore

VLONE

alternate name, see Vlore

VLORE

Lat 40° 27' N; Long 19° 29' E.

Admiralty Chart: 1590
Time Zone: GMT +1 h

Admiralty Pilot: 47
UNCTAD Locode: AL VOA

Principal Facilities:

	P		Y	G		R			

Authority: Seaport of Vlore, Skele, Vlore, Albania, *Tel:* +355 33 29418, *Fax:* +355 33 29418, *Email:* info@portivlore.com, *Website:* www.portivlore.com
Officials: General Director: Platon Arapi.
Pilotage: Compulsory
Traffic: 2005, 403 836 t of cargo handled

Accommodation:

Name	Remarks
Vlore	See [1] below

[1]*Vlore:* One pier with depth alongside of 6.1 m. There is also another pier, suitable only for small vessels. Larger vessels can be worked at anchor in Valona Bay. Good holding ground in parts
Bulk facilities: Specialised equipment for loading salt onto vessels of up to 3000 t has been installed
Tanker facilities: There is a tanker loading berth consisting of mooring buoys in the bay

Lloyd's Agent: Sam Shqip Agencies Ltd, Rruga Skenderbeg 963, Durres, Albania, *Tel:* +355 52 22236, *Fax:* +355 52 25303, *Email:* samshqip@albaniaonline.net, *Website:* www.samer.com/durres

ALGERIA

ALGER

alternate name, see Algiers

ALGIERS

Lat 36° 46' N; Long 3° 3' E.

Admiralty Chart: 2555/855
Time Zone: GMT +1 h

Admiralty Pilot: 45
UNCTAD Locode: DZ ALG

Principal Facilities:

P	Q	Y	G	C	R	L	B	D	T	A

Authority: Entreprise Portuaire d'Alger, 2 Rue d'Angkor, P O Box 259, Algiers, Algeria, *Tel:* +213 21 42 36 16, *Fax:* +213 21 42 36 06, *Email:* epal@portalger.com.dz, *Website:* www.portalger.com.dz

WORMS ALGERIE SHIPPING / WALSHIP S.P.A.

PORT AGENTS — SHIP BROKERS — BUNKER SUPPLY
& MARITIME CONSULTANTS

WORMS ALGERIE SHIPPING / WALSHIP S.P.A.

PORT AGENTS — SHIP BROKERS — BUNKER SUPPLY
& MARITIME CONSULTANTS

When you demand quality and efficiency
WALSHIP is your only reliable partner in the following Algerian ports

GHAZAOUET · ORAN · ARZEW · BETHIOUA · MOSTAGANEM · TENES · ALGIERS · BEJAIA · DJENDJEN · SKIKDA · ANNABA

WALSHIP HEAD OFFICE – ORAN

Address : 02 rue Belkacem Djelloul – 31000 Oran

Phone No: +213 41 33 57 22 / 33 12 31 / 33 40 09 / 33 40 28

Fax No: +213 41 33 10 65 / 33 25 91

E-Mail : **oran@walshipalgerie.com**

CONTACTS :

Mr. M.LARIBI   Mob. + 213 61 20 16 94 /
              DL : + 213 41 33 30 20

Cpt M. GHOMARI : Mob. + 213 61 20 08 80 /
              DL : + 213 41 33 20 87

www.worms-sm.com

WALSHIP GHAZAOUET :   ghazaouet@walshipalgerie.com
WALSHIP ARZEW :   arzew@walshipalgerie.com
WALSHIP BETHIOUA :   bethioua@walshipalgerie.com
WALSHIP MOSTAGANEM : mostaganem@walshipalgerie.com
WALSHIP TENES :   algiers@walshipalgerie.com

WALSHIP ALGIERS :   algiers@walshipalgerie.com
WALSHIP BEJAIA :   bejaia@walshipalgerie.com
WALSHIP DJEN DJEN : djendjen@walshipalgerie.com
WALSHIP ANNABA :   annaba@walshipalgerie.com
WALSHIP SKIKDA :   skikda@walshipalgerie.com

WORMS ALGERIE SHIPPING / WALSHIP S.P.A.

PORT AGENTS — SHIP BROKERS — BUNKER SUPPLY
& MARITIME CONSULTANTS

WORMS ALGERIE SHIPPING / WALSHIP S.P.A.

PORT AGENTS — SHIP BROKERS — BUNKER SUPPLY
& MARITIME CONSULTANTS

Port Security: ISPS compliant. Contact: Achouri Boudjemaa, Tel: +213 21 42 34 06, Fax: +213 21 42 35 15

Approach: North Approach Channel is 176 m wide in depth of 22 m. South Approach Channel is 240 m wide in depth of 16 m. Vessels entering or leaving must follow the channel between no.1 and no.3 buoys on the west side and no.2 and no.4 buoys on the east side. Vessels entering through the south entrance should pass 600 m east of the head of Jetee de Mustapha

Anchorage: No.1 for vessels not carrying dangerous substances
No.2 for vessels carrying gas or dangerous substances
No.3 for vessels with a small tonnage after authorisation by the captain of the port
No.4 for vessels waiting, carrying out repairs or sheltering
Anchoring is prohibited in the eastern part of Baie d'Alger
Depth is 25 to 30 m, good holding ground

Pilotage: Compulsory for all vessels. The pilot is embarked 2.5 cables east of the head of Jetee de Mustapha

Radio Frequency: VHF Channels 16 and 14 for pilot and port services

Weather: Prevailing winds variable. Westerly winds raise the level of the sea in the basins and easterly winds lower it. Levels may be as much as one metre

Maximum Vessel Dimensions: 25 000 t, 11.58 m d, length not restricted

Principal Imports and Exports: Imports: Building materials, Dairy products, Oil, Timber. Exports: Cork, Esparto, Fruit, Minerals, Vegetables, Wine.

Working Hours: 0700-1900, 1900-0100

Accommodation:

Name	Length (m)	Draught (m)	Remarks
Fishing Harbour			
Berth No.1	140	3.75	Fishing vessels
Berth No.2	38	5.9	Fishing vessels
Berth No.3	121	3.75	Fishing vessels
Berth No.4	278	6	Fishing vessels
El Djefna			
Berth No.5	174.5	6.5	General cargo
Berth No.6	137	9.6	General cargo
Berth No.7	185	6.6	General cargo
Berth No.8a	131.5	8	General cargo
El Djezair			
Berth No.8b	131	8	General cargo
Berth No's 9a & 9b	288	8.5–10	General cargo
Berth No.10	125	10	General cargo
Gare Maritime			
Berth No's 11a & 11b	300	8–10	Passengers
Berth No.12	140		Capitainerie
Oued Hamimine			
Berth No.13	167		
Berth No.14	175		
Berth No.15	124	7.3	
Berth No.16	216	8.3	
Ghara Djebilet			
Berth No's 17E & 17W	221	7.3	General cargo
Berth No's 18a & 18b	276	7.3	General cargo
Berth No.19	110	6.3	General cargo
Berth No's 20a & 20b	300	7.5–8.6	General cargo
Bologhine			
Berth No.21	190	6.15	General cargo
Berth No's 22a-22d	556	7.3–9	General cargo
Berth No.22PC	145	9	General cargo
Berth No.23PC	145	6	General cargo
Berth No's 23a-23c	360	5.8–7.3	General cargo
Berth No's 24 & 25	207	6.3	General cargo
Berth No.26	398	8.7	Grain & petroleum
Hadjar			
Berth No's 30a & 30b	337	6.3	
Berth No's 31a-31c	304	8–9.3	
Skikda			
Berth No.32	173	6.2	
Berth No's 33a-33c	435	7.3–10.3	
Berth No.34	171	9.5	
Berth No's 35a & 35b	475	8–10.3	Cereals
Berth No.36	170	6	
Petroleum Port			
Berth No's 37a & 37b	610	10.3	Petroleum products

Bunkering: Algerian Shipping & Chartering S.a.r.l., 13 Rue Omar Boursas, Algiers 16308, Algeria, Tel: +213 21 68 98 28, Fax: +213 21 28 85 60, Email: mail@algerianshipping.com, Website: www.alshic-group.com/algeria/
Algerian Shipping & Chartering S.a.r.l., 13 Rue Omar Boursas, Algiers 16308, Algeria, Tel: +213 21 68 98 28, Fax: +213 21 28 85 60, Email: mail@algerianshipping.com, Website: www.alshic-group.com/algeria/
Bominflot, Bominflot Bunkergesellschaft fur Mineralole mbH & Co. KG, Grosse Baeckerstrasse 11, 20095 Hamburg, Germany, Tel: +49 40 350 930, Fax: +49 40 3509 3116, Email: mail@bominflot.net, Website: www.bominflot.net
BP France S.A., Immeuble le Cervier, 12 Avenue des Beguines, Cergy-Saint-Christophe, 95866 Cergy Pontoise Cedex, France, Tel: +33 1 3422 4000, Fax: +33 1 3422 4417, Email: benoist.grosjean@fr.bp.com, Website: www.bpmarine.com
Entreprise Nationale Commerciale & Distribution, Production Petroliers (NAFTAL), Aeroport Houari Boumediene, P O Box 717, Algiers, Algeria, Tel: +213 6 52252, Fax: +213 6 59485
Medstone Ltd, Suite 305, Cumberland House, 80 Scrubs Lane, London NW10 6RF, United Kingdom, Tel: +44 20 8960 3611, Fax: +44 20 8960 4420, Email: bunkers@medstone.net
Total France S.A., Total Marine Fuels, 51 Esplanade du General de Gaulle, F-92907 Paris la Defense Cedex 10, France, Tel: +33 1 4135 2755, Fax: +33 1 4197 0291, Email: marine.fuels@total.com, Website: www.marinefuels.total.com
Tramp Oil & Marine, World Fuel Services Corporation, 13th Floor, Portland House, Bressenden Place, London SW1E 5BH, United Kingdom, Tel: +44 20 7808 5000, Fax: +44 20 7808 5088, Email: pturner@wfscorp.com, Website: www.wfscorp.com

Trust Marine Enterprises Co. Ltd, 141 Filonos Street, 185 36 Piraeus, Greece, Tel: +30 210 4180083, Fax: +30 210 4136213

Waste Reception Facilities: One deballasting station for dirty ballast

Towage: Four tugs available

Repair & Maintenance: National de Reparation Naval ERENAV, Quai d'Auray No.12, Algiers, Algeria, Tel: +213 21 42 04 00, Fax: +213 21 71 31 72, Email: dep-dg@erenav.com.dz, Website: www.erenav.com.dz Two dry docks: No.1 136 m x 18.5 m x 8 m, No.2 74.3 m x 15.5 m x 5 m

Shipping Agents: Alcomar Sarl, 10 Rue des Frere el Hechmi, Ex Gaston Thomson, Saint Rafael, El Bair, Algiers, Algeria, Tel: +213 21 79 12 90, Fax: +213 21 79 35 05
Algerian Maritime Services, 15 Rue des Freres Bouzid, Bellevue El-Harrach, Algiers 16130, Algeria, Tel: +213 21 52 80 53, Fax: +213 21 52 17 69, Email: ams@wissal.dz, Website: www.ams.com.dz
Algerian Shipping & Chartering S.a.r.l., 13 Rue Omar Boursas, Algiers 16308, Algeria, Tel: +213 21 68 98 28, Fax: +213 21 28 85 60, Email: mail@algerianshipping.com, Website: www.alshic-group.com/algeria/
Societe Algerienne des Etablissements Mory & Cie., 8 Boulevard Colonel Amirouche, Algiers, Algeria, Tel: +213 21 63 56 63, Fax: +213 21 63 56 74, Email: ops-algiers@saem-dz.com
Benmarine Sarl, 115, Lot La Cadat, Les Sources Bir Mandries Algiers, Algiers, Algeria, Tel: +213 21 56 21 38, Fax: +213 21 54 39 45, Email: bemarine.algiers@bemarine.net, Website: www.bemarine.net
CMA-CGM S.A., CMA CGM Algeria, 65 Boulevard Benyoucef Benkhedda (ex Sidi Yahia), Hydra, Algiers 16033, Algeria, Tel: +213 21 54 64 94, Fax: +213 21 54 64 77, Email: age.genmbox@cma-cgm.com, Website: www.cma-cgm.com
CSA S.p.A., 2 Rue Louis Trabut, El Mouradia, Algiers, Algeria, Tel: +213 21 44 71 05, Fax: +213 21 44 71 04, Email: medistar@assila.net, Website: www.csaspa.com
The General Maritime Co (GEMA), Mole El Djefna Quai No.5, P O Box 95, Algiers, Algeria, Tel: +213 21 71 56 69, Fax: +213 21 71 56 70, Website: www.gema.com.dz
Medistar Shipping Agency S.r.l., Rue Ismail Chaalal 18 Bis El Mouradia, Algiers, Algeria, Tel: +213 21 69 85 70, Fax: +213 21 44 71 05, Email: medistar@djazair-connect.com
Mediterranean Shipping Company, MSC Sarl, Cooperative En-Nahar No.11, Les Sources - Bir Mourad Rais, Algiers 16100, Algeria, Tel: +213 21 56 35 30, Fax: +213 21 56 15 35, Email: infoalger@mscalg.com.dz, Website: www.mscgva.ch
A.P. Moller-Maersk Group, Maersk Algerie SpA, 47 Lot Petite Provence, Said Hamdine, Hydra, Algiers 16035, Algeria, Tel: +213 21 60 50 00, Fax: +213 21 60 50 17, Email: algcusimp@maersk.com, Website: www.maerskline.com
Mondial Shipping Co., 23 bis Bd Youcef Zirout, Algiers 16000, Algeria, Tel: +213 21 73 13 48, Fax: +213 21 73 13 45, Email: mondialshipping.alg@wanadoo.dz
MTA/Erhardt, Rue Said Bekel, Algiers, Algeria, Tel: +213 21 42 32 86, Fax: +213 21 42 37 41, Email: algiers@erhardt.es
The National Shipping Co (NASHCO), 1 Rue des Freres, Oukid Square, Port Said, Algiers 16000, Algeria, Tel: +213 21 72 10 79, Fax: +213 21 72 51 16, Email: dgnashco@nashco.com.dz, Website: www.nashco.com.dz
Seacom Agencies, 115 Rue Didouche Mourad, Algiers 16004, Algeria, Tel: +213 21 73 57 40, Fax: +213 21 71 66 97, Email: head-office@seacom-dz.com, Website: www.seacom-dz.com
Societe de Gestion Maritime et de Consignation (SOGEMCO), Cite Bahia 2, E4 le lido, El Mohammadia, Algiers, Algeria, Tel: +213 21 20 57 98, Fax: +213 21 20 58 16, Email: gemdirection@assila.net, Website: www.sogemco.com
Sudcargos Algerie, 17 Av Boudjatit Mahmoud, Kouba, Algiers 16000, Algeria, Tel: +213 21 47 07 00, Fax: +213 21 47 06 96, Email: mboukechoura@sudcargo-algerie.com.dz
Tiba International Algerie, 82 Rue Didouche Mourad, Algiers 16000, Algeria, Tel: +213 21 64 24 45, Fax: +213 21 63 05 50, Email: inhani@tibagroup.com, Website: www.tibagroup.com
Wilhelmsen Ship Services, Barwil Unitor Ship Services, 12 Rue Ali Boumendjel, Algiers 16000, Algeria, Tel: +213 21 73 51 56, Fax: +213 21 73 16 53, Email: barwil.algeria.ops@wilhelmsen.com, Website: www.wilhelmsen.com
Worms Algerie Shipping (Walship) Spa, Cite Sorecal 400, Logts Les Sources, Algiers 16005, Algeria, Tel: +213 21 44 98 10, Fax: +213 21 54 23 93, Email: algiers@walshipalgerie.com, Website: www.worms-sm.com

Surveyors: Bureau Veritas, 21 bis, Rue Mohamed Semani, Hydra, Algiers, Algeria, Tel: +213 21 60 36 73, Fax: +213 21 60 36 73, Website: www.bureauveritas.com
Germanischer Lloyd, City Ain Allah Bat.422B, Apartment No.7 Dely Ibrahim, Algiers 16002, Algeria, Tel: +213 21 47 00 92, Fax: +213 21 47 00 92, Website: www.gl-group.com
Nippon Kaiji Kyokai, Expertises Maritimes, P O Box 119, Algiers, Algeria, Tel: +213 21 72 18 20, Fax: +213 21 72 18 25, Website: www.classnk.or.jp
Societe Generale de Surveillance (SGS), Supervise Algerie S.A., 107 Rue Didouche Mourad, P O Box 242 (Alger-Gare), Algiers 16000, Algeria, Tel: +213 21 65 60 70, Fax: +213 21 73 08 15, Website: www.sgs.com

Medical Facilities: Numerous hospitals and a medical centre for seamen

Airport: Houari Boumediene, 20 km

Railway: AGHA (rail station), approx 500 m. The quays are connected to the national rail network

Development: DP World, in a joint venture with the Port Authority, will redevelop the main container terminal to expand capacity to approx 800 000 TEU's, investing in new cranes and equipment

Lloyd's Agent: Societe Algerienne des Etablissements Mory & Cie., 8 Boulevard Colonel Amirouche, Algiers, Algeria, Tel: +213 21 63 56 63, Fax: +213 21 63 56 74, Email: ops-algiers@saem-dz.com

ANNABA

Lat 36° 53' N; Long 7° 45' E.

Admiralty Chart: 1567		**Admiralty Pilot:** 45	
Time Zone: GMT +1 h		**UNCTAD Locode:** DZ AAE	

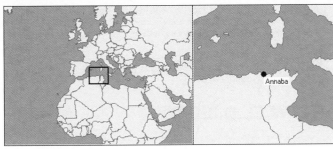

Principal Facilities:

P	Q	Y	G	C	R		B	D	T	A

Tramp Oil & Marine

Wells House, 15-17 Elmfield Road, Bromley,
Kent BR1 1LT, United Kingdom
Phone: +44 20 8315 7777   **Fax:** +44 20 8315 7788
General email: enquiries@tramp-oil.com

See listings for all global offices: **www.tramp-oil.com**

Authority: Entreprise Portuaire de Annaba, Mole Cigogne, P O Box 1232, Annaba 23000, Algeria, *Tel:* +213 38 86 31 31, *Fax:* +213 38 86 54 15, *Email:* epan@annaba-port.com, *Website:* www.annaba-port.com

Port Security: ISPS compliant. Contact: Bounif Amar, Tel: +213.38 80 11 49, Mob: +213 661 32 24 88

Pre-Arrival Information: Advance notice of arrival to Agent and Harbour Master at least 48 h in advance

Approach: Approach channel in the Outer Port 245 m wide and 13.5 m deep

Anchorage: Good anchorage suitable for any vessels is 5 cables E of the harbour entrance in depths of 10-12 m

Pilotage: Compulsory and available 24 h/day, Tel: +213 38 86 45 91, Fax: +213 38 86 42 95. VHF Channels 16 and 14

Radio Frequency: VHF Channel 16 (watching), VHF Channel 14 (traffic)

Traffic: 2007, 5 561 251 t of cargo handled

Maximum Vessel Dimensions: Dry cargo: 60 000 dwt, 225 m loa, 32 m beam, 12.5 m draft

Principal Imports and Exports: Imports: Building materials, Coal, Equipment, General cargo, Oil, Paper, Timber. Exports: Ammonia, Fertilisers, Minerals, Scrap, Steel products.

Working Hours: Sunday to Wednesday 0800-1630. Harbour office 24 h/day

Accommodation:

Name	Length (m)	Depth (m)	Draught (m)	Remarks
Annaba				
Quay 1			8.3	Container, general cargo & ro/ro
Quay 2			8.3	Container, general cargo & ro/ro
Quay 3			8.5	Container, general cargo & ro/ro
Quay 4			8.2	Passengers
Quay 5				General cargo
Quay 6			6.2	General cargo
Quay 7			9.5	General cargo
Quay 8			9.5	General cargo
Quay 9			9.5	General cargo
Quay 10			9.5	General cargo
Quay 11			9.3	Sugar & vegetable oil terminal
Quay 12			9.3	See [1] below
Quay 13			12.5	Coal
Quay 14		9.75		Metallurgical products
Quay 15		11		Metallurgical products
Quay 16		11		Phosphates
Quay 17		11		Phosphates
Quay 18	125	11		Ammonia, fuel & tar
Quay 19	220	9.45		Phosphates
Quay 20	135	9		Sulphur & potash
Quay 22			8.5	Container, general cargo & ro/ro

[1]*Quay 12:* Cereal terminal with grain silo storage cap of 16 000 t

Storage:

Location	Covered (m²)
Annaba	13391

Mechanical Handling Equipment:

Location	Type	Capacity (t)	Qty	Remarks
Annaba	Mult-purp. Cranes	6	18	
Annaba	Mult-purp. Cranes	30	6	on rails
Annaba	Mult-purp. Cranes	80	1	

Bunkering: Algerian Shipping & Chartering S.a.r.l., 13 Rue Omar Boursas, Algiers 16308, Algeria, *Tel:* +213 21 68 98 28, *Fax:* +213 21 28 85 60, *Email:* mail@algerianshipping.com, *Website:* www.alshic-group.com/algeria/
Bominflot, Bominflot Bunkergesellschaft fur Mineralole mbH & Co. KG, Grosse Baeckerstrasse 11, 20095 Hamburg, Germany, *Tel:* +49 40 350 930, *Fax:* +49 40 3509 3116, *Email:* mail@bominflot.de, *Website:* www.bominflot.net
Entreprise Nationale Commerciale & Distribution, Production Petroliers (NAFTAL), Aeroport Houari Boumedienne, P O Box 717, Algiers, Algeria, *Tel:* +213 6 52252, *Fax:* +213 6 59485
Medstone Ltd, Suite 305, Cumberland House, 80 Scrubs Lane, London NW10 6RF, United Kingdom, *Tel:* +44 20 8960 3611, *Fax:* +44 20 8960 4420, *Email:* bunkers@medstone.net
Nourship Shipping Agencies, 11 Boulevard du 1er Novembre 54, Galerie le Magestic, Local No 07, Annaba, Algeria, *Tel:* +213 38 83 59 87, *Fax:* +213 38 86 16 06, *Email:* nourship@nourship.com, *Website:* www.nourship.com
Total France S.A., Total Marine Fuels, 51 Esplanade du General de Gaulle, F-92907 Paris la Defense Cedex 10, France, *Tel:* +33 1 4135 2755, *Fax:* +33 1 4197 0291, *Email:* marine.fuels@total.com, *Website:* www.marinefuels.total.com
Tramp Oil & Marine, World Fuel Services Corporation, 13th Floor, Portland House, Bressenden Place, London SW1E 5BH, United Kingdom, *Tel:* +44 20 7808 5000, *Fax:* +44 20 7808 5088, *Email:* pturner@wfscorp.com, *Website:* www.wfscorp.com

Towage: Three tugs of 1000-3400 hp

Repair & Maintenance: One graving dock with two rolling cradles on slipways, lifting cap 100-200 t. Divers and frogmen available

Ship Chandlers: Nourship Shipping Agencies, 11 Boulevard du 1er Novembre 54, Galerie le Magestic, Local No 07, Annaba, Algeria, *Tel:* +213 38 83 59 87, *Fax:* +213 38 86 16 06, *Email:* nourship@nourship.com, *Website:* www.nourship.com

Shipping Agents: Alshiplink Ltd., 12 Rue Nadjai Nouara, P O Box 853, Annaba 23000, Algeria, *Tel:* +213 38 80 16 48, *Fax:* +213 38 80 14 63, *Email:* ops@alshiplink-dz.com, *Website:* www.alshiplink-dz.com
CMA-CGM S.A., CMA CGM Algeria, Centre d'Affaires Djaouhara, 9 Avenue de l'Aln, Annaba 8000, Algeria, *Tel:* +213 38 84 24 75, *Fax:* +213 38 84 23 86, *Email:* ann.genmbox@cma-cgm.com, *Website:* www.cma-cgm.com
The General Maritime Co (GEMA), Quai Warnier, P O Box 19, Annaba, Algeria, *Tel:* +213 38 86 49 11, *Fax:* +213 38 84 10 63, *Website:* www.gema.com.dz
The National Shipping Co (NASHCO), Bd Ben Abdelmalek, Route de l'Avant-Port, Annaba 23000, Algeria, *Tel:* +213 38 86 71 56, *Fax:* +213 38 86 73 93, *Email:* direc-anb@nashco.com.dz, *Website:* www.nashco.com.dz
Nourship Shipping Agencies, 11 Boulevard du 1er Novembre 54, Galerie le Magestic, Local No 07, Annaba, Algeria, *Tel:* +213 38 83 59 87, *Fax:* +213 38 86 16 06, *Email:* nourship@nourship.com, *Website:* www.nourship.com
Seacom Agencies, Centre d'Affaires Mediterranneen Bureau No.19, Annaba, Algeria, *Tel:* +213 38 84 68 06, *Fax:* +213 38 84 68 16, *Email:* ops-annaba@seacom-dz.com, *Website:* www.seacom-dz.com
Worms Algerie Shipping (Walship) Spa, 1 Rue Zemmouri Ouanessa, P O Box 412, Annaba 23000, Algeria, *Tel:* +213 38 86 84 10, *Fax:* +213 38 86 86 41, *Email:* annaba@walshipalgerie.com, *Website:* www.worms-sm.com

Stevedoring Companies: Groupe Industriel SIDER, Spa, P O Box 342, Annaba 23000, Algeria, *Tel:* +213 38 87 28 83, *Fax:* +213 38 87 29 12, *Email:* dso@sider.dz, *Website:* www.sider.dz

Surveyors: Agency Unimar SARL, 17 Boulevardd Benab delmalek Ramdane, Annaba 23000, Algeria, *Tel:* +213 38 86 56 66, *Fax:* +213 38 86 56 65, *Email:* unimar@caramail.com

Airport: Annaba-Les Salines, 12 km

Lloyd's Agent: Societe Algerienne des Etablissements Mory & Cie., 8 Boulevard Colonel Amirouche, Algiers, Algeria, *Tel:* +213 21 63 56 63, *Fax:* +213 21 63 56 74, *Email:* ops-algiers@saem-dz.com

ARZEW

Lat 35° 51' N; Long 0° 18' W.

Admiralty Chart: 838	**Admiralty Pilot:** 45
Time Zone: GMT +1 h	**UNCTAD Locode:** DZ AZW

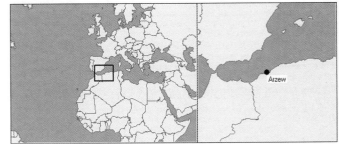

Principal Facilities:

P	Q		G				B		T	A

Key to Principal Facilities:—

A=Airport	**C**=Containers	**G**=General Cargo
B=Bunkers	**D**=Dry Dock	**L**=Cruise

P=Petroleum	**R**=Ro/Ro	**Y**=Dry Bulk
Q=Other Liquid Bulk	**T**=Towage (where available from port)

Tramp Oil & Marine

Wells House, 15-17 Elmfield Road, Bromley,
Kent BR1 1LT, United Kingdom
Phone: +44 20 8315 7777   **Fax:** +44 20 8315 7788
General email: enquiries@tramp-oil.com

See listings for all global offices: **www.tramp-oil.com**

Authority: Entreprise Portuaire d'Arzew, 07 Rue Larbi Tebessi, Arzew, Algeria, *Tel:* +213 41 47 21 27, *Fax:* +213 41 47 21 27, *Email:* contact@arzew-ports.com, *Website:* www.arzew-ports.com

Officials: General Director: N. Hadjioui.

Port Security: ISPS compliant. Contact: Boulilef Si-Aissa, Tel/Fax: +213 41 48 73 66, Email: siaissa2004@yahoo.fr

Approach: There are numerous landmarks and navigational aids, including the oil storage tanks and a conspicuous flare, which are visible for some distance to vessels approaching Arzew Bay. Port approached by a channel, 280 m wide with depths from 10.0 to 13.0 m

Pilotage: Compulsory. Tel: +213 41 47 67 41. For approaches call VHF Channel 16; for berthing manoeuvres/loading purposes call Channels 14 or 12

Accommodation:

Name	Depth (m)	Remarks
Arzew		
Mole III	5–8	Five berths handling general cargoes
Berth P0 (Large Jetty)	10	General cargo
Berth P1 (Large Jetty)	13.5	Vessels up to 50 000 dwt handling crude & condensate
Berth P2 (Large Jetty)	15.5	Vessels up to 100 000 dwt handling crude, condensate & fuel oil
Sea Terminal	26	Vessels up to 250 000 dwt handling crude & condensate
Berth S1 (Secondary Jetty)	10	Vessels up to 15 000 dwt handling refined products & residue
Berth S2 (Secondary Jetty)	11	Vessels up to 25 000 dwt handling refined products & bitumen
Methane Terminal	9.8	Two berths (North and South)
M1 (El Djedid)	13.5	Condensate
M2 (El Djedid)	13.5	LNG
M3 (El Djedid)	13.5	LNG
M4 (El Djedid)	13.5	LNG
M5 (El Djedid)	13.5	LNG
M6 (El Djedid)	13.5	LPG
D1 (El Djedid)	13	LPG
B1 (El Djedid)	23.5	Crude & condensate
B2 (El Djedid)	23.5	Crude & condensate
B3 (El Djedid)	26.5	Crude & condensate

Storage:

Location	Covered (m²)
Arzew	1584

Bunkering: Algerian Shipping & Chartering S.a.r.l., 13 Rue Omar Boursas, Algiers 16308, Algeria, *Tel:* +213 21 68 98 28, *Fax:* +213 21 28 85 60, *Email:* mail@algerianshipping.com, *Website:* www.alshic-group.com/algeria/
Bominflot, Bominflot Bunkergesellschaft fur Mineralole mbH & Co. KG, Grosse Baeckerstrasse 11, 20095 Hamburg, Germany, *Tel:* +49 40 350 930, *Fax:* +49 40 3509 3116, *Email:* mail@bominflot.de, *Website:* www.bominflot.net
Entreprise Nationale Commerciale & Distribution, Production Petroliers (NAFTAL), Aeroport Houari Boumedienne, P O Box 717, Algiers, Algeria, *Tel:* +213 6 52252, *Fax:* +213 6 59485
Medstone Ltd, Suite 305, Cumberland House, 80 Scrubs Lane, London NW10 6RF, United Kingdom, *Tel:* +44 20 8960 3611, *Fax:* +44 20 8960 4420, *Email:* bunkers@medstone.net
Total France S.A., Total Marine Fuels, 51 Esplanade du General de Gaulle, F-92907 Paris la Defense Cedex 10, France, *Tel:* +33 1 4135 2755, *Fax:* +33 1 4197 0291, *Email:* marine.fuels@total.com, *Website:* www.marinefuels.total.com
Tramp Oil & Marine, World Fuel Services Corporation, 13th Floor, Portland House, Bressenden Place, London SW1E 5BH, United Kingdom, *Tel:* +44 20 7808 5000, *Fax:* +44 20 7808 5088, *Email:* pturner@wfscorp.com, *Website:* www.wfscorp.com

Towage: Compulsory for vessels over 1500 gt. Thirteen tugs from 1700 hp to 4120 hp are available. On sea line for berthing or unberthing, two tugs compulsory and three tugs are required for tankers over 50 000 dwt

Shipping Agents: Bemarine Shipping Agency, 5 Rue Abdelhamid Ben Baddis, Arzew, Algeria, *Tel:* +213 41 47 72 95, *Fax:* +213 41 48 60 28, *Email:* bemarine.arzew@bemarine.net, *Website:* www.bemarine.net
Med-Sea Shipping & Maritime Agencies Ltd, 24 Rue des Martyrs, Arzew, Algeria, *Tel:* +213 41 48 88 66, *Fax:* +213 41 48 65 72, *Email:* medsea.arzew@medseashipping.com, *Website:* www.medseashipping.co.uk
Societe de Gestion Maritime et de Consignation (SOGEMCO), 3 Rue des Jardins, Arzew, Algeria, *Tel:* +213 41 47 19 99, *Fax:* +213 41 47 19 99, *Email:* gemarzew@assila.net, *Website:* www.sogemco.com
Worms Algerie Shipping (Walship) Spa, 46 Bd Emir Abdelkader, Arzew 31200,

Algeria, *Tel:* +213 41 47 74 15, *Fax:* +213 41 47 44 61, *Email:* arzew@walshipalgerie.com, *Website:* www.worms-sm.com

Medical Facilities: Hospital at Mohgoune, 5 km

Airport: Es-Senia, 40 km

Lloyd's Agent: Societe Algerienne des Etablissements Mory & Cie., 8 Boulevard Colonel Amirouche, Algiers, Algeria, *Tel:* +213 21 63 56 63, *Fax:* +213 21 63 56 74, *Email:* ops-algiers@saem-dz.com

ARZEW EL DJEDID

harbour area, see under Arzew

BEJAIA

Lat 36° 43' N; Long 5° 4' E.

Admiralty Chart: 1710		**Admiralty Pilot:** 45	
Time Zone: GMT +1 h		**UNCTAD Locode:** DZ BJA	

Principal Facilities:

Tramp Oil & Marine

Wells House, 15-17 Elmfield Road, Bromley,
Kent BR1 1LT, United Kingdom
Phone: +44 20 8315 7777   **Fax:** +44 20 8315 7788
General email: enquiries@tramp-oil.com

See listings for all global offices: **www.tramp-oil.com**

Authority: Entreprise Portuaire de Bejaia, 13 Avenue des Freres Amrani, P O Box 94, Bejaia 06000, Algeria, *Tel:* +213 34 21 18 07, *Fax:* +213 34 20 14 88, *Email:* portbj@portdebejaia.dz, *Website:* www.portdebejaia.com.dz

Officials: General Director: Abdelkader Boumessila, *Email:* aboumessila@portdebejaia.dz.

Port Security: ISPS compliant. Contact: Tahar Bensaada, Tel: +213 34 21 14 12, Fax: +213 34 21 14 06, Email: tahar_bensaada@portdebejaia.dz

Approach: Port approached by a channel 330 m wide in depth of 14 m

Anchorage: Available in Bejaia roadstead which stretches from Cape Carbon to Cape Aokas in depth of 10-20 m. The tanker anchorage is located to the east of the access channel

Pilotage: Compulsory; contact pilot station at the Quai Laferriere via VHF Channel 16 or Tel: +213 34 21 13 45

Traffic: 2007, 14 800 000 t of cargo handled

Maximum Vessel Dimensions: 260 m long

Principal Imports and Exports: Imports: General cargo. Exports: Crude oil.

Working Hours: Saturday to Thursday: 0620-1900 in two shifts. The third shift is optional and operates from 1900-0100

Accommodation:

Name	Length (m)	Depth (m)	Remarks
Bejaia			
Petroleum Berths 1-3 (Avant Port)	770	11.5–13.5	
Quai Central Berths 6 & 7 (Vieux Port)	98	8	
Quai Nord Ouest Berths 9-11 (Vieux Port)	273	8	
Quai de la Casbah Berths 12 & 13 (Vieux Port)	257	8	
Quai Passe Casbah Berth 14 (Passe Casbah)	146	8.5	
Quai Sud Ouest Berths 15 & 16 (Arriere Port)	230	10	

Name	Length (m)	Depth (m)	Remarks
Quai de la Gare Berths 17-19 (Arriere Port)	530	10	
Nouveau Quai Berths 21-24 (Arriere Port)	500	12	See [1] below

[1]*Nouveau Quai Berths 21-24 (Arriere Port):* Container terminal operated by Bejaia Mediterranean Terminal, Bloc Administratif, Nouveau Quai, Port de Bejaia, 06000 Bejaia, Tel: +213 34 22 96 65, Fax: +213 34 22 71 51, Email: info_bmt@bejaiamed.com, Website: www.bejaiamed.com
Equipment includes two 40 t post-panamax cranes, five 36 t RTG's and 360 reefer points

Storage:

Location	Open (m²)	Covered (m²)
Bejaia	400000	17500

Mechanical Handling Equipment:

Location	Type	Capacity (t)	Qty
Bejaia	Mult-purp. Cranes	10–80	7
Bejaia	Forklifts	3–28	43

Bunkering: Algerian Shipping & Chartering S.a.r.l., 13 Rue Omar Boursas, Algiers 16308, Algeria, *Tel:* +213 21 68 98 28, *Fax:* +213 21 28 85 60, *Email:* mail@algerianshipping.com, *Website:* www.alshic-group.com/algeria/
Bominflot, Bominflot Bunkergesellschaft fur Mineralole mbH & Co. KG, Grosse Baeckerstrasse 11, 20095 Hamburg, Germany, *Tel:* +49 40 350 930, *Fax:* +49 40 3509 3116, *Email:* mail@bominflot.de, *Website:* www.bominflot.net
Entreprise Nationale Commerciale & Distribution, Production Petroliers (NAFTAL), Aeroport Houari Boumedienne, P O Box 717, Algiers, Algeria, *Tel:* +213 6 52252, *Fax:* +213 6 59485
Medstone Ltd, Suite 305, Cumberland House, 80 Scrubs Lane, London NW10 6RF, United Kingdom, *Tel:* +44 20 8960 3611, *Fax:* +44 20 8960 4420, *Email:* bunkers@medstone.net
Total France S.A., Total Marine Fuels, 51 Esplanade du General de Gaulle, F-92907 Paris la Defense Cedex 10, France, *Tel:* +33 1 4135 2755, *Fax:* +33 1 4197 0291, *Email:* marine.fuels@total.com, *Website:* www.marinefuels.total.com
Tramp Oil & Marine, World Fuel Services Corporation, 13th Floor, Portland House, Bressenden Place, London SW1E 5BH, United Kingdom, *Tel:* +44 20 7808 5000, *Fax:* +44 20 7808 5088, *Email:* pturner@wfscorp.com, *Website:* www.wfscorp.com

Towage: Six tugs available of 1500-3980 hp

Repair & Maintenance: National de Reparation Naval ERENAV, P O Box 41, Bejaia 06000, Algeria, *Tel:* +213 34 21 16 11, *Fax:* +213 34 21 16 11, *Website:* www.erenav.com.dz Floating dock 190 m long and 70 m wide and has a clear width between fenders of 32 m

Shipping Agents: Algerian Maritime Services, 4 Rue Nacer Benyahia, Bejaia 06000, Algeria, *Tel:* +213 34 20 17 70, *Fax:* +213 34 22 18 38, *Email:* amsbejaia@ams.com.dz, *Website:* www.ams.com.dz
Alshiplink Ltd., 23 avnue des freres amrane, consignataire, Bejaia, Algeria, *Tel:* +213 34 20 28 23, *Fax:* +213 34 20 28 26, *Email:* issabejaia@yahoo.fr, *Website:* www.alshiplink-dz.com
Bemarine Shipping Agency, 6 Rue des Freres Taguelmimt, Bejaia, Algeria, *Tel:* +213 34 22 63 11, *Fax:* +213 34 22 63 17, *Email:* bemarine.bejaia@bemarine.net, *Website:* www.bemarine.net
CMA-CGM S.A., CMA CGM Algeria, Cite Somacob, Bloc B, 2 Etage, Boulevard Krim Belkacem, Bejaia 06000, Algeria, *Tel:* +213 34 21 46 49, *Fax:* +213 34 20 58 75, *Email:* bej.genmbox@cma-cgm.com, *Website:* www.cma-cgm.com
Mediterranean Shipping Company, MSC Sarl, 200 Logements, Batiment a5 308 et 310, Ihaddaden, Bejaia 06000, Algeria, *Tel:* +213 34 21 41 32, *Fax:* +213 34 21 45 59, *Email:* infobejaia@mscalg.com.dz, *Website:* www.mscgva.ch
A.P. Moller-Maersk Group, Maersk Algerie SpA, 18 Lotissement Bouali Sidi Ahmed, Bejaia 06000, Algeria, *Tel:* +213 34 22 16 61, *Fax:* +213 34 20 68 58, *Email:* bjamla@maersk.com, *Website:* www.maerskline.com
The National Shipping Co (NASHCO), Bd Amirouche, Bejaia 6000, Algeria, *Tel:* +213 34 21 14 69, *Fax:* +213 34 20 25 30, *Email:* direc-bej@nashco.com.dz, *Website:* www.nashco.com.dz
Seacom Agencies, 2 Rue Taguelmimt, Bejaia, Algeria, *Tel:* +213 34 22 01 89, *Fax:* +213 34 22 01 93, *Email:* ops-bejaia@seacom-dz.com, *Website:* www.seacom-dz.com
Societe de Gestion Maritime et de Consignation (SOGEMCO), 1 Avenue de l'Aln, Bejaia, Algeria, *Tel:* +213 34 20 72 07, *Fax:* +213 34 20 51 41, *Email:* gembejaia@assila.net, *Website:* www.sogemco.com
Sudcargos Algerie, Bejaia, Algeria, *Tel:* +213 34 21 82 25, *Fax:* +213 34 21 88 64, *Email:* sc-bejaia@sudcargos-algerie.com.dz
Worms Algerie Shipping (Walship) Spa, 05 Place Boucheffa, Bejaia 06000, Algeria, *Tel:* +213 34 22 00 20, *Fax:* +213 34 22 54 77, *Email:* bejaia@walshipalgerie.com, *Website:* www.worms-sm.com

Medical Facilities: Two hospitals and a clinic

Airport: Soummam Airport, 6 km

Lloyd's Agent: Societe Algerienne des Etablissements Mory & Cie., 8 Boulevard Colonel Amirouche, Algiers, Algeria, *Tel:* +213 21 63 56 63, *Fax:* +213 21 63 56 74, *Email:* ops-algiers@saem-dz.com

BENI SAF

Lat 35° 18' N; Long 1° 23' W.

Admiralty Chart: 178	**Admiralty Pilot:** 45
Time Zone: GMT +1 h	**UNCTAD Locode:** DZ BSF

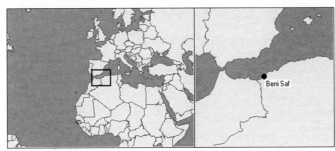

Principal Facilities:

		Y	G				D	A

Authority: Entreprise Portuaire de Beni Saf, Route du Port, Beni Saf, Algeria, *Tel:* +213 43 32 54 68

Approach: Entry difficult during N or NW winds. Port approached by a channel 160 m wide

Anchorage: Anchorage can be obtained outside the port in depths between 15 m and 20 m

Pilotage: Available from Ghazaouet with prior notice; daylight hours only

Weather: Winds W in winter, E in summer

Accommodation:

Name	Length (m)	Depth (m)	Remarks
Beni Saf			See [1] below
West Quay	10	8	See [2] below
Commerce Quay	55	6	

[1]*Beni Saf:* Harbour consists of two jetties. Vessels anchor and secure their sterns to the jetty
[2]*West Quay:* Equipped with a conveyor belt for handling minerals at 500 t/h

Storage: 13 ha of open storage available

Location	Covered (m²)
Beni Saf	1885

Repair & Maintenance: Small dry dock available. Minor repairs only carried out

Airport: Es-Senia or Zenata

Lloyd's Agent: Societe Algerienne des Etablissements Mory & Cie., 8 Boulevard Colonel Amirouche, Algiers, Algeria, *Tel:* +213 21 63 56 63, *Fax:* +213 21 63 56 74, *Email:* ops-algiers@saem-dz.com

BETHIOUA

alternate name, see Arzew

BOLOGHINE

harbour area, see under Algiers

BONE

former name, see Annaba

CHERCHELL

Lat 36° 36' N; Long 2° 11' E.

Admiralty Chart: 1710	**Admiralty Pilot:** 45
Time Zone: GMT +1 h	**UNCTAD Locode:** DZ CHE

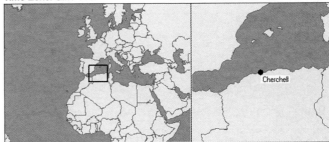

Principal Facilities:

				G					

Authority: Entreprise Portuaire de Mostaganem, Quai du Maghreb, P O Box 131, Mostaganem 27000, Algeria, *Tel:* +213 45 21 17 77, *Fax:* +213 45 21 78 05

Officials: General Director: Mokhtar Sheriff.
Harbour Master: Mohamed Bouabida.

Approach: Port approached by channel 24 m wide. Harbour cannot be entered or left during heavy weather

Anchorage: Anchorage in roadstead entirely exposed and vessels can only anchor in good weather; depth of water 14.6 m, but bottom rocky in many places

Accommodation:

Name	Remarks
Cherchell	Total length of quays 520 m, 3.5-4.2 m d

Lloyd's Agent: Societe Algerienne des Etablissements Mory & Cie., 8 Boulevard Colonel Amirouche, Algiers, Algeria, *Tel:* +213 21 63 56 63, *Fax:* +213 21 63 56 74, *Email:* ops-algiers@saem-dz.com

COLLO

Lat 37° 0' N; Long 6° 33' E.

Admiralty Chart: 1712

Admiralty Pilot: 45

Time Zone: GMT +1 h

UNCTAD Locode: DZ COL

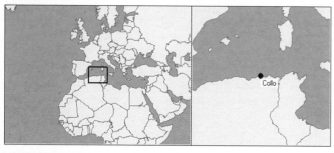

Principal Facilities:

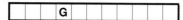

Authority: Entreprise Portuaire de Skikda, Avenue Rezki Rahal, P O Box 65, Skikda 21000, Algeria, *Tel:* +213   38 75 68 27, *Fax:* +213   38 75 20 15, *Email:* epskikda@skikda-port.com, *Website:* www.skikda-port.com

Anchorage: Good anchorage in Baie de Collo with depth of 27.0 m, providing excellent shelter from W and N winds

Accommodation:

Name	Remarks
Collo	See [1] below

[1]*Collo:* Port protected from E winds by a jetty 145 m long. Three small berths totalling 237.5 m in length, 4.2-5.0 m d

Storage: Open storage of 2 ha

Lloyd's Agent: Societe Algerienne des Etablissements Mory & Cie., 8 Boulevard Colonel Amirouche, Algiers, Algeria, *Tel:* +213 21 63 56 63, *Fax:* +213 21 63 56 74, *Email:* ops-algiers@saem-dz.com

DELLYS

Lat 36° 55' N; Long 3° 53' E.

Admiralty Chart: 1710

Admiralty Pilot: 45

Time Zone: GMT +1 h

UNCTAD Locode: DZ DEL

Principal Facilities:

Authority: Entreprise Portuaire de Dellys, Dellys, Algeria, *Tel:* +213 3 21 42 93 77

Port Security: ISPS compliant

Anchorage: The bay of Dellys opens to the N and E giving very good anchorage with a rocky bottom, against winds from the W and NW. The anchorage zone 800 m from shore consists of an area marked by a line joining the points of Dellys and Garrouba with depths from 13 to 24 m

Pilotage: Compulsory for arrivals, sailings and in port movements. Only available during daylight hours

Radio Frequency: Algiers radio gives a 24 h watch, receiving on 500 and 2182 khz and transmitting on 1792 khz. Port Captain obtainable on VHF Channel 16

Weather: Dominant winds from the W and NW

Maximum Vessel Dimensions: Max d 5.49 m, max loa 100 m for commercial vessels and 105 m for ro/ro vessels

Working Hours: 0700-1300, 1300-1900

Accommodation:

Name	Length (m)	Depth (m)	Remarks
Dellys			See [1] below
Berth No.1 (North Quay)	107	6	For commercial vessels
Berth No.4 (South Quay)	129	5.5	For commercial vessels

[1]*Dellys:* Harbour protected from the E by a breakwater. Two quays, North and South with five berths. Ro/ro facilities available for stern ramp vessels

Storage:

Location	Open (m²)
Dellys	17400

Bunkering: Not available but can be obtained from Algiers (88.5 km) or Bejaia (104.6 km)
Algerian Shipping & Chartering S.a.r.l., 13 Rue Omar Boursas, Algiers 16308, Algeria, *Tel:* +213 21 68 98 28, *Fax:* +213 21 28 85 60, *Email:* mail@algerianshipping.com, *Website:* www.alshic-group.com/algeria/
Bominflot, Bominflot Bunkergesellschaft fur Mineralole mbH & Co. KG, Grosse Baeckerstrasse 11, 20095 Hamburg, Germany, *Tel:* +49 40 350 930, *Fax:* +49 40 3509 3116, *Email:* mail@bominflot.de, *Website:* www.bominflot.net
BP France S.A., Immeuble le Cervier, 12 Avenue des Beguines, Cergy-Saint-Christophe, 95866 Cergy Pontoise Cedex, France, *Tel:* +33 1 3422 4000, *Fax:* +33 1 3422 4417, *Email:* benoist.grosjean@fr.bp.com, *Website:* www.bpmarine.com
Entreprise Nationale Commerciale & Distribution, Production Petroliers (NAFTAL), Aeroport Houari Boumedienne, P O Box 717, Algiers, Algeria, *Tel:* +213 6 52252, *Fax:* +213 6 59485
Medstone Ltd, Suite 305, Cumberland House, 80 Scrubs Lane, London NW10 6RF, United Kingdom, *Tel:* +44 20 8960 3611, *Fax:* +44 20 8960 4420, *Email:* bunkers@medstone.net
Total France S.A., Total Marine Fuels, 51 Esplanade du General de Gaulle, F-92907 Paris la Defense Cedex 10, France, *Tel:* +33 1 4135 2755, *Fax:* +33 1 4197 0291, *Email:* marine.fuels@total.com, *Website:* www.marinefuels.total.com
Tramp Oil & Marine, World Fuel Services Corporation, 13th Floor, Portland House, Bressenden Place, London SW1E 5BH, United Kingdom, *Tel:* +44 20 7808 5000, *Fax:* +44 20 7808 5088, *Email:* pturner@wfscorp.com, *Website:* www.wfscorp.com

Medical Facilities: Hospital available, contact agent before arrival of vessel

Airport: Hovari Boumediene, 80 km

Lloyd's Agent: Societe Algerienne des Etablissements Mory & Cie., 8 Boulevard Colonel Amirouche, Algiers, Algeria, *Tel:* +213 21 63 56 63, *Fax:* +213 21 63 56 74, *Email:* ops-algiers@saem-dz.com

DJEN DJEN

Lat 36° 49' N; Long 5° 46' E.

Admiralty Chart: 1712

Admiralty Pilot: 45

Time Zone: GMT +1 h

UNCTAD Locode: DZ DJI

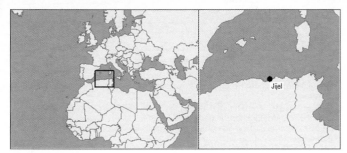

Principal Facilities:

	Y	G	C	R			T	A

Authority: Entreprise Portuaire de Djen Djen, P O Box 87, Jijel 18000, Algeria, *Tel:* +213 34 44 65 64, *Fax:* +213 34 44 52 60, *Email:* epjdjendjen@wissal.dz, *Website:* www.djendjen-port.com.dz

Officials: President: Atmane Mohamed, *Email:* atmane@djendjen-port.com.dz. Harbour Master: Tatare Bader-eddine, *Email:* tatare@djendjen-port.com.dz.

Port Security: ISPS compliant. Contact: Tatar Badr-Eddine, Tel: +213 34 44 55 44, Fax: +213 34 44 55 44, Email: tatar_bader@hotmail.com

Approach: Port approached by a channel 120 m wide in depth of 10-11 m

Pilotage: Compulsory and available 24 h. Vessels should advise ETA to Harbour Master 72 h prior to arrival and confirm on VHF Channel 14 or 16 2 h before arrival at the anchorage area. Pilot boards in pos 36° 51' N; 5° 54' E

Radio Frequency: Pilot on VHF Channel 12. Harbour Master on VHF Channels 16 and 14

Traffic: 2002, 1 753 044 t of cargo handled

Working Hours: 0700-1300, 1300-1900, 1900-0100, 0100-0700 if needed

Accommodation:

Name	Length (m)	Depth (m)	Draught (m)	Remarks
Djen Djen				
General Cargo Quay	769	11		
Mixed Cargo Quay	250	11		Includes a container terminal
Ro/ro Quay		11		Three ro/ro ramps
Western Quay	1060		10.5–18.2	

Mechanical Handling Equipment:

Location	Type	Capacity (t)	Qty
Djen Djen	Mobile Cranes	90	1
Djen Djen	Mobile Cranes	65	3
Djen Djen	Mobile Cranes	28	1
Djen Djen	Forklifts	3–38	25

Towage: One tug of 1500 hp available

Shipping Agents: Algerian Maritime Services, Port de Djendjen, Jijel 18000, Algeria, *Tel:* +213 34 44 58 58, *Fax:* +213 34 44 62 62, *Email:* amsbejaia@ams.dz, *Website:* www.ams.com.dz
Alshiplink Ltd., Jijel, Algeria, *Tel:* +213 34 44 61 00, *Fax:* +213 34 44 61 00, *Email:* djendjen@alshiplink-dz.com
The General Maritime Co (GEMA), Quai Sud, P O Box 89, Jijel, Algeria, *Tel:* +213 34 44 91 52, *Fax:* +213 34 44 91 49, *Website:* www.gema.com.dz
The National Shipping Co (NASHCO), P O Box 33, Jijel 18000, Algeria, *Tel:* +213 34 44 03 24, *Fax:* +213 34 44 03 24, *Email:* djendjen1@nashco.com.dz, *Website:* www.nashco.com.dz
Worms Algerie Shipping (Walship) Spa, Port de Djen Djen, Jijel, Algeria, *Tel:* +213 34 44 55 22, *Fax:* +213 34 44 89 89, *Email:* ops.djendjen@walshipalgerie.net, *Website:* www.worms-sm.com

Medical Facilities: Two hospitals

Airport: Ferhat Abbas Airport, 2 km

Railway: 1.5 km from Jijel and 12 km from Jenjen

Development: DP World, in a joint venture with the Port Authority, will invest in expanding the port over time

Lloyd's Agent: Societe Algerienne des Etablissements Mory & Cie., 8 Boulevard Colonel Amirouche, Algiers, Algeria, *Tel:* +213 21 63 56 63, *Fax:* +213 21 63 56 74, *Email:* ops-algiers@saem-dz.com

EL DJAZAIR

alternate name, see Algiers

EL DJEFNA

harbour area, see under Algiers

GHARA DJEBILET

harbour area, see under Algiers

GHAZAOUET

Lat 35° 5' N; Long 1° 51' W.

Admiralty Chart: 178/2437	**Admiralty Pilot:** 45
Time Zone: GMT +1 h	**UNCTAD Locode:** DZ GHZ

Principal Facilities:

Q	Y	G	C	R	L			T	A

Authority: Entreprise Portuaire de Ghazaouet, P O Box 217, Ghazaouet 13400, Algeria, *Tel:* +213 43 32 32 37, *Fax:* +213 43 32 32 55, *Email:* contact@portdeghazaouet.com, *Website:* www.portdeghazaouet.com

Officials: Harbour Master: Kader Mehabi.
Deputy Harbour Master: Ramdane Mustapha.

Port Security: ISPS compliant. All vessels are protected day and night, watchmen are available

Pre-Arrival Information: Vessel's ETA should be sent 48 h prior to arrival. The following information is required:
Max draft at arrival
Loa
Type and tonnage of cargo
Ship's flag and last port of call
Vsl security (ISPS) information should be sent 24 h prior to arrival
The Algerian flag and vessel's nationality flag are required

Approach: Channel 166 m wide in depth of 16 m

Anchorage: Open anchorage can be obtained off the harbour, N of the breakwater, in depths of 18-22 m; fairly good holding ground of fine sand, not recommended in bad weather

Pilotage: The use of harbour pilots is compulsory for all vessels. There are two pilot boats available. Pilots are available day and night. In very adverse weather conditions the pilot will advise the vessel while in port. Vessels are recommended to keep W of the entrance whilst awaiting a pilot

Radio Frequency: Ghazaouet Port Control on VHF Channel 16, working channel 12

Weather: Prevailing winds W'ly and NW'ly in Winter and E'ly in Summer

Tides: Range of tide 40 cm

Traffic: 2006, 573 099 t of cargo handled

Maximum Vessel Dimensions: 185 m loa, 10.5 m draft

Principal Imports and Exports: Imports: Container cargo, General cargo, Grain, Minerals, Timber, Vegetable oil. Exports: Carobs, Fresh fish, Sulphuric acid, Zinc.

Working Hours: 1st shift 0630-1230, 2nd shift 1230-1900, night shift 2000-0200 (if required)

Accommodation:

Name	Length (m)	Depth (m)	Remarks
Mole d'Alger			
Berths 1-3	300	6.2	See [1] below
Mole Batna			
Berths 4-5	151	7.2	Passenger, cruise & ro/ro vessels
Berth 6	90	7.2	
Mole Constantine			
Berth 7	93	7.2	
Berth 8	105	7.2	General cargo
Berth 9	125	7.2	General cargo, ro/ro & lo/lo
Berth 10	101	7.2	
Mole Djanet			
Berths 11-13	300	7.5	Bulk & dry cargo. Two cranes of 10 t cap
Mole Tlemcen			
Berth 14	120	10.5	Sulphuric acid in bulk, zinc ingots & general cargo
Berths 15-17	289	10.5	See [2] below

[1]*Berths 1-3:* Discharge of vegetable oil, serf, coprah, palm stearine etc
[2]*Berths 15-17:* Bulk cargoes (grain & mineral cargo). Silo facilities with a cap of 30 000 t

Storage: Tank facilities for vegetable oil of 2640 t

Location	Open (m²)	Covered (m²)	Grain (t)
Ghazaouet	105000	960	30000

Mechanical Handling Equipment:

Location	Type	Capacity (t)	Qty
Ghazaouet	Mult-purp. Cranes	30	4
Ghazaouet	Mult-purp. Cranes	90	1
Ghazaouet	Electric Cranes	10	2

Key to Principal Facilities:—				
A=Airport	**C**=Containers	**G**=General Cargo	**P**=Petroleum	**R**=Ro/Ro	**Y**=Dry Bulk
B=Bunkers	**D**=Dry Dock	**L**=Cruise	**Q**=Other Liquid Bulk	**T**=Towage (where available from port)

Location	Type	Capacity (t)	Qty
Ghazaouet	Forklifts	3–28	51

Towage: Compulsory. One tug (Isser 3) and one pilot boat available

Repair & Maintenance: A small slipway is available. Minor repairs only can be carried out

Shipping Agents: CMA-CGM S.A., CMA CGM Ghazaouet, Immeuble Entreprise Portuaire de Ghazaouet, 1 Etage, Ghazaouet 13400, Algeria, *Tel:* +213 43 32 31 23, *Fax:* +213 43 32 31 17, *Website:* www.cma-cgm.com
The National Shipping Co (NASHCO), P O Box 217, Ghazaouet 13000, Algeria, *Tel:* +213 43 32 62 50, *Fax:* +213 43 32 38 40, *Email:* ghz@nashco.com.dz, *Website:* www.nashco.com.dz
Seacom Agencies, Cite Sayah Missoum Bt A2 No.17 Zone 50, Ghazaouet, Algeria, *Tel:* +213 43 32 64 55, *Fax:* +213 43 32 64 55, *Website:* www.seacom-dz.com
Worms Algerie Shipping (Walship) Spa, Entreprise Portuaire de Ghazaouet, P O Box 217, Bureau 107, Ghazaouet 13400, Algeria, *Tel:* +213 43 32 33 03, *Fax:* +213 43 32 33 68, *Email:* ghazaouet@walshipalgerie.com, *Website:* www.worms-sm.com

Medical Facilities: Hospital situated near the port

Airport: Messali Hadj, 50 km

Railway: Ghazaouet Railway Station, situated near to the port

Lloyd's Agent: Societe Algerienne des Etablissements Mory & Cie., 8 Boulevard Colonel Amirouche, Algiers, Algeria, *Tel:* +213 21 63 56 63, *Fax:* +213 21 63 56 74, *Email:* ops-algiers@saem-dz.com

HADJAR

harbour area, see under Algiers

JIJEL

alternate name, see Djen Djen

MESTGHANEM

alternate name, see Mostaganem

MOSTAGANEM

Lat 35° 56' N; Long 0° 4' E.

Admiralty Chart: 822/178   **Admiralty Pilot:** 45
Time Zone: GMT +1 h   **UNCTAD Locode:** DZ MOS

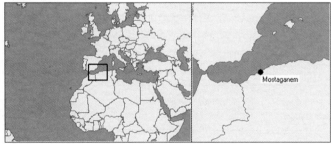

Principal Facilities:

	Y	G	C	R		B		T	

Authority: Entreprise Portuaire de Mostaganem, Quai du Maghreb, P O Box 131, Mostaganem 27000, Algeria, *Tel:* +213 45 21 17 77, *Fax:* +213 45 21 78 05

Officials: General Director: Mokhtar Sheriff.
Harbour Master: Mohamed Bouabida.

Port Security: ISPS compliant. Contact: Moulay Mohamed, Tel/Fax:+213 45 21 19 94, Email: dg@mosta-port.com

Approach: Port approached by a channel 100 m long in depth of 12.0 m

Anchorage: Anchorage to W of harbour entrance in a depth of 25 m

Pilotage: Compulsory. Two pilots; two pilot boats; 24 h service

Radio Frequency: Oran Radio receiving on 2182 kHz and working on 1735 kHz, 24 h service. At Harbour Master's office working on VHF Channel 16

Traffic: 2001, 341 vessels, 951 844 t of cargo handled

Maximum Vessel Dimensions: 180 m loa, 7.62 to 8.23 m d depending on the berth

Working Hours: 0700-0100

Accommodation:

Name	Remarks
Mostaganem	See [1] below

[1]*Mostaganem:* Ten berths available. Vessels arriving after sunset usually wait in the roads until 0600 the next day; vessels can sail at any time. Rail connections on quay. Sugar silo on Maghreb Quay

Storage: Wine storage available

Mechanical Handling Equipment:

Location	Type	Capacity (t)	Qty
Mostaganem	Mult-purp. Cranes	12	5

Bunkering: Gas oil available by truck from Arzew if required

Towage: Two tugs available

Repair & Maintenance: No dry docks available. Minor repairs can be carried out in local workshops

Shipping Agents: The National Shipping Co (NASHCO), Cooperative Colonnel Amirouche B1, Mostaganem, Algeria, *Tel:* +213 45 21 07 86, *Fax:* +213 45 21 98 25, *Email:* direc-mos@nashco.com.dz, *Website:* www.nashco.com.dz
Seacom Agencies, Cite 400 Logements, Route d'Oran A6 4, Mostaganem, Algeria, *Tel:* +213 45 21 80 82, *Fax:* +213 45 21 80 82, *Email:* head-office@seacom-dz.com
Sudcargos Algerie, Mostaganem, Algeria, *Tel:* +213 45 21 09 07, *Fax:* +213 45 21 81 16, *Email:* sud-cargos_mostaganem@yahoo.fr
Worms Algerie Shipping (Walship) Spa, Quai du Maghreb, Port de Mostaganem, Mostaganem 27000, Algeria, *Tel:* +213 45 21 06 64, *Fax:* +213 45 21 91 63, *Email:* mostaganem@walshipalgerie.com, *Website:* www.worms-sm.com

Medical Facilities: All facilities available

Airport: Oran, 80 km

Lloyd's Agent: Societe Algerienne des Etablissements Mory & Cie., 8 Boulevard Colonel Amirouche, Algiers, Algeria, *Tel:* +213 21 63 56 63, *Fax:* +213 21 63 56 74, *Email:* ops-algiers@saem-dz.com

ORAN

Lat 35° 42' N; Long 0° 38' W.

Admiralty Chart: 812   **Admiralty Pilot:** 45
Time Zone: GMT +1 h   **UNCTAD Locode:** DZ ORN

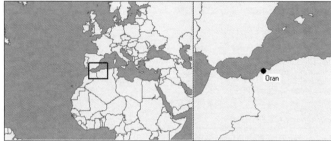

Principal Facilities:

P		Y	G	C	R		B		T	A

Authority: Entreprise Portuaire d'Oran, 1 Rue du 20 Aout, Oran 31000, Algeria, *Tel:* +213 41 33 24 41, *Fax:* +213 41 33 24 98, *Email:* pdg@oran-port.com

Port Security: ISPS compliant. Contact: Bourtal Zarat Ghaouti, Tel: +213 41 39 00 10, Fax: +213 41 39 00 10, Email: bourtal_pfso@oran-port.com

Approach: Eastern Channel 150 m wide in depth of 24 m

Anchorage: Anchorage in the roads in depths up to 40 m

Pilotage: Compulsory. Two 60 hp pilot boats available

Traffic: 2000, 1109 vessels, 3 091 841 t of cargo handled

Working Hours: Sat -Thurs 0700-1900. Availability after these hours upon request

Accommodation: Port protected by two breakwaters and consists of seven basins with water area of 122 ha. There are 37 berths with a quay frontage of 3.5 km, including specialised facilities for handling cargoes such as wine and grain
Container facilities: Container terminal of 11 ha with a storage cap of 4200 TEU's
Bulk facilities: Two grain silo's with storage of 30 000 t and 10 000 t, capable of discharging 4-5000 t/day
Tanker facilities: Two berths operated by Naftal; length 224 m each; 11.58 and 9.75 m d; night berthing possible; water and bunkers available

Name	Length (m)	Draught (m)
Alger		
Berth 1	112	8
Berth 2	112	8
Bejaia		
Beni Saf		

Name	Length (m)	Draught (m)
Senegal		
Berth 1	130	9.15
Berth 4	130	9.15
Berth 5	130	9.15
Conakry		
Berth 6	130	7
Berth 7	130	8.2
Cadix		
Berth 8	138	8.4
Casablanca		
Berth 9	120	8.2
Berth 10	120	6.5
Safi		
Berth 11	140	6.1
Berth 12	140	7.3
Berth 13	140	7.3
Dunkerque		
Berth 14	110	7.5
Berth 15	110	9
Dakar		
Berth 16	200	10
Dar El-Salem		
Berth 17	190	10
Berth 18	190	8.5
Skikda		
Berth 19	120	8
Ghazaouet		
Berth 20	172	9
Berth 21	172	10.5
Genes		
Berth 22	128	12
Gabes		
Berth 23	110	10.5
Berth 24	120	10.5
Berth 25	120	9
Sfax		
Berth 26	100	8.5
Berth 27	100	8.5
Hambourg		
Berth 28	133	9
Berth 29	133	10
Berth 30	134	12
La Havane		
Berth 31	150	12
Le Havre		
Berth 32	140	11
Berth 33	60	9

Storage: Wine storage available

Location	Covered (m²)
Oran	48554

Mechanical Handling Equipment:

Location	Type	Capacity (t)	Qty
Oran	Mobile Cranes	40–80	5
Oran	Shore Cranes	3–6	10

Bunkering: Algerian Shipping & Chartering S.a.r.l., 13 Rue Omar Boursas, Algiers 16308, Algeria, *Tel:* +213 21 68 98 28, *Fax:* +213 21 28 85 60, *Email:* mail@algerianshipping.com, *Website:* www.alshic-group.com/algeria/
Bominflot, Bominflot Bunkergesellschaft fur Mineralole mbH & Co. KG, Grosse Baeckerstrasse 11, 20095 Hamburg, Germany, *Tel:* +49 40 350 930, *Fax:* +49 40 3509 3116, *Email:* mail@bominflot.de, *Website:* www.bominflot.net
Entreprise Nationale Commerciale & Distribution, Production Petroliers (NAFTAL), Aeroport Houari Boumedienne, P O Box 717, Algiers, Algeria, *Tel:* +213 6 52252, *Fax:* +213 6 59485
Medstone Ltd, Suite 305, Cumberland House, 80 Scrubs Lane, London NW10 6RF, United Kingdom, *Tel:* +44 20 8960 3611, *Fax:* +44 20 8960 4420, *Email:* bunkers@medstone.net
Total France S.A., Total Marine Fuels, 51 Esplanade du General de Gaulle, F-92907 Paris la Defense Cedex 10, France, *Tel:* +33 1 4135 2755, *Fax:* +33 1 4197 0291, *Email:* marine.fuels@total.com, *Website:* www.marinefuels.total.com
Tramp Oil & Marine, World Fuel Services Corporation, 13th Floor, Portland House, Bressenden Place, London SW1E 5BH, United Kingdom, *Tel:* +44 20 7808 5000, *Fax:* +44 20 7808 5088, *Email:* pturner@wfscorp.com, *Website:* www.wfscorp.com

Towage: Three tugs of 1000, 1500 and 1700 hp

Repair & Maintenance: Only minor repairs can be effected; three slipways available

Shipping Agents: Algerian Maritime Services, 24 Boulevard de L'aln, Ex Front de Mer, Oran 31000, Algeria, *Tel:* +213 41 39 02 07, *Fax:* +213 41 39 36 66, *Email:* amsoran@ams.com.dz, *Website:* www.ams.com.dz
CMA-CGM S.A., CMA CGM Algeria, 25 Rue Zougai Ali Hai Tafna, Immeuble Victoria Bel Air, Oran 31000, Algeria, *Tel:* +213 41 46 25 87, *Fax:* +213 41 46 23 63, *Email:* ora.genmbox@cma-cgm.com, *Website:* www.cma-cgm.com
Mediterranean Shipping Company, MSC Sarl, 5 Avenue Loubet, Oran, Algeria, *Tel:* +213 41 33 30 89, *Fax:* +213 41 33 56 79, *Email:* infooran@mscalg.com.dz, *Website:* www.mscgva.ch
A.P. Moller-Maersk Group, Maersk Algerie SpA, 113 Bis, Rue Larbi Ben M'Hidi, Oran 31000, Algeria, *Tel:* +213 41 40 44 37, *Fax:* +213 41 40 44 42, *Email:* ornmla@maersk.com, *Website:* www.maerskline.com
Mondial Shipping Co., Oran, Algeria, *Tel:* +213 41 40 01 38, *Fax:* +213 41 40 01 38, *Email:* mondialshipping.om@wanadoo.dz
The National Shipping Co (NASHCO), Oran 31000, Algeria, *Tel:* +213 41 40 10 01, *Fax:* +213 41 40 10 56, *Email:* direc-oran@nashco.com.dz, *Website:* www.nashco.com.dz

Seacom Agencies, 45 Avenue Mohamed Khemisti, Oran, Algeria, *Fax:* +213 41 33 46 29, *Email:* osp-oran@seacom-dz.com, *Website:* www.seacom-dz.com
Societe de Gestion Maritime et de Consignation (SOGEMCO), 2 Boulevard Tripoli, Oran, Algeria, *Tel:* +213 41 39 64 20, *Fax:* +213 41 39 12 55, *Email:* gemoran@assila.net, *Website:* www.sogemco.com
Sudcargos Algerie, Oran, Algeria, *Tel:* +213 41 33 19 56, *Fax:* +213 41 33 33 18, *Email:* oransudcargo@yahoo.fr
Tiba International Algerie, Oran, Algeria, *Tel:* +213 41 41 47 57, *Fax:* +213 41 40 94 08, *Email:* saidm@algeriecom.com
Worms Algerie Shipping (Walship) Spa, 2 Rue Belkacem Djelloul, Oran 31000, Algeria, *Tel:* +213 41 33 57 22, *Fax:* +213 41 33 10 65, *Email:* oran@walshipalgerie.com, *Website:* www.worms-sm.com

Airport: Es-Senia, 6 km

Lloyd's Agent: Societe Algerienne des Etablissements Mory & Cie., 8 Boulevard Colonel Amirouche, Algiers, Algeria, *Tel:* +213 21 63 56 63, *Fax:* +213 21 63 56 74, *Email:* ops-algiers@saem-dz.com

PHILIPPEVILLE

former name, see Skikda

PORT METHANIER

harbour area, see under Skikda

SKIKDA

Lat 36° 52' N; Long 6° 56' E.

Admiralty Chart: 855	**Admiralty Pilot:** 45
Time Zone: GMT +1 h	**UNCTAD Locode:** DZ SKI

Principal Facilities:

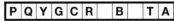

P Q Y G C R　B　T A

Authority: Entreprise Portuaire de Skikda, Avenue Rezki Rahal, P O Box 65, Skikda 21000, Algeria, *Tel:* +213 38 75 68 27, *Fax:* +213 38 75 20 15, *Email:* epskikda@skikda-port.com, *Website:* www.skikda-port.com

Port Security: ISPS compliant. Contact: Abdeladim Mohamed Larbi, Tel: +213 38 75 35 20, Fax: +213 38 75 35 20, Email: abdeladim@skikda-port.com

Documentation: Port Authority;
Inward declaration, Ship's certificates, Crew list, CO2 fire extinguisher, Oil record book, Manifest for dangerous goods, Ship/shore safety check list, Avoidance pollution safety check list.
Police Immigration;
Inward declaration, Declaration of provisions, Declaration of effects and goods, Crew list, List of passengers, Manifest cargo for dangerous goods, Declaration of all weapons and ammunition.
Customs;
Manifest cargo, Crew list, Ship's bonded store list, Narcotic list, Ship's store declaration, Ship's effects declaration

Approach: Approach channel in the Outer Port 100 m long and 15 m deep. The port has a breakwater 1615 m long
New Port: two breakwaters projecting 1737 m NE and 650 m NW

Anchorage: Safe anchorage in the authorised areas of the roads

Baie de Stora affords good protection from the W, but not from NW winds. In bad weather heavy seas roll into Baie de Stora

Anchorage can be obtained for large vessels in good weather SE of Ilot des Singes in depths between 16.5 m and 18.3 m, sand bottom

In winter vessels should anchor further out in depths between 20 m and 22 m. Anchorage can be obtained by small vessels approximately 1.75 cables off the village of Stora in depths between 6 m and 8 m

An anchorage for tankers is situated 1 nautical mile NE of Skikda in depths of over 20 m. Vessels should not obstruct the N and NE approaches to the harbour entrance Anchoring is prohibited in an area extending NE from Ilot des Singes

Pilotage: Compulsory for vessels of 500 gt and above. Pilot boards 1 nautical mile off entrance or at anchorage

Traffic: 2006, 3136 vessels, 22 528 948 t of cargo handled, 12 926 TEU's

Working Hours: First shift: 0600-1220, second shift: 1300-1900, third shift: 2000-0200

Accommodation:

Name	Length (m)	Draught (m)	Remarks
Port Methanier			
General Quay	240	10	
P1	230	12.8	For vessels from 50,000 t to 100,000 t
P2	230	12.8	For vessels from 50,000 t to 100,000 t
P3	260	14.8	For vessels from 50,000 t to 100,000 t
M1	260	11.5	LNG handled from 45 000-90 000 m3
M2	220	11	LNG handled from 45 000-90 000 m3
P5	180	10.5	LPG handled to 40,000 cu m
A1	140	10.5	Ethylene Aromatique - 30,000 cu m
Old Port (Darse Basin)			
Quai Sud Berth No.1	125	6	General cargo handled. Five water hydrants
Quai Sud Berth No.2	135	6	General cargo handled. Ten water hydrants
Quai Sud Berth No.3	140	6	General cargo handled
Quai Sud-Est Berth No.1	130	6	
Quai Sud-Est Berth No.2	140	6	Five water hydrants. One pontoon of 100 t capacity Used by harbour craft
Port of Servitude			
Quai Nord P4	150	8.5	Grain handled by two elevators
Traverse Mole	200	6	Ro/ro berth. North and South berths, each 100 m long
Quai Nord	155	8.5	General cargo handled. Three water hydrants
Quai Est	165	6.5	General cargo handled
Old Port (Avant Basin)			
Avant Port Nord	160	9	General cargo handled. Four water hydrants
Avant Port Sud	80	7	General cargo handled
Chateau Vert Nord Berth No.1	142	10	General cargo handled
Chateau Vert Nord Berth No.2	142	10	General cargo handled
Chateau Vert Sud	142	10	General cargo handled
Old Port			
Grande Jetee, P1	190	11.5	Refinery products handled
Grande Jetee, P2	200	12.5	Refinery products handled
Grande Jetee, P3	230	14	Refinery products handled

Storage: Wine storage available

Location	Open (m2)	Covered (m2)	Grain (t)
Skikda		10253	20000
Port Methanier	29000		
Quai Sud Berth No.1		3817	
Quai Sud Berth No.2		2160	
Quai Sud-Est Berth No.1		323	
Quai Sud-Est Berth No.2		1253	
Quai Nord P4			20000
Avant Port Nord		2160	
Avant Port Sud		540	

Mechanical Handling Equipment:

Location	Type	Capacity (t)	Qty
Skikda	Mult-purp. Cranes	6	8
Skikda	Mult-purp. Cranes		2
Port Methanier	Mobile Cranes	40	1
Quai Sud Berth No.1	Mult-purp. Cranes	6	5
Avant Port Nord	Mult-purp. Cranes	6	3

Bunkering: Algerian Shipping & Chartering S.a.r.l., 13 Rue Omar Boursas, Algiers 16308, Algeria, *Tel:* +213 21 68 98 28, *Fax:* +213 21 28 85 60, *Email:* mail@algerianshipping.com, *Website:* www.alshic-group.com/algeria/

Bominflot, Bominflot Bunkergesellschaft fur Mineralole mbH & Co. KG, Grosse Baeckerstrasse 11, 20095 Hamburg, Germany, *Tel:* +49 40 350 930, *Fax:* +49 40 3509 3116, *Email:* mail@bominflot.de, *Website:* www.bominflot.net

BP France S.A., Immeuble le Cervier, 12 Avenue des Beguines, Cergy-Saint-Christophe, 95866 Cergy Pontoise Cedex, France, *Tel:* +33 1 3422 4000, *Fax:* +33 1 3422 4417, *Email:* benoist.grosjean@fr.bp.com, *Website:* www.bpmarine.com

Entreprise Nationale Commerciale & Distribution, Production Petroliers (NAFTAL), Aeroport Houari Boumedienne, P O Box 717, Algiers, Algeria, *Tel:* +213 6 52252, *Fax:* +213 6 59485

Medstone Ltd, Suite 305, Cumberland House, 80 Scrubs Lane, London NW10 6RF, United Kingdom, *Tel:* +44 20 8960 3611, *Fax:* +44 20 8960 4420, *Email:* bunkers@medstone.net

Total France S.A., Total Marine Fuels, 51 Esplanade du General de Gaulle, F-92907 Paris la Defense Cedex 10, France, *Tel:* +33 1 4135 2755, *Fax:* +33 1 4197 0291, *Email:* marine.fuels@total.com, *Website:* www.marinefuels.total.com

Tramp Oil & Marine, World Fuel Services Corporation, 13th Floor, Portland House, Bressenden Place, London SW1E 5BH, United Kingdom, *Tel:* +44 20 7808 5000, *Fax:* +44 20 7808 5088, *Email:* pturner@wfscorp.com, *Website:* www.wfscorp.com – *Delivery Mode:* barge

Trust Marine Enterprises Co. Ltd, 141 Filonos Street, 185 36 Piraeus, Greece, *Tel:* +30 210 4180083, *Fax:* +30 210 4136213

Repair & Maintenance: Minor repairs can be carried out. There are no drydocks

Shipping Agents: Algerian Maritime Services, 4 Avenue Bachir Boukadoum, Skikda 21000, Algeria, *Tel:* +213 38 76 27 62, *Fax:* +213 38 76 25 09, *Email:* amsskikda@ams.com.da, *Website:* www.ams.com.dz

Compagnie Nationale Algerienne de Navigation, P O Box 116, Skikda, Algeria, *Tel:* +213 38 75 57 54, *Fax:* +213 38 75 67 89

Alshiplink Ltd., Skikda, Algeria, *Tel:* +213 38 76 44 55, *Fax:* +213 38 76 44 55, *Email:* skikda@alshiplink-dz.com

Bemarine Shipping Agency, Route de Collo Beni Malek Bat 5 No.2, Skikda, Algeria, *Tel:* +213 38 75 46 38, *Fax:* +213 38 76 31 74, *Email:* bemarine.skikda@bemarine.net, *Website:* www.bemarine.net

CMA-CGM S.A., CMA CGM Algeria, 6 Avenue Youcef Kadid, P O Box 19, Skikda 21000, Algeria, *Tel:* +213 38 75 43 41, *Fax:* +213 38 76 10 41, *Website:* www.cma-cgm.com

The General Maritime Co (GEMA), Rue de Bejaia, P O Box 116, Skikda, Algeria, *Tel:* +213 38 75 69 18, *Fax:* +213 38 75 69 18, *Website:* www.gema.com.dz

Mediterranean Shipping Company, MSC Sarl, 4 Rue Mustapha Benboulaid, Skikda, Algeria, *Tel:* +213 38 76 45 12, *Fax:* +213 38 75 53 78, *Email:* infoskikda@mscalg.com.dz, *Website:* www.mscgva.ch

A.P. Moller-Maersk Group, Maersk Algerie SpA, 16-18 Centre Commercial 2, Boulevard du 20 Aout 1955, Skikda 21000, Algeria, *Tel:* +213 38 72 25 51, *Fax:* +213 38 72 23 93, *Email:* skimla@maersk.com, *Website:* www.maerskline.com

Mondial Shipping Co., Skikda, Algeria, *Tel:* +213 38 76 29 45, *Fax:* +213 38 75 29 98, *Email:* mondialshipping.ski@wanadoo.dz

The National Shipping Co (NASHCO), P O Box 186, Skikda 21000, Algeria, *Tel:* +213 38 75 30 26, *Fax:* +213 38 75 79 48, *Email:* direc-skd@nashco.com.dz, *Website:* www.nashco.com.dz

Seacom Agencies, Mole du Chateau vert, Skikda, Algeria, *Tel:* +213 38 75 29 22, *Fax:* +213 38 71 66 97, *Email:* head-office@seacom-dz.com

Societe de Gestion Maritime et de Consignation (SOGEMCO), 4 Avenue Brahim Maiza, Skikda, Algeria, *Tel:* +213 38 75 21 48, *Fax:* +213 38 76 24 24, *Email:* gemskikda@assila.net, *Website:* www.sogemco.com

Sudcargos Algerie, Skikda, Algeria, *Tel:* +213 38 75 58 59, *Fax:* +213 38 75 58 69, *Email:* sudcargos_skikda@yahoo.fr

Worms Algerie Shipping (Walship) Spa, Cite Allees du 20 Aout 55, Local No.19, Skikda 21000, Algeria, *Tel:* +213 38 72 17 05, *Fax:* +213 38 72 17 45, *Email:* skikda@walshipalgerie.com, *Website:* www.worms-sm.com

Airport: Annaba or Qacentina, both 80 km

Lloyd's Agent: Societe Algerienne des Etablissements Mory & Cie., 8 Boulevard Colonel Amirouche, Algiers, Algeria, *Tel:* +213 21 63 56 63, *Fax:* +213 21 63 56 74, *Email:* ops-algiers@saem-dz.com

TENES

Lat 36° 31' N; Long 1° 19' E.

Admiralty Chart: 178		**Admiralty Pilot:** 45	
Time Zone: GMT +1 h		**UNCTAD Locode:** DZ TEN	

Principal Facilities:

					G						

Authority: Entreprise Portuaire de Tenes, P O Box 18, Tenes 02200, Algeria, *Tel:* +213 27 76 72 76, *Fax:* +213 27 76 61 77, *Email:* porttenes@yahoo.fr

Officials: President: Hamri Khaldi.
Harbour Master: Lakhdar Brahim, *Email:* asiporttenes@yahoo.fr.

Port Security: ISPS compliant. Contact: Lakhdar Brahim, Tel: +213 27 76 65 89, Fax: +213 27 76 65 89, Email: asiporttenes@yahoo.fr

Approach: Main entry channel through W entrance. Dangerous in heavy weather and care must be taken during strong NW winds. E entrance used for small craft only

Accommodation:

Name	Remarks
Tenes	See [1] below

[1] *Tenes:* Harbour consists of two jetties, North and Southwest, with a detached

breakwater between the heads. Total length of quays 420 m with four berths of 6-7 m d. Rail connections to Southwest Quay

Storage: Wine storage available

Shipping Agents: The General Maritime Co (GEMA), P O Box 22, Tenes, Algeria, *Tel:* +213 27 76 75 67, *Fax:* +213 27 76 65 90, *Website:* www.gema.com.dz

Lloyd's Agent: Societe Algerienne des Etablissements Mory & Cie., 8 Boulevard Colonel Amirouche, Algiers, Algeria, *Tel:* +213 21 63 56 63, *Fax:* +213 21 63 56 74, *Email:* ops-algiers@saem-dz.com

WAHRAN

alternate name, see Oran

ANGOLA

AMBRIZ

Lat 7° 50' S; Long 13° 7' E.

Admiralty Chart: 3448	**Admiralty Pilot:** 2
Time Zone: GMT +1 h	**UNCTAD Locode:** AO AZZ

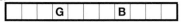

Principal Facilities:

				G			B			

Authority: Porto de Cabinda E.P., Rua do Comercio, Cabinda, Angola, *Tel:* +244 231 223007, *Fax:* +244 231 222464, *Email:* portocab@supernet.ao, *Website:* www.portodecabinda.com

Officials: Director General: Osvaldo Lobo Nascimento.

Anchorage: Outer anchorage may be obtained in a depth of 10 m, anchorage may also be obtained by smaller vessels closer inshore in a depth of 6.7 m

Pilotage: Compulsory, available only during daylight hours

Tides: Mean spring range about 1.3 m, Mean neap range about 0.6 m

Accommodation:

Name	Remarks
Ambriz	See [1] below

[1]*Ambriz:* The harbour consists of a basin 200 m2, dredged to a depth of 5 m with an adjacent quay, and used as a supply base for the oil industry

Bunkering: Diesel oil available

Lloyd's Agent: Core Laboratories Lda (Saybolt Division), Rua Comandante N'Zaji 49, Alvalade, Luanda, Angola, *Tel:* +244 222 321933, *Fax:* +244 222 321933, *Email:* lloyds.sayao@corelab.com, *Website:* www.corelab.com

CABINDA

Lat 5° 33' S; Long 12° 11' E.

Admiralty Chart: 3447	**Admiralty Pilot:** 2
Time Zone: GMT +1 h	**UNCTAD Locode:** AO CAB

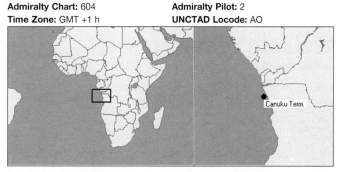

Principal Facilities:

				G			B		A	

Authority: Porto de Cabinda E.P., Rua do Comercio, Cabinda, Angola, *Tel:* +244 231 223007, *Fax:* +244 231 222464, *Email:* portocab@supernet.ao, *Website:* www.portodecabinda.com

Officials: Director General: Osvaldo Lobo Nascimento.

Port Security: ISPS compliant. Contact: Manuel Guimaraes, Tel: +244 231 222474

Approach: The Bay of Cabinda can be entered directly from the sea but due to lack of depth of water caution is needed. A sand bar extends along the coast between Massabi River and the Congo River with a width of 3.2 to 4.8 km

Anchorage: Ocean-going vessels can only anchor some distance from coast in open roads. Official anchorage has a sandy bottom. Safe line of approach found in Portuguese charts. There are wrecks of lighters sunk during cargo operations. Depths at official anchorage between 9.14 m and 10.67 m - open roads subject to heavy swell in season, 3.04 m clearance under keel to be observed

Pilotage: Compulsory. One government pilot available

Weather: At height of dry season (usually March to September) heavy swell predominant; during this swell it is often impossible to work in the roads or alongside pier, resulting in serious congestion (10 days per year). Heavy thunderstorms during rainy season often interfere with work

Tides: Tidal range approx 1.52 m

Traffic: 2006, 230 000 t of cargo handled, 13 387 TEU's

Working Hours: Normal port working hours for all cargoes (weekdays) 0730-1200, 1400-1730. Saturdays 0730-1200. Overtime (weekdays) 1200-1400, 1730-2400 Saturdays overtime 1200-1400, 1400-1730, 1730-2400 Sundays and holidays overtime workable at extra rates, usually 0730-1200

Accommodation:

Name	Length (m)	Depth (m)	Remarks
Cabinda			
Wooden Port Pier	100	3.04	See [1] below

[1]*Wooden Port Pier:* It is possible to work on each side of the pier, but the land side is restricted to light cargo handling in view of the limited cap of outreach of crane. The port operates 28 barges with cap ranging from 100 to 200 t and 17 launches for towing barges and transport

Mechanical Handling Equipment:

Location	Type	Capacity (t)	Qty
Cabinda	Mult-purp. Cranes	12	7

Bunkering: Allmar Ltd, Largro Pedro Benge, Cabinda, Cabinda 205, Angola, *Tel:* +244 913 183353, *Fax:* +244 913 244 2312 221 00, *Email:* ruimass@allmargroup.com, *Website:* www.allmargroup.com
Allmar Ltd, Largro Pedro Benge, Cabinda, Cabinda 205, Angola, *Tel:* +244 913 183353, *Fax:* +244 913 244 2312 221 00, *Email:* ruimass@allmargroup.com, *Website:* www.allmargroup.com

Repair & Maintenance: Sociedade de Representacoes de Cabinda, P O Box 4, Cabinda, Angola, *Tel:* +244 231 222126 Minor repairs

Shipping Agents: Gulf Agency Transportes Agenciamentos e Servicos Lda, Rua de Comercio No.3, Cabinda, Angola, *Tel:* +244 231 223918, *Email:* angola@gacworld.com, *Website:* www.gacworld.com

Airport: Cabinda, 2 km

Lloyd's Agent: Core Laboratories Lda (Saybolt Division), Rua Comandante N'Zaji 49, Alvalade, Luanda, Angola, *Tel:* +244 222 321933, *Fax:* +244 222 321933, *Email:* lloyds.sayao@corelab.com, *Website:* www.corelab.com

CANUKU TERMINAL

Lat 7° 6' S; Long 12° 28' E.

Admiralty Chart: 604	**Admiralty Pilot:** 2
Time Zone: GMT +1 h	**UNCTAD Locode:** AO

Principal Facilities:

P										T	

Authority: SONANGOL P&P, P O Box 2997, Luanda, Angola, *Tel:* +244 2 633261, *Fax:* +244 2 353037

Pre-Arrival Information: Vessels must send ETA 48 h and 24 h prior to arrival or at any time if ETA changes by more than 2 h

Anchorage: Vessels may be directed to anchor 3 miles NE of the FPSO. Vessels must not anchor in any other location due to obstructions on the seabed especially in the vicinity of the FPSO

Pilotage: Compulsory. The pilot boards 2.5 miles NE of the FPSO

Maximum Vessel Dimensions: 150 000 dwt

Accommodation:

Name	Remarks
Canuku Terminal	See [1] below

[1]*Canuku Terminal:* The export vessel moors bow to bow with FPSO 'Ocean Producer', a converted 79 000 dwt tanker, anchored in a depth of approx 83 m.

Key to Principal Facilities:—			
A=Airport	**C**=Containers	**G**=General Cargo	**P**=Petroleum	**R**=Ro/Ro	**Y**=Dry Bulk
B=Bunkers	**D**=Dry Dock	**L**=Cruise	**Q**=Other Liquid Bulk	**T**=Towage (where available from port)

Berthing in daylight only but unberthing may be carried out in darkness by agreement between the FPSO, the export vessel and loading master

Towage: A tug will assist during berthing and throughout the loading operation

Lloyd's Agent: Core Laboratories Lda (Saybolt Division), Rua Comandante N'Zaji 49, Alvalade, Luanda, Angola, *Tel:* +244 222 321933, *Fax:* +244 222 321933, *Email:* lloyds.sayao@corelab.com, *Website:* www.corelab.com

DALIA TERMINAL

Lat 7° 41' S; Long 11° 46' E.

Admiralty Chart: 604	**Admiralty Pilot:** 2
Time Zone: GMT +1 h	**UNCTAD Locode:** AO DAL

Principal Facilities:

P											

Authority: Total E & P Angola, Av. 4 Fevereiro - No.37, Luanda, Angola, *Tel:* +244 222 672000, *Fax:* +244 222 672261, *Website:* www.total.com

Port Security: ISPS compliant

Pre-Arrival Information: Export vessels should forward their ETA with pre-arrival message to the terminal 72 h prior to vessel's arrival via fax and again 4 h prior to arrival on VHF Channels 16 (listening) and 72 (working)

Pilotage: For SPM one Pilot and Berthing Master boards but if in tandem, two Pilots and a Berthing Master will board the export tanker
For FPSO the Pilot and Berthing Master boards the export vessel 3 nautical miles N of the FPSO

Radio Frequency: Listening on VHF Channel 16 and working on VHF Channels 72 and 8

Principal Imports and Exports: Exports: Crude oil, Methanol.

Accommodation:

Name	Remarks
Dalia Terminal	See [1] below

[1]*Dalia Terminal:* Consists of SPM in pos 7° 40' 51" S; 11° 47' 00" E with a loading rate of 6600 m3/h and 'FPSO Dalia' in pos 7° 41' 00" S; 11° 45' 55" E with a loading rate of 7200 m3/h
The terminal is closed to berthing/unberthing 1500-0600

Towage: Available for assistance in berthing and during loading operations

Airport: Luanda International Airport

Lloyd's Agent: Core Laboratories Lda (Saybolt Division), Rua Comandante N'Zaji 49, Alvalade, Luanda, Angola, *Tel:* +244 222 321933, *Fax:* +244 222 321933, *Email:* lloyds.sayao@corelab.com, *Website:* www.corelab.com

ESSUNGO TERMINAL

Lat 6° 20' S; Long 12° 10' E.

Admiralty Chart: 3206	**Admiralty Pilot:** 2
Time Zone: GMT +1 h	**UNCTAD Locode:** AO

Principal Facilities:

P											

Authority: Chevron Panama Inc., P O Box 5897, Luanda, Angola, *Tel:* +244 2 322606, *Fax:* +244 2 321703

Pilotage: Compulsory. The boarding area is 2 miles NW of SPM buoy

Radio Frequency: Essungo Platform on VHF Channels 6 and 72

Accommodation:

Name	Remarks
Essungo Terminal	See [1] below

[1]*Essungo Terminal:* Consists of a SPM equipped with two mooring hawsers and capable of accepting tankers up to 200 000 dwt
Crude oil loaded onto export tanker at rate of approx 80 000 bbls/h
This terminal is only used in the event of an emergency or failure of the Lombo Terminal loading facility

Waste Reception Facilities: There are no garbage disposal or waste oil facilities available

Lloyd's Agent: Core Laboratories Lda (Saybolt Division), Rua Comandante N'Zaji 49, Alvalade, Luanda, Angola, *Tel:* +244 222 321933, *Fax:* +244 222 321933, *Email:* lloyds.sayao@corelab.com, *Website:* www.corelab.com

FUTILA TERMINAL

Lat 5° 27' S; Long 12° 11' E.

Admiralty Chart: 3206	**Admiralty Pilot:** 2
Time Zone: GMT +1 h	**UNCTAD Locode:** AO

Principal Facilities:

P									A

Pilotage: The mooring master boards vessel at the anchorage area

Radio Frequency: Vessels bound for Futila Terminal are required to send ETA advice 72, 48 and 24 h before arrival through their agent in Cabinda. VHF Channels 16 and 12 are monitored continuously

Principal Imports and Exports: Imports: Gasoline. Exports: Diesel.

Accommodation:

Name	Depth (m)	Draught (m)	Remarks
Futila Terminal			
CBM	6.71	4.57	See [1] below

[1]*CBM:* For vessels up to 6400 dwt. Mooring operations usually undertaken 0600-1600

Medical Facilities: Limited medical facilities available only in an emergency

Airport: Cabinda, 35 km

Lloyd's Agent: Core Laboratories Lda (Saybolt Division), Rua Comandante N'Zaji 49, Alvalade, Luanda, Angola, *Tel:* +244 222 321933, *Fax:* +244 222 321933, *Email:* lloyds.sayao@corelab.com, *Website:* www.corelab.com

GIRASSOL TERMINAL

Lat 7° 39' S; Long 11° 41' E.

Admiralty Chart: 604	**Admiralty Pilot:** 2
Time Zone: GMT +1 h	**UNCTAD Locode:** AO

Principal Facilities:

P											

Authority: Total E & P Angola, Av. 4 Fevereiro - No.37, Luanda, Angola, *Tel:* +244 222 672000, *Fax:* +244 222 672261, *Website:* www.total.com

Port Security: ISPS compliant

Pre-Arrival Information: Vessels should advise ETA 72 h, 48 h and 24 h prior to arrival and then must give 4 h prior notice of arrival to the Terminal on VHF Channel 16

Documentation: 1; Crew list, 8 copies
2; Passenger list, 7 copies
3; Stowaway list, 7 copies
4; Vaccination list, 7 copies
5; Aninimal list, 7 copies
6; Stores list, 4 copies
7; Provisions list; 4 copies

8; Crew effects list; 4 copies
9; Maritime declaration of health, 2 copies
10; Original and 5 last port clearance, 1 copy
11; Ports of call list; 7 copies
12; Bonded stores list, 4 copies
13; Narcotics list, 7 copies
14; Arms and Ammunition list, 7 copies
15; Copies and particulars, 5 copies

Pilotage: Compulsory. Pilot boards in the waiting area which has a radius 2 miles, W of the FPSO, centred in pos 7° 40' S; 11° 37' E

Maximum Vessel Dimensions: At FPSO 250 000 dwt. At SPM buoy 400 000 dwt

Working Hours: 24 h/day

Accommodation:

Name	Remarks
Girassol Terminal	See [1] below

[1]*Girassol Terminal:* Consists of a spread moored FPSO 'FPSO Girassol' with a SPM buoy situated 1 mile NNE from it. Berthing takes place 0600-1500 while unberthing is at any time. Export tankers moor to either the SPM or in tandem bow to bow to the FPSO. Cargo transfer is via floating hose arrangements

Bunkering: Not available

Lloyd's Agent: Core Laboratories Lda (Saybolt Division), Rua Comandante N'Zaji 49, Alvalade, Luanda, Angola, *Tel:* +244 222 321933, *Fax:* +244 222 321933, *Email:* lloyds.sayao@corelab.com, *Website:* www.corelab.com

GREATER PLUTONIO TERMINAL

Lat 7° 50' S; Long 12° 7' E.

Admiralty Chart: 604	**Admiralty Pilot:** 2
Time Zone: GMT +1 h	**UNCTAD Locode:** AO

Principal Facilities:

P											

Authority: BP Angola, Avenida Rainha Ginga 87, Luanda, Angola, *Tel:* +244 222 637440, *Fax:* +244 222 637333, *Email:* gpterminal@bp.com, *Website:* www.bp.com

Port Security: ISPS compliant

Pre-Arrival Information: Export tankers should forward their initial ETA via email or fax on departure from previous port. Further updates should be sent 96 h, 72 h, 48 h, 24 h and 4 h prior to arrival

Anchorage: No suitable anchorage available. Vessel's wait in a 10 nautical mile radius holding area centred on pos 7° 36.0' S; 12° 14.0' E

Pilotage: Compulsory except when arriving at or leaving the waiting area. Mooring Master boards in pos 7° 45' S; 12° 09' E

Radio Frequency: Listening on VHF Channel 16 and working on VHF Channel 8

Accommodation:

Name	Remarks
Greater Plutonio Terminal	See [1] below

[1]*Greater Plutonio Terminal:* Consists of 'FPSO Greater Plutonio' with storage cap of 1 770 000 bbls and a CALM/SBM. Mooring operations are usually conducted during daylight hours only

Airport: Luanda International Airport

Lloyd's Agent: Core Laboratories Lda (Saybolt Division), Rua Comandante N'Zaji 49, Alvalade, Luanda, Angola, *Tel:* +244 222 321933, *Fax:* +244 222 321933, *Email:* lloyds.sayao@corelab.com, *Website:* www.corelab.com

LOBITO

Lat 12° 21' S; Long 13° 32' E.

Admiralty Chart: 1215	**Admiralty Pilot:** 2
Time Zone: GMT +1 h	**UNCTAD Locode:** AO LOB

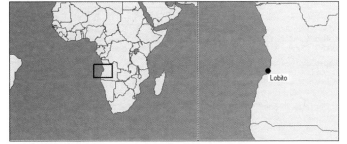

Principal Facilities:

P		Y	G	C	R		B	D	T	A	

Authority: Empresa Portuaria do Lobito E.P., Avenida da Independencia, P O Box 16, Lobito, Angola, *Tel:* +244 272 222710/8, *Fax:* +244 272 222719, *Website:* www.eplobito.com

Officials: General Manager: Dr Jose Carlos Gomes.

Port Security: ISPS compliant. Contact: Vicente Francisco Albano, Fax: +244 272 222718

Approach: Harbour is formed by natural sandspit 4.8 km long and about 731.5 m wide. No inner or outer bars and no currents in harbour area. Depth of approach over 18.2 m. Vessels may enter or leave any time of year, day or night but are not normally berthed during hours of darkness

Pilotage: Compulsory for berthing or sailing, but not compulsory when pilot requested outside harbour entrance. Any manoeuvre inside harbour waters must be with permission of port captain and with pilot aboard

Radio Frequency: VHF Channel 16

Weather: Fair weather conditions with moderate winds

Tides: Rise and fall of tide 1.0-1.83 m

Traffic: 2007, 707 110 t of cargo handled

Maximum Vessel Dimensions: 10.5 m draft

Working Hours: Mon to Fri 0730-1200, 1330-1900; (overtime 2000-0000). Sat 0730-1200 (overtime 1330-1900, 2000-0000). Sun and holidays; all work at overtime rates

Accommodation:

Name	Depth (m)	Remarks
Lobito		See [1] below
Pier No.1	8	
Pier No.2	8.5	
Pier No.3	9	
Pier No.4	9.5	
Pier No.5	10.8	
Pier No.6	10.5	
Pier No.7	10	
Pier No.8	8.5	

[1]*Lobito:* Passenger vessels have preference in berthing. Two concrete quays provide 6 or 8 berths. Containers handled at the general cargo berths. Container yard covering 6000 m2
The terminals for bulk discharge of liquids include a terminal at the end of the South Quay for discharge of wine and two terminals situated on the final section of the South Quay for discharge of petrol and oils for the Sonangol tanks existing within the port areas

Storage: Storage space for up to 64 refrigerated containers. There are seventeen warehouses at the port, the largest of which is 3654 m2. Extensive open storage for containers and minerals in bulk. Cereal silos with a storage cap of 25 000 t

Mechanical Handling Equipment:

Location	Type	Capacity (t)	Qty	Remarks
Lobito	Electric Cranes	3-22	8	At piers 5 & 6
Lobito	Electric Cranes	3-5	8	At piers 1 & 2
Lobito	Electric Cranes	3-22	3	At piers 7 & 8
Lobito	Electric Cranes	3-10	7	At piers 3 & 4

Bunkering: Located at the end of the South Dock, there are two terminals for the reception of bunkers destined for the Sonangol facilities. Fuel and diesel oil available Bominflot, Bominflot Ltd, 5-7 Ravensbourne Road, Bromley, Kent BR1 1HN, United Kingdom, *Tel:* +44 20 8315 5400, *Fax:* +44 20 8315 5429, *Email:* mail@bominflot.co.uk, *Website:* www.bominflot.net

Towage: Two tugs available of 5000 hp and 2800 hp for mooring/unmooring of vessels

Repair & Maintenance: Slipways for vessels up to 1200 t owned by Sorefame who also have a floating drydock with a cap of 2000 t

Shipping Agents: Afritramp, P O Box 143 & 169, Avenida de Mocambique, Lobito 41-47, Angola, *Tel:* +244 272 225102, *Fax:* +244 272 223136, *Email:* sdvamilob@hotmail.com, *Website:* www.afritrampoilfield.com
Jose F Aguiar & Cia Ltda, Rua 15 De Agosto, P O Box Box 31, Lobito, Angola, *Tel:* +244 272 222729, *Fax:* +244 272 223699
Gulf Agency Transportes Agenciamentos e Servicos Lda, Largo Patrice Lumumba 26, 1st Floor, Room 12, Zona Comercial, Lobito, Angola, *Tel:* +244 272 226434, *Fax:* +244 272 226433, *Email:* ops.lobito@gacworld.com, *Website:* www.gacworld.com
A.P. Moller-Maersk Group, Maersk (Angola) Lda, Avenida da Independencia 47, Restinga, Lobito, Angola, *Tel:* +244 272 221962, *Fax:* +244 272 221982, *Email:* lb2mla@maersk.com, *Website:* www.maerskline.com
Orey Comercio e Navegacao S.A., Largo de Restauracao 4, 3rd Floor, Edificio de Alfandega, Lobito, Angola, *Tel:* +244 272 224686, *Fax:* +244 272 224687, *Email:* orey.lobito@ebonet.net, *Website:* www.orey-angola.com
SDV-AMI Angola Lda, Av. de Mocambique 41-47, P O Box 143 & 169, Lobito, Angola, *Tel:* +244 272 223137, *Fax:* +244 272 223136, *Email:* amilobito@ebonet.net

Medical Facilities: Available

Airport: Catumbela, 13 km

Railway: Benguela Railway. The port is connected to the National Rail Network

Lloyd's Agent: Core Laboratories Lda (Saybolt Division), Rua Comandante N'Zaji 49, Alvalade, Luanda, Angola, *Tel:* +244 222 321933, *Fax:* +244 222 321933, *Email:* lloyds.sayao@corelab.com, *Website:* www.corelab.com

LOMBO TERMINAL

Lat 6° 50' S; Long 12° 21' E.

Admiralty Chart: 3206/638/604	**Admiralty Pilot:** 2
Time Zone: GMT +1 h	**UNCTAD Locode:** AO

This terminal is no longer operational

Key to Principal Facilities:—				
A=Airport	**C**=Containers	**G**=General Cargo	**P**=Petroleum	**R**=Ro/Ro	**Y**=Dry Bulk
B=Bunkers	**D**=Dry Dock	**L**=Cruise	**Q**=Other Liquid Bulk	**T**=Towage (where available from port)	

LUANDA

Lat 8° 48' S; Long 13° 13' E.

Admiralty Chart: 3448	**Admiralty Pilot:** 2	
Time Zone: GMT +1 h	**UNCTAD Locode:** AO LAD	

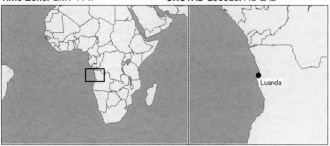

Principal Facilities:

P		Y G C R		B D		A

Authority: Empresa Portuaria de Luanda, Avenue Largo 4 de Fevereiro, P O Box 1229, Luanda, Angola, *Tel:* +244 222 311178, *Fax:* +244 222 311178, *Email:* portoluanda@geral.co.ao

Port Security: ISPS compliant. Contact: Paulo Geronimo Antonio, Tel: +244 222 310355, Fax: +244 222 311950

Approach: Depth at entrance about 27.5 m. No operational navigation marks

Anchorage: Vessels can obtain safe anchorage in Luanda Bay; good holding ground, sand and mud bottom. Several unmarked wrecks and unlit derelict vessels in Luanda Anchorage area

Pilotage: Compulsory only from the entrance of the bay to berth

Traffic: 2007, 5 252 000 t of cargo handled

Working Hours: 0730-1200, 1300-1730. Overtime available

Accommodation:

Name	Length (m)	Depth (m)	Remarks
Luanda			
General Cargo Terminal No.1	460	10.5	Three berths handling general cargo
General Cargo Terminal No.2	365	10.5	Two berths handling general cargo, containers & oil derivatives
Container Terminal No.1			Mainly containers handled but also wine in bulk
Container Terminal No.2	448	10.5	Two berths handling containers
Bulk Terminal	350	10.5	See [1] below
Passenger Terminal	350	3.5–5.5	Four berths handling passengers
Petroleum Support Base	408	12.5	Providing support services to the oil & gas industry

[1]*Bulk Terminal:* Two berths handling bulk cargo, general cargo & containers

Storage:

Location	Covered (m²)	Sheds / Warehouses
General Cargo Terminal No.1	10539	5
General Cargo Terminal No.2	14184	4
Container Terminal No.1	4890	1
Container Terminal No.2	1360	1
Bulk Terminal	13116	5
Passenger Terminal	6520	2

Mechanical Handling Equipment: Only available for discharge of bagged or palletised cargo and loading of empty containers at six berths. Only private hire mobile cranes up to 70 t cap

Location	Type	Capacity (t)	Remarks
Luanda	Mobile Cranes	70	private hire

Bunkering: Sociedade Nacional de Combustiveis de Angola EP (SONANGOL), 8-16 Av. 1 Congresse do MPLA, P O Box 1316, Luanda, Angola, *Tel:* +244 2 33 4143, *Fax:* +244 2 391782, *Website:* www.sonangol.co.ao
The Shell Co. of West Africa Ltd, Avenida 4 de Fevereiro 42, 3 E 5 Andar, Luanda, Angola, *Tel:* +244 2 33 1844, *Fax:* +244 2 33 1848
Bominflot, Bominflot Ltd, 5-7 Ravensbourne Road, Bromley, Kent BR1 1HN, United Kingdom, *Tel:* +44 20 8315 5400, *Fax:* +44 20 8315 5429, *Email:* mail@bominflot.co.uk, *Website:* www.bominflot.net – *Grades:* IFO; MGO
The Shell Co. of West Africa Ltd, Avenida 4 de Fevereiro 42, 3 E 5 Andar, Luanda, Angola, *Tel:* +244 2 33 1844, *Fax:* +244 2 33 1848

Repair & Maintenance: Two small slips available for fishing and small coastal vessels. One floating dock for emergency repairs up to approx 6000 dwt

Shipping Agents: Afritramp, Estrada de Cacuaco 288, Luanda, Angola, *Tel:* +244 222 841549, *Fax:* +244 222 840240, *Email:* afritramp@ao.dti.bollore.com, *Website:* www.afritramp.eu
Jose F Aguiar & Cia Ltda, Av 4 de Fevereiro 18, andar 1, P O Box 761, Luanda, Angola, *Tel:* +244 222 332791, *Fax:* +244 222 332788, *Email:* jfaguiar@ebonet.net
Blue Funnel Angola Ltd., P O Box 1214, Av 4 de Fevereiro, Luanda, Angola, *Tel:* +244

222 310301, *Fax:* +244 222 310879, *Email:* jack.langrishe@hull-blyth.angola, *Website:* www.hull-blyth.com
Casa Maritima-Agentes de Navegacao S.A., Largo 4 de Fevereiro 3, Luanda, Angola, *Tel:* +244 222 310290, *Fax:* +244 222 311159, *Email:* casamaritima@ebonet.net
Gulf Agency Transportes Agenciamentos e Servicos Lda, P O Box 5713, Luanda, Angola, *Tel:* +244 222 441244, *Fax:* +244 222 443993, *Email:* angola@gacworld.com, *Website:* www.gacworld.com
Hull Blyth Group, African Steamship Angola Lda, P O Box 1214, Avenida 4 de Fevereiro 23/24, Luanda, Angola, *Tel:* +244 222 311415, *Fax:* +244 222 310879, *Email:* informacoes@hullblyth-angola.com, *Website:* www.hull-blyth.com
A.P. Moller-Maersk Group, Maersk (Angola) Lda, Rua Major Kanhangulo No.290 R/C, Largo do Ambiente, Luanda, Angola, *Tel:* +244 222 239650, *Email:* angloggen@maersk.com, *Website:* www.maerskline.com
Orey Comercio e Navegacao S.A., Largo 4 de Fevereiro 3, Andar 3, P O Box 583, Luanda, Angola, *Tel:* +244 222 310290, *Fax:* +244 222 310882, *Email:* operations@orey.co.ao, *Website:* www.orey-angola.com
Panalpina Transportes Mundiais, Navegacao & Transitos S.A.R.L., P O Box 3682, Luanda, Angola, *Tel:* +244 222 691000, *Fax:* +244 222 310034, *Email:* info.wasa@panalpina.com, *Website:* www.panalpina.com
Pinto Basto Servicos Maritimos Lda, Edificio Rainha Ginga, Rua Rainha Ginga 187, Luanda, Angola, *Tel:* +244 222 331285, *Fax:* +244 222 338868, *Email:* info@pintobasto-angola.com, *Website:* www.pintobasto.com/angola
SDV-AMI Angola Lda, Estrada de Cacuaco 288, P O Box 2163, Luanda, Angola, *Tel:* +244 222 841266, *Fax:* +244 222 840535, *Email:* carla.leitao@ao.dti.bollore.com
SMI Angola Transportes Maritimos Lda, Largo Bressane, Leite Nr 12, Luanda, Angola, *Tel:* +244 222 392510, *Fax:* +244 222 392510, *Email:* asl@ebonet.net

Surveyors: Bureau Veritas, Rua Joao de Barros No.56, Bairro das Ingombotas, Luanda, Angola, *Tel:* +244 222 311568, *Fax:* +244 222 311009, *Website:* www.bureauveritas.com
Core Laboratories Lda (Saybolt Division), Rua Comandante N'Zaji 49, Alvalade, Luanda, Angola, *Tel:* +244 222 321933, *Fax:* +244 222 321933, *Email:* lloyds.sayao@corelab.com, *Website:* www.corelab.com
Det Norske Veritas A/S, Edificio Monumental, Rua Major Kanhangulo 290, 3 Andar, Luanda, Angola, *Tel:* +244 222 391631, *Fax:* +244 222 392373, *Website:* www.dnv.com
Pinto Basto Servicos Maritimos Lda, Edificio Rainha Ginga, Rua Rainha Ginga 187, Luanda, Angola, *Tel:* +244 222 331285, *Fax:* +244 222 338868, *Email:* info@pintobasto-angola.com, *Website:* www.pintobasto.com/angola
Societe Generale de Surveillance (SGS), SGS Angola Ltd, Rua da Liberdade No.94, Vila Alice, Luanda, Angola, *Tel:* +244 222 264070, *Fax:* +244 222 261200, *Website:* www.sgs.com

Airport: International 4 de Fevereiro, 4 km

Development: Sogester, a joint venture company of A.P. Moller-Maersk affiliate APM Terminals (51%), and Gestao de Fundos (49%), has signed a 20-year concession agreement to operate the container terminal

Lloyd's Agent: Core Laboratories Lda (Saybolt Division), Rua Comandante N'Zaji 49, Alvalade, Luanda, Angola, *Tel:* +244 222 321933, *Fax:* +244 222 321933, *Email:* lloyds.sayao@corelab.com, *Website:* www.corelab.com

MALONGO TERMINAL

Lat 5° 26' S; Long 12° 5' E.

Admiralty Chart: 3447/3285/3206	**Admiralty Pilot:** 2	
Time Zone: GMT +1 h	**UNCTAD Locode:** AO MAL	

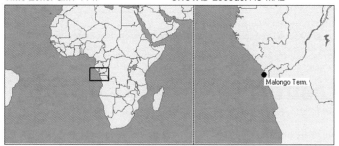

Principal Facilities:

P Q							T A

Authority: Cabinda Gulf Oil Co. Ltd, P O Box 40, Cabinda, Angola, *Tel:* +244 31 391391, *Fax:* +244 31 391391

Approach: Numerous oil structures, drilling rigs and subsea pipelines exist within the Cabinda offshore waters. Masters of vessels calling at Malongo Terminal are advised to navigate with extreme caution and not to enter restricted areas unless directed to do so by berthing pilots

Anchorage: In pos 5° 28' 05" S, 11° 59' 00" E for crude and LPG vessels. Depth of water approx 38 m
In pos 5° 27' 30" S, 12° 09' 00" E for freighters. Depth of water approx 10.5 m

Pilotage: Compulsory. Day or night berthings at SPM berths but daylight only for ship to ship transfers. Unberthing no restrictions

Radio Frequency: Vessels bound for Malongo Terminal are required to send ETA advice at 72, 48 and 24 h intervals (LPG tankers additionally 7 day), through their agent in Cabinda who will advise Cabinda Gulf Oil Co Ltd. Additionally ETA's may be sent directly to Cabinda Gulf Oil Co Ltd via telex: 3160 or 3498 MALONGO AN; via Berge Troll satellite 871/581-1312131 LAGO
For short range communications Cabinda Gulf Oil Co Ltd monitor VHF/SSB channels 24 h/day; call sign: MALONGO TERMINAL
SSB: Monitored 2182 Kcs. Working 2738/2638/2056/2049 Kcs
VHF: Monitored channels 16/12. Working 1-78

Weather: During rainy season (Oct to May) heavy squalls with winds gusting to 50 knots may be experienced
Currents: Generally the current sets towards the north but is seasonally influenced by floodwater from the R Congo. Heavy swells from a south-westerly direction occur during the dry season (June to Sept)

Principal Imports and Exports: Exports: Buthane, Crude oil, LPG.

Accommodation:

Name	Depth (m)	Draught (m)	Remarks
Malongo Terminal			See [1] below
Malongo Export SBM No.1	22.9	16.8	See [2] below
Malongo Export SBM No.2	32		See [3] below
Private Wharves			See [4] below

[1]*Malongo Terminal:* Malongo LPG ship/ship transfer in pos 5° 24' 54" S, 12° 01' 18" E: depth alongside Berge Troll approx 30.5 m, max size of vessel 50 000 dwt. Freighters discharge into lighters at freighter anchorage
[2]*Malongo Export SBM No.1:* Max dwt 140 000. Vessel must maintain 30% dwt at all times. Loading rate of 30 000 bbls/h
[3]*Malongo Export SBM No.2:* Max dwt 325 000, max loa 350.75 m. Vessel must maintain 30% dwt at all times. Loading rate of 40 000 bbls/h
[4]*Private Wharves:* An 'L' shaped jetty 342 m in length used for small coasters and supply boats although subject to heavy swells. Containers transhipped from freighters offloaded here

Mechanical Handling Equipment:

Location	Type	Capacity (t)
Malongo Terminal	Mult-purp. Cranes	15

Towage: Two tugs available for berthing of 22-50 t bollard pull
Medical Facilities: Limited and available in an emergency only
Airport: Cabinda, 35km.
Lloyd's Agent: Core Laboratories Lda (Saybolt Division), Rua Comandante N'Zaji 49, Alvalade, Luanda, Angola, *Tel:* +244 222 321933, *Fax:* +244 222 321933, *Email:* lloyds.sayao@corelab.com, *Website:* www.corelab.com

MOCAMEDES

alternate name, see Namibe

NAMIBE

Lat 15° 9' S; Long 12° 9' E.

Admiralty Chart: 1197
Time Zone: GMT +1 h
Admiralty Pilot: 2
UNCTAD Locode: AO MSZ

Principal Facilities:

P		Y	G	C	R		B		T	A	

Authority: Empresa Portuaria do Namibe E.P., P O Box 16, Namibe, Angola, *Tel:* +244 264 266921, *Fax:* +244 264 266050, *Email:* porto_09namibe@hotmail.com, *Website:* www.portodonamibe.com
Port Security: ISPS compliant
Approach: A natural bay easy of access, particularly for northern calls; for southern calls attention must be paid to Banco Amelia sandbank, which is not marked by lights. Min depth in approach 10.668 m. No inner or outer bars. Vessels may enter or leave bay at any time of year, day or night
Anchorage: Anchorage is indicated by harbour master, passenger vessels having preference
Pilotage: Compulsory and available 24 h. Mooring can only take place until 1900 LT in summer and 1800 LT in winter. Pilot boards in the bay entrance
Radio Frequency: VHF Channels 8, 12, 14 and 16
Weather: Fair weather conditions with moderate winds
Tides: Low tide 0.8 m, high tide 1.3 m
Traffic: 2007, 1 212 000 t of cargo handled
Working Hours: Mon to Fri: 0730-1200, 1400-1730; overtime: 1800-2100. Saturdays: 0730-1130; overtime: 1400-1730. Sundays and holidays: no work

Accommodation:

Name	Length (m)	Remarks
Namibe		
Commercial Quay	870	See [1] below

Name	Length (m)	Remarks
Porto Saco		See [2] below
Tanker Berth		See [3] below

[1]*Commercial Quay:* The quay is divided into three zones, the largest of which is 480 m long in depth of 10.5 m. There is a stacker for containers with cap of 40 t
[2]*Porto Saco:* Porto Saco is the iron-ore loading terminal about 10 km from the general cargo port. Phase I of this project provides the following facilities: loading cap of 3500 t/h; loading installation, Krupp Ardelt conveyor; accommodation for vessels from 150 000 up to 200 000 dwt; max draft at low tide 19 m; length of berthing area 325 m; width of the quay 18 m; height of quay above sea level 5.0 m; max height of loading boom above sea level 31.0 m; height of loading boom above level of quay 26.5 m; max projection of loading boom over berth 29.5 m
The storage area will hold approx 1 200 000 t of ore. Loading undertaken by two heavy cranes transferring the ore from dumps to a conveyor belt. Automatic weighing of ore by machinery and extraction of samples
At Porto Saco the agents of vessels which carry inflammable cargoes must give notice to the Port Captain at Namibe at least two days prior to arrival, indicating quality and quantity of the inflammable products on board. Such notice should always be given in writing and a receipt for delivery of this notice is to be obtained. Tankers are discharged alongside the ore loading terminal
[3]*Tanker Berth:* One berth operated by the Texaco Oil Co., length 480 m and d of 18.78 m; night berthing possible; water and bunkers available

Storage: There are two warehouses with area approx 3650 m2 each, loading and discharging. Two cold stores, one private and the other state-owned

Mechanical Handling Equipment:

Location	Type	Capacity (t)	Qty
Commercial Quay	Mult-purp. Cranes	5–15	3

Cargo Worked: General cargo 8-10 t/gang/h, bagged cargo 15-20 t/gang/h
Bunkering: Fuel oil and blended oils from ChevronTexaco terminal in Porto Saco available at dockside by means of a pipeline. Bunkers and fresh water can be taken during loading operations with delay
Towage: One tug available
Repair & Maintenance: Very limited
Shipping Agents: A.P. Moller-Maersk Group, Maersk (Angola) Lda, Rua Pedro Benge 10, Namibe, Angola, *Tel:* +244 264 250026, *Fax:* +244 264 262367, *Email:* 8xmmlamng@maersk.com, *Website:* www.maerskline.com
Orey Comercio e Navegacao S.A., Largo Espirito Santo 3, Namibe, Angola, *Tel:* +244 264 261680, *Fax:* +244 264 250021, *Email:* orey.namibe@ebonet.net, *Website:* www.orey-angola.com
Medical Facilities: Limited
Airport: Namibe Airport
Lloyd's Agent: Core Laboratories Lda (Saybolt Division), Rua Comandante N'Zaji 49, Alvalade, Luanda, Angola, *Tel:* +244 222 321933, *Fax:* +244 222 321933, *Email:* lloyds.sayao@corelab.com, *Website:* www.corelab.com

PALANCA TERMINAL

Lat 6° 57' S; Long 12° 24' E.

Admiralty Chart: 3206
Time Zone: GMT +1 h
Admiralty Pilot: 2
UNCTAD Locode: AO PAT

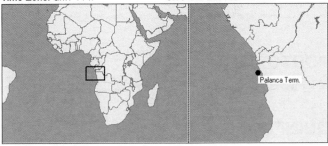

Principal Facilities:

P								T	

Authority: SONANGOL P&P, P O Box 2997, Luanda, Angola, *Tel:* +244 2 633261, *Fax:* +244 2 353037
Port Security: ISPS compliant
Approach: Navigation is prohibited within 1 mile of the production platforms and the SBM. The prohibited area is marked by white light-beacons 19 m in height
Anchorage: Anchorage pos at 6° 55.3' S; 12° 22.5' E in depth of 45 m
Pilotage: Compulsory. Vessels should send ETA 72, 48 and 24 h in advance. Pilot boards approx 2 nautical miles NW of the SBM (6° 57.0' S; 12° 23.9' E)
Radio Frequency: VHF Channels 16 and 67
Principal Imports and Exports: Exports: Crude oil.
Working Hours: There will be no mooring after 1500. If tankers arrival is after this the pilot will board on following day at 0600

Accommodation:

Name	Remarks
Palanca Terminal	See [1] below

[1]*Palanca Terminal:* Two berths at Palanca:
The first is bow to bow with the barge. Loading by two 16'' hoses for tankers up to 180 000 dwt. Rate of loading is 8000 m3/h

---

Key to Principal Facilities:—				
A=Airport	**C**=Containers	**G**=General Cargo	**P**=Petroleum	**R**=Ro/Ro	**Y**=Dry Bulk
B=Bunkers	**D**=Dry Dock	**L**=Cruise	**Q**=Other Liquid Bulk	**T**=Towage (where available from port)	

The second is the SBM buoy. Loading by two 16'' hoses for tankers up to 300 000 dwt. Rate of loading is 6000 m3/h

Towage: Mooring tug assists with berthing

Medical Facilities: Urgent health evacuations to Luanda are carried out at the expense of the vessel

Lloyd's Agent: Core Laboratories Lda (Saybolt Division), Rua Comandante N'Zaji 49, Alvalade, Luanda, Angola, *Tel:* +244 222 321933, *Fax:* +244 222 321933, *Email:* lloyds.sayao@corelab.com, *Website:* www.corelab.com

PORTO AMBOIM

Lat 10° 43' S; Long 13° 45' E.

Admiralty Chart: 1215	**Admiralty Pilot:** 2
Time Zone: GMT +1 h	**UNCTAD Locode:** AO PBN

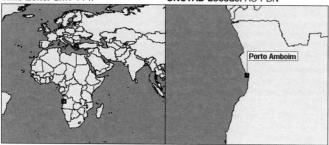

Principal Facilities:

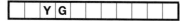

| | Y | G | | | | | | | |

Authority: Companhia do Caminho de Ferro do Amboim, Port Office, Porto Amboim, Angola

Tides: Range 1.3 m

Principal Imports and Exports: Exports: Coffee, Copra, Cotton Wool, Dried Fish, Fish Meal, Fish Oil, Palm Oil, Sisal.

Working Hours: Mon-Fri, 0700-1200, 1400-1700 hrs, Sat, 0700-1200 hrs

Accommodation:

Name	Length (m)	Depth (m)	Apron Width (m)	Remarks
Porto Amboim Jetty	123	2	13	See [1] below

[1]*Jetty:* Vessels anchor approx 350 m from the jetty and work cargo by lighters

Mechanical Handling Equipment:

Location	Type	Capacity (t)	Qty
Porto Amboim	Quay Cranes	5–50	7

Towage: Not available

Medical Facilities: Small hospital

Lloyd's Agent: Core Laboratories Lda (Saybolt Division), Rua Comandante N'Zaji 49, Alvalade, Luanda, Angola, *Tel:* +244 222 321933, *Fax:* +244 222 321933, *Email:* lloyds.sayao@corelab.com, *Website:* www.corelab.com

PORTO SACO

harbour area, see under Namibe

QUINFUQUENA TERMINAL

alternate name, see Essungo Terminal

SOYO

Lat 6° 7' S; Long 12° 16' E.

Admiralty Chart: 3206/658	**Admiralty Pilot:** 2
Time Zone: GMT +1 h	**UNCTAD Locode:** AO SZA

Principal Facilities:

| | P | | G | | | B | T | A | |

Authority: Fina Petroleos de Angola, Quinfuquina Terminal, Marine Division, P O Box 1320, Luanda, Angola

Approach: On the approach to the mouth of the Zaire River, Kwanda Base buoyed channel is on the starboard side of the river mouth, the entrance to the buoyed channel whose max depth is 5.2 m being marked by two entrance buoys in pos 6° 04' 48" S, 12° 20' 08" E. Movement in the channel only during daylight hours

Pilotage: Not available. Assistance given by shore base supply vessel personnel

Tides: Tidal range 1.5 m

Accommodation:

Name	Remarks
Soyo	See [1] below

[1]*Soyo:* Two concrete quays of 200 m each. One metallic quay of 100 m long. Depth alongside 6.0 m at HT. Mainly used by supply vessels, small freighters and fishing vessels

Large freighters anchor on the starboard side of the Zaire River in pos 6° 04' 18" S, 12° 23' 24" E and lighter to supply vessels

Bunkering: Marine diesel available

Towage: Tug/supply vessels available

Medical Facilities: Clinic in base

Airport: Soyo Airport, 5 km

Lloyd's Agent: Core Laboratories Lda (Saybolt Division), Rua Comandante N'Zaji 49, Alvalade, Luanda, Angola, *Tel:* +244 222 321933, *Fax:* +244 222 321933, *Email:* lloyds.sayao@corelab.com, *Website:* www.corelab.com

TAKULA TERMINAL

Lat 5° 13' S; Long 11° 49' E.

Admiralty Chart: 3206/3285	**Admiralty Pilot:** 2
Time Zone: GMT +1 h	**UNCTAD Locode:** AO TAK

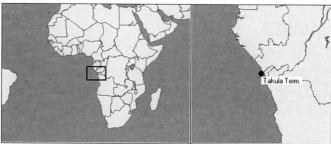

Principal Facilities:

| | P | | | | | | | T | A | |

Authority: Cabinda Gulf Oil Co. Ltd, P O Box 40, Cabinda, Angola, *Tel:* +244 31 391391, *Fax:* +244 31 391391

Approach: Numerous oil structures, drilling rigs and subsea pipelines exist within the Cabinda offshore waters. Masters of vessels calling at Takula Terminal are advised to navigate with extreme caution and not to enter restricted areas unless directed to do so by berthing pilots

Anchorage: N of SBM area in pos 5° 12' 00" S, 11° 47' 30" E. Depth of water approx 70 m

Pilotage: Compulsory. Pilot boards in pos 5° 11.9' S; 11° 47.6' E (1.5 nautical miles NW of the SPM). Berthing and unberthing is possible on a 24 h basis

Weather: During rainy season (Oct to May) heavy squalls with winds gusting to 50 knots may be experienced

Principal Imports and Exports: Exports: Crude oil.

Accommodation:

Name	Remarks
Takula Export SBM No.2	See [1] below

[1]*Takula Export SBM No.2:* Depth at buoy 71.9 m, max vessel 300 000 dwt. Vessels must maintain 30% dwt at all times

Normally all Takula crude production is exported through Malongo Terminal

Cargo Worked: Loading rate between 10-15 000 bbls/h

Towage: Two tugs available for berthing of 22-50 t bollard pull

Medical Facilities: Limited and available in an emergency only

Airport: Cabinda, 35 km

Lloyd's Agent: Core Laboratories Lda (Saybolt Division), Rua Comandante N'Zaji 49, Alvalade, Luanda, Angola, *Tel:* +244 222 321933, *Fax:* +244 222 321933, *Email:* lloyds.sayao@corelab.com, *Website:* www.corelab.com

ANGUILLA

El Dorado Shipping Mall, Water Swamp Road, ANGUILLA
Tel: +1 264 497 1646   Fax: +1 264 497 8050
Email: info@gopetersagency.com
Web: www.gopetersagency.com

ANTIGUA & BARBUDA

ST. JOHN'S

Lat 17° 7' N; Long 61° 50' W.

Admiralty Chart: 2065	**Admiralty Pilot:** 71
Time Zone: GMT -4 h	**UNCTAD Locode:** AG ANU

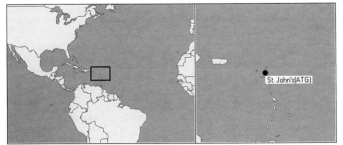

Principal Facilities:

P		Y	G	C	R	L	B		T	A

Authority: Antigua & Barbuda Port Authority, P O Box 1052, St. John's, Antigua & Barbuda, *Tel:* +1268 484 3400, *Fax:* +1268 462 2510, *Email:* abpa@port.gov.ag, *Website:* www.port.gov.ag

Officials: Port Manager: Agatha Dublin, *Email:* dublina@candw.ag. Operations Manager: Hugh Mack.

Port Security: ISPS compliant

Approach: Approach channel 91 m wide in depth of 10.67 m. Turning circle 386 m in diameter

Anchorage: Approx 0.7 nautical miles NNW of Pillar Rock Light in depths of 12.19-13.72 m. Depths of up to 16.46 m two miles N of Sandy Island

Pilotage: Compulsory. Vessels should send ETA 48 h in advance. Pilots board at the channel entrance if proceeding to Deepwater Harbour or 2 miles off Sandy Island if going to Sea Island Berth

Radio Frequency: VHF Channels 16, 14, 13, 9 and 6

Weather: Hurricane season, July to September

Tides: Rise of tide only 0.406 m

Traffic: 2005, 356 752 t of cargo handled

Principal Imports and Exports: Imports: Foodstuffs, Fuel, Machinery & spares, Raw materials, Vehicles. Exports: Clothing, Galvanised sheeting, Paint, Seafood.

Working Hours: Mon-Fri 0700-1200, 1300-1600. Sat 0700-1100. Overtime by arrangement

Accommodation:

Name	Length (m)	Depth (m)	Remarks
St. John's			See [1] below
Deep Water Harbour Jetty	366	10.67	See [2] below
Heritage Quay	152	9.14	Cruise vessels. Two dolphins 61 m apart
Nevis Pier	136	9.14	Cruise vessels. Two dolphins 45.7 m from dock

[1]*St. John's:* Container terminal of 3 ha with storage for 410 TEU's. Two container handlers of 30 & 40 t cap. Seven electrical outlets for reefer containers. Ro/ro facilities available at Deep Water Harbour Jetty and High Point Landing
Bulk facilities: Available at Crabbs Peninsula, Bulk Cement Terminal
Tanker facilities: Two oil berths at Sea Island, length 228.6 m, 13.71 m draft. Night berthing possible. Water and bunkers available
[2]*Deep Water Harbour Jetty:* Consists of three berths handling all imported cargo. Ro/ro facilities available

Storage: Transit shed of 121 m x 30 m at Deep Water Harbour

Mechanical Handling Equipment:

Location	Type	Capacity (t)	Qty
St. John's	Mobile Cranes	140	1

Bunkering: The West Indies Oil Co. Ltd, Friars Hill Road, P O Box 230, St. John's, Antigua & Barbuda, *Tel:* +1268 4620 140, *Fax:* +1268 4620 543, *Email:* info@westindiesoil.com
Chevron Marine Products LLC, Global Marine Products LLC, 1500 Louisiana, 4th Floor, Houston, TX 77002, United States of America, *Tel:* +1 832 8542 988, *Fax:* +1 832 8544 868, *Email:* gulfcbm@chevron.com, *Website:* www.chevron.com – *Grades:* GO – *Delivery Mode:* tank truck

Waste Reception Facilities: Garbage disposal only

Towage: Two 1600 hp tugs are operated by the Port Authority. Private tugs also available

Repair & Maintenance: Antigua Slipway, P O Box 576, English Harbour, St. John's, Antigua & Barbuda, *Tel:* +1268 460 1056, *Fax:* +1268 460 1566, *Email:* antslipway@candw.ag, *Website:* www.antiguaslipway.com For yachts only
Jolly Harbour Marina Antigua, P O Box 1793, St. John's, Antigua & Barbuda, *Tel:* +1268 462 6041, *Fax:* +1268 462 7703, *Email:* jollymarina@candw.ag, *Website:* www.jollyharbourantigua.com For yachts only

Ship Chandlers: Antigua Slipway, P O Box 576, English Harbour, St. John's, Antigua & Barbuda, *Tel:* +1268 460 1056, *Fax:* +1268 460 1566, *Email:* antslipway@candw.ag, *Website:* www.antiguaslipway.com
Geo. W. Bennett Bryson & Co Ltd, P O Box 162, St. John's, Antigua & Barbuda, *Tel:* +1268 480 1200, *Fax:* +1268 462 0170, *Email:* office@brysonsinsurance.com, *Website:* www.brysonsantigua.com

Shipping Agents: Antigua Maritime Agencies Ltd, Milburn House, Old Parham Road, P O Box W1310, St. John's, Antigua & Barbuda, *Tel:* +1268 562 2934, *Fax:* +1268 562 2935, *Email:* aoffice@tropical.com, *Website:* www.tropical.com
Geo. W. Bennett Bryson & Co Ltd, P O Box 162, St. John's, Antigua & Barbuda, *Tel:* +1268 480 1200, *Fax:* +1268 462 0170, *Email:* office@brysonsinsurance.com, *Website:* www.brysonsantigua.com

---

Key to Principal Facilities:—				
A=Airport	**C**=Containers	**G**=General Cargo	**P**=Petroleum	**R**=Ro/Ro	**Y**=Dry Bulk
B=Bunkers	**D**=Dry Dock	**L**=Cruise	**Q**=Other Liquid Bulk	**T**=Towage (where available from port)

Caribbean Forwarders Ltd, Friars Hill Road, P O Box 530, St. John's, Antigua & Barbuda, *Tel:* +1268 462 2955, *Fax:* +1268 480 1120, *Email:* heatherl@candw.ag

CaribSeas Ltd., P O Box 1267, St. John's, Antigua & Barbuda, *Tel:* +1268 462 2744, *Fax:* +1268 462 4864, *Email:* caribsea@candw.ag

Consolidated Maritime Services, P O Box 2478, St. John's, Antigua & Barbuda, *Tel:* +1268 462 1224, *Fax:* +1268 462 1227, *Email:* caribms@candw.ag

Vernon G Edwards, Thames Street, P O Box 82, St. John's, Antigua & Barbuda, *Tel:* +1268 462 2034, *Fax:* +1268 462 2035, *Email:* vedwards@candw.ag

Francis Trading Agency Ltd, P O Box 194, St. John's, Antigua & Barbuda, *Tel:* +1268 462 4555, *Fax:* +1268 462 0849, *Email:* fta@candw.ag

Jasco Agencies Ltd, Rolgen House, Upper St. John's Street, P O Box 2750, St. John's, Antigua & Barbuda, *Tel:* +1268 462 9521, *Fax:* +1268 462 9524, *Email:* jasco@candw.ag, *Website:* www.jasco-ag.net

Stevedoring Companies: Geo. W. Bennett Bryson & Co Ltd, P O Box 162, St. John's, Antigua & Barbuda, *Tel:* +1268 480 1200, *Fax:* +1268 462 0170, *Email:* office@brysonsinsurance.com, *Website:* www.brysonsantigua.com

Vernon G Edwards, Thames Street, P O Box 82, St. John's, Antigua & Barbuda, *Tel:* +1268 462 2034, *Fax:* +1268 462 2035, *Email:* vedwards@candw.ag

Surveyors: Small Ship Consultants Ltd, P O Box 3173, St. John's, Antigua & Barbuda, *Tel:* +1268 460 3414, *Fax:* +1268 460 3414, *Email:* ssc@marinesurveyor.com, *Website:* www.marinesurveyor.com/ssc

Medical Facilities: Holberton Hospital, 7.9 km. Adelin Medical Facility, 1.3 km

Airport: V.C. Bird International, 6 km

Lloyd's Agent: Geo. W. Bennett Bryson & Co Ltd, P O Box 162, St. John's, Antigua & Barbuda, *Tel:* +1268 480 1200, *Fax:* +1268 462 0170, *Email:* office@brysonsinsurance.com, *Website:* www.brysonsantigua.com

ARGENTINA

ALMIRANTE STORNI PIER

harbour area, see under Puerto Madryn

ARROYO SECO

Lat 33° 7' S; Long 60° 31' W.

Admiralty Chart: 1982A	**Admiralty Pilot:** -
Time Zone: GMT -3 h	**UNCTAD Locode:** AR

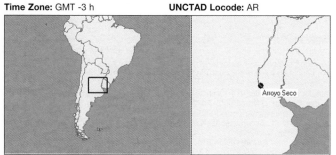

Principal Facilities:

	P	Y			B		

Port Security: ISPS compliant

Anchorage: Anchorage for vessels awaiting berth is between Km 394.7-398.3 left margin, as permitted by the coastguard, usually maximum of four vessels.

Accommodation:

Name	Length (m)	Depth (m)	Remarks
Arroyo Seco			
General Lagos Terminal	140	12–20	See [1] below
Tanker Terminal			See [2] below
Arroyo Seco Terminal	180	13.7	See [3] below

[1]*General Lagos Terminal:* Grain and vegetable oil terminal situated 250 m offshore, with an inclined loading conveyor belt and a viaduct of steel latice work on concrete pilings connecting it to the terminal. Loading rate of approx 2800 t/h for grain, 1500 t/h for by-products and 800 t/h for vegetable oils

[2]*Tanker Terminal:* Belonging to Shell Capsa and is used only by their coastal tankers transporting gas oil and light oils from Buenos Aires. The berth is connected to the shore by a central viaduct which carries the pipelines connected to storage tanks

[3]*Arroyo Seco Terminal:* Vessels up to 275 m loa. Grain loaded at rate of 2400 t/h

Storage:

Location	Grain (t)
General Lagos Terminal	125000

Bunkering: By barge only, fresh water available

Lloyd's Agent: Cooper Brothers S.r.l., Avenida Leandro N. Alem 690, 19th Floor, C1001AAO Buenos Aires, Argentina, *Tel:* +54 11 4311 3121, *Fax:* +54 11 4312 2545, *Email:* argentina@cooperbrosgroup.com, *Website:* www.cooperbrosgroup.com

ATUCHA

Lat 33° 57' S; Long 59° 15' W.

Admiralty Chart: 1982A	**Admiralty Pilot:** 5
Time Zone: GMT -3 h	**UNCTAD Locode:** AR ATU

Principal Facilities:

			G						

Authority: Port Authority of Atucha, P O Box 20, 2800 Lima, Argentina, *Tel:* +54 3487 480 677, *Fax:* +54 3487 480 996, *Email:* pennacchiettio@na-sa.com.ar, *Website:* www.na-sa.com.ar

Officials: Manager: Osvaldo Pennacchietti, *Tel:* +54 3487 480 677, *Email:* pennacchiettio@na-sa.com.ar.
Project Manager: Jose Guala, *Tel:* +54 3487 482 000.

Pilotage: Port pilot service must be requested at Campana Pilot Station and Parana River Pilots at Buenos Aires

Accommodation:

Name	Remarks
Atucha	See [1] below

[1]*Atucha:* Under the jurisdiction of Campana Customs House and Zarate Coastguard. Owned by the Atucha Nuclear Centre, the quay is 33 m in length, 20 m wide with depth approx 13.37 m with two mooring dolphins; specially built for the discharge of heavy material to the Atomic Energy Plant

Lloyd's Agent: Cooper Brothers S.r.l., Avenida Leandro N. Alem 690, 19th Floor, C1001AAO Buenos Aires, Argentina, *Tel:* +54 11 4311 3121, *Fax:* +54 11 4312 2545, *Email:* argentina@cooperbrosgroup.com, *Website:* www.cooperbrosgroup.com

BAHIA BLANCA

Lat 38° 44' S; Long 62° 17' W.

Admiralty Chart: 3755	**Admiralty Pilot:** 5
Time Zone: GMT -3 h	**UNCTAD Locode:** AR BHI

Principal Facilities:

	P	Q	Y	G			B	D		A

Authority: Consorcio de Gestion del Puerto de Bahia Blanca, Av. Dr. Mario M. Guido s/n, Muelle de Carga General, Puerto Ingeniero White, 8103 Ingeniero White, Buenos Aires Province, Argentina, *Tel:* +54 291 457 3213, *Fax:* +54 291 457 3214, *Email:* secretaria@puertobahiablanca.com.ar, *Website:* www.puertobahiablanca.com

Officials: President: Jorge Otharan.
General Manager: Valentin D. Moran.

Port Security: ISPS compliant

Pre-Arrival Information: The following three announcements have to be sent to the Consorcio de Gestion del Puerto de Bahia Blanca containing name of ship, length, beam, depth, arrival draught and estimated departure draught, nrt and gt, origin and destination, type of operation, terminal to visit and estimated cargo to be handled
First announcement to be sent 5 days before arrival
Second announcement or confirmation to be sent 24 h before the expiration of the first announcement
Third announcement to be sent immediately after arrival at the anchorage area

Documentation: General declaration, manifest of cargo, manifest of cargo in transit, ship arrival form 741, clearance from last port if necessary, cabin stores list, deck and engine stores list, crew list, passenger list, list of crews personal effects, arms & ammunition list, maritime health declaration

Approach: The access channel to the port begins at the beacon-buoy 'Rincon' in pos 39° 23' 55.26" S; 61° 29' 01" W. The channel is 97 km long and 190 m wide channel for vessels up to 13.7 m draft

Anchorage: The following positions are anchorage areas for the port of Bahia Blanca:

Alfa: (a) 39° 04' 10" S; 61° 48' 36" W; (b) 39° 05' 12" S; 61° 46' 29" W; (c) 39° 06' 21" S; 61° 46' 36" W; (d) 39° 04' 52" S; 61° 49' 12" W
Bravo: (a) 39° 03' 08" S; 61° 50' 35" W; (b) 39° 04' 06" S; 61° 48' 42" W; (c) 39° 04' 49" S; 61° 49' 17" W; (d) 39° 03' 42" S; 61° 51' 05" W
Charlie: (a) 38° 59' 06" S; 61° 53' 54" W; (b) 38° 59' 30" S; 61° 54' 12" W; (c) 39° 00' 18" S; 61° 51' 06" W; (d) 39° 00' 33" S; 61° 51' 42" W
Delta: (a) 38° 58' 18" S; 61° 56' 00" W; (b) 38° 59' 00" S; 61° 54' 00" W; (c) 39° 59' 24" S; 61° 54' 12" W; (d) 38° 58' 48" S; 61° 56' 12" W

Pilotage: For the access channel, from beacon-buoy 'Rincon' up to buoy 11, pilotage is not compulsory for any vessel
For foreign flag vessels, pilotage is compulsory from buoy 11 up to the ports of Ingeniero White and Galvan
For Argentine flag vessels with any length and a draught up to 8.23 m, pilotage is not compulsory between buoy 11 and buoy 22
For Argentine flag vessels with lengths up to 180 m and draughts up to 8.23 m, pilotage is not compulsory between buoy 22 and the ports of Ingeniero White and Galvan
Pilotage provided by E.S.E.M. S.A., Tel: +54 291 457 1334, Fax: +54 291 457 0114, Email: esemsa@infovia.com.ar and Donmar S.R.L., Tel: +54 291 457 0353, Fax: +54 291 457 0342

Radio Frequency: LPW Radio Bahia Blanca on VHF Channels 16, 26 and 27
Monte Hermoso Radio on VHF Channels 16 and 28
Bahia Blanca Prefectura Naval Argentina L2H on VHF Channel 16 and L2N on VHF Channels 9, 12, 14, 16 and 77
Pilots on VHF Channel 12 and tugs on VHF Channel 08

Weather: Prevailing N'ly, NW'ly and W'ly winds

Traffic: 2007, 12 217 936 t of cargo handled

Principal Imports and Exports: Imports: Fertilisers, Flammables, General cargo. Exports: Frozen fish, Gasoline, Grain, LPG, Petrochemical products, Vegetable oils.

Working Hours: Mon-Fri 0700-1900. Sat 0700-1300. Overtime is available

Accommodation:

Name	Length (m)	Depth (m)	Remarks
Ingeniero White			See [1] below
Toepfer Terminal (Cte. Piedrabuena Pier)		12.8	See [2] below
Bahia Blanca Terminal S.A.			See [3] below
Berth 5/6	300	8.84	See [4] below
Berth 7/8	300	8.84	See [5] below
Berth 9	294	15.24	See [6] below
Cargill S.A.C.I. Terminal		13.7	See [7] below
Break Bulk Cargo Wharf			See [8] below
Profertil S.A. Terminal (Cangrejales Area)		13.72	See [9] below
Mega S.A. Terminal (Cangrejales Area)		13.72	See [10] below
Galvan			
General Cargo Pier			
Berth 1	140	7.62	See [11] below
Berth 2/3	270	11.6	See [12] below
Berth 4			Oleaginosa Moreno Hnos S.A. Terminal. Out of use
Berth 5	249	8.84	See [13] below
Berth 6	120	8.23	See [14] below
Berths 7-11			Out of use
Inflammable Liquid & Gases Terminal			See [15] below
Berth 1	371	12.2	See [16] below
Berth 2	371	12.2	See [17] below
Punta Ciguena & Punta Ancla			See [18] below
Puerto Rosales			See [19] below
Puerto Belgrano			See [20] below

[1] *Ingeniero White:* The principal discharging centre of Bahia Blanca, equipped with modern facilities for handling all classes of cargo
[2] *Toepfer Terminal (Cte. Piedrabuena Pier):* Length between outer mooring dolphins 365 m. Cargoes handled include cereals in bulk, sunflower pellets, sunflower seed and fuel oil. Conveyor belts with mean loading rate of 1000 t/h. Total silo storage cap of 55 000 t
[3] *Bahia Blanca Terminal S.A.:* Tel: +54 291 457 3035, Email: tbbsa@teletel.com.ar. Three berths available
[4] *Berth 5/6:* Cereals in bulk and sunflower seed by conveyor belt at mean loading rate of 1500 t/h
[5] *Berth 7/8:* Cereals in bulk and sunflower seed by conveyor belt at mean loading rate of 1500 t/h
[6] *Berth 9:* Cereals in bulk by conveyor belt at mean loading rate of 1200 t/h
[7] *Cargill S.A.C.I. Terminal:* Length between outer mooring dolphins 280 m. Cargoes handled include cereals in bulk, malt, sunflower pellets and oil. Conveyor belt with mean loading rate of 2400 t/h and rubber hoses for oil seed. Storage cap of 54 000 t (vertical silos), 90 000 t (horizontal silos) and 22 800 m3 (tanks)
[8] *Break Bulk Cargo Wharf:* Berths 17, 18 and 19 form a continuous quay of 450 m. Berth 20 is 210 m long. Depth of berths 18, 19 and 20 is 7.31 m and at berth 17 is 5.8 m. Cargoes handled include frozen fish, cold fruit, cement, machinery etc. Two gantry cranes of 3 t cap and one of 2 t cap as well as two mobile cranes of 15 t and 45 t cap. Three cold storage plants with a total cap of 82 000 m3 at -30°C. Open storage of 18 000 m2 for containers, cars/trucks etc
[9] *Profertil S.A. Terminal (Cangrejales Area):* Urea and ammonia. Conveyor belt (urea) with loading rate of 1250 t/h and one loading arm (ammonia). Storage cap of 150 000 t of urea (horizontal silos) and 30 000 m3 of ammonia (tank)
[10] *Mega S.A. Terminal (Cangrejales Area):* LNG and gasoline. Three loading arms of LNG with loading rate 2000 m3/h and two loading arms of gasoline with loading rate 1000 m3/h. Storage cap of 105 000 m3 for LNG (3 tanks) and 30 000 m3 gasoline (2 tanks)
[11] *Berth 1:* Oleaginosa Moreno Hnos S.A. Terminal. Breakbulk and sometimes dry bulk with portable conveyor belts
[12] *Berth 2/3:* Oleaginosa Moreno Hnos S.A. Terminal. Cereals in bulk, sunflower and

soya bean pellets and oil. Conveyor belt with mean loading rate of 1600 t/h and rubber hoses for oil seed. Total storage cap of 120 000 t (horizontal silos), 20 000 t (vertical silos) and 40 000 m3 (tanks) for sunflower and soya bean oil
[13] *Berth 5:* Breakbulk, containers, fertiliser and sometimes cereals. Two gantry cranes, max lift 35 t. Open storage of 5000 m2
[14] *Berth 6:* Breakbulk and sometimes cereals. Open storage of 4500 m2
[15] *Inflammable Liquid & Gases Terminal:* Operated by Bahia Petroleo S.A., Tel: +54 291 401 0101, Email: administracion@bahiapetroleo.com, Website: www.bahiapetroleo.com
[16] *Berth 1:* Crude oil, oil products, chemical products & caustic soda through pipelines. Five loading arms
[17] *Berth 2:* Chemicals, petrochemicals, oil products & LPG through pipelines. Seven loading arms
[18] *Punta Ciguena & Punta Ancla:* Two SBM's (Punta Ciguena up to 100 000 dwt and Punta Ancla up to 67 500 dwt) in depth of 18.28 m; used by tankers discharging crude oil to the oil tanking terminal
[19] *Puerto Rosales:* Used by launches shuttling crews to/from vessels at anchor and also stores
[20] *Puerto Belgrano:* Principal Argentine Naval Base consisting of an anteport and basin, at the end of which two dry docks are located

Bunkering: Bominflot, Bominflot Bunkergesellschaft fur Mineralole mbH & Co. KG, Floor 6, Reconquista 1048, A1003ABV Buenos Aires, Argentina, Tel: +54 11 4312 0840, Fax: +54 11 4313 8337, Email: mail@bominflot.com.ar, Website: www.bominflot.net – Grades: all grades – Notice: 72 hours – Delivery Mode: barge, truck

Waste Reception Facilities: Special containers are distributed in the port for dry garbage disposal. Sewage disposal has to be arranged with private companies through ship's agent

Towage: Satecna Costa Afuera S.A., 8103 Bahia Blanca, Argentina, Tel: +54 291 457 1619, Fax: +54 291 457 1412, Email: sca@sca-remolcadores.com.ar, Website: www.sca-remolcadores.com.ar
Trans-Ona S.A.M.C.I.F., Agencia Maritima Austral, Acceso Et Muelle Hierro, 8103 Bahia Blanca, Argentina, Tel: +54 291 457 1395, Fax: +54 291 457 1745, Email: operaciones@agencia-austral.com.ar

Repair & Maintenance: Government dry docks at Puerto Belgrano may be used by merchant vessels when not in use by the Navy. Dock No.1, 220 m x 22 m; Dock No.2, 234 m x 35 m
Conyser S.r.l., Avenida Colon 178, 4525409 Bahia Blanca, Argentina, Tel: +54 291 452 5409
Mecanosold S.r.l., Bahia Blanca, Argentina, Tel: +54 291 457 1057, Email: mecanosold@taller.com
Salyco S.A., Bahia Blanca, Argentina, Tel: +54 291 457 1934
Sanym S.A., Bahia Blanca, Argentina, Tel: +54 291 457 0424 Engine repairs
Tallares Navales Malvinas, Bahia Blanca, Argentina, Tel: +54 291 452 7333

Ship Chandlers: Agrioli, Avenida G.Torres 3989, 8103 Ingeniero White, Bahia Blanca, Argentina, Tel: +54 291 457 0141, Fax: +54 291 457 0435, Email: agrioli@infovia.com.ar
Provimar Argentina, Santa Fe 464, 8000 Bahia Blanca, Argentina, Tel: +54 291 451 5246, Fax: +54 291 451 5246, Email: provimar@arnet.com.ar

Shipping Agents: Agencia Maritima Internacional, Belgrano 3328, 8103 Bahia Blanca, Argentina, Tel: +54 291 457 3212, Fax: +54 291 457 3262, Email: amibahiablanca@ocean.com.ar, Website: www.amisa.com
Agencia Maritima Martin Srl, P O Box 335, 8000 Bahia Blanca, Argentina, Tel: +54 291 457 1755, Fax: +54 291 457 0653, Email: email@agencia-martin.com.ar, Website: www.agencia-martin.com.ar
Agencia Maritima Sea White S.R.L., Alte. Brown 3446, Ingeniero White, 8103 Bahia Blanca, Argentina, Tel: +54 291 457 2700, Fax: +54 291 457 2703, Email: agencia@agenciaseawhite.com.ar, Website: www.agenciaseawhite.com.ar
Agencia Maritima Walsh (E. Burton) S.R.L., Grecia 13, Ing. White, B8103 XAA Bahia Blanca, Argentina, Tel: +54 291 457 3080, Fax: +54 291 457 3072, Email: walsh@walsh.com.ar, Website: www.amwalsh.com.ar
Fertimport S.A., Saavedra 636, 7th Floor, B8000DDN Bahia Blanca, Argentina, Tel: +54 291 458 0041/2, Fax: +54 291 455 9654, Email: bbl.fertimport@bunge.com, Website: www.fertimport.com.br

Surveyors: Caliset S.A. (Sucursal Argentina), Bahia Blanca, Argentina, Tel: +54 291 456 5789
Inspectorate, Bahia Blanca, Argentina, Tel: +54 291 455 8071
Societe Generale de Surveillance (SGS), SGS Argentina S.A., Brown 3474, Ingeniero White, 8103 Bahia Blanca, Argentina, Tel: +54 291 457 1311, Fax: +54 291 457 0391, Website: www.sgs.com

Medical Facilities: Various hospitals available

Airport: Bahia Blanca Airport, 18 km

Railway: Connected to national railroad

Development: A new multi-purpose wharf (containers and dry cargo) is under construction at berth 21 in Puerto Ingeniero White, 270 m long in depth of 13.72 m. The construction is about 50% complete and is due to commence operations in May 2005

Lloyd's Agent: Cooper Brothers S.r.l., Avenida Leandro N. Alem 690, 19th Floor, C1001AAO Buenos Aires, Argentina, Tel: +54 11 4311 3121, Fax: +54 11 4312 2545, Email: argentina@cooperbrosgroup.com, Website: www.cooperbrosgroup.com

BARRANQUERAS

Lat 27° 29' S; Long 58° 56' W.

Admiralty Chart: 2039	**Admiralty Pilot:** 5
Time Zone: GMT -3 h	**UNCTAD Locode:** AR BQS

Key to Principal Facilities:—				
A=Airport	**C**=Containers	**G**=General Cargo	**P**=Petroleum	**R**=Ro/Ro	**Y**=Dry Bulk
B=Bunkers	**D**=Dry Dock	**L**=Cruise	**Q**=Other Liquid Bulk	**T**=Towage (where available from port)

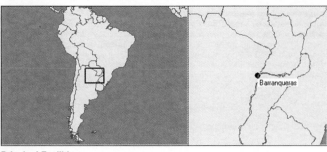

Principal Facilities:

		Y	G	C					A

Authority: Puerto de Barranqueras, Avenida Rio Parana s/n, 3503 Barranqueras, Chaco Province, Argentina, *Tel:* +54 3722 481022, *Fax:* +54 3722 480216, *Website:* webs.advance.com.ar/puertobqras

Port Security: ISPS compliant

Traffic: 2003, 583 000 t of cargo handled

Principal Imports and Exports: Imports: Cement, Iron ore, Manganese. Exports: Cotton.

Accommodation:

Name	Length (m)	Remarks
Barranqueras Quay	800	See [1] below Two grain silos of 1000 t each

[1]*Barranqueras:* There is a grain elevator (storage cap of 105 000 t, fitted with two conveyor belts) situated approx 3 km N of the port which has its own berthing site capable of accommodating two barges on dolphins

Storage:

Location	Covered (m²)	Sheds / Warehouses
Barranqueras	7500	5

Mechanical Handling Equipment:

Location	Type	Capacity (t)	Qty
Barranqueras	Mult-purp. Cranes	27	1
Barranqueras	Mult-purp. Cranes	3	5
Barranqueras	Mult-purp. Cranes	12.5	3

Shipping Agents: Agencia Maritima Transparana S.A., Joaquin V. Gonzalez 385, H3503JWG Barranqueras, Chaco Province, Argentina, *Tel:* +54 3722 485017, *Fax:* +54 3722 485017, *Email:* barranqueras@amtsa.com.ar, *Website:* www.amtsa.com.ar

Airport: Resistencia, 10 km. Corrientes, 24 km

Lloyd's Agent: Cooper Brothers S.r.l., Avenida Leandro N. Alem 690, 19th Floor, C1001AAO Buenos Aires, Argentina, *Tel:* +54 11 4311 3121, *Fax:* +54 11 4312 2545, *Email:* argentina@cooperbrosgroup.com, *Website:* www.cooperbrosgroup.com

BUENOS AIRES

Lat 34° 35' S; Long 58° 22' W.

Admiralty Chart: 1751	**Admiralty Pilot:** 5
Time Zone: GMT -3 h	**UNCTAD Locode:** AR BUE

Principal Facilities:

P	Q	Y	G	C	R	L	B	D	T	A

Authority: Administracion Generale de Puertos, Avenida Ing. Huergo 431 - 1 piso, 1107 Buenos Aires, Argentina, *Tel:* +54 11 4342 1727, *Fax:* +54 11 4342 6836, *Email:* institucionales@puertobuenosaires.gov.ar, *Website:* www.puertobuenosaires.gov.ar

Officials: Port Administrator: LuÝs Angel Diez, *Tel:* +54 11 4342 5621, *Email:* ladiez@puertobuenosaires.gov.ar.
Commercial Manager: Edgardo Vallero, *Tel:* +54 11 4343 2424, *Email:* evallero@puertobuenosaires.gov.ar.

Port Security: ISPS compliant. Container Security Initiative (CSI) designated port

Approach: Most large vessels tend to anchor at Recalada about 30 km S of Montevideo. This is the pilot station for the whole of the River Plate and its tributaries where vessels will often anchor to await further orders or for berths to be vacated Buenos Aires main channel (Punta Indio) starts 2.5 km to the W of the Recalada lightship. The channel is dredged to a depth of 9.77 m on 100 m wide and to 7 m on 200 m width. At a distance of 37 km from the port, the channel reaches the outer roads. Here the channel is 9.14 m deep and 100 m wide. It continues at a depth of 9.75 m until 10 km from the port. Here it divides into two channels. The North Channel connects to Puerto Nuevo and Puerto Madero with a depth of 9.75 m, while the South Channel is dredged to 6.7 m
A channel has been dredged joining N and S Channels between kilometers 9.5 and 11 where the channels diverge
All the channels require constant dredging. Pilotage is compulsory

Anchorage: For Buenos Aires, the outer roads are between the light buoys located between kilometers 25 and 37 with depths of between 5.8-7.9 m. The inner roads are located between light buoys at kilometers 12 and 15. The holding ground is described as soft mud and stone
Approximately 8 km N of La Plata, there is a sector of a circle between true bearings 320° and 040° centred on the East Beacon of kilometer 7.7 of the access channel. This zone is divided into anchorage areas for vessels bound for Buenos Aires, Recalada, ports on the River Parana or La Plata
The anchorage depths are 9.75 m

Pilotage: Compulsory and available from:
Rio Parana Pilots S.A., Tel: +54 11 4331 9111, Fax: +54 11 4331 5201, Email: operaciones@rppilots.com.ar, Website: www.riopar.com.ar
Practicaje Rio de la Plata, Tel: +54 11 4331 7184, Fax: +54 11 4345 5888, Email: pilots@ripla.com.ar, Website: www.riodelaplatapilots.com.ar
Servicio Integral de Practicos S.A. (SIPSA), Email: info@sipsa.com.ar, Website: www.sipsa.com.ar
Pilot boards within the Pilot Boarding Area in Rada La Plata and deep draught vessels within an area bounded by the following positions:
34° 43' 88" S; 57° 46' 73" W
34° 44' 00" S; 57° 46' 43" W
34° 44' 15" S; 57° 45' 12" W
34° 44' 11" S; 57° 44' 83" W

Tides: Mean monthly tidal range is 0.9 m between December and January and is at its lowest between June and July when it is 0.75 m
Outside the port the tidal range varies between 0.15 m and 1.52 m
Southwesterly winds can raise the water level, while northwesterlys can lower the water level

Traffic: 2007, 2195 vessels, 12 276 500 t of cargo handled, 1 153 800 TEU's

Principal Imports and Exports: Imports: Cars, Caustic soda, Chemical products, Coal, Crude oil, Fruit and vegetables, General cargo, Gravel, LPG, Refined oil, Sand, Vegetable oil. Exports: Cars, Caustic soda, Coal, Fruit and vegetables, General cargo, Grain, Gravel, Meat, Oil seed by-products, Sand, Vegetable oil.

Working Hours: Shifts operate as follows: 0700-1300, 1300-1900; and between 1900-0100 and 0100-0700 as overtime

Accommodation:

Name	Length (m)	Depth (m)	Draught (m)	Remarks
Puerto Nuevo (New Port)				
Terminal 1	365		9.75	See [1] below
Terminal 2	450		9.75	See [2] below
Terminal 3	1350	9.7		See [3] below
Terminal 4	795		10.06	See [4] below
Terminal 5	885	8.5–9.75		See [5] below
TERBASA Terminal	585	9.4		See [6] below
South Dock				
Darsena de Propaneros	280	11.9		Operated by Repsol YPF
Darsena de Inflammables		9		Operated by Shell, YPF Repsol and DAPSA. Five berths
Exolgan Container Terminal (Section 1)	1000	9–10		See [7] below

[1]*Terminal 1:* Operated by Terminales Rio de la Plata S.A., Av. Ramon Castillo y Av. Comodoro Py, Puerto Nuevo, Buenos Aires, Tel: +54 11 4319 9500, Fax: +54 11 4315 2700, Email: info@trp.com.ar, Website: www.trp.com.ar
Consists of two berths and two portainer cranes
[2]*Terminal 2:* Operated by Terminales Rio de la Plata S.A., Av. Ramon Castillo y Av. Comodoro Py, Puerto Nuevo, Buenos Aires, Tel: +54 11 4319 9500, Fax: +54 11 4315 2700, Email: info@trp.com.ar, Website: www.trp.com.ar
Consists of two berths and three portainer cranes. Also a 151 m long dedicated berth for feeder/barge traffic with one 35 t luffing crane and in the event of congestion, a sixth berth with 235 m of quay is available to work any vessel equipped with its own cranes. Total of 432 reefer points at terminals 1 & 2
[3]*Terminal 3:* Operated by Terminales Rio de la Plata S.A., Av. Ramon Castillo y Av. Comodoro Py, Puerto Nuevo, Buenos Aires, Tel: +54 11 4319 9500, Fax: +54 11 4315 2700, Email: info@trp.com.ar, Website: www.trp.com.ar
Multi-purpose terminal for containers, cars, ro/ro, general cargo and passenger vessels. Made up of 525 m (three berths) at Basin B-North, 240 m (one berth) at Pierhead 3 and 585 m (three berths) at Basin C-South
[4]*Terminal 4:* Operated by APM Terminals, Av. Edison y Prefectura Naval Argentina, Puerto Nuevo, Buenos Aires, Tel: +54 11 4590 0900, Fax: +54 11 4590 0991, Email: bueapmtmng@apmterminals.com
Multi-purpose terminal handling containerized, unitized, machinery, steel pipes, steel plates, heavy lifts, fruits, paper, livestock, bulk and project cargo. Two mobile cranes, two luffing jib cranes, six reach stackers and 37 forklifts. Warehouse of 9000 m2
[5]*Terminal 5:* Operated by Buenos Aires Container Terminal Services S.A., Tel: +54 11 4510 9800, Fax: +54 11 4510 9821, Email: info@bactssa.com.ar, Website: www.bactssa.com.ar
Made up of Muelle Cabecera 200 m long in depth of 9.75 m, Muelle Principal 500 m long in depth of 9.75 m and Muelle Espigon 185 m long in depth of 8.5 m. Nine RTG's. 480 reefer points
[6]*TERBASA Terminal:* Operated by Terminal Buenos Aires S.A., Tel: +54 11 4311 3589, Fax: +54 11 4311 8031
Grain terminal with storage cap of 175 000 t
[7]*Exolgan Container Terminal (Section 1):* Operated by Exolgan S.A., Alberti 1780, Dock Sud, Avellaneda, Buenos Aires, Tel: +54 11 5811 9100, Fax: +54 11 5811 9124, Email: commercial@exolgan.com, Website: www.exolgan.com

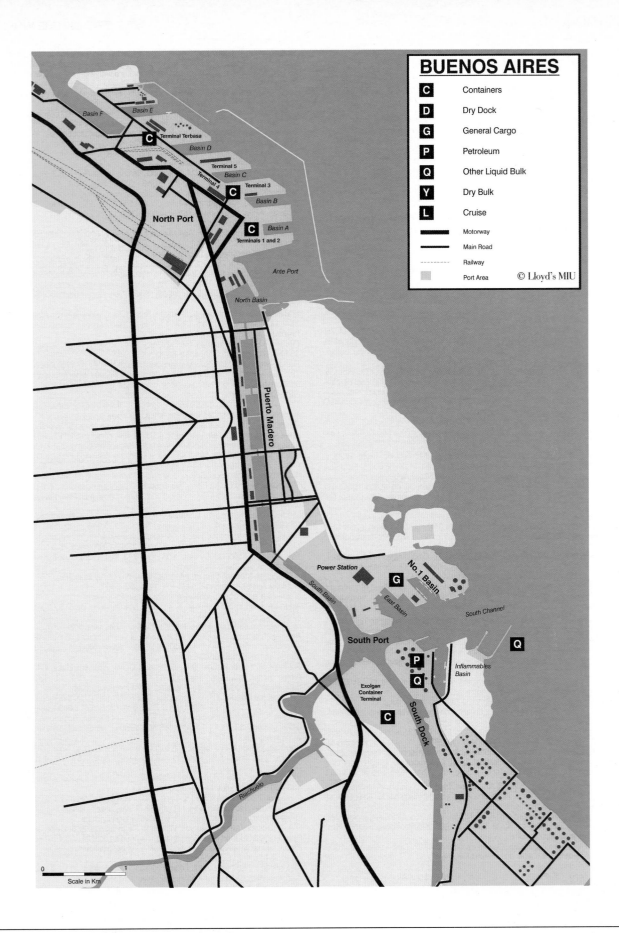

BUENOS AIRES

C	Containers
D	Dry Dock
G	General Cargo
P	Petroleum
Q	Other Liquid Bulk
Y	Dry Bulk
L	Cruise
——	Motorway
——	Main Road
- - - -	Railway
▒	Port Area

© Lloyd's MIU

Basin F

Basin E

Basin D

C Terminal Terbasa

Terminal 5

Terminal 4

Basin C

Terminal 3

C Basin B

North Port

C Basin A

Terminals 1 and 2

Ante Port

North Basin

Puerto Madero

Power Station

G No.1 Basin

South Basin

East Basin

South Channel

South Port

P

Q Inflammables Basin

Q

Exolgan Container Terminal

C

South Dock

Riachuelo

0   1
Scale in Km

MATTINA HNOS S.A.C.I.A.N.

SHIP SUPPLIERS ARGENTINA

G.A. de Lamadrid 434
C1166AAH, Buenos Aires
Argentina

Tel: +54 11 4303 2293/6   Fax: +54 11 4303 2431
Email: pprince@mattina-sa.com.ar

Five berths. Equipment includes three ship-to-shore gantry cranes, one post-panamax gantry crane and fifteen RTG's. 500 reefer points

Bunkering: Bominflot, Bominflot Bunkergesellschaft fur Mineralole mbH & Co. KG, Floor 6, Reconquista 1048, A1003ABV Buenos Aires, Argentina, *Tel:* +54 11 4312 0840, *Fax:* +54 11 4313 8337, *Email:* mail@bominflot.com.ar, *Website:* www.bominflot.net
Coastal Petroleum Argentina S.A., Avenida Corrientes 550 06 Fte, C1043AAS Buenos Aires, Argentina, *Tel:* +54 11 4328 5858, *Fax:* +54 11 4328 6922
Convey S.A., Sarmiento 212, 11th Floor, C1041AAF Buenos Aires, Argentina, *Tel:* +54 11 4331 0766, *Fax:* +54 11 4342 8741, *Email:* convey@convey.com.ar
Maritima Challaco SRL/JRI Comercial Srl, Belgrano Avenida 553, 4th Floor O, 1092 Buenos Aires, Argentina, *Tel:* +54 11 4331 1104, *Fax:* +54 11 4331 1104, *Email:* bunkers@maritimachallaco.com.ar, *Website:* www.maritimachallaco.com.ar
Risler S.A., 28th Floor, Tucuman 540, Capital Federal, 1049 Buenos Aires, Argentina, *Tel:* +54 11 4325 4385, *Fax:* +54 11 4325 3376, *Email:* baires@risler.com.ar, *Website:* www.rislersa.com.ar
Robinson Fletamentos S.A., Lawrence Towers, 25 de Mayo 277, 8 Piso, 1002 Buenos Aires, Argentina, *Tel:* +54 11 5173 1000, *Fax:* +54 11 5173 1074, *Email:* info@robinson.com.ar, *Website:* www.robinson.com.ar
RYTTSA Bunker (Repsol - YPF Trading & Transporte S.A.), Avenida Presidente Roque Saenz Pena 777, 1035 Buenos Aires, Argentina, *Tel:* +54 11 4329 2000, *Fax:* +54 11 4329 5749, *Email:* bunkerbaires@repsolypf.com, *Website:* www.ryttsabunker.com
Sol EC Ltd, P O Box 1759, 1000 Buenos Aires, Argentina, *Tel:* +54 11 4328 2844, *Fax:* +54 11 4328 0742
Sol EC Ltd, Calle Sto.Ponce 2318, Dock Sud, Avellaneda, 1871 Buenos Aires, Argentina, *Tel:* +54 11 42018093/6, *Fax:* +54 11 42227675
Tramp Oil & Marine, Tramp Oil & Marine Argentina, Jeronimo Salguero 2745 71 76, Ciudad Autonoma de Bs.As, C1425DEL Buenos Aires, Argentina, *Tel:* +54 11 4805 7977, *Fax:* +54 11 4804 6922, *Email:* tomsc@tramp-oil.com, *Website:* www.tramp-oil.com
Bominflot, Bominflot Bunkergesellschaft fur Mineralole mbH & Co. KG, Floor 6, Reconquista 1048, A1003ABV Buenos Aires, Argentina, *Tel:* +54 11 4312 0840, *Fax:* +54 11 4313 8337, *Email:* mail@bominflot.com.ar, *Website:* www.bominflot.net – *Grades:* all grades – *Misc:* delivery with own tanker 950t capacity for IFO, MDO, MGO – *Notice:* 72 hours – *Delivery Mode:* tanker
Bominflot, Bominflot Bunkergesellschaft fur Mineralole mbH & Co. KG, Floor 6, Reconquista 1048, A1003ABV Buenos Aires, Argentina, *Tel:* +54 11 4312 0840, *Fax:* +54 11 4313 8337, *Email:* mail@bominflot.com.ar, *Website:* www.bominflot.net

Towage: Abbey Sea Shipping Services, Avenida Alicia Moreau de Justo 1720, 2 Piso, Suite I, C1107AFJ Buenos Aires, Argentina, *Tel:* +54 11 4312 0021, *Fax:* +54 11 4315 3339, *Email:* info@abbeysea.com.ar, *Website:* www.abbeysea.com
Remolcadores Unidos Argentinos S.A.M. y C., Alicia Moreau de Justo 1050, 1st Floor, Suite 228, Dock 7, Puerto Madero, C1107AAV Buenos Aires, Argentina, *Tel:* +54 11 4343 5700, *Fax:* +54 11 4331 7528, *Email:* rua@rua.com.ar, *Website:* www.rua.com.ar
Rio Lujan Navegacion S.A., 25 de Mayo 555, 8th Floor, 1002 Buenos Aires, Argentina, *Tel:* +54 11 4314 8484, *Fax:* +54 11 4313 8983, *Email:* riolujan@ocean.com.ar, *Website:* www.antaresnaviera.com
Satecna Costa Afuera S.A., Reconquista 559, Piso 5, C1003ABK Buenos Aires, Argentina, *Tel:* +54 11 4314 5110, *Fax:* +54 11 4314 5153, *Email:* sca@sca-remolcadores.com.ar, *Website:* www.sca-remolcadores.com.ar
Trans-Ona S.A.M.C.I.F., Gabato 1325, 1157 Buenos Aires, Argentina, *Tel:* +54 11 4301 1807, *Fax:* +54 11 4303 3146, *Website:* www.mar-link.net/usuarios/transona/principal.htm

Repair & Maintenance: Astilleros Alianza S.A., Buenos Aires, Argentina, *Tel:* +54 11 4201 8581, *Fax:* +54 11 4331 9303 One mechanical lift dock of 134 m extreme length
Astilleros Rio Santiago (ARS), Hipolito Yrigoyen Y Don Bosco, 1925 Ensenada, Buenos Aires Province, Argentina, *Tel:* +54 2214 680302, *Fax:* +54 2214 680420, *Email:* secretaria@astillero.gba.gov.ar, *Website:* www.astillero.gba.gov.ar Floating dock with 12 000 t lifting cap and 1000 m of repair berths
Astilleros y Diques S.A. (ASYDISA), Buenos Aires, Argentina, *Tel:* +54 11 4313 0979 One floating dock of 100.75 m extreme length
Cromwell & Cia S.A., California Street 733, 1168 Buenos Aires, Argentina, *Tel:* +54 11 4301 4124, *Fax:* +54 11 4302 7407, *Email:* info@cromwell.com.ar, *Website:* www.cromwell.com.ar Engine repairs
TANDANOR S.A.C.I. y N, Avenida Espana 3091, C1107AMK Buenos Aires, Argentina, *Tel:* +54 11 5554 8300, *Fax:* +54 11 5554 8343, *Email:* info@tandanor.com.ar, *Website:* www.tandanor.com.ar Two dry docks with extreme length of 150 m and 180 m, four floating docks of which the largest is 107 m extreme length and one mechanical lift dock of 220 m length, 32.9 m breadth with a lifting cap of 15 700 t

Ship Chandlers: Ashland Argentina S.A. - Drew Marine Division, Avenida Velez Sarsfield 1940, 1285 Buenos Aires, Argentina, *Tel:* +54 11 4303 1200, *Fax:* +54 11 4303 1880, *Email:* mfisicaro@ashland.com
Buenos Aires Top Co. S.A., California 655, C1168AAA Buenos Aires, Argentina, *Tel:* +54 11 4303 0651, *Fax:* +54 11 4303 0654, *Email:* info@buenosairestop.com, *Website:* www.buenosairestop.com
Casagrande Shipsuppliers Argentina, Casilla de Correo 4902, Correo Central, 1000 Buenos Aires, Argentina, *Tel:* +54 11 4307 0048, *Fax:* +54 11 4307 0035, *Email:* casaship@casagrandeship.com.ar
Holdseal Marine Tape, California 1602, 6th Floor, 1289 Buenos Aires, Argentina, *Tel:* +54 11 4302 8988, *Fax:* +54 11 4302 8988, *Email:* holdseal@uolsinectis.com.ar
London Supply S.A.C.I.F.I., Olga Cossettini, 2nd Floor, 1002 Buenos Aires, Argentina, *Tel:* +54 11 5032 7400, *Fax:* +54 11 5032 7470, *Email:* infopm@londonsupply.net, *Website:* www.londonsupply.net
J.C. Marsano S.r.l., G.A. de la Madrid 334, C1166AAH Buenos Aires, Argentina, *Tel:* +54 11 4301 3424, *Fax:* +54 11 4301 3424, *Email:* jcmarsano@infovia.com.ar
Mattina Hnos. S.A.C.I.A.N., G. A. de la Madrid 434, C1166AAH Buenos Aires, Argentina, *Tel:* +54 11 4303 2293/6, *Fax:* +54 11 4303 2431, *Email:* mdelio@mattina-sa.com.ar, *Website:* www.mattina-sa.com.ar
Navijet S.A., Esmeralda 684, piso 7, 1007 Buenos Aires, Argentina, *Tel:* +54 11 4325 0778, *Fax:* +54 11 4328 4854, *Email:* info@navijetsa.com.ar, *Website:* www.navijetsa.com.ar
Proios S.A., Ministro Brin 774/776, C1158AAH Buenos Aires, Argentina, *Tel:* +54 11 4307 8799, *Fax:* +54 11 4300 5142, *Email:* info@proios.com, *Website:* www.proios.com

Shipping Agents: Abbey Sea Shipping Services, Avenida Alicia Moreau de Justo 1720, 2 Piso, Suite I, C1107AFJ Buenos Aires, Argentina, *Tel:* +54 11 4312 0021, *Fax:* +54 11 4315 3339, *Email:* info@abbeysea.com.ar, *Website:* www.abbeysea.com
Agencia Maritima Dodero S.A., Piedras 77, Piso 3, 1347 Buenos Aires, Argentina, *Tel:* +54 11 4331 7100, *Fax:* +54 11 4331 6737, *Email:* dodero@dodero.sedeco.com.ar, *Website:* www.dodero.com.uy
Agencia Maritima Seaplate S.A., 5th Floor, Maipu 471, C1006ACC Buenos Aires, Argentina, *Tel:* +54 11 5238 9910, *Fax:* +54 11 5238 9911, *Email:* shipagency@seaplate.com.ar, *Website:* www.seaplate.com.ar
Agencia Maritima Silversea S.A., Olga Cossettini, 263-4 floor, 1107 Buenos Aires, Argentina, *Tel:* +54 11 5218 1200, *Fax:* +54 11 5218 1201, *Email:* operations@silversea.com.ar
CMA-CGM S.A., CMA CGM Argentina, Emma De La Barra 353, Piso 1, 1107 Buenos Aires, Argentina, *Tel:* +54 11 5556 1000, *Fax:* +54 11 5556 1050, *Email:* bua.genmbox@cma-cgm.com, *Website:* www.cma-cgm.com
Compania de Navegacion Atlantico Austral S.A., 25 de Mayo 432, 2 Piso, 1002 Buenos Aires, Argentina, *Tel:* +54 11 4312 4896, *Fax:* +54 11 4313 8783, *Email:* buecom@evgegroup.com
Delfino Shipping Agency, San Martin 439, piso 2, P O Box 543, 1004 Buenos Aires, Argentina, *Tel:* +54 11 6320 1000, *Fax:* +54 11 4394 5379, *Email:* admin@delfino.com.ar, *Website:* www.delfino.com.ar
Agencia Maritima Dulce S.A., Tucuman 825, piso 4, 1049 Buenos Aires, Argentina, *Tel:* +54 11 4393 1440, *Fax:* +54 11 4393 4945, *Email:* dulba@dulba.com.ar
Fertimport S.A., 25 de Mayo 501, 7th Floor, Buenos Aires, Argentina, *Tel:* +54 11 5218 9990/1, *Fax:* +54 11 5218 9988, *Email:* bua.fertimport@bunge.com, *Website:* www.fertimport.com.br
Flasa Agency S.A., Avenida Cordoba 883, 5 Piso, 1054 Buenos Aires, Argentina, *Tel:* +54 11 4314 6100, *Fax:* +54 11 4311 2380, *Email:* flasa@flasaagency.com.ar, *Website:* www.mustangcargo.com.ar
Fletamar SAC, Corrientes 327, 4 Piso, 1043 Buenos Aires, Argentina, *Tel:* +54 11 4311 2370, *Fax:* +54 11 4312 5500
Hellas-Mar S.A., 1127 San Martin Street, Suite J, 1004 AAW Buenos Aires, Argentina, *Tel:* +54 11 4311 1384, *Fax:* +54 11 4313 6683, *Email:* operations@hellasmar.com.ar
Inchcape Shipping Services (ISS), Inchcape Shipping Services Argentina S.R.L., Olga Cossettini 263 4th Floor, Capital Federal, C1107CCE Buenos Aires, Argentina, *Tel:* +54 11 5218 1200, *Fax:* +54 11 5218 1201, *Email:* issargentina@iss-shipping.com, *Website:* www.iss-shipping.com
Agencia Maritima Internacional S.A. de C.V., 25 de Mayo 555, piso 20, 1002 Buenos Aires, Argentina, *Tel:* +54 11 4310 2490, *Fax:* +54 11 4310 2455, *Email:* amisa@ocean.com.ar, *Website:* www.amiargentina.com
Maritima de Servicios Srl, The Gral J D Peron 683, 3rd Floor, C1038AAM Buenos Aires, Argentina, *Tel:* +54 11 4322 4902, *Fax:* +54 11 4322 4902, *Email:* maritima@maritima-group.com, *Website:* www.maritima-group.com
Maritima Heinlein S.A., Peru 359, Piso 13, 1067 Buenos Aires, Argentina, *Tel:* +54 11 5382 7067, *Fax:* +54 11 5382 7111, *Email:* heinlein@heinlein.com.ar, *Website:* www.heinlein.com.ar
Mediterranean Shipping Company, MSC Buenos Aires, Bouchard 547, 19th Floor, C1106ABG Buenos Aires, Argentina, *Tel:* +54 11 4316 5100, *Fax:* +54 11 4316 5107, *Email:* info@mscar.mscgva.ch, *Website:* www.mscargentina.com
Mercomar S.A., 25 de Mayo 277, 6 Floor, 1002, C1002ABE Buenos Aires, Argentina, *Tel:* +54 11 4343 3903, *Fax:* +54 11 4343 4017, *Email:* info@mercomar.com.ar, *Website:* www.mercomar.com.ar
A.P. Moller-Maersk Group, Maersk Argentina S.A., Bouchard 557, 19, C1106ABG Buenos Aires, Argentina, *Tel:* +54 11 5382 5800, *Fax:* +54 11 5382 5801, *Email:* argmkt@maersk.com, *Website:* www.maerskline.com
Agencia Maritima Multimar S.A., San Martin 483, piso 5, 1348 Buenos Aires, Argentina, *Tel:* +54 11 4328 3111, *Fax:* +54 11 4325 0904, *Email:* multimar@multimar.com.ar, *Website:* www.multimar.com
Agencia Maritima Mundial S.A., Reconquista 575, piso 1, C1003ABK Buenos Aires, Argentina, *Tel:* +54 11 4313 2390, *Fax:* +54 11 4313 3689, *Email:* agencia@maritimamundial.com.ar
Agencia Maritima Nabsa S.A., Av Paseo Colon 728, 4th Floor, C1063ACU Buenos Aires, Argentina, *Tel:* +54 11 4342 3418, *Fax:* +54 11 4331 5897, *Email:* nabsamain@nabsa.com.ar, *Website:* www.nabsa.com.ar
Navegacion Atlantica S.A., Suipacha 570, 2nd Floor A, 1008 Buenos Aires, Argentina, *Tel:* +54 11 5236 7013, *Fax:* +54 11 5236 7013, *Email:* com@nave.com.ar
Navijet S.A., Esmeralda 684, piso 7, 1007 Buenos Aires, Argentina, *Tel:* +54 11 4325 0778, *Fax:* +54 11 4328 4854, *Email:* info@navijetsa.com.ar, *Website:* www.navijetsa.com.ar
Agencia Maritima Nortemar S.A., Reconquista 575, piso 4/5, C1003 ABK Buenos Aires, Argentina, *Tel:* +54 11 4312 4777, *Fax:* +54 11 4311 7862, *Email:* nortemar@nortemar.com.ar
Platachart S.A., 25 de Mayo 277, piso 9, 1002 Buenos Aires, Argentina, *Tel:* +54 11 4331 0159, *Fax:* +54 11 4342 4808
Robinson Fletamentos S.A., Lawrence Towers, 25 de Mayo 277, 8 Piso, 1002 Buenos Aires, Argentina, *Tel:* +54 11 5173 1000, *Fax:* +54 11 5173 1074, *Email:* info@robinson.com.ar, *Website:* www.robinson.com.ar
S.A. Maritima y Comercial J.R. Williams, Reconquista 336, Dept. J, Capital Federal, Piso 4, 1003 Buenos Aires, Argentina, *Tel:* +54 11 5281 1000, *Fax:* +54 11 5281 1001, *Email:* wimar@jrwilliams.com.ar, *Website:* www.jrwilliams.com.ar
Agencia Maritima Sudocean S.A., 25 de Mayo 555, Piso 19, C1002ABk Buenos Aires, Argentina, *Tel:* +54 11 4310 2300, *Fax:* +54 11 4313 3244, *Email:* sudocean@ocean.com.ar, *Website:* www.sudocean.com
Supermar S.A., Avenida Julio Argentino Roca 672, 9th Floor, C1067ABO Buenos Aires, Argentina, *Tel:* +54 11 5555 0500, *Fax:* +54 11 5555 0514, *Email:* operations@supermar.com.ar, *Website:* www.supermar.com.ar
Topsail Chartering & Trading S.r.l., Tucuman 540, 18th Floor, Suite C, C1049 AAL Buenos Aires, Argentina, *Tel:* +54 11 5556 9091, *Fax:* +54 11 5556 9090, *Email:* topsail@topsail.com.ar, *Website:* www.topsail.com.ar
Transplata S.A., Avenida Cordoba 629, piso 6, 1054 Buenos Aires, Argentina, *Tel:* +54 11 4891 2000, *Fax:* +54 11 4314 1157/75, *Email:* transpla@transplata.com.ar, *Website:* www.transplata.com.ar
JE Turner y Cia S.A., Reconquista 575, Piso 4, C1003ABK Buenos Aires, Argentina, *Tel:* +54 11 4312 6891, *Fax:* +54 11 4312 0416, *Email:* commercial@turner.com.ar, *Website:* www.turner.com.ar
UniOcean Shipping S.A., San Martin 686, 5th Floor, 1004 Buenos Aires, Argentina, *Tel:* +54 11 4314 7050, *Fax:* +54 11 4313 0675, *Email:* info@uniocean.com.ar, *Website:* www.uniocean.com.ar

Stevedoring Companies: Topsail Chartering & Trading S.r.l., Tucuman 540, 18th Floor, Suite C, C1049 AAL Buenos Aires, Argentina, *Tel:* +54 11 5556 9091, *Fax:* +54 11 5556 9090, *Email:* topsail@topsail.com.ar, *Website:* www.topsail.com.ar

Surveyors: ABS (Americas), Avenida Cordoba 950, Piso 13, C1054 AAV Buenos Aires, Argentina, *Tel:* +54 11 4393 6684, *Fax:* +54 11 4393 6618, *Email:* absbuenosaires@eagle.org, *Website:* www.eagle.org

Ascoli & Weil, Tte. Gral. Juan D. Peron 328, 4 Piso, 1038 Buenos Aires, Argentina, *Tel:* +54 11 4342 0081, *Fax:* +54 11 4331 7150, *Email:* ascoliweil@weil.com.ar

Bureau Veritas, 8th & 9th Floor, Avenida Leandro N. Alem 1134, C1001AAT Buenos Aires, Argentina, *Tel:* +54 11 4000 8000, *Fax:* +54 11 4000 8070, *Email:* info.bvbna@ar.bureauveritas.com, *Website:* www.bureauveritas.com

Cooper Brothers S.r.l., Avenida Leandro N. Alem 690, 19th Floor, C1001AAO Buenos Aires, Argentina, *Tel:* +54 11 4311 3121, *Fax:* +54 11 4312 2545, *Email:* argentina@cooperbrosgroup.com, *Website:* www.cooperbrosgroup.com

Det Norske Veritas A/S, Carlos Pellegrini 1023, 4th Floor, C1009ABU Buenos Aires, Argentina, *Tel:* +54 11 4021 4200, *Fax:* +54 11 4021 4201, *Email:* maritime.argentina@dnv.com, *Website:* www.dnv.com

Estudio Lavisse Yusti & Asoc, 25 de Mayo 350 - Piso 9, Ciudad A. de Buenos Aires, Buenos Aires, Argentina, *Tel:* +54 11 4343 5665, *Fax:* +54 11 4343 5665, *Email:* gyusti@lavisse.com.ar

Germanischer Lloyd, Avenida Leandro N. Alem 790, 9th Floor, 1001 Buenos Aires, Argentina, *Tel:* +54 11 4311 2085, *Fax:* +54 11 4314 3786, *Email:* gl-buenos.aires@gl-group.com, *Website:* www.gl-group.com

Hellenic Register of Shipping, Surveys Nickmann & Associates Srl, Esmeralda 923, 10th, 1007 Buenos Aires, Argentina, *Tel:* +54 11 4312 8073, *Fax:* +54 11 4312 0023, *Email:* surveys@sion.com, *Website:* www.hrs.gr

Korean Register of Shipping, Francisco Bilbao 2331, 3 Piso "A", 1406 Capital Federal, Buenos Aires, Argentina, *Tel:* +54 11 4634 0801, *Fax:* +54 11 4633 7684, *Email:* kr-bua@krs.co.kr, *Website:* www.krs.co.kr

Meyer, R.O. Meyer & Associates, 3rd Floor, Office D, Marcelo T. Alvear 429, 1058 Buenos Aires, Argentina, *Tel:* +54 11 4313 8222, *Fax:* +54 11 4313 6882, *Email:* romeyer@meyer-assoc.org, *Website:* www.meyer-assoc.org

Nippon Kaiji Kyokai, Av. Sucre 2074, 2 Piso, UF '9' Beccar, Partido de San Isidro, B1643AQO Buenos Aires, Argentina, *Tel:* +54 11 4765 6600, *Fax:* +54 11 4765 7700, *Email:* bu@classnk.or.jp, *Website:* www.classnk.or.jp

Registro Italiano Navale (RINA), Av. Alicia Moreau de Justo 2030, 1st Floor, Office 119, Buenos Aires, Argentina, *Tel:* +54 11 4314 8666, *Fax:* +54 11 4314 8666, *Email:* buenosaires.office@rina.org, *Website:* www.rina.org

Russian Maritime Register of Shipping, Tte.Gral.Juan Domingo Peron 1730, P.B. Depto.4, 1037 Buenos Aires, Argentina, *Tel:* +54 11 4373 5097, *Fax:* +54 11 4374 5291, *Email:* 277rsar@ciudad.com.ar, *Website:* www.rs-head.spb.ru

G.J. Sigvart Simonsen & Cia SRL, San Martin 424, 1st Floor, 1004 Buenos Aires, Argentina, *Tel:* +54 11 4394 2930, *Fax:* +54 11 4325 5061, *Email:* companymail@simonsen.com.ar

Societe Generale de Surveillance (SGS), SGS Argentina S.A., Alsina 1382, C1088AAJ Buenos Aires, Argentina, *Tel:* +54 11 4124 2060, *Fax:* +54 11 4124 2240, *Email:* ar.contactos@sgs.com, *Website:* www.sgs.com

TANDANOR S.A.C.I. y N, Avenida Espana 3091, C1107AMK Buenos Aires, Argentina, *Tel:* +54 11 5554 8300, *Fax:* +54 11 5554 8343, *Email:* info@tandanor.com.ar, *Website:* www.tandanor.com.ar

Airport: Jorge Newbery, 1 km. Ezeiza, 30 km

Railway: There are good rail connections to and from the port

Lloyd's Agent: Cooper Brothers S.r.l., Avenida Leandro N. Alem 690, 19th Floor, C1001AAO Buenos Aires, Argentina, *Tel:* +54 11 4311 3121, *Fax:* +54 11 4312 2545, *Email:* argentina@cooperbrosgroup.com, *Website:* www.cooperbrosgroup.com

CALETA CORDOVA

harbour area, see under Comodoro Rivadavia

CALETA OLIVARES

harbour area, see under Comodoro Rivadavia

CALETA OLIVIA

harbour area, see under Comodoro Rivadavia

CALETA PAULA

Lat 46° 28' S; Long 67° 29' W.

Admiralty Chart: 552	**Admiralty Pilot:** 5
Time Zone: GMT -3 h	**UNCTAD Locode:** AR

Principal Facilities:

		G							

Authority: Unidad Ejecutora Portuaria de Santa Cruz, Puerto Caleta Paula, Zona Portuaria s/n, 9011 Caleta Olivia, Santa Cruz Province, Argentina, *Tel:* +54 297 485 3342, *Fax:* +54 297 485 3351, *Website:* www.scruz.gov.ar/puertos

Accommodation:

Name	Length (m)	Depth (m)	Remarks
Caleta Paula			
N Quay	453	10.5	For ocean-going vessels up to 140 m loa
NE Quay	170		For fishing vessels or small craft up to 70 m loa

Lloyd's Agent: Cooper Brothers S.r.l., Avenida Leandro N. Alem 690, 19th Floor, C1001AAO Buenos Aires, Argentina, *Tel:* +54 11 4311 3121, *Fax:* +54 11 4312 2545, *Email:* argentina@cooperbrosgroup.com, *Website:* www.cooperbrosgroup.com

CAMPANA

Lat 34° 9' S; Long 58° 57' W.

Admiralty Chart: 1982A	**Admiralty Pilot:** 5
Time Zone: GMT -3 h	**UNCTAD Locode:** AR CMP

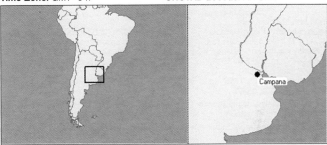

Principal Facilities:

P	Y	G	R	B	T		

Authority: Direccion Provincial de Actividades Portuarias, Campana, Buenos Aires Province, Argentina, *Tel:* +54 3489 437731

Port Security: ISPS compliant

Pilotage: Compulsory. River Plate pilot embarks at Recalada pilot station or at Montevideo Joint Point in pos 35° 03' S; 56° 09' W. Then one River Parana pilot embarks at Zona Comun and sails the vessel up to Campana roads. Harbour pilot in/out

Radio Frequency: W/T and R/T via Pacheco Radio. Zarate Coastguard on VHF Channel 72

Traffic: 2005, 238 207 t of cargo handled

Working Hours: Mon-Fri 0600-1200, 1200-1800. Sat 0600-1200. Overtime available

Accommodation:

Name	Length (m)	Depth (m)	Remarks
Campana			
TenarisSiderca Terminal	185	8.54	See [1] below
Euroamerica Terminal	305	9.75	See [2] below
Desarrollos Portuarios (DEPSA) Wharf	116	9.12	Steel products & general cargo
Maripasa Terminal	225	9.75	See [3] below
Esso S.A.P.A.			
Berth C	50		See [4] below
Berth E	129		See [5] below
Berth G	10		See [6] below
Berth H	70		See [7] below
Carboclor Terminal	70	9.42	See [8] below
Rhasa Terminal	30	10	See [9] below
Tagsa Terminal	30	9.7	See [10] below

[1]*TenarisSiderca Terminal:* Owned by TenarisSiderca, Tel: +54 3489 433100 Discharging bulk iron ore. Average discharge rate of 500 t/h by travelling grab fitted crane, hopper and belt system with outreach of 22 m, airdraft approx 17 m. Also used to load seamless steel pipes using ship's gear

[2]*Euroamerica Terminal:* Operated by Euroamerica S.A., Tel: +54 3489 400400, Fax: +54 3489 427566, Email: euroamerica@euroamerica.com.ar, Website: www.euroamerica.com.ar

Can accommodate two vessels of up to 200 m loa simultaneously. Multi-purpose terminal especially for reefer, forestry, iron & steel products, bagged and bulk cargoes. 30 000 m2 of dry bonded warehouses and 3000 m2 of reefer bonded warehouses

[3]*Maripasa Terminal:* Operated by Euroamerica S.A., Tel: +54 3489 400400, Fax: +54 3489 427566, Email: euroamerica@euroamerica.com.ar, Website: www.euroamerica.com.ar

Cargoes handled include fruit, pipes, paper and other general cargo. 20 000 m2 of dry bonded warehouses and 1000 m2 of reefer bonded warehouses

[4]*Berth C:* Crude & petroleum cargoes for vessels up to 230 m loa & 60 000 dwt

[5]*Berth E:* Crude & petroleum cargoes for vessels up to 150 m loa & 25 000 dwt

[6]*Berth G:* Crude & petroleum cargoes for vessels up to 100 m loa & 10 000 dwt

[7]*Berth H:* Crude & petroleum cargoes for vessels up to 220 m loa & 45 000 dwt

[8]*Carboclor Terminal:* Tel: +54 3489 400765, Fax: +54 3489 422328, Email: info@carboclor.com.ar
Private terminal for liquid bulk chemicals with storage cap of approx 19 620 m3
[9]*Rhasa Terminal:* Naphtha, gasoil, kerosene & liquid fertilizers handled. Tank storage cap of 120 000 m3
[10]*Tagsa Terminal:* Operated by Odfjell Terminals Tagsa S.A., Ribera del Parana de las Palmas km 93.7, Campana, Tel: +54 3489 432153, Fax: +54 3489 427004
Chemical products

Bunkering: Bominflot, Bominflot Bunkergesellschaft fur Mineralole mbH & Co. KG, Floor 6, Reconquista 1048, A1003ABV Buenos Aires, Argentina, *Tel:* +54 11 4312 0840, *Fax:* +54 11 4313 8337, *Email:* mail@bominflot.com.ar, *Website:* www.bominflot.net – *Grades:* all grades – *Notice:* 72 hours – *Delivery Mode:* tanker
BP Marine Americas Inc., 501 Westlake Park Boulevard, Houston, TX 77079, United States of America, *Tel:* +1 281 366 2000, *Email:* firstname.secondname@bp.com
Convey S.A., Sarmiento 212, 11th Floor, C1041AAF Buenos Aires, Argentina, *Tel:* +54 11 4331 0766, *Fax:* +54 11 4342 8741, *Email:* convey@convey.com.ar
Eg3 S.A., 13th Floor, Tucuman 744, 1049 Buenos Aires, Argentina, *Tel:* +54 11 4324 0425, *Fax:* +54 11 4324 0605
ExxonMobil Marine Fuels, Suite 900, One Alhambra Plaza, Coral Gables, FL 33134, United States of America, *Tel:* +1 305 459 6358, *Fax:* +1 305 459 6412, *Email:* emmf@exxonmobil.com, *Website:* www.exxonmobilmarinefuels.com – *Grades:* IFO-180cSt, MGO; MDO – *Notice:* 48 hours – *Delivery Mode:* barge, truck, pipeline
Maritima Challaco SRL/JRI Comercial Srl, Belgrano Avenida 553, 4th Floor O, 1092 Buenos Aires, Argentina, *Tel:* +54 11 4331 1104, *Fax:* +54 11 4331 1104, *Email:* bunkers@maritimachallaco.com.ar, *Website:* www.maritimachallaco.com.ar – *Grades:* MDO; MGO; IFO-180 – *Notice:* 48 hours – *Delivery Mode:* barge, pipeline, truck
RYTTSA Bunker (Repsol - YPF Trading & Transporte S.A.), Avenida Presidente Roque Saenz Pena 777, 1035 Buenos Aires, Argentina, *Tel:* +54 11 4329 2000, *Fax:* +54 11 4329 5749, *Email:* bunkerbaires@repsolypf.com, *Website:* www.ryttsabunker.com
Risler S.A., 28th Floor, Tucuman 540, Capital Federal, 1049 Buenos Aires, Argentina, *Tel:* +54 11 4325 4385, *Fax:* +54 11 4325 3376, *Email:* baires@risler.com.ar, *Website:* www.rislersa.com.ar – *Grades:* all grades, in line blending available – *Parcel Size:* min truck 24-30t, barge 2400t – *Rates:* 200-250t/h – *Notice:* 24 hours – *Delivery Mode:* pipeline, barge, rtw
Sol EC Ltd, P O Box 1759, 1000 Buenos Aires, Argentina, *Tel:* +54 11 4328 2844, *Fax:* +54 11 4328 0742

Towage: Vessels arriving via Mitre Channel do not need tugs for docking but vessels from up river must use a tug for turning 2 to 3 km above or below Campana

Repair & Maintenance: Minor repairs possible

Shipping Agents: Agencia Maritima Internacional, Av. Ing. Rocca 189 9 'C', 2804 Campana, Buenos Aires Province, Argentina, *Tel:* +54 3489 424073, *Fax:* +54 3489 432784, *Email:* amicampana@ocean.com.ar, *Website:* www.amisa.com
Agencia Maritima Transparana S.A., Av. Rocca 189 Piso 3 - Office B, B2804AQP Campana, Buenos Aires Province, Argentina, *Tel:* +54 3489 422685, *Fax:* +54 3489 422685, *Email:* campana@amtsa.com.ar, *Website:* www.amtsa.com.ar
Aguirio Agencia Maritima Srl, J. Dellepiane 688, 2804 Campana, Buenos Aires Province, Argentina, *Tel:* +54 3489 426229, *Fax:* +54 3489 428562, *Email:* aguirio@aguirio.com.ar, *Website:* www.aguirio.com.ar
Agencia Maritima Dulce S.A., Av LN Alem 820, Campana, Buenos Aires Province, Argentina, *Tel:* +54 3489 424414, *Fax:* +54 3489 422014, *Email:* dulca@dulca.com.ar
Agencia Maritima Nabsa S.A., Cristobal Colon 339, B2804FRG Campana, Buenos Aires Province, Argentina, *Tel:* +54 3489 420100, *Fax:* +54 3489 420066, *Email:* campana@nabsa.com.ar, *Website:* www.nabsa.com.ar

Medical Facilities: Municipal hospital and three private clinics

Lloyd's Agent: Cooper Brothers S.r.l., Avenida Leandro N. Alem 690, 19th Floor, C1001AAO Buenos Aires, Argentina, *Tel:* +54 11 4311 3121, *Fax:* +54 11 4312 2545, *Email:* argentina@cooperbrosgroup.com, *Website:* www.cooperbrosgroup.com

COMODORO RIVADAVIA

Lat 45° 51' S; Long 67° 28' W.

Admiralty Chart: 552	Admiralty Pilot: 5
Time Zone: GMT -3 h	UNCTAD Locode: AR CRD

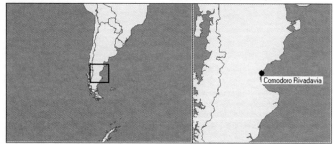

Principal Facilities:

P		G	C		B		T	A	

Authority: Administracion Portuaria del Puerto de Comodoro Rivadavia, Avenida Las Toninas 387, Zona Portuaria, 9000 Comodoro Rivadavia, Chubut Province, Argentina, *Tel:* +54 297 447 3096, *Fax:* +54 297 446 4361, *Email:* administracion@puertocomodororivadavia.com, *Website:* www.puertocomodororivadavia.com

Officials: President: Felix Ernesto Sotomayor, *Email:* administrador@puertocomodororivadavia.com.
Operations Manager: Conrado Marcelo Venter, *Email:* operaciones@puertocomodororivadavia.com.
Harbour Master: Juan Manuel Ghiglione.

Port Security: ISPS compliant

Pilotage: Compulsory. Pilots must proceed from Puerto Madryn as there are none on station locally

Radio Frequency: VHF Channel 16

Traffic: 2005, 89 050 t of cargo handled

Working Hours: 24 h/day

Accommodation:

Name	Length (m)	Depth (m)	Remarks
Comodoro Rivadavia			
Muelle de Ultramar	216	10	General cargo
Muelle Pesquero	100	9.14	Fish
Muelle Pesquero	108	5	Fish
Caleta Cordova			See [1] below
Caleta Olivares			See [2] below

[1]*Caleta Cordova:* Operated by Terminales Maritimas Patagonicas (TERMAP), Democracia 51, Comodoro Rivadavia, Tel: +54 297 447 4400, Fax: +54 297 447 9291, Website: www.termap.com.ar
Situated in pos 45° 43' S; 67° 21' W. Consists of an SBM three miles offshore with loading rate of 3500 m3/h. Depth 29 m for vessels up to 100 000 dwt. There is another installation 1325 m off the Astra beacon. Tankers anchor and moor stern on to six mooring buoys. Loading rate of 1200 m3/h. Depth 10.37 m
[2]*Caleta Olivares:* Situated in pos 45° 46' S; 67° 22' W. Offshore tanker berth comprising four mooring buoys in a depth of 12.8 m. Loading operations are carried out during daylight hours only. A min of 12 h advance notice of arrival must be given to the ships' agents at Comodoro Rivadavia. At present this installation is out of service

Storage:

Location	Open (m²)	Covered (m²)	Sheds / Warehouses
Comodoro Rivadavia	1015	922	2

Mechanical Handling Equipment:

Location	Type	Capacity (t)	Qty
Comodoro Rivadavia	Mobile Cranes	45	1
Comodoro Rivadavia	Mobile Cranes	50	1
Comodoro Rivadavia	Mobile Cranes	7	1
Comodoro Rivadavia	Forklifts	2	1

Bunkering: ExxonMobil Marine Fuels, Suite 900, One Alhambra Plaza, Coral Gables, FL 33134, United States of America, *Tel:* +1 305 459 6358, *Fax:* +1 305 459 6412, *Email:* emmf@exxonmobil.com, *Website:* www.exxonmobilmarinefuels.com – *Grades:* MGO – *Delivery Mode:* truck
Maritima Challaco SRL/JRI Comercial Srl, Belgrano Avenida 553, 4th Floor O, 1092 Buenos Aires, Argentina, *Tel:* +54 11 4331 1104, *Fax:* +54 11 4331 1104, *Email:* bunkers@maritimachallaco.com.ar, *Website:* www.maritimachallaco.com.ar – *Grades:* MDO; MGO; IFO-180 – *Misc:* a pipeline is laid on to the commercial berth to permit bunkers of gas oil from two tanks in the port area – *Delivery Mode:* barge, pipeline, truck

Towage: No tugs required but are available

Shipping Agents: Agencia Maritima Internacional, Francisco Bher No.26 Piso 1, 9000 Comodoro Rivadavia, Chubut Province, Argentina, *Tel:* +54 297 448 0877, *Fax:* +54 297 448 0125, *Email:* amicomodoro@ocean.com.ar, *Website:* www.amisa.com

Medical Facilities: Hospital available

Airport: Local airport with daily service to Buenos Aires

Lloyd's Agent: Cooper Brothers S.r.l., Avenida Leandro N. Alem 690, 19th Floor, C1001AAO Buenos Aires, Argentina, *Tel:* +54 11 4311 3121, *Fax:* +54 11 4312 2545, *Email:* argentina@cooperbrosgroup.com, *Website:* www.cooperbrosgroup.com

CONCEPCION DEL URUGUAY

Lat 32° 28' S; Long 58° 13' W.

Admiralty Chart: 3549	Admiralty Pilot: 5
Time Zone: GMT -3 h	UNCTAD Locode: AR COU

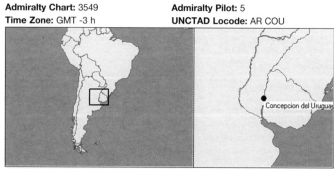

Principal Facilities:

P		Y	G			B		T	A

Authority: Ente Autarquico Puerto Concepcion del Uruguay, Avenida Paysandu 274 (Sur), 3260 Concepcion del Uruguay, Entre Rios Province, Argentina, *Tel:* +54 3442 422191, *Fax:* +54 3442 422191, *Email:* eapcu@puertocdelu.com.ar, *Website:* www.puertocdelu.com.ar

Port Security: ISPS compliant

Approach: Access to the port is by a channel 60 m wide and 1200 m long

Pilotage: Compulsory. River pilots must be requested from Buenos Aires

Radio Frequency: VHF Channels 9, 12, 14 and 16

Traffic: 2004, 321 228 t of cargo handled

Maximum Vessel Dimensions: 225 m loa

Working Hours: Mon-Fri 0700-1300, 1300-1900. Sat 0700-1300. Overtime available

Accommodation:

Name	Length (m)	Remarks
Concepcion del Uruguay		
Berth No.1	35.6	
Berth No.2	66.8	
Berth No's 3 & 4	212	General cargo
Berth No.8	34.5	General cargo
Berth No.9	34.5	General cargo
Berth No.10	34.5	General cargo
Berth No.11	34.5	General cargo
Berth No.12	38.6	General cargo
Berth No.13	38.6	General cargo
Berth No's 14-16	150	Loading of citrus
Berth No's 20-22	90	Grain elevator loading berth with two conveyor belts
Berth No.23	89	Inflammables

Storage:

Location	Open (m²)	Covered (m²)	Sheds / Warehouses	Grain (t)
Concepcion del Uruguay	20000	12500	5	
Berth No's 3 & 4				20000

Mechanical Handling Equipment:

Location	Type	Capacity (t)	Qty
Concepcion del Uruguay	Mobile Cranes	12–45	2
Concepcion del Uruguay	Forklifts	6.3	3

Bunkering: Available from State Oil Co at pier, or by drums from other suppliers

Towage: One tug available of 2700 hp

Repair & Maintenance: Minor repairs possible

Shipping Agents: Agencia Maritima Ghiorzi, Larroque 257, 1st Floor, 3260 Concepcion del Uruguay, Entre Rios Province, Argentina, *Tel:* +54 3442 428395, *Fax:* +54 3442 427103, *Email:* ghiorzi@aghiorzi.com.ar

Medical Facilities: Municipal hospital and two private clinics available

Airport: Concepcion del Uruguay, 10 km

Lloyd's Agent: Cooper Brothers S.r.l., Avenida Leandro N. Alem 690, 19th Floor, C1001AAO Buenos Aires, Argentina, *Tel:* +54 11 4311 3121, *Fax:* +54 11 4312 2545, *Email:* argentina@cooperbrosgroup.com, *Website:* www.cooperbrosgroup.com

DEL GUAZU

Lat 33° 54' S; Long 58° 53' W.

Admiralty Chart: -   **Admiralty Pilot:** -

Time Zone: GMT -3 h   **UNCTAD Locode:** AR

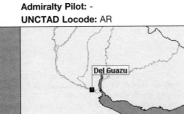

Principal Facilities:

Authority: Del Guazu S.A., Carlos Villate 301, Olivos, B1636BAG Buenos Aires, Argentina, *Tel:* +54 11 4794 4555, *Fax:* +54 11 4794 6959, *Email:* info@delguazu.com, *Website:* www.delguazu.com

Officials: General Manager: Paul Braeken, *Email:* pbraeken@deltadock.com.

Port Security: ISPS compliant

Approach: Through River Plate up to Common Zone, then Martin Garcia Channel and finally Parana Guazu River

Anchorage: Available at Km.171

Pilotage: Compulsory. After River Plate pilot, river pilot is taken on at Common Zone and at approx Km.171 port pilot is boarded

Weather: Temperate, with fog during months of May-June. Frontal passages may cause temporary wind gusts from the S/SE

Tides: Range of 0.6 m subject to wind direction

Principal Imports and Exports: Exports: Corn, Soya, Wheat.

Working Hours: 24 h/day

Accommodation:

Name	Length (m)	Remarks
Del Guazu Berth	200	For cape-size vessels

Storage: Two warehouses, each of 40 000 t cap for wheat

Mechanical Handling Equipment: Two grain bulk loading towers of 1200 t/h each. Conveyor belts travel over the quay

Towage: Available and contracted from Campana

Medical Facilities: Available in Zarate

Airport: Buenos Aires International Airport, 120 km

Lloyd's Agent: Cooper Brothers S.r.l., Avenida Leandro N. Alem 690, 19th Floor, C1001AAO Buenos Aires, Argentina, *Tel:* +54 11 4311 3121, *Fax:* +54 11 4312 2545, *Email:* argentina@cooperbrosgroup.com, *Website:* www.cooperbrosgroup.com

DIAMANTE

Lat 32° 3' S; Long 60° 37' W.

Admiralty Chart: 1982B   **Admiralty Pilot:** 5

Time Zone: GMT -3 h   **UNCTAD Locode:** AR DME

Principal Facilities:

Authority: Ente Autarquico Puerto Diamante, Puerto Nuevo, 3105 Diamante, Entre Rios Province, Argentina, *Tel:* +54 343 498 1424, *Fax:* +54 343 498 1424, *Email:* eptodiamante@arnet.com.ar

Officials: President: Leandro Anibal Blanc.
General Manager: Juan Carlos Favotti, *Email:* juancafavotti@hotmail.com.

Port Security: ISPS compliant

Anchorage: At Diamante Roads there is accommodation for two panamax size vessels

Pilotage: Compulsory. River Plate pilot embarks at Recalada pilot station or at Montevideo Joint Point in pos 35° 03' S; 56° 09' W. Then two River Parana pilots embark at Zona Comun and sail the vessel up to Diamante roads. Harbour pilot in/out

Radio Frequency: VHF Channel 12

Traffic: 2004, 696 086 t of cargo handled

Working Hours: Mon-Fri 0700-1300, 1300-1900. Sat 0700-1300. Overtime available

Accommodation:

Name	Length (m)	Depth (m)	Remarks
Diamante			
Puerto Diamante S.A. Grain Berth	156	5.2	Vessels up to 260 m loa. Average loading rate of 900 t/h
Public Wharf	150		General cargo & solid grains
Barge Berth	60		

Storage:

Location	Open (m²)	Covered (m²)	Sheds / Warehouses	Grain (t)
Diamante	15000			
Puerto Diamante S.A. Grain Berth				60000
Public Wharf		7000	4	

Mechanical Handling Equipment:

Location	Type	Capacity (t)	Qty
Diamante	Mult-purp. Cranes	15	1
Diamante	Forklifts	7	2

Bunkering: ExxonMobil Marine Fuels, Suite 900, One Alhambra Plaza, Coral Gables, FL 33134, United States of America, *Tel:* +1 305 459 6358, *Fax:* +1 305 459 6412, *Email:* emmf@exxonmobil.com, *Website:* www.exxonmobilmarinefuels.com – *Grades:* IFO-180cSt; MGO; MDO – *Notice:* 72 hours – *Delivery Mode:* barge, truck

Repair & Maintenance: Minor repairs only

Medical Facilities: Provincial hospital and private clinic available

Airport: Parana Airport, 50 km

Lloyd's Agent: Cooper Brothers S.r.l., Avenida Leandro N. Alem 690, 19th Floor, C1001AAO Buenos Aires, Argentina, *Tel:* +54 11 4311 3121, *Fax:* +54 11 4312 2545, *Email:* argentina@cooperbrosgroup.com, *Website:* www.cooperbrosgroup.com

Key to Principal Facilities:—			
A=Airport	**C**=Containers	**G**=General Cargo	**P**=Petroleum **R**=Ro/Ro **Y**=Dry Bulk
B=Bunkers	**D**=Dry Dock	**L**=Cruise	**Q**=Other Liquid Bulk **T**=Towage (where available from port)

GALVAN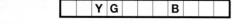

harbour area, see under Bahia Blanca

IBICUY

Lat 33° 44' S; Long 59° 10' W.

Admiralty Chart: -
Time Zone: GMT -3 h

Admiralty Pilot: -
UNCTAD Locode: AR IBY

Principal Facilities:

		Y	G			B		

Authority: Ente Autarquico Puerto Ibicuy, Zona Portuaria Puerto Ibicuy, 2846 Ibicuy, Entre Rios Province, Argentina, *Tel:* +54 3446 498407

Port Security: ISPS compliant. Contact: Carlos Jorge Piter, Tel: +54 3446 429252, Email: ingcarlospiter@hotmail.com

Pilotage: Port pilot to be requested from Campana by the agents well in advance

Working Hours: Mon-Fri 0700-1300, 1300-1900. Sat 0700-1300. Overtime available

Accommodation:

Name	Length (m)	Depth (m)	Remarks
Ibicuy			The port has been closed to shipping since August 2003
Quay	160	7.9	See [1] below

[1]*Quay:* Mainly for exports of woodpulp for vessels up to approx 200 m loa

Storage:

Location	Open (m²)	Covered (m²)	Sheds / Warehouses
Ibicuy	21000	1000	2

Mechanical Handling Equipment:

Location	Type	Qty
Ibicuy	Mobile Cranes	1
Ibicuy	Forklifts	1

Bunkering: Bominflot, Bominflot Bunkergesellschaft fur Mineralole mbH & Co. KG, Floor 6, Reconquista 1048, A1003ABV Buenos Aires, Argentina, *Tel:* +54 11 4312 0840, *Fax:* +54 11 4313 8337, *Email:* mail@bominflot.com.ar, *Website:* www.bominflot.net – *Grades:* all grades – *Notice:* 72 hours – *Delivery Mode:* tanker
BP Marine Americas Inc., 501 Westlake Park Boulevard, Houston, TX 77079, United States of America, *Tel:* +1 281 366 2000, *Email:* firstname.secondname@bp.com
Convey S.A., Sarmiento 212, 11th Floor, C1041AAF Buenos Aires, Argentina, *Tel:* +54 11 4331 0766, *Fax:* +54 11 4342 8741, *Email:* convey@convey.com.ar
Eg3 S.A., 13th Floor, Tucuman 744, 1049 Buenos Aires, Argentina, *Tel:* +54 11 4324 0425, *Fax:* +54 11 4324 0605
ExxonMobil Marine Fuels, Suite 900, One Alhambra Plaza, Coral Gables, FL 33134, United States of America, *Tel:* +1 305 459 6358, *Fax:* +1 305 459 6412, *Email:* emmf@exxonmobil.com, *Website:* www.exxonmobilmarinefuels.com – *Grades:* IFO-180cSt; MGO; MDO – *Delivery Mode:* barge, truck
Maritima Challaco SRL/JRI Comercial Srl, Belgrano Avenida 553, 4th Floor O, 1092 Buenos Aires, Argentina, *Tel:* +54 11 4331 1104, *Fax:* +54 11 4331 1104, *Email:* bunkers@maritimachallaco.com.ar, *Website:* www.maritimachallaco.com.ar – *Grades:* MDO; MGO; IFO-180 – *Delivery Mode:* barge, pipeline, truck
RYTTSA Bunker (Repsol - YPF Trading & Transporte S.A.), Avenida Presidente Roque Saenz Pena 777, 1035 Buenos Aires, Argentina, *Tel:* +54 11 4329 2000, *Fax:* +54 11 4329 5749, *Email:* bunkerbaires@repsolypf.com, *Website:* www.ryttsabunker.com
Risler S.A., 28th Floor, Tucuman 540, Capital Federal, 1049 Buenos Aires, Argentina, *Tel:* +54 11 4325 4385, *Fax:* +54 11 4325 3376, *Email:* baires@risler.com.ar, *Website:* www.rislersa.com.ar – *Grades:* all grades, in line blending available – *Parcel Size:* min truck 24-30t, barge 2400t – *Rates:* 200-250t/h – *Notice:* 24 hours – *Delivery Mode:* pipeline, barge, rtw
Sol EC Ltd, P O Box 1759, 1000 Buenos Aires, Argentina, *Tel:* +54 11 4328 2844, *Fax:* +54 11 4328 0742

Medical Facilities: One small local hospital

Lloyd's Agent: Cooper Brothers S.r.l., Avenida Leandro N. Alem 690, 19th Floor, C1001AAO Buenos Aires, Argentina, *Tel:* +54 11 4311 3121, *Fax:* +54 11 4312 2545, *Email:* argentina@cooperbrosgroup.com, *Website:* www.cooperbrosgroup.com

ING. ROCCA PORT

harbour area, see under La Plata

INGENIERO WHITE

harbour area, see under Bahia Blanca

LA PLATA

Lat 34° 52' S; Long 57° 54' W.

Admiralty Chart: 1751
Time Zone: GMT -3 h

Admiralty Pilot: 5
UNCTAD Locode: AR LPG

Principal Facilities:

P	Q	Y	G		R		B		T	A

Authority: Consorcio de Gestion del Puerto La Plata, St. G. Gaggino y Ortiz de Rosas, 1925 Ensenada, Buenos Aires Province, Argentina, *Tel:* +54 221 460 0203, *Fax:* +54 221 460 0233, *Email:* mrostoll@puertolaplata.com, *Website:* www.puertolaplata.com

Officials: President: Daniel Rodriguez Paz, *Tel:* +54 221 460 1048, *Email:* drodriguez@puertolaplata.com.
General Manager: Rodolfo Rocca, *Tel:* +54 221 460 1159, *Email:* rrocca@puertolaplata.com.
Administration & Finance Manager: Juan Carlos Pozzi, *Email:* jpozzi@puertolaplata.com.
Commercial Manager: Marcello Rostoll, *Tel:* +54 221 460 2196.

Port Security: ISPS compliant

Pilotage: Compulsory and requested from local private companies

Radio Frequency: Coastguard on VHF Channel 9

Traffic: 2005, 5 412 067 t of cargo handled

Maximum Vessel Dimensions: 215 m loa, 30 m breadth. However, special permission can been granted by Coastguard for vessels up to Panama size

Working Hours: Mon-Fri 0700-1300, 1300-1900. Sat 0700-1300

Accommodation:

Name	Length (m)	Depth (m)	Remarks
Grand Dock			
YPF/Repsol Berths 1, 2 & 3	1300	9.12	Situated on E side for oil tankers
YPF/Repsol Berths 6 & 7			See [1] below
Copetro Berths 7 & 8			See [2] below
Berth 9	270		Situated on W side for general cargo
Berths 18/20			General cargo/ferry services
Ing. Rocca Port			
Siderar Berth	154	9.12	See [3] below

[1]*YPF/Repsol Berths 6 & 7:* Situated on W side for loading/discharging chemical products
[2]*Copetro Berths 7 & 8:* Situated on W side. Export of raw petcoke & calcined by one conveyor belt at loading rate of 500 t/h
[3]*Siderar Berth:* For discharge of hot rolled coils coming from Siderar plant at Buitrago (San Nicolas) and export of cold rolled coils and sheets from the adjacent Siderar steel mill

Mechanical Handling Equipment:

Location	Type	Capacity (t)	Qty
Siderar Berth	Shore Cranes	30	2

Bunkering: Bominflot, Bominflot Bunkergesellschaft fur Mineralole mbH & Co. KG, Floor 6, Reconquista 1048, A1003ABV Buenos Aires, Argentina, *Tel:* +54 11 4312 0840, *Fax:* +54 11 4313 8337, *Email:* mail@bominflot.com.ar, *Website:* www.bominflot.net – *Grades:* all grades – *Notice:* 72 hours – *Delivery Mode:* tanker
BP Marine Americas Inc., 501 Westlake Park Boulevard, Houston, TX 77079, United States of America, *Tel:* +1 281 366 2000, *Email:* firstname.secondname@bp.com
Convey S.A., Sarmiento 212, 11th Floor, C1041AAF Buenos Aires, Argentina, *Tel:* +54 11 4331 0766, *Fax:* +54 11 4342 8741, *Email:* convey@convey.com.ar
Eg3 S.A., 13th Floor, Tucuman 744, 1049 Buenos Aires, Argentina, *Tel:* +54 11 4324 0425, *Fax:* +54 11 4324 0605
ExxonMobil Marine Fuels, Suite 900, One Alhambra Plaza, Coral Gables, FL 33134, United States of America, *Tel:* +1 305 459 6358, *Fax:* +1 305 459 6412, *Email:* emmf@exxonmobil.com, *Website:* www.exxonmobilmarinefuels.com – *Grades:* IFO-180cSt; MGO; MDO – *Delivery Mode:* barge, truck
Maritima Challaco SRL/JRI Comercial Srl, Belgrano Avenida 553, 4th Floor O, 1092 Buenos Aires, Argentina, *Tel:* +54 11 4331 1104, *Fax:* +54 11 4331 1104, *Email:* bunkers@maritimachallaco.com.ar, *Website:* www.maritimachallaco.com.ar – *Grades:* MDO; MGO; IFO-180 – *Delivery Mode:* barge, pipeline, truck
RYTTSA Bunker (Repsol - YPF Trading & Transporte S.A.), Avenida Presidente Roque Saenz Pena 777, 1035 Buenos Aires, Argentina, *Tel:* +54 11 4329 2000, *Fax:*

+54 11 4329 5749, *Email:* bunkerbaires@repsolypf.com, *Website:* www.ryttsabunker.com – *Delivery Mode:* pipeline, barge, rtw

Risler S.A., 28th Floor, Tucuman 540, Capital Federal, 1049 Buenos Aires, Argentina, *Tel:* +54 11 4325 4385, *Fax:* +54 11 4325 3376, *Email:* baires@risler.com.ar, *Website:* www.rislersa.com.ar – *Grades:* all grades, in line blending available – *Parcel Size:* min truck 24-30t, barge 2400t – *Rates:* 200-250t/h – *Notice:* 24 hours – *Delivery Mode:* pipeline, barge, rtw

Sol EC Ltd, P O Box 1759, 1000 Buenos Aires, Argentina, *Tel:* +54 11 4328 2844, *Fax:* +54 11 4328 0742

Towage: Four tugs available, two of 2300 hp and two of 3160 hp

Repair & Maintenance: Astilleros Rio Santiago Shipbuilding, Astillero Rio Santiago, H. Irigoyen y Don Bosco, Ensenada, 1925 La Plata, Argentina, *Tel:* +54 221 468 0302, *Fax:* +54 221 468 0420, *Email:* shipyars@satlink.com, *Website:* www.astillerioriosantiago.com All floating repairs available

Shipping Agents: Agencia Maritima Mareas S.A., F. Lavalle 14, Ensenada, B1925BXB La Plata, Argentina, *Tel:* +54 221 460 1233, *Fax:* +54 221 460 1231, *Email:* operac@mareas.com, *Website:* www.mareas.com
Maritima Seghini, G. Gaggino 255, La Plata, Argentina, *Tel:* +54 221 460 1212, *Fax:* +54 221 460 1887, *Email:* marse@maritimaseghini.com.ar

Medical Facilities: Available

Airport: La Plata, 8 km. Buenos Aires, 60 km

Development: Construction of a 850 m container quay with five post-panamax gantries and fifteen RTG's

Lloyd's Agent: Cooper Brothers S.r.l., Avenida Leandro N. Alem 690, 19th Floor, C1001AAO Buenos Aires, Argentina, *Tel:* +54 11 4311 3121, *Fax:* +54 11 4312 2545, *Email:* argentina@cooperbrosgroup.com, *Website:* www.cooperbrosgroup.com

LIMA

Lat 33° 58' S; Long 59° 11' W.

Admiralty Chart: -   **Admiralty Pilot:** -
Time Zone: GMT -3 h   **UNCTAD Locode:** AR

Principal Facilities:

		Y	G		R				

Authority: Delta Dock S.A., Central Atucha Road, Lima, 2806 Zarate, Buenos Aires Province, Argentina, *Tel:* +54 3487 481885, *Fax:* +54 3487 481853, *Email:* terminal@deltadock.com, *Website:* www.deltadock.com

Officials: Commercial Manager: Paul Braeken, *Email:* pbraeken@deltadock.com.

Port Security: Level one, Email: opip@deltadock.com

Pre-Arrival Information: Given through agents

Anchorage: Temporary anchorage is available subject to authorisation of Coast Guard at Km 67.5/69.5 and Km 109-111. It is prohibited to anchor between Km 130-140

Pilotage: Compulsory. Pilots are ordered by agents. River Plate pilot from Recalada to Zona Comun. Parana River Pilot from Zona Comun up to Port (usually ordered by agent from BA or sub agent Zarate). Port pilot usually ordered by sub agent

Weather: Good visibility except in months of May and June with heavy fog during morning hours. During fog no sailing is permitted. Cold fronts may cause strong wind gusts especially from the South and S/East direction with heavy rain showers. Other fronts may cause northern winds

Tides: Range of 0.6 m

Traffic: Approx 75 vessels per year

Maximum Vessel Dimensions: 225 m loa

Principal Imports and Exports: Imports: Bagged fertiliser, Cars. Exports: Agribulk commodities, Cars, Forest products, Soya beans, Steel pipes.

Working Hours: 24 h/day

Accommodation:

Name	Length (m)	Depth (m)	Remarks
Delta Dock			
Main Wharf	172	11.5	See [1] below
Wharf No.2	127	11.5	See [2] below

[1]*Main Wharf:* General cargo, vehicles & grain for vessels up to 225 m loa. Two warehouses, each of 7500 m2 with grain storage of 35 000 t and eight silos each with a cap of 36 000 t. The silos are connected to the wharf by a 1000 m conveyor belt with a cap of 1000 t/h. 22 ha of paved storage area for vehicles and a 2200 m2 warehouse. 4000 m2 warehouse for forest products
[2]*Wharf No.2:* Floating pontoon berth for vessels up to 225 m loa handling general cargo & vehicles when Main Wharf is occupied

Mechanical Handling Equipment:

Location	Type	Qty
Delta Dock	Mobile Cranes	1

Location	Type	Qty
Delta Dock	Forklifts	

Towage: Not compulsory

Medical Facilities: The terminal has an emergency unit equipped with first aid. Ambulance service is given from nearby village of Lima. Serious cases are transferred to public hospital at Zarate, Campana or Buenos Aires

Airport: Buenos Aires and Rosario

Railway: No rail connection inside the terminal

Development: Value added logistics centre is being created

Lloyd's Agent: Cooper Brothers S.r.l., Avenida Leandro N. Alem 690, 19th Floor, C1001AAO Buenos Aires, Argentina, *Tel:* +54 11 4311 3121, *Fax:* +54 11 4312 2545, *Email:* argentina@cooperbrosgroup.com, *Website:* www.cooperbrosgroup.com

MAR DEL PLATA

Lat 38° 1' S; Long 57° 32' W.

Admiralty Chart: 531   **Admiralty Pilot:** 5
Time Zone: GMT -3 h   **UNCTAD Locode:** AR MDQ

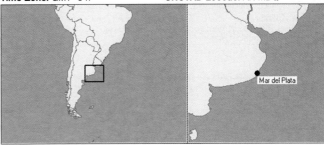

Principal Facilities:

Q	Y	G	C	R	L	B		T	A

Authority: Consorcio Portuario Regional de Mar del Plata, Avenida A y Calle D, Mar del Plata, Buenos Aires Province, Argentina, *Email:* consorcioportuariomdp@speedy.com.ar

Port Security: ISPS compliant

Approach: The port is 4.8 km from the town. It is well sheltered by two breakwaters (the N arm 1099 m long and the S arm 2750 m long). Min depth at entrance and in port is 6.71 m at LW. The depths should be checked as swell and sudden storms can cause considerable differences in depths

Pilotage: Compulsory. Pilot boards vessel in the roads approx 1.5 miles NE of southern breakwater

Radio Frequency: VHF Channel 16

Traffic: 2002, 132 215 t of cargo handled

Maximum Vessel Dimensions: 180 m loa

Principal Imports and Exports: Exports: Fish.

Working Hours: Mon-Fri 0700-1300, 1300-1900. Sat 0700-1300. Overtime available

Accommodation:

Name	Length (m)	Depth (m)	Remarks
Basin A			See [1] below
Basin B			See [2] below
Basin C			Formed by Piers 2 & 3
Berths 12 & 13	276	6.68–8.2	See [3] below
Berth 11	134	4.56	
Berth 10		5.47–7.29	Used or occupied by fishing vessels
Berths 8 & 9			See [4] below
Berth 7	178	8.2	See [5] below
Northern Breakwater Pier			
Pierhead 6	320		Used by passenger & cruise vessels
Southern Breakwater			
Tanker Berth			See [6] below

[1]*Basin A:* Basin A is in the S part of the port and is used by small fishing vessels. It has a syncrolift for repairs and facilities for bunkering
[2]*Basin B:* Formed by Piers 1 & 2 and used by deep-sea trawlers and factory fishing vessels
[3]*Berths 12 & 13:* Grain elevator loading berth leased to Elevadores Mar del Plata Srl. Two loading conveyor belts totalling 800 t/h. This berth is also used by general cargo carriers, passenger vessels and reefer vessels loading fish
[4]*Berths 8 & 9:* Two container terminals operated by Maersk Argentina S.A. and Transplata S.A.
[5]*Berth 7:* Used by ocean-going vessels, reefers and fishing vessels
[6]*Tanker Berth:* Suitable for vessels up to 120 m loa. The berth consists of a central operations platform and two outlying mooring dolphins

Storage:

Location	Grain (t)
Berths 12 & 13	25000

Mechanical Handling Equipment:

Location	Type	Capacity (t)	Qty	Remarks
Mar del Plata	Mobile Cranes	90	7	privately operated

Key to Principal Facilities:—
A=Airport   **C**=Containers   **G**=General Cargo   **P**=Petroleum   **R**=Ro/Ro   **Y**=Dry Bulk
B=Bunkers   **D**=Dry Dock   **L**=Cruise   **Q**=Other Liquid Bulk   **T**=Towage (where available from port)

Bunkering: Bominflot, Bominflot Bunkergesellschaft fur Mineralole mbH & Co. KG, Floor 6, Reconquista 1048, A1003ABV Buenos Aires, Argentina, *Tel:* +54 11 4312 0840, *Fax:* +54 11 4313 8337, *Email:* mail@bominflot.com.ar, *Website:* www.bominflot.net – *Grades:* IFO-180cSt; MGO; MDO – *Delivery Mode:* truck
Convey S.A., Sarmiento 212, 11th Floor, C1041AAF Buenos Aires, Argentina, *Tel:* +54 11 4331 0766, *Fax:* +54 11 4342 8741, *Email:* convey@convey.com.ar
Eg3 S.A., 13th Floor, Tucuman 744, 1049 Buenos Aires, Argentina, *Tel:* +54 11 4324 0425, *Fax:* +54 11 4324 0605
ExxonMobil Marine Fuels, Suite 900, One Alhambra Plaza, Coral Gables, FL 33134, United States of America, *Tel:* +1 305 459 6358, *Fax:* +1 305 459 6412, *Email:* emmf@exxonmobil.com, *Website:* www.exxonmobilmarinefuels.com – *Grades:* MGO; MDO – *Delivery Mode:* truck
Maritima Challaco SRL/JRI Comercial Srl, Belgrano Avenida 553, 4th Floor O, 1092 Buenos Aires, Argentina, *Tel:* +54 11 4331 1104, *Fax:* +54 11 4331 1104, *Email:* bunkers@maritimachallaco.com.ar, *Website:* www.maritimachallaco.com.ar – *Grades:* IFO-180cSt; MDO; MGO – *Delivery Mode:* barge, pipeline, truck
RYTTSA Bunker (Repsol - YPF Trading & Transporte S.A.), Avenida Presidente Roque Saenz Pena 777, 1035 Buenos Aires, Argentina, *Tel:* +54 11 4329 2000, *Fax:* +54 11 4329 5749, *Email:* bunkerbaires@repsolypf.com, *Website:* www.ryttsabunker.com

Towage: Two tugs available of 700-900 hp

Repair & Maintenance: Servicios Portuarios Integrados S.A., 1000 Street between 1001 & 1003, 7600 Mar del Plata, Buenos Aires Province, Argentina, *Tel:* +54 223 489 7150, *Fax:* +54 223 480 9480, *Email:* info@spisa.com.ar, *Website:* www.spisa.com.ar

Shipping Agents: Inda y Garcia S.R.L., Avenida 'A' Zona Fiscal, Mar del Plata, Buenos Aires Province, Argentina, *Tel:* +54 223 480 0340, *Fax:* +54 223 480 0267, *Email:* ingar@lacapitalnet.com.ar

Medical Facilities: Private clinics and hospitals available

Airport: Mar del Plata

Lloyd's Agent: Cooper Brothers S.r.l., Avenida Leandro N. Alem 690, 19th Floor, C1001AAO Buenos Aires, Argentina, *Tel:* +54 11 4311 3121, *Fax:* +54 11 4312 2545, *Email:* argentina@cooperbrosgroup.com, *Website:* www.cooperbrosgroup.com

NECOCHEA

Lat 38° 34' S; Long 58° 43' W.

Admiralty Chart: 531
Time Zone: GMT -3 h

Admiralty Pilot: 5
UNCTAD Locode: AR NEC

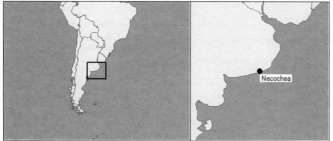

Principal Facilities:

| P | Q | Y | G | | | | B | | T | A |

Authority: Consorcio de Gestion de Puerto Quequen, Avenida Juan de Garay 850, B7631XAF Quequen, Buenos Aires Province, Argentina, *Tel:* +54 2262 450006, *Fax:* +54 2262 450006, *Email:* secretaria@puertoquequen.com, *Website:* www.puertoquequen.com

Officials: President: Mario Goicoechea.
General Manager: Carlos de Pablo Pardo.

Port Security: ISPS compliant

Approach: Two breakwaters protect the entrance of the port at the mouth of the Quequen River; the southern breakwater, 1192 m long running from NW to SE and the northern breakwater, 572 m long, running N to S, leaving a passage between them of 210 m within which there is a channel 120 m wide and dredged to a depth of 12.2 m

Pilotage: Compulsory. Pilot boards in pos 38° 35.70' S; 58° 40.00' W (2 nautical miles SE from the head of the breakwaters)

Radio Frequency: Radio communications 24 h/day via Buenos Aires General Pacheco Radio and Mar del Plata Radio

Tides: MHW 1.57 m, MLW 0.49 m

Maximum Vessel Dimensions: 230 m loa

Principal Imports and Exports: Exports: Grain, Oil.

Working Hours: Mon-Fri 0700-1300, 1300-1900. Sat 0700-1300. Overtime available

Accommodation:

Name	Length (m)	Depth (m)	Remarks
Quequen			See [1] below
Berth No.1	200	12.16	See [2] below
Berth No.2	350		See [3] below
Berth No.3	140	11.85	ACA/FACA grain elevator berth with three dolphins
Berth No's 4 & 5	260	11.55	See [4] below
Berth No.6	110	10.94	See [5] below
Necochea			See [6] below
Berth No's 7 & 8	240	8.5	Used by reefer and fishing vessels
Berth No's 9 & 10	210	9.72	See [7] below

Name	Length (m)	Depth (m)	Remarks
Berth No.11	185	7.6	Fishing trawlers
Berth No.12		7.14	See [8] below

[1]*Quequen:* Situated on the left bank at the mouth of the River Quequen
[2]*Berth No.1:* For loading vegetable oil from tanks by pipeline. Pellets are loaded by portable conveyor belts, each delivering 200 t/h
[3]*Berth No.2:* Operated by ACA/FACA
Loading of agri by-products and discharge of fertiliser
[4]*Berth No's 4 & 5:* Terminal Quequen grain elevator. Vessel berthing on four dolphins. Can accommodate two vessels of up to 140 m loa
[5]*Berth No.6:* Extension of Terminal Quequen grain elevator. Grain and other cargoes can be loaded by vessels up to 230 m loa. Vessels use own gear
[6]*Necochea:* Situated on the right bank at the mouth of the River Quequen
[7]*Berth No's 9 & 10:* Used by vessels discharging/loading general cargo (cement, logs etc) using ship's gear and agri by-products ex trucks using portable conveyor belts. Also for discharging bulk fertilisers by grabs to trucks with ship's gear to NIDERA storage facility of 50 000 m2
[8]*Berth No.12:* Consists of three mooring dolphins permitting vessels up to approx 180 m loa. Used by tankers discharging fuel for power station and also used for grab discharge of fertilisers to trucks

Storage:

Location	Grain (t)
Berth No.3	155000
Berth No's 4 & 5	116000

Mechanical Handling Equipment:

Location	Type	Capacity (t)	Qty
Necochea	Mobile Cranes	25	1

Bunkering: Bominflot, Bominflot Bunkergesellschaft fur Mineralole mbH & Co. KG, Floor 6, Reconquista 1048, A1003ABV Buenos Aires, Argentina, *Tel:* +54 11 4312 0840, *Fax:* +54 11 4313 8337, *Email:* mail@bominflot.com.ar, *Website:* www.bominflot.net – *Grades:* IFO-180cSt; MDO; MGO – *Delivery Mode:* tank truck
Convey S.A., Sarmiento 212, 11th Floor, C1041AAF Buenos Aires, Argentina, *Tel:* +54 11 4331 0766, *Fax:* +54 11 4342 8741, *Email:* convey@convey.com.ar
Eg3 S.A., 13th Floor, Tucuman 744, 1049 Buenos Aires, Argentina, *Tel:* +54 11 4324 0425, *Fax:* +54 11 4324 0605
ExxonMobil Marine Fuels, Suite 900, One Alhambra Plaza, Coral Gables, FL 33134, United States of America, *Tel:* +1 305 459 6358, *Fax:* +1 305 459 6412, *Email:* emmf@exxonmobil.com, *Website:* www.exxonmobilmarinefuels.com – *Grades:* MGO; MDO – *Delivery Mode:* truck
Maritima Challaco SRL/JRI Comercial Srl, Belgrano Avenida 553, 4th Floor O, 1092 Buenos Aires, Argentina, *Tel:* +54 11 4331 1104, *Fax:* +54 11 4331 1104, *Email:* bunkers@maritimachallaco.com.ar, *Website:* www.maritimachallaco.com.ar – *Grades:* IFO-180cSt; MDO; MGO – *Delivery Mode:* barge, pipeline, truck
RYTTSA Bunker (Repsol - YPF Trading & Transporte S.A.), Avenida Presidente Roque Saenz Pena 777, 1035 Buenos Aires, Argentina, *Tel:* +54 11 4329 2000, *Fax:* +54 11 4329 5749, *Email:* bunkerbaires@repsolypf.com, *Website:* www.ryttsabunker.com

Towage: Four tugs available up to 3500 hp

Repair & Maintenance: Minor repairs possible

Shipping Agents: Agencia Maritima Martin Srl, Diagonal San Martin 1167, 7630 Necochea, Argentina, *Tel:* +54 2262 421002, *Fax:* +54 2262 435258, *Email:* necochea@agencia-martin.com.ar, *Website:* www.agencia-martin.com.ar
Agencia Maritima Sea Lion S.A., Avenue 59th No.582, B7630GXQ Necochea, Argentina, *Tel:* +54 2262 435441, *Fax:* +54 2262 437437, *Email:* sealion@sealion.com.ar, *Website:* www.sealion.com.ar
Agencia Pleamar S.A., 68 Street No.2710, 7630 Necochea, Argentina, *Tel:* +54 2262 433336, *Fax:* +54 2262 438007, *Email:* operaciones@pleamar.com.ar, *Website:* www.pleamar.com.ar
Brisamar S.A., 62 Street No.3215, B7630CKW Necochea, Argentina, *Tel:* +54 2262 426165, *Fax:* +54 2262 438960, *Email:* brisamar@brisamar.com.ar, *Website:* www.brisamar.com.ar

Surveyors: Det Norske Veritas A/S, Calle 87 No.368, B7630IWF Necochea, Argentina, *Tel:* +54 2262 425035, *Fax:* +54 2262 524540, *Email:* martin.azcueta@speedy.com.ar, *Website:* www.dnv.com

Medical Facilities: Three private clinics and one municipal hospital at Necochea, and one municipal hospital at Quequen

Airport: Necochea

Lloyd's Agent: Cooper Brothers S.r.l., Avenida Leandro N. Alem 690, 19th Floor, C1001AAO Buenos Aires, Argentina, *Tel:* +54 11 4311 3121, *Fax:* +54 11 4312 2545, *Email:* argentina@cooperbrosgroup.com, *Website:* www.cooperbrosgroup.com

PUERTO ACEVEDO

harbour area, see under Villa Constitucion

PUERTO BELGRANO

harbour area, see under Bahia Blanca

PUERTO DESEADO

Lat 47° 45' S; Long 65° 53' W.

Admiralty Chart: 1302
Time Zone: GMT -3 h

Admiralty Pilot: 6
UNCTAD Locode: AR PUD

Principal Facilities:

			G	C			B	D		A

Authority: Unidad Ejecutora Portuaria de Santa Cruz, Puerto de Puerto Deseado, Zona Portuaria s/n, 9050 Puerto Deseado, Santa Cruz Province, Argentina, *Tel:* +54 297 487 2234, *Fax:* +54 297 487 0914, *Email:* pdeseado@pdeseado.com.ar, *Website:* www.scruz.gov.ar/puertos

Port Security: ISPS compliant

Pilotage: Compulsory for entry or departure. Pilots embark/disembark in approx pos 47° 46.4' S; 65° 50.2' W

Radio Frequency: VHF Channels 12, 14 and 16

Traffic: 2004, 226 434 t of cargo handled

Maximum Vessel Dimensions: 190 m loa

Principal Imports and Exports: Exports: Fish.

Working Hours: Mon-Fri 0700-1300, 1300-1900. Sat 0700-1300. Overtime available

Accommodation:

Name	Length (m)	Depth (m)	Remarks
Puerto Deseado			See [1] below
Berth No.1	129	12	For ocean-going & fishing vessels up to 190 m loa
Berth No.2	146	8–12	Used by ocean-going & fishing vessels
Berth No's 3 & 4	250	8	For ocean-going & fishing vessels of 35-120 m loa

[1]*Puerto Deseado:* There is also a trawler terminal approx 200 m long and a fishing wharf

Storage:

Location	Covered (m²)	Sheds / Warehouses
Puerto Deseado	650	1

Mechanical Handling Equipment:

Location	Type	Capacity (t)	Qty
Puerto Deseado	Mobile Cranes	40	3

Bunkering: Bominflot, Bominflot Bunkergesellschaft fur Mineralole mbH & Co. KG, Floor 6, Reconquista 1048, A1003ABV Buenos Aires, Argentina, *Tel:* +54 11 4312 0840, *Fax:* +54 11 4313 8337, *Email:* mail@bominflot.com.ar, *Website:* www.bominflot.net – *Grades:* MGO – *Delivery Mode:* tank truck, pipeline
ExxonMobil Marine Fuels, Suite 900, One Alhambra Plaza, Coral Gables, FL 33134, United States of America, *Tel:* +1 305 459 6358, *Fax:* +1 305 459 6412, *Email:* emmf@exxonmobil.com, *Website:* www.exxonmobilmarinefuels.com – *Grades:* MGO – *Delivery Mode:* truck
Maritima Challaco SRL/JRI Comercial Srl, Belgrano Avenida 553, 4th Floor O, 1092 Buenos Aires, Argentina, *Tel:* +54 11 4331 1104, *Fax:* +54 11 4331 1104, *Email:* bunkers@maritimachallaco.com.ar, *Website:* www.maritimachallaco.com.ar – *Grades:* MDO; MGO; IFO-180 – *Delivery Mode:* barge, pipeline, truck
RYTTSA Bunker (Repsol - YPF Trading & Transporte S.A.), Avenida Presidente Roque Saenz Pena 777, 1035 Buenos Aires, Argentina, *Tel:* +54 11 4329 2000, *Fax:* +54 11 4329 5749, *Email:* bunkerbaires@repsolypf.com, *Website:* www.ryttsabunker.com

Repair & Maintenance: Coserena S.A., Espana 2595, P O Box 124, 9050 Puerto Deseado, Santa Cruz Province, Argentina, *Tel:* +54 297 487 0660, *Fax:* +54 297 487 0660, *Email:* infopd@coserena.com.ar, *Website:* www.coserena.com.ar Dry dock for vessels up to 87.5 m loa

Shipping Agents: Agencia Maritima Bernard, San Martin 1536, 9050 Puerto Deseado, Santa Cruz Province, Argentina, *Tel:* +54 297 487 2130, *Email:* bernard@maritimabernard.com, *Website:* www.maritimabernard.com

Surveyors: Registro Italiano Navale (RINA), Puerto Deseado, Santa Cruz Province, Argentina, *Tel:* +54 297 467 1148, *Fax:* +54 297 487 2741, *Website:* www.rina.org

Medical Facilities: Available at municipal hospital and private clinic

Airport: 6 miles

Lloyd's Agent: Cooper Brothers S.r.l., Avenida Leandro N. Alem 690, 19th Floor, C1001AAO Buenos Aires, Argentina, *Tel:* +54 11 4311 3121, *Fax:* +54 11 4312 2545, *Email:* argentina@cooperbrosgroup.com, *Website:* www.cooperbrosgroup.com

PUERTO MADRYN

Lat 42° 44' S; Long 65° 2' W.

Admiralty Chart: 3067	**Admiralty Pilot:** 5
Time Zone: GMT -3 h	**UNCTAD Locode:** AR PMY

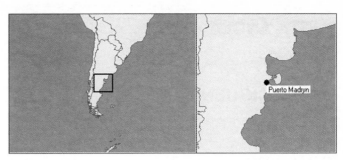

Principal Facilities:

	Y	G	C		L	B			A

Authority: Administracion Portuaria de Puerto Madryn, Muelle Almirante Storni, 9120 Puerto Madryn, Chubut Province, Argentina, *Tel:* +54 2965 451400, *Fax:* +54 2965 452444, *Email:* administracion@appm.com.ar, *Website:* www.appm.com.ar

Officials: General Manager: Hugo Stecconi, *Email:* hstecconi@appm.com.ar.

Port Security: ISPS compliant

Pilotage: Compulsory. Pilot boards approx 1 mile off Almirante Storni pier

Radio Frequency: VHF Channels 12, 14, 16 and 77

Traffic: 2006, 1 231 305 t of cargo handled

Principal Imports and Exports: Imports: Alumina. Exports: Aluminium ingots, Frozen fish, Wool.

Working Hours: Mon-Fri 0700-1300, 1300-1900. Sat 0700-1300. Overtime available

Accommodation:

Name	Length (m)	Depth (m)	Remarks
Almirante Storni Pier			
Berth No.1	217	12.76–16.72	See [1] below
Berth No.2	217	12.76–16.72	See [2] below
Berth No.3	214	10.33–12.76	See [3] below
Berth No.4	300	5.47–10.34	Exclusive use of fishing vessels
Berth No.5	156		
Berth No.6	142		

[1]*Berth No.1:* Bulk berth with a mooring dolphin at 26 m from both ends, accommodating vessels up to 220 m loa. This berth is predominantly used by Aluar S.A. for discharging bulk cargoes at rate of 300 t/h but can also be used by vessels loading general cargo and fruit
[2]*Berth No.2:* For vessels up to 175 m loa. This berth is generally used to load general cargo
[3]*Berth No.3:* A mooring dolphin at 25 m from each end for vessels up to 190 m loa. This berth is used for loading of containers and unloading of general cargo

Storage:

Location	Covered (m²)	Sheds / Warehouses
Puerto Madryn	1714	3

Mechanical Handling Equipment:

Location	Type	Capacity (t)	Qty
Puerto Madryn	Mobile Cranes	45–50	2
Berth No.3	Shore Cranes	6	2

Bunkering: Bominflot, Bominflot Bunkergesellschaft fur Mineralole mbH & Co. KG, Floor 6, Reconquista 1048, A1003ABV Buenos Aires, Argentina, *Tel:* +54 11 4312 0840, *Fax:* +54 11 4313 8337, *Email:* mail@bominflot.com.ar, *Website:* www.bominflot.net – *Grades:* MGO – *Notice:* 72 hours – *Delivery Mode:* tank truck, pipeline
ExxonMobil Marine Fuels, Suite 900, One Alhambra Plaza, Coral Gables, FL 33134, United States of America, *Tel:* +1 305 459 6358, *Fax:* +1 305 459 6412, *Email:* emmf@exxonmobil.com, *Website:* www.exxonmobilmarinefuels.com – *Grades:* MGO – *Notice:* 72 hours – *Delivery Mode:* truck
Maritima Challaco SRL/JRI Comercial Srl, Belgrano Avenida 553, 4th Floor O, 1092 Buenos Aires, Argentina, *Tel:* +54 11 4331 1104, *Fax:* +54 11 4331 1104, *Email:* bunkers@maritimachallaco.com.ar, *Website:* www.maritimachallaco.com.ar – *Grades:* MDO; MGO; IFO-180 – *Notice:* 72 hours – *Delivery Mode:* barge, pipeline, truck

Repair & Maintenance: Minor repairs only

Shipping Agents: Agencia Maritima Martin Srl, G. Maiz 387, 9120 Puerto Madryn, Chubut Province, Argentina, *Tel:* +54 2965 471518, *Fax:* +54 2965 451979, *Email:* madryn@agencia-martin.com.ar, *Website:* www.agencia-martin.com.ar

Medical Facilities: Available at local municipal hospital or private clinic

Airport: Trelew Airport, 67 km

Lloyd's Agent: Cooper Brothers S.r.l., Avenida Leandro N. Alem 690, 19th Floor, C1001AAO Buenos Aires, Argentina, *Tel:* +54 11 4311 3121, *Fax:* +54 11 4312 2545, *Email:* argentina@cooperbrosgroup.com, *Website:* www.cooperbrosgroup.com

PUERTO ROSALES

harbour area, see under Bahia Blanca

Key to Principal Facilities:—					
A=Airport	**C**=Containers	**G**=General Cargo	**P**=Petroleum	**R**=Ro/Ro	**Y**=Dry Bulk
B=Bunkers	**D**=Dry Dock	**L**=Cruise	**Q**=Other Liquid Bulk	**T**=Towage (where available from port)	

PUNTA ANCLA

harbour area, see under Bahia Blanca

PUNTA CIGUENA

harbour area, see under Bahia Blanca

PUNTA COLORADA

Lat 41° 42' S; Long 65° 2' W.

Admiralty Chart: 3067	**Admiralty Pilot:** 5
Time Zone: GMT -3 h	**UNCTAD Locode:** AR PCO

This port is no longer operational

PUNTA LOYOLA

harbour area, see under Rio Gallegos

PUNTA QUILLA

Lat 50° 7' S; Long 68° 24' W.

Admiralty Chart: -	**Admiralty Pilot:** 6
Time Zone: GMT -3 h	**UNCTAD Locode:** AR PQU

Principal Facilities:

P		G		B		A

Authority: Unidad Ejecutora Portuaria de Santa Cruz, Puerto de Punta Quilla, Zona Portuaria s/n, 9300 Punta Quilla, Santa Cruz Province, Argentina, *Tel:* +54 2962 498323, *Fax:* +54 2962 498147, *Email:* ptoptaquilla@santacruz.servisur.com.ar, *Website:* www.scruz.gov.ar/puertos

Approach: Access channel 160 m wide in depth of 15.25 m

Pilotage: Compulsory. Pilot station at Santa Cruz. Agents require 3 h notice for ordering pilot

Radio Frequency: Punta Quilla coastguard on VHF Channel 12

Traffic: 2004, 78 925 t of cargo handled

Maximum Vessel Dimensions: Approx 170 m loa

Working Hours: Mon-Fri 0700-1300, 1300-1900. Sat 0700-1300. Overtime available

Accommodation:

Name	Length (m)	Depth (m)	Remarks
Punta Quilla			
Berth	158	10.03	See [1] below

[1]*Berth:* Predominantly used by fishing vessels. Mooring length extended to 274 m on seaward side, with dolphins 60 m from each end of wharf. Two vessels, each of 130 m loa can berth simultaneously

Mechanical Handling Equipment:

Location	Type	Capacity (t)	Qty
Punta Quilla	Mobile Cranes	50	2
Punta Quilla	Forklifts	4	3

Bunkering: Maritima Challaco SRL/JRI Comercial Srl, Belgrano Avenida 553, 4th Floor O, 1092 Buenos Aires, Argentina, *Tel:* +54 11 4331 1104, *Fax:* +54 11 4331 1104, *Email:* bunkers@maritimachallaco.com.ar, *Website:* www.maritimachallaco.com.ar – *Grades:* MDO; MGO; IFO-180 – *Notice:* 72 hours – *Delivery Mode:* barge, pipeline, truck
RYTTSA Bunker (Repsol - YPF Trading & Transporte S.A.), Avenida Presidente Roque Saenz Pena 777, 1035 Buenos Aires, Argentina, *Tel:* +54 11 4329 2000, *Fax:* +54 11 4329 5749, *Email:* bunkerbaires@repsolypf.com, *Website:* www.ryttsabunker.com

Shipping Agents: Agencia Maritima Internacional, 9 de Julio 867, 9300 Punta Quilla, Santa Cruz Province, Argentina, *Tel:* +54 2962 498373, *Fax:* +54 2962 498337, *Email:* amisantacruz@ocean.com.ar, *Website:* www.amisa.com

Medical Facilities: Provincial hospital available

Airport: Santa Cruz Airport, 10 km

Lloyd's Agent: Cooper Brothers S.r.l., Avenida Leandro N. Alem 690, 19th Floor, C1001AAO Buenos Aires, Argentina, *Tel:* +54 11 4311 3121, *Fax:* +54 11 4312 2545, *Email:* argentina@cooperbrosgroup.com, *Website:* www.cooperbrosgroup.com

QUEQUEN

harbour area, see under Necochea

RAMALLO

Lat 33° 29' S; Long 60° 0' W.

Admiralty Chart: 1982A	**Admiralty Pilot:** 5
Time Zone: GMT -3 h	**UNCTAD Locode:** AR RAM

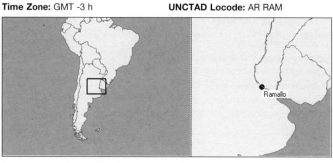

Principal Facilities:

P		Y	G			B		

Authority: Port of Ramallo Authority, Port Office, Ramallo, Argentina, *Tel:* +54 347 488044

Port Security: ISPS compliant

Pilotage: Compulsory. River Plate pilot embarks at Recalada pilot station or at Montevideo Joint Point in pos 35° 03' S; 56° 09' W. Then two River Parana pilots embark at Zona Comun and sails the vessel up to Ramallo roads. Harbour pilot in/out

Maximum Vessel Dimensions: 225 m loa

Principal Imports and Exports: Exports: Grain.

Working Hours: Monday to Friday 0600-1800, Satuirday 0600-1200

Accommodation:

Name	Length (m)	Depth (m)	Remarks
Ramallo			
Muelle Fiscal de Cabotaje	75	9	See [1] below
Puerto Ramallo S.A.	150	11.6	See [2] below

[1]*Muelle Fiscal de Cabotaje:* Operated by Cooperativa Agricola de Ramallo Ltda Grain elevator loading berth at rate of approx 500 t/h by two conveyor belts
[2]*Puerto Ramallo S.A.:* Operated by Glencore S.A.
Grain berth with load rate of 600 t/h

Storage:

Location	Grain (t)
Ramallo	16000
Muelle Fiscal de Cabotaje	16000
Puerto Ramallo S.A.	17000

Bunkering: ExxonMobil Marine Fuels, Suite 900, One Alhambra Plaza, Coral Gables, FL 33134, United States of America, *Tel:* +1 305 459 6358, *Fax:* +1 305 459 6412, *Email:* emmf@exxonmobil.com, *Website:* www.exxonmobilmarinefuels.com – *Grades:* IFO-180cSt; MGO; MDO – *Delivery Mode:* barge, truck

Towage: Not compulsory

Medical Facilities: Available for emergencies only

Development: Bunge is in the process of developing a new grain terminal at the port

Lloyd's Agent: Cooper Brothers S.r.l., Avenida Leandro N. Alem 690, 19th Floor, C1001AAO Buenos Aires, Argentina, *Tel:* +54 11 4311 3121, *Fax:* +54 11 4312 2545, *Email:* argentina@cooperbrosgroup.com, *Website:* www.cooperbrosgroup.com

RIO CULLEN TERMINAL

Lat 52° 48' S; Long 68° 13' W.

Admiralty Chart: 554/1692	**Admiralty Pilot:** 6
Time Zone: GMT -3 h	**UNCTAD Locode:** AR

Principal Facilities:

P									

Authority: Total Austral S.A., Belgrano 801, Rio Grande, Tierra del Fuego, Argentina, *Tel:* +54 2964 430165, *Fax:* +54 2964 425365, *Email:* loading.tdf@totalfinaelf.com

Port Security: ISPS compliant

Anchorage: The recommended waiting zone and anchorage area for tankers is located in pos 52° 54.5' S; 68° 10.0' W in depth of 20 m

Pilotage: Compulsory and carried out by Mooring Master

Radio Frequency: VHF Channels 16 and 69

Weather: The terminal is closed for mooring operations whenever weather conditions exceed wave height of 2.0 m and the wind exceeds 25 knots over a 1 h period

Maximum Vessel Dimensions: 130 000 dwt

Principal Imports and Exports: Exports: Crude oil.

Accommodation:

Name	Remarks
Rio Cullen Terminal	See [1] below

[1]*Rio Cullen Terminal:* Consists of SPM located off the Rio Grande on the E coast of Isla Grande in Tierra del Fuego in depth of 33.5 m

Lloyd's Agent: Cooper Brothers S.r.l., Avenida Leandro N. Alem 690, 19th Floor, C1001AAO Buenos Aires, Argentina, *Tel:* +54 11 4311 3121, *Fax:* +54 11 4312 2545, *Email:* argentina@cooperbrosgroup.com, *Website:* www.cooperbrosgroup.com

RIO GALLEGOS

Lat 51° 37' S; Long 69° 13' W.

Admiralty Chart: -	**Admiralty Pilot:** 6
Time Zone: GMT -3 h	**UNCTAD Locode:** AR RGL

Principal Facilities:

P		Y	G						A

Authority: Unidad Ejecutora Portuaria de Santa Cruz, Puerto de Rio Gallegos, Gobernador Lista 395, 9400 Rio Gallegos, Santa Cruz Province, Argentina, *Tel:* +54 2966 422352, *Fax:* +54 2966 429013, *Email:* claudiobobbio@speedy.com.ar, *Website:* www.scruz.gov.ar/puertos

Officials: Director: Claudio Bobbio.

Approach: Access via North Channel

Pilotage: Compulsory. Pilots should be requested in advance through agents to Nautical S.R.L., Tel: +54 2965 450500, Fax: +54 2965 450500, Email: nautical@infovia.com.ar, in Puerto Madryn at least 5 days before arrival. Vessels southbound usually take the pilot in Puerto Deseado Outer Roads

Radio Frequency: Rio Gallegos Radio: call sign 'LPG' on VHF Channel 26

Working Hours: Mon-Fri 0700-1300, 1300-1900. Sat 0700-1300. Overtime available

Accommodation:

Name	Length (m)	Depth (m)	Remarks
Rio Gallegos			See [1] below
Punta Loyola			See [2] below
Presidente Arturo Illia Quay	200	15	See [3] below

[1]*Rio Gallegos:* Consists of the El Turbio and Fiscal Wharves which are used solely by Argentine vessels engaged in domestic trade up to 140 m loa

[2]*Punta Loyola:* Coal loading facility to ship coal extracted from the Rio Turbio deposits 40 km away. Access viaduct to the quay is 280 m long and 9.8 m wide, carrying a roadway and conveyor belts for loading. Two berths on the quay face, one for loading coal and the other for loading oil

[3]*Presidente Arturo Illia Quay:* Oil and coal loading berth with two outlying mooring dolphins giving an overall length of approx 390 m, able to receive vessels up to 230 m loa

Storage:

Location	Open (m²)	Covered (m²)	Sheds / Warehouses
Rio Gallegos	1300	1920	1

Mechanical Handling Equipment:

Location	Type	Capacity (t)	Qty
Rio Gallegos	Mobile Cranes	60	1
Rio Gallegos	Mobile Cranes	25	1
Rio Gallegos	Mobile Cranes	16	1
Rio Gallegos	Mobile Cranes	15	1
Rio Gallegos	Forklifts		3

Repair & Maintenance: Minor repairs only

Shipping Agents: Agencia Maritima Internacional, Sarmiento 154, 9400 Rio Gallegos, Santa Cruz Province, Argentina, *Tel:* +54 2966 430268, *Fax:* +54 2966 420104, *Email:* amiriogallegos@ocean.com.ar, *Website:* www.amisa.com

Medical Facilities: Public hospital and four private clinics available

Airport: Rio Gallegos Airport

Lloyd's Agent: Cooper Brothers S.r.l., Avenida Leandro N. Alem 690, 19th Floor, C1001AAO Buenos Aires, Argentina, *Tel:* +54 11 4311 3121, *Fax:* +54 11 4312 2545, *Email:* argentina@cooperbrosgroup.com, *Website:* www.cooperbrosgroup.com

RIO GRANDE

Lat 53° 47' S; Long 67° 42' W.

Admiralty Chart: -	**Admiralty Pilot:** -
Time Zone: GMT -3 h	**UNCTAD Locode:** AR RGA

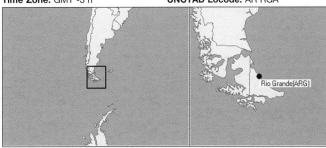

Authority: Port Authority of Rio Grande, Padre Beauviar 531, 9420 Rio Grande, Tierra del Fuego, Argentina, *Tel:* +54 2964 423753, *Fax:* +54 2964 423753, *Email:* gerenciariogrande@speedy.com.ar

Officials: Harbour Master: Guillermo Roberto Izaguirre, *Email:* guillermoizaguirre@speedy.com.ar.

Port Security: ISPS compliant

Shipping Agents: Agencia Maritima Internacional, 9 de Julio 597, 9420 Rio Grande, Tierra del Fuego, Argentina, *Tel:* +54 2964 430249, *Fax:* +54 2964 430700, *Email:* amiriogrande@ocean.com.ar, *Website:* www.amisa.com

Development: It is proposed to build a quay 12 km N of the city, 160 m long with two outlying mooring dolphins for vessels up to 40 000 dwt. The quay will be joined to the shore by a 1620 m long viaduct. Construction is due to resume in 2005

Lloyd's Agent: Cooper Brothers S.r.l., Avenida Leandro N. Alem 690, 19th Floor, C1001AAO Buenos Aires, Argentina, *Tel:* +54 11 4311 3121, *Fax:* +54 11 4312 2545, *Email:* argentina@cooperbrosgroup.com, *Website:* www.cooperbrosgroup.com

ROSARIO

Lat 32° 57' S; Long 60° 38' W.

Admiralty Chart: 1982A/1982B	**Admiralty Pilot:** 6
Time Zone: GMT -3 h	**UNCTAD Locode:** AR ROS

Principal Facilities:

	Q	Y	G			B		A

Authority: Ente Administrador Puerto Rosario, Av. Belgrano 341, 2000 Rosario, Santa Fe Province, Argentina, *Tel:* +54 341 448 7105, *Fax:* +54 341 448 5010, *Email:* rinstitucionales@enapro.com.ar, *Website:* www.enapro.com.ar

Officials: Marketing: Zulma Dinelli.

Port Security: ISPS compliant

Key to Principal Facilities:—

A=Airport	**C**=Containers	**G**=General Cargo	**P**=Petroleum	**R**=Ro/Ro	**Y**=Dry Bulk
B=Bunkers	**D**=Dry Dock	**L**=Cruise	**Q**=Other Liquid Bulk	**T**=Towage (where available from port)

Anchorage: The principal anchorage is between Km 410 and 412. Secondary anchorage between Km 419.5 and 421.5. Auxiliary anchorage between Km 424 and 425

Pilotage: Compulsory. Port pilots stationed at Rosario, Tel/Fax: +54 341 448 3628, Email: rosariopilots@citynet.net.ar

Radio Frequency: VHF Channel 12

Weather: Winds annual average (km/h) Max: 25.9 Min: 9.1

Traffic: 2003, 3 054 539 t of cargo handled

Principal Imports and Exports: Imports: Fertilisers, Iron, Steel. Exports: Grains, Sugar, Vegetable oils.

Working Hours: 24 h/day 365 days per year

Accommodation:

Name	Length (m)	Remarks
Multi-Purpose Terminals		See [1] below
Terminal 1	570	
Terminal 2 (North)	385	
Terminal 2 (South)	653	
Grain Terminals		
Terminal 3	80	See [2] below
Terminal 6	250	See [3] below
Terminal 7	450	See [4] below

[1]*Multi-Purpose Terminals:* Operated by Terminal Puerto Rosario S.A., Av. Belgrano 2015, Rosario, Tel: +54 341 435 5438, Email: info@puertoderosario.com.ar, Website: www.puertoderosario.com.ar
65 ha two terminal facility
[2]*Terminal 3:* Operated by Servicios Portuarios S.A., Tel: +54 341 430 3879, Fax: +54 341 430 3879
Storage cap of 82 000 t with loading cap of 850 t/h
[3]*Terminal 6:* Operated by Servicios Portuarios S.A., Tel: +54 341 481 7774, Fax: +54 341 482 4695
Storage cap of 130 000 t with loading cap of 2000 t/h
[4]*Terminal 7:* Operated by Servicios Portuarios S.A., Tel: +54 341 481 7774, Fax: +54 341 482 4695
One 250 m berth for ocean-going vessels and one 200 m berth for river barges. Storage cap of 80 000 t with loading cap of 3600 t/h

Storage:

Location	Covered (m²)	Grain (t)
Multi-Purpose Terminals	30000	
Terminal 6		120000
Terminal 7		80000

Mechanical Handling Equipment:

Location	Type	Qty
Rosario	Mult-purp. Cranes	2
Rosario	Mobile Cranes	1

Bunkering: Risler S.A., 1st Floor, Risler Building, Avenida Corrientes 809, 2000 Rosario, Santa Fe Province, Argentina, *Tel:* +54 341 4253 388, *Fax:* +54 341 4259 707, *Email:* frisler@risler.com.ar, *Website:* www.rislersa.com.ar
Bominflot, Bominflot Bunkergesellschaft fur Mineralole mbH & Co. KG, Floor 6, Reconquista 1048, A1003ABV Buenos Aires, Argentina, *Tel:* +54 11 4312 0840, *Fax:* +54 11 4313 8337, *Email:* mail@bominflot.com.ar, *Website:* www.bominflot.net – *Grades:* IFO-180cSt; MDO; MGO – *Delivery Mode:* tank truck
Eg3 S.A., 13th Floor, Tucuman 744, 1049 Buenos Aires, Argentina, *Tel:* +54 11 4324 0425, *Fax:* +54 11 4324 0605
ExxonMobil Marine Fuels, Suite 900, One Alhambra Plaza, Coral Gables, FL 33134, United States of America, *Tel:* +1 305 459 6358, *Fax:* +1 305 459 6412, *Email:* emmf@exxonmobil.com, *Website:* www.exxonmobilmarinefuels.com – *Grades:* IFO-180cSt; MDO; MGO – *Delivery Mode:* barge, truck
Maritima Challaco SRL/JRI Comercial Srl, Belgrano Avenida 553, 4th Floor O, 1092 Buenos Aires, Argentina, *Tel:* +54 11 4331 1104, *Fax:* +54 11 4331 1104, *Email:* bunkers@maritimachallaco.com.ar, *Website:* www.maritimachallaco.com.ar – *Grades:* MDO; MGO; IFO-180 – *Delivery Mode:* barge, pipeline, truck
RYTTSA Bunker (Repsol - YPF Trading & Transporte S.A.), Avenida Presidente Roque Saenz Pena 777, 1035 Buenos Aires, Argentina, *Tel:* +54 11 4329 2000, *Fax:* +54 11 4329 5749, *Email:* bunkerbaires@repsolypf.com, *Website:* www.ryttsabunker.com
Risler S.A., 1st Floor, Risler Building, Avenida Corrientes 809, 2000 Rosario, Santa Fe Province, Argentina, *Tel:* +54 341 4253 388, *Fax:* +54 341 4259 707, *Email:* frisler@risler.com.ar, *Website:* www.rislersa.com.ar – *Grades:* all grades, in line blending available – *Misc:* own storage facilities – *Parcel Size:* rtw min 25-30t, barge 950t – *Notice:* 24 hours – *Delivery Mode:* pipeline, barge, road tank wagon
Sol EC Ltd, P O Box 1759, 1000 Buenos Aires, Argentina, *Tel:* +54 11 4328 2844, *Fax:* +54 11 4328 0742

Waste Reception Facilities: Garbage collection as required

Repair & Maintenance: Minor repairs only

Ship Chandlers: Barcelo Hnos Ship Supplies, San Lorenzo 4440, 2000 Rosario, Santa Fe Province, Argentina, *Tel:* +54 341 439 4809, *Fax:* +54 341 430 6869, *Email:* barcelohnos@ciudad.com.ar, *Website:* www.barcelohnos.com.ar
Navy & Co. Argentina, 590 Juan de Garay, 2001 Rosario, Santa Fe Province, Argentina, *Tel:* +54 341 485 1947, *Fax:* +54 341 485 0487, *Email:* navy&co.arg@cablenet.com.ar
Mario Tsioulis S.A., Chacabuco 2014, S2000FIH Rosario, Santa Fe Province, Argentina, *Tel:* +54 341 482 7510, *Fax:* +54 341 485 0006, *Email:* info@tsioulis.com, *Website:* www.tsioulis.com

Shipping Agents: Agencia MarÝtima Silversea S.A., San Martin 440 - First Floor, S2000CJD Rosario, Santa Fe Province, Argentina, *Tel:* +54 341 421 2776, *Fax:* +54 341 421 2776, *Email:* silver@silversea.com.ar, *Website:* www.silversea.com.ar
Agenzia Maritima Delta S.A., San Lorenzo 1035, Piso 8 B, S2000ARW Rosario, Santa Fe Province, Argentina, *Tel:* +54 341 425 6087, *Fax:* +54 341 424 4270, *Email:* delta_agency@ciudad.com.ar

Agencia Maritima Dulce S.A., c/o Upriver SA, Rosario, Santa Fe Province, Argentina, *Tel:* +54 341 421 8833, *Fax:* +54 341 421 8838, *Email:* upriver@upriver.com.ar
Agencia Maritima Nabsa S.A., Buenos Aires 605, S2200CEA Rosario, Santa Fe Province, Argentina, *Tel:* +54 341 425 6252, *Fax:* +54 341 425 6942, *Email:* rosario@nabsa.com.ar, *Website:* www.nabsa.com.ar
Supermar S.A., 27 Febrero 774, S2000EQE Rosario, Santa Fe Province, Argentina, *Tel:* +54 341 481 5462, *Fax:* +54 341 486 0077, *Email:* operations@supermar.com.ar, *Website:* www.supermar.com.ar

Surveyors: Bureau Veritas, 6th Floor - Of. 10 & 11, Sarmiento 819, 2000 Rosario, Santa Fe Province, Argentina, *Tel:* +54 341 530 9880, *Fax:* +54 341 530 9881, *Website:* www.bureauveritas.com
Det Norske Veritas A/S, San Luis 760 Piso 6 Of 2, Santa Fe, S2000BBH Rosario, Santa Fe Province, Argentina, *Tel:* +54 341 424 3732, *Fax:* +54 341 424 4577, *Email:* hantognini@ciudad.com.ar, *Website:* www.dnv.com
Hellenic Register of Shipping, Las Dalias 1950, Rosario, Santa Fe Province, Argentina, *Tel:* +54 341 493 6356, *Fax:* +54 341 493 6356, *Email:* susan@funescoop.com.ar, *Website:* www.hrs.gr

Medical Facilities: Several public and private hospitals available

Airport: Rosario Airport, 35 km

Lloyd's Agent: Cooper Brothers S.r.l., Avenida Leandro N. Alem 690, 19th Floor, C1001AAO Buenos Aires, Argentina, *Tel:* +54 11 4311 3121, *Fax:* +54 11 4312 2545, *Email:* argentina@cooperbrosgroup.com, *Website:* www.cooperbrosgroup.com

SAN ANTONIO ESTE

Lat 40° 49' S; Long 64° 45' W.

Admiralty Chart: 531	**Admiralty Pilot:** 5
Time Zone: GMT -3 h	**UNCTAD Locode:** AR SAE

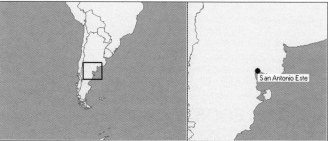

Principal Facilities:

		G	C		B		A

Authority: Terminal de Servicios Portuarios Patagonia Norte S.A., C.C. 78, 8520 San Antonio Este, Rio Negro Province, Argentina, *Tel:* +54 2934 492023, *Fax:* +54 2934 492035, *Email:* info@patagonia-norte.com.ar, *Website:* www.patagonia-norte.com.ar

Officials: Operations Manager: Andres Castro, *Email:* acastro@patagonia-norte.com.ar.

Port Security: ISPS compliant

Pilotage: Compulsory and available at all times. 48 h notice required via agents. Pilot boards in pos 40° 54' S; 64° 57' W

Radio Frequency: VHF Channels 8, 12, 14 and 16

Traffic: 2004, 545 930 t of cargo handled

Maximum Vessel Dimensions: 170 m loa

Principal Imports and Exports: Exports: Fruit.

Working Hours: Mon-Fri 0700-1500, 1500-2300. Overtime available

Accommodation:

Name	Length (m)	Depth (m)	Remarks
Pier			
1 Outer	200	12.1	Fruit export for vessels up to 170 m loa
2 Inner	200	7.9	Fruit export for vessels up to 150 m loa
3 Outer	80	7.9	Fishing vessels
4 Inner	80	6	Fishing vessels

Storage: Three cold stores for fruit prior to loading of 1600 m2, 2300 m2 and 4800 m2

Location	Covered (m²)
San Antonio Este	2130

Mechanical Handling Equipment:

Location	Type	Capacity (t)	Qty
San Antonio Este	Mult-purp. Cranes	27	1
San Antonio Este	Mobile Cranes	30	2

Bunkering: Bominflot, Bominflot Bunkergesellschaft fur Mineralole mbH & Co. KG, Floor 6, Reconquista 1048, A1003ABV Buenos Aires, Argentina, *Tel:* +54 11 4312 0840, *Fax:* +54 11 4313 8337, *Email:* mail@bominflot.com.ar, *Website:* www.bominflot.net – *Grades:* MDO; MGO; IFO-180 – *Notice:* 72 hours – *Delivery Mode:* barge, truck
ExxonMobil Marine Fuels, Suite 900, One Alhambra Plaza, Coral Gables, FL 33134, United States of America, *Tel:* +1 305 459 6358, *Fax:* +1 305 459 6412, *Email:* emmf@exxonmobil.com, *Website:* www.exxonmobilmarinefuels.com – *Grades:* MGO – *Delivery Mode:* truck

Maritima Challaco SRL/JRI Comercial Srl, Belgrano Avenida 553, 4th Floor O, 1092 Buenos Aires, Argentina, *Tel:* +54 11 4331 1104, *Fax:* +54 11 4331 1104, *Email:* bunkers@maritimachallaco.com.ar, *Website:* www.maritimachallaco.com.ar – *Grades:* MDO; MGO; IFO-180 – *Notice:* 72 hours – *Delivery Mode:* barge, pipeline, truck

Shipping Agents: Agencia Maritima Martin Srl, P O Box 95, 8520 San Antonio Este, Rio Negro Province, Argentina, *Tel:* +54 2934 492055, *Fax:* +54 2934 492007, *Email:* saeste@agencia-martin.com.ar, *Website:* www.agencia-martin.com.ar

Medical Facilities: A rural hospital and a private clinic are available at San Antonio Oeste

Airport: San Antonio Este Airport

Lloyd's Agent: Cooper Brothers S.r.l., Avenida Leandro N. Alem 690, 19th Floor, C1001AAO Buenos Aires, Argentina, *Tel:* +54 11 4311 3121, *Fax:* +54 11 4312 2545, *Email:* argentina@cooperbrosgroup.com, *Website:* www.cooperbrosgroup.com

SAN JULIAN

Lat 49° 15' S; Long 67° 40' W.

Admiralty Chart: 3226	**Admiralty Pilot:** 6
Time Zone: GMT -3 h	**UNCTAD Locode:** AR ULA

This port is no longer operational

SAN LORENZO

Lat 32° 43' S; Long 60° 43' W.

Admiralty Chart: 1982B	**Admiralty Pilot:** 5
Time Zone: GMT -3 h	**UNCTAD Locode:** AR SLO

Principal Facilities:

P	Q	Y	G			B		A

Port Security: ISPS compliant

Pilotage: Compulsory. River Plate pilot embarks at Recalada pilot station or at Montevideo Joint Point in pos 35° 03' S; 56° 09' W. Then two River Parana pilots embark at Zona Comun and sail the vessel up to San Lorenzo roads. Harbour pilot in/out

Radio Frequency: VHF Channels 14 and 16

Traffic: 2006, 39 423 000 t of cargo handled

Working Hours: Loading bulk, normal hours 0600-1200, 1200-1800. 1800-2400 and 0000-0600 are overtime hours

Accommodation:

Name	Length (m)	Depth (m)	Remarks
San Martin			
Minera Alumbrera	166	12.46	See [1] below
Terminal 6 (South Berth)	155	12.16	See [2] below
Terminal 6 (North Berth)	161	12.16	See [3] below
Resinfor	55	10.33	See [4] below
El Quebracho	130	9.12	See [5] below
Puerto Fertilizante Quebracho	130	9.5	See [6] below
Petrobras Energia	90		See [7] below
Nidera (IMSA)	150	12.16	See [8] below
El Transito	152	7.8	See [9] below
Pampa	125	12.16	See [10] below
Dempa	125	12.16	See [11] below
San Lorenzo			
Exxon Terminal		7.29	See [12] below
Petrobras Energia S.A.			See [13] below
Jetty 1			Vessels up to 230 m loa
Jetty 2			Coastal craft up to 110 m loa
Jetty 3			Vessels up to 250 m loa
A.C.A.	176	12.16	See [14] below
I.C.I.	60	9.2	See [15] below
Vicentin	140	11.24	See [16] below

[1]*Minera Alumbrera:* Operated by Minera Alumbrera Ltd
For vessels up to 230 m loa. Loading of mineral ore (copper concentrate) at rate of approx 5000-7000 t/day. Berth consists of five berthing dolphins and head/stern mooring dolphins

[2]*Terminal 6 (South Berth):* Operated by Terminal 6 S.A., Tel: +54 3476 438000, Fax: +54 3476 438046, Email: telefonistas@terminal6.com.ar, Website: www.terminal6.com.ar
Four dolphins together with two outlying dolphins for bow and stern moorings. Grain and vegetable proteins loaded via two feeder lines and four loading arms at rate of 800-1000 t/h

[3]*Terminal 6 (North Berth):* Operated by Terminal 6 S.A., Tel: +54 3476 438000, Fax: +54 3476 438046, Email: telefonistas@terminal6.com.ar, Website: www.terminal6.com.ar
Four dolphins and two outlying dolphins. One loading line and two loading arms. Grain loading at 1000 t/h and vegetable proteins at 800 t/h

[4]*Resinfor:* Operated by Resinfor Metanol S.A.
Private berth for vessels up to 240 m loa. Export of methanol and urea formaldehyde resin

[5]*El Quebracho:* Owned by Cargill
Terminal for grain, by-products and vegetable oil for vessels up to 270 m loa

[6]*Puerto Fertilizante Quebracho:* For vessels up to 210 m loa. Consists of three dolphins offering a berthing front of 130 m with two outlying mooring towers, giving an overall length of 270 m and is fitted with hoppers and conveyor belts to permit grab discharge of fertilisers

[7]*Petrobras Energia:* Private berth for loading chemical products belonging to Petrobras Energia S.A. for vessels up to 180 m loa

[8]*Nidera (IMSA):* Operated by Nidera S.A.
Terminal for grain, by-products & vegetable oil

[9]*El Transito:* Operated by Alfred C. Toepfer S.A.
Grain terminal

[10]*Pampa:* Owned by Bunge Argentina S.A., Tel: +54 3476 422045
Private grain berth for vessels up to 270 m loa

[11]*Dempa:* Owned by Bunge Argentina S.A., Tel: +54 3476 422045
Private berth for grain, by-products & vegetable oil for vessels up to 250 m loa

[12]*Exxon Terminal:* Berthing front afforded by two dolphins. Usually coastal and clean product tankers use this berth handling naphtha, kerosene and diesel oil

[13]*Petrobras Energia S.A.:* These berths are served by 4", 6", 8", 10", 12" and 14" pipelines to permit discharge of crude oil as well as petroleum by-products for the nearby refinery

[14]*A.C.A.:* Owned by Asociacion de Cooperativas Argentinas
Private terminal for vessels up to 273 m loa. Storage cap of 240 000 t of grains, 40 000 t of agri by-products and 36 000 t of oil

[15]*I.C.I.:* Owned by I.C.I. (International Chemical Industries) Argentina SAIC
Private terminal for export of various chemical products

[16]*Vicentin:* Owned by Vicentin SAIC, Tel: +54 3476 424899, Fax: +54 3476 425977
Private grain terminal with two conveyor belts of 1200 t/h each

Storage:

Location	Grain (t)
Terminal 6 (South Berth)	528000
El Quebracho	540000
Nidera (IMSA)	335000
El Transito	127000
Pampa	296000
Dempa	150000
Vicentin	254000

Bunkering: Bominflot, Bominflot Bunkergesellschaft fur Mineralole mbH & Co. KG, Floor 6, Reconquista 1048, A1003ABV Buenos Aires, Argentina, *Tel:* +54 11 4312 0840, *Fax:* +54 11 4313 8337, *Email:* mail@bominflot.com.ar, *Website:* www.bominflot.net – *Grades:* IFO-180cSt; MDO; MGO – *Delivery Mode:* tank truck
Eg3 S.A., 13th Floor, Tucuman 744, 1049 Buenos Aires, Argentina, *Tel:* +54 11 4324 0425, *Fax:* +54 11 4324 0605
Maritima Challaco SRL/JRI Comercial Srl, Belgrano Avenida 553, 4th Floor O, 1092 Buenos Aires, Argentina, *Tel:* +54 11 4331 1104, *Fax:* +54 11 4331 1104, *Email:* bunkers@maritimachallaco.com.ar, *Website:* www.maritimachallaco.com.ar – *Grades:* MDO; MGO; IFO-180 – *Delivery Mode:* barge, pipeline, truck
RYTTSA Bunker (Repsol - YPF Trading & Transporte S.A.), Avenida Presidente Roque Saenz Pena 777, 1035 Buenos Aires, Argentina, *Tel:* +54 11 4329 2000, *Fax:* +54 11 4329 5749, *Email:* bunkerbaires@repsolypf.com, *Website:* www.ryttsabunker.com
Risler S.A., 1st Floor, Risler Building, Avenida Corrientes 809, 2000 Rosario, Santa Fe Province, Argentina, *Tel:* +54 341 4253 388, *Fax:* +54 341 4259 707, *Email:* frisler@risler.com.ar, *Website:* www.rislersa.com.ar – *Grades:* all grades – *Parcel Size:* barge 950t, – *Rates:* 250t/h – *Notice:* 24 hours – *Delivery Mode:* barge, pipeline, road tank wagon, wharf
Sol EC Ltd, P O Box 1759, 1000 Buenos Aires, Argentina, *Tel:* +54 11 4328 2844, *Fax:* +54 11 4328 0742

Repair & Maintenance: Minor repairs only

Ship Chandlers: Barcelo Hnos Ship Supplies, San Lorenzo 4440, 2000 Rosario, Santa Fe Province, Argentina, *Tel:* +54 341 439 4809, *Fax:* +54 341 430 6869, *Email:* barcelohnos@ciudad.com.ar, *Website:* www.barcelohnos.com.ar
Claudio A. Polon, Bv. Urquiza 637, 1st Floor, 2200 San Lorenzo, Argentina, *Tel:* +54 3476 423267, *Fax:* +54 3476 427032, *Email:* cpolon@smisl.com.ar, *Website:* www.smisl.com.ar

Shipping Agents: Agencia Maritima el Hauar S.R.L., Mateo Gelvez 457, S2200FIE San Lorenzo, Argentina, *Tel:* +54 3476 427027, *Email:* elhauar@arnet.com.ar, *Website:* www.elhauar.com.ar
Agencia Maritima Internacional, 25 de Mayo 245, 2200 San Lorenzo, Argentina, *Tel:* +54 3476 422089, *Fax:* +54 3476 423653, *Email:* amisanlorenzo@ocean.com.ar, *Website:* www.amisa.com
Agencia Maritima Transparana S.A., Av. San Martin 3888, S2200FPU San Lorenzo, Argentina, *Tel:* +54 3476 428800, *Fax:* +54 3476 426008, *Email:* sanlorenzo@amtsa.com.ar, *Website:* www.amtsa.com.ar
Fertimport S.A., Beron de Astrada, 1331, Prov. de Santa Fe, S2200DGU San Lorenzo, Argentina, *Tel:* +54 3476 432690/1/2, *Fax:* +54 3476 431878, *Email:* slo.fertimport@bunge.com, *Website:* www.fertimport.com.br
Agencia Maritima Nabsa S.A., Cayetano Nerbutti 248, S2202ARD San Lorenzo, Argentina, *Tel:* +54 3476 423749, *Fax:* +54 3476 423345, *Email:* sanlorenzo@nabsa.com.ar, *Website:* www.nabsa.com.ar
Supermar S.A., Building No.656, Salta Street, 2200 San Lorenzo, Argentina, *Tel:* +54 3476 425200, *Fax:* +54 3476 474451, *Email:* operations@supermar.com.ar, *Website:* www.supermar.com.ar

Medical Facilities: Two private clinics

Airport: Rosario Airport, 35 km

Key to Principal Facilities:—					
A=Airport	**C**=Containers	**G**=General Cargo	**P**=Petroleum	**R**=Ro/Ro	**Y**=Dry Bulk
B=Bunkers	**D**=Dry Dock	**L**=Cruise	**Q**=Other Liquid Bulk	**T**=Towage (where available from port)	

Lloyd's Agent: Cooper Brothers S.r.l., Avenida Leandro N. Alem 690, 19th Floor, C1001AAO Buenos Aires, Argentina, *Tel:* +54 11 4311 3121, *Fax:* +54 11 4312 2545, *Email:* argentina@cooperbrosgroup.com, *Website:* www.cooperbrosgroup.com

SAN MARTIN

harbour area, see under San Lorenzo

SAN NICOLAS

Lat 33° 19' S; Long 60° 13' W.

Admiralty Chart: 1982A	**Admiralty Pilot:** 5
Time Zone: GMT -3 h	**UNCTAD Locode:** AR SNS

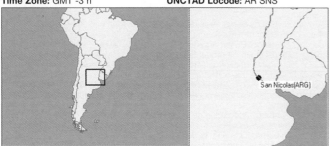

Principal Facilities:

	Y	G			B			A

Authority: Provincial Administration, San Nicolas, Buenos Aires Province, Argentina, *Tel:* +54 3461 460010

Port Security: ISPS compliant

Pilotage: Compulsory. River Plate pilot embarks at Recalada pilot station or at Montevideo Joint Point in pos 35° 03' S; 56° 09' W. Then two River Parana pilots embark at Zona Comun and sail the vessel up to San Nicolas roads. Harbour pilot in/out

Radio Frequency: Coastguard listens on VHF Channel 12

Traffic: 2005, 1 732 743 t of cargo handled

Working Hours: 0600-1200, 1200-1800. Overtime available

Accommodation:

Name	Length (m)	Depth (m)	Remarks
San Nicolas			
Puerto Ing. Buitrago Berths			Operated by SOM S.A.
Berth A	680	6.2	See [1] below
Berth B	320	8.6	See [2] below
Central Termica Power Station	200	9.8	Discharge of coal by two cranes
Grain Elevator	143		See [3] below
Puerto Nuevo	537	8–8.7	See [4] below

[1]*Berth A:* Discharge of iron ore and coal plus loading of coke breeze
[2]*Berth B:* Loading of finished steel products by two 15 t and one 30 t crane
[3]*Grain Elevator:* Operated by Administracion Portuaria Bonaerense (APB) For vessels up to 250 m loa. Loading by two conveyor belts at rate of 700-1400 t/h
[4]*Puerto Nuevo:* Operated by Administracion Portuaria Bonaerense (APB) Cargoes handled include grain, zinc concentrate, steel slabs and billets. A fertilizer plant also operates from this quay

Storage:

Location	Grain (t)
Grain Elevator	77000

Mechanical Handling Equipment:

Location	Type	Capacity (t)	Qty
Puerto Nuevo	Mult-purp. Cranes	20–27	6
Puerto Nuevo	Mobile Cranes	7–30	2

Bunkering: Bominflot, Bominflot Bunkergesellschaft fur Mineralole mbH & Co. KG, Floor 6, Reconquista 1048, A1003ABV Buenos Aires, Argentina, *Tel:* +54 11 4312 0840, *Fax:* +54 11 4313 8337, *Email:* mail@bominflot.com.ar, *Website:* www.bominflot.net – *Grades:* all grades – *Notice:* 72 hours – *Delivery Mode:* tanker Eg3 S.A., 13th Floor, Tucuman 744, 1049 Buenos Aires, Argentina, *Tel:* +54 11 4324 0425, *Fax:* +54 11 4324 0605
Maritima Challaco SRL/JRI Comercial Srl, Belgrano Avenida 553, 4th Floor O, 1092 Buenos Aires, Argentina, *Tel:* +54 11 4331 1104, *Fax:* +54 11 4331 1104, *Email:* bunkers@maritimachallaco.com.ar, *Website:* www.maritimachallaco.com.ar – *Grades:* MDO; MGO; IFO-180 – *Delivery Mode:* barge, pipeline, truck
RYTTSA Bunker (Repsol - YPF Trading & Transporte S.A.), Avenida Presidente Roque Saenz Pena 777, 1035 Buenos Aires, Argentina, *Tel:* +54 11 4329 2000, *Fax:* +54 11 4329 5749, *Email:* bunkerbaires@repsolypf.com, *Website:* www.ryttsabunker.com
Risler S.A., 1st Floor, Risler Building, Avenida Corrientes 809, 2000 Rosario, Santa Fe Province, Argentina, *Tel:* +54 341 4253 388, *Fax:* +54 341 4259 707, *Email:* frisler@risler.com.ar, *Website:* www.rislersa.com.ar – *Grades:* all grades, in line blending available – *Misc:* own storage facilities – *Parcel Size:* min rtw 25-30t, barge 950t – *Notice:* 24 hours – *Delivery Mode:* pipeline, barge, rtw

Sol EC Ltd, P O Box 1759, 1000 Buenos Aires, Argentina, *Tel:* +54 11 4328 2844, *Fax:* +54 11 4328 0742

Repair & Maintenance: Limited repairs only

Shipping Agents: Agencia Maritima Bristol, Almafuerte 341, 2900 San Nicolas, Buenos Aires Province, Argentina, *Tel:* +54 3461 434284, *Fax:* +54 3461 430464, *Email:* bristolsnicolas@arnet.com.ar, *Website:* www.ambristol.com.ar
Alpemar Srl, Francia 190, B2900HVD San Nicolas, Buenos Aires Province, Argentina, *Tel:* +54 3461 424605, *Fax:* +54 3461 429653, *Email:* alpemar@alpemar.com.ar, *Website:* www.alpemar.com.ar
Fertimport S.A., Rivadavia 589, B2900LPK San Nicolas, Buenos Aires Province, Argentina, *Tel:* +54 3461 453330, *Fax:* +54 3461 454344, *Email:* sni.fertimport@bunge.com, *Website:* www.fertimport.com.br

Stevedoring Companies: Compania Argentina de Servicios Portuarios S.A. (CASPORT), Rivadavia 1351, B2900LRA San Nicolas, Buenos Aires Province, Argentina, *Tel:* +54 3461 451415, *Fax:* +54 3461 451417, *Email:* casport@casport.com.ar, *Website:* www.casport.com.ar

Medical Facilities: Available at municipal hospital and private clinics

Airport: Rosario, 60 km

Lloyd's Agent: Cooper Brothers S.r.l., Avenida Leandro N. Alem 690, 19th Floor, C1001AAO Buenos Aires, Argentina, *Tel:* +54 11 4311 3121, *Fax:* +54 11 4312 2545, *Email:* argentina@cooperbrosgroup.com, *Website:* www.cooperbrosgroup.com

SAN PEDRO

Lat 33° 40' S; Long 59° 39' W.

Admiralty Chart: 1982A	**Admiralty Pilot:** 5
Time Zone: GMT -3 h	**UNCTAD Locode:** AR SPD

Principal Facilities:

	Y	G			B			

Authority: Terminal Puerto San Pedro S.A., Av. San Martin 2500, B2930 San Pedro, Buenos Aires Province, Argentina, *Tel:* +54 3329 420999, *Fax:* +54 3329 425279, *Email:* info@tpsp.com.ar, *Website:* www.tpsp.com.ar

Officials: Manager: Fernando Boracchia, *Email:* fboracchia@tpsp.com.ar.

Port Security: ISPS compliant

Pilotage: Compulsory. River Plate pilot embarks at Recalada pilot station or at Montevideo Joint Point in pos 35° 03' S; 56° 09' W. Then two River Parana pilots embark at Zona Comun and sail the vessel up to San Pedro roads. Harbour pilot in/out

Radio Frequency: San Pedro Radio on VHF Channels 16, 25, 27 and 28

Traffic: 2005, 1 127 839 t of cargo handled

Maximum Vessel Dimensions: 225 m loa, 33 m beam

Principal Imports and Exports: Exports: Grain.

Working Hours: Mon-Fri 0600-1200, 1200-1800. Sat 0600-1200. Overtime available

Accommodation:

Name	Length (m)	Depth (m)	Remarks
San Pedro			
Terminal Puerto San Pedro S.A.	220	8.43	Grain terminal
Pierhead	85		See [1] below

[1]*Pierhead:* Occasionally loading bagged grain or bulk agricultural by-products via portable conveyor belts

Storage:

Location	Covered (m²)	Sheds / Warehouses	Grain (t)
San Pedro	2250	3	
Terminal Puerto San Pedro S.A.			204000

Bunkering: ExxonMobil Marine Fuels, Suite 900, One Alhambra Plaza, Coral Gables, FL 33134, United States of America, *Tel:* +1 305 459 6358, *Fax:* +1 305 459 6412, *Email:* emmf@exxonmobil.com, *Website:* www.exxonmobilmarinefuels.com – *Grades:* IFO-180cSt; MDO; MGO – *Misc:* available from Buenos Aires or Campana – *Delivery Mode:* barge, truck

Medical Facilities: Municipal hospital and two private clinics

Lloyd's Agent: Cooper Brothers S.r.l., Avenida Leandro N. Alem 690, 19th Floor, C1001AAO Buenos Aires, Argentina, *Tel:* +54 11 4311 3121, *Fax:* +54 11 4312 2545, *Email:* argentina@cooperbrosgroup.com, *Website:* www.cooperbrosgroup.com

SAN SEBASTIAN TERMINAL

Lat 53° 19' S; Long 68° 16' W.

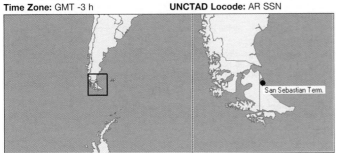

Admiralty Chart: 554	**Admiralty Pilot:** 6
Time Zone: GMT -3 h	**UNCTAD Locode:** AR SSN

Principal Facilities:

P									

Authority: Pan American Fueguina S.A., San Sebastian Terminal, Almirante Brown 1496, 9420 Rio Grande, Tierra del Fuego, Argentina, *Tel:* +54 2964 436061, *Fax:* +54 2964 436061, *Email:* epellegrini@pan-energy.com

Officials: Manager: Edgardo Pellegrini.

Accommodation:

Name	Remarks
San Sebastian Oil Terminal	See [1] below

[1]*San Sebastian Oil Terminal:* Tank storage terminal connected by pipeline to two loading/discharging points where vessels anchor and moor stern-on to five mooring buoys. The outer position at 53° 16' 22" S; 68° 12' 56" W is for loading crude oil. This terminal is operated by Pan American Energy

Lloyd's Agent: Cooper Brothers S.r.l., Avenida Leandro N. Alem 690, 19th Floor, C1001AAO Buenos Aires, Argentina, *Tel:* +54 11 4311 3121, *Fax:* +54 11 4312 2545, *Email:* argentina@cooperbrosgroup.com, *Website:* www.cooperbrosgroup.com

SANTA FE

Lat 31° 38' S; Long 60° 42' W.

Admiralty Chart: 1982B	**Admiralty Pilot:** 5
Time Zone: GMT -3 h	**UNCTAD Locode:** AR SFN

Principal Facilities:

P	Q	Y	G	C		B		T	A

Authority: Ente Administrador Puerto Santa Fe, Cabecera Darsena 1, 3000 Santa Fe, Santa Fe Province, Argentina, *Tel:* +54 342 455 8400, *Fax:* +54 342 455 8392, *Email:* puertosfe@puertosfe.com, *Website:* www.puertosfe.com

Officials: President: Alfredo Cecchi, *Email:* alfredocecchi@puertosfe.com.
Port Manager: Julio Montero, *Tel:* +54 342 453 3997, *Email:* juliomontero@puertosfe.com.

Port Security: ISPS compliant

Approach: Santa Fe is the last important port up the R Parana for ocean-going vessels. Vessels are to enter at very slow speed due to dredge working on access channel. Access permitted 0900-1700 h. Sailing: 0900-1500 h in summer; 0900-1400 h rest of year. Access to port is through channel from river, 6085 m long; the anchorage is below the mouth of this channel

Pilotage: Compulsory. River Plate pilot embarks at Recalada pilot station or at Montevideo Joint Point in pos 35° 03' S; 56° 09' W. Then two River Parana pilots embark at Zona Comun and sail the vessel up to Santa Fe roads. Harbour pilot in/out

Maximum Vessel Dimensions: 202 m loa, 30 m breadth

Working Hours: 0700-1300, 1300-1900

Accommodation:

Name	Length (m)	Depth (m)	Remarks
Santa Fe			See [1] below
Dock No.1	1449	7.31	See [2] below
Dock No.2			Old and out of use
Derivation Channel	2178		See [3] below
Coasting Wharf	810		See [4] below

[1]*Santa Fe:* The port is composed of Dock No.1, Dock No.2, Derivation Channel and

Coasting Wharf. Depending upon the river, frequently in the summer season the max permitted draft to sail by Prefectura is limited by depth existing in the Tacuari Pass Bulk facilities: Grain loading facilities: Unit I, on S end of the W quay of Dock 1 can dock two vessels in 7.31 m. Berth 259 m in length. Storage cap of 50 000 t with loading rate of 700-900 t/h. Eight telescopic chutes served by three conveyor belts. Unit II has storage cap of 10 000 t with loading rate of 500-600 t/h by two lines
[2]*Dock No.1:* Can accommodate seven vessels. The greater part of the general cargo and container cargo is discharged here and there are four large warehouses, well equipped with cranes up to 200 t and sheds. Vegetable oil plant operated by Cia Continental Imp Exp S.A. with cap of 5000 t and pumping cap of 23 000 t/h
[3]*Derivation Channel:* Next to Dock No.2. Open banks. It is not recommended for general use as most of the wharves are used for inflammables. There are a number of dolphins and mooring facilities. W part is reserved for inflammables and Esso SAPA, Shell Mex Argentina and YPF all have oil intakes to storage on the banks. Two deposits for Quebraco logs and for bones. Full rail facilities but not cranes. Vessels awaiting orders or effecting repairs can be laid up on the E side without being charged permanency dues
[4]*Coasting Wharf:* Continuation of the W side of Dock No.1. This is used by river craft etc

Mechanical Handling Equipment:

Location	Type	Capacity (t)	Qty
Santa Fe	Mobile Cranes	200	1
Santa Fe	Mobile Cranes	45	1
Santa Fe	Forklifts	4.5–6	2

Bunkering: Fuel oil available at 72 h notice. As there are no barges, fuel must be taken from tanker trucks
Sol EC Ltd, Zona Rural S/N, Arroyo Seco, 2128 Santa Fe, Santa Fe Province, Argentina, *Tel:* +54 340 2426 711, *Fax:* +54 340 2426 793, *Email:* daniel.pignolo@shell.com, *Website:* www.shell.com

Towage: One tug available of 4000 hp

Repair & Maintenance: Two workshops available for minor repairs

Medical Facilities: Available

Airport: Sauce Viejo, 22 km

Lloyd's Agent: Cooper Brothers S.r.l., Avenida Leandro N. Alem 690, 19th Floor, C1001AAO Buenos Aires, Argentina, *Tel:* +54 11 4311 3121, *Fax:* +54 11 4312 2545, *Email:* argentina@cooperbrosgroup.com, *Website:* www.cooperbrosgroup.com

TIMBUES

Lat 32° 38' S; Long 60° 44' W.

Admiralty Chart: -	**Admiralty Pilot:** 6
Time Zone: GMT -3 h	**UNCTAD Locode:** AR

Principal Facilities:

		Y							

Authority: Noble Argentina S.A., Carlos Pellegrini 1163 Piso 9, C1009ABW Buenos Aires, Argentina, *Tel:* +54 11 4131 7100, *Fax:* +54 11 4131 7120, *Email:* comercial@noblegrain.com, *Website:* www.noblegrain.com.ar

Officials: Managing Director: Alfonso Romero, *Email:* aromero@noblegrain.com.

Maximum Vessel Dimensions: 235 m loa

Principal Imports and Exports: Exports: Corn, Soybeans, Wheat.

Accommodation:

Name	Remarks
Timbues	See [1] below

[1]*Timbues:* Local Office: Brigadier Estanislao Lopez 8514, 2204 Timbues, Tel: +54 3476 495565
Grain river port located on the lower Parana River in Santa Fe Province, approx 35 km N of Rosario and 340 km from Buenos Aires. Three derricks and loading rate of 1600 t/h

Storage:

Location	Grain (t)
Timbues	130000

Lloyd's Agent: Cooper Brothers S.r.l., Avenida Leandro N. Alem 690, 19th Floor, C1001AAO Buenos Aires, Argentina, *Tel:* +54 11 4311 3121, *Fax:* +54 11 4312 2545, *Email:* argentina@cooperbrosgroup.com, *Website:* www.cooperbrosgroup.com

Key to Principal Facilities:—			
A=Airport	**C**=Containers	**G**=General Cargo	**P**=Petroleum **R**=Ro/Ro **Y**=Dry Bulk
B=Bunkers	**D**=Dry Dock	**L**=Cruise	**Q**=Other Liquid Bulk **T**=Towage (where available from port)

USHUAIA

Lat 54° 48' S; Long 68° 13' W.

Admiralty Chart: 554 **Admiralty Pilot:** 6
Time Zone: GMT -3 h **UNCTAD Locode:** AR USH

Principal Facilities:

P		Y	G	C	R	L	B			A

Authority: Direccion Provincial de Puertos de la Provincia de Tierra del Fuego, Avenida Maipu 510, 1 Piso, Puerto Ushuaia, V9410BJL Ushuaia, Tierra del Fuego, Argentina, *Tel:* +54 2901 435200, *Fax:* +54 2901 431443, *Email:* operaciones@puertoushuaia.gov.ar, *Website:* www.puertoushuaia.gov.ar

Officials: President: Sergio Garcia, *Email:* presidencia@puertoushuaia.gov.ar.
Port Manager: Gustavo De Robles, *Email:* gderobles@puertoushuaia.gov.ar.

Port Security: ISPS compliant

Pilotage: Argentine pilot boarding points are as follows:
a) vessels arriving at the eastern end of the Beagle Channel, 1.5 miles off Moat Point or adjacent to Cape San Pio, or in the case of bad weather in the shelter of Slogget Bay
b) if arriving from the west the pilot is taken off Roca Peron at the demarcation of the Chilean/Argentine jurisdiction
c) vessels proceeding from the Chilean port of Puerto Williams take the Argentine Ushuaia port pilot at Les Eclaireurs

Radio Frequency: Ushuaia coastguard on VHF Channel 16

Traffic: 2001, 140 980 t of cargo handled

Working Hours: Shifts of 6 or 8 hours plus overtime available

Accommodation:

Name	Length (m)	Depth (m)	Remarks
Commercial Pier			Containers, fishing vessels & cruise vessels
Berth No.1 (S side)	129	3.1–5	
Berth No.2 (N side)	45	5.2–5.8	
Berth No.3 (S side)	80	5–5.8	
Berth No.4 (N side)	120	5.8–7.5	
Berth No.5 (S side)	120	5.8–7.5	
Berth No.6 (N side)	150	7.5–8.2	
Berth No.7 (S side)	150	7.5–8.2	
Berth No.8 (N side)	200	8.2–10.8	
Berth No.9 (S side)	200	8.2–10.8	
Orion Oil Jetty			See [1] below

[1]*Orion Oil Jetty:* Situated approx 0.5 miles NE of the Commercial Pier. It is a narrow T-shaped jetty extending approx 85 m from the shore with a frontage of 30 m at its head, 10 m width and fitted with outlying mooring points. Used by tankers to discharge gas oil to shore storage tanks

Storage: Bonded warehouse of 1100 m2, also two privately owned warehouses available. Accommodation for approx 800 TEU's and facilities for 30 reefer containers

Mechanical Handling Equipment:

Location	Type	Capacity (t)	Qty
Ushuaia	Reach Stackers	40	1
Ushuaia	Forklifts	2.5–7	3

Bunkering: Bominflot, Bominflot Bunkergesellschaft fur Mineralole mbH & Co. KG, Floor 6, Reconquista 1048, A1003ABV Buenos Aires, Argentina, *Tel:* +54 11 4312 0840, *Fax:* +54 11 4313 8337, *Email:* mail@bominflot.com.ar, *Website:* www.bominflot.net – *Grades:* MGO – gas oil available from Orion Oil Jetty storage tanks – *Delivery Mode:* tank truck, pipeline
ExxonMobil Marine Fuels, Suite 900, One Alhambra Plaza, Coral Gables, FL 33134, United States of America, *Tel:* +1 305 459 6358, *Fax:* +1 305 459 6412, *Email:* emmf@exxonmobil.com, *Website:* www.exxonmobilmarinefuels.com – *Grades:* MGO – *Delivery Mode:* truck
Maritima Challaco SRL/JRI Comercial Srl, Belgrano Avenida 553, 4th Floor O, 1092 Buenos Aires, Argentina, *Tel:* +54 11 4331 1104, *Fax:* +54 11 4331 1104, *Email:* bunkers@maritimachallaco.com.ar, *Website:* www.maritimachallaco.com.ar – *Grades:* MDO; MGO; IFO-180 – *Misc:* gas oil available from Orion Oil Jetty storage tanks – *Delivery Mode:* barge, pipeline, truck
RYTTSA Bunker (Repsol - YPF Trading & Transporte S.A.), Avenida Presidente Roque Saenz Pena 777, 1035 Buenos Aires, Argentina, *Tel:* +54 11 4329 2000, *Fax:* +54 11 4329 5749, *Email:* bunkerbaires@repsolypf.com, *Website:* www.ryttsabunker.com

Repair & Maintenance: Repairs carried out by Naval Dockyard

Ship Chandlers: Mattina Hnos. S.A.C.I.A.N., Heroes de Malvinas 4765, 9410 Ushuaia, Tierra del Fuego, Argentina, *Tel:* +54 2901 422680, *Fax:* +54 2901 422680, *Email:* pprince@usu.mattina-sa.com.ar
Navalia S.r.l., 25 de Mayo 250, Oficina 3, 9410 Ushuaia, Tierra del Fuego, Argentina,

Tel: +54 2901 435616, *Fax:* +54 2901 424470, *Email:* operations@navalia.com.ar, *Website:* www.navalia.com.ar

Shipping Agents: Agencia Maritima Internacional, Gobernador Deloqui 555 - 4th Floor, V9410BDK Ushuaia, Tierra del Fuego, Argentina, *Tel:* +54 2901 431110, *Fax:* +54 2901 431110, *Email:* amiushuaia@ocean.com.ar, *Website:* www.amisa.com
Navalia S.r.l., 25 de Mayo 250, Oficina 3, 9410 Ushuaia, Tierra del Fuego, Argentina, *Tel:* +54 2901 435616, *Fax:* +54 2901 424470, *Email:* operations@navalia.com.ar, *Website:* www.navalia.com.ar

Medical Facilities: Available at municipal hospital and a private clinic

Airport: Ushuaia Airport

Lloyd's Agent: Cooper Brothers S.r.l., Avenida Leandro N. Alem 690, 19th Floor, C1001AAO Buenos Aires, Argentina, *Tel:* +54 11 4311 3121, *Fax:* +54 11 4312 2545, *Email:* argentina@cooperbrosgroup.com, *Website:* www.cooperbrosgroup.com

VILLA CONSTITUCION

Lat 33° 13' S; Long 60° 19' W.

Admiralty Chart: 1982A **Admiralty Pilot:** 5
Time Zone: GMT -3 h **UNCTAD Locode:** AR VCN

Principal Facilities:

		Y	G			B		T	A

Authority: Puerto Villa Constitucion S.R.L., Villa Constitucion, Santa Fe Province, Argentina, *Tel:* +54 3400 470958, *Fax:* +54 3400 470958, *Email:* puertovconstitucion@arnet.com.ar, *Website:* www.puertovconstitucion.com.ar

Officials: President: Cesar Carra.

Port Security: ISPS compliant

Pilotage: Compulsory. River Plate pilot embarks at Recalada pilot station or at Montevideo Joint Point in pos 35° 03' S; 56° 09' W. Then two River Parana pilots embark at Zona Comun and sail the vessel up to Villa Constitucion roads. Harbour pilot in/out

Radio Frequency: Coastguard listens on VHF Channel 9

Working Hours: Normal 0600-1800. Overtime 1800-0600

Accommodation:

Name	Length (m)	Depth (m)	Remarks
Villa Constitucion			
Servicios Portuarios S.A. Wharf (Unit 1)	150	4.86	Tel/Fax: +54 3400 475882/3 Loading of grain from four silo's. Only used occasionally
Servicios Portuarios S.A. Grain Elevator Terminal (Unit II)	165	6.38	See [1] below
Puerto Acevedo (Acindar Steel Wharf)	110	7	See [2] below
Puerto Acevedo (Acindar Iron Ore Wharf)	160	7.6	See [3] below

[1]*Servicios Portuarios S.A. Grain Elevator Terminal (Unit II):* Tel/Fax: +54 3400 475882/3
Two vessels, one each side of loading tower, served by two tubes which can operate either one each side of pier or both on the same side. Storage cap at elevator silos is 55 000 t plus 170 000 t in underground deposits
[2]*Puerto Acevedo (Acindar Steel Wharf):* Operated by Acindar S.A., Tel: +54 11 4719 8500, Fax: +54 11 4719 8501, Email: sac@acindar.com.ar
Steel products (mostly with coils) for vessels up to 180 m loa
[3]*Puerto Acevedo (Acindar Iron Ore Wharf):* Operated by Acindar S.A., Tel: +54 11 4719 8500, Fax: +54 11 4719 8501, Email: sac@acindar.com.ar
Discharge of iron ore at average rate of approx 420 t/h

Mechanical Handling Equipment:

Location	Type	Capacity (t)	Qty
Villa Constitucion	Mult-purp. Cranes	10	1
Villa Constitucion	Mult-purp. Cranes	45	2
Villa Constitucion	Mobile Cranes	12	2
Puerto Acevedo (Acindar Steel Wharf)	Mobile Cranes	12	2

Bunkering: Bominflot, Bominflot Bunkergesellschaft fur Mineralole mbH & Co. KG, Floor 6, Reconquista 1048, A1003ABV Buenos Aires, Argentina, *Tel:* +54 11 4312 0840, *Fax:* +54 11 4313 8337, *Email:* mail@bominflot.com.ar, *Website:* www.bominflot.net – *Grades:* MDO; MGO; IFO-180 – *Delivery Mode:* rtw
Eg3 S.A., 13th Floor, Tucuman 744, 1049 Buenos Aires, Argentina, *Tel:* +54 11 4324 0425, *Fax:* +54 11 4324 0605
ExxonMobil Marine Fuels, Suite 900, One Alhambra Plaza, Coral Gables, FL 33134, United States of America, *Tel:* +1 305 459 6358, *Fax:* +1 305 459 6412, *Email:*

emmf@exxonmobil.com, *Website:* www.exxonmobilmarinefuels.com – *Grades:* IFO-180cSt; MDO; MGO – *Delivery Mode:* barge, truck

Maritima Challaco SRL/JRI Comercial Srl, Belgrano Avenida 553, 4th Floor O, 1092 Buenos Aires, Argentina, *Tel:* +54 11 4331 1104, *Fax:* +54 11 4331 1104, *Email:* bunkers@maritimachallaco.com.ar, *Website:* www.maritimachallaco.com.ar – *Grades:* MDO; MGO; IFO-180 – *Delivery Mode:* barge, pipeline, truck

RYTTSA Bunker (Repsol - YPF Trading & Transporte S.A.), Avenida Presidente Roque Saenz Pena 777, 1035 Buenos Aires, Argentina, *Tel:* +54 11 4329 2000, *Fax:* +54 11 4329 5749, *Email:* bunkerbaires@repsolypf.com, *Website:* www.ryttsabunker.com

Risler S.A., 1st Floor, Risler Building, Avenida Corrientes 809, 2000 Rosario, Santa Fe Province, Argentina, *Tel:* +54 341 4253 388, *Fax:* +54 341 4259 707, *Email:* frisler@risler.com.ar, *Website:* www.rislersa.com.ar – *Grades:* all grades, in line blending available – *Misc:* own storage facilities – *Parcel Size:* min rtw 25-30t, barge 950t – *Delivery Mode:* pipeline, barge, rtw

Sol EC Ltd, P O Box 1759, 1000 Buenos Aires, Argentina, *Tel:* +54 11 4328 2844, *Fax:* +54 11 4328 0742

Towage: One tug of 1850 hp

Repair & Maintenance: Can be effected, if necessary bringing men and equipment from Rosario or Buenos Aires

Ship Chandlers: Soulos S.r.l., Almafuerte 1811, 2919 Villa Constitucion, Santa Fe Province, Argentina, *Tel:* +54 3400 473542, *Fax:* +54 3400 473429, *Email:* soulos@soulos.com.ar, *Website:* www.soulos.com.ar

Medical Facilities: Hospital, various clinics and emergency mobile units are available

Airport: San Nicolas, 30 km

Lloyd's Agent: Cooper Brothers S.r.l., Avenida Leandro N. Alem 690, 19th Floor, C1001AAO Buenos Aires, Argentina, *Tel:* +54 11 4311 3121, *Fax:* +54 11 4312 2545, *Email:* argentina@cooperbrosgroup.com, *Website:* www.cooperbrosgroup.com

VITCO OIL TERMINAL

harbour area, see under Zarate

ZARATE

Lat 34° 5' S; Long 59° 1' W.

Admiralty Chart: 1982A	**Admiralty Pilot:** 5
Time Zone: GMT -3 h	**UNCTAD Locode:** AR ZAE

Principal Facilities:

P	Q	Y	G	C	R		B			

Authority: Port Administration, Zarate, Buenos Aires Province, Argentina, *Tel:* 54 3489

Officials: Manager: Norberto Ferreyra.

Port Security: ISPS compliant

Pilotage: Compulsory. River Plate pilot embarks at Recalada pilot station or at Montevideo Joint Point in pos 35° 03' S; 56° 09' W. Then one River Parana pilot embarks at Zona Comun and sails the vessel up to Zarate roads. Harbour pilot in/out

Radio Frequency: Zarate Prefectura Naval Radio on VHF Channels 14 and 72

Accommodation:

Name	Length (m)	Depth (m)	Remarks
Vitco Oil Terminal			See [1] below
Berth 1	80	11.8	Ocean-going vessels up to approx 200 m loa
Berth 2	30	8.8	River craft up to 110 m loa
Auto Terminal Zarate S.A.			See [2] below
Quay	245	10.6	Vessels up to 230 m loa
Zarate Port S.A.			See [3] below
Berth	118	12.8	

[1]*Vitco Oil Terminal:* Owned by Vitco S.A.
Private oil terminal dealing in home trade imports and exports of crude oil & petroleum by-products

[2]*Auto Terminal Zarate S.A.:* Av. Felix Pagola 2671, Zarate, Tel: +54 3487 429000, Fax: +54 3487 429163, Email: info@atzport.com.ar, Website: www.atzport.com.ar
Total terminal area of 60 ha. 550 000 m2 of paved, fenced and lighted parking lots. 100 000 m2 customs bonded area. 24 000 vehicle storage cap

[3]*Zarate Port S.A.:* Av. Felix Pagola 2007, Zarate, Tel: +54 3487 435114, Fax: +54 3487 423212, Email: zarateport@zport.com.ar, Website: www.zport.com.ar
Private terminal handling general, bulk & container cargo

Bunkering: Bominflot, Bominflot Bunkergesellschaft fur Mineralole mbH & Co. KG, Floor 6, Reconquista 1048, A1003ABV Buenos Aires, Argentina, *Tel:* +54 11 4312 0840, *Fax:* +54 11 4313 8337, *Email:* mail@bominflot.com.ar, *Website:* www.bominflot.net – *Grades:* all grades – *Notice:* 72 hours – *Delivery Mode:* tanker

BP Marine Americas Inc., 501 Westlake Park Boulevard, Houston, TX 77079, United States of America, *Tel:* +1 281 366 2000, *Email:* firstname.secondname@bp.com

Convey S.A., Sarmiento 212, 11th Floor, C1041AAF Buenos Aires, Argentina, *Tel:* +54 11 4331 0766, *Fax:* +54 11 4342 8741, *Email:* convey@convey.com.ar

Eg3 S.A., 13th Floor, Tucuman 744, 1049 Buenos Aires, Argentina, *Tel:* +54 11 4324 0425, *Fax:* +54 11 4324 0605

ExxonMobil Marine Fuels, Suite 900, One Alhambra Plaza, Coral Gables, FL 33134, United States of America, *Tel:* +1 305 459 6358, *Fax:* +1 305 459 6412, *Email:* emmf@exxonmobil.com, *Website:* www.exxonmobilmarinefuels.com – *Grades:* IFO-180cSt, MGO; MDO – *Delivery Mode:* barge, truck

Maritima Challaco SRL/JRI Comercial Srl, Belgrano Avenida 553, 4th Floor O, 1092 Buenos Aires, Argentina, *Tel:* +54 11 4331 1104, *Fax:* +54 11 4331 1104, *Email:* bunkers@maritimachallaco.com.ar, *Website:* www.maritimachallaco.com.ar – *Grades:* MDO; MGO; IFO-180 – *Delivery Mode:* barge, pipeline, truck

RYTTSA Bunker (Repsol - YPF Trading & Transporte S.A.), Avenida Presidente Roque Saenz Pena 777, 1035 Buenos Aires, Argentina, *Tel:* +54 11 4329 2000, *Fax:* +54 11 4329 5749, *Email:* bunkerbaires@repsolypf.com, *Website:* www.ryttsabunker.com

Risler S.A., 28th Floor, Tucuman 540, Capital Federal, 1049 Buenos Aires, Argentina, *Tel:* +54 11 4325 4385, *Fax:* +54 11 4325 3376, *Email:* baires@risler.com.ar, *Website:* www.rislersa.com.ar – *Grades:* all grades, in line blending available – *Parcel Size:* min truck 24-40t, barge 2400t – *Rates:* 200-250t/h – *Notice:* 24 hours – *Delivery Mode:* pipeline barge, rtw

Sol EC Ltd, P O Box 1759, 1000 Buenos Aires, Argentina, *Tel:* +54 11 4328 2844, *Fax:* +54 11 4328 0742

Medical Facilities: One hospital and two private clinics

Lloyd's Agent: Cooper Brothers S.r.l., Avenida Leandro N. Alem 690, 19th Floor, C1001AAO Buenos Aires, Argentina, *Tel:* +54 11 4311 3121, *Fax:* +54 11 4312 2545, *Email:* argentina@cooperbrosgroup.com, *Website:* www.cooperbrosgroup.com

ARUBA

BARCADERA

Lat 12° 28' N; Long 69° 59' W.

Admiralty Chart: 702	**Admiralty Pilot:** 7A
Time Zone: GMT -4 h	**UNCTAD Locode:** AW BAR

Principal Facilities:

P	Q	Y	G		R		B		T	A

Authority: Aruba Ports Authority N.V., Port Administration Building, L.G. Smith Boulevard 23, Oranjestad, Aruba, *Tel:* +297 582 6633, *Fax:* +297 583 2896, *Email:* info@arubaports.com, *Website:* www.arubaportsauthority.com

Officials: Managing Director: Juan Alfonso Boekhoudt, *Email:* juan.boekhoudt@arubaports.com.
Finance Director: Humphrey Tromp, *Email:* humphrey.tromp@arubaports.com.
Nautical Director: John H. Seraus, *Email:* john.seraus@arubaports.com.
Marketing Manager: Richard Lacle, *Email:* richard.lacle@arubaports.com.

Port Security: ISPS compliant. Contact: Gertjan Eerenberg, Tel: +297 582 6633

Pre-Arrival Information: 1) Ship's Particulars:
ship's name and call sign
ship's ETA at Oranjestad or Barcadera pilot station 72 h, 48 h and 24 h prior to arrival
ship's arrival draft and estimated sailing draft
ship's identification number
port of registry and classification society
previous names, if any
type of vessel
gt, nrt, sdwt, loa, beam, depth and summer draught
2) Security Information:
certification date of the International Ship Security Certificate and certifying Authority
security level at which the ship is currently operating
security level at which the ship operated during the last 10 calls at port facilities (listing last 10 port calls and respective security levels)
any special or additional security measures taken by the ship within the peroid of the last 10 calls at port facilities
ship security procedures maintained during any ship-to-ship activity within the period of the last 10 calls at port facilities
any Declarations of Security that were entered into with port facilities or other ship's other practical security related information you can provide
crew list
passenger list
type and quantity of transit cargo (including any dangerous goods)

Key to Principal Facilities:—				
A=Airport	**C**=Containers	**G**=General Cargo	**P**=Petroleum	**R**=Ro/Ro	**Y**=Dry Bulk
B=Bunkers	**D**=Dry Dock	**L**=Cruise	**Q**=Other Liquid Bulk	**T**=Towage (where available from port)

certification date of the ISM/SMC and certifying Authority
3) Mooring Information:
is vessel fitted with bow/stern thruster, twin screw/twin rudder
for ro/ro vessels, is the ship fitted with stern ramp/side shell door or bow ramp
requirements for tug service
are the ship's steering and propulsion systems operational and in good working order
does the ship have any defects/non conformities which may affect safe and efficient cargo or manoeuvring operations
4) Additional for Tankers:
does the vessel have any cargo on board
if not, are the tanks gas free
if not, are the tanks inerted and if yes, what is the percentage o2 and pressure in the tanks
any other relevant information

Documentation: Crew list (5 copies), passenger list (4 copies), stowaways list (5 copies), tobacco/spirits/personal effects (1 copy), stores list (1 copy), arms and ammunition list (1 copy), health documents (1 copy), certificate of deratting (1 copy), bill of ladings (2 copies), manifests freighted (2 copies), manifests unfreighted (2 copies), last port clearance (1 copy)

Approach: Harbour is protected by a coral reef

Pilotage: Compulsory for vessels over 50 gt. Pilot boards in pos 12° 28' 50" N; 70° 01' 00" W

Radio Frequency: Oranjestad Pilot Station on VHF Channels 16 and 11

Weather: Prevailing E'ly winds

Tides: Tidal variation 0.4 m

Maximum Vessel Dimensions: 230 m loa, 9.75 m draft

Working Hours: 24 h/day

Accommodation:

Name	Length (m)	Depth (m)	Draught (m)	Remarks
Barcadera				See [1] below
Dock	353	10.97	9.75	See [2] below

[1]*Barcadera:* Situated 3 miles SE of the Oranjestad Harbour
[2]*Dock:* All non-containerized cargo, break bulk, ro/ro, aggregates, LPG gas and gasoline are handled at this facility . Ro/ro platform of 12 m width in depth of 4.26 m at western end of dock

Storage: Limited storage available

Waste Reception Facilities: Waste oil disposal service provided by private contractors. Tanker trucks utilized for collection and removal. Garbage collection available. Ship's agent to make arrangements

Towage: Two harbour tugs of 2200 hp and 3500 hp respectively, fitted with R/T and VHF are available from Oranjestad. Tug lines are used

Repair & Maintenance: Radio, radar and gyro repairs can be carried out. Local workshops can carry out minor repairs to machinery. Arrangements to be made via ship's agent

Stevedoring Companies: Aruba Stevedoring Co. N.V., Port Administration Building, L.G. Smith Boulevard 23, Oranjestad, Aruba, *Tel:* +297 582 2558, *Email:* astec_admin@setarnet.aw

Medical Facilities: Excellent medical and dental service available

Airport: Queen Beatrix International Airport, 4 km

Lloyd's Agent: Maduro & Curiel's Insurance Services N.V., Schottegatweg Oost No.130, P O Box 305, Curacao, Netherlands Antilles, *Tel:* +599 9 466 1610, *Fax:* +599 9 466 1611, *Email:* violeta.merced@mcb-insurance.com, *Website:* www.mcb-insurance.com

ORANJESTAD

Lat 12° 31' N; Long 70° 2' W.

Admiralty Chart: 1312	**Admiralty Pilot:** 7A
Time Zone: GMT -4 h	**UNCTAD Locode:** AW ORJ

Principal Facilities:

		G	C	R	L	B		T	A

Authority: Aruba Ports Authority N.V., Port Administration Building, L.G. Smith Boulevard 23, Oranjestad, Aruba, *Tel:* +297 582 6633, *Fax:* +297 583 2896, *Email:* info@arubaports.com, *Website:* www.arubaportsauthority.com

Officials: Managing Director: Juan Alfonso Boekhoudt, *Email:* juan.boekhoudt@arubaports.com.
Finance Director: Humphrey Tromp, *Email:* humphrey.tromp@arubaports.com.
Nautical Director: John H. Seraus, *Email:* john.seraus@arubaports.com.
Marketing Manager: Richard Lacle, *Email:* richard.lacle@arubaports.com.

Port Security: ISPS compliant. Contact: Gertjan Eerenberg, Tel: +297 582 6633. The port has its own security guard system which patrols the harbour 24 hours seven days a week

Pre-Arrival Information: 1) Ship's Particulars:
ship's name and call sign
ship's ETA at Oranjestad or Barcadera pilot station 72 h, 48 h and 24 h prior to arrival
ship's arrival draft and estimated sailing draft
ship's identification number
port of registry and classification society
previous names, if any
type of vessel
gt, nrt, sdwt, loa, beam, depth and summer draught
2) Security Information:
certification date of the International Ship Security Certificate and certifying Authority
security level at which the ship is currently operating
security level at which the ship operated during the last 10 calls at port facilities (listing last 10 port calls and respective security levels)
any special or additional security measures taken by the ship within the peroid of the last 10 calls at port facilities
ship security procedures maintained during any ship-to-ship activity within the period of the last 10 calls at port facilities
any Declarations of Security that were entered into with port facilities or other ship's other practical security related information you can provide
crew list
passenger list
type and quantity of transit cargo (including any dangerous goods)
certification date of the ISM/SMC and certifying Authority
3) Mooring Information:
is vessel fitted with bow/stern thruster, twin screw/twin rudder
for ro/ro vessels, is the ship fitted with stern ramp/side shell door or bow ramp
requirements for tug service
are the ship's steering and propulsion systems operational and in good working order
does the ship have any defects/non conformities which may affect safe and efficient cargo or manoeuvring operations
4) Additional for Tankers:
does the vessel have any cargo on board
if not, are the tanks gas free
if not, are the tanks inerted and if yes, what is the percentage o2 and pressure in the tanks
any other relevant information

Documentation: Crew list (5 copies), passenger list (4 copies), stowaways list (5 copies), tobacco/spirits/personal effects (1 copy), stores list (1 copy), arms and ammunition list (1 copy), health documents (1 copy), certificate of deratting (1 copy), bill of ladings (2 copies), manifests freighted (2 copies), manifests unfreighted (2 copies), last port clearance (1 copy)

Approach: Oranjestad harbour is easily accessible for the largest vessels. Ships enter through the western fairway, head-on to wind and current, and motor alongside modern concrete docks. Western entrance 141.7 m (min) in width; eastern entrance 243.8 m tapering to 204.2 m min width. The width of the harbour opposite the 527.2 m dock is 213.4 m; opposite the basins 243.8 m. Depth in the harbour 12 m. Depth in the two basins 10.36 m and alongside the docks, also 10.36 m. In these basins vessels are moored head-on to the prevailing eastern trade winds

Anchorage: Suitable even for deepest draft vessels are located 7 to 8 miles S of Oranjestad in depth of 45 m
Restricted anchorage, the limits of which are shown on British Admiralty Chart 702, extend W of the coast; it is reserved for the use of vessels carrying out repairs and underwater hull cleaning. Special permission to be obtained from Direktie Scheepvaart, Tel: +297 583 5192, Fax: 583 5221

Pilotage: Compulsory for vessels over 50 gt. Pilot boards in the following positions: NW entrance in pos 12° 31' 02" N; 70° 04' 17" W
SE entrance in pos 12° 30' 30" N; 70° 03' 00" W

Radio Frequency: VHF Channel 16, Port Channel 11

Traffic: 2005, 18 422 TEU's handled

Maximum Vessel Dimensions: Vessels up to 312+ m loa with draft of 9.75 m have used facilities

Working Hours: 0700-1200, 1300-1600, 1600-2400. Overtime available at all times

Accommodation:

Name	Length (m)	Depth (m)	Draught (m)	Remarks
Oranjestad				See [1] below
Container Berth	250		9.75	See [2] below
Cruise Berths		9.8–11		See [3] below

[1]*Oranjestad:* The cargo terminal has a total area of 1.4 million sq ft, over 7500 TEU's storage cap and 36 reefer points
[2]*Container Berth:* On weekends the container berth is used as a third mega cruise berth
[3]*Cruise Berths:* Five cruise berths: two mega berths each with their own cruise terminal measure 1910 ft in length and the other two berths sharing one cruise terminal are 1443 ft in length. One additional cruise berth is 557 ft long

Mechanical Handling Equipment:

Location	Type	Capacity (t)	Qty
Container Berth	Container Cranes	50	1

Cargo Worked: 20-30 containers/h

Bunkering: S.E.L. Maduro & Sons Inc., S.E.L. Maduro & Sons (Aruba) Inc., 1 Rockefeller Street, Oranjestad, Aruba, *Tel:* +297 528 2343, *Fax:* +297 582 6136, *Email:* operations@selmaduro.com, *Website:* www.selmaduro.com

Waste Reception Facilities: Waste oil disposal service provided by private contractors. Tanker trucks utilized for collection and removal. Garbage collection available. Ship's agent to make arrangements

Towage: Two harbour tugs of 2200 hp and 3500 hp respectively, fitted with R/T and VHF

Ship Chandlers: S.E.L. Maduro & Sons Inc., S.E.L. Maduro & Sons (Aruba) Inc., 1 Rockefeller Street, Oranjestad, Aruba, *Tel:* +297 528 2343, *Fax:* +297 582 6136, *Email:* operations@selmaduro.com, *Website:* www.selmaduro.com
Ola Ship Supplies N.V., de la Sallestraat 43A, Oranjestad AW, Aruba, *Tel:* +297 583

6599, *Fax:* +297 583 8662, *Email:* ola-ship-supply@setarnet.aw, *Website:* www.olashipsupply.com

Shipping Agents: Admiral Shipping Agency N.V., Weg Seroe Blanco 17-C, P O Box 2488, San Nicolas, Aruba, *Tel:* +297 584 1633, *Fax:* +297 584 1634, *Email:* aruba@admiralshipping.com, *Website:* www.admiralshipping.com
Anthony Veder & Co. N.V., VR Shipping (Aruba) N.V., Frankfijkstraat 1, P O Box 533, Oranjestad, Aruba, *Tel:* +297 5824124, *Fax:* +297 5825988, *Email:* veder@setarnet.aw, *Website:* www.vrshipping.com
Gomez Enterprises, Italiestraat 18, Oranjestad, Aruba, *Tel:* +297 582 3961, *Fax:* +297 582 1466, *Email:* gomarnv@setarnet.aw
Intermodal Container Service, LG Smith Boulevard 82, Boulevard Shopping Centre, P O Box 189, Oranjestad, Aruba, *Tel:* +297 582 4622, *Fax:* +297 582 1627, *Email:* ics@metacorp.aw
Kroonvlag (Aruba) N.V., Rockerfellerstraat 1, P O Box 36, Oranjestad, Aruba, *Tel:* +297 582 3888, *Fax:* +297 582 6136, *Email:* kroonvlagaruba@selmaduro.com
S.E.L. Maduro & Sons Inc., S.E.L. Maduro & Sons (Aruba) Inc., 1 Rockefeller Street, Oranjestad, Aruba, *Tel:* +297 528 2343, *Fax:* +297 582 6136, *Email:* operations@selmaduro.com, *Website:* www.selmaduro.com
Mansun Shipping N.V., Rockerfellerstraat 3, P O Box 377, Oranjestad, Aruba, *Tel:* +297 582 6013, *Email:* kroonvlagaruba@selmaduro.com, *Website:* www.selmaduro.com
Nautilus Shipping & Trading Co. N.V., Caya GF (Betico) Croes 196, P O Box 5246, Offshorex, Oranjestad, Aruba, *Tel:* +297 583 3700, *Fax:* +297 588 2380, *Email:* nautilus@setarnet.aw
Rocargo Services N.V., Lago Heightsstraat 28, P O Box 2527, San Nicolas, Aruba, *Tel:* +297 584 4900, *Fax:* +297 584 4880, *Email:* rocargoaruba@rocargo.com, *Website:* www.rocargo.com

Stevedoring Companies: Aruba Stevedoring Co. N.V., Port Administration Building, L.G. Smith Boulevard 23, Oranjestad, Aruba, *Tel:* +297 582 2558, *Email:* astec_admin@setarnet.aw

Medical Facilities: Excellent medical and dental service available

Airport: Prinses Beatrix International, 4 km

Development: All containerised cargoes are to be moved to Barcadera

Lloyd's Agent: Maduro & Curiel's Insurance Services N.V., Schottegatweg Oost No.130, P O Box 305, Curacao, Netherlands Antilles, *Tel:* +599 9 466 1610, *Fax:* +599 9 466 1611, *Email:* violeta.merced@mcb-insurance.com, *Website:* www.mcb-insurance.com

SAN NICOLAS BAY

Lat 12° 25' N; Long 69° 55' W.

Admiralty Chart: 1412	**Admiralty Pilot:** 7A
Time Zone: GMT -4 h	**UNCTAD Locode:** AW SNL

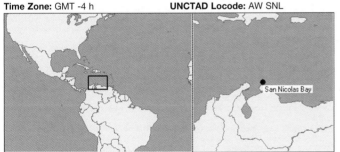

Principal Facilities:

P	Q	Y	G			B		T	A	

OLA
SHIP SUPPLIES N.V.

Prov-Cabin-Bond-
Deck & Engine stores

Email:
ola-ship-supply@setarnet.aw
rwever@olashipsupply.com

P. O. Box 522
De Lasallestraat 43A,
Oranjestad, Aruba, AW
Tel: **+297 583 6599**
Mobile: **+297 593 4800**
Fax: **+297 583 8662**

Authority: Valero Aruba Refining Co. N.V., P O Box 2150, San Nicolas, Aruba, *Tel:* +297 889 4359, *Fax:* +297 889 4554, *Email:* richard.simon@valero.com

Officials: Harbour Master: W. Martinez.

Port Security: ISPS compliant. Contact: Johnny Martes, Tel: +297 589 8235 or Capt. Tom Blanchard, Tel: +297 589 4742

Anchorage: If for any reason a vessel is required to anchor prior to or after berthing the normal anchorage (known as the outer anchorage) is centred in pos 12° 20' N; 70° 04' W, approx 11 miles SW of San Nicolas, in approx 20 fathoms
A secondary anchorage (known as the reef anchorage) is controlled by Valero and vessels should only anchor with their agreement. It is situated off the reef between the eastern exit and western entrance to the inner harbour

Pilotage: Compulsory. Pilots board vessel approx 1-2 miles WSW of the inner harbour entrance for vessels berthing at the inner harbour. Pilots board vessel approx 2-2.5 miles W of the reef berths for vessels berthing at the reef berths. Pilots board vessel 1.5-2 miles SW of the HDS harbour entrance for vessels berthing at the HDS and coke berth

Radio Frequency: All vessels shall advise their ETA 72, 48 and 24 h in advance via telex, fax or email through appointed agents and be able to communicate with 'Valero Marine' on VHF Channels 16, 08 and 79 when within range

Working Hours: 24 h/day

Accommodation:

Name	Draught (m)	Remarks
Inner Harbour		See [1] below
Pier 1 South	11.58	For vessels up to 225.5 m loa
Pier 1 North	11.58	For vessels up to 210.3 m loa
Pier 3 South	12.2	For vessels up to 243.8 m loa
Pier 3 North	12.2	For vessels up to 236.2 m loa
Outer Harbour		
Reef Berth 1	22.8	
Reef Berth 2	32.2	
HDS & Coke Berths		
HDS Berth	9.5	Bulk sulphur loaded at average rate of approx 150 t/h by conveyor belt
Coke Berth	12.2	See [2] below

[1]*Inner Harbour:* Enclosed by a coral reef and has two entrances, both 42 m wide with 13.7 m depth. Vessels normally enter through the W entrance. There is a large refinery situated on shore. Night berthing possible. Slop tank facilities
[2]*Coke Berth:* Petcoke loaded at average rate of approx 1500 t/h by a telescoping ship loader

Bunkering: Chevron Marine Products LLC, Global Marine Products LLC, 1500 Louisiana, 4th Floor, Houston, TX 77002, United States of America, *Tel:* +1 832 8542 988, *Fax:* +1 832 8544 868, *Email:* gulfcbm@chevron.com, *Website:* www.chevron.com – *Grades:* all grades – *Delivery Mode:* pipeline

Towage: Six tugs available of 1200-4520 hp

Repair & Maintenance: Joseph Oduber, Ship Repair Contractor, P O Box 387, San Nicolas, Aruba All kinds of repairs carried out, except those requiring dry docking

Ship Chandlers: Ola Ship Supplies N.V., de la Sallestraat 43A, Oranjestad AW, Aruba, *Tel:* +297 583 6599, *Fax:* +297 583 8662, *Email:* ola-ship-supply@setarnet.aw, *Website:* www.olashipsupply.com

Medical Facilities: Clinic in San Nicolas. Hospital in Oranjestad

Airport: Prinses Beatrix International, 14 km

Lloyd's Agent: Maduro & Curiel's Insurance Services N.V., Schottegatweg Oost No.130, P O Box 305, Curacao, Netherlands Antilles, *Tel:* +599 9 466 1610, *Fax:* +599 9 466 1611, *Email:* violeta.merced@mcb-insurance.com, *Website:* www.mcb-insurance.com

AUSTRALIA

ABBOT POINT

Lat 19° 53' S; Long 148° 4' E.

Admiralty Chart: AUS 255	**Admiralty Pilot:** 15
Time Zone: GMT +10 h	**UNCTAD Locode:** AU ABP

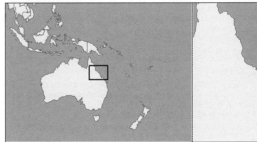

Principal Facilities:

		Y						T		

Authority: Ports Corporation of Queensland, Floor 24, 300 Queen Street, P O Box 409, Brisbane, Qld., Australia 4001, *Tel:* +61 7 3224 7088, *Fax:* +61 7 3224 7234, *Email:* info@pcq.com.au, *Website:* www.pcq.com.au

Officials: Chief Executive Officer: Brad Fish, *Email:* bfish@pcq.com.au.
Communications Manager: Rachel Campbell, *Tel:* +61 7 3224 8863, *Email:* rcampbell@pcq.com.au.

Port Security: ISPS compliant

Approach: Channel depth 17.2 m LWD. A dangerous point is Clark Shoal which extends for approx 3 nautical miles in a north westerly direction from Abbot Point; marked by beacon exhibiting Q(3) 10s

Anchorage: Vessels awaiting berth should anchor in general area approx 2.7 nautical miles N of the wharf

Pilotage: Compulsory. Pilot boards in pos 19° 48.5' S; 148° 05' E. ETA to be confirmed 24 h prior to arrival

Key to Principal Facilities:—			
A=Airport	**C**=Containers	**G**=General Cargo	**P**=Petroleum	**R**=Ro/Ro	**Y**=Dry Bulk
B=Bunkers	**D**=Dry Dock	**L**=Cruise	**Q**=Other Liquid Bulk	**T**=Towage (where available from port)

Radio Frequency: Port working: VHF Channel 12 and 16. Tug working: VHF Channel 6

Weather: SE winds can average 20-30 knots for periods up to two weeks continuously. Winds from between NE and SE, average 15-20 knots for much of the year. Cyclone season Nov/Apr

Tides: Tidal flow normal to wharf at 1-2 knots. MSTR is 2.3 m and MNTR is 0.6 m

Traffic: 2007/08, 169 vessels, 12 475 908 t of bulk cargo exported

Maximum Vessel Dimensions: 300 m loa, 53 m beam, 17.6 m draft

Principal Imports and Exports: Exports: Coal.

Working Hours: Continuous

Accommodation:

Name	Remarks
Abbot Point	See [1] below

[1]*Abbot Point:* Operated by Abbot Point Bulk Coal Pty Ltd., P O Box 207, Bowen, Qld 4805, Tel: +61 7 4786 0300
There is a trestle jetty 2.75 km long with a berthing face of 264 m and depth alongside of 19.4 m LWD. The shiploader has a cap of 4600 t/h and three stacker/reclaimers have an operating cap of 4000 t/h. Two stockpiles with a total cap of 1 250 000 t

Towage: Two tugs available for berthing, each with 50 t bollard pull

Shipping Agents: Barwil Agencies Australia Pty Ltd, P O Box 1055, Townsville, Qld., Australia 4810, *Tel:* +61 7 4721 4955, *Fax:* +61 7 4772 5743, *Email:* townsville@wilhelmsen.com, *Website:* www.wilhelmsen.com

Medical Facilities: Bowen, 40 km S of Abbot Point

Development: Construction of a second 500 m long berth, approx 2.9 km offshore

Lloyd's Agent: Freemans Marine, P O Box 554, Fortitude Valley, Brisbane, Qld., Australia 4006, *Tel:* +61 7 3867 4646, *Fax:* +61 7 3867 4699, *Email:* john.cupitt@freemans.com.au, *Website:* www.freemansmarine.com.au

ADELAIDE

Lat 34° 51' S; Long 138° 34' E.

Admiralty Chart: AUS 137/138	**Admiralty Pilot:** 13
Time Zone: GMT +9.5 h	**UNCTAD Locode:** AU ADL

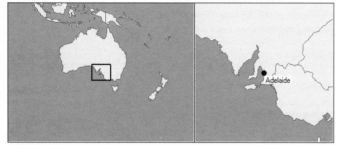

Principal Facilities:

P Q Y G C R L B · T A

Authority: Flinders Ports Proprietary Ltd, 296 St. Vincent Street, P O Box 19, Adelaide, S.A., Australia 5015, *Tel:* +61 8 8447 0611, *Fax:* +61 8 8447 0606, *Email:* flindersports@flindersports.com.au, *Website:* www.flindersports.com.au

Officials: Chief Executive Officer: Vincent Tremaine, *Tel:* +61 8 8447 0633, *Email:* tremaine.vincent@flindersports.com.au.
Chief Financial Officer: Mark Travers, *Tel:* +61 8 8447 0619, *Email:* travers.mark@flindersports.com.au.
General Manager: Capt Carl Kavina, *Tel:* +61 8 8447 0622, *Email:* kavina.carl@flindersports.com.au.
Business Development Manager: Stewart Lammin, *Tel:* +61 8 8447 0627, *Email:* lammin.stewart@flindersports.com.au.
Shipping Manager: Mark Hales, *Email:* hales.mark@flindersports.com.au.

Port Security: ISPS compliant

Approach: The main shipping channel at Outer Harbour, which begins approx 8.5 km W of the main breakwater entrance and extends through the main passenger and freight wharves and ends approx 400 m N of the main container terminal at the Outer Harbour, is dredged to a depth of 14.2 m

Pilotage: Compulsory and available 24 h/day. Pilot boarding ground two miles W of fairway beacon in pos 34° 47.4' S; 138° 22.1' E

Radio Frequency: VHF Channels 6, 8, 12, 16 and 67

Tides: MHWN 1.3 m, MHWS 2.4 m

Traffic: 2007/08, 1134 vessels, 10 297 070 t of cargo handled, 280 121 TEU's

Maximum Vessel Dimensions: Outer Harbour: 288 m loa. Inner Harbour: 206 m loa. Osborne: 206 m loa

Principal Imports and Exports: Imports: Di-ammonium phosphate, Iron and steel, Machinery, Manufactured fertiliser, Motor vehicle parts & accessories, Paper & paper products, Phosphate rock, Timber, Tractors. Exports: Animal feedstuffs, Barley, Container cargo, Copper, Lead, Malt, Meat & meat preparations, Metal waste & scrap, Soda ash, Wheat.

Working Hours: 24 h/day

Accommodation:

Name	Length (m)	Depth (m)	Remarks
Inner Harbour			
Berth No.18	178	10	General cargo
Berth No.19	168	10	General cargo
Berth No.20	163	10	General cargo
Berth No.25	240	10.2	See [1] below
Berth No.27	204	10.9	See [2] below
Berth No.29	245	10	Length of solid wharf 169 m. Bulk loading berth
'H' Berth	304	11.2	See [3] below
'K' Berth	171	7.5	Bulk limestone discharge berth
'M' Berth	218	10.7	Common user tanker berth
Osborne			
Penrice	120	7.5	Loading of bulk soda ash
Osb. 1	208	10	
Outer Harbour			See [4] below
Berth No.1	185	11.5	General cargo
Berth No.2	183	11.2	Passenger terminal & ro/ro
Berth No.3	150	11.2	Motor vehicle terminal
Berth No.4	214	11.2	Motor vehicle terminal
Berth No.6	300	13.2	See [5] below
Berth No.7	210	13.2	Container terminal
Berth No.8	320	16.2	See [6] below

[1]*Berth No.25:* Ro/ro shore ramp. Length of solid wharf 122 m. Currently leased to BHP Billiton
[2]*Berth No.27:* Bulk grain loading berth. Length of solid wharf 142 m. Two travelling loading booms with spouts
[3]*'H' Berth:* Bulk cement/clinker loading berth. Fixed loader with luffing and slewing boom
[4]*Outer Harbour:* Constellation Brands have developed a 20 000 m2 storage and distribution warehouse adjacent to the container terminal
[5]*Berth No.6:* Berth No's 6 and 7 are operated by DP World Adelaide Pty. Ltd., P O Box 207, Port Adelaide, SA 5015, Tel:+61 8 8248 9300, Fax: +61 8 8248 9370, Email: serviceadl@dpworld.com.au, Website: www.dpworld.com.au
Container Terminal. 380 reefer plugs & storage for 5000 TEU's. Ro/ro ramp and on-dock intermodal rail yard
[6]*Berth No.8:* Grain loading wharf capable of handling panamax size bulk vessels

Mechanical Handling Equipment:

Location	Type	Capacity (t)	Qty	Remarks
Berth No.6	Container Cranes	46–60	1	
Berth No.6	Container Cranes	36	1	
Berth No.6	Straddle Carriers		14	at berths 6 & 7
Berth No.6	Forklifts		9	at berths 6 & 7
Berth No.7	Container Cranes	35.5	1	
Berth No.7	Container Cranes	40.6	1	

Bunkering: Diesel and heavy fuel from road tankers available at some berths
BP Australia (Proprietary) Ltd, P O Box 5222, Melbourne, Vic., Australia 3001, *Tel:* +61 3 9268 4111, *Fax:* +61 3 9268 3321, *Email:* gomiasfuelsales@bp.com, *Website:* www.bp.com
Caltex Australia Petroleum Proprietary Ltd, Caltex Australia Petroleum Proprietary Ltd, No 2 Market Street, Sydney, N.S.W., Australia 2000, *Tel:* +61 2 9668 1148, *Fax:* +61 2 9668 1243, *Email:* mnicholl@caltex.com.au, *Website:* www.caltex.com.au
ExxonMobil Marine Fuels, 1 Harbour Front Place, 06-00 Harbour Front, Tower One, Singapore, Republic of Singapore 098633, *Tel:* +65 6885 8998, *Fax:* +65 6885 8794, *Email:* asiapac.marinefuels@exxonmobil.com, *Website:* www.exxonmobilmarinefuels.com – *Grades:* IFO-30; MGO – *Delivery Mode:* barge, tank truck
Shell Australia Ltd, Shell Company of Australia, Marine Centre Oceania, No 8 Redfern Road, Melbourne, Vic., Australia 3123, *Tel:* +61 3 9666 5446, *Fax:* +61 3 8823 4800, *Email:* sal-marine-products@shell.com, *Website:* www.shell.com.au

Waste Reception Facilities: Garbage is collected by a local contractor from 1000 h each day. Oily water and sludge may also be discharged into road tankers for disposal

Towage: Working hours 0830-1700 hrs Monday to Friday, orders for tugs must be lodged at least two hours before towage service is required and no later than 1530 hrs.
Tugs:
Tarpan: 50t bollard pull
Corsair: 43.4t bollard pull
Tapir: 43.4t bollard pull
Tingari: 60t bollard pull
SVITZER, SVITZER Australasia, 4 Victoria Road, Birkenhead, Adelaide, S.A., Australia 5015, *Tel:* +61 8 8449 8466, *Fax:* +61 8 8449 1149, *Email:* info.sa@adsteam.com.au, *Website:* www.svitzer.com

Repair & Maintenance: Structural and engineering repairs can be undertaken by local engineering contractors

Seaman Missions: The Seamans Mission, BISS Seafarers' Centre, 2 Nelson Street, Adelaide, S.A., Australia, *Tel:* +61 8 8447 5733, *Fax:* +61 8 8341 3053

Ship Chandlers: Coast to Coast Services Proprietary Ltd, 987-991 Port Road, Adelaide, S.A., Australia 5014, *Tel:* +61 8 8240 0450, *Fax:* +61 8 8240 0449, *Email:* sales@coast2coastservices.com, *Website:* www.coast2coastservices.com
Quin Marine Proprietary Ltd, 77-89 St Vincent Street, Adelaide, S.A., Australia 5015, *Tel:* +61 8 8440 2800, *Fax:* +61 8 8341 0567, *Email:* quin@quinmarine.com.au, *Website:* www.quinmarine.com.au
Southern Cross Marine Supplies Proprietary Ltd, Suite 5, 149 Brebner Drive, Adelaide, S.A., Australia 5021, *Tel:* +61 8 8235 1052, *Fax:* +61 8 8235 0852, *Email:* gsm@scms.com.au, *Website:* www.scms.com.au

Shipping Agents: ANL Container Line Proprietary Ltd, 306 St. Vincent Street, P O Box 114, Adelaide, S.A., Australia 5015, *Tel:* +61 8 8347 5400, *Fax:* +61 8 8447 1870, *Email:* harvg@anl.com.au, *Website:* www.anl.com.au
Asiaworld Shipping Services Proprietary Ltd, 229B St. Vincent Street, Adelaide, S.A., Australia 5015, *Tel:* +61 8 8447 7855, *Fax:* +61 8 8341 1550, *Email:* aw.adelaide@asiaworld.com.au, *Website:* www.asiaworld.com.au
Barwil Agencies Australia Pty Ltd, P O Box 1559, Adelaide, S.A., Australia 5015, *Tel:*

+61 8 8341 0466, *Fax:* +61 8 8341 0506, *Email:* ptadelaide@wilhelmsen.com, *Website:* www.wilhelmsen.com

Beaufort Shipping Agency Proprietary Ltd, 124 Lipson Street, Adelaide, S.A., Australia 5015, *Tel:* +61 8 8447 1511, *Fax:* +61 8 8241 0519, *Email:* manager.adelaide@beaufortshipping.com, *Website:* www.beaufortshipping.com.au

CMA-CGM S.A., CMA CGM Australia Pty Ltd, 306 St. Vincent Street, P O Box 114, Adelaide, S.A., Australia 5015, *Tel:* +61 8 8347 5410, *Fax:* +61 8 8347 5415, *Website:* www.cma-cgm.com

Gulf Agency Co (Australia) Pty Ltd., Unit 2, 171 Commercial Road, Adelaide, S.A., Australia 5015, *Tel:* +61 8 8240 4096, *Fax:* +61 8 8240 4984, *Email:* shipping.adelaide@gacworld.com, *Website:* www.gacworld.com

A Hartrodt International, 68 Pym Street, Dudley Park, Adelaide, S.A., Australia, *Tel:* +61 8 8343 5100, *Fax:* +61 8 8343 5199, *Email:* adelaide@hartrodt.com.au, *Website:* www.hartrodt.com.au

Hetherington Kingsbury Proprietary Ltd, P O Box 3003, Adelaide, S.A., Australia 5015, *Tel:* +61 8 8240 1414, *Fax:* +61 8 8240 1417, *Email:* hkadl@hksa.com.au, *Website:* www.hksa.com.au

Holyman Marine Agencies, 111 Lipson Street, Adelaide, S.A., Australia 5015, *Tel:* +61 8 8447 1663, *Fax:* +61 8 8240 0552, *Email:* joellutz@hmas.com.au

Inchcape Shipping Services (ISS), Inchcape Shipping Services Pty Ltd, Level 1, 139-145 St Vincent Street, P O Box 107, Adelaide, S.A., Australia 5015, *Tel:* +61 8 8447 4655, *Fax:* +61 8 8447 6139, *Email:* adelaide@iss-shipping.com.au, *Website:* www.iss-shipping.com

K Line Ship Management Co. Ltd, 113 Lipson Street, Adelaide, S.A., Australia 5015, *Tel:* +61 8 8240 1200, *Fax:* +61 8 8240 1133, *Email:* adlsls@klineaus.com.au, *Website:* www.klineaus.com.au

McArthur Shipping & Agency Co Pty Ltd, P O Box 330, Adelaide, S.A., Australia 5015, *Tel:* +61 8 8447 6711, *Fax:* +61 8 8447 8143, *Email:* adelaide@mcaship.com.au, *Website:* www.mcaship.com.au

Mediterranean Shipping Company, MSC (Aust) Pty Ltd., P O Box 363, Adelaide, S.A., Australia 5015, *Tel:* +61 8 8341 1644, *Fax:* +61 8 8341 1899, *Email:* adlinfo@msc.com.au, *Website:* www.msc.com.au

A.P. Moller-Maersk Group, Maersk Australia Pty Ltd, Level 2 Customs House, 220 Commercial Road, Adelaide, S.A., Australia 5015, *Tel:* +61 8 8447 3400, *Fax:* +61 8 8447 4899, *Email:* adlmla@maersk.com, *Website:* www.maerskline.com

Monson Agencies Australia Proprietary Ltd, 124 Lipson Street, P O Box 3133, Adelaide, S.A., Australia 5015, *Tel:* +61 8 8341 2450, *Fax:* +61 8 8341 1495, *Email:* adelaide@monson.com.au, *Website:* www.monson.com.au

C. Piesse & Co. Proprietary Ltd, 1st Floor, 122-130 Carrington Street, Adelaide, S.A., Australia 5000, *Tel:* +61 8 8232 1960, *Fax:* +61 8 8223 7220, *Email:* saust@piesse.com.au

Seatrans Australia Proprietary Ltd, Level 1, 306 St Vincent Street, Adelaide, S.A., Australia 5015, *Tel:* +61 8 8447 6711, *Fax:* +61 8 8447 8143, *Email:* adelaide@mcaship.com.au, *Website:* www.mcaship.com.au

Stevedoring Companies: Patrick Stevedoring, 224 Eastern Parade, Adelaide, S.A., Australia 5015, *Tel:* +61 8 8447 5100, *Fax:* +61 8 8447 4273, *Website:* www.patrick.com.au

P&O Ports, P O Box 155, Adelaide, S.A., Australia 5015, *Tel:* +61 8 8447 5833, *Fax:* +61 8 8447 3183

Surveyors: Australian Ship P & I, No. 1, Unit 5,, Donegal Road, Lonsdale, Adelaide, S.A., Australia 5160, *Tel:* +61 8 8235 2511, *Fax:* +61 8 8326 3045, *Email:* adelaide@ausship.com.au

Nippon Kaiji Kyokai, c/o E.J.C. Carr & Associates Pty Ltd, P O Box 3024, Adelaide, S.A., Australia 5015, *Tel:* +61 8 8447 5924, *Fax:* +61 8 8341 1564, *Website:* www.classnk.or.jp

Airport: Adelaide Airport, 11 km

Lloyd's Agent: Maritime & General Insurance Surveyors Proprietary Ltd, Suite 4, 7 Divett Street, Adelaide, S.A., Australia 5015, *Tel:* +61 8 8341 2552, *Fax:* +61 8 8241 0229, *Email:* maritime-general@adam.com.au

ALBANY

Lat 35° 1' S; Long 117° 53' E.

Admiralty Chart: AUS 109/118   **Admiralty Pilot:** 13
Time Zone: GMT +8 h   **UNCTAD Locode:** AU ALH

Principal Facilities:

P		Y	G		L	B		T		A

Authority: Albany Port Authority, 85 Brunswick Road, Albany, W.A., Australia 6330, *Tel:* +61 8 9892 9000, *Fax:* +61 8 9841 7566, *Email:* apa@albanyport.com.au, *Website:* www.albanyport.com.au

Officials: Chief Executive Officer: Brad Williamson, *Email:* brad.williamson@albanyport.com.au.
Harbour Master: Capt Steve Young, *Email:* steve.young@albanyport.com.au.

Port Security: ISPS compliant

Pre-Arrival Information: Vessel's intending to call at the port need to submit using fax or email the following forms:
1 Application to berth
2 48 h notice of arrival

Both these forms can be found on the website www.albanyport.com.au under Operational Procedures in the Shipping section

Approach: The entrance channel has a width of 550 m with a navigable section of 2 miles long, 145 m wide and a min depth of 12.2 m LWOST. Vessels other than woodchip carriers and panamax size vessels can berth day or night. Woodchip carriers and panamax size vessels must berth in daylight. Vessels intending to proceed to Berth No's 1 & 2 have a draft restriction of 9.80 m

Anchorage: There are seven designated anchorages in King George Sound marked on the Australian Chart 109 and vessels will be allocated appropriate anchorages as directed by the Harbour Master

Pilotage: Compulsory for vessels over 500 gt

Radio Frequency: VHF service on Channel 12. Listening watch maintained on weekdays from 0830-1630 and one hour prior to movements on weekends and public holidays, call sign 'Albany Port'

Weather: Prevailing winds, W to SW in winter, E to SE in summer. Weather patterns are affected by passing frontal depressions that skim the South coast of Western Australia

Tides: Range 1 m, but can be influenced by weather conditions

Traffic: 2007/08, 129 vessels, 3 665 999 t of cargo handled

Maximum Vessel Dimensions: Commercial vessels up to Panamax size. Passenger vessels up to 300 m loa subject to weather conditions

Principal Imports and Exports: Imports: Fertiliser, Fish, Petroleum products. Exports: Grain, Logs, Silica sand, Woodchips.

Working Hours: Pilotage operations at the port are carried out between the hours of 0600-2200. The ports office hours are between 0830-1700. The local stevedoring work force provides the following shifts: 0730-1530, 1530-2330, 2330-0730. Day shift may be extended as required

Accommodation:

Name	Length (m)	Depth (m)	Draught (m)	Remarks
Princess Royal Harbour				See [1] below
Berth No.1	209	10.5	9.8	See [2] below
Berth No.2	172	10.5	9.8	See [3] below
Berth No.3	227	12.2	11.5	See [4] below
Berth No.6	216	12.3	11.5	See [5] below

[1]*Princess Royal Harbour:* Princess Royal Harbour, with the exception of the dredged area at its NE part forming the Port of Albany, is very shallow but affords good shelter for small craft. The Port of Albany is situated on the N side of Princess Royal Harbour and comprises a dolphin berth and three land backed wharves, situated about 6 cables and 1 mile W of King Point, respectively. A Town Jetty extends S and SE into Hanover Bay from the N shore 1 mile NW by W of the Dolphin Berth. The E part of the harbour is protected by Vancouver Peninsula, with Geake Point (35° 03' S; 117° 54' E) at its W extremity. A jetty extends about 60 m NNW from Geake Point with depth alongside of less than 1.4 m. Between Geake Point and Stuarts Head (35° 04' S; 117° 52' E), 1.75 miles SW the coast forms a bay in which depths are generally less than 3 m. South Spit, a drying sandy protuberance, extends NE for about 8 cables on the SW side of this bay. Little Grove Jetty and an extension jetty extend 1.25 cables NE from Stuarts Head. Pagoda Point is situated at the SE extremity of Stuarts Head. The jetties are used by a sailing club and several yellow piles used as markers are laid up to 1.25 miles from Stuarts Head. Between Stuarts Head and Town Jetty 2 miles NNE, the harbour is mainly shoal and W of the area dries out at LW
[2]*Berth No.1:* General & bulk cargo. Transit shed. Land backed wharf. Vessel's use own gear; mobile cranes and forklifts are available at the wharf
[3]*Berth No.2:* General bulk cargo & secured tanker berth. Land backed wharf. Vessels use own gear; mobile cranes, forklifts and bulk cargo hoppers are available at the wharf
[4]*Berth No.3:* Cooperative Bulk Handling Ltd., *Tel:* +61 8 9841 1133, *Fax:* +61 9 9841 8499, *Email:* info@cbh.com.au
Grain loading with airdraft of 14 m at HW. Three shiploaders with a total cap of 1600 t/h working a max of two loaders at a time
[5]*Berth No.6:* Seven dolphins with a fixed woodchip loader. Airdraft of 17 m at HW

Storage:

Location	Cold (m³)
Albany	9800

Mechanical Handling Equipment:

Location	Type	Capacity (t)	Qty
Albany	Mobile Cranes	12	1
Albany	Mobile Cranes	5	1

Bunkering: BP Australia (Proprietary) Ltd, P O Box 5222, Melbourne, Vic., Australia 3001, *Tel:* +61 3 9268 4111, *Fax:* +61 3 9268 3321, *Email:* gomiasfuelsales@bp.com, *Website:* www.bp.com – *Misc:* Marine diesel is available by pipeline at Berth 2 at a rate of approx 100t/h. – *Delivery Mode:* truck

Towage: Two tugs available of 3240 hp and 1900 hp

Repair & Maintenance: 300 t cap slipway available. Small repairs only are dealt with. Hold cleaning is done by contractors. Details available from ship's agents

Seaman Missions: The Seamans Mission, P O Box 1299, Albany, W.A., Australia 6331, *Tel:* +61 8 9841 2440, *Fax:* +61 8 9841 2440, *Email:* albany@mts.org.au

Ship Chandlers: Sealanes, 178 Marine Terrace, Fremantle, W.A., Australia 6162, *Tel:* +61 8 9432 8888, *Fax:* +61 8 9430 4019, *Email:* sea@sealanes.com.au, *Website:* www.sealanes.com.au

Sinwa Imes Pty Ltd., P O Box 1468, Bibra Lake, Fremantle, W.A., Australia 6965, *Tel:* +61 8 9434 3300, *Fax:* +61 8 9434 3322, *Email:* sales-imes@sinwa.com.au, *Website:* www.sinwaglobal.com

Shipping Agents: Barwil Agencies Australia Pty Ltd, P O Box 805, Fremantle, W.A., Australia 6959, *Tel:* +61 8 9336 0900, *Fax:* +61 8 9336 0999, *Email:* fremantle@barwil.com.au, *Website:* www.barwil.com

Stevedoring Companies: P&O Ports, P O Box 226, Fremantle, W.A., Australia 6159, *Tel:* +61 8 9430 0111, *Fax:* +61 8 9335 4215, *Email:* ann.gosling@poports.com.au

Key to Principal Facilities:—			
A=Airport	**C**=Containers	**G**=General Cargo	**P**=Petroleum	**R**=Ro/Ro	**Y**=Dry Bulk
B=Bunkers	**D**=Dry Dock	**L**=Cruise	**Q**=Other Liquid Bulk	**T**=Towage (where available from port)	

Medical Facilities: Hospital available

Airport: 11 km from port for light aircraft only

Railway: No public rail service. Commercial rail operations only

Development: Potential for new berth development for iron ore exports

Lloyd's Agent: Moko Proprietary Ltd, P O Box 685, Willetton, W.A., Australia 6955, *Tel:* +61 8 9354 2248, *Fax:* +61 8 9354 2234, *Email:* kglange@bigpond.com

APPLETON DOCK

harbour area, see under Melbourne

ARDROSSAN

Lat 34° 26' S; Long 137° 54' E.

Admiralty Chart: AUS 139/781	Admiralty Pilot: 13
Time Zone: GMT +9.5 h	UNCTAD Locode: AU ARD

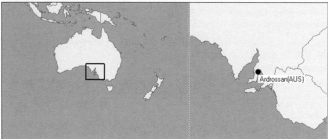

Principal Facilities:

	Y						T	

Authority: ABB Grain Ltd, Old Boat Ramp Road, Ardrossan, S.A., Australia 5571, *Tel:* +61 8 8837 3306, *Fax:* +61 8 8837 3639, *Email:* tim.gurney@abb.com.au, *Website:* www.abb.com.au

Officials: Managing Director: Tim Gurney.

Port Security: ISPS compliant

Approach: The channel depth is 7.62 m at LWOST and has a muddy bottom. There are two departure channels. N Channel has a depth of 9.2 m and SN Channel 8.2 m

Pilotage: Compulsory for all vessels. Boarding ground one mile E of jetty. Pratique is granted at the port by Dept of Health officers who travel by road from Adelaide at shipowner's expense. A pilot usually comes by road from either Adelaide or Wallaroo for vessels to and from the port and returns by road to his respective port

Radio Frequency: VHF Channel 16

Tides: MHWS 3.1 m, MHWN 1.8 m

Traffic: 1999/2000, 31 commercial vessels, 770 473 t of cargo handled

Maximum Vessel Dimensions: 46 000 dwt, 200 m loa

Principal Imports and Exports: Exports: Barley, Dolomite, Salt.

Working Hours: 0800-1600, 1600-2359, 0001-0800

Accommodation:

Name	Length (m)	Depth (m)	Remarks
Ardrossan			
ABB Grain Jetty	409	9.2	See [1] below

[1]*ABB Grain Jetty:* The jetty is 'T' shaped with a conveyor situated in the middle. Loading rates: grain 900 t/h, dolomite ore 2400 t/h, salt 800 t/h. Fixed chute from conveyor belt necessitates warping vessels along the 'T' head during loading. Height from bottom of chute over water low tide is 12.38 m. Therefore both draft and freeboard have to be considered, and in particular height from light loadline to top of hatch coaming. Max outreach of chute is 16.1 m; max height above LW is 16.18 m. Vessels loading bulk grain must be fitted out and passed by the Commonwealth Department of Transport prior to arrival. Surveyors will attend vessel during loading, travelling by road from Adelaide

Towage: Tugs are available from Adelaide and are compulsory for vessels berthing; over 150 m loa one tug and vessels over 182.8 m loa two tugs. Also required for unberthing vessels over 152.4 m one tug and vessels heading N with a draft over 7.32 m

Shipping Agents: Barwil Agencies Australia Pty Ltd, P O Box 1559, Adelaide, S.A., Australia 5015, *Tel:* +61 8 8341 0466, *Fax:* +61 8 8341 0506, *Email:* ptadelaide@wilhelmsen.com, *Website:* www.wilhelmsen.com

Medical Facilities: Available

Lloyd's Agent: Maritime & General Insurance Surveyors Proprietary Ltd, Suite 4, 7 Divett Street, Adelaide, S.A., Australia 5015, *Tel:* +61 8 8341 2552, *Fax:* +61 8 8241 0229, *Email:* maritime-general@adam.com.au

AUCKLAND POINT WHARF

harbour area, see under Gladstone

BALLAST HEAD

Lat 35° 46' S; Long 137° 48' E.

Admiralty Chart: AUS 780	Admiralty Pilot: 13
Time Zone: GMT +9.5 h	UNCTAD Locode: AU BAH

This port is no longer operational

BARNEY POINT

harbour area, see under Gladstone

BARROW ISLAND TERMINAL

Lat 20° 47' S; Long 115° 32' E.

Admiralty Chart: AUS 742	Admiralty Pilot: 17
Time Zone: GMT +8 h	UNCTAD Locode: AU BWB

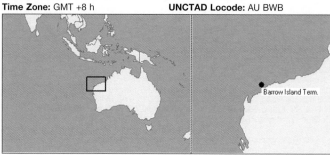

Principal Facilities:

P							T	

Authority: Chevron Australia Proprietary Ltd, P O Box S1580, Perth, W.A., Australia 6845, *Tel:* +61 8 9216 4000, *Fax:* +61 8 9216 4044, *Email:* chevronaustralia@chevron.com, *Website:* www.chevron.com

Officials: Marketing Manager: Neil Theobald, *Tel:* +61 8 9216 4000, *Email:* neil.theobald@chevron.com.

Port Security: ISPS compliant

Pre-Arrival Information: ETA must be communicated to Operators, Tel: +61 8 9216 4210, Fax: +61 8 9216 4044 and Terminal, Tel: +61 8 9184 3749, Fax: +61 8 9184 3799, 96 h, 48 h, 24 h and 12 h before arrival. The first message should include:
Name of tanker and flag
Inmarsat phone number inc. satellite in use (872 or 873)
Inmarsat fax number inc. satellite in use (872 or 873)
Name of P&I club
Cargo requirements in m3 at 15°C
Total quantity and condition of ballast; ballast to be discharged at ChevronTexaco Terminal; ballast loaded in which port
Maximum loading rate through one 12" hose
Arrival draft
Estimated departure draft
Distance bridge to bow in metres
Distance bow to manifold in metres
Are all tanks inerted below 8%
Can vessel carry out closed loading
Master's name as he/she wishes it to appear on the Bills of Lading
Last port of call
Next port of call
Discharge port of Barrow Island crude oil
Confirmation that tanker has a clean bill of health
What electrical voltage has tanker and what socket type
Number of shackles (shots) of cable on each anchor cable
Number and location of mooring wires/ropes on winches and number, location and type of spare mooring ropes
Diameter and breaking strain of mooring ropes/wires and diameter and breaking strain of spare mooring ropes
Are mooring bitts located so that backup lines may be deployed to any of the six mooring buoys and hove in and made fast to the bitts
Diameter and safe working load of bitts
Holding power of mooring winch brakes
Is manifold OCIMF standard
Is tanker fitted with a crane or derrick
Safe working load of crane or derrick
Helicopter landing capability, winch or land on

Approach: The recommended approach to the terminal is to the N and E of Monte Bello Islands

Anchorage: Anchorage can be obtained 2 nautical miles E of the mooring buoys, good holding ground

Pilotage: Compulsory. The Mooring Master boards in pos 20° 48.5' S; 115° 36.1' E (2 nautical miles E of the oil loading mooring buoys)

Radio Frequency: Tankers listen on VHF Channels 16 and 14 when within 100 nautical miles of the Terminal. Barrow Island does not maintain a listening watch on any radio frequency
ChevronTexaco provide portable UHF radio's for communications between the Tanker, Mooring Vessels and the Terminal onshore control room during berthing, loading and unberthing. Channel 1 (469.775 MHz) and Channel 2 (469.800 MHz)

Maximum Vessel Dimensions: Restricted to tankers which have a loaded displacement of 40 000-105 000 t, a max beam of 47 m and a max slab side area of 4838 m2

Working Hours: Round the clock

Accommodation:

Name	Remarks
Barrow Island Terminal	See [1] below

[1]*Barrow Island Terminal:* Crude oil loading terminal. Tankers are berthed to a mooring terminal, comprising six mooring buoys and two swamped moorings located 9.8 km offshore. Min depth of water at the berth is 12.0 m and an under-keel clearance of not less than 1.56 m must be maintained for tankers up to 33 m beam. Tankers must be equipped with a crane or derrick on the starboard side with a min SWL of 10 t There are three storage tanks onshore each with a cap of 200 000 bbls. Loading by submarine pipeline at a rate of 14 700 bbls/h. Loading hose connection is 1 x 12'' dia over the rail hose
Berthing at the Marine Terminal takes place in daylight, during periods of ebb tides unless otherwise approved by the Pilot/Mooring Master. Generally berthing will take place at high water or before low water slack tide, to avoid the period of strongest tidal stream in the middle of the ebb tide. The direction of the tidal stream is approx 245° on flood and 065° on ebb and attains a rate of 1.0 kn at springs. Unberthing takes place at any time, during the ebb tide or at other times as approved by the Pilot/Mooring Master

Towage: A mooring launch assists with berthing, together with a tug with min of 35 t bollard pull

Shipping Agents: Barwil Agencies Australia Pty Ltd, P O Box 1005, Karratha, W.A., Australia 6714, *Tel:* +61 8 9144 2311, *Fax:* +61 8 9144 2008, *Email:* dampier@wilhelmsen.com, *Website:* www.wilhelmsen.com

Lloyd's Agent: Moko Proprietary Ltd, P O Box 685, Willetton, W.A., Australia 6955, *Tel:* +61 8 9354 2248, *Fax:* +61 8 9354 2234, *Email:* kglange@bigpond.com

BELL BAY

harbour area, see under Launceston

BLACKWATTLE BAY

harbour area, see under Sydney

BLUESCOPE STEEL WHARF

harbour area, see under Hastings

BOTANY BAY

Lat 33° 57' S; Long 151° 13' E.

Admiralty Chart: AUS 198/199	**Admiralty Pilot:** 14
Time Zone: GMT +10 h	**UNCTAD Locode:** AU BTB

Principal Facilities:

P	Q		G	C		B		T	A	

Authority: Sydney Ports Corp., Level 8, 207 Kent Street, P O Box 25, Millers Point, N.S.W., Australia 2000, *Tel:* +61 2 9296 4999, *Fax:* +61 2 9296 4742, *Email:* enquiries@sydports.com.au, *Website:* www.sydneyports.com.au

Officials: Chief Executive Officer: Grant Gilfillan, *Tel:* +61 2 9296 4681, *Email:* ggilfillan@sydneyports.com.au.
Corporate Affairs Manager: Kamini Parashar, *Tel:* +61 2 9296 4995, *Email:* kparashar@sydneyports.com.au.
Harbour Master: Capt Robin Heath, *Tel:* +61 2 9296 4650, *Email:* rheath@sydneyports.com.au.
Marketing: Geneveive Bonello, *Tel:* +61 2 9296 4807, *Email:* gbonello@sydneyports.com.au.

Port Security: ISPS compliant

Approach: The channel to the swinging basin and berths at Kurnell has a min depth of 11.2 m. The channel to the Port Botany area is 213 m wide and has a min depth of 15 m. The swinging basin at Brotherson Dock is dredged to 14.4 m

Anchorage: There is no recommended anchorage off the port. Anchoring is at the Master's discretion, however vessels should anchor outside port limits and are requested to anchor at least 3 nautical miles from the coast

Pilotage: Compulsory for all vessels except where the Master holds a Pilotage Exemption Certificate
Sydney Pilot Service Pty Ltd (SPS), Tel: +61 2 9337 6648, Fax: +61 2 9337 4048
Pilot boards in pos 34° 02' S; 151° 18' 08" E. ETA to be confirmed with Botany Harbour Control 4 h prior to arrival and reconfirmed 2 h and 1 h before reaching pilot boarding ground

Radio Frequency: VHF Radio call sign 'Botany Harbour Control'. Channel 16 for calling and 12 for arrival reporting and exchange of information. All traffic movements are controlled on Channel 13

Weather: All berths can be affected by strong winds. There are special mooring points at container berths

Tides: Range of tide 1.6 m MHWS. 1.3 m MHWN

Traffic: 2007/08, 29 200 000 t of cargo handled, 1 778 442 TEU's (includes Sydney)

Principal Imports and Exports: Imports: Bulk liquids, Containers, Crude oil, Machinery, Paper, Petroleum products. Exports: Containers, Cotton, Frozen meat, Wool.

Working Hours: Wharves operate 24 h

Accommodation:

Name	Length (m)	Depth (m)	Remarks
Port Botany			
Port Botany Container Terminal	936	14–14.8	See [1] below
Patrick Terminal	1006	14.2–14.9	See [2] below
Bulk Liquids Berth		18.3	See [3] below
Kurnell			See [4] below
Berth No.1	200	10.3	Vessels up to 185 m loa
Berth No.2	200	10.6	Vessels up to 200 m loa
Berth No.3			See [5] below

[1]*Port Botany Container Terminal:* Operated by DP World Sydney, P O Box 192, Matraville, NSW 2036, Tel: +61 2 9394 0900, Fax: +61 2 9394 0955
Berths 4, 5, 5A and 6. Total terminal area of 38.6 ha. Equipped with three twin-lift and three high-speed, single lift quay cranes, each with a spreader cap of 40 t and heavy lift cap up to 84 t. 376 reefer points
[2]*Patrick Terminal:* Operated by Patrick Stevedores, Gate B110 Penrhyn Road, Port Botany, NSW 2036, Tel: +61 2 9394 0000, Fax: +61 2 9394 0395
Berths 1, 1A, 2, 2A and 3. Total terminal area of 46.1 ha. Equipped with six single-lift quay cranes of which four also have a heavy lift cap of 80 t and 28 straddle carriers. 700 reefer outlets
[3]*Bulk Liquids Berth:* Vessels up to 75 000 dwt (90 000 dwt on application) and 250 m loa. Hazardous and non-hazardous bulk liquids, petrochemicals and gases are transferred by marine loading arms and flexible pipeline to nearby industry storage facilities which are operated by private companies including VOPAK, Origin Energy, Orica Australia Pty Ltd, Terminals Pty Ltd and Elgas Ltd
[4]*Kurnell:* Operated by Caltex Refineries (NSW) Pty Ltd., 2 Solander Street, Kurnell, NSW 2231, Tel: +61 2 9668 1423, Fax: +61 2 9668 1190, Website: www.caltex.com.au
Primarily for crude oil imports as well as other petrochemical products
[5]*Berth No.3:* Multi-buoy mooring with a submarine pipeline to the Caltex shore facility for vessels up to 275 m loa and 11.6 m draft

Bunkering: Available at all Kurnell Berths and by barge moored in Brotherson Dock
BP Australia (Proprietary) Ltd, P O Box 5222, Melbourne, Vic., Australia 3001, *Tel:* +61 3 9268 4111, *Fax:* +61 3 9268 3321, *Email:* gomiasfuelsales@bp.com, *Website:* www.bp.com
Caltex Australia Petroleum Proprietary Ltd, Caltex Australia Petroleum Proprietary Ltd, No 2 Market Street, Sydney, N.S.W., Australia 2000, *Tel:* +61 2 9668 1148, *Fax:* +61 2 9668 1243, *Email:* mnicholl@caltex.com.au, *Website:* www.caltex.com.au
ExxonMobil Marine Fuels, 1 Harbour Front Place, 06-00 Harbour Front, Tower One, Singapore, Republic of Singapore 098633, *Tel:* +65 6885 8998, *Fax:* +65 6885 8794, *Email:* asiapac.marinefuels@exxonmobil.com, *Website:* www.exxonmobilmarinefuels.com – *Grades:* MGO – *Delivery Mode:* tank truck
Shell Australia Ltd, Shell Company of Australia, Marine Centre Oceania, No 8 Redfern Road, Melbourne, Vic., Australia 3123, *Tel:* +61 3 9666 5446, *Fax:* +61 3 8823 4800, *Email:* sal-marine-products@shell.com, *Website:* www.shell.com.au

Towage: Three tugs owned and operated by a private operator are available. Others can be obtained from Sydney on request
PB Towage (Australia) Proprietary Ltd, P O Box 733, Botany, N.S.W., Australia 1455, *Tel:* +61 2 9695 0700, *Fax:* +61 2 9666 6411, *Email:* info@pbtowage.com, *Website:* www.pbtowage.com

Shipping Agents: Barwil Agencies Australia Pty Ltd, P O Box 4097, Sydney, N.S.W., Australia 2001, *Tel:* +61 2 9439 7223, *Fax:* +61 2 9439 8587, *Email:* sydney@wilhelmsen.com, *Website:* www.wilhelmsen.com

Medical Facilities: Arrangements made through agents

Airport: Kingsford Smith, 2 km

Railway: Rail access provided to all container terminals

Development: 1850 m of container wharf space and terminal under construction with opening due 2012

Lloyd's Agent: Freemans Marine, P O Box 36, St. Leonards, N.S.W., Australia 1590, *Tel:* +61 2 9438 2655, *Fax:* +61 2 9436 1367, *Email:* lloyds@freemans.com.au, *Website:* www.freemansmarine.com.au

BOWEN

Lat 20° 1' S; Long 148° 15' E.

Admiralty Chart: AUS 255	**Admiralty Pilot:** 15
Time Zone: GMT +10 h	**UNCTAD Locode:** AU ZBO

This port is no longer open to commercial shipping

Shipping Agents: Neptune Pacific Agency Australia Proprietary Ltd, Ground Floor, South Tower, 527 Gregory Terrace, Bowen, Qld., Australia 4006, *Tel:* +61 7 3332 8560, *Fax:* +61 7 3332 8561

Key to Principal Facilities:—				
A=Airport	**C**=Containers	**G**=General Cargo	**P**=Petroleum	**R**=Ro/Ro	**Y**=Dry Bulk
B=Bunkers	**D**=Dry Dock	**L**=Cruise	**Q**=Other Liquid Bulk	**T**=Towage (where available from port)

BOYNE WHARF

harbour area, see under Gladstone

BRISBANE

Lat 27° 24' S; Long 153° 9' E.

Admiralty Chart: AUS 237/238 **Admiralty Pilot:** 15
Time Zone: GMT +10 h **UNCTAD Locode:** AU BNE

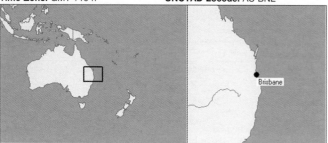

Principal Facilities:

P	Q	Y	G	C	R	L	B		T	A

Authority: Port of Brisbane Corp., 1 Sandpiper Avenue, Fisherman Islands, P O Box 1818, Brisbane, Qld., Australia 4178, *Tel:* +61 7 3258 4888, *Fax:* +61 7 3258 4703, *Email:* info@portbris.com.au, *Website:* www.portbris.com.au

Officials: Chief Executive Officer: Jeff Coleman, *Tel:* +61 7 3258 4774, *Email:* jeff.coleman@portbris.com.au.
General Manager: Gerry Johnstone, *Tel:* +61 7 3258 4830, *Email:* gerry.johnstone@portbris.com.au.
Operations Manager: Peter Keyte, *Tel:* +61 7 3258 4620, *Email:* peter.keyte@portbris.com.au.
Harbour Master: Richard Johnson, *Tel:* +61 7 3860 3552, *Email:* richard.c.johnson@msq.qld.gov.au.

Port Security: ISPS compliant

Approach: Access to the Port of Brisbane is via Moreton Bay, where deep-water channels are a min of 300 m wide from Fairway Beacons to Entrance Beacons, and the min draft is 14 m LAT
The main access to the port is via the NW channel. Port channels and swing basins are maintained at the following depths: NW channel 15.0 m, Spitfire Banks channel 14.0 m, East channel (west) 14.0 m, Bar Cutting (river entrance) 14.0 m (for 6 miles), Fisherman Islands swing basin 14.0 m, Pelican Banks Cutting to Hamilton Reach 9.1 m. Moreton Bay channels are a min of 300 m wide from Fairway Beacons to Entrance Beacons. The Brisbane River Bar Butting (river entrance) is 180 m wide and channels above Fisherman Islands swing basin are 120 m wide. A vessel can navigate the river as far as seven nautical miles from its mouth to upstream Hamilton Reach berths with draft of 10.0 m on any day of the year
All vessels entering Brisbane Port limits must call Brisbane Harbour on VHF Channel 12 at the following times:
(a) when the pilot is on board, giving FWB time, ETA Entrance Beacons, channels used, draft, and, if at anchor, anchor aweigh time
(b) when passing the Fairway Buoy (customs requirement)
(c) 30 minutes prior to passing Entrance Beacons to Bar Cutting
(d) when passing Entrance Beacons, advising all river traffic of time at berth (named) and whether berthing head-up, head-down or swinging (name basin)
(e) after secured alongside, giving time of first line, whether vessel is berthed head-up or head-down, confirm vessel all fast and time of all fast
(f) vessels going to anchor at Brisbane Roads, when anchored, giving anchorage position as a bearing and distance from the Entrance Beacons

Pilotage: Compulsory for every Australian-registered vessel that is 50 m loa or more, any vessel other than an Australian vessel that is 35 m loa or more or any vessel if directed by the Harbour Master. This does not apply to vessels with master's holding a pilotage exemption
The pilot boarding ground is situated three nautical miles SE of Point Cartwright, near Caloundra (pilots may board or disembark outside these limits by prior arrangement)
Requests for pilots should be made via the ship's agent, giving at least 24 h notice
Brisbane Marine Pilots maintain a 24 h listening watch on VHF Channel 12. ETA at the boarding ground should be confirmed at least 2 h before arrival by calling 'Brisbane Harbour' on VHF Channel 12
Pilots embark and disembark using fast, yellow-hulled launches. Vessels are requested to provide a good lee and maintain a speed of 8 knots when embarking or disembarking their pilot
Pilot ladders should be rigged in accordance with SOLAS regulations and ISO standards, 2 m above the water, with two man-ropes and a heaving line standing by
Brisbane Marine Pilots Pty Ltd., Tel: +61 7 3862 2260, Fax: +61 7 3862 2240, Email: operations@brisbanepilots.com.au, Website: www.brisbanepilots.com.au

Radio Frequency: Brisbane Port Control's call sign is 'Brisbane Harbour'. The following VHF channels are used:
VHF Channel 16 - call up, answering and emergencies
VHF Channel 12 - working channel and port operations
VHF Channel 67 - small craft
VHF Channels 6, 8, 9 and 10 - pilots and tugs
VHF Channels 63 and 73 - water, police and coastguard

Tides: In Moreton Bay and the Brisbane River the mean spring rise is 2.16 m above LAT and the mean neap rise is 1.76 m above LAT. The max spring tide is 2.71 m above LAT

Traffic: 2007/08, 2618 commercial vessels & 61 cruise vessels, 30 214 635 t of cargo handled, 942 716 TEU's

Principal Imports and Exports: Imports: Building products, Cement, Crude oil, Electrical equipment, Fertiliser & rural and industrial chemicals, Gypsum & limestone, Household items, Iron & steel, Machinery, Oil seeds, Paper & wood pulp, Timber, Transport equipment & motor vehicles. Exports: Building products, Cereals, Coal, Cotton & cotton seeds, Iron & steel, Meat products, Mineral ores & sands, Paper & wood pulp, Refined oil & gas, Silica sand, Tallow, Timber, Woodchip.

Working Hours: 24 h/day

Accommodation:

Name	Length (m)	Depth (m)	Remarks
Brisbane			See [1] below
Fisherman Islands			See [2] below
Wharf No's 1-3	697	14	See [3] below
Wharf No's 4-6	700	14	See [4] below
Wharf No's 7-9	737	14	See [5] below
Grain Wharf	285	13	See [6] below
Bulk Berth No.1	317	13.5	See [7] below
Caltex Crude Wharf	400	14.3	See [8] below
BP Crude Wharf	329	14.3	See [9] below
Caltex Products Wharf	285	9.8	See [10] below
Clinker Wharf	220	9.8	See [11] below
Shell Wharf	234	11	See [12] below
BP Products Wharf	235	11	See [13] below
Pacific Terminals	208	9	See [14] below
Incitec Pivot North	210	10.1	See [15] below
Incitec Pivot South	220	10.5	See [16] below
Pinkenba Bulk Terminal	360	10.5	See [17] below
Sugar Terminal	270	10.1	See [18] below
Hamilton Wharf No.1	170	10.4	See [19] below
Hamilton Wharf No.2	210	10.4	See [20] below
Hamilton Wharf No.3	170	10.4	See [21] below
Hamilton Wharf No.4	210	10.4	See [22] below
Maritime No.1 (Dolphin Berth)	172	9.1	See [23] below
Maritime Wharf No.2	254	10.4	See [24] below
Maritime Wharf No.3	259	10.4	See [25] below

[1]*Brisbane:* Brisbane Cruise Terminal (Portside Wharf) 236 m long in depth of 9 m LAT, for up to 2500 passengers for base-porting and turnaround ships, Tel: +61 7 3868 5101, Fax: +61 7 3868 5102, Website: www.brisbanecruiseterminal.com.au
A tug base, small craft depot and port control centre are located at Whyte Island, adjacent to Fisherman Island facilities. There are four finger piers comprising eight berths and a heavy lift facility. The port is well served by both road and rail transport
[2]*Fisherman Islands:* There are three container parks operated by Chalmers Industries, P&O Container Park and Patrick Port Services. There is also a 24 h distribution centre, operated by Patrick Port Services. The Brisbane Multimodal Terminal is located behind the container terminals and links the movement of containers by road and rail to the Fisherman Islands wharves
[3]*Wharf No's 1-3:* Operated by Australian Amalgamated Terminals (AAT), Berth 3, Port Drive, Port of Brisbane Qld 4178, Tel: +61 7 3909 3000, Fax: +61 7 3895 2598, Website: www.aat.auz.biz
General cargo wharves handling breakbulk cargo, containers, motor vehicles and other ro/ro cargo. Equipped with one panamax container crane and one mobile harbour crane
[4]*Wharf No's 4-6:* Operated by DP World Brisbane, P O Box 702, Wynnum, Qld 4178, Tel: +61 7 3895 0022, Fax: +61 7 3895 1221
Terminal area of 27 ha with container stacking cap of 7070 TEU's. Equipment includes three panamax, one post-panamax and two super post-panamax container cranes
[5]*Wharf No's 7-9:* Operated by Patrick Terminals, P O Box 734, Wynnum, Qld 4178, Tel: +61 7 3893 8555, Fax: +61 7 3893 8525
Equipment includes four panamax cranes, two post-panamax cranes and 23 straddle carriers
[6]*Grain Wharf:* Operated by GrainCorp Operations, P O Box 349, Wynnum, Qld 4178, Tel: +61 7 3895 1033, Fax: +61 7 3895 1034, Website: www.graincorp.com.au
Grain, woodchips, sugar & cotton-seed exports. Grain loading up to 2200 t/h with silo storage of 60 000 t. Woodchip loading up to 750 t/h. Sugar loading at 700 t/h. Cotton-seed loading at 700 t/h. Sugar/cotton-seed shed of 40 000 t
[7]*Bulk Berth No.1:* Coal terminal operated by Queensland Bulk Handling Pty Ltd., P O Box 348, Wynnum, Qld 4178, Tel: +61 7 3895 6500, Fax: +61 7 3895 1170. Coal exports. Average loading rate of 2000 t/h with stockpile storage of 360 000 t. Receival by rail at 2500 t/h
Cement/clinker plant operated by Sunstate Cement Ltd., P O Box 350, Wynnum, Qld 4178, Tel: +61 7 3895 1199, Fax: +61 7 3895 1198, Email: sunstate@sunstatecement.com.au, Website: www.sunstatecement.com.au. Bulk clinker, gypsum & slag imports. Cement clinker: receival hopper for self-unloading vessels up to 2000 t/h
[8]*Caltex Crude Wharf:* Operated by Caltex Refineries (Qld) Ltd., P O Box 40, Wynnum, Qld 4178, Tel: +61 7 3362 7555, Fax: +61 7 3362 7111, Website: www.caltex.com.au
Crude oil discharge & loading. Crude oil: one 600 mm pipeline with three 250 mm connections. Bunker fuel: one 150 mm pipeline and connection. Discharge at 3000-4000 t/h and load at 250-620 t/h
[9]*BP Crude Wharf:* Operated by BP Refinery (Bulwer Island) Pty Ltd., P O Box 4, Pinkenba, Qld 4008, Tel: +61 7 3243 7333, Fax: +61 7 3243 7502
Crude oil/feedstocks discharge and load/discharge of petroleum products. Crude oil/feedstocks: booms connected to one 500 mm pipeline. Discharge rate 3000 t/h. Petroleum products: one 200 mm boom connected to one 200 mm pipeline. Load/discharge rate 450 t/h
[10]*Caltex Products Wharf:* Operated by Caltex Refineries (Qld) Ltd., P O Box 40, Wynnum, Qld 4178, Tel: +61 7 3362 7555, Fax: +61 7 3362 7111, Website: www.caltex.com.au
Petroleum products. Four 200 mm connections. Discharge/loading rate 200-1000 t/h
[11]*Clinker Wharf:* Operated by Cement Australia, 77 Pamela Street, Bulwer Island, Qld 4008,Tel: +61 7 3632 7800, Fax: +61 7 3632 7820, Website: www.cementaustralia.com.au
Bulk clinker, gypsum & slag imports. Cement clinker: receival hopper with travelling grab crane bucket. Discharge up to 400 t/h. Three storage sheds of 30 000 t, 82 000 t and 5000 t

[12]*Shell Wharf:* Operated by Shell Co of Australia., P O Box 1456, Brisbane, Qld 4001, Tel: +61 7 3364 5399, Fax: +61 7 3364 5273, Website: www.shell.com.au
Petroleum products: two 200 mm white oil lines and one 250 mm black oil. Load/discharge and bunkering rate 200-900 t/h. Two 100 mm bunker lines, load 100 t/h. One 150 mm LPG pipeline, load/discharge 100 t/h
[13]*BP Products Wharf:* Operated by BP Refinery (Bulwer Island) Pty Ltd., P O Box 4, Pinkenba, Qld 4008, Tel: +61 7 3243 7333, Fax: +61 7 3243 7502
Petroleum and bunkering products, load/unload LPG. Petroleum products: two 200 mm booms with two 200 mm pipelines, load/discharge 400-900 t/h (gas oil) and 380 t/h (motor spirits). Slops/tank washings 1500 t cap. One 200 mm boom with 250 mm pipeline for fuel oil bunkers/slops. LPG: (for BP) one 150 mm pipeline for liquid and one 80 mm for vapour (for Origin) one 250 mm pipeline for liquid and one 100 mm for vapour
[14]*Pacific Terminals:* Operated by Pacific Terminals Pty Ltd., 105 Tingira Street, Pinkenba, Qld 4008, Tel: +61 7 3291 8050, Fax: +61 7 3260 1786, Email: ptaqld@pacterm.com, Website: www.pacterm.com
Bulk flammable & combustible liquids. Discharge rate 200-400 t/h. Storage cap of 30 000 m3
[15]*Incitec Pivot North:* Operated by Incitec Pivot, P O Box 140, Morningside, Qld 4170, Tel: +61 7 3867 9337, Fax: +61 7 3867 9323, Email: incitec.info@incitec.com.au, Website: www.incitecpivot.com.au
Bulk fertiliser loaded into three 50 t hoppers using ship or mobile cranes. Storage cap of 50 000 t. Bulk liquids storage: sulphuric acid 17 000 t and caustic 5000 t
[16]*Incitec Pivot South:* Operated by Incitec Pivot, P O Box 140, Morningside, Qld 4170, Tel: +61 7 3867 9337, Fax: +61 7 3867 9323, Email: incitec.info@incitec.com.au, Website: www.incitecpivot.com.au
Bulk liquid & bulk dry cargoes. For dry cargoes fixed gantry ship loader at 200 t/h with storage cap of 50 000 t. Bulk liquid storage of 10 000 t for amonia
[17]*Pinkenba Bulk Terminal:* Jointly operated by Port of Brisbane Corporation and GrainCorp Operations, Tel: +61 7 3895 1033, Fax: +61 7 3895 1034
Grain, silica sand, other dry bulk handling, general cargo, soya-bean meal & fertiliser. Loading rate up to 1200 t/h. Total storage shed cap of 80 000 t, total silo storage cap of 62 000 t & total open area cap of 25 000 t
[18]*Sugar Terminal:* Operated by Queensland Sugar Ltd., Tel: +61 7 3815 0100, Fax: +61 7 3815 0199, Email: info@queenslandsugar.com, Website: www.queenslandsugar.com
Bulk sugar exports & temporary berth available for longer term arrangements. Sugar: mobile gantry loader at rate of 1500 t/h. Storage shed of 120 000 t (80% of capacity available for non-sugar storage). Laydown area available
[19]*Hamilton Wharf No.1:* Operated by P&O Ports Ltd., P O Box 702, Wynnum, Qld 4178, Tel: +61 7 3268 9222, Fax: +61 7 3895 1221, Website: www.poports.com.au
General cargo, cars, containers & bulk cargo. Storage shed of 3300 m2. Portable hoppers available for all wharves
[20]*Hamilton Wharf No.2:* Operated by P&O Ports Ltd., P O Box 702, Wynnum, Qld 4178, Tel: +61 7 3268 9222, Fax: +61 7 3895 1221, Website: www.poports.com.au
General cargo, cars, containers & bulk cargo. Storage shed of 1811 m2 and rail-mounted wharf crane with SWL of 64 t at 15 m radius
[21]*Hamilton Wharf No.3:* Operated by P&O Ports Ltd., P O Box 702, Wynnum, Qld 4178, Tel: +61 7 3268 9222, Fax: +61 7 3895 1221, Website: www.poports.com.au
General cargo, cars, containers & bulk cargo. Storage sheds of 4400 m2
[22]*Hamilton Wharf No.4:* Operated by P&O Ports Ltd., P O Box 702, Wynnum, Qld 4178, Tel: +61 7 3268 9222, Fax: +61 7 3895 1221, Website: www.poports.com.au
General cargo, cars, containers, bulk cargo & sand. Storage sheds of 3400 m2 (storage capacity shared with Berth 3)
[23]*Maritime No.1 (Dolphin Berth):* Operated by Patrick Maritime
Dolphin berth. Bulk oil & chemicals. Direct line to chemical and tallow tank storage. Oil product load/discharge. Storage cap of 14 000 m2
[24]*Maritime Wharf No.2:* Operated by Patrick Maritime
General cargo, cars, containers & bulk cargo. Storage shed of 3400 m2. Rail-mounted wharf crane with SWL of 73.5 t at 11.5 m radius
[25]*Maritime Wharf No.3:* Operated by Patrick Maritime
General cargo, cars, containers & bulk cargo. Storage shed of 4850 m2

Bunkering: Riverside Oil Bunkering Proprietary Ltd, 1 Macquarie Street, New Farm, Brisbane, Qld., Australia 4005, *Tel:* +61 7 3358 2122, *Fax:* +61 7 3358 3386, *Email:* admin@riversidemarine.com.au, *Website:* www.riversidemarine.com.au
Australian Petroleum Proprietary Ltd, Solander Street, Kurnell, Sydney, N.S.W., Australia, *Tel:* +61 2 972 2597, *Fax:* +61 2 981 1159 – *Grades:* FO – *Delivery Mode:* barge, ex-pipe
BP Australia (Proprietary) Ltd, P O Box 5222, Melbourne, Vic., Australia 3001, *Tel:* +61 3 9268 4111, *Fax:* +61 3 9268 3321, *Email:* gomiasfuelsales@bp.com, *Website:* www.bp.com – *Grades:* IFO-180cSt; MGO; other IF grades subject to enquiry – *Notice:* 48 hours – *Delivery Mode:* barge, truck, pipeline
Caltex Australia Petroleum Proprietary Ltd, Caltex Australia Petroleum Proprietary Ltd, No 2 Market Street, Sydney, N.S.W., Australia 2000, *Tel:* +61 2 9668 1148, *Fax:* +61 2 9668 1243, *Email:* mnicholl@caltex.com.au, *Website:* www.caltex.com.au
ExxonMobil Marine Fuels, 1 Harbour Front Place, 06-00 Harbour Front, Tower One, Singapore, Republic of Singapore 098633, *Tel:* +65 6885 8998, *Fax:* +65 6885 8794, *Email:* asiapac.marinefuels@exxonmobil.com, *Website:* www.exxonmobilmarinefuels.com – *Grades:* MGO – *Delivery Mode:* tank truck
Riverside Oil Bunkering Proprietary Ltd, 1 Macquarie Street, New Farm, Brisbane, Qld., Australia 4005, *Tel:* +61 7 3358 2122, *Fax:* +61 7 3358 3386, *Email:* admin@riversidemarine.com.au, *Website:* www.riversidemarine.com.au – *Grades:* all grades – *Parcel Size:* max 1200t – *Rates:* HFO 350t/h, MGO 40t/h – *Notice:* 48 hours – *Delivery Mode:* barge
Shell Australia Ltd, Shell Company of Australia, Marine Centre Oceania, No 8 Redfern Road, Melbourne, Vic., Australia 3123, *Tel:* +61 3 9666 5446, *Fax:* +61 3 8823 4800, *Email:* sal-marine-products@shell.com, *Website:* www.shell.com.au

Towage: PB Towage (Australia) Proprietary Ltd, 18 Howard Smith Drive, P O Box 3420, Brisbane, Qld., Australia 4178, *Tel:* +61 7 3895 2677, *Fax:* +61 7 3895 2688, *Email:* pbbrisbane@pbtowage.com.au, *Website:* www.pbtowage.com
SVITZER, SVITZER Australasia, 20 Howard Smith Drive, Brisbane, Qld., Australia 4178, *Tel:* +61 7 3895 1022, *Fax:* +61 7 3895 1024, *Email:* info.qld@adsteam.com.au, *Website:* www.svitzer.com

Repair & Maintenance: Brisbane Slipways & Engineering Proprietary Ltd, 397 Thynne Road, Colmslie, Qld., Australia 4171, *Tel:* +61 7 3902 3555, *Fax:* +61 7 3902 3500, *Email:* admin@bse.net.au, *Website:* www.bse.net.au Slipway with cap 2500 t
Canniffe Engineering Proprietary Ltd, 190 South Pine Road, Alderley, Brisbane, Qld., Australia 4051, *Tel:* +61 7 3355 7222, *Fax:* +61 7 3355 9433, *Email:* mail@canniffeeng.com.au
Forgacs Cairncross Dockyard, P O Box 425, Bulimba, Qld., Australia 4171, *Tel:* +61 7 3227 0888, *Fax:* +61 7 3399 6164, *Email:* forgacs@cairncross.com.au, *Website:* www.cairncross.com.au

Seaman Missions: The Seamans Mission, P O Box 9260, Wynnum, Qld., Australia 4178, *Tel:* +61 7 3895 1181, *Fax:* +61 7 3348 7409, *Email:* brisbane@mts.org.au

Ship Chandlers: Australian Providoring & Trading Co., P O Box 1185, Eagle Farm, Brisbane, Qld., Australia 4009, *Tel:* +61 7 3268 7727, *Fax:* +61 7 3268 6056, *Email:* shipsup@marinesupply.com.au
O.A.S.I.S. Australia (International) Proprietary Ltd, 1/24 Boolarra Street, Hemmant, Brisbane, Qld., Australia 4174, *Tel:* +61 7 3390 7666, *Fax:* +61 7 3390 4844, *Email:* oasis@oasisintl.net, *Website:* www.oasisintl.net
Southern Cross Marine Supplies Proprietary Ltd, 1/24 Boolarra Street, Brisbane, Qld., Australia QLD 4174, *Tel:* +61 7 3390 4264, *Fax:* +61 7 3348 7003, *Email:* brisbane@scms.com.au

Shipping Agents: ANL Container Line Proprietary Ltd, 6th Floor, 379/391 Queen Street, Brisbane, Qld., Australia 4000, *Tel:* +61 7 3233 2233, *Fax:* +61 7 3233 2232, *Email:* gordona@anal.com.au, *Website:* www.anl.com.au
Asiaworld Shipping Services Proprietary Ltd, Level 1, 232 Boundary Street, Spring Hill, Brisbane, Qld., Australia 4000, *Tel:* +61 7 3839 4235, *Fax:* +61 7 3839 7430, *Email:* aw.brisbane@asiaworld.com.au, *Website:* www.asiaworld.com.au
Barwil Agencies Australia Pty Ltd, P O Box 1252, Brisbane, Qld., Australia 4006, *Tel:* +61 7 3216 0680, *Fax:* +61 7 3252 4953, *Email:* brisbane@barwil.com.au
Beaufort Shipping Agency Proprietary Ltd, 17 MacArthur Avenue, Hamilton, Brisbane, Qld., Australia 4007, *Tel:* +61 7 3268 8272, *Fax:* +61 7 3268 8242, *Email:* manager.brisbane@beaufortshipping.com, *Website:* www.beaufortshipping.com.au
C.& S. Shipping Agency Proprietary Ltd, 470 Lytton Road, Morningside, P O Box 170, Brisbane, Qld., Australia 4170, *Tel:* +61 7 3899 4511, *Fax:* +61 7 3899 4533, *Email:* aus@cnsshipping.com, *Website:* www.cnsshipping.com
CMA-CGM S.A., CMA CGM Australia Pty Ltd, 6th Floor - 379 Queen Street, P O Box 3083, Brisbane, Qld., Australia 4001, *Tel:* +61 7 3233 2250, *Fax:* +61 7 3233 2259, *Website:* www.cma-cgm.com
Djakarta Lloyd Agencies (Australia) Proprietary Ltd, Level 6, 379 Queen Street, P O Box 3083, Brisbane, Qld., Australia 4001, *Tel:* +61 7 3233 2211, *Fax:* +61 7 3233 2232, *Email:* alang@anl.com.au, *Website:* www.anl.com.au
Evergreen Shipping Agency (Australia) Proprietary Ltd, Level 4, 316 Adelaide Street, Brisbane, Qld., Australia 4000, *Tel:* +61 7 3237 7377, *Fax:* +61 7 3237 7399, *Email:* i.mcalpine@evergreen-shipping.com.au, *Website:* www.evergreen-line.com
Five Star Shipping & Agency Co. Proprietary Ltd, 6th Floor, 12 Creek Street, P O Box 2908, Brisbane, Qld., Australia 4000, *Tel:* +61 7 3215 1100, *Fax:* +61 7 3220 0234, *Email:* smyler@cosco.com.au, *Website:* www.fivestarshipping.com.au
Globe Star Shipping Proprietary Ltd, Level 9, 333 Adelaide Street, P O Box 964, Brisbane, Qld., Australia 4000, *Tel:* +61 7 3105 7600, *Fax:* +61 7 3831 9010, *Email:* lawrieu@globestar.com.au, *Website:* www.globestar.com.au
Gulf Agency Co (Australia) Pty Ltd., The Moorings on Rivergate, Unit 1B, 20 Rivergate Place, Murarrie, Qld., Australia 4172, *Tel:* +61 7 3390 6420, *Fax:* +61 7 3348 8255, *Email:* shipping.brisbane@gacworld.com, *Website:* www.gacworld.com
Hanjin Shipping Australia Pty Ltd, 470 Upper Roma Street, Unit 2, Brisbane, Qld., Australia 4000, *Tel:* +61 7 3252 6800, *Fax:* +61 7 3257 3789, *Email:* cthomas@au.hanjin.com, *Website:* www.hanjin.com
A Hartrodt International, 22 Chapman Place, Eagle Farm, P O Box 15 60, Brisbane, Qld., Australia, *Tel:* +61 7 3630 6700, *Fax:* +61 7 3630 6777, *Email:* brisbane@hartrodt.com.au, *Website:* www.hartrodt.com.au
Hetherington Kingsbury Proprietary Ltd, P O Box 155, Brisbane, Qld., Australia 4006, *Tel:* +61 7 3257 0755, *Fax:* +61 7 3257 0622, *Email:* dhislop@hksa.com.au, *Website:* www.hksa.com.au
Holyman Marine Agencies, Evergreen Shipping Agency, Level 4, 316 Adelaide Street, Brisbane, Qld., Australia 4000, *Tel:* +61 7 3237 7377, *Fax:* +61 7 3237 7399, *Email:* bbnemcbiz@evergreen-shipping.com.au, *Website:* www.evergreen-line.com
Horizon Shipping Agencies, Ground Floor, South Tower, Gregory Terrace, Bowens Hills, Brisbane, Qld., Australia 4006, *Tel:* +61 7 3221 8555, *Fax:* +61 7 3221 8588, *Email:* mktg@aalsa.com.au, *Website:* www.aalpas.com
Inchcape Shipping Services (ISS), 44A Borthwick Avenue, Morningside, Qld., Australia 4170, *Tel:* +61 7 3899 6540, *Fax:* +61 7 3899 6541, *Email:* brisbane@iss-shipping.com.au, *Website:* www.iss-shipping.com
McArthur Shipping & Agency Co Pty Ltd, P O Box 155, Albion, Brisbane, Qld., Australia 4010, *Tel:* +61 7 3854 1055, *Fax:* +61 7 3268 5733, *Email:* brisbane@mcaship.com.au, *Website:* www.mcaship.com.au
Mediterranean Shipping Company, MSC (Aust) Pty Ltd., P O Box 739, Morningside, Qld., Australia 4170, *Tel:* +61 7 3909 4666, *Fax:* +61 7 3909 4644, *Email:* bneinfo@msc.com.au, *Website:* www.msc.com.au
Monson Agencies Australia Proprietary Ltd, Level 6, 193 North Quay, Brisbane, Qld., Australia 4000, *Tel:* +61 7 3839 8972, *Fax:* +61 7 3832 7445, *Email:* brisbane@monson.com.au, *Website:* www.monson.com.au
Seatrans Australia Proprietary Ltd, Suite 32, Argyle Place, corner Argyle Street & Sandgate Road, Breakfast Creek, Brisbane, Qld., Australia 4010, *Tel:* +61 7 3262 7466, *Fax:* +61 7 3262 7751, *Email:* brisbane@mcaship.com.au
Swire Shipping Agencies, Level 8, 444 Queen Street, P O Box 2450, Brisbane, Qld., Australia 4000, *Tel:* +61 7 3302 3300, *Fax:* +61 7 3302 1539/3674, *Email:* ssabne@swire.com.au
Worldwide Project Consortium Ltd (WWPC), 30 Napier Street, Ascot, Brisbane, Qld., Australia 4007, *Tel:* +61 7 3268 2021, *Fax:* +61 7 3268 2481, *Email:* headoffice@wwpc.info, *Website:* www.wwpc.info

Stevedoring Companies: Patrick Stevedoring, Maritime Wharf, Macarther Avenue, Hamilton, Qld., Australia 4007, *Tel:* +61 7 3868 9591, *Fax:* +61 7 3268 2532, *Website:* www.patrick.com.au
P&O Ports, P O Box 1087, Wynnum, Qld., Australia 4178, *Tel:* +61 7 3895 9222, *Fax:* +61 7 3909 3096, *Email:* greg.nugent@poports.com.au, *Website:* www.poports.com.au

Surveyors: Australian Ship P & I, P O Box 218, Woodford, Brisbane, Qld., Australia 4514, *Tel:* +61 7 5496 4688, *Fax:* +61 7 5496 4530, *Email:* brisbane@ausship.com.au
BMT WBM Proprietary Ltd, P O Box 203, Spring Hill, Brisbane, Qld., Australia 4004, *Tel:* +61 7 3831 6744, *Fax:* +61 7 3832 3627, *Email:* wbm@wbmpl.com.au, *Website:* www.wbmpl.com.au
Bureau Veritas, 7 Palmer Place, Murarrie, Brisbane, Qld., Australia 4172, *Tel:* +61 7

Key to Principal Facilities:—
A=Airport **C**=Containers **G**=General Cargo **P**=Petroleum **R**=Ro/Ro **Y**=Dry Bulk
B=Bunkers **D**=Dry Dock **L**=Cruise **Q**=Other Liquid Bulk **T**=Towage (where available from port)

3907 7111, *Fax:* +61 7 3890 3716, *Email:* bv.aus@au.bureauveritas.com, *Website:* www.bureauveritas.com

Det Norske Veritas A/S, Suite 3, 57 Cambridge Parade, Manly, Brisbane, Qld., Australia 4179, *Tel:* +61 7 3348 7911, *Fax:* +61 7 3348 7912, *Email:* brisbane@dnv.com, *Website:* www.dnv.com

Nippon Kaiji Kyokai, 12 Arun Drive, Brisbane, Qld., Australia, *Tel:* +61 7 5563 2846, *Fax:* +61 7 5563 2847, *Website:* www.classnk.or.jp

Normarine Service Proprietary Ltd, 63 Bleakley Road, Woodford, Brisbane, Qld., Australia 4514, *Tel:* +61 7 5496 4530, *Fax:* +61 7 5496 4594, *Email:* normarine@normarine.com.au

Airport: Brisbane Airport

Railway: QR, Tel: +61 (7) 3235 2222, operates two Seafreighter services on the North Coast Line, servicing importers and exporters between the BMT and QR terminals at Bundaberg, Gladstone, Mt Miller, Biloela, Rockhampton, Mackay and Townsville

Development: Construction of a new 380 m long container berth (No.10 wharf), to be operated by Patrick Terminals, has commenced and is scheduled to be operational July 2008. When completed, Patrick will vacate Wharf 7 and DP World Brisbane will take it over

A new 210 m general-purpose wharf, to be managed by Port of Brisbane Corporation, will be constructed at Fisherman Islands to handle bulk and break-bulk cargoes and is due to be completed mid 2009

Container berth no's 11 and 12, to be operated by Brisbane Container Terminals (BCT), are expected to be operational by mid-2012 and mid-2014 respectively. Upon completion, BCT will have a total area of 26 ha, a quay length of 660 m with a depth alongside of 14 m

Lloyd's Agent: Freemans Marine, P O Box 554, Fortitude Valley, Brisbane, Qld., Australia 4006, *Tel:* +61 7 3867 4646, *Fax:* +61 7 3867 4699, *Email:* john.cupitt@freemans.com.au, *Website:* www.freemansmarine.com.au

Location	Grain (t)
Broome	16000

Mechanical Handling Equipment:

Location	Type	Capacity (t)	Qty
Broome	Mobile Cranes	30–120	3
Broome	Forklifts	3–30	6

Bunkering: Three bunker outlets on the inner berth and three on the outer berth rated at 120 kl/h

BP Australia (Proprietary) Ltd, P O Box 5222, Melbourne, Vic., Australia 3001, *Tel:* +61 3 9268 4111, *Fax:* +61 3 9268 3321, *Email:* gomiasfuelsales@bp.com, *Website:* www.bp.com

Towage: One tug is available

Shipping Agents: Barwil Agencies Australia Pty Ltd, P O Box 378, Port Hedland, W.A., Australia 6721, *Tel:* +61 8 9173 1809, *Fax:* +61 8 9173 2526, *Email:* pthedland@wilhelmsen.com, *Website:* www.wilhelmsen.com

Inchcape Shipping Services (ISS), Inchcape Shipping Services Pty Ltd, Unit 2, 10 Frederick Street, P O Box 2340, Broome, W.A., Australia 6725, *Tel:* +61 8 9192 6504, *Fax:* +61 8 9192 6548, *Email:* broome@iss-shipping.com.au, *Website:* www.iss-shipping.com

Stevedoring Companies: P&O Ports, P O Box 226, Fremantle, W.A., Australia 6159, *Tel:* +61 8 9430 0111, *Fax:* +61 8 9335 4215, *Email:* ann.gosling@poports.com.au

Medical Facilities: Hospital and a local dental clinic available

Airport: Broome, 9 km

Lloyd's Agent: Moko Proprietary Ltd, P O Box 685, Willetton, W.A., Australia 6955, *Tel:* +61 8 9354 2248, *Fax:* +61 8 9354 2234, *Email:* kglange@bigpond.com

BROOME

Lat 17° 57' S; Long 122° 14' E.

Admiralty Chart: AUS 324	**Admiralty Pilot:** 17
Time Zone: GMT +8 h	**UNCTAD Locode:** AU BME

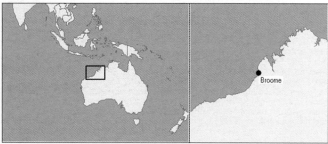

Principal Facilities:

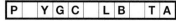

P		Y	G	C		L	B		T	A

Authority: Broome Port Authority, Port of Pearls House, 401 Port Drive, P O Box 46, Broome, W.A., Australia 6725, *Tel:* +61 8 9192 1304, *Fax:* +61 8 9192 1778, *Email:* info@broomeport.com, *Website:* www.broomeport.com

Officials: Chief Executive Officer: Vic Justice, *Tel:* +61 8 9194 3100, *Email:* ceo@broomeport.com.
Administration: Rosemary Braybrook, *Tel:* +61 8 9194 3100.

Port Security: ISPS compliant

Pre-Arrival Information: Vessels should send ETA 7 days in advance with updates 48 h and 24 h prior to arrival

Approach: Entrance channel has a depth of 13 m at LW datum

Anchorage: Anchorage area in Roebuck Bay in close proximity to Broome jetty

Pilotage: Compulsory for all vessels over 150 gt. Vessels should request a pilot 48 h in advance through Broome Port Authority. Pilot boards by pilot launch in the following positions:
Outer Pilot Boarding Station in pos 17° 58' 10" S; 122° 05' 30" E (for all vessels unless otherwise arranged with the Port Authority)
Inner Pilot Boarding Station in pos 18° 00' 73" S; 122° 11' 59" E (for use as agreed between Port Authority and individual ship masters)

Radio Frequency: During office hours 0730-1630 the port maintains a watch on VHF Channel 16 and SSB general marine channel 4620.0 kHz

Weather: Monsoon weather with the rainy tropical summer from November to March

Tides: Tidal range of 9.6 m

Traffic: 2007/08, 404 vessels, 321 357 t of cargo handled

Principal Imports and Exports: Imports: Bitumen, Cement, Fuel, Steel casing. Exports: Livestock.

Working Hours: Available 24 h/day

Accommodation:

Name	Remarks
Broome	See [1] below

[1]*Broome:* The jetty is a steel piled structure with a concrete deck and spring fendering. The outer berth is 331 m long and two inner berths 170 m long and 96 m long. At zero datum it is 12.5 m from the waterline to the deck of the wharf and 11.34 m to the top of the fender system. The port is also used as a supply base for servicing offshore oil and gas activity in the Browse Basin area and by visiting cruise vessels

Storage: Transit shed of 500 m2 and supply base warehouse of 3000 m2

BUNBURY

Lat 33° 20' S; Long 115° 39' E.

Admiralty Chart: AUS 115	**Admiralty Pilot:** 17
Time Zone: GMT +8 h	**UNCTAD Locode:** AU BUY

Principal Facilities:

Q	Y	G		R	L	B		T	A

Authority: Bunbury Port Authority, P O Box 4, Bunbury, W.A., Australia 6231, *Tel:* +61 8 9729 7020, *Fax:* +61 8 9721 8253, *Email:* byport@byport.com.au, *Website:* www.byport.com.au

Officials: Port Superintendent: David Lantry, *Tel:* +61 8 9729 7026, *Email:* david.lantry@byport.com.au.
Harbour Master: Helen Cole, *Tel:* +61 8 9729 7048, *Email:* helen.cole@byport.com.au.

Port Security: ISPS compliant

Approach: Depth at entrance to approach channel 13.4 m

Anchorage: Two main anchorage areas, one with lighthouse bearing 160° T at 5.63 km and breakwater 140° T at 4.51 km in a depth of 16 m and the second with main lighthouse bearing 160° T at 3.22 km and breakwater 120° T at 2.41 km in a depth of 15 m

Pilotage: Compulsory for all vessels except Australian flag with exempt master. Pilot boarding ground in pos 33° 16' 30" S; 115° 36' 30" E
Duty pilot: Tel; +61 8 9721 8370

Radio Frequency: Direct contact on VHF Channel 16, 156.8 mHz although not manned continuously. Working channel 12

Weather: Summer winds moderate E in the morning, later SW sea breezes fresh-strong. Winter winds strong N-WSW. Moderate to heavy swell from the W

Tides: Range of tide, neaps 0.3 m, max springs 1.3 m

Traffic: 2007/08, 337 vessels, 13 658 940 t of cargo handled

Maximum Vessel Dimensions: Outer harbour 225 m loa, 9.2 m draft. Inner harbour 234 m loa, 12.3 m draft

Principal Imports and Exports: Imports: Caustic soda, Edible oil, General cargo, Methanol, Phosphate rock, Potash, Sulphur. Exports: Alumina, Mineral sands, Woodchips.

Working Hours: 0800-1700, 1700-2400, 0000-0800

Accommodation: Harbour is well protected by stone breakwater 1813 m long

Name	Length (m)	Depth (m)	Remarks
Outer Harbour			
Berth No.1	184	9.2	See [1] below
Berth No.2	184	7–8	General cargo & methanol. Methanol storage tanks
Inner Harbour			
Berth No.3	381	12.2	See [2] below
Berth No.4	250	12.7	See [3] below

Name	Length (m)	Depth (m)	Remarks
Berth No.5	240	12.2	See [4] below
Berth No.6	123	12.7	See [5] below
Berth No.8	250	12.4	See [6] below

[1]*Berth No.1:* Bulk & general cargo. Mechanical shiploader rated at 900 t/h. Air draught 14.0 m

[2]*Berth No.3:* Operated by W.A. Chip & Pulp Co Pty Ltd., P O Box 2453, Bunbury WA 6231, *Tel:* +61 8 9721 7411, *Fax:* +61 8 9721 3213, *Email:* bunbury.port@wapres.com.au, *Website:* www.wapres.com.au Woddchips. Mechanical shiploader rated at 1000 t/h and linked to ship side storage

[3]*Berth No.4:* Operated by Alcoa World Alumina Alumina & caustic soda. Mechanical shiploader rated at 2000 t/h and linked to ship side storage, also used for the discharge of caustic soda

[4]*Berth No.5:* Bulk & general cargo. Equipped with mobile hoppers for bulk discharge and a transportable bulk materials shiploader

[5]*Berth No.6:* Operated by Worsley Alumina Pty Ltd. Alumina & caustic soda. Mechanical shiploader rated at 3000 t/h; also used for the discharge of caustic soda

[6]*Berth No.8:* Minerals & other sands. Shoreside storage areas linked to gantry shiploader for mineral sands, silica sand and related products. Loading from storage and from connected road hopper at 2000 t/h

Storage: Large area adjacent to No.5 berth for holding stock, timber, containers etc. Ample open space, minimal warehousing

Bunkering: Furnace oil, marine and light diesel. Available by road tankers BP Australia (Proprietary) Ltd, P O Box 5222, Melbourne, Vic., Australia 3001, *Tel:* +61 3 9268 4111, *Fax:* +61 3 9268 3321, *Email:* gomiasfuelsales@bp.com, *Website:* www.bp.com Shell Australia Ltd, Shell Company of Australia, Marine Centre Oceania, No 8 Redfern Road, Melbourne, Vic., Australia 3123, *Tel:* +61 3 9666 5446, *Fax:* +61 3 8823 4800, *Email:* sal-marine-products@shell.com, *Website:* www.shell.com.au

Waste Reception Facilities: Oily water disposal, limited capacity, by road tanker

Towage: Two tugs available each fitted with fire fighting equipment; Riverwijs Isabelle: 42t bollard pull Riverwijs Grace: 42t bollard pull Riverwijs Dampier Proprietary Ltd, Suite 10, 18 Parry Street, P O Box 1213, Fremantle, W.A., Australia 6160, *Tel:* +61 8 9433 1311, *Fax:* +61 8 9433 1611, *Email:* paul@riversidemarine.com.au

Repair & Maintenance: Limited repairs only

Seaman Missions: The Seamans Mission, 17 Victoria Street, Bunbury, W.A., Australia 6230, *Tel:* +61 8 9721 2370, *Email:* bunbury@mts.org.au

Ship Chandlers: Sealanes, 178 Marine Terrace, Fremantle, W.A., Australia 6162, *Tel:* +61 8 9432 8888, *Fax:* +61 8 9430 4019, *Email:* sea@sealanes.com.au, *Website:* www.sealanes.com.au Sinwa Imes Pty Ltd., P O Box 1468, Bibra Lake, Fremantle, W.A., Australia 6965, *Tel:* +61 8 9434 3300, *Fax:* +61 8 9434 3322, *Email:* sales-imes@sinwa.com.au, *Website:* www.sinwaglobal.com

Shipping Agents: Barwil Agencies Australia Pty Ltd, P O Box 805, Fremantle, W.A., Australia 6959, *Tel:* +61 8 9336 0900, *Fax:* +61 8 9336 0999, *Email:* fremantle@barwil.com.au, *Website:* www.barwil.com Inchcape Shipping Services (ISS), Inchcape Shipping Services Pty Ltd, P O Box 537, Bunbury, W.A., Australia 6230, *Tel:* +61 8 9791 5077, *Fax:* +61 8 9721 9922, *Email:* bunbury@iss-shipping.com.au, *Website:* www.iss-shipping.com Monson Agencies Australia Proprietary Ltd, P O Box 292, Bunbury, W.A., Australia 6231, *Tel:* +61 8 9791 3181, *Fax:* +61 8 9721 9499, *Email:* bunbury@monson.com.au, *Website:* www.monson.com.au

Stevedoring Companies: P&O Ports, P O Box 403, Bunbury, W.A., Australia 6231, *Tel:* +61 8 9791 5992, *Fax:* +61 8 9791 5993, *Email:* glenn.gibson@poports.com.au, *Website:* www.poports.com.au

Surveyors: Griffith WA Services, Bunbury, W.A., Australia, *Tel:* +61 8 9921 2472, *Fax:* +61 8 9921 4452

Medical Facilities: Public and private hospital available

Airport: Bunbury Airport

Railway: Bunbury (fast train to Perth) 2 km from inner harbour

Lloyd's Agent: Moko Proprietary Ltd, P O Box 685, Willetton, W.A., Australia 6955, *Tel:* +61 8 9354 2248, *Fax:* +61 8 9354 2234, *Email:* kglange@bigpond.com

BUNDABERG

Lat 24° 48' S; Long 152° 24' E.

Admiralty Chart: AUS 242/243		**Admiralty Pilot:** 15
Time Zone: GMT +10 h		**UNCTAD Locode:** AU BDB

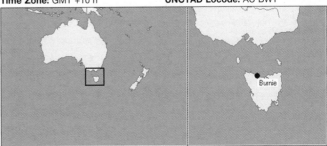
Bundaberg

Principal Facilities:

P	Q	Y	G			B		T	A

Authority: Port of Brisbane Corp., 1 Sandpiper Avenue, Fisherman Islands, P O Box 1818, Brisbane, Qld., Australia 4178, *Tel:* +61 7 3258 4888, *Fax:* +61 7 3258 4703, *Email:* info@portbris.com.au, *Website:* www.portbris.com.au

Officials: Chief Executive Officer: Jeff Coleman, *Tel:* +61 7 3258 4774, *Email:* jeff.coleman@portbris.com.au. General Manager: Gerry Johnstone, *Tel:* +61 7 3258 4830, *Email:* gerry.johnstone@portbris.com.au. Operations Manager: Peter Keyte, *Tel:* +61 7 3258 4620, *Email:* peter.keyte@portbris.com.au. Harbour Master: Richard Johnson, *Tel:* +61 7 3860 3552, *Email:* richard.c.johnson@msq.qld.gov.au.

Port Security: ISPS compliant

Approach: Access to the port is via Hervey Bay, thence to the Burnett River. The depth of water at LAT in the port is 9.5 m from Fairway Beacons to the upper end of the swing basin, then 0.7 m to the Town Reach. The swinging basin has a width of 320 m, a length of 1165 m and a min depth of 8.3 m. The width of the channel from the Fairway Beacons to the swinging basin is 103 m. The max draft of vessels that may enter the port is 9.5 m plus the predicted rise of tide. All vessels are required to have a min keel clearance of 0.9 m Note: vessels are not to pass out through the Sea Reach Leads on the ebb tide

Pilotage: Compulsory. Vessels should send their ETA and max draught to the Harbour Master at least 24 h in advance and subsequent ammendments should be sent immediately. Pilot boards 2.6 nautical miles E of South Head Lt in pos 24° 45' 48" S; 152° 27' 55" E

Radio Frequency: Bundaberg Harbour Control on VHF Channel 16 (distress, safety & calling) and VHF Channel 6 (Bundaberg Harbour Control & pilot vessel)

Tides: Range of tide 3.3 m. MSR 2.9 m, MNR 2 m. Tidal stream in excess of 4 knots may be encountered between New Bundaberg Port and Burnett Heads. The tide sets across channel in the Sea Reaches. An extremely strong northerly set is frequently experienced just seaward of the lighthouse

Traffic: 2006/07, 26 vessels, 473 041 t of cargo handled

Maximum Vessel Dimensions: 200 m loa, 10.99 m draft

Principal Imports and Exports: Imports: Petroleum products. Exports: Bulk raw sugar, Molasses, Wooden poles.

Working Hours: When required, no limit

Accommodation:

Name	Length (m)	Depth (m)	Remarks
Bundaberg			
Sir Thomas Hiley Wharf	191	11	See [1] below
John T. Fisher Wharf	240	9.7	See [2] below

[1]*Sir Thomas Hiley Wharf:* This berth is used for the export of sugar, with a loading rate of 1400 t/h and a storage cap of 300 000 t in two sheds

[2]*John T. Fisher Wharf:* Liquid cargo berth. Pipelines to Mobil Oil Australia Ltd and Bundaberg Molasses Co. Terminals are laid along this 'T' head jetty. The oil terminal has a cap of 24 600 t. The discharge of petroleum products from tank vessels is via a 10'' pipeline at a rate of 900 t/h. Molasses is exported at 285 t/h, from 36 641 t cap bulk tanks through a 15'' pipeline

Mechanical Handling Equipment: Mobile cranes available

Bunkering: BP Australia (Proprietary) Ltd, P O Box 5222, Melbourne, Vic., Australia 3001, *Tel:* +61 3 9268 4111, *Fax:* +61 3 9268 3321, *Email:* gomiasfuelsales@bp.com, *Website:* www.bp.com ExxonMobil Marine Fuels, 1 Harbour Front Place, 06-00 Harbour Front, Tower One, Singapore, Republic of Singapore 098633, *Tel:* +65 6885 8998, *Fax:* +65 6885 8794, *Email:* asiapac.marinefuels@exxonmobil.com, *Website:* www.exxonmobilmarinefuels.com – *Grades:* MGO – *Delivery Mode:* tank truck International Bunker Supplies Proprietary Ltd, Majella, 473 St. Kilda Road, Melbourne, Vic., Australia 3004, *Tel:* +61 3 9211 9360, *Fax:* +61 3 9211 9365, *Email:* bunkers@ibsfuels.com, *Website:* www.ibsfuels.com

Repair & Maintenance: Bundaberg Foundry Engineers Ltd, 4 Gavin Street, Bundaberg, Qld., Australia 4670, *Tel:* +61 7 4150 8700, *Fax:* +61 7 4150 8711, *Email:* results@bfel.com.au, *Website:* www.bfel.com.au

Shipping Agents: Barwil Agencies Australia Pty Ltd, P O Box 5166, Gladstone, Qld., Australia 4680, *Tel:* +61 7 4972 8833, *Fax:* +61 7 4972 8696, *Email:* gladstone@wilhelmsen.com, *Website:* www.wilhelmsen.com

Airport: Hinkler, 21 km

Lloyd's Agent: Freemans Marine, P O Box 554, Fortitude Valley, Brisbane, Qld., Australia 4006, *Tel:* +61 7 3867 4646, *Fax:* +61 7 3867 4699, *Email:* john.cupitt@freemans.com.au, *Website:* www.freemansmarine.com.au

BURNIE

Lat 41° 3' S; Long 145° 54' E.

Admiralty Chart: AUS 163		**Admiralty Pilot:** 14
Time Zone: GMT +10 h		**UNCTAD Locode:** AU BWT

Burnie

Key to Principal Facilities:—				
A=Airport	**C**=Containers	**G**=General Cargo	**P**=Petroleum	**R**=Ro/Ro	**Y**=Dry Bulk
B=Bunkers	**D**=Dry Dock	**L**=Cruise	**Q**=Other Liquid Bulk	**T**=Towage (where available from port)

Principal Facilities:

P	Q	Y	G	C	R	L	B		T	A

Authority: Tasmanian Ports Corp. Proprietary Ltd (TasPorts), P O Box 216, Burnie, Tas., Australia 7320, *Tel:* +61 3 6434 7300, *Fax:* +61 3 6434 7373, *Email:* secretary@tasports.com.au, *Website:* www.tasports.com.au

Officials: Chief Executive Officer: Robert Barnes, *Email:* robert.barnes@tasports.com.au.
Marketing Manager: Charles Scarafiotti, *Email:* charles.scarafiotti@tasports.com.au.

Port Security: ISPS compliant

Approach: The bay is 2 miles wide and 1 mile deep, facing in a N direction. The bottom is sand and clay interspersed with patches of reef and rock particularly in the SE sector of the bay. The port is protected by two breakwaters: the inner, founded at the inner end of Blackman Reef, lies in a 110 degree direction and is 381 m long. The other, an island structure, lies in a 130 degree direction and is 488 m long. The W end of this breakwater bears 045 degrees true, 213 m from the E end of the inner breakwater. The principal danger approaching the port is Blackman Reef, with shallow water extending 1 mile seaward from the W shore of the bay. Vessels approaching the port from the W should, by night, keep in the white sector of Round Hill Point Light until the two blue lights of the main leads come into transit. By day, keep the two orange beacons on the shoulder of Round Hill open to the north and then turn onto the main harbour leads which are in transit 224 degrees true

Anchorage: Vessels may anchor on the main leads in the vicinity of the pilot boarding ground, but it is not advisable to remain at anchor during strong on-shore winds

Pilotage: Compulsory for vessels over 35 m loa. Pilots available 24 h/day. Vessel's should advise ETA at the pilot boarding position 24 h in advance. Pilot boards in pos 41° 01' 62" S; 145° 57' 19" E

Radio Frequency: Coast Station: on VHF Channels 16, 14, 12 and 67
Pilot Vessel and Tugs: on VHF Channels 16, 12, 8, 6 and 67

Tides: 3 m MHHW, 0.5 m MLLW

Traffic: 2007/08, 531 vessels, 4 457 061 t of cargo handled, 206 348 TEU's

Maximum Vessel Dimensions: Max loa 260 m

Principal Imports and Exports: Imports: Bulk commodities, Containerised cargo, Machinery, Petroleum products, Woodpulp. Exports: Bulk minerals, Containerised cargo, Logs, Paper, Timber, Woodchips.

Working Hours: 24 h/day

Accommodation:

Name	Length (m)	Depth (m)	Remarks
Burnie			
Berth No.4	183	10	See [1] below
Berth No.5	213	11	See [2] below
Berth No.6	198	11.5	See [3] below
Berth No.7	219	11.5	See [4] below

[1]*Berth No.4:* At the inshore end is a tidebridge stern loading facility suitable for vessels with their own ramp
[2]*Berth No.5:* Bulk loading berth with 213 m of effective berthage for vessels up to 250 m loa. Loading cap in excess of 1000 t/h. Berth is also suitable for discharge of petroleum products
[3]*Berth No.6:* One storage shed of 1500 m2. This berth has a 80 t cap single lift paceco portainer crane. 201 reefer points
[4]*Berth No.7:* 65 t cap twin lift paceco portainer crane. 114 reefer points. A travelling woodchip shiploader at outer end at 1200 t/h. One storage shed of approx 1784 m2

Storage:

Location	Cold (m³)
Burnie	31279

Mechanical Handling Equipment:

Location	Type	Capacity (t)	Qty
Burnie	Forklifts	30	
Berth No.6	Mult-purp. Cranes	80	1
Berth No.7	Mult-purp. Cranes	65	1

Cargo Worked: 100 containers per shift

Bunkering: Diesel oil and heavy fuel oil is available by road tanker
BP Australia (Proprietary) Ltd, P O Box 5222, Melbourne, Vic., Australia 3001, *Tel:* +61 3 9268 4111, *Fax:* +61 3 9268 3321, *Email:* gomiasfuelsales@bp.com, *Website:* www.bp.com – *Misc:* Diesel can be bunkered via pipeline at berth No.5
ExxonMobil Marine Fuels, 1 Harbour Front Place, 06-00 Harbour Front, Tower One, Singapore, Republic of Singapore 098633, *Tel:* +65 6885 8998, *Fax:* +65 6885 8794, *Email:* asiapac.marinefuels@exxonmobil.com, *Website:* www.exxonmobilmarinefuels.com – *Grades:* MGO – *Delivery Mode:* tank truck

Waste Reception Facilities: Sludge road tankers available. Commercial incinerator for garbage and waste disposal

Towage: Three twin screw tugs available with up to 40 t bollard pull
North Western Shipping & Towage Proprietary Ltd, Inspection Head Wharf, Beauty Point, P O Box 76, Beaconsfield, Tas., Australia 7270, *Tel:* +61 3 6383 4522, *Fax:* +61 3 6383 4604, *Email:* inquiries@nwst.com.au, *Website:* www.nwst.com.au

Repair & Maintenance: Local engineering firms with foundries and extensive machine shops available
Emu Bay Railway Co., Wilson Street, Burnie, Tas., Australia, *Tel:* +61 3 6430 4211, *Fax:* +61 3 6430 4204
The Engineering Co., P O Box 215, Somerset, Burnie, Tas., Australia 7322, *Tel:* +61 3 6435 1556, *Fax:* +61 3 6435 2586, *Email:* theengco@southcom.com.au, *Website:* www.theengco.com.au

Seaman Missions: The Seamans Mission, P O Box 44, Burnie, Tas., Australia 7320, *Tel:* +61 3 6432 2396, *Fax:* +61 3 6432 3658, *Email:* burnie@mts.org.au

Shipping Agents: Barwil Agencies Australia Pty Ltd, P O Box 311, George Town, Tas., Australia 7253, *Tel:* +61 3 6382 4088, *Fax:* +61 3 6382 4099, *Email:* bellbay@wilhelmsen.com, *Website:* www.wilhelmsen.com
Monson Agencies Australia Proprietary Ltd, P O Box 609, Burnie, Tas., Australia

7320, *Tel:* +61 3 6431 9536, *Fax:* +61 3 6431 3326, *Email:* tasmania@monship.com.au, *Website:* www.monson.com.au
C. Piesse & Co. Proprietary Ltd, 1st Floor, JD Loane Building, 100 Wilson Street, P O Box 298, Burnie, Tas., Australia 7320, *Tel:* +61 3 6431 3833, *Fax:* +61 3 6431 1794, *Email:* tas@piesse.com.au

Stevedoring Companies: P&O Ports, P O Box 964, Devonport, Tas., Australia 7310, *Tel:* +61 3 6432 3964, *Fax:* +61 3 6432 3964

Surveyors: Bass Coast Marine Surveyors, Burnie, Tas., Australia, *Tel:* +61 3 6429 3334
Briar Maritime Services Proprietary Ltd, P O Box 338, Ulverstone, Tas., Australia 7315, *Tel:* +61 3 6429 3272, *Fax:* +61 3 6429 3264, *Email:* briarmaritime@bigpond.com, *Website:* www.briarmaritime.com

Medical Facilities: Public and private hospitals

Airport: Wynyard, 20 km

Lloyd's Agent: Freemans Marine, Level 7, 564 St. Kilda Road, Melbourne, Vic., Australia 3004, *Tel:* +61 3 9935 2400, *Fax:* +61 3 9915 0351, *Email:* lloyds@freemans.com.au, *Website:* www.freemansmarine.com.au

BUSSELTON

Lat 33° 38' S; Long 115° 20' E.

Admiralty Chart: AUS 115
Time Zone: GMT +8 h

Admiralty Pilot: 17
UNCTAD Locode: AU BUS

This port is no longer open to commercial shipping

CAIRNS

Lat 16° 55' S; Long 145° 46' E.

Admiralty Chart: AUS 262/263
Time Zone: GMT +10 h

Admiralty Pilot: 15
UNCTAD Locode: AU CNS

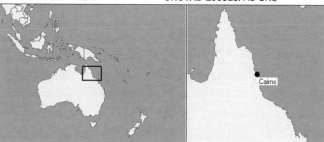

Principal Facilities:

P	Q	Y	G	C		L	B	D	T	A

Authority: Cairns Port Authority, Corner of Grafton & Hartley Streets, P O Box 594, Cairns, Qld., Australia 4870, *Tel:* +61 7 4052 3842, *Fax:* +61 7 4052 1493, *Email:* seaport@cairnsport.com.au, *Website:* www.cairnsport.com.au

Officials: General Manager: Chris Boland, *Tel:* +61 7 4052 3847, *Email:* chris.boland@cairnsport.com.au.
Public Relations Manager: Kerry Egerton, *Tel:* +61 7 4052 3823, *Email:* kerry.egerton@cairnsport.com.au.

Port Security: ISPS compliant

Pre-Arrival Information: Vessels bound for the port are required to advise their ETA to the Seaport Operations Centre at least 72 h prior to arrival and again at 48 h and then every 12 h

Documentation: Manifests: A cargo manifest is required by CPA and Australian Quarantine & Inspection Service. For foreign vessels a cargo manifest is required by Australian Customs Service 48 h in advance. After gaining radio pratique, the master of the ship is required to fill out a Health declaration form. Passengers must fill out a Customs, Quarantine and Wildlife declaration. All international passengers must have current visa and passport. However, if entering the country and leaving on the same vessel in the course of the same voyage, only a passport is required

Approach: Deep water passage to Cairns through the Great Barrier Reef is available via Grafton Passage from the E, which is 34 km long and 8 km wide. Entrance to harbour is by a dredged channel approx 11 km long and 90 m wide with a depth of 8.3 m LAT

Anchorage: Cairns has 91 pile berths located on the eastern side of Trinity Inlet. There are also areas designated for anchorage only, situated N and S of the piles, E of Admiralty Island and in Smith's Creek

Pilotage: Compulsory for internationally registered vessels over 35 m and Australian registered vessels of 50 m unless the Master holds a current pilotage exemption certificate. Pilotage services are available 24 h/day. North Queensland Port Pilots provide pilotage for vessels entering and departing the port. Vessels requiring the services of a pilot should wire their agent or Duty Pilot from the last port of call giving ETA and estimated draft. Pilot boarding ground is approx 4 km seaward of the Fairway beacons at pos 16° 48.7' S; 145° 50.6' E
Maritime Safety Queensland (Port Pilots), Tel: +61 7 4052 7487, Fax: +61 7 4035 5623

Radio Frequency: VHF Channel 16 (156.8 mHz), call sign 'Cairns Harbour' and HF on 4125 kHz

Weather: Prevailing winds from December to August are SE'ly with N'ly winds occurring from September to November

Tides: Tidal planes are MHWS 2.57 m, MHWN 1.88 m, MLWS 0.74 m, MLWN 1.44 m

Traffic: 2007/08, 582 commercial vessels & 87 cruise vessels, 1 196 604 t of cargo handled, 17 515 TEU's

Maximum Vessel Dimensions: 8.5 m draft

Principal Imports and Exports: Imports: Fertiliser, General cargo, LPG, Petroleum products. Exports: Copper concentrate, General cargo, Molasses, Petroleum products, Sugar.

Working Hours: 0001-0700, 0800-1500, 1600-2300. Continuous work is available on request

Accommodation: Large sheltered natural harbour with three swing basins; one adjacent to wharf No.1 with depth of 6.3 m and diameter of 400 m, one adjacent to wharf No.12 with depth of 8.3 m and diameter of 320 m and the other adjacent to the entrance of Smith's Creek with a depth of 5.0 m and diameter of 360 m. The inlet runs on for about 8 km past the city with varying depths

Name	Length (m)	Depth (m)	Remarks
Trinity Inlet			
Berth No.1	80	8.4	See [1] below
Berth No.2	90	8.4	See [2] below
Berth No.3	90	8.4	General cargo & passengers
Berth No.4	95	8.4	General cargo & dry bulk
Berth No.5	70	8.4	General cargo & dry bulk
Berth No.6	170	7	See [3] below
Berth No's 7 & 8	250	9.3	See [4] below
Berth No.10	220	9.2	See [5] below
Berth No.11			Navy berth
Berth No.12	183	9.5	See [6] below
Smiths Creek			
Berth No.1	53.4	5	General cargo for vessels up to 65 m loa

[1]*Berth No.1:* Passengers. Terminal No.1 is located on the second floor of the Trinity Wharf complex and has immigration and customs facilities
[2]*Berth No.2:* Cruise vessels. Passenger Terminal No.2 has immigration and customs facilities
[3]*Berth No.6:* General cargo & containers. Weight restrictions apply to this facility on application
[4]*Berth No's 7 & 8:* General cargo & containers for vessels up to 250 m loa and 40 000 dwt. 12 reefer points located at rear of berth 7
[5]*Berth No.10:* Oil & LPG. Connected by pipelines to several shore tanks. For vessels up to 200 m loa
[6]*Berth No.12:* Bulk sugar & molasses. Bulk sugar terminal served by a traveling gantry loader with an average cap of 1750 t/h. Two sugar storage sheds, each with a cap of 117 000 t of sugar. It is also equipped with a 350 mm pipeline for loading molasses at a discharge rate of approx 400 t/h from molasses tanks with holding cap of 18 600 t for molasses

Storage:

Location	Open (m²)	Covered (m²)
Cairns	27330	4358

Mechanical Handling Equipment: Mobile handling equipment is available from local stevedores or hire contractors

Location	Type	Capacity (t)	Qty
Berth No.6	Mult-purp. Cranes	25.4	1

Bunkering: Quantities of fuel over 30 000 litres can be supplied at No.10 berth. Lesser quantities can be supplied by road tanker at the main berths. A bunkering barge service is offered for quantities up to 700 000 litres. Medium fuel oil and distillate can be supplied
BP Australia (Proprietary) Ltd, P O Box 5222, Melbourne, Vic., Australia 3001, *Tel:* +61 3 9268 4111, *Fax:* +61 3 9268 3321, *Email:* gomiasfuelsales@bp.com, *Website:* www.bp.com
ExxonMobil Marine Fuels, 1 Harbour Front Place, 06-00 Harbour Front, Tower One, Singapore, Republic of Singapore 098632, *Tel:* +65 6885 8998, *Fax:* +65 6885 8794, *Email:* asiapac.marinefuels@exxonmobil.com, *Website:* www.exxonmobilmarinefuels.com – *Grades:* MGO – *Delivery Mode:* tank truck
Shell Australia Ltd, Shell Company of Australia, Marine Centre Oceania, No 8 Redfern Road, Melbourne, Vic., Australia 3123, *Tel:* +61 3 9666 5446, *Fax:* +61 3 8823 4800, *Email:* sal-marine-products@shell.com, *Website:* www.shell.com.au

Waste Reception Facilities: The Port Authority provides daily garbage collection services for both quarantine and non-quarantine garbage as determined by the Department of Primary Industries

Towage: Two tugs available of 15 t bollard pull and 27 t bollard pull. A third can be made available from the Port of Mourilyan if required

Repair & Maintenance: Cairns Slipways, 18-22 Tingira Street, Portsmith, P O Box 5000, Cairns, Qld., Australia 4870, *Tel:* +61 7 4052 7354, *Fax:* +61 7 4035 2332, *Email:* info@cairns-slipways.com.au, *Website:* www.cairns-slipways.com.au Dry dock for vessels up to 60 m and a slipway up to 1100 t
Norship Marine Shipyard, 60-62 Tingara Street, Portsmith, Cairns, Qld., Australia 4870, *Tel:* +61 7 4035 1722, *Fax:* +61 7 4035 1613, *Email:* gm@norship.com.au, *Website:* www.norship.com.au Travel-lift of 120 t cap
Tropical Reef Shiyard Proprietary Ltd, P O Box 44, Cairns, Qld., Australia 4870, *Tel:* +61 7 4051 6877, *Fax:* +61 7 4051 0798, *Email:* trshipyard@iig.com.au, *Website:* www.trshipyard.com.au Slipway for vessels up to 61 m in length or 3000 t. Fully equipped workshop facilities

Ship Chandlers: Southern Cross Marine Supplies Proprietary Ltd, 5 Undine Street, Cairns, Qld., Australia QLD 4879, *Tel:* +61 7 4952 5377, *Email:* cairns@scms.com.au, *Website:* www.scms.com.au

Shipping Agents: Barwil Agencies Australia Pty Ltd, P O Box 1392, Cairns, Qld., Australia 4870, *Tel:* +61 7 4035 4344, *Fax:* +61 7 4035 4006, *Email:* cairns@wilhelmsen.com, *Website:* www.wilhelmsen.com
Gulf Agency Co (Australia) Pty Ltd, P O Box 6041, Cairns, Qld., Australia 4870, *Tel:* +61 7 4041 0569, *Fax:* +61 7 4041 2084, *Email:* shipping.cairns@gacworld.com, *Website:* www.gacworld.com
Inchcape Shipping Services (ISS), Inchcape Shipping Services Pty Ltd, Level 1, 22 Martyn Street, P O Box 621, Cairns, Qld., Australia 4870, *Tel:* +61 7 4051 5211, *Fax:* +61 7 4051 5082, *Email:* cairns@iss-shipping.com.au, *Website:* www.iss-shipping.com

Stevedoring Companies: Northern Shipping & Stevedoring Proprietary Ltd, Dutton Street, Cairns, Qld., Australia 4870, *Tel:* +61 7 4051 7338, *Fax:* +61 7 4031 7191
Perkins Shipping Proprietary Ltd, 153 Lyons Street, P O Box 348, Bungalow, Cairns, Qld., Australia 4870, *Tel:* +61 7 4051 3411, *Fax:* +61 7 4031 5847, *Email:* gfscairns@perkins.com.au, *Website:* www.perkins.com.au

Surveyors: Capt. B. Copland & Associates Proprietary Ltd, Cairns, Qld., Australia, *Tel:* +61 7 4093 7945, *Fax:* +61 7 4093 7729, *Email:* capt.copland@iig.com.au
Det Norske Veritas A/S, Suite F16, The Conservatory, 12-14 Lake Street, Cairns, Qld., Australia 4870, *Tel:* +61 7 4031 4022, *Fax:* +61 7 4031 4122, *Email:* cairns@dnv.com, *Website:* www.dnv.com
Russ Larkin & Associates Proprietary Ltd, Unit 9, 182 Grafton Street, P O Box 5394, Cairns, Qld., Australia 4870, *Tel:* +61 7 4031 6046, *Fax:* +61 7 4031 6041, *Email:* office@russlarkinassociates.com.au, *Website:* www.russlarkinassociates.com.au
Nippon Kaiji Kyokai, c/o D. Olufson Holdings Pty Ltd, 18 Cassia Street, Edge Hill, Cairns, Qld., Australia 4870, *Tel:* 61 7, *Fax:* +61 7 4032 1238, *Website:* www.classnk.or.jp
Stewart Marine Design Proprietary Ltd, P O Box 5014, Cairns, Qld., Australia 4870, *Tel:* +61 7 4053 6402, *Fax:* +61 7 4053 7180, *Email:* admin@smd.com.au, *Website:* www.smd.com.au

Medical Facilities: Two major hospitals located close to the port

Airport: Cairns International Airport, 8 km

Railway: Cairns Railway Station, 4 km

Lloyd's Agent: Freemans Marine, P O Box 554, Fortitude Valley, Brisbane, Qld., Australia 4006, *Tel:* +61 7 3867 4646, *Fax:* +61 7 3867 4699, *Email:* john.cupitt@freemans.com.au, *Website:* www.freemansmarine.com.au

CAPE CUVIER

Lat 24° 13' S; Long 113° 23' E.

Admiralty Chart: AUS 330   **Admiralty Pilot:** 17
Time Zone: GMT +8 h   **UNCTAD Locode:** AU CCU

Principal Facilities:

		Y						T	A

Authority: Dampier Salt Ltd., Lake Macleod Division, P O Box 501, Carnarvon, W.A., Australia 6701, *Tel:* +61 8 9956 3222, *Fax:* +61 8 9956 3200, *Email:* michael.lepage@riotinto.com, *Website:* www.dampiersalt.com.au

Officials: Vice President, Marketing: Michael Le Page.

Port Security: ISPS compliant

Pre-Arrival Information: 1) Current ship's particulars, including:
    (a) Name of vessel
    (b) Previous names if any
    (c) Year and country of build
    (d) Details of last 5 bulk cargoes for determining likelihood of contamination
    (e) Summer dwt, Summer dft, gt/nrt
    (f) Length Between Perpendiculars
    (g) Vessel's telex/fax numbers and email address
2) GA Plan - forecastle head and poop areas, showing winch & mooring layout
3) Number of hatches. Minimum hatch length 12 m
4) Limewashing of holds for salt cargoes (compliance). See RTM guidelines
5) The number of independently operated winches - fore and aft
6) Declaration that winches are well maintained
7) Declaration that winches are not tension set
8) Confirm that winches are not 'split drum reels'
9) Winches to be hydraulic driven and not pure electric
10) Winch brakes: when considerable pressure is applied on the brake hand-wheels, a min 15% of screw thread adjustment must remain on the hand-wheel spindle
11) Declaration that all brake liners are of non-asbestos material
12) Mooring ropes: advise the number, length, material and diameter of ropes. Note that only polypropylene ropes are permitted due to stretch characteristics
13) Number of hours required for deballasting. Pumps to be in good working order
14) Report measurements for your winches
15) Plain, vertical roller leads are required both forward and aft. Leads other than plain roller leads are normally not acceptable
16) All roller leads should be free and in good condition with the centre leads (aft only) being fitted with a 75 mm bar to stop the wires coming off the rollers and damaging the ship's rails when the vessel is trimmed by the stern
17) Whenever a vessel is fitted with angled winches on the after deck, acceptance will be subject to the fitting of the 75 mm safety bars across the central roller fairleads

Documentation: The Australian Customs Service requires the following reports and forms:
1) Ship arrival details (48 h notice)
2) Ship certificate expiry dates (48 h notice)
3) Ship's inward cargo report (Form 1)
4) Crew reports (Forms 13 and 3b)

	Key to Principal Facilities:—					
A=Airport	**C**=Containers	**G**=General Cargo	**P**=Petroleum	**R**=Ro/Ro	**Y**=Dry Bulk	
B=Bunkers	**D**=Dry Dock	**L**=Cruise	**Q**=Other Liquid Bulk	**T**=Towage (where available from port)		

5) Ship's report of arrival (Form 5, Part 1)
6) Crew effects declaration (Form 5, Part 2 and continuation sheet)
7) Report of ship's stores (Form 5, Part 4)

Anchorage: Vessels normally anchor 1-2 miles N to NW from the berth, but due to the variable holding qualities of the whole area it is recommended that the Master exercise the utmost caution when anchoring and whilst laying at anchor

Pilotage: Compulsory and supplied by Dampier Salt Limited as required. Pilot will board by tug approx 1 mile N of berth

Radio Frequency: VHF Channel 16 - call and distress
VHF Channel 6 - terminal working channel
VHF Channel 8 - tug and riggers 'standby' working channels

Weather: Berthing may be delayed due to strong winds or heavy swell and vessels may be required to return to anchor before completion of loading if berth is affected

Tides: The tidal flow at the moorings is approx East/West and may attain strengths of approx 0.5 knots at spring tides

Maximum Vessel Dimensions: Approx 220 m loa. Larger vessels may be accommodated with prior written permission

Principal Imports and Exports: Exports: Gypsum, Salt.

Accommodation:

Name	Remarks
Cape Cuvier	See [1] below

[1]*Cape Cuvier:* The privately operated offshore vessel moorings and loading facilities are situated at the end of a timber-decked jetty in depth of 17.8 m. A central timber-decked wharf head carries a fixed position, stiff arm, slewing and luffing conveyor boom shiploader, with deflector capability for spout trimming. The moorings consist of six buoys fitted with fixed hooks and held to the seabed by concrete clumps backed up by one or more anchors

Towage: Two tugs available, one of 1800 hp and bollard pull 25 t and the other of 1600 hp and bollard pull of 28 t. A mooring launch is also available for assistance

Shipping Agents: Barwil Agencies Australia Pty Ltd, P O Box 805, Fremantle, W.A., Australia 6959, *Tel:* +61 8 9336 0900, *Fax:* +61 8 9336 0999, *Email:* fremantle@barwil.com.au, *Website:* www.barwil.com

Medical Facilities: Regional Hospital at Carnarvon

Airport: Carnarvon Airport

Lloyd's Agent: Moko Proprietary Ltd, P O Box 685, Willetton, W.A., Australia 6955, *Tel:* +61 8 9354 2248, *Fax:* +61 8 9354 2234, *Email:* kglange@bigpond.com

CAPE FLATTERY

Lat 14° 56' S; Long 145° 20' E.

Admiralty Chart: AUS 270/832   **Admiralty Pilot:** 15
Time Zone: GMT +10 h   **UNCTAD Locode:** AU CQP

Principal Facilities:

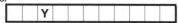

		Y								

Authority: Ports Corporation of Queensland, Floor 24, 300 Queen Street, P O Box 409, Brisbane, Qld., Australia 4001, *Tel:* +61 7 3224 7088, *Fax:* +61 7 3224 7234, *Email:* info@pcq.com.au, *Website:* www.pcq.com.au

Officials: Chief Executive Officer: Brad Fish, *Email:* bfish@pcq.com.au.
Communications Manager: Rachel Campbell, *Tel:* +61 7 3224 8863, *Email:* rcampbell@pcq.com.au.

Port Security: ISPS compliant

Approach: Entrance through the reef for larger vessels can be made by Grafton Passage (East of Cairns) or by any other recommended passage. Dangers include a sand bar which extends from Cape Flattery for approx 2 nautical miles; aft of Berthing Dolphin 6 at the offshore berth where there is a 12 m patch; Decapolis Reef which dries 1.52 m at LW, lies 113°(T), 2.9 nautical miles from Hill 275 on Lookout Point; four foot rock lies 273°(T), 0.8 nautical mile from Decapolis Reef beacon; Jedda wreck lies 203°(T), 1.1 nautical miles from Decapolis Reef beacon; Sim Reefs on the northern side of the recommended track, lies 013°(T) to 033°(T) from Decapolis Reef distance 2.2 nautical miles

Anchorage: The sea bed in the vicinity of the offshore berth consists of rocky slate therefore anchors should be utiized only in an emergency and whilst berthing. Anchors and windlass must be in good working order as this berth may require the use of an anchor whilst berthing alongside. On approaching the port, and if not bething on arrival, vessels should anchor approximately 1-1.5 nautical miles N of the inner harbour leads (No.1 anchorage). If berthing on arrival in good weather, use No.2 anchorage located at 14° 56.8' S, 145° 22.2' E

Pilotage: Compulsory. 48 h notice required with a 24 h update. Pilot boards 3 miles N of the berth or at the anchorage

Radio Frequency: Communications on VHF channel 16, Berthing channel 6

Weather: Winds predominantly SE

Tides: MHWS 2.8 m, MHWN 1.8 m

Traffic: 2007/08, 34 vessels, 1 735 099 t of bulk cargo exported
Maximum Vessel Dimensions: 225 m loa, 32 m beam, 14.5 m draft
Principal Imports and Exports: Exports: Silica sand.
Accommodation:

Name	Remarks
Cape Flattery	See [1] below

[1]*Cape Flattery:* Operated by Cape Flattery Silica Mines Pty Ltd., Tel: +61 7 4043 1111, Fax: +61 7 4043 1110, Email: enquiries@cfsm.com.au, Website: www.cfsm.com.au Offshore wharf and trestle jetty, berth length 230 m, depth 15 m capable of handling panamax size vessels. Travelling shiploader rated at 2000 t/h max

Shipping Agents: Barwil Agencies Australia Pty Ltd, P O Box 1392, Cairns, Qld., Australia 4870, *Tel:* +61 7 4035 4344, *Fax:* +61 7 4035 4006, *Email:* cairns@wilhelmsen.com, *Website:* www.wilhelmsen.com

Lloyd's Agent: Freemans Marine, P O Box 554, Fortitude Valley, Brisbane, Qld., Australia 4006, *Tel:* +61 7 3867 4646, *Fax:* +61 7 3867 4699, *Email:* john.cupitt@freemans.com.au, *Website:* www.freemansmarine.com.au

CAPE LAMBERT

see under Port Walcott

CATHERINE HILL BAY

Lat 33° 10' S; Long 151° 38' E.

Admiralty Chart: AUS 207   **Admiralty Pilot:** 15
Time Zone: GMT +10 h   **UNCTAD Locode:** AU CHB

This port is no longer open to commercial shipping

COFFS HARBOUR

Lat 30° 18' S; Long 153° 9' E.

Admiralty Chart: AUS 363   **Admiralty Pilot:** 14
Time Zone: GMT +10 h   **UNCTAD Locode:** AU CFS

This port is no longer open to commercial shipping

COOKTOWN

Lat 15° 28' S; Long 145° 10' E.

Admiralty Chart: AUS 831   **Admiralty Pilot:** 15
Time Zone: GMT +10 h   **UNCTAD Locode:** AU CTN

This port is no longer open to commercial shipping

COSSACK PIONEER TERMINAL

Lat 19° 35' S; Long 116° 27' E.

Admiralty Chart: AUS 327   **Admiralty Pilot:** 17
Time Zone: GMT +8 h   **UNCTAD Locode:** AU COP

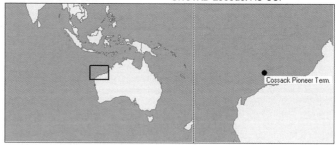

Principal Facilities:

P	Q							T	

Authority: Woodside Energy Ltd, P O Box 188, 240 St Georges Toe, Perth, W.A., Australia 6840, *Tel:* +61 8 9348 4000, *Fax:* +61 8 9214 2777, *Email:* companyinfo@woodside.com.au, *Website:* www.woodside.com.au

Officials: Port Superintendent: John Jenkin, *Email:* john.jenkin@woodside.com.au.

Port Security: Being on offshore terminal all persons visiting the terminal are subject to security screening by Woodside prior to helicopter transfer. All persons boarding the offtake tanker with the Pilot are also subject to Woodside security screening. Crew transfers at the anchorage are subject to customs/immigration screening

Pre-Arrival Information: Agents forward to the vessel a standard format prior to arrival on behalf of the Terminal. The format includes basic arrival details of ETA, draft and displacement; confirmation of ship's operational readiness and load rate; confirmation of manning requirements whilst vessel is at the terminal and that vessel has not had adverse reports since nomination
Pre-arrival information from the Terminal is forwarded via agents and refers to cargo and berthing expectations, anchorages and communications at Port of Dampier

whilst awaiting pilot and pilot boarding requirements. The agents also forward the loading schedule when available

Anchorage: As advised, vessels await pilot at approaches to Port of Dampier. There are no anchorages at the Terminal, however good holding ground can be found at Glomar Shoals about 20 miles E

Pilotage: Compulsory. Boarding area at approaches to the port of Dampier

Radio Frequency: A continuous watch is maintained on VHF Channel 16

Accommodation:

Name	Remarks
Cossack Pioneer Terminal	See [1] below

[1]*Cossack Pioneer Terminal:* Consists of FPSO 'Cossack Pioneer' located approx 35 km E of North Rankin between the Wanaea and Cossack fields. It produces crude oil used as a feedstock for refineries in Australia, the United States and Asia and also produces condensate and natural gas rich in LPG's (propane and butane)
Production capacity is more than 140 000 bbls/day of crude oil and 105 000 000 standard ft3 of gas from five subsea wells on the Wanaea field and one horizontal well in the Cossack field, and 30 000 bbls/day of condensate from the nearby Lambert and Hermes fields
The gas and condensate is sent via subsea pipeline to the North Rankin A platform and then to shore, while the oil is stored onboard the FPSO and offloaded into crude export tankers

Towage: An offshore support vessel attends all offtakes to assist with hose and hawser handling and static towing duties

Lloyd's Agent: Moko Proprietary Ltd, P O Box 685, Willetton, W.A., Australia 6955, *Tel:* +61 8 9354 2248, *Fax:* +61 8 9354 2234, *Email:* kglange@bigpond.com

CRIB POINT JETTY

harbour area, see under Hastings

DALRYMPLE BAY

harbour area, see under Hay Point

DAMPIER

Lat 20° 40' S; Long 116° 42' E.

Admiralty Chart: AUS 58/59
Time Zone: GMT +8 h

Admiralty Pilot: 17
UNCTAD Locode: AU DAM

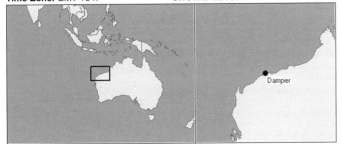

Dampier

Principal Facilities:

P	Q	Y	G	C	R		B		A

Authority: Dampier Port Authority, P O Box 285, Dampier, W.A., Australia 6713, *Tel:* +61 8 9159 6555, *Fax:* +61 8 9159 6557, *Email:* info@dpa.wa.gov.au, *Website:* www.dpa.wa.gov.au

Officials: Chief Executive Officer: Steve Lewis, *Tel:* +61 8 9159 6560, *Email:* stevel@dpa.wa.gov.au.
Harbour Master: John Fewings, *Email:* johnf@dpa.wa.gov.au.

Port Security: ISPS compliant

Pre-Arrival Information: Any vessel intending to enter the port shall notify the Harbour Master at least 24 h prior to arrival or if arriving from a port less than 24 h away, then from that point. This notification also advises the Harbour Master of the vessel's draft and as to whether the equipment and machinery for the navigation and propulsion of the vessel are fully operational, for the purposes of safety, piloting the vessel and if the vessel is to berth at a Company wharf
If Dampier is the first port of entry into Australia, vessels should radio through the normal recognised coast stations, addressing their messages to both their agents and the Dampier Port Authority, Fax: +61 (8) 9159 6558
In the case of vessels arriving from overseas, ETA should be sent 7 days prior to arrival, with their draft and details of cargo to be worked. In the case of all vessels, ETA should be sent 72 h prior to arrival at the pilot boarding ground including in the message, if not previously given, the forward and aft arrival draft and details of cargo to be worked; 48 h prior to intended arrival, with confirmation or any variation of ETA; 24 h prior to arrival confirmation or any variation of ETA should be sent. Coastal vessels may not be able to advise their ETA's in accordance with these rules. Where possible the Master should advise his ETA as soon as is practical
Hamersley Iron Wharves: Every vessel intending to load a cargo of iron ore at Dampier shall, on departure from the last port of call, establish contact with their appointed agent in Dampier advising ETA, quantity of cargo required, deepest departure draft and distance between bottom of keel and top of hatch coaming. 7 days prior to arrival at the port, confirmation or any variation to the above and the loading order by hatches, of the products to be lifted should be sent

Woodside Offshore Petroleum: The following information is required by the Withnell Bay Terminal and is to be sent to the vessel's agent by all tankers using the facility. The tanker's agent is to forward the information to the Woodside Radio Room for distribution: on departure from last port of call (in any event no less than 5 days prior to arrival), answer the Withnell Bay questionnaire; seven days prior to arrival advise ETA and arrival draft at Dampier; three days prior to arrival advise ETA; two days prior to arrival advise ETA, arrival and departure drafts, confirm all cargo systems operational, advise any changes of more than 6 h after 7 day ETA; 24 h prior to arrival confirm ETA and advise any changes of more than 1 h, should be sent to Woodside Radio Telex: AA99571

Approach: The port facilities are situated in sheltered waters and experience only slight seas and occasional low northerly swell in the summer months. The approach channel is 24 km long and recommended for vessels arriving from the N and NE. Ships arriving from the W pass N of Tyrell Rocks situated to the NW of the Monte Bello Islands, and then should pass not less than 8 km to the N of Rosemary Island on the latitude of Legendre Island light. When in a position 9.6 km W of Legendre Island light, course should be altered to the SW to pass into the Archipelago
Vessels intending to load iron ore at Dampier, shall on departure from the last port of call cable HAMIRON AA 99151, Tel: (8) 9143 6000, Fax: (8) 9143 5804

Pilotage: Marine Services WA supply pilotage for Pilbara Iron and Dampier Salt Limited
Woodside Marine supply pilotage to Woodside Energy's Withnell Bay facilities and also to the Dampier Cargo Wharf and Bulk Liquid Berth facilities
Pilotage is compulsory except for vessels of 150 t or less and those Master's who hold a valid Pilotage Exemption
The pilot boarding ground is in pos 20° 24' 0" S; 116° 42' 52.2" E. The pilot may board either by helicopter or pilot cutter. This position must be kept clear except for vessels awaiting a pilot
Vessels should contact their local agents before arrival for pilot boarding and anchoring instructions

Radio Frequency: Dampier Port Communications maintains a continuous watch on VHF Channel 16. All vessels approaching the port or at anchor must also maintain a continuous watch on this frequency. A continuous watch is also maintained on VHF Channel 11, the working channel for general port traffic information

Weather: The cyclone season lasts from November to April

Tides: The tidal streams are weak, the flood flowing to the S, with a max strength of less than one knot at spring tides in the berthing areas. Spring tidal range is 5.3 m, neap tidal range is 3.2 m

Traffic: 2007/08, 4029 vessels, 133 949 276 t of cargo handled

Working Hours: 24 h/day

Accommodation:

Name	Length (m)	Depth (m)	Remarks
Dampier			
Dampier Cargo Wharf			See [1] below
East Intercourse Island Ore Jetty	341	19.5	See [2] below
Parker Point 1 Ore Jetty	269	17.2	See [3] below
Parker Point 2 & 4 Ore Jetty	455	18.8	See [4] below
Parker Point 3 & 5 Ore Jetty	330	18.1	See [5] below
Service Wharf	69	6.7	Imported petroleum products
Withnell Bay LNG Jetty		13.2	See [6] below
Withnell Bay LPG/Condensate Jetty		13.5	See [7] below
Mistaken Island Salt Berth		12	See [8] below

[1]*Dampier Cargo Wharf:* The approach to the wharf has a least depth of 7.5 m LAT. The wharf consists of a concrete deck supported by tubular piles. Access is by a concrete approach bridge 35 m x 9.5 m. Western Berths (No's 1, 3, 5 & 7 totalling 209 m in depth of 10 m) can accept vessels up to 35 000 t displacement and the Eastern Berths (No's 2, 4 & 6 totalling 142 m in depth of 6.5 m) which are suitable for smaller craft ie: supply vessels etc
[2]*East Intercourse Island Ore Jetty:* Operated by Hamersley Iron Pty Ltd., Tel: +61 8 9143 6000, Fax: +61 8 9143 5804, Website: www.riotintoironore.com
The ore jetty consists of a tubular steel pile structure carrying a deck and rail traverse of a slewing boom shiploader. Nine multi-spring dolphins fitted with Yokohama airblock fenders are situated clear of the ore jetty structure, and vessels berth starboard side alongside, mooring to these dolphins. Iron ore is the only product loaded at this facility. Air draft is 24 m LAT from underside boom minus tide. The total length of fendering, No.1 to No.9 dolphins is 429.8 m. The rated cap of the shiploader is 9500 t/h. The jetty is connected to the open sea by a 167.6 m wide departure channel dredged to 15.5 m LAT. The ore loading facility can accommodate vessels in excess of 250 000 dwt. The departure draught from this berth is dependent upon tidal conditions and adequate under keel clearance
[3]*Parker Point 1 Ore Jetty:* Operated by Hamersley Iron Pty Ltd., Tel: +61 8 9143 6000, Fax: +61 8 9143 5804, Website: www.riotintoironore.com
The ore jetty consists of a tubular steel pile structure carrying a deck and rail traverse of a slewing boom shiploader. Eight multi-spring pile dolphins fitted with Yokohama airblock fenders are situated clear of the ore jetty structure, and vessels berth port side alongside, mooring to these dolphins. Iron ore is the only product handled at this facility. The rated cap of the shiploader is 9500 t/h. Air draft is 23 m minus tide from underside boom. The ore jetty is connected to the East Intercourse Island departure channel by a 170 m wide channel dredged to 15.35 m LAT
[4]*Parker Point 2 & 4 Ore Jetty:* Operated by Hamersley Iron Pty Ltd., Tel: +61 8 9143 6000, Fax: +61 8 9143 5804, Website: www.riotintoironore.com
Nine rigid dolphins fitted with Fentek cone fenders are situated as separate structures to the wharf. Vessels berth port side to, and moor to these dolphins. The rated cap of the shiploader is 7500 t/h. Air draft clearance at fender line under boom at LAT 26.3 m
[5]*Parker Point 3 & 5 Ore Jetty:* Operated by Hamersley Iron Pty Ltd., Tel: +61 8 9143 6000, Fax: +61 8 9143 5804, Website: www.riotintoironore.com
Eight rigid dolphins fitted with Fentek cone fenders are situated as separate structures to the wharf. Vessels berth starboard to, and moor to these dolphins. The rated cap of the shiploader is 7500 t/h. Air draft clearance at fender line under boom at LAT is 26.3 m

[6]*Withnell Bay LNG Jetty:* Owned and operated by Woodside Offshore Petroleum, Tel: +61 8 9158 8100, Fax: +61 8 9158 8000

Single berth loading facility for LNG tankers. Six breasting dolphins with double Yokohama fenders and panels extending from LT 0.5 m to LAT +7.1 m comprise the berth face. The loading platform is equipment with four 16" LNG loading/vapour return arms. The berth can accommodate vessels from 190-300 m loa and 30 000-150 000 dwt

[7]*Withnell Bay LPG/Condensate Jetty:* Owned and operated by Woodside Offshore Petroleum, Tel: +61 8 9158 8100, Fax: +61 8 9158 8000

The berth face consists of four breasting dolphins with single, moulded rubber fenders. The loading platform is equipped with two 12" LPG arms with 10"/12" liquid and 6"/8" vapour QC/DC connections and two 12" condensate arms with 10"/12"/16" ANSI 150lb QC/DC connections. The berth can accommodate vessels of 190-300 m loa

[8]*Mistaken Island Salt Berth:* Owned and operated by Dampier Salt Ltd., Tel: +61 8 9143 6870, Fax: +61 8 9143 6844, Website: www.dampiersalt.com.au

Salt loading. berth consisting of a tubular steel pile approach structure carrying a conveyor belt to a fixed cantilever shiploader. Seven multi-spring pile mooring dolphins are situated clear of the shiploader platform. Total length between dolphins is 358.2 m. Vessels may berth either side to, moor to and warp along dolphins using ships winches on fore and aft lines and also central springs attached to No.4 dolphin. Rated cap of shiploader is 3000 t/h. Air draft is 19.5 m from underside boom

Storage:

Location	Open (m²)
Dampier Cargo Wharf	22000

Mechanical Handling Equipment:

Location	Type	Capacity (t)
Dampier Cargo Wharf	Mobile Cranes	150

Bunkering: Shell Australia Ltd, Shell Company of Australia, Marine Centre Oceania, No 8 Redfern Road, Melbourne, Vic., Australia 3123, *Tel:* +61 3 9666 5446, *Fax:* +61 3 8823 4800, *Email:* sal-marine-products@shell.com, *Website:* www.shell.com.au – *Misc:* Diesel is available at Dampier Public Wharf via a direct line – *Delivery Mode:* truck

Waste Reception Facilities: All garbage must be disposed of in the correct manner. All vessels using the Dampier Cargo Wharf must arrange skip bins for all bulk waste to be disposed of. To be arranged via agents

Towage: Hamersley Iron Proprietary Ltd, Port Operations MRU, P O Box 21, Dampier, W.A., Australia 6713, *Tel:* +61 8 9143 5921, *Fax:* +61 8 9143 5982

Mermaid Marine Australia Ltd, Mermaid Road, Dampier, W.A., Australia 6713, *Tel:* +61 8 9183 6600, *Fax:* +61 8 9183 6660, *Email:* dampier@mma.com.au, *Website:* www.mermaidmarine.com.au

Riverwijs Dampier Proprietary Ltd, Suite 10, 18 Parry Street, P O Box 1213, Fremantle, W.A., Australia 6160, *Tel:* +61 8 9433 1311, *Fax:* +61 8 9433 1611, *Email:* paul@riversidemarine.com.au

Repair & Maintenance: A wide range of light engineering, mechanical, electrical, air conditioning, plumbing and referation workshops are located close to port facilities. Instrument and electronic technicians are available with the Shire of Roebourne for repairs and servicing

Seaman Missions: The Seamans Mission, P O Box 263, Dampier, W.A., Australia 6713, *Tel:* +61 8 9183 1424, *Fax:* +61 8 9183 1022, *Email:* info@dampierseafarers.org, *Website:* www.dampierseafarers.org

Ship Chandlers: Sealanes - Fuji, P O Box 186, Karratha, W.A., Australia 6714, *Tel:* +61 8 9185 1422, *Fax:* +61 8 9185 3295, *Email:* sea@sealanes.com.au, *Website:* www.sealanes.com.au

Shipping Agents: Barwil Agencies Australia Pty Ltd, P O Box 1005, Karratha, W.A., Australia 6714, *Tel:* +61 8 9144 2311, *Fax:* +61 8 9144 2008, *Email:* dampier@wilhelmsen.com, *Website:* www.wilhelmsen.com

Beaufort Shipping Agency Proprietary Ltd, Shop 5, Dampier Shopping Centre, Dampier, W.A., Australia 6713, *Tel:* +61 8 9183 0568, *Fax:* +61 8 9183 0564, *Email:* manager.dampier@beaufortshipping.com.au, *Website:* www.beaufortshipping.com.au

Gulf Agency Co (Australia) Pty Ltd., Unit 6, 18 Hedland Place, Karratha, W.A., Australia 6714, *Tel:* +61 8 9183 8627, *Fax:* +61 8 9185 1251, *Email:* shipping.dampier@gacworld.com, *Website:* www.gacworld.com

Inchcape Shipping Services (ISS), Inchcape Shipping Services Pty Ltd, Unit 7, Lot 6/20 Hedland Place, 2nd Floor Ockerby Building, Karratha, W.A., Australia 6714, *Tel:* +61 8 9185 6319, *Fax:* +61 8 9185 2971, *Email:* dampier@iss-shipping.com.au, *Website:* www.iss-shipping.com

McArthur Shipping & Agency Co Pty Ltd, P O Box 191, Karratha, W.A., Australia 6714, *Tel:* +61 8 9185 2121, *Fax:* +61 8 9144 1105, *Email:* mcarthur.kta@wcsa.com.au, *Website:* www.mcaship.com.au

Monson Agencies Australia Proprietary Ltd, P O Box 939, Karratha, W.A., Australia 6714, *Tel:* +61 8 9185 6766, *Fax:* +61 8 9143 1983, *Email:* karratha@monson.com.au, *Website:* www.monson.com.au

Seacorp Agencies, 18 Harriet Way, Karratha, W.A., Australia 6714, *Tel:* +61 8 9144 1192, *Fax:* +61 8 9144 4162, *Email:* seacorpdampier@seacorp.com.au, *Website:* www.seacorp.com.au

Surveyors: Marine Services of WA (Hammersley), Dampier, W.A., Australia, *Tel:* +61 8 9183 1727, *Fax:* +61 8 9183 1422

Mermaid Sound Port & Marine Services Proprietary Ltd, Dampier, W.A., Australia, *Tel:* +61 8 9158 7111, *Fax:* +61 8 9158 7012

Medical Facilities: Karratha General Hospital, 22 km

Airport: Karratha Airport, 15 km

Lloyd's Agent: Moko Proprietary Ltd, P O Box 685, Willetton, W.A., Australia 6955, *Tel:* +61 8 9354 2248, *Fax:* +61 8 9354 2234, *Email:* kglange@bigpond.com

DARLING HARBOUR

harbour area, see under Sydney

DARWIN

Lat 12° 26' S; Long 130° 50' E.

Admiralty Chart: AUS 24/26/27//28	**Admiralty Pilot:** 17	
Time Zone: GMT +9.5 h	**UNCTAD Locode:** AU DRW	

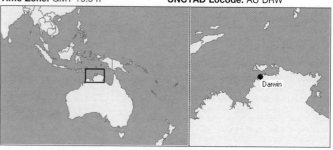

Principal Facilities:

P Q Y G C R L B D T A

Authority: Darwin Port Corp., P O Box 390, Darwin, N.T., Australia 0801, *Tel:* +61 8 8922 0660, *Fax:* +61 8 8922 0666, *Email:* darwinport.dpa@nt.gov.au, *Website:* www.darwinport.nt.gov.au

Officials: Chief Executive Officer: Robert Ritchie, *Tel:* +61 8 8922 0644, *Email:* robert.ritchie@nt.gov.au.

Harbour Master: Capt Bruce Wilson, *Tel:* +61 8 8947 7201, *Email:* bruce.wilson@nt.gov.au.

Port Security: ISPS compliant

Documentation: Primary health report (1 copy), crew list (2 copies), passenger list (2 copies), port of call list (2 copies), crew personal effects list (1 copy), stores list (1 copy), barbers and ships stock (2 copies), animals and pets (1 copy), ships logs, last port clearance

Approach: Least depth in approach channel and quarantine anchorage is 13 m

Anchorage: Good holding ground in sand and/or mud can be had with Channel Rock Buoy bearing between 135°(T) and 145°(T) distant 1500 m or in the Quarantine Anchorage adjacent to 'Q' Buoy

Pilotage: Compulsory for vessels over 25 m loa, unless a valid exemption certificate is held by the master. Pilot boards at Channel Rock Buoy. 24 h and 2 h ETA notice to be given to Harbour Master (local time). By prior arrangement pilot may board one mile N of No.5 buoy for deep draft vessels

Radio Frequency: VHF Channel 16 distress & calling. VHF Channel 10 port working. VHF Channel 12 tug working. VHF Channel 8 or 17 Intership. Call sign is 'Darwin Harbour'. 24 h watch on Channels 16 and 10

Weather: Cyclone season from November to April. During this period all vessels in port will be issued with port procedures which set out in full the various stages of alert and preparation to be observed in the case of an approaching cyclone

Tides: Ranges: springs 7.9 m, neaps 5.1 m

Traffic: 2007/08, 1547 commercial vessels & 45 cruise vessels, 2 729 896 t of cargo handled

Maximum Vessel Dimensions: Vessels up to 300 m loa and 11.0 m draft. Drafts over 12 m may be accepted by prior consultation depending on tidal predictions

Principal Imports and Exports: Imports: Cement clinker, Gas, Lime, Petroleum, Sulphur. Exports: Frozen meat, Iron ore, Livestock, Uranium.

Working Hours: Stevedores work from 0800-2200 (two shifts), extension to 2400 if vessel due to sail. 0001-0700 by arrangement, seven days a week

Accommodation:

Name	Length (m)	Depth (m)	Remarks
Darwin			See [1] below
Berth No.1	142	12	See [2] below
Berth No.2W	150	12	See [3] below
Berth No.2E	150	12	Ro/ro, containers & dry bulk
Berth No.3W	146	9	Cruise & naval vessels
Berth No.3E	146	9	Cruise & naval vessels
Berth No.4W	80	4.5	Fishing
Berth No.4E	100	4.5	Fishing
Fishermen's Wharf	200	4	Fishing
East Arm	740	13–14	See [4] below
Private Wharves			See [5] below

[1]*Darwin:* The fishing harbour mooring basin is a lay-up facility for trawlers, containing 85 berths of either 30, 25 and 20 m. The basin provides cyclone shelter for trawlers and commercial vessels. Access is via a tidal lock operable between tides of 3.2-7.5 m

[2]*Berth No.1:* With mooring dolphins 69 m E and W able to accept vessels up to 250 m loa and 11.5 m draft for discharge of bulk petroleum, sulphuric acid and LPG. Ores and dry bulk cargo can be loaded at a gross rate of up to 600 t/h by a travelling belt loader, having a transit distance of 140 m along the wharf and an outreach of 14 m beyond the fenders

[3]*Berth No.2W:* Ro/ro, containers & dry bulk. Adjacent to this berth the container terminal has fittings for 64 refrigerated containers. Ro/ro facility accessible to all types of ro/ro vessels. It consists of an extendable version of the linkspan ship-to-shore semi-buoyant bridge, 77 m long, connecting with a 30 m x 42 m pontoon and is workable at all tidal levels

[4]*East Arm:* Bulk cargoes, livestock carriers, rig tenders & general cargo vessels

[5]*Private Wharves:* V.B. Perkins has three berths at Frances Bay. Barge Express has two berths at Frances Bay. Rooney Shipping operate a berth at Hudsons Creek. All these berths dry out at LW

Mechanical Handling Equipment:

Location	Type	Capacity (t)	Qty
Darwin	Mobile Cranes	100	
Darwin	Container Cranes	70	1

Bunkering: Most grades of fuels and lubricants available by pipeline ex wharf. Longest possible notice desirable
BP Australia (Proprietary) Ltd, P O Box 5222, Melbourne, Vic., Australia 3001, *Tel:* +61 3 9268 4111, *Fax:* +61 3 9268 3321, *Email:* gomiasfuelsales@bp.com, *Website:* www.bp.com
Caltex Australia Petroleum Proprietary Ltd, Caltex Australia Petroleum Proprietary Ltd, No 2 Market Street, Sydney, N.S.W., Australia 2000, *Tel:* +61 2 9668 1148, *Fax:* +61 2 9668 1243, *Email:* mnicholl@caltex.com.au, *Website:* www.caltex.com.au
ExxonMobil Marine Fuels, 1 Harbour Front Place, 06-00 Harbour Front, Tower One, Singapore, Republic of Singapore 098633, *Tel:* +65 6885 8998, *Fax:* +65 6885 8794, *Email:* asiapac.marinefuels@exxonmobil.com, *Website:* www.exxonmobilmarinefuels.com – *Grades:* MGO – *Delivery Mode:* tank truck, pipeline
Shell Australia Ltd, Shell Company of Australia, Marine Centre Oceania, No 8 Redfern Road, Melbourne, Vic., Australia 3123, *Tel:* +61 3 9666 5446, *Fax:* +61 3 8823 4800, *Email:* sal-marine-products@shell.com, *Website:* www.shell.com.au

Waste Reception Facilities: Private contractors will remove dirty ballast, sludge and chemical waste but quantity is subject to road tanker capacity. Garbage disposal by the Port Authority

Towage: Two tugs of 1400 bhp, 20 t bollard pull; usually joins vessel at Q buoy
SVITZER, SVITZER Australasia, 2nd Floor Fort Hill Wharf Building, Kitchener Drive, Winnellie, N.T., Australia 0821, *Tel:* +61 8 8941 7102, *Fax:* +61 8 8941 7647, *Email:* info.darwin@adsteam.com.au, *Website:* www.svitzer.com

Repair & Maintenance: Darwin Ship Repair & Engineering Proprietary Ltd, Frances Bay Drive, P O Box 4696, Darwin, N.T., Australia 0820, *Tel:* +61 8 8981 4244, *Fax:* +61 8 8981 8729, *Email:* admin@dsre.com.au, *Website:* www.dsre.com.au Extensive docking and repair facilities and operate a 2550 t syncrolift with dimensions 63 m loa, 22.5 m beam, 5 m draft, situated in Frances Bay
Frances Bay Marine, P O Box 39669, Winnellie, N.T., Australia 0821, *Tel:* +61 8 8981 4588, *Fax:* +61 8 8981 4574, *Email:* fbmdtl@bigpond.net.au
Sadgrove's Quay Proprietary Ltd, Frances Bay Drive, P O Box 2651, Darwin, N.T., Australia 0801, *Tel:* +61 8 8981 9625, *Fax:* +61 8 8981 9663, *Email:* sadgrove@d130.aone.net.au Max 70 t travelift

Ship Chandlers: Sealanes-Albatross Proprietary Ltd - Sealanes (1985) Pty Ltd, Lot 3304, Lilwall Road, Darwin Business Park, Berrimah, Palmerston, N.T., Australia 831, *Tel:* +61 8 8947 4888, *Fax:* +61 8 8947 4999, *Email:* orders@nt.sealanes.com.au, *Website:* www.sealanes.com.au
Sinwa Imes Pty Ltd., P O Box 359, Berrimah, Darwin, N.T., Australia 0828, *Tel:* +61 8 8947 4944, *Fax:* +61 8 8947 4955, *Email:* sales.darwin@sinwaglobal.com, *Website:* www.sinwaglobal.com

Shipping Agents: Barwil Agencies Australia Pty Ltd, P O Box 38169, Winnellie, N.T., Australia 0821, *Tel:* +61 8 8947 2882, *Fax:* +61 8 8947 2881, *Email:* darwin@wilhelmsen.com, *Website:* www.wilhelmsen.com
Gulf Agency Co (Australia) Pty Ltd., Unit 3a, 5 Goyder Road, Parap, N.T., Australia 0820, *Tel:* +61 8 8981 7991, *Fax:* +61 8 8981 0142, *Email:* shipping.darwin@gacworld.com, *Website:* www.gacworld.com
Inchcape Shipping Services (ISS), Inchcape Shipping Services Pty Ltd, P O Box 3646, Darwin, N.T., Australia 0820, *Tel:* +61 8 8981 2901, *Fax:* +61 8 8941 1987, *Email:* darwin@iss-shipping.com.au, *Website:* www.iss-shipping.com
Monson Agencies Australia Proprietary Ltd, 11 Ostermann Street, Coconut Grove, Darwin, N.T., Australia 0810, *Tel:* +61 8 8985 3107, *Fax:* +61 8 8985 2106, *Email:* darwin@monson.com.au, *Website:* www.monson.com.au
Swire Shipping Agencies, Fort Hill Wharf, 1 Kitchener Drive, Darwin, N.T., Australia 0801, *Tel:* +61 8 8981 3318, *Fax:* +61 8 8981 3898, *Email:* ssadrw@swire.com.au

Stevedoring Companies: Patrick Stevedoring, East Arm Port, Berrimah Road, Berrimah, N.T., Australia 0801, *Tel:* +61 8 8984 4701, *Fax:* +61 8 8984 4798, *Email:* p.wingrave@patrick.com.au, *Website:* www.patrick.com.au
P&O Ports, P O Box 23, Berrimah, N.T., Australia 0828, *Tel:* +61 8 8922 2300, *Fax:* +61 8 8941 0604, *Email:* darwin.supervisors@poports.com.au, *Website:* www.poports.com.au

Surveyors: Australian Ship P & I, G P O Box 4528, Darwin, N.T., Australia 0801, *Tel:* 61, *Fax:* +61 8 8981 3610, *Email:* darwin@ausship.com.au
Det Norske Veritas A/S, P O Box 4528, Darwin, N.T., Australia 0801, *Tel:* +61 8 8981 9487, *Fax:* +61 8 8981 3610, *Email:* surveys@octa4.net.au

Medical Facilities: Full hospital facilities

Airport: Darwin International, 12 km

Development: Construction of Wickham Point LNG loading jetty consisting of a causeway and trestle extending 1425 m from the shoreline, with a 500 km subsea pipeline connecting to Bayu Undan offshore facilities. First delivery is scheduled for early 2006. Storage facilities will be one tank of 188 000 m3 cap

Lloyd's Agent: Maritime & General Insurance Surveyors Proprietary Ltd, Suite 4, 7 Divett Street, Adelaide, S.A., Australia 5015, *Tel:* +61 8 8341 2552, *Fax:* +61 8 8241 0229, *Email:* maritime-general@adam.com.au

DERBY

Lat 17° 18' S; Long 123° 37' E.

Admiralty Chart: AUS 323	**Admiralty Pilot:** 17
Time Zone: GMT +8 h	**UNCTAD Locode:** AU DRB

The port is no longer operational due to the mine being closed.

DEVONPORT

Lat 41° 10' S; Long 146° 21' E.

Admiralty Chart: AUS 164/799	**Admiralty Pilot:** 14
Time Zone: GMT +10 h	**UNCTAD Locode:** AU DPO

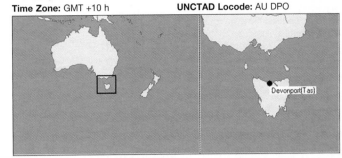

Principal Facilities:

P	Q	Y	G	C	R	L	B		T	A

Authority: Tasmanian Ports Corp. Proprietary Ltd (TasPorts), 48 Formby Road, P O Box 478, Devonport, Tas., Australia 7310, *Tel:* +61 3 6421 4911, *Fax:* +61 3 6421 4988, *Email:* secretary@tasports.com.au, *Website:* www.tasports.com.au

Officials: Chairman: Dr Dan Norton.
Chief Executive Officer: Robert Barnes, *Tel:* +61 3 6421 4911, *Email:* robert.barnes@tasports.com.au.
Port Manager: Charles Black, *Email:* charles.black@tasports.com.au.
Marketing Manager: Charles Scarafiotti, *Email:* charles.scarafiotti@tasports.com.au.
Marketing: Rachel Court.

Port Security: ISPS compliant

Documentation: Prior notification as per Australian Customs requirements

Approach: Depth of entrance channel 9.2 m LAT

Pilotage: Compulsory for overseas vessels. Pilot boards in pos 41° 07' 02" S; 146° 23' 55" E. Pilotage operates 24 h service

Radio Frequency: VHF Channels 16, 12 and 67

Tides: Rise of tide: 3.2 m springs, 2.4 m neaps

Traffic: 2007/08, 850 vessels, 3 263 888 t of cargo handled, 104 930 TEU's

Maximum Vessel Dimensions: 200 m loa, 35.0 m beam, 10.0 m draft

Principal Imports and Exports: Imports: Bulk fuels, Fertiliser, Gypsum, Salt, Wheat. Exports: Agricultural produce, Cement, Tallow.

Working Hours: 24 h/day

Accommodation:

Name	Length (m)	Depth (m)	Remarks
Devonport			
Berth No.1W	87	9.5	See [1] below
Berth No.3W	167	5.5–6.5	See [2] below
Berth No.4W	198	10.2	See [3] below
Berth No.5W	40	5.5	See [4] below
Berth No.1E	115	6.7	See [5] below
Berth No.2E	180	9	See [6] below
Berth No.3E	110	9	See [7] below

[1]Berth No.1W: Bulk cement for vessels up to 195 m loa. Four cement silos of 26 335 t cap
[2]Berth No.3W: General cargo & tallow for vessels up to 200 m loa. One cargo shed of 110 m x 25 m x 7 m high
[3]Berth No.4W: Oil products, wheat, refrigerated, container, general cargo, tallow, livestock and cruise vessels for vessels up to 200 m loa. Two-level freezer and cold store of 7200 m3 refrigerated cap at -23.3°C. Wheat silos located behind the wharf of 11 000 t cap
[4]Berth No.5W: Length 40 m across tee-head for vessels up to 110 m loa. LPG pipelines to storage facility
[5]Berth No.1E: Ro/ro freight fully dedicated to Bass Strait ferry and leased to TT-line. Stern loading ramp. One transit shed of 45 m x 19 m x 6.5 m
[6]Berth No.2E: Has 24.4 m wide ro/ro ramp. Shed of 1760 m2. Berth leased to Patrick Shipping
[7]Berth No.3E: Containers, ro/ro, general cargo. A 25-30 t slewing crane/grab at 32 m

Bunkering: Shell Australia Ltd, Shell Company of Australia, Marine Centre Oceania, No 8 Redfern Road, Melbourne, Vic., Australia 3123, *Tel:* +61 3 9666 5446, *Fax:* +61 3 8823 4800, *Email:* sal-marine-products@shell.com, *Website:* www.shell.com.au – *Delivery Mode:* truck

Towage: North Western Shipping & Towage Proprietary Ltd, Inspection Head Wharf, Beauty Point, P O Box 76, Beaconsfield, Tas., Australia 7270, *Tel:* +61 3 6383 4522, *Fax:* +61 3 6383 4604, *Email:* inquiries@nwst.com.au, *Website:* www.nwst.com.au

Repair & Maintenance: One 400 t slipway, one 100 t slipway and one 10 t slipway

Seaman Missions: The Seamans Mission, Church Street, East Devonport, Tas., Australia 7310, *Tel:* +61 3 6427 9844, *Email:* devonport@mts.org.au

Shipping Agents: Barwil Agencies Australia Pty Ltd, P O Box 311, George Town, Tas., Australia 7253, *Tel:* +61 3 6382 4088, *Fax:* +61 3 6382 4099, *Email:* bellbay@wilhelmsen.com, *Website:* www.wilhelmsen.com
Bass Link Ives Logistics, 14-16 Stony Rise Road, Devonport, Tas., Australia 7310, *Tel:* +61 3 6420 4999, *Fax:* +61 3 6420 4950, *Email:* enquiry@basslink.net.au, *Website:* www.kilogistics.com.au
Inchcape Shipping Services (ISS), Inchcape Shipping Services Pty Ltd, 77 Gunn Street, P O Box 606, Devonport, Tas., Australia 7310, *Tel:* +61 3 6424 3311, *Fax:* +61

Key to Principal Facilities:—				
A=Airport	**C**=Containers	**G**=General Cargo	**P**=Petroleum	**R**=Ro/Ro	**Y**=Dry Bulk
B=Bunkers	**D**=Dry Dock	**L**=Cruise	**Q**=Other Liquid Bulk	**T**=Towage (where available from port)	

3 6424 2511, *Email:* devonport@iss-shipping.com.au, *Website:* www.iss-shipping.com

Stevedoring Companies: Patrick Stevedoring, P. O. Box 299E, East Devonport, Tas., Australia 7310, *Tel:* +61 3 6427 0900, *Fax:* +61 3 6427 0155, *Email:* j.veal@patrick.com.au, *Website:* www.patrick.com.au
P&O Ports, P O Box 964, Devonport, Tas., Australia 7310, *Tel:* +61 3 6432 3964, *Fax:* +61 3 6432 3964

Medical Facilities: Mersey Community Hospital, 8 km

Airport: Pardoe Airport, 8 km

Railway: Access to statewide railway

Lloyd's Agent: Freemans Marine, Level 7, 564 St. Kilda Road, Melbourne, Vic., Australia 3004, *Tel:* +61 3 9935 2400, *Fax:* +61 3 9915 0351, *Email:* lloyds@freemans.com.au, *Website:* www.freemansmarine.com.au

EDEN

Lat 37° 4' S; Long 149° 54' E.

Admiralty Chart: AUS 192
Time Zone: GMT +10 h

Admiralty Pilot: 14
UNCTAD Locode: AU QDN

Principal Facilities:

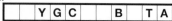

| | Y | G | C | | B | | T | A |

Authority: Port of Eden, Main Jetty, P O Box 137, Snug Cove, Eden, N.S.W., Australia 2551, *Tel:* +61 2 6496 1719, *Fax:* +61 2 6496 3024, *Email:* edenpilot@maritime.nsw.gov.au, *Website:* www.eden.nsw.gov.au

Officials: Harbour Master: Capt Max Saunders.
Harbour Master: Capt Josephine Clark, *Email:* josephine.clark@maritime.nsw.gov.au.

Port Security: ISPS compliant

Pre-Arrival Information: Same as for Port Kembla

Approach: Entrance into Twofold Bay, 36 m at MLLW

Anchorage: Vessels of more than 3000 gt may not anchor inside the port limits without the express permission of the Harbour Master. Vessels awaiting port entry may anchor near the pilot boarding ground in depths of about 35 m

Pilotage: Compulsory for all commercial vessels over 30 m loa. ETA to be sent 7 days, 48 h and 24 h in advance. Pilot boards 1.5 nautical miles E of Lookout Point Light House

Radio Frequency: VHF Channel 16; port working on VHF Channel 8

Weather: The port is open to an easterly swell

Tides: Range of tide, springs 2.0 m

Traffic: 2007/08, 71 vessels, 1 273 113 t of cargo handled

Maximum Vessel Dimensions: 50 000 gt, 11 m draft, 230 m loa

Principal Imports and Exports: Imports: Breakbulk. Exports: Explosives, Logs, Woodchips.

Working Hours: 24 h/day by prior arrangement

Accommodation:

Name	Length (m)	Depth (m)	Remarks
Twofold Bay			
Breakwater Wharf	105	3–8.8	Containers can be handled
Woodchip Loading Berth	275	12.5	See [1] below
Multi-Purpose Wharf	200	12	See [2] below
Mooring Jetty	150		Used by fishing fleet
Eden Main Jetty	200	2–7	Used by fishing fleet

[1]*Woodchip Loading Berth:* Pier extending from the shore with a four buoy mooring system off the end of the pier and five dolphins; berth can accommodate vessels up to 230 m loa and 11 m draft. Loading rate 1200 t/h
[2]*Multi-Purpose Wharf:* Reached via an access jetty 560 m long and 7 m wide. For vessels up to 185 m loa and 10.5 m draft

Storage: An 8 ha hardstand area is available adjacent to the Multi-Purpose Wharf. Approx 1000 m2 of hardstand is available adjacent to the Breakwater Wharf

Mechanical Handling Equipment:

Location	Type	Capacity (t)	Remarks
Eden	Mobile Cranes	20–80	by arrangement

Bunkering: Diesel fuel available by road on Breakwater Wharf
BP Australia (Proprietary) Ltd, P O Box 5222, Melbourne, Vic., Australia 3001, *Tel:* +61 3 9268 4111, *Fax:* +61 3 9268 3321, *Email:* gomiasfuelsales@bp.com, *Website:* www.bp.com
ExxonMobil Marine Fuels, 1 Harbour Front Place, 06-00 Harbour Front, Tower One, Singapore, Republic of Singapore 098633, *Tel:* +65 6885 8998, *Fax:* +65 6885 8794, *Email:* asiapac.marinefuels@exxonmobil.com, *Website:* www.exxonmobilmarinefuels.com – *Grades:* MGO – *Delivery Mode:* tank truck

Port Kembla Marine Fuels, Lot 2, 5 Flinders Street, Port Kembla, N.S.W., Australia 2505, *Tel:* +61 2 4275 3892, *Fax:* +61 2 4274 6507, *Email:* bunkers@pkmf.com, *Website:* www.pkmf.com

Towage: SVITZER, SVITZER Australasia, 12 Weecon Street, Eden, N.S.W., Australia 2551, *Tel:* +61 2 6496 1111, *Fax:* +61 2 6496 3054, *Email:* info.eden@adsteam.com.au, *Website:* www.svitzer.com

Repair & Maintenance: Broadwater Engineering, 200 Imlay Street, Eden, N.S.W., Australia, *Tel:* +61 2 6496 2093 Minor repairs. Slipway facilities for fishing vessels only

Shipping Agents: Barwil Agencies Australia Pty Ltd, P O Box 170, Port Kembla, N.S.W., Australia 2505, *Tel:* +61 2 4275 1500, *Fax:* +61 2 4275 1011, *Email:* ptkembla@wilhelmsen.com, *Website:* www.barwil.com

Medical Facilities: Hospital at Pambula, 15 km

Airport: Merimbula, 17 km

Lloyd's Agent: Freemans Marine, Level 7, 564 St. Kilda Road, Melbourne, Vic., Australia 3004, *Tel:* +61 3 9935 2400, *Fax:* +61 3 9915 0351, *Email:* lloyds@freemans.com.au, *Website:* www.freemansmarine.com.au

ESPERANCE

Lat 33° 52' S; Long 121° 53' E.

Admiralty Chart: AUS 119
Time Zone: GMT +8 h

Admiralty Pilot: 13
UNCTAD Locode: AU EPR

Principal Facilities:

| P | | Y | G | C | R | L | B | | T | A |

Authority: Esperance Port Authority, P O Box 35, Esperance, W.A., Australia 6450, *Tel:* +61 8 9072 3333, *Fax:* +61 8 9071 1312, *Email:* esppa@esperanceport.com.au, *Website:* www.esperanceport.com.au

Officials: Chief Executive Officer: Dennis Parsons, *Email:* dennisparsons@esperanceport.com.au.
Finance Manager: Kevin Fernance, *Email:* kevinfernance@esperanceport.com.au.
Operations Manager: Brant Grundy, *Email:* brantgrundy@esperanceport.com.au.
Public Relations Manager: Richard Grant, *Email:* richardgrant@esperanceport.com.au.
Harbour Master: Capt Jordi Oakley, *Email:* jordioakley@esperanceport.com.au.
Deputy Harbour Master: Capt Julian Thomas, *Email:* julianthomas@esperanceport.com.au.

Port Security: ISPS compliant

Approach: Entrance channel dredged to a depth of 14.5 m

Anchorage: Vessels should anchor in an ENE direction 1.5 nautical mile from the E extreme of the breakwater. Good holding in depths ranging from 14.5 to 27.5 m. Six shackles at least are recommended. Vessel should always be watched, and a pilot ladder rather than an accommodation ladder is recommended due to swell conditions that normally prevail at the anchorage

Pilotage: Compulsory except where exemption certificates are held. Pilot boards 1 nautical mile NE of Cull Island

Radio Frequency: Port VHF Channels 16, 12, 6, 9 and 67. Call sign "Esperance Harbour". Range 40-60 nautical miles. Shore based AIS in service

Tides: HHW 1.1 m. Tidal range of 0.4 m to 1 m

Traffic: 2007/08, 185 vessels, 9 934 127 t of cargo handled

Maximum Vessel Dimensions: 200 000 dwt, 300 m loa, 50 m beam, 18 m draft on No.3 Berth. 76 000 dwt, 230 m loa, 14 m draft on No.1 and 2 Berths

Principal Imports and Exports: Imports: Ammonium nitrate, Fertiliser, Petroleum products. Exports: Grain, Iron ore, Nickel concentrates.

Working Hours: All vessels 0730-1530, 1530-2330, 2330-0730. Iron ore is continuous loading

Accommodation:

Name	Length (m)	Depth (m)	Remarks
Inner Harbour			See [1] below
Berth No.1	244	14.5	See [2] below
Berth No.2	213	14.5	See [3] below
Berth No.3	230	19	See [4] below

[1]*Inner Harbour:* Consists of two landbacked berths able to accommodate fully loaded panamax vessels, so constructed as to form a continuous berth frontage of 457 m. These berths are protected by a breakwater extending 673 m in a NE direction. A 198 m extension in an ENE direction provides additional protection. A third berth is situated on the breakwater with a depth of 19 m alongside and is suitable for capesize vessels loading iron ore
[2]*Berth No.1:* Seven-spout loading gallery supplied by twin sealed conveyors. Grain loading at a max rate of 2500 t/h. Suitable for vessels up to 225 m loa
[3]*Berth No.2:* Suitable for ro/ro using ship's ramp. Shiploader for ores and concentrates at rate of up to 2000 t/h. Suitable for vessels up to panamax size. Petroleum products handled. Pipeline from this berth to tank farm approx 3 km N
[4]*Berth No.3:* For vessels up to 290 m loa (loa up to 300 m subject to Harbour Master's

approval). Iron ore loading rates of up to 4500 t/h are obtained by a travelling shiploader with an outreach suitable for vessel beams of up to 50 m

Mechanical Handling Equipment:

Location	Type	Capacity (t)	Qty
Esperance	Mobile Cranes	8	1
Esperance	Mobile Cranes	18	1

Bunkering: BP Australia (Proprietary) Ltd, P O Box 5222, Melbourne, Vic., Australia 3001, *Tel:* +61 3 9268 4111, *Fax:* +61 3 9268 3321, *Email:* gomiasfuelsales@bp.com, *Website:* www.bp.com – *Notice:* 7 days – *Delivery Mode:* truck
Caltex Australia Petroleum Proprietary Ltd, Caltex Australia Petroleum Proprietary Ltd, No 2 Market Street, Sydney, N.S.W., Australia 2000, *Tel:* +61 2 9668 1148, *Fax:* +61 2 9668 1243, *Email:* mnicholl@caltex.com.au, *Website:* www.caltex.com.au

Waste Reception Facilities: Quarantine waste can be accepted. Sewage and oily water accepted in limited quantities

Towage: Three tugs available;
Cape Le Grand II, 30 t bollard pull
Cape Arid, 30 t bollard pull
Cape Pasley, 65 t bollard pull

Repair & Maintenance: Minor repairs only

Seaman Missions: The Seamans Mission, P O Box 838, Esperance, W.A., Australia 6450, *Tel:* +61 8 9071 6811, *Fax:* +61 8 9071 6822, *Email:* esperance@mts.org.au

Ship Chandlers: Sealanes, 178 Marine Terrace, Fremantle, W.A., Australia 6162, *Tel:* +61 8 9432 8888, *Fax:* +61 8 9430 4019, *Email:* sea@sealanes.com.au, *Website:* www.sealanes.com.au
Sinwa Imes Pty Ltd., P O Box 1468, Bibra Lake, Fremantle, W.A., Australia 6965, *Tel:* +61 8 9434 3300, *Fax:* +61 8 9434 3322, *Email:* sales-imes@sinwa.com.au, *Website:* www.sinwaglobal.com

Shipping Agents: Barwil Agencies Australia Pty Ltd, P O Box 805, Fremantle, W.A., Australia 6959, *Tel:* +61 8 9336 0900, *Fax:* +61 8 9336 0999, *Email:* fremantle@barwil.com.au, *Website:* www.barwil.com
Inchcape Shipping Services (ISS), Inchcape Shipping Services Pty Ltd, P O Box 652, Esperance, W.A., Australia 6450, *Tel:* +61 8 9071 1576, *Fax:* +61 8 9071 4244, *Email:* esperance@iss-shipping.com.au, *Website:* www.iss-shipping.com

Stevedoring Companies: P&O Ports, P O Box 226, Fremantle, W.A., Australia 6159, *Tel:* +61 8 9430 0111, *Fax:* +61 8 9335 4215, *Email:* ann.gosling@poports.com.au

Medical Facilities: Available

Airport: 24 km

Railway: The port is linked to the standard gauge railway system to Kalgoorlie and then on to the West or East coasts

Lloyd's Agent: Moko Proprietary Ltd, P O Box 685, Willetton, W.A., Australia 6955, *Tel:* +61 8 9354 2248, *Fax:* +61 8 9354 2234, *Email:* kglange@bigpond.com

FREMANTLE

Lat 32° 3' S; Long 115° 45' E.

Admiralty Chart: AUS 113/112	**Admiralty Pilot:** 17
Time Zone: GMT +8 h	**UNCTAD Locode:** AU FRE

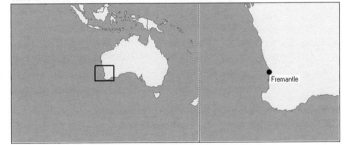

Principal Facilities:

P		Y	G	C	R	L	B		T	A

Authority: Fremantle Ports, 1 Cliff Street, P O Box 95, Fremantle, W.A., Australia 6959, *Tel:* +61 8 9430 3555, *Fax:* +61 8 9336 1391, *Email:* mail@fremantleports.com.au, *Website:* www.fremantleports.com.au

Officials: Harbour Master: Capt Allan Gray, *Tel:* +61 8 9430 3305, *Email:* agray@fremantleports.com.au.

Port Security: ISPS compliant

Pre-Arrival Information: Regulations require that all vessels give the following information of their expected arrival:
(a) 48 h notice of arrival at Fairway Buoy indicating maximum draft, details of hazardous cargo and any requirement for pilot embarkation at the Outer Boarding Ground if the vessel's draft is less than 11.0 m
(b) 24 h notice of arrival at Pilot Boarding Ground
(c) 2 h notice of arrival by VHF
Any variance from the latest advised time should be notified to the Harbour Master as soon as possible

Approach: The channel leading from Gage Roads into Cockburn Sound is 14.7 m deep
The declared depth of the approach channel to Inner Harbour and sections of Inner Harbour area are dredged to 13 m at LW

Pilotage: Pilotage is compulsory except for vessels not exceeding 150 gt and for Master's of vessels which hold current Pilotage Exemption Certificates. Pilots are available 24 h/day
There are two boarding grounds: the first, 3.0 nautical miles WNW of the Fairway

Buoy, is compulsory for vessels drawing 11.0 m draught or greater; the second is in Gage Roads, 1.0 nautical mile west of the Hall Bank Beacon

Radio Frequency: Fremantle Port signal station manned 24 h. Keeps watch principally on VHF Channels 16, 14, 12, 8 and 6. Channels 13 and 6 are exclusively assigned to tug use. Channel 12 for ship/shore contact

Tides: Winter: MHW 1.1 m. Summer: MHW 0.8 m. Not regular, approx one tide a day

Traffic: 2007/08, 1660 commercial vessels & 25 cruise vessels, 26 083 910 t of cargo handled, 580 345 TEU's

Principal Imports and Exports: Imports: Automobiles, Caustic soda, Chemicals, Containers, Fertilisers, General cargo, Petroleum products, Steel, Timber. Exports: Alumina, Containers, Fruit, General cargo, Grains, Livestock, Meat, Minerals, Petroleum products, Wool.

Working Hours: At Inner Harbour, Grain Jetty and Bulk Cargo Jetty: 0730-1430, 1430-2130, 2300-0600
At Refinery Jetty and Alumina Jetty: 0700-1500, 1500-2300, 2300-0700

Accommodation:

Name	Length (m)	Depth (m)	Remarks
Inner Harbour			See [1] below
North Quay			Berths 1, 2, 11 & 12 are common user berths
Berth 1	207	11	Stacking area of 16 130 m2
Berth 2	175	11	Stacking area of 7945 m2
Berths 4-6	526	13	See [2] below
Berth 7-10	726	11–13	See [3] below
Berth 11	196	11	Stacking area of 26 203 m2
Berth 12	233	11	Shed area of 9521 m2 and stacking area of 12 906 m2
Victoria Quay			See [4] below
Berth C	198	11	
Berth D	176	11	
Berth E	230	11	Stacking area of 19 200 m2
Berth F	204	11	
Berth G	206	11	
Berth H	275	11	See [5] below
Outer Harbour			See [6] below
Alcoa World Alumina Refinery Jetty	244	11.6	See [7] below
Kwinana Bulk Terminal			See [8] below
Kwinana Bulk Jetty			Operated by Fremantle Port Authority
Berth No.3	259	13.4	See [9] below
Berth No.4	221	13.4	See [10] below
Kwinana Grain Jetty	291	16.8	See [11] below
Oil Refinery Jetty			See [12] below
No.1 Berth	71.6	14.7	For vessels up to 229 m loa
No.2 Berth	71.6	14.7	For vessels up to 229 m loa
No.3 Berth	71	14.7	For vessels up to 274 m loa

[1]*Inner Harbour:* Situated about 16 km from Rottnest Island, is constructed within the mouth of the Swan River and is protected by two breakwaters. Depth of entrance channel and inner harbour basin is 13 m (depth for berths 4-9 is 13 m, all other berths is 11 m) and is currently dredged to 13 m below LLM. Total length of wharves 3017.5 m (17 berths). Vessels handled are predominantly breakbulk, container, ro/ro, livestock and fishing. Explosives must be unloaded into lighters in Outer Harbour before ship can enter Inner Harbour

[2]*Berths 4-6:* Operated by DP World Fremantle, P O Box 657, Fremantle, WA 6159, Tel: +61 8 9430 0111, Fax: +61 8 9335 4215, Website: www.dpworld.com
Container terminal with a total area of 13.2 ha. 1900 ground slots, 550 reefer points and shed space of 2350 m2

[3]*Berth 7-10:* Operated by Patrick Stevedores, Tel: +61 8 9432 0300, Fax: +61 8 9432 0311, Website: www.patrick.com.au
Total area of 17.8 ha. 2468 container ground slots and 240 reefer points

[4]*Victoria Quay:* Four berths are used for cargo handling and two are used for lay-up. Berths E to H are used predominantly for car carriers as well as passenger cruise vessels, while berths C and D provide limited lay-up. Victoria Quay also provides a passenger terminal combined with a function and exhibition facility at F and G berths. Mobile craneage may be arranged through private operators

[5]*Berth H:* Stacking area of 28 755 m2 (which includes Berth J hardstand)

[6]*Outer Harbour:* Comprises three open deepwater anchorages: Gage Roads, Owen Anchorage and Cockburn Sound. The three together contain 18 907 ha of deep water. There are eight jetty berths handling various special commodities

[7]*Alcoa World Alumina Refinery Jetty:* Operated by Alcoa World Alumina Australia Ltd., Cnr Davy and Marmion Streets, Booragoon WA 6154, Tel: +61 8 9316 5111, Fax: +61 8 9316 5228, Website: www.alcoa.com.au
For vessels up to 200 m loa unloading bulk caustic soda and bulk carriers loading refined alumina by conveyor at average rate of 1000 t/h

[8]*Kwinana Bulk Terminal:* Operated by Fremantle Port Authority
The jetty is 498.32 m long with a berth length of 268.22 m and has a depth alongside of 11 m handling cement clinker, mineral sands, silica sands, coal, iron ore, pig iron and various other materials in association with local industries. The berth has one unloader with a discharge rate of 400 t/h and one with a discharge rate of 1200 t/h. The conveying system has a max loading rate of 2000 t/h

[9]*Berth No.3:* Cargoes handled include phosphate, phosphoric acid, sulphur, ammonium sulphate, potash, ammonia and urea. Two unloaders, one with cap of 1300 t/h and one of 250 t/h

[10]*Berth No.4:* Cargoes handled include refined petroleum, fertilisers, caustic soda, phosphates, ammonia sulphate, sulphuric acid and sulphur. Continuous unloader with a cap of 17 000 t per 22 h working day

[11]*Kwinana Grain Jetty:* Operated by CBH Group, Gayfer House, 30 Delhi Street, West Perth WA 6005, Tel: +61 8 9237 9600, Fax: +61 8 9322 3942, Email: info@cbh.com.au, Website: www.cbh.com.au
For vessels loading bulk grain. Four bulk loaders with designed cap of 5000 t/h

[12]*Oil Refinery Jetty:* Operated by BP Refinery, Mason Road, Kwinana WA 6167, Tel: +61 8 9419 9500, Fax: +61 8 9419 9800, Website: www.bp.com.au
For tankers loading/unloading bulk petroleum products

Key to Principal Facilities:—			
A=Airport	**C**=Containers	**G**=General Cargo	**P**=Petroleum	**R**=Ro/Ro	**Y**=Dry Bulk
B=Bunkers	**D**=Dry Dock	**L**=Cruise	**Q**=Other Liquid Bulk	**T**=Towage (where available from port)	

Mechanical Handling Equipment:

Location	Type	Capacity (t)	Qty	Remarks
North Quay	Mult-purp. Cranes	45–80	3	At berths 7-10
North Quay	Container Cranes	64–67	3	At berths 4-6

Bunkering: Three grades of fuel oil available by pipeline at some Inner Harbour berths, and at the Oil Refinery Jetties and Bulk Cargo Jetty in the Outer Harbour Indian Ocean Shipping Agency, Suite 5, 330 South Terrace, Fremantle, W.A., Australia 6160, *Tel:* +61 8 9430 6266, *Fax:* +61 8 9430 8321, *Email:* ops@indianoceansa.com.au, *Website:* www.indianoceansa.com
BP Australia (Proprietary) Ltd, P O Box 5222, Melbourne, Vic., Australia 3001, *Tel:* +61 3 9268 4111, *Fax:* +61 3 9268 3321, *Email:* gomiasfuelsales@bp.com, *Website:* www.bp.com – *Grades:* MGO; BDO; IFO380-180cSt, other IF grades subject to enquiry – *Notice:* 48 hours – *Delivery Mode:* barge, truck, pipeline
ExxonMobil Marine Fuels, 1 Harbour Front Place, 06-00 Harbour Front, Tower One, Singapore, Republic of Singapore 098633, *Tel:* +65 6885 8998, *Fax:* +65 6885 8794, *Email:* asiapac.marinefuels@exxonmobil.com, *Website:* www.exxonmobilmarinefuels.com – *Grades:* MGO – *Delivery Mode:* tank truck
Shell Australia Ltd, Shell Company of Australia, Marine Centre Oceania, No 8 Redfern Road, Melbourne, Vic., Australia 3123, *Tel:* +61 3 9666 5446, *Fax:* +61 3 8823 4800, *Email:* sal-marine-products@shell.com, *Website:* www.shell.com.au

Waste Reception Facilities: A collection service for all garbage and waste material is available. Oily water from ships can be collected by privately owned road tankers

Towage: All tugs are privately owned and operated. Three tugs are available in the Inner Harbour to assist vessels berthing and two tugs at Outer Harbour berths
Mermaid Marine Australia Ltd, Eagle Jetty, 20 Mews Road, Fremantle, W.A., Australia 6160, *Tel:* +61 8 9431 7431, *Fax:* +61 8 9431 7432, *Email:* corporate@mermaidmarine.com.au, *Website:* www.mma.com.au
Riverwijs Dampier Proprietary Ltd, Suite 10, 18 Parry Street, P O Box 1213, Fremantle, W.A., Australia 6160, *Tel:* +61 8 9433 1311, *Fax:* +61 8 9433 1611, *Email:* paul@riversidemarine.com.au
SVITZER, SVITZER Australasia, 17 Mews Road, Fremantle, W.A., Australia 6160, *Tel:* +61 8 9336 3599, *Fax:* +61 8 9336 3522, *Email:* info.wa@adsteam.com.au, *Website:* www.svitzer.com
Swire Pacific Offshore Services (Private) Ltd, Swire Pacific Offshore Proprietary Ltd, 2nd Floor, Queensgate Centre, Corner Newman & William Street, Fremantle, W.A., Australia 6160, *Tel:* +61 8 9430 5434, *Fax:* +61 8 9430 7849, *Email:* spotty@spotty.com.au, *Website:* www.swire.com.sg

Repair & Maintenance: All types of deck and engine repairs possible

Seaman Missions: The Seamans Mission, The Flying Angel Club, 76 Queen Victoria Street, Fremantle, W.A., Australia 6160, *Tel:* +61 8 9335 5000, *Fax:* +61 8 9335 5321, *Email:* fremantle@mts.org.au

Ship Chandlers: Australian Cruise Ship Supplies Proprietary Ltd (Division of Sealanes (1985) Proprietary Ltd), P O Box 658, Fremantle, W.A., Australia 6959, *Tel:* +61 8 8399 1622, *Fax:* +61 8 8399 1644, *Email:* wmerritt@austcruise.com.au
Liferaft Servicing Group (LSG), 24 Mews Road, Fremantle, W.A., Australia 6160, *Tel:* +61 8 9336 4418, *Fax:* +61 8 9336 4429, *Email:* servicewa@lsg.net.au, *Website:* www.lsg.net.au
Sealanes, 178 Marine Terrace, Fremantle, W.A., Australia 6162, *Tel:* +61 8 9432 8888, *Fax:* +61 8 9430 4019, *Email:* sea@sealanes.com.au, *Website:* www.sealanes.com.au
Sinwa Imes Pty Ltd., P O Box 1468, Bibra Lake, Fremantle, W.A., Australia 6965, *Tel:* +61 8 9434 3300, *Fax:* +61 8 9434 3322, *Email:* sales-imes@sinwa.com.au, *Website:* www.sinwaglobal.com

Shipping Agents: ANL Container Line Proprietary Ltd, Ground Floor, 6 Short Street, Fremantle, W.A., Australia 6160, *Tel:* +61 8 9432 1900, *Fax:* +61 8 9432 1910, *Email:* neatess@anl.com.au, *Website:* www.anl.com.au
Asiaworld Shipping Services Proprietary Ltd, 92 Marine Terrace, Fremantle, W.A., Australia 6160, *Tel:* +61 8 9335 3800, *Fax:* +61 8 9335 3805, *Email:* aw.fremantle@asiaworld.com.au, *Website:* www.asiaworld.com.au
Barwil Agencies Australia Pty Ltd, P O Box 805, Fremantle, W.A., Australia 6959, *Tel:* +61 8 9336 0900, *Fax:* +61 8 9336 0999, *Email:* fremantle@barwil.com.au, *Website:* www.barwil.com
Five Star Shipping & Agency Co. Proprietary Ltd, P O Box 766, Fremantle, W.A., Australia 6160, *Tel:* +61 8 9336 4388, *Fax:* +61 8 9336 3286, *Email:* shipping@vstarcosco.com.au
Gulf Agency Co (Australia) Pty Ltd., P O Box 1770, Fremantle, W.A., Australia 6959, *Tel:* +61 8 9336 4906, *Fax:* +61 8 9433 3459, *Email:* shipping.fremantle@gacworld.com, *Website:* www.gacworld.com
A Hartrodt International, 3 Norfolk Street, P O Box 663, Fremantle, W.A., Australia 6160, *Tel:* +61 8 9335 9866, *Fax:* +61 8 9335 8541, *Email:* fremantle@hartrodt.com.au, *Website:* www.hartrodt.com.au
Hetherington Kingsbury Proprietary Ltd, P O Box 391, Fremantle, W.A., Australia 6160, *Tel:* +61 8 9335 6111, *Fax:* +61 8 9335 3196, *Email:* lrebisz@hksa.com.au, *Website:* www.hksa.com.au
Holyman Marine Agencies, 6 Short Street, Fremantle, W.A., Australia 6160, *Tel:* +61 8 9335 1091, *Fax:* +61 8 9430 7705, *Email:* ryan@norwest-shipping.com.au
Inchcape Shipping Services (ISS), Inchcape Shipping Services Pty Ltd, P O Box 656, Fremantle, W.A., Australia 6163, *Tel:* +61 8 9434 2387, *Fax:* +61 8 9434 2824, *Email:* fremantle@iss-shipping.com.au, *Website:* www.iss-shipping.com
Indian Ocean Shipping Agency, Suite 5, 330 South Terrace, Fremantle, W.A., Australia 6160, *Tel:* +61 8 9430 6266, *Fax:* +61 8 9430 8321, *Email:* ops@indianoceansa.com.au, *Website:* www.indianoceansa.com
K Line Ship Management Co. Ltd, 2 Bannister Street, Fremantle, W.A., Australia 6959, *Tel:* +61 8 9339 4211, *Fax:* +61 8 9430 4155, *Email:* ales@klineaus.com.au
McArthur Shipping & Agency Co Pty Ltd, P O Box 391, Fremantle, W.A., Australia 6959, *Tel:* +61 8 9335 6111, *Fax:* +61 8 9335 3196, *Email:* fremantle@mcaship.com.au, *Website:* www.mcaship.com.au
Mediterranean Shipping Company, MSC (Aust) Pty Ltd., P O Box 1242, Fremantle, W.A., Australia 6959, *Tel:* +61 8 9336 0500, *Fax:* +61 8 9430 6632, *Email:* mscafreinfo@msc.com.au, *Website:* www.msc.com.au
A.P. Moller-Maersk Group, Maersk Australia Pty Ltd, Level 1, 1 Pensioner Guard Road, (CNR Tydeman Road), Fremantle, W.A., Australia 6159, *Tel:* +61 8 9433 9100, *Fax:* +61 8 9433 9190, *Email:* fmnops@maersk.com, *Website:* www.maerskline.com
Monson Agencies Australia Proprietary Ltd, Suite 1, 1 High Street, P O Box 1558, Fremantle, W.A., Australia 6160, *Tel:* +61 8 9335 0000, *Fax:* +61 8 9335 0055, *Email:* fremantle@monson.com.au, *Website:* www.monson.com.au

Pacific Asia Express Proprietary Ltd, Unit 4,, 18 Norfolk Street, Fremantle, W.A., Australia 6160, *Tel:* +61 8 9430 0600, *Fax:* +61 8 9430 0630, *Email:* gg@ilm.com.au, *Website:* www.pae.com.au
Quay West Agencies Proprietary Ltd, Berth 2, 67 Hampton Road, North Quay, P O Box 140, Fremantle, W.A., Australia 6160, *Tel:* +61 8 9437 9284, *Fax:* +61 8 9437 9289, *Email:* qwa@iinet.net.au
Seacorp Agencies, 10 Phillimore Street, Fremantle, W.A., Australia 6160, *Tel:* +61 8 9430 7100, *Fax:* +61 8 9430 7199, *Email:* info@seacorp.com.au, *Website:* www.seacorp.com.au
Seatrans Australia Proprietary Ltd, Suite 2, 18 Norfolk Street, Fremantle, W.A., Australia 6160, *Tel:* +61 8 9335 6111, *Fax:* +61 8 9335 3196, *Email:* lrebisz@hksa.com.au, *Website:* www.hksa.com.au
SMS Shipping, Ground Floor, 2 Birksgate Road, Rous Head, Fremantle, W.A., Australia 6159, *Tel:* +61 8 9430 7666, *Fax:* +61 8 9335 2311, *Email:* mail@smsshipping.com.au, *Website:* www.smsshipping.com.au
Wills Shipping Proprietary Ltd, Level 1, Suite D, 36 Rous Head Road, Fremantle, W.A., Australia 6159, *Tel:* +61 8 9430 5869, *Fax:* +61 8 9430 5141

Stevedoring Companies: Patrick Stevedoring, Berth 1, North Quay, North Fremantle, Fremantle, W.A., Australia 6159, *Tel:* +61 8 9432 0327, *Fax:* +61 8 9430 7705, *Email:* r.redman@patrick.com.au, *Website:* www.patrick.com.au
P&O Ports, P O Box 226, Fremantle, W.A., Australia 6159, *Tel:* +61 8 9430 0111, *Fax:* +61 8 9335 4215, *Email:* ann.gosling@poports.com.au
United Stevedoring Co., P. O. Box 689, Fremantle, W.A., Australia 6959, *Tel:* +61 8 9430 7666, *Fax:* +61 8 9335 2311, *Email:* mail@smsshipping.com.au, *Website:* www.smsshipping.com.au

Surveyors: Det Norske Veritas A/S, Suite 5, Peninsular Offices, 2 Redemptora Road, Henderson, W.A., Australia 6166, *Tel:* +61 8 9437 1411, *Fax:* +61 8 9437 2894, *Email:* wa@dnv.com, *Website:* www.dnv.com
Germanischer Lloyd, Suite 2, 3rd Floor, 26 Queen Street, Fremantle, W.A., Australia 6160, *Tel:* +61 8 9336 1177, *Fax:* +61 8 9336 1178, *Email:* gl-fremantle@gl-group.com, *Website:* www.gl-group.com
Nippon Kaiji Kyokai, 17 Woodlands Way, Fremantle, W.A., Australia 6164, *Tel:* +61 8 9414 8480, *Fax:* +61 8 9414 8490, *Email:* fm@classnk.or.jp, *Website:* www.classnk.or.jp
Registro Italiano Navale (RINA), 6 Vancouver Drive, Canningvale, Perth, W.A., Australia, *Tel:* +61 8 9455 3960, *Fax:* +61 8 9455 4243, *Email:* surveystation.fremantle@rina.org, *Website:* www.rina.org

Medical Facilities: Full hospital facilities available

Airport: Perth International, 35 km

Lloyd's Agent: Moko Proprietary Ltd, P O Box 685, Willetton, W.A., Australia 6955, *Tel:* +61 8 9354 2248, *Fax:* +61 8 9354 2234, *Email:* kglange@bigpond.com

GEELONG

Lat 38° 8' S; Long 144° 20' E.

Admiralty Chart: AUS 157/153		**Admiralty Pilot:** 14	
Time Zone: GMT +10 h		**UNCTAD Locode:** AU GEX	

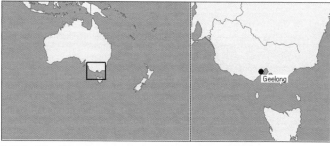

Principal Facilities:

P	Q	Y	G		R	L	B			A

Authority: Asciano Ltd, P O Box 344, Geelong, Vic., Australia 3220, *Tel:* +61 3 5247 0200, *Fax:* +61 3 5221 6883, *Email:* n.kimberley@patrick.com.au, *Website:* www.tollports.com.au

Officials: General Manager: Noel Kimberley.
Finance Manager: Ken Digby, *Email:* ken_digby@toll.com.au.

Port Security: ISPS compliant. Under the provisions of the Maritime Transport Security Act 2003 Geelong Port has produced a Maritime Security Plan for the Port of Geelong which has been approved by the Australian Federal Government. The Port of Geelong will operate under security level 1 as the default level unless otherwise advised by the Federal Government. At level 1 there will be requirements for security to be present at Lascelles and Corio Quay berths at all times while a vessel is at a berth. The security guard will be arranged by Geelong Port and charged to the hirer of the berth

Approach: The approach to Geelong from seaward is through three dredged channels (Point Richards, Wilson Spit and Hopetoun) lit by beacons on either side. They are all 120 m wide through the straight sections

Pilotage: Available from Port Phillip Sea Pilots Pty Ltd., Tel: +61 3 9329 9700, Fax: +61 3 9326 6052, Email: operations@ppsp.com.au. 24 h, VHF Channels 12 and 16

Weather: Wind velocities at times exceed 50 kn, usually in the NW quadrant. Vessels at anchor should keep a constant check on their position

Tides: Spring range 0.8 m. Tide heights are affected greatly by prevailing winds and variations in the barometric pressure. In general low barometric pressure and/or westerly winds increase the height of both high and low water. High barometric pressure and/or easterly winds decrease the height

Traffic: 2007/08, 632 vessels, 10 755 295 t of cargo handled

Maximum Vessel Dimensions: 11.6 m draught

Principal Imports and Exports: Imports: Crude oil, General cargo, Petroleum coke, Petroleum products, Phosphate rock, Potash, Steel, Sulphur. Exports: Bulk & bagged grain, General cargo, Petroleum products, Timber, Woodchips.

Working Hours: 24 h/day

Accommodation: Tanker facilities: Oil pipeline from the Gippsland offshore oilfields to the Shell Refinery at Corio

Name	Length (m)	Depth (m)	Draught (m)	Remarks
Geelong				
Bulk Grain Pier (Berths 1 & 2)	201			See [1] below
Bulk Grain Pier (Berth 3)	168	12.3	11.6	See [2] below
Corio Quay South (Berth 1)	183	11	10.4	General cargo & ro/ro. One shed 125 m x 30.5 m
Corio Quay North (Berths 1 & 2)	375	11	10.4	See [3] below
Corio Quay North (Berth 3)	161	11	10.4	General cargo. One cargo shed of 97.5 m x 27.4 m
Lascelles Berth 1 (Southern)	185	12.3	11.6	See [4] below
Lascelles Berth 2		12.3	11.6	See [5] below
Lascelles Berth 3 (Northern)		12.3	11.6	Dry bulk & fertiliser. Length of berths 2 & 3 total 436 m
Refinery Pier Berths 1-4		12.3	11.6	Chemicals, crude & LPG
Point Wilson Explosives Jetty	168	9.1	8	Dangerous & explosive cargoes
Point Henry Pier	152	12	11.3	See [6] below

[1]*Bulk Grain Pier (Berths 1 & 2):* Bulk grain. Depth at Berth 1 is 10.5 m and at Berth 2 is 12.3 m. Overhead conveyor containing four belts with a total cap of 1600 t/wheat/h. This facility is now redundant with the main loading berth being Bulk Grain Pier No.3 Berth

[2]*Bulk Grain Pier (Berth 3):* Wheat and woodchips for vessels up to 235 m loa. Wheat at 2500 t/h and woodchips at 1000 t/h

[3]*Corio Quay North (Berths 1 & 2):* General cargo & woodchips. One shed 91 m x 30.5 m on Berth 2. Loader for woodchips at 1000 t/h

[4]*Lascelles Berth 1 (Southern):* Dry bulk & general cargo. Shed of 162 m x 53 m exclusively for the use of Pivot Fertilisers

[5]*Lascelles Berth 2:* Dry bulk & fertiliser. Length of berths 2 & 3 total 436 m. Shed of 155 m x 45 m

[6]*Point Henry Pier:* Bulk alumina & petroleum coke. One grab crane of 250 t/h cap

Mechanical Handling Equipment:

Location	Type	Capacity (t)	Qty	Remarks
Corio Quay North (Berths 1 & 2)	Portal Cranes	6	1	
Lascelles Berth 2	Mult-purp. Cranes	20	2	also for Berth 3
Lascelles Berth 3 (Northern)	Mult-purp. Cranes	20	2	also for Berth 2

Bunkering: BP Australia (Proprietary) Ltd, P O Box 5222, Melbourne, Vic., Australia 3001, *Tel:* +61 3 9268 4111, *Fax:* +61 3 9268 3321, *Email:* gomiasfuelsales@bp.com, *Website:* www.bp.com – *Delivery Mode:* barge, truck
Caltex Australia Petroleum Proprietary Ltd, Caltex Australia Petroleum Proprietary Ltd, No 2 Market Street, Sydney, N.S.W., Australia 2000, *Tel:* +61 2 9668 1148, *Fax:* +61 2 9668 1243, *Email:* mnicholl@caltex.com.au, *Website:* www.caltex.com.au
ExxonMobil Marine Fuels, 1 Harbour Front Place, 06-00 Harbour Front, Tower One, Singapore, Republic of Singapore 098633, *Tel:* +65 6885 8998, *Fax:* +65 6885 8794, *Email:* asiapac.marinefuels@exxonmobil.com, *Website:* www.exxonmobilmarinefuels.com – *Grades:* MGO – *Delivery Mode:* tank truck
Shell Australia Ltd, Shell Company of Australia, Marine Centre Oceania, No 8 Redfern Road, Melbourne, Vic., Australia 3123, *Tel:* +61 3 9666 5446, *Fax:* +61 3 8823 4800, *Email:* sal-marine-products@shell.com, *Website:* www.shell.com.au – *Delivery Mode:* barge, truck

Waste Reception Facilities: Contractors available for disposal of dirty ballast and sludge. Garbage pick-up available

Towage: Two diesel tugs up to 2550 bhp

Repair & Maintenance: Abraham Engineering, Geelong, Vic., Australia, *Tel:* +61 3 5278 5980
Seaside Engineering, Geelong, Vic., Australia, *Tel:* +61 3 5243 6557

Seaman Missions: The Seamans Mission, 7 The Esplanade, Geelong, Vic., Australia 3214, *Tel:* +61 3 5278 6985, *Fax:* +61 3 5278 6985, *Email:* geelong@mts.org.au

Shipping Agents: Barwil Agencies Australia Pty Ltd, P O Box 1418, Geelong, Vic., Australia 3220, *Tel:* +61 3 5223 1447, *Fax:* +61 3 5223 1933, *Email:* geelong@wilhelmsen.com, *Website:* www.wilhelmsen.com
Inchcape Shipping Services (ISS), Inchcape Shipping Services Pty Ltd, 172 Latrobe Terrace, Geelong, Vic., Australia 3218, *Tel:* +61 3 5221 8311, *Fax:* +61 3 5221 6055, *Email:* geelong@iss-shipping.com.au, *Website:* www.iss-shipping.com

Stevedoring Companies: P&O Ports, P O Box 397, North Shore, Vic., Australia 3214, *Tel:* +61 3 5272 1833, *Fax:* +61 3 5277 0531
Toll Logistics (New Zealand) Ltd, Geelong, Vic., Australia, *Tel:* +61 3 5226 6200, *Fax:* +61 3 5221 6883, *Email:* richard_redman@toll.com.au
Victorian Regional Stevedores, Geelong, Vic., Australia, *Tel:* +61 3 5272 1833, *Fax:* +61 3 5277 0531

Medical Facilities: Available

Airport: Tullamarine International, 70 km

Railway: Broad gauge rail to Corio Quay

Development: Dual gauge rail (broad and standard gauge) connection to Lascelles Wharf

Lloyd's Agent: Freemans Marine, Level 7, 564 St. Kilda Road, Melbourne, Vic., Australia 3004, *Tel:* +61 3 9935 2400, *Fax:* +61 3 9915 0351, *Email:* lloyds@freemans.com.au, *Website:* www.freemansmarine.com.au

GERALDTON

Lat 28° 46' S; Long 114° 35' E.

Admiralty Chart: AUS 81/333	**Admiralty Pilot:** 17
Time Zone: GMT +8 h	**UNCTAD Locode:** AU GET

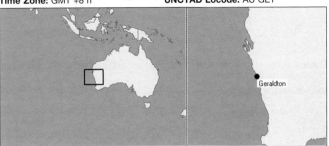

Principal Facilities:

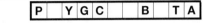

Authority: Geraldton Port Authority, P O Box 1856, Geraldton, W.A., Australia 6531, *Tel:* +61 8 9964 0520, *Fax:* +61 8 9964 0555, *Email:* mail@gpa.wa.gov.au, *Website:* www.gpa.wa.gov.au

Officials: Chief Executive Officer: Peter Klein, *Tel:* +61 8 9964 0537, *Email:* peter.klein@gpa.wa.gov.au.
Commercial Manager: Melanie Davies, *Tel:* +61 8 9964 0535, *Email:* melanie.davies@gpa.wa.gov.au.
Finance Manager: Rick Pochroj, *Tel:* +61 8 9964 0524, *Email:* rick.pochroj@gpa.wa.gov.au.
Operations Manager: Tony Venturini, *Tel:* +61 8 9964 0527, *Email:* tony.venturini@gpa.wa.gov.au.
Harbour Master: Capt Martin North, *Tel:* +61 8 9964 0547, *Email:* martin.north@gpa.wa.gov.au.

Port Security: ISPS compliant. Security Officer boards once vessel alongside

Pre-Arrival Information: Notice of arrival to be advised at least 48 h prior to arrival and updated 24 h and 6 h prior to arrival via fax or email

Documentation: Berthing application form must be completed and lodged 48 h prior to arrival. Form is available from GPA website or vessel's agents in Geraldton

Approach: From seaward the approach is from Racon (G) fairway buoy (28° 46.2' S; 114° 31.7' E) on the Bluff Point leads (28° 45' S; 114° 37' E) bearing 071° 23'. An alternate channel (with the permission of the Harbour Master) for vessels with draughts of not more than 7.5 m is approached from a fairway buoy (28° 41.8' S; 114° 33.3' E) with Bluff Point leads bearing 128°. A dredged channel 2.8 miles long and 180 m wide with 14.2 m depth at the outer end and 12.5 m depth at the inner end, is marked by leading lights and a combination of 10 light beacons and light buoys on each side, through the 7 m areas, into Champion Bay and thence in a southerly direction between breakwaters into Geraldton Harbour

Anchorage: There are twelve designated anchorages off the port as follows:
S1: in pos 28° 47.0' S; 114° 32.2' E
N1: in pos 28° 44.6' S; 114° 32.1' E
N2: in pos 28° 44.6' S; 114° 31.0' E
N3: in pos 28° 43.7' S; 114° 32.5' E
N4: in pos 28° 43.7' S; 114° 31.3' E
N5: in pos 28° 42.7' S; 114° 32.7' E
N6: in pos 28° 42.7' S; 114° 31.6' E
N7: in pos 28° 40.9' S; 114° 33.3' E
N8: in pos 28° 40.9' S; 114° 32.1' E
N9: in pos 28° 39.9' S; 114° 33.6' E
N10: in pos 28° 39.9' S; 114° 32.4' E
QN: in pos 28° 42.5' S; 114° 35.6' E

Pilotage: Compulsory for vessels over 35 m loa and those over 150 gt. Pilot boarding grounds:
(a) in pos 28° 45.5' S; 114° 31' E
(b) in pos 28° 42.0' S; 114° 32' E
Pilotage may be deferred when swell height exceeds 3.0 m or winds in excess of 30 knots
Duty pilot: +61 8 9964 0510

Radio Frequency: Geraldton Harbour VHF Radio 11 or 16 manned during normal working hours (Mon-Fri 0800-1700); weekends and public holidays as required only. Station will be manned 1 h prior to pilot boarding time. If shipping movements in place try calling on VHF Channel 6

Weather: Swell breaks on 7 m areas of reef in swells over 1.5 m

Tides: MHHW 1.1 m, MLLW 0.6 m. Mean sea level influenced by weather conditions

Traffic: 2007/08, 238 vessels, 6 708 871 t of cargo handled

Maximum Vessel Dimensions: Max permitted draught at zero tide is 11.5 m and at plus 1.3 m is 12.8 m. These draughts are subject to conditions of swell. A dynamic underkeel clearance system is utilised to determine max permissible draughts under prevailing conditions. Mariners wishing to load to max draught should obtain permission from the Harbour Master

Principal Imports and Exports: Imports: Fertiliser, Petroleum products. Exports: Bulk grain, Copper ore, General cargo, Iron ore, Livestock, Mineral sands, Talc.

Working Hours: Normally 0800-1700, 1700-2400, 0001-0700 but other flexible arrangements can be made

Key to Principal Facilities:—				
A=Airport	**C**=Containers	**G**=General Cargo	**P**=Petroleum	**R**=Ro/Ro	**Y**=Dry Bulk
B=Bunkers	**D**=Dry Dock	**L**=Cruise	**Q**=Other Liquid Bulk	**T**=Towage (where available from port)

Accommodation:

Name	Length (m)	Depth (m)	Remarks
Geraldton			
Berth No.1	55	8.4	Small vessels
Berth No.2	225	9.6	Multi-purpose & lay-by facilities
Berth No.3	225	13.3	See [1] below
Berth No.4	281	13.3	Mineral sands & iron ore
Berth No.5	220	9.8	Under reconstruction to an iron ore berth
Berth No.6	215	12	General cargo, petroleum, livestock & fertiliser

[1]*Berth No.3:* Grain. Two shiploaders rated at up to 1000 t/h each, horizontal travel 167 m

Storage: Grain storage cap of 783 000 t. Cold storage facilities are available locally through private companies

Mechanical Handling Equipment:

Location	Type	Capacity (t)	Qty
Geraldton	Mobile Cranes	9	
Berth No.4	Gantry Cranes		1
Berth No.6	Mobile Cranes		1

Bunkering: Light diesel fuel oil available at approx 80 t/h by pipeline at No.5 berth only, otherwise by road tanker
BP Australia (Proprietary) Ltd, P O Box 5222, Melbourne, Vic., Australia 3001, *Tel:* +61 3 9268 4111, *Fax:* +61 3 9268 3321, *Email:* gomiasfuelsales@bp.com, *Website:* www.bp.com

Waste Reception Facilities: Incinerator garbage disposal facility available. Road tankers (sullage) available

Towage: Three tugs of 27-47 t bollard pull available, two fitted with firefighting equipment

Repair & Maintenance: Other private light engineering works are located in Geraldton
Geraldton Engineering Co., Geraldton, W.A., Australia Engine and other light repairs

Seaman Missions: The Seamans Mission, Geraldton Flying Angel Club, P O Box 744, Geraldton, W.A., Australia 6531, *Tel:* +61 8 9921 3272, *Fax:* +61 8 9921 2356, *Email:* geraldton@mts.org.au

Ship Chandlers: Sealanes, 178 Marine Terrace, Fremantle, W.A., Australia 6162, *Tel:* +61 8 9432 8888, *Fax:* +61 8 9430 4019, *Email:* sea@sealanes.com.au, *Website:* www.sealanes.com.au
Sinwa Imes Pty Ltd., P O Box 1468, Bibra Lake, Fremantle, W.A., Australia 6965, *Tel:* +61 8 9434 3300, *Fax:* +61 8 9434 3322, *Email:* sales-imes@sinwa.com.au, *Website:* www.sinwaglobal.com

Shipping Agents: Barwil Agencies Australia Pty Ltd, P O Box 805, Fremantle, W.A., Australia 6959, *Tel:* +61 8 9336 0900, *Fax:* +61 8 9336 0999, *Email:* fremantle@barwil.com.au, *Website:* www.barwil.com
Inchcape Shipping Services (ISS), Inchcape Shipping Services Pty Ltd, 241B Lester Avenue, P O Box 209, Geraldton, W.A., Australia 6530, *Tel:* +61 8 9965 3366, *Fax:* +61 8 9965 3388, *Email:* geraldton@iss-shipping.com.au, *Website:* www.iss-shipping.com
Monson Agencies Australia Proprietary Ltd, Level 9 St. George Close, Bluff Point, Geraldton, W.A., Australia 6531, *Email:* geraldton@monson.com.au, *Website:* www.monson.com.au
WA Mercantile Services Pty Ltd, P O Box 2220, Geraldton, W.A., Australia 6531, *Tel:* +61 8 9964 2122, *Fax:* +61 8 9921 4452, *Email:* shipping@wamercantile.com.au

Stevedoring Companies: Co-Operative Bulk Handling Ltd, P O Box 754, Geraldton, W.A., Australia WA 6531, *Tel:* +61 8 9921 9499, *Fax:* +61 8 9921 7463, *Email:* kevin.crouch@cbh.com.au, *Website:* www.cbh.com.au
P&O Ports, P O Box 133, Geraldton, W.A., Australia 6530, *Tel:* +61 8 9921 1634, *Fax:* +61 8 9964 2881
Toll Western Stevedores Pty Ltd, P O Box 140, Fremantle, W.A., Australia 6159, *Tel:* +61 8 9430 6530, *Fax:* +61 8 9430 6532, *Email:* wsfrem@opera.iinet.net.au
United Stevedoring Co., P. O. Box 689, Fremantle, W.A., Australia 6959, *Tel:* +61 8 9430 7666, *Fax:* +61 8 9335 2311, *Email:* mail@smsshipping.com.au, *Website:* www.smsshipping.com.au
WA Mercantile Services Pty Ltd, P O Box 2220, Geraldton, W.A., Australia 6531, *Tel:* +61 8 9964 2122, *Fax:* +61 8 9921 4452, *Email:* shipping@wamercantile.com.au

Medical Facilities: Two fully equipped hospitals

Airport: Greenough Airport, 11 km

Railway: Tracks directly into port for cargo only. No passenger trains

Development: Reconstruction of Berth No.5 from a common user to a dedicated iron ore loading berth; shipments are expected to commence February 2008

Lloyd's Agent: Moko Proprietary Ltd, P O Box 685, Willetton, W.A., Australia 6955, *Tel:* +61 8 9354 2248, *Fax:* +61 8 9354 2234, *Email:* kglange@bigpond.com

GLADSTONE

Lat 23° 50' S; Long 151° 14' E.

Admiralty Chart: AUS 244/245		**Admiralty Pilot:** 15
Time Zone: GMT +10 h		**UNCTAD Locode:** AU GLT

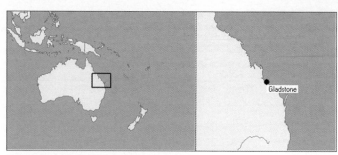

Principal Facilities:

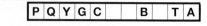

P	Q	Y	G	C		B		T	A

Authority: Gladstone Ports Corp., 19 Yarroon Street, P O Box 259, Gladstone, Qld., Australia 4680, *Tel:* +61 7 4976 1333, *Fax:* +61 7 4972 3045, *Email:* info@gpcl.com.au, *Website:* www.gpcl.com.au

Officials: Chief Executive Officer: Leo Zussino, *Tel:* +61 7 4976 1302, *Email:* zussinol@gpcl.com.au.
Marketing Manager: Lorelei Van Dalen, *Tel:* +61 7 4976 1467, *Email:* vandalenl@gpcl.com.au.
Harbour Master: Capt Michael G Lutze, *Tel:* +61 7 4973 1200, *Email:* mike.g.lutze@msq.qld.gov.au.

Port Security: ISPS compliant

Approach: Entrance channel has least depth of 16.3 m LWD over width of 184 m and a length of 22 km. Depth of water from Fairway Buoy to South Trees is also 16.3 m. The channel between South Trees and Auckland Point Wharf has a width of 180 m, with a depth of 15.8 m LWD. A min of 1.2 m keel clearance is required at all times. Channel designed to cater for 17.0 m draft vessels on any day of year, with greater drafts being available depending on tide. Length and breadth depends upon wharf to which vessel is to proceed. A red and white fairway beacon with a six second flashing white light marks the approach to the harbour entrance, and is situated approx 29 km NW of Bustard Head

Anchorage: Outer harbour anchorage has been gazetted in the vicinity of the Fairway Buoy. Good inner harbour anchorage inside Gatcombe Head approx 0.7 nautical miles S of Bushy Islet in sand and mud, N of Facing Island Leads is available at Harbour Master's discretion

Pilotage: Compulsory for foreign vessels over 35 m loa and Australian vessels over 50 m loa. Pilots board in pos 23° 51.88' S; 151° 32.70' E (2 nautical miles NE of Fairway Lt. Buoy). Pilot requisition must be made at least 24 h in advance, and can be contacted on VHF Channels 16, 10 and 13. Tel: +61 7 4976 8201, Fax: +61 7 4976 8251. Helicopter service also available

Radio Frequency: Harbour radio on VHF Channels 9, 10 and 13

Tides: MHWS 3.91 m, MHWN 3.06 m

Traffic: 2007/08, 1347 vessels, 76 480 082 t of cargo handled

Maximum Vessel Dimensions: 315 m loa, 220 000 dwt, 55 m beam

Principal Imports and Exports: Imports: Bauxite, Break bulk, Bunker oil, Caustic soda, Cement gypsum, Containers, Copper slag, General cargo, Liquid ammonia, Liquid pitch, LPG, Magnetite, Petroleum coke, Petroleum products. Exports: Alumina, Aluminium, Break bulk, Bunker coal, Bunker oil, Calcite, Cement, Cement clinker, Cement gypsum, Coal, Containers, Cotton seed, Fly ash, General cargo, Grain, Limestone, Low sulphur fuel oil, Magnesia, Magnesite, Woodchip.

Working Hours: General cargo and grain: 0800-2100 (meals 1200-1300, 1700-1800). Other cargo: All hours

Accommodation:

Name	Length (m)	Depth (m)	Remarks
Auckland Point Wharf			See [1] below
Berth No.1	173	11.3	See [2] below

Name	Length (m)	Depth (m)	Remarks
Berth No.2	198	11.3	See [3] below
Berth No.3	217	11.3	See [4] below
Berth No.4	172	11.3	See [5] below
South Trees Wharf			See [6] below
Eastern Berth		12.8	See [7] below
Western Berth		12.8	See [8] below
R.G. Tanna Coal Terminal & Clinton Coal Wharf			See [9] below
Barney Point Terminal & Wharf			See [10] below
Boyne Wharf			See [11] below
Fisherman's Landing			See [12] below
Berth No.4	228.5	11.2	See [13] below
Berth No.5	200	11.2	See [14] below

[1]*Auckland Point Wharf:* Owned by Gladstone Ports Corp and operated by Gladstone Ports Corp and other users

[2]*Berth No.1:* Exports magnesia, calcite and woodchip for vessels up to 65 000 dwt. Loading of cargo is by a conveyor system and two mobile gantry loaders capable of 1600 t/h. A stockpile area capable of holding 300 000 t is situated behind the wharf and connected to the gantry loaders by conveyor systems. A smaller bulk stockpile area is also connected to shiploaders

[3]*Berth No.2:* Exports grain for vessels up to 60 000 dwt. Storage shed and two banks of silos capable of storing over 82 000 t of grain are situated behind the wharf and connected by conveyors to two travelling gantry loaders with a combined loading cap of 1600 t/h

[4]*Berth No.3:* For vessels up to 55 000 dwt. This berth is for general cargo, containers, break bulk, magnetite, petroleum products, caustic soda, LPG and cement gypsum. Most of the major oil companies have tank farms for petroleum products behind the wharf

[5]*Berth No.4:* For vessels up to 70 000 dwt. General cargo, containers, break bulk, copper slag, magnetite, fly ash and cement gypsum are handled. 32 reefer points

[6]*South Trees Wharf:* Owned and operated by Queensland Alumina Ltd., Parsons Point, Gladstone, Qld 4680, Tel: +61 7 4976 2211, Fax: +61 7 4976 2300, Website: www.qal.com.au
Total length of South Trees Wharf is 478 m

[7]*Eastern Berth:* Exports alumina and imports bunker fuel oil and caustic soda for vessels up to 80 000 dwt. Alumina is loaded onto vessels using a travelling gantry shiploader at an average rate of 1200 t/h

[8]*Western Berth:* Exports bunker coal and imports bauxite for vessels up to 80 000 dwt. Bauxite is unloaded using two travelling gantry ship unloaders with 'clam shell' grabs at an average unloading rate of 2300 t/h combined

[9]*R.G. Tanna Coal Terminal & Clinton Coal Wharf:* Owned and operated by Gladstone Ports Corp
R.G. Tanna Coal Terminal is located adjacent to the Clinton Industrial Estate. Consists of three berths with total wharf length of 1095 m in depth of 18.8 m for vessels up to 220 000 dwt. Three travelling shiploaders operate at 4000-6000 t/h each and can travel the entire length of the wharf. Stockpile cap is 4.5 million t in 16 stockpiles. Three rail unloading stations allow three trains to unload simultaneously at a rate of 6000 t/h

[10]*Barney Point Terminal & Wharf:* Owned and operated by Gladstone Ports Corp
The wharf is 205 m in length with dolphins at each end, and has a depth of 15 m. Exports coal, magnesite, cottonseed and limestone for vessels up to 90 000 dwt (fully loaded) and 150 000 dwt (part-loaded). Total coal stockpile cap is 400 000 t and coal is unloaded at an unloading station and stockpiled at a rate of 2000 t/h. Coal and other dry bulk cargoes travel via a conveyor system to a travelling gantry shiploader that is capable of loading the cargo at a rate of 2000 t/h

[11]*Boyne Wharf:* Owned by Gladstone Ports Corp and operated by Boyne Smelters Ltd.
The wharf is 250 m long with a depth of 15 m. Exports aluminium and imports petroleum coke, liquid pitch and general cargo for vessels up to 60 000 dwt. Aluminium products are stored on a sealed open area near wharf approach. Liquid pitch is stored in two special tanks adjacent to the wharf. Aluminium products are loaded using the vessel's lifting gear whilst petroleum coke is unloaded using a mobile gantry vacuum unloader at a rate of 400 t/h

[12]*Fisherman's Landing:* Owned by Gladstone Ports Corp and operated by multi-users

[13]*Berth No.4:* Exports cement gypsum, limestone, fly ash, cement clinker, cement and imports caustic soda for vessels up to 25 000 dwt. Cement clinker and fly ash are stored in silos and transported to the wharf via conveyor. Cargoes are then loaded onto vessels using a pivoting radial arm shiploader at rate of 2000 t/h

[14]*Berth No.5:* Exports ultra low sulphur naphtha and light fuel oil and imports liquid ammonia for vessels up to 80 000 dwt (part loaded) or 35 000 dwt (fully loaded). Shale oil products are stored in tanks off site and are pumped to the wharf via pipeline. Liquid ammonia is pumped to an adjacent storage tank via pipeline. Cargoes are loaded onto vessels using two SVT 300 mm hydraulically operated loading arms

Bunkering: BP Australia (Proprietary) Ltd, P O Box 5222, Melbourne, Vic., Australia 3001, Tel: +61 3 9268 4111, Fax: +61 3 9268 3321, Email: gomiasfuelsales@bp.com, Website: www.bp.com
ExxonMobil Marine Fuels, 1 Harbour Front Place, 06-00 Harbour Front, Tower One, Singapore, Republic of Singapore 098633, Tel: +65 6885 8998, Fax: +65 6885 8794, Email: asiapac.marinefuels@exxonmobil.com, Website: www.exxonmobilmarinefuels.com – Grades: MGO – Delivery Mode: tank truck
International Bunker Supplies Proprietary Ltd, Majella, 473 St. Kilda Road, Melbourne, Vic., Australia 3004, Tel: +61 3 9211 9360, Fax: +61 3 9211 9365, Email: bunkers@ibsfuels.com, Website: www.ibsfuels.com – Delivery Mode: barge

Towage: SVITZER, SVITZER Australasia, Macfarlan Drive, Gladstone, Qld., Australia 4680, Tel: +61 7 4972 4500, Fax: +61 7 4972 4493, Email: lfleming@adsteam.com.au, Website: www.svitzer.com

Repair & Maintenance: In water repairs can be carried out to all vessels. Small slipway facilities are available in the Gladstone Marina. Small craft up to 35 m loa, 250 dwt and 8 m beam can be serviced

Seaman Missions: The Seamans Mission, P O Box 370, Gladstone, Qld., Australia 4680, Tel: +61 7 4972 0355, Fax: +61 7 4972 0455, Email: gladstone@mts.org.au

Ship Chandlers: O.A.S.I.S. Australia (International) Proprietary Ltd, 1/24 Boolarra Street, Hemmant, Brisbane, Qld., Australia 4174, Tel: +61 7 3390 7666, Fax: +61 7 3390 4844, Email: oasis@oasisintl.net, Website: www.oasisintl.net
Southern Cross Marine Supplies Proprietary Ltd, Unit 4, 35 Chapple Street, Gladstone, Qld., Australia 4680, Tel: +61 7 4972 1044, Fax: +61 7 4972 1889, Email: gladstone@scms.com.au, Website: www.scms.com.au
Vikki Ship Supplies Proprietary Ltd, P O Box 5488, Gladstone, Qld., Australia 4680, Tel: +61 7 4972 0011, Fax: +61 7 4972 0404, Email: sales@vikkishipsupplies.com.au

Shipping Agents: Barwil Agencies Australia Pty Ltd, P O Box 5166, Gladstone, Qld., Australia 4680, Tel: +61 7 4972 8833, Fax: +61 7 4972 8696, Email: gladstone@wilhelmsen.com, Website: www.wilhelmsen.com
Gulf Agency Co (Australia) Pty Ltd, P O Box 1684, Gladstone, Qld., Australia 4680, Tel: +61 7 4972 8879, Fax: +61 7 4972 8510, Email: shipping.gladstone@gacworld.com, Website: www.gacworld.com
Hetherington Kingsbury Proprietary Ltd, P O Box 308, Gladstone, Qld., Australia 4680, Tel: +61 7 4972 5588, Fax: +61 7 4972 5681, Email: atyrrell@hksa.com.au, Website: www.hksa.com.au
Inchcape Shipping Services (ISS), Inchcape Shipping Services Pty Ltd, Suite 6, 25 Tank Street, P O Box 5010, Gladstone, Qld., Australia 4680, Tel: +61 7 4972 2088, Fax: +61 7 4972 4823, Email: gladstone@iss-shipping.com.au, Website: www.iss-shipping.com
McArthur Shipping & Agency Co Pty Ltd, P O Box 1330, Gladstone, Qld., Australia 4680, Tel: +61 7 4972 4133, Fax: +61 7 4972 5681, Email: gladstone@mcaship.com.au, Website: www.mcaship.com.au
Monson Agencies Australia Proprietary Ltd, P O Box 1622, Gladstone, Qld., Australia 4680, Tel: +61 7 4972 8344, Fax: +61 7 4976 9884, Email: gladstone@monson.com.au, Website: www.monson.com.au
Oceanway Shipping Agency Proprietary Ltd, P O Box 305, Gladstone, Qld., Australia 4680, Tel: +61 7 4972 6388, Fax: +61 7 4972 3440, Email: gladstone@oceanway.com.au, Website: www.oceanway.com.au
PDL Toll, Lower Floor, 33 Goondoon Street, P O Box 5006, Gladstone, Qld., Australia 4680, Tel: +61 7 4972 3811, Fax: +61 7 4972 1563, Email: ian.menzies@pdltoll.com, Website: www.pdltoll.com
Seatrans Australia Proprietary Ltd, 1st Floor, 100 Goondoon Street, Gladstone, Qld., Australia 4680, Tel: +61 7 4972 4133, Fax: +61 7 4927 1309, Email: gladstone@mcaship.com.au, Website: www.mcaship.com.au

Stevedoring Companies: Patrick Stevedoring, Auckland Point Wharf, Gladstone, Qld., Australia 4680, Tel: +61 7 4972 3766, Fax: +61 7 4972 3966, Email: mzwisler@patrick.com.au, Website: www.patrick.com.au
Total Stevedoring Services, Nulgarra, Port Alma Road, Bajool, Gladstone, Qld., Australia QLD 4699, Tel: +61 7 4921 4699, Fax: +61 7 4921 4827, Email: tss@cqnet.com.au

Medical Facilities: Available

Airport: Gladstone Airport, 3 km

Development: Construction of Wiggins Island Coal Terminal expected to commence 2009

Lloyd's Agent: Freemans Marine, P O Box 554, Fortitude Valley, Brisbane, Qld., Australia 4006, Tel: +61 7 3867 4646, Fax: +61 7 3867 4699, Email: john.cupitt@freemans.com.au, Website: www.freemansmarine.com.au

GLEBE ISLAND

harbour area, see under Sydney

GORE BAY TERMINAL

harbour area, see under Sydney

GOVE

Lat 12° 11' S; Long 136° 41' E.

Admiralty Chart: AUS 715	**Admiralty Pilot:** 17
Time Zone: GMT +9.5 h	**UNCTAD Locode:** AU GOV

Principal Facilities:

P	Q	Y	G	C				T	A

Authority: Rio Tinto Alcan, Gove Operations, Foreshore Road, Nhulunbuy, N.T., Australia 0880, Tel: +61 8 8987 5418, Fax: +61 8 8987 5410, Email: shipping.gove@alcan.com, Website: www.riotinto.com/riotintoalcan

Port Security: ISPS compliant

Pre-Arrival Information: ETA's required 10 days, 5 days, 48 h and 24 h prior to arrival (including forward and aft drafts)

	Key to Principal Facilities:—				
	A=Airport	**C**=Containers	**G**=General Cargo	**P**=Petroleum	**R**=Ro/Ro	**Y**=Dry Bulk
	B=Bunkers	**D**=Dry Dock	**L**=Cruise	**Q**=Other Liquid Bulk	**T**=Towage (where available from port)	

For bauxite/alumina/hydrate cargoes: cargo quantity to be loaded and estimated forward and aft drafts; hatch load plan (on proforma supplied)
For bulk liquid cargoes: quantity, product and order of discharge

Approach: There is a good wide approach from a NNE direction to Melville Bay between Bremer Island and English Company's Island

Anchorage: No.1 Anchorage: 2.1 miles WNW of West Woody Island in pos 12° 11' S; 136° 40' E in depth of 15 m
No.2 Anchorage: 2.3 miles NW of West Woody Island in depth of approx 18 m. This anchorage is particularly appropriate for loaded tankers awaiting a berth

Pilotage: Compulsory and usually during daylight hours only; carried out by Rio Tinto Alcan Gove employed pilots

Radio Frequency: Alcan Gove maintains a listening watch on VHF Channel 16 for 24 h/day. The port's working channel is VHF 12, call sign 'Gove Harbour'

Weather: The prevailing wind during the dry season from May to October is SE to S, generally easing with nightfall. Strong winds of up to 55 km/h (30 knots) sometimes occur during this period. Prevailing winds during the monsoon season from November to April are light and variable, mainly from NW. Tropical cyclones which occur occasionally during this period may bring full gale force winds

Tides: HWST 3.7 m, HWNT 2.6 m

Maximum Vessel Dimensions: Export Berth: 245 m loa, 33.2 m beam, 13.2 m air draft, 14.6 m sail draft
Tanker Berth: 275 m loa, 12.8 m air draft
General Cargo Berth: 160 m loa, 25 000 dwt, 10.4 m max draft

Principal Imports and Exports: Imports: Bulk liquids, General cargo. Exports: Alumina, Aluminium hydroxide, Bauxite.

Working Hours: 24 h for bulk and tanker vessels

Accommodation:

Name	Depth (m)	Remarks
Bulk Terminal		See [1] below
Berth No.1 Export Wharf	13.5	See [2] below
Berth No.2 Tanker Wharf	13.6	See [3] below
General Cargo Terminal		See [4] below
Jetty (Berth No.5)		See [5] below

[1]*Bulk Terminal:* Located at the western side of Dundas Point and consists of two in-line berths connected to the shore by light traffic access bridge with the two berths forming the head of a 'T'. The length of the bridge is 982 m
[2]*Berth No.1 Export Wharf:* Bauxite and alumina loading berth for vessels up to 275 m loa and beam of 22-33.2 m. Air draft of 13.9 m at HW. Equipped with a travelling, luffing shiploader with a max rate of 2000 t/h for bauxite and alumina, and is connected by a belt conveyor system to the bauxite stockpiles and to the alumina silos, 4100 and 2950 m distant respectively from the wharf head
[3]*Berth No.2 Tanker Wharf:* Bulk liquids discharge berth for vessels up to 275 m loa with max displacement of 90 000 t. Equipped with three centrally located marine unit unloading arms (two of 8" and one of 10") linked to pipelines supported on a trestle structure for fuel oil, caustic soda and white spirit discharge
[4]*General Cargo Terminal:* Located at the eastern side of Dundas Point, 94 m long and 27.89 m wide, and connected to the shore by an access jetty 287.2 m long and 5.49 m wide. Designed for vessels up to 160 m loa and 25 000 dwt. The SW side (Berth No.3) in depth of 10 m and NE side (Berth No.4) in depth of 11.6 m
[5]*Jetty (Berth No.5):* Public wharf located at the head of Gove Harbour to the north of Harbour Island, managed by Perkins Shipping Pty Ltd., P O Box 1270, Nhulunbuy, NT 0881, Tel: +61 8 8987 1482, Fax +61 8 8987 1968, Website: www.perkins.com.au Length 48 m with depth alongside of 4 m at LAT and includes a ramp suitable for ro/ro barges up to 2000 t. Bunker lines for water and distillate available. Use of the wharf is generally reserved for fishing vessels and ro/ro barges

Mechanical Handling Equipment:

Location	Type	Capacity (t)	Qty
Gove	Mobile Cranes	140	9

Bunkering: Not available

Towage: Two tugs available

Repair & Maintenance: Minor repair facilities are available

Shipping Agents: Barwil Agencies Australia Pty Ltd, P O Box 38169, Winnellie, N.T., Australia 0821, Tel: +61 8 8947 2882, Fax: +61 8 8947 2881, Email: darwin@wilhelmsen.com, Website: www.wilhelmsen.com
Nabalco Shipping, Foreshore Road, Nhulunbury, Gove, Australia 0880, Tel: +61 8 8987 5416, Fax: +61 8 8987 5410, Email: shipping@nabalco.com.au

Medical Facilities: A modern hospital is situated at Nhulunbuy, 14.5 km from the port

Airport: Situated 14.5 km S of main town of Nhulunbuy with daily connecting flights to/from Darwin and Cairns

Lloyd's Agent: Maritime & General Insurance Surveyors Proprietary Ltd, Suite 4, 7 Divett Street, Adelaide, S.A., Australia 5015, Tel: +61 8 8341 2552, Fax: +61 8 8241 0229, Email: maritime-general@adam.com.au

GRIFFIN TERMINAL

Lat 21° 13' S; Long 114° 39' E.

Admiralty Chart: AUS 328		**Admiralty Pilot:** 17	
Time Zone: GMT +8 h		**UNCTAD Locode:** AU GRV	

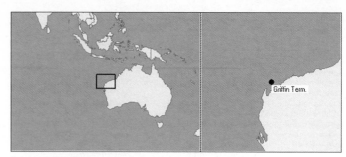

Principal Facilities:

P	Q								

Authority: BHP Billiton Petroleum (Australia) Pty Ltd, G P O Box 86A, Melbourne, Vic., Australia 3001, Tel: +61 3 9609 3015, Fax: +61 3 9609 3333, Website: www.bhpbilliton.com

Pre-Arrival Information: Vessels should advise ETA to the agent and the Terminal's Marine Supervisor 72 h, 48 h and 24 h before arrival giving the following information:
(a) vessel's name and call sign
(b) HF radiotelephone frequencies if so equipped
(c) inmarsat number and satellite in use
(d) arrival draught and trim

Pilotage: Compulsory. The Facility Master boards the export tanker 3 nautical miles from the FPSO

Radio Frequency: A continuous watch is maintained on VHF Channel 72

Maximum Vessel Dimensions: 150 000 dwt

Accommodation:

Name	Remarks
Griffin Terminal	See [1] below

[1]*Griffin Terminal:* Terminal: Tel: +61 8 9159 9013, Fax: +61 8 9159 9016, Email: petgrv.marinesuper@bhpbilliton.com
Oil and gas from the Griffin, Chinook and Scindian fields is produced via the FPSO 'Griffin Venture' . Gas processed on board the vessel is piped 68 km to shore for metering and blending into the Dampier-to-Bunbury Natural Gas Pipeline. The blending plant is 30 km S of Onslow. Natural gas is sold in the Western Australian market under long-term contracts. Crude oil is offloaded from the FPSO to shuttle tankers via a floating hose. Berthing only in daylight hours

Lloyd's Agent: Moko Proprietary Ltd, P O Box 685, Willetton, W.A., Australia 6955, Tel: +61 8 9354 2248, Fax: +61 8 9354 2234, Email: kglange@bigpond.com

GROOTE EYLANDT

alternate name, see Milner Bay

HASTINGS

Lat 38° 17' S; Long 145° 12' E.

Admiralty Chart: AUS 152		**Admiralty Pilot:** 14	
Time Zone: GMT +10 h		**UNCTAD Locode:** AU WEP	

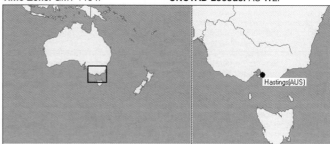

Principal Facilities:

P	Q		G		R		B		T	A

Authority: Patrick, Port of Hastings, Stony Point Road, P O Box 204, Crib Point, Hastings, Vic., Australia 3919, Tel: +61 3 5983 9406, Fax: +61 3 5983 6043, Email: l.ward@patrick.com.au, Website: www.portofhastings.vic.gov.au & www.patrick.com.au

Officials: General Manager: Lindsay Ward.
Harbour Master: Capt Dick Cox, Email: dick.cox@patrick.com.au.

Port Security: ISPS compliant

Approach: Within Western Port Bay are two large islands, French Island in the middle and Phillip Island to seaward, which forms the two approaches to the bay. The Western side is the main entrance marked with fairway buoy ISO.FL.1.0 SEC Racon "Y" - and the only route suitable for large vessels. The navigation channel to Cowes anchorage has a min depth of 14.9 m. The Eastern entrance is narrow and shallow, marked by leads, and suitable only for small vessels with local knowledge
A Naval Gunnery Range is situated south and west of West Head, and active 0930 to 1500 on weekdays. Area R.312B is the area used for surface gunnery practice. Vessels entering or leaving the port should endeavour to keep out of Area R.312B

when it is active. Vessels wishing to transit the area should contact Harbour Control on VHF Channel 16 or 14 for advice on range activity

Anchorage: Main anchorage is at Cowes Roads, between Southern edge Tortoise Head Bank, and Northern shore of Phillip Island. Anchorage is 4 miles in length E-W, and 1.25 miles wide with depths 16 m at Western end decreasing to 11 m at Eastern end
Area adjacent to Long Island Jetty, having least depth of 8.5 m is suitable short term anchorage for medium sized vessels
Area off Stony Point Jetty, having least depth of 10.0 m is suitable short term anchorage for small vessels

Pilotage: Compulsory for all commercial vessels exceeding 30 m loa except those whose master is specifically exempt from pilotage. Pilots for Western Port are available on a 24 h basis. ETA must be given not less than 24 h prior to ship's arrival and again at 4 h before arrival to Port of Hastings and Port Phillip Sea Pilots
Ship's will normally embark their Pilot from a launch, painted orange and showing the signals and lights prescribed for a pilot launch. By day approx 3 miles 180° from West Head and by night in the white sector of McHaffie's Point Light, with Cape Schanck light bearing 295° (white). 38° 34' S; 145° 01' E
Pilots have boarded by helicopter in cases where ship could not supply a safe means of embarkation

Radio Frequency: VHF channels 16 and 14

Tides: The height of tide within the commercial port varies from 2.2 m at neap tides to 3.3 m at springs

Traffic: 2007/08, 200 vessels, 2 842 162 t of cargo handled

Maximum Vessel Dimensions: Max dwt 100 000, max draft (loaded) 15.6 m dependent on tide, max loa 300 m

Principal Imports and Exports: Imports: Steel coil, Steel slab. Exports: Crude oil, LPG, Steel coil.

Accommodation:

Name	Length (m)	Depth (m)	Remarks
Bluescope Steel Wharf			
Berth No.1		12.1	See [1] below
Berth No.2	152	12.1	See [2] below
Stony Point Wharf			See [3] below
Crib Point Jetty			
Berth No.1		15.8	See [4] below
Berth No.2		12.1	See [5] below
Long Island Jetty			
Berth		15.8	See [6] below

[1]*Berth No.1:* Ro/ro berth provides service for vessels with stern door or starboard quarter ramp up to 15 000 dwt. Ramp details: length 28 m (curved), width 8.5 m. Ramp made up of seven sections which are hydraulically operated to allow accommodation of various types of stern loading/unloading vessels
[2]*Berth No.2:* Conventional general cargo wharf, 24 m to 15.6 m wide. Reinforced concrete wharf with wooded fendering. A mooring dolphin is provided 30 m NE. No.2 berth is adjacent and extends in a NE direction from No.1 berth. For vessels up to 200 m loa
[3]*Stony Point Wharf:* Concrete and timber construction with wooded fendering, 190 m long, 6.5 m wide. Depths 2.5 m at S end, 6 m at N end. Used by harbour service craft including two tugs, harbour ferries and small commercial vessels up to 60 m length
[4]*Berth No.1:* Utilised by Trafigura Australia for tankers up to 80 000 dwt. Discharge of motor spirit and automotive diesel to their terminal in Hastings
[5]*Berth No.2:* Decommissioned awaiting future developments. May be used as a repair berth under certain conditions
[6]*Berth:* Utilised by Esso Australia Ltd for vessels up to 165 000 dwt. Export of Gippsland crude oil and LPG

Bunkering: BP Australia (Proprietary) Ltd, P O Box 5222, Melbourne, Vic., Australia 3001, *Tel:* +61 3 9268 4111, *Fax:* +61 3 9268 3321, *Email:* gomiasfuelsales@bp.com, *Website:* www.bp.com
Caltex Australia Petroleum Proprietary Ltd, Caltex Australia Petroleum Proprietary Ltd, No 2 Market Street, Sydney, N.S.W., Australia 2000, *Tel:* +61 2 9668 1148, *Fax:* +61 2 9668 1243, *Email:* mnicholl@caltex.com.au, *Website:* www.caltex.com.au
ExxonMobil Marine Fuels, 1 Harbour Front Place, 06-00 Harbour Front, Tower One, Singapore, Republic of Singapore 098633, *Tel:* +65 6885 8998, *Fax:* +65 6885 8794, *Email:* asiapac.marinefuels@exxonmobil.com, *Website:* www.exxonmobilmarinefuels.com – *Grades:* MGO – *Delivery Mode:* tank truck
Shell Australia Ltd, Shell Company of Australia, Marine Centre Oceania, No 8 Redfern Road, Melbourne, Vic., Australia 3123, *Tel:* +61 3 9666 5446, *Fax:* +61 3 8823 4800, *Email:* sal-marine-products@shell.com, *Website:* www.shell.com.au

Waste Reception Facilities: The Master, Owner or Agent of a ship shall make all arrangements for garbage and rubbish to be collected from ship's within the port and to be delivered to an approved facility for destruction/disposal

Towage: Two tugs available, both of 3800 hp & 50 t bollard pull; they are fitted with VHF radar & fire-fighting equipment

Repair & Maintenance: Crib Point Engineering Proprietary Ltd, Beach Drive, Hastings, Vic., Australia 3915, *Tel:* +61 3 5979 1703, *Fax:* +61 3 5979 3323, *Email:* cpe@cpe.net.au, *Website:* www.cpe.net.au No.2 Crib Point Repair Berth, capable of accommodating vessels up to 95 000 dwt (in ballast), with a depth alongside of 12.8 m. Medium repairs carried out by several local engineering companies
Ocean Engineering Proprietary Ltd, 31 Watts Road, Hastings, Vic., Australia, *Tel:* 61 3, *Fax:* +61 3 5979 3318 No.2 Crib Point Repair Berth, capable of accommodating vessels up to 95 000 dwt (in ballast), with a depth alongside of 12.8 m. Medium repairs carried out by several local engineering companies

Seaman Missions: The Seamans Mission, 26 Bayview Road, P O Box 209, Hastings, Vic., Australia 3915, *Tel:* +61 3 5979 4327, *Fax:* +61 3 5979 4676, *Email:* hastings@mts.org.au

Shipping Agents: Barwil Agencies Australia Pty Ltd, P O Box 361, Melbourne, Vic., Australia 3205, *Tel:* +61 3 9630 0900, *Fax:* +61 3 9630 0999, *Email:* melbourne@barwil.com.au, *Website:* www.barwil.com

Medical Facilities: Available

Airport: Melbourne International, 80 km

Railway: Hastings, 5 km

Lloyd's Agent: Freemans Marine, Level 7, 564 St. Kilda Road, Melbourne, Vic., Australia 3004, *Tel:* +61 3 9935 2400, *Fax:* +61 3 9915 0351, *Email:* lloyds@freemans.com.au, *Website:* www.freemansmarine.com.au

HAY POINT

Lat 21° 17' S; Long 149° 17' E.

Admiralty Chart: AUS 249	**Admiralty Pilot:** 15
Time Zone: GMT +10 h	**UNCTAD Locode:** AU HPT

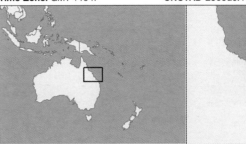

Principal Facilities:

	Y			B	T	A

Authority: Ports Corporation of Queensland, Floor 24, 300 Queen Street, P O Box 409, Brisbane, Qld., Australia 4001, *Tel:* +61 7 3224 7088, *Fax:* +61 7 3224 7234, *Email:* info@pcq.com.au, *Website:* www.pcq.com.au

Officials: Chief Executive Officer: Brad Fish, *Email:* bfish@pcq.com.au. Communications Manager: Rachel Campbell, *Tel:* +61 7 3224 8863, *Email:* rcampbell@pcq.com.au.

Port Security: ISPS compliant

Approach: Approach depths are 13.03 m LAT. Vessels may approach the anchorage area from any easterly direction

Anchorage: While waiting for a berth, vessels should anchor at the anchorage advised by Hay Point Harbour Control, contact by VHF Channel 16, 24 h/day

Pilotage: Compulsory. Pilots are based at Hay Point and require 24 h notice of arrival. Pilots usually board vessel by helicopter if possible
Normal boarding ground is approx 2 nautical miles NE of the Jetty, however, vessels berthing port side to at Hay Point Services berths will be directed to the alternate boarding ground 2 miles SE of the Jetty

Radio Frequency: A continuous watch is maintained on VHF Channel 16 call sign: 'Hay Point Harbour'. VHF Channels 6, 9, 12 and 14 are used for port operations

Weather: The port is situated in the cyclone belt. Season lasts from November to April. During this period cyclone procedures are implemented

Tides: MHWS 5.78 m, MHWN 4.46 m

Traffic: 2007/08, 945 vessels, 80 430 170 t of bulk cargo exported

Maximum Vessel Dimensions: 300 m loa, 56 m beam, 17.5 m draft

Working Hours: 24 h/day in three shifts

Accommodation:

Name	Length (m)	Depth (m)	Remarks
Hay Point Coal Terminal			See [1] below
Berth No.1		16.38	See [2] below
Berth No.2	365	16.68	See [3] below
Dalrymple Bay Coal Terminal			See [4] below
Berth No.1		17.9	
Berth No.2		18.3	
Berth No.3		18.9	

[1]*Hay Point Coal Terminal:* Owned & operated by BHP Billiton Mitsubishi Alliance (BMA)
[2]*Berth No.1:* Used for the export of coking coal from the Bowen Basin coal fields, the berth is situated approx 1.6 km from the shore on a steel piled trestle jetty, together with two mooring and six breasting dolphins at each end giving it a berthing face of 204 m loa. Shiploader has max rate of 4000 t/h
[3]*Berth No.2:* Used for the export of coking coal from the Bowen Basin coal fields, the berth is situated approx 1.6 km from the shore on a steel piled trestle jetty, together with two mooring and six breasting dolphins at each end giving it a berth face of 189 m loa. Shiploader has max rate of 6000 t/h
[4]*Dalrymple Bay Coal Terminal:* Leased from the State Government by Babcock & Brown Infrastructure (BBI), *Website:* www.bbinfrastructure.com
Operated by Dalrymple Bay Coal Terminal Pty Ltd., Martin Armstrong Drive, Hay Point, Qld 4740, Tel: +61 7 4943 8444, Fax: +61 7 4943 8466, Website: www.dbct.com.au
Wharf at the head of a 3.85 km long approach jetty which carries a 3.76 m wide roadway and a conveyor gallery. Vessels from 20 000 to 200 000 dwt can be accommodated. There are eighteen berthing dolphins and four mooring dolphins at Berths 1 & 2 and seven berthing dolphins and four mooring dolphins at Berth 3. Three shiploaders with a loading rate of 7200 t/h

Bunkering: Bunkers are not available at the port. Diesel oil obtainable from small barge depending on weather conditions in anchorage

Waste Reception Facilities: Quarantine waste disposal service for the following types of waste: organic waste, paper, glass, plastic, galley waste, hold sweepings and general waste

Key to Principal Facilities:—					
A=Airport	**C**=Containers	**G**=General Cargo	**P**=Petroleum	**R**=Ro/Ro	**Y**=Dry Bulk
B=Bunkers	**D**=Dry Dock	**L**=Cruise	**Q**=Other Liquid Bulk	**T**=Towage (where available from port)	

Towage: Hay Point Services Berths: two tugs each of 70 t bollard pull and line boats located at Hay Point Tug Harbour. Dalrymple Bay Coal Terminal: two tugs each of 55 t bollard pull and two line boats located at Hay Point Tug Harbour

Shipping Agents: Barwil Agencies Australia Pty Ltd, Shop 4 Valroy Street, Half Tide (M.S. 283), Mackay, Qld., Australia 4740, *Tel:* +61 7 4956 3666, *Fax:* +61 7 4956 3555, *Email:* haypoint@wilhelmsen.com, *Website:* www.wilhelmsen.com

Airport: Mackay, 40 km

Railway: Mackay Railway Station, 40 km. Sarina Railway Station, 26 km

Lloyd's Agent: Freemans Marine, P O Box 554, Fortitude Valley, Brisbane, Qld., Australia 4006, *Tel:* +61 7 3867 4646, *Fax:* +61 7 3867 4699, *Email:* john.cupitt@freemans.com.au, *Website:* www.freemansmarine.com.au

HOBART

Lat 42° 52' S; Long 147° 20' E.

Admiralty Chart: AUS 172/170		**Admiralty Pilot:** 14	
Time Zone: GMT +10 h		**UNCTAD Locode:** AU HBA	

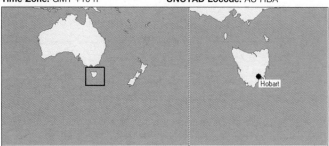

Principal Facilities:

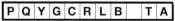

P Q Y G C R L B T A

Authority: Tasmanian Ports Corp. Proprietary Ltd (TasPorts), 1 Franklin Wharf, P O Box 202, Hobart, Tas., Australia 7001, *Tel:* +61 3 6235 1000, *Fax:* +61 3 6231 0693, *Email:* hobart@tasports.com.au, *Website:* www.tasports.com.au

Officials: Chief Executive Officer: Robert Barnes.
Port Manager: Charles Black, *Tel:* +61 3 6421 4911, *Email:* charles.black@tasports.com.au.
Marketing Manager: Charles Scarafiotti, *Tel:* +61 3 6421 4911, *Email:* charles.scarafiotti@tasports.com.au.

Port Security: ISPS compliant

Approach: Channel: River Derwent Entrance, depth 14.1 m; Tasman Bridge, depth 22 m; D'Entrecasteaux Channel, depth 10.2 m; Huon River (S approach to Beaupre Point), depth 22 m; Hospital Bay, depth 8.5 m

Anchorage: May be obtained in any part of the River Derwent, clear of the prohibited anchorages. The safest anchorage is always to be obtained on the W side of the river for the E side is unsafe, especially for small vessels
Anchorage is prohibited in the following areas:
a) Sullivans Cove: to the W of a circle centred on 42° 52.12' S; 147° 20.8' E, from Macquarie No.6 Wharf to the extension of the line of Princes No.4 Wharf
b) within 150 m either side of the Tasman Bridge
c) within the main navigation channel of the Tasman Bridge
d) within 0.5 nm either side of the cable crossing from Blackmans Bay to Halfmoon Bay

Pilotage: Compulsory for all vessels over 35 m loa
For vessels bound for Hobart (including Risdon), the Pilot boarding position is approx 125°(T) by 0.9 nm on an imaginary line E/W along the parallel of Lat 42° 55.5' S across the width of the River Derwent
For vessels bound to either Hobart (Risdon) from the S, via the D'Entrecasteaux Channel, the pilot boarding ground is on a line drawn from the S end of Partridge Island (43° 24.6' S; 147° 06.0' E) to Southport Island
All pilots are stationed at Hobart. The pilot launches are fitted with VHF radio and monitor VHF Channels 12 and 16
The regular pilot boat to Service Zones 'A', 'B' and 'C' of the port is a orange hulled vessel named 'Paringa'. The port calling channel is VHF Channel 12
Special signals: An exempt Master displays by day, a white square flag superior to the berth number. By night, a green over red light, visible all round the horizon. A vessel having a pilot on board displays by day the pilot flag ('H') superior to the berth number and by night displays the green over red lights
The boundaries of the pilotage areas in which pilotage is required are as follows:
Hobart Zone 'A':
a) bounded to the S by an imaginary line E/W along the parallel of Lat 42° 55.5' S across the width of the River Derwent; and
b) to the N by an imaginary line drawn from the diamond shaped beacons, orange in colour, located approx 450 m S of Tasman Bridge in the western shore to another pair of diamond shaped beacons, orange in colour, similarly located on the eastern shore
Hobart Zone 'B':
a) bounded to the S by an imaginary line drawn from the diamond shaped beacons, orange in colour, located approx 450 m S of Tasman Bridge on the western shore to another pair of diamond shaped beacons, orange in colour, similarly located on the eastern shore; and
b) to the N by an imaginary line bearing 082°(T) from Dowsing Point to the eastern point of the River Derwent
Port Huon Zone 'C':
a) to the Hobart Zone 'C' pilotage limit bounded to the S by an imaginary line bearing 223°(T) from the southern end of Partisdge Island to Southport Island; and
b) to the N by an imaginary line bearing 138°(T) from Person Point to Kelly Point

Radio Frequency: Master's of vessels wishing to communicate with the harbour authorities or agents may address messages through the Overseas Telecommunication Commission (OTC) coast radio station Melbourne Radio (VIM)
VIM maintains a 24 h listening watch on the following frequencies: HF 2,182, 4,125, 6,215.5, 8,291 kHz, VHF Channels 16 and 67, Sea phone channels 07 and 27
Traffic lists: HF 2,201, 4,426, 6,507, 8,176 kHz: 0018, 0218, 0618, 1218, 1418, 1618 and 1818 hrs (UTC)
No time signals are transmitted by VIM
Weather forecasts are transmitted daily as follows: 0403, 0803, 2003 hrs (UTC) on the HF traffic list frequencies
All gale, navigational and strong wind warnings are transmitted on the HF traffic list frequencies immediately upon receipt and every 2 hrs on an even number (UTC) times
VHF: The Tasmanian Ports Corporation (Tasports) maintains a port control station in Hobart. The station is manned throughout 24 hrs and a listening watch is kept on Channel 16 (156.8MHz) and Channel 12 (156.6MHz). When contact has been satisfactorily established all traffic must be passed through Channel 12. Vessels can usually establish contact on Channel 16 at ranges in excess of 50 nm from Hobart. This range is extended for vessels passing to the E of Tasmania where contact can be established near Maria Island. Callsign, 'Hobart Port Control' should be used
Small Craft Radio: Coast Radio Hobart (VMT232). This station maintains a listening watch on VHF Channel 16 and HF. The following distress frequencies monitored 24 hrs 7 days as part of the National Coast radio network - 4125 kHz, 6215 kHz and 8291 kHz. Weather forecasts are announced on VHF Channel 16 and provided on Ch 67 & Ch 68 at 0745, 1345 & 1903 7 days

Tides: Tides at Hobart are irregular, the max rise and fall being 1.37 m. See the Australian National Tide Tables

Traffic: 2007/08, 209 commercial vessels & 28 cruise vessels, 2 992 402 t of cargo handled

Working Hours: 24 h/day

Accommodation:

Name	Length (m)	Depth (m)	Remarks
Hobart			
Princes Berth No.1	138	6.9	See [1] below
Princes Berth No.2	100	7.6	See [2] below
Princes Intermediate Berth	65	7.2	See [3] below
Princes Berth No.3	88	8.6	Owned by Commonwealth Government 'CSIRO'
Princes Berth No.4	120	6.8	See [4] below
Elizabeth St Pier (South)	157	7.7	Berthing for small vessels only
Elizabeth St Pier (North)	153	7.2	Berthing for pleasure vessels
Macquarie Berth No.1	169	4.1	See [5] below
Macquarie Berth No.2	154	8.7	See [6] below
Macquarie Berth No.3	174	9.5	See [7] below
Macquarie Berth No.4	244.2	12.6	See [8] below
Macquarie Berth No.5	135	12.6	See [9] below
Macquarie Berth No.6	189	11	See [10] below
Selfs Point, Petroleum Product Discharge Wharf			See [11] below
Spring Bay Berth - Triabunna			See [12] below
Risdon Wharf			See [13] below

[1]*Princes Berth No.1:* Ro/ro berth, with 1650 m2 of wharf apron and a fixed ramp with 40 t axle loadings and the ability to accept vessels up to 22 m beam. Used primarily as a lay-up berth for Antarctic vessels and to accommodate visiting naval vessels
[2]*Princes Berth No.2:* Consists of an inside storage area of 1920 m2 with outside storage of 3269 m2 including an apron area width of 7.6 m. Axle loading 22 t. Used primarily as a cruise ship berth
[3]*Princes Intermediate Berth:* Covers the paddock area and is included in the overall berth length of Princes 2/3
[4]*Princes Berth No.4:* Ro/ro berth, owned by 'CSIRO'. Wheel loading 22 860 kg. Fixed 22.5 t crane, max outreach 20.1 m
[5]*Macquarie Berth No.1:* Berth is used to unload fish for processing in the fish handling centre. Wharf shed is leased to a fish processing company and the Department of Primary Industry (quarantine)
[6]*Macquarie Berth No.2:* Shed space of 6620 m2 with 2295 m2 wharf apron area, 25 t axle loading and five individual cool stores totalling 7680 m3
[7]*Macquarie Berth No.3:* Shed space of 2060 m2 and the wharf apron area is 6500 m2, 25 t axle loading with a stiffened area on apron of 58 t axle loading
[8]*Macquarie Berth No.4:* Back up storage area of 3.6 ha paved to accept 70 t axle loading. The shed is currently leased to the Australian Antarctic Division. The area of the shed is 2600 m2, 120 reefer points. Access is also available via a rail spur
[9]*Macquarie Berth No.5:* Wharf apron width 22.9 m. The wharf shed which has an area of 4510 m2 is leased to a transport company
[10]*Macquarie Berth No.6:* Wharf apron width 43.6 m, transit shed of 4000 m2. There is a fixed ramp facility available
[11]*Selfs Point, Petroleum Product Discharge Wharf:* Consists of a steel pile and concrete decking with a single axle loading on the approach stem of 10 t. The approach stem which is 200 m in length has a between curb width of 3.4 m. The stem head is 100 m in length, width 12 m, with a deck height above CD of 4.08 m. A draft of 14.0 m below CD is available
Four dolphins of 100 t cap each service either end of the wharf with an overall distance apart of 258 m. Each dolphin is fitted with two quick release hooks, connected by gangways to the jetty head. In addition to the quick response fire fighting equipment, the wharf is equipped with two fire-fighting monitors, mounted on 2 x 11 m towers, situated toward the extremities of the stem head. Each monitor is capable of throwing foam/water solution 70 m, with an independent water supply. As each monitor is capable of operating with foam or water, the needs of either product or gas tankers using the wharf will be covered
[12]*Spring Bay Berth - Triabunna:* Operated by Gunns Ltd.
This berth, which is located on the E coast of Tasmania, 85 nm NE of Hobart, is used exclusively for the export of woodchips. The wharf length is 244 m, and 441.9 m over the dolphins. The berth has a declared depth of 11 m and the deck is 4.58 m above CD. The following axel loads apply at this berth 14 t single or 10 t dual at the head and 10 t single and 7.5 t dual at the stem. For 50 000 t bulk carriers
[13]*Risdon Wharf:* Privately owned by Zinifex Ltd

Situated 2 nm above the Tasman Bridge on the W side of the river, this wharf serves the requirements of Zinifex Ltd, formerly Pasminco Metals EZ. Imports of raw and semi-processed materials such as zinc concentrates and phosphate rock etc are discharged via a modern conveyor system and grab discharge utilising a gantry crane with grabs of 12 t cap. Exports of bulk cargo, paragoethite and superphosphate etc are loaded into overseas and interstate vessels by a shiploader facility at 300 t/h. Processed zinc product is consolidated at Macquarie for shipment via the rail network, road transport or vessel

Extensions to the wharf at the N end take the form of a separate berth designed to accommodate specially constructed acid tanker vessels for the export of sulphuric acid in bulk. Length of Berth No's 1 & 2 is 250 m; min depth 9.8 m, height of wharf decking above CD is 3.7 m

Storage: Macquarie No.6 shed has 4000 m2 of undercover general purpose cargo storage available in addition to 3.8 ha of sealed marshalling area with cap for 204 reefer containers

'Tasports Cold Store' has extensive cold and dry storage facilities, and warehousing services tailored to satisfy total supply chain management

Facilities are export registered, accredited by State and federal authorities, and working with exporters and importers in maintaining the quality standards demanded of both domestic and international clients

The Cold Store is able to provide storage, blast freezing, wet fish handling, cross docking, tempering (heating), container loading and unloading all within our fully registered export/import and fish receivers store

Mechanical Handling Equipment: Comprehensive fleet of forklift trucks available for hire seven days a week with capacities ranging from 3.6 t to 32 t. They are available for hire with or without driver, depending on customer requirements. Driver training is available if required and is conducted by a Workplace Standards Authority-accredited trainer

Container crane with 35 t swl at 27.7 m reach and 31.5 t swl at 31 m reach. Lift height of 27 m from wharf. Operational length 340 m

Bunkering: Facilities available at Self's Point Oil Jetty for marine fuel and diesel oil through pipelines. Also available at other berths by road tanker with prior permission Australian Petroleum Proprietary Ltd, Solander Street, Kurnell, Sydney, N.S.W., Australia, Tel: +61 2 972 2597, Fax: +61 2 981 1159 – Grades: MGO – Parcel Size: truck min 30t, pipeline no min – Rates: truck 30t/h, pipeline 100t/h – Notice: 48 hours – Delivery Mode: pipeline, truck

BP Australia (Proprietary) Ltd, P O Box 5222, Melbourne, Vic., Australia 3001, Tel: +61 3 9268 4111, Fax: +61 3 9268 3321, Email: gomiasfuelsales@bp.com, Website: www.bp.com

Caltex Australia Petroleum Proprietary Ltd, Caltex Australia Petroleum Proprietary Ltd, No 2 Market Street, Sydney, N.S.W., Australia 2000, Tel: +61 2 9668 1148, Fax: +61 2 9668 1243, Email: mnicholl@caltex.com.au, Website: www.caltex.com.au

ExxonMobil Marine Fuels, 1 Harbour Front Place, 06-00 Harbour Front, Tower One, Singapore, Republic of Singapore 098633, Tel: +65 6885 8998, Fax: +65 6885 8794, Email: asiapac.marinefuels@exxonmobil.com, Website: www.exxonmobilmarinefuels.com – Grades: MGO – Delivery Mode: tank truck

Waste Reception Facilities: Garbage from all vessels is collected by Tasport's personnel or an approved contractor for disposal under quarantine requirements

Towage: North Western Shipping & Towage Proprietary Ltd, 4 Hornby Road, P O Box 775, Glenorchy, Tas., Australia 7010, Tel: +61 3 6272 3277, Fax: +61 3 6272 4801, Email: inquiries@nwst.com.au, Website: www.nwst.com.au

Repair & Maintenance: Tasmanian Ports Corp. Proprietary Ltd (TasPorts), 1 Franklin Wharf, P O Box 202, Hobart, Tas., Australia 7001, Tel: +61 3 6235 1000, Fax: +61 3 6231 0693, Email: hobart@tasports.com.au, Website: www.tasports.com.au Three slipways of 1200 t, 180 t and 25 t cap

Seaman Missions: The Seamans Mission, 31 Morrison Street, Hobart, Tas., Australia 7000, Tel: +61 3 6234 6016, Fax: +61 3 6234 8155, Email: hobart@mts.org.au

Ship Chandlers: W. Chung Sing & Co. Proprietary Ltd, P O Box 1277, Hobart, Tas., Australia 7001, Tel: +61 3 6234 5033, Fax: +61 3 6234 5354, Email: wchung@chung.com.au, Website: www.chung.com.au

Tasmanian Shipping Supplies, P O Box 20, Sandy Bay, Tas., Australia 7006, Tel: +61 3 6224 2510, Fax: +61 3 6224 2480, Email: tasshipping@fader.com.au, Website: www.tasshipping.com.au

Shipping Agents: Barwil Agencies Australia Pty Ltd, P O Box 311, George Town, Tas., Australia 7253, Tel: +61 3 6382 4088, Fax: +61 3 6382 4099, Email: bellbay@wilhelmsen.com, Website: www.wilhelmsen.com

Hetherington Kingsbury Proprietary Ltd, P O Box 250, Hobart, Tas., Australia 7001, Tel: +61 3 6234 9601, Fax: +61 3 6234 9653, Email: hobart@hksa.com.au, Website: www.hksa.com.au

Horizon Shipping Agencies, Level 1, Macquarie No 3 Shed, Mcquarie Wharf, Hobart, Tas., Australia 7000, Tel: +61 3 6223 7623, Fax: +61 3 6231 4930, Email: hba@horizonshipping.com.au

Inchcape Shipping Services (ISS), Inchcape Shipping Services Pty Ltd, P O Box 1720, Hobart, Tas., Australia 7001, Tel: +61 3 6224 1470, Fax: +61 3 6224 4103, Email: hobart@iss-shipping.com.au, Website: www.iss-shipping.com

McArthur Shipping & Agency Co Pty Ltd, P O Box 250, Hobart, Tas., Australia 7001, Tel: +61 3 6234 9601, Fax: +61 3 6234 9653, Email: tasmania@mcaship.com.au, Website: www.mcaship.com.au

Seatrans Australia Proprietary Ltd, 57B Best Street, Hobart, Tas., Australia 7310, Tel: +61 3 6424 6995, Fax: +61 3 6424 8870, Email: devonport@mcaship.com.au

Stevedoring Companies: Capital Stevedoring, P O Box 202, Hobart, Tas., Australia, Tel: +61 3 6235 1068, Fax: +61 3 6231 0693, Website: www.capitalstevedoring.com.au

P&O Ports, P O Box 271, Hobart, Tas., Australia 7001, Fax: +61 3 6234 7680

Surveyors: Det Norske Veritas A/S, 1 Franklin Wharf, 7th Floor, Hobart, Tas., Australia 7000, Tel: +61 3 6224 8799, Fax: +61 3 6224 8720, Email: hobart@dnv.com, Website: www.dnv.com.au

Medical Facilities: The Royal Hobart Hospital is located within 1 km of the port. Private hospitals also available

Airport: Hobart International Airport, 18 km

Lloyd's Agent: Freemans Marine, Level 7, 564 St. Kilda Road, Melbourne, Vic., Australia 3004, Tel: +61 3 9935 2400, Fax: +61 3 9915 0351, Email: lloyds@freemans.com.au, Website: www.freemansmarine.com

HOLDEN DOCK

harbour area, see under Melbourne

INNISFAIL

Lat 17° 31' S; Long 146° 5' E.

Admiralty Chart: AUS 829	**Admiralty Pilot:** 15
Time Zone: GMT +10 h	**UNCTAD Locode:** AU IFL

This port is no longer open to commercial shipping

INSPECTION HEAD

harbour area, see under Launceston

KARUMBA

Lat 17° 29' S; Long 140° 50' E.

Admiralty Chart: AUS 410	**Admiralty Pilot:** 17
Time Zone: GMT +10 h	**UNCTAD Locode:** AU KRB

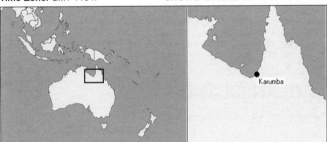

Principal Facilities:

P		Y	G	C					

Authority: Ports Corporation of Queensland, Floor 24, 300 Queen Street, P O Box 409, Brisbane, Qld., Australia 4001, Tel: +61 7 3224 7088, Fax: +61 7 3224 7234, Email: info@pcq.com.au, Website: www.pcq.com.au

Officials: Chief Executive Officer: Brad Fish, Email: bfish@pcq.com.au. Communications Manager: Rachel Campbell, Tel: +61 7 3224 8863, Email: rcampbell@pcq.com.au.

Port Security: ISPS compliant

Pilotage: Pilot boards in pos 17° 25.0' S; 140° 42.6' E (0.8 nautical mile NW of No.1 Lt Bn)

Traffic: 2007/08, 64 vessels, 1 072 791 t of cargo handled

Principal Imports and Exports: Exports: Cattle.

Accommodation:

Name	Remarks
Karumba	See [1] below

[1]Karumba: Located at the mouth of the Norman River in the SE corner of the Gulf of Carpentaria. Privately-owned wharves for the handling of general cargo, livestock, seafood and petroleum

Shipping Agents: Barwil Agencies Australia Pty Ltd, P O Box 1055, Townsville, Qld., Australia 4810, Tel: +61 7 4721 4955, Fax: +61 7 4772 5743, Email: townsville@wilhelmsen.com, Website: www.wilhelmsen.com

Stevedoring Companies: Perkins Shipping Proprietary Ltd, Yappar Street, P O Box 122, Karumba, Qld., Australia 4891, Tel: +61 7 4745 9333, Fax: +61 7 4745 9383, Email: perkins@perkins.com.au, Website: www.perkins.com.au

Lloyd's Agent: Freemans Marine, P O Box 554, Fortitude Valley, Brisbane, Qld., Australia 4006, Tel: +61 7 3867 4646, Fax: +61 7 3867 4699, Email: john.cupitt@freemans.com.au, Website: www.freemansmarine.com.au

KLEIN POINT

Lat 34° 55' S; Long 137° 47' E.

Admiralty Chart: AUS 125/139	**Admiralty Pilot:** 13
Time Zone: GMT +9.5 h	**UNCTAD Locode:** AU KLP

Key to Principal Facilities:—				
A=Airport	**C**=Containers	**G**=General Cargo	**P**=Petroleum	**R**=Ro/Ro	**Y**=Dry Bulk
B=Bunkers	**D**=Dry Dock	**L**=Cruise	**Q**=Other Liquid Bulk	**T**=Towage (where available from port)

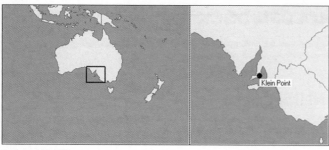

Principal Facilities:

		Y				T	

Authority: Flinders Ports Proprietary Ltd, 3 Diagonal Road, Wallaroo, S.A., Australia 5556, *Tel:* +61 8 8823 2026, *Fax:* +61 8 8823 2026, *Email:* flindersports@flindersports.com.au, *Website:* www.flindersports.com.au

Officials: Business Development Manager: Stewart Lammin, *Tel:* + +61 8 8447 0627, *Email:* lammin.stewart@flindersports.com.au.

Approach: Depth in entrance channel is 6.5 m

Pilotage: Not compulsory

Traffic: 2007/08, 267 vessels, 1 910 079 t of cargo exported

Accommodation:

Name	Length (m)	Depth (m)	Apron Width (m)	Remarks
Klein Point Berth	150	6.5	30	See [1] below

[1]*Berth:* Handling shipments of limestone. Facilities are privately owned by Adelaide Brighton Cement

Towage: Tugs available from Adelaide if required

Lloyd's Agent: Maritime & General Insurance Surveyors Proprietary Ltd, Suite 4, 7 Divett Street, Adelaide, S.A., Australia 5015, *Tel:* +61 8 8341 2552, *Fax:* +61 8 8241 0229, *Email:* maritime-general@adam.com.au

KOOLAN ISLAND

alternate name, see Yampi Sound

KURNELL

harbour area, see under Botany Bay

KWINANA

see under Fremantle

LAMINARIA-CORALLINA TERMINAL

Lat 10° 40' S; Long 126° 0' E.

Admiralty Chart: AUS 312	**Admiralty Pilot:** 17
Time Zone: GMT +9.5 h	**UNCTAD Locode:** AU

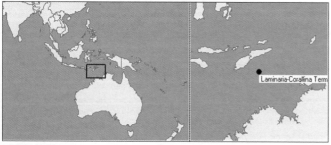

Principal Facilities:

P							

Authority: Woodside Energy Ltd, P O Box 188, 240 St Georges Toe, Perth, W.A., Australia 6840, *Tel:* +61 8 9348 4000, *Fax:* +61 8 9214 2777, *Email:* companyinfo@woodside.com.au, *Website:* www.woodside.com.au

Officials: Port Superintendent: John Jenkin, *Email:* john.jenkin@woodside.com.au.

Pilotage: Compulsory. Vessels should send ETA 72 h, 48 h, 24 h and 12 h in advance to the terminal and the duty pilot via the vessel's agent. Pilot boards in pos 10° 34' S; 125° 59' E

Radio Frequency: VHF Channels 16 and 12

Accommodation:

Name	Remarks
Laminaria-Corallina Terminal	See [1] below

[1]*Laminaria-Corallina Terminal:* Consists of FPSO 'Northern Endeavour' (Fax: +61 (8) 9348 6683) which can produce up to 170 000 bbls of oil a day and has a storage cap of 1 400 000 bbls. The Northern Endeavour is permanently moored between the Laminaria and Corallina fields which allows production on-site, and allows tankers to moor astern of the Northern Endeavour to load the crude oil that Laminaria produces. Crude oil is delivered to the Northern Endeavour from the Laminaria-Corallina fields by a series of subsea pipelines which are connected to four production wells in the Laminaria field, two production wells in Corallina, and a separate gas re-injection well

Lloyd's Agent: Moko Proprietary Ltd, P O Box 685, Willetton, W.A., Australia 6955, *Tel:* +61 8 9354 2248, *Fax:* +61 8 9354 2234, *Email:* kglange@bigpond.com

LAUNCESTON

Lat 41° 26' S; Long 147° 8' E.

Admiralty Chart: AUS 168	**Admiralty Pilot:** 14
Time Zone: GMT +10 h	**UNCTAD Locode:** AU LST

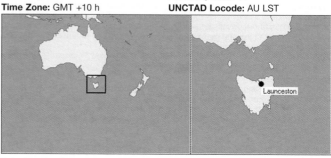

Principal Facilities:

P	Q	Y	G	C	R	L	B		T	A

Authority: Tasmanian Ports Corp. Proprietary Ltd (TasPorts), Locked Bag 4, Georgetown, Launceston, Tas., Australia 7253, *Tel:* +61 3 6380 3011, *Fax:* +61 3 6382 1695, *Email:* bellbay@tasports.com.au, *Website:* www.tasports.com.au

Officials: Chief Executive Officer: Robert Barnes.
Port Manager: Charles Black, *Tel:* +61 3 6421 4911, *Email:* charles.black@tasports.com.au.

Port Security: ISPS compliant

Approach: Vessels over 35 m long must remain North of Lat 41 02 while awaiting a pilot

Anchorage: Outer anchorage in pos 41° 01' S; 146° 45.7' E in depth of 26 m

Pilotage: Compulsory for vessels over 35 m loa. Pilot boarding pos is 41° 01.2' S; 146° 44.3' E

Radio Frequency: Bell Bay Port Control 24 h watch VHF Channels 12 and 16 (8 and 67 on demand)

Weather: Outer anchorage not suitable in strong northerly winds

Tides: Pilot Station: 3.1 m HWS, 2.75 m HWN. George Town: 3.1 m HWS, 3.0 m HWN

Traffic: 2007/08, 445 vessels, 5 512 592 t of cargo handled, 89 458 TEU's

Maximum Vessel Dimensions: 265 m loa. Max permissible draft at LW is 9.0 m, at HW 11.5 m

Principal Imports and Exports: Imports: Alumina, Fuel, General cargo, Manganese ore, Pulp. Exports: Aluminium, Manganese alloys, MDF, Timber products, Woodchips.

Working Hours: 24 h/day

Accommodation:

Name	Length (m)	Depth (m)	Remarks
Bell Bay			On E shore within 7 nautical miles of the entrance
No.1 Comalco Berth (Private)	152	10.8	Alumina & liquid pitch
No.2 Ro/ro & Container Berth	86	8.4	See [1] below
No.3 Berth	152	11.2	See [2] below
No.4 Berth	54	12	See [3] below
No.5 Berth	210	12	See [4] below
No.6 Berth	313	9–12.4	See [5] below
Long Reach			On E shore within 12 nautical miles of the entrance
Thermal Station Berth	26	12.3	Fender dolphins 61 m apart
Woodchip Berth No.1 (North)	217	11.5	See [6] below
Woodchip Berth No.2 (South)	229	11.2	See [7] below
Inspection Head			On W shore within 6.5 nautical miles of the entrance
Wharf	335	9.9	See [8] below

[1]*No.2 Ro/ro & Container Berth:* A specially designed terminal for Bass Strait ships and equipped with stern loading facilities capable of carrying wheeled or mobile cargo in excess of 120 t gross weight. 102 power outlets are provided for 120 freezer containers and a marshalling area of 4.72 ha. Ro/ro ramp of 20 m width and 200 t cap

[2]*No.3 Berth:* For the handling of general & bulk cargoes. Wharf able to carry 140 t loads on suitable transporters. Transit shed space of 744 m2
[3]*No.4 Berth:* For the import of petroleum products & LPG. Tanker terminal with mooring dolphins 245 m apart. Two 250 mm and one 100 mm pipeline
[4]*No.5 Berth:* Operated by Australian Amalgamated Terminals
Container & general cargo. Marshalling area of 2.3 ha and 144 reefer points
[5]*No.6 Berth:* Designed for container, ro/ro, conventional & bulk cargoes. Transit shed space of 2675 m2 and marshalling area of 3.8 ha. Ro/ro ramp, 8.23 m wide with a cap of 100 t. 143 reefer points
[6]*Woodchip Berth No.1 (North):* Consisting of five fender dolphins and two mooring dolphins. Woodchip loader fixed in centre of berth face at 700 t/h
[7]*Woodchip Berth No.2 (South):* Consisting of five fender dolphins and two mooring dolphins. Woodchip loader fixed in centre of berth face at 700 t/h
[8]*Wharf:* Two berths for cruise vessels only, otherwise not used commercially

Storage:

Location	Cold (m³)
Launceston	22864

Mechanical Handling Equipment:

Location	Type	Capacity (t)	Qty
No.2 Ro/ro & Container Berth	Portal Cranes	30	1
No.3 Berth	Mobile Cranes	19	1
No.5 Berth	Mobile Cranes	100	1
No.5 Berth	Container Cranes	24–36	1
No.6 Berth	Portal Cranes	50	1

Cargo Worked: Bulk discharge 350-450 t/h, woodchip loading 900 t/h

Bunkering: Bunker oil available in bulk at Oil Wharf or by road tanker, depending on quantity required
BP Australia (Proprietary) Ltd, P O Box 5222, Melbourne, Vic., Australia 3001, *Tel:* +61 3 9268 4111, *Fax:* +61 3 9268 3321, *Email:* gomiasfuelsales@bp.com, *Website:* www.bp.com
ExxonMobil Marine Fuels, 1 Harbour Front Place, 06-00 Harbour Front, Tower One, Singapore, Republic of Singapore 098633, *Tel:* +65 6885 8998, *Fax:* +65 6885 8794, *Email:* asiapac.marinefuels@exxonmobil.com, *Website:* www.exxonmobilmarinefuels.com – *Grades:* IFO180-380cSt; MGO – *Delivery Mode:* barge, truck, pipeline

Waste Reception Facilities: Quarantine incinerator and commercial waste disposal contractors available

Towage: North Western Shipping & Towage Proprietary Ltd, 4 Hornby Road, P O Box 775, Glenorchy, Tas., Australia 7010, *Tel:* +61 3 6272 3277, *Fax:* +61 3 6272 4801, *Email:* inquiries@nwst.com.au, *Website:* www.nwst.com.au

Seaman Missions: The Seamans Mission, P O Box 55, George Town, Tas., Australia 7253, *Tel:* +61 3 6382 3088, *Fax:* +61 3 6382 2719, *Email:* bellbay@mts.org.au

Shipping Agents: Barwil Agencies Australia Pty Ltd, P O Box 311, George Town, Tas., Australia 7253, *Tel:* +61 3 6382 4088, *Fax:* +61 3 6382 4099, *Email:* bellbay@wilhelmsen.com, *Website:* www.wilhelmsen.com
Pacific Asia Express Proprietary Ltd, 38A Canning Street, Launceston, Tas., Australia 7250, *Tel:* +61 3 6333 0422, *Fax:* +61 3 6333 0288, *Email:* sh.pae@ilm.com.au, *Website:* www.pilship.com

Stevedoring Companies: P&O Ports, 50 Formby Road, Devon Port, Launceston, Tas., Australia 7310, *Tel:* +61 3 6424 6785, *Fax:* +61 3 6424 5453, *Email:* darrell.liddell@poports.com.au, *Website:* www.poports.com.au

Medical Facilities: Launceston General Hospital and Georgetown District Hospital

Airport: Launceston Airport, 1 h drive from port

Railway: The port is serviced by a regular rail (containers) service

Lloyd's Agent: Freemans Marine, Level 7, 564 St. Kilda Road, Melbourne, Vic., Australia 3004, *Tel:* +61 3 9935 2400, *Fax:* +61 3 9915 0351, *Email:* lloyds@freemans.com.au, *Website:* www.freemansmarine.com.au

LEGENDRE TERMINAL

Lat 19° 42' S; Long 116° 43' E.

Admiralty Chart: AUS 327	**Admiralty Pilot:** 17
Time Zone: GMT +8 h	**UNCTAD Locode:** AU LGT

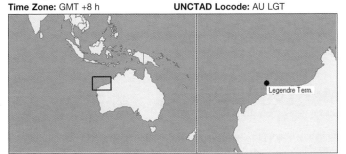

Principal Facilities:

P						T	

Authority: Woodside Energy Ltd, P O Box 188, 240 St Georges Toe, Perth, W.A., Australia 6840, *Tel:* +61 8 9348 4000, *Fax:* +61 8 9214 2777, *Email:* companyinfo@woodside.com.au, *Website:* www.woodside.com.au

Officials: Port Superintendent: John Jenkin, *Email:* john.jenkin@woodside.com.au.

Port Security: Being on offshore terminal all persons visiting the terminal are subject to security screening by Woodside prior to helicopter transfer. All persons boarding the offtake tanker with the Pilot are also subject to Woodside security screening. Crew transfers at the anchorage are subject to customs/immigration screening

Pre-Arrival Information: Agents forward to the vessel a standard format prior to arrival on behalf of the Terminal. The information requested includes basic arrival details of ETA, draft and displacement; confirmation of ship's operational readiness and load rate; confirmation of manning requirements whilst vessel is at the terminal and that vessel has not had adverse reports since nomination
Pre-arrival information from the Terminal is forwarded via agents and refers to cargo and berthing expectations, anchorages and communications at Port of Dampier whilst awaiting pilot and pilot boarding requirements. The agents also forward the loading schedule when available

Anchorage: As advised, vessels await pilot at approaches to port of Dampier. There are no anchorages at the Terminal, however good holding ground can be found at Glomar Shoals about 20 miles NE

Accommodation:

Name	Remarks
Legendre Terminal	See [1] below

[1]*Legendre Terminal:* Consists of FSO 'Karratha Spirit' in depth of 50 m. Nine oil storage tanks of 45 000-120 000 bbls totalling 770 000 bbls with export cap of 650 000 bbls of crude oil in 24 h. Transfer hose from FSO to export tanker of 16" dia, 270 m long, double carcass-type, flotation hose

Towage: An offshore support vessel attends all offtakes to assist with hose and hawser handling and static towing duties

Lloyd's Agent: Moko Proprietary Ltd, P O Box 685, Willetton, W.A., Australia 6955, *Tel:* +61 8 9354 2248, *Fax:* +61 8 9354 2234, *Email:* kglange@bigpond.com

LONG ISLAND POINT JETTY

harbour area, see under Hastings

LONG REACH

harbour area, see under Launceston

LUCINDA

Lat 18° 31' S; Long 146° 19' E.

Admiralty Chart: AUS 259	**Admiralty Pilot:** 15
Time Zone: GMT +10 h	**UNCTAD Locode:** AU LUC

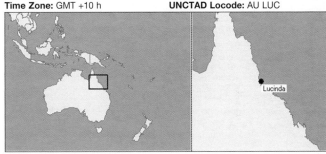

Principal Facilities:

		Y					T	

Authority: Ports Corporation of Queensland, Floor 24, 300 Queen Street, P O Box 409, Brisbane, Qld., Australia 4001, *Tel:* +61 7 3224 7088, *Fax:* +61 7 3224 7234, *Email:* info@pcq.com.au, *Website:* www.pcq.com.au

Officials: Chief Executive Officer: Brad Fish, *Email:* bfish@pcq.com.au.
Communications Manager: Rachel Campbell, *Tel:* +61 7 3224 8863, *Email:* rcampbell@pcq.com.au.

Port Security: ISPS compliant

Approach: The offshore wharf is located 087 degrees(T), 3.1 nautical miles from Lucinda weigh tower. There are no dangers and there is good holding ground everywhere between berth and offshore islands

Anchorage: Offshore wharf anchorage; 18° 30' S, 146° 24'. E. Anchoring is prohibited within 360 m of offshore wharf and approach jetty

Pilotage: Compulsory. Pilotage is arranged through the Duty Pilot at Cairns, Tel: +61 7 4031 9609. Vessels for the offshore berth will be boarded by pilot 1.5 miles NNE of the wharf, off the S entrance bar

Radio Frequency: VHF Channels 16, 12 and 6, call sign 'Lucinda Port'. No regular watch is kept but manned if vessels are due

Tides: MHWS 2.68 m, MHWN 1.85 m

Traffic: 2007/08, 17 vessels, 575 497 t of bulk cargo exported

Maximum Vessel Dimensions: 220 m loa, 45 000 dwt

Principal Imports and Exports: Exports: Raw sugar.

Working Hours: Continuous

Accommodation:

Name	Remarks
Lucinda	See [1] below

[1]*Lucinda:* Operated by Lucinda Bulk Sugar Terminal Organisation
The offshore wharf for handling bulk sugar extends 5.6 km from the shore with a wharf

---

Key to Principal Facilities:—				
A=Airport	C=Containers	G=General Cargo	P=Petroleum	R=Ro/Ro	Y=Dry Bulk
B=Bunkers	D=Dry Dock	L=Cruise	Q=Other Liquid Bulk	T=Towage (where available from port)	

length of 213 m, depth 13.6 m LWD. Sugar handled by conveyor system from three storage sheds with a cap of 231 000 t. Loading rate 2000 t/h

Mechanical Handling Equipment:

Location	Type	Qty	Remarks
Lucinda	Mult-purp. Cranes	1	used for loading of sugar

Towage: Available with notice as tugs come from other ports

Shipping Agents: Barwil Agencies Australia Pty Ltd, P O Box 1055, Townsville, Qld., Australia 4810, *Tel:* +61 7 4721 4955, *Fax:* +61 7 4772 5743, *Email:* townsville@wilhelmsen.com, *Website:* www.wilhelmsen.com

Medical Facilities: Doctor and dentist available

Lloyd's Agent: Freemans Marine, P O Box 554, Fortitude Valley, Brisbane, Qld., Australia 4006, *Tel:* +61 7 3867 4646, *Fax:* +61 7 3867 4699, *Email:* john.cupitt@freemans.com.au, *Website:* www.freemansmarine.com.au

MACKAY

Lat 21° 6' S; Long 149° 13' E.

Admiralty Chart: AUS 250	**Admiralty Pilot:** 15
Time Zone: GMT +10 h	**UNCTAD Locode:** AU MKY

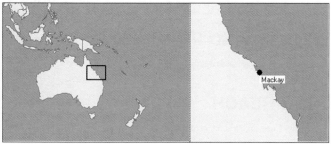

Principal Facilities:

P	Q	Y	G			B		T	A

Authority: Mackay Port Authority, P O Box 3340, North Mackay, Qld., Australia 4740, *Tel:* +61 7 4955 8155, *Fax:* +61 7 4955 2868, *Email:* mpa@mackayports.com, *Website:* www.mackayports.com

Officials: Chief Executive Officer: Jeff Harris.
Executive Assistant: Cathy Swan, *Email:* cswan@mackayports.com.
Operations Manager: John Kraft, *Email:* jkraft@mackayports.com.

Port Security: ISPS compliant

Approach: The width of the entrance channel is 180 m and depth 8.5 m. The swinging basin has a depth of 8.5 m and a width of 510 m. The max draft of vessels that may enter the port can be calculated by dividing the sum of 8.5 m and height of tide by 1.1. Vessels enter harbour on slack water only, which occurs 1-1.5 hours before LW and HW; sailing any time depending on draught and swell conditions at entrance

Anchorage: Recommended anchorage between 1.5-2 miles E of Slade Island

Pilotage: Required for all foreign flag vessels over 35 m loa and Australian flag vessels over 50 m loa. Vessels should send ETA to agents at least 48 h in advance and request pilot 24 h in advance. Pilotage carried out by Port Pilots Queensland. Pilot boards in pos 21° 07' S; 149° 16' E, two nautical miles ESE of the Southern Breakwater

Radio Frequency: VHF Channels 16, 13 and 6

Weather: Prevailing SE'ly winds

Tides: Tidal range of 6.3 m

Traffic: 2007/08, 190 vessels, 2 476 219 t of cargo handled

Maximum Vessel Dimensions: 225 m loa, 32.5 m beam, underkeel clearance rule applies for draft

Principal Imports and Exports: Imports: Fertiliser, Magnetite, Petroleum. Exports: Grain, Sugar.

Working Hours: Monday-Friday 0800-1630

Accommodation:

Name	Length (m)	Depth (m)	Remarks
Mackay			
Berth No.1	208	10.6	See [1] below
Berth No.4	225	10.6	See [2] below
Berth No.5	270	12	Grain, loader rated at 1000 t/h
Love's Jetty		3.4	Consists of 8 berths for passenger & pleasure craft

[1]*Berth No.1:* Petroleum, molasses, tallow, ethanol & general cargo for vessels up to 210 m loa
[2]*Berth No.4:* Refined sugar, loader rated at 500 t/h. One silo of 45 000 t cap

Storage:

Location	Covered (m²)	Grain (t)
Mackay	3000	
Berth No.5		32000

Mechanical Handling Equipment:

Location	Type	Capacity (t)	Qty
Mackay	Mobile Cranes	25	1
Mackay	Forklifts		3
Berth No.5	Mult-purp. Cranes		1

Cargo Worked: Raw sugar up to 2000 t/h. Refined sugar up to 500 t/h. Grain up to 1000 t/h

Bunkering: Midstate Fuel, Harbour Road, Outer Harbour, Mackay, Qld., Australia, *Tel:* +61 79 551 911, *Fax:* +61 79 554 616
BP Australia (Proprietary) Ltd, P O Box 5222, Melbourne, Vic., Australia 3001, *Tel:* +61 3 9268 4111, *Fax:* +61 3 9268 3321, *Email:* gomiasfuelsales@bp.com, *Website:* www.bp.com
Canegrowers Ampol, Harbour Road, Outer Harbour, Mackay, Qld., Australia, *Tel:* +61 7 4972 2597, *Fax:* +61 7 4981 1159 – *Grades:* MGO – *Rates:* 200t/h – *Notice:* 6 hours – *Delivery Mode:* wharf, barge, truck
Midstate Fuel, Harbour Road, Outer Harbour, Mackay, Qld., Australia, *Tel:* +61 79 551 911, *Fax:* +61 79 554 616

Waste Reception Facilities: Garbage disposal daily by the Port Authority. Dirty ballast and chemical waste by road tanker (limited quantities)

Towage: Two tugs of 52 t bollard pull and 42 t bollard pull are available from North Queensland Marine Towage Pty Ltd
SVITZER, SVITZER Australasia, The Harbour Masters Boat Shed, Outer Harbour, Mackay, Qld., Australia 4740, *Tel:* +61 7 4955 1389, *Fax:* +61 7 4955 5498, *Email:* info.qld@adsteam.com.au, *Website:* www.svitzer.com

Repair & Maintenance: NJ Industries, Mackay, Qld., Australia, *Tel:* +61 7 4955 1466
Slipway capable of accepting vessels up to 600 gt

Ship Chandlers: Oasis Australia (Mackay) Proprietary Ltd, 1/44 Elvin Street, Paget, Mackay, Qld., Australia 4740, *Tel:* +61 7 4952 6988, *Fax:* +61 7 4952 6399, *Email:* oasis@oasisintl.net, *Website:* www.oasisintl.net
Southern Cross Marine Supplies Proprietary Ltd, P O Box 5113, No.38 Enterprise Street, Mackay, Qld., Australia 4740, *Tel:* +61 7 4952 5377, *Fax:* +61 7 4952 5416, *Email:* mackay@scms.com.au, *Website:* www.scms.com.au

Shipping Agents: Barwil Agencies Australia Pty Ltd, Shop 4 Valroy Street, Half Tide (M.S. 283), Mackay, Qld., Australia 4740, *Tel:* +61 7 4956 3666, *Fax:* +61 7 4956 3555, *Email:* haypoint@wilhelmsen.com, *Website:* www.wilhelmsen.com
C.& S. Shipping Agency Proprietary Ltd, P O Box 39, Mackay, Qld., Australia 4740, *Tel:* +61 7 4957 5246, *Fax:* +61 7 4957 5276, *Email:* b.cruise@mcaship.com.au
Gulf Agency Co (Australia) Pty Ltd., P O Box 1057, Mackay, Qld., Australia 4740, *Tel:* +61 7 4953 4775, *Fax:* +61 7 4944 1303, *Email:* shipping.mackay@gacworld.com, *Website:* www.gacworld.com
Hetherington Kingsbury Proprietary Ltd, P O Box 39, Mackay, Qld., Australia 4740, *Tel:* +61 7 4957 5246, *Fax:* +61 7 4957 5276, *Email:* mackay@hksa.com.au, *Website:* www.hksa.com.au
Inchcape Shipping Services (ISS), Inchcape Shipping Services Pty Ltd, Houwing House - Unit 2, 105 Alfred Street, P O Box 54, Mackay, Qld., Australia 4740, *Tel:* +61 7 4953 3155, *Fax:* +61 7 4953 3120, *Email:* mackay@iss-shipping.com.au, *Website:* www.iss-shipping.com
McArthur Shipping & Agency Co Pty Ltd, P O Box 102, Mackay, Qld., Australia 4740, *Tel:* +61 7 4951 3877, *Fax:* +61 7 4957 5276, *Email:* mackay@mcaship.com.au, *Website:* www.mcaship.com.au
Monson Agencies Australia Proprietary Ltd, Suite 13, 136 Wood Street, Mackay, Qld., Australia 4740, *Tel:* +61 7 4957 3860, *Fax:* +61 7 4957 6824, *Email:* mackay@monson.com.au, *Website:* www.monson.com.au
Oceanway Shipping Agency Proprietary Ltd, P O Box 6276, Mackay Mail Centre, Mackay, Qld., Australia 4741, *Tel:* +61 7 4944 0566, *Fax:* +61 7 4944 1252, *Email:* mackay@oceanway.com.au, *Website:* www.oceanway.com.au
Seatrans Australia Proprietary Ltd, Unit 3, Riverside Plaza, River Street, Mackay, Qld., Australia 4740, *Tel:* +61 7 4951 3877, *Fax:* +61 7 4951 3214, *Email:* mackay@mcaship.com.au

Stevedoring Companies: Northern Shipping & Stevedoring Proprietary Ltd, Mackay, Qld., Australia, *Tel:* +61 7 4955 6975, *Fax:* +61 7 4955 6587, *Email:* acolborne@bigpond.com

Medical Facilities: All facilities available

Airport: Mackay, 6 km

Railway: Mackay, 5 km

Lloyd's Agent: Freemans Marine, P O Box 554, Fortitude Valley, Brisbane, Qld., Australia 4006, *Tel:* +61 7 3867 4646, *Fax:* +61 7 3867 4699, *Email:* john.cupitt@freemans.com.au, *Website:* www.freemansmarine.com.au

MARIBYNONG

harbour area, see under Melbourne

MARYBOROUGH

Lat 25° 32' S; Long 152° 43' E.

Admiralty Chart: AUS 365/426	**Admiralty Pilot:** 15
Time Zone: GMT +10 h	**UNCTAD Locode:** AU MBH

This port is no longer open to commercial shipping

MELBOURNE

Lat 37° 49' S; Long 144° 55' E.

Admiralty Chart: AUS 154/155	**Admiralty Pilot:** 14
Time Zone: GMT +10 h	**UNCTAD Locode:** AU MEL

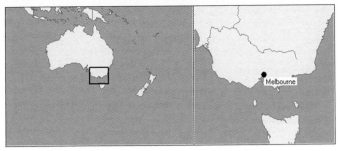

Principal Facilities:

| P | Q | Y | G | C | R | L | B | D | T | A |

Authority: Port of Melbourne Corp., Level 4, 530 Collins Street, Melbourne, Vic., Australia 3000, *Tel:* +61 3 9683 1300, *Fax:* +61 3 9683 1570, *Email:* information@portofmelbourne.com, *Website:* www.portofmelbourne.com.au

Officials: Executive Chairman: Bill Scales, *Email:* bill.scales@portofmelbourne.com. Chief Executive Officer: Stephen Bradford, *Tel:* +61 3 9683 1387, *Email:* stephen.bradford@portofmelbourne.com.
Marketing Manager: Amelia Georgoulos, *Tel:* +61 3 9683 1370, *Email:* amelia.georgoulos@portofmelbourne.com.
Harbour Master: Capt David I. Shennan, *Tel:* +61 3 9683 1463, *Email:* david.shennan@portofmelbourne.com.

Port Security: ISPS compliant

Approach: Fawkner light beacon marks the S end of the 7.2 km long entrance channel leading into Port Melbourne, Williamstown, Webb Dock and the Yarra River mouth; the channel and the river are dredged to 13.1 m as far as 5.6 km above the breakwater light. A Gross Under Keel Clearance of 1.5 m is required at all times when navigating in the channel south of the junction of Williamstown and Port Melbourne channels. (Manoeuvrability Margin 0.9 m & Squat Allowance 0.6 m). A Gross Under Keel Clearance of 1.2 m is required at all times when navigating in channels north of the junction of Williamstown and Port Melbourne channels. (Manoeuvrability Margin 0.6 m & no allowance for Squat). A Gross Under Keel Clearance of 0.6 m is required when manoeuvring within swinging basins, docks and berths. (Manoeuvrability Margin 0.6 m & no allowance for Squat). Vessels over 183 m require 10% of draft in the Yarra River or Webb Dock. Port Phillip South Channel max draught is 11.6 m, or up to 12.1 m with sufficient tide, provided certain criteria are met. Refer to Harbour Master's directions in Operating Handbook. Enquiries should be directed to the Duty Shipping Control Officer at Harbour Control, Tel: +61 3 9644 9700

Anchorage: Safe anchorage may be obtained in an area 2.4 km due S of the breakwater light, extending S and to the W of the Port Melbourne channel. Depth varies from 11-15 m

Pilotage: Compulsory, except for interstate and intrastate vessels whose Masters hold a current Exemption Certificate and a vessel not exceeding 100 t being a vessel employed solely in fishing; or used as a pleasure yacht and not engaged in trading or plying for hire or valuable consideration or the booking of passages by contract
The pilot boarding ground is outside Port Phillip Heads with Port Lonsdale Lighthouse bearing 045° 2.5 nautical miles distance. All pilotage within Port Phillip Bay, the Ports of Melbourne, Geelong and Westernport are supplied by the Port Phillip Sea Pilots Pty Ltd., PO Box 150, North Melbourne, Vic 3051, Tel: +61 3 9329 9700, Fax: +61 3 9326 6052, Email: operations@ppsp.com.au
A pilot station is located at Queenscliff (adjacent to Port Phillip Heads) and at Williamstown. Pilots board vessels from fast cutters

Radio Frequency: Movement of traffic within the Port of Melbourne is controlled by Control Officers operating from Harbour Control who direct all shipping movements in and out of the Port and co-ordinate all ancillary services connected with shipping movements on a 24 h basis
The radio call sign is 'Harbour Control' and the following frequencies and channels are available continuously
156.3 mHz Channel 06 used generally for Interstate Shipping
156.4 mHz Channel 08 pilots and tugs
156.6 mHz Channel 12 Port Philip working channel
156.65 mHz Channel 13 pilots and tugs
156.8 mHz Channel 16 calling and distress
156.375 mHz Channel 67 calling and distress

Weather: Winds are generally W-SW but severe storm squalls are experienced during Nov-Mar

Tides: Port Phillip Heads MHHW 1.4 m, MLHW 1.3 m. Williamstown HHW 0.7 m, LHW 0.6 m

Traffic: 2007/08, 3422 commercial vessels & 44 cruise vessels, 30 822 241 t of cargo handled, 2 256 310 TEU's

Principal Imports and Exports: Imports: Crude oil, Electrical equipment, Machinery & vehicle parts, Motor vehicles. Exports: Cereal grains (rice & wheat), Dairy products, Fruit & vegetables, Motor vehicles, Stockfeeds.

Working Hours: 0730-1430 (with two hours overtime Monday, Tuesday and Wednesday if second shift not available), 1430-2100, 2400-0700. Saturday, 0730-1130. Sundays at overtime rates 0730-1430, 1430-2130

Accommodation: The facilities managed include 493 ha of land, berths, buildings, roads, railways, plant and equipment. There are currently 30 commercial berths at five docks, river wharves and Gellibrand Pier
The berths service two modern, purpose-built international container terminals as well as multi-purpose berths that handle cargoes ranging from timber to motor vehicles and specialised berths for dry cargoes including cement, grain, sugar, fly ash and gypsum, plus dedicated facilities for a variety of liquids from molasses to crude oil and petrochemicals, using the latest handling methods
Station Pier Outer East and Station Pier Outer West have an International Cruise Ship Terminal which is approx 4 km from the Melbourne Central Business District
Tanker facilities: Three oil berths operated by the Port Corporation for vessels up to 289 m long with 11.2 m draft. Night berthing possible depending on vessels length
LPG terminal situated on W side of Breakwater Pier

Name	Length (m)	Depth (m)	Draught (m)	Remarks
South Wharf				
Berth No.26	266	11	10.4	MCF bulk cement berth
Berth No.27	146	9.4	8.8	MCF bulk cement & common user berth
Berth No.28	146	9.4	8.8	Lay-up & common user berth apron
Berth No.29	146	9.4	8.8	Lay-up & common user berth apron
Berth No.33	210	11.6	11	See [1] below
Appleton Dock				
Berth B	192	10.7	10.1	See [2] below
Berth C	192	10.7	10.1	See [3] below
Berth D	200	10.7	10.1	See [4] below
Berth E	137	10.7	10.1	ANL coastal berth (containers)
Berth F	263	11.4	10.8	See [5] below
Swanson Dock				
Berth No's 1-4 West	944	13.1	12.1	See [6] below
Berth No's 1-4 East	884	13.1	12.1	See [7] below
Victoria Dock				
Dock	315	9.4	8.8	Common user general cargo berth
Yarraville				
Berth No.5	148	9.4	8.8	See [8] below
Berth No.6	205	10.2	9.6	Common user bulk cargo berth
Holden Dock				
Oil Berth		13.1	12.1	Oil terminal
Maribyrnong				
Berth No.1		10	9.4	Bulk liquid terminal
Port Melbourne				
Station Pier Inner East	220	10.9	10.3	TT Line-ferry terminal
Station Pier Outer East	223	10.9	10.3	Cruise ship terminal LOA>225 m - Head in only
Station Pier Inner West	95	8	7.4	Cruise ship terminal
Station Pier Outer West	400	10.9	10.3	Cruise ship terminal
Webb Dock				
East No.1 Berth	210	7	6.4	See [9] below
East No.2 Berth	150	7	6.4	Operated by SeaRoad Shipping - Ro/ro Berth
East No.3 Berth	210	10	9.4	See [10] below
East No.4 Berth	280	12.5	11.9	See [11] below
East No.5 Berth	250	12.5	11.9	See [12] below
Williamstown Area				
Breakwater Pier	70			Not used for shipping
Gellibrand Pier		12.1	11.2	See [13] below

[1]*Berth No.33:* Common user berth - two bulk cement terminals
[2]*Berth B:* P&O Automotive & General Stevedoring. General cargo
[3]*Berth C:* P&O Automotive & General Stevedoring. General cargo
[4]*Berth D:* P&O Automotive & General Stevedoring. General cargo
[5]*Berth F:* Common user berth with ABA priority - requires 'Head in' berthing for shiploader use
[6]*Berth No's 1-4 West:* Operated by DP World Melbourne, P O Box 4732, Melbourne, Vic 3001, Tel: +61 3 9687 4266, Fax: +61 3 9687 4482
Dedicated container berths
[7]*Berth No's 1-4 East:* Operated by Patrick Corporation, Tel: +61 3 9688 5600, Fax: +61 3 9687 4318
Dedicated container berths. On-dock rail access
[8]*Berth No.5:* Operated by CSR Ltd., Tel: +61 3 9687 4086
Bulk sugar/gypsum berth. 16 m overlap allowed at each end
[9]*East No.1 Berth:* Operated by TOLL Shipping - Ro/ro Berth, Tel: +61 3 9299 8400, Fax: +61 3 9299 8430
General cargo berth
[10]*East No.3 Berth:* Operated by Patrick Stevedoring, Tel: +61 3 9647 8777, Fax: +61 3 9646 7610
Container and general cargo berth
[11]*East No.4 Berth:* Operated by Patrick Stevedoring, Tel: +61 3 9647 8777, Fax: +61 3 9646 7610
Container and general cargo berth
[12]*East No.5 Berth:* Operated by Patrick Stevedoring, Tel: +61 3 9647 8777, Fax: +61 3 9646 7610
General cargo berth
[13]*Gellibrand Pier:* Operated by Mobil Refiniing Aus. Oil Terminal

Bunkering: Holden Oil Dock and at any berth by barge. Night berthing possible
BHP Transport Proprietary Ltd, Level 27, 600 Bourke Street, P O Box 86A, Melbourne, Vic., Australia 3001, Tel: +61 3 9602421, Fax: +61 3 96092250, Website: www.bhp.com.au/transport
BP Australia (Proprietary) Ltd, P O Box 5222, Melbourne, Vic., Australia 3001, Tel: +61 3 9268 4111, Fax: +61 3 9268 3321, Email: gomiasfuelsales@bp.com, Website: www.bp.com
Chevron Ltd, 500 Collins Street, Melbourne, Vic., Australia, Tel: +61 3 649 4222, Fax: +61 3 629 1609
International Bunker Supplies Proprietary Ltd, Majella, 473 St. Kilda Road, Melbourne, Vic., Australia 3004, Tel: +61 3 9211 9360, Fax: +61 3 9211 9365, Email: bunkers@ibsfuels.com, Website: www.ibsfuels.com
Shell Australia Ltd, Shell Company of Australia, Marine Centre Oceania, No 8 Redfern Road, Melbourne, Vic., Australia 3123, Tel: +61 3 9666 5446, Fax: +61 3 8823 4800, Email: sal-marine-products@shell.com, Website: www.shell.com.au

---

Key to Principal Facilities:—			
A=Airport	**C**=Containers	**G**=General Cargo	**P**=Petroleum	**R**=Ro/Ro	**Y**=Dry Bulk
B=Bunkers	**D**=Dry Dock	**L**=Cruise	**Q**=Other Liquid Bulk	**T**=Towage (where available from port)	

BP Australia (Proprietary) Ltd, P O Box 5222, Melbourne, Vic., Australia 3001, *Tel:* +61 3 9268 4111, *Fax:* +61 3 9268 3321, *Email:* gomiasfuelsales@bp.com, *Website:* www.bp.com – *Grades:* FO; MDO; MGO

Caltex Australia Petroleum Proprietary Ltd, Caltex Australia Petroleum Proprietary Ltd, No 2 Market Street, Sydney, N.S.W., Australia 2000, *Tel:* +61 2 9668 1148, *Fax:* +61 2 9668 1243, *Email:* mnicholl@caltex.com.au, *Website:* www.caltex.com.au

Chevron Australia, 500 Collins Street, Melbourne, Vic., Australia, *Tel:* +61 3 649 4222, *Fax:* +61 3 629 1609 – *Grades:* all grades

ExxonMobil Marine Fuels, 1 Harbour Front Place, 06-00 Harbour Front, Tower One, Singapore, Republic of Singapore 098633, *Tel:* +65 6885 8998, *Fax:* +65 6885 8794, *Email:* asiapac.marinefuels@exxonmobil.com, *Website:* www.exxonmobilmarinefuels.com – *Grades:* IFO180-380cSt; MGO – *Delivery Mode:* barge, tank truck, pipeline

Shell Australia Ltd, Shell Company of Australia, Marine Centre Oceania, No 8 Redfern Road, Melbourne, Vic., Australia 3123, *Tel:* +61 3 9666 5446, *Fax:* +61 3 8823 4800, *Email:* sal-marine-products@shell.com, *Website:* www.shell.com.au – *Grades:* FO; MDO; MGO

Towage: PB Towage (Australia) Proprietary Ltd, Unit 1, 3 Westside Avenue, Port Melbourne, Melbourne, Vic., Australia 3207, *Tel:* +61 3 9645 3688, *Fax:* +61 3 9645 2311, *Email:* meltug@pbtowage.com.au, *Website:* www.pbtowage.com

SVITZER, SVITZER Australasia, 30 South Wharf, 629 Lorimer Street, Melbourne, Vic., Australia 3207, *Tel:* +61 3 9646 0322, *Fax:* +61 3 9646 0217, *Email:* info.vic@adsteam.com.au, *Website:* www.svitzer.com

Repair & Maintenance: Australian Marine Engineering Corp. Consolidated (AMECON), Alfred Graving Dock, Williamstown, Melbourne, Vic., Australia Dry dock 146.2 m x 29.6 m x 7.92 m

Melbourne Marine Services Proprietary Ltd, Melbourne, Vic., Australia, *Tel:* +61 3 9315 2155, *Fax:* +61 3 9315 2276 A floating dock of 156 m x 24 m with a lifting cap of 8000 t

Seaman Missions: The Seamans Mission, Flying Angel Centre, 717 Flinders Street, Melbourne, Vic., Australia 3005, *Tel:* +61 3 9629 7083, *Fax:* +61 3 9629 8450, *Email:* melbourne@mts.org.au

Ship Chandlers: Australian Shipping Supplies (a Division of Tasmanian Shipping Supplies), 6/31 Ascot Vale Road, Ascot Vale, Melbourne, Vic., Australia 3030, *Tel:* +61 3 9372 6112, *Fax:* +61 3 9372 6926, *Email:* sales@ausshipping.com.au, *Website:* www.ausshipping.com.au

BW Technologies, Unit 5, 8-20 Brock Street, Thomastown, Melbourne, Vic., Australia 3074, *Tel:* +61 3 9464 2770, *Fax:* +61 3 9464 2772, *Email:* info@bwtnet.com, *Website:* www.gasmonitors.com

Jotun Australia Pty Ltd, P O Box 105, Altona North, Melbourne, Vic., Australia 3025, *Tel:* +61 3 9314 0722, *Fax:* +61 3 9314 0423, *Email:* sales@jotun.com.au, *Website:* www.jotun.com.au

Liferaft Servicing Group (LSG), P O Box 108, Kingsville, Melbourne, Vic., Australia 3012, *Tel:* +61 3 9362 0011, *Fax:* +61 3 9362 0245, *Email:* vic@liferaftservicing.com.au, *Website:* www.liferaftservicing.com.au

Philip Morris Ltd, 252 Chesterville Road, Moorabbin, Melbourne, Vic., Australia 3184, *Tel:* +61 3 8531 1328, *Fax:* +61 3 8531 1936, *Email:* deborah.oreilly@pmInternational.com

Total Maritime Ship Supply Proprietary Ltd, P O Box 1296, Altona Gate, Melbourne, Vic., Australia 3025, *Tel:* +61 3 9391 0211, *Fax:* +61 3 9391 0266, *Email:* sales@totalmarine.net.au

Wiltrading Proprietary Ltd, 136-140 Hall Street, Spotswood, Melbourne, Vic., Australia 3015, *Tel:* +61 3 9398 0151, *Fax:* +61 3 9360 2244, *Email:* melbourne@wilh.com.au, *Website:* www.wiltrading.com

Shipping Agents: ANL Container Line Proprietary Ltd, Level 7, 432 St. Kilda Road, G P O Box 2238, Melbourne, Vic., Australia 3001, *Tel:* +61 3 9257 0555, *Fax:* +61 3 9257 0619, *Email:* colacog@anl.com.au, *Website:* www.anl.com.au

Asiaworld Shipping Services Proprietary Ltd, Suite 2, 1st Floor, 14 Queens Road, Melbourne, Vic., Australia 3004, *Tel:* +61 3 9866 6955, *Fax:* +61 3 9821 4553, *Email:* aw.melbourne@asiaworld.com.au, *Website:* www.asiaworld.com.au

Barwil Agencies Australia Pty Ltd, P O Box 361, Melbourne, Vic., Australia 3205, *Tel:* +61 3 9630 0900, *Fax:* +61 3 9630 0999, *Email:* melbourne@barwil.com, *Website:* www.barwil.com

Bass Link Ives Logistics, 5 Prohasky Street, Melbourne, Vic., Australia 3207, *Tel:* +61 3 9646 3388, *Fax:* +61 3 9646 2557, *Email:* enquiry@basslink.net.au, *Website:* www.basslink.net.au

Braid Logistics Australia Pty Ltd, Bronson House, Suite 4, 53 Cherry Street, Werribee, Melbourne, Vic., Australia 3043, *Tel:* +61 3 9731 8500, *Fax:* +61 3 9731 8555, *Email:* shane.watson@braidco.com.au, *Website:* www.braidco.com

CMA-CGM S.A., CMA CGM Australia Proprietary Ltd, 432 St Kilda Road, P O Box 2238, Melbourne, Vic., Australia 3004, *Tel:* +61 3 9279 4100, *Fax:* +61 3 9279 4199, *Website:* www.cma-cgm.com

Evergreen Shipping Agency (Australia) Proprietary Ltd, Level 3, 607 Bourke Street, Melbourne, Vic., Australia 3000, *Tel:* +61 3 8628 8888, *Fax:* +61 3 8628 8828, *Email:* melallstaff@evergreen-shipping.com.au, *Website:* www.evergreen-line.com

Five Star Shipping & Agency Co. Proprietary Ltd, Level 1, 535 Flinders Lane, Melbourne, Vic., Australia 3000, *Tel:* +61 3 9258 2600, *Fax:* +61 3 9614 6260, *Email:* pedgley@cosco.com.au, *Website:* www.fivestarshipping.com.au

Gulf Agency Co (Australia) Pty Ltd., Unit B 1.2, 63-85 Turner Street, Melbourne, Vic., Australia 3207, *Tel:* +61 3 9646 8544, *Fax:* +61 3 9646 0785, *Email:* shipping.melbourne@gacworld.com, *Website:* www.gacworld.com

Hanjin Shipping Australia Pty Ltd, Level 1, 100 Albert Road, Melbourne, Vic., Australia 3205, *Tel:* +61 3 9695 0000, *Fax:* +61 3 9682 4799, *Email:* pryan@au.hanjin.com, *Website:* www.hanjin.com

A Hartrodt International, 5-7 Aerolink Drive, P O Box 105, Melbourne, Vic., Australia, *Tel:* +61 3 9330 6666, *Fax:* +61 3 9330 6699, *Email:* melbourne@hartrodt.com.au, *Website:* www.hartrodt.com.au

Hetherington Kingsbury Proprietary Ltd, P O Box 1074, Melbourne, Vic., Australia 3205, *Tel:* +61 3 9699 4122, *Fax:* +61 3 9699 4342, *Email:* chall@hksa.com.au, *Website:* www.hksa.com.au

Holyman Marine Agencies, Holyman House, 188 Bay Street, Melbourne, Vic., Australia 3207, *Tel:* +61 3 9646 7273, *Fax:* +61 3 9646 7274, *Email:* hlmmel@holyman-agencies.com.au

Horizon Shipping Agencies, Level 3,, 448 St Kilda Road, Melbourne, Vic., Australia 3004, *Tel:* +61 3 9861 1300, *Fax:* +61 3 9861 1399, *Email:* mel@horizonshipping>com.au

Inchcape Shipping Services (ISS), Inchcape Shipping Services Pty Ltd, Unit 1, 85 Salmon Street, Melbourne, Vic., Australia 3207, *Tel:* +61 3 8645 6900, *Fax:* +61 3 9681 8372, *Email:* melbourne@iss-shipping.com.au, *Website:* www.iss-shipping.com

Jebsens International (Australia) Proprietary Ltd, Level 4, 250 Queen Street, Melbourne, Vic., Australia 3000, *Tel:* +61 3 9600 0966, *Fax:* +61 3 9600 2660, *Email:* chartering@jebsens.com.au, *Website:* www.jebsens.com

McArthur Shipping & Agency Co Pty Ltd, P O Box 1074, Melbourne, Vic., Australia 3205, *Tel:* +61 3 8217 7275, *Fax:* +61 3 9211 8340, *Email:* melbourne@mcaship.com.au, *Website:* www.mcaship.com.au

Mediterranean Shipping Company, MSC (Aust) Pty Ltd., P O Box 13116, Law Courts, Melbourne, Vic., Australia 8010, *Tel:* +61 3 9254 1444, *Fax:* +61 3 9254 1430, *Email:* melinfo@msc.com.au, *Website:* www.msc.com.au

A.P. Moller-Maersk Group, Maersk Australia Pty Ltd, Level 17, Bourke Place, 600 Bourke Street, Melbourne, Vic., Australia 3000, *Tel:* +61 3 9944 2222, *Fax:* +61 3 9944 2288, *Website:* www.maerskline.com

Monson Agencies Australia Proprietary Ltd, Level 2, 570 St. Kilda Road, Melbourne, Vic., Australia 3205, *Tel:* +61 3 9682 7449, *Fax:* +61 3 9682 7487, *Email:* melbourne@monson.com.au, *Website:* www.monson.com

Neptune Pacific Agency Australia Proprietary Ltd, 3rd Floor, 448 St Kilda Road, Melbourne, Vic., Australia 3004, *Tel:* +61 3 9866 5105, *Fax:* +61 3 9866 5316, *Email:* euan_mccowan@nepship.com

Seatrans Australia Proprietary Ltd, Level 2, Building C, Katherine Square, 535 Flinders Lane, Melbourne, Vic., Australia 3000, *Tel:* +61 3 9621 1444, *Fax:* +61 3 9629 5344, *Email:* melbourne@mcaship.com.au

Stevedoring Companies: Capital Stevedoring, Unit 1/16 Salmon Street, Port Melbourne, P O Box 313, Melbourne, Vic., Australia 3207, *Tel:* +61 3 9203 8040, *Fax:* +61 3 9203 8045, *Email:* secretary@capitalstev.com.au, *Website:* www.capitalstevedoring.com.au

Patrick Corp., 4 Rocklea Drive, Melbourne, Vic., Australia 3207, *Tel:* +61 3 8698 6808, *Fax:* +61 3 8698 6899, *Website:* www.patrick.com.au

Surveyors: Australian Ship P & I, 218 Lorimer Street, Port Melbourne, Melbourne, Vic., Australia 3207, *Tel:* +61 3 6429 3390, *Fax:* +61 3 9646 0308, *Email:* melbourne@ausship.com.au

Berg Shipping Consultancy, 13 Manuela Terrace, Ringwood, Melbourne, Vic., Australia 3134, *Tel:* +61 3 9870 0771, *Fax:* +61 3 9879 4664, *Email:* bsc.melbourne@bigpond.com, *Website:* www.bergshippingconsultancy.com.au

Det Norske Veritas A/S, 1st Floor, 360 Burwood Road, Hawthorn, Melbourne, Vic., Australia 3122, *Tel:* +61 3 9818 4500, *Fax:* +61 3 9818 4103, *Email:* melbourne@dnv.com, *Website:* www.dnv.com

Germanischer Lloyd, P O Box 154, Williamstown, Vic., Australia 3016, *Tel:* +61 3 9397 0547, *Fax:* +61 3 9397 8247, *Website:* www.gl-group.com

Hellenic Register of Shipping, c/o Independent Maritime Services Pty Ltd, 9 Nandina Close, Warrannwood, Melbourne, Vic., Australia 3134, *Tel:* +61 3 9876 7201, *Fax:* +61 3 9812 2216, *Email:* ranjith.munidasa@maritimeserve.com.au, *Website:* www.hrs.gr

Nippon Kaiji Kyokai, P O Box 527, Melbourne, Vic., Australia 3207, *Tel:* +61 3 9646 8747, *Fax:* +61 3 9646 8748, *Website:* www.classnk.or.jp

Medical Facilities: Vessels requiring medical or emergency services may contact Harbour Control who will make the necessary arrangements

Airport: Tullamarine International, 21 km

Railway: Spencer Street Railway Station, 5 km

Lloyd's Agent: Freemans Marine, Level 7, 564 St. Kilda Road, Melbourne, Vic., Australia 3004, *Tel:* +61 3 9935 2400, *Fax:* +61 3 9915 0351, *Email:* lloyds@freemans.com.au, *Website:* www.freemansmarine.com.au

MILNER BAY

Lat 13° 51' S; Long 136° 25' E.

Admiralty Chart: AUS 14		**Admiralty Pilot:** 17	
Time Zone: GMT +9.5 h		**UNCTAD Locode:** AU MIB	

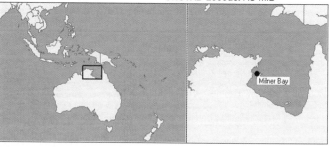

Principal Facilities:

P	Y					T	A

Authority: Groote Eylandt Mining Co. Proprietary Ltd, Port Office, Alyangula, Groote Eylandt, N.T., Australia 0885, *Tel:* +61 8 8987 4284, *Fax:* +61 8 8987 4202, *Email:* gemco.portoffice@bhpbilliton.com, *Website:* www.gemco.com.au

Officials: Harbour Master: Capt K.V. Siethan, *Email:* kv.siethan@bhpbilliton.com.

Port Security: ISPS compliant. The Port of Milner Bay is a secure port and has an approved Port Security Plan. Port security regulations and procedures are handed over to Master's of arriving vessel's by the agent

Pre-Arrival Information: Vessels bound for Groote Eylandt are to radio in their ETA on departure from their last port, seven days before arrival, then at 48 h and 24 h before arriving at Groote Eylandt

Approach: Approaching Groote Eylandt from the northwards, vessels should steer to a position approx 10 miles N of North East Island. This island is rocky on the northern shore and rises to grassy hills behind. A light is exhibited from a tower (Fl 5 sec) and is visible for 15 miles

From this position steer to pass approx 3 miles N of Chasm Island until the recommended track on Chart AUS 14 is reached

The track of 221° passes approx 1 mile E of Brady Rock (Fl (3) 12 sec) and continues on the course until an alteration can be made to bring Bickerton Island Light (Fl 5 sec) ahead on a course of 250°. When 2.3 miles off Hand Islet, alter course to 195° to pass 1.4 miles clear of Connexion Island Light (Fl 2.5 sec). When Connexion Island Light bears 044°(T) x 2.8' alter course to 133°. Remain on this course until Connexion Island Light bears 008°(T) x 3.4', whereupon the vessel should be brought around to steer 270° to pass 0.5 miles to the S of Burley Shoal South Cardinal Buoy (Q6 + Lfl 15 sec). When the jetty bears 058° x 3.7 miles alter course to 040° which will take the vessel to the anchorage and pilot boarding ground

Once in Milner Bay, the vessel should proceed to the anchorage unless otherwise advised to the contrary

Anchorage: The anchorage is located 1.6 miles W of the jetty where there is a sandy bottom under-layed with broken dead coral providing good holding ground in approx 21 m of water

Pilotage: Compulsory. Pilot boarding ground 2 miles W of Milner Bay Jetty

Radio Frequency: The port maintains a radio watch during office hours on VHF Channel 16 and 06, call sign 'MILNER BAY'

Weather: Prevailing SE winds from May to October. SW winds from November to April, the wet season heavy rain squalls and possible cyclones. Early morning heavy fogs may occur in June and July

Tides: Max tidal range of 2.2 m and a mean range of 1.2 m springs

Maximum Vessel Dimensions: 200 m loa, 32 m beam, 12.2 m draft. Max arrival displacement 30 000 t. Vessels with mooring wires are not acceptable

Principal Imports and Exports: Imports: Small quantities of fuel oils. Exports: Manganese ore.

Working Hours: Loading is carried out on a 2 x 12 h shift rotation. One shift starts at 0630 and the other at 1830. Loading is 24 h/day

Accommodation:

Name	Remarks
Milner Bay	See [1] below

[1]*Milner Bay:* Ore loading jetty in depth of 11.5 m at LAT, consists of four breasting dolphins and one long central landing, all of which run in a line bearing 152/332°. The total length between end dolphins is 340 m. Max air draft of 12.9 m HAT. Fixed loader conveyor at rate of 900-1200 t/h. Tankers are usually berthed port side to the berth

Towage: One tug available of 30 t bollard pull

Shipping Agents: Barwil Agencies Australia Pty Ltd, P O Box 38169, Winnellie, N.T., Australia 0821, *Tel:* +61 8 8947 2882, *Fax:* +61 8 8947 2881, *Email:* darwin@wilhelmsen.com, *Website:* www.wilhelmsen.com

Medical Facilities: Small medical centre on Groote Eylandt with doctor, dentist and medical staff on call

Airport: 10 km from port

Lloyd's Agent: Maritime & General Insurance Surveyors Proprietary Ltd, Suite 4, 7 Divett Street, Adelaide, S.A., Australia 5015, *Tel:* +61 8 8341 2552, *Fax:* +61 8 8241 0229, *Email:* maritime-general@adam.com.au

MOURILYAN

Lat 17° 35' S; Long 146° 7' E.

Admiralty Chart: AUS 829	**Admiralty Pilot:** 15
Time Zone: GMT +10 h	**UNCTAD Locode:** AU MOU

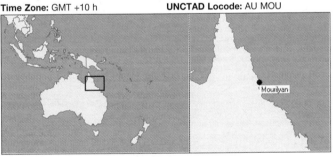

Principal Facilities:

			Y						T			

Authority: Ports Corporation of Queensland, Floor 24, 300 Queen Street, P O Box 409, Brisbane, Qld., Australia 4001, *Tel:* +61 7 3224 7088, *Fax:* +61 7 3224 7234, *Email:* info@pcq.com.au, *Website:* www.pcq.com.au

Officials: Chief Executive Officer: Brad Fish, *Email:* bfish@pcq.com.au.
Communications Manager: Rachel Campbell, *Tel:* +61 7 3224 8863, *Email:* rcampbell@pcq.com.au.

Port Security: ISPS compliant

Approach: Harbour is a land-locked inlet with entrance 91.0 m wide, depth of water 9.6 m LAT. The entrance is only visible between SW and WNW being 201.2 m wide

Anchorage: Anchorage is available on the line of the entrance leads, two miles from the entrance

Pilotage: Compulsory (except when master has obtained exemption). Pilotage arranged through the Duty Pilot at Cairns, *Tel:* +61 7 4031 9609. Pilots board vessels within 2 nautical miles of the harbour entrance. Pilot requisition should be made at least 24 h in advance. Vessels berth or sail at slack water, day or night, depending on draft

Radio Frequency: The pilot vessel is equipped with VHF radio telephone, channels 16 and 12. No regular watch is kept

Tides: MHWS 2.55 m, MHWN 1.89 m, MLWS 0.73 m, MLWN 1.39 m

Traffic: 2007/08, 27 vessels, 527 351 t of cargo exported

Maximum Vessel Dimensions: 185 m loa, 32 m beam, 10.5 m draft

Principal Imports and Exports: Exports: Cattle, Molasses, Raw sugar.

Accommodation:

Name	Length (m)	Depth (m)	Remarks
Mourilyan Bulk Sugar Loading Terminal	193	10	See [1] below

[1]*Bulk Sugar Loading Terminal:* Operated by Mourilyan Bulk Sugar Terminal Organisation

Sugar handled by conveyor system from 187 000 t storage shed via 15 t batch weighing hopper to travelling gantry loader with telescopic chute and adjustable boom; revolving trimmer at foot of tube. Loading rate of 1500 t/h. Four molasses tanks with cap of 3000 t, 11 000 t and 2 x 14 000 t. Rate of delivery to vessels 350 t/h

Towage: Two tugs with bollard pull of 25 t each

Repair & Maintenance: Minor repairs only undertaken

Shipping Agents: Barwil Agencies Australia Pty Ltd, P O Box 1392, Cairns, Qld., Australia 4870, *Tel:* +61 7 4035 4344, *Fax:* +61 7 4035 4006, *Email:* cairns@wilhelmsen.com, *Website:* www.wilhelmsen.com

Lloyd's Agent: Freemans Marine, P O Box 554, Fortitude Valley, Brisbane, Qld., Australia 4006, *Tel:* +61 7 3867 4646, *Fax:* +61 7 3867 4699, *Email:* john.cupitt@freemans.com.au, *Website:* www.freemansmarine.com.au

MUTINEER TERMINAL

Lat 19° 17' S; Long 116° 37' E.

Admiralty Chart: AUS 327	**Admiralty Pilot:** 17
Time Zone: GMT +8 h	**UNCTAD Locode:** AU

Principal Facilities:

P									

Authority: Santos Ltd., Level 28 Forrest Centre, 221 St. Georges Terrace, Perth, W.A., Australia 6000, *Tel:* +61 8 9460 8900, *Fax:* +61 8 9460 8971, *Website:* www.santos.com

Pre-Arrival Information: Incoming export tankers should initially advise Santos's agent and the facility of their ETA 5 days in advance and then 72 h, 48 h, 24 h and 12 h prior to arrival

Pilotage: Compulsory. The pilot/loading master boards approx 2 nautical miles from the FPSO

Radio Frequency: FPSO listens on VHF Channel 16 and works on VHF Channel 72

Maximum Vessel Dimensions: 30 000-140 000 dwt

Principal Imports and Exports: Exports: Crude oil.

Accommodation:

Name	Remarks
Mutineer Terminal	See [1] below

[1]*Mutineer Terminal:* Located in the Mutineer Exeter Field, approx 150 km N of Dampier

Consists of FPSO 'Modec Venture 11' which can store up to 931 650 bbls. Berthing normally takes place during daylight hours only; unberthing anytime

Medical Facilities: Not available at the terminal

Lloyd's Agent: Moko Proprietary Ltd, P O Box 685, Willetton, W.A., Australia 6955, *Tel:* +61 8 9354 2248, *Fax:* +61 8 9354 2234, *Email:* kglange@bigpond.com

NEWCASTLE

Lat 32° 54' S; Long 151° 45' E.

Admiralty Chart: AUS 208	**Admiralty Pilot:** 15
Time Zone: GMT +10 h	**UNCTAD Locode:** AU NTL

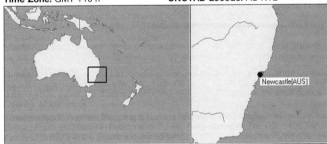

Principal Facilities:

P		Y	G	C	R	L	B	D	T	A

Authority: Newcastle Port Corp., P O Box 663, Newcastle, N.S.W., Australia 2300, *Tel:* +61 2 4985 8222, *Fax:* +61 2 4926 4596, *Email:* mail@newportcorp.com.au, *Website:* www.newportcorp.com.au

Officials: Chief Executive Officer: Gary Webb, *Email:* gary.w@newportcorp.com.au.
Marketing Manager: Priscilla Radice, *Email:* priscilla.r@newportcorp.com.au.
Harbour Master: Tim Turner, *Email:* tim.t@newportcorp.com.au.

Port Security: ISPS compliant

Key to Principal Facilities:—				
A=Airport	**C**=Containers	**G**=General Cargo	**P**=Petroleum	**R**=Ro/Ro	**Y**=Dry Bulk
B=Bunkers	**D**=Dry Dock	**L**=Cruise	**Q**=Other Liquid Bulk	**T**=Towage (where available from port)	

Pre-Arrival Information: Vessel's ETA must be advised by agents 24 h prior to arrival so that a berth can be arranged. All vessels proceeding to the port are required to call Newcastle Harbour on VHF Channel 9, four hours before arrival to confirm ETA

Approach: Entrance protected by two breakwaters, 460 m in width with channel 185 m wide and dredged to a depth of 15.2 m. Steelworks Channel, 180 m wide, depth 15.2 m. Approach to Bulk Berth at Kooragang Island, depth 15.2 m. Depths constantly altering due to siltation and latest information should be obtained from the Harbour Master. Dredging operations are continuous

Pilotage: Compulsory and operates 24 h/day. Pilot boards 3.2 km E of breakwater entrance

Radio Frequency: All movements controlled from Vessel Traffic Information Centre, VHF radio telephone, Channel 9, call sign Newcastle Harbour

Weather: The harbour is sufficiently land-locked to render it safe for vessels in all weathers

Tides: Range of tide 2 m

Traffic: 2007/08, 1537 vessels, 93 314 911 t of cargo handled, 11 396 TEU's

Maximum Vessel Dimensions: 300 m loa, 50 m beam

Principal Imports and Exports: Imports: Alumina, Cement, Fertilisers. Exports: Aluminium, Coal, Concentrates, Iron and steel, Ores, Wheat, Woodchips.

Working Hours: Sunday to Friday, day shift 0800-1500; afternoon shift 1500-2200; night shift 2400-0700. Saturday normal shift 0800-1200, if working to finish a vessel may extend shift by three hours on Saturday and day shift or two hours on afternoon shift

Accommodation:

Name	Length (m)	Depth (m)	Remarks
Newcastle			
Lee Wharf No.5	183	9.7	Used for tie up of naval & cruise vessels
Throsby Basin No.1	183	11	See [1] below
Western Basin No.3	245	11.6	See [2] below
Western Basin No.4	258	11.6	Containers & ro/ro stern ramp, stacking area 1 ha
Eastern Basin No's 1 & 2	484	11.6	See [3] below
Dockyard Berth No.4	300	8.5	Shiprepairs
Dyke Berth No.1	238	12.8	Dolphins for tie-up purposes
Dyke Berth No.2	238	12.8	See [4] below
Dyke Berths No's 4 & 5	558	16.5	See [5] below
Kooragang Island No.2	182	11.6	See [6] below
Kooragang Island No.3	190	13.5	See [7] below
Kooragang Island No's 4, 5 & 6	1080	16.5	See [8] below

[1] *Throsby Basin No.1:* Used for tie up of naval & cruise vessels. Stacking area 1.2 ha, one cargo shed

[2] *Western Basin No.3:* Grain loading berth equipped with four travelling gantry loaders, 1000 t/h cap each. Loading heads operated by the Graincorp Ports Division have a rate of 4000 t/h. Silo storage of 6.2 million bushels. Vessels max loa 250 m, max beam 33 m. Bulk frozen orange juice terminal located at western end of berth

[3] *Eastern Basin No's 1 & 2:* General cargo, stacking area 4 ha. Cargo transit shed 4000 m2

[4] *Dyke Berth No.2:* A transverse single headed bulk loader of 1200 t/h cap has been installed at the facility owned by CBH Resources for ore concentrates. Vessels up to 42 000 dwt can be accommodated at the berth, adjacent to which there is a service wharf for provisioning vessels using the shiploader berth. Covered storage is provided for 15 000 t of copper and zinc concentrates and 10 000 t of silver/lead concentrates

[5] *Dyke Berths No's 4 & 5:* Operated by Port Waratah Coal Services (PWCS) Tel: +61 2 4969 3361, Fax: +61 2 4969 0372, Email: customer.services@pwcs.com.au, Website: www.pwcs.com.au

Steelworks channel coal loading berths, equipped with three travelling A Frame loaders with a combined rate of 7500 t/h. Vessels max loa 290 m, max beam 47 m. Facilities have a cap of 28 million t/year

[6] *Kooragang Island No.2:* Bulk berth with mooring dolphin at each end giving berthing length of 274 m, equipped with two bridge type grabs of 650 t/h cap each, connected to a conveyor system. Facilities for phosphate, cottonseed and liquid cargoes. A wood-chip loading facility operated by Sawmillers Exports Pty Ltd., Tel: +61 49 281436, is incorporated into the system, rate of 700 t/h. Edible oils can also be handled. Vessels max loa 244 m, max beam 33 m. A cement import terminal situated at rear of berth

[7] *Kooragang Island No.3:* Bulk discharge berth for Kooragang Bulk Facilities Ltd with 190 m of berth face capable of accommodating vessels of up to 260 m in length and a depth of 13.5 m. The berth is equipped with 2 x 500 t/h vacuum unloaders for the discharge of alumina and petroleum coke cargoes. The alumina storage silos each have a cap of 35 000 t and the petroleum coke silos each hold 16 000 t. Pneumatic unloaders are installed to prevent pollution by alumina dust. Tank terminal operated by Craig Mostyn used for export of vegetable oils

[8] *Kooragang Island No's 4, 5 & 6:* Coal loader is operated by Port Waratah Coal Services (PWCS), Tel: +61 2 4969 3361, Fax: +61 2 4969 0372, Email: customer.services@pwcs.com.au, Website: www.pwcs.com.au

Designed to load vessels ranging in size from 40 000 to 230 000 dwt, 290 m max loa, 46 m beam. A swinging area of 600 m has been provided adjacent to the wharf. Three shiploaders rated at 10 500 t/h cap

Mechanical Handling Equipment:

Location	Type	Capacity (t)	Qty
Newcastle	Floating Cranes	80	1
Western Basin No.4	Mult-purp. Cranes	35	1

Bunkering: Australian Petroleum Proprietary Ltd, Solander Street, Kurnell, Sydney, N.S.W., Australia, Tel: +61 2 972 2597, Fax: +61 2 981 1159 – Grades: MDO; MGO; FO – Notice: 48 hours – Delivery Mode: truck

BP Australia (Proprietary) Ltd, P O Box 5222, Melbourne, Vic., Australia 3001, Tel: +61 3 9268 4111, Fax: +61 3 9268 3321, Email: gomiasfuelsales@bp.com, Website: www.bp.com

Caltex Australia Petroleum Proprietary Ltd, Caltex Australia Petroleum Proprietary

Ltd, No 2 Market Street, Sydney, N.S.W., Australia 2000, Tel: +61 2 9668 1148, Fax: +61 2 9668 1243, Email: mnicholl@caltex.com.au, Website: www.caltex.com.au

ExxonMobil Marine Fuels, 1 Harbour Front Place, 06-00 Harbour Front, Tower One, Singapore, Republic of Singapore 098633, Tel: +65 6885 8998, Fax: +65 6885 8794, Email: asiapac.marinefuels@exxonmobil.com, Website: www.exxonmobilmarinefuels.com – Grades: MGO – Delivery Mode: tank truck

Shell Australia Ltd, Shell Company of Australia, Marine Centre Oceania, No 8 Redfern Road, Melbourne, Vic., Australia 3123, Tel: +61 3 9666 5446, Fax: +61 3 8823 4800, Email: sal-marine-products@shell.com, Website: www.shell.com.au

Towage: SVITZER, SVITZER Australasia, Dyke Point, Carrington, N.S.W., Australia 2294, Tel: +61 2 4940 0428, Fax: +61 2 4940 0928, Email: info.newcastle@adsteam.com.au, Website: www.svitzer.com

Repair & Maintenance: Floating dock 195 m by 33.5 m with a lifting cap of 15 000 t, capable of accommodating vessels up to 45 000 dwt

Forgacs Cairncross Dockyard, Denison Street, P O Box 90, Carrington, N.S.W., Australia 2294, Tel: +61 2 4962 2866, Fax: +61 2 4962 2848, Email: forgacs@forgacs.com.au, Website: www.forgacs.com.au

Varley Ship Repair, 156 Young Street, Carrington, N.S.W., Australia 2294, Tel: +61 2 4940 8515, Fax: +61 2 4969 5925, Email: shipping@varleygroup.com, Website: www.varleygroup.com

Seaman Missions: The Seamans Mission, 96 Hannell Street, Wickham, N.S.W., Australia 2293, Tel: +61 2 4961 5007, Fax: +61 2 4961 5081, Email: newcastle@mts.org.au

Ship Chandlers: Australian International Marine Services Proprietary Ltd, Unit 2/1, Benjamin Drive, Wickham, Maryland, Newcastle, N.S.W., Australia 2287, Tel: +61 2 4955 8337, Fax: +61 2 4955 9606, Email: newcastle-aims@sinwa.com.au, Website: www.sinwaglobal.com

Port Container Services, P O Box 4051, Kotara East, Newcastle, N.S.W., Australia 2305, Tel: +61 2 9519 5311, Fax: +61 2 4957 9166, Email: sales@portcontainerservices.com.au, Website: www.portcontainerservices.com.au

Southern Cross Marine Supplies Proprietary Ltd, Unit B, 66 The Avenue, Newcastle, N.S.W., Australia NSW 2293, Tel: +61 2 4961 4664, Fax: +61 2 4962 1453, Email: newcastle@scms.com.au

Shipping Agents: Barwil Agencies Australia Pty Ltd, P O Box 2009, Dangar, N.S.W., Australia 2309, Tel: +61 2 4961 5488, Fax: +61 2 4961 1883, Email: newcastle@wilhelmsen.com, Website: www.wilhelmsen.com

Gulf Agency Co (Australia) Pty Ltd., P O Box 1785, Newcastle, N.S.W., Australia 2300, Tel: +61 2 4961 0941, Fax: +61 2 4962 1276, Email: shipping.newcastle@gacworld.com, Website: www.gacworld.com

Hetherington Kingsbury Proprietary Ltd, P O Box 501, Newcastle, N.S.W., Australia 2300, Tel: +61 2 4926 3900, Fax: +61 2 4926 3894, Email: newcastle@hksa.com.au, Website: www.hksa.com.au

Horizon Shipping Agencies, P O Box 44, Wickham, Newcastle, N.S.W., Australia 2293, Tel: +61 2 4969 7988, Fax: +61 2 4969 7995, Email: ntl@aalsa.com.au, Website: www.australasialine.com

Inchcape Shipping Services (ISS), Inchcape Shipping Services Pty Ltd, Suite 3, Level 1, NSW Maritime Building, 8 Cowper Street, P O Box 94, Carrington, N.S.W., Australia 2294, Tel: +61 2 4940 0251, Fax: +61 2 4940 0812, Email: newcastle@iss-shipping.com.au, Website: www.iss-shipping.com

McArthur Shipping & Agency Co Pty Ltd, P O Box 821, Newcastle, N.S.W., Australia 2300, Tel: +61 2 4926 3722, Fax: +61 2 4926 3894, Email: newcastle@mcaship.com.au, Website: www.mcaship.com.au

Monson Agencies Australia Proprietary Ltd, P O Box 121, Waratah, Newcastle, N.S.W., Australia 2298, Tel: +61 2 4967 3629, Fax: +61 2 4960 2649, Email: newcastle@monson.com.au, Website: www.monson.com.au

Seatrans Australia Proprietary Ltd, Suite 2, 4th Floor, Hunter Mall Chambers, 175 Scott Street, Newcastle, N.S.W., Australia 2300, Tel: +61 2 4926 3722, Fax: +61 2 4926 5014, Email: newcastle@mcaship.com

Stevedoring Companies: Newcastle Stevedores Proprietary Ltd, P O Box 525, Newcastle, N.S.W., Australia 2304, Tel: +61 2 4968 8611, Fax: +61 2 4968 8711, Email: newcastle@newcastlestevedores.com.au, Website: www.newcastlestevedores.com.au

P&O Ports, P O Box 499, Newcastle, N.S.W., Australia 2300, Tel: +61 2 4928 0500, Fax: +61 2 4928 4215, Email: wayne.mabbott@poports.com.au, Website: www.poports.com.au

Surveyors: Nippon Kaiji Kyokai, Newcastle, N.S.W., Australia, Tel: +61 2 9975 5361, Fax: +61 2 9975 2574, Website: www.classnk.or.jp

Airport: Newcastle Airport, Williamtown, Tel: +61 2 4928 9800

Railway: The port is connected to the major north/south rail line serving the east coast of Australia. The coal exported from the Hunter Valley is also railed to the port

Development: New coal loading terminal consisting of two berths to be built on 136 ha of former BHP land; scheduled to open in 2009

Lloyd's Agent: Freemans Marine, P O Box 36, St. Leonards, N.S.W., Australia 1590, Tel: +61 2 9438 2655, Fax: +61 2 9436 1367, Email: lloyds@freemans.com.au, Website: www.freemansmarine.com.au

NGANHURRA TERMINAL

Lat 21° 29' S; Long 114° 0' E.

Admiralty Chart: AUS 328		**Admiralty Pilot:** 17
Time Zone: GMT +8 h		**UNCTAD Locode:** AU

Principal Facilities:

P											

Authority: Woodside Energy Ltd, P O Box 517, Karratha, W.A., Australia 6714, Tel: +61 8 9348 4000, Fax: +61 8 9158 8000, Email: john.jenkin@woodside.com.au, Website: www.woodside.com.au

Pre-Arrival Information: ETA's should be forwarded 72 h, 48 h, 24 h and 12 h prior to arrival to the terminal and duty pilot via the vessel's agent

Pilotage: Compulsory for all vessels. Pilot boards in pos 21° 37.80' S; 114° 15.00' E, or between this position and the terminal at the discretion of the pilot with due regard to prevailing conditions

Radio Frequency: Nganhurra Control works on VHF Channel 8

Maximum Vessel Dimensions: 25 000-150 000 dwt except by prior agreement

Principal Imports and Exports: Exports: Crude oil.

Accommodation:

Name	Remarks
Nganhurra Terminal	See [1] below

[1]*Nganhurra Terminal:* Oil is produced through five subsea wells in the Enfield Project, connected to the FPSO vessel 'Nganhurra'. The vessel has a max design production rate of about 100 000 bbls/day and a storage cap of approx 900 000 bbls

Lloyd's Agent: Moko Proprietary Ltd, P O Box 685, Willetton, W.A., Australia 6955, *Tel:* +61 8 9354 2248, *Fax:* +61 8 9354 2234, *Email:* kglange@bigpond.com

NORMANTON

alternate name, see Karumba

OSBORNE

harbour area, see under Adelaide

PORT ALMA

Lat 23° 34' S; Long 150° 51' E.

Admiralty Chart: AUS 247	**Admiralty Pilot:** 15
Time Zone: GMT +10 h	**UNCTAD Locode:** AU PTL

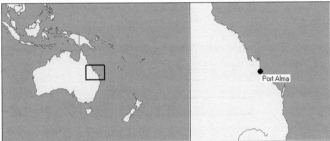

Principal Facilities:

P	Q	Y	G	C				A

Authority: Gladstone Ports Corp., Port Alma Shipping Terminal, P O Box 9, Rockhampton, Qld., Australia 4700, *Tel:* +61 7 4927 2133, *Fax:* +61 7 4922 6096, *Website:* www.gpcl.com.au

Officials: Port Manager: Colin Munro, *Tel:* +61 7 4934 6931.

Port Security: ISPS compliant

Approach: Depth in channel when entered from Keppel Bay has a min of 7.6 m for a distance of approx 488 m. Remainder 7.92 m and over LWOST. The width of the channel is from 91-137 m

Pilotage: Compulsory. Vessels should send their ETA and max draught to Harbour Master at least 24 h in advance and subsequent ammendments should be sent immediately. Pilot boards one nautical mile NE of Timandra Lt buoy in pos 23° 24' 50" S; 151° 00' 90" E

Radio Frequency: VHF Channels 16, 12, 6 and 63. Not watched continuously

Tides: Tidal rise 3.5 m neaps, 4.5 m springs

Traffic: 2007/08, 55 vessels, 168 112 t of cargo handled

Principal Imports and Exports: Imports: Ammonium nitrate, Explosives, Petroleum. Exports: Frozen beef, Salt, Scrap metal, Tallow.

Working Hours: As arranged through agent or Port Authority

Accommodation:

Name	Length (m)	Depth (m)	Remarks
Port Alma			See [1] below
Berth No.1	169	9.7	See [2] below
Berth No.2	122	9.7	See [3] below
Berth No.3	238	9.7	See [4] below

[1]*Port Alma:* The swinging basin has a width of 244 m and a depth of 7.31 m. The max draft of vessels that may enter the port is 11.58 m at HWOST and 7.01 m at LWOST Tanker facilities: Oil Terminal for vessels up to 170 m long with 9.75 m draft

[2]*Berth No.1:* Used for general cargo and frozen meat. Storage shed accommodation 55 m by 12 m is adjacent. Mobile bulk loader can be used on Berths 1 & 2 with a nominal cap of 500 t/h

[3]*Berth No.2:* In a continuous line with Berth 1 providing 291 m of mooring space plus mooring dolphins at each end. Used for containers and general cargo and provided with a 25.4 t stiff-leg crane for handling containers

[4]*Berth No.3:* Consists of four mooring dolphins in line with Berths 1 & 2 with mooring dolphins at both ends. Used for loading salt and discharging petroleum products. Equipped with a shiploader/conveyor with a cap of 1000 t/h

Storage: One shed 55 m x 12 m. Reefer space available

Mechanical Handling Equipment:

Location	Type	Capacity (t)	Qty
Port Alma	Mult-purp. Cranes	25	1
Port Alma	Forklifts	3	1

Repair & Maintenance: Minor repairs available with prior arrangement

Shipping Agents: Barwil Agencies Australia Pty Ltd, P O Box 5166, Gladstone, Qld., Australia 4680, *Tel:* +61 7 4972 8833, *Fax:* +61 7 4972 8696, *Email:* gladstone@wilhelmsen.com, *Website:* www.wilhelmsen.com
Inchcape Shipping Services (ISS), Inchcape Shipping Services Pty Ltd, Unit 11, 174 Quay Street, Central Queensland Mail Centre, P O Box 5181, Rockhampton, Qld., Australia 4700, *Tel:* +61 7 4927 7477, *Fax:* +61 7 4927 8481, *Email:* rockhampton@iss-shipping.com.au, *Website:* www.iss-shipping.com

Medical Facilities: Not available locally, nearest facility at Rockhampton, 70 km

Airport: Rockhampton, 67 km

Lloyd's Agent: Freemans Marine, P O Box 554, Fortitude Valley, Brisbane, Qld., Australia 4006, *Tel:* +61 7 3867 4646, *Fax:* +61 7 3867 4699, *Email:* john.cupitt@freemans.com.au, *Website:* www.freemansmarine.com.au

PORT AUGUSTA

Lat 32° 30' S; Long 137° 47' E.

Admiralty Chart: AUS 136	**Admiralty Pilot:** 13
Time Zone: GMT +9.5 h	**UNCTAD Locode:** AU PUG

This port is no longer open to commercial shipping

PORT BONYTHON

Lat 32° 59' S; Long 137° 46' E.

Admiralty Chart: AUS 136	**Admiralty Pilot:** 13
Time Zone: GMT +9.5 h	**UNCTAD Locode:** AU PBY

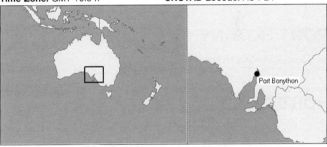

Principal Facilities:

P	Q						T	A

Authority: Santos Ltd Port Bonython, P O Box 344, Whyalla, S.A., Australia 5600, *Tel:* +61 8 8640 3100, *Fax:* +61 8 8640 3200, *Email:* jim.phillips@santos.com, *Website:* www.santos.com

Officials: Co-ordinator: Jim Phillips, *Email:* jim.phillips@santos.com.

Port Security: ISPS compliant

Pre-Arrival Information: The Master or Agent of vessel arriving at the port must give Santos at least 24 h notice of ETA at the pilot boarding ground, and advise the draught fore and aft
Not more than 24 h prior to arrival, the Master or Agent must advise Santos whether, to the best of his knowledge, the vessel's hull is in sound condition and free of leaks

Documentation: All vessels must be in possession of a completed and valid set of safety certificates, ISSC. All officers to be properly qualified and in possession of recognised certificates of competency
All LPG vessels to be in possession of a certificate of fitness under the terms of the IMO code for construction and equipment of ships carrying liquefied gas in bulk, also of an appropriate Classification Society certificate
Complies with International Transport Federation (ITF) Rules and Regulations as are applicable and in operation from time to time. Is entered into a Protection and Indemnity Club (P and I) acceptable to the Buyer and Seller's Representative

Approach: Vessel's approaching from the east should set a course to pass no closer than 10 nautical miles clear of Cape Borda lighthouse from where a course may be set to enter Spencer Gulf between Wedge and Althorpe Island. Tracks can be subject to strong cross sets due to the tides. On entering the Gulf a safe course should be set to pass to the west of Tiparra Reef beacon (30° 04' S; 137 23.5' E). Vessels with local knowledge sometimes pass to the north of Kangaroo Island, using Backstairs Passage and Investigator Strait
Vessel's approaching from the west should set a course to pass 10 nautical miles south of S. Neptune Island lighthouse, and thence into Spencer Gulf by the previously mentioned track. Mariners are cautioned against passing within 5 nautical miles of S. Neptune Island

Anchorage: Inward bound vessels awaiting pilot or customs should anchor in the vicinity of the pilot boarding ground. Water depth is approx 16 m with good holding in sand

Pilotage: Compulsory for all vessels when within the port limits. Pilots board inward bound vessels at a position approx 165°(T) distant 5 nautical miles from the Whyalla Entrance beacon (No.1 Bn.)
Deep draught vessels use the buoyed channel to the east of Fairway Bank. Outward bound, ship's will disembark the pilot at the Entrance Buoy (165° (T) dist. 6.7 nautical miles from No.1 Bn.)

Key to Principal Facilities:—			
A=Airport	**C**=Containers	**G**=General Cargo	**P**=Petroleum	**R**=Ro/Ro	**Y**=Dry Bulk
B=Bunkers	**D**=Dry Dock	**L**=Cruise	**Q**=Other Liquid Bulk	**T**=Towage (where available from port)	

Radio Frequency: VHF Channel 16 is monitored continuously by Santos at Port Bonython and by OneSteel Security at Whyalla

Maximum Vessel Dimensions: Oil tankers 110 000 dwt, LPG carriers 45 000 dwt or 75 000 m3 cap. Larger sizes can be handled at the discretion of the Harbour Master

Principal Imports and Exports: Exports: Crude oil, LPG, Naphtha.

Working Hours: Continuous. Berthing during daylight only

Accommodation:

Name	Depth (m)	Remarks
Port Bonython		Situated on the western shore of Spencer Gulf
Jetty	20	See [1] below

[1]*Jetty:* Concrete loading platform with four breasting dolphins and four mooring dolphins erected on steel piles for loading refrigerated LPG products, crude oil and naphtha. The max allowable displacement for a vessel while berthing at the jetty is 70 000 t

There are ten loading arms, all fitted with hydraulic couplings and quick-release devices. Pennant controls are operated from No's 2, 4, 6 and 9 arms

Max loading rates at the berth are crude oil approx 7000 m3/h, naphtha approx 4200 m3/h, butane approx 1800 m3/h and propane approx 1800 m3/h

Ballast Facilities - Shore Tankage: One receiving tank is available with a normal working cap of 15 000 m3. Prior arrangements with the terminal may allow dirty water discharge as this tank is also used for crude storage. Ballast water containing tank cleaning chemicals or lead contaminants cannot be accepted owing to possible detrimental effects to the plant effluent-treating system and must be retained on board. It is an offence to allow discharge or escape from the ship of any liquid containing oil or other contaminating material

Towage: Two tugs of 3600 hp and 2250 hp available, based at Whyalla

Shipping Agents: Barwil Agencies Australia Pty Ltd, P O Box 162A, Whyalla, S.A., Australia 5600, *Tel:* +61 8 8644 0911, *Fax:* +61 8 8644 0925, *Email:* whyalla@wilhelmsen.com, *Website:* www.wilhelmsen.com

Medical Facilities: First aid available at the jetty. Hospital at Whyalla, approx 45 km

Airport: Approx 45 km

Lloyd's Agent: Maritime & General Insurance Surveyors Proprietary Ltd, Suite 4, 7 Divett Street, Adelaide, S.A., Australia 5015, *Tel:* +61 8 8341 2552, *Fax:* +61 8 8241 0229, *Email:* maritime-general@adam.com.au

PORT BOTANY

harbour area, see under Botany Bay

PORT GILES

Lat 35° 1' S; Long 137° 45' E.

Admiralty Chart: AUS 139/780	**Admiralty Pilot:** 13
Time Zone: GMT +9.5 h	**UNCTAD Locode:** AU PGI

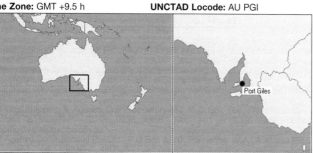

Principal Facilities:

	Y	G		B	T	

Authority: Flinders Ports Proprietary Ltd, 3 Diagonal Road, Wallaroo, S.A., Australia 5556, *Tel:* +61 8 8823 2026, *Fax:* +61 8 8823 2026, *Email:* flindersports@flindersports.com.au, *Website:* www.flindersports.com.au

Officials: Business Development Manager: Stewart Lammin, *Tel:* + +61 8 8447 0627, *Email:* lammin.stewart@flindersports.com.au.

Port Security: ISPS compliant

Approach: Channel has a depth of 13.5 m below CD

Pilotage: Compulsory. Pilot boards 2.5 nautical miles E of sea end of Port Giles jetty

Radio Frequency: VHF Channels 6, 8, 12, 16 and 67

Tides: MHWS 2 m, MHWN 1.2 m

Traffic: 2007/08, 17 vessels, 331 348 t of cargo exported

Maximum Vessel Dimensions: 228 m loa (conditions may be suitable for larger vessels at Port Manager's discretion)

Principal Imports and Exports: Exports: Grain, Seeds.

Working Hours: 0800-1500, 1500-2200 (24 h loading on request)

Accommodation:

Name	Length (m)	Depth (m)	Remarks
Port Giles			
Jetty	255	11.6	See [1] below

[1]*Jetty:* Grain transported from silo's to vessel's side by conventional belt conveyor

capable of handling 1000 t/h. Alongside vessel, elevated gallery with five identical slewing loading booms feeds grain into any hold without movement of ship along berth. Each boom has a max load rate of 500 t/h so that at least two must be used to achieve full ship loading rate. Silo cap of 150 000 t. Road access only

Storage:

Location	Grain (t)
Port Giles	150000

Bunkering: Available by road tanker

Towage: Tugs available from Adelaide

Shipping Agents: Barwil Agencies Australia Pty Ltd, P O Box 1559, Adelaide, S.A., Australia 5015, *Tel:* +61 8 8341 0466, *Fax:* +61 8 8341 0506, *Email:* ptadelaide@wilhelmsen.com, *Website:* www.wilhelmsen.com

Stevedoring Companies: ABB Grain Ltd, Port Giles, S.A., Australia, *Tel:* +61 8 8852 8022, *Fax:* +61 8 8852 8181

Medical Facilities: Hospital and doctor at Yorketown, 17 km

Lloyd's Agent: Maritime & General Insurance Surveyors Proprietary Ltd, Suite 4, 7 Divett Street, Adelaide, S.A., Australia 5015, *Tel:* +61 8 8341 2552, *Fax:* +61 8 8241 0229, *Email:* maritime-general@adam.com.au

PORT HEDLAND

Lat 20° 18' S; Long 118° 34' E.

Admiralty Chart: AUS 52/53/54	**Admiralty Pilot:** 17
Time Zone: GMT +8 h	**UNCTAD Locode:** AU PHE

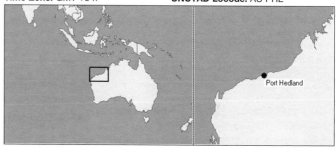

Principal Facilities:

	Y	G			B		T	A

Authority: Port Hedland Port Authority, Wharf Road, P O Box 2, Port Hedland, W.A., Australia 6721, *Tel:* +61 8 9173 0000, *Fax:* +61 8 9173 0060, *Email:* phpa@phpa.com.au, *Website:* www.phpa.com.au

Officials: Chief Executive Officer: Andre Bush, *Email:* andre.bush@phpa.com.au. Harbour Master: Capt Lindsay Copeman, *Email:* lindsay.copeman@phpa.com.au.

Port Security: ISPS compliant

Approach: The inner harbour commences from a line drawn between Hunt Point beacon (No.47) and Airey Point beacon (No.46). It is a secure harbour with a dredged channel, min depth 14.3 m below datum, a turning basin, depth 9.3 m below datum, width 630 m at max. The channel approach is some 26 nautical miles long extending from beacons C1 and C2 to the berths in the inner harbour. The width of channel at the bottom of the sloped sides varies between 183 and 300 m in the port limits and up to 450 m in the pilotage area. Drying coral ledges, covered with a thin layer of sand extend from the shoreline near the harbour entrance for a distance of up to 0.75 nautical miles. A Spoil Bank extends seaward from the foreshore and is situated to the E of the dredged channel. This dries for most of its length acting as a breakwater during E winds. Vessels should approach via the eastern inward route along the track marked by sarus towers

Pilotage: Pilotage is compulsory for all vessels within Port Limits and within a 'Pilotage Area' that extends some 10 nautical miles outside Port Limits. Port Limits embrace all waters up to the High Water Mark within an arc of radius 10 nautical miles from Hunt Point Beacon (47). The Master of any vessel, other than a vessel exempted under the Port's Regulation 51, shall not cause or permit the vessel to enter or depart from or move within the port of the Pilotage Area without first having taken on a pilot, unless authorised to do so by the Harbour Master. Outbound vessels of 150 000 dwt or more will be required to take a pilot beyond Port limits into the outer Pilotage Area. However, if a Master requests the services of a pilot then the port will meet that request where in the opinion of the Harbour Master it is reasonable to do so. If a vessel of 150 000 dwt or less requires extended Pilotage, the Master should request this through the Shipping Agent at the first available opportunity. Vessels under 150 000 dwt may be authorised by the Harbour Master to proceed without a pilot through the outer Pilotage Area. Within Port Limits vessels will require a pilot unless exempted. Pilot usually boards in pos 20° 10' S; 118° 33' E either by helicopter or pilot boat

Radio Frequency: A continuous watch is kept on VHF channel 16 by Port Hedland Harbour Control and vessels should call four hours before arrival at anchorage to confirm their ETA and intended approach track

Weather: The cyclone season is during the summer, November to April and average one per year

Tides: Range of tide up to 7 m

Traffic: 2007/08, 1027 vessels, 130 707 208 t of cargo handled

Maximum Vessel Dimensions: 335 m max loa, 55 m beam, 19.19 m max draft

Principal Imports and Exports: Imports: Bagged cement, Bitumen, Break bulk cargoes, Bulk fuels, Bulk liquid chemicals. Exports: Chrome ore, Copper concentrate, Iron ore, Manganese ore, Salt.

Working Hours: Monday to Friday, day shift 0800-2000, night shift 2000-0800. Saturday, day shift 0800-2000. Sunday, 0800-2000

Accommodation:

Name	Length (m)	Depth (m)	Remarks
Port Hedland			See [1] below
BHP Iron Ore Finucane Island Pier	680	19.2	See [2] below
No.1 Berth	213	11.2	See [3] below
No.3 Berth	183	13.2	See [4] below
BHP Iron Ore Nelson Point	658	19	See [5] below

[1]*Port Hedland:* There are nine berths within the Inner Harbour as follows:
a) three are owned and operated by the Port Authority
b) two (one is a dedicated lay-by berth) are owned and operated by Fortescue Metals Group at Anderson Point
c) four are owned and operated by BHP Billiton Iron Ore (two are located at Nelson Point and two at Finucane Island)

[2]*BHP Iron Ore Finucane Island Pier:* Finucane Island C & D berths are situated on the W side of the harbour and lie SW of Hunt Point Beacon. The berth face is 680 m long and consists of sixteen breasting dolphins. The dredged berthing pocket is 722 m long, 61 m wide with a depth of 19 m below datum. The shiploaders have a combined length of travel of 623 m and an approx load rate of 10 000 t/h. Fresh water and fuel are not available at this berth, except by barge

[3]*No.1 Berth:* Mooring dolphin 58 m from N end. General cargo vessels, tankers and oil rig support vessels up to 230 m loa are catered for. Fresh water and diesel fuel available

PHPA No.2 berth is a 131 m extension to No.1 Berth giving an overall length of 344 m available. There is no bulk loading facilities available on this berth. Fresh water is available but there are no pipeline bunkering facilities

[4]*No.3 Berth:* Situated to the S of No.1 Berth and is constructed of steel piles with a steel and concrete decking; dolphins 46 m ahead and astern to facilitate the mooring of vessels. There is a mooring basin alongside the berth and dolphins which is 275 m in length. Vessels up to 230 m loa may berth. The full length of the wharf is protected by a 'Raykin' fender system. Cargo is handled by forklifts into the shed (which has an area of 1600 m2) or storage area behind the shed, or loaded direct into road trucks. A mechanical bulk loading facility with cap of 2200 t/h is operated by Dampier Salt Ltd. on the wharf. There is also a tanker discharge point. Fresh water available at 50 t/h and diesel at 100 t/h

[5]*BHP Iron Ore Nelson Point:* From a continuous line in a 117 degree-297 degree direction from a position E of the No.3 berth towards Nelson Point. Berth A is the westward berth and is 305 m long; berth B, the eastward berth, is 353 m long; both are of steel pile construction with steel and concrete capping, and are protected by a 'Raykin' fender system. Two shiploaders available with an average loading cap of 6500 t/h each. There is a mooring basin 679 m long, 65 m wide and 19 m deep Bunkers are not available on these berths, although emergency supplies of fresh water may be requested

Mechanical Handling Equipment:

Location	Type	Capacity (t)
Port Hedland	Mobile Cranes	70

Bunkering: BP Australia (Proprietary) Ltd, P O Box 5222, Melbourne, Vic., Australia 3001, *Tel:* +61 3 9268 4111, *Fax:* +61 3 9268 3321, *Email:* gomiasfuelsales@bp.com, *Website:* www.bp.com

Towage: Six tugs up to 3600 bhp with bollard pull of 50 to 53 t
SVITZER, SVITZER Australasia, 1 Wharf Road, P O Box 81, Port Hedland, W.A., Australia 6721, *Tel:* +61 8 9173 1651, *Fax:* +61 8 9173 1343, *Website:* www.svitzer.com

Repair & Maintenance: Minor repairs only can be effected; machine shops available

Seaman Missions: The Seamans Mission, P O Box 261, Port Hedland, W.A., Australia 6721, *Tel:* +61 8 9173 1315, *Fax:* +61 8 9173 2413, *Email:* porthedland@mts.org.au

Ship Chandlers: Sealanes, Lot 71, Richardson Street, Port Hedland, W.A., Australia 6721, *Tel:* +61 8 9173 1244, *Fax:* +61 8 9173 1895, *Email:* sea@sealanes.com.au, *Website:* www.sealanes.com.au

Shipping Agents: Barwil Agencies Australia Pty Ltd, P O Box 378, Port Hedland, W.A., Australia 6721, *Tel:* +61 8 9173 1809, *Fax:* +61 8 9173 2526, *Email:* pthedland@wilhelmsen.com, *Website:* www.wilhelmsen.com
Beaufort Shipping Agency Proprietary Ltd, Inchcape Shipping Services Pty Ltd, 1 Wharf Road, Port Hedland, W.A., Australia 6721, *Tel:* +61 8 9173 2323, *Fax:* +61 8 9173 2450, *Email:* port.hedland@iss-shipping.com.au, *Website:* www.iss-shipping.com
Gulf Agency Co (Australia) Pty Ltd., P O Box 170, Port Hedland, W.A., Australia 6721, *Tel:* +61 8 9173 3014, *Fax:* +61 8 9173 3208, *Email:* shipping.porthedland@gacworld.com, *Website:* www.gacworld.com
Hetherington Kingsbury Proprietary Ltd, P O Box 376, Port Hedland, W.A., Australia 6721, *Tel:* +61 8 9173 2533, *Fax:* +61 8 9173 1458, *Email:* wcsa.phe@wcsa.com.au, *Website:* www.hksa.com.au
Inchcape Shipping Services (ISS), Inchcape Shipping Services Pty Ltd, 1 Wharf Road, P O Box 42, Port Hedland, W.A., Australia 6721, *Tel:* +61 8 9173 2323, *Fax:* +61 8 9173 2450, *Email:* port.hedland@iss-shipping.com.au, *Website:* www.iss-shipping.com
McArthur Shipping & Agency Co Pty Ltd, P O Box 376, Port Hedland, W.A., Australia 6721, *Tel:* +61 8 9173 2533, *Fax:* +61 8 9173 1458, *Email:* pthedland@mcaship.com.au, *Website:* www.mcaship.com.au
Monson Agencies Australia Proprietary Ltd, Shop 14 Port Plaza, 4 Edgar Street, Port Hedland, W.A., Australia 6721, *Tel:* +61 8 9173 4018, *Fax:* +61 8 9173 4019, *Email:* porthedland@monson.com.au, *Website:* www.monson.com.au
Oceanway Shipping Agency Proprietary Ltd, 47 Styles Road, Pretty Pool, P O Box 20, Port Hedland, W.A., Australia 6721, *Tel:* +61 8 9173 4000, *Fax:* +61 8 9173 3777, *Email:* hedland@oceanway.com.au
Seatrans Australia Proprietary Ltd, 2 Wharf Road, Port Hedland, W.A., Australia 6721, *Tel:* +61 8 9173 2533, *Fax:* +61 8 9173 1458, *Email:* wcsa.phe@wcsa.com.au, *Website:* www.hksa.com.au

Medical Facilities: Local doctors and a 100 bed hospital

Airport: Port Hedland International, 11 km

Lloyd's Agent: Moko Proprietary Ltd, P O Box 685, Willetton, W.A., Australia 6955, *Tel:* +61 8 9354 2248, *Fax:* +61 8 9354 2234, *Email:* kglange@bigpond.com

PORT JACKSON

alternate name, see Sydney

PORT KEMBLA

Lat 34° 27' S; Long 150° 53' E.

Admiralty Chart: AUS 194/195
Time Zone: GMT +10 h
Admiralty Pilot: 14
UNCTAD Locode: AU PKL

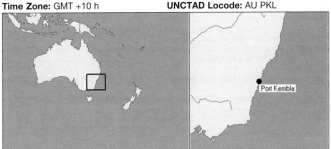

Principal Facilities:

Q	Y	G		R		B		T	A

Authority: Port Kembla Port Corp., P O Box 89, Port Kembla, N.S.W., Australia 2505, *Tel:* +61 2 4275 0100, *Fax:* +61 2 4274 0643, *Email:* enquiries@portkembla.com.au, *Website:* www.portkembla.com.au

Officials: Chief Executive Officer: Dom Figliomeni, *Tel:* +61 2 4275 0101, *Email:* dxf@portkembla.com.au.
General Manager: Kall Dillon, *Tel:* +61 2 4275 0132, *Email:* kjd@portkembla.com.au.
Business Development Manager: Ray Smith, *Tel:* +61 2 4275 0113, *Email:* rxs@portkembla.com.au.

Port Security: ISPS compliant

Approach: Depth at entrance between northern breakwater and eastern breakwater 16.75 m ISLW, width 305 m

Anchorage: Vessels should anchor well clear of the approaches to the port. Foul ground exists close by the Pilot Boarding Ground. Vessels should not anchor between the Islands as this is foul ground
The anchorage off Port Kembla may be unsatisfactory in bad weather. Master's should be prepared to weigh anchor and proceed to sea, especially in SE gales

Pilotage: Compulsory and available 24 h/day. Vessel's should maintain a continuous listening watch on VHF Channel 11 and inform Harbour Control when approaching the pilot boarding position
Pilot Station A: in pos 34° 27' 90" S; 150° 54' 70" E (disembarkation outward-bound and inward-bound embarkation for barge trains and small vessels)
Pilot Station B: in pos 34° 24' 23" S; 150° 57' 62" E (embarkation inward-bound for deep draught (capesize vessels) and vessels arriving from the north or anchorages)
Pilot Station C: in pos 34° 27' 48" S; 150° 59' 15" E (embarkation inward-bound for vessels arriving from the south in fair weather)
Pilot Station D: in pos 34° 26' 00" S; 150° 58' 00" E (alternate pilot station for embarkation/disembarkation in heavy weather)

Radio Frequency: VHF channel 11 for port control - call sign 'Port Kembla Harbour' VHF channel 8 for pilot and tugs

Tides: Range of tide 2 m

Traffic: 2007/08, 756 vessels, 26 591 395 t of cargo handled

Maximum Vessel Dimensions: 295 m loa

Working Hours: 24 h operations

Accommodation:

Name	Length (m)	Draught (m)	Remarks
Inner Harbour			
Berth No.101	215	11.5	See [1] below
Berth No.102	250	16	See [2] below
Berth No.103	200	12.2	See [3] below
Berth No.104	260	16.25	See [4] below
Berth No's 105 & 106	430	13.9–15.7	See [5] below
Berth No.107	290	12.3	See [6] below
Berth No.109		12.2	See [7] below
Berth No.110		11.4	See [8] below
Berth No.111		15.6	See [9] below
Berth No.112		12.8	See [10] below
Berth No.113		11	See [11] below
Outer Harbour			
Berth No.201		8.5–11.67	See [12] below
Berth No's 202-205			See [13] below
Berth No.206		11.2	Bulk liquid facility for vessels up to 180 m loa

[1]*Berth No.101:* Operated by Port Kembla Coal Terminal Ltd., P O Box 823, Wollongong, NSW 2520, Tel: +61 2 4228 0288, Fax: +61 2 4228 7605, Email: info@pkct.com.au, Website: www.pkct.com.au
Vessels up to 225 m loa. One gantry shiploader with nominal loading rate of 1000 t/h
[2]*Berth No.102:* Operated by Port Kembla Coal Terminal Ltd., P O Box 823,

Wollongong, NSW 2520, Tel: +61 2 4228 0288, Fax: +61 2 4228 7605, Email: info@pkct.com.au, Website: www.pkct.com.au

Vessels up to 300 m loa. Two gantry shiploaders with nominal loading rate of 5000 t/h. 850 000 t storage cap

[3]Berth No.103: Currently under construction and due for completion in 2008

[4]Berth No.104: Primarily used for grain. Two gantry shiploaders with combined nominal loading rate of 5000 t/h for vessels up to 300 m loa. Air draught of 17 m. Storage cap of 260 000 t

[5]Berth No's 105 & 106: Operated by Australian Amalgamated Terminals (AAT), P O Box 144, Port Kembla NSW 2505, Tel: +61 2 4221 0925, Fax: +61 2 4221 0950, Email: pk.operations@aat.auz.biz, Website: www.aat.auz.biz

Containers and vehicles for vessels up to 190 m loa

[6]Berth No.107: Operated by Australian Amalgamated Terminals (AAT), P O Box 144, Port Kembla NSW 2505, Tel: +61 2 4221 0925, Fax: +61 2 4221 0950, Email: pk.operations@aat.auz.biz, Website: www.aat.auz.biz

For vessels up to 260 m loa. Used primarily for vehicles

[7]Berth No.109: Private BlueScope wharf for vessels up to 200 m loa. Facilities for loading steel

[8]Berth No.110: Private BlueScope wharf for vessels up to 160 m loa. Facilities for loading steel

[9]Berth No.111: Private BlueScope wharf for vessels up to 300 m loa. Two 15 t travelling transporter grab cranes with gross discharging rate of 500 t/h and one 35 t travelling transporter grab crane with gross discharging rate of 1000 t/h

[10]Berth No.112: Private BlueScope wharf for vessels up to 280 m loa. Facilities for loading steel

[11]Berth No.113: Private BlueScope wharf for vessels up to 200 m loa. Facilities for loading steel

[12]Berth No.201: Discharge berth for petroleum products for vessels up to 225 m loa. Two loading arms

[13]Berth No's 202-205: Operated by Port Kembla Gateway Pty Ltd., P O Box 195, Port Kembla NSW 2505, Tel: +61 2 4276 3566, Fax: +61 2 4274 4765, Email: info@pkgateway.com.au, Website: www.pkgateway.com.au

Berths 202 & 203 for vessels up to 200 m loa with draught of 10.1-10.7 m

Berth 204 for vessels up to 80 m loa with draught of 6.1 m

Berth 205 for vessels up to 80 m loa with draught of 7 m

One 17 t level luffing crane, one 1000 t/h ship loader, dry bulk hoppers, discharge grabs & storage facilities

Cargo Worked: Bulk cargo up to 5000 t/h

Bunkering: Port Kembla Marine Fuels, Lot 2, 5 Flinders Street, Port Kembla, N.S.W., Australia 2505, Tel: +61 2 4275 3892, Fax: +61 2 4274 6507, Email: bunkers@pkmf.com, Website: www.pkmf.com

Port Kembla Marine Fuels, Lot 2, 5 Flinders Street, Port Kembla, N.S.W., Australia 2505, Tel: +61 2 4275 3892, Fax: +61 2 4274 6507, Email: bunkers@pkmf.com, Website: www.pkmf.com – Grades: HFO-380cSt – Delivery Mode: pipeline

Towage: SVITZER, SVITZER Australasia, No. 4 Jetty Foreshore Road, Port Kembla, N.S.W., Australia 2505, Tel: +61 2 4274 6060, Fax: +61 2 4275 2717, Email: info.portkembla@adsteam.com.au, Website: www.svitzer.com

Repair & Maintenance: Garnock Engineering Co. Proprietary Ltd, Shellharbour Road, Kemblawarra, P O Box 199, Port Kembla, N.S.W., Australia 2505, Tel: +61 2 4274 0274, Fax: +61 2 4276 1313, Email: steve@garnock.com.au, Website: www.garnock.com.au Specialised work: Stress relieving, normalising, welding, modifications and services to all types of vessels, shipwright work. Engine repairs Storey & Keers (Ship Repairs) Proprietary Ltd, Lot 5, Shellharbour Road, Port Kembla, N.S.W., Australia 2505, Tel: +61 2 4274 0647, Fax: +61 2 4276 1303, Email: info@storey.com.au, Website: www.storey.com.au

Seaman Missions: The Seamans Mission, P O Box 216, Port Kembla, N.S.W., Australia 2505, Tel: +61 2 4274 6498, Email: portkembla@mts.org.au

Ship Chandlers: Australian International Marine Services Proprietary Ltd, 5 Gibsons Road, Figtree, N.S.W., Australia 2525, Tel: +61 2 2826 3677, Fax: +61 2 9700 0737, Email: portkembla@sinwaglobal.com, Website: www.sinwaglobal.com

Bulbeck Ship Supply Services Proprietary Ltd, 12 Ralph Black Drive, Wollongong, N.S.W., Australia 2500, Tel: +61 2 4226 6166, Fax: +61 2 4226 6188, Email: info@bulbeck.com.au, Website: www.bulbeck.com.au

Shipping Agents: Barwil Agencies Australia Pty Ltd, P O Box 170, Port Kembla, N.S.W., Australia 2505, Tel: +61 2 4275 1500, Fax: +61 2 4275 1011, Email: ptkembla@wilhelmsen.com, Website: www.barwil.com

Beaufort Shipping Agency Proprietary Ltd, 1st Floor, Gateway House, Christy Drive, off Old Port Road, #6 Jetty, Port Kembla, N.S.W., Australia 2505, Tel: +61 2 4275 1899, Fax: +61 2 4274 4622, Email: manager.portkembla@beaufortshipping.com, Website: www.beaufortshipping.com.au

Gulf Agency Co (Australia) Pty Ltd., P O Box 22, Port Kembla, N.S.W., Australia 2505, Tel: +61 2 4274 7017, Fax: +61 2 4274 9239, Email: shipping.portkembla@gacworld.com, Website: www.gacworld.com

Hetherington Kingsbury Proprietary Ltd, 1st Floor, Gateway House, Christy Drive, Outer harbour, Port Kembla, N.S.W., Australia 2505, Tel: +61 2 4276 3533, Fax: +61 2 4276 4344, Email: vkenny@hksa.com.au

Inchcape Shipping Services (ISS), Inchcape Shipping Services Pty Ltd, Ground Floor, Port Kembla Gateway (Nth Wing), No.6 Jetty Christy Drive, P O Box 50, Port Kembla, N.S.W., Australia 2505, Tel: +61 2 4275 2300, Fax: +61 2 4275 2400, Email: port.kembla@iss-shipping.com.au, Website: www.iss-shipping.com

McArthur Shipping & Agency Co Pty Ltd, P O Box 108, Port Kembla, N.S.W., Australia 2505, Tel: +61 2 4276 3533, Fax: +61 2 4276 4344, Email: ptkembla@mcaship.com.au, Website: www.mcaship.com.au

Stevedoring Companies: Illawarra Stevedores Proprietary Ltd, P O Box 88, Port Kembla, N.S.W., Australia 2505, Tel: +61 2 4276 4950, Fax: +61 2 4276 4770, Email: illawarra@illawarrastevedores.com.au, Website: www.illawarrastevedores.com.au

John Wingate & Sons Pty Ltd, Port Kembla, N.S.W., Australia, Tel: +61 2 4276 1782, Fax: +61 2 4276 1380, Email: kwingate@wingates.com.au

P&O Ports, P&O Automotive & General Stevedoring Pty Limited, P O Box 1429, Wollongong, N.S.W., Australia 2505, Tel: +61 2 4222 0200, Fax: +61 2 4225 8938, Email: pkoperations@poports.com.au, Website: www.poports.com

Port Kembla Stevedoring Proprietary Ltd, 18 Beach Street, Wollongong, Port Kembla, N.S.W., Australia NSW 2500, Tel: +61 2 4226 4050, Fax: +61 2 4226 6310, Email: david.wingate@poports.com.au, Website: www.poports.com.au

Toll Stevedoring, No 2 Products Berth, Off Tomthumb Road, Port Kembla, N.S.W.,

Australia 2505, Tel: +61 2 4275 4533, Fax: +61 2 4275 7283, Email: graeme_sargent@toll.com.au, Website: www.toll.com.au

Medical Facilities: Wollongong Hospital, Shellharbour Hospital & Port Kembla Hospital

Airport: Kingsford Smith, 70 km

Railway: The main station is at Wollongong, 3 km

Lloyd's Agent: Freemans Marine, P O Box 36, St. Leonards, N.S.W., Australia 1590, Tel: +61 2 9438 2655, Fax: +61 2 9436 1367, Email: lloyds@freemans.com.au, Website: www.freemansmarine.com.au

PORT KENNEDY

alternate name, see Thursday Island

PORT LATTA

Lat 40° 51' S; Long 145° 23' E.

Admiralty Chart: AUS 790	**Admiralty Pilot:** 14
Time Zone: GMT +10 h	**UNCTAD Locode:** AU PLA

Principal Facilities:

		Y					T	A

Authority: Danbar Marine Services, P O Box 313, Wynyard, Tas., Australia 7325, Tel: +61 3 6272 3277, Fax: +61 3 6272 4801, Email: danbar@southcom.com.au, Website: www.tasports.com.au

Officials: General Manager: David Phillips, Email: david.phillips@tasports.com.au.

Port Security: ISPS compliant

Pre-Arrival Information: All ETA and arrival information to be passed via ship's agent. The pilot radio station is only manned immediately when shipping is due. At all other times no radio contact is available

Approach: Direct approach from open sea

Anchorage: 2 miles NNE from Jetty Head in 28 m

Pilotage: Compulsory for all vessels. Pilot remains on board throughout the vessels stay and also acts as loading master

Radio Frequency: VHF Channels 14 & 16

Weather: Port is affected during strong WNW to E winds

Tides: Range of tide 2.5 m

Traffic: 2000, 46 commercial vessels, 2 234 915 t of cargo handled

Maximum Vessel Dimensions: Max draft 15.25 m plus tide, minus 2.0 m, max length 245 m, max beam 38.5 m; larger vessels by prior consultation

Principal Imports and Exports: Exports: Iron ore concentrate & pellets.

Working Hours: 24 h/day when shipping is alongside

Accommodation:

Name	Remarks
Port Latta	See [1] below

[1]Port Latta: One berth where vessels moor to six buoys 3 m off two protective dolphins. Seven 200 m mooring lines foreward and aft including spring. Two lines to each buoy. Springs to dolphins. Vessels over 100 000 dwt require additional 220 m wire foreward and aft. One iron pellet loader 1828.8 m long, carries an ore conveyor to twin loaders, cap 2300 t/h, each protected by a dolphin

Cargo Worked: 52 800 t/day

Waste Reception Facilities: Nil. Except for garbage, Australian Quarantine Inspection Service now requires all foreign ship garbage to be landed

Towage: Two tugs required for berthing of vessels of 90 000 dwt and over North Western Shipping & Towage Proprietary Ltd, Inspection Head Wharf, Beauty Point, P O Box 76, Beaconsfield, Tas., Australia 7270, Tel: +61 3 6383 4522, Fax: +61 3 6383 4604, Email: inquiries@nwst.com.au, Website: www.nwst.com.au

Repair & Maintenance: Minor repairs can be carried out. Local contractors through an agent

Shipping Agents: Barwil Agencies Australia Pty Ltd, P O Box 311, George Town, Tas., Australia 7253, Tel: +61 3 6382 4088, Fax: +61 3 6382 4099, Email: bellbay@wilhelmsen.com, Website: www.wilhelmsen.com

Surveyors: Briar Maritime Services Proprietary Ltd, P O Box 338, Ulverstone, Tas., Australia 7315, Tel: +61 3 6429 3272, Fax: +61 3 6429 3264, Email: briarmaritime@bigpond.com, Website: www.briarmaritime.com

Medical Facilities: Hospital at Smithton, approx 30 km

Airport: Wynyard, 40 km

Lloyd's Agent: Freemans Marine, Level 7, 564 St. Kilda Road, Melbourne, Vic., Australia 3004, *Tel:* +61 3 9935 2400, *Fax:* +61 3 9915 0351, *Email:* lloyds@freemans.com.au, *Website:* www.freemansmarine.com.au

PORT LINCOLN

Lat 34° 43' S; Long 135° 52' E.

Admiralty Chart: AUS 134	**Admiralty Pilot:** 13
Time Zone: GMT +9.5 h	**UNCTAD Locode:** AU PLO

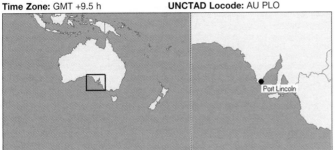

Principal Facilities:

P	Y G	R	B	T	A

Authority: Flinders Ports Proprietary Ltd, P O Box 354, Port Lincoln, S.A., Australia 5606, *Tel:* +61 8 8682 3633, *Fax:* +61 8 8682 6725, *Email:* anderson.phil@flindersports.com.au, *Website:* www.flindersports.com.au

Officials: Operations: Philip Anderson.

Port Security: ISPS compliant

Approach: Depth in Boston Bay approach channel 14.6 m below CD

Pilotage: Compulsory. Pilot boards 1.5 nautical miles ESE of Boston Point

Radio Frequency: VHF Channels 6, 8, 12, 16 and 67

Tides: MHWS 1.54 m, MHWN 1.07 m

Traffic: 2007/08, 79 vessels, 1 076 325 t of cargo handled

Maximum Vessel Dimensions: Oil tankers 182 m loa, grain carriers 262 m loa and fertiliser carriers 196 m loa. 14.7 m max draught

Principal Imports and Exports: Imports: Fertiliser, Fuel. Exports: Grain.

Working Hours: Grain: Sun-Fri 0800-2200. Sat 0800-1200 or 1600 to finish vessel Phosphate: 0800-2300 seven days a week

Accommodation:

Name	Length (m)	Depth (m)	Remarks
Port Lincoln			
Berth No.2	190	8.7	Recreational fishing only
Berth No.3	246		Fishing boats
Berth No's 4 & 5	330	15.2	See [1] below
Berth No.6	250	12.2	Fertiliser & general purpose
Berth No.7	183	8.4	Fishing boats
Berth No.8	77	5.7	Fishing boats
Berth No.9	107	4.6	Ro/ro
Berth No.10	56	.2	Fishing
Kirton Point Jetty	280	9.9	Oil berth with T-head jetty & four mooring dolphins

[1]*Berth No's 4 & 5:* Operated by ABB Grain Ltd
Bulk grain berths with two travelling loaders loading wheat at 2000 t/h, barley at 1750 t/h and oats at 1250 t/h

Mechanical Handling Equipment:

Location	Type	Capacity (t)	Qty
Port Lincoln	Mobile Cranes	20	2
Port Lincoln	Mobile Cranes	9	1
Port Lincoln	Mobile Cranes	33	1

Bunkering: By road tanker to bulk berth. Minor vessel berths have pipelines BP Australia (Proprietary) Ltd, P O Box 5222, Melbourne, Vic., Australia 3001, *Tel:* +61 3 9268 4111, *Fax:* +61 3 9268 3321, *Email:* gomiasfuelsales@bp.com, *Website:* www.bp.com
ExxonMobil Marine Fuels, 1 Harbour Front Place, 06-00 Harbour Front, Tower One, Singapore, Republic of Singapore 098633, *Tel:* +65 6885 8998, *Fax:* +65 6885 8794, *Email:* asiapac.marinefuels@exxonmobil.com, *Website:* www.exxonmobilmarinefuels.com – *Grades:* MGO – *Delivery Mode:* tank truck
Shell Australia Ltd, Shell Company of Australia, Marine Centre Oceania, No 8 Redfern Road, Melbourne, Vic., Australia 3123, *Tel:* +61 3 9666 5446, *Fax:* +61 3 8823 4800, *Email:* sal-marine-products@shell.com.au, *Website:* www.shell.com.au

Towage: Port Lincoln Tugs Proprietary Ltd, 86 Matthew Place, Port Lincoln, S.A., Australia 5606, *Tel:* +61 8 8683 4665

Repair & Maintenance: Slipway for vessels up to 60 m loa with 1800 t max

Seaman Missions: The Seamans Mission, P O Box 73, Port Lincoln, S.A., Australia 5606, *Tel:* +61 8 8683 0036, *Fax:* +61 8 8683 3009, *Email:* portlincoln@mts.org.au

Shipping Agents: Barwil Agencies Australia Pty Ltd, P O Box 162A, Whyalla, S.A., Australia 5600, *Tel:* +61 8 8644 0911, *Fax:* +61 8 8644 0925, *Email:* whyalla@wilhelmsen.com, *Website:* www.wilhelmsen.com
Inchcape Shipping Services (ISS), Inchcape Shipping Services Pty Ltd, Suite 7, 17 Washington Street, P O Box 1592, Port Lincoln, S.A., Australia 5606, *Tel:* +61 8 8682 1011, *Fax:* +61 8 8682 1182, *Email:* port.lincoln@iss-shipping.com.au, *Website:* www.iss-shipping.com
P&O Ports, P O Box 567, Port Lincoln, S.A., Australia 5606, *Tel:* +61 8 8682 1900,

Fax: +61 8 8682 6924, *Email:* lincoln.office@poport.com.au, *Website:* www.poport.com.au

Stevedoring Companies: ABB Grain Ltd, King Street, Port Lincoln, S.A., Australia 5606, *Tel:* +61 8 8682 1888, *Fax:* +61 8 8682 6526, *Email:* ian.bampton@abb.com.au, *Website:* www.abb.com.au
P&O Ports, P O Box 567, Port Lincoln, S.A., Australia 5606, *Tel:* +61 8 8682 1900, *Fax:* +61 8 8682 6924, *Email:* lincoln.office@poport.com.au, *Website:* www.poport.com.au

Airport: 12 km

Railway: Shipping pier connected to railway system

Lloyd's Agent: Maritime & General Insurance Surveyors Proprietary Ltd, Suite 4, 7 Divett Street, Adelaide, S.A., Australia 5015, *Tel:* +61 8 8341 2552, *Fax:* +61 8 8241 0229, *Email:* maritime-general@adam.com.au

PORT PIRIE

Lat 33° 10' S; Long 138° 0' E.

Admiralty Chart: AUS 136	**Admiralty Pilot:** 13
Time Zone: GMT +9.5 h	**UNCTAD Locode:** AU PPI

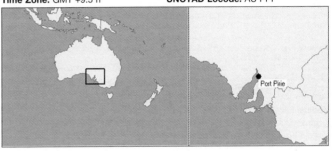

Principal Facilities:

	Y G C		B		T	A

Authority: Flinders Ports Proprietary Ltd, Berth 4, Port Pirie, S.A., Australia 5540, *Tel:* +61 8 8632 1455, *Fax:* +61 8 8632 5918, *Email:* flindersports@flindersports.com.au, *Website:* www.flindersports.com.au

Officials: Operations: Allan Webster, *Email:* webster.allan@flindersports.com.au.

Port Security: ISPS compliant

Approach: Entrance channel 9 miles long, 90 m wide with a depth of 6.4 m above LWOST. Swinging basin 295 m diameter

Anchorage: In pos 30° 04' S; 137° 46' E in a depth of 12 m. The anchorage is open to rough seas from the S but little swell

Pilotage: Compulsory for all non-exempt vessels. Vessels should send requests for pilots to Harbour Master at least 3 h in advance (5 h if pilot required outside office hours)
Pilot boards in the following positions:
Bearing 165°, 5 n miles from Whyalla Entrance No.1 Lt Bn for vessels over 14 m draught
In the vicinity of Port Pirie Pilot Boarding Ground (33° 04' 55" S; 137° 45' 50" E) and 1.7 nautical miles SE of No.1 Lt Bn for vessels less than 14 m draught

Radio Frequency: VHF Channels 6, 8, 12, 16 and 67

Weather: From Jan-Feb freak thunder squalls up to 40-50 knots are known to occur

Tides: MHWS 2.65 m, neaps 1.65 m. Tides are affected by the weather and may be up to 0.60 m above or below prediction

Traffic: 2007/08, 62 vessels, 568 964 t of cargo handled

Maximum Vessel Dimensions: Daylight: max loa 185 m, max beam 28 m. Night: max loa 180 m, max beam 28 m. Vessels larger than these dimensions are subject to Marine Operations General Manager's discretion

Principal Imports and Exports: Imports: Coal, Minerals, Ores. Exports: Grain, Lead, Seeds, Zinc concentrates.

Working Hours: 0800-1500, 1500-2200, 0001-0700 every day. No third shift at the grain berth

Accommodation:

Name	Length (m)	Depth (m)	Remarks
Port Pirie			
Berth No.1	152	5.3	Fishing & recreational vessels
Berth No.2	190	8.2	See [1] below
Berth No.4	107	4.9	Tug berth
Berth No.5	198	8.2	General cargo
Berth No.6	183	8.2	See [2] below
Berth No.7	145	8.2	General cargo & containers
Berth No.8	180	8.2	Lead export
Berth No.9	180	8.2	Lead export & coal import
Berth No.10	158	8.2	Bulk imports. Max air draught 22.1 m

[1]*Berth No.2:* Operated by ABB Grain Ltd.
Grain. Silos are connected to this berth by a conveyor belt terminating in a shipping gallery with five identical slewing loading booms, loading grain at the overall rate of 800 t/h. Storage cap of 3.3 million bushels
[2]*Berth No.6:* Ore exports. Equipped with travelling gantry shiploader handling concentrates and ores. Loading rate of 550-600 t/h. Air draught 12.1 m

Bunkering: BP Australia (Proprietary) Ltd, P O Box 5222, Melbourne, Vic., Australia 3001, *Tel:* +61 3 9268 4111, *Fax:* +61 3 9268 3321, *Email:* gomiasfuelsales@bp.com, *Website:* www.bp.com – *Delivery Mode:* truck
ExxonMobil Marine Fuels, 1 Harbour Front Place, 06-00 Harbour Front, Tower One, Singapore, Republic of Singapore 098633, *Tel:* +65 6885 8998, *Fax:* +65 6885 8794, *Email:* asiapac.marinefuels@exxonmobil.com, *Website:* www.exxonmobilmarinefuels.com – *Grades:* MGO – *Delivery Mode:* tank truck
Shell Australia Ltd, Shell Company of Australia, Marine Centre Oceania, No 8 Redfern Road, Melbourne, Vic., Australia 3123, *Tel:* +61 3 9666 5446, *Fax:* +61 3 8823 4800, *Email:* sal-marine-products@shell.com, *Website:* www.shell.com.au – *Delivery Mode:* truck

Waste Reception Facilities: Removal of garbage is compulsory. There are no facilities for slop reception

Towage: Adsteam Marine Ltd (The Adelaide S.S. Co. Ltd), 24 Forsyth Street, Port Pirie, Whyalla, S.A., Australia 5600, *Tel:* +61 8 8645 8733, *Fax:* +61 8 8645 9959, *Website:* www.svitzer.com

Repair & Maintenance: S.J. Cheesman & Co., 21 George Street, Port Pirie, S.A., Australia 5540, *Tel:* +61 8 8632 1044, *Fax:* +61 8 8632 5399, *Email:* sales@sjcheesman.com.au, *Website:* www.sjcheesman.com.au Minor repairs

Seaman Missions: The Seamans Mission, P O Box 54, Port Pirie, S.A., Australia 5540, *Tel:* +61 8 8632 2057, *Fax:* +61 8 8633 2606, *Email:* portpirie@mts.org.au

Shipping Agents: Barwil Agencies Australia Pty Ltd, P O Box 1559, Adelaide, S.A., Australia 5015, *Tel:* +61 8 8341 0466, *Fax:* +61 8 8341 0506, *Email:* ptadelaide@wilhelmsen.com, *Website:* www.wilhelmsen.com
P&O Ports, P O Box 27, Port Pirie, S.A., Australia 5540, *Tel:* +61 8 8632 3733, *Fax:* +61 8 8632 6724

Stevedoring Companies: ABB Grain Ltd, Port Pirie, S.A., Australia, *Tel:* +61 8 8632 2805, *Fax:* +61 8 8633 0622
P&O Ports, P O Box 27, Port Pirie, S.A., Australia 5540, *Tel:* +61 8 8632 3733, *Fax:* +61 8 8632 6724
Port Pirie Stevedores, Port Pirie, S.A., Australia, *Tel:* +61 8 8633 2708, *Fax:* +61 8 8623 3691

Medical Facilities: Hospital with full facilities available

Airport: 8 km

Lloyd's Agent: Maritime & General Insurance Surveyors Proprietary Ltd, Suite 4, 7 Divett Street, Adelaide, S.A., Australia 5015, *Tel:* +61 8 8341 2552, *Fax:* +61 8 8241 0229, *Email:* maritime-general@adam.com.au

PORT STANVAC

Lat 35° 7' S; Long 138° 28' E.

Admiralty Chart: AUS 125
Time Zone: GMT +9.5 h
This port is no longer operational

Admiralty Pilot: 13
UNCTAD Locode: AU PST

PORT WALCOTT

Lat 20° 35' S; Long 117° 10' E.

Admiralty Chart: AUS 55/56
Time Zone: GMT +8 h

Admiralty Pilot: 17
UNCTAD Locode: AU PWL

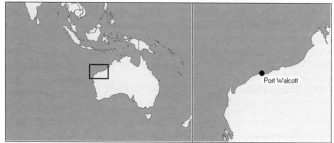

Principal Facilities:

P		Y	G					T	A

Authority: Department of Planning & Infrastructure - Ports, P O Box 402, Fremantle, W.A., Australia 6959, *Tel:* +61 8 9216 8867, *Fax:* +61 8 9216 8982, *Email:* david.heppingstone@dpi.wa.gov.au, *Website:* www.dpi.wa.gov.au

Officials: Harbour Master: David Heppingstone.

Port Security: ISPS compliant

Approach: The approach is marked by five light buoys. The first is in pos 20° 23' 18" S; 117° 25' 30" E and is fitted with a 3 cm Racon-morse code 'K'. From a position about one mile East of this buoy, ships should proceed on a course 183° for seven miles, then 253° for ten miles to the anchorage area. Ships should not attempt to enter via Bass Pass. The departure channel is 35 km long with a width of 270 m and is dredged to a depth of 16 m

Pilotage: For vessels arriving: Vessels proceed to inner pilot boarding ground in pos 20° 33' 5" S; 117° 15' 5" E or to the inner anchorage. Pilotage is not compulsory however, pilots will meet vessels at C.1. beacon in pos 20° 23' 3" S; 117° 26' 5" E if requested. Pilotage is compulsory for all vessels from inner pilotage boarding ground and inner anchorages to berths
For vessels departing: Pilotage is compulsory for all vessels. From the ore jetty vessels depart through an 18 mile departure channel. The pilot departs at C.1. beacon. From the service jetty pilots depart at the inner pilot boarding ground

Radio Frequency: VHF Channel 16 monitored 0830-1200, 1300-1630 Monday to Friday

Weather: Cyclones likely Nov-Mar

Tides: Springs 5.7 m, neaps 1.2 m

Maximum Vessel Dimensions: At Ore Berth No.1, 355 m loa, 50 m beam; No.2, 350 m loa, 55 m beam. At Service Jetty, 180 m loa, approx 32 m beam

Working Hours: 24 h/day

Accommodation:

Name	Remarks
Port Walcott	
Lambert Ore Jetty	See [1] below
Lambert Service Jetty	See [2] below

[1]*Lambert Ore Jetty:* Operated by Pilbara Iron
Extends 2670 m to seawards in a 046 degree direction. It is double sided and capable of handling vessels up to 290 000 dwt. Max beam in No.1 berth is 50 m and No.2 berth 55 m. The depth of water at No.1 is 18.5 m and at No.2 is 19.8 m. Ships should arrange their trim so that there is always a clearance of 1 m when in the berth. Two ship loaders, one designed to operate at 6000 t/h and the other at 9400 t/h. Ships berth 'head out' and are secured to dolphins parallel with the jetty. These dolphins are 7.6 m above LW. The height of the jetty is 18.6 m. Max distance between hatches 234 m at No.1 berth and 236 m at No.2 berth. Berthing of ore carriers is usually carried out 2-3 hours before HW
[2]*Lambert Service Jetty:* The neck is 457 m long and berthing head is 155 m. Off each end of the head is a mooring dolphin some 27 m away. This permits a vessel of about 180 m to the berth. There is a min depth of 10 m at LW. The height of the jetty is 10.67 m. Cargo is handled by ships own gear. The jetty is designed for road transport only. Berthing at the jetty is either at about 2.5 h before or 3.5 h after HW. Tankers berth at the service jetty and discharge is through an 8'' flexible hose located near the centre of the jetty

Mechanical Handling Equipment:

Location	Type
Port Walcott	Mobile Cranes

Towage: Two tugs are available, both of 4200 hp with bollard pull of 62 t

Ship Chandlers: Sealanes - Fuji, P O Box 186, Karratha, W.A., Australia 6714, *Tel:* +61 8 9185 1422, *Fax:* +61 8 9185 3295, *Email:* sea@sealanes.com.au, *Website:* www.sealanes.com.au

Shipping Agents: Barwil Agencies Australia Pty Ltd, P O Box 1005, Karratha, W.A., Australia 6714, *Tel:* +61 8 9144 2311, *Fax:* +61 8 9144 2008, *Email:* dampier@wilhelmsen.com, *Website:* www.wilhelmsen.com

Medical Facilities: Modern hospital, one doctor and a dentist

Airport: Karratha Airport, 67 km

Lloyd's Agent: Moko Proprietary Ltd, P O Box 685, Willetton, W.A., Australia 6955, *Tel:* +61 8 9354 2248, *Fax:* +61 8 9354 2234, *Email:* kglange@bigpond.com

PORTLAND

Lat 38° 21' S; Long 141° 36' E.

Admiralty Chart: AUS 140
Time Zone: GMT +10 h

Admiralty Pilot: 14
UNCTAD Locode: AU PTJ

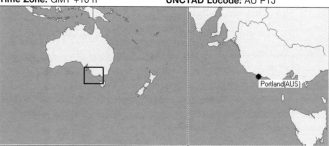

Principal Facilities:

Q	Y	G			B		T	A

Authority: Port of Portland Proprietary Ltd, P O Box 292, Portland, Vic., Australia 3305, *Tel:* +61 3 5525 0900, *Fax:* +61 3 5521 7488, *Email:* info@portofportland.com.au, *Website:* www.portofportland.com.au

Officials: Chief Executive Officer: Scott Paterson, *Tel:* +61 3 5525 0903, *Email:* spaterson@portofportland.com.au
Marine Manager: Vijay Vijayapalan, *Tel:* +61 3 5525 0981, *Email:* vvijayapalan@portofportland.com.au.
Marketing Manager: Jim Cooper, *Tel:* +61 3 5525 0910, *Email:* jcooper@portofportland.com.au
Operations Manager: Peter Moir, *Tel:* +61 3 5525 0964, *Email:* pmoir@portofportland.com.au.

Port Security: ISPS compliant

Pre-Arrival Information: Pre-arrival information should be submitted to the port office directly or through the local agent at least 48 h prior to arrival. For details visit website (www.portofportland.com.au) or contact local agent

Approach: Approach from the W: a safe course into Portland Bay can be maintained by rounding Lawrence Rocks at a distance of 1.4 nautical miles offshore and altering until a course of 330 degrees can be steered, which will clear the S side of the Bay between Point Danger and Portland by 1.3 nautical miles. When Whalers Point Lighthouse bears 270 degrees about 1.2 nautical miles distant, the course can be altered for the harbour entrance. Approach from E: Is a straight course after rounding Lady Julia Percy Island 18 nautical miles from the breakwaters

Anchorage: Portland Bay is clear of all dangers and safe anchorage may be found 1.5 nautical miles N and NE of the main breakwater. Holding ground is good and excellent shelter is obtainable from westerly weather. Anchorage is not recommended in strong E or SE weather, as there may be a confused sea and swell

Pilotage: Compulsory except for exempt Masters. Pilot boards approx 2.1 nautical miles ENE of the main breakwater

Radio Frequency: Maritime VHF operating of channels 12 and 16 is maintained in the Harbour Master's office, call sign 'Portland Port Control'. Listening on channel 16 between 0800-1700 Mon to Fri. After hours and weekends when shipping is expected

Weather: The tidal stream off Portland is feeble and hardly perceptible, and as a general rule is due to wind set. Weather changes are frequent and sudden on the SW coast

Tides: Mean rise and fall is approx 0.7 m, but the prevailing wind has an influence on the tidal range

Traffic: 2007/08, 210 vessels, 3 252 746 t of cargo handled

Maximum Vessel Dimensions: 265 m loa, 12.2 m arrival draught (with tide) and up to 12.8 m departure draught (with tide)

Principal Imports and Exports: Imports: Alumina, Fertiliser product, General cargo, Liquid pitch, Petroleum coke, Sulphuric acid. Exports: Aluminium ingots, General cargo, Grain, Livestock, Logs, Mineral sands, Plantation woodchip.

Working Hours: 24 hours - 0800-1500, 1500-2200 and 2300-0600

Accommodation:

Name	Length (m)	Depth (m)	Draught (m)	Remarks
Portland				See [1] below
K.S. Anderson Wharf No.1 Berth	255	12.5		See [2] below
K.S. Anderson Wharf No.2 Berth	143	11.5		See [3] below
No.5 Berth	240	12.5	12.2	See [4] below
No.6 Berth	229	12	11.5	See [5] below
Smelter Berth	205	12.5	12.2	See [6] below
S.L. Patterson Berth	76	11	10.5	See [7] below

[1]*Portland:* Deep water all-weather port with a harbour basin of 101 ha enclosed by two breakwaters. Entrance to basin 244 m wide. Main breakwater extends 1280 m NS direction with outer extremity in 14.5 m of water. Lee breakwater extends 1179 m E direction

[2]*K.S. Anderson Wharf No.1 Berth:* Bulk loading facilities primarily for grain and woodchips. Two lateral traversing shiploaders operate on the two berths, providing loading rates up to 1200 t/h for various types of grain and woodchip. Graincorp Ltd controls the shore-based grain and woodchip handling. Grain storage cap of 60 000 t. Transit shed of 2550 m2 and open storage space of approx 0.5 ha

[3]*K.S. Anderson Wharf No.2 Berth:* A continuation of No.1 Berth. Bulk loading facilities for grain, liquid pitch & sulphuric acid. Two lateral traversing shiploaders operate on the two berths, providing loading rates up to 1200 t/h for various types of grain and woodchip. Graincorp Ltd controls the shore-based grain and woodchip handling. Grain storage cap of 60 000 t. Transit shed of 5250 m2 and open storage space of approx 0.5 ha

[4]*No.5 Berth:* Breakbulk, ingots, logs, paper pulp, containers, ro/ro, fertilisers, mineral sands, livestock & general cargo. Storage area of 0.9 ha and transit shed of 2550 m2

[5]*No.6 Berth:* Woodchips, breakbulk, logs, ingots, paper pulp, container, ro/ro. fertilisers, livestock & general cargo. Storage area of 0.4 ha

[6]*Smelter Berth:* Dedicated to servicing the import shipping requirements of the Portland Aluminium Smelter - alumina, petroleum coke and aluminium fluoride. Is also capable of handling the export of aluminium ingots

[7]*S.L. Patterson Berth:* Situated on the Lee breakwater, approx 457 m from the seaward end of the breakwater. It is designed for vessels up to 38 000 dwt. It is presently used to accommodate the harbour tugs but can be utilised for vessels/rigs undertaking extensive repairs/surveys

Mechanical Handling Equipment:

Location	Type	Capacity (t)	Qty	Remarks
Portland	Mobile Cranes	10	1	See [1] below

[1]*Portland:* Cranes with larger cap available from private companies

Bunkering: Can be supplied by road transport or by special arrangement with local fuel suppliers. All vessels bunkering require prior approval of the Port management

Waste Reception Facilities: A collection service for domestic and quarantinable garbage is provided at all berths. It is an offence to dump garbage etc. into the waters of Portland harbour

Towage: North Western Shipping & Towage Proprietary Ltd, Slipway Area, P O Box 187, Portland, Vic., Australia 3305, *Tel:* +61 3 5521 7253, *Fax:* +61 3 5521 7259, *Email:* inquiries@onedinmarine.com.au

Repair & Maintenance: John Beever (Australia) Proprietary Ltd, Portland, Vic., Australia, *Tel:* +61 3 5523 2235
Lewmarine Proprietary Ltd, Portland, Vic., Australia, *Tel:* +61 3 5523 1455

Seaman Missions: The Seamans Mission, 61 Cliff Street, Portland, Vic., Australia 3305, *Tel:* +61 3 5523 2776, *Fax:* +61 3 5521 7938, *Email:* portland@mts.org.au

Shipping Agents: Barwil Agencies Australia Pty Ltd, P O Box 361, Melbourne, Vic., Australia 3205, *Tel:* +61 3 9630 0900, *Fax:* +61 3 9630 0999, *Email:* melbourne@barwil.com.au, *Website:* www.barwil.com
Beaufort Shipping Agency Proprietary Ltd, Inchcape Shipping Services Pty Ltd, 93 B Bentinck Street, Portland, Vic., Australia 3305, *Tel:* +61 3 5523 3939, *Fax:* +61 3 5523 5767, *Email:* portland@iss-shipping.com.au, *Website:* www.iss-shipping.com
Inchcape Shipping Services (ISS), Inchcape Shipping Services Pty Ltd, 93B Bentinck Street, P O Box 265, Portland, Vic., Australia 3305, *Tel:* +61 3 5523 3939, *Fax:* +61 3 5523 5767, *Email:* portland@iss-shipping.com.au, *Website:* www.iss-shipping.com
Monson Agencies Australia Proprietary Ltd, Level 1, 2 Gawler Street, P O Box 1222, Portland, Vic., Australia 3305, *Tel:* +61 3 5523 5695, *Fax:* +61 3 5523 6972, *Email:* portland@monson.com.au, *Website:* www.monson.com.au

Stevedoring Companies: Victorian Regional Stevedores, Portland, Vic., Australia, *Tel:* +61 3 5272 1833, *Fax:* +61 3 5277 0531

Medical Facilities: Hospital and medical facilities available

Airport: Local airport with daily flights (morning and evening) to Melbourne on weekdays. On weekends there is a morning flight on Saturday and an evening flight on Sunday. For details visit www.sharpairlines.com.au

Railway: A coach service to Warrnambool connects to a rail service on to Melobourne. For timetables visit www.vline.com.au

Development: There is a proposed development to cater for the export of hardwood chip within the next 12 to 18 months

Lloyd's Agent: Freemans Marine, Level 7, 564 St. Kilda Road, Melbourne, Vic., Australia 3004, *Tel:* +61 3 9935 2400, *Fax:* +61 3 9915 0351, *Email:* lloyds@freemans.com.au, *Website:* www.freemansmarine.com.au

PUFFIN TERMINAL

Lat 12° 17' S; Long 124° 20' E.

Admiralty Chart: AUS 314   **Admiralty Pilot:** 17
Time Zone: GMT +9.5 h   **UNCTAD Locode:** AU
Principal Facilities:

P										

Authority: AED Oil Ltd, P O Box 18199, Collins Street East, Melbourne, Vic., Australia 8003, *Tel:* +61 3 9654 7002, *Fax:* +61 3 9654 7006, *Email:* r.foulds@aedoil.com, *Website:* www.aus-energy.com.au

Port Security: ISPS compliant

Pre-Arrival Information: Export tankers should forward their initial ETA via email or fax to the FPSO on departure from previous port. Further updates should be sent 96 h, 72 h, 48 h, 24 h and 12 h prior to arrival

Anchorage: Export tankers may drift at a distance of at least 10 nautical miles from the terminal if waiting to berth

Pilotage: Compulsory and undertaken by the Mooring Master who boards approx 3 nautical miles from the FPSO

Radio Frequency: Listening on VHF Channel 16 and working on VHF Channels 72 and 68

Principal Imports and Exports: Exports: Crude oil.

Accommodation:

Name	Remarks
Puffin Terminal	See [1] below

[1]*Puffin Terminal:* Consists of FPSO 'Front Puffin' with storage cap of approx 740 000 bbls. Berthing of export tankers only take place during daylight hours. Max loading rate of 30 000 bbls/h

Lloyd's Agent: Moko Proprietary Ltd, P O Box 685, Willetton, W.A., Australia 6955, *Tel:* +61 8 9354 2248, *Fax:* +61 8 9354 2234, *Email:* kglange@bigpond.com

RAPID BAY

Lat 35° 31' S; Long 138° 11' E.

Admiralty Chart: AUS 125   **Admiralty Pilot:** 13
Time Zone: GMT +9.5 h   **UNCTAD Locode:** AU RAB
This port is no longer open to commercial shipping

RISDON

harbour area, see under Hobart

ROCKHAMPTON

alternate name, see Port Alma

SALADIN TERMINAL

Lat 21° 45' S; Long 115° 3' E.

Admiralty Chart: AUS 743   **Admiralty Pilot:** 17
Time Zone: GMT +8 h   **UNCTAD Locode:** AU SMT

Key to Principal Facilities:—

A=Airport	**C**=Containers	**G**=General Cargo
B=Bunkers	**D**=Dry Dock	**L**=Cruise

P=Petroleum	**R**=Ro/Ro **Y**=Dry Bulk
Q=Other Liquid Bulk	**T**=Towage (where available from port)

Principal Facilities:

P							T	

Authority: Chevron Australia Proprietary Ltd, P O Box S1580, Perth, W.A., Australia 6845, *Tel:* +61 8 9216 4000, *Fax:* +61 8 9216 4044, *Email:* chevronaustralia@chevron.com, *Website:* www.chevron.com

Officials: Marketing Manager: Neil Theobald, *Tel:* +61 8 9216 4000, *Email:* neil.theobald@chevron.com.

Pre-Arrival Information: ETA must be communicated to Operators, Tel: +61 8 9216 4210, Fax: +61 8 9216 4044 and Terminal, Tel: +61 8 9184 3832, Fax: +61 8 9184 3899, 96 h, 48 h, 24 h and 12 h before arrival. The first message should include:
Name of tanker and flag
Inmarsat phone number inc. satellite in use (872 or 873)
Inmarsat fax number inc. satellite in use (872 or 873)
Name of P&I club
Cargo requirements in m3 at 15°C
Total quantity and condition of ballast; ballast to be discharged at ChevronTexaco Terminal; ballast loaded in which port
Maximum loading rate through one 12" hose
Arrival draft
Estimated departure draft
Distance bridge to bow in metres
Distance bow to manifold in metres
Are all tanks inerted below 8%
Can vessel carry out closed loading
Master's name as he/she wishes it to appear on the Bills of Lading
Last port of call
Next port of call
Discharge port of Thevenard Blend crude oil
Confirmation that tanker has a clean bill of health
What electrical voltage has tanker and what socket type
Number of shackles (shots) of cable on each anchor cable
Number and location of mooring wires/ropes on winches and number, location and type of spare mooring ropes
Diameter and breaking strain of mooring ropes/wires and diameter and breaking strain of spare mooring ropes
Are mooring bitts located so that backup lines may be deployed to any of the six mooring buoys and hove in and made fast to the bitts
Diameter and safe working load of bitts
Holding power of mooring winch brakes
Is manifold OCIMF standard
Is tanker fitted with a crane or derrick
Safe working load of crane or derrick
Helicopter landing capability, winch or land on

Approach: The approach channel to the Marine Terminal is marked by navigation buoys, fitted with lights and radar reflectors. Tankers should not navigate outside the designated approach channel as areas outside the channel have not been completely surveyed

Pilotage: Compulsory. The Mooring Master boards in pos 21° 24' S; 114° 53' E (2 nautical miles W of the Saladin Lt. Buoy)

Radio Frequency: Tankers listen on VHF Channels 16 and 14 when within 100 nautical miles of the Terminal. Saladin Marine Terminal does not maintain a listening watch on any marine radio channel
ChevronTexaco provide portable UHF radio's for communications between the Tanker and the Terminal onshore control room during berthing, loading and unberthing. Channel 1 (469.775 MHz) and Channel 2 (469.800 MHz)

Maximum Vessel Dimensions: Restricted to tankers which have a loaded displacement of 40 000-180 000 t, a max beam of 47 m and a max slab side area of 6384 m2

Accommodation:

Name	Remarks
Saladin Marine Terminal	See [1] below

[1]*Saladin Marine Terminal:* Used exclusively by tankers loading crude oil from the oil fields surrounding Thevenard Island. The loading terminal is a CBM type consisting of six mooring buoys and two swamp moorings in min depth of 15.6 m. Tankers must be equipped with a crane or derrick on the port side with a min SWL of 10 t. There are three storage tanks onshore each with a cap of 350 000 bbls. Loading by submarine pipeline, 6426 m long. Berthing at the Marine Terminal takes place in daylight, during periods of flood tides unless otherwise approved by the Pilot/Mooring Master. Generally berthing will take place at low water slack tide or before high water slack tide, to avoid the period of strongest tidal stream in the middle of the flood tide. The direction of the tidal stream is approx 120° on flood and 300° on ebb and attains a rate of 1.3 kn at springs. Unberthing takes place at any time, during the flood tide or at other times as approved by the Pilot/Mooring Master

Towage: A mooring launch assists with berthing, together with a tug with min of 35 t bollard pull

Lloyd's Agent: Moko Proprietary Ltd, P O Box 685, Willetton, W.A., Australia 6955, *Tel:* +61 8 9354 2248, *Fax:* +61 8 9354 2234, *Email:* kglange@bigpond.com

SKUA TERMINAL

Lat 12° 30' S; Long 124° 25' E.

Admiralty Chart: AUS 314 **Admiralty Pilot:** 17
Time Zone: GMT +9.5 h **UNCTAD Locode:** AU SKV
This terminal is no longer operational

SMITHS CREEK

harbour area, see under Cairns

SOUTH TREES WHARF

harbour area, see under Gladstone

SPRING BAY

harbour area, see under Hobart

STAG TERMINAL

Lat 20° 17' S; Long 116° 15' E.

Admiralty Chart: AUS 742 **Admiralty Pilot:** 17
Time Zone: GMT +8 h **UNCTAD Locode:** AU

Principal Facilities:

P									

Authority: Apache Energy Ltd, P O Box 477, Perth, W.A., Australia 6872, *Tel:* +61 8 9422 7222, *Fax:* +61 8 9422 7445, *Email:* murray.durham@aus.apachecorp.com, *Website:* www.apachecorp.com

Officials: Business Development Manager: Murray Durham, *Tel:* +61 8 9422 7298, *Mobile Tel:* +61 448775474, *Email:* murray.durham@apachecorp.com.

Pilotage: Compulsory

Radio Frequency: Vessels should contact the Marine Facility on VHF Channel 16 when within 40 nautical miles and confirm ETA

Maximum Vessel Dimensions: 25 000-150 000 dwt

Accommodation:

Name	Remarks
Stag Terminal	See [1] below

[1]*Stag Terminal:* Consists of Central Production Facility (CPF), a CALM buoy situated 1 nautical mile N of the CPF and FSO tanker 'Dampier Spirit'. Loading rate of crude oil from FSO to export tanker of 3240 m3/h

Lloyd's Agent: Moko Proprietary Ltd, P O Box 685, Willetton, W.A., Australia 6955, *Tel:* +61 8 9354 2248, *Fax:* +61 8 9354 2234, *Email:* kglange@bigpond.com

STONY POINT

harbour area, see under Hastings

SWANSON DOCK

harbour area, see under Melbourne

SYDNEY

Lat 33° 51' S; Long 151° 12' E.

Admiralty Chart: AUS 201/202 **Admiralty Pilot:** 14
Time Zone: GMT +10 h **UNCTAD Locode:** AU SYD

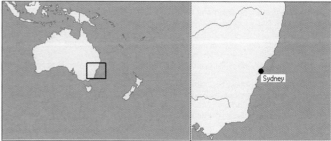

Principal Facilities:

P	Q	Y			R	L	B	D	T	A

Authority: Sydney Ports Corp., Level 8, 207 Kent Street, P O Box 25, Millers Point, N.S.W., Australia 2000, *Tel:* +61 2 9296 4999, *Fax:* +61 2 9296 4742, *Email:* enquiries@sydports.com.au, *Website:* www.sydneyports.com.au

Officials: Chief Executive Officer: Grant Gilfillan, *Tel:* +61 2 9296 4681, *Email:* ggilfillan@sydneyports.com.au.
Corporate Affairs Manager: Kamini Parashar, *Tel:* +61 2 9296 4995, *Email:* kparashar@sydneyports.com.au.
Harbour Master: Capt Robin Heath, *Tel:* +61 2 9296 4650, *Email:* rheath@sydneyports.com.au.
Marketing: Geneveive Bonello, *Tel:* +61 2 9296 4807, *Email:* gbonello@sydneyports.com.au.

Port Security: ISPS compliant

Documentation: List of crew (3), store list (1), ports of call (3), animals carried as cargo (1), animals carried as pets (1), health report, quarantine officials requirement (2)

Approach: Depth at harbour entrance 24.4 m. Western channel 210 m wide, 13.7 m depth at LW and Eastern channel 180 m wide, 10.5 m depth at LW

Anchorage: There is no recommended anchorage off the port. Anchoring is at the Master's discretion, however vessels should anchor outside port limits and are requested to anchor at least 3 nautical miles from the coast. Within the port there are short term anchorages (daylight only)

Pilotage: Compulsory for all vessels except where the Master holds a Pilotage Exemption Certificate
Sydney Pilot Service Pty Ltd (SPS), Tel: +61 2 9337 6648, Fax: +61 2 9337 4048, Website: www.sydneypilotservice.com.au
Pilot boards in pos 33° 50' 68" S; 151° 21' 68" E. ETA to be confirmed on VHF 4 h prior to arrival and reconfirmed 2 h and 1 h before reaching pilot boarding ground

Radio Frequency: VHF Radio call sign 'Harbour Control'. Channel 16 for calling and 12 for arrival confirmation and exchange of information. All vessel movements on Channel 13

Weather: Port protected in all weathers

Tides: MHWS 1.6 m. MHWN 1.3 m

Traffic: 2007/08, 2459 commercial vessels & 101 cruise vessels, 29 176 794 t of cargo handled, 1 778 442 TEU's (includes Botany Bay)

Accommodation:

Name	Length (m)	Depth (m)	Remarks
Darling Harbour			
Wharf 8	335	9.8	See [1] below
Sydney Cove			
Overseas Passenger Terminal	300	10	Cruise terminal with passenger lounge of 465 m2 and customs hall of 1462 m2
Glebe Island			
Berth No's 1 & 2	468	11.9	See [2] below
Berth No.7	229	11.1	See [3] below
Berth No.8	120	9.3	See [4] below
White Bay			Operated by Sydney Ports Corporation
Berth No.2	168	9.8	
Berth No.3	270	10.5	
Berth No.4	274	10.9	
Berth No.5	229	11	11 280 m2 shed
Berth No.6	178	11	
Blackwattle Bay			
Berth	120	5.5	See [5] below
Gore Bay Terminal			See [6] below
Wharf No.1	320	13.7	Vessels up to 265 m loa
Wharf No.2	190	9.7	Vessels up to 190 m loa

[1]*Wharf 8:* Cruise terminal with passenger lounge of 900 m2 and customs hall of 1500 m2
[2]*Berth No's 1 & 2:* Operated by Australian Amalgamated Terminals Pty Ltd (AAT), Sommerville Road, Rozalle, NSW 2039, Tel: +60 2 8755 1200, Fax: +61 2 8755 1204
Dedicated motor vehicle discharge facility with cap to accommodate 5000 vehicles. Operations are gradually being transferred from here to Port Kembla
[3]*Berth No.7:* Common user bulk dry cargo discharge berth
Gypsum Resources Australia (GRA) operates a gypsum storage facility and Sugar Australia Pty Ltd has storage cap for 28 000 t of refined sugar
[4]*Berth No.8:* Common user bulk dry cargo discharge berth
Cement Australia Ltd has storage cap of 40 000 t for bulk cement and Penrice Soda Products Pty Ltd has storage cap of 7500 t for soda ash
[5]*Berth:* Operated by Hanson Australia Pty Ltd., Pyrmont Bridge Road, Glebe, NSW 2037, Tel: +61 2 9323 4000, Fax: +61 2 9323 4500
Used for discharge of bulk concrete aggregate
[6]*Gore Bay Terminal:* Operated by Shell Co. of Australia Ltd., Manns Avenue, Greenwich, NSW 2065, Tel: +61 2 8437 1238, Fax: +61 2 8437 1203
Used for import, export & storage of oil products. Vessels discharge at up to 4000 t/h. 20 bulk storage tanks with a total cap to hold 165 000 t of hydrocarbons

Bunkering: Australia Bunkering Pty Ltd, Suite 604, Level 6, 50 Clarence Street, Sydney, N.S.W., Australia NSW 2000, *Tel:* +61 2 8270 7300, *Fax:* +61 2 8270 7388, *Email:* bunker@ausbunk.com, *Website:* www.ausbunk.com
Australian Petroleum Proprietary Ltd, Solander Street, Kurnell, Sydney, N.S.W., Australia, *Tel:* +61 2 972 2597, *Fax:* +61 2 981 1159
Bridgewater Australia Proprietary Ltd, Level 6, 84 Pitt Street, Sydney, N.S.W., Australia 2000, *Tel:* +61 2 9233 5588, *Fax:* +61 2 9233 5569, *Email:* bunkers@bridgewateraust.com.au, *Website:* www.bridgewateraust.com.au
Caltex Australia Petroleum Proprietary Ltd, Caltex Australia Petroleum Proprietary Ltd, No 2 Market Street, Sydney, N.S.W., Australia 2000, *Tel:* +61 2 9668 1148, *Fax:* +61 2 9668 1243, *Email:* mnicholl@caltex.com.au, *Website:* www.caltex.com.au
Sumitomo Corp., Sumitomo Australia, P O Box 4241, Sydney, N.S.W., Australia 2001, *Tel:* +61 2 9335 3700, *Fax:* +61 2 9335 3775, *Email:* christian.marston@sumitomocorp.co.jp, *Website:* www.sumitomocorp.co.jp
Australian Petroleum Proprietary Ltd, Solander Street, Kurnell, Sydney, N.S.W., Australia, *Tel:* +61 2 972 2597, *Fax:* +61 2 981 1159 – *Grades:* all grades; in line blending available – *Misc:* own storage facilities at Port Botany & Port Jackson – *Parcel Size:* min 100t – *Rates:* max 900t/h ex barge – *Notice:* 48 hours – *Delivery Mode:* ex wharf, barge, truck
BP Australia (Proprietary) Ltd, P O Box 5222, Melbourne, Vic., Australia 3001, *Tel:* +61 3 9268 4111, *Fax:* +61 3 9268 3321, *Email:* gomiasfuelsales@bp.com, *Website:* www.bp.com
Caltex Australia Petroleum Proprietary Ltd, Caltex Australia Petroleum Proprietary Ltd, No 2 Market Street, Sydney, N.S.W., Australia 2000, *Tel:* +61 2 9668 1148, *Fax:* +61 2 9668 1243, *Email:* mnicholl@caltex.com.au, *Website:* www.caltex.com.au
ExxonMobil Marine Fuels, 1 Harbour Front Place, 06-00 Harbour Front, Tower One, Singapore, Republic of Singapore 098633, *Tel:* +65 6885 8998, *Fax:* +65 6885 8794, *Email:* asiapac.marinefuels@exxonmobil.com, *Website:* www.exxonmobilmarinefuels.com – *Grades:* MGO – *Delivery Mode:* tank truck
Shell Australia Ltd, Shell Company of Australia, Marine Centre Oceania, No 8 Redfern Road, Melbourne, Vic., Australia 3123, *Tel:* +61 3 9666 5446, *Fax:* +61 3 8823 4800, *Email:* sal-marine-products@shell.com, *Website:* www.shell.com.au
Sumitomo Corp., Sumitomo Australia, P O Box 4241, Sydney, N.S.W., Australia 2001, *Tel:* +61 2 9335 3700, *Fax:* +61 2 9335 3775, *Email:* christian.marston@sumitomocorp.co.jp, *Website:* www.sumitomocorp.co.jp

Towage: Polaris Marine P/L, 114 Western Crescent, Gladesville, N.S.W., Australia 2111, *Tel:* +61 2 9816 5696, *Fax:* +61 2 9879 6847, *Email:* polarism@pacific.net.au, *Website:* www.polarismarine.com.au
Stannard Brothers Slipway & Engineering Proprietary Ltd, 6/448 Pacific Highway, Artarmon, Sydney, N.S.W., Australia 2064, *Tel:* +61 2 9418 3711, *Fax:* +61 2 9418 3722, *Email:* info@stannard.com.au
SVITZER, SVITZER Australasia & United Salvage, Level 22, Tower 2, 101 Grafton Street, Bondi Junction, Sydney, N.S.W., Australia 2022, *Tel:* +61 2 9369 9200, *Fax:* +61 2 9369 9288, *Email:* info@adsteam.com.au, *Website:* www.svitzer.com
Waratah Towage Proprietary Ltd, 7 Cooper Street, Balmain, Sydney, N.S.W., Australia 2041, *Tel:* +61 2 9818 9400, *Fax:* +61 2 9818 9440, *Email:* info.australasia@svitzer.com, *Website:* www.svitzer.com

Seaman Missions: The Seamans Mission, Flying Angel Seafarers Centre, P O Box Q403, Queen Victoria Building, Sydney, N.S.W., Australia 1230, *Tel:* +61 2 9264 9900, *Fax:* +61 2 9264 9318, *Email:* sydney@mts.org.au

Ship Chandlers: Australian International Marine Services Proprietary Ltd, 4/23 Underwood Avenue, Mascot, N.S.W., Australia 2019, *Tel:* +61 2 9700 0722, *Fax:* +61 2 9700 0737, *Email:* sales.sydney@sinwaglobal.com, *Website:* www.sinwaglobal.com
Liferaft Servicing Group (LSG), 121 Stephen Road, Botany, N.S.W., Australia 2019, *Tel:* +61 2 9666 8066, *Fax:* +61 2 9666 9402, *Email:* nsw@liferaftservicing.com.au
Ocean Services (Australia) Proprietary Ltd, P O Box 491, Lane Cove, 22 Underwood Avenue, Sydney, N.S.W., Australia 2066, *Tel:* +61 2 9316 6255, *Fax:* +61 2 9316 5085, *Email:* mbocean@ozemail.com.au
Sealanes Providors, Unit 6, 198 Young Street, Waterloo, Sydney, N.S.W., Australia 2017, *Tel:* +61 2 8399 1622, *Fax:* +61 2 8399 1644, *Email:* sea@sealanes.com.au
Stanley & Co. (Shipping Providors) Proprietary Ltd, P O Box 345, Alexandria, Sydney, N.S.W., Australia 2015, *Tel:* +61 2 9700 1998, *Fax:* +61 2 9700 1997, *Email:* dkellaway@iimetro.com.au
Wiltrading Proprietary Ltd, P O Box 133, Alexandria, Sydney, N.S.W., Australia 1435, *Tel:* +61 2 9667 4599, *Fax:* +61 2 9669 1181, *Email:* wiltrading@wilh.com.au, *Website:* www.wiltrading.com

Shipping Agents: ANL Container Line Proprietary Ltd, 4th Floor, 131 York Street, Sydney, N.S.W., Australia 2000, *Tel:* +61 2 9225 7333, *Fax:* +61 2 9225 7307, *Email:* wrightb@anl.com.au
Arpeni Merchant Marine Pty Ltd, Level 1, Suite 101, 14 Martin Place, Sydney, N.S.W., Australia 2000, *Tel:* +61 2 9222 9524, *Fax:* +61 2 9222 9529, *Email:* arpeni@bigpond.net.au
Asiaworld Shipping Services Proprietary Ltd, Level 2, 403 Pacific Highway, Artarmon, Sydney, N.S.W., Australia 2064, *Tel:* +61 2 9906 6372, *Fax:* +61 2 9906 1874, *Email:* info@asiaworld.com.au, *Website:* www.asiaworld.com.au
Barbican Marine (Agencies) Proprietary Ltd, Level 23, 60 Margaret Street, P O Box 3283, Sydney, N.S.W., Australia 2001, *Tel:* +61 2 9247 4555, *Fax:* +61 2 9247 4114, *Email:* mstreet@barbican.com.au
Barwil Agencies Australia Pty Ltd, P O Box 4097, Sydney, N.S.W., Australia 2001, *Tel:* +61 2 9439 7223, *Fax:* +61 2 9439 8587, *Email:* sydney@wilhelmsen.com, *Website:* www.wilhelmsen.com
Beaufort Shipping Agency Proprietary Ltd, Level 8, 120 Sussex Street, Sydney, N.S.W., Australia 2000, *Tel:* +61 2 9364 8960, *Fax:* +61 2 9364 8999, *Email:* operations@beaufortshipping.com, *Website:* www.beaufortshipping.com.au
Chess Hanley's Moving & Shipping Pty Ltd, Bessemer Industrial Park, 13 Bessemer Street, Blacktown, Sydney, N.S.W., Australia 2147, *Tel:* +61 2 9671 8400, *Fax:* +61 2 9671 8484, *Email:* sydney@chessmoving.com.au, *Website:* www.chessmoving.com.au
CMA-CGM S.A., CMA CGM Australia Pty Ltd, Suite 75, Lower Deck, 26/32 Pirrama Road, Jones Bay Wharf, Pyrmont, Sydney, N.S.W., Australia 2009, *Tel:* +61 2 9325 7320, *Fax:* +61 2 9325 7329, *Email:* syd.jlhermette@cma-cgm.com, *Website:* www.cma-cgm.com
Cosco Oceania Pty Ltd, Level 2, Cosco House, 101 Sussex Street, Sydney, N.S.W., Australia 2000, *Tel:* +61 2 9373 9588, *Fax:* +61 2 9373 9438, *Email:* coscooceania@cosco.com.au, *Website:* www.cosco.com.au
Evergreen Shipping Agency (Australia) Proprietary Ltd, Level 13, 181 Miller Street, Sydney, N.S.W., Australia 2060, *Tel:* +61 2 9936 5700, *Fax:* +61 2 9936 5710, *Email:* sydemcbiz@evergreen-shipping.com.au, *Website:* www.evergreen-line.com
Globe Star Shipping Proprietary Ltd, 3rd Floor, 89 York Street, P O Box 3946, Sydney, N.S.W., Australia 2000, *Tel:* +61 2 9290 3666, *Fax:* +61 2 9290 1241, *Email:* globestar@att.net.au
Gulf Agency Co (Australia) Pty Ltd., Suite 18 & 19, 2nd Floor, 123 Clarence Street, Sydney, N.S.W., Australia 2000, *Tel:* +61 2 8028 2400, *Fax:* +61 2 9279 0457, *Email:* shipping.sydney@gacworld.com, *Website:* www.gacworld.com
Hanjin Shipping Australia Pty Ltd, 1 Market Street, Level 23-32, Sydney, N.S.W., Australia 2000, *Tel:* +61 2 8226 8000, *Fax:* +61 2 9283 9378, *Email:* daniel_r@au.hanjin.com, *Website:* www.hanjin.com
A Hartrodt International, 7 Coggins Place, P O Box 349, Mascot, Sydney, N.S.W., Australia 2020, *Tel:* +61 2 9364 5900, *Fax:* +61 2 9667 1616, *Email:* sydney@hartrodt.com.au, *Website:* www.hartrodt.com.au
Hetherington Kingsbury Proprietary Ltd, 1st Floor, Unit 4, The Hub, 89-97 Jones Street, Ultimo, P O Box Q293 QVB, Sydney, N.S.W., Australia 1230, *Tel:* +61 2

Key to Principal Facilities:—
A=Airport **C**=Containers **G**=General Cargo **P**=Petroleum **R**=Ro/Ro **Y**=Dry Bulk
B=Bunkers **D**=Dry Dock **L**=Cruise **Q**=Other Liquid Bulk **T**=Towage (where available from port)

92814499, *Fax:* +61 2 92814499, *Email:* shorton@hksa.com.au, *Website:* www.hksa.com.au

Holyman Marine Agencies, Level 13, Bullant Plaza, 181 Miller Street, Sydney, N.S.W., Australia 2000, *Tel:* +61 2 9236 7700, *Fax:* +61 2 9936 5710, *Email:* hlmsyd@holyman-agencies.com.au

Inchcape Shipping Services (ISS), Inchcape Shipping Services Pty Ltd, Suite 1, 1401 Botany Road, Botany, N.S.W., Australia 2019, *Tel:* +61 2 9316 4009, *Fax:* +61 2 9316 4511, *Email:* sydney@iss-shipping.com.au, *Website:* www.iss-shipping.com

K Line Ship Management Co. Ltd, Level 5, 39-41 Chantos Street, St leonards, Sydney, N.S.W., Australia 2065, *Tel:* +61 2 8274 9300, *Fax:* +61 2 9251 0201, *Email:* sydsls@klineaus.com.au, *Website:* www.kline.com.au

McArthur Shipping & Agency Co Pty Ltd, Unit 4, Level 1, The Hub 89-97 Jones Street, Ultimo, Sydney, N.S.W., Australia 1230, *Tel:* +61 2 8217 7271, *Fax:* +61 2 9211 8340, *Email:* mail@mcaship.com.au, *Website:* www.mcaship.com.au

Mediterranean Shipping Company, MSC (Aust) Pty Ltd, Suite 532, 5 Lime Street, King Street Wharf, Sydney, N.S.W., Australia 2000, *Tel:* +61 2 8270 4000, *Fax:* +61 2 8270 4040, *Email:* sydinfo@msc.com.au, *Website:* www.msc.com.au

A.P. Moller-Maersk Group, Maersk Australia Pty Ltd, Level 26, 201-205 Elizabeth Street, Sydney, N.S.W., Australia 2000, *Tel:* +61 2 9696 9696, *Fax:* +61 2 9696 9688, *Website:* www.maerskline.com

Monson Agencies Australia Proprietary Ltd, P O Box 1487, Sydney, N.S.W., Australia 2001, *Tel:* +61 2 8274 9303, *Fax:* +61 2 9251 0201, *Email:* sydney@monson.com.au, *Website:* www.monson.com.au

Neptune Pacific Agency Australia Proprietary Ltd, P O Box 3801, Level 12, 45-47 York Street, Sydney, N.S.W., Australia 2000, *Tel:* +61 2 9235 2999, *Fax:* +61 2 9235 2912, *Email:* neptune_au@nepship.com

Oceanway Shipping Agency Proprietary Ltd, Level 4, Suite 403, St. Thomas House, 781 Pacific Highway, Chatswood, Sydney, N.S.W., Australia 2067, *Tel:* +61 2 9410 1688, *Fax:* +61 2 9410 1876, *Email:* sydney@oceanway.com.au, *Website:* www.oceanway.com.au

Seatrans Australia Proprietary Ltd, Suite 1, Level 3, Link Tower 7-9 Kent Road, Mascot, Sydney, N.S.W., Australia 2020, *Tel:* +61 2 9693 7771, *Fax:* +61 2 9693 7788, *Email:* mail@mcaship.com.au, *Website:* www.mcaship.com.au

Swire Shipping Agencies, Swire House, Level 9, 10 Spring Street, P O Box 3920, Sydney, N.S.W., Australia 2001, *Tel:* +61 2 9272 9333, *Fax:* +61 2 9252 1442, *Email:* csnsw@swireshipping.com, *Website:* www.swireshipping.com

Watt Alexander & Co. Proprietary Ltd, The Rocks, 88 George Street, Sydney, N.S.W., Australia 2000, *Tel:* +61 2 9252 4411, *Fax:* +61 2 9252 4422, *Email:* alexwatt@alexwatt.com, *Website:* www.alexwatt.com

Wills Shipping Proprietary Ltd, Level 1 33-35 Lower Gibbes Street, Chatswood, Sydney, N.S.W., Australia 2067, *Tel:* +61 2 9882 3441, *Fax:* +61 2 9882 2628, *Email:* willsship@willsship.com

Surveyors: ABS (Pacific), Level 3, 53 Walker Street, P O Box 1151, Sydney, N.S.W., Australia 2060, *Tel:* +61 2 9956 7322, *Fax:* +61 2 9954 4233, *Email:* abssydney@eagle.org, *Website:* www.eagle.org

AMD Marine Consulting, P O Box 878, Pymble, Sydney, N.S.W., Australia 2073, *Tel:* +61 2 9484 0288, *Fax:* +61 2 9481 9466, *Email:* amd@amd.com.au, *Website:* www.amd.com.au

AME Mineral Economics, AME House, 342 Kent Street, Sydney, N.S.W., Australia 2000, *Tel:* +61 2 9262 2264, *Fax:* +61 2 9262 2587, *Email:* ame@ame.com.au, *Website:* www.ame.com.au

Australian Ship P & I, 3rd Floor, 43 Hume Street, Crows Nest, Sydney, N.S.W., Australia 2065, *Tel:* +61 2 9439 4877, *Fax:* +61 2 9439 4331, *Email:* ausship@ausship.com.au

M.S. Baveja, P O Box 476, Gordon, Sydney, N.S.W., Australia 2072, *Tel:* +61 2 9418 2286, *Fax:* +61 2 9418 2270, *Email:* austbee@spin.net.au

Burness Corlett - Three Quays (London) Ltd, 2 Grosvenor Place, P O Box 639, Brookvale, Sydney, N.S.W., Australia 2100, *Tel:* +61 2 9938 6199, *Fax:* +61 2 9938 2139, *Email:* bca@dot.net.au, *Website:* www.bctq.com

Det Norske Veritas A/S, Level 7, 124 Walker Street, North Sydney, Sydney, N.S.W., Australia 2060, *Tel:* +61 2 9922 1966, *Fax:* +61 2 9929 8792, *Email:* sydney.station@dnv.com, *Website:* www.dnv.com.au

Germanischer Lloyd, Suite 51 Level 10, 88 Pitt Street, Sydney, N.S.W., Australia 2000, *Tel:* +61 2 9233 1119, *Fax:* +61 2 9233 3315, *Email:* gl-sydney@gl-group.com, *Website:* www.gl-group.com

Korean Register of Shipping, Suite 51, Level 10, 88 Pitt Street, Sydney, N.S.W., Australia 2000, *Tel:* +61 2 9233 1119, *Fax:* +61 2 9233 3315, *Email:* gl-sydney@gl-group.com, *Website:* www.gl-group.com

Nippon Kaiji Kyokai, Suite 201, 90 Mount Street, Sydney, N.S.W., Australia 2060, *Tel:* +61 2 9929 9722, *Fax:* +61 2 9929 9622, *Email:* sy@classnk.or.jp, *Website:* www.classnk.or.jp

Propel Surveyors & Consultants Proprietary Ltd, P O Box 25, Seaforth, Sydney, N.S.W., Australia 2092, *Tel:* +61 2 9948 7243, *Fax:* +61 2 9948 9458, *Email:* propelsg@bigpond.com

Registro Italiano Navale (RINA), Suite 51, Level 10, 88 Pitt Street, Sydney, N.S.W., Australia 2000, *Tel:* +61 2 9233 1119, *Fax:* +61 2 9233 3315, *Email:* gl-sydney@gl-group.com, *Website:* www.gl-group.com

Medical Facilities: Arrangements made through agents

Airport: Kingsford Smith

Railway: Central Station, 3 km from Darling Harbour

Lloyd's Agent: Freemans Marine, P O Box 36, St. Leonards, N.S.W., Australia 1590, *Tel:* +61 2 9438 2655, *Fax:* +61 2 9436 1367, *Email:* lloyds@freemans.com.au, *Website:* www.freemansmarine.com.au

TALISMAN TERMINAL

Lat 19° 40' S; Long 116° 56' E.

Admiralty Chart: AUS 327	**Admiralty Pilot:** 17
Time Zone: GMT +8 h	**UNCTAD Locode:** AU

This terminal is no longer operational

THEVENARD

Lat 32° 8' S; Long 133° 38' E.

Admiralty Chart: AUS 120, 341	**Admiralty Pilot:** 13
Time Zone: GMT +9.5 h	**UNCTAD Locode:** AU THE

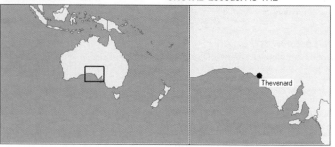

Principal Facilities:

		Y	G			B		T	A

Authority: Flinders Ports Proprietary Ltd, 131 Thevenard Road, Thevenard, S.A., Australia 5690, *Tel:* +61 8 8625 2617, *Fax:* +61 8 8625 3100, *Email:* flindersports@flindersports.com.au, *Website:* www.flindersports.com.au

Officials: Harbour Master: Alun Hodgson, *Email:* hodgson.alun@flindersports.com.au.

Port Security: ISPS compliant

Approach: Depth in Yatala Channel 8.2 m below CD

Anchorage: Inner anchorage available in Murat Bay

Pilotage: Compulsory. Pilot boarding station 1 nautical mile SW of the Entrance Beacon

Radio Frequency: VHF Channels 6, 8, 12, 16 and 67

Weather: Strong southerly sea breezes up to 35 knots during summer months

Tides: MHWS 1.67 m, MHWN 1.08 m

Traffic: 2007/08, 95 vessels, 2 058 598 t of cargo exported

Maximum Vessel Dimensions: Max draft is channel depth plus tide, less keel clearance calculated as: over 8.2 m draft, clearance 90 cm, 8.2 m or less 75 cm, max loa 180 m, max beam 28 m

Principal Imports and Exports: Imports: Fertiliser. Exports: Grain, Gypsum, Salt, Seeds.

Working Hours: Gypsum: 24 h daily. Grain: 24 h daily (24 h shift) or 0800-2200 continuous

Accommodation:

Name	Length (m)	Depth (m)	Remarks
Thevenard			
Jetty	198	9.8	See [1] below

[1]*Jetty:* Operated by ABB Grain Ltd
Consists of one berth on either side (North and South). Grain silos and gypsum storage areas ashore are connected to bulk loading berths on either side of the jetty by a travelling gantry ship loader with a retractable boom, capable of loading 550-750 t/h of wheat, 550 t/h of barley, 500 t/h of oats and 1050 t/h of gypsum. This jetty can only load one side at a time

Bunkering: Shell Australia Ltd, Shell Company of Australia, Marine Centre Oceania, No 8 Redfern Road, Melbourne, Vic., Australia 3123, *Tel:* +61 3 9666 5446, *Fax:* +61 3 8823 4800, *Email:* sal-marine-products@shell.com, *Website:* www.shell.com.au – *Misc:* Diesel avaialble from permanent bunkering facility. FO available by road tanker with prior notice.

Waste Reception Facilities: Ships domestic garbage

Towage: One tug of 20 t bollard pull available

Repair & Maintenance: Minor repairs and welding

Shipping Agents: Barwil Agencies Australia Pty Ltd, P O Box 162A, Whyalla, S.A., Australia 5600, *Tel:* +61 8 8644 0911, *Fax:* +61 8 8644 0925, *Email:* whyalla@wilhelmsen.com, *Website:* www.wilhelmsen.com

Stevedoring Companies: ABB Grain Ltd, Thevenard, S.A., Australia, *Tel:* +61 8 8625 2212, *Fax:* +61 8 8625 3215

Medical Facilities: Local community hospital and two medical and dental practices

Airport: Ceduna, 6 km

Lloyd's Agent: Maritime & General Insurance Surveyors Proprietary Ltd, Suite 4, 7 Divett Street, Adelaide, S.A., Australia 5015, *Tel:* +61 8 8341 2552, *Fax:* +61 8 8241 0229, *Email:* maritime-general@adam.com.au

THURSDAY ISLAND

Lat 10° 35' S; Long 142° 13' E.

Admiralty Chart: AUS 299	**Admiralty Pilot:** 15
Time Zone: GMT +10 h	**UNCTAD Locode:** AU TIS

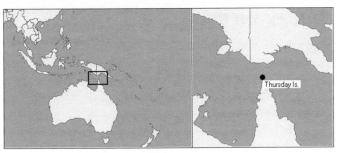

Principal Facilities:

P	Q		G			B	T	A	

Authority: Ports Corporation of Queensland, Floor 24, 300 Queen Street, P O Box 409, Brisbane, Qld., Australia 4001, *Tel:* +61 7 3224 7088, *Fax:* +61 7 3224 7234, *Email:* info@pcq.com.au, *Website:* www.pcq.com.au

Officials: Chief Executive Officer: Brad Fish, *Email:* bfish@pcq.com.au. Communications Manager: Rachel Campbell, *Tel:* +61 7 3224 8863, *Email:* rcampbell@pcq.com.au.

Port Security: ISPS compliant

Approach: Access to the port can be via either of three channels-Normanby Sound, depth 6.3 m, Flinders Passage, depth 3 m, or the Boat Channel, the latter having a depth of only 2.7 m at LWOST, and is only used by vessels with light drafts. There are considerable hazards to navigation in the harbour and the approaches

Anchorage: A safe deep water anchorage to the W of Black Rock and marked Quarantine Anchorage at the entrance to Normandy Sound

Pilotage: Compulsory and arranged through the Duty Pilot at Cairns, Tel: +61 7 4031 9609. Torres Straits pilot boats maintain VHF watch on Channels 12 and 16. Pilots board vessels at the E entrance at Scott Rock, or at the W entrance SW of Tucker Point (Goods Island Lighthouse). Distances from the pilotage boarding ground are 9 km

Radio Frequency: VHF channels 67 and 16. Continuous watch requested on channel 16 between Carpentaria Light Vessel and Wyborn Reef

Tides: MHHW to MLLW range 1.9 m, MLHW to MHLW range 0.5 m

Traffic: 2007/08, 77 876 t of cargo handled

Maximum Vessel Dimensions: Max draft 5.9 m, max loa 113 m

Principal Imports and Exports: Imports: General cargo, Petroleum products. Exports: Fish, Fish products.

Accommodation:

Name	Length (m)	Depth (m)	Remarks
Thursday Island			See [1] below
Main Jetty	30	3.4	See [2] below
Horn Island Jetty	40	4	See [3] below
Fuel Wharf	22	4.4	See [4] below
Engineers Jetty	23	4.3	Primarily used by passenger vessels

[1]*Thursday Island:* The depth of water in Normanby Sound is 6.3 m and in Flinders Passage and Ellis Channel, 3.0 m. The width of the E channel is 152.4 m whilst the W entrance is at least 304.8 m wide. The swinging basin at Thursday Island is between 457.2 and 804.67 m wide and is 6 m in depth, except for one small patch of 5.18 m. The max draft of vessels that may enter the port is 5.45 m at LWOST (1 m clearance required) Vessels of deeper draught could berth, depending upon tidal range at the time

[2]*Main Jetty:* Used for the import and export of all general cargo to and from the island Barge ramp on the western side of the stem

[3]*Horn Island Jetty:* Used for passenger ferries. There is a barge ramp to the E of the berth

[4]*Fuel Wharf:* Used for the supply of bulk distillate, bunkering and fresh water

Mechanical Handling Equipment:

Location	Type	Capacity (t)	Qty
Main Jetty	Mobile Cranes	4	1

Bunkering: Bulk distillate available at the Fuel Wharf and the Horn Island cargo facility

Towage: Tugs available from private operators

Repair & Maintenance: Repairs to small craft only. Slipway of 150 t cap

Shipping Agents: Barwil Agencies Australia Pty Ltd, P O Box 1392, Cairns, Qld., Australia 4870, *Tel:* +61 7 4035 4344, *Fax:* +61 7 4035 4006, *Email:* cairns@wilhelmsen.com, *Website:* www.wilhelmsen.com

Medical Facilities: Hospital available

Airport: Horn Island, 5 km

Lloyd's Agent: Freemans Marine, P O Box 554, Fortitude Valley, Brisbane, Qld., Australia 4006, *Tel:* +61 7 3867 4646, *Fax:* +61 7 3867 4699, *Email:* john.cupitt@freemans.com.au, *Website:* www.freemansmarine.com.au

TOWNSVILLE

Lat 19° 15' S; Long 146° 49' E.

Admiralty Chart: AUS 256/257 **Admiralty Pilot:** 15

Time Zone: GMT +10 h **UNCTAD Locode:** AU TSV

Principal Facilities:

P	Q	Y	G	C	R	L	B		T	A	

Authority: Townsville Port Authority, Benwell Road, P O Box 1031, Townsville, Qld., Australia 4810, *Tel:* +61 7 4781 1500, *Fax:* +61 7 4781 1525, *Email:* info@townsville-port.com.au, *Website:* www.townsville-port.com.au

Officials: Chief Executive Officer: Barry Holden, *Tel:* +61 7 4781 1511, *Email:* bholden@townsville-port.com.au. Harbour Master: John Preston, *Tel:* +61 7 4726 3400.

Port Security: ISPS compliant

Approach: The approach to Cleveland Bay anchorage from the S is clear of dangers, with the exception of Salamander Reef, the Four-foot Rock and the Twenty-foot Rock, all these lying within a radius of 3 nautical miles of Cape Cleveland Lighthouse. To clear these dangers, passing N of them bring Mount Marlow in transit with the extremity of Hawkings Point, bearing 265°T before approaching within 5 nautical miles of Cape Cleveland, which will then bear 252°T. Proceeding into Cleveland Bay, a depth of not less than 8.2 m will be obtained by keeping N of the line Mount Marlow in line with Hawkings Point. Approaching Cleveland Bay from the N, passing E of Magnetic Island, a vessel should keep at least 0.5 nautical mile off Magnetic Island shore to obtain not less than 9.1 m of water at LAT. The shore is steep except for Orchard Rocks off the NE extremity of the island

Anchorage: There is good holding ground everywhere in Cleveland Bay and vessels awaiting pilot should anchor according to draught and as close to the Fairway Beacons as possible, but keeping clear of the line of the prohibited anchorage

Pilotage: Pilotage is compulsory and vessels requiring the service should advise draught and probable time of arrival to their agents from their last port of departure, or advise by radio at least 24 h before arrival. Pilotage is available 24 h/day
The pilot vessel is equipped with VHF radio having international frequencies 8 and 12
Pilot Boarding Ground Bravo in pos 19° 9.5' S; 146° 55.5' E where drafts of up to 10 m are accepted. Pilot Boarding Ground Alpha in pos 19° 6.57' S; 146° 54.16' E for vessels with an arrival draft exceeding 8 m. Drafts between 7 m and 8 m shall require advice from the Duty Pilot as to which pilot boarding ground to use

Radio Frequency: VHF Channels 12 and 16; VHF Channel 67 (small craft); VHF Channels 6, 8, 10 and 13 (pilots and tugs)

Weather: Prevailing winds tend to be E'ly to SE'ly. Cyclone season November to April

Tides: Springs rise from 2.8 m to 4.0 m. Neaps rise from 1.5 m to 2.8 m

Traffic: 2007/08, 705 vessels, 9 833 991 t of cargo handled, 25 472 TEU's

Maximum Vessel Dimensions: 238 m loa

Principal Imports and Exports: Imports: Cement, Fertiliser, General cargo, Nickel ore, Oil, Sulphur, Zinc concentrates. Exports: Cattle, Frozen meat, General cargo, High analysis fertiliser, Minerals, Molasses, Sugar, Sulphuric acid.

Working Hours: General Office: Mon-Fri 0800-1700. Port Services: 24 h/day, 7 days/week

Accommodation:

Name	Length (m)	Depth (m)	Remarks
Townsville			
Berth No.1	250	12.2	See [1] below
Berth No.2	281	12.2	See [2] below
Berth No.3	283	12.2	See [3] below
Berth No.4	220	10.4	See [4] below
Berth No.7	183	10.4	See [5] below
Berth No.8	213	10.1	See [6] below
Berth No.9	248	12.2	See [7] below
Berth No.10	160	9.5	See [8] below
Berth No.11	240	11.9	See [9] below

[1]*Berth No.1:* Vessels up to 238 m loa. It is a dedicated bulk liquids wharf used exclusively by tankers for bulk oil, gas, and sulphuric acid discharge and by all types of vessels for bunkering

[2]*Berth No.2:* Vessels up to 238 m loa. It is used for unloading nickel ore, and is equipped with an ore unloading gantry crane with a 32 t grab which unloads ore from the vessel into hoppers feeding a conveyor system, which carries the ore to the load out site. The berth is leased to M.I.M. Holdings Ltd, and operated by Queensland Nickel Pty Ltd.

[3]*Berth No.3:* Vessels up to 238 m loa. The berth is leased to M.I.M. Holdings Ltd, and is operated by Northern Shipping & Stevedoring Pty Ltd. General purpose wharf equipped with a 25.4 t slewing crane and used for export of lead ingots, refined copper and nickel, livestock and container cargo and imports of fertiliser and container cargo. 1.2 ha is used as storage accommodation for 184 dry containers and Northern Shipping & Stevedoring's terminal has an area of 1.6 ha capable of holding 25 refrigerated containers and 1200 dry containers

[4]*Berth No.4:* Vessels up to 200 m loa, but only on condition that any vessel berthed at Berth No.3 is not closer than the 360 m mark. Multi-purpose wharf equipped with pipelines (cement/molasses imports), and a landing pad supported by steel piling to service stern angle ramp ro/ro vessels importing motor vehicles. The molasses pipeline to this berth is capable of loading up to 400 t/h from four bulk storage tanks totalling 60 000 t. There is also a caustic soda storage tank of 5000 t

[5]*Berth No.7:* Vessels up to 225 m loa. Leased & operated by M.I.M. Holdings Ltd. It

Key to Principal Facilities:—

| A=Airport | C=Containers | G=General Cargo | P=Petroleum | R=Ro/Ro | Y=Dry Bulk |
| B=Bunkers | D=Dry Dock | L=Cruise | Q=Other Liquid Bulk | T=Towage (where available from port) | |

supports a bulk shiploader for mineral concentrates and ores at the rate of 1000 t/h. WMCF also use this berth for fertiliser exports. Covered storage area of 170 000 t. The berth is also equipped with bunker pipelines

[6]*Berth No.8:* Vessels up to 205 m loa. This berth services the export frozen beef trade with cargoes drawn from freezer stores adjacent to the port. It also serves as a general purpose berth, with scrap metal and fertiliser being handled. It has a total area of 0.4 ha and can accommodate 200 containers, 10 of which can be connected to reefer points

[7]*Berth No.9:* Vessels up to 238 m loa. Raw sugar loading berth. A bulk shiploader delivers sugar to carriers at the rate of 2000 t/h from two storage sheds totalling 285 000 t. The berth is also equipped with bulk molasses and bunker pipelines, and is occasionally used by cruise vessels depending upon availability

[8]*Berth No.10:* Vessels up to 152 m loa. A general purpose berth equipped with a 30 t slewing luffing crane and a stern ro/ro ramp. Live cattle are exported over this wharf (by road). Mining materials are exported to Papua New Guinea and Indonesia. An area of 2.6 ha can accommodate 400 containers, 18 of which may be connected to reefer points. The wharf is also used by the Australian Defence Forces from time to time

[9]*Berth No.11:* Vessels up to 195 m loa. This berth is known as the Outer Berth Mineral Concentrates Loading Facility. Lead and zinc concentrates are placed onto a conveyor system by front end loader and transported to the 1350 t/h shiploader. The facility is operated by BHP World Minerals

Storage: Cold storage facilities are operated by Harbourside Coldstores Pty Ltd with a capacity of approx 5000 t adjacent to the port (Boundary Street)

Mechanical Handling Equipment:

Location	Type	Capacity (t)	Qty	Remarks
Berth No.2	Mult-purp. Cranes	32	1	Also operates on Berth 3
Berth No.2	Container Cranes	55	1	Also operates on Berth 3
Berth No.3	Mult-purp. Cranes	25	1	
Berth No.10	Mult-purp. Cranes	30	1	

Bunkering: Bunker fuel oil is available through pipelines at berths 1, 3, 7, 8 and 9. Distillate is available through pipelines at berth 1 subject to oil company approval BP Australia (Proprietary) Ltd, P O Box 5222, Melbourne, Vic., Australia 3001, *Tel:* +61 3 9268 4111, *Fax:* +61 3 9268 3321, *Email:* gomiasfuelsales@bp.com, *Website:* www.bp.com
ExxonMobil Marine Fuels, 1 Harbour Front Place, 06-00 Harbour Front, Tower One, Singapore, Republic of Singapore 098633, *Tel:* +65 6885 8998, *Fax:* +65 6885 8794, *Email:* asiapac.marinefuels@exxonmobil.com, *Website:* www.exxonmobilmarinefuels.com – *Grades:* MGO – *Delivery Mode:* tank truck
Shell Australia Ltd, Shell Company of Australia, Marine Centre Oceania, No 8 Redfern Road, Melbourne, Vic., Australia 3123, *Tel:* +61 3 9666 5446, *Fax:* +61 3 8823 4800, *Email:* sal-marine-products@shell.com, *Website:* www.shell.com.au

Waste Reception Facilities: Can be arranged with 24 h notice

Towage: Pacific Marine Group Proprietary Ltd (PMG), 60 Perkins Street, P O Box 1155, Townsville, Qld., Australia 4810, *Tel:* +61 7 4724 2200, *Fax:* +61 7 4724 2208, *Email:* info@pacificmarinegroup.com.au, *Website:* www.pacificmarinegroup.com.au
SVITZER, P O Box 721, Townsville, Qld., Australia 4810, *Tel:* +61 7 4771 5246, *Fax:* +61 7 4771 3609, *Email:* info.northqld@adsteam.com.au, *Website:* www.svitzer.com

Seaman Missions: The Seamans Mission, The Flying Angel Seafarers' Club, Berth 9, Suter Pier, Townsville, Qld., Australia, *Email:* seafarers.tsv@beyond.net.au

Ship Chandlers: USS-UBS International, Level 2, Port Control Building, Suter Pier, Townsville Port, Townsville, Qld., Australia 4810, *Tel:* +61 7 4721 4341, *Fax:* +61 7 4721 2102, *Email:* info@ubsprov.com.au, *Website:* www.ussubsint.com
Wiltrading Proprietary Ltd, 10-12 Cannan Street, Townsville, Qld., Australia 4810, *Tel:* +61 7 4771 4288, *Fax:* +61 7 4721 1440, *Email:* wiltrading@wilh.com.au, *Website:* www.wiltrading.com

Shipping Agents: Barwil Agencies Australia Pty Ltd, P O Box 1055, Townsville, Qld., Australia 4810, *Tel:* +61 7 4721 4955, *Fax:* +61 7 4772 5743, *Email:* townsville@wilhelmsen.com, *Website:* www.wilhelmsen.com
Inchcape Shipping Services (ISS), Inchcape Shipping Services Pty Ltd, 90A Bundock Street, P O Box 5778, Townsville, Qld., Australia 4810, *Tel:* +61 7 4724 2477, *Fax:* +61 7 4724 2480, *Email:* townsville@iss-shipping.com.au, *Website:* www.iss-shipping.com
McArthur Shipping & Agency Co Pty Ltd, P O Box 1409, Townsville, Qld., Australia 4810, *Tel:* +61 7 4721 1140, *Fax:* +61 7 4721 1635, *Email:* townsville@mcaship.com.au, *Website:* www.mcaship.com.au
Monson Agencies Australia Proprietary Ltd, P O Box 2157, Townsville, Qld., Australia 4810, *Tel:* +61 7 4771 5810, *Fax:* +61 7 4771 6782, *Email:* townsville@monson.com.au, *Website:* www.monson.com.au
Seatrans Australia Proprietary Ltd, Level 5, 75 Denham Street, Townsville, Qld., Australia 4810, *Tel:* +61 7 4721 1140, *Fax:* +61 7 4721 1635, *Email:* townsville@mcaship.com.au

Stevedoring Companies: Coral Sea Shipping Lines Proprietary Ltd, 22 Ross Street, P O Box 2078, Townsville, Qld., Australia 4810, *Tel:* +61 7 4721 1877, *Fax:* +61 7 4721 1414, *Email:* cssl@curtainbros.com.au
Northern Shipping & Stevedoring Proprietary Ltd, P O Box 5740 MC, Townsville, Qld., Australia, *Tel:* +61 7 4771 4111, *Fax:* +61 7 4772 1413, *Email:* nss@ultra.net.au
P&O Ports, Northern Shipping and Stevedoring, P O Box 5740, Townsville, Qld., Australia 4810, *Tel:* +61 7 4771 4111, *Fax:* +61 7 4772 1413, *Email:* nss@nothernshipping.com.au
Total Stevedoring Services, Nulgarra, Port Alma Road, Bajool, Townsville, Qld., Australia 4699, *Tel:* +61 7 4921 4699, *Fax:* +61 7 4921 4837, *Email:* tsskaren@cqnet.com.au

Medical Facilities: Townsville Hospital, 6.5 km

Airport: Townsville Airport, 9.6 km

Railway: Berths 3 and 4 serviced by railway lines integrated with the state railway, Townsville Central Station, 3 km

Development: Dedicated wharf for cruise vessels (Ocean Terminal)

Lloyd's Agent: Freemans Marine, P O Box 554, Fortitude Valley, Brisbane, Qld., Australia 4006, *Tel:* +61 7 3867 4646, *Fax:* +61 7 3867 4699, *Email:* john.cupitt@freemans.com.au, *Website:* www.freemansmarine.com.au

TRINITY INLET

harbour area, see under Cairns

TWOFOLD BAY

harbour area, see under Eden

URANGAN

Lat 25° 17' S; Long 152° 55' E.

Admiralty Chart: AUS 365/426	**Admiralty Pilot:** 15
Time Zone: GMT +10 h	**UNCTAD Locode:** AU URN

This port is no longer open to commercial shipping

USELESS LOOP

Lat 26° 6' S; Long 113° 23' E.

Admiralty Chart: AUS 331	**Admiralty Pilot:** 17
Time Zone: GMT +8 h	**UNCTAD Locode:** AU USL

Principal Facilities:

		Y						A

Authority: Shark Bay Resources Pty Ltd, Level 3, 22 Mount Street, Perth, W.A., Australia 6000, *Tel:* +61 8 9265 8000, *Fax:* +61 8 9265 8080, *Email:* sbr@salt.com.au

Port Security: ISPS compliant

Approach: Vessels from the N proceed direct to Denham Channel. Vessels from the S can navigate through Naturaliste Channel
Denham Channel is 1160 m long, 122 m wide in depth of approx 10.0 m at datum

Anchorage: If loading berth is occupied on arrival, vessels can anchor off berth and close to jetty

Pilotage: Compulsory. Pilot boarding ground is one nautical mile N of Denham Channel Lt. in pos 25° 53.4' S; 113° 14.8' E. Pilotage operates 24 h

Radio Frequency: VHF Channel 16

Tides: Tidal range up to approx 1.5 m

Maximum Vessel Dimensions: Approx 25 000 dwt, approx 183 m loa, max sailing draft is normally 9.75 m but may be improved at pilot's discretion

Working Hours: Around the clock, 7 days a week

Accommodation:

Name	Remarks
Useless Loop	See [1] below

[1]*Useless Loop:* Dolphin type of jetty (berth face 180 m in length) with connecting catwalks between the dolphins. The jetty, which runs in an approx N and S direction, has been established 370 m from Topper Island (Slope Island on chart). The central loading section is joined to the island by a steel framework assembly in association with a conveyor belt system. The conveyor belt is designed to load salt at the rate of 1100 t/h. The stockpiles are on Topper Island (Slope Island)

Cargo Worked: 1100 t/h

Shipping Agents: Barwil Agencies Australia Pty Ltd, P O Box 805, Fremantle, W.A., Australia 6959, *Tel:* +61 8 9336 0900, *Fax:* +61 8 9336 0999, *Email:* fremantle@barwil.com.au, *Website:* www.barwil.com

Medical Facilities: Regional hospital at Carnarvon. Nursing sister/ambulance available on site

Airport: Useless Loop, 3 km

Lloyd's Agent: Moko Proprietary Ltd, P O Box 685, Willetton, W.A., Australia 6955, *Tel:* +61 8 9354 2248, *Fax:* +61 8 9354 2234, *Email:* kglange@bigpond.com

VARANUS ISLAND TERMINAL

Lat 20° 38' S; Long 115° 36' E.

Admiralty Chart: AUS 62/742	**Admiralty Pilot:** 17
Time Zone: GMT +8 h	**UNCTAD Locode:** AU VAR

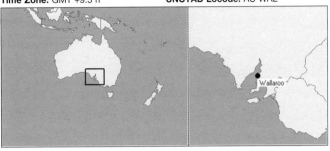

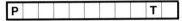

Principal Facilities:

P						T	

Authority: Apache Energy Ltd, P O Box 477, Perth, W.A., Australia 6872, *Tel:* +61 8 9422 7222, *Fax:* +61 8 9422 7445, *Email:* murray.durham@aus.apachecorp.com, *Website:* www.apachecorp.com

Officials: Business Development Manager: Murray Durham, *Tel:* +61 8 9422 7298, *Mobile Tel:* +61 448775474, *Email:* murray.durham@apachecorp.com.

Port Security: ISPS compliant

Pre-Arrival Information: Vessels proceeding to the Varanus Island Loading Terminal should notify Apache Energy Ltd of ETA not less than 96 h before arrival, amending or confirming their ETA at intervals of 48 h and 24 h before arrival

Documentation: Customs requirements prior to arrival:
Masters must send to Agent no later than 72 h prior to arrival (a) Australian customs crew list (Form 3b) in alphabetical order. Only passports can identify documents as the Seaman's book is no longer acceptable (b) Passenger maintenance letter if applicable (c) Ports of call list (Form B921) with at least four ports with arrival/departure dates (d) Certificate expiry dates, load line, safety radio, safety equipment, safety construction, IOPP, CLC insurance, ISM/SMC and Australian Navigation Levy (e) Ship's impending arrival details
On arrival, hand to Agent originals of the following documents with Master's signature and ship's stamp where applicable (a) Customs form B921 ports of call list and ports of loading list (b) Forms 3A and 3B crew report (c) Form 42A report of ship stores (d) Form 5 (part one) ship's report of arrival (e) Form 5 (part two) crew effects declaration (f) Ship's impending arrival details (g) Last port clearance
If the vessel is on a domestic voyage the Agent will require your Customs Transhire envelope and last port clearance that contains the above listed documents
If the vessel is either commencing or completing a domestic voyage, the Agent will require a vessel's completed Customs Bunker Statement form
AQIS requirements prior to arrival: Send to Agent 48 h prior to arrival Quarantine Prearrival Report (Form 006). Send to Agent after completion of ballast water exchange (a) Ballast water uptake/discharge log (Form 026A) (b) Ballast water treatment/exchange log (Form 026B) (c) A statement that you are familiar with AQIS 'foot and mouth' disease requirements
Documents required if the vessel is arriving from another Australian port:
Customs requirements prior to arrival (a) Australian customs crew list (Form 3b) in alphabetical order. Only passports can identify documents as the Seaman's book is no longer acceptable (b) Passenger maintenance letter if applicable (c) Ports of call list (Form B921) with at least four ports with arrival/departure dates (d) Certificate expiry dates, load line, safety radio, safety equipment, safety construction, IOPP, CLC insurance, ISM/SMC and Australian Navigation Levy

Approach: Within the 0.5 nautical mile mooring circle there is a least depth of 20.4 m. Within the conical approach and departure area (060°/240° and 120°/300° boundaries) depths in excess of 20.4 m are found. The max permissible draft of vessels using the CBM Terminal is 17 m

Anchorage: The required anchorage position is 20° 40' S; 115° 40' E

Pilotage: Compulsory. Pilot boards in pos 20° 40' S; 115° 40' E. Berthing by either day or night is at the pilot's discretion and is largely dependent on the prevailing weather conditions

Radio Frequency: Varanus Pilot on VHF Channel 24. Terminal on VHF Channel 74

Weather: The area is subject to strong E'ly winds and associated seas during the winter months (predominantly May-September). The terminal is located within a tropical cyclone region and typically up to five cyclones may track down the Varanus section of coast during the period November-April

Maximum Vessel Dimensions: Approx 140 000 dwt, 300 m loa, 46 m beam, 17 m draft

Accommodation:

Name	Remarks
Varanus Island Terminal	See [1] below

[1]*Varanus Island Terminal:* The onshore terminal is situated on Varanus Island and the CBM Tanker Terminal is situated 2 miles offshore in pos 20° 38' S; 115° 36' E
Varanus Field Superintendent, Tel: +61 8 9422 7301, Fax: +61 8 9422 7317, Email: varanus.fieldsup@aus.apachecorp.com
Onshore Facilities: Three storage tanks with cap of 750 000 bbls. The cargo pumps have a nominal 1654 m3/h cap and the three pumps together export a max 3300 m3/h. The average pumping rate is 18 000 bbls/h
Offshore Facilities: The moorings consist of an eight leg multi-point mooring with four buoyed legs and four swamped legs. A 4200 m long by 762 mm pipeline leads from the shore to the Tanker Terminal. The submarine hose is 73.15 m long

Towage: A tug of min 38 t bollard pull is provided to assist the berthing and departure operations

Medical Facilities: No services available other than dire emergency

Lloyd's Agent: Moko Proprietary Ltd, P O Box 685, Willetton, W.A., Australia 6955, *Tel:* +61 8 9354 2248, *Fax:* +61 8 9354 2234, *Email:* kglange@bigpond.com

VICTORIA DOCK

harbour area, see under Melbourne

WALLAROO

Lat 33° 55' S; Long 137° 37' E.

Admiralty Chart: AUS 777	**Admiralty Pilot:** 13
Time Zone: GMT +9.5 h	**UNCTAD Locode:** AU WAL

Principal Facilities:

	Y	G		B		T	

Authority: Flinders Ports Proprietary Ltd, 3 Diagonal Road, Wallaroo, S.A., Australia 5556, *Tel:* +61 8 8823 2026, *Fax:* +61 8 8823 2026, *Email:* flindersports@flindersports.com.au, *Website:* www.flindersports.com.au

Officials: Business Development Manager: Stewart Lammin, *Tel:* + +61 8 8447 0627, *Email:* lammin.stewart@flindersports.com.au.

Port Security: ISPS compliant

Approach: Approach channel is 6.4 km long, 90 m wide in depth of 8.5 m below CD

Anchorage: Vessels anchor on arrival 1.6 km W of the Fairway Beacon in a depth of 18 m

Pilotage: Compulsory. Pilots (supplied from Adelaide) boarding ground is 2.2 km in 260° direction from the entrance beacon. Vessels over 200 m loa or 30 m beam need two tugs for berthing

Radio Frequency: VHF Channels 6, 8, 12, 16 and 67

Tides: MHWS 1.21 m, MHWN 0.88 m

Traffic: 2007/08, 22 vessels, 315 784 t of cargo handled

Maximum Vessel Dimensions: 230 m loa with beam of 32 m. Panamax vessels of 80 000 dwt able to berth, but due to depth of water and draft restrictions vessels can only be part loaded up to 50 000 dwt

Principal Imports and Exports: Imports: Fertiliser. Exports: Grain, Seeds.

Working Hours: Bulk loader, Sunday to Friday 0800-2200, Saturday 0800-1500

Accommodation:

Name	Length (m)	Depth (m)	Remarks
Wallaroo			
Berth No.1N	84	8.7	
Berth No.2N	290	8.7	See [1] below
Berth No.3N	68	7.2	
Berth No.1S	168	8.7	Fertiliser imports
Berth No.2S	198	8.1	Disused
Berth No.3S	76	7.3	

[1]*Berth No.2N:* Operated by ABB Grain Ltd
Bulk grain loader consists of five identical slewing loading booms with spouts fed by a conveyor system by a bank of silos on shore with a cap of 500 000 bu. Max spout outreach is 20.1 m. Loading rate is 800 t/h

Bunkering: Oil is roaded from Adelaide
BP Australia (Proprietary) Ltd, P O Box 5222, Melbourne, Vic., Australia 3001, *Tel:* +61 3 9268 4111, *Fax:* +61 3 9268 3321, *Email:* gomiasfuelsales@bp.com, *Website:* www.bp.com
ExxonMobil Marine Fuels, 1 Harbour Front Place, 06-00 Harbour Front, Tower One, Singapore, Republic of Singapore 098633, *Tel:* +65 6885 8998, *Fax:* +65 6885 8794, *Email:* asiapac.marinefuels@exxonmobil.com, *Website:* www.exxonmobilmarinefuels.com – *Grades:* MGO – *Delivery Mode:* tank truck
Shell Australia Ltd, Shell Company of Australia, Marine Centre Oceania, No 8 Redfern Road, Melbourne, Vic., Australia 3123, *Tel:* +61 3 9666 5446, *Fax:* +61 3 8823 4800, *Email:* sal-marine-products@shell.com, *Website:* www.shell.com.au

Towage: One tug of 11.5 t bollard pull available

Repair & Maintenance: Available for minor repairs

Shipping Agents: Barwil Agencies Australia Pty Ltd, P O Box 1559, Adelaide, S.A., Australia 5015, *Tel:* +61 8 8341 0466, *Fax:* +61 8 8341 0506, *Email:* ptadelaide@wilhelmsen.com, *Website:* www.wilhelmsen.com
P&O Ports, P O Box 30, Wallaroo, S.A., Australia 5556, *Tel:* +61 8 8823 2202, *Fax:* +61 8 8823 2907

Stevedoring Companies: P&O Ports, P O Box 30, Wallaroo, S.A., Australia 5556, *Tel:* +61 8 8823 2202, *Fax:* +61 8 8823 2907

Medical Facilities: Well equipped hospital

Lloyd's Agent: Maritime & General Insurance Surveyors Proprietary Ltd, Suite 4, 7 Divett Street, Adelaide, S.A., Australia 5015, *Tel:* +61 8 8341 2552, *Fax:* +61 8 8241 0229, *Email:* maritime-general@adam.com.au

Key to Principal Facilities:—				
A=Airport	**C**=Containers	**G**=General Cargo	**P**=Petroleum	**R**=Ro/Ro	**Y**=Dry Bulk
B=Bunkers	**D**=Dry Dock	**L**=Cruise	**Q**=Other Liquid Cargo	**T**=Towage (where available from port)

WEBB DOCK

harbour area, see under Melbourne

WEIPA

Lat 12° 39' S; Long 141° 52' E.

Admiralty Chart: AUS 4
Time Zone: GMT +10 h

Admiralty Pilot: 17
UNCTAD Locode: AU WEI

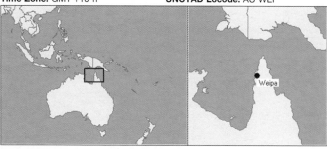

Principal Facilities:

		Y	G			B	T	

Authority: Ports Corporation of Queensland, Floor 24, 300 Queen Street, P O Box 409, Brisbane, Qld., Australia 4001, *Tel:* +61 7 3224 7088, *Fax:* +61 7 3224 7234, *Email:* info@pcq.com.au, *Website:* www.pcq.com.au

Officials: Chief Executive Officer: Brad Fish, *Email:* bfish@pcq.com.au. Communications Manager: Rachel Campbell, *Tel:* +61 7 3224 8863, *Email:* rcampbell@pcq.com.au.

Port Security: ISPS compliant

Approach: The South Channel which is 11.27 km long, 106.06 m bottom width with max dredged depth of 10.8 m LAT (subject to change due to siltation), is marked with beacons for day and night navigation. The width of the channel to Weipa is 152.4 m. There are two natural approach channels to the wharves at Lorim Point. The principal and the deeper being to the N of the Cora Bank, 10.8 m LAT the other being to the S and E of this bank, 7.3 m LAT. A swinging basin 426.7 m in diameter, with least depth of 9.3 m LAT has been dredged from Cora Bank to the E of Lorim Point berth. The swinging basin to the E of Evans Landing Wharf has a width of 335.28 m and a depth of 9.3 m LAT

Anchorage: Anchorage is permitted anywhere in Albatross Bay in a depth of 11.3 m with a soft mud bottom ensuring good holding ground, except in the immediate vicinity of the Fairway Beacon. Anchorage not permitted anywhere within the Embley River except by permission of the Harbour Master

Pilotage: Compulsory and arranged through the Duty Pilot at Cairns, Tel: +61 7 4031 9609. Pilot boards westward of the Fairway Light Beacon; 48 h notice is required. VHF Channel 16

Radio Frequency: Continuous watch on VHF channel 16, call sign 'Weipa Harbour'. Port working, VHF channel 12, tug working, VHF channels 6 and 8

Weather: Monsoonal weather, wet from December to April with variable winds. Dry from May to November with SE trade winds. The port is subject to cyclones from December to April

Tides: MHWS 2.3 m, MLWN 1.6 m

Traffic: 2007/08, 436 vessels, 22 111 499 t of cargo exported

Maximum Vessel Dimensions: 104 865 dwt, 256 m loa, 12.98 m draft

Principal Imports and Exports: Imports: Fuel, General cargo. Exports: Bauxite.

Working Hours: Continuous

Accommodation:

Name	Length (m)	Depth (m)	Remarks
Weipa			See [1] below
Humbug Point Wharf	114	9.5	See [2] below
Lorim Point East Berth		12.3	See [3] below
Lorim Point West Berth		12.3	See [4] below
Evans Landing Wharf	195	9.6	See [5] below

[1]*Weipa:* Operated by Comalco Minerals & Alumina
Max draft of vessels that may enter the port depends upon the tide level, but vessels are required to have 0.9 m keel clearance on departure and 0.6 m on arrival. During the monsoon period the mean sea level is from 0.3 to 0.6 m higher, and in the river the spring rise during strong W winds and heavy rain has been recorded as attaining a height of 3.96 to 4.26 m. This port is developed for the export of bauxite.
The Lorim Point export wharf consists of two berths; Lorim Point East and Lorim Point West. Together they have a total berthing length of 548.6 m, capable of berthing two vessels each of 225 m loa. The depth of water alongside the berths is at present 12.5 m LWOST. The wharf consists of 11 sheet pile, concrete capped, sand filled caissons 15.2 m in diameter, fendered by tubular rubber fendering and interconnected by octagonal steel piling supporting the rail structure for the shiploaders and a light roadway inshore of the loading facility. There are mooring dolphins at each end of the wharf. Bollards and quick release hooks are fitted at intervals along the full length of the wharf and on the dolphins
[2]*Humbug Point Wharf:* Cargo handling wharf for vessels up to 170 m loa and designed to receive heavy equipment
[3]*Lorim Point East Berth:* Serviced by a single travelling, luffing, slewing shiploader and is used for loading raw bauxite and calcined bauxite. Length of travel along berth 164.59 m, max outreach 20.27 m, airdraft at max elevation 18.28 m, loading rates, raw 6000 t/h, calcined 1000 t/h

[4]*Lorim Point West Berth:* Bauxite & heavy fuel for vessels up to 254 m loa. Shiploader with rate of 3500 t/h
[5]*Evans Landing Wharf:* For the discharge of distillate, aviation & motor fuels. Capable of berthing a vessel of up to 191.11 m. The berth consists of six steel piled resilient dolphins. The inner two are larger and strengthened as impact dolphins. Mooring dolphins are established E and W of the berth dolphins. Distillate, mogas and avgas are discharged through a 20 cm line with avgas alternatively discharged through two parallel 7 cm hoses and a 10 cm line

Mechanical Handling Equipment:

Location	Type	Capacity (t)	Qty
Weipa	Mobile Cranes	26	1
Weipa	Mobile Cranes	31	1
Weipa	Mobile Cranes	150	1
Weipa	Mobile Cranes	70	1

Cargo Worked: 71 000 t/day

Bunkering: Limited supplies of distillate only can be arranged in an emergency and only available from Evans Landing Wharf

Towage: Three diesel tugs; bollard pull 2 x 24 t and 1 x 18 t. Only 2 tugs are used, the third tug is stand-by only
SVITZER, SVITZER Australasia, Humbug Point, P O Box 486, Weipa, Qld., Australia 4874, *Tel:* +61 7 4069 7333, *Fax:* +61 7 4069 7041, *Email:* cbusch@adsteam.com.au, *Website:* www.svitzer.com

Shipping Agents: Barwil Agencies Australia Pty Ltd, P O Box 536, Weipa, Qld., Australia 4874, *Tel:* +61 7 4069 7203, *Fax:* +61 7 4069 7221, *Email:* weipa@wilhelmsen.com, *Website:* www.wilhelmsen.com

Stevedoring Companies: Perkins Shipping Proprietary Ltd, C/Humbug Wharf, P O Box 567, Weipa, Qld., Australia 4874, *Tel:* +61 7 4069 7309, *Fax:* +61 7 4069 7233, *Email:* perkins@perkins.com.au, *Website:* www.perkins.com.au

Medical Facilities: Small hospital at Weipa, serious cases can be flown to Cairns

Lloyd's Agent: Freemans Marine, P O Box 554, Fortitude Valley, Brisbane, Qld., Australia 4006, *Tel:* +61 7 3867 4646, *Fax:* +61 7 3867 4699, *Email:* john.cupitt@freemans.com.au, *Website:* www.freemansmarine.com.au

WESTERNPORT

alternate name, see Hastings

WHITE BAY

harbour area, see under Sydney

WHYALLA

Lat 33° 2' S; Long 137° 35' E.

Admiralty Chart: AUS 136
Time Zone: GMT +9.5 h

Admiralty Pilot: 13
UNCTAD Locode: AU WYA

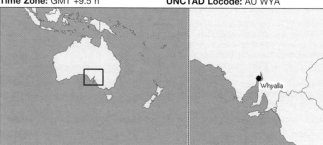

Principal Facilities:

P		Y	G			B		T	A

Authority: OneSteel Whyalla Steelworks, Port Augusta Road, P O Box 21, Whyalla, S.A., Australia 5600, *Tel:* +61 8 8640 4708, *Fax:* +61 8 8640 4756, *Email:* wordenr@onesteel.com, *Website:* www.onesteel.com/onesteel_whyalla

Port Security: ISPS compliant. PSO Officer: Rod Worden, Tel: +61 8 8640 4217, Email: wordenr@onesteel.com

Approach: Inner Harbour Channel is 2 nautical miles long, 120 m wide in depth of 10 m. The Inner Harbour Swing Basin is 304 m diameter in depth of 10 m
Outer Harbour Channel is 1.5 nautical miles long, 122 m wide in depth of 10.7 m. The Outer Harbour Swing Basin has a min 270 m diameter in depth of 10.7 m

Anchorage: It is recommended that vessels not engaged in transhipment anchor in a position south of Lat 33° 04' S, and in the area approx 2-3.5 nautical miles SSE of the Whyalla Port entrance beacon

Pilotage: Compulsory for vessels over 35 m loa. Vessels should send ETA 48 h and 24 h in advance via agent, who will arrange pilotage and towage services. Vessels should advise any alteration in ETA
Pilot boards at the Whyalla Pilot Boarding Ground, 1.7 nautical miles SE of No.1 Lt Bn

Radio Frequency: VHF channels are monitored only when vessel movements are expected, and contact will then be made from the pilot cutter on VHF Channel 16. Subsequent to that, the following channels are used:
VHF Channel 8 for pilotage and berthing

VHF Channel 10 for transhipping
VHF Channel 12 for port operations

Tides: (Jetty and Wharf) HHW 2.5 m, LHW 1.8 m. Gauges on dolphins and wharf show rises

Accommodation:

Name	Length (m)	Depth (m)	Remarks
Whyalla			
Blast Furnace Wharf	701	10.7	See [1] below
No.2 Ore Jetty	274	10.7	See [2] below
Transhipment Points			See [3] below

[1]*Blast Furnace Wharf:* Two berths (Bulk Berth which is serviced by a 26 t stockbridge and Products Berth) situated in the inner harbour on N side of basin for vessels up to 204 m loa. Cargoes handled include steel products and bulk commodities
[2]*No.2 Ore Jetty:* Located in the outer harbour and used exclusively for the loading of bulk iron ore products for vessels usually up to 228 m loa although vessels up to 250 m loa can be considered. Loading rates of 2000 t/h
[3]*Transhipment Points:* There are two transhipment points in the Spencer Gulf for ocean-going vessels loading iron ore:
Cape-size vessels: approx 7.5 nautical miles from Whyalla in pos 33° 09' 12" S; 137° 38' 21" E
Panamax-size vessels: approx 5 nautical miles from Whyalla in pos 33° 06' 12" S; 137° 38' 30" E
The ore is loaded onto two self-unloading barges, tugged to the transhipment point and loaded onto a floating offshore transfer barge, which then transfers the ore to an ocean-going vessel

Bunkering: Available by road tanker from Adelaide at the Products Berth (Inner Harbour) only with 24 h notice
BP Australia (Proprietary) Ltd, P O Box 5222, Melbourne, Vic., Australia 3001, *Tel:* +61 3 9268 4111, *Fax:* +61 3 9268 3321, *Email:* gomiasfuelsales@bp.com, *Website:* www.bp.com
ExxonMobil Marine Fuels, 1 Harbour Front Place, 06-00 Harbour Front, Tower One, Singapore, Republic of Singapore 098633, *Tel:* +65 6885 8998, *Fax:* +65 6885 8794, *Email:* asiapac.marinefuels@exxonmobil.com, *Website:* www.exxonmobilmarinefuels.com – *Grades:* MGO – *Delivery Mode:* tank truck
Shell Australia Ltd, Shell Company of Australia, Marine Centre Oceania, No 8 Redfern Road, Melbourne, Vic., Australia 3123, *Tel:* +61 3 9666 5446, *Fax:* +61 3 8823 4800, *Email:* sal-marine-products@shell.com, *Website:* www.shell.com.au

Waste Reception Facilities: Normal refuse services by a licensed waste transportation contractor are available on request via ship's agent

Towage: Three tugs are available at Whyalla. An additional three tugs are also available from Port Pirie
SVITZER, SVITZER Australasia, 24 Forsyth Street, P O Box 513, Whyalla, S.A., Australia 5600, *Tel:* +61 8 8645 9013, *Fax:* +61 8 8645 9959, *Email:* info.sa@adsteam.com.au, *Website:* www.svitzer.com

Repair & Maintenance: Quirk Engineering & Fabrication, 11 Storey Street, Whyalla, S.A., Australia 4608, *Tel:* +61 8 8645 4002, *Fax:* +61 8 8645 2519, *Email:* admin@quirkeng.com.au Minor repairs

Shipping Agents: Barwil Agencies Australia Pty Ltd, P O Box 162A, Whyalla, S.A., Australia 5600, *Tel:* +61 8 8644 0911, *Fax:* +61 8 8644 0925, *Email:* whyalla@wilhelmsen.com, *Website:* www.wilhelmsen.com

Stevedoring Companies: BIS Industrial Services, 162 Lacey Street, Whyalla, S.A., Australia 5600, *Tel:* +61 8 8645 7355, *Fax:* +61 8 8645 4601
Toll Stevedoring, Port Augusta Road, P O Box 147, Whyalla, S.A., Australia 5600, *Tel:* +61 8 8640 4084, *Fax:* +61 8 8640 4787, *Email:* bill_brodie@toll.com.au

Medical Facilities: Modern hospital, several practitioners

Airport: Whyalla Airport, approx 10 km

Lloyd's Agent: Maritime & General Insurance Surveyors Proprietary Ltd, Suite 4, 7 Divett Street, Adelaide, S.A., Australia 5015, *Tel:* +61 8 8341 2552, *Fax:* +61 8 8241 0229, *Email:* maritime-general@adam.com.au

WILLIAMSTOWN

harbour area, see under Melbourne

WYNDHAM

Lat 15° 27' S; Long 128° 6' E.

Admiralty Chart: AUS 32   **Admiralty Pilot:** 17
Time Zone: GMT +8 h   **UNCTAD Locode:** AU WYN

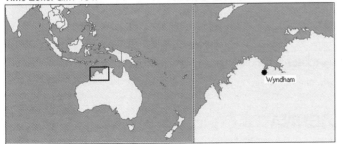

Principal Facilities:

		G	C		B		A

Authority: ORDC Wyndham Port, P O Box 186, Wharf Road, Wyndham, W.A., Australia 6740, *Tel:* +61 8 9161 1203, *Fax:* +61 8 9161 1244, *Email:* ordport@wn.com.au

Officials: Port Manager: Steve Forrest.
Harbour Master: Brian Tod, *Email:* hmordport@westnet.com.au.

Port Security: ISPS compliant

Pre-Arrival Information: Max arrival draft, max displacement, dangerous goods on board

Approach: Navigable in daylight only, ships approach through Cambridge Gulf. Channel (min depth N end Myrmidon Bank 5.5 m and 5.0 m through Middle Gd)

Anchorage: At outer pilot boarding ground

Pilotage: Compulsory for all vessels over 500 gt. Vessels should send request for pilot 7 days in advance, 48 h in advance (giving max draught) and 24 h in advance (stating pilot boarding position required) to the Harbour Master at Wyndham. Pilot boarding ground at Lacrosse Island Light, bearing 351° distant 4.7 miles and Nicholls Point, bearing 214° distant 5.2 miles. Pilotage from both positions is during daylight hours only

Radio Frequency: VHF Channels 16 and 12

Weather: Cyclone season November to April

Tides: (Jetty) HWS 7.3 m, Neaps 5.5 m. Max range 8.5 m

Maximum Vessel Dimensions: Current max displacement 26 000 dwt. Max draft 8.0 m. Max loa 190 m. Larger vessels require clearance from the Harbour Master

Principal Imports and Exports: Imports: Ammonium nitrate, Bulk fuel, Fertilizer, General cargo. Exports: Live cattle, Maize, Molasses, Ore.

Working Hours: Labour available 24 h/day

Accommodation:

Name	Remarks
Wyndham	See [1] below

[1]*Wyndham:* A 450 m long jetty with berthing face of 314 m. The jetty is a piled structure with a concrete deck and spring fendering. A bulk product shiploader is located at the southern end. Air draught from zero datum to underside of loader in horizontal position is 16.4 m. Outreach of luffing boom from face of fendering to pouring spout is 9.7 m. Vessels may be required to move along the berth to facilitate hatch changes

Storage: Bulk sheds: 2 by 4000 m2. General cargo sheds: 3 by 2000 m2

Mechanical Handling Equipment:

Location	Type	Capacity (t)	Qty
Wyndham	Mult-purp. Cranes	5–45	3
Wyndham	Forklifts	2.5–23	6

Bunkering: DFO available by arrangement
ExxonMobil Marine Fuels, 1 Harbour Front Place, 06-00 Harbour Front, Tower One, Singapore, Republic of Singapore 098633, *Tel:* +65 6885 8998, *Fax:* +65 6885 8794, *Email:* asiapac.marinefuels@exxonmobil.com, *Website:* www.exxonmobilmarinefuels.com – *Grades:* MGO – *Delivery Mode:* tank truck, pipeline

Repair & Maintenance: Limited repairs available from local contractors

Medical Facilities: A small modern hospital is located in Wyndham and a doctor is always on call. A dentist is available in Kununurra and visits Wyndham once a fortnight

Airport: Kununura, 99 km

Lloyd's Agent: Moko Proprietary Ltd, P O Box 685, Willetton, W.A., Australia 6955, *Tel:* +61 8 9354 2248, *Fax:* +61 8 9354 2234, *Email:* kglange@bigpond.com

YAMBA

Lat 29° 22' S; Long 153° 18' E.

Admiralty Chart: AUS 812/812   **Admiralty Pilot:** 15
Time Zone: GMT +10 h   **UNCTAD Locode:** AU YBA

Principal Facilities:

		G	C		B	D	T	A

Authority: Port of Yamba, Pilot Station, Pilot Street, Yamba, N.S.W., Australia 2464, *Tel:* +61 2 6646 2002, *Fax:* +61 2 6646 1596, *Email:* yambapilot@maritime.nsw.gov.au, *Website:* www.yamba.nsw.gov.au

Officials: Harbour Master: Capt Alan Jones, *Email:* ajones@maritime.nsw.gov.au.

Port Security: ISPS compliant

Pre-Arrival Information: IMO Number, Draft, LOA, Dangerous Goods Declaration, Crew List

Approach: River port with bar at entrance. Depth over bar 5 m plus tide. The river is buoyed and beaconed and is navigable by vessels of 5.2 m draft as far as Goodwood Island and 4.5 m to Harwood by working the tides

---

Key to Principal Facilities:—				
A=Airport	**C**=Containers	**G**=General Cargo	**P**=Petroleum	**R**=Ro/Ro	**Y**=Dry Bulk
B=Bunkers	**D**=Dry Dock	**L**=Cruise	**Q**=Other Liquid Cargo	**T**=Towage (where available from port)	

Anchorage: One to two nautical miles NE of north breakwater in 15-20 m

Pilotage: Compulsory for all craft of 30 m loa and over and available at all times. Pilot normally boards 1 mile seaward of the breakwater, weather permitting with 72 h and 24 h notice

Radio Frequency: VHF Channel 16, call sign 'Yamba Harbour Control'. Working Channel 12

Weather: NE-SE winds. Occasional tail ends of cyclones

Tides: Max 2 m

Traffic: 2007/08, 44 vessels, 16 203 t of cargo handled

Maximum Vessel Dimensions: Approx 7947 dwt, 5.2 m draft, 119 m length

Principal Imports and Exports: Imports: General cargo, Softwood timber. Exports: General cargo, Logs.

Working Hours: Monday-Friday 0700-1700. Extra shifts if required

Accommodation:

Name	Length (m)	Depth (m)	Draught (m)	Remarks
Yamba				
Goodwood Island Wharf	70	6	6	See [1] below

[1]*Goodwood Island Wharf:* Vessels in excess of 100 m loa can be safely secured. Undercover storage available

Storage:

Location	Open (m²)	Covered (m²)
Goodwood Island Wharf	5000	300

Mechanical Handling Equipment:

Location	Type	Capacity (t)
Yamba	Mobile Cranes	50

Cargo Worked: 1000 t/day of timber, approx 600 t/day of break bulk general

Bunkering: Nearly all grades of fuels and lubricants are available by road through shipping agent

Towage: One tug available of 5 t bollard pull

Repair & Maintenance: Harwood Slipway & Engineering Co.Ltd, 162-164 River Road East, Harwood, N.S.W., Australia 2465, *Tel:* +61 2 6646 4222, *Fax:* +61 2 6646 4472, *Email:* harwoodslipway@bigpond.com, *Website:* www.harwoodslipway.com Slipway capable of slipping a 1100 t barge or 700 t vessel with max length of 48 m

Stevedoring Companies: Tuezeal Pty Ltd, P O Box 283, Maclean, N.S.W., Australia 2463, *Tel:* +61 2 6645 3211, *Fax:* +61 2 6645 2954, *Email:* yamship@bigpond.net.au

Medical Facilities: Hospital and doctors at Maclean and Grafton

Airport: Grafton, 64 km

Railway: Grafton, 65 km from wharf

Lloyd's Agent: Freemans Marine, P O Box 36, St. Leonards, N.S.W., Australia 1590, *Tel:* +61 2 9438 2655, *Fax:* +61 2 9436 1367, *Email:* lloyds@freemans.com.au, *Website:* www.freemansmarine.com.au

YAMPI SOUND

Lat 16° 9' S; Long 123° 45' E.

Admiralty Chart: AUS 733, AUS 40	**Admiralty Pilot:** 17
Time Zone: GMT +8 h	**UNCTAD Locode:** AU YAM

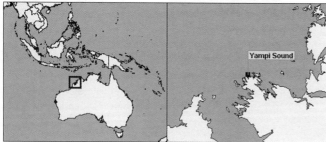

Principal Facilities:

	Y				T	

Port Security: ISPS compliant. Port Security Officer: Colin McCumstie, Tel: +61 8 9423 0853

Approach: Koolan Island is approached from the NW between Irvine and Gibbings Islands, and from the N through Parakeet Channel

Pilotage: Compulsory. The pilot boarding position is approx 9 cables SSW of the western extremity of Tarrant Island in pos 16° 07.6' S; 123° 40.0' E

Tides: Tidal range 8.9 m MLWS-MHWS

Maximum Vessel Dimensions: 225 m loa, 75 000 dwt, 32.3 m beam

Working Hours: 24 h/day subject to tide

Accommodation:

Name	Length (m)	Depth (m)	Remarks
Koolan Island Iron Ore Terminal			Operated by Koolan Iron Ore Pty Ltd
Loading Jetty	377	15	See [1] below

[1]*Loading Jetty:* Consists of two mooring and seven berthing dolphins aligned in a

general SE/NW direction. The shiploader is a fixed, luffing conveyor boom located at the centre dolphin and has an outreach of 19.7 m. It has a normal loading rate of 1500 t/h and a peak rate of 3000 t/h. Berthing is restricted to daylight hours only

Towage: Two tugs and a line boat are available to assist with berthing

Medical Facilities: Nearest hospital at Derby on the mainland

Lloyd's Agent: Moko Proprietary Ltd, P O Box 685, Willetton, W.A., Australia 6955, *Tel:* +61 8 9354 2248, *Fax:* +61 8 9354 2234, *Email:* kglange@bigpond.com

YARRAVILLE

harbour area, see under Melbourne

AUSTRIA

KREMS

Lat 48° 24' N; Long 15° 35' E.

Admiralty Chart: -	**Admiralty Pilot:** -
Time Zone: GMT +1 h	**UNCTAD Locode:** AT KRE

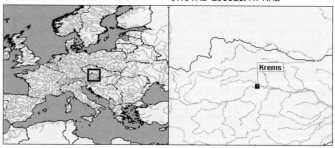

Principal Facilities:

		Y	G	C					

Authority: Mierka Donauhafen Krems Gesellschaft m.b.H. & Co KG, Karl-Mierka-Strasse 7-9, A-3500 Krems, Austria, *Tel:* +43 2732 73571, *Fax:* +43 2732 72571, *Email:* office@mierka.com, *Website:* www.mierka.com

Officials: Managing Director: Hubert Mierka, *Email:* mierka@mierka.com. Marketing Manager: Walter Senk, *Email:* senk@mierka.com.

Traffic: 2006, 40 586 TEU's handled

Working Hours: Mon-Fri 0600-1700. Sat and Sun on request

Accommodation:

Name	Length (m)	Remarks
Krems		See [1] below
Container Terminal	800	See [2] below

[1]*Krems:* Total area of 430 000 m2 consisting of fourteen berths with length of quay totaling 1560 m

[2]*Container Terminal:* Operated by WienCont Krems Kombiterminal GmbH, Karl-Mierka-Strasse 7-9, A-3500 Krems, Tel: +43 2732 81760, Fax: +43 2732 81761, Email: office@wiencont.com, Website: www.wiencont.com Terminal area of 52 000 m2 with 4000 TEU cap

Storage: Free port storage of 280 000 m2

Location	Open (m²)	Covered (m²)
Krems	60000	23000

Mechanical Handling Equipment:

Location	Type	Capacity (t)	Qty
Krems	Floating Cranes		1
Krems	Mobile Cranes	10	2
Krems	Gantry Cranes	40–50	2
Krems	Reach Stackers		2

Lloyd's Agent: Transpack GmbH, Brunner Strasse 14/10, A-1210 Vienna, Austria, *Tel:* +43 1 278 2622, *Fax:* +43 1 278 2624, *Email:* office@transpack.co.at, *Website:* www.transpack.co.at

VIENNA

Lat 48° 13' N; Long 16° 22' E.

Admiralty Chart: -	**Admiralty Pilot:** -
Time Zone: GMT +1 h	**UNCTAD Locode:** AT VIE

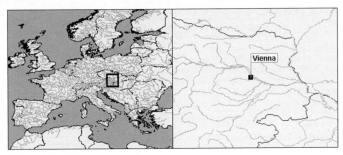

Principal Facilities:

	Y	G	C	R				

Authority: Wiener Hafen GmbH & Co KG, Seitenhafenstrasse 15, A-1023 Vienna, Austria, *Tel:* +43 1 72716-0, *Fax:* +43 1 7271 6200, *Email:* office@wienerhafen.com, *Website:* www.wienerhafen.com

Officials: Managing Director: Walter Edinger, *Tel:* +43 1 7271 6111.
Marketing Manager: Gerhard Lehnert, *Tel:* +43 1 7271 6127, *Email:* lehnert@wienerhafen.com

Traffic: 2007, 1 639 843 t of cargo handled, 323 424 TEU's

Accommodation:

Name	Length (m)	Remarks
Vienna		Total area of the port is 350 ha with quays totaling 5000 m
Freudenau		Km post 120. Includes a car terminal and a container terminal
WienCont Containerterminal GmbH	650	See [1] below
Albern		See [2] below
Lobau		Km post 1916.4. Transhipment & storage of mineral oil products
Vienna Marina		Km post 1926.3. Recreational crafts
DDSG Port Vienna		Km post 1929.5-1928.4. Passenger shipping centre

[1]*WienCont Containerterminal GmbH:* Freudenauer Hafenstrasse 12, A-1020 Vienna, Tel: +43 1 72772-0, Fax: +43 1 72772-19, Email: office@wiencont.com, Website: www.wiencont.com
Equipment includes one 40 t cap gantry for barge handling. 10 reefer points. 277 320 TEU's handled in 2006
[2]*Albern:* Km post 1918.3. Terminal for building materials and transhipment & storage of grain

Storage:

Location	Open (m²)	Covered (m²)
Vienna	270000	70000

Mechanical Handling Equipment:

Location	Type	Capacity (t)	Qty
Vienna	Mult-purp. Cranes	30	2
Vienna	Mobile Cranes	33	2
Vienna	Gantry Cranes	45	3
Vienna	Reach Stackers		9
Vienna	Forklifts	3–5	38

Waste Reception Facilities: Available

Shipping Agents: Astra Transportagentur G.m.b.H., Sonnwendgasse 21, A-1100 Vienna, Austria, *Tel:* +43 1 60184-0, *Fax:* +43 1 6018 4177, *Email:* marina.horak@astra.at
CargoCompass Schiffahrtsagentur GmbH, Suite 339, 1st Floor, DDSG Shipping Center, Handelskai 265, A-1020 Vienna, Austria, *Tel:* +43 1 7283 4840, *Fax:* +43 1 728 3482, *Email:* cargocompass@netway.at
Centranaut Transportagentur GmbH, Gregor-Mendel Strasse 2-4, A-1180 Vienna, Austria, *Tel:* +43 1 3165 1114, *Fax:* +43 1 3165 1119, *Email:* masean@magnet.at
CMA-CGM S.A., CMA CGM Austria GmbH, Rennweg 46-50, A-1030 Vienna, Austria, *Tel:* +43 1 798 3978, *Fax:* +43 1 798 9120, *Email:* vie.genmbox@cma-cgm.com, *Website:* www.cma-cgm.com
Dolphin Shipping Transportagentur GmbH, Wiedner Hauptstrasse 120-124, A-1130 Vienna, Austria, *Tel:* +43 1 877 9611, *Fax:* +43 1 877 9610, *Email:* office@dolphin-shipping.at, *Website:* www.dolphin-shipping.at
Euromar Transportagentur GmbH, Sonnendgasse 21/4 Strasse, A-1100 Vienna, Austria, *Tel:* +43 1 605920, *Fax:* +43 1 60592 ext. 220, *Email:* office@euromar.at
Express AG, Express-Interfracht, Wohllebengasse 18, A-1040 Vienna, Austria, *Tel:* +43 1 5015 6253, *Fax:* +43 1 5015 6404, *Email:* office@spex.at, *Website:* www.spex.at
Far Freight GmbH, Neubaugasse 44/2/10, A-1070 Vienna, Austria, *Tel:* +43 1 712 8436, *Fax:* +43 1 712 8436, *Email:* office@far-freight.com, *Website:* www.far-freight.com
G. Glaser Schiffahrtskontor, Handelskai 265, A-1020 Vienna, Austria, *Tel:* +43 1 728 1860, *Fax:* +43 1 728 9713, *Email:* g.glaser@aon.at
Marineways GmbH, Hohlweggasse 30, A-1030 Vienna, Austria, *Tel:* +43 1 798 3978, *Fax:* +43 1 798 9120, *Email:* vie.genmbox@cma-cgm.com, *Website:* www.cma-cgm.com
Mediterranean Shipping Company, Mediterranean Shipping Company Austria GmbH, Muthgasse 36, A-1190 Vienna, Austria, *Tel:* +43 1 369 6910, *Fax:* +43 1 36969 1030, *Email:* vienna@mscaustria.com, *Website:* www.mscgva.ch
Multimar Seetrachtenkontor GmbH, Wiedner Gürtel 32, A-1040 Vienna, Austria, *Tel:* +43 1 504 1425, *Fax:* +43 1 504 1430, *Email:* office@multimar.at

Reedereikontor Meridian GmbH, Seidengasse 9-11, 1070 Vienna, Austria, *Tel:* +43 1 521 2900, *Fax:* +43 1 5212 9190, *Email:* info@rkm.com, *Website:* www.rkm.com
Safe Shipping A/S, Handelskai 265, A-1020 Vienna, Austria, *Tel:* +43 1 728 5222, *Fax:* +43 1 728 5221, *Email:* fin@safeshipping.at, *Website:* www.safeshipping.at
Enrico Sperco & Sohn GmbH, Reedereienvertretung Sonnwendgasse 21, Strasse 4, A-1100 Vienna, Austria, *Tel:* +43 1 601 983, *Fax:* +43 1 60001 84177, *Email:* office@sperco.at
TLS GmbH, Meidlinger Hauptstrasse 63/4, A-1120 Vienna, Austria, *Tel:* +43 1 813 0203, *Fax:* +43 1 813 2482, *Email:* klaus.egermann@tls.at

Surveyors: Bureau Veritas, Apostelgasse 25-27, A-1030 Vienna, Austria, *Tel:* +43 1 713 1568-0, *Fax:* +43 1 7131 56830, *Email:* office@at.bureauveritas.com, *Website:* www.bureauveritas.com
Germanischer Lloyd, Markgraf-Rudigerstrasse 6, A-1150 Vienna, Austria, *Tel:* +43 1 9824 303, *Fax:* +43 1 9825 184, *Email:* gl-vienna@gl-group.com, *Website:* www.gl-group.com
Russian Maritime Register of Shipping, Hofzeile 19/3, A-1190 Vienna, Austria, *Tel:* +43 1 368 1567, *Fax:* +43 1 3692 8021, *Email:* 250rs-aus@netway.at, *Website:* www.rs-head.spb.ru

Lloyd's Agent: Transpack GmbH, Brunner Strasse 14/10, A-1210 Vienna, Austria, *Tel:* +43 1 278 2622, *Fax:* +43 1 278 2624, *Email:* office@transpack.co.at, *Website:* www.transpack.co.at

AZERBAIJAN

BAKU

Lat 40° 22' N; Long 49° 50' E.

Admiralty Chart: -	**Admiralty Pilot:** -
Time Zone: GMT +4 h	**UNCTAD Locode:** AZ BAK

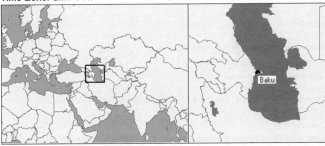

Principal Facilities:

P		Y	G	C	R	L	B		T	A

Authority: Baku International Sea Trading Port, 72 Uzeir Hadjibeyov Street, 370010 Baku, Republic of Azerbaijan, *Tel:* +994 12 493 0268, *Fax:* +994 12 493 3672, *Email:* office@bakuseaport.az, *Website:* www.bakuseaport.az

Officials: General Director: Elchin Mirzayev.
Harbour Master: Shamistan Hasanov.

Port Security: ISPS compliant

Pilotage: Compulsory for all foreign vessels

Traffic: 2001, 1292 vessels, 4 560 851 t of cargo handled

Maximum Vessel Dimensions: 12 000 dwt

Principal Imports and Exports: Imports: Cement, Chemicals, Crude oil, General cargo, Oil products, Salt. Exports: Crude oil, General cargo, Metal, Oil products.

Working Hours: 24 h/day

Accommodation:

Name	Length (m)	Depth (m)	Remarks
Baku			See [1] below
Main Cargo Terminal	866	7	See [2] below
Ferry Terminal	144	7	See [3] below
Dubendi Oil Terminal			See [4] below
Passenger Terminal	340		See [5] below

[1]*Baku:* Container terminal equipped with 42 t container forklift, 40 t reachstacker, two terminal tractors, six trailers & three small forklifts up to 3 t. Container freight station of 1600 m2
[2]*Main Cargo Terminal:* Consists of six berths (one ro/ro quay) handling general, containerized as well as bulk export/import and transit cargoes
[3]*Ferry Terminal:* Provides services for railway & ro/ro ferries across the Caspian Sea to Turkmenbashi and Aktau as well as regular services to Iran
[4]*Dubendi Oil Terminal:* Located 50 km E of Baku for vessels up to 12 000 dwt and consists of two jetties, each 150 m long. The terminal is involved in the handling of crude oil shipped from Kazakhstan's major oil field Tengiz. Also oil products from Turkmenistan and Azerbaijan's local market are discharged daily. Storage cap of 120 000 m3
[5]*Passenger Terminal:* Used by foreign and local passenger vessels cruising between ports of Caspian countries

Storage: Bonded warehouse of 21 000 m2

Location	Open (m²)	Covered (m²)	Sheds / Warehouses
Main Cargo Terminal	24000	10600	5

Key to Principal Facilities:—

A=Airport	**C**=Containers	**G**=General Cargo	**P**=Petroleum	**R**=Ro/Ro	**Y**=Dry Bulk
B=Bunkers	**D**=Dry Dock	**L**=Cruise	**Q**=Other Liquid Bulk	**T**=Towage (where available from port)	

Mechanical Handling Equipment:

Location	Type	Capacity (t)	Qty
Main Cargo Terminal	Portal Cranes	5–40	16
Main Cargo Terminal	Forklifts	1.5–10	

Bunkering: Two bunker boats available

Towage: Five tugs available

Shipping Agents: Baku Inflot Shipping Agency, 58 PR Neftyanikoy, AZ-370010 Baku, Republic of Azerbaijan, *Tel:* +994 12 493 5132, *Fax:* +994 12 493 5132, *Email:* gkmp@caspar.baku.az, *Website:* www.caspar.baku.az
Blue Water Shipping A/S, Wellington Heights, 8 Shakhbazi Street, 1006 Baku, Republic of Azerbaijan, *Tel:* +994 12 497 5830/2, *Fax:* +994 12 498 8164, *Email:* bws@bws.az, *Website:* www.bws.dk
CMA-CGM S.A., CMA CGM Kaspian, 113 A. Aslanov Street, 1000 Baku, Republic of Azerbaijan, *Tel:* +994 12 437 5492, *Fax:* +994 12 498 0991, *Email:* xxx@cma-cgm.com, *Website:* www.cma-cgm.com
Formag Ltd, Lermontov Street 3, 1006 Baku, Republic of Azerbaijan, *Tel:* +994 12 490 5859, *Fax:* +994 12 490 6768, *Email:* baku@formag-group.com, *Website:* www.formag-group.com
Lyonel A. Makzume Shipping AG, 97 Neftchilar Prospekti, AZ-370004 Baku, Republic of Azerbaijan, *Tel:* +994 12 598 0081, *Fax:* +994 12 598 0083, *Email:* lambaku@azerin.com

Stevedoring Companies: Blue Water Shipping A/S, Wellington Heights, 8 Shakh-bazi Street, 1006 Baku, Republic of Azerbaijan, *Tel:* +994 12 497 5830/2, *Fax:* +994 12 498 8164, *Email:* bws@bws.az, *Website:* www.bws.dk

Surveyors: ABS (Europe), Office No.10, City Mansion, 153 Azadlig Avenue, Baku, Republic of Azerbaijan, *Tel:* +994 12 436 1046, *Fax:* +994 12 436 1065, *Email:* absbaku@eagle.org
Bureau Veritas, Bureau Veritas Azeri L.C.C., Bashir Safaroghu Street 191, No.42/44, Baku, Republic of Azerbaijan, *Tel:* +994 12 497 3526, *Fax:* +994 12 497 3529, *Email:* fuad.mammadov@bureauveritas.com.az, *Website:* www.bureauveritas.com
Det Norske Veritas A/S, Veli Mammadov Street 10/12, 370004 Baku, Republic of Azerbaijan, *Tel:* +994 12 497 4335, *Fax:* +994 12 497 4340, *Email:* baku@dnv.com, *Website:* www.dnv.com
Noble Denton Group, Noble Denton Azerbaijan, 31/33 Asaf Zeynally Street, Old City, 1000 Baku, Republic of Azerbaijan, *Tel:* +994 12 497 0453, *Fax:* +994 12 497 0453, *Email:* awardle@nobledenton.az, *Website:* www.nobledenton.com
Russian Maritime Register of Shipping, 119 ul. Vidady, Baku, Republic of Azerbaijan, *Tel:* +994 12 494 1386, *Fax:* +994 12 498 7994, *Website:* www.rs-head.spb.ru

Medical Facilities: Hospital, 1 km

Airport: Baku International Airport, 30 km

Railway: Baku-Tovarnaya, 3 km

Lloyd's Agent: Vitsan Co. Ltd, Ceyhun Selimov Street No.7/129, AZ1078 Baku, Republic of Azerbaijan, *Tel:* +994 12 430 5388, *Fax:* +994 12 497 6893, *Email:* office@vitsan.baku.az, *Website:* www.vitsan.com.tr

BAHAMAS

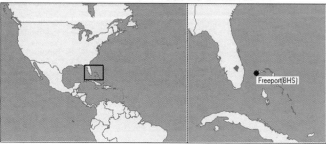

SW
SHARON WILSON & CO.

COUNSEL & ATTORNEYS-AT-LAW · NOTARIES PUBLIC

East Shirley Street at Highland Terrace, P.O. Box SS-19145, Nassau, BAHAMAS
TELEPHONE: (242) 394-8744　FACSIMILE: (242) 394-6556
EMAIL: info@sharonwilsonco.com　WEB: www.sharonwilsonco.com

FREEPORT

Lat 26° 31' N; Long 78° 46' W.

Admiralty Chart: 398	**Admiralty Pilot:** 70
Time Zone: GMT -5 h	**UNCTAD Locode:** BS FPO

Principal Facilities:

P	Q	Y	G	C	R	L	B		T	A

Authority: Freeport Harbour Company, Fishing Hole Road, Queens Highway, P O Box F-42465, Freeport, Grand Bahama Island, Bahamas, *Tel:* +1242 352 9651, *Fax:* +1242 352 4764, *Email:* jones.raymond@fcp.com.bs

Officials: Chief Executive Officer: Chris Gray, *Tel:* +1242 350 8050, *Email:* gray.chris@fcp.com.bs.
Port Director: Capt Orlando Forbes, *Email:* forbes.orlando@fhc.com.bs.
Marketing Manager: Raymond L. Jones, *Tel:* +1242 350 8055.

Port Security: ISPS compliant. Container Security Initiative (CSI) designated port

Pre-Arrival Information: "U.S./Canada citizens who have applied for but not yet received passports can nevertheless temporarily enter and depart from the United States by air with a government issued photo identification and Department of State official proof of application for a passport through September 30, 2007." To enter The Bahamas, citizens from countries other than the U.S. and Canada require a Passport that must be valid for six (6) months beyond the dates of travel and/or a valid Bahamas Visa. You must also possess a return or onward journey ticket and proof of funds to support the visit

Approach: The entrance channel and turning basin are dredged to a depth of 16 m

Anchorage: Vessels may anchor W of the harbour entrance in depths of 14.6-18.3 m. This anchorage is not recommended for vessels over 100 000 dwt. The seabed of sand and limestone rock provides good holding ground

Pilotage: Compulsory in harbour for passenger vessels and for other vessels of 500 gt and over; vessels should cable their ETA and draft at least 24 h before arrival (72 h for bunkering vessels). Vessels bound for Freeport should proceed to the pilot station in pos 26° 31.2' N; 78° 46' W

Radio Frequency: A continuous watch is maintained by Freeport Harbour control tower on VHF Channels 16 and 14, 156.80 mHz

Weather: Freeport, Grand Bahama, one of the Islands Of The Bahamas has a temperate climate ranging from 80-90°F with high humidity in the summer months to 70-80°F in the winter. Nighttime temperatures are generally cooler by 5-7°. In the more northerly islands (Grand Bahama), winter temperatures are approx 5° lower than the southern islands. Sea surface temperatures vary between 74° in February and 84° in August

Maximum Vessel Dimensions: 310 m loa, 14 m draft

Principal Imports and Exports: Imports: Building materials, Electrical appliances, Electronic goods, Electronic products, Foodstuffs, Vehicles. Exports: Aggregate rock, Sand, Seafood.

Working Hours: 0800-1200, 1300-1700. Overtime rates from 1800-2200. Sat 0800-1200; overtime from 1300-1700 and overtime rates from 1800-2200. Sun (overtime) 0800-1200, 1300-1700, 1800-2200

Accommodation: Container facilities: terminal operated by Freeport Container Port Ltd., P O Box F-42465, Freeport, Tel: +1 242 350 8000, Fax: +1 242 348 1201, Email: commercial.marketing@fcp.com.bs, Website: www.freeportcontainerport.com. Consists of three berths totalling 1036 m with depth alongside of 15.5 m. Equipment includes ten super post-panamax quay cranes, two mobile harbour cranes and 59 straddle carriers. 49 ha stacking area
Two passenger terminals: Terminal 1 approx 19 400 sq ft, Terminal 2 approx 18 824 sq ft for cruise vessels
Bulk facilities: Operated by Bahama Rock at Basin No.3 and Island Construction at Berth 14
Tanker facilities: Bahamas Oil Refining Corp (BORCO), operate two offshore jetties. The longer one of 975 m has a depth of 28 m on the seaward side and 19.8 m on the shore side and the inner one is 640 m long with a berth depth of 16.76 m, capable of berthing tankers up to 550 000 dwt. Liquefied gas terminal at Berth No.13 operated by Shell Bahamas Co Ltd

Name	Length (m)	Depth (m)	Remarks
Lucayan Harbour/Freeport Harbour			
Berth No.1	233	10	Cruise vessels, ro/ro
Berth No.2	100	10	Multi-purpose, ro/ro
Berth No.3	200	10	Cruise vessels, ro/ro
Berth No's 4 & 5	350	11.8	Cruise vessels, general cargo
Berth No's 6, 7 & 8	400	8.4	Cruise vessels, ro/ro
Berth No.10	100	8	Containers
Berth No.11	121	8	
Berth No.12	300	11	Lay-up berth
Berth No.13	117	8.3	
Berth No.14	200	8	LPG

Storage: Freeport Harbour Company owns 10 193 m2 of transit sheds and warehouses. Ample open storage area available of 7 acres

Mechanical Handling Equipment:

Location	Type	Qty
Freeport	Forklifts	17

Bunkering: PDVSA Bahamas Oil Refining Co. (BORCO), Bahamas Oil Refining Co. (BORCO), West Sunrise Highway, Freeport 42435, Grand Bahama Island, Bahamas, *Tel:* +1242 3528 864, *Fax:* +1242 3523 537, *Email:* ghall@borcoltd.com
Bominflot, Bominflot do Brazil Comercio Ltda, Avenida Almirante Barosso 63/1809, 20031-003 Rio de Janeiro, Brazil, *Tel:* +55 21 2220 4773, *Fax:* +55 21 2262 2651, *Email:* mail@bominflot.com.br, *Website:* www.bominflot.net – *Delivery Mode:* barge, pipeline
North Star Shipping Agency, P O Box 44631, Suite 10, Jasmine Corp Center, Alcester Road, Freeport, Grand Bahama Island, Bahamas, *Tel:* +1242 352 2730, *Fax:* +1242 352 2746, *Email:* ops@ns-ship.com, *Website:* www.ns-ship.com
PDVSA Bahamas Oil Refining Co. (BORCO), Bahamas Oil Refining Co. (BORCO), West Sunrise Highway, Freeport 42435, Grand Bahama Island, Bahamas, *Tel:* +1242 3528 864, *Fax:* +1242 3523 537, *Email:* ghall@borcoltd.com – *Misc:* complete bunkering services provided – *Delivery Mode:* barge, pipeline
PDVSA Deltaven S.A., Urbanizacion El Vinedo, Avenida Bolivar Cruce Con Calle 137, C.C. Camoruco (Anexo), 1 Piso, Oficina 2, Valencia-Edo, Carabobo 2001, Venezuela,

Tel: +58 241 8203 157, Fax: +58 241 8203 116, Email: davilass@pdvsa.com, Website: www.pdvsa.com

Waste Reception Facilities: Sanitation Services Ltd, Freeport, Grand Bahama Island, Bahamas, Tel: +1242 352 9721

Towage: Seven harbour tugs available through shipping agent or harbour control, each of 3500 hp & 40 t bollard pull
SVITZER, Freepoint Tug & Towing Services, 4 Milton Street, P O Box F-43550, Freeport, Grand Bahama Island, Bahamas, Tel: +1242 352 3060, Fax: +1242 352 4114, Website: www.svitzer.com

Repair & Maintenance: Grand Bahama Shipyard Ltd, The Fishing Hole Road, P O Box F-42498-411, Freeport, Grand Bahama Island, Bahamas, Tel: +1242 350 4000, Fax: +1242 350 4010, Email: mail@gbshipyard.com, Website: www.gbshipyard.com
One dry dock 270 m long with lifting cap of 30 000 t and one dry dock 300 m long with lifting cap of 82 500 t. Two finger piers

Ship Chandlers: Lucaya Shipping & Trading Co. Ltd, P O Box F-3240, Freeport, Grand Bahama Island, Bahamas, Tel: +1242 352 9744, Fax: +1242 352 2246, Email: luship@coralwave.com, Website: www.lucayashipping.net
North Star Shipping Agency, P O Box 44631, Suite 10, Jasmine Corp Center, Alcester Road, Freeport, Grand Bahama Island, Bahamas, Tel: +1242 352 2730, Fax: +1242 352 2746, Email: ops@ns-ship.com, Website: www.ns-ship.com

Shipping Agents: Darvikson Ltd, Peachtree Street & Forest Avenue, P O Box F-42520, Freeport, Grand Bahama Island, Bahamas, Tel: +1242 352 7821, Fax: +1242 352 5263, Email: jackbahl@freeporttransfer.com
DBA Seaport Agencies (Bahamas), 24 Logwood Road, 2nd Floor, MSC Bahamas Building, P O Box F-40553, Freeport, Grand Bahama Island, Bahamas, Tel: +1242 352 6516, Fax: +1242 352 6519, Email: seaportteam@seaportagencies.com
Freeport Ship Services Ltd, 8 Logwood Road, P O Box F-40423, Freeport, Grand Bahama Island, Bahamas, Tel: +1242 351 4343, Fax: +1242 351 4332, Email: info@freeportshipservices.com, Website: www.freeportshipservices.com
Global United Limited, Global Maritime Center, P O Box F-43259, Freeport, Grand Bahama Island, Bahamas, Tel: +1242 352 2328, Fax: +1242 351 2329, Email: globalunited@gulbahamas.com, Website: www.gulbahamas.com
International Shipping Agency Ltd, Freeport Harbour Complex, Building 2, Suite 9, P O Box F-40302, Freeport, Grand Bahama Island, Bahamas, Tel: +1242 351 4754, Fax: +1242 351 4854, Email: info@isabahamas.com, Website: www.isabahamas.com
Lucaya Shipping & Trading Co. Ltd, P O Box F-3240, Freeport, Grand Bahama Island, Bahamas, Tel: +1242 352 9744, Fax: +1242 352 2246, Email: luship@coralwave.com, Website: www.lucayashipping.net
Mediterranean Shipping Company, MSC Bahamas Ltd., 24 Logwood Road, Freeport, Grand Bahama Island, Bahamas, Tel: +1242 351 1158, Fax: +1242 351 7684, Email: mscbahamas@msc-bahamas.com, Website: www.mscbahamas.com
A.P. Moller-Maersk Group, Maersk Bahamas Ltd, P O Box F-42465, Freeport Container Port, Freeport, Grand Bahama Island, Bahamas, Tel: +1242 350 8088, Fax: +1242 350 8099, Email: fpoops@maersk.com, Website: www.maerskline.com
North Star Shipping Agency, P O Box 44631, Suite 10, Jasmine Corp Center, Alcester Road, Freeport, Grand Bahama Island, Bahamas, Tel: +1242 352 2730, Fax: +1242 352 2746, Email: ops@ns-ship.com, Website: www.ns-ship.com
Professional Brokers Agency Co. Ltd, P O Box F-42330, Freeport, Grand Bahama Island, Bahamas, Tel: +1242 351 3839, Fax: +1242 351 2713, Email: ogreenepba@batelnet.bs
Tanja Enterprises Co. Ltd, Queens Highway Suite 1, Freeport Harbour Area, P O Box F-43259, Freeport, Grand Bahama Island, Bahamas, Tel: +1242 352 2328, Fax: +1242 352 2329, Email: globalunited@gulbahamas.com, Website: www.gulbahamas.com
United Shipping Co. Ltd, Harbour Port Building, P O Box F42552, Freeport, Grand Bahama Island, Bahamas, Tel: +1242 352 9315, Fax: +1242 352 2754, Email: gulops@gulbahamas.com, Website: www.gulbahamas.com

Surveyors: K L S Marine Surveying, P O Box F-43711, Freeport, Grand Bahama Island, Bahamas, Tel: +1242 352 9163, Fax: +1242 351 3407, Email: gbahamasurveyor@yahoo.com
West Atlantic Marine Ltd, DMG Marine Centre, 12 Shelley Street, Queens Highway, Freeport, Grand Bahama Island, Bahamas, Tel: +1242 352 8371, Fax: +1242 352 9014, Email: wamcodgow@coralwave.com, Website: www.westatlanticmarine.net

Medical Facilities: Rand Memorial Hospital, Tel: +1 242 352 6735 and two private clinics; Sunrise Medical Clinic, Tel: +1 242 373 3333 and Lucayan Medical Centre East, Tel: +1 242 373 7411

Airport: Grand Bahama International Airport, 8 km

Development: Expansion of the Freeport Container Terminal will add 500 m of berth, 35 acres of container marshalling area, six gantry cranes and 35 straddle carriers and is expected to take two years

Lloyd's Agent: West Atlantic Marine Ltd, DMG Marine Centre, 12 Shelley Street, Queens Highway, Freeport, Grand Bahama Island, Bahamas, Tel: +1242 352 8371, Fax: +1242 352 9014, Email: wamcodgow@coralwave.com, Website: www.westatlanticmarine.net

LUCAYAN HARBOUR

harbour area, see under Freeport

NASSAU

Lat 25° 4' N; Long 77° 19' W.

Admiralty Chart: 1452
Time Zone: GMT -5 h

Admiralty Pilot: 70
UNCTAD Locode: BS NAS

Principal Facilities:

P	Q		G	C	R	L	B		T	A

Authority: Nassau Port Authority, Port Department, P O Box N-8175, Nassau, New Providence Island, Bahamas, Tel: +1242 322 8832, Fax: +1242 322 5545, Email: portaja@batelnet.bs

Officials: Port Administrator: Anthony Allens, Tel: +1242 322 8832.

Port Security: ISPS compliant

Approach: Lighthouse situated on W end of Paradise Island at entrance to harbour, but water tower light, situated on a hill in Nassau called F. Lauderdale, is a better approach light as it is easier to locate

Pilotage: Compulsory. Nassau Harbour Pilots, Tel: +1 242 322 2049 & +1 242 322 8832. Pilots board vessels in the anchorage NW of lighthouse, VHF Channel 16

Working Hours: 0900-1700

Accommodation:

Name	Remarks
Nassau	See [1] below

[1]Nassau: Union wharf has five berths including one 95.4 m long with 5.49 m draft; the other four are nearly always occupied by local cargo vessels on a permanent allocation basis
There is a deep harbour able to handle vessels of all sizes. Channel depth at opening 11.79 m. Main channel and turning basin 11.6 m, channel north of artificial island 8.44 m, channel to Union Wharf 5.09 m, main channel length 1311 m, turning circle 518 m diam (depths given at MLW). One pier, length (accessible to deep draft vessels) 390 m north side, 314 m south side; apron width 7.31 m. An artificial island, length 1128 m, width 384 m, covering an area of 98 acres and with a concrete bridge connecting the Island to the mainland. Two breakwaters: western, length 945 m; eastern, length 182.9 m
The port is an important centre for cruise vessels and the Prince George Wharf has eleven berths for this purpose. In bad weather cruise ships proceed to SW anchorage at Clifton Pier
No lighters, but passenger ships' tenders may be used if available. Launches available

Storage: Privately owned cool room and freezer 3 miles from docks

Bunkering: Available by truck or coaster if sufficient notice given, otherwise vessels should bunker at Freeport
Shell Bahamas Ltd, Boulevard House, 87 Thompson Boulevard, P O Box N-3717, Nassau, New Providence Island, Bahamas, Tel: +1242 322 3252, Fax: +1242 325 0721
Chevron Marine Products LLC, Global Marine Products LLC, 1500 Louisiana, 4th Floor, Houston, TX 77002, United States of America, Tel: +1 832 8542 988, Fax: +1 832 8544 868, Email: gulfcbm@chevron.com, Website: www.chevron.com – Grades: GO – Delivery Mode: tank truck
ExxonMobil Marine Fuels, Suite 900, One Alhambra Plaza, Coral Gables, FL 33134, United States of America, Tel: +1 305 459 6358, Fax: +1 305 459 6412, Email: emmf@exxonmobil.com, Website: www.exxonmobilmarinefuels.com – Grades: ADO – Delivery Mode: truck
Shell Bahamas Ltd, Boulevard House, 87 Thompson Boulevard, P O Box N-3717, Nassau, New Providence Island, Bahamas, Tel: +1242 322 3252, Fax: +1242 325 0721

Towage: Three tugs available for berthing and unberthing cruise ships and freighters in Nassau harbour, and oil tankers at Clifton Pier

Shipping Agents: Bahmar Agencies Ltd, P O Box SS6369, Nassau, New Providence Island, Bahamas, Tel: +1242 323 8804, Fax: +1242 323 7487
Cavalier Shipping Ltd, Arawak Cay, West Bay Street, P O Box N-7109, Nassau, New Providence Island, Bahamas, Tel: +1242 328 3103, Fax: +1242 323 8866, Email: stephen@arawakstevedoring.com
Container Terminals Ltd, John Alfred Dock Bay Street, P O Box N8183, Nassau, New Providence Island, Bahamas, Tel: +1242 322 1012, Fax: +1242 323 7566, Email: kwallace@tropical.com, Website: www.tropical.com
R.H. Curry & Co. Ltd, P O Box N-8168, Nassau, New Providence Island, Bahamas, Tel: +1242 322 8681, Fax: +1242 325 3731, Email: operations@rhcurry.com, Website: www.rhcurry.com
R.R. Farrington & Sons Co. Ltd, P O Box N-93, Union Dock, Nassau, New Providence Island, Bahamas, Tel: +1242 322 2203, Fax: +1242 322 4669, Email: rrfarrington@coralwave.com
Global United Limited, Global Maritime Center, P O Box F-43259, Freeport, Grand Bahama Island, Bahamas, Tel: +1242 352 2328, Fax: +1242 351 2329, Email: globalunited@gulbahamas.com, Website: www.gulbahamas.com
A.P. Moller-Maersk Group, Maersk Bahamas Ltd, Bay Street & Victoria Avenue, Nassau, New Providence Island, Bahamas, Tel: +1242 350 8088, Fax: +1242 350 8099, Email: fpoops@maersk.com, Website: www.maerskline.com
Tanja Enterprises Co. Ltd, Saunders Beach, Plaza on the Way, Suite 3, West Bay Street, P O Box CB13838, Nassau, New Providence Island, Bahamas, Tel: +1242 377 0164, Fax: +1242 377 1258, Email: gulnassau@gulbahamas.com, Website: www.gulbahamas.com
United Shipping Co. Ltd, United Shipping Co. Nassau Ltd, P O Box N4005, Nassau, New Providence Island, Bahamas, Tel: +1242 322 1340/2951, Fax: +1242 323 8779, Email: operations@unitedshippingnassau.com

Key to Principal Facilities:—				
A=Airport	**C**=Containers	**G**=General Cargo	**P**=Petroleum	**R**=Ro/Ro	**Y**=Dry Bulk
B=Bunkers	**D**=Dry Dock	**L**=Cruise	**Q**=Other Liquid Bulk	**T**=Towage (where available from port)	

Surveyors: Bahamas Maritime Authority, P O Box N-4679, Nassau, New Providence Island, Bahamas, *Tel:* +1242 394 3024, *Fax:* +1242 394 3014, *Email:* nassau@bahamasmaritime.com, *Website:* www.bahamasmaritime.com

Airport: Windsor Field Airport

Lloyd's Agent: DMG International Marine Services Agency, Dowdeswell Street, Nassau, New Providence Island, Bahamas, *Tel:* +1242 356 6701, *Fax:* +1242 356 6697, *Email:* dmgintladmin@coralwave.com, *Website:* www.westatlanticmarine.net

SOUTH RIDING POINT

Lat 26° 37' N; Long 78° 13' W.

Admiralty Chart: 390	**Admiralty Pilot:** 70
Time Zone: GMT -5 h	**UNCTAD Locode:** BS SRP

South Riding Point

Principal Facilities:

P						B		T	A	

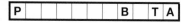

Authority: South Riding Point Holding Ltd, P O Box F-42530, Freeport, Grand Bahama Island, Bahamas, *Tel:* +1242 353 4471/6, *Fax:* +1242 353 4573, *Email:* sridingpoint@netscape.net

Officials: Vice President, Operations: Jaime Vargas, *Email:* jaime_vargas_2001@yahoo.com.
Terminal Manager: Delton Russell, *Email:* delton_russell@yahoo.com.

Port Security: ISPS compliant

Documentation: Crew list (5 copies), stores list (3 copies), crew declaration forms (3 copies), bills of lading (4 copies), cargo manifests (3 copies)

Pilotage: Compulsory and performed by berthing masters. Boarding point 3 miles S of Sea Island

Radio Frequency: Contact established on channel 16, tugs/pilots on channel 73 and terminal oil operations on channel 74

Tides: Max tidal range 1.05 m

Maximum Vessel Dimensions: 500 000 dwt, max d 27.5 m

Working Hours: 24 h/day throughout the year

Accommodation:

Name	Depth (m)	Remarks
South Riding Point		See [1] below
Berth No.1	30.48	See [2] below
Berth No.2	25.9	See [3] below

[1]*South Riding Point:* Crude oil storage and transhipment terminal. Two berth sea island 1219 m offshore. Both berths have self levelling gangways. Crude oil shore tank cap of 5 200 000 bbls
[2]*Berth No.1:* Vessels of 50 000 to 500 000 dwt; equipped with four 16'' dia chicksan loading arms
[3]*Berth No.2:* Vessels of 35 000 to 150 000 dwt with a max loa of 274 m; equipped with four 12'' dia loading arms

Bunkering: PDVSA Bahamas Oil Refining Co. (BORCO), Bahamas Oil Refining Co. (BORCO), West Sunrise Highway, Freeport 42435, Grand Bahama Island, Bahamas, *Tel:* +1242 3528 864, *Fax:* +1242 3523 537, *Email:* ghall@borcoltd.com – *Misc:* complete bunkering services provided – *Delivery Mode:* barge, pipeline
PDVSA Deltaven S.A., Urbanizacion El Vinedo, Avenida Bolivar Cruce Con Calle 137, C.C. Camoruco (Anexo), 1 Piso, Oficina 2, Valencia-Edo, Carabobo 2001, Venezuela, *Tel:* +58 241 8203 157, *Fax:* +58 241 8203 116, *Email:* davilass@pdvsa.com, *Website:* www.pdvsa.com
Shell Bahamas Ltd, Boulevard House, 87 Thompson Boulevard, P O Box N-3717, Nassau, New Providence Island, Bahamas, *Tel:* +1242 322 3252, *Fax:* +1242 325 0721

Towage: Three tugs available each of 4200 hp, bollard pull 45 t

Shipping Agents: Global United Limited, Global Maritime Center, P O Box F-43259, Freeport, Grand Bahama Island, Bahamas, *Tel:* +1242 352 2328, *Fax:* +1242 351 2329, *Email:* globalunited@gulbahamas.com, *Website:* www.gulbahamas.com

Medical Facilities: The Rand Memorial Hospital, Freeport has a 24 h emergency service

Airport: International Airport, 56 km

Lloyd's Agent: West Atlantic Marine Ltd, DMG Marine Centre, 12 Shelley Street, Queens Highway, Freeport, Grand Bahama Island, Bahamas, *Tel:* +1242 352 8371, *Fax:* +1242 352 9014, *Email:* wamcodgow@coralwave.com, *Website:* www.westatlanticmarine.net

BAPCO WHARVES

harbour area, see under Sitra

HIDD

see under Mina Sulman

MINA SULMAN

Lat 26° 12' N; Long 50° 36' E.

Admiralty Chart: 3735/6/7/8	**Admiralty Pilot:** 63
Time Zone: GMT +3 h	**UNCTAD Locode:** BH MIN

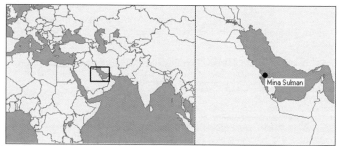

Mina Sulman

Principal Facilities:

		G	C	R	L	B	D	T	A	

Wilhelmsen Ships Service

Almoayed Wilhelmsen
Mina Sulman Industrial Area No.5, Gate 301, Road 4306, Manama, BAHRAIN
TEL: +973 1781 3000   FAX: +973 1781 3011
EMAIL: wss.bahrain@wilhelmsen.com
WEB: www.wilhelmsen.com

Ships Agency & Logistics

Authority: Customs & Ports Affairs, Directorate General of Ports, P O Box 453, Manama, Kingdom of Bahrain, *Tel:* +973 1772 5555, *Fax:* +973 1772 9709, *Email:* brnport@batelco.com.bh, *Website:* www.bahrainports.gov.bh

Port Security: ISPS compliant

Documentation: International declaration of health, crew list (five copies), ship's report, cargo gear register, cargo manifest submitted by agent 3 days prior to ship's arrival

Approach: The inner approach channel into Mina Sulman is 3 nautical miles long, 150 m wide and has a depth of 9.75-10.5 m

Anchorage: Vessels normally anchor in the vicinity of No.27 buoy in pos 26° 10' N, 50° 47' E

Pilotage: Compulsory. Pilot boards at Sitra Anchorage Beacon

Radio Frequency: To contact Mina Sulman Port Control vessels should use VHF Channels 16 and 74. Vessels calling at Mina Sulman should advise agents via Bahrain Radio, call sign A9M, advising ETA, draught, hatch distribution and any requirements with as much notice as possible, Tel: +973 1788 3939, Email: bmoc@btc.com.bh

Tides: Height of tide 0.3 m LW and 2.5 m HW during the year

Traffic: 2005, 871 vessels, 3 243 000 t of cargo handled, 192 731 TEU's

Working Hours: Conventional cargo berths: Sat-Thurs 0700-2200 unless agent requests overtime. Container terminal: 24 h/day

Accommodation:

Name	Length (m)	Depth (m)	Draught (m)	Remarks
Mina Sulman				See [1] below
Finger Pier	800		9	Ten berths
Conventional Berths	900	11		Three 300 m berths
Container Berths	600	11		Two 300 m berths
Coastal Quay	285	7		
Ro/ro Ramp			5.5	15.5 m wide

[1]*Mina Sulman:* Managed and operated by APM Terminals Bahrain, P O Box 50490, Hidd, Tel: +973 1736 5500, Fax: +973 1772 8253, Email: bahapmtcom@apmterminals.com, Website: www.apmterminals.com

Storage: 120 000 m2 of closed shed warehousing, 18 000 m2 of opensided shed space and 2 422 000 m2 of open storage. Extensive privately run cold storage facilities

Mechanical Handling Equipment:

Location	Type	Capacity (t)	Qty
Container Berths	Container Cranes	30.5	2
Container Berths	Container Cranes	35	2

Bunkering: Bahrain Petroleum Co. (BAPCO), P O Box 25555, Awali, Bahrain, Kingdom of Bahrain, *Tel:* +973 1770 4040, *Fax:* +973 1770 4070, *Email:* info@bapco.net, *Website:* www.bapco.com.bh

Waste Reception Facilities: Garbage collection available and arranged through ship's agent

Towage: Two 1600 hp and two 800 hp berthing tugs available

Repair & Maintenance: Aeradio Technical Services WLL, P O Box 26803, Mina Salman Industrial Area, Manama, Kingdom of Bahrain, *Tel:* +973 1772 7790, *Fax:* +973 1770 6444, *Email:* aeradio@batelco.com.bh, *Website:* www.aeradio.com
Arab Shipbuilding & Repair Yard Co. (ASRY), P O Box 50110, Hidd, Kingdom of Bahrain, *Tel:* +973 1767 1111, *Fax:* +973 1767 0236, *Email:* asryco@batelco.com.bh, *Website:* www.asry.net One graving dock of 375 m x 75 m for vessels up to 500 000 dwt. Two floating docks, one of 252 m x 45.2 m with lifting cap of 33 000 t and one of 227 m x 41.2 m with lifting cap of 30 000 t. Also eight repair berths with drafts of 8-11 m

Seaman Missions: The Seamans Mission, Bahrain International Seafarers' Society, P O Box 15007, Manama, Kingdom of Bahrain, *Tel:* +973 1772 8521, *Fax:* +973 1772 8266, *Email:* biss@batelco.com.bh

Ship Chandlers: Dana Marine Supplies, P O Box 15774, Manama, Kingdom of Bahrain, *Tel:* +973 1721 2656, *Fax:* +973 1721 5728, *Email:* danamsup@batelco.com.bh

Shipping Agents: Almoayed Barwil Ltd, Mina Sulman Industrial Area 5, Road 4306, P O Box 26411, Manama, Kingdom of Bahrain, *Tel:* +973 1781 3000, *Fax:* +973 1781 3011, *Website:* www.wilhelmsen.com
Alsharif Shipping Agency, P O Box 1322, Manama, Kingdom of Bahrain, *Tel:* +973 1751 5050, *Fax:* +973 1751 5051, *Email:* general@bahragents.com, *Website:* www.alsharifbahrain.com
Bahrain Marine Supply Co., P O Box 584, Manama, Kingdom of Bahrain, *Tel:* +973 1772 7114, *Fax:* +973 1772 7509, *Email:* shipcare@intercol.com, *Website:* www.intercol.com
Consolidated Shipping Services Group (CSS), Office No.1, Block No.318, Building

No.21, Old Palace Avenue, P O Box 2209, Manama, Kingdom of Bahrain, *Tel:* +973 1754 0106, *Fax:* +973 1754 0107, *Email:* info@cslbahrain.com, *Website:* www.cssgroupsite.com
Fakhro Shipping Agency Ltd, P O Box 5826, Manama, Kingdom of Bahrain, *Tel:* +973 1782 7940, *Fax:* +973 1782 7945, *Email:* fsabah@batelco.com.bh
Gulf Agency Co. (Bahrain) W.L.L, P O Box 412, Manama, Kingdom of Bahrain, *Tel:* +973 1733 9777, *Fax:* +973 1732 0498, *Email:* bahrain@gacworld.com, *Website:* www.gacworld.com
Inchcape Shipping Services (ISS), P O Box 828, Majlis Al Ta'awon Highway, Sitra, Kingdom of Bahrain, *Tel:* +973 1773 9601, *Fax:* +973 1773 5284, *Email:* lloydsagency.bahrain@iss-shipping.com, *Website:* www.iss-shipping.com
International Agencies Co. Ltd, Ali Alwazzan Building, Al-Khalifa Avenue, P O Box 584, Manama, Kingdom of Bahrain, *Tel:* +973 1772 7114, *Fax:* +973 1772 7509, *Email:* shipcare@intercol.com, *Website:* www.intercol.com
National Shipping Agency, 2nd Floor, Almatrook Building, Diplomatic Area, P O Box 762, Manama, Kingdom of Bahrain, *Tel:* +973 1751 5070, *Fax:* +973 1751 5074, *Email:* general@bahragents.com, *Website:* www.alsharifbahrain.com
Union Logistics Co., P O Box 30344, Manama, Kingdom of Bahrain, *Tel:* +973 1740 2848, *Fax:* +973 1740 2866

Surveyors: ABS (Europe), Room 301, Salahuddin Building, Al-Fateh Road, P O Box 155, Manama, Kingdom of Bahrain, *Tel:* +973 1725 5414, *Fax:* +973 1725 6837, *Email:* absmanama@eagle.org
Bureau Veritas, Flat No.11, Building No.574, Road 1111, Manama, Kingdom of Bahrain, *Tel:* +973 1787 7574, *Fax:* +973 1787 7576, *Website:* www.bureauveritas.com
Det Norske Veritas A/S, Manama Centre Entrance No.1, 4th Floor Apartment 406 & 407, P O Box 783, Manama, Kingdom of Bahrain, *Tel:* +973 1721 2552, *Fax:* +973 1721 1696, *Email:* bhr@dnv.com, *Website:* www.dnv.com

Medical Facilities: First aid clinic at Mina Sulman and a government hospital is situated 10 minutes drive from the port, in addition to other special hospitals and clinics

Airport: Bahrain International Airport, 9 km

Development: New port being constructed at Hidd (Khalifa bin Sulman Port) to be run by APM Terminals Bahrain, consisting of two 300 m long container berths, a 300 m long multi-purpose berth for ro/ro and lo/lo traffic and up to three additional 300 m long berths for general cargo. On expected completion at end 2008, Bahrain will transfer most of its maritime operations out of Mina Sulman to the new port. The exception is a few vessels will visit Mina Sulman to carry wheat and chicken feed respectively to the Bahrain Flour Mills Company and the Delmon Poultry Company

Lloyd's Agent: Inchcape Shipping Services (ISS), P O Box 828, Majlis Al Ta'awon Highway, Sitra, Kingdom of Bahrain, *Tel:* +973 1773 9601, *Fax:* +973 1773 5284, *Email:* lloydsagency.bahrain@iss-shipping.com, *Website:* www.iss-shipping.com

SITRA

Lat 26° 9' N; Long 50° 37' E.

Admiralty Chart: 3735/6/7/8	**Admiralty Pilot:** 63
Time Zone: GMT +3 h	**UNCTAD Locode:** BH SIT

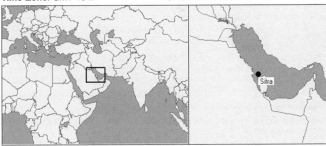

Principal Facilities:

P	Q						T	A

Authority: The Bahrain Petroleum Co. B.S.C., Bahrain Refinery, Bahrain, Kingdom of Bahrain, *Tel:* +973 1770 4040, *Fax:* +973 1770 4070, *Email:* info@bapco.net, *Website:* www.bapco.com.bh

Port Security: ISPS compliant

Approach: Unattended light-vessel, painted red with the word Bahrain painted in large white letters lies at lat 26° 33' N; long 51° 35' E. Channel from here to moorings well-marked with System 'A' buoys
Bahrain Approach Beacon (lat 26° 22' N; long 50° 47' E), steel pile structure 15 m high, flashes red light every 1.5 seconds. South Cardinal Buoy (lat 26° 10.3' N; long 50° 42.9' E)

Anchorage: Vessels not immediately berthing at BAPCO wharves should anchor 1 mile S of No.27 buoy

Pilotage: Compulsory for vessels berthing/unberthing. Mooring masters board vessels 3 cables SE of Sitra Beacon. Masters of all vessels are to maintain a continuous watch on VHF Channels 16 and 74 for Bahrain Port Control

Radio Frequency: All vessels should establish radio contact with BAPCO via 'Bahrain Radio' (A9M) at least 48 h prior to arrival giving a firm ETA, arrival draft and their requirement for bunker fuels. VHF Channel 74

Weather: Hot and humid during May-September. Prevailing NW'ly winds. Strong gusts may develop with no visible warning

Working Hours: 24 h/day

Key to Principal Facilities:—			
A=Airport	**C**=Containers	**G**=General Cargo	**P**=Petroleum	**R**=Ro/Ro	**Y**=Dry Bulk
B=Bunkers	**D**=Dry Dock	**L**=Cruise	**Q**=Other Liquid Bulk	**T**=Towage (where available from port)	

Accommodation:

Name	Depth (m)	Remarks
BAPCO Wharves		See [1] below
No.1 Island Wharf		See [2] below
Berth No.5	14	See [3] below
Berth No.6	13.26	See [4] below
No.2 Wharf		See [5] below
Berth No.1	13.5	See [6] below
Berth No.2	13.5	See [7] below
Berth No.3	11.89	See [8] below
Berth No.4	11.89	See [9] below
Coastal Tanker Wharf		See [10] below
Berth No.7	5.48	See [11] below
Private Wharves		
Aluminium Bahrain (ALBA)		See [12] below
Gulf Industrial Investment Co (GIIC)		See [13] below

[1]*BAPCO Wharves:* Bahrain National Gas Co. B.S.C. (BANAGAS), PO Box 29099, Rifa'a, Bahrain, Tel: +973 1775 6222
Operates a plant producing butane and propane which are exported over BAPCO's wharf
Gulf Petrochemical Industries Co. B.S.C. (GPIC), PO Box 26730, Manama, Bahrain, Tel: +973 1773 1777
Operates a plant producing refrigerated liquid ammonia and methanol which are exported from Sitra Wharf at berths 1 & 2
[2]*No.1 Island Wharf:* Consists of one main central platform supported on steel piles with four interconnected mooring dolphins, two positioned to the NW and two to the SE, giving the wharf an overall length of 281 m
[3]*Berth No.5:* For vessels up to 274 m loa and 110 000 dwt with max sailing draft of 12.85 m. Naphtha, gasoline, kerosene, diesel and fuel oil handled
[4]*Berth No.6:* For vessels up to 274 m loa and 110 000 dwt with max sailing draft of 12.85 m. Naphtha, gasoline, kerosene, diesel and fuel oil handled
[5]*No.2 Wharf:* Pile driven 'T' head structure with three interconnecting dolphins, two positioned to the NW and one to the SE giving the wharf an overall length of 508 m. This wharf is connected by a road trestle (512 m) to a causeway 3 miles from the Main Island of Sitra
[6]*Berth No.1:* For vessels up to 250 m loa and 80 000 dwt with max sailing draft of 12.35 m. Naphtha, gasoline, kerosene, diesel, fuel oil, RLPG, ammonia and methanol handled
[7]*Berth No.2:* For vessels up to 250 m loa and 80 000 dwt with max sailing draft of 12.35 m. Asphalt, naphtha, gasoline, kerosene, diesel, fuel oil, RLPG, ammonia and methanol handled
[8]*Berth No.3:* For vessels up to 171 m loa and 34 000 dwt with max sailing draft of 10.36 m (10.97 m may be permitted under suitable tidal conditions). Asphalt, naphtha, gasoline, kerosene, diesel and fuel oil handled
[9]*Berth No.4:* For vessels up to 160 m loa and 25 000 dwt with max sailing draft of 10.36 m. Asphalt, naphtha, gasoline, kerosene, diesel, fuel oil and RLPG handled
[10]*Coastal Tanker Wharf:* Pile driven structure fendered on it's eastern side only and connected by a catwalk to the causeway. At it's outer end is a warping dolphin
[11]*Berth No.7:* For vessels up to 73.1 m loa with max draft 4.88 m. Asphalt and diesel handled
[12]*Aluminium Bahrain (ALBA):* Tel: +973 1783 0000, Fax: +973 1783 0083, Email: helpdesk@aluminiumbahrain.com, Website: www.aluminiumbahrain.com
Two berths: one for importing alumina and exporting calcined coke, taking vessels up to 60 000 dwt and one for importing liquid pitch, calcined coke and green coke, taking vessels up to 25 000 dwt. Export of metals is shipped via containers through Mina Sulman, Manama
[13]*Gulf Industrial Investment Co (GIIC):* Tel: +973 1767 3311, Fax: +973 1767 5258
There is a deepwater jetty with head 300 m long and 35 m wide and two mooring dolphins capable of accommodating vessels of up to 100 000 dwt. Ore is unloaded by grabs and finished pellets can also be exported

Towage: Two tugs available for berthing

Medical Facilities: Vessel's agents handle all personnel from vessels requiring medical attendance

Airport: Bahrain International Airport, 20 km

Lloyd's Agent: Inchcape Shipping Services (ISS), P O Box 828, Majlis Al Ta'awon Highway, Sitra, Kingdom of Bahrain, *Tel:* +973 1773 9601, *Fax:* +973 1773 5284, *Email:* lloydsagency.bahrain@iss-shipping.com, *Website:* www.iss-shipping.com

BANGLADESH

CHALNA

alternate name, see Mongla

CHITTAGONG

Lat 22° 19' N; Long 91° 49' E.

Admiralty Chart: 84	**Admiralty Pilot:** 21
Time Zone: GMT +6 h	**UNCTAD Locode:** BD CGP

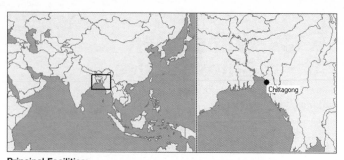

Principal Facilities:

P	Q	Y	G	C	R		B	D	T	A

Tramp Oil & Marine

Wells House, 15-17 Elmfield Road, Bromley,
Kent BR1 1LT, United Kingdom
Phone: +44 20 8315 7777   **Fax:** +44 20 8315 7788
General email: enquiries@tramp-oil.com

See listings for all global offices: **www.tramp-oil.com**

Authority: Chittagong Port Authority, Bandar Bhaban Saltgola Road, P O Box 2013, Chittagong 4100, Bangladesh, *Tel:* +880 31 252 2229, *Fax:* +880 31 251 0889, *Email:* cmancpa@globalctg.net, *Website:* www.cpa.gov.bd

Officials: President: Commodore Muhammed Farooque.
Deputy Conservator: Capt Nazmul Alam, *Email:* capt.nazmul@gmail.com.
Harbour Master: Capt Zafarullah Chowdhury, *Email:* akmz_5@yahoo.com.
Secretary: Syed Farhad Uddin Ahmed, *Email:* secycpa@globalctg.net.

Port Security: ISPS compliant

Approach: The seaward approach to the port is northwards of the 10 fathom contour in pos 22° 24' N; 91° 3" E. The distance to the pilot ground from the south patches shoal is 46 nautical miles on direct course
The following are navigation aids which guide vessels approaching the port:
St. Martin's Island Light House in pos 22° 37' 52" N; 92° 19' 24" E
Coxs Bazar Light House in pos 21° 26' 00" N; 91° 58' 30" E
Kutubdia Light House in pos 21° 52' 18" N; 91° 50' 36" E
Norman's Point Light House in pos 22° 10' 39" N; 91° 49' 30" E
Patenga Light House in pos 22° 13' 34" N; 91° 48' 15" E
Position of Outer Bar Buoys:
Outer Bar Buoy No.3 (Stbd side) in pos 22° 12' 39" N; 91° 47' 49" E
Outer Bar Buoy No.4 (Port side) in pos 22° 12' 56" N; 91° 47' 44" E

Anchorage: Three designated anchorage areas with good holding ground:
Anchorage 'A' (for vessels over 30 ft draught) is formed by extending two lines up to port limit, one having bearing 337° 45' and the other 310° 30' form the point having 22° 12' 30" N; 91° 47' 00" E
Anchorage 'B' (for vessels entering the port within 24 h) is formed in between 4th and 5th line having bearing 234° extended up to port limit from the previous point
Anchorage 'C' (for vessels lightering and other vessels not scheduled to enter the port within 24 h) is between 4th and 5th line having bearing 234° & 157° respectively, extended up to port limit from point 22° 12' 00" N; 91° 47' 12" E
The space between 3rd and 4th lines is prohibited anchorage

Pilotage: Compulsory for ocean-going vessels. Pilot boards approx 2 nautical miles seaward of the Outer Bar buoy

Radio Frequency: Port Radio Control Room maintains watch on VHF Channels 12 and 16 over 24 h

Weather: Generally good conditions except occasional cyclonic storms during October and November

Tides: The tides are semi diurnal with prominent diurnal effect. Tidal range at Petenga is 1.5-5.5 m, at Khal No.10 is 1.5-4.8 m and at Sadarghat is 1.2-4.2 m

Traffic: 2007, 27 629 235 t of cargo handled, 958 020 TEU's

Maximum Vessel Dimensions: Max loa 188 m, max draft 9.2 m for vessels able to enter port. Vessels exceeding limits may lighten at outer anchorage area about 2 nautical miles from the Karnaphuli estuary

Principal Imports and Exports: Imports: Cement, Cement clinker, Chemicals, Coal, Edible oil, Fertilizer, Foodgrain, General cargo, Iron materials, Salt, Sugar. Exports: Fertilizer, Frozen foods, Garments, Hides & skins, Jute & jute products, Molasses, Naptha, Tea.

Working Hours: Two shift vessel works: 0730-1700 (breaks 1200-1400 on Fridays and 1200-1330 on all other working days). 2000-0400 (break 2230-2300)
Three shift vessel works: 0730-1600 (breaks 1230-1400 on Fridays and 1230-1330 on all other working days). 1600-2345 (break 2000-2030). 2345-0730 (break 0400-0430)

Accommodation:

Name	Remarks
Ocean-Going Vessel Berths	See [1] below
Coaster & Inland Vessel Berths	See [2] below
LPG Shore Terminal	See [3] below

[1]*Ocean-Going Vessel Berths:* Ten general cargo berths and six container berths operated by CPA. Container terminal quay length of 450 m with 210 reefer points
Cement Clinker Jetty for vessels up to 167. 63 m loa
Grain Silo Main Jetty for vessels up to 185.91 m loa
T.S.P. Jetty for vessels up to 175.25 m loa
DDJ/1 and DDJ/2: two or more vessels having a total of 302 m loa and draft not exceeding 7 m may be berthed
Chittagong Urea Fertilizer Jetty for vessels up to 176 m loa and loaded up to a max draft of 8.5 m
KAFCO-1 (Urea) & KAFCO-2 (Ammonia): for vessels up to 185.91 m loa and loaded up to a max draft of 9.14 m
River Mooring No.3: for vessels up to 182.87 m loa and 7.61 m draft with dry cargo and edible oil for overside work
River Mooring No.4: with pontoon and shore connection for vessels up to 170.67 m loa and 9.14 m draft with edible oil and POL in bulk
River Mooring No.5: with pontoon and shore connection for vessels up to 185.91 m loa and 9.14 m draft with POL
River Mooring No.6: with pontoon and shore connection for vessels up to 185.91 m loa and 9.14 m draft with POL
Dolphin Oil Jetty: for vessels up to 185.91 m loa and 9.14 m draft for discharging crude oil
River Mooring No.8: for vessels up to 185.91 m loa and 8 m draft with dry bulk cargo for handling through lighters
River Mooring No.9: for vessels up to 185.91 m loa and 6 m draft for vessel repairs/laying off
[2]*Coaster & Inland Vessel Berths:* Lighter Jetty No.1: 122 m jetty face at Sadarghat for coasters and inland vessels up to 70 m loa with day cargo
Lighter Jetty No.2: with pontoon and shore connection (at New Mooring) for coasters and inland vessels up to 76 m loa with dry cargo
Lighter Jetty No.3: with pontoon and shore connection (Jumana) for inland tankers and vessels up to 76 m loa with edible oil & POL in bulk
Lighter Jetty No.4: with pontoon and shore connection (Megna) for inland tankers and vessels up to 75 m loa with POL in bulk
Lighter Jetty No.5: with pontoon and shore connection (ITT) for inland tankers and vessels up to 75 m loa with with edible oil in bulk
Lighter Jetty No.6: with cement concrete Jetty (Padma) for inland tankers and vessels up to 70 m loa for POL in bulk
[3]*LPG Shore Terminal:* Privately operated by Premier L.P. Gas Ltd
Vessels are moored/berthed in between four mooring buoys in draft of 9.2 m approx 4 km from the shore terminal. Cargo is transferred from the vessel to the shore terminal via two underground pipelines of 10" and 6" dia. Storage cap at shore terminal of 5000 m3

Storage: Break bulk: Protected Area: Nine transit sheds totalling 52 069 m2, warehouses (A, B, D, F, P, R, O) totalling 26 746 m2. two car sheds totalling 5082 m2 and open storage totalling 90 000 m2. Outside Protected Area: Six warehouses totalling 32 500 m2 and open storage of 200 000 m2
Container storage at conventional berths: Holding cap of 9657 TEU's, 18 yards totalling 212 238 m2 and 11 container freight stations totalling 86 168 m2
Container Terminal: Holding cap of 6408 m2, container freight station of 12 700 m2 and container storage yard of 150 000 m2

Mechanical Handling Equipment:

Location	Type	Capacity (t)	Qty	Remarks
Chittagong	Mobile Cranes	6–50	28	breakbulk
Chittagong	Shore Cranes	2–3	26	breakbulk
Chittagong	Straddle Carriers	35	25	container
Chittagong	Forklifts	3–5	46	breakbulk
Chittagong	Forklifts	7–42	28	container

Bunkering: Available at the oil moorings and from oil barges
Burmah Eastern Ltd, 4 Strand Road, P O Box 4, Chittagong, Bangladesh, *Tel:* +880 31 201 851
Meghna Petroleum Ltd, 58 Agrabad Commercial Area, P O Box 108, Chittagong, Bangladesh, *Tel:* +880 31 502848
Burmah Eastern Ltd, 4 Strand Road, P O Box 4, Chittagong, Bangladesh, *Tel:* +880 31 201 851
Cockett Marine Oil Ltd, Carrick House, 36 Station Square, Petts Wood, Kent BR5 1NA, United Kingdom, *Tel:* +44 1689 883 400, *Fax:* +44 1689 877 666, *Email:* enquiries@cockett.com, *Website:* www.cockettgroup.com
Meghna Petroleum Ltd, 58 Agrabad Commercial Area, P O Box 108, Chittagong, Bangladesh, *Tel:* +880 31 502848
Tramp Oil & Marine, World Fuel Services Corporation, 13th Floor, Portland House, Bressenden Place, London SW1E 5BH, United Kingdom, *Tel:* +44 20 7808 5000, *Fax:* +44 20 7808 5088, *Email:* pturner@wfscorp.com, *Website:* www.wfscorp.com

Towage: Tugs available up to 3150 bhp

Repair & Maintenance: Chittagong Dry Dock Limited, East Patenga, Chittagong, Bangladesh, *Tel:* +880 31 740922, *Fax:* +880 31 740974, *Email:* drydock@spnetctg.com Dry dock of 182 m x 27 m x 13 m with max cap 16 500 dwt. Specialised work: plate, pipe and machining
Marine Traders, Chittagong, Bangladesh, *Tel:* +880 31 504483
Ship Repair (Bangladesh) Ltd, Chittagong, Bangladesh, *Tel:* +880 31 500794/6

Ship Chandlers: K.M. Chisti Enterprises, c/o Hashim Showdagar Mosjid Building 1st Floor, 471/472 Strand Road, KB Dovash Lane, Goshaildanga, Chittagong 4100, Bangladesh, *Tel:* +880 31 727477, *Fax:* +880 31 710894, *Email:* supply@kmchistigroup.net, *Website:* www.kmchistigroup.net
S & S Ship Management, House No.6, Road No.1, Block-H, Halishahar Housing Estate, PC Road, Chittagong, Bangladesh, *Tel:* +880 31 656044, *Fax:* +880 31 812337, *Email:* sssmanagement@yahoo.com, *Website:* www.interport.org
Seaways Bonded Warehouse Ltd, Jiban Bima Bhaban 4th Floor, 1053 Sheikh Mujib Road, Abrabad Commercial Area, Chittagong 4100, Bangladesh, *Tel:* +880 31 718722, *Fax:* +880 31 711045, *Email:* seaways@bdonline-ctg.com
Seaways Marine Suppliers, Shahajadi Chamber, 7th Floor, 1331/B, Sk. Mujib Road, Agrabad, Chittagong 4100, Bangladesh, *Tel:* +880 31 724878, *Fax:* +880 31 714736, *Email:* seaways@globalctg.net, *Website:* www.seawaysgroup-bd.com
Sovhan Marine Syndicate, 3rd Floor, Arp Bhaban, 107 Agrabad C/A, Chittagong, Bangladesh, *Tel:* +880 31 710790, *Fax:* +880 31 723185, *Email:* sovhan@abnetbd.com, *Website:* www.smssmsgroup.net
Trust Marine Services, 102 Strand Road, Bangla Bazar, Chittagong 4100, Bangladesh, *Tel:* +880 31 712174, *Fax:* +880 31 713792, *Email:* info@trustmarine.com, *Website:* www.trustmarine.com
Western Marine Services Ltd, HBFC Building Ground Floor, 1/D Agrabad Commercial Area, Chittagong 4100, Bangladesh, *Tel:* +880 31 712177, *Fax:* +880 31 720248, *Email:* wms@bbts.net, *Website:* www.wms.com.bd

Shipping Agents: 7 Seas International, Progressive Tower (6th Floor), Agrabad C/A, Chittagong, Bangladesh, *Tel:* +880 31 815455, *Fax:* +880 31 811147, *Email:* nazmul@ctgel.net
AMMS International Ltd, 5th Floor, Daar-E-Shahidi, 69 Agrabad C/A, Chittagong, Bangladesh, *Tel:* +880 31 717516, *Fax:* +880 31 710274, *Email:* amms@techno-bd.net
Aquamarine Ltd, 58 Agrabad CA, P O Box 748, Chittagong, Bangladesh, *Tel:* +880 31 715804, *Fax:* +880 31 710878, *Email:* aml@spnetctg.com
Bangladesh Shipping Corp., BSC Bhaban, Saltgola Road, P O Box 641, Chittagong 4100, Bangladesh, *Tel:* +880 31 713277, *Fax:* +880 31 710506, *Email:* bsc-cht@spnetctg.com, *Website:* www.bsc.gov.bd
Barber Marine Team Sendirian Berhad, Sadharan Bima Sadan, 2nd Floor, 102 Agrabad C/A, Chittagong 4100, Bangladesh, *Tel:* +880 31 712483, *Fax:* +880 31 713983, *Email:* unicorn@globalctg.net, *Website:* www.unicornship.com
Baridhi Shipping Lines Ltd, 3/F Hrc Bhaban, 64-66 Agrabad Com. Area, Agrabad, Chittagong 4100, Bangladesh, *Tel:* +880 31 726142, *Fax:* +880 31 710625, *Email:* cgg@hrcbd.com
Birds Bangladesh Agencies Ltd, 103 Agrabad CA, P O Box 60, Chittagong, Bangladesh, *Tel:* +880 31 715200, *Fax:* +880 31 710012, *Email:* birds@spnetctg.com
Brothers Enterprise, 2 City Corp. Market 2nd Floor, South Halishahar, Bandartila, Chittagong 4218, Bangladesh, *Tel:* +880 31 742020, *Fax:* +880 31 800642, *Email:* lily@spctnet.com
Crown Navigation Co (Private) Ltd, 3rd Floor, Jiban Bima Bhaban, 1053 SK Mujib Road, Chittagong 4100, Bangladesh, *Tel:* +880 31 711271/72, *Fax:* +880 31 710167/037, *Email:* info@chowdhurygroup.com, *Website:* www.chowdhurygroup.com
Everett Bangladesh (Private) Ltd, Pine View, 1st Floor, 100 Agrabad CA, Chittagong 4100, Bangladesh, *Tel:* +880 31 711041/4, *Fax:* +880 31 710668, *Email:* everett@globalctg.net
Goldview Shipping Ltd, 3rd Floor, Ibrahim Building, 60, Agrabad C/A, Chittagong 4100, Bangladesh, *Tel:* +880 31 710054, *Fax:* +880 31 710342, *Email:* gvsl@techno-bd.net
Haque & Sons Ltd, Rummana Haque Tower, 1267/A Goshail Danga, Agrabad C/A, Chittagong, Bangladesh, *Tel:* +880 31 716214, *Fax:* +880 31 710530, *Email:* haqsonsctg@haqsons.com, *Website:* www.haqsons.com
Interport Ship Agents Ltd (ISA), HBFC Building, 1/D Agrabad Commercial Area, Chittagong 4100, Bangladesh, *Tel:* +880 31 252 5064/5, *Fax:* +880 31 728262, *Email:* chittagong@interport.org, *Website:* www.interport.org
Jardine Shipping Services, Ayub Trade Centre, 5th Floor, S/E Corner, 1269/B, Shekh Mujib Road, Agrabad Commercial Area, Chittagong 4100, Bangladesh, *Tel:* +880 31 714271, *Fax:* +880 31 811965, *Email:* gen_jssb@neksus.com, *Website:* www.jardine-shipping.com
JBS Associates, Arup Bhaban (4th Floor), 107 Agrabad C/A, Chittagong, Bangladesh, *Tel:* +880 31 725937, *Fax:* +880 31 715216, *Email:* jbs@jbsbd.net
JF (Bangladesh) Ltd, Finlay House 11, Agrabad Commercial Area, Chittagong 4100, Bangladesh, *Tel:* +880 31 716321, *Fax:* +880 31 710006, *Email:* lloyds@jfbdltd.com, *Website:* www.jfbd.com
Lutful Seaways Ltd, RB Court, 3rd Floor, 54 Agrabad C/A, Chittagong 4100, Bangladesh, *Tel:* +880 31 718825, *Fax:* +880 31 711864, *Email:* lutful2@bttb.net.bd, *Website:* www.lutfulgroup.com
Majestic Shipping Ltd, 26 Agrabad C/A, Chittagong, Bangladesh, *Tel:* +880 31 812534, *Fax:* +880 31 814655, *Email:* msl@spnetctg.com, *Website:* www.majestic-shipping.net
Maritime Services Ltd, 1st Floor, Jahan Building No.3, 79 Agrabad C/A, Chittagong 4100, Bangladesh, *Tel:* +880 31 711554, *Fax:* +880 31 710911, *Email:* info@zedandzed.com, *Website:* www.zedandzed.com
MM Ispahani Ltd, Ispahani Building, Sk Mujib Road, Agrabad CA, P O Box 80, Chittagong, Bangladesh, *Tel:* +880 31 716153, *Fax:* +880 31 710471, *Email:* ispiship@ispahanibd.com, *Website:* www.ispahani.com
A.P. Moller-Maersk Group, Maersk Bangladesh Ltd, 58 Agrabad C/A, 3rd Floor, P O Box 748, Chittagong 4100, Bangladesh, *Tel:* +880 31 726556, *Fax:* +880 31 710875, *Email:* banordmng@maersk.com, *Website:* www.maerskline.com
Ocean International Ltd, Bengal Ship House, 73 Agrabad CA, Chittagong 4100, Bangladesh, *Tel:* +880 31 722351, *Fax:* +880 31 710925, *Email:* ocean@ctpath.net
Omnitrans International Ltd, JIban Bima Road, Agrabad, Chittagong, Bangladesh, *Tel:* +880 31 713146, *Fax:* +880 31 710473, *Email:* omni@bangla.net, *Website:* www.enemomni.com
QC Container Line Ltd, Shafi Bhaban, 3rd Floor, 1216A Sk Mujib Road, Agrabad C/A, Chittagong 4100, Bangladesh, *Tel:* +880 2 9551015, *Fax:* +880 2 9560666, *Email:* info@qcsl.ctg.qc-group.com
Regensea Lines Ltd, 2nd Floor, Ispahani Building, Bangabandhu Road, Agrabad, Chittagong, Bangladesh, *Tel:* +880 31 714984, *Fax:* +880 31 710541/0148, *Email:* ctsrsl@spnetctg.com
S & S Ship Management, House No.6, Road No.1, Block-H, Halishahar Housing Estate, PC Road, Chittagong, Bangladesh, *Tel:* +880 31 656044, *Fax:* +880 31 812337, *Email:* sssmanagement@yahoo.com, *Website:* www.interport.org
Santa Shipping Lines, 5th Floor, 161 Saber Plaza, Strand Road, Agrabad, Chittagong, Bangladesh, *Tel:* +880 31 815299, *Fax:* +880 31 815269, *Email:* shipping@santagroup-bd.com, *Website:* www.santagroup-bd.com
Sea Borne (Private) Ltd, P O Box 748, Chittagong 4001, Bangladesh, *Tel:* +880 31 726105/106, *Fax:* +880 31 715803, *Email:* sbpl@spnetctg.com
Seabird Shipping Agencies Ltd, 3rd Floor, Arup Bhaban, 107 Agrabad C/A, Chittagong, Bangladesh, *Tel:* +880 31 710790, *Fax:* +880 31 723185, *Email:* seabird@smssmsgroup.net
Seacom Shipping Lines Ltd, Taher Chamber (2nd Floor), 10 Agrabad, Commercial Area, Chittagong, Bangladesh, *Tel:* +880 31 711611/5, *Fax:* +880 31 710612, *Email:* seacom@seacomgroup.com, *Website:* www.seacomgroup.com
Sealift Maritime Co., 2nd Floor, Ibrahim Building, 60 Agrabad Commercial Areas, P O Box 1174, Chittagong 4100, Bangladesh, *Tel:* +880 31 711329, *Fax:* +880 31 710912, *Email:* sealift@colbd.net, *Website:* www.sealift.bd.com
Shoreline Services Ltd, Delowar Bhaban 3rd Floor, 104 Agrabad Commercial Area, Chittagong 4100, Bangladesh, *Tel:* +880 31 812814/5, *Fax:* +880 31 711268, *Email:* shoreline@shorelinebd.com, *Website:* www.shorelinebd.com

Key to Principal Facilities:—
A=Airport **C**=Containers **G**=General Cargo **P**=Petroleum **R**=Ro/Ro **Y**=Dry Bulk
B=Bunkers **D**=Dry Dock **L**=Cruise **Q**=Other Liquid Bulk **T**=Towage (where available from port)

Sigma Shipping Lines, Al-Islam Chamber (2nd Floor), 91 Agrabad Commercial Area, Chittagong 4100, Bangladesh, *Tel:* +880 31 711317, *Fax:* +880 31 810536, *Email:* bablu@sigmaship.net, *Website:* www.sigmaship.net

Sovhan Marine Syndicate, 3rd Floor, Arp Bhaban, 107 Agrabad C/A, Chittagong, Bangladesh, *Tel:* +880 31 710790, *Fax:* +880 31 723185, *Email:* sovhan@abnetbd.com, *Website:* www.smssmsgroup.net

SW Shipping Ltd, Rashid Building, Strand Road, P O Box 12, Chittagong 4100, Bangladesh, *Tel:* +880 31 716274, *Fax:* +880 31 710245, *Email:* swsl@spnetcgt.com

Trans Enem Enterprises Ltd, Ispahani Building, 3rd Floor, Sk Mujib Road, Agrabad Commercial Area, Chittagong 4000, Bangladesh, *Tel:* +880 31 726627, *Fax:* +880 31 814724, *Email:* jlm.ctg@gmail.com

Transmarine Logistics Ltd, Shafi Bhaban, 4th Floor, SK Mujib Road, Agrabad CA, Chittagong, Bangladesh, *Tel:* +880 31 710646, *Fax:* +880 31 710847, *Email:* ctgtml@spnetctg.com

Surveyors: ABS (Pacific), 5th Floor, Daar-E-Shahidi Building, 69 Agrabad Commercial Area, Chittagong 4001, Bangladesh, *Tel:* +880 31 714349, *Fax:* +880 31 710968, *Email:* ABSChittagong@eagle.org, *Website:* www.eagle.org

Bureau Veritas, Shahjadi Chamber (5th Floor), 1331/B Sk Mujib Road, Chittagong 4100, Bangladesh, *Tel:* +880 31 815403, *Fax:* +880 31 816518, *Email:* bv.bangladesh@in.bureauveritas.com, *Website:* www.bureauveritas.com

Germanischer Lloyd, HBFC Building, 4th Floor, 1/D Agrabad Commercial Area, Chittagong 4100, Bangladesh, *Tel:* +880 31 713759, *Fax:* +880 31 710851, *Email:* gl-chittagong@gl-group.com, *Website:* www.gl-group.com

Henderson International (LLC), Henderson International (Bangladesh) Ltd, House No 306/B, 1st Floor, Road No. 2 CDA R/A, Agrabad, Chittagong 4100, Bangladesh, *Tel:* +880 31 723681, *Fax:* +880 31 501128, *Email:* info@hendersongroup.com, *Website:* www.hendersongroup.com

Nippon Kaiji Kyokai, Chittagong, Bangladesh, *Tel:* +880 31 726260, *Fax:* +880 31 726261, *Email:* cg@classnk.or.jp, *Website:* www.classnk.or.jp

Western Marine Services Ltd, HBFC Building Ground Floor, 1/D Agrabad Commercial Area, Chittagong 4100, Bangladesh, *Tel:* +880 31 712177, *Fax:* +880 31 720248, *Email:* wms@bbts.net, *Website:* www.wms.com.bd

Medical Facilities: Port Authority hospital available for ships crew. Public and private hospitals also available

Airport: Shah Amanat International Airport, 8 km

Railway: Chittagong Railway Station, 5 km

Lloyd's Agent: JF (Bangladesh) Ltd, Finlay House 11, Agrabad Commercial Area, Chittagong 4100, Bangladesh, *Tel:* +880 31 716321, *Fax:* +880 31 710006, *Email:* lloyds@jfbdltd.com, *Website:* www.jfbd.com

MONGLA

Lat 22° 31' N; Long 89° 35' E.

Admiralty Chart: 732	**Admiralty Pilot:** 21
Time Zone: GMT +6 h	**UNCTAD Locode:** BD MGL

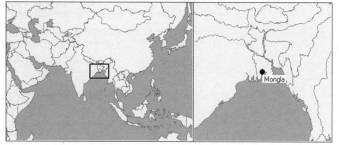

Principal Facilities:

Q	Y	G	C		B		T	A

Authority: Mongla Port Authority, P O Box Mongla Port 9351, Bagerhat District, Mongla, Bangladesh, *Tel:* +880 41 762331 & 761997, *Email:* mpa@bttb.net.bd, *Website:* www.monglaport.gov.bd

Port Security: ISPS compliant

Documentation: Last port clearance; international load line certificate; safety radio telegraphy certificate/GMDSS certificate; safety equipment certificate; safety construction certificates; cargo gear register and relative inspection certificate; ship's register; international oil pollution prevention certificate; competency certificate of officers; CDC for master, officers & crews; article of agreement; deratting exemption certificate; light dues receipt; crew list (12 copies); master's declaration on ship's properties (3 copies)

Approach: Bar at entrance to Pussur River has a min depth of 6.0 m at CD

Anchorage: At the anchorage there are eight swinging mooring buoys in depths of 5.5 to 14.0 m with good holding ground of sand and mud. A further 21 more vessels can safely be anchored within 10 km working range

Pilotage: The pilotage ground extends from the fairway buoy in approx pos 21° 26.9' N; 89° 34.4' E to the northern limit of the port (up to a line drawn between pos 22° 38' N; 89° 40' E)

The lighted buoy painted 'Mongla Fairway' and fitted with a radar reflector flashing white every 10 secs, makes the approach to the pilotage ground reasonably easy and safe. From the fairway buoy to the pilotage ground (near Hiron Point) the channel is marked by 9 pairs of lighted buoys with radar reflectors. Master's of vessels before approaching the pilotage ground, should await instructions from the Hiron Point pilot station

Vessels approaching Mongla Port should send their ETA and draft to their respective agents and to Port Khulna via Khalna Radio (call sign S3E) at least 24 h before their actual time of arrival at the fairway buoy. On receipt of the ETA directly from the ship, the pilot is detailed in order of priority of arrivals. Further instructions are issued by the pilot himself on VHF. On or before arrival at the fairway buoy, the Master is to contact the Hiron Point pilot station on W/T (call sign S3K) or on VHF Channel 16 for bar crossing instructions

Radio Frequency: Khulna Port Control, Mongla Harbour Control and New Port Control Radio Station maintains 24 h watch. VHF Channels 16 and 11

Tides: Tides are semi diurnal with spring rise between max 2.8 m in winter to max 3.35 m during the monsoon. During monsoon current may attain strength up to 6 knots

Traffic: 2007/08, 722 840 t of cargo handled, 20 885 TEU's

Maximum Vessel Dimensions: 200 m loa with permissible draft varying from day to day up to 8 m

Principal Imports and Exports: Imports: Cement, Cement clinker, Fertilizer, General cargo, Grain, Wood pulp. Exports: Jute, Jute products, Shrimps.

Working Hours: Around the clock in two shifts: 0700-1900, 1900-0700

Accommodation:

Name	Length (m)	Depth (m)	Remarks
Mongla			
Wharf	920	6.1	See [1] below
			See [2] below

[1]*Mongla:* The port also consists of 7 single swinging moorings, 14 anchor berths and 7 private jetties

[2]*Wharf:* Incorporating five jetties (J1-J5) for ocean-going vessels, each 183 m long, although only two vessels of more than 182.8 m loa can be accommodated at any one time. Three container yards in operation covering an area of 35 752 m2 with holding cap of 2180 TEU's. 120 reefer points

Storage: Four transit sheds of 4907 m2 each, two warehouses of 9815 m2 and open storage of approx 10 000 m2

Mechanical Handling Equipment:

Location	Type	Capacity (t)	Qty
Mongla	Mult-purp. Cranes	5	7
Mongla	Mobile Cranes	10–30	10
Mongla	Straddle Carriers	32	3
Mongla	Forklifts	2–5	27

Cargo Worked: Up to 150 t/gang/shift

Bunkering: Limited quantity of LDO can be supplied with 48 h notice

Waste Reception Facilities: Garbage disposal available by contractors licensed by Port Authority

Towage: Three powerful tugs and one fire-fighting tug are available

Repair & Maintenance: Minor repairs arranged. Repair facilities are also available at Khulna Shipyard, 40 km away

Shipping Agents: Interport Ship Agents Ltd (ISA), N-1 Main Road, Mongla, Bangladesh, *Tel:* +880 41 760583, *Fax:* +880 41 786044, *Email:* mongla@interport.com, *Website:* www.interport.org

QC Container Line Ltd, 55/1 Ahsan Ahmed Road, Khulna 9100, Bangladesh, *Tel:* +880 41 724426/721742, *Fax:* +880 41 725684, *Email:* qcsl@khulna.bangla.net, *Website:* www.qc-group.com

Stevedoring Companies: Gafur Brothers & Co., Mongla, Bangladesh, *Tel:* +880 41 731446

Khulna Traders, Mongla, Bangladesh, *Tel:* +880 41 723920

Pussur Shipping Ltd, Mongla, Bangladesh, *Tel:* +880 41 725706

Medical Facilities: Port Authority operates a 25 bed hospital; also hospitals and private clinic are available at Khulna City, 45 km from port

Airport: Jessore Airport, 110 km

Railway: Khulna Railway Station, 45 km

Lloyd's Agent: JF (Bangladesh) Ltd, Finlay House 11, Agrabad Commercial Area, Chittagong 4100, Bangladesh, *Tel:* +880 31 716321, *Fax:* +880 31 710006, *Email:* lloyds@jfbdltd.com, *Website:* www.jfbd.com

BARBADOS

BRIDGETOWN

Lat 13° 6' N; Long 59° 37' W.

Admiralty Chart: 502/2485	**Admiralty Pilot:** 71
Time Zone: GMT -4 h	**UNCTAD Locode:** BB BGI

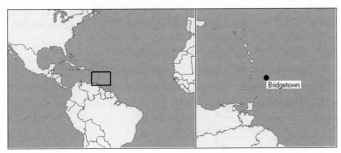

Principal Facilities:

P	Q	Y	G	C		L	B	D	T	A

ERIC HASSELL & SON LTD.

ERICA LUKE
MANAGING DIRECTOR

(246) 436 - 6102 (W)
(246) 822 - 3459 (M)
EMAIL: erica@erichassell.com.bb

SHIPPING AGENTS
STEVEDORING CONTRACTORS
FREIGHT FORWARDERS

TEL: 246 436 6102 FAX: 246 429 3416
WEB: www.erichassell.com.bb

Authority: Barbados Port Inc., University Row, Princess Alice Highway, Bridgetown, Barbados, *Tel:* +1246 430 4700, *Fax:* +1246 429 5348, *Email:* administrator@barbadosport.com, *Website:* www.barbadosport.com

Officials: Chairman: Larry Tatem.
Chief Executive Officer: Everton Walters, *Email:* ewalters@barbadosport.com.
Managing Director: Kenneth Atherley, *Email:* katherley@barbadosport.com.
Public Relations Manager: Frieda Nicholls, *Tel:* +1246 430 5170, *Email:* fnicholls@barbadosport.com.
Harbour Master: Richard Alleyne, *Email:* ralleyne@barbadosport.com.

Port Security: ISPS compliant

Documentation: Crew list (6 copies), passenger list (6 copies), health certificate, ship information (4 copies), vaccination report, deratting certificate, manifest (2 copies), last port clearance, stores list (2 copies), crew declaration list, animal declaration list, form A (3 copies)

Anchorage: Carlisle Bay is an open roadstead about 2 km in width and 0.8 km deep, with good shelter from prevailing winds. Vessels may anchor in depths of 7.0 m upwards

Pilotage: Compulsory. The pilot position is located 0.8 km W of the Fairway Buoy. Watch kept on VHF Channels 12 and 16

Weather: Winds NE to SE

Tides: Max rise 0.6 m

Traffic: 2007, 1 314 698 t of cargo handled, 99 622 TEU's

Principal Imports and Exports: Imports: Clothing, Electrical appliances, Leather goods, Manufactured goods, Vehicles. Exports: Alcoholic beverages, Builders hardware, Finished structures & parts, Food preparations, Meal & flour of cereals.

Working Hours: Mon-Fri: 0700-1600, 1600-2300, 2300-0700 (for containers only). Saturday and Sunday - overtime. Only cruise vessels are accommodated on holidays

Accommodation:

Name	Length (m)	Depth (m)	Remarks
Bridgetown			See [1] below
Cross Berth	121		
Berth No's 2 & 3	366	11	
Berth No.4	184	11	
Berth No.5	100		

[1]*Bridgetown:* Container handling is carried out on Berths 3, 4 and 5. Next to Berths 4 and 5 is a container park covering 47 348 m2 with storage for up to 16 000 TEU's
A 156 m long quay, dredged to 6.8 m is reserved for inter-island vessels
A 307 m sugar berth and other bulk facilities with 183 m of berthing space
The Esso Jetty, located outside the breakwater, can accommodate tankers up to 244 m loa and 11.6 m draught
The Arawak Cement Plant can accommodate ship's up to 121 m loa and 9.0 m draught
Outside of the Bridgetown Port, there are three oil berths:
Needham's Point, for crude oil imports, can accept ship's up to 193 m loa and 11.6 m draught
Oistins Bay is dedicated to the import of aviation fuel and can accommodate tankers up to 172 m loa and 10.0 m draught
Spring Garden is an LPG facility for vessels up to 103 m loa and 4.9 m draught

Storage:

Location	Covered (m²)	Sheds / Warehouses
Bridgetown	14000	3

Mechanical Handling Equipment:

Location	Type	Capacity (t)	Qty
Bridgetown	Mobile Cranes	104	1
Bridgetown	Container Cranes	40	1
Bridgetown	Straddle Carriers	40	8
Bridgetown	Reach Stackers	45	2

Cargo Worked: Break bulk approx 20 t/h. Containers approx 22 lifts/h

Bunkering: Shell Eastern Caribbean Service Ltd, Collymore Rock, St. Michael, Bridgetown, Barbados, *Tel:* +1246 431 4800, *Fax:* +1246 436 9722
Chevron Marine Products LLC, Global Marine Products LLC, 1500 Louisiana, 4th Floor, Houston, TX 77002, United States of America, *Tel:* +1 832 8542 988, *Fax:* +1 832 8544 868, *Email:* gulfcbm@chevron.com, *Website:* www.chevron.com – *Grades:* GO
ExxonMobil Marine Fuels, Mailpoint 31, ExxonMobil House, Ermyn Way, Leatherhead, Surrey KT22 8UX, United Kingdom, *Tel:* +44 1372 222 000, *Fax:* +44 1372 223 922, *Email:* marine.fuels@exxonmobil.com, *Website:* www.exxonmobil.com – *Grades:* IFO30-380cSt; MGO – *Rates:* 150-300t/h – *Notice:* 24 hours – *Delivery Mode:* pipeline
Shell Eastern Caribbean Service Ltd, Collymore Rock, St. Michael, Bridgetown, Barbados, *Tel:* +1246 431 4800, *Fax:* +1246 436 9722

Waste Reception Facilities: Skips available for solid waste removal to incinerator within port facility

Towage: Compulsory for vessels over 1000 nrt. Two tugs available of 4640 hp and 5500 hp

Ship Chandlers: Anchor Ship Chandlery, c/o Hanschell Inniss Ltd, P O Box 143, Bridgetown, Barbados, *Tel:* +1246 436 6650, *Fax:* +1246 427 6938, *Email:* barbados_shipchand@goddent.com, *Website:* www.hanschellinnissltd.com

Shipping Agents: BE Customs Agency, Groung Floor Docklands Place, Cavans Lane, Bridgetown 11156, Barbados, *Tel:* +1246 228 3067, *Fax:* +1246 228 3067, *Email:* sbecustomsagency@caribsurf.com
The Booth Steamship Co. (B'dos) Ltd, 1st Floor, Bridge House, Cavans Lane, P O Box 263, Bridgetown, Barbados, *Tel:* +1246 436 6094, *Fax:* +1246 426 0484, *Email:* info@boothsteamship.com, *Website:* www.boothsteamship.com
BSF Enterprises, 18 Coles Building, Lower Baystreet, Bridgetown, Barbados, *Tel:* +1246 430 0801, *Fax:* +1246 430 0831, *Email:* bsfenterprises@caribsurf.com
Dacosta Mannings Inc., Brandons Complex, Brandons, St Michael, Bridgetown, Barbados, *Tel:* +1246 430 4800, *Fax:* +1246 431 0051, *Email:* agittens@dmishipping.com, *Website:* www.dmishipping.com
Goddards Shipping & Tours Ltd, Goddards Complex, Fontabelle Road, St Michael, Bridgetown, Barbados, *Tel:* +1246 426 9918, *Fax:* +1246 426 7322, *Email:* gst_shipagent@goddent.com, *Website:* www.goddardsadventures.com
Eric Hassell & Son Ltd, Carlisle House, Hincks Street, Bridgetown, Barbados, *Tel:* +1246 436 6102, *Fax:* +1246 429 3416, *Email:* info@erichassell.com.bb, *Website:* www.erichassell.com.bb
H Jason Jones & Co. Ltd, Kensington Fontabel, St Michael, P O Box 141, Bridgetown, Barbados, *Tel:* +1246 429 7209, *Fax:* +1246 429 2011, *Email:* ninniss@kensingtoncourt.com
Marine Trading Ltd, Bay Street, P O Box 425, Bridgetown, Barbados, *Tel:* +1246 426 1292, *Fax:* +1246 429 8121, *Email:* marinetrading@sunbeach.net
R.M. Jones & Co. Ltd, Whitepark Road, Bridgetown, Barbados, *Tel:* +1246 426 2152, *Fax:* +1246 427 6798, *Email:* shipping@rmjones.com.bb
Robulk Agencies Inc, James Fort Building, Hincks Street, Bridgetown, Barbados, *Tel:* +1246 228 8575, *Fax:* +1246 228 8591, *Email:* shipping@robulk.com, *Website:* www.robulk.com
Sea Freight Agencies (B'dos) Ltd, James Fort Building, Hincks Street, Bridgetown, Barbados, *Tel:* +1246 429 9688, *Fax:* +1246 429 5107, *Email:* management@seafrt.com, *Website:* www.seafrt.com

Stevedoring Companies: The Booth Steamship Co. (B'dos) Ltd, 1st Floor, Bridge House, Cavans Lane, P O Box 263, Bridgetown, Barbados, *Tel:* +1246 436 6094, *Fax:* +1246 426 0484, *Email:* info@boothsteamship.com, *Website:* www.boothsteamship.com
Eric Hassell & Son Ltd, Carlisle House, Hincks Street, Bridgetown, Barbados, *Tel:* +1246 436 6102, *Fax:* +1246 429 3416, *Email:* info@erichassell.com.bb, *Website:* www.erichassell.com.bb
Marine Trading Ltd, Bay Street, P O Box 425, Bridgetown, Barbados, *Tel:* +1246 426 1292, *Fax:* +1246 429 8121, *Email:* marinetrading@sunbeach.net
Sea Freight Agencies (B'dos) Ltd, James Fort Building, Hincks Street, Bridgetown, Barbados, *Tel:* +1246 429 9688, *Fax:* +1246 429 5107, *Email:* management@seafrt.com, *Website:* www.seafrt.com

Surveyors: Bureau Veritas, Little Chimney, Clermont, St.James, Bridgetown, Barbados, *Tel:* +1246 425 1206, *Fax:* +1246 427 6798, *Website:* www.bureauveritas.com

Medical Facilities: Port health officers and medical doctors available; modern hospital approx 6 km

Airport: Grantley Adams International, 21 km

Lloyd's Agent: G M Yeadon Group Inc., P O Box 3084, Holetown, St. James, Barbados, *Tel:* +1246 434 5272, *Fax:* +1246 436 7730, *Email:* info@gmyeadon.com, *Website:* www.gmyeadon.com

---

Key to Principal Facilities:—
A=Airport   **C**=Containers   **G**=General Cargo   **P**=Petroleum   **R**=Ro/Ro   **Y**=Dry Bulk
B=Bunkers   **D**=Dry Dock   **L**=Cruise   **Q**=Other Liquid Bulk   **T**=Towage (where available from port)

ANTWERP

Lat 51° 15' N; Long 4° 23' E.

Admiralty Chart: 139   **Admiralty Pilot:** 28

Time Zone: GMT +1 h   **UNCTAD Locode:** BE ANR

Principal Facilities:

P Q Y G C R L B D T A

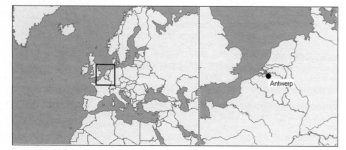

Authority: Antwerp Port Authority, Havenhuis, Entrepotkaai 1, B-2000 Antwerp, Belgium, *Tel:* +32 3 205 2011, *Fax:* +32 3 205 2028, *Email:* info@haven.antwerpen.be, *Website:* www.portofantwerp.com

Officials: President: Marc Van Peel, *Tel:* +32 3 205 2307, *Email:* marc.vanpeel@haven.antwerpen.be.
Chief Executive Officer: Eddy Bruyninckx, *Tel:* +32 3 205 2316, *Email:* eddy.bruyninckx@haven.antwerpen.be.
Commercial Director: Luc Arnouts, *Tel:* +32 3 205 2246, *Email:* luc.arnouts@haven.antwerpen.be.
Harbour Master: Jan Verbist, *Tel:* +32 3 205 2186, *Email:* jan.verbist@haven.antwerpen.be.

Port Security: ISPS compliant. Container Security Initiative (CSI) designated port

Approach: Access to the river via the Wielingen Channel, via Scheur Channel or via the Oostgat Channel. The max permitted draught for vessels entering the port up to December 1990 was 15 m. The max size of the vessel, through, is dependent on tidal conditions. Vessels up to 11.9 m draught are no longer dependent upon the state of the tide and can enter and leave the port at any time

Anchorage: For vessels on the river, anchorage can be obtained at Flushing roads, Everingen, Terneuzen and Springergeul and in emergency near Hansweert, Schaar van Waarde and Schaar van de Noord
For vessels awaiting locks, anchorage is possible at Schaar oud Doel, Liefkenshoek, Meestoof and Oosterweel

Pilotage: Compulsory, except for vessels in ballast of less than 2.2 m draught. For information on pilot services contact: Pilot Service (Loodswezen), Tavernierkaai 5, B-2000 Antwerp, Tel: +32 3 222 0811
In the port docks, a dock pilot from BRABO can be called upon for assistance with piloting, mooring and unmooring, Tel: +32 3 205 9430, Fax: +32 3 205 9431, Email: info@brabo.com, Website: www.brabo.com

Radio Frequency: Pilot cutter on station VHF channel 16, Flushing Radio VHF channel 14, Kruisschans and Zandvliet Radio channel 12, port coordination service VHF channel 18, Ostend Radio VHF channel 16

Tides: Range of tide 4.27 m to 4.57 m

Traffic: 2007, 16 689 sea-going vessels, 182 896 788 t of cargo handled, 8 176 614 TEU's

Working Hours: Day shift 0800-1200, 1230-1545. Morning shift 0600-1000, 1030-1345. Afternoon shift 1400-1800, 1830-2145. Night shift 2200-0200, 0230-0545

Accommodation: The port of Antwerp is situated 68 km from the North Sea and stretches along the banks of the River Scheldt over a distance of 21 km. It is 45 km from Brussels and is easily accessible by road and rail and handily placed for many industrialised regions of W Europe. Inland navigation accounts for much traffic to and from the port, being linked with 1500 km of Belgian waterways and also the large European waterways network
The port consists of three parts: berths along the River Scheldt, the Right Bank Docks and the Left Bank Docks

Name	Length (m)	Depth (m)	Remarks
Right Bank Docks			
Amerikadok	2355	7.5–14.6	
Albertdok	5124	9.5–12	
2 Havendok	1680	10.7	
3 Havendok	2110	11.6–14.7	
Leopolddok	1000	11.3	See [1] below
Hansadok	5243	12–15.2	
4 Havendok	2350	12–13.2	
5 Havendok	4495	12	See [2] below
Industriedok	1640	12	
Marshalldok	3656	12	
6 Havendok	3785	15.2	See [3] below
Graandok	1213	6.2–10.2	
Churchilldok	5036	15.2	See [4] below
Kanaaldok B1	3249	16.7	
Kanaaldok B2	800	16.7	See [5] below
Kanaaldok B3	2549	15.2	
Delwaidedok	4660	16.7	See [6] below
Left Bank Docks			
Waaslandkanaal	2680	18	
Zuidelijk Insteedok		18	
Noordelijk Insteekdok		18	
Droeldok	1200	18	
Vrasenedok	4400	18	
Deurganckdok			See [7] below
Scheldt Quays			See [8] below

[1]*Leopolddok:* Includes a bulk terminal (Quay 209), operated by Sea-Invest N.V., Tel: +32 9 255 0211, Fax: +32 9 259 0894, Email: cdabt-gent@sea-invest.be, Website: www.sea-invest.be, with 28 t mobile cranes and two warehouses of 8400 m2 each

[2]5 *Havendok:* Includes a general cargo terminal totalling 1200 m (Quays 301-315) with draft of 11.3 m, operated by PSA Hesse-Noord Natie, Napelsstraat 79, B-2000 Antwerp, Tel: +32 3 260 6111, Fax: +32 3 260 6200, Email: info@psahnn.be, Website: www.psahnn.be, with three gantry cranes and three mobile cranes
[3]6 *Havendok:* Includes a general cargo terminal totalling 1200 m (Quays 332-344) with draft of 14 m, operated by PSA Hesse-Noord Natie, Napelsstraat 79, B-2000 Antwerp, Tel: +32 3 260 6111, Fax: +32 3 260 6200, Email: info@psahnn.be, Website: www.psahnn.be, with nine gantry cranes and two mobile cranes
Includes a bulk terminal handling minerals in bulk and liquids, operated by Sea-Invest N.V., Tel: +32 9 255 0211, Fax: +32 9 259 0894, Email: cdabt-gent@sea-invest.be, Website: www.sea-invest.be
[4]*Churchilldok:* Includes a multi-purpose terminal, handling steel, paper and other breakbulk cargoes using specialized cranes and rolling equipment, totalling 1665 m (Quays 466-484) with draft of 14 m, operated by DP World Antwerp N.V., Niewe Weg 1, Haven 1053, B-2070 Zwijndrecht, Tel: +32 3 730 3300, Fax: +32 3 730 3301, Website: www.dpworld.be, with eighteen cranes of 10-100 t cap and covered warehousing totalling 60 000 m2
Includes a container terrminal with quay length of 1100 m (Quays 402-428) with draft of 13 m, operated by PSA Hesse-Noord Natie, Napelsstraat 79, B-2000 Antwerp, Tel: +32 3 260 6111, Fax: +32 3 260 6200, Email: info@psahnn.be, Website: www.psahnn.be, with three container cranes and three mobile cranes. 147 reefer points
[5]*Kanaaldok B2:* Includes a bulk terminal for coal & non-ferrous concentrates and various dry bulk cargoes (Quay 510), operated by Sea-Invest N.V., Tel: +32 9 255 0211, Fax: +32 9 259 0894, Email: cdabt-gent@sea-invest.be, Website: www.sea-invest.be, with five gantry cranes of 25 t, two warehouses of 5000 m2 and 7500 m2 and seven silo's of 8000 m3 each
[6]*Delwaidedok:* Includes MSC Home Container Terminal totalling 2140 m (Quays 702-730) with draft of 15 m, operated by PSA Hesse-Noord Natie, Napelsstraat 79, B-2000 Antwerp, Tel: +32 3 260 6111, Fax: +32 3 260 6200, Email: info@psahnn.be, Website: www.psahnn.be, with twenty one gantry cranes and three mobile cranes. 1220 reefer points
Includes a container terminal totalling 1305 m (Quays 732-748) with draft of 15 m, operated by DP World Antwerp N.V., Niewe Weg 1, Haven 1053, B-2070 Zwijndrecht, Tel: +32 3 730 3300, Fax: +32 3 730 3301, Website: www.dpworld.be, with five cranes of 60-120 t cap, thirty five straddle carriers and covered warehousing totalling 41 000 m2
Includes a bulk terminal for solid fuel and iron ore (Quay 750), operated by Sea-Invest N.V., Tel: +32 9 255 0211, Fax: +32 9 259 0894, Email: cdabt-gent@sea-invest.be, Website: www.sea-invest.be. Quay length of 1000 m with discharging cap of 70 000 t/day
[7]*Deurganckdok:* The entire West side of the Deurganckdok forms the Deurganck Container Terminal (Quays 1732-1742), operated by PSA Hesse-Noord Natie, Napelsstraat 79, B-2000 Antwerp, Tel: +32 3 260 6111, Fax: +32 3 260 6200, Email: info@psahnn.be, Website: www.psahnn.be. The first phase has a quay length of 1680 m with draft of 15.5 m. Eight container cranes and 860 reefer points. Once it is fully operational it will have a quay length of 2750 m with a total area of around 200 ha
The entire East side of the Deurganckdok forms the Antwerp Gateway Container Terminal (Quays 1700-1718), operated by DP World Antwerp N.V., Niewe Weg 1, B-2070 Zwijndrecht, Tel: +32 3 730 3379, Fax: +32 3 730 4000, Website: www.antwerpgateway.be. The first phase (now operational) has a quay length of 1650 m with draft of 16 m and is equipped with six super post-panamax gantry cranes of 65-95 t cap. Once it is fully operational it will have a total quay length of 2470 m and a total area of 126 ha
[8]*Scheldt Quays:* Includes Europa Container Terminal totalling 1180 m with draft of 13.5 m (Quays 851-869), operated by PSA Hesse-Noord Natie, Napelsstraat 79, B-2000 Antwerp, Tel: +32 3 260 6111, Fax: +32 3 260 6200, Email: info@psahnn.be, Website: www.psahnn.be, with six gantry cranes, one rail gantry crane and one mobile crane. 648 reefer points
Includes Noordzee Container Terminal totalling 1125 m with draft of 14.5 m (Quays 901-915), operated by PSA Hesse-Noord Natie, Napelsstraat 79, B-2000 Antwerp, Tel: +32 3 260 6111, Fax: +32 3 260 6200, Email: info@psahnn.be, Website: www.psahnn.be, with ten gantry cranes and one rail gantry crane. 808 reefer points

Storage: Over 5 000 000 m2 of covered storage space

Mechanical Handling Equipment:

Location	Type	Capacity (t)	Qty
Antwerp	Floating Cranes	40–800	3
Antwerp	Mobile Cranes	100	10

Bunkering: Agaat Bunkering B.V., Boterhamvaartweg 2, Dok 138, 2030 Antwerp, Belgium, *Tel:* +32 3 542 4184, *Fax:* +32 3 544 8883, *Email:* agaat@agaat.com
Atlas Bunkering Services BVBA, Van Noortstraat 10, B-2018 Antwerp, Belgium, *Tel:* +32 3 2056550, *Fax:* +32 3 2056555, *Email:* atlasbunkering@pandora.be, *Website:* www.atlasbunkering.com
Balkan & Black Sea Shipping Co., Balkan & Black Sea Shipping Co. (Belgium) N.V., 6 Orgelstraat, B-2000 Antwerp, Belgium, *Tel:* +32 3 201 9080, *Fax:* +32 3 233 4302, *Email:* g.petrov@bbss.be, *Website:* www.bbss.uk.com
Belgian Shell S.A., Avenue Arnaud Fraiteur 15, 1050 Brussels, Belgium, *Tel:* +32 2 5089 111, *Fax:* +32 2 5110 571, *Email:* joris.bosschaert@shell.com, *Website:* www.shell.be
Ch de Wit N.V., Haven 40A, Madrasstraat 5, B-2030 Antwerp, Belgium, *Tel:* +32 3 2313 636, *Fax:* +32 3 2102 868, *Email:* info@dewit-bunkering.com, *Website:* www.dewit-bunkering.com
Condor Bunkering & Onyx N.V., Boterhamvaartweg 2, Dock 138, 2030 Antwerp, Belgium, *Tel:* +32 3 6468 018, *Fax:* +32 3 6446 326, *Email:* condor.bunkering@pandora.be
Dynamic Oil Services N.V., Frankrijklei 37, P O Box 5, 2000 Antwerp, Belgium, *Tel:* +32 3 7072 685, *Fax:* +32 3 7072 688, *Email:* jmc.vander.heijden@hetnet.nl
ExxonMobil Corp., ExxonMobil Marine & Fuels, Polderdijkweg 3B, Haven 447, B-2030 Antwerp, Belgium, *Tel:* +32 3 5433 798, *Fax:* +32 3 5433 740, *Email:* marine.fuels@exxonmobil.com, *Website:* www.exxonmobil.com
Oilchart International N.V., Plantinkaai 13, 2000 Antwerp, Belgium, *Tel:* +32 3 2325 234, *Fax:* +32 3 2336 745, *Email:* info@oilchart.com, *Website:* www.oilchart.com
OW Bunker (Belgium) N.V., Ellermanstraat 14, B-2060 Antwerp, Belgium, *Tel:* +32 3 2068 640, *Fax:* +32 3 2068 645, *Email:* owbunker@owbunker.be, *Website:* www.owbunker.com
Van Stappen Bunkering Services N.V., Vosseschijnstraat Kaai 140, 2030 Antwerp, Belgium, *Tel:* +32 3 645 5298, *Fax:* +32 3 6416 375, *Email:* vanstappen@vanstappen.be, *Website:* www.vanstappen.be
Victrol NV, Elzasweg 13, 2030 Antwerp, Belgium, *Tel:* +32 3 5400 570, *Fax:* +32 3 5412 605, *Email:* info@victrol.be, *Website:* www.victrol.be
Wiljo Energy, Wiljo NV, Amsterdamstraat 30, B-2000 Antwerp, Belgium, *Tel:* +32 3 232 3910, *Fax:* +32 3 232 5647, *Email:* wiljo@wiljo.be, *Website:* www.wiljo.be
(Aegean) Bunkers at Sea, Vlasmarkt 11, P O Box 3, B-2000 Antwerp, Belgium, *Tel:* +32 3 202 3060, *Fax:* +32 3 541 4021, *Email:* aegeanbas@ampni.com, *Website:* www.ampni.com
OW Bunker (Belgium) N.V., Tavernierkaai 2, BE 2000 Antwerp, Belgium, *Tel:* +32 3 288 3600, *Fax:* +32 3 475 9671, *Email:* owbunker@owbunker.be, *Website:* www.owbunker.com
Wiljo Energy, Wiljo NV, Amsterdamstraat 30, B-2000 Antwerp, Belgium, *Tel:* +32 3 232 3910, *Fax:* +32 3 232 5647, *Email:* wiljo@wiljo.be, *Website:* www.wiljo.be

Waste Reception Facilities: Apart from these facilities there are a number of firms with mobile reception facilities for oily and chemical waste
Antwerp Cleaning & Storage (ACS), Antwerp, Belgium, *Tel:* +32 3 542 3290, *Fax:* +32 3 541 3755
Antwerp Waste Management, Antwerp, Belgium, *Tel:* +32 3 561 0120, *Fax:* +32 3 568 8099
ASBA, Antwerp, Belgium, *Tel:* +32 3 233 1883, *Fax:* +32 3 231 5594
Belgian Oil Services N.V., Haven 261, Blauwe Weg 7, B-2030 Antwerp, Belgium, *Tel:* +32 3 543 5959, *Fax:* +32 3 543 5960, *Email:* inform@bosserv.com, *Website:* www.bos-antwerp.com
Booy Clean Belgium, Schouwkenbtraat 10, B-2030 Antwerp, Belgium, *Tel:* +32 3 541 1211, *Fax:* +32 3 541 7173
EWACS, Antwerp, Belgium, *Tel:* +32 3 755 4308, *Fax:* +32 3 755 1568
General Tank Storage (GTS), Antwerp, Belgium, *Tel:* +32 3 541 1280, *Fax:* +32 3 541 3163
Pasec Port N.V., Oosterweelsteenweg 58, B-2030 Antwerp, Belgium, *Tel:* +32 3 546 4150, *Fax:* +32 3 542 3113, *Email:* info@pasecport.com, *Website:* www.pasecport.com

Towage: For towage inside the docks, tug service is provided by the Port Authority with nine tugs, Tel: +32 3 229.6711, Fax: +32 3 229 6710, Email: sleepbedrijf@haven.antwerpen.be
Antwerp Towage N.V., Tavernierkaai 2, 5th Floor, B-2000 Antwerp, Belgium, *Tel:* +32 3 212 1000, *Fax:* +32 3 212 1009, *Email:* info@antwerp-towage.com, *Website:* www.antwerp-towage.com
Scheldt Towage Co. S.A., St.Michielskaai 31, B-2000 Antwerp, Belgium, *Tel:* +32 3 237 3681, *Fax:* +32 3 216 2530
Union de Remorquage et de Sauvetage S.A., Italielei 3, P O Box 2, B-2000 Antwerp, Belgium, *Tel:* +32 3 545 1120, *Fax:* +32 3 541 7007, *Email:* info@urs.be, *Website:* www.urs.be

Repair & Maintenance: Antwerp Shiprepair N.V., Haven 403, Industrieweg 11, B-2030 Antwerp, Belgium, *Tel:* +32 3 540 1211, *Fax:* +32 3 540 1200, *Email:* info@asr.be, *Website:* www.asr.be Six dry docks: No.1 146 m x 18 m, No.2 166 m x 21 m, No.3 193 m x 26 m, No.4 207 m x 27 m, No.5 255 m x 39 m, No.6 312 m x 50 m for vessels up to 180 000 dwt. Repair quays totaling 3000 m with max draught 9 m

Seaman Missions: The Seamans Mission, Italielei 72, B-2000 Antwerp, Belgium, *Tel:* +32 3 605 4188, *Email:* mtsantwerp@skynet.be

Ship Chandlers: AFR Safety Services, 40 Selsaetentuinwijk, B-2160 Wommelgem, Belgium, *Tel:* +32 3 354 3748, *Fax:* +32 3 353 9064, *Email:* henry.schroons@telenet.be, *Website:* afrsafetyservices.com Manager: Henry Schroons
Brabo Enterprises, Kleine Molenweg 220, Stabroek, B-2940 Antwerp, Belgium, *Tel:* +32 3 297 9490, *Fax:* +32 3 297 9491, *Email:* info@brabo-enterprises.be, *Website:* www.brabo-enterprises.be
C.L.S. General Suppliers S.A., Genuastraat 9-11, B-2000 Antwerp 1, Belgium, *Tel:* +32 3 232 8300, *Fax:* +32 3 231 0132, *Email:* cls.generalsuppliers@telenet.be
Delta & Co. N.V., Westpoort 51-59, B-2070 Antwerp, Belgium, *Tel:* +32 3 542 0190, *Fax:* +32 3 541 8322, *Email:* info@deltaco.be, *Website:* www.deltaco.be
K. Gjertsen & Co. N.V., Heizegemweg 11, B-2030 Antwerp 3, Belgium, *Tel:* +32 3 541 7240, *Fax:* +32 3 541 7172, *Email:* info@gjertsen.be
Gylstorff & Co., Bredabaan 391, Brasschaat, B-2930 Antwerp, Belgium, *Tel:* +32 3 225 1616, *Fax:* +32 3 231 1814, *Email:* info@gylstorff.com, *Website:* www.gylstorff.com
Jagomar Shipstores N.V., Haven 403, Industrieweg 11, B-2030 Antwerp 3, Belgium, *Tel:* +32 3 540 1254, *Fax:* +32 3 540 1225, *Email:* kubo@klevenberg.com, *Website:* www.klevenberg.com
Kubo Supply Services, Haven 403, Industrieweg 11, B-2030 Antwerp, Belgium, *Tel:* +32 3 540 1254, *Fax:* +32 3 540 1225, *Email:* kubo@klevenberg.com, *Website:* www.klevenberg.com
Proios Maritime N.V., Westport 51-57, Zwijndrecht, B-2070 Antwerp, Belgium, *Tel:* +32 3 231 4845, *Fax:* +32 3 233 3868, *Email:* info@proios.be, *Website:* www.proios.be
Radio Holland Group, Radio Holland Belgium, Noordersingel 17, B-2140 Antwerp, Belgium, *Tel:* +32 3 320 9960, *Fax:* +32 3 320 9961, *Email:* info@radioholland.be, *Website:* www.radioholland.be
Van Hulle Shipsuppliers N.V., Bredastraat 139, B-2060 Antwerp 6, Belgium, *Tel:* +32 3 231 8950, *Fax:* +32 3 233 0040, *Email:* info@vanhulleships.be, *Website:* www.vanhulleships.be
Vets Shipstores N.V., Wilmarsdonksteenweg 11, Haven 259, B-2030 Antwerp 3, Belgium, *Tel:* +32 3 541 0284, *Fax:* +32 3 541 9936, *Email:* sales@vets.be
Wells & Mommaerts N.V., Noorderlaan 123, B-2030 Antwerp 3, Belgium, *Tel:* +32 3 542 2180, *Fax:* +32 3 542 6263, *Email:* stores@wells-mommaerts.be

Shipping Agents: Boeckmans Belgie N.V., Van Meterenkaai 1, P O Box 4, B-2000 Antwerp, Belgium, *Tel:* +32 3 202 0202, *Fax:* +32 3 202 0393, *Email:* info@boeckmans.be, *Website:* www.boeckmans.be Managing Director: Anthony Durot Email: anthony.durot@boeckmans.be
ACSA, Generaal Lemanstraat 82-92, B-2600 Antwerp, Belgium, *Tel:* +32 3 545 3511, *Fax:* +32 3 545 3605, *Email:* mail@acsa.be, *Website:* www.acsa.be
Agence Maritime Delpierre S.A., Agence Maritime Delpierre b.v.b.a., Oude Leeuwenrui 39, B-2000 Antwerp, Belgium, *Tel:* +32 3 248 5620, *Fax:* +32 3 237 9702, *Email:* info@delpierre.be, *Website:* www.amd-med.com
Agence Maritime Lalemant N.V., Lalemant Antwerpen NV, Friendship Building,

Rijnkaai 37, B-2000 Antwerp, Belgium, *Tel:* +32 3 610 0616, *Fax:* +32 3 610 0617, *Email:* info@lalemant-antwerp.com, *Website:* www.lalemant.com
AGS Shipping (Europe) N.V., Noorderlaan 127A, B-2030 Antwerp, Belgium, *Tel:* +32 3 543 2312, *Fax:* +32 3 543 2268, *Email:* agseurope@agseurope.com, *Website:* www.agseurope.com
Ahlers & Partners, Noorderlaan 139, B-2030 Antwerp, Belgium, *Tel:* +32 3 543 7211, *Fax:* +32 3 542 0023, *Email:* info@ahlers.com, *Website:* www.ahlers.be
Antwerp Freight Agencies N.V., Century Center, De Keyserlei 58-60, P O Box 61, B-2018 Antwerp, Belgium, *Tel:* +32 3 203 6900, *Fax:* +32 3 233 3497, *Email:* mgt@evergreen-shipping.be
Aseco Belgium N.V., Antwerp Tower, De Keyserlei 5, P O Box 35, B-2000 Antwerp, Belgium, *Tel:* +32 3 244 2777, *Fax:* +32 3 244 2755, *Email:* asecobe@be.linernet.com
ASMAR N.V., Oude Leeuwenrui 25/27, B-2000 Antwerp, Belgium, *Tel:* +32 3 205 3400, *Fax:* +32 3 205 3489, *Email:* info@multimodal.be, *Website:* www.dkt.be
Balkan & Black Sea Shipping Co., Balkan & Black Sea Shipping Co. (Belgium) N.V., 6 Orgelstraat, B-2000 Antwerp, Belgium, *Tel:* +32 3 201 9080, *Fax:* +32 3 233 4302, *Email:* g.petrov@bbss.be, *Website:* www.bbss.uk.com
Belgian Navigation Agencies (BNA) N.V., Ankerrui 13, B-2000 Antwerp, Belgium, *Tel:* +32 3 233 6446, *Fax:* +32 3 231 4848, *Email:* brokers@antshipchart.be
Belgo-Iberian Maritime N.V., Schouwkensstraat 9, Haven 200, B-2030 Antwerp, Belgium, *Tel:* +32 3 545 9161, *Fax:* +32 3 545 9171, *Email:* bim@belgo.be, *Website:* www.belgo.be
Belgo-Ruys N.V., Haven 200, Schouwkensstraat 9, B-2030 Antwerp, Belgium, *Tel:* +32 3 545 9191, *Fax:* +32 3 540 6150, *Email:* ruys@belgo.be, *Website:* www.belgo.be
John P Best & Co. N.V., Cassiersstraat 5, B-2060 Antwerp, Belgium, *Tel:* +32 3 221 2700, *Fax:* +32 3 234 3676, *Email:* jpbest.be@sdsbo.com, *Website:* www.delmasbelgium.be
Best & Osterrieth N.V., Cassiersstraat 5, B-2060 Antwerp, Belgium, *Tel:* +32 3 221 2900, *Fax:* +32 3 226 4058, *Email:* vincent.maldague@sdsbo.com, *Website:* www.sdsbo.com
CMA-CGM S.A., CMA CGM Belgium N.V ., Stijfselrui 36, 4th Floor, Box No.2, B-2000 Antwerp, Belgium, *Tel:* +32 3 202 3911, *Fax:* +32 3 202 3699, *Email:* ant.genmbox@cma-cgm.com, *Website:* www.cma-cgm.com
COBELFRET N.V., Sneeuwbeslaan 14, Wilrijk, B-2610 Antwerp, Belgium, *Tel:* +32 3 829 9100, *Fax:* +32 3 825 4507, *Email:* info@cobelfret.be, *Website:* www.cobelfret.com
Coil-Tainer Ltd c/o Hemisphere Logistics Bvba, Keizerstraat 76, B-2000 Antwerp, Belgium, *Tel:* +32 3 204 0835, *Fax:* +32 3 226 5410, *Email:* info@hemisphere.be, *Website:* www.coil-tainer.com
Coli Shipping & Transport N.V., Keizerstraat 20-22, 3rd Floor, B-2000 Antwerp, Belgium, *Tel:* +32 3 213 0795, *Fax:* +32 3 233 4326, *Email:* info@coli.be, *Website:* www.coli-shipping.com
Conti-Lines N.V., Generaal Lemanstraat 82-92, Berchem, B-2600 Antwerp, Belgium, *Tel:* +32 3 545 3511, *Fax:* +32 3 545 3512, *Email:* mail@conti7.be, *Website:* www.conti7.be
De Keyser Thornton N.V., Oude Leeuwenrui 25/27, B-2000 Antwerp, Belgium, *Tel:* +32 3 205 3100, *Fax:* +32 3 205 3132, *Email:* info@multimodal.be, *Website:* www.dekeyserthornton.com
Deckers & Wirtz (D&W) Agencies N.V., Noorderlaan 127A, 31241 Antwerp, Belgium, *Tel:* +32 3 543 2290, *Fax:* +32 3 543 2299, *Email:* a.wendrickx@deckerswirtz.be, *Website:* www.deckerswirtz.be
Durot Shipping N.V., Van Meterenkaai 1, P O Box 6, B-2000 Antwerp, Belgium, *Tel:* +32 3 202 0303, *Fax:* +32 3 202 0396, *Email:* durot@durot.be, *Website:* www.durot.be
Alec Eiffe N.V. & Others, Ahlers Logistic and Maritime Services, Noorderlaan 139, B-2030 Antwerp, Belgium, *Tel:* +32 3 543 7611, *Fax:* +32 3 542 0023, *Email:* info@ahlers.com, *Website:* www.ahlers.com
ELAN N.V., St Pietersvliet 7, B-2000 Antwerp, Belgium, *Tel:* +32 3 305 2950, *Fax:* +32 3 226 7843, *Email:* erik.vandesande@elannv.be
Eurokor Logistics BVBA, Verbindingsdock OK 13, B-2000 Antwerp, Belgium, *Tel:* +32 3 232 5058, *Fax:* +32 3 232 5186, *Email:* ekl@eurokor.be
Armando Farina b.v.b.a, Van Cucyckstraat 1, B-2000 Antwerp, Belgium, *Tel:* +32 3 231 5650, *Fax:* +32 3 231 3520, *Email:* info@farina.be, *Website:* www.farina.be
Giani & Muller N.V., Kanaaldijk 35, Schoten, B-2900 Antwerp, Belgium, *Tel:* +32 3 231 7620, *Fax:* +32 3 232 2425, *Email:* info@foldgroup.com, *Website:* www.foldgroup.com
Great White Fleet Ltd, Chiquita International, Rijnkaai 37, B-2000 Antwerp, Belgium, *Tel:* +32 3 203 7000, *Fax:* +32 3 203 7300, *Email:* talktochiquita@chiquita.com, *Website:* www.chiquita.com
A Hartrodt International, Suikerrui 5, P O Box 2, B-2000 Antwerp, Belgium, *Tel:* +32 3 202 4050, *Fax:* +32 3 234 3338, *Email:* postmaster@hartrodt.be, *Website:* www.hartrodt.be
HNN Logistics N.V., Kruisweg K650, B-2040 Antwerp, Belgium, *Tel:* +32 3 5604 900, *Fax:* +32 3 5604 919, *Email:* info@psahnn.be, *Website:* www.psahnn.be
Kersten Hunik & Co. N.V., Haven 40, Kattendijkdok Oostkaai 1, B-2030 Antwerp, Belgium, *Tel:* 32 3, *Fax:* +32 3 231 9074, *Email:* vanderrvloedt@kersten-hunik.be, *Website:* www.kersten-hunik.be
Inchcape Shipping Services (ISS), Kipdorp 57, B-2000 Antwerp, Belgium, *Tel:* +32 3 204 0811, *Fax:* +32 3 231 1126, *Email:* issanrops@iss-shipping.com, *Website:* www.iss-shipping.com
ISA (International Shipping Agencies) N.V., Rijnpoortvest 4, P O Box 4, B-2000 Antwerp, Belgium, *Tel:* +32 3 222 1555, *Fax:* +32 3 222 1534, *Email:* isa@isacnan.be
K Line (Europe) Ltd, Guelinxstraat 20, B-2060 Antwerp, Belgium, *Tel:* +32 3 221 2140, *Fax:* +32 3 232 8486, *Email:* keuanrinfo@be.kline.com, *Website:* www.kline.be
Kennedy Hunter N.V., Generaal Lemanstraat 82-92, B-2600 Antwerp, Belgium, *Tel:* +32 3 545 3939, *Fax:* +32 3 545 3920, *Email:* mail@kennedy.be, *Website:* www.kennedy.be
KGMX Customs & Agencies N.V., Rietschoorvelden 20, B-2170 Antwerp, Belgium, *Tel:* +32 3 640 9356, *Fax:* +32 3 640 9351, *Email:* marc.breugelmans@ritel.be
L&N Shipping Agency, Klein Zuidland No 4, B-2030 Antwerp, Belgium, *Tel:* +32 3 542 0100, *Fax:* +32 3 542 4744, *Email:* info@tcl.be, *Website:* www.tcl.be
MacAndrews & Co Ltd, Cassiersstraat 5, 2060 Antwerp 6, Belgium, *Tel:* +32 3 221 2420, *Fax:* +32 3 475 9042, *Email:* ldeclerck@macandrews.com, *Website:* www.macandrews.com
Maxx Logistics N.V., Rietschoorvelden 20, B-2170 Antwerp, Belgium, *Tel:* +32 3 640 9380, *Fax:* +32 3 640 9360, *Email:* info@maxx.be, *Website:* www.maxx.be
Mediterranean Shipping Company, MSC Belgium, Noordlaan 127a, B-2030 Antwerp, Belgium, *Tel:* +32 3 543 2200, *Fax:* +32 3 543 2550, *Email:* info@mscbelgium.com, *Website:* www.mscbelgium.com
A.P. Moller-Maersk Group, Maersk Benelux B.V., De Gerlachekaai 20, B-2000 Antwerp, Belgium, *Tel:* +32 3 205 1515, *Fax:* +32 3 232 1144, *Email:* beladm@maersk.com, *Website:* www.maerskline.com
Muller Liner Agencies N.V., Yang Ming Belgium, Stijfselrui 44, B-2200 Antwerp, Belgium, *Tel:* +32 3 202 6464, *Fax:* +32 3 202 6494, *Email:* info@yml.be, *Website:* www.yml.com
Neptumar N.V., St Pietersvliet 15, B-2000 Antwerp, Belgium, *Tel:* +32 3 220 0270, *Fax:* +32 3 222 0290, *Email:* neptumar@neptumar.be, *Website:* www.neptumar.dk
Neptune Shipping N.V., Ankerrui 2, B-2000 Antwerp, Belgium, *Tel:* +32 3 224 5628, *Fax:* +32 3 225 0902, *Email:* info@rhenus.be, *Website:* www.rhenus.be
Newman Shipping & Agency Co. N.V., Stijfselrui 44, P O Box 17, B-2000 Antwerp, Belgium, *Tel:* +32 3 222 1511, *Fax:* +32 3 222 1610, *Email:* newman@newman.be, *Website:* www.newman.be
OMT Overseas Maritime Transport N.V., Brouwersvliet 33, P O Box 3, B-2000 Antwerp, Belgium, *Tel:* +32 3 203 5700, *Fax:* +32 3 203 5728, *Email:* info@omt.be, *Website:* www.omt.be
Rhenus Agencies N.V., Noordersingel 21, B-2140 Antwerp, Belgium, *Tel:* +32 3 224 5640, *Fax:* +32 3 225 5988, *Email:* info@be.rhenus.com, *Website:* www.rhenus.com
Rijn-en Kanaalvaart Reederij N.V., Houtdok-Noordkaai 25a, BE-2030 Antwerp, Belgium, *Tel:* +32 3 222 4211, *Fax:* +32 3 234 1840, *Email:* rke@rke.be, *Website:* www.rke.be
Scaldis Salvage & Marine Contractors N.V., North Trade Building, Noorderlaan 133, P O Box 31, B-2030 Antwerp, Belgium, *Tel:* +32 3 541 6955, *Fax:* +32 3 541 8193, *Email:* mail@scaldis-smc.com, *Website:* www.scaldis-smc.com
Schellen Shipping N.V., Keizerstraat 70, B-2000 Antwerp, Belgium, *Tel:* +32 3 229 0020, *Fax:* +32 3 233 4876, *Email:* info@schellenshipping.be, *Website:* www.schellenshipping.be
Seahorse N.V., St Pietersvliet 3, P O Box 13, B-2000 Antwerp, Belgium, *Tel:* +32 3 226 1005, *Fax:* +32 3 226 1839, *Email:* seahorse@seahorse.be
Seatrade Reefer Chartering N.V., Atlantic House, 4th Floor, Noorderlaan 147, P O Box 10012, B-2030 Antwerp, Belgium, *Tel:* +32 3 544 9493, *Fax:* +32 3 544 9300, *Email:* mailbox@seatrade.com, *Website:* www.seatrade.com
Star Shipping Agencies Antwerp N.V., Ankerrui 9, B-2000 Antwerp, Belgium, *Tel:* +32 3 205 1770, *Fax:* +32 3 205 1766, *Email:* info@be.zim.com, *Website:* www.zim.com
Stute-Montan BVBA, Ernest van Dijckkaai 15-17, 2000 Antwerp, Belgium, *Tel:* +32 3 206 8170, *Fax:* +32 3 233 8758, *Email:* stute.montan@stute.be
Teamwork Agencies N.V., Stijfselrui 44, B-2000 Antwerp, Belgium, *Tel:* +32 3 202 4800, *Fax:* +32 3 202 4813, *Email:* teamwork@burgergroup.be, *Website:* www.royalburgergroup.com
Trimar N.V., Antwerp Tower, De Keyserlei 5, 2nd Floor, P O Box 49, B-2000 Antwerp, Belgium, *Tel:* +32 3 222 6800, *Fax:* +32 3 222 6828, *Email:* o.henne@portsupport.com, *Website:* www.unamar.be
TRS Agencies N.V., Cadixstraat 7/4, B-2000 Antwerp, Belgium, *Tel:* +32 3 213 9545, *Fax:* +32 3 226 1501, *Email:* info@trseurope.com, *Website:* www.trseurope.com
Hugo Trumpy (Agencies) bvba, Plantinkaai 6, B-2000 Antwerp, Belgium, *Tel:* +32 3 201 6600, *Fax:* +32 3 201 6609, *Email:* info@brointermed.be
Unimar Zeetransport N.V., Kipdorp 45-47, B-2000 Antwerp, Belgium, *Tel:* +32 3 234 6290, *Fax:* +32 3 234 6264, *Email:* rf@unimar.be
United Antwerp Maritime Agencies Unamar N.V., Oude Leeuwenreui 25-27, Antwerp, Belgium, *Tel:* +32 3 303 4801, *Fax:* +32 3 303 4801, *Email:* unamar@unamar.be, *Website:* www.unamar.be
Unithai Agencies (Europe) B.V., Van Doosselaere & Acthen BVBA, Poseidon Building, St Pietersvliet 15, B-2000 Antwerp, Belgium, *Tel:* +32 3 220 0510, *Fax:* +32 3 231 4574, *Email:* vda@vando.be, *Website:* www.unithai.com
Van Doosselaere & Achten bvba, Sint Pietersvliet 15, B-2000 Antwerp, Belgium, *Tel:* +32 3 220 0484, *Fax:* +32 3 234 0361, *Email:* vda@vando.be
Van Ommeren Antwerpen N.V., Stijfselrui 44, B-2000 Antwerp, Belgium, *Tel:* +32 3 221 4211, *Fax:* +32 3 202 4813, *Email:* info@burgergroup.be, *Website:* www.burgergroup.com
Vinke & Co. N.V., Noorderlaan 139, B-2000 Antwerp, Belgium, *Tel:* +32 3 543 7670, *Fax:* +32 3 543 7421, *Email:* info@ahlers.com, *Website:* www.ahlers.com
VO Agencies N.V., Rijnpoortvest 4 bus 2, B-2000 Antwerp, Belgium, *Tel:* +32 3 221 4211, *Fax:* +32 3 232 9334, *Email:* voagencies@burgergroup.be
Vopak Agencies B.V., Italielei 3, B-2000 Antwerp, Belgium, *Tel:* +32 3 221 4422, *Fax:* +32 3 226 6261, *Email:* agencies.antwerp@vopak.com, *Website:* www.vopak.com
Walina N.V., De Keyserlei 5, P O Box 35, B-2018 Antwerp, Belgium, *Tel:* +32 3 244 2795, *Fax:* +32 3 244 2860, *Email:* walina@be.linernet.com
Waterfront Shipping bvba, Luithagen-Haven 9, B-2030 Antwerp, Belgium, *Tel:* +32 3 544 9550, *Fax:* +32 3 544 9367, *Email:* info@waterfrontshipping.be, *Website:* www.waterfrontshipping.com
Wilhelmsen Ship Services, Barwil Unitor Ship Services, Sint-Laureiskaai 9, B-2000 Antwerp, Belgium, *Tel:* +32 3 206 9580, *Fax:* +32 3 227 3444, *Email:* barwil.antwerp@wilhelmsen.com, *Website:* www.wilhelmsen.com
Zebra Transport N.V., St. Pietersvliet 15, B-2000 Antwerp, Belgium, *Tel:* +32 3 220 0550, *Fax:* +32 3 220 0551, *Email:* ak@vando.be, *Website:* www.anlloyd.be/Comp_home/Z/ZEBRA/index.html
Zim Integrated Shipping Services Ltd, Ankerrui 9, B-2000 Antwerp, Belgium, *Tel:* +32 3 304 1700, *Fax:* +32 3 304 1714, *Email:* info@be.zim.com, *Website:* www.zim.com

Surveyors: ABS (Europe), 9th Floor, St. Katelijnevest 72, Meirbrug 1, P O Box 38, B-2000 Antwerp, Belgium, *Tel:* +32 3 203 4020, *Fax:* +32 3 233 5857, *Email:* absantwerp@eagle.org, *Website:* www.eagle.org
van der Avoirt N.V., Sneeuwbeslaan 6, B-2610 Antwerp, Belgium, *Tel:* +32 3 827 3931, *Fax:* +32 3 827 3983, *Email:* vda@avoirt.be
Bureau Veritas, Mechelsesteenweg 128-136, B-2018 Antwerp, Belgium, *Tel:* +32 3 247 9400, *Fax:* +32 3 247 9499, *Email:* info@be.bureauveritas.com, *Website:* www.bureauveritas.com
C.I.M.S. International N.V., Noorderlaan 115, B-2030 Antwerp 3, Belgium, *Tel:* +32 3 542 0315, *Fax:* +32 3 542 5481, *Email:* blomme@cims-surveys.com, *Website:* www.cims-surveys.com
Cunningham Lindsey Marine Ltd, North Trade Building, Noorderlaan 133, P O Box 16, B-2030 Antwerp, Belgium, *Tel:* +32 3 541 4539, *Fax:* +32 3 541 4643, *Email:* info@cl-be.com, *Website:* www.cunninghamlindsey.com
Det Norske Veritas A/S, Duboisstraat 39, P O Box 1, B-2060 Antwerp, Belgium, *Tel:* +32 3 206 6510, *Fax:* +32 3 231 6745, *Email:* antwerp.maritime@bmv.com, *Website:* www.dnv.com
DP Survey Group N.V., Baarbeek 1, Zwijndrecht, B-2070 Antwerp, Belgium, *Tel:* +32 3 295 1050, *Fax:* +32 3 295 1069, *Email:* info@dpsurveys.com, *Website:* www.dpsurveys.com
General Surveys BVBA, General Surveys, 74 Griffier Schobbenslaan, B-2140 Ant-

werp, Belgium, *Tel:* +32 3 236 4984, *Fax:* +32 3 271 1574, *Email:* info@gensur.be, *Website:* www.gensur.be

Germanischer Lloyd, Noorderlaan 147, B-2030 Antwerp, Belgium, *Tel:* +32 3 646 0416, *Fax:* +32 3 646 0064, *Email:* gl-antwerp@gl-group.com, *Website:* www.gl-group.com

Hellenic Register of Shipping, Noorderlaan 31A, B-2030 Antwerp, Belgium, *Tel:* +32 3 225 0128, *Fax:* +32 3 231 9353, *Email:* info@marinetechnical.be, *Website:* www.hrs.gr

IMCS BVBA, 19 Bataviastraat, B-2000 Antwerp, Belgium, *Tel:* +32 3 458 2930, *Fax:* +32 3 457 7966, *Email:* imcs@imcs.be, *Website:* www.imcs-group.com

Intermodal Transportation Services Inc., Garden Square, Laarstraat 16, 2610 Antwerp, Belgium, *Tel:* +32 3 290 1000, *Fax:* +32 3 290 1011

Mutual Insurance Claims Office, Belcrownlaan 13, 2100 Antwerp, Belgium, *Tel:* +32 3 231 6604, *Fax:* +32 3 233 0530, *Email:* office@mico-ant.be

Nippon Kaiji Kyokai, Amsterdamstraat 14, B-2000 Antwerp, Belgium, *Tel:* +32 3 231 1342, *Fax:* +32 3 232 9177, *Email:* classnkaw@skynet.be, *Website:* www.classnk.or.jp

Russian Maritime Register of Shipping, Tavernierbuilding, Tavernierkaai 2, B-2000 Antwerp, Belgium, *Tel:* +32 3 213 3834, *Fax:* +32 3 233 8665, *Website:* www.rs-head.spb.ru

Scandinavian Underwriters Agency, SCUA Americas Inc., Belcrownlaan 13, B-2100 Antwerp, Belgium, *Tel:* +32 3 231 0693, *Fax:* +32 3 233 6701, *Email:* office@scua-ant.be

Societe Generale de Surveillance (SGS), SGS Belgium N.V., SGS House, Noorderlaan 87, B-2030 Antwerp, Belgium, *Tel:* +32 3 545 4490, *Fax:* +32 3 545 4479, *Email:* dirk.hellesmans@sgs.com, *Website:* www.sgs.com

Sparks Surveyors N.V., 29 Noorderlaan, B-2030 Antwerp, Belgium, *Tel:* +32 3 646 3560, *Fax:* +32 3 646 4064, *Email:* info@sparks-surveyors.com, *Website:* www.sparks-surveyors.com

Touw-Jansen N.V., North Trade Building, Noorderlaan 133, B-2030 Antwerp, Belgium, *Tel:* +32 3 542 1444, *Fax:* +32 3 542 4667, *Email:* antouw-info@pophost.eunet.be

Van Ameyde International B.V., N.V. Bureau Van Ameyde, Burcht Singelberg, Blok C, Ketenislaan 1 - Antwerpen Haven, B-9130 Kallo, Belgium, *Tel:* +32 3 216 4990, *Fax:* +32 3 216 4996, *Email:* antwerpen@ameydemarine.be, *Website:* www.vanameyde.com

Van Sluys & Bayet N.V., Haven 505, Kruisschansweg 11, B-2040 Antwerp 4, Belgium, *Tel:* +32 3 543 9080, *Fax:* +32 3 543 9085, *Email:* HSmitz_VSB@its-belgium.be

Medical Facilities: Medical attention available at port facilities. All hospital facilities in the city

Airport: Deurne Airport

Development: Work has started on deepening of the Westerschelde, the River Scheldt estuary through to the Belgium/Netherlands border, that will eventually allow containerships up to 12 000 TEU's to sail unhindered to the Port of Antwerp. The third deepening of the Westerschelde will see a min guaranteed water depth of 14.7 m, which will allow for ships with a draught of 13.1 m. Currently, the max draught limit is 11.5 m

Lloyd's Agent: N.V. Beeckman De Vos, Stijfselrui 44 / b.5, B-2000 Antwerp, Belgium, *Tel:* +32 3 201 1250, *Fax:* +32 3 231 5599, *Email:* info@bdv.be

BECO DOCK

harbour area, see under Brussels

BRUGES

Lat 51° 13' N; Long 3° 13' E.

Admiralty Chart: 1874   **Admiralty Pilot:** 28
Time Zone: GMT +1 h   **UNCTAD Locode:** BE BGS

Principal Facilities:

P		Y	G			B		A

Authority: Port Authority Bruges-Zeebrugge (MBZ) N.V., P. Vandammehuis, Isabellalaan 1, B-8380 Zeebrugge, Belgium, *Tel:* +32 50 543211, *Fax:* +32 50 543224, *Email:* mbz@zeebruggeport.be, *Website:* www.portofzeebrugge.be

Officials: Chairman: Joachim Coens, *Tel:* +32 50 543215, *Email:* jc@mbz.be. Harbour Master: Alain Van Mullem, *Tel:* +32 50 543341, *Email:* avm@mbz.be.

Port Security: ISPS compliant

Accommodation: Baudouin Canal, from bridge at Dudzele to entrance of West Dock is 4.95 km long with 7 m depth
Tanker facilities: Privately owned terminals for vessels with a max width of 28 m and a max d of 6.75 m

Name	Length (m)	Depth (m)
East Dock		
Quenastkaai No's 921, 922 & 923	389	8
Kaap Hoornkaai No's 924 & 925	228	8
Albertakaai No.926	148	8
West Dock		
Graaf Visartkaai No's 927, 928 & 929	315	8
Julius Sabbekaai	520	8
Industrial Dock	1080	5
Junction Lock	115	4

Storage: Port Authority: One shed of 1500 m2 and 25 ha of open storage. Private: Six sheds totalling 20 500 m2

Mechanical Handling Equipment:

Location	Type	Capacity (t)	Qty
Bruges	Mult-purp. Cranes	5	4
Bruges	Mult-purp. Cranes	30	5

Bunkering: Available by trucks or barges

Repair & Maintenance: Small repairs can be arranged

Airport: Ostend Airport, 30 km

Lloyd's Agent: N.V. Beeckman De Vos, Stijfselrui 44 / b.5, B-2000 Antwerp, Belgium, *Tel:* +32 3 201 1250, *Fax:* +32 3 231 5599, *Email:* info@bdv.be

BRUSSELS

Lat 50° 49' N; Long 4° 18' E.

Admiralty Chart: 139   **Admiralty Pilot:** 28
Time Zone: GMT +1 h   **UNCTAD Locode:** BE BRU

Principal Facilities:

		G		B		T	A

Authority: Port de Bruxelles-Haven van Brussel, Place des Armateurs 6, B-1000 Brussels, Belgium, *Tel:* +32 2 420 6700, *Fax:* +32 2 420 6974, *Email:* portdebruxelles@port.irisnet.be, *Website:* www.portdebruxelles.irisnet.be

Officials: Managing Director: Charles Huygens, *Email:* chuygens@port.irisnet.be. Marketing Manager: Genevieve Origer, *Email:* goriger@port.irisnet.be. Harbour Master: Luc Delprat, *Email:* ldelprat@port.irisnet.be.

Port Security: ISPS compliant

Approach: There are two large sea locks on the maritime canal, the first being the Wintam lock which connects directly with the Scheldt river and the second being the Zemst lock which is located midway along the canal. From the Wintam sea lock to Brussels outer port is 32 km for vessels up to 4500 t

Pilotage: Compulsory on the canal and available from Antwerp

Radio Frequency: Wintam and Zemst locks, VHF Channel 68

Working Hours: 0800-1600

Accommodation:

Name	Depth (m)	Remarks
Vergote Dock		121.4 ha, 1 km long, 119.78 m broad, 6.48 m deep
Quai des Steamers		Breadth of 74.97 m. Railway connections
Quai des Armateurs		Breadth of 74.97 m. Railway connections
Beco Dock		See [1] below
Quai des Materiaux	6.5	Connected by rail with maritime station
Avant Port		See [2] below

[1]*Beco Dock:* Connecting port with Brussels-Charleroi canal, length 728.2 m, breadth 42.4 m, depth 3.5 m
[2]*Avant Port:* 2.1 km of quays, a two-storey warehouse 200 m in length. Eleven electric cranes from 3 t to 10 t. Railway lines connect with Schaerbeek Station

Storage: Public warehouse of five storeys (T.I.R. Complex), 179.8 m long, 59.73 m broad

Mechanical Handling Equipment:

Location	Type	Capacity (t)	Qty
Quai des Steamers	Mult-purp. Cranes	10	7
Quai des Armateurs	Mult-purp. Cranes	4	5

Key to Principal Facilities:—				
A=Airport	**C**=Containers	**G**=General Cargo	**P**=Petroleum	**R**=Ro/Ro	**Y**=Dry Bulk
B=Bunkers	**D**=Dry Dock	**L**=Cruise	**Q**=Other Liquid Bulk	**T**=Towage (where available from port)	

Bunkering: Petrofina S.A., 52 Rue de l'Industrie, B-1040 Brussels, Belgium, *Tel:* +32 2 2339111, *Fax:* +32 2 2882445

Texaco Belgium N.V., 25 Avenue Arnaud Fraiteur, B-1050 Brussels, Belgium, *Tel:* +32 2 6399 111, *Fax:* +32 2 6399 911, *Email:* sara.muef@d-bnl.be, *Website:* www.d-bnl.be

Total Belgium, Handelsstraat 93, Rue de Commerce, 1040 Brussels, Belgium, *Tel:* +32 2 2889 254, *Fax:* +32 2 2889 962, *Email:* rm.be-mkt-marine-fuels-arazone@total.com, *Website:* www.total.com

Belgian Shell S.A., Avenue Arnaud Fraiteur 15, 1050 Brussels, Belgium, *Tel:* +32 2 5089 111, *Fax:* +32 2 5110 571, *Email:* joris.bosschaert@shell.com, *Website:* www.shell.be

Waste Reception Facilities: Garbage disposal available

Towage: Available from private companies

Shipping Agents: Kennedy Hunter N.V., Leon Monnoyerkaai 11, B-1000 Brussels, Belgium, *Tel:* +32 2 245 1500, *Fax:* +32 2 216 2088, *Email:* brussel@kennedy.be, *Website:* www.kennedy.be

Stevedoring Companies: Ceres S.A., Av. de Vilvorde 300, B-1130 Brussels, Belgium, *Tel:* +32 2 240 0600, *Fax:* +32 2 242 4390, *Email:* ceres@ceres.be, *Website:* www.ceres.be

Smet S.A., Quai L. Monnoyer 11, B-1000 Brussels, Belgium, *Tel:* +32 2 245 4030, *Fax:* +32 2 245 2455, *Email:* info@smet.biz

Surveyors: Bureau Veritas, Building 6 - 2nd Floor, Boulevard Paepsem 22, B-1070 Brussels, Belgium, *Tel:* +32 2 520 2090, *Fax:* +32 2 520 2030, *Email:* bvqi@be.bureauveritas.com, *Website:* www.bureauveritas.com

Medical Facilities: Local hospital

Airport: Zaventhem International Airport, 17 km

Lloyd's Agent: N.V. Beeckman De Vos, Stijfselrui 44 / b.5, B-2000 Antwerp, Belgium, *Tel:* +32 3 201 1250, *Fax:* +32 3 231 5599, *Email:* info@bdv.be

BRUSSELS-SCHELDT SEA CANAL

Admiralty Chart: 120/139/1874   **Admiralty Pilot:** 28
Time Zone: GMT +1 h   **UNCTAD Locode:** BE

Authority: Waterwegen en Zeekanaal N.V., Oostdijk 110, B-2830 Willebroek, Belgium, *Tel:* +32 3 860 6211, *Fax:* +32 3 860 6278, *Email:* info@wenz.be, *Website:* www.wenz.be

Officials: Managing Director: Leo Clinckers, *Tel:* +32 3 860 6274, *Email:* leo.clinckers@wenz.be.

Commercial Manager: Lut Verschingel, *Tel:* +32 3 860 6331, *Email:* lut.verschingel@wenz.be.

Harbour Master: Capt F.G. Norbert Van Hoecke, *Tel:* +32 3 860 6294, *Email:* norbert.vanhoecke@wenz.be.

Port Security: Nieuwe Zeesluis Wintam Lock is ISPS compliant. Ship ISPS compliance questionnaire should be sent to: Fax: +32 2 233 7628 or Email: ispsbelgium.reg9@minfin.fed.be

Documentation: Clearance can be effected whilst the ship is at anchor, awaiting the tide at Oosterweel Anchorage (Antwerp Roads). The following forms are required for port clearance:
crew list (2 copies)
ship's stores/bonded stores list/crew declaration (1 copy)
tonnage certificate (1 copy)

Approach: Flushing & Antwerp Roads: It is possible to anchor at the Flushing Anchorage or at Oosterweel awaiting the tide. The ship then has to proceed upstream on the incoming tide, arriving at Wintam Locks at high water. The lock is situated just W of the point where the River Rupel flows into the River Scheldt. The lock is the access point to the Brussels-Scheldt Sea Canal which leads to Brussels
Wintam Lock: 250 m long with width of 25 m. Only wooden or standard fenders are allowed in the lock
Brussels-Scheldt Sea Canal to Berth: Before arriving at the berth the following bridges and lock are passed:
a) Nijverheidsbrug (Puurs) with max width 50 m and no airdraft limitation
b) Boulevardbrug (Willebroek) with max width 17.66 m and no airdraft limitation
c) Spoorbrug Willebroek with max width 19.9 m and no airdraft limitation
d) Vredesbrug with max width 35 m and max airdraft 32 m
e) Ringbrug (Expressbrug) Willebroek with max width 50 m and max airdraft 32 m
f) Hefbrug Tesselt (Willebroek) with max width 35 m and max airdraft 32 m
g) Jan Bogaertbrug (Kapelle op den Bos) with max width 44 m and no airdraft limitation
h) Sluis Zemst (Lock) with max length of 205 m and max width of 24 m (depending on ship's loa and traffic, the lock can be divided into two parts using only one part with max length of 96 m)
i) Hefbrug Humbeek Sas with max width 35 m and max airdraft 32 m
j) Hefbrug Grimbergen (Verbrande Brug) with max width 35 m and max airdraft 32 m

Pilotage: Compulsory. Pilot to be ordered at least 2 h in advance via Nieuwe Zeesluis Wintam (lock), Fax: +32 3 860 6306, Email: sluismeesters.wintam@wenz.be

Radio Frequency: VHF Channels 10, 20 and 68

Maximum Vessel Dimensions: From Nieuwe Zeesluis Wintam to Ruisbroek: max loa 180 m, max beam 23.5 m, max draft 8.5 m (depending on berth) and max airdraft 48 m
From Ruisbroek to Spoorbrug Willebroek: max loa 140 m, max beam 16.5 m, max draft 6 m (depending on berth) and max airdraft 32 m
From Spoorbrug Willebroek to Brussels: max loa 140 m, max beam 16.5 m, max draft 5.8 m (depending on berth) and max airdraft 32 m

Accommodation:

Name	Length (m)	Depth (m)	Remarks
Brussels-Scheldt Sea Canal			
Quay BVBA Mark de Smedt	195	6	See [1] below

Name	Length (m)	Depth (m)	Remarks
Quay Denayer Papier NV/CMI	200	4–5.5	See [2] below
New Quay G&G International NV	236	6	See [3] below
Passenger Quay Willebroek	58	4.5	See [4] below
Quay 3 Fonteinen	133	2.8	See [5] below
Quay Alural-Clijmans	110	4.5	See [6] below
Quay Maxit-Bel NV	158	5.5	See [7] below
Belgian Oil Storage	540	2.8	See [8] below
Belgian Scrap Terminal NV	350	3.5–5.5	See [9] below
Quay Binst	88	5.5	See [10] below
Quay Bos van AA	97	3.5	See [11] below
Quay Calandro	360	2.5–4	See [12] below
Quay DD Shipping NV Grimbergen	215	6	See [13] below
Quay DD Shipping NV Puurs/ex Grace	201	9	See [14] below
Quay de Wip	301	4.5	See [15] below
Quay Deckx NV	114	4.5	See [16] below
Quay Eternit Platenafdeling	206	6.5	See [17] below
Quay G&G International NV	122	4	See [18] below
Quay Hessenatie Logistics-IBO (Cargovil Container Terminal)	150	5.5	See [19] below
Quay Intershipping NV	200	9	See [20] below
Quay Hellegat	346	8.5–9	See [21] below
Quay Kanaalbus	81	3	See [22] below
Quay Kemira	236	6.5	See [23] below
Quay Koekoekx Gebroeders NV	857	2.5	See [24] below
Quay Matramat NV	139	6	See [25] below
Quay Mouterij Albert NV	580	6.5–7	See [26] below
Quay Parmentier	121	4.5	See [27] below
Quay Prebeton NV	179	5.5	See [28] below
Quay Promat International NV	140	6	See [29] below
RCT Verbeke NV	300	2.5–9	See [30] below
Quay Prayon NV	600	6.5–8.5	See [31] below
Quay Star	140	6	See [32] below
Quay TCT Belgium NV	230	8	See [33] below
Quay Tessenderlo Chemie	310	2.5	See [34] below
Quay Total Belgium	166	5.5	See [35] below
Quay Valomac NV	201	6	See [36] below
Quay Van Gansewinkel NV	129	4.5	See [37] below
Quay Willebroek Beton NV	100	3.5	See [38] below
Quay Ex-Euro Union Metal	35	4.5	See [39] below
Quay Ex-Fontaines	219	2.6	See [40] below
Quay Wachtplaats Zemst Met Drinkwaterautomaat	224	4.2	See [41] below
Waiting Quay Willebroek	140	5	See [42] below
Waiting Quay Zemst	209	2.5–3	See [43] below
Waterwegen en Zeekanaal NV	156	4	See [44] below

[1]*Quay BVBA Mark de Smedt:* In pos 50° 55' 50" N; 4° 24' 42" E. Operated by BVBA Mark de Smedt, Westvaartdijk 75, B-1850 Grimbergen, Tel: +32 2 252 0714, Fax: +32 2 252 1103

[2]*Quay Denayer Papier NV/CMI:* In pos 51° 03' 46" N; 4° 21' 52" E. Operated by Denayer Papier NV, Mechelsesteenweg 19, B-2830 Willebroek, Tel: +32 3 886 7101, Fax: +32 3 886 7110

[3]*New Quay G&G International NV:* In pos 51° 02' 39" N; 4° 21' 42" E. Operated by G&G International NV, Molenweg 109, B-2830 Willebroek, Tel: +32 3 860 2011, Fax: +32 3 886 5804

[4]*Passenger Quay Willebroek:* In pos 51° 03' 55" N; 4° 21' 51" E. Operated by Waterwegen en Zeekanaal NV, Afdeling Zeekanaal, Oostdijk 110, B-2830 Willebroek, Tel: +32 3 860 6270, Fax: +32 3 860 6278

[5]*Quay 3 Fonteinen:* In pos 50° 55' 19" N; 4° 25' 08" E. Operated by Waterwegen en Zeekanaal NV, Afdeling Zeekanaal, Oostdijk 110, B-2830 Willebroek, Tel: +32 3 860 6270, Fax: +32 3 860 6278

[6]*Quay Alural-Clijmans:* In pos 51° 02' 26" N; 4° 21' 35" E. Operated by Alural Belgium NV, J. De Blockstraat 69, B-2830 Willebroek, Tel: +32 3 860 7200, Fax: +32 3 886 0634

[7]*Quay Maxit-Bel NV:* In pos 50° 56' 57" N; 4° 24' 48" E. Operated by Maxit-Bel NV, Oostvaartdijk 10, B-1850 Grimbergen, Tel: +32 2 254 7854, Fax: +32 2 254 7855

[8]*Belgian Oil Storage:* In pos 50° 54' 45" N; 4° 24' 54" E. Operated by Van der Sluijs Groep NV, Wiedauwkaai 75, B-9000 Ghent, Tel: +32 9 257 0420

[9]*Belgian Scrap Terminal NV:* In pos 51° 04' 20" N; 4° 21' 51" E. Operated by Belgian Scrap Terminal NV, Boomsesteenweg 170, B-2830 Willebroek, Tel: +32 3 860 9480, Fax: +32 3 860 9485

[10]*Quay Binst:* In pos 50° 59' 32" N; 4° 22' 40" E. Operated by Waterwegen en Zeekanaal NV, Afdeling Zeekanaal, Oostdijk 110, B-2830 Willebroek, Tel: +32 3 860 6270, Fax: +32 3 860 6278

[11]*Quay Bos van AA:* In pos 50° 59' 13" N; 4° 23' 03" E. Operated by DD Shipping NV, Gentsesteenweg 1, B-9520 Vlierzele, Tel: +32 53 822211, Fax: +32 53 822214

[12]*Quay Calandro:* In pos 51° 01' 02" N; 4° 21' 56" E. Operated by Waterwegen en Zeekanaal NV, Afdeling Zeekanaal, Oostdijk 110, B-2830 Willebroek, Tel: +32 3 860 6270, Fax: +32 3 860 6278

[13]*Quay DD Shipping NV Grimbergen:* In pos 50° 56' 48" N; 4° 24' 53" E. Operated by DD Shipping NV, Gentsesteenweg 1, B-9520 Vlierzele, Tel: +32 53 822211, Fax: +32 53 822214

[14]*Quay DD Shipping NV Puurs/ex Grace:* In pos 51° 05' 24" N; 4° 20' 44" E. Operated by DD Shipping NV, Gentsesteenweg 1, B-9520 Vlierzele, Tel: +32 53 822211, Fax: +32 53 822214

[15]*Quay de Wip:* In pos 51° 06' 39" N; 4° 17' 56" E. Operated by Waterwegen en

Zeekanaal NV, Afdeling Zeekanaal, Oostdijk 110, B-2830 Willebroek, Tel: +32 3 860 6270, Fax: +32 3 860 6278

[16]*Quay Deckx NV:* In pos 51° 05' 02" N; 4° 21' 06" E. Operated by Deckx Algemene Ondernemingen NV, Goormansdijk 15, B-2480 Dessel, Tel: +32 14 377672, Fax: +32 14 377677

[17]*Quay Eternit Platenafdeling:* In pos 51° 00' 33" N; 4° 21' 55" E. Operated by Eternit NV, Kuiermanstraat 1, B-1880 Kapelle o/d Bos, Tel: +32 15 717171, Fax: +32 15 717179

[18]*Quay G&G International NV:* In pos 51° 02' 39" N; 4° 21' 42" E. Operated by G&G International NV, Molenweg 109, B-2830 Willebroek, Tel: +32 3 860 2011, Fax: +32 3 886 5804

[19]*Quay Hessenatie Logistics-IBO (Cargovil Container Terminal):* In pos 50° 56' 42" N; 4° 25' 21" E. Operated by Hessenatie Logistics, Schalienstraat 3, B-2000 Antwerp, Tel: +32 3 216 5900, Fax: +32 3 216 5990

[20]*Quay Intershipping NV:* In pos 51° 06' 01" N; 4° 18' 47" E. Operated by Intershipping NV, Beenhouwerstraat 1, B-2830 Heindonk, Tel: +32 3 886 5390, Fax: +32 3 886 0799

[21]*Quay Hellegat:* In pos 51° 05' 38" N; 4° 20' 15" E. Operated by Waterwegen en Zeekanaal NV, Afdeling Zeekanaal, Oostdijk 110, B-2830 Willebroek, Tel: +32 3 860 6270, Fax: +32 3 860 6278

[22]*Quay Kanaalbus:* In pos 50° 55' 33" N; 4° 25' 02" E. Operated by Waterwegen en Zeekanaal NV, Afdeling Zeekanaal, Oostdijk 110, B-2830 Willebroek, Tel: +32 3 860 6270, Fax: +32 3 860 6278

[23]*Quay Kemira:* In pos 51° 04' 40" N; 4° 21' 36" E. Operated by Fertura NV, Goormansdijk 9, B-2480 Dessel

[24]*Quay Koekoekx Gebroeders NV:* In pos 50° 55' 19" N; 4° 25' 12" E. Operated by Koekoekx Gebr., Steenkaai 39, B-1800 Vilvoorde, Tel: +32 2 251 6970, Fax: +32 2 251 6948

[25]*Quay Matramat NV:* In pos 51° 02' 56" N; 4° 21' 45" E. Operated by Matramat NV, Molenweg 102, B-2830 Willebroek, Tel: +32 3 866 5226, Fax: +32 3 866 5227

[26]*Quay Mouterij Albert NV:* In pos 51° 05' 29" N; 4° 20' 27" E. Operated by Mouterij Albert NV, Kanaaldijk, B-2870 Ruisbroek, Tel: +32 3 860 0411, Fax: +32 3 886 8399

[27]*Quay Parmentier:* In pos 50° 55' 45" N; 4° 24' 51" E. Operated by Hout Import Bois Cesar Parmentier NV, Houtkaai 10, B-1800 Vilvoorde, Tel: +32 2 216 0276, Fax: +32 2 245 3420

[28]*Quay Prebeton NV:* In pos 51° 03' 02" N; 4° 21' 47" E. Operated by Prebeton NV, Oostdijk 114, B-2830 Willebroek, Tel: +32 3 866 0167, Fax: +32 3 886 6178

[29]*Quay Promat International NV:* In pos 51° 01' 12" N; 4° 21' 39" E. Operated by Promat International NV, Bormstraat 24, B-2830 Tisselt, Tel: +32 15 718162, Fax: +32 15 718129

[30]*RCT Verbeke NV:* In pos 51° 04' 27" N; 4° 21' 48" E. Operated by RCT Verbeke NV, Boomsesteenweg 180, B-2830 Willebroek, Tel: +32 3 886 3711, Fax: +32 3 886 8235

[31]*Quay Prayon NV:* In pos 51° 05' 11" N; 4° 20' 53" E. Operated by Prayon NV, Gansbroekstraat 31, B-2870 Ruisbroek, Tel: +32 3 860 9200, Fax: +32 3 886 3083

[32]*Quay Star:* In pos 50° 56' 34" N; 4° 24' 60" E. Operated by Jan Stellaert NV, Brusselsesteenweg 26, B-1785 Brussegem, Tel: +32 2 460 1470, Fax: +32 2 460 3796

[33]*Quay TCT Belgium NV:* In pos 51° 04' 15" N; 4° 21' 58" E. Operated by TCT Belgium NV, Victor Dumonlaan 12, B-2830 Willebroek, Tel: +32 3 880 2700, Fax: +32 3 880 2718

[34]*Quay Tessenderlo Chemie:* In pos 50° 56' 22" N; 4° 24' 59" E. Operated by Tessenderlo Chemie, Marius Duchestraat 260, B-1800 Vilvoorde, Tel: +32 2 255 6211, Fax: +32 2 255 6334

[35]*Quay Total Belgium:* In pos 50° 57' 05" N; 4° 24' 43" E. Operated by Total Belgium, Handelsstraat 93, B-1040 Brussels, Tel: +32 2 288 9111

[36]*Quay Valomac NV:* In pos 50° 56' 10" N; 4° 24' 49" E. Operated by Valomac, Westvaartdijk 83Z, B-1850 Grimbergen, Tel: +32 2 253 2184, Fax: +32 2 253 2184

[37]*Quay Van Gansewinkel NV:* In pos 51° 05' 04" N; 4° 21' 10" E. Operated by Van Gansewinkel NV, Nijverheidsstraat 2, B-2870 Puurs, Tel: +32 70 223100, Fax: +32 70 223101

[38]*Quay Willebroek Beton NV:* In pos 51° 02' 18" N; 4° 21' 38" E. Operated by Willebroek Beton NV, Brielen 1, B-2830 Willebroek, Tel: +32 3 866 2166, Fax: +32 3 886 5768

[39]*Quay Ex-Euro Union Metal:* In pos 50° 55' 26" N; 4° 25' 10" E. Operated by Waterwegen en Zeekanaal NV, Afdeling Zeekanaal, Oostdijk 110, B-2830 Willebroek, Tel: +32 3 860 6270, Fax: +32 3 860 6278

[40]*Quay Ex-Fontaines:* In pos 50° 55' 00" N; 4° 25' 06" E. Operated by Waterwegen en Zeekanaal NV, Afdeling Zeekanaal, Oostdijk 110, B-2830 Willebroek, Tel: +32 3 860 6270, Fax: +32 3 860 6278

[41]*Quay Wachtplaats Zemst Met Drinkwaterautomaat:* In pos 50° 59' 32" N; 4° 22' 40" E. Operated by Waterwegen en Zeekanaal NV, Afdeling Zeekanaal, Oostdijk 110, B-2830 Willebroek, Tel: +32 3 860 6270, Fax: +32 3 860 6278

[42]*Waiting Quay Willebroek:* In pos 51° 04' 22" N; 4° 21' 58" E. Operated by Waterwegen en Zeekanaal NV, Afdeling Zeekanaal, Oostdijk 110, B-2830 Willebroek, Tel: +32 3 860 6270, Fax: +32 3 860 6278

[43]*Waiting Quay Zemst:* In pos 50° 59' 33" N; 4° 22' 40" E. Operated by Waterwegen en Zeekanaal NV, Afdeling Zeekanaal, Oostdijk 110, B-2830 Willebroek, Tel: +32 3 860 6270, Fax: +32 3 860 6278

[44]*Waterwegen en Zeekanaal NV:* In pos 51° 03' 09" N; 4° 21' 48" E. Operated by Waterwegen en Zeekanaal NV, Afdeling Zeekanaal, Oostdijk 110, B-2830 Willebroek, Tel: +32 3 860 6270, Fax: +32 3 860 6278

Bunkering: Available by truck or barge and arranged through ship agent

Waste Reception Facilities: Arranged via ship agent

Towage: Vessels with loa over 120 m require one tug
Vessels with beam over 17 m and a bowthruster require one tug
Vessels with beam over 17 m and no bowthruster require two tugs
Vessels with draft over 7 m and no bowthruster require two tugs
Vessels with draft over 7 m and a bowthruster require one tug
Tugs must be ordered at least 2 h in advance via Nieuwe Zeesluis Wintam, Fax: +32 3 860 6306, Email: sluismeesters.wintam@wenz.be

Lloyd's Agent: N.V. Beeckman De Vos, Stijfselrui 44 / b.5, B-2000 Antwerp, Belgium, *Tel:* +32 3 201 1250, *Fax:* +32 3 231 5599, *Email:* info@bdv.be

GENK

Lat 50° 56' N; Long 5° 30' E.

Admiralty Chart: -	**Admiralty Pilot:** -
Time Zone: GMT +1 h	**UNCTAD Locode:** BE GNK

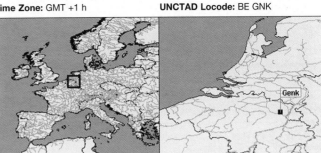

Principal Facilities:

		Y	G	C				

Authority: Haven Genk, Kolenhavenstraat 6, B-3600 Genk, Belgium, *Tel:* +32 89 300660, *Fax:* +32 89 300670, *Email:* info@havengenk.be, *Website:* www.havengenk.be

Officials: Chief Executive Officer: Paul Harmans, *Email:* paul.harmans@havengenk.be.
Commercial Manager: Michelle Neels, *Tel:* +32 89 360052, *Email:* michelle.neels@havengenk.be.
Harbour Master: Johan Harmans, *Tel:* +32 89 300674, *Email:* johan.harmans@havengenk.be.

Accommodation:

Name	Length (m)	Remarks
Genk Quay	500	See [1] below

[1]*Genk:* Bulk, general & container cargo handled. Terminal area of 7 ha. Storage cap of 5000 TEU's. Dedicated coal terminal. Three weighbridges

Storage:

Location	Open (m²)	Covered (m²)
Genk	10000	8000

Mechanical Handling Equipment:

Location	Type	Capacity (t)	Qty
Genk	Portal Cranes	50	1
Genk	Reach Stackers		3

Lloyd's Agent: N.V. Beeckman De Vos, Stijfselrui 44 / b.5, B-2000 Antwerp, Belgium, *Tel:* +32 3 201 1250, *Fax:* +32 3 231 5599, *Email:* info@bdv.be

GENT

alternate name, see Ghent

GHENT

Lat 51° 5' N; Long 3° 44' E.

Admiralty Chart: 120	**Admiralty Pilot:** 28
Time Zone: GMT +1 h	**UNCTAD Locode:** BE GNE

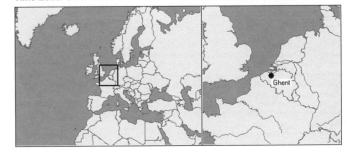

Principal Facilities:

P	Q	Y	G	C	R	L	B	D	T	A

Key to Principal Facilities:—

A=Airport	**C**=Containers	**G**=General Cargo	**P**=Petroleum	**R**=Ro/Ro	**Y**=Dry Bulk
B=Bunkers	**D**=Dry Dock	**L**=Cruise	**Q**=Other Liquid QL	**T**=Towage (where available from port)

Authority: Ghent Port Company AMC, John Kennedylaan 32, B-9042 Ghent, Belgium, *Tel:* +32 9 251 0550 & 251 0457, *Fax:* +32 9 251 5406 & 251 6062, *Email:* info@havengent.be, *Website:* www.portofghent.be

Officials: Chairman: Sas van Rouveroij, *Email:* sas.van.rouveroij@gent.be. General Manager: Eugeen van Craeyvelt, *Email:* e.vancraeyvelt@havengent.be. Commercial Director: Dirk Becquart, *Email:* d.becquart@havengent.be.

Port Security: ISPS compliant

Documentation: Crew list (2 copies), passenger list (1 copy), crew effects declaration (2 copies), bonded stores list (2 copies)
Upon arrival in Ghent the following documents are required:
Cargo documents
International tonnage certificate
Dangerous cargo declaration
All necessary ship documents for port state control

Approach: The canal from Terneuzen to Ghent has a length of 31 km (of which 15 km on Belgian territory), a width of 150-200 m and depth of 13.5 m. The sealock in Terneuzen has a length of 290 m, a width of 40 m and depth of 13.5 m

Pilotage: Available from official Ministry of Transport pilots, Loodswezen, Motorstraat 109, Ghent, Tel: +32 9 251 1759. Vessels bound for Ghent take on a sea pilot off the Belgian coast at the A1 buoy and proceed to Flushing. The sea pilot is then replaced by a canal pilot who conducts the vessel through the Western Scheldt and the sealock at Terneuzen to the port of Ghent

Radio Frequency: Port Radio, VHF Channels 11 and 5

Weather: Prevailing W winds

Tides: Ghent itself is a tideless, freshwater port

Traffic: 2007, 25 103 244 t of maritime cargo handled

Maximum Vessel Dimensions: Vessels with the following dimensions are allowed to enter the Terneuzen lock without restrictions: length 265 m by 34 m by 12.50 m draft; for vessels with draught over 11.75 m notice must be given to the Harbour Master of Terneuzen at least 24 h before arrival

Principal Imports and Exports: Imports: Cars, Coal, Grain, Iron ore, Minerals, Ro/ro cargo. Exports: Agribulk, Scrap & metal waste, Steel products.

Working Hours: Normal hours 0745-1130, 1330-1700. Overtime available with possibility of working on Saturdays, Sundays and holidays

Accommodation: SIFFERDOK: Handling and storage of bulk goods by C.B.M. N.V., Skaldenstraat 1, B-9042 Ghent, Tel: +32 9 255 0211, Fax: +32 9 259 0895, at quays 0900-0950
Storage, transhipment and processing of deep frozen fruit juice concentrates by Citrus Coolstore N.V., Alphonse Sifferdok 99, B-9000 Ghent, Tel: +32 9 255 9255, Fax: +32 9 251 4515, at quays 0980 and 0990 and by Louis Dreyfus Citrus Juice Terminal, Sifferdok Kaai 1010, B-9000 Ghent, Tel: +32 9 250 9195, Fax: +32 9 250 9198, Email: ldbelcitrus@louisdreyfus.com, at quay 1010
Storage and transhipment of cereals and derivatives by Euro-Silo N.V., John Kennedylaan 19, B-9000 Ghent, Tel: +32 9 251 2141, Fax: +32 9 251 6074, Email: info@eurosilo.be, Website: www.eurosilo.be, at quays 0965-0970
Handling of iron & steel products, motor vehicles, lo/lo, cereals, bagged goods, timber, paper pulp, containers and frozen products by Stukwerkers Havenbedrijf N.V., Port Arthurlaan 40, B-9000 Ghent, Tel: +32 9 251 2545, Fax: +32 9 251 6181, Email: hq@stukwerkers.com, Website: www.stukwerkers.com; Terminal 1 at quays 0830-0840 and Terminal 2 at quays 1000, 1030 & 1040
RODENHUIZEDOK: Storage and transhipment of cereals, seeds and derivatives by Euro-Silo N.V., Pleitstraat, B-9042 Ghent, Tel: +32 9 251 2141, Fax: +32 9 251 6074, Email: info@eurosilo.be, Website: www.eurosilo.be
Handling and storage of liquid bulk by Oiltanking Ghent N.V., Haven 4560A - Moervaartkaai 12, B-9042 Ghent, Tel: +32 9 342 2727, Fax: +32 9 342 2737, Email: commerce.belgium@oiltanking.com, Website: www.oiltanking.com, between Rodenhuizedok and Moervaart
GROOTDOK, NOORDDOK, MIDDENDOK & ZUIDDOK: Handling and storage of bulk goods by C.B.M. N.V., Skaldenstraat 1, B-9042 Ghent, Tel: +32 9 255 0211, Fax: +32 9 259 0895, at Zuiddok quays 0440-0470, at Middendok quays 0560-0580 and 0630-0650 and at Noorddok quays 0660-0745
Drying, pulverizing and breaking of minerals, manganese ore and screening and breaking of calcinated petroleum coke by Ensagent N.V., De Farmanstr 39, B-9000 Ghent, Tel: +32 9 251 1335, Fax: +32 9 251 6461 at Middendok quays 0550-0570
Handling of sand and gravel and other bulk goods by Georges Kesteleyn N.V., Zuiddokweg 430, B-9000 Ghent, Tel: +32 9 223 2981, Fax: +32 9 233 0509, at Zuiddok quays 0410-0430
Transhipment, transport and storage of agricultural products and general cargo by Ghent Transport & Storage N.V., Tel: +32 9 251 6464, Fax: +32 9 251 1052, at Middendok quays 0600-0620
Import and export of glues and storage, transhipment and distribution of liquids and solids by Sea Tank Terminal N.V., Middendok Kaai 540, B-9000 Ghent, Tel: +32 9 255 5666, Fax: +32 9 255 5660, at Zuiddok quays 0480-0510, at Grootdok quays 0520-0530 and at Middendok quay 0540
Handling and storage of bulk cargo by Manuport N.V., Port Arthurlaan 172, B-9000 Ghent, Tel: +32 9 218 2509, Fax: +32 9 251 0184, at Grootdok quays 0270-0290

Handling of iron & steel products, motor vehicles, ro/ro, lo/lo, cereals, bagged goods, logs, timber, paper pulp, containers and frozen products by Stukwerkers Havenbedrijf N.V., Port Arthurlaan 40, B-9000 Ghent, Tel: +32 9 251 2545, Fax: +32 9 251 6181, Email: hq@stukwerkers.com, Website: www.stukwerkers.com, at Grootdok quays 0290, 0300, 0310, 0335, 0340, 0345, 0350 & 0360
MERCATORDOK: Ro/ro terminal DFDS Tor Line, Doornzelestraat 71, B-9000 Ghent, Tel: +32 9 269 1260, Fax: +32 9 233 5016, Website: www.dfdstorline.com, at quays 2120-2220
Handling of iron & steel products, motor vehicles, ro/ro, lo/lo, cereals, bagged goods, logs, timber, paper pulp, containers and frozen products by Stukwerkers Havenbedrijf N.V., Port Arthurlaan 40, B-9000 Ghent, Tel: +32 9 251 2545, Fax: +32 9 251 6181, Email: hq@stukwerkers.com, Website: www.stukwerkers.com, at quays 2020-2110 and handling of containers by Intermodal Platform Ghent N.V., Tel: +32 9 255 9790, Fax: +32 9 218 5363, at quays 2030-2040

Name	Length (m)	Depth (m)	Remarks
Ghent			See [1] below
Sifferdok	4741	12.5–13.5	See [2] below
Rodenhuizedok	790	13.5	See [3] below
Grootdok, Noorddok, Middendok & Zuiddok	6856	13	See [4] below
Mercatordok	1813	13.5	See [5] below
Seacanal			See [6] below

[1]*Ghent:* Other docks have depths of water from 3.5 m to 7 m but are less used for maritime navigation. Barge traffic is an important aspect of the port through the European canal system
[2]*Sifferdok:* This dock offers facilities for grain and derivatives; storage for bulk cargoes such as pyrites, coal, ores, phosphates etc. There is also equipment for handling fertilisers, storage for deep frozen fruit juice and containers can be handled. Four grain elevators up to 700 t/h and four grain loading towers up to 1000 t/h and three spiral conveyors
[3]*Rodenhuizedok:* This dock is mainly used for grain and derivatives and also for tanker operations where there are two jetties for tankers up to 80 000 dwt. Equipment includes three grain elevators up to 700 t/h, three loading towers of 800 t/h and a mobile crane of 1600 t/h cap
[4]*Grootdok, Noorddok, Middendok & Zuiddok:* General cargo docks but also specialised berths for handling fertilisers, cement, liquid non petroleum products and ro/ro operations. Reefer sheds with cap of 76 000 m3. Equipment also includes two spiral conveyors for loading
[5]*Mercatordok:* Multi-purpose dock consisting of steel and forest products, Honda car terminal, Ro/ro Terminal and inland container terminal IPG (Intermodal Platform Ghent)
[6]*Seacanal:* Quay length of 4097 m in depth of 13.5 m and 185 m in depth of 8.75 m. As well as linking the port to the sea, this section also acts partly as an industrial dock, serving private industries established along the bank of the canal. Several chemical plants are established along the canal as well as a steel plant with an ore and coal terminal of 1 150 000 t storage cap. Another coal terminal with storage cap of 3 000 000 t is situated on the right bank

Storage: Open storage of 78 ha and liquid products storage of 800 000 m3

Location	Covered (m3)	Grain (t)	Cold (m3)
Ghent	173000	1220000	76000

Mechanical Handling Equipment:

Location	Type	Capacity (t)	Qty
Ghent	Floating Cranes	25	1
Sifferdok	Mult-purp. Cranes	35	2
Sifferdok	Mult-purp. Cranes	10	4
Grootdok, Noorddok, Middendok & Zuiddok	Mult-purp. Cranes	35	2
Grootdok, Noorddok, Middendok & Zuiddok	Mult-purp. Cranes	40	1
Grootdok, Noorddok, Middendok & Zuiddok	Mult-purp. Cranes	5	2
Grootdok, Noorddok, Middendok & Zuiddok	Mult-purp. Cranes	8	4
Grootdok, Noorddok, Middendok & Zuiddok	Mobile Cranes		7
Mercatordok	Mobile Cranes		1
Seacanal	Mult-purp. Cranes	7	1
Seacanal	Mult-purp. Cranes	35	1
Seacanal	Mult-purp. Cranes	25	2
Seacanal	Mult-purp. Cranes	20	2
Seacanal	Mult-purp. Cranes	12	3
Seacanal	Mult-purp. Cranes	3	1

Bunkering: Full bunkering facilities are available from several companies, delivery by barge or road tanker
Associated Bunkeroil Contractors N.V., P.de Smet de Nayerplein 8, 9000 Ghent, Belgium, *Tel:* +32 10 436 0533, *Fax:* +32 10 436 0439, *Email:* info@abc-house.com
Associated Bunkeroil Contractors N.V., P.de Smet de Nayerplein 8, 9000 Ghent, Belgium, *Tel:* +32 10 436 0533, *Fax:* +32 10 436 0439, *Email:* info@abc-house.com
Atlas Bunkering Services BVBA, Beethovenlaan 105C, 3335 BE Zwijndrecht, Belgium, *Tel:* +32 3 205 6550, *Fax:* +32 3 205 6555, *Email:* atlasbunkering@pandora.be
Belgian Trading & Bunkering BVBA, Madrasstraat 5, Haven 40, 2030 Antwerp,

Belgium, *Tel:* +32 3 229 9060, *Fax:* +32 3 233 3475, *Email:* mail@btb-bunkering.com, *Website:* www.btb-bunkering.com

Bominflot, Bominflot B.V., Zuurbes 5, 3069 NL Rotterdam, Netherlands, *Tel:* +31 10 2518 551, *Fax:* +31 10 2281 898, *Email:* bunkers@bominflot.nl, *Website:* www.bominflot.net

BP Belgium NV - BP Marine Fuels, Uitbreidingstraat 60-62, Quinten, 2600 Berchem, Belgium, *Tel:* +32 3 2868 254, *Fax:* +32 3 2866 299, *Email:* catherine.konings@bp.com, *Website:* www.bp.com

BP Marine Ltd, Building D, 1st Floor, Chertsey Road, Sunbury-on-Thames, Middlesex TW16 7LN, United Kingdom, *Tel:* +44 1932 762 000, *Fax:* +44 1932 739 001, *Email:* uk-fuels@bp.com, *Website:* www.bp.com

Calpam B.V., Waalhaven ZZ 12, 3088 HH Rotterdam, Netherlands, *Tel:* +31 10 217 1663, *Fax:* +31 10 412 3493, *Email:* info@calpam.nl, *Website:* www.calpam.nl

Ch de Wit N.V., Haven 40A, Madrasstraat 5, B-2030 Antwerp, Belgium, *Tel:* +32 3 2313 636, *Fax:* +32 3 2102 868, *Email:* info@dewit-bunkering.com, *Website:* www.dewit-bunkering.com

Chemoil Corp., Chemoil Europe B.V., Montevideo 5th Floor, Otto Reuchlinweg 1088, 3072 MD Rotterdam, Netherlands, *Tel:* +31 10 2929 933, *Fax:* +31 10 4829 190, *Email:* eumarketing@chemoil.com, *Website:* www.chemoil.com

Dynamic Oil Services N.V., Frankrijklei 37, P O Box 5, 2000 Antwerp, Belgium, *Tel:* +32 3 7072 685, *Fax:* +32 3 7072 688, *Email:* jmc.vander.heijden@hetnet.nl

ExxonMobil Marine Fuels, Mailpoint 31, ExxonMobil House, Ermyn Way, Leatherhead, Surrey KT22 8UX, United Kingdom, *Tel:* +44 1372 222 000, *Fax:* +44 1372 223 922, *Email:* marine.fuels@exxonmobil.com, *Website:* www.exxonmobil.com – *Grades:* IFO30-380cSt; MDO; MGO – *Delivery Mode:* barge

Frisol Bunkering B.V., Frisol B.V., Scheepmakerij 250, P O Box 160, 3330 MB Zwijndrecht, Netherlands, *Tel:* +31 78 6485 630, *Fax:* +31 78 6485 648, *Email:* bunkering@frisol.com, *Website:* www.frisol.com

Kinematic Energy B.V., Weena 290, 3012 NJ Rotterdam, Netherlands, *Tel:* 31 10, *Fax:* +31 10 282 1333, *Email:* bunkers@kinematic-energy.com

Oilchart International N.V., Plantinkaai 13, 2000 Antwerp, Belgium, *Tel:* +32 3 2325 234, *Fax:* +32 3 2336 745, *Email:* info@oilchart.com, *Website:* www.oilchart.com

Postoils B.V., P O Box 639, Pernis, 3195 ZG Rotterdam, Netherlands, *Tel:* +31 10 231 44 70, *Fax:* +31 10 485 89 35, *Email:* sales@postoils.nl, *Website:* www.postoils.nl

Texaco Belgium N.V., 25 Avenue Arnaud Fraiteur, B-1050 Brussels, Belgium, *Tel:* +32 2 6399 111, *Fax:* +32 2 6399 911, *Email:* sara.muef@d-bnl.be, *Website:* www.d-bnl.be

Total France S.A., Total Marine Fuels, 51 Esplanade du General de Gaulle, F-92907 Paris la Defense Cedex 10, France, *Tel:* +33 1 4135 2755, *Fax:* +33 1 4197 0291, *Email:* marine.fuels@total.com, *Website:* www.marinefuels.total.com – *Grades:* IFO30-380cSt – *Misc:* own storeage facilities, operates a refinery at Flushing – *Parcel Size:* min 25t – *Notice:* 24-48 hours – *Delivery Mode:* barge

Trefoil Trading B.V., Glashaven 49, 3011 XG Rotterdam, Netherlands, *Tel:* +31 10 4113 315, *Fax:* +31 10 4129 989, *Email:* bunkers@trefoil.nl

Van Stappen Bunkering Services N.V., Vosseschijnstraat Kaai 140, 2030 Antwerp, Belgium, *Tel:* +32 3 645 5298, *Fax:* +32 3 6416 375, *Email:* vanstappen@vanstappen.be, *Website:* www.vanstappen.be

Wiljo Energy, Wiljo NV, Amsterdamstraat 30, B-2000 Antwerp, Belgium, *Tel:* +32 3 232 3910, *Fax:* +32 3 232 5647, *Email:* wiljo@wiljo.be, *Website:* www.wiljo.be – *Grades:* all grades – *Delivery Mode:* barge

Waste Reception Facilities: Belgian Oil Services N.V., Haven 261, Blauwe Weg 7, B-2030 Antwerp, Belgium, *Tel:* +32 3 543 5959, *Fax:* +32 3 543 5960, *Email:* inform@bosserv.com, *Website:* www.bos-antwerp.com

Towage: Unie van Redding-en Sleepdienst Belgie N.V. (U.R.S.), Ghent, Belgium, *Tel:* +32 9 251 0553, *Fax:* +32 9 251 5690

Repair & Maintenance: Port Service BVBA, Wiedauwkaai 64B, B-9000 Ghent, Belgium, *Tel:* +32 9 258 2181, *Fax:* +32 9 258 0903, *Email:* info@portservice.be, *Website:* www.portservice.be Two dry docks available of 130 m by 13 m and 75 m by 11 m. All types of engine and hull repairs carried out

Ship Chandlers: Wells & Mommaerts N.V., Ham 225, B-9000 Ghent, Belgium, *Tel:* +32 9 223 9258, *Fax:* +32 9 225 6653, *Email:* stores@wells-mommaerts.be

Shipping Agents: Boeckmans Belgie N.V., Van Meterenkaai 1, P O Box 4, B-2000 Antwerp, Belgium, *Tel:* +32 3 202 0202, *Fax:* +32 3 202 0393, *Email:* info@boeckmans.be, *Website:* www.boeckmans.be Managing Director: Anthony Durot Email: anthony.durot@boeckmans.be

Agence Maritime Lalemant N.V., Lalemant Ghent N.V., Doornzelestraat 71, B-9000 Ghent, Belgium, *Tel:* +32 9 235 5611, *Fax:* +32 9 223 8499, *Email:* info@lalemant.com, *Website:* www.lalemant.com

Agro-Maas N.V., Voorhavenlaan 14T, B-9000 Ghent, Belgium, *Tel:* +32 9 345 8977, *Fax:* +32 9 345 7795, *Email:* logics5@agromaas.be, *Website:* www.agromaas.be

Cargill N.V., Moervaartkaai 1, B-9042 Ghent, Belgium, *Tel:* +32 9 342 2250, *Fax:* +32 9 345 5125, *Email:* cargillagency-belgium@cargill.com, *Website:* www.cargill.com

COBELFRET Port Agencies N.V., Farmanstraat 40, B-9000 Ghent, Belgium, *Tel:* +32 9 251 5262, *Fax:* +32 9 251 7972, *Email:* agency.gent@cobelfret.com, *Website:* www.cobelfret.com

DFDS Tor Line AB, Doornzelestraat 71, B-9000 Ghent, Belgium, *Tel:* +32 9 269 1260, *Fax:* +32 9 233 5016

Gans Transport BVBA, John Kennedylaan 31a, B-9042 Ghent, Belgium, *Tel:* +32 9 255 7879, *Fax:* +32 9 251 7885

Ghent Transport & Storage N.V., Henri Farmanstraat 43, Middendok Noord Kaaien 600-620, B-9000 Ghent, Belgium, *Tel:* +32 9 251 6464, *Fax:* +32 9 251 1052, *Email:* info@gtsghent.be, *Website:* www.gtsghent.be

Herfurth & Co. N.V., Stapelplein 38, B-9000 Ghent, Belgium, *Tel:* +32 9 269 0396, *Fax:* +32 9 269 0397

Kennedy Hunter N.V., Muidenpoort 30, B-9000 Ghent, Belgium, *Tel:* +32 9 251 3991, *Fax:* +32 9 251 3963, *Email:* gent@kennedy.be, *Website:* www.kennedy.be

Kesteleyn Georges N.V., Zuiddokweg 50, B-9000 Ghent, Belgium, *Tel:* +32 9 223 2981, *Fax:* +32 9 233 0509, *Email:* info@kesteleyn.be

Osterrieth Maritime Cy, Stapelplein 38, B-9000 Ghent, Belgium, *Tel:* +32 9 269 0396, *Fax:* +32 9 269 0397

Promar Agencies (Belgium) N.V., Alphonse Sifferlaan Haven 0850A, B-9000 Ghent, Belgium, *Tel:* +32 9 251 6363, *Fax:* +32 9 251 6123, *Email:* ghent@promar-agencies.be, *Website:* www.promar-agencies.be

SSM Coal Ltd, Pinksterbloemstraat 35, B-9030 Ghent, Belgium, *Tel:* +32 9 236 5030, *Fax:* +32 9 227 5167, *Email:* ghent@ssmcoal.com, *Website:* www.ssmcoal.com

Stukwerkers Havenbedrijf N.V., Port Arthurlaan 40, B-9000 Ghent, Belgium, *Tel:* +32

9 251 2545, *Fax:* +32 9 251 6181, *Email:* hq@stukwerkers.com, *Website:* www.stukwerkers.com

Vopak Agencies B.V., Pleitstraat 3, B-9042 Ghent, Belgium, *Tel:* +32 9 342 0000, *Fax:* +32 9 342 0001, *Email:* agencies.ghent@vopak.com, *Website:* www.vopak.com

Stevedoring Companies: Cargill N.V., Moervaartkaai 1, B-9042 Ghent, Belgium, *Tel:* +32 9 342 2250, *Fax:* +32 9 345 5125, *Email:* cargillagency-belgium@cargill.com, *Website:* www.cargill.com

C.B.M. N.V., Skaldenstraat 1, B-9042 Ghent, Belgium, *Tel:* +32 9 255 0211, *Fax:* +32 9 259 0895, *Email:* cdgent@sea-invest.be, *Website:* www.sea-invest.be

Ensagent N.V., Farmanstraat 39, B-9000 Ghent, Belgium, *Tel:* +32 9 255 0211, *Fax:* +32 9 259 0895, *Email:* ludo.de.nijs@sea-invest.be, *Website:* www.seainvest.be

Euro-Silo N.V., John Kennedylaan 19, B-9000 Ghent, Belgium, *Tel:* +32 9 251 2141, *Fax:* +32 9 251 6074, *Email:* info@eurosilo.be, *Website:* www.eurosilo.be

Ghent Coal Terminal N.V., Skaldenstraat 1, B-9042 Ghent, Belgium, *Tel:* +32 9 255 0211, *Fax:* +32 9 259 0895, *Email:* info@sea-invest.be, *Website:* www.sea-invest.be

Ghent Transport & Storage N.V., Henri Farmanstraat 43, Middendok Noord Kaaien 600-620, B-9000 Ghent, Belgium, *Tel:* +32 9 251 6464, *Fax:* +32 9 251 1052, *Email:* info@gtsghent.be, *Website:* www.gtsghent.be

Kesteleyn Georges N.V., Zuiddokweg 50, B-9000 Ghent, Belgium, *Tel:* +32 9 223 2981, *Fax:* +32 9 233 0509, *Email:* info@kesteleyn.be

Locachim N.V., Skaldenstraat 1, 9042 Ghent, Belgium, *Tel:* +32 9 255 5666, *Fax:* +32 9 255 5660, *Email:* info@sea-tankterminal.com, *Website:* www.sea-invest.be

Manuport N.V., Port Arthurlaan 172, B-9000 Ghent, Belgium, *Tel:* +32 9 218 2500, *Fax:* +32 9 218 2501, *Email:* info@manuportgroup.com, *Website:* www.manuportgroup.com

Oiltanking, Moervaartkaai 12, B-9042 Ghent, Belgium, *Tel:* +32 9 342 2727, *Fax:* +32 9 342 2737, *Email:* commerce.belgium@oiltanking.com, *Website:* www.oiltanking.com

Sea-Invest N.V., Skaldenstraat 1, B-9042 Ghent, Belgium, *Tel:* +32 9 255 0211, *Fax:* +32 9 259 0894, *Email:* cd-gent@sea-invest.be, *Website:* www.sea-invest.be

Stukwerkers Havenbedrijf N.V., Port Arthurlaan 40, B-9000 Ghent, Belgium, *Tel:* +32 9 251 2545, *Fax:* +32 9 251 6181, *Email:* hq@stukwerkers.com, *Website:* www.stukwerkers.com

Medical Facilities: Several hospitals in vicinity of port

Airport: Zaventem International Airport, 60 km

Railway: All quays are railway connected

Development: At the beginning of 2008 Ghent Container Terminal signed the concession contract with Ghent Port Company AMC for the construction and operation of a multimodal sea-going/inland navigation container terminal in the port of Ghent. It will be situated on the south side of the Kluizendok and take up a surface area of almost 16 ha that is being developed in two phases. Total capacity is expected to reach 300 000 TEU's/year. 240 m of quay are planned for the handling of inland vessels and 216 m of quay for short sea services. The terminal will be equipped with a railway connection in 2010. It will start up in October 2008

Lloyd's Agent: N.V. Beeckman De Vos, Stijfselrui 44 / b.5, B-2000 Antwerp, Belgium, *Tel:* +32 3 201 1250, *Fax:* +32 3 231 5599, *Email:* info@bdv.be

HEMIKSEM

Lat 51° 9' N; Long 4° 20' E.

| **Admiralty Chart:** - | **Admiralty Pilot:** 28 |
| **Time Zone:** GMT +1 h | **UNCTAD Locode:** BE HEX |

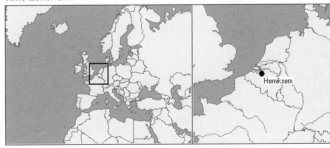

Principal Facilities:

P								A

Authority: Vopak Terminal Hemiksem, Terlochtweg 60-64, B-2620 Hemiksem, Belgium, *Tel:* +32 3 870 6240, *Fax:* +32 3 887 8665, *Email:* vth.terminal@vopak.com, *Website:* www.vopak.com

Officials: Terminal Manager: Rene Ruthgeerts, *Email:* rene.ruthgeerts@vopak.com.

Maximum Vessel Dimensions: 15 000 dwt (ocean-going), 9000 dwt (inland waterways), 174 m loa

Working Hours: 24 h/day on demand

Accommodation:

Name	Length (m)	Draught (m)	Remarks
Hemiksem Jetty	106	9.58	See [1] below

[1]*Jetty:* 'T' jetty with dolphins at either end for chemicals and lubricating oils. 77 storage tanks with cap of 107 000 m3

Airport: Deurne Airport

Lloyd's Agent: N.V. Beeckman De Vos, Stijfselrui 44 / b.5, B-2000 Antwerp, Belgium, *Tel:* +32 3 201 1250, *Fax:* +32 3 231 5599, *Email:* info@bdv.be

Key to Principal Facilities:—		
A=Airport	**C**=Containers	**G**=General Cargo
B=Bunkers	**D**=Dry Dock	**L**=Cruise
P=Petroleum	**R**=Ro/Ro	**Y**=Dry Bulk
Q=Other Liquid Bulk	**T**=Towage (where available from port)	

LIEGE

Lat 50° 38' N; Long 5° 34' E.

Admiralty Chart: -   **Admiralty Pilot:** -
Time Zone: GMT +1 h   **UNCTAD Locode:** BE LGG

Principal Facilities:

P		Y	G	C	R			A

Authority: Port Autonome de Liege, Quai de Maestricht 14, B-4000 Liege, Belgium, *Tel:* +32 4 232 9797, *Fax:* +32 4 223 1109, *Email:* portdeliege@skynet.be, *Website:* www.portdeliege.be

Officials: General Manager: Emile-Louis Bertrand.
Communications Manager: Helene Thiebaut, *Tel:* +32 4 232 9785, *Email:* h.thiebaut@portdeliege.be.

Port Security: ISPS compliant

Approach: Depth on Albert Canal from Antwerp to Liege is 3.4 m. Merksem bridge on Albert Canal, 6.7 m air draught and Arches bridge on River Meuse has 7 m air draught upon 26 m wide

Pilotage: Compulsory to Antwerp for all sea-going vessels, except for vessels in ballast drawing less than 2.2 m. Sea pilots are available from Wandelaar pilot station and Scheldt river pilot at Flushing Roads

Weather: Prevailing SW'ly winds

Traffic: 2007, 15 788 667 t of water traffic handled and 21 243 665 t of global traffic (rail, road and water) handled

Maximum Vessel Dimensions: Barges up to 2500 t, trains of tugged barges up to 4500 t and coasters up to 3000 t

Working Hours: Two shifts from 0600-2200

Accommodation:

Name	Remarks
Liege	See [1] below

[1]*Liege:* Liege Port Authority manages 31 public port areas (366 ha) along the River Meuse and Albert Canal
26 km of quayside including a container terminal at Renory with a 50 t gantry crane, a 50 t mobile crane and a 50 t forklift. Container shuttles to Antwerp and Rotterdam
Ro/ro quay at Seraing for loads up to 1200 t
Bulk facilities: All quays have facilities to load and discharge bulk cargoes. Also silos for storage of sand and gravel with cap of 60 000 t and for grain with cap of 50 000 m3
Tanker facilities: Oil terminal at Souverain-Wandre with an area of 59 ha. Nine wharves for tankers up to 2200 t. Storage tank cap of 200 000 m3
A covered dock - yacht marina with 130 berths

Storage:

Location	Covered (m²)	Sheds / Warehouses
Liege	115000	54

Shipping Agents: Somef S.A., Rue de l'Ile Monsin 87, B-4020 Liege, Belgium, *Tel:* +32 4 264 8430, *Fax:* +32 4 264 8539, *Email:* sales@somef.be, *Website:* www.somef.be

Medical Facilities: All medical facilities are available in Liege

Airport: Liege Airport, 10 km

Railway: Guillemins TGV Station, 5 km

Development: Liege Port Authority is developing a multimodal logistic park of 100 ha called 'Liege Trilogiport', located on the banks of the Albert Canal near the borders of Germany & the Netherlands. The multimodal platform of Liege Trilogiport will include the following facilities:
A container terminal of 15 ha
A quayside of 1750 m
Regular container shuttle to Antwerp and Rotterdam. Antwerp can be reached within 15 h sail / Rotterdam within 24 h navigation. Excellent connections to the European navigable network, railway network, road network. Customs services
The assets of Liege Trilogiport are highly important: connections with rail network and road network accessibility to push convoys up to 4 500 t and to coasters up to 2500 t. 56 million inhabitants within a radius of 250 km, 60% of the European purchasing power within a radius of 500 km. Strategic location near new Eastern European markets

Lloyd's Agent: N.V. Beeckman De Vos, Stijfselrui 44 / b.5, B-2000 Antwerp, Belgium, *Tel:* +32 3 201 1250, *Fax:* +32 3 231 5599, *Email:* info@bdv.be

NIEUWPOORT

Lat 51° 8' N; Long 2° 44' E.

Admiralty Chart: 1872/1873   **Admiralty Pilot:** 28
Time Zone: GMT +1 h   **UNCTAD Locode:** BE NIE

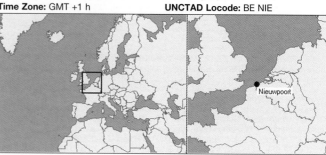

Principal Facilities:

		G		B		A

Authority: Afdeling Kust, Vrijhavenstraat 3, B-8400 Ostend, Belgium, *Tel:* +32 59 554211, *Fax:* +32 59 507037, *Email:* kust@vlaanderen.be, *Website:* www.afdelingkust.be

Officials: Managing Director: Bernard De Putter, *Tel:* +32 59 554207, *Email:* bernard.deputter@mow.vlaanderen.be.
Public Relations Manager: John Pauwels, *Tel:* +32 59 554202, *Email:* johnv.pauwels@mow.vlaanderen.be.
Harbour Master: Capt Ronald Kreps.

Approach: Harbour entrance formed by two parallel piers placed NW-SE, giving access to inner harbour through straight channel

Anchorage: Good anchorage available in roads

Pilotage: Compulsory for all vessels except those in ballast drawing less than 2.2 m. Pilot station at inner end of W Pier. VHF Channel 9

Tides: Tidal range 4-5 m

Traffic: 1997, 750 vessels

Maximum Vessel Dimensions: 5.4 m draft, 82 m loa

Accommodation:

Name	Remarks
Nieuwpoort	See [1] below

[1]*Nieuwpoort:* Commercial wharf 1200 m long in depth of 2.5 m for sand and gravel. Three yacht harbours with berths for approx 2000 yachts. Three locks at the head of the harbour giving access to the inland waterway system

Mechanical Handling Equipment:

Location	Type	Capacity (t)	Qty
Nieuwpoort	Mult-purp. Cranes	5	1
Nieuwpoort	Mult-purp. Cranes	3	1

Bunkering: Light and heavy gas oil available

Repair & Maintenance: Small repairs only

Medical Facilities: Hospital at Veurne, 10 km

Airport: Ostend Airport, 10 km

Railway: Veurne, 10 km. Ostend, 20 km

Lloyd's Agent: N.V. Beeckman De Vos, Stijfselrui 44 / b.5, B-2000 Antwerp, Belgium, *Tel:* +32 3 201 1250, *Fax:* +32 3 231 5599, *Email:* info@bdv.be

OOSTENDE

alternate name, see Ostend

OSTEND

Lat 51° 13' N; Long 2° 55' E.

Admiralty Chart: 1872/1873   **Admiralty Pilot:** 28
Time Zone: GMT +1 h   **UNCTAD Locode:** BE OST

Principal Facilities:

	Y	G	C	R	L	B		T	A

Authority: AG Haven Oostende, Slijkensesteenweg 2, B-8400 Ostend, Belgium, *Tel:* +32 59 340711, *Fax:* +32 59 340710, *Email:* info@portofoostende.be, *Website:* www.portofoostende.be

Officials: Managing Director: Paul Gerard, *Email:* paul.gerard@portofoostende.be. Marketing Manager: Patrick De Bruyne, *Email:* patrick.debruyne@portofoostende.be.
Harbour Master: Capt Ronald Kreps, *Email:* harbour.master@portofoostende.be.

Port Security: ISPS compliant. PFSO: Ronald Kreps, Email: harbour.master@portofoostende.be

Pilotage: Compulsory

Radio Frequency: Traffic control on VHF Channel 09

Tides: Tidal range of 4-5 m in outer harbour

Traffic: 2006, 7 812 375 t of cargo handled, 231 364 passengers

Maximum Vessel Dimensions: 130 m loa, 7.2 m draft. Larger vessels up to 160 m loa and 8.5 m draft may be accepted upon advice from pilot/harbour master

Principal Imports and Exports: Imports: Clay, Coal, Containers, Ro/ro, Sand, Wood. Exports: Containers, Ro/ro.

Working Hours: 1st Shift: 0600-1000, 1030-1346. Day Shift: 0800-1200, 1230-1546. 2nd Shift: 1400-1800, 1830-2146. 3rd Shift: 2200-0200, 0230-0546

Accommodation:

Name	Length (m)	Depth (m)	Draught (m)	Remarks
Outer Harbour				
Deepwater Quay (Berth No's 204-206)	360	8–12		
Cockerill Quay (Berth No's 201-203)	320	10–14	10	
Oosteroever				
Berth 602	120	5.5–9.5		Containers
Natien Quay				
Berth 101	120	5.8–9.8		Fast ferry berth
Berth 102	130	5.8–9.8		
Berth 103-104	250	8–12		Cruise vessels
Berth 105	165	7.5–11.5		Ro/ro berth with side loader
Zeewezen Dock				Turning basin of 250 m diameter
Berth 501	190	8–12		Ro/ro berth
Berth 502	170	8–12		Ro/ro berth
Berth 503	110	5.6–9.3		Containers
Inner Harbour				See [1] below
Vlotdock (Berth No's 301-310)	1250	7–8	7.2	
Houtdock & Zwaaidock (Berth No's 311-324)	910	7	7.2	
Canal (Berth No's 700-770)				See [2] below

[1] *Inner Harbour:* Lock Derney (VHF Channel 10) 128 m long, 18 m breadth, 4.5 m depth MLWS, for vessels up to 124 m loa, 17.4 m wide and 7.2 m draft. Conterdam bridge between Vlotdock and Houtdock, 18 m wide
[2] *Canal (Berth No's 700-770):* Via Doksluis (VHF Channel 10): for vessels up to 110 m loa, 17 m beam & 5.4 m draft

Storage: Open and covered storage available, no refrigerated space

Mechanical Handling Equipment:

Location	Type	Capacity (t)	Qty
Ostend	Mult-purp. Cranes	8	3
Ostend	Container Cranes	100	1

Bunkering: All kinds of fuel can be delivered
Associated Bunkeroil Contractors N.V., P.de Smet de Nayerplein 8, 9000 Ghent, Belgium, *Tel:* +32 10 436 0533, *Fax:* +32 10 436 0439, *Email:* info@abc-house.com
Atlas Bunkering Services BVBA, Van Noortstraat 10, B-2018 Antwerp, Belgium, *Tel:* +32 3 2056550, *Fax:* +32 3 2056555, *Email:* atlasbunkering@pandora.be, *Website:* www.atlasbunkering.com
Bominflot, Bominflot B.V., Zuurbes 5, 3069 NL Rotterdam, Netherlands, *Tel:* +31 10 2518 551, *Fax:* +31 10 2281 898, *Email:* bunkers@bominflot.nl, *Website:* www.bominflot.net
BP Belgium NV - BP Marine Fuels, Uitbreidingstraat 60-62, Quinten, 2600 Berchem, Belgium, *Tel:* +32 3 2868 254, *Fax:* +32 3 2866 299, *Email:* catherine.konings@bp.com, *Website:* www.bp.com
ExxonMobil Marine Fuels, Mailpoint 31, ExxonMobil House, Ermyn Way, Leatherhead, Surrey KT22 8UX, United Kingdom, *Tel:* +44 1372 222 000, *Fax:* +44 1372 223 922, *Email:* marine.fuels@exxonmobil.com, *Website:* www.exxonmobil.com – *Grades:* IFO30-380cSt; MDO; MGO; In line blending available – *Delivery Mode:* barge, truck
Oilchart International N.V., Plantinkaai 13, 2000 Antwerp, Belgium, *Tel:* +32 3 2325 234, *Fax:* +32 3 2336 745, *Email:* info@oilchart.com, *Website:* www.oilchart.com
Texaco Belgium N.V., 25 Avenue Arnaud Fraiteur, B-1050 Brussels, Belgium, *Tel:* +32 2 6399 111, *Fax:* +32 2 6399 911, *Email:* sara.muef@d-bnl.be, *Website:* www.d-bnl.be
Total Belgium, Handelsstraat 93, Rue de Commerce, 1040 Brussels, Belgium, *Tel:* +32 2 2889 254, *Fax:* +32 2 2889 962, *Email:* rm.be-mkt-marine-fuels-arazone@total.com, *Website:* www.total.com
Wiljo Energy, Wiljo NV, Amsterdamstraat 30, B-2000 Antwerp, Belgium, *Tel:* +32 3 232 3910, *Fax:* +32 3 232 5647, *Email:* wiljo@wiljo.be, *Website:* www.wiljo.be

Waste Reception Facilities: Oil and garbage disposal available

Towage: Two tugs available up to 30 t bollard pull from OSMA N.V.

Repair & Maintenance: All types of deck and engine repairs available

Ship Chandlers: General Stores N.V., Zandvoordestraat 492, B-8400 Ostend, Belgium, *Tel:* +32 59 702503, *Fax:* +32 59 808810, *Email:* info@generalstores.be

Shipping Agents: Ferryways N.V., Esplanadestraat 10, B-8400 Ostend, Belgium, *Tel:* +32 59 342220, *Fax:* +32 59 342229, *Email:* info@ferryways.be, *Website:* www.ferryways.com

Stevedoring Companies: Searoad Stevedores, Esplanadestraat 10, B-8400 Ostend, Belgium, *Tel:* +32 59 342220, *Fax:* +32 59 342229, *Email:* commercial@ferryways.be, *Website:* www.ferryways.com
Ter Polder N.V., Zwaaidok 2, B-8400 Ostend, Belgium, *Tel:* +32 59 331133, *Fax:* +32 59 331433, *Email:* agency@terpolder.be, *Website:* www.terpolder.be

Medical Facilities: Three main hospitals available in Ostend

Airport: Ostend Airport, 10 km

Railway: Railway station in the port next to the cruise berth

Development: In the Outer Harbour Berths 607-609 are being reconstructed for the purpose of a new aggregates terminal to be operated by NHM N.V.

Lloyd's Agent: N.V. Beeckman De Vos, Stijfselrui 44 / b.5, B-2000 Antwerp, Belgium, *Tel:* +32 3 201 1250, *Fax:* +32 3 231 5599, *Email:* info@bdv.be

VERGOTE DOCK

harbour area, see under Brussels

ZEEBRUGGE

Lat 51° 19' N; Long 3° 12' E.

Admiralty Chart: 1872/1874   **Admiralty Pilot:** 28
Time Zone: GMT +1 h   **UNCTAD Locode:** BE ZEE

Principal Facilities:

P	Q	Y	G	C	R	L	B		T	A

Authority: Port Authority Bruges-Zeebrugge (MBZ) N.V., P. Vandammehuis, Isabellalaan 1, B-8380 Zeebrugge, Belgium, *Tel:* +32 50 543211, *Fax:* +32 50 543224, *Email:* mbz@zeebruggeport.be, *Website:* www.portofzeebrugge.be

Officials: Chairman: Joachim Coens, *Tel:* +32 50 543215, *Email:* jc@mbz.be. Harbour Master: Alain Van Mullem, *Tel:* +32 50 543341, *Email:* avm@mbz.be.

Port Security: ISPS compliant. Container Security Initiative (CSI) designated port

---

Key to Principal Facilities:—
A=Airport   **C**=Containers   **G**=General Cargo   **P**=Petroleum   **R**=Ro/Ro   **Y**=Dry Bulk
B=Bunkers   **D**=Dry Dock   **L**=Cruise   **Q**=Other Liquid Bulk   **T**=Towage (where available from port)

Approach: The entrance is protected by two breakwaters (Western 4450 m long and Eastern 4100 m long) and is formed by the 'Pas van het Zand' channel, 2000 m long and 600 m wide, branching off from the Wielingen and Scheur passes, dredged to a depth of 13.5 m at LLWS over a width of 300 m, in a NW-SE direction

Anchorage: Available in pos 51° 22' 30" N; 2° 53' 30" E

Pilotage: Compulsory. Vessels waiting to call at Zeebrugge should acknowledge 'Wandelaar Pilot Station' of their ETA or via their local agent
The position of Wandelaar Pilot Station is 51° 22' 25" N; 2° 43' 00" E. Pilot service, Tel: +32 50 545072, Fax: +32 50 550410

Radio Frequency: Port control on VHF Channels 13 and 71. VTC Centre on VHF Channel 9

Weather: Occasional winter storms. Prevailing SW winds

Tides: Mean range 3.65 m, spring range 4.3 m, neap range 2.78 m

Traffic: 2007, 42 077 236 t of cargo handled, 2 020 723 TEU's

Maximum Vessel Dimensions: VLCC, 320 000 dwt, 16 m d, length unlimited, beam 55 m in outer harbour. Max length 400 m, 15.9 m d, beam 48 m in inner harbour

Working Hours: 0600-1400, 1400-2200, 2200-0600. Other times can be arranged

Accommodation:

Name	Length (m)	Depth (m)	Remarks
Outer Port			See [1] below
P&O North Sea Ferries (Quay No's 106-108)	530	7.2	See [2] below
Swedish Quay Terminal (Quay No's 702, 703 & 705)	825	15	See [3] below
Britannia Dock Terminal (Quay No's 608, 609, 612 & 613)		10	See [4] below
Wielingendok Terminals (Quay No's 140-144)	1000	15	See [5] below
Container Handling Zeebrugge (Quay No's 202-207)	1050	15	See [6] below
Fluxys LNG Terminal (Quay 615)	380	13	See [7] below
Albert II Dock South (Quay No's 120-122)	900	16	See [8] below
Inner Port			See [9] below
Canada Terminal (Quay No's 525, 527, 530 & 531)	606	15	See [10] below
Belgian New Fruit Wharf Terminal (Quay No's 401-403 & 411-412)	1103	14.5	See [11] below
Combined Terminal Operators Terminal			See [12] below
Multi-Purpose Terminal	900	13.5	See [13] below
Leopold II Mole			Quays 103-105
ICO Car Terminal	900	13.5	See [14] below
Tameco Terminal (Quay No's 415-416)		6.5–14	See [15] below
Toyota Terminal (Quay No's 525-527)		8–15	See [16] below
Bastenaken Terminal (Quay No's 501-505)	780		Operated by International Car Operators (ICO N.V.)

[1]*Outer Port:* Protected by two long breakwaters. All container and short-sea ro/ro vessels berth in the outer port
[2]*P&O North Sea Ferries (Quay No's 106-108):* Ro/ro cargo operated by P&O North Sea Ferries, Tel: +32 50 542266, Fax: +32 50 542288, Email: freight.zeebrugge@ponsf.be
Receives the daily services to Hull (passengers & freight) as well as the freight only services to Tees. Linkspan with 2 x SWL to 180 t
[3]*Swedish Quay Terminal (Quay No's 702, 703 & 705):* Ro/ro cargo operated by SeaRo Terminal N.V., Alfred Ronsestraat 100, B-8380 Zeebrugge, Tel: +32 50 557100, Fax: +32 50 557109, Email:searo@searo.be, Website: www.searo.be
Two linkspans (1 x SWL 100 t and 1 x SWL 130 t)
[4]*Britannia Dock Terminal (Quay No's 608, 609, 612 & 613):* Ro/ro cargo operated by SeaRo Terminal N.V., Alfred Ronsestraat 100, B-8380 Zeebrugge, Tel: +32 50 557100, Fax: +32 50 557109, Email: searo@searo.be, Website: www.searo.be
Three jetties (190, 200 & 288 m long). Three linkspans with SWL to 140 t
[5]*Wielingendok Terminals (Quay No's 140-144):* SeaRo Terminal, Alfred Ronsestraat 100, B-8380 Zeebrugge, Tel: +32 50 557100, Fax: +32 50 557109, Email: searo@searo.be, Website: www.searo.be, operates the Wielingendok forest products terminal (Quay No's 140-143)
80 000 m2 dedicated intermodal & distribution warehouses
Ro/ro freight quay (Quay No.144) operated by PSA-Hesse-Noord Natie Zeebrugge, New Yorklaan 11, B-8380 Zeebrugge, Tel: +32 50 543611, Fax: +32 50 547520, Email: info@psahnn.be, Website: www.psahnn.be
Handling the ro/ro vessels of Dart Line, offering three departures/day from Zeebrugge to Dartford
[6]*Container Handling Zeebrugge (Quay No's 202-207):* Containers operated by PSA-Hesse-Noord Natie Zeebrugge, New Yorklaan 11, B-8380 Zeebrugge, Tel: +32 50 543611, Fax: +32 50 547520, Email: info@psahnn.be, Website: www.psahnn.be
Container terminal of 420 000 m2 and ro/ro terminal of 79 000 m2. Equipment includes eight gantry cranes (three of which are super post-panamax)
[7]*Fluxys LNG Terminal (Quay 615):* Operated by Fluxys LNG N.V., Tel: +32 50 366611, Fax: +32 50 366609, Email: info@fluxyslng.net, Website: www.fluxyslng.net
For vessels up to 350 m loa, 55 m beam and 12 m draft with an unloading cap of up to 12 000 m3/h. Three storage tanks with an overall cap up to 261 000 m3
[8]*Albert II Dock South (Quay No's 120-122):* Operated by APM Terminals Zeebrugge N.V., Leopold II-Dam Kaai 120, B-8380 Zeebrugge, Tel: +32 50 502500, Fax: +32 50 502551, Email: zeeapmtadm@apmterminals.com, Website: www.apmterminals.be
Equipment includes seven super-post panamax quay cranes and twenty three straddle carriers. 784 reefer points

[9]*Inner Port:* The Pierre Vandamme lock (length 500 m, width 57 m and depth up to 18.5 m) provides access to the inner port which has two major docks. The Northern Dock with depth up to 14 m and the Southern Canal Dock with depth up to 18.5 m
[10]*Canada Terminal (Quay No's 525, 527, 530 & 531):* Ro/ro cargo operated by SeaRo Terminal N.V., Alfred Ronsestraat 100, B-8380 Zeebrugge, Tel: +32 50 557100, Fax: +32 50 557109, Email: searo@searo.be, Website: www.searo.be
49 ha hardstanding area (including the Wallenius Wilhelmsen Lines Terminal). One pontoon for handling vessels which are equipped with a stern ramp; deepsea vessels are handled through quarter ramp. Three car ramps and one mobile crane
[11]*Belgian New Fruit Wharf Terminal (Quay No's 401-403 & 411-412):* Operated by Belgian New Fruit Wharf (B.N.F.W.), Tel: +32 50 543111, Fax: +32 50 547231, Email: bnfw@sea-invest.be
Fruit, conventional & containers. Six cold storage warehouses with total surface area of 42 242 m2 and two deep freeze warehouses with a total storage cap of 132 000 m3. The terminal is equipped with three conveyors, by which the cardboard boxes are transported through a spiral conveyor, fully sheltered, from the hold to the warehouse. Next to this four mobile cranes, reach stackers and forklift trucks are used
[12]*Combined Terminal Operators Terminal:* Operated by Combined Terminal Operators (C.T.O.) N.V., Tel: +32 50 542411, Fax: +32 50 546098, Email: general@cto.be, Website: www.cto.be
[13]*Multi-Purpose Terminal:* Quays 404 & 406-410 handling sugar, forest products, iron & steel, fruit & vegetables and other general cargo
[14]*ICO Car Terminal:* Quays 405-409 operated by International Car Operators (ICO N.V.)
[15]*Tameco Terminal (Quay No's 415-416):* Liquid bulk terminal operated by Tameco N.V., J. Verschaveweg 100, B-8380 Zeebrugge, Tel: +32 50 557055, Fax: +32 50 547415
Berth lengths 200 m + 90 m. Eleven storage tanks with total cap of 25 000 m3 for the storage and handling of liquid food products and non-hazardous chemicals
[16]*Toyota Terminal (Quay No's 525-527):* Two jetties operated by Toyota Vehicle Logistics Centre, Aziestraat 2, B-8380 Zeebrugge, Tel: +32 50 288902, Fax: +32 50 288945, Email: koen.vandersteegen@toyota-europe.com

Bunkering: StatoilHydro ASA, Gassco AS, Barlenhuisstraat 1, Kaai 524, B-8380 Zeebrugge, Belgium, *Tel:* +32 50 461611, *Fax:* +32 50 599004, *Email:* info@gassco.no, *Website:* www.gassco.no
OW Bunker (Belgium) N.V., Tavernierkaai 2, BE 2000 Antwerp, Belgium, *Tel:* +32 3 288 3600, *Fax:* +32 3 475 9671, *Email:* owbunker@owbunker.be, *Website:* www.owbunker.com
Wiljo Energy, Wiljo NV, Amsterdamstraat 30, B-2000 Antwerp, Belgium, *Tel:* +32 3 232 3910, *Fax:* +32 3 232 5647, *Email:* wiljo@wiljo.be, *Website:* www.wiljo.be

Towage: Five tugs available of 1500 to 4000 hp, permanently; others obtainable at short notice

Repair & Maintenance: Flanders Ship Repair N.V., Noordzeestraat 14, B-8380 Zeebrugge, Belgium, *Tel:* +32 50 337050, *Fax:* +32 50 335304, *Email:* info@fsr.be, *Website:* www.fsr.be Dry dock for vessels up to 106 m loa and 4500 t lifting cap
SDS Verheye N.V., Boomkorstraat 7-8, 8380 Zeebrugge, Belgium, *Tel:* +32 50 544541, *Fax:* +32 50 545837, *Email:* info@gardec.be, *Website:* www.gardec.be Dry dock of 40 m with lifting cap 600 t

Ship Chandlers: Brabo Enterprises, Brabo Coastal, Noordzeestraat 14, Zeebrugge, Belgium, *Tel:* +32 50 471687, *Fax:* +32 50 471688, *Website:* www.brabo-enterprises.be
Wells & Mommaerts N.V., Boomkorstraat 2, B-8380 Zeebrugge, Belgium, *Tel:* +32 50 546981, *Fax:* +32 50 547398, *Email:* wells-mommaerts.zbg@ping.be

Shipping Agents: Boeckmans Belgie N.V., Van Meterenkaai 1, P O Box 4, B-2000 Antwerp, Belgium, *Tel:* +32 3 202 0202, *Fax:* +32 3 202 0393, *Email:* info@boeckmans.be, *Website:* www.boeckmans.be Managing Director: Anthony Durot Email: anthony.durot@boeckmans.be
Agence Maritime Lalemant N.V., Tijdokstraat 12, 8380 Zeebrugge, Belgium, *Tel:* +32 50 544266, *Fax:* +32 50 546601, *Email:* zeebrugge@lalemant.com, *Website:* www.lalemant.com
Algemeen Expeditiebedrijf Zeebrugge b.v.b.a, Doverlaan 7, B-8380 Zeebrugge, Belgium, *Tel:* +32 50 545308, *Fax:* +32 50 546161, *Email:* gilbert@aezforward.be
Beltraf N.V., Kustlaan 176, 8380 Zeebrugge, Belgium, *Tel:* +32 50 551501, *Fax:* +32 50 551301, *Email:* beltraf@skynet.be
CMA-CGM S.A., CMA CGM Belgium N.V ., c/o Ochz Terminal, New Yorklaan 11, P O Box 10, B-8380 Zeebrugge, Belgium, *Tel:* +32 50 842372, *Fax:* +32 50 842346, *Email:* zbr.agency@cma-cgm.com, *Website:* www.cma-cgm.com
Eagle N.V., Karveelstraat 18, B-8380 Zeebrugge, Belgium, *Tel:* +32 50 558855, *Fax:* +32 50 546599, *Email:* rik.steen@maritserv.com
Flamar bvba, Vissersstraat 27/33, B-8380 Zeebrugge, Belgium, *Tel:* +32 50 542054, *Fax:* +32 50 547069, *Email:* info@flamar.com, *Website:* www.flamar.com
Herfurth & Co. N.V., Doverlaan No 7, 8380 Zeebrugge, Belgium, *Tel:* +32 50 590556, *Fax:* +32 50 598620, *Email:* zeemar.be@sdsbo.com, *Website:* www.sdsbo.com
Kennedy Hunter N.V., Britse Kaai 8, B-8000 Zeebrugge, Belgium, *Tel:* +32 50 348330, *Fax:* +32 50 348368, *Email:* zeebrugge@kennedy.be, *Website:* www.kennedy.be
MG Agency, Zeedijk 38, B-8380 Zeebrugge, Belgium, *Tel:* +32 50 552575, *Fax:* +32 50 546183, *Email:* info@zeebrugeagents.com, *Website:* www.zeebruggeagents.com
RBZ N.V., Vismijnstraat 17, B-8380 Zeebrugge, Belgium, *Tel:* +32 50 542090, *Fax:* +32 50 545168, *Email:* agency@rbz.be, *Website:* www.rbz.be
Wetrex N.V., Karveelstraat 18, B-8380 Zeebrugge, Belgium, *Tel:* +32 50 558866, *Fax:* +32 50 545969, *Email:* luc@maritserv.com, *Website:* www.wetrex.com
Zeebrugge Shipping & Bunkering S.A., Kiwiweg 80, B-8380 Zeebrugge, Belgium, *Tel:* +32 50 542411, *Fax:* +32 50 546098, *Email:* agency@zsb.be, *Website:* www.zsb.be
Zeemar N.V., Dover Laan 7, B-8380 Zeebrugge, Belgium, *Tel:* +32 50 590550, *Fax:* +32 50 598620, *Email:* zeemar.be@sdsbo.com, *Website:* www.herfurth-group.com

Stevedoring Companies: Belgian New Fruit Wharf, Kiwiweg 120, Nieuw Zeelandkaai 401 - 403, 8380 Zeebrugge, Belgium, *Tel:* +32 50 543111, *Fax:* +32 50 545397, *Email:* bnfw@sea-invest.be, *Website:* www.sea-invest.be
Borlix N.V., Lanceloot Blondeellaan 15, Prins Filipsdok - Kaai 303, B-8380 Zeebrugge, Belgium, *Tel:* +32 50 544861, *Fax:* +32 50 544942, *Email:* info@borlix.be, *Website:* www.borlix.be
Combined Terminal Operators (C.T.O.) N.V., Kiwiweg 80, 8380 Zeebrugge, Belgium, *Tel:* +32 50 542488, *Fax:* +32 50 546098, *Email:* general@cto.be, *Website:* www.cto.be
Flanders Cold Center, Zeebrugge, Belgium, *Tel:* +32 50 559027, *Fax:* +32 50 550797

Flanders Container Terminals N.V., Leopold 11 Dam, 8380 Zeebrugge, Belgium, *Tel:* +32 50 559111, *Fax:* +32 50 559191, *Email:* info@katoennatie.com

Fluxys N.V., Henri Victor Wolvenstraat 3, B-8380 Zeebrugge, Belgium, *Tel:* +32 50 366611, *Fax:* +32 50 366609, *Email:* francis.vanderwalla@fluxys.net, *Website:* www.fluxys.net

Hanson Belgium Aggregates N.V., Lanceloot Blondeellaan 1, B-8380 Zeebrugge, Belgium, *Tel:* +32 50 557474, *Fax:* +32 50 544321, *Email:* herman.dhoore@hanson.biz, *Website:* www.hanson.be

Ocean Container Terminal Hessenatie Zeebrugge, New Yorklaan, 11, B-8380 Zeebrugge, Belgium, *Tel:* +32 50 543611, *Fax:* +32 50 547520, *Email:* jack.reyniers@psnhnn.be, *Website:* www.portofzeebrugge.be

P & O North Sea Ferries, Zeebrugge, Belgium, *Tel:* +32 50 542266, *Fax:* +32 50 542288, *Email:* freight.zeebrugge@ponsf.com

SeaRo Terminal N.V., Alfred Ronsestraat 100, B-8380 Zeebrugge, Belgium, *Tel:* +32 50 557100, *Fax:* +32 50 557109, *Email:* searo@searo.be, *Website:* www.searo.be

StatoilHydro ASA, Gassco AS, Barlenhuisstraat 1, Kaai 524, B-8380 Zeebrugge, Belgium, *Tel:* +32 50 461611, *Fax:* +32 50 599004, *Email:* info@gassco.no, *Website:* www.gassco.no

Zeebrugse Visveiling N.V., Noordzeestraat 201, B-8380 Zeebrugge, Belgium, *Tel:* +32 50 544120, *Fax:* +32 50 545018, *Email:* info@zv.be, *Website:* www.zv.be

Surveyors: Burex Enterprises N.V., Bosterhoutstraat 5, 8760 Zeebrugge, Belgium, *Tel:* +32 50 624003, *Email:* varia@burex.be, *Website:* www.burex.be

Coppernicus Recycling, Zeebrugge, Belgium, *Tel:* +32 50 621759

Exco N.V., Rederskaai 29, B-8380 Zeebrugge, Belgium, *Tel:* +32 50 545433, *Fax:* +32 50 547882, *Email:* exco@exco.be, *Website:* www.exco.be

ITS Inc., Zeebrugge, Belgium, *Tel:* +32 50 547838, *Fax:* +32 50 547839, *Email:* claims.zeebrugge@its-surveys.com

Van Ameyde International B.V., Noordelijk Insteekdok, USA Kaai, B-8380 Zeebrugge, Belgium, *Tel:* +32 50 550890, *Fax:* +32 50 547870, *Email:* zeebrugge@ameydemarine.be, *Website:* www.vanameyde.com

Medical Facilities: First aid facility, Tel: +32 (50) 546515. Hospitals at Bruges, Blankenberge and Knokke

Airport: Ostend Airport, 25 km

Railway: All Zeebrugge terminals have on-site rail connections

Lloyd's Agent: N.V. Beeckman De Vos, Stijfselrui 44 / b.5, B-2000 Antwerp, Belgium, *Tel:* +32 3 201 1250, *Fax:* +32 3 231 5599, *Email:* info@bdv.be

BELIZE

BELIZE CITY

Lat 17° 29' N; Long 88° 12' W.

Admiralty Chart: 522	**Admiralty Pilot:** 69A
Time Zone: GMT -6 h	**UNCTAD Locode:** BZ BZE

Principal Facilities:

P		G	C	R		B		T	A

Authority: Port of Belize Ltd, P O Box 2674, Caesar Ridge Road, Belize City, Belize, *Tel:* +501 227 2439, *Fax:* +501 227 3571, *Email:* info@portofbelize.com, *Website:* www.portofbelize.com

Officials: Chief Executive Officer: Raineldo D. Guerrero, *Email:* rdguerrero@portofbelize.com.

Deputy Chief Executive Officer: Franzine A. Waight, *Email:* fawaight@portofbelize.com.

Operations Manager: Kenrick M. Richards, *Email:* kmrichards@portofbelize.com.

Port Security: ISPS compliant

Documentation: Crew list (6 copies), passenger list (6 copies), arms and ammunition (3 copies), stores list (4 copies), crew's declarations (2 copies), crew's vaccinations (1 copy), International Maritime Health Declaration and clearance from last port, manifest copies (12). Vessel's papers and certificates should be available on request

Approach: Access channel 4600 m long and 120 m wide. Turning basin is 600 m long & 340 m wide

Anchorage: Depths in the harbour anchorage vary due to a natural slope. For example vessels drawing 4.27 m anchor within 0.4 km; 6.1 m, 1.6 km and so on S Certain designated anchorages; Middle Ground in 6.4 m, Buckle Rocks in 8.23 m, Goff's Caye in 6.1 m. Masters should consult with pilots

Pilotage: Compulsory, *Tel:* +501 227 2439, *Fax:* +501 227 3571, *Email:* info@portofbelize.com. Vessels should advise ETA 24 h before arrival. Pilot boards in pos 17° 19.52' N; 88° 00.05' W, approx 2.3 nautical miles E of English Cay Lt

Radio Frequency: VHF Channels 16 and 12

Weather: Winter winds average 360° northerly at 9 knots and in summer 90° easterly at 11 knots. Hurricane season from June 1 to November 30

Tides: Tidal range of 2.5 ft

Traffic: 2007, 256 vessels, 722 796 t of cargo handled, 39 191 TEU's

Principal Imports and Exports: Imports: Electrical appliances, Foodstuffs, Fuel, Industrial equipment, Vehicles. Exports: Bananas, Citrus concentrate, Fish, Garments, Lumber, Sugar.

Working Hours: Office Hours: Mon-Fri: 0800-1700. Terminal Operations: Mon-Sun 24 h/day

Accommodation:

Name	Length (m)	Draught (m)	Remarks
Belize City			See [1] below
Quay	67	10	
Ro/ro Berth	25		
Commerce Bight			
Quay	27	7	

[1]*Belize City:* Low berth facility with two breakwaters, wharf length of 150 m and draft of 2 m

Storage: Warehouse of 7000 m2. Two container yards of 31 000 m2 and 19 000 m2. 24 reefer points

Mechanical Handling Equipment:

Location	Type	Capacity (t)	Qty
Belize City	Mult-purp. Cranes	55–100	3

Bunkering: Esso Standard Oil, Caesar Ridge Road, Loyola Park, Belize City, Belize, *Tel:* +501 227 7323

Shell Belize Ltd, SOL Belize, P O Box 608, Belize City, Belize, *Tel:* +501 2 230 406, *Fax:* +501 2 230 704, *Email:* solbelize@btl.net, *Website:* www.solpetroleum.com

Chevron Marine Products LLC, Global Marine Products LLC, 1500 Louisiana, 4th Floor, Houston, TX 77002, United States of America, *Tel:* +1 832 8542 988, *Fax:* +1 832 8544 868, *Email:* gulfcbm@chevron.com, *Website:* www.chevron.com – *Grades:* GO – *Delivery Mode:* tank truck

Esso Standard Oil, Caesar Ridge Road, Loyola Park, Belize City, Belize, *Tel:* +501 227 7323 – *Misc:* supplies bunkering facilities on a 24 hour basis – *Notice:* 24 hours

Shell Belize Ltd, SOL Belize, P O Box 608, Belize City, Belize, *Tel:* +501 2 230 406, *Fax:* +501 2 230 704, *Email:* solbelize@btl.net, *Website:* www.solpetroleum.com

Shipping Agents: Belize Estate Co. Ltd, 1 Slaughterhouse Road, P O Box 151, Belize City, Belize, *Tel:* +501 223 0641, *Fax:* +501 223 1367, *Email:* kia@btl.net

Belize Shipping Agency, 95 Albert Street, Belize City, Belize, *Tel:* +501 227 0530, *Fax:* +501 227 0529, *Email:* bzeshipag@btl.net

Eurocaribe Shipping Services Ltd, 14 Fort Street, P O Box 281, Belize City, Belize, *Tel:* +501 223 3140, *Fax:* +501 223 1657, *Email:* eurocaribecargo@btl.net

Marine & Services Ltd, P O Box 611, 95 Albert Street, Belize City, Belize, *Tel:* +501 227 2112, *Fax:* +501 227 5404, *Email:* marserve@btl.net, *Website:* www.marineservices.bz

S.J. Turton Agencies Ltd, 71 North Front Street, Belize City, Belize, *Tel:* +501 227 7288, *Fax:* +501 227 2797

Medical Facilities: Available

Airport: Phillip Goldson International, 16 km

Lloyd's Agent: Belize Estate Co. Ltd, 1 Slaughterhouse Road, P O Box 151, Belize City, Belize, *Tel:* +501 223 0641, *Fax:* +501 223 1367, *Email:* kia@btl.net

BIG CREEK

Lat 16° 30' N; Long 88° 24' W.

Admiralty Chart: 1797	**Admiralty Pilot:** 69A
Time Zone: GMT -6 h	**UNCTAD Locode:** BZ BGK

Principal Facilities:

			Y	G	C				

Authority: Port of Big Creek, Independence, Stann Creek, Belize, *Tel:* +501 523 2003, *Fax:* +501 523 2201, *Email:* info@portofbigcreek.com, *Website:* www.portofbigcreek.com

Pre-Arrival Information: Vessels should advise ETA via agent 48 h prior to arrival

Approach: Buoyed and dredged entrance 1.5 km long with min depth of 7 m

Anchorage: The vessel anchorage position is 16° 26.03' N; 88° 21.13' W

Pilotage: Compulsory. Pilot boards in pos 16° 25.83' N; 88° 21.83' W (in the vicinity of Lt buoy 2)

Accommodation:

Name	Length (m)	Depth (m)	Remarks
Big Creek			See [1] below
Quay	133	6.7	See [2] below

[1]*Big Creek:* Owned by Banana Enterprise Ltd (BEL), Email: bananaentp@btl.net
[2]*Quay:* Handling dry & refrigerated containers, breakbulk cargo, fresh produce and grain

Lloyd's Agent: Belize Estate Co. Ltd, 1 Slaughterhouse Road, P O Box 151, Belize City, Belize, *Tel:* +501 223 0641, *Fax:* +501 223 1367, *Email:* kia@btl.net

COMMERCE BIGHT

harbour area, see under Belize City

Key to Principal Facilities:—					
A=Airport	**C**=Containers	**G**=General Cargo	**P**=Petroleum	**R**=Ro/Ro	**Y**=Dry Bulk
B=Bunkers	**D**=Dry Dock	**L**=Cruise	**Q**=Other Liquid Bulk	**T**=Towage (where available from port)	

BENIN

COTONOU

Lat 6° 21' N; Long 2° 25' E.

Admiralty Chart: 1380
Admiralty Pilot: 1
Time Zone: GMT +1 h
UNCTAD Locode: BJ COO

Cotonou

Principal Facilities:

| P | Q | Y | G | C | R | | B | | T | A | |

Tramp Oil & Marine

Wells House, 15-17 Elmfield Road, Bromley,
Kent BR1 1LT, United Kingdom
Phone: +44 20 8315 7777   **Fax:** +44 20 8315 7788
General email: enquiries@tramp-oil.com

See listings for all global offices: **www.tramp-oil.com**

INTER-SEAS BENIN (ISB) SARL

Carre 361 - 362, Rue du Gouverneur Felix Eboue Von Euraf
Cotonou, BENIN
Tel: +229 21 31 45 06
Fax: +229 21 31 45 08
Email: isb@intnet.bj / mail@pharaon-telecom.net
Contact : Mr AHYI Etienne

SHIPPING AGENTS

Authority: Port Autonome de Cotonou, P O Box 927, Cotonou, Republic of Benin, *Tel:* +229 2131 5280, *Fax:* +229 2131 2891, *Email:* pac@leland.bj, *Website:* www.portdecotonou.com

Port Security: ISPS compliant

Approach: Channel depth 12.0 m. Fairway buoy in pos bearing 106° from the red beacon to the west quay

Anchorage: The anchorage is one nautical mile SE of the Lighthouse in a depth of about 14.0 m. It affords good holding ground having a sandy bed

Pilotage: Compulsory for vessels entering or leaving port over 150 nrt. Working hours 0600 to 2400. Pilot requests must be made to the harbour master's office at least three working hours in advance or before 1830 for night movements

Radio Frequency: Operating on VHF Channel 16 or radio telephone on 2182 khz

Weather: Prevailing winds blow from the SW

Tides: Range of tide 1.0 m, neap 0.2 m, springs 1.95 m

Traffic: 2006, 5 073 000 t of cargo handled

Maximum Vessel Dimensions: Max d 10.0 m, max loa 210 m

Principal Imports and Exports: Imports: Cereals, Fertiliser, Manufactured goods, Rice, Wheat. Exports: Cotton, Cotton seed, Crude oil, Vegetable oil.

Accommodation:

Name	Depth (m)	Remarks
Cotonou		
Commercial Quay	10–11	See [1] below
Eastern Jetty		See [2] below

[1]*Commercial Quay:* Six conventional berths of 155-180 m long, one container berth 220 m long and one ro/ro quay. Container storage of 65 000 m2 available
[2]*Eastern Jetty:* One berth for tankers and bulk carriers 200 m long, one berth for vegetable oil tankers 160 m long and one berth for fishing vessels 100 m long

Storage: 49 050 m2 of bonded warehouses, 6300 m2 of unbonded warehouses and 296 500 m2 of open storage. Two cold rooms available for refrigerated goods

Location	Open (m²)
Cotonou	296500

Mechanical Handling Equipment:

Location	Type	Capacity (t)	Qty
Cotonou	Mobile Cranes	50	1

Cargo Worked: 1200 t/day for stacked merchandise and 900 t/day for breakbulk, 3000 t/day for clinker, 230 TEU's

Bunkering: Wilson International Ltd, C/120 Jericho, Cotonou, Republic of Benin, *Tel:* +229 9764 4569, *Fax:* +229 2132 3549, *Email:* wilsonltd1@yahoo.com
Addax Bunkering Services, c/o Addax BV, 12 Rue Michel-Servet, P O Box 404, 1211 Geneva 12, Switzerland, *Tel:* +41 22 702 9040, *Fax:* +41 22 702 9100, *Email:* abs@aogltd.com
Bominflot, Bominflot Bunkergesellschaft fur Mineralole mbH & Co. KG, Grosse Baeckerstrasse 11, 20095 Hamburg, Germany, *Tel:* +49 40 350 930, *Fax:* +49 40 3509 3116, *Email:* mail@bominflot.de, *Website:* www.bominflot.net
BP France S.A., Immeuble le Cervier, 12 Avenue des Beguines, Cergy-Saint-Christophe, 95866 Cergy Pontoise Cedex, France, *Tel:* +33 1 3422 4000, *Fax:* +33 1 3422 4417, *Email:* benoist.grosjean@fr.bp.com, *Website:* www.bpmarine.com
Total France S.A., Total Marine Fuels, 51 Esplanade du General de Gaulle, F-92907 Paris la Defense Cedex 10, France, *Tel:* +33 1 4135 2755, *Fax:* +33 1 4197 0291, *Email:* marine.fuels@total.com, *Website:* www.marinefuels.total.com
Tramp Oil & Marine, World Fuel Services Corporation, 13th Floor, Portland House, Bressenden Place, London SW1E 5BH, United Kingdom, *Tel:* +44 20 7808 5000, *Fax:* +44 20 7808 5088, *Email:* pturner@wfscorp.com, *Website:* www.wfscorp.com – *Grades:* all grades

Towage: Compulsory for vessels over 500 gt. Three tugs of 1400-2000 hp available

Repair & Maintenance: Direction d'Exploitation des Installations de Peche, Cotonou, Republic of Benin, *Tel:* +229 2131 2762 Minor repairs available

Ship Chandlers: A10 Marine Sarl, Hall des Armateurs, Bureau No 12, Port de Pecche, Cotonou, Republic of Benin, *Tel:* +229 2131 6432, *Fax:* +229 2131 6432, *Email:* ama10@firstnet1.com, *Website:* www.beninweb.org/a10marine

Shipping Agents: Africa Asia Agency, Ilot 544, Parcelle K Guinkome, Rue de la Grande Gare OCBN, P O Box 080956, Cotonou, Republic of Benin, *Tel:* +229 2131 4965, *Fax:* +229 2131 5251
Afritramp, Boulevard de France, Cotonou, Republic of Benin, *Tel:* +229 2131 3793, *Fax:* +229 2131 1246, *Email:* stephane.moteyen@bj.dti.bollore.com, *Website:* www.afritrampoilfield.com
Agence de Transit et Logistique - Atral S.A., 06 Akpakpa, P O Box 2671, Cotonou, Republic of Benin, *Tel:* +229 2133 4031, *Email:* atralshipping@firstnet1.com
Compagnie Beninoise de Navigation Maritime (COBENAM), P O Box 2032, Cotonou, Republic of Benin, *Tel:* +229 2131 4987, *Fax:* +229 2131 3642
Doba Shipping International & Trade, Siege Social Ex Immeuble Mercedes, En Face du Stade Rene Pleven, Akpakpa, Cotonou, Republic of Benin, *Tel:* +229 2131 8435, *Fax:* +229 2133 5079, *Email:* dsidoba@yahoo.fr
GAC-GETMA, Parcelle K, Lot 544, Guinkomey, P O Box 4338, Cotonou, Republic of Benin, *Tel:* +229 2132 8162, *Fax:* +229 2132 8172, *Email:* gac-getma.benin@gacworld.com, *Website:* www.gacworld.com
Geodis Overseas, c/o Atral Benin, P O Box 2671 Akpakra, Cotonou, Republic of Benin, *Tel:* +229 2133 4031, *Fax:* +229 2133 3906, *Email:* atral@firstnet.bg
Grimaldi Benin, Port de Peche, P O Box 01, P O Box 5401, Cotonou, Republic of Benin, *Tel:* +229 2131 6728, *Fax:* +229 2131 6729, *Email:* grimaldi@grimaldi-benin.com, *Website:* www.grimaldi-benin.com
Groupe Kajebau, Lot 1153 Haie-Vive, P O Box 452, Cotonou, Republic of Benin, *Tel:* +229 2130 5034, *Fax:* +229 2130 9006, *Email:* kajebau@yahoo.fr
Groupe Navitrans, Lot 544 Parcelle K Guinkome, Cotonou, Republic of Benin, *Tel:* +229 2131 4965, *Fax:* +229 2131 5251, *Email:* euipment@navitrans-benin.com, *Website:* www.navitrans.fr
Inter-Seas Benin (ISB) Sarl, Carre 361-362, Rue du Gouverneur Felix Eboue Von Euraf, Cotonou, Republic of Benin, *Tel:* +229 2131 4506, *Fax:* +229 2131 4508, *Email:* isb@intnet.bj
Intermodal Shipping Agencies S.A., Shipping House, Boulevard de France, Cotonou, Republic of Benin, *Tel:* +229 2131 3181, *Fax:* +229 2131 3013
Maguesto Sarl, 121 St. Michel, P O Box 06-2662, Cotonou, Republic of Benin, *Tel:* +229 2132 8230, *Fax:* +229 2132 8230, *Email:* maguesto@intnet.bj
Mediterranean Shipping Company, MSC Benin, P O Box 132, Cotonou, Republic of Benin, *Tel:* +229 2131 5690, *Fax:* +229 2131 3437, *Email:* info@mscbj.mscgva.ch, *Website:* www.mscgva.ch
A.P. Moller-Maersk Group, Maersk Benin S.A., P O Box 2826, Cotonou, Republic of Benin, *Tel:* +229 2131 4330, *Fax:* +229 2131 5660, *Email:* cooordimpcus@maersk.com, *Website:* www.maerskline.com
SAGA Benin, Zone Portuaire, Boulevard de France, P O Box 1733, Cotonou, Republic of Benin, *Tel:* +229 2131 2119, *Fax:* +229 2131 3409, *Email:* azeez.bori@bj.dti.bollore.com
SDV Benin S.A., Boulevard de France, Cotonou, Republic of Benin, *Tel:* +229 2131 2357, *Fax:* +229 2131 5926, *Email:* sdvb10@calva.com
Sitt Benin, Tokp Hoho, derriere Cine Vog, P O Box 2527, Cotonou, Republic of Benin, *Tel:* +229 2131 8573, *Fax:* +229 2131 8640, *Email:* sitt@intnet.bj
Societe Inter-Continentale d'Affrements et d'Agence Maritime (SICAAM S.A.), P O Box 3043, Cotonou, Republic of Benin, *Tel:* +229 2131 4862, *Fax:* +229 2131 4855, *Email:* sicamship@yahoo.fr
Supermaritime Benin S.A., P O Box 489, Lot 137, Villa Vignon/Face Ecole Primaire Camp Guezo, Cotonou, Republic of Benin, *Tel:* +229 2130 9203, *Fax:* +229 2130 9004, *Email:* supmar@intnet.bj, *Website:* www.supermaritime.com
Westport S.A., Scoa Gbeto, P O Box 03-4376, Cotonou, Republic of Benin, *Tel:* +229 2131 7722, *Fax:* +229 2131 2909, *Email:* westport@firstnet1.com

Surveyors: Bureau Veritas, Zone Residentielle, Lot No.2, Imm. Face a L'ancienne Maison de la Radio, Cotonou, Republic of Benin, *Tel:* +229 2130 2013, *Fax:* +229 2130 0182, *Website:* www.bureauveritas.com
Societe Generale de Surveillance (SGS), SGS Benin SA, Les Cocotiers, Lot L/19, P O Box 08-0605, Cotonou, Republic of Benin, *Tel:* +229 2130 0709, *Fax:* +229 2130 1946, *Website:* www.sgs.com

Medical Facilities: National hospital and private clinics

Airport: 5 km from port

Lloyd's Agent: Omega Marine Benin, Cotonou, Republic of Benin, *Tel:* +229 2132 1764, *Fax:* +229 2132 7315, *Email:* omega-benin@omega-marine.com

BERMUDA

FREEPORT

Lat 32° 19' N; Long 64° 50' W.

Admiralty Chart: 332   **Admiralty Pilot:** 70
Time Zone: GMT -4 h   **UNCTAD Locode:** BM FPT

Principal Facilities:

P	Y			L	B		T	A

Authority: Department of Marine & Ports Services, P O Box HM 180, Hamilton, Bermuda HM AX, *Tel:* +1441 295 6575, *Fax:* +1441 295 5523, *Email:* frichardson@gov.bm, *Website:* www.gov.bm

Officials: Director: Francis Richardson.
Manager: Kathayann Woodley, *Email:* kswoodley@gov.bm.
Harbour Master: David Simmons, *Email:* dcsimmons@gov.bm.

Port Security: ISPS compliant

Documentation: Crew list (5 copies), crew declaration (1 copy), passenger list (5 copies), report of ship's stores (1 copy), declaration of health (1 copy), clearance from vessel's last port of call (1 copy), bermuda vessel report (1 copy), cargo manifests (4 copies)

Approach: Following pilot boarding, vessels enter the Narrows Channel in depth of 11.6-12.5 m. On clearing the Narrows Channel vessels may take either the North Channel in depth of 11.6-12.5 m or the South Channel in depth of 8.8-9.8 m to Freeport

Anchorage: Murrays Anchorage: limiting draft of 36 ft, exposed
The Great Sound: limiting draft of 34 ft, sheltered from the SW direction, used mainly by passenger liners
Five Fathom Hole: unlimited draft, exposed

Pilotage: The pilot boarding area is at the Sea Buoy in pos 32° 22.9' N; 64° 37.0' W. Pilots are ordered by Agent on receipt of vessels ETA. Pilotage is confined to daylight hours only

Radio Frequency: All communications regarding shipping movements in and out of Bermuda are handled by Bermuda Harbour Radio, call sign 'ZBM' which has been designated as Rescue Co-ordination Centre (RCC) aand Vessel Traffic Services (VTS) station for the area
A 24 h listening watch is maintained on VHF Channels 16 and 70. Pilot working channel on VHF Channel 12 and tugs use VHF Channel 10

Weather: Prevailing winds are NW'ly (winter) and SW'ly (summer)

Tides: Tidal range of 1.5 m

Maximum Vessel Dimensions: Max draft 10.4 m

Accommodation:

Name	Length (m)	Draught (m)	Remarks
Freeport			Situated in the N of Ireland Island
King's Wharf	300	10.4	See [1] below
South Basin	305	9	See [2] below
Commercial Jetty	243	9.1	See [3] below

[1]*King's Wharf:* Situated on the SE side of the North Breakwater of North Basin. Used by cruise vessels
[2]*South Basin:* Admiralty berthing area situated at the SW end of the NW wall
[3]*Commercial Jetty:* Situated at the end of the NW wall for vessels up to 183 m loa. Used for bulk cement and by Shell Company of Bermuda for bunkering. Also used as a lay berth for minor repairs

Bunkering: The Shell Company of Bermuda Ltd, Rubis Energy Bermuda Ltd, P O Box GE2, St. George, St. George's Island, Bermuda GE BX, *Tel:* +1441 2971 577, *Fax:* +1441 2978 472, *Email:* corporate@rubis-bermuda.com – *Grades:* MDO – *Misc:* own storage facilities – *Rates:* 50-300t/h – *Notice:* 48 hours – *Delivery Mode:* pipeline, truck

Towage: Two tugs of 3200 hp and one tug of 1200 hp

Repair & Maintenance: All types of minor deck and engine repairs can be carried out

Medical Facilities: Hamilton, 10 km

Airport: 22 km from port

Lloyd's Agent: Freisenbruch-Meyer Group, 75 Front Street, Hamilton, Bermuda HM 12, *Tel:* +1441 296 3600, *Fax:* +1441 295 6209, *Email:* jsykes@fmgroup.bm, *Website:* www.fmgroup.bm

HAMILTON

Lat 32° 18' N; Long 64° 47' W.

Admiralty Chart: 1073   **Admiralty Pilot:** 70
Time Zone: GMT -4 h   **UNCTAD Locode:** BM BDA

Principal Facilities:

	G	C	R	L	B		T	A	

Authority: Department of Marine & Ports Services, P O Box HM 180, Hamilton, Bermuda HM AX, *Tel:* +1441 295 6575, *Fax:* +1441 295 5523, *Email:* frichardson@gov.bm, *Website:* www.gov.bm

Officials: Director: Francis Richardson.
Manager: Kathayann Woodley, *Email:* kswoodley@gov.bm.
Harbour Master: David Simmons, *Email:* dcsimmons@gov.bm.

Port Security: ISPS compliant

Documentation: Crew list (5 copies), crew declaration (1 copy), passenger list (5 copies), report of ship's stores (1 copy), declaration of health (1 copy), clearance from vessel's last port of call (1 copy), bermuda vessel report (1 copy), cargo manifests (4 copies)

Approach: From Five Fathom Hole through Narrows Channel into Murray's Anchorage, thence along the North Shore into Grassy Bay, thence through Dundonald Channel and Two Rock Passage into Hamilton Harbour. Depth at entrance 8.53 m MLW

Anchorage: Murrays Anchorage: limiting draft of 36 ft, exposed
The Great Sound: limiting draft of 34 ft, sheltered from the SW direction, used mainly by passenger liners
Five Fathom Hole: unlimited draft, exposed

Pilotage: The pilot boarding area is at the Sea Buoy in pos 32° 22.9' N; 64° 37.0' W. Pilots are ordered by Agent on receipt of vessels ETA. Pilotage is confined to daylight hours only

Radio Frequency: All communications regarding shipping movements in and out of Bermuda are handled by Bermuda Harbour Radio, call sign 'ZBM' which has been designated as Rescue Co-ordination Centre (RCC) aand Vessel Traffic Services (VTS) station for the area
A 24 h listening watch is maintained on VHF Channels 16 and 70. Pilot working channel on VHF Channel 12 and tugs use VHF Channel 10

Weather: Prevailing winds NW'ly (winter) and SW'ly (summer)

Tides: Tidal range 1.5 m

Maximum Vessel Dimensions: Max draft 7.92 m

Working Hours: Regular: Mon-Fri 0800-1200, 1300-1630
Overtime: Mon-Fri 1730-2200. Sat 0800-1200, 1300-1600. Sun 0800-1200, 1300-1630, 1730-2200

Accommodation:

Name	Length (m)	Depth (m)	Draught (m)	Remarks
Hamilton				See [1] below
Berth No.1	155	8.5	7.9	For cruise vessels
Berth No's 5 & 6	192	8.5	7.9	For cruise vessels
Berth No's 7 & 8	412	8.5		See [2] below

[1]*Hamilton:* The harbour comprises 750 m of wharfage with 71 500 ft2 of shed space. Cruise ships are accommodated at two berths with a max d of 7.9 m, or at the anchorages. One tender available with a cap of 750 passengers
Containers are handled at Berth No's 7 & 8, max d 7.9 m; loading and discharging by two mobile cranes with cap of 225 t and 250 t. Only 20 ft containers may be handled. Ro/ro facilities at Berth No's 6 & 7
[2]*Berth No's 7 & 8:* For general cargo and container vessels. Max draft at Berth 7 is 7.9 m and at Berth 8 is 5.2 m. Ro/ro vessels use Berth 7. Storage for 700 TEU's, 64 reefer points

Mechanical Handling Equipment:

Location	Type	Capacity (t)	Qty
Berth No's 7 & 8	Mobile Cranes	225	1
Berth No's 7 & 8	Mobile Cranes	165	1

Key to Principal Facilities:—				
A=Airport	**C**=Containers	**G**=General Cargo	**P**=Petroleum	**R**=Ro/Ro	**Y**=Dry Bulk
B=Bunkers	**D**=Dry Dock	**L**=Cruise	**Q**=Other Liquid Bulk	**T**=Towage (where available from port)	

Cargo Worked: Stevedoring Services Ltd labour force: approx 65 men or 2 gangs. General cargo is discharged at a rate of 10 to 12 t/hatch/h. Stevedoring rates quoted on application

Bunkering: Hampton Bermuda (Bunkering), Suite 402, International Centre, 26 Bermudiana Street, Pembroke, Hamilton, Bermuda HM 11, *Tel:* +1441 2950 902, *Fax:* +1441 2952 165, *Email:* bunkers@hamptonmtl.ca
ExxonMobil Marine Fuels, Suite 900, One Alhambra Plaza, Coral Gables, FL 33134, United States of America, *Tel:* +1 305 459 6358, *Fax:* +1 305 459 6412, *Email:* emmf@exxonmobil.com, *Website:* www.exxonmobilmarinefuels.com – *Grades:* MGO – *Misc:* own storage facilities – *Parcel Size:* 100-600t – *Rates:* 80t/h – *Notice:* 48 hours – *Delivery Mode:* truck
Hampton Bermuda (Bunkering), Suite 402, International Centre, 26 Bermudiana Street, Pembroke, Hamilton, Bermuda HM 11, *Tel:* +1441 2950 902, *Fax:* +1441 2952 165, *Email:* bunkers@hamptonmtl.ca
The Shell Company of Bermuda Ltd, Rubis Energy Bermuda Ltd, P O Box GE2, St. George, St. George's Island, Bermuda GE BX, *Tel:* +1441 2971 577, *Fax:* +1441 2978 472, *Email:* corporate@rubis-bermuda.com – *Grades:* MDO – *Misc:* own storage facilities – *Rates:* 50-300t/h – *Notice:* 48 hours – *Delivery Mode:* pipeline, truck

Towage: Three tugs available; two of 3200 hp and one of 1200 hp

Repair & Maintenance: Minor repairs to ocean-going vessels can be effected, as well as emergency temporary repairs carried out in the anchorages. There are slipways to handle yachts

Shipping Agents: AM Services Ltd, Belvedere Building, 69 Pitts Road, P O Box HM2452, Pembroke HM 08, Hamilton, Bermuda HMJX, *Tel:* +1441 295 0850, *Fax:* +1441 292 3704, *Email:* amsl@northrock.bm
Atlantic Maritime Services Ltd, 3 Crown Hill, P O Box 1524, Hamilton, Bermuda 5, *Tel:* +1441 238 2203, *Fax:* +1441 238 2203
Bermuda Forwarders Ltd, 2 Mills Creek Park, P O Box HM 511, Hamilton, Bermuda HM CX, *Tel:* +1441 292 4600, *Fax:* +1441 292 1859, *Email:* info@bermudaforwarders.com, *Website:* www.bermudaforwarders.com
Bermuda Ocean Shipping Services Ltd, P O Box HM 1114, Hamilton, Bermuda HM EX, *Tel:* +1441 295 7090, *Fax:* +1441 292 8069, *Email:* lblee@boss.bm, *Website:* www.boss.bm
Container Ship Management Ltd, 14 Par-La-Ville Road, P O Box HM 2266, Hamilton, Bermuda HM JX, *Tel:* +1441 295 1624, *Fax:* +1441 295 3781, *Email:* csm@csm.bm

Medical Facilities: Hamilton, 2 km

Airport: Kindley Field International, 16 km

Lloyd's Agent: Freisenbruch-Meyer Group, 75 Front Street, Hamilton, Bermuda HM 12, *Tel:* +1441 296 3600, *Fax:* +1441 295 6209, *Email:* jsykes@fmgroup.bm, *Website:* www.fmgroup.bm

ST. GEORGE'S

Lat 32° 23' N; Long 64° 40' W.

Admiralty Chart: 1315/868   **Admiralty Pilot:** 70
Time Zone: GMT -4 h   **UNCTAD Locode:** BM SGE

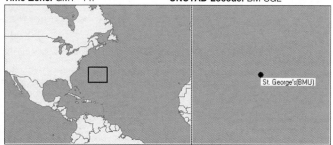
St. George's (BMU)

Principal Facilities:

P		Y	G		R	L	B		T	A	

Authority: Department of Marine & Ports Services, P O Box HM 180, Hamilton, Bermuda HM AX, *Tel:* +1441 295 6575, *Fax:* +1441 295 5523, *Email:* frichardson@gov.bm, *Website:* www.gov.bm

Officials: Director: Francis Richardson.
Manager: Kathayann Woodley, *Email:* kswoodley@gov.bm.
Harbour Master: David Simmons, *Email:* dcsimmons@gov.bm.

Port Security: ISPS compliant

Documentation: Crew list (5 copies), crew declaration (1 copy), passenger list (5 copies), report of ship's stores (1 copy), declaration of health (1 copy), clearance from vessel's last port of call (1 copy), bermuda vessel report (1 copy), cargo manifests (4 copies)

Approach: From Five Fathom Hole through the Town Cut Channel, depth 8.53 m MLW

Anchorage: Murrays Anchorage: limiting draft of 36 ft, exposed
The Great Sound: limiting draft of 34 ft, sheltered from the SW direction, used mainly by passenger liners
Five Fathom Hole: unlimited draft, exposed

Pilotage: The pilot boarding area is at the Sea Buoy in pos 32° 22.9' N; 64° 37.0' W. Pilots are ordered by Agent on receipt of vessels ETA. Pilotage is confined to daylight hours only

Radio Frequency: All communications regarding shipping movements in and out of Bermuda are handled by Bermuda Harbour Radio, call sign 'ZBM' which has been designated as Rescue Co-ordination Centre (RCC) aand Vessel Traffic Services (VTS) station for the area
A 24 h listening watch is maintained on VHF Channels 16 and 70. Pilot working channel on VHF Channel 12 and tugs use VHF Channel 10

Maximum Vessel Dimensions: Max draft 7.92 m

Accommodation:

Name	Length (m)	Depth (m)	Draught (m)	Remarks
St. George's				
Ordnance Island	107	8.3	7.9	Cruise vessels
Pennos	229	9.1	7.9	See [1] below
Esso Oil Terminal			10.4	See [2] below

[1]*Pennos:* Cruise & cargo vessels. Ro/ro's accommodated
[2]*Esso Oil Terminal:* Operated by Esso Bermuda, on the end of a 100 m pier, situated on the S side of Murray's Anchorage. Tankers up to 230 m loa can be accommodated

Bunkering: ExxonMobil Marine Fuels, Suite 900, One Alhambra Plaza, Coral Gables, FL 33134, United States of America, *Tel:* +1 305 459 6358, *Fax:* +1 305 459 6412, *Email:* emmf@exxonmobil.com, *Website:* www.exxonmobilmarinefuels.com – *Grades:* MGO – *Delivery Mode:* truck
Hampton Bermuda (Bunkering), Suite 402, International Centre, 26 Bermudiana Street, Pembroke, Hamilton, Bermuda HM 11, *Tel:* +1441 2950 902, *Fax:* +1441 2952 165, *Email:* bunkers@hamptonmtl.ca
The Shell Company of Bermuda Ltd, Rubis Energy Bermuda Ltd, P O Box GE2, St. George, St. George's Island, Bermuda GE BX, *Tel:* +1441 2971 577, *Fax:* +1441 2978 472, *Email:* corporate@rubis-bermuda.com – *Grades:* MDO – *Misc:* own storage facilities – *Rates:* 50-300t/h – *Notice:* 48 hours – *Delivery Mode:* pipeline, truck

Towage: Two tugs of 3200 hp and one tug of 1200 hp

Repair & Maintenance: Some marine repairs available. Marine slip of 1000 t cap. Emergency temporary repairs can be done at anchorage
Wm. F. Meyer & Co. Ltd Bermuda Machine & Casting Ltd, P O Box 20, St. George, St. George's Island, Bermuda, *Tel:* +1441 297 1712

Shipping Agents: Meyer Agencies Ltd, Admiral's Level, Somers Wharf, 14 Water Street, St. George, St. George's Island, Bermuda GE BX, *Tel:* +1441 297 2303, *Fax:* +1441 292 1583, *Email:* meyershipping@meyer.bm, *Website:* www.meyer.bm

Medical Facilities: Hamilton, 10 km

Airport: 2 km from port

Lloyd's Agent: Freisenbruch-Meyer Group, 75 Front Street, Hamilton, Bermuda HM 12, *Tel:* +1441 296 3600, *Fax:* +1441 295 6209, *Email:* jsykes@fmgroup.bm, *Website:* www.fmgroup.bm

BRAZIL

ALUMAR

Lat 2° 41' S; Long 44° 22' W.

Admiralty Chart: 535   **Admiralty Pilot:** 5
Time Zone: GMT -3 h   **UNCTAD Locode:** BR ALU

Alumar

Principal Facilities:

		Y				B		T	A	

Authority: Consorcio de Aluminio do Maranhao - ALUMAR, P O Box 661, 65095-050 Sao Luis MA, Brazil, *Tel:* +55 98 216 1392, *Website:* www.alumar.com.br

Approach: Access channel is 3 miles long with min width of 120 m and dredged to 7 m. There is a turning basin of 400 m dia

Anchorage: Waiting area in pos 2° 28.4' S; 44° 23.5' W

Pilotage: Compulsory

Traffic: 2005, 156 vessels, 4 644 867 t of cargo handled

Maximum Vessel Dimensions: 10.5 m draft
Principal Imports and Exports: Imports: Bauxite. Exports: Alumina.
Accommodation:

Name	Length (m)	Remarks
Alumar Wharf	252	Terminal located 8 km from Itaqui See [1] below

[1]*Wharf:* Consists of two berths with one berth designed to receive bauxite from the Trombetas mines in Amazonia with unloading cap of approx 1200 t/h, whilst the other berth is for exporting alumina at rate of 1500 t/h. Mooring dolphin 50 m from the W end of the wharf and a mooring buoy 110 m from the W end of the wharf

Bunkering: Available by barge with advance notice
Towage: Two tugs available of 1830 hp
Medical Facilities: Sao Luis Hospital
Airport: Approx 18 km
Lloyd's Agent: Inspect Consultoria Ltda (Sao Luis), Av Dos Portugueses, 31 Vila Embratel, 65085-580 Sao Luis MA, Brazil, *Tel:* +55 98 3242 4016, *Email:* inspectconsultoria@br.inter.net

ANGRA DOS REIS

Lat 23° 0' S; Long 44° 18' W.

Admiralty Chart: 433	**Admiralty Pilot:** 5
Time Zone: GMT -3 h	**UNCTAD Locode:** BR ADR

Principal Facilities:

	Y	G		R		B		T	

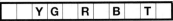

Tramp Oil & Marine

Wells House, 15-17 Elmfield Road, Bromley,
Kent BR1 1LT, United Kingdom
Phone: +44 20 8315 7777　**Fax:** +44 20 8315 7788
General email: enquiries@tramp-oil.com

See listings for all global offices: **www.tramp-oil.com**

Authority: Companhia Docas do Rio de Janeiro, Gerencia Porto de Angra dos Reis RJ, Avenida dos Reis Magos s/n, 23900-000 Angra dos Reis RJ, Brazil, *Tel:* +55 24 3365 0602, *Fax:* +55 24 3365 0273
Port Security: ISPS compliant
Approach: The access channel is 150 m wide commencing from where the N and S channels meet. Max depth of water is 14 m. The manoeuvring basin is 320 m wide with a depth of 10 m
Pilotage: Compulsory between the anchorage and any berth or between Imboassica Island and Saracura Island. Requisition for pilot can be made up to 2 h in advance
Tides: Range of tide 1.8 m
Traffic: 2006, 14 728 000 t of cargo handled
Maximum Vessel Dimensions: 200 m loa, 8.9 m draft, 29 000 dwt
Accommodation:

Name	Remarks
Angra dos Reis	See [1] below

[1]*Angra dos Reis:* The docks are 400 m long, of which 340 m is for berthing vessels, 9 m max draft at HW and 8 m at LW. Two suction grain dischargers with a rate of 60 t/h. There are also two privately owned mechanical conveyors for hire, each with an 80 t/h cap

Storage: Three warehouses with a total area of 5372 m2, eight yards with a total area of 21 020 m2 and a 17 unit silo cap 4200 t
Mechanical Handling Equipment:

Location	Type	Capacity (t)	Qty
Angra dos Reis	Floating Cranes	80	1
Angra dos Reis	Mult-purp. Cranes		12

Location	Type	Capacity (t)	Qty
Angra dos Reis	Forklifts		17

Bunkering: Tramp Oil & Marine, World Fuel Services Corporation, 13th Floor, Portland House, Bressenden Place, London SW1E 5BH, United Kingdom, *Tel:* +44 20 7808 5000, *Fax:* +44 20 7808 5088, *Email:* pturner@wfscorp.com, *Website:* www.wfscorp.com – *Grades:* all grades – *Delivery Mode:* barge, pipeline, truck
Towage: There are three tugs available of 320-650 hp
Repair & Maintenance: Minor repairs only
Medical Facilities: Hospital
Lloyd's Agent: Inspect Consultoria Ltda (Rio de Janeiro), Avenida Rio Branco 37, Grupo 1902 Centro, 20090-003 Rio de Janeiro RJ, Brazil, *Tel:* +55 21 2263 3330, *Fax:* +55 21 2253 9322, *Email:* inspectconsultoria@br.inter.net, *Website:* www.inspectconsultoria.com.br

ANTONINA

harbour area, see under Paranagua

ARACAJU

Lat 10° 55' S; Long 37° 2' W.

Admiralty Chart: 3976	**Admiralty Pilot:** 5
Time Zone: GMT -3 h	**UNCTAD Locode:** BR AJU

Principal Facilities:

P		G			B		A	

Tramp Oil & Marine

Wells House, 15-17 Elmfield Road, Bromley,
Kent BR1 1LT, United Kingdom
Phone: +44 20 8315 7777　**Fax:** +44 20 8315 7788
General email: enquiries@tramp-oil.com

See listings for all global offices: **www.tramp-oil.com**

Authority: Empresa Administradora de Portos de Sergipe, Travessa Baltazar Goes 86, Ed. Estado de Sergipe - 8 andar - Centro, 49010-500 Aracaju SE, Brazil, *Tel:* +55 79 3224 1855
Port Security: ISPS compliant
Approach: The approach channel is 100 m wide and 2400 m in length. Depth at the bar is 4 m
Anchorage: Depth at the anchorage is 12 m
Pilotage: Compulsory, 24 h notice required
Traffic: 2002, 2 886 743 t of cargo handled
Accommodation:

Name	Length (m)	Depth (m)	Draught (m)	Remarks
Aracaju				See [1] below
Concrete Docks	96	5–7		See [2] below
Commercial Quay	340		10.5	

[1]*Aracaju:* Tanker facilities: Carmopolis Terminal operated by Petrobas, Dutos E Terminais da Bahia, Sergipe E Alagoas (DTBASA), Tel: +55 79 3243 2611, Fax: +55 79 3243 1735
Located 9 km S of Aracaju. Crude oil loading seaberth in pos 11° 02' 53" S; 37° 00' 47" W in a depth of 18 m. Tankers are moored to buoys and loading is effected by a submarine pipeline extending 7.5 km from the shore. Vessels up to 115 000 dwt, max loa 300 m, 15 m draft can be accommodated in favorable conditions. Mooring during daylight hours only
[2]*Concrete Docks:* The height of the dock surface from the water level is 4 m at LT and 1.07 m at HT

Storage: General cargo warehouse of 2500 m2. Urea silo of 35 000 m3

Key to Principal Facilities:—			
A=Airport	**C**=Containers	**G**=General Cargo	**P**=Petroleum	**R**=Ro/Ro	**Y**=Dry Bulk
B=Bunkers	**D**=Dry Dock	**L**=Cruise	**Q**=Other Liquid Bulk	**T**=Towage (where available from port)

Mechanical Handling Equipment:

Location	Type	Capacity (t)	Qty
Aracaju	Mult-purp. Cranes	30	1
Aracaju	Forklifts	2	1

Bunkering: Tramp Oil & Marine, World Fuel Services Corporation, 13th Floor, Portland House, Bressenden Place, London SW1E 5BH, United Kingdom, *Tel:* +44 20 7808 5000, *Fax:* +44 20 7808 5088, *Email:* pturner@wfscorp.com, *Website:* www.wfscorp.com – *Grades:* all grades – *Delivery Mode:* barge, pipeline, truck

Repair & Maintenance: Small repairs only

Medical Facilities: There are several hospitals and first-aid services available

Airport: Santa Maria, 13 km

Lloyd's Agent: Inspect Consultoria Ltda (Recife), Rua Padre Carapuceiro 412/603, Boa Viagem, 51020-280 Recife PE, Brazil, *Tel:* +55 81 9952 5868, *Email:* inspectrecife@terra.com.br

ARACRUZ

alternate name, see Portocel

ARATU

Lat 12° 47' S; Long 38° 29' W.

Admiralty Chart: 545   **Admiralty Pilot:** 5
Time Zone: GMT -3 h   **UNCTAD Locode:** BR ARB

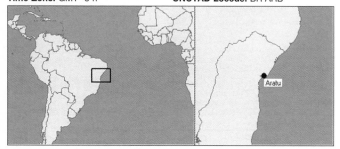

Principal Facilities:

P	Q	Y					T	A

Authority: Companhia das Docas do Estado da Bahia (CODEBA), Porto de Aratu, Via Matoim s/n, Baia de Aratu, 43800-000 Candeias BA, Brazil, *Tel:* +55 71 3602 5711, *Fax:* +55 71 3602 5705, *Email:* portoaratu@codeba.com.br, *Website:* www.codeba.com.br

Port Security: ISPS compliant

Pilotage: Compulsory

Traffic: 2007, 6 747 827 t of cargo handled

Accommodation:

Name	Length (m)	Depth (m)	Remarks
Solid Bulk Terminal (TGS)			
North Berth	153.2	12	Max 200 m loa
South Berth	202.6	11.5	Max 250 m loa
Liquid Bulk Terminal (TGL)			
North Berth		12	Max 220 m loa
South Berth		11	Max 170 m loa
Liquid Gas Terminal (TPG)			
Berth	70	12	Max 297 m loa

Towage: Available

Airport: Dois de Julho Airport, 43 km

Lloyd's Agent: Inspect Consultoria Ltda (Recife), Rua Padre Carapuceiro 412/603, Boa Viagem, 51020-280 Recife PE, Brazil, *Tel:* +55 81 9952 5868, *Email:* inspectrecife@terra.com.br

AREIA BRANCA

see under Salineiro Terminal

ATALAIA DOCK

harbour area, see under Vitoria

BARAO DE TEFFE

harbour area, see under Paranagua

BARRA DO RIACHO

alternate name, see Portocel

BELEM

Lat 1° 26' S; Long 48° 29' W.

Admiralty Chart: 397   **Admiralty Pilot:** 5
Time Zone: GMT -3 h   **UNCTAD Locode:** BR BEL

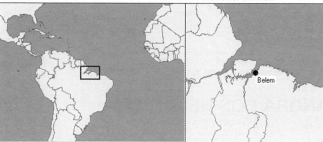

Principal Facilities:

P	Q	Y	G	C	R	L	B	D	T	A

Tramp Oil & Marine

Wells House, 15-17 Elmfield Road, Bromley,
Kent BR1 1LT, United Kingdom
Phone: +44 20 8315 7777   **Fax:** +44 20 8315 7788
General email: enquiries@tramp-oil.com

See listings for all global offices: **www.tramp-oil.com**

Authority: Companhia Docas do Para, Porto de Belem, Av. Marechal Hermes s/n, Cais do Porto, 66010-000 Belem PA, Brazil, *Tel:* +55 91 3216 2073, *Fax:* +55 91 3216 2042, *Email:* pedroamaral@cdp.com.br, *Website:* www.cdp.com.br

Officials: Port Administrator: Pedro Paulo Amaral.

Port Security: ISPS compliant

Approach: The approach to Belem is entered via the Baia de Marajo which is at the mouth of the River Para
Canal do Mosqueiro, the channel leading to Belem is entered between Ponta do Chapeau - Virado and Ilha Tatuoca 4.25 nautical miles SSW - extending 18 nautical miles S to the wharves. There are three entrance channels into the Baia de Guajara. One for deepsea vessels and large coasters, one for small coasters and river craft and one with a shallow, dividing it into two and connecting to the main channel on the eastern side. The main approach channel begins off Val-de-Caes and is about 3 miles long. It's width varies from 90-180 m and at spring tides the depth is 8 m

Anchorage: (a) Vessels with a draught greater than 8 m anchor off Icoaraci where they can work cargo to lighters, depth 10.06 m. This is situated 10 miles N of Belem. There are lighters of 50-500 t available and tugs for towing them. Stevedores come from Belem
(b) Impounded vessels anchor off Val-de-Caes (3 miles N of Belem), depth 7.92 m
(c) Vessels undergoing repairs anchor off the Naval base dock at Val-de-Caes
(d) Vessels with a draught less than 8 m anchor at Val-de-Caes - co-ordinates: 01° 24.01' S; 48° 30' W and 01° 21.03' S; 48° 29.03' W
The anchorage off the port of Belem is in depths of up to 8.5 m but the current is very strong
The anchorages have good holding ground. It must be noted that the banks and channels in the Baia de Guajara are subject to continual change

Pilotage: Pilotage between Salinopolis and the port is compulsory and pilots board vessels approx 7 nautical miles N of the Salinas lighthouse in about 11 fathoms. There are twelve pilots employed on the Salinopolis to Belem area of the river

Weather: Tropical. Frequent rain from January to June with an annual rainfall of 107"

Tides: Tidal range of 3.33 m

Traffic: 2007, 11 466 980 t of cargo handled, 67 141 TEU's

Principal Imports and Exports: Imports: Refined fuel products, Wheat. Exports: Metallic silicon, Nuts, Pepper, Timber.

Working Hours: 24 h available if required

Accommodation:

Name	Length (m)	Depth (m)	Remarks
Belem			
Berths 1-2	300	3–5	River craft
Berths 3-4	342	3–6.7	River craft
Berths 5-7	385	3–6.7	Coastal vessels
Berth No.8	100	6.7	See [1] below

Name	Length (m)	Depth (m)	Remarks
Berth No.9		2.5	River craft
Berth No.10			River craft
Berths 11-12	261	6.7	See [2] below
Grain Terminal	110	7.3	

[1]*Berth No.8:* Coastal vessels with occasional foreign vessels. Warehouse for imported cargo
[2]*Berths 11-12:* Overseas vessels. Warehouse for imported cargoes

Mechanical Handling Equipment:

Location	Type	Capacity (t)	Qty
Belem	Floating Cranes	200	1
Belem	Electric Cranes	6–13.2	16

Bunkering: Tramp Oil & Marine, World Fuel Services Corporation, 13th Floor, Portland House, Bressenden Place, London SW1E 5BH, United Kingdom, *Tel:* +44 20 7808 5000, *Fax:* +44 20 7808 5088, *Email:* pturner@wfscorp.com, *Website:* www.wfscorp.com – *Grades:* all grades – *Delivery Mode:* pipeline, barge, truck

Towage: There are no tugs for docking/undocking. Naval tugs may be used in an emergency. Private tugs are available

Ship Chandlers: Comercial Calhau Ltda, Trav Angustura 1.852, 66080-180 Belem, Brazil, *Tel:* +55 91 3276 0138, *Fax:* +55 91 3276 5182, *Email:* calhau@amazon.com.br

Shipping Agents: Agencia Maritima Brandao Filhos Ltda, Avenida Conselheiro Furtado 2865, P O Box 1904, Belem, Brazil, *Tel:* +55 91 3259 2591, *Fax:* +55 91 3269 5500, *Email:* belem@brandao.com.br
Atlas Maritime Ltda, Avenida Alcindo Cacela 1264, SL 1002/1003, Nazare, 66060-000 Belem PA, Brazil, *Tel:* +55 91 3246 7300, *Fax:* +55 91 3246 7011, *Email:* atlas_belem@atlasmaritime.com.br, *Website:* www.atlasmaritime.com.br
CMA-CGM S.A., CMA CGM do Brasil Agencia Maritima, Av. Governador Jose Malcher 815, 6 Andar Nazare, Ed Paladium Center, 66035-100 Belem PA, Brazil, *Tel:* +55 91 3202 9500, *Fax:* +55 91 3223 0533, *Email:* brb.genmbox@cma-cgm.com, *Website:* www.cma-cgm.com
Consulmar Agencia Maritima Ltda, Avenida Marechal hermes 368, Bairro Reduto, CEP 66053-150, Belem, Brazil, *Tel:* +55 91 3241 1608, *Fax:* +55 91 3242 6624
Corymar Agencia Maritima Ltd, Rua Santo Antonio 316, Conj 501 Centro, 66010-090 Belem PA, Brazil, *Tel:* +55 91 3222 4973, *Fax:* +55 91 3223 9432, *Email:* willbel@williams.com.br, *Website:* www.williams.com.br
LBH Brasil, Av. Gov. Jose Malcher 815 - Conj 801, Ed Palladium Center, Bairro Nazare, 66055-260 Belem PA, Brazil, *Tel:* +55 91 4006 6855, *Fax:* +55 91 4006 6864, *Email:* brazblm@lbhbrasil.com.br, *Website:* www.brazshipping.com.br
Oceanus Agencia Maritima S.A., Av. Senador Lemos 443 - R 909, 66050-000 Belem PA, Brazil, *Tel:* +55 91 3212 7600, *Fax:* +55 91 3242 9833, *Email:* agency.blm@oceanus.com.br, *Website:* www.oceanus.com.br
Wilson Sons Agencia Maritima Ltda, Av. Governador Magalhaes Barata 651, Edificio Belem Office Center Sala 610, Bairro Nazare, 66063-240 Belem PA, Brazil, *Tel:* +55 91 4009 0050, *Fax:* +55 91 4009 0051, *Email:* agebe@wilsonsons.com.br, *Website:* www.wilsonsons.com.br

Surveyors: Nippon Kaiji Kyokai, Hw Engenharia e Comercio Ltda, Rodovia Arthur Bernardes 397, 66115-000 Belem PA, Brazil, *Tel:* +55 91 3244 2877, *Fax:* +55 91 3244 0252, *Website:* www.classnk.or.jp

Airport: Val-de-Caes International, 5 km

Lloyd's Agent: Inspect Consultoria Ltda (Recife), Rua Padre Carapuceiro 412/603, Boa Viagem, 51020-280 Recife PE, Brazil, *Tel:* +55 81 9952 5868, *Email:* inspectrecife@terra.com.br

CABEDELO

Lat 6° 58' S; Long 34° 50' W.

Admiralty Chart: 960	**Admiralty Pilot:** 5
Time Zone: GMT -3 h	**UNCTAD Locode:** BR CDO

Principal Facilities:

P		Y	G	C	R		T	

Authority: Companhia Docas da Paraiba, Porto de Cabedelo, Rua Presidente Joao Pessoa s/n, 58310-000 Cabedelo PA, Brazil, *Tel:* +55 83 3228 2805, *Fax:* +55 83 3228 2619

Port Security: ISPS compliant

Approach: 6 km long, 150 m wide with a depth of 8 m. The turning basin is 700 m long, 300 m wide with a depth of 10 m

Anchorage: Anchorage in the vicinity of the breakwater has depths of water from 9 to 15 m at LT and at the anchorage S of the docks, the depth is 4.6 m at LT

Pilotage: Compulsory. Request for pilot should be radioed 12 h in advance. While waiting for pilots, vessels should anchor ENE from the light beacon at a distance of 1.3 km where the depth of water is 10 m, but care should be taken to avoid some stony parts at the bottom

Traffic: 2005, 156 800 t of cargo handled

Principal Imports and Exports: Imports: Coal, Corn, Petroleum products, Soya beans. Exports: Bentonite, Cotton, Fruit, Mica, Sisal.

Accommodation:

Name	Remarks
Cabedelo	See [1] below

[1]*Cabedelo:* The dock space is 602 m long, 20 m wide with a depth of 10 m. The height of the dock surface from water level at LT is 3.42 m and at HT is 0.58 m
Container handling area of 10 000 m2 and a ro/ro ramp

Storage: Eight warehouses totalling 16 000 m2 and a general cargo shed of 1310 m2

Location	Open (m2)
Cabedelo	8496

Mechanical Handling Equipment:

Location	Type	Capacity (t)	Qty
Cabedelo	Mult-purp. Cranes	6	5
Cabedelo	Forklifts		27

Towage: Two tugs available

Repair & Maintenance: Metalurgica Heim is the only small repair shop in the area

Shipping Agents: Agencia Maritima Cabo Branco Ltda, Rua Presidente Joao Pessoa 19 - Centro, Cabedelo, Brazil, *Tel:* +55 83 3228 3284, *Fax:* +55 83 3228 3127, *Email:* info@agcabobranco.com.br, *Website:* www.agcabobranco.com.br
Corymar Agencia Maritima Ltd, Avenida Presidente Joao Pessoa 61, 58310-000 Cabedelo PB, Brazil, *Tel:* +55 83 3228 1350, *Fax:* +55 83 3228 1092, *Email:* willcbd@williams.com.br, *Website:* www.williams.com.br
Heytor Gusmao Comercio e Representacoes Ltda, Rua Presidente Joao Pessoa 21, CEP 58310-000 Cabedelo, Brazil, *Tel:* +55 83 3228 3030, *Fax:* +55 83 3228 2033, *Email:* heygus@heytorgusmao.com.br, *Website:* www.heytorgusmao.com.br
LBH Brasil, Rua Pastor Jose Alves de Oliveira 516 - Sala 104, 58310-000 Cabedelo PB, Brazil, *Tel:* +55 83 3228 1575, *Fax:* +55 83 3228 1575, *Email:* brazcbl@lbhbrasil.com.br, *Website:* www.brazshipping.com.br
Ultramar Agencia Maritima Ltda, Rua Presidente Joao Pessoa 19, 58310-000 Cabedelo, Brazil, *Tel:* +55 83 3228 3284, *Fax:* +55 83 3228 3127, *Website:* www.ultramargroup.com
Wilson Sons Agencia Maritima Ltda, Pca. Getulio Vargas 99 - Centro, 58130-000 Cabedelo PB, Brazil, *Tel:* +55 83 3228 8844, *Fax:* +55 83 3228 8848, *Email:* opere@wilsonsons.com.br, *Website:* www.wilsonsons.com.br

Medical Facilities: There is a hospital at Cabedelo and a larger one at Joao Pessoa

Lloyd's Agent: Inspect Consultoria Ltda (Recife), Rua Padre Carapuceiro 412/603, Boa Viagem, 51020-280 Recife PE, Brazil, *Tel:* +55 81 9952 5868, *Email:* inspectrecife@terra.com.br

CAPUABA DOCK

harbour area, see under Vitoria

FORNO

Lat 23° 1' S; Long 42° 0' W.

Admiralty Chart: 3971	**Admiralty Pilot:** 5
Time Zone: GMT -3 h	**UNCTAD Locode:** BR FNO

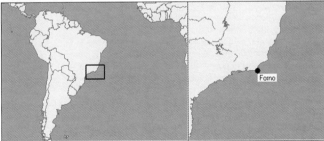

Principal Facilities:

		Y	G					

Authority: Companhia Municipal da Administracao Portuaria, Porto de Forno, Rua Santa Cruz 100, 28930-000 Arraial do Cabo RJ, Brazil, *Tel:* +55 24 622 1185, *Fax:* +55 24 622 1185, *Email:* portodoforno@mar.com.br

Approach: Vessels pass through the bar between Cabo Frio Island and Porcos Island

Tides: Rise of tide 0.7 m

Traffic: 2005, 567 976 t of cargo handled

Accommodation:

Name	Remarks
Forno	See [1] below

[1]*Forno:* The harbour has three berths with total berthing length of 300 m with depth alongside of 10 m. Vessels up to 36 000 dwt engaged in the coastal trade only can be accommodated. Two berths handle solid bulks. Specific goods such as salt and caustic soda are handled; raw materials essential to the Companhia Nacional de Alcalis Installation

---

	Key to Principal Facilities:—				
A=Airport	**C**=Containers	**G**=General Cargo	**P**=Petroleum	**R**=Ro/Ro	**Y**=Dry Bulk
B=Bunkers	**D**=Dry Dock	**L**=Cruise	**Q**=Other Liquid Bulk	**T**=Towage (where available from port)	

Storage:

Location	Covered (m²)
Forno	5000

Mechanical Handling Equipment:

Location	Type	Capacity (t)	Qty
Forno	Mult-purp. Cranes	6	3

Lloyd's Agent: Inspect Consultoria Ltda (Rio de Janeiro), Avenida Rio Branco 37, Grupo 1902 Centro, 20090-003 Rio de Janeiro RJ, Brazil, *Tel:* +55 21 2263 3330, *Fax:* +55 21 2253 9322, *Email:* inspectconsultoria@br.inter.net, *Website:* www.inspectconsultoria.com.br

FORTALEZA

Lat 3° 45' S; Long 38° 30' W.

Admiralty Chart: 526		**Admiralty Pilot:** 5
Time Zone: GMT -3 h		**UNCTAD Locode:** BR FOR

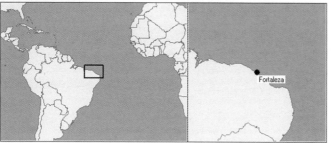

Principal Facilities:

P Q Y G C R L B T A

Tramp Oil & Marine

Wells House, 15-17 Elmfield Road, Bromley, Kent BR1 1LT, United Kingdom

Phone: +44 20 8315 7777　**Fax:** +44 20 8315 7788

General email: enquiries@tramp-oil.com

See listings for all global offices: **www.tramp-oil.com**

Authority: Companhia Docas do Ceara, Praca Amigos da Marinha s/n, Mucuripe, 60182-640 Fortaleza CE, Brazil, *Tel:* +55 85 3263 2267, *Fax:* +55 85 3266 5241, *Email:* docasdoceara@docasdoceara.com.br, *Website:* www.docasdoceara.com.br

Port Security: ISPS compliant

Approach: The entrance channel is 1000 m long, 100 m wide in depth of 10 m. Manoeuvring basin 500 m wide in depth of 7-10 m

Anchorage: Available in pos 3° 40' 3" S; 38° 29' 5" W in a depth of 11 m

Pilotage: Compulsory. Pilot boards from a red motor launch off the end of the breakwater

Radio Frequency: VHF Channel 16

Weather: SE and E winds

Tides: Max 2.6 m, average 2 m

Traffic: 2005, 4 448 409 t of cargo handled

Maximum Vessel Dimensions: 190 m loa, 70 000 dwt, 10 m draft

Principal Imports and Exports: Imports: Bulk oil, Malt in bags, Wheat. Exports: Cashew nuts, Cotton, Fish, Lobster tails, Textiles.

Working Hours: 0700-1300, 1300-1900, 1900-0100, 0100-0700

Accommodation:

Name	Length (m)	Depth (m)	Remarks
Commercial Wharf			
Berth 101	220	5–8	See [1] below
Berth 102	197	5–8	See [2] below
Berth 103	210	10	See [3] below
Berth 104	210	10	See [4] below
Berth 105	210	10	See [5] below
Petroleum Pier			See [6] below
Fishing Wharf			210 m long in depth of 3-5 m

[1]*Berth 101:* Situated in front of warehouse A1, from mooring dolphin 1 to mooring dolphin 8. For Petrobras tugs, fishing boats and long haul vessels that do not require deep draught for docking

[2]*Berth 102:* Situated in front of warehouse A2, from mooring dolphin 8 to mooring dolphin 17. For Petrobras tugs, fishing boats and long haul vessels that do not require deep draught for docking

[3]*Berth 103:* Situated in front of warehouse A3, from mooring dolphin 17 to mooring dolphin 24. For docking of coastal and long haul vessels

[4]*Berth 104:* Situated in front of warehouse A4, from mooring dolphin 24 to mooring dolphin 31. For docking of coastal and long haul vessels

[5]*Berth 105:* Situated in front of warehouse A5, from mooring dolphin 31 to mooring dolphin 38. For docking of coastal and long haul vessels

[6]*Petroleum Pier:* Access bridge 853 m long and docking platform 90 m long. Petroleum and other products are discharged through shore lines on the quay from two mooring berths. The inner berth has a depth of 11 m and outer berth has a depth of 12 m

Storage: Five warehouses (A1-A5), each of 6000 m2. Two open storage areas for containers, one behind warehouses A3-A4 of 50 000 m2 and one behind warehouse A5 of 60 000 m2. Privately owned silo storage

Mechanical Handling Equipment:

Location	Type	Capacity (t)	Qty
Fortaleza	Mult-purp. Cranes	15	6

Cargo Worked: General cargo break bulk approx 25 t/h/gang

Bunkering: Tramp Oil & Marine, World Fuel Services Corporation, 13th Floor, Portland House, Bressenden Place, London SW1E 5BH, United Kingdom, *Tel:* +44 20 7808 5000, *Fax:* +44 20 7808 5088, *Email:* pturner@wfscorp.com, *Website:* www.wfscorp.com – *Grades:* all grades – *Delivery Mode:* barge, pipeline, truck

Towage: Four tugs of 1050-2200 hp

Repair & Maintenance: Industria Naval do Ceara Ltda (hull, equipment and motor repairs); Federal Railway System S.A. (heavy machinery repairs and marine repairs only in cases of emergency)
Mecanica Industrial e Maritime Ltda, Fortaleza, Brazil Mechanical, electronic and refrigerator repairs
Mechanics and Salvage Netuno Ltd, Fortaleza, Brazil Engines and equipments, also provide divers for hull requirements
Retifica Sao Paulo, Fortaleza, Brazil Motor and equipment repairs
Tecno-Mecanica Norte S.A. - TECNORTE, Fortaleza, Brazil Metal containers for petroleum by-products and compressed gas

Ship Chandlers: Nordsee Ship Supplies, Rua Engenheiro Placido Coelho Jr, No 78 Bairro, Vicente Pizon, 60 155-480 Fortaleza, Brazil, *Tel:* +55 85 3249 3227, *Fax:* +55 85 3249 3222, *Email:* nordsee@emsbrazil.com, *Website:* www.emsbrazil.com
Servmar-Servicos Maritimos Ltda, Rua Olga Barroso N 108, Mucuripe, 60175-390 Fortaleza, Brazil, *Tel:* +55 85 3262 7866, *Fax:* +55 85 3262 2012, *Email:* servmar@servmar.com.br, *Website:* www.servmar.com.br

Shipping Agents: Agencia Maritima Brandao Filhos Ltda, Rua Oswaldo Cruz 1 - Sala 412, Meireles, 60120-002 Fortaleza, Brazil, *Tel:* +55 85 3242 1818, *Fax:* +55 85 3242 1442, *Email:* santana1@brandao.com.br, *Website:* www.brandao.com.br
V. Castro & Cia Ltda, Suite 1/2, Avenida Rui Barbosa 780, Shopping Malaui, 60115-222 Fortaleza, Brazil, *Tel:* +55 85 3261 4433, *Fax:* +55 85 3264 2074, *Email:* vcastro@vcastro.com.br, *Website:* www.vcastro.com.br
CMA-CGM S.A., CMA CGM do Brasil Agencia Maritima, Rua Costa Barros 915 - Sls 1301/1303, Centro, 60160-280 Fortaleza CE, Brazil, *Tel:* +55 85 4006 8999, *Fax:* +55 85 4006 8953, *Email:* brf.genmbox@cma-cgm.com, *Website:* www.cma-cgm.com
Consulmar Agencia Maritima Ltda, Room 407, 915 Costa Barros, Edano Building, Centro, 60160-280 Fortaleza, Brazil, *Tel:* +55 85 3254 4566, *Fax:* +55 85 3254 4732, *Email:* consuopra@ultranet.com.br
Corymar Agencia Maritima Ltd, Avenida Monsenhor Tabosa 111, 1st Floor Room 14, Vicente de Castro Neto Building, 60165-000 Fortaleza CE, Brazil, *Tel:* +55 85 3219 9370, *Fax:* +55 85 3219 0045, *Email:* willfor@williams.com.br, *Website:* www.williams.com.br
A.P. Moller-Maersk Group, Maersk Brasil Ltda, Av Santos Dumont 1789, Sala 1301-1305, 60150-160 Fortaleza CE, Brazil, *Tel:* +55 85 3486 1900, *Fax:* +55 85 3486 1901, *Email:* brzcrcftz@maersk.com, *Website:* www.maerskline.com
Transatlantic Carriers (Agenciamentos) Ltda, Av Dom Luiz, Suite 628, Fortaleza, Brazil, *Tel:* +55 85 3264 0040, *Fax:* +55 85 3264 0040, *Email:* operations@transcar-fortaleza.com.br
Wilson Sons Agencia Maritima Ltda, Ed. Ebano Centro Comercial, Rua Costa Barros 915 - Salas 1101, 1103, 1105, 60160-280 Fortaleza CE, Brazil, *Tel:* +55 85 4005 6151, *Fax:* +55 85 4005 6161, *Email:* agefz@wilsonsons.com.br, *Website:* www.wilsonsons.com.br

Medical Facilities: Available

Airport: Pinto Martins Airport, 10 km

Railway: REFESA-with connection to the port

Lloyd's Agent: Inspect Consultoria Ltda (Sao Luis), Av Dos Portugueses, 31 Vila Embratel, 65085-580 Sao Luis MA, Brazil, *Tel:* +55 98 3242 4016, *Email:* inspectconsultoria@br.inter.net

GEBIG

Lat 23° 3' S; Long 44° 14' W.

Admiralty Chart: 433		**Admiralty Pilot:** 5
Time Zone: GMT -3 h		**UNCTAD Locode:** BR GEB

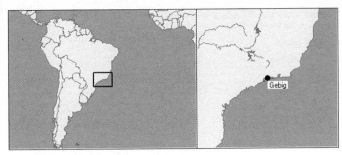

Principal Facilities:

P					B	T		

Tramp Oil & Marine

Wells House, 15-17 Elmfield Road, Bromley,
Kent BR1 1LT, United Kingdom
Phone: +44 20 8315 7777   **Fax:** +44 20 8315 7788
General email: enquiries@tramp-oil.com

See listings for all global offices: **www.tramp-oil.com**

Authority: Dutos e Terminals do Sudeste, Terminal Gerencia da Baia da Ilha Grande (GEBIG), BR 101 Km. 81 Jacuacanga, 23900 Angra dos Reis RJ, Brazil, *Tel:* +55 24 3361 2255, *Fax:* +55 24 3361 2519

Port Security: ISPS compliant

Pre-Arrival Information: ETA must be radioed by all Petrobras chartered vessels 72 h and 48 h prior to arrival to Petrobras as well as to the Agent. Confirmation as well as any changes in ETA must be radioed 24 h prior to arrival

Approach: The access channel from anchorage to the maneuvering area (near the pier) is approx 8.75 miles long, 350 m wide and 25 m deep

Anchorage: For tankers awaiting a berth or for lighterage anchorage is within a circle of 1 mile radius, its centre near Ponta de Acaia, with Laje Branca Lt. bearing 075°(T) 2.8 miles away

Pilotage: Compulsory. Pilot boards 3.2 km WSW of Ponta Acaia, the W point of Ilha Grande. ETA should be signalled 72 h in advance stating last port of call and draught, then confirmed 48 h and 24 h before arrival

Radio Frequency: VHF Channel 16

Tides: Local and diurnal tidal rise is approx 1.2 m above MLWS at neaps and 1.7 m in MHWS

Maximum Vessel Dimensions: 500 000 dwt, 25 m draft

Working Hours: 24 h/day

Accommodation:

Name	Length (m)	Depth (m)	Remarks
Gebig			See [1] below
Outer Berth (P1)	570	30	See [2] below
Inner Berth (P2)	570	36	See [3] below

[1]*Gebig:* L-shaped pier accommodating oil tankers up to 500 000 dwt, projecting from Ponta do Leme, approx 1318 m long in a east-westerly direction, with two berths
[2]*Outer Berth (P1):* Four 20" loading arms for oil and ballast & one 12" loading arm for diesel oil and fuel oil
[3]*Inner Berth (P2):* Four 16" loading arms for oil and ballast & one 12" loading arm for diesel oil and fuel oil

Bunkering: Tramp Oil & Marine, World Fuel Services Corporation, 13th Floor, Portland House, Bressenden Place, London SW1E 5BH, United Kingdom, *Tel:* +44 20 7808 5000, *Fax:* +44 20 7808 5088, *Email:* pturner@wfscorp.com, *Website:* www.wfscorp.com – *Grades:* all grades – *Notice:* 48 hours – *Delivery Mode:* barge, pipeline, truck

Towage: Three tugs available of 3720 hp

Medical Facilities: If required, emergency medical aid may be summoned

Lloyd's Agent: Inspect Consultoria Ltda (Rio de Janeiro), Avenida Rio Branco 37, Grupo 1902 Centro, 20090-003 Rio de Janeiro RJ, Brazil, *Tel:* +55 21 2263 3330, *Fax:* +55 21 2253 9322, *Email:* inspectconsultoria@br.inter.net, *Website:* www.inspectconsultoria.com.br

GUAIBA ISLAND

harbour area, see under Sepetiba

GUAMARE TERMINAL

Lat 4° 52' S; Long 36° 21' W.

Admiralty Chart: 3955	**Admiralty Pilot:** 5
Time Zone: GMT -3 h	**UNCTAD Locode:** BR

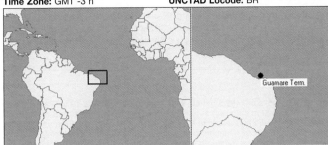

Principal Facilities:

P									

Authority: Petrobras Dutos e Terminais do Norte e Nordeste, Rodovia PE 60, Km.10 s/n, 54500-000 Ipojuca PE, Brazil, *Tel:* +55 81 527 1077

Port Security: ISPS compliant

Anchorage: The recommended anchorage is in pos 4° 51' 05" S; 36° 23' 00" W in depth of 17 m

Pilotage: All maneuvers are performed by the ship's captain, assisted by a Mooring Master of the Terminal, who comes onboard at the anchorage

Accommodation:

Name	Remarks
Guamare Terminal	See [1] below

[1]*Guamare Terminal:* The DTNEST/SEGUAM offshore terminal is a single berth of five mooring buoys named Quadro de Boias de Ubarana, where vessels up to 116 000 dwt can moor after dropping both its anchors. The terminal loads tankers with crude oil generated in the fields of Rio Grande do Norte State, including offshore production. The total storage cap of the terminal is 172 000 m3

Lloyd's Agent: Inspect Consultoria Ltda (Recife), Rua Padre Carapuceiro 412/603, Boa Viagem, 51020-280 Recife PE, Brazil, *Tel:* +55 81 9952 5868, *Email:* inspectrecife@terra.com.br

ILHA DA MADEIRA

harbour area, see under Sepetiba

ILHA DO PRINCIPE TERMINAL

harbour area, see under Vitoria

ILHA GUAIBA

harbour area, see under Sepetiba

ILHEUS

Lat 14° 47' S; Long 39° 1' W.

Admiralty Chart: 551	**Admiralty Pilot:** 5
Time Zone: GMT -3 h	**UNCTAD Locode:** BR IOS

Principal Facilities:

P	Q	Y	G	C	R	L	B		T	A

Authority: Companhia das Docas do Estado da Bahia (CODEBA), Porto de Ilheus, Rua Rotary s/n, Cidade Nova, 45650-000 Ilheus BA, Brazil, *Tel:* +55 73 3231 1200, *Fax:* +55 73 3231 3318, *Email:* portoilheus@codeba.com.br, *Website:* www.codeba.com.br

Port Security: ISPS compliant

Key to Principal Facilities:—				
A=Airport	**C**=Containers	**G**=General Cargo	**P**=Petroleum	**R**=Ro/Ro	**Y**=Dry Bulk
B=Bunkers	**D**=Dry Dock	**L**=Cruise	**Q**=Other Liquid Bulk	**T**=Towage (where available from port)	

Approach: The artificial basin is formed by a breakwater 1922 m long, the first 650 m bearing NE, followed by a curve of 162 m leading to the last part bearing N and 1110 m long. The approach channel is 200 m wide and 1150 m long bearing N, its axis at 165 m from the protecting breakwater and commencing at the Ponta do Molhe (light beacon). The manoeuvring basin is 200 m wide and 10 m in depth

Pilotage: Compulsory. Any request for a pilot should be made at least 4 h in advance

Traffic: 2007, 756 246 t of cargo handled

Maximum Vessel Dimensions: Max gt 17 000 t, 210 m max loa

Principal Imports and Exports: Exports: Cocoa beans, Cocoa products, Graphite.

Working Hours: Monday to Saturday 0700-1100, 1300-1700. Overtime can be arranged

Accommodation:

Name	Remarks
Ilheus	See [1] below

[1]*Ilheus:* The docks are 432.5 m long with a depth alongside of 10 m. There is also a wooden pier 70 m long with a depth alongside of 6.0 m. The height of the dock surface from the water level is 4 m at LT and 1.5 m at HT. The main terminal attends to the export of cocoa beans from the most important cocoa producing region of Brazil. Of the other two terminals, one is for the handling of inflammables destined for all S parts, of Bahia, for N parts of Minas Gerais and for the state of Espirito Santo, and the remaining terminal handles liquid petroleum gas also destined to the same regions as the inflammables
There is 7000 m2 of container storage space with one 32 t cap crane available

Storage:

Location	Covered (m²)	Sheds / Warehouses
Ilheus	16000	2

Mechanical Handling Equipment:

Location	Type	Capacity (t)	Qty
Ilheus	Mult-purp. Cranes	3	3
Ilheus	Mult-purp. Cranes	6	2

Bunkering: Petrobras Bunkering, Avenida Republica do Chile 65, 20 andar, sala 2001-H, 20035-913 Rio de Janeiro, Brazil, *Tel:* +55 21 3224 3290, *Fax:* +55 21 2262 8134, *Email:* bunker@petrobras.com.br, *Website:* www.petrobras.com.br – *Grades:* MGO – *Delivery Mode:* truck

Towage: Three tugs of 650, 750 and 1500 hp

Repair & Maintenance: Repair shops available for small repairs or emergencies

Shipping Agents: Bahiaship Agencia Maritima Ltda, Room 206/7, Praca Jose Marcelino 14, CEP 45660-000 Ilheus, Brazil, *Tel:* +55 73 3231 7979, *Fax:* +55 73 3231 7972, *Email:* bahiaship@bahiaship.com.br

Medical Facilities: Six hospitals and adequate medical attention is available

Airport: 3 km from city

Lloyd's Agent: Inspect Consultoria Ltda (Recife), Rua Padre Carapuceiro 412/603, Boa Viagem, 51020-280 Recife PE, Brazil, *Tel:* +55 81 9952 5868, *Email:* inspectrecife@terra.com.br

IMBITUBA

Lat 28° 14' S; Long 48° 39' W.

Admiralty Chart: 549   **Admiralty Pilot:** 5
Time Zone: GMT -3 h   **UNCTAD Locode:** BR IBB

Principal Facilities:

P	Q	Y	G	C	R		B		T	

Authority: Companhia Docas de Imbituba, Porto de Imbituba, Av. Presidente Vargas s/n, 88780-000 Imbituba SC, Brazil, *Tel:* +55 48 3255 0080, *Fax:* +55 48 3255 0701, *Email:* jeziel@cdiport.com.br, *Website:* www.cdiport.com.br

Officials: Port Administrator: Jeziel Pamato de Souza.
Marketing Manager: Marcio Nunes, *Email:* marcio@cdiport.com.br.

Port Security: ISPS compliant

Approach: Consists of an artificial basin open to the NNW and protected by a breakwater on its E side, which projects 850 m NNW from Ponta da Imbituba. Access to the port is via the N channel between the beach and rocks in min depth of 10 m, or the S channel between the rocks and the breakwater in min depth of 12 m

Pilotage: Compulsory. Pilot may be contacted on VHF Channel 16 with ETA to be given 24 h prior to arrival via radio "PPF", and confirmed or adjusted 12 h prior to arrival

Weather: Prevailing NE'ly and SW'ly winds

Tides: Tidal range 0.8 m

Traffic: 2007, 1 467 817 t of cargo handled

Maximum Vessel Dimensions: 200 m loa, 9.5 m draft

Principal Imports and Exports: Imports: Coal coke, Corn, Fertiliser, Salt, Soda ash. Exports: Containers, Frozen products, Sugar.

Working Hours: 24 h/day

Accommodation:

Name	Length (m)	Depth (m)	Remarks
Imbituba			See [1] below
Berth No.1	140	9.43	Liquid bulk, frozen cargo, general cargo & containers
Berth No.2	168	9.43	Liquid bulk, frozen cargo, general cargo & containers
Berth No.3	245	9.43	Solid bulk & containers
Berth No.4	24	7–9.43	Ro/ro terminal. Platform of 96 m2

[1]*Imbituba:* Container terminal operated by Santos Brasil, of 25 855 m2

Storage:

Location	Covered (m²)
Imbituba	6000

Mechanical Handling Equipment:

Location	Type	Capacity (t)	Qty
Imbituba	Mult-purp. Cranes	10	1

Bunkering: Marine gas oil is available on request in small deliveries by tank trucks; fuel oil not available

Towage: One tug of 1680 bhp available

Ship Chandlers: Sea Star Ship Suppliers Ltd, Travessa Dona Adelina No. 35 Paqueta, 11013-130 Santos, Brazil, *Tel:* +55 13 3232 5757, *Fax:* +55 13 3233 3211, *Email:* seastartrans@uol.com.br, *Website:* www.seastarsantos.com.br

Shipping Agents: Agencia Maritima Imbituba Ltda, Av. Dr. Joao Rimsa 170, Centro, 88780-000 Imbituba SC, Brazil, *Tel:* +55 48 3255 0116, *Fax:* +55 48 3255 0426, *Email:* agmil@maritimaimbituba.com.br, *Website:* www.maritimaimbituba.com.br
Corymar Agencia Maritima Ltd, Rua Nereu Ramos 124, Room 02, Centro, 88780-000 Imbituba SC, Brazil, *Tel:* +55 48 3255 0262, *Fax:* +55 48 3255 0458, *Email:* willibt@williams.com.br, *Website:* www.williams.com.br
Oceanus Agencia Maritima S.A., Rua Dr. Joao Rimsa 174 S/2, 88780-000 Imbituba SC, Brazil, *Tel:* +55 48 3255 2317, *Email:* agency.imb@oceanus.com.br, *Website:* www.oceanus.com.br
Agencia Maritima Orion Ltda, Rua Nereu Ramos 815, Sala 209, Centro, Imbituba, Brazil, *Tel:* +55 53 2125 4400, *Fax:* +55 53 2125 4444, *Email:* orion@imb.amorion.com.br, *Website:* www.amorion.com.br
Supermar S.A., Rua Nereu Ramos 124 sala 04, CEP88780-000 Imbituba, Brazil, *Tel:* +55 48 3255 8092, *Fax:* +55 48 3255 8025, *Email:* imbituba@supermar.com.br, *Website:* www.supermar.com.br
Wilson Sons Agencia Maritima Ltda, Avenida Santa Catarina 353, Sala 101 - Centro, 88780-000 Imbituba SC, Brazil, *Tel:* +55 48 3255 6619, *Fax:* +55 48 3255 2468, *Email:* agency.imbituba@wilsonsons.com.br, *Website:* www.wilsonsons.com.br

Medical Facilities: One hospital available. Major facilities at Florianopolis, 100 km

Lloyd's Agent: Inspect Santos Consultoria e Peritagens Ltda, Av. Conselheiro Nebias, 726 - sala 114, Boqueirao, 11045-002 Santos SP, Brazil, *Tel:* +55 13 3234 5246, *Fax:* +55 13 3235 2250, *Email:* inspect@inspect.com.br

ITAJAI

Lat 26° 53' S; Long 48° 40' W.

Admiralty Chart: 549   **Admiralty Pilot:** 5
Time Zone: GMT -3 h   **UNCTAD Locode:** BR ITJ

Principal Facilities:

P	Q		G	C	R	L	B		T	A	

Tramp Oil & Marine

Wells House, 15-17 Elmfield Road, Bromley,
Kent BR1 1LT, United Kingdom
Phone: +44 20 8315 7777   **Fax:** +44 20 8315 7788
General email: enquiries@tramp-oil.com

See listings for all global offices: **www.tramp-oil.com**

Authority: Porto de Itajai, Rua Blumenau 05, 88305-101 Itajai SC, Brazil, *Tel:* +55 47 3341 8000, *Fax:* +55 47 3341 8075, *Email:* atendimento@portoitajai.com.br, *Website:* www.portoitajai.com.br

Officials: Executive Director: Marcelo Werner Salles, *Email:* marcelo@portoitajai.com.br.
Superintendent: Eliane Neves Rebello, *Email:* elianerebello@portoitajai.com.br.
Business Manager: Leonidas Ferreira, *Email:* negocios@portoitajai.com.br.

Port Security: ISPS compliant

Approach: The access channel is 3.2 km long with a breadth of 100 m and dredged to a depth of 10 m. The bar channel is 1.5 km long with a breadth of 100 m and dredged to a depth of 10 m. The evolution basin is 700 m long and 250 m wide, dredged to a depth of 10 m

Anchorage: Anchorage in pos 26° 54' 09" S; 48° 36' 32" N in a depth of 10 m

Pilotage: Compulsory. Pilot boards one mile E of the Cabecudas Lighthouse. Pilot Station may be contacted on VHF Channel 16

Weather: Under certain conditions involving N or NE winds, following a long period of rain, the bar becomes impracticable due to the outflow of the Itajai-Acu River

Tides: Tidal range 1 m

Traffic: 2007, 7 309 884 t of cargo handled

Maximum Vessel Dimensions: 207 m loa, 10.0 m draft

Principal Imports and Exports: Imports: Chemical products, Machinery & motors. Exports: Frozen products, Machinery & motors, Paper, Sugar, Textiles, Tobacco, Wood.

Working Hours: 0700-1300, 1300-1900, 1900-0100, 0100-0700

Accommodation:

Name	Remarks
Itajai	See [1] below

[1]*Itajai:* Length of docks is 740 m comprising five berths with depths alongside of 10.0 m. 25 000 m3 container storage area with fourteen 37 t cap and one 12 t cap forklifts for stacking
Container terminal operated by Terminal de Conteineres do Vale do Itajai (TECONVI), Rua Felipe Schmidt 480, Centro, 88301-041 Itajai SC, Tel: +55 47 3341 9800, Website: www.teconvi.com, comprising two dedicated private berths and one public berth
Private terminal for refrigerated cargoes operated by Braskarne Com. Arm. Gerais Ltda., Tel: +55 47 3344 8200, Fax: +55 47 3344 8219. Refrigerated warehousing cap of 7500 t and wharves up to 180 m length and 9 m draft

Storage: Container storage area of 38 000 m2 with another 25 550 m2 for pre-stacking. There are two interior customs stations: one for dry cargo with a covered storage area of 31 500 m2, open storage area of 121 450 m2 and a container terminal of 42 500 m2, the other is for refrigerated cargo with an area of 65 000 m3, allowing storage at temperatures up to -25°C

Mechanical Handling Equipment:

Location	Type	Capacity (t)	Qty
Itajai	Mobile Cranes		1
Itajai	Reach Stackers	40	13
Itajai	Forklifts	37	6
Itajai	Forklifts	7	8
Itajai	Forklifts	3.5	4
Itajai	Forklifts	3	28
Itajai	Forklifts	1	4
Itajai	Forklifts	5	2
Itajai	Forklifts	2.5	11

Cargo Worked: Sawn timber 18 t/gang/h, bagged sugar 20 t/gang/h, palletised cargoes 25 t/gang/h, kraft paper 50 t/gang/h, container 15-20 units/gang/h

Bunkering: Tramp Oil & Marine, World Fuel Services Corporation, 13th Floor, Portland House, Bressenden Place, London SW1E 5BH, United Kingdom, *Tel:* +44 20 7808 5000, *Fax:* +44 20 7808 5088, *Email:* pturner@wfscorp.com, *Website:* www.wfscorp.com – *Grades:* all grades – *Delivery Mode:* barge, pipeline, truck

Towage: Three tugs; one of 1680 hp and two of 2000 hp

Repair & Maintenance: Corena S.A., Itajai, Brazil Repair facilities

Ship Chandlers: Exportadora Sao Francisco Ltda, Rua Alfredo Trompowski 404, Vila Operaria, Itajai, Brazil, *Tel:* +55 47 3348 2443, *Fax:* +55 47 3444 2400, *Email:* exportadora@exportadora-sf.com.br

Shipping Agents: Atlas Maritime Ltda, Rua Gil Stein Ferreira 100, CJ 1203 Centro, 88301-210 Itajai SC, Brazil, *Tel:* +55 47 3349 0005, *Fax:* +55 47 3349 3335, *Email:* atlas_itajai@atlasmaritime.com.br, *Website:* www.atlasmaritime.com.br
CMA-CGM S.A., CMA CGM do Brasil Agencia Maritima, Av Coronel Marcos Konder 1177, Salas 603, 701-703, Centro, 88301-303 Itajai SC, Brazil, *Tel:* +55 47 3344 7300, *Fax:* +55 47 3344 7327, *Email:* itj.genmbox@cma-cgm.com, *Website:* www.cma-cgm.com

Corymar Agencia Maritima Ltd, Rua Dr. Pedro Ferreira 155, Room 1006-A, Genesio M.Lins Building, 88301-030 Itajai SC, Brazil, *Tel:* +55 47 3348 4199, *Fax:* +55 47 3348 4742, *Email:* willitj@williams.com.br, *Website:* www.williams.com.br
Agencia de Vapores Grieg S.A., Av Joca Brandao 1313, andar 8, salas 801/806, 88301-301 Itajai SC, Brazil, *Tel:* +55 47 3348 5612, *Fax:* +55 47 3348 4869, *Email:* griegitj@grieg.com.br, *Website:* www.grieg.com.br
Lachmann Logistica Ltda, Rua Almirante Tamandade 100/Centro, CEP 88301-260 Itajai, Brazil, *Tel:* +55 47 3348 6767, *Fax:* +55 47 3348 4002, *Email:* lachmann.itj@lachmann.com.br
A.P. Moller-Maersk Group, Maersk Brasil Ltda, Rua Dagoberto Nogueira 100, Edificio Torre Azul, 14 andar, 88301-060 Itajai SC, Brazil, *Tel:* +55 47 3045 8300, *Fax:* +55 47 3045 8301, *Email:* brzcrcitj@maersk.com, *Website:* www.maerskline.com
Oceanus Agencia Maritima S.A., Rua Almirante Tamandare 100, 88301-430 Itajai SC, Brazil, *Tel:* +55 47 3341 5900, *Fax:* +55 47 3341 5999, *Email:* agency.itj@oceanus.com.br, *Website:* www.oceanus.com.br
Agencia Maritima Orion Ltda, Rua Gil Stein Ferreira 357, Room 401/402, Centro, 88301-210 Itajai, Brazil, *Tel:* +55 47 2104 6400, *Fax:* +55 47 2104 6444, *Email:* orion@itj.amorion.com.br, *Website:* www.amorion.com.br
Agencia Maritima Osny S.A., Rua Alfredo Elcke 341, P O Box 292, Barra do Rio, CEP 88305-300 Itajai, Brazil, *Tel:* +55 47 3348 2800, *Fax:* +55 47 3348 2032, *Email:* anapaula@osny.com.br, *Website:* www.osny.com.br
Rocha Top Terminais e Operatores Portuarios Ltda, Rua Pedro Ferreira 180, CEP 8801-030 Itajai, Brazil, *Tel:* +55 47 3348 8332, *Fax:* +55 47 3348 8188, *Email:* fcezar@rochatop.com.br
Sernaval Agencia Maritima, Tijucas, 625 Centro-Cep, CEP 88301-101 Itajai, Brazil, *Tel:* +55 47 3348 0572, *Fax:* +55 47 3348 6910, *Email:* julio.boticelli@sernaval.com.br
Seven Stars Containers (Afretamento) Ltd, Avenida Ministro Victor Konder 400, 88301-700 Itajai, Brazil, *Tel:* +55 47 3348 6933, *Fax:* +55 47 3348 6934, *Email:* supervisor@sevenstars.com.br
Transatlantic Carriers (Agenciamentos) Ltda, Av Marcos Konder 1207, Suite 99, Itajai, Brazil, *Tel:* +55 47 3346 9300, *Fax:* +55 47 3241 2114, *Email:* ricardo@transcar-itajai.com.br
Unimar Agenciamentos Maritimos Ltda, Rua Gil Stein Ferreira 357, Sala 101, CEP88302-210 Itajai, Brazil, *Tel:* +55 47 3346 6421, *Fax:* +55 47 3348 3109, *Email:* unimar-itajai@unimar-agency.com.br

Surveyors: Nippon Kaiji Kyokai, Surveyor Inspecoes Tecnicas Ltda, Rua Dr. Pedro Ferreira, 155-18 andar, Sala 1813, 88301-030 Itajai SC, Brazil, *Tel:* +55 47 3348 4139, *Fax:* +55 47 3348 4139, *Website:* www.classnk.or.jp

Medical Facilities: There is one hospital available

Airport: Navegantes, 20 km

Lloyd's Agent: Inspect Santos Consultoria e Peritagens Ltda, Av. Conselheiro Nebias, 726 - sala 114, Boqueirao, 11045-002 Santos SP, Brazil, *Tel:* +55 13 3234 5246, *Fax:* +55 13 3235 2250, *Email:* inspect@inspect.com.br

ITAQUI

Lat 2° 34' S; Long 44° 21' W.

Admiralty Chart: 535		**Admiralty Pilot:** 5	
Time Zone: GMT -3 h		**UNCTAD Locode:** BR ITQ	

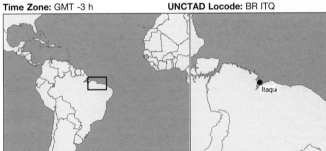

Principal Facilities:

P	Q	Y	G	C	R		B		T	A

Tramp Oil & Marine

Wells House, 15-17 Elmfield Road, Bromley,
Kent BR1 1LT, United Kingdom
Phone: +44 20 8315 7777   **Fax:** +44 20 8315 7788
General email: enquiries@tramp-oil.com

See listings for all global offices: **www.tramp-oil.com**

Authority: Empresa Maranhense de Administracao Portuaria (EMAP), Porto de Itaqui, 65085-370 Sao Luis MA, Brazil, *Tel:* +55 98 3216 6000, *Fax:* +55 98 3216 6060, *Email:* itaqui@emap.ma.gov.br, *Website:* www.portodoitaqui.ma.gov.br

Officials: President: Antonio Carlos Lago, *Email:* antoniocarlos@emap.ma.gov.br.

Port Security: ISPS compliant

Approach: Access channel is 125 000 m long, 1800 m width in min depth of 23 m

Key to Principal Facilities:—				
A=Airport	**C**=Containers	**G**=General Cargo	**P**=Petroleum	**R**=Ro/Ro	**Y**=Dry Bulk
B=Bunkers	**D**=Dry Dock	**L**=Cruise	**Q**=Other Liquid Bulk	**T**=Towage (where available from port)

Anchorage: In pos 2° 35' 30" S; 44° 22' 24" W in a depth of 21.5 m

Pilotage: Compulsory

Radio Frequency: VHF Channel 16

Tides: Max range 7.1 m, medium range 5.4 m

Principal Imports and Exports: Imports: Diesel oil, Fertilizers, General cargo. Exports: Aluminium, Ingots, Iron ore, Manganese, Pellets, Pig iron, Soy beans, Timber.

Working Hours: 0730-1130, 1330-1930, 1930-2300, 0000-0730

Accommodation:

Name	Length (m)	Depth (m)	Remarks
Itaqui			
Berth 101	239	9	
Berth 102	239	10	
Berth 103	239	13	
Berth 104	200	14.5	
Berth 105	280	18.9	
Berth 106	420	19	Oil tankers up to 200 000 dwt

Storage: Open storage area of 42 000 m2, general cargo warehouse of 7500 m2, solid granary inflatable warehouse of 3000 m2, vertical and horizontal silo's for grain totalling 20 000 t, liquid granary storage tanks with cap of 210 000 m3

Mechanical Handling Equipment:

Location	Type	Capacity (t)	Qty
Itaqui	Mult-purp. Cranes	64	1
Itaqui	Mobile Cranes	6.3	

Cargo Worked: Iron ore 200 000 t/day, bauxite 1900 t/day, aluminium 1500 t/day

Bunkering: Tramp Oil & Marine, World Fuel Services Corporation, 13th Floor, Portland House, Bressenden Place, London SW1E 5BH, United Kingdom, *Tel:* +44 20 7808 5000, *Fax:* +44 20 7808 5088, *Email:* pturner@wfscorp.com, *Website:* www.wfscorp.com – *Grades:* all grades – *Delivery Mode:* barge, pipeline, truck

Towage: Available

Ship Chandlers: Exportadora Star Ltda, Avenida dos Portugueses No. 10, Bairro Bacanga, 65.080-580 Sao Luiz, Brazil, *Tel:* +55 98 3273 3086, *Fax:* +55 98 3273 3087, *Email:* starstor@elogica.com.br

Shipping Agents: Corymar Agencia Maritima Ltd, Rua Inacio de Xavier Carvalho 161 - Room 505, 65020-450 Sao Luis MA, Brazil, *Tel:* +55 98 3221 1488, *Fax:* +55 98 3222 6194, *Email:* willslz@williams.com.br, *Website:* www.williams.com.br
Inchcape Shipping Services (ISS), ISS Marine Services Ltda, Av Colares Moreira 10, Edif Sao Luis Multiempresarial, 9 Andar, Sala, 635075-441 Sao Luis MA, Brazil, *Tel:* +55 98 3227 7338, *Fax:* +55 98 3227 7674, *Email:* iss.saoluis@iss-shipping.com, *Website:* www.iss-shipping.com
N. Magioli Agencia Maritima Ltda, Rua Cel. Euripedes Bezerra - Quadra 14 C/01-B, Jardim Eldorado - Turu, 65066-260 Sao Luis MA, Brazil, *Tel:* +55 98 3226 6404, *Fax:* +55 98 3226 4528, *Email:* magioli@magioli.com, *Website:* www.magioli.com
Rodos Agencia Maritima Ltda, Avenida Maestro Joao Nunes 12, Centro Empresarial Mendes Frota - Sala 403, 65076-200 Sao Luis MA, Brazil, *Tel:* +55 98 3235 4457, *Fax:* +55 98 3235 4610, *Email:* rodos.slm@rodos.com.br, *Website:* www.rodos.com.br
Wilson Sons Agencia Maritima Ltda, Rua Juno Qd 22 - 5th Floor, Ed. Manhattan Center - SL 505 - Renascenca II, 65075-740 Sao Luis MA, Brazil, *Tel:* +55 98 3235 2529, *Fax:* +55 98 3235 4269, *Email:* agesl@wilsonsons.com.br, *Website:* www.wilsonsons.com.br

Stevedoring Companies: Companhia Operadora Portuaria do Itaqui (COPI), Av. dos Portugueses s/n, 65085-370 Itaqui, Brazil, *Tel:* +55 98 3232 3434, *Fax:* +55 98 3222 8921, *Email:* s.hermes@copi-portodoitaqui.com.br
Costa Norte Maritima Ltda, Avenida dos Portugueses 2001, 65085-570 Sao Luis, Brazil, *Tel:* +55 98 3242 0044, *Fax:* +55 98 3242 0055, *Email:* costanorte@cnorte.com.br
Pedreiras Transportes do Maranhao Ltda, Porto do Itaqui s/n, 65085-370 Sao Luis, Brazil, *Tel:* +55 98 3232 3334, *Fax:* +55 98 3232 3508, *Email:* pedra@elo.com.br, *Website:* www.pedreirastransportes.com.br

Medical Facilities: Nearest hospital 10 km from port

Airport: Tirirical, 18 km

Railway: CFN and EFC railways

Lloyd's Agent: Inspect Consultoria Ltda (Sao Luis), Av Dos Portugueses, 31 Vila Embratel, 65085-580 Sao Luis MA, Brazil, *Tel:* +55 98 3242 4016, *Email:* inspectconsultoria@br.inter.net

LAGOA PARDA TERMINAL

Lat 19° 42' S; Long 39° 50' W.

Admiralty Chart: 3973	**Admiralty Pilot:** 5
Time Zone: GMT -3 h	**UNCTAD Locode:** BR

Principal Facilities:

P							T		

Authority: Petrobras E&P ES/GEPRO, Regencia Rod. BR 101, Km. 67.5, 29930-000 Sao Mateus ES, Brazil, *Tel:* +55 27 763 2112, *Fax:* +55 27 763 3525

Anchorage: The recommended anchorage area to wait for the dawn or to wait for orders is in pos 19° 42' 30" S; 39° 50' 00" W in depth of approx 16 m

Pilotage: Compulsory. The mooring master boards approx one nautical mile SE of the buoy

Radio Frequency: VHF Channel 16

Weather: Predominant winds are NNE/ENE from October to March and SSE/SW from April to September

Working Hours: Loading during daylight only

Accommodation:

Name	Remarks
Lagoa Parda Terminal	See [1] below

[1]*Lagoa Parda Terminal:* Comprises a set of four mooring buoys for tankers up to 30 000 dwt with max draft of 13 m. The terminal handles the loading of all oil production from the land wells and those from both the State of Espirito Santo continental platform and the production fields in the South of Bahia. The product is stored in four tanks with a cap of 10 000 m3 each

Towage: There is a contracted tug to assist vessels during mooring and unmooring manoeuvres

Medical Facilities: Available in emergencies only

Lloyd's Agent: Inspect Consultoria Ltda (Rio de Janeiro), Avenida Rio Branco 37, Grupo 1902 Centro, 20090-003 Rio de Janeiro RJ, Brazil, *Tel:* +55 21 2263 3330, *Fax:* +55 21 2253 9322, *Email:* inspectconsultoria@br.inter.net, *Website:* www.inspectconsultoria.com.br

MACAPA

Lat 0° 2' N; Long 51° 2' W.

Admiralty Chart: 2189	**Admiralty Pilot:** 5
Time Zone: GMT -3 h	**UNCTAD Locode:** BR MCP

Principal Facilities:

P		Y	G		R				A

Authority: Companhia Docas do Para, Porto de Macapa, Av. Claudio Lucio Monteiro 1380, 68925-000 Santana PA, Brazil, *Tel:* +55 96 3281 1092, *Fax:* +55 96 3281 4000, *Website:* www.cdp.com.br

Port Security: ISPS compliant

Approach: Via the N channel approx 276 km long. Outer bar 9.75 m draft at LW, 11.28 m at HW

Anchorage: There are two anchorages: Fazendinha in pos 00° 04' 06" S; 51° 06' 45" W and Santana in pos 00° 03' 31" S; 51° 11' 43" W

Pilotage: Compulsory. Pilots board at Fazendinha Pilot Station in pos 0° 04' 06" S, 51° 06' 45" W

Weather: Frequent heavy rain, Jan to June

Tides: Rain season 2.5 m to 3.7 m. Dry season 2.4 m to 3.4 m

Traffic: 2005, 1 524 345 t of cargo handled

Maximum Vessel Dimensions: 56 683 dwt, 12 m draft, 223.25 m loa

Principal Imports and Exports: Exports: Manganese ore, Plywood, Sawn timber, Vegetable oil.

Working Hours: Four shifts 0700-1100, 1300-1700, 1900-2300, 0100-0600. At Icomi Wharf 0000-1200, 1300-2300

Accommodation:

Name	Length (m)	Depth (m)	Remarks
Macapa			
New Pier	200	13	General cargo
Icomi Wharf	247	10	See [1] below

[1]*Icomi Wharf:* A manganese ore loading pier, operated by Industria e Comercio de Minerios (ICOMI), consisting of a floating structure supported by 48 rectangular steel pontoons, equipped to load ore carriers at up to 400 t/h. Palm oil may be loaded

Storage: Port Authority warehouse of 2800 m2; general cargo warehouse of 1500 m2 and open warehouse for timber

Mechanical Handling Equipment:

Location	Type	Capacity (t)	Qty
New Pier	Forklifts	3	1
Icomi Wharf	Mult-purp. Cranes	40	1

Cargo Worked: Manganese ore 8800 t/day, plywood and timber 900 t/day

Shipping Agents: LBH Brasil, Rua Av. Feliciano Coelho 365-A, Bairro Trem, 68901-025 Macapa AP, Brazil, *Tel:* +55 96 2101 6855, *Fax:* +55 96 3223 8097, *Email:* brazmcp@lbhbrasil.com.br, *Website:* www.brazshipping.com.br
Wilson Sons Agencia Maritima Ltda, Maria Colares No.1865, Nova Brazilia, 68900-020 Macapa AP, Brazil, *Tel:* +55 96 3283 4021, *Fax:* +55 96 3283 4018, *Email:* wsonsmacapa@terra.com.br, *Website:* www.wilsonsons.com.br

Medical Facilities: General hospital at Macapa. First aid hospital at Santana and a hospital at Serra do Navio, both owned by ICOMI

Airport: 22 km from Santana

Lloyd's Agent: Inspect Consultoria Ltda (Sao Luis), Av Dos Portugueses, 31 Vila Embratel, 65085-580 Sao Luis MA, Brazil, *Tel:* +55 98 3242 4016, *Email:* inspectconsultoria@br.inter.net

MACEIO

Lat 9° 40' S; Long 35° 44' W.

Admiralty Chart: 960	**Admiralty Pilot:** 5
Time Zone: GMT -3 h	**UNCTAD Locode:** BR MCZ

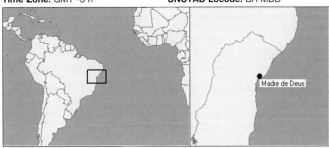

Principal Facilities:

P	Q	Y	G		L			T	A

Authority: Administracao do Porto de Maceio, Rua S'a e Albuquerque s/n, Jaragua, 57025-180 Maceio AL, Brazil, *Tel:* +55 82 3231 1999, *Fax:* +55 82 3231 2975, *Email:* jabsonlevino@portodemaceio.com.br, *Website:* www.portodemaceio.com.br

Port Security: ISPS compliant

Approach: Light in pos 9° 41' 07" S; 35° 41' W, visible 21 miles, height 26 m. White 1-sec flash, eclipse 9-sec, red 1-sec flash, eclipse 9-sec. Harbour protected by a breakwater 3 km long. The approach channel is 80 m wide with depths of 10-14 m but care should be taken to avoid the shoals existing to the NE of the Peixe-Pau buoy. The manoeuvring basin is 400 m long, 350 m wide and 10 m deep. The bar is unobstructed with depths of water from 10.7-15.7 m. Continuous dredging inside port

Anchorage: Inner anchorage protected by the mole from NE winds which prevail during summer. Good holding ground, fine sand, westward of head of breakwater

Pilotage: Compulsory. Pilots board off Baixio de Peixe Pau

Weather: From June to September moderate or fresh SW winds may raise heavy seas, from which vessels are only partially protected and are liable to range and surge against quay due to rebound of swell. Ships alongside sometimes obliged to use additional fenders, owing to the construction of the mole, ie, projecting concrete platform and pillars over steel piles

Tides: Range of tide 2.6 m

Traffic: 2005, 3 353 324 t of cargo handled

Maximum Vessel Dimensions: 30 000 dwt

Working Hours: Normal 0700-1100, 1300-1700. Overtime 1700-1900, 1900-2300, 0100-0500, 0500-0700, including Saturdays

Accommodation:

Name	Length (m)	Depth (m)	Remarks
Maceio			See [1] below
Sugar & Molasses Berth	250	10	
Salegma Wharf	228	9	Bulk wheat is discharged by pneumatic equipment
Oil Berth	250	10	Night berthing possible. Water available
Chemical Marine Terminal	1300	7.6	Loading platform 132 m long

[1]*Maceio:* The docks total 750 m in length and depth alongside is 10 m. The height of the dock surface from water level is 4.13 m at LT and 1.33 m at HT

Storage:

Location	Covered (m²)	Sheds / Warehouses
Maceio	7600	5

Mechanical Handling Equipment:

Location	Type	Capacity (t)	Qty
Maceio	Mult-purp. Cranes	10	7
Maceio	Mobile Cranes	5	1

Towage: One tug of 1680 hp

Repair & Maintenance: Fives Lille do Brasil (Fives CAIL Group), Rua Teodoro Sampaio, 1020 7 andar, Sala 702, P O Box 05 406 050, Sao Paulo, Brazil, *Tel:* +55 11 3061 1619, *Fax:* +55 11 3898 1473, *Email:* fiveslillebrasil@uol.com.br, *Website:* www.fiveslille.com Engine, heavy equipment repairs and all types of boiler work
Mecania Pesada Continental S.A., Maceio, Brazil Repair facilities

Mecanica Industrial e Maritime Ltda, Fortaleza, Brazil Mechanical, electronic and refrigerator repairs
Nova Fundicao Alagoana Ltda, Maceio, Brazil Soldering and motor equipment

Shipping Agents: Corymar Agencia Maritima Ltd, Rua Barao de Jaragua 292, P O Box 1009, 57025-140 Maceio AL, Brazil, *Tel:* +55 82 3223 2299, *Fax:* +55 82 3221 9710, *Email:* willmcz@williams.com.br, *Website:* www.williams.com.br
Irmaos Britto Representacoes e Comercio Ltda, Rua Sa Albuquerque 454, Bairro Jaragua, CEP57025-180 Maceio, Brazil, *Tel:* +55 82 3221 0009, *Fax:* +55 82 3221 6951, *Email:* ibritto@ibritto.com.br, *Website:* www.ibritto.com.br

Medical Facilities: There is a hospital and first aid services are available

Airport: Palmares, 30 km

Lloyd's Agent: Inspect Consultoria Ltda (Recife), Rua Padre Carapuceiro 412/603, Boa Viagem, 51020-280 Recife PE, Brazil, *Tel:* +55 81 9952 5868, *Email:* inspectrecife@terra.com.br

MADRE DE DEUS

Lat 12° 45' S; Long 38° 37' W.

Admiralty Chart: 545	**Admiralty Pilot:** 5
Time Zone: GMT -3 h	**UNCTAD Locode:** BR MDD

Principal Facilities:

P	Q					B		T	A

Authority: Petrobras Transporte S.A., Commercial Pipeline & Terminal Management, Av. Presidente Vargas 328/6o andar - Centro, 20091-060 Rio de Janeiro RJ, Brazil, *Tel:* +55 21 3211 9285, *Fax:* +55 21 3211 9301, *Email:* comercial_transpetro@petrobrass.com.br, *Website:* www.transpetro.com.br

Officials: Manager: Andre Jose Lepsch, *Email:* lepsch@petrobrass.com.br.
Commercial Manager: Luiz Marcio Garcia, *Email:* luiz.marcio@petrobrass.com.br.
Co-ordinator: Carlos Maligo

Port Security: ISPS compliant

Pre-Arrival Information: Vessel's have to inform their ETA 72 h, 48 h and 24 h in advance directly to their agents by telex or fax
The vessel must send the terminal the following information by fax to the agent before mooring:
(a) ship's name
(b) flag
(c) total length
(d) dwt
(e) draft fore and aft
(f) quantity and type of cargo onboard
(g) loading/unloading flow
(h) quantity of ballast and slop aboard
(i) requested fuel supply
(j) inert gas system conditions
(k) number of tanks with cargo
The following documents are required by the authorities to release the ship on arrival:
(a) crew list
(b) passenger list in transit/disembarking
(c) list of weapons, munitions and narcotics
(d) vaccination list
(e) maritime statement of health
(f) list of material onboard
(g) list of provisions
(h) cargo manifest
(i) cargo waybill
(j) list of crew's personal belongings
(k) baggage statement of passengers leaving the ship
(l) bill of lading

Approach: Access to the terminal is by a channel 6 miles long with min depth of 12 m, marked with light buoys starting in pos 12° 49' 02'' S; 38° 34' W and ending in the maneuvring basin in front of the pier

Pilotage: Compulsory for vessels making for Madre de Deus terminal from the anchorage in Salvador. Pilotage operates 24 h/day. Request for pilotage must be made at least 4 h in advance
Vessels waiting for a pilot must anchor in the area marked by a circle with the centre in pos 12° 57' 10'' S; 38° 33' 05'' W and radius of 0.25 mile in depth of 16-46 m
Pilot boards at the anchorage, SW of the Panela bank in pos 12° 58' 10'' S; 38° 32' 22'' W, in Salvador harbour

Radio Frequency: VHF Channel 16

Weather: Prevailing winds are SE'ly in February and October and E'ly in December and January. S'ly winds normally blow when there is a full or new moon and the waters in the bay are rougher. In July and September there are occasional strong winds. It is very unusual to have winds strong enough to stop maneuvers ar the terminal

Key to Principal Facilities:—				
A=Airport	**C**=Containers	**G**=General Cargo	**P**=Petroleum	**R**=Ro/Ro	**Y**=Dry Bulk
B=Bunkers	**D**=Dry Dock	**L**=Cruise	**Q**=Other Liquid Bulk	**T**=Towage (where available from port)	

Accommodation:

Name	Depth (m)	Remarks
Madre de Deus		See [1] below
Pier PP1	13	See [2] below
Pier PP2	13	Vessels up to 120 000 t and 275 m loa (day) 240 m loa (night)
Pier PP3	10.5	See [3] below
Pier PP4	22	See [4] below
Pier PS1	8.3	See [5] below
Pier PS2	4.2	Allocated to lighters, tugs & motor boats and MF and MGO supplies

[1]*Madre de Deus:* Madre de Deus Sea Terminal, Tel: +55 71 804 1216, Fax: +55 71 804 3355

[2]*Pier PP1:* Vessels up to 120 000 t and 275 m loa (day) 240 m loa (night). Two 12" arms for loading and unloading dark products; two 8" arms and a 12" arm for loading and unloading naphtha, gasoline, diesel, alcohol, lubes and other light products. There are another two arms for refrigerated LPG ship operations, one 10" (liquid stage) and the other 8" (steam stage)

[3]*Pier PP3:* Vessels up to 31 000 t . Two 8" arms for light products, one 10" arm for handling dark products and another 6" arm at the end of the pier for supplying ships

[4]*Pier PP4:* Vessels up to 120 000 t and 275 m loa (day) 240 m loa (night). Only dark products are handled with three 16" arms for loading and unloading crude, fuel, gasoil, diluent and ballast

[5]*Pier PS1:* LPG vessels up to 10 000 t. An 8" arm for pressurized, refrigerated and semi-refrigerated LPG operations, a 6" arm to receive steam return, another two 6" and 4" hand arms for loading lighters and tugs with MF's and MGO respectively. It also has an outlet for a 6" suction pipe for both products

Bunkering: All kinds of marine fuel oil or diesel oil directly through pipes

Towage: Two tugs available for berthing/unberthing. When more than two are required they will be contracted

Medical Facilities: Medical and dental facilities are available in Salvador

Airport: Approx 50 km

Lloyd's Agent: Inspect Consultoria Ltda (Recife), Rua Padre Carapuceiro 412/603, Boa Viagem, 51020-280 Recife PE, Brazil, *Tel:* +55 81 9952 5868, *Email:* inspectrecife@terra.com.br

MALHADO

alternate name, see Ilheus

MANAUS

Lat 3° 9' S; Long 60° 1' W.

Admiralty Chart: 2229
Admiralty Pilot: 5
Time Zone: GMT -4 h
UNCTAD Locode: BR MAO

Principal Facilities:

P	Q	Y	G	C	R	L	B		T	A

Tramp Oil & Marine

Wells House, 15-17 Elmfield Road, Bromley,
Kent BR1 1LT, United Kingdom
Phone: +44 20 8315 7777   **Fax:** +44 20 8315 7788
General email: enquiries@tramp-oil.com

See listings for all global offices: **www.tramp-oil.com**

Authority: Sociedade de Navegacao, Portos e Hidrovias do Estado do Amazonas, Rua Marques de Santa Cruz 25, Centro, 69005-050 Manaus AM, Brazil, *Tel:* +55 92 3621 4300, *Fax:* +55 92 3635 9464, *Website:* www.portodemanaus.com.br

Port Security: ISPS compliant

Approach: No approach channel marked due to exceptionally good navigable conditions on the Rio Negro

Anchorage: For vessels over 3000 gt in pos 03° 09' 00" S; 60° 01' 48" W
For vessels under 3000 gt in pos 03° 09' 00" S; 60° 02' 12" W
Vessels in quarantine in pos 03° 08' 48" S; 59° 55' 48" W

Pilotage: Compulsory. Pilots join vessel at Belem and make the round voyage back to Belem. Vessels entering via North Channel take a pilot at Santana. No pilots from Barra Norte to Santana
Praticagem dos Rios Ocidentais da Amazonia Ltda., Tel: +55 92 3624 2164, Fax: +55 92 3624 2406, Email: proa@argo.com.br
Unipilot, Tel: +55 91 3242 5508, Fax: +55 91 3241 1110, Email: linesio@unipilot.com
Nortepilot - Empresa de Praticagem do Norte S/C Ltda., Tel/Fax: +55 91 3242 7589, Email: nortepilot@interconect.com.br

Radio Frequency: Sanilopolis Radio or Rio Radio. There is also Barbados Radio Station at Belem

Weather: Occasional sudden squalls with heavy rain and strong winds

Tides: Non tidal

Traffic: 2005, 14 901 347 t of cargo handled

Maximum Vessel Dimensions: Entry to the Amazon via the North Channel max draft 30 ft, via Belem draft 29 ft with a length up to 175 m and draft 24 ft with a length up to 210 m

Principal Imports and Exports: Imports: Crude oil, Electrical components, Grain, Malted grain, Milk powder. Exports: Brazil nuts, Cocoa products, Lumber, Motorcycles, Pepper, Razors.

Accommodation:

Name	Length (m)	Remarks
Manaus		See [1] below
T-Jetty		Floating roadway to two floating stages
Easterly	272	
Westerly	362.7	
Stone Jetty	500	
Moageria Berth		Discharge of bulk grain at rate of 30 t/h
Copam Refinery Berth		See [2] below

[1]*Manaus:* Passage across Barra Norte to be made at HW only. Berthing and unberthing preferably takes place at Manaus in daylight

[2]*Copam Refinery Berth:* A floating pontoon with buoy moorings ahead and astern. Vessel berths starboard side to, using port anchor. Facilities for crude discharge. Products only loaded. No dirty ballast facilities

Mechanical Handling Equipment:

Location	Type	Capacity (t)	Qty
Manaus	Floating Cranes	100	1
Manaus	Floating Cranes	15	1
Manaus	Mobile Cranes	9–50	6
Manaus	Electric Cranes	3.2	3
Manaus	Forklifts	3–25	23

Bunkering: Tramp Oil & Marine, World Fuel Services Corporation, 13th Floor, Portland House, Bressenden Place, London SW1E 5BH, United Kingdom, *Tel:* +44 20 7808 5000, *Fax:* +44 20 7808 5088, *Email:* pturner@wfscorp.com, *Website:* www.wfscorp.com – *Grades:* all grades – *Notice:* 7 days – *Delivery Mode:* barge, pipeline, truck

Waste Reception Facilities: Depending on the quantity, the local refinery is able to receive sludge. Garbage removal by barge is available

Towage: One tug of 1680 hp and one tug of 210 hp available

Repair & Maintenance: Limited facilities available

Shipping Agents: Atlas Maritime Ltda, Avenida Rio Jutai, 486 Quadra 48, CJ Vieiralves, Bairro Nossa Senhora das Gralas, CEP 69053-020 Manaus, Brazil, *Tel:* +55 92 3622 8050, *Fax:* +55 92 3622 8051, *Email:* atlas_manaus@atlasmaritime.com.br, *Website:* www.atlasmaritime.com.br
CMA-CGM S.A., CMA CGM do Brasil Agencia Maritima, Rua Vila Amazonas 10 Cj Vila Amazonas, Bairro N. Sra. das Gracas, 69057-240 Manaus AM, Brazil, *Tel:* +55 92 3642 1117, *Fax:* +55 92 3642 1146, *Email:* bmn.genmbox@cma-cgm.com, *Website:* www.cma-cgm.com
Corymar Agencia Maritima Ltd, Avenida Eduardo Ribeiro 520, 7th Floor Room 11, Centro, 69010-000 Manaus AM, Brazil, *Tel:* +55 92 3234 8910, *Fax:* +55 92 3234 7628, *Email:* willamazon@williams.com.br, *Website:* www.williams.com.br
Inchcape Shipping Services (ISS), Av Eduardo Ribeiro 520-13 andar, Salas 1301/1302, Centro, 69010-000 Manaus AM, Brazil, *Tel:* +55 92 3234 4991, *Fax:* +55 92 3234 4830, *Email:* gilberto.costa@iss-shipping.com, *Website:* www.iss-shipping.com
LBH Brasil, Av. Eduardo Ribeiro 520 Sala 1106, Ed. Manaus Shopping Center, CEP 69010-901 Manaus AM, Brazil, *Tel:* +55 92 2101 6855, *Fax:* +55 92 2101 6865, *Email:* brazmao@lbhbrasil.com.br, *Website:* www.brazshipping.com.br
Martrade Agencia Maritima Ltd, Av Teres, 439 ltos, Cachoeirnha, Manaus, Brazil, *Tel:* +55 92 3663 2303, *Fax:* +55 92 3663 2228, *Email:* macrade@terra.com.br
A.P. Moller-Maersk Group, Maersk Brasil Brasmar Ltda, Rua 41, Numero 858 - Conj. 31 de Marco, 69077-410 Manaus AM, Brazil, *Tel:* +55 92 3614 0100, *Fax:* +55 92 3631 7211, *Email:* ftzopsgen@maersk.com, *Website:* www.maerskline.com
Nortemar Agencia Maritima Ltda, Avenida Castelo Branco 2070/E, Cachoeirinha, Manaus, Brazil, *Tel:* +55 92 3611 5202, *Fax:* +55 92 3611 7990, *Email:* nortemar@internext.com.br

Medical Facilities: Doctors and hospital facilities available

Airport: Eduardo Gomes, 15 km

Development: Development of a 600 000 m2 container facility

Lloyd's Agent: Inspect Consultoria Ltda (Manaus), Rua Barao de Anajatuba No.7, Cond. Laranjeiras, Flores, 69058-110 Manaus AM, Brazil, *Tel:* +55 92 8138 0704, *Fax:* +55 92 3642 2096, *Email:* inspectmanaus@osite.com.br

MIRAMAR

Lat 1° 24' S; Long 48° 29' W.

Admiralty Chart: 397	**Admiralty Pilot:** 5
Time Zone: GMT -3 h	**UNCTAD Locode:** BR

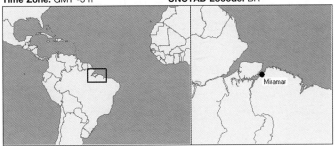

Principal Facilities:

P	Q					B		A	

Authority: Companhia Docas do Para, Terminal Petroquimico de Miramar, Rod. Arthur Bernardes s/n, 66115-000 Val-de-Caes PA, Brazil, *Tel:* +55 91 257 0808, *Fax:* +55 91 257 1563, *Email:* ailton@cdp.com.br, *Website:* www.cdp.com.br

Officials: Port Administrator: Jose Barros Leite.

Pilotage: Compulsory

Accommodation:

Name	Length (m)	Draught (m)	Remarks
Oil Terminal			
Pier No.1	80	7.9	
Pier No.2	40	7.9	230 m long with the four dolphins

Storage: 92 tanks with total cap of 206 847m3

Bunkering: Gas oil and MDO available alongside by tanker truck

Airport: Val-de-Caes International, 2.5 km

Lloyd's Agent: Inspect Consultoria Ltda (Sao Luis), Av Dos Portugueses, 31 Vila Embratel, 65085-580 Sao Luis MA, Brazil, *Tel:* +55 98 3242 4016, *Email:* inspectconsultoria@br.inter.net

MUCURIPE

alternate name, see Fortaleza

MUNGUBA

Lat 1° 5' S; Long 52° 23' W.

Admiralty Chart: 2204	**Admiralty Pilot:** 5
Time Zone: GMT -3 h	**UNCTAD Locode:** BR MGU

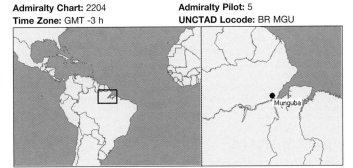

Principal Facilities:

		Y	G						A	

Authority: Jari Celulose S.A., Vila Munguba s/n, 68240-000 Monte Dourado PA, Brazil, *Tel:* +55 93 3736 6201, *Fax:* +55 93 3736 1180

Port Security: ISPS compliant

Documentation: Crew list (4 copies), passenger list (4 copies), ships general info (6 copies), certificate list (2 copies), bonded stores list (2 copies), provisions list (2 copies), personal effects list (2 copies), maritime declaration of health (1 copy), crew vaccination list (2 copies), list of ports of call (2 copies)

Approach: Draught restriction on the Jari River, January to June of 8.53 m; July to December 7.62 m. Time of transit from the mouth of the Jari River to the port is about 5.5 h

Pilotage: Compulsory. Pilot boards at Fazendinha, near Macapa, in pos 0° 40' 36" S; 51° 06' 45" W. Navigation of the Jari River during daylight hours only

Radio Frequency: VHF Channel 16

Weather: Frequent heavy rains from January to June

Tides: Range of tide, rainy season 0.3 m to 1.0 m; dry season 0.8 m to 1.3 m

Maximum Vessel Dimensions: 42 000 dwt, max draft 10.5 m, 196.5 m loa

Principal Imports and Exports: Imports: Caustic soda, Chemical products, Salt, Sulphur. Exports: Bauxite, Kaolin, Woodpulp.

Working Hours: 0700-1100, 1300-2300, 0000-0600

Accommodation:

Name	Length (m)	Depth (m)	Remarks
Munguba			
General Cargo Pier (Facel)	156	12	
Bulk Cargo Pier (Salt Pier)	150		Discharge of salt, sulphur & caustic soda
Bulk Cargo Pier (Cadam Pier)	200	12	See [1] below

[1]*Bulk Cargo Pier (Cadam Pier):* Loading kaolin & bauxite. The shiploader has a rate of 500 t/h and an air draught of 12 m. There is a small ro/ro ramp for barge use only

Storage:

Location	Covered (m²)	Sheds / Warehouses
Munguba	9416	2

Mechanical Handling Equipment:

Location	Type	Capacity (t)	Qty
Munguba	Mobile Cranes	50	2

Cargo Worked: Bulk kaolin 9600 t/day, bulk bauxite 12 000 t/day, woodpulp 8000 t/day

Medical Facilities: Hospital at Monte Dourado; serious cases are treated at Belem

Airport: Monte Dourado, 30 km

Lloyd's Agent: Inspect Consultoria Ltda (Sao Luis), Av Dos Portugueses, 31 Vila Embratel, 65085-580 Sao Luis MA, Brazil, *Tel:* +55 98 3242 4016, *Email:* inspectconsultoria@br.inter.net

NATAL

Lat 5° 47' S; Long 35° 11' W.

Admiralty Chart: 504	**Admiralty Pilot:** 5
Time Zone: GMT -3 h	**UNCTAD Locode:** BR NAT

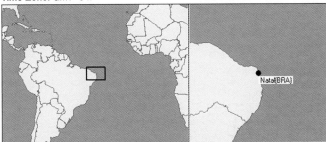

Principal Facilities:

P	Q	Y	G	C		L	B		A	

Authority: Companhia Docas do Rio Grande do Norte (CODERN), Av. Eng Hildebrando de Gois 220, Ribeira, 59010-700 Natal RN, Brazil, *Tel:* +55 84 3211 5311, *Fax:* +55 84 3221 6072, *Email:* codmkt@zaz.com.br, *Website:* www.codern.com.br

Officials: President: Carlos Ivan da Camara Ferreira de Melo.

Port Security: ISPS compliant

Documentation: Ship's characteristics (type, overall length, beam, draft), shipowner's identification & type of cargo, cargo manifest, bill of lading

Approach: The access channel is 3 km long, 100 m wide in depth of 10 m. The bottom consists of sand and mud and is free of any rocks. The manoeuvring basin is 250 m wide, 400 m long and 10 m deep

Anchorage: No.1 Anchorage for vessels awaiting berth: located between 5° 45' 00" S and 5° 45' 15" S and between 35° 10' 00" W and 35° 10' 30" W
No.2 Anchorage for quarantine vessels: located between 5° 45' 24" S and 5° 45' 36" S and between 35° 11' 06" W and 35° 11' 24" W

Pilotage: Compulsory. Pilot boards in pos 5° 45' 06" S: 35° 10' 30" W, Tel: +55 84 211 8483

Radio Frequency: VHF Channel 16

Weather: Winds predominantly ESE with only small variations from E to SE

Tides: Max 2.8 m

Traffic: 2005, 4 529 838 t of cargo handled

Maximum Vessel Dimensions: 204 m loa, 30 m beam

Principal Imports and Exports: Imports: Corn, Cotton, Machinery, Oil products, Wheat. Exports: Fruit, Sugar.

Working Hours: 24 h/day

Accommodation:

Name	Length (m)	Depth (m)	Remarks
Natal			See [1] below
Quay	540	11.5	See [2] below

[1]*Natal:* The Dunas oil pier, owned by Petrobras and used in bulk liquid transactions is situated approx 50 m N of the quay

---

Key to Principal Facilities:—			
A=Airport	**C**=Containers	**G**=General Cargo	
B=Bunkers	**D**=Dry Dock	**L**=Cruise	

P=Petroleum	**R**=Ro/Ro	**Y**=Dry Bulk
Q=Other Liquid Bulk	**T**=Towage (where available from port)	

[2]*Quay:* 90 reefer points. Container area of 15 000 m2. Bulk cargo unloaded by crane at rate of 350 t/h

Storage: Two holding warehouses of 1800 m2 each and two adjacent storage rooms of 456 m2 and 380 m2. Open storage available. The port has a cold storage plant for 2000 t

Mechanical Handling Equipment: Two top loaders with cap of 37 t

Location	Type	Capacity (t)	Qty
Natal	Forklifts	1.5–7	31

Bunkering: Fuel oil and diesel oil available from tank trucks

Waste Reception Facilities: Domestic garbage facilities only

Shipping Agents: CMA-CGM S.A., CMA CGM do Brasil Agencia Maritima, Av. Senador Salgado Filho 2190 Sala 128, Lagoa Nova, 59075-000 Natal RN, Brazil, *Tel:* +55 84 3206 5314, *Fax:* +55 84 3206 5314, *Email:* nat.flopes@cma-cgm.com, *Website:* www.cma-cgm.com
Corymar Agencia Maritima Ltd, Avenida Hildebrando de Gois 220, Codern Ribeira, 59010-700 Natal RN, Brazil, *Tel:* +55 84 3222 5791, *Fax:* +55 84 3221 2337, *Email:* willnat@williams.com.br, *Website:* www.williams.com.br

Stevedoring Companies: Grande Moinho Potiguar, Natal, Brazil, *Tel:* +55 84 3220 5345, *Fax:* +55 84 3220 5331, *Email:* jfilho@mdb.com.br
Modallink-Logistica e Operacoes Portuarias Ltda, Natal, Brazil, *Tel:* +55 84 3221 2020, *Fax:* +55 84 3611 2010, *Email:* modallink@digi.com.br
Porto Flash, Natal, Brazil, *Tel:* +55 84 3211 2781, *Email:* maisa.natal@cabugisat.com.br
Superservice-Inspecoes e Operacoes Portuarias Ltda, Natal, Brazil, *Tel:* +55 84 3201 2343, *Email:* sservice@zaz.com.br

Medical Facilities: Medical services and hospitals available in Natal. Nearest hospital, 2 km

Airport: 14 km from port

Railway: The harbour is connected to other northeastern states through the Northeastern Railway Company-CFN

Development: Entrance channel and berths to be dredged to 12.5 m; scheduled to be finished end of 2008, by which time the port will be able to accept vessels up to 45 000 dwt

Lloyd's Agent: Inspect Consultoria Ltda (Recife), Rua Padre Carapuceiro 412/603, Boa Viagem, 51020-280 Recife PE, Brazil, *Tel:* +55 81 9952 5868, *Email:* inspectrecife@terra.com.br

NAVEGANTES

Lat 26° 53' S; Long 48° 39' W.

Admiralty Chart: 549	**Admiralty Pilot:** 5
Time Zone: GMT -3 h	**UNCTAD Locode:** BR NVT

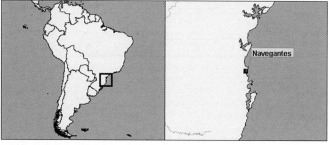

Principal Facilities:

		G	C				A

Authority: Portonave S/A Terminais Portuarios de Navegantes, Av. Joao Sacavem 85, 88375-000 Navegantes SC, Brazil, *Tel:* +55 47 2104 3300, *Fax:* +55 47 2104 3301, *Website:* www.portodenavegantes.net

Port Security: ISPS compliant

Accommodation:

Name	Length (m)	Depth (m)	Remarks
Navegantes Quay	900	12	Four berths

Mechanical Handling Equipment:

Location	Type	Qty
Navegantes	Mobile Cranes	2
Navegantes	Post Panamax	3
Navegantes	Transtainers	8
Navegantes	Reach Stackers	2

Airport: Navegantes International Airport, 2 km

Lloyd's Agent: Inspect Santos Consultoria e Peritagens Ltda, Av. Conselheiro Nebias, 726 - sala 114, Boqueirao, 11045-002 Santos SP, Brazil, *Tel:* +55 13 3234 5246, *Fax:* +55 13 3235 2250, *Email:* inspect@inspect.com.br

NITEROI

Lat 22° 53' S; Long 43° 7' W.

Admiralty Chart: 566	**Admiralty Pilot:** 5
Time Zone: GMT -3 h	**UNCTAD Locode:** BR NTR

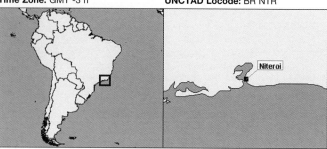

Principal Facilities:

	Y	G			B	T	A

Authority: Companhia Docas do Rio de Janeiro, Porto do Rio de Janeiro, Avenida Rodrigues Alves 20, 4 andar - Praca Maua, 20081-000 Rio de Janeiro RJ, Brazil, *Tel:* +55 21 2291 2122, *Fax:* +55 21 2516 1958, *Email:* suprio@portosrio.gov.br, *Website:* www.portosrio.gov.br

Documentation: 1: General declaration
2: Crew list
3: Crew personal effects list
4: Disembarking passenger list
5: Transit passengers list
6: Negative passenger list
7: Passenger list
8: Stores list
9: Cargo manifest
10: Maritime health declaration
11: Health certificate (from last port)
12: Maritime police pass

Pilotage: Compulsory, the pilot boards at Rio de Janiero station

Principal Imports and Exports: Imports: Wheat. Exports: Frozen fish.

Accommodation:

Name	Length (m)	Depth (m)
Niteroi		
Niteroi Quay	436	2–5

Storage: Two internal warehouses 22 x 75 m each with an area of 1650 m2 and an open storage area of 20 000 m2, there is also a wheat silo with a storage capacity of 15 000t

Bunkering: Fuel oil of all grades available by lighter only

Towage: Available

Repair & Maintenance: Enavi Reparos Navais Ltda, Avenida Contorno 169-Barreto, 24110-200 RJ Niteroi, Brazil, *Tel:* +55 21 2199 8044, *Fax:* +55 21 2624 1662, *Email:* enavi@enavi.com.br, *Website:* www.enavi.com.br Almirante Alexandrino floating dock 215 m x 35 m with lifting cap of 20 000 t. Almirante Guilem floating dock 200 m x 32.8 m with lifting cap of 18 000 t. Jose Rebelo floating dock 70 m x 17 m with lifting cap of 1800 t. Henrique Lage dry dock 184 m x 27 m. Orlando Barbosa dry dock 136 m x 17.43 m. Berthing facilities of 850 m

Airport: Rio de Janeiro

Lloyd's Agent: Inspect Consultoria Ltda (Rio de Janeiro), Avenida Rio Branco 37, Grupo 1902 Centro, 20090-003 Rio de Janeiro RJ, Brazil, *Tel:* +55 21 2263 3330, *Fax:* +55 21 2253 9322, *Email:* inspectconsultoria@br.inter.net, *Website:* www.inspectconsultoria.com.br

PARANAGUA

Lat 25° 30' S; Long 48° 31' W.

Admiralty Chart: 231	**Admiralty Pilot:** 5
Time Zone: GMT -3 h	**UNCTAD Locode:** BR PNG

Principal Facilities:

P	Q	Y	G	C	R		B		T	A

Tramp Oil & Marine

Wells House, 15-17 Elmfield Road, Bromley,
Kent BR1 1LT, United Kingdom
Phone: +44 20 8315 7777   **Fax:** +44 20 8315 7788
General email: enquiries@tramp-oil.com

See listings for all global offices: **www.tramp-oil.com**

NAVETEC
MARINE WORKSHOP AND SHIP REPAIR

Av Bento Rocha, 717 Rocio, 83221-565 Paranagua, BRAZIL
TEL: +55 41 3422-8373   FAX: +55 41 3424-1518
EMAIL: navetec@onda.com.br
WEB: www.navetec.page.tl

**Navetec is your reliable ship repairer at Paranaguá and neighbouring
ports of Antonina, São Francisco do Sul and Itajaí.**

Authority: Administracao dos Portos de Paranagua e Antonina, Rua Antonio Pereira 161, 83221-030 Paranagua PR, Brazil, *Tel:* +55 41 3420 1100, *Fax:* +55 41 3422 5324, *Email:* appasac@pr.gov.br, *Website:* www.portosdoparana.com.br

Officials: Marketing Director: Ruy Alberto Zibeti, *Email:* diremp@pr.gov.br.

Port Security: ISPS compliant

Approach: Vessels arriving approach the bar and embark pilot at the waiting buoy. The distance from the bar to the docks is 18 nautical miles. There are three channels to the harbour, the N channel, used by coasters and fishing craft, and the SE channel, depth 10 m, 4500 m long and 150 m wide, used by deep-sea vessels; max official draft for crossing the bar during spring tide 9.45 m (brackish), and during neap tide 8.84 m (brackish). The S channel has been dredged to 12 m. Vessels can enter at any time except those of over 10.66 m draft. The manoeuvring basin is 600 m wide and 12 m deep

Anchorage: Outer roads in depths of 15-20 m or the inner roads in a depth of 14 m

Pilotage: Compulsory between the buoy off Ilha do Mel, awaiting pilot, to any point of berthing. Pilot must be requested at least 4 h in advance

Radio Frequency: VHF Channels 16, 13 and 10

Weather: Southerly winds

Tides: Range of tide 2.3 m

Traffic: Paranagua: 2007, 38 225 388 t of cargo handled, 595 261 TEU's
Antonina: 2007, 626 224 t of cargo handled

Principal Imports and Exports: Imports: Barley, Fertiliser, Hardware, Wheat. Exports: Chickens, Coffee, Cotton, Frozen meat, Kraft paper, Oil & pellets, Soya beans, Steel, Wood.

Working Hours: Normal day shift 0700-1100, 1300-1700. Normal night shift 1900-2300, 0001-0400. No night shift on Sundays or holidays

Accommodation:

Name	Length (m)	Depth (m)	Draught (m)	Remarks
Paranagua				See [1] below
Berth No.201		9.44		Wheat & barley
Berth No.202		9.44		Paper & timber
Berth No.203		8.23		Paper & timber
Berth No.204		8.23		Frozen general cargo
Berth No.205		8.23		Frozen general cargo
Berth No.206		8.23		Grain
Berth No.207		8.23		General cargo
Berth No's 208 & 209		7.61		General cargo. Ro/ro, fertiliser & salt at berth 209
Berth No's 210 & 211		8.23		General cargo. Fertiliser & salt at berth 211
Berth No.211A		8.23		Fertiliser
Berth No.212		10.05		Soya beans
Berth No.213		10.05		Soya beans
Berth No.214		10.05		Soya beans
Berth No's 215 & 216	655	12		See [2] below
Cattalini Private Terminal	244		7–12	See [3] below
Antonina				See [4] below
Barao de Teffe Terminal		5.79		See [5] below

Name	Length (m)	Depth (m)	Draught (m)	Remarks
Ponta do Felix Terminal	360			See [6] below

[1] *Paranagua:* Tanker facilities: Inflammables Pier: comprises two piers, one 143 m long and the other 184 m long. The 184 m pier can berth two vessels simultaneously, one vessel on the internal side and the other on the external side. Another characteristic of this pier is that a third vessel can be berthed alongside

[2] *Berth No's 215 & 216:* Container terminal operated by Terminal de Conteineres de Paranagua S.A. (TCP), Caixa Postal 169, 83203-970 Paranagua PR, Tel: +55 41 3420 3300, Fax: +55 41 3420 3327, Email: tcp@tcp.com.br, Website: www.tcp.com.br Equipment includes two panamax cranes of 40 t cap, one post-panamax crane of 40 t cap and seven RTG's of 40.6 t cap. 324 reefer points. Warehouse of 12 000 m2

[3] *Cattalini Private Terminal:* Operated by Cattalini Terminais Maritimos Ltda., 2677 Cel. Santa Rita St., 83221-240 Paranagua PR, Tel: +55 41 3420 3500, Fax: +55 41 3423 3442, Email: cattalini@cattaliniterminais.com.br, Website: www.cattaliniterminais.com.br
Private pier which allows berthing of two 50 000 dwt vessels simultaneously for liquid bulk cargoes

[4] *Antonina:* Port of Antonina, Tel: +55 41 3432 1448, Fax: +55 41 3432 1442

[5] *Barao de Teffe Terminal:* For vessels up to 155 m loa with two warehouses of 2436 m2 and 1056 m2

[6] *Ponta do Felix Terminal:* Operated by Terminais Portuarios da Ponta do Felix S.A., Rua Eng. Luiz Augusto de Leao Fonseca 1520, 83370-000 Antonina PR, Tel: +55 41 3432 8000, Fax: +55 41 3432 8015, Email: pontadofelix@pontadofelix.com.br, Website: www.pontadofelix.com.br
Access is through the Paranagua Bay canal which is 5.4 nautical miles long in depth of 10 m. Supports the docking of two vessels simultaneously, of which 210 m are intended for forest products and containers, and 150 m for refrigerated cargoes. Consolidation area for 2300 containers with 200 reefer points. There are three general cargo warehouses, one of 2500 m2 with 10 000 m3 cap and two of 3125 m2 with 18 000 m3 cap each. Equipment includes electronic semi-automatic weighing devices with max cap up to 60 t, pallet bridge type cranes with max cap of 7 t, forklifts with max cap of 12 t and reach stacker equipment for container moving

Storage: Two refrigerated warehouses of 4400 m2 and 5500 m2

Location	Open (m²)	Covered (m²)	Sheds / Warehouses
Paranagua	65000	61000	24

Mechanical Handling Equipment:

Location	Type	Capacity (t)	Qty
Paranagua	Floating Cranes	100	1
Paranagua	Mult-purp. Cranes	130	16

Cargo Worked: General cargo 250-2500 t/day

Bunkering: Tramp Oil & Marine, World Fuel Services Corporation, 13th Floor, Portland House, Bressenden Place, London SW1E 5BH, United Kingdom, *Tel:* +44 20 7808 5000, *Fax:* +44 20 7808 5088, *Email:* pturner@wfscorp.com, *Website:* www.wfscorp.com – *Grades:* all grades – *Misc:* fresh water available – *Delivery Mode:* barge, pipeline, truck

Waste Reception Facilities: Only by trucks while berthed

Towage: Wilson Sons Agencia Maritima Ltda, Rua Tuiuti 58, 1st & 2nd Floors, 11010-220 Santos SP, Brazil, *Tel:* +55 13 3211 2300, *Fax:* +55 13 3219 5250, *Email:* agest@wilsonsons.com.br, *Website:* www.wilsonsons.com.br

Repair & Maintenance: Brasil Maritima, Paranagua, Brazil, *Tel:* +55 41 3422 4590 J. Monteiro, Paranagua, Brazil, *Tel:* +55 41 3422 1020, *Fax:* +55 41 3422 6351 Navetec, Avenida Bento Rocha, 717 Rocio, 83221-565 Paranagua PR, Brazil, *Tel:* +55 41 3422 8373, *Fax:* +55 41 3424 1518, *Email:* navetec@brturbo.com.br

Ship Chandlers: Millennium General Ship Services, Rue Xavier da Silva 47, 83203-620 Paranagua, Brazil, *Tel:* +55 41 3424 2001, *Fax:* +55 41 3424 3725, *Email:* millennium@mgss.com.br, *Website:* www.mgss.com.br
Newport Ship Chandler Ltda, Rua Guanandis 363, Jardim, Samambaia, 83212-310 Paranagua, Brazil, *Tel:* +55 41 3427 3444, *Fax:* +55 41 3427 3692, *Email:* newport@brturbo.com, *Website:* www.nechandler.com.br
Polynave Marine Supplies Ltd, 1065 Rua Manoel Pereira, 83203-765 Paranagua, Brazil, *Tel:* +55 41 3425 5648, *Fax:* +55 41 3422 6934, *Email:* polynave@uol.com.br
Vapo's - Lizott & Cia. Ltda, Rua Arthur Bernardes 945, 83206-110 Paranagua, Brazil, *Tel:* +55 41 3422 2967, *Fax:* +55 41 3423 2836, *Email:* vapo@lol.com.br, *Website:* www.eurosull.com.br

Shipping Agents: Atlas Maritime Ltda, Avenida Coronel Jose Lobo 727/895, Costeira, 83203-310 Paranagua, Brazil, *Tel:* +55 41 3422 0101, *Fax:* +55 41 3422 1240, *Email:* atlas_paranagua@atlasmaritime.com.br, *Website:* www.atlasmaritime.com.br
CMA-CGM S.A., CMA CGM do Brasil Agencia Maritima, Av. Coronel Jose Lobo 218, Costeira, 83203-340 Paranagua PR, Brazil, *Tel:* +55 41 3420 3100, *Fax:* +55 41 3420 3114, *Email:* pga.ccorrea@cma-cgm.com, *Website:* www.cma-cgm.com
Corymar Agencia Maritima Ltd, Williams Shipping Agency, Rua Joao Eugenio 613, 1st Floor Room 1-2, Palacio do Cafezinho Building, 83203-380 Paranagua PR, Brazil, *Tel:* +55 41 3422 7266, *Fax:* +55 41 3422 7386, *Email:* willpga@williams.com.br, *Website:* www.williams.com.br
Fertimport S.A., Rua Manoel Correa, 1195, Paranagua, Brazil, *Tel:* +55 41 3423 4142, *Fax:* +55 41 3422 2185, *Email:* pga.fertimport@bunge.com.br
Agencia de Vapores Grieg S.A., Av Arthur de Abreu 29, andar 6, 83203-480 Paranagua PR, Brazil, *Tel:* +55 41 3423 1123, *Fax:* +55 41 3423 4516, *Email:* griegpga@grieg.com.br, *Website:* www.grieg.com.br
A.P. Moller-Maersk Group, Maersk Brasil Ltda, Rua Nestor Victor 800, 83203-540 Paranagua PR, Brazil, *Tel:* +55 41 3038 5400, *Fax:* +55 41 3038 5400, *Email:* brzcrcitj@maersk.com, *Website:* www.maerskline.com
Oceanus Agencia Maritima S.A., Av. Rodrigues Alves 800 - 6th Floor, 83203-170 Paranagua PR, Brazil, *Tel:* +55 41 3423 1066, *Fax:* +55 41 3423 3481, *Email:* agency.png@oceanus.com.br, *Website:* www.oceanus.com.br
Agencia Maritima Orion Ltda, Rua Manoel Correa 1345, Alto Sao Sebastiao, 83206-030 Paranagua, Brazil, *Tel:* +55 41 3420 3700, *Fax:* +55 41 3422 4987, *Email:* orion@png.amorion.com.br, *Website:* www.amorion.com.br
Rocha Top Terminais e Operadores Portuarios Ltda, Rua Joao Eugenio 922, P O Box

---

Key to Principal Facilities:—
A=Airport   **C**=Containers   **G**=General Cargo   **P**=Petroleum   **R**=Ro/Ro   **Y**=Dry Bulk
B=Bunkers   **D**=Dry Dock   **L**=Cruise   **Q**=Other Liquid Bulk   **T**=Towage (where available from port)

05, CEP 83203-400 Paranagua, Brazil, *Tel:* +55 41 3420 2300, *Fax:* +55 41 3420 2397/96, *Email:* shipping@rochatop.com.br, *Website:* www.rochatop.com.br

Seatrade Agencia Maritima Ltda, Av Porturia, c/h Bairro Dom Pedro II, Paranagua, Brazil, *Tel:* +55 41 3423 2031, *Fax:* +55 41 3422 0766, *Email:* charles@png.seatrade.com.br, *Website:* www.seatrade.com.br

Supermar S.A., Rua Manuel Pereira 990, Leblon, CEP83203-765 Paranagua, Brazil, *Tel:* +55 41 3422 6856, *Email:* paranagua@supermar.com.br

Transatlantic Carriers (Agenciamentos) Ltda, Avenida Cel Jose Lobo, 407, CEP 83203-310 Paranagua, Brazil, *Tel:* +55 41 3423 1266, *Fax:* +55 41 3423 6361, *Email:* transcar@transcar-png.com.br

Agencia Maritima Transatlantica Ltda, Rua Nestor Vitor 800, P O Box 112, CEP 83200-260 Paranagua, Brazil, *Tel:* +55 41 3423 1233, *Fax:* +55 41 3423 2393, *Email:* tranship@bsi.com.br

Unimar Agenciamentos Maritimos Ltda, Rua Soares Gomes 999 Leblon, CEP83203-470 Paranagua, Brazil, *Tel:* +55 41 3423 3950, *Fax:* +55 41 3423 1375, *Email:* unimar-paranagua@unimar-agency.com.br

V Morel S.A., Avenida Arthur de Abreu 29, 6 Andar cjs.4/5, CEP83203-480 Paranagua, Brazil, *Tel:* +55 41 3423 4611, *Fax:* +55 41 3422 7111, *Email:* paranagua@vmorel.com.br, *Website:* www.vmorel.com.br

Wilson Sons Agencia Maritima Ltda, Rua Rodrigues Alves 759 - Centro, 83203-170 Paranagua PR, Brazil, *Tel:* +55 41 2152 1400, *Fax:* +55 41 2152 1440, *Email:* agepg@wilsonsons.com.br, *Website:* www.wilsonsons.com.br

Surveyors: Det Norske Veritas A/S, Paranagua, Brazil, *Tel:* +55 41 3423 2425, *Fax:* +55 41 3423 2425, *Website:* www.dnv.com

Nippon Kaiji Kyokai, Avenue Arthur de Abreu 29, 10th Floor, Suite 01/02, 83203-210 Paranagua PR, Brazil, *Tel:* +55 41 3423 2425, *Fax:* +55 41 3422 2483, *Email:* pandb@sul.com.br

Medical Facilities: Hospital and medical facilities are available

Airport: Afonso Pena, 90 km

Lloyd's Agent: Inspect Santos Consultoria e Peritagens Ltda, Av. Conselheiro Nebias, 726 - sala 114, Boqueirao, 11045-002 Santos SP, Brazil, *Tel:* +55 13 3234 5246, *Fax:* +55 13 3235 2250, *Email:* inspect@inspect.com.br

PAUL DOCK

harbour area, see under Vitoria

PECEM

Lat 3° 33' S; Long 38° 49' W.

Admiralty Chart: 526/3957	**Admiralty Pilot:** 5
Time Zone: GMT -3 h	**UNCTAD Locode:** BR PEC

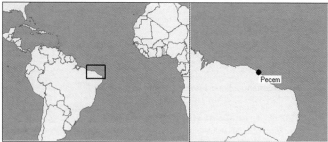

Principal Facilities:

P	Q	Y	G	C					

Authority: Companhia de Integracao Portuaria do Ceara (CEARAPORTOS), Esplanada do Pecem s/n, Terminal Portuario do Pecem, 62674-000 Sao Goncalo do Amarante CE, Brazil, *Tel:* +55 85 3315 1122, *Fax:* +55 85 3315 1045, *Email:* cearaportos@cearaportos.ce.gov.br, *Website:* www.cearaportos.ce.gov.br

Port Security: ISPS compliant

Pilotage: Compulsory. Vessels should send ETA 24 h in advance, and advise any subsequent changes. Pilot boards in pos 3° 28.5' S; 38° 47.8' W (0.8 nautical mile NE of the Fairway Lt buoy)

Radio Frequency: VHF Channels 16 and 10

Traffic: 2007, 2 205 361 t of cargo handled, 143 667 TEU's

Accommodation:

Name	Length (m)	Depth (m)	Remarks
Pecem			See [1] below
Pier No.1	350	15.5	Container, bulk & general cargo
Pier No.2	336.6	16–17	Petroleum products
LNG Terminal			See [2] below

[1]*Pecem:* Port protected by an L-shaped breakwater 1768 m long
[2]*LNG Terminal:* The LNG carrier 'Golar Spirit' serves as a floating import terminal with a storage cap of 129 000 m3

Storage:

Location	Open (m²)	Covered (m²)	Sheds / Warehouses
Pecem	380000	16250	2

Stevedoring Companies: Ceara Terminal Operator Ltda, Esplanada do Pecem s/n, Bloco B - Sala 4, 62674-000 Sao Goncalo do Amarante CE, Brazil, *Tel:* +55 85 3315

1515, *Fax:* +55 85 3315 1002, *Email:* cto-pecem@cto-pecem.com.br, *Website:* www.cto-pecem.com.br

Lloyd's Agent: Inspect Consultoria Ltda (Sao Luis), Av Dos Portugueses, 31 Vila Embratel, 65085-580 Sao Luis MA, Brazil, *Tel:* +55 98 3242 4016, *Email:* inspectconsultoria@br.inter.net

PELOTAS

Lat 31° 45' S; Long 52° 15' W.

Admiralty Chart: 3063/556	**Admiralty Pilot:** 5
Time Zone: GMT -3 h	**UNCTAD Locode:** BR PET

Principal Facilities:

		G						A	

Authority: Superintendencia de Portos e Hidrovias do Rio Grande do Sul, Divisao do Porto de Pelotas, Rua Benjamin Constant 215, 96010-020 Pelotas RS, Brazil, *Tel:* +55 53 278 7322, *Fax:* +55 53 278 7333, *Email:* portopel@sph.rs.gov.br, *Website:* www.portopelotas.rs.gov.br

Approach: The bar of Lagoa dos Patos is the access to the port

Pilotage: Round trip Rio Grande-Pelotas, according to gross tonnage. Sundays, holidays and nights, +20% (in addition to bar pilotage entering Rio Grande). Pilotage from Rio Grande and back is compulsory

Traffic: 2005, 305 490 t of cargo handled

Accommodation:

Name	Remarks
Pelotas	See [1] below

[1]*Pelotas:* The length of the quay is 500 m. The depth alongside the quay is 5.18 m max. Vessels have to enter and clear at the Capitania and Customs House at Rio Grande. Max permitted draft on sailing from Rio Grande to Pelotas is 3.66 m

Airport: 11.2 km from port

Lloyd's Agent: Inspect Santos Consultoria e Peritagens Ltda, Av. Conselheiro Nebias, 726 - sala 114, Boqueirao, 11045-002 Santos SP, Brazil, *Tel:* +55 13 3234 5246, *Fax:* +55 13 3235 2250, *Email:* inspect@inspect.com.br

POLVO TERMINAL

Lat 23° 5' S; Long 41° 0' W.

Admiralty Chart: 3971	**Admiralty Pilot:** 5
Time Zone: GMT -3 h	**UNCTAD Locode:** BR

Principal Facilities:

P									

Authority: Devon Energy do Brasil Ltda, Av. Atlantica 1130, 17th Floor, Copacabana, 22021-000 Rio de Janeiro RJ, Brazil, *Tel:* +55 21 2127 2920, *Email:* andreyassumpcao@dvn.com, *Website:* www.devonenergy.com

Port Security: ISPS compliantaxi

Pre-Arrival Information: ETA to be forwarded to FPSO 72 h prior to arrival with updates every 24 h and any other time if the ETA is to be revised by more than 12 h

Pilotage: Compulsory by Mooring Master

Maximum Vessel Dimensions: 60 000-150 000 dwt

Principal Imports and Exports: Exports: Crude oil.

Accommodation:

Name	Remarks
Polvo Terminal	See [1] below

[1]*Polvo Terminal:* Consists of 'FPSO Polvo'. Average loading rate of 7500 m3/h. Mooring during daylight hours only

Lloyd's Agent: Inspect Consultoria Ltda (Rio de Janeiro), Avenida Rio Branco 37, Grupo 1902 Centro, 20090-003 Rio de Janeiro RJ, Brazil, *Tel:* +55 21 2263 3330, *Fax:* +55 21 2253 9322, *Email:* inspectconsultoria@br.inter.net, *Website:* www.inspectconsultoria.com.br

PONTA DA MADEIRA

Lat 2° 33' S; Long 44° 22' W.

Admiralty Chart: 535	**Admiralty Pilot:** 5
Time Zone: GMT -3 h	**UNCTAD Locode:** BR PMA

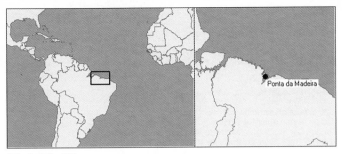

Principal Facilities:

	Y				T	A	

Authority: Vale, Praia Mole SC, Brazil, *Tel:* +55 27 3333 5624, *Fax:* +55 27 3333 5293

Port Security: ISPS compliant

Approach: The access channel starts around 12 miles S of pos 01° 34.9' S; 43° 50.8' W. It is 55 miles long and divided into the following parts:
(a) from the pair of light buoys 1 and 2 to abeam of buoy 6, being 7.6 miles long, along 208°-28°
(b) from light buoy 6 until 1.8 miles beyond buoy 14, being 11.6 miles long, along 238°-58°
(c) from 1.8 miles after buoy 14 to the pair of buoys 19 and 24, being 33.6 miles long, along 213°-33°
The width of the channel is 1000 m along almost all of its extension except between the pair of light buoys 1 and 2, the pair of light buoys 3 and 4, the pair of light buoys 5 and 10, the pair of light buoys 9 and 14 and the pair of light buoys 17 and 22 where the min width is 480 m
The min depth of the channel is 23 m except between light buoys 17 and 22 where it is 25 m

Anchorage: If all anchorage areas (inner and outer) are occupied, vessels must anchor in the outside anchorage area, located N-NE of buoy 2 in the entrance of the channel
Area 1: between buoys 6 and 10, reserved for vessels bound for TMPM in part cargo having a draft above 11 m and also for vessels that are the subject of dispute and those under extensive repairs. The area is limited by a rectangle in the following coordinates: 01° 58.5' S; 44° 07.0' W, 01° 55.5' S; 44° 09.0' W, 01° 49.2' S; 43° 58.4' W, 01° 51.8' S; 43° 56.5' W
Area 2: between buoys 16 and 18, intended for loaded vessels with draft above 20 m waiting for tide conditions to pass buoys 14 and 10, and also buoys 4 and 2. The area is limited by the polygon in the following coordinates: 02° 02.9' S; 44° 03.4' W, 02° 05.4' S; 44° 03.4' W, 02° 06.0' S; 44° 07.2' W, 02° 04.4' S; 44° 06.1' W
Area 3: between buoys 18 and 15, intended for loaded vessels with draft above 20 m waiting for tide conditions to pass buoys 14 and 10, and also buoys 4 and 2 when Area 2 is occupied. The area is limited by the polygon in the following coordinates: 02° 08.3' S; 44° 08.7' W, 02° 10.9' S; 44° 09.0' W, 02° 12.1' S; 44° 10.0' W, 02° 12.1' S; 44° 11.0' W
Area 4: reserved for vessels with a max draft of 11 m waiting to berth. The north area is located abeam buoys 20 and 22 and the south area is located between buoy 22 and the lighthouses of Sao Marcos and Aracagi and is limited by the following coordinates: 02° 19.25' S; 44° 12.2' W, 02° 21.39' S; 44° 09.61' W, 02° 24.38' S; 44° 12.8' W, 02° 27.4' S; 44° 17.2' W, 02° 26.58' S; 44° 19.4' W
Area 5: reserved for vessels with a max draft of 11 m waiting to berth. It is located next to the pair of buoys 17 and 22 and is limited by the following coordinates: 02° 22.2' S; 44° 20.3' W, 02° 25.0' S; 44° 21.3' W, 02° 24.4' S; 44° 22.2' W, 02° 20.1' S; 44° 20.4' W
Area 6: for vessels with a draft less than 11 m and displacement of 80 000 t. It is necessary to get authorization from the Harbour Master and is limited by the following coordinates: 02° 26.6' S; 44° 24.5' W, 02° 29.2' S; 44° 24.0' W, 02° 30.6' S; 44° 25.4' W, 02° 29.8' S; 44° 26.0' W
Area 7: for vessels with a draft less than 11 m and displacement of 80 000 t. It is necessary to get authorization from the Harbour Master and is limited by the following coordinates: 02° 33.6' S; 44° 25.0' W, 02° 34.0' S; 44° 23.6' W, 02° 35.5' S; 44° 24.3' W, 02° 34.8' S; 44° 25.7' W
Area 8: used for loading/unloading explosives and fuel. It is necessary to get authorization from the Harbour Master and is limited by the following coordinates: 02° 35.4' S; 44° 26.0' W, 02° 34.8' S; 44° 25.7' W, 02° 35.5' S; 44° 24.3' W, 02° 36.8' S; 44° 24.8' W, 02° 36.2' S; 44° 26.0' W

Pilotage: Compulsory. Vessels with draft over 11 m must take on pilot between buoys 17 and 22. Vessels with draft less than 11 m must take on pilot at the pilot station in pos 02° 28.9' S; 44° 22.2' W

Radio Frequency: VHF Channel 16

Tides: Tides in Sao Marcos Bay are semi diurnal

Traffic: 2005, 572 vessels, 74 421 597 t of cargo handled

Working Hours: 24 h/day

Accommodation:

Name	Length (m)	Depth (m)	Remarks
Ponta da Madeira			See [1] below
Pier No.1	320	23	See [2] below
Pier No.2	280	18	See [3] below
Pier No.3	571	21	See [4] below

[1]*Ponta da Madeira:* Ore is transported by a rail link 890 km long from the mines in the Carajas region
[2]*Pier No.1:* Max 420 000 dwt. Four berthing dolphins and six mooring dolphins. One shiploader at 16 000 t/h. Max air draft 22.4 m
[3]*Pier No.2:* Max 155 000 dwt. One shiploader at 8000 t/h with max air draft of 18 m and one shiploader (loading copper only) at 1320 t/h with max air draft of 11 m
[4]*Pier No.3:* Max of one vessel up to 200 000 dwt or two vessels up to 125 000 dwt at south part and 75 000 dwt at north part. Twenty eight berthing dolphins. One shiploader at 8000 t/h with max air draft of 22.4 m

Towage: The use of tugs is compulsory and available

Shipping Agents: Oceanus Agencia Maritima S.A., Av. Maestro Joao Nunes, Quadra 19 - Lote 2, Rooms 1009/1013, 65076-200 Sao Luis MA, Brazil, *Tel:* +55 98 3227 9460, *Fax:* +55 98 3227 9462, *Email:* tramp.slz@oceanus.com.br, *Website:* www.oceanus.com.br

Medical Facilities: Sao Luis Hospital

Airport: Tirirical, 26 km

Lloyd's Agent: Inspect Consultoria Ltda (Sao Luis), Av Dos Portugueses, 31 Vila Embratel, 65085-580 Sao Luis MA, Brazil, *Tel:* +55 98 3242 4016, *Email:* inspectconsultoria@br.inter.net

PONTA DO UBU

Lat 20° 47' S; Long 40° 35' W.

Admiralty Chart: 551	**Admiralty Pilot:** 5
Time Zone: GMT -3 h	**UNCTAD Locode:** BR POU

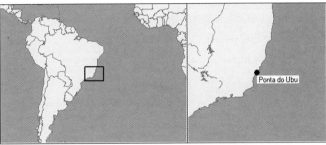

Principal Facilities:

	Y	G			B		T	A	

Authority: Samarco Mineracao S.A., Terminal de Ponta Ubu, Rodovia do Sol (ES 060) - Km 14, Ponta Ubu, 29230-000 Anchieta ES, Brazil, *Tel:* +55 27 3361 9330, *Fax:* +55 27 3361 9474, *Website:* www.portodeubu.com.br

Approach: The channel is 2.8 km long and 210 m wide reaching 600 m in the turning basin and 150 m in the pier vicinity, depth in channel is maintained at min of 19 m

Pilotage: Compulsory. Pilot boards in anchorage area 20° 46' 24" S; 40° 32' 33" W. Anchorage instructions must be requested from Marine Operations 4 h prior to arrival at boarding area, or when within VHF range, Channel 16. The master of an arriving vessel is required to cable his notice of ETA 15 days, or when departing from previous port if sailing distance is less than 15 days, then 5 days, 48 h and 24 h prior to ETA to supply specific information

Radio Frequency: Marine Operations Station monitored 24 h/day. VHF Channel 16, 156.8 mHz (calling); working channels 156.375 mHz, 156.65 mHz and 156.7 mHz

Traffic: 2005, 16 853 855 t of cargo handled

Maximum Vessel Dimensions: 308 m loa

Working Hours: 24 h/day

Accommodation:

Name	Length (m)	Depth (m)	Remarks
Ponta do Ubu			See [1] below
Pier	313	15–19	See [2] below

[1]*Ponta do Ubu:* A privately owned iron ore terminal consisting of a breakwater protected pier
[2]*Pier:* Pier projects from the E portion of the breakwater to a distance of 685 m from the shore with berths on both E and W sides. A mobile rail mounted shiploader has a 41.6 m fixed length boom with 280° turning angle and 19.5 m air draft, giving nominal loading cap of 8700-9000 t/h for pellets and filter cake. Stockpile cap of 1 000 000 t of pellets and 500 000 t of concentrate

Bunkering: Only available by barge from Vitoria

Towage: Compulsory. Two tugs of 1680 hp and 22 t bollard pull are permanently based at the Terminal. Further tugs are on call if required

Shipping Agents: LBH Brasil, Av. AtÝlio Rauta 877, Bairro Justica, 29230-000 Anchieta ES, Brazil, *Tel:* +55 28 3536 1547, *Fax:* +55 28 3536 3623, *Email:* brazubu@lbhbrasil.com.br, *Website:* www.brazshipping.com.br

Medical Facilities: Nearest facilities at Guarapari, 15 km. Modern hospitals at Vitoria

Airport: Vitoria, 64 km

Lloyd's Agent: Inspect Consultoria Ltda (Rio de Janeiro), Avenida Rio Branco 37, Grupo 1902 Centro, 20090-003 Rio de Janeiro RJ, Brazil, *Tel:* +55 21 2263 3330, *Fax:* +55 21 2253 9322, *Email:* inspectconsultoria@br.inter.net, *Website:* www.inspectconsultoria.com.br

PORTO ALEGRE

Lat 30° 2' S; Long 51° 13' W.

Admiralty Chart: 3063/3969	**Admiralty Pilot:** 5
Time Zone: GMT -3 h	**UNCTAD Locode:** BR POA

Key to Principal Facilities:—					
A=Airport	**C**=Containers	**G**=General Cargo	**P**=Petroleum	**R**=Ro/Ro	**Y**=Dry Bulk
B=Bunkers	**D**=Dry Dock	**L**=Cruise	**Q**=Other Liquid Bulk	**T**=Towage (where available from port)	

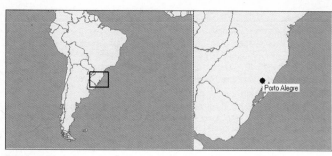

Principal Facilities:

| P | Q | Y | G | C | | | B | | T | A | |

Authority: Superintendencia de Portos e Hidrovias do Rio Grande do Sul, Avenida Maua 1050, Bairro Centro, 90010-110 Porto Alegre RS, Brazil, *Tel:* +55 51 3211 4849, *Fax:* +55 51 3225 8954, *Email:* portopoa@sph.rs.gov.br, *Website:* www.portoportoalegre.com.br

Port Security: ISPS compliant

Approach: The approach to the port is made through eight channels, the biggest being Feitoria (120 m wide) between Pelotas and Rio Grande, the other seven being within the entrance to the port. The artificial channels are:
Itapua Channel 4.97 km long and 115 m width, Campista Channel 1.9 km long and 85 m width, Junco Channel 12.3 km long and 85 m width, Belem Channel 7.8 km long and 85 m width, Leitao Channel 7.7 km long and 85 m width, Pedras Brancas Channel 1.95 km long and 85 m width, Cristal Channel 2.5 km long and 85 m width
The manoeuvring basin is 450 m wide and 5.8 m deep

Anchorage: In front of the Maua section, length 4 km, beam 600 m, depth 10 m

Pilotage: Compulsory in the Lagoa dos Patos and in the port itself. Pilot requisition should be made 12 h in advance. Pilotage for Pelotas and Rio Grande is available at Porto Alegre

Radio Frequency: VHF Channel 16

Traffic: 2006, 12 275 000 t of cargo handled

Maximum Vessel Dimensions: The official draft for a vessel entering the port is 5.18 m, max length 245 m

Principal Imports and Exports: Imports: Fertiliser, Paper, Salt, Soya bean oil. Exports: Lumber, Soya bean meal, Steel, Woodpulp.

Working Hours: 0730-1130, 1300-1700 (normal time). 1700-2300, 0000-0400 (overtime). Sat is a normal working day

Accommodation:

Name	Length (m)	Depth (m)	Remarks
Porto Alegre			See [1] below
Maua Section (Central Zone)	3240	4–6	There is 1390 m of quay space where small river and lake crafts can go alongside
Navegantes Section	2500	5–6	See [2] below
Marcilio Dias Section	2260	4–5	Mainly used by smaller craft

[1]*Porto Alegre:* Bulk facilities: There are terminals at the port for the handling of bulk solids. CESA Terminal has a silo cap of 18 750 t, rate 200 t/h; SAMRIG Terminal, silo cap 18 000 t, rate 200 t/h; CIAGRAN Terminal, silo cap 50 000 t, rate 500 t/h
[2]*Navegantes Section:* This section has 300 m of quay where ro/ro vessels are handled

Storage: Refrigerated space of 9400 m2

Location	Covered (m²)
Porto Alegre	66153

Mechanical Handling Equipment:

Location	Type	Capacity (t)	Qty
Porto Alegre	Mult-purp. Cranes	70	15
Porto Alegre	Forklifts		18

Cargo Worked: Paper 1800 t/day with two gangs, iron & steel 1500 t/day with three gangs, fertilizer 1900 t/day with two gangs and general cargo 900 t/day with three gangs

Bunkering: Marbrax marine lubricants are delivered by trucks in drums to the berth. Three days notice is required. Fresh water is also available
ExxonMobil Marine Fuels, Suite 900, One Alhambra Plaza, Coral Gables, FL 33134, United States of America, *Tel:* +1 305 459 6358, *Fax:* +1 305 459 6412, *Email:* emmf@exxonmobil.com, *Website:* www.exxonmobilmarinefuels.com – *Grades:* IFO30-180cSt; MGO; MDO – *Delivery Mode:* barge, truck, pipeline
Petrobras Bunkering, Avenida Republica do Chile 65, 20 andar, sala 2001-H, 20035-913 Rio de Janeiro, Brazil, *Tel:* +55 21 3224 3290, *Fax:* +55 21 2262 8134, *Email:* bunker@petrobras.com.br, *Website:* www.petrobras.com.br – *Grades:* MGO – *Notice:* 7 days – *Delivery Mode:* truck

Towage: Four privately owned tugs of 250-400 hp and one Government tug of 1680 hp

Repair & Maintenance: Estaleiro So, Padre Cacique 2893, 90180-240 Porto Alegre, Brazil, *Tel:* +55 51 3249 4890, *Fax:* +55 51 3249 5087

Shipping Agents: Atlas Maritime Ltda, Avenida Carlos Gomes 1155, CJ 301, Auxiliadore, 90480-004 Porto Alegre RS, Brazil, *Tel:* +55 51 3332 5575, *Fax:* +55 51 3332 5260, *Email:* atlas_portoalegre@atlasmaritime.com.br, *Website:* www.atlasmaritime.com.br
CMA-CGM S.A., CMA CGM do Brasil Agencia Maritima, Av. Carlos Gomes 1340 / Sala 503, Bela Vista, 90480-001 Porto Alegre RS, Brazil, *Tel:* +55 51 3021 9100, *Fax:* +55 51 3328 4491, *Email:* bpa.genmbox@cma-cgm.com, *Website:* www.cma-cgm.com

Fertimport S.A., Rua Moura Azevedo 125, Porto Alegre, Brazil, *Tel:* +55 51 3346 1488, *Fax:* +55 51 3344 3664, *Email:* liner-poa@ferimport.infonet.com
Agencia de Vapores Grieg S.A., Av Julio de Castilhos 132, sala 503, 90030-130 Porto Alegre RS, Brazil, *Tel:* +55 51 3286 1911, *Fax:* +55 51 3286 1911, *Email:* griegpoa@grieg.com.br, *Website:* www.grieg.com.br
Grimaldi Cia de Navigazione do Brasil Ltda, Avenida Maua 2011, 21st Floor Room 1202, Porto Alegre, Brazil, *Tel:* +55 51 3228 1112, *Fax:* +55 51 3228 3097, *Email:* grimpoa@uol.com.br
Lachmann Logistica Ltda, Avenida Maua, 2011/803/804, Centro, CEP 90030-000 Porto Alegre, Brazil, *Tel:* +55 51 3211 1570, *Fax:* +55 51 3228 4176, *Email:* lachmann.poa@lachmann.com.br
Mediterranean Shipping Company, MSC do Brasil Ltda, Rua Sete de Setembro 745, 7 andar, Centro, 90010-190 Porto Alegre RS, Brazil, *Tel:* +55 51 3535 1800, *Fax:* +55 51 3535 1827, *Email:* distribution@mscbr.com.br, *Website:* www.mscgva.ch
Agencia Maritima Orion Ltda, Avenida Benjamin Constant 1258, Sala 101, Bairro Floresta, Porto Alegre, Brazil, *Tel:* +55 51 3373 5100, *Fax:* +55 51 3373 5110, *Email:* orion@poa.amorion.com.br
Supermar S.A., Avenida Maua, 2011 Suite 1401/1106, CEP90030-080 Porto Alegre, Brazil, *Tel:* +55 51 3012 5974, *Fax:* +55 51 3012 5975, *Email:* portoalegre@supermar.com.br, *Website:* www.supermar.com.br
Unimar Agenciamentos Maritimos Ltda, Rua Germano Petersen Junior 101, 5 Andar, CEP90540-140 Porto Alegre, Brazil, *Tel:* +55 51 3343 2458, *Fax:* +55 51 3343 0866, *Email:* unimar-portoalegre@unimar-agency.com.br
Wilson Sons Agencia Maritima Ltda, Avenida Pernambuco 1652, 2nd Floor, 90240-002 Porto Alegre RS, Brazil, *Tel:* +55 51 3325 5277, *Fax:* +55 51 3325 5377, *Email:* agepa@wilsonsons.com.br, *Website:* www.wilsonsons.com.br

Medical Facilities: Good hospital and doctors available

Airport: Salgado Filho International, 3 km

Railway: Rede Ferrouiaria Federal S.A., 1 km

Lloyd's Agent: Inspect Santos Consultoria e Peritagens Ltda, Av. Conselheiro Nebias, 726 - sala 114, Boqueirao, 11045-002 Santos SP, Brazil, *Tel:* +55 13 3234 5246, *Fax:* +55 13 3235 2250, *Email:* inspect@inspect.com.br

PORTO CHIBATAO

Lat 3° 10' S; Long 59° 59' W.

Admiralty Chart: 2229	**Admiralty Pilot:** 5
Time Zone: GMT -4 h	**UNCTAD Locode:** BR

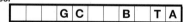

Principal Facilities:

| | | G | C | | | B | | T | A |

Authority: Porto Chibatao Navegacao e Comercio Ltda., Rua Zebu 201, Colonia Oliveira Machado, 69073-670 Manaus AM, Brazil, *Tel:* +55 92 2129 1900, *Fax:* +55 92 3624 2809, *Email:* portochibatao@portochibatao.com.br, *Website:* www.portochibatao.com.br

Officials: President: Jose Ferreira de Oliveira, *Email:* passarao@portochibatao.com.br.

Pilotage: Compulsory

Maximum Vessel Dimensions: 13 m draft

Accommodation:

Name	Length (m)	Depth (m)	Remarks
Porto Chibatao			Located on the left side of the Rio Negro river
Floating Dock	150	10–15	See [1] below

[1]*Floating Dock:* For vessels up to 200 m loa at outer face and 150 m loa at the inner face

Storage:

Location	Covered (m²)	Sheds / Warehouses
Porto Chibatao	3930	2

Mechanical Handling Equipment:

Location	Type	Capacity (t)	Qty
Porto Chibatao	Reach Stackers	30–45	6

Bunkering: Available ex barge

Towage: Two tugs available

Medical Facilities: Available

Airport: Eduardo Gomes, 18 km

Lloyd's Agent: Inspect Consultoria Ltda (Manaus), Rua Barao de Anajatuba No.7, Cond. Laranjeiras, Flores, 69058-110 Manaus AM, Brazil, *Tel:* +55 92 8138 0704, *Fax:* +55 92 3642 2096, *Email:* inspectmanaus@osite.com.br

PORTO VELHO

harbour area, see under Rio Grande

PORTOCEL

Lat 19° 51' S; Long 40° 3' W.

Admiralty Chart: 551
Time Zone: GMT -3 h
Admiralty Pilot: 5
UNCTAD Locode: BR PCL

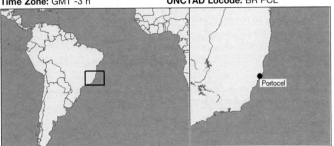

Principal Facilities:

	Y	G				T	A	

Authority: Terminal Especializado de Barra do Riacho S.A., Caminho da Barra do Riacho s/n, 29197-000 Aracruz ES, Brazil, *Tel:* +55 27 3270 4444, *Fax:* +55 27 3270 4433, *Email:* msc@portocel.com.br, *Website:* www.portocel.com.br

Officials: Director: Carlos Gilberto Marques.

Port Security: ISPS compliant

Approach: The approach channel to the terminal has a course of 065° and is approx 150 m wide and 670 m long in depth of 11.5-13.5 m. Vessels must be aware of the submarine pipeline at the end of the S breakwater

Anchorage: Vessels must anchor in a circular area of one mile diameter situated approx 2 miles E of the port entrance in pos 19° 50' 30" S; 40° 02' 00" W in depth of 20 m

Pilotage: Compulsory to and from the Terminal. Pilots must be requested 6 h in advance from Vitoria. Pilot boards in pos 19° 50' 30" S; 40° 02' 00" W

Radio Frequency: Vitoria on VHF Channel 14 and standby channel 16 for calls on a 24 h basis. The radio communication with Portocel can also be made on channels 10 and/or 12

Weather: During the summer the predominant wind is NE'ly and in winter SW'ly and NW'ly. Velocities during the year seldom affect the vessel's manoeuver and operation

Tides: Max rise 1.6 m

Traffic: 2004, 185 vessels, 3 050 866 t of woodpulp exported

Maximum Vessel Dimensions: 200 m loa, 45 000 dwt, 35 m beam

Principal Imports and Exports: Exports: Woodpulp.

Working Hours: 24 h/day

Accommodation:

Name	Length (m)	Depth (m)	Draught (m)	Remarks
Portocel				See [1] below
Berth No.1	230	11.8	10.3	
Berth No.2	200	11.8	10.3	
Darseus	150	5.5	4	

[1]*Portocel:* The harbour is protected by two breakwaters. The northern breakwater has a total length of 850 m and the southern breakwater totals 1420 m long
Most of Aracruz Celulose S.A. pulp production is exported through this port and also Celulose Nipo-Brasileira S.A. (CENIBRA)
Portocel is a terminal which specializes in the handling of woodpulp. Besides that, the terminal also handles logs, salt, steel coils, sodium sulphate, granite/marble, hydrogen peroxide and other cargoes which are compatible with woodpulp

Storage: Five warehouses for the storage of woodpulp

Location	Covered (m²)
Portocel	40000

Mechanical Handling Equipment:

Location	Type	Capacity (t)	Qty
Portocel	Forklifts	7	24

Towage: One conventional tug to help the manoeuver to and from the terminal. Tugs must be requested from Vitoria

Stevedoring Companies: Brazcargo Servicos Maritimos Ltda, Portocel, Brazil, *Tel:* +55 27 3200 3064, *Fax:* +55 27 3324 8276

Medical Facilities: Sao Camilo Hospital, Aracruz City

Airport: Vitoria, 70 km

Railway: CVRD linked to the port

Development: Construction of a new berth in 2008

Lloyd's Agent: Inspect Consultoria Ltda (Rio de Janeiro), Avenida Rio Branco 37, Grupo 1902 Centro, 20090-003 Rio de Janeiro RJ, Brazil, *Tel:* +55 21 2263 3330, *Fax:* +55 21 2253 9322, *Email:* inspectconsultoria@br.inter.net, *Website:* www.inspectconsultoria.com.br

PRAIA MOLE

Lat 20° 17' S; Long 40° 14' W.

Admiralty Chart: 521
Time Zone: GMT -3 h
Admiralty Pilot: 5
UNCTAD Locode: BR PRM

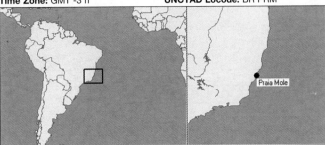

Principal Facilities:

	Y			B		T	A	

Authority: Vale, Praia Mole SC, Brazil, *Tel:* +55 27 3333 5624, *Fax:* +55 27 3333 5293

Approach: Access to Coal Terminal is through a channel 4100 m long, min width of 150 m and max depth of 18 m. Turning basin of 250 m radius

Pilotage: Compulsory

Tides: Max range 1.6 m

Traffic: 2005, 17 765 493 t of cargo handled

Maximum Vessel Dimensions: 250 000 dwt, 300 m loa

Working Hours: 24 h/day

Accommodation:

Name	Length (m)	Depth (m)	Draught (m)	Remarks
Coal Terminal				Operated by Vale
Berth No.1	330	15.7		See [1] below
Berth No.2	400	18	17.2	See [2] below
Steel Products Terminal				See [3] below
Berth 1	214.5	14.5	13.5	
Berth 2	201.2	14.5	13.5	
Berth 3	222.5	14.5	13.5	

[1]*Berth No.1:* For vessels up to 270 m loa and 170 000 dwt
[2]*Berth No.2:* For vessels up to 400 m loa and 250 000 dwt
[3]*Steel Products Terminal:* Operated by a consortium of three steel mills; Ulsimas, Acominas & C.S.T.

Storage: Five yards, each of 250 000 t cap

Mechanical Handling Equipment: Three ship unloaders at rate of 1800 t/h each, two stackers at rate of 2200 t/h and one reclaimer at 2200 t/h, three swivel cranes of 25 t cap and five gantry cranes of 42 t cap

Bunkering: Tramp Oil & Marine, World Fuel Services Corporation, 13th Floor, Portland House, Bressenden Place, London SW1E 5BH, United Kingdom, *Tel:* +44 20 7808 5000, *Fax:* +44 20 7808 5088, *Email:* pturner@wfscorp.com, *Website:* www.wfscorp.com – *Grades:* all grades – *Delivery Mode:* barge, pipeline, truck

Towage: Vale, Praia Mole SC, Brazil, *Tel:* +55 27 3333 5624, *Fax:* +55 27 3333 5293

Medical Facilities: First aid clinic in the port. Hospital, 10 km

Airport: Vitoria, 12 km

Railway: EFVM, in the port

Lloyd's Agent: Inspect Santos Consultoria e Peritagens Ltda, Av. Conselheiro Nebias, 726 - sala 114, Boqueirao, 11045-002 Santos SP, Brazil, *Tel:* +55 13 3234 5246, *Fax:* +55 13 3235 2250, *Email:* inspect@inspect.com.br

RECIFE

Lat 8° 3' S; Long 34° 52' W.

Admiralty Chart: 969
Time Zone: GMT -3 h
Admiralty Pilot: 5
UNCTAD Locode: BR REC

Key to Principal Facilities:—
A=Airport   **C**=Containers   **G**=General Cargo   **P**=Petroleum   **R**=Ro/Ro   **Y**=Dry Bulk
B=Bunkers   **D**=Dry Dock   **L**=Cruise   **Q**=Other Liquid Bulk   **T**=Towage (where available from port)

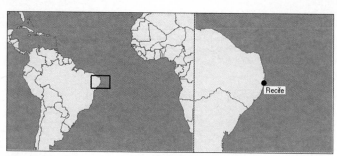

Principal Facilities:

P	Q	Y	G	C	R	L	B		T	A

Tramp Oil & Marine

Wells House, 15-17 Elmfield Road, Bromley,
Kent BR1 1LT, United Kingdom
Phone: +44 20 8315 7777   **Fax:** +44 20 8315 7788
General email: enquiries@tramp-oil.com

See listings for all global offices: **www.tramp-oil.com**

Sea Survey do Brasil Ltda

Rua Carlos Pereira Falca 1145, Apt 701
Ed. Ranata Dias Boa
Viagem, Recife 51021-350 PE, BRAZIL

Tel: +55 81 332 85 507
Fax: +55 81 332 85 507
Email: seasurve@elogica.com.br

Authority: Administracao do Porto do Recife, Praca Comunidade Luso Brasileira 70, Bairro do Recife, 50030-280 Recife PE, Brazil, *Tel:* +55 81 3419 1900, *Fax:* +55 81 3224 2848, *Email:* portodorecife@portodorecife.pe.gov.br, *Website:* www.portodorecife.pe.gov.br

Officials: President: Capt Alexandre De Oliveira Catao, *Tel:* +55 81 3419 1901, *Email:* alexandre.catao@portodorecife.pe.gov.br.
Commercial Manager: Sergio Albino Pimentel, *Tel:* +55 81 3419 1910, *Email:* sergio.pimentel@portodorecife.pe.gov.br.
Harbour Master: Alcione Goncalves, *Tel:* +55 81 3424 7111.

Port Security: ISPS compliant

Approach: The approach channel is a natural channel 3.4 km long, 260 m wide and 10 m deep at HT. The manoeuvring basin width varies from 160 m to 475 m, the depth of water being between 8 m and 10 m

Pilotage: Compulsory and starts at the breakwater Banco Ingles. It is provided by the Associacao dos Praticos do Estado de Pernambuco, Tel: +55 81 3224 1104

Radio Frequency: Olinda Radio, call sign 'PPO', Working, VHF Channels 27, 23 and 16

Tides: Range of tide 2.6 m

Traffic: 2005, 2 429 381 t of cargo handled

Maximum Vessel Dimensions: 220 m loa, 10 m draft

Principal Imports and Exports: Imports: Barley, Corn, Fertilizer, Petcoke, Wheat. Exports: Cement & clinker, Sugar.

Working Hours: Normal: 0800-1400, 1400-2000, 2000-0200, 0200-0800

Accommodation:

Name	Length (m)	Draught (m)	Remarks
Recife			See ¹ below
Berth No.0	180	10	Sugar terminal
Berth No.1	160	10	Grain terminal
Berth No.2	228.5	12	Containers
Berth No.3	162.9	12	Solid bulk
Berth No.4	200.3	12	Solid bulk
Berth No.5	221.4	12	General cargo
Berth No.6	196.6	12	General cargo
Berth No.7	137	8	General cargo
Berth No.8	120	8	General cargo
Berth No.9	239.9	10	Grain terminal

Name	Length (m)	Draught (m)	Remarks
Berth No.10	150	10	General cargo
Berth No.11	158.3	8	General cargo
Berth No.12	150	9	General cargo
Berth No.13	150	9	General cargo
Berth No.14	156.4	9	Reefer cargo
Berth No.15	183.4	8	Reefer cargo

¹*Recife:* Container Terminal with an area of 75 500 m2. One 32 t portable container crane, two 30.5 t container transporters and two forklifts of 30 and 40 t
Bulk facilities: For the discharge of grain there are two pneumatic unloaders with a discharging rate of 300 t/h. There is a terminal with two silos for storing 200 000 t of bulk demerara sugar which can be loaded at the rate of 1000 t/h
Tanker facilities: Two oil berths. Lengths 200 m; 8.5 m and 9.5 m draft. Night berthing possible depending on vessel's draft. Water and bunkers available

Storage: There are thirteen warehouses inside the port area with a total cap of 36 145 m2, three warehouses outside the port area with a cap of 16 778 m2 and 1658 m2 of refrigerated space with a cap of 600 t

Location	Grain (t)
Recife	38500

Mechanical Handling Equipment:

Location	Type	Capacity (t)	Qty
Recife	Mobile Cranes		3
Recife	Electric Cranes	3.2–25	7
Recife	Transtainers	30	1
Recife	Forklifts	2.5–40	15

Bunkering: Marbrax marine lubricants are available and delivered in drums to the vessel by truck. Three days' notice is required. Fresh water is also supplied. If a bunkering call is expected to take place from the last port of call it is advisable to obtain a sailing pass mentioning Recife as a port of call. This will facilitate the handling of formalities by the harbour master
ExxonMobil Marine Fuels, Suite 900, One Alhambra Plaza, Coral Gables, FL 33134, United States of America, *Tel:* +1 305 459 6358, *Fax:* +1 305 459 6412, *Email:* emmf@exxonmobil.com, *Website:* www.exxonmobilmarinefuels.com
Tramp Oil & Marine, World Fuel Services Corporation, 13th Floor, Portland House, Bressenden Place, London SW1E 5BH, United Kingdom, *Tel:* +44 20 7808 5000, *Fax:* +44 20 7808 5088, *Email:* pturner@wfscorp.com, *Website:* www.wfscorp.com – *Grades:* all grades – *Delivery Mode:* barge, pipeline, truck

Towage: Two tugs available, plus two on station at Suape

Repair & Maintenance: Mario Cirelli, Recife, Brazil Diesel motors and injection pumps
Cormeletro Don e Ltda, Recife, Brazil Motor repairs and industrial chromium plating
Fabrica & Fundicao Capunga, Recife, Brazil Repair and casting of propellers
Fabrica Fundicao Pernambucana, Recife, Brazil Electrical repairs
Fundicao Recife Ltda, Recife, Brazil Marine repairs
Leon Heimer Industries & Com Ltda, Mascarenhas de Morais 310, P O Box 51150-000, Recife, Brazil, *Tel:* +55 81 3305 5500, *Email:* contact@heimer.com.br, *Website:* www.heimer.com.br Motor and generator repairs and soldering
Industria & Comercio Santoro S.A., Recife, Brazil Motor repairs
Oficina Mecanica Sao Marcos, Recife, Brazil Mechanical repairs
Oficina Belens, Recife, Brazil Electrical repairs
Oficina Internacional, Recife, Brazil Marine repairs
Herberto Ramos Industries & Com. S.A., Recife, Brazil Marine repairs
Retifica Imperial, Recife, Brazil Motor repairs
Oficina Romana, Recife, Brazil Marine repairs
Leonardo Jose dos Santos & Co., Recife, Brazil Boiler repairs and hull and equipment soldering
Usina Siderurguca Lubax S.A., Recife, Brazil Marine repairs
Volvo Norte do Brasil Ltda, Recife, Brazil Engine and motor reconditioning

Ship Chandlers: Exportadora Star Ltda, Rua Apolo No. 43, 50.030-220 Recife, Brazil, *Tel:* +55 81 3424 7988, *Fax:* +55 81 3224 0146, *Email:* starstor@elogica.com.br
Ocean Nautica Ltda, Avenida Barbosa Lima 149, 50030-330 Recife, Brazil, *Tel:* +55 81 3224 4487, *Fax:* +55 81 3224 8083, *Email:* ocean@oceanautica.com.br

Shipping Agents: CMA-CGM S.A., CMA CGM do Brasil Agencia Maritima, Av. Marques de Olinda 126 sala 100 Ed. Citibank, Recife Antigo, 50030-000 Recife PE, Brazil, *Tel:* +55 81 3224 8814, *Fax:* +55 81 3224 0373, *Email:* rce.laraujo@cma-cgm.com, *Website:* www.cma-cgm.com
Comercio e Navegacao E. Batista Ltda, Rua Vigario Tenorio 105 - Sala 702, 50030-010 Recife, Brazil, *Tel:* +55 81 3224 4144, *Fax:* +55 81 3224 2032, *Email:* ebatista@ebatista.com.br, *Website:* www.ebatista.com.br
Consulmar Agencia Maritima Ltda, Rua Ribeiro de Brito 590, 51021-310 Recife, Brazil, *Tel:* +55 81 3465 6645, *Fax:* +55 81 3465 6645, *Email:* recife.sales@for.consulmar.com.br
Corymar Agencia Maritima Ltd, Avenida Eng. Antonio de Goes 449, 9th Floor, Pina, 51110-000 Recife PE, Brazil, *Tel:* +55 81 3327 9200, *Fax:* +55 81 3465 4555, *Email:* williams@williams.com.br, *Website:* www.williams.com.br
Fertimport S.A., Avenida Marques de Olinda 126, suites 103/106, 50030-901 Recife, Brazil, *Tel:* +55 81 3224 8433, *Fax:* +55 81 3224 6266, *Email:* rec.fertimport@bunge.com, *Website:* www.fertimport.com.br
LBH Brasil, Rua Ribeiro de Brito 830 - Sala 604, Boa Viagem, 51021-310 Recife PE, Brazil, *Tel:* +55 81 2138 6855, *Fax:* +55 81 2138 6850, *Email:* brazrcf@lbhbrasil.com.br, *Website:* www.brazshipping.com.br
Mediterranean Shipping Company, MSC do Brasil Ltda, Avenida Engenheiro Antonio de Goes No. 60, 18th Floor - Bairro 'Pina', 51010-000 Recife PE, Brazil, *Tel:* +55 81 3228 9200, *Fax:* +55 81 3228 9217, *Website:* www.mscgva.ch
Pennant Servicos Maritimos Ltd, Rua Vigaro Tenorio 105, cj102, CEP 50030-010 Recife, Brazil, *Tel:* +55 81 3224 9780, *Fax:* +55 81 3224 9992, *Email:* pennrce@pennant.br
Thom & Cia. Ltda, Rua da Moeda 63, Cidade, 5003-040 Recife PE, Brazil, *Tel:* +55 81 2101 1622, *Fax:* +55 81 3224 4808, *Email:* central@thomecia.com.br
Transatlantic Carriers (Agenciamentos) Ltda, Av Marques de Olinda 126, Suite 101, Recife, Brazil, *Tel:* +55 81 3221 6440, *Fax:* +55 81 3224 3560, *Email:* management@transcar-recife.com.br

Wilson Sons Agencia Maritima Ltda, Rua Mariz e Barros 71, Bairro do Recife, 50030-120 Recife PE, Brazil, *Tel:* +55 81 3419 1300, *Fax:* +55 81 3419 1301, *Email:* agere@wilsonsons.com.br, *Website:* www.wilsonsons.com.br
Windrose-Servicos Maritimos e Representacoes Ltda, Rua Vigario Tenorio 105, sala 404, CEP 50030-010 Recife, Brazil, *Tel:* +55 81 3224 7484, *Fax:* +55 81 3224 0218, *Email:* windrose@elogica.com

Surveyors: Sea Survey do Brasil Ltda, Apartment 701, Edificio Renata Dias Boa Viagem, Rua Carlos Pereira Falca 1145, 51021-350 Recife PE, Brazil, *Tel:* +55 81 3328 5507, *Fax:* +55 81 3328 5507, *Email:* seasurve@elogica.com.br

Medical Facilities: Several hospitals

Airport: Guararapes, 21 km

Lloyd's Agent: Inspect Consultoria Ltda (Recife), Rua Padre Carapuceiro 412/603, Boa Viagem, 51020-280 Recife PE, Brazil, *Tel:* +55 81 9952 5868, *Email:* inspectrecife@terra.com.br

RIO DE JANEIRO

Lat 22° 55' S; Long 43° 12' W.

Admiralty Chart: 3970/566	**Admiralty Pilot:** 5
Time Zone: GMT -3 h	**UNCTAD Locode:** BR RIO

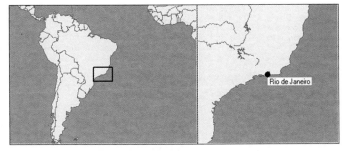

Principal Facilities:

P	Q	Y	G	C	R	L	B	D	T

Authority: Companhia Docas do Rio de Janeiro, Porto do Rio de Janeiro, Avenida Rodrigues Alves 20, 4 andar - Praca Maua, 20081-000 Rio de Janeiro RJ, Brazil, *Tel:* +55 21 2291 2122, *Fax:* +55 21 2516 1958, *Email:* suprio@portosrio.gov.br, *Website:* www.portosrio.gov.br

Port Security: ISPS compliant

Approach: The main approach channel is 200 m wide with a depth of 17 m at LT. The approach channel to the container terminals docks is approx 150 m wide commencing near the Pier Maua up to the respective manoeuvring basin. The depth of water is 10 m in this channel. The approach channel to the Pier Maua, Gamboa and Sao Cristovao is approx 300 m wide for the full length of the docks, with a depth of 6 m to 12 m. The approach channel to the Caju docks is 80 m wide all along the docks with a depth of 5.8 m. Vessels entering or leaving port by way of the main channel have right of way over vessels, launches, towboats and other craft navigating outside of this channel

Pilotage: Pilotage service is compulsory for vessels of any tonnage carrying petroleum, propane or explosives and for foreign vessels of any draught. Pilot boards vessel 0.5 nautical miles S of a line between the Ilha de Villegagnon Lt and the Church on Ilha do Boa Viagem. Deep draught vessels are boarded 2 nautical miles N of Ilha Rasa or at any anchorage in the Baia de Guanabara

Radio Frequency: Pilot requisition also may be made by radiogram via Station PPR-Rio Radio, in the frequencies 17.194, 13.105 and 8.364 kHz or through VHF Channel 16; for pilotage and other purposes, using Channels 11 and 12

Tides: Rise of tide 1.6 m

Traffic: 2006, 16 544 000 t of cargo handled

Working Hours: Day Period: 1st shift 0700-1100, 1100-1200 (meal hour); 2nd shift 1200-1600 extended from 1600-1900. Night period: 1st shift 1900-2300, 2300-2400 (meal hour); 2nd shift 2400-0400 extended from 0400-0700

Accommodation:

Name	Length (m)	Draught (m)	Remarks
Rio de Janeiro			See [1] below
Pier Maua	880	7.3–10.1	
Gamboa Docks	3175	7.2–10.3	Comprising warehouses No's 1 to 18
Sao Cristovao Docks	1350	6–8.5	Comprising warehouses No's 22, 23, 24 and 30
Caju Docks	1300	5.2–6.4	Comprising warehouses 31 to 33
Coal & Ore Docks	765	11.5–15	See [2] below

[1]*Rio de Janeiro:* Container facilities: Terminal 1, operated by Libra Terminals, Tel: +55 21 2585 8585, Fax: +55 21 2585 8569, Email: dtl@terminal1rio.com.br, Website: www.terminal1rio.com.br. Two berths available on dock 545 m long in depth of 12 m with 155 000 m2 container storage area and 250 reefer points
Terminal 2 (Multiterminals Container Terminal), operated by Multi-Rio Operacoes Portuarias, Rua Mayrink Veiga, 4-16 andar - Centro, 20090-050 Rio de Janeiro RJ, Tel: +55 21 3289 4800, Fax: +55 21 3890 3143, Email: info.multirio@multiterminais.com.br, Website: www.multiterminais.com.br. Berth length of 520 m in depth of 11 m
Ro/ro terminal also operated by Multiterminals
Tanker facilities: Shell has a terminal at Governor's Island, depth of water 9.8 m. Esso also has a terminal here with a water depth of 10 m. Petrobras have several terminals at Torgua (22° 48' 3" S; 43° 08' 09" W): S Dock Island, depth 17 m; N Dock Island, depth 10.2 m; Butadiene Dock Island, depth 8.5 m and Redonda Island Pier (LPG) 8.5 m at LT
[2]*Coal & Ore Docks:* Operated by Companhia Siderurgica Nacional (CSN). Storage cap of 400 000 t of ore at rate of 4000 t/h

Storage: Three grain mills have an aggregate cap of 75 000 t. There are also eight outer warehouses with a total area of 97 257 m2. Heavy lift storage yards adjoin the container storage yards. One cold storage warehouse with a cap of 66 240 m3 with a handling rate of 2000 cases of fruit per h. Explosives and inflammables are stored at Ilha do Braco Forte (Island depot) with 1335 m2 for inflammables, with two depots for explosives, each of 25 m2

Mechanical Handling Equipment:

Location	Type	Qty
Rio de Janeiro	Floating Cranes	2
Rio de Janeiro	Mult-purp. Cranes	104
Rio de Janeiro	Mobile Cranes	13
Rio de Janeiro	Forklifts	204

Bunkering: Max size of vessel at bunkering berths is up to 274.31 m in length and from 5.79 m to 10.06 m loaded draft. Fresh water is also available. Marbrax marine lubricants are available subject to three days notice. Max size of vessel at bunkering berth is 109.72 m (Redonda Island) with varying draft at the following berths: PP-1,

---

Key to Principal Facilities:—

A=Airport	**C**=Containers	**G**=General Cargo	**P**=Petroleum	**R**=Ro/Ro	**Y**=Dry Bulk
B=Bunkers	**D**=Dry Dock	**L**=Cruise	**Q**=Other Liquid Bulk	**T**=Towage (where available from port)

15.85 m; PP-2, 11.89 m; PS-1, 10.36 m; PS-2, 8.23 m; PA-B, 8.53 m and IR, 7.01 m.
Bominflot, Bominflot do Brazil Comercio Ltda, Avenida Almirante Barosso 63/1809, 20031-003 Rio de Janeiro, Brazil, *Tel:* +55 21 2220 4773, *Fax:* +55 21 2262 2651, *Email:* mail@bominflot.com.br, *Website:* www.bominflot.net
Petrobras Bunkering, Avenida Republica do Chile 65, 20 andar, sala 2001-H, 20035-913 Rio de Janeiro, Brazil, *Tel:* +55 21 3224 3290, *Fax:* +55 21 2262 8134, *Email:* bunker@petrobras.com.br, *Website:* www.petrobras.com.br
Tramp Oil & Marine, Tramp Oil (Brasil) Ltda, Avenida Rio Branco 181, Room 3004, 20040 Rio de Janeiro 007, Brazil, *Tel:* +55 21 2169 7000, *Fax:* +55 21 2169 7007, *Email:* rio@wfscorp.com, *Website:* www.wfscorp.com
Bominflot, Bominflot do Brazil Comercio Ltda, Avenida Almirante Barosso 63/1809, 20031-003 Rio de Janeiro, Brazil, *Tel:* +55 21 2220 4773, *Fax:* +55 21 2262 2651, *Email:* mail@bominflot.com.br, *Website:* www.bominflot.net
ExxonMobil Marine Fuels, Suite 900, One Alhambra Plaza, Coral Gables, FL 33134, United States of America, *Tel:* +1 305 459 6358, *Fax:* +1 305 459 6412, *Email:* emmf@exxonmobil.com, *Website:* www.exxonmobilmarinefuels.com
Shell Marine Products, Avenida das Americas, 4200, Bloco 5 / 2 Andar, Barra da Tijuca, 22640-102 Rio de Janeiro, Brazil, *Tel:* +55 21 3984 8385, *Fax:* +55 11 3472 8003, *Email:* antonio.ribeiro@shell.com, *Website:* www.shell.com
Tramp Oil & Marine, World Fuel Services Corporation, 13th Floor, Portland House, Bressenden Place, London SW1E 5BH, United Kingdom, *Tel:* +44 20 7808 5000, *Fax:* +44 20 7808 5088, *Email:* pturner@wfscorp.com, *Website:* www.wfscorp.com – *Grades:* all grades – *Delivery Mode:* barge, pipeline, truck

Towage: There are 11 tugs available from 310 to 3200 hp as well as those belonging to Petrobas. 20 to 50 t cap lighters are available for transporting cargo
SVITZER, Rio Wijsmuller Ltd, Praia do Flamengo 154, 2nd Floor - Flamengo, 22210-030 Rio de Janeiro RJ, Brazil, *Tel:* +55 21 2555 2800, *Fax:* +55 21 2555 2945, *Website:* www.svitzer.com

Repair & Maintenance: EMAQ-Verolme Estaleiros S.A., Rio de Janeiro, Brazil, *Tel:* +55 21 2396 1530, *Fax:* +55 21 2396 2903
Ishikawajima do Brasil Estaleiros S.A., Rue General Gurjao 2, Rio de Janeiro, Brazil, *Tel:* +55 21 2585 5445, *Fax:* +55 21 2580 8826
Sermetal Estaleiros Ltda., Rua General Gurjao, 2, Caju, 20931-040 Rio de Janeiro, Brazil, *Tel:* +55 21 2585 9400, *Fax:* +55 21 2580 5331, *Email:* sermetal@sermetal.net, *Website:* www.sermetal.net
Soebin Industria Naval S.A., Rio de Janeiro, Brazil, *Tel:* +55 21 2717 2323, *Fax:* +55 21 2717 4925

Ship Chandlers: Akti Marine Supply, Av. Venezuela 3 / 13 andar, Centro, 20081-311 Rio de Janeiro RJ, Brazil, *Tel:* +55 21 2104 8500, *Fax:* +55 21 2518 4373, *Email:* commerciali@aktimarine.com.br, *Website:* www.aktimarine.com.br
Ashland Brasil Ltda, Avenida Paris No. 676 - Bonsucesso, 21.041-020 Rio de Janeiro, Brazil, *Tel:* +55 21 2560 3330, *Fax:* +55 21 2560 1538, *Email:* jfcavalcante@ashland.com
Boa Praca Importadora e Exportadora Ltda, Rua do Arroz No. 89, Mercado Sao Sebastiao, Penha, 21011-070 Rio de Janeiro, Brazil, *Tel:* +55 21 2584 7509, *Fax:* +55 21 2584 2488, *Email:* bpnav@boapraca.com.br, *Website:* www.boapraca.com.br
Cesario Marine Service Import e Export Ltda, 15th Floor, Avenida Rio Branco No. 4, 20090-003 Rio de Janeiro, Brazil, *Tel:* +55 21 2233 2289, *Fax:* +55 21 2233 2036, *Email:* riodejaneiro@cesariomarine.com.br
Draft Marine Supply Ltd, Rua do Trigo No. 66, Penha, 21011-690 Rio de Janeiro, Brazil, *Tel:* +55 21 2584 9595, *Fax:* +55 21 2584 9695, *Email:* draft@draftmarine.com.br, *Website:* www.draftmarine.com.br
Extecil Equipamentos Contra Incendio e Salvatagem Ltda, Rua Teixeira Ribeiro No. 229, Ramos, 21.040-240 Rio de Janeiro, Brazil, *Tel:* +55 21 2123 2100, *Fax:* +55 21 2123 2112, *Email:* extecil@rio.com.br
Mapamar Comcercio e Servicos Ltda, Rua Ricardo Machado 156A, Sao Cristovao, 20921-270 Rio de Janeiro, Brazil, *Tel:* +55 21 3295 2600, *Fax:* +55 21 3860 7029, *Email:* cabranco@mapamar.com.br, *Website:* www.mapamar.com.br
Provedor Rio Fornecimentos Maritimos Ltda (Former Penn Ship do Brasil), Rua Galvao No.148, Barreto, Niteroi, 24110-260 Rio de Janeiro, Brazil, *Tel:* +55 21 2620 3783, *Fax:* +55 21 2622 8917, *Email:* comercial@provedorrio.com.br

Shipping Agents: Abaco Shipping Agency, Venezuela Av.27, 7th Floor, 20081-310 Rio de Janeiro, Brazil, *Tel:* +55 21 2223 1511, *Fax:* +55 21 2223 0978, *Email:* abaco@abacorio.com, *Website:* www.abacorio.com
CMA-CGM S.A., CMA CGM do Brasil Agencia Maritima, Av. Presidente Wilson 231, Sala 1402 Castelo, 20030-905 Rio de Janeiro RJ, Brazil, *Tel:* +55 21 2272 9581, *Fax:* +55 21 2517 3176, *Email:* brj.genmbox@cma-cgm.com, *Website:* www.cma-cgm.com
Corymar Agencia Maritima Ltd, Rua Dom Gerardo 63, Grupo 1406/07 Centro, 20090-030 Rio de Janeiro RJ, Brazil, *Tel:* +55 21 2263 7515, *Fax:* +55 21 2263 7794, *Email:* willrio@williams.com.br, *Website:* www.williams.com.br
Coryrio Agenciamentos, Afretamentos e Operador Portuario Ltda, Avenida Rio Branco 4, Andar 11, P O Box 774, 20096-900 Rio de Janeiro, Brazil, *Tel:* +55 21 2223 3222, *Fax:* +55 21 2233 2469, *Email:* cory@cory-br.com.br, *Website:* www.cory-br.com.br
Fertimport S.A., Avenida Rio Branco 4, 12th Floor, 20096-900 Rio de Janeiro, Brazil, *Tel:* +55 21 3232 5900, *Fax:* +55 21 2518 0663, *Email:* operations-rio.fertimport@bunge.com, *Website:* www.fertimport.com.br
Agencia de Vapores Grieg S.A., Rua da Assembleia 11, andar 8, 20011-001 Rio de Janeiro RJ, Brazil, *Tel:* +55 21 2533 8383, *Fax:* +55 21 2533 9402, *Email:* griegrio@grieg.com.br, *Website:* www.grieg.com.br
Inchcape Shipping Services (ISS), ISS Marine Services Ltd., Rua Sao Bento 9, 4 Andar, Centro, 20090-010 Rio de Janeiro RJ, Brazil, *Tel:* +55 21 2518 5756, *Fax:* +55 21 2518 6778, *Email:* issrio@iss-shipping.com, *Website:* www.iss-shipping.com
Kadmos Shipping Enterprises, Office 202, 61 Rosario Street, 20041-002 Rio de Janeiro, Brazil, *Tel:* +55 21 2223 1004, *Fax:* +55 21 2283 3857, *Email:* kadmos@kadmos.com.br, *Website:* www.kadmos.com.br
Lachmann Logistica Ltda, Rua Sao Bento No.8, 3rd Floor, CEP 20090 010 Rio de Janeiro, Brazil, *Tel:* +55 21 3849 5700, *Fax:* +55 21 3849 5830, *Email:* lachmann.rio@lachmann.com.br, *Website:* www.lachmann.com.br
LBH Brasil, Av. Ayrton Senna 1850 - 4 andar - Conj 411, Ed Barra Plaza, Barra da Tijuca, 22775-001 Rio de Janeiro RJ, Brazil, *Tel:* +55 21 2196 6855, *Fax:* +55 21 2196 6890, *Email:* brazrio@lbhbrasil.com.br, *Website:* www.brazshipping.com.br
Marship Agenciamentos Ltd, Av Presidente Vargas 529, piso 9, CEP 20071-003 Rio de Janeiro, Brazil, *Tel:* +55 21 2221 1435, *Fax:* +55 21 2221 3444, *Email:* marship@transcar-rio.com.br
Mediterranean Shipping Company, MSC do Brasil Ltda, Rua Marechal Floriano 19 - 23rd Floor, 20080-003 Rio de Janeiro RJ, Brazil, *Tel:* +55 21 2271 2500, *Fax:* +55 21 2516 2680, *Email:* distribution@mscbr.com.br, *Website:* www.mscgva.ch
A.P. Moller-Maersk Group, Maersk Brasil Ltda, Praia do Flamengo 154, 2 Andar, Flamengo, 22210-906 Rio de Janeiro RJ, Brazil, *Tel:* +55 21 2555 2800, *Fax:* +55 21 2555 2948, *Email:* brzcrcrio@maersk.com, *Website:* www.maerskline.com
Oceanus Agencia Maritima S.A., Rua Sao Bento 08 - 3rd Floor, 20090-010 Rio de Janeiro RJ, Brazil, *Tel:* +55 21 3849 5700, *Fax:* +55 21 3849 5858, *Email:* agency@oceanus.com.br, *Website:* www.oceanus.com.br
Pennant Servicos Maritimos Ltd, Av Presidente Vargas 446, piso 15, CEP 20071-000 Rio de Janeiro, Brazil, *Tel:* +55 21 2233 8785, *Fax:* +55 21 2263 6316, *Email:* pennrio@pennant.com.br, *Website:* www.pennant.com.br
Sulnorte Servicos Maritimos Ltda, SLS 1304 & 1308, Avenida Venezuela 3, 13 Andar, 21081-311 Rio de Janeiro, Brazil, *Tel:* +55 21 2104 8500, *Fax:* +55 21 2263 4373, *Email:* sulnorte@sulnorte.com.br, *Website:* www.sulnorte.com.br
Transatlantic Carriers (Agenciamentos) Ltda, Av Presidentes Vargas 529, 9th Floor, Rio de Janeiro, Brazil, *Tel:* +55 21 2223 4222, *Fax:* +55 21 2221 3444, *Email:* mcampos@transcar-rio.com.br
Wilson Sons Agencia Maritima Ltda, Avenida Rio Branco 25, 4th Floor, P O Box 21007, 20090-902 Rio de Janeiro, Brazil, *Tel:* +55 21 2126 4222, *Fax:* +55 21 2206 4269, *Email:* agerj@wilsonsons.com.br, *Website:* www.wilsonsons.com.br

Stevedoring Companies: Oceanus Agencia Maritima S.A., Rua Sao Bento 08 - 3rd Floor, 20090-010 Rio de Janeiro RJ, Brazil, *Tel:* +55 21 3849 5700, *Fax:* +55 21 3849 5858, *Email:* agency@oceanus.com.br, *Website:* www.oceanus.com.br
Wilson Sons Agencia Maritima Ltda, Rua Dom Gerardo 64 - 2nd Floor, 20090-030 Rio de Janeiro RJ, Brazil, *Tel:* +55 21 2223 9950, *Fax:* +55 21 2223 9993, *Email:* agerj@wilsonsons.com.br, *Website:* www.wilsonsons.com.br

Surveyors: ABS (Americas), Avenida Venezuela 3, 16 Andar, P O Box 21142, 20081-311 Rio de Janeiro, Brazil, *Tel:* +55 21 2518 3535, *Fax:* +55 21 2518 1328, *Email:* absriodejaneiro@eagle.org, *Website:* www.eagle.org
Bureau Veritas, Bureau Veritas do Brazil, Praca Pio X, 17-9 andar Centro, 20040-020 Rio de Janeiro RJ, Brazil, *Tel:* +55 21 2206 9200, *Fax:* +55 21 2233 9253, *Email:* bv.rio@br.bureauveritas.com, *Website:* www.bureauveritas.com
C-Mar America Inc., C-Mar do Brasil Ltda, Edificio Marins Sala 307, Rod. Amaral Peixoto 4741 Centro, Rio Das Ostras, 28890-000 Rio de Janeiro, Brazil, *Tel:* +55 21 2760 6123, *Fax:* +55 21 2760 8457, *Email:* brasil@c-mar.com, *Website:* www.c-mar.com
Det Norske Veritas A/S, Rua Sete de Setembro 111, 12th Floor, 20050-006 Rio de Janeiro RJ, Brazil, *Tel:* +55 21 2517 7232, *Fax:* +55 21 3722 7571, *Email:* rio.maritime@dnv.com, *Website:* www.dnv.com
Forecastle Cons Tecnica e Rep Maritimas Ltda, Avenida Passos No.101, Sala 1606 Centro, 20051-040 Rio de Janeiro RJ, Brazil, *Tel:* +55 21 2233 6795, *Fax:* +55 21 2263 5639, *Email:* focsle@ccard.com.br
Germanischer Lloyd, Rua Sete de Setembro, 55-24 andar, 20050-004 Rio de Janeiro RJ, Brazil, *Tel:* +55 21 2221 9403, *Fax:* +55 21 2509 5352, *Email:* gl-rio.de.janeiro@gl-group.com, *Website:* www.gl-group.com
Hellenic Register of Shipping, c/o Pirani & Associates, Rua Visconde de Piraja, 303 gr. 711, 22410-001 Rio de Janeiro RJ, Brazil, *Tel:* +55 21 2525 6625, *Fax:* +55 21 2227 4008, *Email:* pirani@uninet.com.br, *Website:* www.hrs.gr
Nippon Kaiji Kyokai, Avenida das Americas 1650, Block 2 Sala 220 Barra da Tijuca, 20020-010 Rio de Janeiro RJ, Brazil, *Tel:* +55 21 2484 9656, *Fax:* +55 21 2533 7535, *Email:* rj@classnk.or.jp, *Website:* www.classnk.or.jp
Noble Denton Group, Noble Denton & Associates Services Maritimos Ltda, Edificio Rodolpho de Paoli, Avenida Nilo Pecanha 50 - 2701, 20020-906 Rio de Janeiro, Brazil, *Tel:* +55 21 3084 1720, *Fax:* +55 21 3084 1716, *Email:* andrew.theophanatos@nobledenton.com.br, *Website:* www.nobledenton.com
Picolo E Associados Ltd, Avenida Rio Branco 45, Suite 2412, 20090 003 Rio de Janeiro, Brazil, *Tel:* +55 21 2263 5751, *Fax:* +55 21 2253 5604, *Email:* picolo@radnet.com.br
Pirani & Associates, Rua Visconde de Piraja, 303 Gr 711, 20090/RJ Rio de Janeiro, Brazil, *Tel:* +55 21 2525 6625, *Fax:* +55 21 2227 4008, *Email:* pirani@uninet.com.br
Planave S/A Estudos E Projectos de Engenharia, Rua Costa Ferreira 106, 20221-240 Rio de Janeiro, Brazil, *Tel:* +55 21 2223 3177, *Fax:* +55 21 2263 5523, *Email:* planave@montreal.com.br
Registro Italiano Navale (RINA), Av Rio Branco 50, 5 andar, 20090-002 Rio de Janeiro RJ, Brazil, *Tel:* +55 21 2518 7545, *Fax:* +55 21 2263 6126, *Email:* rinabrasil@rinabrasil.com.br, *Website:* www.rina.org
Sealink Consultoria Tecnica & Comercial Ltda, Suite 213 Saude, 3 Venezuela Avenue, 20081-310 Rio de Janeiro, Brazil, *Tel:* +55 21 2253 4874, *Fax:* +55 21 2516 2406, *Email:* sealink@terra.com.br

Medical Facilities: Several hospitals

Lloyd's Agent: Inspect Consultoria Ltda (Rio de Janeiro), Avenida Rio Branco 37, Grupo 1902 Centro, 20090-003 Rio de Janeiro RJ, Brazil, *Tel:* +55 21 2263 3330, *Fax:* +55 21 2253 9322, *Email:* inspectconsultoria@br.inter.net, *Website:* www.inspectconsultoria.com.br

RIO GRANDE

Lat 32° 10' S; Long 52° 5' W.

Admiralty Chart: 2002
Admiralty Pilot: 5
Time Zone: GMT -3 h
UNCTAD Locode: BR RIG

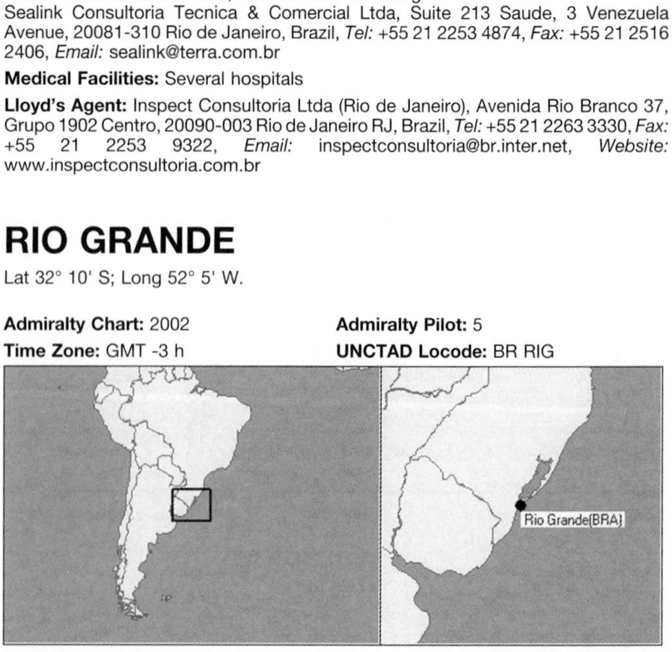

Principal Facilities:

P	Q	Y	G	C		B		T

Tramp Oil & Marine

Wells House, 15-17 Elmfield Road, Bromley,
Kent BR1 1LT, United Kingdom
Phone: +44 20 8315 7777   **Fax:** +44 20 8315 7788
General email: enquiries@tramp-oil.com

See listings for all global offices: **www.tramp-oil.com**

SAMPAYO NICKHORN S.A.

Sampayo Nickhorn S/A
Agent - Port Operator - Logistic Provider
www.sampayo.com.br – sampayo@sampayo.com.br
Ports attendance in Brazil
Rio Grande - Porto Alegre - Tramandai
Head Office Contact: 55 53 3231-1477
Mr. Thiago Bouchut Palacio - Commercial Manager 55 53 9976-6484
Mr. Paulo Veleda Moraes - Operations Manager 55 53 9976-6474
75 Years of tradition on shipping service

Authority: Superintendencia de Portos e Hidrovias do Rio Grande do Sul, Porto de Rio Grande, Avenida Honorio Bicalho s/n, P O Box 198, 96201-020 Rio Grande RS, Brazil, *Tel:* +55 53 3231 1366, *Fax:* +55 53 3231 1857, *Email:* suprg@portoriogrande.com.br, *Website:* www.portoriogrande.com.br

Officials: Managing Director: Newton Quintas, *Email:* nquintas@portoriogrande.com.br.
Harbour Master: Bercilio Da Silva, *Email:* bercilio@portoriogrande.com.br.

Port Security: ISPS compliant

Approach: The bar of Lagoa dos Patos is the access to the ports of Rio Grande, Pelotas and Porto Alegre, located at the S end of Lagoa dos Patos with a max permitted draft on bar of 11.58 m. The access channel is 11 km long, its width varying from 200 m to 300 m with a depth of 12.19 m. The manoeuvring basin is 200 m wide with a depth of water of 7.92 m in front of Porto Novo and 5.18 m in front of Porto Velho. At the bar in the vicinity of the breakwaters the depth of water varies from 8 m to 12 m. From the breakwaters to the entrance of the channel of access to Porto Novo, the channel is marked with buoys and the depth of water varies from 9 m to 17 m

Anchorage: Area Alpha: It is prohibited to anchor in this area. In emergencies the Port Superintendent may authorize anchorage of one vessel up to 190 m loa and max draft of 12.19 m
Areas Bravo, Charlie and Delta: It is forbidden to anchor in these areas
Area Echo: Anchorage is allowed for vessels up to 190 m loa and max draft of 9.14 m
Area Foxtrot: Anchorage is forbidden
Area Golf: Anchorage allowed for vessels up to 6.7 m draft. It is divided into three areas depending on length of vessel. Golf 1 for vessels up to 120 m loa, Golf 2 for vessels up to 190 m loa and Golf 3 for vessels up to 225 m loa

Pilotage: Compulsory, Tel: +55 (53) 3231 2233, Email: rgpilots@rgpilots.com.br. Pilots board off the whistle buoy about 1.6 km E of the breakwaters. ETA must be notified 24 h in advance and confirmed not less than 12 h before arrival. Radio message should be sent via PPJ radio station-500 kHz frequency. VHF Channel 16

Weather: Predominant SE and NE winds

Traffic: 2007, 26 700 000 t of cargo handled

Working Hours: 0730-1130, 1300-1700, 1700-1900, 1900-2300, 0001-0400, 0400-0600. Work during the midday meal now is restricted to passenger vessels only or those loading refrigerated cargo

Accommodation:

Name	Length (m)	Depth (m)	Remarks
Porto Velho			See [1] below
Porto Novo			Quay 1952 m long in depth of 9.15 m
CESA Terminal			See [2] below
Ro/ro Berth			Mooring 56 to 50. 136 000 m2 storage yard for vehicles
Solid/Liquid Bulk Berth			Between moorings 44 and 37
Container Berths			See [3] below
Fertilizer Berths			See [4] below
Super Porto			
Copesul Terminal	70	10.05	See [5] below
Petrobras Terminal	318	10.05	Oil & bunkers

Name	Length (m)	Depth (m)	Remarks
Adubos Trevo Terminal	360	12.2	Fertilizer & chemical products
Bunge Alimentos Terminal	412	12.2	See [6] below
Bianchini Terminal	300	12.2	See [7] below
Tergrasa Terminal	1080	12.2	See [8] below
Termasa Terminal	200	12.2	See [9] below
Transbordo Dolphins	180	12.2	
Tecon Rio Grande Terminal	850	12.2	See [10] below
Leal Santos Alim Terminal	70	7.95	
Marinha Terminal	300	9.15	

[1]*Porto Velho:* Quay 640 m long in depth of 4.6 m. This dock is used by fishing vessels and lake lighters discharging meal to trucks and passenger vessels
[2]*CESA Terminal:* Moorings 62 to 56. Loading/unloading of solid bulk. Storage of grains (soy, corn, wheat, barley)
[3]*Container Berths:* Between moorings 37 and 14. Three exclusive berths and one berth for barges (TEFLU)
[4]*Fertilizer Berths:* Between moorings 14 and 0. Three berths (one for barges). Loading/unloading of fertilizers (raw materials and by-products)
[5]*Copesul Terminal:* Storage facilities for hydrocarbon liquids, pressurized storage for propylene, gas storage and related facilities
[6]*Bunge Alimentos Terminal:* Tel: +55 53 3233 7000, Fax: +55 53 3234 1230. Export of grain, bran & oils
[7]*Bianchini Terminal:* Tel: +55 53 3234 1262, Fax: +55 53 3234 1262, Email: bianchini@vetorialnet.com.br. Cereals
[8]*Tergrasa Terminal:* Tel: +55 53 3234 1500, Fax: +55 53 3234 1500, Email: tergrasa@tergrasa.com.br, Website: www.termasa.com.br. Quay length of 450 m for ships and 630 m for barges. Wheat & soya
[9]*Termasa Terminal:* Tel: +55 53 3234 1500, Fax: +55 53 3234 1500, Email: termasa@termasa.com.br, Website: www.termasa.com.br. Grain
[10]*Tecon Rio Grande Terminal:* Operated by Tecon Rio Grande S.A., Tel: +55 53 3234 3000, Fax: +55 53 3234 1501, Email: webmaster@tecon.com.br, Website: www.tecon.com.br
Three berths. Equipment includes four post panamax cranes, four RTG's and fourteen reach stackers. Paved area of 235 000 m2. 1050 reefer points

Bunkering: Tramp Oil & Marine, World Fuel Services Corporation, 13th Floor, Portland House, Bressenden Place, London SW1E 5BH, United Kingdom, *Tel:* +44 20 7808 5000, *Fax:* +44 20 7808 5088, *Email:* pturner@wfscorp.com, *Website:* www.wfscorp.com – *Grades:* all grades – *Misc:* fresh water available – *Delivery Mode:* barge, pipeline, truck

Towage: Eleven tugs available of 520 hp to 4426 hp

Repair & Maintenance: Irmaos Fernandes Ltda, Rio Grande, Brazil Generalised mechanics
Cia. Estaleiros Rio Grande S.A., Rio Grande, Brazil Engine, hull and equipment repairs

Ship Chandlers: Brasil Sul, Rua Riachuelo 1, 96200-390 Rio Grande RS, Brazil, *Tel:* +55 53 3232 4497, *Fax:* +55 53 3232 3192, *Email:* brasisul@vetorialnet.com.br, *Website:* www.brasilsulprovedora.com
Polynave Marine Supplies Ltd, 19 Rua Riachuelo, 96200-390 Rio Grande, Brazil, *Tel:* +55 53 3232 1496, *Fax:* +55 53 3231 3712, *Email:* polynave@vetorial.net

Shipping Agents: Atlas Maritime Ltda, Avenida Silva Paes 266 - Centro, 96200-340 Rio Grande RS, Brazil, *Tel:* +55 53 3233 5400, *Fax:* +55 53 3231 4488, *Email:* atlas_riogrande@atlasmaritime.com.br, *Website:* www.atlasmaritime.com.br
CMA-CGM S.A., CMA CGM do Brasil Agencia Maritima, Rua Luiz Lorea 419 s.01, Centro, 96200-350 Rio Grande RS, Brazil, *Tel:* +55 53 2125 2100, *Fax:* +55 53 2125 2119, *Email:* brg.amartin@cma-cgm.com, *Website:* www.cma-cgm.com
Corymar Agencia Maritima Ltd, Rua Franciso Marques 178, 96200-150 Rio Grande RS, Brazil, *Tel:* +55 53 3232 1377, *Fax:* +55 53 3232 4516, *Email:* corymar@corymar.com.br, *Website:* www.corymar.com.br
Cranston Transportes Integrados Ltda, Rua Marechal Floriano, 122 Centro, CEP 96200-380 Rio Grande, Brazil, *Tel:* +55 53 3231 1515, *Fax:* +55 53 3231 1200, *Email:* tony.rig@cranwood.com.br
Fertimport S.A., Carlos Gomez 658, 96200-460 Rio Grande, Brazil, *Tel:* +55 53 3231 2488, *Fax:* +55 53 3231 3708, *Email:* fertrgd@fertimport.infonet.com, *Website:* www.fertimport.com.br
Mediterranean Shipping Company, MSC do Brazil Ltda, Rua Marechal Floriano Peixoto 122, Centro, 96200-380 Rio Grande RS, Brazil, *Tel:* +55 53 3035 9800, *Fax:* +55 53 3035 9805, *Email:* distribution@mscbr.com.br, *Website:* www.mscgva.ch
A.P. Moller-Maersk Group, Maersk Brasil Ltda, Rua Zalony 160, Salas 701/702, Centro, 96200-070 Rio Grande RS, Brazil, *Tel:* +55 53 3035 8800, *Fax:* +55 53 3035 8840, *Email:* brzcrcnvm@maersk.com, *Website:* www.maerskline.com
Oceanus Agencia Maritima S.A., Rua Francisco Marques 183, 96200-150 Rio Grande RS, Brazil, *Tel:* +55 53 3231 1355, *Fax:* +55 53 3231 1976, *Email:* agency.rig@oceanus.com.br, *Website:* www.oceanus.com.br
Agencia Maritima Orion Ltda, Rua Aquidaban 623, 170 SL 303/304, 96200-480 Rio Grande, Brazil, *Tel:* +55 53 2125 4400, *Fax:* +55 53 2125 4444, *Email:* orion@rgd.amorion.com.br, *Website:* www.amorion.com.br
Sampayo Nickhorn S.A., Rua Riachuelo 197, Andar 1, P O Box 165, 96200-390 Rio Grande, Brazil, *Tel:* +55 53 3231 1477, *Fax:* +55 53 3231 3131, *Email:* sampayo@sampayo.com.br, *Website:* www.sampayo.com.br
Supermar S.A., Rua General Neto 273, CEP 96200-010 Rio Grande, Brazil, *Tel:* +55 53 3231 1122, *Fax:* +55 53 3231 1722, *Email:* riogrande@supermar.com.br, *Website:* www.supermar.com.br
Unimar Agenciamentos Maritimos Ltda, Rua Zolony 10, Sala 1304, Centro, Rio Grande, Brazil, *Tel:* +55 53 3231 1104, *Fax:* +55 53 3231 3875, *Email:* apaes@rig.unimar-agency.com.br
V Morel S.A., Rua Zalony 160, 7 Andar, cj 707/708, 96200-070 Rio Grande, Brazil, *Tel:* +55 53 3232 4329, *Fax:* +55 53 3232 6135, *Email:* vmorel@vmorel.com.br, *Website:* www.vmorel.com.br
Wilson Sons Agencia Maritima Ltda, Rua Riachuelo 201/205, 96200-390 Rio Grande RS, Brazil, *Tel:* +55 53 3233 7700, *Fax:* +55 53 3231 1246, *Email:* agerg@wilsonsons.com.br, *Website:* www.wilsonsons.com.br

---

Key to Principal Facilities:—				
A=Airport	**C**=Containers	**G**=General Cargo	**P**=Petroleum	**R**=Ro/Ro	**Y**=Dry Bulk
B=Bunkers	**D**=Dry Dock	**L**=Cruise	**Q**=Other Liquid Bulk	**T**=Towage (where available from port)	

Surveyors: Det Norske Veritas A/S, Zalony 160, Route 1001, 96200-070 Rio Grande, Brazil, *Tel:* +55 53 3231 2970, *Fax:* +55 53 3231 3306, *Email:* consunav@consunav.com.br, *Website:* www.consunav.com.br

Nippon Kaiji Kyokai, Consunav Consultoria e Projetos Navais Ltda, Rua Zalony 160 - Sala 1001, 96200-070 Rio Grande RS, Brazil, *Tel:* +55 53 3231 2970, *Fax:* +55 53 3231 3306, *Email:* consunav@consunav.com.br, *Website:* www.consunav.com.br

Registro Italiano Navale (RINA), Rua Zalony No.160 Sala 1001, Centro, CEP 96200-070 Rio Grande, Brazil, *Tel:* +55 53 3231 2970, *Fax:* +55 53 3231 3306, *Email:* consunav@consunav.com.br, *Website:* www.consunav.com.br

Medical Facilities: Two hospitals

Lloyd's Agent: Inspect Santos Consultoria e Peritagens Ltda, Av. Conselheiro Nebias, 726 - sala 114, Boqueirao, 11045-002 Santos SP, Brazil, *Tel:* +55 13 3234 5246, *Fax:* +55 13 3235 2250, *Email:* inspect@inspect.com.br

SALINEIRO TERMINAL

Lat 4° 49' S; Long 37° 2' W.

Admiralty Chart: 526/3955	**Admiralty Pilot:** 5
Time Zone: GMT -3 h	**UNCTAD Locode:** BR

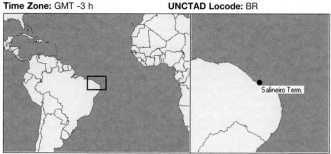

Principal Facilities:

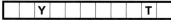

Authority: Terminal Salineiro de Areia Branca, Cais Tertuliano Fernandes 81, 59655-000 Areia Branca RN, Brazil, *Tel:* +55 84 3332 2168, *Fax:* +55 84 3332 2399, *Email:* codern@uol.com.br, *Website:* www.codern.com.br

Port Security: ISPS compliant

Approach: The access channel is about 15 km long with min depth 11 m and variable width of between 400 m and 1000 m. This channel is closed for night navigation

Pilotage: Compulsory. Pilot boards in pos 4° 43' 36" S; 36° 55' 36" W

Weather: From January to June the wind blows weakly from the NE; between June and October the wind blows strongly from the East, usually more intensely during August; in November and December the wind also blows from the East, although not as intensely. The rainy season known in the region as winter, starts in January and ends in May

Tides: Max 3.8 m, min 2.2 m

Principal Imports and Exports: Exports: Salt.

Accommodation:

Name	Remarks
Salineiro Terminal	See [1] below

[1]*Salineiro Terminal:* Areia Branca Salt company terminal, also known as Port Island, is an artificial structure set in the open sea, located 26 km NE of Areia Branca. It ships out salt produced in the cities of Macau, Grossos, Mossoro and Areia Branca. Salt is shifted by ferry boats run by private companies with an average daily shifting of 7000 t/boat according to tide. The terminal has three mechanical unloaders which unload the ferry boats, two of them hold up to 350 t/h and the other up to 450 t/h. The salt can be stocked in the Island or taken straight into the vessel through the rollers which are 432 m long at a rate of 1500 t/h

Towage: Available

Lloyd's Agent: Inspect Consultoria Ltda (Recife), Rua Padre Carapuceiro 412/603, Boa Viagem, 51020-280 Recife PE, Brazil, *Tel:* +55 81 9952 5868, *Email:* inspectrecife@terra.com.br

SALVADOR

Lat 12° 57' S; Long 38° 30' W.

Admiralty Chart: 545	**Admiralty Pilot:** 5
Time Zone: GMT -3 h	**UNCTAD Locode:** BR SSA

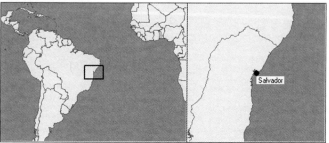

Principal Facilities:

P		Y	G	C	R	L	B		T	A	

Authority: Companhia das Docas do Estado da Bahia (CODEBA), Porto de Salvador, Avenida da Franca 1551, Comercio, 40010-000 Salvador BA, Brazil, *Tel:* +55 71 3320 1299, *Fax:* +55 71 3243 9269, *Email:* portosalvador@codeba.com.br, *Website:* www.codeba.com.br

Officials: Marketing Manager: Marcelo da Gama Lobo, *Email:* marcelo.lobo@codeba.com.br.

Port Security: ISPS compliant

Approach: The approach channel is 400 m wide, and the manoeuvring basin 700 m wide. All vessels entering or leaving the port, and drawing 8.5 m must use the N channel (the entrance facing dock No.2 runs into shallow water).The mean depth of water in the channel of access to the dock warehouses is 10 m, except opposite shed No.2 where the maximum depth of water is 7.3 m. From the point where the pilot boards or from the anchorage to the port, attention must be paid to the Banco da Panela shoal (min depth 4.98 m), the extremities of which are marked by three luminous buoys

The average depth of water in the channel leading to the dock warehouses is 10 m. The dock quays are sheltered by two breakwaters, the southern breakwater, 1000 m in length, juts out NW from the shore with the other breakwater running N/S, one running parallel with the shore for just over 0.5 miles and some 700 m off the docks

Anchorage: The Monte Serrat anchorage, north of Banco da Panela, has a depth of 13 m with a mud bottom

The inspection area of the 4 Port Health Authorities, Federal Receipt and Maritime Police is defined by a radius of one mile around the point of co-ordinates 12° 58' 07'' S; 38° 32' 18'' W, and the area around 12° 55' 56'' S; 38° 31' 37'' W. Vessels may only come alongside after clearance by the Federal Receipt, Port Health Authorities and Federal Police. The free anchorage coincides with the pilotage waiting area and permitted anchorage (Monte Serrat)

Inside the breakwater and to the south of Fort Sao Marcelo there is an exclusive anchorage for the mooring of LASH vessel barges

Pilotage: Compulsory for all foreign vessels

Tides: Tidal range of 2.5 m

Traffic: 2007, 23 090 307 t of cargo handled, 230 270 TEU's

Working Hours: Port working hours 0700-1100, 1300-1700. Saturdays 0700-1100. Overtime can be arranged

Accommodation:

Name	Length (m)	Depth (m)	Draught (m)	Remarks
Salvador				See [1] below
Commercial Wharf	1420		10	See [2] below
Commercial Wharf	238	7.86		Four berths for coastal vessels
New Quay	270			Lash barges unloaded
Ten Metre Quay	370		10	See [3] below

[1]*Salvador:* The area between the breakwaters is the turning basin with depths of 8-12 m

[2]*Commercial Wharf:* Import and export cargo handled at five berths. Vessels drawing 7.86 m are kept off the wharf by 5 m wide pontoons which allows a draught of 10 m. No railway lines. Passenger terminal at north end of the wharf

[3]*Ten Metre Quay:* Vegetable oil handled by lighters. Container yard. At the end of the wharf there is a fixed loading belt for magnesite at 150 t/h. Other bulk ores by buckets Ro/ro berth, max draught 7.9 m for bow or stern, berth to a ramp with a heavy lift crane. Railway connections

Storage: There are nine warehouses - 15 000 m2. Two tanks for vegetable oil. Three yards roofed over - 60 000 m2

Location	Cold (m³)
Salvador	2300

Mechanical Handling Equipment:

Location	Type	Capacity (t)	Qty
Salvador	Floating Cranes	100	1
Salvador	Mult-purp. Cranes	40	30
Salvador	Mobile Cranes	66	1
Salvador	Transtainers		2
Salvador	Forklifts	30	42
Salvador	Yard Tractors		7
New Quay	Mult-purp. Cranes	6	4
Ten Metre Quay	Mult-purp. Cranes	30	2

Bunkering: Available from lighters

ExxonMobil Marine Fuels, Suite 900, One Alhambra Plaza, Coral Gables, FL 33134, United States of America, *Tel:* +1 305 459 6358, *Fax:* +1 305 459 6412, *Email:* emmf@exxonmobil.com, *Website:* www.exxonmobilmarinefuels.com – *Grades:* IFO30-180cSt; MGO; MDO – *Delivery Mode:* barge, truck, pipeline

Petrobras Bunkering, Avenida Republica do Chile 65, 20 andar, sala 2001-H, 20035-913 Rio de Janeiro, Brazil, *Tel:* +55 21 3224 3290, *Fax:* +55 21 2262 8134, *Email:* bunker@petrobras.com.br, *Website:* www.petrobras.com.br – *Grades:* all grades, in line blending available – *Misc:* own storage facilities – *Rates:* 300-400t/h – *Delivery Mode:* barge, pipeline, truck

Towage: Nineteen tugs available of 720-2100 hp

Ship Chandlers: Avesmar Marine Supply (Peca Rapido Comercio Import Export Ltda, Avenida Oscar Pontes No. 11, Agua de Meninos, Bahia, 40460-130 Salvador, Brazil, *Tel:* +55 71 3242 3855, *Fax:* +55 71 3242 5006, *Email:* valeriano@cpunet.com.br, *Website:* www.avesmar.com

International Marine Services Ltda, Avenida Beira Mar 181, Galpao 04, 40420-340 Salvador, Brazil, *Tel:* +55 71 3315 0977, *Fax:* +55 71 3315 0980, *Email:* imarineservices@uol.com.br

Shipping Agents: Bahiaship Agencia Maritima Ltda, Edif Suerdieck, andar 8, CJ 801, Avenida Estado Unidos 14, P O Box 1959, CEP 40010 Salvador, Brazil, *Tel:* +55 71 3243 8011, *Fax:* +55 71 3243 3125, *Email:* eduardo@bahiaship.com.br

Brisamar Agencias Maritimas S.A., Avenida Estados Unidos 397, andar 6, salas 601/4, CEP 40018-900 Salvador, Brazil, *Tel:* +55 71 3242 7011, *Fax:* +55 71 3241 0518, *Email:* brisamar@zaz.com.br

CMA-CGM S.A., CMA CGM do Brasil Agencia Maritima, Rua Miguel Calmon 555, Sl.613 pte, Comercio, 40015-010 Salvador BA, Brazil, *Tel:* +55 71 3327 2510, *Fax:* +55 71 2104 9773, *Email:* sla.vandrade@cma-cgm.com, *Website:* www.cma-cgm.com

Corymar Agencia Maritima Ltd, Rua Miguel Calmon 19, Room 1001, P O Box 1022, 40015-010 Salvador BA, Brazil, *Tel:* +55 71 3241 5122, *Fax:* +55 71 3243 9048, *Email:* willssa@williams.com.br, *Website:* www.williams.com.br

LBH Brasil, Rua Miguel Calmon 555, Sala 505, Ed. Citibank, 40015-010 Salvador BA, Brazil, *Tel:* +55 71 3186 6455, *Fax:* +55 71 3186 6450, *Email:* brazssa@lbhbrasil.com.br, *Website:* www.brazshipping.com.br

Link Insurance Services Brasil Ltda, Estr do Coco Km 7.5, Cond Marina Riverside C8/212, Lauro de Freitas, 42700-000 Salvador, Brazil, *Tel:* +55 71 3379 7818, *Fax:* +55 71 3369 1377, *Email:* inspect@lisbrasil.com.br, *Website:* www.lisbrasil.co.br

Mediterranean Shipping Company, MSC do Brasil Ltda, Avenue Professor Magalhaes 1752 - 12th Floor, Bairro Pituba, Salvador BA, Brazil, *Tel:* +55 71 3242 5422, *Fax:* +55 71 3242 5422, *Email:* distribution@mscbr.com.br, *Website:* www.mscgva.ch

A.P. Moller-Maersk Group, Maersk Brasil Ltda, Rua Portugal 5/7 - 13 andar, Edificio Status - Comercio, 40015-000 Salvador BA, Brazil, *Tel:* +55 71 3319 9400, *Fax:* +55 71 3326 0396, *Email:* ssaops@maersk.com, *Website:* www.maerskline.com

Oceanus Agencia Maritima S.A., Av. Estados Unidos 555, 7th Floor - Room 712, 40015-010 Salvador BA, Brazil, *Tel:* +55 71 3241 4990, *Fax:* +55 71 3243 5633, *Email:* agency.ssa@oceanus.com.br, *Website:* www.oceanus.com.br

Pennant Servicos Maritimos Ltd, Av Estados Unidos 397, cj 601/604, piso 6, CEP 40018-900 Salvador, Brazil, *Tel:* +55 71 3242 7011, *Fax:* +55 71 3241 0518, *Email:* pennssa@pennant.com.br

Star Ship Agencia Maritma Ltda, Av. Estados Unidos No.4, Room 611 - Comercio, 40010-020 Salvador, Brazil, *Tel:* +55 71 3242 5444, *Fax:* +55 71 3242 5917, *Email:* starship-ba@starship-ba.com.br, *Website:* www.starship-ba.com.br

Transcargo Servicios Maritimos Ltd, 5/7 Rua Portugal, 13 Andar, Conj 1301-1305, CEP 40015-000 Salvador, Brazil, *Tel:* +55 71 3326 2110, *Fax:* +55 71 3326 0396, *Email:* almir.xavier@transcargoba.com.br

Wilson Sons Agencia Maritima Ltda, Rua Miguel Calmon 555, 401/407 Comercio, 40015-010 Salvador BA, Brazil, *Tel:* +55 71 2104 9766, *Fax:* +55 71 3241 8709, *Email:* agesv@wilsonsons.com.br, *Website:* www.wilsonsons.com.br

Surveyors: Det Norske Veritas A/S, Rua Dr.Jose Peroba 149 - Sala 1101, Ed.Centro Empresarial Eldorado-Stiep, 41770-790 Salvador BA, Brazil, *Tel:* +55 71 3341 5332, *Fax:* +55 71 3272 1993, *Email:* salvador@dnv.com, *Website:* www.dnv.com

Airport: Dois de Julho Airport, 40 km

Lloyd's Agent: Inspect Consultoria Ltda (Recife), Rua Padre Carapuceiro 412/603, Boa Viagem, 51020-280 Recife PE, Brazil, *Tel:* +55 81 9952 5868, *Email:* inspectrecife@terra.com.br

SANTA CLARA

Lat 29° 54' S; Long 51° 22' W.

Admiralty Chart: -	**Admiralty Pilot:** -
Time Zone: GMT -3 h	**UNCTAD Locode:** BR SCS

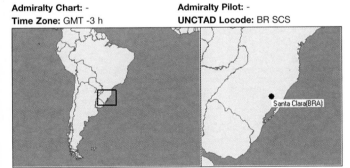

Principal Facilities:

	Q	Y				B		A	

Authority: Companhia Petroquimica do Sul, Br.386 Rod.Tabai/Canoas Km 419, Polo Petroquimico do Sul, 95853-000 Triunfo RS, Brazil, *Tel:* +55 51 457 1100, *Fax:* +55 51 457 1369

Port Security: ISPS compliant

Documentation: Vessels form "c" and check list for safety system

Approach: Navigation through Porto Alegre to Santa Clara must be done during daylight hours and vessels must pass under a bridge with a max air draft of 34 m. The terminal access channel has a length of 7.5 km, bottom width of 50 m and a depth of 6.75 m

Pilotage: Compulsory

Radio Frequency: VHF Channels 16 and 12, call sign 'Santa Clara'

Weather: Winds changing from freak to strong winds (over 100KM/h).

Maximum Vessel Dimensions: Max loa 155 m, max draft 5.2 m, max beam 30 m, max air draft 34 m. Longer vessels may be accommodated with prior agreement with Authorities

Working Hours: 24 h/day

Accommodation:

Name	Length (m)	Remarks
Santa Clara Pier No.1	42	See [1] below Used exclusively for the loading of petrochemicals

Name	Length (m)	Remarks
Pier No.2	42	Used for loading butane gas, propylene & butadiene
Pier No.3		See [2] below

[1]*Santa Clara:* There is a turning basin 320 m by 520 m with an irregular form and two dolphins where vessels can berth to await when loading berths are occupied

[2]*Pier No.3:* Mainly used for the discharge of coal, but also has the capability to purify and load butadiene, propylene and propane

Cargo Worked: Benzene 300 t/h, butadiene 300 t/h, butane 300 t/h, propane 180 t/h, ethyl-benzene 170 t/h, ethylene 140 t/h, toluene 100 t/h and xylene 100 t/h

Bunkering: Petrobras Bunkering, Avenida Republica do Chile 65, 20 andar, sala 2001-H, 20035-913 Rio de Janeiro, Brazil, *Tel:* +55 21 3224 3290, *Fax:* +55 21 2262 8134, *Email:* bunker@petrobras.com.br, *Website:* www.petrobras.com.br – *Grades:* MGO; lubes – *Delivery Mode:* truck

Waste Reception Facilities: Able to recieve sludge, chemical waste, garbage disposal duly selected, dirty ballast (except caustic soda, acid residues and salt water ballast).

Medical Facilities: At Porto Alegre, 55 km by road

Airport: Salgado Filho International, 50 km

Development: A new berth under construction for general /dry cargo and containers

Lloyd's Agent: Inspect Santos Consultoria e Peritagens Ltda, Av. Conselheiro Nebias, 726 - sala 114, Boqueirao, 11045-002 Santos SP, Brazil, *Tel:* +55 13 3234 5246, *Fax:* +55 13 3235 2250, *Email:* inspect@inspect.com.br

SANTANA

alternate name, see Macapa

SANTAREM

Lat 2° 25' S; Long 54° 42' W.

Admiralty Chart: 2229	**Admiralty Pilot:** 5
Time Zone: GMT -4 h	**UNCTAD Locode:** BR STM

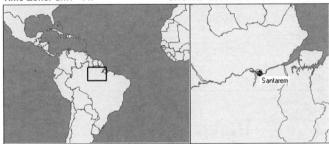

Principal Facilities:

		Y	G						A	

Authority: Companhia Docas do Para, Porto de Santarem, Av. Cuiaba s/n, Bairro Vera Paz, 68040-400 Santarem PA, Brazil, *Tel:* +55 93 3523 4693, *Fax:* +55 93 3523 4693, *Email:* aposan@cdp.com.br, *Website:* www.cdp.com.br

Officials: Port Administrator: Celso Angelo de Castro Lima.

Port Security: ISPS compliant

Documentation: Crew list (6 copies), passenger list (6 copies), ships general info (5 copies), certificate list (3 copies), bonded stores list (2 copies), provision list (2 copies), personal effects list (2 copies), maritime declaration of health (2 copies), list of ports of call (2 copies), crew vaccination list (2 copies)

Approach: Access channel is 1200 m wide with a depth of 18 m. The manoeuvring basin, commencing at Ponta Negra is 800 m wide in front of the quays

Pilotage: Compulsory. Pilot boards at either Belem or Santana

Weather: Frequent rain from January to June

Tides: Tides average 7.5 m throughout the year at the pier

Traffic: 2007, 2 240 132 t of cargo handled

Maximum Vessel Dimensions: 16 666 gt, 8.8 m draft, 185.4 m loa

Principal Imports and Exports: Exports: Lumber.

Working Hours: 0700-1100, 1300-1700. Overtime can be arranged

Accommodation:

Name	Length (m)	Depth (m)	Remarks
Santarem Pier	220	6–10	Berthing possible on both sides of the pier
Secondary Dock	170	6–10	Three platforms and three levels

Storage:

Location	Covered (m²)	Sheds / Warehouses
Santarem	3000	2

Key to Principal Facilities:—					
A=Airport	**C**=Containers	**G**=General Cargo	**P**=Petroleum	**R**=Ro/Ro	**Y**=Dry Bulk
B=Bunkers	**D**=Dry Dock	**L**=Cruise	**Q**=Other Liquid Bulk	**T**=Towage (where available from port)	

Mechanical Handling Equipment:

Location	Type	Capacity (t)	Qty
Santarem	Mult-purp. Cranes	6	2
Santarem	Mobile Cranes	9	1

Cargo Worked: 30 t/gang/h

Repair & Maintenance: Two repair shops with slipways to accommodate vessels up to 200 gt

Shipping Agents: LBH Brasil, Travessa 15 de Agosto 20 - Sala 209, Ed. Marques Pinto, Centro, 68005-300 Santarem PA, Brazil, *Tel:* +55 93 2101 6855, *Fax:* +55 93 2101 6858, *Email:* brazstm@lbhbrasil.com.br, *Website:* www.brazshipping.com.br

Medical Facilities: Available

Lloyd's Agent: Inspect Consultoria Ltda (Sao Luis), Av Dos Portugueses, 31 Vila Embratel, 65085-580 Sao Luis MA, Brazil, *Tel:* +55 98 3242 4016, *Email:* inspectconsultoria@br.inter.net

SANTOS

Lat 23° 56' S; Long 46° 20' W.

Admiralty Chart: 19

Admiralty Pilot: 5

Time Zone: GMT -3 h

UNCTAD Locode: BR SSZ

Principal Facilities:

P Q Y G C R L B D T A

Authority: Companhia Docas do Estado de Sao Paulo (CODESP), Autoridade Portuaria de Santos, Avenida Conselheiro Rodrigues Alves s/n, 11015-900 Santos SP, Brazil, *Tel:* +55 13 3233 6565, *Fax:* +55 13 3233 3080, *Email:* cmmgerencia@portodesantos.com.br, *Website:* www.portodesantos.com

Officials: President: Jose di Bella Filho, *Tel:* +55 13 3233 6565, *Email:* dpdiret@portodesantos.com.br.
Director: Paulino Moreira da Silva Vicente, *Tel:* +55 13 3233 6565.
Commercial Director: Carlos Helmut, *Tel:* +55 13 3233 6565.
Finance Director: Alencar Costa, *Tel:* +55 13 3233 6565.
Marketing Manager: Wagner Moreira Goncalves, *Tel:* +55 13 3233 6565, *Email:* wagnermgoncalves@portodesantos.com.br.

Port Security: ISPS compliant. Container Security Initiative (CSI) designated port

Documentation: Crew list, passenger list, tobacco/spirits/personal effects list, stores list, arms & ammunition list, health documents or certificates, certificate of deratting, load line certificate, tonnage certificate, certificate of nationality, safety equipment certificate, cargo gear certificate, bill of ladings, cargo manifests

Approach: The harbour is formed on the E by the Island of Santo Amaro and on the W by the Island of Sao Vicente, and is served by calm and safe waters all year round. The approach channel is 300-700 m wide with a min depth of 12 m. The manoeuvring basin is 200 m wide

Anchorage: Internal Berthage (for vessels with max draft of 9 m, only during daylight period) between the following positions:
23° 55' 48" S; 46° 19' 00" W
23° 55' 40" S; 46° 19' 00" W
23° 55' 39" S; 46° 19' 24" W
23° 55' 34" S; 46° 19' 24" W
Anchorage No.1 (for warships only) between the following positions:
23° 59' 24" S; 46° 20' 12" W
23° 59' 24" S; 46° 20' 48" W
24° 00' 00" S; 46° 20' 48" W
24° 00' 00" S; 46° 20' 24" W
Anchorage No.2 (for vessels needing sanitary inspection or clearance, crew debarkation/embarkation, workshops and materials, max of 3 h stay) between the following positions:
24° 00' 45" S; 46° 20' 10" W
24° 00' 45" S; 46° 19' 42" W
24° 01' 30" S; 46° 20' 30" W
24° 01' 30" S; 46° 19' 42" W
Anchorage No.3 (for vessels with defined berthing schedule within next 24 h) between the following positions:
24° 03' 00" S; 46° 20' 48" W
24° 06' 00" S; 46° 22' 09" W
24° 06' 00" S; 46° 18' 36" W
24° 05' 18" S; 46° 18' 36" W
Anchorage No.4 (for vessels with defined berthing schedule within next 24 h) between the following positions:

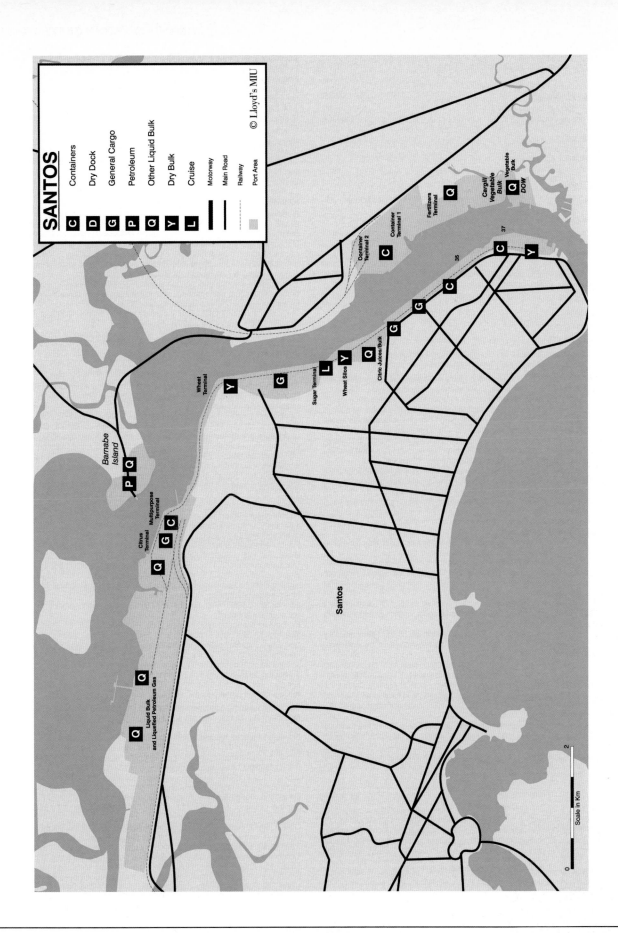

SANTOS

- C Containers
- D Dry Dock
- G General Cargo
- P Petroleum
- Q Other Liquid Bulk
- Y Dry Bulk
- L Cruise

Motorway
Main Road
Railway
Port Area

© Lloyd's MIU

Barnabe Island

Wheat Terminal

Sugar Terminal

Wheat Silos

Citric Juices/Bulk

Container Terminal 2

Container Terminal 1

Fertilizers Terminal

Cargill Vegetable Bulk

Vegetable Bulk

DOW

35

37

Citrus Terminal

Multipurpose Terminal

Liquid Bulk and Liquefied Petroleum Gas

Santos

Scale in Km

0   2

24° 06' 00" S; 46° 22' 06" W
24° 06' 00" S; 46° 18' 36" W
24° 05' 18" S; 46° 18' 36" W
24° 05' 18" S; 46° 15' 00" W
24° 10' 00" S; 46° 15' 00" W
24° 10' 00" S; 46° 19' 24" W
Anchorage No.5 (for vessels not scheduled for Port of Santos) between the following positions:
24° 10' 00" S; 46° 19' 24" W
24° 10' 00" S; 46° 15' 00" W
24° 05' 18" S; 46° 15' 00" W
24° 05' 18" S; 46° 10' 00" W
24° 15' 00" S; 46° 10' 00" W
24° 15' 00" S; 46° 19' 24" W
Anchorage No.6 (for vessels in quarantine) between the following positions:
24° 05' 00" S; 46° 24' 27" W
24° 05' 00" S; 46° 22' 45" W
24° 07' 12" S; 46° 25' 27" W
24° 07' 12" S; 46° 23' 42" W
The above coordinates refer to Nautical Chart No's 1701 and 1711

Pilotage: Compulsory. Requisition for pilot should be made 2 h in advance prior to arrival at pilot station on VHF Channel 16. Pilotage service, Tel: +55 13 3261 5800, Fax: +55 13 3261 5098, Email: praticos@bignet.com.br

Radio Frequency: VHF Channel 16 (pilot station)

Weather: Heavy mist in the mornings during the winter and rainy season

Tides: Average tidal variation 1.5 m

Traffic: 2007, 80 775 867 t of cargo handled, 2 169 432 TEU's

Working Hours: The port operates 24 h/day and the work is organised into four shifts of 6 h each (Christmas and New Year no work after 1900)

Accommodation: Container & ro/ro facilities: There is a container terminal (Tecon, operated by Santos Brasil S.A., Website: www.santosbrasil.com.br) at Conceicaozinho on the left bank of the river, on the opposite side to the Port's main dock areas. It covers an area of 484 000 m2 with three berths totalling 760 m in depth of 13.7 m and is equipped with five container gantry cranes of 35 t cap on the quay and various yard gantries, front handlers, tractors and trailers etc. There are three large warehouses for storage of unstuffed cargoes, a centre for container repair and maintenance and 1250 points for refrigerated containers. The terminal has road and rail connections with the city of Sao Paulo and other interior locations
Terminal 37, operated by Libra Terminals, Tel: +55 13 3071 3606, Fax: +55 13 3071 3605, Email: rarten@t37.com.br, Website: www.t37.com.br, with five berths available totalling 1110 m in depth of 10-13.5 m and a 164 000 m2 container yard with 916 reefer points. Equipment includes five dockside cranes, fourteen reach stackers and six RTG's
Ro/ro facilities are available on berths at the Saboo part of the quayside with 9.6 m depth and Shed 35 with 11 m depth
Bulk facilities: Steel Works: Owned by Companhia Siderurgica Paulista (COSIPA) who have their own terminal at Piacaguera. There are two quays each 300 m long with a depth of 10 m accommodating two vessels each simultaneously. Quay No.1 for the loading of steel products for export. Quay No.2 for the discharge of iron ore and coal by two discharging units rated at 1200 t/h and two conveyor belts extending for 1 km into the stockpiles
Fertiliser quay: two berths totalling 567 m in depth of 13.5 m. There are six warehouses, each with a cap of 30 000 t. Eleven electric cranes equipped with automatic buckets and two belt transporting systems
The Macuco Novo quay has a length of 280 m in depth of 13 m. There are four warehouses (total area of 38 154 m2) connected to the quayside by conveyor transporters and loaders
Tanker facilities: The Barnabe Island Terminal is used for the loading and discharging of inflammable liquids (benzene, gasoline, gas oil, kerosene etc). Length 302 m with a max draft of 10 m. This island is connected to the right side at Alemoa, by means of two oil ducts, one for gasoline and the other for diesel oil and kerosene. These oil ducts are 4640 m long with an importing cap of 226 m3/h and exporting cap of 135 m3/h
The Alemoa Tanker Terminal for vessels up to 60 000 dwt and 243 m loa has two berths for vessels known as Pier 1A and Pier 2A which are used as loading or discharge for products and LPG. Pier 1A is for the exclusive service of PETROBRAS and Pier 2A is shared with other chemical companies. At the inner side, two more piers are used only for loading barges with bunkers for vessels

Name	Remarks
Santos	See [1] below
Private Wharves	See [2] below

[1]*Santos:* 53 public berths totalling 11 673 m and 10 private berths totalling 1413 m Depth alongside the docks varies from 5 to 13.5 m; Inflammables Island (Barnabe), 10 m; Alamoa Terminal, 12 m; Saboo Quay, 10 m; Conceicaozinha Terminal, 13.5 m (All HWS). Depth in the NE part of the recommended anchorage varies between 10 m and 13 m. Dock space available is 10 800 m of which 6700 m is for general cargoes. Special warehouses for inspection and sorting of coffee. Facilities are available for the handling of bulk maize, bagged sugar, bulk sugar, cotton, bulk wheat, iron ore, coal and bulk fertiliser
[2]*Private Wharves:* At Cubatao: COSIPA, 300 m long in depth of 10 m for bulk solids and general cargo. ULTRAFERTIL, 294 m long in depth of 10 m for bulk solids and liquids
On Santo Amaro Island: DOW CHEMICAL, 253 m long in depth of 10 m for bulk liquids. CUTRALE, 286 m long in depth of 9 m for bulk orange juice. CARGIL, 250 m long in depth of 13 m for soya beans and pellets of citric pulp and soya

Mechanical Handling Equipment:

Location	Type	Capacity (t)	Qty
Santos	Mobile Cranes	140	8
Santos	Portal Cranes	32	85
Santos	Transtainers	30	6
Santos	Forklifts	45	

Bunkering: ExxonMobil Marine Fuels, Suite 900, One Alhambra Plaza, Coral Gables, FL 33134, United States of America, *Tel:* +1 305 459 6358, *Fax:* +1 305 459 6412, *Email:* emmf@exxonmobil.com, *Website:* www.exxonmobilmarinefuels.com
Tramp Oil & Marine, World Fuel Services Corporation, 13th Floor, Portland House, Bressenden Place, London SW1E 5BH, United Kingdom, *Tel:* +44 20 7808 5000, *Fax:* +44 20 7808 5088, *Email:* pturner@wfscorp.com, *Website:* www.wfscorp.com – *Grades:* all grades – *Delivery Mode:* barge, pipeline, truck

Towage: Companhia Navegacao das Lagoas, Santos, Brazil, *Tel:* +55 13 3219 5482
Metalnave Comercio E Industria S.A., Santos, Brazil, *Tel:* +55 13 3219 5681
Sulnorte Servicos Maritimos Ltda, Pca Barao do Rio Branco 142/143, Salas 14, 11010-040 Santos, Brazil, *Tel:* +55 13 3211 5040, *Fax:* +55 13 3211 5041, *Email:* santos@sulnorte.com.br, *Website:* www.sulnorte.com.br
Wilson Sons Agencia Maritima Ltda, Rua Tuiuti 58, 1st & 2nd Floors, 11010-220 Santos SP, Brazil, *Tel:* +55 13 3211 2300, *Fax:* +55 13 3219 5250, *Email:* agest@wilsonsons.com.br, *Website:* www.wilsonsons.com.br

Repair & Maintenance: Coimbra Ltda, Rua Amador Bueno 447, 11013-152 Santos, Brazil, *Tel:* +55 13 3221 1441, *Fax:* +55 13 3233 1577, *Email:* marine@coimbra-brazil.com.br, *Website:* www.coimbra-brazil.com.br Services; general ship repair. Deck machinery:- Cranes; electro-hydraulic specialists, winches & windlass, hatch covers, hydraulic systems, spare parts, cargo gear survey & load tests, specialists structural repairs for cranes. Metal steel works:- tanks & structures, pressure boilers & piping, deck & hull repairs, any kind of welding. Electric services:- Electromotors & generators rewinding & service station. Electronic services:- automation systems, computer service, radio station, gyro compass, satelite navigation system, autopilot. Other services:- diving services & inspection.
Metalock do Brasil Ltda, Rua Visconde do Rio Branco 20/26, 11013-030 Santos, Brazil, *Tel:* +55 13 3226 4686, *Fax:* +55 13 3226 4680, *Email:* santos@metalock.com.br, *Website:* www.metalock.com.br Engine repairs
Ofremarte Ltda, Santos, Brazil, *Tel:* +55 13 3232 6737, *Fax:* +55 13 3232 8291
Wilson Sons Agencia Maritima Ltda, Rua Tuiuti 58, 1st & 2nd Floors, 11010-220 Santos SP, Brazil, *Tel:* +55 13 3211 2300, *Fax:* +55 13 3219 5250, *Email:* agest@wilsonsons.com.br, *Website:* www.wilsonsons.com.br

Ship Chandlers: Agelopoulos Maritima Ltda, Praca Azevedo Junior 20, SP 11010-030 Santos, Brazil, *Tel:* +55 13 3219 3926, *Fax:* +55 13 3216 1105, *Email:* atlasmarine@uol.com.br
Chapinter Marine Supply Exportadora Ltda, Avenida Sao Francisco 423, 11013-203 Santos, Brazil, *Tel:* +55 13 3233 6888, *Fax:* +55 13 3233 6888, *Email:* chapintermarine@terra.com.br, *Website:* www.chapintermarine.com.br
DSF-Servicos e Fornecedora de Navios Ltda, R. Santos Dumont 133/135, 11015-231 Santos, Brazil, *Tel:* +55 13 3227 5566, *Fax:* +55 13 3231 0655, *Email:* info@dsfservicos.com.br, *Website:* www.dsfservicos.com.br
Extecil Santos Comercio e Mant. De equip de Seguranca e Salvatagem Ltda, Avenida Conselheiro Nebias 106, 11015 -00 Santos, Brazil, *Tel:* +55 13 3224 5050, *Fax:* +55 13 3234 5050, *Email:* naval@extecilsantos.com.br, *Website:* www.extecilsantos.com.br
Extintec - Extintores e Equipamentos de Seg. Industrial Ltda, Rua Joao Guerra 190, 11015 - 130 Santos, Brazil, *Tel:* +55 13 3234 4422, *Fax:* +55 13 3232 8121, *Email:* extintec@extintec.com.br, *Website:* www.extintec.com.br
Paulo Fernandes Ship Suppliers Ltda, Rua Gal. Camara No. 366, 11.010-122 Santos, Brazil, *Tel:* +55 13 3232 4091, *Fax:* +55 13 3235 3302, *Email:* paulonande@uol.com.br
Mansueto Pierotti & Filhos Ltda, Rua Mansueto Pierotti n 36, 11.010-918 Santos, Brazil, *Tel:* +55 13 3213 4646, *Fax:* +55 13 3213 4647, *Email:* mp@mansuetopierotti.com.br, *Website:* www.mansuetopierotti.com.br
Nordsee Ship Supplies, Rua Joao Pessoa n 447/449, 11013-003 Santos, Brazil, *Tel:* +55 13 3223 3080, *Fax:* +55 13 3223 9749, *Email:* nordsee@terra.com.br, *Website:* www.emsbrazil.com
Pellegrini Fornecedora de Navios Ltda, P O Box No. 35, 11.001-970 Santos, Brazil, *Tel:* +55 13 3261 3075, *Fax:* +55 13 3261 1484, *Email:* pellegrn@terra.com.br
Sea Star Ship Suppliers Ltd, Travessa Dona Adelina No. 35 Paqueta, 11013-130 Santos, Brazil, *Tel:* +55 13 3232 5757, *Fax:* +55 13 3233 3211, *Email:* seastartrans@uol.com.br, *Website:* www.seastarsantos.com.br
Turbogen do Brasil Reparos Navais Ltda, Rua Joao Guerra 194, 11015 - 130 Santos, Brazil, *Tel:* +55 13 3232 6217, *Fax:* +55 13 3232 8121, *Email:* turbogen@turbogen.com.br, *Website:* www.turbogen.com.br

Shipping Agents: Agelopoulos Maritima Ltda, Praca Azevedo Junior 20, SP 11010-030 Santos, Brazil, *Tel:* +55 13 3219 3926, *Fax:* +55 13 3216 1105, *Email:* atlasmarine@uol.com.br
Agencia Maritima Atlantico Sul Ltda - AMAS, Rua Quinzw de Novembro 65, 5 andar, CJ 52, CEP 11010-150 Santos, Brazil, *Tel:* +55 13 3219 8996, *Fax:* +55 13 3219 4540, *Email:* amas@amassantos.com.br, *Website:* www.amassantos.com.br
Atlas Maritime Ltda, Rua XV de Novembro 152, CEP 11010-151 Santos, Brazil, *Tel:* +55 13 3219 9705, *Fax:* +55 13 3219 2486, *Email:* atlas_santos@atlasmaritime.com.br, *Website:* www.atlasmaritime.com.br
Beacon & South Atlantic Agenciamentos Ltda, 55 6th Floor, Rua do Comercio, Santos, Brazil, *Tel:* +55 13 3219 4455, *Fax:* +55 13 3219 1100, *Email:* directoria@beaconsouth.com.br
CMA-CGM S.A., CMA CGM do Brasil Agencia Maritima, Praca da Republica 65, Terreo - Centro, 11013-010 Santos SP, Brazil, *Tel:* +55 13 3226 7059, *Fax:* +55 13 3226 7060, *Email:* ssz.genmbox@cma-cgm.com, *Website:* www.cma-cgm.com
Compass Containers e Shipping Services Ltda, Avenida Marg Dir da Via Anchieta 1050, 11090-000 Santos, Brazil, *Tel:* +55 13 3230 8595, *Fax:* +55 13 3230 8873, *Email:* compass@compass.com.br, *Website:* www.compass.com.br
Cone Sul Agencia de Navegacao Ltda, 34 Rua Martim Afonso Street, 1st Floor, 11010-060 Santos SP, Brazil, *Tel:* +55 13 3224 7444, *Fax:* +55 13 3222 2805, *Email:* conesul@conesulagencia.com.br, *Website:* www.conesulagencia.com.br
Conquest Logistica e Consultoria Aduaneria Ltda, Rua Bras Cubas, No.9 -5o Andar, salas 11A a 14, 11013-161 Santos, Brazil, *Tel:* +55 13 3221 6959, *Fax:* +55 13 3235 5100, *Email:* comercial@conquestlogistica.com.br, *Website:* www.conquestlogistica.com.br
Corymar Agencia Maritima Ltd, Rua Braz Cubas 37, Conj. 86, 11013-161 Santos SP, Brazil, *Tel:* +55 13 3222 9334, *Fax:* +55 13 3235 1063, *Email:* willssz@williams.com.br, *Website:* www.williams.com.br
Deep Sea Shipping Agency, Ruia Riachuelo, 82 cj. 21, Centro, 11.010-020 Santos, Brazil, *Tel:* +55 13 3219 1074, *Fax:* +55 13 3219 3607, *Email:* deepsea@deepsea-agency.com
Fertimport S.A., Rua Frei Gaspar 22, 8th Floor, P O Box 316, 11010-090 Santos, Brazil, *Tel:* +55 13 3201 9000, *Fax:* +55 13 3201 9130, *Email:* commercial.fertimport@bunge.com, *Website:* www.fertimport.com.br

Agencia de Vapores Grieg S.A., Rua Augusto Severo 7, andar 4, 11010-919 Santos SP, Brazil, *Tel:* +55 13 3219 7373, *Fax:* +55 13 3219 7944, *Email:* griegsts@grieg.com.br, *Website:* www.grieg.com.br

Inchcape Shipping Services (ISS), Praca Barao de Rio Branco 14, 2 Andar, Sala 22, Centro, 10010-921 Santos SP, Brazil, *Tel:* +55 13 3219 8463, *Fax:* +55 13 3219 8463, *Email:* isssantos@iss-shipping.com, *Website:* www.iss-shipping.com

LBH Brasil, Rua Paulo Bueno Wolf 1 - Conj 83, Centro Empresarial Costa Verde, 11030-381 Santos SP, Brazil, *Tel:* +55 13 2101 8655, *Fax:* +55 13 2101 8607, *Email:* brazsts@lbhbrasil.com.br, *Website:* www.brazshipping.com.br

Mediterranean Shipping Company, MSC do Brasil Ltda, Av. Senador Feijo 14 - 3rd Floor, Centro, 11015-500 Santos SP, Brazil, *Tel:* +55 13 3211 9500, *Fax:* +55 13 3211 9527, *Email:* distribution@mscbr.com.br, *Website:* www.mscgva.ch

Mercotrade Agencia Maritima Ltda, Avenida Senador Geijo 14, 7 andar, 11015-500 Santos, Brazil, *Tel:* +55 13 2102 6644, *Fax:* +55 13 3219 7997, *Email:* mercotrade@mercotrade.com.br, *Website:* www.mercotrade.com.br

A.P. Moller-Maersk Group, Maersk Brasil Ltda, Pca Rui Barbosa 26/27, 11010-130 Santos SP, Brazil, *Tel:* +55 13 3211 7800, *Fax:* +55 13 3211 7801, *Email:* sszopsgen@maersk.com, *Website:* www.maerskline.com

Norsul Barwil Agencies Maritimas Ltd, Barwil Brazil Ltd, Rua XV de Novembro 124, CEP 11015-500 Santos, Brazil, *Tel:* +55 13 3219 1822, *Fax:* +55 13 3219 5291, *Email:* barwil.santos@barwil.com, *Website:* www.barwilunitor.com

Oceanus Agencia Maritima S.A., R. Cidade de Toledo 13, 11010-010 Santos SP, Brazil, *Tel:* +55 13 3202 2000, *Fax:* +55 13 3219 1194, *Email:* agency.ssz@oceanus.com.br, *Website:* www.oceanus.com.br

Rocha Top Terminais e Operadores Portuarios Ltda, Praca Antonio Teles No 15, 1st Floor, 11013-020 Santos, Brazil, *Tel:* +55 13 3226 9500, *Fax:* +55 13 3226 9509, *Email:* dbirkett@rochatop.co.br, *Website:* www.rochatop.co.br

Sudamericana Agencia Maritima do Brasil Ltd, Libra Ltd, Rua dras Cudas 37, Piso 5, 11013-161 Santos, Brazil, *Tel:* +55 13 3213 9600, *Fax:* +55 13 3216 9688, *Email:* aclaudino@libra.com.br, *Website:* www.libra.com.br

Sulnorte Servicos Maritimos Ltda, SLS 1304 & 1308, Avenida Venezuela 3, 13 Andar, 21081-311 Rio de Janeiro, Brazil, *Tel:* +55 21 2104 8500, *Fax:* +55 21 2263 4373, *Email:* sulnorte@sulnorte.com.br, *Website:* www.sulnorte.com.br

Transatlantic Carriers (Agenciamentos) Ltda, P O Box 730, CEP 11010-921 Santos, Brazil, *Tel:* +55 13 3219 7171, *Fax:* +55 13 3219 6800, *Email:* julio@transcar-sts.com.br

Tropical Agencia Maritima Ltd, Pca da Republica 22, Andar 1, Centro, CEP 11013-010 Santos, Brazil, *Tel:* +55 13 3222 8840, *Fax:* +55 13 3234 7141, *Email:* tropical@tropmar.com.br, *Website:* www.tropmar.com.br

Unimar Agenciamentos Maritimos Ltda, Praca Correa de Melo 09 Centro, CEP11013-220 Santos, Brazil, *Tel:* +55 13 3235 7890, *Fax:* +55 13 3234 8030, *Email:* unimar-santos@unimar-agency.com.br, *Website:* www.unimar-agency.com.br

V Morel S.A., Rua Frei Gaspar 22, 10 Andar, cj 101, 11010-090 Santos, Brazil, *Tel:* +55 13 3213 5222, *Fax:* +55 13 3213 5225, *Email:* vmorel@vmorel.com.br, *Website:* www.vmorel.com.br

Wilson Sons Agencia Maritima Ltda, Rua Tuiuti 58, 1st & 2nd Floors, 11010-220 Santos SP, Brazil, *Tel:* +55 13 3211 2300, *Fax:* +55 13 3219 5250, *Email:* agest@wilsonsons.com.br, *Website:* www.wilsonsons.com.br

Stevedoring Companies: Bussola, Santos, Brazil, *Tel:* +55 13 3232 4122, *Fax:* +55 13 3233 9035

Eurobras, General Camara 141, 3rd Floor, 11010-906 Santos, Brazil, *Tel:* +55 13 3222 4545, *Fax:* +55 13 3202 8290, *Email:* marketing@rodrimar.com.br, *Website:* www.rodrimar.com.br

Oceanus Agencia Maritima S.A., R. Cidade de Toledo 13, 11010-010 Santos SP, Brazil, *Tel:* +55 13 3202 2000, *Fax:* +55 13 3219 1194, *Email:* agency.ssz@oceanus.com.br, *Website:* www.oceanus.com.br

Tropical Agencia Maritima Ltd, Pca da Republica 22, Andar 1, Centro, CEP 11013-010 Santos, Brazil, *Tel:* +55 13 3222 8840, *Fax:* +55 13 3234 7141, *Email:* tropical@tropmar.com.br, *Website:* www.tropmar.com.br

V. Morel, Rua Frei Gaspar 22, 10 andar - cj. 101, 11010-090 Santos, Brazil, *Tel:* +55 13 3213 5222, *Fax:* +55 13 3213 5225, *Email:* vmorel@vmorel.com.br, *Website:* www.vmorel.com.br

Wilson Sons Agencia Maritima Ltda, Rua Tuiuti 58, 1st & 2nd Floors, 11010-220 Santos SP, Brazil, *Tel:* +55 13 3211 2300, *Fax:* +55 13 3219 5250, *Email:* agest@wilsonsons.com.br, *Website:* www.wilsonsons.com.br

Surveyors: Bureau Veritas, Av. Ana Costa No.151, Conjuto No.52, Villa Mathias, 11060-001 Santos SP, Brazil, *Tel:* +55 13 3228 5200, *Fax:* +55 13 3233 1905, *Email:* sidney.santos@br.bureauveritas.com, *Website:* www.bureauveritas.com

Det Norske Veritas A/S, Av. Conselheiro Nebias 793 Conj. 53, Boqueirao, 11045-003 Santos SP, Brazil, *Tel:* +55 13 3288 2729, *Fax:* +55 13 3288 3739, *Email:* san@dnv.com, *Website:* www.dnv.com

Germanischer Lloyd, Avenida Ana Costa 484 Conj. 713, SP 11060-002 Santos SP, Brazil, *Tel:* +55 13 3288 1608, *Fax:* +55 13 3288 1608, *Email:* gl-santos@gl-group.com, *Website:* www.gl-group.com

Nippon Kaiji Kyokai, Rua Rio Grande do Norte 99 - Apt.21, 11065-460 Santos SP, Brazil, *Tel:* +55 13 3251 8716, *Fax:* +55 13 3225 2251, *Email:* mcsb@uol.com.br, *Website:* www.classnk.or.jp

Registro Italiano Navale (RINA), Rua Goias 28, Bairro Boqueira, Santos, Brazil, *Tel:* +55 13 3223 2033, *Fax:* +55 13 3221 4234, *Email:* consultsafeport@terra.com.br, *Website:* www.rina.org

Medical Facilities: Several local hospitals available

Airport: Congonhas Airport, 65 km

Railway: The railways of Ferrovias Brasil S.A. and Mrs Logistica connect Santos to Sao Paulo

Development: Cereal Sul is building a new grain terminal with a storage cap of approx 36 000 t to handle various solid bulk cargoes especially soy; scheduled to be open mid 2007

Lloyd's Agent: Inspect Santos Consultoria e Peritagens Ltda, Av. Conselheiro Nebias, 726 - sala 114, Boqueirao, 11045-002 Santos SP, Brazil, *Tel:* +55 13 3234 5246, *Fax:* +55 13 3235 2250, *Email:* inspect@inspect.com.br

SAO FRANCISCO DO SUL

Lat 26° 14' S; Long 48° 38' W.

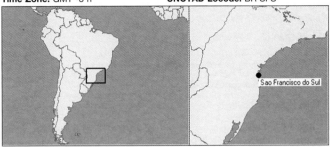

Admiralty Chart: 555	**Admiralty Pilot:** 5
Time Zone: GMT -3 h	**UNCTAD Locode:** BR SFS

Principal Facilities:

	Y	G	C		B		T	A

Tramp Oil & Marine

Wells House, 15-17 Elmfield Road, Bromley,
Kent BR1 1LT, United Kingdom
Phone: +44 20 8315 7777   **Fax:** +44 20 8315 7788
General email: enquiries@tramp-oil.com

See listings for all global offices: **www.tramp-oil.com**

Authority: Administracao do Porto de Sao Francisco do Sul, Rua Engenheiro Leite Ribeiro 782, P O Box 71-Centro, 89240-000 Sao Francisco do Sul SC, Brazil, *Tel:* +55 47 3471 1200, *Fax:* +55 47 3471 1211, *Email:* porto@apsfs.sc.gov.br, *Website:* www.apsfs.sc.gov.br

Officials: President: Paulo Cesar Cortes Corsi, *Email:* paulocorsi@apsfs.sc.gov.br. Commercial Director: Joao Carlos Goncalves, *Email:* joaocarlos@apsfs.sc.gov.br.

Port Security: ISPS compliant

Approach: The access channel is 9.3 km long, 150 m wide with a depth of 10 m. The Evolution Basin has a length of 525 m, width of 400 m and a depth of 10 m. Night navigation is only allowed for vessels up to 8.5 m draft

Anchorage: There are four designated anchorage areas. Between 'Parcel da Torre' and 'Lage Grande de Baixo' for vessels up to 9 m draft. 900 m NE from 'Lage Grande de Baixo' for vessels over 9 m draft. Between 'Pontal Tricheira' and buoy 'Coroa dos Pampas' for vessels carrying dangerous cargoes or quarantined and between 'Laje do Abrev de Dentro' and 'Lage do Sueco' for small vessels

Pilotage: Compulsory. Pilots board in pos 26° 14' 17" S; 48° 41' 33" W, approx 5.6 km from the Ilha Paz. ETA must be sent 24 h ahead and can be corrected at 12 h. Pilots can be called on VHF Channel 16 or at Travessa Pratico Severino N de Oliveira 18, *Tel:* +55 47 444 0002 & +55 47 444 0278

Radio Frequency: Agents can be contacted via Paranagua or Santos Radio or on VHF channel 16

Weather: Visibility generally fair all year round

Tides: Mean tide level 0.84 m

Traffic: 2007, 8 386 004 t of cargo handled

Maximum Vessel Dimensions: Max draft 12 m

Principal Imports and Exports: Imports: General cargo, Soya beans. Exports: Chickens, Paper, Soya bean products, Textiles, Timber.

Working Hours: Regular hours 0700-1100, 1300-1700. Overtime 1700-1900, 1900-2300, 0001-0400

Accommodation:

Name	Length (m)	Depth (m)	Remarks
Sao Francisco			
Berth 101	275	11	Grain & containers
Berth 102	175	10	Container cargo
Berth 103	150	9	General cargo
Berth 201	150	8	
Berth 301	290	12	See [1] below

[1]*Berth 301:* Operated by Terminal Santa Catarina S.A. (TESC), Engineer Avenue Leite Ribeiro 99, Centro, 89204-000 Sao Francisco do Sul SC, *Tel:* +55 47 3471-2121, *Fax:* +55 47 3471-2141, *Email:* tesc@terminalsc.com.br, *Website:* www.terminalsc.com.br
Containers & general cargo

Storage: Three warehouses for general cargo, two of 4000 m2 each and one of 1213 m2. Five vegetable oil silo's, storage cap of 9156 m3. Open storage of 150 000 m2 for containers

Key to Principal Facilities:—			
A=Airport	**C**=Containers	**G**=General Cargo	**P**=Petroleum	**R**=Ro/Ro	**Y**=Dry Bulk
B=Bunkers	**D**=Dry Dock	**L**=Cruise	**Q**=Other Liquid Bulk	**T**=Towage (where available from port)

Location	Grain (t)
Sao Francisco do Sul	115000

Mechanical Handling Equipment:

Location	Type	Capacity (t)	Qty
Sao Francisco do Sul	Mult-purp. Cranes	7	2
Sao Francisco do Sul	Mobile Cranes	40	2
Sao Francisco do Sul	Forklifts	7	30

Bunkering: Fuel oil, diesel and gasoline are supplied by trucks
Tramp Oil & Marine, World Fuel Services Corporation, 13th Floor, Portland House, Bressenden Place, London SW1E 5BH, United Kingdom, *Tel:* +44 20 7808 5000, *Fax:* +44 20 7808 5088, *Email:* pturner@wfscorp.com, *Website:* www.wfscorp.com – *Grades:* all grades – *Delivery Mode:* barge, pipeline, truck

Towage: Four tugs of 250, 545, 1010 and 1680 hp

Repair & Maintenance: Minor repairs are made in small local workshops
Pereira Correa e Cia Ltda, Sao Francisco do Sul, Brazil, *Tel:* +55 47 3444 0014
Santos Reparos Navais e Containers Ltda, Sao Francisco do Sul, Brazil, *Tel:* +55 47 3444 0671
Tavares Companhia de Torneados, Sao Francisco do Sul, Brazil, *Tel:* +55 47 3444 0500

Ship Chandlers: Exportadora Sao Francisco Ltda, Rua Marcilio Dias 40, Sala 01, 89240-000 Sao Francisco do Sul, Brazil, *Tel:* +55 47 3444 2051, *Fax:* +55 47 3444 2420, *Email:* exportadora@exportadora-sf.com.br, *Website:* www.exportadora-sf.com.br

Shipping Agents: CMA-CGM S.A., CMA CGM do Brasil Agencia Maritima, Travessa Major Lucio Caldeira 54, Centro, 89240-000 Sao Francisco do Sul SC, Brazil, *Tel:* +55 47 3442 1393, *Fax:* +55 47 3442 2485, *Email:* sfd.apedroni@cma-cgm.com, *Website:* www.cma-cgm.com
Empresa Maritima e Comercial Ltda, Rua Hercilio Luz 79, Centro, Edif Torre Szul, Sao Francisco do Sul, Brazil, *Tel:* +55 47 3444 2730, *Fax:* +55 47 3444 2085, *Email:* e.rocha@douat.com.br
Fertimport S.A., Rodovia Olivio Nobrega 6500, Sao Francisco do Sul, Brazil, *Tel:* +55 47 3444 3868, *Fax:* +55 47 3444 4668, *Email:* sfs.fertimport@bunge.com.br
Oceanus Agencia Maritima S.A., Rua Marcilio Dias 40 - Room 8, 89240-000 Sao Francisco do Sul SC, Brazil, *Tel:* +55 47 3442 3563, *Fax:* +55 47 3442 1333, *Email:* agency.sfs@oceanus.com.br, *Website:* www.oceanus.com.br
Agencia Maritima Orion Ltda, Rua Almirante Guilhem 02, Room 110, Centro, 89240-000 Sao Francisco do Sul, Brazil, *Tel:* +55 47 3444 2156, *Fax:* +55 47 3444 2356, *Email:* orion@sfs.amorion.com.br, *Website:* www.amorion.com.br
Rocha Top Terminais e Operatores Portuarios Ltda, Rua Babitonga 71, CEP 89240-000 Sao Francisco do Sul, Brazil, *Tel:* +55 47 3444 2469, *Fax:* +55 47 3444 2260, *Email:* arsampario@rochatop.com.br
Seatrade Agencia Maritima Ltda, Joaquim Santiago 157 centro, CEP89240-000 Sao Francisco do Sul, Brazil, *Tel:* +55 47 3444 2037, *Fax:* +55 47 3444 2436, *Email:* seatrade@seatrade.com.br, *Website:* www.seatrade.com.br
Seven Stars Containers (Afretamento) Ltd, Rua Almirante Guilhem 02, Room 4, Sao Francisco do Sul, Brazil, *Tel:* +55 47 3444 2324, *Fax:* +55 47 3444 2314, *Email:* paulo@sfs.sevenstars.com.br
Supermar S.A., Rua Marcilio Dias 40 Suite 03, CEP89240-000 Sao Francisco do Sul, Brazil, *Tel:* +55 47 3444 6681, *Fax:* +55 47 3444 6684, *Email:* sfs@supermar.com.br, *Website:* www.supermar.com.br
Unimar Agenciamentos Maritimos Ltda, Praca de Bandeira 17, Centro, CEP89240-000 Sao Francisco do Sul, Brazil, *Tel:* +55 47 3343 2458, *Fax:* +55 47 3343 0866, *Email:* unimar-saofrancisco@unimar-agency.com.br
Wilson Sons Agencia Maritima Ltda, Praca Getulio Vargas 70 - Centro, 89240-000 Sao Francisco do Sul SC, Brazil, *Tel:* +55 47 3471 2460, *Fax:* +55 47 3471 2402, *Email:* agesf@wilsonsons.com.br, *Website:* www.wilsonsons.com.br

Medical Facilities: Local hospital or medical services in Joinville, 45 km

Airport: Joinville Airport, 62 km

Lloyd's Agent: Inspect Santos Consultoria e Peritagens Ltda, Av. Conselheiro Nebias, 726 - sala 114, Boqueirao, 11045-002 Santos SP, Brazil, *Tel:* +55 13 3234 5246, *Fax:* +55 13 3235 2250, *Email:* inspect@inspect.com.br

SAO LUIS

alternate name, see Itaqui

SAO SEBASTIAO

Lat 23° 48' S; Long 45° 24' W.

Admiralty Chart: 3970	**Admiralty Pilot:** 5
Time Zone: GMT -3 h	**UNCTAD Locode:** BR SSO

Principal Facilities:

P		Y	G			B		T	

Authority: Companhia Docas de Sao Sebastiao, Av. Dr. Altino Arantes 410, 11600-000 Sao Sebastiao SP, Brazil, *Tel:* +55 12 3892 1899, *Fax:* +55 12 3892 1599, *Email:* rogerio4@ig.com.br, *Website:* www.dersa.sp.gov.br/porto

Officials: Manager: Ernesto F Cardoso.

Port Security: ISPS compliant

Documentation: Crew list (10 copies) and two copies each of deck and engine, cabin stores and personal effects

Approach: The access channel through the N bar is marked by buoys and has a width of 550 m, commencing in the vicinity of Ponta das Canas, ending up within the manoeuvring basin. The access channel through the S bar is also marked by buoys with a width of 250 m, commencing in the vicinity of Ponta da Sela, ending up within the manoeuvring basin. The depth of the access channels to the N and S bars is 25 m. Vessels drawing over 10.5 m should avoid entering the N bar due to the varying levels of the bottom. In the manoeuvring basin vessels up to 300 000 dwt can easily manoeuvre

Anchorage: Within port boundaries designated by pilots. Tankers anchor in depths of 25-35 m, good holding ground

Pilotage: Compulsory in the channel between Ponta da Sela and Ponta das Canas, except for vessels of Brazilian flag with less than 60 000 dwt. Inside the port area pilotage is compulsory for shifting vessels between anchorage to any berth or for leaving the berth, involving vessels of over 200 gt. Request for pilot should be made 24 h in advance. Should the vessel be destined for the Petrobras terminal, ETA must be confirmed 3 h ahead of time

Radio Frequency: VHF Channel 16

Weather: Winter squalls, strong winds and currents running from N to S. During changes in season sudden winds of 30 knots are known to arise from the SW causing currents of 5 knots. During these winds oil operations cease

Tides: Range of tide 1.2 m

Traffic: 2006, 47 686 000 t of cargo handled

Principal Imports and Exports: Imports: Containers, Crude oil, Methanol, Soda ash, Sodium sulphate, Wheat. Exports: Containers, General cargo, Palletized asbestos, Refined products, Steel products.

Working Hours: 0700-1300, 1300-1900, 1900-0100, 0100-0700

Accommodation:

Name	Length (m)	Depth (m)	Remarks
Sao Sebastiao			See [1] below
Berth 101	150	8.2	See [2] below
Berth 201	51	7.2	

Name	Length (m)	Depth (m)	Remarks
Berth 202	75	6.2	
Berth 203	86	4.2	

[1]*Sao Sebastiao:* Tanker facilities: Operated by Petrobras, Terminal Maritimo Almirante Barroso (TEBAR), Ave Guarda-Mor Lobo Viana 1111, Sao Sebastiao, Tel: +55 12 3892 1510, Fax: +55 12 3892 2558. Consists of a pier 1690 m long, branching out into two piers, forming the letter 'T'. The North Pier is 395 m long, providing berths for two vessels from 65 000 to 150 000 dwt, the inside berth (PP-4) in a depth of 13.7 m and outside berth (PP-3) in a depth of 19 m. The South Pier is 510 m long, providing berths for two vessels from 155 000 to 300 000 dwt, the inside berth (PP-2) in a depth of 19 m and the outside berth (PP-1) in a depth of 26 m

[2]*Berth 101:* Commercial quay. General cargo, ro/ro & bulk facilities available

Storage: There are three warehouses with a total area of 2531 m2 and an external warehouse of 16 000 m2 which is 800 m away from the docks

Mechanical Handling Equipment:

Location	Type	Capacity (t)	Qty
Sao Sebastiao	Mobile Cranes	25	4
Sao Sebastiao	Forklifts		10

Cargo Worked: Loading steel rebars 6000 t/day, bulk soda ash and sodium sulphate 8000 t/day, asbestos on pallets 1600 t/day

Bunkering: Tramp Oil & Marine, World Fuel Services Corporation, 13th Floor, Portland House, Bressenden Place, London SW1E 5BH, United Kingdom, *Tel:* +44 20 7808 5000, *Fax:* +44 20 7808 5088, *Email:* pturner@wfscorp.com, *Website:* www.wfscorp.com – *Grades:* all grades – *Misc:* fresh water available – *Delivery Mode:* barge, pipeline, truck

Waste Reception Facilities: Tebar Terminal has reasonable facilities for receipt of liquids such as dirty ballast, sludge, tank washing etc. Applications to be made 48 h in advance to reserve shore tank space. Cap of main tank is 1800 m3

Towage: Three tugs available. There are also two privately owned tugs based at the dry cargo dock

Ship Chandlers: Mansueto Pierotti & Filhos Ltda, R. Antonio Goulart Marmo No. 58, 11600-000 Sao Sebastiao, Brazil, *Tel:* +55 13 3213 4646, *Fax:* +55 13 3213 4647, *Email:* geraldo@mansuetopierotti.com.br, *Website:* www.mansuetopierotti.com.br
Sea Star Ship Suppliers Ltd, Travessa Dona Adelina No. 35 Paqueta, 11013-130 Santos, Brazil, *Tel:* +55 13 3232 5757, *Fax:* +55 13 3233 3211, *Email:* seastartrans@uol.com.br, *Website:* www.seastarsantos.com.br

Shipping Agents: Cone Sul Agencia de Navegacao Ltda, 34 Rua Martim Afonso Street, 1st Floor, 11010-060 Santos SP, Brazil, *Tel:* +55 13 3224 7444, *Fax:* +55 13 3222 2805, *Email:* conesul@conesulagencia.com.br, *Website:* www.conesulagencia.com.br
Deep Sea Shipping Agency, Rua Duque de Caxias 188, Sala 15 - 2 Piso, Centro, 11600-000 Sao Sebastiao, Brazil, *Tel:* +55 12 3893 2247, *Fax:* +55 12 3892 3760, *Email:* mail@deepsea-agency.com, *Website:* www.deepsea-agency.com
D.A. McNeill Agencia Maritima Ltda, Rua Sebastiao Silvestre Neves NR, 153 Sao Sebastiao, P O Box 186, 11600-000 Sao Sebastiao, Brazil, *Tel:* +55 12 3892 1558, *Fax:* +55 12 3892 1788, *Email:* damcneil@uol.com.br
Pronave-Agentes de Comercio Exterior Ltda., Rua Vitorino Goncalves dos Santos 168 - Sala 04, 11600-000 Sao Sebastiao, Brazil, *Tel:* +55 12 3892 1499, *Fax:* +55 12 3892 2431, *Email:* pronave@pronave.com.br, *Website:* www.pronave.com.br
Wilson Sons Agencia Maritima Ltda, Rua Auta Pinder 114 - Centro, 11600-000 Sao Sebastiao SP, Brazil, *Tel:* +55 12 3891 2200, *Fax:* +55 12 3891 2201, *Email:* agess@wilsonsons.com.br, *Website:* www.wilsonsons.com.br

Stevedoring Companies: H.F. Comercial e Maritima Ltda., Sao Sebastiao, Brazil, *Tel:* +55 12 3892 2067, *Fax:* +55 12 3892 2713
D.A. McNeill Agencia Maritima Ltda, Rua Sebastiao Silvestre Neves NR, 153 Sao Sebastiao, P O Box 186, 11600-000 Sao Sebastiao, Brazil, *Tel:* +55 12 3892 1558, *Fax:* +55 12 3892 1788, *Email:* damcneil@uol.com.br
Pronave-Agentes de Comercio Exterior Ltda., Rua Vitorino Goncalves dos Santos 168 - Sala 04, 11600-000 Sao Sebastiao, Brazil, *Tel:* +55 12 3892 1499, *Fax:* +55 12 3892 2431, *Email:* pronave@pronave.com.br, *Website:* www.pronave.com.br
Wilport Operadores Portuarios S/A, Sao Sebastiao, Brazil, *Tel:* +55 12 3892 1688, *Fax:* +55 12 3892 1427

Medical Facilities: Hospital and private doctors available. Contact agents in order to obtain medical attendance

Development: The port is to start handling containers as an overflow port for nearby Santos

Lloyd's Agent: Inspect Santos Consultoria e Peritagens Ltda, Av. Conselheiro Nebias, 726 - sala 114, Boqueirao, 11045-002 Santos SP, Brazil, *Tel:* +55 13 3234 5246, *Fax:* +55 13 3235 2250, *Email:* inspect@inspect.com.br

SAO TORQUATO TERMINAL

harbour area, see under Vitoria

SEPETIBA

Lat 22° 56' S; Long 43° 50' W.

Admiralty Chart: 431		**Admiralty Pilot:** 5	
Time Zone: GMT -3 h		**UNCTAD Locode:** BR SPB	

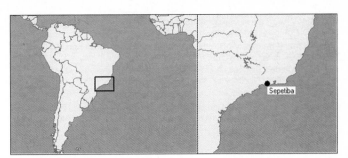

Principal Facilities:

Y	G	C	R		B		T	A

Tramp Oil & Marine

Wells House, 15-17 Elmfield Road, Bromley, Kent BR1 1LT, United Kingdom
Phone: +44 20 8315 7777　　**Fax:** +44 20 8315 7788
General email: enquiries@tramp-oil.com

See listings for all global offices: **www.tramp-oil.com**

Authority: Companhia Docas do Rio de Janeiro, Gerencia do Porto de Sepetiba, Estrada da Ilha da Madeira - Km 18, 23854-410 Itaguai RJ, Brazil, *Tel:* +55 21 2688 1402, *Fax:* +55 21 2688 1287

Port Security: ISPS compliant

Approach: The approach channel is 14 km long and 23 m deep, the entrance being marked by two light buoys, besides those which are stationed along the channel and manoeuvring basin. The channel's width varies from 280 m up to Buoy No.7, 580 m up to Buoy No.9, decreasing to 330 m on the final approach to the manoeuvring basin which is 1.8 nautical miles long with an average width of 0.5 nautical miles. Advice of ETA is required six days, 48 and 24 h and when within VHF range
Vessels bound to Ilha da Madeira follow the access channel which is 20 m wide and dredged to 18 m from the bay entrance to the manoeuvring basin, 540 m long by 400 m wide in a depth of 11 m

Anchorage: Vessels waiting for Ilha da Madeira may anchor at designated anchorages in depths of 10-12 m

Pilotage: Compulsory. Pilot boards vessel in pos 23° 08' 39" S, 44° 04' 36" W. The lower platform of the gangway must be 5 m above the water level, especially for vessels of 40 000 dwt and over

Radio Frequency: Vessels are requested to contact Sepetiba Marine Operations directly. VHF Channel 16 (calling) and 11, 12 and 13 (working)

Tides: Range of tide 1.8 m

Accommodation:

Name	Length (m)	Depth (m)	Remarks
Ilha da Madeira			
Coal Terminal	540	12–15	See [1] below
Container Terminal	810	14.5	See [2] below
Ilha Guaiba			
Iron Ore Terminal	470	19–24	See [3] below

[1]*Coal Terminal:* Operated by Companhia Siderurgica Nacional (CSN)
A mooring pier in pos 22° 56' S; 43° 5' W. This pier permits the berthing of either one 90 000 dwt on one side and one 65 000 dwt on the other, or two 45 000 dwt at the north side. Coal is unloaded by means of gantry equipment with clam shell scoops directly to the conveyor belts which will take it over the access bridge to the storage yard, or directly to the wagon-loading silo. For this purpose the port unit is equipped with two unloaders with 1500 t/h cap each; and two for 800 t/h. The alumina suction system can handle 300 t/h. Transport of these products is performed by two conveyor belts with cap for up to 4500 t/h, total belt length is 14 km. The train loading silo has two 680 m3 units each capable of handling 2000 t/h. 2 500 000 m2 of yard space allowing for storage of 5 050 000 t of coal

[2]*Container Terminal:* Three berths managed by Sepetiba Tecon S.A., *Tel:* +55 21 2688 9232, Fax: +55 21 2688 9235, Email: comercial@sepetibatecon.com.br, Website: www.sepetibatecon.com.br
Total area of 400 000 m2. Terminal includes two post-panamax cranes, two mobile harbour cranes and seven reach stackers

[3]*Iron Ore Terminal:* An iron ore exporting terminal operated by Mineracoes Brasileiras Reunidas S.A.
Can accommodate vessels up to 300 000 dwt. Loading equipment available with a cap of 7000 t/h. Height of the pier surface from water level is 7.22 m at LT and 5 m at HT. Terminal has yard with 1 700 000 t cap

Bunkering: Tramp Oil & Marine, World Fuel Services Corporation, 13th Floor, Portland House, Bressenden Place, London SW1E 5BH, United Kingdom, *Tel:* +44 20 7808 5000, *Fax:* +44 20 7808 5088, *Email:* pturner@wfscorp.com, *Website:* www.wfscorp.com – *Grades:* all grades – *Delivery Mode:* barge, pipeline, truck

Towage: Three tugs available of 4000 hp. Berthing and unberthing must always be assisted by two towboats, both with a bollard pull force corresponding to the vessel proceeding to the ore pier. The towboats commence accompanying the vessel at

Key to Principal Facilities:—					
A=Airport	**C**=Containers	**G**=General Cargo	**P**=Petroleum	**R**=Ro/Ro	**Y**=Dry Bulk
B=Bunkers	**D**=Dry Dock	**L**=Cruise	**Q**=Other Liquid Bulk	**T**=Towage (where available from port)	

Buoy No's 7 and 8 (for vessels drawing over 13.71 m). Berthing will also be assisted by two launches for handling the mooring lines

Repair & Maintenance: Minor repairs only. More serious repairs will be attended to by Verolme at Angra dos Reis or at Rio de Janeiro

Medical Facilities: First aid and minor medical treatment available at Mangaratiba, 8 km from Guaiba. All else must be attended to at Rio de Janeiro

Airport: Rio de Janeiro, 95 km

Lloyd's Agent: Inspect Consultoria Ltda (Rio de Janeiro), Avenida Rio Branco 37, Grupo 1902 Centro, 20090-003 Rio de Janeiro RJ, Brazil, *Tel:* +55 21 2263 3330, *Fax:* +55 21 2253 9322, *Email:* inspectconsultoria@br.inter.net, *Website:* www.inspectconsultoria.com.br

SUAPE

Lat 8° 23' S; Long 34° 58' W.

Admiralty Chart: 3978   **Admiralty Pilot:** 5
Time Zone: GMT -3 h   **UNCTAD Locode:** BR SUA

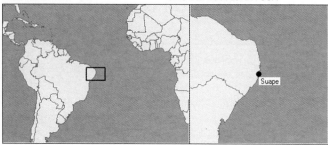

Principal Facilities:

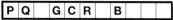

| P | Q | | G | C | R | | B | | | |

Tramp Oil & Marine

Wells House, 15-17 Elmfield Road, Bromley,
Kent BR1 1LT, United Kingdom
Phone: +44 20 8315 7777   **Fax:** +44 20 8315 7788
General email: enquiries@tramp-oil.com

See listings for all global offices: **www.tramp-oil.com**

Authority: Suape Complexo Industrial Portuario, Rodovia PE-60, Km-10, Engenho Massangana, 55590-972 Ipojuca PE, Brazil, *Tel:* +55 81 3527 5000, *Fax:* +55 81 3527 5064, *Email:* suape@suape.pe.gov.br, *Website:* www.suape.pe.gov.br

Officials: Antonio Uchoa.
President: Fernando Bezerra Coelho, *Tel:* +55 81 3527 5000, *Email:* presidencia@suape.pe.gov.br.
Business Manager: Sidnei Aires, *Tel:* +55 81 3527 5000, *Email:* sidnei.aires@suape.pe.gov.br.

Port Security: ISPS compliant

Approach: The access channel has a depth of 16.5 m

Pilotage: Compulsory. Pilot boards in pos 8° 23.03' S; 34° 55.95' W

Radio Frequency: VHF Channel 16

Traffic: 2007, 241 757 TEU's handled

Accommodation:

Name	Length (m)	Depth (m)	Remarks
Outer Port			Formed by an L-shaped breakwater 2950 m long
Liquid Granary Pier No.1	250	14	Two berths for vessels up to 45 000 dwt
Liquid Granary Pier No.2	386	14.5	Two berths for vessels up to 90 000 dwt
Multi-Purpose Quay	343		See [1] below
Inner Port			
Suape Container Terminal	660	15.5	See [2] below
Public Dock	275	15.5	Multi-purpose

[1]*Multi-Purpose Quay:* Two berths for methane vessels up to 135 000 m3. East berth in depth of 15.5 m and West berth in depth of 10 m
[2]*Suape Container Terminal:* Two berths managed by Tecon Suape S.A., Avenida Portuaria s/n, Porto de Suape, 55590-000 Ipojuca PE, Tel: +55 81 3527 5200, Fax: +55 81 3527 5203, Email: comercial@teconsuape.com, Website: www.teconsuape.com
Terminal area of 29 ha with container yard of 13.5 ha and 520 reefer points

Mechanical Handling Equipment:

Location	Type	Qty
Suape Container Terminal	Panamax	2
Suape Container Terminal	Post Panamax	2
Suape Container Terminal	RTG's	4
Suape Container Terminal	Reach Stackers	7

Bunkering: Tramp Oil & Marine, World Fuel Services Corporation, 13th Floor, Portland House, Bressenden Place, London SW1E 5BH, United Kingdom, *Tel:* +44 20 7808 5000, *Fax:* +44 20 7808 5088, *Email:* pturner@wfscorp.com, *Website:* www.wfscorp.com – Grades: all grades – Delivery Mode: barge, pipeline, truck

Surveyors: Sea Survey do Brasil Ltda, Apartment 701, Edificio Renata Dias Boa Viagem, Rua Carlos Pereira Falca 1145, 51021-350 Recife PE, Brazil, *Tel:* +55 81 3328 5507, *Fax:* +55 81 3328 5507, *Email:* seasurve@elogica.com.br Director: Stanislav Zrncic

Development: Tecon Suape to gain an extra berth from the port authority leading to the purchase of at least two more post-panamax ship to shore gantry cranes

Lloyd's Agent: Inspect Consultoria Ltda (Recife), Rua Padre Carapuceiro 412/603, Boa Viagem, 51020-280 Recife PE, Brazil, *Tel:* +55 81 9952 5868, *Email:* inspectrecife@terra.com.br

TERMISA TERMINAL

alternate name, see Salineiro Terminal

TRAMANDAI

Lat 30° 0' S; Long 50° 5' W.

Admiralty Chart: 3969   **Admiralty Pilot:** 5
Time Zone: GMT -3 h   **UNCTAD Locode:** BR TRM

Principal Facilities:

| P | Q | | | | | | | | |

Tramp Oil & Marine

Wells House, 15-17 Elmfield Road, Bromley,
Kent BR1 1LT, United Kingdom
Phone: +44 20 8315 7777   **Fax:** +44 20 8315 7788
General email: enquiries@tramp-oil.com

See listings for all global offices: **www.tramp-oil.com**

Authority: Petroleo Brasileiro S.A., Terminal Maritimo Almirante Soares Dutra (TEDUT), P O Box 19, 95590 Tramandai RS, Brazil, *Tel:* +55 51 3221 2888, *Fax:* +55 51 3261 1342, *Email:* rprazeres@petrobras.com.br

Port Security: ISPS compliant. Port Facility Security Officer, Tel: +55 51 9712 7022 or +55 51 9955 3387 (24 h)

Pre-Arrival Information: Vessels bound for Tramandai should inform their ETA 72 h, 48 h and 24 h prior to arrival to their agents. The communications at Tramandai roads can be carried out by VHF Channel 9 or 11

Anchorage: Three anchorage areas available with holding ground of sand and mud
ALFA: one nautical mile radius from pos 29° 57' 42" S; 50° 04' 24" W for vessels bound for SPM No.1
BRAVO: one nautical mile radius from pos 29° 59' 24" S; 50° 02' 30" W for vessels bound for SPM No.2
CHARLIE: one nautical mile radius from pos 29° 57' 30" S; 50° 01' 54" W for vessels awaiting orders

Pilotage: There are no pilots at Tramandai. The Terminal provides a Mooring Master duly trained whose service is compulsory to assist Master's of ships approaching, mooring, unmooring and carrying out ship operations as Loading Master. Boarding is usually done in the anchorage area. Mooring can only be performed during daylight, although unmooring can be performed at any time, including nighttime

Radio Frequency: VHF Channels 16, 9 or 11

Weather: Winds predominantly from N and NE direction. A strong swell may prevent operations; if wave height exceeds 3.5 m emergency disconnecting of hoses will take place, even at night

Tides: Non-tidal

Maximum Vessel Dimensions: SPM No.1: 200 000 t max displacement, 16 m max draft, 140 m max distance between bow-manifold
SPM No.2: 200 000 t max displacement, 18 m max draft, 180 m max distance between bow-manifold

Principal Imports and Exports: Imports: Condensate, Crude oil, Naphtha. Exports: Gas oil, Gasoline.

Working Hours: Round the clock

Accommodation:

Name	Remarks
Tramandai	Two single point moorings
SPM No.1	See [1] below
SPM No.2	See [2] below

[1]*SPM No.1:* In pos 30° 00' 36" S; 50° 05' 54" W. Vessels up to 200 000 t max displacement, 16 m draft can be accommodated. Import of naphtha and condensate and export of gas oil. The floating hoses string consists of 25 units of 20" double carcass hose

[2]*SPM No.2:* In pos 30° 01' 36" S; 50° 05' 12" W. Vessels up to 200 000 t max displacement, 18 m draft can be accommodated. Import of crude oil and condensate. The outer floating hoses string consists of 29 units of 20" double carcass hose and the inner floating hoses string consists of 25 units of 20" double carcass hose

Bunkering: Tramp Oil & Marine, World Fuel Services Corporation, 13th Floor, Portland House, Bressenden Place, London SW1E 5BH, United Kingdom, *Tel:* +44 20 7808 5000, *Fax:* +44 20 7808 5088, *Email:* pturner@wfscorp.com, *Website:* www.wfscorp.com

Medical Facilities: There are public and private hospitals available for emergencies. For further details the agent should be contacted in advance

Airport: Porto Alegre International Airport, 120 km

Lloyd's Agent: Inspect Santos Consultoria e Peritagens Ltda, Av. Conselheiro Nebias, 726 - sala 114, Boqueirao, 11045-002 Santos SP, Brazil, *Tel:* +55 13 3234 5246, *Fax:* +55 13 3235 2250, *Email:* inspect@inspect.com.br

TROMBETAS

Lat 1° 28' S; Long 56° 23' W.

Admiralty Chart: 2229   **Admiralty Pilot:** 5
Time Zone: GMT -4 h   **UNCTAD Locode:** BR TMT

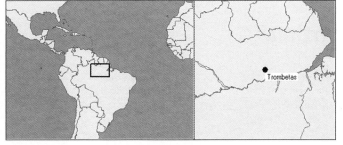

Principal Facilities:

		Y	G				T		

Authority: Mineracao Rio do Norte S.A. (MRN), Porto Trombetas, 68275-000 Oriximina PA, Brazil, *Tel:* +55 93 549 7006, *Fax:* +55 93 549 1482, *Email:* juarezbarbosa@mrn.com.br, *Website:* www.mrn.com.br

Officials: Manager: Juarez Barbosa.

Port Security: ISPS compliant

Approach: Amazon River N Bar: 11.58 m draft at HW, 8.53 m draft at LW. Trombetas River: 11.58 m max draft during the dry season (October-January). The draft may be reduced according to the level of the river. All drafts in fresh water and subject to confirmation by vessel's agent. Up-bound vessels are not permitted to enter the Trombetas River without prior clearance by MRN

Anchorage: Two waiting vessels can be secured to mooring buoys about 2.9 km downstream from the berth. A secondary waiting area is located W of the mouth of the Trombetas River in pos 1° 54' S; 55° 40' W

Pilotage: Compulsory from Macapa (Fazendinha) to Trombetas with two pilots on board who stay on duty during the loading period. Vessels contact AMSANAV Santana on VHF Channel 16, with ETA at least 24 h before arrival

Radio Frequency: The terminal can be contacted on VHF Channel 14

Weather: Short, heavy rain showers are common from January to June. From July to December E and ESE winds predominate followed by NE winds back to SW with persistent showers. Wind speed 10 knots

Traffic: 2000, 231 vessels, 11 158 746 t of bauxite handled

Maximum Vessel Dimensions: Max dwt 60 000 t, max draft 11.58 m, max loa 260 m

Principal Imports and Exports: Exports: Bauxite.

Working Hours: 24 h/day, Sundays and holidays included

Accommodation:

Name	Length (m)	Remarks
Trombetas		See [1] below
Bauxite Loading Pier	100	See [2] below
General Cargo Floating Wharf		350 m downstream from the bulk berth. Operated by MRN

[1]*Trombetas:* Tankers discharge at a floating pier situated about 400 m upstream from the bulk berth
[2]*Bauxite Loading Pier:* Can load ore carriers up to panamax size. Max air draft (the distance from the waterline to the top of the hatches coaming) of 13.5 m at HW. Four concrete dolphins upon metal piling and four mooring buoys. One vessel can be loaded at a time. Max loading rate is 6000 t/h, average rate is 3000 t/h

Cargo Worked: 28 000 t/day for dry and wet bauxite

Towage: Two tugs of 26 t bollard pull available

Repair & Maintenance: Minor repairs undertaken by MRN workshop in emergencies

Medical Facilities: Emergency facilities available at the MRN hospital

Lloyd's Agent: Inspect Consultoria Ltda (Sao Luis), Av Dos Portugueses, 31 Vila Embratel, 65085-580 Sao Luis MA, Brazil, *Tel:* +55 98 3242 4016, *Email:* inspectconsultoria@br.inter.net

TUBARAO

Lat 20° 17' S; Long 40° 15' W.

Admiralty Chart: 521   **Admiralty Pilot:** 5
Time Zone: GMT -3 h   **UNCTAD Locode:** BR TUB

Principal Facilities:

P		Y	G			B		T	A

Tramp Oil & Marine

Wells House, 15-17 Elmfield Road, Bromley, Kent BR1 1LT, United Kingdom
Phone: +44 20 8315 7777   **Fax:** +44 20 8315 7788
General email: enquiries@tramp-oil.com

See listings for all global offices: **www.tramp-oil.com**

Authority: Vale, Praia Mole SC, Brazil, *Tel:* +55 27 3333 5624, *Fax:* +55 27 3333 5293

Port Security: ISPS compliant

Approach: Channel is 3800 m long, width 285 m with max draft of 20 m plus tide

Anchorage: Available between the following positions:
a) 20° 17' 30" S; 40° 13' 26" W
b) 20° 18' 24" S; 40° 13' 19" W
c) 20° 19' 01" S; 40° 14' 01" W
d) 20° 18' 06" S; 40° 14' 13" W

Pilotage: Compulsory. The pilot boards in pos 20° 20' 00" S; 40° 14' 13" W

Radio Frequency: VHF Channels 12 and 16

Weather: NE wind prevails at the port, however SW wind occurs mainly during winter. No ships come alongside when wind is blowing at 60 km/h or more. The max wave height is 1.5 m with NE wind and 2.5 m on the rare occasions the SW blows

Tides: On average the tidal variation is small with two flood tides and two ebb tides occuring daily. The rise of tide is approx 1.4 m

Traffic: 2006, 103 626 000 t of cargo handled

Working Hours: 24 h/day

Accommodation:

Name	Length (m)	Depth (m)	Remarks
Tubarao			
Pier 1 (North Side)	390	16.5	See [1] below
Pier 1 (South Side)	390	15.6	See [2] below
Pier 2	400	24	See [3] below

Key to Principal Facilities:—				
A=Airport	**C**=Containers	**G**=General Cargo	**P**=Petroleum	**R**=Ro/Ro	**Y**=Dry Bulk
B=Bunkers	**D**=Dry Dock	**L**=Cruise	**Q**=Other Liquid Bulk	**T**=Towage (where available from port)

Name	Length (m)	Depth (m)	Remarks
TPD Terminal			
Pier 3	280	16	See [4] below
Pier 4	225	12.5	See [5] below
TGL Terminal			
Pier 5	124.5	12.5	See [6] below

[1]*Pier 1 (North Side):* Loading of iron ore & pig iron for vessels up to 320 m loa and 200 000 dwt. Equipped with one shiploader of 6000 t/h and one shiploader of 8000 t/h. Max arrival draft of 14 m and sailing draft of 15.2 m + tide height at the moment of event

[2]*Pier 1 (South Side):* Loading of iron ore & pig iron for vessels up to 285 m loa and 170 000 dwt. Equipped with one shiploader of 6000 t/h and one shiploader of 8000 t/h. Max arrival draft of 14 m and sailing draft of 15.5 m + tide height at the moment of event

[3]*Pier 2:* For vessels up to 350 m loa and 365 000 dwt. Equipped with two shiploaders of up to 16 000 t/h each. Max arrival draft of 14 m and sailing draft of 20 m + tide height at the moment of event

[4]*Pier 3:* Loading grain and cereals in bulk for vessels up to 280 m loa and 150 000 dwt. Equipped with four shiploaders of up to 3000 t/h each. Max arrival draft of 14 m and sailing draft of 14.7 m + tide height at the moment of event

[5]*Pier 4:* Fertilisers, containers, pallets, general cargo & ro/ro for vessels up to 230 m loa and 50 000 dwt. Max draft of 12 m + tide height at the moment of event. Two mobile cranes with a cap of 64 t, a 600 t/h hopper (for fertilizers & other solid bulk products) coupled to a 1800 t/h conveyor belt and a 350 t/h hopper for truck loading

[6]*Pier 5:* Liquid bulk terminal for vessels up to 181 m loa and 40 000 dwt. Max draft of 11.35 m, operated by Petrobras and C.V.R.D.

Bunkering: Tramp Oil & Marine, World Fuel Services Corporation, 13th Floor, Portland House, Bressenden Place, London SW1E 5BH, United Kingdom, *Tel:* +44 20 7808 5000, *Fax:* +44 20 7808 5088, *Email:* pturner@wfscorp.com, *Website:* www.wfscorp.com – *Grades:* all grades – *Delivery Mode:* barge, pipeline, truck

Towage: The use of tugs on manoeuvrings of vessels which proceed to the port is compulsory

Repair & Maintenance: California Servicos Subaquaticos Ltda, Tubarao, Brazil, *Tel:* +55 27 3229 1921

SIMB-Reparos Navais Ltda, Tubarao, Brazil, *Tel:* +55 27 3226 0899

Medical Facilities: For emergency services the terminal keeps a medical station equipped with an ambulance to take emergency cases to Vitoria

Airport: Vitoria, 25 km

Railway: Vitoria Minas Railroad transports the iron ore from Itabira to Tubarao Port

Lloyd's Agent: Inspect Santos Consultoria e Peritagens Ltda, Av. Conselheiro Nebias, 726 - sala 114, Boqueirao, 11045-002 Santos SP, Brazil, *Tel:* +55 13 3234 5246, *Fax:* +55 13 3235 2250, *Email:* inspect@inspect.com.br

VILA DO CONDE

Lat 1° 33' S; Long 48° 45' W.

Admiralty Chart: 2204   **Admiralty Pilot:** 5
Time Zone: GMT -3 h   **UNCTAD Locode:** BR VLC

Principal Facilities:

	Y	G	C		B		A

Authority: Companhia Docas do Para, Porto de Vila do Conde, Rodovia PA-481, Km 2,3, Vila dos Cabanos, 68447-000 Barcarena PA, Brazil, *Tel:* +55 91 3754 1343, *Fax:* +55 91 3754 1026, *Email:* leite@cdp.com.br, *Website:* www.cdp.com.br

Officials: Port Administrator: Olivio Antonio Pantoja Gomes.

Port Security: ISPS compliant

Documentation: Crew list (6 copies), passenger list (6 copies), ships general info (6 copies), certificate list (3 copies), bonded stores list (2 copies), provision list (2 copies), personal effects list (2 copies), maritime declaration of health (2 copies), crew vaccination list (2 copies), ports of call (2 copies)

Approach: The access channel to the Port of Vila do Conde is the same as for the Port of Belem with draft of 9 to 10.5 m as far as to the front of the Island of Mosqueiro. From there onwards vessels proceed to the Port of Vila do Conde via the Bay of Marajo. The turning basin has an area of 4 km of width and depths of 15 to 20 m. There are no buoys

Anchorage: In pos 01° 32' 00" S; 48° 46' 00" W in depth of 15 to 22 m with bottom of mud and sand

Pilotage: Pilot usually ordered through vessel's Belem Agent, ETA at least 48 h in advance and confirming not less than 24 h prior to arrival. Vessels can apply direct to Pilot Station (on condition that local radio station is operating). Telegraphic address "Praticagem-Salinopolis", and call sign of Salinopolis (or Salinas) Radio Station is PPL. Pilot Station, Fax: +55 91 823 2141. Pilot boards at a point 7 miles North of Salinas Lighthouse (00° 29' 06" S; 46° 23' 01" W); a red motor-launch is used. Launch carries a red flag with a black "P" painted on each side and on cabin roof. If pilot boat not in position on arrival of vessel, position 7 miles North of the light is

a safe anchorage. Masters who do not know area should approach Salinas with caution

Radio Frequency: Radio Station is PPL. Salinopolis Pilot Station on VHF Channel 16, working on Channel 11. Operates 24 hours. Suggested that ship contacts Belem Agent through Barbados Radio and this is also usual way that vessels are contacted by Belem. An alternative to Barbados Radio is United States radio station at Chatham, Virginia

Weather: Prevailing winds: NE'ly

Tides: MHWS: 3.04 m, MLWS: 0.30 m, MHWN: 2.47 m, MLWN: 0.86 m, Max tide (flow tide): 2.36 m, Min tide (ebb tide): 0.69 m

Traffic: 2007, 15 862 752 t of cargo handled, 28 913 TEU's

Principal Imports and Exports: Imports: Alumina, Coke, Pencil pitch. Exports: Aluminium ingots.

Working Hours: Continuous

Accommodation:

Name	Length (m)	Draught (m)	Remarks
Vila do Conde			See [1] below
Left Pier	291	16–20	Two berths for general & solid bulk cargo
Right Pier	127	16–20	Two berths for general & liquid bulk cargo

[1]*Vila do Conde:* Consists of a 550 m long pier, linked to the land by a 450 m long bridge. Equipment includes a pneumatic ship unloader for alumina and coke operating at 500 t/h through two parallel suction systems. The facilities are operated by ALBRAS-Aluminio Brasileiro S.A., exporting aluminium ingots

Container terminal operated by Conteneres de Vila do Conde (CONVICON), Tel: +55 91 3754 1271, Email: convicon@convicon.com.br, Website: www.convicon.com.br, for vessels up to 75 000 dwt. Equipment includes three reach stackers and one 100 t harbour mobile crane

Mechanical Handling Equipment:

Location	Type	Capacity (t)	Qty
Vila do Conde	Mult-purp. Cranes	12	1

Cargo Worked: Alumina 4000 t/day, coke 2500 t/day, aluminium 1500 t/gang/day

Bunkering: Small quantities can be delivered by barges from Belem

Waste Reception Facilities: The agent provides this through private companies

Repair & Maintenance: Small repairs (painting and welding) can be made by repairers near the Port. A larger repair facility can be found in Belem

Medical Facilities: Small local clinic. Several hospitals in Belem

Airport: Val-de-Caes International, 52 km. There is a seaplane landing area in the N part of Canal da Ilha das Oncas

Lloyd's Agent: Inspect Consultoria Ltda (Sao Luis), Av Dos Portugueses, 31 Vila Embratel, 65085-580 Sao Luis MA, Brazil, *Tel:* +55 98 3242 4016, *Email:* inspectconsultoria@br.inter.net

VITORIA

Lat 20° 18' S; Long 40° 20' W.

Admiralty Chart: 521   **Admiralty Pilot:** 5
Time Zone: GMT -3 h   **UNCTAD Locode:** BR VIX

Principal Facilities:

P		Y	G	C	R	L	B		T	A

Authority: Companhia Docas do Espirito Santo, Av. Getulio Vargas 556 - Centro, 29010-040 Vitoria ES, Brazil, *Tel:* +55 27 3132 7314, *Fax:* +55 27 3132 7313, *Email:* falaporto@codesa.gov.br, *Website:* www.portodevitoria.com.br

Officials: Commercial Manager: Fabio Falce, *Email:* ffalce@codesa.gov.br.

Port Security: ISPS compliant

Approach: Access channel is 7500 m long, 75-215 m wide with max depth of 10.5 m

Pilotage: Compulsory. VHF Channel 16

Tides: Average tide of 1.04 m

Traffic: 2004, 6 936 558 t of cargo handled

Maximum Vessel Dimensions: 242 m loa, 32.4 m breadth

Principal Imports and Exports: Imports: Coal, Machinery, Wheat, Wood. Exports: Cocoa products, Coffee, Soya, Steel products, Woodpulp.

Working Hours: General cargo quays 0700-1100, 1300-1700, 1700-1900, 1900-2300, 0000-0400, 0400-0600. Work on Sunday 0700-1100, 1300-1700

Accommodation:

Name	Length (m)	Depth (m)	Remarks
Commercial Dock			Handles mainly general, breakbulk & bagged cargoes
Berth 101	179.7	9.2	Coffee
Berth 102	196.8	9.15	Cellulose & paper
Berth 103	211.4	8.2	Wheat & general cargo
Berth 104	123	7.1	Back-up vessels & tugs
Capuaba Dock			
Berth 201	202	10.67	
Berth 202	185	10.67	12 800 m2 stockyard
Berth 203	178	10.67	See [1] below
Berth 204	190	10.67	See [2] below
Berth 205		9.24	Vessels up to 148 m loa
Atalaia Dock			
Berth 207		9.5	Vessels up to 180 m loa
Paul Dock			
Berth 206	260	9.75	Multi-purpose berth with stockyard of 25 000 m2
Berth 905	160	10.06	See [3] below
Jaburuna Inlet & Saco do Aribiri			
Jarubuna Inlet	850	14.5	Stockyard of 860 000 m2
Saco do Aribiri	1800	13	Stockyard of 800 000 m2
Portuary Vila Velha	250	10.5	
Sao Torquato Terminal			
Berth 902		8.23	See [4] below
Ilha do Principe Terminal			
Berth 906		6.7	Vessels up to 130 m loa

[1]*Berth 203:* Customs warehouse of 8000 m2 and stockyard of 16 000 m2
[2]*Berth 204:* Customs warehouse of 8000 m2 and stockyard of 50 000 m2
[3]*Berth 905:* Pig iron for panamax vessels up to 74 000 t loaded to a max of 52 000 t. Car unloader and ship loader with cap of 900 t/h. The Aroaba Yard, 27 km from Paul Quay, can receive up to 150 000 t of pig iron
[4]*Berth 902:* Liquid fuel terminal for vessels up to 162 m loa. Fuel tanks of 50 000 m3

Storage:

Location	Grain (t)
Berth 201	128000

Mechanical Handling Equipment:

Location	Type	Capacity (t)	Qty
Berth 101	Mult-purp. Cranes	3.2	4
Berth 102	Mult-purp. Cranes	3.2	4
Berth 103	Mult-purp. Cranes	6.3	2
Berth 201	Mult-purp. Cranes	12	1
Berth 201	Mult-purp. Cranes	6	2
Berth 202	Mult-purp. Cranes	12	1
Berth 202	Mult-purp. Cranes	6	2
Berth 203	Mult-purp. Cranes	40	2
Berth 203	Mult-purp. Cranes	12	1
Berth 204	Mult-purp. Cranes	40	2
Jarubuna Inlet	Transtainers	40	20
Saco do Aribiri	Transtainers	40	20

Cargo Worked: Loading rates: Coffee approx 25 to 30 t/h/gang, timber approx 10 t/h/gang, slab steel, pig iron etc an average of 50 t/h/gang

Bunkering: ExxonMobil Marine Fuels, Suite 900, One Alhambra Plaza, Coral Gables, FL 33134, United States of America, *Tel:* +1 305 459 6358, *Fax:* +1 305 459 6412, *Email:* emmf@exxonmobil.com, *Website:* www.exxonmobilmarinefuels.com
Tramp Oil & Marine, World Fuel Services Corporation, 13th Floor, Portland House, Bressenden Place, London SW1E 5BH, United Kingdom, *Tel:* +44 20 7808 5000, *Fax:* +44 20 7808 5088, *Email:* pturner@wfscorp.com, *Website:* www.wfscorp.com – *Grades:* all grades – *Delivery Mode:* barge, pipeline, truck

Towage: There are 13 tugs available between 650 to 3000 hp. Rates on application There are also two cargo pontoons of 300 and 400 t operating between Vitoria and the Tubarao Terminal

Repair & Maintenance: Auremar Servicos Maritimos Ltda, Avenida Nossa Senhora dos Navegantes, Vitoria, Brazil, *Tel:* +55 27 3222 4366
Brashol Mecanica Ltda, Vitoria, Brazil, *Tel:* +55 27 3227 1144
California Servicos Subaquaticos Ltda, Vitoria, Brazil, *Tel:* +55 27 3229 1921
Capixaba Eletro Instrumentacao Naval (CEIN), Vitoria, Brazil, *Tel:* +55 27 3222 1471
Industria Comercio Ltda (Tecnave), Vitoria, Brazil, *Tel:* +55 27 3226 0899
Mariner Servicos Subaquaticos Ltda, Vitoria, Brazil, *Tel:* +55 27 3223 1400

Ship Chandlers: Ocean Bay Catering Solutions Ltd., Rua Rosa Amarela 20, Quadra 18, Bairro Novo Mexico, 29104-020 Vila Velha ES, Brazil, *Tel:* +55 27 9849 1574, *Fax:*

+55 27 3299 8640, *Email:* oceanbay@oceanbay.com.br, *Website:* www.oceanbay.com.br Commercial Manager: Juan Victor
Aalborg Importadora e Exportadora Ltda, Primeira Avenida No.13, Cobilandia, 29111-160 Vilha Velha ES, Brazil, *Tel:* +55 27 3316 0345, *Fax:* +55 27 3316 0346, *Email:* aalborg.vix@zaz.com.br, *Website:* www.aalborg.com.br
Boa Praca Importadora e Exportadora Ltda, Rua Gil Martins de Oliveira 55, Santa Lucia, 29056-300 Vitoria, Brazil, *Tel:* +55 27 3357 1400, *Fax:* +55 27 3235 2954, *Email:* bpnav@boapraca.com.br, *Website:* www.boapraca.com.br
Nau - L.M. Neffa Comercial Exportadora e Importadora, Rua Coronel Vicente Peixoto N 95, 29010-280 Vitoria, Brazil, *Tel:* +55 27 3322 1144, *Fax:* +55 27 3223 5746, *Email:* nau@terra.com.br, *Website:* www.lmneffa.com.br
Sea Horse Ship Supplier, Rua 16, No. 107 - Castelo Branco, 29140-790 Cariacica, Brazil, *Tel:* +55 27 3326 3123, *Fax:* +55 27 3326 7465, *Email:* seahorse@uol.com.br
Tax Free Com. Import Export Ltda, Rua Castro Alves No. 52, Bairro Planalto, 29.118-360 Vila Velha, Brazil, *Tel:* +55 27 3326 2358, *Fax:* +55 27 3326 2301, *Email:* tax-free@uol.com.br

Shipping Agents: Agencia Maritima Ltd, Avenida Jeronimo Monteiro 1000, Suite 1701/1704, CEP 29010-004 Vitoria, Brazil, *Tel:* +55 27 2122 7000, *Fax:* +55 27 2122 7001, *Email:* transcarvix@transcargroup.com.br, *Website:* www.transcar.com.br
Corymar Agencia Maritima Ltd, Avenida Jeronimo Monteiro 240, Ruralbank Building Room 1210, P O Box 329, 29010-002 Vitoria ES, Brazil, *Tel:* +55 27 3223 0238, *Fax:* +55 27 3223 2441, *Email:* willvix@williams.com.br, *Website:* www.williams.com.br
Fertimport S.A., Av Americo Buaiz, 501, cj 603, 29050-911 Vitoria, Brazil, *Tel:* +55 27 3334 6800, *Fax:* +55 27 3334 6810, *Email:* operations.vix.fertimport@bunge.com, *Website:* www.fertimport.com.br
Lachmann Logistica Ltda, Rua Dr. Eurico de Aguiar, 888/1304 Santa Lucia, CEP 29055-280 Vitoria, Brazil, *Tel:* +55 27 3225 5663, *Fax:* +55 27 3225 7075, *Email:* agency.vix@lachmann.com.br, *Website:* www.lachmann.com.br
LBH Brasil, Av. Americo Buaiz 501 û Cj 1005, Ed. Victoria Office Tower û Torre Leste, Enseada do Sua, 29050-911 Vitoria ES, Brazil, *Tel:* +55 27 2122 8655, *Fax:* +55 27 3345 6575, *Email:* brazvix@lbhbrasil.com.br, *Website:* www.brazshipping.com.br
Mediterranean Shipping Company, MSC do Brazil Ltda, Av. Carlos Lindemberg s/n, Nossa Sra da Penha, 29110-902 Vila Velha ES, Brazil, *Tel:* +55 27 2104 9500, *Fax:* +55 27 2123 1801, *Email:* distribution@mscbr.com.br, *Website:* www.mscgva.ch
A.P. Moller-Maersk Group, Maersk Brasil Ltda, Av.Nsa Sra. dos Navegantes 451, Sala 412 - Edificio Petro Tower, Enseada do Sua, 29050-335 Vitoria ES, Brazil, *Tel:* +55 27 3334 7200, *Fax:* +55 27 3334 7200, *Email:* brzcrcrio@maersk.com, *Website:* www.maerskline.com
Oceanus Agencia Maritima S.A., Rua Eurico de Aguiar 888, 13th Floor - Room 1303/1304, 29056-200 Vitoria ES, Brazil, *Tel:* +55 27 3225 5663, *Fax:* +55 27 3225 7075, *Email:* agency.vix@oceanus.com.br, *Website:* www.oceanus.com.br
Pennant Servicos Maritimos Ltd, Av. Jeronimo Monteiro, 1000 - 5th floor 522, 29014-900 Vitoria, Brazil, *Tel:* +55 27 2124 7300, *Fax:* +55 27 2124 7313, *Email:* pennvix@pennant.com.br, *Website:* www.pennant.com.br
Port Shipping Agencia Maritima Ltda, Jeronimo Monteiro Avenue 1000, Gr. 918/920 - Centro, 29014-900 Vitoria, Brazil, *Tel:* +55 27 3222 2055, *Fax:* +55 27 3222 4414, *Email:* portshipping@portshipping.com.br, *Website:* www.portshipping.com.br
Poseidon Maritima Ltda, Rua da Garcia 320, Praia do Canto, P O Box 660, 29045-560 Vitoria, Brazil, *Tel:* +55 27 3227 5499, *Fax:* +55 27 3227 8597, *Email:* poseidon@poseidon.com.br, *Website:* www.poseidon.com.br
Prado Agencia Maritima Ltd, Rua Alberto de Oliveira Santos 42, Room No.1005, P O Box 1087, CEP 29010-901 Vitoria, Brazil, *Tel:* +55 27 3322 5922, *Fax:* +55 27 3322 0998, *Email:* prado@prado.com.br, *Website:* www.prado.com.br
Rodos Agencia Maritima Ltda, Rua Eugenio Netto 488, Ed. Praia Office - Salas 1110/1111/1112, Praia do Canto, 29055-270 Vitoria, Brazil, *Tel:* +55 27 3200 3474, *Fax:* +55 27 3325 1825, *Email:* rodos@rodos.com.br, *Website:* www.rodos.com.br
Transregional Shipping Agency Ltd, Avenida Jeronimo Monteiro 1000, Sl. 1218/1220, 29014-900 Vitoria ES, Brazil, *Tel:* +55 27 2124 6161, *Fax:* +55 27 3223 7059, *Email:* transregional@transregional.com.br, *Website:* www.transregional.com.br
Wilson Sons Agencia Maritima Ltda, Avenida Princesa Isabel 599 - 9th Floor, 29010-361 Vitoria ES, Brazil, *Tel:* +55 27 3232 1422, *Fax:* +55 27 3222 1297, *Email:* agevi@wilsonsons.com.br, *Website:* www.wilsonsons.com.br

Surveyors: Bureau Veritas, Rua Carlos Eduardo Monteiro de Lemos 262 - Sala 206, Jardim da Penha, 29060-120 Vitoria ES, Brazil, *Tel:* +55 27 3135 3000, *Fax:* +55 27 3135 3025, *Email:* bv.vitoria@br.bureauveritas.com, *Website:* www.bureauveritas.com
Det Norske Veritas A/S, Vitoria, Brazil, *Tel:* +55 27 3345 6696, *Fax:* +55 27 3345 6417, *Email:* vit@dnv.com, *Website:* www.dnv.com

Medical Facilities: Good hospitals and medical treatment available

Airport: Vitoria, 8 km

Lloyd's Agent: Inspect Consultoria Ltda (Rio de Janeiro), Avenida Rio Branco 37, Grupo 1902 Centro, 20090-003 Rio de Janeiro RJ, Brazil, *Tel:* +55 21 2263 3330, *Fax:* +55 21 2253 9322, *Email:* inspectconsultoria@br.inter.net, *Website:* www.inspectconsultoria.com.br

---

Key to Principal Facilities:—				
A=Airport	**C**=Containers	**G**=General Cargo	**P**=Petroleum	**R**=Ro/Ro	**Y**=Dry Bulk
B=Bunkers	**D**=Dry Dock	**L**=Cruise	**Q**=Other Liquid Bulk	**T**=Towage (where available from port)	

BRITISH INDIAN OCEAN TERRITORY

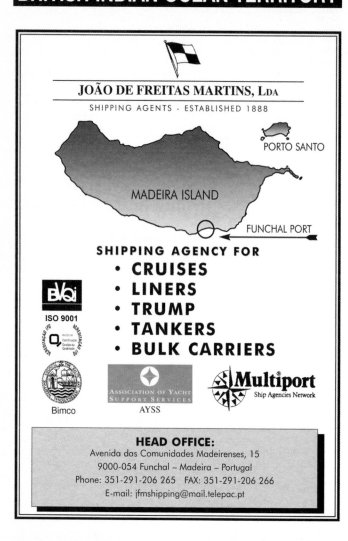

JOÃO DE FREITAS MARTINS, Lda

SHIPPING AGENTS · ESTABLISHED 1888

PORTO SANTO

MADEIRA ISLAND

FUNCHAL PORT

SHIPPING AGENCY FOR
- **CRUISES**
- **LINERS**
- **TRUMP**
- **TANKERS**
- **BULK CARRIERS**

ISO 9001

Bimco   AYSS   **Multiport** Ship Agencies Network

HEAD OFFICE:
Avenida das Comunidades Madeirenses, 15
9000-054 Funchal – Madeira – Portugal
Phone: 351-291-206 265 FAX: 351-291-206 266
E-mail: jfmshipping@mail.telepac.pt

BRUNEI

KUALA BELAIT

Lat 4° 35' N; Long 114° 11' E.

Admiralty Chart: 2109
Time Zone: GMT +8 h
Admiralty Pilot: 31
UNCTAD Locode: BN KUB

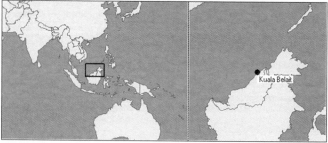

Principal Facilities:

P	Q		G			B	D		A

Authority: Ports Department, Kuala Belait 6020, Brunei Darussalam, *Tel:* +673 3 335298, *Fax:* +673 3 342619

Officials: Port Director: Pengiran Abdul Rahman Ismail.
Port Officer: Mohd Shaharini Abdullah.
Port Officer: Helmi Bin Haji Talib.

Port Security: ISPS compliant

Approach: Depth at bar ranges from 0.5 m at very low tides to around 2 m at average high tides

Anchorage: There is ample anchorage in the stream for vessels which can enter the river

Pilotage: Available from Bandar Seri Begawan

Working Hours: 0800-1200, 1330-1700

Accommodation:

Name	Length (m)	Depth (m)	Remarks
Kuala Belait			See [1] below
Government Wharf	91	.6	
Another Wharf	325	2.4	

[1]*Kuala Belait:* The port is mainly used by the Brunei Shell Petroleum Co Ltd

Storage:

Location	Covered (m²)
Kuala Belait	1500

Cargo Worked: 300-350 t/day

Bunkering: Fuel services available

Repair & Maintenance: Kuala Belait Shipyard Sendirian Berhad, Lot 3318 Tanjong Rassau, P O Box 745, Kuala Belait 6007, Brunei Darussalam, *Tel:* +673 3 334559, *Fax:* +673 3 335225 Engine repairs

Surveyors: Bureau Veritas, P O Box 1259, Kuala Belait KA 1131, Brunei Darussalam, *Tel:* +673 3 330265, *Fax:* +673 3 334749, *Email:* bv_bvqi_kb@brunet.bn, *Website:* www.bureauveritas.com
Germanischer Lloyd, Kuala Belait, Brunei Darussalam, *Tel:* +673 3 340845, *Fax:* +673 3 340843, *Email:* gl-brunei@gl-group.com, *Website:* www.gl-group.com

Medical Facilities: Available at Government hospital

Airport: Bandar Seri Begawan, 90km

Lloyd's Agent: Jasra Harrisons Shipping & Agency Services Sendirian Berhad, P O Box 16, Kuala Belait, Bandar Seri Begawan KA1189, Brunei Darussalam, *Tel:* +673 2 231515, *Email:* jasrains@brunet.bn

LUMUT

Lat 4° 39' N; Long 114° 26' E.

Admiralty Chart: 2109
Time Zone: GMT +8 h
Admiralty Pilot: 31
UNCTAD Locode: BN LUM

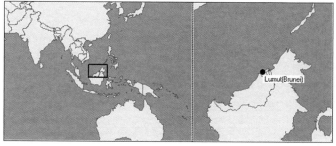

Principal Facilities:

Q							T	A

Authority: Brunei Shell Petroleum Co. Sendirian Berhad, Seria 7082, Brunei Darussalam, *Tel:* +673 3 378443, *Fax:* +673 3 378428, *Email:* shu-hua.chung@shell.com, *Website:* www.bsp.com.bn

Port Security: ISPS compliant

Anchorage: Three miles N of the berth in depth of 21-25 m bounded by pos 4° 45' N and 4° 46' N; 114° 26' E and 114° 28' E

Pilotage: Compulsory. Pilot boards 2 nautical miles N of the berth

Radio Frequency: Lumut Control may be contacted on VHF Channel 71 or 73 from 20 mile range

Tides: Max tidal range is 2.4 m

Working Hours: 24 h/day

Accommodation:

Name	Remarks
Lumut	See [1] below

[1]*Lumut:* The BLNG terminal consists of a 2.4 mile long jetty extending from the LNG plant. Limiting weather conditions restrict the berthing and mooring of vessels in berths
The side loading berth is capable of accommodating vessels up to 135 000 m3 and 11.3 m d loading through a midships manifold
Detailed design restrictions of vessels mooring, manifold and cargo equipment apply to the berth. All prospective vessels details must be vetted by BLNG and BSP Marine Department before vessels may be accepted to the side loading berth

Towage: Berthing on side berth is with two or three 55 t bollard pull tractor propulsion tugs

Medical Facilities: In emergencies only by arrangement with Agent

Airport: Bandar Seri Begawan, 90 km from Kuala Belait

Lloyd's Agent: Jasra Harrisons Shipping & Agency Services Sendirian Berhad, P O Box 16, Kuala Belait, Bandar Seri Begawan KA1189, Brunei Darussalam, *Tel:* +673 2 231515, *Email:* jasrains@brunet.bn

MUARA PORT

Lat 5° 2' N; Long 115° 5' E.

Admiralty Chart: 2134 **Admiralty Pilot:** 31
Time Zone: GMT +8 h **UNCTAD Locode:** BN MUA

Principal Facilities:

P		Y	G	C	R		B		T	A	

Jasra Harrisons Sdn. Bhd

Junction of Jalan McArthur and Jalan Kianggeh
P.O.Box 2255, Bandar Seri Begawan BS8674
BRUNEI DARUSSALAM

TEL: 00 673 2242361 - 64 FAX: 00 673 2232537
EMAIL: jhsbshpgmgr@brunet.bn

SHIPPING AGENTS

Authority: Port of Muara, Jalan Pelabuhan, Muara BT 1728, Brunei Darussalam, *Tel:* +673 2 770222, *Fax:* +673 2 774226, *Email:* ports@brunet.bn, *Website:* www.ports.gov.bn

Officials: Port Director: Souyono Salamat.
Commercial Manager: Fadzillah Yaakub.
Marketing: Marsalinawati Haji Omar Ali, *Email:* lisa.omarali@gmail.com.

Port Security: ISPS compliant

Documentation: Notice of arrival to Ports Department and copy to relevant government agencies
Crew list and passenger list (for cruise vessels)
Cargo manifest for Ports and Custom Department

Approach: The only approach to Muara Port for ocean-going vessels is through the dredged channel of Tanjong Pelompong. The channel is dredged to 12.5 m below CD and is 2651 m long and 122 m wide at the sea bed. Training banks were constructed 2012 m long on the western side of the entrance channel and 457 m long on the eastern side. These banks are built of sand and stone rubber, topped with large blocks of stone weighing up to 4 t each. Both banks slope downwards as they proceed from Tanjong Pelompong spit into South China Sea

Anchorage: Outer harbour in pos 5° 35' N, 115° 06' E. Inner harbour in pos 4° 54' 07" N, 115° 04' 06" E. Tanjong Selirong (for loading logs) in pos 5° 01' 36" N, 115° 04' 12" E

Pilotage: Pilotage services are provided by the Marine Department. Application for pilots can be made by giving at least 24 h notice of arrival. Vessel's are requested to report to the Marine signal station on VHF Channel 16, call sign 'Muara Harbour' at least 1 h before arrival and listen on the above channel for information on pilotage and berthing

Radio Frequency: The Muara signal station is manned 24 h and can be contacted through VHF Channel 16 at any time

Weather: Monsoon season is from November to March

Tides: 0.2 m at LT, 2.2 m at HT

Traffic: 2005, 1 768 620 t of cargo handled, 108 103 TEU's

Maximum Vessel Dimensions: 12.5 m draft

Principal Imports and Exports: Imports: Cement, Foodstuffs, General cargo, Rice, Steel. Exports: Garments, Scrap steel.

Working Hours: 24 h/day

Accommodation:

Name	Length (m)	Draught (m)	Remarks
Muara Port			See [1] below
Conventional Berths	611	12.5	See [2] below
Muara Container Terminal	250	12.5	See [3] below

[1]*Muara Port:* A tanker terminal is operated by Brunei Shell Petroleum in Muara harbour
[2]*Conventional Berths:* Four berths handling general cargo, vehicles, steel pipes & building materials. Also one additional finger pier 87 m long in depth of 5.2 m
[3]*Muara Container Terminal:* Two berths. Container freight station of 5000 m2. 156 reefer points

Storage: Three general cargo transit sheds totalling 12 950 m2, four warehouses for long storage totalling 16 630 m2, 2 ha of container yard, 2 ha of open storage and two cement silos for dry bulk cement with cap of 8000 t

Mechanical Handling Equipment:

Location	Type	Capacity (t)	Qty
Muara Port	Mult-purp. Cranes	6	1
Muara Port	Mobile Cranes	75	
Muara Container Terminal	Panamax	40	2

Bunkering: Brunei Shell Marketing Co., Ground & 12th Floor, PGGMB Building, Jalan Kianggeh, Bandar Seri Begawan BS8111, Brunei Darussalam, *Tel:* +673 2 244 739, *Fax:* +673 2 240 470, *Email:* aslie.lakim@shell.com, *Website:* www.bsm.com.bn – *Misc:* high speed diesel available in small quantities

Towage: Two tugs of 20 t bollard pull owned by Marine Department

Shipping Agents: Archipelago Development Corp. Sendirian Berhad, Unit 3-5, Latifuddin Complex, Spg 168-38, Jalan Tutong, Bandar Seri Begawan 3619, Brunei Darussalam, *Tel:* +673 2 221383, *Fax:* +673 2 220106, *Email:* info@archipelago2002.com, *Website:* www.archibn.com
Boustead Shipping Agencies Sendirian Berhad, Km.1 Jalan Tutong 4A, 1st Floor Princess HRH Norain Complex, Simpang 9, P O Box 2716, Bandar Seri Begawan 2628, Brunei Darussalam, *Tel:* +673 2 221434, *Fax:* +673 2 221484, *Email:* boussip@brunet.bn, *Website:* www.bousteadshipping.com.my
B.T. Forwarding Co., P O Box 1777, Bandar Seri Begawan BS8673, Brunei Darussalam, *Tel:* +673 2 222933, *Fax:* +673 2 238716, *Website:* www.beeseng.com
Jasra Harrisons Shipping & Agency Services Sendirian Berhad, P O Box 16, Kuala Belait, Bandar Seri Begawan KA1189, Brunei Darussalam, *Tel:* +673 2 231515, *Email:* jasrains@brunet.bn

Stevedoring Companies: Abd Saman Ahmad Freight Forwarding, Muara, Brunei Darussalam, *Tel:* +673 2 448278, *Fax:* +673 2 448267
Brunei Transporting Co., P O Box 1528, Bandar Seri Begawan, Muara BS8673, Brunei Darussalam, *Tel:* +673 2 231621, *Fax:* +673 2 231622, *Email:* brutco@brunet.bn, *Website:* www.bruneitransport.com
D & J Transport Services, Muara, Brunei Darussalam, *Tel:* +673 2 445087, *Fax:* +673 2 445088
Sabli Shipping & Forwarding Agencies, 21 Lambak Kanan Industrial Estate, Muara BB 1714, Brunei Darussalam, *Tel:* +673 2 391122, *Fax:* +673 2 391600, *Email:* sabligrp@brunet.bn
Syarikat Haji Mohammad Moktal, Muara, Brunei Darussalam, *Tel:* +673 2 420185, *Fax:* +673 2 420186
Syarikat Pemunggahan Hj Buang & Anak2, Muara, Brunei Darussalam, *Tel:* +673 2 770107, *Fax:* +673 2 770298
Syarikat Pemunggahan Tiga Muara, Muara, Brunei Darussalam, *Tel:* +673 2 770096, *Fax:* +673 2 770097

Surveyors: Bureau Veritas, Al Warasah Commercial Centre, Lot 3672, EDR 3364, 2nd Floor, Units S1 & S2, Muara BT 1328, Brunei Darussalam, *Tel:* +673 2 771499, *Fax:* +673 2 771533, *Email:* bv_bvqi_mu@brunet.bn, *Website:* www.bureauveritas.com

Medical Facilities: Muara Health Centre, 1 km. General Hospital, 28 km

Airport: Brunei International Airport, 19 km

Lloyd's Agent: Jasra Harrisons Shipping & Agency Services Sendirian Berhad, P O Box 16, Kuala Belait, Bandar Seri Begawan KA1189, Brunei Darussalam, *Tel:* +673 2 231515, *Email:* jasrains@brunet.bn

SERIA TERMINAL

Lat 4° 37' N; Long 114° 19' E.

Admiralty Chart: 2109 **Admiralty Pilot:** 31
Time Zone: GMT +8 h **UNCTAD Locode:** BN SER

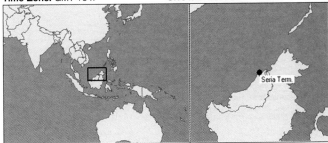

Principal Facilities:

P					B		T	A	

Authority: Brunei Shell Petroleum Co. Sendirian Berhad, Seria 7082, Brunei Darussalam, *Tel:* +673 3 378443, *Fax:* +673 3 378428, *Email:* shu-hua.chung@shell.com, *Website:* www.bsp.com.bn

Port Security: ISPS compliant

Documentation: Last port of clearance, inward cargo manifest (3 copies), crew list (6 copies), maritime declaration of health (2 copies), vaccination list (2 copies), ship store list (3 copies), crew effects declaration list (3 copies), passenger list (3 copies) and copies of ship's valid certificates

Anchorage: A tanker anchorage is located approx 3 miles N of the SBM berths in an area contained within 4° 45' N and 4° 47' N; 114° 17' E and 114° 19' E in depth of 35 m. Tankers should not anchor at any other locations due to the presence of many submarine pipelines throughout the oil field and adjoining areas

Pilotage: Compulsory. Pilot boards approx 2 miles N of the SBM's. Berthing master remains on board throughout loading operations. ETA must be confirmed at least 48 h prior to arrival. VHF Channel 16 and 13

	Key to Principal Facilities:—				
	A=Airport	**C**=Containers	**G**=General Cargo	**P**=Petroleum	**R**=Ro/Ro	**Y**=Dry Bulk
	B=Bunkers	**D**=Dry Dock	**L**=Cruise	**Q**=Other Liquid Bulk	**T**=Towage (where available from port)	

Radio Frequency: Arriving vessels should contact Seria Terminal on VHF Channel 13 when in range

Weather: Berthing operations are, as a rule, suspended when wind speeds exceed 25 knots

Tides: Average tide height 1.3 m

Working Hours: 24 h/day

Accommodation:

Name	Draught (m)	Remarks
Seria Terminal		See [1] below
SBM No.1	17.4	See [2] below
SBM No.2	15.85	See [3] below

[1]*Seria Terminal:* Crude oil loading terminal. Two single buoy moorings located approx 5.4 miles from the coast, connected to the shore installations by submarine pipelines
[2]*SBM No.1:* Designed to accommodate vessels up to 320 000 dwt. Berthing and unberthing is carried out night and day. Max loading rate is 4300 m3/h
[3]*SBM No.2:* Designed to accommodate vessels up to 320 000 dwt. Berthing and unberthing is carried out night and day. Max loading rate (condensate only) is 2500 m3/h

Bunkering: Not available at Seria but can be obtained from Miri with 3 days prior notice

Towage: Not available on a routine basis. In an emergency one or more of the tugs working in the oil field would be available

Medical Facilities: Available in cases of emergency only by arrangement with agent

Airport: Bandar Seri Begawan, 90 km from Kuala Belait

Lloyd's Agent: Jasra Harrisons Shipping & Agency Services Sendirian Berhad, P O Box 16, Kuala Belait, Bandar Seri Begawan KA1189, Brunei Darussalam, *Tel:* +673 2 231515, *Email:* jasrains@brunet.bn

TANJONG SALIRONG

Lat 4° 54' N; Long 115° 6' E.

Admiralty Chart: 2134

Admiralty Pilot: 31

Time Zone: GMT +8 h

UNCTAD Locode: BN TAS

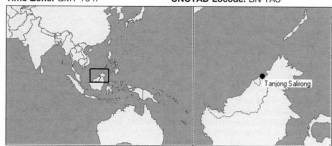

Principal Facilities:

			G						

Authority: Port of Tanjong Salirong, Marine Department, HM Customs Building, Bandar Seri Begawan, Brunei Darussalam

Pilotage: Not compulsory but available if required with 24 h notice

Tides: Range of tide 2 m

Accommodation:

Name	Remarks
Tanjong Salirong	See [1] below

[1]*Tanjong Salirong:* Open roadstead. Vessels load in river anchorage 12 miles above the outer bar at the mouth of the Brunei River. Max permissible draught of vessels is 6.1 m. Loading of logs is the principal cargo handled

Lloyd's Agent: Jasra Harrisons Shipping & Agency Services Sendirian Berhad, P O Box 16, Kuala Belait, Bandar Seri Begawan KA1189, Brunei Darussalam, *Tel:* +673 2 231515, *Email:* jasrains@brunet.bn

BULGARIA

BALCHIK

harbour area, see under Varna

BOURGAS

Lat 42° 29' N; Long 27° 27' E.

Admiralty Chart: 2399

Admiralty Pilot: 24

Time Zone: GMT +2 h

UNCTAD Locode: BG BOJ

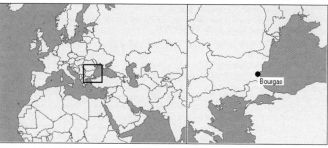

Principal Facilities:

P	Q	Y	G	C	R		B	D	T	A

Authority: Port of Bourgas, 1 Prince Alexander Battenberg Street, 8000 Bourgas, Bulgaria, *Tel:* +359 56 840293, *Fax:* +359 56 822156, *Email:* headoffice@port-burgas.com, *Website:* www.port-burgas.com

Officials: Executive Director: Argir Boyadzhiev, *Tel:* +359 56 822222.
Finance Director: Stoyan Angelov, *Tel:* +359 56 822250, *Email:* st_angelov@port-burgas.com.
Harbour Master: Zhivko Petrov.
Marketing: Tanyo Ivanov, *Tel:* +359 56 822066, *Email:* ivanov@port-burgas.com.

Port Security: ISPS compliant

Documentation: Crew list (6 copies), passenger list (6 copies), crew effects and money list (4 copies), store list (4 copies), cargo manifest (4 copies), health declaration

Approach: Safe in fairway, depth 14 m. Attention must be paid to navigational hazard South Buoy, 1 mile E of breakwater light. Harbour Control on VHF Channel 16 may be contacted for guidance

Anchorage: Area 1 (for vessels up to 150 m loa):
42° 28' 12" N; 27° 29' 19" E
42° 27' 82" N; 27° 29' 19" E
42° 27' 52" N; 27° 29' 79" E
42° 27' 32" N; 27° 29' 79" E
42° 27' 32" N; 27° 30' 59" E
42° 28' 12" N; 27° 30' 59" E
42° 28' 12" N; 27° 29' 19" E
Area 2 (for tankers up to 5000 gt):
42° 28' 12" N; 27° 30' 69" E
42° 27' 52" N; 27° 30' 69" E
42° 27' 52" N; 27° 31' 29" E
42° 28' 12" N; 27° 31' 29" E
42° 28' 12" N; 27° 30' 69" E
Area 3 (for vessels over 150 m loa):
42° 30' 02" N; 27° 32' 09" E
42° 29' 42" N; 27° 32' 09" E
42° 29' 42" N; 27° 33' 49" E
42° 29' 42" N; 27° 33' 49" E
42° 30' 02" N; 27° 32' 09" E
Area 4 (for tankers over 5000 gt)
42° 30' 02" N; 27° 33' 49" E
42° 29' 42" N; 27° 33' 49" E
42° 29' 42" N; 27° 34' 89" E
42° 30' 02" N; 27° 34' 89" E
42° 30' 02" N; 27° 33' 49" E
Area 5 (quarantine & dangerous cargo):
42° 28' 22" N; 27° 32' 29" E
42° 28' 22" N; 27° 32' 69" E
42° 27' 82" N; 27° 32' 69" E
42° 27' 72" N; 27° 32' 29" E
42° 28' 22" N; 27° 32' 29" E

Pilotage: Compulsory. 24 h notice needed for deep sea pilotage. Pilot boards 4 cables from breakwater or in the roads, if at anchor. Pilot station on VHF Channel 14

Radio Frequency: Berthing instructions on VHF Channel 16 and 14. Bourgas Radio Station on VHF Channel 16 and 28

Maximum Vessel Dimensions: Bulk Vessels: 60 000 dwt, 11.5 m d, 252 m loa. Tankers: 100 000 dwt, 12.65 m d, 261 m loa

Principal Imports and Exports: Imports: Coal, Crude oil, General cargo, Ore & concentrates. Exports: Fertilizer, Metals, Oil products.

Working Hours: General cargo 0530-1415, 1415-2300. Bulk, metals and containers 24 h/day

Accommodation:

Name	Length (m)	Draught (m)	Remarks
Port East			General & bulk cargoes handled
Berth No.1	160	9.7	Discontinued
Berth No.2	160	9.2	Discontinued
Berth No.3	155	7.1	Discontinued
Berth No.4	155	6.8	Discontinued
Berth No.5	155	7.2	Discontinued
Berth No.6	155	6.8	
Berth No.11	132	7.2	
Berth No.12	175	8.1	
Berth No.13	175	7.3	
Port Bulk Cargoes			Handling coal, coke, ores & concentrates etc
Berth No.17	180	11	
Berth No.18	180	11	
Berth No.19	180	11	
Berth No.20	180	11	
Berth No.20A		6.5	Oils, chemicals & ethanol
Port West			See [1] below
Berth No.21A	220	8.2	
Berth No.21B	60	8.5	
Berth No.22	200	11	
Berth No.23	200	11	
Berth No.24	200	11	
Berth No.25	120	6.1	
Terminal 2A			See [2] below
Berth No.30	195	11.5	
Berth No.31	230	14.5	
Berth No.32	280	15.5	
Berth No.33	87	11.5	

[1]*Port West:* Ro/ro & container traffic. Cold storage of 7000 m2. Container yard at Berths 23 and 24 of approx 60 000 m2 with 1330 ground slots. 50 reefer points
[2]*Terminal 2A:* Handling bulk cargoes such as coal, coke, ores & concentrates, clinker etc

Storage:

Location	Open (m²)	Covered (m²)
Port East	50000	44500
Port Bulk Cargoes	49000	5000
Port West	191000	11000
Terminal 2A	108000	

Mechanical Handling Equipment:

Location	Type	Capacity (t)	Qty
Port East	Mobile Cranes	25–50	4
Port East	Portal Cranes	10–20	26
Port Bulk Cargoes	Portal Cranes	10–20	8
Port West	Mobile Cranes	25–100	2
Port West	Portal Cranes	10–40	13
Port West	Reach Stackers	37–42	2
Terminal 2A	Portal Cranes	20–50	4

Bunkering: Burgas Bunker, 6, 6th September Street, 8000 Bourgas, Bulgaria, *Tel:* +359 56 843 877, *Fax:* +359 56 845 137, *Email:* bs_bunker@bitex.com
Litshipping Ltd, 11 Antim 1 Street 2nd Floor, 8000 Bourgas, Bulgaria, *Tel:* +359 56 840 404, *Fax:* +359 56 840 408, *Email:* litshipping@mbox.contact.bg
Moniks Marine Services Ltd, Industrialna Street 33, 8000 Bourgas, Bulgaria, *Tel:* +359 56 840 824, *Fax:* +359 56 842 085, *Email:* moniks.marine.services@gmail.com, *Website:* www.moniks.com
Transimpex Bunker, 1 Fotinov Street, 8000 Bourgas, Bulgaria, *Tel:* +359 56 857321, *Fax:* +359 56 844298, *Email:* shipchandler@bs.transimpex.bg, *Website:* www.transimpex.bg
Burgas Bunker, 6, 6th September Street, 8000 Bourgas, Bulgaria, *Tel:* +359 56 843 877, *Fax:* +359 56 845 137, *Email:* bs_bunker@bitex.com
Cosmos Shipping AD, 6 Petko Karavelov Street, 9000 Varna, Bulgaria, *Tel:* +359 52 622274, *Fax:* +359 52 622275, *Email:* bunker@cosmosltd.com, *Website:* www.cosmosltd.com
Moniks Marine Services Ltd, Industrialna Street 33, 8000 Bourgas, Bulgaria, *Tel:* +359 56 840 824, *Fax:* +359 56 842 085, *Email:* moniks.marine.services@gmail.com, *Website:* www.moniks.com
Navigation Maritime Bulgare Ltd (NAVIBULGAR), 1 Primorski Boulevard, Chervenoarmeiski, 9000 Varna, Bulgaria, *Tel:* +359 52 633 100, *Fax:* +359 52 633 033, *Email:* office@navbul.com, *Website:* www.navbul.com
Petromar Ltd, 32 Tzar Simeon Street, Floor 4, 9000 Varna, Bulgaria, *Tel:* +359 52 609287, *Fax:* +359 52 609288, *Email:* office@petromar-bg.com, *Website:* www.petromar-bg.com
Seatrade Ltd, 33A, Knyaz Boris 1 Boulevard, 9000 Varna, Bulgaria, *Tel:* +359 52 601981, *Fax:* +359 52 901982
Swift Sea Services Ltd, 25 Tzar Simeon Street, Office 408, 9000 Varna, Bulgaria, *Tel:* +359 52 630 547, *Fax:* +359 52 630 747, *Email:* sss@nat.bg
Tramp Oil & Marine, World Fuel Services Corporation, 13th Floor, Portland House, Bressenden Place, London SW1E 5BH, United Kingdom, *Tel:* +44 20 7808 5000, *Fax:* +44 20 7808 5088, *Email:* pturner@wfscorp.com, *Website:* www.wfscorp.com
Transimpex Bunker, 1 Fotinov Street, 8000 Bourgas, Bulgaria, *Tel:* +359 56 857321, *Fax:* +359 56 844298, *Email:* shipchandler@bs.transimpex.bg, *Website:* www.transimpex.bg

Waste Reception Facilities: Tankers to proceed under clean ballast only. Bilges are taken by barge. Daily garbage service

Towage: Tugs from 600-2400 hp available, Port of Bourgas

Repair & Maintenance: Bourgas Shipyards Co. Ltd, Komlushka Mizima 1, 8002 Bourgas, Bulgaria, *Tel:* +359 56 853365, *Fax:* +359 56 852303, *Email:* bship@unacs.bg, *Website:* www.bourgasshipyards.com Repair and conversion of vessels up to 185 m x 26 m x 5 m, max 6300 t. Shiprepair slipway 200 m. Yard has access to 400 m outfitting quay and 250 m shiprepair quay

Ship Chandlers: Transimpex Bunker, 1 Fotinov Street, 8000 Bourgas, Bulgaria, *Tel:* +359 56 857321, *Fax:* +359 56 844298, *Email:* shipchandler@bs.transimpex.bg, *Website:* www.transimpex.bg
Vistamar Ltd, 52 Chataldja Street Pobeda Road, 8000 Bourgas, Bulgaria, *Tel:* +359 56 843675, *Fax:* +359 56 843678, *Email:* office@vistamarltd.com, *Website:* www.vistamarltd.com

Shipping Agents: Bulkam Sea Trading Ltd, 5 Ferdinandova Street, BG-8000 Bourgas, Bulgaria, *Tel:* +359 56 840670, *Fax:* +359 56 840588, *Email:* mail@bulkam.com, *Website:* www.bulkam.com
Economou International Shipping Agencies Ltd, 10th Floor, Industrialna Strasse 3, Port of Bourgas, 8000 Bourgas, Bulgaria, *Tel:* +359 56 844637, *Fax:* +359 56 844567, *Email:* economou@alba-bg.com, *Website:* www.economou.gr
Inflot Bulgarian Shipping Agency, 57 Ferdinandova Street, Bourgas, Bulgaria, *Tel:* +359 56 844762, *Fax:* +359 56 844762, *Email:* inflotbs@bs.spnet.net
Karimex Shipping Agency Bourgas, Floor 1, ENTR V, 46 Sheinovo Street, 8000 Bourgas, Bulgaria, *Tel:* +359 56 843701, *Fax:* +359 56 841768, *Email:* karimex1@digicom.bg
Mela Shipping & Forwarding Ltd, 34 Antim I Street, 8000 Bourgas, Bulgaria, *Tel:* +359 56 843723, *Fax:* +359 56 843724, *Email:* mela@mela-shipping.com, *Website:* www.mela-shipping.com
Navigation Maritime Bulgare Ltd (NAVIBULGAR), NAVIAGENT, 1 Kniaz Alexander Batemberg, 8000 Bourgas, Bulgaria, *Tel:* +359 56 879716, *Fax:* +359 56 841738, *Email:* burgasagency@burgas.navbul.com, *Website:* www.navbul.com
Stenamar Co. Ltd, 6, 6th September Street, Bourgas, Bulgaria, *Tel:* +359 56 840828, *Email:* stenamar@stenmar.com
Unimasters Logistics Ltd, 3th Floor, 1A Bulair Street, BG-8000 Bourgas, Bulgaria, *Tel:* +359 56 843780, *Fax:* +359 56 843797, *Email:* bourgas@fidelitas.bg, *Website:* www.fidelitas.bg
Wilhelmsen Ship Services, Barwil Unimasters Ltd, 25 Dr. Nider Street, 8000 Bourgas, Bulgaria, *Tel:* +359 56 843796, *Fax:* +359 56 840390, *Email:* bourgas@barwil.bg, *Website:* www.barwilunitor.com

Surveyors: Black Sea Cargo Inspection Ltd, ulica Ferdinandova 5, 8000 Bourgas, Bulgaria, *Tel:* +359 56 843015, *Fax:* +359 56 842247
Cargo Inspections Group (CIG), Operations Centre, Ferdinandova Street 5, 8000 Bourgas, Bulgaria, *Tel:* +359 56 840169, *Fax:* +359 56 840132, *Email:* ops@cargoinspections.com, *Website:* www.cargoinspections.com
Cargo Survey & Software (CCS) Ltd, 32 Vazrajdane Street, 8000 Bourgas, Bulgaria, *Tel:* +359 56 841771, *Fax:* +359 56 843479, *Email:* office@cargo-survey.com, *Website:* www.cargo-survey.com
International Naval Surveys Bureau, 11 Varazhdane Street, 8000 Bourgas, Bulgaria, *Tel:* +359 56 840518, *Fax:* +359 56 840519, *Email:* insb_bg@infotel.bg

Medical Facilities: Five hospitals available

Airport: Bourgas Airport, 8 km

Railway: Central railway station is situated 200 m from the port's main gate

---

Key to Principal Facilities:—

A=Airport	**C**=Containers	**G**=General Cargo
B=Bunkers	**D**=Dry Dock	**L**=Cruise

P=Petroleum	**R**=Ro/Ro	**Y**=Dry Bulk
Q=Other Liquid Bulk	**T**=Towage (where available from port)	

Lloyd's Agent: Fidelitas Ltd, 40 Graf Ignatiev Street, 9000 Varna, Bulgaria, *Tel:* +359 52 665 5111, *Fax:* +359 52 600453, *Email:* ognyan.kostov@fidelitas.bg, *Website:* www.fidelitas.bg

BURGAS

alternate name, see Bourgas

LESPORT

harbour area, see under Varna

LOM

Lat 43° 50' N; Long 23° 12' E.

Admiralty Chart: -	Admiralty Pilot: -
Time Zone: GMT +2 h	UNCTAD Locode: BG LOM

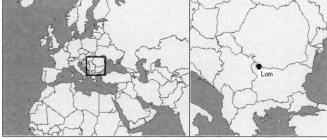

Principal Facilities:

		Y	G			B			

Authority: Port Complex of Lom, 21 Pristanishtna Street, 3600 Lom, Bulgaria, *Tel:* +359 971 60300, *Fax:* +359 971 60301

Accommodation:

Name	Remarks
Lom	See [1] below

[1]*Lom:* The port comprises thirteen berths. Berths 1, 2 and 3 are allocated at the Danube. Berths 4 to 9 are allocated at the west side of the harbour basin. Furthermore, there is one berth at the south side (No.10) and three berths (No's 11, 12 and 13) at the east side of the harbour basin

Main commodities handled are iron ore, coal, fertilizers and urea (in bulk), grain (bulk, direct handling from ship to waggon), cement (bags and big bags), rolling stock, machinery and project cargo, iron and steel (breakbulk), other general cargo and raw materials for car tyre production (unloading in bulk, bagging in big bags)

Storage:

Location	Open (m²)	Covered (m²)
Lom	36000	4800

Mechanical Handling Equipment:

Location	Type	Capacity (t)	Qty
Lom	Shore Cranes	5–20	26

Bunkering: Transimpex Bunker, 1 Nechaev Sqr, 3600 Lom, Bulgaria, *Tel:* +359 2 9172 131, *Fax:* +359 2 9516 641, *Email:* marine@transimpex.bg, *Website:* www.transimpex.bg

Burgas Bunker, 6, 6th September Street, 8000 Bourgas, Bulgaria, *Tel:* +359 56 843 877, *Fax:* +359 56 845 137, *Email:* bs_bunker@bitex.com

Transimpex Bunker, 1 Nechaev Sqr, 3600 Lom, Bulgaria, *Tel:* +359 2 9172 131, *Fax:* +359 2 9516 641, *Email:* marine@transimpex.bg, *Website:* www.transimpex.bg

Railway: Connected to the hinterland by an electrified railway track to the Bulgarian railway system

Lloyd's Agent: Fidelitas Ltd, 40 Graf Ignatiev Street, 9000 Varna, Bulgaria, *Tel:* +359 52 665 5111, *Fax:* +359 52 600453, *Email:* ognyan.kostov@fidelitas.bg, *Website:* www.fidelitas.bg

VARNA

Lat 43° 11' N; Long 27° 54' E.

Admiralty Chart: 2285	Admiralty Pilot: 24
Time Zone: GMT +2 h	UNCTAD Locode: BG VAR

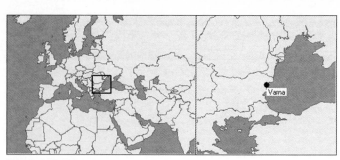

Principal Facilities:

P	Q	Y	G	C	R	L	B	D	T	A

Authority: Port of Varna EAD, 1 Slaveikov Square, 9000 Varna, Bulgaria, *Tel:* +359 52 692232, *Fax:* +359 52 632953, *Email:* headoffice@port-varna.bg, *Website:* www.port-varna.bg

Officials: Executive Director: Danail Papazov, *Email:* dpapazov@port-varna.bg. Finance Director: Andrian Atanasov, *Tel:* +359 52 692402, *Email:* aatanasov@port-varna.bg.

Operations Director: Alexander Stankov, *Tel:* +359 52 692233, *Email:* astankov@port-varna.bg.

Technical Director: Marian Gospodinov, *Tel:* +359 52 692230, *Email:* mgospodinov@port-varna.bg.

Marketing Manager: Velichka Georgieva, *Tel:* +359 52 692550, *Email:* vgeorgieva@port-varna.bg.

Harbour Master: Capt Bogdan Bogdanov, *Tel:* +359 52 684922, *Email:* bogdanov@marad.bg.

Port Security: ISPS compliant

Pre-Arrival Information: ETA's: At least 24 h prior to arrival. All vessels (excluding warships) shall give a written final notice via the ship agent to the Executive Agency 'Maritime Administration', Varna Directorate and to the port operator

Notice of Readiness: 7 day and 5 day notices. Final 3 day notice for the call, but not later than 24 h prior to arrival in the port. After arrival in the port, whether the vessel is on berth or anchorage, the master shall give notice of readiness for handling to the port operator via ship agent

Documentation: General declaration, cargo declaration, ship stores declaration, crew personal effects declaration, crew list, passenger list, maritime declaration of health

Approach: Two access channels to Varna West: Channel No.1 with draft of 11.5 m and Channel No.2 with draft of 11 m

Vessels with loa over 200 m, beam over 26 m and gt over 20 000 t pass the channels during daylight only

Anchorage: Two anchorages at Varna roadstead. Winter anchorage from Oct 1 to May 1 and summer anchorage from May 1 to Oct 1

Pilotage: Compulsory for vessels over 100 gt. Varna Pilot Station, Tel: +359 52 602448, Fax: +359 52 602445

Radio Frequency: All vessels within the territorial waters of Bulgaria, the roads or inland waterways shall maintain a double VHF radio watch on VHF Channel 16 (156.800 mHz) for calls and distress

Operational channels: Varna Radio on VHF Channel 26, Traffic Tower on VHF Channel 11 and Pilots on VHF Channel 14

Weather: Conditions do not hinder the year-round navigation and stevedoring activities. Winds vary in terms of direction and force

Tides: Negligible

Traffic: 2007, 6 622 000 t of cargo handled, 99 713 TEU's

Principal Imports and Exports: Imports: Coal, Containerized cargo, Grain, Ore & ore concentrates, Petro-coke, Phosphates, Sugar. Exports: Clinker cement, Containerized cargo, Fertilizers, Fibre-board, Grain, Kaolin, Quartz sand, Soda, Sulphuric acid.

Working Hours: 24 h/day

Accommodation:

Name	Length (m)	Depth (m)	Remarks
Varna East			See [1] below
Berth No.1P	177	7.8–8	Passengers
Berth No.1	177	6.7–7.8	
Berth No.2	129	5.8–6.1	
Berth No.3	169	6.5–6.8	
Berth No.4	169	6.5–7	

Name	Length (m)	Depth (m)	Remarks
Berth No.5	169	7.4	
Berth No.6	143	8–10.8	
Berth No.7	179	11–11.3	
Berth No.8	146	10	
Berth No.9	204	9.5–10	
Berth No.10	145	9.2	
Berth No.11	110	7	
Berth No.12	241	7.5	
Berth No.13	220	7	
Varna West			See [2] below
Berth No.1	240	10.5	
Berth No.2	200	10.5	
Berth No.3	135	10.5	
Berth No.4	140	10.5	
Berth No.5	155	10.5	
Berth No.6	210	9	
Berth No.7	153	9.7	
Berth No.8	160	9.7	
Berth No.9	160	9.8–10.4	
Berth No.10	162	10.5	
Berth No.0	213	7.4	
Berth No.11	220	8.5	
Berth No.12	162	9.5–10	
Berth No.13	160	9.5–10	
Berth No.14	160	9.2–10	
Berth No.15	168	9.6–10	
Berth No.16	230	9	
Berth No.17	200	8.7	
Balchik			Handling grain, edible oils & livestock
Berth No.1	164	7.6	
Lesport			See [3] below

[1]*Varna East:* Handling bulk goods (grain, sugar, kaolin, scrap metal, ores and ore concentrates etc), general cargo (fibre-boards, pipes, cellulose, beans, rice in bags, metals etc), liquid bulks (molasses), containers and passengers

[2]*Varna West:* Handling bulk goods (coal, coke, petro-coke, soda ash, phosphates, clinker, cement, copper concentrates, quartz sand, fertilizers, gypsum, sugar etc), general cargo (soda ash, fertilizers, metals, equipment, timber & forest products etc), liquid bulks (sulphuric acid, liquid fertilizer, caustic soda) and containers. Max air draught of 41.72 m

[3]*Lesport:* Operated by Lesport Plc, P O Box 232, 9000 Varna, Tel: +359 52 483011, Fax: +359 52 482396, Email: lesport@triada.bg. Multi-purpose port terminal

Storage: Total storage area of 318 300 m2 (open and closed)
Varna East: open storage of 49 800 m2 and closed storage of 41 500 m2
Varna West: open storage of 191 000 m2 and closed storage of 36 000 m2
Balchik: open storage of 4200 m2
Storage Base: open storage of 16 000 m2 and closed storage of 15 000 m2

Mechanical Handling Equipment: One shiploader for bulk grain, one unloader for molasses, one belt conveyor with three shiploaders for soda and urea, one shiploader for bulk chemicals, thee loaders with belt conveyors, one loading facility for liquid chemicals, one shiploader for sulphuric acid and one shiploader for caustic soda
Mobile Equipment: 37 bucket loaders, 80 forklifts, 1 reachstacker and 300 units of other equipment

Location	Type	Capacity (t)	Qty
Varna	Container Cranes	30.5	1
Varna	Container Cranes	35	2
Varna	Portal Cranes	5–32	58

Cargo Worked: Grain import 5000 t/day, grain export 2500 t/day, metals 2500 t/day, coal/ores/bulk discharging 8000 t/day, bags discharging 600 t/day, bags loading 2000 t/day, containers 12-15 moves/h

Bunkering: Atlas Marine Co. Ltd, 10 Druzki Street, 9000 Varna, Bulgaria, Tel: +359 52 633 550, Fax: +359 52 633 549, Email: atlas@varna.net
Bon Marine S.A., 3 Vardar Street, P O Box 67, 9000 Varna, Bulgaria, Tel: +359 52 687 000, Fax: +359 52 632 149, Email: office@bonmar.bg, Website: www.bonmarine.com
Cosmos Shipping AD, 6 Petko Karavelov Street, 9000 Varna, Bulgaria, Tel: +359 52 622274, Fax: +359 52 622275, Email: bunker@cosmosltd.com, Website: www.cosmosltd.com
Moniks Marine Services Ltd, Plamen Chrisstov, 6 Krali Marko Street, 9000 Varna, Bulgaria, Tel: +359 52 605599, Fax: +359 52 601154, Email: mail@moniks.com, Website: www.moniks.com
Navigation Maritime Bulgare Ltd (NAVIBULGAR), 1 Primorski Boulevard, Chervenoarmeiski, 9000 Varna, Bulgaria, Tel: +359 52 633 100, Fax: +359 52 633 033, Email: office@navbul.com, Website: www.navbul.com
Seaborne Ltd, 40 Graf Ignatiev Street, 9000 Varna, Bulgaria, Tel: +359 52 6655 205, Fax: +359 52 601 708, Email: sales@seaborne.bg, Website: www.seaborne.bg
Seatrade Ltd, 33A, Knyaz Boris 1 Boulevard, 9000 Varna, Bulgaria, Tel: +359 52 601981, Fax: +359 52 901982
Swift Sea Services Ltd, 25 Tzar Simeon Street, Office 408, 9000 Varna, Bulgaria, Tel: +359 52 630 547, Fax: +359 52 630 747, Email: sss@nat.bg
Transimpex Bunker, 22 Sofia Street, 9000 Varna, Bulgaria, Tel: +359 52 602329, Fax: +359 52 602342, Email: corporate@vn.transimpex.bg, Website: www.transimpex.bg
Zodiac Shipping Ltd, 10 Druzki Street, 9000 Varna, Bulgaria, Tel: +359 52 600650, Fax: +359 52 600879, Email: zodiac@triada.bg
Atlas Marine Co. Ltd, 10 Druzki Street, 9000 Varna, Bulgaria, Tel: +359 52 633 550, Fax: +359 52 633 549, Email: atlas@varna.net
Bon Marine S.A., 3 Vardar Street, P O Box 67, 9000 Varna, Bulgaria, Tel: +359 52 687 000, Fax: +359 52 632 149, Email: office@bonmar.bg, Website: www.bonmarine.com
Burgas Bunker, 6, 6th September Street, 8000 Bourgas, Bulgaria, Tel: +359 56 843 877, Fax: +359 56 845 137, Email: bs_bunker@bitex.com
Cosmos Shipping AD, 6 Petko Karavelov Street, 9000 Varna, Bulgaria, Tel: +359 52 622274, Fax: +359 52 622275, Email: bunker@cosmosltd.com, Website: www.cosmosltd.com
Moniks Marine Services Ltd, Plamen Chrisstov, 6 Krali Marko Street, 9000 Varna,

Bulgaria, Tel: +359 52 605599, Fax: +359 52 601154, Email: mail@moniks.com, Website: www.moniks.com
Navigation Maritime Bulgare Ltd (NAVIBULGAR), 1 Primorski Boulevard, Chervenoarmeiski, 9000 Varna, Bulgaria, Tel: +359 52 633 100, Fax: +359 52 633 033, Email: office@navbul.com, Website: www.navbul.com
Petromar Ltd, 32 Tzar Simeon Street, Floor 4, 9000 Varna, Bulgaria, Tel: +359 52 609287, Fax: +359 52 609288, Email: office@petromar-bg.com, Website: www.petromar-bg.com
Seaborne Ltd, 40 Graf Ignatiev Street, 9000 Varna, Bulgaria, Tel: +359 52 6655 205, Fax: +359 52 601 708, Email: sales@seaborne.bg, Website: www.seaborne.bg
Seatrade Ltd, 33A, Knyaz Boris 1 Boulevard, 9000 Varna, Bulgaria, Tel: +359 52 601981, Fax: +359 52 901982
Swift Sea Services Ltd, 25 Tzar Simeon Street, Office 408, 9000 Varna, Bulgaria, Tel: +359 52 630 547, Fax: +359 52 630 747, Email: sss@nat.bg
Tramp Oil & Marine, World Fuel Services Corporation, 13th Floor, Portland House, Bressenden Place, London SW1E 5BH, United Kingdom, Tel: +44 20 7808 5000, Fax: +44 20 7808 5088, Email: pturner@wfscorp.com, Website: www.wfscorp.com
Transimpex Bunker, 22 Sofia Street, 9000 Varna, Bulgaria, Tel: +359 52 602329, Fax: +359 52 602342, Email: corporate@vn.transimpex.bg, Website: www.transimpex.bg

Waste Reception Facilities: Available

Towage: Nine tugs up to 1200 hp and one tug up to 1600 hp available

Repair & Maintenance: Bulyard Shipbuilding Industry AD, South Industrial Zone, 9000 Varna, Bulgaria, Tel: +359 52 613192, Fax: +359 52 613179, Email: office@bulyard.com, Website: www.bulyard.com
MTG-Dolphin PLC, 8 Drazki Street, 9000 Bulgaria, Tel: +359 52 602074, Fax: +359 52 632963, Email: info@dolphin1.bg, Website: www.dolphin1.bg Two floating docks: No 1 - 205 m x 31.5 m with lifting cap of 18 000 t. No 2 - 150 m x 24.4 m with lifting cap of 8500 t
Odessos Shiprepair Yard S.A., Island Zone, 9000 Varna, Bulgaria, Tel: +359 52 601107, Fax: +359 52 608289, Email: commdept@odessos-yard.bg, Website: www.odessos-yard.bg Dry dock 240 m x 27 m x 10 m for vessels up to 30 000 gt. Floating dock No.1 106 m x 19 m x 5.3 m with cap 4100 t. Floating dock No.2 160 m x 27 m x 5.8 m with cap 12 000 t. Repair quays of 1200 m with max draught 7.5 m
TEREM - KRZ Flotski Arsenal - Varna Ltd, P O Box 135, 9000 Varna, Bulgaria, Tel: +359 52 370261, Fax: +359 52 370277, Email: krz-fa@krz-fa.com, Website: www.krz-fa.com

Ship Chandlers: SeaMar Services Ltd, Atanas Moskov Blvd. 20, Jambo Office Building, 9000 Varna, Bulgaria, Tel: +359 52 730842, Fax: +359 52 750095, Email: office@seamar-services.com, Website: www.seamar-services.com Managing Director: Miroslav Minov
Bulmar Consult Ltd, Zpz Bulmar Building, 9000 Varna, Bulgaria, Tel: +359 52 554161, Fax: +359 52 554160, Email: bulmar@bulmarconsult.com, Website: www.bulmarconsult.com
Ciconia Ltd, 27 Tzar Simeon 1st Street, 9000 Varna, Bulgaria, Tel: +359 52 634629, Fax: +359 52 634617, Email: ciconia@ciconia.net, Website: www.ciconia.net
Gama 95 Ltd, 2A James Bouchier Street, 1st Floor, Apartment 1, 9002 Varna, Bulgaria, Tel: +359 52 302169, Fax: +359 52 300745, Email: gama95@technolink.com, Website: www.gamaltd.hit.bg
Giab 44 Ltd, 128 8th Primorski polk Boulevard, 3rd Floor, Room 321, 9000 Varna, Bulgaria, Tel: +359 52 304878, Fax: +359 52 305404, Email: office@giab44com, Website: www.giab44.com
Karavela Ltd, 16 Han Krum Street, Floor 2, 9000 Varna, Bulgaria, Tel: +359 52 612919, Fax: +359 52 633111, Email: karavela@abv.bg
Moniks Marine Services Ltd, Plamen Chrisstov, 6 Krali Marko Street, 9000 Varna, Bulgaria, Tel: +359 52 605599, Fax: +359 52 601154, Email: mail@moniks.com, Website: www.moniks.com
Petromar Ltd, 32 Tzar Simeon 1st Street, 9000 Varna, Bulgaria, Tel: +359 52 609287, Fax: +359 52 609288, Email: office@petromar-bg.com, Website: www.petromar-bg.com
Seny Ltd, 27 Tzar Simeon 1st Street, 9000 Varna, Bulgaria, Tel: +359 52 600162, Fax: +359 52 630172, Email: office@senyltd.com, Website: www.senyltd.com
Transimpex Bunker, 22 Sofia Street, 9000 Varna, Bulgaria, Tel: +359 52 602329, Fax: +359 52 602342, Email: corporate@vn.transimpex.bg, Website: www.transimpex.bg
Vistamar Ltd, 5A Sofia Street, 9000 Varna, Bulgaria, Tel: +359 52 653533, Fax: +359 52 653533, Email: varna@vistamarltd.com, Website: www.vistamar.com

Shipping Agents: Bon Marine Shipping Agency Ltd, 5 Vardar Street, Bon Marine House, BG-9000 Varna, Bulgaria, Tel: +359 52 687187, Fax: +359 52 632149, Email: bmcont@bonmar.bg, Website: www.bonmarine.com
BSM Shipping Ltd, 7 Radko Dimitriev Street, 9000 Varna, Bulgaria, Tel: +359 52 602286, Fax: +359 52 606860, Email: office@bsmbg.com, Website: www.bsmbg.com
Cosmos Shipping AD, 6 Petko Karavelov Street, 9000 Varna, Bulgaria, Tel: +359 52 622274, Fax: +359 52 622275, Email: bunker@cosmosltd.com, Website: www.cosmosltd.com
Deta Maritime Ltd, 16 Gabrovo Street, BG-9000 Varna, Bulgaria, Tel: +359 52 630711, Fax: +359 52 630712, Email: detamaritime@varna.net
Economou International Shipping Agencies Ltd, 1st Floor, 14 Alexander Malinov Street, 9000 Varna, Bulgaria, Tel: +359 52 683855, Fax: +359 52 612066, Email: eisa@eisa-varna.com, Website: www.economou.gr
Inflot Bulgarian Shipping Agency, 21 Kap Petko Voivoda Street, Varna, Bulgaria, Tel: +359 52 362365, Fax: +359 52 362465, Email: inflot@mbox.digsys.bg, Website: www.inflot.buldata.com
KM&D Ltd, 33 Tzar Asen Street, Varna, Bulgaria, Tel: +359 52 686080/83, Fax: +359 52 686099, Email: kmandd@kmandd.com, Website: www.kmandd.com
Mediterranean Shipping Company, MSC Bulgara Ltd, 6 Pliska Street, 9000 Varna, Bulgaria, Tel: +359 52 681122, Fax: +359 52 681121, Email: info@msc.bg, Website: www.mscgva.ch
A.P. Moller-Maersk Group, Maersk Bulgaria Ltd, Building B1, Office 301, Business Park Varna, 9009 Varna, Bulgaria, Tel: +359 52 663031, Fax: +359 52 663000, Email: varmng@maersk.com, Website: www.maerskline.com
Navigation Maritime Bulgare Ltd (NAVIBULGAR), NAVIAGENT, 1 Primorski Boulevard, 9000 Varna, Bulgaria, Tel: +359 52 632937, Fax: +359 52 632916, Email: agency@navbul.com, Website: www.navbul.com
Stenamar Co. Ltd, 9 Tsaribrod Street, 9000 Varna, Bulgaria, Tel: +359 52 645670, Fax: +359 52 645671, Email: stenamar@stenamar.com, Website: www.stenamar.com

---

Key to Principal Facilities:—

A=Airport	**C**=Containers	**G**=General Cargo	**P**=Petroleum	**R**=Ro/Ro	**Y**=Dry Bulk
B=Bunkers	**D**=Dry Dock	**L**=Cruise	**Q**=Other Liquid Bulk	**T**=Towage (where available from port)	

Steorra LLC, 46 Raiko Jinzifov Street, BG-9000 Varna, Bulgaria, *Tel:* +359 52 681745, *Fax:* +359 52 681747, *Email:* steorra@steorra.bg, *Website:* www.steorra.bg

Trident Freight Ltd, 46 Raiko Jinzifov Street, 9000 Varna, Bulgaria, *Tel:* +359 52 681721, *Fax:* +359 52 601310, *Email:* trident@trident-freight.bg, *Website:* www.trident-freight.bg

Unishipping International Ltd, 5th Floor, Rooms 501-511, 25 Tzar Simeon Street, 9000 Varna, Bulgaria, *Tel:* +359 52 606759, *Fax:* +359 52 606758, *Email:* info@unishipping.net, *Website:* www.unishipping.net

Zodiac Shipping Ltd, 10 Druzki Street, 9000 Varna, Bulgaria, *Tel:* +359 52 600650, *Fax:* +359 52 600879, *Email:* zodiac@triada.bg

Stevedoring Companies: Lesport plc, P O Box 232, 9000 Varna, Bulgaria, *Tel:* +359 52 483011, *Fax:* +359 52 482396, *Email:* lesport@triada.bg

Surveyors: Bulcargo Ltd, 7 Vassil Drumev Street, Appartment 1, 9002 Varna, Bulgaria, *Tel:* +359 52 642060, *Fax:* +359 52 642060, *Email:* survey@bulcargo.com, *Website:* www.bulcargo.com

Bulmar Consult Ltd, Zpz Bulmar Building, 9000 Varna, Bulgaria, *Tel:* +359 52 554161, *Fax:* +359 52 554160, *Email:* bulmar@bulmarconsult.com, *Website:* www.bulmarconsult.com

Bureau Veritas, 7-9 Buzludzha Street, Floor 3, 9000 Varna, Bulgaria, *Tel:* +359 52 602309, *Fax:* +359 52 602310, *Email:* officevarna@bg.bureauveritas.com, *Website:* www.bureauveritas.com

Hellenic Register of Shipping, c/o Kalimbassieris Maritime Co Ltd, 6 Tsar Simeon I Street, 9000 Varna, Bulgaria, *Tel:* +359 52 600338, *Fax:* +359 52 601740, *Email:* kalmar_vn@triada.bg, *Website:* www.hrs.gr

Koraboimpex Group PLC, 128 Osmi Primorski Polk Boulevard, 9000 Varna, Bulgaria, *Tel:* +359 52 301864, *Fax:* +359 52 301838, *Email:* koraboimpex@net-bg.net, *Website:* www.koraboimpex.com

Russian Maritime Register of Shipping, P O Box 175, 9000 Varna, Bulgaria, *Tel:* +359 52 632118, *Fax:* +359 52 632118, *Email:* 252rs-bol@triada.bg, *Website:* www.rs-head.spb.ru

Vilmar Control Ltd, 33 Bratya Georgievich Street, 9000 Varna, Bulgaria, *Tel:* +359 52 601674, *Fax:* +359 52 601676, *Email:* office@vilmar-control.com, *Website:* www.vilmar-control.com

Medical Facilities: Hospital available close to the port

Airport: Varna Airport, 10 km

Railway: Bulgarian State Railways (BDZ), good rail access to the port

Lloyd's Agent: Fidelitas Ltd, 40 Graf Ignatiev Street, 9000 Varna, Bulgaria, *Tel:* +359 52 665 5111, *Fax:* +359 52 600453, *Email:* ognyan.kostov@fidelitas.bg, *Website:* www.fidelitas.bg

CAMBODIA

KOMPONG SOM

former name, see Sihanoukville

PHNOM PENH

Lat 11° 36' N; Long 104° 54' E.

Admiralty Chart: -	Admiralty Pilot: 30
Time Zone: GMT +7 h	UNCTAD Locode: KH PNH

Principal Facilities:

		G	C		B		T	A

Authority: Phnom Penh Autonomous Port (PPAP), 2 Baksei Cham Krong Street, Sangkat Wat Phnom, Khan Daun Penh, Phnom Penh, Cambodia, *Tel:* +855 23 427802, *Fax:* +855 23 427802, *Website:* www.ppap.com.kh

Officials: General Director: Hei Bavy, *Tel:* +855 23 12 812762.

Pre-Arrival Information: ETA required 48 h in advance

Documentation: Ship arrival, manifest

Anchorage: Available in harbour area

Pilotage: Compulsory for incoming and outgoing vessels up and down the stream of the Mekong River. The pilots are under direct control of the Habour Master

Radio Frequency: VHF Channels 16 and 14

Working Hours: 24 h/day

Accommodation:

Name	Length (m)	Depth (m)	Draught (m)	Remarks
Phnom-Penh Berth	300	6–14	4.2–5.2	See [1] below

[1]*Phnom-Penh:* Passenger terminal for both domestic and international passenger vessels

Storage:

Location	Open (m²)	Covered (m²)	Sheds / Warehouses
Phnom Penh	27000	3455	11

Mechanical Handling Equipment:

Location	Type	Capacity (t)	Qty
Phnom Penh	Floating Cranes		2
Phnom Penh	Mobile Cranes	2–100	36

Bunkering: Diesel and fuel oil available from barges (private terminal)

Waste Reception Facilities: Available

Towage: Two tugs of 380 hp and 560 hp are available

Shipping Agents: Angkor Logistics (Cam) Co Ltd, No.19 Street 420 - Sangkat Boeng Trabek, Khan Chamkarmorn, Phnom Penh, Cambodia, *Tel:* +855 23 222828, *Fax:* +855 23 993839, *Email:* info@angkorlogistics.com, *Website:* www.angkorlogistics.com

Bright Shipping Agency Pte Ltd, 305 AE3-BE3 Mae Tse Tong Boulevard, Phnom Penh, Cambodia, *Tel:* +855 23 218911, *Fax:* +855 23 218912, *Email:* dnasales@camnet.com.kh

EWS Agency Co. Ltd, 163 Kampuchea Krom (Street 128), Phnom Penh 12252, Cambodia, *Tel:* +855 23 882496, *Fax:* +855 23 885024, *Email:* paulyap@online.com.kh

Feeder Shipping Agency Co Ltd, Office 460, Suite 466 Sangkat Tunle Basac, Khan Chamkamorn, Phnom Penh, Cambodia, *Tel:* +855 23 213883/4, *Fax:* +855 23 213885, *Email:* rclpnh@rclgroup.com, *Website:* www.rclgroup.com

Haven Shipping Agency Ltd, House 312AE0, Preah Movivong Boulevard, Group 40 Sangkat Chaktomuk, Khan Daun Penh, Phnom Penh, Cambodia, *Tel:* +855 23 723088, *Fax:* +855 23 723303, *Email:* pnh.genmbox@cma-cgm.com

ITL Logistics (Cambodia) Pte Ltd, 3, 306 St.Sangkat Boeung Keng Kong 1, Khan Chamcamon, Phnom Penh, Cambodia, *Tel:* +855 23 213118, *Fax:* +855 23 215901, *Email:* kent@itl.com.kh

Kampuchea Shipping Agency & Brokers, 109 & 02Eo, Corner of Preah Sisowath and Seng Thuon Street, Sangkat wat Phnom, Khan Daun Penh, Phnom Penh, Cambodia, *Tel:* +855 23 725419, *Fax:* +855 23 426457, *Email:* kamsab@online.com.kh, *Website:* www.kamsab.com.kh

MCC Transport Private Ltd, 313 Sisowath Quay, South Wing, Hotel Cambodiana, Phnom Penh, Cambodia, *Tel:* +855 23 216744, *Fax:* +855 23 213843, *Email:* cbosal@maersk.com, *Website:* www.mcc.com.sg

Mercury Freight Cambodia Ltd, Unit 9A - Century Plaza, USSR Street, Phnom Penh, Cambodia, *Tel:* +855 23 890189, *Fax:* +855 23 890289, *Email:* cambodia@mercuryfreight.com, *Website:* www.mercuryfreight.com

A.P. Moller-Maersk Group, Maersk (Cambodia) Ltd, Regency Office Complex Zone, No.8A Inter Continental Hotel, 298 Mao Tse Toung, Phnom Penh, Cambodia, *Tel:* +855 23 424705, *Fax:* +855 23 424711, *Email:* cboops@maersk.com, *Website:* www.maerskline.com

National Shipping Lines of (Cambodia) Ltd, 355-357 Kampuchea Krom Boulevard(St 128), Sangkat Mittapheap, Khan 7 Makara, Phnom Penh 12252, Cambodia, *Tel:* +855 23 880816, *Fax:* +855 23 880817, *Email:* nslc.mgr@sklgroup.com, *Website:* www.sklgroup.com

Pacific Crown Shipping, 254 Monivong Boulevard, I0C building, Unit F1-R03, Phnom Penh, Cambodia, *Tel:* +855 23 211966/9, *Fax:* +855 23 211965, *Email:* pacificcrown@camnet.com.kh

SDV Cambodge, House 22 Street 240, P O Box 463, Phnom Penh, Cambodia, *Tel:* +855 23 427955, *Fax:* +855 23 224753, *Email:* m.sovann@sdv.com, *Website:* www.sdv.com

SHA Transport Express Co Ltd, 389 Eo - Street 128 (Kampuchea Krom Boulevard), Sangkat Phsa Depo III, Khan Toulkork, Phnom Penh, Cambodia, *Tel:* +855 23 987892, *Fax:* +855 23 987782, *Email:* info@shatransportexpress.com, *Website:* www.shatransportexpress.com

Surveyors: Eurogal GSL Surveys Ltd, Eurogal Surveys (Cambodia) Ltd, #293E0, Tep Pan (St 182), Sangkat Teuk Laak II Khan Toul Kork, Phnom Penh, Cambodia, *Tel:* +855 23 881963, *Fax:* +855 23 881964, *Email:* cambodia@eurogal-surveys.com, *Website:* www.eurogal-surveys.com

Medical Facilities: Several hospitals in the town

Airport: Phnom-Penh International Airport

Lloyd's Agent: Eurogal GSL Surveys Ltd, Eurogal Surveys (Cambodia) Ltd, #293E0, Tep Pan (St 182), Sangkat Teuk Laak II Khan Toul Kork, Phnom Penh, Cambodia, *Tel:* +855 23 881963, *Fax:* +855 23 881964, *Email:* cambodia@eurogal-surveys.com, *Website:* www.eurogal-surveys.com

SIHANOUKVILLE

Lat 10° 38' N; Long 103° 30' E.

Admiralty Chart: 3967/2103	Admiralty Pilot: 30
Time Zone: GMT +7 h	UNCTAD Locode: KH SHV

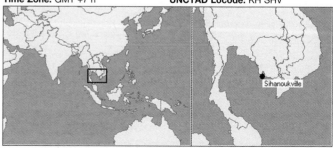

Principal Facilities:

P		Y	G	C		L	B		T	A

Authority: Sihanoukville Autonomous Port (PAS), Vithei Phe Street, Sihanoukville, Cambodia, *Tel:* +855 34 390455/6, *Fax:* +855 34 933693 & 399395, *Email:* market@pas.gov.kh, *Website:* www.pas.gov.kh

Officials: Chief Executive Officer: Lou Kim Chhun.
Marketing Director: Norng Soyeth.
Technical Director: Chea Yuthdyka.
Harbour Master: May Marith, *Tel:* +855 34 390460, *Email:* pheng@pas.gov.kh.

Port Security: Port security service with guards on watch

Pre-Arrival Information: Vessel's characteristics or ship's particulars, kind and tonnage of cargo for Sihanoukville, vessel's ETA and master's requests are required by Harbour Master's Dept. 48 h, 24 h or at least 6 h before the time of vessel's arrival at Sihanoukville Port anchorage

Documentation: Entry permit (arranged by KAMSAB, official shipping agency)
Last port clearance certificate
5 lists of last port of call (at least 10 last ports)
5 declarations of arrival
15 import cargo manifests
3 bills of lading
2 transit cargo manifests
7 crew lists
7 passenger lists
3 lists of vessel's provisions
3 lists of crew personnel effects
1 copy of maritime declaration of health
1 copy of vaccination list
1 copy of drugs & narcotic list
1 copy of fresh water origin
3 cargo plans
1 copy of valid original ship's certificates (collect only one time from ship's maiden call)
Derat exemption certificate (to be inspected by quarantine officers)
International Certificates (to be consulted and should be presented one copy each, on maiden call of any vessel in Sihanoukville Autonomous Port:
Certificate of vessel's registration
International load line certificate
International tonnage certificate
International oil pollution prevention certificate
Cargo vessel safety equipment certificate
Cargo vessel safety radio certificate
Minimum safe manning certificate

Approach: Southern Channel: in pos 10° 36' 58" N; 103° 28' 54" E, for vessels over 7 m draft
Northern Channel: in pos 10° 38' 94" N; 103° 28' 76" E, for vessels less than 7 m draft

Anchorage: There are three entry anchorages and one waiting anchorage inside the port area for deeper draft vessels:
South Anchorage in pos 10° 36.0' N; 103° 28.5' E for vessels over 7 m draft
North Anchorage in pos 10° 39' 30" N; 103° 29.0' E for vessels under 7 m draft
Tanker Anchorage in pos 10° 39' 05" N; 103° 25.7' E for all tankers
Inner Anchorage in pos 10° 39' 06" N; 103° 29' 65" E reserved for emergency or temporary anchorage and terminal shifting

Pilotage: Compulsory for all vessels. Pilot boards at South Anchorage in pos 10° 36.0' N; 103° 28.5' E or North Anchorage in pos 10° 39' 30" N; 103° 29' 00" E. Berthing day and night by North Channel for vessels less than 7 m draft. Vessels over 7 m draft, night time berthing should be requested to Harbour Master's Dept. one day before vessel's arrival time

Radio Frequency: All vessels can communicate with Pilot Station by international sound signal at any time and by walkie-talkie on VHF Channel 16 (156.80 mHz) during working hours (0700-1130, 1400-1730)

Weather: SW monsoon from June to October and NE monsoon from November to February

Tides: Range of 1.2 m

Traffic: 2006, 912 vessels, 1 586 791 t of cargo handled

Maximum Vessel Dimensions: At berth 8.5 m draft, at tanker wharf 4.2 m draft, at oil terminal 9.2 m draft

Principal Imports and Exports: Imports: Construction materials, Containers, Fabric/material for garment industry, Fuel, Machinery. Exports: Containers, Garments, Textile goods.

Working Hours: 0700-1130, 1300-1730, 1900-2330. 24 h service for container vessels or any special contracted vessels

Accommodation:

Name	Depth (m)	Remarks
Commercial Jetty (Old Pier)		See ¹ below
Berth No.1	9–13	On W part of pier for vessels up to 150 m loa
Berth No.2	8–8.5	On E part of pier for vessels up to 100 m loa
Berth No.3	9–13	On W part of pier for vessels up to 150 m loa
Berth No.4	8–8.5	On E part of pier for vessels up to 100 m loa
New Quay		Container handling & other heavy goods. Total length of 350 m
Berth No.5	7	On E part for vessels up to 150 m loa
Berth No.6	6.5	On E part for vessels up to 150 m loa
Container Terminal (Berth No's 7-9)	9.5	On E part for feeder container ships over 100 m loa with 5 ha paved container yard

Name	Depth (m)	Remarks
Tanker Terminals		See ² below

¹*Commercial Jetty (Old Pier):* General cargo, container handling & passenger vessels. Both sides of pier (E and W) are 290 m long
²*Tanker Terminals:* One small pier 53 m long for tankers less than 80 m loa and 4.2 m draft
CMB: in pos 10° 43' N; 103° 32' 44" E for tankers up to 110 m loa with max draft of 6 m
Deep draft tanker terminal: in pos 10° 43' 00" N; 103° 31' 80" E for tankers up to 9.2 m draft
PTT: in pos 10° 29' 50" N; 103° 36' 62" E, reserved for PTT company for tankers up to 2000 dwt

Storage: Five warehouses totalling 36 000 m2 for loose cargo storage, open storage area of 56 000 m2 with storage cap up to 100 000 t and container yard of 96 000 m2 with storage cap up to 7500 TEU's
Inland container depot (ICD) of 16 ha, located in the W part of Phnom Penh suburb along the national road No.4, 15 km from Phnom Penh International Airport

Mechanical Handling Equipment: Two mobile harbour cranes of 64 t cap, two RTG's of 40.6 t cap, six super stackers of 45 t cap, two empty stackers of 7.5 t cap, seventeen 20' & 40' trailers, five shore cranes of 10-50 t cap, ten forklifts of 5-25 t cap and ten trucks of 10-20 t cap

Bunkering: Available in small quantities

Waste Reception Facilities: Collection service is available. Dustmen come on board on the first day of the ship's stay at wharf, and every 5 days or on the request of Master or Agent

Towage: Five tugs available of 800-1800 hp; also one pilot boat, one mooring boat and two speed boats

Repair & Maintenance: Minor repairs only can be undertaken at dock

Shipping Agents: MS Overseas Transport Co. Ltd, Sangkat, 3 Khan Mittaphcap, Sihanoukville, Cambodia, *Tel:* +855 34 933769, *Fax:* +855 34 933769
Pacific Crown Shipping, 1B Ekareach Street Kram 3, Mondul 3, Sangkat II, Khan Mittapheap, Sihanoukville, Cambodia, *Tel:* +855 34 933762, *Fax:* +855 34 933759, *Email:* pcssih@camintel.com

Medical Facilities: Emergency services available at the port. Advance notice required for serious cases to arrange transportation to Phnom Penh. Local doctors and hospital are available. Crews require cholera and yellow fever certificates

Airport: Sihanoukville Airport, 18 km. Phnom Penh International Airport, 226 km

Railway: Railway connects the port to Phnom Penh, 262 km away

Lloyd's Agent: Eurogal GSL Surveys Ltd, Eurogal Surveys (Cambodia) Ltd, #293E0, Tep Pan (St 182), Sangkat Teuk Laak II Khan Toul Kork, Phnom Penh, Cambodia, *Tel:* +855 23 881963, *Fax:* +855 23 881964, *Email:* cambodia@eurogal-surveys.com, *Website:* www.eurogal-surveys.com

CAMEROON

DOUALA

Lat 4° 3' N; Long 9° 42' E.

Admiralty Chart: 1456	**Admiralty Pilot:** 2
Time Zone: GMT +1 h	**UNCTAD Locode:** CM DLA

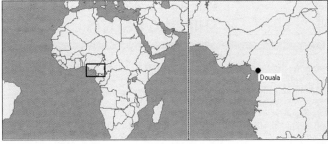

Principal Facilities:

P		Y	G	C	R		B	D	T	A

Key to Principal Facilities:—

A=Airport	**C**=Containers	**G**=General Cargo	**P**=Petroleum	**R**=Ro/Ro	**Y**=Dry Bulk
B=Bunkers	**D**=Dry Dock	**L**=Cruise	**Q**=Other Liquid Bulk	**T**=Towage (where available from port)	

Authority: Port Authority of Douala (PAD), P O Box 4020, Douala, Cameroon, *Tel:* +237 3342 7322, *Fax:* +237 3342 6797, *Email:* portdouala@iccnet2000.com

Officials: Managing Director: Emmanuel Etoundi Oyono.
Deputy Managing Director: Ewodo Noah Simon Pierre.

Port Security: ISPS compliant

Approach: The entrance is well marked. The min depth of the approach channel is 10.5 m; length of channel 24 km. Max safe draft from 6.4 m NT to 8.0 m ST. The first buoy, called 'A' buoy, is positioned at 3° 45' N, 9° 24' E (white light 6 seconds) and Base Buoy, 3° 54' N, 9° 32' E (white light), at which vessels await the pilot

Pilotage: Pilot working hours 24 h/day. Request for pilot for berthing, sailing or all other movements in port is done by Agent during port meetings held as follows: Monday to Saturday 1000 and 1600. Sunday and Holidays 1000
Pilot cannot be ordered out of port meetings nor directly from vessel. Ships are advised of shifting by a port notice remitted through Agents

Radio Frequency: Port control on VHF Channel 16

Tides: Range of tide 1.85 m to 2.9 m

Traffic: 2006, 200 251 TEU's handled

Maximum Vessel Dimensions: 230 m loa, max draft 6.2 m + tide

Principal Imports and Exports: Imports: Alumina, Cement, Chemicals, Clinker, Fertiliser, Flour, Iron & steel, Refined oil, Rice, Vehicles, Wheat. Exports: Aluminium, Bananas, Cocoa, Coffee, Cotton, Logs, Rubber, Sawn timber.

Working Hours: 0730-1700, 1730-0630

Accommodation:

Name	Remarks
Douala	See [1] below
Berth No.1	Multi-purpose & scrap
Berth No.2	Alumina, petcoke & pitch
Berth No.3	Palm oil & wine in bulk
Berth No.4	Conventional cargo
Berth No.5	Conventional cargo
Berth No.6	Conventional cargo
Berth No.7	Conventional cargo
Berth No.8	Conventional cargo
Berth No.9	Conventional cargo
Berth No.10	Conventional cargo
Berth No.11	Conventional cargo
Berth No.12	Fruit
Berth No.13	Wheat in bulk
Berth No.14	Dockyard
Berth No.15	Containers
Berth No.16	Ro/ro
Berth No.17	Ro/ro

[1]*Douala:* Container & ro/ro terminal (berth no's 15-17), operated by Douala International Container Terminal, P O Box 3945, Douala, Tel: +237 3342 1185, Fax: +237 3343 3900, Email: cmrpj@apmterminals.com, Website: www.apmterminals.com, with 660 m of berth and 17 ha container yard with two railheads and a ro/ro ramp. Equipment includes two gantry cranes. 120 reefer points

Storage: Berth No.2: six alumina silos of 1600 t cap each
Berth No's 2 & 3: four palm oil tanks of 2100 t cap each
Berth No's 3, 4 & 5: warehouse of 4000 m2
Berth No.6: warehouses of 4000 m2 and 2800 m2
Berth No.7: three warehouses of 5600 m2 each
Berth No.8: warehouses of 2000 m2 and 3600 m2
Berth No's 9 & 10: warehouse of 4000 m2
Berth No.11: warehouse of 1875 m2

Bunkering: Africa Shipping & Stevedoring Agency (ASSA), Boulevard Leclerc, Harbour Zone, P O Box 15167, Douala, Cameroon, *Tel:* +237 3340 5499, *Fax:* +237 3340 5579, *Email:* assa@globalnet2.net, *Website:* www.assacam.com
BP Cameroun S.A., P O Box 1055, Douala, Cameroon, *Tel:* +237 2242 0131, *Fax:* +237 2242 7653
Societe Shell du Cameroun, 5 Rue Tamaris, Bonadibong, Akwa, Douala, Cameroon, *Tel:* +237 422415, *Fax:* +237 426031
Bominflot, Bominflot Bunkergesellschaft fur Mineralole mbH & Co. KG, Grosse Baeckerstrasse 11, 20095 Hamburg, Germany, *Tel:* +49 40 350 930, *Fax:* +49 40 3509 3116, *Email:* mail@bominflot.de, *Website:* www.bominflot.net
BP France S.A., Immeuble le Cervier, 12 Avenue des Beguines, Cergy-Saint-Christophe, 95866 Cergy Pontoise Cedex, France, *Tel:* +33 1 3422 4000, *Fax:* +33 1 3422 4417, *Email:* benoist.grosjean@fr.bp.com, *Website:* www.bpmarine.com
Cockett Marine Oil Ltd, Carrick House, 36 Station Square, Petts Wood, Kent BR5 1NA, United Kingdom, *Tel:* +44 1689 883 400, *Fax:* +44 1689 877 666, *Email:* enquiries@cockett.com, *Website:* www.cockettgroup.com
ExxonMobil Marine Fuels, Mailpoint 31, ExxonMobil House, Ermyn Way, Leatherhead, Surrey KT22 8UX, United Kingdom, *Tel:* +44 1372 222 000, *Fax:* +44 1372 223 922, *Email:* marine.fuels@exxonmobil.com, *Website:* www.exxonmobil.com
Societe Shell du Cameroun, 5 Rue Tamaris, Bonadibong, Akwa, Douala, Cameroon, *Tel:* +237 422415, *Fax:* +237 426031
Total France S.A., Total Marine Fuels, 51 Esplanade du General de Gaulle, F-92907 Paris la Defense Cedex 10, France, *Tel:* +33 1 4135 2755, *Fax:* +33 1 4197 0291, *Email:* marine.fuels@total.com, *Website:* www.marinefuels.total.com
Tramp Oil & Marine, World Fuel Services Corporation, 13th Floor, Portland House, Bressenden Place, London SW1E 5BH, United Kingdom, *Tel:* +44 20 7808 5000, *Fax:* +44 20 7808 5088, *Email:* pturner@wfscorp.com, *Website:* www.wfscorp.com – *Grades:* MGO; IFO-180cSt – *Delivery Mode:* ex pipe, truck

Waste Reception Facilities: Sludge reception by private companies

Towage: One sea-going tug of 2000 hp and two harbour tugs of 800 hp and 1000 hp. One tug is usually supplied for berthing or departure, additional if required is ordered by Agent during port meeting or on pilot request
Swire Pacific Offshore Services (Private) Ltd, Swire Pacific Offshore Africa S.A., 2nd Floor Immeuble Gicam, Vallee des Ministres, Bonanjo, Douala, Cameroon, *Tel:* +237 3342 2433, *Fax:* +237 3342 2822, *Email:* florent.kirchhoff@swire-cm.com, *Website:* www.swire.com.sg

Repair & Maintenance: Cameroon Shipyard & Industrial Engineering Ltd, Quai des Reparations Navales, Zone Portuaire Amont, P O Box 2389, Douala, Cameroon, *Tel:* +237 3340 3488, *Fax:* +237 3340 6199, *Email:* enquiries@cnicyard.com, *Website:* www.cnicyard.com One floating dock of 180 m x 33 m x 7.8 m with lifting cap of 10 000 t, capable of accepting vessels up to 30 000 dwt and two small floating docks with cap of 1000 t and 500 t for vessels up to 65 m loa and 13 m beam. Repair quays 200 m in length

Ship Chandlers: ETS Meitang, 734 Rue Tobie Kouoh, P O Box 2651, Douala, Cameroon, *Tel:* +237 3343 0847, *Fax:* +237 3342 1016, *Email:* meitangh@yahoo.fr
Nontcho Marine Services, Rue King Bell Bali, P O Box 9622, Douala, Cameroon, *Tel:* +237 7477 6965, *Fax:* +237 3342 4904, *Email:* nontchoservices@yahoo.fr
The NYL Company, Douala 3983, Cameroon, *Fax:* +237 3342 9018, *Email:* thenylcompany@yahoo.fr
Tchambia Ship Suppliers, P O Box 2449, Douala, Cameroon, *Tel:* +237 3343 9030, *Fax:* +237 3343 9030, *Email:* tchambiaship@yahoo.fr
Tefon Oilfield Services, P O Box 842, Douala, Cameroon, *Tel:* +237 3343 9574, *Fax:* +237 3343 9574, *Email:* operations@tefonservices.com

Shipping Agents: Assistance Maritime Internationale, Terminal Ayal du Port de Douala, P O Box 3086, Douala, Cameroon, *Tel:* +237 3342 8334 & 3342 1610, *Fax:* +237 3342 3281, *Email:* infos@ami-cameroun.com, *Website:* www.ami-cameroun.com

Societe Camatrans Cameroun, Rue Kitchener, P O Box 263, Douala, Cameroon, *Tel:* +237 3342 4750, *Fax:* +237 3342 8851

Cameroon Shipping Lines S.A. (CAMSHIP), Centre des Affaires Maritimes, P O Box 4054, Douala, Cameroon, *Tel:* +237 3342 0038, *Fax:* +237 3342 2181, *Email:* agencies@camshipinc.com

Eagle Cameroun, P O Box 2604, Douala, Cameroon, *Tel:* +237 3340 6202, *Fax:* +237 3340 8269, *Email:* eaglecmr@yahoo.fr & bohimboetota@yahoo.fr

GAC-GETMA, Avenue du General de Gaulle, P O Box 4144, Douala, Cameroon, *Tel:* +237 33 430820, *Fax:* +237 33 430777, *Email:* gac-getma.cameroon@gacworld.com, *Website:* www.gacworld.com

Geodis Cameroun, P O Box 284, Douala, Cameroon, *Tel:* +237 3342 4051, *Fax:* +237 3342 4274, *Email:* geodis@geodiscameroun.com, *Website:* www.geodiscameroun.com

Groupe Navitrans, Avenue du General de Gaulle, P O Box 12823, Douala, Cameroon, *Tel:* +237 3343 1550, *Fax:* +237 3342 1130, *Email:* info@messinaline-cm.com, *Website:* www.navitrans.fr

Mediterranean Shipping Company, MSC Cameroun S.A., Rue de la Base Navale, P O Box 1506, Douala, Cameroon, *Tel:* +237 3343 9148, *Fax:* +237 3343 1405, *Email:* info@msccm.mscgva.ch, *Website:* www.mscgva.ch

A.P. Moller-Maersk Group, Maersk Cameroun S.A., 2 Maersk Place - Zone Udeac, P O Box 12414, Douala, Cameroon, *Tel:* +237 3342 1145, *Fax:* +237 3342 1186, *Email:* dlacusmng@maersk.com, *Website:* www.maerskline.com

SAGA-Cameroon, 5 Boulevard de la Liberte, P O Box 320, Douala, Cameroon, *Tel:* +237 3342 8196, *Fax:* +237 3342 9815, *Email:* jean-claude.sorin@cm.dti.bollore.com

SDV Cameroun, P O Box 263, Douala, Cameroon, *Tel:* +237 3342 1036, *Fax:* +237 3342 8851, *Email:* sdvshipping.douala@cm.dti.bollore.com

Socomar Cameroun, Boulevard Udeac, P O Box 12351, Douala, Cameroon, *Tel:* +237 3342 4550, *Fax:* +237 3342 6818

Socopao Cameroun, P O Box 215, Douala, Cameroon, *Fax:* +237 3342 4515, *Email:* cameroun/sc62@dms.calva.com

Sud Maritime S.A., 678 Avenue General de Gaulle, Douala 12416, Cameroon, *Tel:* +237 3342 3880, *Fax:* +237 3342 4904, *Email:* sudmar@sudmar.com

Supermaritime Cameroun S.A., P O Box 3631, Douala, Cameroon, *Tel:* +237 3342 5452, *Fax:* +237 3342 5439, *Email:* supermaritime@douala1.com, *Website:* www.supermaritime.com

Tefon Oilfield Services, P O Box 842, Douala, Cameroon, *Tel:* +237 3343 9574, *Fax:* +237 3343 9574, *Email:* operations@tefonservices.com

Transcap Shipping, Rue de la Motte Piquet, P O Box 4059, Douala, Cameroon, *Tel:* +237 3342 7214, *Fax:* +237 3342 1031

Surveyors: Bureau Veritas, P O Box 830, Douala, Cameroon, *Tel:* +237 3342 1218, *Fax:* +237 3342 1686, *Website:* www.bureauveritas.com

Medical Facilities: Port dispensary and clinics

Airport: Douala International Airport, 10 km

Lloyd's Agent: Omega Marine Cameroon, Douala, Cameroon, *Email:* omega-cameroon@omega-marine.com

EBOME TERMINAL

Lat 2° 48' N; Long 9° 50' E.

Admiralty Chart: 1888	**Admiralty Pilot:** 2
Time Zone: GMT +1 h	**UNCTAD Locode:** CM EBT

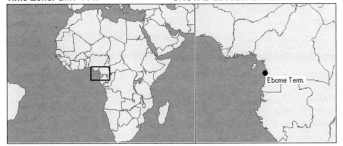

Principal Facilities:

P							A

Authority: Perenco Cameroon S.A., Avenue Ahmadou Ahidjo, P O Box 1225, Douala, Cameroon, *Tel:* +237 3342 3291, *Fax:* +237 3342 4359, *Email:* om_ebome@cm.perenco.com

Port Security: ISPS compliant

Pre-Arrival Information: Vessel's should send ETA to the Operations and Terminal Manager 72 h prior to arrival or as soon as possible if the previous port is less than 72 h away, together with the following information:
a) vessel's name and flag
b) ETA (local time)
c) grade and quantity of cargo to be loaded
d) max loading rate acceptable
e) lifting cap of derrick (SWL) or crane
f) size of vessel's manifold flanges
g) distance bow/cargo manifold
h) ISPS information
ETA should be confirmed or amended 48 h and 24 h prior to arrival

Anchorage: A circular area of 1 mile radius is located within a centre in pos 02° 48' 23.13" N; 09° 47' 07.57" E (approx 2 miles W of loading buoy)

Pilotage: Compulsory and provided by Douala. Pilot boards in the anchorage area 1 nautical mile W of the SPM, dependent on weather conditions

Radio Frequency: When approaching, vessels should contact the terminal on VHF Channel 16 or 13 (permanently on watch). Working channel 13

Maximum Vessel Dimensions: Max dwt 180 000 t

Accommodation:

Name	Remarks
Ebome Terminal	Consists of one storage vessel 'La Lobe' and one SPM loading buoy for export of crude oil

Airport: The nearest airport is located 4 km from Douala

Lloyd's Agent: Omega Marine Cameroon, Douala, Cameroon, *Email:* omega-cameroon@omega-marine.com

KOLE TERMINAL

Lat 4° 13' N; Long 8° 34' E.

Admiralty Chart: 1860/3433	**Admiralty Pilot:** 2
Time Zone: GMT +1 h	**UNCTAD Locode:** CM KOL

Principal Facilities:

P								T	

Authority: Total E&P Cameroun, P O Box 2214, Douala, Cameroon, *Tel:* +237 3342 1366, *Fax:* +237 3340 0020

Port Security: ISPS compliant

Pre-Arrival Information: Tankers should notify Total E&P Cameroun of their arrival by radio 72, 48 and 24 h in advance. Thereafter, they should give notice of any appreciable change in the forecast timetable. On notifying their ETA the Captain shall communicate the following information to the Terminal:
Flag name
Coming from
Destination
Quantity to load
Duration of de-ballasting if not concurrently with loading
Maximum loading rate
Safe working load of derrick or crane
Dimensions of manifold flanges
Distance from bow to middle manifold
Captain's Name
Dwt, gt, nrt

Documentation: Shipping Documents: bill of lading, quality and quantity certificate, certificate of origin, time sheet, ulage report, distribution of documents, receipt for sample, cargo manifest
Other Documents: notice of readiness (if the vessel does not wish to establish its own, or if its form is not accepted by the terminal), acknowledgement receipt of port and safety regulations, arrival information sheet, ship/shore safety check list (jointly signed), watch request to monitor buoy and hoses, safety requirements

Approach: Vessels should not navigate within the prohibited areas near the oil installations

Anchorage: Anchorage can be obtained 2 miles SW of loading buoy KLB2 in a depth of 38 m within the quadrilateral determined by the following coordinates:
4° 12.3' N; 8° 33' E
4° 12.3' N; 8° 34' E
4° 11.3' N; 8° 33' E
4° 11.3' N; 8° 34' E

Pilotage: Compulsory. Services rendered by a pilot from Cameroon Ports Authority. Pilot boards 2 miles SW of the loading point KLB2 in pos 4° 12' N; 8° 32' E, and will act as mooring master, remaining on board throughout operations. ETA should be advised 72, 48 and 24 h prior to arrival, with confirmation 24 h prior

Radio Frequency: A constant watch is maintained on VHF Channel 16. Working on VHF Channels 11 and 12

Tides: Semi diurnal

Traffic: 2003, 33 vessels, 3 400 000 t of crude oil exported

Maximum Vessel Dimensions: 22 m draught at KLB2 and 16 m draught at KLB1

Principal Imports and Exports: Exports: Crude oil.

Working Hours: Berthing 0600-1600

Accommodation:

Name	Remarks
Kole Terminal	See [1] below

[1]*Kole Terminal:* Consists of two loading buoys (KLB1 & KLB2) and a floating storage facility (SEREPCA 1 call sign TJCJ). They are connected by 3000 m and 1600 m long sea lines
KLB1 (IMODCO): in pos 4° 14' 57" N; 8° 33' 07" E, emergency loading point designed for the mooring of tankers up to 150 000 dwt in depth of 23.5 m (at present this is not operative)
KLB2 (BLUEWATER): in pos 4° 13' 21" N; 8° 33' 31" E, designed for the mooring and loading of tankers of 50 000-310 000 dwt in depth of 30.5 m. Loading can be performed at a max flow of 4000 t/h

Towage: One tug boat available, supplied by terminal

Key to Principal Facilities:—					
A=Airport	**C**=Containers	**G**=General Cargo	**P**=Petroleum	**R**=Ro/Ro	**Y**=Dry Bulk
B=Bunkers	**D**=Dry Dock	**L**=Cruise	**Q**=Other Liquid Bulk	**T**=Towage (where available from port)	

Medical Facilities: If required cases can be transported to hospitals at Douala

Lloyd's Agent: Omega Marine Cameroon, Douala, Cameroon, *Email:* omega-cameroon@omega-marine.com

KOME-KRIBI 1 TERMINAL

Lat 2° 55' N; Long 9° 48' E.

Admiralty Chart: 1322	**Admiralty Pilot:** 2	
Time Zone: GMT +1 h	**UNCTAD Locode:** CM	

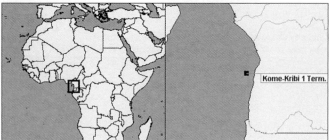

Principal Facilities:

P									

Authority: Cameroon Oil Transportation Co. S.A. (COTCO), P O Box 3738, Douala, Cameroon

Port Security: ISPS compliant

Pre-Arrival Information: Export tankers should send an initial ETA message via email, fso.cotco.mooringmaster@exxonmobil.com, to the marine terminal when they start on passage with updates 96, 72, 48 and 24 h prior to arrival

When within 50 nautical miles of the marine terminal, the export tanker should maintain a listening watch on VHF Channels 9 and 16

Anchorage: 4 miles off the marine terminal in depth of approx 51 m

Pilotage: Compulsory. The Mooring Master gives the Export Tanker's Master a boarding position in terms of bearing and distance from marine terminal

Radio Frequency: Listening on VHF Channel 16 and operating on VHF Channel 9 throughout 24 h

Principal Imports and Exports: Exports: Crude oil.

Accommodation:

Name	Remarks
Kome-Kribi 1 Marine Terminal	See [1] below

[1]*Kome-Kribi 1 Marine Terminal:* Export terminal for petroleum derived from Chad consisting of a FSO permanently connected by the stern to a SPM and then connected to the shore by a submarine pipeline. Mooring operations are normally conducted during daylight hours only, unmooring throughout 24 h. Max loading rate of 50 000 bbls/h

Towage: Two 80 t bollard pull tugs available

Lloyd's Agent: Omega Marine Cameroon, Douala, Cameroon, *Email:* omega-cameroon@omega-marine.com

KRIBI

Lat 2° 56' N; Long 9° 55' E.

Admiralty Chart: 1322	**Admiralty Pilot:** 2
Time Zone: GMT +1 h	**UNCTAD Locode:** CM KBI

Principal Facilities:

		G					A	

Authority: Port Authority of Douala (PAD), P O Box 4020, Douala, Cameroon, *Tel:* +237 3342 7322, *Fax:* +237 3342 6797, *Email:* portdouala@iccnet2000.com

Officials: Managing Director: Emmanuel Etoundi Oyono.
Deputy Managing Director: Ewodo Noah Simon Pierre.

Port Security: ISPS compliant

Accommodation:

Name	Remarks
Kribi	One wharf 250 m in length

Storage: Stacking area of 2500 m2

Location	Covered (m²)
Kribi	6200

Mechanical Handling Equipment:

Location	Type	Capacity (t)	Qty
Kribi	Mult-purp. Cranes	10	1
Kribi	Mult-purp. Cranes	25	1

Airport: Kribi National Airport

Lloyd's Agent: Omega Marine Cameroon, Douala, Cameroon, *Email:* omega-cameroon@omega-marine.com

LIMBE

Lat 4° 0' N; Long 9° 12' E.

Admiralty Chart: 1455	**Admiralty Pilot:** 2
Time Zone: GMT +1 h	**UNCTAD Locode:** CM LIM

Principal Facilities:

Q	G			B			

Authority: Port Authority of Douala (PAD), P O Box 4020, Douala, Cameroon, *Tel:* +237 3342 7322, *Fax:* +237 3342 6797, *Email:* portdouala@iccnet2000.com

Officials: Managing Director: Emmanuel Etoundi Oyono.
Deputy Managing Director: Ewodo Noah Simon Pierre.

Working Hours: 0730-1200, 1430-1800. Saturday closed

Accommodation:

Name	Remarks
Limbe	See [1] below

[1]*Limbe:* Depth at entrance 12.8-16.5 m. Depths in harbour 9.1-12.8 m. Depths at the four anchorage berths 12.8-16.5 m. Loading and discharging by barges and dumb lighters. Seven motor barges and 14 dumb lighters varying from 40-150 t cap and seven tugs available. There are two self-propelled and two dumb oil barges for discharge of palm oil only. One lighter wharf at Bota equipped with electric cranes. Lighterage, wharfage and handling are carried out by, and all labour on board ships is provided by Cameroon National Ports Authority. No container handling. Anchor berths are signalled from end of Bota wharf

Bunkering: Bominflot, Bominflot Bunkergesellschaft fur Mineralole mbH & Co. KG, Grosse Baeckerstrasse 11, 20095 Hamburg, Germany, *Tel:* +49 40 350 930, *Fax:* +49 40 3509 3116, *Email:* mail@bominflot.de, *Website:* www.bominflot.net
ExxonMobil Marine Fuels, Mailpoint 31, ExxonMobil House, Ermyn Way, Leatherhead, Surrey KT22 8UX, United Kingdom, *Tel:* +44 1372 222 000, *Fax:* +44 1372 223 922, *Email:* marine.fuels@exxonmobil.com, *Website:* www.exxonmobil.com
Total France S.A., Total Marine Fuels, 51 Esplanade du General de Gaulle, F-92907 Paris la Defense Cedex 10, France, *Tel:* +33 1 4135 2755, *Fax:* +33 1 4197 0291, *Email:* marine.fuels@total.com, *Website:* www.marinefuels.total.com
Tramp Oil & Marine, World Fuel Services Corporation, 13th Floor, Portland House, Bressenden Place, London SW1E 5BH, United Kingdom, *Tel:* +44 20 7808 5000, *Fax:* +44 20 7808 5088, *Email:* pturner@wfscorp.com, *Website:* www.wfscorp.com – *Grades:* MGO; IFO-180cSt – *Delivery Mode:* ex pipe, truck

Shipping Agents: Cameroon Shipping Lines S.A. (CAMSHIP), P O Box 209, Limbe, Cameroon, *Tel:* +237 3333 3399, *Fax:* +237 3333 3399, *Email:* agencies@camship.com

Development: Cameroon Shipyard & Industrial Engineering Ltd is developing a shiprepair facility on a 45 ha site

Lloyd's Agent: Omega Marine Cameroon, Douala, Cameroon, *Email:* omega-cameroon@omega-marine.com

LIMBOH TERMINAL

Lat 4° 0' N; Long 9° 8' E.

Admiralty Chart: 1455	**Admiralty Pilot:** 2
Time Zone: GMT +1 h	**UNCTAD Locode:** CM LIT

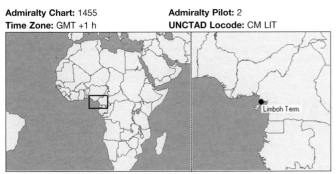

Principal Facilities:

P											

Authority: Societe Nationale de Raffinage, Limbe, Cameroon

Port Security: ISPS compliant

Pilotage: Pilot boards 1 mile S of the SBM

Radio Frequency: The refinery keeps radio watch on VHF channel 14 and should be contacted 2 h prior to arrival

Maximum Vessel Dimensions: 90 000 dwt, 243.5 m loa

Accommodation:

Name	Remarks
Cap Limboh	See [1] below

[1]*Cap Limboh:* Single buoy mooring in a depth of 21 m, connected to the refinery on shore by a submarine pipeline. Loading or discharging is through a 16'' hose and a min 10 t cap port side derrick is required
There is a jetty at the refinery with a depth of 12 m at the seaward end

Lloyd's Agent: Omega Marine Cameroon, Douala, Cameroon, *Email:* omega-cameroon@omega-marine.com

MOUDI TERMINAL

Lat 4° 8' N; Long 8° 27' E.

Admiralty Chart: 1860	**Admiralty Pilot:** 2
Time Zone: GMT +1 h	**UNCTAD Locode:** CM MOU

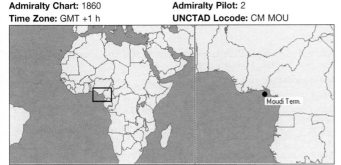

Principal Facilities:

P											

Authority: Perenco Cameroon S.A., Avenue Ahmadou Ahidjo, P O Box 1225, Douala, Cameroon, *Tel:* +237 3342 3291, *Fax:* +237 3342 4359, *Email:* om_ebome@cm.perenco.com

Port Security: ISPS compliant

Anchorage: The anchorage for vessels waiting to berth is 3.2 km ENE of the terminal

Pilotage: Compulsory. Pilot boards at the anchorage. Vessels ETA should be transmitted via Douala Radio or Ship Agent 72, 48 and 24 h before arrival

Radio Frequency: Douala Radio 2182 kHz and VHF Channel 16. Vessels should make contact with the terminal on Channel 13 when 100 km away

Maximum Vessel Dimensions: Max dwt 280 000 t

Accommodation:

Name	Remarks
Moudi Terminal	See [1] below

[1]*Moudi Terminal:* Single buoy mooring and a 225 000 dwt storage tanker Moudi in a depth of 57 m. Berthing normally during daylight, unberthing anytime. Vessels load using 24'' floating hoses and two 16'' tanker rail hoses for connection to tanker manifold. No deballasting facilities available

Lloyd's Agent: Omega Marine Cameroon, Douala, Cameroon, *Email:* omega-cameroon@omega-marine.com

VICTORIA

alternate name, see Limbe

CANADA

ALBERT MATAIS TERMINAL

harbour area, see under La Baie

ALCAN TERMINALS

harbour area, see under Kitimat

ANNACIS AUTO TERMINALS

harbour area, see under Fraser River Port

ANSE-AU-FOULON

harbour area, see under Quebec

ARGENTIA

Lat 47° 18' N; Long 53° 59' W.

Admiralty Chart: 4737	**Admiralty Pilot:** 50
Time Zone: GMT -3.5 h	**UNCTAD Locode:** CA NWP

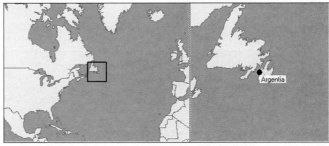

Principal Facilities:

		Y	G	C	R	L	B		T	

Authority: Argentia Port Corp., P O Box 95, Argentia, NL, Canada A0B 1W0, *Tel:* +1 709 227 5502, *Fax:* +1 709 227 5592, *Email:* k.browne@argentia.ca, *Website:* www.argentia.nf.ca

Officials: General Manager: Ken Browne, *Tel:* +1 709 227 5518.
Manager: Marion King.
Marketing Manager: Harvey Brenton, *Tel:* +1 709 227 5518, *Email:* w.brenton@argentia.ca.

Port Security: ISPS compliant

Pre-Arrival Information: Internationally registered vessels must provide 96 h pre-arrival notice

Approach: The harbour is entered between Low Room Point and Broad Cove Point and extends 3 km SW to the head of Sandy Cove

Anchorage: Available 1.6 km from Fleet Dock

Pilotage: Not compulsory, but licensed pilots available if needed. Pilot boards off Argentia in pos 47° 20' 00" N; 54° 06' 30" W. ETA to be sent 12 h and 3 h prior to arrival. Pilot messages can be passed through, Tel: +1 877 272 3477, Fax: +1 877 745 3477

Radio Frequency: Placentia Traffic operates on VHF Channels 12 and 14

Weather: The navigation season is year-round

Tides: Rise of tide 1.9 m MWST, 1.45 m MWNT

Principal Imports and Exports: Imports: Automobiles, General cargo, Lumber. Exports: Fish, Scrap metal.

Accommodation:

Name	Length (m)	Depth (m)	Remarks
Argentia			See [1] below
Fleet Dock Berth 1	150	11	
Fleet Dock Berth 2	155	11	
Fleet Dock Berth 3	130	8.5	Heavy lift
Marine Atlantic Berth 6	20		
Marine Atlantic Berth 7	185	10–13.3	
Navy Dock Berth 8	95	7.4–11	

Key to Principal Facilities:—			
A=Airport	**C**=Containers	**G**=General Cargo	**P**=Petroleum **R**=Ro/Ro **Y**=Dry Bulk
B=Bunkers	**D**=Dry Dock	**L**=Cruise	**Q**=Other Liquid Bulk **T**=Towage (where available from port)

Name	Length (m)	Depth (m)	Remarks
Navy Dock Berth 9	95	7.4–11	

[1]*Argentia:* Argentia Harbour is located on the east side of Placentia Bay

Mechanical Handling Equipment:

Location	Type	Capacity (t)	Qty
Argentia	Mobile Cranes	200	1

Bunkering: Fuel is available from a variety of providers by tanker truck

Waste Reception Facilities: Arrangements must be made through Agent for garbage and waste oil disposal

Towage: Not usually necessary but three tugs from Come by Chance can be arranged

Repair & Maintenance: Local contractors can perform minor repairs. Major repairs must be undertaken by companies from nearby St. John's or Marystown

Shipping Agents: Canadian Maritime Agency Ltd, 4 Refinery Road, P O Box 119, Come by Chance, NL, Canada A0B 1N0, *Tel:* +1 709 463 4717, *Fax:* +1 709 463 8737, *Email:* opscbc@canadianmaritime.nf.ca, *Website:* www.canadianmaritime.com

Medical Facilities: Placentia Health Care Complex, 6.5 km

Lloyd's Agent: Hayes Stuart Inc., 297 Duke Street, Montreal, Que., Canada H3C 2M2, *Tel:* +1 514 866 1801, *Fax:* +1 514 866 1259, *Email:* montreal@hayesstuart.com, *Website:* www.hayesstuart.com

BAIE COMEAU

alternate name, see Comeau Bay

BARRACK POINT TERMINAL

harbour area, see under Saint John

BATHURST

Lat 47° 37' N; Long 65° 38' W.

Admiralty Chart: 4768	**Admiralty Pilot:** 65
Time Zone: GMT -4 h	**UNCTAD Locode:** CA BAT

Principal Facilities:

		G		B		A

Authority: The MI'K MAG Port of Bathurst Inc., 132 Main Street, Bathurst, N.B., Canada E2A 1A4, *Tel:* +1 506 545 9222, *Fax:* +1 506 545 9224

Port Security: ISPS compliant

Approach: Depth in entrance channel 3.7 m at LW plus 2.1 m springs and 1.2 m neaps

Anchorage: Anchorage area 2 or 3 miles off harbour entrance

Pilotage: Compulsory. Atlantic Pilotage Authority has a 24 h centralised pilot dispatch centre in Halifax, Tel: +1 877 272 3477 (toll free) and +1 902 426 7610 (inmarsat), Fax: +1 877 745 3477 (toll free) and +1 902 426 7236 (inmarsat), Email: dispatch@atlanticpilotage.com

Maximum Vessel Dimensions: 5.0 m d

Accommodation:

Name	Length (m)	Depth (m)	Remarks
Bathurst(NB)			See [1] below
Consolidated Bathurst Wharf	152	6.1	See [2] below
Transport Canada Wharf	122	6.4	

[1]*Bathurst(NB):* There are a number of wharves, but only two in good enough condition to accommodate ocean-going vessels
[2]*Consolidated Bathurst Wharf:* Situated on W side of the river, approx 152.4 m in length with depth alongside of 6.1 m LW; equipped with a shed. Rail tracks on wharf

Mechanical Handling Equipment:

Location	Type
Bathurst	Mobile Cranes

Bunkering: Imperial Oil (Anjou) Ltd, 7100 Jean-Talon Street East, Anjou, Que., Canada H1M 3R8, *Tel:* +1 450 6497 519, *Fax:* +1 450 6497 821, *Email:* christian.beaunoyer@esso.ca, *Website:* www.imperialoil.com – *Grades:* MDO
Irving Oil Co. Ltd, 10 Sydney Street, P O Box 1421, Saint John, N.B., Canada E2L 4K1, *Tel:* +1 888 3101 924, *Fax:* +1 506 2023 868, *Email:* webinquiries@irvingoil.com, *Website:* www.irvingoilco.com – *Grades:* MDO

Repair & Maintenance: Minor repairs possible

Shipping Agents: Seacrest Shipping Agency, 1980 Wellington Avenue, Bathurst, N.B., Canada E2A 4X8, *Tel:* +1 506 546 4391, *Fax:* +1 506 548 2709, *Email:* seacrest@nb.sympatico.ca

Airport: West Bathurst, 8 km

Lloyd's Agent: Hayes Stuart Inc., 297 Duke Street, Montreal, Que., Canada H3C 2M2, *Tel:* +1 514 866 1801, *Fax:* +1 514 866 1259, *Email:* montreal@hayesstuart.com, *Website:* www.hayesstuart.com

BAYSIDE

Lat 45° 10' N; Long 67° 8' W.

Admiralty Chart: 352	**Admiralty Pilot:** 59
Time Zone: GMT -4 h	**UNCTAD Locode:** CA BAS

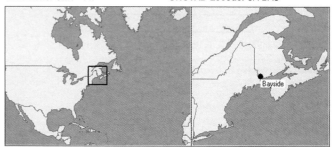

Principal Facilities:

		G		B		

Authority: Bayside Port Corp., 108 Champlain Drive, P O Box 341, St. Stephen, N.B., Canada E5B 2Y2, *Tel:* +1 506 529 3503, *Fax:* +1 506 529 3504, *Email:* baysideport@nb.aibn.com

Officials: Port Manager: David Senan.

Port Security: ISPS compliant

Approach: Channel depth in the St. Croix River is 21.3 m

Pilotage: Not compulsory

Weather: Ice conditions prevail in the St. Croix River from January to March, during which time the river is usually closed to shipping

Tides: Range of tide 7.6 m

Principal Imports and Exports: Imports: Fish, Fruit, Gypsum, Meat. Exports: Dairy, Fish, Fruit, Lumber, Meat, Potatoes.

Accommodation:

Name	Length (m)	Depth (m)	Remarks
Bayside Wharf	240	8.5	See [1] below Government Wharf at Sand Point

[1]*Bayside:* Inner berthage of 80 m with depth of 6.5 m available. Laydown area of 27 875 m2

Bunkering: Fuel and diesel oil can be obtained from Saint John with 24 h advance notice

Lloyd's Agent: Hayes Stuart Inc., 297 Duke Street, Montreal, Que., Canada H3C 2M2, *Tel:* +1 514 866 1801, *Fax:* +1 514 866 1259, *Email:* montreal@hayesstuart.com, *Website:* www.hayesstuart.com

BEAUPORT

harbour area, see under Quebec

BECANCOUR

Lat 46° 23' N; Long 72° 22' W.

Admiralty Chart: 4789	**Admiralty Pilot:** 65
Time Zone: GMT -5 h	**UNCTAD Locode:** CA BEC

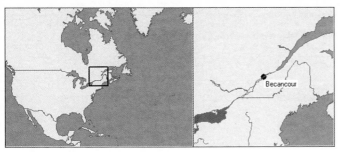

Principal Facilities:

Q	Y	G	C	R		B		T	A

Authority: Societe du Parc Industriel et Portuaire de Becancour, 1000 Arthur-Sicard Boulevard, Becancour, Que., Canada G9H 2Z8, *Tel:* +1 819 294 6656, *Fax:* +1 819 294 9020, *Email:* spipb@spipb.com, *Website:* www.spipb.com

Officials: President: Guy Leblanc, *Email:* gleblanc@spipb.com.
Co-ordinator: Manon Blais, *Email:* mblais@spipb.com.

Port Security: ISPS compliant

Pre-Arrival Information: A berth reservation form is available on the website www.spipb.com and must be completed and returned at least 5 days prior to arrival

Approach: Ship approach to the port facilities is from Buoy C-21 for westbound 'upstream' traffic, and from Buoy C-23 for eastbound 'downstream' traffic
The approach channel leads southwards for approx 1.6 km towards berth B1 and then into a large basin measuring approx 560 m x 575 m, within which berths B2, B3, B4 and B5 are located

Anchorage: One anchorage off Berth B1, an anchorage at Batiscan 16 km E of port or at Three Rivers, 8 km W of port, all in a depth of 10.67 m

Pilotage: Pilotage is mandatory. Maritime traffic is subject to the Pilotage Act. Ships must use the services of a pilot upstream of Les Escoumins. They must send 24 hours advance notice to the Montreal pilot station of their estimated time of arrival (ETA) at Les Escoumins if their point of origin is east of the strait of Belle-Isle or the Cabot Strait. A second notice must be given 12 hours before ETA and final conformation 6 hours before arrival. In the case of vessels arriving from points west of the Strait of Belle-Isle, the Cabot Strait or the Canso Strait, only the 12 hours and 6 hours advance notice are required. The pilot boat service at the Les Escoumins pilot station maintains a 24-hour listening watch on VHF 156.45, channel 9. Additional information on pilotage service may be obtained by contacting the Director of Operations, Laurentian Pilotage Authority

Radio Frequency: Vessel Traffic Services on VHF Channel 11, 156.55 mhz

Tides: Max tidal range is approx 0.3 m

Traffic: 2006, 132 vessels, 1 700 000 t of cargo handled

Principal Imports and Exports: Imports: Alumina, Bauxite, Chrome ore, Coal, Coke, Magnesite, Quartz, Salt calcium, Sodium chloride. Exports: Caustic liquids, Lumber.

Working Hours: 24 h/day

Accommodation:

Name	Length (m)	Depth (m)	Remarks
Becancour			See [1] below
Berth 1	244	10.67	Open, paved, well lit
Berth 2	150	10.67	Open, paved, well lit, ro/ro ramp 21 m wide
Berth 3	219	10.67	Open, paved, well lit
Berth 4	214	10.67	Open, paved, well lit
Berth 5	292	10.67	See [2] below

[1]*Becancour:* Private port and industrial park covering some 4900 ha of land. The principal materials handled include alumina, coke and magnesite
[2]*Berth 5:* Smelter plant, suction discharge 1100 t/h. Alumina and coke discharged by two pneumatic suction systems

Storage: 14 ha of paved, lit open storage

Mechanical Handling Equipment:

Location	Type	Capacity (t)
Becancour	Mobile Cranes	400

Cargo Worked: Approx 20 000 t/day

Bunkering: ExxonMobil Marine Fuels, Suite 900, One Alhambra Plaza, Coral Gables, FL 33134, United States of America, *Tel:* +1 305 459 6358, *Fax:* +1 305 459 6412, *Email:* emmf@exxonmobil.com, *Website:* www.exxonmobilmarinefuels.com
Imperial Oil (Anjou) Ltd, 7100 Jean-Talon Street East, Anjou, Que., Canada H1M 3R8, *Tel:* +1 450 6497 519, *Fax:* +1 450 6497 821, *Email:* christian.beaunoyer@esso.ca, *Website:* www.imperialoil.com
Kildair Service Ltd, 92 Chemin Delangis, St. Paul de Joliette, Que., Canada J0K 3E0, *Tel:* +1 450 7568 091, *Fax:* +1 450 7564 783, *Email:* info@kildair.com, *Website:* www.kildair.com
Petro Canada Products Ltd, 11701 Sherbrooke Street East, Montreal, Que., Canada H1B 1C3, *Tel:* +1 613 657 1004, *Fax:* +1 514 640 8365, *Email:* elliott@petro-canada.ca, *Website:* www.petro-canada.ca
Reiter Petroleum Inc, Suite 900, 625 President Kennedy, Montreal, Que., Canada H3A 1K2, *Tel:* +1 514 8782 563, *Fax:* +1 514 8783 463, *Email:* bunkers@reiterpet.com, *Website:* www.reiterpet.com
Shell Canada Products Ltd, 10501 Sherbroke Street East, Montreal, Que., Canada H1B 1B3, *Tel:* +1 514 6409 897, *Fax:* +1 514 6451 490, *Email:* patrick.st-laurent@shell.com, *Website:* www.shell.com
Ultramar Canada Inc., 2200 McGill College Avenue, Montreal, Que., Canada H3A 3L3, *Tel:* +1 514 4996 111, *Fax:* +1 514 4996 320, *Email:* wholesale@ultramar.ca, *Website:* www.ultramar.ca

Towage: Ocean Remorquage Trois-Rivieres Inc, P O Box 1963, Three Rivers, Que., Canada G1K 7M1, *Tel:* +1 819 377 4374, *Fax:* +1 819 377 4434, *Email:* ort@groupocean.com, *Website:* www.groupocean.com

Repair & Maintenance: Contact Shipping Agents

Stevedoring Companies: Quebec Port Terminals Inc., 355 Boul. Alphonse-Deshaies, Becancour, Que., Canada G9H 2Y7, *Tel:* +1 819 294 9911, *Fax:* +1 819 294 2601, *Email:* info@qsl.com, *Website:* www.qsl.com

Medical Facilities: Five hospitals in the area

Airport: Three Rivers, 27 km

Railway: A railway line links the port facilities to the CN railway network

Lloyd's Agent: Hayes Stuart Inc., 297 Duke Street, Montreal, Que., Canada H3C 2M2, *Tel:* +1 514 866 1801, *Fax:* +1 514 866 1259, *Email:* montreal@hayesstuart.com, *Website:* www.hayesstuart.com

BEDFORD BASIN

harbour area, see under Halifax

BELLEDUNE

Lat 47° 55' N; Long 65° 51' W.

Admiralty Chart: 4768	**Admiralty Pilot:** 65
Time Zone: GMT -4 h	**UNCTAD Locode:** CA BEL

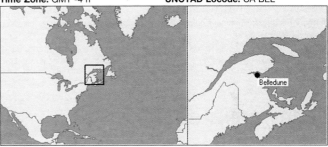

Principal Facilities:

P	Q	Y	G		R		B		T	A

Authority: Belledune Port Authority, 112 Shannon Drive, Belledune, N.B., Canada E8G 2W2, *Tel:* +1 506 522 1200, *Fax:* +1 506 522 0803, *Email:* info@portofbelledune.ca, *Website:* www.portofbelledune.ca

Officials: Chief Executive Officer: Rayburn Doucett, *Email:* doucett@portofbelledune.ca.
Operations Director: Wynford Goodman, *Email:* goodman@portofbelledune.ca.

Port Security: ISPS compliant

Approach: The harbour is approached from the NE in Chaleur Bay and entered between Belledune Point and the outer end of the breakwater, 4 cables NW. The approach channel has a width of 145 m and a water depth of 11.6 m

Anchorage: Anchorage can be obtained approx 1-2 miles N of the harbour breakwater in depths of 20-25 m

Pilotage: The users of shipping services at this port require non-Canadian ships to use the services of an APA licensed pilot. The services of Atlantic Pilotage Authority licensed pilots are available through ship's agent 24 h/day. Alternatively, a 24 h centralised pilot dispatch centre in Halifax, Tel: +1 877 272 3477 (toll free) and +1 902 426 7610 (inmarsat), Fax: +1 877 745 3477 (toll free) and +1 902 426 7236 (inmarsat), Email: dispatch@atlanticpilotage.com. Pilot boat meets arriving vessels between 1.5 and 2 miles NE of the breakwater

Radio Frequency: VHF Channels 16, 65A and 11 are designated for the Port of Belledune

Tides: Rise of tides: 1.83 m ST, 1.07 m NT; tidal currents seldom exceed one knot

Traffic: 2007, 1 850 000 t of cargo handled

Maximum Vessel Dimensions: 80 000 dwt, 12.65 m draft, 270 m loa

Principal Imports and Exports: Imports: Coal, Forest products, Lead concentrates, Petroleum products. Exports: Aggregates, Forest products, Gypsum, Lead ingots, Other general & break bulk cargo, Peat moss, Rock, Sulphuric acid, Zinc & copper concentrates.

Working Hours: Bulk cargoes and liquid products 24 h/day. General cargo 0800-2100

Accommodation:

Name	Length (m)	Depth (m)	Remarks
Belledune			See [1] below
Xstrata Zinc/BMS Dry/Liquid Bulk Berth	155	10.4	See [2] below
NB Power Coal Berth	307	14.4	See [3] below
M.D. Young Terminal	455		See [4] below
West		10.1	
East		11.5	

[1]*Belledune:* A receiving pipe on the berth linked to a tank farm. BMS also has a sulphuric acid pipeline
[2]*Xstrata Zinc/BMS Dry/Liquid Bulk Berth:* Operated by Xstrata Zinc, Brunswick Smelter, 692 Main Street, Belledune, NB E8G 2M1, Tel: +1 506 522 7014, Fax: +1 506 522 7090, Website: www.xstrata.com
For vessels up to 40 000 dwt. Used for import/export of concentrate minerals, mainly

zinc, lead and copper concentrates and to export sulphuric acid. Equipped with a ship unloader rated at 1800 t/h

[3]*NB Power Coal Berth:* Operated by Energie NB Power Corp., Belledune Generating Station, 1558 Main Street, Belledune, NB E8G 2M3, Tel: +1 506 522 2400, Fax: +1 506 522 2424, Website: www.energienb.ca
Coal wharf for vessels up to 100 000 dwt
[4]*M.D. Young Terminal:* Operated by Eastern Canada Stevedoring, Port of Belledune, 261 Shannon Drive, Unit 2, Belledune, NB E8G 2W1, Tel: +1 506 522 1800, Fax: +1 506 522 1803, Email: info@qsl.com, Website: www.qsl.com
Bulk & general cargo for vessels up to 50 000 dwt

Storage: Open storage of 13.5 ha with one storage shed of 6500 m2 and one of 2700 m2

Mechanical Handling Equipment:

Location	Type	Capacity (t)
Belledune	Mult-purp. Cranes	27

Bunkering: Available by road tanker only

Towage: Two tugs of 1000 hp and 3000 hp

Repair & Maintenance: Minor repairs can be locally arranged

Shipping Agents: Calypso Marine, 110 Shannon Drive, Belledune, N.B., Canada E8G 2W2, *Tel:* +1 506 522 2161, *Fax:* +1 506 522 2162, *Email:* calypso@nb.aibn.com
Fundy Shipping Ltd, 111-5 Brunswick Street, P O Box 5183, Dalhousie, N.B., Canada E8C 1G5, *Tel:* +1 506 684 3373, *Fax:* +1 506 684 5311, *Email:* funbro@nbnet.nb.ca
Goodfellow Shipping Agency Ltd, 255 Harbour Road, East Marine Terminal, Dalhousie, N.B., Canada E8C 1X3, *Tel:* +1 506 684 3321, *Fax:* +1 506 684 2825, *Email:* goodship@nbnet.nb.ca

Stevedoring Companies: Eastern Canada Stevedoring Inc, 261 Shannon Drive, Unit 2, Belledune, N.B., Canada E8G 2W1, *Tel:* +1 506 522 1800, *Fax:* +1 506 522 1803, *Email:* info@qsl.com, *Website:* www.qsl.com

Medical Facilities: Regional Hospital Centre, Bathurst, about 30 km

Airport: Bathurst, 35 km

Railway: The port connects to the New Brunswick East Coast Railway line, 8 km

Lloyd's Agent: Hayes Stuart Inc., 297 Duke Street, Montreal, Que., Canada H3C 2M2, *Tel:* +1 514 866 1801, *Fax:* +1 514 866 1259, *Email:* montreal@hayesstuart.com, *Website:* www.hayesstuart.com

BERRY POINT SITE

harbour area, see under Vancouver

BICKERDIKE TERMINAL

harbour area, see under Montreal

BOTWOOD

Lat 49° 9' N; Long 55° 19' W.

Admiralty Chart: 285	**Admiralty Pilot:** 50
Time Zone: GMT -3.5 h	**UNCTAD Locode:** CA BWD

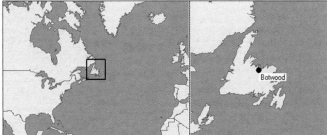

Principal Facilities:

P	Q	Y	G			B		A

Authority: Transport Canada, Atlantic Region, P O Box 236, Botwood, NL, Canada A0H 1E0, *Tel:* +1 709 489 8860, *Website:* www.tc.gc.ca

Officials: Harbour Master: Cyril Lanning.

Port Security: ISPS compliant

Approach: Deep water approaches

Anchorage: Good anchorage in Botwood harbour about 0.4 km off the wharves in depths of 18.3 to 36.6 m, mud or small gravel bottom

Pilotage: Compulsory. The pilot boarding station from May 31 to December 14 depending on ice conditions is in pos 49° 23' N, 55° 09' W and from December 15 to May 30 depending on ice conditions, pos 47° 33' N, 52° 37' W. Vessels should advise ETA at least 12 h in advance and confirmed 3 h in advance. Pilots at Bay of Exploits on VHF Channel 16 and Saint John's on VHF Channels 16 and 11 (156.8 and 156.55 mHz)

Weather: Although ice may be a problem from late January to late April, it is now considered to be an all year-round port. Canadian Coast Guard ice-breakers, when available, assist vessels in and out of the harbour during the winter season

Tides: Tidal range of 1.43 m

Principal Imports and Exports: Imports: Caustic soda, Clean fuels, General cargo, Sulphur. Exports: Fish, Newsprint.

Working Hours: Three 8 h shifts. Sat ordinary working day. Sun, work optional

Accommodation:

Name	Length (m)	Depth (m)	Remarks
Botwood			
Transit Wharf	83	8.9	Public
Oil Dock	42	5.9	Public. Operated by Ultramar with lines to a tank farm
Abitibi-Price	142	8.2–9.4	
Irving Oil	12	8.2	

Mechanical Handling Equipment:

Location	Type
Botwood	Mult-purp. Cranes

Bunkering: No bunker 'C' fuel oil for vessels, but light diesel oil available in any quantity by tank truck

Waste Reception Facilities: Arrangements must be made through Agent for garbage and waste oil disposal

Repair & Maintenance: Minor repairs and welding can be done. No drydock or slip

Shipping Agents: Montship Inc., Connaught Hall, 175 Water Street, P O Box 310, Botwood, NL, Canada A0H 1E0, *Tel:* +1 709 257 2421, *Fax:* +1 709 257 2142, *Email:* dbutt.montship@nf.sympatico.ca, *Website:* www.montship.ca

Medical Facilities: Hospital facilities in Grand Falls, 35 km and Botwood

Airport: Gander, 86 km

Lloyd's Agent: Hayes Stuart Inc., 297 Duke Street, Montreal, Que., Canada H3C 2M2, *Tel:* +1 514 866 1801, *Fax:* +1 514 866 1259, *Email:* montreal@hayesstuart.com, *Website:* www.hayesstuart.com

BOUCHERVILLE TERMINAL

harbour area, see under Montreal

BURLINGTON NORTHERN SANTA FE

harbour area, see under Vancouver

CAMPBELL RIVER

see under Duncan Bay

CANADA PLACE

harbour area, see under Vancouver

CANAPORT

see under Saint John

CANTERM CANADIAN TERMINALS

harbour area, see under Montreal

CARAQUET

Lat 47° 48' N; Long 65° 1' W.

Admiralty Chart: 4768	**Admiralty Pilot:** 65
Time Zone: GMT -4 h	**UNCTAD Locode:** CA CAQ

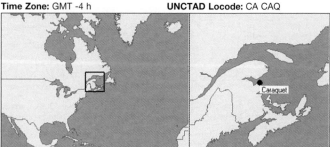

Principal Facilities:

			G			B	T	A

Authority: Le Comite du Port de Caraquet Inc., 26 Rue du Quai, Caraquet, N.B., Canada E1W 1B6, *Tel:* +1 506 727 6145, *Fax:* +1 506 727 2020, *Email:* cpc@nb.aibn.com

Officials: Manager: Rufin Doiron.

Approach: Depth of channel 5.5 m at low tide everwhere, rising to 6.5 m at high tide.

Anchorage: Sheltered anchorage in a depth of 16.5 m

Pilotage: Not compulsory. Pilot boards vessel at buoy "EE Shippegan North". Atlantic Pilotage Authority has a 24 h centralised pilot dispatch centre in Halifax, Tel: +1 877 272 3477 (toll free) and +1 902 426 7610 (inmarsat), Fax: +1 877 745 3477 (toll free) and +1 902 426 7236 (inmarsat), Email: dispatch@atlanticpilotage.com

Radio Frequency: VHF Channel 16

Weather: NW winds predominant especially in fall and winter

Tides: Range of tide 2.1 m ST, 1.6 m NT

Maximum Vessel Dimensions: 140 m long, with maximum draft loaded 6.5 m.

Working Hours: 0800-1700 with overtime as required

Accommodation:

Name	Length (m)	Depth (m)
Caraquet		
West Pierhead	165	7
East Pierhead	90	7

Mechanical Handling Equipment:

Location	Type	Capacity (t)
Caraquet	Mult-purp. Cranes	150

Cargo Worked: Would depend on goods handling

Bunkering: Fuel and diesel oil available by truck

Waste Reception Facilities: Garbage disposal available on request

Towage: Small tug available

Repair & Maintenance: L'Industrie Marine de Caraquet Ltee (Caraquet Yacht Inc.), 2265 rue du Quai, Caraquet, B.C., Canada E1W 1B7, *Tel:* +1 506 727 0166, *Fax:* +1 506 727 7522, *Email:* info@caraquetyacht.com
Dugas Equipment Ltd, 80 Boulevard St-Pierre Establishment, Caraquet, B.C., Canada E1W 1A9, *Tel:* +1 506 727 2220, *Fax:* +1 506 727 0952, *Email:* info@dugasequipement.ca, *Website:* www.dugasequipement.ca

Medical Facilities: Local hospital, 1 km from port. Regional Hospital Bathurst, 80 km

Airport: Pokemouche, 6 km

Railway: C.N.R. at Bathurst, 80 km

Lloyd's Agent: Hayes Stuart Inc., 297 Duke Street, Montreal, Que., Canada H3C 2M2, *Tel:* +1 514 866 1801, *Fax:* +1 514 866 1259, *Email:* montreal@hayesstuart.com, *Website:* www.hayesstuart.com

CASCADIA TERMINAL

harbour area, see under Vancouver

CATALINA

Lat 48° 31' N; Long 53° 4' W.

Admiralty Chart: 4733/4734
Time Zone: GMT -3.5 h

Admiralty Pilot: 50
UNCTAD Locode: CA CAT

Principal Facilities:

		P		Y	G							

Authority: Harbour Authority of Catalina, P O Box 87, Catalina, NL, Canada A0C 1J0, *Tel:* +1 709 469 2441

Approach: Min depth in channel to Catalina Harbour is 9.1 m. Channel to the NE arm is 60 m wide and has a least depth of 5.5 m

Anchorage: Anchorage can be obtained within the harbour in depths ranging from 7.3 m to 9.1 m

Pilotage: Not compulsory but local pilots are available if required

Principal Imports and Exports: Imports: Coal, General cargo, Oil, Salt. Exports: Fish.

Accommodation:

Name	Length (m)	Depth (m)	Remarks
Catalina			See [1] below
Government Wharf	75	6.1	Storage shed available

[1]*Catalina:* Main port facilities are located in the NE arm of the harbour. In the SW arm there is the Fishery Products Wharf, 134 m long with a depth alongside of 3.7 m. A jetty, 61 m in length, extends from this wharf and has a max depth alongside of 5.2 m. A fish processing plant is serviced by conveyor belt from the wharf
Tanker facilities: Irving Oil Co jetty located in the SW arm of the harbour, depth alongside 4.9 m. Storage tanks on the shore

Medical Facilities: Doctor available in the port area. Hospital at Bonavista, 20 km

Lloyd's Agent: Hayes Stuart Inc., 297 Duke Street, Montreal, Que., Canada H3C 2M2, *Tel:* +1 514 866 1801, *Fax:* +1 514 866 1259, *Email:* montreal@hayesstuart.com, *Website:* www.hayesstuart.com

CENTERM

harbour area, see under Vancouver

CHANDLER

Lat 48° 21' N; Long 64° 40' W.

Admiralty Chart: 4768
Time Zone: GMT -5 h

Admiralty Pilot: 65
UNCTAD Locode: CA CHR

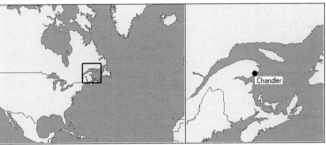

Principal Facilities:

			G			B			

Authority: Transport Canada, Champlain Harbour Station, 901 Cap Diamant 4th Floor, Quebec, Que., Canada G1K 4K1, *Tel:* +1 418 648 4103, *Fax:* +1 418 648 7980, *Website:* www.tc.gc.ca

Officials: Regional Manager: Andre Roy, *Tel:* +1 418 648 7213, *Email:* royan@tc.gc.ca.
Harbour Master: Michel Petit, *Tel:* +1 418 648 3640.

Port Security: ISPS compliant

Approach: No hazards and good anchorage. Channel depth 8 m at extreme LT. Icebreaker assistance available in winter if necessary

Pilotage: Not compulsory but recommended. Pilots available from Atlantic Pilotage Authority which has a 24 h centralised pilot dispatch centre in Halifax, Tel: +1 877 272 3477 (toll free) and +1 902 426 7610 (inmarsat), Fax: +1 877 745 3477 (toll free) and +1 902 426 7236 (inmarsat), Email: dispatch@atlanticpilotage.com

Tides: Range of tide 1.2 m

Traffic: 2005, 3 vessels, 3928 t of cargo handled

Working Hours: Mon to Fri 0800-1700. Overtime as required. Holidays and weekends on notice only

Accommodation:

Name	Length (m)	Depth (m)	Remarks
Chandler			See [1] below
Government Wharf	150	9	

[1]*Chandler:* Located on the S shore of the Gaspe peninsula at the entrance to Chaleur Bay. The cargo transhipped is limited almost exclusively to salt

Storage:

Location	Open (m²)
Chandler	8400

Bunkering: Diesel oil is available. Fuel oil can be brought in by rail wagon

Medical Facilities: Hospital in the town

Lloyd's Agent: Hayes Stuart Inc., 297 Duke Street, Montreal, Que., Canada H3C 2M2, *Tel:* +1 514 866 1801, *Fax:* +1 514 866 1259, *Email:* montreal@hayesstuart.com, *Website:* www.hayesstuart.com

CHARLOTTETOWN

Lat 46° 13' N; Long 63° 7' W.

Admiralty Chart: 1651
Time Zone: GMT -4 h

Admiralty Pilot: 50
UNCTAD Locode: CA CHA

Key to Principal Facilities:—			
A=Airport	**C**=Containers	**G**=General Cargo	**P**=Petroleum	**R**=Ro/Ro	**Y**=Dry Bulk
B=Bunkers	**D**=Dry Dock	**L**=Cruise	**Q**=Other Liquid Bulk	**T**=Towage (where available from port)	

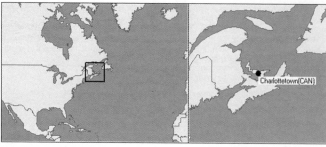

Principal Facilities:

P	Y G		L B		A

Authority: Charlottetown Harbour Authority Inc, P O Box 1117, Charlottetown, P.E.I., Canada C1A 7M8, *Tel:* +1 902 566 7974, *Fax:* +1 902 566 7980, *Email:* rswitzer.chai@pei.aibn.com, *Website:* www.historiccharlottetownseaport.com

Officials: Terminal Operations Manager: Ron Switzer, *Email:* rswitzer.chai@pei.aibn.com.

Port Security: ISPS compliant

Approach: The 8 mile approach channel has depths of not less than 10.98 m in the fairway, which is marked by light buoys and leading lights

Anchorage: Anchorage inside harbour in pos 46° 13' N; 63° 08' W, average depth of 9.15 m

Pilotage: Compulsory

Tides: Tidal range of 1.75 m

Traffic: 2005, 23 cruise vessels

Principal Imports and Exports: Imports: Aggregate, Agricultural fertilizer, Petroleum products. Exports: Potatoes.

Accommodation:

Name	Length (m)	Depth (m)	Remarks
Charlottetown			Primarily used by cruise vessels
East Berth	183	13	
South Berth	70	13	

Bunkering: Available by truck
Imperial Oil (Dartmouth) Ltd, P O Box 1010, Dartmouth, N.S., Canada B2Y 4RI, *Tel:* +1 902 420 6872, *Fax:* +1 902 420 6996
Irving Oil Co. Ltd, 10 Sydney Street, P O Box 1421, Saint John, N.B., Canada E2L 4K1, *Tel:* +1 888 3101 924, *Fax:* +1 506 2023 868, *Email:* webinquiries@irvingoil.com, *Website:* www.irvingoilco.com

Repair & Maintenance: Corrigan's Welding & Wood Stoves, Corrigan's Stove Centre, 100 Kensington Road, Charlottetown, P.E.I., Canada C1A 5J5, *Tel:* +1 902 629 1205, *Fax:* +1 902 629 1205, *Email:* corriganscentre@pei.aibn.com
Ben Livingstone & Sons, P O Box 444, Charlottetown, P.E.I., Canada C1A 7K7, *Tel:* +1 902 892 2561, *Fax:* +1 902 892 4096, *Email:* pliving@eastlink.ca
Ken Newbury & Sons Ltd, 58 Spring Road, Charlottetown, P.E.I., Canada C1A 5Z9, *Tel:* +1 902 892 8897, *Fax:* +1 902 368 3537

Medical Facilities: Ample hospital facilities available

Airport: Charlottetown Airport, 4 km

Lloyd's Agent: Hayes Stuart Inc., 1000 Windmill Road, Suite 19, Dartmouth, N.S., Canada B3B 1L7, *Tel:* +1 902 468 2651, *Fax:* +1 902 468 4315, *Email:* halifax@hayesstuart.com, *Website:* www.hayesstuart.com

CHATHAM

Lat 47° 2' N; Long 65° 28' W.

Admiralty Chart: 4765		**Admiralty Pilot:** 65	
Time Zone: GMT -4 h		**UNCTAD Locode:** CA CHN	

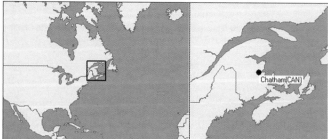

Principal Facilities:

P	Y G			B	T A

Authority: Province of New Brunswick, Department of Economic Development & Tourism, P O Box 6000, Fredericton, N.B., Canada E3B 5H1, *Tel:* +1 506 453 6464

Approach: Depth at entrance 7.2 m LW

Pilotage: Compulsory. Pilot boards off Escuminac Breakwater using motor boat. From December 10 until ice breaks up, pilot boards at Eddy Point if vessels coming from Atlantic, and at St. Lawrence River ports in other cases. Atlantic Pilotage Authority rates for the Miramichi Pilotage Area

Tides: ST rise 1.75 m, NT rise 1.22 m

Maximum Vessel Dimensions: A 7.2 m d can be taken in and out safely

Principal Imports and Exports: Exports: Lumber, Paper.

Accommodation:

Name	Length (m)	Depth (m)	Remarks
Chatham			
Millbank	105	10.67	
Chatham	179	8.8	
New Brunswick Hydro	30	6.1	
Marine Terminal	91	7.2	See [1] below
Northwood Panelboard	152	7.2	
Station Wharf	136	8.2	

[1]*Marine Terminal:* Dolphin on upper end; used for petroleum products and bulk cement

Storage:

Location	Covered (m²)	Sheds / Warehouses
Chatham	3888	1

Mechanical Handling Equipment:

Location	Type
Chatham	Mobile Cranes

Bunkering: Fuel and diesel oil by tank wagon

Towage: Not necessary, but tugs available

Airport: Chatham Airport, 5 km

Lloyd's Agent: Hayes Stuart Inc., 297 Duke Street, Montreal, Que., Canada H3C 2M2, *Tel:* +1 514 866 1801, *Fax:* +1 514 866 1259, *Email:* montreal@hayesstuart.com, *Website:* www.hayesstuart.com

CHEMAINUS

Lat 48° 55' N; Long 123° 42' W.

Admiralty Chart: -		**Admiralty Pilot:** 25	
Time Zone: GMT -8 h		**UNCTAD Locode:** CA CHM	

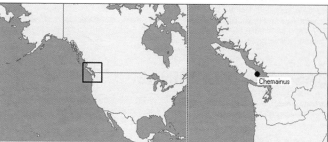

Principal Facilities:

	Y				T A

Authority: Weyerhaeuser Chemainus Sawmill, P O Box 540, 2860 Victoria Street, Chemainus, B.C., Canada V0R 1K0, *Tel:* +1 250 246 3221, *Fax:* +1 250 246 5128

Port Security: ISPS compliant

Approach: The approaches to the port are deep and danger free so long as the track indicated by the leading mark is maintained. However, a 14 m patch lies 365.7 m N of Bare Point and Hospital Reef, off the west side of the harbour entrance; it has depths of 9.6 m close to the leading lines. Owing to the presence of extensive booming grounds within Chemainus Bay, there is inadequate swinging room for large vessels to anchor

Anchorage: Vessels awaiting berth usually anchor in Houstoun Passage to the W of Southerly Point in a depth of about 21.9 m, sand and mud bottom, sheltered with adequate swinging room

Pilotage: Compulsory. Pilot obtained off Race Rocks or Royal Roads. Pacific Pilotage Authority

Radio Frequency: Coast Guard on VHF Channel 16 and vessel traffic on VHF Channel 11

Principal Imports and Exports: Exports: Lumber.

Working Hours: 24 h/day

Accommodation:

Name	Length (m)	Depth (m)
Chemainus		
Chemainus Sawmill Wharf	170	9.1–15.8

Towage: Tugs available

Medical Facilities: Hospital and doctor's office within walking distance

Airport: Nanaimo Airport, 14 km

Lloyd's Agent: McLarens Canada (Vancouver), 505 1100 Melville Street, Vancouver, B.C., Canada V6E 4A6, *Tel:* +1 604 681 7107, *Fax:* +1 604 681 8125, *Email:* philip.vardon@mclarens.ca, *Website:* www.mclarens.ca

CHURCHILL

Lat 58° 47' N; Long 94° 13' W.

Admiralty Chart: 4406	**Admiralty Pilot:** 50
Time Zone: GMT -6 h	**UNCTAD Locode:** CA CHV

Principal Facilities:

P		Y	G			B		T	A

Authority: Hudson Bay Port Company, Port of Churchill, P O Box 217, Churchill, Man., Canada R0B 0E0, *Tel:* +1 204 675 8823, *Fax:* +1 204 675 2550, *Email:* shutchins@omnitrax.com

Officials: General Manager: Lyle Fetterly.
Assistant General Manager: Shane Hutchins.

Port Security: ISPS compliant

Documentation: Crew lists (3 copies), passenger lists (3 copies if applicable), ship stores lists (3 copies), two quarantine certificates, personal effects list, arms and ammunition list, stowaways list, vessels official documents, cargo documents Arctic Waters Pollution Prevention certificate required for vessels arriving at Churchill

Approach: Min channel depth at LW is 7.1 m
Coast Guard Services: A coast guard traffic centre (Nordreg Canada) is located at Iqaluit, N.W.T. and provides a service for the support of vessels navigating the waters of Hudson Strait and Bay. Up-to-date information on ice conditions, advise on routes, aids to navigation and icebreaker assistance is available throughout the navigation season. Icebreaker assistance should be requested well in advance through Nordreg Canada although one is normally stationed in Hudson Strait area

Anchorage: Masters of smaller vessels may consult Harbour Authorities regarding possible short-term anchorage inside the harbour. The recommended anchorage for larger vessels is 1-3 miles NW to NE of the fairway buoy in 11-14 fathoms over sand and mud. This anchorage is exposed and vessels in light condition may drag, particularly in strong NE winds. Masters are advised to weigh anchor and stand out to sea when gales are expected, until the weather moderates. Vessels should not anchor off the harbour entrance because the ebb tide is strong and there is a danger of dragging ashore should an unexpected NE gale develop

Pilotage: Compulsory for merchant vessels entering or shifting berth in Churchill harbour. The pilot boards from a tug in the vicinity of the fairway light buoy, weather permitting. Masters can arrange for a pilot by contacting their Agent at Churchill or calling directly to the pilot boat H.M. Wilson on VHF

Radio Frequency: Churchill operates remote from Thunder Bay Coast Guard Radio VBA around the clock during the navigation season. VHF Channels 16, 26 and 12

Tides: The ranges of mean tides and large tides at Churchill harbour are 3.4 m and 4.8 m

Principal Imports and Exports: Imports: Diesel oil, General cargo. Exports: Grain, Lumber, Other bulk commodities.

Working Hours: Monday to Friday: 0800-1200, 1300-1700. Saturday and evenings: time and a half payable; Sunday: double time payable; holidays: triple time payable

Accommodation:

Name	Length (m)	Depth (m)	Remarks
Churchill			See ¹ below
Wolfe Berth	844	10–11	Shed of 144.8 x 52.72 available
Grain Berth No.1		9.3–10	
Grain Berth No.2		9.3–10	
Dalgliesh Berth		9.3–10	
Coastal Berth	91	5.2–6.1	

¹*Churchill:* Bulk facilities: Bulk grain handling facilities available. Elevator, cap 140 000 t equipped with galleries to wharf, four belts and 23 spouts for loading three vessels up to 15 000 t simultaneously at the rate of 1680 t/h or two vessels over 15 000 t. The spouts have a reach of 25.9 m to 27.4 m and in the case of vessels with large beam width, extensions can be added
Tanker facilities: Operated by Imperial Oil Co. A manifold (raised face flange) is installed alongside Dalgliesh berth to accommodate 8'' (inside dia) discharge hose from vessel. 6'' dia steel pipeline to tank farm of 46 000 m3 cap ashore

Storage:

Location	Open (m²)
Wolfe Berth	23225

Mechanical Handling Equipment:

Location	Type	Capacity (t)	Qty
Churchill	Mult-purp. Cranes	100	1

Bunkering: Arctic diesel fuel available but heavier bunker fuel or coal can be delivered to ship-side by rail if ordered well in advance

Waste Reception Facilities: Not available

Towage: Two tugs available; one of 3000 bhp and one of 600 bhp
Repair & Maintenance: No dry docks or slips for large vessels. Good machine shop available operated by Canada Ports Corporation; also diver and diving gear
Medical Facilities: Available
Airport: Churchill Airport, 9 km (Ministry of Transport)
Railway: Hudson Bay Railway. Tel:(204) 627 2007 Fax:(204) 623 3095
Lloyd's Agent: McLarens Canada (Toronto), 600 Alden Road, Suite 600, Markham, Toronto, Ont., Canada L3R 0E7, *Tel:* +1 905 946 9995, *Fax:* +1 905 946 0171, *Email:* roger.bickers@mclarens.ca, *Website:* www.mclarens.ca

COLLINGWOOD

Lat 44° 30' N; Long 80° 14' W.

Admiralty Chart: -	**Admiralty Pilot:** -
Time Zone: GMT -5 h	**UNCTAD Locode:** CA COL

Principal Facilities:

	Y	G				D		A

Authority: Transport Canada, 4900 Yonge Street, Suite 300, Toronto, Ont., Canada M2N 6A5, *Tel:* +1 416 952 0154, *Fax:* +1 416 952 0159, *Email:* taylodd@tc.gc.ca, *Website:* www.tc.gc.ca

Officials: General Director: Debra Taylor, *Email:* taylodd@tc.gc.ca.

Approach: The port is entered through a 609.6 m dredged channel which is not less than 61 m wide and dredged to a depth of 6.5 m, marked by red and green buoys. There is a turning basin for vessels up to 244 m

Anchorage: Limited anchorage within harbour

Pilotage: Not compulsory

Radio Frequency: VHF channels 26 and 16

Weather: Strong W winds can be hazardous

Maximum Vessel Dimensions: 6.5 m d, 225 m loa

Accommodation:

Name	Remarks
Collingwood	See ¹ below

¹*Collingwood:* Artificial harbour protected by breakwaters. The narrow elevator wharf, 392.2 m length lies approx 131.1 m westward to the eastern breakwater and parallel to it. A mooring crib, to the southward of and in line with the wharf provides a berthing face of approx 396.2 m. The depth alongside is 6.5 m. Between this wharf and the breakwater is a landfill area on which the elevator is built. The south end of the elevator wharf, combined with a small wharf 83.8 m long with a depth of 4.9 m alongside and extending at right angles to the breakwater, provides an enclosure used as a small boat basin. To the south of this basin is a government wharf consisting of four dolphins, providing a berth 152.9 m in length with a depth of 5.2 m alongside

Medical Facilities: Collingwood General and Marine Hospital
Airport: Collingwood Airport, 8 km
Lloyd's Agent: McLarens Canada (Toronto), 600 Alden Road, Suite 600, Markham, Toronto, Ont., Canada L3R 0E7, *Tel:* +1 905 946 9995, *Fax:* +1 905 946 0171, *Email:* roger.bickers@mclarens.ca, *Website:* www.mclarens.ca

COME BY CHANCE

Lat 47° 48' N; Long 54° 1' W.

Admiralty Chart: 4739	**Admiralty Pilot:** 50
Time Zone: GMT -3.5 h	**UNCTAD Locode:** CA CBC

Principal Facilities:

P						B		T	

Key to Principal Facilities:—					
A=Airport	**C**=Containers	**G**=General Cargo	**P**=Petroleum	**R**=Ro/Ro	**Y**=Dry Bulk
B=Bunkers	**D**=Dry Dock	**L**=Cruise	**Q**=Other Liquid Bulk	**T**=Towage (where available from port)	

Authority: North Atlantic Refinery Ltd, P O Box 40, Come by Chance, NL, Canada A0B 1N0, *Tel:* +1 709 463 8811, *Fax:* +1 709 463 8076, *Email:* communications@na-refining.nf.ca, *Website:* www.na-refining.nf.ca

Anchorage: Three vessel anchor berths for tankers over 80 000 dwt; Berth A, off Bordeaux Island in a depth of 73 m; Berth B, off Woody Island in a depth of 79 m; Berth C, off Bar Haven Island in a depth of 51 m. Two vessel anchor berths for tankers up to 60 000 dwt; Berths D and E, both off Whiffin Head in a depth of 26 m. These anchorages will be assigned at the discretion of the pilot

Pilotage: Compulsory. Zone A Pilot Boarding station in vicinity of Coombes Rk in 47° 42' 18" N, 54° 03' 18" W for vessels less than 223 m in length. Zone B for all vessels greater than 223 m in length, pilot boards off Argentia in pos 47° 20' 00" N, 54° 06' 30" W. ETA to be sent 12 h prior to arrival to St. John's Pilotage with confirmation 3 h prior

Radio Frequency: VHF Channel 16. In port movements monitored on VHF Channel 12, call sign "Placentia Traffic". Other channels used are VHF Channel 6 (tugs), 11 (pilotage) and 14

Weather: Prevailing SW wind in summer, NW in winter. Gales can sometimes restrict the movements of vessels. Fog is experienced from April to July, usually when the wind is from a southerly direction

Tides: Range of tide 1.7 m to 2.6 m. Prolonged S winds can increase the range

Principal Imports and Exports: Imports: Crude oil. Exports: Refined petroleum products.

Accommodation:

Name	Remarks
Come by Chance	See [1] below

[1]*Come by Chance:* L-shaped jetty extending 914 m from the shore with a berthing length at the head of 463 m, two berths are available
Berth No.1 can accommodate tankers of 27 000-326 000 dwt in a depth of 30.5 m, max d 27.4 m; equipment includes four 16'' arms for unloading and one 10'' arm for bunkering
Berth No.2 can accommodate tankers of 5000-80 000 dwt in a depth of 15.8 m, max d 14.6 m; used mainly for refined products; equipment includes four 10'' arms for cargo operations and one 8'' arm for bunkering
Dirty ballast facilities are available at each berth

Storage: Crude oil storage cap of 3 400 000 bbls. Intermediate and finished products storage cap of 3 600 000 bbls

Bunkering: All types are available at the oil terminal wharf by prior arrangement at rate of 600 t/h
ExxonMobil Marine Fuels, Suite 900, One Alhambra Plaza, Coral Gables, FL 33134, United States of America, *Tel:* +1 305 459 6358, *Fax:* +1 305 459 6412, *Email:* emmf@exxonmobil.com, *Website:* www.exxonmobilmarinefuels.com
Imperial Oil (Dartmouth) Ltd, P O Box 1010, Dartmouth, N.S., Canada B2Y 4RI, *Tel:* +1 902 420 6872, *Fax:* +1 902 420 6996

Towage: Two tugs available

Shipping Agents: Canadian Maritime Agency Ltd, 4 Refinery Road, P O Box 119, Come by Chance, NL, Canada A0B 1N0, *Tel:* +1 709 463 4717, *Fax:* +1 709 463 8737, *Email:* opscbc@canadianmaritime.nf.ca, *Website:* www.canadianmaritime.com

Medical Facilities: Hospital at Clarenville, 48 km

Lloyd's Agent: Hayes Stuart Inc., 297 Duke Street, Montreal, Que., Canada H3C 2M2, *Tel:* +1 514 866 1801, *Fax:* +1 514 866 1259, *Email:* montreal@hayesstuart.com, *Website:* www.hayesstuart.com

COMEAU BAY

Lat 49° 14' N; Long 68° 8' W.

Admiralty Chart: 4778
Time Zone: GMT -4 h
Admiralty Pilot: 65
UNCTAD Locode: CA BCO

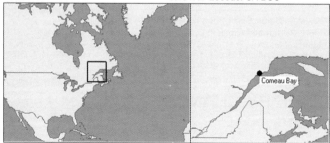

Principal Facilities:

	Y	G		R		B		T	A	

Authority: Baie Comeau Port Authority, P O Box 331, Baie Comeau, Que., Canada G4Z 2H1, *Tel:* +1 418 296 4296, *Fax:* +1 418 296 9582, *Email:* lavoisi@tc.gc.ca, *Website:* www.tc.gc.ca

Officials: Port Manager: Simon Lavoie.

Port Security: ISPS compliant

Approach: Depth in approach at LW 8.2 m. Icebreaker assistance available in winter if necessary

Pilotage: Not compulsory for public wharves but recommended

Tides: Range of tide 2.7 m neaps and 3.8 m springs

Traffic: 2002, 5 900 000 t of cargo handled

Maximum Vessel Dimensions: 8.2 m draft is permissible at lowest LW

Working Hours: Mon to Fri 0800-1700. Overtime as required. Holidays and weekends on notice only

Accommodation:

Name	Length (m)	Depth (m)	Remarks
Public Harbour			See [1] below
Public Wharf No.1	155	9	
Public Wharf No.2	155	8.5	
Public Wharf No.3	135	8.5	Not used at present
Public Wharf No.4	220	8.7	Ro/ro wharf owned by Transport Quebec
Private Harbour			
Wharf No.1	180	7.1	Operated by Paper Co. of Quebec & Ontario
Wharf No.2	164	10.1	See [2] below
Wharf No.3	179	10.1	See [3] below
Wharf No.4	168	10.1	See [4] below
Wharf No.5	178	12.2	Operated by Cargill Grain Co Ltd
Wharf No.6	178	11.6	Operated by Cargill Grain Co Ltd
Wharf No.7	212	8.4	Operated by Cargill Grain Co Ltd

[1]*Public Harbour:* The public wharf extends NE, then to the north which forms a basin protecting the four berths inside the public harbour. A floating mobile and adjustable ro/ro ramp is situated near the inner end of the public wharf with a cap of 400 t
[2]*Wharf No.2:* Operated by Canadian Reynolds Metals. Equipped with two pneumatic unloaders for alumina and coke (two storage tanks for alumina of 40 000 t and one for coke of 5000 t). Connectors for the handling of petroleum products are located approx 64 m from the outer end of the berth
[3]*Wharf No.3:* Opeated by Canadian Reynolds Metals. An extension of Wharf No.2 where there is a storage shed and a dock office
[4]*Wharf No.4:* Operated by Canadian Reynolds Metals. Used only for loading; three cargo sheds available

Storage: Cargill Grain terminal consists of a grain elevator with a cap of 441 784 t for wheat and several silos

Location	Open (m²)
Comeau Bay	6000

Bunkering: ExxonMobil Marine Fuels, Suite 900, One Alhambra Plaza, Coral Gables, FL 33134, United States of America, *Tel:* +1 305 459 6358, *Fax:* +1 305 459 6412, *Email:* emmf@exxonmobil.com, *Website:* www.exxonmobilmarinefuels.com
Imperial Oil (Anjou) Ltd, 7100 Jean-Talon Street East, Anjou, Que., Canada H1M 3R8, *Tel:* +1 450 6497 519, *Fax:* +1 450 6497 821, *Email:* christian.beaunoyer@esso.ca, *Website:* www.imperialoil.com
Kildair Service Ltd, 92 Chemin Delangis, St. Paul de Joliette, Que., Canada J0K 3E0, *Tel:* +1 450 7568 091, *Fax:* +1 450 7564 783, *Email:* info@kildair.com, *Website:* www.kildair.com
Shell Canada Products Ltd, 10501 Sherbroke Street East, Montreal, Que., Canada H1B 1B3, *Tel:* +1 514 6409 897, *Fax:* +1 514 6451 490, *Email:* patrick.st-laurent@shell.com, *Website:* www.shell.ca

Towage: One tug available but towage is not compulsory for public wharves. Private wharves require tug assistance

Medical Facilities: Hospital available

Airport: Municipal Airport, 29 km

Lloyd's Agent: Hayes Stuart Inc., 297 Duke Street, Montreal, Que., Canada H3C 2M2, *Tel:* +1 514 866 1801, *Fax:* +1 514 866 1259, *Email:* montreal@hayesstuart.com, *Website:* www.hayesstuart.com

CONTRECOEUR

Lat 45° 53' N; Long 73° 12' W.

Admiralty Chart: 4791
Time Zone: GMT -5 h
Admiralty Pilot: 65
UNCTAD Locode: CA COC

Principal Facilities:

		Y				B		

Authority: Contrecoeur Maritime Terminal Inc., 1920 Marie-Victorin, Contrecoeur, Que., Canada J0L 1C0, *Tel:* +1 450 587 2073, *Fax:* +1 450 587 8570, *Email:* corp@logistec.com

Port Security: ISPS compliant

Approach: Approach channel has a min depth of 10.67 m

Pilotage: Pilots board at Three Rivers, Sorel or Montreal

Working Hours: Monday-Friday 0800-1600. Saturday or Sunday work must be confirmed by 1300 on Friday to allow for scheduling of crews. Overtime is available from 1600-2400 and 0000-0800 for bulk material

Accommodation:

Name	Length (m)	Depth (m)	Remarks
Contrecoeur			See [1] below
Berth No.1	229	11.3	Two travelling towers with a lifting cap of 30 t
Berth No.2	148	6.7	

[1] *Contrecoeur:* Dispatcher Transfer Dock with complete facilities for transhipping iron ore and other bulk products transported on the St. Lawrence River. Operated by Logistec Stevedoring Inc

Storage:

Location	Open (m²)	Covered (m²)
Berth No.1	7796	3750
Berth No.2	4621	

Bunkering: BP Marine Americas Inc., 501 Westlake Park Boulevard, Houston, TX 77079, United States of America, *Tel:* +1 281 366 2000, *Email:* firstname.secondname@bp.com
Bunkerina International Inc., 11 3rd Avenue South, Roxboro, Montreal, Que., Canada H8Y 2L3, *Tel:* +1 514 806 2760, *Fax:* +1 514 683 2760
ExxonMobil Marine Fuels, Suite 900, One Alhambra Plaza, Coral Gables, FL 33134, United States of America, *Tel:* +1 305 459 6358, *Fax:* +1 305 459 6412, *Email:* emmf@exxonmobil.com, *Website:* www.exxonmobilmarinefuels.com – *Grades:* IFO40-380cSt; MDO – *Delivery Mode:* truck
Hampton Bunkering Ltd, Suite 615, 999 de Maisonneuve Boulevard West, Montreal, Que., Canada H3A 3L4, *Tel:* +1 514 2882 818, *Fax:* +1 514 2829 279, *Email:* bunkers@hamptonmtl.ca
ICS Petroleum, ICS Petroleum (Montreal) Ltd, Suite 302, 430 Ste-Helene Street, Montreal, Que., Canada H2Y 2K7, *Tel:* +1 514 849 1223, *Fax:* +1 514 849 0517, *Email:* bunkers@ics-mtl.com, *Website:* www.icspet.com
Imperial Oil (Anjou) Ltd, 7100 Jean-Talon Street East, Anjou, Que., Canada H1M 3R8, *Tel:* +1 450 6497 519, *Fax:* +1 450 6497 821, *Email:* christian.beaunoyer@esso.ca, *Website:* www.imperialoil.com
Kildair Service Ltd, 92 Chemin Delangis, St. Paul de Joliette, Que., Canada J0K 3E0, *Tel:* +1 450 7568 091, *Fax:* +1 450 7564 783, *Email:* info@kildair.com, *Website:* www.kildair.com
Petro Canada Products Ltd, 11701 Sherbrooke Street East, Montreal, Que., Canada H1B 1C3, *Tel:* +1 613 657 1004, *Fax:* +1 514 640 8365, *Email:* elliott@petro-canada.ca, *Website:* www.petro-canada.ca
Reiter Petroleum Inc, Suite 900, 625 President Kennedy, Montreal, Que., Canada H3A 1K2, *Tel:* +1 514 8782 563, *Fax:* +1 514 8783 463, *Email:* bunkers@reiterpet.com, *Website:* www.reiterpet.com
Universal Maritime Agency & Trading Co. Ltd (Umatco), 2444 Marisa Ct., Mississauga, Ont., Canada, *Tel:* +1 905 823 4638, *Fax:* +1 905 823 3938, *Email:* umatco@sympatico.ca

Repair & Maintenance: Available at Montreal

Railway: Canadian Railway (CN)

Lloyd's Agent: Hayes Stuart Inc., 297 Duke Street, Montreal, Que., Canada H3C 2M2, *Tel:* +1 514 866 1801, *Fax:* +1 514 866 1259, *Email:* montreal@hayesstuart.com, *Website:* www.hayesstuart.com

CORNER BROOK

Lat 48° 57' N; Long 57° 56' W.

Admiralty Chart: 4741   **Admiralty Pilot:** 50
Time Zone: GMT -3.5 h   **UNCTAD Locode:** CA CBK

Principal Facilities:

P		Y	G	C		L	B		A

Authority: Corner Brook Port Corp., P O Box 1165, Suite 206-10, Main Street, Corner Brook, NL, Canada A2H 6T2, *Tel:* +1 709 634 6600, *Fax:* +1 709 634 6620, *Email:* info@cornerbrookport.com, *Website:* www.cornerbrookport.com

Officials: Chief Executive Officer: Jacqueline Chow, *Email:* jchow@cornerbrookport.com.
Business Development Manager: Rebecca Hefferton, *Email:* rhefferton@cornerbrookport.com.
Operations Manager: Chris Power, *Tel:* +1 709 637 4282, *Email:* cpower@cornerbrookport.com.

Port Security: ISPS compliant

Documentation: General declaration (4 copies), crew effects declaration (3 copies), ship stores declaration (3 copies), immigration crew list (3 copies), marine declaration of health (1 copy), port clearance from previous port

Approach: Pilots will advise regarding a submarine cable which enters the waters of Humber Arm at Wild Cove and continues out of the Bay via Frenchman's Head and South Head

Anchorage: Good anchorages in the outer bay; the most suitable is off Petitpas Cove in 27.5-36.6 m

Pilotage: Compulsory and available from Atlantic Pilotage Authority which has a 24 h centralised pilot dispatch centre in Halifax, *Tel:* +1 877 272 3477 (toll free) and +1 902 426 7610 (inmarsat), *Fax:* +1 877 745 3477 (toll free) and +1 902 426 7236 (inmarsat), *Email:* dispatch@atlanticpilotage.com

Tides: Tidal range of 1.9 m

Working Hours: Corner Brook Pulp and Paper Ltd. premises: three gangs 0800-1200, 1230-1630; two gangs 1630-2030, 2100-0100. Overtime possible

Accommodation:

Name	Length (m)	Depth (m)	Remarks
Corner Brook			See [1] below
Seal Head Wharf	361	9.1–13.1	One transit shed of 65.3 m x 37.3 m
North Star Cement Wharf	121	5.18–7.31	Partly laden tankers of T-2 class discharge here

[1] *Corner Brook:* Corner Brook Pulp and Paper Ltd. wharves consist of four continuous berths, total length 503 m; min depth of 8.53 m in No.1 berth; elsewhere 9.14-9.75 m at LW. Three storage sheds, each approx 182.87 m x 45.71 m; total cap 33 000 t of mill products. Mobile crane of cap 11-8 t. Bulk facilities available
Tanker facilities: Three discharging piers with drafts of 6.7 m, 7.92 m and 9.14 m. There is no night berthing or sailing for oil tankers for Humbermouth

Storage:

Location	Covered (m²)	Sheds / Warehouses
Seal Head Wharf	2425	1

Mechanical Handling Equipment:

Location	Type	Capacity (t)	Qty
Corner Brook	Mobile Cranes	220	2

Bunkering: Bunker 'C' available at Corner Brook Pulp and Paper Ltd, No.4 berth, 24 h notice required. Marine diesel fuel, gas oil and lubricants available by truck delivery

Waste Reception Facilities: Available locally

Towage: Corner Brook Pulp & Paper Co., P O Box 2001, Corner Brook, NL, Canada A2H 6J4, *Tel:* +1 709 637 3322, *Fax:* +1 709 637 3469, *Email:* gvandusen@cb.kruger.com, *Website:* www.cbppl.com

Repair & Maintenance: Minor emergency repairs

Shipping Agents: Canadian Maritime Agency Ltd, 4 Refinery Road, P O Box 119, Come by Chance, NL, Canada A0B 1N0, *Tel:* +1 709 463 4717, *Fax:* +1 709 463 8737, *Email:* opscbc@canadianmaritime.nf.ca, *Website:* www.canadianmaritime.com
Western Dock Services, P O Box 1002, Corner Brook, NL, Canada A2H 6J3, *Tel:* +1 709 632 8590, *Fax:* +1 709 639 7922, *Email:* batten@wds.nf.ca

Medical Facilities: Hospital with full medical services

Airport: Deer Lake, 51 km

Lloyd's Agent: Hayes Stuart Inc., 297 Duke Street, Montreal, Que., Canada H3C 2M2, *Tel:* +1 514 866 1801, *Fax:* +1 514 866 1259, *Email:* montreal@hayesstuart.com, *Website:* www.hayesstuart.com

CORNWALL

Lat 45° 1' N; Long 74° 43' W.

Admiralty Chart: 4793   **Admiralty Pilot:** 65
Time Zone: GMT -5 h   **UNCTAD Locode:** CA CWL

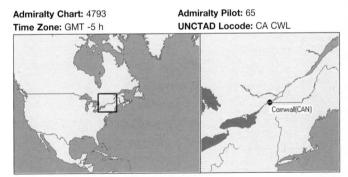

Principal Facilities:

P	Q		G			B			A

Authority: Transport Canada, 4900 Yonge Street, Suite 300, Toronto, Ont., Canada M2N 6A5, *Tel:* +1 416 952 0154, *Fax:* +1 416 952 0159, *Email:* taylodd@tc.gc.ca, *Website:* www.tc.gc.ca

Officials: General Director: Debra Taylor, *Email:* taylodd@tc.gc.ca.

Port Security: ISPS compliant

Approach: The Cornwall Channel is marked by buoys and has a least width of 137.2 m with a least depth of 8.2 m. It branches from the Seaway channel S of the Colquhoun Islands

Pilotage: Compulsory

Radio Frequency: Through Cardinal (VDQ)

Weather: Prevailing W winds

Maximum Vessel Dimensions: 228 m loa

Principal Imports and Exports: Imports: Caustic soda, Wood pulp. Exports: Lumber, Wood pulp.

Key to Principal Facilities:—			
A=Airport	**C**=Containers	**G**=General Cargo	**P**=Petroleum	**R**=Ro/Ro	**Y**=Dry Bulk
B=Bunkers	**D**=Dry Dock	**L**=Cruise	**Q**=Other Liquid Bulk	**T**=Towage (where available from port)	

Accommodation:

Name	Length (m)	Depth (m)	Remarks
Cornwall(Ont)			See [1] below
Cornwall Wharf	175	8.2	A turning area extending 274.5 m S

[1]*Cornwall(Ont):* Tanker facilities: Universal Terminals Ltd has facilities for discharging petroleum and liquid chemicals and an 8 acre tank farm

Storage:

Location	Open (m²)	Covered (m²)	Sheds / Warehouses
Cornwall Wharf	2785	4275	1

Mechanical Handling Equipment:

Location	Type
Cornwall Wharf	Mobile Cranes

Bunkering: BP Marine Americas Inc., 501 Westlake Park Boulevard, Houston, TX 77079, United States of America, *Tel:* +1 281 366 2000, *Email:* firstname.secondname@bp.com

Bunkerina International Inc., 11 3rd Avenue South, Roxboro, Montreal, Que., Canada H8Y 2L3, *Tel:* +1 514 806 2760, *Fax:* +1 514 683 2760

ExxonMobil Marine Fuels, Suite 900, One Alhambra Plaza, Coral Gables, FL 33134, United States of America, *Tel:* +1 305 459 6358, *Fax:* +1 305 459 6412, *Email:* emmf@exxonmobil.com, *Website:* www.exxonmobilmarinefuels.com

Hampton Bunkering Ltd, Suite 615, 999 de Maisonneuve Boulevard West, Montreal, Que., Canada H3A 3L4, *Tel:* +1 514 2882 818, *Fax:* +1 514 2829 279, *Email:* bunkers@hamptonmtl.ca

ICS Petroleum, ICS Petroleum (Montreal) Ltd, Suite 302, 430 Ste-Helene Street, Montreal, Que., Canada H2Y 2K7, *Tel:* +1 514 849 1223, *Fax:* +1 514 849 0517, *Email:* bunkers@ics-mtl.com, *Website:* www.icspet.com

Imperial Oil (Anjou) Ltd, 7100 Jean-Talon Street East, Anjou, Que., Canada H1M 3R8, *Tel:* +1 450 6497 519, *Fax:* +1 450 6497 821, *Email:* christian.beaunoyer@esso.ca, *Website:* www.imperialoil.com

Kildair Service Ltd, 92 Chemin Delangis, St. Paul de Joliette, Que., Canada JOK 3EO, *Tel:* +1 450 7568 091, *Fax:* +1 450 7564 783, *Email:* info@kildair.com, *Website:* www.kildair.com

Petro Canada Products Ltd, 11701 Sherbrooke Street East, Montreal, Que., Canada H1B 1C3, *Tel:* +1 613 657 1004, *Fax:* +1 514 640 8365, *Email:* elliott@petro-canada.ca, *Website:* www.petro-canada.ca

Reiter Petroleum Inc, Suite 900, 625 President Kennedy, Montreal, Que., Canada H3A 1K2, *Tel:* +1 514 8782 563, *Fax:* +1 514 8783 463, *Email:* bunkers@reiterpet.com, *Website:* www.reiterpet.com

Universal Maritime Agency & Trading Co. Ltd (Umatco), 2444 Marisa Ct., Mississauga, Ont., Canada, *Tel:* +1 905 823 4638, *Fax:* +1 905 823 3938, *Email:* umatco@sympatico.ca – *Grades:* IFO

Repair & Maintenance: B. & W. Bingley Steel Works Ltd, P O Box 727, Cornwall, Ont., Canada K6H 5T5, *Tel:* +1 613 933 1365, *Fax:* +1 613 938 7578 Repairs to boilers, engines and hulls

Medical Facilities: Available

Airport: Montreal International, 96 km

Lloyd's Agent: McLarens Canada (Toronto), 600 Alden Road, Suite 600, Markham, Toronto, Ont., Canada L3R 0E7, *Tel:* +1 905 946 9995, *Fax:* +1 905 946 0171, *Email:* roger.bickers@mclarens.ca, *Website:* www.mclarens.ca

COWICHAN BAY

Lat 48° 45' N; Long 123° 36' W.

Admiralty Chart: 4920	**Admiralty Pilot:** 25
Time Zone: GMT -8 h	**UNCTAD Locode:** CA CCB

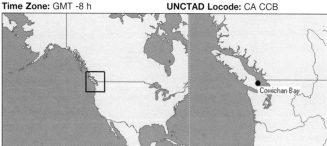

Principal Facilities:

		Y			B			

Authority: Westcan Terminals Ltd, P O Box 131, 5105 Tzouhalem Road, Duncan, B.C., Canada V9L 3X1, *Tel:* +1 250 748 5206, *Fax:* +1 250 748 2932, *Email:* cbaywest@island.net, *Website:* www.westcan.ws

Port Security: ISPS compliant

Approach: Cowichan Bay is entered from Satellite Channel S of Separation Point and extends 4.8 km W, terminating in a large mud flat formed by the Cowichan and Koksilah River estuaries. The approaches to the deep sea berths in the SW corner of the bay on the edge of the mud flat are wide, deep and free from hazards

Anchorage: Eight permanent anchorages are available in depths of approx 40-50 m on a line starting 700 m SSW of Skinner Point and ranging with three designated anchorages along the N side of Cowichan Bay to Separation Point; and then on the S side of Satellite Channel with five anchorages from Separation Point to 1000 m N of Hatch Point. Anchorage can also be afforded to small vessels (excluding deep sea

or commercial vessels) at Genoa Bay in depths of 4.6-11 m which has a rock marked by a beacon in the middle of its entrance, and two other rock hazards nearby

Pilotage: Compulsory. Pacific Pilotage Authority

Principal Imports and Exports: Exports: Lumber.

Accommodation:

Name	Length (m)	Depth (m)	Remarks
Cowichan Bay Docks			Operated by Westcan Terminals Ltd
Berth No.1 (S)	155	9.3	
Berth No.2 (N)	198	8.3	See [1] below
Fishermen's Wharf			Capacity for 55 fishing boats & pleasure craft

[1]*Berth No.2 (N):* Concrete filled steel pile mooring dolphin installed 15.24 m off the end

Storage: Paved area of about 8 ha adjacent to the docks used for lumber assembly and storage

Bunkering: Diesel fuel, gasoline and other petroleum products are available in moderate quantities by road tanker at berth. Larger quantities and heavy fuels are available from Vancouver by barge

Medical Facilities: Cowichan District Hospital at Duncan, 10 km

Lloyd's Agent: McLarens Canada (Vancouver), 505 1100 Melville Street, Vancouver, B.C., Canada V6E 4A6, *Tel:* +1 604 681 7107, *Fax:* +1 604 681 8125, *Email:* philip.vardon@mclarens.ca, *Website:* www.mclarens.ca

CROFTON

Lat 48° 52' N; Long 123° 38' W.

Admiralty Chart: -	**Admiralty Pilot:** 25
Time Zone: GMT -8 h	**UNCTAD Locode:** CA CRO

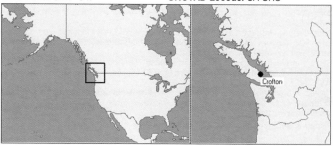

Principal Facilities:

		Y				T	A

Authority: Transport Canada, Harbours & Ports Department, 620-800 Burrard Street, Vancouver, B.C., Canada V6Z 2JB, *Tel:* +1 604 666 5399, *Fax:* +1 604 666 2961, *Website:* www.tc.gc.ca

Port Security: ISPS compliant

Approach: The approaches to the berths are deep and free of danger but occasional strong E winds can make berthing difficult and necessitate the use of tugs

Pilotage: Compulsory. Pacific Pilotage Authority

Radio Frequency: Coast Guard on VHF Channel 16 and vessel traffic on VHF Channel 11

Maximum Vessel Dimensions: 45 295 dwt, 201 m loa

Principal Imports and Exports: Exports: Forest products.

Working Hours: 24 h/day

Accommodation:

Name	Length (m)	Depth (m)	Remarks
Stuart Channel Wharves			Ship's gear used at all berths
Berth No.1	170	12	See [1] below
Berth No.2	152	12.2	
Berth No.3	138	12	See [2] below

[1]*Berth No.1:* Berths 1 & 2 operated by Catalyst Paper Corp., PO Box 70, Crofton, B.C. V0R 1R0, Tel: +1 250 246 6100, Fax: +1 250 246 6300, Website: www.catalystpaper.com, serve the adjoining Crofton Pulp & Paper Mill

[2]*Berth No.3:* Operated by TimberWest Forest Corp., 8359 Crofton Road, PO Box 40, Crofton, B.C. V0R 1R0, Tel: +1 250 246 3234, Fax: +1 250 246 9300, Email: ulleyw@timberwest.com, Website: www.timberwest.com

Storage: Open storage area of 9.2 ha

Location	Covered (m²)
Berth No.1	1040
Berth No.2	2600
Berth No.3	843

Towage: Available

Medical Facilities: Available

Airport: Nanaimo Airport, 20 km

Lloyd's Agent: McLarens Canada (Vancouver), 505 1100 Melville Street, Vancouver, B.C., Canada V6E 4A6, *Tel:* +1 604 681 7107, *Fax:* +1 604 681 8125, *Email:* philip.vardon@mclarens.ca, *Website:* www.mclarens.ca

DALHOUSIE

Lat 48° 4' N; Long 66° 22' W.

Admiralty Chart: 4769
Time Zone: GMT -4 h

Admiralty Pilot: 65
UNCTAD Locode: CA DHS

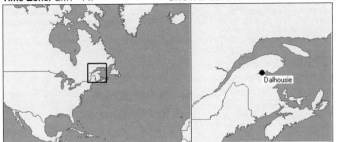

Principal Facilities:

	P		Y	G			B			A

Authority: Port of Dalhousie Inc., 221 Harbour Road, Dalhousie, N.B., Canada E8C 1 X3, *Tel:* +1 506 684 2530, *Fax:* +1 506 684 5617

Port Security: ISPS compliant

Approach: A draft of 10.4 m can be taken in or out of the channel

Anchorage: Secure and ample anchorage grounds; best anchorage is anywhere E of N side of Middle Ground in depths of 18.3 to 27.5 m

Pilotage: Pilots meet vessels off Maguasha Quarantine Buoy, mouth of Restigouche River. Atlantic Pilotage Authority has a 24 h centralised pilot dispatch centre in Halifax, Tel: +1 877 272 3477 (toll free) and +1 902 426 7610 (inmarsat), Fax: +1 877 745 3477 (toll free) and +1 902 426 7236 (inmarsat), Email: dispatch@atlanticpilotage.com

Tides: Range of tide 2.1 to 2.8 m

Maximum Vessel Dimensions: 70 947 dwt, 234.6 m loa

Principal Imports and Exports: Imports: Coal, Petroleum. Exports: Ore concentrates, Paper.

Accommodation:

Name	Length (m)	Depth (m)	Remarks
Dalhousie			
West Wharf	335	10.3	Petroleum, coal & ore concentrates
East Wharf	340	9.7	Mainly paper shipments
New Brunswick International Paper Company's Wharf(Moffat wharf)	152	7.3–8.2	See [1] below

[1]*New Brunswick International Paper Company's Wharf(Moffat wharf):* With 8.2 m depth up to 131.1-160 m mark and 7.3 m depth from 131.1-160 m mark alongside at LW. Railway tracks; water main; electric light and power; no cranes or hoists; used for paper and sulphur.

Storage:

Location	Covered (m²)	Sheds / Warehouses
East Wharf	10370	1

Mechanical Handling Equipment:

Location	Type
Dalhousie	Mobile Cranes

Bunkering: Fuel and diesel oils can be secured in emergency

Repair & Maintenance: Minor repairs only

Medical Facilities: Available

Airport: Restigouche Municipal Airport, 11 km

Lloyd's Agent: Hayes Stuart Inc., 297 Duke Street, Montreal, Que., Canada H3C 2M2, *Tel:* +1 514 866 1801, *Fax:* +1 514 866 1259, *Email:* montreal@hayesstuart.com, *Website:* www.hayesstuart.com

DARTMOUTH

harbour area, see under Halifax

DUKE POINT

harbour area, see under Nanaimo

DUNCAN BAY

Lat 50° 5' N; Long 125° 17' W.

Admiralty Chart: 4920
Time Zone: GMT -8 h

Admiralty Pilot: 25
UNCTAD Locode: CA DCN

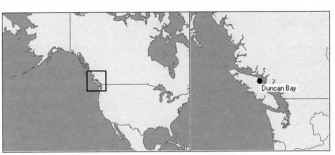

Principal Facilities:

		Y	G						

Authority: Duncan Bay Port Authority, P O Box 2000, Campbell River, B.C., Canada V9W 5C9, *Tel:* +1 250 287 5200, *Fax:* +1 250 287 5577

Officials: General Manager: Mick Pom.

Approach: Channel dredged to 9.1 m at LW

Anchorage: Anchorage can be obtained in the middle of Duncan Bay in a depth of 27 m; bottom sand; sheltered from all winds except from a NW direction

Tides: Range of tide 4.9 m at ST

Principal Imports and Exports: Exports: Paper, Woodpulp.

Accommodation:

Name	Length (m)	Depth (m)	Remarks
Duncan Bay			Dedicated to the adjoining Elk Falls Pulp & Paper Mill
Paper Wharf	152	4.6	
Pulp Wharf	152	3.6–7.8	
Barge Terminal		4–7.5	Coal transshipment

Medical Facilities: Hospital at Campbell River

Lloyd's Agent: McLarens Canada (Vancouver), 505 1100 Melville Street, Vancouver, B.C., Canada V6E 4A6, *Tel:* +1 604 681 7107, *Fax:* +1 604 681 8125, *Email:* philip.vardon@mclarens.ca, *Website:* www.mclarens.ca

DUNCAN WHARF

harbour area, see under Port Alfred

ESTUAIRE

harbour area, see under Quebec

EUROCAN TERMINALS

harbour area, see under Kitimat

FAIRVIEW COVE

harbour area, see under Halifax

FIBRECO TERMINAL

harbour area, see under Vancouver

FORESTVILLE

Lat 48° 48' N; Long 69° 4' W.

Admiralty Chart: 310
Time Zone: GMT -4 h

Admiralty Pilot: 65
UNCTAD Locode: CA FRV

This port is no longer open to commercial shipping

FRASER RIVER PORT

Lat 49° 12' N; Long 122° 55' W.

Admiralty Chart: 576
Time Zone: GMT -8 h

Admiralty Pilot: 25
UNCTAD Locode: CA NWE

Key to Principal Facilities:—			
A=Airport	**C**=Containers	**G**=General Cargo	**P**=Petroleum	**R**=Ro/Ro	**Y**=Dry Bulk
B=Bunkers	**D**=Dry Dock	**L**=Cruise	**Q**=Other Liquid Bulk	**T**=Towage (where available from port)	

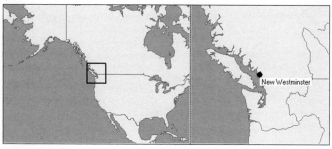

Principal Facilities:

Q	Y	G	C	R		B		T	A

Authority: Port Metro Vancouver, 400-625 Agnes Street, New Westminster, B.C., Canada V3M 5Y4, *Tel:* +1 604 524 6655, *Fax:* +1 604 524 1127, *Email:* fraserport@frpa.com, *Website:* www.frpa.com

Officials: Chief Executive Officer: Capt Gordon Houston.

Port Security: ISPS compliant

Approach: 11.5 m draft on a 3.5 m tide

Anchorage: Available N of Sand Heads

Pilotage: Compulsory under Pacific Pilotage Authority, from Sandheads at mouth of river to Pitt River, 8 km above New Westminster. Pilotage boarding station is maintained within 1.6 km seaward of Sandhead lighthouse at entrance to river. For further information and charges contact Pacific Pilotage Authority, Tel: +1 604 666 6771, Fax: +1 604 666 1647

Radio Frequency: VHF Channel 74

Traffic: 2007, 4 157 947 t of international cargo and 30 673 837 t of domestic cargo handled, 191 402 TEU's

Maximum Vessel Dimensions: 245 m loa, 32.3 m beam, 11.5 m draft

Working Hours: 24 h, 7 days a week

Accommodation:

Name	Length (m)	Depth (m)	Remarks
Fraser Surrey Docks			See [1] below
Berths 2-3	548		
Berth 4			See [2] below
Berth 6			See [3] below
Berth 7-8	457	11.4	See [4] below
Berth 9	244	11.4	
Berth 10	145		See [5] below
WWL Vehicle Services Canada Ltd			See [6] below
Berth 1	213	11	
Berth 2	213	10.6	A 32 m section for heavy lifts
Private Wharves			See [7] below

[1]*Fraser Surrey Docks:* Operated by Fraser Surrey Docks LP, 11060 Elevator Road, Surrey BC V3V 2R7, Tel: +1 604 581 2233, Fax: +1 604 581 6488, Email: interact@fsd.bc.ca, Website: www.fsd.bc.ca. Eight berths with drafts up to 11.4 m for general cargo and containers. Almost 35 000 m2 of closed storage space and 44.5 ha of outside storage. The port is serviced by rail and road connections that span the continent. Water, supplies, telephone and power available at all berths

[2]*Berth 4:* Has a 4645 m2 shed alongside to handle paper and forest products and some general cargo as well as a 2787 m2 shed to handle steel products

[3]*Berth 6:* Barge ramp with 50 t cap. Central location allows easy access to storage sheds and yards

[4]*Berth 7-8:* With mooring dolphins 47.75 m off each end and a scow berth at the south end to facilitate cargo movements

[5]*Berth 10:* Bulk carrier tie-up consisting of three dolphins. Has approach trestle

[6]*WWL Vehicle Services Canada Ltd:* Tel: +1 604 521 6681, Fax: +1 604 522 7783. Ro/ro facility; automobile terminal with cap for 22 000 vehicles. Served by rail. Water, telephone and power available

[7]*Private Wharves:* Fraser Wharves Ltd, automobile import centre for Canadian Motor Industries Ltd with storage for approx 15 000 vehicles; dock 152.4 m long, depth 10.67 m alongside. Water, telephone and power available

LeHigh Cement Ltd., 182 m concrete loading facility with a depth alongside of 7.6 m. Rate of loading 350 t/h. Water, telephone and power available

Seaspan Coastal Intermodal, provides truck and rail ferry service to Vancouver Island and consists of two working berths and three lay-over berths

Mechanical Handling Equipment:

Location	Type	Capacity (t)	Qty
Berths 2-3	Mult-purp. Cranes	50	1
Berths 2-3	Mult-purp. Cranes	40	1
Berths 2-3	Panamax		2

Bunkering: ExxonMobil Marine Fuels, Suite 900, One Alhambra Plaza, Coral Gables, FL 33134, United States of America, *Tel:* +1 305 459 6358, *Fax:* +1 305 459 6412, *Email:* emmf@exxonmobil.com, *Website:* www.exxonmobilmarinefuels.com – *Grades:* all grades – *Delivery Mode:* barge, truck

ICS Petroleum, ICS Petroleum Ltd., P O Box 12115, Suite 2360, 555 West Hastings Street, Vancouver, B.C., Canada V6B 4N6, *Tel:* +1 604 6856 221, *Fax:* +1 604 6857 352, *Email:* bunkers@ics-vcr.com, *Website:* www.icspet.com – *Grades:* all grades – *Delivery Mode:* barge, truck

Imperial Oil (Burnaby) Ltd, International Marine Sales, 4720 Kingsway, Burnaby, B.C., Canada V5H 4N2, *Tel:* +1 604 451 5955, *Fax:* +1 604 451 5950 – *Grades:* all grades – *Delivery Mode:* barge, truck

Marine Petrobulk Ltd, 10 Pemberton Avenue, Vancouver, B.C., Canada V7P 2R1, *Tel:* +1 604 9874 415, *Fax:* +1 604 9873 824, *Email:* tbrewster@marinepetro.com, *Website:* www.marinepetrobulk.com – *Grades:* all grades – *Delivery Mode:* barge, truck

Waste Reception Facilities: Garbage disposal available

Towage: Harken Towing Co. Ltd, 1990 Argue Avenue, P O Box 7, Coquitlam, B.C., Canada V3C 3V5, *Tel:* +1 604 942 8511, *Fax:* +1 604 942 4914, *Email:* harken@harkentowing.com, *Website:* www.harkentowing.com

Rivtow Marine Inc., SMIT Marine Canada Inc., 2285 Commissioner Street, P O Box 3650, Vancouver, B.C., Canada V6B 3Y8, *Tel:* +1 604 255 1133, *Fax:* +1 604 251 0213, *Email:* info.canada@smit.com, *Website:* www.smit.com

Seaspan International Ltd, 10 Pemberton Avenue, Vancouver, B.C., Canada V7P 2R1, *Tel:* +1 604 988 3111, *Fax:* +1 604 984 1613, *Email:* info@seaspan.com, *Website:* www.seaspan.com

Westminster Tug Boats, 617-713 Columbia Street, New Westminster, B.C., Canada V3M 1B2, *Tel:* +1 604 522 4604, *Fax:* +1 604 522 7298, *Email:* westug@telus.net

Repair & Maintenance: Engine repairs only

Airport: Vancouver International Airport, 29 km

Railway: Canadian National, CP Rail, Burlington Northern and Southern Railway

Lloyd's Agent: McLarens Canada (Vancouver), 505 1100 Melville Street, Vancouver, B.C., Canada V6E 4A6, *Tel:* +1 604 681 7107, *Fax:* +1 604 681 8125, *Email:* philip.vardon@mclarens.ca, *Website:* www.mclarens.ca

GASPE

Lat 48° 50' N; Long 64° 29' W.

Admiralty Chart: -		**Admiralty Pilot:** 65	
Time Zone: GMT -5 h		**UNCTAD Locode:** CA GPE	

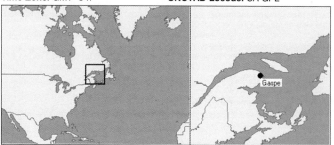

Principal Facilities:

P		G		B	T	A

Authority: Transport Canada, Champlain Harbour Station, 901 Cap Diamant 4th Floor, Quebec, Que., Canada G1K 4K1, *Tel:* +1 418 648 4103, *Fax:* +1 418 648 7980, *Website:* www.tc.gc.ca

Officials: Regional Manager: Andre Roy, *Tel:* +1 418 648 7213, *Email:* royan@tc.gc.ca.

Harbour Master: Michel Petit, *Tel:* +1 418 648 3640.

Port Security: ISPS compliant

Approach: Min depth at entrance 19.8-21.3 m. Depth on bar 8.2 m. Inner harbour 9.1-12.2 m. Outer harbour 21.3-24.4 m. Icebreaker available in winter if necessary

Anchorage: Good anchorage in inner or outer harbours

Pilotage: Not compulsory but recommended

Tides: Range 1.22 m (neap), 1.52 m (spring)

Traffic: 2005, 16 vessels, 78 000 t of cargo handled

Working Hours: Mon to Fri 0800-1700. Overtime as required. Holidays and weekends on notice only

Accommodation:

Name	Length (m)	Depth (m)	Remarks
Gaspe			See [1] below
Berth No.1	180	10	
Berth No.2	175	8	

[1]*Gaspe:* Cargo primarily handled includes sulphuric acid, petroleum products, copper and salt. Ultramar Oil and Irving Oil have pipelines on the wharf. There is also a pipeline for loading of sulphuric acid

Storage:

Location	Open (m²)
Gaspe	5600

Mechanical Handling Equipment:

Location	Type
Gaspe	Mult-purp. Cranes

Bunkering: Only on application. Fuel and diesel oil from several oil companies stations

Towage: Tugs available

Repair & Maintenance: Minor hull and machinery repairs possible

Medical Facilities: Gaspe Hospital

Airport: 9 km from port

Lloyd's Agent: Hayes Stuart Inc., 297 Duke Street, Montreal, Que., Canada H3C 2M2, *Tel:* +1 514 866 1801, *Fax:* +1 514 866 1259, *Email:* montreal@hayesstuart.com, *Website:* www.hayesstuart.com

GEORGETOWN

Lat 46° 11' N; Long 62° 32' W.

Admiralty Chart: 4765	Admiralty Pilot: 65
Time Zone: GMT -4 h	UNCTAD Locode: CA GGW

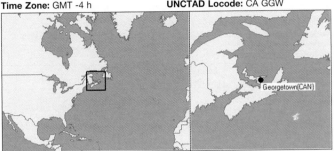

Principal Facilities:

		G		B		A	

Authority: Transport Canada, Atlantic Region, P O Box 197, Georgetown, P.E.I., Canada C0A 1L0, *Tel:* +1 902 652 2770, *Fax:* +1 902 652 2915, *Website:* www.tc.gc.ca

Officials: Harbour Master: Leslie King.

Port Security: ISPS compliant

Approach: Approach channel in depth of 10.97 m

Anchorage: Safe anchorage is available

Pilotage: Atlantic Pilotage Authority

Radio Frequency: VCA Charlottetown 156.8 mcs, 2182 mHz

Tides: Range of tide 1.52 m springs, 1.07 m neaps

Accommodation:

Name	Length (m)	Depth (m)	Remarks
Georgetown Marine Terminal (Railway Wharf)			Carries a frost-proof shed 49 m x 12 m
East	200	8	
West	262	8	

Storage:

Location	Covered (m²)	Sheds / Warehouses
Georgetown	600	1

Mechanical Handling Equipment:

Location	Type	Capacity (t)
Georgetown	Mobile Cranes	45

Bunkering: Diesel and fuel oil available by tank wagon

Repair & Maintenance: Local shipyards carry out repairs to hull and engine

Airport: Charlottetown Airport, 61 km

Lloyd's Agent: Hayes Stuart Inc., 1000 Windmill Road, Suite 19, Dartmouth, N.S., Canada B3B 1L7, *Tel:* +1 902 468 2651, *Fax:* +1 902 468 4315, *Email:* halifax@hayesstuart.com, *Website:* www.hayesstuart.com

GEORGIA PACIFIC CORP TERMINAL

harbour area, see under Point Tupper

GOOSE BAY

Lat 53° 21' N; Long 60° 25' W.

Admiralty Chart: -	Admiralty Pilot: 50
Time Zone: GMT -4 h	UNCTAD Locode: CA GOO

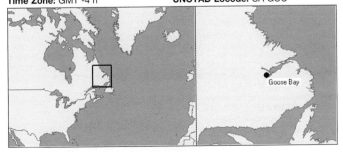

Principal Facilities:

P		G	C	R		B		A	

Authority: Works, Services & Transportation, Govt. of Newfoundland & Labrador, P O Box 8700, St. John's, NL, Canada A1B 4J6, *Tel:* +1 709 729 3676, *Fax:* +1 709 729 4285, *Email:* davidsalter@gov.nl.ca, *Website:* www.tw.gov.nl.ca

Officials: Communications Director / Manager: David Salter.

Port Security: ISPS compliant

Documentation: General declaration (4 copies), crew effects declaration (3 copies), ship stores declaration (3 copies), immigration crew list (3 copies), marine declaration of health (1 copy), port clearance from previous port

Approach: Sandy Point Channel at the entrance to Goose Bay and 24 km from the dock has a navigable width of 61 m and a charted depth of 7.6 m. Depths vary from year to year and current information should be obtained from the Harbour Master. Groves Point Channel at the entrance to Terrington Basin from Goose Bay and 2.4 km from Main Dock has a depth of 9.4 m and a width of 91 m

Pilotage: Available but not compulsory. Vessels should send ETA 12 h and 6 h in advance to Atlantic Pilotage Authority which has a 24 h centralised pilot dispatch centre in Halifax, Tel: +1 877 272 3477 (toll free) and +1 902 426 7610 (inmarsat), Fax: +1 877 745 3477 (toll free) and +1 902 426 7236 (inmarsat), Email: dispatch@atlanticpilotage.com

Tides: Rise and fall of tide 0.76 m

Accommodation:

Name	Length (m)	Depth (m)	Remarks
Goose Bay			See [1] below
Main Public Wharf	244		See [2] below
Public Wharf No.2		5.4–7.1	Situated 0.6 km NW of the main wharf

[1]*Goose Bay:* Containers can be offloaded onto dock. Ro/ro traffic can be accommodated

[2]*Main Public Wharf:* With depths of 7.4 m at face and 9.2 m at 6.0 m off face; the harbour master should be consulted for details.

Storage:

Location	Covered (m²)	Sheds / Warehouses
Goose Bay	1022	1

Mechanical Handling Equipment:

Location	Type
Goose Bay	Mobile Cranes

Bunkering: Ample supplies of diesel oil by pipeline

Waste Reception Facilities: Not available

Repair & Maintenance: Minor repairs in emergency. No drydock

Medical Facilities: Hospital with doctor and medical services, 2.5 km

Airport: 2.5 km

Lloyd's Agent: Hayes Stuart Inc., 297 Duke Street, Montreal, Que., Canada H3C 2M2, *Tel:* +1 514 866 1801, *Fax:* +1 514 866 1259, *Email:* montreal@hayesstuart.com, *Website:* www.hayesstuart.com

GRAND BANK

Lat 47° 6' N; Long 55° 45' W.

Admiralty Chart: 4734	Admiralty Pilot: 65
Time Zone: GMT -3.5 h	UNCTAD Locode: CA GRB

Principal Facilities:

P		G			B		A	

Authority: Grand Bank Harbour Authority, 10 Lower Water Street, P O Box 88, Grand Bank, NL, Canada A0E 1W0, *Tel:* +1 709 832 0255, *Fax:* +1 709 832 2055, *Email:* f6gbha1@nf.aibn.com

Officials: President: Eric Miller.
Harbour Master: George Snook, *Email:* geo-glo@hotmail.com.

Approach: The approach channel is currently being dredged to a depth of 8 m. The angle of approach is 254°(T)

Anchorage: Depth at anchorage 9.1 m

Pilotage: Can be arranged

Radio Frequency: Call sign CHC-442, VHF Channel 74

Weather: Winds from N/E are not suitable for lower end of harbour

Tides: 2 m LWOST, HWOST 2.1 m

Maximum Vessel Dimensions: 350 ft loa

Principal Imports and Exports: Imports: Fish, Road salt.

Working Hours: Mon-Fri 0800-1700

Key to Principal Facilities:—				
A=Airport	**C**=Containers	**G**=General Cargo	**P**=Petroleum	**R**=Ro/Ro	**Y**=Dry Bulk
B=Bunkers	**D**=Dry Dock	**L**=Cruise	**Q**=Other Liquid Bulk	**T**=Towage (where available from port)

Accommodation:

Name	Length (m)	Depth (m)	Remarks
Grand Bank			See [1] below
Western Pier	73	4.3	The deck of the berth has an elevation of about 1.2 m
Fish Wharf	75	4.9	Situated on the E side of the harbour
Private Wharves			Six floating docks

[1]*Grand Bank:* There is a marginal wharf located on the W side of the harbour and a public wharf in the S
Tanker facilities: Diesel, gas & propane by prior notice

Storage: One storage shed of 1080 m3 cap

Bunkering: Fuel and diesel oil available by tank truck

Waste Reception Facilities: Garbage and waste oil tank

Repair & Maintenance: Fortune Marine Service Centre Ltd, Harbour Drive, Fortune, NL, Canada A0E 1P0, *Tel:* +1 709 832 0737, *Fax:* +1 709 832 1479, *Email:* burinpeninsulamarine@nfaibn.com

Surveyors: Peer Less Marine Survey, Grand Bank, NL, Canada, *Tel:* +1 709 279 2686, *Fax:* +1 709 279 2686

Medical Facilities: Hospital and Medical Clinic in the town

Airport: Winterland Airstrip, 40 km

Lloyd's Agent: Hayes Stuart Inc., 297 Duke Street, Montreal, Que., Canada H3C 2M2, *Tel:* +1 514 866 1801, *Fax:* +1 514 866 1259, *Email:* montreal@hayesstuart.com, *Website:* www.hayesstuart.com

GRANDE-ANSE

harbour area, see under La Baie

GREAT LAKES

Pilotage: See under St. Lawrence Seaway. Available from Great Lakes Pilotage Authority Ltd., 202 Pitt Street, PO Box 95, Cornwall Ont. K6H 5R9, Tel: +1 613 932 2995, Fax: +1 613 932 3793

Accommodation:

Name	Remarks
Great Lakes	See [1] below

[1]*Great Lakes:* The Great Lakes consist of five freshwater lakes bordering on Canada and the United States of America
The largest, Lake Superior, has a length of 563 km and a width of 257 km; Lake Huron is 331 by 294 km; Lake Michigan 494 by 190 km; Lake Erie 388 by 92 km and Lake Ontario 311 by 85 km
The Great Lakes Connection Channels comprise the waterways from Lake Superior to Lakes Michigan, Huron and Lake Erie including Pelee Passage, St Mary's River, Straits of Mackinac, St Clair River, Lake St Clair and Detroit River. Construction as authorized provides channel depths varying from 8.19 to 9.10 m below LW datum depending on the exposure of the channel and the hardness of the bottom material. These depths are designed to permit a max draft of 7.92 m when the ruling lake is at its LW datum. Actual safe draft will depend on the levels of the Great Lakes and on the clearance and safety allowances established by individual vessel operators
For information on ports situated on the Great Lakes, see under the respective ports in the Canada and United States sections

Lloyd's Agent: McLarens Canada (Toronto), 600 Alden Road, Suite 600, Markham, Toronto, Ont., Canada L3R 0E7, *Tel:* +1 905 946 9995, *Fax:* +1 905 946 0171, *Email:* roger.bickers@mclarens.ca, *Website:* www.mclarens.ca

GROS CACOUNA

Lat 47° 56' N; Long 69° 30' W.

Admiralty Chart: 4783

Time Zone: GMT -5 h

Admiralty Pilot: 65

UNCTAD Locode: CA GCA

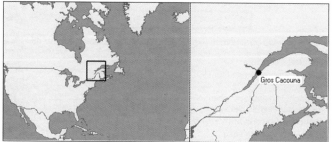

Principal Facilities:

		Y	G		B		A

Authority: Transport Canada, Champlain Harbour Station, 901 Cap Diamant 4th Floor, Quebec, Que., Canada G1K 4K1, *Tel:* +1 418 648 4103, *Fax:* +1 418 648 7980, *Website:* www.tc.gc.ca

Officials: Regional Manager: Andre Roy, *Tel:* +1 418 648 7213, *Email:* royan@tc.gc.ca.
Harbour Master: Michel Petit, *Tel:* +1 418 648 3640.

Port Security: ISPS compliant

Approach: Channel width of 170 m in depth of 10.2 m

Pilotage: Compulsory

Tides: Range of tide is 5.6 m springs

Traffic: 2005, 40 vessels, approx 323 000 t of cargo handled

Working Hours: Mon to Fri 0800-1700. Overtime as required. Holidays and weekends on notice only

Accommodation:

Name	Length (m)	Depth (m)	Remarks
Gros Cacouna			See [1] below
Berth No.1	141	10.2	Cargoes handled include lumber & cement
Berth No.2	141	10.2	Cargoes handled include lumber & cement

[1]*Gros Cacouna:* Artificial harbour located on the SW end of Cacouna Island, joined by road to the mainland

Storage:

Location	Open (m²)	Covered (m²)
Gros Cacouna	100000	2741

Mechanical Handling Equipment:

Location	Type
Gros Cacouna	Mult-purp. Cranes

Bunkering: Diesel oil can be obtained on request

Stevedoring Companies: Quebec Port Terminals Inc., 200 Avenue du Port, Cacouna, Que., Canada G0L 1G0, *Tel:* +1 418 862 9753, *Fax:* +1 418 862 9485, *Email:* info@qsl.com, *Website:* www.qsl.com

Medical Facilities: Riviere du Loup Hospital, 3 km

Airport: Riviere du Loup

Lloyd's Agent: Hayes Stuart Inc., 297 Duke Street, Montreal, Que., Canada H3C 2M2, *Tel:* +1 514 866 1801, *Fax:* +1 514 866 1259, *Email:* montreal@hayesstuart.com, *Website:* www.hayesstuart.com

HALIFAX

Lat 44° 39' N; Long 63° 35' W.

Admiralty Chart: 4752/3/4/5

Time Zone: GMT -4 h

Admiralty Pilot: 59

UNCTAD Locode: CA HAL

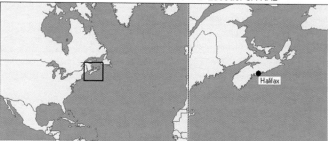

Principal Facilities:

P	Q	Y	G	C	R	L	B	D	T	A

Authority: Halifax Port Authority, P O Box 336, Halifax, N.S., Canada B3J 2P6, *Tel:* +1 902 426 8222, *Fax:* +1 902 426 7335, *Email:* mkt@portofhalifax.ca, *Website:* www.portofhalifax.ca

Officials: Chief Executive Officer: Karen Oldfield, *Email:* koldfield@portofhalifax.ca.
Commercial Director: Paul DuVoisin, *Email:* pduvoisin@portofhalifax.ca.
Operations Manager: Ches Carter, *Tel:* +1 902 426 1796, *Email:* cxc@portofhalifax.ca.

Port Security: ISPS compliant. Container Security Initiative (CSI) designated port

Approach: The harbour is naturally well sheltered with a very large inner 'Bedford Basin'. Controlling depth in channels of approach is 18.1 m at LW, but charted depths indicate a channel of 21.34 m is available at LW as far as The Narrows, inner limit of the area of general cargo piers

Pilotage: Compulsory. 12 h notice of ETA required, confirmed or corrected three hours before arrival to Atlantic Pilotage Authority which has a 24 h centralised pilot dispatch centre in Halifax, Tel: +1 877 272 3477 (toll free) and +1 902 426 7610 (inmarsat), Fax: +1 877 745 3477 (toll free) and +1 902 426 7236 (inmarsat), Email: dispatch@atlanticpilotage.com. Pilots board in vicinity of Inner Automatic Light and Whistle buoy, approx 3 km NE of Chebucto Head

Radio Frequency: Halifax Marine Radio 500 or 2182 kHz, VHF on 156.8, working channel 26, 161.9 and 157.3 mHz

Weather: It is an all-weather port, free of ice in the winter season

Tides: Tides rise 1.98 m springs and 1.37 m neaps

Traffic: 2007, 12 238 908 t of cargo handled, 490 071 TEU's

Principal Imports and Exports: Imports: Automobiles, Crude Oil, Mixed containerised cargo, Refined petroleum. Exports: Automobiles, Flour, Grain, Gypsum, Mixed containerised cargo, Refined petroleum.

Working Hours: 0800-1200, 1300-1700, 1800-2200 or 1800-0500 or to a finish 2400-0800 (Meals 1200-1300, 1700-1800, 2300-2400, 0500-0800 but 0400-0430 if working 2400-0800). Passenger vessels may start work 0700 instead of 0800. Work commencement 2400 only applies to terminal operations, ro/ro operations, non-ship work and container ship work wherever covered by agreement
Sat, Sun and holidays: work performed against payment of overtime except on non-working days

Accommodation: Halifax Grain Elevator Ltd., 951 South Bland Street, Halifax, NS B3H 4S5, Tel: +1 902 421 1714, Fax: +1 902 420 0343, Email: hfxgrain@aol.com.
Storage cap of 140 000 t of wheat
Tanker facilities: Nine berths operated by Imperial Oil Ltd and Irving Oil Co. Night berthing possible, also water and bunkers (by special arrangement at one berth where slop tank facilities are also available)

Name	Length (m)	Depth (m)	Remarks
Seawall (Public)			See [1] below
Berth No.20	221.5	12.2	
Berth No.21	178	12.2	Cruise pavilion
Berth No.22	212	12.2	
Ocean Terminals (Public)			Operated by Halifax Port Authority
Berth No.23	213	9.9	See [2] below
Berth No.24	142	8.9	See [3] below
Berth No.25 (Pier A)	171	11.2	Open pier (marine leg for receiving grain)
Berth No.26 (Pier A)	210	11.2	
Berth No.27 (Pier A)	210	12.2	Forest products
Berth No.28 (Pier A)	171	12.2	Six grain towers capable of delivering 50 000 bu/h
Berth No.30 (Pier A1)	190.5	8.5–13.1	
Berth No.31 (Pier A1)	190.5	13.1	
Berth No.33 (Pier A1)	190.5	12.2	Heated shed
Berth No.34 (Pier A1)	190.5	8.3	Heated shed
South End Container Terminal (Public)			See [4] below
Berth 36 (Pier B)	190.5	13.9	
Berth 37 (Pier B)	190.5	14.1	
Berth 39 (Pier B)	190.5	11.3	
Berth 41 (Pier C)	300	16	
Berth 42 (Pier C)	300	16	
Richmond Terminals (Public)			See [5] below
Berth No.9	213	9.1	See [6] below
Berth No.9a	241	8.8	See [7] below
Richmond Offshore Terminals (Public)			See [8] below
Berth No.9b	216	9.1	
Berth No.9c	140	8.9	
Area No.9d			Open area of 21 306 m2
Fairview Cove Container Terminal (Public)			See [9] below
East Berth	330	13.7	
West Berth	330	13.7	
Bedford Basin (Private)			
National Gypsum Wharf	197	10	See [10] below
Imperial Oil Wharves, Dartmouth (Private)			Owned by Imperial Oil Ltd., Tel: +1 902 420 6872, Fax: +1 902 420 6996
Imperial Oil Dock 3	67	11	Bunkering
Imperial Oil Dock 4	122	10.4	Bunkering, refinery & storage tanks
Imperial Oil Dock 5	67	14.9	Bunkering
Autoport, Eastern Passage (Private)			See [11] below
Floating Dock	201	13.7	40.5 ha for vehicle storage owned by CN

[1]*Seawall (Public):* Primary cruise ship facility operated by Halifax Port Authority
[2]*Berth No.23:* It is equipped for direct loading from rail to ship. Cargoes handled include container, ro/ro, breakbulk and heavy-lift
[3]*Berth No.24:* Berth for working cargoes that require open space such as steel, project cargoes and heavy-lift operations. It is equipped with a rail siding immediatley adjacent to the pier to facilitate direct loading to ship
[4]*South End Container Terminal (Public):* Operated by Halterm Ltd., P O Box 1057, Halifax NS B3J 2X1, Tel: +1 902 421 1778, Fax: +1 902 429 3193, Email: info@halterm.com, Website: www.halterm.com
Total terminal area of 29.2 ha (5 ha at Pier B and 24.2 ha at Pier C). Cargoes handled include container, ro/ro, breakbulk, heavy-lift
[5]*Richmond Terminals (Public):* Multi-user facility adjacent to CN's Halifax Intermodal Terminal
[6]*Berth No.9:* Operated by IT International Telecom, 3481 North Marginal Road, Pier 9, Halifax NS B3K 5M8, Tel: +1 902 422 5594, Fax: +1 902 425 0225, Website: www.ittelecom.com
Bulk, breakbulk, container & project cargoes
[7]*Berth No.9a:* Operated by Scotia Terminals Ltd., Pier 9A, Halifax NS, Tel: +1 902 422 2478, Fax: +1 902 422 2378, Email: ops@scotiaterminals.com, Website: www.scotiaterminals.com
Container, breakbulk, project & heavy lift cargoes
[8]*Richmond Offshore Terminals (Public):* Multi-user supply base operated by EnCana Corporation Offshore Supply Base, 3657 North Marginal Road, Halifax NS B3K 5M4, Tel: +1 902 492 5778, Fax: +1 902 422 4329
[9]*Fairview Cove Container Terminal (Public):* Operated by Cerescorp Co., P O Box 8958, Halifax NS B3K 5M6, Tel: +1 902 453 4590, Fax: +1 902 454 4772, Email: cwhidden@cerescorp.com, Website: www.ceresglobal.com
70 acre terminal situated at the entrance to Bedford Basin. 300 reefer outlets, storage space for 9 000 TEU's and on-dock double stack rail service. Container, ro/ro, breakbulk and heavy lift cargoes handled
[10]*National Gypsum Wharf:* Owned and operated by National Gypsum (Canada) Ltd.,

200 Wrights Cove Road, Milford Station NS, Tel: +1 902 468 7455, Fax: +1 902 468 3505
Raw gypsum delivery from rail to ship
[11]*Autoport, Eastern Passage (Private):* Operated by Autoport Ltd., P O Box 9, Eastern Passage NS B3G 1M4, Tel: +1 902 465 6050, Fax: +1 902 465 6007, Email: autoport@autoport.ca

Storage:

Location	Open (m²)	Covered (m²)
Berth No.20		5213
Berth No.21		4613
Berth No.22		5529
Berth No.23		4706
Berth No.24	4459	
Berth No.25 (Pier A)	4960	
Berth No.26 (Pier A)	2690	8519
Berth No.27 (Pier A)	6387	
Berth No.28 (Pier A)	4170	
Berth No.30 (Pier A1)	8419	
Berth No.31 (Pier A1)	8419	
Berth No.33 (Pier A1)		5743
Berth No.34 (Pier A1)	1858	3620
Berth 42 (Pier C)		2780
Berth No.9	4530	8185
Berth No.9a	1393	5603
Berth No.9b		5875
Berth No.9c	9290	

Mechanical Handling Equipment:

Location	Type	Capacity (t)	Qty
South End Container Terminal (Public)	Container Cranes	36	2
South End Container Terminal (Public)	Container Cranes	40	2
South End Container Terminal (Public)	Post Panamax	55	2
South End Container Terminal (Public)	Yard Tractors		28
Fairview Cove Container Terminal (Public)	Container Cranes	40	3
Fairview Cove Container Terminal (Public)	Super Post Panamax	65	3
Fairview Cove Container Terminal (Public)	Yard Tractors		19

Bunkering: ExxonMobil Marine Fuels, Suite 900, One Alhambra Plaza, Coral Gables, FL 33134, United States of America, Tel: +1 305 459 6358, Fax: +1 305 459 6412, Email: emmf@exxonmobil.com, Website: www.exxonmobilmarinefuels.com – Grades: IFO40-380cSt; MDO; MGO – Delivery Mode: barge, truck, pipeline
Imperial Oil (Dartmouth) Ltd, P O Box 1010, Dartmouth, N.S., Canada B2Y 4RI, Tel: +1 902 420 6872, Fax: +1 902 420 6996
Irving Oil Co. Ltd, 10 Sydney Street, P O Box 1421, Saint John, N.B., Canada E2L 4K1, Tel: +1 888 3101 924, Fax: +1 506 2023 868, Email: webinquiries@irvingoil.com, Website: www.irvingoilco.com

Towage: SVITZER, Eastern Canada Towing Co, P O Box 337, Halifax, N.S., Canada B3J 2N7, Tel: +1 902 423 7381, Fax: +1 902 423 5123, Email: ectug@svitzerwijsmuller.com, Website: www.svitzer.com

Repair & Maintenance: Irving Shipbuilding Inc., Halifax Shipyard, 3099 Barrington Street, P O Box 9110, Halifax, N.S., Canada B3K 5M7, Tel: +1 902 423 9271, Fax: +1 902 422 5253, Email: marketing@irvingshipbuilding.com, Website: www.irvingshipbuilding.com

Seaman Missions: The Seamans Mission, P O Box 27114, Halifax, N.S., Canada B3H 4M8, Tel: +1 902 422 7790, Fax: +1 902 420 9786

Ship Chandlers: Blue Water Agencies Ltd, 40 Topple Drive, Dartmouth, N.S., Canada B3B 1L6, Tel: +1 902 468 4900, Fax: +1 902 468 4901, Email: shipstores@bluewateragencies.ca, Website: www.bluewateragencies.ca
Karlo Corp. - Marine Group, 10 Morris Drive, Burnside Industrial Park, Halifax, N.S., Canada B3B 1K8, Tel: +1 902 468 9547, Fax: +1 902 468 6274, Email: canada@karlogroup.com, Website: www.karlogroup.com
Mercator Ship Supplies Ltd, 38 Payzant Avenue, Burnside Industrial Park, Dartmouth, N.S., Canada B3B 1Z6, Tel: +1 902 481 1661, Fax: +1 902 481 8548, Email: shipsupply@halifax.seagulf.com, Website: www.seagulf.com
Seagulf (Maritimes) Ltd, 38 Payzant Avenue, Burnside Industrial Park, Dartmouth, N.S., Canada B3B 1Z6, Tel: +1 902 481 1661, Fax: +1 902 481 8548, Email: shipsupply@halifax.seagulf.com, Website: www.seagulf.com

Shipping Agents: Furncan Marine Ltd, 1505 Barrington Street, Suite 1302, Halifax, N.S., Canada B3J 3K5, Tel: +1 902 423 6111, Fax: +1 902 423 0177, Email: ops@furncanmarine.com, Website: www.furncanmarine.com
Holmes Maritime Inc., 1345 Hollis Street, Halifax, N.S., Canada B3J 1T8, Tel: +1 902 422 0400, Fax: +1 902 422 9439, Email: info@holmesmaritime.com, Website: www.holmesmaritime.com
Inchcape Shipping Services (ISS), 38 Payzant Avenue, Dartmouth, N.S., Canada B3B 1Z6, Tel: +1 902 465 3361, Fax: +1 902 465 3376, Email: iss.halifax@iss-shipping.com, Website: www.@iss-shipping.com
I.H. Mathers & Son Ltd, 1525 Birmingham Street, Halifax, N.S., Canada B3J 2J6, Tel: +1 902 429 5680, Fax: +1 902 429 5221, Email: info@ihmathers.com, Website: www.ihmathers.com
McLean Kennedy Inc., 2000 Barrington Street, Suite 920, Cogswell Tower, Halifax, N.S., Canada D3J 3K1, Tel: +1 902 423 8136, Fax: +1 902 429 1326, Email: ops@fkwarren.ca
Montship Inc., Suite 1502, Purdy's Wharf Tower 1, 1959 Upper Water Street, Halifax, N.S., Canada B3J 3N2, Tel: +1 902 420 9184, Fax: +1 902 422 6010, Email: ktyler@montship.ca, Website: www.montship.ca

Key to Principal Facilities:—				
A=Airport	**C**=Containers	**G**=General Cargo	**P**=Petroleum	**R**=Ro/Ro	**Y**=Dry Bulk
B=Bunkers	**D**=Dry Dock	**L**=Cruise	**Q**=Other Liquid Cargo	**T**=Towage (where available from port)	

Norton Lilly International Inc., 119 Dorothea Drive, Dartmouth, N.S., Canada B2W 2E7, *Tel:* +1 902 461 1405, *Fax:* +1 902 466 4637, *Email:* hal-ops@nortonlilly.com, *Website:* www.nortonlilly.com

Pickford & Black, Suite 920, Cogswell Tower, 2000 Barrington Street, Halifax, N.S., Canada B3J 2X1, *Tel:* +1 902 423 9191, *Fax:* +1 902 429 1326, *Email:* pickops@pickford-black.ns.ca

Protos Shipping Ltd, 1660 Hollis Street, Suite 902, Halifax, N.S., Canada B3J 1V7, *Tel:* +1 902 421 1211, *Fax:* +1 902 425 4336, *Email:* bbetts@halifax.protos.ca, *Website:* www.protos.ca

Robert Reford Inc., Suite 1302, 1505 Barrington Street, Halifax, N.S., Canada B3J 3K5, *Tel:* +1 902 423 6111, *Fax:* +1 902 423 0177, *Email:* info@reford.ca

Seabridge International Shipping Inc., 2000 Barrington Street, Suite 1200, Halifax, N.S., Canada B3J 3K1, *Tel:* +1 902 425 5500, *Fax:* +1 902 425 0877, *Email:* halifax@seabridge.ca, *Website:* www.seabridge.ca

F.K. Warren Ltd, 2000 Barrington Street, Suite 920, Cogswell Tower, P O Box 1117, Halifax, N.S., Canada B3J 2X1, *Tel:* +1 902 423 8136, *Fax:* +1 902 429 1326, *Email:* ops@fkwarren.ca, *Website:* www.fkwarren.ca

Stevedoring Companies: Ceres Marine Terminals Incorporated, Cerescorp Company, Fairview Cove Container Terminal, 4755 Barrington Street Station A, P O Box 8958, Halifax, N.S., Canada B3K 5M6, *Tel:* +1 902 453 4590, *Fax:* +1 902 454 4772, *Email:* ceres@ceresglobal.com, *Website:* www.cereglobal.com

Furncan Marine Ltd, 1505 Barrington Street, Suite 1302, Halifax, N.S., Canada B3J 3K5, *Tel:* +1 902 423 6111, *Fax:* +1 902 423 0177, *Email:* ops@furncanmarine.com, *Website:* www.furncanmarine.com

Halterm Ltd, P O Box 1057, Halifax, N.S., Canada B3J 2X1, *Tel:* +1 902 421 1778, *Fax:* +1 902 429 3193, *Email:* drose@halterm.com

Pickford & Black, Suite 920, Cogswell Tower, 2000 Barrington Street, Halifax, N.S., Canada B3J 2X1, *Tel:* +1 902 423 9191, *Fax:* +1 902 429 1326, *Email:* pickops@pickford-black.ns.ca

Surveyors: ABS (Americas), Metropolitan Place, 99 Wyse Road, Suite 1470, Dartmouth, N.S., Canada B3A 1L9, *Tel:* +1 902 423 6236, *Fax:* +1 902 423 9697, *Email:* abshalifax@eagle.org

Allswater Marine Consultants Ltd, 1111 Bedford Highway, Bedford, N.S., Canada B4A 1B9, *Tel:* +1 902 444 7447, *Fax:* +1 902 444 7449, *Email:* office@allswater.com, *Website:* www.allswater.com

Bureau Veritas, 1000 Windmill Road, Dartmouth, N.S., Canada B3B 1L7, *Tel:* +1 902 468 2651, *Fax:* +1 902 468 4315, *Email:* halifax@hayesstuart.com, *Website:* www.hayesstuart.com

Det Norske Veritas A/S, 99 Wyse Road, Suite 900, Dartmouth, N.S., Canada B3A 4S5, *Tel:* +1 902 464 0905, *Fax:* +1 902 464 0516, *Email:* halifax@dnv.com, *Website:* www.dnv.com

MacDonnell Group, P O Box 2045, Station M, 1505 Barrington Street, Halifax, N.S., Canada B3J 2Z1, *Tel:* +1 902 425 3980, *Fax:* +1 902 423 7593, *Email:* adowthwa@mgnet.com

Nippon Kaiji Kyokai, c/o Hayes Stuart Atlantic Inc, 1000 Windmill Road, Suite 19, Dartmouth, N.S., Canada B3B 1L7, *Tel:* +1 902 468 2651, *Fax:* +1 902 468 4315, *Email:* halifax@hayesstuart.com, *Website:* www.classnk.or.jp

Pickford & Black, Suite 920, Cogswell Tower, 2000 Barrington Street, Halifax, N.S., Canada B3J 2X1, *Tel:* +1 902 423 9191, *Fax:* +1 902 429 1326, *Email:* pickops@pickford-black.ns.ca

Silver Agencies, P O Box 1088, Halifax, N.S., Canada B3J 2X1, *Tel:* +1 902 423 7158, *Fax:* +1 902 484 6497, *Email:* survey@silvers.ca, *Website:* www.silvers.ca

Universal Marine Consultants (Maritimes) Ltd, Suite 214, 15 Dartmouth Road, Bedford, N.S., Canada B4A 3X6, *Tel:* +1 902 835 2283, *Fax:* +1 902 835 1493, *Email:* info@universalmarine.ca, *Website:* www.universalmarine.ca

Medical Facilities: Four hospitals close at hand

Airport: Halifax, 35 km

Railway: The port is connected to CN Rail with twice daily departures for Montreal, Toronto, Chicago and beyond. The port is connected to Central Canada and the US Midwest with double stacked container trains. All major cargo terminals within the port have on-dock rail

Lloyd's Agent: Hayes Stuart Inc., 1000 Windmill Road, Suite 19, Dartmouth, N.S., Canada B3B 1L7, *Tel:* +1 902 468 2651, *Fax:* +1 902 468 4315, *Email:* halifax@hayesstuart.com, *Website:* www.hayesstuart.com

HAMILTON

Lat 43° 14' N; Long 79° 51' W.

Admiralty Chart: -   **Admiralty Pilot:** -

Time Zone: GMT -5 h   **UNCTAD Locode:** CA HAM

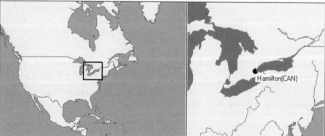

Principal Facilities:

P	Q	Y	G			B	D	T	A

Authority: Hamilton Port Authority, Harbour Administration Building, 605 James Street North, Hamilton, Ont., Canada L8L 1K1, *Tel:* +1 905 525 4330, *Fax:* +1 905 528 6554, *Email:* info@hamiltonport.ca, *Website:* www.hamiltonport.ca

Officials: Chief Executive Officer: Bruce Wood, *Email:* bwood@hamiltonport.ca.

Port Security: ISPS compliant

Approach: A good land-locked harbour on Great Lakes, divided from lake by natural sand barrier; access by Burlington Channel (clear width available 91.44 m, 8.84 m d). The triangular area enclosed is 7.24 km long by up to 4.83 km wide and is sheltered from all winds; depths in general are from 6.71 m to 8.23 m in the slips to over 24.38 m in mid-harbour. Facilities are designed to accommodate the largest lake carriers and those using the St Lawrence Seaway

Pilotage: Contact the Great Lakes Pilotage Authority at St Catherines, Tel: 934 1253

Radio Frequency: Monitoring on VHF Channel 12

Traffic: 2007, 11 782 656 t of cargo handled

Working Hours: 0800-1200, 1300-1700, 1800-2200 or 2300. Overtime, weekdays after 1800, all day Sat, Sun and holidays. Night work by arrangement

Accommodation:

Name	Length (m)	Depth (m)	Draught (m)	Remarks
Hamilton Port Authority Commercial Cargo Piers				
Pier 8 (Centennial Terminal)			8.2	See [1] below
Pier 10				See [2] below
Berth 104	397		8.2	
Berth 107	300		8.2	
Pier 11			8.2	See [3] below
East	396		8.2	
North	344		8.2	
Pier 12				See [4] below
12 E	352		8.2	
12 N	252		8.2	
12 W	396		8.2	
Pier 14				See [5] below
14 N	252		8.2	
14 W	352		8.2	
Pier 23				
23 N	378		8.2	See [6] below
23 S	347		8.2	Liquid bulk cargoes
Pier 25	550	8.2		See [7] below
Pier 26	300		8.2	See [8] below
Stelco Piers				
Pier 16	701	8.23–9.5		
Pier 17	1219	8.23		
Pier 18	304	8.2		

[1]*Pier 8 (Centennial Terminal):* Operated by Great Lakes Stevedoring Co Ltd., Tel: +1 905 529 2355, Fax: +1 905 529 2356
Berths 82, 84, 86 & 87. Steel & general cargo

[2]*Pier 10:* Operated by Hamilton Harbour Terminals Inc., Tel: +1 905 529 0200, Fax: +1 905 529 5604
Steel & general cargo

[3]*Pier 11:* Operated by Montank Transit Inc., Tel: +1 905 529 1339, Fax: +1 905 529 8634
Dry & liquid bulk cargo

[4]*Pier 12:* Operated by Federal Marine Terminals, Tel: +1 905 528 8741, Fax: +1 905 528 9332
Bulk, steel & general cargo

[5]*Pier 14:* Operated by Federal Marine Terminals, Tel: +1 905 528 8741, Fax: +1 905 528 9332
Bulk, steel & general cargo

[6]*23 N:* Operated by Dofasco Inc., 1330 Burlington Street East, P O Box 2460, Hamilton Ont L8N 3J5, Tel: +1 905 544 3761, Website: www.dofasco.ca
Steel cargoes

[7]*Pier 25:* Operated by James Richardson International and Agrico Canada Ltd., Tel: +1 905 544 4971, Fax: +1 905 544 7113
Two berths available for grain

[8]*Pier 26:* Operated by Lafarge Slag, 139 Windermere Road, Hamilton Ont L8H 3Y2, Tel: +1 905 547 2133, Fax: +1 905 545 3308
Slag

Storage: Tank storage for oils; open spaces for coal, sand etc; bridges for unloading ore, coal and scrap

Location	Covered (m²)
Hamilton	59272

Mechanical Handling Equipment:

Location	Type	Capacity (t)	Qty
Hamilton	Shore Cranes	150	1
Hamilton	Shore Cranes	250	2

Bunkering: Provmar Fuels Inc., Station C, P O Box 3355, Hamilton, Ont., Canada L8H 7L4, *Tel:* +1 905 5499 402, *Fax:* +1 905 5499 929, *Email:* inquiries@provmar.com, *Website:* www.provmar.com

Provmar Fuels Inc., Station C, P O Box 3355, Hamilton, Ont., Canada L8H 7L4, *Tel:* +1 905 5499 402, *Fax:* +1 905 5499 929, *Email:* inquiries@provmar.com, *Website:* www.provmar.com – *Grades:* IFO; MDO

Towage: McKeil Marine Ltd, 208 Hillyard Street, Hamilton, Ont., Canada L8L 6B6, *Tel:* +1 905 528 4780, *Fax:* +1 905 528 6144, *Email:* info@mckeil.com, *Website:* www.mckeilmarine.com

Repair & Maintenance: Canadian Westinghouse Ltd, 717 Woodward Avenue, Hamilton, Ont., Canada Operates marine service locations for all types and makes of electrical equipment 24 h/day

Clare Moore Ltd, 601 Burlington Street E, Hamilton, Ont., Canada

Hamilton Boiler Works, 105 Cascade Street, Hamilton, Ont., Canada L8E 3B7, *Tel:* +1 905 561 4233, *Fax:* +1 905 561 3488, *Email:* info@hamiltonboilerworks.com, *Website:* www.hamiltonboilerworks.com

Heddle Marine Service Inc., 208 Hillyard Street, Hamilton, Ont., Canada L8L 6B6, *Tel:*

+1 905 528 2635, *Fax:* +1 905 522 5230, *Email:* heddlemarine@bellnet.ca, *Website:* www.heddlemarine.com Operate a dry dock of 122 m x 19.8 m

Seaman Missions: The Seamans Mission, Group Box 12, 600 Ferguson Street North, Hamilton, Ont., Canada L8L 4Z9, *Tel:* +1 905 528 8681, *Fax:* +1 905 529 4090

Shipping Agents: CMC Currie Maritime Corp., Suite 110, 93 Skyway Avenue, Etobicoke, Ont., Canada M9W 6N6, *Tel:* +1 416 674 7111, *Fax:* +1 416 674 8555, *Email:* ops@curriemaritime.com

Stevedoring Companies: Federal Marine Terminals Inc., P O Box 528, Hamilton, Ont., Canada L8L 7W9, *Tel:* +1 905 528 8741, *Fax:* +1 905 528 9332, *Email:* fedmar@fedmar.com, *Website:* www.fedmar.com
Great Lakes Stevedoring Co Ltd, Pier 12 Fednav Building, P O Box 57120, Hamilton, Ont., Canada L8P 4W9, *Tel:* +1 905 529 2355, *Fax:* +1 905 529 2356, *Email:* info@qsl.com, *Website:* www.qsl.com

Medical Facilities: Three hospitals available

Airport: Toronto International, 48 km

Development: Renovation of Piers 12 and 14, transforming the area into a modern international terminal

Lloyd's Agent: McLarens Canada (Toronto), 600 Alden Road, Suite 600, Markham, Toronto, Ont., Canada L3R 0E7, *Tel:* +1 905 946 9995, *Fax:* +1 905 946 0171, *Email:* roger.bickers@mclarens.ca, *Website:* www.mclarens.ca

HAVRE ST. PIERRE

Lat 50° 14' N; Long 63° 36' W.

Admiralty Chart: 4774	**Admiralty Pilot:** 65
Time Zone: GMT -5 h	**UNCTAD Locode:** CA HSP

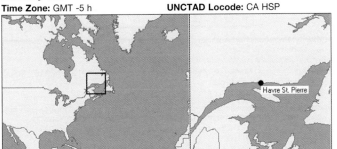

Principal Facilities:

		Y	G				A

Authority: Corporation de Developpement et de Gestion du Port de Havre-Saint-Pierre, Havre St. Pierre, Que., Canada G0G 1P0

Port Security: ISPS compliant

Approach: Deep water channel in depth of 14.6 m. Good anchorage and no hazards

Pilotage: Compulsory. Pilot station at Les Escoumins

Tides: Range of tide 1.9 m to 2.36 m springs, 1.45 m neaps

Traffic: 2005, 147 vessels, 3 100 000 t of cargo handled

Working Hours: Mon to Fri 0800-1700. Overtime as required. Holidays and weekends on notice only

Accommodation:

Name	Length (m)	Depth (m)	Remarks
Havre St. Pierre			The port operates from April to January
Berth No.1	93	7.5	
Berth No.2	46	7.5	

Storage:

Location	Open (m²)	Covered (m²)
Havre St. Pierre	65	225

Mechanical Handling Equipment: Cranes up to 30 t available on request. Cranes over 30 t may be available with delay

Repair & Maintenance: Minor repairs only

Medical Facilities: Hospital nearby, 1 km

Airport: Havre St Pierre, 3 km

Lloyd's Agent: Hayes Stuart Inc., 297 Duke Street, Montreal, Que., Canada H3C 2M2, *Tel:* +1 514 866 1801, *Fax:* +1 514 866 1259, *Email:* montreal@hayesstuart.com, *Website:* www.hayesstuart.com

HOCHELAGA TERMINAL

harbour area, see under Montreal

HOLYROOD

Lat 47° 24' N; Long 53° 8' W.

Admiralty Chart: 4733/4734	**Admiralty Pilot:** 50
Time Zone: GMT -3.5 h	**UNCTAD Locode:** CA HOD

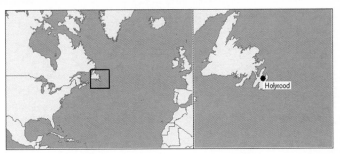

Principal Facilities:

P						B		A

Authority: Transport Canada, Atlantic Region, P O Box 383, Holyrood, NL, Canada A0A 2R0, *Tel:* +1 709 2296 510, *Fax:* +1 709 2296 510, *Email:* mcdonac@tc.gc.ca, *Website:* www.tc.gc.ca

Officials: Harbour Master: Regina Hepditch.
Operations Officer: Cynthia Mcdonald, *Tel:* + +1 709 7726 197, *Email:* mcdonac@tc.gc.ca.

Port Security: ISPS compliant

Approach: Depth in channel is 11.9 m

Anchorage: Good anchorage can be obtained in Holyrood Bay in the South Arm in depths ranging from 29 m to 33 m and in the North Arm in depths of 18 m to 20 m

Pilotage: Compulsory. Pilot boards 1 mile NNE of Harbour Main Point. Request for pilot should be made 12 h in advance of ETA to Atlantic Pilotage Authority which has a 24 h centralised pilot dispatch centre in Halifax, *Tel:* +1 877 272 3477 (toll free) and +1 902 426 7610 (inmarsat), *Fax:* +1 877 745 3477 (toll free) and +1 902 426 7236 (inmarsat), *Email:* dispatch@atlanticpilotage.com

Weather: Conception Bay normally fills with ice between mid January and March and clears between mid March and mid April. Coastguard icebreaker assistance is available upon request

Tides: Range of tide 1.5 m ST, 1.0 m NT

Accommodation:

Name	Remarks
Holyrood	See ¹ below

¹*Holyrood:* There are various small Government wharves within the harbour area but the principal berths are used for tankers
Ultramar Canada Wharf, T-shaped jetty with a berthing face of 85 m. Vessels of up to 213 m loa and 9.8 m d can be accommodated
Holyrood Generating Plant Wharf, owned by Newfoundland and Labrador Hydro, 66 m long with a depth alongside of 15.2 m; used for oil cargoes for the generating plant

Bunkering: Imperial Oil (Dartmouth) Ltd, P O Box 1010, Dartmouth, N.S., Canada B2Y 4RI, *Tel:* +1 902 420 6872, *Fax:* +1 902 420 6996
Irving Oil Co. Ltd, 10 Sydney Street, P O Box 1421, Saint John, N.B., Canada E2L 4K1, *Tel:* +1 888 3101 924, *Fax:* +1 506 2023 868, *Email:* webinquiries@irvingoil.com, *Website:* www.irvingoilco.com
Ultramar Canada Inc., 2200 McGill College Avenue, Montreal, Que., Canada H3A 3L3, *Tel:* +1 514 4996 111, *Fax:* +1 514 4996 320, *Email:* wholesale@ultramar.ca, *Website:* www.ultramar.ca – *Grades:* IFO; MDO

Shipping Agents: Canadian Maritime Agency Ltd, 4 Refinery Road, P O Box 119, Come by Chance, NL, Canada A0B 1N0, *Tel:* +1 709 463 4717, *Fax:* +1 709 463 8737, *Email:* opscbc@canadianmaritime.nf.ca, *Website:* www.canadianmaritime.com

Medical Facilities: Hospital at St. John's, approx 55 km

Airport: St. John's, 55 km

Lloyd's Agent: Hayes Stuart Inc., 297 Duke Street, Montreal, Que., Canada H3C 2M2, *Tel:* +1 514 866 1801, *Fax:* +1 514 866 1259, *Email:* montreal@hayesstuart.com, *Website:* www.hayesstuart.com

ISAAC'S HARBOUR

Lat 45° 10' N; Long 61° 39' W.

Admiralty Chart: 729	**Admiralty Pilot:** 59
Time Zone: GMT -4 h	**UNCTAD Locode:** CA

This port is no longer open to commercial shipping

JAMES RICHARDSON INTERNATIONAL TERMINAL

harbour area, see under Vancouver

KITIMAT

Lat 54° 0' N; Long 128° 42' W.

Admiralty Chart: 4931	**Admiralty Pilot:** 26
Time Zone: GMT -8 h	**UNCTAD Locode:** CA KTM

Key to Principal Facilities:—			
A=Airport	**C**=Containers	**G**=General Cargo	**P**=Petroleum **R**=Ro/Ro **Y**=Dry Bulk
B=Bunkers	**D**=Dry Dock	**L**=Cruise	**Q**=Other Liquid Bulk **T**=Towage (where available from port)

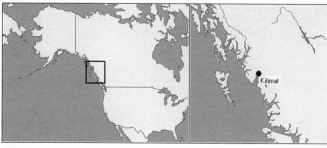

Principal Facilities:

Q	Y	G	C	R		B		T	A

Authority: District of Kitimat, Port of Kitimat, 270 City Centre, Kitimat, B.C., Canada V8C 2H7, *Tel:* +1 250 632 8900, *Fax:* +1 250 632 4995, *Email:* info@city.kitimat.bc.ca, *Website:* www.portofkitimat.com

Port Security: ISPS compliant

Approach: Approach to the port from the south is via Larado Sound, Larado Channel, Campania Sound, Whale or Squally Channels and thence via Douglas Channel; from the north via Brown Passage, Grenville Channel and Douglas Channel. The route is approx 192 km to the open sea

Anchorage: Anchorage is available at the head of the harbour in Kitimat Arm. Alternatively there are anchorage areas at Emilia Anchorage, 14 nautical miles from the harbour area; Kitkiata Inlet, approx 23 nautical miles S of the harbour area

Pilotage: Compulsory. Pacific Pilotage Authority. Pilotage authority requires 48 h notice to allow pilot to meet vessel at Triple Island or Cape Beale

Radio Frequency: Prince Rupert Vessel Traffic Services operates on VHF Channels 11 and 71. Local marine traffic communicates on VHF Channel 6

Tides: Average tidal range 4.0 m

Maximum Vessel Dimensions: 320 000 dwt

Principal Imports and Exports: Imports: Alumina, Condensate, Petroleum coke. Exports: Aggregate, Aluminium ingots, Kraft paper.

Working Hours: Alcan: 0000-0800, 0800-1600, 1600-2400. Eurocan: 0730-1930, 1930-0730. Methanex: 0600-1800, 1800-0600

Accommodation:

Name	Length (m)	Depth (m)	Remarks
Alcan Terminals			See [1] below
Berth No.1	229.5	10.67	See [2] below
Berth No.2			Used for Kemano Passenger Ferry
Methanex Terminal			See [3] below
Berth	430	12	See [4] below
Eurocan Terminals			See [5] below
Berth No.1 (southern)	137	14	
Berth No.2 (northern)	137	10.9	

[1] *Alcan Terminals:* Operated by Alcan Primary Metal-BC, P O Box 1800, Kitimat, Tel: +1 250 639 8677, Fax: +1 250 639 8127
Imports of bulk alumina, pitch, coke and fluoride. Exports of aluminium ingots
[2] *Berth No.1:* Mooring dolphins are located S of the Terminal and can accommodate vessels up to 175 m loa
[3] *Methanex Terminal:* Operated by Methanex Corporation, PO Box 176, Kitimat BC V8C 2G7, Tel: +1 250 639 9292, Fax: +1 250 639 3262, Website: www.methanex.com
[4] *Berth:* Cargoes handled include methanol, for vessels up to 177 m loa. The loading platform with two pads on either side of the wharf has mooring dolphins north and south. The distance between breasting pads is approx 78 m and the overall length between dolphins is approx 300 m
[5] *Eurocan Terminals:* Operated by Eurocan Pulp & Paper Co., Tel: +1 250 632 6111, Fax: +1 250 639 3583
Both berths have mooring dolphins at each end. A chip-loading facility with a cap of 265 t/h is located at the N end of the terminal. Storage warehouse cap of 73 200 m2 or 40 000 t of paper. Commodities: linerboard and sackkraft paper

Bunkering: Available by truck with 48 h notice

Waste Reception Facilities: Garbage disposal available. No facilities available for International garbage

Towage: Two tugs available of 1800 hp

Repair & Maintenance: Kitimat Iron & Metal Works Ltd, 752 Enterprise Avenue, Kitimat, B.C., Canada V8C 2E6, *Tel:* +1 250 632 6776, *Fax:* +1 250 632 4334, *Email:* kitiron@monarch.net Repair facilities
Weslund Industrial, 318 Railway Avenue, Kitimat, B.C., Canada V8C 2G2, *Tel:* +1 250 632 6106, *Fax:* +1 250 632 4248, *Email:* bprice@emcoltd.com, *Website:* www.westlund.ca Repair facilities
West Fraser Electro/Mechanical Ltd, 3937 22nd Avenue, Prince George, B.C., Canada V2N 1B7, *Tel:* +1 250 563 4330, *Fax:* +1 250 563 9492, *Website:* www.west-fraser.com Repair facilities
Westburnedirect.com, 716 Enterprise Avenue, Kitimat, B.C., Canada V8C 2E6, *Tel:* +1 250 632 2148, *Fax:* +1 250 632 4452, *Email:* wendy.pigeon@westburne.ca, *Website:* www.westburnedirect.ca Repair facilities
Zanron Fabrication & Machine Co. Ltd, 256 - 3rd Street, Kitimat, B.C., Canada V8C 2B8, *Tel:* +1 250 632 2181, *Fax:* +1 250 632 6049, *Email:* zanron@zanron.com, *Website:* www.zanron.com Repair facilities

Surveyors: Danforth Marine Surveyors, 57 Teal Street, Kitimat, B.C., Canada V8C 1K9, *Tel:* +1 250 632 3366, *Fax:* +1 250 632 3372
Saybolt Italia S.r.l., 616 Commercial Avenue, Kitimat, B.C., Canada, *Tel:* +1 250 632 2711, *Fax:* +1 250 632 2799, *Website:* www.saybolt.com
Societe Generale de Surveillance (SGS), Kitimat, B.C., Canada, *Tel:* +1 250 632 4190, *Fax:* +1 250 632 4192, *Email:* enquiries@sgs.com, *Website:* www.sgs.com

Medical Facilities: Kitimat General Hospital and city centre medical clinic

Airport: Northwest Regional Airport, Terrace-Kitimat, 45 km
Railway: Serviced by Canadian National Rail
Lloyd's Agent: McLarens Canada (Vancouver), 505 1100 Melville Street, Vancouver, B.C., Canada V6E 4A6, *Tel:* +1 604 681 7107, *Fax:* +1 604 681 8125, *Email:* philip.vardon@mclarens.ca, *Website:* www.mclarens.ca

LA BAIE

Lat 48° 19' N; Long 70° 52' W.

Admiralty Chart: 4780		**Admiralty Pilot:** 65
Time Zone: GMT -5 h		**UNCTAD Locode:** CA LBA

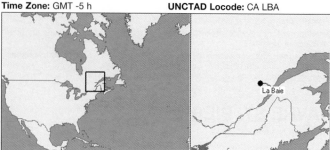

Principal Facilities:

P	Q	Y	G			B		T	A

Authority: Saguenay Port Authority, 6600 Quai-Marcel-Dionne Road, Ville de la Baie, Que., Canada G7B 3N9, *Tel:* +1 418 697 0250, *Fax:* +1 418 697 0243, *Email:* info@portsaguenay.ca, *Website:* www.portsaguenay.ca

Officials: General Manager: Alain Bouchard, *Tel:* +1 418 697 0246, *Email:* abouchard@portsaguenay.ca.

Port Security: ISPS compliant

Documentation: Vessel declaration (A-6 in and out) for foreign vessels and 1-C Form (in and out) for domestic vessels. Manifest of cargo-loading and unloading
These documents must be forwarded by the agency 48 h after the loading/unloading of cargo from a vessel

Anchorage: Vessels for Grande Anse Marine Terminal may anchor at St Fulgence, 2 miles upstream from the Grande Anse Terminal

Pilotage: Compulsory. Pilots board vessels that are westerly-bound at Escoumins and easterly bound at Quebec City. A min notice of 24 h of ship's ETA is required

Radio Frequency: VHF Channel 14 (156.7 mHz)

Weather: Prevailing winds from WSE for both terminals

Tides: Range of tide 1-6 m

Traffic: 2006, 324 000 t of cargo handled

Working Hours: Grand-Anse: 0800-1700, 1800-2200, overtime available. Albert Maltais: 24 h/day

Accommodation:

Name	Length (m)	Depth (m)	Remarks
Grande-Anse Marine Terminal			
Wharf	286	13.8	See [1] below
Albert Maltais Marine Terminal			This terminal is presently not active
Berth	40	9.1	Two dolphins 91 m apart

[1] *Wharf:* General cargo terminal with two berths and 5.85 ha of open storage

Storage:

Location	Covered (m²)	Sheds / Warehouses
Wharf	5715	1

Mechanical Handling Equipment:

Location	Type	Capacity (t)	Qty	Remarks
Grande-Anse Marine Terminal	Mult-purp. Cranes	165	1	See [1] below

[1] *Grande-Anse Marine Terminal:* owned by St. Lawrence Stevedoring Co Ltd

Cargo Worked: Lumber 125 m3/gang/h, granite 8 blocs/gang/h, woodpulp 130 t/gang/h, coal 190 t/gang/h, paper 80 t/gang/h

Bunkering: Ultramar Canada Inc., 2200 McGill College Avenue, Montreal, Que., Canada H3A 3L3, *Tel:* +1 514 4996 111, *Fax:* +1 514 4996 320, *Email:* wholesale@ultramar.ca, *Website:* www.ultramar.ca – *Grades:* MDO – *Delivery Mode:* truck

Towage: Available privately from Alcan, Tel: +1 418 544 9643, Fax: +1 418 544 9622

Repair & Maintenance: Canmec, 1750 La Grande, Chicoutimi, Que., Canada G7K 1H7, *Tel:* +1 418 543 6161, *Fax:* +1 418 543 5564, *Email:* info@canmec.com, *Website:* www.canmec.com Repair facilities
Fjordtech Industrie Inc., 2760 Boulevard de la Grande-Baie Nord, Ville de la Baie, Que., Canada G7B 3N8, *Tel:* +1 418 544 7091, *Fax:* +1 418 544 3739, *Email:* info@fjordtech.qc.ca, *Website:* www.fjordtech.qc.ca Repair facilities
Hydraulic Metal Enr., Ville de la Baie, Que., Canada, *Tel:* +1 418 544 6431, *Fax:* +1 418 544 5427 Repair facilities

Stevedoring Companies: Quebec Port Terminals Inc., 6700 Ch. du Quai-Marcel-Dionne, Ville Saguenay, Que., Canada G7B 3N9, *Tel:* +1 418 544 7341, *Fax:* +1 418 544 2236, *Email:* info@qsl.com, *Website:* www.qsl.com

Surveyors: Certispec Services Inc., 2813 Murray Street, Port Moody, B.C., Canada V3H 1X3, *Tel:* +1 604 469 9180, *Fax:* +1 604 469 0993, *Email:* information@certispec.com, *Website:* www.certispec.com
Societe Generale de Surveillance (SGS), Service de Surveillance SGS Inc., P O Box 1606, Quebec, La Baie, Canada G1K 7J8, *Tel:* +1 418 661 6624, *Fax:* +1 418 661 7319, *Email:* enquiries@sgs.com, *Website:* www.sgs.com

Medical Facilities: Chicoutimi Hospital and Ville de la Baie Hospital

Airport: Bagotville, 20 km

Railway: Canadian National, 16 km

Lloyd's Agent: Hayes Stuart Inc., 297 Duke Street, Montreal, Que., Canada H3C 2M2, *Tel:* +1 514 866 1801, *Fax:* +1 514 866 1259, *Email:* montreal@hayesstuart.com, *Website:* www.hayesstuart.com

LADYSMITH

Lat 48° 59' N; Long 123° 47' W.

Admiralty Chart: 576
Time Zone: GMT -8 h
Admiralty Pilot: 25
UNCTAD Locode: CA LAD

This port is no longer opan to commercial shipping

LAKEFIELD ST. TERMINAL

harbour area, see under Montreal

LAURIER TERMINAL

harbour area, see under Montreal

LEVIS

harbour area, see under Quebec

LISCOMB

Lat 45° 0' N; Long 62° 0' W.

Admiralty Chart: 729
Time Zone: GMT -4 h
Admiralty Pilot: 59
UNCTAD Locode: CA

This port is no longer open to commercial shipping

LITTLE NARROWS

Lat 45° 59' N; Long 60° 59' W.

Admiralty Chart: 4748
Time Zone: GMT -4 h
Admiralty Pilot: 65
UNCTAD Locode: CA LIN

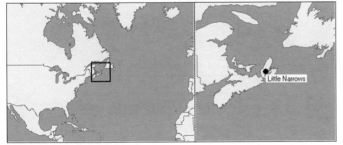

Principal Facilities:

		Y							

Authority: Little Narrows Gypsum Co Ltd., 79 Main Street, RR#1, Little Narrows, N.S., Canada B0E 1T0, *Tel:* +1 902 756 2081, *Fax:* +1 902 756 2493

Port Security: ISPS compliant

Approach: Vessels enter the Bras d'Or Lake through the Great Bras d'Or Channel, 8.3 m max d

Pilotage: Compulsory. Atlantic Pilotage Authority. Pilots despatched from Eddy Point Traffic Control Office who require 24, 12 and 6 h ETA's

Working Hours: Loading round the clock

Accommodation:

Name	Length (m)	Draught (m)	Remarks
Little Narrows			Port only used for loading gypsum
Private Wharf	144	8.7	See [1] below

[1]*Private Wharf:* Max size of vessel 10 000 t. Equipped with belt conveyor loading rate approx 1000 t/h

Bunkering: Available at Sydney, 109.4 km

Lloyd's Agent: Hayes Stuart Inc., 1000 Windmill Road, Suite 19, Dartmouth, N.S., Canada B3B 1L7, *Tel:* +1 902 468 2651, *Fax:* +1 902 468 4315, *Email:* halifax@hayesstuart.com, *Website:* www.hayesstuart.com

LIVERPOOL

Lat 44° 3' N; Long 64° 43' W.

Admiralty Chart: -
Time Zone: GMT -4 h
Admiralty Pilot: 59
UNCTAD Locode: CA LIV

Principal Facilities:

P		Y	G			B	D	T	

Authority: Mersey Seafoods Ltd, P O Box 1290, Liverpool, N.S., Canada B0T 1K0, *Tel:* +1 902 354 3467, *Fax:* +1 902 354 2319, *Email:* raymond@merseyseafoods.com

Officials: Sales & Marketing Manager: Bill Muirhead, *Tel:* +1 902 364 2266, *Email:* bill.muirhead@ns.sympatico.ca.
Harbour Master: Raymond Bush, *Tel:* +1 902 364 2266.

Port Security: ISPS compliant

Approach: Controlling LW depths are 3.7 m Liverpool and 7.92 m Brooklyn

Pilotage: Not compulsory but available from Atlantic Pilotage Authority which has a 24 h centralised pilot dispatch centre in Halifax, *Tel:* +1 877 272 3477 (toll free) and +1 902 426 7610 (inmarsat), *Fax:* +1 877 745 3477 (toll free) and +1 902 426 7236 (inmarsat), *Email:* dispatch@atlanticpilotage.com

Weather: SE through NE gales cause large breakers to form in outer harbour.

Tides: Tidal range of 2.3 max and an average of 1.8

Maximum Vessel Dimensions: 5.31 m max d

Accommodation:

Name	Length (m)	Depth (m)	Remarks
Liverpool			Berth available for small coastal tankers
Government Wharf	112	3.35	Bulk cargo facilities available
Private Wharves			See [1] below

[1]*Private Wharves:* Steel & Engine Products Ltd Wharf, 182.9 m long with depth of 4.57 m alongside at LW used for fitting out and repairing vessels. At Brooklyn: Bowater Mersey Paper Co's Paper Wharf, length 146.30 m with 7.92 m depth at LW equipped with shed 134.1 m by 30.48 m. Mersey Paper Co's Coal Wharf, length 121.9 m with depth 7.92 m at LW equipped with an electric crane with clamshell bucket

Mechanical Handling Equipment:

Location	Type
Liverpool	Mobile Cranes

Bunkering: Imperial Oil (Dartmouth) Ltd, P O Box 1010, Dartmouth, N.S., Canada B2Y 4RI, *Tel:* +1 902 420 6872, *Fax:* +1 902 420 6996 – *Grades:* MDO – *Delivery Mode:* truck
Irving Oil Co. Ltd, 10 Sydney Street, P O Box 1421, Saint John, N.B., Canada E2L 4K1, *Tel:* +1 888 310 1924, *Fax:* +1 506 2023 868, *Email:* webinquiries@irvingoil.com, *Website:* www.irvingoilco.com – *Grades:* MDO – *Delivery Mode:* truck

Towage: Two tugs available for light towing

Repair & Maintenance: Steel & Engine Products Ltd, 72 Market Street, Liverpool, N.S., Canada B0T 1K0, *Tel:* +1 902 354 3483, *Fax:* +1 902 354 4308

Surveyors: Silver Agencies, P O Box 1088, Halifax, N.S., Canada B3J 2X1, *Tel:* +1 902 423 7158, *Fax:* +1 902 484 6497, *Email:* survey@silvers.ca, *Website:* www.silvers.ca
Universal Marine Consultants (Maritimes) Ltd, Suite 214, 15 Dartmouth Road, Bedford, N.S., Canada B4A 3X6, *Tel:* +1 902 835 2283, *Fax:* +1 902 835 1493, *Email:* info@universalmarine.ca, *Website:* www.universalmarine.ca

Medical Facilities: Queens General Hospital in Liverpool

Lloyd's Agent: Hayes Stuart Inc., 1000 Windmill Road, Suite 19, Dartmouth, N.S., Canada B3B 1L7, *Tel:* +1 902 468 2651, *Fax:* +1 902 468 4315, *Email:* halifax@hayesstuart.com, *Website:* www.hayesstuart.com

LONG HARBOUR

Lat 47° 27' N; Long 53° 49' W.

Admiralty Chart: 4733/4734/4738
Time Zone: GMT -3.5 h
Admiralty Pilot: 50
UNCTAD Locode: CA LOH

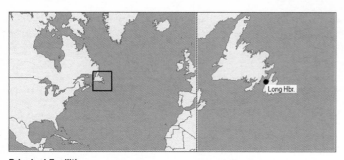

Principal Facilities:

		G		B	T	

Authority: Transport Canada, Atlantic Region, P O Box 63, Long Harbour, NL, Canada A0B 2JO, *Tel:* +1 709 228 2014, *Email:* emurphy@esdnl.ca, *Website:* www.tc.gc.ca

Officials: Harbour Master: Edna Murphy.

Approach: Depth in main channel 11.3 m

Anchorage: Anchorage can be obtained just outside the channel in a depth of 18 m

Pilotage: Not compulsory but can be arranged

Maximum Vessel Dimensions: 259 m long, 31.4 m beam, 10.4 m d

Accommodation:

Name	Length (m)	Depth (m)	Remarks
Long Harbour			
Government Wharf	37	2.4	Suitable for small vessels only
The Erco Wharf	488	10.98	See [1] below

[1]*The Erco Wharf:* With a dolphin extension 38 m long, joined to the wharf by a catwalk. The outer 213 m on the N side of the wharf is used for unloading by means of a conveyor. The loading berth in least depth of 6.4 m is on the inner end of the S side with an overhead pipeline used for loading

Bunkering: Fuel oil and diesel oil can be brought in by road tanker from St. John's if required

Towage: Three tugs available from Come by Chance

Shipping Agents: Canadian Maritime Agency Ltd, 4 Refinery Road, P O Box 119, Come by Chance, NL, Canada A0B 1N0, *Tel:* +1 709 463 4717, *Fax:* +1 709 463 8737, *Email:* opscbc@canadianmaritime.nf.ca, *Website:* www.canadianmaritime.com

Medical Facilities: Nearest hospital at Placentia or Markland

Lloyd's Agent: Hayes Stuart Inc., 297 Duke Street, Montreal, Que., Canada H3C 2M2, *Tel:* +1 514 866 1801, *Fax:* +1 514 866 1259, *Email:* montreal@hayesstuart.com, *Website:* www.hayesstuart.com

LONG POND

Lat 47° 31' N; Long 52° 58' W.

Admiralty Chart: 4733/4734	**Admiralty Pilot:** 50
Time Zone: GMT -3.5 h	**UNCTAD Locode:** CA LOP

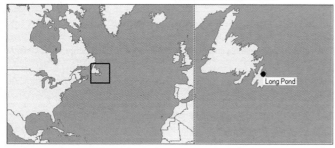

Principal Facilities:

P		Y	G			B		A

Authority: Transport Canada, Atlantic Region, 24 Stanley's Road, Conception Bay South, NL, Canada A1W 5H8, *Tel:* +1 709 834 1744, *Fax:* +1 709 834 1078, *Website:* www.tc.gc.ca

Officials: Harbour Master: Paul Trickett.

Port Security: ISPS compliant

Approach: The channel is dredged to a depth of 7.9 m and the entrance marked by light-buoys. Mariners should not attempt to enter Long Pond without local knowledge

Pilotage: Not compulsory but can be arranged through St. John's if required

Tides: Range of tide 1.38 m

Maximum Vessel Dimensions: Max loa 152.4 m, max d 8.08 m

Principal Imports and Exports: Imports: Cement, Grain, Petroleum products. Exports: Talc concentrates.

Accommodation:

Name	Length (m)	Depth (m)	Remarks
Long Pond			See [1] below
Government Wharf	245	6.9	See [2] below

[1]*Long Pond:* The harbour area is protected by two breakwaters, between which the width of the dredged channel is 50 m. Yachting facilities are available at the port. Facilities exist for tankers and there are storage tanks near to the wharf
[2]*Government Wharf:* Used primarily for bulk cargoes. There is a dredged turning area extending 135 m off the wharf with a depth of 8.2 m. Heavy lift crane pad on wharf built for 200 t mobile crane at min radius

Mechanical Handling Equipment:

Location	Type
Long Pond	Mobile Cranes

Bunkering: Available by road tanker at Government Wharf

Waste Reception Facilities: Arrangements must be made through Agent for garbage and waste oil disposal

Shipping Agents: Canadian Maritime Agency Ltd, 4 Refinery Road, P O Box 119, Come by Chance, NL, Canada A0B 1N0, *Tel:* +1 709 463 4717, *Fax:* +1 709 463 8737, *Email:* opscbc@canadianmaritime.nf.ca, *Website:* www.canadianmaritime.com

Medical Facilities: Local clinics available

Airport: St. John's, 25 km

Lloyd's Agent: Hayes Stuart Inc., 297 Duke Street, Montreal, Que., Canada H3C 2M2, *Tel:* +1 514 866 1801, *Fax:* +1 514 866 1259, *Email:* montreal@hayesstuart.com, *Website:* www.hayesstuart.com

LOUIS-HIPPOLYTE-LAFONTAINE SECTOR

harbour area, see under Montreal

LOWER COVE TERMINAL

harbour area, see under Saint John

LUNENBURG

Lat 44° 22' N; Long 64° 18' W.

Admiralty Chart: -	**Admiralty Pilot:** 59
Time Zone: GMT -4 h	**UNCTAD Locode:** CA LUN

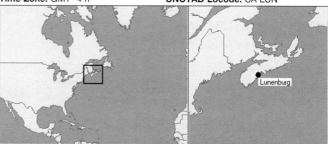

Principal Facilities:

	Y	G			B		

Authority: Harbour Authority of Lunenburg, P O Box 748, Lunenburg, N.S., Canada B0J 2C0, *Tel:* +1 902 634 3470, *Fax:* +1 902 634 3899, *Email:* bruces@eastlink.ca

Officials: Harbour Master: Bruce Saunders.

Approach: Controlling depth at LW in channel approach and entrance has been dredged to 6.4 m and that draft can be taken in and out

Pilotage: Not compulsory but available from Atlantic Pilotage Authority which has a 24 h centralised pilot dispatch centre in Halifax, Tel: +1 877 272 3477 (toll free) and +1 902 426 7610 (inmarsat), Tel: +1 877 745 3477 (toll free) and +1 902 426 7236 (inmarsat), Email: dispatch@atlanticpilotage.com

Tides: Range of tide 1.98 m springs, 1.52 m neaps

Working Hours: 0800-1200, 1300-1700

Accommodation:

Name	Remarks
Lunenburg	See [1] below

[1]*Lunenburg:* Good anchorage in harbour. There are two terminals named Railway Wharf and Fisherman's Wharf

Mechanical Handling Equipment:

Location	Type
Lunenburg	Mult-purp. Cranes

Bunkering: Imperial Oil (Dartmouth) Ltd, P O Box 1010, Dartmouth, N.S., Canada B2Y 4RI, *Tel:* +1 902 420 6872, *Fax:* +1 902 420 6996 – *Delivery Mode:* truck
Irving Oil Co. Ltd, 10 Sydney Street, P O Box 1421, Saint John, N.B., Canada E2L

4K1, *Tel:* +1 888 3101 924, *Fax:* +1 506 2023 868, *Email:* webinquiries@irvingoil.com, *Website:* www.irvingoilco.com – *Delivery Mode:* truck

Repair & Maintenance: Lunenburg Foundry Engineering Ltd, 53 Falkland Street, P O Box 1240, Lunenburg, N.S., Canada B0J 2C0, *Tel:* +1 902 634 8827, *Fax:* +1 902 634 8886, *Email:* mail@lunenburgfoundry.com, *Website:* www.lunenburgfoundry.com Repair to hulls and machinery

Medical Facilities: Hospital in Lunenburg town

Lloyd's Agent: Hayes Stuart Inc., 1000 Windmill Road, Suite 19, Dartmouth, N.S., Canada B3B 1L7, *Tel:* +1 902 468 2651, *Fax:* +1 902 468 4315, *Email:* halifax@hayesstuart.com, *Website:* www.hayesstuart.com

LYNNTERM

harbour area, see under Vancouver

MAISONNEUVE TERMINAL

harbour area, see under Montreal

MARATHON

Lat 48° 45' N; Long 86° 23' W.

Admiralty Chart: -	**Admiralty Pilot:** -
Time Zone: GMT -5 h	**UNCTAD Locode:** CA MAR

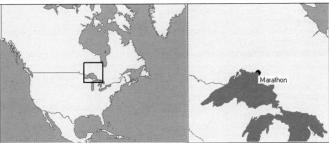

Principal Facilities:

		G						A	

Authority: James River Marathon Ltd, PO Bag JR, Mill Road, Marathon, Ont., Canada, *Tel:* +1 807 229 0297, *Fax:* +1 807 229 0349

Port Security: ISPS compliant

Maximum Vessel Dimensions: 16 797 dwt, 164 m loa

Principal Imports and Exports: Imports: Bunker c oil, Caustic Soda, Coal. Exports: Woodpulp.

Working Hours: Woodpulp, Mon-Fri 0800-1700

Accommodation:

Name	Length (m)	Depth (m)
Marathon		
Marathon Wharf	140	6

Storage:

Location	Covered (m²)
Marathon	5560

Cargo Worked: 1600 t/day of woodpulp

Medical Facilities: Wilson Memorial Hospital

Airport: Marathon Airport, 10 km

Railway: Canadian Pacific Rail, 1 km

Lloyd's Agent: McLarens Canada (Toronto), 600 Alden Road, Suite 600, Markham, Toronto, Ont., Canada L3R 0E7, *Tel:* +1 905 946 9995, *Fax:* +1 905 946 0171, *Email:* roger.bickers@mclarens.ca, *Website:* www.mclarens.ca

MARYSTOWN

Lat 47° 10' N; Long 55° 9' W.

Admiralty Chart: 4737	**Admiralty Pilot:** 50
Time Zone: GMT -3.5 h	**UNCTAD Locode:** CA MTN

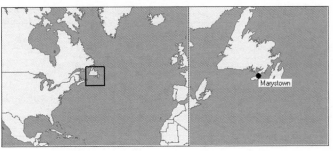

Principal Facilities:

P		G			B	D	

Authority: Marystown Port Authority, P O Box 337, Marystown, NL, Canada A0E 2M0, *Tel:* +1 709 279 3725, *Fax:* +1 709 279 3690

Officials: Operations Manager: Cynthia McDonald.
Harbour Master: William Power.

Port Security: ISPS compliant

Pilotage: Not compulsory but can be arranged

Accommodation:

Name	Length (m)	Depth (m)	Remarks
Marystown			
Government Wharf	36	6.2	See [1] below
Private Wharves			See [2] below

[1]*Government Wharf:* Equipped with a transit shed. A fixed red light is shown from the rear of the shed
Facilities exist for refined petroleum products
[2]*Private Wharves:* The Fisheries Products Wharves are located in Lower Mooring Cove in the NW part of Mortier Bay. The main wharf is 55 m long and 14 m wide with 10.7 m depth of water alongside the outer end. A breakwater wharf lies about 30 m NE of the main wharf. A smaller wharf with an outer face 21 m long and 5.5 m depth of water alongside, lies about 43 m SE of the main wharf

Bunkering: Available by road tanker at Government Wharf

Repair & Maintenance: An oil rig servicing base operated by Kiewit is situated on the NE side of Mortier Bay. There is an L-shaped wharf extending 115 m from Cow Head; this allows for alongside repair and service work. The outer end of the wharf is 44 m long and 20 m wide, semi-submersible platforms with drafts up to 15 m can be accommodated

Shipping Agents: Canadian Maritime Agency Ltd, 4 Refinery Road, P O Box 119, Come by Chance, NL, Canada A0B 1N0, *Tel:* +1 709 463 4717, *Fax:* +1 709 463 8737, *Email:* opscbc@canadianmaritime.nf.ca, *Website:* www.canadianmaritime.com

Medical Facilities: Marystown Hospital, 10 km

Lloyd's Agent: Hayes Stuart Inc., 297 Duke Street, Montreal, Que., Canada H3C 2M2, *Tel:* +1 514 866 1801, *Fax:* +1 514 866 1259, *Email:* montreal@hayesstuart.com, *Website:* www.hayesstuart.com

MATANE

Lat 48° 50' N; Long 67° 32' W.

Admiralty Chart: 4777	**Admiralty Pilot:** 65
Time Zone: GMT -4 h	**UNCTAD Locode:** CA MNE

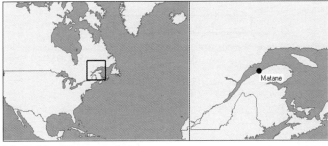

Principal Facilities:

	Y	G			B		A	

Authority: Transport Canada, Champlain Harbour Station, 901 Cap Diamant 4th Floor, Quebec, Que., Canada G1K 4K1, *Tel:* +1 418 648 4103, *Fax:* +1 418 648 7980, *Website:* www.tc.gc.ca

Officials: Regional Manager: Andre Roy, *Tel:* +1 418 648 7213, *Email:* royan@tc.gc.ca.
Harbour Master: Michel Petit, *Tel:* +1 418 648 3640.

Port Security: ISPS compliant

Anchorage: Anchorage in 9.15 m, about 0.8 km offshore and 18.3 km a little farther out, the bottom being sand and clay

Pilotage: Not compulsory but available

Weather: Prevailing winds usually E-NE during spring, SW wind frequent during summer and in autumn NW wind becomes more common

Tides: Tide rises from 2.74 m to 4.26 m

Working Hours: Mon to Fri 0800-1700. Overtime as required. Holidays and weekends on notice only

Key to Principal Facilities:—				
A=Airport	**C**=Containers	**G**=General Cargo	**P**=Petroleum	**R**=Ro/Ro	**Y**=Dry Bulk
B=Bunkers	**D**=Dry Dock	**L**=Cruise	**Q**=Other Liquid Bulk	**T**=Towage (where available from port)

Accommodation:

Name	Length (m)	Depth (m)	Remarks
Matane			See [1] below
Berth No.1	186	10	Commercial berth
Berth No.2	92	4.9	
Berth No.3	134	4	

[1]*Matane:* The harbour is open year round, but occasionally assistance of icebreakers may be required

Storage:

Location	Open (m²)
Matane	33779

Mechanical Handling Equipment: Cranes available on request

Bunkering: Fuel and diesel oil delivered by tank trucks, also bunker coal
Shell Canada Products Ltd, 10501 Sherbrooke Street East, Montreal, Que., Canada H1B 1B3, *Tel:* +1 514 6409 897, *Fax:* +1 514 6451 490, *Email:* patrick.st-laurent@shell.com, *Website:* www.shell.ca

Stevedoring Companies: Quebec Port Terminals Inc., 1620 Rue de Matane-sur-Mer, P O Box 576, Matane, Que., Canada G4W 3P5, *Tel:* +1 418 562 7166, *Fax:* +1 418 562 7270, *Email:* info@qsl.com, *Website:* www.qsl.com

Medical Facilities: Local hospital

Airport: Mont-Joli

Lloyd's Agent: Hayes Stuart Inc., 297 Duke Street, Montreal, Que., Canada H3C 2M2, *Tel:* +1 514 866 1801, *Fax:* +1 514 866 1259, *Email:* montreal@hayesstuart.com, *Website:* www.hayesstuart.com

METHANEX TERMINAL

harbour area, see under Kitimat

MIDLAND

Lat 44° 45' N; Long 79° 56' W.

Admiralty Chart: -	**Admiralty Pilot:** -
Time Zone: GMT -5 h	**UNCTAD Locode:** CA MID

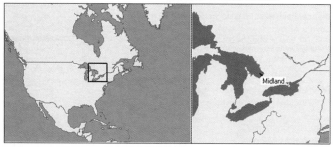

Principal Facilities:

		Y	G		L	B		A	

Authority: Midland Harbour, 527 Len Self Boulevard, Midland, Ont., Canada L4R 5N6, *Tel:* +1 705 526 4610, *Fax:* +1 705 526 9971, *Email:* towncoms@town.midland.on.ca

Officials: Harbour Master: Reck Leaney.
Assistant: Madelaine Twitchin.

Port Security: ISPS compliant

Approach: Depth at entrance 7.31 m

Pilotage: Not compulsory

Traffic: Approx 30-40 vessels per season

Maximum Vessel Dimensions: 213 m loa

Working Hours: 24 h/day during shipping season

Accommodation:

Name	Remarks
Midland	See [1] below

[1]*Midland:* There are two major commercial docks:
Unimin Canada Ltd., Tel: +1 705 526 5479, Fax: +1 705 526 7161, handles silica sand
There is also a grain elevator operated by ADM-Ogilvie
The port is also used by cruise vessels

Bunkering: Fuel oil available; diesel oil delivered by tank trucks at any dock

Medical Facilities: Hospital available, 1 mile

Airport: Barrie Airport, 50 km

Lloyd's Agent: McLarens Canada (Toronto), 600 Alden Road, Suite 600, Markham, Toronto, Ont., Canada L3R 0E7, *Tel:* +1 905 946 9995, *Fax:* +1 905 946 0171, *Email:* roger.bickers@mclarens.ca, *Website:* www.mclarens.ca

MONT LOUIS

Lat 49° 14' N; Long 65° 44' W.

Admiralty Chart: 1623	**Admiralty Pilot:** 65
Time Zone: GMT -5 h	**UNCTAD Locode:** CA MOL

This port is no longer open to commercial shipping

MONTREAL

Lat 45° 30' N; Long 73° 33' W.

Admiralty Chart: 4792	**Admiralty Pilot:** 65
Time Zone: GMT -5 h	**UNCTAD Locode:** CA MTR

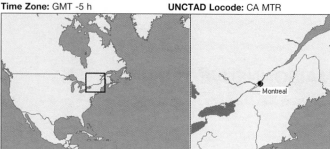

Principal Facilities:

P	Q	Y	G	C	R	L	B		T	A

Authority: Montreal Port Authority, Port of Montreal Building, 2100 Pierre-Dupuy Avenue, Wing No.1, Montreal, Que., Canada H3C 3R5, *Tel:* +1 514 283 7011, *Fax:* +1 514 283 0829, *Email:* info@port-montreal.com, *Website:* www.port-montreal.com

Officials: Chief Executive Officer: Patrice M. Pelletier, *Email:* pelletierpm@port-montreal.com.
Harbour Master: Capt Jean-Luc Bedard, *Tel:* +1 514 283 7020, *Email:* bedardjl@port-montreal.com.

Port Security: ISPS compliant. Container Security Initiative (CSI) designated port

Approach: All ocean-going vessels (unless trading under a Canadian Coastwise Licence) proceeding up the St. Lawrence Seaway must stop at Montreal for various clearances and inspections. Seaway equipment, radio telephones etc, are available for purchase or rental through Steamship Agents in Montreal
The limits of Montreal Harbour extend from Victoria Bridge to a line corresponding with the upstream boundary of Sorel Harbour and abeam with St Joseph River
The min depth of the Ship Channel from the St. Lawrence to Quebec is 9.14 m LWOST with a mean rise of 4.88 m. Dredging has increased the depth to 12.19 m in the North Traverse Channel on the east side of Ile d'Orleans. The min width is 304.8 m
From Quebec to Montreal the min depth of the Ship Channel is 11.0 m with a min width of 243.8 m in the straight sections and up to 457.1 m in the curved

Anchorage: For long durations ample anchorages are available for all types of vessels at Lanoraie, which is located 8.05 km upstream from Sorel Harbour. In the immediate port area vessels may anchor at Montreal East, Pointe-aux-Trembles and opposite Grain Elevator No.4

Pilotage: Compulsory. St. Lawrence Pilotage District No 1-1 (Montreal Harbour Pilot); District No.1 (Quebec to Montreal) and District No.2 (Les Escoumins to Quebec). River pilots board inbound vessels at Anse-Aux-Basques near Les Escoumins and stay on board as far as Quebec, where pilots are changed for the sector of the river to Trois Rivieres. Pilots are again changed at Trois Rivieres for the final sector to Montreal. River pilots will dock/undock vessels on arrival and departure but any intervening moves within the harbour limits will be undertaken by harbour pilots. See also the St. Lawrence Seaway and Great Lakes Pilotage Section

Weather: Although the port is open all year round, night navigation may not be possible from mid-December to early April when the summer buoys are removed. Due to the ice conditions frequently encountered during winter months, it is customary for vessels coming to Montreal to be ice-strengthened

Tides: Tidal effects do not reach as far as Montreal but a strong current which flows between St. Helen's Island and the west bank of the river attains an average of 4-5 knots. The rate of the current decreases gradually further downstream

Traffic: 2007, 26 018 508 t of cargo handled, 1 363 021 TEU's

Working Hours: Mon to Fri 0800-1700. Saturdays and weekdays from 1800 to 2200 at time and a half. Sundays and holidays at double time. Night work by arrangement

Accommodation:

Name	Length (m)	Depth (m)	Remarks
Cast Terminal			See [1] below
Berth No.77	249	10.7	
Berth No.78	175	10.7	
Berth No.79	245	10.7	
Berth No.80	69	10.7	
Maisonneuve Terminal			See [2] below
Berth No.66	200	10.7	Equipped with 9.6 m wide ro/ro ramp
Berth No.67	232	10.7	
Berth No.68	195	10.7	
Berth No.70	200	10.7	
Racine Terminal			See [3] below
Berth No.57S	265	8.2	
Berth No.57N	200	9.8	
Berth No.58	163	10.7	

Name	Length (m)	Depth (m)	Remarks
Berth No.59	152	10.7	
Berth No.60	152	10.7	
Berth No.61	182	10.7	
Berth No.62	245	10.7	
Berth No.64	285	9.1	
Bickerdike Terminal			See [4] below
B1	182.9	7.6–8.8	Open space of 9409 m2 and shed area of 5828 m2
B2	186.6	8.8	Open space of 6960 m2 and shed area of 5828 m2
B3	197.5	8.8	Open space of 13 546 m2
B4	200.2	8.8	Open space of 7993 m2 and shed area of 6347 m2
B5	186.6	8.8	Open space of 7234 m2 and shed area of 7050 m2
B6	198.8	8.8	Open space of 9377 m2 and shed area of 7050 m2
B7	174	8.8	Open area of 4800 m2
B8	183	8.8	See [5] below
12N	152.4	8.8–10.7	Open space of 1937 m2
Laurier Terminal			See [6] below
Berth No.36	163.6	9.1	Open area of 7561 m2
Berth No.37	183.4	9.4	Open area of 8723 m2
Berth No.39	183.4	9.4	Open area of 8722 m2 and shed area of 5222 m2
Berth No.40	185.6	9.4–10.7	Open area of 9237 m2 and shed area of 5222 m2
Berth No.41	192.1	10.7	Open area of 7030 m2 and shed area of 5490 m2
Berth No.42	195.3	10.7	Open area of 25 677 m2 and shed area of 7023 m2
Berth No.43	265.6	10.2	Open space of 31 082 m2
Pie IX Terminal			See [7] below
Berth No.46	143.6	10.7	Open area of 5812 m2 and shed area of 3904 m2
Berth No.48	158	10.4	Open area of 26 160 m2. 9.1 m wide ro/ro ramp
Berth No.49	183	10.4	Open area of 10 540 m2 and shed area of 7042 m2
Louis-Hippolyte-Lafontaine Sector			See [8] below
Berth No.71	198.1	10.7	Open area of 27 305 m2 and shed area of 4638 m2
Berth No.72	171.8	10.7	Open area of 23 436 m2
Montreal-East Sector			See [9] below
Berth No.98	146.5	10.7	
Berth No.99	146.5	9.14–10.7	
Berth No.100	146.5	9.14	
Hochelaga Terminal			See [10] below
Berth No.50	190.2	10.4–10.7	Open area of 14 689 m2 and shed area of 3607 m2
Berth No.51	239.6	10.7	Open area of 14 590 m2 and shed area of 8445 m2
Berth No.52	338	10.7	See [11] below
Boucherville Terminal			General cargo terminal with an area of 4.2 ha
Berth No.73	192.9	10.7	See [12] below
Berth No.74	192.9	10.7	
Grain Terminal			See [13] below
Berth No's 54 & 55	395	10.7	Loading berths at 5500 t/h
Berth No.56	245	8.2	Unloading berth at 3000 t/h
Lakefield St. Terminal			See [14] below
Berth No.34	143.3	9.1	Open space of 7240 m2
Berth No.35	168.7	9.1	Open space of 11 203 m2
Berth No.97	202.3	9.1	Open space of 4900 m2
Terminal Norcan Inc			See [15] below
Berth No.74	192.9	10.7	Oil berth
Canterm Canadian Terminals			See [16] below
Berth No.94	238.1	10.7	Bunker and oil berth
Terminal Montreal Est (T.M.E.) Ltd			See [17] below
Berth No's 95, 96 & 97	404.8	9.1–10.7	Oil & bunkering berths
Shell Canada Products Ltd.			See [18] below
Berth 103S	189.6	10.7	Oil berth
Berth 103N	189.6	8.7	Bunker berth
Ultramar Ltd.			See [19] below
Berth No's 105 & 106	232.6	9.4	Oil berth
Petro-Canada			Operated by Petro-Canada, Tel: +1 514 640 8202
Berth No's 109 & 110E	278	10.7	Oil berth

[1]*Cast Terminal:* Container terminal operated by Cast Terminal Co., 305 Curatteau Street, Montreal Que H1L 6R6, Tel: +1 514 257 3040, Fax: +1 514 257 3077
Area of terminal 23 ha. Two 60 t and two 50 t dockside gantry cranes, six 40 t rubber tyred gantry cranes, eight 40 t top pick front-end loaders and twelve 2-30 t forklifts
[2]*Maisonneuve Terminal:* Container and general cargo terminal operated by Termont Terminal Inc., P O Box 36, Succ. K, Section 68, Port de Montreal, Montreal Que H1N 3K9, Tel: +1 514 254 0526, Fax: +1 514 251 1952, Email: info@termont.com, Website: www.termont.com
Covers an area of 18.2 ha. Three 30-40 t dockside gantry cranes, six 40 t yard gantry cranes, eight 40 t top handlers, three 30 t forklifts and 22 tractors
[3]*Racine Terminal:* Container terminal operated by Racine Terminal (Montreal) Co., P O Box 360, Station K, Montreal Que H1N 3L3, Tel: +1 514 257 3040, Fax: +1 514 257 3077
Area of terminal 25 ha. Three 60 t dockside gantry cranes, two 40 t dockside gantry

cranes, seven 35 t yard gantry cranes, ten 40 t top lifts, one empty container handler, 32 tractors, 31 chassis and 240 outlets for temperature-controlled containers
[4]*Bickerdike Terminal:* Container and general cargo terminal operated by Empire Stevedoring Co Ltd., 500 Place D'Armes, Suite 2800, Montreal Que H2Y 2W2, Tel: +1 514 288 2222, Fax: +1 514 288 1148
Two container berths (B7 and B8) cover an area of 9.6 ha with one dockside gantry crane of 35 t and one dockside gantry crane of 40 t, eight 30-40 t lifters, four 40 t yard gantry cranes, nine 50-200 t mobile cranes, 95 3-20 t forklifts and 36 outlets for temperature-controlled containers
Berths B1-B6 and 12N are general cargo berths leased on a short-term basis
[5]*B8:* Equipped with 16 m wide ro/ro ramp. Open area of 4800 m2
[6]*Laurier Terminal:* General cargo and bulk terminal operated by Logistec Stevedoring Inc., 360 St. Jacques Street, Suite 1500, Montreal Que H2Y 1P5, Tel: +1 514 844 9381, Fax: +1 514 842 1262, Email: info@logistec.com
[7]*Pie IX Terminal:* General cargo and bulk terminal operated by Logistec Stevedoring Inc., 360 St. Jacques Street, Suite 1500, Montreal Que H2Y 1P5, Tel: +1 514 844 9381, Fax: +1 514 842 1262, Email: info@logistec.com
[8]*Louis-Hippolyte-Lafontaine Sector:* Bulk terminal operated by Logistec Stevedoring Inc., 360 St. Jacques Street, Suite 1500, Montreal Que H2Y 1P5, Tel: +1 514 844 9381, Fax: +1 514 842 1262, Email: info@logistec.com
[9]*Montreal-East Sector:* Bulk terminal operated by Logistec Stevedoring Inc., 360 St. Jacques Street, Suite 1500, Montreal Que H2Y 1P5, Tel: +1 514 844 9381, Fax: +1 514 842 1262, Email: info@logistec.com
[10]*Hochelaga Terminal:* General cargo terminal operated by Logistec Stevedoring Inc., 360 St. Jacques Street, Suite 1500, Montreal Que H2Y 1P5, Tel: +1 514 844 9381, Fax: +1 514 842 1262, Email: info@logistec.com
[11]*Berth No.52:* Open area of 25 151 m2 and shed area of 9868 m2. Ro/ro ramp for vessels with quarter stern ramp
[12]*Berth No.73:* Equipped with a 9.6 m wide ro/ro ramp. Open space of 42 100 m2 and shed area of 1836 m2
[13]*Grain Terminal:* Operated by Montreal Port Authority with storage cap of 260 000 t
[14]*Lakefield St. Terminal:* Dry bulk terminal operated by Canadian Salt Co Ltd., Tel: +1 514 630 0900, Fax: +1 514 694 2451
Total area of 4.8 ha
[15]*Terminal Norcan Inc:* Operated by Terminal Norcan Inc., Tel: +1 514 253 2222, Fax: +1 514 251 0848, Email: carrier@vif.com
[16]*Canterm Canadian Terminals:* Operated by CanTerm Canadian Terminals Inc., 2775 Georges V. Avenue, Montreal-East Que H1L 6J7, Tel: +1 514 645 6526, Fax: +1 514 645 8048, Email: canterm@canterm.com, Website: www.canterm.com
[17]*Terminal Montreal Est (T.M.E.) Ltd:* Operated by Terminal Montreal Est (T.M.E.) Ltd., 9980 Notre-Dame Est, Montreal Que H1L 3R4, Tel: +1 514 640 9361, Fax: +1 514 645 0138
[18]*Shell Canada Products Ltd.:* Operated by Shell Canada Products Ltd., Tel: +1 514 640 3259
[19]*Ultramar Ltd.:* Operated by Ultramar Ltd., 7000 Marien Avenue, Montreal East Que H1B 4W3, Tel: +1 514 640 2342

Bunkering: Hampton Bunkering Ltd, Suite 615, 999 de Maisonneuve Boulevard West, Montreal, Que., Canada H3A 3L4, *Tel:* +1 514 2882 818, *Fax:* +1 514 2829 279, *Email:* bunkers@hamptonmtl.ca
ICS Petroleum, ICS Petroleum (Montreal) Ltd, Suite 302, 430 Ste-Helene Street, Montreal, Que., Canada H2Y 2K7, *Tel:* +1 514 849 1223, *Fax:* +1 514 849 0517, *Email:* bunkers@ics-mtl.com, *Website:* www.icspet.com
Petro Canada Products Ltd, 11701 Sherbrooke Street East, Montreal, Que., Canada H1B 1C3, *Tel:* +1 613 657 1004, *Fax:* +1 514 640 8365, *Email:* elliott@petro-canada.ca, *Website:* www.petro-canada.ca
Poros Shipping Agencies Inc., 1015 Beaver Hall Hill, Suite 310, Montreal, Que., Canada H2Z 1S1, *Tel:* +1 514 866 7438, *Fax:* +1 514 866 4949, *Email:* ops@porosshipping.com, *Website:* www.porosshipping.com
Reiter Petroleum Inc, Suite 900, 625 President Kennedy, Montreal, Que., Canada H3A 1K2, *Tel:* +1 514 8782 563, *Fax:* +1 514 8783 463, *Email:* bunkers@reiterpet.com, *Website:* www.reiterpet.com
Shell Canada Products Ltd, 10501 Sherbroke Street East, Montreal, Que., Canada H1B 1B3, *Tel:* +1 514 6409 897, *Fax:* +1 514 6451 490, *Email:* patrick.st-laurent@shell.com, *Website:* www.shell.ca
Triton Marine Fuels Canada Inc., 4148 A Saint Catherine Street West, Suite 109, Westmount, Que., Canada H3Z OA2, *Tel:* +1 450 4434 422, *Fax:* +1 450 4434 340, *Email:* bunkers@tritoncnd.com
Ultramar Canada Inc., 2200 McGill College Avenue, Montreal, Que., Canada H3A 3L3, *Tel:* +1 514 4996 111, *Fax:* +1 514 4996 320, *Email:* wholesale@ultramar.ca, *Website:* www.ultramar.ca
BP Marine Americas Inc., 501 Westlake Park Boulevard, Houston, TX 77079, United States of America, *Tel:* +1 281 366 2000, *Email:* firstname.secondname@bp.com
Bunkerina International Inc., 11 3rd Avenue South, Roxboro, Montreal, Que., Canada H8Y 2L3, *Tel:* +1 514 806 2760, *Fax:* +1 514 683 2760
ExxonMobil Marine Fuels, Suite 900, One Alhambra Plaza, Coral Gables, FL 33134, United States of America, *Tel:* +1 305 459 6358, *Fax:* +1 305 459 6412, *Email:* emmf@exxonmobil.com, *Website:* www.exxonmobilmarinefuels.com
Hampton Bunkering Ltd, Suite 615, 999 de Maisonneuve Boulevard West, Montreal, Que., Canada H3A 3L4, *Tel:* +1 514 2882 818, *Fax:* +1 514 2829 279, *Email:* bunkers@hamptonmtl.ca
ICS Petroleum, ICS Petroleum (Montreal) Ltd, Suite 302, 430 Ste-Helene Street, Montreal, Que., Canada H2Y 2K7, *Tel:* +1 514 849 1223, *Fax:* +1 514 849 0517, *Email:* bunkers@ics-mtl.com, *Website:* www.icspet.com
Imperial Oil (Anjou) Ltd, 7100 Jean-Talon Street East, Anjou, Que., Canada H1M 3R8, *Tel:* +1 450 6497 519, *Fax:* +1 450 6497 821, *Email:* christian.beaunoyer@esso.ca, *Website:* www.imperialoil.com
Kildair Service Ltd, 92 Chemin Delangis, St. Paul de Joliette, Que., Canada JOK 3EO, *Tel:* +1 450 7568 091, *Fax:* +1 450 7564 783, *Email:* info@kildair.com, *Website:* www.kildair.com
Petro Canada Products Ltd, 11701 Sherbrooke Street East, Montreal, Que., Canada H1B 1C3, *Tel:* +1 613 657 1004, *Fax:* +1 514 640 8365, *Email:* elliott@petro-canada.ca, *Website:* www.petro-canada.ca
Reiter Petroleum Inc, Suite 900, 625 President Kennedy, Montreal, Que., Canada H3A 1K2, *Tel:* +1 514 8782 563, *Fax:* +1 514 8783 463, *Email:* bunkers@reiterpet.com, *Website:* www.reiterpet.com
Shell Canada Products Ltd, 10501 Sherbroke Street East, Montreal, Que., Canada

Key to Principal Facilities:—				
A=Airport	**C**=Containers	**G**=General Cargo	**P**=Petroleum	**R**=Ro/Ro	**Y**=Dry Bulk
B=Bunkers	**D**=Dry Dock	**L**=Cruise	**Q**=Other Liquid Bulk	**T**=Towage (where available from port)

H1B 1B3, *Tel:* +1 514 6409 897, *Fax:* +1 514 6451 490, *Email:* patrick.st-laurent@shell.com, *Website:* www.shell.ca
Ultramar Canada Inc., 2200 McGill College Avenue, Montreal, Que., Canada H3A 3L3, *Tel:* +1 514 4996 111, *Fax:* +1 514 4996 320, *Email:* wholesale@ultramar.ca, *Website:* www.ultramar.ca
Universal Maritime Agency & Trading Co. Ltd (Umatco), 2444 Marisa Ct., Mississauga, Ont., Canada, *Tel:* +1 905 823 4638, *Fax:* +1 905 823 3938, *Email:* umatco@sympatico.ca

Waste Reception Facilities: Urgence Marine Inc., Section 110N, P O Box 511, Montreal, Que., Canada H1B 5P3, *Tel:* +1 514 640 3138, *Fax:* +1 514 640 4509, *Email:* marine@urgencemarine.com, *Website:* www.urgencemarine.com

Towage: McAllister Towing & Salvage Inc., Section 57, Port de Montreal, Notre Dame Street, Montreal, Que., Canada H1N 3L3, *Tel:* +1 514 849 2221, *Fax:* +1 514 849 7231, *Email:* orm@groupocean.com, *Website:* www.groupocean.com
McKeil Marine Ltd, 2 Boul St.Jean Baptiste, Montreal, Que., Canada H1B 3Z4, *Tel:* +1 514 640 4970, *Fax:* +1 514 640 1905, *Email:* sales@mckeil.com

Repair & Maintenance: Genivar, 5858 Cote des Neiges Road, Floor 4, Montreal, Que., Canada H3S 1Z1, *Tel:* +1 514 340 0046, *Fax:* +1 514 340 1337, *Email:* marlene.casciaro@genivar.com, *Website:* www.genivar.com
Mount Royal/Walsh Inc., 2101 Aird Avenue, Montreal, Que., Canada H1V 2W3, *Tel:* +1 514 255 3301, *Fax:* +1 514 255 8851, *Email:* mrw@mrw-group.com, *Website:* www.mrw-group.com Engine repairs
Navamar Inc, 10150 Notre Dame E, Montreal, Que., Canada H1B 2T7, *Tel:* +1 514 989 0048, *Fax:* +1 514 989 9314, *Email:* info@navamar.com, *Website:* www.navamar.com

Seaman Missions: The Seamans Mission, P O Box 128, Place d'Armes, Montreal, Que., Canada H2Y 3E9, *Tel:* +1 514 849 3234, *Fax:* +1 514 849 2874, *Email:* marinershouse@rapidweb.ca

Ship Chandlers: Andros Marine Supplies, Andros Building, 1700 Norman, Lachine, Que., Canada H8S 1A9, *Tel:* +1 514 637 3726, *Fax:* +1 514 637 3759, *Email:* info@androsmarine.ca, *Website:* www.androsmarine.ca
Clipper Ship Supply Ltd, 770 Mill Street, Montreal, Que., Canada H3C 1Y3, *Tel:* +1 514 937 9561, *Fax:* +1 514 935 7203, *Email:* supply@clippership.ca, *Website:* www.clippership.ca
Corsan Marine (1998) Inc., 10500 Cote de Liesse, Suite 115, Montreal, Que., Canada H8T 1A4, *Tel:* +1 514 631 8117, *Fax:* +1 514 631 8116, *Email:* corsan@corsanmarine.com, *Website:* www.corsanmarine.com
Hellas Ship Supply Inc., 1700 Norman Street, Lachine, Que., Canada H8S 1A9, *Tel:* +1 514 637 3760, *Fax:* +1 514 637 3764, *Email:* theomar@iprimus.ca
Karlo Corp. - Marine Group, Karlo Building, 2225 Leclaire Street, Montreal, Que., Canada H1V 3A3, *Tel:* +1 514 255 5017, *Fax:* +1 514 255 6888, *Email:* canada@karlogroup.com, *Website:* www.karlogroup.com
North Star Ship Chandler Inc., 2016 Richardson Street, Montreal, Que., Canada H3K 1G7, *Tel:* +1 514 932 2947, *Fax:* +1 514 932 9884, *Email:* northstar@total.net, *Website:* www.northstarship.ca
Seagulf Marine Industries Inc., 815 Mill Street, Montreal, Que., Canada H3C 1Y5, *Tel:* +1 514 935 6933, *Fax:* +1 514 935 3665, *Email:* shipsupply@montreal.seagulf.com, *Website:* www.seagulf.com

Shipping Agents: Amican Navigation Inc., 300 Rue St. Sacrement, Suite 218, Montreal, Que., Canada H2Y 1X4, *Tel:* +1 514 844 2632, *Fax:* +1 514 844 1843, *Email:* amican@cam.org
Andersen-Sima Maritime Inc, 1 McGill Street, Suite 214, Montreal, Que., Canada H2Y 4A3, *Tel:* +1 514 285 9070, *Fax:* +1 514 285 9072, *Email:* ansima@colba.net
APL Ltd, 615 Rene Levesque Boulevard West, Suite 640, Montreal, Que., Canada H3B 1P5, *Tel:* +1 514 845 3125, *Fax:* +1 514 845 0081, *Email:* doug_mccullough@apl.com, *Website:* www.apl.com
B&K Shipping Agency Ltd, 360 St.Jacques, Montreal, Que., Canada H2Y 1P7, *Tel:* +1 514 842 7983, *Fax:* +1 514 849 2696, *Email:* ship.bk@sympatico.ca
Braemar Shipping Inc., 1750 Richardson Street, Suite 3113, Montreal, Que., Canada H3K 1G6, *Tel:* +1 514 925 9031, *Fax:* +1 514 925 9041, *Email:* mail@braemarship.com
Canadian Maritime Agency Ltd, 4 Refinery Road, P O Box 119, Come by Chance, NL, Canada A0B 1N0, *Tel:* +1 709 463 4717, *Fax:* +1 709 463 8737, *Email:* opscbc@canadianmaritime.nf.ca, *Website:* www.canadianmaritime.com
Canfornav Inc., 315 de la Commune Street West, Montreal, Que., Canada H2Y 2E1, *Tel:* +1 514 284 9193, *Fax:* +1 514 499 1030, *Email:* chartering@canfornav.com, *Website:* www.canfornav.com
Chartwell Shipping, 276 St.Jacques Street, Suite 728, Montreal, Que., Canada H2Y 1N3, *Tel:* +1 514 849 7705, *Fax:* +1 514 849 4009, *Email:* shipbrokers@chartwellshipping.ca
CMA-CGM S.A., CMA CGM (Canada) Inc, Suite 1330 - 13th Floor, 740 Notre-Dame Street West, Montreal, Que., Canada H3C 3X6, *Tel:* +1 514 908 7001, *Fax:* +1 514 908 7142, *Email:* cda.lpoirier@cma-cgm.com, *Website:* www.cma-cgm.com
Colley Motorships Ltd, 1751 rue Richardson, Suite 3112, Montreal, Que., Canada H3K 1G6, *Tel:* +1 514 939 2366, *Fax:* +1 514 939 2316, *Email:* tdobesch@colleyms.com
Contimar Maritime Inc., 465 St. Jean Street, Suite 1001, Montreal, Que., Canada H2Y 2R6, *Tel:* +1 514 499 0091, *Fax:* +1 514 499 1595, *Email:* conti@metz.ca
Cross Marine Inc., 500 Place D'Armes, Suite 2800, Montreal, Que., Canada H2Y 2W2, *Tel:* +1 514 288 2242, *Fax:* +1 514 228 2066, *Email:* operations@crossmarine.com
Danfor Shipping & Trading Inc, 560 Wiseman Avenue, Montreal, Que., Canada H2V 3J8, *Tel:* +1 514 270 3729, *Fax:* +1 514 270 3729, *Email:* hj.peterson@sympatico.ca
Echo Freight Inc., 305 Saint Louis Street, Montreal, Que., Canada H2Y 1A7, *Tel:* +1 514 333 3380, *Fax:* +1 514 333 4959, *Email:* rates@echofreight.com, *Website:* www.echofreight.com
Fednav International Ltd, 1000 rue de La Gauchetiere Ouest, Suite 3500, Montreal, Que., Canada H3B 4W5, *Tel:* +1 514 878 6500, *Fax:* +1 514 878 6642, *Email:* info@fednav.com, *Website:* www.fednav.com
Gibson Canadian & Global Inc, 1 Westmount Square, Suite 711, Montreal, Que., Canada H3Z 2P9, *Tel:* +1 514 933 7371, *Fax:* +1 514 937 1774, *Email:* chartering@gibson.ca
Gresco Ltd, 299 de la Commune Street W, Montreal, Que., Canada H2Y 2E1, *Tel:* +1 514 842 4051, *Fax:* +1 514 845 6055, *Email:* agency@gresco.net
Hampton Shipagency, 999 de Maisonneuve Boulevard West, Suite 615, Montreal, Que., Canada H3A 3L4, *Tel:* +1 514 288 2818, *Fax:* +1 514 282 9279, *Email:* brokering@hamptonmtl.ca
Inchcape Shipping Services (ISS), 620 Bord du Lac, Suite 304, Dorval, Que., Canada H9S 2B6, *Tel:* +1 514 861 1216, *Fax:* +1 514 861 1113, *Email:* iss.montreal@iss-shipping.com, *Website:* www.iss-shipping.com
Jonker Navigation Corporation, 465 St Jean Street, Suite 505, Montreal, Que., Canada H2Y 2R6, *Tel:* +1 514 288 6034, *Fax:* +1 514 288 6062, *Email:* info@jonkernavigation.com
Laden Maritime Inc, Montreal World Trade Centre, 393 St.Jacques Street, Suite 365, Montreal, Que., Canada H2Y 1N9, *Tel:* +1 514 284 4202, *Fax:* +1 514 284 1791, *Email:* laden@lade-maritime.com
McLean Kennedy Inc., 368 Notre Dame Street West, Montreal, Que., Canada H2Y 1T9, *Tel:* +1 514 849 6111, *Fax:* +1 514 849 0649, *Email:* agency@mcleankennedy.ca, *Website:* www.mcleankennedy.ca
Mediterranean Shipping Company, MSC Canada Inc, 360 St Jacques Street, Suite 900, Montreal, Que., Canada H2Y 1P5, *Tel:* +1 514 844 3711, *Fax:* +1 514 844 4272, *Email:* msccanada@mscca.mscgva.ch, *Website:* www.mscgva.ch
Merada Transportation Ltd, 1255 University Street, Suite 310, Montreal, Que., Canada H3B 3B4, *Tel:* +1 514 875 5344, *Fax:* +1 514 875 5537, *Email:* merada@generation.net
A.P. Moller-Maersk Group, Maersk Canada Inc, 740 Notre Dame Street West, Suite 790, Montreal, Que., Canada H3C 3X6, *Tel:* +1 514 871 0210, *Fax:* +1 514 871 8269, *Email:* monsal@maersk.com, *Website:* www.maerskline.com
Montreal Marine Services Ltd, 50 Rue de la Barre, Suite 111, Longueuil, Que., Canada J4K 5G2, *Tel:* +1 450 646 3448, *Fax:* +1 450 646 3449, *Email:* operations@montrealmarine.ca, *Website:* www.montrealmarine.ca
Montship Inc., Suite 1000, 360 rue Saint-Jacques, Montreal, Que., Canada H2Y 1R2, *Tel:* +1 514 286 4646, *Fax:* +1 514 286 4650, *Email:* sdohring@montship.ca, *Website:* www.montship.ca
Norton Lilly International Inc., 465 Rue St-Jean, Suite 708, Montreal, Que., Canada H2Y 2R6, *Tel:* +1 514 223 2944, *Email:* mtr-ops@nortonlilly.com, *Website:* www.nortonlilly.com
Poros Shipping Agencies Inc., 1015 Beaver Hall Hill, Suite 310, Montreal, Que., Canada H2Z 1S1, *Tel:* +1 514 866 7438, *Fax:* +1 514 866 4949, *Email:* ops@porosshipping.com, *Website:* www.porosshipping.com
Protos Shipping Ltd, 740 Notre Dame Street West, Suite 1245, Montreal, Que., Canada H3C 3X6, *Tel:* +1 514 866 7799, *Fax:* +1 514 866 7077, *Email:* info@protos.ca, *Website:* www.protos.ca
Robert Reford Inc., Suite 1777, 2 Place Alexis Nihon, 3500 de Maisonneuve West, Montreal, Que., Canada H3Z 3C1, *Tel:* +1 514 845 5201, *Fax:* +1 514 845 6490, *Email:* ops@reford.ca, *Website:* www.robertreford.com
Scandia Shipping Canada Inc., 1130 Sherbrooke West, Suite PH1, Montreal, Que., Canada, *Tel:* +1 514 879 9222, *Fax:* +1 514 879 9260, *Email:* chartering@scandia.ca, *Website:* www.scandia.ca
Seabridge International Shipping Inc., 401 Notre Dame east, Montreal, Que., Canada H2Y 1C9, *Tel:* +1 514 393 9100, *Fax:* +1 514 393 1515, *Email:* montreal@seabridge.ca, *Website:* www.seabridge.ca
Seanautic Marine Inc., 20 rue Saint-Paul Ouest, Suite 201, Montreal, Que., Canada H2Y 1Y7, *Tel:* +1 514 287 1812, *Fax:* +1 514 287 9202, *Email:* infomtl@seanauticmarine.com, *Website:* www.seanauticmarine.com
Westward Shipping Ltd, Suite 1217, 360 St. Jaques Street, Montreal, Que., Canada H2Y 1P5, *Tel:* +1 514 877 0101, *Fax:* +1 514 877 0088, *Email:* sales@westwardmtl.com, *Website:* www.westwardshipping.com

Stevedoring Companies: Calogeras Master Supplies Inc, 8533 Delmeade Road, Montreal, Que., Canada H4T 1M1, *Tel:* +1 514 931 0341, *Fax:* +1 514 931 1147, *Email:* supplies@calmas.com
Ceres Marine Terminals Incorporated, Cerescorp Company, P O Box 444, Station K, Montreal, Que., Canada H1N 3L4, *Tel:* +1 514 254 3511, *Fax:* +1 514 254 8004, *Email:* ceres@ceresglobal.com, *Website:* www.ceresglobal.com
Empire Stevedoring Co Ltd, 500 Place d'Armes, Suite 2800, Montreal, Que., Canada H2Y 2W2, *Tel:* +1 514 288 2222, *Fax:* +1 514 288 1148, *Email:* goro@empstev.com
Logistec Stevedoring Inc., 360 St.Jacques Street, Suite 1500, Montreal, Que., Canada H2Y 1P5, *Tel:* +1 514 844 9381, *Fax:* +1 514 842 1262, *Email:* info@logistec.com, *Website:* www.logistec.com

Surveyors: Bureau Veritas, 410 Rue St-Nicolas, Suite 014, Montreal, Que., Canada H2Y 2P5, *Tel:* +1 514 288 6515, *Fax:* +1 514 288 9471, *Website:* www.bureauveritas.com
Crawford & Company, Marine Surveyors & Loss Adjusters, 404 Boulevard Decarie, Bureau 300, Montreal, Que., Canada, *Tel:* +1 514 748 7300, *Fax:* +1 514 748 2228, *Email:* lacostm0@crawco.ca, *Website:* www.crawfordandcompany.com
Det Norske Veritas A/S, 1100 Cremazie Boulevard East, Suite 415, Montreal, Que., Canada H2P 2X2, *Tel:* +1 514 861 0660, *Fax:* +1 514 861 7557, *Email:* montreal@dnv.com, *Website:* www.dnv.com
Germanischer Lloyd, 300 St. Sacrement, Suite 530, Montreal, Que., Canada H2Y 1X4, *Tel:* +1 514 287 7102, *Fax:* +1 514 287 7525, *Email:* gl-montreal@gl-group.com, *Website:* www.gl-group.com
Hayes Stuart Inc., 297 Duke Street, Montreal, Que., Canada H3C 2M2, *Tel:* +1 514 866 1801, *Fax:* +1 514 866 1259, *Email:* montreal@hayesstuart.com, *Website:* www.hayesstuart.com
R. MacDonald Marine Engineers & Ship Surveyors Ltd, 120 Longmore, Pointe Claire, Montreal, Que., Canada H9S 5A3, *Tel:* +1 514 630 0966, *Fax:* +1 514 695 8036, *Email:* ron.macdonald@sympatico.ca
Nippon Kaiji Kyokai, Suite 1340, 1 Westmount Square, Westmount, Que., Canada H3Z 2P9, *Tel:* +1 514 846 9414, *Fax:* +1 514 846 9433, *Email:* mt@classnk.or.jp, *Website:* www.classnk.or.jp
Societe Generale de Surveillance (SGS), SGS Canada Inc, 11000A Sherbrooke Est, Unit 33, Montreal, Que., Canada H1B 5W1, *Tel:* +1 514 645 8754, *Fax:* +1 514 640 3039, *Email:* enquiries@sgs.com, *Website:* www.sgs.com

Airport: Dorval International Airport, 24 km

Railway: The Port of Montreal operates a railway network with 100 km of track serving most of the marine terminals and berths, and connections are made with the main line railways, CN North America and CP Rail System to all parts of Canada and the United States. Modern highways also link the port to other major industrial centres in North America

Lloyd's Agent: Hayes Stuart Inc., 297 Duke Street, Montreal, Que., Canada H3C 2M2, *Tel:* +1 514 866 1801, *Fax:* +1 514 866 1259, *Email:* montreal@hayesstuart.com, *Website:* www.hayesstuart.com

MULGRAVE

Lat 45° 35' N; Long 61° 23' W.

Admiralty Chart: 4758　　　　**Admiralty Pilot:** 65
Time Zone: GMT -4 h　　　　**UNCTAD Locode:** CA MUL

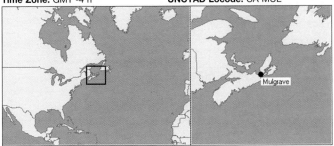

Principal Facilities:

		Y	G		B		T	A	

Authority: Strait of Canso Superport Corp. Ltd, P O Box 238, Mulgrave, N.S., Canada B0E 2G0, *Tel:* +1 902 747 2078, *Fax:* +1 902 747 2453, *Email:* timgilfoy@straitsuperport.com, *Website:* www.straitsuperport.com

Officials: Chief Executive Officer: Tim Gilfoy, *Email:* timgilfoy@straitsuperport.com. Operations: Ralph Hadley, *Email:* ralphhadley@straitsuperport.com.

Port Security: ISPS compliant

Approach: Approach channel 800 m wide in depth of 12.2 m

Anchorage: There is good anchorage sheltered from NW winds in 10.7-13.7 m with mud bottom, off the mouth of Venus Cove, with Macnair Point 365.8 m away in line with Port Hastings, bearing 347°

Pilotage: Compulsory

Radio Frequency: VHF Channel 14

Working Hours: 0800-1700. Overtime occasionally worked under special conditions

Accommodation:

Name	Remarks
Mulgrave	See [1] below

[1]*Mulgrave:* Wharf has two berths providing lengths of 275 m and 150 m. Laydown areas of 8000 m2 and 10 000 m2 exist adjacent to these berths and the latter is subtended at an angle enabling vessels of more than 200 m loa easy access

Storage:

Location	Open (m²)
Mulgrave	10950

Bunkering: Available

Towage: Eastern Canada Towing Limited, 1549 Lower Water Street, P O Box 337, Halifax, N.S., Canada B3J 2N7, *Tel:* +1 902 423 7381, *Fax:* +1 902 423 5123, *Email:* ectug@ectug.com, *Website:* www.svitzer.com

Repair & Maintenance: East Coast Hydraulics & Machinery Co. Ltd, P O Box 130, Mulgrave, N.S., Canada B0E 2G0, *Tel:* +1 902 747 3133, *Fax:* +1 902 747 2388, *Email:* echm@ns.aliantzinc.ca, *Website:* www.eastcoasthydraulics.com Minor repairs Mulgrave Machine Works Ltd, 34 England Avenue, P O Box 280, Mulgrave, N.S., Canada B0E 2G0, *Tel:* +1 902 747 2157, *Fax:* +1 902 747 2227, *Email:* mmw@mulgravemachineworks.ca, *Website:* www.mulgravemachineworks.ca Minor repairs

Stevedoring Companies: Strait of Canso Superport Corp. Ltd, P O Box 238, Mulgrave, N.S., Canada B0E 2G0, *Tel:* +1 902 747 2078, *Fax:* +1 902 747 2453, *Email:* timgilfoy@straitsuperport.com, *Website:* www.straitsuperport.com

Medical Facilities: Strait Richmond, 25 mins. St. Martha's Regional, 30 mins

Airport: Port Hastings, 10 mins

Railway: 5 mins from port

Lloyd's Agent: Hayes Stuart Inc., 1000 Windmill Road, Suite 19, Dartmouth, N.S., Canada B3B 1L7, *Tel:* +1 902 468 2651, *Fax:* +1 902 468 4315, *Email:* halifax@hayesstuart.com, *Website:* www.hayesstuart.com

NANAIMO

Lat 49° 10' N; Long 123° 56' W.

Admiralty Chart: 4920/4957/4958　　　**Admiralty Pilot:** 25
Time Zone: GMT -8 h　　　　**UNCTAD Locode:** CA NNO

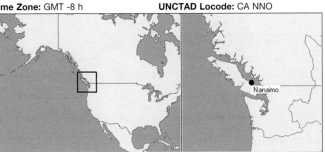

Principal Facilities:

P		G	C	R	L	B		T	A

Authority: Nanaimo Port Authority, P O Box 131, Nanaimo, B.C., Canada V9R 5K4, *Tel:* +1 250 753 4146, *Fax:* +1 250 753 4899, *Email:* info@npa.ca, *Website:* www.npa.ca

Officials: Chief Executive Officer: Bernie Dumas.
Finance Manager: Ian Marr, *Email:* imarr@npa.ca.
Marketing Manager: Douglas Peterson, *Email:* dougp@npa.ca.
Harbour Master: Andrew Pitcher, *Email:* apitch@npa.ca.

Port Security: ISPS compliant

Documentation: Crew list (3 copies), passenger list (1 copy), ship stores (3 copies), crew declarations (3 copies), quarantine certificate (1 copy), manifest from previous ports

Approach: Min controlling depth for inner harbour 9 m over Meakin Channel and 7 m over Middle Bank at LW

Anchorage: Seven deep water anchorages E of Newcastle and protection islands:
49° 10' 01" N; 123° 54' 16" W in depth of 14 m for vessels up to 180 m loa
49° 10' 22" N; 123° 54' 00" W in depth of 55 m for vessels up to 200 m loa
49° 10' 44" N; 123° 53' 42" W in depth of 70 m for vessels up to 200 m loa
49° 10' 43" N; 123° 54' 20" W in depth of 40 m for vessels up to 200 m loa
49° 11' 13.4" N; 123° 54' 15" W in depth of 40 m for vessels up to 300 m loa
49° 11' 47" N; 123° 54' 10" W in depth of 80 m for vessels up to 250 m loa
49° 12' 10" N; 123° 54' 42.8" W in depth of 40 m for vessels up to 280 m loa

Pilotage: Pilot boards off William Head, Victoria. Pacific Pilotage Authority, *Tel:* +1 604 666 6771

Radio Frequency: Nanaimo Radio, VHF channel 87, VBJ 40

Tides: Mean tidal range 3.2 m. Max large tide range 4.9 m

Traffic: 2007, 1 760 000 t of cargo handled

Maximum Vessel Dimensions: Max draft 13.5 m

Principal Imports and Exports: Imports: Forest products, Kaolin, Petroleum products. Exports: Forest products, Lumber, Pulp.

Working Hours: Loading 24 h/day except Christmas Day, New Year's Day and Labour Day

Accommodation:

Name	Length (m)	Depth (m)	Remarks
Nanaimo			See [1] below
Coastal Intermodal	106	7.62	
Nanaimo Assembly Wharf			See [2] below
Berth A	182	10.1	
Berth B	182	12.4	Ro/ro facility
Berth C	182	11.7	
Coastwise Berth	61	4.8	With a 60 t barge ramp
Island Timberlands			
Harmac E	137	10.4	Multi-use berth
Harmac W	115	10	Pulp terminal
Duke Point Deep Sea Terminal			See [3] below

[1]*Nanaimo:* Visiting Vessel Pier-Cruise Ship Facility is a floating pier length 180 m, width 11.6 m with a freeboard of 1.28 m from deck to water and minimum water depth of 8.5 m alongside. Can accommodate vessels with a displacement of 3000 t and 113 m in length. Larger vessels may be accommodated subject to the harbour master's approval. Full facilities are available. Warehouse space of 8300 m2 is available
Tanker facilities: Imperial Oil Wharf, 48.76 m long with 6.14 m depth alongside; Petro Canada, 33.53 m long with 4.88 m depth alongside
[2]*Nanaimo Assembly Wharf:* Forest products & general cargo. 15 ha paved open storage area
[3]*Duke Point Deep Sea Terminal:* Located 3 km S of Nanaimo, is an industrial site including a 28 ha terminal facility with one deep-sea berth used for the shipment of forest products and containers. Berth 'D', 170 m long with 13.5 m depth alongside. Vessels of up to 243 m loa can be accommodated. 100 t cap ro/ro ramp for barge loading and unloading located adjacent to Berth 'D'

Storage:

Location	Covered (m²)	Sheds / Warehouses
Nanaimo Assembly Wharf	8332	3

Mechanical Handling Equipment:

Location	Type	Capacity (t)	Qty
Nanaimo Assembly Wharf	Mobile Cranes		
Duke Point Deep Sea Terminal	Container Cranes	40	1

Bunkering: ExxonMobil Marine Fuels, Suite 900, One Alhambra Plaza, Coral Gables, FL 33134, United States of America, *Tel:* +1 305 459 6358, *Fax:* +1 305 459 6412, *Email:* emmf@exxonmobil.com, *Website:* www.exxonmobilmarinefuels.com – *Delivery Mode:* truck, barge
ICS Petroleum, ICS Petroleum Ltd., P O Box 12115, Suite 2360, 555 West Hastings Street, Vancouver, B.C., Canada V6B 4N6, *Tel:* +1 604 6856 221, *Fax:* +1 604 6857 352, *Email:* bunkers@ics-vcr.com, *Website:* www.icspet.com – *Delivery Mode:* truck, barge
Imperial Oil (Burnaby) Ltd, International Marine Sales, 4720 Kingsway, Burnaby, B.C., Canada V5H 4N2, *Tel:* +1 604 451 5955, *Fax:* +1 604 451 5950 – *Delivery Mode:* truck, barge
Marine Petrobulk Ltd, 10 Pemberton Avenue, Vancouver, B.C., Canada V7P 2R1, *Tel:* +1 604 9874 415, *Fax:* +1 604 9873 824, *Email:* tbrewster@marinepetro.com, *Website:* www.marinepetrobulk.com – *Delivery Mode:* truck, barge

Towage: Tugs always available and join vessel at Gallows Point, Protection Island

---

Key to Principal Facilities:—				
A=Airport	**C**=Containers	**G**=General Cargo	**P**=Petroleum	**R**=Ro/Ro	**Y**=Dry Bulk
B=Bunkers	**D**=Dry Dock	**L**=Cruise	**Q**=Other Liquid Bulk	**T**=Towage (where available from port)	

Stevedoring Companies: Canadian Stevedoring Co. Ltd, Nanaimo, B.C., Canada, *Tel:* +1 250 753 1810, *Fax:* +1 250 754 2100
Westcan Stevedoring Ltd, P O Box 81, 11 Port Way, Nanaimo, B.C., Canada V9R 5K4, *Tel:* +1 250 754 7701, *Fax:* +1 250 754 8187, *Email:* naw@westcan.ws

Medical Facilities: Regional general hospital

Airport: Nanaimo Regional Airport, 15 km

Railway: E & N Railway siding into Nanaimo Assembly Wharf.

Lloyd's Agent: McLarens Canada (Vancouver), 505 1100 Melville Street, Vancouver, B.C., Canada V6E 4A6, *Tel:* +1 604 681 7107, *Fax:* +1 604 681 8125, *Email:* philip.vardon@mclarens.ca, *Website:* www.mclarens.ca

NAVY ISLAND TERMINAL

harbour area, see under Saint John

NEPTUNE TERMINALS

harbour area, see under Vancouver

NEW WESTMINSTER

alternate name, see Fraser River Port

NEWCASTLE

Lat 47° 0' N; Long 65° 33' W.

Admiralty Chart: 4762
Time Zone: GMT -4 h
Admiralty Pilot: 65
UNCTAD Locode: CA NCT

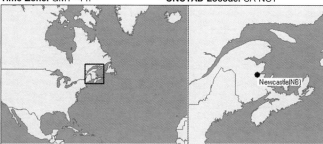

Principal Facilities:

P		G		B		A

Authority: Miramichi Port Committee Inc., P O Box 569, 10 Jane Street, Miramichi, N.B., Canada E1V 3T7, *Tel:* +1 506 622 0918, *Fax:* +1 506 622 0907, *Email:* mpci@nb.aibn.com

Officials: President: Richard G. Hare.

Pilotage: See under Chatham

Working Hours: 24 h/day, 7 days a week

Accommodation:

Name	Length (m)	Depth (m)	Remarks
Miramichi			See [1] below
Imperial Oil	152	10.67	Petroleum products
Miramichi Marine Terminal	313	9	Rail tracks; fresh water
Irving Oil	60	6.7	
Acadia Forest Products	216	6.7	
Miramichi Timber Resources	30	5.79	Petroleum products

[1]*Miramichi:* The port also includes the wharves at Nelson opposite Newcastle. A steel drawbridge, through which large vessels can pass, connects the two. Icebreaker assistance in winter. Controlling depth in the channel is 5.49 m. ST rise 1.37 m, NT rise 0.91 m. A draft of 6.4 m can be taken in or out

Storage:

Location	Open (m²)	Covered (m²)	Sheds / Warehouses
Miramichi Marine Terminal	9000	12625	2

Mechanical Handling Equipment:

Location	Type
Newcastle	Mobile Cranes

Bunkering: No coal. Oil from tank cars by arrangement

Repair & Maintenance: Castle Machine Works Ltd, 142 Roger Street, Miramichi, N.B., Canada E1V 3M3, *Tel:* +1 506 622 0752, *Fax:* +1 506 622 0477, *Email:* info@castlemachineworks.ca, *Website:* www.castlemachineworks.ca Engineers, machinists, welders and fabricators

Medical Facilities: Miramichi Hospital

Airport: Chatham, 10 km

Railway: Rail siding at port; CN/CP Rail

Lloyd's Agent: Hayes Stuart Inc., 297 Duke Street, Montreal, Que., Canada H3C 2M2, *Tel:* +1 514 866 1801, *Fax:* +1 514 866 1259, *Email:* montreal@hayesstuart.com, *Website:* www.hayesstuart.com

OSHAWA

Lat 43° 51' N; Long 78° 49' W.

Admiralty Chart: -
Time Zone: GMT -5 h
Admiralty Pilot: -
UNCTAD Locode: CA OSH

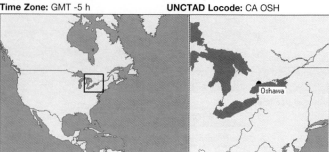

Principal Facilities:

		Y	G	R				A

Authority: Oshawa Harbour Commission, 1050 Farewell Street, Oshawa, Ont., Canada L1H 6N6, *Tel:* +1 905 576 0400, *Fax:* +1 905 576 5701, *Email:* info@portofoshawa.ca, *Website:* www.portofoshawa.ca

Officials: Chief Executive Officer: Donna Taylor.

Port Security: ISPS compliant

Approach: Channel depth 8.23 m

Pilotage: Arranged by ship's agent

Traffic: 2007, 238 773 t of cargo handled

Maximum Vessel Dimensions: Seaway size

Principal Imports and Exports: Imports: Asphalt, Calcium, Chloride, Fuel oil, Gasoline, General cargo, Gypsum, Steel. Exports: General cargo, Steel.

Working Hours: General Cargo 0800-2200, 7 days a week. Bulk cargo 24 h/day, 7 days a week

Accommodation:

Name	Length (m)	Depth (m)	Remarks
Oshawa			
Berth	433	8.2	See [1] below

[1]*Berth:* Dry bulk, general cargo & transhipment of steel products. Four domes capable of holding up to 10 534 m2

Storage: Two warehouses with 100 000 sq ft of covered storage

Location	Open (m²)
Oshawa	32515

Mechanical Handling Equipment: Cranes rented locally up to 650 t cap

Cargo Worked: Bulk cargo 4000-6000 short t (24 h discharged). General cargo 20-120 short t/gang/h

Stevedoring Companies: Oshawa Stevedoring Inc., 1050 Farewell Street, Oshawa, Ont., Canada L1H 6N6, *Tel:* +1 905 728 9299, *Fax:* +1 905 728 7898, *Email:* info@qsl.com, *Website:* www.qsl.com

Medical Facilities: Oshawa General Hospital

Airport: Oshawa Municipal Airport, 10 km

Railway: Canadian National (CN Rail) connections

Lloyd's Agent: McLarens Canada (Toronto), 600 Alden Road, Suite 600, Markham, Toronto, Ont., Canada L3R 0E7, *Tel:* +1 905 946 9995, *Fax:* +1 905 946 0171, *Email:* roger.bickers@mclarens.ca, *Website:* www.mclarens.ca

OWEN SOUND

Lat 44° 35' N; Long 80° 57' W.

Admiralty Chart: -
Time Zone: GMT -5 h
Admiralty Pilot: -
UNCTAD Locode: CA OWS

Principal Facilities:

P	Q	Y	G			B		A

Authority: Transport Canada, 4900 Yonge Street, Suite 300, Toronto, Ont., Canada M2N 6A5, *Tel:* +1 416 952 0154, *Fax:* +1 416 952 0159, *Email:* taylodd@tc.gc.ca, *Website:* www.tc.gc.ca

Officials: General Director: Debra Taylor, *Email:* taylodd@tc.gc.ca.

Port Security: ISPS compliant

Approach: Depth of approach and harbour entrance is 7.16 m

Pilotage: Not compulsory. VHF Channels 16 and 26

Maximum Vessel Dimensions: 190 m loa, 6.8 m d

Accommodation:

Name	Remarks
Owen Sound	See [1] below

[1]*Owen Sound:* West side has 487.6 m of wharf with 6.7 m of water, used for grain shipments and winter lay-up for grain vessels. East pier outer section, 426.7 m long, 6.8 m deep, used by tankers and bulk carriers. East pier inner section is 548.6 m long with 5.4 m of water, used by small craft
Bulk facilities: Salt, gravel and potash offloaded by ships gear at East pier outer section. Great Lakes elevator dock, 6.8 m depth alongside with storage cap of 110 000 t
Tanker facilities: Calcium chloride discharged at East pier outer section

Bunkering: Available

Medical Facilities: Owen Sound General hospital

Airport: Wiarton Airport, 50 km

Lloyd's Agent: McLarens Canada (Toronto), 600 Alden Road, Suite 600, Markham, Toronto, Ont., Canada L3R 0E7, *Tel:* +1 905 946 9995, *Fax:* +1 905 946 0171, *Email:* roger.bickers@mclarens.ca, *Website:* www.mclarens.ca

PARRY SOUND

Lat 45° 22' N; Long 80° 3' W.

Admiralty Chart: -   **Admiralty Pilot:** -
Time Zone: GMT -5 h   **UNCTAD Locode:** CA PRS

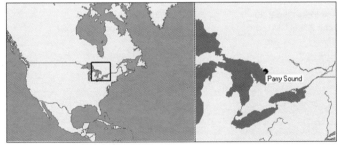

Principal Facilities:

P		Y	G		L			A

Authority: Town of Parry Sound, 52 Seguin Street, Parry Sound, Ont., Canada P2A 1B4, *Tel:* +1 705 746 2101, *Fax:* +1 705 746 7461, *Email:* info@townofparrysound.com, *Website:* www.townofparrysound.com

Port Security: ISPS compliant

Approach: Hazardous channel with rock bottom in 8-9 m depth. Entrance to inner harbour 6-7 m depth

Anchorage: Within the inner harbour in about 8-9 m depth

Pilotage: Compulsory only for foreign vessels

Radio Frequency: VHF Channels 16 (working), 26 (ship to shore) and 68 (ship to ship)

Weather: Prevailing W'ly winds. In strong SW winds narrow entry from Big to Little Sound is difficult

Traffic: 1998, 10 vessels, 143 420 t of salt handled

Maximum Vessel Dimensions: 225 m loa, 6.7 m d

Principal Imports and Exports: Exports: Salt.

Accommodation:

Name	Remarks
Parry Sound	See [1] below

[1]*Parry Sound:* Two salt-loading docks: North American Salt with a 40 000 t storage cap and Sifto Canada Inc with a 50 000 t cap. Southwestern Sales also operates a 200 000 t limestone dock at nearby Depot Harbour
The port is also used by cruise vessels

Medical Facilities: Parry Sound Health Center

Airport: Georgian Bay Airport, 20 km S of Parry Sound

Lloyd's Agent: McLarens Canada (Toronto), 600 Alden Road, Suite 600, Markham, Toronto, Ont., Canada L3R 0E7, *Tel:* +1 905 946 9995, *Fax:* +1 905 946 0171, *Email:* roger.bickers@mclarens.ca, *Website:* www.mclarens.ca

PICTOU

Lat 45° 41' N; Long 62° 43' W.

Admiralty Chart: 4765   **Admiralty Pilot:** 65
Time Zone: GMT -4 h   **UNCTAD Locode:** CA PTO

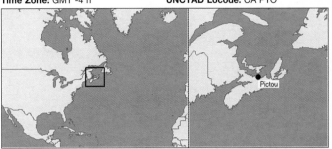
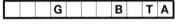

Principal Facilities:

		G		B	T	A

Authority: Pictou Marine Terminals, P O Box 1709, Pictou, N.S., Canada B0K 1H0, *Tel:* +1 902 485 9280, *Fax:* +1 902 485 9281, *Email:* straitline@truroreload.com, *Website:* www.pictoumarineterminals.com

Officials: Harbour Master: Peter MacKay, *Email:* pmackay@truroreload.com.

Port Security: ISPS compliant for bulk cargoes and cruise ships

Pre-Arrival Information: Fax information to +1 902 485 9281

Documentation: A6 in duplicate, clearance from last port, E1 in duplicate, 414 in duplicate, immigration form 200 in duplicate, Q25 in duplicate, fumigation & de-rat, loadline, inspection certificate, safety equipment certificate, radio & telephone certificate, certificate of registry, if first port in Canada - ocean bills for goods to be discharged in Canada, proof of P+I required

Approach: Channel depth of 6.4 m LW and 8 m HW, 120 m wide at lighthouse (Pictou Light-Moodie Point)

Anchorage: Preferred anchorage in pos 45° 45' N; 62° 25' E

Pilotage: Not compulsory but may be arranged via Coast Guard Canada Radio (VCO-Sydney), 12 h and 6 h before boarding. Pilot boards in pos 45° 42.5' N; 62° 33.6' W

Radio Frequency: Sydney Coast Guard Radio (VCO) on VHF Channel 16

Weather: Available from Environment Canada

Tides: Rise of tide 1.68 m springs, 1.37 m neaps

Principal Imports and Exports: Imports: Bagged fertiliser, Breakbulk cargoes. Exports: Aggregate, Fishery products, Lumber, Pulpwood, Rock, Steel components, Treated poles, Woodpulp.

Working Hours: 0800-2200

Accommodation:

Name	Length (m)	Depth (m)
Pier C		
South Berth	180	6.4–11.3
North Berth	180	6.4–11.3
Pier End	30	6.4–11.3
Quay Wall Wharf		
Berth	212	6

Storage: 55 m x 25 m unheated storage building on Pier C. 6000 m2 fenced open storage

Mechanical Handling Equipment:

Location	Type	Capacity (t)
Pictou	Mobile Cranes	250
Pictou	Forklifts	

Bunkering: Imperial Oil (Dartmouth) Ltd, P O Box 1010, Dartmouth, N.S., Canada B2Y 4RI, *Tel:* +1 902 420 6872, *Fax:* +1 902 420 6996 – *Grades:* IFO; HFO – *Delivery Mode:* truck
Irving Oil Co. Ltd, 10 Sydney Street, P O Box 1421, Saint John, N.B., Canada E2L 4K1, *Tel:* +1 888 3101 924, *Fax:* +1 506 2023 868, *Email:* webinquiries@irvingoil.com, *Website:* www.irvingoilco.com – *Grades:* IFO; HFO – *Delivery Mode:* truck

Waste Reception Facilities: Suction trucks available. Domestic and international garbage arranged with agent

Towage: Available

Stevedoring Companies: Straitline Stevedoring, 37A Water, Pictou, N.S., Canada B0K 1H0, *Tel:* +1 902 485 9280, *Fax:* +1 902 485 9281, *Email:* straitline@truroreload.com

Surveyors: J.B. McGuire Marine Associates Ltd, Water Street, Pictou, N.S., Canada B0K1H0, *Tel:* +1 902 485 8055, *Fax:* +1 902 485 4300

Medical Facilities: Aberdeen Hospital, 15 km. Doctor available locally

Airport: Trenton Municipal Airport, 20 km. Halifax International Airport, 100 km

Railway: Cape Breton & Central Nova RR, 15 km to nearest siding

Lloyd's Agent: Hayes Stuart Inc., 1000 Windmill Road, Suite 19, Dartmouth, N.S., Canada B3B 1L7, *Tel:* +1 902 468 2651, *Fax:* +1 902 468 4315, *Email:* halifax@hayesstuart.com, *Website:* www.hayesstuart.com

---

Key to Principal Facilities:—		
A=Airport	**C**=Containers	**G**=General Cargo	**P**=Petroleum	**R**=Ro/Ro	**Y**=Dry Bulk
B=Bunkers	**D**=Dry Dock	**L**=Cruise	**Q**=Other Liquid Bulk	**T**=Towage (where available from port)	

POINT TUPPER

Lat 45° 36' N; Long 61° 22' W.

Admiralty Chart: 4758	**Admiralty Pilot:** 65
Time Zone: GMT -4 h	**UNCTAD Locode:** CA PTU

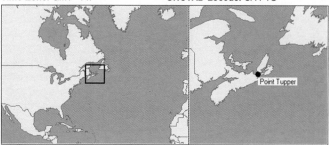

Principal Facilities:

P		Y	G			B			

Authority: Port Authority of Point Tupper, Point Tupper, N.S., Canada

Accommodation: Tanker facilities: Kaneb Pipe Line Partners Wharf, situated at Wright Point is T-shaped, extending 228.6 m from the shore with a sectional face 609.6 m long, parallel to the straight. This wharf accommodates vessels in excess of 325 000 t, 304.8 m in length and 21.3 m d for products and crude. Tankers up to 50 000 t can be berthed inside the NW extension of the wharf

Name	Remarks
Point Tupper	See [1] below
Georgia Pacific Corp Terminal	See [2] below
Point Tupper Marine Coal Terminal	450 m long with an outer face 190 m long. Coal unloaded from E-crane with a duty cycle rating of 27 t

[1]*Point Tupper:* There are several small craft anchorages west of Eddy Point in Critchett Cove and Byers Cove on the SW shore of the Strait, on the NE shore in Bear Cove, NW of Bear Island, off Madden Cove and off Cass Cove. However, these anchorages are exposed to some winds and have poor holding grounds

[2]*Georgia Pacific Corp Terminal:* Consists of seven dolphins connected by a catwalk, having a total length of 335.3 m with depth alongside of 8.2 m at LW; capable of mooring a vessel of 214 m loa. Gypsum is loaded by conveyor

Nova Scotia Forest Industries has a T-shaped wharf 129.5 m long at the face with a min depth of 7.9 m alongside

Bunkering: NuStar Energy LP, NuStar Terminals Canada Partnership, 4090 Port Malcom Road, Point Tupper, N.S., Canada B9A 1Z5, *Tel:* +1 902 6251 711, *Fax:* +1 902 6253 098, *Email:* richard.hanlon@nustarenergy.com, *Website:* www.valero.com
ExxonMobil Marine Fuels, Suite 900, One Alhambra Plaza, Coral Gables, FL 33134, United States of America, *Tel:* +1 305 459 6358, *Fax:* +1 305 459 6412, *Email:* emmf@exxonmobil.com, *Website:* www.exxonmobilmarinefuels.com
Imperial Oil (Dartmouth) Ltd, P O Box 1010, Dartmouth, N.S., Canada B2Y 4RI, *Tel:* +1 902 420 6872, *Fax:* +1 902 420 6996
Statia Terminals Inc., Suite 295, 800 Fairway Drive, Deerfield Beach, FL 33441, United States of America, *Tel:* +1 954 698 0705, *Fax:* +1 954 698 0706 – *Grades:* all grades – *Delivery Mode:* pipe

Shipping Agents: Canadian Maritime Agency Ltd, 4 Refinery Road, P O Box 119, Come by Chance, NL, Canada A0B 1N0, *Tel:* +1 709 463 4717, *Fax:* +1 709 463 8737, *Email:* opscbc@canadianmaritime.nf.ca, *Website:* www.canadianmaritime.com

Lloyd's Agent: Hayes Stuart Inc., 1000 Windmill Road, Suite 19, Dartmouth, N.S., Canada B3B 1L7, *Tel:* +1 902 468 2651, *Fax:* +1 902 468 4315, *Email:* halifax@hayesstuart.com, *Website:* www.hayesstuart.com

POINTE AU PIC

Lat 47° 37' N; Long 70° 8' W.

Admiralty Chart: 4783	**Admiralty Pilot:** 65
Time Zone: GMT -5 h	**UNCTAD Locode:** CA PPC

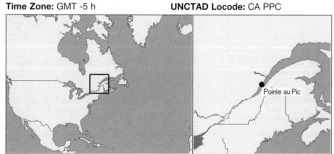

Principal Facilities:

			G						

Authority: Transport Canada, Champlain Harbour Station, 901 Cap Diamant 4th Floor, Quebec, Que., Canada G1K 4K1, *Tel:* +1 418 648 4103, *Fax:* +1 418 648 7980, *Website:* www.tc.gc.ca

Officials: Regional Manager: Andre Roy, *Tel:* +1 418 648 7213, *Email:* royan@tc.gc.ca.
Harbour Master: Michel Petit, *Tel:* +1 418 648 3640.

Port Security: ISPS compliant

Approach: Channel depth of 7.9 m

Anchorage: Good anchorage can be obtained off Murray Bay in a depth of 21.9 m

Pilotage: Compulsory. Pilot station at Les Escoumins

Tides: Range of tide 6.4 m ST, 2.4 m NT. A strong flood current is experienced off the wharf after the tide has begun to ebb and also in the reverse direction following the end of the ebb

Traffic: 2005, 12 vessels, 66 000 t of cargo handled

Principal Imports and Exports: Exports: Paper, Woodpulp

Working Hours: Mon to Fri 0800-1700. Overtime as required. Holidays and weekends on notice only

Accommodation:

Name	Length (m)	Depth (m)
Pointe au Pic Berth No.1	120	7.9

Storage:

Location	Open (m²)	Covered (m²)
Pointe au Pic	10000	1935

Mechanical Handling Equipment:

Location	Type	Capacity (t)	Qty
Pointe au Pic	Mult-purp. Cranes	20	1

Stevedoring Companies: Quebec Port Terminals Inc., 500 Chemin du Havre, La Malbaie, Que., Canada G5A 2Y9, *Tel:* +1 418 665 4485, *Fax:* +1 418 665 2292, *Email:* info@qsl.com, *Website:* www.qsl.com

Medical Facilities: Hospital at La Malbaie, 3.2 km

Lloyd's Agent: Hayes Stuart Inc., 297 Duke Street, Montreal, Que., Canada H3C 2M2, *Tel:* +1 514 866 1801, *Fax:* +1 514 866 1259, *Email:* montreal@hayesstuart.com, *Website:* www.hayesstuart.com

PORT ALBERNI

Lat 49° 14' N; Long 125° 0' W.

Admiralty Chart: 4944	**Admiralty Pilot:** 25
Time Zone: GMT -8 h	**UNCTAD Locode:** CA PAB

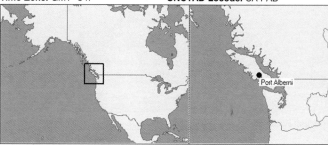

Principal Facilities:

	Y	G	C		L			A	

Authority: Port Alberni Port Authority, 2750 Harbour Road, Port Alberni, B.C., Canada V9Y 7X2, *Tel:* +1 250 723 5312, *Fax:* +1 250 723 1114, *Email:* bmadelung.papa@telus.net, *Website:* www.portalberniportauthority.ca

Officials: Chief Executive Officer: Brad Madelung.

Port Security: ISPS compliant. Transport Canada approved Security Plan in place

Pre-Arrival Information: Please contact the Terminal Manager's office at least 24 h prior to arrival, Tel: +1 250 723 7922

Approach: Deepwater approach from Barkley Sound via Alberni Inlet, 48 km distance, average width 1.6 km with depths up to 25 m. Controlling depth 18.3 m

Anchorage: Three anchorages in the inner harbour with a min depth of 18 m

Pilotage: Compulsory, contact through Vancouver radio. Pilot boards at Cape Beale, Barkley Sound. Vessel Traffic Management System: Tofino Traffic VHF 156.55 mHz (11) Pacific Pilotage Authority

Weather: Port is ice free in winter with a moderate climate. Generally the surface is calm and no ocean swell is experienced. At times when strong southerly winds occur, wave heights to 1 meter can be experienced. Usually high winds are rare.

Tides: Tides rise 3.5 m springs, 2.5 m neaps

Maximum Vessel Dimensions: Panamax size vessels with a max draught of 12.2 m

Principal Imports and Exports: Exports: Forest products.

Working Hours: 24 Hrs

Accommodation:

Name	Length (m)	Depth (m)	Remarks
Port Alberni			See [1] below
Berth No.1	320	11.4	
Berth No.2	320	11.4	

Name	Length (m)	Depth (m)	Remarks
Berth No.3	183	12.2	
Private Wharves			See [2] below

[1]*Port Alberni:* Containers can be handled upon special arrangements with terminal manager. There are no dock container cranes in the port
[2]*Private Wharves:* Smaller wharves and floats available, also storage sheds and storage ground. No deep sea bunkering facilities except by tank vehicle

Storage: Warehouses capable of storing 9000 t, floodlit with 24 h security

Location	Covered (m²)	Sheds / Warehouses
Port Alberni	4645	4

Mechanical Handling Equipment:

Location	Type	Capacity (t)	Qty
Port Alberni	Mobile Cranes	50	
Port Alberni	Forklifts		18

Cargo Worked: Lumber (forest product) average of 4000-8000 t/shift

Repair & Maintenance: Port Machine Works Ltd, 3726 Fourth Avenue, Port Alberni, B.C., Canada V9Y 4H8, *Tel:* +1 250 723 8165, *Fax:* +1 250 723 0277, *Email:* les@portmachine.ca, *Website:* www.portmachine.ca

Stevedoring Companies: Canadian Stevedoring Co. Ltd, Port Alberni, B.C., Canada, *Tel:* +1 250 753 1810, *Fax:* +1 250 754 2100
Empire International, Port Alberni, B.C., Canada, *Tel:* +1 250 758 8122
Westcan Stevedoring, Port Alberni, B.C., Canada, *Tel:* +1 250 753 5166

Surveyors: Mitchell Fothergill Marine Surveys, 2717 Murray Street, Port Moody, Nanaimo, B.C., Canada V3H 1X1, *Tel:* +1 604 939 4885, *Fax:* +1 604 939 2289, *Email:* surveys@bcmariner.com, *Website:* www.bcmariner.com

Medical Facilities: West Coast General Hospital in Port Alberni

Airport: Port Alberni Airport, 10 km

Railway: Rail line into Port Alberni, runs alongside Port Alberni terminals. E & N Railway.

Lloyd's Agent: McLarens Canada (Vancouver), 505 1100 Melville Street, Vancouver, B.C., Canada V6E 4A6, *Tel:* +1 604 681 7107, *Fax:* +1 604 681 8125, *Email:* philip.vardon@mclarens.ca, *Website:* www.mclarens.ca

PORT ALFRED

Lat 48° 20' N; Long 70° 52' W.

Admiralty Chart: 4785   **Admiralty Pilot:** 65
Time Zone: GMT -5 h   **UNCTAD Locode:** CA PAF

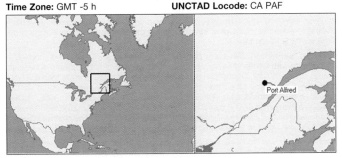

Principal Facilities:

P	Q	Y	G			B		T	A

Authority: Alcan Smelters & Chemicals Ltd, P O Box 10, Ville de la Baie, Que., Canada G7B 3R1, *Tel:* +1 418 544 9674 & 9643, *Fax:* +1 418 544 9622, *Email:* pa.agency@alcan.com, *Website:* www.alcan.com

Officials: Superintendent: Claude Chateauneuf.

Approach: Ha Ha Bay is a deep natural harbour 10 km long, affording room for a considerable number of vessels and is sheltered from all but easterly winds. Deep water in all approaches. Navigation all year round

Pilotage: Compulsory from or to Escoumins or Quebec. St. Lawrence Pilotage District No.2. VHF Radio Channel 9. An ETA min notice of 48 h then confirmed at 24 h, then four hours before arrival at Escoumins
All vessels of 500 gt and over, towing vessels and vessels carrying pollutant or dangerous goods, approaching the Eastern Canada Traffic Zone must inform Ecareg Canada by radio via any convenient Canadian Coast Guard Radio Station, all information in respect of the vessel and then obtain a traffic clearance
All masters should be supplied with a copy of 'Eastern Canada Traffic Zone Regulations' before proceeding to a port within the eastern waters of Canada

Tides: Rise of tide 6.3 m at HWS, 5 m at HWM, 1.8 m neaps

Traffic: Approx 140 vessels per year

Maximum Vessel Dimensions: Vessels up to 245 m can be berthed safely

Principal Imports and Exports: Imports: Alumina, Bauxite, Coke, Fluorspar. Exports: Aluminium ingots, Newsprint paper.

Working Hours: Bulk cargo at Duncan Wharf around-the-clock

Accommodation: Vessels awaiting berthing facilities anchor off Anse a Philippe (48° 21' N; 70° 53' W). Canadian National Railways, the Roberval and Saguenay Railway and road transport maintain freight and passenger service to and from Quebec City, Montreal, Arvida, Kenogami and the Lake St. John district

Name	Length (m)	Depth (m)	Remarks
Powell Wharf			Transit shed of 304.8 m x 15.2 m
South Side No.1		9.72	South Side Berths 1 & 2 total 346.8 m long
South Side No.2		10.97	
North Side No.4	146	10.8	Liquid unloading berth
Duncan Wharf			See [1] below
Berth No.1	190	11.25	
Berth No.2	195.5	11.25	

[1]*Duncan Wharf:* For unloading bauxite coke, fluorspar, alumina, bulk ore and salt (bulk). Two electric gantry towers of 500 t/h each. Also two electric unloading towers handling 1000 t each per hour

Mechanical Handling Equipment:

Location	Type	Capacity (t)	Qty
Powell Wharf	Mult-purp. Cranes	4	2

Bunkering: No coal and no fuel. Diesel oil by special arrangement. Tank truck delivery
ExxonMobil Marine Fuels, Suite 900, One Alhambra Plaza, Coral Gables, FL 33134, United States of America, *Tel:* +1 305 459 6358, *Fax:* +1 305 459 6412, *Email:* emmf@exxonmobil.com, *Website:* www.exxonmobilmarinefuels.com
Kildair Service Ltd, 92 Chemin Delangis, St. Paul de Joliette, Que., Canada J0K 3E0, *Tel:* +1 450 7568 091, *Fax:* +1 450 7564 783, *Email:* info@kildair.com, *Website:* www.kildair.com
Petro Canada Products Ltd, 11701 Sherbrooke Street East, Montreal, Que., Canada H1B 1C3, *Tel:* +1 613 657 1004, *Fax:* +1 514 640 8365, *Email:* elliott@petro-canada.ca, *Website:* www.petro-canada.ca
Reiter Petroleum Inc, Suite 900, 625 President Kennedy, Montreal, Que., Canada H3A 1K2, *Tel:* +1 514 8782 563, *Fax:* +1 514 8783 463, *Email:* bunkers@reiterpet.com, *Website:* www.reiterpet.com
Shell Canada Products Ltd, 10501 Sherbroke Street East, Montreal, Que., Canada H1B 1B3, *Tel:* +1 514 6409 897, *Fax:* +1 514 6451 490, *Email:* patrick.st-laurent@shell.com, *Website:* www.shell.ca
Ultramar Canada Inc., 2200 McGill College Avenue, Montreal, Que., Canada H3A 3L3, *Tel:* +1 514 4996 111, *Fax:* +1 514 4996 320, *Email:* wholesale@ultramar.ca, *Website:* www.ultramar.ca

Waste Reception Facilities: Dirty ballast and sludge could be available but very expensive to dispose of. Garbage disposal available

Towage: Two tugs available of 2400 hp and 3000 hp. Tugs are compulsory for all vessels over 3000 gt docking or undocking at Duncan Wharf and for tankers above 5000 gt

Repair & Maintenance: Fjordtech Industrie Inc., 2760 Boulevard de la Grande-Baie Nord, Ville de la Baie, Que., Canada G7B 3N8, *Tel:* +1 418 544 7091, *Fax:* +1 418 544 3739, *Email:* info@fjordtech.qc.ca, *Website:* www.fjordtech.qc.ca Repair facilities

Stevedoring Companies: Alcan Stevedores, Port Alfred, Que., Canada, *Tel:* +1 418 544 9697, *Fax:* +1 418 544 9616

Medical Facilities: Local hospital available, 1.6 km

Airport: Bagotville Airport, 9.6 km

Railway: Roberval Saguenay with service into the port

Lloyd's Agent: Hayes Stuart Inc., 297 Duke Street, Montreal, Que., Canada H3C 2M2, *Tel:* +1 514 866 1801, *Fax:* +1 514 866 1259, *Email:* montreal@hayesstuart.com, *Website:* www.hayesstuart.com

PORT ALICE

Lat 50° 23' N; Long 127° 27' W.

Admiralty Chart: -   **Admiralty Pilot:** 25
Time Zone: GMT -8 h   **UNCTAD Locode:** CA PAC

Principal Facilities:

P		Y	G			B		T	A

Authority: Western Pulp Ltd Partnership, P O Box 2000, Port Alice, B.C., Canada V0N 2N0, *Tel:* +1 604 284 3331, *Fax:* +1 604 284 6631

Approach: Controlling channel depth from entrance of Quatsino Sound to dock, 44 m

Anchorage: Good anchorage about half a mile from Company's dock in 60-62 m

Pilotage: Compulsory. British Columbia Pilot Authority. Pilot boards off Cape Beale, Barkley Sound, at S end of Vancouver Island. Master should advise 'Pilots Victoria' via radio station VAK giving their ETA at Cape Beale or Quatsino Sound

Radio Frequency: VHF Channel 6, 156.3 mHz

Maximum Vessel Dimensions: 29 500 dwt, draft 10.77 m

Working Hours: 12 h/day

Key to Principal Facilities:—			
A=Airport	**C**=Containers	**G**=General Cargo	**P**=Petroleum	**R**=Ro/Ro	**Y**=Dry Bulk
B=Bunkers	**D**=Dry Dock	**L**=Cruise	**Q**=Other Liquid Bulk	**T**=Towage (where available from port)	

Accommodation:

Name	Remarks
Port Alice	See [1] below

[1]*Port Alice:* Private port. A draft of 8.53 m can be handled alongside the dock and a vessel of 160 m in length can be berthed with safety

Bulk facilities: Bulk carriers with draft 10.67 m and 162.2 m length are berthed 4.88 m from dock by means of fender logs. Gantry for monck cranes extended over apron of dock

Tanker facilities: Oil tankers with draft of 10.67 m and 176.77 m length berth against berthing scow, positioned between dock and tanker, width of scow 10.67 m

Cargo Worked: Pulp 1500 t/day

Bunkering: Diesel oil in limited quantity: fuel oil emergency only, from gravity hose on dock. Ship must supply hose from dock to ship

Towage: Two tugs of 335 hp assist in berthing operations if required

Repair & Maintenance: Minor repairs at plant machine shop

Medical Facilities: Provincial 10 bed hospital. Physician in attendance

Airport: Port Hardy, 56 km

Lloyd's Agent: McLarens Canada (Vancouver), 505 1100 Melville Street, Vancouver, B.C., Canada V6E 4A6, *Tel:* +1 604 681 7107, *Fax:* +1 604 681 8125, *Email:* philip.vardon@mclarens.ca, *Website:* www.mclarens.ca

PORT AUX BASQUES

Lat 47° 34' N; Long 59° 7' W.

Admiralty Chart: -	**Admiralty Pilot:** 50
Time Zone: GMT -3.5 h	**UNCTAD Locode:** CA PBQ

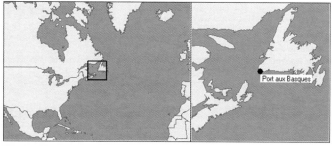

Principal Facilities:

			G		B			

Authority: Harbour Authority of Port aux Basques, P O Box 1380, Port aux Basques, NL, Canada A0M 1C0, *Tel:* +1 709 695 7975, *Fax:* +1 709 695 9485, *Email:* haportauxbasques@nf.aibn.com

Documentation: General declaration (4 copies), crew effects declaration (3 copies), ship stores declaration (3 copies), immigration crew list (3 copies), marine declaration of health (1 copy), port clearance from previous port

Approach: The best approach is from the SE where the water is deep and free from hazards

Pilotage: Not compulsory. Pilots are available by contacting Atlantic Pilotage Authority which has a 24 h centralised pilot dispatch centre in Halifax, Tel: +1 877 272 3477 (toll free) and +1 902 426 7610 (inmarsat), Fax: +1 877 745 3477 (toll free) and +1 902 426 7236 (inmarsat), Email: dispatch@atlanticpilotage.com

Radio Frequency: VHF Channel 11

Tides: Tidal range 1.6 m

Maximum Vessel Dimensions: 7036 dwt, 119 m loa

Accommodation:

Name	Length (m)	Depth (m)	Remarks
Port aux Basques			See [1] below
South Wharf	169	7.3–9.1	See [2] below
North Wharf	166	6.4	See [3] below
Marine Atlantic Ferry Terminal			
C Wharf	122	6.7	one crane available
E Wharf	192	6.4	
W Wharf		5.8	consists of a line of dolphins

[1]*Port aux Basques:* There are two Government jetties joined at the inner end, one is 52 m long with a least depth of 3.7 m and the other 90 m long with a least depth of 4.9 m along the outside. There are also several smaller berths

[2]*South Wharf:* Located on the W side of the port and operated by Marine Atlantic

[3]*North Wharf:* Located on the W side of the port and operated by Marine Atlantic

Bunkering: Fuel oil available

Waste Reception Facilities: Not available

Repair & Maintenance: Minor repairs undertaken

Medical Facilities: Hospital available

Lloyd's Agent: Hayes Stuart Inc., 297 Duke Street, Montreal, Que., Canada H3C 2M2, *Tel:* +1 514 866 1801, *Fax:* +1 514 866 1259, *Email:* montreal@hayesstuart.com, *Website:* www.hayesstuart.com

PORT CARTIER

Lat 50° 2' N; Long 66° 47' W.

Admiralty Chart: 4778	**Admiralty Pilot:** 65
Time Zone: GMT -4 h	**UNCTAD Locode:** CA PCA

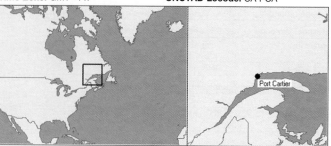

Principal Facilities:

P		Y	G			B		T	A

Authority: Quebec Cartier Mining Company, 24 Boulevard des Iles, Bureau 201, Port Cartier, Que., Canada G5B 2H3, *Tel:* +1 418 766 2000, *Fax:* +1 418 768 2344, *Email:* port@qcmines.com, *Website:* www.qcmines.com

Officials: Harbour Master: Danny Labrie, *Tel:* +1 418 766 2000 ext.2197, *Email:* labrie.danny@qcmines.com.

Port Security: ISPS compliant. Marine Facility Security Officer (MFSO): Danny LaBrie or Veronic Allard-Vermette, Tel: +1 418 766 2000 ext.2335 (24 h)
If a security incident or breach of security should occur it should be reported to the Vessel Agency or Main Gate/Security Office who shall report the incident or breach by calling the Port Authority/Harbour Master and the FSO from the Security and Emergency Contact List above. The FSO will direct any additional calls to be made from the other numbers on the list. The designated Ship Security Officer has the obligation to monitor access to the vessel. Vessel's crew members are not authorized to enter nor leave the terminal without having proper I.D. card with photograph. The personnel responsible for security surveillance can verify their identification with the crew list at their disposal

Pre-Arrival Information: Customs requires at least 96 h prior arrival, crew list and pre clearance. Information to be sent by Fax: +1 418 768 2344 or Email: port@qcmines.com

Approach: Sailing directions Canadian 'St Lawrence Pilot'. Canadian Charts 1212, 1218 and 1226. When vessels are 36 h from Port Cartier they are required to keep W/T watch on VHF (Escoumins Traffic Control). Radio for traffic from Port Cartier. W/T frequency calling 500 kHz. Cable Address: 'Cartier'
Harbour entrance 152.4 m wide with radar reflectors on both sides. Approach channel dredged to 16.61 m at LW for a width of 121.9 m; depth in harbour from entrance 15.24 m at LW

Pilotage: Compulsory. St Lawrence Pilotage District No.3. Pilots will be supplied in accordance with Compagnie Miniere Quebec Cartier pilotage conditions. All vessels should advise ETA 72, 48 and 24 h before arrival. If any change of more than one hour occurs in ETA at any time after transmission of 24 h ETA, vessel should send a corrected ETA immediately. Vessels proceeding to Port Cartier should advise tonnage of cargo required in the 72 h ETA. In the 24 h ETA the estimated time required for pumping ballast after arriving alongside should be included. Any change in ballast pumping time, for any reason should be radioed to the Port Official immediately

Radio Frequency: Port Office operates on a 24 h basis; working frequency 156.6 mHz Channel 12. Tugs and pilot working frequency 156.35 mHz Channel 7a

Tides: Rise in tide 3.35 m at springs, 2.13 m at neaps

Traffic: 400-450 vessels per year

Maximum Vessel Dimensions: 304 m loa, 53 m breadth. Vessels of 100 000 dwt and over must not have a draught exceeding 10.1 m fwd and 11.6 m aft

Principal Imports and Exports: Imports: Bentonite, Coke breeze, Dolomite, Limestone, Magnesiumeze. Exports: Iron ore, Wheat.

Working Hours: Port is in continuous operation 24 h/day, 7 days a week for iron ore operations. Grain operations are left to the sole discretion of Les Silos Port Cartier

Accommodation: Bulk facilities: Compagnie Miniere Quebec Cartier have installed ore loading equipment with a cap of 7000 t/h. Vessels accepting delivery of ore must conform in construction to port's requirements. Grain unloading berth is capable of discharging 80 000 bu/h

Tanker facilities: Facilities for oil receiving are located at Berth No's 1, 2, 3 and 4

Name	Remarks
North Wall	See [1] below
South Wall	See [2] below

[1]*North Wall:* Total berthing length of 761.9 m with 15.24 m depth alongside. Berth No.1 is the Westerly 304.8 m of the North Wall; Berth No.4 is the Easterly 457.1 m of the North Wall. Berth No's 1 and 4 are for ore loading and Berth No.5 is for discharging bentonite

[2]*South Wall:* Total berthing length of 451 m with 15.24 m depth alongside. Berth No.2 is the Westerly half of the South Wall and Berth No.3 is the Easterly half of the South Wall. Berth No.6 at extreme east end of harbour is used to receive bulk cargo from self-unloading vessels
All bollards on the N and S Walls (except those at Berth No's 2 and 6) are 1.22 m in diameter and all mooring ropes and wires should have eyes at least 2.44 m in diameter

Mechanical Handling Equipment: Stiff leg crane of 180 t cap

Bunkering: ExxonMobil Marine Fuels, Suite 900, One Alhambra Plaza, Coral Gables, FL 33134, United States of America, *Tel:* +1 305 459 6358, *Fax:* +1 305 459 6412, *Email:* emmf@exxonmobil.com, *Website:* www.exxonmobilmarinefuels.com – *Grades:* IFO30-380cSt; MDO; MGO – *Delivery Mode:* barge, pipe

Imperial Oil (Anjou) Ltd, 7100 Jean-Talon Street East, Anjou, Que., Canada H1M 3R8, *Tel:* +1 450 6497 519, *Fax:* +1 450 6497 821, *Email:* christian.beaunoyer@esso.ca, *Website:* www.imperialoil.com

Kildair Service Ltd, 92 Chemin Delangis, St. Paul de Joliette, Que., Canada J0K 3E0, *Tel:* +1 450 7568 091, *Fax:* +1 450 7564 783, *Email:* info@kildair.com, *Website:* www.kildair.com

Ultramar Canada Inc., 2200 McGill College Avenue, Montreal, Que., Canada H3A 3L3, *Tel:* +1 514 4996 111, *Fax:* +1 514 4996 320, *Email:* wholesale@ultramar.ca, *Website:* www.ultramar.ca – *Grades:* MDO – *Misc:* no coal – *Rates:* 900t/h – *Delivery Mode:* pipeline

Towage: Compulsory for vessels over 300 ft loa; otherwise at Port Official's option. Two tugs of 3800 hp are available

Repair & Maintenance: Bouchard & Blanchette Marine, 356 rue Evangeline, Seven Islands, Que., Canada G4R 2N3, *Tel:* +1 418 968 2505, *Fax:* +1 418 968 2059, *Email:* bouchard.blanchette@bbmarine.ca, *Website:* www.bbmarine.ca

Stevedoring Companies: Quebec Port Terminals Inc., 175 Boul. du Portage-des-Mousses, P O Box 38, Port Cartier, Que., Canada G5B 2G7, *Tel:* +1 418 766 5412, *Fax:* +1 418 766 0149, *Email:* info@qsl.com, *Website:* www.qsl.com

Medical Facilities: C.L.S.C. des Sept-Rivieres, Tel: +1 (418) 766 2715

Airport: Sept Iles, 65 km

Lloyd's Agent: Hayes Stuart Inc., 297 Duke Street, Montreal, Que., Canada H3C 2M2, *Tel:* +1 514 866 1801, *Fax:* +1 514 866 1259, *Email:* montreal@hayesstuart.com, *Website:* www.hayesstuart.com

PORT COLBORNE

Lat 42° 52' N; Long 79° 14' W.

Admiralty Chart: -	**Admiralty Pilot:** -
Time Zone: GMT -5 h	**UNCTAD Locode:** CA PCO

Principal Facilities:

P	Y	G		B	A	

Authority: City of Port Colborne, 66 Charlotte Street, Port Colborne, Ont., Canada L3K 3C8, *Tel:* +1 905 835 2900, *Fax:* +1 905 835 2969, *Email:* cao@city.portcolborne.on.ca, *Website:* www.city.portcolborne.on.ca

Port Security: ISPS compliant

Approach: Sailing directions: Canadian 'Great Lakes Pilot', Volume 1, Canadian Chart 2042 (Port Weller to Port Colborne). Limiting depth in the channel from Port Colborne piers to Bridge 21 and 20 is 8.23 m. From Bridge 21 and 20 north to Rameys Bend the limiting depth in the channel is 8.23 m. The Welland Canal will accommodate vessels not exceeding 222.5 m in overall length and 23.16 m in extreme breadth. Permissible draft is 7.92 m

Pilotage: Vessels over 250 gt are required to carry a pilot. Pilots are available at Port Weller (upbound) and Sarnia (downbound). Supervisor of pilots located at St Catherines

Accommodation:

Name	Length (m)	Depth (m)	Remarks
Port Colborne			See [1] below
Wharf 11	120	8.23	See [2] below
Wharf 12	547	8.23	Stone and sand (tunnel and belt conveyor)
Wharf 13	304	7.62	Grain and grain products (elevator)
Wharf 15	259	4.27	Sand (self-unloaders)
Wharf 16	451	8.2	See [3] below
Wharf 17	341	8.2	See [4] below
Wharf 18	502	8.2	See [5] below
Wharf 19	502	8.2	Grain elevator with 63 000 t cap
Wharf 20	274	4.72–5.79	See [6] below

[1]*Port Colborne:* Road and rail links to Toronto, Hamilton, Buffalo and thence all major cities
[2]*Wharf 11:* Dolphin berth. Grain discharge into hopper (ships equipment)
[3]*Wharf 16:* Stone and marine diesel oil (belt conveyor, 7"-8" pipeline). Storage cap of 27 000 t
[4]*Wharf 17:* Unloading and loading bulk cargo (ships equipment). Storage cap of 225 000 t
[5]*Wharf 18:* Marine diesel fuel, coal. Imperial Oil with storage cap of 170 000 bbls
[6]*Wharf 20:* Grain elevator of 84 000 t cap and a loading cap of 2800 t/h

Bunkering: Supplies available including bunker and diesel fuel

Repair & Maintenance: Repairs may be performed to hull and machinery above water by local firms

Fraser Marine & Industrial, 1 Chestnut Street, Port Colborne, Ont., Canada L3K 1R3, *Tel:* +1 905 8345 644, *Email:* dross@algonet.com, *Website:* www.frasermarineandindustrial.com

Medical Facilities: Port Colborne General Hospital

Airport: Buffalo Airport, 40 km

Lloyd's Agent: McLarens Canada (Toronto), 600 Alden Road, Suite 600, Markham, Toronto, Ont., Canada L3R 0E7, *Tel:* +1 905 946 9995, *Fax:* +1 905 946 0171, *Email:* roger.bickers@mclarens.ca, *Website:* www.mclarens.ca

PORT HARDY

Lat 50° 43' N; Long 127° 29' W.

Admiralty Chart: -	**Admiralty Pilot:** 25
Time Zone: GMT -8 h	**UNCTAD Locode:** CA PHY

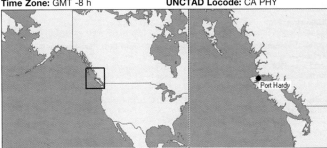

Principal Facilities:

P		G		L	B		A	

Authority: Port Hardy Harbour Authority, P O Box 68, Port Hardy, B.C., Canada V0N 2P0, *Tel:* +1 250 949 6332, *Fax:* +1 250 949 6037, *Email:* phfloats@cablerocket.com

Officials: Harbour Master: Pat McPhee.

Accommodation:

Name	Remarks
Port Hardy	See [1] below

[1]*Port Hardy:* Natural harbour. Seagate Wharf 61 m long with depths alongside ranging from 3.4 m to 7.3 m. Anchorage can be obtained approx 550 m ENE of the pier. There is a boat basin S of the pier with a depth of 3.2 m
Tanker facilities: Facilities exist for the unloading of fuel
The port is an important centre for the fishing industry and has a large cannery. The port is also now being used as a stop on the cruiseships itinerary

Bunkering: Supplies of fuel oil are available

Repair & Maintenance: Minor repairs can be undertaken

Medical Facilities: Hospital in the town

Airport: Port Hardy Airport

Lloyd's Agent: McLarens Canada (Vancouver), 505 1100 Melville Street, Vancouver, B.C., Canada V6E 4A6, *Tel:* +1 604 681 7107, *Fax:* +1 604 681 8125, *Email:* philip.vardon@mclarens.ca, *Website:* www.mclarens.ca

PORT HARMON

alternate name, see Stephenville

PORT HAWKESBURY

Lat 45° 36' N; Long 61° 21' W.

Admiralty Chart: 4758	**Admiralty Pilot:** 65
Time Zone: GMT -4 h	**UNCTAD Locode:** CA PHW

Principal Facilities:

P		Y	G			B		

Authority: Strait of Canso Superport Corp. Ltd, P O Box 238, Mulgrave, N.S., Canada B0E 2G0, *Tel:* +1 902 747 2078, *Fax:* +1 902 747 2453, *Email:* timgilfoy@straitsuperport.com, *Website:* www.straitsuperport.com

Officials: Chief Executive Officer: Tim Gilfoy, *Email:* timgilfoy@straitsuperport.com. Operations: Ralph Hadley, *Email:* ralphhadley@straitsuperport.com.

Key to Principal Facilities:—			
A=Airport	**C**=Containers	**G**=General Cargo	**P**=Petroleum	**R**=Ro/Ro	**Y**=Dry Bulk
B=Bunkers	**D**=Dry Dock	**L**=Cruise	**Q**=Other Liquid Bulk	**T**=Towage (where available from port)

Port Security: ISPS compliant

Approach: Approach channel 800 m wide in depth of 12.2 m

Pilotage: Compulsory

Radio Frequency: VHF Channel 16

Accommodation:

Name	Length (m)	Depth (m)	Remarks
Port Hawkesbury Government Wharf	146	6.7	See [1] below With an 'L' end 31.1 m in length

[1]*Port Hawkesbury:* There is good anchorage, sheltered from NW winds in 10.7-13.7 m off the mouth of Venue Cove
The roadstead off the mouth of Ship Harbour, outside Premier Shoal, has depths of 12.2-18.3 m. Sand, gravel and mud bottom. Except near the head of the harbour, there is secure anchorage for small vessels in 6.1 m of water. Mud bottom. The port is open to NNW winds which frequently blow directly through the Strait and cause a heavy short sea

Bunkering: Statia Terminals Inc., Suite 295, 800 Fairway Drive, Deerfield Beach, FL 33441, United States of America, *Tel:* +1 954 698 0705, *Fax:* +1 954 698 0706

Repair & Maintenance: Breton Industry & Marine Ltd, Port Hawkesbury, N.S., Canada
Port Hawkesbury Marine Railway Co., Port Hawkesbury, N.S., Canada Operates two cradles near Point Tupper. The larger cradle is 51.8 m long and 11.6 m wide inside uprights with a max lift of 800 t. Hull and machinery repairs can be undertaken

Shipping Agents: F.K. Warren Ltd, 20 Mackintosh Street, Port Hawkesbury, N.S., Canada B9A 3K5, *Tel:* +1 902 625 2823, *Fax:* +1 902 625 3940, *Email:* ops@pth.fkwarren.ca, *Website:* www.fkwarren.ca

Railway: The Cape Breton and Central Nova Scotia Railway

Lloyd's Agent: Hayes Stuart Inc., 1000 Windmill Road, Suite 19, Dartmouth, N.S., Canada B3B 1L7, *Tel:* +1 902 468 2651, *Fax:* +1 902 468 4315, *Email:* halifax@hayesstuart.com, *Website:* www.hayesstuart.com

PORT MELLON

Lat 49° 31' N; Long 123° 29' W.

Admiralty Chart: -	**Admiralty Pilot:** 25
Time Zone: GMT -8 h	**UNCTAD Locode:** CA PML

Principal Facilities:

		Y	G					T	A	

Authority: Howe Sound Pulp & Paper Ltd Partnership, General Delivery, Port Mellon, B.C., Canada V0N 2S0, *Tel:* +1 604 884 5223, *Fax:* +1 604 884 2170, *Email:* hsppcomments@hspp.ca, *Website:* www.hspp.ca

Officials: President: Mac Palmiere, *Email:* mac.palmiere@hspp.ca.
Harbour Master: Bob Crosby, *Email:* bob.crosby@hspp.ca.

Port Security: ISPS compliant

Approach: Depth in channel is 9.8 m at LW

Pilotage: Compulsory. Pilots board off Victoria or from last British Columbia port

Tides: Range of tide 4.9 m ST, 3.4 m NT

Maximum Vessel Dimensions: 45 295 dwt, 201.6 m loa

Principal Imports and Exports: Exports: Newsprint, Woodpulp.

Working Hours: Mon-Fri 0745-2330. Limited weekend coverage

Accommodation:

Name	Length (m)	Depth (m)	Remarks
Port Mellon			Private port. Various bulk cargoes can be handled
Main Wharf	190	10.1	See [1] below
Private Wharves			H.S.L.P. is a private wharf

[1]*Main Wharf:* Vessels are loaded and discharged by ship's own gear

Towage: Squamish tugs, Seaspan or Rivtow provide berthing assistance

Repair & Maintenance: Minor repairs can be effected by the company machine shops

Medical Facilities: First aid facilities on site. Hospital within 30 km

Airport: Vancouver International Airport, 60 km

Lloyd's Agent: McLarens Canada (Vancouver), 505 1100 Melville Street, Vancouver, B.C., Canada V6E 4A6, *Tel:* +1 604 681 7107, *Fax:* +1 604 681 8125, *Email:* philip.vardon@mclarens.ca, *Website:* www.mclarens.ca

PORT MOODY

harbour area, see under Vancouver

PORT SAGUENAY

harbour area, see under Port Alfred

PORT WELLER

Lat 43° 13' N; Long 79° 12' W.

Admiralty Chart: -	**Admiralty Pilot:** -
Time Zone: GMT -5 h	**UNCTAD Locode:** CA PWE

Principal Facilities:

		Y	G			B	D	T	

Authority: St. Lawrence Seaway Management Corp., 508 Glendale Avenue, P O Box 370, St. Catharines, Ont., Canada L2R 6V8, *Tel:* +1 905 641 1932, *Fax:* +1 905 641 5721, *Email:* bhodgson@seaway.ca, *Website:* www.greatlakes-seaway.com

Officials: Marketing Director: Bruce Hodgson, *Tel:* +1 905 641 1932 Ext.5436.

Approach: Sailing directions: Canadian 'Great Lakes Pilot', Vol 1. Canadian chart 2042 (Port Weller to Port Colborne). Channel depth: limiting depth at entrance and through the Welland Ship Canal is 8.23 m. Permissible draft is 8.0 m. The locks will accommodate vessels not exceeding 222.5 m in overall length and 23.16 m in extreme breadth

Pilotage: Master of vessels requiring pilotage service in the Port Weller-Sarnia area should send a notice of their arrival by radio-telephone so as to avoid any delay in waiting for a pilot. When westbound, master should order a pilot 4 h in advance of the ETA at Port Weller through Prescott (VBR) radio. When eastbound, masters should order a pilot 4 h in advance of their ETA at Lake Huron Lt Buoys or Rogers City. Both an accommodation ladder and a Jacob's ladder are required to assist pilots boarding vessels at Port Weller

Radio Frequency: Traffic control Seaway Welland on VHF Channel 14

Accommodation: The harbour consists of two embankments projecting out into Lake Ontario and forming the entrance to the Canal and Lock No.1
A section of the west entrance wall, 392.6 m long and 8.23 m deep which is used for sand storage. The southerly embankment is 103 6 m and used by Fourum Transport Ltd. The northerly is 135.6 m long and used by Seaway Terminal Co. The remaining 153.4 m is not in use for cargo handling purposes. Part of the East Harbour is leased to McKeil Work Boats Ltd
All vessels entering the Welland Canal from Lake Ontario, or vessels from Lake Erie to Lake Ontario, via the Canal, use this port but no steamship line makes it a regular port of call for discharging or loading freight. The highway connects with St Catharines which is 5.5 km away

Name	Length (m)	Depth (m)	Remarks
Port Weller Harbour E Berth No.1	194	8.23	See [1] below
Port Weller Harbour W Berth No.1	392	8.23	Coal, sand, zircon ore, bulk sugar (self-unloaders only)

[1]*Berth No.1:* Various and sundry partial cargoes (self-unloaders or rented cranes)

Bunkering: Provmar Fuels Inc., Station C, P O Box 3355, Hamilton, Ont., Canada L8H 7L4, *Tel:* +1 905 5499 402, *Fax:* +1 905 5499 929, *Email:* inquiries@provmar.com, *Website:* www.provmar.com – *Delivery Mode:* barge, truck

Waste Reception Facilities: Ballast water controls in effect. Garbage removal available. Mobile reception facilities available for slops

Towage: McKeil Marine Ltd, 208 Hillyard Street, Hamilton, Ont., Canada L8L 6B6, *Tel:* +1 905 528 4780, *Fax:* +1 905 528 6144, *Email:* info@mckeil.com, *Website:* www.mckeilmarine.com

Repair & Maintenance: Seaway Marine & Industrial Inc., 340 Lakeshore Road East, St. Catharines, Ont., Canada L2M 0A2, *Tel:* +1 905 934 7759, *Fax:* +1 905 934 5588, *Website:* www.seamind.ca Graving dock 228.6 m long, 24.38 m wide, depth over sill 9.15 m. There is also a fitting out berth 365.8 m long

Medical Facilities: General Hospital and Hotel Dieu at St Catharines

Lloyd's Agent: McLarens Canada (Toronto), 600 Alden Road, Suite 600, Markham, Toronto, Ont., Canada L3R 0E7, *Tel:* +1 905 946 9995, *Fax:* +1 905 946 0171, *Email:* roger.bickers@mclarens.ca, *Website:* www.mclarens.ca

POWELL RIVER

Lat 49° 52' N; Long 124° 33' W.

Admiralty Chart: -
Admiralty Pilot: 25
Time Zone: GMT -8 h
UNCTAD Locode: CA POW

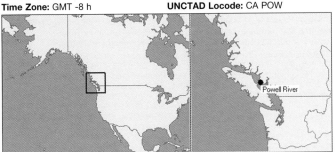

Principal Facilities:

P	Q		G			B		T	A	

Authority: District of Powell River Municipal Wharfinger, West View Harbour, 6910 Duncan Street, Powell River, B.C., Canada V8A 1V4, *Tel:* +1 604 485 5244, *Fax:* +1 604 485 5286, *Email:* jparsons@cdpr.bc.ca

Approach: All vessels docking are notified in advance by radio on 2366 kHz to which berth they may proceed. Breakwaters shelter some of the berths and prevent silting from the river. Channel depth 9.1-10.7 m LW

Anchorage: Anchorage may be obtained SW of the wharves but is exposed to westerly winds. No anchoring allowed by submerged pipeline, running 823 m out from SW corner of the mill. The pipeline is clearly marked on shore

Pilotage: Compulsory. Pilots board at Victoria or Vancouver. Pacific Pilotage Authority

Radio Frequency: Norske Skog Canada Ltd. maintain a 24 h watch on VHF Channel 10, call sign VJK 76

Maximum Vessel Dimensions: 43 082 dwt, 199.4 m loa, 10.3 m d

Working Hours: 0800-2400. Oil carriers 24 h, berthing and unberthing 24 h

Accommodation:

Name	Length (m)	Depth (m)	Remarks
Powell River			See [1] below
Pier A		9	See [2] below
Pier D (Shore Quay)	179	7.6	Used for the barge loading of pulp and paper products
Government Tanker Wharf (Westview)	83	9.4	See [3] below

[1]*Powell River:* Facilities to serve the paper mills, pulp mills and sawmills of Norske Skog Canada Ltd., 6270 Yew Street, Powell River BC V8A 4Z7, Tel: +1 604 483 3722
[2]*Pier A:* Two berths each 148.2 m long (only one berth is fully operational). It is used for the shipment of newsprint and pulp. SE winds may cause difficulties when docking and undocking on Berth 1 but tugs are available to assist
[3]*Government Tanker Wharf (Westview):* Operated by the District of Powell River. One oil company has pipelines from the wharf to storage tanks ashore. There are facilities to offload and store liquid propane. Fresh water from mains on wharf. There is a public barge loading wharf 4 km S of the tanker wharf which has a movable ramp with a 50 t cap; warehousing available. Close to the tanker wharf is a shelter for small craft which has been constructed by rock breakwaters. Another harbour for small craft, also protected by rock breakwaters is situated N of the tanker wharf

Bunkering: Diesel oil and gasoline available at Westview

Towage: Catalyst Paper Corp., 16th Floor, 250 Howe Street, Vancouver, B.C., Canada V6C 3R8, *Tel:* +1 604 654 4000, *Fax:* +1 604 654 4048, *Email:* contactus@catalystpaper.com, *Website:* www.catalystpaper.com
Westview Navigation Ltd, 3515 Marine Avenue, Powell River, B.C., Canada V8A 2H5, *Tel:* +1 604 485 5051

Repair & Maintenance: Underwater inspection and repair can be carried out by local divers. Other hull, engine, electrical and electronic repairs can be done by local firms. Minor repairs arranged with Norske Skog Canada Ltd. There are also facilities available for the repair of small craft including a marine railway

Medical Facilities: General hospital and medical clinic

Airport: 15 km from port

Lloyd's Agent: McLarens Canada (Vancouver), 505 1100 Melville Street, Vancouver, B.C., Canada V6E 4A6, *Tel:* +1 604 681 7107, *Fax:* +1 604 681 8125, *Email:* philip.vardon@mclarens.ca, *Website:* www.mclarens.ca

POWELL WHARF

harbour area, see under Port Alfred

PRESCOTT

Lat 44° 42' N; Long 75° 31' W.

Admiralty Chart: 4793
Admiralty Pilot: 65
Time Zone: GMT -5 h
UNCTAD Locode: CA PRE

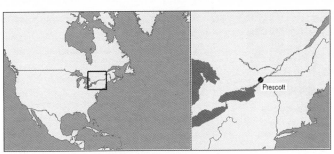

Principal Facilities:

		Y	G					T	A	

Authority: Port of Prescott, P O Box 520, Prescott, Ont., Canada K0E 1TO, *Tel:* +1 613 925 4228, *Fax:* +1 613 925 5022, *Email:* generalinfo@portofprescott.com, *Website:* www.portofprescott.com

Officials: General Manager: Bob Hennessy.

Port Security: ISPS compliant

Pilotage: Available with 4 h notice

Traffic: 2005, 436 884 t of cargo handled

Accommodation:

Name	Draught (m)	Remarks
Prescott		See [1] below
Loading Slip 'A'	8.23	See [2] below
Unloading Slip 'B'	8.23	See [3] below

[1]*Prescott:* The port has a land area of approx 35 ha of which 17 ha are occupied by commercial port and grain activities
Grain elevator has a storage cap of 5 600 000 bu with unloading rate of 2750 t/h and loading rate of 1800 t/h
[2]*Loading Slip 'A':* River front dock length of 144 m, port dock length of 183 m and grain elevator dock 'A' length of 282 m
[3]*Unloading Slip 'B':* Harbour front dock length of 442 m and grain elevator dock length of 399 m

Towage: North Channel Marine, Prescott, Ont., Canada, *Tel:* +1 613 925 2817

Repair & Maintenance: Prescott Machine and Welding Ltd, County Road 2, Prescott, Ont., Canada, *Tel:* +1 613 925 4277, *Fax:* +1 613 925 1256

Medical Facilities: Nearest hospital at Brockville, Ontario. Ambulance service at Prescott

Airport: Ottawa International Airport, 90 km

Railway: Served by Canadian Pacific and Canadian National Railways

Lloyd's Agent: McLarens Canada (Toronto), 600 Alden Road, Suite 600, Markham, Toronto, Ont., Canada L3R 0E7, *Tel:* +1 905 946 9995, *Fax:* +1 905 946 0171, *Email:* roger.bickers@mclarens.ca, *Website:* www.mclarens.ca

PRINCE RUPERT

Lat 54° 19' N; Long 130° 22' W.

Admiralty Chart: 4935/4936/4937
Admiralty Pilot: 26
Time Zone: GMT -8 h
UNCTAD Locode: CA PRR

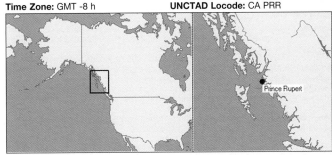

Principal Facilities:

P	Q	Y	G		R	L	B		T	A	

Authority: Prince Rupert Port Authority, 200-215 Cow Bay Road, Prince Rupert, B.C., Canada V8J 1A2, *Tel:* +1 250 627 8899, *Fax:* +1 250 627 8980, *Email:* pcorp@rupertport.com, *Website:* www.rupertport.com

Officials: Chief Executive Officer: Don H. Krusel, *Email:* dkrusel@rupertport.com. Manager: Barry Bartlett, *Tel:* +250 627 2509, *Mobile Tel:* +250 627 9693, *Email:* bbartlett@rupertport.com. Harbour Master: Gary Paulson, *Email:* gpaulson@rupertport.com

Port Security: ISPS compliant

Approach: Entry is from the S between Digby and Kaien Islands. Controlling depths in approach channel 35.0 m

Anchorage: Available within harbour limits in depths of 36.6 m LW and allocated by the Harbour Master. Additional anchorages outside harbour limits in the vicinity of Prescott, Stephens and Lucy Islands

Pilotage: Compulsory. 48 h notice required. Pacific Pilotage Authority. Pilot boards vessels at Triple Island, Tree Knob group, Brown passage, 41.6 km from port. VTS system in operation on VHF Channel 71, compulsory for vessels of 20 m loa and over within harbour limits

Key to Principal Facilities:—				
A=Airport	**C**=Containers	**G**=General Cargo	**P**=Petroleum	**R**=Ro/Ro	**Y**=Dry Bulk
B=Bunkers	**D**=Dry Dock	**L**=Cruise	**Q**=Other Liquid Bulk	**T**=Towage (where available from port)	

Radio Frequency: Prince Rupert Marine Communications and Vessel Traffic Services operate on VHF Channels 11 and 71. Prince Rupert Coast Guard Radio on VHF Channel 16

Weather: Prince Rupert harbour is subject to violent gusts of wind from the mountain slopes during SE gales, which are prevalent during the autumn and winter months. The harbour is ice-free year round

Tides: Range of tide 7.7 m ST, 4.9 m NT

Traffic: 2007, 10 600 000 t of cargo handled

Maximum Vessel Dimensions: 250 000 dwt

Principal Imports and Exports: Imports: Slack wax. Exports: Barley, Coal, Grain by-products, Lumber, Pulp, Wheat.

Working Hours: Continuous if required

Accommodation: Large, deep and sheltered harbour; easy access and well lighted; can be entered at all times and at all seasons. Entrance 457 m wide, 40-44 m deep

Name	Length (m)	Depth (m)	Draught (m)	Remarks
Prince Rupert (Inner Harbour)				
Fairview Container Terminal	400	16		See [1] below
Atlin Dock	100			See [2] below
Northland Dock	340			See [3] below
Westview Terminal	309		12.2	See [4] below
Ocean Dock	151		7.3	See [5] below
Ridley Island				
Grain Export Terminal		14.5		See [6] below
Coal Terminal			22	See [7] below

[1]*Fairview Container Terminal:* Operated by Maher Terminals of Canada Corp., Scott Road, Off Of Highway 16 West, Prince Rupert, Tel: +1 250 624 2124, Fax: +1 250 624 2323, Website: www.mahercanada.com

[2]*Atlin Dock:* Min depth of 5 m for vessels up to 7500 gt. Cruise terminal with visitor reception centre, retail and office space, a passenger exchange area and customs clearance area

[3]*Northland Dock:* Cruise berth consisting of eight mooring and breasting dolphins and a 40 m floating dock for passenger handling operations. Min depth of 14 m for vessels up to 300 m loa and 100 000 dwt

[4]*Westview Terminal:* Owned by the Prince Rupert Port Authority. 6 ha site presently leased for seasonal commercial fishing operations

[5]*Ocean Dock:* Restricted to vessels of 15 m loa or 5000 t displacement

[6]*Grain Export Terminal:* Operated by Prince Rupert Grain Ltd., 200 Cow Bay Road, Prince Rupert BC V8J 1A2, Tel: +1 250 627 8777, Fax: +1 250 627 8541
One berth for vessels up to 145 000 dwt. Storage cap of 202 000 t. 17 km of terminal rail trackage. Eight shipping bins and three tower-mounted loading spouts can load wheat or barley at rate of up to 4000 t/h

[7]*Coal Terminal:* Operated by Ridley Terminals Inc., P O Box 8000, Prince Rupert BC V8J 4H3, Tel: +1 250 624 9511, Fax: +1 250 624 4990, Website: www.rti.ca
Dolphin type berth with berthing dolphins of 150 m and mooring dolphins of 370 m for vessels up to 250 000 dwt, 325 m loa, 50 m beam and 22 m draft. The terminal is equipped with two quadrant slewing shiploaders with a loading rate of 4500 t/h cap each. On-site storage cap of 1 200 000 t

Mechanical Handling Equipment:

Location	Type	Capacity (t)	Qty	Remarks
Prince Rupert	Floating Cranes	50	1	
Prince Rupert	Mobile Cranes	60	3	See [1] below
Fairview Container Terminal	Super Post Panamax		3	

[1]*Prince Rupert:* Owned by Skeena Cranes Ltd

Bunkering: Various oil companies have small berths in the port. There are plans for a fuelling station to be located at Fairview Terminal. Contact Port Authority
ICS Petroleum, ICS Petroleum Ltd., P O Box 12115, Suite 2360, 555 West Hastings Street, Vancouver, B.C., Canada V6B 4N6, Tel: +1 604 6856 221, Fax: +1 604 6857 352, Email: bunkers@ics-vcr.com, Website: www.icspet.com – Grades: MGO; HFO – Notice: must be well in advance – Delivery Mode: barge, truck

Waste Reception Facilities: Garbage is removed on request and only after permission granted by Environment Canada. Garbage is placed in dumpsters and removed by a private contractor. At present there are no facilities to handle international garbage

Towage: Private tugs, boatmen and linesmen are available for berthing assistance

Repair & Maintenance: Minor repairs can be effected to hull and machinery. McLean slipway and boatbuilding works can haul out and repair small boats

Shipping Agents: Montship Inc., 120 Gull Crescent, Prince Rupert, B.C., Canada V8J 4G5, Tel: +1 250 624 9668, Fax: +1 250 624 6783, Email: norship@citytel.net
G.W. Nickerson, 30 342-3rd Avenue West, Prince Rupert, B.C., Canada V8J 3P4, Tel: +1 250 624 5233, Fax: +1 250 624 5855, Email: operations@nicson.biz
Rupert Marine Shipping, 239 4th Avenue East, Prince Rupert, B.C., Canada V8J 1N4, Tel: +1 250 624 5339, Fax: +1 250 624 4329, Email: shipping@citytel.net
T.N.C. Agencies Canada Ltd, 1617 2nd Avenue West, Prince Rupert, B.C., Canada V8J 1J5, Tel: +1 250 624 4447, Fax: +1 250 632 4460, Email: princerupert@transmarine.com, Website: www.transmarine.com

Stevedoring Companies: Canadian Stevedoring Co. Ltd, Prince Rupert, B.C., Canada, Tel: +1 250 624 5243, Fax: +1 250 627 1868

Surveyors: IMS Marine Surveyors Ltd, Suite 223, 3823 Henning Drive, Burnaby, B.C., Canada V5C 6P3, Tel: +1 604 298 9968, Fax: +1 604 298 4862, Email: office@ims-van.com, Website: www.ims-van.com
Quality Marine Surveyors Ltd, P O Box 1105, Prince Rupert, B.C., Canada V8J 4H6, Tel: +1 250 624 4138, Fax: +1 250 627 4238, Email: quality@citytel.net
Societe Generale de Surveillance (SGS), SGS Canada Inc., P O Box 1082, Prince Rupert, B.C., Canada V8J 4H6, Tel: +1 250 624 9745, Fax: +1 250 627 8437, Email: princer@sgs.ca, Website: www.sgs.com

Medical Facilities: Full facilities available at Prince Rupert Regional Hospital, Tel: +1 (250) 624 2171

Airport: Digby Is., 4 km

Railway: Located at the terminus of the Canadian National Railway's northern line

Development: Expansion of the Fairview Container Terminal to a 2 million TEU handling capability is scheduled for completion by 2010

Lloyd's Agent: McLarens Canada (Vancouver), 505 1100 Melville Street, Vancouver, B.C., Canada V6E 4A6, Tel: +1 604 681 7107, Fax: +1 604 681 8125, Email: philip.vardon@mclarens.ca, Website: www.mclarens.ca

PUGSLEY TERMINAL

harbour area, see under Saint John

QUEBEC

Lat 46° 49' N; Long 71° 12' W.

Admiralty Chart: 4785/4786
Admiralty Pilot: 65
Time Zone: GMT -5 h
UNCTAD Locode: CA QUE

Principal Facilities:

P	Q	Y	G	C	R	L	B	D	T	A

Authority: Quebec Port Authority, 150 Dalhousie Street, P O Box 80, Station Haute-Ville, Quebec, Que., Canada G1R 4M8, Tel: +1 418 648 4956, Fax: +1 418 648 4160, Email: marketing@portquebec.ca, Website: www.portquebec.ca

Officials: Chief Executive Officer: Ross Gaudreault, Email: ross.gaudreault@portquebec.ca.
Marketing Manager: Patrick Robitaille, Email: patrick.robitaille@portquebec.ca.
Harbour Master: Michel Petit, Email: michel.petit@portquebec.ca.
Administrative Assistant: Josianne Miclette.

Port Security: ISPS compliant

Approach: Approach channel of the Traverses, 50 km below Quebec has a depth of 12.2 m LW plus 4.5 m average tide. The 200 ha Port and Industrial Area is accessible throughout the year

Anchorage: Anchorage in harbour prohibited without permission of Harbour Master

Pilotage: Compulsory from Les Escoumins and upstream. Vessels are required to send notice to the Montreal pilot station 24 h before ETA at Les Escoumins if their point of origin is E of the Strait of Belle-Isle or Cabot Strait. A second notice must be given 12 h before ETA and final confirmation 6 h prior to arrival. Pilot vessels at the Les Escoumins station maintain a continuous listening watch on VHF Channel 9
Laurentian Pilotage Authority, PO Box 247, Quebec, G1K 7M6, Tel: +1 418 648 3556, Fax: +1 418 649 6414

Radio Frequency: Harbour Master on VHF Channel 77

Weather: Prevailing winds W, force 3-4. Ice in the river from December 15 to the end of March

Tides: Spring rise 6.4 m, neaps 3.2 m

Traffic: 2007, 26 800 000 t of cargo handled

Maximum Vessel Dimensions: 16.7 m draft for refinery terminal and 15 m draft for other terminals

Principal Imports and Exports: Imports: Alumina, Chemicals, Coke, Fertilizers, Grain, Iron ore, Nickel, Oil, Sugar. Exports: Grain, Iron ore, Jet fuel, Mill scale, Newsprint, Zinc.

Working Hours: 0800-1600 (rest 1200-1300), 1600-2400 (rest 2000-2100), 0000-0800 (rest 0400-0500)

Accommodation: Bulk facilities: Four bridge towers cap 3100 t/h and one SA conveyor belt ship loader and travelling stacker of 2500 t/h spread along 850 m of quayage with depths from 12.2 m to 15 m at LW
Tanker facilities: Five public berths with depths from 11.3 m to 15 m. Public liquid terminal operated by IMTT-Quebec with a storage cap of 202 000 m3

Name	Length (m)	Depth (m)	Remarks
Vieux-Port (Public)			
Berth No.4	240	3.8–5.4	Tourist vessels
Berth No.5	180	5.1–5.6	Tourist vessels
Berth No.14	178	7	Port Services
Berth No.17	210	7.5	Coast Guard
Mole V	72	3.3–4.8	Tourist vessels
Tanguay		3.3–4.8	Tourist vessels
Renaud 2		3.3–4.8	Tourist vessels
Renaud 1		3.3–4.8	Tourist vessels
Noad		3.3–4.8	Tourist vessels
Buteau	92	3.3–4.8	Tourist vessels
Marques	69	2.8–4.3	Tourist vessels
Berth No.19	192	8	Harbour cruises
Berth No.20	342	7.5	Repair & wintering
Estuaire (Public)			
Berth No.18	240.8	11	Grain unloading
Berth No.21	206	11.7	Passengers & visiting vessels
Berth No.22	325	10.7	Passengers & visiting vessels. Cruise terminal
Berth No.24	167.6	10	Not in use
Berth No.25	222.5	10.7	General cargo
Berth No.26	240.8	11	General cargo
Berth No.27	293.2	12	Ro/ro & general cargo
Berth No.28	277.4	12	Grain loading
Berth No.29	304.8	11.3	Grain unloading
Berth No.30	224	10	General cargo
Berth No.31	224	8	General cargo
Beauport (Public)			
Berth No.50	300	12	Liquid & solid bulk
Berth No.51	235	12.5	Solid & liquid bulk
Berth No.52	260	12.5	Solid & liquid bulk
Berth No.53	325	15.5	Solid & liquid bulk
Anse-au-Foulon (Public)			
Berth No.101	198.1	11.3	General cargo
Berth No.102	134.1	11.3	General cargo & solid bulk
Berth No.103	210.9	12	General cargo & solid bulk
Berth No.104	210.9	10.3	General cargo
Berth No.105	195.4	11.3	General cargo & solid bulk
Berth No.106	195.4	11.3	General cargo & solid bulk
Berth No.107	173.1	11.3	Liquid & solid bulk
Berth No.108	180.1	11.3	Liquid & solid bulk
Davie Industries Inc (Private)			
Berth No.70	152.2	7.9	Lay-by berth/Shipyard
Berth No.71	121.9	7.6	Lay-by berth/Shipyard
Berth No.72	106.6	7	Outfitting wharf/Shipyard
Berth No.73	164	8.3	Outfitting wharf/Shipyard
Berth No.74	141	4	Outfitting wharf/Shipyard
Berth No.75	168.8	6	Floating dry dock/Shipyard
Berth No.76	182.8	5.3	Lay-by berth/Shipyard
Berth No.77	169.9	5.8	Lay-by berth/Shipyard
Societe Des Traversiers (Private)			
Berth No.82	96	7.1	Ferry terminal
Berth No.92	140	6.1	Ferry terminal
Ville de Quebec (Private)			
Berth No.91	140	5	Excursion boats
Ultramar (Private)			Refinery (private)
Berth No.86	295	10.6	Loading petroleum products
Berth No.87	335	16.7	Unloading crude oil
Daishowa Paper (Private)			Stadacona paper (private)
Berth No.46	210	6.7	Forest products
Berth No.47	205	6.7	Forest products
Canadian Coast Guard (Private)			
Berth No.93	96.9	10.2	
Berth No.94	98.2	10.2	
Berth No.95	99.7	10.2	Service boats & cruise ships
Berth No.96	73.5	10.2	
Berth No.97	135.9	10.4	
Berth No.98	57.9	10.4	

Bunkering: Shell Canada Products Ltd, 130 Rue Dalhousie, 1st Stage, Quebec, Que., Canada G1K 7P6, *Email:* pierre.fortin@shell.com, *Website:* www.shell.ca
Shell Canada Products Ltd, 130 Rue Dalhousie, 1st Stage, Quebec, Que., Canada G1K 7P6, *Email:* pierre.fortin@shell.com, *Website:* www.shell.ca

Waste Reception Facilities: Available on request. Contact Harbour Master

Towage: Le Groupe Ocean Inc., Suite 510, 105 Rue Abraham-Martin, P O Box 1963, Quebec, Que., Canada G1K 7M1, *Tel:* +1 418 694 1414, *Fax:* +1 418 692 4572, *Email:* info@groupocean.com

Repair & Maintenance: Chantier Maritime Montmagny Inc, 19 Avenue des Canotiers, Montmagny, Quebec, Que., Canada G5V 2B9, *Tel:* +1 418 248 7977, *Fax:* +1 418 248 7466
Davie Yards Inc, 22 George-D.-Davie Street, Levis, Que., Canada G6V 8V5, *Tel:* +1 418 837 5841, *Fax:* +1 418 835 1017, *Email:* marketing@davie.ca, *Website:* www.davie.ca Two dry docks and repair quays of 2000 m with max draught 9.15 m at low tide
Verrault Navigation Inc., Quebec, Que., Canada, *Tel:* +1 418 729 3733, *Fax:* +1 418 729 3285, *Email:* verronav@quebectel.com, *Website:* www.groupeverreault.com One dry dock of 252 m x 26 m and one floating dock of 36.5 m x 17.5 m

Shipping Agents: Lower St Lawrence Ocean Agencies Ltd, Station B, P O Box 248, Quebec, Que., Canada G1K 7A6, *Tel:* +1 418 692 2850, *Fax:* +1 418 692 2854, *Email:* lolaqbc@lola.ca, *Website:* www.lola.ca
Ramsay Greig & Co. Ltd, 2 Rue Nouvelle-France, Station B, P O Box 40, Quebec, Que., Canada G1K 7A2, *Tel:* +1 418 525 8171, *Fax:* +1 418 525 9940, *Email:* quebec.ops@ramsey-greig.com, *Website:* www3.logistec.com

Stevedoring Companies: Logistec Stevedoring Inc., 2 Nouvelle France, Quebec, Que., Canada G1K 8P7, *Tel:* +1 418 522 7161, *Fax:* +1 418 525 9940, *Email:* fvannell@logistec.com, *Website:* www.logistec.com
Quebec Stevedoring Co. Ltd, 961 Boulevard Champlain, P O Box 1502, Quebec, Que., Canada G1K 7H6, *Tel:* +1 418 522 4701, *Fax:* +1 418 522 2695, *Email:* info@qsl.com, *Website:* www.qsl.com
St. Lawrence Stevedoring, Quai 51, P O Box 1525, Quebec, Que., Canada G1K 7H6, *Tel:* +1 418 661 8477, *Fax:* +1 418 661 5074, *Email:* info@qsl.com, *Website:* www.qsl.com

Surveyors: Bureau Veritas, Bureau Veritas (Canada) Inc, 1561 du Tertre, Quebec, Que., Canada G1W 4N7, *Tel:* +1 418 650 0076, *Fax:* +1 418 650 0180, *Email:* michel.dionne@ca.bureauveritas.com, *Website:* www.bureauveritas.com

Medical Facilities: Hospital, 2 km

Airport: Quebec, 20 km

Railway: Canadian National Railway and Canadian Pacific to all terminals

Lloyd's Agent: Hayes Stuart Inc., 297 Duke Street, Montreal, Que., Canada H3C 2M2, *Tel:* +1 514 866 1801, *Fax:* +1 514 866 1259, *Email:* montreal@hayesstuart.com, *Website:* www.hayesstuart.com

RACINE TERMINAL

harbour area, see under Montreal

RICHELIEU RIVER

harbour area, see under Sorel

RIDLEY ISLAND

harbour area, see under Prince Rupert

RIMOUSKI

Lat 48° 28' N; Long 68° 30' W.

Admiralty Chart: 4777		**Admiralty Pilot:** 65	
Time Zone: GMT -5 h		**UNCTAD Locode:** CA RIM	

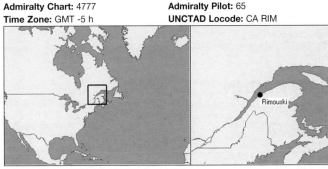

Principal Facilities:

P		G			B		A

Authority: Transport Canada, P O Box 493, Rimouski, Que., Canada G5L 7C5, *Tel:* +1 418 722 3011, *Fax:* +1 418 722 3007, *Email:* caronm@tc.gc.ca, *Website:* www.tc.gc.ca

Officials: Harbour Master: Michel Caron.

Port Security: ISPS compliant

Pre-Arrival Information: 48 h advance notice required before date of arrival at dock

Approach: A dredged channel leads in from deep water to the wharf with a least depth of 4.3 m in the channel and 5.6 m at berthage section 3-4 and 5

Anchorage: Anchorage in Rimouski Roads off the wharf and E end of Barnabe Island

Pilotage: Not compulsory but pilots available. St Lawrence Pilotage District No.3

Traffic: 2006, 71 vessels, 230 000 t of cargo handled

Key to Principal Facilities:—			
A=Airport	**C**=Containers	**G**=General Cargo	
B=Bunkers	**D**=Dry Dock	**L**=Cruise	
P=Petroleum	**R**=Ro/Ro	**Y**=Dry Bulk	
Q=Other Liquid Bulk	**T**=Towage (where available from port)		

Working Hours: Mon to Fri 0800-1700. Overtime as required. Holidays and weekends on notice only

Accommodation:

Name	Length (m)	Draught (m)	Remarks
Rimouski			Petroleum & general cargo handled
Berth No.1	210	7.3	
Berth No.3	125	7.3	
Berth No.4	150	7.3	
Berth No.5	150	7.3	
Berth No.6	113	4.3	
Berth No.7	255	4.3	
Berth No.8	30	3.5	

Storage:

Location	Open (m²)	Covered (m²)
Rimouski	30000	209

Mechanical Handling Equipment:

Location	Type	Capacity (t)	Qty
Rimouski	Mult-purp. Cranes	50	1

Bunkering: Diesel and gas lines available

Towage: Not available

Repair & Maintenance: Only minor repairs can be made

Stevedoring Companies: Quebec Port Terminals Inc., Rue du Quai, Rimouski, Que., Canada, *Tel:* +1 418 723 6897, *Email:* info@qsl.com, *Website:* www.qsl.com

Medical Facilities: Hospital in Rimouski

Airport: Rimouski Airport, 0.5 mile. Mont Joli Regional Airport, approx 20 miles

Railway: Via Rail Canada

Lloyd's Agent: Hayes Stuart Inc., 297 Duke Street, Montreal, Que., Canada H3C 2M2, *Tel:* +1 514 866 1801, *Fax:* +1 514 866 1259, *Email:* montreal@hayesstuart.com, *Website:* www.hayesstuart.com

ROBERTS BANK

harbour area, see under Vancouver

RODNEY TERMINAL

harbour area, see under Saint John

ROGERS SUGAR DOCK

harbour area, see under Vancouver

RUPERT INLET

Lat 50° 33' N; Long 127° 34' W.

Admiralty Pilot: 25

Time Zone: GMT -8 h   **UNCTAD Locode:** CA RUI

This port is no longer open to commercial shipping

SAINT JOHN

Lat 45° 16' N; Long 66° 4' W.

Admiralty Chart: 4749/4750   **Admiralty Pilot:** 59
Time Zone: GMT -4 h   **UNCTAD Locode:** CA SJB

Principal Facilities:

| P | Q | Y | G | C | R | L | B | | T | A | |

Authority: Saint John Port Authority, 111 Water Street, Saint John, N.B., Canada E2L 0B1, *Tel:* +1 506 636 4869, *Fax:* +1 506 636 4443, *Email:* port@sjport.com, *Website:* www.sjport.com

Officials: Chief Executive Officer: Capt Alwyn G. Soppitt, *Tel:* +1 506 636 5377, *Email:* asoppitt@sjport.com.
Harbour Master: Capt John McCann, *Tel:* +1 506 636 4884, *Email:* jmccann@sjport.com.

Port Security: ISPS compliant

Documentation: Crew list (3 copies), vessel report (5 copies), health documents (1 copy), cargo manifest (3 sets), dangerous goods manifest (3 sets), ships certificates (expiry dates reviewed), ships stores (3 copies), crew declaration (3 copies)

Approach: Main channel has a width of 183 m and a depth of 9.14 m at LW

Anchorage: There are three main anchorages located to the S of Partridge Island. Alpha: in min depth of 11.0 m and Bravo: in min depth of 18.0 m, both located SW of Partridge Island and Charlie: in min depth of 31.0 m for deeper draught vessels located SSE of Partridge Island

Pilotage: Compulsory. 12 h advance notice should be sent, giving vessel's ETA, which must be confirmed or corrected 4 h prior to arrival. Pilot boards vessel at harbour entrance within a radius of 13 km from Partridge Island. Provided by Atlantic Pilotage Authority which has a 24 h centralised pilot dispatch centre in Halifax, Tel: +1 877 272 3477 (toll free) and +1 902 426 7610 (inmarsat), Fax: +1 877 745 3477 (toll free) and +1 902 426 7236 (inmarsat), Email: dispatch@atlanticpilotage.com

Traffic: 2007, 27 030 000 t of cargo handled, 46 574 TEU's

Working Hours: Mon-Fri 0800-1200, 1300-1700. Overtime 0001-0400, 1900-2300 at time and half
Sat 0001-0400, 0800-1200, 1300-1700 at time and half and 1900-2300 at 3 for 1
Sun 0800-1200, 1300-1700 at double time

Accommodation: Main channel depth 9.14 m LT and 17.67 m HT. Courtenay Bay channel 6.5 m LT and 14.7 m HT. Berths vary from 10.4 m to 12.8 m CD. The harbour is safe, always accessible and is ice-free year-round. Port specialises in petroleum, drybulk cargoes, forest products and containers. Specialised facilities include the Forest Products Terminal (FORTERM) providing the largest roofed-over terminal in Canada, Barrack Point Potash Terminal operated by Furncan Marine Ltd giving an annual throughput of 1 500 000 t and Rodney Container Terminal which provides 900 m of berth space and is served by two portainer cranes. Cruise vessels are at a dedicated facility at Pugsley Terminal. The port is served by two rail systems and has major highway links to Canada and the United States

Name	Length (m)	Depth (m)	Remarks
Pugsley Terminal			
North Berth	89	10.4	
Berth A/B	298	10.4	Cruise facility
Berth C	232	10.4	See [1] below
Lower Cove Terminal			Bulk, container & general cargo handled
Berth	245	10.7	Open area of 9.4 ha
Barrack Point Potash Terminal			Potash and rock salt handled
Berth	290	12.2	See [2] below
Long Wharf Terminal			General and bulk cargo
Berth A	182	9.1	
Berth B/C	280	10.7	
Rodney Container Terminal			See [3] below
Slip Berth	295	12.2	Equipped for starboard quarter ramps
Margin Berths	608	12.2	
Terminal 11/12			General & bulk cargo
Berth 11	68	10.4	
Berth 12	263	9.1	One shed of 6900 m2
Navy Island Forest Products Terminal			See [4] below
Berth 1A/B	378	10.4	
Berth 2B	200	10.4	
Berth 3A/B	313	10.4	
Private Facilities			See [5] below

[1]*Berth C:* Breakbulk cargoes. 6100 m2 of insulated and heated sheds
[2]*Berth:* Operated by Furncan Marine Ltd., P O Box 6340, Station A, Saint John NB E2L 3Z5, Tel: +1 506 636 4320, Fax: +1 506 635 4328
Potash loaded at rate of 2700 t/h. One shed of 9750 m2 and one of 12 561 m2 for bulk storage only
[3]*Rodney Container Terminal:* Operated by BTI (Brunswick Terminals Inc), 12 King Street West, Saint John NB E2M 7Y5, Tel: +1 506 635 4500, Fax: +1 506 635 4515, Email: cdoiron@logistec.com
[4]*Navy Island Forest Products Terminal:* Operated by Forest Products Terminal Corporation Ltd (Forterm), P O Box 3518, Station B, Saint John NB E2M 4Y1, Tel: +1 506 635 1910, Fax: +1 506 635 8638, Website: www.forterm.com

Forest products, general cargo and containers. Open area of 6.5 ha

[5]*Private Facilities:* Courtney Bay Oil Terminal: used for the export of refined products from the Irving Oil Refinery

Crosby Molasses: multi-purpose liquid bulk operation with a 26 000 t storage tank

Canaport Marine Terminal: ULCC's transfer petroleum cargo at a monobuoy offshore

Bay Ferries Terminal: used by vessel Princess of Acadia which crosses the Bay of Fundy from Saint John to Digby

Storage:

Location	Covered (m²)	Sheds / Warehouses
Navy Island Forest Products Terminal	48200	4

Mechanical Handling Equipment:

Location	Type	Capacity (t)	Qty
Saint John	Mult-purp. Cranes	40	2
Saint John	Mult-purp. Cranes	84	8
Saint John	Mobile Cranes		
Rodney Container Terminal	Container Cranes	45	

Cargo Worked: 500 t/gang/h for forest products, 26 moves/h/crane for containers, 2000 t/h for bulk

Bunkering: Irving Oil Co. Ltd, 10 Sydney Street, P O Box 1421, Saint John, N.B., Canada E2L 4K1, *Tel:* +1 888 3101 924, *Fax:* +1 506 2023 868, *Email:* webinquiries@irvingoil.com, *Website:* www.irvingoilco.com
Irving Oil Co. Ltd, 340 Loch Lomond Road, P O Box 1260, Saint John, N.B., Canada E2L 4H6, *Tel:* +1 506 6322 000, *Fax:* +1 506 2023 284, *Email:* nicole.bardeau@irvingoil.com, *Website:* www.irvingoil.com
Imperial Oil (Dartmouth) Ltd, P O Box 1010, Dartmouth, N.S., Canada B2Y 4RI, *Tel:* +1 902 420 6872, *Fax:* +1 902 420 6996 – *Grades:* GO subject to enquiry, lubes – *Delivery Mode:* truck
Irving Oil Co. Ltd, 10 Sydney Street, P O Box 1421, Saint John, N.B., Canada E2L 4K1, *Tel:* +1 888 3101 924, *Fax:* +1 506 2023 868, *Email:* webinquiries@irvingoil.com, *Website:* www.irvingoilco.com

Towage: Atlantic Towing Ltd, 2nd Floor, 300 Union Street, P O Box 5777, Saint John, N.B., Canada E2L 4M3, *Tel:* +1 506 648 2750, *Fax:* +1 506 648 2752, *Email:* chartering@atlantow.com, *Website:* www.atlantictowing.com

Seaman Missions: The Seamans Mission, P O Box 3934, Station 'B', Saint John, N.B., Canada E2M 5E6, *Tel:* +1 506 635 1731

Ship Chandlers: Blue Water Agencies Ltd, 1216 S & Cove Road, Unit 805, Saint John, N.B., Canada E2M 5V8, *Tel:* +1 506 672 1700, *Fax:* +1 506 672 1704, *Email:* shipstores@bluewateragencies.ca, *Website:* www.bluewateragencies.ca

Shipping Agents: Canadian Maritime Agency Ltd, 4 Refinery Road, P O Box 119, Come by Chance, NL, Canada A0B 1N0, *Tel:* +1 709 463 4717, *Fax:* +1 709 463 8737, *Email:* opscbc@canadianmaritime.nf.ca, *Website:* www.canadianmaritime.com
Furncan Marine Ltd, P O Box 6340, Station A, Saint John, N.B., Canada EL2 3Z5, *Tel:* +1 506 632 1090, *Fax:* +1 506 636 8924, *Website:* www.furncanmarine.com
HE Kane Agencies Ltd, 20 King Street, P O Box 6489, Saint John, N.B., Canada E2L 4R9, *Tel:* +1 506 632 0945, *Fax:* +1 506 634 2802, *Email:* kane@nb.aibn.com
Kent Line Ltd, 300 Union Street, P O Box 66, Saint John, N.B., Canada E2L 3X1, *Tel:* +1 506 632 1660, *Fax:* +1 506 634 4200, *Email:* sales@kentline.com, *Website:* www.kentline.com
McLean Kennedy Inc., 10 Kings Street West, Unit 6, Saint John, N.B., Canada E2M 7Y5, *Tel:* +1 506 635 1303, *Fax:* +1 506 634 1933, *Email:* info@snb.fkwarren.ca, *Website:* www.fkwarren.ca
Montship Inc., Rodney Container Terminal, Shed 8, 10 King Street West Unit 2, Saint John, N.B., Canada E2M 7Y5, *Tel:* +1 506 658 1066, *Fax:* +1 506 648 9992, *Email:* ops@montshipmaritime.com, *Website:* www.montship.ca
F.K. Warren Ltd, 10 King Street West, Unit-6, Saint John, N.B., Canada E2M 7Y5, *Tel:* +1 506 635 1303, *Fax:* +1 506 634 1933, *Email:* info@snb.fkwarren.ca, *Website:* www.fkwarren.ca

Stevedoring Companies: Brunswick Terminals Inc., 10 King Street W, Unit 8, Saint John, N.B., Canada E2M 7Y5, *Tel:* +1 506 635 4500, *Fax:* +1 506 635 4515
Courtenay Stevedoring Ltd, Saint John, N.B., Canada, *Tel:* +1 506 633 3333, *Fax:* +1 506 632 6415
Furncan Marine Ltd, P O Box 6340, Station A, Saint John, N.B., Canada EL2 3Z5, *Tel:* +1 506 632 1090, *Fax:* +1 506 636 8924, *Website:* www.furncanmarine.com

Surveyors: Michael Dunn, P O Box 1437, Shediac, Saint John, N.B., Canada E4P 2G7, *Tel:* +1 506 532 0284, *Fax:* +1 506 532 6727, *Email:* mjdal@nbnet.nb.ca

Medical Facilities: Saint John Regional Hospital

Airport: Saint John, 24 km

Lloyd's Agent: Hayes Stuart Inc., 297 Duke Street, Montreal, Que., Canada H3C 2M2, *Tel:* +1 514 866 1801, *Fax:* +1 514 866 1259, *Email:* montreal@hayesstuart.com, *Website:* www.hayesstuart.com

SANDY BEACH

alternate name, see Gaspe

SARNIA

Lat 42° 59' N; Long 82° 25' W.

Admiralty Chart: -   **Admiralty Pilot:** -
Time Zone: GMT -5 h   **UNCTAD Locode:** CA SNI

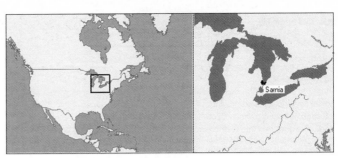

Principal Facilities:

P		Y	G			B		T	A

Authority: Port of Sarnia, 100 Seaway Road, P O Box 325, Sarnia, Ont., Canada N7T 7J2, *Tel:* +1 519 337 5121, *Fax:* +1 519 344 5598, *Email:* harbourmaster@sarship.com

Officials: Harbour Master: Allan Columbus.

Port Security: ISPS compliant

Accommodation:

Name	Remarks
Sarnia	See [1] below

[1]*Sarnia:* Including docks at Point Edward, there are more than 16.1 km of waterfront along the St Clair River. Depths in channel, harbour and alongside principal wharves are sufficient for vessels navigating Lake Huron
Government Docks, 317 m long, and the easterly 304.8 m is a cargo facility with several sheds in depth of 7.3 m
The Sarnia Elevator Co berth has a length of 274.3 m with depth of 7.3 m alongside. Main elevator cap of 3 000 000 bu with annex and country elevator totalling 2 780 000 bu. Docks served by five rail tracks
CNR-CSL Joint Dock at Point Edward is the most northerly marine terminal in the Sarnia area. It has a least depth of 7.0 m alongside
To the south of the CNR-CSL facility is a large dredged basin with mooring dolphins on the east and west side, operated by the Ministry of Transport principally for winter vessel lay-up. 518.1 m of berthing is provided on the east side of this slip. To the SE is another such basin
Several private wharves are located further south along the east bank of the St Clair River to Corunna, about 9.7 km distant. These wharves are owned by oil and petrochemical firms and others are owned by Reid Aggregates, Cope Ltd; also Belton Lumber Co and Mueller Brass Works have a rail car ferry slip. Ontario Hydro has a wharf for coal unloading located at Courtright, about 24.1 km south of Sarnia
Tanker facilities: Facilities are operated by Imperial Oil Ltd, Sun Oil Co, Polysar Ltd, Dow Chemical Co and Shell Canada Ltd

Bunkering: ExxonMobil Marine Fuels, Suite 900, One Alhambra Plaza, Coral Gables, FL 33134, United States of America, *Tel:* +1 305 459 6358, *Fax:* +1 305 459 6412, *Email:* emmf@exxonmobil.com, *Website:* www.exxonmobilmarinefuels.com – *Grades:* IFO40-380cSt; MDO – *Delivery Mode:* pipeline

Towage: Sandrin Services Inc., 150 Exmouth Street, Sarnia, Ont., Canada N7T 5M3, *Tel:* +1 519 336 5588, *Fax:* +1 519 336 5659, *Email:* service@sandrininc.com, *Website:* www.sandrininc.com

Repair & Maintenance: Slip available for major marine repairs including work on hull, boiler and engine. Repair companies are Sandrin Bros (1968) Ltd and Shelley Machine & Marine Ltd

Shipping Agents: Sarnia Shipping, 100 Seaway Road, P O Box 123, Sarnia, Ont., Canada N7T 7H8, *Tel:* +1 519 344 9984, *Fax:* +1 519 344 5598, *Email:* ops@sarship.com

Airport: Sarnia

Lloyd's Agent: McLarens Canada (Toronto), 600 Alden Road, Suite 600, Markham, Toronto, Ont., Canada L3R 0E7, *Tel:* +1 905 946 9995, *Fax:* +1 905 946 0171, *Email:* roger.bickers@mclarens.ca, *Website:* www.mclarens.ca

SASKATCHEWAN WHEAT POOL

harbour area, see under Vancouver

SAULT STE. MARIE

Lat 46° 30' N; Long 84° 21' W.

Admiralty Chart: -   **Admiralty Pilot:** -
Time Zone: GMT -5 h   **UNCTAD Locode:** CA SSM

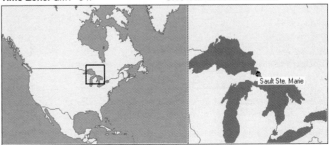

Principal Facilities:

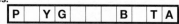

P		Y	G			B		T	A	

Authority: Port of Sault Ste. Marie, 67 Golf Range Crescent, Sault Ste. Marie, Ont., Canada P6A 6A4, *Tel:* +1 705 9460 800, *Fax:* +1 705 9465 775, *Email:* rlamon@shaw.ca

Officials: Director: Ron Lamon, *Tel:* + +1 705 9460 800, *Email:* rlamon@shaw.ca.

Port Security: ISPS compliant

Pilotage: Not compulsory. Pilots available on 6 h notice

Radio Frequency: Ship to shore communications through VBB on either AM or FM radio. Telephone call VBB using 2182 mc/s on AM R/T or call VBB using 156.8 mc/s on FM R/T. Duplex calls may be carried on both AM or FM through VBB

Principal Imports and Exports: Imports: Petroleum Products.

Accommodation:

Name	Length (m)	Depth (m)	Remarks
Sault Ste. Marie			See [1] below
East Face Wharf	91	6.1	See [2] below
South Face Wharf	95	6.1	See [3] below
Seaway Pier	152	5.49	See [4] below
Private Wharves			See [5] below

[1]*Sault Ste. Marie:* Tanker facilities: Gulf Oil Canada Ltd, berthing length E side 121.9 m, depth 5.64 m
[2]*East Face Wharf:* No tug is necessary to berth or unberth at the dock in good weather
[3]*South Face Wharf:* No tug is necessary to berth or unberth at the dock in good weather
[4]*Seaway Pier:* Mobile lifting equipment available. The pier is mostly used for berthing for minor repairs or for waiting for a berth at the Algoma Steel Corp Dock. No refrigerated space. Fresh water and provisions available
[5]*Private Wharves:* The Algoma Steel Corporation Dock: This dock is situated above the Canadian Canal and the following berths are available. (a) Coal and ore dock with combined length of 853.4 m. (b) a commercial dock 121.9 m long on the west side of the slip. (c) a limestone dock which is 'L' shaped. It is 108.2 m long on the west side and 137.1 m long on the south side. The dock is used for loading finished steel. All the berths have a depth of 6.55 m. Only vessels carrying material consigned to or being shipped from the Algoma Steel Corp, have access to these docks

Storage: Storage space is available for lease, contact Regional Manager

Location	Covered (m²)
Sault Ste. Marie	985

Bunkering: Light bunker available at all berths via tank trucks. Bunker 'C' available only at Lime Island, 80 km down river and open all navigation season

Towage: Purvis Marine Ltd, 1 Pim Street, Sault Ste. Marie, Ont., Canada P6A 3G3, *Tel:* +1 705 253 3038, *Fax:* +1 705 253 5232, *Email:* info@purvismarine.com, *Website:* www.purvismarine.com

Repair & Maintenance: Purvis Marine Ltd, 1 Pim Street, Sault Ste. Marie, Ont., Canada P6A 3G3, *Tel:* +1 705 253 3038, *Fax:* +1 705 253 5232, *Email:* info@purvismarine.com, *Website:* www.purvismarine.com

Medical Facilities: Available

Airport: Sault Ste Marie, 24 km

Lloyd's Agent: McLarens Canada (Toronto), 600 Alden Road, Suite 600, Markham, Toronto, Ont., Canada L3R 0E7, *Tel:* +1 905 946 9995, *Fax:* +1 905 946 0171, *Email:* roger.bickers@mclarens.ca, *Website:* www.mclarens.ca

SEPT ILES

alternate name, see Seven Islands

SEVEN ISLANDS

Lat 50° 12' N; Long 66° 22' W.

Admiralty Chart: 4776	**Admiralty Pilot:** 65
Time Zone: GMT -5 h	**UNCTAD Locode:** CA SEI

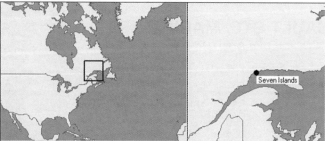

Principal Facilities:

P		Y	G	C	R		B		T	A	

Authority: Port of Sept-Iles, 1 Quai Mgr Blanche, Seven Islands, Que., Canada G4R 5P3, *Tel:* +1 418 968 1235, *Fax:* +1 418 962 4445, *Email:* portsi@portsi.com, *Website:* www.portsi.com

Officials: President: Pierre Gagnon, *Tel:* +1 418 961 1223, *Email:* pgagnon@portsi.com.

Corporate Affairs Manager: Patsy Keays.
Harbour Master: Shawn Grant, *Tel:* +1 418 961 1229, *Email:* sgrant@portsi.com.

Port Security: ISPS compliant

Documentation: Quarantine form (2 copies), crew list (3 copies), report inward (3 copies), crew declaration (3 copies), ship's stores (3 copies), clearance from last port (1 copy)

Anchorage: The designated anchorage area is defined by the triangle formed from the following points: Position 1 in 50° 11.6' N; 066° 25.0' W, Position 2 in 50° 13.1' N; 066° 29.7' W, Position 3 in 50° 10.5' N; 066° 29.7' W

Pilotage: Private docking masters always available. Vessels should signal their ETA to Wabush Marine Services, Lower St. Lawrence Oceans Agencies Ltd or IOC Marine Services requesting berthing instructions 96 h before arrival. Pilots and tugs are compulsory at all berths

Radio Frequency: Escoumins Traffic, Canadian Coast Guard Station, on VHF Channel 14, operates 24 h/day

Weather: Prevailing NNW'ly winds

Tides: Range of tide 3.5 m springs, 1.67 m neaps, 2.5 m average

Traffic: 2007, 21 367 838 t of cargo handled

Maximum Vessel Dimensions: No restriction on vessels in the bay

Principal Imports and Exports: Imports: Alumina, Bentonite, Dolomite, Petcoke. Exports: Aluminium ingots, Iron ore.

Working Hours: 24 h/day

Accommodation:

Name	Length (m)	Depth (m)	Remarks
Seven Islands			
Tug Basin		6.5	See [1] below
No.2 Dock	488	18	See [2] below
No's 4 & 5 Docks	487	11	See [3] below
No.7 Dock	183	8.5	General cargo & bulk. Sheds. Port owned
No.8 Dock	98	12	Petroleum wharf operated by Esso Imperial
No.11 Dock	30	4	Winter storage park
No's 14 & 15 Docks	244	8	General cargo. Port Authority owned
No's 30 & 31 Docks	488	15.5	Iron ore & fuel. Port Authority owned
No.40 Dock	260	14	See [4] below
No.41 Dock	141	9	See [5] below

[1]*Tug Basin:* Owned by Iron Ore Company of Canada. Two 5400 hp tugs
[2]*No.2 Dock:* Iron ore. Owned by Iron Ore Company of Canada. Conveyors & shiploaders
[3]*No's 4 & 5 Docks:* Bulk & general cargo. Owned by Iron Ore Company of Canada. Derrick crane, bulk unloader, conveyors & hoppers
[4]*No.40 Dock:* Bulk & general cargo. 100 t MHB and conveyors. Port Authority owned
[5]*No.41 Dock:* Railcar ferry wharf. 100 t MHB and conveyors. Port Authority owned

Storage: Pointe-aux-Basques Terminal: one shed of 7000 m2. La Relance Terminal (Pointe-Noire): 120 000 m2 of open storage

Mechanical Handling Equipment:

Location	Type	Capacity (t)	Qty
Seven Islands	Mult-purp. Cranes	100	1
Seven Islands	Mult-purp. Cranes	135	1

Bunkering: Most grades of oil readily available. Arrangements must be made through agents
ExxonMobil Marine Fuels, Suite 900, One Alhambra Plaza, Coral Gables, FL 33134, United States of America, *Tel:* +1 305 459 6358, *Fax:* +1 305 459 6412, *Email:* emmf@exxonmobil.com, *Website:* www.exxonmobilmarinefuels.com – *Grades:* imper
Imperial Oil (Anjou) Ltd, 7100 Jean-Talon Street East, Anjou, Que., Canada H1M 3R8, *Tel:* +1 450 6497 519, *Fax:* +1 450 6497 821, *Email:* christian.beaunoyer@esso.ca, *Website:* www.imperialoil.com
Kildair Service Ltd, 92 Chemin Delangis, St. Paul de Joliette, Que., Canada J0K 3E0, *Tel:* +1 450 7568 091, *Fax:* +1 450 7564 783, *Email:* info@kildair.com, *Website:* www.kildair.com
Shell Canada Products Ltd, 10501 Sherbroke Street East, Montreal, Que., Canada H1B 1B3, *Tel:* +1 514 6409 897, *Fax:* +1 514 6451 490, *Email:* patrick.st-laurent@shell.com, *Website:* www.shell.ca

Waste Reception Facilities: No discharge of domestic or international waste is permitted at the port

Towage: Two tugs, each of 5400 hp are available and compulsory at all wharves

Repair & Maintenance: Bouchard & Blanchette Marine, 356 rue Evangeline, Seven Islands, Que., Canada G4R 2N3, *Tel:* +1 418 968 2505, *Fax:* +1 418 968 2059, *Email:* bouchard.blanchette@bbmarine.ca, *Website:* www.bbmarine.ca

Stevedoring Companies: Logistec Ltd, P O Box 159, Seven Islands, Que., Canada G4R 4K3, *Tel:* +1 418 962 7638, *Fax:* +1 418 962 7815, *Email:* fvanell@logistec.com, *Website:* www.logistec.com
Porlier Express Ltd, 315, avenue Otis, Seven Islands, Que., Canada G4R 1K9, *Tel:* +1 418 962 3073, *Fax:* +1 418 962 3067, *Email:* porlex@globetrotter.net, *Website:* www.porlier.com
Quebec Port Terminals Inc., 149 Rue Maltais, Seven Islands, Que., Canada G4R 3J8, *Tel:* +1 418 968 4707, *Fax:* +1 418 968 6910, *Email:* info@qsl.com, *Website:* www.qsl.com

Medical Facilities: Available from Sept-Iles Regional Hospital, Tel: +1 (418) 962 9761

Airport: Sept-Iles Airport, 12 km

Development: Superbulk terminal in development stage in Pointe-Noire area

Lloyd's Agent: Hayes Stuart Inc., 297 Duke Street, Montreal, Que., Canada H3C 2M2, *Tel:* +1 514 866 1801, *Fax:* +1 514 866 1259, *Email:* montreal@hayesstuart.com, *Website:* www.hayesstuart.com

SHEET HARBOUR

Lat 44° 51' N; Long 62° 27' W.

Admiralty Chart: 4748   **Admiralty Pilot:** 59

Time Zone: GMT -4 h   **UNCTAD Locode:** CA SHH

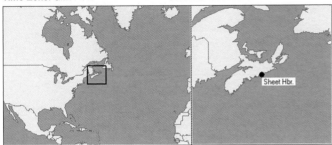

Principal Facilities:

	Y	G		B		

Authority: ERW Holdings Ltd, 715 Highway 224, RR 1, Sheet Harbour, N.S., Canada B0J 3B0, *Tel:* +1 902 885 2336, *Email:* johnb.kelly@ns.sympatico.ca

Officials: General Manager: John Kelly.

Port Security: ISPS compliant

Pilotage: Not compulsory but pilots supplied by Atlantic Pilotage Authority which has a 24 h centralised pilot dispatch centre in Halifax, Tel: +1 877 272 3477 (toll free) and +1 902 426 7610 (inmarsat), Fax: +1 877 745 3477 (toll free) and +1 902 426 7236 (inmarsat), Email: dispatch@atlanticpilotage.com

Tides: LWOST 0.49 m above CD, HWOST 1.92 m above CD

Maximum Vessel Dimensions: 180 m loa, 9.5 m d

Principal Imports and Exports: Exports: Woodpulp.

Accommodation:

Name	Length (m)	Depth (m)	Remarks
Sheet Harbour			
Nova Scotia Business Development Wharf	152	10	With a buoy on each end for securing large vessels.

Storage: 12 acre common user area

Mechanical Handling Equipment:

Location	Type
Sheet Harbour	Mobile Cranes

Bunkering: Imperial Oil (Dartmouth) Ltd, P O Box 1010, Dartmouth, N.S., Canada B2Y 4RI, *Tel:* +1 902 420 6872, *Fax:* +1 902 420 6996 – *Grades:* IFO; MDO – *Delivery Mode:* truck
Irving Oil Co. Ltd, 10 Sydney Street, P O Box 1421, Saint John, N.B., Canada E2L 4K1, *Tel:* +1 888 3101 924, *Fax:* +1 506 2023 868, *Email:* webinquiries@irvingoil.com, *Website:* www.irvingoilco.com – *Grades:* IFO; MDO – *Delivery Mode:* truck

Medical Facilities: Hospital in Sheet Harbour

Lloyd's Agent: Hayes Stuart Inc., 1000 Windmill Road, Suite 19, Dartmouth, N.S., Canada B3B 1L7, *Tel:* +1 902 468 2651, *Fax:* +1 902 468 4315, *Email:* halifax@hayesstuart.com, *Website:* www.hayesstuart.com

SHELLBURN TERMINAL

harbour area, see under Vancouver

SHIP HARBOUR

Lat 44° 45' N; Long 62° 45' W.

Admiralty Chart: 729   **Admiralty Pilot:** 59

Time Zone: GMT -4 h   **UNCTAD Locode:** CA

This port is no longer open to commercial shipping

SOREL

Lat 46° 2' N; Long 73° 6' W.

Admiralty Chart: 4790   **Admiralty Pilot:** 65

Time Zone: GMT -5 h   **UNCTAD Locode:** CA SOR

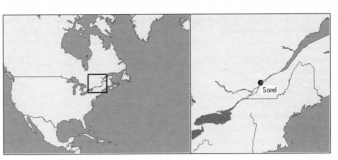

Principal Facilities:

	Y	G			B	D	T	

Authority: Transport Canada, 15 Prince Street, Sorel, Que., Canada J3P 4J4, *Tel:* +1 450 746 4316, *Fax:* +1 450 746 4332, *Website:* www.tc.gc.ca

Officials: Manager: Andre Cardin.

Port Security: ISPS compliant

Approach: From St Lawrence Ship Channel there is a clear approach for 10.67 m draft vessels to the outer docks. Depths are reduced to CD and must be used as guidance only. For up to date information refer to Canada Marine Chart No.1338 (Sorel Harbour)

Anchorage: Safe and commodious anchorage in the St Lawrence River off Sorel in a basin 14.5 km long by 0.8 km wide with a depth of 9.14 to 15.24 m

Pilotage: Compulsory. St Lawrence Pilotage District No.1

Radio Frequency: St Lawrence River Marine Traffic, control call system VFN Sorel and VBK Three Rivers

Weather: In icy conditions channel may close a few days during the winter

Traffic: 2005, 288 vessels, 5 200 000 t of cargo handled

Maximum Vessel Dimensions: Max d 10.67 m, max loa 223.5 m

Working Hours: 24 h/day

Accommodation: Bulk facilities: Open storage at the public wharves for 10 000 t. Steel and concrete grain elevators at Les Elevators de Sorel Stee, 5 500 000 bu cap. Fer et Titane du Quebec operate one electric mobile bridge, for ore 900 t/h. Grain loading 4400 t/h, discharge 2000 t/h

Name	Length (m)	Depth (m)
Transport Canada (Public)		
Section 5	182	7.6
Section 6	106	5.5
Section 7	152	8.53
Section 8	160	6.1
Section 9	60	6.1
Section 10	160	6.1
Les Elevateurs de Sorel Limitee (Private)		
Section 11	152	7.32
Section 12	106	7.32
Section 13	76	7.32
Section 14	187	8.3
Section 15	189	10.67
GEC Alsthom Inc (Private)		
Section 19	182	9.1
Fer & Titane du Quebec Wharves (Private)		
Sections 20 & 21	335	9.14
Richelieu River (Private)		
Section 16	106	4.88
Section 17	213	4.88

Mechanical Handling Equipment:

Location	Type	Capacity (t)
Sorel	Mobile Cranes	150

Bunkering: Shell Canada Products Ltd, 80 Rue George, P O Box 246, Sorel, Que., Canada G3R 5N7, *Email:* pierre.fortin@shell.com, *Website:* www.shell.ca
BP Marine Americas Inc., 501 Westlake Park Boulevard, Houston, TX 77079, United States of America, *Tel:* +1 281 366 2000, *Email:* firstname.secondname@bp.com
Bunkerina International Inc., 11 3rd Avenue South, Roxboro, Montreal, Que., Canada H8Y 2L3, *Tel:* +1 514 806 2760, *Fax:* +1 514 683 2760
ExxonMobil Marine Fuels, Suite 900, One Alhambra Plaza, Coral Gables, FL 33134, United States of America, *Tel:* +1 305 459 6358, *Fax:* +1 305 459 6412, *Email:* emmf@exxonmobil.com, *Website:* www.exxonmobilmarinefuels.com
Hampton Bunkering Ltd, Suite 615, 999 de Maisonneuve Boulevard West, Montreal, Que., Canada H3A 3L4, *Tel:* +1 514 2882 818, *Fax:* +1 514 2829 279, *Email:* bunkers@hamptonmtl.ca
ICS Petroleum, ICS Petroleum (Montreal) Ltd, Suite 302, 430 Ste-Helene Street, Montreal, Que., Canada H2Y 2K7, *Tel:* +1 514 849 1223, *Fax:* +1 514 849 0517, *Email:* bunkers@ics-mtl.com, *Website:* www.icspet.com
Imperial Oil (Anjou) Ltd, 7100 Jean-Talon Street East, Anjou, Que., Canada H1M 3R8, *Tel:* +1 450 6497 519, *Fax:* +1 450 6497 821, *Email:* christian.beaunoyer@esso.ca, *Website:* www.imperialoil.com
Kildair Service Ltd, 92 Chemin Delangis, St. Paul de Joliette, Que., Canada J0K 3EO, *Tel:* +1 450 7568 091, *Fax:* +1 450 7564 783, *Email:* info@kildair.com, *Website:* www.kildair.com
Petro Canada Products Ltd, 11701 Sherbrooke Street East, Montreal, Que., Canada H1B 1C3, *Tel:* +1 613 657 1004, *Fax:* +1 514 640 8365, *Email:* elliott@petro-canada.ca, *Website:* www.petro-canada.ca
Reiter Petroleum Inc, Suite 900, 625 President Kennedy, Montreal, Que., Canada

Key to Principal Facilities:—				
A=Airport	**C**=Containers	**G**=General Cargo	**P**=Petroleum	**R**=Ro/Ro	**Y**=Dry Bulk
B=Bunkers	**D**=Dry Dock	**L**=Cruise	**Q**=Other Liquid Bulk	**T**=Towage (where available from port)	

H3A 1K2, *Tel:* +1 514 8782 563, *Fax:* +1 514 8783 463, *Email:* bunkers@reiterpet.com, *Website:* www.reiterpet.com
Shell Canada Products Ltd, 80 Rue George, P O Box 246, Sorel, Que., Canada G3R 5N7, *Email:* pierre.fortin@shell.com, *Website:* www.shell.ca
Universal Maritime Agency & Trading Co. Ltd (Umatco), 2444 Marisa Ct., Mississauga, Ont., Canada, *Tel:* +1 905 823 4638, *Fax:* +1 905 823 3938, *Email:* umatco@sympatico.ca

Towage: Ocean Remorquage Sorel Inc, 130 chemin des Patriotes, Sorel, Que., Canada J3P 2L2, *Tel:* +1 450 742 4882, *Fax:* +1 450 742 9590, *Email:* knichol@groupocean.com

Shipping Agents: Sorel Maritime Agencies Inc, 201 Montcalm, Suite 106, St. Joseph de Sorel, Sorel, Que., Canada J3R 1B9, *Tel:* +1 450 743 3585, *Fax:* +1 450 743 0727, *Email:* agency@sorel-maritime.qc.ca, *Website:* www.sorel-maritime.qc.ca

Medical Facilities: Doctors and hospital facilities

Lloyd's Agent: Hayes Stuart Inc., 297 Duke Street, Montreal, Que., Canada H3C 2M2, *Tel:* +1 514 866 1801, *Fax:* +1 514 866 1259, *Email:* montreal@hayesstuart.com, *Website:* www.hayesstuart.com

SOURIS

Lat 46° 21' N; Long 62° 15' W.

Admiralty Chart: 4419	**Admiralty Pilot:** 65
Time Zone: GMT -4 h	**UNCTAD Locode:** CA SOU

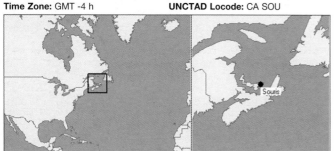

Principal Facilities:

		G		B		A

Authority: Souris Harbour Authority Inc., P O Box 339, Souris, P.E.I., Canada C0A 2B0, *Tel:* +1 902 687 7209, *Fax:* +1 902 687 7210, *Email:* shai@pei.aibn.com, *Website:* www.sourisharbourauthority.com

Officials: President: Denis Thibodeau.
Port Manager: Art MacDonald.

Approach: Breakwater protecting the entrance to the port. Approach channel 100 m wide in depth of 8 m

Pilotage: Not compulsory but available from Atlantic Pilotage Authority, Tel: +1 877 272 3477, Email: dispatch@atlanticpilotage.com

Weather: Generally ice free during the winter season. Upon request, icebreaker support is available if required

Accommodation:

Name	Remarks
Souris	See [1] below

[1]*Souris:* Comprises five wharves: Fisherman's Wharf, Eastpac Wharf, USFN's Wharf, Marine Terminal and Breakwater Wharf
The primary user of the port is the fishing industry although aggregate and potatoes are also shipped through the port. There is also a recreational marina operated by the Town of Souris
The Transport Canada Ferry Terminal is operated by CTMA

Storage: Transit shed available

Bunkering: Imperial Oil (Dartmouth) Ltd, P O Box 1010, Dartmouth, N.S., Canada B2Y 4RI, *Tel:* +1 902 420 6872, *Fax:* +1 902 420 6996 – *Grades:* IFO; MDO – *Delivery Mode:* truck
Irving Oil Co. Ltd, 10 Sydney Street, P O Box 1421, Saint John, N.B., Canada E2L 4K1, *Tel:* +1 888 3101 924, *Fax:* +1 506 2023 868, *Email:* webinquiries@irvingoil.com, *Website:* www.irvingoilco.com – *Grades:* IFO; MDO – *Delivery Mode:* truck

Repair & Maintenance: Minor repairs available

Medical Facilities: Available

Airport: Charlottetown Airport, 80 km

Lloyd's Agent: Hayes Stuart Inc., 1000 Windmill Road, Suite 19, Dartmouth, N.S., Canada B3B 1L7, *Tel:* +1 902 468 2651, *Fax:* +1 902 468 4315, *Email:* halifax@hayesstuart.com, *Website:* www.hayesstuart.com

SQUAMISH

Lat 49° 41' N; Long 123° 10' W.

Admiralty Chart: -	**Admiralty Pilot:** 25
Time Zone: GMT -8 h	**UNCTAD Locode:** CA SQA

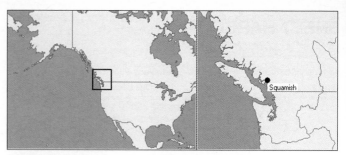

Principal Facilities:

	Y	G			B		T	A

Authority: Squamish Terminals Ltd, 37500 Third Avenue, P O Box 1520, Squamish, B.C., Canada V8B 0B1, *Tel:* +1 604 892 3511, *Fax:* +1 604 892 5623, *Email:* doug_hackett@sqterminals.com, *Website:* www.sqterminals.com

Officials: Chief Executive Officer: Ron Anderson, *Tel:* +604 892 3511 Ext.326, *Email:* ron_anderson@sqterminals.com.
Operations Manager: Joe Webber, *Tel:* +604 892 3511 Ext.307, *Email:* joe_webber@sqterminals.com.

Port Security: ISPS compliant

Approach: Through Howe Sound, no limitation to navigation day or night

Pilotage: Available from Pacific Pilotage, Vancouver

Maximum Vessel Dimensions: 212 m loa, 50 000 dwt

Accommodation:

Name	Length (m)	Draught (m)	Remarks
Squamish			Located at the head of Howe Sound and covers 17 ha
Berth No.1	137	11.6	
Berth No.2	152.4	12.2	

Storage:

Location	Covered (m²)	Sheds / Warehouses
Squamish	47380	3

Mechanical Handling Equipment: 'Boxcar Special' lift trucks for unloading railcars and a 28 000 lb cap Hyster lift truck for transfer of cargo into storage areas and from storage to alongside vessel or onto trailers

Bunkering: Available by truck or from barges

Towage: Squamish Tug Boat Co., P O Box 1099, Squamish, B.C., Canada V0N 3G0, *Tel:* +1 604 898 3733

Medical Facilities: Modern regional hospital

Airport: Vancouver International Airport, 90 km

Railway: CN Rail

Lloyd's Agent: McLarens Canada (Vancouver), 505 1100 Melville Street, Vancouver, B.C., Canada V6E 4A6, *Tel:* +1 604 681 7107, *Fax:* +1 604 681 8125, *Email:* philip.vardon@mclarens.ca, *Website:* www.mclarens.ca

ST. ANDREWS

Lat 45° 4' N; Long 67° 3' W.

Admiralty Chart: 352	**Admiralty Pilot:** 59
Time Zone: GMT -3.5 h	**UNCTAD Locode:** CA SAD

This port is no longer open to commercial shipping

ST. JOHN'S

Lat 47° 33' N; Long 52° 42' W.

Admiralty Chart: 4736	**Admiralty Pilot:** 50
Time Zone: GMT -3.5 h	**UNCTAD Locode:** CA SJF

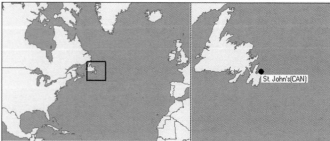

Principal Facilities:

P		Y	G	C	R	L	B		A

Authority: St. John's Port Authority, 1 Water Street, P O Box 6178, St. John's, NL, Canada A1C 5X8, *Tel:* +1 709 738 4782, *Fax:* +1 709 738 4784, *Email:* info@sjpa.com, *Website:* www.sjpa.com

Officials: Chief Executive Officer: Sean Hanrahan, *Tel:* +1 709 738 4780.
Business Development Manager: Bob McCarthy, *Tel:* +1 709 738 4770.

Port Security: ISPS compliant

Documentation: Crew list (3 copies), passenger list, stowaways list, tobacco/spirits/personal effects list, safety equipment, tonnage certificate, nationality certificate, cargo documents (3 copies of customs cargo manifest), cargo list of dangerous goods, ship's stores

Approach: Entrance to the port is from the open Atlantic and gained through a navigational channel, 91 m width in depth of 11.8 m at LT

Pilotage: Compulsory and necessary from entrance to harbour. 12 h advance notice should be send through 'Pilots, Halifax' giving ship's ETA which must be confirmed or corrected not less than 4 h prior to ETA. Atlantic Pilotage Authority ship to shore communications through St. John's Marine Radio VON on various frequencies. Pilot station and pilot boats equipped with VHF Channels 16 and 11

Tides: Range of tide 1.3 m ST

Traffic: 2007, 1 483 486 t of cargo handled, 117 599 TEU's

Working Hours: 24 h if required, After normal working hours call Canadian Coast Guard, St. John's Traffic Centre, Tel: +1 709 772 2083 for Duty Harbour Master's instructions

Accommodation: Tanker facilities: operated by Petro-Canada and Irving Oil Ltd, night berthing possible; water and bunkers available

Name	Depth (m)	Remarks
Main Terminal		See [1] below
Berth No.1	3	
Berth No.2	7.7	General, container, ro/ro
Berth No.3	9.1	
Berth No.4	8.4	
Berth No.5	8.8	
Marginal Wharf		See [2] below
Berth No.6	6.1	
Berth No.7	7.9	
Berth No.8	7.9	
Berth No.9	7.3	
Berth No.10	9.1	
Berth No.11	9.1	
A. Harvey Offshore Ltd (Pier 12, 14, 15 & 16)		See [3] below
Berth No.12	7.3	
Berth No.14	5.8	
Berth No.15	8.2	
Berth No.16	7.6	
Pier 17		See [4] below
Berth No.17	10.5	
Pier 18		See [5] below
Berth No.18	16.9	
Pier 19, 20 & 21		See [6] below
Berth No.19	5.8	
Berth No.20	5.5	
Berth No.21	8.5	
Mobil Oil Offshore Supply Base (Pier 22)		Operated by Mobil Oil Ltd Petroleum/bunkering. Total length of 153 m
Berth No.22	6.7	
Irving Oil (Pier 23)		See [7] below
Berth No.23	5.8	
Irving Oil (Pier 24)		See [8] below
Berth No.24	9.5	
Pier 25		See [9] below
Berth No.25	9.5	
Dept. of National Defence HMCS Cabot (Piers 26 & 27)		Operated by Dept. of National Defence General cargo & naval reserve facility. Total length of 214 m
Berth No.26	6.7	
Berth No.27	5.5	
Dept. of Fisheries & Oceans (Piers 28 & 29)		Operated by Govt. of Canada General cargo. Total length of 183 m
Berth No.28	5.2	
Berth No.29	5.2	
Canadian Coast Guard (Piers 30 & 31)		Operated by Govt. of Canada General cargo and search & rescue. Total length of 282 m
Berth No.30	5.2	
Berth No.31	7	
NEWDOCK		See [10] below
Berth No.34		
Berth No.35	7.6	
Berth No.36	5.8	
Berth No.37	6.7	

[1] *Main Terminal:* Operated by Oceanex (1997) Inc., Tel: +1 709 726 2507, Email: getchegary@oceanex.com, Website: www.oceanex.com Containerised and ro/ro (general consumer goods). Total length of berths 800 m
[2] *Marginal Wharf:* Operated by St. John's Port Authority Cruise vessels, lay-up, general ship supplies & repairs. Total length of 870 m
[3] *A. Harvey Offshore Ltd (Pier 12, 14, 15 & 16):* Operated by A. Harvey & Co Ltd., Pier 14, 71 Water Street, St. John's NL A1C 1A1, Tel: +1 709 570 7060, Fax: +1 709 570 7068, Email: gcunningham@aharvey.nf.ca, Website: www.aharvey.com/marine Offshore oil supply/service base & bulk cargo storage. Total length of 533 m
[4] *Pier 17:* Operated by St. John's Port Authority Multi-purpose facility - general cargo, offshore supply base. Total length of 180 m
[5] *Pier 18:* Operated by St. John's Port Authority Loading/offloading petroleum and bunkering products & other bulk liquids. Dolphins
[6] *Pier 19, 20 & 21:* Operated by St. John's Port Authority Offloading facility for commercial fishing vessels. Total length of 335 m
[7] *Irving Oil (Pier 23):* Operated by Irving Oil Ltd

Petroleum/bunkering. Total length of 115 m
[8] *Irving Oil (Pier 24):* Operated by Irving Oil Ltd Petroleum/bunkering. Total length of 69 m
[9] *Pier 25:* Operated by Province of Newfoundland and Labrador General cargo & marine safety training facility. Total length of 137 m
[10] *NEWDOCK:* Operated by NEWDOCK Ltd General cargo. Marine synchrolift facility with repair cap of 3600 gt and marine graving dock facility with cap to handle vessels up to approx 174 m loa

Mechanical Handling Equipment:

Location	Type	Capacity (t)	Qty
Main Terminal	Mult-purp. Cranes	100	2

Bunkering: ExxonMobil Marine Fuels, Suite 900, One Alhambra Plaza, Coral Gables, FL 33134, United States of America, Tel: +1 305 459 6358, Fax: +1 305 459 6412, *Email:* emmf@exxonmobil.com, *Website:* www.exxonmobilmarinefuels.com – *Grades:* MGO – *Delivery Mode:* barge, truck, pipeline
Imperial Oil (Dartmouth) Ltd, P O Box 1010, Dartmouth, N.S., Canada B2Y 4RI, *Tel:* +1 902 420 6872, *Fax:* +1 902 420 6996 – *Grades:* GO; lubes – *Delivery Mode:* truck
Petro Canada Products Ltd, 11701 Sherbrooke Street East, Montreal, Que., Canada H1B 1C3, *Tel:* +1 613 657 1004, *Fax:* +1 514 640 8365, *Email:* elliott@petro-canada.ca, *Website:* www.petro-canada.ca – *Grades:* MDO – *Delivery Mode:* tank, barge
Ultramar Canada Inc., 2200 McGill College Avenue, Montreal, Que., Canada H3A 3L3, *Tel:* +1 514 4996 111, *Fax:* +1 514 4996 320, *Email:* wholesale@ultramar.ca, *Website:* www.ultramar.ca – *Grades:* MDO – *Delivery Mode:* tank, barge

Repair & Maintenance: St. John's Dockyard Ltd (NEWDOCK), 475 Water Street, St. John's, NL, Canada A1E 6B5, *Tel:* +1 709 758 6800, *Fax:* +1 709 758 6824, *Email:* admin@newdock.nf.ca, *Website:* www.newdock.nf.ca One graving dock of 175.2 m x 22.5 m and one synchrolift of 91 m x 17 m for vessels up to 3600 gt

Ship Chandlers: Blue Water (Newfoundland) Ltd, 127 Clyde Avenue, Mount Pearl, NL, Canada A1N 4R9, *Tel:* +1 709 754 8900, *Fax:* +1 709 754 8901, *Email:* bluewater@nfld.com, *Website:* www.bluewateragencies.ca
Campbells Ships Supplies, 689 Water Street West, P O Box 274, St. John's, NL, Canada A1C 5J2, *Tel:* +1 709 726 6932, *Fax:* +1 709 739 9890, *Email:* order@campbellship.com, *Website:* www.campbellship.com
Karlo Corp. - Marine Group, 1 Duffy Place, St. John's, NL, Canada A1B 4M6, *Tel:* +1 709 738 1811, *Fax:* +1 709 738 1812, *Email:* canada@karlogroup.com

Shipping Agents: Avalon Customs Brokers, Suite 301, 4th Floor, 60 Water Street, P O Box 5774, St. John's, NL, Canada A1C 5X3, *Tel:* +1 709 576 4761, *Fax:* +1 709 576 0159, *Email:* acb@aharvey.nf.ca, *Website:* www.aharvey.com
Blue Peter Marine Agencies Ltd, 125 New Gower Street, P O Box 6030, St. John's, NL, Canada A1C 5X9, *Tel:* +1 709 726 2440, *Fax:* +1 709 726 2444, *Email:* clancy@bluepeter.nf.ca
Canadian Maritime Agency Ltd, 4 Refinery Road, P O Box 119, Come by Chance, NL, Canada A0B 1N0, *Tel:* +1 709 463 4717, *Fax:* +1 709 463 8737, *Email:* opscbc@canadianmaritime.nf.ca, *Website:* www.canadianmaritime.com
Hf Eimskipafelag Islands, Eimskip Canada Inc., 33 Pippy Place, Suite 305, St. John's, NL, Canada A1B 3X2, *Tel:* +1 709 754 7222, *Fax:* +1 709 754 7999, *Email:* kro@eimskip.ca, *Website:* www.eimskip.com
A. Harvey & Co. Ltd, P O Box 5128, 60 Water Street, St. John's, NL, Canada A1C 5V6, *Tel:* +1 709 726 8000, *Fax:* +1 709 726 9891, *Email:* rchp@aharvey.nf.ca, *Website:* www.aharvey.com/marine
F.K. Warren Ltd, 162 Duckworth Street, P O Box 5514, St. John's, NL, Canada A1C 5W4, *Tel:* +1 709 754 4872, *Fax:* +1 709 726 7165, *Email:* ops@fkwarren.ca, *Website:* www.fkwarren.ca

Surveyors: Det Norske Veritas A/S, 140 Water Street, Suite 902, St. John's, NL, Canada A1C 6H6, *Tel:* +1 709 753 8370, *Fax:* +1 709 753 8372, *Email:* stjohns@dnv.com, *Website:* www.dnv.com
Germanischer Lloyd, St. John's, NL, Canada, *Tel:* +1 709 753 8370, *Fax:* +1 709 753 8372, *Website:* www.gl-group.com
Nippon Kaiji Kyokai, St. John's, NL, Canada, *Tel:* +1 709 739 6888, *Fax:* +1 709 739 4971, *Website:* www.classnk.or.jp
Noble Denton Group, Noble Denton Canada Ltd, Suite 902, Fortis Building, 139 Water Street, St. John's, NL, Canada A1C 1B2, *Tel:* +1 709 739 0119, *Fax:* +1 709 739 0190, *Email:* ndimmell@nobledenton.nf.ca, *Website:* www.nobledenton.com

Medical Facilities: Health Sciences Centre, Tel: +1 (709) 777 6300. St. Clare's Mercy Hospital, Tel: +1 (709) 777 5000

Airport: St. John's, 4 km

Lloyd's Agent: Hayes Stuart Inc., 297 Duke Street, Montreal, Que., Canada H3C 2M2, *Tel:* +1 514 866 1801, *Fax:* +1 514 866 1259, *Email:* montreal@hayesstuart.com, *Website:* www.hayesstuart.com

STANOVAN TERMINAL

harbour area, see under Vancouver

STEPHENVILLE

Lat 48° 31' N; Long 58° 32' W.

Admiralty Chart: 283		**Admiralty Pilot:** 65	
Time Zone: GMT -3.5 h		**UNCTAD Locode:** CA STV	

Key to Principal Facilities:—				
A=Airport	**C**=Containers	**G**=General Cargo	**P**=Petroleum	**R**=Ro/Ro	**Y**=Dry Bulk
B=Bunkers	**D**=Dry Dock	**L**=Cruise	**Q**=Other Liquid Bulk	**T**=Towage (where available from port)

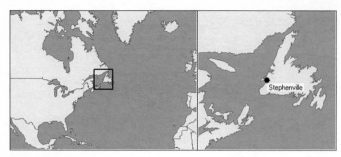

Principal Facilities:

P	Q	Y	G					T	A

Authority: Port Harmon Authority Ltd, P O Box 100, Stephenville, NL, Canada A2N 2Y7, *Tel:* +1 709 643 5626, *Fax:* +1 709 643 6130, *Email:* portharmonauth@nf.aibn.com, *Website:* www.portharmonauthority.ca

Officials: President: Cec Stein.
Port Manager: Jim Cochrane.

Port Security: ISPS compliant

Documentation: General declaration (4 copies), crew effects declaration (3 copies), ship stores declaration (3 copies), immigration crew list (3 copies), marine declaration of health (1 copy), port clearance from previous port

Approach: Access to the turning basin and harbour is through a 72 m wide by 2100 m long dredged channel with a limiting depth of 10.4 m

Anchorage: There are several anchorages in the Bay St George

Pilotage: Compulsory

Radio Frequency: VHF Channel 16

Weather: Navigational season is year round with occasional icebreaker assistance during winter months

Tides: Tidal range 1.7 m

Working Hours: 24 h/day

Accommodation:

Name	Length (m)	Depth (m)	Remarks
Stephenville			See [1] below
Wharf No.1	293	7.8–9.1	Situated on the E shore of the harbour

[1]*Stephenville:* The harbour and channel are protected by two rubble mound breakwaters. The North breakwater is 410 m long and 5.5 m wide and the South breakwater is 136 m long and 5.0 m wide. The least depth of water reported in the channel is 10.4 m and 10.1 m at wharf face

Storage:

Location	Open (m²)
Stephenville	10000

Mechanical Handling Equipment:

Location	Type
Stephenville	Mobile Cranes

Waste Reception Facilities: Garbage disposal available

Towage: Montreal Shipping Inc., P O Box 597, Stephenville, NL, Canada A2N 3B4, *Tel:* +1 709 643 5753, *Fax:* +1 709 643 9738, *Email:* rgreer@montship.ca, *Website:* www.montship.ca

Repair & Maintenance: Minor repairs only

Shipping Agents: Canadian Maritime Agency Ltd, 4 Refinery Road, P O Box 119, Come by Chance, NL, Canada A0B 1N0, *Tel:* +1 709 463 4717, *Fax:* +1 709 463 8737, *Email:* opscbc@canadianmaritime.nf.ca, *Website:* www.canadianmaritime.com
Montship Inc., 165 Main Street, P O Box 597, Stephenville, NL, Canada A2N 3B4, *Tel:* +1 709 643 5753, *Fax:* +1 709 643 9738, *Email:* bpartridge.montship@nfld.net, *Website:* www.montship.ca

Medical Facilities: Hospital, 8 km

Airport: 4 km

Lloyd's Agent: Hayes Stuart Inc., 297 Duke Street, Montreal, Que., Canada H3C 2M2, *Tel:* +1 514 866 1801, *Fax:* +1 514 866 1259, *Email:* montreal@hayesstuart.com, *Website:* www.hayesstuart.com

STEWART

Lat 55° 55' N; Long 130° 0' W.

Admiralty Chart: -	**Admiralty Pilot:** 26
Time Zone: GMT -8 h	**UNCTAD Locode:** CA STW

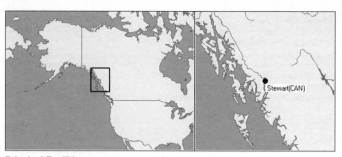

Principal Facilities:

	Y	G			B		A

Authority: Stewart Harbour Authority, P O Box 544, Stewart, B.C., Canada V0T 1W0, *Tel:* +1 250 636 2802, *Fax:* +1 250 636 2628, *Email:* evzell@hotmail.com

Officials: President: Gody Appenzeller.
Harbour Manager: Aaron van der Nobelen.

Port Security: ISPS compliant

Anchorage: Good anchorage holding ground off Stewart in 25-30 fathoms; available for vessels loading logs

Pilotage: Compulsory from Triple Island Pilot Boarding Station

Radio Frequency: see Prince Rupert

Maximum Vessel Dimensions: 40 000 dwt

Principal Imports and Exports: Exports: Copper ore, Raw logs.

Accommodation:

Name	Length (m)	Depth (m)	Remarks
Stewart			
Government & Arrow Dock			Reconstruction of these two docks are being considered
Bulk Terminal	244	12.2	See [1] below

[1]*Bulk Terminal:* Mooring buoys are located at either end. Gold and silver ore concentrates handled

Bunkering: Diesel fuel available

Airport: 3.2 km

Lloyd's Agent: McLarens Canada (Vancouver), 505 1100 Melville Street, Vancouver, B.C., Canada V6E 4A6, *Tel:* +1 604 681 7107, *Fax:* +1 604 681 8125, *Email:* philip.vardon@mclarens.ca, *Website:* www.mclarens.ca

STUART CHANNEL WHARVES

harbour area, see under Crofton

SYDNEY

Lat 46° 9' N; Long 60° 12' W.

Admiralty Chart: 4748	**Admiralty Pilot:** 65
Time Zone: GMT -4 h	**UNCTAD Locode:** CA SYD

Principal Facilities:

P		Y	G	C	R	L	B	D	T	A

Authority: Port of Sydney, P O Box 327, Sydney, N.S., Canada B1P 6H2, *Tel:* +1 902 564 6882, *Fax:* +1 902 564 0911, *Email:* information@sydneyport.ca, *Website:* www.portofsydney.ca

Officials: General Manager: Donald Rowe, *Tel:* +1 902 564 8452, *Email:* don@sydneyport.ca.
Marketing Manager: Bernadette MacNeil, *Tel:* +1 902 564 4377, *Email:* bernadette@sydneyport.ca.

Port Security: ISPS compliant

Approach: Maximum draft in harbour channel is 11.7 m and in harbour is 13.7 m

Pilotage: Compulsory. The pilot boards vessel at 46° 18' N; 60° 08' W. The pilot boat is equipped with VHF Channels 16 and 11. Atlantic Pilotage Authority has a 24 h centralised pilot dispatch centre in Halifax, Tel: +1 877 272 3477 (toll free) and +1 902 426 7610 (inmarsat), Fax: +1 877 745 3477 (toll free) and +1 902 426 7236 (inmarsat), Email: dispatch@atlanticpilotage.com

Tides: Range of tide 0.9 m to 1.4 m

Working Hours: 24 h/day

Accommodation:

Name	Length (m)	Depth (m)	Remarks
Sydney			See [1] below
Sydney Marine Terminal	275	12	See [2] below
Sydney Steel Corp Dock No.3	213	12.5	
Sydney Steel Corp Dock No.4	218	12.5	
International Coal Wharf	180		See [3] below
Syd-Port Industrial Port			See [4] below
North Sydney			See [5] below

[1]*Sydney:* Located in Cabot Strait at the NE shore of Cape Breton Island
[2]*Sydney Marine Terminal:* Operated by Sydney Ports Corp Inc., P O Box 327, Sydney NS B1P 6H2, Tel: +1 902 564 6882
Handling cruise ships, project cargo, break bulk, bulk and fuel and is located on the East side of the south arm of the harbour
[3]*International Coal Wharf:* Operated by Emera Corp
Mainly used for importing coal and has a radial self-trimming ship loader for export bulk cargo
[4]*Syd-Port Industrial Port:* Situated on the Westmount side of Sydney Harbour and used for bulk handling, containers and heavy lift cargoes. Also used as a cruise line terminal, for petroleum and liquid cargoes and by the fishing industry. Open storage is available and the offshore industry is also served
[5]*North Sydney:* Mainland terminus for Marine Atlantic who operate daily passenger and freight services to Newfoundland. Private wharves handle fresh and frozen fish and are used for general cargo

Bunkering: Diesel and gas oil available. Bunker oil available on request with advance notice. Diesel, lubricating oils and gas oil available from all petroleum supplies

Towage: Available upon request

Repair & Maintenance: North Sydney Marine Railway Ltd Ship Repair & Drydock Facilities, North Sydney, N.S., Canada, *Tel:* +1 902 794 2844 Machine shop and cradles for vessels up to 1000 long t and travel lift with cap of 150 t

Shipping Agents: Greer Shipping Agency, P O Box 512, Sydney, N.S., Canada B1P 6H2, *Tel:* +1 902 539 1180
Lorway Shipping Co Ltd., P O Box 277, 183 Charlotte Street, Sydney, N.S., Canada B1P 6H1, *Tel:* +1 902 562 2880, *Fax:* +1 902 539 6028, *Email:* marineservice@ns.sympatico.ca

Airport: Sydney Airport, 11 km

Lloyd's Agent: Hayes Stuart Inc., 1000 Windmill Road, Suite 19, Dartmouth, N.S., Canada B3B 1L7, *Tel:* +1 902 468 2651, *Fax:* +1 902 468 4315, *Email:* halifax@hayesstuart.com, *Website:* www.hayesstuart.com

TADOUSSAC

Lat 48° 8' N; Long 69° 42' W.

Admiralty Chart: 1370	**Admiralty Pilot:** 65
Time Zone: GMT -5 h	**UNCTAD Locode:** CA TAD

This port is no longer open to commercial shipping

THOROLD

Lat 43° 5' N; Long 79° 10' W.

Admiralty Chart: -	**Admiralty Pilot:** -
Time Zone: GMT -5 h	**UNCTAD Locode:** CA THD

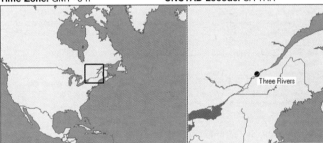

Principal Facilities:

	Y	G					A

Authority: Industrial Docks & Supplies Ltd, P O Box 98, Thorold, Ont., Canada L2V 3Y7, *Tel:* +1 905 227 1884, *Fax:* +1 905 227 5760, *Email:* moore-mccleary@computan.on.ca

Port Security: ISPS compliant

Documentation: Canada Customs forms - A6, A6A, bill of lading, ship's crew list, ship's provisions

Approach: Sailing directions: Canadian CEN 300, 302, 303. Canadian Chart 2042. Channel depth: max permissible draft in Welland Canal and approaches is 8.0 m

Pilotage: Great Lakes Pilot Authority

Radio Frequency: Ship-to-shore communications via Prescott (VBR) or Buffalo (WBL). VHF Channel 6

Weather: Prevailing westerly winds

Working Hours: Mon-Fri 0600-2400. Other hours available

Accommodation:

Name	Length (m)	Depth (m)	Remarks
Thorold			
Wharf No.5	152	5.5	
Wharf No.6	342	7.8	See [1] below

[1]*Wharf No.6:* Dock wall 121.9 m long. Various bulk and general commodities handled such as bauxite, ores, petroleum coke & coke breeze

Storage: Open paved storage available; also dry inside quonsets (44 400 ft2) and dry warehouse (47 000 ft2)

Mechanical Handling Equipment: Two 165 t crawler cranes and a stacking conveyor

Cargo Worked: Bulk or bagged materials via shore based crawler cranes, self-unloading bulk vessels and shore-based heavy lifts

Waste Reception Facilities: Ballast water controls in effect. Garbage removal available. Mobile reception facilities available for slops

Towage: Available if required

Stevedoring Companies: Great Lakes Stevedoring Co Ltd, 1281 Old Thorold Stone Road, P O Box 98, Thorold, Ont., Canada L2V 3Y7, *Tel:* +1 905 227 1884, *Fax:* +1 905 227 5760, *Email:* info@qsl.com, *Website:* www.qsl.com

Medical Facilities: St Catharines General and Hotel Dieu both situated in St Catharines

Airport: Toronto International Airport, 60 miles. Hamilton Airport, 35 miles. Buffalo Airport, 45 miles

Lloyd's Agent: McLarens Canada (Toronto), 600 Alden Road, Suite 600, Markham, Toronto, Ont., Canada L3R 0E7, *Tel:* +1 905 946 9995, *Fax:* +1 905 946 0171, *Email:* roger.bickers@mclarens.ca, *Website:* www.mclarens.ca

THREE RIVERS

Lat 46° 19' N; Long 72° 32' W.

Admiralty Chart: 4789	**Admiralty Pilot:** 65
Time Zone: GMT -5 h	**UNCTAD Locode:** CA TRR

Principal Facilities:

Q	Y	G		R		B		T	A

Authority: Trois-Rivieres Port Authority, 1545 du Fleuve, Suite 300, P O Box 999, Three Rivers, Que., Canada G9A 6K4, *Tel:* +1 819 378 2887, *Fax:* +1 819 378 2487, *Email:* adm_gen@porttr.com, *Website:* www.porttr.com

Officials: Chief Executive Officer: Gaetan Boivin, *Tel:* +1 819 378 2887 ext.22, *Email:* boivin@porttr.com.
Vice President, Marketing: Jacques Paquin, *Tel:* +1 819 378 2887 ext.28, *Email:* paquin@porttr.com.
Operations Manager: Rejean Nadeau, *Tel:* +1 819 378 2887 ext.25, *Email:* nadeau@porttr.com.
Harbour Master: Paul Gendron, *Tel:* +1 819 378 2887 ext.24, *Email:* gendron@porttr.com.

Port Security: ISPS compliant

Anchorage: Anchorage 3.2 km up river. Depth at entrance is that of St Lawrence Ship Channel, dredged to 11.3 m at LW. Max rise and fall 0.3 m. Navigation season: all year round. Vessels should be reinforced for ice between January and March

Pilotage: Compulsory. St Lawrence Pilotage District No.1. Pilots board at Anse-Aux-Basques, near Les Escoumins, to bring the vessels to Quebec where pilots are exchanged for the trip to Trois Rivieres

Radio Frequency: VHF Channel 13

Tides: Max rise and fall 0.3 m

Traffic: 2007, 2 500 000 t of cargo handled

Maximum Vessel Dimensions: Max d 11.0 m at LW

Principal Imports and Exports: Imports: Alumina, Aluminium ingots, China clay, Coal tar pitch, Coke, Grain, Molasses, Paper & paper products, Petroleum products, Salt. Exports: Grain, Newsprint.

Working Hours: Normal hours: Monday-Friday 0800-1200, 1300-1700; overtime 1800-2200 or 2300. Saturdays 0800-1200, 1300-1700, double time paid. Sundays 0800-1200, 1300-1700, double time paid. Night work by arrangement

Accommodation:

Name	Length (m)	Depth (m)	Remarks
Three Rivers			See [1] below
Berth No.1A	152	9.1	
Berth No.1B			
Berth No.2	122	9.1	
Berth No.3	218	9.1	
Berth No.4	117	5.5	

Key to Principal Facilities:—					
A=Airport	**C**=Containers	**G**=General Cargo	**P**=Petroleum	**R**=Ro/Ro	**Y**=Dry Bulk
B=Bunkers	**D**=Dry Dock	**L**=Cruise	**Q**=Other Liquid Bulk	**T**=Towage (where available from port)	

Name	Length (m)	Depth (m)	Remarks
Berth No.6	91	5.5	
Berth No.7	91	5.5	
Berth No.9	99	4.6	
Berth No.10	251	10.7	
Berth No.11	229	10.7	Ro/ro ramp available
Berth No.13	184	9.1	Ro/ro ramp available
Berth No.14	152	10.7	
Berth No.15	122	10.7	
Berth No.16	175	10.7	
Berth No.17	221	10.7	
Berth No.19	221	10.7	
Berth No.20	221	10.7	

[1]*Three Rivers:* CP Rail and trucking companies connect with various industrial shipping centres of Quebec
Containers handled by shore cranes
Bulk facilities: Two berths, 428 m of wharves for ore and dry/liquid bulk facilities. Conveyor belts available for loading and unloading operations. There is a grain elevator on berth 16 with a loading cap of 2150 t/h and storage facilities for 110 000 t. A terminal for handling and storage of alumina and calcined coke with static storage cap of approx 100 000 t. A pitch liquefaction centre is also in operation
Tanker facilities: Sections 14, 19 and 20 offer facilities for tankers

Storage:

Location	Open (m²)	Covered (m²)
Berth No.1A		3555
Berth No.1B		2962
Berth No.2	4528	
Berth No.9		4706
Berth No.10		4672
Berth No.11	27481	8449
Berth No.14		14194
Berth No.19	35858	8697

Bunkering: Shell Canada Products Ltd, Suite 412, 25 des Forges, Three Rivers, Que., Canada G9A 06AZ, *Email:* pierre.fortin@shell.com, *Website:* www.shell.ca
BP Marine Americas Inc., 501 Westlake Park Boulevard, Houston, TX 77079, United States of America, *Tel:* +1 281 366 2000, *Email:* firstname.secondname@bp.com
Bunkerina International Inc., 11 3rd Avenue South, Roxboro, Montreal, Que., Canada H8Y 2L3, *Tel:* +1 514 806 2760, *Fax:* +1 514 683 2760
ExxonMobil Marine Fuels, Suite 900, One Alhambra Plaza, Coral Gables, FL 33134, United States of America, *Tel:* +1 305 459 6358, *Fax:* +1 305 459 6412, *Email:* emmf@exxonmobil.com, *Website:* www.exxonmobilmarinefuels.com
Hampton Bunkering Ltd, Suite 615, 999 de Maisonneuve Boulevard West, Montreal, Que., Canada H3A 3L4, *Tel:* +1 514 2882 818, *Fax:* +1 514 2829 279, *Email:* bunkers@hamptonmtl.ca
ICS Petroleum, ICS Petroleum (Montreal) Ltd, Suite 302, 430 Ste-Helene Street, Montreal, Que., Canada H2Y 2K7, *Tel:* +1 514 849 1223, *Fax:* +1 514 849 0517, *Email:* bunkers@ics-mtl.com, *Website:* www.icspet.com
Imperial Oil (Anjou) Ltd, 7100 Jean-Talon Street East, Anjou, Que., Canada H1M 3R8, *Tel:* +1 450 6497 519, *Fax:* +1 450 6497 821, *Email:* christian.beaunoyer@esso.ca, *Website:* www.imperialoil.com
Kildair Service Ltd, 92 Chemin Delangis, St. Paul de Joliette, Que., Canada JOK 3EO, *Tel:* +1 450 7568 091, *Fax:* +1 450 7564 783, *Email:* info@kildair.com, *Website:* www.kildair.com
Petro Canada Products Ltd, 11701 Sherbrooke Street East, Montreal, Que., Canada H1B 1C3, *Tel:* +1 613 657 1004, *Fax:* +1 514 640 8365, *Email:* elliott@petro-canada.ca, *Website:* www.petro-canada.ca
Reiter Petroleum Inc, Suite 900, 625 President Kennedy, Montreal, Que., Canada H3A 1K2, *Tel:* +1 514 8782 563, *Fax:* +1 514 8783 463, *Email:* bunkers@reiterpet.com, *Website:* www.reiterpet.com
Shell Canada Products Ltd, Suite 412, 25 des Forges, Three Rivers, Que., Canada G9A 06AZ, *Email:* pierre.fortin@shell.com, *Website:* www.shell.ca
Universal Maritime Agency & Trading Co. Ltd (Umatco), 2444 Marisa Ct., Mississauga, Ont., Canada, *Tel:* +1 905 823 4638, *Fax:* +1 905 823 3938, *Email:* umatco@sympatico.ca

Towage: Ocean Remorquage Trois-Rivieres Inc, P O Box 1963, Three Rivers, Que., Canada G1K 7M1, *Tel:* +1 819 377 4374, *Fax:* +1 819 377 4434, *Email:* ort@groupocean.com, *Website:* www.groupocean.com

Shipping Agents: Lower St Lawrence Ocean Agencies Ltd, P O Box 304, Three Rivers, Que., Canada G9A 5G4, *Tel:* +1 819 376 6611, *Fax:* +1 819 376 6140, *Email:* lolabcr@lola.ca

Stevedoring Companies: Logistec Stevedoring Inc., 2075 Notre-Dame, Three Rivers, Que., Canada G9A 4Y7, *Tel:* +1 819 379 0811, *Fax:* +1 819 379 2996, *Email:* info@logistec.com, *Website:* www.logistec.com
Prommel Inc., 3450 Boul Gene-H.-Kruger, Three Rivers, Que., Canada G9A 5G1, *Tel:* +1 819 379 3311, *Fax:* +1 819 379 5584, *Email:* info@prommel.com, *Website:* www.prommel.com

Airport: 8 km from city

Lloyd's Agent: Hayes Stuart Inc., 297 Duke Street, Montreal, Que., Canada H3C 2M2, *Tel:* +1 514 866 1801, *Fax:* +1 514 866 1259, *Email:* montreal@hayesstuart.com, *Website:* www.hayesstuart.com

THUNDER BAY

Lat 48° 25' N; Long 89° 13' W.

Admiralty Chart: -		**Admiralty Pilot:** -	
Time Zone: GMT -6 h		**UNCTAD Locode:** CA THU	

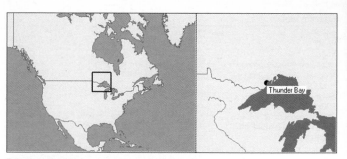

Principal Facilities:

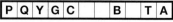

P	Q	Y	G	C			B		T	A

Authority: Thunder Bay Port Authority, 100 Main Street, Thunder Bay, Ont., Canada P7B 6R9, *Tel:* +1 807 345 6400, *Fax:* +1 807 345 9058, *Email:* tbport@tbaytel.net, *Website:* www.portofthunderbay.ca

Officials: Chief Executive Officer: Tim Heney, *Email:* tim@tbport.on.ca.
Harbour Master: Guy Jarvis, *Tel:* +1 807 346 7389, *Email:* guy@tbport.on.ca.

Port Security: ISPS compliant

Approach: Main channels have a depth of 8.2 m. Consult Canadian Hydrographic Chart No.2314

Pilotage: Foreign vessels require pilots while underway in port. Pilots are otherwise required in accordance with the Great Lakes Pilotage Regulations

Radio Frequency: Coast Guard radio VBA provides a complete information service to mariners. All vessels entering or leaving port, or engaged in vessel transits within the port, must contact Coast Guard radio VBA. VHF Channel 12 is used as working frequency by vessels in port waters

Weather: Navigation season usually from the end of March through to early January. Salt water vessels must clear port by mid December so as to exit seaway before Seaway Clearance Date (variable date - contact Seaway Authority)

Traffic: 2007, 8 490 000 t of cargo handled

Maximum Vessel Dimensions: 7.9 m draft

Working Hours: 24 h/day

Accommodation:

Name	Length (m)	Remarks
Thunder Bay		See [1] below
Keefer Terminal	750	See [2] below
Valley Camp Inc.		See [3] below
Thunder Bay Terminals	262	See [4] below

[1]*Thunder Bay:* Grain Terminals: Nine grain terminals with a total storage cap of 1 400 000 t. Wheat, durum, coarse grains, oilseeds, feed grains, peas and other pulses as well as various grain by-products are handled with loading rates of 1000-3400 t/h
Agricore United., Tel: +1 807 345 7351, operates two distinct facilities with different specialization totalling 500 000 t
Canadian Malting Co Ltd., Tel: +1 807 343 5460, operate a 62 800 t elevator and a 275 000 t/year malt production facility
Cargill Limited, Tel: +1 807 623 6724, operate a 176 000 t grain handling facility
Parrish & Heimbecker Ltd., Tel: +1 807 345 5822, operate a multi-product terminal with 40 000 t storage
Richardson Terminals Ltd., Tel: +1 807 343 5570, have a 208 500 t cap terminal capable of handling all varieties
Saskatchewan Wheat Pool, Tel: +1 807 344 8261, operates the Pool 7 complex and offers services for all grains through a 362 600 t facility
Western Grain By-Products, Tel: +1 807 623 8500, handle a wide range of speciality crops and offer custom bagging at their 40 000 t facility
Liquid Bulk Facilities: Petro Canada Inc., Tel: +1 807 622 8701 operate petroleum terminals
There are two chemical companies with storage facilities: General Chemical Co., Tel: +1 807 622 4346, receives calcium chloride from Southern Ontario which is offloaded into storage tanks for distribution throughout Northwestern Ontario and Dow Chemical Canada, Tel: +1 807 577 8429, receives caustic soda by rail from Alberta which is offloaded into large storage tanks for local use and for further shipment to Eastern Canada and the United States
[2]*Keefer Terminal:* Tel: +1 807 345 6400, Fax: +1 807 345 9058, E-mail: tbport@tbaytel.net
General cargo, lumber, steel, machinery, bagged goods, large project cargoes, heavy lifts
[3]*Valley Camp Inc.:* Tel: +1 807 622 6464, Fax: +1 807 623 7872, Email: valcamp@tbaytel.net
Three cargo handling areas with a free flowing dry-bulk transfer system, a bulk commodity dock with cranes and a dry bulk handling facility. Vessels up to 304 m can be handled at the docks which are 550 m and 201 m in length. Outside ground storage for over 2 000 000 t of cargo
[4]*Thunder Bay Terminals:* Tel: +1 807 625 7800, Fax: +1 807 623 5740
Transfer of low sulphur bituminous and lignite coal from mines in British Columbia, Alberta and Saskatchewan to Ontario Hydro's thermal generating stations. The facility also handles metallurgical coal as well as other dry bulk commodities such as potash, urea and various agri-products

Bunkering: Petro Canada Products Ltd, 11701 Sherbrooke Street East, Montreal, Que., Canada H1B 1C3, *Tel:* +1 613 657 1004, *Fax:* +1 514 640 8365, *Email:* elliott@petro-canada.ca, *Website:* www.petro-canada.ca – *Grades:* MDO

Waste Reception Facilities: Thunder Bay Marine Services, Thunder Bay, Ont., Canada, *Tel:* +1 807 344 9221

Towage: Gravel & Lake Services Ltd, P O Box 2180, Thunder Bay, Ont., Canada P7B 5E8, *Tel:* +1 807 345 7305, *Fax:* +1 807 345 8377
Thunder Bay Tug Services Ltd, 600-100 Main Street, Thunder Bay, Ont., Canada P7B 6R9, *Tel:* +1 807 343 4784, *Fax:* +1 807 768 1239, *Email:* sdawson@tbaytel.net

Repair & Maintenance: Lakehead Marine & Industrial Inc., P O Box 10634, 401 Shipyard Drive, Thunder Bay, Ont., Canada P7B 6V1, *Tel:* +1 807 683 6261, *Fax:* +1 807 683 3607, *Email:* info@lakemind.ca, *Website:* www.lakemind.ca Full service dry dock and vessel repair facility

Seaman Missions: The Seamans Mission, Suite 450, 100 Main Street, Thunder Bay, Ont., Canada P7B 6R9, *Tel:* +1 807 344 8241, *Fax:* +1 807 345 3135, *Email:* flyingangel@tbaytel.net

Stevedoring Companies: Empire Stevedoring Co Ltd, 100 Main Street, P O Box 29070, Thunder Bay, Ont., Canada P7B 6P9, *Tel:* +1 807 346 5700, *Fax:* +1 807 346 6868, *Email:* empstev@tbaytel.net, *Website:* www.empirestevedoring.com

Surveyors: Crawford & Company, 395 Fort William Road, Thunder Bay, Ont., Canada P7B 2Z5, *Tel:* +1 807 344 1800, *Fax:* +1 807 344 1803, *Email:* geoff.sullivan@crawco.ca, *Website:* www.crawfordandcompany.com
Kam River Inspection Services Ltd, Thunder Bay, Ont., Canada, *Tel:* +1 807 577 9565
Societe Generale de Surveillance (SGS), SGS Supervision Services Inc., Thunder Bay, Ont., Canada, *Tel:* +1 807 475 8955, *Website:* www.sgs.com

Medical Facilities: Three general hospitals

Airport: Thunder Bay Airport, approx 30 mins

Railway: Served by Canadian National and Canadian Pacific Railways

Lloyd's Agent: McLarens Canada (Toronto), 600 Alden Road, Suite 600, Markham, Toronto, Ont., Canada L3R 0E7, *Tel:* +1 905 946 9995, *Fax:* +1 905 946 0171, *Email:* roger.bickers@mclarens.ca, *Website:* www.mclarens.ca

TORONTO

Lat 43° 39' N; Long 79° 21' W.

Admiralty Chart: -	**Admiralty Pilot:** -
Time Zone: GMT -5 h	**UNCTAD Locode:** CA TOR

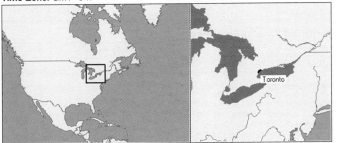

Principal Facilities:

Y	G	C	R	L	B		T	A	

Authority: Toronto Port Authority, 60 Harbour Street, Toronto, Ont., Canada M5J 1B7, *Tel:* +1 416 863 2000, *Fax:* +1 416 863 0495, *Email:* info@torontoport.com, *Website:* www.torontoport.com

Officials: Chief Executive Officer: Lisa Raitt, *Tel:* +1 416 863 2016, *Email:* lraitt@torontoport.com.
Chief Financial Officer: Alan Paul, *Tel:* +1 416 863 2082, *Email:* apaul@torontoport.com.
Harbour Master: Angus Armstrong, *Tel:* +1 416 863 2026, *Email:* aarmstrong@torontoport.com.
Marketing: James Fox, *Tel:* +1 416 863 2010, *Email:* jfox@@torontoport.com.

Port Security: ISPS compliant. Full security 24 h/day - 7 days a week. Canada customs bonded warehouses and yard

Pre-Arrival Information: Advance notice required for berthing as far in advance as possible, estimated date and time of arrival, departure and nature of cargo, if any to be handled. Such requests are required by Fax: +1 416 462 1612 or Email: alefebvr@logistec.com

Approach: The Eastern Gap is the main channel entrance with a depth of 8.2 m. Vessels using gap must not exceed a speed of 6 knots

Anchorage: All anchorages allotted by the Harbour Master

Pilotage: Available from St. Lawrence Pilotage Authority

Radio Frequency: Call on VHF Channel 16, working channel VHF Channel 12

Traffic: 2006, 2 154 913 t of cargo handled

Maximum Vessel Dimensions: Max d 8.23 m, max loa 222.5 m

Principal Imports and Exports: Imports: Bulk cargo, General cargo, Heavy lift, Project cargo, Steel. Exports: General cargo, Heavy lift, Machinery, Project cargo.

Working Hours: Monday to Friday 0800-1200, 1300-1700. Overtime 1800-2200, Saturday, Sunday and holidays

Accommodation:

Name	Remarks
Toronto	See [1] below

[1]*Toronto:* Excellent land-locked harbour with two channel entrances, of which the eastern one is the main shipping entrance. Each is dredged to seaway depth. 19.2 km of docks include facilities for the handling of bulk and general cargoes
The Port Authority operates two general cargo terminals with berthage of 3490 m at max seaway depth and with a total of 80 230 m2 of warehouse space and 356 500 m2 of outside storage area. All berths and the container centre are connected to two trans-continental railway systems by 56 km of waterfront track and Canada Customs offices are on location. The movement of cargo is controlled by computerised inventory and release system. Private cranes ranging in cap from 20 t to 150 t are available by arrangement
Container & ro/ro facilities: Marine Terminal 51, container distribution centre, total length of berth 884 m in depth alongside of 8.23 m with special container handling

equipment including a mobile container crane capable of direct ship loading and discharging. 57 000 m2 of dry storage. There are two berths to handle ro/ro traffic

Storage:

Location	Open (m²)	Covered (m²)
Toronto	356500	80230

Mechanical Handling Equipment:

Location	Type	Capacity (t)	Qty	Remarks
Toronto	Mult-purp. Cranes	300	1	shear legs
Toronto	Mult-purp. Cranes	50	1	
Toronto	Mobile Cranes		6	
Toronto	Mobile Cranes	200	1	See [1] below
Toronto	Container Cranes	50	7	

[1]*Toronto:* used for container handling

Cargo Worked: Up to 2400 t/day

Bunkering: Sheella Bunker Supply, 20 Teesdale Place, Suite 1006, Toronto, Ont., Canada M1L-1L1, *Tel:* +1 416 4180 934, *Fax:* +1 416 6986 989, *Email:* sheellabunker@rogers.com
Provmar Fuels Inc., Station C, P O Box 3355, Hamilton, Ont., Canada L8H 7L4, *Tel:* +1 905 5499 402, *Fax:* +1 905 5499 929, *Email:* inquiries@provmar.com, *Website:* www.provmar.com – *Grades:* all grades – *Delivery Mode:* truck

Towage: Great Lakes Marine Contracting Ltd, 220 North Tower Drive, Black Creek, Black Creek, WI 54106, United States of America, *Tel:* +1 920 984 4303
McKeil Work Boats Ltd, Toronto, Ont., Canada, *Tel:* +1 416 643 1821

Repair & Maintenance: Ship repairs carried out afloat only; nearest dry dock is 41.6 km across the lake at Port Weller, entrance to the Welland Ship Canal which links Lake Ontario with Lake Erie

Seaman Missions: The Seamans Mission, Pier 51, 8 Unwin Avenue, Toronto, Ont., Canada M5A 1A1, *Tel:* +1 416 469 5391, *Fax:* +1 416 469 1602, *Email:* toangels@sympatico.ca

Shipping Agents: Inchcape Shipping Services (ISS), 125 Carleton Street, P O Box 29066, St. Catharines, Ont., Canada L2R 7P9, *Tel:* +1 905 688 6124, *Fax:* +1 905 688 6304, *Email:* iss.toronto@iss-shipping.com, *Website:* www.iss-shipping.com
McLean Kennedy Inc., Toronto, Ont., Canada, *Tel:* +1 905 794 2246, *Fax:* +1 905 794 9036, *Email:* hjaffer@mcleankennedy.ca
Mediterranean Shipping Company, MSC Canada Inc, 300 The East Mall, Suite 402, Etobicoke, Ont., Canada M9B 6B7, *Tel:* +1 416 231 6434, *Fax:* +1 416 231 0281, *Email:* msccanada@mscca.mscgva.ch, *Website:* www.mscgva.ch
A.P. Moller-Maersk Group, Maersk Canada Inc, 2576 Matheson Boulevard East, Mississauga, Ont., Canada L4W 5H1, *Tel:* +1 905 624 5585, *Fax:* +1 905 624 3585, *Email:* torsal@maersk.com, *Website:* www.maerskline.com
Protos Shipping Ltd, 701 Evans Avenue, Suite 700, Toronto, Ont., Canada M9C 1A3, *Tel:* +1 416 621 4381, *Fax:* +1 416 626 1311, *Email:* info@protos.ca, *Website:* www.protos.ca
Robert Reford Inc., 425 Adelaide Street West, Suite 303, Toronto, Ont., Canada M5V 3C1, *Tel:* +1 514 867 5207, *Fax:* +1 514 845 6490, *Email:* ops@reford.ca, *Website:* www.robertreford.com
Seabridge International Shipping Inc., 18 King Street East, Suite 902, Toronto, Ont., Canada M5C 1C4, *Tel:* +1 416 862 7600, *Fax:* +1 416 862 5453, *Email:* toronto@seabridge.ca, *Website:* www.seabridge.ca
Seanautic Marine Inc., 703 Evans Avenue, Toronto, Ont., Canada M9C 5E9, *Tel:* +1 416 620 7224, *Fax:* +1 416 620 7073, *Email:* infotor@seanauticmarine.com, *Website:* www.seanauticmarine.com
Westward Shipping Ltd, 55 Town Centre Court, Suite 632, Toronto, Ont., Canada M1P 4X4, *Tel:* +1 416 290 0554, *Fax:* +1 416 290 0559, *Email:* westward@bellnet.ca, *Website:* www.westwardshipping.com

Surveyors: Crawford & Company, Suite 700, 505 Consumers Road, Toronto, Ont., Canada M2J 4V8, *Tel:* +1 416 499 9950, *Fax:* +1 416 499 9263, *Email:* roland.paxton@crawco.ca, *Website:* www.crawfordandcompany.com
Matthews-Daniel Services (Bermuda) Ltd, Matthews-Daniel International (Canada) Ltd, 20 Bay Street 1025, Toronto, Ont., Canada M5J 2N8, *Tel:* +1 416 594 2424, *Fax:* +1 416 594 1623, *Website:* www.matdan.com

Medical Facilities: Doctor and hospital services available

Airport: Toronto Island, 10 km

Railway: All principal berths are rail-served. CN and CP Rail on site

Lloyd's Agent: McLarens Canada (Toronto), 600 Alden Road, Suite 600, Markham, Toronto, Ont., Canada L3R 0E7, *Tel:* +1 905 946 9995, *Fax:* +1 905 946 0171, *Email:* roger.bickers@mclarens.ca, *Website:* www.mclarens.ca

TRANS MOUNTAIN PIPELINE WEST-RIDGE TERMINAL

harbour area, see under Vancouver

TROIS RIVIERES

alternate name, see Three Rivers

TUKTOYAKTUK

Lat 69° 26' N; Long 133° 3' W.

Admiralty Chart: 2177	**Admiralty Pilot:** 12
Time Zone: GMT -8 h	**UNCTAD Locode:** CA TUK

Key to Principal Facilities:—

A=Airport	**C**=Containers	**G**=General Cargo	**P**=Petroleum	**R**=Ro/Ro	**Y**=Dry Bulk
B=Bunkers	**D**=Dry Dock	**L**=Cruise	**Q**=Other Liquid Bulk	**T**=Towage (where available from port)

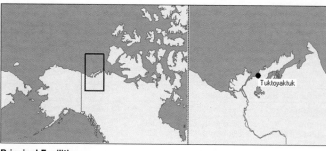

Principal Facilities:

P		G C		B		T A

Authority: Northern Transportation Company Limited (NTCL), 42003 MacKenzie Highway, Hay River, N.W.T., Canada XOE OR9, *Tel:* +1 867 8745 100, *Fax:* +1 867 8745 103, *Email:* ntcl@ntcl.com, *Website:* www.ntcl.com

Officials: President: Cameron Clement.
Vice President: Rick Connors.
Director: Capt Terry Camsell.
Director: Capt David Day.
Director: Lynette Storoz.
General Manager: Gary Latimer.
Manager: Greg Whitlock.
Marketing Manager: Sunny Munroe, *Tel:* +1 867 4442441, *Email:* smunroe@ntcl.com

Port Security: ISPS compliant

Approach: Narrow entrances with strong streams. Depth in main channel max 4 m d; channel well marked with buoys for 24 km seaward

Pilotage: Contact Coastguard Radio 'INUVIK NWT', 5803 mHz

Maximum Vessel Dimensions: Max loa 200 m, max d 4.0 m

Working Hours: 24 h/day

Accommodation:

Name	Length (m)	Depth (m)	Remarks
Tuktoyaktuk			Local Office, Tel: +1 867 977 2442, Fax: +1 867 977 2410
Wharf	335.2	3–6.1	Two ramps for landing craft at the transit depot

Storage: Open storage of 4.6 ha

Location	Covered (m²)	Sheds / Warehouses
Tuktoyaktuk	1672	1

Bunkering: Imperial Oil (Burnaby) Ltd, International Marine Sales, 4720 Kingsway, Burnaby, B.C., Canada V5H 4N2, *Tel:* +1 604 451 5955, *Fax:* +1 604 451 5950

Towage: Available

Medical Facilities: Nursing station with two resident nurses

Airport: Local airport, 1.6 km

Lloyd's Agent: McLarens Canada (Edmonton), 4208 97 Street, Suite 103, Edmonton, Alta., Canada T6E 5Z1, *Email:* roger.bickers@mclarens.ca, *Website:* www.mclarens.ca

VALLEYFIELD

Lat 45° 13' N; Long 74° 5' W.

Admiralty Chart: -	**Admiralty Pilot:** -
Time Zone: GMT -5 h	**UNCTAD Locode:** CA VLF

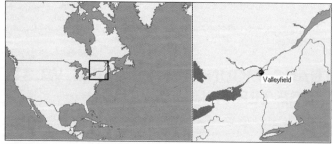

Principal Facilities:

P Q Y G		R		B		A

Authority: Port of Valleyfield, 950 Gerard-Cadieux Boulevard, Suite 100, Valleyfield, Que., Canada J6T 6L4, *Tel:* +1 450 373 4021, *Fax:* +1 450 373 4026, *Email:* info@portvalleyfield.com, *Website:* www.portvalleyfield.com

Officials: General Manager: Michel Gadoua, *Email:* mgadoua@portvalleyfield.com.
Executive Assistant: Isabelle Viau, *Email:* iviau@portvalleyfield.com.

Port Security: ISPS compliant

Pre-Arrival Information: This information can be obtained from ship's agents

Pilotage: Compulsory. Great Lakes pilotage at St. Lambert Lock (Montreal)

Weather: Normal winds. Ice from January to March when Seaway is closed

Traffic: 2006, 475 087 t of cargo handled

Principal Imports and Exports: Imports: Bauxite, General cargo, Industrial Salt, Liquid bulk, Road salt, Steel. Exports: General cargo, Other liquid bulk, Slag stone, Sulphuric acid.

Working Hours: 0800-1700. Overtime as needed

Accommodation:

Name	Length (m)	Depth (m)	Remarks
Valleyfield			
North West Dock	482	8	See [1] below
South Dock	274	8	See [2] below
North East Dock	350	8	See [3] below

[1]*North West Dock:* Operated by Valleytank Inc., 950 Gerard-Cadieux Blvd, Suite 600, Valleyfield Que J6T 6L4, Tel: +1 450 371 1781, Fax: +1 450 371 8613, Email: management@valleytank.ca, Website: www.valleytank.ca
Handling of liquid bulk cargo. 28 tanks with total cap of 22 300 m3
[2]*South Dock:* Operated by Valport Maritime Services Inc., 950 Gerard-Cadieux Blvd, Suite 500, Valleyfield Que J6T 6L4, Tel: +1 450 377 6686, Fax: +1 450 377 2521, Email: info@valport.ca, Website: www.valport.ca
Dry bulk & general cargo
[3]*North East Dock:* Operated by Valport Maritime Services Inc., 950 Gerard-Cadieux Blvd, Suite 500, Valleyfield Que J6T 6L4, Tel: +1 450 377 6686, Fax: +1 450 377 2521, Email: info@valport.ca, Website: www.valport.ca
Dry bulk & general cargo

Storage: 34 storage reservoirs for liquid bulk cargo with a total cap of 36 683 m3

Location	Open (m²)	Covered (m²)	Sheds / Warehouses
Valleyfield	77500	14700	3

Mechanical Handling Equipment:

Location	Type	Capacity (t)	Qty
Valleyfield	Mult-purp. Cranes	100	1

Cargo Worked: 6000-7000 t dry bulk/day

Bunkering: BP Marine Americas Inc., 501 Westlake Park Boulevard, Houston, TX 77079, United States of America, *Tel:* +1 281 366 2000, *Email:* firstname.secondname@bp.com
Bunkerina International Inc., 11 3rd Avenue South, Roxboro, Montreal, Que., Canada H8Y 2L3, *Tel:* +1 514 806 2760, *Fax:* +1 514 683 2760
ExxonMobil Marine Fuels, Suite 900, One Alhambra Plaza, Coral Gables, FL 33134, United States of America, *Tel:* +1 305 459 6358, *Fax:* +1 305 459 6412, *Email:* emmf@exxonmobil.com, *Website:* www.exxonmobilmarinefuels.com
Hampton Bunkering Ltd, Suite 615, 999 de Maisonneuve Boulevard West, Montreal, Que., Canada H3A 3L4, *Tel:* +1 514 2882 818, *Fax:* +1 514 2829 279, *Email:* bunkers@hamptonmtl.ca
ICS Petroleum, ICS Petroleum (Montreal) Ltd, Suite 302, 430 Ste-Helene Street, Montreal, Que., Canada H2Y 2K7, *Tel:* +1 514 849 1223, *Fax:* +1 514 849 0517, *Email:* bunkers@ics-mtl.com, *Website:* www.icspet.com
Imperial Oil (Anjou) Ltd, 7100 Jean-Talon Street East, Anjou, Que., Canada H1M 3R8, *Tel:* +1 450 6497 519, *Fax:* +1 450 6497 821, *Email:* christian.beaunoyer@esso.ca, *Website:* www.imperialoil.com
Kildair Service Ltd, 92 Chemin Delangis, St. Paul de Joliette, Que., Canada JOK 3EO, *Tel:* +1 450 7568 091, *Fax:* +1 450 7564 783, *Email:* info@kildair.com, *Website:* www.kildair.com
Petro Canada Products Ltd, 11701 Sherbrooke Street East, Montreal, Que., Canada H1B 1C3, *Tel:* +1 613 657 1004, *Fax:* +1 514 640 8365, *Email:* elliott@petro-canada.ca, *Website:* www.petro-canada.ca
Reiter Petroleum Inc, Suite 900, 625 President Kennedy, Montreal, Que., Canada H3A 1K2, *Tel:* +1 514 8782 563, *Fax:* +1 514 8783 463, *Email:* bunkers@reiterpet.com, *Website:* www.reiterpet.com
Universal Maritime Agency & Trading Co. Ltd (Umatco), 2444 Marisa Ct., Mississauga, Ont., Canada, *Tel:* +1 905 823 4638, *Fax:* +1 905 823 3938, *Email:* umatco@sympatico.ca

Waste Reception Facilities: Dry garbage disposal available

Repair & Maintenance: Repair shops available locally

Medical Facilities: Modern hospital within 5 mins

Airport: Dorval International Airport, 40 km

Railway: CN and CSX serve the port

Lloyd's Agent: Hayes Stuart Inc., 297 Duke Street, Montreal, Que., Canada H3C 2M2, *Tel:* +1 514 866 1801, *Fax:* +1 514 866 1259, *Email:* montreal@hayesstuart.com, *Website:* www.hayesstuart.com

VANCOUVER

Lat 49° 17' N; Long 123° 6' W.

Admiralty Chart: 4962/4963/4964/4965	**Admiralty Pilot:** 25
Time Zone: GMT -8 h	**UNCTAD Locode:** CA VAN

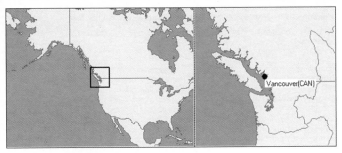

Principal Facilities:

P	Q	Y	G	C	R	L	B	D	T	A

Authority: Port Metro Vancouver, 100 The Pointe, 999 Canada Place, Vancouver, B.C., Canada V6C 3T4, *Tel:* +1 604 665 9000, *Email:* info@vfpa.ca, *Website:* www.vfpa.ca

Officials: Chairman: Sarah Morgan-Silvester.
Chief Executive Officer: Capt Gordon Houston, *Tel:* +1 604 665 9000, *Email:* gordon.houston@vfpa.ca.
Harbour Master: Yoss Leclerc, *Email:* harbour_master@vfpa.ca.

Port Security: ISPS compliant. Container Security Initiative (CSI) designated port

Approach: The principal approach is from the S through the Strait of Juan de Fuca separating Canada and the United States, then around the southern tip of Vancouver Island through Haro Strait between the many Gulf Islands, and the Strait of Georgia
Access to Vancouver from the N is usually made by vessels calling at northern British Columbia or Alaskan ports, through the sheltered Inside Passage, a route which includes Queen Charlotte Strait, Johnstone Strait, through Seymour Narrows and into the Strait of Georgia

Pilotage: Compulsory and managed by Pacific Pilotage Authority, Tel: +1 604 666 6771, Fax: +1 604 666 1647. Pilots may board inbound vessels at three pilot stations
Brotchie Ledge (Victoria Pilot Station) Buoy in approx pos 48 22.5' N; 123 23.5' W which is the main pilot station for Vancouver and used for all Juan de Fuca inbound traffic
Triple Island (near Prince Rupert) in pos 54 17.7' N; 130 52.7' W, used for vessels approaching from the north
Cape Beale in pos 48 47.2' N; 125 23.5' W, used mainly for W coast Vancouver Island ports
12 h notice is required to obtain a pilot at Brotchie Ledge with confirmation of ETA not less than 4 h prior to arrival, and 48 h notice is required at Triple Island

Radio Frequency: VHF Channel 12 for Vancouver Traffic Services

Tides: Mixed diurnal type, with mean range of 3.1 m and max of 5 m. Deep-sea vessels transiting under the Second Narrows Bridges do so during periods of operation established either side of high and low water slack and based on a limiting rate of tidal current of 2 knots and a tidal height of 2.13 m or more

Traffic: 2007, 82 700 000 t of cargo handled, 2 307 289 TEU's

Maximum Vessel Dimensions: 259 588 dwt, 328.6 m loa

Principal Imports and Exports: Imports: Iron, Metals, Phosphate rock, Raw sugar, Salt, Steel. Exports: Coal and coke, Copper ores, Fodder and feedstuffs, Grain, Lumber, Potash, Sulphur, Woodpulp.

Working Hours: 24 h/day, seven days a week. No work on Labour Day, Christmas Day and New Year's Day

Accommodation: The port of Vancouver encompasses three main areas: Burrard Inlet, Roberts Bank and English Bay
Burrard Inlet (between First and Second Narrows): First Narrows has a controlling depth of 15.0 m at LNT and an air draft of 60.0 m at HHW under Lions Gate Bridge. Distance between bridge towers is 457 m and the navigation channel is 396 m wide. Vessels can transit First Narrows 24 h/day. There are six restricted-use anchorages in this area
Burrard Inlet (above Second Narrows): Second Narrows with both a highway and rail

bridge across, is a movement restricted area. Large vessels are restricted to transiting the narrows at times published by the Harbour Master. Vessels over 6500 t displacement must be escorted by two tugs during transit of the bridges. The navigable channel width at the bridges is 137 m and air draft is 44 m at HHW. Four anchorages are available above Second Narrows
Roberts Bank: Man-made harbour on the Strait of Georgia, 25 nautical miles S of Burrard Inlet. Westshore Terminals has two berths for coal loading and Deltaport Container Terminal has two berths
English Bay: Forms the main anchorage area for the port with fifteen numbered anchorages, all anchorages assigned by the Harbour Master

Name	Length (m)	Depth (m)	Draught (m)	Remarks
Cascadia Terminal				
Berth No.1	274	15.2		Cereals. Storage of 280 000 t
Rogers Sugar Dock				Owned by BC Sugar
Berth	144	9.1		
Berry Point Site				
Berth No.1	213	12.7		
Berth No.2	170	12.7		
Berth No.3	185	12.7		
Berth No.4	185	12.7		
Canada Place (Cruise Ship Terminal)				
East Berth	314	8.4		
North Berth	135	8.4		
West Berth	326	8.4		
CXY Chemicals				
Berth No.1		10.66		See [1] below
Centerm				See [2] below
Berth No.1	364	12		General cargo
Berth No.2	200	12		General cargo
Berth No.3	200	12.19		General cargo
Berth No.4	183	12.19		General cargo
Berth No.5	322	12.2		Containers
Berth No.6	322	15.5		Containers
Burlington Northern Santa Fe				See [3] below
Deep Sea Berth	200	10		
Barge Berth	120	6.5		
Dow Chemical Terminal				
Lynnterm No.4 Berth	200	11.6		See [4] below
Fibreco Terminal				See [5] below
Berth	137	11.5		Including mooring dolphins 265 m
Imperial Oil IOCO Terminal				
Berth		10.1		See [6] below
Lynnterm				See [7] below
Main Street Dock				See [8] below
Berth	122	5		
Neptune Bulk Terminals				See [9] below
Berth No.1	230		15.2	See [10] below
Berth No.2	230		14.6	See [11] below
Berth No.3	250		13.4	See [12] below
Pacific Elevators				See [13] below
Berth No.1		9.6		See [14] below
Berth No.2		13.7		See [15] below
Berth No.4	305	10.2		
Petro-Canada Terminal				Petroleum products
West Berth		12		See [16] below
East Berth	40	6		
Pier 94				
West Berth	183	6		
East Berth	110	9		
JRI (James Richardson International) Terminal				
Berth	180	15.24		Canadian grain with storage of 108 000 t
Saskatchewan Wheat Pool				See [17] below
Berth No.1	230	15.5		
Berth No.2	230	15.5		
Shellburn Terminal				Petroleum products
Outer Berth	122	8.9		
Inner Berth	94	5.2		Mooring dolphins 154 m apart
Stanovan Terminal				Petroleum products
Berth No.1	85	12.5		Mooring dolphins 216 m apart
Trans Mountain Pipeline Westridge Terminal				Crude petroleum, petroleum products & jet fuel
Berth	92	11		See [18] below
United Grain Growers				Grain & grain products. Storage of 102 070 t
West Berth	213	11.7		
East Berth	213	13.6		
Vancouver Wharves				See [19] below
Berth No's 1,2 & 3	411	11.3–13.7		

Key to Principal Facilities:—
A=Airport	**C**=Containers	**G**=General Cargo
B=Bunkers	**D**=Dry Dock	**L**=Cruise

P=Petroleum	**R**=Ro/Ro
Q=Other Liquid Bulk	**T**=Towage (where available from port)

Y=Dry Bulk

Name	Length (m)	Depth (m)	Draught (m)	Remarks
Berth No's 4 & 5	396	12.8		
Vanterm				See [20] below
Berth No.1	286	15.2		Containers
Berth No.2	286	15.2		Containers
Berth No.3	228	15.2		Containers
Berth No.4	183	15.2		Combo/conventional vessels
Berth No.5	91	15.2		Combo/conventional vessels
Port Moody				
Pacific Coast Terminals Co Ltd				See [21] below
Berth No.1	237		12	Petrochemical liquids & sulphur
Berth No.2	293		12	Sulphur
Roberts Bank				
Deltaport Container Terminal	670	15.85		See [22] below
Westshore Terminals				See [23] below

[1]*Berth No.1:* Length 152 m plus mooring floats 243 m apart
Imports of bulk sea salt and exports of caustic soda and sodium chlorate
[2]*Centerm:* Operated by DP World Vancouver, 777 Centennial Road, Vancouver BC V6A 1A3, Tel: +1 604 255 5151, Fax: +1 604 662 8464, Website: www.dpworld.com
Container, forest products, breakbulk & general cargoes. Three sheds totalling 30 000 m2 and container storage of 9600 TEU's. Lumber and general cargo staging area
[3]*Burlington Northern Santa Fe:* Operated by Empire Stevedoring
Steel, breakbulk, pulp, newsprint & lumber
[4]*Lynnterm No.4 Berth:* Caustic soda solution (storage 40 000 t, loading at 1200 t/h), ethylene dichloride (storage 30 000 t, loading at 1000 t/h) and ethylene glycol (storage 17 000 t, loading at 800 t/h)
[5]*Fibreco Terminal:* Fibreco Exports Inc., 1209 McKeen Avenue, North Vancouver BC V7P 3H9, Tel: +1 604 980 6543, Fax: +1 604 984 2593, Website: www.fibreco.com
Loading of wood-chips for vessels up to 42 000 dwt. The bulk loader has a cap of 1200 t/h
[6]*Berth:* Petroleum products. Length 165 m with mooring dolphins for tankers up to 35 000 dwt
[7]*Lynnterm:* Wood pulp, lumber, plywood, steel, containers, project & general cargo
Four berths totalling 915 m in depth 15 m. Four warehouses totalling 56 000 m2
[8]*Main Street Dock:* Primarily used as a lay-by berth for smaller vessels like tugs & barges
[9]*Neptune Bulk Terminals:* Neptune Bulk Terminals (Canada) Ltd., P O Box 86367, North Vancouver BC V7L 4K6, Tel: +1 604 985 7461, Fax: +1 604 985 8941, Email: inquiries@nbtcl.bc.ca, Website: www.neptuneterminals.com
Products handled include metallurgical and thermal coal, potash, feed pellets, chemical fertilizers, canola oil and phosphate rock
[10]*Berth No.1:* Coal berth for vessels up to 180 000 dwt. Two quadrant shiploaders rated at 2700 t/h each. Air draft 19 m
[11]*Berth No.2:* Dry bulk berth for vessels up to 80 000 dwt. Two quadrant shiploaders rated at 2200 t/h each. Air draft 19 m
[12]*Berth No.3:* Dry bulk berth for vessels up to 65 000 dwt. Travelling shiploader at rate of 2500 t/h for potash and 1200 t/h for agricultural. Air draft 17.7 m
[13]*Pacific Elevators:* Canola, malting barley, feed barley, rye, peas, flax and pellets
[14]*Berth No.1:* Lay-berth. Dock face of 185 m plus bollards on overhang
[15]*Berth No.2:* Loading berth. Dock face of 215 m plus bollards on overhang
[16]*West Berth:* Length 43 m plus mooring/breasting dolphins
[17]*Saskatchewan Wheat Pool:* Wheat, durum wheat, canola, barley & grain by-products. Storage of 240 000 t
[18]*Berth:* 305 m between extreme mooring dolphins
[19]*Vancouver Wharves:* Products handled include mineral concentrates, liquids, methanol, pulp and paper, sulphur, potash, fertilizers and other dry bulk commodities at five berths
[20]*Vanterm:* Vanterm Container Terminal operated by Terminal Systems Inc (TSI), 1300 Stewart Street, Vancouver BC V5L 4X5, Tel: +1 604 251 9200, Fax: +1 604 251 9214, Email: vtcyservices@tsi.bc.ca, Website: www.tsi.bc.ca
Located on the S shore of Burrard Inlet in the Vancouver Inner Harbour with a total area of 76 acres, comprises two 286 m berths and one 228 m berth. This terminal is designed to handle third generation container vessels using the most modern concepts in container handling and container freight station of 11 613 m2; storage area for 9200 TEU's
[21]*Pacific Coast Terminals Co Ltd:* 2300 Columbia Street, Port Moody BC V3H 5J9, Tel: +1 604 939 7371, Fax: +1 604 936 6850, Email: pctinfo@pct.ca, Website: www.pct.ca
Sulphur, ethylene glycol & styrene monomer
[22]*Deltaport Container Terminal:* Operated by Terminal Systems Inc (TSI), 2 Roberts Bank Road, Delta BC V4M 4G5, Tel: +1 604 215 5700, Fax: +1 604 215 570, Email: dpcyservices@tsi.bc.ca, Website: www.tsi.bc.ca
Two berths. 40 ha container terminal (to be expanded to 65 ha) with storage for 13 000 TEU's. 600 reefer points. On-dock rail intermodal yard
[23]*Westshore Terminals:* Operated by Westshore Terminals Ltd., 1 Roberts Bank, Delta BC V4M 4G5, Tel: +1 604 946 4491, Fax: +1 604 946 1388, Website: www.westshore.com
Coal and coke terminals located on a total of approx 100 ha of reclaimed land on Fraser River flatlands S of Vancouver. Connected to the mainland by a 5 km causeway, permitting road and rail access. There are two loading berths suitable for handling coal and coke. Bulk carriers up to 260 000 dwt can be accommodated at Berth No.1 and up to 150 000 dwt at Berth No.2. Equipment installed for coal handling includes three stacker/reclaimers and two rotary rail car dumpers

Mechanical Handling Equipment:

Location	Type	Capacity (t)	Qty
Centerm	Post Panamax	45–50	5
Vanterm	Container Cranes		5
Vanterm	Super Post Panamax	65	2
Deltaport Container Terminal	Post Panamax		6
Deltaport Container Terminal	Super Post Panamax	65	1

Bunkering: C.H. Cates & Sons Ltd, 10 Pemberton Avenue, Vancouver, B.C., Canada V7P 2R1, *Tel:* +1 604 988 2161, *Fax:* +1 604 988 6060, *Email:* info@seaspan.com, *Website:* www.seaspan.com
ICS Petroleum, ICS Petroleum Ltd., P O Box 12115, Suite 2360, 555 West Hastings Street, Vancouver, B.C., Canada V6B 4N6, *Tel:* +1 604 6856 221, *Fax:* +1 604 6857 352, *Email:* bunkers@ics-vcr.com, *Website:* www.icspet.com
Marine Petrobulk Ltd, 10 Pemberton Avenue, Vancouver, B.C., Canada V7P 2R1, *Tel:* +1 604 9874 415, *Fax:* +1 604 9873 824, *Email:* tbrewster@marinepetro.com, *Website:* www.marinepetrobulk.com
ExxonMobil Marine Fuels, Suite 900, One Alhambra Plaza, Coral Gables, FL 33134, United States of America, *Tel:* +1 305 459 6358, *Fax:* +1 305 459 6412, *Email:* emmf@exxonmobil.com, *Website:* www.exxonmobilmarinefuels.com – *Grades:* IFO40-380cSt; MDO – *Delivery Mode:* barge
ICS Petroleum, ICS Petroleum Ltd., P O Box 12115, Suite 2360, 555 West Hastings Street, Vancouver, B.C., Canada V6B 4N6, *Tel:* +1 604 6856 221, *Fax:* +1 604 6857 352, *Email:* bunkers@ics-vcr.com, *Website:* www.icspet.com – *Grades:* all grades – *Rates:* barge 300t/h, truck 50t/h – *Delivery Mode:* barge, truck
Imperial Oil (Burnaby) Ltd, International Marine Sales, 4720 Kingsway, Burnaby, B.C., Canada V5H 4N2, *Tel:* +1 604 451 5955, *Fax:* +1 604 451 5950 – *Grades:* all grades – *Misc:* own storage facilities – *Notice:* 72 hours – *Delivery Mode:* barge, truck
Marine Petrobulk Ltd, 10 Pemberton Avenue, Vancouver, B.C., Canada V7P 2R1, *Tel:* +1 604 9874 415, *Fax:* +1 604 9873 824, *Email:* tbrewster@marinepetro.com, *Website:* www.marinepetrobulk.com – *Grades:* all grades – *Misc:* owns and operates 3 bunker barges – *Rates:* 300t/h – *Delivery Mode:* barge, truck

Towage: C.H. Cates & Sons Ltd, 10 Pemberton Avenue, Vancouver, B.C., Canada V7P 2R1, *Tel:* +1 604 988 2161, *Fax:* +1 604 988 6060, *Email:* info@seaspan.com, *Website:* www.seaspan.com
Seaspan International Ltd, 10 Pemberton Avenue, Vancouver, B.C., Canada V7P 2R1, *Tel:* +1 604 988 3111, *Fax:* +1 604 984 1613, *Email:* info@seaspan.com, *Website:* www.seaspan.com

Repair & Maintenance: Dollarton Shipyard, 3829 Dollarton Highway, Vancouver, B.C., Canada V7G 1A1, *Tel:* +1 604 929 0866, *Fax:* +1 604 929 3898, *Email:* ds@alliedship.com, *Website:* www.alliedship.com
Vancouver Shipyards Co. Ltd, 50 Pemberton Avenue, Vancouver, B.C., Canada V7P 2R2, *Tel:* +1 604 988 6361, *Fax:* +1 604 990 3290, *Email:* info@vanship.com, *Website:* www.vanship.com Floating dock of 220 m x 45.8 m with lifting cap of 36 000 t. Also a syncrolift marine elevator with lifting cap of 1500 t

Seaman Missions: Flying Angel Club, 401 East Waterfront Road, Vancouver, B.C., Canada V6A 4G9, *Tel:* +1 604 253 4421, *Fax:* +1 604 253 0874, *Email:* missionvanc@flyingangel.ca, *Website:* www.flyingangel.ca

Ship Chandlers: Ava Hi Seas Ship Suppliers Ltd, 1668 West 75th Avenue, Vancouver, B.C., Canada V6P 6G2, *Tel:* +1 604 264 1474, *Fax:* +1 604 264 1475, *Email:* avahi@telus.net
Karlo Corp. - Marine Group, 2459 Beta Avenue, Burnaby, Vancouver, B.C., Canada V5C 5N1, *Tel:* +1 604 205 5466, *Fax:* +1 604 205 5488, *Email:* canada@karlogroup.com, *Website:* www.karlogroup.com
LAM Marine Supplies, 765 East Cordova Street, Vancouver, B.C., Canada V6A 1M2, *Tel:* +1 604 255 6236, *Fax:* +1 604 255 6234, *Email:* info@lammarine.ca, *Website:* www.lammarine.ca
MAAS Hugdahl (Canada) Ltd, 3440 Bridgeway Street, Vancouver, B.C., Canada V5K 1B6, *Tel:* +1 604 294 5765, *Fax:* +1 604 294 5766, *Email:* sales@maashugdahl.com
Triton Marine Supply (Div. Triton Marine Group Inc.), 3440 Bridgeway Street, Vancouver, B.C., Canada V5K 1B6, *Tel:* +1 604 294 4444, *Fax:* +1 604 294 5879, *Email:* tms@tritonmarine.com, *Website:* www.tritonmarine.com
T.S.E. Ship Chandler Ltd, 1875 Franklin Street, Vancouver, B.C., Canada V5L 1P9, *Tel:* +1 604 685 9265, *Fax:* +1 604 687 0967, *Email:* office@tsesupply.com
United Maritime Suppliers Inc., 1854 Franklin Street, Vancouver, B.C., Canada V5L 1P8, *Tel:* +1 604 255 6525, *Fax:* +1 604 255 1212, *Email:* ums@unitedmaritime.com

Shipping Agents: Anglo Canadian Shipping Co., Suite 1100, 900 West Hastings Street, Vancouver, B.C., Canada V6C 1E5, *Tel:* +1 604 683 4221, *Fax:* +1 604 688 3401, *Email:* medbulk@anglo-vcr.com, *Website:* www.anglocanadian.ca
CMA-CGM S.A., CMA CGM (Canada) Inc, 1177 West Hastings Street, Suite 1720, Vancouver, B.C., Canada V6E 2K3, *Tel:* +1 604 681 0987, *Fax:* +1 604 681 6835, *Email:* cda.dthomas@cma-cgm.com, *Website:* www.cma-cgm.com
Empire Shipping Co. Ltd, 611 Alexander Street, Suite 316, Vancouver, B.C., Canada V6A 1E1, *Tel:* +1 604 255 1116, *Fax:* +1 604 255 1152, *Email:* office@vnc.empireship.com, *Website:* www.empireshipping.ca
Greer Shipping Ltd, Suite 600, 900 West Hastings Street, Vancouver, B.C., Canada V6C 1E5, *Tel:* +1 604 891 7447, *Fax:* +1 604 891 7446, *Email:* rec@greer.com, *Website:* www.greer.com
Grieg Star Shipping (Canada) Ltd, 900 -1111 West Hastings Street, Vancouver, B.C., Canada V6E 2J3, *Tel:* +1 604 661 2000, *Fax:* +1 604 685 0242, *Email:* starvcr@starshipping.com, *Website:* www.starshipping.com
International Chartering Services Ltd, Suite 2360, 555 West Hasting Street, P O Box 12115, Vancouver, B.C., Canada V6B 4N6, *Tel:* +1 604 685 6221, *Fax:* +1 604 685 7329, *Email:* rita@ics-vcr.com
Mason Agency Ltd, 1550 United Kingdom Building, 409 Granville Street, Vancouver, B.C., Canada V6C 1T2, *Tel:* +1 604 689 8628, *Fax:* +1 604 689 8230, *Email:* masonagency@bcshipping.ca
McLean Kennedy Inc., Suite 1451, 409 Granville Street, Vancouver, B.C., Canada V6c 1T2, *Fax:* +1 604 688 6713, *Email:* jmorris@mcleankennedy.ca, *Website:* www.mcleankennedy.ca
Mediterranean Shipping Company, MSC Canada Inc, 789 W. Pender Street, Suite 1530, Vancouver, B.C., Canada V6C 1H2, *Tel:* +1 604 688 9494, *Fax:* +1 604 688 9499, *Email:* msccanada@mscca.mscgva.ch, *Website:* www.mscgva.ch
A.P. Moller-Maersk Group, Maersk Canada Inc, 1185 West Georgia Street, Suite 1605, Vancouver, B.C., Canada V6E 4E6, *Tel:* +1 604 687 1530, *Fax:* +1 604 687 1580, *Email:* vnrsal@maersk.com, *Website:* www.maerskline.com
Montship Inc., Suite 800, 1111 West Hastings Street, Vancouver, B.C., Canada V6E 2J3, *Tel:* +1 604 640 7400, *Fax:* +1 604 685 7707, *Email:* dwylie@montship.ca, *Website:* www.montship.ca

Norton Lilly International Inc., 1130 West Pender Street, Suite 828, Vancouver, B.C., Canada V6E 4A4, *Tel:* +1 604 669 8866, *Fax:* +1 604 669 5606, *Email:* van-ops@nortonlilly.com, *Website:* www.nortonlilly.com

Quay Cruise Agencies, 134 Abbot Street, Suite 604, Vancouver, B.C., Canada V6B 2K4, *Tel:* +1 604 681 5131, *Fax:* +1 604 681 5181, *Email:* ops@quaycruise.bc.ca

Robert Reford Inc., 2360- 555 West Hastings Street, P O Box 12115, Vancouver, B.C., Canada V6B 4N6, *Tel:* +1 604 687 2624, *Fax:* +1 604 681 5679, *Email:* vanops@redford.ca, *Website:* www.robertreford.com

Seabridge International Shipping Inc., 744 West Hastings Street, Suite 527, Van-couver, B.C., Canada V6C 1A5, *Tel:* +1 604 602 6666, *Fax:* +1 604 602 6661, *Email:* vancouver@seabridge.ca, *Website:* www.seabridge.ca

SMI Marine Ltd, Suite 118, 2465 Beta Avenue, Vancouver, B.C., Canada V6C 1A9, *Tel:* +1 604 685 0131, *Fax:* +1 604 685 2241, *Email:* smivcr@axion.net

Westward Shipping Ltd, 2208 - 13353 Commerce Parkway, Richmond, Vancouver, B.C., Canada V6V 3A1, *Tel:* +1 604 273 6141, *Fax:* +1 604 273 4300, *Email:* vancouveroffice@westwardshipping.com, *Website:* www.westwardshipping.com

World Trade Systems (WTS) Agencies Inc., 1166 Alberni Street, Suite 503, Van-couver, B.C., Canada V6E 3Z3, *Tel:* +1 604 681 9242, *Fax:* +1 604 681 6732, *Email:* leilani.gunaratna@wtsa.com, *Website:* www.wtsa.com

Surveyors: F.I. Hopkinson Marine Surveyors, 1225 Riverside Drive North, Van-couver, B.C., Canada V7H 1V6, *Tel:* +1 604 924 4903, *Fax:* +1 604 924 4906, *Email:* marsurv@allstream.net Managing Director: Ian F. Hopkinson

Acres International Ltd, 700-1066 W Hastings Street, Vancouver, B.C., Canada V6E 3X2, *Tel:* +1 604 683 9141, *Fax:* +1 604 683 9148, *Email:* vancouver@hatchenergy.com, *Website:* www.hatchenergy.com

Aker Yards Marine Inc., 1818 Cornwall Avenue, Vancouver, B.C., Canada V6J 1C7, *Tel:* +1 604 730 4200, *Fax:* +1 604 730 4297, *Email:* info@akermarine.com, *Website:* www.akermarine.com

All Points Marine Surveyors, 36-2662 Morningstar Crescent, Vancouver, B.C., Canada V5S 4P4, *Tel:* +1 604 873 9407, *Fax:* +1 604 874 4430, *Email:* robertsj@direct.ca, *Website:* www.marinesurveyor.com/allpoints

Associated Marine Surveyors Ltd, 19 East 33rd Avenue, Vancouver, B.C., Canada V5V 2Z3, *Tel:* +1 604 879 1069, *Fax:* +1 604 879 1069, *Email:* tonyrepard@shaw.ca, *Website:* www.marinesurveyor.ca

BC Research Inc., 3650 Wesbrook Mall, Vancouver, B.C., Canada V6S 2L2, *Tel:* +1 604 224 4331, *Fax:* +1 604 224 0540, *Email:* info@bcresearch.com, *Website:* www.bcresearch.com

B.C. Supercargoes' Association, 206 3711 Delbrook Avenue, Vancouver, B.C., Canada V7N 3Z4, *Tel:* +1 604 878 1258, *Fax:* +1 604 904 6545, *Email:* admin@supercargoes.bc.ca, *Website:* www.supercargoes.bc.ca

BMT Fleet Technology Ltd, 611 Alexander Street, Suite 412, Vancouver, B.C., Canada V6A 1E1, *Tel:* +1 604 253 0955, *Fax:* +1 604 253 5023, *Email:* fleet@fleetech.com, *Website:* www.fleetech.com

Bureau Veritas, 535 Thurlow Street, Suite 801, Vancouver, B.C., Canada V6E 3L2, *Tel:* +1 604 689 1355, *Fax:* +1 604 689 1356, *Website:* www.bureauveritas.com

Crawford & Company, 2985 Virtual Way, Suite 280, Vancouver, B.C., Canada V5M 4X7, *Tel:* +1 604 436 2277, *Fax:* +1 604 436 1211, *Email:* brian.gielty@crawco.ca, *Website:* www.crawfordandcompany.com

Det Norske Veritas A/S, 804-1112 W. Pender Street, Vancouver, B.C., Canada V6E 2S1, *Tel:* +1 604 689 7425, *Fax:* +1 604 689 7450, *Email:* vancouver@dnv.com, *Website:* www.dnv.com

Germanischer Lloyd, #222, 7455 132nd Street, Surrey, B.C., Canada V3W 1J8, *Tel:* +1 604 502 9972, *Fax:* +1 604 502 9982, *Email:* gl-vancouver@gl-group.com, *Website:* www.gl-group.com

IMS Marine Surveyors Ltd, Suite 223, 3823 Henning Drive, Burnaby, B.C., Canada V5C 6P3, *Tel:* +1 604 298 9968, *Fax:* +1 604 298 4862, *Email:* office@ims-van.com, *Website:* www.ims-van.com

Marine Design Associates Ltd, 4489 Stonehaven Avenue, Vancouver, B.C., Canada V7G 1E7, *Tel:* +1 604 929 5404, *Fax:* +1 604 929 5405, *Email:* marinesurveyor@shaw.ca, *Website:* www.marinedesign.net

Nippon Kaiji Kyokai, Suite 902, Pender Place, 700 West Pender Street, Vancouver, B.C., Canada V6C 1G8, *Tel:* +1 604 685 2121, *Fax:* +1 604 685 7631, *Email:* vc@classnk.or.jp, *Website:* www.classnk.or.jp

Westmar Consultants Inc., 233 West 1st Street, Suite 400, Vancouver, B.C., Canada V7M 1B3, *Tel:* +1 604 985 6488, *Fax:* +1 604 985 2581

Airport: Vancouver International Airport

Railway: CN North America, CP Rail System, BC Rail, Burlington Northern

Development: Construction of a third container berth at Deltaport increasing length overall to 1135 m; scheduled for completion in the third quarter of 2009

Lloyd's Agent: McLarens Canada (Vancouver), 505 1100 Melville Street, Vancouver, B.C., Canada V6E 4A6, *Tel:* +1 604 681 7107, *Fax:* +1 604 681 8125, *Email:* philip.vardon@mclarens.ca, *Website:* www.mclarens.ca

VANTERM

harbour area, see under Vancouver

VICTORIA

Lat 48° 25' N; Long 123° 23' W.

Admiralty Chart: 4959

Time Zone: GMT -8 h

Admiralty Pilot: 25

UNCTAD Locode: CA VIC

Principal Facilities:

		G		L	B	D	T	A

Authority: Greater Victoria Harbour Authority, 202-468 Belleville Street, Victoria, B.C., Canada V8V 1W9, *Tel:* +1 250 383 8300, *Fax:* +1 250 383 8322, *Email:* gvha@victoriaharbour.org, *Website:* www.victoriaharbour.org

Officials: Chief Executive Officer: Paul Servos, *Tel:* +1 250 383 8300 Ext.225, *Email:* pservos@victoriaharbour.org.
Business Development Manager: Darryl Anderson, *Tel:* +1 250 383 8300 Ext.248, *Email:* danderson@victoriaharbour.org.
Harbour Master: Dave Featherby, *Tel:* +1 250 363 3625, *Email:* feathed@tc.gc.ca.

Port Security: ISPS compliant

Approach: The harbour entrance to the S of Victoria has a deep, wide, open approach; the only hazard is Brotchie Ledge, 900 m SE of the outer end of the harbour entrance breakwater. There are beacons on the outer end of the breakwater and also on Brotchie Ledge

Anchorage: Royal Roads Anchorage provides six permanent anchorages 3.7 km SW of Victoria harbour entrance. Plumper Sound Anchorage, 39 nautical miles NNE of Victoria, situated between North and South Pender Islands and Mayne and Saturna Islands, has four permanent and one temporary anchorage. Senanus Island Anchorage contains one permanent anchorage in protected waters, 47 nautical miles NW of Victoria and situated in Brentwood Bay off Saanich Inlet
Constance Bank Temporary Anchorage in pos 48° 20' 40" N, 123° 21' 20" W. Pilot not required to proceed to or from this anchorage provided (a) inbound vessels wishing to use this anchorage must request a Pilotage Waiver through their Agent 12 h in advance of ETA (b) outbound vessels using this anchorage must request a Pilotage Waiver through their Agent prior to departing the anchorage (c) any vessel using this anchorage without receiving a Pilotage Waiver will be assessed pilotage dues and may be prosecuted. Vancouver Traffic controls and assists waived vessels to this anchorage
Captains Passage Anchorage: in pos 48° 49' N, 123° 25' W consists of two holding anchorages 67 km N of Victoria. Pilotage is required and it is restricted to vessels up to 200 m loa
Fulford Harbour Anchorage: in pos 48° 44.68' N, 123° 25.33' W consists of one anchorage 65 km N of Victoria in depth of 34 m. Pilotage is required and it is restricted to vessels up to 180 m loa

Pilotage: Compulsory. Pacific Pilotage Authority. Pilot boards at Fairway Buoy, 3.22 km S of harbour entrance breakwater. VHF Channels 17 and 16 (calling) and 17 and 08 (working)

Traffic: 2007, 15 cargo vessels, 177 cruise vessels and 344 656 passengers

Working Hours: Shift schedule for deepsea ship and dock work on cargo operations. First shift 0100-0430, 0500-0800; second shift 0800-1200, 1300-1700; third shift 1700-2100, 2130-0100

Accommodation:

Name	Remarks
Victoria	
Ogden Point	See [1] below
Fisherman's Wharf	See [2] below
Government Street/Ship Point	See [3] below
Wharf Street to Johnson Street	See [4] below

[1]*Ogden Point:* Consists of Pier A and Pier B totalling four docks. The facility has become a major destination for cruise vessels in the North West. Ogden Point is also an important depot for fiber optic cable repairs. A heliport provides direct services to Seattle, Vancouver and Vancouver International Airport

[2]*Fisherman's Wharf:* Located east of Shoal Point and provides moorage for visiting recreational vessels, 'live aboards', fishing vessels and float homes

[3]*Government Street/Ship Point:* Located in Victoria's city centre. There is 100 m of float space available at this facility or at the Ship's Point dock moorage for vessels up to 75 m. A large pier is located between the Causeway floats and the Wharf Street floats. Attached to the south side of the pier is a float that is used by pleasure and some commercial vessels for pick-up and drop-off. Canadian fishing vessels are not permitted to berth at the float. Areas at this facility are sometimes reserved for special events, pocket cruise ships and larger pleasure yachts

[4]*Wharf Street to Johnson Street:* This facility consists of 450 m of floats and is the major facility for yachts and transient vessels in the summer months. There is a customs dock at this facility located immediately below Wharf Street

Bunkering: ExxonMobil Marine Fuels, Suite 900, One Alhambra Plaza, Coral Gables, FL 33134, United States of America, *Tel:* +1 305 459 6358, *Fax:* +1 305 459 6412, *Email:* emmf@exxonmobil.com, *Website:* www.exxonmobilmarinefuels.com – *Grades:* all grades in moderate quantities – *Misc:* heavy fuel and large amounts available by barge from Vancouver – *Delivery Mode:* barge, truck

ICS Petroleum, ICS Petroleum (Montreal) Ltd, Suite 302, 430 Ste-Helene Street, Montreal, Que., Canada H2Y 2K7, *Tel:* +1 514 849 1223, *Fax:* +1 514 849 0517, *Email:* bunkers@ics-mtl.com, *Website:* www.icspet.com – *Grades:* all grades in moderate quantities – *Misc:* heavy fuel and large amounts available by barge from Vancouver – *Delivery Mode:* barge, truck

Imperial Oil (Burnaby) Ltd, International Marine Sales, 4720 Kingsway, Burnaby, B.C., Canada V5H 4N2, *Tel:* +1 604 451 5955, *Fax:* +1 604 451 5950 – *Grades:* all grades in moderate quantities – *Misc:* heavy fuel and large amounts available by barge from Vancouver – *Delivery Mode:* barge, truck

Marine Petrobulk Ltd, 10 Pemberton Avenue, Vancouver, B.C., Canada V7P 2R1, *Tel:* +1 604 9874 415, *Fax:* +1 604 9873 824, *Email:* tbrewster@marinepetro.com, *Website:* www.marinepetrobulk.com – *Grades:* all grades in moderate quantities – *Misc:* heavy fuel and large amounts available by barge from Vancouver – *Delivery Mode:* barge, truck

Waste Reception Facilities: Shore facilities available to handle international garbage with 48 h notice

Towage: Two harbour tugs; one of 450 hp and one of 500 hp are readily available Seaspan International Ltd, 345 Harbour Road, Victoria, B.C., Canada V9A 3S2, *Tel:* +1 250 920 7924, *Fax:* +1 250 920 7925, *Website:* www.seaspan.com

Repair & Maintenance: Point Hope Maritime, 345 Harbour Road, Victoria, B.C., Canada V9A 3S2, *Tel:* +1 250 385 3623, *Fax:* +1 250 385 3166, *Email:* info@pointhopemaritime.com, *Website:* www.pointhopemaritime.com Floating dry dock of 200 t cap

Victoria Shipyards, 825 Admirals Road, Victoria, B.C., Canada V9A 2P1, *Tel:* +1 250 995 6510, *Fax:* +1 250 995 6599, *Email:* info@vicship.com, *Website:* www.vicship.com

Shipping Agents: Dowell Marine Shipping Services Inc., 325 Woodside Place, Okotoks, Victoria, B.C., Canada T1S 1L9, *Tel:* +1 403 995 0115, *Fax:* +1 403 995 0115, *Email:* office@dowellmarine.com, *Website:* www.dowellmarine.com

Surveyors: Marine Design Associates Ltd, 307-1625 Oak Bay Avenue, Victoria, B.C., Canada V8R 1B1, *Tel:* +1 250 384 4191, *Fax:* +1 250 381 1143, *Email:* info@marinedesign.net, *Website:* www.marinedesign.net

Medical Facilities: Victoria General Hospital and Royal Jubilee Hospital

Airport: Victoria International Airport, 30 km

Lloyd's Agent: McLarens Canada (Vancouver), 505 1100 Melville Street, Vancouver, B.C., Canada V6E 4A6, *Tel:* +1 604 681 7107, *Fax:* +1 604 681 8125, *Email:* philip.vardon@mclarens.ca, *Website:* www.mclarens.ca

VIEUX-PORT

harbour area, see under Quebec

WEYMOUTH

Lat 44° 27' N; Long 66° 1' W.

Admiralty Chart: 352
Time Zone: GMT -4 h
Admiralty Pilot: 59
UNCTAD Locode: CA WEY

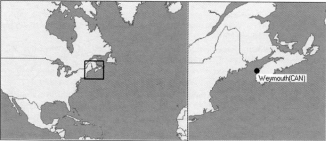

Principal Facilities:

			G		B		A

Approach: Depth of 7.6 m at HW. Approach channel to the main wharf, 122 m long, 9.1 m wide. River dredged to 2.7 m at LW

Anchorage: Good anchorage 0.4 km NW of Fairway Buoy

Pilotage: Available

Tides: Tidal range of 4.79 m

Maximum Vessel Dimensions: 6.7 m max d

Accommodation:

Name	Length (m)	Depth (m)	Remarks
Weymouth Wharf No.1	85	2.9	See [1] below

[1]*Weymouth:* Depth at entrance 7 62 m in dredged eastern channel at OT and 4.27 m in western channel. Depth in harbour 7.92 m. Max safe draft 6.7 m. Assembly area of 1380 m2

Due to siltation in both the harbour entrance and port facility, activity has been limited to fishing vessels and barging of pulpwood/hardwood

Mechanical Handling Equipment:

Location	Type
Weymouth	Mobile Cranes

Bunkering: Imperial Oil (Dartmouth) Ltd, P O Box 1010, Dartmouth, N.S., Canada B2Y 4RI, *Tel:* +1 902 420 6872, *Fax:* +1 902 420 6996 – *Misc:* can be obtained from Halifax, Digby or Yarmouth – *Delivery Mode:* truck

Irving Oil Co. Ltd, 10 Sydney Street, P O Box 1421, Saint John, N.B., Canada E2L 4K1, *Tel:* +1 888 3101 924, *Fax:* +1 506 2023 868, *Email:* webinquiries@irvingoil.com, *Website:* www.irvingoilco.com – *Delivery Mode:* truck

Medical Facilities: Available at Digby, 30 km

Airport: Yarmouth Airport, 80 km

Lloyd's Agent: Hayes Stuart Inc., 1000 Windmill Road, Suite 19, Dartmouth, N.S., Canada B3B 1L7, *Tel:* +1 902 468 2651, *Fax:* +1 902 468 4315, *Email:* halifax@hayesstuart.com, *Website:* www.hayesstuart.com

WHIFFEN HEAD

Lat 47° 46' N; Long 54° 1' W.

Admiralty Chart: 4737
Time Zone: GMT -3.5 h
Admiralty Pilot: 50
UNCTAD Locode: CA WHH

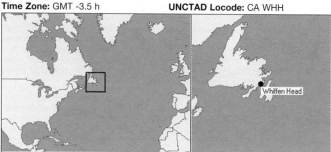

Principal Facilities:

P							

Authority: IMTT-Newfoundland Ltd, P O Box 451, Whiffen Head Road, Arnold's Cove, NL, Canada A0B 1A0, *Tel:* +1 709 463 4688, *Fax:* +1 709 463 4752, *Email:* hgkelly@imtt.nf.ca, *Website:* www.imtt.com

Officials: Terminal Manager: Howard Kelly.

Port Security: Fully secure, 24 h manned facility

Accommodation:

Name	Remarks
Whiffen Head	See [1] below

[1]*Whiffen Head:* Dedicated facility to receiving crude oil from petroleum production offshore Newfoundland for transshipment to major refining centers in North America Two deepwater jetties with high volume transfer capabilities to and from tank storage. Jetties can handle tankers up to 155 000 dwt with a draft of 17 m

Storage: Six tanks; 3.0 million barrels total working cap

Shipping Agents: Canadian Maritime Agency Ltd, 4 Refinery Road, P O Box 119, Come by Chance, NL, Canada A0B 1N0, *Tel:* +1 709 463 4717, *Fax:* +1 709 463 8737, *Email:* opscbc@canadianmaritime.nf.ca, *Website:* www.canadianmaritime.com

Lloyd's Agent: Hayes Stuart Inc., 297 Duke Street, Montreal, Que., Canada H3C 2M2, *Tel:* +1 514 866 1801, *Fax:* +1 514 866 1259, *Email:* montreal@hayesstuart.com, *Website:* www.hayesstuart.com

WINDSOR

Lat 42° 19' N; Long 83° 3' W.

Admiralty Chart: -
Time Zone: GMT -5 h
Admiralty Pilot: -
UNCTAD Locode: CA WND

Principal Facilities:

P	Q	Y	G			B		T	A

Authority: Windsor Port Authority, 251 Goyeau Street, Suite 502, Windsor, Ont., Canada N9A 6V2, *Tel:* +1 519 258 5741, *Fax:* +1 519 258 5905, *Email:* wpa@portwindsor.com, *Website:* www.portwindsor.com

Officials: Chief Executive Officer: David S.H. Cree, *Email:* dcree@portwindsor.com. Harbour Master: William A. Marshall, *Email:* bmarshall@portwindsor.com.

Port Security: ISPS compliant

Approach: The shipping channel is Seaway depth

Anchorage: There is an anchorage able to handle three seaway depth vessels. Permission to use the anchorage must be obtained from the Sarnia Traffic Centre

Pilotage: Available from Great Lakes Pilotage Authority Ltd., *Tel:* +1 613 932 2991

Radio Frequency: Contact Harbour Master on VHF Channel 16 during working hours. For 24 h contact, *Tel:* +1 519 258 5741

Tides: River not subject to tidal influence

Traffic: 2007, 5 125 442 t of cargo handled

Maximum Vessel Dimensions: 306.2 m loa, 32 m beam

Principal Imports and Exports: Imports: Building machines, Coal, Gravel.

Working Hours: 24 h/day

Accommodation:

Name	Remarks
Windsor	See [1] below
Private Wharves	See [2] below

[1]*Windsor:* Harbour front is approx 22 km in length and includes a large number of facilities operated by various companies

Modern transit sheds, loading and unloading facilities owned by Morterm Limited, 1601 Lincoln Road, (PO Box 2186), Windsor Ont N8Y 4Y9, Tel: +1 519 973 8200, Fax: +1 519 973 7234, Email: bmckeown@morterm.com. The Morterm Terminal has a slip frontage of 731.5 m and is equipped with a mobile crane of 400 t cap. Bonded area and warehouses available

Bulk facilities: Available at several berths

Tanker facilities: Marine fueling facility operated by Sterling Marine Fuels, P O Box 7218, 3565 Russell Street, Windsor Ont N9E 3Z1, Tel: +1 519 253 4694, Fax: +1 519 253 5120, Email: sterling@wincom.net

[2]*Private Wharves:* Canadian Salt Company (Ojibway Site), Tel: +1 519 966 2142: 222.5 m long, T dock, 7.9 m depth

Windsor Grain Terminal: 396.2 m long, T dock, full seaway depth

Morterm: slip 731.5 m long and 60.9 m wide, 228.6 m docking on river

Southwestern Sales, West Dock, Tel: +1 519 735 9822, Fax: +1 519 735 1913, Email: southwstrn@aol.com: 427 m dockage, 8.2 m depth

Lafarge Construction Materials, Tel: +1 519 256 4904, Fax: +1 519 256 8857: 335 m dock, seaway depth

Essroc Italcementi Group, Tel: +1 519 253 4651, Fax: +1 519 256 4509/The Dunn Group, Tel: +1 519 727 3838, Fax: +1 519 727 3675: 304.8 m dock, 7.9 m depth

Ford Motor, Tel: +1 519 257 4540: 548.6 m dock, 7.5 m depth

Southwestern Sales, East Dock, Tel: +1 519 735 9822, Fax: +1 519 735 1913, Email: southwstrn@aol.com: 213 m dock, 8.5 m depth

Storage: Total of 24 000 m2 of storage space

Mechanical Handling Equipment:

Location	Type	Capacity (t)	Qty
Windsor	Mult-purp. Cranes	228	
Windsor	Forklifts		55

Bunkering: Sterling Marine Fuels, 3565 Russel Street, P O Box 7218, Windsor, Ont., Canada N9C 3Z1, *Tel:* +1 519 2534 694, *Fax:* +1 519 2535 120, *Email:* sterling@wincom.net

Sterling Marine Fuels, 3565 Russel Street, P O Box 7218, Windsor, Ont., Canada N9C 3Z1, *Tel:* +1 519 2534 694, *Fax:* +1 519 2535 120, *Email:* sterling@wincom.net

Towage: Not required but available

Surveyors: Clarke Surveyors Inc., 2535 Lesperance Road, Tecumseh, Ont., Canada N8N 2X1, *Tel:* +1 519 258 4166, *Fax:* +1 519 258 3874, *Email:* jhannon@clarkesurveyors.com, *Website:* www.clarkesurveyors.com

Verhaegen Stubberfield Hartley Brewer Bezaire Inc., Windsor, Ont., Canada, *Tel:* +1 519 258 1772, *Fax:* +1 519 258 1791, *Email:* windsor.office@vshbbsurveys.com

Medical Facilities: Windsor Regional Hospital, Tel: +1 519 257 5100

Hotel-Dieu Grace Hospital, Tel: +1 519 973 4444

Airport: Windsor International, 15 km

Railway: ETR with various connections

Development: 18 ha and 8 ha waterfront sites available for lease from the Port Authority

Lloyd's Agent: McLarens Canada (Toronto), 600 Alden Road, Suite 600, Markham, Toronto, Ont., Canada L3R 0E7, *Tel:* +1 905 946 9995, *Fax:* +1 905 946 0171, *Email:* roger.bickers@mclarens.ca, *Website:* www.mclarens.ca

WOODFIBRE

Lat 49° 40' N; Long 123° 15' W.

Admiralty Chart: -	**Admiralty Pilot:** 25
Time Zone: GMT -8 h	**UNCTAD Locode:** CA WOO

Principal Facilities:

		G						

Authority: Western Pulp Ltd Partnership, P O Box 5000, Squamish, B.C., Canada V0N 3G0, *Tel:* +1 604 892 6600, *Fax:* +1 604 892 6603

Pilotage: Compulsory. Pilots board off Victoria

Maximum Vessel Dimensions: 41 808 dwt, 200.9 m loa

Principal Imports and Exports: Exports: Unitised baled pulp.

Working Hours: 0800-1700, 1800-2200

Accommodation:

Name	Remarks
Woodfibre	See [1] below

[1]*Woodfibre:* Two wharves owned by Western Pulp Ltd Partnership with berthing frontage of 132 m in depth alongside of 10.4 m LW

Lloyd's Agent: McLarens Canada (Vancouver), 505 1100 Melville Street, Vancouver, B.C., Canada V6E 4A6, *Tel:* +1 604 681 7107, *Fax:* +1 604 681 8125, *Email:* philip.vardon@mclarens.ca, *Website:* www.mclarens.ca

YARMOUTH

Lat 43° 50' N; Long 66° 7' W.

Admiralty Chart: -	**Admiralty Pilot:** 59
Time Zone: GMT -4 h	**UNCTAD Locode:** CA YOI

Principal Facilities:

Y	G	C	R		B		A

Authority: Port of Yarmouth, 233 Water Street, Yarmouth, N.S., Canada B5A 1M1, *Tel:* +1 902 742 1803, *Fax:* +1 902 742 3107, *Email:* yarmouth@swsda.com, *Website:* www.portofyarmouth.com

Officials: Port Manager: Dave Whiting, *Email:* dwhiting@swsda.com.

Harbour Master: Garth Atkinson, *Tel:* +1 902 742 4289, *Email:* gb97@eastlink.ca.

Port Security: ISPS compliant

Pre-Arrival Information: Contact wharfinger/harbour master Garth Atkinson, Tel: +1 902 742 4289

Approach: The dredged channel of Yarmouth Harbour begins in the outer reaches at a width of 180 m, narrowing to a min width of 100 m at 'Bug Light' and continuing past the tanker terminal for 2500 m to the Port's 'Old Public Wharf'. Depth is maintained at approx 6.6 m LWOST with some variance at times due to siltation

Pilotage: Optional but recommended for ship's with master's unfamiliar with the harbour

Tides: Tidal range of 5 m

Traffic: 2003, 120 vessels

Maximum Vessel Dimensions: 130 m loa, 5.4 m draft

Principal Imports and Exports: Imports: Fish products. Exports: .

Working Hours: 24 h/day

Accommodation:

Name	Length (m)	Depth (m)	Remarks
Yarmouth			
Ferry Terminal	115		Operated by Bay Ferries
Old Public Wharf (Outer Berth)	121	5.1–5.8	
Old Public Wharf (Inner Berth)	80	2.1	
Marginal Wharf	106.7	1.2–1.9	
Lobster Rock Marine Terminal (Outer Berth)	152	5.8–6.4	
Lobster Rock Marine Terminal (Western Inner Berth)	100	5.8–6.4	
Lobster Rock Marine Terminal (Eastern Inner Berth)	31	5.8–6.4	

Mechanical Handling Equipment:

Location	Type	Capacity (t)	Qty	Remarks
Yarmouth	Mobile Cranes	40	1	available for hire

Bunkering: Available by tank truck with min 24 h advance notice

Irving Oil Co. Ltd, 10 Sydney Street, P O Box 1421, Saint John, N.B., Canada E2L 4K1, *Tel:* +1 888 3101 924, *Fax:* +1 506 2023 868, *Email:* webinquiries@irvingoil.com, *Website:* www.irvingoilco.com

Waste Reception Facilities: Garbage disposal available by private contractor

Repair & Maintenance: Machine shops equipped for minor repairs, also electronic repairs

Medical Facilities: Regional hospital with helipad in Yarmouth

Airport: Yarmouth Airport, 3 km

Lloyd's Agent: Hayes Stuart Inc., 1000 Windmill Road, Suite 19, Dartmouth, N.S., Canada B3B 1L7, *Tel:* +1 902 468 2651, *Fax:* +1 902 468 4315, *Email:* halifax@hayesstuart.com, *Website:* www.hayesstuart.com

Key to Principal Facilities:—			
A=Airport	**C**=Containers	**G**=General Cargo	**P**=Petroleum	**R**=Ro/Ro	**Y**=Dry Bulk
B=Bunkers	**D**=Dry Dock	**L**=Cruise	**Q**=Other Liquid Bulk	**T**=Towage (where available from port)

CAPE VERDE

MINDELO

Lat 16° 53' N; Long 24° 59' W.

Admiralty Chart: 367   **Admiralty Pilot:** 1

Time Zone: GMT -1 h   **UNCTAD Locode:** CV MIN

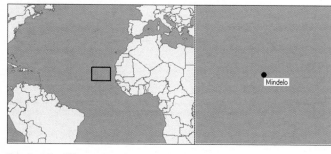

Principal Facilities:

P | Y G C R L B D T A

Authority: Empresa Nacional de Administracao dos Portos S.A. (ENAPOR), P O Box 82, Mindelo, St. Vincent Island, Republic of Cape Verde, *Tel:* +238 230 7500, *Fax:* +238 230 1433, *Email:* portogrande@enapor.cv, *Website:* www.enapor.cv

Officials: Port Administrator: Jorge Humberto Pimenta Mauricio.

Port Security: ISPS compliant. Port Facility Security Officer: Capt. Jose Julio Soares, Email: josejulio@enapor.com

Documentation: Bunkering & other purposes: 1 copy maritime declaration of health, 5 copies of crew, 5 copies passengers, 3 copies stores, 2 copies crew effects list
For discharging (generals etc): as above plus 3 copies B/L and 3 manifests
For discharging (tankers): as above plus 3 copies B/L and 3 manifests
Also 2 copies each dry/origin/quantity/quality certificates requested for tankers

Approach: Approach from N or S. No hazards or sand bars

Anchorage: Situated on the NE of the island at 16° 53' N; 25° 01' W in a depth of 36.3 m

Pilotage: Compulsory inwards, for harbour movements and berth shifts. Optional outwards. 24 h notice of ETA required. Vessel to contact pilot station by VHF Channel 16 two hours prior to arrival. Pilot meets vessel at entrance anchorage

Radio Frequency: St. Vincent Radio (call sign D4A) 500 kHz; VHF Channel 16 or 8469 Mcs and listening on 8 mHz

Weather: Trade winds cool and humid from the NE, harmattan from the E from October to June and monsoon rain from SSW from August to October

Tides: Range of tide 1.2 m

Traffic: 2007, 2286 vessels, 15 561 TEU's handled

Principal Imports and Exports: Imports: Building materials, Foodstuffs, Fuels. Exports: Bananas, Cloth, Fish.

Working Hours: 24 h/day as necessary

Accommodation:

Name	Length (m)	Depth (m)
Porto Grande		
Berth No.1	315	11.5
Berth No.2	315	11.5
Berth No.3	235	12
Berth No.4	235	12
Berth No.5	100	8.5
Berth No.6	122	6.5
Berth No.7	60	4.5
Berth No.8	106.7	3.5
Passenger Terminal A	120	4
Passenger Terminal B	50	4
Passenger Terminal C	65	4

Storage: Refrigerated storage available

Location	Open (m²)	Covered (m²)	Sheds / Warehouses
Mindelo	30620	7000	5

Mechanical Handling Equipment:

Location	Type	Capacity (t)	Qty
Porto Grande	Mult-purp. Cranes	35	2
Porto Grande	Mult-purp. Cranes	80	1
Porto Grande	Forklifts	2.5–45	15

Cargo Worked: 15/20 t/gang/h for bagged cargo, 20/25 t/gang/h for bulk cargo

Bunkering: AAB Shipping Agencia Viking Lda, 37 Rua Libertadores de Africa, P O Box 448, Mindelo, St. Vincent Island, Republic of Cape Verde, *Tel:* +238 231 7118, *Fax:* +238 231 7120, *Email:* viking@cvtelecom.cv
Shell Cabo Verde S.a.r.l., Avenida Amilcar Cabral, P O Box 4, Mindelo, St. Vincent Island, Republic of Cape Verde, *Tel:* +238 2307 600, *Fax:* +238 2326 629, *Email:* antonio.m.moeda@scv.simis.com
Cockett Marine Oil Ltd, Carrick House, 36 Station Square, Petts Wood, Kent BR5 1NA, United Kingdom, *Tel:* +44 1689 883 400, *Fax:* +44 1689 877 666, *Email:* enquiries@cockett.com, *Website:* www.cockettgroup.com – *Grades:* all grades – *Delivery Mode:* barge, truck
Enacol S.a.r.l., P O Box 1, S. Vicente, Praia, Santiago Island, Republic of Cape Verde, *Tel:* +238 2306 060, *Fax:* +238 2609 030, *Email:* angelogoncalves@enacol.cv
ExxonMobil Marine Fuels, Mailpoint 31, ExxonMobil House, Ermyn Way, Leatherhead, Surrey KT22 8UX, United Kingdom, *Tel:* +44 1372 222 000, *Fax:* +44 1372 223 922, *Email:* marine.fuels@exxonmobil.com, *Website:* www.exxonmobil.com

Towage: Compulsory for docking/undocking of vessels over 2000 gt. Five tugs available of 600-2930 hp

Repair & Maintenance: Cabnave - Estaleiros Navais de Cabo Verde, Matiota, P O Box 188, Mindelo, St. Vincent Island, Republic of Cape Verde, *Tel:* +238 232 1930,

Fax: +238 232 1935, *Email:* cabnavesarl@mail.cvtelecom.cv Dry dock for vessels up to 110 m loa, 18 m beam, 2800 t lifting cap. Four slipways for smaller craft. Vessels up to 5000 dwt can be accommodated. The yard is designed to provide support for fishing fleets and oil exploration vessels working in the area, as well as accommodating merchant vessels

Shipping Agents: Agencia Nacional de Viagens S.A. (ANV), Avenida da Republica 15/17, P O Box 16 & 142, Mindelo, St. Vincent Island, Republic of Cape Verde, *Tel:* +238 232 1115, *Fax:* +238 232 1445, *Email:* anvsv@cvtelecom.cv, *Website:* www.anv.cv Chief Operating Officer: Anibal Duarte Mobile Tel: +238 994 1160
AAB Shipping Agencia Viking Lda, 37 Rua Libertadores de Africa, P O Box 448, Mindelo, St. Vincent Island, Republic of Cape Verde, *Tel:* +238 231 7118, *Fax:* +238 231 7120, *Email:* viking@cvtelecom.cv
Cabo Verde Shipping Agency Lda, Rua Angola, Predio Miguel Coutinho R/C, Mindelo, St. Vincent Island, Republic of Cape Verde, *Tel:* +238 232 2750, *Fax:* +238 232 2751
Manoel Gomes Madeira (Sucrs) Ltda, Rua Patrice Lumumba 02, Mindelo, St. Vincent Island, Republic of Cape Verde, *Tel:* +238 232 1785, *Fax:* +238 232 2617, *Email:* mamoelgmadeira@cvtelecom.cv
A.P. Moller-Maersk Group, Maersk Line, Mindelo, St. Vincent Island, Republic of Cape Verde, *Tel:* +238 232 3649, *Fax:* +238 232 2617, *Email:* manoelgmadeira@cvtelecom.cv, *Website:* www.maerskline.com

Stevedoring Companies: ENAPOR-Porto Grande, Mindelo, St. Vincent Island, Republic of Cape Verde, *Tel:* +238 232 4414, *Fax:* +238 232 1433, *Email:* portogrande@enapor.cv
Agencia Nacional de Viagens S.A. (ANV), Avenida da Republica 15/17, P O Box 16 & 142, Mindelo, St. Vincent Island, Republic of Cape Verde, *Tel:* +238 232 1115, *Fax:* +238 232 1445, *Email:* anvsv@cvtelecom.cv, *Website:* www.anv.cv

Surveyors: Bureau Veritas, Mindelo, St. Vincent Island, Republic of Cape Verde, *Tel:* +238 232 3503, *Fax:* +238 232 7200, *Website:* www.bureauveritas.com
Det Norske Veritas A/S, Mindelo, St. Vincent Island, Republic of Cape Verde, *Tel:* +238 231 5292, *Fax:* +238 231 2055, *Website:* www.dnv.com
International Shipping & Engineering Service, Mindelo, St. Vincent Island, Republic of Cape Verde, *Tel:* +238 231 7024, *Fax:* +238 231 7126, *Email:* silvioduarte@mail.cvtelecom.cv

Medical Facilities: Hospital with modern facilities

Airport: San Pedro Airport, 10 km

Lloyd's Agent: Agencia Nacional de Viagens S.A. (ANV), Avenida da Republica 15/17, P O Box 16 & 142, Mindelo, St. Vincent Island, Republic of Cape Verde, *Tel:* +238 232 1115, *Fax:* +238 232 1445, *Email:* anvsv@cvtelecom.cv, *Website:* www.anv.cv

PALMEIRA

harbour area, see under Sal Island

PORTO GRANDE

harbour area, see under Mindelo

PORTO NOVO (CPV)

Lat 17° 1' N; Long 25° 4' W.

Admiralty Chart: 367   **Admiralty Pilot:** 1
Time Zone: GMT -1 h   **UNCTAD Locode:** CV PON

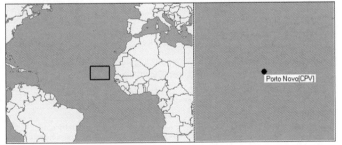

Principal Facilities:

				G						

Authority: Empresa Nacional de Administracao dos Portos S.A. (ENAPOR), P O Box 39, Porto Novo, Novo, S. Antao Island, Republic of Cape Verde, *Tel:* +238 222 1254, *Fax:* +238 222 1469, *Email:* portonovo@enapor.cv, *Website:* www.enapor.cv

Officials: Manager: Manuel R Gomes, *Email:* mrgomes69@hotmail.com.

Accommodation:

Name	Length (m)	Depth (m)
Porto Novo		
Berth No.1	133.6	7
Berth No.2	52	4.5
Berth No.3	43	3.5
Berth No.4	16	2.5

Mechanical Handling Equipment:

Location	Type	Capacity (t)	Qty
Porto Novo	Mult-purp. Cranes	3	1
Porto Novo	Forklifts	3–5	3

Shipping Agents: AAB Shipping Agencia Viking Lda, 37 Rua Libertadores de Africa, P O Box 448, Mindelo, St. Vincent Island, Republic of Cape Verde, *Tel:* +238 231 7118, *Fax:* +238 231 7120, *Email:* viking@cvtelecom.cv

Lloyd's Agent: Agencia Nacional de Viagens S.A. (ANV), Avenida da Republica 15/17, P O Box 16 & 142, Mindelo, St. Vincent Island, Republic of Cape Verde, *Tel:* +238 232 1115, *Fax:* +238 232 1445, *Email:* anvsv@cvtelecom.cv, *Website:* www.anv.cv

PRAIA

Lat 14° 54' N; Long 23° 31' W.

Admiralty Chart: 367   **Admiralty Pilot:** 1
Time Zone: GMT -1 h   **UNCTAD Locode:** CV RAI

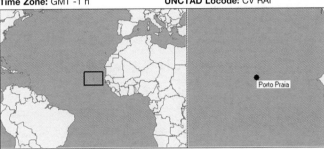

Principal Facilities:

Q	Y	G	C	R		B		T	A

Authority: Empresa Nacional de Administracao dos Portos S.A. (ENAPOR), P O Box 87, Praia, Santiago Island, Republic of Cape Verde, *Tel:* +238 260 9060, *Fax:* +238 263 3899, *Website:* www.enapor.cv

Officials: Port Administrator: Jose Manuel Fortes.

Port Security: ISPS compliant. Port Facility Security Officer: Capt. Antonio S. Ramos Pina

Documentation: For discharging (generals etc): 1 copy maritime declaration of health, 5 copies of crew, 5 copies passengers, 3 copies stores, 2 copies crew effects list, 3 copies B/L, 3 manifests
For discharging (gas): as above plus copies of dry/origin/quantity/quality certificates

Approach: Entrance from N or S. No hazards or sand bars. Pilot to be contacted by VHF Channel 16 for instructions 2 h prior to arrival

Anchorage: Vessels of any size can be accommodated at anchorage

Pilotage: Compulsory inwards for harbour movements and berth shifts. Optional outwards. Pilot boards vessel near lighthouse 'Farol Dona Maria Pia'. Master must contact pilot station on VHF two hours before arrival

Radio Frequency: St. Vincent Radio (call sign D4A) 500 kHz; VHF Channel 16 or 8469 Mcs and listening on 8 mHz

Weather: With strong NE winds little protection is afforded by the shore and there is a considerable swell. Rainy season July to November

Tides: Range of tide 1.22 m

Traffic: 2007, 1133 vessels, 28 003 TEU's handled

Principal Imports and Exports: Imports: Building materials, Foodstuffs. Exports: Bananas.

Working Hours: Normal 0800-1700. Overtime 1700-1900

Accommodation:

Name	Length (m)	Depth (m)	Remarks
Porto Praia			
Berth No.1	217	9	
Berth No.2	31.4	7.5	
Berth No.3	80	5	
Berth No.4	80	5	
Berth No.5	55	3	Fishing

Storage:

Location	Open (m²)	Covered (m²)	Sheds / Warehouses
Praia	16000	8700	4

Mechanical Handling Equipment:

Location	Type	Capacity (t)	Qty
Praia	Mult-purp. Cranes	10–35	3
Praia	Forklifts	3–45	15

Cargo Worked: 15-20 t/gang/h for bagged cargo, 20-25 t/gang/h for bulk cargo

Bunkering: Not available except small quantities of gas oil can be supplied by truck alongside pier
Enacol S.a.r.l., P O Box 1, S. Vicente, Praia, Santiago Island, Republic of Cape Verde, *Tel:* +238 2306 060, *Fax:* +238 2609 030, *Email:* angelogoncalves@enacol.cv

Towage: One 600 hp tug available for mooring and unmooring vessels at quay

---

Key to Principal Facilities:—

A=Airport	**C**=Containers	**G**=General Cargo	**P**=Petroleum	**R**=Ro/Ro	**Y**=Dry Bulk
B=Bunkers	**D**=Dry Dock	**L**=Cruise	**Q**=Other Liquid Bulk	**T**=Towage (where available from port)	

Shipping Agents: AAB Shipping Agencia Viking Lda, 32 Rua Candido dos Reis, Predio Senna Sport, Praia, Santiago Island, Republic of Cape Verde, *Tel:* +238 991 2053, *Fax:* +238 991 5055, *Email:* viking@cvtelecom.cv

CSA Shipping Agency, Rua Visconde S. Januario, No.12 Plato, P O Box 501, Praia, Santiago Island, Republic of Cape Verde, *Tel:* +238 261 1179, *Fax:* +238 261 1198, *Email:* csa.com@cvtelecom.cv

Diallo & Macedo Compania Navebacad Lda, Avenida Cidade de Lisboa, P O Box 281-C, Praia, Santiago Island, Republic of Cape Verde, *Tel:* +238 261 9988, *Fax:* +238 261 6244, *Email:* diallomacedo@hotmail.com

Manoel Gomes Madeira (Sucrs) Ltda, Rua Serpa Pinto 57, R/C, Praia, Santiago Island, Republic of Cape Verde, *Tel:* +238 261 9770, *Fax:* +238 261 9838, *Email:* manoelgmadeira@cvtelecom.cv

A.P. Moller-Maersk Group, Maersk Line, Praia, Santiago Island, Republic of Cape Verde, *Tel:* +238 261 9838, *Fax:* +238 261 9770, *Email:* cverep@maersk.com, *Website:* www.maerskline.com

Agencia Nacional de Viagens S.A. (ANV), Agencia Nacional de Viagens S.A. (ANAV-PRAIA), Rua Serpa Pinto, P O Box 58, Praia, Santiago Island, Republic of Cape Verde, *Tel:* +238 260 3100, *Fax:* +238 261 2162, *Email:* anavpraia@cvtelecom.cv, *Website:* www.anv.cv

Medical Facilities: One modern hospital

Airport: Francisco Mendes, 7 km

Development: Plans include an extension to Berth No.1, construction of a new breakwater and construction of a new container terminal

Lloyd's Agent: Agencia Nacional de Viagens S.A. (ANV), Avenida da Republica 15/17, P O Box 16 & 142, Mindelo, St. Vincent Island, Republic of Cape Verde, *Tel:* +238 232 1115, *Fax:* +238 232 1445, *Email:* anvsv@cvtelecom.cv, *Website:* www.anv.cv

SAL ISLAND

Admiralty Chart: 367/369

Admiralty Pilot: 1

Time Zone: GMT -1 h

UNCTAD Locode: CV SID

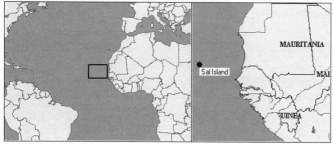

Principal Facilities:

P		G	C	R			T	A

Authority: Empresa Nacional de Administracao dos Portos S.A. (ENAPOR), Palmeira, Sal Island, Republic of Cape Verde, *Tel:* +238 241 1348, *Fax:* +238 241 1348, *Website:* www.enapor.cv

Port Security: ISPS compliant. Port Facility Security Officer: Capt. Daniel Delgado, Email: daniel_delgado@hotmail.com

Documentation: For discharging (generals etc): 1 copy maritime declaration of health, 5 copies of crew, 5 copies passengers, 3 copies stores, 2 copies crew effects list, 3 copies B/L, 3 manifests

For discharging (tankers): as above plus 2 copies each dry/origin/quantity/quality certificates

Approach: Vessels can enter from N or S but pilot must fly from St. Vincent to board vessel to indicate anchorage or assist with mooring at Palmeira Bay

Pilotage: Compulsory. Vessels must contact St. Vincent through Agents for a pilot with at least 72 h notice

Radio Frequency: St. Vincent Radio (call sign D4A) 500 kHz; VHF Channel 16 or 8469 Mcs and listening on 8 mHz

Tides: Range of tide 1.22 m

Traffic: 2007, 398 vessels, 4928 TEU's handled

Principal Imports and Exports: Imports: Building materials, Foodstuffs. Exports: Fish, Salt.

Working Hours: 0800-1300, 1400-1900

Accommodation:

Name	Length (m)	Depth (m)
Palmeira		
Berth No.1	60	4.1
Berth No.2	30	2
Berth No.3	34	1

Storage:

Location	Open (m²)	Covered (m²)	Sheds / Warehouses
Palmeira	5605	450	1

Mechanical Handling Equipment:

Location	Type	Capacity (t)	Qty
Palmeira	Mult-purp. Cranes		1
Palmeira	Forklifts	3	7

Cargo Worked: 15-20 t/gang/h bagged cargo

Towage: Tugs available from Mindelo or Praia

Medical Facilities: Small hospital available

Airport: Amilcar Cabral International

Development: Expansion and modernisation of the port in two phases:
Phase 1 consists of an extension to the existing piers and construction of a ro/ro ramp
Phase 2 involves construction of a new jetty

Lloyd's Agent: Agencia Nacional de Viagens S.A. (ANV), Avenida da Republica 15/17, P O Box 16 & 142, Mindelo, St. Vincent Island, Republic of Cape Verde, *Tel:* +238 232 1115, *Fax:* +238 232 1445, *Email:* anvsv@cvtelecom.cv, *Website:* www.anv.cv

ST. VINCENT

see under Mindelo

CAYMAN ISLANDS

CAYMAN BRAC

Lat 19° 44' N; Long 79° 47' W.

Admiralty Chart: 462

Admiralty Pilot: 70

Time Zone: GMT -5 h

UNCTAD Locode: KY CYB

Principal Facilities:

P		G	C	R		B		A

Authority: Port Authority of the Cayman Islands, P O Box 9, The Creek, Cayman Brac KY2-2301, Cayman Islands, *Tel:* +1345 948 0428, *Fax:* +1345 948 0408, *Email:* bracport@candw.ky

Officials: Port Superintendent: Capt Edgar Ashton Bodden, *Email:* ashton@caymanport.com.

Port Security: ISPS compliant

Anchorage: Available in the following positions:
19° 41.6' N; 79° 53.4' W in depth of 21 m
19° 40.9' N; 79° 53.2' W in depth of 23 m
19° 40.7' N; 79° 54.1' W in depth of 24 m

Pilotage: Available on request, Tel: +1345 916 5262, Email: tatum@candw.ky or hgasbrac@candw.ky

Pilot boards in pos 19° 43' N; 79° 53' W or 19° 40' N; 79° 53' W, and remains on board during all berthing, unberthing and lightening operations, together with two assistants and two riggers to handle the fenders. These men may be relieved if lightening operations are prolonged. Mooring can take place by day or night

Radio Frequency: VHF Channel 16

Weather: Trade winds NE to SE

Tides: Range of tide 0.25 m

Principal Imports and Exports: Imports: Building materials, General cargo.

Working Hours: Mon-Fri 0800-1700. Sat 0800-1200

Accommodation:

Name	Remarks
Cayman Brac	See [1] below

[1]*Cayman Brac:* Two berths in harbour, one 61 m long accommodating vessels up to a max forward draft of 3 m, and the other also 61 m in length to take vessels up to 4.5 m draft. Container and ro/ro vessels can be accommodated

Cayman Brac and the nearby Little Cayman Island are used for the purpose of lightening operations between tankers. Officials board tankers by launches from the shore. Oil transfer operations are carried out off both islands and the service tanker keeps in the lee of the larger tanker being lightened. The vessels are separated by floating fenders supplied by the Company. Oil transfer is by two 10'' hoses and the max discharge rate permitted is 5000 t/h. Operations are only occasionally interrupted due to bad weather and the amount of mooring lines between the two vessels may vary depending on conditions

Storage: Limited amount of storage available

Mechanical Handling Equipment:

Location	Type	Capacity (t)	Qty
Cayman Brac	Mobile Cranes	20	1

Cargo Worked: 300 t/day

Bunkering: Available by truck

Waste Reception Facilities: Garbage disposal available

Medical Facilities: Faith Hospital

Airport: Gerard Smith International, 10 miles

Lloyd's Agent: Leroy B. Whorms Sr. & Associates (Marine Surveyors) Ltd, P O Box 2584 GT, George Town KY1-1103, Grand Cayman, Cayman Islands, *Tel:* +1345 949 9210, *Fax:* +1345 949 9210, *Email:* lloyds@candw.ky

GEORGE TOWN

Lat 19° 18' N; Long 81° 23' W.

Admiralty Chart: 462

Time Zone: GMT -5 h

Admiralty Pilot: 70

UNCTAD Locode: KY GEC

Principal Facilities:

| P | Q | | G | C | R | L | B | | A |

West Indian Shipping Ltd

West Indian Marine Group

PO Box 31194 SMB
2nd Floor, Panton House, 24 Warwick Drive,
Grand Cayman, CAYMAN ISLANDS KY1-1205
Tel: 1-345-9457126   Fax: 1-345-9450613
Managing Director - John Mackenzie
Email: john.mackenzie@wishipping.com
Web: www.wimarine.com

SHIPPING

West Indian Shipping Ltd. is a liner shipping and port agent, operating liner shipping services with world wide shipping connections from Mobile in Alabama, Jacksonville and Port Everglades in Florida and Kingston, Jamaica to George Town, Grand Cayman, Cayman Islands and Panama.

We are also port agents and ship owner's agents handling all aspects of vessel and ship owner's port agency representation. We also specialize in the logistics and handling of project cargoes, scrap metal, bulk construction aggregates and heavy lift cargoes.

Authority: Cayman Islands Port Authority, P O Box 1358, George Town KY1-1108, Grand Cayman, Cayman Islands, *Tel:* +1345 949 2055, *Fax:* +1345 949 5820, *Email:* info@caymanport.com, *Website:* www.caymanport.com

Officials: Port Director: Paul Hurlston, *Email:* phurlston@caymanport.com.
Deputy Port Director: Clement Reid, *Email:* creid@caymanport.com.
Administrative Assistant: Katherine Smalldon, *Email:* ksmalldon@caymanport.com.

Port Security: ISPS compliant. PFSO: Joseph Woods Jr., *Email:* pfso@caymanport.com

Documentation: Customs:
a) clearance from last port (original)
b) ship information sheet - pre-arrival notification (2 copies)
c) maritime declaration of health
d) stores list
e) crew list
f) crew effects declaration
g) passenger list
h) embarking crew/passenger list
i) disembarking passenger/crew list
Immigration:
a) clearance from last port (original)
b) ship information sheet - pre arrival notification (2 copies)
c) maritime declaration of health
d) crew list
e) passenger list
f) embarking crew/passenger list
g) disembarking passenger/crew list
Ship's Agent:
a) ship information sheet - pre-arrival notification (3 copies)
b) crew list
c) passenger list

Anchorage: Anchorage area off the port for large vessels in a depth of 15 m

Pilotage: Available on request from Bodden Shipping Agents and Cayman Islands Shipping

Radio Frequency: Cayman Port Authority operates on SSB 8294.0 between 0800-1630. Round the clock watch on VHF channel 16, call sign 'Port Security'

Weather: Prevailing NE winds. Hurricane season between June and November

Traffic: 2007, 38 889 TEU's handled, 1 725 647 cruise passengers

Maximum Vessel Dimensions: 139 m loa, 6000 dwt, 6.5 m draught

Working Hours: Office Hours: Mon-Fri 0830-1630. Sat 0830-1200
General Cargo Working: Sun-Sat 0600-1800
Bulk Cargo (Aggregate) Working: Sun-Sat 0600-1800

Accommodation:

Name	Length (m)	Depth (m)	Remarks
George Town			See [1] below
North Pier	61	6.5	Ro/ro
South Pier	134	5	Lo/lo
West Pier	73	4	Lo/lo

[1]*George Town:* There are five anchorages for cruise vessels:
Anchorage No.1: in pos 19° 17' 88" N; 81° 23' 02" W
Anchorage No.2: in pos 19° 18' 18.3" N; 81° 23' 30.9" W
Anchorage No.3: in pos 19° 18' 45.8" N; 81° 23' 46.3" W
Anchorage No.4: in pos 19° 17' 63.9" N; 81° 23' 30.6" W
Anchorage No.5: in pos 19° 18' 76.0" N; 81° 23' 58.0" W
Royal Walter Cruise Terminal for cruise passengers

Storage: Covered storage of 1858 m2 and open storage of 13 acres. Storage cap of 800 TEU's. 27 reefer points

Mechanical Handling Equipment:

Location	Type	Qty
George Town	Mult-purp. Cranes	3
George Town	Forklifts	4
George Town	Yard Tractors	14

Bunkering: Marine diesel fuel available for small cargo vessels by hose pipe Chevron Marine Products LLC, Global Marine Products LLC, 1500 Louisiana, 4th Floor, Houston, TX 77002, United States of America, *Tel:* +1 832 8542 988, *Fax:* +1 832 8544 868, *Email:* gulfcbm@chevron.com, *Website:* www.chevron.com – *Grades:* GO – *Delivery Mode:* tank truck

Shipping Agents: Cayman Freight Shipping Services, Mirco Commerce Centre, Industrial Park, P O Box 1372, Grand Cayman, Cayman Islands, *Tel:* +1345 949 4977, *Fax:* +1345 949 8402, *Email:* ivyjulio@candw.ky, *Website:* www.seaboardmarinecayman.ky
Thompson Shipping Co. Ltd, Eastern Avenue, P O Box 188, George Town 33142, Grand Cayman, Cayman Islands, *Tel:* +1345 949 8044, *Fax:* +1345 945 1234, *Email:* info@thompsonshipping.com, *Website:* www.thompsonshipping.com
West Indian Shipping Ltd, 2nd Floor, Anton House, 24 Warwick Drive, Grand Cayman, Cayman Islands, *Tel:* +1345 945 7126, *Fax:* +1345 945 0613

Stevedoring Companies: Shelbys Agency & Stevedoring Ltd, P O Box 458, George Town, Grand Cayman, Cayman Islands, *Tel:* +1345 949 2101, *Fax:* +1345 949 8692

Surveyors: Cayman Islands Registry, 2nd Floor Strathvale House, 90 North Church Street, P O Box 2256, George Town KY1 1107, Grand Cayman, Cayman Islands, *Tel:* +1345 949 8831, *Fax:* +1345 949 8849, *Email:* cisrky@cishipping.com, *Website:* www.cishipping.com
Nippon Kaiji Kyokai, P O Box 1610, George Town, Grand Cayman, Cayman Islands, *Tel:* +1345 947 8425, *Fax:* +1345 947 3289, *Website:* www.classnk.or.jp

Medical Facilities: Small hospital in the town

Airport: Owen Robert Airport, 2 km

Lloyd's Agent: Leroy B. Whorms Sr. & Associates (Marine Surveyors) Ltd, P O Box 2584 GT, George Town KY1-1103, Grand Cayman, Cayman Islands, *Tel:* +1345 949 9210, *Fax:* +1345 949 9210, *Email:* lloyds@candw.ky

CHILE

L&R Abogados

Apoquindo Ave. 3001 10th floor, Las Condes, Santiago - CHILE
Zip code 7550227
Phone: +56 2 498 2800
Fax: +56 2 498 2900
Email: rrozas@blr.cl
Web: www.blr.cl

ANTOFAGASTA

Lat 23° 39' S; Long 70° 23' W.

Admiralty Chart: 4223/4227

Time Zone: GMT -4 h

Admiralty Pilot: 7

UNCTAD Locode: CL ANF

Key to Principal Facilities:—			
A=Airport	**C**=Containers	**G**=General Cargo	**P**=Petroleum	**R**=Ro/Ro	**Y**=Dry Bulk
B=Bunkers	**D**=Dry Dock	**L**=Cruise	**Q**=Other Liquid Bulk	**T**=Towage (where available from port)

Principal Facilities:

| P | Q | Y | G | C | R | | B | | T | A | |

Authority: Empresa Portuaria Antofagasta, Avenida Grecia s/n, P O Box 190, Antofagasta, Chile, *Tel:* +56 55 223587, *Fax:* +56 55 223171, *Email:* epa@puertoantofagasta.cl, *Website:* www.puertoantofagasta.cl

Officials: General Manager: Alvaro Fernandez Slater, *Email:* afernandez@puertoantofagasta.cl.

Port Security: ISPS compliant

Pilotage: Compulsory in or out

Radio Frequency: 2182 kHz and 500 kHz

Tides: Range of tide 1.5 m

Traffic: 2006 3 341 271 t of cargo handled

Principal Imports and Exports: Imports: General cargo, Wheat. Exports: Fishmeal, Minerals.

Working Hours: Three shifts 0700-1500, 1500-2300, 2300-0700

Accommodation:

Name	Length (m)	Depth (m)	Remarks
Antofagasta			See [1] below
Berth No's 1, 2 & 3	600	9.14	
Berth No's 4 & 5	185	9.1	See [2] below
Berth No.6	130	9.46	
Berth No.7	220	11.28	

[1]*Antofagasta:* Excellent artificial harbour owned by the State. Roadstead exposed to heavy S and W ocean swell, effects of which may be exaggerated by strong winds. Anchorage in about 27.5 to 74 m, uneven and rocky bottom. Cargo no longer handled by lighters

Inside the portworks vessels go alongside and use one bow anchor and 82 to 137 m of chain. The entry to the portworks is 150 m wide and min depth at approaches 18 m. Depth inside varies from 9.14 to 27.43 m. There are seven berths
Tanker facilities: Two oil berths. Lengths 170.7 m and 182.9 m, 10.06 m draft and 9.75 m draft respectively. Night berthing possible. One berth for small vessels to discharge liquefied gas. Water and bunkers available
All berths are served by road and rail links
[2]*Berth No's 4 & 5:* Berths 4-7 operated by Antofagasta Terminal Internacional (ATI), Tel: +56 55 432350, Fax: +56 55 432355, Email: terminal@atiport.cl, Website: www.atiport.cl

Storage: Three storage sheds, two of 5000 m2 and one of 4000 m2, also one Bolivian transit shed of 3100 m2

Location	Open (m²)
Antofagasta	52550

Mechanical Handling Equipment:

Location	Type	Capacity (t)	Qty
Antofagasta	Mobile Cranes	12	6
Antofagasta	Mobile Cranes	5	8

Cargo Worked: Discharge rate, general cargo 500 to 1000 t/day. Port loading rate about 1000 t/day

Bunkering: Agencias Universales S.A. (AGUNSA), Condell 1949, P O Box 763, Antofagasta, Chile, *Tel:* +56 55 263419, *Fax:* +56 55 225487, *Email:* agunsaanf@agunsa.cl, *Website:* www.agunsa.com
Ian Taylor y Compania S.A., Avenida Grecia 583, Oficina 22, Antofagasta, Chile, *Tel:* +56 55 262563, *Fax:* +56 55 265580, *Email:* antofagasta@iantaylor.com, *Website:* www.iantaylorgroup.com
Compania de Petroleos de Chile Copec S.A. (COPEC), Avenida Jorge Montt 2300, P O Box 2532-691, Vina del Mar, Chile, *Tel:* +56 32 2324 326, *Fax:* +56 32 2699 651, *Email:* bunkers@copec.cl, *Website:* www.copec.cl

Towage: Ian Taylor y Compania S.A., Avenida Grecia 583, Oficina 22, Antofagasta, Chile, *Tel:* +56 55 262563, *Fax:* +56 55 265580, *Email:* antofagasta@iantaylor.com, *Website:* www.iantaylorgroup.com
Ultramar Agencia Maritima Ltda, Pasaje San Guillermo No.121, P O Box 109, Quintero, Chile, *Tel:* +56 32 293 0927, *Fax:* +56 32 293 0265, *Email:* quintero@ultramar.cl, *Website:* www.ultramar.cl

Ship Chandlers: Gandara Chile S.A., Calle Eduardo Orchard #1200, Antofagasta, Chile, *Tel:* +56 55 472479, *Fax:* +56 55 472480, *Email:* antofagasta@gandarachile.cl, *Website:* www.gandarachile.cl
J.V.G. General Shipchandlers S.A., Condell No 2377, Office No 301, Antofagasta, Chile, *Tel:* +56 55 263428, *Fax:* +56 55 263428, *Email:* jvgantofagasta@terra.cl, *Website:* www.jvg.cl

Shipping Agents: Agencias Maritimas Agental Ltda, Calle M.A. Matta 1839, Piso 6, Of 601-D, Edificio el Obelisco, Antofagasta, Chile, *Tel:* +56 55 493620, *Fax:* +56 55 493644, *Email:* agentanf@agental.cl, *Website:* www.agental.cl
Agencias Maritimas Broom y Cia. Ltda, Latorre 2274, Antofagasta, Chile, *Tel:* +56 55 269083, *Fax:* +56 55 265765, *Email:* manageranf@ajbroom.cl, *Website:* www.ajbroom.cl

Agencias Universales S.A. (AGUNSA), Condell 1949, P O Box 763, Antofagasta, Chile, *Tel:* +56 55 263419, *Fax:* +56 55 225487, *Email:* agunsaanf@agunsa.cl, *Website:* www.agunsa.com
Maritima Valparaiso Chile S.A., Edificio El Obelisco, Avenida Manuel Antonio Matta, No.1839 Oficina 1201 A, Antofagasta, Chile, *Tel:* +56 55 283693, *Fax:* +56 55 227729, *Email:* antofagasta@anf.marval.cl, *Website:* www.marval.cl
Sudamericana Agencias Aereas y Maritimas S.A. (SAAM), M.A. Matta 1839, Oficina 701, Antofagasta, Chile, *Tel:* +56 55 204000, *Fax:* +56 55 251392, *Email:* antofagasta@saamsa.com, *Website:* www.saam.cl
Ian Taylor y Compania S.A., Avenida Grecia 583, Oficina 22, Antofagasta, Chile, *Tel:* +56 55 262563, *Fax:* +56 55 265580, *Email:* antofagasta@iantaylor.com, *Website:* www.iantaylorgroup.com
Ultramar Agencia Maritima Ltda, P O Box 1210, Antofagasta, Chile, *Tel:* +56 55 263399, *Fax:* +56 55 227341, *Email:* antofagasta@ultramar.cl, *Website:* www.ultramar.cl

Stevedoring Companies: Sudamericana Agencias Aereas y Maritimas S.A. (SAAM), M.A. Matta 1839, Oficina 701, Antofagasta, Chile, *Tel:* +56 55 204000, *Fax:* +56 55 251392, *Email:* antofagasta@saamsa.com, *Website:* www.saam.cl
Ian Taylor y Compania S.A., Avenida Grecia 583, Oficina 22, Antofagasta, Chile, *Tel:* +56 55 262563, *Fax:* +56 55 265580, *Email:* antofagasta@iantaylor.com, *Website:* www.iantaylorgroup.com

Medical Facilities: Hospital and private facilities available

Airport: Cerro Moreno, 40 km

Lloyd's Agent: Gibbs & Cia SAC, Marchant Pereira 367, 5th Floor, Santiago 664 0622, Chile, *Tel:* +56 2 269 6364, *Fax:* +56 2 269 6395, *Email:* secretaria@gibbs.cl, *Website:* www.gibbs.cl

ARICA

Lat 18° 28' S; Long 70° 19' W.

Admiralty Chart: 4217		**Admiralty Pilot:** 7	
Time Zone: GMT -4 h		**UNCTAD Locode:** CL ARI	

Principal Facilities:

| P | | Y | G | C | | | B | | T | A | |

Authority: Empresa Portuaria Arica, Avenida Maximo Lira No.389, P O Box 932, Arica, Chile, *Tel:* +56 58 202080, *Fax:* +56 58 202090, *Email:* puertoarica@puertoarica.cl, *Website:* www.puertoarica.cl

Officials: Port Manager: Mario Moya, *Email:* mmoya@puertoarica.cl.
Marketing Manager: Yuny Arias, *Email:* yarias@puertoarica.cl.

Port Security: ISPS compliant

Pilotage: Compulsory

Radio Frequency: VHF Channel 16, 2182 kHz

Traffic: 2007, 1 528 725 t of cargo handled, 87 335 TEU's

Working Hours: Three shifts 0800-1600, 1600-2300, 2300-0630. 50% surcharge for working Sundays and holidays

Accommodation:

Name	Length (m)	Draught (m)	Remarks
Arica			See [1] below
Berth No.1	114	4	
Berth No.2	200	4.9	
Berth No.3	200	8.2	
Berth No.4	170	9.3	
Berth No.5	170	8.6	
Berth No.6	200	9.75	

[1]*Arica:* Operated by Terminal Puerto Arica S.A., Av. Maximo Lira 389, Arica, Tel: +56 58 202000, Fax: +56 58 202005, Email: tpa@tpa.cl, Website: www.tpa.cl
Artificial mole and sheltered roadstead for tankers. Pipe line from Sica Sica, Bolivia, in operation exporting about 90 000 t of crude oil monthly. Captain of the Port and Agents should be advised by wireless of ETA and whether carrying explosives
There are two tanker installations each consisting of three stern buoys. One is for the loading of Bolivian crude and is situated 1 km from the end of the mole bearing 39°. Vessels of 50 000 dwt can be accommodated in a depth of 13.11 m. Loading rate 9000 bbls/h through a 16'' pipeline with on shore storage of 700 000 bbls. The other installation is in San Martin Bay in a depth of 13.72 m. The pipeline is 10'' diameter with onshore storage of 60 000 bbls. Daytime berthing only at both installations with sailing anytime
Railways to La Paz, Bolivia and Tacna, Peru

Storage:

Location	Open (m²)	Covered (m²)
Arica	177375	28248

Mechanical Handling Equipment:

Location	Type	Capacity (t)	Qty
Arica	Mult-purp. Cranes	30	5
Arica	Mobile Cranes	100	1

Cargo Worked: Bulk cargo 1500 t/shift, other cargoes 150-200 t shift

Bunkering: Agencias Universales S.A. (AGUNSA), Arturo Prat 391, Floor 15, Office 154, Edificio Empresarial, P O Box 28-D, Arica, Chile, *Tel:* +56 58 231077, *Fax:* +56 58 230088, *Email:* agunsaari@agunsa.cl, *Website:* www.agunsa.cl
Ian Taylor y Compania S.A., Arturo Prat 391, Oficina 151-152, 15 Piso, Arica, Chile, *Tel:* +56 58 232151, *Fax:* +56 58 252638, *Email:* arica@iantaylor.com, *Website:* www.iantaylorgroup.com
Compania de Petroleos de Chile Copec S.A. (COPEC), Avenida Jorge Montt 2300, P O Box 2532-691, Vina del Mar, Chile, *Tel:* +56 32 2324 326, *Fax:* +56 32 2699 651, *Email:* bunkers@copec.cl, *Website:* www.copec.cl – *Grades:* MDO; IFO; in line blending available – *Misc:* own storage facilities – *Rates:* 40-100t/h – *Notice:* 48 hours – *Delivery Mode:* truck
ExxonMobil Marine Fuels, Suite 900, One Alhambra Plaza, Coral Gables, FL 33134, United States of America, *Tel:* +1 305 459 6358, *Fax:* +1 305 459 6412, *Email:* emmf@exxonmobil.com, *Website:* www.exxonmobilmarinefuels.com – *Grades:* MGO – *Notice:* 48 hours – *Delivery Mode:* truck
Ian Taylor y Compania S.A., Arturo Prat 391, Oficina 151-152, 15 Piso, Arica, Chile, *Tel:* +56 58 232151, *Fax:* +56 58 252638, *Email:* arica@iantaylor.com, *Website:* www.iantaylorgroup.com

Towage: Three tugs available
Ian Taylor y Compania S.A., Arturo Prat 391, Oficina 151-152, 15 Piso, Arica, Chile, *Tel:* +56 58 232151, *Fax:* +56 58 252638, *Email:* arica@iantaylor.com, *Website:* www.iantaylorgroup.com

Repair & Maintenance: Slipway for small craft

Shipping Agents: Agencias Maritimas Agental Ltda, Arturo Prat 391, Piso 14, Of.145 - Edificio Empresarial, Arica, Chile, *Tel:* +56 58 255710, *Fax:* +56 58 255712, *Email:* agentari@agental.cl, *Website:* www.agental.cl
Agencias Maritimas Broom y Cia. Ltda, Baquedano 731 - Of. 809, Arica, Chile, *Tel:* +56 58 250410, *Fax:* +56 58 253399, *Email:* arica@ajbroom.cl, *Website:* www.ajbroom.cl
Agencias Universales S.A. (AGUNSA), Arturo Prat 391, Floor 15, Office 154, Edificio Empresarial, P O Box 28-D, Arica, Chile, *Tel:* +56 58 231077, *Fax:* +56 58 230088, *Email:* agunsaari@agunsa.cl, *Website:* www.agunsa.cl
Maritima Valparaiso Chile S.A., Edificio Empressarial, Arturo Prat No.391, 6th Floor, Oficina 63, Arica, Chile, *Tel:* +56 58 251696, *Fax:* +56 58 254650, *Email:* jdroguett@ari.marval.cl, *Website:* www.marval.cl
Mediterranean Shipping Company, MSC Arica, Thompson 102, Oficina 301, Arica, Chile, *Tel:* +56 58 594400, *Fax:* +56 58 594490, *Website:* www.mscchile.com
A.P. Moller-Maersk Group, Maersk Chile S.A., Arturo Prat 391, Oficinas 131-132 - Edificio Empresarial, Arica, Chile, *Tel:* +56 58 231288, *Fax:* +56 58 231289, *Email:* chlopsarc@maersk.com, *Website:* www.maerskline.com
Sudamericana Agencias Aereas y Maritimas S.A. (SAAM), Prat 391, 8 Piso, Edificio Empresarial, Arica, Chile, *Tel:* +56 58 207000, *Fax:* +56 58 232901, *Email:* arica@saamsa.com, *Website:* www.saam.cl
Ian Taylor y Compania S.A., Arturo Prat 391, Oficina 151-152, 15 Piso, Arica, Chile, *Tel:* +56 58 232151, *Fax:* +56 58 252638, *Email:* arica@iantaylor.com, *Website:* www.iantaylorgroup.com
Ultramar Agencia Maritima Ltda, 18 de Septiembre No.112, P O Box 12-d, Arica, Chile, *Tel:* +56 58 231126, *Fax:* +56 58 231096, *Email:* arica@ultramar.cl, *Website:* www.ultramar.cl

Stevedoring Companies: Naviera Portuaria Arica S.A., Colon 203, Arica, Chile, *Tel:* +56 58 231715, *Fax:* +56 58 231949, *Email:* comercialarica@naviport.cl, *Website:* www.naviport.cl
Sudamericana Agencias Aereas y Maritimas S.A. (SAAM), Prat 391, 8 Piso, Edificio Empresarial, Arica, Chile, *Tel:* +56 58 207000, *Fax:* +56 58 232901, *Email:* arica@saamsa.com, *Website:* www.saam.cl
Ian Taylor y Compania S.A., Arturo Prat 391, Oficina 151-152, 15 Piso, Arica, Chile, *Tel:* +56 58 232151, *Fax:* +56 58 252638, *Email:* arica@iantaylor.com, *Website:* www.iantaylorgroup.com
Ultramar Agencia Maritima Ltda, 18 de Septiembre No.112, P O Box 12-d, Arica, Chile, *Tel:* +56 58 231126, *Fax:* +56 58 231096, *Email:* arica@ultramar.cl, *Website:* www.ultramar.cl

Medical Facilities: Available

Airport: Chacalluta, 17 km

Railway: Railway in the port which goes to La Paz in Bolivia

Development: Construction of an additional berth with draft of 12.5 m for vessels over 200 m loa

Lloyd's Agent: Gibbs & Cia SAC, Marchant Pereira 367, 5th Floor, Santiago 664 0622, Chile, *Tel:* +56 2 269 6364, *Fax:* +56 2 269 6395, *Email:* secretaria@gibbs.cl, *Website:* www.gibbs.cl

BARQUITO

see under Chanaral

CABO NEGRO

Lat 52° 57' S; Long 70° 47' W.

Admiralty Chart: 1694	**Admiralty Pilot:** 6
Time Zone: GMT -4 h	**UNCTAD Locode:** CL CNX

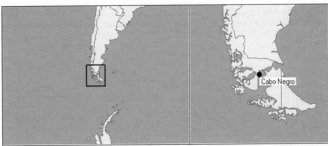

Principal Facilities:

Q				B	T	

Authority: Empresa Portuaria Austral, B. O'Higgins 1385, Punta Arenas, Chile, *Tel:* +56 61 711210, *Fax:* +56 61 711233, *Email:* portspuq@epa.co.cl, *Website:* www.epa.co.cl

Officials: General Manager: Eduardo Manzanares Castesc, *Email:* emanzanares@epa.co.cl.
Assistant General Manager: Rosita Sanchez, *Email:* rsanchez@epa.co.cl.

Pilotage: Compulsory. Arranged from Punta Arenas. Vessels berth during daylight hours only but are able to sail at night at the discretion of the pilot

Traffic: 2006, 3 862 474 t of cargo handled

Accommodation:

Name	Remarks
Cabo Negro	See [1] below

[1]*Cabo Negro:* Liquefield Gas & Methanol Terminal: Pier extends 120 m from the shore with a berthing platform 40 m long at its head, together with two mooring dolphins. Vessels up to 25 000 gt, max loa 170 m can be accommodated. Draught limitation for berthing is 9.8 m and max permissible draught on departure is 12.8 m. Loading rate of 1000 t/h
New 455 m long jetty used by Methanex and ENAP for vessels up to 100 000 dwt
Delivery of LPG can also be made by coastal tanker from Puerto Percy, across the Magellan Strait. No deballasting or inerting facilities; clean ballast may be discharged into the sea. Storage tanks on the shore have a cap for 200 000 bbls of propane and 100 000 bbls of butane

Bunkering: Compania de Petroleos de Chile Copec S.A. (COPEC), Avenida Jorge Montt 2300, P O Box 2532-691, Vina del Mar, Chile, *Tel:* +56 32 2324 326, *Fax:* +56 32 2699 651, *Email:* bunkers@copec.cl, *Website:* www.copec.cl

Towage: Compulsory for vessels over 2000 gt; vessels over 17 000 gt may be required to use a second tug. Tugs are stationed at Punta Arenas

Lloyd's Agent: Gibbs & Cia SAC, Marchant Pereira 367, 5th Floor, Santiago 664 0622, Chile, *Tel:* +56 2 269 6364, *Fax:* +56 2 269 6395, *Email:* secretaria@gibbs.cl, *Website:* www.gibbs.cl

CALBUCO

Lat 41° 45' S; Long 73° 9' W.

Admiralty Chart: 4247	**Admiralty Pilot:** 7
Time Zone: GMT -4 h	**UNCTAD Locode:** CL CBC

Principal Facilities:

	Y				T	

Authority: Portuaria Cabo Froward S.A., Urriola 87 Floor 3, Valparaiso, Chile, *Tel:* +56 41 271 1091, *Fax:* +56 41 271 1638, *Email:* info@froward.cl, *Website:* www.froward.cl

Officials: General Manager: Jaime Vargas Barahona, *Email:* jbarahona@froward.cl.
Commercial Manager: Alex Reitzsch Winkler, *Email:* awinkler@froward.cl.
Operations Manager: Miguel Munoz Munoz, *Email:* miguelm@froward.cl.

Anchorage: Anchorage A in pos 37° 02' 53" S; 73° 10' 05" W
Anchorage B in pos 37° 03' 17.85" S; 73° 10' 05" W
Anchorage C in pos 37° 03' 42.7" S; 73° 10' 05" W

Pilotage: Compulsory

Traffic: 2004, 45 vessels, 1 697 340 t of cargo handled

Accommodation:

Name	Remarks
Calbuco Terminal	Bulk cargo for vessels up to 230 m loa
Jureles Terminal	Bulk cargo for vessels up to 238 m loa and 70 000 dwt
Puchoco Terminal	Bulk cargo for vessels up to 250 m loa and 65 000 dwt

Key to Principal Facilities:—				
A=Airport	**C**=Containers	**G**=General Cargo	**P**=Petroleum	**R**=Ro/Ro	**Y**=Dry Bulk
B=Bunkers	**D**=Dry Dock	**L**=Cruise	**Q**=Other Liquid Bulk	**T**=Towage (where available from port)

Towage: Two tugs available of 1200 hp

Lloyd's Agent: Gibbs & Cia SAC, Marchant Pereira 367, 5th Floor, Santiago 664 0622, Chile, *Tel:* +56 2 269 6364, *Fax:* +56 2 269 6395, *Email:* secretaria@gibbs.cl, *Website:* www.gibbs.cl

CALDERA

Lat 27° 4' S; Long 70° 53' W.

Admiralty Chart: 4231/4225
Admiralty Pilot: 7

Time Zone: GMT -4 h
UNCTAD Locode: CL CLD

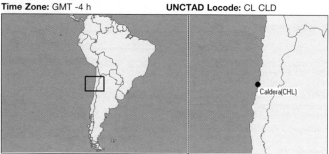

Caldera(CHL)

Principal Facilities:

P		Y	G				B		T	A	

Authority: Gobernacion Maritima, Whell Wright 441, Caldera, Chile, *Tel:* +56 52 315551, *Fax:* +56 52 315276, *Email:* caldera@directemar.cl

Officials: Harbour Master: Luis Tagle.

Port Security: ISPS compliant

Documentation: Clearance from last port (original), cargo manifest (5 copies), crew list (3 copies), personal effects list (3 copies), stores list (3 copies), port of call (3 copies), P&I entry certificate (2 copies), health declaration (3 copies), ship's particulars (3 copies), negative list (3 copies), arrival conditions (original)

Anchorage: a) 27° 02' 12" S; 70° 50' 12" W
b) 27° 02' 28" S; 70° 49' 54" W
c) 27° 02' 31" S; 70° 50' 32" W
d) 27° 02' 46" S; 70° 50' 14" W
Good holding ground with sandy bottom. Best anchorage is 800 m in line with mechanised mole in depth of 20 m. Reference S.H.O.A. No.3001. Forbidden zone marked on charts

Pilotage: Compulsory for all vessels moored to mechanised mole and for foreign vessels mooring in roads or close to head of Fiscal Mole (one pilot needed)

Radio Frequency: Continuous watch maintained on VHF Channel 16, 2185 kc. Playa Ancha, 500 kc for route information

Weather: Prevailing SW winds, heavy swells in winter

Tides: Range of tide 1.5 m

Principal Imports and Exports: Imports: Gas oil. Exports: Fishflour, Fishmeal, Fresh fruit, Vegetable products.

Working Hours: First shift 0800-1530, second shift 1530-2300, third shift 2300-0630

Accommodation:

Name	Length (m)	Draught (m)	Remarks
Caldera			See [1] below
Fiscal Mole	112	3.5	See [2] below
Playa Blanca			See [3] below
Punta Caleta Quay	165	11.88	See [4] below
Punta Padrones Quay	240	12.4	See [5] below

[1]*Caldera:* Some vessels with a draft up to 7 m can go near the Fiscal Quay by the stern and work from this quay where they may moor. Loading/discharging effected by lighters from mole to ship
Tanker facilities: There is one terminal owned by COPEC, capable of handling vessels of 35 000 gt, 14 m draft, 200 m loa, discharging through an 8'' pipeline, rated at 300 t/h. Operating 24 h
[2]*Fiscal Mole:* Situated about 0.9 km SE from Point Caldera. Max size of vessel 2000 gt and 110 m loa. Lighters, tugs and minor craft can moor alongside. General cargo and also shipment of ores worked through this mole
[3]*Playa Blanca:* Pontoon. Situated at Calderilla, can handle vessels up to 10 m draft and 200 m loa. Shipments of fishmeal and fishflour
[4]*Punta Caleta Quay:* For vessels up to 17 000 dwt. This quay is used for loading fresh fruit and general cargo
[5]*Punta Padrones Quay:* Owned by Minera Contractual Candelaria, used to load copper concentrate at rate of 1200 t/h

Mechanical Handling Equipment:

Location	Type	Capacity (t)	Qty
Caldera	Floating Cranes	7	1

Bunkering: Compania de Petroleos de Chile Copec S.A. (COPEC), Avenida Jorge Montt 2300, P O Box 2532-691, Vina del Mar, Chile, *Tel:* +56 32 2324 326, *Fax:* +56 32 2699 651, *Email:* bunkers@copec.cl, *Website:* www.copec.cl – *Grades:* MDO; IFO; in line blending available – *Misc:* own storage facilities – *Rates:* 40-100t/h – *Notice:* 48 hours – *Delivery Mode:* truck
ExxonMobil Marine Fuels, Suite 900, One Alhambra Plaza, Coral Gables, FL 33134, United States of America, *Tel:* +1 305 459 6358, *Fax:* +1 305 459 6412, *Email:* emmf@exxonmobil.com, *Website:* www.exxonmobilmarinefuels.com – *Grades:* all grades except MDO – *Delivery Mode:* pipeline, truck

Towage: One tug available

Shipping Agents: Agencias Maritimas del Norte S.A., Agencias Maritimas de Caldera Ltda, Punta Caleta s/n, Caldera, Chile, *Tel:* +56 52 316111, *Fax:* +56 52 316118, *Email:* seiviport.caldera@terra.cl
Ultramar Agencia Maritima Ltda, Avenida Arturo Prat 058, P O Box 139, Caldera 1570000, Chile, *Tel:* +56 52 316428, *Fax:* +56 52 316412, *Email:* caldera@ultramar.cl, *Website:* www.ultramar.cl

Stevedoring Companies: Agencias Maritimas del Norte S.A., Agencias Maritimas de Caldera Ltda, Punta Caleta s/n, Caldera, Chile, *Tel:* +56 52 316111, *Fax:* +56 52 316118, *Email:* seiviport.caldera@terra.cl
Ultramar Agencia Maritima Ltda, Avenida Arturo Prat 058, P O Box 139, Caldera 1570000, Chile, *Tel:* +56 52 316428, *Fax:* +56 52 316412, *Email:* caldera@ultramar.cl, *Website:* www.ultramar.cl

Medical Facilities: Local hospital available

Airport: Chamonate, 68 km

Lloyd's Agent: Gibbs & Cia SAC, Marchant Pereira 367, 5th Floor, Santiago 664 0622, Chile, *Tel:* +56 2 269 6364, *Fax:* +56 2 269 6395, *Email:* secretaria@gibbs.cl, *Website:* www.gibbs.cl

CALETA CLARENCIA

Lat 52° 54' S; Long 70° 9' W.

Admiralty Chart: 1694
Admiralty Pilot: 6

Time Zone: GMT -4 h
UNCTAD Locode: CL CLR

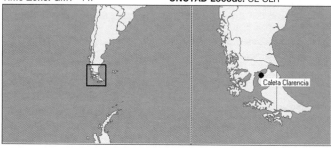

Caleta Clarencia

Principal Facilities:

P						T	

Authority: Empresa Portuaria Austral, B. O'Higgins 1385, Punta Arenas, Chile, *Tel:* +56 61 711210, *Fax:* +56 61 711233, *Email:* portspuq@epa.co.cl, *Website:* www.epa.co.cl

Officials: General Manager: Eduardo Manzanares Castesc, *Email:* emanzanares@epa.co.cl.
Assistant General Manager: Rosita Sanchez, *Email:* rsanchez@epa.co.cl.

Approach: Limiting draught for vessels at entrance to Gente Grande Bay is 10.97 m at LWST

Pilotage: Compulsory

Tides: Range of tide 1.5 m ST, 0.45 m NT. Double tidal effect with a 2.5 h difference producing four high waters a day

Accommodation:

Name	Remarks
Caleta Clarencia	See [1] below

[1]*Caleta Clarencia:* Tanker Terminal: Berth for the loading of crude oil comprising four mooring buoys in a depth of about 12 m with submarine pipelines connecting to oil storage tanks on the shore. Vessels up to max loa 250 m and max draft of 10.97 m can be accommodated. The berth is equipped with two 16'' lines with 12'' flexible on each for loading. Deballasting facilities, using a third line with a 10'' flexible are available at the terminal; clean ballast may be discharged into the sea. Due to the 10.97 m draught restriction, larger vessels usually complete loading cargo at Gregorio oil terminal

Towage: One tug to provide assistance with mooring is available

Lloyd's Agent: Gibbs & Cia SAC, Marchant Pereira 367, 5th Floor, Santiago 664 0622, Chile, *Tel:* +56 2 269 6364, *Fax:* +56 2 269 6395, *Email:* secretaria@gibbs.cl, *Website:* www.gibbs.cl

CALETA PATILLOS

Lat 20° 45' S; Long 70° 12' W.

Admiralty Chart: 4222
Admiralty Pilot: 7

Time Zone: GMT -4 h
UNCTAD Locode: CL CAL

Caleta Patillos

Principal Facilities:

		Y			B		A

Authority: Salinas de Punta de Lobos S.A.M., Caleta Patillos, Chile, *Tel:* +56 57 423007, *Fax:* +56 57 426831

Approach: Patillos Cove is entered between Punta Patillos and Punta Cotitira

Anchorage: Anchorage can be obtained off the S shore of the cove in depths ranging from 23.8 m to 29.3 m

Pilotage: Compulsory. Pilot will come from Iquique where notice of ETA should be sent. Vessels normally berth and unberth during daylight hours only

Traffic: 2006, 3 965 979 t of cargo handled

Accommodation:

Name	Length (m)	Depth (m)	Draught (m)	Remarks
Caleta Patillos				See [1] below
Pier	220	18.3	14.3	See [2] below

[1]*Caleta Patillos:* Privately owned facilities for loading salt in bulk
[2]*Pier:* Six mooring buoys at the head. The pier is equipped with a conveyor and fixed loader which has a loading rate of 24 000 t/day. The vessel is required to move along the pierhead in order to load each hatch

Bunkering: Compania de Petroleos de Chile Copec S.A. (COPEC), Avenida Jorge Montt 2300, P O Box 2532-691, Vina del Mar, Chile, *Tel:* +56 32 2324 326, *Fax:* +56 32 2699 651, *Email:* bunkers@copec.cl, *Website:* www.copec.cl

Airport: Diego Aracena, 20 km

Lloyd's Agent: Gibbs & Cia SAC, Marchant Pereira 367, 5th Floor, Santiago 664 0622, Chile, *Tel:* +56 2 269 6364, *Fax:* +56 2 269 6395, *Email:* secretaria@gibbs.cl, *Website:* www.gibbs.cl

CASTRO

Lat 42° 29' S; Long 73° 46' W.

Admiralty Chart: 3749	**Admiralty Pilot:** 7
Time Zone: GMT -4 h	**UNCTAD Locode:** CL WCA

Principal Facilities:

			G		R			A

Authority: Gobernacion Maritima de Castro, Avda. Pedro Montt 85, Castro, Chile, *Tel:* +56 65 631200, *Fax:* +56 65 631296, *Email:* cpcastro@directemar.cl

Radio Frequency: VHF Channel 16 and 88

Maximum Vessel Dimensions: Max loa 150 m

Principal Imports and Exports: Exports: Frozen sea products, Preserved shellfish, Salmon.

Working Hours: 0800-2000

Accommodation:

Name	Length (m)	Depth (m)	Remarks
Castro			The port is used mainly by coastal vessels
Fiscal Wharf	70	6	See [1] below

[1]*Fiscal Wharf:* No cranes; vessels use ship's own gear. Lighters are available

Cargo Worked: Approx 400 t per 12 h

Medical Facilities: Small hospital in the town

Airport: Gamboa Airport, 4 km

Lloyd's Agent: Gibbs & Cia SAC, Marchant Pereira 367, 5th Floor, Santiago 664 0622, Chile, *Tel:* +56 2 269 6364, *Fax:* +56 2 269 6395, *Email:* secretaria@gibbs.cl, *Website:* www.gibbs.cl

CHACABUCO

Lat 45° 28' S; Long 72° 50' W.

Admiralty Chart: -	**Admiralty Pilot:** 7
Time Zone: GMT -4 h	**UNCTAD Locode:** CL CHB

Principal Facilities:

P		Y	G	C	R	L	B			A

Authority: Empresa Portuaria Chacabuco, Recinto Portuario s/n, Puerto Chacabuco, Chile, *Tel:* +56 67 351139, *Fax:* +56 67 351174, *Email:* info@chacabucoport.cl, *Website:* www.chacabucoport.cl

Officials: President: Luis Musalem.
Director General: Javier Vergara.
Vice President: Silvia Moreno.
General Manager: Enrique Runin.

Port Security: ISPS compliant

Anchorage: Good anchorage can be obtained SE of Chacabuco Bay in depths ranging from 40 m to 50 m

Pilotage: Compulsory for all foreign vessels

Radio Frequency: Transmission and reception on 156.8 kHz

Weather: Generally SW strong winds with occasional NW'lys

Traffic: 2006, 467 476 t of cargo handled

Principal Imports and Exports: Exports: Frozen fish, Lead concentrates, Wool, Zinc.

Working Hours: 24 h/day

Accommodation:

Name	Depth (m)	Remarks
Chacabuco		See [1] below
Dock No.1	9.6	See [2] below
Dock No.2	7.62	One berth of 52 m and two berths of 32 m for vessels up to 165 m loa

[1]*Chacabuco:* Floating pontoon of 288 m2 used by small craft, tenders, fishing vessels etc
Discharge line for LPG available S of the offshore tanker berth for vessels up to 750 gt
[2]*Dock No.1:* Length 71.5 m without dolphin and 114 m with dolphin for vessels of up to 180 m loa

Storage: Refrigerated warehouse with cap up to 2500 t

Mechanical Handling Equipment:

Location	Type
Chacabuco	Mobile Cranes

Bunkering: Compania de Petroleos de Chile Copec S.A. (COPEC), Avenida Jorge Montt 2300, P O Box 2532-691, Vina del Mar, Chile, *Tel:* +56 32 2324 326, *Fax:* +56 32 2699 651, *Email:* bunkers@copec.cl, *Website:* www.copec.cl – *Grades:* MDO; IFO; in line blending available – *Misc:* own storage facilities – *Rates:* 40-100t/h – *Notice:* 48 hours – *Delivery Mode:* truck
Ian Taylor y Compania S.A., Agencia Maritimas Unidas S.A., Terminal de Transbordadores s/n, Puerto Chacabuco, Chile, *Tel:* +56 67 351151, *Fax:* +56 67 351202, *Email:* ageuco@agemar.cl

Towage: Ian Taylor y Compania S.A., Agencia Maritimas Unidas S.A., Terminal de Transbordadores s/n, Puerto Chacabuco, Chile, *Tel:* +56 67 351151, *Fax:* +56 67 351202, *Email:* ageuco@agemar.cl

Shipping Agents: Agencias Maritimas Broom y Cia. Ltda, Diego Portales s/n, Puerto Chacabuco, Chile, *Tel:* +56 67 351134, *Fax:* +56 67 351134, *Email:* broomuco@ajbroom.cl, *Website:* www.ajbroom.cl
Sudamericana Agencias Aereas y Maritimas S.A. (SAAM), Bernardo O'Higgins 089, Puerto Chacabuco, Chile, *Tel:* +56 67 351179, *Fax:* +56 67 351178, *Email:* chacabuco@saamsa.com, *Website:* www.saam.cl
Ian Taylor y Compania S.A., Agencia Maritimas Unidas S.A., Terminal de Transbordadores s/n, Puerto Chacabuco, Chile, *Tel:* +56 67 351151, *Fax:* +56 67 351202, *Email:* ageuco@agemar.cl
Ultramar Agencia Maritima Ltda, Juan Jose Latorre 087, Puerto Chacabuco, Chile, *Tel:* +56 67 351208, *Fax:* +56 67 351166, *Email:* chacabuco@ultramar.cl, *Website:* www.ultramar.cl

Stevedoring Companies: Ian Taylor y Compania S.A., Agencia Maritimas Unidas S.A., Terminal de Transbordadores s/n, Puerto Chacabuco, Chile, *Tel:* +56 67 351151, *Fax:* +56 67 351202, *Email:* ageuco@agemar.cl

Medical Facilities: Small hospital at Puerto Aysen, 15 km

Airport: Coyhaique, 70 km

Lloyd's Agent: Gibbs & Cia SAC, Marchant Pereira 367, 5th Floor, Santiago 664 0622, Chile, *Tel:* +56 2 269 6364, *Fax:* +56 2 269 6395, *Email:* secretaria@gibbs.cl, *Website:* www.gibbs.cl

Key to Principal Facilities:—				
A=Airport	**C**=Containers	**G**=General Cargo	**P**=Petroleum	**R**=Ro/Ro	**Y**=Dry Bulk
B=Bunkers	**D**=Dry Dock	**L**=Cruise	**Q**=Other Liquid Bulk	**T**=Towage (where available from port)	

CHANARAL

Lat 26° 21' S; Long 70° 38' W.

Admiralty Chart: 3079
Time Zone: GMT -4 h

Admiralty Pilot: 7
UNCTAD Locode: CL CNR

Principal Facilities:

P		Y	G	C		B		T	A	

Authority: Codelco-Chile Division Salvador Interacid Ltda., Panamericana Norte s/n, Barquito, Chanaral, Chile, *Tel:* +56 52 488520 & 488517, *Fax:* +56 52 472933

Officials: Manager: W. Carmona.

Port Security: ISPS compliant

Documentation: Clearance from last port (original), cargo manifest (5 copies), crew list (3 copies), personal effects list (3 copies), stores list (3 copies), port of call (3 copies), P&I entry certificate (2 copies), health declaration (3 copies), ship's particulars (3 copies), negative list (3 copies), arrival conditions (original)

Approach: The harbour is open to NW

Anchorage: a) bearing 110°, 0.7 miles from Punta Piedra Blanca
b) bearing 140°, 0.7 miles from Punta Piedra Blanca
c) bearing 125°, 1 mile from Punta Piedra Blanca
reference S.H.O.A. No.3001. Forbidden zone marked on charts

Pilotage: Compulsory. One pilot needed

Radio Frequency: VHF Channel 16, HF 2182 kc and 500 kc. Playa Ancha station for en route information

Weather: Bad weather can be experienced during May and June

Tides: Range of tide 1 m

Traffic: 2000, 76 vessels, 550 000 t of cargo handled

Maximum Vessel Dimensions: 68 930 dwt, max draft 12.8 m, max loa 250 m, max beam 36 m

Principal Imports and Exports: Imports: Chemical products, General cargo, Iron & steel, Mining machinery. Exports: Copper cathodes, Copper concentrate, Copper scrap, Seaweed.

Working Hours: Three shifts: 0800-1530, 1530-2300, 2300-0630

Accommodation:

Name	Remarks
Chanaral	See [1] below

[1]*Chanaral:* Coldelco-Chile has a mechanical loading plant at Point Piedra Blanca. Air draft 11.2 m, loading arm extension 17.5 m, max loa 250 m. Vessels come alongside and are moored to buoys on which they manoeuvre fore and aft as the plant has only one loading arm. The company also has a small mole for loading and discharging goods

Pan American Highway runs through both Chanaral and Barquito and is completely paved to Arica in the N and Puerto Montt in the S

Tanker facilities: Terminal Petrolero Codelco Barquito. Vessels tie up to three buoys and connect to a 10'' flexible hose on the port side. Discharge is rated at 400 t/h and working is continuous

Sulphuric acid terminal in front of Codelco's terminal

Narrow gauge State Railway runs from Chanaral to Iquique in the N and southwards to La Calera which is the junction to the Santiago/Valparaiso Railway (wide gauge)

Mechanical Handling Equipment: Two 35 t spreaders for containers

Location	Type	Capacity (t)	Qty
Chanaral	Forklifts	3.5	8

Cargo Worked: 600 t/gang/shift

Bunkering: ExxonMobil Marine Fuels, Suite 900, One Alhambra Plaza, Coral Gables, FL 33134, United States of America, *Tel:* +1 305 459 6358, *Fax:* +1 305 459 6412, *Email:* emmf@exxonmobil.com, *Website:* www.exxonmobilmarinefuels.com
Petroleos Marinos de Chile Ltda (PMC), P. O. Box 34, Puchuncavi, V Region, Santiago, Chile, *Tel:* +56 32 2796 550, *Fax:* +56 32 2796 233, *Email:* bunkers@pmchile.cl

Towage: Two tugs available in summer season

Shipping Agents: Agencias Maritimas del Norte S.A., Panamericana Norte s/n, Chanaral, Chile, *Tel:* +56 52 480006, *Fax:* +56 52 480161, *Email:* jorpol.chanaral@jorpol.cl, *Website:* www.jorpol.cl
Agencias Universales S.A. (AGUNSA), Calle Comercio 168, Chanaral, Chile, *Tel:* +56 52 480346, *Fax:* +56 52 481193, *Email:* agenciachanaral@agunsa.cl, *Website:* www.agunsa.com

Stevedoring Companies: Agencias Maritimas del Norte S.A., Panamericana Norte s/n, Chanaral, Chile, *Tel:* +56 52 480006, *Fax:* +56 52 480161, *Email:* jorpol.chanaral@jorpol.cl, *Website:* www.jorpol.cl
Agencias Universales S.A., Calle Comercio 168, Chanaral, Chile, *Tel:* +56 52 480346, *Fax:* +56 52 481193, *Email:* psepulveda@agunsa.cl, *Website:* www.agunsa.com

Medical Facilities: Local hospital

Airport: Chanaral, 2 km

Lloyd's Agent: Gibbs & Cia SAC, Marchant Pereira 367, 5th Floor, Santiago 664 0622, Chile, *Tel:* +56 2 269 6364, *Fax:* +56 2 269 6395, *Email:* secretaria@gibbs.cl, *Website:* www.gibbs.cl

COQUIMBO

Lat 29° 57' S; Long 71° 21' W.

Admiralty Chart: 3080
Time Zone: GMT -4 h

Admiralty Pilot: 7
UNCTAD Locode: CL CQQ

Principal Facilities:

	Y	G	C	R	L	B		T	A	

Authority: Empresa Portuaria Coquimbo, Melgarejo 676, P O Box 10 D, Coquimbo, Chile, *Tel:* +56 51 313606, *Fax:* +56 51 326146, *Email:* ptocqq@entelchile.net, *Website:* www.puertocoquimbo.cl

Officials: General Manager: Miguel Zuvic Mujica, *Email:* mzuvic@puertocoquimbo.cl.

Port Security: ISPS compliant

Documentation: Clearance from last port (original), cargo manifest (5 copies), crew list (3 copies), personal effects list (3 copies), stores list (3 copies), port of call (3 copies), P&I entry certificate (2 copies), health declaration (3 copies), ship's particulars (3 copies), negative list (3 copies), arrival conditions (original)

Approach: The harbour is open to NW

Anchorage: A in pos 29° 56' 27" S; 71° 19' 26" W
B in pos 29° 56' 22" S; 71° 19' 26" W
C in pos 29° 56' 18" S; 71° 19' 07" W
D in pos 29° 56' 40" S; 71° 19' 07" W
E in pos 29° 57' 16" S; 71° 18' 55" W
reference S.H.O.A. No.4120. Forbidden zone marked on charts

Pilotage: Compulsory (two pilots are compulsory for vessels over 220 m loa and one pilot for unberthing)

Radio Frequency: VHF Channel 16, HF 2182

Weather: Well protected bay, moderate swell in winter, predominant SW wind; considered one of the safest harbours in the country

Tides: Range of tide 1.5 m

Traffic: 2006, 237 799 t of cargo handled

Principal Imports and Exports: Imports: Corn, General cargo, Wheat. Exports: Canned fish, Copper concentrate, Eucaliptus pulplogs, Fishmeal, Fresh fruit, Manganese, Trioxide of arsenic.

Working Hours: Three shifts: 0800-1530, 1530-2300, 2300-0630

Accommodation:

Name	Length (m)	Draught (m)	Remarks
Coquimbo			
Berth No.1	159	9.26	General cargo
Berth No.2	219	9.37	Bulk cargo & container vessels

Storage:

Location	Open (m²)	Covered (m²)	Sheds / Warehouses
Coquimbo	32921	2500	1

Mechanical Handling Equipment:

Location	Type	Capacity (t)	Qty
Coquimbo	Mobile Cranes	40	1
Coquimbo	Portal Cranes	5	3
Coquimbo	Forklifts	2–4	12

Bunkering: Ian Taylor y Compania S.A., Jorge Carle y Cia. Ltd, Aldunate 700, Coquimbo, Chile, *Tel:* +56 51 315744, *Fax:* +56 51 321858, *Email:* ptocqbo@jcarle.cl, *Website:* www.jcarle.cl
Compania de Petroleos de Chile Copec S.A. (COPEC), Avenida Jorge Montt 2300, P O Box 2532-691, Vina del Mar, Chile, *Tel:* +56 32 2324 326, *Fax:* +56 32 2699 651, *Email:* bunkers@copec.cl, *Website:* www.copec.cl – *Grades:* MDO; IFO; in line blending available – *Misc:* own storage facilities – *Rates:* 40-100t/h – *Notice:* 48 hours – *Delivery Mode:* truck
Ian Taylor y Compania S.A., Jorge Carle y Cia. Ltd, Aldunate 700, Coquimbo, Chile, *Tel:* +56 51 315744, *Fax:* +56 51 321858, *Email:* ptocqbo@jcarle.cl, *Website:* www.jcarle.cl

Towage: Two tugs of 1700 hp and 3500 hp in summer season and one tug of 3500 hp from March-December
Ian Taylor y Compania S.A., Jorge Carle y Cia. Ltd, Aldunate 700, Coquimbo, Chile, *Tel:* +56 51 315744, *Fax:* +56 51 321858, *Email:* ptocqbo@jcarle.cl, *Website:* www.jcarle.cl

Repair & Maintenance: Astilleros Servel Ltda, Regimiento Coquimbo 230, Coquimbo, Chile, *Tel:* +56 51 329543, *Fax:* +56 51 315751

Shipping Agents: Agencias Maritimas del Norte S.A., Avenida Costanera No.841, Coquimbo, Chile, *Tel:* +56 51 321023, *Fax:* +56 51 313687, *Email:* jorpol@jorpol.cl, *Website:* www.jorpol.cl

Agencias Universales S.A. (AGUNSA), Aldunate 700, Coquimbo, Chile, *Tel:* +56 51 323855, *Fax:* +56 51 312225, *Email:* agunsacoq@agunsa.cl, *Website:* www.agunsa.com

Sudamericana Agencias Aereas y Maritimas S.A. (SAAM), Melgarejo 720, Coquimbo, Chile, *Tel:* +56 51 324139, *Fax:* +56 51 322715, *Email:* coquimbo@saamsa.com, *Website:* www.saam.cl

Ian Taylor y Compania S.A., Jorge Carle y Cia. Ltd, Aldunate 700, Coquimbo, Chile, *Tel:* +56 51 315744, *Fax:* +56 51 321858, *Email:* ptocqbo@jcarle.cl, *Website:* www.jcarle.cl

Ultramar Agencia Maritima Ltda, Aldunate 544, Coquimbo, Chile, *Tel:* +56 51 314000, *Fax:* +56 51 320611, *Email:* coquimbo@ultramar.cl, *Website:* www.ultramar.cl

Stevedoring Companies: Aga Larraguibel y Cia. Ltd, Argandona 320, Coquimbo, Chile, *Tel:* +56 51 313116, *Fax:* +56 51 314929, *Email:* agente@larraguibel.cl, *Website:* www.larraguibel.cl

Agencia de Aduana Jorge Wilson A. y Cia. Ltda, Jose Santiago Aldunate 763, Coquimbo, Chile, *Tel:* +56 51 311251, *Fax:* +56 51 311212

Agencias Maritimas del Norte S.A., Avenida Costanera No.841, Coquimbo, Chile, *Tel:* +56 51 321023, *Fax:* +56 51 313687, *Email:* jorpol@jorpol.cl, *Website:* www.jorpol.cl

Agencias Universales S.A., Aldunate 700, Coquimbo, Chile, *Tel:* +56 51 323855, *Fax:* +56 51 312225, *Email:* agunsacoq@agunsa.cl, *Website:* www.agunsa.com

Jorge Carle y Cia. Ltd, Jose Santiago Aldunate 641, Coquimbo, Chile, *Tel:* +56 51 313293, *Fax:* +56 51 319922

Sudamericana Agencias Aereas y Maritimas S.A. (SAAM), Melgarejo 720, Coquimbo, Chile, *Tel:* +56 51 324139, *Fax:* +56 51 322715, *Email:* coquimbo@saamsa.com, *Website:* www.saam.cl

Ian Taylor y Compania S.A., Jorge Carle y Cia. Ltd, Aldunate 700, Coquimbo, Chile, *Tel:* +56 51 315744, *Fax:* +56 51 321858, *Email:* ptocqbo@jcarle.cl, *Website:* www.jcarle.cl

Medical Facilities: First aid clinic in the port. San Pablo Hospital, 3 km

Airport: La Florida Airport, 20 km

Railway: Ferronor S.A. (cargo service), 5 km

Lloyd's Agent: Gibbs & Cia SAC, Marchant Pereira 367, 5th Floor, Santiago 664 0622, Chile, *Tel:* +56 2 269 6364, *Fax:* +56 2 269 6395, *Email:* secretaria@gibbs.cl, *Website:* www.gibbs.cl

CORONEL

Lat 37° 2' S; Long 73° 10' W.

Admiralty Chart: 3082	**Admiralty Pilot:** 7
Time Zone: GMT -4 h	**UNCTAD Locode:** CL CNL

Principal Facilities:

	Y	G	C		B		A

Authority: Compania Puerto de Coronel S.A., Avenida Carlos Prats No.40, Coronel, Chile, *Tel:* +56 41 271 0303, *Fax:* +56 41 271 0555, *Email:* gerencia@puertodecoronel.cl, *Website:* www.puertodecoronel.cl

Officials: General Manager: Alberto Miranda Guerra, *Email:* aguerra@puertodecoronel.cl.
Commercial Manager: Jorge Hinojosa, *Email:* jhinojosa@puertodecoronel.cl.

Port Security: ISPS compliant

Pilotage: Compulsory

Traffic: 2007, 2 747 184 t of cargo handled

Maximum Vessel Dimensions: 220 m loa, 70 000 dwt, 13 m draft

Principal Imports and Exports: Imports: Coal, Industrial products, Wheat. Exports: Logs, Sawn lumber, Wood pulp.

Working Hours: 24 h/day

Accommodation:

Name	Length (m)	Depth (m)	Draught (m)
Coronel			
Berth No.1	190	14	13
Berth No.2	172	14	13
Berth No.3	172	12	11.4

Storage: Pulp warehouses with 30 000 m2 of storage for up to 120 000 t
Warehouse of 21 178 m2 for storage of dry cut lumber, boards and finished wood products with a cap of 42 500 m3
Other warehouses totalling 64 000 m2 are allotted for green cut woods and other low-volume cargos

West of the central road is a paved yard for the storage of a variety of cargos such as green sawed lumber, containers or logs

Bunkering: Compania de Petroleos de Chile Copec S.A. (COPEC), Avenida Jorge Montt 2300, P O Box 2532-691, Vina del Mar, Chile, *Tel:* +56 32 2324 326, *Fax:* +56 32 2699 651, *Email:* bunkers@copec.cl, *Website:* www.copec.cl

Medical Facilities: Available

Airport: Concepcion, 30 km

Development: Two new piers are being constructed, one for containers and the other for discharge of coal

Lloyd's Agent: Gibbs & Cia SAC, Marchant Pereira 367, 5th Floor, Santiago 664 0622, Chile, *Tel:* +56 2 269 6364, *Fax:* +56 2 269 6395, *Email:* secretaria@gibbs.cl, *Website:* www.gibbs.cl

CORRAL

Lat 39° 52' S; Long 73° 25' W.

Admiralty Chart: 4245	**Admiralty Pilot:** 7
Time Zone: GMT -4 h	**UNCTAD Locode:** CL CRR

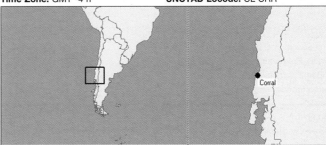

Principal Facilities:

		Y	G				T	A

Authority: Portuaria Corral S.A., Avenida Arturo Prat 588, Valdivia, Chile, *Tel:* +56 63 291305, *Fax:* +56 63 291396, *Email:* cpvaldivia@directemar.cl, *Website:* www.portuariacorral.cl

Officials: Port Captain: Renzo Cuneo.

Anchorage: There are three anchorages for vessels of differing draught (with positions from Roca El Conde Light)
a) approx 5 cables ENE with max draught 8 m
b) approx 2.5 cables E with max draught 6.5 m
c) approx 4.5 cables SE with max draught 5 m
All vessels with draughts exceeding 8 m must anchor outside port limits

Pilotage: Available

Principal Imports and Exports: Exports: Logs, Woodchips.

Working Hours: 24 h/day

Accommodation:

Name	Remarks
Corral Harbour	See [1] below
Las Mulatas	See [2] below

[1]*Corral Harbour:* Small, moderately secure, depth 17 m; affected by strong currents at times, is the ocean entrance to Valdivia, which lies about 19.2 km up the river; average depth in channel 9.75 m.
All cargo discharged at Port Corral into lighters is then towed up river to Valdivia. Three lighters of 300 t each available
[2]*Las Mulatas:* Wharf of 120 m long, S of Valdivia town. Vessels up to 180-229 m loa and 9.75-12.2 m draft can navigate the river to work there by means of barges

Towage: Available and necessary
Ian Taylor y Compania S.A., Arturo Prat 391, Oficina 151-152, 15 Piso, Arica, Chile, *Tel:* +56 58 232151, *Fax:* +56 58 252638, *Email:* arica@iantaylor.com, *Website:* www.iantaylorgroup.com

Stevedoring Companies: Servicios Portuarios Reloncavi Ltd, Corral, Chile, *Tel:* +56 63 471281, *Email:* rechevarria@reloncavi.cl, *Website:* www.reloncavi.cl

Medical Facilities: Available

Airport: Pichoy, 28 km

Railway: Station, 19 km

Lloyd's Agent: Gibbs & Cia SAC, Marchant Pereira 367, 5th Floor, Santiago 664 0622, Chile, *Tel:* +56 2 269 6364, *Fax:* +56 2 269 6395, *Email:* secretaria@gibbs.cl, *Website:* www.gibbs.cl

ENAEX TERMINAL

harbour area, see under Mejillones

GREGORIO

Lat 52° 38' S; Long 70° 11' W.

Admiralty Chart: 1693	**Admiralty Pilot:** 6
Time Zone: GMT -4 h	**UNCTAD Locode:** CL BAG

Key to Principal Facilities:—				
A=Airport	**C**=Containers	**G**=General Cargo	**P**=Petroleum	**R**=Ro/Ro	**Y**=Dry Bulk
B=Bunkers	**D**=Dry Dock	**L**=Cruise	**Q**=Other Liquid Bulk	**T**=Towage (where available from port)

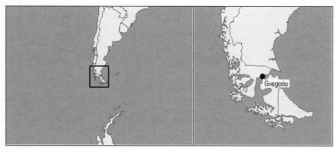

Principal Facilities:

P					B	T	

Authority: Empresa Portuaria Austral, B. O'Higgins 1385, Punta Arenas, Chile, *Tel:* +56 61 711210, *Fax:* +56 61 711233, *Email:* portspuq@epa.co.cl, *Website:* www.epa.co.cl

Officials: General Manager: Eduardo Manzanares Castesc, *Email:* emanzanares@epa.co.cl.
Assistant General Manager: Rosita Sanchez, *Email:* rsanchez@epa.co.cl.

Pilotage: Compulsory. Arranged from Punta Arenas. Vessels berth during daylight hours only but are able to sail at night at the discretion of the pilot. All mooring and unmooring must be done at slack water

Radio Frequency: VHF Channel 16

Tides: Range of tide 1.65 m at ST

Accommodation:

Name	Remarks
Gregorio	See [1] below

[1]*Gregorio:* Berth for the loading of crude oil comprising four mooring buoys in a depth of 25 m with submarine pipelines connecting to a large number of storage tanks on the shore. Vessels up to max loa 250 m and max draft of 14.9 m can be accommodated. The berth is equipped with two 16'' lines for loading and two lines for deballasting with 10'' and 8'' flexibles
There is a pier located 3.6 km SW of the terminal used by small tankers

Bunkering: Compania Maritima de Punta Arenas S.A., Calle Independencia 830, P O Box 337, Punta Arenas, Chile, *Tel:* +56 61 241752, *Fax:* +56 61 247514 – *Grades:* MGO – *Rates:* truck 40t/h, pipeline/barge 100t/h – *Notice:* 24 hours – *Delivery Mode:* pipeline, barge, truck
Compania de Petroleos de Chile Copec S.A. (COPEC), Avenida Jorge Montt 2300, P O Box 2532-691, Vina del Mar, Chile, *Tel:* +56 32 2324 326, *Fax:* +56 32 2699 651, *Email:* bunkers@copec.cl, *Website:* www.copec.cl – *Grades:* MDO; IFO; in line blending available – *Misc:* own storage facilities – *Rates:* 40-100t/h – *Notice:* 48 hours – *Delivery Mode:* truck
ExxonMobil Marine Fuels, Suite 900, One Alhambra Plaza, Coral Gables, FL 33134, United States of America, *Tel:* +1 305 459 6358, *Fax:* +1 305 459 6412, *Email:* emmf@exxonmobil.com, *Website:* www.exxonmobilmarinefuels.com – *Grades:* MGO – *Notice:* 48 hours – *Delivery Mode:* truck

Towage: Compulsory for large tankers. Tugs are stationed at Punta Arenas

Lloyd's Agent: Gibbs & Cia SAC, Marchant Pereira 367, 5th Floor, Santiago 664 0622, Chile, *Tel:* +56 2 269 6364, *Fax:* +56 2 269 6395, *Email:* secretaria@gibbs.cl, *Website:* www.gibbs.cl

GUARELLO

Lat 50° 21' S; Long 75° 20' W.

Admiralty Chart: 4258	**Admiralty Pilot:** 6
Time Zone: GMT -4 h	**UNCTAD Locode:** CL GUR

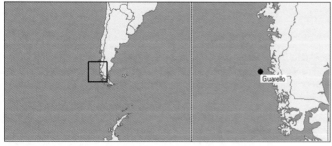

Principal Facilities:

		Y							

Authority: Guarello Port Authority, Port Office, Guarello, Chile

Approach: Entry is by either the Trinidad Channel or Concepcion Channel and also by the Messier Strait into the West Channel and Contreras Fjord

Anchorage: Anchorage can be obtained off the port in the centre of Corbeta Papudo Bay in a depth of 18.3 m

Pilotage: Compulsory. The pilot will remain on board vessel during loading operations

Weather: A wind from the NW can make berthing difficult

Principal Imports and Exports: Exports: Limestone.

Accommodation:

Name	Remarks
Guarello	See [1] below

[1]*Guarello:* Facilities for the loading of limestone operated by Cia de Acero del Pacifico S.A. Platform and dolphin berth equipped with a rotating crane and loading arm. Vessels up to 200 m loa can be accommodated. The loader operates at a rate of 800 t/h and vessels must shift along the berth so as to present all hatches under the arm

Lloyd's Agent: Gibbs & Cia SAC, Marchant Pereira 367, 5th Floor, Santiago 664 0622, Chile, *Tel:* +56 2 269 6364, *Fax:* +56 2 269 6395, *Email:* secretaria@gibbs.cl, *Website:* www.gibbs.cl

GUAYACAN

Lat 29° 58' S; Long 71° 22' W.

Admiralty Chart: 3080	**Admiralty Pilot:** 7
Time Zone: GMT -4 h	**UNCTAD Locode:** CL GYC

Principal Facilities:

		Y					T	A

Authority: Compania Minera del Pacifico S.A., Pedro Pablo Munoz 675, La Serena, Chile, *Tel:* +56 51 208000, *Fax:* +56 51 208140, *Email:* cmpsa@cmp.cl, *Website:* www.cmp.cl

Officials: Commercial Manager: German Gajardo.

Documentation: Clearance from last port (original), cargo manifest (5 copies), crew list (3 copies), personal effects list (3 copies), stores list (3 copies), port of call (3 copies), P&I entry certificate (2 copies), health declaration (3 copies), ship's particulars (3 copies), negative list (3 copies), arrival conditions (original)

Approach: Depth at entrance varies between 42 and 66 m. The entrance is 731.4 m wide which broadens inside to 1.6 km and extends 2 km in SE direction. Approach to Herradura Bay is a fishing zone and caution must be maintained during navigation

Anchorage: A in pos 29° 56' 27" S; 71° 19' 26" W
B in pos 29° 56' 22" S; 71° 19' 26" W
C in pos 29° 56' 18" S; 71° 19' 07" W
D in pos 29° 56' 40" S; 71° 19' 07" W
E in pos 29° 57' 16" S; 71° 18' 55" W
reference S.H.O.A. No.4120. Forbidden zone marked on charts

Pilotage: Compulsory. Vessels must pick up pilots in Coquimbo Bay (two pilots are compulsory for vessels over 220 m loa and one pilot for unberthing)

Radio Frequency: VHF Channel 16, HF 2182

Weather: Well protected bay, moderate swell in winter, predominant SW wind

Tides: Range of tide 1.5 m

Traffic: 2006, 2 319 122 t of cargo handled

Principal Imports and Exports: Exports: Fine ores, Iron ore, Lump ore, Pellet feed.

Working Hours: 24 h/day including Sundays and holidays

Accommodation:

Name	Length (m)	Draught (m)	Remarks
Guayacan			
Ore Pier	268	16.2	See [1] below

[1]*Ore Pier:* Loading system by conveyor belt with loading rate of 3000 t/h. Moveable loading tower of 118.9 m on pier. Loading boom extends 24 m from the face of the pier and can be retracted 10 m. Open storage areas available. Max air draft of 19 m

Storage: Open storage for 1 100 000 t

Towage: One tug of 3500 hp

Repair & Maintenance: Astilleros Servel Ltda, Regimiento Coquimbo 230, Coquimbo, Chile, *Tel:* +56 51 329543, *Fax:* +56 51 315751

Medical Facilities: San Pablo Hospital, 2 km

Airport: La Florida Airport, 18 km

Railway: Private railway from Romeral mine

Lloyd's Agent: Gibbs & Cia SAC, Marchant Pereira 367, 5th Floor, Santiago 664 0622, Chile, *Tel:* +56 2 269 6364, *Fax:* +56 2 269 6395, *Email:* secretaria@gibbs.cl, *Website:* www.gibbs.cl

HUASCO

Lat 28° 27' S; Long 71° 14' W.

Admiralty Chart: 3079	**Admiralty Pilot:** 7
Time Zone: GMT -4 h	**UNCTAD Locode:** CL HSO

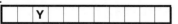

Principal Facilities:

	Y			B	T	A

Authority: Compania Minera del Pacifico S.A./Empresa Electrica Guacolda S.A., Brasil Street No.1050, Vallenar, Chile, *Tel:* +56 51 208950, *Fax:* +56 51 208902, *Email:* cphuasco@directemar.cl

Port Security: ISPS compliant

Documentation: Clearance from last port (original), cargo manifest (5 copies), crew list (3 copies), personal effects list (3 copies), stores list (3 copies), port of call (3 copies), P&I entry certificate (2 copies), health declaration (3 copies), ship's particulars (3 copies), negative list (3 copies), arrival conditions (original)

Approach: Situated between Point Negra and Guacolda Peninsula-exposed to the North and includes the Port of Huasco and Maritime Terminals, Guacolda

Anchorage: Vessels can anchor in a depth of 58.6 m in the centre of the bay; anchorage of 18.3 m, 500 m N of Cayo Blanco Island

Pilotage: Compulsory. Pilot station - 045° Guacolda lighthouse, 1600 m (two pilots are compulsory for vessels over 220 m loa and one pilot for unberthing)

Radio Frequency: VHF Channel 16, HF 2182

Weather: Well protected bay except for N/NW winds, strong winds SW frequently occur during the afternoon but do not disturb loading activities

Tides: Range of tide 1.68 m

Traffic: 2006, 6 907 870 t of cargo handled

Principal Imports and Exports: Imports: Coal. Exports: Iron ore pellets.

Working Hours: 24 h/day including Sundays and holidays

Accommodation:

Name	Length (m)	Draught (m)	Remarks
Huasco			
Guacolda I (Empresa Electrica Guacolda S.A.)	240	13.5	See [1] below
Guacolda II (Cia. Minera del Pacifico S.A.)	315	22	See [2] below

[1]*Guacolda I (Empresa Electrica Guacolda S.A.):* This quay is used for discharge of bulk coal by two cranes of 770 t/h each with three reception hoppers on the pier. The cargo can be carried from the berth using conveyor belt to storage areas 2000 m away

[2]*Guacolda II (Cia. Minera del Pacifico S.A.):* This terminal is used for loading iron ore in bulk, using a conveyor belt with a rate of 3500 t/h

Bunkering: Ian Taylor y Compania S.A., Serrano 286, Huasco, Chile, *Tel:* +56 51 531629, *Fax:* +56 51 531629, *Email:* taycocld@entelchile.net, *Website:* www.iantaylorgroup.com
Compania de Petroleos de Chile Copec S.A. (COPEC), Avenida Jorge Montt 2300, P O Box 2532-691, Vina del Mar, Chile, *Tel:* +56 32 2324 326, *Fax:* +56 32 2699 651, *Email:* bunkers@copec.cl, *Website:* www.copec.cl

Towage: One tug of 3500 hp
Ian Taylor y Compania S.A., Serrano 286, Huasco, Chile, *Tel:* +56 51 531629, *Fax:* +56 51 531629, *Email:* taycocld@entelchile.net, *Website:* www.iantaylorgroup.com

Repair & Maintenance: Small repairs possible

Shipping Agents: Agencias Maritimas del Norte S.A., Craig 246, P O Box 78, Huasco, Chile, *Tel:* +56 51 531156, *Fax:* +56 51 531013, *Email:* jorpol.huasco@jorpol.cl, *Website:* www.jorpol.cl
Ian Taylor y Compania S.A., Serrano 286, Huasco, Chile, *Tel:* +56 51 531629, *Fax:* +56 51 531629, *Email:* taycocld@entelchile.net, *Website:* www.iantaylorgroup.com
Ultramar Agencia Maritima Ltda, P O Box 73, Huasco, Chile, *Tel:* +56 51 531366, *Fax:* +56 51 531286, *Email:* huasco@ultramar.cl, *Website:* www.ultramar.cl

Stevedoring Companies: Agencias Maritimas del Norte S.A., Craig 246, P O Box 78, Huasco, Chile, *Tel:* +56 51 531156, *Fax:* +56 51 531013, *Email:* jorpol.huasco@jorpol.cl, *Website:* www.jorpol.cl
Ian Taylor y Compania S.A., Serrano 286, Huasco, Chile, *Tel:* +56 51 531629, *Fax:* +56 51 531629, *Email:* taycocld@entelchile.net, *Website:* www.iantaylorgroup.com
Ultramar Agencia Maritima Ltda, P O Box 73, Huasco, Chile, *Tel:* +56 51 531366, *Fax:* +56 51 531286, *Email:* huasco@ultramar.cl, *Website:* www.ultramar.cl

Medical Facilities: Small modern hospital

Airport: Vallenar, 50 km

Railway: Private railway from Los Colorados mine

Lloyd's Agent: Gibbs & Cia SAC, Marchant Pereira 367, 5th Floor, Santiago 664 0622, Chile, *Tel:* +56 2 269 6364, *Fax:* +56 2 269 6395, *Email:* secretaria@gibbs.cl, *Website:* www.gibbs.cl

INTERACID TERMINAL

harbour area, see under Mejillones

IQUIQUE

Lat 20° 12' S; Long 70° 9' W.

Admiralty Chart: 3076	**Admiralty Pilot:** 7
Time Zone: GMT -4 h	**UNCTAD Locode:** CL IQQ

Principal Facilities:

P	Q	Y	G	C		B		T	A

Authority: Empresa Portuaria Iquique, Avenida Jorge Barrera 62, Iquique, Chile, *Tel:* +56 57 400100, *Fax:* +56 57 413176, *Email:* epi@epi.cl, *Website:* www.epi.cl

Officials: General Manager: Alfredo Leiton Arbea, *Email:* alfredo.leiton@epi.cl.

Port Security: ISPS compliant

Pre-Arrival Information: Estimated time of arrival should be notified 72, 48, 24, and 6 hours in advance

Approach: Depth in bay 36.6 m

Anchorage: Good anchorage can be obtained in depths ranging from 15-25 m

Pilotage: Compulsory

Radio Frequency: VHF Channel 62

Tides: Range of tide 0.8 m LHW, 1.5 m HHW

Traffic: 2007, 665 vessels, 2 593 993 t of cargo handled, 263 451 TEU's

Principal Imports and Exports: Imports: Chemicals, General cargo, Machinery, Shredded steel, Soya oil, Sulphur, Vehicles, Wheat. Exports: Cathodes, Copper bars, Fishmeal, Fishoil.

Working Hours: 0800-1530, 1530-2300, 2300-0630

Accommodation:

Name	Length (m)	Depth (m)	Remarks
Molo di Abrigo			
Dock No.1	184	9.3	
Dock No.2	214	9.2	
Fishing Dock	130	8	
Espigon			See [1] below
Dock No.3	335		
Dock No.4	280		

[1]*Espigon:* Operated by Iquique Terminal Internacional S.A. (ITI), San Martin 255, Oficina 151, Oficina Edificio Empressarial, Iquique, Tel: +56 57 396000, Email: terminal@iti.cl, Website: www.iti.cl

Storage: Two warehouses providing a total of 9680 m3, open storage of 64 315 m3 owned by Port Authority. Privately owned refrigerated cap of 1500 t only by special request

Mechanical Handling Equipment:

Location	Type	Qty
Dock No.1	Mobile Cranes	1
Espigon	Mobile Cranes	2

Bunkering: Ian Taylor y Compania S.A., Bolivar 471, Iquique, Chile, *Tel:* +56 57 421126, *Fax:* +56 57 420369, *Email:* iquique@iantaylorgroup.com, *Website:* www.iantaylorgroup.com
Compania de Petroleos de Chile Copec S.A. (COPEC), Avenida Jorge Montt 2300, P O Box 2532-691, Vina del Mar, Chile, *Tel:* +56 32 2324 326, *Fax:* +56 32 2699 651, *Email:* bunkers@copec.cl, *Website:* www.copec.cl

Towage: Six tugs available
Sagemar Ltda, Tarapaca No.123, Iquique, Chile, *Tel:* +56 57 390900, *Fax:* +56 57 427635, *Email:* gonzalo@matamala@sagemar.cl
Sudamericana Agencias Aereas y Maritimas S.A. (SAAM), Patricio Lynch 145, Iquique, Chile, *Tel:* +56 57 407700, *Fax:* +56 57 429035, *Email:* iquique@saamsa.com, *Website:* www.saam.cl
Ian Taylor y Compania S.A., Bolivar 471, Iquique, Chile, *Tel:* +56 57 421126, *Fax:* +56 57 420369, *Email:* iquique@iantaylorgroup.com, *Website:* www.iantaylorgroup.com

Repair & Maintenance: Astilleros Marco Chilena Ltda, Recinto Portuario s/n, Iquique, Chile, *Tel:* +56 57 532501, *Fax:* +56 57 532507, *Website:* www.marcochilena.cl One slipway for vessels up to 300 t

Ship Chandlers: Iquique Ship Services, Avenida Gomez Carrentildeo 2420, Iquique, Chile, *Tel:* +56 57 318865, *Fax:* +56 57 318865, *Email:* info@isserv.cl

Shipping Agents: Agencias Maritimas Agental Ltda, Sotomayor 625, Oficina 1101, Iquique, Chile, *Tel:* +56 57 510867, *Fax:* +56 57 510866, *Email:* agentiqq@agental.cl, *Website:* www.agental.cl
Agencias Maritimas Broom y Cia. Ltda, Manzana V. Terrazas 2 y 2A, Barrio Industrial, Zona Franca, Iquique, Chile, *Tel:* +56 57 412616, *Fax:* +56 57 411254, *Email:* manageriqq@ajbroom.cl, *Website:* www.ajbroom.cl
Agencias Universales S.A. (AGUNSA), Ramirez 411, P O Box 297, Iquique, Chile, *Tel:* +56 57 428266, *Fax:* +56 57 428230, *Email:* agunsaiqq@agunsa.cl, *Website:* www.agunsa.com
Maritima Valparaiso Chile S.A., Edificio Empressarial, San Martin No.255, Oficina

Key to Principal Facilities:—

A=Airport	**C**=Containers	**G**=General Cargo
B=Bunkers	**D**=Dry Dock	**L**=Cruise

P=Petroleum	**R**=Ro/Ro	**Y**=Dry Bulk
Q=Other Liquid Bulk	**T**=Towage (where available from port)

131, 13th Floor, Iquique, Chile, *Tel:* +56 57 423981, *Fax:* +56 57 470263, *Email:* manuelespinoza@iqq.marval.cl, *Website:* www.marval.cl

Mediterranean Shipping Company, MSC Iquique, 151-A Jose de San Martin Street, Iquique, Chile, *Tel:* +56 57 524300, *Fax:* +56 57 427770, *Website:* www.mscchile.com

A.P. Moller-Maersk Group, Maersk Chile S.A., Serrano 389, Oficina 605, Iquique, Chile, *Tel:* +56 57 425475, *Fax:* +56 57 411471, *Email:* chlsaliqq@maersk.com, *Website:* www.maerskline.com

Sudamericana Agencias Aereas y Maritimas S.A. (SAAM), Patricio Lynch 145, Iquique, Chile, *Tel:* +56 57 407700, *Fax:* +56 57 429035, *Email:* iquique@saamsa.com, *Website:* www.saam.cl

Ian Taylor y Compania S.A., Bolivar 471, Iquique, Chile, *Tel:* +56 57 421126, *Fax:* +56 57 420369, *Email:* iquique@iantaylorgroup.com, *Website:* www.iantaylorgroup.com

Ultramar Agencia Maritima Ltda, San Martin 151, P O Box 2, Iquique, Chile, *Tel:* +56 57 414380, *Fax:* +56 57 423652, *Email:* iquique@ultramar.cl, *Website:* www.ultramar.cl

Stevedoring Companies: Ian Taylor y Compania S.A., Bolivar 471, Iquique, Chile, *Tel:* +56 57 421126, *Fax:* +56 57 420369, *Email:* iquique@iantaylorgroup.com, *Website:* www.iantaylorgroup.com

Medical Facilities: General hospital, three private clinics and private doctors also available

Airport: Diego Aracena, 40 km

Railway: Empresa de Ferrocarriles del Estado, approx 3 km

Lloyd's Agent: Gibbs & Cia SAC, Marchant Pereira 367, 5th Floor, Santiago 664 0622, Chile, *Tel:* +56 2 269 6364, *Fax:* +56 2 269 6395, *Email:* secretaria@gibbs.cl, *Website:* www.gibbs.cl

LAS MULATAS

harbour area, see under Corral

LAS SALINAS

see under Valparaiso

LENADURA

harbour area, see under Punta Arenas

LIRQUEN

Lat 36° 42' S; Long 72° 59' W.

Admiralty Chart: 4248   **Admiralty Pilot:** 7
Time Zone: GMT -4 h   **UNCTAD Locode:** CL LQN

Principal Facilities:

	Y	G	C		B		T	A	

Authority: Puerto de Lirquen S.A., Recinto Muelle s/n, Lirquen, Chile, *Tel:* +56 41 240 6000, *Fax:* +56 41 238 4657, *Email:* lirquen@puerto.cl, *Website:* www.puerto.cl

Officials: General Manager: Juan Manuel Gutierrez Philippi, *Email:* juan.gutierrez@puerto.cl.
Operations Manager: Jorge Baksai Marquez, *Email:* jorge.baksai@puerto.cl.
Harbour Master: Oscar Ortiz, *Tel:* +56 41 238 4550.

Port Security: ISPS compliant

Pre-Arrival Information: ETA to be sent 24 h in advance to pilot. 72 h, 48 h, 24 h and 12 h in advance concerning requirements

Documentation: Cargo manifest (5 copies), general declaration (5 copies), crew list (5 copies), personal effects (5 copies), stores list (5 copies)

Approach: Entry direct from open sea. Many trawlers operate in the area

Anchorage: Available in the following positions:
36° 41' 54" S; 73° 00' 28" W
36° 41' 54" S; 72° 59' 50" W
36° 42' 24" S; 73° 00' 28" W

Pilotage: Compulsory for all foreign vessels. Available from Talcahuano; request from Agency

Radio Frequency: VHF Channel 16

Weather: Winds in summer SSW, in winter NNE

Traffic: 2007, 5 530 202 t of cargo handled, 203 578 TEU's

Maximum Vessel Dimensions: 60 000 dwt

Principal Imports and Exports: Imports: Containers, Fertiliser, General cargo. Exports: Containers, Logs, Newsprint, Sawn timber, Woodpulp.

Working Hours: Three shifts 0800-1530, 1530-2300, 2300-0630. Special 0630-0800

Accommodation:

Name	Length (m)	Draught (m)	Remarks
Pier No.1			See [1] below
Berth No.1	220	12.8	
Berth No.2	210	11.37	
Berth No.3	200	9.6	
Berth No.4	160	7.39	
Pier No.2			
Berth No.5	200	15.49	
Berth No.6	200	12.11	

[1]*Pier No.1:* Conveyor belt system at rate of 7200 t/day cap for unloading of bulk products

Storage: Open storage: paved storage of 235 192 m2 and stabilized storage of 69 735 m2
Covered storage: warehouses and sheds totalling 136 714 m2

Mechanical Handling Equipment:

Location	Type	Capacity (t)	Qty
Lirquen	Mobile Cranes	100	3
Lirquen	Forklifts	4–16	67

Bunkering: Compania de Petroleos de Chile Copec S.A. (COPEC), Avenida Jorge Montt 2300, P O Box 2532-691, Vina del Mar, Chile, *Tel:* +56 32 2324 326, *Fax:* +56 32 2699 651, *Email:* bunkers@copec.cl, *Website:* www.copec.cl

Towage: Six tugs available from Talcahuano, each of 1340 hp

Medical Facilities: Hospital, 1 km from pier

Airport: Carriel Sur, 28 km

Railway: Access from the north and south

Development: Additional open storage areas (aprox 15 000 m2) and covered areas (aprox 8000 m2) will be carried out in 2007

Lloyd's Agent: Gibbs & Cia SAC, Marchant Pereira 367, 5th Floor, Santiago 664 0622, Chile, *Tel:* +56 2 269 6364, *Fax:* +56 2 269 6395, *Email:* secretaria@gibbs.cl, *Website:* www.gibbs.cl

MEJILLONES

Lat 23° 6' S; Long 70° 28' W.

Admiralty Chart: 3076   **Admiralty Pilot:** 7
Time Zone: GMT -4 h   **UNCTAD Locode:** CL MJS

Principal Facilities:

	Y			B		A

Authority: Compania Portuaria Mejillones S.A., Napoleon 3010 Of.71, Las Condes, Santiago, Chile, *Tel:* +56 2 334 2840, *Fax:* +56 2 334 2841, *Email:* portmej@netline.cl, *Website:* www.mejillones.com

Port Security: ISPS compliant

Pilotage: Compulsory for all vessels who should advise ETA to the Port Captain 24 h prior to arrival, Tel: +56 (55) 621513, Email: cpmejillones@directemar.cl
Pilot boards for Enaex Terminal and Mejillones Terminal in pos 23° 04.6' S; 70° 26.1' W
Pilot boards for Interacid Terminal and Puerto Angamos in pos 23° 03.5' S; 70° 24.0' W
Pilot boards for Michilla Terminal in pos 22° 43.0' S; 70° 19.0' W

Radio Frequency: VHF Channel 16

Tides: Range of tide 1.5 m

Accommodation:

Name	Remarks
Terminal 1 (Puerto Angamos)	See [1] below
Michilla Terminal	See [2] below
Interacid Terminal	See [3] below
Enaex Terminal	See [4] below

[1]*Terminal 1 (Puerto Angamos):* Longitudinal 5500, Mejillones, Tel: +56 55 357000, Fax: +56 55 357014, Website: www.puertoangamos.cl
Handling of metal copper, general cargo and containers. Three berths, two of which correspond to a "finger pier" dock with min depth of 14 m and the third berth is a quay with vertical face on a sheetpile basis with min depth of 12 m
[2]*Michilla Terminal:* Private terminal operated by Minera Michilla S.A., Tel: +56 55 637617, Website: www.michilla.cl
Import of sulphuric acid for vessels up to 180 m loa and 10 m draft. Sulphuric acid is discharged through a 6" floating pipeline through the ship's pumps to tanks ashore with a cap of 7000 t, at a max rate of 350 t/h

[3]*Interacid Terminal:* Private terminal operated by Interacid Chile Ltda., Parque Industrial 6500, Mejillones, Tel: +56 55 621792, Website: www.interacid.cl Vessels up to 30 000 dwt for storage and dispatch of sulphuric acid. Storage cap of 40 000 t (two 20 000 t tanks)

[4]*Enaex Terminal:* Private terminal operated by Enaex S.A., Renato Sanchez 3859, Las Condes, Santiago, Tel: +56 2 210 6600, Fax: +56 2 206 6752, Email: enaex@enaex.cl, Website: www.enaex.cl Explosives for vessels up to 185 m loa

Mechanical Handling Equipment:

Location	Type	Capacity (t)	Qty
Terminal 1 (Puerto Angamos)	Mobile Cranes	100	1

Bunkering: Compania de Petroleos de Chile Copec S.A. (COPEC), Avenida Jorge Montt 2300, P O Box 2532-691, Vina del Mar, Chile, *Tel:* +56 32 2324 326, *Fax:* +56 32 2699 651, *Email:* bunkers@copec.cl, *Website:* www.copec.cl – *Grades:* MDO; IFO; in line blending available – *Misc:* own storage facilities – *Rates:* 40-100t/h – *Notice:* 48 hours – *Delivery Mode:* truck

Shipping Agents: Sudamericana Agencias Aereas y Maritimas S.A. (SAAM), Antonio Varas 129, Mejillones, Chile, *Tel:* +56 55 622902, *Fax:* +56 55 622916, *Email:* mejillones@saamsa.cl, *Website:* www.saam cl
Ultramar Agencia Maritima Ltda, Camino a Chacaya s/n, Mejillones, Chile, *Tel:* +56 55 621140, *Fax:* +56 55 621966, *Website:* www.ultramar.cl

Airport: Cerro Moreno, 37 km

Lloyd's Agent: Gibbs & Cia SAC, Marchant Pereira 367, 5th Floor, Santiago 664 0622, Chile, *Tel:* +56 2 269 6364, *Fax:* +56 2 269 6395, *Email:* secretaria@gibbs.cl, *Website:* www.gibbs.cl

MICHILLA TERMINAL

harbour area, see under Mejillones

PENCO

harbour area, see under Talcahuano

POLICARPO TORO TERMINAL

harbour area, see under San Antonio

PUERTO ANGAMOS

harbour area, see under Mejillones

PUERTO MONTT

Lat 41° 28' S; Long 72° 57' W.

Admiralty Chart: 1313
Time Zone: GMT -4 h
Admiralty Pilot: 7
UNCTAD Locode: CL PMC

Principal Facilities:

P		Y	G	C	R	L	B		T	A	

Authority: Empresa Portuaria Puerto Montt, Avenida Angelmo 1673, Puerto Montt, Chile, *Tel:* +56 65 253263, *Fax:* +56 65 252247, *Email:* info@empormontt.cl, *Website:* www.empormontt.cl

Officials: General Manager: Patricio Campana Cuello, *Email:* pcampana@empormontt.cl.
Operations Manager: Alfredo Bustos Iturrieta, *Tel:* +56 65 257643, *Email:* abustos@empormontt.cl.

Port Security: ISPS compliant

Approach: Bay divided into two parts, W side formed by Tenglo Channel and Caleta Angelmo (commercial port), and the outer port (Puerto Montt Bay) with mouth 4.68 km wide. The outer port is surrounded by a bank of sand which extends 45 to 140 m outside the coast. This harbour, depth over 20 m to 50 m in centre, is suitable for any kind of vessel. In very bad weather refuge found inside Tenglo Channel at Caleta Angelmo, a well protected place, depth 7 to 8 m, site chosen for new commercial port of Puerto Montt

Anchorage: Anchorage in Puerto Montt Bay in pos 41° 26' 8" S; 72° 56' 8" W

Pilotage: Compulsory. To anchor in bay, moor to quays or anchor inside channel, pilot to be awaited one mile out of bay. VHF Channel 16 in Port Captain's office

Weather: Predominant winds N-S

Traffic: 2005, 1 055 105 t of cargo handled

Maximum Vessel Dimensions: 230 m loa

Working Hours: 0800-1600, 1600-2400, 2400-0800

Accommodation:

Name	Length (m)	Depth (m)	Remarks
Puerto Montt			See [1] below
Berth No.1	240	9.3	
Berth No.2	145	7.5	

[1]*Puerto Montt:* Tanker facilities: Four buoys available: (a) max length 180 m, 12.2 m depth; (b) max length 60 m, 3.66 m depth

Storage: 80 000 m2 of port yard for lumber or container storage

Location	Covered (m²)
Puerto Montt	15000

Mechanical Handling Equipment:

Location	Type	Capacity (t)	Qty
Puerto Montt	Electric Cranes	3	3
Puerto Montt	Electric Cranes	5	2

Cargo Worked: 7000 t fertiliser in bulk

Bunkering: Ian Taylor y Compania S.A., Agencia Maritimas Unidas S.A., Avenida Angalmo 2147, Puerto Montt, Chile, *Tel:* +56 65 270712, *Fax:* +56 65 254224, *Email:* agemar@agemar.cl, *Website:* www.agemar.cl
Compania de Petroleos de Chile Copec S.A. (COPEC), Avenida Jorge Montt 2300, P O Box 2532-691, Vina del Mar, Chile, *Tel:* +56 32 2324 326, *Fax:* +56 32 2699 651, *Email:* bunkers@copec.cl, *Website:* www.copec.cl – *Grades:* MDO; IFO; in line blending available – *Misc:* own storage facilities – *Rates:* 40-100t/h – *Notice:* 48 hours – *Delivery Mode:* truck
ExxonMobil Marine Fuels, Suite 900, One Alhambra Plaza, Coral Gables, FL 33134, United States of America, *Tel:* +1 305 459 6358, *Fax:* +1 305 459 6412, *Email:* emmf@exxonmobil.com, *Website:* www.exxonmobilmarinefuels.com – *Grades:* MGO – *Delivery Mode:* truck
Ian Taylor y Compania S.A., Agencia Maritimas Unidas S.A., Avenida Angalmo 2147, Puerto Montt, Chile, *Tel:* +56 65 270712, *Fax:* +56 65 254224, *Email:* agemar@agemar.cl, *Website:* www.agemar.cl

Towage: One 4200 hp and one 2650 hp tug. Two motor boats for mooring
Ian Taylor y Compania S.A., Agencia Maritimas Unidas S.A., Avenida Angalmo 2147, Puerto Montt, Chile, *Tel:* +56 65 270712, *Fax:* +56 65 254224, *Email:* agemar@agemar.cl, *Website:* www.agemar.cl

Repair & Maintenance: Astilleros Jaras S.A., Puerto Montt, Chile, *Tel:* +56 65 258580, *Fax:* +56 65 258081
Maestranza Naviera Tenglo Ltda, Casilla 15, Arturo Prat, Canal Beagle, Caldera, Chile, *Tel:* +56 52 315200, *Fax:* +56 52 315414, *Email:* astilleros@mnavales.cl, *Website:* www.maestranzasnavales.cl

Ship Chandlers: Gandara Chile S.A., Angelmo 1750, Puerto Montt, Chile, *Tel:* +56 65 255019, *Fax:* +56 65 257186, *Email:* pmontt@gandarachile.cl, *Website:* www.gandarachile.cl

Shipping Agents: Agencias Maritimas Broom y Cia. Ltda, Angelmo 1676, Puerto Montt, Chile, *Tel:* +56 65 250990, *Fax:* +56 65 266188, *Email:* broompmc@ajbroom.cl, *Website:* www.ajbroom.cl
Agencias Universales S.A. (AGUNSA), Camino El Tepual Km 1.3 Ruta 226, Puerto Montt, Chile, *Tel:* +56 65 254262, *Fax:* +56 65 254262, *Email:* agunsaptm@agunsa.cl, *Website:* www.agunsa.com
A.P. Moller-Maersk Group, Maersk Chile S.A., Concepcion 120, Oficina 502, Edificio Dona Encarnacion, Puerto Montt, Chile, *Tel:* +56 65 310128, *Fax:* +56 65 340806, *Email:* chlsalpmc@maersk.com, *Website:* www.maerskline.com
Sudamericana Agencias Aereas y Maritimas S.A. (SAAM), Ruta 5 Camino a Pargua s/n, Puerto Montt, Chile, *Tel:* +56 65 324500, *Fax:* +56 65 311445, *Email:* pmontt@saamsa.com, *Website:* www.saam.cl
Ian Taylor y Compania S.A., Agencia Maritimas Unidas S.A., Avenida Angalmo 2147, Puerto Montt, Chile, *Tel:* +56 65 270712, *Fax:* +56 65 254224, *Email:* agemar@agemar.cl, *Website:* www.agemar.cl
Ultramar Agencia Maritima Ltda, Av. Diego Portales 870 - Piso 2, Puerto Montt, Chile, *Tel:* +56 65 341040, *Fax:* +56 65 341042, *Email:* ptomontt@ultramar.cl, *Website:* www.ultramar.cl

Stevedoring Companies: Servicios Portuarios Reloncavi, Puerto Montt, Chile, *Tel:* +56 65 325100, *Email:* supervisorpmc@reloncavi.cl, *Website:* www.reloncavi.cl
Ian Taylor y Compania S.A., Agencia Maritimas Unidas S.A., Avenida Angalmo 2147, Puerto Montt, Chile, *Tel:* +56 65 270712, *Fax:* +56 65 254224, *Email:* agemar@agemar.cl, *Website:* www.agemar.cl
Ultraport, Puerto Montt, Chile, *Tel:* +56 65 341040, *Fax:* +56 65 341042

Medical Facilities: Hospital and clinic available

Airport: El Tepual, 15 km

Lloyd's Agent: Gibbs & Cia SAC, Marchant Pereira 367, 5th Floor, Santiago 664 0622, Chile, *Tel:* +56 2 269 6364, *Fax:* +56 2 269 6395, *Email:* secretaria@gibbs.cl, *Website:* www.gibbs.cl

PUERTO NATALES

Lat 51° 43' S; Long 72° 31' W.

Admiralty Chart: -
Time Zone: GMT -4 h
Admiralty Pilot: 6
UNCTAD Locode: CL PNT

Key to Principal Facilities:—				
A=Airport	**C**=Containers	**G**=General Cargo	**P**=Petroleum	**R**=Ro/Ro	**Y**=Dry Bulk
B=Bunkers	**D**=Dry Dock	**L**=Cruise	**Q**=Other Liquid Bulk	**T**=Towage (where available from port)	

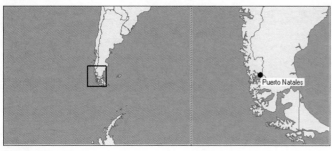

Principal Facilities:

		G	R				A

Authority: Port Captain, Puerto Natales, Chile, *Tel:* +56 61 411570, *Fax:* +56 61 411409

Approach: Through the various fjords and passes of the Patagonian Channels

Anchorage: Anchorage can be obtained in mid channel, NW of the port in a depth of 30 m

Pilotage: Compulsory. Pilots can be requested through the Port Captains at Punta Arenas or Valparaiso

Accommodation:

Name	Depth (m)	Remarks
Puerto Natales		
Muelle Arturo Prat	5.2	See [1] below
Muelle Terminal Maritimo	9	See [2] below

[1]*Muelle Arturo Prat:* Extending 108 m from the shore with a berthing face 31 m long. No cranes on the pier, vessels use ships own gear. General cargo is handled
[2]*Muelle Terminal Maritimo:* Located 100 m SE of the general cargo pier, the longer side having a length of 115 m and the shorter side 32 m. There are three berthing dolphins off the pier; vessels up to 8.8 m draft can be accommodated

Medical Facilities: Hospital in the town

Airport: Local airport with connecting flights to Punta Arenas

Lloyd's Agent: Gibbs & Cia SAC, Marchant Pereira 367, 5th Floor, Santiago 664 0622, Chile, *Tel:* +56 2 269 6364, *Fax:* +56 2 269 6395, *Email:* secretaria@gibbs.cl, *Website:* www.gibbs.cl

PUERTO PERCY

Lat 52° 55' S; Long 70° 17' W.

Admiralty Chart: 1694	**Admiralty Pilot:** 6
Time Zone: GMT -4 h	**UNCTAD Locode:** CL PPY

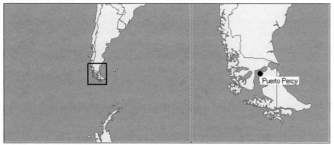

Principal Facilities:

	Q				B		

Authority: Empresa Portuaria Austral, B. O'Higgins 1385, Punta Arenas, Chile, *Tel:* +56 61 711210, *Fax:* +56 61 711233, *Email:* portspuq@epa.co.cl, *Website:* www.epa.co.cl

Officials: General Manager: Eduardo Manzanares Castesc, *Email:* emanzanares@epa.co.cl.
Assistant General Manager: Rosita Sanchez, *Email:* rsanchez@epa.co.cl.

Pilotage: Compulsory. Arranged from Punta Arenas. Berthing during daylight hours only

Weather: Persistent strong winds prevail at the terminal; most common from the SW and NW during spring and summer

Tides: Range of tide 1.5 m ST, 0.45 m NT

Accommodation:

Name	Remarks
Puerto Percy	See [1] below

[1]*Puerto Percy:* Liquefied Gas Terminal: Berth for loading LPG comprising four mooring buoys in a depth of 11 m with submarine pipelines connecting to the shore facilities. Vessels of up to max loa 130 m and max draft of 9.14 m can be accommodated. Gas is loaded at the rate of 250 t/h through a 10'' line. Vessels should be ready to disconnect hoses in good time if the weather deteriorates
There is a pier located to the SSW of the mooring buoys used by small LPG carriers
The port is normally only used for coastwise shipments

Bunkering: Fuel oil can be supplied from a tank barge at a rate of 700 t/h

Lloyd's Agent: Gibbs & Cia SAC, Marchant Pereira 367, 5th Floor, Santiago 664 0622, Chile, *Tel:* +56 2 269 6364, *Fax:* +56 2 269 6395, *Email:* secretaria@gibbs.cl, *Website:* www.gibbs.cl

PUERTO VENTANAS

Lat 32° 45' S; Long 71° 30' W.

Admiralty Chart: 1314	**Admiralty Pilot:** 7
Time Zone: GMT -4 h	**UNCTAD Locode:** CL VNT

Principal Facilities:

P		Y	G	C	R		B		A

Authority: Puerto Ventanas S.A., Calle Malaga 120, Piso 5, Las Condes, Santiago, Chile, *Tel:* +56 2 228 4113, *Fax:* +56 2 228 4213, *Email:* pventanas@pvsa.cl, *Website:* www.puertoventanas.cl

Officials: General Manager: Gamaliel Villalobos Aranda, *Email:* gamaliel.villalobos@pvsa.cl.
Commercial Manager: Sergio Azocar Velez, *Email:* sergio.azocar@pvsa.cl.
Operations Manager: Alvaro Larenas Letelier, *Email:* alvaro.larenas@pvsa.cl.
Harbour Master: Rodrigo Pulgar, *Email:* rodrigo.pulgar@pvsa.cl.

Port Security: ISPS compliant

Anchorage: Available in Quintero Bay in pos 32° 45' 10" S, 71° 30' 00" W in depth of 20-38 m

Pilotage: Compulsory

Radio Frequency: VHF Channel 16, 156.00 mHz Quintero Radio

Tides: Range of tide 1.3 m

Traffic: 2006, 3 548 500 t of cargo handled

Maximum Vessel Dimensions: 240 m loa, 14.3 m draft

Principal Imports and Exports: Imports: Bauxite, Clinker, Coal, Corn, Wheat. Exports: Copper mineral concentrates, Gold concentrates, Onions, Tomatoes.

Working Hours: 24 h/day, 7 days/week

Accommodation:

Name	Length (m)	Draught (m)	Remarks
Puerto Ventanas			
Berth No.1	125	8.17	Liquid bulk for vessels up to 12 000 dwt
Berth No.2	200	9.52	Solid & liquid bulk for vessels up to 30 000 dwt
Berth No.3	200	11.5	Bulk & general cargo for vessels up to 45 000 dwt
Berth No.5	240	14.3	Bulk & general cargo for vessels up to 70 000 dwt

Storage: Open storage for bulk cargo of 3500 m2 and for general cargo of 3500 m2. Warehousing for bulk cargo of 45 000 t

Mechanical Handling Equipment:

Location	Type	Capacity (t)	Qty
Puerto Ventanas	Mult-purp. Cranes	30	2

Bunkering: Available either by pipeline via bunkering manifolds to vessels berthed at Puerto Ventanas or by two mini tankers with a 3100 t rated cap to vessels at adjacent ports such as Valparaiso, San Antonio, Quintero and Los Vicos, Tel: +56 32 796550, Fax: +56 32 796233, Email: hpizarro@gener.cl
Compania de Petroleos de Chile Copec S.A. (COPEC), Avenida Jorge Montt 2300, P O Box 2532-691, Vina del Mar, Chile, *Tel:* +56 32 2324 326, *Fax:* +56 32 2699 651, *Email:* bunkers@copec.cl, *Website:* www.copec.cl – *Grades:* MDO; IFO; in line blending available – *Misc:* own storage facilities – *Rates:* 40-100t/h – *Notice:* 48 hours – *Delivery Mode:* truck
ExxonMobil Marine Fuels, Suite 900, One Alhambra Plaza, Coral Gables, FL 33134, United States of America, *Tel:* +1 305 459 6358, *Fax:* +1 305 459 6412, *Email:* emmf@exxonmobil.com, *Website:* www.exxonmobilmarinefuels.com
Petroleos Marinos de Chile Ltda (PMC), P. O. Box 34, Puchuncavi, V Region, Santiago, Chile, *Tel:* +56 32 2796 550, *Fax:* +56 32 2796 233, *Email:* bunkers@pmchile.cl

Waste Reception Facilities: Garbage disposal by trucks. For liquid disposal and sludge, tanks reception delivered by trucks

Towage: Ultramar Agencia Maritima Ltda, Pasaje San Guillermo No.121, P O Box 109, Quintero, Chile, *Tel:* +56 32 293 0927, *Fax:* +56 32 293 0265, *Email:* quintero@ultramar.cl, *Website:* www.ultramar.cl

Medical Facilities: Hospitals available

Airport: Torquemada, 60 km

Railway: Ventanas, 1 km (cargo only)

Lloyd's Agent: Gibbs & Cia SAC, Marchant Pereira 367, 5th Floor, Santiago 664 0622, Chile, *Tel:* +56 2 269 6364, *Fax:* +56 2 269 6395, *Email:* secretaria@gibbs.cl, *Website:* www.gibbs.cl

PUERTO WILLIAMS

Lat 54° 56' S; Long 67° 37' W.

Admiralty Chart: 3425	**Admiralty Pilot:** 6
Time Zone: GMT -4 h	**UNCTAD Locode:** CL WPU

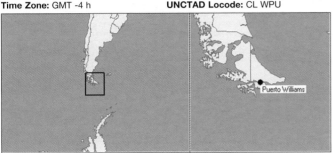

Principal Facilities:

P					B	T	A	

Authority: Gobernacion Maritime de Puerto Williams, Puerto Williams, Chile, *Tel:* +56 61 621090, *Fax:* +56 61 621090, *Email:* cpwilliams@directemar.cl

Officials: Harbour Master: Domingo Hormazabal Figueroa.

Port Security: ISPS compliant

Approach: Through Beagle Channel

Anchorage: Good anchorage 574 m off Punta Gusano in depth of 31 m

Pilotage: Compulsory. Pilots can be requested through Port Captains at Punta Arenas or Valparaiso

Radio Frequency: VHF Channel 16

Weather: Variable with westerly winds, port well protected and normally calm

Working Hours: 24 h/day

Accommodation:

Name	Remarks
Puerto Williams	See [1] below

[1]*Puerto Williams:* T-shaped mole extending 66 m from shore. T-head 8 m wide, berthing face 86 m long with depth alongside of 4.57 m

Mechanical Handling Equipment:

Location	Type	Capacity (t)	Qty
Puerto Williams	Mobile Cranes	6	1

Bunkering: Limited quantities available by pipeline

Towage: Towage can be requested from Punta Arenas

Shipping Agents: Ultramar Agencia Maritima Ltda, Arturo Prat 035, Puerto Williams, Chile, *Tel:* +56 61 621049, *Fax:* +56 61 621049, *Email:* pleslie@ultramar.cl, *Website:* www.ultramar.cl

Medical Facilities: Naval hospital nearby

Airport: Guardiamarina Zanartu Airport

Lloyd's Agent: Gibbs & Cia SAC, Marchant Pereira 367, 5th Floor, Santiago 664 0622, Chile, *Tel:* +56 2 269 6364, *Fax:* +56 2 269 6395, *Email:* secretaria@gibbs.cl, *Website:* www.gibbs.cl

PUNTA ARENAS

Lat 53° 10' S; Long 70° 54' W.

Admiralty Chart: 1694	**Admiralty Pilot:** 6
Time Zone: GMT -4 h	**UNCTAD Locode:** CL PUQ

Principal Facilities:

P	Q	Y	G	C	R	L	B		T	A

Authority: Empresa Portuaria Austral, B. O'Higgins 1385, Punta Arenas, Chile, *Tel:* +56 61 711210, *Fax:* +56 61 711233, *Email:* portspuq@epa.co.cl, *Website:* www.epa.co.cl

Officials: General Manager: Eduardo Manzanares Castesc, *Email:* emanzanares@epa.co.cl.
Assistant General Manager: Rosita Sanchez, *Email:* rsanchez@epa.co.cl.

Port Security: ISPS compliant

Anchorage: Good and extensive anchorage in Punta Arenas Bay in depths of 40-50 m and 22 to 27.4 m of water within 1.2 km of end of Fiscal Mole

Pilotage: Compulsory. Pilots available for vessels passing through the Strait of Magellan and/or Patagonian Channels. Vessels crossing the Strait from Pacific to Atlantic must embark pilots at Punta Arenas Roads; they disembark at Possesion Bay, east entrance Magellan Strait (lat 52° 17' 5" S; long 69° 14' W). For the transit from Atlantic to Pacific, same procedure vice versa. For vessels proceeding to the various oil and liquefied gas terminals in the vicinity of Punta Arenas, a Magellan Strait Pilot is required and also a port pilot at the respective berth. Masters of vessels intending to enter the Strait must request pilots 24 h prior to ETA

Radio Frequency: Transmissions on 156 800 mHz, 500, 2182, 4322 & 8694 kHz. Listening on 156 800 mHz, 500, 2182, 4181.6 & 8363.8 kHz

Weather: Weather variable, strong winds and choppy seas in summer; frequent gales, rain and snow in winter

Tides: Rise and fall of spring tides is about 1.83 m

Traffic: 2006, 475 103 t of cargo handled

Maximum Vessel Dimensions: 8.23 m max draft at head of mole, 9 m aft of mole. In extension of 160 m, max draught decreasing to 4.27 m

Principal Imports and Exports: Exports: Fish, General cargo, Meat, Mineral products, Wool.

Working Hours: 24 h/day

Accommodation:

Name	Length (m)	Draught (m)	Remarks
Punta Arenas			
Arturo Prat Terminal	542	8.23	
Jose de los Santos Mardones Terminal			See [1] below
Lenadura			See [2] below

[1]*Jose de los Santos Mardones Terminal:* L-shaped pier located 4.5 km N of Punta Arenas for general cargo. Exterior front of 150 m in depth of 16 m and interior of 126 m in depth of 12 m. Bunkers available by truck
[2]*Lenadura:* Petroleum products berth located 6.4 km S of Punta Arenas, comprising three mooring buoys. Vessels up to 175 m loa, 7 m draft can be accommodated. Berthing during daylight hours only

Storage:

Location	Open (m²)	Covered (m²)	Cold (m³)
Punta Arenas	7000	5572	500

Mechanical Handling Equipment:

Location	Type	Capacity (t)	Qty
Punta Arenas	Mult-purp. Cranes	2	1
Punta Arenas	Mobile Cranes	10	2
Punta Arenas	Forklifts	15	1

Bunkering: Agencias Universales S.A. (AGUNSA), Avenida Independencia 772, P O Box 60-D, Punta Arenas, Chile, *Tel:* +56 61 241065, *Fax:* +56 61 228239, *Email:* agunsapta@agunsa.cl, *Website:* www.agunsa.com
Ian Taylor y Compania S.A., 21 de Mayo 1668, Punta Arenas 1222, Chile, *Tel:* +56 61 242340, *Fax:* +56 61 228842, *Email:* mailboxpuq@taylor.cl, *Website:* www.iantaylorgroup.com
Compania Maritima de Punta Arenas S.A., Calle Independencia 830, P O Box 337, Punta Arenas, Chile, *Tel:* +56 61 241752, *Fax:* +56 61 247514 – *Grades:* MGO – *Rates:* truck 40t/h, pipeline/barge 100t/h – *Notice:* 24 hours – *Delivery Mode:* pipeline, barge, truck
Compania de Petroleos de Chile Copec S.A. (COPEC), Avenida Jorge Montt 2300, P O Box 2532-691, Vina del Mar, Chile, *Tel:* +56 32 2324 326, *Fax:* +56 32 2699 651, *Email:* bunkers@copec.cl, *Website:* www.copec.cl – *Grades:* MDO; IFO; in line blending available – *Misc:* own storage facilities – *Rates:* 40-100t/h – *Notice:* 48 hours – *Delivery Mode:* truck
ExxonMobil Marine Fuels, Suite 900, One Alhambra Plaza, Coral Gables, FL 33134, United States of America, *Tel:* +1 305 459 6358, *Fax:* +1 305 459 6412, *Email:* emmf@exxonmobil.com, *Website:* www.exxonmobilmarinefuels.com – *Grades:* MGO – *Notice:* 48 hours – *Delivery Mode:* truck
Ian Taylor y Compania S.A., 21 de Mayo 1668, Punta Arenas 1222, Chile, *Tel:* +56

Key to Principal Facilities:—

A=Airport	**C**=Containers	**G**=General Cargo
B=Bunkers	**D**=Dry Dock	**L**=Cruise

P=Petroleum	**R**=Ro/Ro	**Y**=Dry Bulk
Q=Other Liquid Bulk	**T**=Towage (where available from port)

61 242340, *Fax:* +56 61 228842, *Email:* mailboxpuq@taylor.cl, *Website:* www.iantaylorgroup.com

Towage: Remolcadores Ultragas Ltda, Avenida El Bosque Norte 500, 20th Floor, Las Condes, Santiago 755-0092, Chile, *Tel:* +56 2 630 1190, *Fax:* +56 2 334 3043, *Email:* operations@ultratug.com, *Website:* www.ultratug.com

Repair & Maintenance: Asmar Shipbuilding & Ship Repair Company, Avenida Bulnes 05275, P O Box 110-D, Punta Arenas, Chile, *Tel:* +56 61 214151, *Fax:* +56 61 211143, *Email:* asmarmag@asmar.cl, *Website:* www.asmar.cl General Manager: Gabriel Barros Email: gbarros@asmar.cl Marine railway with lifting cap of 4000 t, 6 m draft. Two ships simultaneously, max loa 130 m, max beam 24 m

Ship Chandlers: Galicia Ship Suppliers, El Ovejero 298, Punta Arenas, Chile, *Tel:* +56 61 200105, *Fax:* +56 61 200104, *Email:* galiciaship@hotmail.com & galiciaship@123.cl

Gandara Chile S.A., Maipu 501, Punta Arenas, Chile, *Tel:* +56 61 221323, *Email:* parenas@gandarachile.cl, *Website:* www.gandarachile.cl

Shipping Agents: Agencias Maritimas Broom y Cia. Ltda, Roca 924, Punta Arenas, Chile, *Tel:* +56 61 203400, *Fax:* +56 61 203420, *Email:* managerpuq@ajbroom.cl, *Website:* www.ajbroom.cl

Agencias Universales S.A. (AGUNSA), Avenida Independencia 772, P O Box 60-D, Punta Arenas, Chile, *Tel:* +56 61 241065, *Fax:* +56 61 228239, *Email:* agunsapta@agunsa.cl, *Website:* www.agunsa.com

Inchcape Shipping Services (ISS), Magallanes 974, Punta Arenas, Chile, *Tel:* +56 61 244592, *Fax:* +56 61 247514, *Email:* isspuntarenas@iss-shipping.com, *Website:* www.iss-shipping.com

Sudamericana Agencias Aereas y Maritimas S.A. (SAAM), Independencia 736, Punta Arenas, Chile, *Tel:* +56 61 294600, *Fax:* +56 61 226061, *Email:* servicioalcliente@saamsa.com

Ian Taylor y Compania S.A., 21 de Mayo 1668, Punta Arenas 1222, Chile, *Tel:* +56 61 242340, *Fax:* +56 61 228842, *Email:* mailboxpuq@taylor.cl, *Website:* www.iantaylorgroup.com

Ultramar Agencia Maritima Ltda, P O Box 44-d, Independencia 865, Punta Arenas, Chile, *Tel:* +56 61 204800, *Fax:* +56 61 226664, *Email:* puntaarenas@ultramar.cl, *Website:* www.ultramar.cl

Stevedoring Companies: Ian Taylor y Compania S.A., 21 de Mayo 1668, Punta Arenas 1222, Chile, *Tel:* +56 61 242340, *Fax:* +56 61 228842, *Email:* mailboxpuq@taylor.cl, *Website:* www.iantaylorgroup.com

Surveyors: Det Norske Veritas A/S, Inave SMI Ltda, P O Box 568, Punta Arenas, Chile, *Tel:* +56 61 214032, *Fax:* +56 61 214032, *Email:* inave@ctcinternet.cl, *Website:* www.dnv.com

Medical Facilities: Supplied by ships agents

Airport: Presidente Carlos Ibanez del Campo, 25 km

Lloyd's Agent: Gibbs & Cia SAC, Marchant Pereira 367, 5th Floor, Santiago 664 0622, Chile, *Tel:* +56 2 269 6364, *Fax:* +56 2 269 6395, *Email:* secretaria@gibbs.cl, *Website:* www.gibbs.cl

QUINTERO

Lat 32° 46' S; Long 71° 30' W.

Admiralty Chart: 1314	Admiralty Pilot: 7
Time Zone: GMT -4 h	UNCTAD Locode: CL QTV

Principal Facilities:

P	Q	Y	G			B			

Authority: Gobernacion Maritima de Valparaiso, Armada de Chile Capitan de Puerto Quintero, Avenida 21 Mayo s/n, Quintero, Chile, *Tel:* +56 32 293 0057, *Fax:* +56 32 293 0057, *Email:* cpquintero@directemar.cl

Officials: Harbour Master: Javier Chappuzeau Guzman.

Port Security: ISPS compliant

Approach: Quintero Bay is entered between Point Ventanilla and Point Liles

Anchorage: Anchorage can be obtained in the bay clear of the prohibited areas in depths ranging from 14.6 m to 20 m

Pilotage: Compulsory, *Tel:* +56 32 293 0057, *Fax:* +56 32 293 1043, *Email:* praccpqtr@directemar.cl. ETA should be sent to agent 72 h before arrival, with confirmation 24 h before arrival. Pilots board in pos 32° 44.86' S; 71° 31.87' W.

Radio Frequency: VHF Channels 16,70 and 85

Traffic: 2006, 13 060 250 t of cargo handled

Working Hours: 24 h/day

Accommodation:

Name	Remarks
Quintero	See [1] below

[1]*Quintero:* Pier about 725 m long with depths alongside ranging from 9.8 m to 19 m. On the S side of the pier is a berth with four dolphins, providing frontage of 180 m, accommodating vessels up to 160 m loa and 9.1 m draft. Copper concentrates are handled by belt conveyor for loading at the rate of 1000 t/h. The berth is also used

for discharging bulk grain but vessels have to move along the berth to unload each hatch, owing to the fixed loading tower

A coal berth is situated on the N side of the pier and vessels of up to 135 m loa can be accommodated. It is equipped with a travelling discharging tower, fitted with a grab on an overhead rail and extending 13.5 m from the quayside. Discharge rate is 300 t/h into a hopper, onto a belt conveyor to the stockpiles

Tanker facilities: Oil terminal operated by Empresa Nacional de Petroleo (ENAP) at Plaza de la Herradura. Three offshore mooring buoys provide berths for tankers up to 50 000 dwt to load and discharge petroleum products; max permissible draught is 18 m

A single buoy mooring is situated 2.6 km offshore and is equipped with floating pipelines. Tankers up to 200 000 dwt can berth in a depth of 47 m; max permissible length is 342 m and up to 25.5 m draft. Discharge rate of about 8000 t/h

ENAP have a pier 200 m long which is used for service craft

Three mooring buoys situated near the tanker buoys for gas carriers up to 15 000 dwt and 11 m draft. Discharge rate of 240 m3/h

There is a smaller berth used for loading copper ore, vessels up to 95 m loa can be accommodated with max draft at HW of 5.2 m. There are also fish canneries and fishmeal plants

Bunkering: Agencias Universales S.A. (AGUNSA), Pasaje Ida Schubert 944, P O Box 62, Quintero, Chile, *Tel:* +56 32 293 0069/255 6370, *Fax:* +56 32 293 0835, *Email:* agunsaqtv@agunsa.cl, *Website:* www.agunsa.com

Ian Taylor y Compania S.A., Pasaje Ida Schubert 959, Quintero, Chile, *Tel:* +56 32 293 0529, *Fax:* +56 32 293 4708, *Email:* evaras@taylor.cl, *Website:* www.iantaylorgroup.com

Compania de Petroleos de Chile Copec S.A. (COPEC), Avenida Jorge Montt 2300, P O Box 2532-691, Vina del Mar, Chile, *Tel:* +56 32 2324 326, *Fax:* +56 32 2699 651, *Email:* bunkers@copec.cl, *Website:* www.copec.cl – *Grades:* MDO; IFO; in line blending available – *Misc:* own storage facilities – *Rates:* 40-100t/h – *Notice:* 48 hours – *Delivery Mode:* truck

ExxonMobil Marine Fuels, Suite 900, One Alhambra Plaza, Coral Gables, FL 33134, United States of America, *Tel:* +1 305 459 6358, *Fax:* +1 305 459 6412, *Email:* emmf@exxonmobil.com, *Website:* www.exxonmobilmarinefuels.com

Petroleos Marinos de Chile Ltda (PMC), P. O. Box 34, Puchuncavi, V Region, Santiago, Chile, *Tel:* +56 32 2796 550, *Fax:* +56 32 2796 233, *Email:* bunkers@pmchile.cl

Ian Taylor y Compania S.A., Pasaje Ida Schubert 959, Quintero, Chile, *Tel:* +56 32 293 0529, *Fax:* +56 32 293 4708, *Email:* evaras@taylor.cl, *Website:* www.iantaylorgroup.com

Towage: Ian Taylor y Compania S.A., Pasaje Ida Schubert 959, Quintero, Chile, *Tel:* +56 32 293 0529, *Fax:* +56 32 293 4708, *Email:* evaras@taylor.cl, *Website:* www.iantaylorgroup.com

Shipping Agents: Agencias Maritimas Agental Ltda, Pasaje Ida Schubert 959, Quintero, Chile, *Tel:* +56 32 293 4526, *Fax:* +56 32 293 4708, *Email:* agentqtr@agental.cl, *Website:* www.agental.cl

Agencias Universales S.A. (AGUNSA), Pasaje Ida Schubert 944, P O Box 62, Quintero, Chile, *Tel:* +56 32 293 0069/255 6370, *Fax:* +56 32 293 0835, *Email:* agunsaqtv@agunsa.cl, *Website:* www.agunsa.com

Sudamericana Agencias Aereas y Maritimas S.A. (SAAM), Fernandez Mella 87, Quintero, Chile, *Tel:* +56 32 293 0366, *Fax:* +56 32 293 0929, *Email:* quintero@saamsa.com, *Website:* www.saam.cl

Ian Taylor y Compania S.A., Pasaje Ida Schubert 959, Quintero, Chile, *Tel:* +56 32 293 0529, *Fax:* +56 32 293 4708, *Email:* evaras@taylor.cl, *Website:* www.iantaylorgroup.com

Ultramar Agencia Maritima Ltda, Pasaje San Guillermo No.121, P O Box 109, Quintero, Chile, *Tel:* +56 32 293 0927, *Fax:* +56 32 293 0265, *Email:* quintero@ultramar.cl, *Website:* www.ultramar.cl

Stevedoring Companies: Sudamericana Agencias Aereas y Maritimas S.A. (SAAM), Fernandez Mella 87, Quintero, Chile, *Tel:* +56 32 293 0366, *Fax:* +56 32 293 0929, *Email:* quintero@saamsa.com, *Website:* www.saam.cl

Ian Taylor y Compania S.A., Pasaje Ida Schubert 959, Quintero, Chile, *Tel:* +56 32 293 0529, *Fax:* +56 32 293 4708, *Email:* evaras@taylor.cl, *Website:* www.iantaylorgroup.com

Ultramar Agencia Maritima Ltda, Pasaje San Guillermo No.121, P O Box 109, Quintero, Chile, *Tel:* +56 32 293 0927, *Fax:* +56 32 293 0265, *Email:* quintero@ultramar.cl, *Website:* www.ultramar.cl

Lloyd's Agent: Gibbs & Cia SAC, Marchant Pereira 367, 5th Floor, Santiago 664 0622, Chile, *Tel:* +56 2 269 6364, *Fax:* +56 2 269 6395, *Email:* secretaria@gibbs.cl, *Website:* www.gibbs.cl

SAN ANTONIO

Lat 33° 36' S; Long 71° 37' W.

Admiralty Chart: 3073	Admiralty Pilot: 7
Time Zone: GMT -4 h	UNCTAD Locode: CL SAI

Principal Facilities:

P	Q	Y	G	C	R		B		T	

Authority: Empresa Portuaria San Antonio, Alan Macowan 0245, Barrancas, San Antonio 2662845, Chile, *Tel:* +56 35 586000, *Fax:* +56 35 586015, *Email:* aespinosa@sanantonioport.com, *Website:* www.sanantonioport.com

Officials: General Manager: Alvaro Espinosa Almarza.

Port Security: ISPS compliant

Anchorage: Vessels must anchor in pos 090° and 1.3 miles from the edge of the south breakwater in 28 m of water. The bottom is sand and mud

Pilotage: Compulsory. Pilot boards vessel about one mile outside the port. Vessels should await pilots with engines stopped in pos bearing 060° and one mile from Panul Lighthouse

Radio Frequency: Port control on VHF Channel 16, 24 h/day

Weather: W to SW winds

Tides: Range of tide 1.25 m

Traffic: 2007, 12 640 889 t of cargo handled, 650 697 TEU's

Principal Imports and Exports: Imports: Chemical products, Grain, Heavy industrial equipment, Vehicles. Exports: Agricultural products, Copper bars, Fruit.

Working Hours: 0800-15:30, 1530-2300 and 2300-0630, seven days a week. Work from 0630-0800 is overtime and normally used only if vessel scheduled to complete operations within this period

Accommodation:

Name	Length (m)	Draught (m)	Remarks
South Mole Terminal			See [1] below
Berth No's 1-3	769	11.3–12.4	
Espigon Terminal			See [2] below
Berth No's 4-5	341	9.45	
Berth No's 6-7	321	6.8–7.93	
North Terminal			See [3] below
Berth No.8	230	11	
Policarpo Toro Terminal			See [4] below
Berth No.9	190	10	

[1]*South Mole Terminal:* Operated by San Antonio Terminal Internacional, Avda. Ramon Barros Luco 1613 Piso 13, San Antonio, Tel: +56 35 201600, Fax: +56 35 201660, Email: box@stiport.com, Website: www.stiport.com
Three vessels can be berthed simultaneously. Yard area of over 25 ha with 1536 reefer points. Specialises in containers
[2]*Espigon Terminal:* Operated by Empresa Portuaria San Antonio
Solid and liquid bulk cargo, containerisation cargo & break bulk cargo
[3]*North Terminal:* Operated by Puerto Panul S.A., Av. Nunez de Fonseca 440, San Antonio, Tel: +56 35 355900, Fax: +56 35 355930, Email: aperez@puertopanul.cl
Bulk terminal for vessels up to 60 000 dwt. One level-luffing crane
[4]*Policarpo Toro Terminal:* Operated by Empresa Portuaria San Antonio
Liquid bulk cargoes for vessels up to 190 m loa

Storage:

Location	Covered (m²)	Sheds / Warehouses
South Mole Terminal	5000	2
Espigon Terminal	5100	3

Mechanical Handling Equipment:

Location	Type	Capacity (t)	Qty
South Mole Terminal	Container Cranes	60	2
South Mole Terminal	Container Cranes	40	2
South Mole Terminal	RTG's	30	2
South Mole Terminal	Reach Stackers	40	13
Espigon Terminal	Mult-purp. Cranes	100	1
Espigon Terminal	Reach Stackers	40	7

Cargo Worked: Copper 120 t/h/shift, wheat pellets 300 t/h/shift, general cargo 30-40 t/h/shift, containers 30-35 TEU's/h/shift, bulk salt 100-120 t/h/shift, drums 35-40 t/h/shift

Bunkering: Agencias Universales S.A. (AGUNSA), Av. Angamos 1546, Barrancas, P O Box 903, San Antonio, Chile, *Tel:* +56 35 212542, *Fax:* +56 35 211880, *Email:* agunsasai@agunsa.cl, *Website:* www.agunsa.com
Ian Taylor y Compania S.A., Avenida Angamos 1170, San Antonio, Chile, *Tel:* +56 35 212421, *Fax:* +56 35 211376/213749, *Email:* mailboxsai@taylor.cl, *Website:* www.iantaylorgroup.com
Compania de Petroleos de Chile Copec S.A. (COPEC), Avenida Jorge Montt 2300, P O Box 2532-691, Vina del Mar, Chile, *Tel:* +56 32 2324 326, *Fax:* +56 32 2699 651, *Email:* bunkers@copec.cl, *Website:* www.copec.cl

Towage: Six tugs of 1000-2500 hp available
Ian Taylor y Compania S.A., Avenida Angamos 1170, San Antonio, Chile, *Tel:* +56 35 212421, *Fax:* +56 35 211376/213749, *Email:* mailboxsai@taylor.cl, *Website:* www.iantaylorgroup.com

Repair & Maintenance: Three workshops for minor repairs. Major repairs at Valparaiso

Ship Chandlers: Gandara Chile S.A., 21 de Mayo 1040, San Antonio, Chile, *Tel:* +56 35 231696, *Fax:* +56 35 231696, *Email:* santonio@gandarachile.cl, *Website:* www.gandarachile.cl
Zuany Group Co., Avenida Esperidion Vera 1522, San Antonio, Chile, *Tel:* +56 35 232030, *Fax:* +56 35 233952, *Email:* zuany@ctcreuna.cl, *Website:* www.zuanygroup.com

Shipping Agents: Agencias Maritimas Broom y Cia. Ltda, Barros Luco 1431, San Antonio, Chile, *Tel:* +56 35 211997, *Fax:* +56 35 212807, *Email:* managersai@ajbroom.cl, *Website:* www.ajbroom.cl
Agencias Universales S.A. (AGUNSA), Av. Angamos 1546, Barrancas, P O Box 903, San Antonio, Chile, *Tel:* +56 35 212542, *Fax:* +56 35 211880, *Email:* agunsasai@agunsa.cl, *Website:* www.agunsa.com
A.P. Moller-Maersk Group, Maersk Chile S.A., Av. Ramon Barros Luco 1613, Piso 12, Torre Bioceanica, Barrancas, San Antonio, Chile, *Tel:* +56 35 203600, *Fax:* +56 35 231009, *Email:* chlopsvsl@maersk.com, *Website:* www.maerskline.com
Sudamericana Agencias Aereas y Maritimas S.A. (SAAM), Calle Bernardo O'Higgins

2263, San Antonio, Chile, *Tel:* +56 35 201000, *Fax:* +56 35 285096, *Email:* santonio@saamsa.com, *Website:* www.saam.cl
Ian Taylor y Compania S.A., Avenida Angamos 1170, San Antonio, Chile, *Tel:* +56 35 212421, *Fax:* +56 35 211376/213749, *Email:* mailboxsai@taylor.cl, *Website:* www.iantaylorgroup.com
Ultramar Agencia Maritima Ltda, Av. El Molo 097, San Antonio, Chile, *Tel:* +56 35 203000, *Fax:* +56 35 211949, *Email:* sanantonio@ultramar.cl, *Website:* www.ultramar.cl

Stevedoring Companies: Agencias Universales S.A. (AGUNSA), Av. Angamos 1546, Barrancas, P O Box 903, San Antonio, Chile, *Tel:* +56 35 212542, *Fax:* +56 35 211880, *Email:* agunsasai@agunsa.cl, *Website:* www.agunsa.com
Ian Taylor y Compania S.A., Avenida Angamos 1170, San Antonio, Chile, *Tel:* +56 35 212421, *Fax:* +56 35 211376/213749, *Email:* mailboxsai@taylor.cl, *Website:* www.iantaylorgroup.com

Medical Facilities: Hospital and clinics available

Airport: Aeropuerto Internacional Arturo Merino Benitez, 130 km

Railway: Ramal Alameda-San Antonio (exclusive for loading) which connects with the South Network Troncal

Lloyd's Agent: Gibbs & Cia SAC, Marchant Pereira 367, 5th Floor, Santiago 664 0622, Chile, *Tel:* +56 2 269 6364, *Fax:* +56 2 269 6395, *Email:* secretaria@gibbs.cl, *Website:* www.gibbs.cl

SAN VICENTE

Lat 36° 44' S; Long 73° 7' W.

Admiralty Chart: 4249	**Admiralty Pilot:** 7
Time Zone: GMT -4 h	**UNCTAD Locode:** CL SVE

Principal Facilities:

P	Q	Y	G	C		B		T	A

Authority: San Vicente Terminal Internacional S.A. (SVTI), Avenida Latorre 1590, Talcahuano, Chile, *Tel:* +56 41 250 3600, *Fax:* +56 41 255 6992, *Email:* customer@svti.cl, *Website:* www.svti.cl

Officials: General Manager: Felipe Barison Kahn, *Email:* fbarison@svti.cl.
Commercial Manager: Eduardo Gonzalez, *Email:* egonzalez@svti.cl.

Port Security: ISPS compliant

Pilotage: Compulsory for all foreign vessels

Radio Frequency: VHF Channel 16, 2182 kc. Monitored continuously

Weather: Little protection from winds particularly in summer when prevailing winds are S and SW. The N part of the bay offers good shelter from N and NW storms during the winter with swell from the ocean coming inside when the wind is W

Tides: Range of tide 1.8 m

Maximum Vessel Dimensions: 220 m loa, 12 m draft

Principal Imports and Exports: Imports: Fertilizers, General cargo, Machinery. Exports: Fishmeal, Frozen fish, Logs, Steel, Sugar beet, Woodchips, Woodpulp.

Working Hours: 0800-1530, 1530-2300, 2300-0600 with two hours overtime if necessary

Accommodation:

Name	Length (m)	Depth (m)	Draught (m)	Apron Width (m)	Remarks
San Vicente					See [1] below
Berth 1	200	11.5	11.28		
Berth 2	200	11.89	11.28		
Berth 3	200	12.5	11.89		
CAP Pier	373	7.62–9.91		27	See [2] below

[1]*San Vicente:* 2000 TEU ground slots and 256 reefer points
Two terminals owned by Petrox S.A., Tel: +56 41 250 6000, Fax: +56 41 241 0775 with mooring buoys in N part of bay. Terminal B: for crude and fuel oil. Max 12.8 m draft, max length 250 m. Terminal C: for clean products. Max 11 m draft, max length 200 m. No night berthing. Vessels up to 80 000 dwt. Liquefied gas is now discharged through terminal C. Vessels up to 10 000 dwt can be accommodated
[2]*CAP Pier:* Owned by Cia. Siderurgica Huachipato S.A., Avda. Gran Bretana 2910, Talcahuano, Tel: +56 41 255 4455, Fax: +56 41 250 2870, Email: huachipato@csh.cl, Website: www.huachipato.cl
One ship can berth each side; depths alongside are 7.62 m on the S side and 9.91 m on the N side, but as there is usually a swell running it is advisable to make allowance for the rise and fall of the vessel while alongside. The distance between bollard No's 1 to 8 is 154 m. N side of pier used mainly for handling bulk cargoes such as iron ore, limestone and coal for the plant; mechanical grabber and conveyor belts installed. N side of pier can also be used for handling general cargo when not required by owners. Railway spurs of S side, no cranes. There is also a discharge tower on berths 1 & 2 and a conveyor system used for loading on berth No.2

Key to Principal Facilities:—			
A=Airport	**C**=Containers	**G**=General Cargo	**P**=Petroleum	**R**=Ro/Ro	**Y**=Dry Bulk
B=Bunkers	**D**=Dry Dock	**L**=Cruise	**Q**=Other Liquid Bulk	**T**=Towage (where available from port)

Storage:

Location	Covered (m²)
San Vicente	62000

Mechanical Handling Equipment:

Location	Type	Capacity (t)	Qty
San Vicente	Mobile Cranes	100	3
San Vicente	Reach Stackers		10
San Vicente	Forklifts	3–16	35

Bunkering: Compania de Petroleos de Chile Copec S.A. (COPEC), Avenida Jorge Montt 2300, P O Box 2532-691, Vina del Mar, Chile, *Tel:* +56 32 2324 326, *Fax:* +56 32 2699 651, *Email:* bunkers@copec.cl, *Website:* www.copec.cl – *Grades:* MDO; IFO; in line blending available – *Misc:* own storage facilities – *Rates:* 40-100t/h – *Notice:* 48 hours – *Delivery Mode:* truck
ExxonMobil Marine Fuels, Suite 900, One Alhambra Plaza, Coral Gables, FL 33134, United States of America, *Tel:* +1 305 459 6358, *Fax:* +1 305 459 6412, *Email:* emmf@exxonmobil.com, *Website:* www.exxonmobilmarinefuels.com – *Grades:* all grades except MDO – *Rates:* IFO 180t/h, MGO 450t/h – *Delivery Mode:* pipeline, truck

Towage: Three tugs available

Medical Facilities: Higueras, 5 km. Other hospitals in Concepcion and Talcahuano

Airport: Carriel Sur Airport, 15 km

Railway: Passenger stations in Talcahuano, 4 km and in Concepcion, 17 km

Lloyd's Agent: Gibbs & Cia SAC, Marchant Pereira 367, 5th Floor, Santiago 664 0622, Chile, *Tel:* +56 2 269 6364, *Fax:* +56 2 269 6395, *Email:* secretaria@gibbs.cl, *Website:* www.gibbs.cl

TALCAHUANO

Lat 36° 41' S; Long 73° 5' W.

Admiralty Chart: 4248	**Admiralty Pilot:** 7
Time Zone: GMT -4 h	**UNCTAD Locode:** CL TAL

Talcahuano

Principal Facilities:

P Q Y G C R B D T A

Authority: Empresa Portuaria Talcahuano, Avenida Blanco Encalada 547, Talcahuano, Chile, *Tel:* +56 41 279 7600, *Fax:* +56 41 279 7626, *Email:* eportuaria@puertotalcahuano.cl, *Website:* www.puertotalcahuano.cl

Officials: General Manager: Luis Alberto Rosenberg, *Email:* larosenberg@puertotalcahuano.cl.
Commercial Manager: Raul Ojeda, *Email:* rojeda@puertotalcahuano.cl.

Port Security: ISPS compliant

Approach: The port is situated in Concepcion bay which has two entrances, divided by the Island of Quiriquina. The smaller entrance Boca Chica, which is not recommended has a depth of 12.19 to 13.79 m, and the larger, Boca Grande, a depth of 35.05 to 39.62 m. Close to land is shallow water with a soft mud bottom

Anchorage: S of Belen lighthouse in 10 m

Pilotage: Compulsory for all foreign vessels

Radio Frequency: International frequency 2182 kc and VHF Channel 16, both watched continuously

Weather: Good weather for 6-8 months with winds from the SW. Between May to October there can be banks of mist on the coast

Tides: Range of tide 1.8 m

Principal Imports and Exports: Imports: General cargo, Machinery. Exports: Fishmeal, Logs, Lumber, Newsprint rolls, Sawn timber, Steel products, Woodpulp.

Working Hours: 0800-1530, 1530-2300, 2300-0600 with two hours overtime when necessary

Accommodation:

Name	Length (m)	Depth (m)	Remarks
Talcahuano			See [1] below
Berth No.1	155	8.84	See [2] below
Penco Pier	1500		See [3] below

[1]*Talcahuano:* There is an important Naval base at the port within which Molo 500 is used commercially in all its extension of 500 m and a depth of 8.23 m accommodating up to two vessels at a time
[2]*Berth No.1:* With adjacent railways sidings. Containers are discharged to trucks using ships gear. Ro/ro vessels use Berth No.1
[3]*Penco Pier:* Owned by Muelles de Penco S.A., Tel: +56 41 245 1091, Fax: +56 41 245 2253, Email: mpenco@muellesdepenco.cl
At the head it has a section 27 m long and 11 m wide accommodating one berthing site with a depth of 10.06 m. It has four mooring buoys. The pier is provided with a conveyor belt for carrying the product to the storage yards at cap of 250 t/h

Storage: One general cargo warehouse of 3267 m2 and two of 1000 m2. 31 620 m2 of storage yards for depositing cargo

Location	Covered (m²)	Sheds / Warehouses
Talcahuano	3264	
Penco Pier	15400	3

Mechanical Handling Equipment:

Location	Type	Capacity (t)	Qty
Talcahuano	Floating Cranes	180	1
Talcahuano	Mult-purp. Cranes	6	2

Cargo Worked: Fishmeal (in bulk) 300 t/h, (in bags) 30 t; timber 100 t/h; logs 100-150 t/h; woodpulp 45 t/h

Bunkering: Ian Taylor y Compania S.A., Blanco Encalada 444, Office 408, Talcahuano, Chile, *Tel:* +56 41 242 7353, *Fax:* +56 41 242 7354, *Email:* talcahuano@iantaylor.com, *Website:* www.iantaylorgroup.com
Compania de Petroleos de Chile Copec S.A. (COPEC), Avenida Jorge Montt 2300, P O Box 2532-691, Vina del Mar, Chile, *Tel:* +56 32 2324 326, *Fax:* +56 32 2699 651, *Email:* bunkers@copec.cl, *Website:* www.copec.cl – *Grades:* MDO; IFO; in line blending available – *Misc:* own storage facilities – *Rates:* 40-100t/h – *Notice:* 48 hours – *Delivery Mode:* truck
ExxonMobil Marine Fuels, Suite 900, One Alhambra Plaza, Coral Gables, FL 33134, United States of America, *Tel:* +1 305 459 6358, *Fax:* +1 305 459 6412, *Email:* emmf@exxonmobil.com, *Website:* www.exxonmobilmarinefuels.com – *Grades:* all grades except MDO – *Rates:* IFO 180t/h, MGO 450t/h – *Notice:* 5 days – *Delivery Mode:* pipeline, truck
Ian Taylor y Compania S.A., Blanco Encalada 444, Office 408, Talcahuano, Chile, *Tel:* +56 41 242 7353, *Fax:* +56 41 242 7354, *Email:* talcahuano@iantaylor.com, *Website:* www.iantaylorgroup.com

Towage: Empresa Portuaria Talcahuano, Avenida Blanco Encalada 547, Talcahuano, Chile, *Tel:* +56 41 279 7600, *Fax:* +56 41 279 7626, *Email:* eportuaria@puertotalcahuano.cl, *Website:* www.puertotalcahuano.cl
Ian Taylor y Compania S.A., Blanco Encalada 444, Office 408, Talcahuano, Chile, *Tel:* +56 41 242 7353, *Fax:* +56 41 242 7354, *Email:* talcahuano@iantaylor.com, *Website:* www.iantaylorgroup.com

Repair & Maintenance: Asmar Shipbuilding & Ship Repair Company, Avenida Jorge Montt 250, P O Box 104, Talcahuano, Chile, *Tel:* +56 41 274 4100, *Fax:* +56 41 274 4017, *Email:* administrador@asmar.cl, *Website:* www.asmar.cl Manager: Carlos Fanta Email: cfanta@asmar.cl Dry dock No.1 175 m x 21.5 m x 8.25 m for vessels up to 18 000 dwt. Dry dock No.2 242 m x 33.8 m x 10.5 m for vessels up to 95 000 dwt. Four floating docks: 'Mery' 120.7 m x 16.5 m x 7 m with lifting cap of 3500 t, 'Mutilla' 120.7 m x 16.5 m x 7 m with lifting cap of 3500 t, 'Gutierrez' 80 m x 16 m x 6.5 m with lifting cap of 1200 t, 'Manterola' 66 m x 10.6 m x 5.5 m with lifting cap of 1000 t
Chile Services Management S.A., Av. Francia 1001, Valparaiso, Chile, *Tel:* +56 32 221 0766, *Fax:* +56 32 222 8995, *Email:* andre.quint@csmchile.cl, *Website:* www.csmchile.cl
Astilleros Marco Chilena Ltda, Recinto Portuario s/n, San Vicente, Talcahuano, Chile, *Tel:* +56 41 254 3331, *Fax:* +56 41 254 2905, *Email:* msmartin@marco.cl, *Website:* www.marcochilena.cl

Ship Chandlers: Gandara Chile S.A., Gomez Carreno 3197, Talcahuano, Chile, *Tel:* +56 41 259 3371, *Fax:* +56 41 259 3370, *Email:* talcahuano@gandarachile.cl, *Website:* www.gandarachile.cl
J.V.G. General Shipchandlers S.A., Avenida Argentina No.235, Talcahuano, Chile, *Tel:* +56 41 254 3694, *Fax:* +56 41 254 1423, *Email:* ivgsa@entelchile.cnet

Shipping Agents: Agencias Maritimas Agental Ltda, Perez Gactua 355, Piso 3, Talcahuano, Chile, *Tel:* +56 41 254 6124, *Fax:* +56 41 254 6169, *Email:* agenttho@agental.cl, *Website:* www.agental.cl
Agencias Maritimas Broom y Cia. Ltda, Jaime Repullo 1815, Sector Huertos Familiares, Talcahuano, Chile, *Tel:* +56 41 257 9110, *Fax:* +56 41 257 7864, *Email:* managertho@ajbroom.cl, *Website:* www.ajbroom.cl
Agencias Universales S.A. (AGUNSA), Av. Latorre 839, San Vicente, P O Box 567, Talcahuano, Chile, *Tel:* +56 41 254 3961, *Fax:* +56 41 254 4947, *Email:* mcontreras@agunsa.cl, *Website:* www.agunsa.com
Maritima Valparaiso Chile S.A., Edificio Don Cristobal, Avenida Blanco Encalada No.444, Oficina 611, Talcahuano, Chile, *Tel:* +56 41 254 7339, *Fax:* +56 41 254 8913, *Email:* mlatorre@tlc.marval.cl, *Website:* www.marval.cl
Sudamericana Agencias Aereas y Maritimas S.A. (SAAM), Avenida Blanco 444, Oficina 801, 8 Piso, Talcahuano, Chile, *Tel:* +56 41 254 6045, *Fax:* +56 41 254 2610, *Email:* talcahuano@saamsa.com, *Website:* www.saam.cl
Ian Taylor y Compania S.A., Blanco Encalada 444, Office 408, Talcahuano, Chile, *Tel:* +56 41 242 7353, *Fax:* +56 41 242 7354, *Email:* talcahuano@iantaylor.com, *Website:* www.iantaylorgroup.com
Ultramar Agencia Maritima Ltda, Blanco Encalada No.444, P O Box 577, Oficina 401,

4 Piso, Talcahuano, Chile, *Tel:* +56 41 250 7700, *Fax:* +56 41 254 2931, *Email:* talcahuano@ultramar.cl, *Website:* www.ultramar.cl

Stevedoring Companies: Ian Taylor y Compania S.A., Blanco Encalada 444, Office 408, Talcahuano, Chile, *Tel:* +56 41 242 7353, *Fax:* +56 41 242 7354, *Email:* talcahuano@iantaylor.com, *Website:* www.iantaylorgroup.com
Ultramar Agencia Maritima Ltda, Blanco Encalada No.444, P O Box 577, Oficina 401, 4 Piso, Talcahuano, Chile, *Tel:* +56 41 250 7700, *Fax:* +56 41 254 2931, *Email:* talcahuano@ultramar.cl, *Website:* www.ultramar.cl

Medical Facilities: Three hospitals available in Talcahuano

Airport: Carriel Sur, 9 km

Railway: Passenger station in Concepcion, 17 km

Lloyd's Agent: Gibbs & Cia SAC, Marchant Pereira 367, 5th Floor, Santiago 664 0622, Chile, *Tel:* +56 2 269 6364, *Fax:* +56 2 269 6395, *Email:* secretaria@gibbs.cl, *Website:* www.gibbs.cl

TOCOPILLA

Lat 22° 5' S; Long 70° 14' W.

Admiralty Chart: 4223/4224   **Admiralty Pilot:** 7
Time Zone: GMT -4 h   **UNCTAD Locode:** CL TOQ

Principal Facilities:

P	Q	Y	G			B		T	A

Authority: Armada de Chile, Barros Arana s/n, Tocopilla, Chile, *Tel:* +56 55 813279, *Fax:* +56 55 813279, *Email:* cptocopilla@directemar.cl, *Website:* www.directemar.cl

Officials: Port Captain: Ignacio Rojas Gajardo.

Port Security: ISPS compliant

Documentation: Crew list (5 copies), stores list (5 copies), crew personal effects list (5 copies), health declaration (1 copy), cargo manifest in transit (2 copies)

Approach: Bay 3.2 km wide at entrance with a bight of 1.2 km, ample and deep; depths from 15 m to 45 m. In S, moderate depths

Anchorage: Anchorage can be obtained in depths ranging from 15 m to 30 m in pos:
a) 22° 04' 28" S; 70° 12' 52" W
b) 22° 04' 28" S; 70° 12' 33" W
c) 22° 04' 52" S; 70° 12' 33" W
d) 22° 04' 47" S; 70° 12' 52" W

Pilotage: Compulsory in and out. For anchoring, mooring/unmooring to buoy or nitrate mole, pilot must be awaited. One pilot always available

Radio Frequency: VHF Channel 16 (Tocopilla radio) and VHF Channel 6 (pilot)

Weather: Frequent fog and exposed to strong NW winds

Traffic: 2006, 2 838 204 t of cargo handled

Maximum Vessel Dimensions: 250 m loa, 80 000 dwt, 14.38 m draft

Principal Imports and Exports: Imports: Coal, Petroleum, Sulphuric acid, Urea. Exports: Fishmeal, Nitrate, Sulphate & potash chloride.

Working Hours: Three shifts: 0800-1530, 1530-2300, 2300-0630

Accommodation:

Name	Draught (m)	Remarks
Tocopilla		
Electroandina Pier	14.38	See [1] below
SIT	10.5	See [2] below

[1]*Electroandina Pier:* Operated by Agental Ltda. Max 250 m loa.. Coal, petroleum, sulphuric acid, fishmeal, containers & general cargo
[2]*SIT:* Operated by SIT S.A. Max 213 m loa, max air draft 11.5 m. Nitrate, sulphate & potash chloride in bulk. Cargo is transported by conveyor belts at rate of 400-800 t/h

Mechanical Handling Equipment:

Location	Type	Capacity (t)	Qty
Electroandina Pier	Mult-purp. Cranes	30	2
SIT	Mult-purp. Cranes	5	2

Cargo Worked: Coal discharge rate 750-900 t/h, fuel discharge rate 800-1100 m3/h, diesel discharge rate 500-800 m3/h

Bunkering: Ian Taylor y Compania S.A., B & M Agencia Maritima Ltda, Sargento Aldea 1250, Tocopilla, Chile, *Tel:* +56 55 813296, *Fax:* +56 55 812746, *Email:* b.m.toc@bm-maritima.cl, *Website:* www.bmchile.cl
Compania de Petroleos de Chile Copec S.A. (COPEC), Avenida Jorge Montt 2300, P O Box 2532-691, Vina del Mar, Chile, *Tel:* +56 32 2324 326, *Fax:* +56 32 2699 651, *Email:* bunkers@copec.cl, *Website:* www.copec.cl

Towage: Ian Taylor y Compania S.A., B & M Agencia Maritima Ltda, Sargento Aldea 1250, Tocopilla, Chile, *Tel:* +56 55 813296, *Fax:* +56 55 812746, *Email:* b.m.toc@bm-maritima.cl, *Website:* www.bmchile.cl

Remolcadores Tocopilla S.A., Tocopilla, Chile, *Tel:* +56 55 813006, *Fax:* +56 55 813099

Repair & Maintenance: Only small workshop available

Shipping Agents: Agencias Maritimas Agental Ltda, Policarpo Toro 0277, Vila Las Rocas, Tocopilla, Chile, *Tel:* +56 55 813006, *Fax:* +56 55 813099, *Email:* agenttoc@agental.cl, *Website:* www.agental.cl
Agencias Universales S.A. (AGUNSA), Direccion 21 de Mayo 1317, Tocopilla, Chile, *Tel:* +56 55 813006, *Fax:* +56 55 813099, *Email:* agenttoc@agental.cl, *Website:* www.agunsa.com
Ian Taylor y Compania S.A., B & M Agencia Maritima Ltda, Sargento Aldea 1250, Tocopilla, Chile, *Tel:* +56 55 813296, *Fax:* +56 55 812746, *Email:* b.m.toc@bm-maritima.cl, *Website:* www.bmchile.cl

Stevedoring Companies: Ian Taylor y Compania S.A., B & M Agencia Maritima Ltda, Sargento Aldea 1250, Tocopilla, Chile, *Tel:* +56 55 813296, *Fax:* +56 55 812746, *Email:* b.m.toc@bm-maritima.cl, *Website:* www.bmchile.cl

Medical Facilities: Public hospital and three clinics

Airport: Barriles Airport

Lloyd's Agent: Gibbs & Cia SAC, Marchant Pereira 367, 5th Floor, Santiago 664 0622, Chile, *Tel:* +56 2 269 6364, *Fax:* +56 2 269 6395, *Email:* secretaria@gibbs.cl, *Website:* www.gibbs.cl

VALPARAISO

Lat 33° 1' S; Long 71° 38' W.

Admiralty Chart: 1314/4242   **Admiralty Pilot:** 7
Time Zone: GMT -4 h   **UNCTAD Locode:** CL VAP

Principal Facilities:

P	Q	Y	G	C	R	L	B	D	T	A

Authority: Empresa Portuaria Valparaiso, Avenida Errazuriz 25, Valparaiso, Chile, *Tel:* +56 32 244 8800, *Fax:* +56 32 222 4190, *Email:* comercial@epv.cl, *Website:* www.portvalparaiso.cl

Officials: General Manager: Harald Jaeger Karl, *Tel:* +56 32 244 8811.
Communications Manager: Pamela San Martin, *Tel:* +56 32 244 8820, *Email:* psanmartin@epv.cl.

Port Security: ISPS compliant

Documentation: Despatch (1 copy), light dues certificate (1 copy), port cargo manifest of Valparaiso (4 copies), transhipment cargo manifest (7 copies), passenger lists for port (3 copies), fumigation certificate (1 copy), crew lists (18 copies), personal effects list (1 copy), passenger baggage declaration (2 per passenger), passenger lists for transit (3 copies)

Anchorage: Anchorage outside artificial port in 27.5 to 46 m. Important to secure good anchorage due to strong winds and heavy swells. Contact Harbour Master on arrival for anchorage etc (24 h notice)

Pilotage: Compulsory. Pilot must be awaited near Punta de Angeles. Vessels reception is made approx 2.5 cables off the breakwater on a bearing of 009° from the breakwater head light

Radio Frequency: VHF Channel 16, 2182 kHz

Weather: No complete protection against N winds. Prevailing winds, S in spring and summer which sometimes interferes with traffic in bay. In winter N winds prevail. Work stops only for a few days in the year. Fog experienced especially from March to May

Tides: Range of tide 1.5 m

Traffic: 2007, 9 713 720 t of cargo handled, 845 234 TEU's

Principal Imports and Exports: Imports: Chemical products, Foodstuffs, Vehicles. Exports: Copper, Frozen food, Fruit.

Key to Principal Facilities:—				
A=Airport	**C**=Containers	**G**=General Cargo	**P**=Petroleum	**R**=Ro/Ro **Y**=Dry Bulk
B=Bunkers	**D**=Dry Dock	**L**=Cruise	**Q**=Other Liquid Bulk	**T**=Towage (where available from port)

Working Hours: Three shifts 0800-1530, 1530-2300, 2300-0630

Accommodation:

Name	Length (m)	Draught (m)	Remarks
Valparaiso			See [1] below
Berth No's 1-3	620	11.4	
Berth No's 4-5	365	9.4	
Berth No.6	185.7	8.5	
Berth No.7	125	6.19	
Berth No.8	235	8.5	

[1]*Valparaiso:* Terminal 1: (Berths 1-5) handling container and multi-purpose cargo, operated by Terminal Pacifico Sur Valparaiso S.A., Antonio Varas 2, Floor 3, Valparaiso, Tel: +56 32 227 5800, Fax: +56 32 227 5813, Website: www.tpsv.cl. Covers 15.6 ha with 20 000 m2 of warehouse space
Terminal 2: (Berths 6-8) handling container and multi-purpose cargo operated by EPV Valparaiso Passenger Terminal, Urriola 87, Valparaiso, Tel: +56 32 259 4073, Fax: +56 32 222 1389, Email: info@vtp.cl, Website: www.vtp.cl, located one mile from the berths with an area of 4200 m2
LAS SALINAS: Three offshore terminals for tankers with limiting draughts of 18.3 m and 12.2 m respectively. Vessels berth during daylight hours only. Bulk liquid cargo terminal in operation equipped with several storage tanks

Storage:

Location	Open (m²)	Covered (m²)	Sheds / Warehouses
Valparaiso	86184	25534	8

Mechanical Handling Equipment:

Location	Type	Capacity (t)	Qty
Valparaiso	Mult-purp. Cranes	36	1
Valparaiso	Mobile Cranes	100	2
Valparaiso	Container Cranes	80	2
Valparaiso	Reach Stackers	20	11

Bunkering: Agencias Universales S.A. (AGUNSA), Urriola 87, Piso 2, Valparaiso, Chile, *Tel:* +56 32 221 7333, *Fax:* +56 32 225 7586, *Email:* agunsavlp@agunsa.cl, *Website:* www.agunsa.com
Ian Taylor y Compania S.A., Prat 827, Office 301, Valparaiso, Chile, *Tel:* +56 32 226 1000, *Fax:* +56 32 226 1100, *Email:* info@iantaylorgroup.com, *Website:* www.iantaylor.com
Compania de Petroleos de Chile Copec S.A. (COPEC), Avenida Jorge Montt 2300, P O Box 2532-691, Vina del Mar, Chile, *Tel:* +56 32 2324 326, *Fax:* +56 32 2699 651, *Email:* bunkers@copec.cl, *Website:* www.copec.cl

Waste Reception Facilities: Only liquid and sludge disposal. Tanks reception delivered to trucks

Towage: Six tugs available of 750-4000 hp
Ian Taylor y Compania S.A., Prat 827, Office 301, Valparaiso, Chile, *Tel:* +56 32 226 1000, *Fax:* +56 32 226 1100, *Email:* info@iantaylorgroup.com, *Website:* www.iantaylor.com

Repair & Maintenance: Asmar Shipbuilding & Ship Repair Company, Prat 856, Floor 13, Edificio Rapa Nui, P O Box 150, Valparaiso, Chile, *Tel:* +56 32 227 2000, *Fax:* +56 32 226 0158, *Email:* rrpp@asmar.cl, *Website:* www.asmar.cl Executive Director: Carlos Santa Email: csanta@asmar.cl
Chile Services Management S.A., Av. Francia 1001, Valparaiso, Chile, *Tel:* +56 32 221 0766, *Fax:* +56 32 222 8995, *Email:* andre.quint@csmchile.cl, *Website:* www.csmchile.cl
Pacifico Ship Repairs - Marine, Morris 642, Valparaiso, Chile, *Tel:* +56 32 259 6393, *Fax:* +56 32 259 6393, *Email:* contact@pacificoship.cl, *Website:* www.pacificoship.cl
Servicios Maritimos Progremar Ltda, Pocuro 1036, Valparaiso, Chile, *Tel:* +56 32 223 0613, *Fax:* +56 32 223 4547, *Email:* infotech@progremar.cl, *Website:* www.progremar.cl Afloat repairs, turbochargers, refrigeration, hydraulic, pumps, electrical motor rewinding, welding, pneumatics and air compressed systems, under floating repairs, engine room cleaning, tank cleaning, general cleaning and painting, technical supply, CO2 system
SOCIBER Ltda - Sociedad Iberoamericana de Reparaciones Navales Ltda, Blanco 1199, 9th Floor, Valparaiso, Chile, *Tel:* +56 32 221 3032, *Fax:* +56 32 225 4162, *Email:* informatica@sociber.cl, *Website:* www.sociber.cl Engine repairs

Ship Chandlers: Gandara Chile S.A., Calle Cerri ekl Plomo 3729, Parque Industrial Curauma de Placilla, Valparaiso, Chile, *Tel:* +56 32 229 4200, *Fax:* +56 32 229 4201, *Email:* admin@gandarachile.cl, *Website:* www.gandarachile.cl
J.V.G. General Shipchandlers S.A., P O Box 127, Valparaiso, Chile, *Tel:* +56 32 223 0200, *Fax:* +56 32 223 8983, *Email:* jvg-prov-maritimo@entelchile.net, *Website:* www.jvg.cl
Sermapi Marine Supply Services, Avenida Rodriguez No.624, Valparaiso, Chile, *Tel:* +56 32 225 5429, *Fax:* +56 32 284 9931, *Email:* sermapi@terra.cl
Unicorn Marine Supply Ltda, Valparaiso, Chile, *Tel:* +56 32 225 3814, *Fax:* +56 32 223 6916, *Email:* unicorn@entelchile.net
Valparaiso Ship Services S.A., Templeman 550, Cerro Con cion, Valparaiso 2374525, Chile, *Tel:* +56 32 225 6540, *Fax:* +56 32 225 4483, *Email:* valpaship@hotmail.com, *Website:* www.valparaisoshipservice.cl

Shipping Agents: Agencias Maritimas Agental Ltda, Almirante Seforet 70, Of.25, Edificio Capitania, Valparaiso, Chile, *Tel:* +56 32 222 1617, *Fax:* +56 32 229 3554, *Email:* agentvap@agental.cl, *Website:* www.agental.cl
Agencias Maritimas Broom y Cia. Ltda, Errazuriz 629, 3rd & 4th Floor, Valparaiso, Chile, *Tel:* +56 32 226 8200, *Fax:* +56 32 221 3308, *Email:* operations@ajbroom.cl, *Website:* www.ajbroom.cl
Agencias Universales S.A. (AGUNSA), Urriola 87, Piso 2, Valparaiso, Chile, *Tel:* +56 32 221 7333, *Fax:* +56 32 225 7586, *Email:* agunsavlp@agunsa.cl, *Website:* www.agunsa.com
Inchcape Shipping Services (ISS), Arturo Prat 639, Valparaiso, Chile, *Tel:* +56 32 221 7681, *Fax:* +56 32 223 9632, *Email:* isschile@iss-shipping.com, *Website:* www.iss-shipping.com
Maritima Valparaiso Chile S.A., 5th Floor, Almirante Gomez Carrerio 49, Valparaiso, Chile, *Tel:* +56 32 223 4124, *Fax:* +56 32 223 4126, *Email:* pespinoza@marval.cl, *Website:* www.marval.cl

Mediterranean Shipping Company, MSC Iquique, 151-A Jose de San Martin Street, Iquique, Chile, *Tel:* +56 57 524300, *Fax:* +56 57 427770, *Website:* www.mscchile.com
Sudamericana Agencias Aereas y Maritimas S.A. (SAAM), Blanco 895, Valparaiso, Chile, *Tel:* +56 32 220 1102, *Fax:* +56 32 225 0089, *Email:* servicioalcliente@saamsa.com, *Website:* www.saamsa.com
Ian Taylor y Compania S.A., Prat 827, Office 301, Valparaiso, Chile, *Tel:* +56 32 226 1000, *Fax:* +56 32 226 1100, *Email:* info@iantaylorgroup.com, *Website:* www.iantaylor.com
Terminal Pacifico Sur Valparaiso S.A., Avenida Antonio Varas No. 2, Piso 3, Valparaiso, Chile, *Tel:* +56 32 227 5800, *Fax:* +56 32 227 5813, *Email:* contact@tps.cl, *Website:* www.tps.cl
Ultramar Agencia Maritima Ltda, Cochrane No.813, P O Box 52-v, Piso 8, Valparaiso, Chile, *Tel:* +56 32 220 2000, *Fax:* +56 32 225 6607, *Email:* valparaiso@ultramar.cl, *Website:* www.ultramar.cl

Stevedoring Companies: Sudamericana Agencias Aereas y Maritimas S.A. (SAAM), Blanco 895, Valparaiso, Chile, *Tel:* +56 32 220 1102, *Fax:* +56 32 225 0089, *Email:* servicioalcliente@saamsa.com, *Website:* www.saamsa.com
Ian Taylor y Compania S.A., Prat 827, Office 301, Valparaiso, Chile, *Tel:* +56 32 226 1000, *Fax:* +56 32 226 1100, *Email:* info@iantaylorgroup.com, *Website:* www.iantaylor.com

Surveyors: ABS (Americas), Pudeto 351, Oficina 13, Piso 5, P O Box 3159, Valparaiso, Chile, *Tel:* +56 32 225 3743, *Fax:* +56 32 221 0510, *Email:* absvalparaiso@eagle.org, *Website:* www.eagle.org
Det Norske Veritas A/S, Avenida Libertad 1405, Of.1602, P O Box 766, Vina del Mar, Valparaiso, Chile, *Tel:* +56 32 299 1202, *Fax:* +56 32 299 1203, *Email:* vpo@dnv.com, *Website:* www.dnv.com
Germanischer Lloyd, Libertad 1405, Oficina 1502, Edificio Torre Coraceros, Vina del Mar, Valparaiso, Chile, *Tel:* +56 32 268 8323, *Fax:* +56 32 269 0110, *Email:* gl-valparaiso@gl-group.com, *Website:* www.gl-group.com
Nippon Kaiji Kyokai, Av. Nueva Libertad 1405, Of.1703, Vina del Mar, Valparaiso, Chile, *Tel:* +56 32 246 0202, *Fax:* +56 32 246 0078, *Email:* vp@classnk.or.jp, *Website:* www.classnk.or.jp
Southern Shipmanagement (Chile) Ltda, Tecnopacifico Building, Blanco 937 4to Piso, Valparaiso, Chile, *Tel:* +56 32 232 7500, *Fax:* +56 32 225 6471, *Email:* southship@ssm.cl, *Website:* www.ssm.cl

Medical Facilities: Aleman Hospital, Van Buren Hospital, Hoseg Hospital, Valparaiso Hospital and Baron Clinic Hospital

Airport: Rodelillo, 12 km

Railway: Ferrocarriles del Pacifico S.A. is next to the port

Lloyd's Agent: Gibbs & Cia SAC, Marchant Pereira 367, 5th Floor, Santiago 664 0622, Chile, *Tel:* +56 2 269 6364, *Fax:* +56 2 269 6395, *Email:* secretaria@gibbs.cl, *Website:* www.gibbs.cl

CHINA

AMOY

former name, see Xiamen

ANLAN

harbour area, see under Wenzhou

ANQING

Lat 30° 31' N; Long 117° 2' E.

Admiralty Chart: 2947	**Admiralty Pilot:** 32
Time Zone: GMT +8 h	**UNCTAD Locode:** CN AQG

Principal Facilities:

P	Y	G	C		B	T	

Authority: Anqing City Port Administration, 7 Yanjiang Zhong Road, Central, Anqing, Anhui Province 246030, People's Republic of China, *Tel:* +86 556 551 4810, *Website:* www.aqport.net

Port Security: ISPS compliant

Anchorage: General cargo anchorage in depth of 6-10 m

Pilotage: Compulsory and available 24 h. Pilot boards vessel at the anchorage

Radio Frequency: VHF Channel 10

Traffic: 2005, 10 500 000 t of cargo handled

Accommodation:

Name	Length (m)	Depth (m)	Remarks
Anqing			
Berth No.1	66	6	Crude oil for vessels up to 5000 dwt
Berth No.2	90	6–10	Crude oil for vessels up to 10 000 dwt
Berth No.3	90	6–10	Crude oil for vessels up to 10 000 dwt
Berth No.4	66	6	Crude oil for vessels up to 5000 dwt
Berth No.5	90	6	Product oil for vessels up to 10 000 dwt
Berth No.6	66	7	Product oil for vessels up to 6000 dwt
Berth No.7	65	6	Product oil for vessels up to 2400 dwt
Berth No.11	67.2	6.5	General cargo for vessels up to 5000 dwt
Berth No.13	36	4.8	Coal for vessels up to 1500 dwt
Berth No.14	36	4	Coal for vessels up to 1500 dwt
Berth No's 15-16	150	6–10	General & bulk cargo for vessels up to 6000 dwt
Berth No.17	76.8	4	Fuel oil for vessels up to 1500 dwt
Berth No.18	50	4	Ore for vessels up to 1500 dwt
Berth No.19	50	5	For vessels up to 3000 dwt
Berth No.20	60	5	Sand for vessels up to 5000 dwt
Xiaonanmen	50	2–5	General & bulk cargo for vessels up to 500 dwt
Paoshanying	40	6	Sand for vessels up to 1500 dwt
Container Berth	190	6–10	See [1] below

[1]*Container Berth:* Container, general cargo & bulk cargo for vessels up to 10 000 dwt

Storage: Container yard of 12 191 m2

Location	Open (m²)	Covered (m²)
Anqing	18721	7331

Mechanical Handling Equipment:

Location	Type	Capacity (t)	Qty
Anqing	Floating Cranes	15	1
Berth No.1	Shore Cranes	3	2
Berth No.2	Shore Cranes	3	1
Berth No.11	Shore Cranes	5	2
Berth No.13	Shore Cranes	3	1
Berth No.14	Shore Cranes	3	1
Berth No's 15-16	Shore Cranes	5	2
Berth No.17	Shore Cranes	3	1
Berth No.20	Shore Cranes	5	2
Xiaonanmen	Shore Cranes	3	2
Paoshanying	Shore Cranes	3	1
Container Berth	Shore Cranes	4–10	2

Bunkering: Available

Towage: Six tugs available of 98-1000 hp

Shipping Agents: China Marine Shipping Agency Co. Ltd, China Marine Shipping Agency Anhui Anqing Company, 2nd Floor, Hualian Building B, Huxin South Road, Anqing, Anhui Province, People's Republic of China, *Tel:* +86 556 551 4825, *Fax:* +86 556 551 4193, *Email:* huzhonghong@sinotrans-aq.com

Airport: Hefei Airport

Lloyd's Agent: Huatai Surveyors & Adjusters Co., 14th Floor, China Re Building, No.11 Jin Rong Avenue, Xicheng District, Beijing 100140, People's Republic of China, *Tel:* +86 10 6657 6577, *Fax:* +86 10 6657 6502, *Email:* agency.bj@huatai-serv.com, *Website:* www.huatai-serv.com

AOFENG

harbour area, see under Fuzhou

ASHIHE

harbour area, see under Harbin

BAGONGSHAN

harbour area, see under Huainan

BAHE

Lat 30° 24' N; Long 115° 1' E.

Admiralty Chart: 2947
Time Zone: GMT +8 h
Admiralty Pilot: 32
UNCTAD Locode: CN

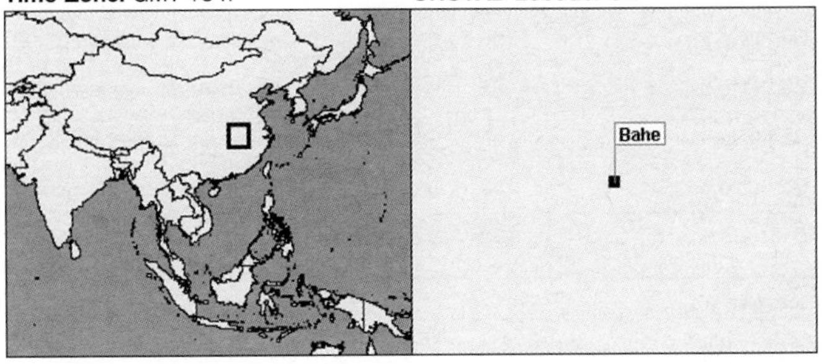

Principal Facilities:

		Y	G						

Accommodation:

Name	Remarks
Bahe	Two berths for vessels up to 1000 dwt handling sand, coal, grain and salt

Storage: Open and covered storage available

Mechanical Handling Equipment: Cargo handling cranes available

Lloyd's Agent: Huatai Surveyors & Adjusters Co., 14th Floor, China Re Building, No.11 Jin Rong Avenue, Xicheng District, Beijing 100140, People's Republic of China, *Tel:* +86 10 6657 6577, *Fax:* +86 10 6657 6502, *Email:* agency.bj@huatai-serv.com, *Website:* www.huatai-serv.com

BAILIANJING

harbour area, see under Chuansha

BAOSHAN

harbour area, see under Shanghai

BAOZHEN

harbour area, see under Chongming

BASUO

Lat 19° 6' N; Long 108° 37' E.

Admiralty Chart: 3893
Time Zone: GMT +8 h
Admiralty Pilot: 30
UNCTAD Locode: CN BAS

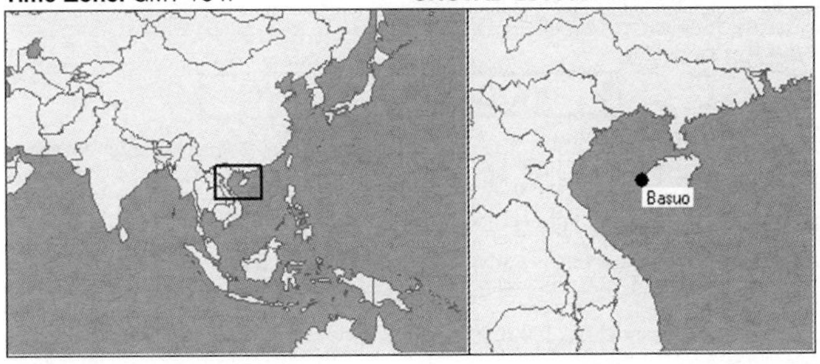

Principal Facilities:

P	Q	Y	G			B		T	

Authority: Basuo Port Administration, Haigang Road, Dongfang, Hainan Province 572600, People's Republic of China, *Tel:* +86 898 2552 2512, *Fax:* +86 898 2552 1054

Port Security: ISPS compliant

Approach: Harbour Channel 1.8 km long, 120 m wide in depth of 9 m

Anchorage: Dangerous cargo anchorage in depth of 9 m and pilot anchorage in depth of 11 m

Pilotage: Compulsory and available during daytime only. Pilot boards at the Pilot Anchorage

Radio Frequency: VHF Channel 16

Tides: Average tidal range of 1.48 m

Traffic: 2003, 4 300 000 t of cargo handled

Principal Imports and Exports: Imports: Cement, Coal, Fertilizer, Grain, Steel products, Sugar. Exports: General cargo, Local products, Ore, Silica sand.

Key to Principal Facilities:—			
A=Airport	**C**=Containers	**G**=General Cargo	**P**=Petroleum	**R**=Ro/Ro	**Y**=Dry Bulk
B=Bunkers	**D**=Dry Dock	**L**=Cruise	**Q**=Other Liquid Bulk	**T**=Towage (where available from port)	

Working Hours: 0730-1130 and 1430-1730

Accommodation:

Name	Length (m)	Depth (m)	Remarks
Basuo			
Berth No.1	175	9	Ore for vessels up to 20 000 dwt
Berth No.2	196	9	Ore for vessels up to 20 000 dwt
Berth No.3	185	9	Break bulk for vessels up to 20 000 dwt
Berth No.4	185	9	General cargo for vessels up to 20 000 dwt
Berth No.5	250	9	General cargo for vessels up to 20 000 dwt
Berth No.6	150	9	LPG for vessels up to 20 000 dwt

Storage:

Location	Open (m²)	Covered (m²)
Basuo	44357	12000

Mechanical Handling Equipment:

Location	Type	Capacity (t)	Qty
Berth No.3	Shore Cranes	10	2
Berth No.4	Shore Cranes	10	3

Towage: Two tugs available

Railway: There are railways for passenger and cargo transport from Basuo to Shilu (54 km), Hanagliu (63 km), Lingtou (50 km) and Sanya (164 km)

Lloyd's Agent: Huatai Surveyors & Adjusters Co., 14th Floor, China Re Building, No.11 Jin Rong Avenue, Xicheng District, Beijing 100140, People's Republic of China, *Tel:* +86 10 6657 6577, *Fax:* +86 10 6657 6502, *Email:* agency.bj@huatai-serv.com, *Website:* www.huatai-serv.com

BAYUQUAN

harbour area, see under Yingkou

BEIHAI

Lat 21° 27' N; Long 109° 3' E.

Admiralty Chart: 41   **Admiralty Pilot:** 30
Time Zone: GMT +8 h   **UNCTAD Locode:** CN BHY

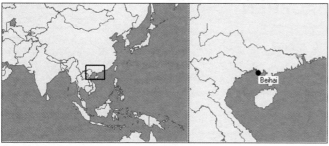

Principal Facilities:

	P		Y	G	C			B		T	

Authority: Beihai Port Group Co Ltd, 75 Haijiao Avenue, Beihai, Guangxi Province 536000, People's Republic of China, *Tel:* +86 779 303 4011, *Website:* www.bhport.cn

Port Security: ISPS compliant

Approach: The main channel extends from the Pilotage and Quarantine Anchorage and has a length of 14.6 km, width of 500-2000 m and 6-10.5 m depth. No reefs or sand bars
The Shibuling channel is 1300 m long, 90 m wide at the bottom and 6.3 m depth
The Waisha west harbour channel is approx 1200 m long, 60-80 m wide at the bottom and 2.8-3.5 m depth

Anchorage: No.1 Anchorage in depth of 9 m for vessels up to 15 000 dwt
No.2 Anchorage in depth of 7 m for vessels up to 10 000 dwt
No.3 Anchorage in depth of 5 m for vessels up to 5000 dwt

Pilotage: Compulsory and available during daytime only. Pilot boards vessel at No.1 buoy

Radio Frequency: VHF Channel 16, call sign: Beihai Radio

Tides: Average tidal range of 2.52 m

Traffic: 2005, 7 670 000 t of cargo handled

Accommodation:

Name	Length (m)	Depth (m)	Remarks
Beihai			
Berth No's 1-2	370	9.5	See [1] below
Berth No's 3-4	433	10.8-12	See [2] below

[1]*Berth No's 1-2:* General, bulk & chemical cargo for vessels up to 15 000 dwt

[2]*Berth No's 3-4:* Containers, bulk & general cargo for vessels up to 35 000 dwt

Storage:

Location	Open (m²)	Covered (m²)
Beihai	220000	21624

Mechanical Handling Equipment:

Location	Type	Capacity (t)	Qty
Berth No's 1-2	Shore Cranes	10	2
Berth No's 1-2	Shore Cranes	5	1
Berth No's 3-4	Mult-purp. Cranes	40	1
Berth No's 3-4	Shore Cranes	16	1
Berth No's 3-4	Shore Cranes	10	2

Bunkering: Available

Towage: Two tugs of 2960 hp, one tug of 720 hp and two tugs of 200 hp

Repair & Maintenance: Minor repairs available

Shipping Agents: China Marine Shipping Agency Co. Ltd, China Marine Shipping Agency Guangxi Beihai Company, Sinotrans Building, 9 Chengdu Road, Beihai, Guangxi Province 536000, People's Republic of China, *Tel:* +86 779 391 1066, *Fax:* +86 779 391 1069, *Email:* agency@gx163.net, *Website:* www.sinoagent.com
Sino-Continental, Beihai Branch, 145 Haijiao Road, Beihai, Guangxi Province 536000, People's Republic of China, *Tel:* +86 779 390 3461, *Fax:* +86 779 390 3647, *Email:* beihai@sino-continental.com, *Website:* www.sino-continental.com

Lloyd's Agent: Huatai Surveyors & Adjusters Co., 14th Floor, China Re Building, No.11 Jin Rong Avenue, Xicheng District, Beijing 100140, People's Republic of China, *Tel:* +86 10 6657 6577, *Fax:* +86 10 6657 6502, *Email:* agency.bj@huatai-serv.com, *Website:* www.huatai-serv.com

BEIJIAO

Lat 22° 54' N; Long 113° 10' E.

Admiralty Chart: -   **Admiralty Pilot:** -
Time Zone: GMT +8 h   **UNCTAD Locode:** CN BJO

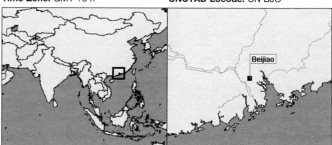

Principal Facilities:

		Y	G	C					

Authority: Beijiao Port Freight Corp. Ltd, 8 South Gangqian Road, Beijiao Town Industrial Park, Shunde, Guangdong Province, People's Republic of China, *Tel:* +86 757 2665 9068, *Fax:* +86 757 2665 2816, *Email:* info@bjport.com, *Website:* www.bjport.com

Accommodation:

Name	Length (m)	Remarks
Beijiao		
Berth	300	See [1] below

[1]*Berth:* Container, general & bulk cargo. Container yard of 80 000 m2, bulk cargo yard of 15 000 m2 and warehouses totaling 8000 m2

Mechanical Handling Equipment:

Location	Type	Capacity (t)	Qty
Beijiao	Mult-purp. Cranes	10–40	6
Beijiao	Reach Stackers	45	2
Beijiao	Forklifts	2–25	

Lloyd's Agent: Huatai Surveyors & Adjusters Co., Room 802, Jun Yuan Mansion, 155 Tian He East Road, Guangzhou, Guangdong Province 510620, People's Republic of China, *Tel:* +86 20 3881 2306, *Fax:* +86 20 3881 2470, *Email:* agency.gz@huatai-serv.com, *Website:* www.huatai-serv.com

BEILIANG

Lat 38° 58' N; Long 121° 48' E.

Admiralty Chart: 1255/3694   **Admiralty Pilot:** 32
Time Zone: GMT +8 h   **UNCTAD Locode:** CN

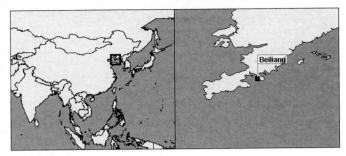

Principal Facilities:

P	Q	Y	G	C				T	

Authority: Beiliang Group, 50 Lu Xun Road, Zhongshan District, Dalian, Liaoning Province 116001, People's Republic of China, *Tel:* +86 411 8270 8238, *Fax:* +86 411 8270 9318, *Website:* www.beiliang.com

Port Security: ISPS compliant

Approach: The main navigation fairway has a depth of 13.5-15.1 m

Pilotage: Compulsory

Accommodation:

Name	Length (m)	Depth (m)	Remarks
Beiliang			See [1] below
Berth No.1	192	12.4	See [2] below
Berth No.2	350.5	15.8	See [3] below
Berth No's 3 & 4		12.4	See [4] below
Berth No.5	242	12.4	See [5] below
Berth No.6	242	12.4	See [6] below
Oil Wharf			See [7] below
Berth No's 7 & 10	269		For tankers of 1000-30 000 dwt
Berth No's 8 & 9	376		See [8] below

[1]*Beiliang:* Vegetable oil wharf equipped with six loading arms, handling crude soybean oil, palm oil, rapeseed oil etc for tankers up to 30 000 dwt. There are four pipelines connecting the wharf, with a nominal diameter of 300 mm each. The max load/discharge rate is 1600 t/h. 29 storage tanks offer a total storage cap of 153 800 m3

[2]*Berth No.1:* Multi-purpose berth including containers for vessels up to 50 000 dwt. Container freight station of 11 ha with 84 reefer points

[3]*Berth No.2:* Bulk & general cargo for vessels up to 80 000 dwt. Grain is discharged at max rate of 2000 t/h by two shipunloaders. There are a total of 274 grain silos with a total storage cap up to 1 500 000 t

[4]*Berth No's 3 & 4:* Bulk cargo for vessels up to 50 000 dwt with two shiploaders providing max loading cap of 4000 t/h

[5]*Berth No.5:* Bulk & general cargo with two shiploaders providing max loading cap of 2000 t/h

[6]*Berth No.6:* Bulk & general cargo with two shiploaders providing max loading cap of 2000 t/h

[7]*Oil Wharf:* Petrochemical wharf operated by Dalian Beiliang Petrochemical Co Ltd (BLPC), Beiliang Port Economic & Technological Development Zone, Dalian, Tel: +86 411 8899 9119, Fax: +86 411 8733 6058, Email: shihua@beiliang.com, Website: www.beiliangshihua.com
Consists of nineteen loading arms on four berths capable of handling such oil products as gasoline, diesel, naphtha, kerosene, fuel oil and LPG

[8]*Berth No's 8 & 9:* Berth No.8 for tankers of 10 000-100 000 dwt and Berth No.9 for tankers of 5000-50 000 dwt

Storage:

Location
Beiliang

Mechanical Handling Equipment:

Location	Type	Capacity (t)	Qty	Remarks
Beiliang	Container Cranes	40	1	at berth 1
Beiliang	Shore Cranes	40	2	at berth 1
Beiliang	Shore Cranes	10–16	4	at berths 5 & 6

Towage: Two tugs available of 3400 hp

Airport: International Airport, 35 km

Railway: There are two rail tracks connecting with the container freight station

Lloyd's Agent: Huatai Surveyors & Adjusters Co., 14th Floor, China Re Building, No.11 Jin Rong Avenue, Xicheng District, Beijing 100140, People's Republic of China, *Tel:* +86 10 6657 6577, *Fax:* +86 10 6657 6502, *Email:* agency.bj@huatai-serv.com, *Website:* www.huatai-serv.com

BEILUN

harbour area, see under Ningbo

BEIMEN

harbour area, see under Ezhou

BEIPEI

Lat 29° 49' N; Long 106° 26' E.

Admiralty Chart: -	**Admiralty Pilot:** -
Time Zone: GMT +8 h	**UNCTAD Locode:** CN

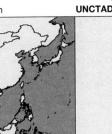

Principal Facilities:

	Y	G				T	

Accommodation:

Name	Remarks
Beipei	See [1] below

[1]*Beipei:* Consists of nineteen berths handling grain, cement, timber, coal, construction materials and non-metallic ores

Storage:

Location	Open (m²)	Covered (m²)
Beipei	37800	680

Mechanical Handling Equipment:

Location	Type	Capacity (t)
Beipei	Mult-purp. Cranes	15

Towage: Available

Lloyd's Agent: Huatai Surveyors & Adjusters Co., 14th Floor, China Re Building, No.11 Jin Rong Avenue, Xicheng District, Beijing 100140, People's Republic of China, *Tel:* +86 10 6657 6577, *Fax:* +86 10 6657 6502, *Email:* agency.bj@huatai-serv.com, *Website:* www.huatai-serv.com

BENGBU

Lat 32° 56' N; Long 117° 21' E.

Admiralty Chart: -	**Admiralty Pilot:** -
Time Zone: GMT +8 h	**UNCTAD Locode:** CN BFU

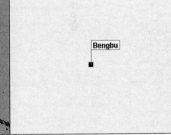

Principal Facilities:

P		Y	G				T	

Authority: Bengbu Harbour Administration, 1 Shengping Street, Central District, Bengbu, Anhui Province 233000, People's Republic of China

Accommodation:

Name	Remarks
Bengbu	Consists of twenty two berths handling grain, coal, petroleum, iron & steel and fertilisers

Storage:

Location	Covered (m²)	Sheds / Warehouses
Bengbu	23181	5

Mechanical Handling Equipment:

Location	Type	Capacity (t)
Bengbu	Mult-purp. Cranes	20

Towage: Available

Lloyd's Agent: Huatai Surveyors & Adjusters Co., 14th Floor, China Re Building, No.11 Jin Rong Avenue, Xicheng District, Beijing 100140, People's Republic of China, *Tel:* +86 10 6657 6577, *Fax:* +86 10 6657 6502, *Email:* agency.bj@huatai-serv.com, *Website:* www.huatai-serv.com

Key to Principal Facilities:—				
A=Airport	**C**=Containers	**G**=General Cargo	**P**=Petroleum	**R**=Ro/Ro	**Y**=Dry Bulk
B=Bunkers	**D**=Dry Dock	**L**=Cruise	**Q**=Other Liquid Bulk	**T**=Towage (where available from port)	

BINHAI

Lat 34° 0' N; Long 119° 50' E.

Admiralty Chart: 1253   **Admiralty Pilot:** 32
Time Zone: GMT +8 h   **UNCTAD Locode:** CN

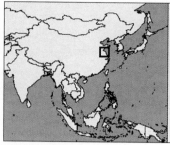

Principal Facilities:

P		Y	G							

Authority: Binhai Harbour Administration, 143 Fudong Zhong Road, Binhai, Jiangsu Province 224500, People's Republic of China

Accommodation:

Name	Remarks
Binhai	See [1] below

[1]*Binhai:* There are numerous berths for vessels up to 200 dwt handling coal, petroleum, salt, grain and general cargo

Storage: Open and covered storage areas available

Mechanical Handling Equipment:

Location	Type	Capacity (t)
Binhai	Mult-purp. Cranes	5

Lloyd's Agent: Huatai Surveyors & Adjusters Co., 14th Floor, China Re Building, No.11 Jin Rong Avenue, Xicheng District, Beijing 100140, People's Republic of China, *Tel:* +86 10 6657 6577, *Fax:* +86 10 6657 6502, *Email:* agency.bj@huatai-serv.com, *Website:* www.huatai-serv.com

BOZHONG FIELD

Admiralty Chart: 1250   **Admiralty Pilot:** 32
Time Zone: GMT +8 h   **UNCTAD Locode:** CN

Principal Facilities:

P										

Anchorage: BZ 25-1 Terminal: The anchorage area is contained within the following coordinates:
38° 18' 12" N; 119° 12' 24" E
38° 19' 00" N; 119° 13' 12" E
38° 20' 30" N; 119° 11' 36" E
38° 19' 42" N; 119° 10' 48" E
BZ 34 Terminal: The anchorage area is contained within the following coordinates:
38° 16' N; 119° 41' E
38° 16' N; 119° 44' E
38° 13' N; 119° 41' E
38° 13' N; 119° 44' E

Pilotage: Compulsory

Radio Frequency: BZ 25-1 Terminal: Listening on VHF Channel 16 and working on VHF Channel 67
BZ 34 Terminal keeps a continuous dual watch on VHF Channels 67 and 16 throughout 24 h

Accommodation:

Name	Remarks
BZ 25-1 Terminal	See [1] below
BZ 34 Terminal	See [2] below

[1]*BZ 25-1 Terminal:* In pos 38° 14' N; 119° 09' E. Operated by China Offshore Oil Bohai Corporation, Tel: +86 22 2580 1700, Fax: +86 22 2580 9547
Consists of six wellheads and the FPSO 'Hai Yang Shi You 113', moored in approx depth of 18 m and has a storage cap of 973 300 bbls of crude oil. Vessels of 40 000-120 000 dwt can be accommodated with berthing/unberthing during daylight hours only
[2]*BZ 34 Terminal:* In pos 38° 07' N; 119° 33' E. Operated by Japan China Oil Development Corporation (JCODC), Tel: +86 22 2579 2081, Fax: +86 22 2579 2078
Consists of three wellhead platforms, a fixed tower SPM and FPSU 'Bohai Chang Qing Hao', moored in a depth of 17.6 m, accommodating vessels of 15 000-110 000 dwt. Mooring/unberthing during daylight hours only

Lloyd's Agent: Huatai Surveyors & Adjusters Co., 14th Floor, China Re Building, No.11 Jin Rong Avenue, Xicheng District, Beijing 100140, People's Republic of China, *Tel:* +86 10 6657 6577, *Fax:* +86 10 6657 6502, *Email:* agency.bj@huatai-serv.com, *Website:* www.huatai-serv.com

BZ 25-1 TERMINAL

harbour area, see under Bozhong Field

BZ 34 TERMINAL

harbour area, see under Bozhong Field

CANTON

former name, see Guangzhou

CAOFEIDIAN

Lat 38° 55' N; Long 118° 30' E.

Admiralty Chart: 1250   **Admiralty Pilot:** 32
Time Zone: GMT +8 h   **UNCTAD Locode:** CN
Principal Facilities:

P										

Accommodation:

Name	Remarks
Caofeidian Field	
CFD 11 Terminal	See [1] below

[1]*CFD 11 Terminal:* Operated by China Offshore Oil Bohai Corp., P O Box 501, Tanggu District, Tianjin 300456, Tel: +86 22 2580 1700, Fax: +86 22 2580 9547
In pos 38° 46' N; 118° 42' E. Consists of ten wellheads, two wellhead platforms and FPSO 'Hai Yang Shi You 112', in depth of approx 20-24 m, exporting crude oil and accommodating vessels of 30 000-150 000 dwt. Storage cap of 990 000 bbls. Berthing/unberthing during daylight hours only
The anchorage area is contained within the following coordinates:
38° 45' 32" N; 118° 44' 19" E
38° 45' 32" N; 118° 45' 41" E
38° 44' 28" N; 118° 45' 41" E
38° 44' 28" N; 118° 44' 19" E
The FPSO listens on VHF Channel 16 and works on VHF Channel 67

Development: Plans are for:
Two 300 000 t oil berths
Sixteen coal berths, each able to handle 50 000-100 000 t at a time
Four ore berths with cap of 250 000-400 000 t
One LNG berth

Lloyd's Agent: Huatai Surveyors & Adjusters Co., 14th Floor, China Re Building, No.11 Jin Rong Avenue, Xicheng District, Beijing 100140, People's Republic of China, *Tel:* +86 10 6657 6577, *Fax:* +86 10 6657 6502, *Email:* agency.bj@huatai-serv.com, *Website:* www.huatai-serv.com

CAOFEIDIAN FIELD

see under Caofeidian

CFD 11 TERMINAL

harbour area, see under Caofeidian

CHANGDE

Lat 29° 2' N; Long 111° 40' E.

Admiralty Chart: -   **Admiralty Pilot:** -
Time Zone: GMT +8 h   **UNCTAD Locode:** CN CDE

Principal Facilities:

		Y	G					A

Authority: Changde Harbour Administration, Dahe Street, Changde, Hunan Province 415000, People's Republic of China

Accommodation:

Name	Remarks
Changde	See [1] below

[1]*Changde:* Consists of eight operational areas: Daximen, Jiaje, Lolukou, Central District, Yanguan, Nanzhan, Deshan and Daguxiang
Cargoes handled include grain, coal, fertiliser and construction materials

Storage: Open and covered storage areas available

Towage: Available

Airport: Doumuhu Airport

Lloyd's Agent: Huatai Surveyors & Adjusters Co., 14th Floor, China Re Building, No.11 Jin Rong Avenue, Xicheng District, Beijing 100140, People's Republic of China, *Tel:* +86 10 6657 6577, *Fax:* +86 10 6657 6502, *Email:* agency.bj@huatai-serv.com, *Website:* www.huatai-serv.com

CHANGJIAGANG

former name, see Zhangjiagang

CHANGJIANG

harbour area, see under Lanxi

CHANGSHA

Lat 28° 11' N; Long 112° 58' E.

Admiralty Chart: 2947	**Admiralty Pilot:** 32
Time Zone: GMT +8 h	**UNCTAD Locode:** CN CSX

Principal Facilities:

	P		Y	G	C				A	

Authority: Changsha Harbour Administration Bureau, 82 Wuyi Xi Road, Changsha, Hunan Province 410005, People's Republic of China

Accommodation:

Name	Remarks
Changsha	Cargoes handled at the port include grain, coal, fertiliser, ores and salt

Storage: Open and covered storage areas available

Shipping Agents: CMA-CGM S.A., CMA CGM Changsha, Room 807, Yada Times Square, 456 Wuyi Road (E), Changsha, Hunan Province 410100, People's Republic of China, *Tel:* +86 731 233 8868, *Fax:* +86 731 233 8865, *Email:* scx.genmbox@cma-cgm.com, *Website:* www.cma-cgm.com

Airport: Changsha Huanghua International Airport

Lloyd's Agent: Huatai Surveyors & Adjusters Co., 14th Floor, China Re Building, No.11 Jin Rong Avenue, Xicheng District, Beijing 100140, People's Republic of China, *Tel:* +86 10 6657 6577, *Fax:* +86 10 6657 6502, *Email:* agency.bj@huatai-serv.com, *Website:* www.huatai-serv.com

CHANGSHOU TERMINAL

harbour area, see under Chongqing

CHANGSHU

Lat 31° 38' N; Long 120° 44' E.

Admiralty Chart: -	**Admiralty Pilot:** 32
Time Zone: GMT +8 h	**UNCTAD Locode:** CN CGU

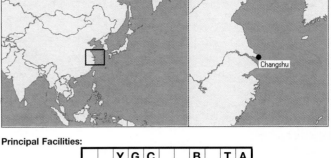

Principal Facilities:

	Y	G	C		B		T	A

Authority: Changshu Xinghua Port Co Ltd, No.1 Xinghua Gangqu, Changshu, Jiangsu Prov. 215513, People's Republic of China, *Tel:* +86 512 5269 5858, *Fax:* +86 512 5269 5072, *Email:* fang.wang@cxp.com.cn, *Website:* www.cxp.com.cn

Port Security: ISPS compliant

Anchorage: Quarantine anchorage in pos 31° 47' 05" N; 120° 54' 57" E in depth of 8.5 m

Pilotage: Compulsory. Pilot boards at Baoshan Anchorage

Radio Frequency: VHF Channel 20

Tides: Max 5.75 m, min 0.36 m

Maximum Vessel Dimensions: 50 000 dwt

Accommodation:

Name	Length (m)	Depth (m)	Remarks
Changshu			
Changshu Xinghua Berths	1500	13	See [1] below

[1]*Changshu Xinghua Berths:* Eight berths for vessels up to 50 000 dwt handling containers, general cargo, breakbulk, refrigerated, project, liquid & dangerous cargoes

Storage: Container yard for up to 2500 TEU's. Warehousing available

Location	Open (m²)	Covered (m²)
Changshu	159050	36370

Mechanical Handling Equipment:

Location	Type
Changshu Xinghua Berths	Container Cranes
Changshu Xinghua Berths	Reach Stackers
Changshu Xinghua Berths	Forklifts

Bunkering: Available

Towage: Three tugs of 3200 hp

Ship Chandlers: Changshu Ocean Shipping Supply Co. Ltd, Room 911, Binjiang International Building, 88 Tonggang Road, Changshu, Jiangsu Prov. 215513, People's Republic of China, *Tel:* +86 512 5152 3030, *Fax:* +86 512 5229 5911, *Email:* cssupso@hotmail.com

Shipping Agents: China Marine Shipping Agency Co. Ltd, China Marine Shipping Agency Jiangsu Changshu Company Limited, 2nd Floor, Tower B, Changshu Port United Inspection Service Ctr, Xinghua Port Area, Changshu, Jiangsu Prov., People's Republic of China, *Tel:* +86 512 5229 1901, *Fax:* +86 512 5229 1901, *Email:* changshu@sinoagent.com
Pen-Wallem Shipping Services Co Ltd, Changshu, Jiangsu Prov., People's Republic of China, *Tel:* +86 512 5229 0350, *Fax:* +86 512 5229 0359, *Email:* wallemschu@pen-wallem.com, *Website:* www.pen-wallem.com
Tongsheng International Shipping Agencies, Changshu Tongsheng International Shipping Agency Co Ltd, 4-B Floor, Commercial Center Economic Development Zone, 27 Fenglin Road, Changshu, Jiangsu Prov. 215500, People's Republic of China, *Tel:* +86 512 5286 8029, *Fax:* +86 512 5286 8033, *Email:* changshu@tongsheng.net.cn, *Website:* www.tongshengshipping.com

Airport: Wuxi Airport, 55 km

Lloyd's Agent: Huatai Surveyors & Adjusters Co., 14th Floor, China Re Building, No.11 Jin Rong Avenue, Xicheng District, Beijing 100140, People's Republic of China, *Tel:* +86 10 6657 6577, *Fax:* +86 10 6657 6502, *Email:* agency.bj@huatai-serv.com, *Website:* www.huatai-serv.com

CHANGZHOU

Lat 23° 3' N; Long 113° 25' E.

Admiralty Chart: -	**Admiralty Pilot:** 32
Time Zone: GMT +8 h	**UNCTAD Locode:** CN CZX

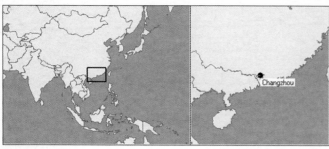

Principal Facilities:

		Y	G	C		B		T	A

Authority: Changzhou Port Co Ltd., Administration Office, Weitang Town New District, Changzhou, Jiangsu Province 213128, People's Republic of China, *Tel:* +86 519 8577 0881

Port Security: ISPS compliant

Pilotage: Compulsory

Radio Frequency: VHF Channels 6 and 16

Tides: Average tidal range of 2 m

Traffic: 2005, 3 890 000 t of cargo handled, 33 200 TEU's

Accommodation:

Name	Length (m)	Depth (m)	Remarks
Changzhou			
Changzhou Terminal	327	11	See [1] below

[1]*Changzhou Terminal:* Four berths handling bulk, container & general cargo for vessels up to 45 000 dwt

Storage:

Location	Open (m²)	Covered (m²)
Changzhou	150000	6000

Mechanical Handling Equipment:

Location	Type	Capacity (t)	Qty
Changzhou Terminal	Shore Cranes	5–40	4

Bunkering: Available

Towage: One tug of 1960 hp

Shipping Agents: China Marine Shipping Agency Co. Ltd, China Marine Shipping Agency Changzhou Company Limited, 101 Customs Building, 85 Hehai Mid Road, Xinbei District, Changzhou, Jiangsu Province 213022, People's Republic of China, *Tel:* +86 519 8513 6680, *Fax:* +86 519 8513 6690, *Email:* sinoagtcz@pub.cz.jsinfo.net, *Website:* www.sinoagent.com

Airport: Changzhou Airport

Lloyd's Agent: Huatai Surveyors & Adjusters Co., 14th Floor, China Re Building, No.11 Jin Rong Avenue, Xicheng District, Beijing 100140, People's Republic of China, *Tel:* +86 10 6657 6577, *Fax:* +86 10 6657 6502, *Email:* agency.bj@huatai-serv.com, *Website:* www.huatai-serv.com

CHAOTIANMEN TERMINAL

harbour area, see under Chongqing

CHAOZHOU

Lat 23° 37' N; Long 117° 6' E.

Admiralty Chart: 854	**Admiralty Pilot:** 32
Time Zone: GMT +8 h	**UNCTAD Locode:** CN COZ

Principal Facilities:

P		Y	G	C				A

Port Security: ISPS compliant

Pilotage: Compulsory for all foreign vessels, Tel: +86 768 780 8182, Fax: +86 768 780 8182. Pilot boards in the following positions:
a) Datang Coal Terminal in pos 23° 31.00' N; 117° 09.00' E
b) Saibaimen Gangwu Working Zone in pos 23° 31.50' N; 117° 06.50' E
c) Huafeng Huyu LPG Terminal in pos 23° 30.50' N; 117° 11.00' E

Radio Frequency: VHF Channel 16

Accommodation:

Name	Remarks
Chaozhou	
Sanbaimen	See [1] below
Zhelin	See [2] below

[1]*Sanbaimen:* Seven docks consisting of a 50 000 t gas dock, a 5000 t container dock, a 5000 t gas dock, a 3000 t grain dock, a 1000 t container dock, a 5000 t multi-purpose freight dock and a coal dock
[2]*Zhelin:* Consists of a 500 t dock for seafood, two 16 000 t anchorage grounds and a 50 000 t gas dock

Airport: Shantou Airport, 30 km

Lloyd's Agent: Huatai Surveyors & Adjusters Co., 14th Floor, China Re Building, No.11 Jin Rong Avenue, Xicheng District, Beijing 100140, People's Republic of China, *Tel:* +86 10 6657 6577, *Fax:* +86 10 6657 6502, *Email:* agency.bj@huatai-serv.com, *Website:* www.huatai-serv.com

CHEFOO

former name, see Yantai

CHENGLINGJI

Lat 29° 26' N; Long 113° 8' E.

Admiralty Chart: 2947	**Admiralty Pilot:** 32
Time Zone: GMT +8 h	**UNCTAD Locode:** CN CLJ

Principal Facilities:

	Q	Y	G	C		B		T	

Authority: Chenglingji Port (Group) Ltd., Port Administration Office, 2 Changjiang Road, Yueyang, Hunan Province 414002, People's Republic of China, *Tel:* +86 730 856 1761

Anchorage: Lu Xi Zhou Anchorage in pos 29° 28' N; 113° 28' E in depth of 5 m

Pilotage: Compulsory

Radio Frequency: VHF Channel 14

Traffic: 2005, 9 350 000 t of cargo handled, 68 000 TEU's

Accommodation:

Name	Length (m)	Depth (m)	Remarks
Chenglingji			See [1] below
Main Cargo Terminal	752	10	Thirty three berths for vessels up to 5000 dwt
Foreign Trade Wharf	320	5.5	Two berths for vessels up to 5000 dwt

[1]*Chenglingji:* Main cargoes include petroleum, ores, coal steel & agricultural products

Storage: Container yard cap of 1500 TEU's

Location	Open (m²)	Covered (m²)
Chenglingji	90136	10500

Mechanical Handling Equipment:

Location	Type	Capacity (t)	Qty
Chenglingji	Shore Cranes	15	1
Chenglingji	Shore Cranes	40	1

Bunkering: Available

Towage: Four 500 hp tugs and one 300 hp tug

Airport: Changsha Huanghua International Airport, 135 km

Lloyd's Agent: Huatai Surveyors & Adjusters Co., 14th Floor, China Re Building, No.11 Jin Rong Avenue, Xicheng District, Beijing 100140, People's Republic of China, *Tel:* +86 10 6657 6577, *Fax:* +86 10 6657 6502, *Email:* agency.bj@huatai-serv.com, *Website:* www.huatai-serv.com

CHINKIANG

former name, see Zhenjiang

CHINWANGTAO

former name, see Qinhuangdao

CHIWAN

Lat 22° 28' N; Long 113° 53' E.

Admiralty Chart: 342/343	**Admiralty Pilot:** 30
Time Zone: GMT +8 h	**UNCTAD Locode:** CN CWN

赤湾集装箱码头有限公司
CHIWAN CONTAINER TERMINAL
SHENZHEN CHINA
WWW.CWCCT.COM

YOUR MOST ESTABLISHED GATEWAY
TO AND FROM SOUTH CHINA

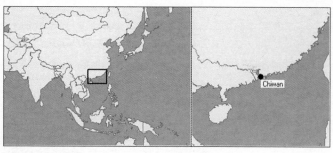

Principal Facilities:

	Y	G	C		B		T	

Authority: Shenzhen Chiwan Wharf Holdings Ltd, Chiwan, Shenzhen, Guangdong Province 518068, People's Republic of China, *Tel:* +86 755 2669 4222, *Fax:* +86 755 2668 4117, *Website:* www.szcwh.com

Port Security: ISPS compliant. Container Security Initiative (CSI) designated port

Pre-Arrival Information: Vessel's should send ETA 72 h, 48 h and 24 h in advance

Approach: Chiwan approach channel 1 km long in depth of 12.5 m. Kaifeng approach channel in depth of 13 m

Anchorage: Good anchorage can be obtained in four designated areas in depths ranging from 7 m to 13 m

Pilotage: Compulsory. Pilot boards in pos 22° 23' 40" N; 113° 53' 65" E (Urnston Roads) and 22° 18' 98" N; 113° 50' 26" E (Longguxi Hangdao)

Radio Frequency: VHF Channels 11 and 73

Tides: Average tidal range of 1.36 m

Traffic: 2006, 5 260 000 TEU's handled at Chiwan Container Terminal

Accommodation:

Name	Length (m)	Depth (m)	Draught (m)	Remarks
Chiwan				
Berth No.1	180	9.6		Max 15 000 dwt. Bulk & general cargo
Berth No.2	200	10.6		Max 25 000 dwt. Bulk & general cargo
Berth No.3	70	8.6		Max 15 000 dwt. General cargo
Berth No.4	66	8.6		Max 15 000 dwt. General cargo
Berth No.5	216	12.5		Max 35 000 dwt. Bulk & general cargo
Berth No.6	218	12.5		Max 35 000 dwt. Bulk & general cargo
Berth No.7	300	13		Max 60 000 dwt. Bulk & general cargo
Berth No.8	270	13		See [1] below
Chiwan Container Terminal				See [2] below
Berth No.9	325	14–16	14.5	Max 65 000 dwt. Container cargo
Berth No.10	325	14–16	14.5	Max 65 000 dwt. Container cargo
Berth No.11	350	15		Max 65 000 dwt. Container cargo
Berth No.12		16		Container cargo

[1]*Berth No.8:* Max 60 000 dwt. Container, bulk & general cargo
[2]*Chiwan Container Terminal:* Chiwan Container Terminal Co Ltd., 11th Floor, Marine Building Chiwan, Shenzhen 518068, Tel: +86 755 2669 4168, Fax: +86 755 2669 4435, Email: wuzm@cwcct.com, Website: www.cwcct.com
Stacking yard of 450 000 m2 with cap for 55 000 TEU's. 666 reefer points

Storage:

Location	Covered (m²)
Chiwan	156000

Mechanical Handling Equipment:

Location	Type	Capacity (t)	Qty
Chiwan	Mult-purp. Cranes	40	
Chiwan Container Terminal	Post Panamax	40.5–60	35
Chiwan Container Terminal	RTG's		108

Bunkering: Available

Towage: Five tugs up to 3000 hp are available
Shenzhen Chiwan Shipping Co, 5/F, Building B1, Chiwan Port Area, Chiwan, People's Republic of China, *Tel:* +86 755 2681 7313, *Fax:* +86 755 2669 4243

Shipping Agents: Atlanta Shipping Agency Ltd, Room 202, Chiwan Harbour, Container Office Building, Chiwan, People's Republic of China, *Tel:* +86 755 2669 4896, *Fax:* +86 755 2669 4854, *Email:* jessiechang@atlanta.com.mo

Railway: A railway links the port to the Guangzhou-Shenzhen railway and the national rail network

Development: All bulk cargo operations will be moved out of Chiwan Port to nearby Humen Port, making Chiwan a 100% container port

Lloyd's Agent: Huatai Surveyors & Adjusters Co., Room 802, Jun Yuan Mansion, 155 Tian He East Road, Guangzhou, Guangdong Province 510620, People's Republic of China, *Tel:* +86 20 3881 2306, *Fax:* +86 20 3881 2470, *Email:* agency.gz@huatai-serv.com, *Website:* www.huatai-serv.com

CHIZHOU

Lat 30° 39' N; Long 117° 27' E.

Admiralty Chart: 2947	**Admiralty Pilot:** 32
Time Zone: GMT +8 h	**UNCTAD Locode:** CN

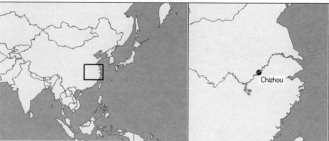

Principal Facilities:

	Y	G	C		B		T	

Authority: Chizhou Port Corp., 88 Qi jiang North Road, Guichi City, Anhui Province 247000, People's Republic of China, *Tel:* +86 566 212 1992, *Fax:* +86 566 212 1992, *Email:* czgqhb01@126.com, *Website:* www.czport.com

Port Security: ISPS compliant

Anchorage: Nizhou Anchorage in depth of 10-22 m

Pilotage: Compulsory. Pilot boards at Wu Songkou

Radio Frequency: VHF Channel 14

Traffic: 2005, 3 830 000 t of cargo handled

Accommodation:

Name	Length (m)	Depth (m)	Remarks
Chizhou			
Laogang Terminal	1740	8	Eleven berths for vessels up to 5000 dwt
Jiangkou Terminal	460	9	Two berths for vessels up to 5000 dwt

Storage:

Location	Open (m²)	Covered (m²)
Chizhou	204200	12200

Mechanical Handling Equipment:

Location	Type	Capacity (t)	Qty
Chizhou	Floating Cranes	15	1

Bunkering: Available

Towage: Four tugs available

Shipping Agents: China Marine Shipping Agency Co. Ltd, China Marine Shipping Agency Anhui Chizhou Company, No. 99 Donghu Road, Guichi City, Anhui Province, People's Republic of China, *Tel:* +86 566 551 4191, *Fax:* +86 566 551 4193, *Email:* sinotrans@mail.hf.ah.cn

Lloyd's Agent: Huatai Surveyors & Adjusters Co., 14th Floor, China Re Building, No.11 Jin Rong Avenue, Xicheng District, Beijing 100140, People's Republic of China, *Tel:* +86 10 6657 6577, *Fax:* +86 10 6657 6502, *Email:* agency.bj@huatai-serv.com, *Website:* www.huatai-serv.com

CHONGMING

Lat 31° 37' N; Long 121° 23' E.

Admiralty Chart: -	**Admiralty Pilot:** 32
Time Zone: GMT +8 h	**UNCTAD Locode:** CN CMG

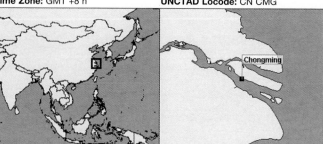

Principal Facilities:

		Y	G					

Authority: Chongming Shipping Administration, 59 Nanmen Road, Chongming County, Shanghai, Shanghai Province 202150, People's Republic of China

Accommodation:

Name	Remarks
Chongming	See [1] below

[1]*Chongming:* Consists of five harbour areas: Baozhen, Xinhe, Nanmen, Xinjian and Niupeng
Cargoes handled include coal, ores, general cargo, timber and iron & steel

Storage: Open and covered storage areas are available

Lloyd's Agent: Huatai Surveyors & Adjusters Co., 14th Floor, China Re Building, No.11 Jin Rong Avenue, Xicheng District, Beijing 100140, People's Republic of China, *Tel:* +86 10 6657 6577, *Fax:* +86 10 6657 6502, *Email:* agency.bj@huatai-serv.com, *Website:* www.huatai-serv.com

CHONGQING

Lat 29° 34' N; Long 106° 35' E.

Admiralty Chart: -   **Admiralty Pilot:** -
Time Zone: GMT +8 h   **UNCTAD Locode:** CN CKG

Principal Facilities:

	Y	G	C	R			T		

Authority: Chongqing Port (Group) Co Ltd., 18 Xinyi Street, Yuzhongqu District, Chongqing, Sichuan Province, People's Republic of China, *Tel:* +86 23 6383 5551, *Fax:* +86 23 6383 7693, *Website:* www.cqg.com.cn

Approach: Draft limitation in channel 2.7-2.9 m

Radio Frequency: VHF Channel 16

Traffic: 2005, 9 500 000 t of cargo handled, 170 100 TEU's

Principal Imports and Exports: Imports: Fertilizer, General cargo, Grain, Ore, Petroleum. Exports: Coal, Local products, Pig iron.

Accommodation:

Name	Depth (m)	Remarks
Jiulongpo Terminal		
Wharf 1	2.9	
Wharf 2	4	
Wharf 3	4	
Wharf 4	4	
Wharf 5	4	
Wharf 6	4	
Wharf 7	4	
Oil Wharf	4	
Miscellaneous Wharf	4	
Container Wharf	4	
Lanjiantuo Terminal		
Scrap Goods Wharf	2.9	
General Cargo Wharf	2.9	
Mao'ertuo Terminal		
Phosphorite Wharf	4	
General Cargo Wharf	4	
Dangerous Cargo Wharf	4	
Chaotianmen Terminal		
Hongyanku	4	
Passenger Wharf	4	
Cuntan International Container Terminal		
Berths	5	Three 3000 dwt berths & a ro/ro terminal
Jiangbei Terminal		
Dayuwan	2.9	
Wailiang	4	
Hexinguobo	4	
Changshou Terminal		
Baishawan	4	
Yangjiaobao	5	

Mechanical Handling Equipment:

Location	Type	Capacity (t)	Qty
Jiulongpo Terminal	Mult-purp. Cranes	180	34
Lanjiantuo Terminal	Mult-purp. Cranes	16	12
Mao'ertuo Terminal	Mult-purp. Cranes	16	5
Chaotianmen Terminal	Mult-purp. Cranes	5	2
Jiangbei Terminal	Mult-purp. Cranes	16	3
Changshou Terminal	Mult-purp. Cranes	3	2

Towage: Eleven tugs available from 160-1960 hp

Shipping Agents: CMA-CGM S.A., CMA CGM Chongqing, 2102A Metropolitan Tower, 68 Zourong Road, Central District, Chongqing, Sichuan Province 400010, People's Republic of China, *Tel:* +86 23 6380 9822, *Fax:* +86 23 6380 0469, *Email:* cqh.genmbox@cma-cgm.com, *Website:* www.cma-cgm.com
K Line Ship Management Co. Ltd., 'K' Line (China) Ltd, Room 3012 Metropolitan Tower, 68 Zourong Road, Yuzhong District, Chongqing, Sichuan Province 400012, People's Republic of China, *Tel:* +86 23 6372 5550, *Fax:* +86 23 6372 5551, *Website:* www.kline.co.jp
Young Carrier Co. Ltd., Room 1107, 68 Zou Rong Road, Chongqing, Sichuan Province 400010, People's Republic of China, *Tel:* +86 23 6380 5671, *Fax:* +86 23 6380 5670, *Email:* spike.li@yml.com.cn, *Website:* www.yml.com.cn

Surveyors: China Classification Society, No.6, 3rd Xiang Shanxi Road, Chongqing, Sichuan Province 400011, People's Republic of China, *Tel:* +86 23 6382 7124, *Fax:* +86 23 6384 2535, *Email:* ccscq@ccs.org.cn, *Website:* www.ccs.org.cn

Development: Three more 3000 dwt container berths and a further ro/ro terminal to be onstructed at Cuntan International Container Terminal and is scheduled for completion in 2009
Shanghai International Port Group is to build a 13-berth terminal in Chongqing. The project in the Chayuan port area includes the construction of twelve 3000 t multi-purpose berths and a ro/ro terminal

Lloyd's Agent: Huatai Surveyors & Adjusters Co., 14th Floor, China Re Building, No.11 Jin Rong Avenue, Xicheng District, Beijing 100140, People's Republic of China, *Tel:* +86 10 6657 6577, *Fax:* +86 10 6657 6502, *Email:* agency.bj@huatai-serv.com, *Website:* www.huatai-serv.com

CHUANSHA

Lat 31° 12' N; Long 121° 41' E.

Admiralty Chart: 1199   **Admiralty Pilot:** 32
Time Zone: GMT +8 h   **UNCTAD Locode:** CN

Principal Facilities:

	Y	G						

Authority: Chuansha Shipping Administration, 5219 Shangchuan Road, Chuansha County, Shanghai, Shanghai Province 201200, People's Republic of China

Accommodation:

Name	Remarks
Chuansha	See [1] below

[1]*Chuansha:* Consists of six harbour areas: Bailianjing, Chusha Town, Chuanyanghe, Donggou, Gaoqiao and Yangjing
Cargoes handled include ores, coal and general cargo

Storage: Open and covered storage areas available

Lloyd's Agent: Huatai Surveyors & Adjusters Co., 14th Floor, China Re Building, No.11 Jin Rong Avenue, Xicheng District, Beijing 100140, People's Republic of China, *Tel:* +86 10 6657 6577, *Fax:* +86 10 6657 6502, *Email:* agency.bj@huatai-serv.com, *Website:* www.huatai-serv.com

CHUANYANGHE

harbour area, see under Chuansha

DA CHAN BAY

Lat 22° 33' N; Long 113° 52' E.

Admiralty Chart: -   **Admiralty Pilot:** 30
Time Zone: GMT +8 h   **UNCTAD Locode:** CN

Key to Principal Facilities:—
A=Airport   **C**=Containers   **G**=General Cargo   **P**=Petroleum   **R**=Ro/Ro   **Y**=Dry Bulk
B=Bunkers   **D**=Dry Dock   **L**=Cruise   **Q**=Other Liquid Bulk   **T**=Towage (where available from port)

Da Chan Bay Terminal One
大铲湾码头（一期）

YOUR NO. 1 CHOICE FOR
CONTAINER TERMINAL FACILITIES IN SOUTH CHINA

华 南 首 选 集 装 箱 码 头

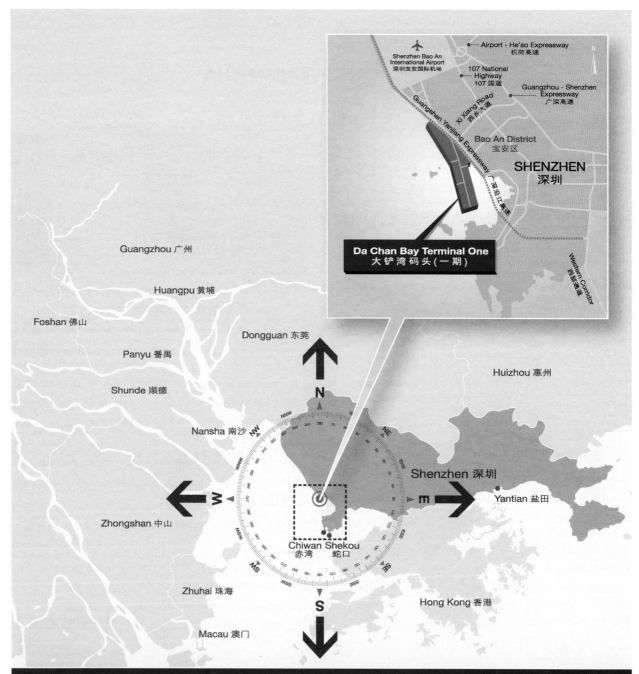

Da Chan Bay Terminal One 大铲湾码头(一期)

Da Chan Bay Terminal One, Xi Xiang, Bao An District, Shenzhen, PRC   Zip Code 518102   中国深圳市宝安区西乡大铲湾码头一期 邮编：518102
Tel/电话：(86) 755 2902 2888   Fax/传真：(86) 755 2902 2828
E-mail/电邮：commercial@DaChanBayOne.com   Website/网址：www.DaChanBayOne.com

Principal Facilities:

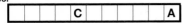

			C				A

Authority: Da Chan Bay Terminal One, Xi Xiang, Bao An District, Shenzhen, Guangdong Province 518102, People's Republic of China, *Tel:* +86 755 2902 2888, *Fax:* +86 755 2902 2828, *Email:* commercial@dachanbayone.com, *Website:* www.dachanbayone.com

Approach: Tonggu Channel - SZ Western Port Channel
East Lamma Channel - Urmstron Road - Longgu Channel - SZ Western Port Channel

Anchorage: No.4 anchorage, to the west of Black Point of HK, with an area of 3.3 km2 and depth of 12-20 m
No.8 anchorage, in the west of Guishan Island, with 18.69 km2 water area and 10 m depth

Pilotage: Compulsory. Pilot boards in pos 22° 23' 40" N; 113° 53' 65" E (Urnston Roads) and 22° 18' 98" N; 113° 50' 26" E (Longguxi Hangdao)

Radio Frequency: Call sign 'Shenzhen VTS' listen on VHF Channel 69

Weather: Subtropical Zone Oceanic Monsoonal Climate. The annual average wind speed is 3.7 m/s. There is about 0.8 typhoon each year on average. The annual average number of days with the visibility below 1 km is 10.4 days. Foggy days mostly take place in the period from October to the next April. The annual average relative humidity is 78%

Tides: Irregular tide phenomenon of half-day tide with the average tide range of 132 cm, maximum tide range of 285 cm. The movement forms of the tides are reciprocating stream. The flood tide direction is NW to N, and the ebb tide direction is SE to S. The annual average wave of the terminal basin is only 0.2 m

Maximum Vessel Dimensions: No limit to vessel length

Working Hours: 24 h/day, 365 days

Accommodation:

Name	Length (m)	Depth (m)	Remarks
Da Chan Bay Terminal 1	1830	15.5	See [1] below

[1]*Terminal 1:* Five container berths. Total area of 112 ha with 816 reefer points

Storage: Around 75 ha in year 2009

Mechanical Handling Equipment: Tandem 40 type quayside crane (outreach 67.7 m): 12 pcs
Electrical rubber tyred gantry crane (one over six high and one plus six wide): 30 pcs
Tandem 40 type quayside crane: 26 pcs
Electrical rubber tyred gantry crane: 108 pcs

Towage: Four (more to come in the future)

Airport: Shenzhen Bao An International Airport, 10 km

Development: The berths will be dredged up to 18 m in the future

Lloyd's Agent: Huatai Surveyors & Adjusters Co., Room 802, Jun Yuan Mansion, 155 Tian He East Road, Guangzhou, Guangdong Province 510620, People's Republic of China, *Tel:* +86 20 3881 2306, *Fax:* +86 20 3881 2470, *Email:* agency.gz@huatai-serv.com, *Website:* www.huatai-serv.com

DABUQIAO

harbour area, see under Xiangtan

DAFENG

Lat 33° 12' N; Long 120° 25' E.

Admiralty Chart: 1253	**Admiralty Pilot:** 32
Time Zone: GMT +8 h	**UNCTAD Locode:** CN

Principal Facilities:

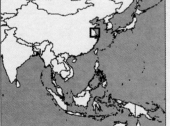

		Y	G				

Authority: Dafeng Harbour Administration, 63 Renmin South Road, Dafeng, Jiangsu Province 224100, People's Republic of China

Accommodation:

Name	Remarks
Dafeng	See [1] below

[1]*Dafeng:* Numerous berths for vessels up to 120 dwt
Cargoes handled include coal, ores, iron & steel, timber, grain, fertiliser and cotton

Storage: Open and covered storage areas available

Mechanical Handling Equipment:

Location	Type	Capacity (t)
Dafeng	Mult-purp. Cranes	10

Lloyd's Agent: Huatai Surveyors & Adjusters Co., 14th Floor, China Re Building, No.11 Jin Rong Avenue, Xicheng District, Beijing 100140, People's Republic of China, *Tel:* +86 10 6657 6577, *Fax:* +86 10 6657 6502, *Email:* agency.bj@huatai-serv.com, *Website:* www.huatai-serv.com

DAGANG

harbour area, see under Dalian

DAHUA

harbour area, see under Dalian

DAIREN

former name, see Dalian

DALIAN

Lat 38° 55' N; Long 121° 39' E.

Admiralty Chart: 3695/3696/3697	**Admiralty Pilot:** 32
Time Zone: GMT +8 h	**UNCTAD Locode:** CN DLC

Principal Facilities:

P		Y	G	C	R		B	D	T	A

Authority: Dalian Port Corp. Ltd, 1 Gangwan Street, Zhongshan District, Dalian, Liaoning Province 116004, People's Republic of China, *Tel:* +86 411 8263 7873, *Fax:* +86 411 8280 7148, *Email:* dgtxc@mail.dlptt.ln.cn, *Website:* www.portdalian.com

Officials: General Manager: Sun Hong.

Port Security: ISPS compliant

Approach: Draft limitation in Dagang Channel is 10.0 m and in Ganjingzi Channel is 8.5 m

Anchorage: No.1 Ship Anchorage in depth of 7.0-18.0 m for vessels up to 10 000 t and used for quarantine, haven, provisions & fresh water, pilot, repairing.
No.2 Ship Anchorage in depth of 7.0-18.0 m for vessels up to 10 000 t and used for quarantine, haven, provisions & fresh water, pilot, repairing.
Anchorage for oil tankers in depth of 7.0-18.0 m for vessels up to 10 000 t and used for quarantine, haven, provisions & fresh water, pilot, repairing.
Anchorage for New Port (Nianyuwan) in depth of 18.0 m for vessels up to 10 000 t and used for quarantine, haven, provisions & fresh water, pilot, repairing

Pilotage: Compulsory and available 24 h/day. Pilot boards vessel at the anchorage

Radio Frequency: VHF Channel 25 and 13

Tides: Average tidal range of 2.5 m

Traffic: 2006, 200 460 000 t of cargo handled, 3 212 000 TEU's

Working Hours: Round the clock. Office hours are 0800-1200, 1400-1700

Accommodation:

Name	Length (m)	Depth (m)	Draught (m)	Remarks
Dagang (Old Port)				
Berth No.1	180	9		See [1] below
Berth No.2	133	6.8		See [2] below
Berth No.3	133	5.8		See [3] below
Berth No.4	134	6.8		See [4] below
Berth No.5	150	6.4		See [5] below
Berth No.6	196	8.8		See [6] below
Berth No.7	140	8.9		See [7] below
Berth No.8	220	10		Grain for vessels up to 25 000 dwt
Berth No.9	246	11		Wheat for vessels up to 25 000 dwt
Berth No.10	250	12		Fertiliser for vessels up to 60 000 dwt
Berth No.11	236	10.7		See [8] below
Berth No.12	236	10.7		See [9] below
Berth No.13	196	7.7		See [10] below

Name	Length (m)	Depth (m)	Draught (m)	Remarks
Berth No.14	100	7.3		See [11] below
Berth No.15	150	7.3		See [12] below
Berth No.16	180	8.5		See [13] below
Berth No.17	180	8.8		Ore for vessels up to 10 000 dwt
Berth No.18	246	10.4		Ore for vessels up to 25 000 dwt
Berth No.19	180	9		See [14] below
Berth No.20	210	9		See [15] below
Berth No.21	216	8.8		See [16] below
Berth No.22	135	9		Containers for vessels up to 5000 dwt
Berth No.23	135	9		Containers for vessels up to 5000 dwt
Berth No.24	180	10.6		Containers for vessels up to 10 000 dwt
Berth No.25	180	10.9		Coal for vessels up to 10 000 dwt
Berth No.26	246	11.1		Coal for vessels up to 25 000 dwt
Berth No.27	180	8.6		See [17] below
Berth No.28	180	9		See [18] below
Berth No.29	123	8.9		Ore for vessels up to 5000 dwt
Berth No.30	123	8.9		See [19] below
Xianglujiao				
Berth No.1	150	8		See [20] below
Berth No.2	257	8		See [21] below
Berth No.3	250	7		See [22] below
Berth No.4	150	6.6		See [23] below
Berth No.5	190	7		See [24] below
Berth No.6	210	9.6		See [25] below
Berth No.7	220	9.4		See [26] below
Berth No.8	180	7.8		See [27] below
Siergou				
Berth No.1	180	9.3		See [28] below
Berth No.2	170	9.6		See [29] below
Berth No.3	190	9.1		See [30] below
Berth No.4	180	7.1		See [31] below
Ganjingzi				
Berth No.1	230	9.1		See [32] below
Berth No.2	210	9.7		Grain for vessels up to 10 000 dwt
Oil Terminal (Berth No.15)				For tankers of 30 000-50 000 dwt
Dalianwan				
Berth No.1	227	10.9		See [33] below
Berth No.2	235	11.2		See [34] below
Berth No.3	270	9.7		Coal for vessels up to 30 000 dwt
Xingang				
Berth No.1	421	17.5		Crude oil for vessels up to 175 000 dwt
Berth No.2	406	16.5		Crude oil for vessels up to 100 000 dwt
Berth No.3	175	11		See [35] below
Berth No.4	175	11		See [36] below
Berth No.5	175	11		See [37] below
Berth No.6	150	6.5		See [38] below
Berth No.10				Vessels up to 10 000 dwt
Berth No's 11 & 12				See [39] below
Dayaowan				
Berth No.0	310	15.5		Bulk cargo for vessels up to 80 000 dwt
Berth No.1	240	12.1		Grain for vessels up to 50 000 dwt
Berth No.2	240	12.1		Grain for vessels up to 50 000 dwt
Berth No's 3-7	1459	14		See [40] below
Berth No's 11-14	1380		13.9–16	See [41] below
Dalian Automobile Terminal	640			See [42] below
Dahua				
Berth No.1	57	6		See [43] below
Berth No.2	197	8.7		See [44] below
Berth No.3	174	8.7		See [45] below
Berth No.4	60	5.6		See [46] below
Ganxiaodong				
Berth No.1	110	6.5		Oil for vessels up to 5000 dwt
Berth No.2	145	9.3		Oil for vessels up to 10 000 dwt
Berth No.3	290	13.2		Oil for vessels up to 80 000 dwt
Ganxiaoxi				
Berth No.4	300	12		Oil for vessels up to 50 000 dwt
Berth No.5	140	9.5		Oil for vessels up to 10 000 dwt
Berth No.6	115	7		Oil for vessels up to 5000 dwt
Ganshun				
Berth No.1	232	8.5		Oil & LPG for vessels up to 10 000 dwt

Name	Length (m)	Depth (m)	Draught (m)	Remarks
Berth No.2	183	8.5		Oil for vessels up to 7000 dwt
Berth No.3	165	7		Oil for vessels up to 5000 dwt
Jingu				
Berth No.1	141	5.7		See [47] below

[1]Berth No.1: Soybean & general cargo for vessels up to 10 000 dwt
[2]Berth No.2: General cargo & passenger for vessels up to 3000 dwt
[3]Berth No.3: General cargo & passenger for vessels up to 3000 dwt
[4]Berth No.4: General cargo & passenger for vessels up to 3000 dwt
[5]Berth No.5: General cargo & passenger for vessels up to 5000 dwt
[6]Berth No.6: General cargo for vessels up to 7000 dwt
[7]Berth No.7: General cargo & passenger for vessels up to 3000 dwt
[8]Berth No.11: General cargo for vessels up to 10 000 dwt
[9]Berth No.12: General cargo for vessels up to 10 000 dwt
[10]Berth No.13: General cargo & passenger for vessels up to 3000 dwt
[11]Berth No.14: General cargo & passenger for vessels up to 3000 dwt
[12]Berth No.15: General cargo for vessels up to 5000 dwt
[13]Berth No.16: General cargo for vessels up to 10 000 dwt
[14]Berth No.19: General cargo for vessels up to 5000 dwt
[15]Berth No.20: General cargo for vessels up to 10 000 dwt
[16]Berth No.21: General cargo for vessels up to 10 000 dwt
[17]Berth No.27: General cargo & grain for vessels up to 10 000 dwt
[18]Berth No.28: General cargo & grain for vessels up to 10 000 dwt
[19]Berth No.30: General cargo & grain for vessels up to 10 000 dwt
[20]Berth No.1: Steel, timber & general cargo for vessels up to 10 000 dwt
[21]Berth No.2: Steel, grain & general cargo for vessels up to 7000 dwt
[22]Berth No.3: Steel, timber & general cargo for vessels up to 5000 dwt
[23]Berth No.4: Steel, timber & general cargo for vessels up to 5000 dwt
[24]Berth No.5: Grain & general cargo for vessels up to 7000 dwt
[25]Berth No.6: Grain & general cargo for vessels up to 20 000 dwt
[26]Berth No.7: Steel, grain & general cargo for vessels up to 10 000 dwt
[27]Berth No.8: Steel, timber, grain & general cargo for vessels up to 7000 dwt
[28]Berth No.1: Diesel & crude oil for vessels up to 20 000 dwt
[29]Berth No.2: Diesel & crude oil for vessels up to 20 000 dwt
[30]Berth No.3: Petrol & crude oil for vessels up to 30 000 dwt
[31]Berth No.4: Petrol & crude oil for vessels up to 20 000 dwt
[32]Berth No.1: Coal & grain for vessels up to 10 000 dwt
[33]Berth No.1: Dangerous & general cargo for vessels up to 30 000 dwt
[34]Berth No.2: Coal & general cargo for vessels up to 30 000 dwt
[35]Berth No.3: General cargo for vessels up to 20 000 dwt
[36]Berth No.4: General cargo & coal for vessels up to 20 000 dwt
[37]Berth No.5: General cargo & ore for vessels up to 20 000 dwt
[38]Berth No.6: Diesel oil & LPG for vessels up to 3000 dwt
[39]Berth No's 11 & 12: Petroleum products & liquid chemicals for vessels up to 5000 dwt
[40]Berth No's 3-7: Dalian Container Terminal Co Ltd (DCT), Tel: +86 411 8759 7543, Fax: +86 411 8759 7387, Website: www.dct.com.cn
Comprises five berths in Dayaowan district with yard area of 27 601 m2. Thirteen quay cranes, 33 yard cranes, stacking cap of 30 566 TEU's and 896 reefer points
[41]Berth No's 11-14: Dalian Port Container Terminal Co Ltd (DPCM), Tel: +86 411 8759 5000, Fax: +86 411 8759 5018, Website: www.dpcmterminal.com
Four container berths. Equipment includes four 65 t cap quay cranes and twelve 41 t cap RTG's
[42]Dalian Automobile Terminal: Total land area of approx 540 000 m2, equipped with two berths for ro/ro vessels and has an annual handling cap of 600 000 vehicles
[43]Berth No.1: General cargo for vessels up to 1000 dwt
[44]Berth No.2: General cargo for vessels up to 10 000 dwt
[45]Berth No.3: General cargo for vessels up to 10 000 dwt
[46]Berth No.4: General cargo for vessels up to 10 000 dwt
[47]Berth No.1: Oil, LPG & bulk chemicals for vessels up to 5000 dwt

Storage:

Location	Open (m²)	Covered (m²)
Dalian	716000	319000

Mechanical Handling Equipment:

Location	Type	Capacity (t)	Qty
Dalian	Floating Cranes	200	1
Dalian	Floating Cranes	100	1
Dalian	Floating Cranes	63	1
Berth No.5	Shore Cranes	5	2
Berth No.6	Shore Cranes	5	2
Berth No.8	Shore Cranes	10	2
Berth No.9	Shore Cranes	10	3
Berth No.10	Shore Cranes	25	3
Berth No.10	Shore Cranes	10	3
Berth No.11	Shore Cranes	10	3
Berth No.12	Shore Cranes	10	3
Berth No.14	Shore Cranes	10	1
Berth No.15	Shore Cranes	10	1
Berth No.16	Shore Cranes	20	3
Berth No.17	Shore Cranes	10	2
Berth No.18	Shore Cranes	10	3
Berth No.19	Shore Cranes	27.5	1
Berth No.19	Shore Cranes	5	2
Berth No.20	Shore Cranes	10	3
Berth No.21	Shore Cranes	10	3
Berth No.22	Mult-purp. Cranes	27.5	1
Berth No.23	Mult-purp. Cranes	80	1
Berth No.24	Shore Cranes	10	3
Berth No.25	Shore Cranes	10	3
Berth No.26	Shore Cranes	10–27.5	6
Berth No.27	Shore Cranes	10	2

Location	Type	Capacity (t)	Qty
Berth No.28	Shore Cranes	10	1
Berth No.29	Shore Cranes	10	3
Berth No.1	Shore Cranes	10	2
Berth No.2	Shore Cranes	10	2
Berth No.3	Shore Cranes	10	2
Berth No.4	Shore Cranes	10	1
Berth No.5	Shore Cranes	10	2
Berth No.6	Mult-purp. Cranes	25	2
Berth No.7	Shore Cranes	10	4
Berth No.8	Shore Cranes	10	4
Berth No.1	Shore Cranes	10	3
Berth No.2	Shore Cranes	10	6
Berth No.3	Shore Cranes	15	2
Berth No.1	Shore Cranes	16	3

Bunkering: China Marine Bunker Supply Co., 13F Qian Cun Mansion A, No.2, 5th Block, Anzhen Xili, Chaoyang District, Beijing 100029, People's Republic of China, *Tel:* +86 10 6443 0717, *Fax:* +86 10 6443 0708, *Email:* business@chimbusco.com.cn, *Website:* www.chimbusco.com.cn – *Grades:* IFO120-380cSt; MGO
ExxonMobil Marine Fuels, 1 Harbour Front Place, 06-00 Harbour Front, Tower One, Singapore, Republic of Singapore 098633, *Tel:* +65 6885 8998, *Fax:* +65 6885 8794, *Email:* asiapac.marinefuels@exxonmobil.com, *Website:* www.exxonmobilmarinefuels.com – *Grades:* MDO; MGO; IFO – *Delivery Mode:* barge
Promar Energy Private Ltd, Farrer Road, P O Box 0019, Singapore, Republic of Singapore 912801, *Tel:* +65 6635 4395, *Fax:* +65 6260 4902

Towage: Harbour tugs up to 4200 hp are available

Repair & Maintenance: COSCO (Dalian) Shipyard, 80 Zhong Yuan Road, Dalian, Liaoning Province 116113, People's Republic of China, *Fax:* +86 411 8760 1117, *Website:* www.cosco-shipyard.com One 300 000 dwt floating dock, one 180 000 dwt floating dock, one 80 000 dwt dry dock and nine repair berths including 300 000 dwt wharf and 10 000 t slipway
Dalian Shipyard, P O Box 3, 1 Yanhai Street, Xigang District, Dalian, Liaoning Province 116005, People's Republic of China, *Tel:* +86 411 8263 7627, *Fax:* +86 411 8263 3461, *Email:* ds@mail.dlptt.ln.cn, *Website:* www.dlsy.com Two drydocks of 169 m x 21.6 m x 10.2 m and 134 m x 15.6 m x 8.4 m. Vessels up to 15 000 dwt and 5000 dwt respectively can be accommodated

Ship Chandlers: Dalian Friendship (Group) Co. Ltd, Ocean Shipping Supply Corp., No.91 Renmin Road, Dalian, Liaoning Province 116001, People's Republic of China, *Tel:* +86 411 8264 6435, *Fax:* +86 411 8280 3962, *Email:* supco@mail.dlptt.ln.cn, *Website:* www.dlsupco.com.cn
Dalian Lian-Da Shipping Supply Co. Ltd, No.7-2 Huanghai West Road, Economical Development Zone, Dalian, Liaoning Province 116600, People's Republic of China, *Tel:* +86 411 8761 5198, *Fax:* +86 411 8764 6898, *Email:* dalianlianda@sohu.com, *Website:* www.dalianlianda.com
Dalian New Port Ocean Shipping Supply Corp., Yingbin Road, New Port, Dalian, Liaoning Province 116601, People's Republic of China, *Tel:* +86 411 8759 6521, *Fax:* +86 411 8280 8898, *Email:* n.dragon@263.net
Dalian Ocean Shipping Co Supply Department, 100 Yanhai Street, Xigang District, Dalian, Liaoning Province, People's Republic of China, *Tel:* +86 411 8442 1485, *Fax:* +86 411 8442 1487, *Email:* office@dlgy-cosco.cn, *Website:* www.dlgy-cosco.cn

Shipping Agents: Ben Line Agencies Ltd, Room 1007, Dalian Gold Name Commercial Tower, 68 Renmin Road, Zhong Shan District, Dalian, Liaoning Province 116001, People's Republic of China, *Tel:* +86 411 8273 0981, *Fax:* +86 411 8273 0980, *Email:* dlc.ops@benline.com.cn, *Website:* www.benlineagencies.com
Chiao Feng Shipping Ltd, Room 1605A, The Times Building, 7 Harbor Street, Zhong Shan District, Dalian, Liaoning Province 116001, People's Republic of China, *Tel:* +86 411 8279 8148, *Fax:* +86 411 8279 8399, *Email:* dalian@chiaofeng.com.cn, *Website:* www.chiaofeng.com.hk
China Marine Shipping Agency Co. Ltd, China Marine Shipping Agency Liaoning Company Limited, 2/16th Floor, Guoyun Building, 85 Renmin Road, Dalian, Liaoning Province 116001, People's Republic of China, *Tel:* +86 411 8255 1171, *Fax:* +86 411 8280 3858, *Email:* sinoagentdl@sinoagent.com, *Website:* www.sinoagent.com
China Ocean Shipping Agency, 11th & 12th Floors Shum Yip Building, 2 Gangwan Street, Zhongshan District, Dalian, Liaoning Province 116001, People's Republic of China, *Tel:* +86 411 8251 3888, *Fax:* +86 411 8263 7169, *Email:* info@cosco-logisticsdl.com, *Website:* www.pendal.com.cn
CMA-CGM S.A., CMA CGM Dalian, Room 2701, Xi Wang Tower, 136 Zhongshan Road, Zhongshan District, Dalian, Liaoning Province 116001, People's Republic of China, *Tel:* +86 411 8800 8000, *Fax:* +86 411 8800 8100, *Email:* dln.genmbox@cma-cgm.com, *Website:* www.cma-cgm.com
GAC Forwarding & Shipping (Shanghai) Ltd, 69 Yucai Street, Zhongshan District, Dalian, Liaoning Province, People's Republic of China, *Tel:* +86 411 8279 4777, *Fax:* +86 411 8270 5095, *Email:* freight.dalian@gacworld.com, *Website:* www.gacworld.com
K Line Ship Management Co. Ltd, 'K' Line (China) Ltd, Room 1005, Dalian Asia Pacific Finance Centre, 55 Renmin Road, Dalian, Liaoning Province 116001, People's Republic of China, *Tel:* +86 411 8899 5838, *Fax:* +86 411 8280 4947, *Website:* www.kline.co.jp
Minsheng International Shipping Agency Co, Room 912 & 916, Kanoi Mansion, 61 People Road, Zhongshan District, Dalian, Liaoning Province, People's Republic of China, *Tel:* +86 411 8265 1676, *Fax:* +86 411 8265 1606, *Email:* benj@minshengdl.com
Pen-Wallem Shipping Services Co Ltd, Dalian, Liaoning Province, People's Republic of China, *Tel:* +86 411 8271 1212, *Fax:* +86 411 8271 1122, *Email:* dalian@pen-wallem.com
Sinotrans (HK) Logistics Ltd, Room 1603, Sinotrans Mansion, 85 Ren Min Road, Dalian, Liaoning Province 116001, People's Republic of China, *Tel:* +86 411 8255 1216, *Fax:* +86 411 8280 3858, *Email:* dalian@sinotrans-logistics.com, *Website:* www.sinotrans-logistics.com
Sun Hing Shipping Co Ltd, Room A, 17/F, Liyuan Mansion, 16-18 Mingze Street, Zhongshan District, Dalian, Liaoning Province 116001, People's Republic of China, *Tel:* +86 411 8281 8353, *Fax:* +86 411 8281 6008, *Website:* www.sunhinggroup.com
THI (Hong Kong) Ltd, Shum Yip Building, Room A311, 2 Gangwan Street, Zhongshan Dist, Dalian, Liaoning Province 116001, People's Republic of China, *Tel:* +86 411 8270 7454, *Fax:* +86 411 8212 8288, *Email:* thedal@thi-group.com, *Website:* www.thi-group.com
United Transportation (HK) Ltd, Room 1605A, The Times Building, 7 Harbor Street, Zhong Shan District, Dalian, Liaoning Province 116001, People's Republic of China, *Tel:* +86 411 8279 8148, *Fax:* +86 411 8279 8399, *Email:* utlotal@netvigator.com
Young Carrier Co. Ltd, The Bank Center, Room 2401, Dalian Gold Name Tower, 68 Renmin Road, Dalian, Liaoning Province, People's Republic of China, *Tel:* +86 411 6262 8000, *Fax:* +86 411 8273 6889, *Email:* ymldlc@yml.com.cn

Surveyors: China Classification Society, 8-9th Floor, 29 Changjiang Road, Zhongshan District, Dalian, Liaoning Province 116001, People's Republic of China, *Tel:* +86 411 8264 9060, *Fax:* +86 411 8263 0848, *Email:* ccsdl@ccs.org.cn, *Website:* www.ccs.org.cn
Dalian Trust Maritime Survey Co. Ltd, Room 403, 57-2 Chaoyang Street, Zhongshan District, Dalian, Liaoning Province 116001, People's Republic of China, *Tel:* +86 411 8279 9967, *Fax:* +86 411 8279 9969, *Email:* ibschina@online.ln.cn, *Website:* www.css1999.com
Det Norske Veritas A/S, 21st Floor, Senmao Building, 147 Zhongshan Road, Dalian, Liaoning Province 116011, People's Republic of China, *Tel:* +86 411 8360 3028, *Fax:* +86 411 8360 3018, *Email:* mchcn420@dnv.com, *Website:* www.dnv.com
Germanischer Lloyd, Room 1015, Summit Building, 4 Shanghai Road, Dalian, Liaoning Province 116001, People's Republic of China, *Tel:* +86 411 8263 2762, *Fax:* +86 411 8263 2142, *Email:* gl-dalian@gl-group.com, *Website:* www.gl-group.com
Korean Register of Shipping, Room J, 22nd Floor Chinabank Plaza, No.15 Renmin Road, Zhongshan District, Dalian, Liaoning Province, People's Republic of China, *Tel:* +86 411 8210 8701, *Fax:* +86 411 8210 8707, *Email:* kr-dln@krs.co.kr, *Website:* www.krs.co.kr
Nippon Kaiji Kyokai, 21F Senmao Building, 147 Zhongshan Road, Xigang District, Dalian, Liaoning Province 116011, People's Republic of China, *Tel:* +86 411 8369 4144, *Fax:* +86 411 8369 4154, *Email:* zd@classnk.or.jp, *Website:* www.classnk.or.jp
Union Bureau of Shipping, 2-6-3 Huaxiang Weiyena Building, 57 Chaoyang Street, Zhongshanqu, Dalian, Liaoning Province, People's Republic of China, *Tel:* +86 411 8273 8640, *Fax:* +86 411 8273 8943, *Email:* ubsho@online.ln.cn, *Website:* www.ubsho.com

Medical Facilities: Dalian Railway Hospital, International Seamen's Ward, Tel: +86 (411) 203478

Airport: Dalian Airport

Development: Dalian Port Container Terminal Co Ltd has signed a 50-year agreement to acquire, construct and manage Berth No's 11-16 at Dalian Dayaowan Phase II. When completed in 2008 it will have 2097 m of quay and depths alongside of 13.5-17.8 m
Construction of an ore terminal operated by Dalian Ore Terminals Ltd consisting of two berths totalling 886 m in depth of 23 m with three ship unloaders
Construction of a bulk terminal at Changxing Island consisting of two berths for vessels up to 70 000 dwt and one berth for vessels up to 50 000 dwt

Lloyd's Agent: Huatai Surveyors & Adjusters Co., Room 1107, Dalian Asia Pacific Finance Centre, 55 Renmin Road, Zhongshan District, Dalian, Liaoning Province 116001, People's Republic of China, *Tel:* +86 411 8281 1122, *Fax:* +86 411 8281 1133, *Email:* agency.dl@huatai-serv.com, *Website:* www.huatai-serv.com

DANDONG

Lat 40° 8' N; Long 124° 24' E.

Admiralty Chart: 1251	**Admiralty Pilot:** 32
Time Zone: GMT +8 h	**UNCTAD Locode:** CN DDG

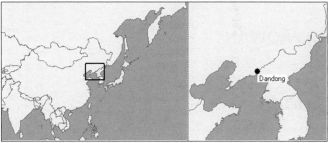

Principal Facilities:

	Y	G	C	R		B		T	

Authority: Dandong Port Authority, 7 Xingwu Road, Dandong, Liaoning Province 118000, People's Republic of China, *Tel:* +86 415 312 2088, *Fax:* +86 415 312 3512, *Website:* www.dandongport.com

Port Security: ISPS compliant

Approach: Draft limitation in Dadong Channel is 12.5 m (summer) 11 m (winter) and Langtou Channel is 5.5 m (summer) 4.2 m (winter)

Anchorage: Outer Anchorage in pos 39° 32' 00" N; 123° 55' 00" E in depth of 15 m Dadong Anchorage in pos 39° 39' 05" N; 124° 04' 08" E in depth of 10 m

Pilotage: Compulsory. Pilot boards vessel at pilotage anchorage

Radio Frequency: VHF Channel 16 and 11

Weather: Ice conditions occur in the river from the end of October or mid November until late March or early April, when the river is closed to shipping

Accommodation:

Name	Length (m)	Depth (m)	Remarks
Dandong			
Berth No.2	190	11	General & bulk cargo for vessels up to 30 000 dwt
Berth No.3	190	13	General & bulk cargo for vessels up to 55 000 dwt

---

Key to Principal Facilities:—
A=Airport　　**C**=Containers　　**G**=General Cargo　　**P**=Petroleum　　**R**=Ro/Ro　　**Y**=Dry Bulk
B=Bunkers　　**D**=Dry Dock　　**L**=Cruise　　**Q**=Other Liquid Bulk　　**T**=Towage (where available from port)

Name	Length (m)	Depth (m)	Remarks
Berth No.4	190	10.5	General & bulk cargo for vessels up to 30 000 dwt
Berth No.5	190	7.5	General & container cargo for vessels up to 5000 dwt
Langtou			
Berth No.1	130	5	General & bulk cargo for vessels up to 1000 dwt
Berth No.2	130	6	General & bulk cargo for vessels up to 2000 dwt
Berth No.3	150	6.5	General & bulk cargo for vessels up to 3000 dwt
Berth No.4	150	6.5	General & bulk cargo for vessels up to 3000 dwt

Storage: Container yard of 8000 m2

Location	Open (m²)	Covered (m²)
Dandong	550000	10000

Mechanical Handling Equipment:

Location	Type	Capacity (t)	Qty
Berth No.2	Shore Cranes	15	2
Berth No.3	Shore Cranes	15	2
Berth No.4	Shore Cranes	15	2
Berth No.5	Container Cranes	35	1
Berth No.5	Shore Cranes	30	1
Berth No.1	Shore Cranes	15	1
Berth No.2	Shore Cranes	15	2
Berth No.3	Shore Cranes	15	2
Berth No.4	Shore Cranes	15	2

Bunkering: Available

Towage: Four tugs of 600-3200 hp

Shipping Agents: China Marine Shipping Agency Co. Ltd, China Marine Shipping Agency Dandong Liaoning, No. 11 Jangcheng Street, Dandong, Liaoning Province, People's Republic of China, *Tel:* +86 415 213 1087, *Fax:* +86 415 212 3124, *Email:* cnddg@sinoagent.com

Lloyd's Agent: Huatai Surveyors & Adjusters Co., 14th Floor, China Re Building, No.11 Jin Rong Avenue, Xicheng District, Beijing 100140, People's Republic of China, *Tel:* +86 10 6657 6577, *Fax:* +86 10 6657 6502, *Email:* agency.bj@huatai-serv.com, *Website:* www.huatai-serv.com

DATUAN

harbour area, see under Nanhui

DAXIE

harbour area, see under Ningbo

DAYAOWAN

harbour area, see under Dalian

DIDONG

harbour area, see under Zhaoqing

DIGANG

Lat 31° 6' N; Long 118° 0' E.

Admiralty Chart: 2412	**Admiralty Pilot:** 32
Time Zone: GMT +8 h	**UNCTAD Locode:** CN

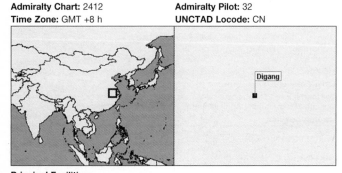

Principal Facilities:

		Y	G						

Authority: Digang Harbour Administration, Digang Town, Wuhu, Anhui Province 241201, People's Republic of China

Accommodation: Cargoes handled include coal, iron & steel, grain, fertiliser and ores

Name	Remarks
Digang	Nineteen berths totalling 375 m for vessels up to 1500 dwt
Xingang	Seven berths totalling 227 m for vessels up to 1500 dwt

Storage: Open and covered storage areas available

Lloyd's Agent: Huatai Surveyors & Adjusters Co., 14th Floor, China Re Building, No.11 Jin Rong Avenue, Xicheng District, Beijing 100140, People's Republic of China, *Tel:* +86 10 6657 6577, *Fax:* +86 10 6657 6502, *Email:* agency.bj@huatai-serv.com, *Website:* www.huatai-serv.com

DINGHAI

harbour area, see under Zhoushan

DIXI

harbour area, see under Zhaoqing

DONGCHANG

harbour area, see under Shanghai

DONGDU

harbour area, see under Xiamen

DONGFANG

former name, see Basuo

DONGGOU

harbour area, see under Chuansha

DONGGUAN

Lat 23° 3' N; Long 113° 43' E.

Admiralty Chart: -	**Admiralty Pilot:** 30
Time Zone: GMT +8 h	**UNCTAD Locode:** CN DGG

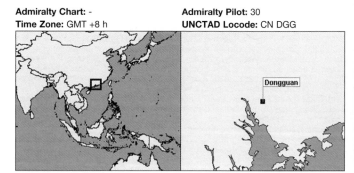

Principal Facilities:

		Y	G						

Port Security: ISPS compliant

Accommodation:

Name	Remarks
Dongguan	Numerous berths for vessels up to 500 dwt handling coal and ores

Shipping Agents: China Marine Shipping Agency Co. Ltd, China Marine Shipping Agency Guangdong Company Limited Dongguan Branch, 6th Floor, Sinotrans Building, 17 Guantai Road, Dongguan, Guangdong Province, People's Republic of China, *Tel:* +86 769 2245 2628, *Fax:* +86 769 2248 1663, *Email:* dongguan@sinoagentgd.com
CMA-CGM S.A., CMA CGM Dongguan, Room 806 Hunghei Commercial Building, 23 Guantai Road, Huangcun District, Dongguan, Guangdong Province 523011, People's Republic of China, *Tel:* +86 769 2238 1834, *Fax:* +86 769 2238 1824, *Email:* dgu.genmbox@cma-cgm.com, *Website:* www.cma-cgm.com
Young Carrier Co. Ltd, Room 502, Fangzhong Building, Eastern Town Road,

Dongguan, Guangdong Province 523008, People's Republic of China, *Tel:* +86 769 2250 0205, *Fax:* +86 769 2248 6895, *Email:* dongguan@ymlchina.com

Lloyd's Agent: Huatai Surveyors & Adjusters Co., 14th Floor, China Re Building, No.11 Jin Rong Avenue, Xicheng District, Beijing 100140, People's Republic of China, *Tel:* +86 10 6657 6577, *Fax:* +86 10 6657 6502, *Email:* agency.bj@huatai-serv.com, *Website:* www.huatai-serv.com

DONGLIAN

Lat 22° 44' N; Long 114° 37' E.

Admiralty Chart: 3026	**Admiralty Pilot:** 30
Time Zone: GMT +8 h	**UNCTAD Locode:** CN

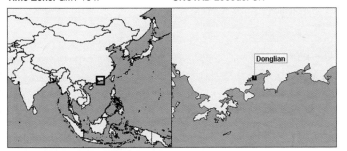

Principal Facilities:

	P	Q						T	

Authority: The CNOOC & Shell Petrochemicals Co Ltd, Dayawan Petrochemical Industrial Park, Huizhou, Guangdong Province 516086, People's Republic of China, *Tel:* +86 752 368 2228, *Fax:* +86 752 368 1188, *Email:* luo.peter@cnoocshell.com, *Website:* www.cnoocshell.com

Pre-Arrival Information: Vessel's should advise ETA via agent or owner 10 days, 7 days, 5 days, 72 h, 48 h and 24 h prior to arrival at the pilot station. Vessel's should then advise CSPC Logistics and Huizhou MSA by VHF 2 h prior to arrival at the pilot station. The ETA message should contain the following information:
a) vessel's name
b) flag
c) master's name
d) ETA
e) discharge/load rate
f) cargo
g) loa
h) dwt
i) draught

Anchorage: No.1 centred on pos 22° 38.75' N; 114° 41.35' E with a radius of 300 m in depth of 12 m
No.2 centred on pos 22° 38.35' N; 114° 41.65' E with a radius of 300 m in depth of 12 m

Pilotage: Compulsory for all foreign flag vessels, for domestic vessels calling at the terminal for the first time, for domestic vessels over 200 000 dwt carrying dangerous cargo and other domestic vessels whose Master is not approved by the CSPC Marine team. Pilot boards in pos 22° 39.80' N; 114° 41.10' E

Maximum Vessel Dimensions: 178 m loa, 40 000 dwt, 9 m draft

Accommodation:

Name	Length (m)	Depth (m)	Remarks
Donglian			
Berth No.1	250	9.85	See [1] below
Berth No.2	267	9.85	See [2] below
Berth No.3	267	9.85	See [3] below

[1]*Berth No.1:* Petrochemicals & LPG for vessels up to 150 m loa & 12 500 dwt
[2]*Berth No.2:* Petrochemicals for vessels up to 150 m loa & 12 500 dwt
[3]*Berth No.3:* Petrochemicals for vessels up to 178 m loa & 40 000 dwt

Towage: Two 3600 hp and one 1800 hp tugs available

Medical Facilities: Available

Lloyd's Agent: Huatai Surveyors & Adjusters Co., Room 802, Jun Yuan Mansion, 155 Tian He East Road, Guangzhou, Guangdong Province 510620, People's Republic of China, *Tel:* +86 20 3881 2306, *Fax:* +86 20 3881 2470, *Email:* agency.gz@huatai-serv.com, *Website:* www.huatai-serv.com

DONGSHAN

Lat 23° 45' N; Long 117° 31' E.

Admiralty Chart: 1767	**Admiralty Pilot:** 32
Time Zone: GMT +8 h	**UNCTAD Locode:** CN DSN

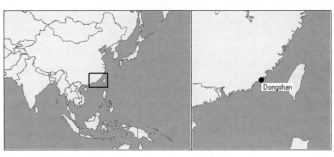

Principal Facilities:

	Y	G	C		B			

Authority: Dongshan Port Authority, Dongshan, Fujian Province, People's Republic of China, *Tel:* +86 596 562 2374

Approach: Draft limitation in channel is 8.0 m

Anchorage: No.1 Anchorage in pos 23° 45' 00" N; 117° 35' 00" E in depth of 10-15 m for medium to large size vessels
No.2 Anchorage in pos 23° 45' 00" N; 117° 34' 18" E in depth of 10-15 m for medium to large size vessels
No.3 Anchorage within the following pos 21° 29' 32" N; 109° 05' 16" E, 21° 29' 49" N; 109° 05' 16" E, 21° 29' 43" N; 109° 05' 49" E, 21° 29' 59" N; 109° 05' 49" E in depth of 5 m for vessels up to 5000 dwt
No.4 Anchorage in pos 23° 45' 42" N; 117° 30' 18" E in depth of 8 m for medium to small size vessels
Quarantine Anchorage in pos 23° 43.8' N; 117° 34.3' E in depth of 10-15 m for medium to large size vessels

Pilotage: Compulsory and available 10 h during the day. Pilot boards vessel in pos 23° 43.8' N; 117° 33.3' E

Radio Frequency: VHF Channel 9

Tides: Average tidal range of 2.2 m

Accommodation:

Name	Length (m)	Depth (m)	Remarks
Dongshan			
Si02 Sand Berth	120	7.2	Silica sand for vessels up to 7000 dwt
General Cargo Berth	115	5.5	General cargo & container for vessels up to 5000 dwt
Oil Berth	152	5.2	Petroleum for vessels up to 3000 dwt
Donggu Sand Berth	120	6.5	Silica sand for vessels up to 5000 dwt

Storage: Container yard of 5000 m2

Location	Open (m²)	Covered (m²)
Dongshan	12000	2020

Mechanical Handling Equipment:

Location	Type	Capacity (t)	Qty
Dongshan	Mult-purp. Cranes	5	2
Dongshan	Mult-purp. Cranes	40	1
General Cargo Berth	Container Cranes	16	1
General Cargo Berth	Shore Cranes	8	2

Bunkering: Available

Shipping Agents: China Marine Shipping Agency Co. Ltd, China Marine Shipping Agency Fujian Zhangzhou Company Dongshan Office, 3rd Floor, Sinotrans Building, Wuliting, Tongling Town, Dongshan, Fujian Province, People's Republic of China, *Tel:* +86 596 562 0474, *Fax:* +86 596 562 3516, *Email:* lwy909@sohu.com

Lloyd's Agent: Huatai Surveyors & Adjusters Co., 14th Floor, China Re Building, No.11 Jin Rong Avenue, Xicheng District, Beijing 100140, People's Republic of China, *Tel:* +86 10 6657 6577, *Fax:* +86 10 6657 6502, *Email:* agency.bj@huatai-serv.com, *Website:* www.huatai-serv.com

DONGTAI

Lat 32° 50' N; Long 120° 18' E.

Admiralty Chart: 1641	**Admiralty Pilot:** 32
Time Zone: GMT +8 h	**UNCTAD Locode:** CN

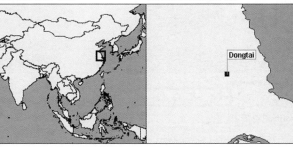

Key to Principal Facilities:—

A=Airport	**C**=Containers	**G**=General Cargo	**P**=Petroleum	**R**=Ro/Ro	**Y**=Dry Bulk
B=Bunkers	**D**=Dry Dock	**L**=Cruise	**Q**=Other Liquid Bulk	**T**=Towage (where available from port)

Principal Facilities:

P	Y	G						

Authority: Dongtai Harbour Administration, Central City, Dongtai, Jiangsu Province 224200, People's Republic of China

Accommodation:

Name	Remarks
Dongtai	See [1] below

[1]*Dongtai:* Numerous berths for vessels up to 150 dwt handling coal, ores, iron & steel, cement, timber, grain, cotton and petroleum

Storage: Open and covered storage areas available

Mechanical Handling Equipment:

Location	Type	Capacity (t)
Dongtai	Mult-purp. Cranes	15

Lloyd's Agent: Huatai Surveyors & Adjusters Co., 14th Floor, China Re Building, No.11 Jin Rong Avenue, Xicheng District, Beijing 100140, People's Republic of China, *Tel:* +86 10 6657 6577, *Fax:* +86 10 6657 6502, *Email:* agency.bj@huatai-serv.com, *Website:* www.huatai-serv.com

EZHOU

Lat 30° 24' N; Long 114° 49' E.

Admiralty Chart: 2947	**Admiralty Pilot:** 32
Time Zone: GMT +8 h	**UNCTAD Locode:** CN EZH

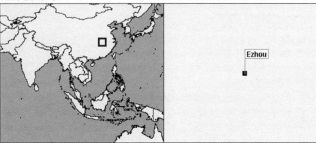

Principal Facilities:

P		Y	G						

Accommodation:

Name	Remarks
Zhouwei	Numerous berths available handling ores, petroleum, chemical products and coal
Beimen	Numerous berths available handling passengers, general cargo and iron & steel
Xiongjiagou	See [1] below

[1]*Xiongjiagou:* Numerous berths available handling iron & steel, construction materials and chemical products

Mechanical Handling Equipment:

Location	Type	Capacity (t)
Ezhou	Mult-purp. Cranes	15

Lloyd's Agent: Huatai Surveyors & Adjusters Co., 14th Floor, China Re Building, No.11 Jin Rong Avenue, Xicheng District, Beijing 100140, People's Republic of China, *Tel:* +86 10 6657 6577, *Fax:* +86 10 6657 6502, *Email:* agency.bj@huatai-serv.com, *Website:* www.huatai-serv.com

FANGCHENG

Lat 21° 36' N; Long 108° 19' E.

Admiralty Chart: 41	**Admiralty Pilot:** 30
Time Zone: GMT +8 h	**UNCTAD Locode:** CN FAN

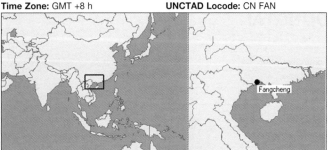

Principal Facilities:

	Y	G	C		B	T	

Authority: Fangcheng Port Group Co Ltd, Port Administration Office, 22 Youyi Road, Fangchenggang, Guangxi Province 538001, People's Republic of China, *Tel:* +86 770 289 8141, *Fax:* +86 770 282 2663, *Website:* www.fcport.com.cn

Port Security: ISPS compliant

Approach: Approach channel 6.1 nautical miles long, in three sections: Sanya 160 m wide and 16 m depth, Xixian 125 m wide and 11 m depth and Niutou 125 m wide and 11 m depth

Anchorage: Pilot and Quarantine Anchorage in pos 21° 27' 56" N; 108° 21' 13" E in depth of 12.0 m, sand with good holding ground.
No.6 buoy anchorage in pos 21° 32' 44" N; 108° 21' 30" E, depth 7-11 m, mud and sand with good holding ground

Pilotage: Compulsory and available during daytime only

Radio Frequency: VHF Channel 16 on 24 h service

Tides: Average tidal range of 2.25 m, minimum 0.79 m, maximum 4.5 m

Traffic: 2005, 20 060 000 t of cargo handled

Principal Imports and Exports: Imports: Coal, Fertiliser, General, Grain, Steel, Sugar. Exports: Cement, General, Ore, Timber.

Working Hours: 24 h/day

Accommodation:

Name	Length (m)	Depth (m)	Remarks
Fangcheng			
Berth No.1	180	8.5	General cargo for vessels up to 10 000 dwt
Berth No.2	180	8.5	General cargo for vessels up to 10 000 dwt
Berth No.3	180	9	Bulk cargo for vessels up to 15 000 dwt
Berth No.4	180	9	Bulk cargo for vessels up to 15 000 dwt
Berth No.5	180	9.6	Bulk & general cargo for vessels up to 15 000 dwt
Berth No.6	210	11.4	Bulk cargo for vessels up to 25 000 dwt
Berth No.7	180	11.4	Bulk, coal & ore cargoes for vessels up to 30 000 dwt
Berth No.8	220	11.4	Bulk cargo for vessels up to 30 000 dwt
Berth No.9	256	13.6	Bulk cargo for vessels up to 50 000 dwt
Berth No.10	242	11.65	Container cargo for vessels up to 25 000 dwt
Berth No.11	256	13.6	Grain for vessels up to 50 000 dwt
Cement Berth	165	7.5	Cement for vessels up to 10 000 dwt
Xingzhong Berth	441	7.5	Five general cargo berths for vessels up to 5000 dwt

Storage:

Location	Open (m²)	Covered (m²)
Fangcheng	160000	55000

Mechanical Handling Equipment:

Location	Type	Capacity (t)	Qty
Berth No.1	Shore Cranes	10	2
Berth No.2	Shore Cranes	25	1
Berth No.2	Shore Cranes	10	2
Berth No.3	Shore Cranes	10	1
Berth No.3	Shore Cranes	16	1
Berth No.4	Shore Cranes	10	2
Berth No.5	Shore Cranes	10	2
Berth No.5	Shore Cranes	16	2
Berth No.6	Shore Cranes	10	2
Berth No.6	Shore Cranes	16	2
Berth No.7	Shore Cranes	10	2
Berth No.7	Shore Cranes	16	2
Berth No.8	Shore Cranes	10	2
Berth No.8	Shore Cranes	16	1
Berth No.9	Mult-purp. Cranes	25	6
Berth No.10	Container Cranes	40	2
Berth No.11	Shore Cranes	25	2

Bunkering: Available

Towage: Seven tugs of 670-3840 hp

Ship Chandlers: Fangchenggang Ocean Shipping Supply & Duty Free Co. Ltd, No.9 Friendship Road, Fangchenggang, Guangxi Province 538001, People's Republic of China, *Tel:* +86 770 282 2608, *Fax:* +86 770 282 3323, *Email:* supply@shipservice.org

Shipping Agents: Chiao Feng Shipping Ltd, Room 708, 7/F Foreign Trade Building, Friendship Avenue, Fangcheng, People's Republic of China, *Tel:* +86 770 289 2260, *Fax:* +86 770 289 2272, *Email:* fangcheng@chiaofeng.com.cn, *Website:* www.chiaofeng.com.hk
China Marine Shipping Agency Co. Ltd, China Marine Shipping Agency Guangxi Fangcheng Company, Sinotrans Building, Xinggang Road, Fangchenggang, Guangxi Province, People's Republic of China, *Tel:* +86 770 282 2792, *Fax:* +86 770 282 2537, *Email:* fangchenggang@sinoagent.com, *Website:* www.sinoagent.com
Sino-Continental, Fangcheng Branch, 9th Floor Insurance Building, 8 Friendship Road, Gangkou District, Fangchenggang, Guangxi Province 538001, People's Republic of China, *Tel:* +86 770 283 1074, *Fax:* +86 770 283 1075, *Email:* fangcheng@sino-continental.com, *Website:* www.sino-continental.com

Airport: Nanning International Airport, 160 km

Railway: The Nanning-Fangcheng railroad is linked to the national rail system via the Hunan-Guangxi railroad

Lloyd's Agent: Huatai Surveyors & Adjusters Co., 14th Floor, China Re Building, No.11 Jin Rong Avenue, Xicheng District, Beijing 100140, People's Republic of China, *Tel:* +86 10 6657 6577, *Fax:* +86 10 6657 6502, *Email:* agency.bj@huatai-serv.com, *Website:* www.huatai-serv.com

FENGCHENG

harbour area, see under Fengxian

FENGJIE

Lat 31° 2' N; Long 109° 31' E.

Admiralty Chart: -	**Admiralty Pilot:** -
Time Zone: GMT +8 h	**UNCTAD Locode:** CN

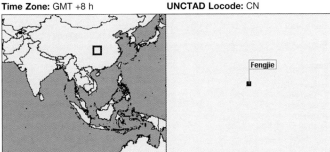

Principal Facilities:

		Y	G					T	

Authority: Fengjie Harbour Administration, 38 Dananmen, Fengjie, Sichuan Province 634600, People's Republic of China

Accommodation:

Name	Remarks
Fengjie	Numerous berths for vessels up to 3000 dwt handling passengers, coal and general cargo

Storage: Open and covered storage areas available

Mechanical Handling Equipment:

Location	Type	Capacity (t)
Fengjie	Mult-purp. Cranes	5

Towage: Available

Lloyd's Agent: Huatai Surveyors & Adjusters Co., 14th Floor, China Re Building, No.11 Jin Rong Avenue, Xicheng District, Beijing 100140, People's Republic of China, *Tel:* +86 10 6657 6577, *Fax:* +86 10 6657 6502, *Email:* agency.bj@huatai-serv.com, *Website:* www.huatai-serv.com

FENGXIAN

Lat 30° 55' N; Long 121° 26' E.

Admiralty Chart: 1602	**Admiralty Pilot:** 32
Time Zone: GMT +8 h	**UNCTAD Locode:** CN

Principal Facilities:

		Y	G						

Authority: Fengxian Shipping Administration, 8 Nanhang Road, Nanqiao Town, Fengxian County, Shanghai, Shanghai Province 201400, People's Republic of China

Accommodation: Cargoes handled include ore, grain, coal and iron & steel

Name	Remarks
Nanqiao Area	Numerous berths for vessels up to 100 dwt
Fengcheng Area	Numerous berths for vessels up to 100 dwt

Lloyd's Agent: Huatai Surveyors & Adjusters Co., 14th Floor, China Re Building, No.11 Jin Rong Avenue, Xicheng District, Beijing 100140, People's Republic of China, *Tel:* +86 10 6657 6577, *Fax:* +86 10 6657 6502, *Email:* agency.bj@huatai-serv.com, *Website:* www.huatai-serv.com

FOOCHOW

former name, see Fuzhou

FOSHAN

Lat 23° 2' N; Long 113° 6' E.

Admiralty Chart: -	**Admiralty Pilot:** -
Time Zone: GMT +8 h	**UNCTAD Locode:** CN FOS

Principal Facilities:

P		Y	G						A

Authority: Foshan Harbour Administration, 4 Nandi Road, Foshan, Guangdong Province 528000, People's Republic of China

Accommodation: Cargoes handled include coal, timber, petroleum, grain, ore and general cargo

Name	Remarks
Jiebian	Several berths handling coal for vessels up to 100 dwt
Nandi	Six berths for vessels up to 200 dwt
Xinshi	Four berths for vessels up to 1000 dwt

Shipping Agents: China Marine Shipping Agency Co. Ltd, China Marine Shipping Agency Guangdong Foshan Company, 88 Qianjin Road, Lanshi, Foshan, Guangdong Province, People's Republic of China, *Tel:* +86 757 8310 2562, *Fax:* +86 757 8310 1002, *Email:* chenxiaomin-fs@transgd.com.cn

CMA-CGM S.A., CMA CGM Foshan, Room 3018-3020 Baihua Plaza, 33 Zu Miao Road, Foshan, Guangdong Province 528000, People's Republic of China, *Tel:* +86 757 8328 7636, *Fax:* +86 757 8328 7861, *Email:* fsh.mho@cma-cgm.com, *Website:* www.cma-cgm.com

A Hartrodt International, Foshan Representative Office, Room 2603-05 Bai Hua Plaza, No. 33 Zumiao Road, Foshan, Guangdong Province 528000, People's Republic of China, *Tel:* +86 757 8330 7910, *Fax:* +86 757 8330 7912, *Email:* foshan@hartrodt.com.hk

Airport: Foshan Airport

Lloyd's Agent: Huatai Surveyors & Adjusters Co., Room 802, Jun Yuan Mansion, 155 Tian He East Road, Guangzhou, Guangdong Province 510620, People's Republic of China, *Tel:* +86 20 3881 2306, *Fax:* +86 20 3881 2470, *Email:* agency.gz@huatai-serv.com, *Website:* www.huatai-serv.com

FUJIN

Lat 47° 15' N; Long 132° 1' E.

Admiralty Chart: -	**Admiralty Pilot:** -
Time Zone: GMT +8 h	**UNCTAD Locode:** CN FUJ

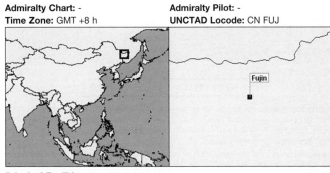

Principal Facilities:

		Y	G						

Authority: Fujin Harbour Administration, North End Xinkai Road, Fujin, Helongjiang Province, People's Republic of China

Accommodation:

Name	Remarks
Fujin	See [1] below

[1]*Fujin:* Four berths for vessels up to 3000 dwt handling passengers, coal, timber, grain and general cargo

Storage: Open and covered storage areas available

Mechanical Handling Equipment: Cranes available

Key to Principal Facilities:—

A=Airport	**C**=Containers	**G**=General Cargo	**P**=Petroleum	**R**=Ro/Ro	**Y**=Dry Bulk
B=Bunkers	**D**=Dry Dock	**L**=Cruise	**Q**=Other Liquid Bulk	**T**=Towage (where available from port)

Lloyd's Agent: Huatai Surveyors & Adjusters Co., 14th Floor, China Re Building, No.11 Jin Rong Avenue, Xicheng District, Beijing 100140, People's Republic of China, *Tel:* +86 10 6657 6577, *Fax:* +86 10 6657 6502, *Email:* agency.bj@huatai-serv.com, *Website:* www.huatai-serv.com

FULING

Lat 29° 42' N; Long 107° 20' E.

Admiralty Chart: -   **Admiralty Pilot:** -
Time Zone: GMT +8 h   **UNCTAD Locode:** CN FLG

Principal Facilities:

P		Y	G					

Authority: Fuling Harbour Administration, 164 Zhongshan Dong Road, Fuling, Sichuan Province 648000, People's Republic of China

Accommodation:

Name	Remarks
Fuling	See [1] below

[1]*Fuling:* Numerous berths available handling petroleum, coal, iron & steel, fertiliser and manufactured goods

Storage: Open and covered storage areas available

Mechanical Handling Equipment:

Location	Type	Capacity (t)
Fuling	Mult-purp. Cranes	15

Lloyd's Agent: Huatai Surveyors & Adjusters Co., 14th Floor, China Re Building, No.11 Jin Rong Avenue, Xicheng District, Beijing 100140, People's Republic of China, *Tel:* +86 10 6657 6577, *Fax:* +86 10 6657 6502, *Email:* agency.bj@huatai-serv.com, *Website:* www.huatai-serv.com

FUZHOU

Lat 26° 3' N; Long 119° 18' E.

Admiralty Chart: 2419   **Admiralty Pilot:** 32
Time Zone: GMT +8 h   **UNCTAD Locode:** CN FOC

Principal Facilities:

Q	Y	G	C		B	D	T	A

Authority: Fuzhou Municipal Port Authority, 3 Gangkou Road, Mawei District, Fuzhou, Fujian Province 350015, People's Republic of China, *Tel:* +86 591 8368 2312, *Fax:* +86 591 8368 2674, *Website:* www.fpa.gov.cn

Port Security: ISPS compliant

Approach: From the pilotage and quarantine anchorage at the entry of the Min River to Mawei Harbour, the channel is 50 km long and with the high tide it can accommodate vessels up to 20 000 t. The channel from Mawei to Taijian harbour is 17 km long and can accommodate vessels up to 1000 t

Anchorage: Guantou Anchorage: in pos 26° 06' 45" N; 119° 33' 00" E in depth of 6-10 m for vessels of 3000-10 000 dwt
Tingjiang Anchorage: in pos 26° 04' 00" N; 109° 30' 45" E in depth of 6-8 m for vessels of 3000-8000 dwt
Maoyu Anchorage: in pos 25° 59' 00" N; 119° 28' 00" E in depth of 6-9.5 m for vessels of 3000-10 000 dwt
Yingqian Anchorage: in pos 25° 58' 30" N; 109° 27' 15" E in depth of 4-6 m for vessels of 1000-2000 dwt

Pilotage: Compulsory and available during daytime only. Pilot boards vessel at the Baita Pilot Anchorage

Radio Frequency: VHF Channel 16

Tides: Average tidal range of 4.2 m

Traffic: 2006, 88 495 000 t of cargo handled, 1 012 000 TEU's

Working Hours: 24 h/day in three shifts

Accommodation:

Name	Length (m)	Depth (m)	Draught (m)	Remarks
Mawei				
General Cargo Berth	592	6–8		General cargo for vessels up to 10 000 dwt
Container Berth No.1	220	11		Containers for vessels up to 15 000 dwt
Container Berth No.2	220	11		Containers for vessels up to 15 000 dwt
Container Berth No.3	190	11		Containers for vessels up to 15 000 dwt
Container Berth No.4	190	11		Containers for vessels up to 15 000 dwt
Container Berth No.5	170	11		Containers for vessels up to 7500 dwt
Songmen				
Berth No.1	171	11.9		Coal for vessels up to 15 000 dwt
Berth No.2	162	11.9		Grain for vessels up to 5000 dwt
Jiangyin				
Fuzhou Jiangyin International Container Terminal	375		14	See [1] below
Qingzhou				
Fuzhou Qingzhou Container Terminal	519		11.5	See [2] below
Aofeng				
Fuzhou Aofeng Container Terminal	156		6.5	See [3] below

[1]*Fuzhou Jiangyin International Container Terminal:* Operated by Fuzhou International Container Terminal Co Ltd., Xinjiang Road, Fuqing City, Fujian Province 350309, Tel: +86 591 8596 6698, Fax: +86 591 8596 6665, Website: www.fict.cn
[2]*Fuzhou Qingzhou Container Terminal:* Operated by Fuzhou Qingzhou Container Terminal Co Ltd., Tel: +86 591 8398 5651, Fax: +86 591 8398 6897, Website: www.fqct.com
Terminal area of 28 ha consisting of three berths totalling 519 m. Container stacking yard cap of 12 000 TEU's, container freight station of 8200 m2 and 228 reefer points. Four quay cranes and twelve yard cranes
[3]*Fuzhou Aofeng Container Terminal:* Terminal area of 38 000 m2 consisting of two berths totalling 156 m. Container stacking yard cap of 1200 TEU's and 20 reefer points. One fixed crane and two reach stackers

Storage:

Location	Open (m²)	Covered (m²)
Fuzhou	140000	110000

Mechanical Handling Equipment:

Location	Type	Capacity (t)	Qty
Fuzhou	Floating Cranes	60	1
General Cargo Berth	Shore Cranes	40	1
General Cargo Berth	Shore Cranes	10	4
Berth No.1	Shore Cranes	10	1
Fuzhou Jiangyin International Container Terminal	Container Cranes		5
Fuzhou Jiangyin International Container Terminal	RTG's		12
Fuzhou Jiangyin International Container Terminal	Reach Stackers		2
Fuzhou Qingzhou Container Terminal	Mult-purp. Cranes		12
Fuzhou Qingzhou Container Terminal	Container Cranes		4
Fuzhou Aofeng Container Terminal	Container Cranes		1
Fuzhou Aofeng Container Terminal	Reach Stackers		2

Bunkering: Available

Towage: Three tugs of 1600-3400 hp

Shipping Agents: China Marine Shipping Agency Co. Ltd, China Marine Shipping gency Fujian Company Limited (Fuzhou), 15th Floor, Yifa Building, No. 111 Wusi Road, Fuzhou, Fujian Province, People's Republic of China, *Tel:* +86 591 8368 0233, *Fax:* +86 591 8368 2445, *Email:* fjmarket@sinoagent.com
China Ocean Shipping Agency, 12th Floor World Wide Plaza, 158 Wusi Road, Fuzhou, Fujian Province 350003, People's Republic of China, *Tel:* +86 591 8781 3803, *Fax:* +86 591 8780 9600, *Email:* penfuz@pub1.fz.fj.cn, *Website:* www.penavicofz.com.cn
CMA-CGM S.A., CMA CGM Fuzhou, Room 2102/2103, 21F Worldwide Plaza, 158 Wusi Road, Fuzhou, Fujian Province 350001, People's Republic of China, *Tel:* +86 591 8766 2222, *Fax:* +86 591 8750 1586, *Email:* foc.genmbox@cma-cgm.com, *Website:* www.cma-cgm.com
Ever Concord Lines Ltd, YaQing Metropolitan Financial Plaza, Unit 21-A, 21st Floor, 43 East Street, Fuzhou, Fujian Province 350001, People's Republic of China, *Tel:* +86 591 8752 6705, *Fax:* +86 591 8752 5209

K Line Ship Management Co. Ltd, 'K' Line (China) Ltd, 12F, Worldwide Plaza, 158 Wusi Road, Fuzhou, Fujian Province 350003, People's Republic of China, *Tel:* +86 591 8780 7206, *Fax:* +86 591 8780 1785, *Website:* www.kline.co.jp

Mediterranean Shipping Company, MSC (Hong Kong) Ltd, Unit 04, 32nd Floor, Worldwide Plaza, 158 Wusi Road, Fuzhou, Fujian Province 350003, People's Republic of China, *Tel:* +86 591 8787 0746, *Fax:* +86 591 8787 0740, *Email:* msc@mschkg.com, *Website:* www.mschongkong.com

Sun Hing Shipping Co Ltd, Room 7-B3, 7/F, Office Block, Fortune Building, 168 Hudong Road, Fuzhou, Fujian Province 350001, People's Republic of China, *Tel:* +86 591 8785 6266, *Fax:* +86 591 8785 6378, *Website:* www.sunhinggroup.com

United Transportation (HK) Ltd, Room J 13 Floor, Block A, Huakai Fugui Building, 8 Dongda Road, Fuzhou, Fujian Province, People's Republic of China, *Tel:* +86 591 8333 2051, *Fax:* +86 591 8761 2128, *Email:* utlotal@netvigator.com

Young Carrier Co. Ltd, Unit 3006 30th Fl, Worldwide Plaza, 158 Wusi Road, Fuzhou, Fujian Province, People's Republic of China, *Tel:* +86 591 8780 8387, *Fax:* +86 591 8780 8386, *Email:* ymlfoc@yml.com.cn, *Website:* www.yml.com.tw

Surveyors: China Classification Society, 6E New Metropolis Financial Square, 43 East Street, Gulou District, Fuzhou, Fujian Province 350001, People's Republic of China, *Tel:* +86 591 2830 8555, *Fax:* +86 591 8750 1950, *Email:* ccsfz@ccs.org.cn, *Website:* www.ccs.org.cn

Medical Facilities: Fuzhou Majiang Hospital

Airport: Fuzhou Changle International Airport

Railway: Special purpose railway in Mawei Harbour and Kuiqi operational area is connected to the Fuzhou-Mawei railway and leads to the National railway network

Development: A total of five berths are to be constructed at Fuzhou Jiangyin International Container Terminal

Lloyd's Agent: Huatai Surveyors & Adjusters Co., 14th Floor, China Re Building, No.11 Jin Rong Avenue, Xicheng District, Beijing 100140, People's Republic of China, *Tel:* +86 10 6657 6577, *Fax:* +86 10 6657 6502, *Email:* agency.bj@huatai-serv.com, *Website:* www.huatai-serv.com

GANJINGZI

harbour area, see under Dalian

GANSHUN

harbour area, see under Dalian

GANXIAODONG

harbour area, see under Dalian

GANXIAOXI

harbour area, see under Dalian

GANZHOU

Lat 25° 51' N; Long 114° 55' E.

Admiralty Chart: -   **Admiralty Pilot:** -
Time Zone: GMT +8 h   **UNCTAD Locode:** CN

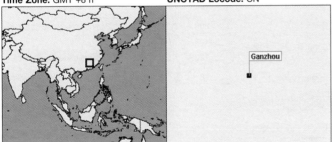

Principal Facilities:

	Y	G					

Authority: Ganzhou Harbour & Shipping Administration, 41 Lianxi Road, Ganzhou, Jiangxi Province 341000, People's Republic of China

Accommodation:

Name	Remarks
Guijiaowei	See [1] below
Yongjinmen	See [2] below
Jianchunmen	See [3] below
Mojiaoshang	See [4] below

[1]*Guijiaowei:* Numerous berths for vessels up to 100 dwt. Open and covered storage areas available, as well as cranes

[2]*Yongjinmen:* Numerous berths for vessels up to 100 dwt. Open and covered storage areas available, as well as cranes

[3]*Jianchunmen:* Four berths for vessels up to 50 dwt. Open and covered storage areas available, as well as cranes

[4]*Mojiaoshang:* Eight berths for vessels up to 300 dwt. Open and covered storage areas available, as well as cranes

Lloyd's Agent: Huatai Surveyors & Adjusters Co., 14th Floor, China Re Building, No.11 Jin Rong Avenue, Xicheng District, Beijing 100140, People's Republic of China, *Tel:* +86 10 6657 6577, *Fax:* +86 10 6657 6502, *Email:* agency.bj@huatai-serv.com, *Website:* www.huatai-serv.com

GAOGANG

alternate name, see Taizhou

GAOLAN

harbour area, see under Zhuhai

GAOQIAO

harbour area, see under Chuansha

GAOTING

harbour area, see under Zhoushan

GAOYANG

harbour area, see under Shanghai

GONGQING

harbour area, see under Shanghai

GUANGDONG TERMINAL

Lat 22° 34' N; Long 114° 26' E.

Admiralty Chart: -   **Admiralty Pilot:** -
Time Zone: GMT +8 h   **UNCTAD Locode:** CN

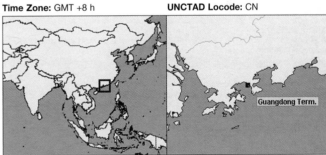

Principal Facilities:

Q							

Authority: Guangdong Dapeng LNG Co Ltd., 11/F Times Financial Centre, 4001 Shennan Road, Shenzhen, Guangdong Province 518034, People's Republic of China, *Tel:* +86 755 3332 6888, *Fax:* +86 755 3332 6887, *Email:* info@dplng.com, *Website:* www.dplng.com

Principal Imports and Exports: Imports: LNG.

Accommodation:

Name	Length (m)	Remarks
Guangdong Terminal		Total land area of 40 ha
Berth	450	See [1] below

[1]*Berth:* LNG supplied by Australia Northwest Shelf LNG Venture for LNG carriers up to 145 000 m3 cap. Three 160 000 m3 storage tanks

Lloyd's Agent: Huatai Surveyors & Adjusters Co., Room 802, Jun Yuan Mansion, 155 Tian He East Road, Guangzhou, Guangdong Province 510620, People's Republic of China, *Tel:* +86 20 3881 2306, *Fax:* +86 20 3881 2470, *Email:* agency.gz@huatai-serv.com, *Website:* www.huatai-serv.com

Key to Principal Facilities:—			
A=Airport	**C**=Containers	**G**=General Cargo	**P**=Petroleum	**R**=Ro/Ro	**Y**=Dry Bulk
B=Bunkers	**D**=Dry Dock	**L**=Cruise	**Q**=Other Liquid Bulk	**T**=Towage (where available from port)

GUANGZHOU

Lat 23° 6' N; Long 113° 14' E.

Admiralty Chart: 3620/3646-7/346
Admiralty Pilot: 30
Time Zone: GMT +8 h
UNCTAD Locode: CN CAN

Principal Facilities:

P		Y	G	C	R		B		T	A

Authority: Guangzhou Port Group Co. Ltd, 531 Gang Qian Lu, Huangpu District, Guangzhou, Guangdong Province 510700, People's Republic of China, *Tel:* +86 20 8227 9412, *Fax:* +86 20 8227 0868, *Email:* yw-jzx@gzport.com, *Website:* www.gzport.com

Port Security: ISPS compliant

Approach: Channel from Guishan Island at the river entrance to the harbour consists of 8 sections, 114.5 km in length -
1) Guishan channel, 18.5 km length, depth 10 m, natural
2) Linding channel, 45 km length, depth 10.5 m, artificial
3) Chuanbi channel, length 13 km, depth 9 m, natural
4) Dahu channel, length 8.6 m, depth 9 m, natural
5 & 6) Nizhou and Lianhuashan channels, length 20.6 m, depth 9 m, artificial
7) Chisha channel, length 5.5 m, depth 9 m, artificial
8) Dahazhou channel, length 3.3 km, depth 8 m, artificial
The Linding and Lianhuashan channels are artificially maintained for the Huangpu harbour

Anchorage: Dahaozhou anchorage (D1) in pos 23° 02' 01" N; 113° 30' 45" E in depth of 9.5 m, mud and sand with good holding ground, lightening
Dazaozhou anchorage (D2) in pos 23° 03' 14" N; 113° 29' 57" E in depth of 9.5 m, mud and sand with good holding ground, lightening
Dahu anchorage (H1) in pos 22° 50' 36" N; 113° 34' 24" E in depth of 10.7 m, mud and sand with good holding ground, lightening & haven
Dahu anchorage (H2) in pos 22° 50' 56" N; 113° 34' 12" E in depth of 11.5 m, mud and sand with good holding ground, lightening & haven
Dahu anchorage (H3) in pos 22° 51' 16" N; 113° 34' 00" E in depth of 11.5 m, mud and sand with good holding ground, lightening & haven
Dahu anchorage (H4) in pos 22° 51' 48" N; 113° 33' 41" E in depth of 6.9 m, mud and sand with good holding ground, lightening & haven
F1 in pos 23° 05' 36.8" N; 113° 25' 48.4" E in depth of 9 m, mud with good holding ground, lightening
P2 in pos 23° 05' 29" N; 113° 27' 03.7" E in depth of 9 m, mud with good holding ground, lightening
P3 in pos 23° 05' 31.7" N; 113° 26' 51.5" E in depth of 9 m, mud with good holding ground, lightening
P4 in pos 23° 05' 33.8" N;113° 26' 39" E in depth of 9 m, mud with good holding ground, lightening
P5 in pos 23° 05' 35.2" N; 113° 26' 06" E in depth of 9 m, mud with good holding ground, lightening

Pilotage: Compulsory for all foreign vessels entering and leaving the port. Pilot boards as follows:
Large Vessel Anchorage: centred on pos 22° 05.0' N; 113° 53.5' E
Guishan Large Vessel Anchorage: centred on pos 22° 08.4' N; 113° 48.4' E
Guishan Pilot Anchorage: centred on pos 22° 07.9' N; 113° 46.3' E
Zhu Jiang Zhoutou Pilot Anchorage: centred on pos 22° 07.3' N; 113° 40.5' E
Dadanwei Pilot Anchorage (Large Vessels): centred on pos 21° 57.60' N; 113° 59.10' E
Wai Lingding Works Area Pilot Anchorage: centred on pos 22° 05.5' N; 114° 00.5' E

Radio Frequency: Port Authority on VHF Channels 16, 13 and 77. Pilots on VHF Channel 71

Weather: Prevailing winds NE'ly and SW'ly monsoons

Tides: Average tidal range of 2.22 m

Traffic: 2007, 7 100 000 TEU's handled (includes Nansha)

Principal Imports and Exports: Imports: Coal, Fertiliser, General, Grain, Ore, Petroleum, Steel products. Exports: General, Grain, Rice.

Working Hours: Round the clock. Office hours are 0800-1200, 1400-1700

Accommodation:

Name	Length (m)	Depth (m)	Remarks
Huangpu Old Terminal			
Berth No.1	199	9	Iron ore for vessels up to 10 000 dwt
Berth No.2	200	9	General cargo for vessels up to 10 000 dwt
Berth No.3	100	6	General cargo for vessels up to 5000 dwt
Berth No.4	200	9	General cargo for vessels up to 10 000 dwt

Name	Length (m)	Depth (m)	Remarks
Berth No.5	200	9	General cargo for vessels up to 10 000 dwt
Berth No.6	178	9	Fertilizer for vessels up to 10 000 dwt
Berth No.7	178	9	General cargo for vessels up to 10 000 dwt
Berth No.8	179	9	General cargo for vessels up to 10 000 dwt
Huangpu New Terminal			
Berth No.1	220	12.5	Grain for vessels up to 35 000 dwt
Berth No.2	176	11	Fertilizer for vessels up to 20 000 dwt
Berth No.3	176	11	Steel & general cargo for vessels up to 20 000 dwt
Berth No.4	176	11	Steel & general cargo for vessels up to 20 000 dwt
Berth No.5	176	11	Steel & ore for vessels up to 20 000 dwt
Xingang Container Terminal	659	12.5	See [1] below
Xinsha			
Berth No.1	210	12.5	Coal & ore for vessels up to 35 000 dwt
Berth No.2	200	12.5	Coal & ore for vessels up to 35 000 dwt
Berth No.3	200	12.5	General cargo for vessels up to 35 000 dwt
Berth No.4	210	12.5	Fertilizer for vessels up to 35 000 dwt
Berth No.5	180	12.5	General cargo for vessels up to 35 000 dwt
Berth No.6	220	12.5	Grain for vessels up to 35 000 dwt
Xinsha Container Terminal	640	12.5	See [2] below
Hongshengsha			
Berth No.1	180	9	Bulk cargo for vessels up to 10 000 dwt
Berth No.2	165	9	General cargo for vessels up to 10 000 dwt
Berth No.3	174	9	General cargo for vessels up to 10 000 dwt
Xiji			
Berth No.1	220	12.5	Coal & ore for vessels up to 35 000 dwt
Berth No.2	220	12.5	Coal & ore for vessels up to 35 000 dwt
Sino-Pec			
Oil Terminal	287	9.5	Crude oil for vessels up to 24 000 dwt
Guangdong			
Oil Terminal	132	8	Fuel & gasoline for vessels up to 24 000 dwt
Fangcun Terminal Inner III			
Berth No's 1-2	280	5.8	General cargo for vessels up to 3000 dwt
Fangcun Terminal Inner IV			
Berth No's 1-2	286	7	Containers for vessels up to 5000 dwt
Henan Lijiao Terminal			
Berth No's 1-3	350	6	General cargo for vessels up to 5000 dwt
Panyu Nansha Terminal			
Berth No.1	200	7.5	General cargo for vessels up to 30 000 dwt
Berth No.2	200	7.5	Containers for vessels up to 30 000 dwt
Zhongran Oil Terminal			
Berth No.1	120	7	Fuel & gasoline for vessels up to 5000 dwt
Berth No.2	78	5	Fuel & gasoline for vessels up to 1000 dwt
Humen Power Plant			
Oil Terminal	239	10.6	Gasoline for vessels up to 10 000 dwt
Shajiao Power Plant Terminal			
Berth A	205	13.1	Coal for vessels up to 35 000 dwt
Berth B	261	13	Coal for vessels up to 35 000 dwt
Berth C	290	14	Coal for vessels up to 40 000 dwt
Zhudian	275	13	Coal for vessels up to 40 000 dwt

[1]*Xingang Container Terminal:* Operated by Guangzhou Container Terminal Co Ltd., Tel: +86 20 8225 6388, Fax: +86 20 8221 2858, Email: marketing@gct.com.cn, Website: www.gct.com.cn
Three container berths
[2]*Xinsha Container Terminal:* Operated by Guangzhou Container Terminal Co Ltd., Tel: +86 20 8225 6388, Fax: +86 20 8221 2858, Email: marketing@gct.com.cn, Website: www.gct.com.cn
Three container berths

Storage:

Location	Open (m²)	Covered (m²)
Guangzhou	880000	350000

Mechanical Handling Equipment:

Location	Type	Qty
Xingang Container Terminal	Mult-purp. Cranes	16
Xingang Container Terminal	Container Cranes	6
Xinsha Container Terminal	Mult-purp. Cranes	12
Xinsha Container Terminal	Container Cranes	4

Bunkering: BP Hong Kong Ltd, 21st Floor, Super Ocean Financial Centre, 067 West Yan An Road, Shanghai, Shanghai Province, People's Republic of China, *Tel:* +86 21 6278 4858, *Fax:* +86 21 6275 7702, *Email:* lucn@bp.com
China Marine Bunker Supply Co., 13F Qian Cun Mansion A, No.2, 5th Block, Anzhen Xili, Chaoyang District, Beijing 100029, People's Republic of China, *Tel:* +86 10 6443 0717, *Fax:* +86 10 6443 0708, *Email:* business@chimbusco.com.cn, *Website:* www.chimbusco.com.cn – *Grades:* IFO120-380cSt; MGO
ExxonMobil Marine Fuels, 1 Harbour Front Place, 06-00 Harbour Front, Tower One, Singapore, Republic of Singapore 098633, *Tel:* +65 6885 8998, *Fax:* +65 6885 8794, *Email:* asiapac.marinefuels@exxonmobil.com, *Website:* www.exxonmobilmarinefuels.com – *Grades:* MDO; MGO; IFO – *Delivery Mode:* barge

Towage: Nine tugs available of 3200-4000 hp

Repair & Maintenance: CSSC Guangzhou Dockyards, 1 Wenchuan Road, Huangpu, Guangzhou, Guangdong Province 510727, People's Republic of China, *Tel:* +86 20 8239 8266, *Fax:* +86 20 8239 7534, *Email:* shiprepair@gzdock.com, *Website:* www.gzdock.com
Guangzhou Huangpu Shipbuilding Co. Ltd, P O Box 1047, Changzhouzhen, Huangpu, Guangzhou, Guangdong Province, People's Republic of China, *Tel:* +86 20 8220 1345, *Fax:* +86 20 8220 1387 Repairs available for ocean-going vessels at 2000 m long waterfront
Guangzhou Shipyard International Co. Ltd, No.40 South Fangcun Road, P O Box 105, Bai He Dong, Guangzhou, Guangdong Province, People's Republic of China, *Tel:* +86 20 8189 1712, *Fax:* +86 20 8189 1575, *Email:* gsi@chinagsi.com, *Website:* www.chinagsi.com 480 m ship repair quay and a 10 000 t dry dock
Guangzhou Wenchong Shipyard, Guangzhou, Guangdong Province 510727, People's Republic of China, *Tel:* +86 20 8238 9933, *Fax:* +86 20 8239 9338, *Website:* www.wenchongshipyard.com Two dry docks at Huangpu with dimensions 200 m x 28 m x 11 m and 185 m x 24 m x 9.5 m accommodating vessels up to 25 000 dwt and 15 000 dwt respectively. A drydock of 300 m x 62 m. Dry docks: 'Nantong' 270 m x 48 m for vessels up to 150 000 dwt and 'Yuan Tong' 230 m x 44 m for vessels up to 80 000 dwt. Quays of 1000 m with max draught 11 m

Ship Chandlers: China National Ship Supply & Service (Group) Co. Ltd, Room 301, No.253 Dasha Road (E), Guangzhou, Guangdong Province 510700, People's Republic of China, *Tel:* +86 20 8323 99421, *Fax:* +86 20 8323 99451, *Email:* cnssgz@tom.com
Guangzhou Huangpu Ocean Shipping Supply Co. Ltd, 96 Haiyuan Road, Huangpu 510700, People's Republic of China, *Tel:* +86 20 8227 9995, *Fax:* +86 20 8229 0556, *Email:* hpsupco@21cn.com
Man Sang (China) Co. Ltd, Hai Yuan Road 96, Huangpu, Guangzhou, Guangdong Province, People's Republic of China, *Tel:* +86 20 6266 0648, *Fax:* +86 20 8249 4636, *Email:* gz@mansangco.com

Shipping Agents: Ben Line Agencies Ltd, Room 1902, Dongshan Plaza, 69 Xian Lie Road Central, Guangzhou, Guangdong Province 510095, People's Republic of China, *Tel:* +86 20 8760 7413, *Fax:* +86 20 8730 3484, *Email:* can.general@benline.com.cn, *Website:* www.benlineagencies.com
China Marine Shipping Agency Co. Ltd, China Marine Shipping Agency Guangdong Company Limited, 17th Floor, 97 Haiyuan Road, Huangpu, Guangzhou, Guangdong Province 510700, People's Republic of China, *Tel:* +86 20 8710 2100, *Fax:* +86 20 8710 2120, *Email:* ops@sinoagentgd.com, *Website:* www.sinoagentgd.com
CMA-CGM S.A., CMA CGM Guangzhou, Room 1106-1109 Guangzhou Intl Electric Complex, 403 Huan Shi Dong Road, Guangzhou, Guangdong Province 510095, People's Republic of China, *Tel:* +86 20 8732 2896, *Fax:* +86 20 8732 2535, *Email:* ggz.genmbox@cma-cgm.com, *Website:* www.cma-cgm.com
Guangzhou International Shipping Agency Ltd, 1003/27 Haiyuan Road, Huangpu Area, Guangzhou, Guangdong Province, People's Republic of China, *Tel:* +86 20 8229 3663, *Fax:* +86 20 8229 0077, *Email:* optn@isacogz.com.cn, *Website:* www.isaco.com.cn
Jardine Shipping Services, Room 903 T.P. Plaza, 9/109 Liu Hua Road, Guangzhou, Guangdong Province 510010, People's Republic of China, *Tel:* +86 20 8667 5529, *Fax:* +86 20 8669 2796, *Email:* raymond.cheng@jsa.com.hk, *Website:* www.jardine-shipping.com
K Line Ship Management Co. Ltd, 'K' Line (China) Ltd, Room 2406-2407, Guangzhou International Electronics Tower, 403 Huan Shi Road East, Guangzhou, Guangdong Province 510095, People's Republic of China, *Tel:* +86 20 8732 7001, *Fax:* +86 20 8732 1663, *Website:* www.kline.co.jp
Seven Seas Shipping & Transport Co., Room 1015, Fu Li Building No.23, Zhongshan 8 Road, Guangzhou, Guangdong Province, People's Republic of China, *Tel:* +86 20 8119 4476, *Fax:* +86 20 8119 4475, *Email:* nader@7seaschina.com, *Website:* www.7seasjordan.com
Sino-Continental, Guangzhou Branch, Room 409 4th Floor Waiyun Building, 97 Haiyuan Road, Huangpu, Guangzhou, Guangdong Province 510700, People's Republic of China, *Tel:* +86 20 8227 4665, *Fax:* +86 20 8227 4386, *Email:* guangzhou@sino-continental.com, *Website:* www.sino-continental.com
Sun Hing Shipping Co Ltd, Unit B, 19/F, Tower A, Guangdong International Hotel, 339 Huanshi Dong Lu, Guangzhou, Guangdong Province 510060, People's Republic of China, *Tel:* +86 20 8331 1145, *Fax:* +86 20 8331 1144, *Website:* www.sunhinggroup.com
Swire Shipping (Agencies) Ltd, Room 1121, Dongshan Plaza, 69 Xian Lie Road, Guangzhou, Guangdong Province, People's Republic of China, *Tel:* +86 20 8732 1225, *Fax:* +86 20 8732 1552, *Email:* swiresal@pub.guangzhou.gd.cn
TES International Transport (China) Ltd, Room 3005, 30/F Guangdong Foreign Economy & Trade Building, 351 Tainhe Road, Guangzhou, Guangdong Province

510130, People's Republic of China, *Tel:* +86 20 8364 9652, *Fax:* +86 20 8364 9697, *Website:* www.teschina.com.hk

Surveyors: Bureau Veritas, 116 Tiyu Dong Road, Unit 802 East Tower, Fortune Plaza, Tian He District, Guangzhou, Guangdong Province 510602, People's Republic of China, *Tel:* +86 20 3893 1150, *Website:* www.bureauveritas.com
China Classification Society, 40 Haitianswang, Hongde Road, Guangzhou, Guangdong Province 510235, People's Republic of China, *Tel:* +86 20 3434 5769, *Fax:* +86 20 3434 5108, *Email:* ccsgz@ccs.org.cn, *Website:* www.ccs.org.cn
Det Norske Veritas A/S, Room 902-903 West Tower, Fortune Plaza, 114-118 Tiyu Road East, Guangzhou, Guangdong Province 510620, People's Republic of China, *Tel:* +86 20 3893 1231, *Fax:* +86 20 3893 1252, *Email:* mchcn222@dnv.com, *Website:* www.dnv.com
Germanischer Lloyd, Room 2911, The Metro Plaza Building, 183 Tian He Bei Road, Guangzhou, Guangdong Province 510075, People's Republic of China, *Tel:* +86 20 8755 5157, *Fax:* +86 20 8755 5076, *Email:* gl-guangzhou@gl-group.com, *Website:* www.gl-group.com
Nippon Kaiji Kyokai, Room 5703, CITIC Plaza, 233 Tian He North Road, Guangzhou, Guangdong Province 510060, People's Republic of China, *Tel:* +86 20 3877 0693, *Fax:* +86 20 3877 0716, *Email:* zg@classnk.or.jp, *Website:* www.classnk.or.jp
Registro Italiano Navale (RINA), c/o Guangzhou Shipyard International Co Ltd, 40 Fang Cun Road South, Guangzhou, Guangdong Province 510 382, People's Republic of China, *Tel:* +86 20 8189 1712, *Fax:* +86 20 8156 1095, *Email:* surveystation.guangzhou@rina.org, *Website:* www.rina.org

Medical Facilities: Hospital available

Airport: Guangzhou Airport

Railway: The port railroads are connected with the national rail network by Beijing-Guangzhou, Guangzhou-Shenzhen and Guangzhou-Sanshui railroads

Lloyd's Agent: Huatai Surveyors & Adjusters Co., Room 802, Jun Yuan Mansion, 155 Tian He East Road, Guangzhou, Guangdong Province 510620, People's Republic of China, *Tel:* +86 20 3881 2306, *Fax:* +86 20 3881 2470, *Email:* agency.gz@huatai-serv.com, *Website:* www.huatai-serv.com

GUICHENG

Lat 23° 5' N; Long 109° 35' E.

Admiralty Chart: -	**Admiralty Pilot:** -
Time Zone: GMT +8 h	**UNCTAD Locode:** CN GCE

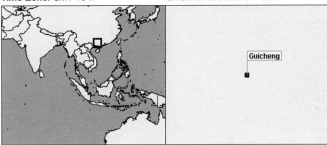

Principal Facilities:

		Y	G				T	

Accommodation:

Name	Remarks
Guicheng	See ¹ below

¹*Guicheng:* Numerous berths for vessels up to 1000 dwt handling passengers, coal, ore, iron & steel, grain, sugar and fertiliser

Storage: Open and covered storage areas available

Towage: Available

Lloyd's Agent: Huatai Surveyors & Adjusters Co., 14th Floor, China Re Building, No.11 Jin Rong Avenue, Xicheng District, Beijing 100140, People's Republic of China, *Tel:* +86 10 6657 6577, *Fax:* +86 10 6657 6502, *Email:* agency.bj@huatai-serv.com, *Website:* www.huatai-serv.com

GUIJIAOWEI

harbour area, see under Ganzhou

HAICANG

harbour area, see under Xiamen

HAIHE PORT

harbour area, see under Xingang

Key to Principal Facilities:—

A=Airport	**C**=Containers	**G**=General Cargo	**P**=Petroleum	**R**=Ro/Ro	**Y**=Dry Bulk
B=Bunkers	**D**=Dry Dock	**L**=Cruise	**Q**=Other Liquid Bulk	**T**=Towage (where available from port)

HAIKOU

Lat 20° 1' N; Long 110° 16' E.

Admiralty Chart: 37
Time Zone: GMT +8 h
Admiralty Pilot: 30
UNCTAD Locode: CN HAK

Principal Facilities:

| P | | Y | G | C | R | | B | | T | A |

Authority: Hainan Port Affairs Bureau, Haikou, Hainan Province 570311, People's Republic of China, *Tel:* +86 898 6862 3518, *Fax:* +86 898 6865 4972, *Email:* hkport@hainan.net, *Website:* www.hk-port.com

Port Security: ISPS compliant

Approach: Draft limitation in outer channel is 9.5 m and inner channel is 7.4 m

Anchorage: No.1 Anchorage: in pos 20° 06' 09" N; 110° 16' 12" E in depth of 25 m
No.2 Anchorage: in pos 20° 05' 06" N; 110° 15' 40" E in depth of 30 m
No.3 Anchorage: in pos 20° 05' 16" N; 110° 17' 07" E in depth of 12 m
No.4 Anchorage: in pos 20° 05' 16" N; 110° 16' 57" E in depth of 14 m
No.5 Anchorage: in pos 20° 45' 09" N; 110° 16' 08" E in depth of 11 m
No.6 Anchorage: in pos 20° 05' 09" N; 110° 13' 11" E in depth of 16 m

Pilotage: Compulsory and available 24 h. Pilot boards vessel at Pilot Anchorage

Radio Frequency: VHF Channel 16

Tides: Average tidal range of 1.1 m

Traffic: 2003, 13 300 000 t of cargo handled

Principal Imports and Exports: Imports: Building materials, Coal, Fertilizer, General cargo, Grain, Petroleum, Steel. Exports: Local products, Rubber, Sugar, Tea.

Accommodation:

Name	Length (m)	Depth (m)	Remarks
Haikou			
Berth No's 1-2	120	3.6	General cargo for vessels up to 500 dwt
Berth No's 4-5	190	3.6	General cargo for vessels up to 1000 dwt
Berth No.6	110	6.5	General cargo for vessels up to 5000 dwt
Berth No's 7-8	210	3	Ferries up to 500 dwt
Berth No.9	96	6	General cargo for vessels up to 3000 dwt
Berth No.10	116	6	General cargo for vessels up to 3000 dwt
Berth No.11	67.2	6.5	General cargo for vessels up to 5000 dwt
Berth No.12	109	8	General cargo for vessels up to 5000 dwt
Berth No.13	36	4.8	Coal for vessels up to 1500 dwt
Berth No.14	150	8	General cargo for vessels up to 5000 dwt
Berth No.17	196	10.2	General cargo for vessels up to 10 000 dwt
Berth No.18	196	10.2	General cargo for vessels up to 10 000 dwt

Storage: Container yard of 10 300 m2

Location	Open (m²)	Covered (m²)
Haikou	63599	28209

Mechanical Handling Equipment:

Location	Type	Capacity (t)	Qty
Haikou	Floating Cranes	50	1
Berth No's 1-2	Shore Cranes	10	1
Berth No.6	Shore Cranes	10	3
Berth No.11	Shore Cranes	5	2
Berth No.13	Shore Cranes	3	1
Berth No.17	Shore Cranes	10	1
Berth No.18	Shore Cranes	10	1

Bunkering: Available

Towage: Two tugs of 3600 hp

Repair & Maintenance: Facilities are available for minor repairs

Ship Chandlers: Haikou Port Ocean Shipping Supply Co. Ltd, 908/BF, 45 Heping Nan Road, Haikou, Hainan Province 570000, People's Republic of China, *Tel:* +86 898 6535 5014, *Fax:* +86 898 6534 3704

Shipping Agents: China Marine Shipping Agency Co. Ltd, China Marine Shipping Agency Hainan Company, 141 Binhai Street, Xiuying District, Haikou, Hainan

Province, People's Republic of China, *Tel:* +86 898 6866 2279, *Fax:* +86 898 6866 6664, *Email:* hainan@sinoagent.com
CMA-CGM S.A., CMA CGM Haikou, Room 501, Sinotrans Building, 141 Binhai Street, Xiuying District, Haikou, Hainan Province 570311, People's Republic of China, *Tel:* +86 898 6866 3809, *Fax:* +86 898 6866 3980, *Email:* hku.eliu@cma-cgm.com, *Website:* www.cma-cgm.com

Airport: Haikou Airport

Development: Work to start in 2006 on two breakwaters and the area behind them will be reclaimed from the sea to create two container berths; scheduled to be completed in 2008

Lloyd's Agent: Huatai Surveyors & Adjusters Co., 14th Floor, China Re Building, No.11 Jin Rong Avenue, Xicheng District, Beijing 100140, People's Republic of China, *Tel:* +86 10 6657 6577, *Fax:* +86 10 6657 6502, *Email:* agency.bj@huatai-serv.com, *Website:* www.huatai-serv.com

HAIMEN

Lat 28° 41' N; Long 121° 26' E.

Admiralty Chart: 1759
Time Zone: GMT +8 h
Admiralty Pilot: 32
UNCTAD Locode: CN HME

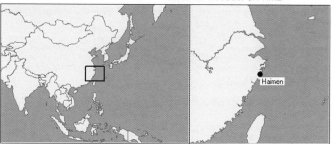

Principal Facilities:

| | Y | G | C | | B | | T | |

Authority: Taizhou Port Co Ltd., 38 Jiangbin Road, Jiaojiang District, Taizhou, Jiangsu Province 311800, People's Republic of China, *Tel:* +86 576 888 1387

Approach: Draft in Haimen Channel is 6.8 m

Anchorage: Pilot Quarantine Anchorage and Lightening Anchorage in depth of 9 m

Pilotage: Compulsory and available 24 h. Pilot boards vessel at Pilot Quarantine Anchorage

Radio Frequency: VHF Channel 11

Tides: Average tidal range of 4 m

Principal Imports and Exports: Imports: Containers, Grain, Timber. Exports: Cement, Coal, General cargo.

Accommodation:

Name	Length (m)	Depth (m)	Remarks
Haimen			
Foreign Trade Berth	244	7	General cargo & containers for vessels up to 10 000 dwt
Berth No.1	105	6	Coal for vessels up to 3000 dwt
Berth No.3 (E)	98	6	General cargo for vessels up to 3000 dwt
Berth No.3 (W)	67	7	General cargo for vessels up to 1000 dwt
Berth No.4	72	5	General cargo for vessels up to 1000 dwt
Berth No.5	95	5	General cargo for vessels up to 1000 dwt
Passenger Berth	168	5	Passengers for vessels up to 1000 dwt
Materials Bureau	71	5.8	For vessels up to 3000 dwt
Oil Berth	93	7	Oil for vessels up to 3000 dwt
Generating Station	215	6	Coal for vessels up to 5000 dwt

Storage: Container yard of 30 000 m2

Location	Open (m²)	Covered (m²)
Haimen	20702	9759

Mechanical Handling Equipment:

Location	Type	Capacity (t)	Qty
Foreign Trade Berth	Shore Cranes	25	1
Foreign Trade Berth	Shore Cranes	8	1
Foreign Trade Berth	Shore Cranes	16	1
Foreign Trade Berth	Shore Cranes	35	1
Berth No.1	Shore Cranes	15	3
Berth No.3 (E)	Shore Cranes	15	3
Berth No.3 (W)	Shore Cranes	16	3

Bunkering: Available

Towage: Two tugs of 600 hp

Ship Chandlers: Taizhou Foreign Shipping Supply Co., 197 Zhongshan West Road, Jiaojing, Taizhou, Jiangsu Province 318000, People's Republic of China, *Tel:* +86 576 888 2917, *Fax:* +86 576 888 1834, *Email:* tzdfjcn@sina.com

Lloyd's Agent: Huatai Surveyors & Adjusters Co., 14th Floor, China Re Building, No.11 Jin Rong Avenue, Xicheng District, Beijing 100140, People's Republic of China, *Tel:* +86 10 6657 6577, *Fax:* +86 10 6657 6502, *Email:* agency.bj@huatai-serv.com, *Website:* www.huatai-serv.com

HAITIAN

harbour area, see under Xiamen

HANGCHOW

former name, see Zhapu

HANGTOU

harbour area, see under Nanhui

HANGZHOU

Lat 30° 15' N; Long 120° 10' E.

Admiralty Chart: 2946　　　　　**Admiralty Pilot:** 32
Time Zone: GMT +8 h　　　　　　**UNCTAD Locode:** CN HGH

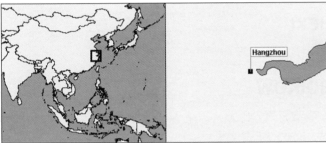

Principal Facilities:

		Y	G						

Accommodation: Cargoes handled include ore, coal, iron & steel, grain, timber, salt, sand, stone and limestone

Name	Remarks
Qiantang River Area	Vessels up to 500 dwt
Grand Canal Area	Vessels up to 300 dwt

Storage: Open and covered storage areas are available

Shipping Agents: CMA-CGM S.A., CMA CGM Hangzhou, Room 1208, Jiahua International Bus Centre, 20 Hangda Road, Hangzhou, Zhejiang Province 310007, People's Republic of China, *Tel:* +86 571 8717 4799, *Fax:* +86 571 8717 4798, *Email:* hzu.genmbox@cma-cgm.com, *Website:* www.cma-cgm.com
Mediterranean Shipping Company, MSC (Hong Kong) Ltd, Room 2205, Tower A, Zhongda Plaza, Hangzhou, Zhejiang Province 310003, People's Republic of China, *Tel:* +86 571 8577 7737, *Fax:* +86 571 8577 7261, *Email:* mschz@nprc.mschkg.com, *Website:* www.mschongkong.com
Sun Hing Shipping Co Ltd, Room 812, 157 Qing Chun Road, Hangzhou, Zhejiang Province 310006, People's Republic of China, *Tel:* +86 571 8721 8564, *Fax:* +86 571 8721 8562, *Website:* www.sunhinggroup.com

Lloyd's Agent: Huatai Surveyors & Adjusters Co., 14th Floor, China Re Building, No.11 Jin Rong Avenue, Xicheng District, Beijing 100140, People's Republic of China, *Tel:* +86 10 6657 6577, *Fax:* +86 10 6657 6502, *Email:* agency.bj@huatai-serv.com, *Website:* www.huatai-serv.com

HANKOW

former name, see Wuhan

HARBIN

Lat 45° 44' N; Long 126° 36' E.

Admiralty Chart: -　　　　　　　**Admiralty Pilot:** -
Time Zone: GMT +8 h　　　　　　**UNCTAD Locode:** CN HRB

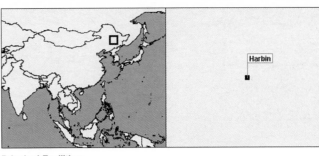

Principal Facilities:

		Y	G					T	

Authority: Harbin Harbour Administration, 1 Haiyuan Street, Taiping District, Harbin, Heilongjiang Province 150050, People's Republic of China

Accommodation:

Name	Remarks
Harbin	See [1] below

[1]*Harbin:* Consists of four harbour areas: Sankeshu, Ashihe, Zhengyanghe and Hulanhe
Cargoes handled include coal, ore and timber

Storage: Open and covered storage areas available

Towage: Tugs available

Shipping Agents: CMA-CGM S.A., CMA CGM Harbin, Room 323 Huating Hotel, 403 Huayuan Street, Nangang District, Harbin, Heilongjiang Province 150001, People's Republic of China, *Tel:* +86 451 5367 0748, *Fax:* +86 451 5367 0108, *Email:* hbi.genmbox@cma-cgm.com, *Website:* www.cma-cgm.com

Lloyd's Agent: Huatai Surveyors & Adjusters Co., 14th Floor, China Re Building, No.11 Jin Rong Avenue, Xicheng District, Beijing 100140, People's Republic of China, *Tel:* +86 10 6657 6577, *Fax:* +86 10 6657 6502, *Email:* agency.bj@huatai-serv.com, *Website:* www.huatai-serv.com

HECHUAN

Lat 29° 59' N; Long 106° 16' E.

Admiralty Chart: -　　　　　　　**Admiralty Pilot:** -
Time Zone: GMT +8 h　　　　　　**UNCTAD Locode:** CN

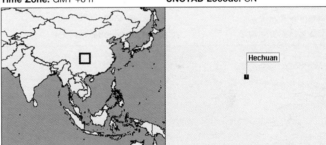

Principal Facilities:

P		Y	G						

Authority: Hechuan Wharf & Ferry Administration, 143 Kangtong Street, Heyang Town, Hechuan, Sichuan Province 631520, People's Republic of China

Accommodation:

Name	Remarks
Hechuan	See [1] below

[1]*Hechuan:* Numerous berths available handling ore, grain, coal, construction materials, fertiliser and petroleum

Storage: Open and covered storage areas available

Mechanical Handling Equipment:

Location	Type	Capacity (t)
Hechuan	Mult-purp. Cranes	6

Lloyd's Agent: Huatai Surveyors & Adjusters Co., 14th Floor, China Re Building, No.11 Jin Rong Avenue, Xicheng District, Beijing 100140, People's Republic of China, *Tel:* +86 10 6657 6577, *Fax:* +86 10 6657 6502, *Email:* agency.bj@huatai-serv.com, *Website:* www.huatai-serv.com

HEFEI

Lat 31° 51' N; Long 117° 16' E.

Admiralty Chart: 2946　　　　　**Admiralty Pilot:** 32
Time Zone: GMT +8 h　　　　　　**UNCTAD Locode:** CN HFE

Key to Principal Facilities:—				
A=Airport	**C**=Containers	**G**=General Cargo	**P**=Petroleum	**R**=Ro/Ro	**Y**=Dry Bulk
B=Bunkers	**D**=Dry Dock	**L**=Cruise	**Q**=Other Liquid Bulk	**T**=Towage (where available from port)	

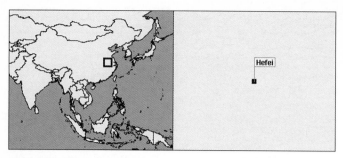

Principal Facilities:

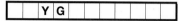

| | | Y | G | | | | | | | |

Authority: Hefei Harbour Administration, 31 Chaohu Road, Hefei, Anhui Province 230001, People's Republic of China

Accommodation:

Name	Remarks
Hefei	See [1] below

[1]*Hefei:* Numerous berths for vessels up to 300 dwt handling iron & steel, ore, timber, fertiliser, coal, grain and general cargo

Storage: Open and covered storage areas available

Shipping Agents: CMA-CGM S.A., CMA CGM Hefei, Room 902, Sinotrans Mansion, 385 Huangshan Road, Hefei, Anhui Province 230022, People's Republic of China, *Tel:* +86 551 366 1111, *Fax:* +86 551 366 3333, *Email:* hef.genmbox@cma-cgm.com, *Website:* www.cma-cgm.com
K Line Ship Management Co. Ltd, 'K' Line (China) Ltd, Room 819, Holiday Inn Hotel, 1104 Changjiang East Road, Hefei, Anhui Province 230011, People's Republic of China, *Tel:* +86 551 220 1156, *Fax:* +86 551 220 6261, *Website:* www.kline.co.jp

Lloyd's Agent: Huatai Surveyors & Adjusters Co., 14th Floor, China Re Building, No.11 Jin Rong Avenue, Xicheng District, Beijing 100140, People's Republic of China, *Tel:* +86 10 6657 6577, *Fax:* +86 10 6657 6502, *Email:* agency.bj@huatai-serv.com, *Website:* www.huatai-serv.com

HEIHE

Lat 50° 14' N; Long 127° 28' E.

Admiralty Chart: -

Admiralty Pilot: -

Time Zone: GMT +8 h

UNCTAD Locode: CN HEK

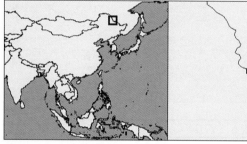

Principal Facilities:

| | | | G | | R | | | | | |

Authority: Heihe Port Authority, 4 Wangsu Street, Heihe, Heilongjiang, People's Republic of China, *Tel:* +86 456 822 3841

Accommodation:

Name	Remarks
Heihe	Several berths for ro/ro and general cargo vessels up to 1000 dwt

Storage: Open and covered storage areas available

Lloyd's Agent: Huatai Surveyors & Adjusters Co., 14th Floor, China Re Building, No.11 Jin Rong Avenue, Xicheng District, Beijing 100140, People's Republic of China, *Tel:* +86 10 6657 6577, *Fax:* +86 10 6657 6502, *Email:* agency.bj@huatai-serv.com, *Website:* www.huatai-serv.com

HENGYANG

Lat 26° 53' N; Long 112° 37' E.

Admiralty Chart: -

Admiralty Pilot: -

Time Zone: GMT +8 h

UNCTAD Locode: CN HNY

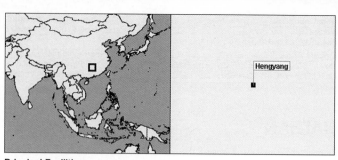

Principal Facilities:

| | | Y | G | | | | | | | |

Authority: Hengyang Harbour Administration, 50 Xiangjiang Bei Road, Hengyang, Hunan Province, People's Republic of China

Accommodation:

Name	Remarks
Hengyang	See [1] below

[1]*Hengyang:* Numerous cargo and passenger wharves handling ore, timber, coal, fertiliser and construction materials

Storage: Open and covered storage areas available

Lloyd's Agent: Huatai Surveyors & Adjusters Co., 14th Floor, China Re Building, No.11 Jin Rong Avenue, Xicheng District, Beijing 100140, People's Republic of China, *Tel:* +86 10 6657 6577, *Fax:* +86 10 6657 6502, *Email:* agency.bj@huatai-serv.com, *Website:* www.huatai-serv.com

HEPING

harbour area, see under Xiamen

HEXI

harbour area, see under Xiangtan

HOIKOW

former name, see Haikou

HONG KONG

Lat 22° 17' N; Long 114° 9' E.

Admiralty Chart: 4117-23/4127-28

Admiralty Pilot: 30

Time Zone: GMT +8 h

UNCTAD Locode: CN HKG

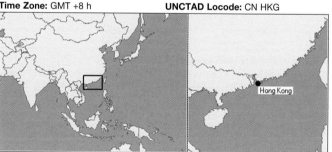

Principal Facilities:

| P | Q | Y | G | C | R | L | B | D | T | A |

Authority: Hong Kong Marine Department, 22nd Floor, Harbour Building, 38 Pier Road, P O Box 4155, Hong Kong, Hong Kong, *Tel:* +852 2542 3711, *Fax:* +852 2541 7194, *Email:* mdenquiry@mardep.gov.hk, *Website:* www.mardep.gov.hk

Port Security: ISPS compliant. Container Security Initiative (CSI) designated port

Pre-Arrival Information: All vessels with the exception of
(a) a locally licensed vessel
(b) ferries plying regularly between Hong Kong SAR and Pearl River Delta Ports and Macau
are required to forward their pre-arrival notifications to the Vessel Traffic Centre (VTC) of the Marine Department by Fax: +852 2359 4264 (24 hours) not less than 24 h before the intended entry of the vessel into Hong Kong waters or immediately after leaving its last port of call, where that vessel takes less than 24 h for that intended entry

Approach: The harbour can be approached from both the E and W, both approaches having compulsory traffic separation schemes in force. The Western Harbour area is approached via the deep water East Lamma Channel being the main access to Kwai Chung Container Port, Western Anchorage and the Central Harbour area via the Northern Fairway
To the E the Central Harbour area is approached via the Tathong Channel through Lai Yue Mun pass into the Eastern and Hung Hom fairways. This Eastern approach is restricted to vessels of 10.97 m draft

Anchorage: There are 19 'A' class and 10 'B' class moorings laid within the port of Hong Kong for commercial shipping. 'A' class moorings are suitable for vessels of a length not exceeding 183 m and 'B' class moorings for vessels not exceeding 137 m. Harbour moorings include 19 special moorings to which vessels can remain secured during tropical storms. The following anchorages are established within the waters of Hong Kong for specified purposes:
1) Quarantine Anchorages:
(a) Eastern Quarantine Anchorage
(b) Western Quarantine Anchorage
2) Dangerous Goods Anchhorages:
(a) Kau Yi Chau Dangerous Goods Anchorage
(b) Tsuen Wan Dangerous Goods Anchorage
(c) Western Dangerous Goods Anchorage
(d) Rocky Harbour Dangerous Goods Anchorage
(e) Junk Bay Dangerous Goods Anchorage
(f) Mirs Bay Dangerous Goods Anchorage
(g) South Lamma Dangerous Goods Anchorage
(h) Reserved Dangerous Goods Anchorage
3) Service Anchorages:
(a) Ma Wan Anchorage
(b) Pun Shan Shek Anchorage
(c) Western Anchorage No.1
(d) Western Anchorage No.2
(e) Western Anchorage No.3
(f) North Lamma Anchorage
(g) North-west Lamma Anchorage
(h) Yau Ma Tei Anchorage
(i) Kellett Anchorage No.1
(j) Kellett Anchorage No.2
(k) Kellett Anchorage No.3
(l) Sham Shui Kok Anchorage No.1
(m) Sham Shui Kok Anchorage No.2
4) Naval Anchorage

Pilotage: Compulsory pilotage for:
(a) vessels over 3000 gt
(b) vessels over 1000 gt proceeding to and from container terminal, oil and power company wharfs
(c) vessels over 1000 gt carrying dangerous goods (Cat. 1, 2 & 5)

(d) vessels over 1000 gt proceeding to and from Government mooring buoy
(e) vessels over 300 gt, dead ship or disabled ship
(f) gas carriers
Pilots available 24 h/day from the Hong Kong Pilots Association Ltd., Tel: +852 2803 0840, Fax: +852 2803 0859, Email: hkpilots@netvigator.com
The pilot boarding stations are:
Ha Mei Wan, west of Lamma Island, in pos 22° 12.0' N; 114° 05.3' E
Tathong Channel in pos 22° 16.0' N; 114° 15.7' E
Urmston Road in pos 22° 23.5' N; 113° 53.5' E
Tolo Channel in pos 22° 29.6' N; 114° 19.7' E
Ngan Chau in East Lamma Channel in pos 22° 13.1' N; 114° 09.7' E

Radio Frequency: Where the master of a vessel in the waters of Hong Kong is to report to the Vessel Traffic Centre he should use the VHF channel appropriate to the VHF sector in which the vessel is presently located in those waters:
VHF Channel 67 for Western Approaches, VHF Channel 12 for Eastern Approaches, VHF Channel 14 for Harbour, VHF Channel 74 for Kwai Chung Container Terminals and VHF Channel 20 for Navigational Warning

Traffic: 2007, 245 433 000 t of cargo handled, 23 880 000 TEU's

Working Hours: The Vessel Traffic Centre operates 24 h/day

Accommodation: Bulk facilities: There are two major power stations which receive cargoes of coal and other necessary materials
Po Lo Tsui on Lamma Island, owned by Hong Kong Electric Co Ltd., Tel: +852 2982 6274, Fax: +852 2982 1654, Email: mail@hec.com.hk, Website: www.hec.com.hk, can accommodate vessels up to 100 000 dwt and 262 m loa. Depth alongside berth is 13.9 m. Cargo handling is undertaken by two grab type unloaders and three 1500 t/h continuous unloaders
China Light and Power Co operates two berths at Castle Peak Power Station in Tuen Mun for vessels up to 140 000 dwt. Berth length of 545 m and two dolphins allow the simultaneous mooring of two vessels having draughts up to 17.0 m. Coal handling equipment includes two 1500 t/h grab unloaders and two 1500 t/h continuous unloaders
Green Island Cement Co Ltd., Tel: +852 2440 5111, Fax: +852 2441 3421, Email: info@gich.com.hk, Website: www.gich.com.hk, has three berths at Tap Shek Kok. A main jetty of 270 m with a depth of 14.0 m, having fifteen 70 t mooring bollards, can berth vessels up to 60 000 dwt. An auxiliary jetty of 275 m with a depth of 14.0 m has three 25 t mooring bollards. The third berth is for lighters with 4.5 m draft
HUD Bulk, a division of Hong Kong United Dockyards Ltd., Tel: +852 2497 5181, have shore based bagging facilities for free flowing bulk commodities. Facilities include four Richard Simon & Sons 'Containerpacks' each rated at 2000 x 50 kg bags/h, reception hoppers fitted with spill screens and de-lumping equipment, two mono-tower quayside cranes with hoist speeds of 6 m/minute at 10 t cap. Accommodation is for vessels up to and including panamax size with drafts in excess of 13.5 m. Storage cap of 2000 m2 of covered warehouse space for bags is available
Tanker facilities: Eight oil berths with lengths ranging from 60.9 m to 250 m. The principal terminals are as follows:
Shell Terminal, Tel: +852 2432 8704. At Tsing Yi, accommodation for vessels up to 110 000 dwt with limit on max draft 14.5 m
ExxonMobil Terminal, Tel: +852 3197 8274. Situated on Tsing Yi Island, accommodation for vessels up to 120 000 dwt with limit on max draft 14.6 m
Caltex Terminal, Tel: +852 2431 2414. At Tsing Yi Island, accommodation for vessels up to 235 m loa, 60 000 dwt with limit of max draft 12.6 m
China Resources Petrochems (Group) Co Ltd., Tel: +852 2431 2962. At Tsing Yi, accommodation for vessels up to 250 m loa, 80 000 dwt with limit of max draft 14.0 m
LPG facilities exist at the terminals operated by Shell, ExxonMobil, Caltex, CRC and Hong Kong Oil

Name	Length (m)	Depth (m)	Remarks
Hong Kong			See [1] below
Container Terminals 1, 2 & 5	1082	14	See [2] below
Container Terminals 4, 6, 7 & 8 (east)			See [3] below
Container Terminal 3	305	14	See [4] below
Container Terminal 8 (west)	740	15.5	See [5] below
Container Terminal 9	1940	15.5	See [6] below
River Trade Terminal	3000		See [7] below
Ocean Terminal		9–11	See [8] below

[1]*Hong Kong:* All 29 moorings (mid-stream operations) in the harbour for ocean-going vessels are government owned. 19 are 'A' class, for vessels up to 183 m loa and the remainder are 'B' Class, for vessels up to 137 m loa. To book any of these moorings contact Vessel Traffic Centre, Tel: +852 2858 2107, Fax: +852 2858 6646. Goods are loaded and discharged by lighters working from Public Cargo Working Areas in Wan Chai, Western District, New Yaumatei, Kwun Tong, Stonecutters Island, Rambler Channel, Cha Kwo Ling, Tuen Mun and Chai Wan. The total sea frontage of Public Cargo Working Areas, managed by the Cargo Handling Section, amounts to 6992 m
There is an extensive traffic of river vessels and ferries which operate between Hong Kong, Macau, Guangzhou and other Chinese coastal ports. The China Ferry Terminal in Tsim Sha Tsui operates to 20 destinations in China. The Hong Kong-Macau Ferry Terminal in Central District has ten hydrofoil docking platforms
[2]*Container Terminals 1, 2 & 5:* Operated by Modern Terminals Ltd. (MTL), Berth One, Kwai Chung, Hong Kong, Tel: +852 2115 3838, Fax: +852 2115 3232, Email: cad@modernterminals.com, Website: www.modernterminals.com
[3]*Container Terminals 4, 6, 7 & 8 (east):* Operated by Hong Kong International Terminals Ltd. (HIT), Terminal 4, Container Port Road South, Kwai Chung, Hong Kong, Tel: +852 2619 7557, Fax: +852 2612 0083, Email: gca@hph.com, Website: www.hit.com.hk
Jointly operate Terminal 8 (east) with COSCO
Total quay length at Terminals 4, 6 and 7 of 3292 m in depth of 12.5-15.5 m (ten ship berths and four barge berths). Total area of 92 ha
Total quay length at Terminal 8 (East) of 1088 m in depth of 15.5 m (two ship berths and four-five barge berths). Total area of 30 ha
[4]*Container Terminal 3:* Operated by DP World Hong Kong Ltd., Berth 3, Kwai Chung Container Terminal, Kwai Chung, Hong Kong, Tel: +852 2489 5005, Fax: +852 2614 4791, Email: inquiry.hkg@dpworld.com, Website: www.dpworld.com

Total terminal area of 16.7 ha with yard stacking cap of 10 872 TEU's. 378 reefer points

[5]*Container Terminal 8 (west):* Operated by Asia Container Terminals Ltd., Main Office Building, Container Terminal 8 West, Container Port Road South, Kwai Chung, Hong Kong, Tel: +852 2276 8000, Fax: +852 3101 1536, Email: act-hotline@act.com.hk, Website: www.asiacontainerterminals.com

Two berths with total terminal area of 28.54 ha

[6]*Container Terminal 9:* Four berths (each 310 m long) operated by Modern Terminals Ltd. (MTL), Berth One, Kwai Chung, Hong Kong, Tel: +852 2115 3838, Fax: +852 2115 3232, Email: cad@modernterminals.com, Website: www.modernterminals.com

Two berths (each 350 m long) operated by Hong Kong International Terminals Ltd. (HIT), Terminal 4, Container Port Road South, Kwai Chung, Hong Kong, Tel: +852 2619 7557, Fax: +852 2612 0083, Email: gca@hph.com, Website: www.hit.com.hk

[7]*River Trade Terminal:* Operated by River Trade Terminal Co Ltd., Terminal Office Building, 201 Lung Mun Road, Tuen Mun, N.T., Hong Kong, Tel: +852 2122 7878, Fax: +852 2122 7438, Email: corp_com@rttc.com.hk, Website: www.rttc.com.hk

Located at Tuen Mun. Terminal area of 7 000 000 ft2 and forty nine berths. Container and breakbulk operations for inbound, outbound and transshipment cargo. 408 reefer points

[8]*Ocean Terminal:* Tel: +852 2118 8951, Fax: +852 2736 2481, Email: kwkwan@terminal.harbourcity.com.hk, Website: www.oceanterminal.com.hk

Finger pier of 381 m loa orientated E-W, and of open piled construction. Berths are provided symmetrically about the pier centreline on both its north and south side. It is the sole cruise terminal in Hong Kong. The terminal building of 58 m width extends from the shore westwards along the centreline of the pier for 305 m

Mechanical Handling Equipment:

Location	Type	Capacity (t)	Qty	Remarks
Container Terminals 1, 2 & 5	Container Cranes		19	
Container Terminals 1, 2 & 5	RTG's		75	
Container Terminals 4, 6, 7 & 8 (east)	RTG's		122	90 at terminals 4, 6 & 7. 32 at terminal 8 (east)
Container Terminals 4, 6, 7 & 8 (east)	Quay Cranes		42	33 at terminals 4, 6 & 7. 9 at terminal 8 (east)
Container Terminal 3	RTG's		8	
Container Terminal 3	Shore Cranes		4	
Container Terminal 8 (west)	Container Cranes		8	
Container Terminal 8 (west)	RTG's		20	
Container Terminal 9	Container Cranes		14	at Modern berths
Container Terminal 9	Container Cranes		9	at HIT berths
Container Terminal 9	RTG's		48	at Modern berths
River Trade Terminal	RTG's		40	
River Trade Terminal	Quay Cranes		30	
River Trade Terminal	Reach Stackers		12	
River Trade Terminal	Forklifts	2.5–15	26	

Bunkering: Bominflot, Bomin Bunker Oil Ltd, Room 604-605, 6/F, Centre Point, 181-185 Gloucester Road, Wanchai, Hong Kong, Hong Kong, *Tel:* +852 2891 7799, *Fax:* +852 2893 1636, *Email:* bunkers@bomin.hk, *Website:* www.bominflot.net

BP Hong Kong Ltd, 22nd Floor, Devon House, 979 Kings Road, Taikoo Place, Quarry Bay, Hong Kong, Hong Kong, *Tel:* +852 2586 8899, *Fax:* +852 2586 8981, *Email:* kantk@bp.com, *Website:* www.bp.com

Callany Ltd, 19th Floor, China Resources Building, 26 Harbour Road, Wanchai, Hong Kong, Hong Kong, *Tel:* +852 25937420, *Fax:* +852 28024121, *Email:* win@crpetro-chem.com, *Website:* www.crpetro-chem.com

Candia Shipping (HK) Ltd, Suite 1411, Melbourne Plaza, 33 Queens Road Central, Hong Kong, Hong Kong, *Tel:* +852 2521 5348, *Fax:* +852 845 2571

Chevron Hong Kong Ltd, Chevron Hong Kong Ltd., 42nd Floor Central Plaza, 18 Harbour Road, P O Box 147, Wanchai, Hong Kong, Hong Kong, *Tel:* +852 2802 8338, *Fax:* +852 2511 2316, *Email:* gmphkb@chevron.com, *Website:* www.chevron.com

Chevron Marine Products LLC, 42/F., Central Plaza, 18 Harbour Road, Wanchai, Hong Kong, Hong Kong, *Tel:* +852 2582 7723, *Fax:* +852 2524 8418, *Email:* hkfuels@chevron.com, *Website:* www.chevron.com

Feoso Oil Ltd, 10th Floor, Feoso Building, 877 Lai Chi Kok Road, Kowloon, Hong Kong, Hong Kong, *Tel:* +852 3162 3888, *Fax:* +852 3162 3600, *Email:* feosobkr@feoso.com.hk, *Website:* www.feoso.com.hk

Frisol Bunkering Hong Kong Ltd, 33 Floor Hopewell Centre, 183 Queen's Road East, Wanchai, Hong Kong, Hong Kong, *Tel:* +852 2529 3122, *Fax:* +852 2527 3318, *Email:* bunker@frisol.com.hk, *Website:* www.frisol.com

Hong Kong Fuels Ltd, 11 Floor, Jonism Place, 228 Queen's Road East, Hong Kong, Hong Kong, *Tel:* +852 2234 0088, *Fax:* +852 2234 0078, *Email:* operations@hongkongfuels.com.hk

Mainway Petroleum Ltd, 7 Floor, 9 Chatham Road South, Tsimshatsui, Kowloon, Hong Kong, Hong Kong, *Tel:* +852 2367 8787, *Fax:* +852 2367 8777, *Email:* davidlau@mainwaygroup.com

Marsco Corp., Room 701, Alliance Building, 130-6 Connaught Road, Hong Kong, Hong Kong, *Tel:* +852 2545 0343, *Fax:* +852 2541 8431

Marubeni Hong Kong & South China Ltd, 20th Floor, Tower 1, Admiralty Centre, 18 Harcourt Road, Hong Kong, Hong Kong, *Tel:* +852 2861 2922, *Fax:* +852 2865 2396, *Email:* hkgcomm@hkg.marubenicorp.com, *Website:* www.marubeni.com

New Asia Energy Ltd, Room 1101, Asia Standard Tower, 59-65 Queens Road, Hong Kong, Hong Kong, *Tel:* +852 2530 0833, *Fax:* +852 2810 9722

Oil Shipping B.V., Oil Shipping (Hong Kong), 17/F., The Phoenix, No 21-25 Luard, Wanchai, Hong Kong, Hong Kong, *Tel:* +852 2520 0157, *Fax:* +852 2865 1700, *Email:* oshk@wfscorp.com, *Website:* www.wfscorp.com

OW Bunker China Ltd, Room 1710 - 11, Shui On Centre, 6 - 8 Harbour Road, Wanchai, Hong Kong, Hong Kong, *Tel:* +852 2866 6254, *Fax:* +852 2866 9590, *Email:* owbchina@owbunker.com.hk, *Website:* www.owbunker.com

Singapore Petroleum Co. Ltd, Singapore Petroleum Co. (HK) Ltd, 908 China Resources Building, 26 Harbour Road, Hong Kong, Hong Kong, *Tel:* +852 2511 0693, *Fax:* +852 2511 0867, *Email:* hkspc@spc-hk.com.hk, *Website:* www.spc.com.sg

Sino United International Petroleum Ltd, 21st Floor Ngan House, 210 Des Voeux Road, Hong Kong, Hong Kong, *Tel:* +852 2851 9292, *Fax:* +852 2851 7799, *Email:* swong@nwtbb.com

Soaring Dragon Enterprise Ltd, Room 1208, Central Plaza, Harbour Road, Wanchai, Hong Kong, Hong Kong, *Tel:* +852 2519 3882, *Fax:* +852 2511 3130, *Email:* business@soaringdragon.com.hk, *Website:* www.soaringdragon.com.hk

South Horizons International Petroleum Ltd, O.W. Bunker China Ltd, Room 1710 - 11,, Shui On Centre, 6 - 8 Harbour Road, Wanchai, Hong Kong, Hong Kong, *Tel:* +852 2866 6254, *Fax:* +852 2866 9590, *Email:* owbchina@owbunker.com.hk, *Website:* www.owbunker.com

Vermont Marine Bunkering Ltd, 31st Floor, Room 3101, 3107-3110, Yat Chau International Plaza, 118 Connaught Road West, Hong Kong, Hong Kong, *Tel:* +852 2803 0608, *Fax:* +852 2527 3851, *Email:* vermont@vermont.com.hk

Wilhelmsen Ship Services, Barwil Agencies Ltd, Rooms 1104-6 11 Floor Lu Plaza, 2 Wing Yip Street, Kwun Tung Kowloon, Hong Kong, Hong Kong, *Tel:* +852 2880 1688, *Fax:* +852 2880 5058, *Email:* hong.kong@wilhelmsen.com, *Website:* www.wilhelmsen.com

Waste Reception Facilities: A domestic and operational refuse collection service is provided by the Marine Department for all ocean-going and local vessels in the harbour. A chemical waste treatment centre is in operation on Tsing Yi Island for receiving oil and chemical wastes from vessels

Towage: The Hongkong Salvage & Towage Co. Ltd, 2nd Floor, HUD Administration Building, Sai Tso Wan Road, Tsing Yi Island, Hong Kong, Hong Kong, *Tel:* +852 2427 7477, *Fax:* +852 2480 5894, *Email:* hkst@hktug.com, *Website:* www.hktug.com

Repair & Maintenance: The Hong Kong Shipyard Ltd., 98 Tam Kon Shan Road, North Tsing Yi, New Territories, Hong Kong, Hong Kong, *Tel:* +852 2436 1138, *Fax:* +852 2436 2011, *Email:* hksyd@hkf.com, *Website:* www.hkf.com Syncrolift of 90 m x 20 m with a lifting cap up to 3400 t

HUD Group, TYTL 108, Sai Tso Wan Road, Tsing Yi Island, New Territories, Hong Kong, Hong Kong, *Tel:* +852 2431 2828, *Fax:* +852 2433 0180, *Email:* shiprepair@hud.com.hk, *Website:* www.hud.com.hk Length 290 m (over blocks 270 m) x 41 m x 10 m with 350 t cap floating heavy lift crane

Yiu Lian Dockyards Ltd, 1-7 Sai Tso Wan Road, Tsing Yi Island, New Territories, Hong Kong, Hong Kong, *Tel:* +852 2541 0988, *Fax:* +852 2815 0702, *Email:* yldockhk@yiulian.com.hk, *Website:* www.yiulian.com.hk Floating dock of 305 m x 45.8 m x 15 m for vessels up to 180 000 dwt

Seaman Missions: The Seamans Mission, 2 Container Port Road, Kwai Chung, Hong Kong, Hong Kong, *Tel:* +852 2410 8240, *Fax:* +852 2410 8617, *Email:* seamenkc@netvigator.com

Ship Chandlers: AIK Friend Ltd, Shop Floor, Good Luck Mansion, 41 Po Tuck Street, 101 Hill Road, Hong Kong, Hong Kong, *Tel:* +852 2818 8073, *Fax:* +852 2818 8142, *Email:* aikltd@netvigator.com

Dickson General Appliances Ltd, 2nd Floor, Feoso Building, 877 Lai Chi Kok Road, Kowloon, Hong Kong, Hong Kong, *Tel:* +852 2415 0513, *Email:* dicksong@dicksonship.com.hk

Fortune Ship-Chandlers Co. Ltd, 12 Ground Floor, Tung On Street, Mongkok, Kowloon, Hong Kong, Hong Kong, *Tel:* +852 2544 3429, *Fax:* +852 2542 3905, *Email:* info@hkfortuneship-chandlers.com, *Website:* www.hkfortuneship-chandlers.com

Goldrich International Co., Shop 3A, Ground Floor, Connaught Garden, 155 Connaught Road West, Hong Kong, Hong Kong, *Tel:* +852 2541 3897, *Fax:* +852 2541 9140, *Email:* grlntl@netvigator.com

Hsing Loong Co. Ltd, 220-248 Texaco Road, Suite 1209, Tsuen Wan Industrial Centre, Tsuen Wan, Hong Kong, Hong Kong, *Tel:* +852 2545 0877, *Fax:* +852 2815 1765, *Email:* davidnie@hotmail.com, *Website:* hsingloongroup.tripod.com

Kemklen Technical Services Ltd, 1701- 02 East Town Building, 41 Lockhart Road, Wanchai, Hong Kong, Hong Kong, *Tel:* +852 2861 2812, *Fax:* +852 2861 1168, *Email:* ktssales@turbokts.com, *Website:* www.turbokts.com

Man Sang (China) Co. Ltd, Shop A G/F, Good Prospect Factory Building, 33-35 Wong Chuk Hang Road, Hong Kong, Hong Kong, *Tel:* +852 2858 9622, *Fax:* +852 2858 9569, *Email:* hk@mansangco.com, *Website:* www.mansangco.com

Ming Ocean & Co., Ground Floor, 32 Man Ying Street, Yaumatei, Kowloon, Hong Kong, Hong Kong, *Tel:* +852 2332 5677, *Fax:* +852 2728 6839, *Email:* mingocn@netvigator.com

Ocean Marine Supply Ltd, Ground Floor, Kam Teem Industrial Building, 135/6 Connaught Road West, Hong Kong, Hong Kong, *Tel:* +852 2549 4698, *Fax:* +852 2559 8768, *Email:* omsltdhk@biznetvigator.com, *Website:* www.oceanmarinesupply.com

Sims Trading Co. Ltd, 10th Floor, DCH Building, 20 Kai Cheung Road, Kowloon Bay, Hong Kong, Hong Kong, *Tel:* +852 2375 0768, *Fax:* +852 2375 0172, *Email:* ssd@sims.com.hk, *Website:* www.simshk.com

United Shipchandlers Ltd, 8th Floor, Tung Cheong Industrial Building, 177-181 Yeung Uk Road, Tsuen Wan, Hong Kong, Hong Kong, *Tel:* +852 2816 7228, *Fax:* +852 2816 7107, *Email:* info@unitedshipchandlers.com

Wei Hsing Marine Co. Ltd, Shop 9, Tak Hay Building, Yau Ma Tei, Kowloon, Hong Kong, Hong Kong, *Tel:* +852 2780 6268, *Fax:* +852 2771 6066, *Email:* weihsing@hk.super.net

Wing Fung Hong Kong Trading Co. Ltd, Unit A, Ground Floor, Prosperity Centre, "77-81 Container Port Road, Kwai Chung", Hong Kong, Hong Kong, *Tel:* +852 2332 6317, *Fax:* +852 2388 8042, *Email:* wfhktrdg@wftrdg.biz.com.hk

Shipping Agents: Ben Line Agencies Ltd, Room 2702, Bonham Trade Centre, 50 Bonham Strand, Sheung Wan, Hong Kong, Hong Kong, *Tel:* +852 2893 4307, *Fax:* +852 2893 4377, *Email:* mngt@benline.com.hk, *Website:* www.benlineagencies.com

Eternity Shipping Agencies Ltd (ESAL), 1302 Shun Tak Centre West Tower, 168-200 Connaught Road, Hong Kong, Hong Kong, *Tel:* +852 2545 1212, *Fax:* +852 2541 2085, *Email:* eternity@esal.com.hk, *Website:* www.esal.com.hk

GMT Shipping Line Ltd, 18th Floor, Harbour Commercial Building, 122-124 Connaught Road Central, Sheung Wan, Hong Kong, Hong Kong, *Tel:* +852 2581 1800, *Fax:* +852 2851 8399, *Email:* commercial@gmtshipping.com, *Website:* www.gmtshipping.com

Gulf Agency Co. (Hong Kong) Ltd, P O Box 69559, Kwun Tong Post Office, Hong Kong, Hong Kong, *Tel:* +852 2723 6306, *Fax:* +852 2723 3413, *Email:* hongkong@gacworld.com, *Website:* www.gacworld.com

A Hartrodt International, Flat 816 8th Floor Block B Southmark, 11 Yip Hing Street, Wong Chuk Hang, Hong Kong, Hong Kong, *Tel:* +852 2812 2928, *Fax:* +852 2812 2777, *Email:* info@hartrodt.com.hk

Hongkong Company Ltd, Room 1103-4, Li Po Chun Chambers, 189 Des Voeux

Road, Central, Hong Kong, Hong Kong, *Tel:* +852 2534 4800, *Fax:* +852 2815 1344, *Email:* hkadmin@cngr.com.hk, *Website:* www.cngr.com.hk
Inchcape Shipping Services (ISS), Inchcape Shipping Services (Hong Kong) Ltd, Units 1802-1805 18th Floor, 3 Lockhart Road, Wanchai, Hong Kong, Hong Kong, *Tel:* +852 2786 1155, *Fax:* +852 2744 3240, *Email:* iss.hongkong@iss-shipping.com, www.iss-shipping.com
Interocean Shipping Co. Ltd, 4th Floor, Harbour Commercial Building, 122 Connaught Road Central, Hong Kong, Hong Kong, *Tel:* +852 2541 2624/7, *Fax:* +852 2541 6449, *Email:* interocean@vol.net
A.P. Moller-Maersk Group, Maersk Hong Kong Ltd, 16-19/F, One Kowloon, 1-11 Wang Yuen Street, Kowloon Bay, Hong Kong, Hong Kong, *Tel:* +852 3765 3765, *Fax:* +852 2972 0679, *Website:* www.maerskline.com
Penavico (Hong Kong) Ltd, Room 4008-09, 40/F, Cosco Tower, 183 Queen's Road Central, Hong Kong, Hong Kong, *Tel:* +852 2559 1996, *Fax:* +852 2549 8622, *Email:* penavico@penavico.com.hk, *Website:* www.cosco.com.hk
Shenship Logistics Ltd, 2nd Floor, No.8 Jordan Road, Kowloon, Hong Kong, Hong Kong, *Tel:* +852 26272920, *Fax:* +852 2185 1120, *Email:* info@shenship.com, *Website:* www.shenship.com
Shenzhen Integrity International Logistics Co Ltd, Flat A 13th Floor Hillier Commercial Boulevard, 65-67 Bonham Street, Hong Kong, Hong Kong, *Tel:* +852 2135 6686, *Fax:* +852 2135 6686, *Email:* frank@szintegrity.com, *Website:* www.szintegrity.com
Sinotrans (HK) Logistics Ltd, 18th Floor, 9 Des Voeux Road West, Hong Kong, Hong Kong, *Tel:* +852 2559 7911, *Fax:* +852 2581 3336, *Email:* mail@sinotrans-logistics.com, *Website:* www.sinotrans-logistics.com
Star Shipping Agencies Ltd, 15th & 17th Floors, Allied Kajima Building, 138 Gloucester Road, Wanchai, Hong Kong, Hong Kong, *Tel:* +852 2823 5888, *Fax:* +852 2528 6744, *Email:* leung.llewellyn@starshiphk.com, *Website:* www.sunhinggroup.com
Wallem Shipping Agencies Limited, Wallem Shipping (Hong Kong) Limited, 12th Floor, Warwick House East, Taikoo Place, 979 King's Road, Quarry Bay, Hong Kong, Hong Kong, *Tel:* +852 2876 8500, *Fax:* +852 2876 1500, *Email:* wshk@wallem.com, *Website:* www.wallem.com/hongkong
Wilhelmsen Ship Services, Barwil Agencies Ltd, Rooms 1104-6 11 Floor Lu Plaza, 2 Wing Yip Street, Kwun Tung Kowloon, Hong Kong, Hong Kong, *Tel:* +852 2880 1688, *Fax:* +852 2880 5058, *Email:* hong.kong@wilhelmsen.com, *Website:* www.wilhelmsen.com
Yi Tong Container Line, Yi Tong Lines Co. Ltd, Room 2501-6, 25th Floor, ING Tower, 308-320 Des Voeux Road Central, Sheung Wan, Hong Kong, Hong Kong, *Tel:* +852 2881 6038, *Fax:* +852 2881 7721, *Email:* yitonghk@netvigator.com, *Website:* www.yitonghk.com.hk

Stevedoring Companies: Fat Kee Stevedores Ltd, Room 415, Phase I, MTL Warehouse Building, Berth 1, Container Port Road, Kwai Chung, Hong Kong, Hong Kong, *Tel:* +852 2487 6287, *Fax:* +852 2420 6719, *Email:* fkshghk@fksteve.com, *Website:* www.fkstev.com

Surveyors: Bureau Veritas, Room 2704, Vicwood Plaza, 199 Des Voeux Road C, P O Box 5046, Hong Kong, Hong Kong, *Tel:* +852 2815 1863, *Fax:* +852 2815 3428, *Email:* miranda.kwan@hk.bureauveritas.com, *Website:* www.bureauveritas.com
Carmichael & Clarke Co. Ltd, 17th Floor Jade Centre, 98 Wellington Street, Hong Kong, Hong Kong, *Tel:* +852 2581 2678, *Fax:* +852 2581 2722, *Email:* carmi@hkstar.com, *Website:* www.carmichaelandclarke.com
China Classification Society, Room 2904-2905, 29th Floor, West Tower, Shun Tak Centre, 168-200 Connaught Road, Hong Kong, Hong Kong, *Tel:* +852 2547 6181, *Fax:* +852 2858 2629, *Email:* ccshk@ccs.biz.com.hk, *Website:* www.ccs.org.cn
Det Norske Veritas A/S, Room 1704-7, 17th Floor, New York Life Tower, Windsor House, 311 Gloucester Road, Causeway Bay, Hong Kong, Hong Kong, *Tel:* +852 2865 3332, *Fax:* +852 2865 3513, *Email:* mchhk220@dnv.com, *Website:* www.dnv.com
Germanischer Lloyd, Room 918, 9/F., Star House, 3 Salisbury Road, Tsim Sha Tsui, Kowloon, Hong Kong, Hong Kong, *Tel:* +852 2317 1980, *Fax:* +852 2314 7003, *Email:* gl-hong.kong@gl-group.com, *Website:* www.gl-group.com
Intertek Testing Services, Unit C, 9/F Garment Centre, 576 Castle Peak Road, Kowloon, Hong Kong, Hong Kong, *Tel:* +852 2197 1838, *Fax:* +852 2307 0373, *Email:* gen.info@intertek.com, *Website:* www.intertek.com
Lloyd's Register, Lloyd's Register Asia, Suite 3501 China Merchants Tower, Shun Tak Centre, 168-200 Connaught Road Central, Hong Kong, Hong Kong, *Tel:* +852 2287 9333, *Fax:* +852 2526 2921, *Email:* hong-kong@lr.org, *Website:* www.lr.org
Andrew Moore & Associates Ltd, 2703 Universal Trade Centre, 3 Artbuthnot Road, Central, Hong Kong, Hong Kong, *Tel:* +852 2861 3313, *Fax:* +852 2865 6571, *Email:* lloydsagency@andrew-moore.com, *Website:* www.andrew-moore.com
Nippon Kaiji Kyokai, Room 3705, Shun Tak Centre, West Tower, 200 Connaught Road, Hong Kong, Hong Kong, *Tel:* +852 2517 7023, *Fax:* +852 2857 7401, *Email:* hn@classnk.or.jp, *Website:* www.classnk.or.jp
Registro Italiano Navale (RINA), Unit 1703 17th Floor Golden Centre, 188 Des Voeux Road Central, Hong Kong, Hong Kong, *Tel:* +852 2866 3433, *Fax:* +852 2861 2676, *Email:* hongkong.office@rina.org, *Website:* www.rina.org
Toplis & Harding (HK) Ltd, 14/F Shanghai Ind Investment Building, 48-62 Hennessy Road, Wanchai, Hong Kong, Hong Kong, *Tel:* +852 2866 7744, *Fax:* +852 2858 2633, *Email:* general@toplishk.com
Union Star Surveyors Ltd, 10/F MTL Berth 1, Kwai Chung, Hong Kong, Hong Kong, *Tel:* +852 2424 5521, *Fax:* +852 2489 2704, *Email:* unionstarsur@ctimail.com
J.D. Wort & Co. Ltd, Suite B6, 29th Floor, Causeway Centre, 28 Harbour Road, Hong Kong, Hong Kong, *Tel:* +852 2802 1019, *Fax:* +852 2827 2355, *Email:* jdwco@netvigator.com

Medical Facilities: Available from Port Health, *Tel:* 2572 2841

Airport: Hong Kong International Airport

Lloyd's Agent: Andrew Moore & Associates Ltd, 2703 Universal Trade Centre, 3 Artbuthnot Road, Central, Hong Kong, Hong Kong, *Tel:* +852 2861 3313, *Fax:* +852 2865 6571, *Email:* lloydsagency@andrew-moore.com, *Website:* www.andrew-moore.com

HONGSHENGSHA

harbour area, see under Guangzhou

HUAIAN

Lat 33° 30' N; Long 119° 8' E.

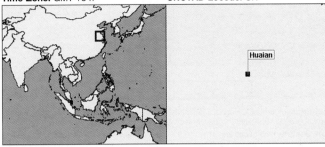

Admiralty Chart: 3480	**Admiralty Pilot:** 32
Time Zone: GMT +8 h	**UNCTAD Locode:** CN

Principal Facilities:

		Y	G						

Accommodation:

Name	Remarks
Huaian	Numerous berths available handling ore, coal, grain and salt

Storage: Open storage area available

Mechanical Handling Equipment:

Location	Type	Capacity (t)
Huaian	Mult-purp. Cranes	12

Lloyd's Agent: Huatai Surveyors & Adjusters Co., 14th Floor, China Re Building, No.11 Jin Rong Avenue, Xicheng District, Beijing 100140, People's Republic of China, *Tel:* +86 10 6657 6577, *Fax:* +86 10 6657 6502, *Email:* agency.bj@huatai-serv.com, *Website:* www.huatai-serv.com

HUAINAN

Lat 32° 40' N; Long 117° 0' E.

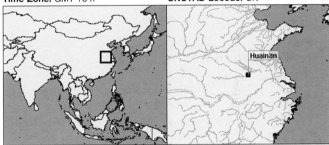

Admiralty Chart: -	**Admiralty Pilot:** -
Time Zone: GMT +8 h	**UNCTAD Locode:** CN

Principal Facilities:

		Y	G						

Authority: Huainan Shipping Administration, Longhu Zhong Road, Huainan, Anhui Province 232007, People's Republic of China

Accommodation:

Name	Remarks
Huainan	See [1] below

[1]*Huainan:* Consists of three harbour areas: Tianjiaan, Bagongshan and Lizuizi. Vessels up to 500 dwt handling grain, coal, clay, iron & steel, cement, timber and sand

Storage: Open and covered storage areas available

Lloyd's Agent: Huatai Surveyors & Adjusters Co., 14th Floor, China Re Building, No.11 Jin Rong Avenue, Xicheng District, Beijing 100140, People's Republic of China, *Tel:* +86 10 6657 6577, *Fax:* +86 10 6657 6502, *Email:* agency.bj@huatai-serv.com, *Website:* www.huatai-serv.com

HUANGDAO

see under Qingdao

HUANGHUA

Lat 38° 22' N; Long 117° 20' E.

Admiralty Chart: 1250	**Admiralty Pilot:** 32
Time Zone: GMT +8 h	**UNCTAD Locode:** CN HHA

Key to Principal Facilities:—					
A=Airport	**C**=Containers	**G**=General Cargo	**P**=Petroleum	**R**=Ro/Ro	**Y**=Dry Bulk
B=Bunkers	**D**=Dry Dock	**L**=Cruise	**Q**=Other Liquid Bulk	**T**=Towage (where available from port)	

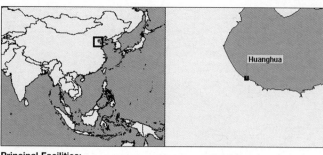

Principal Facilities:

	Y	G				T	A	

Authority: Huanghua Harbour Administration, Xincun Village, Huanghua, Hebei Province 061110, People's Republic of China, *Website:* www.huanghuaport.com

Port Security: ISPS compliant

Pre-Arrival Information: Notice of ETA required 72 h, 48 h and 24 h before arrival

Approach: The channel is dredged to 11 m but is subject to siltation

Anchorage: No.1 Anchorage (pilot and quarantine) in depth of approx 9 m
No.2 Anchorage (pilot and quarantine) in depth of approx 13 m
No.3 Anchorage in depth of approx 15 m

Pilotage: Compulsory for foreign vessels and available 24 h. Pilots board in anchorages 1 and 2

Weather: Ice is present for approx 3 months of the year

Maximum Vessel Dimensions: 225 m loa, 32.2 m beam, 8.5 m draught

Principal Imports and Exports: Exports: Coal.

Accommodation:

Name	Remarks
Huanghua	Three berths available for the export of coal, the largest being 280 m long in depth of 14 m

Storage: Available

Towage: Available

Airport: Tianjin Airport

Lloyd's Agent: Huatai Surveyors & Adjusters Co., 14th Floor, China Re Building, No.11 Jin Rong Avenue, Xicheng District, Beijing 100140, People's Republic of China, *Tel:* +86 10 6657 6577, *Fax:* +86 10 6657 6502, *Email:* agency.bj@huatai-serv.com, *Website:* www.huatai-serv.com

HUANGPU

harbour area, see under Guangzhou

HUANGSHI

Lat 30° 13' N; Long 115° 5' E.

Admiralty Chart: 2947   **Admiralty Pilot:** 32
Time Zone: GMT +8 h   **UNCTAD Locode:** CN HSI

Principal Facilities:

	Y	G	C		B		T	A	

Authority: Huangshi Port (Group) Ltd., Port Administration Office, 7 Jiaotong Road, Huangshi, Hubei Province 435000, People's Republic of China, *Tel:* +86 714 624 3765, *Fax:* +86 714 625 3662, *Website:* www.hsport.com

Approach: Draft limitation in channel 4 m during dry season and 14 m during flood season

Anchorage: Daoshifu anchorage in depths of 10-15 m for vessels up to 5000 dwt

Pilotage: Compulsory and available 0500-2100. Pilot boards vessel at Huangshi Anchorage

Radio Frequency: VHF Channel 23

Traffic: 2005, 3 500 000 t of cargo handled

Principal Imports and Exports: Exports: Cement, Coal, Grain, Metal, Steel, Stone.

Accommodation:

Name	Length (m)	Depth (m)	Remarks
Huangshi Foreign Trade Terminal	588	4	See [1] below

Name	Length (m)	Depth (m)	Remarks
Xishaishan Terminal	320	4	Two berths for vessels up to 1500 dwt

[1]*Foreign Trade Terminal:* Two berths. General cargo & container for vessels up to 5000 dwt

Storage:

Location	Open (m²)	Covered (m²)
Huangshi	68000	60000

Mechanical Handling Equipment:

Location	Type	Capacity (t)	Qty
Huangshi	Floating Cranes	15	1
Foreign Trade Terminal	Mult-purp. Cranes	25	1
Foreign Trade Terminal	Mult-purp. Cranes	5	2

Bunkering: Available

Towage: Four tugs of 300-800 hp

Airport: Wuhan Tianhe International Airport

Lloyd's Agent: Huatai Surveyors & Adjusters Co., 14th Floor, China Re Building, No.11 Jin Rong Avenue, Xicheng District, Beijing 100140, People's Republic of China, *Tel:* +86 10 6657 6577, *Fax:* +86 10 6657 6502, *Email:* agency.bj@huatai-serv.com, *Website:* www.huatai-serv.com

HUATONG

harbour area, see under Xiuyu

HUINAN

harbour area, see under Nanhui

HUISHAN

harbour area, see under Shanghai

HUIYANG

former name, see Huizhou

HUIZHOU

Lat 22° 42' N; Long 114° 34' E.

Admiralty Chart: 3026   **Admiralty Pilot:** 30
Time Zone: GMT +8 h   **UNCTAD Locode:** CN HUI

Principal Facilities:

P	Q	Y	G	C		B		T	

Authority: Huizhou Port Affairs Group Co. Ltd, Quanwan Port Complex Area, Daya Bay, Huizhou, Guangdong Province 516081, People's Republic of China, *Tel:* +86 752 557 4940, *Fax:* +86 752 557 4941, *Email:* hzgwgs@hzport.com, *Website:* www.hzport.com

Port Security: ISPS compliant

Anchorage: Crude oil tanker anchorage in pos 22° 33' N; 114° 41' E in depth of 18.4 m
30 000 dwt anchorage in pos 22° 35' 54" N; 114° 36' 44" E in depth of 13 m
Dangerous cargo anchorage in pos 22° 35' 30" N; 114° 36' 00" E in depth of 12 m

Pilotage: Compulsory. Pilot boards in pos 22° 31' 50" N; 144° 44' 60" E

Radio Frequency: VHF Channel 11

Accommodation:

Name	Length (m)	Depth (m)	Remarks
Quanwan Port Zone Huizhou Port Industrial Corp Ltd (HPIC) Berths	1386	12	See [1] below

[1] *Huizhou Port Industrial Corp Ltd (HPIC) Berths:* Multi-purpose facility of 52 ha which handles non-containerised goods such as refined oil and LPG in addition to bulk cargo and containers. Consists of five oil & gas berths and four multi-purpose berths

Storage:

Location	Covered (m²)
Huizhou Port Industrial Corp Ltd (HPIC) Berths	7200

Mechanical Handling Equipment:

Location	Type	Capacity (t)	Qty
Huizhou Port Industrial Corp Ltd (HPIC) Berths	Mult-purp. Cranes	15	2
Huizhou Port Industrial Corp Ltd (HPIC) Berths	Mult-purp. Cranes	45	4
Huizhou Port Industrial Corp Ltd (HPIC) Berths	Mobile Cranes		4
Huizhou Port Industrial Corp Ltd (HPIC) Berths	RTG's		2

Bunkering: Available

Towage: Five tugs up to 3200 hp

Shipping Agents: Awards Shipping Agency Ltd, Bo Mei Tang Building, 919 Mai Xing Road, Huizhou, Guangdong Province 516000, People's Republic of China, *Tel:* +86 752 256 9485/8, *Fax:* +86 752 256 9490, *Email:* dannyche@awards.com.cn, *Website:* www@awarda.com.hk
China Marine Shipping Agency Co. Ltd, China Marine Shipping Agency Guangdong Huizhou Company, No. 9 An Hui Street, Daya Bay Economic Developing Zone, Huizhou, Guangdong Province, People's Republic of China, *Tel:* +86 752 556 0903, *Fax:* +86 752 557 8591, *Email:* huizhou@sinoagentgd.com
CMA-CGM S.A., CMA CGM Huizhou, 610 Bomeitang Building, 13 Mai Xing Road, Huizhou, Guangdong Province 516000, People's Republic of China, *Tel:* +86 752 226 9373, *Fax:* +86 752 227 0122, *Email:* hui.genmbox@cma-cgm.com, *Website:* www.cma-cgm.com

Airport: Shenzhen Huangtian Airport

Development: Hutchison Port Holdings and Huizhou Port Affairs Group Co Ltd. have formed a joint venture 'Huizhou Port International Container Terminals' to build two 50 000 t container berths in the Quanwan Port Zone of Huizhou with a total berth length of 800 m, a yard area of 60 ha and depth alongside of 15.2 m

Lloyd's Agent: Huatai Surveyors & Adjusters Co., Room 802, Jun Yuan Mansion, 155 Tian He East Road, Guangzhou, Guangdong Province 510620, People's Republic of China, *Tel:* +86 20 3881 2306, *Fax:* +86 20 3881 2470, *Email:* agency.gz@huatai-serv.com, *Website:* www.huatai-serv.com

HUIZHOU TERMINAL

Lat 21° 21' N; Long 115° 25' E.

Admiralty Chart: 1968/3489
Time Zone: GMT +8 h
Admiralty Pilot: 30
UNCTAD Locode: CN

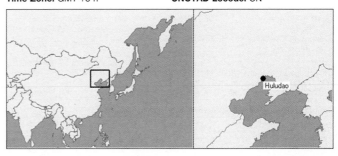

Principal Facilities:

P						T	

Authority: CACT Operators Group, 15-21 Floor, Offshore Petroleum Building, No.1 Industry Road 2, Shekou Special Industrial Zone, Shenzhen, Guangdong Province 518069, People's Republic of China, *Tel:* +86 755 669 1608, *Fax:* +86 755 669 1606, *Email:* ricci@actog.com

Anchorage: Waiting area 3.75 nautical miles SE of the FPSO. Anchorage is not recommended

Pilotage: Compulsory. Mooring master usually boards vessel from helicoptor near or at the waiting area or sometimes in favourable weather conditions from a supply vessel. Mooring during daylight hours only

Accommodation:

Name	Remarks
Huizhou Terminal	See [1] below

[1] *Huizhou Terminal:* Comprises four lighted production platforms connected to FPSO 'Nan Hai Fa Xian' in depth of 116 m. Crude oil is offloaded to tankers of 60 000-160 000 dwt

Towage: Available

Lloyd's Agent: Huatai Surveyors & Adjusters Co., Room 802, Jun Yuan Mansion, 155 Tian He East Road, Guangzhou, Guangdong Province 510620, People's Republic of China, *Tel:* +86 20 3881 2306, *Fax:* +86 20 3881 2470, *Email:* agency.gz@huatai-serv.com, *Website:* www.huatai-serv.com

HULANHE

harbour area, see under Harbin

HULUDAO

Lat 40° 43' N; Long 120° 59' E.

Admiralty Chart: -
Admiralty Pilot: -
Time Zone: GMT +8 h
UNCTAD Locode: CN

Principal Facilities:

P		Y	G			B		

Authority: Port Authority of Huludao, Port Office, Huludao, Liaoning Province, People's Republic of China

Pilotage: Compulsory and available 0800-1700

Radio Frequency: VHF Channels 13 and 16

Tides: Average range of 2.05 m

Accommodation:

Name	Length (m)	Depth (m)	Remarks
Huludao Berth	170	10	See [1] below

[1] *Berth:* For vessels up to 12 500 dwt. Cargoes handled include general cargo, grain, zinc ingots, cement & chemicals

Storage:

Location	Open (m²)
Huludao	110000

Bunkering: Available

Shipping Agents: China Marine Shipping Agency Co. Ltd, China Marine Shippinjg Agency Liaoning Company Limited Huludao Branch, Room 9001-2, 9th Floor, Kouan Building, New Zone, Longgang District, Huludao, Liaoning Province, People's Republic of China, *Tel:* +86 429 823 0333, *Fax:* +86 429 312 7020, *Email:* tang-chuan@china.com

Development: One berth of 20 000 dwt cap and one berth of 35 000 dwt cap are under construction
Another six berths will be built under the second-phase expansion

Lloyd's Agent: Huatai Surveyors & Adjusters Co., 14th Floor, China Re Building, No.11 Jin Rong Avenue, Xicheng District, Beijing 100140, People's Republic of China, *Tel:* +86 10 6657 6577, *Fax:* +86 10 6657 6502, *Email:* agency.bj@huatai-serv.com, *Website:* www.huatai-serv.com

HUMEN

Lat 22° 48' N; Long 113° 40' E.

Admiralty Chart: -
Admiralty Pilot: 30
Time Zone: GMT +8 h
UNCTAD Locode: CN HMN

Key to Principal Facilities:—		
A=Airport	**C**=Containers	**G**=General Cargo
B=Bunkers	**D**=Dry Dock	**L**=Cruise

P=Petroleum	**R**=Ro/Ro	**Y**=Dry Bulk
Q=Other Liquid Cargo	**T**=Towage (where available from port)	

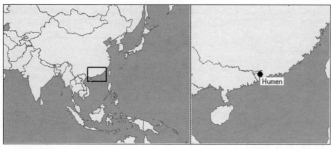

Principal Facilities:

P		Y	G	C					

Authority: Port Authority of Humen, Port Office, Humen, People's Republic of China

Pilotage: Compulsory. Huangpu pilot for Zhujiang Channel and Dongguan pilot for Humen Channel

Radio Frequency: VHF Channels 9, 16 and 11

Accommodation:

Name	Length (m)	Depth (m)	Remarks
Humen			
Shajiao Wharf	270	13	Coal for vessels up to 60 000 dwt
Shatian Wharf	160	6.8	Oil & chemical products for vessels up to 5000 dwt
Dongguan Container Terminal	678	14.3	See [1] below

[1]*Dongguan Container Terminal:* Operated by PSA Dongguan Container Terminal Co Ltd., Shatian Harbour District, Humen Port, Dongguan 523980, Tel: +86 769 8866 6181, Email: lliu@psa.com.sg
Two 50 000 t container berths. Area of 48.5 ha

Mechanical Handling Equipment:

Location	Type	Qty
Dongguan Container Terminal	Container Cranes	6

Development: Two more container berths are being built, and are expected to commence operations in 2010

Lloyd's Agent: Huatai Surveyors & Adjusters Co., 14th Floor, China Re Building, No.11 Jin Rong Avenue, Xicheng District, Beijing 100140, People's Republic of China, *Tel:* +86 10 6657 6577, *Fax:* +86 10 6657 6502, *Email:* agency.bj@huatai-serv.com, *Website:* www.huatai-serv.com

JIAMUSI

Lat 46° 48' N; Long 130° 21' E.

Admiralty Chart: - **Admiralty Pilot:** -
Time Zone: GMT +8 h **UNCTAD Locode:** CN JMU

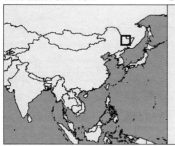

Principal Facilities:

	Y	G	C				T		

Authority: Jiamusi Harbour Administration, 1 Heping Road, Qianjin District, Jiamusi, Heilongjiang Province 154002, People's Republic of China

Accommodation:

Name	Remarks
Jiamusi	Several berths for vessels up to 1000 dwt handling coal, timber, ore and general cargo

Storage: Open and covered storage areas available

Mechanical Handling Equipment:

Location	Type	Capacity (t)
Jiamusi	Mult-purp. Cranes	40

Towage: Available

Lloyd's Agent: Huatai Surveyors & Adjusters Co., 14th Floor, China Re Building, No.11 Jin Rong Avenue, Xicheng District, Beijing 100140, People's Republic of China, *Tel:* +86 10 6657 6577, *Fax:* +86 10 6657 6502, *Email:* agency.bj@huatai-serv.com, *Website:* www.huatai-serv.com

JIANCHUNMEN

harbour area, see under Ganzhou

JIANGAN

harbour area, see under Wuhu

JIANGBEI TERMINAL

harbour area, see under Chongqing

JIANGMEN

Lat 22° 40' N; Long 113° 5' E.

Admiralty Chart: - **Admiralty Pilot:** -
Time Zone: GMT +8 h **UNCTAD Locode:** CN JMN

Principal Facilities:

			G	C					

Authority: Jiangmen International Container Terminals, Gaosha Wei, Baishi Administration Zone, Jiangmen, Guangdong Province 529030, People's Republic of China, *Tel:* +86 750 329 2300, *Fax:* +86 750 329 2313, *Email:* com@jmct.com.cn, *Website:* www.jmct.com.cn

Officials: General Manager: Danny Lee, *Email:* jmct@jmct.com.cn.

Port Security: ISPS compliant

Accommodation:

Name	Remarks
Jiangmen International Container Terminal	Total area of 12.5 ha. Berthing length of 623 m in depth of 3-4.5 m. Container freight station. Also handles reefer and dangerous cargo

Storage:

Location	Covered (m²)	Sheds / Warehouses
Jiangmen International Container Terminal	10000	10

Mechanical Handling Equipment:

Location	Type	Qty
Jiangmen International Container Terminal	Mult-purp. Cranes	11
Jiangmen International Container Terminal	Container Cranes	4

Shipping Agents: China Marine Shipping Agency Co. Ltd, China Marine Shipping Agency Guangdong Company Limited Jiangmen Branch, 3rd Floor, 14 Wufu Street6, Beijiaoxincheng, Jiangmen, Guangdong Province, People's Republic of China, *Tel:* +86 750 327 5501, *Fax:* +86 750 321 1515, *Email:* jiangmen@transgd.com.cn
CMA-CGM S.A., CMA CGM Jiangmen, Room 723, Jinhua Commercial Building, 61 Donghua Road 1, Jiangmen, Guangdong Province 529000, People's Republic of China, *Tel:* +86 750 339 2751, *Fax:* +86 750 339 2761, *Email:* jgn.genmbox@cma-cgm.com, *Website:* www.cma-cgm.com
Sea Well Shipping Ltd, Sec 1, 41 Feng-Le Road, Jiangmen, Guangdong Province 529000, People's Republic of China, *Tel:* +86 750 310 2109, *Fax:* +86 750 310 2106, *Email:* yml@yml-jiangmen.com

Lloyd's Agent: Huatai Surveyors & Adjusters Co., Room 802, Jun Yuan Mansion, 155 Tian He East Road, Guangzhou, Guangdong Province 510620, People's Republic of China, *Tel:* +86 20 3881 2306, *Fax:* +86 20 3881 2470, *Email:* agency.gz@huatai-serv.com, *Website:* www.huatai-serv.com

JIANGYIN

Lat 31° 55' N; Long 120° 15' E.

Admiralty Chart: 1641 **Admiralty Pilot:** 32
Time Zone: GMT +8 h **UNCTAD Locode:** CN JIA

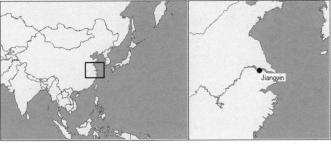

Principal Facilities:

| P | Q | Y | G | C | | B | | T | |

Authority: Jiangyin Port Group Co Ltd, 581 Tongjiang North Road, Jiangyin, Jiangsu Province 214433, People's Republic of China, *Tel:* +86 510 8602 1881, *Fax:* +86 510 8602 1238, *Email:* office@jyport.com.cn, *Website:* www.jyport.com.cn

Port Security: ISPS compliant

Pilotage: Compulsory and available during daytime only. Pilot boards vessel at Baoshan Anchorage

Radio Frequency: VHF Channel 69

Tides: Max tidal range of 3.39 m

Traffic: 2005, 15 000 000 t of cargo handled, 48 600 TEU's

Accommodation:

Name	Length (m)	Depth (m)	Remarks
Jiangyin			
Berth No.1	300	10.5	See [1] below
Berth No.2	152	8	See [2] below
Berth No.4	180	10.5	General cargo, timber & steel for vessels up to 50 000 dwt
Liaohe Berth	275	9.5	Chemicals & oils for vessels up to 25 000 dwt
Sinopec Jiangsu Petrochem Changshan Branch			
Berth No.1	80	7	Chemicals & lube oils for vessels up to 5000 dwt
Berth No.2	180	9.5	Chemicals & oils for vessels up to 25 000 dwt
Berth No.3	180	9.5	Chemicals, oils & LPG for vessels up to 25 000 dwt
Wuxi Lyon Petrochem Co Ltd			
Lyon	174	9.5	LPG for vessels up to 25 000 dwt

[1]*Berth No.1:* Timber, steel, molten sulphur, ore & containers for vessels up to 50 000 dwt
[2]*Berth No.2:* General cargo, timber, steel & phosphoric acid for vessels up to 15 000 dwt

Storage: Container yard of 7000 m2

Location	Open (m²)	Covered (m²)
Jiangyin	25000	53000

Mechanical Handling Equipment:

Location	Type	Capacity (t)	Qty
Jiangyin	Floating Cranes	100	1
Jiangyin	Floating Cranes	60	1
Berth No.1	Shore Cranes	10	5
Berth No.2	Shore Cranes	10	2
Berth No.4	Shore Cranes	40	1
Berth No.4	Shore Cranes	10	2

Bunkering: China Marine Bunker Supply Co., 13F Qian Cun Mansion A, No.2, 5th Block, Anzhen Xili, Chaoyang District, Beijing 100029, People's Republic of China, *Tel:* +86 10 6443 0717, *Fax:* +86 10 6443 0708, *Email:* business@chimbusco.com.cn, *Website:* www.chimbusco.com.cn – *Grades:* IFO120-380cSt; MGO

Towage: Two tugs of 980 hp and one of 400 hp

Repair & Maintenance: Chengxi Shipyard Co. Ltd, 1 Hengshan Road, Jiangyin, Jiangsu Province 214433, People's Republic of China, *Tel:* +86 510 8166 8888, *Fax:* +86 510 8166 8166, *Email:* cssc.cxsy@public1.wx.js.cn, *Website:* www.chengxi.com Floating docks: Chang Shan 189 m x 28 m x 1 5m with lifting cap of 13 000 t, Zhong Shan 158 m x 24.5 m x 12.4 m with lifting cap of 6500 t, Heng Shan 257 m long with lifting cap of 26 000 t, Jin Shan 256 m long with lifting cap of 18 580 t

Ship Chandlers: Jiangyin General Shipchandler Co. Ltd, No.181 Binjiang Middle Road, Jiangyin, Jiangsu Province 214431, People's Republic of China, *Tel:* +86 510 8685 5991, *Fax:* +86 510 8685 5992, *Email:* jysupco@pub.wx.jsinfo.net

Shipping Agents: China Marine Shipping Agency Co. Ltd, China Marine Shipping Agency Jiangsu Jiangyin Company Limited, 581 Tongjiang North Road, Jiangyin, Jiangsu Province, People's Republic of China, *Tel:* +86 510 8602 2544, *Fax:* +86 510 8602 1372, *Email:* email@sinoagentjy.com

Surveyors: Det Norske Veritas A/S, Chengxi Site Office, 1 Heng Shan Road, Jiangyin, Jiangsu Province, People's Republic of China, *Tel:* +86 510 8611 9361, *Fax:* +86 510 8611 9361, *Email:* mchcn335@dnv.com, *Website:* www.dnv.com Germanischer Lloyd, Room 308, Building 1, New Century Garden, South Street, Jiangyin, Jiangsu Province 214400, People's Republic of China, *Tel:* +86 510 8688 7966, *Fax:* +86 510 8687 7665, *Email:* gl-jiangyin@gl-group.com, *Website:* www.gl-group.com

Lloyd's Agent: Huatai Surveyors & Adjusters Co., 14th Floor, China Re Building, No.11 Jin Rong Avenue, Xicheng District, Beijing 100140, People's Republic of China, *Tel:* +86 10 6657 6577, *Fax:* +86 10 6657 6502, *Email:* agency.bj@huatai-serv.com, *Website:* www.huatai-serv.com

JIEBIAN

harbour area, see under Foshan

JINGTANG

harbour area, see under Tangshan

JINGU

harbour area, see under Dalian

JINGZHOU

Lat 30° 21' N; Long 112° 12' E.

Admiralty Chart: 2947 | **Admiralty Pilot:** 32
Time Zone: GMT +8 h | **UNCTAD Locode:** CN JGZ

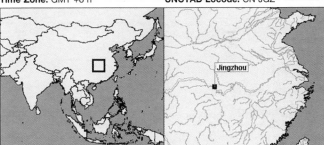

Principal Facilities:

| P | | Y | G | C | | B | | A | |

Authority: Jingzhou Port (Group) Ltd., 23 Qi Jiang Road, Shashi, Hubei Province 434000, People's Republic of China, *Tel:* +86 716 821 3095, *Fax:* +86 716 821 3095, *Website:* www.jzgwjt.com

Traffic: 2005, 1 820 000 t of cargo handled, 22 308 TEU's

Accommodation:

Name	Length (m)	Depth (m)	Remarks
Jingzhou			
Yanka Terminal	700	7	Four berths for vessels up to 3000 dwt
Chengqu Terminal	5000	3	Nine berths for vessels up to 3000 dwt

Storage:

Location	Open (m²)	Covered (m²)
JIngzhou	111000	37200

Mechanical Handling Equipment:

Location	Type	Capacity (t)
JIngzhou	Mult-purp. Cranes	40

Bunkering: Available

Airport: Shashi & Yichang Airport

Lloyd's Agent: Huatai Surveyors & Adjusters Co., 14th Floor, China Re Building, No.11 Jin Rong Avenue, Xicheng District, Beijing 100140, People's Republic of China, *Tel:* +86 10 6657 6577, *Fax:* +86 10 6657 6502, *Email:* agency.bj@huatai-serv.com, *Website:* www.huatai-serv.com

JINSHAN

Lat 30° 43' N; Long 121° 19' E.

Admiralty Chart: 1199 | **Admiralty Pilot:** 32
Time Zone: GMT +8 h | **UNCTAD Locode:** CN

Key to Principal Facilities:—			
A=Airport	**C**=Containers	**G**=General Cargo	**P**=Petroleum	**R**=Ro/Ro	**Y**=Dry Bulk
B=Bunkers	**D**=Dry Dock	**L**=Cruise	**Q**=Other Liquid Bulk	**T**=Towage (where available from port)

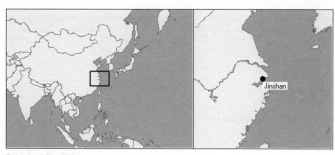

Principal Facilities:

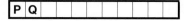

| P | Q | | | | | | | | | | |

Authority: Shanghai Petrochemical Co. Ltd, 48 Jinyi Road, Jinshan District, Shanghai, Shanghai Province 200540, People's Republic of China, *Tel:* +86 21 5794 3931, *Fax:* +86 21 5794 1741, *Email:* spc@spc.com.cn, *Website:* www.spc.com.cn

Officials: President: Rong Guangdao.

Anchorage: Quarantine Anchorage centred at pos 30° 38' 02" N; 121° 20' 19" E

Pilotage: Pilot boards at the Quarantine Anchorage

Radio Frequency: Jinshan Harbour Control on VHF Channel 8

Accommodation:

Name	Remarks
Jinshan	See [1] below

[1]*Jinshan:* Tanker terminals serving the Shanghai Petrochemical Plant. One pier capable of taking 25 000 t class tankers with crude oil. Three smaller berths have been completed to accommodate 5000 t class vessels, two are 126 m long with a depth alongside of 8.6 m and 9 m respectively and the other is 76 m long and 5.2 m depth. These berths are designed to handle chemical products. There are large oil storage tanks and the terminal can receive 2.5 million t of crude oil per year

Lloyd's Agent: Huatai Surveyors & Adjusters Co., 14th Floor, China Re Building, No.11 Jin Rong Avenue, Xicheng District, Beijing 100140, People's Republic of China, *Tel:* +86 10 6657 6577, *Fax:* +86 10 6657 6502, *Email:* agency.bj@huatai-serv.com, *Website:* www.huatai-serv.com

JINSHI

Lat 29° 37' N; Long 111° 51' E.

Admiralty Chart: 2947	**Admiralty Pilot:** 32
Time Zone: GMT +8 h	**UNCTAD Locode:** CN

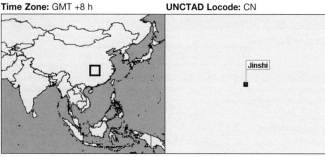

Principal Facilities:

| | Y | G | | | | | | | |

Authority: Jinshi Harbour Administration, 47 Renmin Road, Jinshi, Hunan Province 415400, People's Republic of China

Accommodation:

Name	Remarks
Jinshi	See [1] below

[1]*Jinshi:* Five cargo handling areas: Liugongqiao, Salt Area, Qijiaxiang, Wangjiaqiao and Yaopodu
Numerous berths for vessels up to 700 dwt handling passengers, salt, ore, textiles and agricultural products

Storage: Open and covered storage areas available

Mechanical Handling Equipment:

Location	Type
Jinshi	Mult-purp. Cranes

Lloyd's Agent: Huatai Surveyors & Adjusters Co., 14th Floor, China Re Building, No.11 Jin Rong Avenue, Xicheng District, Beijing 100140, People's Republic of China, *Tel:* +86 10 6657 6577, *Fax:* +86 10 6657 6502, *Email:* agency.bj@huatai-serv.com, *Website:* www.huatai-serv.com

JINZHOU

Lat 40° 45' N; Long 121° 6' E.

Admiralty Chart: 1248	**Admiralty Pilot:** 32
Time Zone: GMT +8 h	**UNCTAD Locode:** CN JNZ

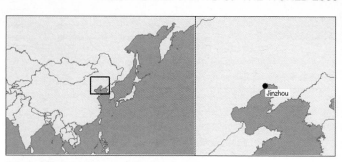

Principal Facilities:

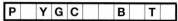

| P | | Y | G | C | | | B | | T | |

Authority: Jinzhou Port Co. Ltd, No.1 Section, 1 Jingang Street, Jinzhou, Liaoning Province 121007, People's Republic of China, *Tel:* +86 416 312 7123, *Fax:* +86 416 358 2841, *Email:* jzp@jinzhouport.com, *Website:* www.jinzhouport.com

Port Security: ISPS compliant

Approach: Main navigation channel is 7750 m long in depth of 11-14 m

Anchorage: No.1 Anchorage in pos 40° 42' 24" N; 121° 06' 30" E in depth of 9.5 m and used for quarantine, awaiting berth and pilot
No.2 Anchorage in pos 40° 33' 00" N; 121° 26' 30" E in depth of 11.0 m and used for vessels awaiting berth

Pilotage: Compulsory. Available 24 h in summer and daytime only in winter. Pilot boards in pos 40° 42.4' N; 121° 06.5' E

Radio Frequency: VHF Channel 16

Tides: Average tidal range of 2.63 m

Principal Imports and Exports: Imports: General cargo, Oil, Ore. Exports: Cement, General cargo, Grain.

Accommodation:

Name	Length (m)	Depth (m)	Remarks
Cargo Berths			
Berth No.103	217.4	10.7	General cargo for vessels up to 10 000 dwt
Berth No.104	189.7	10.7	General cargo for vessels up to 10 000 dwt
Berth No.105	151.8	10.7	General cargo & containers for vessels up to 10 000 dwt
Berth No.106	230.2	12.7	General cargo for vessels up to 30 000 dwt
Berth No.107	150	7.5	General cargo for vessels under 3000 dwt
Berth No.201	262	12	General cargo & containers for vessels up to 30 000 dwt
Berth No.202	280	14	General cargo for vessels up to 50 000 dwt
Oil Berths			
Berth No.101	356	14	Oil for vessels up to 50 000 dwt
Berth No.102	241.4	10.4	Oil & liquid chemical cargo for vessels up to 10 000 dwt

Storage: Container yard of 8000 m2

Location	Open (m²)	Covered (m²)	Sheds / Warehouses	Grain (t)
Jinzhou	80000	3600	1	28800

Mechanical Handling Equipment:

Location	Type	Capacity (t)	Qty
Berth No.103	Shore Cranes	10	2
Berth No.104	Shore Cranes	10	2
Berth No.105	Shore Cranes	10	2
Berth No.105	Shore Cranes	16	1
Berth No.106	Shore Cranes	16	1
Berth No.106	Shore Cranes	10	2
Berth No.201	Shore Cranes	10	1
Berth No.201	Shore Cranes	40	1
Berth No.201	Shore Cranes	16	1
Berth No.202	Shore Cranes	16	6

Bunkering: BP Hong Kong Ltd, 21st Floor, Super Ocean Financial Centre, 067 West Yan An Road, Shanghai, Shanghai Province, People's Republic of China, *Tel:* +86 21 6278 4858, *Fax:* +86 21 6275 7702, *Email:* lucn@bp.com

Towage: Three tugs of 2000-3700 hp

Ship Chandlers: Jinzhou Foreign Supply Co., 24 Section, 3 Shanghai Road, Jinzhou, Liaoning Province 121000, People's Republic of China, *Tel:* +86 416 212 2358, *Fax:* +86 416 212 3041

Shipping Agents: China Marine Shipping Agency Co. Ltd, China Marine Shipping Agency Liaoning Company Limited Jinzhou Branch, No. 14, Section 4, Nanjing Road, Jinzhou, Liaoning Province, People's Republic of China, *Tel:* +86 416 357 0752, *Fax:* +86 416 358 1107, *Email:* sinoagnt@mail.jzptt.ln.cn, *Website:* www.sinoagentsh.com

Lloyd's Agent: Huatai Surveyors & Adjusters Co., 14th Floor, China Re Building, No.11 Jin Rong Avenue, Xicheng District, Beijing 100140, People's Republic of China, *Tel:* +86 10 6657 6577, *Fax:* +86 10 6657 6502, *Email:* agency.bj@huatai-serv.com, *Website:* www.huatai-serv.com

JIUJIANG

Lat 29° 43' N; Long 115° 59' E.

Admiralty Chart: 2947	**Admiralty Pilot:** 32
Time Zone: GMT +8 h	**UNCTAD Locode:** CN JIU

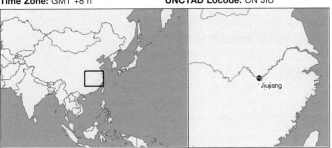

Principal Facilities:

		Y	G	C		B		T	

Authority: Jiujiang Port (Group) Ltd., 37 Binjiang Road, Jiujiang, Jiangxi Province 332000, People's Republic of China, *Tel:* +86 792 822 2011, *Fax:* +86 792 822 4783

Approach: Draft limitation in channel is 4.0 m during dry season and 7.2 m during flood season

Anchorage: Guanjiapai anchorage of mud and sand in depths of 3-15 m for vessels up to 5000 dwt

Pilotage: Compulsory and available during daytime only. Pilot boards at Jiujiang Anchorage

Radio Frequency: VHF Channels 12, 16 and 21

Traffic: 2005, 9 280 000 t of cargo handled, 46 200 TEU's

Working Hours: Heavy and bulk cargo 0700-1600, 1800-0700. Bagged cargo 0700-1600, 1600-2400

Accommodation:

Name	Length (m)	Depth (m)	Remarks
Jiujiang			
Foreign Trade Terminal	271	5	Two berths for vessels up to 5000 dwt
Longkaihe Terminal	121	4	Two berths for vessels up to 3000 dwt
Sanjiaoxian Terminal	163	3.5	Three berths for vessels up to 3000 dwt

Storage:

Location	Open (m²)	Covered (m²)
Jiujiang	171000	30000

Mechanical Handling Equipment:

Location	Type	Capacity (t)	Qty
Jiujiang	Floating Cranes	3–15	4

Bunkering: Available

Towage: Four tugs of 300-1200 hp

Shipping Agents: China Marine Shipping Agency Co. Ltd, China Marine Shipping Agency Jiangxi Jiujiang Company, No. 191 Lushan Road, Jiujiang, Jiangxi Province 322000, People's Republic of China, *Tel:* +86 792 822 4605, *Fax:* +86 792 822 6406, *Email:* jjsinoagent@yahoo.com, *Website:* www.sinotrans.com
China Sailing International Shipping Agency Ltd, Room 1302-A, Viewing Lake Mansion, Huan Chen Road, Jiujiang, Jiangxi Province 332000, People's Republic of China, *Tel:* +86 792 812 9636, *Fax:* +86 792 812 5018, *Email:* xiongwb@hastrans.com, *Website:* www.chinasailing.com.cn

Lloyd's Agent: Huatai Surveyors & Adjusters Co., 14th Floor, China Re Building, No.11 Jin Rong Avenue, Xicheng District, Beijing 100140, People's Republic of China, *Tel:* +86 10 6657 6577, *Fax:* +86 10 6657 6502, *Email:* agency.bj@huatai-serv.com, *Website:* www.huatai-serv.com

JIULONGPO TERMINAL

harbour area, see under Chongqing

JIUZHOU

harbour area, see under Zhuhai

JUNGONGLU

harbour area, see under Shanghai

KUNSHAN

Lat 31° 22' N; Long 120° 56' E.

Admiralty Chart: 1619	**Admiralty Pilot:** 32
Time Zone: GMT +8 h	**UNCTAD Locode:** CN KUS

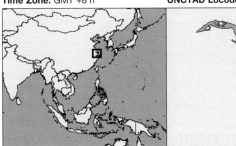

Principal Facilities:

		Y							

Authority: Kunshan Harbour Administration, 13 Xiaoma Road, Yushan Town, Kunshan, Jiangsu Province 215300, People's Republic of China

Accommodation:

Name	Remarks
Kunshan	Numerous berths available handling grain, coal and ore

Storage: Open and covered storage areas available

Mechanical Handling Equipment:

Location	Type	Capacity (t)
Kunshan	Mult-purp. Cranes	32

Lloyd's Agent: Huatai Surveyors & Adjusters Co., 14th Floor, China Re Building, No.11 Jin Rong Avenue, Xicheng District, Beijing 100140, People's Republic of China, *Tel:* +86 10 6657 6577, *Fax:* +86 10 6657 6502, *Email:* agency.bj@huatai-serv.com, *Website:* www.huatai-serv.com

LAIZHOU

Lat 37° 23' N; Long 119° 57' E.

Admiralty Chart: -	**Admiralty Pilot:** 32
Time Zone: GMT +8 h	**UNCTAD Locode:** CN LAI

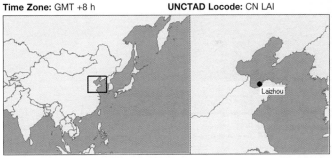

Principal Facilities:

		Y	G		R		B		T

Authority: Laizhou Port Authority, 1 Haigang Road, Special Industrial District, Sanshan Island, Laizhou, Shandong Province, People's Republic of China, *Tel:* +86 535 278 2350, *Fax:* +86 535 278 2028

Pilotage: Compulsory and available 24 h. Pilot boards vessel at No.3 buoy

Radio Frequency: VHF Channel 16

Tides: Average tidal range of 1.61 m

Accommodation:

Name	Length (m)	Depth (m)	Remarks
Laizhou			
Berth No.1	190.9	9.8	Bulk & general cargo for vessels up to 10 000 dwt
Berth No.2	76.7	7.2	Bulk & general cargo for vessels up to 3000 dwt
Berth No.3	79.7	7.2	Bulk & general cargo for vessels up to 3000 dwt
Berth No.4	162.8	7.2	Ro/ro cargo for vessels up to 3000 dwt

Storage:

Location	Open (m²)	Covered (m²)
Laizhou	45540	1440

Key to Principal Facilities:—				
A=Airport	**C**=Containers	**G**=General Cargo	**P**=Petroleum	**R**=Ro/Ro	**Y**=Dry Bulk
B=Bunkers	**D**=Dry Dock	**L**=Cruise	**Q**=Other Liquid Bulk	**T**=Towage (where available from port)	

Mechanical Handling Equipment:

Location	Type	Capacity (t)	Qty
Berth No.1	Shore Cranes	10	2
Berth No.2	Shore Cranes	10	1
Berth No.3	Shore Cranes	10	1

Bunkering: Available at berth and anchorage

Towage: Two tugs of 1500 hp and one tug of 3000 hp

Shipping Agents: China Marine Shipping Agency Co. Ltd, China Marine Shipping Agency Shandong Company Limited Laizhou Branch, Room 106, 105 Customs Building, Laizhou Building, Laizhou, Shandong Province, People's Republic of China, *Tel:* +86 535 278 3226, *Fax:* +86 535 278 3226, *Email:* gfsdcd_laizhou@sinotrans.com

Lloyd's Agent: Huatai Surveyors & Adjusters Co., 14th Floor, China Re Building, No.11 Jin Rong Avenue, Xicheng District, Beijing 100140, People's Republic of China, *Tel:* +86 10 6657 6577, *Fax:* +86 10 6657 6502, *Email:* agency.bj@huatai-serv.com, *Website:* www.huatai-serv.com

LAN SHUI TERMINAL

alternate name, see Liuhua Terminal

LANGTOU

harbour area, see under Dandong

LANJIANTUO TERMINAL

harbour area, see under Chongqing

LANSHAN

Lat 35° 5' N; Long 119° 21' E.

Admiralty Chart: 1253
Time Zone: GMT +8 h

Admiralty Pilot: 30
UNCTAD Locode: CN LSN

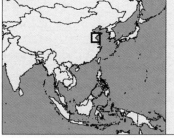

Principal Facilities:

P		Y	G					T	

Authority: Lanshan Port Authority, Lanshan 276808, People's Republic of China, *Tel:* +86 633 843 1046, *Fax:* +86 633 843 1033, *Website:* www.lsport.com.cn

Pilotage: Compulsory
Working Hours: 24 h/day

Accommodation:

Name	Length (m)	Draught (m)	Remarks
Lanshan			
Berth No.3	178	7.5	General & bulk cargo for vessels up to 10 000 dwt
Berth No.4	220	10.2	General & bulk cargo for vessels up to 40 000 dwt
Berth No.5	130	7.5	General & bulk cargo for vessels up to 10 000 dwt
Berth No.6	180	8.5	General & bulk cargo for vessels up to 30 000 dwt
Berth No.8 (Vopak Terminal)	200	11	See [1] below
Berth No.9	240	13.3	General & bulk cargo for vessels up to 70 000 dwt
Berth No.10			Under construction

[1]*Berth No.8 (Vopak Terminal):* Tel: +86 633 263 5388, Email: brian.davies@vopak.com, Website: www.vopak.com
Tankers up to 50 000 dwt handling petroleum products, chemical and specialist products such as sulphuric acid, latex, carbon black and bitumen. Total tank storage cap of 107 800 m3

Storage: Open and covered storage areas available
Mechanical Handling Equipment: Numerous cranes available
Towage: Four tugs available
Shipping Agents: China Marine Shipping Agency Co. Ltd, China Marine Shipping Agency Shandong Company Limited Lanshan Branch, Sinotrans Building, Shenglan

East Road, Lanshan Port, Rizhao, Shandong Province 276808, People's Republic of China, *Tel:* +86 633 288 2001, *Fax:* +86 633 288 1323, *Email:* sinoagnt@163169.net
Tongsheng International Shipping Agencies, Rizhao Tongsheng International Shipping Agency Co Ltd, Lanshan Branch, Shenglan East Road, Lanshan District, Rizhao, Shandong Province 276808, People's Republic of China, *Tel:* +86 633 223 6728, *Fax:* +86 633 223 6729, *Email:* tongsheng@tongshengrz.com, *Website:* www.tongshengshipping.com

Lloyd's Agent: Huatai Surveyors & Adjusters Co., 14th Floor, China Re Building, No.11 Jin Rong Avenue, Xicheng District, Beijing 100140, People's Republic of China, *Tel:* +86 10 6657 6577, *Fax:* +86 10 6657 6502, *Email:* agency.bj@huatai-serv.com, *Website:* www.huatai-serv.com

LANXI

Lat 30° 20' N; Long 115° 7' E.

Admiralty Chart: 2947
Time Zone: GMT +8 h

Admiralty Pilot: 32
UNCTAD Locode: CN

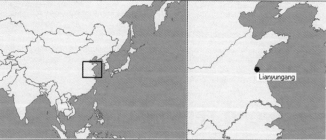

Principal Facilities:

P		Y	G						

Accommodation:

Name	Remarks
Lanxi	See [1] below
Changjiang Area	Berths for vessels of 500-3000 dwt
Nianyuwei Area	Mainly used for storage and transhipment of sand

[1]*Lanxi:* Cargoes handled include sand, fertiliser, coal, iron & steel, petroleum and manufactured goods

Storage: Open and covered storage areas available
Lloyd's Agent: Huatai Surveyors & Adjusters Co., 14th Floor, China Re Building, No.11 Jin Rong Avenue, Xicheng District, Beijing 100140, People's Republic of China, *Tel:* +86 10 6657 6577, *Fax:* +86 10 6657 6502, *Email:* agency.bj@huatai-serv.com, *Website:* www.huatai-serv.com

LAOTANGSHAN

harbour area, see under Zhoushan

LIANYUNGANG

Lat 34° 44' N; Long 119° 27' E.

Admiralty Chart: 878
Time Zone: GMT +8 h

Admiralty Pilot: 32
UNCTAD Locode: CN LYG

Principal Facilities:

		Y	G	C			B	D	T	

Authority: Lianyungang Port Authority, 99 Zhongshan Road, Lianyungang, Jiangsu Province 222046, People's Republic of China, *Tel:* +86 518 8238 3193, *Fax:* +86 518 8233 1261, *Website:* www.lygport.com.cn

Port Security: ISPS compliant

Anchorage: No.1 Quarantine and Pilot Anchorage in pos 34° 48.5' N; 119° 47.0' E with 13-15 m depth and of mud and sandy bottom
No.2 Quarantine and Pilot Anchorage in pos 34° 47.3' N; 119° 34.1' E with 7-9 m depth and of mud bottom
No.3 Quarantine and Pilot Anchorage for vessels under 5000 gt in pos 34° 45.3' N; 119° 31.6' E

Pilotage: Compulsory and available 24 h. Pilot boards vessel at No.1, No.2 or No.3 anchorage

Radio Frequency: VHF Channels 69 and 16

Tides: Average tidal range of 5.2 m during summer and 4.62 m during winter

Traffic: 2006, 72 322 000 t of cargo handled, 1 302 300 TEU's handled

Accommodation:

Name	Length (m)	Depth (m)	Remarks
Lianyungang			
Berth No.1	156	7.9	See [1] below
Berth No.2	153	6.2	General & bulk cargo for vessels up to 7500 dwt
Berth No.3	142	6.5	General & bulk cargo for vessels up to 10 000 dwt
Berth No.4	180	8.2	General & bulk cargo for vessels up to 10 000 dwt
Berth No.5	188	8.1	See [2] below
Berth No.6	190	7.7	General & bulk cargo for vessels up to 75 000 dwt
Berth No.8	130	8.6	General & bulk cargo for vessels up to 75 000 dwt
Berth No.9	260	11.4	See [3] below
Berth No.10	200	11	Repair berth for vessels up to 44 000 dwt
Berth No.11	210	12.3	See [4] below
Berth No.12	182	7.7	See [5] below
Berth No.14	162	8.2	See [6] below
Berth No.16	182	9.2	See [7] below
Berth No.31	250	10.6	See [8] below
Berth No.32	290	9.8	General cargo & containers for vessels up to 75 000 dwt
Berth No.33	280	10.5	See [9] below
Berth No.34	280		Under reconstruction
Berth No.35	215	11	See [10] below
Berth No.36	235	11	See [11] below
Berth No.38	236	12.6	Coal for vessels up to 50 000 dwt
Berth No.39	240	13.5	Coal for vessels up to 50 000 dwt
Berth No.61	190	11.5	See [12] below
Berth No.62	190	10.5	General & bulk cargo for vessels up to 50 000 dwt
Berth No.63	180	10.7	General & bulk cargo for vessels up to 25 000 dwt
Berth No.64	180	10	General & bulk cargo for vessels up to 16 500 dwt
Berth No.65	180	10.1	See [13] below
Berth No.66	180	10.1	General & bulk cargo for vessels up to 16 500 dwt
Kang Yun Oil Berth	220	7	MFO, MDO & LPG for vessels up to 7500 dwt

[1]Berth No.1: General, bulk & chemical cargo for vessels up to 11 500 dwt
[2]Berth No.5: General cargo, bulk cargo, iron ore, steel slabs & bitumen for vessels up to 75 000 dwt
[3]Berth No.9: General cargo, bulk cargo, fertiliser, sulphur & alumina for vessels up to 75 000 dwt
[4]Berth No.11: General cargo, bulk cargo, sulphur & alumina for vessels up to 75 000 dwt
[5]Berth No.12: General cargo, bulk cargo, molten sulphur & alumina for vessels up to 75 000 dwt
[6]Berth No.14: Coal pitch, rock phosphate & molten sulphur for vessels up to 25 000 dwt
[7]Berth No.16: Chemicals, LPG, palm oil & alcohol for vessels up to 22 500 dwt
[8]Berth No.31: General cargo, containers & molten sulphur for vessels up to 75 000 dwt. Lianyungang New Oriental Container Terminal Co Ltd., Website: www.lnoct.com, operate container berths at Berth No's 31 and 32
[9]Berth No.33: Grain, barley, soybeans & wheat for vessels up to 75 000 dwt
[10]Berth No.35: General cargo, timber, iron ore, coke, pig iron & rock phosphate for vessels up to 20 000 dwt
[11]Berth No.36: Timber, iron ore, pig iron, coke & metal concentrates for vessels up to 80 000 dwt
[12]Berth No.61: General cargo, bulk cargo, coke & chemicals for vessels up to 70 000 dwt
[13]Berth No.65: General cargo, bulk cargo & asphalt for vessels up to 50 000 dwt

Storage:

Location	Open (m²)	Covered (m²)
Lianyungang	803416	75478

Mechanical Handling Equipment:

Location	Type	Capacity (t)	Qty
Lianyungang	Floating Cranes	200	1
Berth No.1	Shore Cranes	10	5
Berth No.2	Shore Cranes	10	5
Berth No.3	Shore Cranes	10	5
Berth No.4	Shore Cranes	10	5
Berth No.5	Shore Cranes	10	2
Berth No.5	Shore Cranes	16	3
Berth No.6	Shore Cranes	16	3
Berth No.6	Shore Cranes	10	2
Berth No.8	Shore Cranes	10	6
Berth No.9	Shore Cranes	10	6
Berth No.11	Shore Cranes	10	6
Berth No.12	Shore Cranes	10	6
Berth No.31	Container Cranes	45	2

Location	Type	Capacity (t)	Qty
Berth No.32	Container Cranes	45	2
Berth No.35	Shore Cranes	25	6
Berth No.36	Shore Cranes	25	6
Berth No.61	Shore Cranes	25	2
Berth No.61	Shore Cranes	10	8
Berth No.62	Shore Cranes	25	2
Berth No.62	Shore Cranes	10	8
Berth No.63	Shore Cranes	16	6
Berth No.63	Shore Cranes	25	2
Berth No.64	Shore Cranes	25	2
Berth No.64	Shore Cranes	16	3
Berth No.65	Shore Cranes	16	8
Berth No.65	Shore Cranes	25	2
Berth No.66	Shore Cranes	16	4
Berth No.66	Shore Cranes	25	2

Bunkering: China Marine Bunker Supply Co., 13F Qian Cun Mansion A, No.2, 5th Block, Anzhen Xili, Chaoyang District, Beijing 100029, People's Republic of China, *Tel:* +86 10 6443 0717, *Fax:* +86 10 6443 0708, *Email:* business@chimbusco.com.cn, *Website:* www.chimbusco.com.cn – *Grades:* IFO120-380cSt; MGO

Towage: Available up to 3200 hp

Repair & Maintenance: Drydock for repairs to foreign vessels available. There are workshops for engineering, hull works etc

Ship Chandlers: Lianyungang Ocean Shipping Supply Co. Ltd, No.131 Zhongshan Road, Lianyungang, Jiangsu Province 222046, People's Republic of China, *Tel:* +86 518 8233 1013, *Fax:* +86 518 8233 2461, *Email:* lygsupco@public.lyg.js.cn, *Website:* www.issalygsupco.net
Lianyungang Ship Supplier Co Ltd, 1-5 Building Zhonghua Road, Lianyungang, Jiangsu Province 222042, People's Republic of China, *Tel:* +86 518 8232 2588, *Fax:* +86 518 8232 3089, *Email:* supply@shipsupplier.com.cn, *Website:* www.shipsupplier.com.cn

Shipping Agents: China Marine Shipping Agency Co. Ltd, China Marine Shipping Agency Lianyungang Company Limited, Sinoagent Garden, 6 Zhongshan Road (W), Xugou, Lianyungang, Jiangsu Province 222042, People's Republic of China, *Tel:* +86 518 8231 0246, *Fax:* +86 518 8231 9748, *Email:* cnlyg@sinoagent.com, *Website:* www.sinoagentsh.com
China Ocean Shipping Agency, 87 Haitang Road (S), Xugou, Lianyungang, Jiangsu Province 222042, People's Republic of China, *Tel:* +86 518 8223 1007, *Fax:* +86 518 8231 1842, *Email:* fangyr@penavicolyg.com, *Website:* www.penavicolyg.com
CMA-CGM S.A., CMA CGM Lianyungang, A611 Land Bridge International Business Building, 188 North Haitang Road, Lianyungang, Jiangsu Province 222042, People's Republic of China, *Tel:* +86 518 8223 6201, *Fax:* +86 518 8223 6203, *Email:* ygg.genmbox@cma-cgm.com, *Website:* www.cma-cgm.com
Lianyungang Philhua Shipping Agency Co Ltd, Unit B510, Land Bridge International Business Building, 188 Haitang Road (North), Lianyungang, Jiangsu Province 222042, People's Republic of China, *Tel:* +86 518 8542 8018, *Fax:* +86 518 8542 8028, *Email:* agency@philhua.com, *Website:* www.philhua.com
Sun Hing Shipping Co Ltd, Room 302, 3/F, Shipping Company Ltd, Zhong Hua Road, Lianyungang, Jiangsu Province 222042, People's Republic of China, *Tel:* +86 518 8230 0398, *Fax:* +86 518 8230 0398, *Website:* www.sunhinggroup.com
Tongsheng International Shipping Agencies, Lianyungang Tongsheng International Shipping Agency Co Ltd, Room 617-626, 369 Zhongshan Road, Xugou, Lianyungang, Jiangsu Province 222042, People's Republic of China, *Tel:* +86 518 8232 7972, *Fax:* +86 518 8232 7971, *Email:* lyg@tongsheng.net.cn, *Website:* www.tongshengshipping.com
Young Carrier Co. Ltd, Room 207 Area A, Dluqiao Int Business Mansion, 188 Haitang North Road, Lianyungang, Jiangsu Province, People's Republic of China, *Tel:* +86 518 8223 1672, *Fax:* +86 518 8223 1185, *Email:* slender.zhao@yml.com.cn

Railway: The Longhai railroad links the port to eleven provinces

Lloyd's Agent: Huatai Surveyors & Adjusters Co., 14th Floor, China Re Building, No.11 Jin Rong Avenue, Xicheng District, Beijing 100140, People's Republic of China, *Tel:* +86 10 6657 6577, *Fax:* +86 10 6657 6502, *Email:* agency.bj@huatai-serv.com, *Website:* www.huatai-serv.com

LIUGONGQIAO

harbour area, see under Jinshi

LIUHUA TERMINAL

Lat 20° 50' N; Long 115° 42' E.

Admiralty Chart: 3489	**Admiralty Pilot:** 30
Time Zone: GMT +8 h	**UNCTAD Locode:** CN

Liu Hua Term.

Principal Facilities:

P							T	

Key to Principal Facilities:—					
A=Airport	**C**=Containers	**G**=General Cargo	**P**=Petroleum	**R**=Ro/Ro	**Y**=Dry Bulk
B=Bunkers	**D**=Dry Dock	**L**=Cruise	**Q**=Other Liquid Bulk	**T**=Towage (where available from port)	

Authority: CNOOC China Ltd, 17th Floor, Finances Centre, Tai Zi Road, Shekou Industrial Zone, Shenzhen, Guangdong Province 518067, People's Republic of China, *Tel:* +86 755 2667 1212, *Fax:* +86 755 2667 1211, *Email:* ming-chen@aopc.com.cn, *Website:* www.cnoocltd.com

Pilotage: Compulsory. Mooring Master normally boards vessel by helicoptor at the waiting area centred in pos 20° 44' N; 115° 38' E

Radio Frequency: The FPSO maintains a radio watch on VHF Channel 16

Principal Imports and Exports: Exports: Crude oil.

Accommodation:

Name	Remarks
Liuhua Terminal	See [1] below

[1]*Liuhua Terminal:* Consists of offshore loading berth FPSO 'Nan Hai Sheng Li' for export tankers of 35 000-140 000 dwt loading crude oil. Vessels moored in daylight only. Loading rate of approx 30 000 bbls/h

Towage: Two tug/supply vessels available to aid in berthing

Lloyd's Agent: Huatai Surveyors & Adjusters Co., Room 802, Jun Yuan Mansion, 155 Tian He East Road, Guangzhou, Guangdong Province 510620, People's Republic of China, *Tel:* +86 20 3881 2306, *Fax:* +86 20 3881 2470, *Email:* agency.gz@huatai-serv.com, *Website:* www.huatai-serv.com

LIZUIZI

harbour area, see under Huainan

LONGKOU

Lat 37° 39' N; Long 120° 19' E.

Admiralty Chart: 2119
Time Zone: GMT +8 h

Admiralty Pilot: 32
UNCTAD Locode: CN LKU

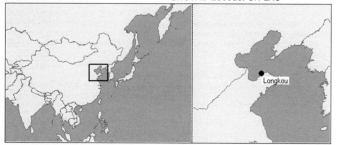

Principal Facilities:

	Y	G	C		B		T	A	

Authority: Longkou Port Group Co Ltd, 24 Huanhai Road, Longkou, Shandong Province 265700, People's Republic of China, *Tel:* +86 535 884 2091, *Fax:* +86 535 884 1137, *Email:* lkgbgs@163.com, *Website:* www.lkport.com

Officials: General Manager: Meng Xing Gang.

Port Security: ISPS compliant

Approach: Draft limitation in main channel is 12 m

Anchorage: Quarantine Pilot Anchorage: in depth of 8.6 m for quarantine and pilot. No.1 Anchorage in depth of 10-15 m for lightening. No.2 Anchorage in depth of 10-15 m for lightening

Pilotage: Compulsory and available 24 h. Pilot boards vessel at the Quarantine Pilot Anchorage

Radio Frequency: VHF Channel 16

Tides: Average tidal range of 1.36 m

Maximum Vessel Dimensions: 70 000 dwt

Working Hours: 24 h/day

Accommodation:

Name	Length (m)	Depth (m)	Remarks
Longkou			
Berth No.1	180	10.3	General & bulk cargo for vessels up to 16 000 dwt
Berth No.2	120	7.5	General cargo for vessels up to 5000 dwt
Berth No.3	100	6.7	General & bulk cargo for vessels up to 3000 dwt
Berth No.4	100	6.7	General & bulk cargo for vessels up to 3000 dwt
Berth No.5	103.9	6.8	General cargo for vessels up to 3000 dwt
Berth No.6	103.9	6.8	General cargo for vessels up to 3000 dwt
Berth No.7	47	4	General cargo for vessels up to 1000 dwt
Berth No.8	47	4	General cargo for vessels up to 1000 dwt
Berth No.9	131	7.5	General cargo for vessels up to 5000 dwt
Berth No.10	131	7.5	General cargo for vessels up to 5000 dwt
Berth No.11	275	14	See [1] below

Name	Length (m)	Depth (m)	Remarks
Berth No.12	218	14	General & bulk cargo for vessels up to 50 000 dwt
Berth No.13	217	14	General cargo for vessels up to 50 000 dwt
Berth No.16	180	10.3	Containers for vessels up to 16 000 dwt
Berth No.17	180	10.3	General cargo for vessels up to 16 000 dwt
Berth No.18	178	10	General & bulk cargo for vessels up to 16 000 dwt
Berth No.19	177	10.1	Coal for vessels up to 16 000 dwt
Berth No.20	130	7.8	Dangerous cargo for vessels up to 5000 dwt

[1]*Berth No.11:* Presently under construction. Grain for vessels up to 50 000 dwt

Storage: Storage area of 720 000 m2

Mechanical Handling Equipment:

Location	Type	Capacity (t)	Qty
Berth No.1	Portal Cranes	10	3
Berth No.2	Portal Cranes	10	3
Berth No.7	Portal Cranes	10	1
Berth No.8	Portal Cranes	10	1
Berth No.9	Portal Cranes	10	1
Berth No.10	Portal Cranes	10	2
Berth No.11	Portal Cranes	16	3
Berth No.12	Portal Cranes	16	4
Berth No.13	Portal Cranes	16	2
Berth No.16	Mult-purp. Cranes	80	1
Berth No.16	Container Cranes	40	2
Berth No.16	RTG's	30.5	2
Berth No.18	Portal Cranes	16	3
Berth No.19	Portal Cranes	10	3

Bunkering: Available at berth and anchorage

Towage: Three tugs up to 3500 hp are available

Repair & Maintenance: Basic repairs available

Shipping Agents: China Marine Shipping Agency Co. Ltd, China Marine Shipping Agency Shandong Company Limited Longkou Branch, 96 Huanhai Road, Longkou, Shandong Province, People's Republic of China, *Tel:* +86 535 881 2403, *Fax:* +86 535 881 2475, *Email:* gfsdcd_longkou@sinotrans.com

Airport: 50 km from port

Lloyd's Agent: Huatai Surveyors & Adjusters Co., 14th Floor, China Re Building, No.11 Jin Rong Avenue, Xicheng District, Beijing 100140, People's Republic of China, *Tel:* +86 10 6657 6577, *Fax:* +86 10 6657 6502, *Email:* agency.bj@huatai-serv.com, *Website:* www.huatai-serv.com

LONGWAN

harbour area, see under Wenzhou

LONGWU

harbour area, see under Shanghai

LONGYAN

Lat 37° 24' N; Long 122° 37' E.

Admiralty Chart: 1254
Time Zone: GMT +8 h

Admiralty Pilot: 32
UNCTAD Locode: CN

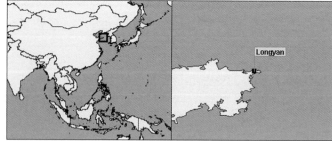

Principal Facilities:

	Y	G	C				T		

Accommodation:

Name	Remarks
Longyan	See [1] below

[1]*Longyan:* Consists of three berths of over 10 000 dwt, five berths over 5000 dwt and two specialized container berths

Storage: Open and covered storage areas available

Mechanical Handling Equipment:

Location	Type	Capacity (t)
Longyan	Mult-purp. Cranes	25

Towage: Available

Lloyd's Agent: Huatai Surveyors & Adjusters Co., 14th Floor, China Re Building, No.11 Jin Rong Avenue, Xicheng District, Beijing 100140, People's Republic of China, *Tel:* +86 10 6657 6577, *Fax:* +86 10 6657 6502, *Email:* agency.bj@huatai-serv.com, *Website:* www.huatai-serv.com

LUCHAO

harbour area, see under Nanhui

LUFENG TERMINAL

Lat 21° 38' N; Long 116° 2' E.

Admiralty Chart: -	**Admiralty Pilot:** -
Time Zone: GMT +8 h	**UNCTAD Locode:** CN

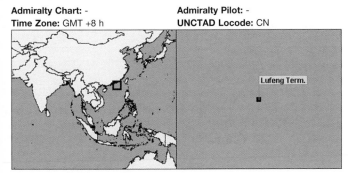

Principal Facilities:

P										

Authority: Lufeng 22-1 Statoil (Orient) Inc, 20/F Times Plaza No.1, Taizi Road, Shekou, Guangdong Province 518067, People's Republic of China, *Tel:* +86 755 2685 5335, *Fax:* +86 755 2685 5331, *Website:* www.statoil.com

Pilotage: Mooring Master boards lifting tanker 5 nautical miles from FPSO

Maximum Vessel Dimensions: 35 000 -150 000 dwt

Working Hours: 24 h/day

Accommodation:

Name	Remarks
Lufeng Terminal	Consists of FPSO 'Munin' in depth of approx 330 m. Vessels moor in daylight hours only

Lloyd's Agent: Huatai Surveyors & Adjusters Co., Room 802, Jun Yuan Mansion, 155 Tian He East Road, Guangzhou, Guangdong Province 510620, People's Republic of China, *Tel:* +86 20 3881 2306, *Fax:* +86 20 3881 2470, *Email:* agency.gz@huatai-serv.com, *Website:* www.huatai-serv.com

LUZHOU

Lat 28° 53' N; Long 105° 26' E.

Admiralty Chart: -	**Admiralty Pilot:** -
Time Zone: GMT +8 h	**UNCTAD Locode:** CN LZU

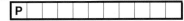

Principal Facilities:

	Y	G	C				T	A	

Authority: Luzhou Harbour Administration, Xinma Road, Central District, Luzhou, Sichuan Province 646000, People's Republic of China

Traffic: 2005, 21 500 TEU's handled

Accommodation:

Name	Length (m)	Depth (m)	Remarks
Luzhou Berth	65	2.9	See [1] below Max 3000 dwt handling container & bulk cargoes

[1]*Luzhou:* Situated in Longmatan district on the N bank of the Yangtze

Storage: Container yard of 60 000 m2

Location	Covered (m²)
Luzhou	2500

Mechanical Handling Equipment:

Location	Type	Capacity (t)
Luzhou	Mult-purp. Cranes	40

Towage: Available

Stevedoring Companies: Sichuan Changtong Port Co Ltd., Luzhou, Sichuan Province, People's Republic of China, *Tel:* +86 830 279 2999, *Website:* www.lzict.com

Airport: Luzhou Lantian Airport

Lloyd's Agent: Huatai Surveyors & Adjusters Co., 14th Floor, China Re Building, No.11 Jin Rong Avenue, Xicheng District, Beijing 100140, People's Republic of China, *Tel:* +86 10 6657 6577, *Fax:* +86 10 6657 6502, *Email:* agency.bj@huatai-serv.com, *Website:* www.huatai-serv.com

MA'ANSHAN

Lat 31° 49' N; Long 118° 32' E.

Admiralty Chart: 2946	**Admiralty Pilot:** 32
Time Zone: GMT +8 h	**UNCTAD Locode:** CN MAA

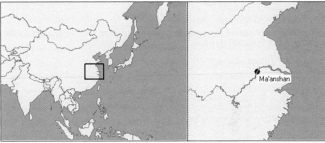

Principal Facilities:

	Y		C				T	A

Authority: Ma'anshan Port (Group) Co Ltd., 47 Qi Jiang Road, Anshan, Anhui Province 243000, People's Republic of China, *Tel:* +86 555 284 5963, *Email:* masport@masport.com.cn, *Website:* www.masport.com.cn

Port Security: ISPS compliant

Pilotage: Compulsory and available 24 h

Radio Frequency: VHF Channel 13

Tides: Max 1.1 m, min 0.6 m

Traffic: 2005, 15 690 000 t of cargo handled, 37 100 TEU's

Accommodation:

Name	Length (m)	Depth (m)	Remarks
Ma'anshan Terminal	2412	7.4	Thirteen berths for vessels up to 5000 dwt

Storage:

Location	Open (m²)	Covered (m²)
Ma'anshan	20300	4630

Mechanical Handling Equipment:

Location	Type	Capacity (t)
Ma'anshan	Mult-purp. Cranes	40

Bunkering: Available

Towage: Four 1200 hp tugs

Shipping Agents: China Marine Shipping Agency Co. Ltd, China Marine Shipping Agency Anhui Maanshan Company, No. 298 Huashan Road, Maanshan, Anhui Province, People's Republic of China, *Tel:* +86 555 247 3947, *Fax:* +86 555 249 2343, *Email:* maanshan@sinoagent.com

Airport: Nanjing Lukou International Airport and Wuhu Airport

Lloyd's Agent: Huatai Surveyors & Adjusters Co., 14th Floor, China Re Building, No.11 Jin Rong Avenue, Xicheng District, Beijing 100140, People's Republic of China, *Tel:* +86 10 6657 6577, *Fax:* +86 10 6657 6502, *Email:* agency.bj@huatai-serv.com, *Website:* www.huatai-serv.com

MABIANZHOU

Lat 22° 40' N; Long 114° 39' E.

Admiralty Chart: 3026	**Admiralty Pilot:** 30
Time Zone: GMT +8 h	**UNCTAD Locode:** CN

Key to Principal Facilities:—				
A=Airport	**C**=Containers	**G**=General Cargo	**P**=Petroleum	**R**=Ro/Ro	**Y**=Dry Bulk
B=Bunkers	**D**=Dry Dock	**L**=Cruise	**Q**=Other Liquid Bulk	**T**=Towage (where available from port)

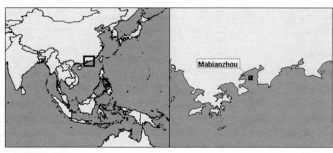

Principal Facilities:

P								T	

Authority: The CNOOC & Shell Petrochemicals Co Ltd, Dayawan Petrochemical Industrial Park, Huizhou, Guangdong Province 516086, People's Republic of China, *Tel:* +86 752 368 2228, *Fax:* +86 752 368 1188, *Email:* luo.peter@cnoocshell.com, *Website:* www.cnoocshell.com

Anchorage: Centred on pos 22° 31.2' N; 114° 45.7' E in depth of 15 m

Pilotage: Compulsory. Berthing during daylight hours only

Maximum Vessel Dimensions: 294 m loa, 150 000 dwt

Accommodation:

Name	Length (m)	Depth (m)	Draught (m)	Remarks
Mabianzhou Dolphin Berth	412	14.8	13.3	See ¹ below

¹*Dolphin Berth:* Import of condensate or naphtha feedstock. Transferred to petrochemicals complex at Daya Bay by an 11 km undersea pipeline

Towage: Three tugs available

Medical Facilities: Available

Lloyd's Agent: Huatai Surveyors & Adjusters Co., Room 802, Jun Yuan Mansion, 155 Tian He East Road, Guangzhou, Guangdong Province 510620, People's Republic of China, *Tel:* +86 20 3881 2306, *Fax:* +86 20 3881 2470, *Email:* agency.gz@huatai-serv.com, *Website:* www.huatai-serv.com

MACAU

Lat 22° 12' N; Long 113° 33' E.

Admiralty Chart: 341

Admiralty Pilot: 30

Time Zone: GMT +8 h

UNCTAD Locode: CN MFM

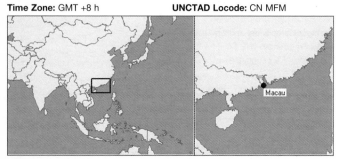

Principal Facilities:

P	Q		G	C			B			A	

Authority: Macau Maritime Administration, Quartel dos Mouros, Calcada da Barra, P O Box 47, Macau, Macau, *Tel:* +853 2855 9922, *Fax:* +853 2851 1986, *Email:* cpm@macau.ctm.net, *Website:* www.marine.gov.mo

Port Security: ISPS compliant

Approach: Access channel to Inner Harbour is 45 m wide in depth of 3.5 m below CD with max air draught of 30 m
Access channel to Outer Harbour is 120 m wide in depth of 4.4 m below CD with max air draught of 30 m
Access channel to Ka-Ho Port is 75 m wide in depth of 4 m below CD

Anchorage: Outer anchorage in pos 22° 09' N; 113° 36.50' E in depth of 4 m. The anchorage area is defined by the parallels of 22° 08.30' N and 22° 09.70' N and by the meridians of 113° 36.01' E and 113° 37.00' E or within the radius of 0.4 nautical mile with the centre on pos 22° 07.30' N; 113° 36.55' E

Pilotage: Compulsory. Pilots should be requested from the Macau Maritime Administration through vessels port agent

Radio Frequency: Macau radio on 156.8 mHz (channel 16) and 156.5 mHz (channel 10)

Weather: Typhoon season April-October

Tides: Tidal range 0.5-3.5 m

Traffic: 2000, 47 356 vessels, 1 852 042 t of cargo handled

Maximum Vessel Dimensions: 105 m loa, 5588 dwt, 5.77 m draft

Principal Imports and Exports: Imports: Food, Fuel, Machinery & equipment. Exports: , Textiles, Toys.

Working Hours: 24 h/day

Accommodation:

Name	Length (m)	Depth (m)	Draught (m)	Remarks
Macau				
Macau Fuel Terminal (Ka-Ho Port)	110	6		Tankers & LPG vessels. Tel: +853 2887 0132, Fax: +853 2888 1036
Macauport Container Terminal (Ka-Ho Port)	306.4			See ¹ below
Maritime Harbour (Outer Harbour)		6	4.4	See ² below
Inner Harbour Berths		4		Berth lengths between 30 m and 130 m

¹*Macauport Container Terminal (Ka-Ho Port):* Operated by Macauport S.A., P O Box 1306, Macau, Tel: +853 2887 0558, Fax: +853 2887 0602, Email: mcp@macau.ctm.net, Website: www.macauport.com.mo
Total area of 49 524 m2 with container yard area of 23 828 m2 and CFS of 2850 m2
²*Maritime Harbour (Outer Harbour):* Managed by S.T.D.M. Shipping Dept., Tel: +853 2879 0722, Fax: +853 2872 6234
Passenger vessels. Consists of one long berth approx 270 m long and twelve berths for high-speed craft

Mechanical Handling Equipment:

Location	Type	Capacity (t)	Qty
Macauport Container Terminal (Ka-Ho Port)	Mobile Cranes	35	1

Bunkering: Fuel oil and MDO only available from Hong Kong by barge

Waste Reception Facilities: Garbage disposal available

Repair & Maintenance: Macau Government Dockyard, Macau, Macau, *Tel:* +853 2833 5946, *Fax:* +853 2831 7030 Repair facilities

Shipping Agents: Vinda International Express Ltd, 12th Floor, Talent Commercial Centre, Macau, Macau, *Tel:* +853 2832 9290, *Fax:* +853 2832 2807, *Email:* vinda@macau.ctm.net

Medical Facilities: Two fully equipped hospitals

Airport: Macau International Airport, 7 km

Lloyd's Agent: Andrew Moore & Associates Ltd, 2703 Universal Trade Centre, 3 Artbuthnot Road, Central, Hong Kong, Hong Kong, *Tel:* +852 2861 3313, *Fax:* +852 2865 6571, *Email:* lloydsagency@andrew-moore.com, *Website:* www.andrew-moore.com

MACUN

Lat 19° 57' N; Long 110° 3' E.

Admiralty Chart: 3991

Admiralty Pilot: 30

Time Zone: GMT +8 h

UNCTAD Locode: CN

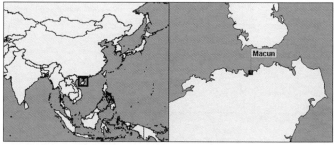

Principal Facilities:

P		Y							

Radio Frequency: VHF Channel 16

Accommodation:

Name	Remarks
Macun	Coal berths for vessels up to 35 000 dwt and also transhipment of petroleum

Mechanical Handling Equipment:

Location	Type
Macun	Mult-purp. Cranes

Lloyd's Agent: Huatai Surveyors & Adjusters Co., 14th Floor, China Re Building, No.11 Jin Rong Avenue, Xicheng District, Beijing 100140, People's Republic of China, *Tel:* +86 10 6657 6577, *Fax:* +86 10 6657 6502, *Email:* agency.bj@huatai-serv.com, *Website:* www.huatai-serv.com

MAJIAHE

harbour area, see under Xiangtan

MAOCAOJIE

Lat 29° 4' N; Long 112° 18' E.

Admiralty Chart: -
Admiralty Pilot: -
Time Zone: GMT +8 h
UNCTAD Locode: CN

Principal Facilities:

		Y	G						

Accommodation:

Name	Remarks
Maocaojie	Cargoes handled include grain, ore, coal, cotton and fertiliser
Songquhongdao Area	Vessels up to 500 dwt
Nanmao Canal Area	Vessels up to 100 dwt

Storage: Open and covered storage areas available
Lloyd's Agent: Huatai Surveyors & Adjusters Co., 14th Floor, China Re Building, No.11 Jin Rong Avenue, Xicheng District, Beijing 100140, People's Republic of China, *Tel:* +86 10 6657 6577, *Fax:* +86 10 6657 6502, *Email:* agency.bj@huatai-serv.com, *Website:* www.huatai-serv.com

MAO'ERTUO TERMINAL

harbour area, see under Chongqing

MAOMING

harbour area, see under Shuidong

MAWAN

Lat 22° 29' N; Long 113° 52' E.

Admiralty Chart: 342/343
Admiralty Pilot: 30
Time Zone: GMT +8 h
UNCTAD Locode: CN MWN

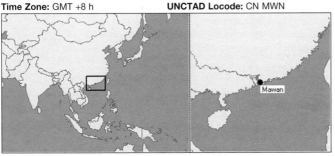

Principal Facilities:

	P		Y	G	C			B		T	

Authority: Haixin Harbour Development Co. Ltd, Mawan 518052, People's Republic of China, *Tel:* +86 755 2669 3751, *Fax:* +86 755 2669 3757
Approach: Draft limitation in the channel is 12.3 m
Pilotage: Compulsory and available 24/h. Pilot boards in pos 22° 23' 40" N; 113° 53' 65" E (Urnston Roads) and 22° 18' 98" N; 113° 50' 26" E (Longguxi Hangdao)
Radio Frequency: VHF Channels 16 and 11
Tides: Average tidal range of 1.36 m
Traffic: 2003, 16 870 000 t of cargo handled
Accommodation:

Name	Length (m)	Depth (m)	Remarks
Mawan			
Berth No.1	237	10	Bulk & general cargo
Berth No.2	237	12.5	Bulk & general cargo
Berth No.3a	150	7.5	Bulk & general cargo
Berth No.3b	120	7	Bulk & general cargo
Berth No.3c	150	7.5	Bulk & general cargo
Berth No.4	226	11	Bulk & general cargo

Name	Length (m)	Depth (m)	Remarks
Berth No's 0, 5, 6 & 7	1388	12.5–17	See [1] below
Dovechem Berth No.1	230	10.8	Chemicals
Dovechem Berth No.2	120	6	Chemicals

[1]*Berth No's 0, 5, 6 & 7:* Container terminal operated by China Merchants Holdings (International) Co Ltd., Tel: +86 755 2688 6723, Fax: +86 755 2688 6722, Email: linxinduo@cmhk.com, Website: www.cmhico.com

Storage:

Location	Open (m²)	Covered (m²)
Mawan	80000	21000

Mechanical Handling Equipment:

Location	Type	Capacity (t)	Qty
Berth No.1	Mult-purp. Cranes	45	1
Berth No.2	Mult-purp. Cranes	10	1
Berth No.2	Mult-purp. Cranes	25	1
Berth No.2	Mult-purp. Cranes	16	3
Berth No.3a	Mult-purp. Cranes	10	1
Berth No.3c	Mult-purp. Cranes	45	1
Berth No.4	Mult-purp. Cranes	15	1
Berth No.4	Mult-purp. Cranes	16	1
Berth No.4	Mult-purp. Cranes	10	2
Berth No's 0, 5, 6 & 7	Container Cranes		12
Berth No's 0, 5, 6 & 7	RTG's		40

Bunkering: Available at both berth and anchorage
Towage: Five tugs available
Shenzhen Huxing Tugboat Co. Ltd, Haixing Building, Mawan Port Area, Mawan 518052, People's Republic of China, *Tel:* +86 755 2669 3753, *Fax:* +86 755 2667 6593
Development: Berth No.7 due to be delivered in September 2007
Lloyd's Agent: Huatai Surveyors & Adjusters Co., 14th Floor, China Re Building, No.11 Jin Rong Avenue, Xicheng District, Beijing 100140, People's Republic of China, *Tel:* +86 10 6657 6577, *Fax:* +86 10 6657 6502, *Email:* agency.bj@huatai-serv.com, *Website:* www.huatai-serv.com

MAWEI

harbour area, see under Fuzhou

MEIZHOUWAN

harbour area, see under Xiuyu

MINSHENG

harbour area, see under Shanghai

MISHIDU

harbour area, see under Songjiang

MOJIAOSHANG

harbour area, see under Ganzhou

NANCHANG

Lat 28° 40' N; Long 115° 53' E.

Admiralty Chart: 2947
Admiralty Pilot: 32
Time Zone: GMT +8 h
UNCTAD Locode: CN KHN

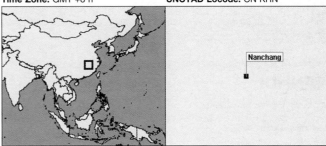

Key to Principal Facilities:—			
A=Airport	**C**=Containers	**G**=General Cargo	**P**=Petroleum	**R**=Ro/Ro	**Y**=Dry Bulk
B=Bunkers	**D**=Dry Dock	**L**=Cruise	**Q**=Other Liquid Bulk	**T**=Towage (where available from port)

Principal Facilities:

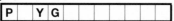

| P | | Y | G | | | | | | | |

Authority: Nanchang Harbour Administration, Yanjiang Bei Road, Nanchang, Jiangxi Province 330008, People's Republic of China

Accommodation:

Name	Remarks
Nanchang	Cargoes handled include coal, petroleum, iron & steel, sand, timber, fertiliser and grain

Storage: Open and covered storage areas available

Shipping Agents: CMA-CGM S.A., CMA CGM Nanchang, Room 2008, Jiangxin International Building, 88 Beijing Road West, Nanchang, Jiangxi Province 332000, People's Republic of China, *Tel:* +86 791 630 4709, *Fax:* +86 791 630 4721, *Email:* ncg.kfang@cma-cgm.com, *Website:* www.cma-cgm.com

Lloyd's Agent: Huatai Surveyors & Adjusters Co., 14th Floor, China Re Building, No.11 Jin Rong Avenue, Xicheng District, Beijing 100140, People's Republic of China, *Tel:* +86 10 6657 6577, *Fax:* +86 10 6657 6502, *Email:* agency.bj@huatai-serv.com, *Website:* www.huatai-serv.com

NANDI

harbour area, see under Foshan

NANHAI

Lat 23° 6' N; Long 113° 11' E.

Admiralty Chart: -	**Admiralty Pilot:** -
Time Zone: GMT +8 h	**UNCTAD Locode:** CN NAH

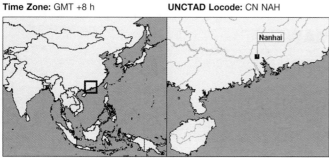

Principal Facilities:

| | | | | C | | | | | | |

Authority: Nanhai International Container Terminals, Sanshan Port Economic Development Zone, Nanhai 528251, People's Republic of China, *Tel:* +86 757 8670 0019, *Fax:* +86 757 8670 0020, *Email:* nict@nict.com.cn

Accommodation:

Name	Length (m)	Depth (m)	Remarks
Nanhai			See [1] below
Quay	420	8	See [2] below

[1]*Nanhai:* Located at the Sanshan Economic Development Zone
[2]*Quay:* 5000 t off-dock refrigerated warehouse and a 6000 m2 all-weather CFS warehouse

Mechanical Handling Equipment:

Location	Type	Qty
Quay	Mult-purp. Cranes	4
Quay	Mobile Cranes	4
Quay	RTG's	6
Quay	Forklifts	27

Lloyd's Agent: Huatai Surveyors & Adjusters Co., 14th Floor, China Re Building, No.11 Jin Rong Avenue, Xicheng District, Beijing 100140, People's Republic of China, *Tel:* +86 10 6657 6577, *Fax:* +86 10 6657 6502, *Email:* agency.bj@huatai-serv.com, *Website:* www.huatai-serv.com

NANHUI

Lat 31° 3' N; Long 121° 45' E.

Admiralty Chart: 1602	**Admiralty Pilot:** 32
Time Zone: GMT +8 h	**UNCTAD Locode:** CN

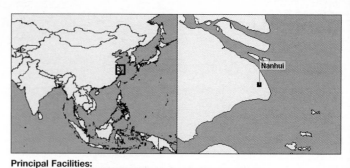

Principal Facilities:

| P | | Y | G | | | | | | | |

Accommodation:

Name	Remarks
Nanhui	See [1] below

[1]*Nanhui:* The port has six operational areas: Zhoupu, Hangtou, Xinchang, Huinan, Datuan and Luchao
Cargoes handled include general cargo, timber, ore, coal and petroleum

Lloyd's Agent: Huatai Surveyors & Adjusters Co., 14th Floor, China Re Building, No.11 Jin Rong Avenue, Xicheng District, Beijing 100140, People's Republic of China, *Tel:* +86 10 6657 6577, *Fax:* +86 10 6657 6502, *Email:* agency.bj@huatai-serv.com, *Website:* www.huatai-serv.com

NANJING

Lat 32° 3' N; Long 118° 47' E.

Admiralty Chart: 1642	**Admiralty Pilot:** 32
Time Zone: GMT +8 h	**UNCTAD Locode:** CN NKG

Principal Facilities:

| P | | Y | G | C | R | | B | | T | A |

Authority: Nanjing Port Group Co., 19 Jiangbian Road, Nanjing, Jiangsu Province 210011, People's Republic of China, *Tel:* +86 25 5858 2721, *Fax:* +86 25 5882 3898, *Email:* juban@njp.com.cn, *Website:* www.njp.com.cn

Port Security: ISPS compliant

Approach: The main channel has a 9.7 m draught

Anchorage: Qixia anchorage and Yizheng anchorage for oil tankers. Yizheng has a depth of 12 m, mud and sand bottom with good holding ground. Vessels to 50 000 dwt. It is also used as a quarantine anchorage
Xinshengyu anchorage can accommodate up to three 10 000 dwt vessels at any one time
Danian waiting berth, 32° 14.5' N; 119° 19' E, and joint inspection anchorage located at Siyuangou which can accommodate six 10 000 dwt vessels at any one time. Depth 13 to 16 m. Bottom mud and sand - good holding ground
No.5 co.anchorage, depth 12 m, mud and sand bottom, good holding ground, vessels to 50 000 dwt and is used as a lightening anchorage

Pilotage: Compulsory - Pilotage upriver is in two stages. First from the mouth of the Yangtze River to Baoshan, which is by Shanghai pilots. The second stage is from Baoshan to Nanjing, which is by Nanjing pilots.
The distance from Changjiang entrance to Baoshan is 53 miles. Baoshan is located 3 miles upriver. The vessel may have to anchor here for Nanjing pilots, they board on arrival and the Shanghai pilot disembarks. The vessel continues without stopping, which is a distance of 177 miles to Nanjing. When the vessel anchors at the Nanjing Waiting or Quarantine anchorage the pilot leaves and the berthing pilot boards
At least two days notice of application for pilotage

Weather: The port is ice free. The prevailing wind in Spring and Summer is E/SE, and Autumn and Winter is N/NE
Strong winds July, August and September when effected by typhoons. Fog in Autumn and Winter

Tides: Tidal range: min 0.02 m, max 1.47 m

Traffic: 2006, 100 910 000 t of cargo handled

Principal Imports and Exports: Imports: Equipment, Iron ore, Steel, Timber. Exports: Animal feedstuffs, Chemical products, Cotton, General, Oil products.

Accommodation:

Name	Length (m)	Depth (m)	Remarks
Yangzi Petrochemical Berth No.11	90	16	Petrochemical products for vessels up to 15 000 dwt

Name	Length (m)	Depth (m)	Remarks
Berth No.12	70	16	Petrochemical products for vessels up to 5000 dwt
Berth No.14	110	25	Petrochemical products for vessels up to 15 000 dwt
Yizheng			
Berth No.605	90	9	Petrochemical products for vessels up to 15 000 dwt
Berth No.608	90	9	Petrochemical products for vessels up to 5000 dwt
Berth No.612	123	9	Petrochemical products for vessels up to 35 000 dwt
Berth No.614	110	9	Petrochemical products for vessels up to 20 000 dwt
Nanjing Oil Refinery			
Berth No.6	100	9	Product oil for vessels up to 24 000 dwt
Berth No.7	90	9	Product oil for vessels up to 24 000 dwt
Berth No.10	100	9	Product oil for vessels up to 35 000 dwt
Berth No.11	100	9	Product oil for vessels up to 25 000 dwt
Berth No.12	100	9	Product oil for vessels up to 35 000 dwt
No.1 Chemical Plant			
Jinyan	90	9	Petrochemical products for vessels up to 5000 dwt
Jinyan No.1	90	9	Petrochemical products for vessels up to 5000 dwt
Xinshengwei			
Berth No.400	186	13	General cargo for vessels up to 15 000 dwt
Berth No.401	124	13	General cargo for vessels up to 15 000 dwt
Berth No.402	180	13	General cargo for vessels up to 35 000 dwt
Berth No.403	180	13	General cargo for vessels up to 15 000 dwt
Berth No.702	90	13	Ore for vessels up to 25 000 dwt
Berth No.703	180	13	Ore for vessels up to 25 000 dwt
Berth No.704	184	13	Ore for vessels up to 35 000 dwt
Berth No.705	90	13	Ore for vessels up to 25 000 dwt
Berth No.706	90	13	Ore for vessels up to 25 000 dwt
Berth No.707	90	13	Ore for vessels up to 25 000 dwt
Berth No.708	180	13	Ore for vessels up to 25 000 dwt
Berth No.709	180	13	Ore for vessels up to 35 000 dwt
Nanjing International Container Terminal			See [1] below
Berth No.404	186	13	Container cargo for vessels up to 25 000 dwt
Berth No.405	224	13	Container cargo for vessels up to 25 000 dwt
Nanjing Longtan Container Terminal			See [2] below
Berths	910	12	See [3] below

[1]*Nanjing International Container Terminal:* Operated by Nanjing International Container Terminal Services Co Inc., Tel: +86 25 8580 2210, Website: www.nicc2000.com

[2]*Nanjing Longtan Container Terminal:* Operated by Nanjing Port Longtan Container Terminal Co., Tel: +86 25 5858 3900, Website: www.lct2005.com

[3]*Berths:* Container terminal consisting of five berths (three 50 000 dwt berths and two 1000 dwt berths). Container yard area of 930 000 m2

Storage: Container yard of 100 000 m2

Location	Open (m^2)	Covered (m^2)
Nanjing	120000	30000

Mechanical Handling Equipment:

Location	Type	Capacity (t)	Qty
Nanjing	Floating Cranes	63	4
Berth No.400	Shore Cranes	10	2
Berth No.400	Shore Cranes	25	2
Berth No.401	Shore Cranes	25	2
Berth No.401	Shore Cranes	40	2
Berth No.402	Shore Cranes	40	2
Berth No.402	Shore Cranes	25	2
Berth No.403	Shore Cranes	25	2
Berth No.403	Shore Cranes	10	3
Berth No.702	Shore Cranes	10	3
Berth No.703	Shore Cranes	10	3
Berth No.704	Shore Cranes	10	3
Berth No.705	Shore Cranes	10	3
Berth No.706	Shore Cranes	10	4
Berth No.707	Shore Cranes	10	4
Berth No.708	Shore Cranes	10	4
Berth No.404	Mult-purp. Cranes	30	1

Location	Type	Capacity (t)	Qty
Berth No.405	Mult-purp. Cranes	30	1

Bunkering: China Marine Bunker Supply Co., 13F Qian Cun Mansion A, No.2, 5th Block, Anzhen Xili, Chaoyang District, Beijing 100029, People's Republic of China, *Tel:* +86 10 6443 0717, *Fax:* +86 10 6443 0708, *Email:* business@chimbusco.com.cn, *Website:* www.chimbusco.com.cn – *Grades:* IFO120-380cSt; MGO

Towage: Eleven tugs available of 1320-2640 hp

Repair & Maintenance: Jinling Shipyard, 55 Yanjing Road, Xiaguan District, Nanjing, Jiangsu Province 210015, People's Republic of China, *Tel:* +86 25 5878 5115, *Fax:* +86 25 5878 1075, *Website:* www.jl-shipyard.com.cn
Jinling Shipyard, 55 Yanjing Road, Xiaguan District, Nanjing, Jiangsu Province 210015, People's Republic of China, *Tel:* +86 25 5878 2179, *Fax:* +86 25 5878 1075, *Website:* www.jl-shipyard.com.cn

Ship Chandlers: Nanjing Ocean Shipping Supply Corp., 18th Floor No.17, Han Zhong Road, Nanjing, Jiangsu Province 210005, People's Republic of China, *Tel:* +86 25 8473 3109, *Fax:* +86 25 8322 3071, *Email:* njosscpa@public1.ptt.js.cn

Shipping Agents: China Marine Shipping Agency Co. Ltd, China Marine Shipping Agency Jiangsu Company Limited (Nanjing), 6th Floor, 129 Zhonghua Road, Nanjing, Jiangsu Province 210001, People's Republic of China, *Tel:* +86 25 5237 7807, *Fax:* +86 25 5224 5794, *Email:* shipping@sinotrans-js.com, *Website:* www.sinotrans-js.com
CMA-CGM S.A., CMA CGM Nanjing, F23, Zhidi Plaza, 55 North Hongwu Road, Nanjing, Jiangsu Province 210018, People's Republic of China, *Tel:* +86 25 8689 0368, *Fax:* +86 25 8689 0398, *Email:* jng.genmbox@cma-cgm.com, *Website:* www.cma-cgm.com

Surveyors: China Classification Society, 12 Jiang Jia Yuan, Nanjing, Jiangsu Province 210011, People's Republic of China, *Tel:* +86 25 5883 8006, *Fax:* +86 25 5880 2499, *Website:* www.ccs.org.cn
Det Norske Veritas A/S, Jinling Site Office, c/o Nanjing Jinling Shipyard, 55 Yan Jiang Road, Nanjing, Jiangsu Province 210015, People's Republic of China, *Tel:* +86 25 5878 3692, *Fax:* +86 25 5879 4996, *Email:* mchcn331@dnv.com, *Website:* www.dnv.com
Germanischer Lloyd, Room 501, 15# Jingcheng Garden, 30 Gui Yun Tang, Nanjing, Jiangsu Province 210003, People's Republic of China, *Tel:* +86 25 5880 0364, *Fax:* +86 25 5883 9250, *Email:* gl-nanjing@gl-group.com, *Website:* www.gl-group.com

Airport: Nanjing Airport

Development: Newly constructed general cargo terminal operated by Nanjing Longtan Tianyu Terminal Co Ltd, scheduled to be operational August 2007

Lloyd's Agent: Huatai Surveyors & Adjusters Co., 14th Floor, China Re Building, No.11 Jin Rong Avenue, Xicheng District, Beijing 100140, People's Republic of China, *Tel:* +86 10 6657 6577, *Fax:* +86 10 6657 6502, *Email:* agency.bj@huatai-serv.com, *Website:* www.huatai-serv.com

NANMEN

harbour area, see under Chongming

NANPU

harbour area, see under Shanghai

NANQIAO

harbour area, see under Fengxian

NANSHA

Lat 22° 50' N; Long 113° 34' E.

Admiralty Chart: 343		**Admiralty Pilot:** 30	
Time Zone: GMT +8 h		**UNCTAD Locode:** CN NSA	

Principal Facilities:

P	Y	G	C		B		T	

Authority: Guangzhou Port Group Co. Ltd, 531 Gang Qian Lu, Huangpu District, Guangzhou, Guangdong Province 510700, People's Republic of China, *Tel:* +86 20 8227 9412, *Fax:* +86 20 8227 0868, *Email:* yw-jzx@gzport.com, *Website:* www.gzport.com

Pilotage: Compulsory and available 24 h. Pilot boards at the Guangzhou and Huangpu Pilot Station or via the Hong Kong and Urmston Road Pilot Stations

Key to Principal Facilities:—			
A=Airport	**C**=Containers	**G**=General Cargo	**P**=Petroleum	**R**=Ro/Ro	**Y**=Dry Bulk
B=Bunkers	**D**=Dry Dock	**L**=Cruise	**Q**=Other Liquid Bulk	**T**=Towage (where available from port)

Radio Frequency: VHF Channel 11

Tides: Average tidal range of 1.59 m

Traffic: 2005, 1 080 000 TEU's handled

Maximum Vessel Dimensions: 200 m loa, 50 000 dwt, 10.5 m draft

Accommodation:

Name	Length (m)	Depth (m)	Remarks
Nansha			
Nanwei Deepwater Wharf	425	7.5	Container & general cargo for vessels up to 30 000 dwt
Lianhe Container Wharf	1400	14.5	See [1] below
Guangzhou South China Oceangate Container Terminal (Berth No's 5-10)	2100	14.5	Operated by Guangzhou South China Oceangate Container Terminal Co Ltd

[1]*Lianhe Container Wharf:* Operated by Nansha Stevedoring Co. Ltd of Guangzhou Port, Nansha New Terminal, Sea Port Avenue, Longxue Island, Nansha Development District, Guangzhou 511462, Tel: +86 20 3466 0660, Fax: +86 20 3466 0600, Email: ywb@gnict.com, Website: www.gnict.com
Four berths for vessels up to 50 000 dwt. Container yard area of 900 000 m2. 1080 reefer points

Mechanical Handling Equipment:

Location	Type	Capacity (t)	Qty
Nanwei Deepwater Wharf	Shore Cranes	50	1
Nanwei Deepwater Wharf	Shore Cranes	10	3
Nanwei Deepwater Wharf	Shore Cranes	40	1

Bunkering: Available

Towage: Tugs available of 1200-4200 hp

Shipping Agents: China Marine Shipping Agency Co. Ltd, China Marine Shipping Agency Guangdong Company Limited Nansha Branch, Room 212, Port Building, 587 Jingang Road, Nansha, Panyu, Guangdong Province 511457, People's Republic of China, *Tel:* +86 20 8468 8700, *Fax:* +86 20 8468 1059, *Email:* nansha@sinoagentgd.com, *Website:* www.sinoagentgd.com

Stevedoring Companies: Guangzhou Nansha Tung Fat Cargo Terminal Ltd, Guangqian Road, Nansha, Panyu, Guangzhou, Guangdong Province, People's Republic of China, *Tel:* +86 20 8468 0396, *Fax:* +86 20 8468 0395, *Email:* nstfct@public.guangzhou.gd.cn, *Website:* www.fkstev.com

Lloyd's Agent: Huatai Surveyors & Adjusters Co., Room 802, Jun Yuan Mansion, 155 Tian He East Road, Guangzhou, Guangdong Province 510620, People's Republic of China, *Tel:* +86 20 3881 2306, *Fax:* +86 20 3881 2470, *Email:* agency.gz@huatai-serv.com, *Website:* www.huatai-serv.com

NANTONG

Lat 32° 0' N; Long 120° 48' E.

Admiralty Chart: 1619

Admiralty Pilot: 32

Time Zone: GMT +8 h

UNCTAD Locode: CN NTG

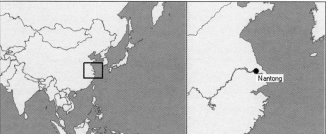

Principal Facilities:

P Q Y G C   B D T A

Authority: Nantong Port Group Co Ltd, 12 Qingnian Road (W), Nantong, Jiangsu Province 226006, People's Republic of China, *Tel:* +86 513 8355 9358, *Fax:* +86 513 8355 9359, *Email:* ntpa@public.nt.js.cn, *Website:* www.ntport.com.cn

Officials: Director: Shi Boxiang.

Port Security: ISPS compliant

Approach: Tongzhousha East Waterway: A deep fresh water channel near the north bank in depth of 10-50 m. Draft limitation is 9.7 m

Anchorage: Anchorage No.1 in depth of 10-15 m with a mud and sand bottom with good holding ground
Anchorage No.2 in depth of 10-15 m with a mud and sand bottom with good holding ground
Lightering Anchorage in depth of 12 m with a mud and sand bottom with good holding ground

Pilotage: Compulsory. Pilots board at Baoshan Anchorage from sunrise to sunset

Radio Frequency: VHF Channel 69 for vessel traffic service

Weather: Typhoon season is July to September. Variable winds. Gales may suddenly occur, mainly in winter

Tides: Max tidal range 4.01 m

Traffic: 2006, 103 860 000 t of cargo handled

Principal Imports and Exports: Imports: Chemicals, Coal, Grain, LNG, Oil, Ore, Steel, Timber. Exports: Cement, Clothing, Cotton, Dolomite, General cargo, Rice, Salt, Steel, Textiles.

Accommodation:

Name	Length (m)	Depth (m)	Remarks
Nantong			
Langshan Berth No.1	180.4	10.5	General & bulk cargo for vessels up to 14 000 dwt
Langshan Berth No.2	180.4	10.5	General & bulk cargo for vessels up to 14 000 dwt
Langshan Berth No.3	187	11	General & bulk cargo for vessels up to 25 000 dwt
Langshan Floating Berth	40	10	General & bulk cargo for vessels up to 1000 dwt
Huaneng Coal Berth	200	10	Coal for vessels up to 25 000 dwt
Huaneng No.2 Coal Berth	230	4.5	Coal for vessels up to 1000 dwt
Material Bureau Berth	90	8	Timber & general cargo for vessels up to 5000 dwt
Grain Bureau Berth	192	10.5	Grain & forage for vessels up to 25 000 dwt
Grain Bureau Berth	180	10.5	Grain & forage for vessels up to 25 000 dwt
Bunker Company Berth	90	8	Oil for vessels up to 5000 dwt
Yaogang Petroleum Berth	124	10	Petroleum & chemicals for vessels up to 10 000 dwt
Yaogang Berth No.5	200	11	Bulk cargo for vessels up to 25 000 dwt
Yaogang Berth No.6	180	10.5	Bulk cargo for vessels up to 13 000 dwt
Yaogang Berth No.7	180	10.5	Bulk cargo for vessels up to 13 000 dwt
Tongzhou Berth No's 3-4	232	10	General cargo for vessels up to 16 000 dwt
Tongzhou Berth No.5	90	8.5	General cargo for vessels up to 3000 dwt
Tongzhou Berth No.7	70	7	Bulk cargo for vessels up to 3000 dwt
Tiansheng Berth No.1	65	4.5	Coal for vessels up to 2000 dwt
Tiansheng Berth No.2	65	4.5	Coal for vessels up to 2000 dwt
Container Berth	180	10.5	Containers for vessels up to 10 000 dwt
Nacks Berths	512	9	General cargo for vessels up to 25 000 dwt
Xingda Berth	361	10.5	See [1] below
Huayang Berth	70		Liquid chemicals for vessels up to 10 000 dwt
Jiamin, Yujing & Qianhong Berths	260		Oil & chemicals for vessels up to 25 000 dwt
Huifeng Berth	270		Oil & chemicals for vessels up to 25 000 dwt
Huitong Berth	210	10	Oil & chemicals for vessels up to 25 000 dwt
Jianhai Berth	180		Oil & chemicals for vessels up to 25 000 dwt
Rugao Dongfang Berth	270	10.5	Oil & chemicals for vessels up to 35 000 dwt
Shenhua Berth	139		Oil & chemicals for vessels up to 5000 dwt
Huayang LNG Berth	180	10	LNG for vessels up to 25 000 dwt
Container Terminal	440		See [2] below

[1]*Xingda Berth:* General, bulk & container cargo for vessels up to 25 000 dwt
[2]*Container Terminal:* Operated by Nantong Port Container Terminal Co Ltd (NTCT), Tel: +86 513 8516 6666, Fax: +86 513 8516 6100, Website: www.ntctnet.com

Storage:

Location	Open (m²)	Covered (m²)
Nantong	110000	27000

Mechanical Handling Equipment:

Location	Type	Capacity (t)	Qty
Langshan Berth No.1	Shore Cranes	10	3
Langshan Berth No.2	Shore Cranes	10	3
Langshan Berth No.3	Shore Cranes	10	3
Huaneng Coal Berth	Mult-purp. Cranes	30	1
Huaneng Coal Berth	Shore Cranes	16	3
Huaneng No.2 Coal Berth	Shore Cranes	8	1
Material Bureau Berth	Shore Cranes	5	1
Grain Bureau Berth	Shore Cranes	16	1
Grain Bureau Berth	Shore Cranes	10	4
Bunker Company Berth	Shore Cranes	2.5	1
Yaogang Berth No.5	Shore Cranes	16	3
Yaogang Berth No.6	Shore Cranes	16	2

Location	Type	Capacity (t)	Qty
Tongzhou Berth No's 3-4	Floating Cranes	10	1
Tongzhou Berth No's 3-4	Floating Cranes	63	1
Tongzhou Berth No's 3-4	Shore Cranes	10	3
Tongzhou Berth No's 3-4	Shore Cranes	40	1
Tongzhou Berth No.7	Floating Cranes	5	2
Tiansheng Berth No.1	Floating Cranes	5	1
Tiansheng Berth No.2	Floating Cranes	5	1
Container Berth	Container Cranes	30.5	1
Container Terminal	Container Cranes		3
Container Terminal	Transtainers		5

Bunkering: China Marine Bunker Supply Co., 13F Qian Cun Mansion A, No.2, 5th Block, Anzhen Xili, Chaoyang District, Beijing 100029, People's Republic of China, *Tel:* +86 10 6443 0717, *Fax:* +86 10 6443 0708, *Email:* business@chimbusco.com.cn, *Website:* www.chimbusco.com.cn – *Grades:* IFO120-380cst; MGO

Towage: Ten tugs available of 1500-4600 hp

Repair & Maintenance: Nantong Ocean Ship Engineering Co. Ltd (NOSEC), South of Rengang, Nantong, Jiangsu Province 226005, People's Republic of China, *Tel:* +86 513 8351 4351, *Fax:* +86 513 8352 9283, *Email:* nosec@public.nt.js.cn Dry docks: 'Nantong' 270 m x 48 m for vessels up to 150 000 dwt and 'Yuan Tong' 230 m x 44 m for vessels up to 80 000 dwt. Quays of 1000 m with max draught 11 m

Ship Chandlers: Nantong Ocean Shipping Supply Co., Room 202, No.22 Wai Tan Xiao Qu, Nantong, Jiangsu Province 226006, People's Republic of China, *Tel:* +86 513 8351 1063, *Fax:* +86 513 8353 0992, *Email:* ntsupco@pub.nt.jsinfo.net

Shipping Agents: China Marine Shipping Agency Co. Ltd, China Marine Shipping Agency Nantong Company Limited, 41 Qing Nian Xi Lu, Nantong, Jiangsu Province, People's Republic of China, *Tel:* +86 513 8351 9134, *Fax:* +86 513 8352 7077, *Email:* sinoagt@pub.nt.jsinfo.net
China Ocean Shipping Agency, 59 West Waihuan Road, Nantong, Jiangsu Province 226006, People's Republic of China, *Tel:* +86 513 8355 8595, *Fax:* +86 513 8355 8522, *Website:* www.penavicont.com.cn
CMA-CGM S.A., CMA CGM Nantong, 2nd Floor, Sinotrans Building, 41 West Qingnian Road, Nantong, Jiangsu Province, People's Republic of China, *Tel:* +86 513 8352 4757, *Fax:* +86 513 8350 0467, *Email:* ntg.genmbox@cma-cgm.com, *Website:* www.cma-cgm.com

Surveyors: Det Norske Veritas A/S, NACKS Site Office, c/o Nantong COSCO KHI Ship Engineering Co Ltd, 117 Linjiang Road, Nantong, Jiangsu Province 226005, People's Republic of China, *Tel:* +86 513 8353 9859, *Fax:* +86 513 8353 9859, *Email:* mchcn330@dnv.com, *Website:* www.dnv.com

Medical Facilities: The No.1 People's Hospital, 2 km

Airport: Nantong Airport, domestic flights only

Lloyd's Agent: Huatai Surveyors & Adjusters Co., 14th Floor, China Re Building, No.11 Jin Rong Avenue, Xicheng District, Beijing 100140, People's Republic of China, *Tel:* +86 10 6657 6577, *Fax:* +86 10 6657 6502, *Email:* agency.bj@huatai-serv.com, *Website:* www.huatai-serv.com

NIANYUWEI

harbour area, see under Lanxi

NINGBO

Lat 29° 52' N; Long 121° 33' E.

Admiralty Chart: 1592	**Admiralty Pilot:** 32
Time Zone: GMT +8 h	**UNCTAD Locode:** CN NGB

Principal Facilities:

P	Q	Y	G	C		B		T	A

Authority: Ningbo Port Group Ltd, 496 Yanjiang Road E., Zhenhai District, Ningbo, Zhejiang Province 315200, People's Republic of China, *Tel:* +86 574 8769 5250, *Fax:* +86 574 8769 5523, *Email:* npa_office@nbport.com.cn, *Website:* www.nbport.com.cn

Officials: Director: Li Linghong.

Port Security: ISPS compliant

Anchorage: Qiliyu anchorage between the following pos 29° 59' 18" N-30° 00' 18" N and 121° 46' 30" E-121° 47' 30" E in depth of 9 m for vessels of 3000-5000 dwt

Jintang anchorage between the following pos 30° 00' 00" N-30° 02' 30" N and 121° 48' 12" E-121° 50' 00" E in depth of 13.4 m for vessels up to 10 000 dwt
Xiachi anchorage between the following pos 29° 44' 30" N-29° 46' 30" N and 122° 20' 30" E-122° 23' 00" E in depth of 17.2 m for vessels of 10 000-300 000 dwt

Pilotage: Compulsory. Pilot boards in the following positions:
Qili Anchorage in pos 30° 01.50' N; 121° 46.40' E
Xiazhi Men Northern Anchorage in pos 29° 45.50' N; 122° 21.50' E
In pos 29° 51.58' N; 122° 12.95' E

Radio Frequency: VHF Channel 16

Tides: Ningbo: max 3.62 m, min 0.92 m. Zhenhai: max 3.51 m, min 0.02 m. Beilun: max 3.36 m, min 0.4 m

Traffic: 2007, 9 360 000 TEU's handled

Working Hours: Mon-Fri 0730-1130, 1200-1600

Accommodation:

Name	Length (m)	Depth (m)	Remarks
Ningbo			
Berth No's 1-13	344	5.5	General cargo for vessels up to 3000 dwt
Zhenhai			
Berth No.1	130	7	Coal for vessels up to 3000 dwt
Berth No.2	180	9.5	Coal for vessels up to 10 000 dwt
Berth No.3	180	9.5	Coal for vessels up to 10 000 dwt
Berth No.4	170	9.5	General cargo for vessels up to 10 000 dwt
Berth No.5	180	9.5	General cargo for vessels up to 10 000 dwt
Berth No.6	180	9.5	General cargo for vessels up to 10 000 dwt
Berth No's 7-8	248	7	General cargo for vessels up to 3000 dwt
Berth No.9	180	9.5	General cargo for vessels up to 10 000 dwt
Berth No.14	50	7	Liquid chemicals for vessels up to 5000 dwt
Berth No.16	128	9	Liquid chemicals for vessels up to 10 000 dwt
Berth No.17	349	14	Liquid chemicals for vessels up to 50 000 dwt
Berth No.18	340	14	Liquid chemicals for vessels up to 50 000 dwt
Beilun			
Ningbo Beilun International Container Terminal	900	13.5	See [1] below
Coal Terminal	414	13.5	Two berths handling coal for vessels up to 50 000 dwt
Berth No.1	351	18.2	Ore & coal for vessels up to 140 000 dwt
Berth No.2	360	20.5	Ore & coal for vessels up to 200 000 dwt
Berth No's 3-5	650	12	Ore for vessels up to 25 000 dwt
Berth No.6	248	13.5	General & bulk cargo for vessels up to 50 000 dwt
Daxie			See [2] below
Berth No's 1-4	1500	17.5	
ZRCC Berths			
Berth No.1	510	20.5	Crude oil for vessels up to 250 000 dwt
Berth No.2	305	13	Crude & product oil for vessels up to 50 000 dwt
Berth No.3	305	13	Crude & product oil for vessels up to 50 000 dwt
Berth No.4	93	8	Product oil for vessels up to 3000 dwt
Berth No.5	177	10	Product oil for vessels up to 5000 dwt

[1]*Ningbo Beilun International Container Terminal:* Operated jointly by HPH and Ningbo Port Group Ltd., Bei Ji Xing Road, Beilun Port, Ningbo 315800, Tel: +86 574 2769 7838, Website: www.nbct.com.cn
Consists of three berths with total area of 756 888 m2. Stacking cap of 39 591 TEU's and 992 reefer points
[2]*Daxie:* Container terminal operated by China Merchants International Terminals Co Ltd., Port District D, Daxie Development Zone, Ningbo 315812, Tel: +86 574 8671 9818, Fax: +86 574 8671 9820, Email: business@cmict.com.cn, Website: www.cmict.com.cn

Storage:

Location	Open (m²)	Covered (m²)
Ningbo	550000	110000

Mechanical Handling Equipment:

Location	Type	Capacity (t)	Qty
Berth No's 1-13	Shore Cranes	5	3
Berth No's 1-13	Shore Cranes	40	1
Berth No's 1-13	Shore Cranes	20	1
Berth No's 1-13	Shore Cranes	4	4
Berth No.2	Shore Cranes	10	5
Berth No.3	Shore Cranes	10	5
Berth No.4	Shore Cranes	10	2
Berth No.5	Shore Cranes	40	1

Key to Principal Facilities:—				
A=Airport	**C**=Containers	**G**=General Cargo	**P**=Petroleum	**R**=Ro/Ro	**Y**=Dry Bulk
B=Bunkers	**D**=Dry Dock	**L**=Cruise	**Q**=Other Liquid Bulk	**T**=Towage (where available from port)	

Location	Type	Capacity (t)	Qty
Berth No.5	Shore Cranes	25–30	2
Berth No.6	Shore Cranes	10	3
Berth No.9	Shore Cranes	10	3
Ningbo Beilun International Container Terminal	Container Cranes		10
Ningbo Beilun International Container Terminal	RTG's		32
Ningbo Beilun International Container Terminal	Reach Stackers		9
Coal Terminal	Shore Cranes	10	6
Berth No.6	Shore Cranes	10	1
Berth No.6	Shore Cranes	16	2

Bunkering: Available at berths and anchorages

Towage: Eight tugs from 3200-4200 hp

Ship Chandlers: Golden Beach China Shipping Marine Service Co. Ltd, Room 501, Tower B, No.7 Lane 39 Huatai Street, Ningbo, Zhejiang Province 315040, People's Republic of China, *Tel:* +86 574 8771 8306, *Fax:* +86 574 8771 7516, *Email:* mail@friendship.com, *Website:* www.friendshipmarine.com
Ningbo Ocean Shipping Supply Co. Ltd, 252 Mayuan Road, Ningbo, Zhejiang Province 315012, People's Republic of China, *Tel:* +86 574 8712 1139, *Fax:* +86 574 8712 6844, *Email:* nbwlgy@chinaissa.com, *Website:* www.cnshipsupply.com

Shipping Agents: Awards Shipping Agency Ltd, 7/F Petroleum Building, 618 Zhenming Road, Ningbo, Zhejiang Province 315010, People's Republic of China, *Tel:* +86 574 8717 1590/6, *Fax:* +86 574 8717 1635, *Email:* ivyzhu@awards-nb.com
Chiao Feng Shipping Ltd, Room 1307-8, 13/F, PICC Building, 50 Da Lai Street, Ningbo, Zhejiang Province 315010, People's Republic of China, *Tel:* +86 574 8719 0958, *Fax:* +86 574 8719 0950, *Email:* ningbo@chiaofeng.com.cn, *Website:* www.chiaofeng.com.hk
China Marine Shipping Agency Co. Ltd, China Marine Shipping Agency Ningbo Company Limited, No. 69 Jiefang South Road, Ningbo, Zhejiang Province 315010, People's Republic of China, *Tel:* +86 574 8732 1470, *Fax:* +86 574 8732 1105, *Email:* shipping@sinoagentnb.com, *Website:* www.sinoagentnb.com
China Sailing International Shipping Agency Ltd, Room 811, China Hong International Centre, 717 Zhongxing Road, Ningbo, Zhejiang Province 315040, People's Republic of China, *Tel:* +86 574 8785 5182, *Fax:* +86 574 8785 5177, *Email:* shipping@chinasailing-ngb.com.cn, *Website:* www.chinasailing.com.cn
CMA-CGM S.A., CMA CGM Ningbo, 27/F Portman Tower, 48 Caihong Road (N), Ningbo, Zhejiang Province 315040, People's Republic of China, *Tel:* +86 574 8773 1818, *Fax:* +86 574 8770 8450, *Email:* ngp.genmbox@cma-cgm.com, *Website:* www.cma-cgm.com
A Hartrodt International, Room 709 Waitan Building, No.132 Renmin Road, Ningbo, Zhejiang Province 315000, People's Republic of China, *Tel:* +86 574 8772 9158, *Fax:* +86 574 8772 9166, *Email:* ningbo@hartrodt.com.cn
K Line Ship Management Co. Ltd, 'K' Line (China) Ltd, Room 1706-1707, PICC Building, 151 Yaohang Jie, Ningbo, Zhejiang Province, People's Republic of China, *Tel:* +86 574 8730 1527, *Fax:* +86 574 8719 7366, *Website:* www.kline.co.jp
Mediterranean Shipping Company, MSC (Hong Kong) Ltd, Suite 01, 29th Floor, Portman Tower, 48 Caihong Road (N), Ningbo, Zhejiang Province 315040, People's Republic of China, *Tel:* +86 574 8797 2888, *Fax:* +86 574 8705 1591, *Email:* msc@nprc.mschkg.com, *Website:* www.mschongkong.com
Ningbo International Shipping Agency Ltd, Ningbo, Zhejiang Province 315040, People's Republic of China, *Tel:* +86 574 8773 1266, *Fax:* +86 574 8773 1277, *Email:* shipping@isaconb.com.cn, *Website:* www.isaco.com.cn
Pen-Wallem Shipping Services Co Ltd, Ningbo, Zhejiang Province, People's Republic of China, *Tel:* +86 574 2786 8695, *Fax:* +86 574 2786 8690, *Email:* wallemning@pen-wallem.com
Sinotrans (HK) Logistics Ltd, Room 2115, DTIC CAC International Business Building, 181 Zhong Shan East Road, Ningbo, Zhejiang Province 315000, People's Republic of China, *Tel:* +86 574 8725 4828, *Fax:* +86 574 8725 4817, *Email:* ningbo@sinotrans-logistics.com, *Website:* www.sinotrans-logistics.com
Sun Hing Shipping Co Ltd, 12th Floor, East Building, 2 Zhongshan West Road, Ningbo, Zhejiang Province 305010, People's Republic of China, *Tel:* +86 574 8726 2042, *Fax:* +86 574 8726 3255, *Website:* www.sunhinggroup.com
United Transportation (HK) Ltd, Room 1307-1308, 13F Picc Building, 151 Yaohang Street, Ningbo, Zhejiang Province 315010, People's Republic of China, *Tel:* +86 574 8719 1344, *Fax:* +86 574 8719 0950, *Email:* utlotal@netvigator.com

Airport: Lishe Airport

Railway: The Hangzhou-Ningbo railroad joins all the port areas to the Shanghai-Hangzhou and Zhejing-Jianxi railroads

Development: Construction has started on Berth No.7 for containers at Beilun with length of 310 m in depth of 15 m
Construction of a new chemical and oil products terminal on Daxie Island with 23 storage tanks totaling 204 000 m3, to be operated by Stolthaven Ningbo, scheduled to come onstream in 2008

Lloyd's Agent: Huatai Surveyors & Adjusters Co., 14th Floor, China Re Building, No.11 Jin Rong Avenue, Xicheng District, Beijing 100140, People's Republic of China, *Tel:* +86 10 6657 6577, *Fax:* +86 10 6657 6502, *Email:* agency.bj@huatai-serv.com, *Website:* www.huatai-serv.com

NIUPENG

harbour area, see under Chongming

PANYU TERMINAL

Lat 20° 51' N; Long 114° 42' E.

Admiralty Chart: -	Admiralty Pilot: 30
Time Zone: GMT +8 h	UNCTAD Locode: CN

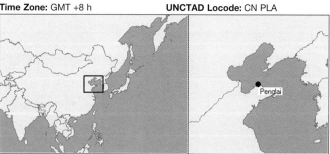

Principal Facilities:

P								

Authority: Devon Energy China Ltd, 8th Floor, Times Plaza, Shekou, Shenzhen, Guangdong Province 518067, People's Republic of China, *Tel:* +86 755 2682 1128, *Fax:* +86 755 2682 0364

Pilotage: Compulsory. Vessels should advise ETA to agents and operators 96 h prior to arrival, and copied directly to the Terminal via Inmarsat. The initial ETA message should contain the following information:
(a) Vessel's name and call sign
(b) ETA
(c) Vessel's flag and port of registry
(d) Registered owner and Captain's name (in full)
(e) Last port of call and next port of call
(f) Last 2 cargoes transported
(g) Quantity of cargo required at the Terminal
(h) If SBT or BT, and quantity of ballast on arrival (% of SDW)
(i) Quantity of cargo on board if partially loaded
(j) Arrival draught (fore and aft)
Pilot boards 5 nautical miles leeward of the Terminal. The mooring master will board the vessel on arrival by helicopter

Radio Frequency: VHF Channels 16 and 77

Maximum Vessel Dimensions: 35 000-150 000 dwt

Principal Imports and Exports: Exports: Crude oil.

Accommodation:

Name	Remarks
Panyu Terminal	See [1] below

[1]*Panyu Terminal:* Located approx 200 km S of Hong Kong. Consists of FPSO 'Hai Yang Shi You 111' in depth of 103 m. Loading rate for crude oil of approx 30 000 bbls/h. Normally operations carried out during daylight hours only

Medical Facilities: None available at the terminal

Lloyd's Agent: Huatai Surveyors & Adjusters Co., Room 802, Jun Yuan Mansion, 155 Tian He East Road, Guangzhou, Guangdong Province 510620, People's Republic of China, *Tel:* +86 20 3881 2306, *Fax:* +86 20 3881 2470, *Email:* agency.gz@huatai-serv.com, *Website:* www.huatai-serv.com

PENGLAI

Lat 37° 49' N; Long 120° 43' E.

Admiralty Chart: 1255	Admiralty Pilot: 32
Time Zone: GMT +8 h	UNCTAD Locode: CN PLA

Principal Facilities:

	Y	G					T	

Authority: Penglai Port Authority, Technical Development District, Penglai, Shandong Province, People's Republic of China, *Tel:* +86 535 597 1423

Pilotage: Compulsory and available 0600-1800. Pilot boards at anchorage

Radio Frequency: VHF Channel 13

Accommodation:

Name	Length (m)	Depth (m)	Remarks
Penglai Berth No.1	100	5.5	Vessels up to 1000 dwt

Name	Length (m)	Depth (m)	Remarks
Berth No.2	120	8	Vessels up to 5000 dwt
Berth No.3	180	10	Vessels up to 10 000 dwt
Berth No.4	330	13	Under construction

Storage:

Location	Open (m²)	Covered (m²)
Penglai	35000	2770

Mechanical Handling Equipment:

Location	Type	Capacity (t)	Qty
Berth No.2	Shore Cranes	10	1
Berth No.3	Shore Cranes	10	3

Towage: One tug available of 3400 hp

Shipping Agents: China Marine Shipping Agency Co. Ltd, China Marine Shipping Agency Shandong Company Limited Penglai Branch, 185 Beihuan Road, Penglai, Shandong Province, People's Republic of China, *Tel:* +86 535 562 7277, *Fax:* +86 535 562 7277, *Email:* gfsdcd_penglai@sinotrans.com

Lloyd's Agent: Huatai Surveyors & Adjusters Co., 14th Floor, China Re Building, No.11 Jin Rong Avenue, Xicheng District, Beijing 100140, People's Republic of China, *Tel:* +86 10 6657 6577, *Fax:* +86 10 6657 6502, *Email:* agency.bj@huatai-serv.com, *Website:* www.huatai-serv.com

PINGHU

Lat 30° 41' N; Long 121° 0' E.

Admiralty Chart: 1199	**Admiralty Pilot:** 32
Time Zone: GMT +8 h	**UNCTAD Locode:** CN PNU

Principal Facilities:

			Y	G								

Authority: Pinghu Shipping Administration, 56 Nanlangxia, Chengguan Town, Pinghu, Zhejiang Province 221300, People's Republic of China

Accommodation:

Name	Remarks
Pinghu	See [1] below

[1]*Pinghu:* Numerous berths available for vessels up to 120 dwt handling agricultural products, raw materials, fuel, salt and stones

Storage: Open and covered storage areas available

Mechanical Handling Equipment:

Location	Type	Capacity (t)
Pinghu	Mult-purp. Cranes	5

Lloyd's Agent: Huatai Surveyors & Adjusters Co., 14th Floor, China Re Building, No.11 Jin Rong Avenue, Xicheng District, Beijing 100140, People's Republic of China, *Tel:* +86 10 6657 6577, *Fax:* +86 10 6657 6502, *Email:* agency.bj@huatai-serv.com, *Website:* www.huatai-serv.com

QHD 32-6 TERMINAL

harbour area, see under Qinhuangdao Field

QIANWAN

see under Qingdao

QIJIAXIANG

harbour area, see under Jinshi

QILI

harbour area, see under Wenzhou

QINGDAO

Lat 36° 5' N; Long 120° 19' E.

Admiralty Chart: 876	**Admiralty Pilot:** 32
Time Zone: GMT +8 h	**UNCTAD Locode:** CN TAO

Principal Facilities:

P		Y	G	C			B	D	T	A	

Authority: Qingdao Port (Group) Co Ltd, 6 Gangqing Road, Qingdao, Shandong Province 266011, People's Republic of China, *Tel:* +86 532 8298 2011, *Fax:* +86 532 8282 2878, *Email:* president@qdport.com, *Website:* www.qdport.com

Officials: Chairman: Chang Dechuan.

Port Security: ISPS compliant

Approach: The Dagang channel draught is 13 m. The Qianwan channel draught is 14 m

Anchorage: Inner Anchorage between the following pos 36° 06' 00" N; 120° 14' 30" E, 36° 06' 00" N; 120° 16' 50" E, 36° 04' 18" N; 120° 14' 30" E, 36° 04' 18" N; 120° 16' 50" E in depth of 5-38 m, mud and sand bottom with good holding ground for vessels up to 10 000 dwt
Outer Anchorage No.1 between the following pos 36° 00' 46" N; 120° 20' 41" E, 36° 00' 46" N; 120° 21' 58" E, 36° 00' 12" N; 120° 20' 51" E, 36° 00' 12" N; 120° 21' 42" E in depth of 5-38 m, mud and sand bottom with good holding ground for vessels up to 200 000 dwt
Outer Anchorage No.2 between the following pos 35° 57' 30" N; 120° 21' 54" E, 35° 57' 30" N; 120° 22' 42" E, 35° 58' 54" N; 120° 21' 24" E, 35° 58' 54" N; 120° 23' 36" E in depth of 12-20.6 m, mud and sand bottom with good holding ground for vessels up to 10 000 dwt
Outer Anchorage No.3 between the following pos 35° 57' 30" N; 120° 24' 30" E, 35° 57' 30" N; 120° 26' 30" E, 35° 58' 54" N; 120° 25' 18" E, 35° 58' 54" N; 120° 27' 18" E in depth of 14-20 m, mud and sand bottom with good holding ground for vessels up to 10 000 dwt

Pilotage: Compulsory and available 24 h/day. Pilot boards within No.2 Precautionary Area bounded by the following positions:
36° 01.77' N; 120° 19.29' E
36° 01.12' N; 120° 19.10' E
36° 00.89' N; 120° 20.30' E
36° 01.57' N; 120° 20.49' E

Weather: Ice is occasionally experienced from end January to mid February but does not impede navigation

Tides: Max tidal range of 4.66 m, min tidal range of 0.28 m

Traffic: 2007, 9 460 000 TEU's handled

Principal Imports and Exports: Imports: Coal, Corn, Cotton, Crude oil, Hardwood, Peanut oil. Exports: Fertiliser, Grain, Metal ores, Steel, Timber.

Accommodation:

Name	Length (m)	Depth (m)	Remarks
Qingdao			See [1] below
Dagang Company of Qingdao Port	5789		See [2] below
Oil Port Company of Qingdao Port			See [3] below
Qingdao Qianwan Container Terminal	3400	14.5–17.5	See [4] below
Qiangang Company			See [5] below
Xigang Company	582		See [6] below

[1]*Qingdao:* Consists of three port areas: Old Port Area, Huangdao Oil Port Area and Qianwan New Port
[2]*Dagang Company of Qingdao Port:* Tel: +86 532 8298 3789, Email: ywb.dg@qdport.com
Consists of six wharves with twenty six berths. There are ten berths over 10 000 t and twelve berths of 5000 t handling containers, grain, alumina, fertilizer and bulk cargo bagging operations
[3]*Oil Port Company of Qingdao Port:* Tel: +86 532 8298 8230, Email: bgs.yg@qdport.com
Two crude oil docks and two fuel oil docks with oil storage cap over 2 970 000 m3. Berth No.60 for 5000-30 000 t vessels, Berth No.61 for 15 000-70 000 t vessels and Berth No.62 for 80 000-280 000 t vessels
[4]*Qingdao Qianwan Container Terminal:* Operated by Qingdao Qianwan Container Terminal Co Ltd., Fenjin 4th Road, Port of Qianwan, Huangdao District, Qingdao 266500, Tel: +86 532 8298 8888, Fax: +86 532 8298 8927, Email: marketing@qqct.com.cn, Website: qqct.com.cn
Consists of eight berths. Equipment includes thirty four container cranes and 77 RTG's
[5]*Qiangang Company:* Tel: +86 532 8298 8131, Email: qg@qdport.com
Consists of three wharves and seven deepwater berths. Mainly involved in loading/unloading of coal and iron ore
[6]*Xigang Company:* Tel: +86 532 8298 8085, Email: bgs.xg@qdport.com

Key to Principal Facilities:—			
A=Airport	**C**=Containers	**G**=General Cargo	**P**=Petroleum	**R**=Ro/Ro	**Y**=Dry Bulk
B=Bunkers	**D**=Dry Dock	**L**=Cruise	**Q**=Other Liquid Bulk	**T**=Towage (where available from port)	

Handling a variety of general and bulk cargo such as paper pulp, steel, alumina, sulphur, iron ore, lumber, fertilizer and grain

Bunkering: China Marine Bunker Supply Co., 13F Qian Cun Mansion A, No.2, 5th Block, Anzhen Xili, Chaoyang District, Beijing 100029, People's Republic of China, *Tel:* +86 10 6443 0717, *Fax:* +86 10 6443 0708, *Email:* business@chimbusco.com.cn, *Website:* www.chimbusco.com.cn – *Grades:* IFO120-380cSt; MGO
Daitsin International Marine Ltd, Suite 209, 133 Yanan 3rd Road, Qingdao, Shandong Province 266071, People's Republic of China, *Tel:* +86 532 386 9731, *Fax:* +86 532 386 8573

Towage: Two tugs of 1000 hp, two of 1670 hp and five of 3200 hp

Repair & Maintenance: Qingdao Beihai Shipbuilding Heavy Industry Co. Ltd, No.369 Lijiang East Road, Qingdao Economic & Technical Development Zone, Qingdao, Shandong Province 266520, People's Republic of China, *Tel:* +86 532 8675 6188, *Fax:* +86 532 8675 6199, *Email:* bhrepair@public.qd.sd.cn, *Website:* www.bhshipyard.com.cn One 100 000 t floating dock, one 25 000 t dry dock and one 15 000 t dry dock. Also 840 m of deep water wharves

Ship Chandlers: Peninsular Star Marine Service (Qingdao) Co Ltd., Flat 3, Room No.102, Phoenix Garden, Qingdao, Shandong Province, People's Republic of China, *Tel:* +86 532 8276 6598, *Fax:* +86 532 8597 0149, *Email:* qd@psmsmarine.com, *Website:* www.psmsmarine.com
Qingdao Fanyuan Shipping Supply Co Ltd., 3 Dagangwei 1 Road, Qingdao, Shandong Province, People's Republic of China, *Tel:* +86 532 8285 5367, *Fax:* +86 532 8285 5367, *Email:* shipstore@qdfanyuan.com, *Website:* www.qdfanyuan.com
Qingdao Foreign Shipping Supply General Corp., 12 Xinjiang Road, Qingdao, Shandong Province 266011, People's Republic of China, *Tel:* +86 532 8282 1277, *Fax:* +86 532 8281 2677, *Email:* qdshipsupply@vip.163.com, *Website:* www.qdshipsupply.com
Qingdao Ocean Shipping Supply Co. Ltd, Room 1006, Penavico Building, 101 Huanghe East Road, Qingdao, Shandong Province, People's Republic of China, *Tel:* +86 532 8690 9288, *Fax:* +86 532 8690 9897, *Email:* sunnyliu@public.qd.sd.cn, *Website:* www.oceanshippingsupply.com
Qingdao (Qianwan) Ocean Shipping Supply Co. Ltd, 5th Floor, 18 Ningguo No.1 Road, Qingdao, Shandong Province 266000, People's Republic of China, *Tel:* +86 532 8571 1906, *Fax:* +86 532 8575 0908, *Email:* sales@supplier-qianwan.com, *Website:* www.supplier-qianwan.com

Shipping Agents: Ben Line Agencies Ltd, Room 703, 76 Xiang Ganag Zhong Lu, Qingdao, Shandong Province 266701, People's Republic of China, *Tel:* +86 532 8575 7064, *Fax:* +86 532 8576 8915, *Email:* tao.jzhang@benline.com.cn, *Website:* www.benlineagencies.com
Blue Water Shipping A/S, Room 714, Times Square, No.52 Hongkong Middle Road, Qingdao, Shandong Province 266071, People's Republic of China, *Tel:* +86 532 8597 0531, *Fax:* +86 532 9597 0532, *Email:* bwsqdao@bws.dk, *Website:* www.bws.dk
Chiao Feng Shipping Ltd, 16/F, Times Square, 52 Hong Kong Middle Road, Qingdao, Shandong Province 266071, People's Republic of China, *Tel:* +86 532 8575 7880, *Fax:* +86 532 8575 7137, *Email:* qingdao@chiaofeng.com.cn, *Website:* www.chiaofeng.com.hk
China Marine Shipping Agency Co. Ltd, China Marine Shipping Agency Shandong Company Limited (Qingdao), 10th Floor, Sinotrans Building, 5 Henan Road, Qingdao, Shandong Province 266001, People's Republic of China, *Tel:* +86 532 8289 7866, *Fax:* +86 532 8289 7816, *Email:* sinoagentqingdao@sinotrans.com, *Website:* www.sinotrans.com
CMA-CGM S.A., CMA CGM Qingdao, Room 1210-8, Yizhong Holiday Inn, 76 Hongkong Zhong Road, Qingdao, Shandong Province 266071, People's Republic of China, *Tel:* +86 532 8577 7100, *Fax:* +86 532 8575 9277, *Email:* qgd.genmbox@cma-cgm.com, *Website:* www.cma-cgm.com
GAC Forwarding & Shipping (Shanghai) Ltd, Room 605, Zhongtianheng Building, 8 Fuzhou Road (S), Qingdao, Shandong Province, People's Republic of China, *Tel:* +86 532 8571 8651, *Fax:* +86 532 8571 8653, *Email:* arthur.hu@gacworld.com, *Website:* www.gacworld.com
Hanjin Shipping Co. Ltd, Shangdong Hanjin Shipping Co. Ltd, No.1 Office Building, 3rd Floor Qingdao Pacific Plaza, 35 Dong hai Road, Qingdao, Shandong Province, People's Republic of China, *Tel:* +86 532 8571 7795, *Fax:* +86 532 8571 8137, *Email:* helenwu@shabb.hanjin.com, *Website:* www.hanjin.com
K Line Ship Management Co. Ltd, 'K' Line (China) Ltd, 20F B Huaren International Building, 2 Shandong Road, Qingdao, Shandong Province, People's Republic of China, *Tel:* +86 532 8386 5858, *Fax:* +86 532 8387 2733, *Website:* www.kline.co.jp
Mediterranean Shipping Company, MSC (Hong Kong) Ltd, 38th Floor, Qingdao International Finance Center, 59 Hong Kong Middle Road, Qingdao, Shandong Province 266071, People's Republic of China, *Tel:* +86 532 8909 6000, *Fax:* +86 532 8909 6572, *Email:* msc@nprc.mschkg.com, *Website:* www.mschongkong.com
Minsheng International Shipping Agency Co, Room 1, 10th Floor, Tower A, Shenye Centre Building, 9 Shandong Road, Shan Ong Prov, Qingdao, Shandong Province, People's Republic of China, *Tel:* +86 532 8584 4901, *Fax:* +86 532 8501 3991, *Email:* minshengqd@qd-public.sd.cninfo.net
Pen-Wallem Shipping Services Co Ltd, Qingdao, Shandong Province, People's Republic of China, *Tel:* +86 532 8309 5066, *Fax:* +86 532 8309 5067, *Email:* wallemqing@pen-wallem.com, *Website:* www.wallem.com
Sun Hing Shipping Co Ltd, Room D, Block B, 12/F, Jindu Garden, 18 Donghai Road, Qingdao, Shandong Province 266071, People's Republic of China, *Tel:* +86 532 8583 0831, *Fax:* +86 532 8584 1957, *Website:* www.sunhinggroup.com
TES International Transport (China) Ltd, Room 1010 Zhonggang Building, No.16 Fuzhou Nan Road, Shinan District, Qingdao, Shandong Province, People's Republic of China, *Tel:* +86 532 8578 3960, *Fax:* +86 532 8578 3957, *Website:* www.teschina.com.hk
World Marine Corp, Qingdao Port Captain Station, Qingdao, Shandong Province, People's Republic of China, *Tel:* +86 532 8506 5586, *Fax:* +86 532 8506 5587, *Email:* wmarqq@sina.com
Young Carrier Co. Ltd, Frenghe Plaza, Room B7406, 12 Xiangang Middle Road, Qingdao, Shandong Province, People's Republic of China, *Tel:* +86 532 8502 6024, *Fax:* +86 532 8502 6021, *Email:* ymltao@public.qd.sd.cn

Stevedoring Companies: Blue Water Shipping A/S, Room 714, Times Square, No.52 Hongkong Middle Road, Qingdao, Shandong Province, People's Republic of China, *Tel:* +86 532 8597 0531, *Fax:* +86 532 9597 0532, *Email:* bwsqdao@bws.dk, *Website:* www.bws.dk

Surveyors: Bureau Veritas, Room 1708 Sunshine Tower, 61 Hong Kong Middle Road, Qingdao, Shandong Province 266071, People's Republic of China, *Tel:* +86 532 8576 5207, *Fax:* +86 532 8573 8122, *Website:* www.bureauveritas.com
China Classification Society, 7-9th Floor Galaxy Building, 29 Shandong Road, Qingdao, Shandong Province 266071, People's Republic of China, *Tel:* +86 532 8501 6478, *Fax:* +86 532 8501 6456, *Email:* ccsqd@public.qd.sd.cn, *Website:* www.ccs.org.cn
Det Norske Veritas A/S, Qingdao, Shandong Province, People's Republic of China, *Tel:* +86 532 8571 2212, *Fax:* +86 532 8571 2375, *Email:* mchcn426@dnv.com, *Website:* www.dnv.com
Korean Register of Shipping, Room C, 14th Floor Jinguang Building, Jindu garden, 37 Donghai Road, Qingdao, Shandong Province, People's Republic of China, *Tel:* +86 532 8572 3247, *Fax:* +86 532 8572 7637, *Email:* kr-qdo@krs.co.kr, *Website:* www.krs.co.kr
Nippon Kaiji Kyokai, Room 1318 Crowne Plaza Qingdao, 76 Xiang Gang Zhong Lu, Qingdao, Shandong Province 266071, People's Republic of China, *Tel:* +86 532 8576 5023, *Fax:* +86 532 8576 5053, *Email:* zq@classnk.or.jp, *Website:* www.classnk.or.jp

Airport: Qingdao Airport

Development: Liquid chemical dock being constructed at Oil Port consisting of two berths. One handling liquid chemical vessels under 50 000 t will be in use shortly. The other one which is designed for handling liquid chemical vessels under 80 000 t will be built later
Development of a new container terminal to be operated by DP World China Qingdao Ltd consisting of four berths with a quay length of 1320 m, set to commence operations in 2009
China Marine Qingdao Terminal, *Website:* www.cmhico.com, will have a quay length of approx 2272 m with draft of 15-17 m, to consist of six container berths (2 x 100 000 dwt, 3 x 30 000 dwt and 1 x 20 000 dwt) and two 30 000 dwt multi-purpose cargo handling berths. One 100 000 dwt container berth and one 30 000 dwt multi-purpose berth are scheduled to be delivered by the second half of 2006 and all berths are scheduled to be built by 2010
On November 16 2007 a contract was signed between QQCT and Pan Asia International Shipping Limited (Hong Kong) to establish Qingdao New Qianwan Container Terminal Co Ltd (QQCTN) to develop and operate the 3408 m container quay on the southern coast of Qianwan Bay. Together with the existing 3400 m quay in the northern side, there will be 6800 m quay for container operations and a whole capacity of 14 million TEU's. QQCTN will build the 3408 m quay into 10 berths (four from Phase IV, another four from DP World and two from Pan Asia), and the deepest berth will reach 20 m. Phase IV construction was started in September 2007 and four berths will be ready by the end of 2008. The joint venture will integrate the 3400 m quay under the operation of QQCT and the 3408 m quay under the construction of QQCTN into one body

Lloyd's Agent: Huatai Surveyors & Adjusters Co., Room AB, 9th Floor, No.9 Building, Pacific Plaza, 35 Donghai Western Road, Qingdao, Shandong Province 266071, People's Republic of China, *Tel:* +86 532 8502 3303, *Fax:* +86 532 8502 3828, *Email:* agency.qd@huatai-serv.com, *Website:* www.huatai-serv.com

QINGLAN

Lat 19° 35' N; Long 110° 53' E.

Admiralty Chart: 3991	**Admiralty Pilot:** 30
Time Zone: GMT +8 h	**UNCTAD Locode:** CN QLN

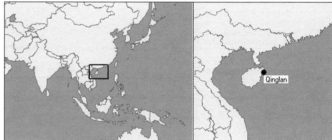

Principal Facilities:

P		Y	G						

Authority: Port Authority of Qinglan, Port Office, Qinglan, People's Republic of China

Pilotage: Compulsory and available during daylight only

Radio Frequency: VHF Channels 16 and 11

Tides: Average range of 1.1 m

Accommodation:

Name	Length (m)	Depth (m)	Remarks
Qinglan			
Berth No.3	110	4.5	General cargo for vessels up to 5000 dwt

Mechanical Handling Equipment:

Location	Type	Capacity (t)	Qty
Berth No.3	Shore Cranes	25	4
Berth No.3	Shore Cranes	8	1

Lloyd's Agent: Huatai Surveyors & Adjusters Co., 14th Floor, China Re Building, No.11 Jin Rong Avenue, Xicheng District, Beijing 100140, People's Republic of China, *Tel:* +86 10 6657 6577, *Fax:* +86 10 6657 6502, *Email:* agency.bj@huatai-serv.com, *Website:* www.huatai-serv.com

QINGZHOU

harbour area, see under Fuzhou

QINHUANGDAO

Lat 39° 55' N; Long 119° 38' E.

Admiralty Chart: 3378
Time Zone: GMT +8 h

Admiralty Pilot: 32
UNCTAD Locode: CN SHP

Principal Facilities:

P	Y	G	C		B	D	T	A

Authority: Qinhuangdao Port Group Co Ltd, 35 Haibin Road, Qinhuangdao, Hebei Province 066002, People's Republic of China, *Tel:* +86 335 309 4924, *Fax:* +86 335 309 3522, *Email:* qhdgww@portqhd.com, *Website:* www.portqhd.com

Officials: Chief Executive Officer: Xing Luzhen.
Marketing Manager: Fan Guangzhi, *Tel:* +86 335 309 3640, *Email:* fanguangzhi@portqhd.com.

Port Security: ISPS compliant

Approach: Draft limitation of 16.5 m in the main and eastern channel and 13.5 m in the western channel

Anchorage: Eastern Anchorage located in a sector area with Nanshan Tou Lighthouse as its centre, lying between the true bearings of 110° and 135° and between two arcs of 3 and 7 miles in radius. Mud and sand bottom in depth of 11-15.5 m for vessels up to 50 000 dwt
Western Anchorage located in a sector area with Nanshan Tou Lighthouse as its centre, lying between the true bearings of 165° and 190° and between two arcs of 3 and 8 miles in radius. Mud and sand bottom in depth of 10-14 m for vessels up to 50 000 dwt
Oil Tanker Anchorage located in a sector area with Nanshan Tou Lighthouse as its centre, lying between the true bearings of 100° and 110° and between two arcs of 3 and 7 miles in radius. Bottom of mud and sand in depth of 11.7-15 m for vessels up to 50 000 dwt

Pilotage: Compulsory. Pilot service is available 24 h. Pilot boards vessel at the quarantine anchorage

Radio Frequency: VHF Channel 16

Weather: Ice conditions occur mid-January to mid-February. The port is kept open with icebreaker assistance

Tides: Tidal range: maximum 2.45 m, minimum 0.11 m, average 1.28 m

Traffic: 2006, 201 867 000 t of cargo handled of which coal amounted to 176 500 000 t, 200 007 TEU's

Principal Imports and Exports: Imports: Coal, Fruit, General cargo, Grain, Livestock, Oil, Ore. Exports: Cement, Fertiliser, Grain, Iron, Minerals, Steel, Sugar, Timber.

Working Hours: Four harbour stevedoring companies operate in the port giving a 24 h/day service. This is operated with a two shift system of 0730-1930 and 1930-0730. Sundays and holidays included

Accommodation:

Name	Length (m)	Depth (m)	Remarks
Qinhuangdao			
Berth No.10	256.3	14	Containers for vessels up to 50 000 dwt
Berth No.11	256	14	General cargo for vessels up to 50 000 dwt
Berth No.12	227	14	Corn for vessels up to 50 000 dwt
Berth No.13	227	14	General cargo for vessels up to 50 000 dwt
Berth No.14	231.7	14	General cargo for vessels up to 50 000 dwt
Berth No.15	231.7	14	General cargo for vessels up to 50 000 dwt
Berth No.16	172	11	General cargo for vessels up to 10 000 dwt
Berth No.17	256	11	General cargo for vessels up to 15 000 dwt
Berth No.18	205.7	11	General cargo for vessels up to 15 000 dwt
Berth No.19	205.7	11	General cargo for vessels up to 15 000 dwt
Berth No.203	307.5	14	Coal for vessels up to 50 000 dwt
Berth No.204	307.5	14	Coal for vessels up to 50 000 dwt
Berth No.301	340	17	Coal for vessels up to 100 000 dwt
Berth No.302	235	12.5	Coal for vessels up to 35 000 dwt
Berth No.704	215	12.5	Coal for vessels up to 35 000 dwt
Berth No.705	215	12.5	Coal for vessels up to 35 000 dwt
Berth No.706	341	17	Coal for vessels up to 100 000 dwt
Oil Port			See [1] below
Berth No.101			See [2] below
Berth No.102			See [3] below
Berth No.103			See [4] below
Berth No.104			Oil products for vessels up to 3000 dwt

[1] *Oil Port:* A 1152 km long oil pipeline and a 368 km long pipeline closely link the dock of Qinhuangdao Oilport with Daqing Oilfield and Yanshan Petrochemical Corporation of Beijing. The oil port is equipped with 3 loading bridges for railway wagons, which can allow 3 railway wagons to load and unload simultaneously. 280 000 m3 of self-owned oil tanks plus 1 009 000 m3 oil tanks on the harbour periphery serve the oil port
[2] *Berth No.101:* Crude oil & other oil products for vessels up to 20 000 dwt
[3] *Berth No.102:* Crude oil & other oil products for vessels up to 20 000 dwt
[4] *Berth No.103:* Crude oil & other oil products for vessels up to 50 000 dwt

Storage: Coal stacking area of 2 498 000 m2. Container yard of 60 000 m2

Mechanical Handling Equipment:

Location	Type	Capacity (t)	Qty
Qinhuangdao	Floating Cranes	70	1
Berth No.11	Shore Cranes	10	6
Berth No.13	Shore Cranes	10	3
Berth No.14	Shore Cranes	16	9
Berth No.15	Shore Cranes	16	9
Berth No.16	Shore Cranes	10	3
Berth No.18	Shore Cranes	10	4

Bunkering: Available at both berth and anchorage, not available at the tanker and dangerous cargo jetties
BP Hong Kong Ltd, 21st Floor, Super Ocean Financial Centre, 067 West Yan An Road, Shanghai, Shanghai Province, People's Republic of China, *Tel:* +86 21 6278 4858, *Fax:* +86 21 6275 7702, *Email:* lucn@bp.com
ExxonMobil Marine Fuels, 1 Harbour Front Place, 06-00 Harbour Front, Tower One, Singapore, Republic of Singapore 098633, *Tel:* +65 6885 8998, *Fax:* +65 6885 8794, *Email:* asiapac.marinefuels@exxonmobil.com, *Website:* www.exxonmobilmarinefuels.com – *Grades:* MDO; MGO; IFO – *Delivery Mode:* barge

Towage: Twelve tugs available up to 4700 hp

Repair & Maintenance: Shanhaiguan Shipyard, Shanhaiguan, Qinhuangdao, Hebei Province, People's Republic of China, *Tel:* +86 335 508 1131, *Fax:* +86 335 508 1350, *Email:* business@shgshipyard.com, *Website:* www.shgshipyard.com Three dry docks of 170 m x 28 m x 9.1 m, 240 m x 39 m x 11.4 m and 340 m x 64 m x 12.8 m. Also seven berthing quays totalling 1574 m

Ship Chandlers: Qinhuangdao Foreign Supply General Corp., No.28 Haibin Road, Qinhuangdao, Hebei Province 66002, People's Republic of China, *Tel:* +86 335 341 5900, *Fax:* +86 335 342 4817, *Email:* supco@heinfo.net, *Website:* www.ship-foreign-supply.com
Runtong Marine Supply & Engineering Service Co. Ltd, 12 Xueshan Road, Development Zone, Qinhuangdao, Hebei Province 066004, People's Republic of China, *Tel:* +86 335 591 0190/8, *Fax:* +86 335 850 0886, *Email:* info@runtongmarine.com, *Website:* www.runtongmarine.com

Shipping Agents: China Marine Shipping Agency Co. Ltd, China Marine Shipping Agency Qinhuangdao Company, 38 Youyi Road, Qinhuangdao, Hebei Province, People's Republic of China, *Tel:* +86 335 342 8424, *Fax:* +86 335 341 3622, *Email:* sinoagt@heinfo.net, *Website:* www.sinotrans.com
China Ocean Shipping Agency, 25 Haibin Street, Qinhuangdao, Hebei Province 066002, People's Republic of China, *Tel:* +86 335 340 8007, *Fax:* +86 335 340 8058, *Email:* lx@penavico-qhd.com
CMA-CGM S.A., CMA CGM Qinhuangdao, Room 728, Jinyang Building, 197 Hebei Street, Haigang District, Qinhuangdao, Hebei Province 066002, People's Republic of China, *Tel:* +86 335 302 2006, *Fax:* +86 335 302 2002, *Email:* qin.ccao@cma-cgm.com, *Website:* www.cma-cgm.com

Surveyors: China Classification Society, 73 Donggang Road, Haigang District, Qinhuangdao, Hebei Province 066002, People's Republic of China, *Fax:* +86 335 323 5068, *Email:* ccsqh@ccs.org.cn, *Website:* www.ccs.org.cn

Airport: Tianjin Airport

Railway: Rail links are provided to the Beijing-Shenyang railroad and thus into northern China. Electrified rail links operate between Beijing and Qinhuangdao and Datong and Qinhuangdao, this is solely for coal transportation
Port network which consists of 147 km and marshall yards - connect to four main lines

Lloyd's Agent: Huatai Surveyors & Adjusters Co., 14th Floor, China Re Building, No.11 Jin Rong Avenue, Xicheng District, Beijing 100140, People's Republic of China, *Tel:* +86 10 6657 6577, *Fax:* +86 10 6657 6502, *Email:* agency.bj@huatai-serv.com, *Website:* www.huatai-serv.com

Key to Principal Facilities:—				
A=Airport	**C**=Containers	**G**=General Cargo	**P**=Petroleum	**R**=Ro/Ro	**Y**=Dry Bulk
B=Bunkers	**D**=Dry Dock	**L**=Cruise	**Q**=Other Liquid Bulk	**T**=Towage (where available from port)	

QINHUANGDAO FIELD

Admiralty Chart: 1250
Time Zone: GMT +8 h
Principal Facilities:

P									

Admiralty Pilot: 32
UNCTAD Locode: CN

Authority: China Offshore Oil Bohai Corp., P O Box 501, Tanggu District, Tianjin, Tianjin Municipality 300456, People's Republic of China, *Tel:* +86 22 2580 1700, *Fax:* +86 22 2580 9547

Anchorage: The anchorage area is contained within the following coordinates:
39° 01' 43" N; 119° 13' 15" E
39° 02' 43" N; 119° 15' 40" E
39° 01' 44" N; 119° 16' 19" E
39° 00' 44" N; 119° 13' 52" E

Pilotage: Compulsory

Radio Frequency: The FPSO listens on VHF Channel 16 and works on VHF Channel 67

Accommodation:

Name	Remarks
QHD 32-6 Terminal	See [1] below

[1]*QHD 32-6 Terminal:* In pos 39° 07' N; 119° 12' E. Consists of six wellheads and FPSO 'Bohai Shi Ji', moored in depth of 20.2 m and accommodating vessels up to 120 000 dwt. Storage cap of 1 000 000 bbls. Berthing/unberthing during daylight hours only

Lloyd's Agent: Huatai Surveyors & Adjusters Co., 14th Floor, China Re Building, No.11 Jin Rong Avenue, Xicheng District, Beijing 100140, People's Republic of China, *Tel:* +86 10 6657 6577, *Fax:* +86 10 6657 6502, *Email:* agency.bj@huatai-serv.com, *Website:* www.huatai-serv.com

QINZHOU

Lat 21° 57' N; Long 108° 37' E.

Admiralty Chart: 3990
Time Zone: GMT +8 h
Admiralty Pilot: 30
UNCTAD Locode: CN QZH

Principal Facilities:

P	Q	Y	G	C				T	

Authority: Qinzhou Port (Group) Co Ltd, Qinzhou Port, Qinzhou, Guangxi Province, People's Republic of China, *Tel:* +86 777 388 8511, *Fax:* +86 777 388 9058

Anchorage: Available in pos 21° 28' 28" N; 108° 30' 51" E in depth of 11 m

Pilotage: Compulsory. Pilot boards in pos 21° 29' 47" N; 108° 32' 18" E

Radio Frequency: VHF Channels 16 and 11

Tides: Max 5.2 m, min 0.81 m

Traffic: 2006, 7 520 000 t of cargo handled, 43 484 TEU's

Accommodation:

Name	Length (m)	Depth (m)	Remarks
Qinzhou			
Guangming Petroleum Wharf	180	12	Product oil & alcohol for vessels up to 30 000 dwt
Legou Wharf	360	12	Bulk & general cargo for vessels up to 30 000 dwt
Zhongshan Wharf	100	5	Bulk & general cargo for vessels up to 2000 dwt
Guoxing LPG Wharf	120	8	LPG for vessels up to 5000 dwt
China Petrochemical Wharf	180	12	Product oil & LPG for vessels up to 30 000 dwt

Mechanical Handling Equipment:

Location	Type	Capacity (t)	Qty
Legou Wharf	Mult-purp. Cranes	16	4
Legou Wharf	Mult-purp. Cranes	30	1

Towage: One tug of 900 hp and one tug of 2600 hp

Shipping Agents: China Marine Shipping Agency Co. Ltd, China Marine Shipping Agency Guangxi Qinzhou Company Limited, Sinoagent Qinzhou Building, Kouan-xincun, Qinzhou, Guangxi Province, People's Republic of China, *Tel:* +86 777 239 5508, *Fax:* +86 777 239 5398, *Email:* qinzhou@sinoagent.com

Lloyd's Agent: Huatai Surveyors & Adjusters Co., 14th Floor, China Re Building, No.11 Jin Rong Avenue, Xicheng District, Beijing 100140, People's Republic of China, *Tel:* +86 10 6657 6577, *Fax:* +86 10 6657 6502, *Email:* agency.bj@huatai-serv.com, *Website:* www.huatai-serv.com

QUANZHOU

Lat 24° 54' N; Long 118° 35' E.

Admiralty Chart: 1786
Time Zone: GMT +8 h
Admiralty Pilot: 32
UNCTAD Locode: CN QZJ

Principal Facilities:

P	Y	G	C			B		T	

Authority: Quanzhou Port Authority, Quanzhou, Fujian Province, People's Republic of China, *Tel:* +86 595 2258 2725, *Fax:* +86 595 2258 2725, *Website:* www.qzgw.com

Port Security: ISPS compliant

Approach: Draft limitation in Houzhou Channel is 9.5 m

Anchorage: Xiangzhijiao Anchorage in pos 24° 47' 30" N; 118° 47' 30" E

Pilotage: Compulsory and available 8 h during daytime only. Pilot boards:
a) in pos 24° 47' 50" N; 118° 47' 55" E (Xiangzhi Pilot Anchorage)
b) in pos 24° 29' 51" N; 118° 31' 95" E (Weitou Wan)
c) Shenhu Wan: quarantine anchorage bounded by the following positions:
24° 38' 57" N; 118° 41' 76" E
24° 38' 80" N; 118° 42' 42" E
24° 38' 52" N; 118° 42' 54" E
24° 38' 28" N; 118° 41' 88" E

Radio Frequency: VHF Channel 16

Tides: Average tidal range of 4.52 m

Traffic: 2005, 630 000 TEU's handled

Accommodation:

Name	Length (m)	Depth (m)	Remarks
Quanzhou			
Houzhu Berth No.1	80	2.5	General cargo for vessels up to 500 dwt
Houzhu Berth No.3	102	4	General cargo for vessels up to 1000 dwt
Houzhu Berth No.4	124	5	General cargo for vessels up to 3000 dwt
Houzhu Berth No.5	152	7	General cargo for vessels up to 5000 dwt
General Cargo Berth	193	10	General cargo for vessels up to 10 000 dwt
Oil Berth	152	5.2	Petroleum for vessels up to 3000 dwt
Crude Oil Berth	450	15.5	Crude oil for vessels up to 150 000 dwt
Quanzhou Pacific Container Terminal	970	15.1	See [1] below

[1]*Quanzhou Pacific Container Terminal:* Tel: +86 595 8868 2999, Fax: +86 595 8868 2888, Email: master@qpct.com.cn, Website: www.qpct.com.cn
Four container berths

Storage: Container yard of 10 000 m2

Location	Open (m²)	Covered (m²)
Quanzhou	43800	8448

Mechanical Handling Equipment:

Location	Type	Capacity (t)	Qty
Houzhu Berth No.5	Shore Cranes	10	2
General Cargo Berth	Shore Cranes	10	2

Bunkering: China Marine Bunker Supply Co., 13F Qian Cun Mansion A, No.2, 5th Block, Anzhen Xili, Chaoyang District, Beijing 100029, People's Republic of China, *Tel:* +86 10 6443 0717, *Fax:* +86 10 6443 0708, *Email:* business@chimbusco.com.cn, *Website:* www.chimbusco.com.cn – *Grades:* IFO120-380cSt; MGO

Towage: Two tugs of 980-2300 hp

Shipping Agents: China Marine Shipping Agency Co. Ltd, China Marine Shipping Agency Fujian Company Limited Quanzhou Branch, 6th Floor, International Trade Building, Citong East Road, Quanzhou, Fujian Province, People's Republic of China, *Tel:* +86 595 2210 6825, *Fax:* +86 595 2211 0104, *Email:* sinoagent@public.qz.fj.cn, *Website:* www.sinoagent.com
China Ocean Shipping Agency, 21st Floor, The Industrial Bank Building, Fengze Street, Quanzhou, Fujian Province 362000, People's Republic of China, *Tel:* +86 595 2298 9650, *Fax:* +86 595 2289 5165, *Email:* hubin@qz.penavicofj.com

CMA-CGM S.A., CMA CGM Quanzhou, 10/F Waidai Building, Tian'an Road, Quanzhou, Fujian Province 362000, People's Republic of China, *Tel:* +86 595 2218 2899, *Fax:* +86 595 2218 2668, *Email:* qzh.genmbox@cma-cgm.com, *Website:* www.cma-cgm.com

Lianfeng Shipping Co. Ltd, Room 1202, Minmetals Mansion, Quanxiu Road, Quanzhou, Fujian Province, People's Republic of China, *Tel:* +86 595 2257 7809, *Fax:* +86 595 2257 7810, *Email:* 1fship@public.qz.fj.cn

Development: Quanzhou Pacific Container Terminal Co. will construct a new container berth and build a new multi-purpose berth. The two new berths are expected to be built by 2008

Lloyd's Agent: Huatai Surveyors & Adjusters Co., 14th Floor, China Re Building, No.11 Jin Rong Avenue, Xicheng District, Beijing 100140, People's Republic of China, *Tel:* +86 10 6657 6577, *Fax:* +86 10 6657 6502, *Email:* agency.bj@huatai-serv.com, *Website:* www.huatai-serv.com

RIZHAO

Lat 35° 29' N; Long 119° 29' E.

Admiralty Chart: 1253

Admiralty Pilot: 30

Time Zone: GMT +8 h

UNCTAD Locode: CN RZH

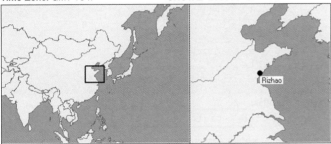

Principal Facilities:

P		Y	G	C			B		T	

Authority: Shijiu Harbour Administration, Huanghai 1 Road, Rizhao, Shandong Province 276826, People's Republic of China, *Tel:* +86 633 838 3668, *Fax:* +86 633 838 2282, *Website:* www.rzport.com

Port Security: ISPS compliant

Approach: Draft limitation in Coal Wharf Channel is 15 m and in General Cargo Wharf Channel is 11 m

The channel is divided into two sections:

The first section is connected elliptically to the turning basin which is SW of the coal wharf. It is 2400 m in length and 200 m width, dredged to 15 m. There is a 500 m wide ancilliary channel on either side of this section. The second section starts where the dredged section ends and runs to the anchorage, It is a natural waterway, 4300 m in length and 3000 m width, mud bottom and 15-18 m depth

The channel for the general cargo wharves is 4100 m length, 120 m width with a depth of 11 m

Anchorage: Anchorage Area No.1 is within the boundary formed by the following four points:
35° 21' 80" N; 119° 38' 62" E
35° 20' 82" N; 119° 40' 97" E
35° 18' 90" N; 119° 39' 78" E
35° 19' 87" N; 119° 37' 45" E

Anchorage Area No.2 is within the boundary formed by the following four points:
35° 20' 82" N; 119° 40' 97" E
35° 19' 85" N; 119° 43' 33" E
35° 17' 92" N; 119° 42' 13" E
35° 18' 90" N; 119° 39' 78" E

Anchorage Area No.3 is within the boundary formed by the following four points:
35° 17' 15" N; 119° 37' 73" E
35° 16' 17" N; 119° 40' 08" E
35° 14' 23" N; 119° 38' 90" E
35° 15' 22" N; 119° 36' 53" E

Anchorage Area No.4 is within the boundary formed by the following four points:
35° 16' 17" N; 119° 40' 08" E
35° 15' 20" N; 119° 42' 43" E
35° 13' 27" N; 119° 41' 25" E
35° 14' 23" N; 119° 38' 90" E

Anchorage Area No.5 for vessels over 100 000 dwt and 16 m draught is within the boundary formed by the following four points:
35° 17' 70" N; 119° 48' 50" E
35° 16' 72" N; 119° 50' 85" E
35° 14' 80" N; 119° 49' 65" E
35° 15' 73" N; 119° 47' 30" E

Pilotage: Compulsory and available 24 h. Pilot boards in the following positions:
a) for vessels over 100 000 dwt and 16 m draught the pilot boarding position (No.2) is within a circle of 750 m radius centered on pos 35° 16.48' N; 119° 46.68' E
b) for all other vessels pilot boarding position (No.1) is within a circle of 750 m radius centered on pos 35° 18.57' N; 119° 37.45' E

Radio Frequency: VHF Channel 16

Weather: Main wind is from the NE quadrant. Ice free. Fog April to July

Tides: Average tidal range of 2.98 m, max 4.9 m, spring 4.5 m, neap 3.5 m

Traffic: 2006, 110 074 000 t of cargo handled

Principal Imports and Exports: Imports: Fertiliser, General cargo, Steel products. Exports: Agricultural products, Coal, Grain.

Working Hours: 24 h/day

Accommodation:

Name	Length (m)	Depth (m)	Remarks
Rizhao			
Berth No.1	130	6.9	Petroleum & general cargo for vessels up to 5000 dwt
Berth No.2	238	8.5	Petroleum & chemicals for vessels up to 10 000 dwt
Berth No.3	180	9.5	General cargo for vessels up to 15 000 dwt
Berth No.4	200	10.5	Bulk cement for vessels up to 25 000 dwt
Berth No.5	171	10.1	General cargo for vessels up to 40 000 dwt
Berth No.6	171	11	Containers for vessels up to 40 000 dwt
Berth No.7	189	11	General cargo for vessels up to 60 000 dwt
Berth No.8	171	11	General cargo for vessels up to 60 000 dwt
Berth No.9	187	11	General cargo & iron ore for vessels up to 60 000 dwt
Coal Berth A	230	16.5	Coal for vessels up to 60 000 dwt
Coal Berth B	280	16.5	Coal for vessels up to 150 000 dwt

Storage: Coal storage space of 270 000 m2 and container yard of 3000 m2

Location	Open (m²)	Covered (m²)
Rizhao	220000	22000

Mechanical Handling Equipment:

Location	Type	Capacity (t)	Qty
Rizhao	Floating Cranes	150	1
Berth No.1	Mobile Cranes		1
Berth No.3	Shore Cranes	10	2
Berth No.5	Shore Cranes	10	3
Berth No.5	Shore Cranes	16	1
Berth No.6	Mult-purp. Cranes	31	2
Berth No.7	Shore Cranes	10	4
Berth No.7	Shore Cranes	16	4
Berth No.8	Shore Cranes	16	4
Berth No.8	Shore Cranes	10	4
Berth No.9	Shore Cranes	10	4
Berth No.9	Shore Cranes	16	4

Bunkering: Available

Towage: Four tugs available of 3200-4200 hp

Repair & Maintenance: Available

Ship Chandlers: Rizhao Lanshan Ocean Shipping Supply Co., Lanshan Port, Rizhao, Shandong Province 276808, People's Republic of China, *Tel:* +86 633 288 6098, *Fax:* +86 633 288 6888, *Email:* supcols@lanshansupply.com

Rizhao Ocean Shipping Supply Co. Ltd, 82 Haibin Road 2, Rizhao, Shandong Province 276826, People's Republic of China, *Tel:* +86 633 833 2001, *Fax:* +86 633 833 2001, *Email:* rzsupco@163169.net

Shipping Agents: China Marine Shipping Agency Co. Ltd, China Marine Shipping Agency Shandong Company Limited Rizhao Branch, 63 Huanghai Road 2, Shijiu, Rizhao, Shandong Province, People's Republic of China, *Tel:* +86 633 832 3486, *Fax:* +86 633 833 1998, *Email:* sinorz@vip.sina.com

China Ocean Shipping Agency, Rizhao, Shandong Province, People's Republic of China, *Tel:* +86 633 832 1752, *Fax:* +86 633 833 1116, *Website:* www.penavicorz.com

Tongsheng International Shipping Agencies, Rizhao Tongsheng International Shipping Agency Co Ltd, 105 Huanghai No.1 Road, Rizhao, Shandong Province 276826, People's Republic of China, *Tel:* +86 633 221 1336, *Fax:* +86 633 221 1337, *Email:* tongsheng@tongshengrz.com, *Website:* www.tongshengshipping.com

Lloyd's Agent: Huatai Surveyors & Adjusters Co., 14th Floor, China Re Building, No.11 Jin Rong Avenue, Xicheng District, Beijing 100140, People's Republic of China, *Tel:* +86 10 6657 6577, *Fax:* +86 10 6657 6502, *Email:* agency.bj@huatai-serv.com, *Website:* www.huatai-serv.com

RONGQI

Lat 22° 41' N; Long 113° 13' E.

Admiralty Chart: -

Admiralty Pilot: -

Time Zone: GMT +8 h

UNCTAD Locode: CN ROQ

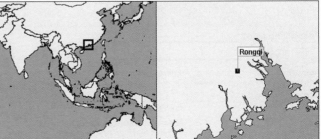

Key to Principal Facilities:—			
A=Airport	**C**=Containers	**G**=General Cargo	**P**=Petroleum	**R**=Ro/Ro	**Y**=Dry Bulk
B=Bunkers	**D**=Dry Dock	**L**=Cruise	**Q**=Other Liquid Cargo	**T**=Towage (where available from port)

Principal Facilities:

		Y	G						

Authority: Rongqi Harbour Administration, Changti, Rongqi Town, Shunde, Guangdong Province 528000, People's Republic of China

Accommodation:

Name	Remarks
Rongqi	See [1] below

[1]*Rongqi:* Numerous berths available for vessels up to 5000 dwt handling coal, ore, grain and manufactured goods

Storage: Open and covered storage areas available

Lloyd's Agent: Huatai Surveyors & Adjusters Co., Room 802, Jun Yuan Mansion, 155 Tian He East Road, Guangzhou, Guangdong Province 510620, People's Republic of China, *Tel:* +86 20 3881 2306, *Fax:* +86 20 3881 2470, *Email:* agency.gz@huatai-serv.com, *Website:* www.huatai-serv.com

SAIQI

Lat 26° 56' N; Long 119° 41' E.

Admiralty Chart: 1754　　　**Admiralty Pilot:** 32
Time Zone: GMT +8 h　　　**UNCTAD Locode:** CN

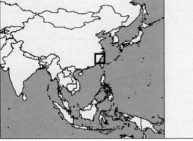

Principal Facilities:

	P		Y	G					

Authority: Saiqi Harbour Administration, Jiefang Road, Saiqi, Fujian Province 355001, People's Republic of China

Accommodation:

Name	Remarks
Saiqi	See [1] below

[1]*Saiqi:* Numerous berths available fior vessels up to 1300 dwt handling passengers, petroleum, coal, grain, ore and fertiliser

Storage: Open and covered storage areas available

Mechanical Handling Equipment:

Location	Type
Saiqi	Mult-purp. Cranes

Lloyd's Agent: Huatai Surveyors & Adjusters Co., 14th Floor, China Re Building, No.11 Jin Rong Avenue, Xicheng District, Beijing 100140, People's Republic of China, *Tel:* +86 10 6657 6577, *Fax:* +86 10 6657 6502, *Email:* agency.bj@huatai-serv.com, *Website:* www.huatai-serv.com

SANBING

Lat 31° 32' N; Long 117° 44' E.

Admiralty Chart: 2946　　　**Admiralty Pilot:** 32
Time Zone: GMT +8 h　　　**UNCTAD Locode:** CN

Principal Facilities:

		Y							

Authority: Sanbing Shipping Administration, Shanpengwan, Sanbing Town, Chaohu, Anhui Province 238000, People's Republic of China

Accommodation:

Name	Remarks
Sanbing	Numerous berths available for vessels up to 100 dwt handling ore materials

Storage: Open and covered storage areas available

Mechanical Handling Equipment:

Location	Type	Capacity (t)
Sanbing	Mult-purp. Cranes	3

Lloyd's Agent: Huatai Surveyors & Adjusters Co., 14th Floor, China Re Building, No.11 Jin Rong Avenue, Xicheng District, Beijing 100140, People's Republic of China, *Tel:* +86 10 6657 6577, *Fax:* +86 10 6657 6502, *Email:* agency.bj@huatai-serv.com, *Website:* www.huatai-serv.com

SANBU

Lat 22° 28' N; Long 112° 45' E.

Admiralty Chart: 1555　　　**Admiralty Pilot:** 30
Time Zone: GMT +8 h　　　**UNCTAD Locode:** CN SBU

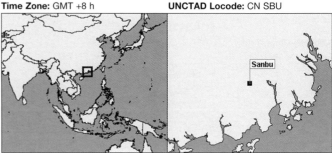

Principal Facilities:

	P		Y	G					

Authority: Sanbu Harbour Administration, 1 Harbour Road, Sanbu Town, Kaiping, Guangdong Province 529300, People's Republic of China

Accommodation:

Name	Remarks
Sanbu	See [1] below

[1]*Sanbu:* Numerous berths available for vessels up to 500 dwt handling petroleum, coal, ore, cement and fertiliser

Lloyd's Agent: Huatai Surveyors & Adjusters Co., Room 802, Jun Yuan Mansion, 155 Tian He East Road, Guangzhou, Guangdong Province 510620, People's Republic of China, *Tel:* +86 20 3881 2306, *Fax:* +86 20 3881 2470, *Email:* agency.gz@huatai-serv.com, *Website:* www.huatai-serv.com

SANKESHU

harbour area, see under Harbin

SANYA

Lat 18° 11' N; Long 109° 28' E.

Admiralty Chart: 3893　　　**Admiralty Pilot:** 30
Time Zone: GMT +8 h　　　**UNCTAD Locode:** CN SYX

Principal Facilities:

		Y	G	C			B		T	A

Authority: Sanya Port Administration, Sheng Li Road, Sanya, Hainan Province, People's Republic of China, *Tel:* +86 898 8827 4031

Port Security: ISPS compliant

Approach: Length of channel 1.1 km in depth of 7 m

Anchorage: Pilot Anchorage in pos 18° 11' N; 109° 26' E in depth of 20-28 m

Pilotage: Compulsory and available 24 h. Pilot boards vessel at Pilotage Anchorage

Radio Frequency: VHF Channel 16

Tides: Average tidal range of 0.79 m

Traffic: 2003, 600 000 t of cargo handled

Principal Imports and Exports: Imports: Cement, Coal, Grain, Steel. Exports: Local products, Rubber, Salt, Sugar.

Accommodation:

Name	Length (m)	Depth (m)	Remarks
Sanya			
Berth No.3	91.5	4.5	General cargo for vessels up to 1500 dwt
Berth No's 4-5	250	4.2	General cargo for vessels up to 1000 dwt
Berth No's 6-7	260	6.4	General cargo for vessels up to 5000 dwt

Storage: Container yard of 5000 m2

Location	Open (m²)	Covered (m²)
Sanya	51000	9034

Mechanical Handling Equipment:

Location	Type	Capacity (t)	Qty
Berth No.3	Shore Cranes	15	2
Berth No's 4-5	Shore Cranes	36	2
Berth No's 6-7	Shore Cranes	10	2

Bunkering: Available at berth and anchorage

Towage: One tug of 400 hp

Airport: Sanya Airport

Lloyd's Agent: Huatai Surveyors & Adjusters Co., 14th Floor, China Re Building, No.11 Jin Rong Avenue, Xicheng District, Beijing 100140, People's Republic of China, *Tel:* +86 10 6657 6577, *Fax:* +86 10 6657 6502, *Email:* agency.bj@huatai-serv.com, *Website:* www.huatai-serv.com

SHANGHAI

Lat 31° 15' N; Long 121° 30' E.

Admiralty Chart: 1601/1602/1603/1144	**Admiralty Pilot:** 32
Time Zone: GMT +8 h	**UNCTAD Locode:** CN SHA

Principal Facilities:

P		Y	G	C	R	L	B	D	T	A

Authority: Shanghai International Port (Group) Co Ltd, 18 Yangshupu Road, Shanghai, Shanghai Province 200082, People's Republic of China, *Tel:* +86 21 6329 0660, *Fax:* +86 21 6321 7936, *Email:* admin@portshanghai.com.cn, *Website:* www.portshanghai.com.cn

Officials: Chairman: Lu Haihu.

Port Security: ISPS compliant. Container Security Initiative (CSI) designated port

Pre-Arrival Information: Vessel Traffic Service: Compulsory for all foreign vessels, all vessels of 1000 gt and over, vessels of excessive beam or LOA or towed vessels of 1000 dwt and over, passenger vessels carrying 12 passengers or more and tankers of 500 dwt and over including oil tankers, chemical tankers and liquefied gas carriers
The VTS area encompasses the waters bordered by the following lines:
(a) Changjiang Kou No.256 Lt. Buoy (31° 07.57' N; 122° 15.58' E) and No.5 Lt. Buoy (31° 03.22' N; 122° 08.18' E)
(b) Changjiang and Liuhe Kou harbour limits
(c) Line between the upper points of Chaolin ferry terminal on Huangpu Jiang
Wusong VTS, Tel: +86 21 5667 1249, Fax: +86 21 5667 4045
Shanghai MSA, Tel: +86 21 5393 1419, Fax: +86 21 5393 1420
Reporting lines have been established as follows:
(a) L1: between Niupi Jiao Lt Bn (31° 08.44' N; 122° 15.12' E), Changjiang Kou Lt V (31° 06.04' N; 122° 28.09' E) and Nanzhi Lt V (30° 58.58' N; 122° 10.89' E)
(b) L2: between No.256 Lt Buoy and No.5 Lt Buoy
(c) L3: Liuhe Kou harbour limits
(d) L4: between Wusong Kou Hetang Lt (31° 23.80' N; 121° 31.11' E) and No.101 Lt Buoy (31° 23.66' N; 121° 31.51' E)
(e) L5: between the upper points of Chaolin ferry terminal and Huangpu Jiang
Vessels should report to Shanghai MSA before 1600 LT of the day before arrival at the port, via agent, owners or operators, stating the following:
(a) vessel's name
(b) nationality
(c) loa
(d) gt
(e) draught
(f) maximum height
(g) last port
(h) destination/berth/anchorage
(i) ETA
(j) type and quantity of cargo
(k) number of passengers and crew
Vessels should report to Wusong VTS when passing the reporting lines on the appropriate VHF channel stating the following:

(a) vessel's name
(b) time of passing reporting line
(c) ETA of next reporting line
Vessels should report to Wusong VTS on the appropriate VHF channel before moving stating the following
(a) vessel's name
(b) name of berth or anchorage
(c) berth of destination
Vessels should report to Wusong VTS on the appropriate VHF channel when movement, anchoring or berthing has been completed, stating the following:
(a) vessel's name
(b) time of anchoring or securing
(c) name of berth or anchorage
Vessels should report to Shanghai MSA before 1600 LT of the day before departure, via agent, owners or operators, stating the following:
(a) vessel's name
(b) nationality
(c) loa
(d) gt
(e) draught
(f) maximum height
(g) next port
(h) destination/berth/anchorage
(i) ETA
(j) type and quantity of cargo
(k) number of passengers and crew
Vessels should report to Wusong VTS on the appropriate VHF channel before getting underway, stating the vessel's name and position
Any of the following should be immediately reported on the appropriate VHF channel
(a) any defect in an aid to navigation
(b) involvement in a maritime casualty
(c) any pollution incident
(d) any condition that may impair a vessel's ability to navigate or manoeuvre
(e) any hazard to navigation
(f) any adverse weather conditions including reduction in visibility
The VTS provides traffic safety information, hydrometeorology information, navigational assistance, anchorage arrangements and other information on request. Daily safety information is broadcast every even hour (LT) and when an emergency situation exists

Approach: Draft limitation at mouth of the Yangtze River Channel is 10.5 m FW
South Channel has three shoal areas with a min depth of 6 m. The Huangpu River Channel is 10 m depth to Zhanghuabang, 8 m depth to Longhua and 7 m depth to Minhang

Anchorage: Changjiangkou Anchorage in depth of 10-14 m, mud with good holding ground - in pos 30° 56' N; 122° 25' E, 30° 56' N; 122° 32' E, 31° 00' N; 122° 25' E, 31° 00' N; 122° 32' E
Luhuashan Anchorage in depth of 22-33 m, mud with good holding ground - in pos 30° 47' N; 122° 37' E, 30° 47' N; 122° 38' E, 30° 48' N; 122° 37' E, 30° 48' N; 122° 38' E
Wusong Anchorage in depth of 5-17 m, mud and sand, with good holding ground - among buoys Q5, Q4, 29 and 31

Pilotage: Compulsory and available 24 h, Email: pilots@public4.sta.net.cn, Website: www.sh-pilots.com.cn. Vessel's should request pilot and advise ETA via agent 72 h before arrival, and update daily with draught betwee 0900-1000 LT. Pilot boarding positions:
North Channel (Beicao Hangdao):
No.1(N) in pos 31° 07' 30" N; 122° 25' 50" E
No.1(S) in pos 31° 05' 00" N; 122° 25' 50" E
No.2(N) in pos 31° 07' 80" N; 122° 36' 60" E
No.2(S) in pos 31° 04' 60" N; 122° 36' 60" E
South Channel (Nancao Hangdao):
No.3(N) in pos 31° 03' 00" N; 122° 18' 80" E
No.3(S) in pos 31° 01' 40" N; 122° 18' 40" E
For Yangshan vessels should contact pilots on VHF Channel 63 or 69 when approaching Y1 Lt buoy (30° 32' 61" N; 122° 19' 63" E) or Y22 Lt buoy (30° 41' 67" N; 122° 15' 23" E). The pilot boards either at No.1 Anchorage (30° 25' 40" N; 122° 45' 70" E) or No.1 Quarantine Anchorage (30° 29' 00" N; 122° 29' 30" E)

Radio Frequency: VHF Channel 11 or 27

Tides: Average tidal range of 2.14 m. Maximum 4.24 m

Traffic: 2007, 560 000 000 t of cargo handled, 26 150 000 TEU's

Principal Imports and Exports: Imports: Bulk grain, Bulk ore, General, Steel, Timber. Exports: Agricultural products, Chemical products, General, Oil products, Textiles.

Working Hours: Round the clock. Office hours are 0800-1200, 1400-1700

Accommodation:

Name	Length (m)	Depth (m)	Remarks
Waigaoqiao			
Shanghai Zhendong Container Terminal	1566		See [1] below
Shanghai East Container Terminal	1250	14.2	See [2] below
Shanghai Mingdong Container Terminal	1110	12.8	See [3] below
Shanghai Pudong Container Terminal	900	12	See [4] below
Wusong			
Zhanghuabang	784	12.5	See [5] below
Jungong	857	10.5	See [6] below
Baoshan	640	9.4	See [7] below
Yangshan			
Berths	4200	16	See [8] below
Minsheng			See [9] below
Berths	738	10	See [10] below
Nanpu			See [11] below
Gaoyang			See [12] below

Key to Principal Facilities:—

A=Airport	**C**=Containers	**G**=General Cargo	**P**=Petroleum	**R**=Ro/Ro	**Y**=Dry Bulk
B=Bunkers	**D**=Dry Dock	**L**=Cruise	**Q**=Other Liquid Bulk	**T**=Towage (where available from port)	

Name	Length (m)	Depth (m)	Remarks
Coal Branch			See [13] below
Berths	2008		See [14] below
Xinhua			See [15] below
Berths	1584	10.5	See [16] below
Zhanghuabang			See [17] below
Berths	540		See [18] below
Jungong			See [19] below
Berths	743		See [20] below
Baoshan			See [21] below
Berths	780		See [22] below
Longwu			See [23] below
Berth No.1	167	8.5	Max 10 000 dwt
Berth No.2	167	8.5	Max 10 000 dwt
Berth No.3	167	8.5	Max 10 000 dwt
Berth No.4	167	8.5	Max 10 000 dwt
Berth No.5	167	8.5	Max 10 000 dwt
Berth No.6	167	8.5	Max 10 000 dwt
Berth No.7	180	8.5	Max 10 000 dwt
Berth No.8	180	8.5	Max 10 000 dwt
Luojing			See [24] below
Unloading Quay		11	Max 180 000 dwt
Loading Quay		8	Can accommodate vessels on both of its sides
Coal Terminal	721		Five berths
Ore, Coal & Steel Terminal	2720		See [25] below
Passenger Transport Corporation			See [26] below
Berths	1121		Consists of eight berths of 7000-10 000 t
Haitong International Automobile Terminal			See [27] below
Berth	219.4	14	See [28] below

[1]*Shanghai Zhendong Container Terminal:* Operated by Shanghai Zhendong Container Terminal Co Ltd., 1299 Ganghua Road, Pudong, Shanghai 200137, Tel: +86 21 5040 7878, Fax: +86 21 5041 1299, Website: www.spcwt.com
Consists of five container berths and is equipped with 13 quay cranes
[2]*Shanghai East Container Terminal:* Operated by Shanghai East Container Terminal Management Co Ltd., 1 Gangjian Road, Pudong New Area, Shanghai 200137, Tel: +86 21 6868 5966, Fax: +86 21 6868 5225, Email: office@sect.com.cn, Website: www.sect.com.cn
Four berths for container vessels and two berths for barges. Total land area of 1 550 000 m2 and yard area of 707 800 m2. There are a total of fourteen quay cranes consisting of twelve cranes with lifting cap of 61 t and two barge cranes with lifting cap of 40 t. Also there are 48 RTG's of 40-50 t cap
[3]*Shanghai Mingdong Container Terminal:* Operated by Shanghai Mingdong Container Terminals Ltd., 999 Gangjian Road, Pudong New Area, Shanghai 200137, Tel: +86 21 3898 4888, Fax: +86 21 6868 5888, Website: www.smct.com.cn
Four container berths for vessels up to 50 000 t. Equipment includes twelve super post-panamax cranes and 48 RTG's
Also two barge berths totaling 190 m for vessels up to 3000 t
[4]*Shanghai Pudong Container Terminal:* Operated by Shanghai Pudong International Container Terminals Ltd., 88 Yanggao No.1 Road (N), Pudong New Area, Shanghai 200131, Tel: +86 21 5861 3635, Fax: +86 21 5861 1238, Website: www.spict.com
Three container berths. Equipment includes ten container cranes and 36 RTG's
[5]*Zhanghuabang:* Operated by Shanghai Container Terminals Ltd (SCT), 4333 Yixian Road, Shanghai 200940, Tel: +86 21 5644 1988, Fax: +86 21 5644 1566, Website: www.sctport.com.cn (a 50/50 joint venture between Shanghai Port Container Co Ltd and Hutchison Port Holdings Ltd)
Three berths with total area of 303 036 m2. Stacking cap of 22 000 TEU's. Eight container cranes and 22 RTG's
[6]*Jungong:* Operated by Shanghai Container Terminals Ltd (SCT), 4333 Yixian Road, Shanghai 200940, Tel: +86 21 5644 1988, Fax: +86 21 5644 1566, Website: www.sctport.com.cn (a 50/50 joint venture between Shanghai Port Container Co Ltd and Hutchison Port Holdings Ltd)
Four berths with total area of 303 839 m2. Stacking cap of 23 000 TEU's. Seven container cranes and 20 RTG's
[7]*Baoshan:* Operated by Shanghai Container Terminals Ltd (SCT), 4333 Yixian Road, Shanghai 200940, Tel: +86 21 5644 1988, Fax: +86 21 5644 1566, Website: www.sctport.com.cn (a 50/50 joint venture between Shanghai Port Container Co Ltd and Hutchison Port Holdings Ltd)
Three berths with total area of 218 051 m2. Stacking cap of 15 000 TEU's. Five container cranes and 12 RTG's
[8]*Berths:* Operated by Shanghai Shengdong International Container Terminal Co Ltd., 1 Tonghui Road, Luchaogang Town, Nanhui District, Shanghai 201308
Office address: Administrative Centre, Yangshan Deepwater Port Area, Tel: +86 21 6828 8888, Fax: +86 21 6828 9800, Email: admin@shsict.com, Website: www.shsict.com
Consists of twelve container berths. The berths are equipped with 34 container cranes and 108 RTG's
[9]*Minsheng:* Minsheng Controlled Co Ltd., 3 Minsheng Road, Pudong New Area, Shanghai 200135, Tel: +86 21 5885 3675
Specialises in the handling, storage, transport and transfer of imported bulk grains, oils and feeds as well as exported rice and other bulk and break-bulk cargoes
[10]*Berths:* Four 10 000 t berths. Covers an area of 174 000 m2 and has two silo's with a total volume of 170 000 m3, which can store 120 000 t of grain. Equipped with two scraper ship unloaders with a rated speed up to 1000 t/h. More than 200 handling machines, including 10 t and 16 t gantry cranes, ship loaders
[11]*Nanpu:* Nanpu Branch Ltd., 1 Lianyungang Road, Pudong New Area, Shanghai 200126, Tel: +86 21 5883 8640, Fax: +86 21 5880 0901
Mainly engaged in handling and transfer of wood, iron & steel and other bulk and break-bulk cargoes
Consists of Bailianjing Terminal and Tangkou Terminal. Four 10 000 t deepwater berths and two 1000 t berths. 43 000 m2 storage yard and more than 80 special loading and unloading machines
[12]*Gaoyang:* Gaoyang Branch Ltd., 19, Lane 888, Dong Da Ming Road, Shanghai 200082, Tel: +86 21 6512 3322, Fax: +86 21 6537 8465
Bulk and break-bulk terminals
[13]*Coal Branch:* Coal Branch Ltd., 78 Tangqiao Road, Pudong New Area, Shanghai 200127, Tel: +86 21 5881 1350, Fax: +86 21 5881 0516
Specialises in handling coal, sand and gravel
[14]*Berths:* Consists of seventeen berths, eight of which are of 10 000 t. Covers an area of 573 500 m2. Storage yards totaling 204 000 m2
[15]*Xinhua:* Xinhua Co Ltd., 1 Yuanshen Road, Pudong, Shanghai 200120, Tel: +86 21 5885 5588, Fax: +86 21 5885 2077
Cargoes handled include metallic ores, bulk chemical fertilizers and bulk cargoes
[16]*Berths:* Consists of nine 10 000 t berths. Land area of 422 000 m2. Over one hundred machines such as gantry cranes, container forklifts, large-sized loaders, excavators and various hoisters and horizontal conveyors
[17]*Zhanghuabang:* Zhanghuabang Co Ltd., 4177 Yixian Road, Shanghai, Tel: +86 21 5682 1616, Fax: +86 21 5644 0324, Email: zhbsh@public2.sta.net.cn
Specialises in handling bulk and heavy cargo, containers and steel products
[18]*Berths:* Consists of three 10 000 t berths. Land area of 200 000 m2. Over ninety handling machines of various types, and the max lifting cap of crane is 40 t
[19]*Jungong:* Jungong Road Branch Ltd., 4501 Jungong Road, Shanghai 200438, Tel: +86 21 5682 1616, Fax: +86 21 5644 1795
Specialises in handling bulk and break-bulk cargoes including iron, steel, pulp, vehicles, bulk items and equipment, containers etc
[20]*Berths:* Consists of four 10 000 t multi-purpose berths. Covers an area of 251 000 m2. Equipped with eight gantry cranes and 154 handling machines of varioust types. 6304 m long exclusive railroad directly extending to the terminal berth. Total area of warehouses and storage yards amounts to 143 000 m2
[21]*Baoshan:* Baoshan Terminal Branch Ltd., 1875 Mudanjiang Road, Baoshan District, Shanghai 201900, Tel: +86 21 5660 1310, Fax: +86 21 5660 1394, Email: jlb@portbs.com, Website: www.portbs.com
Handling, storage, transport and agency service for containers, bulk and break-bulk cargoes, steel products and massive items
[22]*Berths:* Consists of three berths of 10 000 t and two berths of 1000 t. Port area of 525 000 m2 and land area of 270 000 m2. Container yard inside the port of 104 000 m2 and outside the port of 100 000 m2. Storage area of 34 000 m2. There are more than 100 portal cranes, container forklifts and other cranes, pallet forklifts, container trailers and lorries of different loading capacities, including two 40 t portal cranes, one 90 t cross-country crane and one 45 t tyre crane
[23]*Longwu:* Longwu Port Co., Tel: +86 21 6434 2300, Fax: +86 21 6434 5662, Email: longwu@public1.sta.net.cn, Website: www.longwuport.com
Cargoes handled include steel, grain, construction materials and containers. Storage area of 216 000 m2 and seven warehouses totalling 48 000 m2
[24]*Luojing:* Luojing Subsidiary Co Ltd., 8 Shigang Road, Yuepu Town (Chengqiao), Baoshan District, Shanghai 200942, Tel: +86 21 5615 0090, Fax: +86 21 5615 1325
Specialises in handling of bulk cargoes
Land area of 500 000 m2 and is equipped with eleven large-sized machines, fifty mobile machines and nearly 9 km long belt conveyer systems
[25]*Ore, Coal & Steel Terminal:* Total of nine berths consisting of 2 x 200 000 t berths for ores, 1 x 70 000 t berth for coal and 6 x 30 000-50 000 t berths for steel products
[26]*Passenger Transport Corporation:* Passenger Transport Corp Ltd., 8 Yangshupu Road, Shanghai 200082, Tel: +86 21 6546 0730, Fax: +86 21 6541 8720
Specialises in passenger traffic and handling of domestic freight. It is situated in the North Bund Area and has a terminal waterfront of 1,121m and eight berths of 7,000-10,000 tonnage
[27]*Haitong International Automobile Terminal:* Haitong International Automobile Terminal Co Ltd., 3988 Zhouhai Road, Pudong New Area, Shanghai 200137, Tel: +86 21 5848 0808, Fax: +86 21 5848 2649
Specialises in ro/ro traffic
[28]*Berth:* Land area of 265 000 m2. Special yard capable of parking 7000 cars

Bunkering: Bominflot, Room 805, 400 Middle Zhejiang Road, Huangpu, Shanghai, Shanghai Province 200001, People's Republic of China, *Tel:* +86 21 6351 2072, *Fax:* +86 21 6351 3996, *Email:* bominchina@online.sh.cn, *Website:* www.bominflot.net
Cockett Marine Oil Ltd, Cockett Marine Oil (Asia) Pte.Ltd, Shanghai Representative Office, 828 Zhang Yang Road, 14H Huadu Mansion, Shanghai, Shanghai Province 200120, People's Republic of China, *Tel:* +86 21 5081 6933, *Fax:* +86 21 5081 6960, *Email:* shanghai@cockettasiachina.com, *Website:* www.cockettgroup.com
A/S Dan-Bunkering Ltd, Shanghai Rep. Office, Room 2706, CITIC Square, 1168 Nan Jing Road West, Shanghai, Shanghai Province 200041, People's Republic of China, *Tel:* +86 21 6135 2700, *Fax:* +86 21 6135 2701, *Email:* shanghai@dan-bunkering.com.cn, *Website:* www.dan-bunkering.dk
OW Bunker China Ltd, O.W. Bunker China Ltd Shanghai Rep Office, 12th Floor, Unit F, Majesty Tower, 138 Pudong Avenue, Shanghai, Shanghai Province 200120, People's Republic of China, *Tel:* +86 21 5130 2288, *Fax:* +86 21 5130 2299, *Email:* owbshanghai@owbunker.com, *Website:* www.owbunker.com
China Marine Bunker Supply Co., 13F Qian Cun Mansion A, No.2, 5th Block, Anzhen Xili, Chaoyang District, Beijing 100029, People's Republic of China, *Tel:* +86 10 6443 0717, *Fax:* +86 10 6443 0708, *Email:* business@chimbusco.com.cn, *Website:* www.chimbusco.com.cn – *Grades:* IFO120-380cSt; MGO
Cockett Marine Oil Ltd, Cockett Marine Oil (Asia) Pte.Ltd, Shanghai Representative Office, 828 Zhang Yang Road, 14H Huadu Mansion, Shanghai, Shanghai Province 200120, People's Republic of China, *Tel:* +86 21 5081 6933, *Fax:* +86 21 5081 6960, *Email:* shanghai@cockettasiachina.com, *Website:* www.cockettgroup.com
ExxonMobil Marine Fuels, 1 Harbour Front Place, 06-00 Harbour Front, Tower One, Singapore, Republic of Singapore 098633, *Tel:* +65 6885 8998, *Fax:* +65 6885 8794, *Email:* asiapac.marinefuels@exxonmobil.com, *Website:* www.exxonmobilmarinefuels.com – *Grades:* MDO; MGO; IFO – *Delivery Mode:* barge
OW Bunker China Ltd, O.W. Bunker China Ltd Shanghai Rep Office, 12th Floor, Unit F, Majesty Tower, 138 Pudong Avenue, Shanghai, Shanghai Province 200120, People's Republic of China, *Tel:* +86 21 5130 2288, *Fax:* +86 21 5130 2299, *Email:* owbshanghai@owbunker.com, *Website:* www.owbunker.com

Towage: Twenty five tugs available of 1670-5200 hp

Repair & Maintenance: China Shipping International Shipyard Co Ltd (Changxing), Xing Kai Gang, Chang Xing Island, Shanghai, Shanghai Province 201913, People's Republic of China, *Tel:* +86 21 5685 1166, *Fax:* +86 21 5685 0057, *Email:* mail@cxshipyard.com, *Website:* www.cxshipyard.com Floating dock 'CSIS Mt. Putuo Shan' of 80 000 t cap and floating dock 'CSIS Mt. Jiuhaua Shan' of 10 000 t cap, together with a 3000 m wharf
Huarun Dadong Dockyard Co. Ltd, 7th Floor Cimic Tower, 1090 Century Boulevard, Shanghai, Shanghai Province, People's Republic of China, *Tel:* +86 21 5836 3555,

Fax: +86 21 5836 5841, *Email:* info@hrdd.com.cn, *Website:* www.hrdd.com.cn Dadong floating dock for vessels up to 200 000 dwt. Huadong floating dock for vessels up to 150 000 dwt. Xingdong floating dock for vessels up to 80 000 dwt. Rundong floating dock for vessels up to 50 000 dwt. Also six repair jetties over 1350 m

Jiangnan Shipyard (Group) Co. Ltd, P O Box 3206, 2 Gaoxiong Road, Shanghai, Shanghai Province 200011, People's Republic of China, *Tel:* +86 21 6315 1818, *Fax:* +86 21 6289 4035, *Email:* jninfo@jnshipyard.com.cn, *Website:* www.jnshipyard.com.cn Three dry docks for vessels up to 80 000 dwt, 25 000 dwt and 3000 dwt

Shanghai Lifeng Shipyard, Sanlin Pudong New Area, Shanghai, Shanghai Province 200124, People's Republic of China, *Tel:* +86 21 5841 6606, *Fax:* +86 21 5841 1000, *Email:* li-feng@online.sh.cn, *Website:* www.lifeng-shipyard.com Two floating docks: Huangshang 190 m x 28.8 m and 13 000 t cap and Huangshan 164 m x 27.4 m and 9000 t cap

Shanghai Lixin Shipyard, 330 Dong Tang Road, Pu Dong, Shanghai, Shanghai Province 201208, People's Republic of China, *Tel:* +86 21 5861 2772, *Fax:* +86 21 5861 2769, *Email:* lxsy1924@sh163.net, *Website:* www.lixin-shipyard.com.cn Two floating docks: Pudong 222.5 m x 47 m with lifting cap 22 000 t and Lushan 157 m x 23.4 m with lifting cap 6500 t

Ship Chandlers: Runtong Marine Supply & Engineering Service Co. Ltd, Rooms 1301-1303, Building No.3, 251 Songhuajiang Road, Shanghai, Shanghai Province 200093, People's Republic of China, *Tel:* +86 21 6538 1199, *Fax:* +86 21 6538 0899, *Email:* shanghai@runtongmarine.com, *Website:* www.runtongmarine.com Customer Services: Lavender Chen

China National Ship Supply & Service (Group) Co. Ltd, 2nd Floor, 88 Chenhang Highway, Pudong, Shanghai, Shanghai Province 200124, People's Republic of China, *Tel:* +86 21 519 03835, *Fax:* +86 21 5190 3837, *Email:* sales@cnss.com.cn, *Website:* www.csss.com.cn

Golden Beach China Shipping Marine Service Co. Ltd, 16 Zhaojiazhai, Fengcheng Road, Yangpu, Shanghai, Shanghai Province 200093, People's Republic of China, *Tel:* +86 21 6570 4630, *Fax:* +86 21 6570 4649, *Email:* mail@friendshipmarine.com, *Website:* www.friendshipmarine.com

Golden Harvest Shipping Service Co. Ltd, 516 Linqing Road, Yangpu District, Shanghai, Shanghai Province 200090, People's Republic of China, *Tel:* +86 21 6584 3468, *Fax:* +86 21 6584 2994, *Email:* ghssco@public7.sta.net.cn, *Website:* www.cn-goldenharvest.com

Goldenwaves Marine Services & Trading Ltd, Room 202-201, 117 Songnan Bacun, Baoshan District, Shanghai, Shanghai Province, People's Republic of China, *Tel:* +86 21 5521 7780, *Fax:* +86 21 5521 7782, *Email:* goldenwaves@goldenwavesmarine.com, *Website:* www.goldenwavesmarine.com

Leader Marine Trading (HK) Co. Ltd, Suite 616, Cimic Tower, 1090 Century Avenue, Shanghai, Shanghai Province 200120, People's Republic of China, *Tel:* +86 21 5835 1816, *Fax:* +86 21 5836 1681, *Email:* zhang@leadermarine.com

Man Sang (China) Co. Ltd, No.266 Miao Pu Road, Pudong, Shanghai, Shanghai Province, People's Republic of China, *Tel:* +86 21 5885 8780, *Fax:* +86 21 5885 4238, *Email:* shanghai@mansangco.com

Seagle Marine Service Co Ltd., Room 801, No.41 Lane, 1318 Changlin Road, Shanghai, Shanghai Province 200443, People's Republic of China, *Tel:* +86 21 3387 4180, *Fax:* +86 21 3387 4182, *Email:* seaglemarine@163.com, *Website:* seaglemarine.com

Shanghai MakeFine Marine Co Ltd., 52 Dongtangjiazhai, Hongyicun, Wanggang, Pudong New District, Shanghai, Shanghai Province 201201, People's Republic of China, *Tel:* +86 21 5026 3120, *Fax:* +86 21 5026 3121, *Email:* marine@makefine.cn, *Website:* www.makefine.cn

Shanghai Ocean Shipping Supply Co. Ltd, 359 Daming Road East, Shanghai, Shanghai Province 200080, People's Republic of China, *Tel:* +86 21 6541 8141, *Fax:* +86 21 6545 0540, *Email:* supcosh@hotmail.com, *Website:* www.supcosh.com

Sunlee Hong Engineering & Supply Co. Ltd, Sunlee Hong (Shanghai) Co. Ltd, Huamin Empire Plaza, Room 23D, No.726 Yan'an Road (West), Shanghai, Shanghai Province 200050, People's Republic of China, *Tel:* +86 21 5238 0896, *Fax:* +86 21 5238 0996, *Email:* slhchina@online.sh.cn, *Website:* www.sunleehong.com

Sunshine Shipping Service Co. Ltd, Room 101, No.3 Lane 3329, Hong Mei Road, Shanghai, Shanghai Province 201103, People's Republic of China, *Tel:* +86 21 6401 6907, *Fax:* +86 21 6401 6900, *Email:* xieshen@online.sh.cn, *Website:* www.vsunshine.com

Shipping Agents: APC-Realco (HK) Ltd, Room 808, Fuhai Building, 1318 Sichuan Bei Lu, Shanghai, Shanghai Province, People's Republic of China, *Tel:* +86 21 6364 2789, *Fax:* +86 21 6364 0861, *Email:* andyyang@realco-cn.com, *Website:* www.realco.com.tw

Awards Shipping Agency Ltd, 18F (A) 760 Dongchangzhi Road, Shanghai, Shanghai Province 200082, People's Republic of China, *Tel:* +86 21 6535 6135, *Fax:* +86 21 6535 5698, *Email:* pqi@awards-sh.com

Ben Line Agencies Ltd, Room 345, Shanghai Bund 12 Building, 12 Zhong Shan Dong Yi Road, Shanghai, Shanghai Province 200002, People's Republic of China, *Tel:* +86 21 6329 6568, *Fax:* +86 21 6329 5628, *Email:* shg.mngt@benline.com.cn, *Website:* www.benlineagencies.com

Bernhard Schulte Shipmanagement (China) Co. Ltd, 1-3 F, Block 7, 1690 Cai Lun Road, Zhang Jiang, Pu Dong, Shanghai, Shanghai Province 201203, People's Republic of China, *Tel:* +86 21 6106 1333, *Fax:* +86 21 6106 1300, *Email:* eurasia.shanghai@eurasiagroup.com, *Website:* www.eurasiagroup.com

Braid Logistics Australia Pty Ltd, Room 5A 14th Floor, N 888 Yi Shan Road, Kin Ying Tower, Caoheijin Hi Tech Park, Shanghai, Shanghai Province 200233, People's Republic of China, *Tel:* +86 21 6485 6283, *Fax:* +86 21 6485 6282, *Email:* sissi@braidco.com, *Website:* www.braidco.com

Chiao Feng Shipping Ltd, Room 502-3 Shanghai Trade Square, 188 Si Ping Road, Shanghai, Shanghai Province 200080, People's Republic of China, *Tel:* +86 21 6521 6668, *Fax:* +86 21 6522 5943, *Email:* shanghai@chiaofeng.com.cn, *Website:* www.chiaofeng.com.hk

China Marine Shipping Agency Co. Ltd, China Marine Shipping Agency Shanghai Company Limited, Room No 203, Sinotrans Mansior, 188 Fujian Zhong Road, Shanghai, Shanghai Province 200001, People's Republic of China, *Tel:* +86 21 6375 7190, *Fax:* +86 21 6375 7197, *Email:* pln.ops.agtsh@sinotrans.com, *Website:* www.sinoagentssh.com

China Ocean Shipping Agency, 3rd Floor, No.13 Zhongshan Road (E), Shanghai, Shanghai Province 200080, People's Republic of China, *Tel:* +86 21 6329 0088, *Fax:* +86 21 6329 1519, *Email:* shenhd@coscologistics.sh.cn

China Sailing International Shipping Agency Ltd, 18 Yangshupu Road, Shanghai, Shanghai Province 200082, People's Republic of China, *Tel:* +86 21 6547 2288, *Fax:* +86 21 6586 3030, *Email:* service@chinasailing.com.cn, *Website:* www.chinasailing.com.cn

CMA-CGM S.A., CMA CGM China, 39F & 3506 Bund Centre, 222 Yan'an Road East, Shanghai, Shanghai Province 200002, People's Republic of China, *Tel:* +86 21 2306 9696, *Fax:* +86 21 6335 2500, *Email:* shg.genmbox@cma-cgm.com, *Website:* www.cma-cgm.com

CnC Marine Service & Engineering Ltd, Room 902, Kunlun Office Building, 393 Changshou Road, Shanghai, Shanghai Province 200060, People's Republic of China, *Tel:* +86 21 6266 9877, *Fax:* +86 21 6266 9994, *Email:* cncmarine@online.sh.cn, *Website:* www.cncmarine.com

Crew & Ships Management International, 18th Floor, A Block B, 1089 Pudong Avenue, Shanghai, Shanghai Province 200135, People's Republic of China, *Tel:* +86 21 6853 3795, *Fax:* +86 21 6855 0345, *Email:* cmi-china@cmi.net.cn, *Website:* www.cmi.gr

GAC Forwarding & Shipping (Shanghai) Ltd, 1109A-1110 Cross Tower, 318 Fuzhou Road, Shanghai, Shanghai Province 200001, People's Republic of China, *Tel:* +86 21 6391 2777, *Fax:* +86 21 6391 2206, *Email:* china@gacworld.com, *Website:* www.gacworld.com

GMT Shipping Line Ltd, Room 1702 Shanghai Xin Cheng Mansion No.167, Jiang Ning Road, Shanghai, Shanghai Province 200041, People's Republic of China, *Tel:* +86 21 5213 3068, *Email:* philip.young@gmtshipping.com, *Website:* www.gmtshipping.com

A Hartrodt International, Room 610, He Nan Road South, Central Place, Shanghai, Shanghai Province 200002, People's Republic of China, *Tel:* +86 21 6374 2488, *Fax:* +86 21 6374 1620, *Email:* shanghai@hartrodt.com.cn

Inchcape Shipping Services (ISS), Unit 1001, Tower No.1, Resource Plaza, 268 Zhongshan South Road, Shanghai, Shanghai Province 200010, People's Republic of China, *Tel:* +86 21 6332 1166, *Fax:* +86 21 6360 2115, *Email:* iss.shanghai@iss-shipping.com, *Website:* www.iss-shipping.com

Jardine Shipping Services, Unit 602, K Wah Centre, 1010 Huai Hai Zhong Road, Shanghai, Shanghai Province 200031, People's Republic of China, *Tel:* +86 21 5405 1777, *Fax:* +86 21 5405 1590, *Email:* jameswang@jsash.com.cn, *Website:* www.jardine-shipping.com

K Line Ship Management Co. Ltd, 'K' Line (China) Ltd, Room 2101, K Wah Center, 1010 Huaihai Zhong Road, Shanghai, Shanghai Province 200031, People's Republic of China, *Tel:* +86 21 5405 0099, *Fax:* +86 21 5405 1199, *Email:* shabcusvc@cn.kline.com, *Website:* www.kline.co.jp

Mediterranean Shipping Company, MSC (Hong Kong) Ltd, 5th Floor, Marine Tower, 1 Pu Dong Avenue, Shanghai, Shanghai Province 200120, People's Republic of China, *Tel:* +86 21 6104 3333, *Fax:* +86 21 6886 1059, *Email:* msc@nprc.mschkg.com, *Website:* www.mschongkong.com

Minsheng International Shipping Agency Co, 6-7th Floor, 137 Haining Road, Hongkou District, Shanghai, Shanghai Province, People's Republic of China, *Tel:* +86 21 6356 8218, *Fax:* +86 21 6356 0380, *Email:* msco@minshengsh.com, *Website:* www.msshipping.cn

NCL Shipping Agencies Ltd, Unit 1109-1110, Pidemco Tower, 318 Fuzhou Road, Huangpu District, Shanghai, Shanghai Province 200001, People's Republic of China, *Tel:* +86 21 6391 2727, *Fax:* +86 21 6391 2525, *Email:* shnmng@shn.nclshipping.com

Pen-Wallem Shipping Services Co Ltd, 10th Floor, Alison international Tower, 8 Fu You Road, Shanghai, Shanghai Province 200010, People's Republic of China, *Tel:* +86 21 6330 8618, *Fax:* +86 21 6320 1636, *Email:* wshops@pen-wallem.com, *Website:* www.wallem.com

Shanghai Changjiang International Shipping Agency (SCISA), 935 South Zhongshan Road, Shanghai, Shanghai Province 200011, People's Republic of China, *Tel:* +86 21 6318 7697, *Fax:* +86 21 6318 8165, *Email:* scisa@scisa.com.cn, *Website:* www.scisa.com.cn

Shanghai-Gdynia International Transportation Agency Co. Ltd, 27th Floor, Gong Shan Lian Building, 55 Yan An Road, Shanghai, Shanghai Province 200002, People's Republic of China, *Tel:* +86 21 6336 0465, *Fax:* +86 21 6336 1236, *Email:* oper@sga.com.cn

Shanghai United International Ocean Shipping Agency Co Ltd, 908 Doing Da Ming Road, Shanghai, Shanghai Province 200082, People's Republic of China, *Tel:* +86 21 6595 3888, *Fax:* +86 21 6595 0001, *Email:* shpg@unisco.com.cn, *Website:* www.unisco.com.cn

Sinotrans (HK) Logistics Ltd, Room 407-408 Jiu An Plaza, 258 Tong Ren Road, Shanghai, Shanghai Province 200040, People's Republic of China, *Tel:* +86 21 6289 1222, *Fax:* +86 21 6247 0222, *Email:* shanghai@sinotrans-logistics.com, *Website:* www.sinotrans-logistics.com

Sun Hing Shipping Co Ltd, Room 1905 World Trade Tower, 500 Guangdong Road, Shanghai, Shanghai Province 200001, People's Republic of China, *Tel:* +86 21 6350 0808, *Fax:* +86 21 6350 0303, *Website:* www.sunhinggroup.com

Swire Shipping (Agencies) Ltd, 712 Shanghai Dynasty Business Centre, 457 Wulumuqi Road North, Shanghai, Shanghai Province 200040, People's Republic of China, *Tel:* +86 21 6249 5398, *Fax:* +86 21 6249 5399, *Email:* lucy@uninet.com.cn

TES International Transport (China) Ltd, Room 311 Long Jiang Commercial Centre, 260 Nan Xun Road, Hongkou District, Shanghai, Shanghai Province, People's Republic of China, *Tel:* +86 21 6357 8706, *Fax:* +86 21 6357 8707, *Website:* www.teschina.com.hk

Tongsheng International Shipping Agencies, Shanghai Tongsheng International Shipping Agency Co Ltd, Room 427, 4/F, 110 Huangpu Road, Shanghai, Shanghai Province 200080, People's Republic of China, *Tel:* +86 21 6306 2959, *Fax:* +86 21 6306 4939, *Email:* shanghai@tongsheng.net.cn, *Website:* www.tongshengshipping.com

V-Grow Logistics (Shanghai) Co Ltd, Suite 1502-03, 100 Zyunyi Road, City Centre, Tower A, Shanghai, Shanghai Province 200051, People's Republic of China, *Tel:* +86 21 6237 0862, *Fax:* +86 21 6237 0863, *Email:* weimin.yang@v-grow.com, *Website:* www.v-grow.com

V. Ship Agency, 188 Si Ping Road, 1609, Trade Square, Shanghai, Shanghai Province 200086, People's Republic of China, *Tel:* +86 21 5240 2398, *Fax:* +86 21 5240 2398, *Email:* agency.china@vships.cn, *Website:* www.vships.com

World Marine Corp, Room 606 Friendship Building, 26 Sichuan Road (South), Shanghai, Shanghai Province 200002, People's Republic of China, *Tel:* +86 21 6374 5585, *Fax:* +86 21 6328 7502, *Email:* wmarsh@publics.sta.net.cn, *Website:* www.worldmarine.gr

Young Carrier Co. Ltd, Harbour Plaza, 30th Floor, 18 XI Zang Road (Middle), Shanghai, Shanghai Province 200001, People's Republic of China, *Tel:* +86 21 5385 2099, *Fax:* +86 21 5385 2082, *Email:* ymlsha@online.sh.cn

Key to Principal Facilities:—
A=Airport **C**=Containers **G**=General Cargo **P**=Petroleum **R**=Ro/Ro **Y**=Dry Bulk
B=Bunkers **D**=Dry Dock **L**=Cruise **Q**=Other Liquid Bulk **T**=Towage (where available from port)

Surveyors: ABS (Pacific), 500 North Cheng Du Road, Lucky Target Square, Shanghai, Shanghai Province 200003, People's Republic of China, *Tel:* +86 21 6322 6285, *Fax:* +86 21 6322 9649, *Email:* absshanghai@eagle.org
Bureau Veritas, 5th Floor, Wah Tai Mansion, 388 Zhao Jia Bang Road, Shanghai, Shanghai Province 200031, People's Republic of China, *Tel:* +86 21 6415 9881, *Fax:* +86 21 6415 9880, *Website:* www.bureauveritas.com
China Classification Society, 1234 Pudong Da Dao, Shanghai, Shanghai Province 200135, People's Republic of China, *Tel:* +86 21 5885 1234, *Fax:* +86 21 5885 2626, *Email:* ccssh@ccs.org.cn, *Website:* www.ccs.org.cn
CnC Marine Service & Engineering Ltd, Room 902, Kunlun Office Building, 393 Changshou Road, Shanghai, Shanghai Province 200060, People's Republic of China, *Tel:* +86 21 6266 9877, *Fax:* +86 21 6266 9994, *Email:* cncmarine@online.sh.cn, *Website:* www.cncmarine.com
Det Norske Veritas A/S, House No. 9, 1591 Hong Qiao Road, Shanghai, Shanghai Province 200336, People's Republic of China, *Tel:* +86 21 3208 4518, *Fax:* +86 21 6278 8090, *Email:* mchcn320@dnv.com, *Website:* www.dnv.com
Eurogal GSL Surveys Ltd, Room 710, Ai Hua Business Centre, 400 Wan Ping Road (South), Shanghai, Shanghai Province 200023, People's Republic of China, *Tel:* +86 21 5424 7622, *Fax:* +86 21 5424 7633, *Email:* esisha@online.sh.cn, *Website:* www.eurogal-surveys.com
Germanischer Lloyd, Room 1201, Central Plaza, 381 Huaihai M. Road, Shanghai, Shanghai Province 200020, People's Republic of China, *Tel:* +86 21 6391 5858, *Fax:* +86 21 6391 5822, *Email:* gl-shanghai@gl-group.com, *Website:* www.gl-group.com
International Shipping Bureau (ISB), 1 Pudong Avenue, 1204 Marine Tower, Shanghai, Shanghai Province 200120, People's Republic of China, *Tel:* +86 21 6886 0181, *Fax:* +86 21 6886 0182, *Email:* shang@isbchina.cn, *Website:* www.isbship.com
J & A Marine Consultant Limited, Room 306, Mansion B World Centre, 18 Tao Lin Road, Pudong, Shanghai, Shanghai Province 200135, People's Republic of China, *Tel:* +86 21 5851 6712, *Fax:* +86 21 5851 3739, *Email:* info@jamarine.com, *Website:* www.jamarine.com
Korean Register of Shipping, Zao Feng Universe Building, 14 Floor H, NO.1800 Zhong Shan West Road, Shanghai, Shanghai Province, People's Republic of China, *Tel:* +86 21 6440 1041, *Fax:* +86 21 6440 1312, *Email:* kr-shi@krs.co.kr, *Website:* www.krs.co.kr
Nippon Kaiji Kyokai, Room 2208, International Trade Centre, 2201 Yan An West Road, Shanghai, Shanghai Province 200336, People's Republic of China, *Tel:* +86 21 6270 3089, *Fax:* +86 21 6219 5699, *Email:* sc@classnk.or.jp, *Website:* www.classnk.or.jp
Polish Register of Shipping, No 107 Yangdan Road, Floor 13 B Yangdang Building, Shanghai, Shanghai Province 200020, People's Republic of China, *Tel:* +86 21 3310 0338, *Fax:* +86 21 3310 0338, *Email:* shanghai@prs.pl, *Website:* www.prs.pl
Registro Italiano Navale (RINA), Unit #05-03, Office Complex, Equatorial Shanghai, 65 Yan'an Road West, Shanghai, Shanghai Province 200040, People's Republic of China, *Tel:* +86 21 6248 2604, *Fax:* +86 21 6248 2605, *Email:* shanghai.office@rina.org, *Website:* www.rina.org
Shanghai Marine Technology Services Co. Ltd, Room 2007, Shencheng Building, No.22 Juye Road, Shanghai, Shanghai Province 200135, People's Republic of China, *Tel:* +86 21 3882 0373, *Fax:* +86 21 5851 2546, *Email:* sst66@online.sh.cn

Medical Facilities: Available

Airport: Hongqiao International Airport, 30 km

Development: Another 10-12 berths are planned at Yangshan by 2013
An LNG terminal at Yangshan is set to become operational in Spring 2009 with three 160 000 m3 storage tanks

Lloyd's Agent: Huatai Surveyors & Adjusters Co., 14-A World Plaza, 855 Pudong South Road, Shanghai, Shanghai Province 200120, People's Republic of China, *Tel:* +86 21 5836 9707, *Fax:* +86 21 5836 9709, *Email:* agency.sh@huatai-serv.com, *Website:* www.huatai-serv.com

SHANTOU

Lat 23° 21' N; Long 116° 42' E.

Admiralty Chart: 854
Admiralty Pilot: 32
Time Zone: GMT +8 h
UNCTAD Locode: CN SWA

Principal Facilities:

| P | Q | Y | G | C | | B | | T | A |

Authority: Shantou Port Group Corp., 3 Shangping Road, Shantou, Guangdong Province 515041, People's Republic of China, *Tel:* +86 754 8827 5421, *Fax:* +86 754 8829 7654, *Email:* spg@stport.com, *Website:* www.stport.com

Port Security: ISPS compliant

Approach: Draft limitation in Luyu Channel is 6.0 m, length 4.6 nautical miles, width 500 m

Anchorage: Fourteen anchorages in depths of 5.5-6.0 m; bottom of mud with good holding ground.
No.1: 23° 20' 43" N; 116° 43' 38" E in depth of 5.8 m
No.2: 23° 20' 49" N; 116° 43' 11" E in depth of 5.5 m
No.3: 23° 20' 51" N; 116° 42' 51" E in depth of 5.5 m
No.4: 23° 20' 54" N; 116° 42' 31" E in depth of 5.5 m
No.5: 23° 20' 55" N; 116° 42' 10" E in depth of 8 m
No.6: 23° 20' 57" N; 116° 41' 50" E in depth of 8 m
No.7: 23° 20' 57" N; 116° 41' 28" E in depth of 8 m
No.11: 23° 20' 36" N; 116° 39' 24" E in depth of 7.5 m
No.12: 23° 20' 32" N; 116° 39' 06" E in depth of 7.5 m
No.13: 23° 20' 30" N; 116° 38' 46" E in depth of 7.5 m
No.14: 23° 20' 28" N; 116° 38' 26" E in depth of 7.5 m
No.5 buoy: 23° 20' 52" N; 116° 40' 23" E in depth of 8 m
No.7 buoy: 23° 20' 53.5" N; 116° 40' 13.5" E in depth of 7.5 m
No.9 buoy: 23° 20' 49" N; 116° 39' 59" E in depth of 7.5 m

Pilotage: Compulsory and available 24 h. Pilot boards in pos 23° 17' N; 116° 48' E

Radio Frequency: VHF Channel 11

Tides: Range 0.55 to 2.63 m

Traffic: 2005, 17 500 000 t of cargo handled, 103 000 TEU's

Principal Imports and Exports: Imports: Cement, Fertiliser, Machinery, Oranges, Steel products, Wheat. Exports: General, Oranges.

Accommodation:

Name	Length (m)	Depth (m)	Remarks
Shantou			
Shantou International Container Terminal	460	7.5	See [1] below
Berth No.4	125.5	5.5	General cargo for vessels up to 5000 dwt
Berth No.5	110	5.5	Containers for vessels up to 5000 dwt
Berth No.6	110	6.5	General cargo for vessels up to 5000 dwt
Berth No.8	140	6	Passengers for vessels up to 5000 dwt
Berth No.9	96	6	General cargo for vessels up to 3000 dwt
Berth No.10	116	6	General cargo for vessels up to 3000 dwt
Guang Ao Berth	265	10	See [2] below
Shantou Cement Berth	145	7.5	Cement & stone for vessels up to 15 000 dwt
Mashan Berth	150	9.5	Coal for vessels up to 5000 dwt
Aotou Berth	160	7.5	Oil & LNG for vessels up to 5000 dwt
Caltex Berth	230	11	LPG for vessels up to 50 000 dwt
Haiyang Berth	120	6.5	For vessels up to 3000 dwt
Yuechang Berth	100	4.5	Chemicals & LPG for vessels up to 2000 dwt
Zhuchi Berth	100	4.5	Oil & LPG for vessels up to 5000 dwt

[1]*Shantou International Container Terminal:* Operated by Shantou International Container Terminals Ltd., Tel: +86 754 8893 9888, Fax: +86 754 8893 9880, Email: sict@sict.com.cn, Website: www.sict.com.cn
Total area of 42.5 ha with stacking cap of 20 000 TEU's and 300 reefer points
[2]*Guang Ao Berth:* General cargo, containers & soybean for vessels up to 20 000 dwt

Storage:

Location	Open (m²)	Covered (m²)
Shantou	60000	20000

Mechanical Handling Equipment:

Location	Type	Capacity (t)	Qty
Shantou International Container Terminal	Mobile Cranes		1
Shantou International Container Terminal	Container Cranes		3
Shantou International Container Terminal	RTG's		6
Shantou International Container Terminal	Forklifts		10
Berth No.4	Shore Cranes	10	2
Berth No.5	Shore Cranes	35	1
Guang Ao Berth	Shore Cranes	10	2
Guang Ao Berth	Shore Cranes	40	1
Mashan Berth	Shore Cranes	16	3

Bunkering: Available at berth and anchorage

Towage: Five tugs of 600-3400 hp

Repair & Maintenance: Available

Shipping Agents: Asia Shipping Ltd, Room 801, Haifu Building, Chaoyang Block, Shantou, Guangdong Province, People's Republic of China, *Tel:* +86 754 8893 9988, *Fax:* +86 754 8893 9977, *Email:* stasia@pub.shantou.gd.cn
Awards Shipping Agency Ltd, Chaoshan Galaxy Building, Time Plaza Western 1503, Shantou, Guangdong Province 515041, People's Republic of China, *Tel:* +86 754 8848 5508, *Fax:* +86 754 8848 5500, *Email:* leowong@awards.com.cn
China Marine Shipping Agency Co. Ltd, China Marine Shipping Agency Guangdong Shantou Company, No. 9 Jinsha Road, Shantou, Guangdong Province, People's Republic of China, *Tel:* +86 754 8868 7818, *Fax:* +86 754 8867 1555, *Email:* shipping.st@sinoagent.com
CMA-CGM S.A., CMA CGM Shantou, Room 702-3, MSA Building, 47 Haibin Road, Shantou, Guangdong Province 515041, People's Republic of China, *Tel:* +86 754 8852 9166, *Fax:* +86 754 8855 5191, *Email:* swa.genmbox@cma-cgm.com, *Website:* www.cma-cgm.com

Shantou Ping Ye International Freight Corp. Ltd, 20 Floor, Huaqiao Commercial Bank Building, No 127 Jinsha East Road, Shantou, Guangdong Province 515041, People's Republic of China, *Tel:* +86 754 8889 8555, *Fax:* +86 754 8889 0555, *Email:* generalmail@pingye.com.cn, *Website:* www.pingye.com.cn

Airport: Shantou Airport

Lloyd's Agent: Huatai Surveyors & Adjusters Co., Room 802, Jun Yuan Mansion, 155 Tian He East Road, Guangzhou, Guangdong Province 510620, People's Republic of China, *Tel:* +86 20 3881 2306, *Fax:* +86 20 3881 2470, *Email:* agency.gz@huatai-serv.com, *Website:* www.huatai-serv.com

SHANWEI

Lat 22° 48' N; Long 115° 20' E.

Admiralty Chart: 1372	**Admiralty Pilot:** 30
Time Zone: GMT +8 h	**UNCTAD Locode:** CN SWE

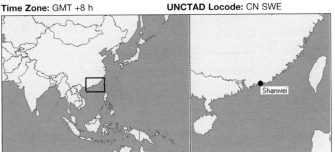

Principal Facilities:

P	Y	G	C		B		

Authority: Shanwei Harbour Administration, Shanwei, Guangdong Province, People's Republic of China, *Tel:* +86 660 332 8777

Anchorage: Pilotage anchorage in pos 22° 44.5' N; 115° 13.0' E in depth of 9.6 m

Pilotage: Compulsory and available daytime only, Pilot boards in pos 22° 45' N; 115° 13' E

Radio Frequency: VHF Channel 11

Tides: Max tidal range 1.9 m, min 0.1 m

Accommodation:

Name	Length (m)	Depth (m)	Remarks
Shanwei			
Ocean Dock	225	7.5	See [1] below

[1]*Ocean Dock:* Packaged cargo, container cargo & edible oil in bulk for vessels up to 5000 dwt

Storage: Container yard with 20 000 TEU cap

Location	Open (m²)	Covered (m²)
Shanwei	10000	20000

Mechanical Handling Equipment:

Location	Type	Capacity (t)	Qty
Ocean Dock	Shore Cranes	5	2
Ocean Dock	Shore Cranes	35	1

Bunkering: Available

Lloyd's Agent: Huatai Surveyors & Adjusters Co., Room 802, Jun Yuan Mansion, 155 Tian He East Road, Guangzhou, Guangdong Province 510620, People's Republic of China, *Tel:* +86 20 3881 2306, *Fax:* +86 20 3881 2470, *Email:* agency.gz@huatai-serv.com, *Website:* www.huatai-serv.com

SHEKOU

Lat 22° 29' N; Long 113° 54' E.

Admiralty Chart: 342/343	**Admiralty Pilot:** 30
Time Zone: GMT +8 h	**UNCTAD Locode:** CN SHK

Principal Facilities:

P	Y	G	C		B	T	A

Authority: China Merchants Port Service (Shenzhen) Co. Ltd, 8/F SKP Building, Shekou, Shenzhen, Guangdong Province 518067, People's Republic of China, *Tel:* +86 755 2668 8828, *Fax:* +86 755 2669 8113

Port Security: ISPS compliant. Container Security Initiative (CSI) designated port

Pre-Arrival Information: Vessel's should send ETA 72 h, 48 h and 24 h in advance

Approach: Draft limitation in channel is 12.5 m

Pilotage: Compulsory and available 24 h/day. Pilot boards in pos 22° 23' 40" N; 113° 53' 65" E (Urnston Roads) and 22° 18' 98" N; 113° 50' 26" E (Longguxi Hangdao)

Radio Frequency: VHF Channels 11 and 8

Tides: Average tidal range of 1.36 m

Traffic: 2007, 3 300 000 TEU's handled at Shekou Container Terminal

Accommodation:

Name	Length (m)	Depth (m)	Remarks
Shekou			
Passenger Berth	605	4.5	
Tanker Berth	260	6.5	
Berth No.1	152	7.5	General cargo & containers for vessels up to 5000 dwt
Berth No.2	170	8.8	General cargo & containers for vessels up to 15 000 dwt
Berth No.3	195	9.5	General cargo & containers for vessels up to 15 000 dwt
Berth No.4	236	10.5	See [1] below
Berth No.5	90	4.6	General & bulk cargo for vessels up to 3000 dwt
Berth No.6	176	7	General & bulk cargo for vessels up to 5000 dwt
Berth No.7	186	9.2	General & bulk cargo for vessels up to 15 000 dwt
Berth No.8	270	12	General & bulk cargo for vessels up to 35 000 dwt
Berth No.9	300	12.8	General & bulk cargo for vessels up to 76 000 dwt
Shekou Container Terminal	2550	14–16	See [2] below

[1]*Berth No.4:* General cargo, bulk cargo & cement for vessels up to 35 000 dwt
[2]*Shekou Container Terminal:* Shekou Container Terminals Ltd., Jetty Three, Harbor Road, Shekou 518069, Tel: +86 755 2685 1375, Fax: +86 755 2685 2820, Email: marketing@sctcn.com, Website: www.sctcn.com
Seven berths

Storage:

Location	Open (m²)	Covered (m²)
Shekou	140000	40000

Mechanical Handling Equipment:

Location	Type	Capacity (t)	Qty
Berth No.1	Shore Cranes	10	3
Berth No.1	Shore Cranes	35	1
Berth No.2	Shore Cranes	35	1
Berth No.2	Shore Cranes	10	3
Berth No.3	Shore Cranes	10	3
Berth No.4	Shore Cranes	10	5
Berth No.5	Shore Cranes	10	5
Berth No.7	Shore Cranes	10	6
Berth No.8	Shore Cranes	10	6
Berth No.9	Shore Cranes	10	2
Berth No.9	Shore Cranes	16	2
Shekou Container Terminal	Panamax		4
Shekou Container Terminal	Post Panamax		24
Shekou Container Terminal	Super Post Panamax		4
Shekou Container Terminal	RTG's		82

Bunkering: Available at berth and anchorage

Towage: Four tugs available
Shenzhen Lianda Towing & Tug Co. Ltd, 6/F, Merchants Port Shipping Center, Southern Harbour Road, Shekou Industy Area, Shenzhen, Guangdong Province, People's Republic of China, *Tel:* +86 755 2668 6899, *Fax:* +86 755 2669 1055

Repair & Maintenance: Yiu Lian Dockyards Ltd, Yiu Lian Dockyards (Shekou) Ltd, Jetty Three, Lian Yang Road, Shekou, Guangdong Province 518068, People's Republic of China, *Tel:* +86 755 2686 9999, *Fax:* +86 755 2668 4860, *Email:* yiuliansk@yiulian.com, *Website:* www.yiulian.com One floating dock of 240.5 m x 36 m x 6 m for vessels up to 70 000 dwt and one floating dock of 190 m x 27.8 m x 6 m for vessels up to 30 000 dwt

Shipping Agents: China Marine Shipping Agency Co. Ltd, China Marine Shipping Agency Shenzhen Company Limited, Room B.C.D, 21st Floor, Seaview Square, No. 18 Taizi Road, Shekou, Guangdong Province 518067, People's Republic of China, *Tel:* +86 755 2681 5113, *Fax:* +86 755 2681 5157, *Email:* agent@sinoagentsz.com
China Ocean Shipping Agency, 1,8,9 Floor Lianhe Building, Nanhai Road, Shekou, Shenzhen, Guangdong Province 518066, People's Republic of China, *Tel:* +86 755 2668 8998, *Fax:* +86 755 2668 9946, *Email:* hq@penavicosz.com.cn, *Website:* www.penavicosz.com
A Hartrodt International, Shenzhen Representative Office, Room 1804-05, Golden Business Centre, No.2028 Shennan Road East, Shenzhen, Guangdong Province 518007, People's Republic of China, *Tel:* +86 755 8215 7758, *Fax:* +86 755 8215 7761, *Email:* shenzhen@hartrodt.com.hk
Pen-Wallem Shipping Services Co Ltd, Shenzhen, Guangdong Province, People's Republic of China, *Tel:* +86 755 2682 0681, *Fax:* +86 755 2682 0680, *Email:* wszen@wallem.com

Key to Principal Facilities:—				
A=Airport	**C**=Containers	**G**=General Cargo	**P**=Petroleum	**R**=Ro/Ro	**Y**=Dry Bulk
B=Bunkers	**D**=Dry Dock	**L**=Cruise	**Q**=Other Liquid Bulk	**T**=Towage (where available from port)	

Shenzhen Integrity International Logistics Co Ltd, 14th Floor, China Merchants deu Centre Road, Shekou, Guangdong Province, People's Republic of China, *Tel:* +86 755 2681 9792, *Fax:* +86 755 2688 3229, *Email:* ken@szintegrity.com
Shenzhen United International Shipping Agency Co. Ltd, 32nd Floor, Times Plaza, 1 Taizi Road, Shekou, Guangdong Province 518067, People's Republic of China, *Tel:* +86 755 2667 1084, *Fax:* +86 755 2681 1699, *Email:* affairs5@sunisco.com

Airport: Shenzhen International Airport, 30 km

Development: Construction of an additional berth at Shekou Container Terminal making eight berths in all

Lloyd's Agent: Huatai Surveyors & Adjusters Co., Room 802, Jun Yuan Mansion, 155 Tian He East Road, Guangzhou, Guangdong Province 510620, People's Republic of China, *Tel:* +86 20 3881 2306, *Fax:* +86 20 3881 2470, *Email:* agency.gz@huatai-serv.com, *Website:* www.huatai-serv.com

SHENJIAMEN

harbour area, see under Zhoushan

SHIDAO

Lat 36° 52' N; Long 122° 25' E.

Admiralty Chart: -	**Admiralty Pilot:** 32
Time Zone: GMT +8 h	**UNCTAD Locode:** CN SHD

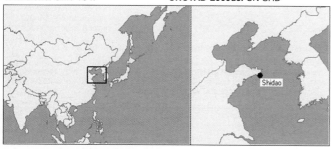

Principal Facilities:

		Y	G	C			B		T		

Port Security: ISPS compliant

Pilotage: Compulsory and available for 12 h during the day. Pilot boards vessel at the Pilot Anchorage

Radio Frequency: VHF Channel 16

Tides: Average tidal range of 1.68 m

Accommodation:

Name	Length (m)	Draught (m)	Remarks
Shidao			
Old Port	400	5	General cargo for vessels up to 10 000 dwt
New Port	800	11	General & container cargo for vessels up to 50 000 dwt

Storage:

Location	Open (m²)	Covered (m²)
Shidao	16450	1784

Mechanical Handling Equipment:

Location	Type	Capacity (t)	Qty
New Port	Shore Cranes	10	6
New Port	Shore Cranes	30	1

Bunkering: Available at berth and anchorage

Towage: One tug available

Shipping Agents: China Marine Shipping Agency Co. Ltd, China Marine Shipping Agency Shandong Company Limited Shidao Branch, Huanghai North Road, Shidao, Shandong Province, People's Republic of China, *Tel:* +86 631 728 7990, *Fax:* +86 631 737 5616, *Email:* sinoagentshidao@163.com

Lloyd's Agent: Huatai Surveyors & Adjusters Co., 14th Floor, China Re Building, No.11 Jin Rong Avenue, Xicheng District, Beijing 100140, People's Republic of China, *Tel:* +86 10 6657 6577, *Fax:* +86 10 6657 6502, *Email:* agency.bj@huatai-serv.com, *Website:* www.huatai-serv.com

SHIJIUSUO

see under Rizhao

SHILONG

Lat 23° 6' N; Long 113° 49' E.

Admiralty Chart: 346	**Admiralty Pilot:** 30
Time Zone: GMT +8 h	**UNCTAD Locode:** CN SHL

Principal Facilities:

			Y	G					

Authority: Shilong Harbour Administration, Shilong, Guangdong Province, People's Republic of China

Accommodation:

Name	Remarks
Shilong	See [1] below

[1]*Shilong:* There are thirty berths in the port totalling 941 m long. Cargoes handled include passengers, coal, ore, fertiliser and manufactured goods

Storage:

Location	Open (m²)	Covered (m²)
Shilong	32826	12000

Mechanical Handling Equipment:

Location	Type	Capacity (t)
Shilong	Mult-purp. Cranes	8

Lloyd's Agent: Huatai Surveyors & Adjusters Co., Room 802, Jun Yuan Mansion, 155 Tian He East Road, Guangzhou, Guangdong Province 510620, People's Republic of China, *Tel:* +86 20 3881 2306, *Fax:* +86 20 3881 2470, *Email:* agency.gz@huatai-serv.com, *Website:* www.huatai-serv.com

SHIPU

Lat 29° 11' N; Long 121° 51' E.

Admiralty Chart: 1759	**Admiralty Pilot:** 32
Time Zone: GMT +8 h	**UNCTAD Locode:** CN

Principal Facilities:

			Y	G					

Authority: Xiangshan Harbour Administration, 1 Yugang Nan Road, Shipu Town, Xiangshan, Zhejiang Province, People's Republic of China

Accommodation:

Name	Remarks
Shipu	See [1] below

[1]*Shipu:* Numerous berths available for vessels up to 5000 dwt handling general cargo, grain and cement

Storage: Open and covered storage areas available

Lloyd's Agent: Huatai Surveyors & Adjusters Co., 14th Floor, China Re Building, No.11 Jin Rong Avenue, Xicheng District, Beijing 100140, People's Republic of China, *Tel:* +86 10 6657 6577, *Fax:* +86 10 6657 6502, *Email:* agency.bj@huatai-serv.com, *Website:* www.huatai-serv.com

SHIQIAO

Lat 22° 55' N; Long 113° 21' E.

Admiralty Chart: -	**Admiralty Pilot:** 30
Time Zone: GMT +8 h	**UNCTAD Locode:** CN PNY

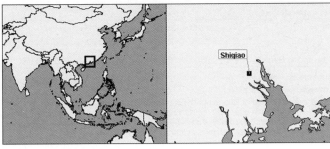

Principal Facilities:

		Y	G	C				

Authority: Shiqiao Harbour Administration, 1 Haibang Xi, Shiqiao Town, Fanyu, Guangdong Province 511400, People's Republic of China

Accommodation:

Name	Remarks
Shiqiao	Numerous berths available handling bulk, general and container cargo

Storage: Open and covered storage areas available

Mechanical Handling Equipment:

Location	Type	Capacity (t)
Shiqiao	Mult-purp. Cranes	5

Lloyd's Agent: Huatai Surveyors & Adjusters Co., Room 802, Jun Yuan Mansion, 155 Tian He East Road, Guangzhou, Guangdong Province 510620, People's Republic of China, *Tel:* +86 20 3881 2306, *Fax:* +86 20 3881 2470, *Email:* agency.gz@huatai-serv.com, *Website:* www.huatai-serv.com

SHUIDONG

Lat 21° 29' N; Long 111° 4' E.

Admiralty Chart: 3892	**Admiralty Pilot:** 30
Time Zone: GMT +8 h	**UNCTAD Locode:** CN SDG

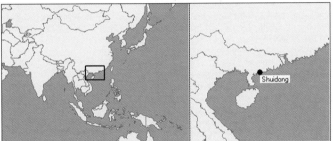

Principal Facilities:

	P	Q		G	C		B		T	

Authority: Shuidong Port Authority, Administration Office, 1 Qiaonan Road, Shuidong, Guangdong Province 525400, People's Republic of China

Approach: Draft limitation in channel is 7 m

Pilotage: Compulsory. For port pilot boards in pos 21° 23' 07" N; 111° 07' 46" E and for SBM pilot boards in pos 21° 14' 07" N; 111° 08' 45" E

Radio Frequency: VHF Channel 16

Tides: Average tidal range of 1.75 m

Accommodation:

Name	Length (m)	Depth (m)	Remarks
Harbour Bureau			
5000 t Berth	90	6.5	Base oil for vessels up to 5000 dwt
10 000 t Berth	139	7	General cargo & containers for vessels up to 10 000 dwt
Maoming			
3000 t Berth	151	7	Product oil for vessels up to 3000 dwt
7000 t Berth	140	7	LPG for vessels up to 7000 dwt
20 000 t Berth	243	7	General cargo & containers for vessels up to 20 000 dwt
30 000 t Berth	276	7	Product oil & chemicals for vessels up to 30 000 dwt
250 000 t SBM		19.6	Crude oil for vessels up to 280 000 dwt

Storage: Container yard of 2000 m2

Location	Open (m²)	Covered (m²)
Shuidong	40000	7000

Mechanical Handling Equipment:

Location	Type	Capacity (t)	Qty
10 000 t Berth	Shore Cranes	35	1
10 000 t Berth	Shore Cranes	5	1
20 000 t Berth	Shore Cranes	40	1
20 000 t Berth	Shore Cranes	16	1

Bunkering: BP Hong Kong Ltd, 21st Floor, Super Ocean Financial Centre, 067 West Yan An Road, Shanghai, Shanghai Province, People's Republic of China, *Tel:* +86 21 6278 4858, *Fax:* +86 21 6275 7702, *Email:* lucn@bp.com
China Marine Bunker Supply Co., 13F Qian Cun Mansion A, No.2, 5th Block, Anzhen Xili, Chaoyang District, Beijing 100029, People's Republic of China, *Tel:* +86 10 6443 0717, *Fax:* +86 10 6443 0708, *Email:* business@chimbusco.com.cn, *Website:* www.chimbusco.com.cn – *Grades:* IFO120-380cSt; MGO

Towage: Five tugs of 900-3400 hp

Lloyd's Agent: Huatai Surveyors & Adjusters Co., Room 802, Jun Yuan Mansion, 155 Tian He East Road, Guangzhou, Guangdong Province 510620, People's Republic of China, *Tel:* +86 20 3881 2306, *Fax:* +86 20 3881 2470, *Email:* agency.gz@huatai-serv.com, *Website:* www.huatai-serv.com

SHUNDE

Lat 22° 43' N; Long 113° 13' E.

Admiralty Chart: 3026	**Admiralty Pilot:** 30
Time Zone: GMT +8 h	**UNCTAD Locode:** CN SUD

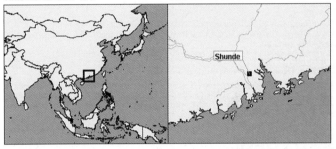

Principal Facilities:

		Y		C				

Authority: Shunde Container Terminal Co Ltd., Shunde, Guangdong Province, People's Republic of China, *Tel:* +86 757 2662 1339, *Fax:* +86 757 2661 2928, *Website:* www.shundeport.com

Accommodation:

Name	Remarks
Shunde	Consists of ten berths for container and bulk cargoes with vessel cap up to 2000 dwt

Storage: Six import and export warehouses

Mechanical Handling Equipment:

Location	Type	Capacity (t)	Qty
Shunde	Quay Cranes	40	11

Shipping Agents: China Marine Shipping Agency Co. Ltd, China Marine Shipping Agency Guangdong Company Limited Shunde Branch, No. 10 Jiangnan Road, Ronggui, Shunde, Guangdong Province, People's Republic of China, *Tel:* +86 757 2881 5333, *Fax:* +86 757 2881 5338, *Email:* sdtrans@sinotrans-shunde.com
CMA-CGM S.A., CMA CGM Shunde, Room 501-504, Hongjian Building, Feng Xiang South Road, Ronggui Town, Shunde, Guangdong Province 528303, People's Republic of China, *Tel:* +86 757 2881 9228, *Fax:* +86 757 2881 9236, *Email:* ush.genmbox@cma-cgm.com, *Website:* www.cma-cgm.com

Lloyd's Agent: Huatai Surveyors & Adjusters Co., Room 802, Jun Yuan Mansion, 155 Tian He East Road, Guangzhou, Guangdong Province 510620, People's Republic of China, *Tel:* +86 20 3881 2306, *Fax:* +86 20 3881 2470, *Email:* agency.gz@huatai-serv.com, *Website:* www.huatai-serv.com

SIERGOU

harbour area, see under Dalian

SIJING

harbour area, see under Songjiang

SILJIAO

harbour area, see under Zhoushan

Key to Principal Facilities:—			
A=Airport	**C**=Containers	**G**=General Cargo	
B=Bunkers	**D**=Dry Dock	**L**=Cruise	
P=Petroleum	**R**=Ro/Ro	**Y**=Dry Bulk	
Q=Other Liquid Bulk	**T**=Towage (where available from port)		

SONGJIANG

Lat 31° 0' N; Long 121° 13' E.

| **Admiralty Chart:** 3480 | **Admiralty Pilot:** 32 |
| **Time Zone:** GMT +8 h | **UNCTAD Locode:** CN SNG |

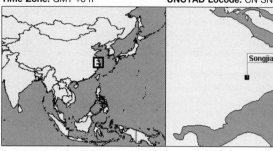

Principal Facilities:

		Y	G						

Authority: Songjiang Shipping Administration, 26 Renmin Qiao Road, Songjiang, Shanghai Province 201600, People's Republic of China

Accommodation:

Name	Remarks
Songjiang	See [1] below

[1]*Songjiang:* Consists of four harbour areas: Songjiang (berths for vessels up to 1000 dwt), Mishidu (berths for vessels up to 100 dwt), Sijing (berths for vessels up to 60 dwt) and Youdun
Cargoes handled include grain, coal, ore, fertiliser and general cargo

Storage: Open and covered storage areas available

Lloyd's Agent: Huatai Surveyors & Adjusters Co., 14th Floor, China Re Building, No.11 Jin Rong Avenue, Xicheng District, Beijing 100140, People's Republic of China, *Tel:* +86 10 6657 6577, *Fax:* +86 10 6657 6502, *Email:* agency.bj@huatai-serv.com, *Website:* www.huatai-serv.com

SONGMEN

harbour area, see under Fuzhou

SONGQUHONGDAO

harbour area, see under Maocaojie

SONGXIA

Lat 25° 41' N; Long 119° 35' E.

| **Admiralty Chart:** 2413/1761 | **Admiralty Pilot:** 32 |
| **Time Zone:** GMT +8 h | **UNCTAD Locode:** CN SON |

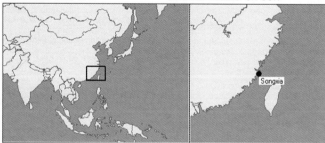

Principal Facilities:

		Y				B	T		

Authority: Port Authority of Songxia, Port Office, Songxia, People's Republic of China

Anchorage: Anchorage area established within an area bounded by the following positions:
25° 46' 68" N; 119° 48' 32" E
25° 46' 68" N; 119° 49' 51" E
25° 47' 76" N; 119° 49' 51" E
25° 47' 76" N; 119° 48' 32" E

Pilotage: Compulsory. Pilotage area bounded by the following positions:
25° 44' 03" N; 119° 40' 66" E
25° 44' 23" N; 119° 42' 32" E
25° 44' 73" N; 119° 41' 97" E
25° 44' 47" N; 119° 39' 82" E

Tides: Average range of 2.43 m

Accommodation:

Name	Length (m)	Depth (m)	Remarks
Songxia			
Yuanhong Berth	230	11.4	Vessels up to 30 000 dwt

Bunkering: Available

Towage: One tug of 2200 hp

Lloyd's Agent: Huatai Surveyors & Adjusters Co., 14th Floor, China Re Building, No.11 Jin Rong Avenue, Xicheng District, Beijing 100140, People's Republic of China, *Tel:* +86 10 6657 6577, *Fax:* +86 10 6657 6502, *Email:* agency.bj@huatai-serv.com, *Website:* www.huatai-serv.com

SWATOW

former name, see Shantou

TAICANG

Lat 31° 27' N; Long 121° 5' E.

| **Admiralty Chart:** 1619 | **Admiralty Pilot:** 32 |
| **Time Zone:** GMT +8 h | **UNCTAD Locode:** CN TAG |

Principal Facilities:

P	Q		G	C			B		T	

Authority: Taicang Port Authority, Taicang, Jiangsu Province 215400, People's Republic of China, *Tel:* +86 512 5352 3455, *Fax:* +86 512 5354 5078, *Website:* www.tcport.gov.cn

Approach: Draft limitation in channel is 10.5 m

Pilotage: Compulsory

Radio Frequency: VHF Channels 6 and 10

Tides: Average tidal range of 2.17 m

Accommodation:

Name	Length (m)	Depth (m)	Remarks
Taicang			
Taicang Terminal	2030	12	See [1] below
Berth	100	6	See [2] below
Jiangsu Yangtze Petrochemical Berth No.1	330	9	LPG, methanol, toluene, xylene for vessels up to 30 000 dwt
Jiangsu Yangtze Petrochemical Berth No.2	100	6	For vessels up to 3000 dwt
Mobil Taicang Berth	221	8.3	LPG & lube base oil for vessels up to 25 000 dwt

[1]*Taicang Terminal:* Operated by Taicang International Container Terminal Co Ltd., No.1 East Tonggang Road, Fuqiao, Taicang City 215434, Tel: +86 512 5371 0088, Fax: +86 512 5371 0099, Email: cdd@taicangterminals.com (containers) bbd@taicangterminals.com (breakbulk), Website: www.taicangterminals.com
Six berths handling container cargo & two berths handling breakbulk cargo for vessels up to 50 000 dwt
[2]*Berth:* LPG, toluene,xylene & methanol for vessels up to 300 dwt

Storage:

Location	Open (m²)	Covered (m²)
Taicang	76000	5400

Mechanical Handling Equipment:

Location	Type	Qty
Taicang Terminal	Mult-purp. Cranes	4
Taicang Terminal	Container Cranes	7

Bunkering: Available

Towage: Two tugs available

Shipping Agents: China Marine Shipping Agency Co. Ltd, China Marine Shipping Agency Taicang, 88 Jinzhou Road, Taicang, Jiangsu Province, People's Republic of China, *Tel:* +86 512 5357 3598, *Fax:* +86 512 5357 3590, *Email:* taicang@sinotrans-js.com, *Website:* www.sinotrans.com
China Ocean Shipping Agency, 7 floor, Century Fortune Mansion No 86, 12 Shanghai East Road, Taicang, Jiangsu Province 215400, People's Republic of China, *Tel:* +86 512 5359 1283, *Fax:* +86 512 5359 1285, *Email:* ptcoffc@pub.sz.jsinfo.net, *Website:* www.penavicotc.com

Tongsheng International Shipping Agencies, Taicang Tongsheng International Shipping Agency Co Ltd, 3/F 6 South Taiping Road, Taicang, Jiangsu Province 215400, People's Republic of China, *Tel:* +86 512 5893 0500, *Fax:* +86 512 5358 6103, *Email:* taicang@tongsheng.net.cn, *Website:* www.tongshengshipping.com

Lloyd's Agent: Huatai Surveyors & Adjusters Co., 14th Floor, China Re Building, No.11 Jin Rong Avenue, Xicheng District, Beijing 100140, People's Republic of China, *Tel:* +86 10 6657 6577, *Fax:* +86 10 6657 6502, *Email:* agency.bj@huatai-serv.com, *Website:* www.huatai-serv.com

TAIPING

Lat 22° 49' N; Long 113° 40' E.

Admiralty Chart: 346	**Admiralty Pilot:** 30
Time Zone: GMT +8 h	**UNCTAD Locode:** CN TAP

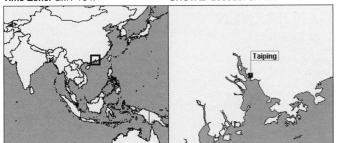

Principal Facilities:

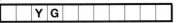

		Y	G						

Authority: Taiping Harbour Administration, 14 Changdi Road, Humen Town, Dongwan, Guangdong Province 511761, People's Republic of China

Accommodation:

Name	Remarks
Taiping	See [1] below

[1]*Taiping:* No.1 Operational Area for vessels up to 600 dwt. No.2 Operational Area for vessels up to 600 dwt. No.3 Operational Area for vessels up to 600 dwt. No.4 Operational Area for vessels up to 600 dwt
Cargoes handled include ore, cement and manufactured goods

Lloyd's Agent: Huatai Surveyors & Adjusters Co., Room 802, Jun Yuan Mansion, 155 Tian He East Road, Guangzhou, Guangdong Province 510620, People's Republic of China, *Tel:* +86 20 3881 2306, *Fax:* +86 20 3881 2470, *Email:* agency.gz@huatai-serv.com, *Website:* www.huatai-serv.com

TAIXING

Lat 32° 9' N; Long 120° 0' E.

Admiralty Chart: 1641	**Admiralty Pilot:** 32
Time Zone: GMT +8 h	**UNCTAD Locode:** CN

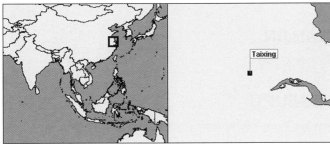

Principal Facilities:

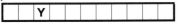

			Y						

Authority: Taixing Harbour Administration, 8 Station Road, Taixing, Jiangsu Province 225400, People's Republic of China

Accommodation:

Name	Remarks
Taixing	Numerous berths available for vessels up to 1000 dwt handling coal and ore

Storage: Open and covered storage areas available

Mechanical Handling Equipment:

Location	Type	Capacity (t)
Taixing	Mult-purp. Cranes	20

Lloyd's Agent: Huatai Surveyors & Adjusters Co., 14th Floor, China Re Building, No.11 Jin Rong Avenue, Xicheng District, Beijing 100140, People's Republic of China, *Tel:* +86 10 6657 6577, *Fax:* +86 10 6657 6502, *Email:* agency.bj@huatai-serv.com, *Website:* www.huatai-serv.com

TAIZHOU

Lat 32° 25' N; Long 119° 25' E.

Admiralty Chart: 1642	**Admiralty Pilot:** 32
Time Zone: GMT +8 h	**UNCTAD Locode:** CN TZO

Principal Facilities:

Q	Y	G	C			B		T	A

Authority: Taizhou Port Co Ltd., Gaogang District, Taizhou, Jiangsu Province 225321, People's Republic of China, *Tel:* +86 523 8698 1379, *Fax:* +86 523 8698 1848, *Email:* taizhouport@sohu.com, *Website:* www.taizhouport.com

Port Security: ISPS compliant

Pilotage: Compulsory and available during daytime only. Pilot boards vessel at the Baoshan Anchorage

Radio Frequency: VHF Channel 14

Tides: Average tidal range of 1.19 m

Traffic: 2005, 15 810 000 t of cargo handled, 39 900 TEU's

Accommodation:

Name	Length (m)	Depth (m)	Remarks
Taizhou			
Berth No.5	68	8	General cargo for vessels up to 5000 dwt
Berth No.6	65	6	Passengers for vessels up to 3000 dwt
Berth No.7	65	6	Passengers for vessels up to 3000 dwt
Zhenhai Berth	186.7	17	General cargo for vessels up to 25 000 dwt
Synthesize Berth (Taizhou)	80	8	General cargo for vessels up to 5000 dwt
Synthesize Berth (Yangwan)	330	15	General cargo & containers for vessels up to 15 000 dwt
LPG Berth	130	7.5	LPG for vessels up to 1500 dwt

Storage:

Location	Open (m²)	Covered (m²)
Taizhou	241000	7929

Mechanical Handling Equipment:

Location	Type	Capacity (t)	Qty
Taizhou	Floating Cranes	60	1
Taizhou	Floating Cranes	8	2
Berth No.5	Shore Cranes	10	2
Zhenhai Berth	Shore Cranes	5–25	3
Synthesize Berth (Yangwan)	Shore Cranes	40	1
Synthesize Berth (Yangwan)	Shore Cranes	10	3

Bunkering: Available at berth and anchorage

Towage: One tug of 800 hp and one tug of 2640 hp

Shipping Agents: China Marine Shipping Agency Co. Ltd, China Marine Shipping Agency Jiangzhou Taizhou Company Limited, No. 16 Changjiang Road, Kouan Town, Gaogang District, Taizhou, Jiangsu Province 225321, People's Republic of China, *Tel:* +86 523 8210 3153, *Fax:* +86 523 8210 3159, *Email:* tzcd@sinotrans-ty.com
China Sailing International Shipping Agency Ltd, Room 1702 Mansion Jiangong Fenghuang Road 68, Taizhou, Jiangsu Province 225300, People's Republic of China, *Tel:* +86 523 8689 0221, *Fax:* +86 523 8689 0195, *Email:* taizhou@chnsl-yz.com, *Website:* www.chinasailing.com.cn
Tongsheng International Shipping Agencies, Taizhou Tongsheng International Shipping Agency Co Ltd, 16 Changjiang Road, Gaogang District, Taizhou, Jiangsu Province 225321, People's Republic of China, *Tel:* +86 523 8210 3133, *Fax:* +86 523 8210 3178, *Email:* taizhou@tongsheng.net.cn, *Website:* www.tongshengshipping.com

Airport: Changzhou Airport

Lloyd's Agent: Huatai Surveyors & Adjusters Co., 14th Floor, China Re Building, No.11 Jin Rong Avenue, Xicheng District, Beijing 100140, People's Republic of China, *Tel:* +86 10 6657 6577, *Fax:* +86 10 6657 6502, *Email:* agency.bj@huatai-serv.com, *Website:* www.huatai-serv.com

---

Key to Principal Facilities:—			
A=Airport	**C**=Containers	**G**=General Cargo	**P**=Petroleum **R**=Ro/Ro **Y**=Dry Bulk
B=Bunkers	**D**=Dry Dock	**L**=Cruise	**Q**=Other Liquid Bulk **T**=Towage (where available from port)

TANGSHAN

Lat 39° 13' N; Long 119° 1' E.

Admiralty Chart: 1219
Time Zone: GMT +8 h
Admiralty Pilot: 32
UNCTAD Locode: CN TAS

Principal Facilities:

		Y			B		T	

Authority: Tangshan Harbour Administration, Wangtan, Leting County, Tangshan, Hebei Province 063600, People's Republic of China, *Tel:* +86 315 291 4059

Port Security: ISPS compliant

Approach: Depth in channel is 10.5 m

Anchorage: Jingtanggang Anchorage in pos 39° 09' 48" N; 119° 07' 08" E in depth of 13-15 m

Pilotage: Compulsory and available 24 h. Pilot boards vessel at Jingtang Port Anchorage

Radio Frequency: VHF Channel 16

Tides: Average tidal range of 1.98 m

Accommodation:

Name	Length (m)	Depth (m)	Remarks
Jingtang			
Berth No.1	252	11.8	Cement for vessels up to 35 000 dwt
Berth No.2	180	9.6	Coking coal for vessels up to 20 000 dwt
Berth No.3	185	9.8	Coal for vessels up to 15 000 dwt
Berth No.4	202	9.6	Dangerous & general cargo for vessels up to 15 000 dwt
Berth No.5	202	9.6	General cargo for vessels up to 35 000 dwt
Berth No.6	195	9.8	Coal for vessels up to 20 000 dwt
Berth No.7	183	9.6	Coal & general cargo for vessels up to 20 000 dwt
Berth No.8	183	10.5	Coal & general cargo for vessels up to 35 000 dwt
Berth No.9	210	10.3	Salt & general cargo for vessels up to 25 000 dwt
Berth No.10	305	10.5	General & bulk cargo for vessels up to 35 000 dwt
Berth No.11	252	11.8	Containers for vessels up to 35 000 dwt
Berth No.34	262	11.5	Propylene for vessels up to 25 000 dwt

Storage:

Location	Open (m²)
Tangshan	250000

Mechanical Handling Equipment:

Location	Type	Capacity (t)	Qty
Berth No.5	Shore Cranes	16	3
Berth No.7	Shore Cranes	10	2
Berth No.8	Shore Cranes	10	3
Berth No.9	Shore Cranes	10	1
Berth No.10	Shore Cranes	16	2

Bunkering: Available at berths

Towage: One tug of 2080 hp and one tug of 4000 hp

Ship Chandlers: Tangshan Foreign Supply-Service Co., Jingtang Harbour, Tangshan, Hebei Province 63611, People's Republic of China, *Tel:* +86 315 291 4423, *Fax:* +86 315 291 4889, *Email:* jtport@heinfo.net

Shipping Agents: China Marine Shipping Agency Co. Ltd, China Marine Shipping Agency Hebei Tangshan Company, No. 14 Meiyi Road, Tangshan, Hebei Province, People's Republic of China, *Tel:* +86 315 291 4550, *Fax:* +86 315 291 4297, *Email:* sinoagnt@heinfo.net
China Ocean Shipping Agency, 3rd Floor Penavico Building, 36-10 Xueyuan Road, Tangshan, Hebei Province, People's Republic of China, *Email:* office@penavicots.com, *Website:* www.penavicots.com
Tongsheng International Shipping Agencies, Tangshan Tongsheng International Shipping Agency Co Ltd, Jingtag Port, Tangshan, Hebei Province 063611, People's Republic of China, *Tel:* +86 315 291 1491, *Fax:* +86 315 291 1491, *Email:* tangshan@tongsheng.net.cn, *Website:* www.tongshengshipping.com

Development: New coal berth scheduled to start operations July 2007

Lloyd's Agent: Huatai Surveyors & Adjusters Co., 14th Floor, China Re Building, No.11 Jin Rong Avenue, Xicheng District, Beijing 100140, People's Republic of China, *Tel:* +86 10 6657 6577, *Fax:* +86 10 6657 6502, *Email:* agency.bj@huatai-serv.com, *Website:* www.huatai-serv.com

TANJIAHU

harbour area, see under Xiangtan

TIANJIAAN

harbour area, see under Huainan

TIANJIAZHEN

Lat 29° 54' N; Long 115° 24' E.

Admiralty Chart: 2947
Time Zone: GMT +8 h
Admiralty Pilot: 32
UNCTAD Locode: CN

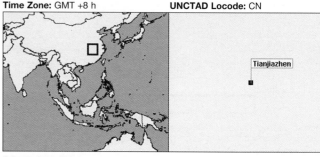

Principal Facilities:

		Y	G					

Authority: Wuxue Harbour Administration, Tianzhen, Wuxue, Hubei Province 436400, People's Republic of China

Accommodation:

Name	Remarks
Tianjiazhen	See [1] below

[1]*Tianjiazhen:* Numerous berths available for vessels up to 1000 dwt handling ore, cement and construction materials

Storage: Open and covered storage areas available

Mechanical Handling Equipment:

Location	Type	Capacity (t)
Tianjiazhen	Mult-purp. Cranes	5

Lloyd's Agent: Huatai Surveyors & Adjusters Co., 14th Floor, China Re Building, No.11 Jin Rong Avenue, Xicheng District, Beijing 100140, People's Republic of China, *Tel:* +86 10 6657 6577, *Fax:* +86 10 6657 6502, *Email:* agency.bj@huatai-serv.com, *Website:* www.huatai-serv.com

TIANJIN

see under Xingang

TIENIUPU

harbour area, see under Xiangtan

TONGJIANG

Lat 47° 38' N; Long 132° 30' E.

Admiralty Chart: -
Time Zone: GMT +8 h
Admiralty Pilot: -
UNCTAD Locode: CN TOJ

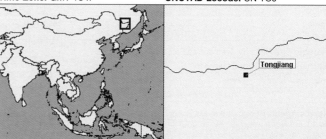

Principal Facilities:

		Y	G		R				

Authority: Tongjiang Port Authority, Tongjiang, Heilongjiang Province, People's Republic of China, *Tel:* +86 454 292 2154

Accommodation:

Name	Remarks
Tongjiang	See [1] below

[1]*Tongjiang:* Four berths available for vessels up to 5000 dwt handling coal, general cargo, passengers and ro/ro

Storage: Open and covered storage areas available

Mechanical Handling Equipment:

Location	Type	Capacity (t)
Tongjiang	Mult-purp. Cranes	16

Lloyd's Agent: Huatai Surveyors & Adjusters Co., 14th Floor, China Re Building, No.11 Jin Rong Avenue, Xicheng District, Beijing 100140, People's Republic of China, *Tel:* +86 10 6657 6577, *Fax:* +86 10 6657 6502, *Email:* agency.bj@huatai-serv.com, *Website:* www.huatai-serv.com

TONGLING

Lat 30° 57' N; Long 117° 40' E.

Admiralty Chart: 2946	**Admiralty Pilot:** 32
Time Zone: GMT +8 h	**UNCTAD Locode:** CN TOL

Principal Facilities:

		Y	G	C		B		T	

Authority: Tongling Port (Group) Co Ltd., Administration Office, Henggang, Tongling, Anhui Province 244000, People's Republic of China, *Tel:* +86 562 382 5106

Port Security: ISPS compliant

Pilotage: Compulsory and available during daytime only. Pilot boards at Liuhe Anchorage

Radio Frequency: VHF Channel 11

Traffic: 2005, 3 520 000 t of cargo handled

Accommodation:

Name	Length (m)	Depth (m)	Remarks
Tongling			
Foreign Trade Berth	231	10	See [1] below
Hengang Terminal	900	8	Seven berths for vessels up to 5000 dwt

[1]*Foreign Trade Berth:* Pig iron, river sand, cement, coal etc for two vessels simultaneously up to 5000 dwt

Storage:

Location	Open (m²)	Covered (m²)
Tongling	95000	6500

Mechanical Handling Equipment:

Location	Type	Capacity (t)	Qty
Foreign Trade Berth	Shore Cranes	10	2
Foreign Trade Berth	Shore Cranes	40	1

Bunkering: Available

Towage: One tug of 428 hp and one tug of 500 hp

Lloyd's Agent: Huatai Surveyors & Adjusters Co., 14th Floor, China Re Building, No.11 Jin Rong Avenue, Xicheng District, Beijing 100140, People's Republic of China, *Tel:* +86 10 6657 6577, *Fax:* +86 10 6657 6502, *Email:* agency.bj@huatai-serv.com, *Website:* www.huatai-serv.com

TSAMKONG

former name, see Zhanjiang

TSINGTAO

former name, see Qingdao

WAIGAOQIAO

harbour area, see under Shanghai

WAN XIAN

alternate name, see Wanzhou

WANGJIAQIAO

harbour area, see under Jinshi

WANZHOU

Lat 30° 48' N; Long 108° 22' E.

Admiralty Chart: -	**Admiralty Pilot:** -
Time Zone: GMT +8 h	**UNCTAD Locode:** CN

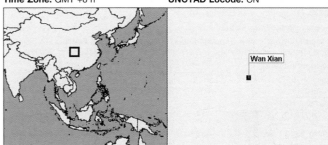

Principal Facilities:

P		Y	G	C	R		B		A

Authority: Chongqing Wanzhou Port (Group) Co Ltd., Wanzhou, Sichuan Province, People's Republic of China, *Tel:* +86 23 5829 5315, *Fax:* +86 23 5881 2934, *Email:* wzg@wzg.com.cn, *Website:* www.wzg.com.cn

Anchorage: Hongxigou Anchorage in depth of 13 m
Chenjiaba Anchorage in depth of 13 m

Traffic: 2005, 4 900 000 t of cargo handled, 11 800 TEU's

Accommodation:

Name	Length (m)	Depth (m)	Remarks
Wanzhou			See [1] below
Hongxigou Terminal	1300	10	Six berths for vessels up to 3000 dwt

[1]*Wanzhou:* The port consists of a number of facilities spread over an area of 26 km2 with 22 berths handling a variety of cargoes such as crude oil & derivatives, natural gas, coal, iron & steel, grain, non-metal ore, fertiliser, medical products and vehicles

Storage:

Location	Open (m²)	Covered (m²)
Wanzhou	25000	3000

Mechanical Handling Equipment:

Location	Type	Capacity (t)
Wanzhou	Mult-purp. Cranes	40

Bunkering: Available

Airport: Wanzhou Airport

Railway: A 3 km long railway line running from Hongxigou Terminal is linked to Wanzhou's main railway station

Development: Construction of Jiangnan Tuokou Container Terminal with four 3000 dwt berths; scheduled to be completed 2008

Lloyd's Agent: Huatai Surveyors & Adjusters Co., 14th Floor, China Re Building, No.11 Jin Rong Avenue, Xicheng District, Beijing 100140, People's Republic of China, *Tel:* +86 10 6657 6577, *Fax:* +86 10 6657 6502, *Email:* agency.bj@huatai-serv.com, *Website:* www.huatai-serv.com

WEIHAI

Lat 37° 30' N; Long 122° 7' E.

Admiralty Chart: 1260	**Admiralty Pilot:** 32
Time Zone: GMT +8 h	**UNCTAD Locode:** CN WEI

Key to Principal Facilities:—				
A=Airport	**C**=Containers	**G**=General Cargo	**P**=Petroleum	**R**=Ro/Ro	**Y**=Dry Bulk
B=Bunkers	**D**=Dry Dock	**L**=Cruise	**Q**=Other Liquid Bulk	**T**=Towage (where available from port)	

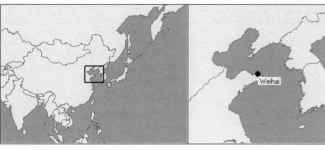

Principal Facilities:

	Y	G	C		B		T	

Authority: Weihai Harbour Bureau, 53 Haibin Middle Road, Weihai, Shandong Province 264200, People's Republic of China, *Tel:* +86 631 523 3253, *Fax:* +86 631 523 2512, *Website:* www.portweihai.com

Port Security: ISPS compliant

Approach: Draft limitation in Weihai Channel is 9.5 m and in Southern Port is 9-11 m

Anchorage: Quarantine Anchorage 1 mile NE of the N extremity of Liugong Dao in depth of approx 20 m, bottom of mud and sand with good holding ground

Pilotage: Compulsory and available 24 h. Pilots board in the quarantine anchorage

Radio Frequency: VHF Channel 16

Tides: Average tidal range of 1.35 m

Principal Imports and Exports: Imports: Chemicals, Coal, Fertilizer, Petroleum, Steel, Timber. Exports: Fruit, Glass, Light industry goods, Salt, Sand, Textiles.

Accommodation:

Name	Length (m)	Depth (m)	Remarks
Weihai			
Berth No.4	117	7	Passengers for vessels up to 5000 dwt
Berth No.5	117	7	Passengers for vessels up to 5000 dwt
Berth No.9	96	6	General cargo for vessels up to 3000 dwt
Berth No.10	200	11	General cargo for vessels up to 20 000 dwt
Berth No.11	225	11.8	Containers for vessels up to 30 000 dwt
Berth No.12	200	11	General cargo for vessels up to 20 000 dwt

Storage:

Location	Covered (m²)
Weihai	3500

Mechanical Handling Equipment:

Location	Type	Capacity (t)	Qty
Berth No.10	Shore Cranes	10	4
Berth No.11	Shore Cranes	40	2
Berth No.11	Shore Cranes	10	2
Berth No.12	Shore Cranes	10	2

Bunkering: Available at berth and anchorage

Towage: One tug of 1670 hp and one of 4000 hp

Ship Chandlers: Weihai Ocean Shipping Supply Co. Ltd, 119-18 Tongyi Road, Weihai, Shandong Province 264200, People's Republic of China, *Tel:* +86 631 521 7507, *Fax:* +86 631 522 2856, *Email:* weihaigongying@163.com

Shipping Agents: China Marine Shipping Agency Co. Ltd, China Marine Shipping Agency Shandong Company Limited Weihai Branch, 28 Haibin Middle Road, Weihai, Shandong Province, People's Republic of China, *Tel:* +86 631 530 9631, *Fax:* +86 631 532 8603, *Email:* sinowh@vip.sina.com
China Ocean Shipping Agency, Weihai, Shandong Province 264206, People's Republic of China, *Tel:* +86 631 590 0116, *Fax:* +86 631 590 0111, *Email:* penavicoweihai@vip.163.com
CMA-CGM S.A., CMA CGM Weihai, Room 1201, 12F Weisheng Building, 46 Haibin Road, Weihai, Shandong Province, People's Republic of China, *Tel:* +86 631 528 8277, *Fax:* +86 631 521 5377, *Email:* wei.gcai@cma-cgm.com, *Website:* www.cma-cgm.com

Lloyd's Agent: Huatai Surveyors & Adjusters Co., 14th Floor, China Re Building, No.11 Jin Rong Avenue, Xicheng District, Beijing 100140, People's Republic of China, *Tel:* +86 10 6657 6577, *Fax:* +86 10 6657 6502, *Email:* agency.bj@huatai-serv.com, *Website:* www.huatai-serv.com

WENZHOU

Lat 28° 0' N; Long 120° 40' E.

Admiralty Chart: 1763	**Admiralty Pilot:** 32
Time Zone: GMT +8 h	**UNCTAD Locode:** CN WNZ

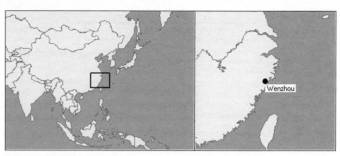

Principal Facilities:

	Y	G	C		B		T	A

Authority: Wenzhou Port Group, Mahang Wharf, Wangjiang Road, Wenzhou, Zhejiang Province 325000, People's Republic of China, *Tel:* +86 577 8818 6775, *Fax:* +86 577 8823 0420, *Email:* office@wzport.com, *Website:* www.wzport.com

Port Security: ISPS compliant

Anchorage: Huangdaao Quarantine Anchorage in pos 27° 56' 30" N; 121° 06' 41" E in depth of 7 m; mud bottom with good holding ground

Pilotage: Compulsory and only available for 8 h during the day. Pilot boards at the following positions:
In pos 27° 56' 00" N; 121° 07' 00" E (Huangdaao Quarantine Anchorage)
In pos 28° 02' 55" N; 121° 11' 98" E

Radio Frequency: VHF Channels 11, 13 and 16

Tides: Average tidal range of 3.92 m

Working Hours: 0000-0800, 0800-1600, 1600-2400

Accommodation:

Name	Length (m)	Depth (m)	Remarks
Wenzhou			
Berth No.1	86	6.1	General cargo for vessels up to 3000 dwt
Berth No.2	72	5.9	General cargo for vessels up to 2000 dwt
Berth No.3	82	5.9	General cargo for vessels up to 3000 dwt
Berth No.4	84	6.6	General cargo for vessels up to 3000 dwt
Berth No.5	90	6.15	General cargo for vessels up to 5000 dwt
Berth No.6	86	5.4	Sand for vessels up to 500 dwt
Anlan	95	4.6	General cargo for vessels up to 2000 dwt
Longwan	425	9	See [1] below
Yangfushan	481	7.2	See [2] below
Qili	582	8–13	See [3] below

[1]*Longwan:* Operated by Longwan Container Co Ltd., Tel: +86 577 8663 6951, Fax: +86 577 8663 6003, Website: www.lwct.com.cn
General cargo & containers for vessels up to 10 000 dwt
[2]*Yangfushan:* Operated by Yangfushan Port Co Ltd., Tel: +86 577 8813 8899, Fax: +86 577 8813 2127, Email: yfs@wzport.com, Website: www.yfsport.com
Coal & containers
[3]*Qili:* Operated by Qili Container Co Ltd., Tel: +86 577 6267 7787, Fax: +86 577 6267 7780, Email: info@qlct.com, Website: www.qlct.com.cn
Container terminal

Storage: Container yard of 2000 m2

Location	Open (m²)	Covered (m²)
Wenzhou	17800	15300

Mechanical Handling Equipment:

Location	Type	Capacity (t)	Qty	Remarks
Wenzhou	Shore Cranes	16	1	at berths 1-6
Wenzhou	Shore Cranes	25	5	at berths 1-6
Anlan	Shore Cranes	5	3	
Anlan	Shore Cranes	16	1	
Longwan	Shore Cranes	16	2	
Longwan	Shore Cranes	10	30	
Longwan	Shore Cranes	30	1	

Bunkering: Available at berth and anchorage

Towage: Five tugs available up to 650 hp

Shipping Agents: CMA-CGM S.A., CMA CGM Wenzhou, Rm 02.03 East, 28th Floor, Intl Trade Ctr, 8 Liming Road West, Wenzhou, Zhejiang Province 325003, People's Republic of China, *Tel:* +86 577 8886 2201, *Fax:* +86 577 8886 2203, *Email:* wnz.genmbox@cma-cgm.com, *Website:* www.cma-cgm.com
Sun Hing Shipping Co Ltd, Room 317 Fujian Hotel, 11 Hong Dian North Road, Wenzhou, Zhejiang Province 325003, People's Republic of China, *Tel:* +86 577 8833 4953, *Fax:* +86 577 8833 4953, *Website:* www.sunhinggroup.com
Wenzhou Port Freight Forwarding & Shipping Agency Co Ltd, Third Floor of Port Building, 138 Maxingseng Street, Wenzhou, Zhejiang Province, People's Republic of China, *Tel:* +86 577 8819 2571, *Fax:* +86 577 8818 2983, *Email:* ghcd@wzport.com

Airport: Wenzhou Airport

Lloyd's Agent: Huatai Surveyors & Adjusters Co., 14th Floor, China Re Building, No.11 Jin Rong Avenue, Xicheng District, Beijing 100140, People's Republic of China, *Tel:* +86 10 6657 6577, *Fax:* +86 10 6657 6502, *Email:* agency.bj@huatai-serv.com, *Website:* www.huatai-serv.com

WUHAN

Lat 30° 35' N; Long 114° 19' E.

Admiralty Chart: 2947   **Admiralty Pilot:** 32

Time Zone: GMT +8 h   **UNCTAD Locode:** CN WUH

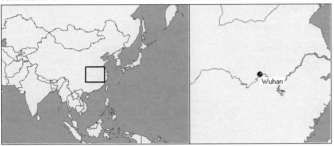

Principal Facilities:

		G	C	R		B		A

Authority: Wuhan Port Group Co Ltd, 91 Yanjiang Road, Wuhan, Hubei Province 430014, People's Republic of China, *Tel:* +86 27 8282 4776, *Fax:* +86 27 8282 4776, *Website:* www.wuhanport.com

Anchorage: Qingshanxia anchorage in depths ranging from 7-15 m for vessels up to 7000 dwt

Pilotage: Compulsory and is undertaken from 0600-2000. Pilot boards vessel at Qingshanxia Anchorage

Radio Frequency: VHF Channel 16

Traffic: 2005, 26 440 000 t of cargo handled

Accommodation:

Name	Length (m)	Depth (m)	Remarks
Wuhan			
Qingshan Foreign Trade Berth	420	12	General cargo for three vessels simultaneously up to 5000 dwt
Hanyang Berth No's 7-12	620	8	See [1] below
Wuhan International Terminal			See [2] below

[1]*Hanyang Berth No's 7-12:* General cargo for five vessels simultaneously up to 3000 dwt

[2]*Wuhan International Terminal:* Tel: +86 27 8698 3333, Fax: +86 27 8698 0000, Email: service@witport.com, Website: www.witport.com
Two berths handling containers. Stacking yard area of 45 000 m2

Storage:

Location	Open (m²)	Covered (m²)
Wuhan	388665	45880

Mechanical Handling Equipment:

Location	Type	Capacity (t)	Qty
Qingshan Foreign Trade Berth	Shore Cranes	10	2
Qingshan Foreign Trade Berth	Shore Cranes	40	1
Hanyang Berth No's 7-12	Shore Cranes	40	2

Bunkering: Available at berth and anchorage

Repair & Maintenance: China Shipbuilding Trading (Wuhan) Co Ltd., 250 Jianghan Road, Wuhan, Hubei Province 430013, People's Republic of China, *Tel:* +86 27 8277 0644, *Fax:* +86 27 8281 4292, *Email:* cstcwh@public.wh.hb.cn, *Website:* www.cstcwh.com

Shipping Agents: China Marine Shipping Agency Co. Ltd, China Marine Shipping Agency Shanghai Company Limited Wuhan Branch, 611 Jianshe Road, Hankou, Wuhan, Hubei Province, People's Republic of China, *Tel:* +86 27 8362 0283, *Fax:* +86 27 8361 7432, *Email:* sinoaghb@public.wh.hb.cn
China Sailing International Shipping Agency Ltd, Room 701 Mansion Fuxin Shanghui, 186 Xinhua Road, Jianghang District, Wuhan, Hubei Province 430022, People's Republic of China, *Tel:* +86 27 8548 3301, *Fax:* +86 27 8548 3273, *Website:* www.chinasailing.com.cn
CMA-CGM S.A., CMA CGM Wuhan, Room 2502-2503, Wuhan Inter. Business Tower, 186 Xinhua Avenue, Wuhan, Hubei Province 430022, People's Republic of China, *Tel:* +86 27 8535 0728, *Fax:* +86 27 8535 0729, *Email:* whu.genmbox@cma-cgm.com, *Website:* www.cma-cgm.com
A Hartrodt International, Room 310, No.134 YanJiang Road, Wuhan, Hubei Province 430014, People's Republic of China, *Tel:* +86 27 8284 9321, *Fax:* +86 27 8282 2423, *Email:* wuhan@hartrodt.com.cn
K Line Ship Management Co. Ltd, 'K' Line (China) Ltd, Room 1605, China Merchants Bank Tower, 518 Construction Road, Wuhan, Hubei Province 430022, People's Republic of China, *Tel:* +86 27 5950 0986, *Fax:* +86 27 5950 0987, *Website:* www.kline.co.jp
Young Carrier Co. Ltd, Room 2511 New World International Trade Tower, 568 Jianshe Avenue, Wuhan, Hubei Province 430022, People's Republic of China, *Tel:* +86 27 6885 0911, *Fax:* +86 27 6885 0915, *Email:* spike.li@yml.com.cn, *Website:* www.yml.com.cn

Surveyors: China Classification Society, 128 Liujiaoting New Road, Qiaokou District, Wuhan, Hubei Province 430022, People's Republic of China, *Tel:* +86 27 8586 4947, *Fax:* +86 27 8585 6274, *Email:* ccswh@ccs.org.cn, *Website:* www.ccs.org.cn
Det Norske Veritas A/S, Room 1008, Wuhan International Trade Commerce Centre, 566 Jian She Avenue, Wuhan, Hubei Province 430022, People's Republic of China, *Tel:* +86 27 8579 9725, *Fax:* +86 27 8571 8426, *Email:* mchcn323@dnv.com, *Website:* www.dnv.com
Germanischer Lloyd, Dongsha Mansion A-18B, 122 Zhongbei Road, Wuchang District, Wuhan, Hubei Province 430070, People's Republic of China, *Tel:* +86 27 5980 8958, *Fax:* +86 27 5980 8959, *Email:* gl-wuhan@gl-group.com, *Website:* www.gl-group.com

Airport: Wuhan Tianhe International Airport

Lloyd's Agent: Huatai Surveyors & Adjusters Co., 14th Floor, China Re Building, No.11 Jin Rong Avenue, Xicheng District, Beijing 100140, People's Republic of China, *Tel:* +86 10 6657 6577, *Fax:* +86 10 6657 6502, *Email:* agency.bj@huatai-serv.com, *Website:* www.huatai-serv.com

WUHU

Lat 31° 20' N; Long 118° 22' E.

Admiralty Chart: 2946   **Admiralty Pilot:** 32

Time Zone: GMT +8 h   **UNCTAD Locode:** CN WHI

Principal Facilities:

		Y	G	C		B		T	

Authority: Wuhu Port (Group) Co Ltd., Wuhu, Anhui Province, People's Republic of China, *Tel:* +86 553 584 0501, *Fax:* +86 553 584 0510, *Website:* www.wuhuport.com

Port Security: ISPS compliant

Anchorage: Wuhu Anchorage in depths of 8-12 m in mud and sand for vessels from 10 000-15 000 dwt

Pilotage: Compulsory and available 0800-1700. Pilot boards at Wuhu Harbour Master Station

Radio Frequency: VHF Channel 9

Tides: Average tidal range of 0.1 m

Traffic: 2005, 18 500 000 t of cargo handled, 64 200 TEU's

Working Hours: 0730-1130, 1330-0230

Accommodation:

Name	Length (m)	Depth (m)	Remarks
Jiangan			
Berth No.5	65	5.8	General cargo for vessels up to 3000 dwt
Berth No.6	35	4	General cargo for vessels up to 1500 dwt
Berth No.8	90	20.9	Passengers for vessels up to 3000 dwt
Berth No.11	35	6	Cement for vessels up to 1500 dwt
Berth No.12	61	14.8	General cargo
Berth No.13	36	7.9	Project cargo for vessels up to 1500 dwt
Zhujiaqiao			
Berth No.15	72	4.8	Ore for vessels up to 1500 dwt
Berth No.16	60	6.4	Ore for vessels up to 3000 dwt
Berth No.17	402	9	Bulk cargo & containers
Yugang			
Berth No.29	188	4.5	General cargo for vessels up to 1500 dwt
Berth No.32	82	4.5	Coal for vessels up to 3000 dwt

Storage: Container yard of 26 000 m2

Location	Open (m²)	Covered (m²)
Wuhu	121000	35150

Mechanical Handling Equipment:

Location	Type	Capacity (t)	Qty
Wuhu	Floating Cranes	15	1
Berth No.6	Shore Cranes	3	1
Berth No.11	Shore Cranes	3	1
Berth No.13	Shore Cranes	15	1
Berth No.15	Shore Cranes	3	2
Berth No.16	Shore Cranes	5	1

Key to Principal Facilities:—		
A=Airport	**C**=Containers	**G**=General Cargo
B=Bunkers	**D**=Dry Dock	**L**=Cruise

P=Petroleum	**R**=Ro/Ro	**Y**=Dry Bulk
Q=Other Liquid Bulk	**T**=Towage (where available from port)	

Location	Type	Capacity (t)	Qty
Berth No.16	Shore Cranes	25	1
Berth No.17	Shore Cranes	16	1
Berth No.17	Shore Cranes	10	1
Berth No.29	Shore Cranes	5	2
Berth No.29	Shore Cranes	10	2

Bunkering: Available

Towage: Five tugs available up to 980 hp

Shipping Agents: China Marine Shipping Agency Co. Ltd, China Marine Shipping Agency Anhui Wuhu Company, 4th Floor, 67 Zheshan Road (West), Wuhu, Anhui Province 241001, People's Republic of China, *Tel:* +86 553 585 1855, *Fax:* +86 553 585 6021, *Email:* wuhu@sinoagent.com

Surveyors: Det Norske Veritas A/S, c/o Wuhu Shipyard, 41 Changjiang Road, Wuhu, Anhui Province, People's Republic of China, *Tel:* +86 553 387 8991, *Fax:* +86 553 387 8991, *Website:* www.dnv.com

Airport: Nanjing Lukou International Airport and Hefei Luogang Airport

Lloyd's Agent: Huatai Surveyors & Adjusters Co., 14th Floor, China Re Building, No.11 Jin Rong Avenue, Xicheng District, Beijing 100140, People's Republic of China, *Tel:* +86 10 6657 6577, *Fax:* +86 10 6657 6502, *Email:* agency.bj@huatai-serv.com, *Website:* www.huatai-serv.com

WUXUE

Lat 29° 51' N; Long 115° 33' E.

Admiralty Chart: 2947	**Admiralty Pilot:** 32
Time Zone: GMT +8 h	**UNCTAD Locode:** CN

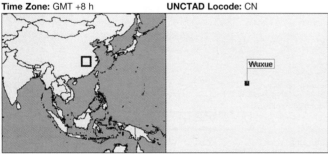

Principal Facilities:

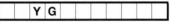

Y G

Authority: Wuxue Harbour Administration, 205 Hejie, Wuxue, Hubei Province 436400, People's Republic of China

Accommodation:

Name	Remarks
Wuxue	Numerous berths and pontoons available handling coal, sand and construction materials

Storage: Open and covered storage areas available

Lloyd's Agent: Huatai Surveyors & Adjusters Co., 14th Floor, China Re Building, No.11 Jin Rong Avenue, Xicheng District, Beijing 100140, People's Republic of China, *Tel:* +86 10 6657 6577, *Fax:* +86 10 6657 6502, *Email:* agency.bj@huatai-serv.com, *Website:* www.huatai-serv.com

WUZHOU

Lat 23° 29' N; Long 111° 16' E.

Admiralty Chart: -	**Admiralty Pilot:** -
Time Zone: GMT +8 h	**UNCTAD Locode:** CN WUZ

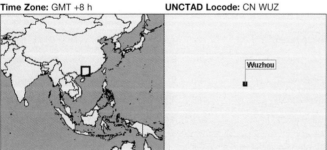

Principal Facilities:

Y G

Authority: Wuzhou Harbour Administration, 59 Nandi Road, Wuzhou, Guangxi Province 543000, People's Republic of China

Accommodation:

Name	Remarks
Wuzhou	See [1] below

[1]*Wuzhou:* Numerous berths available for vessels up to 500 dwt handling passengers, coal, manufactured goods, fertiliser, ore and cement

Storage: Open and covered storage areas available

Lloyd's Agent: Huatai Surveyors & Adjusters Co., 14th Floor, China Re Building, No.11 Jin Rong Avenue, Xicheng District, Beijing 100140, People's Republic of China, *Tel:* +86 10 6657 6577, *Fax:* +86 10 6657 6502, *Email:* agency.bj@huatai-serv.com *Website:* www.huatai-serv.com

XIAMEN

Lat 24° 27' N; Long 118° 4' E.

Admiralty Chart: 3449/3452	**Admiralty Pilot:** 32
Time Zone: GMT +8 h	**UNCTAD Locode:** CN XMN

Principal Facilities:

Y G C   B   T A

Authority: Xiamen Municipal Port Authorities, Harbour Building, 127 Dongdu Road, Xiamen, Fujian Province 361012, People's Republic of China, *Tel:* +86 592 561 4889, *Fax:* +86 592 561 2682, *Website:* www.portxiamen.com.cn

Port Security: ISPS compliant

Approach: Draft limitation in Houyu Channel is 8 m

Anchorage: Pilot and Quarantine Anchorage in pos 24° 24' 30" N; 118° 05' 16" E in depth of 12 m

Pilotage: Compulsory and available during daytime only. Pilot boards vessel at Pilot Anchorage

Radio Frequency: VHF Channels 16, 12 and 25

Tides: Average tidal range of 3.98 m

Traffic: 2006, 77 921 000 t of cargo handled, 4 018 700 TEU's

Accommodation:

Name	Length (m)	Depth (m)	Draught (m)	Remarks
Haicang				
Xiamen International Container Terminal (XICT)	640	13.3		See [1] below
Xiamen Songyu Container Terminal	1246	17		Three berths. 50-50 joint venture between APM Terminals and Xiamen Port Group
Heping				
Berth No.1	100	7.9		See [2] below
Berth No.2	100	8.4		See [3] below
Berth No.3	120	9.9		See [4] below
Container Berth	212	11		Containers for vessels up to 15 000 dwt
Dongdu				
Berth No.2	254	11.7		Grain for vessels up to 50 000 dwt
Berth No.3	190	11.7		See [5] below
Berth No.4	166	9.5		See [6] below
Berth No's 12-16	976		13.5	See [7] below
Haitian				See [8] below
Berth No.5	260	13.4		
Berth No.6	170	12.2		
Berth No.7	177	12.2		
Berth No.8	303	13.3		
Berth No.9	190	13.3		
Berth No.10	207	13.8		
Berth No.11	203	13.8		

[1]*Xiamen International Container Terminal (XICT):* Operated by Xiamen International Container Terminals Ltd., Tel: +86 592 689 0888, Fax:+86 592 689 0601, Email: xict@xict.com.cn, Website: www.xict.com.cn
Consists of three berths with total area of 48 ha
[2]*Berth No.1:* General cargo & passengers for vessels up to 10 000 dwt
[3]*Berth No.2:* General cargo & passengers for vessels up to 5000 dwt
[4]*Berth No.3:* General cargo & passengers for vessels up to 10 000 dwt
[5]*Berth No.3:* Bulk fertilizer for vessels up to 15 000 dwt
[6]*Berth No.4:* General cargo for vessels up to 10 000 dwt
[7]*Berth No's 12-16:* Operated by Xiamen New World Xiangyu Terminals Co Ltd (NWXY), No.8 Xiangyu Load, Huli District, Xiamen 361006, Tel: +86 592 562 5888, Fax: +86 592 603 5674, Email: xyqbus@nwxy.com, Website: www.nwxy.com
Total area of 488 000 m2. Container freight station of 7110 m2. Yard stacking cap of 30 250 TEU's
[8]*Haitian:* Operated by Xiamen Haitian Container Terminals Ltd (XHCT), Tel: +86 592 582 9716, Fax: +86 592 562 7135, Email: wys@xhct.com.cn, Website: www.xhct.com.cn
Container terminal with stacking area of 330 000 m2 and warehouse space of 9345 m2. 1052 reefer points

Storage: Container yard of 70 000 m2

Location	Open (m²)	Covered (m²)
Xiamen	378837	51053

Mechanical Handling Equipment:

Location	Type	Capacity (t)	Qty
Xiamen	Floating Cranes	60	1
Xiamen	Floating Cranes	100	1
Xiamen International Container Terminal (XICT)	Mult-purp. Cranes		2
Xiamen International Container Terminal (XICT)	Mobile Cranes		3
Xiamen International Container Terminal (XICT)	Container Cranes		6
Xiamen International Container Terminal (XICT)	RTG's		22
Xiamen International Container Terminal (XICT)	Forklifts		15
Berth No.1	Shore Cranes	1.5	2
Berth No.2	Shore Cranes	1.5	2
Berth No.3	Shore Cranes	3–5	2
Container Berth	Container Cranes	30.5	1
Berth No.2	Shore Cranes	10	3
Berth No.3	Shore Cranes	10	3
Berth No.4	Shore Cranes	10	3
Berth No's 12-16	Container Cranes	40–45	9
Berth No's 12-16	RTG's	35–41	21
Berth No's 12-16	Reach Stackers	41–45	3
Haitian	Container Cranes	30.5–61	6
Haitian	RTG's		28
Haitian	Straddle Carriers		11

Bunkering: China Marine Bunker Supply Co., 13F Qian Cun Mansion A, No.2, 5th Block, Anzhen Xili, Chaoyang District, Beijing 100029, People's Republic of China, *Tel:* +86 10 6443 0717, *Fax:* +86 10 6443 0708, *Email:* business@chimbusco.com.cn, *Website:* www.chimbusco.com.cn – *Grades:* IFO120-380cSt; MGO

Towage: Two tugs of 1670 hp and one tug of 4140 hp

Ship Chandlers: Xiamen A-One Ocean Shipping Supply Co. Ltd, 128 Dongdu Road, Xiamen, Fujian Province 361012, People's Republic of China, *Tel:* +86 592 6031100, *Fax:* +86 592 561 4267, *Email:* a-one@xmshipsupplier.com, *Website:* www.xmshipsupplier.com

Shipping Agents: Awards Shipping Agency Ltd, Room F-P 10/F Bonded Goods Market Building, Bonded Goods Market Building, 88 Xiangyu Road, Hull District, Xiamen, Fujian Province 361006, People's Republic of China, *Tel:* +86 592 575 0858, *Fax:* +86 592 575 0851, *Email:* larry@awards-xm.com
Ben Line Agencies Ltd, B3, 17/F, Great Power Building, No.9 Hubin Xi Road, Fujian, Xiamen, Fujian Province 361004, People's Republic of China, *Tel:* +86 592 239 7990, *Fax:* +86 592 239 7718, *Email:* xmn.general@benline.com.cn, *Website:* www.benlineagencies.com
Chiao Feng Shipping Ltd, 3A Yinlong Building, 258 Dongdu Road, Xiamen, Fujian Province 361012, People's Republic of China, *Tel:* +86 592 268 5666, *Fax:* +86 592 268 5665, *Email:* xiamen@chiaofeng.com.cn, *Website:* www.chiaofeng.com.hk
China Marine Shipping Agency Co. Ltd, China Marine Shipping Agency Fujian Company Limited Xiamen Branch, 3rd Floor, Haitian Logistics Center, No. 1 Haitian Road, Huli District, Xiamen, Fujian Province 361006, People's Republic of China, *Tel:* +86 592 567 8702, *Fax:* +86 592 567 8123, *Email:* ops@sinoagentxm.com, *Website:* www.sinotrans.com
China Ocean Shipping Agency, Shipping Centre, 809 Songyu Road, Central, Haicang District, Xiamen, Fujian Province 361026, People's Republic of China, *Tel:* +86 592 689 7331, *Fax:* +86 592 689 7335, *Email:* pcc@penavicoxm.com, *Website:* www.penavicoxm.com
CMA-CGM S.A., CMA CGM Xiamen, 22nd Floor, International Plaza, 8 Lujiang Road, Xiamen, Fujian Province 361000, People's Republic of China, *Tel:* +86 592 266 6666, *Fax:* +86 592 266 6600, *Email:* xia.genmbox@cma-cgm.com, *Website:* www.cma-cgm.com
Everwin Shipping (Xiamen) Co Ltd, Suite N, 7th Floor, Bonded Market Building, 88 Xiangyu Road, Xiamen, Fujian Province, People's Republic of China, *Tel:* +86 592 560 5523, *Fax:* +86 592 602 5640, *Email:* info@everwinshipping.com, *Website:* www.everwinshipping.com
GAC Forwarding & Shipping (Shanghai) Ltd, Room 0401 Bingo City, 57 Hubin Bei Road, Xiamen, Fujian Province, People's Republic of China, *Tel:* +86 592 566 6520, *Fax:* +86 592 566 6523, *Email:* david.huang@gacworld.com, *Website:* www.gacworld.com
K Line Ship Management Co. Ltd, 'K' Line (China) Ltd, Room 2715-2716, Bank Center, 189 Xiahe Road, Xiamen, Fujian Province 361003, People's Republic of China, *Tel:* +86 592 239 4588, *Fax:* +86 592 239 4760, *Website:* www.kline.co.jp
Lianfeng Shipping Co. Ltd, Room 209 Huicheng Commercial Complex, 839 Xia He Road, Xiamen, Fujian Province, People's Republic of China, *Tel:* +86 592 508 7201, *Fax:* +86 592 508 7203, *Email:* xmnlfhj@public.xm.fj.cn
Mediterranean Shipping Company, MSC (Hong Kong) Ltd, 23rd Floor, Zhongmin Building, 72 North Hubin Road, Xiamen, Fujian Province 361012, People's Republic of China, *Tel:* +86 592 535 0222, *Fax:* +86 592 536 1376, *Email:* msc@mschkg.com, *Website:* www.mschongkong.com
Pen-Wallem Shipping Services Co Ltd, Xiamen, Fujian Province, People's Republic of China, *Tel:* +86 592 318 8138, *Fax:* +86 592 318 8133, *Email:* waixia@pen-wallem.com, *Website:* www.pen-wallem.com
Sun Hing Shipping Co Ltd, Unit 6-7, 29/F, The Bank Centre, 189 Xiahe Road, Xiamen, Fujian Province 361033, People's Republic of China, *Tel:* +86 592 239 8239, *Fax:* +86 592 239 9239, *Website:* www.sunhinggroup.com
Xiamen Globelink China Logistics Ltd, Unit G, 9th Floor International Plaza, 8 Lujiang

Road, Xiamen, Fujian Province 361006, People's Republic of China, *Tel:* +86 592 211 9888, *Fax:* +86 592 207 9111, *Website:* www.china-logistics.com
Young Carrier Co. Ltd, The Bank Center, Room 03-07, 30th Floor, 189 Xiamen Road, Xiamen, Fujian Province, People's Republic of China, *Tel:* +86 592 239 5567, *Fax:* +86 592 239 6660, *Email:* ymlxmn@xpublic.fz.fj.cn

Surveyors: Huatai Surveyors & Adjusters Co., Room 1603, Atlantic Centre 9, West Hubin Road, Xiamen, Fujian Province 361003, People's Republic of China, *Tel:* +86 592 268 1230, *Fax:* +86 592 268 1235, *Email:* xiamen@huatai-serv.com

Airport: Xiamen International Airport

Railway: Xiamen is joined to the national railway system by the Yingtan-Xiamen railroad

Development: Cosco Pacific and CMA CGM will build two container terminals in the Haicang area. The Cosco Pacific Terminal will offer a quay length of 1500 m, while the CMA CGM terminal will consist of two 370 m berths

Lloyd's Agent: Huatai Surveyors & Adjusters Co., 14th Floor, China Re Building, No.11 Jin Rong Avenue, Xicheng District, Beijing 100140, People's Republic of China, *Tel:* +86 10 6657 6577, *Fax:* +86 10 6657 6502, *Email:* agency.bj@huatai-serv.com, *Website:* www.huatai-serv.com

XIANGFAN

Lat 32° 0' N; Long 112° 8' E.

Admiralty Chart: -	**Admiralty Pilot:** -
Time Zone: GMT +8 h	**UNCTAD Locode:** CN

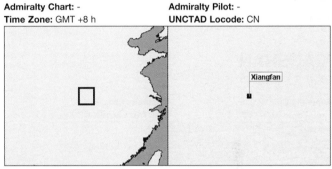

Principal Facilities:

		Y	G						

Authority: Xiangfan Shipping Administration, 14 Danjiang Road, Xiangfan, Hubei Province 441000, People's Republic of China

Accommodation:

Name	Remarks
Xiangfan	See [1] below

[1]*Xiangfan:* Numerous berths available for vessels up to 500 dwt handling fertiliser, construction materials, ore and cotton

Storage: Open and covered storage areas available

Mechanical Handling Equipment:

Location	Type	Capacity (t)
Xiangfan	Mult-purp. Cranes	8

Lloyd's Agent: Huatai Surveyors & Adjusters Co., 14th Floor, China Re Building, No.11 Jin Rong Avenue, Xicheng District, Beijing 100140, People's Republic of China, *Tel:* +86 10 6657 6577, *Fax:* +86 10 6657 6502, *Email:* agency.bj@huatai-serv.com, *Website:* www.huatai-serv.com

XIANGLUJIAO

harbour area, see under Dalian

XIANGTAN

Lat 27° 51' N; Long 112° 53' E.

Admiralty Chart: -	**Admiralty Pilot:** -
Time Zone: GMT +8 h	**UNCTAD Locode:** CN XTA

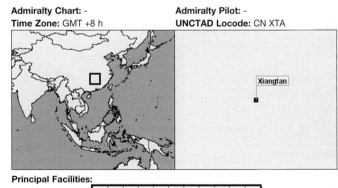

Principal Facilities:

			Y	G					

Key to Principal Facilities:—			
A=Airport	**C**=Containers	**G**=General Cargo	**P**=Petroleum **R**=Ro/Ro **Y**=Dry Bulk
B=Bunkers	**D**=Dry Dock	**L**=Cruise	**Q**=Other Liquid Bulk **T**=Towage (where available from port)

LLOYD'S LIST PORTS OF THE WORLD 2009

Authority: Xiangtan Harbour Administration, Shaoshan Xi Road, Xiangtan, Hunan Province 411100, People's Republic of China

Accommodation:

Name	Remarks
Xiangtan	
Majiahe	Four wharves handling construction materials & cement
Tieniupu	Two wharves handling ore
Tanjiahu	Four berths handling coal & ore for vessels up to 500 dwt
Dabuqiao	Four berths handling sand & stone
Hexi	Numerous berths handling iron and steel, fertiliser, cement, grain & timber
Yijiawan	Five wharves handling coal, sand, stone & general cargo

Storage: Open and covered storage areas available

Lloyd's Agent: Huatai Surveyors & Adjusters Co., 14th Floor, China Re Building, No.11 Jin Rong Avenue, Xicheng District, Beijing 100140, People's Republic of China, *Tel:* +86 10 6657 6577, *Fax:* +86 10 6657 6502, *Email:* agency.bj@huatai-serv.com, *Website:* www.huatai-serv.com

XIANGYU

harbour area, see under Xiamen

XIAOSHAN

Lat 30° 9' N; Long 120° 15' E.

Admiralty Chart: 2946
Time Zone: GMT +8 h
Admiralty Pilot: 32
UNCTAD Locode: CN XIS

Principal Facilities:

P		Y	G						

Authority: Xiaoshan Shipping Administration, 91 Xiaoxi Road, Chengxiang Town, Xiaoshan, Zhejiang Province 311200, People's Republic of China

Accommodation:

Name	Remarks
Xiaoshan	See [1] below

[1]Xiaoshan: Numerous berths available for vessels up to 40 dwt handling grain, ore, coal, fertiliser, timber, iron & steel, cement, petroleum and salt

Lloyd's Agent: Huatai Surveyors & Adjusters Co., 14th Floor, China Re Building, No.11 Jin Rong Avenue, Xicheng District, Beijing 100140, People's Republic of China, *Tel:* +86 10 6657 6577, *Fax:* +86 10 6657 6502, *Email:* agency.bj@huatai-serv.com, *Website:* www.huatai-serv.com

XIASHI

Lat 30° 32' N; Long 120° 41' E.

Admiralty Chart: 2946
Time Zone: GMT +8 h
Admiralty Pilot: 32
UNCTAD Locode: CN

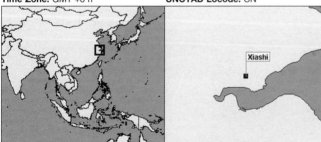

Principal Facilities:

		Y	G						

Authority: Haining Shipping Administration, 25 Jianshe Road, Xiashi Town, Haining, Zhejiang Province 314400, People's Republic of China

Accommodation:

Name	Remarks
Xiashi	Numerous berths for vessels up to 100 dwt

Mechanical Handling Equipment:

Location	Type	Capacity (t)
Xiashi	Mult-purp. Cranes	5

Lloyd's Agent: Huatai Surveyors & Adjusters Co., 14th Floor, China Re Building, No.11 Jin Rong Avenue, Xicheng District, Beijing 100140, People's Republic of China, *Tel:* +86 10 6657 6577, *Fax:* +86 10 6657 6502, *Email:* agency.bj@huatai-serv.com, *Website:* www.huatai-serv.com

XIJI

harbour area, see under Guangzhou

XINCHANG

harbour area, see under Nanhui

XINGANG

Lat 38° 59' N; Long 117° 45' E.

Admiralty Chart: 2653/2654
Time Zone: GMT +8 h
Admiralty Pilot: 32
UNCTAD Locode: CN XGG

Principal Facilities:

P		Y	G	C			B	D	T	A

Authority: Tianjin Port (Group) Co Ltd, 35 Xingang Road No.2, Tanggu, Tianjin, Tianjin Municipality 300456, People's Republic of China, *Tel:* +86 22 2579 3466, *Fax:* +86 22 2570 9747, *Email:* waishichu@ptacn.com, *Website:* www.ptacn.com

Officials: Chairman: Yu Rumin.

Port Security: ISPS compliant

Approach: The main channel is dredged to a depth of 12 m. The channel is 12 nautical miles long with a width of 180 m. Draught limitation 10 m. Dredging is carried out when necessary

Anchorage: Dagu North Anchorage: 4 miles ENE of Dagu Light in depth of 7-14 m for vessels with draught less than 10.5 m (excluding vessels with dangerous cargo, tankers and bulk chemical vessels)
Dagu South Anchorage: 4 miles ESE of Dagu Light in depth of 11-16 m for vessels with dangerous cargoes of draught over 8 m and other vessels over 10 m draught
Dagu Tanker Anchorage: 1.5 miles S of Dagu Light in depth of 8-11 m for tankers and bulk chemical vessels with draught less than 8 m
Vessels over 100 000 dwt: 12 miles ESE of Dagu Light in depth of 19-22 m

Pilotage: Compulsory for foreign flag vessels, available 24 h - pilots board at Dagu anchorage

Radio Frequency: Pilotage on VHF Channel 71. Foreign vessel agency on VHF Channel 11

Tides: Tidal range max 4.37 m. Average 2.48 m

Traffic: 2006, 257 597 000 t of cargo handled, 5 950 000 TEU's

Maximum Vessel Dimensions: 50 000 dwt

Principal Imports and Exports: Imports: Equipment, Fertilizer, General cargo, Grain, Steel. Exports: Coal, Coke, Manufactured goods, Non-metal ore, Salt.

Working Hours: Round the clock

Accommodation: Container facilities: Tianjin Orient Container Terminals Co Ltd., (TOCT), Tel: +86 22 2570 0710, Email: toct@toct.com.cn, Website: www.toct.com.cn, operate four berths totalling 1150 m long with draft of 14 m with eight container cranes of 35-40 t cap, nineteen RTG's and two reach stackers
Tianjin Five Continents International Container Terminal Co Ltd., Tel: +86 22 2570 1539, Fax: +86 22 2570 7540, Website: www.5ict.com, operate four berths (1 x 50 000 dwt, 2 x 40 000 dwt and 1 x 25 000 dwt) totalling 1202 m long with draft of 15.7 m with twelve container cranes and twenty five RTG's and RMG's
Bulk facilities: Bulk cargo facilities are under construction in the South Harbour area of the port. Two terminals, one for vessels up to 50 000 dwt and one for vessels up to 15 000 dwt are now in operation
Tanker facilities: One petroleum wharf. Numerous oil storage tanks have been built in recent years

Name	Length (m)	Depth (m)	Remarks
New Port			See [1] below
Berth No.0101	175	7	General cargo handled for vessels up to 7000 dwt
Berth No.0102	175	7	General cargo handled for vessels up to 7000 dwt
Berth No.0103	175	7	General cargo handled for vessels up to 7000 dwt
Berth No.0106	201	10.5	Bulk cargo handled for vessels up to 10 000 dwt
Berth No.0207	184	8.5	General cargo for vessels up to 10 000 dwt
Berth No.0208	182	8.3	General cargo for vessels up to 10 000 dwt
Berth No.0209	176	9	General cargo for vessels up to 10 000 dwt
Berth No.0210	176	9	General cargo for vessels up to 10 000 dwt
Berth No.0211	176	9	General cargo for vessels up to 10 000 dwt
Berth No.0212	252	11	General cargo and grain for vessels up to 20 000 dwt
Berth No.0213	251	11	See [2] below
Berth No.0214	189	8.5	General cargo for vessels up to 10 000 dwt
Berth No.0215	184	8.5	General cargo for vessels up to 10 000 dwt
Berth No.0416	187	8	General cargo for vessels up to 10 000 dwt
Berth No.0417	185	8	General cargo for vessels up to 10 000 dwt
Berth No.0418	182	8.5	General cargo for vessels up to 10 000 dwt
Berth No.0419	179	9.2	General cargo for vessels up to 10 000 dwt
Berth No.0420	179	9.2	Steel handled for vessels up to 10 000 dwt
Berth No.0522	177	9	General cargo for vessels up to 10 000 dwt
Berth No.0523	177	9	General cargo for vessels up to 10 000 dwt
Berth No.0524	176	9	General cargo for vessels up to 10 000 dwt
Berth No.0525	233	9	General cargo for vessels up to 10 000 dwt
Berth No.0526	233	9	General cargo for vessels up to 10 000 dwt
Berth No.0624	398	10	Container cargo handled for vessels up to 10 000 dwt
Berth No.0627	300	11	Container cargo handled for vessels up to 20 000 dwt
Berth No.0628	300	11	Container cargo handled for vessels up to 20 000 dwt
Berth No.0629	295	11	Container cargo handled for vessels up to 20 000 dwt
Berth No.0930	780	10.5	Container cargo handled for vessels up to 25 000 dwt
Berth No.0931		10.5	Container cargo handled for vessels up to 25 000 dwt
Berth No.0932		10.5	Container cargo handled for vessels up to 25 000 dwt
Berth No.0933		10.5	Container cargo handled for vessels up to 25 000 dwt
Berth No.0934	170	10	Container cargo handled for vessels up to 10 000 dwt
Berth No.0935	186	11.5	Ore cargo handled for vessels up to 10 000 dwt
Berth No.0936	187	11.5	For vessels up to 15 000 dwt
Berth No.0937	187	11.5	For vessels up to 15 000 dwt
Berth No.0938	187	11.5	For vessels up to 15 000 dwt
Berth No.0939	187	11.5	For vessels up to 15 000 dwt
Berth No.0940	187	10	For vessels up to 15 000 dwt
Berth No.01A1	311	8.5	Passenger terminal for vessels up to 10 000 dwt
Berth No.01A2	311	8.5	Passenger terminal for vessels up to 10 000 dwt
Bunker Supply	186	9.2	For vessels up to 10 000 dwt
Sinor	205	11.5	For vessels up to 38 000 dwt
Southern No.1	212	10	For vessels up to 15 000 dwt
Southern No.2	212	10	For vessels up to 15 000 dwt
Southern No.3	212	10	Edible oil handled for vessels up to 15 000 dwt
Southern No.4	308	13.5	Edible oil handled for vessels up to 50 000 dwt
9706 Factory	200	4.5	See [3] below
Landing Stage	181	5	General cargo for vessels up to 2000 dwt
Loading Terminal	252	7.5	General cargo for vessels up to 5000 dwt
Food & Oil Factory	250	5	Food & oil for vessels up to 2000 dwt
Haihe Port			
Berth No.0305	115	6	General cargo for vessels up to 3000 dwt
Berth No.0306	115	6	General cargo for vessels up to 3000 dwt

Name	Length (m)	Depth (m)	Remarks
Berth No.0307	200	6	General cargo for vessels up to 6000 dwt
Berth No.0308	148	6	General cargo for vessels up to 6000 dwt
Berth No.0309	131	6	General cargo for vessels up to 5000 dwt
Berth No.0310	136	6	General cargo for vessels up to 5000 dwt
Berth No.0311	219	6	General cargo for vessels up to 5000 dwt

[1]*New Port:* Situated in Bohai Bay at the mouth of the Haihe River. The new port lies on the north bank and is man made. Protected by two breakwaters - 5.4 km and 8 km length with a width of 1.3 km

[2]*Berth No.0213:* Grain in bulk for vessels up to 20,000 dwt. Pneumatic sucker - 8 x 750 t/h

[3]*9706 Factory:* Oil & chemicals handled for vessels up to 3000 dwt. Pump - 10 x 160 t/h

Storage: Warehousing 309 097 sq m . Numerous oil storage tanks

Location	Open (m²)
Xingang	1141897

Mechanical Handling Equipment:

Location	Type	Capacity (t)	Qty
Xingang	Floating Cranes	200	1
Xingang	Floating Cranes	120	1
Xingang	Mult-purp. Cranes	150	
Xingang	Container Cranes	40	13
Xingang	Forklifts		
Xingang	Yard Tractors		
Berth No.0101	Mult-purp. Cranes	25	2
Berth No.0102	Mult-purp. Cranes	16	2
Berth No.0103	Mult-purp. Cranes	10	3
Berth No.0207	Mult-purp. Cranes	10	3
Berth No.0208	Mult-purp. Cranes	10	1
Berth No.0209	Mult-purp. Cranes	10	3
Berth No.0210	Mult-purp. Cranes	10	4
Berth No.0211	Mult-purp. Cranes	10	2
Berth No.0212	Mult-purp. Cranes	20	1
Berth No.0212	Mult-purp. Cranes	10	4
Berth No.0213	Mult-purp. Cranes		1
Berth No.0214	Mult-purp. Cranes	20	1
Berth No.0215	Mult-purp. Cranes	10	5
Berth No.0416	Mult-purp. Cranes	10	3
Berth No.0417	Mult-purp. Cranes	10	2
Berth No.0418	Mult-purp. Cranes	10	3
Berth No.0419	Mult-purp. Cranes	35	2
Berth No.0420	Mult-purp. Cranes	10	6
Berth No.0522	Mult-purp. Cranes	10	2
Berth No.0522	Mult-purp. Cranes	23	1
Berth No.0523	Mult-purp. Cranes	10	3
Berth No.0524	Mult-purp. Cranes	10	2
Berth No.0525	Mult-purp. Cranes	10	4
Berth No.0525	Mult-purp. Cranes	23	1
Berth No.0526	Mult-purp. Cranes	10	3
Berth No.0624	Mult-purp. Cranes	30	3
Berth No.0627	Mult-purp. Cranes	30	2
Berth No.0628	Mult-purp. Cranes	30	2
Berth No.0629	Mult-purp. Cranes	30	2
Berth No.0930	Mult-purp. Cranes	30	3
Berth No.0935	Mult-purp. Cranes	16	10
Berth No.0935	Mult-purp. Cranes	25	2
Berth No.0936	Mult-purp. Cranes	10	4
Landing Stage	Mult-purp. Cranes	25	1
Loading Terminal	Mult-purp. Cranes	25	1
Berth No.0310	Mult-purp. Cranes	10	2
Berth No.0311	Mult-purp. Cranes	10	2

Cargo Worked: Coke 5-7000 t per day, coke 7-10 000 t per day (4 gangs), ore 2500 t per day,
packaged cargo 700 t per day. Discharging rate - packaged cargo 700 t per day, grain/fertilisers 2500-3000 t per day

Bunkering: A special pier is in operation for refuelling 10 000 t class vessels
BP Hong Kong Ltd, 21st Floor, Super Ocean Financial Centre, 067 West Yan An Road, Shanghai, Shanghai Province, People's Republic of China, *Tel:* +86 21 6278 4858, *Fax:* +86 21 6275 7702, *Email:* lucn@bp.com
ExxonMobil Marine Fuels, 1 Harbour Front Place, 06-00 Harbour Front, Tower One, Singapore, Republic of Singapore 098633, *Tel:* +65 6885 8998, *Fax:* +65 6885 8794, *Email:* asiapac.marinefuels@exxonmobil.com, *Website:* www.exxonmobilmarinefuels.com – *Grades:* MDO; MGO; IFO – *Delivery Mode:* barge
Shell China Ltd, Floor 32, China World Tower 2, International Trade Center, No.1 Jian Guo Men Wai Avenue, Beijing 100004, People's Republic of China, *Tel:* +86 10 6505 4501, *Fax:* +86 10 6505 4011, *Email:* order-china@shell.com, *Website:* www.shell.com

Towage: Twenty tugs available of 980-3200 hp

Repair & Maintenance: Bohai Shipyard (Tianjin) Co. Ltd, P O Box 501, Tanggu, Tianjin, Tianjin Municipality 300456, People's Republic of China, *Tel:* +86 22 2580 0222, *Fax:* +86 22 2580 7973, *Email:* bosembew@public.tpt.ti.cn Graving dock of 156 m x 42 m x 9 m, cap of 25 000 dwt. Floating dock of 195 m x 35 m x 9.5 m, cap of 60 000 dwt

---

Key to Principal Facilities:—

A=Airport	**C**=Containers	**G**=General Cargo	**P**=Petroleum **R**=Ro/Ro **Y**=Dry Bulk
B=Bunkers	**D**=Dry Dock	**L**=Cruise	**Q**=Other Liquid Bulk **T**=Towage (where available from port)

Ship Chandlers: Tianjin Ocean Shipping Supply Co. Ltd, 6 Mi Xingang, Tianjin, Tianjin Municipality 300456, People's Republic of China, *Tel:* +86 22 2579 3731, *Fax:* +86 22 2579 7504, *Email:* supcotj@starinfo.net.cn, *Website:* www.tjsupco.cn

Shipping Agents: Ben Line Agencies Ltd, Room 2401, 24th Floor, Tianjin Finance Building, Commercial Tower, 123 Weidi Road, Hexi District, Tianjin, Tianjin Municipality 300074, People's Republic of China, *Tel:* +86 22 2840 1560, *Fax:* +86 22 2840 7563, *Email:* tsn.gwang@benline.com.cn, *Website:* www.benlineagencies.com
Chiao Feng Shipping Ltd, Room 3506, The Exchange Tower, 189 Naning Road, Hexi District, Tianjin, Tianjin Municipality 300042, People's Republic of China, *Tel:* +86 22 2311 0308, *Fax:* +86 22 2311 2122, *Email:* tianjin@chiaofeng.com.cn, *Website:* www.chiaofeng.com.hk
China Marine Shipping Agency Co. Ltd, China Marine Shipping Agency Tianjin Company Limited, 86 Xingang Road, Tanggu District, Tianjin, Tianjin Municipality 300450, People's Republic of China, *Tel:* +86 22 2571 4344, *Fax:* +86 22 2571 9651, *Email:* agent@sinoagenttj.com, *Website:* www.sinoagenttj.com
China Ocean Shipping Agency, 5 Xuzhou Road, He Xi District, Tianjin, Tianjin Municipality 300042, People's Republic of China, *Email:* pentj@penavicotj.com, *Website:* www.penavicotj.com
CMA-CGM S.A., CMA CGM Tianjin, Room 1808 Tianjin International Building, 75 Nanjing Road, Tianjin, Tianjin Municipality 300050, People's Republic of China, *Tel:* +86 22 2313 9777, *Fax:* +86 22 2330 3589, *Email:* tjn.genmbox@cma-cgm.com, *Website:* www.cma-cgm.com
K Line Ship Management Co. Ltd, 'K' Line (China) Ltd, Room 9A, Ping'an Building, 59 Ma Chang Road, He Xi District, Tianjin, Tianjin Municipality 300203, People's Republic of China, *Tel:* +86 22 8558 9280, *Fax:* +86 22 8558 9282, *Website:* www.kline.co.jp
Mediterranean Shipping Company, MSC (Hong Kong) Ltd, 35th Floor, Tianjin Riverfront Square, 81 Shi Yi Jing Road, Hedong District, Tianjin, Tianjin Municipality 300171, People's Republic of China, *Tel:* +86 22 2425 7555, *Fax:* +86 22 2410 9801, *Email:* msc@nprc.mschkg.com, *Website:* www.mschongkong.com
Pen-Wallem Shipping Services Co Ltd, Tianjin Heping District, Tianjin, Tianjin Municipality, People's Republic of China, *Tel:* +86 22 2311 7858, *Fax:* +86 22 2311 7878, *Email:* wallemtian@pen-wallem.com, *Website:* www.pen-wellem.com
Sinotrans (HK) Logistics Ltd, Room 401, 80 Qufu Road, Heping District, Tianjin, Tianjin Municipality 300042, People's Republic of China, *Tel:* +86 22 2303 6240, *Fax:* +86 22 2303 6267, *Email:* tianjin@sinotrans-logistics.com, *Website:* www.sinotrans-logistics.com
Sun Hing Shipping Co Ltd, 57 Chengdu Road, Heping District, Tianjin, Tianjin Municipality 300050, People's Republic of China, *Tel:* +86 22 2312 3183, *Fax:* +86 22 2312 3180, *Website:* www.sunhinggroup.com
TES International Transport (China) Ltd, Room 0710 North Financial Building, 5 Youyi Road, Hexi District, Tianjin, Tianjin Municipality 300201, People's Republic of China, *Tel:* +86 22 2883 50223, *Fax:* +86 22 2883 50256
Tongsheng International Shipping Agencies, Tianjin Tongsheng International Shipping Agency Co Ltd, Room 601, Tianwai Building, 1111 Xingang Road, Tanggu District, Tianjin, Tianjin Municipality 300456, People's Republic of China, *Tel:* +86 22 2571 5686, *Fax:* +86 22 2571 6855, *Email:* xingang@tongshengshipping.com, *Website:* www.tongshengshipping.com
Velikar Enterprises Ltd, Hexi District, Tianjin, Tianjin Municipality, People's Republic of China, *Tel:* +86 22 8837 2181, *Fax:* +86 22 8837 2181, *Email:* vickyzhang@velikar.com, *Website:* www.velikar.com
World Marine Corp, Tiangin/Xingang Port Captain Station, Xingang, People's Republic of China, *Tel:* +86 22 2587 1503, *Fax:* +86 22 2587 1503, *Email:* wmarxg@starinfo.net.cn

Surveyors: China Classification Society, A Building, Ming Zhu Yuan, 11 Nanhai Road, Tianjin, Tianjin Municipality 300457, People's Republic of China, *Tel:* +86 22 6202 2888, *Fax:* +86 22 6202 2666, *Email:* ccstj@ccs.org.cn, *Website:* www.ccs.org.cn
Det Norske Veritas A/S, Room 3516, Golden Emperor Building, 20 Nanjing Road, Hexi District, Tianjin, Tianjin Municipality 300202, People's Republic of China, *Tel:* +86 22 2332 0616, *Fax:* +86 22 2332 0626, *Email:* mchcn423@dnv.com, *Website:* www.dnv.com
Russian Maritime Register of Shipping, Room 503, Block B, Haowei Mansion No.8, The 3rd Avenue, Tianjin, Tianjin Municipality 300457, People's Republic of China, *Tel:* +86 22 6529 2980, *Fax:* +86 22 6529 2981, *Website:* www.rs-head.spb.ru

Medical Facilities: Port hospital available

Airport: Tianjin Airport, 35 km

Railway: Available inside the port area, connecting to the national line. The first international railway container line went into operation on 23 November 1997 in Tianjin. The railway line is 200 metres away from the container port.
The Corporation handles transport business along three railway lines - Tianjin to Russia then Europe, Tianjin to Mongolia then Russia and Europe, Tianjin to Kazakhstan then Central Asia and Europe

Development: Construction of a new $98 million ro/ro terminal, to be operated by TPG Global Ro-Ro Terminal Co. Ltd. Designed to handle 500,000 vehicles a year, the new terminal will includes two ro/ro berths for cars, high and heavy ro/ro equipment and static cargoes. Construction of the new terminal in Tianjin Port's North Harbour is due to start mid-August 2007. The plan is to have one berth open by end of 2007 and the whole terminal by October 2008
DP World and the Tianjin Port Group Co. Ltd. will invest $500 million to develop the man-made Island Phase 2 Container Terminal. The project, in the Bohai Area, includes plans for a 140 ha terminal area with a 1400 m quay length, and an annual handling cap of 2.2 million TEU's. Reclamation work for the development is already underway and operations are scheduled to begin in 2011

Lloyd's Agent: Huatai Surveyors & Adjusters Co., Room 501, E8B, Binhai Finance Zone, 20 Guang Chang East Road, Teda, Tianjin, Tianjin Municipality 300457, People's Republic of China, *Tel:* +86 22 6622 0723, *Fax:* +86 22 6622 0725, *Email:* agency.tj@huatai-serv.com, *Website:* www.huatai-serv.com

XINHE

harbour area, see under Chongming

XINHUA

harbour area, see under Shanghai

XINHUI

Lat 22° 31' N; Long 113° 2' E.

Admiralty Chart: -	**Admiralty Pilot:** -	
Time Zone: GMT +8 h	**UNCTAD Locode:** CN XIN	

Principal Facilities:

P	Q	Y	G	C		B		T	

Authority: Xinhui Port Authority, Gangkou Road, Xin Shi District, Xinhui, Guangdong Province, People's Republic of China, *Tel:* +86 750 639 0512, *Fax:* +86 750 639 0512

Pilotage: Compulsory and available 24 h. Pilot boards vessel at Zhuhai Pilot Anchorage

Tides: Average tidal range of 1.55 m

Accommodation:

Name	Length (m)	Depth (m)	Remarks
Xinhui			
Berth No.1	262.5	8	See [1] below
Niuguling Gas Berth	103	6	LPG & chemical products for vessels up to 3000 dwt

[1]Berth No.1: General cargo, asphalt & containers for vessels up to 5000 dwt

Storage: Container yard of 15 000 m2

Location	Open (m²)	Covered (m²)
Xinhui	80000	30000

Mechanical Handling Equipment:

Location	Type	Capacity (t)	Qty
Berth No.1	Shore Cranes	10	2
Berth No.1	Shore Cranes	35	1

Bunkering: Available

Towage: Available

Shipping Agents: China Marine Shipping Agency Co. Ltd, China Marine Shipping Agency Guangdong Company Limited Xinhui Branch, No. D17, Longxing Garden, Huicheng Town, Xinhui, Guangdong Province 529100, People's Republic of China, *Tel:* +86 750 668 5990, *Fax:* +86 750 668 8370, *Email:* xinhui@sinoagentgd.com, *Website:* www.sinoagentgd.com

Lloyd's Agent: Huatai Surveyors & Adjusters Co., Room 802, Jun Yuan Mansion, 155 Tian He East Road, Guangzhou, Guangdong Province 510620, People's Republic of China, *Tel:* +86 20 3881 2306, *Fax:* +86 20 3881 2470, *Email:* agency.gz@huatai-serv.com, *Website:* www.huatai-serv.com

XINJIAN

harbour area, see under Chongming

XINSHA

harbour area, see under Guangzhou

XINSHENGWEI

harbour area, see under Nanjing

XINSHI

harbour area, see under Foshan

XIONGJIAGOU

harbour area, see under Ezhou

XIUYU

Lat 25° 13' N; Long 118° 59' E.

Admiralty Chart: 1761   **Admiralty Pilot:** 32
Time Zone: GMT +8 h   **UNCTAD Locode:** CN XIU

Principal Facilities:

P	Q	Y	G	C		B		T	

Authority: Putian Port Group Co Ltd., Xiuyu Town, Putian City, Fujian Province 351158, People's Republic of China, *Tel:* +86 594 569 1210, *Fax:* +86 594 569 7630, *Email:* ptgwsw1210@126.com

Anchorage: Middle Road Anchorage in pos 25° 08.5' N; 118° 59.7' E in depth of 18 m for shelter
No.1 Pilot Anchorage in pos 25° 03' N; 119° 03' E in depth of 13 m
No.2 Pilot Anchorage in pos 25° 01.5' N; 119° 02.8' E in depth of 31 m
Working Anchorage in pos 25° 12.3' N; 118° 59.4' E in depth of 15 m

Pilotage: Compulsory and available 12 h. Pilot boards in pos 25° 03' N; 119° 03' E

Radio Frequency: VHF Channel 16

Tides: Average tidal range of 5.11 m

Principal Imports and Exports: Imports: Coal, Food, Food oil, Machinery equipment, Small arms trade, Wood. Exports: Local minerals, Salt, Timber.

Working Hours: 24 h/day

Accommodation:

Name	Length (m)	Depth (m)	Remarks
Xiuyu			
LNG Terminal	390	13.6	'T' type pier with terminal cap of 100 000 dwt
Meizhouwan			
35 000 t Berth	304	13.8	See [1] below
10 000 t Berth	213	9.6	General cargo & containers for vessels up to 10 000 dwt
3000 t Berth	149	6.5	General cargo & containers for vessels up to 3000 dwt
Huatong			
Chemical Pontoon Jetty	40	7.2	Chemicals for vessels up to 3000 dwt

[1]*35 000 t Berth:* General cargo, coal & containers for vessels up to 35 000 dwt

Storage: Open storage of 226 300 m2. Three 4320 m2 warehouses and two 3600 m2 warehouses. Container yard of 1500 m2

Mechanical Handling Equipment:

Location	Type	Capacity (t)	Qty
Xiuyu	Floating Cranes	30	1
Xiuyu	Mobile Cranes	8–25	5
Xiuyu	Portal Cranes	10–40	5

Bunkering: Available
China Marine Bunker Supply Co., 13F Qian Cun Mansion A, No.2, 5th Block, Anzhen Xili, Chaoyang District, Beijing 100029, People's Republic of China, *Tel:* +86 10 6443 0717, *Fax:* +86 10 6443 0708, *Email:* business@chimbusco.com.cn, *Website:* www.chimbusco.com.cn – *Grades:* IFO120-380cSt; MGO

Towage: Three tugs of 600-3400 hp

Medical Facilities: Clinics available

Lloyd's Agent: Huatai Surveyors & Adjusters Co., 14th Floor, China Re Building, No.11 Jin Rong Avenue, Xicheng District, Beijing 100140, People's Republic of China, *Tel:* +86 10 6657 6577, *Fax:* +86 10 6657 6502, *Email:* agency.bj@huatai-serv.com, *Website:* www.huatai-serv.com

YA XIAN

alternate name, see Sanya

YANCHENG

Lat 33° 23' N; Long 120° 7' E.

Admiralty Chart: 3480   **Admiralty Pilot:** 32
Time Zone: GMT +8 h   **UNCTAD Locode:** CN YCG

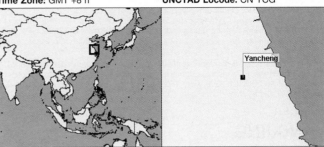

Principal Facilities:

		Y	G						

Authority: Yancheng Harbour Administration, 195 Jianjun Zhong Road, Yancheng, Jiangsu Province 224001, People's Republic of China

Accommodation:

Name	Remarks
Yancheng	See [1] below

[1]*Yancheng:* Numerous berths available for vessels up to 200 dwt handling iron & steel, coal, ore, timber, cement, fertiliser, grain and salt

Storage: Open and covered storage areas available

Lloyd's Agent: Huatai Surveyors & Adjusters Co., 14th Floor, China Re Building, No.11 Jin Rong Avenue, Xicheng District, Beijing 100140, People's Republic of China, *Tel:* +86 10 6657 6577, *Fax:* +86 10 6657 6502, *Email:* agency.bj@huatai-serv.com, *Website:* www.huatai-serv.com

YANGFUSHAN

harbour area, see under Wenzhou

YANGJIANG

Lat 21° 51' N; Long 111° 56' E.

Admiralty Chart: 1555   **Admiralty Pilot:** 30
Time Zone: GMT +8 h   **UNCTAD Locode:** CN YJI

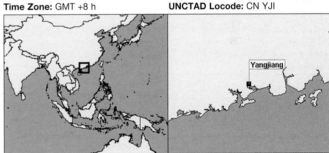

Principal Facilities:

P	Q	Y	G						

Authority: Yangjiang Harbour Administration, Shijuetou, Xingang Road, Yangjiang, Guangdong Province 529500, People's Republic of China, *Tel:* +86 662 382 1717

Port Security: ISPS compliant

Anchorage: In pos 21° 33' 00" N; 111° 47' 32" E in depth of 10 m

Pilotage: Compulsory

Working Hours: 24 h/day

Accommodation:

Name	Length (m)	Depth (m)	Draught (m)	Remarks
Yangjiang				
Oil/LPG Berth	226	10	8.5	Oil & LPG for vessels up to 20 000 dwt
General Cargo Berth	308	9	8	General cargo for vessels up to 10 000 dwt

Storage: Oil and LPG storage tanks available

Location	Open (m²)	Covered (m²)
General Cargo Berth	62638	13036

Key to Principal Facilities:—
A=Airport **C**=Containers **G**=General Cargo **P**=Petroleum **R**=Ro/Ro **Y**=Dry Bulk
B=Bunkers **D**=Dry Dock **L**=Cruise **Q**=Other Liquid Bulk **T**=Towage (where available from port)

Mechanical Handling Equipment:

Location	Type	Capacity (t)	Qty
General Cargo Berth	Shore Cranes	5–35	4

Shipping Agents: China Marine Shipping Agency Co. Ltd, China Marine Shipping Agency Guangdong Yangjiang Company Ltd, 30 Chuangye Road, Yangjiang, Guangdong Province, People's Republic of China, *Tel:* +86 662 342 2130, *Fax:* +86 662 342 2132, *Email:* sinoagent-yj@public.yangjiang.gd.cn
CMA-CGM S.A., CMA CGM Yangjiang, Room 611, World Trade Centre, 18 Wan Fu Road, Jiang Cheng District, Yangjiang, Guangdong Province 529500, People's Republic of China, *Tel:* +86 662 323 8222, *Fax:* +86 662 322 2066, *Email:* yji.mlin@cma-cgm.com, *Website:* www.cma-cgm.com

Lloyd's Agent: Huatai Surveyors & Adjusters Co., Room 802, Jun Yuan Mansion, 155 Tian He East Road, Guangzhou, Guangdong Province 510620, People's Republic of China, *Tel:* +86 20 3881 2306, *Fax:* +86 20 3881 2470, *Email:* agency.gz@huatai-serv.com, *Website:* www.huatai-serv.com

YANGJING

harbour area, see under Chuansha

YANGPU

Lat 19° 42' N; Long 109° 20' E.

Admiralty Chart: 3990/3991	**Admiralty Pilot:** 30
Time Zone: GMT +8 h	**UNCTAD Locode:** CN YPG

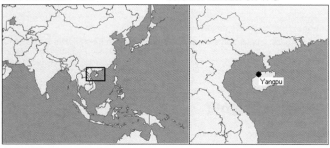

Principal Facilities:

		Y	G	C		B	T	

Authority: Yangpu Harbour Administration Co. Ltd, Administration Office, Yangpu Eco & Development Zone, Yangpu 578101, People's Republic of China, *Tel:* +86 890 882 2292, *Fax:* +86 890 882 2292

Port Security: ISPS compliant

Pilotage: Compulsory and available 0800-1800. Pilot boards at the pilot anchorage

Radio Frequency: VHF Channel 14 for the port and VHF Channels 16 and 8 for the harbour master

Tides: Average tidal range of 1.81 m

Accommodation:

Name	Draught (m)	Remarks
Yangpu		
Berth No.1	7	Inner working berth for vessels up to 3000 dwt
Berth No.2	10.8	General & bulk cargo for vessels up to 20 000 dwt
Berth No.3	10.8	General & bulk cargo for vessels up to 20 000 dwt
Berth No.4	13.2	Containers for vessels up to 35 000 dwt
Berth No.5	13.2	Containers for vessels up to 35 000 dwt
Berth No.6	13.2	Containers for vessels up to 35 000 dwt

Storage:

Location	Open (m²)	Covered (m²)
Yangpu	120000	27000

Mechanical Handling Equipment:

Location	Type	Capacity (t)	Qty
Berth No.1	Shore Cranes	16	1
Berth No.1	Shore Cranes	40	1
Berth No.2	Shore Cranes	10	3

Bunkering: Available at berth and anchorage

Towage: One tug of 2600 hp and one tug of 3900 hp

Lloyd's Agent: Huatai Surveyors & Adjusters Co., 14th Floor, China Re Building, No.11 Jin Rong Avenue, Xicheng District, Beijing 100140, People's Republic of China, *Tel:* +86 10 6657 6577, *Fax:* +86 10 6657 6502, *Email:* agency.bj@huatai-serv.com, *Website:* www.huatai-serv.com

YANGZHOU

Lat 32° 22' N; Long 119° 22' E.

Admiralty Chart: 1619	**Admiralty Pilot:** 32
Time Zone: GMT +8 h	**UNCTAD Locode:** CN YZH

Principal Facilities:

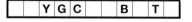

	Y	G	C		B		T	

Authority: Yangzhou Port (Group) Co Ltd., Yangzhou, Jiangsu Province, People's Republic of China, *Tel:* +86 514 8752 7699

Port Security: ISPS compliant

Pilotage: Compulsory and available during daytime only. Pilot boards vessel at Baoshan Channel

Radio Frequency: VHF Channels 13 and 6

Tides: Max tidal range of 2.1 m

Traffic: 2005, 11 790 000 t of cargo handled, 157 000 TEU's

Accommodation:

Name	Length (m)	Depth (m)	Remarks
Yangzhou			
Berth No.1	370	11	Containers & general cargo for vessels up to 15 000 dwt
Berth No.2	300	12	General cargo for vessels up to 10 000 dwt
Floating Berth	180	10	General cargo for vessels up to 10 000 dwt

Storage: Container yard of 50 000 m2

Location	Open (m²)	Covered (m²)
Yangzhou	220000	32000

Mechanical Handling Equipment:

Location	Type	Capacity (t)	Qty
Yangzhou	Floating Cranes	30	1
Berth No.1	Shore Cranes	30	1
Berth No.1	Shore Cranes	10	2
Berth No.2	Shore Cranes	35	1
Berth No.2	Shore Cranes	10	2
Floating Berth	Shore Cranes	8	3

Bunkering: Available

Towage: One tug of 2640 hp and one tug of 3600 hp

Shipping Agents: China Marine Shipping Agency Co. Ltd, China Marine Shipping Agency Jiangsu Yangzhou Company Limited, 4th Floor, Shuili Building, Wencheng West Road, Yangzhou, Jiangsu Province 225003, People's Republic of China, *Tel:* +86 514 8736 2449, *Fax:* +86 514 8732 6949, *Email:* yzsinoagt@pub.yz.jsinfo.net, *Website:* www.sinoagent.com
China Ocean Shipping Agency, 141 Wenchang West Road, Yangzhou, Jiangsu Province 225012, People's Republic of China, *Tel:* +86 514 8780 2289, *Fax:* +86 514 8785 3399, *Email:* penyz@public.yz.js.cn, *Website:* www.penavicoyz.com
China Sailing International Shipping Agency Ltd, Room 307 Mansion Weiheng/Lanyuan District B, Yangzhou, Jiangsu Province 225009, People's Republic of China, *Tel:* +86 514 8510 6850, *Fax:* +86 514 8510 6860, *Email:* chnsl@chinasailing-yz.com.cn, *Website:* www.chinasailing.com.cn

Development: Construction of Berth No's 3 (multi-purpose) and 4 (containers) scheduled to be completed 2005

Lloyd's Agent: Huatai Surveyors & Adjusters Co., 14th Floor, China Re Building, No.11 Jin Rong Avenue, Xicheng District, Beijing 100140, People's Republic of China, *Tel:* +86 10 6657 6577, *Fax:* +86 10 6657 6502, *Email:* agency.bj@huatai-serv.com, *Website:* www.huatai-serv.com

YANGZI

harbour area, see under Nanjing

YANTAI

Lat 37° 33' N; Long 121° 22' E.

Admiralty Chart: 1260	**Admiralty Pilot:** 32
Time Zone: GMT +8 h	**UNCTAD Locode:** CN YNT

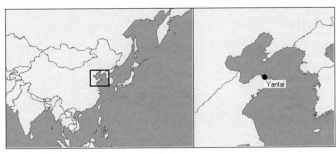

Principal Facilities:

P	Y	G	C	R		B		T	A	

Authority: Yantai Port Group Co Ltd, 155 Bei Ma Road, Yantai, Shandong Province 264000, People's Republic of China, *Tel:* +86 535 674 3176, *Fax:* +86 535 674 2151, *Email:* zhengsch@yantaiport.com.cn, *Website:* www.yantaiport.com.cn

Officials: General Manager: Shao Bo Ji, *Email:* jishb@yantaiport.com.cn.
Assistant General Manager: Yuan Le Ma, *Tel:* +86 535 674 2538, *Email:* mayl@yantaiport.com.cn.
Business Development Manager: Zheng Song Chang.

Approach: The port has two principal fairways:
Bei Hangdao leading to No.3 Basin which has a least depth of 15.4 m. A branch leads NW to the area N of No.4 Pier with a least depth of 7.3 m; a second branch leads WSW to No.1 Basin with a least depth of 12.8 m.
Nan Hangdao leading to East Basin which has a least depth of 8 m

Anchorage: No.1 pilot and quarantine anchorage is situated off the N channel of the outer harbour in depths of 10.5-14.5 m in the eastern part and 7-9 m in the western part accommodating vessels up to 20 000 t. No.2 pilot and quarantine anchorage is located 8 nautical miles NE of the harbour in depth of 17 m accommodating vessels up to 20 000 t. The tanker cargo/oil transferring anchorage is N of Zhifu Island in depth of 18 m accommodating vessels over 20 000 t. The sheltered anchorage is S of Danzi Island and Kongtong Island in depths of 7-9 m accommodating vessels up to 10 000 t

Pilotage: Compulsory and available 24 h. Pilot boards vessel at the anchorage

Radio Frequency: VHF Channel 11

Tides: Average tidal range of 1.64 m

Traffic: 2006, 60 756 000 t of cargo handled, 1 049 000 TEU's

Principal Imports and Exports: Imports: Building materials, Fertilizer, Logs, Provisions. Exports: Coal, Cotton, Fruit, Mineral powders.

Accommodation:

Name	Length (m)	Depth (m)	Remarks
DP World Yantai Container Terminal			
Berths 61 & 62	573	14	See [1] below
Yantai Gantong Container Terminal			
Berths 38 & 39	730	14	See [2] below
No.1 District			
Berth No.11	182	6.3	Max 3000 dwt. Coal
Berth No.12	140	6.3	Max 3000 dwt. Chemicals
Berth No.13	180	6.5	Max 3000 dwt. General cargo
Berth No.14	180	6.9	Max 3000 dwt. General cargo
Berth No.15	180	9.9	Max 10 000 dwt. Bulk & general cargo
Berth No.16	180	9.9	Max 10 000 dwt. Bulk & general cargo
Berth No.17	180	9.9	Max 10 000 dwt. Bulk & general cargo
Berth No.18	125	7.9	Max 5000 dwt. Containers
Berth No.19	112	6.9	Max 3000 dwt. Containers
No.2 District			
Berth No.21	230	11.3	Max 16 000 dwt. Coal
Berth No.22	195	11.3	Max 25 000 dwt. Timber
Berth No.23	195	12	Max 25 000 dwt. Timber
Berth No.24	210	11.3	Max 25 000 dwt. Chemicals & fertilizers
Berth No.25	170	10.3	Max 10 000 dwt. Bulk & general cargo
Berth No.26	236	10.3	Max 16 000 dwt. Bulk & general cargo
Passenger Berths			
K1	162	6.9	Max 3000 dwt. Passengers & general cargo
K2	126	6.9	Max 3000 dwt. Passengers & general cargo
K3	140	6.9	Max 5000 dwt. Passengers & general cargo
K4	141	6.9	Max 5000 dwt. Passengers & general cargo
K5	112	6.9	Max 3000 dwt. Passengers & general cargo
Edible Oil Berth			
D6	80	5	Max 1000 dwt. Edible oil

[1]*Berths 61 & 62:* Operated by DP World Yantai Co Ltd., Tel: +86 535 674 0888, Fax: +86 535 674 5556, Email: simon.huang@dpworld.com
Two berths for post-panamax vessels
[2]*Berths 38 & 39:* Operated by Yantai Rising Dragon International Container Terminal

Ltd. (YRDICT), 78 Gangwan Dadao, Yantai 264000, Tel: +86 535 674 0956, Fax: +86 535 674 1307, Email: service@ictsiyantai.com, Website: www.ictsiyantai.com
Two container berths. Container yard area of 16 ha with back-up area of 17 ha. Container freight station of 4500 m2. 222 reefer points

Storage:

Location	Open (m²)	Covered (m²)
Yantai	33000	24000

Mechanical Handling Equipment:

Location	Type	Capacity (t)	Qty
Yantai	Floating Cranes	63	1
Yantai	Mult-purp. Cranes	16	
DP World Yantai Container Terminal	Container Cranes	55	4
DP World Yantai Container Terminal	RTG's		3
Yantai Gantong Container Terminal	Post Panamax		6
Yantai Gantong Container Terminal	RTG's		12

Bunkering: BP Hong Kong Ltd, 21st Floor, Super Ocean Financial Centre, 067 West Yan An Road, Shanghai, Shanghai Province, People's Republic of China, *Tel:* +86 21 6278 4858, *Fax:* +86 21 6275 7702, *Email:* lucn@bp.com
China Marine Bunker Supply Co., 13F Qian Cun Mansion A, No.2, 5th Block, Anzhen Xili, Chaoyang District, Beijing 100029, People's Republic of China, *Tel:* +86 10 6443 0717, *Fax:* +86 10 6443 0708, *Email:* business@chimbusco.com.cn, *Website:* www.chimbusco.com.cn – *Grades:* IFO120-380cSt; MGO
Shell China Ltd, Floor 32, China World Tower 2, International Trade Center, No.1 Jian Guo Men Wai Avenue, Beijing 100004, People's Republic of China, *Tel:* +86 10 6505 4501, *Fax:* +86 10 6505 4011, *Email:* order-china@shell.com, *Website:* www.shell.com

Towage: Ten harbour tugs up to 3200 hp

Ship Chandlers: Yantai Ocean Shipping Supply Co., No.19 Haigang Road, Yantai, Shandong Province 264000, People's Republic of China, *Tel:* +86 535 624 6361, *Fax:* +86 535 628 7104

Shipping Agents: China Marine Shipping Agency Co. Ltd, China Marine Shipping Agency Shandong Yantai Company, 2 Jianshe Road, Yantai, Shandong Province 264000, People's Republic of China, *Tel:* +86 535 624 5886, *Fax:* +86 535 624 7190, *Email:* sinoagt@public.ytptt.sd.cn, *Website:* www.sinotrans.com
CMA-CGM S.A., CMA CGM Yantai, Room 1105, 9 Nanda Street, Jindu Mansion, Yantai, Shandong Province 264001, People's Republic of China, *Tel:* +86 535 661 5168, *Fax:* +86 535 621 8610, *Email:* yti.genmbox@cma-cgm.com, *Website:* www.cma-cgm.com
Sun Hing Shipping Co Ltd, Room 909, Yili Mansion, 80 Chaoyang Street, Yantai, Shandong Province 264000, People's Republic of China, *Tel:* +86 535 662 2445, *Fax:* +86 535 662 2228, *Website:* www.sunhinggroup.com
THI (Hong Kong) Ltd, International Financial Nation, Room 1618, 16th Floor, 166 Jie Fang Road, Yantai, Shandong Province 264001, People's Republic of China, *Tel:* +86 535 662 0851, *Fax:* +86 535 662 0852, *Email:* thiyat@thi-group.com

Surveyors: Det Norske Veritas A/S, 70 Zhifu East Road, Zhifu Island, Yantai, Shandong Province 264000, People's Republic of China, *Tel:* +86 535 682 8431, *Fax:* +86 535 682 8430, *Website:* www.dnv.com

Airport: Yantai Airport, 30 km

Lloyd's Agent: Huatai Surveyors & Adjusters Co., 14th Floor, China Re Building, No.11 Jin Rong Avenue, Xicheng District, Beijing 100140, People's Republic of China, *Tel:* +86 10 6657 6577, *Fax:* +86 10 6657 6502, *Email:* agency.bj@huatai-serv.com, *Website:* www.huatai-serv.com

YANTIAN

Lat 22° 35' N; Long 114° 16' E.

Admiralty Chart: 3544/939	**Admiralty Pilot:** 30
Time Zone: GMT +8 h	**UNCTAD Locode:** CN YTN

Principal Facilities:

		G	C	R		B		T		

Authority: Shenzhen Yantian Port Group Co. Ltd, Yantian Port, Sha Tou Jiao, Shenzhen, Guangdong Province 518081, People's Republic of China, *Tel:* +86 755 2529 1055, *Fax:* +86 755 2529 0641, *Email:* wuc@ytport.com, *Website:* www.ytport.com

Port Security: ISPS compliant. Container Security Initiative (CSI) designated port

Approach: Draft limitation in channel is 12 m, access is through Dapeng Bay with depths of 14-20 m

Anchorage: No's 1 and 2 Anchorages in depth of 16-17 m for vessels up to 50 000 dwt

Key to Principal Facilities:—
A=Airport   **C**=Containers   **G**=General Cargo   **P**=Petroleum   **R**=Ro/Ro   **Y**=Dry Bulk
B=Bunkers   **D**=Dry Dock   **L**=Cruise   **Q**=Other Liquid Bulk   **T**=Towage (where available from port)

a) temporary anchorage -22° 35' 40" N; 114° 12' 54" E, depth 15 m, mud and sand with good holding ground, to 10 000 dwt, awaiting pilot
b) No.1 quarantine anchorage -
22° 25' 40" N; 114° 31' 48" E
22° 21' 30" N; 114° 34' 07" E
22° 23' 50" N; 114° 38' 37" E
22° 27' 30" N; 114° 35' 12" E
depth 17 m, mud and sand with good holding ground, for vessels less than 50 000 dwt
c) No.2 quarantine anchorage -
22° 34' 25" N; 114° 21' 43" E
22° 35' 27" N; 114° 23' 47" E
22° 33' 38" N; 114° 25' 29" E
22° 31' 57" N; 114° 23' 10" E
depth 16 m, mud and sand with good holding ground, for vessels over 50 000 dwt
d) No.3 quarantine anchorage -
22° 33' 34" N; 114° 25' 44" E
22° 34' 34" N; 114° 26' 06" E
22° 33' 36" N; 114° 27' 41" E
22° 33' 35" N; 114° 27' 41" E
22° 31' 35" N; 114° 26' 38" E
22° 33' 45" N; 114° 26' 38" E
depth 11 m, mud and sand with good holding ground, for vessels under 50 000 dwt
e) No.4 anchorage -
22° 35' 38" N; 114° 24' 14" E
22° 33' 40" N; 114° 24' 14" E
22° 33' 40" N; 114° 25' 24" E
22° 34' 58" N; 114° 25' 24" E
depth 13 m, mud and sand with good holding ground, for vessels with dangerous cargo

Pilotage: Compulsory. Pilot boards at Yantian Port Area in pos 22° 34' 09" N; 114° 20' 58" E, Shenzhen Port No.5 Anchorage in pos 22° 34' 74" N; 114° 19' 40" E or Daya Wan No.2 Quarantine Anchorage in pos 22° 36' 48" N; 114° 35' 00" E

Radio Frequency: VHF Channels 11 and 16

Weather: In winter, subject to NE monsoons; in summer, typhoons

Tides: Average tidal range of 1.03 m. Maximum range 2.57 m

Traffic: 2006, 8 865 000 TEU's handled

Accommodation:

Name	Length (m)	Depth (m)	Remarks
Yantian			
Container Terminal (West)	4815	14–16	See [1] below

[1]*Container Terminal (West):* Operated by Yantian International Container Terminals Ltd., Yantian Port, Sha Tou Jiao, Shenzhen 518081, Tel: +86 755 2529 0888, Fax: +86 755 2529 1188, Website: www.yict.com.cn
Five 50 000 t container berths in depth of 14-15 m with 20 container cranes and 88 yard cranes
Eight 100 000 t container berths in depth of 16 m with 18 container cranes and 66 yard cranes

Bunkering: Available at berth

Towage: Three tugs available of 1800-3400 hp

Shipping Agents: Atlanta Shipping Agency Ltd, Room 501-4, YICT Office Building, Yantian Port, Shenzhen, Yantian, Shenzhen Guangdong Province, People's Republic of China, *Tel:* +86 755 2529 0815, *Fax:* +86 755 2529 0814, *Email:* carolwu@atlanta.com.mo
China Marine Shipping Agency Co. Ltd, China Marine Shipping Agency Shenzhen Company Limited Yantian Branch, Room 1201, Haigang Building, Yantian, Shenzhen Guangdong Province, People's Republic of China, *Tel:* +86 755 2529 0262, *Fax:* +86 755 2529 0264, *Email:* agent@sinoagentsz.com
K Line Ship Management Co. Ltd, 'K' Line (China) Ltd, Room 413-415, Waiting Building, Yantian Port, Tou Jiao, Shenzhen, Guangdong Province 518081, People's Republic of China, *Tel:* +86 755 2529 2749, *Fax:* +86 755 2529 0750, *Website:* www.kline.co.jp
Young Carrier Co. Ltd, Room 505-508, Waiting Building, Yantian Port, Yantian, Shenzhen Guangdong Province 518081, People's Republic of China, *Tel:* +86 755 2529 1956, *Fax:* +86 755 2529 1110, *Email:* szterminal@ymlchina.com

Railway: Railway Services Department (RSD) handles all rail transport activities from the port

Development: Expansion of container terminal (West) with the construction of two more container berths to be completed by end of 2009
Shenzhen Yantian Port Group and Hutchison Port Holdings have signed an agreement for the joint construction and development of the Shenzhen Yantian East Port Phase I container terminal project which will cover a total area of 138.5 ha and be operated by Yantian International Container Terminals Ltd. It will have a total quay length of 1442 m split between four deepwater berths; two 6600 TEU berths and two 9500 TEU berths

Lloyd's Agent: Huatai Surveyors & Adjusters Co., Room 802, Jun Yuan Mansion, 155 Tian He East Road, Guangzhou, Guangdong Province 510620, People's Republic of China, *Tel:* +86 20 3881 2306, *Fax:* +86 20 3881 2470, *Email:* agency.gz@huatai-serv.com, *Website:* www.huatai-serv.com

YAOPODU

harbour area, see under Jinshi

YIBIN

Lat 28° 46' N; Long 104° 37' E.

Admiralty Chart: -	**Admiralty Pilot:** -
Time Zone: GMT +8 h	**UNCTAD Locode:** CN

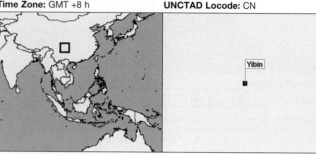

Principal Facilities:

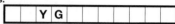

		Y	G						

Authority: Yibin Bureau of Communication, Yifu Street, Yibin, Sichuan Province 644000, People's Republic of China

Accommodation:

Name	Remarks
Yibin	See [1] below

[1]*Yibin:* Consists of three harbour areas: Changjiang River Area, Jinsha River Area and Minjiang River Area
Cargoes handled include ore, coal, bamboo, timber and general cargo

Storage: Open and covered storage areas available

Mechanical Handling Equipment:

Location	Type	Capacity (t)
Yibin	Mult-purp. Cranes	3

Lloyd's Agent: Huatai Surveyors & Adjusters Co., 14th Floor, China Re Building, No.11 Jin Rong Avenue, Xicheng District, Beijing 100140, People's Republic of China, *Tel:* +86 10 6657 6577, *Fax:* +86 10 6657 6502, *Email:* agency.bj@huatai-serv.com, *Website:* www.huatai-serv.com

YICHANG

Lat 30° 42' N; Long 111° 18' E.

Admiralty Chart: 2947	**Admiralty Pilot:** 32
Time Zone: GMT +8 h	**UNCTAD Locode:** CN YIC

Principal Facilities:

		Y	G	C			B		A

Authority: Yichang Port (Group) Ltd., Yichang, Hubei Province 443003, People's Republic of China, *Tel:* +86 717 696 6606, *Website:* www.ycp.com.cn

Traffic: 2005, 4 710 000 t of cargo handled, 12 100 TEU's

Accommodation:

Name	Length (m)	Depth (m)	Remarks
Yichang			See [1] below
Central Terminal	130	3	Two berths for vessels up to 3000 dwt
Zhicheng Terminal	1037	6	See [2] below
Linjiangping Terminal	267	5	Ten berths for vessels up to 5000 dwt

[1]*Yichang:* Situated at the dividing line between the upper and middle reaches of the Yangtze handling breakbulk cargo, containers and passengers
[2]*Zhicheng Terminal:* Twenty two berths for vessels up to 3000 dwt handling coal, phosphorus ores & metal ores

Storage:

Location	Open (m²)	Covered (m²)
Yichang	174000	15423

Bunkering: Available

Shipping Agents: CMA-CGM S.A., CMA CGM Yichang, Room 2303, Qingjiang Tower, 95 Dongshan Avenue, Yichang, Hubei Province 443000, People's Republic of China, *Tel:* +86 717 631 9076, *Fax:* +86 717 631 9075, *Email:* yic.genmbox@cma-cgm.com, *Website:* www.cma-cgm.com

Airport: Yichang Airport

Lloyd's Agent: Huatai Surveyors & Adjusters Co., 14th Floor, China Re Building, No.11 Jin Rong Avenue, Xicheng District, Beijing 100140, People's Republic of China, *Tel:* +86 10 6657 6577, *Fax:* +86 10 6657 6502, *Email:* agency.bj@huatai-serv.com, *Website:* www.huatai-serv.com

YIJIAWAN

harbour area, see under Xiangtan

YINGKOU

Lat 40° 41' N; Long 122° 14' E.

Admiralty Chart: 1262/2991	**Admiralty Pilot:** 32
Time Zone: GMT +8 h	**UNCTAD Locode:** CN YIK

Principal Facilities:

P	Q	Y	G	C		B		T	

Authority: Yingkou Port Group, No.1 New Port Avenue, Bayuquan District, Yingkou, Liaoning Province 115007, People's Republic of China, *Tel:* +86 417 626 9335, *Fax:* +86 417 615 1523, *Website:* www.ykport.com.cn

Port Security: ISPS compliant

Approach: Draft limitation in Yingkou Channel is 6.0 m and Bayuquan Channel is 10.5 m

Anchorage: Yingkou Anchorage in depth of 9.5 m for vessels up to 10 000 dwt and used for quarantine and pilot
Lightening Anchorage in depth of 10.0 m for vessels up to 10 000 dwt and used for lightening
Bayuquan Quarantine Anchorage in depth of 13.5 m for vessels up to 60 000 dwt and used for large vessel lightening
Bayuquan Pilot Anchorage in depth of 11.0 m for vessels up to 20 000 dwt and used for smaller vessels and pilot

Pilotage: Compulsory. Pilotage is undertaken day and night. Pilot boards vessel at pilot anchorage in pos 40° 31.5' N; 122° 00' E

Radio Frequency: VHF Channels 16 and 18

Tides: Average tidal range of 2.56 m

Traffic: 2006, 94 774 000 t of cargo handled, 1 011 000 TEU's

Principal Imports and Exports: Imports: Fertilizer, General bulk goods, Iron and steel. Exports: Magnesium ore, Maize, Sorghum, Talc.

Accommodation:

Name	Length (m)	Depth (m)	Remarks
Yingkou			
No.2 Terminal N	131	6.2	Max 3000 dwt. General & bulk cargo
No.2 Terminal Middle & S	240	6.2	Max 3000 dwt. General & bulk cargo
No.2 Terminal Grain	85	6.5	Max 3000 dwt. Grain
No.3 Terminal E	123	6.5	Max 3000 dwt. General & bulk cargo
No.3 Terminal W	121	6	Max 3000 dwt. General & bulk cargo
No.4 Terminal 1000 t	80	5	Max 1000 dwt. General & bulk cargo
Bayuquan			
Berth No.0	140	8	Max 5000 dwt. General & bulk cargo
Berth No.1	187	11	Max 15 000 dwt. General & bulk cargo
Berth No.2	182	11	Max 15 000 dwt. General & bulk cargo
Berth No.3	212	11	Max 15 000 dwt. General & bulk cargo
Berth No.4	154	11	Max 5000 dwt. Container & general cargo
Berth No.5	155	11	Max 5000 dwt. Container & general cargo
Berth No.6	212	11	Max 15 000 dwt. General & bulk cargo
Berth No.7	182	11	Max 15 000 dwt. General & bulk cargo
Berth No.8	187	11	Max 15 000 dwt. General & bulk cargo
Berth No.9	150	8	Max 10 000 dwt. General & bulk cargo
Coal	289	11	Max 30 000 dwt. General cargo, bulk cargo & coal
LPG	36	5.5	Max 3000 dw. LPG & chemicals

Storage:

Location	Open (m²)	Covered (m²)
Yingkou	240000	270000
Bayuquan		77000

Bunkering: Available at Yingkou berths

Towage: Eight tugs ranging from 600-3400 hp

Ship Chandlers: Yingkou Foreign Supply Co. Ltd, Yingkou Economic & Technological Development Zone, Xingang Road, Yingkou, Liaoning Province 115007, People's Republic of China, *Tel:* +86 417 614 0752, *Fax:* +86 417 614 0921, *Email:* office@yksupco.com

Shipping Agents: China Marine Shipping Agency Co. Ltd, China Marine Shipping Agency Liaoning Company Limited Yingkou Branch, Sinotrans Building, Tianshan Street, Bayuquan District, Yingkou, Liaoning Province, People's Republic of China, *Tel:* +86 417 615 2917, *Fax:* +86 417 615 1809, *Email:* yangchengli@sinotrans-yk.com, *Website:* www.sinoagent.com
CMA-CGM S.A., CMA CGM Yingkou, Room 901, Waidai Building, 1 Xingangda Road, Bayuquan District, Yingkou, Liaoning Province 115007, People's Republic of China, *Tel:* +86 417 615 5977, *Fax:* +86 417 615 5966, *Email:* yik.awang@cma-cgm.com, *Website:* www.cma-cgm.com

Railway: The Changchun-Dabian railway is 9 km from the port

Lloyd's Agent: Huatai Surveyors & Adjusters Co., 14th Floor, China Re Building, No.11 Jin Rong Avenue, Xicheng District, Beijing 100140, People's Republic of China, *Tel:* +86 10 6657 6577, *Fax:* +86 10 6657 6502, *Email:* agency.bj@huatai-serv.com, *Website:* www.huatai-serv.com

YIYANG

Lat 28° 34' N; Long 112° 19' E.

Admiralty Chart: -	**Admiralty Pilot:** -
Time Zone: GMT +8 h	**UNCTAD Locode:** CN

Principal Facilities:

		Y	G						

Authority: Yiyang Harbour Administration, Qiaonan, Yiyang, Hunan Province 413000, People's Republic of China

Accommodation:

Name	Remarks
Yiyang	See [1] below

[1]*Yiyang:* Numerous berths available for vessels up to 500 dwt handling ore, fertiliser, iron & steel, coal, grain and construction materials

Storage: Open and covered storage areas available

Mechanical Handling Equipment:

Location	Type	Capacity (t)
Yiyang	Mult-purp. Cranes	16

Lloyd's Agent: Huatai Surveyors & Adjusters Co., 14th Floor, China Re Building, No.11 Jin Rong Avenue, Xicheng District, Beijing 100140, People's Republic of China, *Tel:* +86 10 6657 6577, *Fax:* +86 10 6657 6502, *Email:* agency.bj@huatai-serv.com, *Website:* www.huatai-serv.com

YONGJINMEN

harbour area, see under Ganzhou

Key to Principal Facilities:—				
A=Airport	**C**=Containers	**G**=General Cargo	**P**=Petroleum	**R**=Ro/Ro	**Y**=Dry Bulk
B=Bunkers	**D**=Dry Dock	**L**=Cruise	**Q**=Other Liquid Bulk	**T**=Towage (where available from port)	

YOUDUN

harbour area, see under Songjiang

YUANJIANG

Lat 28° 50' N; Long 112° 22' E.

Admiralty Chart: 2947
Time Zone: GMT +8 h

Admiralty Pilot: 32
UNCTAD Locode: CN

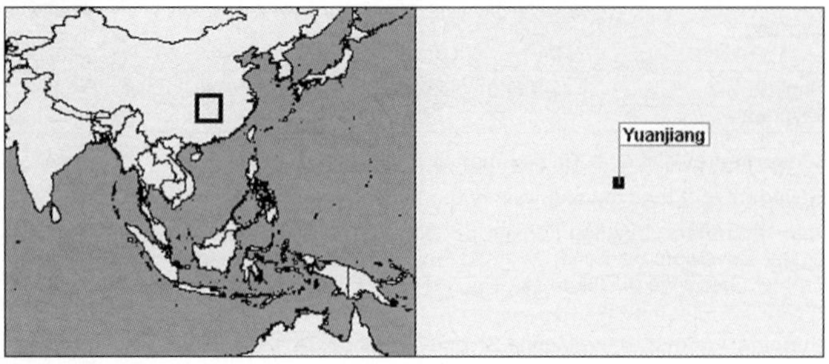

Principal Facilities:

P		Y	G						

Authority: Yuanjiang Harbour & Shipping Administration, Qionghu Town, Yuanjiang, Hunan Province 413100, People's Republic of China

Accommodation:

Name	Remarks
Yuanjiang	See [1] below

[1]*Yuanjiang:* Numerous berths available for vessels up to 500 dwt handling passengers, ore, coal, petroleum, iron & steel, grain and timber

Storage: Open and covered storage areas available

Lloyd's Agent: Huatai Surveyors & Adjusters Co., 14th Floor, China Re Building, No.11 Jin Rong Avenue, Xicheng District, Beijing 100140, People's Republic of China, *Tel:* +86 10 6657 6577, *Fax:* +86 10 6657 6502, *Email:* agency.bj@huatai-serv.com, *Website:* www.huatai-serv.com

YUGANG

harbour area, see under Wuhu

ZHANGHUABANG

harbour area, see under Shanghai

ZHANGJIABU

Lat 37° 1' N; Long 122° 11' E.

Admiralty Chart: 1254
Time Zone: GMT +8 h

Admiralty Pilot: 32
UNCTAD Locode: CN

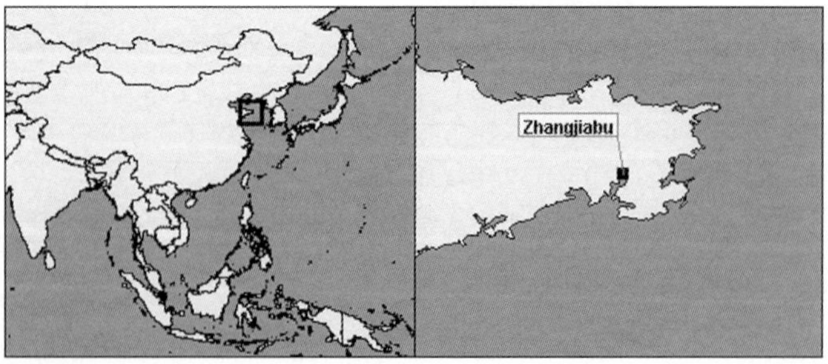

Principal Facilities:

P		Y	G						

Authority: Zhangjiabu Port Administration, Bukou Town, Wendeng, Shandong Province 264406, People's Republic of China

Accommodation:

Name	Remarks
Zhangjiabu	See [1] below

[1]*Zhangjiabu:* Three berths available for vessels up to 1000 dwt handling ore, coal, petroleum, fertiliser, timber, salt, grain and general cargo

Storage: Open and covered storage areas available

Lloyd's Agent: Huatai Surveyors & Adjusters Co., 14th Floor, China Re Building, No.11 Jin Rong Avenue, Xicheng District, Beijing 100140, People's Republic of China, *Tel:* +86 10 6657 6577, *Fax:* +86 10 6657 6502, *Email:* agency.bj@huatai-serv.com, *Website:* www.huatai-serv.com

ZHANGJIAGANG

Lat 31° 57' N; Long 120° 23' E.

Admiralty Chart: 1619
Time Zone: GMT +8 h

Admiralty Pilot: 32
UNCTAD Locode: CN ZJG

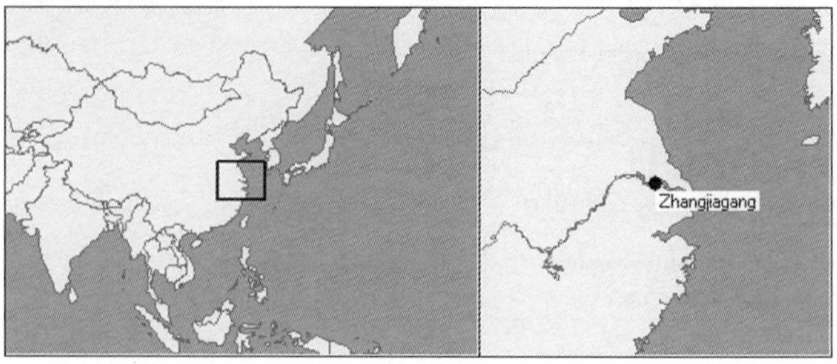

Principal Facilities:

P		Y	G	C		B		T	

Authority: Zhangjiagang Port Group Co Ltd, Harbour District, Zhangjiagang, Jiangsu Province 215633, People's Republic of China, *Tel:* +86 512 5833 1701, *Website:* www.zjgport.com.cn

Port Security: ISPS compliant

Anchorage: Zhangjiagang Anchorage in depth of 15 m; bottom of sand and mud with good holding ground

Pilotage: Compulsory and available during daytime only. Pilot boards at the Baoshan Anchorage

Radio Frequency: VHF Channel 11

Tides: Average tidal range of 2.62 m

Traffic: 2006, 455 900 TEU's handled

Accommodation:

Name	Length (m)	Depth (m)	Remarks
Zhangjiagang			
Berth No.1	256	14	Max 30 000 dwt. General cargo
Berth No.2		14	Max 30 000 dwt. General cargo
Berth No.4	256	14	Max 30 000 dwt. Bulk cargo
Berth No.5		14	Max 30 000 dwt. Bulk cargo
Berth No.6	180	14	Max 30 000 dwt. General & bulk cargo
Berth No.7	180	14	Max 30 000 dwt. General & bulk cargo
Berth No.8	215	14	Max 30 000 dwt. General & bulk cargo
Berth No.9	185	14	Max 30 000 dwt. General & bulk cargo
Berth No.10	196	14	Max 30 000 dwt. General & bulk cargo
Berth No's 15-16	510	10	See [1] below
Coal Berth	180	14	Max 30 000 dwt. Coal
Donggang Berth No.14	190	14	Max 30 000 dwt. General & bulk cargo
Jianghai Berth No.1	180	14	Max 30 000 dwt. Food & edible
Jianghai Berth No.2	200	14	Max 30 000 dwt. Food & edible
Changshan Berth	90	7.5	Max 5000 dwt. Chemicals (liquid)
Chemicals Berth	90	7.5	Max 7000 dwt. Chemicals (liquid)

[1]*Berth No's 15-16:* Operated by Zhangjiagang Win Hanverky Container Terminal Co Ltd., Tel: +86 512 5833 2511, Fax: +86 512 5833 2064, Website: www.zwtnet.com Container terminal

Storage:

Location	Open (m²)	Covered (m²)
Zhangjiagang	400000	55000

Mechanical Handling Equipment:

Location	Type	Capacity (t)	Qty
Zhangjiagang	Floating Cranes	16	1
Zhangjiagang	Floating Cranes	32	1
Zhangjiagang	Mult-purp. Cranes	35	
Berth No's 15-16	Container Cranes		3
Berth No's 15-16	Transtainers		4

Bunkering: China Marine Bunker Supply Co., 13F Qian Cun Mansion A, No.2, 5th Block, Anzhen Xili, Chaoyang District, Beijing 100029, People's Republic of China, *Tel:* +86 10 6443 0717, *Fax:* +86 10 6443 0708, *Email:* business@chimbusco.com.cn, *Website:* www.chimbusco.com.cn – *Grades:* IFO120-380cSt; MGO

Towage: Three tugs of 960 hp are available

Ship Chandlers: Zhangjiagang River & Ocean Shipping Supply Center, The End of Tian Tai North Road, Gang Qu Town, Zhangjiagang, Jiangsu Province 215633, People's Republic of China, *Tel:* +86 512 5833 7288, *Fax:* +86 512 5833 7188, *Email:* Louislg2002@hotmail.com

Shipping Agents: China Marine Shipping Agency Co. Ltd, China Marine Shipping Agency Zhangjiagang Company Limited, 45 Changjiang Mid Road, Jingang Town, Zhangjiagang, Jiangsu Province 215633, People's Republic of China, *Tel:* +86 512 5833 2515, *Fax:* +86 512 5833 1481, *Email:* sinoagent@sinotrans-zjg.com, *Website:* www.sinotrans-zjg.com
CMA-CGM S.A., CMA CGM Zhangjiagang, Room 911 Guotai Mansion, Renmin Road Middle, Zhangjiagang, Jiangsu Province 215600, People's Republic of China, *Tel:* +86 512 5818 5507, *Fax:* +86 512 5818 5627, *Email:* gzg.genmbox@cma-cgm.com, *Website:* www.cma-cgm.com
Jiangsu Jinmao Storage & Transport Co., Central Xiang Shan Road, Gang Qu Zhen, Zhangjiagang, Jiangsu Province 251633, People's Republic of China, *Tel:* +86 512 5839 3480, *Fax:* +86 512 5839 3481, *Email:* nkgmng@maersk.com
Tongsheng International Shipping Agencies, Zhangjiagang Tongsheng International Shipping Agency Co Ltd, 4/F,2 Shuangshan Road, Gangqu Town, Zhangjiagang, Jiangsu Province 215633, People's Republic of China, *Tel:* +86 512 5893 0500, *Fax:* +86 512 5893 0511, *Email:* zjg@tongsheng.net.cn, *Website:* www.tongshengshipping.com

Lloyd's Agent: Huatai Surveyors & Adjusters Co., 14th Floor, China Re Building, No.11 Jin Rong Avenue, Xicheng District, Beijing 100140, People's Republic of China, *Tel:* +86 10 6657 6577, *Fax:* +86 10 6657 6502, *Email:* agency.bj@huatai-serv.com, *Website:* www.huatai-serv.com

ZHANGZHOU

Lat 24° 24' N; Long 118° 3' E.

Admiralty Chart: 1767	**Admiralty Pilot:** 32
Time Zone: GMT +8 h	**UNCTAD Locode:** CN ZZU

Principal Facilities:

	Y	G	C	R		B		T	A

Authority: Zhangzhou China Merchants Port Co. Ltd, Zhangzhou, Fujian Province 363105, People's Republic of China, *Tel:* +86 596 685 8888, *Fax:* +86 596 685 8555, *Email:* xz@zcmp.com.cn, *Website:* www.zcmp.com.cn

Officials: General Manager: Liu Enhuai.

Port Security: ISPS compliant

Pre-Arrival Information: Obtain vessel's pre-arrival information through ship agency

Approach: Channel depth of 10.1 m

Anchorage: Shares the same anchorage with Xiamen Terminals. Water area of 19.6 km2, including 1.5 km2 anchorage for vessels of 50 000-100 000 dwt

Pilotage: Compulsory and available 24 h/day. Pilot boards vessel at anchorage or on the terminal

Radio Frequency: VHF Channel 16

Weather: Belongs to subtropical monsoonal wet weather

Tides: Regular half-day tide; average high tide of 5.46 m, average low tide of 1.47 m and average tidal difference of 3.99 m

Maximum Vessel Dimensions: Cape-size vessels can be berthed

Principal Imports and Exports: Imports: Cereals, Containers, Iron ore, Lumber, Steel. Exports: Cereals, Containers, Sand, Steel.

Working Hours: 24 h/day

Accommodation:

Name	Length (m)	Depth (m)	Remarks
Zhangzhou			
Berth No's 1-2	547	17.5	Containers
Berth No.3	267	12.5	Multi-purpose
Berth No's 4-5	410	13.2	Multi-purpose
Berth No's 7-9	780	17.5	General & bulk
Berth No.14	120	6	Mineral building materials for vessels of 7000-10 000 dwt

Storage: Storage centre occupies an area of 160 000 m2 consisting of two 8200 m2 warehouses, one 7800 m2 container freight station, eight 15 000 m3 silos and a yard of over 20 000 m2

Mechanical Handling Equipment:

Location	Type	Capacity (t)	Qty
Zhangzhou	Mobile Cranes	16–25	5
Zhangzhou	Container Cranes	35.5–50	4
Zhangzhou	RTG's	41	4
Zhangzhou	Portal Cranes	10–40	10

Location	Type	Capacity (t)	Qty
Zhangzhou	Reach Stackers	40–45	3
Zhangzhou	Forklifts	3–15	34

Bunkering: Available

Waste Reception Facilities: Available

Towage: Available

Shipping Agents: China Marine Shipping Agency Co. Ltd, China Marine Shipping Agency Fujian Zhangzhou Company, 4th Floor, Port Building, Zhaoshangju Developing Zone, Zhangzhou, Fujian Province, People's Republic of China, *Tel:* +86 596 230 0596, *Fax:* +86 596 685 2596, *Email:* sinotrag@public.zzptt.fj.com
China Ocean Shipping Agency, 2nd Floor Zhangzhou Harbour Building, 95 Yanan Road (N), Zhangzhou, Fujian Province 363000, People's Republic of China, *Tel:* +86 596 203 3973, *Fax:* +86 596 202 8622, *Email:* penavico@public.zzptt.fj.cn, *Website:* www.penavicozz.com.cn
CMA-CGM S.A., CMA CGM Zhangzhou, Room C, 9th Floor CTS Commercial Building, 38 Yan'an North Road, Zhangzhou, Fujian Province 363000, People's Republic of China, *Tel:* +86 596 202 3488, *Fax:* +86 596 202 3399, *Email:* zan.ihang@cma-cgm.com, *Website:* www.cma-cgm.com

Medical Facilities: 5 mins drive to a hospital

Airport: Gaoqi International Airport

Development: Deepening of the approach channel for vessels of 100 000-150 000 dwt

Lloyd's Agent: Huatai Surveyors & Adjusters Co., 14th Floor, China Re Building, No.11 Jin Rong Avenue, Xicheng District, Beijing 100140, People's Republic of China, *Tel:* +86 10 6657 6577, *Fax:* +86 10 6657 6502, *Email:* agency.bj@huatai-serv.com, *Website:* www.huatai-serv.com

ZHANJIANG

Lat 21° 10' N; Long 110° 24' E.

Admiralty Chart: 3349	**Admiralty Pilot:** 30
Time Zone: GMT +8 h	**UNCTAD Locode:** CN ZHA

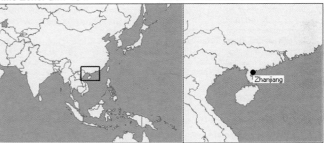

Principal Facilities:

P	Q	Y	G	C	R		B		T	A

Authority: Zhanjiang Port Group Co. Ltd, Seaport Building, 1 Youyi Road, Zhanjiang, Guangdong Province 524027, People's Republic of China, *Tel:* +86 759 225 5516, *Fax:* +86 759 228 0814, *Email:* zhangy@zjport.com, *Website:* www.zjport.com

Officials: Chairman: Riqiang Zheng.
Chief Executive Officer: Yi Zhang.

Port Security: ISPS compliant

Approach: Channel 35 km long from Naozhou Island with depth of 17 m at HW and 14.6 m at LW

Pilotage: Compulsory and available 24 h

Radio Frequency: VHF Channel 16

Tides: Average tidal range of 2.14 m

Traffic: 2006, 81 728 000 t of cargo handled

Maximum Vessel Dimensions: 14 m draught

Principal Imports and Exports: Imports: Fertilizer, Grain, Ironstone, Petroleum, Steel. Exports: Bauxite, General cargo, Non-metallic ores, Woodchips.

Working Hours: 0000-0800, 0800-1600, 1600-2400

Accommodation:

Name	Length (m)	Depth (m)	Remarks
No.1 District			
Berth No.101	188	10.3	Max 15 000 dwt. General cargo
Berth No.102	188	10.3	Max 15 000 dwt. General cargo
Berth No.103	188	10.3	Max 15 000 dwt. General cargo
Berth No.104	189	10.3	Max 15 000 dwt. General cargo
Berth No's 106 & 107	164	5	Max 1000 dwt. General cargo
Berth No.108	135	7.3	Max 5000 dwt. General cargo
Berth No.109	135	7.3	Max 5000 dwt. General cargo
No.2 District			
Berth No.201	138	12.5	Max 50 000 dwt. Crude oil
Berth No.202	479	18.6	Max 300 000 dwt. Crude oil
Berth No.205	75	2	Max 500 dwt. Product oil

Key to Principal Facilities:—			
A=Airport	**C**=Containers	**G**=General Cargo	**P**=Petroleum	**R**=Ro/Ro	**Y**=Dry Bulk
B=Bunkers	**D**=Dry Dock	**L**=Cruise	**Q**=Other Liquid Bulk	**T**=Towage (where available from port)	

Name	Length (m)	Depth (m)	Remarks
No.3 District			
Berth No.300	202	12	Max 35 000 dwt. Coal
Berth No.301	170	10	Max 10 000 dwt. Ore
Berth No.302	174	10	Max 10 000 dwt. General cargo
Berth No.303	200	10	Max 15 000 dwt. Ore
Berth No.304	200	10	Max 15 000 dwt. Ore
No.4 District			
Berth No.401	191	11	Max 15 000 dwt. Steel
Berth No.402	180	11	Max 15 000 dwt. Fertilizer
Berth No.403	200	11	Max 15 000 dwt. Grain
Berth No.404	275	12	Max 35 000 dwt. Bulk grain
Berth No.405	200	11	Max 15 000 dwt. General cargo
Berth No.406	194	11	Max 15 000 dwt. General cargo
Berth No.407	214	11.3	Max 20 000 dwt. Bulk & general cargo
Berth No.408	274	10.7	Max 20 000 dwt. Bulk & general cargo
Berth No.409	273	10.7	Max 20 000 dwt. Bulk & general cargo
Berth No.410	198	11.3	Max 20 000 dwt. Containers
Berth No.411	198	11.3	Max 20 000 dwt. Containers

Storage: Warehousing storage of more than 60 000 m2 with cap of over 1 500 000 t at one time

Mechanical Handling Equipment:

Location	Type	Capacity (t)	Qty
Zhanjiang	Container Cranes	46	2

Bunkering: BP Hong Kong Ltd, 21st Floor, Super Ocean Financial Centre, 067 West Yan An Road, Shanghai, Shanghai Province, People's Republic of China, *Tel:* +86 21 6278 4858, *Fax:* +86 21 6275 7702, *Email:* lucn@bp.com
China Marine Bunker Supply Co., 13F Qian Cun Mansion A, No.2, 5th Block, Anzhen Xili, Chaoyang District, Beijing 100029, People's Republic of China, *Tel:* +86 10 6443 0717, *Fax:* +86 10 6443 0708, *Email:* business@chimbusco.com.cn, *Website:* www.chimbusco.com.cn – *Grades:* IFO120-380cSt; MGO
ExxonMobil Marine Fuels, 1 Harbour Front Place, 06-00 Harbour Front, Tower One, Singapore, Republic of Singapore 098633, *Tel:* +65 6885 8998, *Fax:* +65 6885 8794, *Email:* asiapac.marinefuels@exxonmobil.com, *Website:* www.exxonmobilmarinefuels.com – *Grades:* MDO; MGO; IFO – *Delivery Mode:* barge

Towage: Nine tugs ranging from 400-3200 hp

Repair & Maintenance: Zhanjiang Ocean Ship Repair Co., Zhanjiang, Guangdong Province, People's Republic of China, *Tel:* +86 759 228 9575, *Fax:* +86 759 228 9576

Ship Chandlers: Zhanjiang Ocean Shipping Supply Co. Ltd, No.2 Renmin Road South, Zhanjiang, Guangdong Province 524001, People's Republic of China, *Tel:* +86 759 228 5233, *Fax:* +86 759 222 1386, *Email:* info@zjsupco.com, *Website:* www.zjsupco.com

Shipping Agents: China Marine Shipping Agency Co. Ltd, China Marine Shipping Agency Guangdong Zhanjiang Company, Foreign Trade Building, 1 Renmin Road East 1, Zhanjiang, Guangdong Province 524001, People's Republic of China, *Tel:* +86 759 223 7344, *Fax:* +86 759 228 0869, *Email:* zhanjiang@sinoagentgd.com, *Website:* www.sinoagentgd.com
China Ocean Shipping Agency, 7 Renmin Road (E.1), Zhanjiang, Guangdong Province 524001, People's Republic of China, *Tel:* +86 759 238 1068, *Email:* shipping@penavicozj.com.cn, *Website:* www.penavicozj.com.cn
CMA-CGM S.A., CMA CGM Zhangjiang, Room 901 Huaqiao Building, Renmin South Road, Xiashan District, Zhanjiang, Guangdong Province 524000, People's Republic of China, *Tel:* +86 759 221 8223, *Fax:* +86 759 221 8221, *Email:* zhg.genmbox@cma-cgm.com, *Website:* www.cma-cgm.com
Sino-Continental, Zhanjiang Branch, Room B-5 Building A Conton Bay Hotel, 16 Remin South Road, Xiashan District, Zhanjiang, Guangdong Province 524001, People's Republic of China, *Fax:* +86 759 222 9299, *Email:* zhanjiang@sino-continental.com, *Website:* www.sino-continental.com
Zhanjiang International Shipping Agency Ltd, 7th Floor, Haigang Mansion, Youyi Road, Xiashan Area, Zhanjiang, Guangdong Province 524027, People's Republic of China, *Tel:* +86 759 225 6689, *Fax:* +86 759 225 6809, *Email:* operation@isacozj.com.cn, *Website:* www.isaco.com.cn

Medical Facilities: Harbour hospital, 100 m

Airport: Zhanjiang Airport, 10 km

Railway: The Litong-Zhanjiang railroad links to the national rail system

Development: Phase III of the channel dredging project
A jetty will be extended from Berth No.411 to build a 150 000 dwt ironstone berth with a length of 410 m

Lloyd's Agent: Huatai Surveyors & Adjusters Co., Room 802, Jun Yuan Mansion, 155 Tian He East Road, Guangzhou, Guangdong Province 510620, People's Republic of China, *Tel:* +86 20 3881 2306, *Fax:* +86 20 3881 2470, *Email:* agency.gz@huatai-serv.com, *Website:* www.huatai-serv.com

ZHAOQING

Lat 23° 3' N; Long 112° 26' E.

Admiralty Chart: -	**Admiralty Pilot:** -
Time Zone: GMT +8 h	**UNCTAD Locode:** CN ZQG

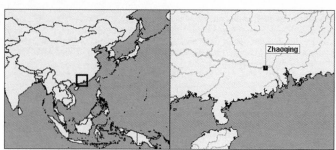

Principal Facilities:

		Y	G						

Authority: Zhaoqing Harbour Administration, 2 Jiangbin Xi Road, Zhaoqing, Guangdong Province 526020, People's Republic of China

Accommodation:

Name	Remarks
Zhaoqing	Cargoes handled include ore, coal, fertiliser and grain
Dixi	Two berths for vessels up to 500 dwt
Didong	Eleven berths for vessels up to 1000 dwt

Storage: Open and covered storage areas available

Mechanical Handling Equipment:

Location	Type	Capacity (t)
Zhaoqing	Mult-purp. Cranes	35

Shipping Agents: CMA-CGM S.A., CMA CGM - Zhaoqing, Room 1404-1405, Development Plaza, 75 Tian Ning North Road, Zhaoqing, Guangdong Province, People's Republic of China, *Tel:* +86 758 231 2029, *Fax:* +86 758 231 2030, *Email:* zqg.kpeng@cma-cgm.com, *Website:* www.cma-cgm.com

Lloyd's Agent: Huatai Surveyors & Adjusters Co., Room 802, Jun Yuan Mansion, 155 Tian He East Road, Guangzhou, Guangdong Province 510620, People's Republic of China, *Tel:* +86 20 3881 2306, *Fax:* +86 20 3881 2470, *Email:* agency.gz@huatai-serv.com, *Website:* www.huatai-serv.com

ZHAPU

Lat 30° 35' N; Long 121° 5' E.

Admiralty Chart: 1143/1199	**Admiralty Pilot:** 32
Time Zone: GMT +8 h	**UNCTAD Locode:** CN ZAP

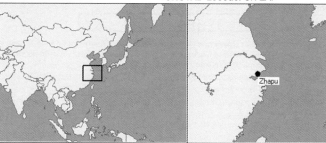

Principal Facilities:

P	Q	Y	G	C		B		T	

Authority: Zhapu Port Authority, Port Administration Office, Huhang Road, Pinghu, Zhejiang Province 314201, People's Republic of China, *Tel:* +86 573 552 2035, *Fax:* +86 573 552 2035

Pilotage: Compulsory and available for 7 h during the day. The anchorage area at the Zhapu pilot boarding place is bounded by the following positions:
30° 34.20' N; 121° 04.83' E
30° 34.20' N; 121° 05.46' E
30° 32.42' N; 121° 05.46' E
30° 32.42' N; 121° 04.83' E

Radio Frequency: VHF Channel 8

Tides: Average tidal range of 4.69 m

Accommodation:

Name	Length (m)	Depth (m)	Remarks
Zhapu			
Berth	232	11.3	General & oil cargo for vessels up to 25 000 dwt

Storage: Container yard of 6000 m2

Location	Open (m²)	Covered (m²)
Zhapu	6000	5000

Mechanical Handling Equipment:

Location	Type	Capacity (t)	Qty
Berth	Shore Cranes	40	1
Berth	Shore Cranes	10	3

Bunkering: Available

Towage: Four tugs available of 2400-3400 hp

Lloyd's Agent: Huatai Surveyors & Adjusters Co., 14th Floor, China Re Building, No.11 Jin Rong Avenue, Xicheng District, Beijing 100140, People's Republic of China, *Tel:* +86 10 6657 6577, *Fax:* +86 10 6657 6502, *Email:* agency.bj@huatai-serv.com, *Website:* www.huatai-serv.com

ZHENGYANGHE

harbour area, see under Harbin

ZHENHAI

harbour area, see under Ningbo

ZHENJIANG

Lat 32° 13' N; Long 119° 24' E.

Admiralty Chart: 1642　　　　　　**Admiralty Pilot:** 32
Time Zone: GMT +8 h　　　　　　**UNCTAD Locode:** CN ZHE

Principal Facilities:

| P | Q | Y | G | C | | | B | | T | A |

Authority: Zhenjiang Port (Group) Co Ltd, 19 Changjiang Road, Zhenjiang, Jiangsu Province 212001, People's Republic of China, *Tel:* +86 511 8527 4892, *Fax:* +86 511 8527 7837, *Website:* www.zhenjiangport.com

Port Security: ISPS compliant

Anchorage: Luochengzhou Anchorage in depth of 11 m; bottom of mud and sand with good holding ground

Pilotage: Compulsory and available during daytime only. Pilot boards at Liuhe Anchorage

Radio Frequency: VHF Channels 11, 16 and 23

Tides: Average tidal range of 0.94 m

Traffic: 2006, 35 000 000 t of cargo handled, 100 000 TEU's

Principal Imports and Exports: Imports: Coal, Oil products, Ore, Scrap, Timber. Exports: Cotton, General cargo, Grain.

Accommodation:

Name	Length (m)	Depth (m)	Remarks
No.2 District			
Berth No.1	278	11	Max 30 000 dwt. Ore
Berth No.2	205	11	Max 30 000 dwt. Bulk cargo
Berth No.3	183	11	Max 30 000 dwt. General cargo
Berth No.4	183	11	Max 30 000 dwt. General cargo
Berth No.5	183	11	Max 30 000 dwt. General cargo
No.3 District			
Berth No.6	210	11	Max 30 000 dwt. General cargo
Berth No.7	220	11	Max 30 000 dwt. Containers
Berth No.8	180	11	Max 30 000 dwt. General & bulk cargo
Berth No.9	180	11	Max 30 000 dwt. General & bulk cargo
Jianbi Oil Berth	234	8.1	Max 10 000-25 000 dwt. Two berths for product oil

Storage:

Location	Open (m²)	Covered (m²)
Zhenjiang	580000	120000

Mechanical Handling Equipment:

Location	Type	Capacity (t)
Zhenjiang	Mult-purp. Cranes	40

Bunkering: Available from Chang Jiang Bunker Supply Station

Towage: One tug of 3400 hp, two tugs of 1960 hp, two tugs of 1670 hp and three tugs of 980 hp

Ship Chandlers: Zhenjiang Ocean Shipping Supply Co. Ltd, 98 Zhongshan West Road, Zhenjiang, Jiangsu Province 212004, People's Republic of China, *Tel:* +86 511 8589 8088, *Fax:* +86 511 8589 8333, *Email:* zjossc@pub.zj.jsinfo.net, *Website:* www.cnossc.com

Shipping Agents: China Marine Shipping Agency Co. Ltd, China Marine Shipping Agency Zhengjiang Company Limited, 12th Floor, Foreign Trade Building, No 98 Zhongshan Road West, Zhenjiang, Jiangsu Province 212004, People's Republic of China, *Tel:* +86 511 8524 2330, *Fax:* +86 511 8524 2177, *Email:* sinoagentzj@263.net, *Website:* www.sinotranszj.com

Airport: Lukou International Airport in Nanjing, 80 km. Changzhou Airport, 50 km

Lloyd's Agent: Huatai Surveyors & Adjusters Co., 14th Floor, China Re Building, No.11 Jin Rong Avenue, Xicheng District, Beijing 100140, People's Republic of China, *Tel:* +86 10 6657 6577, *Fax:* +86 10 6657 6502, *Email:* agency.bj@huatai-serv.com, *Website:* www.huatai-serv.com

ZHONGSHAN

Lat 22° 31' N; Long 113° 21' E.

Admiralty Chart: -　　　　　　**Admiralty Pilot:** -
Time Zone: GMT +8 h　　　　　　**UNCTAD Locode:** CN ZSN

Principal Facilities:

| P | | Y | G | C | | | | |

Authority: Zhongshan Port & Shipping Enterprise Group Ltd, Port & Shipping Building, 3 Yanjiang East 1 Road, Zhongshan, Guangdong Province 528437, People's Republic of China, *Tel:* +86 760 8559 8777, *Fax:* +86 760 8559 6108, *Email:* ghjt@zhongshanshipping.com, *Website:* www.zhongshanshipping.com

Approach: Depth in channel ranges from 9 m to 15 m

Traffic: 2006, 1 173 400 TEU's handled

Maximum Vessel Dimensions: 5000 dwt

Accommodation:

Name	Length (m)	Draught (m)	Remarks
Zhongshan			
Foreign Service Harbour	210	5	Container & bulk cargo for vessels up to 3000 dwt
Port & Shipping Enterprise Group Ltd	821	5	Container & bulk cargo for vessels up to 3000 dwt
Shanhai Port	93.5	5	Container & bulk cargo for vessels up to 3000 dwt
Unicizers Ind. Co Ltd	135	7	Chemicals for vessels up to 5000 dwt
Power Plant Berth	100	5	Oils for vessels up to 5000 dwt

Storage: Warehouses available

Shipping Agents: China Marine Shipping Agency Co. Ltd, China Marine Shipping Agency Guangdong Co. Ltd Zhongshan Branch, Zhongshan Harbour Foreign Trade Service Port, Zhongshan, Guangdong Province, People's Republic of China, *Tel:* +86 760 8531 0668, *Fax:* +86 760 8338 1218, *Email:* zhongshan@sinoagentgd.com
CMA-CGM S.A., CMA CGM Zhongshan, Room 1801-1802, Bank of China Tower, 18 Zhong Shan San Road, Zhongshan, Guangdong Province 528400, People's Republic of China, *Tel:* +86 760 8831 7529, *Fax:* +86 760 8831 7264, *Email:* zsn.genmbox@cma-cgm.com, *Website:* www.cma-cgm.com
Mediterranean Shipping Company, MSC (Hong Kong) Ltd, Room 2011-2013, 20/F, Bank of China Tower, 18 Zhongshan Three Road, Zhongshan, Guangdong Province 528043, People's Republic of China, *Tel:* +86 760 8822 3971, *Fax:* +86 760 8822 3978, *Email:* msc@mschkg.com, *Website:* www.mschongkong.com
Mighty Ocean Shipping Ltd, Ground Floor, 19 Nang Bou Building, Yue Lai Nang Bo Ai Er Road, Zhongshan, Guangdong Province, People's Republic of China, *Tel:* +86 760 8332 6611, *Fax:* +86 760 8881 1733, *Email:* moslzhn@pub.zhongshan.gd.cn
Agencia de Navegacao Yat Fat Lda, Unit 612, Building 2, Holiday Plaza, Zhongshan, Guangdong Province, People's Republic of China, *Tel:* +86 760 8531 0123, *Fax:* +86 760 8531 0999, *Email:* yatfat@macau.ctm.net
Young Carrier Co. Ltd, Unit A-106, 28 Zhong Shan 3rd Road, Zhongshan, Guangdong Province 528403, People's Republic of China, *Tel:* +86 760 8830 5030, *Fax:* +86 760 8830 5031, *Email:* zhongshan@ymlchina.com

Lloyd's Agent: Huatai Surveyors & Adjusters Co., Room 802, Jun Yuan Mansion, 155 Tian He East Road, Guangzhou, Guangdong Province 510620, People's Republic of China, *Tel:* +86 20 3881 2306, *Fax:* +86 20 3881 2470, *Email:* agency.gz@huatai-serv.com, *Website:* www.huatai-serv.com

ZHOUPU

harbour area, see under Nanhui

Key to Principal Facilities:—				
A=Airport	**C**=Containers	**G**=General Cargo	**P**=Petroleum	**R**=Ro/Ro	**Y**=Dry Bulk
B=Bunkers	**D**=Dry Dock	**L**=Cruise	**Q**=Other Liquid Bulk	**T**=Towage (where available from port)

ZHOUSHAN

Lat 30° 0' N; Long 122° 6' E.

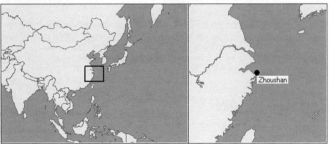

Admiralty Chart: 1126   **Admiralty Pilot:** 32
Time Zone: GMT +8 h   **UNCTAD Locode:** CN ZOS

Principal Facilities:

P		Y	G	C	R		B		T	A	

Authority: Zhoushan Port Administrative Bureau, 1 Ding Harbor Terminal, Zhoushan, Zhejiang Province, People's Republic of China, *Tel:* +86 580 202 7799, *Fax:* +86 580 202 7915, *Website:* www.zsport.com.cn

Port Security: ISPS compliant

Approach: The east channel runs to the East China Sea via the Luotou waterway and the Xiazhimen approach channel, which, with a breadth of 750 m at the narrowest point and a depth of 17.9 m (21.4-22.4 m at high water) at the shallowest point outside the entrance, allows 150 000 t vessels to come into and out of the port freely and 200 000 t vessels to tide into the port

The south channel, having a water depth of 16 m at the shallowest point and navigable for 100 000 t vessels, extends in a southerly direction along the Luotou waterway and the Tiaozhoumen approach channel and connects Zhoushan port with the ports on the coast of Zhejiang and Fujian provinces

The west channel leads to the Hangzhou Bay via the Jintang waterway and the Xihoumen approach channel and is accessible to vessels of 35 000 t and below

Anchorage: Luhuashan anchorage (N): for lightering, sheltering and anchoring temporarily in pos 30° 45' 00" N; 122° 38' 16" E, 30° 46' 21" N; 122° 38' 16" E, 30° 47' 26" N; 122° 38' 52" E, 30° 48' 24" N; 122° 38' 45" E, 30° 48' 24" N; 122° 38' 22" E, 30° 48' 08" N; 122° 38' 59" E, 30° 45' 00" N; 122° 38' 59" E in depth of 18-56 m
Luhuashan anchorage (S): water area of 0.6 nm radius centered on pos 30° 50' 54" N; 122° 37' 30" E in depth of 19-28 m
Luhuashan anchorage's fresh & live aquatic products delivery spot: in pos 30° 49' 12" N; 122° 36' 30" E, 30° 49' 12" N; 122° 37' 00" E, 30° 49' 00" N; 122° 37' 00" E, 30° 49' 00" N; 122° 36' 30" E in depth of 2-4.5 m
Huangxing anchorage: for fresh & live aquatic products delivery spot in pos 30° 12' 00" N; 122° 38' 00" E, 30° 12' 00" N; 122° 38' 12" E, 30° 11' 30" N; 122° 38' 12" E, 30° 11' 30" N; 122° 38' 00" E in depth of 5-8 m
Chenqianshan anchorage (N): waiting anchorage for joint inspection of domestic vessels (second-grade trading port in Shensi) in pos 30° 44' 18" N; 122° 48' 15" E, 30° 44' 30" N; 122° 48' 15" E, 30° 44' 30" N; 122° 48' 30" E, 30° 44' 18" N; 122° 48' 30" E in depth of 40 m
Chenqianshan anchorage (S): waiting anchorage for joint inspection of domestic vessels (second-grade trading port in Shensi) in pos 30° 42' 24" N; 122° 48' 30" E, 30° 42' 38" N; 122° 48' 30" E, 30° 42' 38" N; 122° 48' 48" E, 30° 42' 24" N; 122° 48' 48" E in depth of 17-20 m
Jinjishan anchorage: waiting anchorage for joint inspection of domestic vessels (second-grade trading port in Shensi) in pos 30° 45' 09" N; 122° 25' 43" E, 30° 45' 24" N; 122° 25' 43" E, 30° 45' 24" N; 122° 26' 06" E, 30° 45' 09" N; 122° 26' 06" E in depth of 5-7 m
Gaoting joint inspection anchorage: joint inspection anchorage for domestic vessels (second-grade trading port in Daishan) in pos 30° 14' 41" N; 122° 06' 12" E, 30° 15' 04" N; 122° 06' 12" E, 30° 15' 04" N; 122° 06' 40" E, 30° 14' 41" N; 122° 06' 40" E in depth of 8.4-20 m
Putuoshan foreign passenger vessel joint inspection anchorage: joint inspection anchorage for foreign passenger vessel with water area of 250 m radius centered in pos 29° 57' 36" N; 122° 23' 30" E in depth of 11.8 m
Mazhi joint inspection and lightering anchorage (S): joint inspection, lightering, anchoring of vessels to be traded in pos 29° 55' 30" N; 122° 16' 30" E, 29° 54' 00" N; 122° 16' 30" E, 29° 54' 00" N; 122° 13' 30" E, 29° 52' 30" N; 122° 13' 30" E, 29° 52' 00" N; 122° 12' 00" E, 29° 54' 00" N; 122° 12' 42" E, 29° 55' 30" N; 122° 12' 42" E in depth of 10.4-45 m
Aoshan joint inspection anchorage: water area of 800 m radius centered in pos 29° 51' 36" N; 122° 12' 54" E in depth of 33-54 m
Yeyashan joint inspection anchorage: in pos 30° 01' 46" N; 121° 59' 15" E, 30° 00' 36" N; 122° 00' 22" E, 29° 59' 31" N; 122° 59' 03" E, 30° 00' 00" N; 122° 58' 36" E, 30° 01' 24" N; 122° 58' 48" E in depth of 20-32 m
Xiazhimen anchorage (N): pilotage anchorage in pos 29° 46' 30" N; 121° 20' 30" E, 29° 46' 30" N; 122° 23' 00" E, 29° 44' 30" N; 122° 23' 00" E, 29° 44' 30" N; 122° 20' 30" E in depth of 17-24 m
Xiazhimen anchorage (S): pilotage anchorage in pos 29° 43' 30" N; 121° 20' 00" E, 29° 42' 12" N; 122° 23' 00" E, 29° 41' 36" N; 122° 23' 00" E, 29° 41' 36" N; 122° 20' 00" E in depth of 19.5-23 m
Xixiezhi anchorage (NE): sheltering in pos 29° 59' 36" N; 122° 03' 03" E, 29° 59' 12" N; 122° 03' 03" E, 29° 59' 45" N; 122° 23' 30" E, 29° 59' 12" N; 122° 03' 30" E in depth of 16-35 m
Mazhi dangerous cargo anchorage: anchoring of dangerous cargo vessels of 500 t and above in pos 29° 56' 36" N; 122° 14' 00" E, 29° 55' 54" N; 122° 14' 00" E, 29° 56' 10" N; 122° 16' 00" E, 29° 55' 54" N; 122° 16' 00" E in depth of 11-15 m
Pingyangpu anchorage: anchoring and sheltering of small vessels in pos 29° 57' 51" N; 122° 13' 56" E, 29° 57' 45" N; 122° 13' 52" E, 29° 57' 29" N; 122° 14' 38" E, 29° 57' 24" N; 122° 14' 39" E in depth of 3-4 m
Duntou anchorage: anchoring and sheltering of small vessels in pos 29° 57' 06" N;

122° 15' 12" E, 29° 56' 47" N; 122° 15' 42" E, 29° 56' 42" N; 122° 15' 37" E, 29° 57' 00" N; 122° 15' 07" E in depth of 2-4 m
Xiaozhushan anchorage (E): sheltering in pos 30° 00' 28" N; 122° 05' 22" E, 30° 00' 30" N; 122° 05' 48" E, 30° 00' 12" N; 122° 05' 23" E, 30° 00' 22" N; 122° 05' 46" E in depth of 3.5-7.8 m
Dawukui anchorage (S): sheltering and anchoring of vessels to be traded in pos 29° 59' 36" N; 122° 05' 36" E, 29° 59' 36" N; 122° 06' 24" E, 29° 59' 12" N; 122° 05' 48" E, 29° 59' 12" N; 122° 06' 24" E in depth of 14-37 m
Dawukui anchorage (E): sheltering of oil tankers and dangerous cargo vessels in pos 30° 00' 00" N; 122° 06' 17" E, 30° 00' 00" N; 122° 06' 25" E, 29° 59' 42" N; 122° 06' 22" E, 29° 59' 42" N; 122° 06' 35" E in depth of 3-7 m
Mazhi dangerous cargo handling anchorage: water area of 215 m radius centered in pos 29° 55' 57" N; 122° 16' 06" E in depth of 10 m
Mazhishan outer anchorage: anchoring of larger vessels in pos 30° 26' 31" N; 122° 45' 27" E, 30° 25' 13" N; 122° 44' 20" E, 29° 24' 15" N; 122° 45' 50" E, 29° 25' 33" N; 122° 46' 58" E in depth of 29-35 m
Mazhishan pilotage anchorage: water area of 1000 m radius centered in pos 30° 37' 00" N; 122° 32' 42" E in depth of 23 m
Jintang anchorage: pilotage, sheltering and waiting in pos 30° 00' 00" N; 121° 49' 04" E, 30° 00' 00" N; 121° 49' 32" E, 30° 00' 30" N; 121° 50' 00" E, 30° 02' 00" N; 121° 50' 00" E, 30° 02' 30" N; 122° 49' 32" E, 30° 02' 30" N; 122° 48' 36" E, 30° 00' 30" N; 122° 48' 36" E in depth of 10-20 m
Anchorage for lightering of crude oil tankers (outside Xiazhimen): water area of 1852 m radius centered in pos 29° 42' 12" N; 122° 32' 42" E in depth of 24 m

Pilotage: Compulsory and available 12 h during the day, Tel: +86 580 206 7230, Fax: +86 580 206 7216
Pilot boards in the following positions:
Qili Anchorage in pos 30° 01.50' N; 121° 46.40' E
Xiazhi Men Northern Anchorage in pos 29° 45.50' N; 122° 21.50' E
In pos 29° 51.58' N; 122° 12.95' E

Radio Frequency: VHF Channel 16

Traffic: 2004, 73 593 000 t of cargo handled

Accommodation: The port is divided into the following eight areas:
1) DINGHAI is located in the urban area of Dinghai district on Zhoushan main island. It extends to Yangluoshan light beacon and Lengkenzui in the west and to Goushanpu in the east. 57.4 km usable deepwater shoreline consisting of nine operational zones (Dinghai, Waiyangluo, Qingleitou, Wayaowan, Panzhi, Changzhi, Aoshan, Yongdong and Zhairuoshan)
2) SHENJIAMEN is situated east of Goushanpu. 14.3 km usable deepwater shoreline consisting of five operational zones (Duntou, Putuoshan, Donggang, Liuheng and Liuheng)
3) LAOTANGSHAN lies west of Yangluoshan light beacon and Lengkenzui. 36 km usable deepwater shoreline including 7 km at Yeyashan and 14.5 km on Jintang island, consisting of eight operational zones (Laotangshan, Jintang I, Jintang II, Jintang III, Cezi, Mamu, Lidiao and Waidiao)
4) GAOTING includes Daishan main island and the islands of Dachangtu, Xiaochangtu and Xiushan. 25.6 km usable deepwater shoreline consisting of four operational zones (Gaoting Old Operational Zone, Gaoting New Operational Zone, Daidong and Xiushan
5) SILJIAO covers Sijiao, Majishan, Jinji and Huanglong Islands. 11 km usable deepwater shoreline consisting of two operational zones (Lizhushan and Majishan)
6) QUSHAN includes Qushan Main Island and the Islands of Xiaoqushan and Huangzeshan and consists of two operational zones and 18 km of usable deepwater shoreline
7) LUHUASHAN on Luhuashan Island has one operational zone and 3.5 km of usable deepwater shoreline
8.YANGSHAN consisting of Dayangshan and Xiaoyangshan Islands with one operational zone and 3.3 km of usable deepwater shoreline

Name	Length (m)	Depth (m)	Remarks
Public Berths			
Dinghai			
Dinghai Passenger Terminal Berth No.1	60	6	See [1] below
Dinghai Passenger Terminal Berth No.2	60	6	See [2] below
Dinghai Passenger Terminal Berth No.3	60	6	See [3] below
Dinghai Passenger Terminal Berth No's 4, 5, 6 & 7	30	4	Passenger berths operated by Zhoushan Port Haitong Passenger Transport Co Ltd for vessels up to 500 t
Wayaowan Berth	104	6	See [4] below
Zhoushan Port Hailong Co Berth No.1	18	2	See [5] below
Zhoushan Port Hailong Co Berth No.2	74	3	See [6] below
Zhoushan Port Haitong Tug & Barge Co Berth No's 1, 2 & 3	36	9	Tug berths operated by Zhoushan Port Haitong Tug & Barge Co Ltd for tugs up to 500 t
Shenjiamen			
Shenjiamen Berth No.4	97	6	See [7] below
Putuoshan Passenger Terminal Fixed Berth	180	14	See [8] below
Putuoshan Passenger Terminal Berth No's 1, 2 & 3	36	7	Passenger berths operated by Zhoushan Port Haitong Passenger Transport Co Ltd for vessels up to 500 t
Laotangshan			
Laotangshan (Phase I) Berth	250	10.5	See [9] below
Laotangshan (Phase II) Berth No.1	186	11.5	See [10] below
Laotangshan (Phase II) Berth No.2	137	11.5	See [11] below

Name	Length (m)	Depth (m)	Remarks
Laotangshan (Phase III) Berth	302	15	See [12] below
Other Berths of 3000 t & above			
Dinghai			
Dinghai Power Plant Coal Unloading Berth	110	10	Coal berth operated by Zhoushan Power Co for vessels up to 3000 t
Fuxing Xixiezhi Oil Depot Berth	100	12	See [13] below
Longzhou Petrochemical Changsheng Oil Depot Berth	100	7.5	Oil products berth operated by Zhoushan Longzhou Petrochemical Co Ltd for vessels up to 3000 t
Qinfeng Stevedoring Co No.5 Berth	105	7	See [14] below
Shuangyang Oil Depot Berth	135	7.6	See [15] below
Xingzhong Oil Co No.1 Berth	555	20	See [16] below
Xingzhong Oil Co No.2 Berth	340	12	See [17] below
Xingzhong Oil Co No.3 Berth	230	9.5	See [18] below
Gangkoupu Coal Yard Berth	72	10	See [19] below
Zhoushan Power Plant Berth	208	10	Coal berth operated by Zhoushan Power Co for vessels up to 10 000 t
Zhoushan Economic Development Zone No.1 Berth	98	7	See [20] below
Zhoushan Oil Co Gangkoupu No.1 Berth	86	7	See [21] below
Zhoushan Oil Co Gangkoupu No.2 Berth	72	7	See [22] below
Zhoushan Tongda Co Ximatou Berth	50	6	See [23] below
Shenjiamen			
Banshengdong Oil Depot Berth	152	4	See [24] below
Banshengdong Oil Depot Berth	69	11.6	See [25] below
Zhangqigang Oil Depot Berth	84	9.5	Oil products berth operated by Zhoushan Jinhui Oil Co Ltd for vessels up to 5000 t
Lujiazhi Oil Depot Berth	133	7.5	See [26] below
Sinopec Mazhi Berth	173	6.8	See [27] below
Gaoting			
Daishan Power Co Pumen Power Plant Berth	102	8	Coal berth operated by Daishan Power Co for vessels up to 3000 t
Langjizui Power Plant Berth	50	8	Coal berth operated by Daishan Power Co for vessels up to 3000 t
Langjizui Cargo Berth	102	6	See [28] below
Daishan Crude Oil Transshipment Berth	225	11.5	See [29] below
Siljiao			
Majishan Unloading Berth	456	23	See [30] below
Majishan Loading Berth	275	11.2	See [31] below
Gouqi Oil Depot Berth	61	8.5	See [32] below

[1]*Dinghai Passenger Terminal Berth No.1:* Passenger berth operated by Zhoushan Port Haitong Passenger Transport Co Ltd for vessels up to 3000 t

[2]*Dinghai Passenger Terminal Berth No.2:* Passenger berth operated by Zhoushan Port Haitong Passenger Transport Co Ltd for vessels up to 3000 t

[3]*Dinghai Passenger Terminal Berth No.3:* Passenger berth operated by Zhoushan Port Haitong Passenger Transport Co Ltd for vessels up to 1000 t

[4]*Wayaowan Berth:* General cargo berth operated by Zhoushan Port Hailong Stevedoring & Transport Co Ltd for vessels up to 5000 t

[5]*Zhoushan Port Hailong Co Berth No.1:* General cargo berth operated by Zhoushan Port Hailong Stevedoring & Transport Co Ltd for vessels up to 200 t

[6]*Zhoushan Port Hailong Co Berth No.2:* General cargo berth operated by Zhoushan Port Hailong Stevedoring & Transport Co Ltd for vessels up to 500 t

[7]*Shenjiamen Berth No.4:* General cargo berth operated by Zhoushan Port Haixing Stevedoring & Storage & Transport Co Ltd for vessels up to 3000 t

[8]*Putuoshan Passenger Terminal Fixed Berth:* Passenger berth operated by Zhoushan Port Hailong Passenger Transport Co Ltd for vessels of 3000-10 000 t

[9]*Laotangshan (Phase I) Berth:* General cargo berth operated by Zhoushan Port Haitong Transshipment & Storage Co Ltd for vessels up to 15 000 t

[10]*Laotangshan (Phase II) Berth No.1:* Coal berth operated by Zhoushan Port Haitong Transshipment & Storage Co Ltd for vessels up to 25 000 t

[11]*Laotangshan (Phase II) Berth No.2:* Coal berth operated by Zhoushan Port Haitong Transshipment & Storage Co Ltd for vessels up to 7000 t

[12]*Laotangshan (Phase III) Berth:* Multi-purpose berth operated by Zhoushan Port Haitong Transshipment & Storage Co Ltd for vessels of 50 000-80 000 t

[13]*Fuxing Xixiezhi Oil Depot Berth:* Oil products berth operated by Zhoushan Fuxing Energy Co Ltd for vessels up to 18 000 t

[14]*Qinfeng Stevedoring Co No.5 Berth:* General cargo berth operated by Dinghai Qinfeng Stevedoring & Transport Co Ltd for vessels up to 3000 t

[15]*Shuangyang Oil Depot Berth:* Oil products berth operated by Petrochina Haiguang Oil Marketing Co Ltd for vessels up to 3000 t

[16]*Xingzhong Oil Co No.1 Berth:* Oil products berth operated by Sinochem Xingzhong Oil Staging (Zhoushan) Co Ltd for vessels up to 250 000 t

[17]*Xingzhong Oil Co No.2 Berth:* Oil products berth operated by Sinochem Xingzhong Oil Staging (Zhoushan) Co Ltd for vessels up to 100 000 t

[18]*Xingzhong Oil Co No.3 Berth:* Oil products berth operated by Sinochem Xingzhong Oil Staging (Zhoushan) Co Ltd for vessels up to 12 500 t

[19]*Gangkoupu Coal Yard Berth:* Coal berth operated by Zhoushan Fuels Transport & Marketing Co Ltd for vessels up to 3000 t

[20]*Zhoushan Economic Development Zone No.1 Berth:* General cargo berth operated by Zhoushan Economic Development Zone Sunchang Storage & Transport Co Ltd for vessels up to 3000 t

[21]*Zhoushan Oil Co Gangkoupu No.1 Berth:* Oil products berth operated by Sinopec Zhejiang Zhoushan Oil Co for vessels up to 5000 t

[22]*Zhoushan Oil Co Gangkoupu No.2 Berth:* Oil products berth operated by Sinopec Zhejiang Zhoushan Oil Co for vessels up to 3000 t

[23]*Zhoushan Tongda Co Ximatou Berth:* Ro/ro berth operated by Zhoushan Tongda Maritime Transport Co Ltd for vessels up to 3000 t

[24]*Banshengdong Oil Depot Berth:* Oil products berth operated by Sinopec Zhejiang Zhoushan Putuo Oil Co for vessels up to 5000 t

[25]*Banshengdong Oil Depot Berth:* Oil products berth operated by Zhejiang Oil Co Putuo Oil Storage & Transport Co for vessels up to 30 000 t

[26]*Lujiazhi Oil Depot Berth:* Oil products berth operated by Petrochina Zhejiang Zhoushan Marketing Co for vessels up to 5000 t

[27]*Sinopec Mazhi Berth:* Oil products berth operated by Sinopec Putuo Mazhi Oil Depot for vessels up to 3000 t

[28]*Langjizui Cargo Berth:* General cargo berth operated by Daishan Xinhai Stevedoring & Transport Co Ltd for vessels up to 3000 t

[29]*Daishan Crude Oil Transshipment Berth:* Oil products berth operated by Shanghai Petroleum Co Ltd Oil Storage & Transshipment Co for vessels up to 20 000 t

[30]*Majishan Unloading Berth:* Mineral ore berth operated by Shanghai Baosteel Group Shensi Majishan Port Area for vessels up to 250 000 dwt

[31]*Majishan Loading Berth:* Mineral ore berth operated by Shanghai Baosteel Group Shensi Majishan Port Area for vessels up to 35 000 t

[32]*Gouqi Oil Depot Berth:* Oil products berth operated by Sinopec Zhejiang Zhoushan Oil Co for vessels up to 3000 t

Bunkering: China Marine Bunker Supply Co., 13F Qian Cun Mansion A, No.2, 5th Block, Anzhen Xili, Chaoyang District, Beijing 100029, People's Republic of China, *Tel:* +86 10 6443 0717, *Fax:* +86 10 6443 0708, *Email:* business@chimbusco.com.cn, *Website:* www.chimbusco.com.cn – *Grades:* IFO120-380cSt; MGO

Towage: Five tugs of 3200-4000 hp

Ship Chandlers: Zhoushan Ocean Shipping Supply Co. Ltd, No.29 Ren Min Zhong Road, Zhoushan, Zhejiang Province 316000, People's Republic of China, *Tel:* +86 580 202 5835, *Fax:* +86 580 202 5835, *Email:* zsbh@mail.zsptt.zj.cn, *Website:* www.zsissa.com

Shipping Agents: China Marine Shipping Agency Co. Ltd, China Marine Shipping Agency Zhoushan Company Limited, 10th Floor, Zhoushan Building, 66 Huancheng East Road, Zhoushan, Zhejiang Province, People's Republic of China, *Tel:* +86 580 204 1372, *Fax:* +86 580 202 7801, *Email:* zscw@mail.zsptt.zj.cn
Zhoushan International Shipping Agency Ltd, 1701/17/B Xingluting Apartment, Wreath City South Road, Dinghai, Zhoushan, Zhejiang Province 316000, People's Republic of China, *Fax:* +86 580 206 0953, *Email:* zhangzq@isaconb.com.cn, *Website:* www.isaco.com.cn

Airport: Putuoshan Airport, located on Zhujiajian Island

Lloyd's Agent: Huatai Surveyors & Adjusters Co., 14th Floor, China Re Building, No.11 Jin Rong Avenue, Xicheng District, Beijing 100140, People's Republic of China, *Tel:* +86 10 6657 6577, *Fax:* +86 10 6657 6502, *Email:* agency.bj@huatai-serv.com, *Website:* www.huatai-serv.com

ZHOUWEI

harbour area, see under Ezhou

ZHUHAI

Lat 22° 16' N; Long 113° 34' E.

Admiralty Chart: 1557/3026/341	**Admiralty Pilot:** 30
Time Zone: GMT +8 h	**UNCTAD Locode:** CN ZUH

Principal Facilities:

P	Q	Y	G	C		B		T	A

Authority: Zhuhai Gaolan Port Economic Zone, Taiping Bay, Nanshui Township, Zhuhai, Guangdong Province 519050, People's Republic of China, *Tel:* +86 756 726 8118, *Fax:* +86 756 726 8789, *Website:* www.zhhiz.cn

Officials: Commissioner of Maritime Affairs: Lan Sheng Giau.

Anchorage: Guishan loading/unloading anchorage between the following pos 22° 07' 36" N; 113° 48' 20" E and 22° 08' 00" N; 113° 48' 20" E in depth of 15-17 m Jiuzhou anchorage between the following pos 22° 14' 08" N; 113° 37' 50" E, 22° 13' 30" N; 113° 36' 45" E and 22° 12' 20" N; 113° 36' 48" N in depth of 4 m Touzhou pilot station between the following pos 22° 08' 06" N; 113° 40' 54" E, 22°

06' 36" N; 113° 40' 45" E, 22° 08' 42" N; 113° 40' 12" E and 22° 07' 06" N; 113° 40' 45" E in depth of 6-7 m

Touzhou waiting anchorage between the following pos 22° 05' 14" N; 113° 45' 00" E, 22° 04' 04" N; 113° 45' 24" E, 22° 04' 09" N; 113° 43' 00" E and 22° 03' 02" N; 113° 43' 26" E in depth of 11-13 m

Gaolan No.1 anchorage between the following pos 21° 51' 18" N; 113° 15' 45" E, 21° 51' 18" N; 113° 21' 00" E, 21° 48' 36" N; 113° 21' 00" E and 21° 48' 36" N; 113° 15' 45" E in depth of 14 m

Gaolan No.2 anchorage between the following pos 21° 53' 56" N; 113° 10' 06" E, 21° 53' 56" N; 113° 10' 56" E, 21° 52' 54" N; 113° 11' 48" E and 21° 52' 54" N; 113° 10' 56" E in depth of 6 m

Pilotage: For Zhuhai and Jiuzhou pilotage is compulsory and pilot boards within the following anchorage areas:
(a) vessels between 6-12 m draught in pos 22° 03.6' N; 113° 44.0' E
(b) vessels less than 6 m draught in pos 22° 07.6' N; 113° 40.4' E
(c) vessels less than 4 m draught in pos 22° 13.6' N; 113° 37.0' E
For Gaolan pilotage is compulsory and pilot boards within the following anchorage areas:
(a) vessels between 6-13 m draught in pos 21° 49.5' N; 113° 14.5' E
(b) vessels less than 6 m draught in pos 21° 53.0' N; 113° 12.0' E

Radio Frequency: VHF Channel 16

Tides: Average tidal range of 1.07 m

Traffic: 2005, 18 000 000 t of cargo handled

Accommodation:

Name	Length (m)	Depth (m)	Remarks
Zhuhai			
Dayuwan Terminal	130	6	LPG, bulk chemicals & oil for vessels up to 5000 dwt
Multi-Buoy Oil Terminal		15	Product oil for vessels up to 50 000 dwt
Jovo-Arco LPG Terminal	330	13.5	LPG for vessels up to 50 000 dwt
Iwatani LPG Terminal	330	12.5	LPG for vessels up to 50 000 dwt
Gaolan			
Zhuhai International Container Terminal	410	11	See [1] below
Jiuzhou			
Zhuhai International Container Terminal	703	5	See [2] below

[1]*Zhuhai International Container Terminal:* Operated by Zhuhai International Container Terminals (Gaolan) Ltd., Terminal Main Building, Gaolan, Zhuhai Port, Zhuhai 519050, Tel: +86 756 726 8828, Fax: +86 756 726 8603, Email: gaolan@zictg.com.cn, Website: www.hdp.com.hk/eng/zhuhai_gaolan.html
Terminal area of 20.8 ha for vessels up to 25 000 t. Container freight station.
[2]*Zhuhai International Container Terminal:* Operated by Zhuhai International Container Terminals (Jiuzhou) Ltd., Tel: +86 756 322 0000, Fax:+86 756 335 5993, Website: www.zictj.com.cn
Total area of 15.4 ha. Container freight station. Feeder service to Hong Kong and Yantian for transhipment

Storage:

Location	Covered (m²)	Sheds / Warehouses
Zhuhai International Container Terminal	14000	7

Mechanical Handling Equipment:

Location	Type	Qty
Zhuhai International Container Terminal	Mobile Cranes	6
Zhuhai International Container Terminal	Quay Cranes	6
Zhuhai International Container Terminal	Forklifts	24
Zhuhai International Container Terminal	RTG's	7
Zhuhai International Container Terminal	Quay Cranes	2
Zhuhai International Container Terminal	Straddle Carriers	7
Zhuhai International Container Terminal	Forklifts	30

Bunkering: Available for foreign vessels

Towage: Tugs available at Gaolan and Jiuzhou

Ship Chandlers: Zhuhai Ocean Shipping Supply Co., Jiuzhou Harbour, Zhuhai, Guangdong Province 519015, People's Republic of China, *Tel:* +86 756 336 4619, *Fax:* +86 756 333 3904, *Email:* ossco904@sina.com.cn

Shipping Agents: Atlanta Shipping Agency Ltd, Room 503, 5th Floor Hong Ta Da Xia, Shui Wan Lu, Ji Da, Zhuhai, Guangdong Province, People's Republic of China, *Tel:* +86 756 336 2386, *Fax:* +86 756 336 3822, *Email:* katherinekan@atlanta.com.mo
China Marine Shipping Agency Co. Ltd, China Marine Shipping Agency Zhuhai Company Limited, 3A, 1st Flat Block 17, Jizhou Garden, 455 Qing Lu South Road, Zhuhai, Guangdong Province, People's Republic of China, *Tel:* +86 756 322 8250, *Fax:* +86 756 322 8200, *Email:* sinoagent@pub.zhuhai.gd.cn, *Website:* www.sinoagent.com
CMA-CGM S.A., CMA CGM Zhuhai, Room 1007, Yindo Hotel, Yuehai East Road, Zhuhai, Guangdong Province 519020, People's Republic of China, *Tel:* +86 756 888 5113, *Fax:* +86 756 888 5229, *Email:* zhh.genmbox@cma-cgm.com, *Website:* www.cma-cgm.com
Mighty Ocean Shipping Ltd, Room 1806, Ever Bright International Trade Centre, Haibinnanlu, Jida, Zhuhai, Guangdong Province, People's Republic of China, *Tel:* +86 756 332 8410, *Fax:* +86 756 332 8415, *Email:* zhuhai@mighty-ocean.com

Sea Well Shipping Ltd, Aite Commercial Building Unit A5-A6, 9th Floor, 69-71 Lianhua Road, Gongbei, Zhuhai, Guangdong Province 519020, People's Republic of China, *Tel:* +86 756 889 6038, *Fax:* +86 756 889 6036, *Email:* yml@yml-zhuhai.com
Agencia de Navegacao Yat Fat Lda, Room 1105 Yindo Hotel, Yuehai Road, Gongbei, Guangdong, Zhuhai, Guangdong Province, People's Republic of China, *Tel:* +86 756 815 3571, *Fax:* +86 756 815 3573, *Email:* yatfat@macau.ctm.net

Airport: Zhuhai Airport

Development: Zhuhai International Container Terminals (Gaolan) has received approval to embark on the Phase II project which involves the construction of two new 50 000 t container berths with a total quay length of 824 m and depth alongside of 15 m. The first berth will be operational by end 2008 and the second berth in March 2009

Lloyd's Agent: Huatai Surveyors & Adjusters Co., Room 802, Jun Yuan Mansion, 155 Tian He East Road, Guangzhou, Guangdong Province 510620, People's Republic of China, *Tel:* +86 20 3881 2306, *Fax:* +86 20 3881 2470, *Email:* agency.gz@huatai-serv.com, *Website:* www.huatai-serv.com

ZHUJIAQIAO

harbour area, see under Wuhu

ZHUZHOU

Lat 27° 50' N; Long 113° 8' E.

Admiralty Chart: -	**Admiralty Pilot:** -
Time Zone: GMT +8 h	**UNCTAD Locode:** CN ZUU

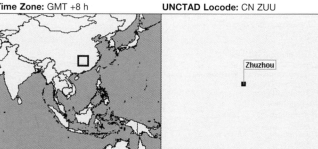

Principal Facilities:

		Y	G				

Authority: Zhuzhou Harbour Administration, 30 Fangzhi Xi Road, Zhuzhou, Hunan Province 412000, People's Republic of China

Accommodation:

Name	Remarks
Zhuzhou	See [1] below

[1]*Zhuzhou:* Numerous berths available for vessels up to 1000 dwt handling coal, fertiliser, ore, grain, sand and general cargo

Lloyd's Agent: Huatai Surveyors & Adjusters Co., 14th Floor, China Re Building, No.11 Jin Rong Avenue, Xicheng District, Beijing 100140, People's Republic of China, *Tel:* +86 10 6657 6577, *Fax:* +86 10 6657 6502, *Email:* agency.bj@huatai-serv.com, *Website:* www.huatai-serv.com

CHRISTMAS ISLAND

FLYING FISH COVE

Lat 10° 25' S; Long 105° 43' E.

Admiralty Chart: AUS 920	**Admiralty Pilot:** 34
Time Zone: GMT +7 h	**UNCTAD Locode:** CX FFC

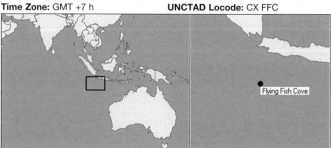

Principal Facilities:

P		Y	G			B		A

Authority: Christmas Island Port, P O Box 445, Christmas Island, Christmas Island 6798, *Tel:* +672 891 648434, *Fax:* +672 891 648435, *Email:* westernci@pulau.cx

Officials: Harbour Master: Andrew Butterworth.

Pre-Arrival Information: Contact Port Authority or local agent at least 48 h prior to arrival

Pilotage: Compulsory for merchant vessels. Pilot boards 1 mile W of Smith Point

Radio Frequency: VHF Channel 16. All radio communication via Perth or Singapore Radio

Weather: SE trades prevail April to November. Unsettled W winds and swells December to March which can prevent mooring. Swells may occasionally affect mooring even during SE trade season

Tides: Range of tide 2 m

Maximum Vessel Dimensions: 35 000 dwt, for bulk vessels loading rock phosphates

Principal Imports and Exports: Imports: General cargo.

Working Hours: Weekdays 0700-1100, 1200-1600. Overtime available

Accommodation:

Name	Remarks
Flying Fish Cove	See [1] below

[1]*Flying Fish Cove:* Open Roadstead. Vessels moor in Flying Fish Cove at buoys laid in deep water. General cargo discharged by powered lighters. One warehouse for general cargo. One crane of 20 t cap and one of 4 t used only for transhipment from wharf to lighters

Tanker facilities: Vessels berth at buoys. Discharge effected through two floating hoses 6'' and 8'' into bulk oil tanks situated on various parts of the island

Storage: Limited but available with prior written request

Mechanical Handling Equipment:

Location	Type	Capacity (t)	Qty
Flying Fish Cove	Mult-purp. Cranes	20	1

Cargo Worked: General cargo 500-600 t/day

Bunkering: Limited supplies of diesel oil in emergency only

Medical Facilities: Fully staffed hospital available. Serious cases which cannot be handled can be flown to mainland Australia or Singapore

Airport: Flights to Perth (Monday and Tuesday). Flights to Denpaser (Saturday)

Lloyd's Agent: N & R Marine Surveying Proprietary Ltd, 690 Seaview Drive, Christmas Island, Christmas Island 6798, *Email:* nrsurvey@runbox.com

COLOMBIA

BARRANQUILLA

Lat 10° 57' N; Long 74° 46' W.

Admiralty Chart: 2261	**Admiralty Pilot:** 7
Time Zone: GMT -5 h	**UNCTAD Locode:** CO BAQ

Principal Facilities:

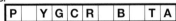

P | Y | G | C | R | | B | | T | A

Authority: Sociedad Portuaria Regional de Barranquilla S.A., Carrera 38 Calle 1, Orilla Del Rio, P O Box 3140, Barranquilla, Colombia, *Tel:* +57 5 371 6200, *Fax:* +57 5 371 6310, *Email:* info@sprb.com.co, *Website:* www.sprb.com.co

Officials: Chief Executive Officer: Fernando Arteta, *Email:* farteta@sprb.com.co. Commercial Director: Enrique Carvajales, *Email:* ecarvajales@sprb.com.co. Port Captain: Capt Jorge Reyes, *Email:* jreyes@sprb.com.co.

Port Security: ISPS compliant

Pilotage: Compulsory. Pilot boarding area 1.5 miles WNW of the breakwater in pos 11° 07' N; 74° 52.5' W

Weather: Prevailing NE winds from November-April

Tides: River fluctuates about 1 m dependant upon dry or rainy season

Traffic: 2006, 845 vessels, 3 641 948 t of cargo handled

Principal Imports and Exports: Imports: Cement, Coal, Containers, Fertiliser, General cargo, Iron, Wood pulp in bales. Exports: Cement, Coal, Containers, Fertiliser, General cargo, Iron, Wood pulp in bales.

Working Hours: 24 h/day

Accommodation:

Name	Length (m)	Draught (m)	Remarks
Barranquilla			See [1] below
Wharf	1058	9.9	See [2] below

[1]*Barranquilla:* The terminal has an extension of 88 ha, including a dock of 43 ha
Consists of the following ten terminals:
Patio Industrial Malambo S.A. (PIMSA)
Zona Franca Industrial Barranquilla
Sociedad Portuaria Regional Barranquilla
Mitchell Mar
VOPAK
Cementos Argos
Monomeros Colombo-Venezolana
Siderurgica del Norte
Sociedad Portuaria del Norte
Base Naval Barranquilla
List of operators include:
Sociedad Portuaria Regional Barranquilla, Tel: +57 5 371 6209, Email: priveira@sprb.com.co
Gran Puerto Ltda, Tel: +57 5 379 9610, Email: cayala@sprb.com.co
OSI Trademar S.A.-Operadora Servicios Integrales, Tel: +57 5 379 4992, Email: cjaramillo@sprb.com.co
Serteport Servicios Tecnicos Portuarios, Tel: +57 5 379 0349, Email: jredondo@gsacol.com
Transportes Max Paez S.A., Tel: +57 5 379 9605, Email: gerencia@tmaxpaez.com
Yale Group S.A., Tel: +57 5 379 4052
Alpopular S.A. Almacen General de Deposito, Tel: +57 5 374 0266, Email: luis.chica@alpopula.com.co
Graneles del Caribe S.A., Tel: +57 1 640 9666, Email: ahogadopp@algranel.com.co
Aserbuques del Atlantico Ltda, Tel: +57 5 360 0339, Email: serbuque@metrotel.net.co
Operaciones Portuarias Car E.U., Tel: +57 5 344 3171, Email: mrpbq@metrotel.net.co
[2]*Wharf:* Six berths. Capable of receiving six vessels simultaneously (with a max of 240 m loa, 45 m beam and draught of 9.14 m in fresh water). The terminal also offers a 550 lineal wharf for barge operations

Storage: Containers: storage area of 225 000 m3, storage cap of 5000 TEU's and 54 reefer points
General cargo: 9721 m2 of fenced yard, 39 400 m2 storage yard, five warehouses totaling 22 466 m2, a specialized 5400 m2 warehouse for steel and a specialized warehouse for coffee
Solid bulk cargo: eight warehouses totaling 24 155 m2 suitable for storing 60 000 t, a horizontal silo with a 15 000 t cap and a horizontal silo with a 22 000 t cap
Coal: storage area of 60 000 m2

Mechanical Handling Equipment:

Location	Type	Capacity (t)	Qty
Barranquilla	Mult-purp. Cranes	100	2
Barranquilla	Mobile Cranes	104	1
Barranquilla	Mobile Cranes	64	1

Bunkering: Codis S.A., Via 40 69-140, Barranquilla, Colombia, *Tel:* +57 5 3690 641, *Fax:* +57 5 3690 642, *Email:* sales@codis.com.co, *Website:* www.codis.com.co
Mobil de Colombia S.A., Carrera 46 No 48-11, Barranquilla, Colombia, *Tel:* +57 5 632 0418, *Fax:* +57 5 349 0142
Organizacion Terpel S.A., Calle 66 # 67-123, Barranquilla 00000000000, Colombia, *Tel:* +57 5 3697300, *Fax:* +57 5 3600 363/3440 011, *Email:* info@terpel.com, *Website:* www.terpel.com

Petroleos del Milenio C.I. Ltd, Carrera 87 No 85-81, Barranquilla, Colombia, *Tel:* +57 5 373 0888, *Fax:* +57 5 668 5603, *Email:* petromil@petromil.com

Areda Marine Fuel C.I.S.A., Areda Marine Fuel C.I.S.A., Barrio Albornoz, cra 46 #2-22, Muelle Matteucci, Cartagena, Colombia, *Tel:* +57 5 6573 742, *Fax:* +57 5 6767 266, *Email:* sales@aredamarine.com, *Website:* www.aredamarine.com – *Grades:* IFO; MGO – *Parcel Size:* barge 250t min, truck 30t min – *Delivery Mode:* barge, truck

C.I. Intracol S.A., Diag 21a, 53-94 Bosque Calle Buenos Aires, Cartagena, Colombia, *Tel:* +57 5 662 7127, *Fax:* +57 5 662 7127

ExxonMobil Marine Fuels, Suite 900, One Alhambra Plaza, Coral Gables, FL 33134, United States of America, *Tel:* +1 305 459 6358, *Fax:* +1 305 459 6412, *Email:* emmf@exxonmobil.com, *Website:* www.exxonmobilmarinefuels.com – *Delivery Mode:* truck

Mobil de Colombia S.A., Carrera 46 No 48-11, Barranquilla, Colombia, *Tel:* +57 5 632 0418, *Fax:* +57 5 349 0142

Petroleos del Milenio C.I. Ltd, Carrera 87 No 85-81, Barranquilla, Colombia, *Tel:* +57 5 373 0888, *Fax:* +57 5 668 5603, *Email:* petromil@petromil.com

Refineria del Nare S.A., Carrera 13A No 125-81, Barrio Multicentro, Bogota, Colombia, *Tel:* +57 1 612 2300, *Fax:* +57 1 612 4631, *Email:* refinare@andinet.com

Towage: Two tugs available up to 1200 hp

Shipping Agents: Aduanera Colombiana SIA S.A., Calle 38, A Norte 3N-66, Barrio Prados del Norte, P O Box 2254, Cali, Colombia, *Tel:* +57 2 654 1185/89, *Fax:* +57 2 665 6273, *Email:* operations@aduanera.com.co, *Website:* www.aduanera.com.co

Agencia Maritima del Caribe, Carrera 77B 57-141, Office 706-707, Barranquilla, Colombia, *Tel:* +57 5 360 3200, *Fax:* +57 5 353 4035, *Email:* acarbonell@agefront.com

Agencia Maritima Transmares Ltda, Cra. 30 Avenida Hamburgo, Edificio Adminstrativo Zona Franca, Piso 2, Barranquilla, Colombia, *Tel:* +57 5 370 4800, *Fax:* +57 5 370 5770, *Email:* transbaq@transmares.com.co, *Website:* www.transmares.com.co

Aquarius Shipping Colombia Ltda, Carrera 51B No.82-254, Oficina 56 Piso 4, Barranquilla, Colombia, *Tel:* +57 5 378 2686, *Fax:* +57 5 378 2676, *Email:* baq@aquarius.com.co, *Website:* www.aquarius.com.co

Cia Transportadora S.A., Carrera 54 68-196, Edificio Prado, Oficina 704, P O Box 286, Barranquilla, Colombia, *Tel:* +57 5 358 9719, *Fax:* +57 5 243 4578, *Email:* barranquilla@ciatransportadora.com, *Website:* www.ciatransportadora.com

Global Maritime Transportation Agency, Calle 84 # 50 - 10, Oficina 201, Barranquilla, Colombia, *Tel:* +57 5 373 8195/6, *Fax:* +57 5 373 8170, *Email:* ramiroanaya@gmtagency.com, *Website:* www.gmtagency.com

Global Shipping Agencies S.A., Sociedad Portuaria Regional de Barranquilla, Calle 1 Carerra 38 Oficina 7, Edificio David Arango, Barranquilla, Colombia, *Tel:* +57 5 379 0004, *Fax:* +57 5 379 0003, *Email:* info@gsacol.com, *Website:* www.gsacol.com

A.P. Moller-Maersk Group, Maersk Colombia S.A., Calle 77B No. 7 No.57-141, Oficina 305, Edificio Centro Empresarial de las Americas, Barranquilla, Colombia, *Tel:* +57 5 360 2936, *Fax:* +57 5 360 7315, *Email:* baqsal@maersk.com, *Website:* www.maerskline.com

Surveyors: Societe Generale de Surveillance (SGS), SGS Colombia S.A., Autopista Aeropuerto Km8, P O Box 3505, Barranquilla, Colombia, *Tel:* +57 5 342 3255, *Fax:* +57 5 342 2268, *Website:* www.sgs.com

Airport: Ernesto Cortissoz Airport, 5 km. Served by major airlines

Lloyd's Agent: Crawford Colombia Ltda, Carrera 13 No.71-69, Bogota 94754, Colombia, *Tel:* +57 1 347 6349, *Fax:* +57 1 347 6349, *Email:* lloydsagency@crawfordcolombia.com, *Website:* www.crawfordandcompany.com

BUENAVENTURA

Lat 3° 54' N; Long 77° 5' W.

Admiralty Chart: 2319	**Admiralty Pilot:** 7
Time Zone: GMT -5 h	**UNCTAD Locode:** CO BUN

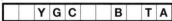

Principal Facilities:

	Y	G	C		B		T	A	

Authority: Sociedad Portuaria Regional de Buenaventura S.A., Avenida Portuaria, Edificio de Administracion, Piso 3, Buenaventura AA 478 10765, Colombia, *Tel:* +57 2 241 0700/9, *Fax:* +57 2 242 2475, *Email:* yahairad@sprbun.com, *Website:* www.puertobuenaventura.com

Officials: General Manager: Domingo Chinea.
Commercial Manager: Fernando Aulestia Marin, *Email:* fernandoa@sprbun.com.

Port Security: ISPS compliant

Documentation: Port Captain: clearance from last port, crew list, passenger list (if any), stores list, dangerous cargo list
Immigration: crew list
Health Official: vaccination list
Agriculture Dept: stores list

Approach: Channel depth 10.06 m, 7.62 m at LT

Anchorage: On the N side of the channel between buoys 17, 15 and 13 in depths of 10.06 to 21.33 m

Pilotage: Compulsory for all vessels over 500 gt. Pilot boarding takes place at fairway buoy in pos 3° 47' 39.1" N; 77° 19' 08.4" W

Radio Frequency: Port Captain: VHF Channel 16. Pilots on VHF channel 16 and 68

Weather: Humid climate, winds from E and W, max velocity 10 knots

Tides: Range of tide 4.4 m. Soft muddy bottom

Traffic: 2007, 10 000 000 t of cargo handled, 720 000 TEU's

Maximum Vessel Dimensions: Least depth is about 6.1 m over an outer bar, vessels drawing up to 9.5 m can reach the inner harbour during HT

Principal Imports and Exports: Imports: Fertiliser, Gasoline, Metals, Soya beans, Urea, Wheat. Exports: Coffee, Molasses, Sugar.

Working Hours: 24 h/day

Accommodation:

Name	Remarks
Buenaventura	See [1] below

[1]*Buenaventura:* In general the harbour offers good protection with adequate turning space and anchorage. The terminal consists of a marginal wharf 2126 m long, plus a 200 m angled berth at the W end. Thirteen ships of average length can be accommodated allowing 168 m of berthing space each along the marginal wharf. Depth alongside wharf 10.0 m
Wharf 13 operated by Grupo Portuario S.A.: 150 m long handling bulk solids, loose cargo, automobiles and containers. Three specialized warehouses for storage of bulk solids covering a total area of 8110 m2 and two sheds adapted for storage of general cargo
Container facilities: Container terminal operated by Terminal Especializado de Contenedores de Buenaventura S.A. (TECSA), Tel: 57 2 241 5949, Fax: 57 2 241 5887, Email: tecsa@tecbuenaventura.com, Website: www.tecbuenaventura.com. Equipment includes four container cranes (two post-panamax) and sixteen RTG's
Bulk facilities: Equipment for loading sugar at 180 t/h. Mechanical system for unloading bulk cereals and minerals
Road and railway connection to the hinterland

Storage: Nine warehouses totalling 76 541 m2, six sheds totalling 39 157 m2 and eight yards totalling 102 374 m2. No refrigerated space

Mechanical Handling Equipment:

Location	Type	Capacity (t)	Qty
Buenaventura	Mult-purp. Cranes	75	1
Buenaventura	Mult-purp. Cranes	50	1
Buenaventura	Mult-purp. Cranes	130	1
Buenaventura	Mult-purp. Cranes	16	3

Cargo Worked: 500 t/shift, 2500 t/day

Bunkering: Areda Marine Fuel C.I.S.A., Areda Marine Fuel C.I.S.A., Barrio Albornoz, cra 46 #2-22, Muelle Matteucci, Cartagena, Colombia, *Tel:* +57 5 6573 742, *Fax:* +57 5 6767 266, *Email:* sales@aredamarine.com, *Website:* www.aredamarine.com – *Grades:* IFO; MGO – *Parcel Size:* 30t min – *Delivery Mode:* truck

C.I. Intracol S.A., Diag 21a, 53-94 Bosque Calle Buenos Aires, Cartagena, Colombia, *Tel:* +57 5 662 7127, *Fax:* +57 5 662 7127 – *Delivery Mode:* truck

Cockett Marine Oil Ltd, Carrick House, 36 Station Square, Petts Wood, Kent BR5 1NA, United Kingdom, *Tel:* +44 1689 883 400, *Fax:* +44 1689 877 666, *Email:* enquiries@cockett.com, *Website:* www.cockettgroup.com – *Grades:* all grades – *Notice:* 72 hours – *Delivery Mode:* truck

ExxonMobil Marine Fuels, Suite 900, One Alhambra Plaza, Coral Gables, FL 33134, United States of America, *Tel:* +1 305 459 6358, *Fax:* +1 305 459 6412, *Email:* emmf@exxonmobil.com, *Website:* www.exxonmobilmarinefuels.com – *Grades:* MGO – *Delivery Mode:* truck

Mobil de Colombia S.A., Carrera 46 No 48-11, Barranquilla, Colombia, *Tel:* +57 5 632 0418, *Fax:* +57 5 349 0142 – *Delivery Mode:* truck

Refineria del Nare S.A., Carrera 13A No 125-81, Barrio Multicentro, Bogota,

Colombia, *Tel:* +57 1 612 2300, *Fax:* +57 1 612 4631, *Email:* refinare@andinet.com
– *Delivery Mode:* truck

Towage: Four tugs available of 1800-2300 hp

Shipping Agents: Aduanera Colombiana SIA S.A., Calle 38, A Norte 3N-66, Barrio Prados del Norte, P O Box 2254, Cali, Colombia, *Tel:* +57 2 654 1185/89, *Fax:* +57 2 665 6273, *Email:* operations@aduanera.com.co, *Website:* www.aduanera.com.co
Agencia Maritima Barlovento S.A., Edif Banco De Bogota, piso 2, Of 201, Calle 1, 2A-31, Buenaventura, Colombia, *Tel:* +57 2 241 8926, *Fax:* +57 2 241 7809, *Email:* barl-bun@pop.colombianet.net
Agencia Maritima Transmares Ltda, Calle 3 No.3-83, Oficina 205, Edificio Felix Alomia, Buenaventura, Colombia, *Tel:* +57 2 241 8740, *Fax:* +57 2 241 8746, *Email:* transbun@transmares.com.co, *Website:* www.transmares.com.co
Aquarius Shipping Colombia Ltda, Calle 7 No.3-11 Oficina 1704, Eidifico Pacific Trade Center, Buenaventura, Colombia, *Tel:* +57 2 241 7580, *Fax:* +57 2 241 7576, *Email:* bun@aquarius.com.co, *Website:* www.aquarius.com.co
Cia Transportadora S.A., Carrera 2 2-03, Apardado 548, Buenaventura, Colombia, *Tel:* +57 2 241 8123, *Fax:* +57 2 241 8122, *Email:* buenaventura@ciatransportadora.com, *Website:* www.ciatransportadora.com
Frontier Agencia MarÝtima, Calle 7, No. 7-11, Oficinas 1101-B, Piso 11, Edificio Pacific Trade Center, Buenaventura, Colombia, *Tel:* +57 2 242 6850, *Fax:* +57 2 242 6851, *Email:* layala@agefront.com, *Website:* www.agefront.com
Global Shipping Agencies S.A., Carrera 3 #7-22, Oficina 1903, Edificio Pacific Trade Center, Buenaventura, Colombia, *Tel:* +57 2 241 8079, *Fax:* +57 2 242 2129, *Email:* bvt@gsacol.com, *Website:* www.gsacol.com
HSAC Gerleinco Logistica EU, Calle 8A 3-313, Edificio Gerleinco, Buenaventura, Colombia, *Tel:* +57 2 241 5082, *Fax:* +57 2 243 3799, *Email:* gerlein@bun.gerlein.com.co
Maritrans S.A., Calle Cubarado 3-19, Oficina 202, Buenaventura, Colombia, *Tel:* +57 2 242 4384, *Fax:* +57 2 242 2847, *Email:* maritbun@telesat.com.co
Mediterranean Shipping Company, MSC Buenaventura, Edificio Banco de Bogota - Piso 2, Calle 1, No.2a-25, Buenaventura, Colombia, *Tel:* +57 2 241 8926, *Fax:* +57 2 241 7809, *Email:* info@msc-colombia.com.co, *Website:* www.mscgva.ch
A.P. Moller-Maersk Group, Maersk Colombia S.A., Calle 7A No.3-11, Oficina 12-02, Edificio Pacific Trade Center, Buenaventura, Colombia, *Tel:* +57 2 241 1400, *Fax:* +57 2 241 8683, *Website:* www.maerskline.com
Seaway Ltda, Carrera 2 No. 1-20, Office No.209 Edificio Cascajal, Buenaventura, Colombia, *Tel:* +57 2 241 6506, *Fax:* +57 2 241 6343, *Email:* seaway@seaway-ltda.com, *Website:* www.seaway-ltda.com

Surveyors: Bureau Veritas, Edificio Roldan, Calle 7 No.3-50 Ofic. 208, Cauca, Buenaventura, Colombia, *Tel:* +57 2 241 8190, *Fax:* +57 2 241 8191, *Email:* cre.buenaventura@co.bureauveritas.com, *Website:* www.bureauveritas.com

Medical Facilities: Available

Airport: Local airport, 18 km

Development: International Container Terminal Services Inc. has completed an agreement to develop a new $180 million container terminal with a capacity to handle 700 000 TEU's a year. Construction is scheduled to begin November 2007, and officials expect the terminal to be operational in 18 to 24 months

Lloyd's Agent: Crawford Colombia Ltda, Carrera 13 No.71-69, Bogota 94754, Colombia, *Tel:* +57 1 347 6349, *Fax:* +57 1 347 6349, *Email:* lloydsagency@crawfordcolombia.com, *Website:* www.crawfordandcompany.com

CARTAGENA

Lat 10° 24' N; Long 75° 31' W.

Admiralty Chart: 2434	**Admiralty Pilot:** 7A
Time Zone: GMT -5 h	**UNCTAD Locode:** CO CTG

Principal Facilities:

P Q Y G C R L B D T A

Authority: Sociedad Portuaria de Cartagena S.A., Manga Terminal Maritimo, Cartagena AA 7954, Colombia, *Tel:* +57 5 660 8071, *Fax:* +57 5 650 2239, *Email:* comercial@sprc.com.co, *Website:* www.puertocartagena.com

Officials: General Manager: Capt Alfonso Salas Trujillo, *Email:* gerencia@sprc.com.co.
Marketing Director: Giovanni Benedetti, *Email:* gbenedetti@sprc.com.co.
Operations Director: Gustavo Florez, *Email:* gflorez@sprc.com.co.

Port Security: ISPS and Bio-Terrorism Act compliant. Container Security Initiative (CSI) designated port. Antinarcotics and explosives detection procedures

Pre-Arrival Information: Vessels ETA should be advised 72, 48, 24 and 12 h prior to the arrival to the agent. The message should include vessels name, ETA in local time, arrival drafts, number of crew including master and any special requirements such as additional tug, portside berthing etc

Approach: From the outer fairway lightbuoy, the route leads between No's 1 and 2 lightbuoys and then between No's 3 and 4 lightbuoys, moored 0.5 nm and 0.25 nm WSW respectively, off the S point of Isla Tierra Bomba on which stands Fuerte de San Fernando in pos 10° 19.3' N; 75° 35.4' W thence; with positions relative to this point: between No.5 lightbuoy, 0.2 nm ESE and a beacon marking the N point of the island on which Fuerte San Jose stands, 0.275 nm SE; between No's 6 and 7 lightbuoys, 0.5 nm ESE S of No.9 lightbuoy in pos 10° 19.2' N; 75° 33.9' W marking Bajo Carreya, with a least depth of 5.5 m over it
The bottom of the harbour is mainly soft mud and shoals with depths of up to 3.7 m over them are easily distinguished as far as Banco Santa Cruz in pos 10° 20' N; 75° 31' W

Anchorage: Anchorage area available in front of Tierrabomba Island

Pilotage: The pilot will board at any hour, up to 1 nm W of the sea buoy. It is a national regulation that all vessels must have a pilot for entering the bay. If the vessel is bound for the port terminal, the pilot will berth in one operation, unless there is no berth, when anchorage will be taken in approx 17.7 m of water, 1500 m off the two piers
There are 10 pilots available, the station is situated at the entrance of Boca Chica, on San Fernando Island in approx 10° 19.6' N; 75° 34.8' W
The pilots have a VHS radio station and stand by 24 h/day, frequencies monitored are VHF Channels 11 and 16
Sound signals for vessels requesting a pilot should be made as follows: three blast for a cargo vessel and four for a tanker

Radio Frequency: Port communications on VHF Channels 16 and 11

Weather: Prevailing winds NE

Tides: Range of tide 0.5 m

Traffic: 2007, 7 116 687 t of cargo handled, 795 380 TEU's

Maximum Vessel Dimensions: 340 m loa, 14 m draft

Principal Imports and Exports: Imports: Chemicals, Food products, Machinery, Paper, Parts, Raw materials, Synthetic resins, Tiles. Exports: Cars, Chemical products, Coffee, Fruit & vegetables, Nickel, Oil, Resins, Textiles, Tiles.

Working Hours: Office hours: 0700-2000. Vessel working: 24 h/day

Accommodation:

Name	Length (m)	Depth (m)
Cartagena		
Berth No.1	202	8.9
Berth No.2	202	11
Berth No.3	182	11
Berth No.4	130	8.9
Berth No.5	202	12
Berth No.6	182	12
Berth No.7	270	13.5
Berth No.8	268	13.5
Ro/ro 1	40	11
Ro/ro 2	40	11

Storage: Warehouse 1: 7760 m2. Warehouse 2: 7186 m2. Warehouse 3: 7763 m2. Warehouse 4: 2246 m2. Warehouse 5: 2178 m2. Roofed area of 976 m2. Loose cargo area of 12 583 m2. Container area of 103 934 m2

Mechanical Handling Equipment:

Location	Type	Capacity (t)	Qty
Cartagena	Mobile Cranes	100	4
Cartagena	Post Panamax	40–60	2
Cartagena	Super Post Panamax	50–70	5
Cartagena	RTG's	40	24
Cartagena	Reach Stackers	40	17

Bunkering: Areda Marine Fuel C.I.S.A., Areda Marine Fuel C.I.S.A., Barrio Albornoz, cra 46 #2-22, Muelle Matteucci, Cartagena, Colombia, *Tel:* +57 5 6573 742, *Fax:* +57 5 6767 266, *Email:* sales@aredamarine.com, *Website:* www.aredamarine.com

Key to Principal Facilities:—				
A=Airport	**C**=Containers	**G**=General Cargo	**P**=Petroleum	**R**=Ro/Ro	**Y**=Dry Bulk
B=Bunkers	**D**=Dry Dock	**L**=Cruise	**Q**=Other Liquid Bulk	**T**=Towage (where available from port)	

Caribbean Worldwide Shipping Service Agency Ltda (CARIBBSA), Bocagrande, Carrera 3, No.8-129 Edificio Centro Ejecutivo Building, Suite 15-02, Cartagena, Colombia, *Tel:* +57 5 665 5780, *Fax:* +57 5 665 2966, *Email:* marineoperations@caribbsa.com, *Website:* www.caribbsa.com

C.I. Bunkercol, Edificio Banco Popular Oficina 505, Cartagena, Colombia, *Tel:* +57 95 664 5067, *Fax:* +57 95 664 1853, *Website:* www.grupoorco.com

C.I. Intracol S.A., Diag 21a, 53-94 Bosque Calle Buenos Aires, Cartagena, Colombia, *Tel:* +57 5 662 7127, *Fax:* +57 5 662 7127

Areda Marine Fuel C.I.S.A., Areda Marine Fuel C.I.S.A., Barrio Albornoz, cra 46 #2-22, Muelle Matteucci, Cartagena, Colombia, *Tel:* +57 5 6573 742, *Fax:* +57 5 6767 266, *Email:* sales@aredamarine.com, *Website:* www.aredamarine.com – *Grades:* IFO; MGO – *Parcel Size:* IFO 150t min, MGO 60t min – *Delivery Mode:* barge

C.I. Intracol S.A., Diag 21a, 53-94 Bosque Calle Buenos Aires, Cartagena, Colombia, *Tel:* +57 5 662 7127, *Fax:* +57 5 662 7127 – *Delivery Mode:* barge

Cockett Marine Oil Ltd, Carrick House, 36 Station Square, Petts Wood, Kent BR5 1NA, United Kingdom, *Tel:* +44 1689 883 400, *Fax:* +44 1689 877 666, *Email:* enquiries@cockett.com, *Website:* www.cockettgroup.com – *Grades:* all grades – *Notice:* 72 hours – *Delivery Mode:* barge

Codis S.A., Via 40 69-140, Barranquilla, Colombia, *Tel:* +57 5 3690 641, *Fax:* +57 5 3690 642, *Email:* sales@codis.com.co, *Website:* www.codis.com.co – *Delivery Mode:* barge

ExxonMobil Marine Fuels, Suite 900, One Alhambra Plaza, Coral Gables, FL 33134, United States of America, *Tel:* +1 305 459 6358, *Fax:* +1 305 459 6412, *Email:* emmf@exxonmobil.com, *Website:* www.exxonmobilmarinefuels.com – *Delivery Mode:* truck

Mobil de Colombia S.A., Carrera 46 No 48-11, Barranquilla, Colombia, *Tel:* +57 5 632 0418, *Fax:* +57 5 349 0142 – *Delivery Mode:* barge

Petroleos del Milenio C.I. Ltd, Carrera 87 No 85-81, Barranquilla, Colombia, *Tel:* +57 5 373 0888, *Fax:* +57 5 668 5603, *Email:* petromil@petromil.com – *Delivery Mode:* barge

Refineria del Nare S.A., Carrera 13A No 125-81, Barrio Multicentro, Bogota, Colombia, *Tel:* +57 1 612 2300, *Fax:* +57 1 612 4631, *Email:* refinare@andinet.com – *Delivery Mode:* barge

Towage: Coremar Group, Bosque, Diagonal 23 56-152, Abajo Purina, P O Box 505, Cartagena, Colombia, *Tel:* +57 5 662 6570, *Fax:* +57 5 662 7592, *Email:* comercial@coremar.com, *Website:* www.coremar.com

Repair & Maintenance: Astilleros Cartagena & Cia Ltda, Carretera a Mamonal, Albornoz Carrera 56, Cartagena, Colombia, *Tel:* +57 5 668 5025, *Email:* asticar@latinmail.com

Coremar Group, Bosque, Diagonal 23 56-152, Abajo Purina, P O Box 505, Cartagena, Colombia, *Tel:* +57 5 662 6570, *Fax:* +57 5 662 7592, *Email:* comercial@coremar.com, *Website:* www.coremar.com

COTECMAR, Via Mamonal Km 9, Cartagena, Colombia, *Tel:* +57 5 6685033 ext 161, *Fax:* +57 5 668 5297, *Email:* jef-com@cotecmar.com, *Website:* www.cotecmar.com

Francisco J. Escamilla E.U., Alto Bosque Calle Sena No.21B-122 Transv 49, Cartagena, Colombia, *Tel:* +57 5 669 0147, *Fax:* +57 5 672 2027, *Email:* franciscoescamilla@costa.net.co

Ship Chandlers: Caribbean Worldwide Shipping Service Agency Ltda (CARIBBSA), Bocagrande, Carrera 3, No.8-129 Edificio Centro Ejecutivo Building, Suite 15-02, Cartagena, Colombia, *Tel:* +57 5 665 5780, *Fax:* +57 5 665 2966, *Email:* marineoperations@caribbsa.com, *Website:* www.caribbsa.com

Jaime Rozo Gomez & Cia. Ltda, Tr.48 No.21, 85 Nilo Street, El Bosque, P O Box 11-06, Cartagena, Colombia, *Tel:* +57 5 662 3916, *Fax:* +57 5 669 0750, *Email:* jrozoycia@enred.com, *Website:* www.therozogroup.com.pa

Shipping Agents: Aduanera Colombiana SIA S.A., Calle 38, A Norte 3N-66, Barrio Prados del Norte, P O Box 2254, Cali, Colombia, *Tel:* +57 2 654 1185/89, *Fax:* +57 2 665 6273, *Email:* operations@aduanera.com.co, *Website:* www.aduanera.com.co

Agencia Maritima Altamar, La Matuna, 12-05 Edificio Concasa, Oficina 1405, Cartagena 2117, Colombia, *Tel:* +57 5 664 0000, *Fax:* +57 5 664 0512, *Email:* altamar@altamaragency.com, *Website:* www.altmaragency.com

Agencia Maritima Barlovento S.A., Via Mamonal Km2, Carrera 56, Suite 3, A183, Cartagena, Colombia, *Tel:* +57 5 667 1111, *Fax:* +57 5 667 0953, *Email:* barloctg@enred.com

Agencia Maritima Grancolombiana S.A., Manga, Avenida 2 con Asamblea Esquina, Casa Velez Daniels No. 26 95, Cartagena, Colombia, *Tel:* +57 5 660 7715, *Fax:* +57 5 660 8120, *Email:* favarela@amg.com.co

Agencia Maritima Transmares Ltda, Manga, Tercer Callejon, No. 26-55,, Edificio Don Eloy,, Segundo Piso, Cartagena, Colombia, *Tel:* +57 5 660 6474, *Fax:* +57 5 660 6691 Ext:102, *Email:* transcart@transmares.com.co, *Website:* www.transmares.com.co

Agencia MarÝtima Internacional, Manga Carrera 29 28-50, Cartagena, Colombia, *Tel:* +57 5 660 7810, *Fax:* +57 5 660 8134, *Email:* amicar@telecartagena.com

Agencia Oceanic Ltda, Manga, Avenida Jimenez 19-49, Calle 26, Cartagena, Colombia, *Tel:* +57 5 660 6358/660 6216, *Fax:* +57 5 660 6267, *Email:* oceanica@oceanicaltd.com, *Website:* www.oceanicaltd.com

Agentes MarÝtimos del Caribe Internacional Ltda., Matuna, Edificio Banco Popular, Oficinas 1204, Cartagena, Colombia, *Tel:* +57 5 664 3619, *Fax:* +57 5 664 0125, *Email:* amcpchap@ctgred.net.co

Altas Shipping Services S.A., Avenida Miramar, Calle 24 #23-57, Barrio Manga, Cartagena, Colombia, *Fax:* +57 5 660 9411, *Email:* operations@atlasshipping.com.co, *Website:* www.atlasshipping.com.co

Americana de Carga Ltda, Avenida El Dorado No 84A-55 Local A240, Bogota, Colombia, *Tel:* +57 1 416 2680, *Fax:* +57 1 410 7239, *Email:* jairo@grupoamericana.com.co

Aquarius Shipping Colombia Ltda, Manga Avenida Miraar, Calle del Pastelillo No.24-107, Cartagena, Colombia, *Tel:* +57 5 660 5246, *Fax:* +57 5 660 5721, *Email:* ctg@aquarius.com.co

Caribbean Worldwide Shipping Service Agency Ltda (CARIBBSA), Bocagrande, Carrera 3, No.8-129 Edificio Centro Ejecutivo Building, Suite 15-02, Cartagena, Colombia, *Tel:* +57 5 665 5780, *Fax:* +57 5 665 2966, *Email:* marineoperations@caribbsa.com, *Website:* www.caribbsa.com

Cia Transportadora S.A., La Manuna, Edificio Banco Popular Piso 7, Oficina 704/706, Apartardo Aero 26, Cartagena, Colombia, *Tel:* +57 5 664 1020, *Fax:* +57 5 664 0130, *Email:* cartegena@ciatransportadora.com, *Website:* www.ciatransportadora.com

Coremar Group, Bosque, Diagonal 23 56-152, Abajo Purina, P O Box 505, Cartagena, Colombia, *Tel:* +57 5 662 6570, *Fax:* +57 5 662 7592, *Email:* comercial@coremar.com, *Website:* www.coremar.com

Frontier Agencia MarÝtima, Manga, Calle 26, No. 21-111 Avenida Alfonso, Araujo,

Cartagena, Colombia, *Tel:* +57 5 660 4459, *Fax:* +57 5 660 4466, *Email:* mcavelier@agefront.com, *Website:* www.agefront.com

Eduardo L. Gerlein S.A., Manga, Carrera 10 24-46, Cartagena, Colombia, *Tel:* +57 5 660 4861, *Fax:* +57 5 660 4701, *Email:* gerlein@ctg.gerlein.com.co

Global Shipping Agencies S.A., Sociedad Portuaria Regional de Cartagena, Barrio Manga, Cartagena, Colombia, *Tel:* +57 5 660 8888, *Fax:* +57 5 660 9015, *Email:* ctg@gsacol.com, *Website:* www.gsacol.com

Jaime Rozo Gomez & Cia. Ltda, Tr.48 No.21, 85 Nilo Street, El Bosque, P O Box 11-06, Cartagena, Colombia, *Tel:* +57 5 662 3916, *Fax:* +57 5 669 0750, *Email:* jrozoycia@enred.com, *Website:* www.therozogroup.com.pa

HSAC Gerleinco Logistica EU, Gerleinco Building Carrera 20, 24-46, Hanga, Cartagena, Colombia, *Tel:* +57 5 660 4861, *Fax:* +57 5 660 4701, *Email:* gerlein@ctg.gerlein.com.co

Maritrans S.A., Matuna, Edificio Caja Agraria Piso 3, Oficina 316, Cartagena, Colombia, *Tel:* +57 5 664 0071, *Fax:* +57 5 664 0069, *Email:* maritctg@enred.com

Mediterranean Shipping Company, MSC Cartagena, Via Mamonal Km 2, Carrera 56 #3 A183, Cartagena, Colombia, *Tel:* +57 5 667 1111, *Fax:* +57 5 667 0953, *Email:* info@msc-colombia.com.co, *Website:* www.mscgva.ch

A.P. Moller-Maersk Group, Maersk Colombia S.A., Carrera 2 No 9-145 Of. 1401, Cartagena, Colombia, *Tel:* +57 5 659 5000, *Fax:* +57 5 665 2674, *Email:* ctgsal@maersk.com, *Website:* www.maerskline.com

Mundinaves Ltd, La Matuna Calle 35, Edificio City Bank, Oficina 13F-13G, Cartagena, Colombia, *Tel:* +57 5 664 4188, *Fax:* +57 5 664 7571, *Email:* mundinaves@ctgred.net.co

Navegar, Mamonal Km 2, Carrera 56 3A-183, Cartagena, Colombia, *Tel:* +57 5 657 1321, *Fax:* +57 5 657 3339, *Email:* navemarctg@colnvmr.com

Rozo & Cia Ltda, Bosque Transversal 48 21-85, Cartagena, Colombia, *Tel:* +57 5 662 3221, *Fax:* +57 5 669 0750, *Email:* jroycia@ctgred.net.co

Servinaves Ltda, Getsemani, Calle 25, 10B-70 Pisa 2, Calle Larga, Cartagena, Colombia, *Tel:* +57 5 664 5051, *Fax:* +57 5 664 0194, *Email:* srvnaves@ctgred.net.co

Stevedoring Companies: Caribbean Worldwide Shipping Service Agency Ltda (CARIBBSA), Bocagrande, Carrera 3, No.8-129 Edificio Centro Ejecutivo Building, Suite 15-02, Cartagena, Colombia, *Tel:* +57 5 665 5780, *Fax:* +57 5 665 2966, *Email:* marineoperations@caribbsa.com, *Website:* www.caribbsa.com

Surveyors: ABS (Americas), Edificio Banco Del Estado Of. 10-01, Avenida Daniel Lemaitre, Cartagena, Colombia, *Tel:* +57 5 664 7781, *Fax:* +57 5 664 8448, *Email:* abscartagena@eagle.org, *Website:* www.eagle.org

Caribbean Worldwide Shipping Service Agency Ltda (CARIBBSA), Bocagrande, Carrera 3, No.8-129 Edificio Centro Ejecutivo Building, Suite 15-02, Cartagena, Colombia, *Tel:* +57 5 665 5780, *Fax:* +57 5 665 2966, *Email:* marineoperations@caribbsa.com, *Website:* www.caribbsa.com

COTECMAR, Via Mamonal Km 9, Cartagena, Colombia, *Tel:* +57 5 6685033 ext 161, *Fax:* +57 5 668 5297, *Email:* jef-com@cotecmar.com, *Website:* www.cotecmar.com

Germanischer Lloyd, Edificio Banco Popular, Oficina 503, Calle 32 No. 26-13, La Matuna, Cartagena, Colombia, *Tel:* +57 5 664 3256, *Fax:* +57 5 664 1309, *Email:* gl-cartagena@gl-group.com, *Website:* www.gl-group.com

Nippon Kaiji Kyokai, Calle 4 No.2-49 Bocagrande, Cartagena, Colombia, *Tel:* +57 5 665 5848, *Website:* www.classnk.or.jp

Medical Facilities: Full hospital facilities available

Airport: Rafael Nunez, 10 km

Development: A new Mega Container Terminal, Contecar S.A., will be developed into a 3 000 000 TEU/year facility with 14 gantries, 60 RTG's and a 240 acre yard. The 1st stage is to be developed late 2009 to early 2010
Dredging of main channel to 17 m draught

Lloyd's Agent: Crawford Colombia Ltda, Carrera 13 No.71-69, Bogota 94754, Colombia, *Tel:* +57 1 347 6349, *Fax:* +57 1 347 6349, *Email:* lloydsagency@crawfordcolombia.com, *Website:* www.crawfordandcompany.com

COVENAS

Lat 9° 25' N; Long 75° 41' W.

Admiralty Chart: 1277		**Admiralty Pilot:** 7A	
Time Zone: GMT -5 h		**UNCTAD Locode:** CO CVE	

Principal Facilities:

P					B	T	

ISACOL S.A.
SHIP AGENTS

Bocagrande Carrera 3ra #6A-100
Torre Empresarial Ofc 10-01
Cartagena, Colombia
Phones
+57 5 6655100
+57 5 6656990
Fax
+57 5 6655569
mobile
+57 314 5242982
e-mail
commercial@isacol.com
web
www.isacol.com

"Sailing the extra mile"

Authority: Empresa Colombiana de Petroleos, P O Box 1107, Cucuta, Colombia, *Tel:* +57 75 760260, *Fax:* +57 75 760422

Port Security: ISPS compliant

Pre-Arrival Information: Notice of ETA to be sent 72 h, 48 h, 24 h and 12 h in advance

Approach: Roca Morrosquillo Buoy in pos 9° 35.5' N, 75° 59.5' W. Vessels may pass either side in depth of 48 m

Anchorage: Anchorage Area limited by the following points:
9° 31.42' N; 76° 48.48' W
9° 33.18' N; 75° 48.48' W
9° 33.18' N; 75° 50.30' W
9° 31.42' N; 75° 50.30' W
Quarantine Area limited by the following points:
9° 34.00' N; 75° 51.00' W
9° 34.00' N; 75° 51.30' W
9° 33.00' N; 75° 51.30' W
9° 33.00' N; 75° 51.00' W

Pilotage: Compulsory, 24 h service. Pilots board in pos 9° 32' 30" N; 75° 50' 00" W

Radio Frequency: VHF Channel 77

Traffic: 2001, 14 900 560 t of cargo handled

Principal Imports and Exports: Exports: Crude oil.

Working Hours: 24 h/day

Accommodation:

Name	Draught (m)	Remarks
Covenas		
Tanker Loading Unit 1	17.07	See [1] below
Tanker Loading Unit 2	17.3	See [2] below
Tanker Loading Unit 3	17.07	See [3] below

[1]*Tanker Loading Unit 1:* SPM in pos 9° 29' 46" N; 75° 44' 15" W for vessels up to 300 m loa. Connection through two 16" hoses with max loading rate of 40 000 bbls/h
[2]*Tanker Loading Unit 2:* SPM in pos 9° 29' 36" N; 75° 45' 36" W for vessels up to 320 m loa. Connection through three 16" hoses with max loading rate of 60 000 bbls/h
[3]*Tanker Loading Unit 3:* SPM in pos 9° 31' 45" N; 75° 47' 11" W for vessels up to 300 m loa. Connection through one 16" hose with max loading rate of 18 000 bbls/h

Bunkering: Areda Marine Fuel C.I.S.A., Areda Marine Fuel C.I.S.A., Barrio Albornoz, cra 46 #2-22, Muelle Matteucci, Cartagena, Colombia, *Tel:* +57 5 6573 742, *Fax:* +57 5 6767 266, *Email:* sales@aredamarine.com, *Website:* www.aredamarine.com – *Grades:* IFO; MGO – *Parcel Size:* 30t min – *Delivery Mode:* truck

Towage: Two 7000 bhp tugs available for berthing assistance

Shipping Agents: Aduanera Colombiana SIA S.A., Calle 38, A Norte 3N-66, Barrio Prados del Norte, P O Box 2254, Cali, Colombia, *Tel:* +57 2 654 1185/89, *Fax:* +57 2 665 6273, *Email:* operations@aduanera.com.co, *Website:* www.aduanera.com.co

Medical Facilities: Closest full medical facility is Cartagena

Lloyd's Agent: Crawford Colombia Ltda, Carrera 13 No.71-69, Bogota 94754, Colombia, *Tel:* +57 1 347 6349, *Fax:* +57 1 347 6349, *Email:* lloydsagency@crawfordcolombia.com, *Website:* www.crawfordandcompany.com

MAMONAL

Lat 10° 19' N; Long 75° 30' W.

Admiralty Chart: 2434
Time Zone: GMT -5 h
Admiralty Pilot: 7A
UNCTAD Locode: CO MAM

Principal Facilities:

P						B	D	T	A

Authority: Sociedad Portuaria de Cartagena S.A., Manga Terminal Maritimo, Cartagena AA 7954, Colombia, *Tel:* +57 5 660 8071, *Fax:* +57 5 650 2239, *Email:* comercial@sprc.com.co, *Website:* www.puertocartagena.com

Officials: General Manager: Capt Alfonso Salas Trujillo, *Email:* gerencia@sprc.com.co.
Marketing Director: Giovanni Benedetti, *Email:* gbenedetti@sprc.com.co.
Operations Director: Gustavo Florez, *Email:* gflorez@sprc.com.co.

Approach: Entrance through tbe Boca Chica Channel, max draft 14 m

Anchorage: One mile SW of the pier

Pilotage: Compulsory. Pilot boards off the fairway buoy. A mooring master takes over 0.5 mile off the pier

Radio Frequency: VHF Channels 16 and 10

Maximum Vessel Dimensions: Max dwt 85 000 t, max draft 11.58 m, max loa 260 m

Accommodation:

Name	Depth (m)	Remarks
Mamonal		
Refinery Terminal	12.19	Two mooring dolphins & four breasting dolphins
Private Wharves		See [1] below

[1]*Private Wharves:* Nestor Pineda Terminal, Tel: +57 5 668 5400/1, Fax: +57 5 668 5273
Contecar Terminal, Tel: +57 5 668 6067, Fax: +57 5 668 5882
H & A Trading Colombia Terminal, Tel: +57 5 668 6041, Fax: +57 5 668 5496

Cargo Worked: Fuel oil 2400 t/h, diesel oil 1100 t/h

Bunkering: Fuel oil available by pipeline at both terminals
C.I. Intracol S.A., Diag 21a, 53-94 Bosque Calle Buenos Aires, Cartagena, Colombia, *Tel:* +57 5 662 7127, *Fax:* +57 5 662 7127
Codis S.A., Via 40 69-140, Barranquilla, Colombia, *Tel:* +57 5 3690 641, *Fax:* +57 5 3690 642, *Email:* sales@codis.com.co, *Website:* www.codis.com.co
ExxonMobil Marine Fuels, Suite 900, One Alhambra Plaza, Coral Gables, FL 33134, United States of America, *Tel:* +1 305 459 6358, *Fax:* +1 305 459 6412, *Email:* emmf@exxonmobil.com, *Website:* www.exxonmobilmarinefuels.com – *Delivery Mode:* truck
Mobil de Colombia S.A., Carrera 46 No 48-11, Barranquilla, Colombia, *Tel:* +57 5 632 0418, *Fax:* +57 5 349 0142
Petroleos del Milenio C.I. Ltd, Carrera 87 No 85-81, Barranquilla, Colombia, *Tel:* +57 5 373 0888, *Fax:* +57 5 668 5603, *Email:* petromil@petromil.com
Refineria del Nare S.A., Carrera 13A No 125-81, Barrio Multicentro, Bogota, Colombia, *Tel:* +57 1 612 2300, *Fax:* +57 1 612 4631, *Email:* refinare@andinet.com

Towage: Available

Repair & Maintenance: COTECMAR, Via Mamonal Km 9, Cartagena, Colombia, *Tel:* +57 5 6685033 ext 161, *Fax:* +57 5 668 5297, *Email:* jef-com@cotecmar.com, *Website:* www.cotecmar.com

Shipping Agents: Aduanera Colombiana SIA S.A., Calle 38, A Norte 3N-66, Barrio Prados del Norte, P O Box 2254, Cali, Colombia, *Tel:* +57 2 654 1185/89, *Fax:* +57 2 665 6273, *Email:* operations@aduanera.com.co, *Website:* www.aduanera.com.co

Medical Facilities: Bocagrande Hospital, 30 km

Airport: Rafael Nunez Airport

Lloyd's Agent: Crawford Colombia Ltda, Carrera 13 No.71-69, Bogota 94754, Colombia, *Tel:* +57 1 347 6349, *Fax:* +57 1 347 6349, *Email:* lloydsagency@crawfordcolombia.com, *Website:* www.crawfordandcompany.com

POZOS COLORADOS TERMINAL

Lat 11° 9' N; Long 74° 15' W.

Admiralty Chart: 1276
Time Zone: GMT -5 h
Admiralty Pilot: 7A
UNCTAD Locode: CO POC

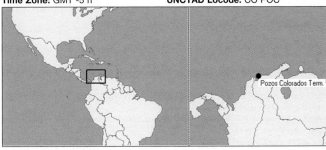

Principal Facilities:

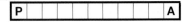

P									A

Authority: Pozos Colorados Terminal, Terminal Pozos Colorados, Santa Marta, Colombia

Port Security: ISPS compliant

Pilotage: Compulsory. Mooring master boards vessels approx 1 mile seaward of the mooring buoys and will remain on board throughout operations

Accommodation:

Name	Remarks
Pozos Colorados Terminal	See [1] below

[1]*Pozos Colorados Terminal:* Tanker terminal. Vessels secure to seven mooring buoys located about 320 m offshore in a depth of 16.8 m. Tankers of up to 70 000 dwt, 13.7 m draft can be accommodated. Pumping rate via submarine pipeline is 10 000 bbls/h.

Key to Principal Facilities:—

A=Airport	**C**=Containers	**G**=General Cargo	**P**=Petroleum	**R**=Ro/Ro	**Y**=Dry Bulk
B=Bunkers	**D**=Dry Dock	**L**=Cruise	**Q**=Other Liquid Bulk	**T**=Towage (where available from port)	

Shore deballasting facilities handling up to 84 000 bbls are available with advance notice. There are storage tanks on shore with a cap of 750 000 bbls

Shipping Agents: Aduanera Colombiana SIA S.A., Calle 38, A Norte 3N-66, Barrio Prados del Norte, P O Box 2254, Cali, Colombia, *Tel:* +57 2 654 1185/89, *Fax:* +57 2 665 6273, *Email:* operations@aduanera.com.co, *Website:* www.aduanera.com.co

Medical Facilities: Hospital and doctors at Santa Marta

Airport: Simon Bolivar International, 1 km

Lloyd's Agent: Crawford Colombia Ltda, Carrera 13 No.71-69, Bogota 94754, Colombia, *Tel:* +57 1 347 6349, *Fax:* +57 1 347 6349, *Email:* lloydsagency@crawfordcolombia.com, *Website:* www.crawfordandcompany.com

PUERTO BOLIVAR

Lat 12° 16' N; Long 71° 57' W.

Admiralty Chart: 2267	**Admiralty Pilot:** 7A
Time Zone: GMT -5 h	**UNCTAD Locode:** CO PBO

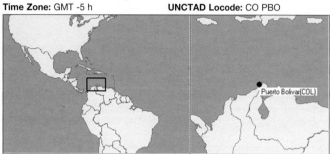

Principal Facilities:

P		Y	G	C	R			T	A

ISACOL S.A.
SHIP AGENTS
"Sailing the extra mile"

Bocagrande Carrera 3ra #6A-100
Torre Empresarial Ofc 10-01
Cartagena, Colombia
Phones
+57 5 6655100
+57 5 6656990
Fax
+57 5 6655569
mobile
+57 314 5242982
e-mail
commercial@isacol.com
web
www.isacol.com

Authority: Cerrejon, Carrera 54 No.72-80, Barranquilla, Colombia, *Tel:* +57 5 350 6400, *Fax:* +57 5 350 2110, *Email:* cerrejonmarketing@cerrejoncoal.com, *Website:* www.cerrejoncoal.com

Officials: Port Manager: Ricardo Acosta, *Email:* ricardo.acosta@cerrejoncoal.com.

Port Security: ISPS compliant

Approach: Dredged channel 4 km long, 265 m wide with a depth of 19 m

Anchorage: Vessels may anchor in the area included in the following coordinates in depth of approx 27-30 m
12° 16' 30" N; 71° 59' 30" W
12° 19' 00" N; 71° 59' 30" W
12° 19' 00" N; 71° 02' 00" W
12° 16' 30" N; 72° 02' 00" W

Pilotage: Compulsory. Pilot usually boards from a tug 1.25 miles NW of the Puerto Bolivar Light-buoy

Radio Frequency: Puerto Bolivar Radio Room, 24 h/day, VHF Channels 16 and 14, manoeuvres on Channel 13

Weather: Prevailing NE winds, velocity approx 25-35 knots

Traffic: 2003, 22 700 000 t of cargo handled

Principal Imports and Exports: Imports: General cargo. Exports: Coal, General cargo.

Working Hours: 24 h/day, seven days a week

Accommodation:

Name	Length (m)	Draught (m)	Remarks
Puerto Bolivar			
Coal Berth		17	See [1] below
Commodity Pier (East side)	278	9	Fuel oil for tankers up to 25 000 dwt
Commodity Pier (West side)	278	11	General cargo

[1]*Coal Berth:* Vessels up to 300 m loa. One shiploader at rate of 4800 t/h. Open storage cap of 700 000 t

Towage: Four tugs; three of 4000 hp and one of 3000 hp

Shipping Agents: Aduanera Colombiana SIA S.A., Calle 38, A Norte 3N-66, Barrio Prados del Norte, P O Box 2254, Cali, Colombia, *Tel:* +57 2 654 1185/89, *Fax:* +57 2 665 6273, *Email:* operations@aduanera.com.co, *Website:* www.aduanera.com.co Caribbean Worldwide Shipping Service Agency Ltda (CARIBBSA), Bocagrande, Carrera 3, No.8-129 Edificio Centro Ejecutivo Building, Suite 15-02, Cartagena, Colombia, *Tel:* +57 5 665 5780, *Fax:* +57 5 665 2966, *Email:* marineoperations@caribbsa.com, *Website:* www.caribbsa.com

Stevedoring Companies: Caribbean Worldwide Shipping Service Agency Ltda (CARIBBSA), Bocagrande, Carrera 3, No.8-129 Edificio Centro Ejecutivo Building, Suite 15-02, Cartagena, Colombia, *Tel:* +57 5 665 5780, *Fax:* +57 5 665 2966, *Email:* marineoperations@caribbsa.com, *Website:* www.caribbsa.com

Medical Facilities: 24 h medical centre

Airport: Ernesto Cortissoz Airport, served by major airlines

Lloyd's Agent: Crawford Colombia Ltda, Carrera 13 No.71-69, Bogota 94754, Colombia, *Tel:* +57 1 347 6349, *Fax:* +57 1 347 6349, *Email:* lloydsagency@crawfordcolombia.com, *Website:* www.crawfordandcompany.com

PUERTO PRODECO

harbour area, see under Puerto Zuniga

PUERTO ZUNIGA

Lat 11° 9' N; Long 74° 13' W.

Admiralty Chart: 1276	**Admiralty Pilot:** 7A
Time Zone: GMT -5 h	**UNCTAD Locode:** CO

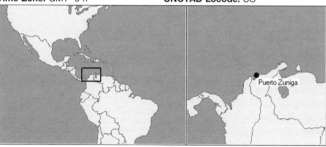

Principal Facilities:

		Y						T	A

Authority: Sociedad Portuaria de Santa Marta, Carrera 1a. No.10A-12, Santa Marta AA 655, Colombia, *Tel:* +57 5 421 1311, *Fax:* +57 5 421 2161, *Email:* spsm@spsm.com.co, *Website:* www.spsm.com.co

Officials: General Manager: Mauricio Suarez, *Email:* msuarez@spsm.com.co. Marketing Manager: Rodolfo Schmulson, *Email:* rschmulson@spsm.com.co.

Port Security: ISPS compliant

Pre-Arrival Information: The Master of the vessel is required to send immediately upon receiving instructions from the Owner or his Charterer (or upon departure from the previous port), the first ETA notice to Puerto Prodeco. Further ETA notices are to be sent 7, 5, 3, 2 and 1 day(s) prior to arrival at Puerto Prodeco, in addition to any other ETA notices required in the Charter Party. Furthermore the Master shall immediately inform Puerto Prodeco of any deviation in excess of 24 h to the aforementioned ETA . The Master is required to notify Puerto Prodeco of his stowage plan and loading sequence as soon as possible but not later than 72 h prior to arrival. The loading sequence must be take into consideration:
(a) a max of 2 rotations per hold and minimum shifting of cranes
(b) a max requirement of 1 (hold) separation between the loading cranes at all times

Pilotage: Compulsory. Pilot boarding position 0.5 nautical mile due S of the Morro Grande Light. Santa Marta port control station and pilots can be contacted on VHF Channels 11, 16 and 74

Principal Imports and Exports: Exports: Coal.

Working Hours: 24 h/day

Accommodation:

Name	Depth (m)	Draught (m)	Remarks
Puerto Prodeco			See [1] below
Alpha	21	18	See [2] below
Bravo	12.5	10.5	See [3] below

[1]*Puerto Prodeco:* Open roadstead port for coal export. Coal is transported from central Colombia by rail to the port. Loading takes place at anchorage at two mooring places called 'Alpha' and 'Bravo' by way of barges which are initially loaded at Prodeco's conveyor belt pier and then towed alongside the vessel, where coal is then grab loaded with either one of the three floating cranes
[2]*Alpha:* Located 2.5 miles from Prodeco's pier with the following four mooring buoys:
Buoy 1 in pos 11° 08' 00" N; 74° 17' 00" W
Buoy 2 in pos 11° 08' 00" N; 74° 15' 00" W
Buoy 3 in pos 11° 05' 00" N; 74° 15' 00" W
Buoy 4 in pos 11° 07' 00" N; 74° 17' 00" W
[3]*Bravo:* Located 1.5 miles from Prodeco's pier with the following mooring buoy:
Buoy 1 in pos 11° 06' 19" N; 74° 15' 13" W

Mechanical Handling Equipment:

Location	Type	Qty
Puerto Prodeco	Floating Cranes	3

Towage: One tug is available

Medical Facilities: Hospital and doctors at Santa Marta

Airport: Simon Bolivar International, 1 km

Lloyd's Agent: Crawford Colombia Ltda, Carrera 13 No.71-69, Bogota 94754, Colombia, *Tel:* +57 1 347 6349, *Fax:* +57 1 347 6349, *Email:* lloydsagency@crawfordcolombia.com, *Website:* www.crawfordandcompany.com

SAN ANDRES

Lat 12° 33' N; Long 81° 41' W.

Admiralty Chart: 1511	**Admiralty Pilot:** 69A
Time Zone: GMT -5 h	**UNCTAD Locode:** CO ADZ

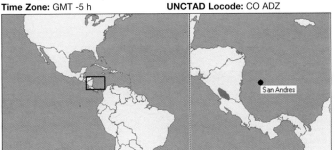

Principal Facilities:

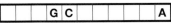

		G	C			A	

Authority: The Port Captain, Avenue Francisco Newball, San Andres, Colombia, *Tel:* +57 25613, *Fax:* +57 25613

Port Security: ISPS compliant

Documentation: Vessel certificate, cargo manifest, crew list, captain's licence, crew's licence, mail list, armament list

Approach: Channel depth 4.57 m

Pilotage: Compulsory. Pilot needed from Buoy No.1. Service only available during daylight hours

Radio Frequency: VHF Channels 16 or 71

Traffic: 1999, 60 061 t of cargo handled

Maximum Vessel Dimensions: 1800 t max dwt, 3.96 m max draft

Principal Imports and Exports: Imports: Foodstuffs, Household electrical appliances. Exports: Seafood.

Working Hours: 0800-1800

Accommodation:

Name	Remarks
San Andres	Muelle Departamental, 450 m long with depth alongside of 3.96 m

Storage: Two warehouses of 40 000 m3 and one of 50 000 m3 are available. Another warehouse of 30 000 m3 is located near to the airport. Open storage area of 3000 m3

Mechanical Handling Equipment:

Location	Type	Capacity (t)
San Andres	Mult-purp. Cranes	50

Cargo Worked: Approx 700 t/day

Medical Facilities: One public hospital and two private clinics

Airport: Gustavo Rojas Pinilla

Lloyd's Agent: Crawford Colombia Ltda, Carrera 13 No.71-69, Bogota 94754, Colombia, *Tel:* +57 1 347 6349, *Fax:* +57 1 347 6349, *Email:* lloydsagency@crawfordcolombia.com, *Website:* www.crawfordandcompany.com

SANTA MARTA

Lat 11° 15' N; Long 74° 12' W.

Admiralty Chart: 2267	**Admiralty Pilot:** 7A
Time Zone: GMT -5 h	**UNCTAD Locode:** CO SMR

Principal Facilities:

	Y	G	C	R	L	B		T	A	

ISACOL S.A.
SHIP AGENTS

"Sailing the extra mile"

Bocagrande Carrera 3ra #6A-100
Torre Empresarial Ofc 10-01
Cartagena, Colombia
Phones
+57 5 6655100
+57 5 6656990
Fax
+57 5 6655569
mobile
+57 314 5242982
e-mail
commercial@isacol.com
web
www.isacol.com

Authority: Sociedad Portuaria de Santa Marta, Carrera 1a. No.10A-12, Santa Marta AA 655, Colombia, *Tel:* +57 5 421 1311, *Fax:* +57 5 421 2161, *Email:* spsm@spsm.com.co, *Website:* www.spsm.com.co

Officials: General Manager: Mauricio Suarez, *Email:* msuarez@spsm.com.co. Marketing Manager: Rodolfo Schmulson, *Email:* rschmulson@spsm.com.co.

Port Security: ISPS compliant

Documentation: Pollution certificate, sanitary certificate, load line, cargo ship safety equipment certificate, cargo gear inspection certificate

Approach: This bay is easy of access in all weathers by day or night and is well protected from prevailing winds, possessing a natural inner harbour of about 121 ha of water with a varying depth from 7.92 to 24.38 m

Anchorage: Anchorage in safety anywhere in the harbour and bay

Pilotage: Available round the clock, VHF Channels 11 and 16

Radio Frequency: VHF Channels 16 and 11

Weather: Strong NE trade winds may be expected during the first three months of the year, and heavy rain from August-November

Traffic: 2007, 6 400 000 t of cargo handled, 93 000 TEU's

Maximum Vessel Dimensions: At Piers: 240 m loa, 12 m draft

Principal Imports and Exports: Imports: Chemical products, General cargo, Grain, Machinery, Paper, Vehicles. Exports: Bananas, Coal, Coffee, Vegetable oil.

Working Hours: 24 h/day

Accommodation:

Name	Length (m)	Depth (m)	Remarks
Santa Marta			
Berth No.1	100	6.1	
Berth No.2	180	11	
Berth No.3	141	11	
Berth No.4	232	12.2	
Berth No.5	94	6.1	
Berth No.6	154	18.3	
Berth No.7	154	10.7	See [1] below

[1]*Berth No.7:* Carbosan coal loader with loading rate of approx 20 000 t/day

Storage:

Location	Open (m²)	Covered (m²)	Grain (t)
Santa Marta	76113	21353	60300

Mechanical Handling Equipment:

Location	Type	Capacity (t)	Qty
Santa Marta	Mult-purp. Cranes	70	1
Santa Marta	Mult-purp. Cranes	20	2
Santa Marta	Mobile Cranes	100	1
Santa Marta	Forklifts	7	8
Santa Marta	Forklifts	40	3
Santa Marta	Forklifts	20	1
Santa Marta	Forklifts	3	38

Cargo Worked: Average of 7444 t/day

Bunkering: Areda Marine Fuel C.I.S.A., Areda Marine Fuel C.I.S.A., Barrio Albornoz, cra 46 #2-22, Muelle Matteucci, Cartagena, Colombia, *Tel:* +57 5 6573 742, *Fax:* +57 5 6767 266, *Email:* sales@aredamarine.com, *Website:* www.aredamarine.com – *Grades:* IFO, MGO – *Rates:* 30t Min – *Delivery Mode:* truck

C.I. Intracol S.A., Diag 21a, 53-94 Bosque Calle Buenos Aires, Cartagena, Colombia, *Tel:* +57 5 662 7127, *Fax:* +57 5 662 7127 – *Delivery Mode:* truck

ExxonMobil Marine Fuels, Suite 900, One Alhambra Plaza, Coral Gables, FL 33134, United States of America, *Tel:* +1 305 459 6358, *Fax:* +1 305 459 6412, *Email:* emmf@exxonmobil.com, *Website:* www.exxonmobilmarinefuels.com – *Delivery Mode:* truck

Mobil de Colombia S.A., Carrera 46 No 48-11, Barranquilla, Colombia, *Tel:* +57 5 632 0418, *Fax:* +57 5 349 0142 – *Delivery Mode:* truck

Petroleos del Milenio C.I. Ltd, Carrera 87 No 85-81, Barranquilla, Colombia, *Tel:* +57 5 373 0888, *Fax:* +57 5 668 5603, *Email:* petromil@petromil.com – *Delivery Mode:* truck

Refineria del Nare S.A., Carrera 13A No 125-81, Barrio Multicentro, Bogota, Colombia, *Tel:* +57 1 612 2300, *Fax:* +57 1 612 4631, *Email:* refinare@andinet.com – *Delivery Mode:* truck

Waste Reception Facilities: Sludge and garbage disposal available by truck

Towage: Four tugs of 2000-4000 bhp available

Repair & Maintenance: Minor repairs, *Tel:* +57 5 421 6867

Key to Principal Facilities:—			
A=Airport	**C**=Containers	**G**=General Cargo	**P**=Petroleum	**R**=Ro/Ro	**Y**=Dry Bulk
B=Bunkers	**D**=Dry Dock	**L**=Cruise	**Q**=Other Liquid Bulk	**T**=Towage (where available from port)	

Shipping Agents: Aduanera Colombiana SIA S.A., Calle 38, A Norte 3N-66, Barrio Prados del Norte, P O Box 2254, Cali, Colombia, *Tel:* +57 2 654 1185/89, *Fax:* +57 2 665 6273, *Email:* operations@aduanera.com.co *Website:* www.aduanera.com.co
Agencia Maritima Transmares Ltda, Avenida del Ferrocarril 1C-119, Bodega 3, Interior Zona Franca Comercial, Santa Marta, Colombia, *Tel:* +57 5 421 2429, *Fax:* +57 5 421 1877, *Email:* info@transmares.com.co, *Website:* www.transmares.com.co
Aquarius Shipping Colombia Ltda, Calle 15 No.1C-54, Oficina 509 Edificio Pevesca, Santa Marta, Colombia, *Tel:* +57 5 431 2162, *Fax:* +57 5 431 2320, *Email:* sma@aquarius.com.co
Caribbean Worldwide Shipping Service Agency Ltda (CARIBBSA), Suite 905, Bahia Centro Building, Santa Marta, Colombia, *Tel:* +57 5 421 0424, *Fax:* +57 5 421 3769, *Email:* operationsma@caribbsa.com, *Website:* www.caribbsa.com
Cia Transportadora S.A., Calle 15 1C-54, Oficina 508, Edificio Pevesca, Santa Marta, Colombia, *Tel:* +57 5 421 2948, *Fax:* +57 5 421 0274, *Email:* santamarta@ciatransportadora.com, *Website:* www.ciatransportadora.com

Stevedoring Companies: Caribbean Worldwide Shipping Service Agency Ltda (CARIBBSA), Suite 905, Bahia Centro Building, Santa Marta, Colombia, *Tel:* +57 5 421 0424, *Fax:* +57 5 421 3769, *Email:* operationsma@caribbsa.com, *Website:* www.caribbsa.com

Medical Facilities: Available

Airport: Simon Bolivar, 12 km

Lloyd's Agent: Crawford Colombia Ltda, Carrera 13 No.71-69, Bogota 94754, Colombia, *Tel:* +57 1 347 6349, *Fax:* +57 1 347 6349, *Email:* lloydsagency@crawfordcolombia.com, *Website:* www.crawfordandcompany.com

TUMACO

Lat 1° 51' N; Long 78° 44' W.

Admiralty Chart: 2799	**Admiralty Pilot:** 7
Time Zone: GMT -5 h	**UNCTAD Locode:** CO TCO

Principal Facilities:

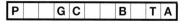

| P | | G | C | | B | | T | A |

ISACOL S.A.
SHIP AGENTS

"Sailing the extra mile"

Bocagrande Carrera 3ra #6A-100
Torre Empresarial Ofc 10-01
Cartagena, Colombia
Phones
+57 5 6655100
+57 5 6656990
Fax
+57 5 6655569
mobile
+57 314 5242982
e-mail
commercial@isacol.com
web
www.isacol.com

Authority: Sociedad Portuaria Regional de Tumaco S.A., Terminal Maritimo, Tumaco, Colombia, *Tel:* +57 30 272457, *Fax:* +57 30 272457

Port Security: ISPS compliant

Documentation: Last port clearance, full set cargo manifest with copies B/L (5 copies), crew list (5 copies), store list (5 copies), health declaration (1 copy)

Anchorage: In pos 1° 53.00' N, 78° 48.25' W in depth of 30 m

Pilotage: Compulsory for the oil terminal. Pilot boards at Sea Buoy No.1 in pos 1° 51.8' N; 78° 48.6' W

Radio Frequency: Port Captain's office on VHF Channel 16

Weather: Prevailing SW'ly winds

Tides: Tide variations 2.44 to 3.66 m. Soft muddy bottom

Traffic: 2003, 1 066 927 t of cargo handled

Working Hours: 24 h/day

Accommodation:

Name	Length (m)	Depth (m)	Remarks
Tumaco			See [1] below
Marginal Wharf	300	9.14	Providing berthing space for two medium-sized vessels

[1]*Tumaco:* There is a private oil terminal at Pindo for the shipment of crude from the Orito Fields, situated 3.25 miles offshore in a depth of 27.43 m, for vessels up to 50 000 dwt with normal loading rate of 25 000 bbls/h

Storage: Dry cargo storage in warehouse for approx 7000 t. Refrigerated space also available

Bunkering: Available by truck and barge

Towage: Available

Repair & Maintenance: Minor repairs only

Medical Facilities: Available

Airport: 1.8 km

Lloyd's Agent: Crawford Colombia Ltda, Carrera 13 No.71-69, Bogota 94754, Colombia, *Tel:* +57 1 347 6349, *Fax:* +57 1 347 6349, *Email:* lloydsagency@crawfordcolombia.com, *Website:* www.crawfordandcompany.com

TURBO

Lat 8° 4' N; Long 76° 44' W.

Admiralty Chart: 1277	**Admiralty Pilot:** 7
Time Zone: GMT -5 h	**UNCTAD Locode:** CO TRB

Principal Facilities:

| | | | G | | | | | | A |

Authority: Capitania del Puerto, Avenida la Playa, Turbo, Colombia, *Tel:* +57 94 827 9371, *Fax:* +57 94 827 9372

Officials: Harbour Master: Marco Antonio Olier Mendoza.

Port Security: ISPS compliant

Documentation: Clearance from last port, bill of ladings (5 copies and 1 original when not sent by email to agents), crew list (7 copies), maritime health declaration (2 copies), in bound cargo manifest (7 copies), transit cargo manifest (1 copy), ship's in ballast manifest (7 copies if needed), list of last port of call (4 copies), passenger list (5 copies), personal effects list (5 copies), stores list (5 copies), yellow fever vaccination list (2 copies), negatives list (5 copies eg firearms, ammunition, animals, dangerous cargo, stowaways, plants)
If it is the first visit of the vessel in Turbo it is necessary to show ship's particulars (1 copy) and international tonnage certificate (1 copy)
If it is not the first visit it is advisable to present a pink copy of the last report received in Turbo to the Harbour Master representative
Valid original vessel documents: Register, P&I Policy Certificate of Entry, IOPP Certificate, Derat Certificate, Load Line Certificate, Safety Equipment Certificate, Safety Radio Certificate, Cargo Gear Book, Safety Management Certificate & DOC

Anchorage: 1.5 mile W of Punta Las Vacas Light. Vessels can arrive at the station at any time but should approach with caution due to small vessels crossing the gulf

Pilotage: Compulsory for vessels over 200 gt and provided by Consorcio Piluraba, Tel/Fax: +57 (94) 827 3213. Pilot boards at Punta de Las Vacas in pos 08° 04' 13" N; 76° 46' 36" W, 08° 04' 13" N; 76° 45' 33" W, 08° 03' 09" N; 76° 45' 36" W, 08° 03' 09" N; 76° 46' 36" W

Radio Frequency: Harbour Master on VHF Channel 16, Coast Guard Station on VHF Channel 16, Pilot Station on VHF Channels 16 and 11, Turbaduana Agency on VHF Channel 16, Naser Agency on VHF Channel 16

Traffic: 1999, 1 893 774 t of cargo handled

Working Hours: 24 h/day

Accommodation:

Name	Remarks
Turbo	See [1] below

[1]*Turbo:* The only cargo activity is loading of bananas from barges and tankers arriving with agricultural chemicals who then discharge into barges. This is all done in the following anchorage areas:
Dry season (December to May) Boca del Rio Leoncito area:
08° 00' 18" N; 76° 51' 33" W
07° 59' 50" N; 76° 51' 18" W
08° 00' 18" N; 76° 50' 45" W
08° 00' 06" N; 76° 50' 48" W
Rainy season (May to December) Rio Leon area:
07° 56' 48" N; 76° 47' 48" W
07° 56' 48" N; 76° 46' 37" W
07° 57' 28" N; 76° 46' 20" W
07° 56' 00" N; 76° 47' 54" W

Repair & Maintenance: Electrical motor repairs and some workshop repairs can be done ashore

Medical Facilities: Hospital available

Airport: Turbo Airport, 20 mins by speedboat from pilot station

Lloyd's Agent: Crawford Colombia Ltda, Carrera 13 No.71-69, Bogota 94754, Colombia, *Tel:* +57 1 347 6349, *Fax:* +57 1 347 6349, *Email:* lloydsagency@crawfordcolombia.com, *Website:* www.crawfordandcompany.com

COMOROS

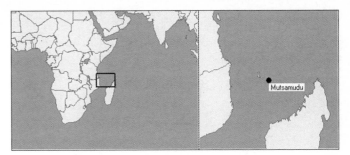

MORONI

Lat 11° 42' S; Long 43° 15' E.

Admiralty Chart: 563   **Admiralty Pilot:** 39

Time Zone: GMT +3 h   **UNCTAD Locode:** KM YVA

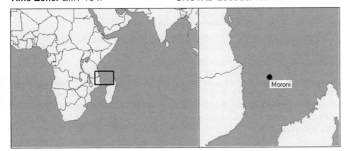

Principal Facilities:

P		Y	G	C					A

Authority: The Port of Moroni, P O Box 651, Moroni, Grand Comore, Comoros, *Tel:* +269 773 2546 & 773 2174

Anchorage: In pos 11° 41' S; 43° 14' E, 2.5 cables from Souazo Island

Pilotage: Compulsory for vessels over 30 m loa. 18 h notice required by telex

Radio Frequency: 6216 mHz from 0730-1430 on Mon-Sat

Tides: Varying from 1.2 m to 4.5 m

Maximum Vessel Dimensions: 9.5 m d at roads

Principal Imports and Exports: Imports: Cement, Meat, Rice, Salt, Sugar, Timber. Exports: Vanilla.

Working Hours: Mon-Thurs 0730-1430. Fri 0730-1100. Sat 0730-1200. Overtime on Fri, Sat and Sun until 1600

Accommodation:

Name	Remarks
Moroni	See [1] below

[1]*Moroni:* Open roadstead. Anchorage zone very narrow for ocean-going vessels and the holding ground is not good. The anchorage should be approached with caution as the depths decrease rapidly. Vessels anchor in 22-35 m. Discharging and loading by lighters and dhows. There is a berth 70 m long in depth of 4 m to handle lighters etc, equipped with two cranes

Mechanical Handling Equipment:

Location	Type	Capacity (t)	Qty
Moroni	Mult-purp. Cranes	18	1
Moroni	Mult-purp. Cranes	5	1

Cargo Worked: 550 t/day for bagged cargo and 300 t/day for conventional cargo

Shipping Agents: Societe Comorienne de Consignation et de Transit, A 5636, Caltex, Boite Cedex, P O Box 483, Moroni, Grand Comore, Comoros, *Tel:* +269 773 1783, *Fax:* +269 773 0737, *Email:* scct2000@yahoo.fr
Societe de Representation et de Navigation, MZI de Mavouna, P O Box 2493, Moroni, Grand Comore, Comoros, *Tel:* +269 773 0377, *Fax:* +269 773 0377, *Email:* sornav.moroni@snpt.km
Spanfreight Shipping SARL, P O Box 1007, Moroni, Grand Comore, Comoros, *Tel:* +269 773 5132, *Fax:* +269 773 0632, *Email:* ebmaritime@snpt.km

Medical Facilities: Hospital available

Airport: Hahaya Airport, 25 km

Development: Gulftainer has signed a 15 year agreement to operate, manage and upgrade the port

Lloyd's Agent: Harold J. Thomson (Indoceanic Services Ltd), 7 Rue Ambroise Croizat, Le Port 97420, Reunion, *Tel:* +262 262 433333, *Fax:* +262 262 420310, *Email:* lloydsr@indoceanic.com, *Website:* www.indoceanic.com

MUTSAMUDU

Lat 12° 10' S; Long 44° 24' E.

Admiralty Chart: 563   **Admiralty Pilot:** 39

Time Zone: GMT +3 h   **UNCTAD Locode:** KM MUT

Principal Facilities:

P		G	R			T	A

Authority: Socopotram, P O Box 11, Mutsamudu, Anjouan Island 205, Comoros, *Tel:* +269 771 0143

Anchorage: Two anchorages in depths between 35 and 46 m

Pilotage: Compulsory

Radio Frequency: SSB 6210.4 mHz. VHF Channel 16

Principal Imports and Exports: Imports: Cement, Flour, Iron, Rice, Sugar. Exports: Vanilla, Ylang extract.

Working Hours: Mon-Thurs 0730-1430. Fri 0730-1100. Sat 0730-1200

Accommodation: Tanker facilities: There are two mooring buoys available for coastal tankers off Pointe Patsy. Anchorage terminal for tankers up to 6000 dwt comprising three mooring buoys

Name	Length (m)	Depth (m)	Remarks
Quay No.1			A 10 m length of Quay No.1 is for ro/ro's
Berth 1A	173	9	Used for foreign trade
Berth 1B	66	4.5	Used by coasters
Berth 1C			At the shore end of the quay dries at LW
Quay No.2			See [1] below

[1]*Quay No.2:* To the south of No.1, is 82 m long with a depth of 3.7 m and used for inter-island vessels

Mechanical Handling Equipment:

Location	Type	Capacity (t)	Qty
Mutsamudu	Mult-purp. Cranes	40	1

Cargo Worked: 500 t/day of bagged cargo and 300 t/day of conventional cargo

Towage: One tug of 10 t bollard pull available

Shipping Agents: Anjouan Stevedoring Co., P O Box 234, Mutsamudu, Anjouan Island, Comoros, *Tel:* +269 771 1365, *Fax:* +269 771 1365, *Email:* legal@anjouanstevedoring.com
Rainbow Shipping Agency, Twaman Djema, P O Box 176, Mutsamudu, Anjouan Island, Comoros, *Tel:* +269 771 1678, *Fax:* +269 771 1678, *Email:* indoceanic.mutsa@snpt.km
Societe Comorienne de Consignation et de Transit, P O Box 43, Anjouan Island, Comoros, *Tel:* +269 771 0000, *Fax:* +269 771 0000
Socopatram Comores, P O Box 11/205, Mutsamudu, Anjouan Island, Comoros, *Tel:* +269 771 0143, *Fax:* +269 771 1055

Stevedoring Companies: Anjouan Stevedoring Co., P O Box 234, Mutsamudu, Anjouan Island, Comoros, *Tel:* +269 771 1365, *Fax:* +269 771 1365, *Email:* legal@anjouanstevedoring.com

Medical Facilities: Available

Airport: Ouani Airport, 7 km

Development: Gulftainer has signed a 15 year agreement to operate, manage and upgrade the port

Lloyd's Agent: Harold J. Thomson (Indoceanic Services Ltd), 7 Rue Ambroise Croizat, Le Port 97420, Reunion, *Tel:* +262 262 433333, *Fax:* +262 262 420310, *Email:* lloydsr@indoceanic.com, *Website:* www.indoceanic.com

CONGO

BANANA

Lat 6° 1' S; Long 12° 24' E.

Admiralty Chart: 658/3206   **Admiralty Pilot:** 2

Time Zone: GMT +1 h   **UNCTAD Locode:** CD BNW

Key to Principal Facilities:—				
A=Airport	**C**=Containers	**G**=General Cargo	**P**=Petroleum	**R**=Ro/Ro	**Y**=Dry Bulk
B=Bunkers	**D**=Dry Dock	**L**=Cruise	**Q**=Other Liquid Bulk	**T**=Towage (where available from port)	

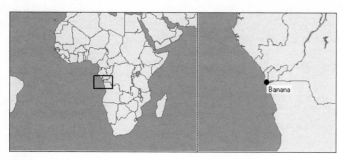

Principal Facilities:

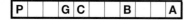

| P | | G | C | | B | | A |

Authority: Office National des Transports (ONATRA), Boulevard du 30 Juin, P O Box 98, Kinshasa, Democratic Republic of Congo, *Tel:* +243 12 24781

Officials: Manager: Otshudi Olomo.
Harbour Master: Bosenge Isanya.

Documentation: Crew list (7 copies), vaccination list, bonded stores list, personal effects list, arms & ammunition list, narcotics list, passenger list, last port of call list, stowaways list, health officer declaration, original of last port of clearance

Approach: See Admiralty Charts 638 and 3206 (Admiralty Pilot 2)

Anchorage: Sea anchorage is approx 5 miles W of Moita Seca Lt in approx 10 fathoms of wake and about 12 miles from Stella Buoy. General cargo vessels are recommended to anchor 1 mile W of Stella Buoy. During this time VHF Channel 16 should be on stand-by for any instructions

Pilotage: Compulsory for vessels over 500 gt. Pilot boards vessel from 0600 local time at Banana Pilot Station, 1 mile S of 'Pointe Francaise'

Radio Frequency: Stand-by on VHF Channel 16 for any instructions

Weather: Rainy season from October 15 to May 15. During heavy rainfall all operations are suspended

Tides: Range of tide 1.52 m. Westerly currents of 4-5 knots are experienced, depending on season

Traffic: 2001, 568 vessels (including tugs), 16 237 t of cargo handled

Principal Imports and Exports: Imports: Containers, General cargo, Petroleum products. Exports: Containers, General cargo, Petroleum products.

Working Hours: 1st shift: 0630-1430, 2nd shift: 1430-2230, 3rd shift: 2230-0630. Overtime on 2nd and 3rd shifts and on Sundays/holidays

Accommodation:

Name	Length (m)	Depth (m)	Remarks
Banana			See [1] below
Quay	75	5.49	See [2] below

[1]*Banana:* Tankers discharge or load petroleum products at anchor in Congo River between Buoys 12 and 14 and between Buoys 14 and 16. Vessels should use both anchors with approx eight shackles of chain. Pusher barges are moored alongside the vessel for loading/discharging operations. The barges are equipped with 8'' hoses and have a receiving rate up to 400 t/h. No tank cleaning facilities. A barge provided by the oil company is available for dirty ballast on special request
The oil refinery of SOCIR is located at Moanda, NE of Banana town
[2]*Quay:* Loading/discharging is carried out by ship's own gear. Vessels exceeding the depth alongside the wharf are handled at anchor in the river between Buoys 12 and 14 by supply boats

Storage: Covered storage available

Mechanical Handling Equipment:

Location	Type	Capacity (t)	Qty
Banana	Mult-purp. Cranes	6	2
Banana	Forklifts	4	2

Bunkering: Fuel oil and diesel oil is supplied by SOCIR barges. Bunkering is not to interfere with cargo operations

Medical Facilities: Limited medical facilities are available at Muanda Hospital, 15 km. Transfer is possible to a specialised hospital at Kinshasa

Airport: Muanda Airport, 15 km

Lloyd's Agent: Congo Containers sprl, P O Box 134, 6 Avenue de la Poste, Matadi 29001, Democratic Republic of Congo, *Email:* lloyds.matadi@ic.cd

BOMA

Lat 5° 51' S; Long 13° 3' E.

Admiralty Chart: 657   **Admiralty Pilot:** 2
Time Zone: GMT +1 h   **UNCTAD Locode:** CD BOA

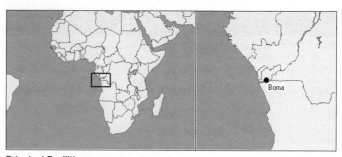

Principal Facilities:

| | Y | G | C | | | D | T | A |

Authority: Office National des Transports (ONATRA), Avenue Makhuku No.1, P O Box 143, Boma, Democratic Republic of Congo

Officials: Harbour Master: Bazonga Baza Marc.

Documentation: Five copies each of: crew list, bonded stores list, narcotics list, crew personal effects list, passenger list, arms & ammunition list, stowaways list, animals list, provisions/stores list, ports of call list + maritime declaration of health

Anchorage: Three anchorage positions available off the port in depth of 10-15 m

Pilotage: Congolese pilots available 0600-1800. No night navigation allowed

Radio Frequency: Pilot station standing by on VHF Channel 16

Traffic: 2001, 50 006 t of cargo handled

Maximum Vessel Dimensions: 200 m loa, 23 ft draft

Principal Imports and Exports: Imports: Building materials, Containers, Fish, Malt, Onions, Rice, Salt, Vehicles. Exports: Coffee, Sawn timber, Timber.

Working Hours: 24 h/day

Accommodation:

Name	Length (m)	Depth (m)	Remarks
Boma			
Berth No.1	175	6.8	
Berth No.2	155	6.4	
Berth No.3	155	6.1	
Berth No.4			Not available at present

Storage: Open and covered storage available

Mechanical Handling Equipment:

Location	Type	Qty
Boma	Shore Cranes	4

Towage: One old tug available

Shipping Agents: Agence Maritime Internationale du Congo Ltd, Quai du Commerce, P O Box 356, Boma, Democratic Republic of Congo, *Tel:* +243 810 338001, *Email:* amicongo@mat-ic.cd

Medical Facilities: No medical facilities at the port but four hospitals nearby

Airport: Boma Airport, 2 km

Lloyd's Agent: Congo Containers sprl, P O Box 134, 6 Avenue de la Poste, Matadi 29001, Democratic Republic of Congo, *Email:* lloyds.matadi@ic.cd

MATADI

Lat 5° 49' S; Long 13° 27' E.

Admiralty Chart: 657   **Admiralty Pilot:** 2
Time Zone: GMT +1 h   **UNCTAD Locode:** CD MAT

Principal Facilities:

| P | Q | Y | G | C | R | | B | | T | A |

Authority: Office National des Transports (ONATRA), P O Box 242, Matadi, Democratic Republic of Congo

Officials: Manager: Mangumbu Mbemba.
Harbour Master: Mfinda Nleba.

Documentation: Five copies each of: crew list, bonded stores list, narcotics list, crew personal effects list, passenger list, arms & ammunition list, stowaways list, animals list, provisions/stores list, ports of call list + maritime declaration of health

Approach: Vessels have to pass the 'Devil's Cauldron' (5 km before Matadi) with an average current rate of 8 knots
Allowed official draft on the river: 21 ft HT up-river (FW) and 22 ft HT down-river (FW)

Anchorage: Anchorage can be obtained at Ango-Ango in a depth of 15 m and Ikungulu in depth of 18.3 m

Pilotage: Compulsory and available in daylight only 0600-1800

Radio Frequency: The pilot station is on stand-by on VHF Channel 16

Weather: Rainy season Sept 15 to May 15. Prevailing winds are W'ly

Traffic: 2001, 284 vessels, 1 031 589 t of cargo handled

Maximum Vessel Dimensions: 200 m loa, 22 ft draft

Principal Imports and Exports: Imports: Bitumen, Chemicals, Coke, Containers, Fertilisers, Frozen goods, Iron, Maize flour, Malt, Metals, Onions, Rice, Salt, Sugar, Wheat flour, White cement. Exports: Cocoa, Coffee, Kernel oil, Logs, Rubber, Sawn wood, Tobacco.

Working Hours: 1st shift: 0630-1430, 2nd shift: 1430-2230, 3rd shift: 2230-0630

Accommodation:

Name	Length (m)	Depth (m)	Remarks
Matadi			Ro/ro vessels accessible at berths 5, 6 and 7
Berth No.1	149		
Berth No.2	161		
Berth No.3	155		
Berth No.4	158		
Berth No.5	156		
Berth No.6	176		
Berth No.7	184		
Berth No.8	149	10	
Berth No.9	167		
Berth No.10	143	10	
Ango Ango			
SEP-Congo	183	9–14	

Storage: Covered storage: Warehouse A of 5000 m2, Warehouse B of 5000 m2, Warehouse C of 5000 m2, Warehouse D of 2000 m2, Warehouse H of 14 700 m2, Warehouse I of 16 180 m2 and Warehouse J of 16 180 m2
Open storage: ABC Yard of 15 000 m2, Venise Yard of 12 000 m2 and Kala Kala Yard of 40 000 m2
No refrigerated storage. Private silo's at Midema, 0.5 km from port

Mechanical Handling Equipment:

Location	Type	Capacity (t)	Qty
Matadi	Electric Cranes	3–6	8
Matadi	Electric Cranes	1–3	35
Matadi	Forklifts	2.5–12	65

Bunkering: Fuel oil, gas oil, Mogas, Avgas, Jet A1 and HV1 available from SEP-Congo

Towage: One tug of 344 cv

Shipping Agents: Afritramp, 6 Rue de la Poste, P O Box 36, Matadi, Democratic Republic of Congo, *Tel:* +243 894 6770, *Fax:* +243 880 4334, *Email:* emambu@matic.cd, *Website:* www.afritrampoilfield.com
A.P. Moller-Maersk Group, Maersk Congo RDC, 20 Avenue de la Poste, Ville Basse, P O Box 99, Matadi, Democratic Republic of Congo, *Tel:* +243 9 940140, *Fax:* +243 9 975314, *Email:* drccusmng@maersk.com, *Website:* www.maerskline.com

Medical Facilities: Not available at the port. Nearest private hospital is 'La Patience', 0.5 km

Airport: Tshimpi, 17 km

Railway: Chemin de Fer/Onatra, 0.5 km

Lloyd's Agent: Congo Containers sprl, P O Box 134, 6 Avenue de la Poste, Matadi 29001, Democratic Republic of Congo, *Email:* lloyds.matadi@ic.cd

MOANDA TERMINAL

Lat 5° 58' S; Long 12° 8' E.

Admiralty Chart: 3206

Time Zone: GMT +1 h

Admiralty Pilot: 2

UNCTAD Locode: CD MNB

Principal Facilities:

P								A

Authority: Moanda International Oil Co., Kinshasa, Democratic Republic of Congo, *Email:* zmoore@cd.perenco.com

Port Security: ISPS compliant

Pre-Arrival Information: Vessel's should advise ETA preferably via email to the Terminal, Moanda Office and via vessel's agent in Kinshasa 72 h, 48 h and 24 h in advance stating the following:
a) vessel's name
b) ETA
c) master's name
d) estimated arrival draught (fore and aft) and displacement

e) if vessel is proceeding to any port(s) prior to Moanda, and if so, any delays anticipated
f) cargo requirements
g) agent's name

Documentation: Crew list (7 copies), vaccination list, bonded stores list, personal effects list, arms & ammunition list, narcotics list, passenger list, last port of call list, stowaways list, health officer declaration, original of last port of clearance

Approach: Owing to the presence of oil wells and submarine pipelines vessels should not enter in the area bounded by lines joining the following positions:
(a) 5° 46.5' S; 12° 12.5' E
(b) 5° 49.5' S; 12° 09' E
(c) 6° 00' S; 12° 09' E
(d) 6° 00' S; 12° 18' E
(e) 5° 53.5' S; 12° 18' E

Anchorage: May be obtained in a designated anchorage area 2 miles N of the SPM

Pilotage: Compulsory. Mooring Master boards:
a) 2.5 nautical miles NW of FSO Kalamu
b) at the anchorage, a circle of radius 0.5 nautical mile centered on pos 5° 56' 60" S; 12° 07' 00" E

Radio Frequency: A 24 h watch is maintained by the storage tanker on VHF Channel 16 and export vessels are usually able to make contact on this channel at a distance of 20-30 miles

Weather: Wind and swell are mostly from a SW'ly direction with a heavy swell from March until September

Tides: A NW current is experienced with an average rate of 3 to 4 knots. The current is greatly affected by the flow of water from the Congo River, and when the water level in the river is high, a rate of 7 knots may be attained

Traffic: 2001, 36 tankers, 1 672 519 t of crude oil exported

Maximum Vessel Dimensions: 125 000 dwt, 55 ft draught, no length restriction

Principal Imports and Exports: Exports: Crude oil.

Working Hours: Loading of tankers is carried out continuously during the day and night, Sundays and holidays

Accommodation:

Name	Remarks
Moanda Terminal	See [1] below

[1]*Moanda Terminal:* Located 16.9 km WSW of Kupundji Light. Tankers of up to 150 000 dwt can be accommodated. Consists of an SPM and FSO 'Kalamu' moored in a depth of 27 m. The installations are connected by numerous submarine oil pipelines. Berthing is only permitted during daylight hours but vessels can sail at night

Cargo Worked: Max loading rate available for transfer operations is 13 500 bbls/h

Medical Facilities: Limited medical facilities are available in Muanda Hospital. Transfer is possible to a specialised hospital at Kinshasa

Airport: Muanda Airport, 15 km from Banana Port

Lloyd's Agent: Congo Containers sprl, P O Box 134, 6 Avenue de la Poste, Matadi 29001, Democratic Republic of Congo, *Email:* lloyds.matadi@ic.cd

CONGO, THE

DJENO TERMINAL

Lat 4° 56' S; Long 11° 54' E.

Admiralty Chart: 3206

Time Zone: GMT +1 h

Admiralty Pilot: 2

UNCTAD Locode: CG DJE

Principal Facilities:

P					B		T	A

Authority: Total E&P Congo, P O Box 761, Pointe Noire, The Congo, *Tel:* +242 94 20 41, *Fax:* +242 94 60 00

Anchorage: Vessels anchor at Pointe Noire roads

Pilotage: Compulsory. Pilot boards off Pointe Noire. VHF Channel 16

Radio Frequency: Watch kept on 500 and 2182 kHz between 0600 and 1800 hours, call sign TNA

Weather: Rainy season extends from November to May

Tides: Range of tide 1.6 m

Maximum Vessel Dimensions: Max dwt 140 000 t fully loaded, 240 000 dwt half loaded, max d 16.0 m

Working Hours: 24 h/day as required

Key to Principal Facilities:—			
A=Airport	**C**=Containers	**G**=General Cargo	**P**=Petroleum	**R**=Ro/Ro	**Y**=Dry Bulk
B=Bunkers	**D**=Dry Dock	**L**=Cruise	**Q**=Other Liquid Bulk	**T**=Towage (where available from port)	

Accommodation:

Name	Remarks
Djeno Terminal	See [1] below

[1]*Djeno Terminal:* Single buoy mooring 15.3 km SSE of Pointe Noire. The mooring is 3.8 km from the shore in a depth of 23 m. Loading is carried out via two 20'' flexible hoses at the rate of 8000 m3/h. Berthing and unberthing day or night

Bunkering: Available at Pointe Noire

Towage: Three tugs of 1800 hp, 1000 hp and 600 hp available from Pointe Noire

Airport: 5 km from Pointe Noire port

Lloyd's Agent: Omega Marine Congo, P O Box 4051, Pointe Noire, The Congo, *Email:* omega-congo@omega-marine.com

POINTE NOIRE

Lat 4° 47' S; Long 11° 50' E.

Admiralty Chart: 3285   **Admiralty Pilot:** 2
Time Zone: GMT +1 h   **UNCTAD Locode:** CG PNR

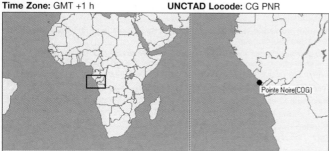

Principal Facilities:

P	Q	Y	G	C	R			T	A

Authority: Port Autonome de Pointe Noire, P O Box 711, Pointe Noire, The Congo, *Tel:* +242 94 00 52, *Fax:* +242 94 20 42, *Website:* www.congoport-papn.com

Port Security: ISPS compliant

Documentation: Crew list (4 copies), passenger list (4 copies), ports of call (4 copies), stores list (2 copies), cargo manifest (5 copies), narcotics list, arms list, crew personal effects list (2 copies), animals list, master's copy of B/L, dangerous goods declaration, vaccination list

Approach: You are clear of the sand bars if passing more than 2 miles W of the breakwater. All sand bars are W of the breakwater, min depth 3.0 m, channel depth 11.0 m

Anchorage: For general cargo vessels anchorage is either 1 mile N of the breakwater in a depth of 14 m or 1 mile N of the Fairway Buoy in a depth of 12-13 m

Pilotage: Compulsory for all vessels over 100 gt, available day and night. VHF Channel 16. Pilot boards one mile N of the green channel light buoy

Radio Frequency: VHF Channel 16, 24 h service

Weather: Winds usually SSW, force 2-4

Tides: Range of tide 1.6 m

Traffic: 2005, 3 300 000 t of cargo handled

Maximum Vessel Dimensions: For tanker berth max loa is 230 m with a d of 10.2 m. For manganese berth max loa is up to 200 m with a d of 10.46 m

Principal Imports and Exports: Imports: Manufactured products. Exports: Crude oil, Timber.

Working Hours: 0700-1200, 1430-1700. Extended hours may be worked, 0700-1200 and 1300-1900

Accommodation:

Name	Length (m)	Depth (m)	Remarks
Pointe Noire			See [1] below
Quay D	720		See [2] below
Quay G	520		See [3] below
Mole Quay	350	9.45	See [4] below

[1]*Pointe Noire:* Bulk facilities: Ore berth is G3. No air draught restriction. Manganese berth with moving conveyor
Tanker facilities: One berth inside harbour in depth of 11.0 m, discharging oil products. One liquefied gas terminal inside the port owned by Hydrocongo
[2]*Quay D:* Five berths for general cargo with the following depths: D1 7.9 m, D2-4 8.7 m, D5 9.4 m
[3]*Quay G:* Comprising two general cargo berths with the following depths: G1 9.45 m, G2-3 10.46-13.2 m
[4]*Mole Quay:* Comprises two berths (No's 7 and 8) for the export of timber

Storage: Timber stacking area of 8.9 ha

Location	Open (m²)	Covered (m²)	Cold (m³)
Pointe Noire	380442	120000	5230

Mechanical Handling Equipment: Private cranes available only. A special crane for very heavy products can be rented from Bouygues Offshore

Location	Type	Capacity (t)	Qty	Remarks
Pointe Noire	Mult-purp. Cranes	20	2	for timber terminal

Cargo Worked: Timber approx 1500 t/day, eucalyptus 3000 t/day

Towage: Compulsory for vessels over 130 m loa. One tug of 1800 hp and one of 900 hp available. For vessels over 160 m loa two tugs are compulsory

Repair & Maintenance: Gestion Nouvelle des Chantiers et Ateliers du Congo, P O Box 1155, Pointe Noire, The Congo, *Tel:* +242 94 03 63, *Fax:* +242 94 39 50, *Email:* contact@gncac.net, *Website:* www.gncac.net Slipway for vessels of 600 dwt, max loa 35.0 m, beam 15.45 m, max d 5.0 m

Ship Chandlers: S.A.M. Congo - Daron Shipchandler, P O Box 95, Pointe Noire, The Congo, *Tel:* +242 94 09 21, *Fax:* +242 94 40 45, *Email:* sam-cg-pnr@daron-shipchandler.com, *Website:* www.daron-shipchandler.com

Shipping Agents: Afritramp, Avenue de Loango, P O Box 616, Pointe Noire, The Congo, *Tel:* +242 94 70 40, *Fax:* +242 94 34 04, *Email:* afritramp.pnr@cg.dti.bollore.com, *Website:* www.afritrampoilfield.com
GAC-GETMA, P O Box 1032, Pointe Noire, The Congo, *Email:* gac-getma.congo@gacworld.com, *Website:* www.gacworld.com
A.P. Moller-Maersk Group, Maersk Congo S.A., 15 Avenue Kaat Matou, Pointe Noire, The Congo, *Tel:* +242 94 21 41, *Fax:* +242 94 23 25, *Email:* cgosvd@maersk.com, *Website:* www.maerskline.com
SAGA-Congo, 18 Rue Du Prophet Lassy-Zephirin, P O Box 674, Pointe Noire, The Congo, *Tel:* +242 94 10 16, *Fax:* +242 94 37 06, *Email:* jean-pierre.sancerne@cg.dti.bollore.com
Samariti Sarl, P O Box 5049, Pointe Noire, The Congo, *Tel:* +242 94 71 30, *Fax:* +242 94 56 77, *Email:* samariti-marcel@cg.celtelplus.com
Socopao-Congo, P O Box 664, Pointe Noire, The Congo, *Tel:* +242 94 38 14, *Fax:* +242 94 38 14, *Email:* guillaume.de-chastellux@cg.dti.bollore.com

Medical Facilities: Two hospitals and three private clinics, 2-3 km from port

Airport: Agosthino Neto, 5 km

Railway: Station, 1 km

Lloyd's Agent: Omega Marine Congo, P O Box 4051, Pointe Noire, The Congo, *Email:* omega-congo@omega-marine.com

YOMBO TERMINAL

Lat 4° 27' S; Long 11° 6' E.

Admiralty Chart: 604   **Admiralty Pilot:** 2
Time Zone: GMT +1 h   **UNCTAD Locode:** CG

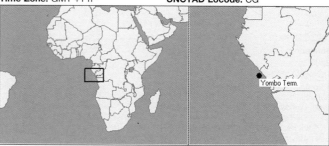

Principal Facilities:

P							T	

Authority: CMS Nomeco Congo Inc., P O Box 212, Pointe Noire, The Congo, *Tel:* +242 942470, *Fax:* +242 941376, *Email:* ebilongo@cg.perenco.com

Port Security: ISPS compliant

Pre-Arrival Information: Vessel's should send ETA message 72 h, 48 h and 24 h in advance and give notice of any change of ETA when a change of more than 2 h occurs. The 72 h message should be sent by fax or email to the Operators, stating the information required in the Terminal Regulations handbook
Vessel's should maintain a continuous listening watch on 2182 kHz RT and VHF Channel 12 when not less than 12 h from the terminal. Watch should be maintained whilst the vessel is at the anchorage awaiting berthing

Pilotage: Compulsory. The Mooring Master boards (weather permitting) 4 nautical miles N of the FPSO in pos 4° 24.0' S; 11° 07.00' E

Accommodation:

Name	Remarks
Yombo Terminal	See [1] below

[1]*Yombo Terminal:* Consists of FPSO 'Conkouati' which is connected by submarine pipeline to platforms Yombo A and Yombo B, 1.5 miles SSW and 1.5 miles SW respectively from the terminal, which can accommodate tankers up to 155 000 dwt, 280 m loa, 53 m beam and 15 m loaded draft

Towage: Tugs are provided for mooring and unmooring, remaining secured to the tanker throughout the loading operation

Lloyd's Agent: Omega Marine Congo, P O Box 4051, Pointe Noire, The Congo, *Email:* omega-congo@omega-marine.com

COOK ISLANDS

AVATIU

Lat 21° 12' S; Long 159° 47' W.

Admiralty Chart: NZ 9558   **Admiralty Pilot:** 62
Time Zone: GMT +10 h   **UNCTAD Locode:** CK RAR

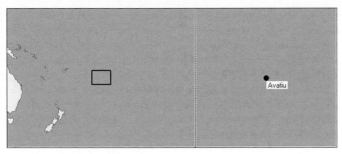

Principal Facilities:

P		G	C	R		B		T	A

Authority: Cook Islands Ports Authority, P O Box 84, Rarotonga, Cook Islands, *Tel:* +682 21921, *Fax:* +682 21191, *Email:* andrewm@ports.co.ck, *Website:* www.ports.co.ck

Officials: General Manager: Andrew McBirney.
Harbour Master: John Fallon.

Port Security: ISPS compliant

Documentation: Clearance from last port, crew list, stores list, passenger list, health declaration and cargo manifest

Anchorage: Off Avarua Harbour in depth of 35 m

Pilotage: Not compulsory, although pilot available and recommended for first visit

Radio Frequency: Radio Rarotonga '2KR' continuous watch on 2182 and 4125, VHF Channel 16

Weather: Unpredictable swells up to 3 m at times. Anchor watch is advisable when vessel is on roads

Tides: Range of tide 0.55 m to 0.915 m

Traffic: 2001, 44 vessels, 10 000 t of break bulk, 15 000 t of bulk fuel & 1200 TEU's

Maximum Vessel Dimensions: 90 m loa, 3000 dwt, 5.8 m draught

Principal Imports and Exports: Imports: Building materials, Foodstuffs, Fuel, Vehicles.

Working Hours: Monday to Saturday 0700--2200

Accommodation:

Name	Length (m)	Depth (m)
Avatiu		
Outer Berth	135	6
Inner Berth	127	5.5

Storage: Sheds and warehouses available

Mechanical Handling Equipment:

Location	Type	Capacity (t)	Qty
Avatiu	Mobile Cranes	15	1
Avatiu	Forklifts	25	1
Avatiu	Forklifts	20	1

Cargo Worked: Average 30 m3/h, 15 TEU's/h using ship's gear

Bunkering: ExxonMobil Marine Fuels, 1 Harbour Front Place, 06-00 Harbour Front, Tower One, Singapore, Republic of Singapore 098633, *Tel:* +65 6885 8998, *Fax:* +65 6885 8794, *Email:* asiapac.marinefuels@exxonmobil.com, *Website:* www.exxonmobilmarinefuels.com – *Grades:* MGO – *Delivery Mode:* tank truck, pipeline

Waste Reception Facilities: Garbage disposal available

Towage: One tug available of 4.5 t bollard pull

Repair & Maintenance: Rarotonga Welding & Steel Construction Ltd, P O Box 949, Rarotonga, Cook Islands, *Tel:* +682 26445, *Fax:* +682 26445

Stevedoring Companies: Cook Islands General Transport Ltd, 1 Happy Valley Road, Takuvaine, P O Box 326, Rarotonga, Cook Islands, *Tel:* +682 24441, *Fax:* +682 24446, *Email:* movers@cigt.co.ck Manager: Jessie Sword Mobile Tel: +682 55242
Hawaii-Pacific Maritime Ltd, P O Box 435, Avarua, Rarotonga, Cook Islands, *Tel:* +682 27185, *Fax:* +682 27186, *Email:* hipacmar@oyster.net.ck

Medical Facilities: Hospital, 4 km

Airport: Rarotonga International Airport, 1 km

Lloyd's Agent: Cook Islands General Transport Ltd, 1 Happy Valley Road, Takuvaine, P O Box 326, Rarotonga, Cook Islands, *Tel:* +682 24441, *Fax:* +682 24446, *Email:* movers@cigt.co.ck

COSTA RICA

CALDERA

Lat 9° 54' N; Long 84° 42' W.

Admiralty Chart: 1931
Time Zone: GMT -6 h

Admiralty Pilot: 8
UNCTAD Locode: CR CAL

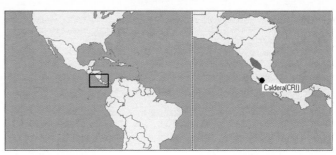

Principal Facilities:

P	Y	G	C	R		B		T	A

Authority: Sociedad Portuaria de Caldera (SPC) S.A., P O Box 168-5400, Puntarenas, Costa Rica, *Tel:* +506 2634 4003, *Fax:* +506 2634 4595, *Email:* d.chinea@spcaldera.com, *Website:* www.spcaldera.com

Officials: General Manager: Domingo Segundo Chinea.

Pilotage: Compulsory. Pilot boards approx 2 miles SW of the breakwater

Traffic: 2006, 2 982 737 t of cargo handled

Working Hours: 24 h/day

Accommodation:

Name	Length (m)	Depth (m)	Remarks
Caldera			See [1] below
Berth 1	210	11	Vessels up to 25 000 dwt
Berth 2	150	10	Vessels up to 15 000 dwt
Berth 3	130	7	Vessels up to 5000 dwt

[1]*Caldera:* Modern concrete quay 490 m in length containing three berths
Containers are handled with modern equipment. There are 20 reefer points for refrigerated containers. Ro/ro cargoes also handled
Bulk facilities: Discharge system with pneumatic suction units and silos with cap of 15 000 t for storage
Tanker facilities: Mooring buoy 304.8 m offshore, connected to five large storage tanks by 6'' submarine pipelines

Storage:

Location	Open (m²)
Caldera	25000

Mechanical Handling Equipment:

Location	Type	Capacity (t)
Caldera	Mobile Cranes	127
Caldera	Forklifts	35

Bunkering: Chevron Marine Products LLC, Global Marine Products LLC, 1500 Louisiana, 4th Floor, Houston, TX 77002, United States of America, *Tel:* +1 832 8542 988, *Fax:* +1 832 8544 868, *Email:* gulfcbm@chevron.com, *Website:* www.chevron.com – *Grades:* GO; FO – *Delivery Mode:* tank truck
Cockett Marine Oil Ltd, Carrick House, 36 Station Square, Petts Wood, Kent BR5 1NA, United Kingdom, *Tel:* +44 1689 883 400, *Fax:* +44 1689 877 666, *Email:* enquiries@cockett.com, *Website:* www.cockettgroup.com – *Grades:* all grades – *Notice:* 72 hours – *Delivery Mode:* pipeline, road tank wagon

Towage: Two tugs available; compulsory for berthing and unberthing

Shipping Agents: Corporacion Improsa S.A., Paso Ancho, Corporacion Improsa Building, 2 Floor, 4-2300 San Jose, Costa Rica, *Tel:* +506 2586 9540, *Fax:* +506 2227 0300, *Email:* martin.nielsen@improsa.com, *Website:* www.improsa.com

Medical Facilities: Port clinic, or at a hospital 17 km distant

Airport: San Jose International Airport, 90 km

Lloyd's Agent: G.W.F. Franklin S.A., Diagonal Esquina Noreste de la Nunciatura, Contiguo Galeria de Arte 99, Rohrmoser, San Jose, Costa Rica, *Tel:* +506 2296 7001, *Fax:* +506 2322 2067, *Email:* franklin@ice.co.cr, *Website:* www.franklin.com.gt

GOLFITO

Lat 8° 38' N; Long 83° 11' W.

Admiralty Chart: 1932
Time Zone: GMT -6 h

Admiralty Pilot: 8
UNCTAD Locode: CR GLF

Principal Facilities:

P		G				B			A

Key to Principal Facilities:—
A=Airport   **C**=Containers   **G**=General Cargo   **P**=Petroleum   **R**=Ro/Ro   **Y**=Dry Bulk
B=Bunkers   **D**=Dry Dock   **L**=Cruise   **Q**=Other Liquid Bulk   **T**=Towage (where available from port)

Authority: Instituto Costarricense de Puertos del Pacifico (INCOP), Caldera, Costa Rica, *Tel:* +506 2634 4151, *Fax:* +506 2634 4134, *Email:* dportuaria@incop.go.cr, *Website:* www.incop.go.cr

Officials: Administration & Finance Manager: Gonzalo Corrales. Project Manager: Natalia Alvarez.

Approach: Min draft in approaches 9.14 m. No bars

Pilotage: No light. Launch can be sent to guide vessels if requested on radio system. VHF Channel 16

Tides: From January to June tide of about 2.8 m. From June to December tide of about 3.1 m

Working Hours: 24 h/day

Accommodation:

Name	Remarks
Golfito	See [1] below
Private Wharves	See [2] below

[1]*Golfito:* One wharf affording two berths accommodates vessels drawing max 7.31 m at banana pier and 7.92 m at general cargo pier. Facilities for loading and unloading (grabs, pallets and hysters), fuel discharged by pipeline at cargo berth. Rail spur on wharf, direct loading to rail trucks

[2]*Private Wharves:* Operated by Transportes Maritimos, Ministerio de Obras Publicas (MOP), Gobierno de Costa Rica

Cargo Worked: 21 t/h/gang

Bunkering: Chevron Marine Products LLC, Global Marine Products LLC, 1500 Louisiana, 4th Floor, Houston, TX 77002, United States of America, *Tel:* +1 832 8542 988, *Fax:* +1 832 8544 868, *Email:* gulfcbm@chevron.com, *Website:* www.chevron.com – *Grades:* GO; FO – *Delivery Mode:* tank truck
Cockett Marine Oil Ltd, Carrick House, 36 Station Square, Petts Wood, Kent BR5 1NA, United Kingdom, *Tel:* +44 1689 883 400, *Fax:* +44 1689 877 666, *Email:* enquiries@cockett.com, *Website:* www.cockettgroup.com – *Grades:* all grades – *Notice:* 72 hours – *Delivery Mode:* pipeline, road tank wagon

Repair & Maintenance: Carried out by Cia Bananera de Costa Rica

Airport: Golfito

Lloyd's Agent: G.W.F. Franklin S.A., Diagonal Esquina Noreste de la Nunciatura, Contiguo Galeria de Arte 99, Rohrmoser, San Jose, Costa Rica, *Tel:* +506 2296 7001, *Fax:* +506 2322 2067, *Email:* franklin@ice.co.cr, *Website:* www.franklin.com.gt

PUERTO LIMON

Lat 10° 0' N; Long 83° 3' W.

Admiralty Chart: 1798	**Admiralty Pilot:** 7A
Time Zone: GMT -6 h	**UNCTAD Locode:** CR LIO

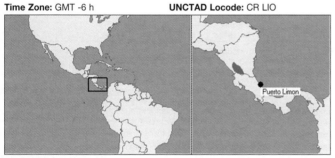

Principal Facilities:

P	Q	Y	G	C	R	L	B		T	A

Authority: Caribbean Coast Port Authority (JAPDEVA), P O Box 1320-7300, Limon, Costa Rica, *Tel:* +506 2795 4747, *Fax:* +506 2795 0728, *Email:* fpecou@japdeva.go.cr, *Website:* www.japdeva.go.cr

Officials: Port Manager: Danny Morris, *Tel:* +506 758 0567, *Email:* dmorris@japdeva.go.cr.
Marketing Manager: Felix Pecou, *Tel:* +506 758 2456.
Marketing: Walter Anderson.

Approach: Hazard free entrance in depth of 14 m

Anchorage: Anchorage between Uvita Island and Port installations

Pilotage: Five pilots available, 24 h/day

Radio Frequency: VHF Channel 16

Weather: Tropical and humid climate with temperatures ranging from 25°-32° C

Traffic: 2007, 9 920 617 t of cargo handled, 842 903 TEU's

Maximum Vessel Dimensions: 210 m loa, 9.0 m draft, 27 802 dwt

Working Hours: 24 h/day

Accommodation:

Name	Length (m)	Depth (m)	Remarks
Puerto Limon			See [1] below
Limon			
Berths	1219	7–10	Seven berths
Moin			
Berths	993	10–12	Six berths

[1]*Puerto Limon:* Consists of two facilities approx 7 km apart. The container terminal is located in the older facility of Port Limon and the port also specialises in ro/ro and cruise ship vessels, in addition to general cargoes

Storage:

Location	Open (m²)	Covered (m²)
Puerto Limon	21000	18758

Mechanical Handling Equipment:

Location	Type	Capacity (t)	Qty
Limon	Container Cranes	35–40	2
Limon	Straddle Carriers		4
Limon	Forklifts		57

Cargo Worked: 200 t of general cargo/gang/working day

Bunkering: Chevron Marine Products LLC, Global Marine Products LLC, 1500 Louisiana, 4th Floor, Houston, TX 77002, United States of America, *Tel:* +1 832 8542 988, *Fax:* +1 832 8544 868, *Email:* gulfcbm@chevron.com, *Website:* www.chevron.com – *Grades:* GO; FO – *Delivery Mode:* tank truck
Cockett Marine Oil Ltd, Carrick House, 36 Station Square, Petts Wood, Kent BR5 1NA, United Kingdom, *Tel:* +44 1689 883 400, *Fax:* +44 1689 877 666, *Email:* enquiries@cockett.com, *Website:* www.cockettgroup.com – *Grades:* all grades – *Notice:* 72 hours – *Delivery Mode:* pipeline, road tank wagon
Refinadora Costaricense de Petroleos S.A., P O Box 4351-100, San Jose, Costa Rica, *Tel:* +506 2257 6544, *Fax:* +506 2222 6118 – *Grades:* DO; MDO; IFO180-380cSt – *Misc:* own storage facilities – *Parcel Size:* MDO min 20t, FO min 50t max 2000t – *Rates:* FO 100t/h – *Notice:* 24 hours – *Delivery Mode:* truck, wharf

Towage: Three tugs available; two of 1800 hp and one of 2200 hp

Repair & Maintenance: Minor repairs by local workshops

Shipping Agents: Corporacion Improsa S.A., Paso Ancho, Corporacion Improsa Building, 2 Floor, 4-2300 San Jose, Costa Rica, *Tel:* +506 2586 9540, *Fax:* +506 2227 0300, *Email:* martin.nielsen@improsa.com, *Website:* www.improsa.com
Inter-Moves SG Global S.A., P O Box 11990-1000, San Jose, Costa Rica, *Tel:* +506 2258 0018, *Fax:* +506 2256 5705, *Website:* www.intermoves-sgcr.com
Mediterranean Shipping Company, MSC Costa Rica S.A., Edificio Cerro Chato, Pino No.2, La Uraca, San Jose, Costa Rica, *Tel:* +506 2291 5535, *Fax:* +506 2291 5540, *Email:* msccr@msc-costarica.co.cr, *Website:* www.mscgva.ch
Representaciones B y A S.A., P O Box 812, San Jose, Costa Rica, *Tel:* +506 2240 0210, *Fax:* +506 2241 1755, *Email:* byasacr@racsa.co.cr, *Website:* www.byasa.co.cr

Medical Facilities: Local hospital

Airport: El Coco, 4 km from Limon and 11 km from Moin

Lloyd's Agent: G.W.F. Franklin S.A., Diagonal Esquina Noreste de la Nunciatura, Contiguo Galeria de Arte 99, Rohrmoser, San Jose, Costa Rica, *Tel:* +506 2296 7001, *Fax:* +506 2322 2067, *Email:* franklin@ice.co.cr, *Website:* www.franklin.com.gt

PUERTO MOIN

harbour area, see under Puerto Limon

PUNTARENAS

Lat 9° 59' N; Long 84° 51' W.

Admiralty Chart: 1931	**Admiralty Pilot:** 8
Time Zone: GMT -6 h	**UNCTAD Locode:** CR PAS

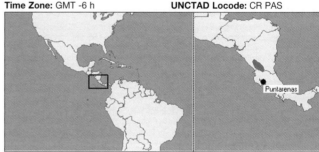

Principal Facilities:

P		G		L	B		A

Authority: Instituto Costarricense de Puertos del Pacifico (INCOP), Caldera, Costa Rica, *Tel:* +506 2634 4151, *Fax:* +506 2634 4134, *Email:* dportuaria@incop.go.cr, *Website:* www.incop.go.cr

Officials: Administration & Finance Manager: Gonzalo Corrales. Project Manager: Natalia Alvarez.

Pilotage: Available. Pilot boards in pos 9° 57' 32" N; 84° 48' 04" W

Traffic: 2006, 117 954 t of cargo handled

Accommodation:

Name	Remarks
Puntarenas	See [1] below

[1]*Puntarenas:* Outer roadstead, in open sea, with sufficient depth for the largest vessels. Good anchorage. Depth inside pier 7.31 m LW, 9.14 m HW, outside pier 8.23 m LW, 10.67 m HW. Agents recommend that inward vessels, berthed to load, should not draw more than 7.31 m. Pier takes two vessels at a time, length inner side 109.7 m, outer side 137.2 m giving all the facilities and security of modern wharfage. Four breast or mooring buoys anchored to cement blocks alongside the pier. Crane, gangway and slings. No elevators. Six railroad tracks run into pier. Discharging is made directly into the railroad cars. Electric railway connects Puntarenas with San Jose, 128 km away

Tanker facilities: One oil berth, length 149.3 m with 7.31 m d. Night berthing possible. Water and bunkers available

Bunkering: Chevron Marine Products LLC, Global Marine Products LLC, 1500 Louisiana, 4th Floor, Houston, TX 77002, United States of America, *Tel:* +1 832 8542 988, *Fax:* +1 832 8544 868, *Email:* gulfcbm@chevron.com, *Website:* www.chevron.com – *Grades:* GO; FO – *Delivery Mode:* tank truck
Cockett Marine Oil Ltd, Carrick House, 36 Station Square, Petts Wood, Kent BR5 1NA, United Kingdom, *Tel:* +44 1689 883 400, *Fax:* +44 1689 877 666, *Email:* enquiries@cockett.com, *Website:* www.cockettgroup.com – *Grades:* all grades – *Notice:* 72 hours – *Delivery Mode:* pipeline, road tank wagon
Refinadora Costaricense de Petroleos S.A., P O Box 4351-100, San Jose, Costa Rica, *Tel:* +506 2257 6544, *Fax:* +506 2222 6118 – *Grades:* DO; MDO; IFO180-380cSt – *Parcel Size:* max 150t – *Delivery Mode:* truck

Repair & Maintenance: Available

Airport: San Jose International Airport

Lloyd's Agent: G.W.F. Franklin S.A., Diagonal Esquina Noreste de la Nunciatura, Contiguo Galeria de Arte 99, Rohrmoser, San Jose, Costa Rica, *Tel:* +506 2296 7001, *Fax:* +506 2322 2067, *Email:* franklin@ice.co.cr, *Website:* www.franklin.com.gt

CROATIA

BAKAR

harbour area, see under Rijeka

BRSICA

harbour area, see under Rasa

DUBROVNIK

Lat 42° 38' N; Long 18° 7' E.

Admiralty Chart: 683
Time Zone: GMT +1 h
Admiralty Pilot: 47
UNCTAD Locode: HR DBV

Principal Facilities:

P		Y	G	C	R	L			T	A

Authority: Port Authority of Dubrovnik, Obala Pape Ivana Pavla II. 1, 20000 Dubrovnik, Republic of Croatia, *Tel:* +385 20 313333, *Fax:* +385 20 418551, *Email:* padubrovnik@portdubrovnik.hr, *Website:* www.portdubrovnik.hr

Officials: General Manager: Vlaho Durkovic, *Email:* dpa.vlaho@portdubrovnik.hr. Marketing Manager: Kristina Laptalo, *Tel:* +385 20 313331, *Email:* dpa.kristina@portdubrovnik.hr.
Harbour Master: Capt Ivan Filippi, *Tel:* +385 20 418988.

Port Security: ISPS compliant

Approach: The port is approached from SW through Velika vrata, the S entrance to Kolocepski Kanal and then by passing either N or S of Daksa Inlet (42° 40' N; 18° 04' E)

Anchorage: Anchorage can be obtained about 0.8 miles WNW of Kantafig light, between Daksa Island and mainland, in a depth of 42 m. Vessels may anchor off the old city harbour, between Lokrum Island and the mainland. This area can accommodate cruise vessels and has a depth of 38 m but should not be used during winter months when exposed to strong S winds

Pilotage: Compulsory for vessels exceeding 500 gt. Dubrovacki Peljar, Tel/Fax: +385 20 419307. Vessels should request pilots 24 h prior to arrival. The pilot boards 7 nautical miles N of Hridi light (42° 39.1' N; 18° 03.2' E)

Radio Frequency: Radio Dubrovnik, call sign 9AD. Pilot Station calling on VHF Channel 16 and working on VHF Channel 12. Harbour Control calling on VHF Channel 16 and working on VHF Channels 10, 4 and 7. Port Authority calling on VHF Channel 16 and working on VHF Channel 9

Weather: Prevailing winds NE and SE

Tides: Max 0.5 m

Traffic: 2003, 480 cruise vessels with 395 000 passengers, 24 025 t of cargo handled

Maximum Vessel Dimensions: Passenger vessels up to 300 m loa with draft 6-11 m, width no limit

Working Hours: 0600-1300, 1400-2100

Accommodation:

Name	Length (m)	Draught (m)
Dubrovnik		
Berth No.1	250	11.5
Berth No.2	250	8
Berth No.3	300	7
Berth No.4	200	7

Storage: Cement silo of 3000 t

Location	Covered (m²)
Dubrovnik	7000

Mechanical Handling Equipment:

Location	Type	Capacity (t)	Qty
Dubrovnik	Mult-purp. Cranes	25	1

Cargo Worked: Timber 500 m3/day. General cargo 400 t/day

Waste Reception Facilities: On request trucks available for collecting garbage, dirty ballast water, oil bilge water, sludge from fuel oil purifier

Towage: Tugs can be arranged with 72 h notice from Ploce or Split

Ship Chandlers: Adria-Dubrovnik-Co d.o.o., Obala pape Ivana Pavla II No.1, 20000 Dubrovnik, Republic of Croatia, *Tel:* +385 20 419059, *Fax:* +385 20 419022, *Email:* adria.dubrovnik@provimar.es, *Website:* www.provimar.es

Shipping Agents: Jadroagent d.d., Obala pape Ivana Pavla II No. 1, P O Box 183, 20000 Dubrovnik, Republic of Croatia, *Tel:* +385 20 419000, *Fax:* +385 20 419029, *Email:* dubrovnik@jadroagent.hr, *Website:* www.jadroagent.com
Posejdon Shipping Agency Ltd, Dubrovnik, Republic of Croatia, *Tel:* +385 20 313101, *Fax:* +385 20 418455, *Email:* posejdon@du.hinet.hr, *Website:* www.posejdon.hr

Medical Facilities: Available at local hospital

Airport: Cilipi Airport, 17 km

Lloyd's Agent: Jadroagent d.d., Trg Ivana Koblera 2, 51000 Rijeka, Republic of Croatia, *Tel:* +385 51 780500, *Fax:* +385 51 215357, *Email:* info@jadroagent.hr, *Website:* www.jadroagent.hr

FIUME

alternate name, see Rijeka

GAZENICA

harbour area, see under Zadar

HVAR

Lat 43° 16' N; Long 16° 27' E.

Admiralty Chart: 269
Time Zone: GMT +1 h
Admiralty Pilot: 47
UNCTAD Locode: HR HVA

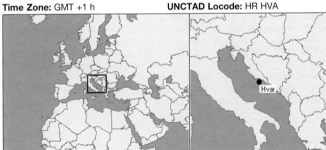

Principal Facilities:

			G		L				

Authority: Lucka Ispostava Hvar, Fabrika bb, 21450 Hvar, Republic of Croatia, *Tel:* +385 21 741007

Accommodation:

Name	Depth (m)	Remarks
Hvar		The port serves mainly cruise vessels
Quay	5	

Lloyd's Agent: Jadroagent d.d., Trg Ivana Koblera 2, 51000 Rijeka, Republic of Croatia, *Tel:* +385 51 780500, *Fax:* +385 51 215357, *Email:* info@jadroagent.hr, *Website:* www.jadroagent.hr

JADRANSKI NAFTOVOD

harbour area, see under Omisalj

Key to Principal Facilities:—					
A=Airport	**C**=Containers	**G**=General Cargo	**P**=Petroleum	**R**=Ro/Ro	**Y**=Dry Bulk
B=Bunkers	**D**=Dry Dock	**L**=Cruise	**Q**=Other Liquid Bulk	**T**=Towage (where available from port)	

KARDELJEVO

alternate name, see Ploce

KORCULA

Lat 42° 48' N; Long 17° 8' E.

Admiralty Chart: 683   **Admiralty Pilot:** 47
Time Zone: GMT +1 h   **UNCTAD Locode:** HR KOR

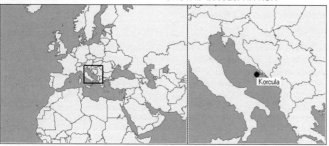

Principal Facilities:

			G				T	

Authority: Lucka Kapetanija Korcula, 20270 Korcula, Korcula Island, Republic of Croatia, *Tel:* +385 20 711178, *Email:* li-korcula@pomorstvo.hr

Officials: Harbour Master: Capt Vojko Trojan.

Anchorage: In pos 42° 58.2' N, 17° 08.3' E with min depth in approaches of 29 m

Pilotage: Compulsory. West station in pos 42° 58.4' N, 17° 06' E and East station in pos 42° 58' N, 17° 13' E. VHF Channel 16

Radio Frequency: Dubrovnik Radio call sign 9AD. Calling on VHF Channel 16 and working on VHF Channels 9 and 12

Weather: Strong NNE winds during Autumn and Winter

Traffic: 2000, 4038 t of cargo handled

Principal Imports and Exports: Imports: Steel plates. Exports: Hatch covers.

Working Hours: 0700-1500

Accommodation:

Name	Length (m)	Depth (m)	Remarks
Korcula			
East berth	100	5.1	Ferries
West berth	150	6.7	Passenger vessels

Cargo Worked: 150 t/day

Waste Reception Facilities: Garbage disposal available

Towage: Available from Ploce or Split with 72 h advanced notice required

Repair & Maintenance: Shipyard Leda, Domince b.b., P O Box 42, 20260 Korcula, Korcula Island, Republic of Croatia, *Tel:* +385 20 715307, *Fax:* +385 20 715308, *Email:* info@shipyard-leda.hr, *Website:* www.shipyard-leda.hr Repair facilities

Surveyors: Croatian Register of Shipping, Ulica 58.15, 20270 Vela Luka, Republic of Croatia, *Tel:* +385 20 813120, *Fax:* +385 20 813120, *Email:* crs-korcula@crs.hr, *Website:* www.crs.hr

Medical Facilities: Available at local hospital

Lloyd's Agent: Jadroagent d.d., Trg Ivana Koblera 2, 51000 Rijeka, Republic of Croatia, *Tel:* +385 51 780500, *Fax:* +385 51 215357, *Email:* info@jadroagent.hr, *Website:* www.jadroagent.hr

KOROMACNO

harbour area, see under Rasa

MASLENICA

Lat 44° 13' N; Long 15° 32' E.

Admiralty Chart: 515   **Admiralty Pilot:** 47
Time Zone: GMT +1 h   **UNCTAD Locode:** HR MAS
This port is closed at present due the entrace being blocked by a destroyed bridge

OMISALJ

Lat 45° 13' N; Long 14° 33' E.

Admiralty Chart: 1996   **Admiralty Pilot:** 47
Time Zone: GMT +1 h   **UNCTAD Locode:** HR OMI

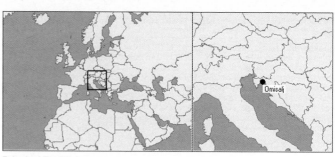

Principal Facilities:

P	Q					B	T	A

Authority: Lucka Ispostava Omisalj, Put mora 1, 51513 Omisalj, Republic of Croatia, *Tel:* +385 51 842053, *Fax:* +385 51 842219, *Email:* li-omisalj@pomorstvo.hr

Officials: Harbour Master: Capt Darijo Sokota.

Approach: The port is approached by Vela Vrata between Istra Peninsula and Cres Island. A traffic separation scheme is established in Vela Vrata

Anchorage: For tankers and vessels carrying dangerous cargo enclosed by following positions: 45° 14.6' N; 14° 29.24' E, 45° 15.6' N; 14° 27.6' E, 45° 17.48' N; 14° 28.0' E, 45° 16.6' N; 14° 31.48' E
For vessels carrying liquefied gas anchorage is in radius of 2.7 km from pos 45° 11.6' N; 14° 28.42' E in depth of 54-62 m
During strong NE gales vessels may be forced to seek shelter under the lee of Krk Island

Pilotage: Compulsory. Rates are based on gt. VHF Channel 9

Weather: Prevailing NE'ly and SE'ly winds. In winter NE winds may reach hurricane force

Traffic: 2005, 110 tankers, 7 005 829 t of crude oil and petrochemicals

Principal Imports and Exports: Imports: Crude oil & chemicals. Exports: Chemicals.

Accommodation:

Name	Draught (m)	Remarks
Jadranski Naftovod		See [1] below
Jetty A	11.5	See [2] below
Jetty B	15	See [3] below

[1]*Jadranski Naftovod:* Tel: +385 51 206200, Fax: +385 51 842273, Email: bruno.jankovic@janaf.hr, Website: www.janaf.hr
Two T shaped piers each 127 m long fitted with fenders and sliding hooks and equipped with four 16" unloading arms for discharging crude oil. Distance between each pier about 370 m. Height of platforms above sea level is 7.35 m with depth alongside of 29 m, allowing tankers of up to 350 000 dwt to discharge safely. Use of fire-fighting tugs for tankers during loading/discharging is compulsory
[2]*Jetty A:* For gas carriers up to 15 000 m3 cap equipped with 8" loading arms for ethylene and VCM
[3]*Jetty B:* For chemical tankers up to 60 000 dwt, equipped with 8" loading arms for fuel oil, caustic soda and EDC liquid

Mechanical Handling Equipment:

Location	Type	Capacity (t)	Qty
Omisalj	Mult-purp. Cranes	2	4

Bunkering: Available by barge from Rijeka on completion of discharge and at anchorage. Jadroagent, Tel: +385 (51) 211794, Fax: 215357

Waste Reception Facilities: Liquid residues are acceptable into 5 m3 shore slop tank. Inflammable gases may be disposed. Garbage removal is not available

Towage: Available from Rijeka

Airport: Rijeka, 7 km

Railway: Rijeka, 30 km

Lloyd's Agent: Jadroagent d.d., Trg Ivana Koblera 2, 51000 Rijeka, Republic of Croatia, *Tel:* +385 51 780500, *Fax:* +385 51 215357, *Email:* info@jadroagent.hr, *Website:* www.jadroagent.hr

PLOCE

Lat 43° 2' N; Long 17° 25' E.

Admiralty Chart: 269   **Admiralty Pilot:** 47
Time Zone: GMT +1 h   **UNCTAD Locode:** HR PLE

Principal Facilities:

P	Q	Y	G	C	R			T	

Authority: Port of Ploce Authority, Trg Kralja Tomislava 21, 20340 Ploce, Republic of Croatia, *Tel:* +385 20 603180, *Fax:* +385 20 670271, *Email:* lucka-uprava-ploce1@du.t-com.hr, *Website:* www.port-authority-ploce.hr

Officials: Executive Director: Tomislav Batur, *Tel:* +385 20 603281, *Email:* batur@port-authority-ploce.hr.
Harbour Master: Capt Ivo Matkovic, *Tel:* +385 20 679008.
Marketing: Svemir Zekulic, *Email:* zekulic@port-authority-ploce.hr.

Port Security: ISPS compliant. PFSO: Capt. Ivan Maric, Tel: +385 20 603184, Fax: +385 20 603184, Email: pfso-maric@port-authority-ploce.hr

Pre-Arrival Information: All vessels bound for Port of Ploce must send their ETA to Ploce Port Control Centre, either direct or through the Ship's Agent 48 h prior to arrival or as soon as after departure from last port. Changes to ETA must be reported as soon as practicable but not less than 24 h prior to entering Port of Ploce
Standard ETA Message:
1. Name of ship
2. International call sign
3. Flag and port of registry
4. Name of registered owner of vessel
5. Name of operator of vessel
6. Classification Society
7. IMO number
8. MMSI number
9. gt
10. Year of build
11. Deadweight
12. Length overall, max breadth, max.arrival draft
13. Cargo on board (vessels with dangerous cargoes must provide name of each dangerous cargo carried, the United Nations (UN) numbers where they exist, the IMO hazard classes in accordance with the IMDG, IBC and IGC Codes and, where appropriate, the class of the ship as defined by the INF Code, the quantities of such goods and their location on board and, if they are being carried in cargo transport units other than tanks, the identification number thereof, confirmation that a list or manifest or appropriate loading plan giving details of the dangerous or polluting goods carried and of their location on the ship is on board, address from which detailed information on the cargo may be obtained
14. Agent's name
15. Last port of call
16. Next port of call
17. Location/position at time of report
18. ETA (LT Croatia)
19. Number of crew and passengers - crew list including: name, rank, nationality, residence (country & city), age, position or duties on vessel, place and date of sign on, number of crew leaving/boarding vessel in this port); non-crew and passenger list
20. Notification of type and amount of waste and residues (notification should only be made by vessels other than recreational craft and small fishing vessels)
21. Ballast water reporting form ISPS
ETA message must also include details of the vessel's International Ship Security Certificate (ISSC) and the follwing information:
a) Date of issue and date of expiry of the vessel's ISSC
b) Name of flag administration/recognised that issued ISSC certificate
c) Declaration that the approved ship security plan is being implemented
d) The name and 24 h contact information for the Company Security Officer and Ship Security Officer
e) Ten past ports of call, date/time of departure, security level in these ports, special and additional measures taken in these ports
f) Security level on board

Approach: The port is entered through a dredged channel marked by lights and light buoys, which leads NNE between the high Visnjica Peninsula on the W side and the low broken and shoal coast of the mouth of the Neretva River. The Vlaska channel is entered approx 7 cables SSE of Cape Visnjica and leads NE to a single berth oil terminal on the NW side of the channel
West or NW Approach: Vessels are required to pass at least 1 nautical mile clear of Rt. Visnjica Light structure (43° 02.4' N; 17° 25.3' E), until the bearing of the axis of the entrance channel. Large vessels are advised to remain in pilot boarding position about 2 nautical miles SW from Point Visnjica until boarding pilot. When leaving the entrance channel bound W or NW, vessels are required to round Rt. Visnjica at a distance of 0.5 nautical miles to avoid incoming traffic. Vessels are prohibited from passing each other in the entrance channel. Vessels leaving the channel take precedence over vessels entering

Anchorage: Available in the area limited by the following positions:
43° 02.5' N; 17° 23.7' E
43° 00.8' N; 17° 22.7' E
43° 03.2' N; 17° 18.9' E
43° 04.7' N; 17° 21.0' E
Malo More-Soline Bay is prohibited for anchorage due to undersea pipelines
Vessels are not allowed to anchor east of the line, which connects Kunova Cove on Peninsula Peljesac with pos 43° 03' N; 17° 24' E on the coast

Pilotage: Available on a 24 h basis, Tel: +385 98 243932. VHF Channel 12
Port Pilotage: Compulsory for vessels over 500 gt and yachts over 1000 gt. Final notice of ETA and request for pilot must be made to Port of Ploce Authority on VHF Channels 9 or 16 at least 1 h before arrival at pilot's boarding position. Pilot boards vessel about 2.0 nautical miles WSW from Point Visnjica in pos 43° 01' N; 17° 23' E
Coastal Pilotage: Compulsory for gas carriers (LPG & LNG) and chemical tankers with noxious liquid substances onboard. Notice of ETA and request for pilot must be made to the Port of Ploce Authority at least 6 h prior to arrival at the pilot boarding position 43° 05' N; 17° 00' E

Radio Frequency: Split Radio on 2182 kHz and 518 kHz, Dubrovnik Radio on 2182 kHz and 2615 kHz, both on VHF Channel 16
Port of Ploce Authority listens on VHF Channels 16 and 9 and operates on VHF Channel 9
Pilots operate on VHF Channel 12
Mooring and Tug Service operates on VHF Channel 14
Oil Terminal Operators operate on VHF Channel 11
Harbour Master's Office listens on VHF Channel 16 and works on VHF Channel 10

Weather: Prevailing winds are from NE and SE and can reach strong gale force in the winter season, as well as N-W wind during summer makes manoeuvring difficult in the entrance of the basin
Vessels are not allowed to navigate in Vlaska Channel when winds over 10 m/s blow N/S or winds over 14 m/s blow E/W

Tides: 0.27 m LAT, 1.04 m HAT, 0.10 m MLLW, 0.35 m MHHW

Traffic: 2007, 4 214 736 t of cargo handled

Maximum Vessel Dimensions: Dry cargo vessels: 255 m loa, 32.26 m breadth, 13 m draft, 66 000 dwt
Tankers: 220 m loa, 28.5 m breadth, 10.2 m draft
River Neretva (Port Metkovic): max airdraft 14.0 m, 80 m loa, 4.5 m draft
The maximum dimensions mentioned above do not necessarily apply to all berths, quays or areas within the port. The maximum permissible draft is raised up to 13.00 m on high tide and seawater density (1.0250) and for vessel calling and sailing at quay No.5 berth 11

Principal Imports and Exports: Imports: Alumina, Coal, Coke, Containerised goods, Iron ore. Exports: Aluminium products, Steel products, Timber.

Working Hours: Monday to Saturday 0600-2200. Overtime 2200-0600 against 50% extra

Accommodation:

Name	Length (m)	Depth (m)	Draught (m)	Remarks
Ploce				See [1] below
General Cargo Terminal			10	Loading of steels 400 t/working hatch-day
Dry Bulk Cargo Terminal	510	10.9–13.2	10.55–13	See [2] below
Loose Load Terminal	180	10.1	9.8	See [3] below
Liquid Cargo Terminals	220	10.6–10.9	10.2	See [4] below
Alumina Silo	132	10.1	9.8	See [5] below

[1]*Ploce:* Specialised terminals for bulk and liquid cargoes, timber and livestock. Modern railway connections to Sarajevo, Budapest, Prague and Bucharest. Excellent road connections to hinterland and all parts of the country. Berthing space for eleven ocean-going vessels
[2]*Dry Bulk Cargo Terminal:* Coal, iron ore & petroleum coke. Loading 30 000-50 000 t/day, discharging 8000-10 000 t/day
[3]*Loose Load Terminal:* Wheat, corn & soya. Loading up to 35 000 t/day, discharging 3000 t/day. Storage cap of 35 000 t
[4]*Liquid Cargo Terminals:* Two cargo terminals located in Vlaska Channel. Fuel oil & chemical products. Tank cap of 118 565 m3
Terminal Operators:
NTF (Naftni Terminali Federacije d.o.o.), Tel: +385 20 679455, Fax: +385 20 679942, Email: ntf@du.t-com.hr
Luka Ploce Trgovina, Lucka cesta bb, 20340 Ploce, Tel: +385 20 679023, Fax: +385 20 679039, Email: ivica.milicevic@lpt-ploce.hr, Website: www.lpt-ploce.hr
[5]*Alumina Silo:* Cap of 20 000 t with loading at rate of 800 t/h

Storage: Storage cap of 50 000 m3 at wood terminal, dry bulk storage cap of 300 000 t, petrolcoke silo of 10 000 t cap and cold storage warehouse of 920 t cap

Location	Open (m²)	Covered (m²)
General Cargo Terminal	153925	35834

Mechanical Handling Equipment:

Location	Type	Capacity (t)	Qty
Ploce	Floating Cranes	100	1
Ploce	Mult-purp. Cranes	5–10	15
Ploce	Mobile Cranes	50	1
Ploce	Mobile Cranes	25	3

Waste Reception Facilities: Dirty ballast water max 300 m3 into road tankers. Garbage removal is compulsory. Fumigation available

Towage: Two tugs of 2900 kw and 1180 kw are available. All tankers are obliged to use two tugs for mooring/unmooring

Repair & Maintenance: Luka Ploce Trgovina Ltd, Lucka Cesta bb, 20340 Ploce, Republic of Croatia, *Tel:* +385 20 679023, *Fax:* +385 20 679039, *Email:* marija.vuckovic@lpt-ploce.hr, *Website:* www.lpt-ploce.hr Minor repairs only

Ship Chandlers: Tankerkomerc dd Zadar, Trg Kralja Tomislava 22, HR 20340 Ploce, Republic of Croatia, *Tel:* +385 20 679267, *Fax:* +385 20 679251, *Email:* tankerkomerc@tankerkomerc.htnet.hr, *Website:* www.tankerkomerc.hr

Shipping Agents: Capris Agency Ltd, Trg Kralja Tomislava 22, 20340 Ploce, Republic of Croatia, *Tel:* +385 20 676336, *Fax:* +385 20 676337, *Email:* capris-croatia@du.htnet.hr, *Website:* www.capris.si
Jadroagent d.d., PP 5, 20430 Ploce, Republic of Croatia, *Tel:* +385 20 679964, *Fax:* +385 20 679118, *Email:* ploce@jadroagent.hr, *Website:* www.jadoragent.com
A.P. Moller-Maersk Group, Maersk Croatia d.o.o., Trg Kralja Tomislava 20, 20340 Ploce, Republic of Croatia, *Tel:* +385 20 414304, *Fax:* +385 20 691513, *Email:* crosal@maersk.com, *Website:* www.maerskline.com
Transagent International Shipping & Forwarding Agency Ltd, Neretvanskih gusara 12, Ploce, Republic of Croatia, *Tel:* +385 20 679846, *Fax:* +385 20 679725, *Email:* transagent.ploce@transagent.hr

Stevedoring Companies: Port of Ploce, Trg Kralja Tomislava 21, 20340 Ploce, Republic of Croatia, *Tel:* +385 20 679601, *Fax:* +385 20 679103, *Email:* ured-direktora@luka-ploce.hr, *Website:* www.port-authority-ploce.hr

Medical Facilities: Nearest hospitals in Split and Dubrovnik, 120 km. Ambulance Ploce, Tel: +385 20 679702

Airport: Split, 140 km. Dubrovnik, 140 km

Railway: Railway connections to Sarajevo, Budapest, Prague and Bucharest

Development: Additional cargo storage and handling facilities are under construction as follows:
A multi-purpose container terminal will be located at South Pier No.V and will be built

---

Key to Principal Facilities:—				
A=Airport	**C**=Containers	**G**=General Cargo	**P**=Petroleum	**R**=Ro/Ro	**Y**=Dry Bulk
B=Bunkers	**D**=Dry Dock	**L**=Cruise	**Q**=Other Liquid Bulk	**T**=Towage (where available from port)

in phases. Phase I, which will be built as part of the project will consist of a storage facility and handling area (total 65 300 m3) with a cap of 60 000 TEU's/year. The terminal is planned to be in use end of 2009

A solid bulk cargo terminal is planned to be constructed in the southeast part of the port area, on the right side of the Vlaska Channel. The terminal will have an import cap of 5.0 million t of coal, coke, iron and bauxite per year. The quay length is expected to be 350 m with the ability to accommodate vessels up to 80 000 dwt (panamax). Scheduled to be functional in 2011

Lloyd's Agent: Jadroagent d.d., Trg Ivana Koblera 2, 51000 Rijeka, Republic of Croatia, *Tel:* +385 51 780500, *Fax:* +385 51 215357, *Email:* info@jadroagent.hr, *Website:* www.jadroagent.hr

PLOMIN

Lat 45° 8' N; Long 14° 12' E.

Admiralty Chart: 2719	**Admiralty Pilot:** 47
Time Zone: GMT +1 h	**UNCTAD Locode:** HR PLM

Principal Facilities:

	Y		R		B		T	A	

Authority: TE Plomin, 52234 Plomin, Republic of Croatia, *Tel:* +385 52 863180, *Fax:* +385 52 863491, *Email:* zivko.tetina@hep.hr, *Website:* www.hep.hr

Officials: Port Manager: Zivko Tetina.

Port Security: ISPS compliant

Anchorage: In pos 44° 55' N, 14° 06' E or in Bay of Rijeka, depending on the Harbour Master

Pilotage: Compulsory for vessels over 500 gt, Tel: +385 98 254355. VHF Channel 12

Radio Frequency: Rijeka Radio call sign '9AR'. VHF Channel 16

Weather: Berthing is not available if wind exceeds 10 m/s or visibility is less than 1000 m or waves ampl over 1.0 m. Coal discharge to be stopped if wind exceeds 20 m/s

Traffic: 2002, 13 vessels, 857 347 t of coal handled

Principal Imports and Exports: Imports: Coal.

Working Hours: Mon-Fri 0800-1500. The coal terminal works round the clock

Accommodation:

Name	Length (m)	Depth (m)	Remarks
Plomin			
Coal Terminal	210	15	See [1] below
Ro/ro Berth	90	5.8–6	

[1]*Coal Terminal:* Concrete offshore wharf situated 1.6 nautical miles inside Plomin Bay for vessels up to 225 m loa, 32.25 m beam and 13.2 m draft. One unloader averaging 650-700 t/h, max 1000 t/h

Storage: Storage of 240 000 t cap

Bunkering: Available at Rijeka

Waste Reception Facilities: Garbage collection is compulsory

Towage: Compulsory. Navigation inside Plomin Bay is allowed only during daylight hours

Medical Facilities: Available at Labin, 15 km

Airport: Pula, 60 km

Lloyd's Agent: Jadroagent d.d., Trg Ivana Koblera 2, 51000 Rijeka, Republic of Croatia, *Tel:* +385 51 780500, *Fax:* +385 51 215357, *Email:* info@jadroagent.hr, *Website:* www.jadroagent.hr

PULA

Lat 44° 53' N; Long 13° 50' E.

Admiralty Chart: 1426	**Admiralty Pilot:** 47
Time Zone: GMT +1 h	**UNCTAD Locode:** HR PUY

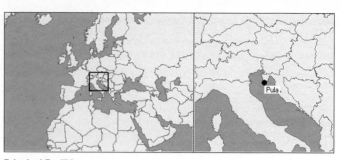

Principal Facilities:

	Y	G	C	R	L	B		T	A	

Authority: Lucka Uprava Pula, Kandlerova 42, 52100 Pula, Republic of Croatia, *Tel:* +385 52 383160, *Fax:* +385 52 383162, *Email:* info@lup.hr, *Website:* www.lup.hr

Officials: Port Manager: Davor Barbic. Harbour Master: Josip Lazaric.

Port Security: ISPS compliant

Anchorage: Anchorage can be obtained in the outer harbour, about 0.4 miles W of St. Andria Island in depth of 12-14 m

Pilotage: Compulsory for vessels over 500 gt

Radio Frequency: Harbour Master's Office on VHF Channel 10, 24 h/day. Pilot station on VHF Channels 12 and 18

Tides: Range of 1.5 m

Traffic: 2005, 476 vessels, 866 099 t of cargo handled

Maximum Vessel Dimensions: 7.0 m max d

Working Hours: Mon-Fri 0800-1800. Overtime available

Accommodation:

Name	Length (m)	Draught (m)	Remarks
Pula			See [1] below
Rijeka Quay	150	4	Cruise vessels handled
Ugljen Quay	160	6.5	
Cement Quay	146	6	Bagged cement 500 t/day
Uljanik Shipyard			See [2] below

[1]*Pula:* Harbour well protected from all winds by a breakwater. Depth at entrance 15-35 m.
[2]*Uljanik Shipyard:* Uljanik Shipyard, Flaciusova 1, 52100 Pula, Tel: +385 52 373000, Fax: +385 52 535098, Email: shipyard@uljanik.hr, Website: www.uljanik.hr
180 m long, 6.5 m d & 270 m long, 7.0 m d

Storage:

Location	Open (m²)	Covered (m²)
Pula	85000	25000

Mechanical Handling Equipment:

Location	Type	Capacity (t)	Qty
Pula	Floating Cranes	120	1
Cement Quay	Mult-purp. Cranes	15	1
Uljanik Shipyard	Mult-purp. Cranes	200	

Cargo Worked: Average of 800 t/day

Bunkering: Limited quantities available by truck

Waste Reception Facilities: Garbage removal every second day

Towage: Available from Rijeka

Repair & Maintenance: Tehnomont Brodogradiliste Ltd, Fizela 6, 52100 Pula, Republic of Croatia, *Tel:* +385 52 386011, *Fax:* +385 52 386328, *Email:* info@tehnomont.hr, *Website:* www.tehnomont.hr Repair of vessels up to 60 m x 16 m
Uljanik Brodogradiliste d.d., Flaciusova 1, 52100 Pula, Republic of Croatia, *Tel:* +385 52 374450, *Fax:* +385 52 374504, *Email:* uljanik@uljanik.hr, *Website:* www.uljanik.hr

Shipping Agents: Jadroagent d.d., PP 57, 52100 Pula, Republic of Croatia, *Tel:* +385 52 210431, *Fax:* +385 52 211799, *Email:* jadroagent-pula@jadroagent.hr, *Website:* www.jadroagent.com

Surveyors: Croatian Register of Shipping, Forum 5, 52100 Pula, Republic of Croatia, *Tel:* +385 52 223152, *Fax:* +385 52 214487, *Email:* crs-pula@crs.hr, *Website:* www.crs.hr
Det Norske Veritas A/S, Det Norske Veritas Adriatica Ltd, Ruziceva 32, 51000 Pula, Republic of Croatia, *Tel:* +385 52 211776, *Fax:* +385 52 211274, *Email:* pulaoffice@dnv.com, *Website:* www.dnv.com

Medical Facilities: Available

Airport: Istarski Aerodrom, 6 km

Lloyd's Agent: Jadroagent d.d., Trg Ivana Koblera 2, 51000 Rijeka, Republic of Croatia, *Tel:* +385 51 780500, *Fax:* +385 51 215357, *Email:* info@jadroagent.hr, *Website:* www.jadroagent.hr

RAGUSA

alternate name, see Dubrovnik

RASA

Lat 45° 2' N; Long 14° 4' E.

Admiralty Chart: 1426　　　　　　　**Admiralty Pilot:** 47
Time Zone: GMT +1 h　　　　　　　**UNCTAD Locode:** HR RAS

Principal Facilities:

		Y	G					T	A

Authority: Lucka Kapetanija Rasa, 52224 Trget, Republic of Croatia, *Tel:* +385 52 875 127, *Fax:* +385 52 875 127, *Email:* li-rasa@pomorstvo.hr

Officials: Harbour Master: Josip Zupicic, *Tel:* +385 52 875 127.

Port Security: ISPS compliant

Pre-Arrival Information: Notice of arrival to be sent 24 h in advance

Documentation: Notice of arrival, ballast water report, IMDG report, waste report, IMO crew and passenger list, ISSG

Anchorage: Anchorage can be obtained S of Cape Traget in pos 45° 01' N; 14° 03' 30" E in depths ranging from 14 m to 16 m. Dropping anchor in vicinity of Koromacno is forbidden due to underwater cables

Pilotage: Compulsory for vessels over 500 gt, from anchorage to the berth

Radio Frequency: VHF Channels 10 and 16

Weather: Strong NE winds during winter

Tides: Up to 0.6 m

Traffic: 2005, 133 vessels, 289 450 t of cargo handled

Maximum Vessel Dimensions: Max d at timber quay 10 m, max d at livestock quays 6 m

Principal Imports and Exports: Imports: Coal, Gypsum, Slag. Exports: Cement, Livestock, Timber.

Working Hours: Mon-Fri 0700-2300. Sat 0700-1500

Accommodation:

Name	Length (m)	Depth (m)	Remarks
Rasa			See [1] below
Brsica Timber Terminal	164	8.5	Allows two vessels to load simultaneously
Livestock Pier	25	6	See [2] below
Koromacno			See [3] below
Loading Berth	96	5.1–6	Cement loaded at max rate of 300 t/h. Pneumatic system
Discharge Berth	110	6.1–10	See [4] below

[1]*Rasa:* A safe harbour in naturally protected bay, with depth of approx 40 m
[2]*Livestock Pier:* Shed for 2500 sheep, open stable for 350 cows and 200 m2 hay storage
[3]*Koromacno:* Operated by Holcim Hrvatska doo, Tel: +385 52 876900, Fax: +385 52 876221
Situated outside Rasa Bay handling cement, coal, slag & gypsum
[4]*Discharge Berth:* Discharge rate of 1500 t/day. One movable 12 t shore crane

Storage:

Location	Open (m²)
Brsica Timber Terminal	150000

Mechanical Handling Equipment:

Location	Type	Capacity (t)	Qty
Rasa	Shore Cranes	5	2

Cargo Worked: 1000 m3 of sawn timber gang/day, 500 t of bulk cargo gang/shift

Towage: Available from Rijeka

Shipping Agents: Jadroagent d.d., Trget, HR 52224 Rasa, Republic of Croatia, *Tel:* +385 52 875006, *Fax:* +385 52 875106, *Email:* rasa@jadroagent.hr, *Website:* www.jadroagent.com

Stevedoring Companies: Luka Rijeka, Terminal Rasa, Rasa, Republic of Croatia, *Tel:* +385 52 875090, *Fax:* +385 52 875027

Medical Facilities: Pula hospital, 30 km

Airport: Pula, 28 km

Railway: In the port

Lloyd's Agent: Jadroagent d.d., Trg Ivana Koblera 2, 51000 Rijeka, Republic of Croatia, *Tel:* +385 51 780500, *Fax:* +385 51 215357, *Email:* info@jadroagent.hr, *Website:* www.jadroagent.hr

RIJEKA

Lat 45° 19' N; Long 14° 26' E.

Admiralty Chart: 1996　　　　　　　**Admiralty Pilot:** 47
Time Zone: GMT +1 h　　　　　　　**UNCTAD Locode:** HR RJK

Principal Facilities:

P	Q	Y	G	C	R	L		D	T	A

Authority: Port of Rijeka Authority, Riva 1, 51000 Rijeka, Republic of Croatia, *Tel:* +385 51 212974, *Fax:* +385 51 331764, *Email:* rijeka.gateway@portauthority.hr, *Website:* www.portauthority.hr/rijeka

Officials: Executive Director: Bojan Hlaca, *Tel:* +385 51 351111.
Marketing Manager: Snijezana Papes, *Tel:* +385 51 351117, *Email:* marketing.ri@portauthority.hr.
Harbour Master: Zdeslav Mastrovic, *Tel:* +385 51 351116, *Email:* portcaptain.ri@portauthority.hr.

Port Security: ISPS compliant

Pre-Arrival Information: The Master of the vessel, or the Agent, should send the notice of arrival (not less than 24 h before arrival or immediately on departure from last port of call if less than 24 h), on a form required, to the Harbour Master's Office and the Port Authority by fax and/or electronic mail
The notice of arrival should include:
a) necessary details about ship and cargo
b) necessary details about dangerous goods, if any
c) data on the state of security on the vessel
d) information about ship's waste
e) information about ballast water treatment
Master shall give notice to the Port of Rijeka Authority (VTMS Centre Rijeka) on VHF Channel 09 of the exact time of arrival to anchorage or location for taking aboard a pilot at least 2 h before the arrival and re-confirm the time of srrival immediately before entry into the Vela vrata passage

Documentation: Crew list (6 copies), passenger list (5 copies), stores list (3 copies), arms & ammunition list (2 copies), narcotic list (2 copies), health declaration (1 copy), crew/passenger private manifests (2 copies), manifest of goods (3 copies)

Approach: Well sheltered harbour. Breakwaters 1754 and 420 m. Width of entrance 270 m; width of entrance to Susak Basin 43 m. Depth at entrance 40 m; in mid-harbour 20 to 28 m; at quays 6 to 10 m. Bay of Bakar, 4700 m long, 700 m wide, average depth 26 m, at entrance 44 m. Entrance to Bay of Bakar is 400 m wide

Anchorage: Vessels are permitted to use the eastern and western anchorage in depths of 54-64 m. Liquid cargo and dangerous cargo vessels should proceed to the tanker anchorage (in the eastern part of Rijeka Bay). Liquefied gas carriers should anchor in the SE part of Rijeka Bay in depth of 62 m

Pilotage: Croatia Pilot, Tel: +385 51 213748, Fax: +385 51 337914
Harbour pilotage is compulsory for vessels over 500 gt. Sundays and holidays at 100% extra, Saturdays at 50% extra and overtime up to 30% extra. Pilotage of LPG and chemical carriers at 40% extra. Vessels with crude oil and derivatives at 20% extra
Coastal pilotage according to agreement: compulsory for LPG and chemical carriers. Tel: +385 51 337913, Fax: +385 51 337914. VHF Channel 12

Radio Frequency: Rijeka radio call sign 9AR. Calling on VHF Channel 9 and working on VHF Channels 16 and 24. Harbour Master on VHF Channel 10

Weather: Prevailing winds SE and NE

Tides: 0.3-0.5 m

Traffic: 2007, 13 212 464 t of cargo handled, 145 040 TEU's

Working Hours: Mon-Fri 0630-1430, 1430-2230. Overtime 2230-0630. Sat and Sun overtime rates apply

Accommodation:

Name	Remarks
Rijeka	See [1] below
Rijeka port basin	
Zagreb Quay	Timber & general cargo
Bratislava Quay	Soda, salt & fertilizers
Prague Quay	General & heavy cargo
Visin Quay	General & heavy cargo
Budapest Quay	Cereals & oil seed terminal
Orlando Quay	Refrigerated cargo terminal
Vienna Quay	Mixed cargo
De Francheschi Quay	Mixed cargo
Rijeka Basin Breakwater	Passenger, general & bulk cargo terminal
Susak port basin	
Senj Quay	Timber & general cargo
Ruzic Quay	Mixed cargo
Susak Basin Breakwater	Timber & bulk cargo
Kostrena Quay	Container & ro/ro terminal
Riva Galioti	Ro/ro cargo
Bakar port basin	
Podbok Quay	Bulk & loose cargo

Key to Principal Facilities:—			
A=Airport	**C**=Containers	**G**=General Cargo	**P**=Petroleum	**R**=Ro/Ro	**Y**=Dry Bulk
B=Bunkers	**D**=Dry Dock	**L**=Cruise	**Q**=Other Liquid Bulk	**T**=Towage (where available from port)	

Name	Remarks
Goranin Quay	General, loose & ro/ro cargo

[1]*Rijeka:* A berth for loading LPG situated at Srscica, near Urinj tanker terminal is 68 m long with 10 m depth alongside and can accommodate vessels up to 4500 dwt. Loading rate is approx 200 t/h through a 6" flexible hose

Storage: Covered surface storage of 113 000 m2 for general cargo and 53 000 m2 for timber. Tanks for discharge of vegetable oil of 3600 m3. Phosphate terminal, cap 15 000 t. Refrigerated storage units capable of storing 2500 t of fruit and 500 t of fish and meat. 57 000 t silo for grain and soya

Location	Open (m²)	Grain (t)
Rijeka	150000	57000

Mechanical Handling Equipment:

Location	Type	Capacity (t)	Qty
Rijeka	Floating Cranes	30	1
Rijeka	Floating Cranes	100	1
Rijeka	Mobile Cranes	32	42
Rijeka	Electric Cranes	5	64
Rijeka	Forklifts	12	130

Waste Reception Facilities: Garbage removal is compulsory. One shore tank (2000 gross t cap) for oily/ballast water at Bakar Petrol Berth for tankers only. Discharging through one 12" line at 200-300 m3/h. One boat capable of collecting 1000 t of oil residues or ballast/bilge water directly from vessels

Towage: Jadranski Pomorski Servis d.d., Verdieva 19, 51000 Rijeka, Republic of Croatia, *Tel:* +385 51 355000, *Fax:* +385 51 355060, *Email:* jps@jps.hr, *Website:* www.jps.hr

Repair & Maintenance: Shipyard Viktor Lenac Ltd, Martinscica bb, P O Box 210, 51001 Rijeka, Republic of Croatia, *Tel:* +385 51 405555, *Fax:* +385 51 217175, *Email:* viktor.mgt@lenac.hr, *Website:* www.lenac.hr

Ship Chandlers: A.M.E.C. d.o.o. Rijeka, Osjecka 47, 51000 Rijeka, Republic of Croatia, *Tel:* +385 51 500770, *Fax:* +385 51 500799, *Email:* amec@amec.hr
Ben Ship Supply d.o.o., Riva Bodili 1/VI, HR 51000 Rijeka, Republic of Croatia, *Tel:* +385 51 214712, *Fax:* +385 51 320870, *Email:* benship@benship.hr
Tankerkomerc dd Zadar, AK Miosica 9, HR 51000 Rijeka, Republic of Croatia, *Tel:* +385 51 373047, *Fax:* +385 51 373067, *Email:* shipsupply@tankerkomerc.hr, *Website:* www.tankerkomerc.hr

Shipping Agents: Adriatica d.o.o., Verdieva 6/VI, 51000 Rijeka, Republic of Croatia, *Tel:* +385 51 214511, *Fax:* +385 51 214300, *Email:* adriatica-ri@ri.htnet.hr Managing Director: Ivan Marovic
Agemar S.r.l., Riva 8, 51000 Rijeka, Republic of Croatia, *Tel:* +385 51 324740, *Fax:* +385 51 324741, *Email:* agemar-rijeka@ri.t-com.hr, *Website:* www.agemar.it
Astro Shipping Agency, F. L. Guardia No.27, 51000 Rijeka, Republic of Croatia, *Tel:* +385 51 325963, *Fax:* +385 51 325964, *Email:* astro-rijeka@hi.t-com.hr
Capris Agency Ltd, Agaticeva 2, 51000 Rijeka, Republic of Croatia, *Tel:* +385 51 317170, *Fax:* +385 51 212706, *Email:* capris-cro@ri.htnet.hr, *Website:* www.capris.si
CB Maritime Ltd., Riva 4 / I, P O Box 172, 51000 Rijeka, Republic of Croatia, *Tel:* +385 51 376001, *Fax:* +385 51 376005, *Email:* contact@cbmaritime.hr, *Website:* www.cbmaritime.hr
CMA-CGM S.A., CMA-CGM Croatia doo, Zrtava Fasizma 2, 2nd Floor, HR-51000 Rijeka, Republic of Croatia, *Tel:* +385 51 327595, *Fax:* +385 51 327570, *Email:* rjk.genmbox@cma-cgm.com, *Website:* www.cma-cgm.com
Garma doo, Trpimirova 4, HR-51000 Rijeka, Republic of Croatia, *Tel:* +385 51 211287, *Fax:* +385 51 213687, *Email:* garma@inet.hr, *Website:* www.garma.hr
Interagent doo, Barciceva 1, HR-51000 Rijeka, Republic of Croatia, *Tel:* +385 51 213464, *Fax:* +385 51 336540
Jadroagent d.d., Trg Ivana Koblera 2, 51000 Rijeka, Republic of Croatia, *Tel:* +385 51 780500, *Fax:* +385 51 215357, *Email:* info@jadroagent.hr, *Website:* www.jadroagent.hr
Lotus Shipping Agencies SAL, Nikola Tesla 9/1, 51000 Rijeka, Republic of Croatia, *Fax:* +385 51 323937, *Email:* rijeka@lotusshipping.com
Media Mare doo, Trpimirova 4, 51000 Rijeka, Republic of Croatia, *Tel:* +385 51 330280, *Fax:* +385 51 330278, *Email:* mediamare@mediamare.hr, *Website:* www.mediamare.hr
Mediterranean Shipping Company, MSC Croatia Ltd, Trpimirova 4/II, 51000 Rijeka, Republic of Croatia, *Tel:* +385 51 356920, *Fax:* +385 51 356930, *Email:* info@rij.msccroatia.com, *Website:* www.mscgva.ch
A.P. Moller-Maersk Group, Maersk Croatia d.o.o., Fiorello la Guardia 13, 51000 Rijeka, Republic of Croatia, *Tel:* +385 51 324410, *Fax:* +385 51 332379, *Email:* crosal@maersk.com, *Website:* www.maerskline.com
Tankerkomerc dd Zadar, AK Miosica 9, HR 51000 Rijeka, Republic of Croatia, *Tel:* +385 51 373047, *Fax:* +385 51 373067, *Email:* shipsupply@tankerkomerc.hr, *Website:* www.tankerkomerc.hr
Tradeways d.o.o., Riva Bodulia 1, 51000 Rijeka, Republic of Croatia, *Fax:* +385 51 321909, *Email:* tradeways.rijeka@ri.htnet.hr, *Website:* www.tradeways.si
Transadria Shipping Agency, Riva Boduli 1, P O Box 290, 51000 Rijeka, Republic of Croatia, *Tel:* +385 51 213235, *Fax:* +385 51 211002, *Email:* agency@transadria.hr, *Website:* www.transadria.hr
Transagent International Shipping & Forwarding Agency Ltd, Verdieva 6, P O Box 100, HR-51000 Rijeka, Republic of Croatia, *Tel:* +385 51 325510, *Email:* operations.rjk@transagent.hr, *Website:* www.transagent.hr

Surveyors: ABS (Europe), c/o Jadroagent, Trg. Ivana Koblera 2, 51000 Rijeka, Republic of Croatia, *Tel:* +385 51 333019, *Fax:* +385 51 211339, *Email:* absrijeka@eagle.org, *Website:* www.eagle.org
Adria Control Ltd, Adria Control Rijeka Ltd, Zagrebacka1, 51000 Rijeka, Republic of Croatia, *Tel:* +385 51 315581, *Fax:* +385 51 315580, *Email:* acrijeka@ri.htnet.hr, *Website:* www.adriacontrol.com
Bureau Veritas, Riva 16/V, 51000 Rijeka, Republic of Croatia, *Tel:* +385 51 213672, *Fax:* +385 51 211067, *Email:* office.croatia@hr.bureauveritas.com, *Website:* www.bureauveritas.com
Croatian Register of Shipping, Candekova 8b, 51000 Rijeka, Republic of Croatia, *Tel:* +385 51 671811, *Fax:* +385 51 671917, *Email:* crs-rijeka@crs.hr, *Website:* www.crs.hr
Det Norske Veritas A/S, Ruziceva 32, 51000 Rijeka, Republic of Croatia, *Tel:* +385

51 227057/58, *Fax:* +385 51 227055, *Email:* rijekaoffice@dnv.com, *Website:* www.dnv.com
EDOC Ltd, Kresimirova 8/II, 51000 Rijeka, Republic of Croatia, *Tel:* +385 51 214498, *Fax:* +385 51 214626, *Email:* edoc@edoc.hr, *Website:* www.edoc.hr
IMCS BVBA, Gajeva 8, 51000 Rijeka, Republic of Croatia, *Tel:* +385 51 424571/400250, *Fax:* +385 51 400250, *Email:* imcs-jadran1@ri.htnet.hr, *Website:* www.imcs-group.com
Jadroagent d.d., Trg Ivana Koblera 2, 51000 Rijeka, Republic of Croatia, *Tel:* +385 51 780500, *Fax:* +385 51 215357, *Email:* info@jadroagent.hr, *Website:* www.jadroagent.hr
G. Meden, Raspora Spanca 3, 51000 Rijeka, Republic of Croatia, *Tel:* +385 51 651458, *Fax:* +385 51 675818, *Email:* gmeden@rijeka.ritch.hr
Narval d.o.o., J.P. Kamova 95, 51000 Rijeka, Republic of Croatia, *Tel:* +385 51 400617, *Fax:* +385 51 400616, *Email:* info@narval.hr, *Website:* www.narval.hr
Russian Maritime Register of Shipping, Korzo 2A/1V, 51000 Rijeka, Republic of Croatia, *Tel:* +385 51 323823, *Fax:* +385 51 211492, *Email:* 275rs-hor@ri.htnet.hr, *Website:* www.rs-head.spb.ru
Societe Generale de Surveillance (SGS), SGS Adriatica d.d., Fiorello la Guardia 13, P O Box 270, 51000 Rijeka, Republic of Croatia, *Tel:* +385 51 333611, *Fax:* +385 51 333483, *Email:* enquiries@sgs.com, *Website:* www.sgs.com
Vodaric, Captain V. Vodaric & Son, Drenovski Put 30, H-51000 Rijeka, Republic of Croatia, *Tel:* +385 51 500250, *Fax:* +385 51 500252, *Email:* capt-vodaric@ri.tel.hr, *Website:* www.capt-vodaric.cjb.net

Medical Facilities: All kinds available

Airport: Rijeka, 28 km. Pula, 100 km

Lloyd's Agent: Jadroagent d.d., Trg Ivana Koblera 2, 51000 Rijeka, Republic of Croatia, *Tel:* +385 51 780500, *Fax:* +385 51 215357, *Email:* info@jadroagent.hr, *Website:* www.jadroagent.hr

ROVIGNO

alternate name, see Rovinj

ROVINJ

Lat 45° 5' N; Long 13° 38' E.

Admiralty Chart: 1426		**Admiralty Pilot:** 47	
Time Zone: GMT +1 h		**UNCTAD Locode:** HR ROV	

Principal Facilities:

						G							A

Authority: Lucka Uprava Rovinj, Obala Aldo Rismondo 2, 52210 Rovinj, Republic of Croatia, *Tel:* +385 52 814166, *Fax:* +385 52 814166, *Email:* info@port-rovinj.hr, *Website:* www.port-rovinj.hr

Officials: General Manager: Ing Donald Schiozzi, *Email:* donald@port-rovinj.hr. Harbour Master: Giorgio Bastijancic, *Tel:* +385 52 811132.

Port Security: ISPS compliant

Pilotage: Available

Radio Frequency: VHF Channels 16 and 09

Weather: During winter winds usually NE and SE, during summer NW

Tides: Tidal range 1.5 m

Traffic: Approx 40 000 passengers per year plus approx 350 000 passengers in local traffic

Working Hours: 0700-2200. Overtime available

Accommodation:

Name	Remarks
Rovinj	See [1] below

[1]*Rovinj:* Old Harbour S of town is well protected (for passengers and coastal vessels). Two berths for cargo vessels are at the N port, depth 4.5 m alongside

Storage: Open storage of 10 000 m2. Refrigerated warehouse for 3000 t of cargo

Location	Open (m²)
Rovinj	10000

Mechanical Handling Equipment: Auto-cranes are available

Waste Reception Facilities: Limited quantities in drums only

Medical Facilities: Available

Airport: Pula, 40 km

Railway: Kanfanar, 25 km

Lloyd's Agent: Jadroagent d.d., Trg Ivana Koblera 2, 51000 Rijeka, Republic of Croatia, *Tel:* +385 51 780500, *Fax:* +385 51 215357, *Email:* info@jadroagent.hr, *Website:* www.jadroagent.hr

SIBENIK

Lat 43° 44' N; Long 15° 54' E.

Admiralty Chart: 2773

Time Zone: GMT +1 h

Admiralty Pilot: 47

UNCTAD Locode: HR SIB

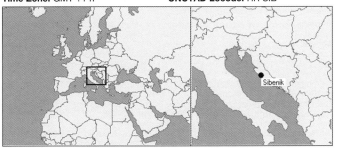

Principal Facilities:

Q	Y	G		R		B		T	A

Authority: Lucka Uprava Sibenik, Obala Hrvatske Mornarice 4, 22000 Sibenik, Republic of Croatia, *Tel:* +385 22 213033, *Fax:* +385 22 200362, *Email:* lucka-uprava-sibenik@si.htnet.hr, *Website:* www.lukasibenik.hr

Officials: Director: Marijan Petkovic.
General Manager: Davor Skugor.

Port Security: ISPS compliant

Approach: Through Dvainka passage, min depth 23 m. All vessels over 50 gt must apply for permission to enter the St. Ante Channel by using VHF Channel 71. Vessels may enter channel only when authorised by one green light (one red light means channel is closed)

Anchorage: Anchorage for Sibenik Port limited by the following points: 43° 40' 30" N, 15° 52' 45" E; 43° 41' 25" N, 15° 52' 45" E; 43° 40' 40" N, 15° 53' 50" E and 43° 40' 00" N, 15° 53' 40" E

Pilotage: Harbour pilot compulsory for all vessels over 500 gt from entrance of the channel. Pilot station situated one mile S of the red buoy marking the entrance to the channel. Pilot working on VHF Channel 12
Branko Pilot, *Tel:* +385 22 354277, *Fax:* +385 22 354277, *Email:* info@branko-pilot.hr, *Website:* www.branko-pilot.hr. Boarding in pos 43° 42' N; 15° 52' E. For vessels with dangerous cargo boarding in pos 43° 38' 07" N; 15° 52' 03" E

Radio Frequency: VHF Channels 12 and 16. Harbour Master's Office on VHF Channels 10, 16, 18 and 84

Weather: NW prevailing winds during summer and NE & SE during other seasons

Tides: Max tide 0.6 m

Traffic: 2005, 336 vessels, 1 434 221 t of cargo handled

Maximum Vessel Dimensions: 45 000 dwt, 220 m loa, 32 m beam, 10 m draft

Principal Imports and Exports: Imports: Phosphate, Potash. Exports: Clay, Fertiliser, Timber.

Working Hours: Three shifts 0700-1500, 1500-2300 and 2300-0700 only with grabs. Timber handled during daylight only 0700-1800

Accommodation:

Name	Length (m)	Depth (m)	Draught (m)	Remarks
Sibenik				See [1] below
Timber (Lukadrvo) Terminal	294	6.5		Two berths
Rogac Terminal	450	7–8		See [2] below
Phosphate (Dobrika) Terminal	225		9.6	Covered warehouse cap of 120 000 t. One ship loader of 400 t/h cap
Ro/ro Pier	100		7	

[1]*Sibenik:* Well sheltered harbour. Entrance through a channel 2.2 km long. Berthing Quays of 1625 m, depth from 5.2-10 m
[2]*Rogac Terminal:* Three berths handling fertilisers and aluminium metals

Storage:

Location	Open (m²)	Covered (m²)	Sheds / Warehouses
Timber (Lukadrvo) Terminal	51000	9200	
Rogac Terminal	15000	5000	2
Ro/ro Pier	10000		

Mechanical Handling Equipment:

Location	Type	Capacity (t)	Qty
Rogac Terminal	Mult-purp. Cranes	5	3
Rogac Terminal	Mult-purp. Cranes	7	2

Cargo Worked: Phosphates 4000 t/day, timber 150 m3/hatch/day, bagged fertilizers 250 t/hatch/day

Bunkering: Diesel and gas oil available in small quantities with advanced notice

Waste Reception Facilities: Garbage collected in plastic bags

Towage: One tug available and compulsory for vessels over 2500 dwt entering or leaving the harbour. Transiting St. Ante Channel vessels over 10 000 dwt require one tug and over 20 000 dwt two tugs. One tug is available from Split with advance notice

Repair & Maintenance: Repair yard, Sibenik, *Tel:* +385 22 333399, *Fax:* +385 22 336117

Shipping Agents: Jadroagent d.d., Fra Jerolima Milete 8, 1st floor, 22000 Sibenik, Republic of Croatia, *Tel:* +385 22 212570/1, *Fax:* +385 22 212682, *Email:* sibenik@jadroagent.hr, *Website:* www.jadoragent.com
Sartija Nautika doo, Obala Franje Tudmana 14, HR-22000 Sibenik, Republic of Croatia, *Tel:* +385 22 214605, *Fax:* +385 22 214611, *Email:* sn@sartija-nautika.hr

Stevedoring Companies: Luka Sibenik, Obala Hrvatske Mornariche 4, 22000 Sibenik, Republic of Croatia, *Tel:* +385 22 213033, *Fax:* +385 22 212133, *Email:* luka@lukasibenik.hr, *Website:* www.lukasibenik.hr

Surveyors: Croatian Register of Shipping, Mandalinskih zrtava 16e, 22000 Sibenik, Republic of Croatia, *Tel:* +385 22 214975, *Fax:* +385 22 200830, *Email:* crs-sibenik@crs.hr, *Website:* www.crs.hr

Medical Facilities: Medical service and hospitalization available

Airport: Split, 50 km

Lloyd's Agent: Jadroagent d.d., Trg Ivana Koblera 2, 51000 Rijeka, Republic of Croatia, *Tel:* +385 51 780500, *Fax:* +385 51 215357, *Email:* info@jadroagent.hr, *Website:* www.jadroagent.hr

SPALATO

alternate name, see Split

SPLIT

Lat 43° 30' N; Long 16° 27' E.

Admiralty Chart: 269

Time Zone: GMT +1 h

Admiralty Pilot: 47

UNCTAD Locode: HR SPU

Principal Facilities:

P	Q	Y	G		R	L	B	D	T	A

Key to Principal Facilities:—

A=Airport	**C**=Containers	**G**=General Cargo	**P**=Petroleum	**R**=Ro/Ro	**Y**=Dry Bulk
B=Bunkers	**D**=Dry Dock	**L**=Cruise	**Q**=Other Liquid Bulk	**T**=Towage (where available from port)

Boktuljin put bb, POB 305
21000 Split CROATIA
switchboard: +385 21 558 558
fax: +385 21 558 555/556
main email: ssm@ssm.t-com.hr
website: www.ssm.hr

• Crew and Technical Management
Freight Forwarding • Commercial Management
Broking • Consultancy • Technical Support
Maritime Training • Ship Supplying
• Travel Agency • Shipping Agency

Authority: Lucka Uprava Split, Gat Sv. Duje 1, 21000 Split, Republic of Croatia, *Tel:* +385 21 390222, *Fax:* +385 21 390239, *Email:* lucka-uprava-split@st.htnet.hr, *Website:* www.portsplit.com

Officials: General Manager: Branko Grgic, *Email:* branko.grgic@portsplit.com. Harbour Master: Boais Natosic.

Port Security: ISPS compliant

Approach: The recommended approach to both North and South ports is through the Splitska Vrata channel which is deep and marked by lights and light buoys

Anchorage: Anchorage for all vessels arriving in South and North Port can be obtained 0.5-1.0 miles off the South Port breakwater

Pilotage: Compulsory for vessels over 500 gt. Split Pilot, Tel: +385 21 338320. VHF Channel 12

Radio Frequency: Split Radio on VHF Channel 16

Weather: NE winds can reach gale force in winter which makes for difficult berthing in North Harbour

Tides: Range up to 0.5 m

Traffic: 2004, 2 581 931 t of cargo handled

Maximum Vessel Dimensions: 200 m loa, 10.7 m max draft for general cargo vessels, 11.28 m for grain and 11.6 m for tankers

Principal Imports and Exports: Imports: Bananas, Cement, Coal, Frozen food, Iron products, Salt, Wood products. Exports: Cement, Frozen fish, Grains, Salt.

Working Hours: 24 h/day

Accommodation:

Name	Remarks
Split	See [1] below

[1]*Split:* The port of Split comprises Sjeverna Splitska Luka (N Harbour of Split) including Vranjic, Sucurac (also Adriachem) and Sveti Kajo. The S port, now mainly used by passenger vessels, is well protected by breakwater and the N port by a natural fjord. Berthing quays of 2535 m for 15 ocean-going vessels, 10.67 m d max. Ore berths equipped with cranes for grab discharge of bulk cargo. If ordered in good time, floating crane of lifting cap 350 t is available. Grain elevator at max rate of 2500 t/day. Loading and discharging of tankers at two berths. Floating cranes for heavy lifts up to 60 t
Two berths for bulk cement: SV Juraj, 200 m long and 9.8 m d and SV Kajo, 220 m long and 8.2 m d
Tanker facilities: Available at Solin Ina Petronafta berth, 11.6 m max d and at Brizine berth, 8.5 m d
Liquefied Gas Terminals: Dolphin berth, Adriachem Kastel Sucurac, 80 m long, 9.7 m d
Railway connections to all parts of Europe
There are facilities for shipbreaking at the port

Storage:

Location	Open (m²)	Covered (m²)	Grain (t)
Split	150000	30000	32000

Mechanical Handling Equipment:

Location	Type	Capacity (t)	Qty
Split	Floating Cranes	350	1
Split	Mult-purp. Cranes	7	
Split	Forklifts	2–22	

Bunkering: Only minor quantities of diesel oil

Waste Reception Facilities: Slop is acceptable with advance notice (no chemical residues). 5000 m3 slop tank at Ina Petronafta. Garbage disposal is compulsory Adriatic Blizna Trogir, A.Starcevica Street 16, 21220 Trogir, Republic of Croatia, *Tel:* +385 21 885643, *Fax:* +385 21 885639, *Email:* adriatic-blizna@st.htnet.hr, *Website:* www.cursor.hr/pa.nsf/Pages/adriablizna-trog
Cian Split, Split, Republic of Croatia, *Tel:* +385 21 540190, *Fax:* +385 21 540199, *Email:* cian@st.htnet.hr

Towage: Brodospas d.d., Obala Lazareta 2, P O Box 495, 21000 Split, Republic of Croatia, *Tel:* +385 21 405111, *Fax:* +385 21 344368, *Email:* brodospas@brodospas.hr, *Website:* www.brodospas.net

Repair & Maintenance: Shipyard Trogir, Put Brodograditelja 16, P O Box 41, 21220 Trogir, Republic of Croatia, *Tel:* +385 21 881303, *Fax:* +385 21 881881, *Email:* repairsales@brodotrogir.hr, *Website:* www.brodotrogir.hr Chairman: Josko Buble
Shipyard Trogir, Put Brodograditelja 16, P O Box 41, 21220 Trogir, Republic of Croatia, *Tel:* +385 21 883333, *Fax:* +385 21 881881, *Email:* repairsales@brodotrogir.hr, *Website:* www.brodotrogir.hr Chairman: Josko Buble
Shipyard Trogir, Put Brodograditelja 16, P O Box 41, 21220 Trogir, Republic of Croatia, *Tel:* +385 21 881303, *Fax:* +385 21 883406, *Email:* repairsales@brodotrogir.hr, *Website:* www.brodotrogir.hr Chairman: Josko Buble

Shipyard Trogir, Put Brodograditelja 16, P O Box 41, 21220 Trogir, Republic of Croatia, *Tel:* +385 21 883333, *Fax:* +385 21 883406, *Email:* repairsales@brodotrogir.hr, *Website:* www.brodotrogir.hr Chairman: Josko Buble
Brodogradiliste Brodosplit Shipbuilding, Brodosplit Shipyard, Put Supavla 21, P O Box 517, 21000 Split, Republic of Croatia, *Tel:* +385 21 382784, *Fax:* +385 21 391173, *Email:* brodospli-bso@bso.brodosplit.hr, *Website:* www./brodosplit-bso.hr/en-contact.php
Brodoremont Vranjic, Kreoimirova 137, 21 211 Split, Republic of Croatia, *Tel:* +385 21 211360, *Fax:* +385 21 211276 Floating dock with lifting cap of 4500 t

Ship Chandlers: Split Ship Management Ltd, SSM House, Boktuljin Put b.b., 21000 Split, Republic of Croatia, *Tel:* +385 21 558546, *Fax:* +385 21 558555, *Email:* ssm.chartering@ssm.hnet.hr, *Website:* www.ssm.hr
Tankerkomerc dd Zadar, Kopilica 62, HR 21000 Split, Republic of Croatia, *Tel:* +385 21 338337, *Fax:* +385 21 339080, *Email:* tankerkomerc@tankerkomerc.htnet.hr, *Website:* www.tankerkomerc.hr

Shipping Agents: Bandic Ltd., Smiljanica 2, 2nd Floor, HR-21000 Split, Republic of Croatia, *Tel:* +385 21 544265, *Fax:* +385 21 544277, *Email:* bandic@bandic.hr, *Website:* www.bandic.hr
Capris Agency Ltd, Vidilice 5, 21000 Split, Republic of Croatia, *Tel:* +385 21 572722, *Fax:* +385 21 572723, *Email:* capris.croatia.split@email.t-com.hr, *Website:* www.capris.si
Jadroagent d.d., PP 166, Split, Republic of Croatia, *Tel:* +385 21 460999, *Fax:* +385 21 460848, *Email:* split@jadroagent.hr, *Website:* www.jadroagent.com
Split Ship Management Ltd, SSM House, Boktuljin Put b.b., 21000 Split, Republic of Croatia, *Tel:* +385 21 558546, *Fax:* +385 21 558555, *Email:* ssm.chartering@ssm.hnet.hr, *Website:* www.ssm.hr
Tankerkomerc dd Zadar, Kopilica 62, HR 21000 Split, Republic of Croatia, *Tel:* +385 21 338337, *Fax:* +385 21 339080, *Email:* tankerkomerc@tankerkomerc.htnet.hr, *Website:* www.tankerkomerc.hr

Surveyors: Bureau Veritas, Kralja Zvonimira 14, P O Box 227, 21000 Split, Republic of Croatia, *Tel:* +385 21 323024, *Fax:* +385 21 482871, *Email:* tihomir.kezic@hr.bureauveritas.com, *Website:* www.bureauveritas.com
Cadea doo, Trg M Pavlinovica 6, 21000 Split, Republic of Croatia, *Tel:* +385 21 490151, *Fax:* +385 21 490154, *Email:* info@cadea.hr, *Website:* www.cadea.hr
Conmar, Marina Drzica 8, 21000 Split, Republic of Croatia, *Tel:* +385 21 323010, *Fax:* +385 21 323012, *Email:* conmar@conmar.hr, *Website:* www.conmar.hr
Croatian Register of Shipping, Marasoviceva 67, P O Box 187, 21000 Split, Republic of Croatia, *Tel:* +385 21 408110, *Fax:* +385 21 358159, *Email:* crs-split@crs.hr, *Website:* www.crs.hr
Det Norske Veritas A/S, c/o Brodosplit Shipyard, Put Supavla 19, 21000 Split, Republic of Croatia, *Tel:* +385 21 392550, *Fax:* +385 21 392505, *Email:* splitoffice@dnv.com, *Website:* www.dnv.com
Germanischer Lloyd, Osjecka 8, HR-21000 Split, Republic of Croatia, *Tel:* +385 21 548149, *Fax:* +385 21 548150, *Email:* gl-split@gl-group.com, *Website:* www.gl-group.com
Hellenic Register of Shipping, c/o Conmar d.o.o., Marina Drzica 8, P O Box 245, 21000 Split, Republic of Croatia, *Tel:* +385 21 323010, *Fax:* +385 21 323012, *Email:* conmar@st.hinet.hr, *Website:* www.conmar.hr
Nippon Kaiji Kyokai, Split, Republic of Croatia, *Tel:* +385 21 358933, *Fax:* +385 21 358159, *Website:* www.classnk.or.jp

Medical Facilities: Two general hospitals

Airport: Kastela Airport, 20 km

Railway: 200 m walking distance

Lloyd's Agent: Jadroagent d.d., Trg Ivana Koblera 2, 51000 Rijeka, Republic of Croatia, *Tel:* +385 51 780500, *Fax:* +385 51 215357, *Email:* info@jadroagent.hr, *Website:* www.jadroagent.hr

SUSAK

harbour area, see under Rijeka

ZADAR

Lat 44° 7' N; Long 15° 14' E.

Admiralty Chart: 2711 **Admiralty Pilot:** 47
Time Zone: GMT +1 h **UNCTAD Locode:** HR ZAD

Principal Facilities:

P	Q	Y	G		R	L		D	T	A

Authority: Lucka Uprava Zadar, Liburnska Obala 6/1, 23000 Zadar, Republic of Croatia, *Tel:* +385 23 250520, *Fax:* +385 23 250666, *Email:* lucka.uprava.zadar@zd.htnet.hr, *Website:* www.port-authority-zadar.hr

Officials: General Manager: Ivica Buric.
Harbour Master: Capt Milivoj Maricic, *Tel:* +385 23 254882.

Port Security: ISPS compliant

Approach: Old Port: Well sheltered harbour, easy of access, with 7.01 m depth at entrance, which is 70 m wide between Zadar Peninsula and the breakwater Zadar-Gazenica Commercial Port: 2.5 miles S of Zadar, 80 m wide approach channel leads from Zadar Channel to Gazenica. A light buoy moored 900 m SE of Point Kolovare marks the N side of the channel

Anchorage: Anchorage can be obtained 0.5 miles, 245° from green port light on the N part of the Zadar Peninsula, in a depth of about 40 m
Separate anchorage for tankers carrying dangerous cargoes is available in an area between the following positions: 44° 07' 12" to 44° 08' 36" N and 15° 08' 24" to 15° 10' 24" E

Pilotage: Compulsory for all vessels over 500 gt. Pilots board approaching vessels at the anchorage, about 5 cables W of the Green light at the W entrance to the old port, or the separate anchorage allocated to tankers carrying dangerous cargoes. Available on VHF Channel 12
Coastal pilotage is compulsory for tankers carrying dangerous cargoes and pilots board/disembark from vessels in 44° 23' 18" N, 14° 34' 36" E near Grujica Lighthouse. 24 h notice of ETA at pilot position is requested together with confirmation of ETA no less than 12 h in advance

Radio Frequency: Rijeka call sign 9AR; Split call sign 9AS. Available on VHF Channels 16 and 10

Weather: When entering the new basin at Gazenica, S and NW winds could affect navigation

Traffic: 2005, 205 vessels, 412 159 t of cargo handled

Principal Imports and Exports: Imports: Bulk liquid chemicals, Fruit, Jute, Liquefied gas, Pulp, Softwood, Soya beans. Exports: Hardwood, Logs, Maize, Petrochemicals, Softwood.

Working Hours: 0700-1400, 1500-2200. Sat overtime rates apply

Accommodation:

Name	Length (m)	Depth (m)	Draught (m)	Remarks
Old port				See [1] below
Gazenica Commercial Port				See [2] below
Northern dry cargo terminal	144	8.5		
Southern dry cargo terminal	155	7.2–10		
Soya bean terminal	150	15	11.6	See [3] below
Tanker berth	60	11–15	8.7–10.7	See [4] below

[1]*Old port:* 969 m of wharfage and 10 moorings, mainly used by coastal and passenger vessels of 6.7 m max d
[2]*Gazenica Commercial Port:* Contains four berths, comprising two dry cargo terminals, a soya bean terminal and a tanker terminal
[3]*Soya bean terminal:* The discharging rate is 150 t/h and storage cap is 77 000 t. In the same berth tankers of 11.5 m max d can be accommodated to discharge vegetable oil
[4]*Tanker berth:* The storage cap is 25 000 m3 for vegetable oils, 20 000 m3 for fuel oil, 15 000 m3 for oil derivates, 12 000 m3 for chemicals and 9000 m3 for vinyl chloride monomer. The discharging rate is between 150-300 t/h

Storage: Refrigerated storage for fruit only of 3500 m2

Location	Open (m²)	Covered (m²)
Zadar	200000	31500

Mechanical Handling Equipment:

Location	Type	Capacity (t)	Qty
Zadar	Mobile Cranes	100	1
Zadar	Mobile Cranes	32	2
Zadar	Mobile Cranes	7	1
Zadar	Mobile Cranes	9	1

Waste Reception Facilities: Up to 400 m3 of slop, dirty ballast water and mineral oil residue can be accepted. Garbage disposal may be arranged

Towage: One tug of 880 kw. Additional tugs from Sibenik or Split with 10 h advance notice

Repair & Maintenance: Nauta Lamjana d.d., Velan Lamjana bb, P O Box 3, 27200 Kali, Republic of Croatia, *Tel:* +385 23 208711, *Fax:* +385 23 281051, *Email:* info@nauta-lamjana.hr Floating dock of 155 m x 23.4 m with lifting cap of 8500 t

Ship Chandlers: Tankerkomerc dd Zadar, Obala Kneza Trpimira 2, HR 23000 Zadar, Republic of Croatia, *Tel:* +385 23 204830, *Fax:* +385 23 333912, *Email:* tankerkomerc@tankerkomerc.hr, *Website:* www.tankerkomerc.hr

Shipping Agents: Capris Agency Ltd, I.Brlic Mazuranic 23, 23000 Zadar, Republic of Croatia, *Tel:* +385 23 332610, *Fax:* +385 23 332108, *Email:* globalagent@post.t-com.hr, *Website:* www.capris.si
Jadroagent d.d., P O Box 210, 23000 Zadar, Republic of Croatia, *Tel:* +385 23 251052, *Fax:* +385 23 250647, *Email:* zadar@jadroagent.hr, *Website:* www.jadoragent.com
Tankerkomerc dd Zadar, Obala Kneza Trpimira 2, HR 23000 Zadar, Republic of Croatia, *Tel:* +385 23 204830, *Fax:* +385 23 333912, *Email:* tankerkomerc@tankerkomerc.hr, *Website:* www.tankerkomerc.hr

Surveyors: Croatian Register of Shipping, Ivana Mazuranica 2, 23000 Zadar, Republic of Croatia, *Tel:* +385 23 235981, *Fax:* +385 23 235788, *Email:* crs-zadar@crs.hr, *Website:* www.crs.hr

Medical Facilities: All kinds available

Airport: Zadar Airport, 12 km

Lloyd's Agent: Jadroagent d.d., Trg Ivana Koblera 2, 51000 Rijeka, Republic of Croatia, *Tel:* +385 51 780500, *Fax:* +385 51 215357, *Email:* info@jadroagent.hr, *Website:* www.jadroagent.hr

ZARA

alternate name, see Zadar

CUBA

30 DE NOVIEMBRE DOCK

harbour area, see under Santiago

ANTILLA

Lat 20° 50' N; Long 75° 44' W.

Admiralty Chart: -	**Admiralty Pilot:** 70
Time Zone: GMT -5 h	**UNCTAD Locode:** CU ANT

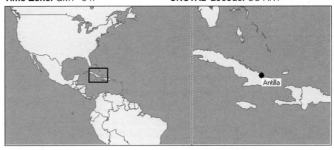

Principal Facilities:

		G		B	T

Authority: Empresa Terminales Mambisas de Antilla, Antilla, Cuba

Approach: Nipe Bay, suitable for large vessels with max d up to 22.86 m and length up to 400 m

Anchorage: Point Salinas anchorage: About nine vessels can be accommodated in this anchorage with max d of 9.1 to 17 m and length up to 170 m
Corojal anchorage: Only three vessels can be accommodated with d of 6.09 m and length of 145 m
Antilla Anchorage No.2: Can accommodate only one vessel, with d of 7.1 m and length of 152.4 m

Pilotage: Compulsory. Pilot taken on board one mile NE of Point Mayari in pos 20° 47' 46" N; 75° 32' 15" W

Tides: Tidal variation averages 2.25 to 2.5 feet

Maximum Vessel Dimensions: Max length 186 m, max d 6.71 m

Principal Imports and Exports: Imports: Diesel oil, Gasoline, General cargo. Exports: Molasses, Sugar.

Accommodation:

Name	Length (m)	Draught (m)	Remarks
Antilla			
Pier No.4			See [1] below
Coastal Pier	136	6.1	Used for discharging oil and cereal and loading molasses
Bacaladera Dock	170		See [2] below
Preston			See [3] below
Felton			See [4] below

[1]*Pier No.4:* Loading of bagged raw sugar and molasses and unloading of general cargo. North Side has d of 4.88 m at base and 6.71 m at head with length of 170 m. South Side has d of 6.1 m at base and 6.71 m at head with length of 170 m
[2]*Bacaladera Dock:* Used for discharging liquid asphalt. 3.05 m d at bow and 3.66 m d at stern
[3]*Preston:* In pos 20° 46' N; 75° 40' W. On S side of Nipe Bay can take vessels up to 146 m, 6.1 m d at Preston Pier. Water available by pipeline
[4]*Felton:* In pos 20° 44' 45" N; 75° 35' 40" W. On S side of Nipe Bay. Manoeuvres are limited to daylight hours with wind force 3 or less. Vessels with length smaller than 153 m can operate with d up to 8.53 m. Vessels over 153 m and up to 170 m operate with d of 7.92 m. Vessels are berthed to four steel dolphins and two mooring buoys. One electric shore crane used mainly for discharge of bulk raw materials

Bunkering: Empresa Consignataria Mambisa (ECM), Payret Building, No. 65 San Jose Street, P O Box 174, Havana, Cuba, *Tel:* +53 7 862 7138, *Fax:* +53 7 833 8111, *Email:* ecm@mambisa.transnet.cu – *Grades:* FO; MDO – *Parcel Size:* 50t – *Delivery Mode:* railroad tankcar

Towage: Available from Authority. Not compulsory

Medical Facilities: Antilla hospital

Lloyd's Agent: Marinter S.A., Edificio 'Playa', Calle 12, 105e/1ra y 3ra piso, Miramar, Havana, Cuba, *Tel:* +53 7 204 9742, *Fax:* +53 7 204 9743, *Email:* havana@marintercu.com, *Website:* www.cubaweb.cu/marintersa/marinter.html

---

Key to Principal Facilities:—				
A=Airport	**C**=Containers	**G**=General Cargo	**P**=Petroleum	**R**=Ro/Ro	**Y**=Dry Bulk
B=Bunkers	**D**=Dry Dock	**L**=Cruise	**Q**=Other Liquid Bulk	**T**=Towage (where available from port)

ANTONIO MACEO DOCK

harbour area, see under Santiago

ARACELIO IGLESIAS TERMINAL

harbour area, see under Havana

BAHIA HONDA

Lat 22° 58' N; Long 83° 10' W.

Admiralty Chart: -
Time Zone: GMT -5 h
Admiralty Pilot: 70
UNCTAD Locode: CU BHO

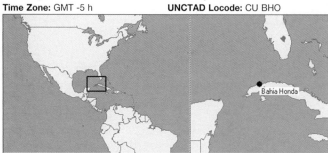

Principal Facilities:

			G							

Authority: Port Authority of Bahia Honda, Ministerio del Transporte, Havana, Cuba
Approach: Entrance channel has sandy bottom by eastern side and rocky bottom by western side. Approx 150 m wide. Max draft at LW at entrance or on bar 8.53 m, max length 147 m. Vessels may enter or leave during daylight only. Tugs not needed for entry operations
Anchorage: There is only one anchorage for vessels of 8.53 m d. Max length permitted 130 m
Pilotage: Compulsory. Pilot taken on and returned to Mariel
Accommodation:

Name	Length (m)	Draught (m)	Remarks
Bahia Honda			
Ciro Redondo Berth	130	6.71	See [1] below

[1]*Ciro Redondo Berth:* Used as a base for dismantling of vessels & loading scrap iron

Lloyd's Agent: Marinter S.A., Edificio 'Playa', Calle 12, 105e/1ra y 3ra piso, Miramar, Havana, Cuba, *Tel:* +53 7 204 9742, *Fax:* +53 7 204 9743, *Email:* havana@marintercu.com, *Website:* www.cubaweb.cu/marintersa/marinter.html

BARACOA

Lat 20° 21' N; Long 74° 29' W.

Admiralty Chart: -
Time Zone: GMT -5 h
Admiralty Pilot: 70
UNCTAD Locode: CU BCA

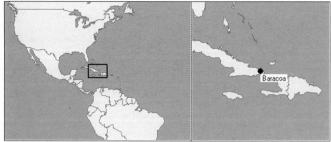

Principal Facilities:

		G				T	A			

Authority: Port Authority of Baracoa, P O Box 27, c/o Empresa Nacional de Cabotaje, Baracoa, Cuba
Pilotage: Pilot boards 2 miles in front of the port of Moa
Tides: Average of 2-3 feet between high and low tides
Accommodation:

Name	Remarks
Baracoa	See [1] below

[1]*Baracoa:* The entrance channel is straight. Vessels up to 100 m long and 6.1 m d may enter through channel, only in daylight hours. There is no pier at this port and vessels anchor at bay for performing operations. There are several barges with 100 t cap

Storage: Warehouse cap for 1000 t of general cargo
Towage: Available from Authority. Not compulsory
Medical Facilities: Baracoa general hospital
Airport: Gustavo Rizo Airport
Lloyd's Agent: Marinter S.A., Edificio 'Playa', Calle 12, 105e/1ra y 3ra piso, Miramar, Havana, Cuba, *Tel:* +53 7 204 9742, *Fax:* +53 7 204 9743, *Email:* havana@marintercu.com, *Website:* www.cubaweb.cu/marintersa/marinter.html

BOQUERON

Lat 19° 59' N; Long 75° 7' W.

Admiralty Chart: -
Time Zone: GMT -5 h
Admiralty Pilot: 70
UNCTAD Locode: CU BOQ

Principal Facilities:

	Q	Y	G					T		

Authority: Empresa Terminales Mambisas del Oriente, Boqueron, Cuba
Approach: The entrance has a muddy bottom and two slight turns
Pilotage: Pilot boards the vessel one mile from buoy No.1 at the entrance to the port
Maximum Vessel Dimensions: Vessels up to 170 m in length with a max draft of 5.79 m can enter the port
Accommodation:

Name	Length (m)	Draught (m)	Remarks
Boqueron			See [1] below
Boqueron Pier	152	5.79	See [2] below

[1]*Boqueron:* Commercial vessels, though permitted passage through the lower bay, are not permitted to put in there as the entire area constitutes the United States Naval Station
[2]*Boqueron Pier:* Molasses operations are carried out on N side, with bulk raw sugar on the S side. Operations performed during daylight hours only

Towage: Available from Authority. Not compulsory
Lloyd's Agent: Marinter S.A., Edificio 'Playa', Calle 12, 105e/1ra y 3ra piso, Miramar, Havana, Cuba, *Tel:* +53 7 204 9742, *Fax:* +53 7 204 9743, *Email:* havana@marintercu.com, *Website:* www.cubaweb.cu/marintersa/marinter.html

BUFADERO PIER

harbour area, see under Nuevitas

CABANAS

Lat 23° 0' N; Long 82° 59' W.

Admiralty Chart: -
Time Zone: GMT -5 h
Admiralty Pilot: 70
UNCTAD Locode: CU CAB

Principal Facilities:

	Q	Y	G					T		

Authority: Port Authority of Cabanas, P O Box 5, Empresa Consignataria Mambisa, Mariel, Cuba
Pilotage: Compulsory. Pilot taken on and returned to Mariel
Accommodation:

Name	Remarks
Cabanas	See [1] below

[1]Cabanas: Depth at entrance 6.7 m. No tugs needed for entry manoeuvres. Vessels enter/leave during daylight only. Pablo de la Torriente Brau dock 109.7 m long, 5.79 m d, where vessels with max length of 137.2 m are allowed to dock. It is used for the shipment of raw sugar. Railway connections. Max draft for ships at anchorage 5.79 m. Two molasses storage tanks, cap 400 000 gallons. Two vessels can be loaded simultaneously
The port of Cabanas is presently out of service

Towage: Available from Authority

Lloyd's Agent: Marinter S.A., Edificio 'Playa', Calle 12, 105e/1ra y 3ra piso, Miramar, Havana, Cuba, *Tel:* +53 7 204 9742, *Fax:* +53 7 204 9743, *Email:* havana@marintercu.com, *Website:* www.cubaweb.cu/marintersa/marinter.html

CAIBARIEN

Lat 22° 32' N; Long 79° 28' W.

Admiralty Chart: 1217   **Admiralty Pilot:** 70
Time Zone: GMT -5 h   **UNCTAD Locode:** CU CAI

Principal Facilities:

			G					T		

Authority: Empresa Terminales Mambisas del Centro Este, Caibarien, Cuba

Pilotage: Pilot boards the vessel 0.5 mile from Catalina buoy at the entrance to Frances Cay anchorage

Accommodation:

Name	Remarks
Caibarien	See [1] below

[1]Caibarien: Operations are carried out at Frances Cay anchorage by lighters. It is 25.6 km from Caibarien. This anchorage is easily accessible. The bottoms are of mud and sand, and the Port Buoy anchorage bottom is of stone but free of reefs. Vessels may enter or sail from the anchorage with any draft up to 10.67 m. When vessels have a draft of less than 6.1 m they must proceed to the inner anchorage (La Caldera). If more than 6.1 m but less than 7.92 m they proceed to the outer anchorage (La Poza), and those over 7.92 m and up to a max of 10.06 m proceed to the third anchorage (Port Buoy). Vessels may enter at any time and tugs are not necessary for entering/sailing manoeuvres
At Caibarien itself, there are nine piers. These piers are used for the shipment of raw sugar in barges which are then towed to the Frances Cay anchorages where the vessels are loaded. All the piers with the exception of Maritima Pier which has a draft of 2.59 m, have 2.13 m alongside

Storage: The Pita Afianzado Pier is used by the Customs House to receive general cargo, jute bags and any other import cargo, and also for storing sugar when necessary. There are 28 warehouses which have a total cap of 242 280 m3

Towage: Available from Authority. Not compulsory

Repair & Maintenance: There are repair shops at this port, but due to the distance between the port and the anchorages, it is difficult and costly to perform anything more than minor repairs

Medical Facilities: Caibarien hospital

Lloyd's Agent: Marinter S.A., Edificio 'Playa', Calle 12, 105e/1ra y 3ra piso, Miramar, Havana, Cuba, *Tel:* +53 7 204 9742, *Fax:* +53 7 204 9743, *Email:* havana@marintercu.com, *Website:* www.cubaweb.cu/marintersa/marinter.html

CARDENAS

Lat 23° 3' N; Long 81° 12' W.

Admiralty Chart: -   **Admiralty Pilot:** 70
Time Zone: GMT -5 h   **UNCTAD Locode:** CU CAR

Principal Facilities:

			G						T	A

Authority: Empresa Terminales Mambisas de Matanzas, Cardenas, Cuba

Approach: The entrance channel has a muddy bottom and due to the amount of mud deposited in this channel, the max draft which is permissible is 5.2 m and the max length approx 170.7 m. Vessels may enter or leave during daylight only

Principal Imports and Exports: Imports: Bagged fertiliser, Flour, General cargo, Lumber, Woodpulp. Exports: Bagged refined sugar.

Accommodation:

Name	Length (m)	Draught (m)
Cardenas Pier	319	5.2

Towage: Available from Authority. Not compulsory

Medical Facilities: Cardenas civil hospital

Airport: Varadero, 20 km

Lloyd's Agent: Marinter S.A., Edificio 'Playa', Calle 12, 105e/1ra y 3ra piso, Miramar, Havana, Cuba, *Tel:* +53 7 204 9742, *Fax:* +53 7 204 9743, *Email:* havana@marintercu.com, *Website:* www.cubaweb.cu/marintersa/marinter.html

CASILDA

Lat 21° 45' N; Long 79° 59' W.

Admiralty Chart: -   **Admiralty Pilot:** 70
Time Zone: GMT -5 h   **UNCTAD Locode:** CU CAS

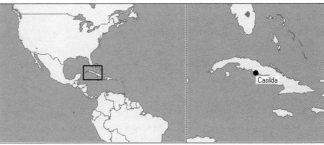

Principal Facilities:

			G					T		

Authority: Empresa Terminales Mambisas del Centro Este, Casilda, Cuba

Approach: The entrance channel to the port has a muddy bottom with a very dangerous 'S' shaped turn. Vessels may enter or sail with a max of 7.62 m d and a max length of 170 m

Pilotage: Pilot boards vessel in pos 21° 37' 36" N; 79° 52' 32" W which is one mile SW of the Blanco Cay lighthouse

Tides: Tidal variation of 2 feet

Principal Imports and Exports: Imports: Caustic soda, Crude oil, General cargo, Petroleum, Wood, Woodpulp. Exports: Alcohol, Bagged raw & refined sugar.

Working Hours: Mon to Sat 0600-1000, 1200-1600

Accommodation:

Name	Remarks
Casilda	See [1] below

[1]Casilda: There is an L-shaped pier, the W side of which is 158 m and the S side (tanker pier) is 119 m. Both sides can handle vessels up to 170 m with a draft of 7.62 m on the W side and 7.0 m (bow) 7.32 m (stern) on the S side. The pier has railway tracks along its length and, at the paved W side, trucking operations can be effected. Vessels may enter or leave during daylight hours only

Storage: There are two warehouses with a total storage cap for 70 000 bags of sugar

Towage: Available from Authority. Not compulsory

Medical Facilities: Trinidad city hospital

Lloyd's Agent: Marinter S.A., Edificio 'Playa', Calle 12, 105e/1ra y 3ra piso, Miramar, Havana, Cuba, *Tel:* +53 7 204 9742, *Fax:* +53 7 204 9743, *Email:* havana@marintercu.com, *Website:* www.cubaweb.cu/marintersa/marinter.html

CAYO MOA

Lat 20° 41' N; Long 74° 54' W.

Admiralty Chart: -   **Admiralty Pilot:** 70
Time Zone: GMT -5 h   **UNCTAD Locode:** CU MOA

Key to Principal Facilities:—			
A=Airport	**C**=Containers	**G**=General Cargo	**P**=Petroleum	**R**=Ro/Ro	**Y**=Dry Bulk
B=Bunkers	**D**=Dry Dock	**L**=Cruise	**Q**=Other Liquid Bulk	**T**=Towage (where available from port)	

Principal Facilities:

| | | G | | | | | T | A | |

Authority: Port Authority of Cayo Moa, Ministerio del Transporte, Havana, Cuba

Approach: Entrance channel is 1560 m long, 200-750 m wide and 12.2 m depth. It is almost straight with two very slight turns and entry or sailing is during daylight only

Pilotage: Pilot boards vessel two miles off the port entrance

Accommodation:

Name	Length (m)	Draught (m)	Remarks
Cayo Moa			
Moa Pier No.1	152	10.97	See [1] below
Moa Pier No.2	170	10.97	See [2] below

[1]*Moa Pier No.1:* Cargoes handled include import of bulk sulphur and general cargo and export of nickel and cobalt concentrate
[2]*Moa Pier No.2:* Cargoes handled include import of bulk sulphur and general cargo and export of nickel and cobalt concentrate

Towage: One tug available

Repair & Maintenance: Minor repairs only by mining enterprise

Medical Facilities: Moa Hospital

Airport: Orestes Acosta Airport

Lloyd's Agent: Marinter S.A., Edificio 'Playa', Calle 12, 105e/1ra y 3ra piso, Miramar, Havana, Cuba, *Tel:* +53 7 204 9742, *Fax:* +53 7 204 9743, *Email:* havana@marintercu.com, *Website:* www.cubaweb.cu/marintersa/marinter.html

CIENFUEGOS

Lat 22° 8' N; Long 80° 27' W.

Admiralty Chart: 444	**Admiralty Pilot:** 70
Time Zone: GMT -5 h	**UNCTAD Locode:** CU CFG

Principal Facilities:

| P | Q | Y | G | | | B | | T | A | |

Authority: Empresa Terminales Mambisas del Centro Este, Cienfuegos, Cuba

Approach: At the entrance there are two sharp turns; at Pasa Caballos and the W part of Cayo Carenas. It has a muddy bottom. Vessels drawing up to 11.55 m and with a length up to 207 m may enter through the channel

Anchorage: North Anchorage: Bottom is soft mud. Min d of anchorage is 12.19 m. Used for awaiting berths, bunkers, water etc and also can discharge or load by means of barges
General Anchorage: Bottom is soft mud. Max d of 10.97 m and is used for awaiting berths, bunkers, water, provisions etc and can also discharge or load by means of barges
Quarantine and Explosive Anchorage: Bottom is soft mud, having d of 15.25 m

Pilotage: Pilot boards the vessel one mile SW of Los Colorados lighthouse in pos 22° 01' 33" N; 80° 26' 53" W. Service available 24 h

Accommodation:

Name	Length (m)	Apron Width (m)	Remarks
Cienfuegos			
Tricontinental Pier	207	43	See [1] below
Pablo E. Guzman Pier			See [2] below
Citric Dock			See [3] below
Molasses Terminal Berth			See [4] below
ICP Submarine Pipeline			Located E of Point Majagua. Vessels berth to three mooring buoys aft, to discharge fuel oil, d even keel 11.58 m
Olimpia Medina Pier			See [5] below

Name	Length (m)	Apron Width (m)	Remarks
Fertilisers Plant Submarine Pipeline			See [6] below
Thermoelectric Plant Submarine Pipeline			See [7] below

[1]*Tricontinental Pier:* Located SE of Ramirez Cove. The east side has d of 10.52 m and is specially conditioned for loading bulk raw sugar and has two cranes mounted on rails, each one capable of loading 600 t/h. Berthing length at east side is only 165 m. The west side has d of 10.52 m and is used for discharge of cereals
[2]*Pablo E. Guzman Pier:* Located E of Point Arenas. The west side (east out of service) is 186 m long with d of 8.84 m (bow) 9.14 m (stern). Berthing operations can only be performed during daylight hours. Used for discharge of petroleum products and supplying diesel oil
[3]*Citric Dock:* Berth No's 3 and 4, lengths 140 m with d even keel of 9.75 m (No.3) and 9.45 m (No.4). Located E of Tricontinental Pier. Berth No.5 still under construction
[4]*Molasses Terminal Berth:* Located S of Point Arenas. Loading of molasses is performed through three connections, each 8'' diameter. Vessels berth to four dolphins and two mooring buoys. Docking effected only during daylight hours
[5]*Olimpia Medina Pier:* Located at Marsillan Cove. Berth No.1, length 170 m with d even keel of 7.92 m. Berth No.2, length 170 m with d at east end 7.62 m and at west end 7.92 m. Berth No.3, length 170 m with d of 5.79 m
[6]*Fertilisers Plant Submarine Pipeline:* Vessels berth to three mooring buoys aft to discharge naphta in d of 9.45 m. Berthing operations performed only in daylight
[7]*Thermoelectric Plant Submarine Pipeline:* Vessels berth to three mooring buoys aft and one buoy fore to discharge fuel oil, d of 10.97 m. Berthing operations performed only in daylight

Bunkering: Empresa Consignataria Mambisa (ECM), Payret Building, No. 65 San Jose Street, P O Box 174, Havana, Cuba, *Tel:* +53 7 862 7138, *Fax:* +53 7 833 8111, *Email:* ecm@mambisa.transnet.cu – *Grades:* FO; MDO – *Parcel Size:* 325t – *Delivery Mode:* barge, pipeline

Towage: Available from Authority. Not compulsory

Repair & Maintenance: Only light repairs possible

Medical Facilities: Cienfuegos general hospital

Airport: Jaime Gonzalez Airport

Lloyd's Agent: Marinter S.A., Edificio 'Playa', Calle 12, 105e/1ra y 3ra piso, Miramar, Havana, Cuba, *Tel:* +53 7 204 9742, *Fax:* +53 7 204 9743, *Email:* havana@marintercu.com, *Website:* www.cubaweb.cu/marintersa/marinter.html

COMANDER TURCIOS LIMA

harbour area, see under Havana

FELTON

harbour area, see under Antilla

FRANK PAIS PIER

harbour area, see under Santiago

GUAYABAL

Lat 20° 42' N; Long 77° 37' W.

Admiralty Chart: -	**Admiralty Pilot:** 70
Time Zone: GMT -5 h	**UNCTAD Locode:** CU GYB

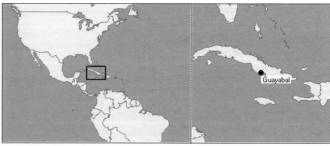

Principal Facilities:

| | | | G | | | | | | |

Authority: Empresa Terminales Mambisas del Centro Este, Guayabal, Cuba

Approach: The entrance channel has a depth of 13.7 m and a width of 319 m at one part. Also at this point is a turn of approx 20° where some precautions must be taken. There is a dredged channel at the entrance to the pier 2474 m long and 60 m wide

Pilotage: The pilot boards the vessel at the entrance of Cuatro Reales channel in pos 20° 27' 00" N; 78° 00' 30" W

Accommodation:

Name	Length (m)	Remarks
Guayabal		
Guayabal Pier	170	See [1] below

[1]*Guayabal Pier:* For vessels up to 190 m. Max draft allowed is 9.45 m for vessels sailing at HT. Fuel oil, molasses and alcohol are handled on the east side where vessels are permitted with a max d of 8.23 m provided that when undocking max d does not exceed 7.62 m. Loading of bulk sugar is handled on the west side and vessels with a length up to 150 m can dock with a d of 9.14 m, vessels with length 150-170 m can dock with d of 7.62 m and vessels over 170 m can dock with d of 7.32 m

Lloyd's Agent: Marinter S.A., Edificio 'Playa', Calle 12, 105e/1ra y 3ra piso, Miramar, Havana, Cuba, *Tel:* +53 7 204 9742, *Fax:* +53 7 204 9743, *Email:* havana@marintercu.com, *Website:* www.cubaweb.cu/marintersa/marinter.html

HABANA

alternate name, see Havana

HAIPHONG TERMINAL

harbour area, see under Havana

HAVANA

Lat 23° 8' N; Long 82° 21' W.

Admiralty Chart: 414
Admiralty Pilot: 70
Time Zone: GMT -5 h
UNCTAD Locode: CU HAV

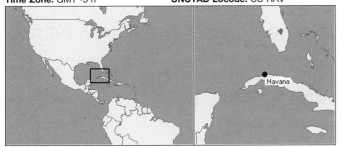

Principal Facilities:

P Q Y G C R L B D T A

Authority: Empresa Terminales Mambisas de La Habana, Havana, Cuba

Port Security: ISPS compliant

Approach: The entrance channel has a mud bottom. There are no hazards except a strong current, which has to be taken into consideration when entering. Max d throughout bay (except refinery quay) 12.8 m at LW. Tankers may enter drawing up to 11.43 m as they take a special course once they are in the bay

Anchorage: The max draft at the main anchorage is 10.6 m

Pilotage: Compulsory. Pilot boards approx 1 mile from port; contact on VHF Channel 13

Radio Frequency: Vessels navigating to Cuba can communicate with Mambisa Havana through CLA Havana radiotelegraphy station which relays the message immediately by telex. Vessels approaching Havana can communicate by VHF radio: pilot station, channel 13 and Mambisa Agency, channel 12. Both channels are open 24 h/day

Tides: Average range of tide 0.45 m

Maximum Vessel Dimensions: Max d 11.43 m, max loa 230 m (dry cargo)

Working Hours: Mon to Sat 0700-1300, 1300-1900

Accommodation:

Name	Length (m)	Draught (m)	Remarks
Andres Gonzalez Lines Dock			See [1] below
Berth No.1 (east)	332	9	
Berth No.2 (west)	170	6.8	
Sierra Maestra Terminal			See [2] below
Pier 1 (north side)	201	8.84–9.75	
Pier 1 (south side)	201	9.14–9.75	
Pier 2 (north side)	201	9.14–9.75	
Pier 2 (south side)	183	9.14–9.75	
Pier 3 (north side)	190	9.14–9.75	
Pier 3 (south side)	171	8.23–9.75	
Margarito Iglesias Terminal			See [3] below
Pier 1 (north side)	135	6.1	
Pier 1 (south side)	135	6.1	
Pier 2 (north side)	135	6.1	
Pier 2 (south side)	135	6.1	
Pier 3 (north side)	135	5.49	
Pier 3 (south side)	135	5.49	
Havana Central Pier			See [4] below

Name	Length (m)	Draught (m)	Remarks
Aracelio Iglesias Terminal			See [5] below
Juan Manuel Diaz Terminal			See [6] below
Osvaldo Sanchez Docks			See [7] below
Dock No.1	130	4.88	
Dock No.2	155	5.49	
Haiphong Terminal			See [8] below
Berth No.1	160	9.75	
Berth No.2	160	9.75	
Berth No.3	160	9.75	
Berth No.4	200	9.75	
Berth No.5	170	8.08–8.6	
Manuel Porto Dapena Terminal			See [9] below
Berth No.1	140	7.62	
Berth No.2	165	9.39	
Comander Turcios Lima Grain Elevator			See [10] below
Jose Antonio Echeverria Pier			See [11] below
Facilidades Maritimas Dock			See [12] below
Puerto Pesquero de La Habana			See [13] below
Pier 1	260	7.92	
Pier 1A	137	7.92	
Pier 2	130	7.92	
Pier 3	200	7.92	
Pier 3A	89	7.92	
Pier 4	160	7.32	
Pier 5	137	7.92	
Pier 6	137	4.78	
Floating Dock (east side)	127	6.71	
Floating Dock (west side)	128	6.7	
Nico Lopez Oil Terminal			See [14] below
Nico Lopez Pier No.1 (north side)	313	10.67	
Nico Lopez Pier No.1 (south side)	302	11.4	
Nico Lopez Pier No.2 (north side)	302	11.43	
Nico Lopez Pier No.2 (south side)	302	11.43	
Muelle Nico Lopez No.3	100	4	

[1]*Andres Gonzalez Lines Dock:* This dock is used for the discharge of fertilizers, bulk coal and machinery and is equipped with an overhead crane

[2]*Sierra Maestra Terminal:* There is one warehouse at each of the piers and all have rail connections. The terminal is used for loading and discharge of general cargo

[3]*Margarito Iglesias Terminal:* All piers have rail connections. The terminal used for loading and discharging of general cargo

[4]*Havana Central Pier:* This pier is used for discharge and loading of general cargo. North Side is 132 m long with d of 4.57 m (base) 9.14 m (head). South side is 146 m long with d of 7.3 m (base) 9.75 m (head). It is forbidden to dock vessels over 100 m long when there are vessels docked at S side of Margarito Iglesias Pier 3 unless those vessels do not exceed 80 m in length. Pier has a sheltered warehouse cap of 21 285 m3 and a railroad siding connected with main track

[5]*Aracelio Iglesias Terminal:* This terminal, used in the discharge and loading of general cargo, consists of a dock and a pier. The dock is 174.6 m long and 13.41 m wide, and drafts alongside range from 6.7 to 8.53 m. Dock has one sheltered warehouse with cap of 110 463 m3
Pier (north side), length 157.8 m, width 36 m, drafts 8.23 m (base) 10.05 m (head). Pier (south side), length 137 m, width 31.7 m, drafts 8.23 m (base) 10.36 m (head). Pier has a sheltered warehouse with a cap of 30 880 m3
Both dock and pier have railroad siding connecting with the main track

[6]*Juan Manuel Diaz Terminal:* The terminal, used in discharge and loading of general cargo, consists of two docks and one pier. Dock No.3, 158.8 m in length, width 17.07 m, drafts 6.71 m (bow) 7.92 m (stern). Dock has a sheltered warehouse with a cap of 50 230 m3
Pier (north side), length 152.4 m, width 38.1 m, drafts 6.1 m (base) 7.01 m (head). Pier (south side), length 161.5 m, width 38.1 m, drafts 7.31 m (base) 10.25 m (head). Pier has sheltered warehouse with cap of 39 821 m3
Dock No.2, length 146.6 m, width 9.45 m, drafts 5.79 m (bow) 7.32 m (stern). Dock has a sheltered warehouse with cap of 112 471 m3
Both docks and pier have railroad sidings connecting with main track

[7]*Osvaldo Sanchez Docks:* These docks are used chiefly in discharge of lumber. The docks have sheltered warehouses with combined cap of 101, 713, 731 and 47 m3. There are no sidings but suitable for trucking operations

[8]*Haiphong Terminal:* Consists of five berths, No.4 being used mainly for docking and operating of ro/ro vessels. Cargoes handled include general cargo, lumber, structural steel, steel scrap, transport etc

[9]*Manuel Porto Dapena Terminal:* Suitable for loading and discharging of general cargo, lumber, refrigerated cargoes etc. There are also installations for the discharge of used lubricating oil and petroleum products

[10]*Comander Turcios Lima Grain Elevator:* Consists of one pier, length 237 m, width 9 m with d even keel of 9.6 m. Handles all kinds of bulk grain with the exception of durum wheat and also general cargo, refrigerated cargoes, containers etc are discharged at this dock

[11]*Jose Antonio Echeverria Pier:* Used for discharging of bulk grains, equipped with elevator and silos which have a storage cap of approx 20 000 t. Length 152 m, width 79 m with d of 8.84 m (bow) 9.14 m (centre) 9.75 m (stern). Vessels usually dock port side to pier

[12]*Facilidades Maritimas Dock:* Length 248 m, width 8 m with d 8.2 m (bow) 8.84 m (stern). Usually vessels dock port side to dock; used for loading molasses and the discharge of tallow and chemicals. Rail sidings

[13]*Puerto Pesquero de La Habana:* Owned and operated by Cuban Fisheries Ministry with large refrigerated warehouse. Facilities frequently used to handle the import and export of refrigerated cargoes other than fish

Key to Principal Facilities:—
A=Airport	**C**=Containers	**G**=General Cargo
B=Bunkers	**D**=Dry Dock	**L**=Cruise

P=Petroleum	**R**=Ro/Ro	**Y**=Dry Bulk
Q=Other Liquid Bulk	**T**=Towage (where available from port)	

[14]*Nico Lopez Oil Terminal:* Used exclusively for the discharge of crude oil and petroleum by-products

Storage:

Location	Grain (t)
Comander Turcios Lima Grain Elevator	30000
Jose Antonio Echeverria Pier	20000

Mechanical Handling Equipment:

Location	Type	Capacity (t)	Qty
Havana	Floating Cranes	35	3
Havana	Floating Cranes	100	1
Havana	Mult-purp. Cranes	30	
Haiphong Terminal	Mult-purp. Cranes	8	12

Bunkering: Empresa Consignataria Mambisa (ECM), Payret Building, No. 65 San Jose Street, P O Box 174, Havana, Cuba, *Tel:* +53 7 862 7138, *Fax:* +53 7 833 8111, *Email:* ecm@mambisa.transnet.cu

Empresa Consignataria Mambisa (ECM), Payret Building, No. 65 San Jose Street, P O Box 174, Havana, Cuba, *Tel:* +53 7 862 7138, *Fax:* +53 7 833 8111, *Email:* ecm@mambisa.transnet.cu – *Grades:* FO; MDO – *Misc:* service available 24 hours a day, seven days a week through – *Delivery Mode:* barge

Repair & Maintenance: Astilleros del Caribe (ASTICAR), Ensenada de Potes y Atares, Habana Vieja, P O Box 10100, Havana, Cuba, *Tel:* +53 7 866 0172/3, *Fax:* +53 7 866 0174, *Email:* mkt@asticar.telemar.cu Floating dock of 4500 t cap
CDM Havana Shipyard, P O Box 6651, Zona Postal 6, Havana, Cuba, *Tel:* +53 7 833 8158, *Fax:* +53 7 833 8751, *Email:* aag@cdmhav.get.cma.net, *Website:* www.cdmhav.cubaweb.cu One graving dock 153 m x 27 m, cap 15 000 dwt. Two floating docks: 100 m x 21 m for vessels up to 4500 t and 227 m x 37 m for vessels up to 22 000 t. Repair quays of 1100 m

Shipping Agents: Empresa Consignataria Mambisa (ECM), Payret Building, No. 65 San Jose Street, P O Box 174, Havana, Cuba, *Tel:* +53 7 862 7138, *Fax:* +53 7 833 8111, *Email:* ecm@mambisa.transnet.cu
Laemar, Tte Rey Nr 60 esq San Ignacio, Edif Santo Angel, 1 er Piso A, Habana Vieja, Havana 10100, Cuba, *Tel:* +53 7 866 0343, *Fax:* +53 7 866 0840, *Email:* laemar@laemar.com.cu
Marinter S.A., Edificio 'Playa', Calle 12, 105e/1ra y 3ra piso, Miramar, Havana, Cuba, *Tel:* +53 7 204 9742, *Fax:* +53 7 204 9743, *Email:* havana@marintercu.com, *Website:* www.cubaweb.cu/marintersa/marinter.html
Navemar S.A., Monserrate 261, 6 Piso, E/San Juan de Dios y Empedrado, Havana, Cuba, *Tel:* +53 7 861 5786, *Fax:* +53 7 860 9534, *Email:* hav.genmbox@cma-cgm.com
Perez S.A., Monserrate 261, piso 5, E/San Juan de Dios y Empedrado, Havana 10200, Cuba, *Tel:* +53 7 860 8223, *Fax:* +53 7 860 8225, *Email:* havana@perezyciacu.com

Surveyors: Bureau Veritas, Calle 21 - No 4, Vedado, Havana, Cuba, *Tel:* +53 7 833 3418, *Fax:* +53 7 833 3903, *Email:* bvhavana@bveritas.co.cu, *Website:* www.bureauveritas.com
Germanischer Lloyd, Linea No.5, 8th Floor, Vedado, Havana 10400, Cuba, *Tel:* +53 7 833 3440, *Fax:* +53 7 833 3064, *Email:* gl-havana@gl-group.com, *Website:* www.gl-group.com
Hellenic Register of Shipping, c/o Jaguey Maritima, Linea No.756, e/Paceoy 2, Municipio Plaza de la Revolucion, Havana, Cuba, *Tel:* +53 7 880 1313, *Email:* chipre@cubacel.net, *Website:* www.hrs.gr
Nippon Kaiji Kyokai, Linea No.5, 8th Floor, Vedado, Havana, Cuba, *Tel:* +53 7 833 3440, *Fax:* +53 7 833 3064, *Website:* www.classnk.or.jp
Registro Italiano Navale (RINA), Linea No.5, 8th floor, Vedado, Havana, Cuba, *Tel:* +53 7 833 3440, *Fax:* +53 7 833 3064, *Website:* www.rina.org

Medical Facilities: Cira Garcia Hospital

Airport: Jose Marti International, 15 km

Lloyd's Agent: Marinter S.A., Edificio 'Playa', Calle 12, 105e/1ra y 3ra piso, Miramar, Havana, Cuba, *Tel:* +53 7 204 9742, *Fax:* +53 7 204 9743, *Email:* havana@marintercu.com, *Website:* www.cubaweb.cu/marintersa/marinter.html

ISABELA DE SAGUA

Lat 22° 57' N; Long 80° 1' W.

Admiralty Chart: -	Admiralty Pilot: 70
Time Zone: GMT -5 h	UNCTAD Locode: CU IDS

Principal Facilities:

		G			B	T	

Authority: Empresa Terminales Mambisas del Centro Este, Isabela de Sagua, Cuba
Approach: Through channel from outward to inward by stages. Bottom is sandy and coral reef, hard rock, mud and clay. Turns not dangerous except in narrow portions where both the current and kind of bottom make them dangerous

Anchorage: Inner Anchorage No.1, located about 300 m NW from the piers. Max d allowed 7.31 to 7.62 m depending on vessels length. Vessels load or discharge at this anchorage by means of barges
Inner Anchorage No.2, located close to and S of Palomino Cay. Max d allowed is 4.57 m. Vessels load and discharge at this anchorage by means of barges, but it is chiefly used for vessels awaiting berth
Outer Anchorage, located E of Del Cristo Cay and about 8 miles from Isabela Vessels can load safely up to 10.06 m d with length of 190 m. Loading or discharging is effected by means of barges

Pilotage: Pilot boards vessel at about 1-2 miles from buoy No's 1 and 2 which mark the port entrance

Maximum Vessel Dimensions: Max drafts for vessels entering is 7.62 m. Vessels of length up to 180 m have entered this port. Vessels can usually enter or sail during daylight hours only

Principal Imports and Exports: Imports: Bagged fertiliser, Bagged malt, Bagged milk, General cargo. Exports: Bagged sugar, General cargo, Molasses.

Accommodation:

Name	Length (m)	Draught (m)	Remarks
Isabela de Sagua			
Amezaga Pier (SW side)	140	6.71	See [1] below
Alfert Pier (E side)	137	5.49–6.1	See [2] below
Begueristain Pier	165	4.88	See [3] below

[1]*Amezaga Pier (SW side):* Cargo handled includes general, bagged, raw & refined sugar
[2]*Alfert Pier (E side):* Cargo handled includes general, molasses & bagged sugar
[3]*Begueristain Pier:* This pier is out of service due to shallowness alongside

Bunkering: Small quantities of gas oil can be delivered by tank trucks when vessel is berthed at Amezaga Dock

Towage: Tugs available

Repair & Maintenance: Minor repairs only. Larger repairs at Sagua la Grande

Medical Facilities: Sagua la Grande Hospital

Lloyd's Agent: Marinter S.A., Edificio 'Playa', Calle 12, 105e/1ra y 3ra piso, Miramar, Havana, Cuba, *Tel:* +53 7 204 9742, *Fax:* +53 7 204 9743, *Email:* havana@marintercu.com, *Website:* www.cubaweb.cu/marintersa/marinter.html

JOSE ANTONIO ECHEVERRIA PIER

harbour area, see under Havana

JUAN MANUEL DIAZ

harbour area, see under Havana

JUCARO

Lat 21° 37' N; Long 78° 51' W.

Admiralty Chart: 3866	Admiralty Pilot: 70
Time Zone: GMT -5 h	UNCTAD Locode: CU JUC

Principal Facilities:

			G					T		

Authority: Empresa Terminales Mambisas del Centro Este, Jucaro, Cuba
Approach: Entrance through Breton Channel during day or night. Bottom is rocky sand and has no turns. Max d 8.84 m with no length limitations
Pilotage: Pilot boards vessel at entrance to Breton Channel in pos 21° 08' 18" N; 79° 30' 24" W
Working Hours: Mon to Sat 0600-1000, 1200-1600

Accommodation:

Name	Remarks
Jucaro	See [1] below

[1]*Jucaro:* All work takes place at anchorages
Anchorage No.1, located S of Obispo Cay, d of 7.32 m with no length limitations
Anchorage No.2, located SE of Obispo Cay, d of 8.23 m with no length limitations
Anchorage No.3, located 1 mile toward the E of No.2 anchorage, d of 9.14 m with no length limitations
All three anchorages handle the export of bagged refined sugar

Towage: Available from Authority
Medical Facilities: Two hospitals in the nearby city of Ciego de Avila

Lloyd's Agent: Marinter S.A., Edificio 'Playa', Calle 12, 105e/1ra y 3ra piso, Miramar, Havana, Cuba, *Tel:* +53 7 204 9742, *Fax:* +53 7 204 9743, *Email:* havana@marintercu.com, *Website:* www.cubaweb.cu/marintersa/marinter.html

LUIS F. MENA GIL DOCK

harbour area, see under Santiago

MANATI

Lat 21° 22' N; Long 76° 49' W.

Admiralty Chart: -	**Admiralty Pilot:** 70
Time Zone: GMT -5 h	**UNCTAD Locode:** CU MNT

Principal Facilities:

	Q	Y	G				T	

Authority: Empresa Terminales Mambisas del Centro Este, Manati, Cuba

Approach: Entrance channel is narrow and deep with average depths from 15.24 to 18.29 m, with the exception of a pass near Carenero Shoal, where depth is 11.58 m at LT. It's bottom is irregular, part sandy

Accommodation:

Name	Remarks
Manati	See [1] below

[1]*Manati:* 'L' shaped pier, length 141.7 m. Pier has an east and west side but only the east side is used, max d 9.45 m. Railroad tracks of double standard and a single narrow gauge track. It is not possible to operate trucks at this pier. Port used for exports of sugar from the Argelia Libre sugar mill

Storage: There is only one warehouse, cap for storage of approx 100 000 bags of sugar

Towage: Available from Authority

Repair & Maintenance: Minor repairs only

Lloyd's Agent: Marinter S.A., Edificio 'Playa', Calle 12, 105e/1ra y 3ra piso, Miramar, Havana, Cuba, *Tel:* +53 7 204 9742, *Fax:* +53 7 204 9743, *Email:* havana@marintercu.com, *Website:* www.cubaweb.cu/marintersa/marinter.html

MANUEL PORTO DAPENA TERMINAL

harbour area, see under Havana

MANZANILLO

Lat 20° 21' N; Long 77° 7' W.

Admiralty Chart: -	**Admiralty Pilot:** 70
Time Zone: GMT -5 h	**UNCTAD Locode:** CU MZO

Principal Facilities:

P		Y	G				T	A

Authority: Empresa Terminales Mambisas del Oriente, Manzanillo, Cuba

Approach: Madrona Channel: This channel has sharp and narrow turns with soft mud bottom. Max draft for vessels entering channel 10.06 m. Vessels must await favourable tide. No tug boat necessary
Palomino Channel: Turns less difficult than Madrona Channel. Soft mud bottom, max 6.1 m d, no tug boat necessary. Vessels should enter and sail only during hours of daylight

Pilotage: Compulsory. Pilot taken on at Cape Cruz in pos 19° 49' 12" N; 77° 45' 12" W

Accommodation:

Name	Remarks
Manzanillo	See [1] below

[1]*Manzanillo:* All operations take place at anchorage using barges
Inner Anchorage No.1, located in pos 20° 21' 54" N; 77° 08' 24" W, length 180 m with d of 6.4 m. Cargoes handled are import of general cargo and export of bagged raw sugar
Outward Anchorage No.2, located in pos 20° 22' 36" N; 77° 08' 40" W, length 180 m with d of 8.53 m. Cargoes handled are import of general cargo and export of bagged raw sugar
Outward Anchorage No.3, located in pos 20° 23' 30" N; 77° 09' 18" W, length 180 m with d of 10.06 m. Cargoes handled are import of general cargo and export of bagged raw sugar
Tanker facilities: A submarine pipeline anchorage is situated in pos 20° 21' 12" N; 77° 10' 21" W about 3.2 km from shore. Vessels up to 8.5 m d are moored to four dolphins by Terminals Mambisas tugboats. Cargoes handled are discharge of kerosene, gasoline and diesel oil

Towage: Small tugs available

Repair & Maintenance: Minor repairs can be carried out. Mechanic and foundry shop

Medical Facilities: Manzanillo Hospital

Airport: Manzanillo

Lloyd's Agent: Marinter S.A., Edificio 'Playa', Calle 12, 105e/1ra y 3ra piso, Miramar, Havana, Cuba, *Tel:* +53 7 204 9742, *Fax:* +53 7 204 9743, *Email:* havana@marintercu.com, *Website:* www.cubaweb.cu/marintersa/marinter.html

MARGARITO IGLESIAS TERMINAL

harbour area, see under Havana

MARIEL

Lat 23° 1' N; Long 82° 45' W.

Admiralty Chart: 411	**Admiralty Pilot:** 70
Time Zone: GMT -5 h	**UNCTAD Locode:** CU MAR

Principal Facilities:

P		Y	G				T	

Authority: Empresa Terminales Mambisas del Mariel, Mariel, Cuba

Port Security: ISPS compliant

Approach: The entrance channel is approx 60 m wide and a max of 9.45 m d. Vessels can enter and sail day and night

Pilotage: Compulsory. Pilot boards vessel one mile off buoy No.1 which marks the port entrance

Working Hours: Mon to Sat 0700-1300, 1300-1900, 1900-0100

Accommodation:

Name	Length (m)	Draught (m)
Mariel		
Sugar Bulk Terminal	178	8.53–9.14
Andres Gonzalez Lines Dock	170	8.53
Rene Arcay Pier (north side)	109	7.92
Osvaldo Sanchez Pier (west side)	170	8.53
Osvaldo Sanchez Pier (east side)	170	7.62–8.23
General Cargo Pier	170	8.53

Towage: Available

Lloyd's Agent: Marinter S.A., Edificio 'Playa', Calle 12, 105e/1ra y 3ra piso, Miramar, Havana, Cuba, *Tel:* +53 7 204 9742, *Fax:* +53 7 204 9743, *Email:* havana@marintercu.com, *Website:* www.cubaweb.cu/marintersa/marinter.html

Key to Principal Facilities:—			
A=Airport	**C**=Containers	**G**=General Cargo	**P**=Petroleum	**R**=Ro/Ro	**Y**=Dry Bulk
B=Bunkers	**D**=Dry Dock	**L**=Cruise	**Q**=Other Liquid Bulk	**T**=Towage (where available from port)	

MATANZAS

Lat 23° 3' N; Long 81° 34' W.

Admiralty Chart: 411

Admiralty Pilot: 70

Time Zone: GMT -5 h

UNCTAD Locode: CU QMA

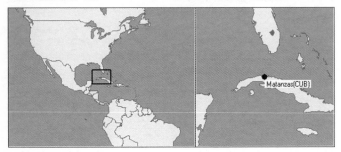

Principal Facilities:

Q	Y	G							

Authority: Empresa Terminales Mambisas de Matanzas, Matanzas, Cuba

Port Security: ISPS compliant

Approach: North channel 15.2 m max depth with a muddy bottom; South Channel 24.4 m max depth with a rocky bottom; Centre Channel is seldom used as has only 9.14 m max d. Vessels of any draft can enter the ample anchorages in Matanzas Bay

Pilotage: Pilot boards vessel approx 2.5 miles after the port mouth is sailed past, in front of the first port pier

Accommodation:

Name	Length (m)	Draught (m)	Remarks
Matanzas			See [1] below
Jesus Menendez Pier	242	8.5	See [2] below
Frank Pais Pier	162	6.4	See [3] below
Reynold Garcia Pier (north side)	170	10.4	See [4] below
Reynold Garcia Pier (south side)	212	11.6	Cargo handled includes the export of bulk raw sugar, dextrana and rayon
Morales Bayona Pier	180	11	See [5] below
Jose Luis Dubrocq Pier			
Berth No.1	152	9.75	See [6] below
Berth No.2	152	8.8	Cargoes handled similar to No.1 berth

[1]*Matanzas:* Five separate berthing installations, all located on the NW shore bay
[2]*Jesus Menendez Pier:* Presently no operations are performed at this pier due to the bad conditions of its solid dolphins
[3]*Frank Pais Pier:* Only the SW side is used. Cargo handled includes discharge of fuel and diesel oil, gasoline and kerosene
[4]*Reynold Garcia Pier (north side):* Cargo handled includes the import of dry cargo and export of bagged refined sugar, dextrana, licors etc
[5]*Morales Bayona Pier:* At this installation tanker vessels berth to two solid dolphins and two mooring buoys fore and aft. Cargo handled includes export of molasses and alcohol
[6]*Berth No.1:* Four overhead cranes for discharging of bulk fertilisers. Cargo handled includes import of general cargo, bulk fertilisers, bagged cargoes, lumber and export of general cargo

Repair & Maintenance: Minor repairs

Medical Facilities: Matanzas Civil Hospital

Lloyd's Agent: Marinter S.A., Edificio 'Playa', Calle 12, 105e/1ra y 3ra piso, Miramar, Havana, Cuba, *Tel:* +53 7 204 9742, *Fax:* +53 7 204 9743, *Email:* havana@marintercu.com, *Website:* www.cubaweb.cu/marintersa/marinter.html

MOA

alternate name, see Cayo Moa

NICARO

Lat 20° 43' N; Long 75° 33' W.

Admiralty Chart: -

Admiralty Pilot: 70

Time Zone: GMT -5 h

UNCTAD Locode: CU ICR

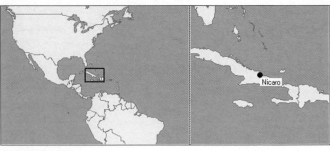

Principal Facilities:

		G						A	

Authority: Port Authority of Nicaro, Ministerio del Transporte, Havana, Cuba

Approach: The entrance to Nicaro is risky for vessels over 107 m due to narrowness and sharp turns, some of nearly 90°. Vessels of this length, up to max allowed of 156 m require tug assistance and all vessels should enter or sail during daylight hours

Anchorage: No.1 located about 1200 m SW of Point Gorda with d of 9.14 m. No.2 located about 1000 m NE of pier head with d of 9.14 m

Accommodation:

Name	Length (m)	Draught (m)	Remarks
Nicaro			
Nicaro Pier (north side)	156	9.14	See [1] below
Nicaro Pier (south side)	156	6.71–9.14	See [2] below

[1]*Nicaro Pier (north side):* Cargo handled includes general cargo, fuel oil, diesel oil and liquid ammonia
[2]*Nicaro Pier (south side):* Cargo handled includes anthracite coal, nickel and general cargo

Medical Facilities: Nicaro Hospital

Airport: Nicaro Airport

Lloyd's Agent: Marinter S.A., Edificio 'Playa', Calle 12, 105e/1ra y 3ra piso, Miramar, Havana, Cuba, *Tel:* +53 7 204 9742, *Fax:* +53 7 204 9743, *Email:* havana@marintercu.com, *Website:* www.cubaweb.cu/marintersa/marinter.html

NICO LOPEZ OIL TERMINAL

harbour area, see under Havana

NUEVA GERONA

Lat 21° 55' N; Long 82° 46' W.

Admiralty Chart: 3867

Admiralty Pilot: 70

Time Zone: GMT -5 h

UNCTAD Locode: CU GER

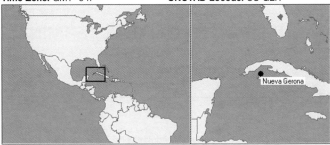

Principal Facilities:

		G					A	

Authority: Port Authority of Nuevo Gerona, Ministerio del Transporte, Isla de Pinoa, Nueva Gerona, Cuba

Approach: Entrance is from the Batabano Gulf; the channel can take vessels up to 5.64 m d

Anchorage: Anchorage can be obtained off the mouth of the Las Casas River in a depth of 6.7 m

Pilotage: Compulsory. Pilot boards at Punta Frances, off the W coast of Isla de Pinos. Entry or sailing can be performed day or night. Advance notice of ETA is advisable to all authorities and agents

Tides: Range of tide 0.3 m

Accommodation:

Name	Remarks
Nueva Gerona	See [1] below

[1]*Nueva Gerona:* Main Pier 61 m long accommodating vessels up to 90 m loa, 4.5 m d; used for loading fruit. Larger vessels can be loaded at the anchorage; two barges and one small tug are available for this purpose
There are other small wharves with depths alongside of 2.7 m. Daily ferry service to Surgidero de Batabano on the S coast of the mainland, where there are road and rail connections to Havana

Medical Facilities: Hospital in the town

Airport: Rafael Perez Airport

Lloyd's Agent: Marinter S.A., Edificio 'Playa', Calle 12, 105e/1ra y 3ra piso, Miramar, Havana, Cuba, *Tel:* +53 7 204 9742, *Fax:* +53 7 204 9743, *Email:* havana@marintercu.com, *Website:* www.cubaweb.cu/marintersa/marinter.html

NUEVITAS

Lat 21° 33' N; Long 77° 16' W.

Admiralty Chart: -	**Admiralty Pilot:** 70
Time Zone: GMT -5 h	**UNCTAD Locode:** CU NVT

Principal Facilities:

P	Q	Y	G			B		T	A	

Authority: Empresa Terminales Mambisas del Centro Este, Nuevitas, Cuba

Approach: The entrance is through a narrow and crooked channel between Point Sotavento and Practicos, 11.2 km long. Vessels may safely use it but great care has to be taken due to the narrowness and sharp turns of the entrance and the velocity of the tidal currents

Anchorage: There are ample anchorage zones close to the place of operations where vessels have a good swing area. Anchorages are used as waiting places when piers are occupied, although occasionally loading or discharging operations are performed

Pilotage: The pilot boards vessel in the vicinity of Point Practicos at about one mile N of buoy No.1 which marks the port entrance

Maximum Vessel Dimensions: Max draft with which vessels can enter and sail is up to 10.39 m with max length of 195 m

Working Hours: Mon to Sat 0700-1300, 1300-1900

Accommodation:

Name	Length (m)	Draught (m)	Remarks
Pastelillo Pier			Vessels can be supplied with fuel and diesel oil at this pier
North Side	188	10.06	Used for sugar & general cargo
South Side	174	10.06	Used by tankers, apart from those using naphta
Cement Dock			See [1] below
Bufadero Pier			See [2] below
Tarafa			See [3] below
Pier B (North Side)	146	6.4–7.92	
Pier B (South Side)	146	6.1–7.92	
Pier C (North West Side)	133	7.92–8.23	
Pier C (South East Side)	133	7.62–7.92	
Pier D (North West Side)	234	8.23	
Pier D (South Side)	180	6.1–8.23	

[1]*Cement Dock:* Length 84 m with draft even keel of 6.1 m. Bulk cement is shipped by means of a pneumatic system
[2]*Bufadero Pier:* This concrete pier is used only by tanker vessels up to 110 m in length for discharging liquid asphalt. Only the S side of the pier is used
[3]*Tarafa:* This terminal consists of three solid concrete piers each with railroad sidings connected with main track. Cargo handled includes general cargo, machinery, fresh and canned fruits, cement, bagged cargo and sugar etc

Bunkering: Fuel oil is available only at Pastelillo Pier if advance notice is given

Towage: Available from Port Authority

Repair & Maintenance: There is a repair shop available

Medical Facilities: Nuevitas Regional Hospital

Airport: Camaguey, 79 km

Lloyd's Agent: Marinter S.A., Edificio 'Playa', Calle 12, 105e/1ra y 3ra piso, Miramar, Havana, Cuba, *Tel:* +53 7 204 9742, *Fax:* +53 7 204 9743, *Email:* havana@marintercu.com, *Website:* www.cubaweb.cu/marintersa/marinter.html

OSVALDO SANCHEZ DOCKS

harbour area, see under Havana

PASTELILLO PIER

harbour area, see under Nuevitas

PRESTON

harbour area, see under Antilla

PUERTO CARUPANO

harbour area, see under Puerto Padre

PUERTO PADRE

Lat 21° 17' N; Long 76° 32' W.

Admiralty Chart: -	**Admiralty Pilot:** 70
Time Zone: GMT -5 h	**UNCTAD Locode:** CU PPA

Principal Facilities:

P	Q		G							

Authority: Empresa Terminales Mambisas del Centro Este, Puerto Padre, Cuba

Approach: The entrance channel is funnel shaped at mouth; it has two turns, but the one to take into consideration when manoeuvring vessels over 160 m is 'Carenero' turn although vessels with a length of 172.2 m have entered this port. Entrance marked by No's 1 and 2 buoys; length of channel about 7.2 km up to main anchorage. Width of channel 219.4 m max, 137.2 m min. Depth on bar 8.23 m. The bottom is rocky in entrance channel and muddy in the bay. Owing to current in channel vessels must await slack water for entering and sailing

Pilotage: Pilot boards vessel at not less than one mile off buoy No.1 at the entrance to the port in pos 21° 16' 42" N; 76° 32' 42" W

Maximum Vessel Dimensions: Max length is 170 m. Vessels up to 168 m can enter or sail at all times and have a max draft of 7.6 m; vessels over 168 m have a max draft of 7.3 m and must enter or sail in daylight

Accommodation:

Name	Length (m)	Draught (m)	Remarks
Puerto Carupano			See [1] below
Pier No.1	159	8.53	See [2] below
Pier No.2	170	9.14	See [3] below
Pier No.3	183	9.14	See [4] below

[1]*Puerto Carupano:* Loading and/or discharging operations are carried out at Puerto Carupano (Cayo Juan Claro) approx 3 miles from Puerto Padre
[2]*Pier No.1:* Cargo handled includes import and export of general cargo
[3]*Pier No.2:* Cargo handled includes the export of molasses and alcohol and the import of fuel oil
[4]*Pier No.3:* Cargo handled at this pier is the export of bulk raw sugar by mechanical means

Cargo Worked: Molasses average pumping rate 50 000 gall/h. Fuel oil discharging rate 45 000 gall/h. Gas oil discharging rate 35 000 gall/h

Repair & Maintenance: No repair shop but in case of winch damage or any other light repairs, work can be carried out at the Sugar Mill 'Central Antonio Guiteras' repair shop

Medical Facilities: Puerto Padre Municipal Hospital

Lloyd's Agent: Marinter S.A., Edificio 'Playa', Calle 12, 105e/1ra y 3ra piso, Miramar, Havana, Cuba, *Tel:* +53 7 204 9742, *Fax:* +53 7 204 9743, *Email:* havana@marintercu.com, *Website:* www.cubaweb.cu/marintersa/marinter.html

PUNTA GORDA

harbour area, see under Nuevitas

ROLANDO ROCA PACHECO PIER

harbour area, see under Santiago

ROMERO PIER

harbour area, see under Santiago

Key to Principal Facilities:—				
A=Airport	**C**=Containers	**G**=General Cargo	**P**=Petroleum	**R**=Ro/Ro	**Y**=Dry Bulk
B=Bunkers	**D**=Dry Dock	**L**=Cruise	**Q**=Other Liquid Bulk	**T**=Towage (where available from port)

SANTA LUCIA

Lat 22° 41' N; Long 83° 58' W.

Admiralty Chart: 1217
Admiralty Pilot: 70
Time Zone: GMT -5 h
UNCTAD Locode: CU

Principal Facilities:

		Y						T		

Authority: Empresa Terminales Mambisas del Mariel, Santa Lucia Port Authority, Empresa Terminales, Mambisas D Mariel, Mariel, Cuba

Approach: Anchorage port. Entrance to the onshore port facilities and the smaller anchorages is through the Pasa Honda Channel which is 200 m wide; least depth over bar of 5.2 m. The channel is marked by light buoys and contains two bends with dangerous narrows. Channel to lighter wharf is 50 m wide with a least depth of 4.9 m

Pilotage: Compulsory. Pilot arranged through Mariel with advance notice and will board off Pasa Honda. Channel navigated during daylight hours only

Tides: Range of tide 0.45 m

Accommodation:

Name	Remarks
Santa Lucia	See [1] below

[1]*Santa Lucia:* Three designated anchorage berths for loading copper mineral and the discharge of sulphur in bulk
Anchorage No.1 (La Poza): Length 140 m with d of 4.72 m. Anchorage No.2 (El Quebrado): Length 140 m with d of 5.49 m. Anchorage No.3 (Open Sea): Length is unlimited with d of 8.84 m
Patricio Lumumba Pier: Length 85 m with d of 4.72 m

Towage: One tug available

Medical Facilities: Clinic available in the town. Hospital at Pinar del Rio

Lloyd's Agent: Marinter S.A., Edificio 'Playa', Calle 12, 105e/1ra y 3ra piso, Miramar, Havana, Cuba, *Tel:* +53 7 204 9742, *Fax:* +53 7 204 9743, *Email:* havana@marintercu.com, *Website:* www.cubaweb.cu/marintersa/marinter.html

SANTIAGO

Lat 20° 1' N; Long 75° 49' W.

Admiralty Chart: 443
Admiralty Pilot: 70
Time Zone: GMT -5 h
UNCTAD Locode: CU SCU

Principal Facilities:

P	Q	Y	G				B		T	A

Authority: Empresa Terminales Mambisas del Oriente, Santiago de Cuba, Cuba

Approach: The entrance to the port and the channel itself is narrow with some turns

Anchorage: Inner Anchorage: Located from the N of Ratones Cay up to the W of buoy No.20. Can accommodate vessels up to 214 m in length and 9.14 m draft
Outer Anchorage: Located W of Punta Gorda and just in front of refinery piers. Can accommodate vessels up to 214 m in length and 10.97 m draft and is used mainly by tankers

Pilotage: Pilot boards vessel one mile off the port mouth

Maximum Vessel Dimensions: Vessels up to 214 m, with 10.9 m draft can enter during the morning, with vessels up to 183 m at other times

Working Hours: Mon to Sat 0700-1300, 1300-1900

Accommodation:

Name	Length (m)	Draught (m)	Remarks
Luis F. Mena Gil Dock			
East Berth	145	6.71	See [1] below

Name	Length (m)	Draught (m)	Remarks
Centre Berth	145	8.69	See [2] below
West Berth	100	7.01	See [3] below
West Extreme Berth	140	6.1–7.01	Cargo handled includes general cargo and cement
30 de Noviembre Dock			See [4] below
Berth No.3	163	7.92	
Berth No.4	163	8.23	
Rolando Roca Pacheco Pier			
North Side	160	8.69	General cargo
South Side	160	8.69	General cargo
Romero Pier			
East Side	100	4.57–5.18	See [5] below
West Side	100	5.79–6.4	See [6] below
Antonio Maceo Dock			See [7] below
South Side	221	9.14	
North Side			See [8] below
Fabrica de Cemento Dock			See [9] below
Refinery Hermanos Diaz Pier			Length 214 m with draft of 10.97 m. Used for discharge of oil
Frank Pais Pier			See [10] below

[1]*East Berth:* Cargo handled includes light general cargo, molasses and petroleum sub-products
[2]*Centre Berth:* Cargo handled includes bagged raw sugar, general and heavy cargo
[3]*West Berth:* Cargo handled includes bagged raw sugar, general cargo and sometimes lubricating oil
[4]*30 de Noviembre Dock:* Operations can only be effected during daylight hours
[5]*East Side:* Cargo handled includes general cargo, bagged cement and refrigerated cargo
[6]*West Side:* Cargo handled includes general cargo, bagged cement and refrigerated cargo
[7]*Antonio Maceo Dock:* Located in front of a modern cold storage house which makes it appropriate for operating refrigerated vessels loading frozen fish
[8]*North Side:* At present not in operation as draft work has not yet finished
[9]*Fabrica de Cemento Dock:* Used only for loading cement and all operations are performed by trucks. Due to bad condition of dock vessels are not permitted to berth alongside
[10]*Frank Pais Pier:* Vessels berth to eight solid buoys for discharge of bulk grain. No limitation on vessel length but draft up to 9.1 m max. Cap of silos 8200 t. Conveyor and pipeline available

Mechanical Handling Equipment:

Location	Type	Capacity (t)	Qty
Santiago	Floating Cranes	35	1
Santiago	Mult-purp. Cranes	16	10

Bunkering: Empresa Consignataria Mambisa (ECM), Payret Building, No. 65 San Jose Street, P O Box 174, Havana, Cuba, *Tel:* +53 7 862 7138, *Fax:* +53 7 833 8111, *Email:* ecm@mambisa.transnet.cu – *Grades:* FO; MDO – *Delivery Mode:* barge, pipeline

Towage: Available from Port Authority

Repair & Maintenance: Damex Shipbuilding & Engineering, Km 7.5, Carretera de Punta Gorda, Santiago de Cuba, Cuba, *Tel:* +53 22 686101, *Fax:* +53 22 688101, *Email:* damex@damex.ciges.inf.cu, *Website:* www.damex.biz

Medical Facilities: Santiago Provincial Hospital

Airport: Santiago de Cuba, 3 km

Lloyd's Agent: Marinter S.A., Edificio 'Playa', Calle 12, 105e/1ra y 3ra piso, Miramar, Havana, Cuba, *Tel:* +53 7 204 9742, *Fax:* +53 7 204 9743, *Email:* havana@marintercu.com, *Website:* www.cubaweb.cu/marintersa/marinter.html

SIERRA MAESTRA TERMINAL

harbour area, see under Havana

TANAMO

Lat 20° 42' N; Long 75° 20' W.

Admiralty Chart: -
Admiralty Pilot: 70
Time Zone: GMT -5 h
UNCTAD Locode: CU TAN

Principal Facilities:

			G							A	

Authority: Empresa Terminales Mambisas de Antilla, Tanamo, Cuba

Approach: The entrance channel is shaped like an 'S' with rocky and muddy bottoms in many parts. There are 90° turns. Also narrow and dangerous parts

Pilotage: Pilot boards vessel about one mile off the port entrance

Maximum Vessel Dimensions: Max length 180 m with max draft of 10.67 m. Vessels over 157.2 m length require the assistance of a tugboat for entering/sailing manoeuvres

Accommodation:

Name	Length (m)	Draught (m)	Remarks
Punta Gorda Pier			See [1] below
North Side	157	4.17–6.1	
South Side	157	5.79–6.71	

[1]*Punta Gorda Pier:* Cargo handled includes the export of raw sugar, refined sugar and molasses

Airport: Cayo Mambi

Lloyd's Agent: Marinter S.A., Edificio 'Playa', Calle 12, 105e/1ra y 3ra piso, Miramar, Havana, Cuba, *Tel:* +53 7 204 9742, *Fax:* +53 7 204 9743, *Email:* havana@marintercu.com, *Website:* www.cubaweb.cu/marintersa/marinter.html

TARAFA

harbour area, see under Nuevitas

VITA

Lat 21° 5' N; Long 75° 57' W.

Admiralty Chart: 3865
Admiralty Pilot: 70
Time Zone: GMT -5 h
UNCTAD Locode: CU VIT

Principal Facilities:

P	Q		G							

Authority: Empresa Terminales Mambisas de Antilla, Vita, Cuba

Approach: Entry to the bay is through a narrow channel. Vessels over 130 m in length require the assistance of a tug

Anchorage: Vita anchorage is located about 190 m from the pier. Recommended only to medium sized vessels as insufficient swinging area

Pilotage: Compulsory. Pilot boards 3 miles from entrance channel; entry and sailing during daylight hours only

Weather: Strong N winds can make entry difficult

Principal Imports and Exports: Imports: Bagged fertiliser, Jute bales. Exports: Bagged raw sugar, Molasses.

Accommodation:

Name	Remarks
Vita Pier (North Side)	See [1] below

[1]*Vita Pier (North Side):* Length 150 m with draft even keel of 7.92 m. Cargo handled includes export of bagged raw sugar and molasses

Medical Facilities: Hospital at Santa Lucia

Lloyd's Agent: Marinter S.A., Edificio 'Playa', Calle 12, 105e/1ra y 3ra piso, Miramar, Havana, Cuba, *Tel:* +53 7 204 9742, *Fax:* +53 7 204 9743, *Email:* havana@marintercu.com, *Website:* www.cubaweb.cu/marintersa/marinter.html

CYPRUS

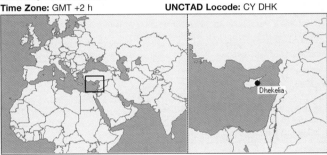

Christodoulos G. Vassiliades & Co
Advocates-Legal Consultants

Ledra House, 15 Agiou Pavlou Street
Agios Andreas, 1105 Nicosia, Cyprus

Mailing Address:
P.O. Box 24444, 1703 Nicosia, Cyprus

Tel: 357-22556677
Fax: 357-22556688
E-mail: info@vasslaw.com
Website: www.vasslaw.com

DHEKELIA

Lat 34° 59' N; Long 33° 44' E.

Admiralty Chart: 850/851
Admiralty Pilot: 49
Time Zone: GMT +2 h
UNCTAD Locode: CY DHK

Principal Facilities:

P								T	A

Authority: Electricity Authority of Cyprus, 15 Foti Pitta Street, P O Box 24506, Lefkosia 1399, Cyprus, *Tel:* +357 2284 5000, *Fax:* +357 2276 0735, *Email:* eac@eac.com.cy, *Website:* www.eac.com.cy

Port Security: ISPS compliant

Documentation: Crew list, vessel's particulars, cargo declaration

Pilotage: Compulsory. Pilot available through the harbour master at Larnaca

Accommodation:

Name	Depth (m)	Remarks
Dhekelia		
Fuel Oil Berth	14	See [1] below

[1]*Fuel Oil Berth:* Open roadstead. Heavy fuel oil for vessels up to 225 m loa and 12.5 m draught. A submarine pipeline 651 m x 12 inch extends from the shore from power station 'B'

Towage: Available

Medical Facilities: Hospital facilities available

Airport: Larnaca Airport, 20 km

Lloyd's Agent: Orphanides & Murat Ltd, P O Box 71200, Limassol 3841, Cyprus, *Tel:* +357 2556 6099, *Fax:* +357 2556 1231, *Email:* rotacy@globalsoftmail.com, *Website:* www.orphanidesandmurat.com

FAMAGUSTA

Lat 35° 7' N; Long 33° 56' E.

Admiralty Chart: 848
Admiralty Pilot: 49
Time Zone: GMT +2 h
UNCTAD Locode: CY FMG

Key to Principal Facilities:—				
A=Airport	**C**=Containers	**G**=General Cargo	**P**=Petroleum	**R**=Ro/Ro	**Y**=Dry Bulk
B=Bunkers	**D**=Dry Dock	**L**=Cruise	**Q**=Other Liquid Bulk	**T**=Towage (where available from port)	

Principal Facilities:

| P | Q | Y | G | C | R | | | T | A |

Authority: Department of Ports, Ministry of Communications & Works, Famagusta, 10 Mersin, Turkey, *Tel:* +90 392 366 2627, *Fax:* +90 392 366 6465

Pre-Arrival Information: Master's to cable ETA 24 h before arrival to agents

Approach: Approach channel to outer harbour 10.3 m deep and mean width at entrance 183.87 m

Anchorage: Outer anchorage has a depth of 11 to 15 m

Pilotage: Compulsory for vessels over 300 gt. Four pilots available. Call pilots on VHF Channel 16 during normal working hours

Radio Frequency: Northern Cyprus Radio on VHF Channel 16 during office hours

Weather: Occasional storms mainly from the NE, E and SE

Tides: Range of tide 0.45 m

Maximum Vessel Dimensions: Outer Harbour: 220 m loa (130 m loa for ro/ro vessels), 9.15 m draught
Inner Harbour: 110 m loa, 6.7 m draught

Principal Imports and Exports: Imports: Foodstuffs, General cargo, Oil. Exports: Citrus fruit, Household goods, Manufactured goods, Potatoes, Textiles.

Working Hours: 0800-1200, 1300-1700, 1800-2300

Accommodation:

Name	Length (m)	Depth (m)	Remarks
Famagusta			
Outer Harbour	655	9.75	See [1] below
			Anchorage for vessels having up to 6.7 m draught
Inner Harbour	540	7.3	See [2] below

[1]*Famagusta:* Containers can be handled at the general cargo berths. Ro/ro vessels with stern or side doors can be accommodated
Bulk facilities: Vessels up to 3000 dwt discharged with mobile grab cranes. Two pneumatic conveyors of 60 t/h cap also available
Tanker facilities: Pumping arrangements at No.1 Berth, Outer Harbour
[2]*Inner Harbour:* Anchorage suitable for small vessels only, max depth 3.5 m

Storage:

Location	Open (m²)	Covered (m²)
Outer Harbour	33220	9189
Inner Harbour	1025	8726

Mechanical Handling Equipment:

Location	Type	Capacity (t)	Qty
Famagusta	Floating Cranes	60	1
Famagusta	Mult-purp. Cranes	36	1
Famagusta	Mobile Cranes	5	7
Famagusta	Mobile Cranes	10	7
Famagusta	Mobile Cranes	17	7
Famagusta	Container Cranes	36	1
Famagusta	Forklifts	40	

Cargo Worked: 3000-5000 t/day

Towage: Four tugs available of 1200, 600, 410 and 150 hp respectively. One fitted with fire fighting equipment

Repair & Maintenance: Minor repairs may be effected. Two small slipways available for vessels up to 600 t

Shipping Agents: A&S Atun Group, 24 Istiklal Caddesi, Famagusta, P O Box 81, 10 Mersin, Turkey, *Tel:* +90 392 366 5322, *Fax:* +90 392 366 3988, *Email:* info@atun.com, *Website:* www.atun.com

Medical Facilities: It is advisable to include in ETA message to agents whether any medical attention is required. Hospital and private clinic facilities available

Airport: Ercan, 53 km

Lloyd's Agent: Catoni Persa Supervision Expertise and Controlling S.A., Gundogdu Mahallesi 5786, Sokak No.2, 33040 Mersin, Turkey, *Tel:* +90 324 234 9595, *Fax:* +90 324 234 9596, *Email:* cpmersin@catonipersa.com.tr

KALECIK

Lat 35° 19' N; Long 33° 59' E.

Admiralty Chart: -	**Admiralty Pilot:** 49
Time Zone: GMT +2 h	**UNCTAD Locode:** CY KAL

Principal Facilities:

| P | | Y | G | | | | | T | A |

Authority: Department of Ports, Ministry of Communications & Works, Famagusta, 10 Mersin, Turkey, *Tel:* +90 392 366 2627, *Fax:* +90 392 366 6465

Pre-Arrival Information: Master's to cable ETA 24 h before arrival to agents

Approach: No hazards or sand bars exist in the approach. Vessels can enter from either direction

Anchorage: Anywhere within the limits of Gastria Bay

Pilotage: Not compulsory

Radio Frequency: Northern Cyprus Radio on VHF Channel 16 during office hours

Weather: Occasional storms mainly from the NE, E and SE

Tides: Range of tide 0.45 m

Maximum Vessel Dimensions: 80-90 m loa, 8 m draught

Accommodation:

Name	Length (m)	Depth (m)	Remarks
Kalecik			
Pier	42	6	See [1] below
Tanker terminal			See [2] below

[1]*Pier:* Installation suitable for loading/unloading of bulk and bagged cargoes at max rate of 250 t/h
[2]*Tanker terminal:* Tanker terminal with underwater pipelines extending 410 m into the sea, operated by Cyprus Turkish Petroleum Products Co Ltd
Second tanker terminal with underwater pipelines extending 500 m into the sea, operated by Altinbas Petroleum Co Ltd

Cargo Worked: Tankers 1000 t/shift, conveyor 250 t/h

Towage: Not available. Tugs from Famagusta if required

Medical Facilities: It is advisable to include in ETA message to agents whether any medical attention is required. Hospital and private clinic facilities available

Airport: Ercan, 73 km

Lloyd's Agent: Catoni Persa Supervision Expertise and Controlling S.A., Gundogdu Mahallesi 5786, Sokak No.2, 33040 Mersin, Turkey, *Tel:* +90 324 234 9595, *Fax:* +90 324 234 9596, *Email:* cpmersin@catonipersa.com.tr

KARAVOSTASSI

Lat 35° 8' N; Long 32° 49' E.

UNCTAD Locode: CY KAR

This port is no longer open to commercial shipping

KYRENIA

Lat 35° 20' N; Long 33° 19' E.

Admiralty Chart: 849	**Admiralty Pilot:** 49
Time Zone: GMT +2 h	**UNCTAD Locode:** CY KYR

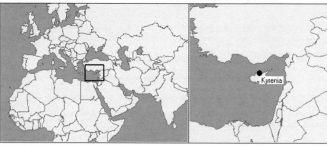

Principal Facilities:

| | | G | | R | | B | | T | A |

Authority: Department of Ports, Ministry of Communications & Works, Famagusta, 10 Mersin, Turkey, *Tel:* +90 392 366 2627, *Fax:* +90 392 366 6465

Approach: Port entrance has a width of 180 m in depth of 5.5 m

Pilotage: Compulsory for vessels over 300 gt. Pilot maintains watch on VHF Channel 16 during working hours

Radio Frequency: Northern Cyprus Radio, VHF Channel 16 during official working hours

Weather: Occasional storms mainly from the N, NW, NE and E

Tides: Range of tide 0.45 m

Traffic: Approx 3100 vessels and over 320 000 passengers annually

Maximum Vessel Dimensions: 110 m loa, 5.5 m draught

Working Hours: Winter 0800-1200, 1300-1700. Summer 0730-1400 except Mondays which are 0730-1400, 1530-1700 (Outside these hours with prior notice to pilot)

Accommodation:

Name	Length (m)	Depth (m)	Remarks
Kyrenia			
Tourism Harbour (New Port)	707	3–8	Eight quays for passenger, ferries & ro/ro vessels

Bunkering: Supplied by the Cyprus Turkish Petroleum Co Ltd from road tankers

Towage: Two tugs of 150 hp and 350 hp

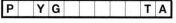

Repair & Maintenance: Minor deck and engine repairs can be carried out at local workshops or at Gemyat Delta Marina

Medical Facilities: State hospital within 5 mins drive

Airport: Ercan, 37 km

Lloyd's Agent: Catoni Persa Supervision Expertise and Controlling S.A., Gundogdu Mahallesi 5786, Sokak No.2, 33040 Mersin, Turkey, *Tel:* +90 324 234 9595, *Fax:* +90 324 234 9596, *Email:* cpmersin@catonipersa.com.tr

LARNACA

Lat 34° 55' N; Long 33° 38' E.

Admiralty Chart: 848
Time Zone: GMT +2 h

Admiralty Pilot: 49
UNCTAD Locode: CY LCA

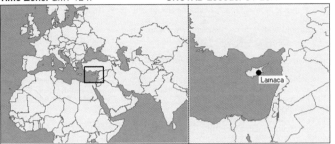

Principal Facilities:

| P | Q | Y | G | C | R | L | B | | T | A |

Authority: Cyprus Ports Authority, P O Box 40290, Larnaca 6017, Cyprus, *Tel:* +357 2481 5225, *Fax:* +357 2463 5630, *Email:* laport@cpa.gov.cy, *Website:* www.cpa.gov.cy

Officials: Port Manager: Capt Pambis Vassiliou.

Port Security: ISPS compliant

Pre-Arrival Information: 24 h before arrival inform through agent: ETA, loa, max draft and cargo on board

Approach: Approach channel dredged to 13 m depth with a min width of 160 m

Anchorage: Anchorage is in an open roadstead with no draft limitation

Pilotage: Compulsory. Vessels are not allowed to enter the port or berth at the mooring buoys outside the breakwater unless permission is granted

Radio Frequency: VHF Channels 16 and 14

Weather: Prevailing winds E'ly in winter and SW'ly in summer. During the winter period winds may affect the anchorage area

Tides: 0.60 m is the max tide you can reach

Maximum Vessel Dimensions: 220 m loa, 11.4 m draught

Principal Imports and Exports: Imports: Bulk grain, Consumer goods, Fertilizer, General cargo, Iron, Timber. Exports: Gypsum stone, Potatoes.

Working Hours: 0730-2300. Container operations service on a 24 h basis

Accommodation:

Name	Length (m)	Depth (m)	Draught (m)	Remarks
Larnaca				
South Quay	340	12		General cargo & containers
North Quay	326	10		General cargo & containers
Oil Terminal				Mooring on buoys at open roadstead
C.P.R.L.	215		12.7	Oil tankers. Three buoys
Petrolina	200		12.5	Oil tankers. Two buoys
Mobil	150		9.5	Gas tankers. Three buoys
Synergas	140		8.5	Gas tankers. Three buoys
INTERGAZ	155		9	Gas tankers. Three buoys

Storage:

Location	Open (m²)	Covered (m²)	Sheds / Warehouses
Larnaca	150000	18000	3

Mechanical Handling Equipment:

Location	Type	Capacity (t)	Qty	Remarks
Larnaca	Mobile Cranes	40	1	can serve both quays
Larnaca	Forklifts	2–40	27	
South Quay	Panamax	40	2	
South Quay	Quay Cranes	45	1	
North Quay	Quay Cranes	35	1	

Bunkering: Petrolina Holdings Public Ltd, Petrolina Holdings Public Ltd, Lefkaritis House, 1 Kilkis Street, Larnaca 6015, Cyprus, *Tel:* +357 2484 8000, *Fax:* +357 2465 7173, *Email:* info@petrolina.com.cy, *Website:* www.petrolina.com.cy
Ajax Offshore Bunkering Services Ltd, 124 Ayias Paraskevis Street, Yermasoyia, P

O Box 54548, Limassol 3725, Cyprus, *Tel:* +357 25 899 000, *Fax:* +357 25 312 477, *Email:* bunkers@ajaxbunkering.com, *Website:* www.edtoffshore.com
BP Cyprus Ltd, 6 Ayios Procopios Street, P O Box 2441, Nicosia 1521, Cyprus, *Tel:* +357 22 0239 3166, *Fax:* +357 22 0278 1272 – *Grades:* IFO-180-380cSt – *Delivery Mode:* barge, pipeline, truck
ExxonMobil Marine Fuels, Mailpoint 31, ExxonMobil House, Ermyn Way, Leatherhead, Surrey KT22 8UX, United Kingdom, *Tel:* +44 1372 222 000, *Fax:* +44 1372 223 922, *Email:* marine.fuels@exxonmobil.com, *Website:* www.exxonmobil.com – *Grades:* IFO30-IF60, IF180cSt; MGO – *Delivery Mode:* truck
Island Oil Ltd, Island Oil Holdings Ltd, 145-149 Chr. Hadjipavlou Street, 2nd Floor Christiel Building, Limassol 3036, Cyprus, *Tel:* +357 2588 9000, *Fax:* +357 2574 5466, *Email:* bunkers@island-oil.com, *Website:* www.island-oil.com – *Grades:* IFO-180cSt; MGO; in line blending available – *Parcel Size:* no min – *Rates:* 150t/h – *Notice:* 24 hours – *Delivery Mode:* barge, truck
E.J. Papadakis Ltd, P O Box 50024, Limassol 3600, Cyprus, *Tel:* +357 2534 9000, *Fax:* +357 2534 9001, *Email:* papadaki@cytanet.com.cy – *Grades:* IFO60-180cSt; MGO – *Parcel Size:* min 15t, max 500t – *Rates:* 100t/h – *Notice:* 24 hours – *Delivery Mode:* barge, truck
Petrolina Ltd, Franglinou Roosevelt Avenue 126 B, P O Box 50042, Limassol 3600, Cyprus, *Tel:* +357 2536 2670, *Fax:* +357 2536 9060, *Email:* info@petrolina.com.cy – *Grades:* IFO-160cSt; MGO; in line blending available – *Parcel Size:* min 10t, max 350t – *Rates:* 40t/h – *Notice:* 24 hours – *Delivery Mode:* truck

Waste Reception Facilities: Garbage collection service is available

Towage: Three tugs available with bollard pull up to 35 t

Repair & Maintenance: Minor repairs only

Ship Chandlers: Loucas Kokkinos Ship Suppliers Ltd, 133A Franklin Roosevelt Avenue, Limassol 3508, Cyprus, *Tel:* +357 2556 7332, *Fax:* +357 2556 6154, *Email:* loukinos@globalsoftmail.com
E.A.P. Philiastides, Suite 402 4th Floor, 4 Cleovoulou Papakyriakou, Philikos Court, P O Box 40328, Larnaca 6303, Cyprus, *Tel:* +357 2466 2314, *Fax:* +357 2463 7915, *Email:* sales.eapmarine@cytanet.com.cy
Theseas Savva Ltd, 118 Franklin Roosevelt Avenue, P O Box 50114, Larnaca 3601, Cyprus, *Tel:* +357 2556 5899, *Fax:* +357 2556 2917, *Email:* theseas@cytanet.com.cy

Shipping Agents: Francoudi & Stephanou Ltd, 14B Makarios III Avenue, P O Box 40025, Larnaca 6300, Cyprus, *Tel:* +357 2465 2032, *Fax:* +357 2462 7794, *Email:* zedep@cytanet.com.cy, *Website:* www.francoudi.com Operations Manager: Antonakis Nicolaou
GAP Vassilopoulos Group, 17 Artemidos Avenue, Sonic House, P O Box 43014, Larnaca CY-6025, Cyprus, *Tel:* +357 2462 5610, *Fax:* +357 2462 5656, *Email:* info@gapgroup.com, *Website:* www.gapgroup.com

Medical Facilities: Larnaca General Hospital, 5 km

Airport: Larnaca International Airport, 7 km

Lloyd's Agent: Orphanides & Murat Ltd, P O Box 71200, Limassol 3841, Cyprus, *Tel:* +357 2556 6099, *Fax:* +357 2556 1231, *Email:* rotacy@globalsoftmail.com, *Website:* www.orphanidesandmurat.com

LIMASSOL

Lat 34° 39' N; Long 33° 0' E.

Admiralty Chart: 849
Time Zone: GMT +2 h

Admiralty Pilot: 49
UNCTAD Locode: CY LMS

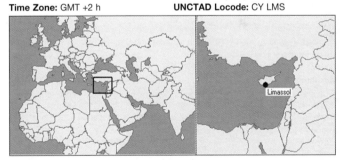

Principal Facilities:

| P | | Y | G | C | R | L | B | D | T | A |

Key to Principal Facilities:—
A=Airport **C**=Containers **G**=General Cargo **P**=Petroleum **R**=Ro/Ro **Y**=Dry Bulk
B=Bunkers **D**=Dry Dock **L**=Cruise **Q**=Other Liquid Bulk **T**=Towage (where available from port)

Authority: Cyprus Ports Authority, P O Box 53331, Limassol 3302, Cyprus, *Tel:* +357 2581 9200, *Fax:* +357 2556 6374, *Email:* limassol.port@cpa.gov.cy, *Website:* www.cpa.gov.cy

Officials: Port Manager: Capt Christos Matsis.

Port Security: ISPS compliant

Pre-Arrival Information: 24 h before arrival inform through agent: ETA, loa, max draft and cargo on board
Ship pre-arrival security information form to be sent 24 h prior to entry into the port

Documentation: Crew list (5 copies), passenger list (6 copies), maritime health declaration (1 copy), crew declaration (1 copy), stores list (1 copy), general declaration (1 copy)

Approach: Breakwater-sheltered port. Approach channel dredged to 15 m. There is a distance of 250 m between the ends of its breakwaters

Anchorage: Anchorage may be obtained 1 mile ENE from the south breakwater in depths of 10-75 m

Pilotage: Compulsory. Pilot boards vessel at least one nautical mile from the port entrance

Radio Frequency: VTS on VHF Channel 9 and pilots on VHF Channel 10

Weather: Prevailing winds WSW'ly in summer and E'ly in winter

Tides: Range of tide 0.6 m

Traffic: 2006, 4 317 000 t of cargo handled, 360 800 TEU's

Maximum Vessel Dimensions: 300 m loa, 13.5 m draught

Principal Imports and Exports: Imports: General cargo in containers, Grain, Iron, Timber. Exports: Citrus, Foodstuffs, General cargo in containers, Grapes.

Working Hours: 0730-2300. For container operations service on a 24 h basis

Accommodation: Cruise vessels may berth anywhere in the port
Conventional buoy berths for oil discharging at Moni (Electricity Authority of Cyprus), Moni Cement Plant and Akrotiri (BSBA)

Name	Length (m)	Depth (m)	Remarks
Multi-Purpose/Bulk Berths			
North Quay	430	11	
West Quay	450	11–13	
Container/RoRo Berths			
East Container Terminal	480	11	Terminal area of 22 ha
West Container Terminal	620	14	Terminal area of 23 ha
Ro/ro Berth	50	14	

Storage: Stacking area for containers of 345 000 m2 and container freight station of 35 800 m2

Location	Open (m²)	Covered (m²)	Cold (m³)
Limassol	158000	39760	72000

Mechanical Handling Equipment:

Location	Type	Capacity (t)	Qty
Limassol	Mobile Cranes	20–35	3
Limassol	Transtainers	40	4
Limassol	Straddle Carriers	40	7
Limassol	Forklifts	2.5–20	88
East Container Terminal	Gantry Cranes	40	2

Location	Type	Capacity (t)	Qty
West Container Terminal	Panamax	40	2
West Container Terminal	Post Panamax	45	2

Bunkering: Ajax Offshore Bunkering Services Ltd, 124 Ayias Paraskevis Street, Yermasoyia, P O Box 54548, Limassol 3725, Cyprus, *Tel:* +357 25 899 000, *Fax:* +357 25 312 477, *Email:* bunkers@ajaxbunkering.com, *Website:* www.edtoffshore.com
Albo Shipping Ltd, 81 Omonias Avenue, M&A House, 4th Floor, Office 42, P O Box 58324, Limassol 3733, Cyprus, *Tel:* +357 2556 5245, *Fax:* +357 2556 5329, *Email:* alboship@logos.cy.net
Bunkernet Ltd, 6 Evagoras Papachristophorou Street, P O Box 59649, Limassol CY 4011, Cyprus, *Tel:* +357 25 828915, *Fax:* +357 25 342213, *Email:* sales@bunkernet.com.cy, *Website:* www.bunkernet.com.cy
DalcyOil Ltd, P O Box 53672, Limassol 3317, Cyprus, *Tel:* +357 25 585121, *Fax:* +357 25 590338, *Email:* dalcy.c@brand9.com
DAP Shipping Agency Ltd, 51 Stingos Street, P O Box 7181, Limassol CY - 3313, Cyprus, *Tel:* +357 2557 1888, *Fax:* +357 2557 3397, *Email:* dapcy@spidernet.com.cy, *Website:* www.dap.com.cy
Enoil Ltd, Iris House, 8 John Kennedy Street, Kanika Enaerios Complex, Limassol 3772, Cyprus, *Tel:* +357 25 585 615, *Fax:* +357 25 581 614
Evrasia Bunker Ltd, Corner Spyrou Araouzou and Koumandarias Street, Tonia II Court, 4th Floor Office 4B, Limassol 3036, Cyprus, *Tel:* +357 2576 0376, *Fax:* +357 2534 1803, *Email:* info@evrasiabunker.com, *Website:* www.evrasiabunker.com
Interbunker Management Ltd, Office 3, Othon Court, 4 Vasili Vryonidi Street, P O Box 51121, Limassol 3501, Cyprus, *Tel:* +357 2587 8870, *Fax:* +357 2587 8871, *Email:* boris@interbunker.com, *Website:* www.interbunker.com
Island Oil Ltd, Island Oil Holdings Ltd, 145-149 Chr. Hadjipavlou Street, 2nd Floor Christiel Building, Limassol 3036, Cyprus, *Tel:* +357 2588 9000, *Fax:* +357 2574 5466, *Email:* bunkers@island-oil.com, *Website:* www.island-oil.com
Lavar Shipping Co. Ltd, P O Box 50407, Limassol 3604, Cyprus, *Tel:* +357 2581 8600, *Fax:* +357 2536 5269, *Email:* info@lavargroup.com.cy, *Website:* www.lavargroup.com
M.Y. Bunkers Ltd, P O Box 52452, Limassol 4064, Cyprus, *Tel:* +357 2531 3698, *Fax:* +357 2531 0197, *Email:* mail@mybunkers.com, *Website:* www.mybunkers.com
N.L. Transoil Ltd / Ladis Ltd, Libra Tower, 23 Olympion Street, Office 2401, Limassol 3730, Cyprus, *Tel:* +357 25 871 373, *Fax:* +357 25 734 464, *Email:* transoil@cylink.com.cy, *Website:* www.transoil-holdings.com
E.J. Papadakis Ltd, P O Box 50024, Limassol 3600, Cyprus, *Tel:* +357 2534 9000, *Fax:* +357 2534 9001, *Email:* papadaki@cytanet.com.cy
Petrolina Ltd, Franglinou Roosevelt Avenue 126 B, P O Box 50042, Limassol 3600, Cyprus, *Tel:* +357 2536 2670, *Fax:* +357 2536 9060, *Email:* info@petrolina.com.cy
SKP Enterprises Ltd, Ayias Phylaxeos 205, Limassol 8083, Cyprus, *Tel:* +357 2538 6476, *Fax:* +357 2538 6286, *Email:* skpbunkers@cytanet.com.cy
Tramp Oil & Marine, Tramp Oil & Marine (Med) Ltd, P O Box 56384, Limassol 3306, Cyprus, *Tel:* +357 25 873524, *Fax:* +357 25 311505, *Email:* cyprus@tramp-oil.com, *Website:* www.tramp-oil.com
Transbunker Co., 4th Floor, Vashiotis Business Center, 156 28th Octovriou & Iakovou Tompazi Streets, Limassol 3107, Cyprus, *Tel:* +357 2585 9740, *Fax:* +357 2535 3595, *Email:* bunkerholdings@transbunker.com, *Website:* www.bunkerholdings.com
Yevraziya Bunker Trading Co., Evrasia Bunker Ltd, 2 E. Pallikarides Street, Suncourt, Office A1, Limassol 3106, Cyprus, *Tel:* +357 2558 6765, *Fax:* +357 2559 1836, *Email:* info@hijet.com, *Website:* www.evrasia.com.cy
Ajax Offshore Bunkering Services Ltd, 124 Ayias Paraskevis Street, Yermasoyia, P O Box 54548, Limassol 3725, Cyprus, *Tel:* +357 25 899 000, *Fax:* +357 25 312 477, *Email:* bunkers@ajaxbunkering.com, *Website:* www.edtoffshore.com
BP Cyprus Ltd, 6 Ayios Procopios Street, P O Box 2441, Nicosia 1521, Cyprus, *Tel:* +357 22 0239 3166, *Fax:* +357 22 0278 1272
Enoil Ltd, Iris House, 8 John Kennedy Street, Kanika Enaerios Complex, Limassol 3772, Cyprus, *Tel:* +357 25 585 615, *Fax:* +357 25 581 614
ExxonMobil Marine Fuels, Mailpoint 31, ExxonMobil House, Ermyn Way, Leatherhead, Surrey KT22 8UX, United Kingdom, *Tel:* +44 1372 222 000, *Fax:* +44 1372 223 922, *Email:* marine.fuels@exxonmobil.com, *Website:* www.exxonmobil.com
Island Oil Ltd, Island Oil Holdings Ltd, 145-149 Chr. Hadjipavlou Street, 2nd Floor Christiel Building, Limassol 3036, Cyprus, *Tel:* +357 2588 9000, *Fax:* +357 2574 5466, *Email:* bunkers@island-oil.com, *Website:* www.island-oil.com
M.Y. Bunkers Ltd, P O Box 52452, Limassol 4064, Cyprus, *Tel:* +357 2531 3698, *Fax:* +357 2531 0197, *Email:* mail@mybunkers.com, *Website:* www.mybunkers.com
E.J. Papadakis Ltd, P O Box 50024, Limassol 3600, Cyprus, *Tel:* +357 2534 9000, *Fax:* +357 2534 9001, *Email:* papadaki@cytanet.com.cy
Petrolina Holdings Public Ltd, Petrolina Holdings Public Ltd, Lefkaritis House, 1 Kilkis Street, Larnaca 6015, Cyprus, *Tel:* +357 2484 8000, *Fax:* +357 2465 7173, *Email:* info@petrolina.com.cy, *Website:* www.petrolina.com.cy
Tramp Oil & Marine, World Fuel Services Corporation, 13th Floor, Portland House, Bressenden Place, London SW1E 5BH, United Kingdom, *Tel:* +44 20 7808 5000, *Fax:* +44 20 7808 5088, *Email:* pturner@wfscorp.com, *Website:* www.wfscorp.com
Yevraziya Bunker Trading Co., Evrasia Bunker Ltd, 2 E. Pallikarides Street, Suncourt, Office A1, Limassol 3106, Cyprus, *Tel:* +357 2558 6765, *Fax:* +357 2559 1836, *Email:* info@hijet.com, *Website:* www.evrasia.com.cy

Waste Reception Facilities: Garbage collection service is available
Sludge, oily waste and bilge water facilities available in port and at anchorage

Towage: Three tugs available; two of 3500 bhp (35 t bollard pull) and one of 1320 bhp (16.5 t bollard pull)

Repair & Maintenance: Famalift Shipyard Ltd, New Port Area, P O Box 51903, Limassol 3509, Cyprus, *Tel:* +357 2539 2060, *Fax:* +357 2539 3362, *Email:* info@famagroup.com.cy, *Website:* www.famagroup.com.cy Floating dock 63 m long with max lifting cap of 1360 t. Repair quay 60 m long with max draught 7.3 m

Seaman Missions: The Seamans Mission, P O Box 6885, Limassol 3310, Cyprus, *Tel:* +357 2566 0009, *Fax:* +357 2566 0009, *Email:* cypmts@spidernet.com.cy

Ship Chandlers: Michalakis Michaelides, 107A Franklin Roosevelt Avenue, Limassol 3011, Cyprus, *Tel:* +357 2557 8377, *Fax:* +357 2556 8655, *Email:* mmichael@globalsoftmail.com Managing Director: Michalakis Michaelides Mobile Tel: +357 99407496
Rodou Charalambous & Son Ltd, P O Box 56912, Limassol 3311, Cyprus, *Tel:* +357 2533 7015, *Fax:* +357 2538 7513, *Email:* rodoucha@logosnet.cy.net

GMS Trading Ltd, 53 Pafou Street, Omonia, P O Box 55113, Limassol 3820, Cyprus, *Tel:* +357 2587 3732, *Fax:* +357 2587 3733, *Email:* info@gms.com.cy, *Website:* www.gms.com.cy

Loucas Kokkinos Ship Suppliers Ltd, 133A Franklin Roosevelt Avenue, Limassol 3508, Cyprus, *Tel:* +357 2556 7332, *Fax:* +357 2556 6154, *Email:* loukinos@globalsoftmail.com

Lavar Shipping Co. Ltd, P O Box 50407, Limassol 3604, Cyprus, *Tel:* +357 2581 8600, *Fax:* +357 2536 5269, *Email:* info@lavargroup.com.cy, *Website:* www.lavargroup.com

Nimi Ship Suppliers, 97 Omonias Avenue, P O Box 58461, Limassol 3734, Cyprus, *Tel:* +357 2581 9000, *Fax:* +357 2556 1674, *Email:* nimi@logos.cy.net

E.A.P. Philiastides, 1st Floor Suite 102, Eden Beach House, 28th Oktovriou Street, P O Box 52112, Limassol 4061, Cyprus, *Tel:* +357 2535 1555, *Fax:* +357 2534 1100, *Email:* eapmarine@cytanet.com.cy

Stamatis Baroutis Ltd, 56/58 Ghalileos Street, P O Box 53273, Limassol 3301, Cyprus, *Tel:* +357 2556 9266, *Fax:* +357 2557 8516, *Email:* barbouti@cytanet.com.cy

Theseas Savva Ltd, 118 Franklin Roosevelt Avenue, P O Box 50114, Limassol 3601, Cyprus, *Tel:* +357 2556 5899, *Fax:* +357 2556 2917, *Email:* theseas@cytanet.com.cy

Shipping Agents: Albo Shipping Ltd, 81 Omonias Avenue, M&A House, 4th Floor, Office 42, P O Box 58324, Limassol 3733, Cyprus, *Tel:* +357 2556 5245, *Fax:* +357 2556 5329, *Email:* alboship@logos.cy.net

Amathus Aegeas Ltd, 2 Syntagmatos Square, P O Box 50046, Limassol 3600, Cyprus, *Tel:* +357 2536 2145, *Fax:* +357 2535 1271, *Email:* info@amathusaegeas.com.cy

Atteshlis Shipping Ltd, Atteshlis House, 37 Galileor Street, P O Box 51335, Limassol CY-3504, Cyprus, *Tel:* +357 2588 1000, *Fax:* +357 2556 4550, *Email:* ymllim@atteshlis.com

G.& J. Balkan Shipping & Trade Agency Ltd, 1st Floor, Office 1, 54 Omonia Avenue, P O Box 1025, Limassol 3500, Cyprus, *Tel:* +357 2535 2151/2, *Fax:* +357 2537 9580, *Email:* james@cytanet.com.cy

Bellapais Shipping Co. Ltd, P O Box 51281, Omonia Avenue & Eves Street, Limassol CY-3503, Cyprus, *Tel:* +357 2556 6762, *Fax:* +357 2557 6817, *Email:* bellashi@spidernet.com.cy

Blue Ice Navigation Co Ltd., 30B Omonias Avenue, Ground Floor, P O Box 57460, Limassol 3316, Cyprus, *Tel:* +357 2556 1160, *Fax:* +357 2557 6217, *Email:* info@blueice.com.cy, *Website:* www.blueice.com.cy

Comarine Ltd., P O Box 50624, Limassol 3608, Cyprus, *Tel:* +357 2587 5588, *Fax:* +357 2558 9593, *Email:* info@comarine.com.cy, *Website:* www.comarine.com.cy

Cyprian Seaways Agencies Ltd, 83 Franklin Roosevelt Avenue, 3rd Floor, P O Box 56839, Limassol CY-3011, Cyprus, *Tel:* +357 2556 2002, *Fax:* +357 2557 7024, *Email:* gaclma@gac.com.cy, *Website:* www.gacworld.com

The Cyprus Shipping Co. Ltd, 115 Omonia Avenue, Paroutis Building, 2nd & 3rd Floors, P O Box 50073, Limassol CY-3600, Cyprus, *Tel:* +357 2587 7677, *Fax:* +357 2557 1113, *Email:* main@cyprus-shipping.com.cy

DAP Shipping Agency Ltd, 51 Stingos Street, P O Box 7181, Limassol CY - 3313, Cyprus, *Tel:* +357 2557 1888, *Fax:* +357 2557 3397, *Email:* dapcy@spidernet.com.cy, *Website:* www.dap.com.cy

Francoudi & Stephanou Ltd, The Maritime Centre, 141 Omonia Avenue, P O Box 51490, Limassol 3506, Cyprus, *Tel:* +357 2586 7190, *Fax:* +357 2557 5763, *Email:* t@francoudi.com

G.A.P. Vassilopoulos Group, P O Box 55507, Limassol 3317, Cyprus, *Tel:* +357 2587 7737, *Fax:* +357 2556 5982, *Email:* shipagency@gapgroup.com, *Website:* www.gapgroup.com

Gulf Agency Co. (Cyprus) Ltd, 83 Franklin Roosevelt Avenue, P O Box 51141, Limassol CY-3502, Cyprus, *Tel:* +357 2520 9100, *Fax:* +357 2520 9201, *Email:* cyprus@gacworld.com, *Website:* www.gacworld.com

Hull Blyth Group, Hull Blyth Araouzos Ltd, 147 Chr. Hadjipavlou Street, P O Box 50017, Limassol 3600, Cyprus, *Tel:* +357 2536 2223, *Fax:* +357 2574 7662, *Email:* shipping@hba.com.cy, *Website:* www.hba.com.cy

G. Kirzis & Co., 126 Franklin Roosevelt Avenue, P O Box 18, Limassol, Cyprus, *Tel:* +357 2536 0333, *Fax:* +357 2536 0338, *Email:* g.kirzis1@cytanet.com.cy

Lavar Shipping Co. Ltd, P O Box 50407, Limassol 3604, Cyprus, *Tel:* +357 2581 8600, *Fax:* +357 2536 5269, *Email:* info@lavargroup.com.cy, *Website:* www.lavargroup.com

Manda Navigation Co. Ltd, 81 Omonia Avenue, P O Box 51432, Limassol, Cyprus, *Tel:* +357 2556 7070, *Fax:* +357 2556 7919, *Email:* lim.genmbox@cma-cgm.com

Mediterranean Shipping Company, MSC (Cyprus) Ltd, Cleovoulou Building, 57 Omonias Avenue, P O Box 55705, Limassol 3780, Cyprus, *Tel:* +357 2583 5300, *Fax:* +357 2556 3887, *Email:* info@msccy.com.cy, *Website:* www.mscgva.ch

A.P. Moller-Maersk Group, Maersk Cyprus Ltd, 86 Franklin Roosevelt Avenue, Limassol 3011, Cyprus, *Tel:* +357 2587 7171, *Fax:* +357 2587 7200, *Email:* lloops@maersk.com, *Website:* www.maerskline.com

Nasitas Ltd, P O Box 125, 4 Irinis Street, Limassol, Cyprus, *Tel:* +357 2534 4500, *Fax:* +357 2534 4788, *Email:* nasitas.ltd@cytanet.com.cy

Panship Agencies Ltd, 135 Omonia Avenue, UAD Court, 1st Floor, P O Box 55560, Limassol CY-3780, Cyprus, *Tel:* +357 2556 4444, *Fax:* +357 2557 8012, *Email:* panship@panship.com.cy

Paradise Cruises Ltd, 38 Kitiou Kyprianou Street, P O Box 15738, Limassol 3601, Cyprus, *Tel:* +357 2535 7604, *Fax:* +357 2537 0298, *Email:* cruises@paradise.com.cy, *Website:* www.paradise.com.cy

Seascope Navigation Ltd, P O Box 3253, Limassol 3301, Cyprus, *Tel:* +357 2584 1000, *Fax:* +357 2556 9624, *Email:* admin@seascope.com.cy, *Website:* www.seascope.com.cy

Senator Agency (Cyprus) Ltd, 126 Franklin Roosevelt Avenue, P O Box 56823, Limassol, Cyprus, *Tel:* +357 2537 4230, *Fax:* +357 2537 4229, *Email:* central@senatoragencies.com.cy

Shiptrans Shipping & Trading Agency Ltd, Cleovoulou Building, 57 Omonia Avenue, Limassol 3052, Cyprus, *Tel:* +357 2537 0393, *Fax:* +357 2537 9887, *Email:* shiptran@cytanet.com.cy

Shoham (Cyprus) Ltd, P O Box 50230, Limassol 3602, Cyprus, *Tel:* +357 2556 3890, *Fax:* +357 2556 8990, *Email:* mail@shoham.com.cy, *Website:* www.shoham.com.cy

Solomonides Shipping Ltd, 140B Franklin Roosevelt Avenue, P O Box 50259, Limassol 3602, Cyprus, *Tel:* +357 2556 7000, *Fax:* +357 2557 7005, *Email:* shipping@solomonides.eu, *Website:* www.solomonides.eu

Stevedoring Companies: Amathus Aegeas Ltd, 2 Syntagmatos Square, P O Box 50046, Limassol 3600, Cyprus, *Tel:* +357 2536 2145, *Fax:* +357 2535 1271, *Email:* info@amathusaegeas.com.cy

Lavar Shipping Co. Ltd, P O Box 50407, Limassol 3604, Cyprus, *Tel:* +357 2581 8600, *Fax:* +357 2536 5269, *Email:* info@lavargroup.com.cy, *Website:* www.lavargroup.com

Mantovani Navigation Ltd, P O Box 50001, Limassol 3600, Cyprus, *Tel:* +357 2536 2045, *Fax:* +357 2537 7842, *Email:* mantocy@logos.cy.net, *Website:* www.almantovani.com

Solomonides Shipping Ltd, 140B Franklin Roosevelt Avenue, P O Box 50259, Limassol 3602, Cyprus, *Tel:* +357 2556 7000, *Fax:* +357 2557 7005, *Email:* shipping@solomonides.eu, *Website:* www.solomonides.eu

Surveyors: Bureau Veritas, P O Box 53421, Limassol 3302, Cyprus, *Tel:* +357 2572 5350, *Fax:* +357 2572 5351, *Email:* danos.georgiadis@bureauveritas.com, *Website:* www.bureauveritas.com

Cyprus Bureau of Shipping, Corner Sp., Araouzou & Koumantarias Street, Tonia Court Two, 2nd Floor, P O Box 50214, Limassol CY 3602, Cyprus, *Tel:* +357 2537 6418, *Fax:* +357 2535 6432, *Email:* cbs@cbs.com.cy, *Website:* www.cbs.com.cy

Dafnis Navigation Ltd, 1 Archbishop Kyprianou Street, P O Box 50555, Limassol 3607, Cyprus, *Tel:* +357 2536 0001, *Fax:* +357 2536 5000, *Email:* info@dafnisgroup.com

Det Norske Veritas A/S, 120 Gladstonos & Filokyprou Street, Foloune House E2, P O Box 56628, Limassol 3309, Cyprus, *Tel:* +357 2581 7824, *Fax:* +357 2534 5501, *Email:* limassol.office@dnv.com, *Website:* www.dnv.com

Elias Marine Consultants Ltd, Maximos Court, Block B, 6th Floor, Leontios A Avenue, P O Box 51455, Limassol 3505, Cyprus, *Tel:* +357 2533 5529, *Fax:* +357 2580 0801, *Email:* emco@eliasmarine.com, *Website:* www.eliasmarine.com

Eurogal GSL Surveys Ltd, Suite 101, 118 Anexartisias Street, P O Box 54189, Limassol 3040, Cyprus, *Tel:* +357 2576 3340, *Fax:* +357 2576 3360, *Email:* eurogal@spidernet.com.cy, *Website:* www.eurogal-surveys.com

Germanischer Lloyd, Pamelva Building, 1st Floor, Office No.108, Corner Anastasi Sioukri & Griva Digheni, Limassol 3105, Cyprus, *Tel:* +357 2536 1393, *Fax:* +357 2536 4590, *Email:* gl-limassol@gl-group.com, *Website:* www.gl-group.com

Gyro Survey Bureau, 1 Nikis Street, Pakova Centre, Suite 104, P O Box 53432, Limassol 3302, Cyprus, *Tel:* +357 2558 7050, *Fax:* +357 2558 4944, *Email:* gyro@cytanet.com.cy

Hanseatic Marine Consult, 111 Spyrou Araouzou Street, Limassol 3036, Cyprus, *Tel:* +357 2534 5111, *Fax:* +357 2534 2879, *Email:* management@hanseatic.com.cy

International Register of Shipping (BSS), 137 Gladstone Street, Office 202, Taitou Court, P O Box 7401, Limassol, Cyprus, *Tel:* +357 2574 7638, *Fax:* +357 2574 7894, *Email:* isbcy@spidernet.com.cy, *Website:* www.intlreg.com

International Shipping Bureau (ISB), ISB Management Ltd, Office 202, Taitou Court, 137 Gladstonos Street, Limassol 3032, Cyprus, *Tel:* +357 2574 7638, *Fax:* +357 2574 7894, *Email:* isbcy@spidernet.com.cy, *Website:* www.isbship.com

Nippon Kaiji Kyokai, Elias Consultancy Services Ltd, Maximos Court, Block B, 7th Floor, Leontios A Avenue, P O Box 53265, Limassol 3301, Cyprus, *Tel:* +357 2580 0700, *Fax:* +357 2580 0701, *Email:* elco@elco.com.cy, *Website:* www.eliasmarine.com

Russian Maritime Register of Shipping, 10 Evangelistrias Street, Levanco Tower 1, Room 304, 3rd Floor, Limassol, Cyprus, *Tel:* +357 2534 2166, *Fax:* +357 2534 2166, *Email:* rs-cyprus@cytanet.com.cy, *Website:* www.rs-head.spb.ru

Medical Facilities: First aid unit in the port. Limassol General Hospital, 8 km

Airport: Paphos, 56 km. Larnaca, 70 km

Development: The design of a new Passenger Terminal of 8000 m2 is in progress and the commencement of works is expected to begin in 2008 with an estimated cost of 25M Euros
Entrance channel and turning circle will be dredged to 17 m and the berths at the west container terminal will be dredged to 16 m
The quay in the west basin will be extended by 500 m to a total length of 800 m

Lloyd's Agent: Orphanides & Murat Ltd, P O Box 71200, Limassol 3841, Cyprus, *Tel:* +357 2556 6099, *Fax:* +357 2556 1231, *Email:* rotacy@globalsoftmail.com, *Website:* www.orphanidesandmurat.com

MONI ANCHORAGE

Lat 34° 42' N; Long 33° 12' E.

Admiralty Chart: 849	**Admiralty Pilot:** 49
Time Zone: GMT +2 h	**UNCTAD Locode:** CY MOI

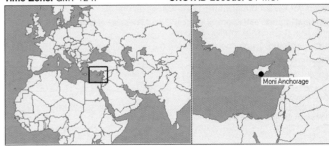

Principal Facilities:

P							T	A

Authority: Electricity Authority of Cyprus, 15 Foti Pitta Street, P O Box 24506, Lefkosia 1399, Cyprus, *Tel:* +357 2284 5000, *Fax:* +357 2276 0735, *Email:* eac@eac.com.cy, *Website:* www.eac.com.cy

Port Security: ISPS compliant

Documentation: Crew list, vessel's particulars, cargo declaration

Pilotage: Compulsory. Pilot available through the Port Manager at Limassol; prior notice is required

Tides: Tidal range 0.8 m

Working Hours: 0730-1430

Key to Principal Facilities:—			
A=Airport	**C**=Containers	**G**=General Cargo	**P**=Petroleum	**R**=Ro/Ro	**Y**=Dry Bulk
B=Bunkers	**D**=Dry Dock	**L**=Cruise	**Q**=Other Liquid Bulk	**T**=Towage (where available from port)	

Accommodation:

Name	Depth (m)	Remarks
Moni		
Fuel Oil Berth	18.3	See [1] below

[1]*Fuel Oil Berth:* Open roadstead. Heavy fuel oil for vessels up to 213 m loa and 12 m draught. Supply through a pipeline of 1204 m x 12 inch. Daylight docking only

Towage: Available from Limassol

Medical Facilities: Hospital facilities available in Limassol

Airport: Larnaca Airport, 60 km

Lloyd's Agent: Orphanides & Murat Ltd, P O Box 71200, Limassol 3841, Cyprus, *Tel:* +357 2556 6099, *Fax:* +357 2556 1231, *Email:* rotacy@globalsoftmail.com, *Website:* www.orphanidesandmurat.com

PAPHOS

Lat 34° 45' N; Long 32° 25' E.

Admiralty Chart: 849/775		**Admiralty Pilot:** 49	
Time Zone: GMT +2 h		**UNCTAD Locode:** CY PFO	

This port is no longer open to commercial shipping

Shipping Agents: GAP Vassilopoulos Group, Ellados Avenue, & Olgas Xinaridou, Paphos 8020, Cyprus, *Tel:* +357 26 950 093, *Fax:* +357 26 923 887, *Email:* info@gapgroup.com, *Website:* www.gapgroup.com

VASSILIKO BAY

Lat 34° 42' N; Long 33° 20' E.

Admiralty Chart: 849		**Admiralty Pilot:** 49	
Time Zone: GMT +2 h		**UNCTAD Locode:** CY VAS	

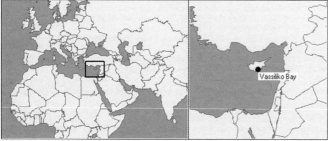

Principal Facilities:

P	Q	Y	G		R		B		T	A	

Authority: Cyprus Ports Authority, 23 Crete Street, P O Box 22007, Nicosia 1516, Cyprus, *Tel:* +357 2281 7200, *Fax:* +357 2276 5420, *Email:* cpa@cpa.gov.cy, *Website:* www.cpa.gov.cy

Port Security: ISPS compliant

Documentation: Crew list, vessel's particulars, cargo declaration

Approach: Vessels approach from a SE direction, max draught 8.5 m

Pilotage: Available on request and contact through VHF Channel 8

Tides: Range of tide 0.65 m

Traffic: 2005, 1 199 000 t of cargo handled

Maximum Vessel Dimensions: 170 m loa, 8.5 m draught

Principal Imports and Exports: Imports: Coal, Minerals, Petroleum, Soya, Sulphuric acid. Exports: Cement, Clinker, Minerals.

Working Hours: Cargo operations round the clock. Marine services 0700-2300

Accommodation:

Name	Length (m)	Depth (m)	Draught (m)	Remarks
Vassiliko Bay				
Main Quay	360	9	8.5	See [1] below
Western Quay	125	9	8.5	
Fuel Oil Berth (SPM)		32		See [2] below

[1]*Main Quay:* Cement bulk loading facility with loading rate of 5000 t day
[2]*Fuel Oil Berth (SPM):* Open roadstead berth. Heavy fuel oil for vessels up to 260 m loa and 13.9 m draught. Daylight docking only

Storage: Two tanks of 8000 t cap for storage of sulphuric acid

Location	Open (m²)
Vassiliko Bay	55000

Mechanical Handling Equipment:

Location	Type	Capacity (t)	Qty
Vassiliko Bay	Mobile Cranes	30	3
Vassiliko Bay	Mobile Cranes	80	1

Bunkering: Ajax Offshore Bunkering Services Ltd, 124 Ayias Paraskevis Street, Yermasoyia, P O Box 54548, Limassol 3725, Cyprus, *Tel:* +357 25 899 000, *Fax:* +357 25 312 477, *Email:* bunkers@ajaxbunkering.com, *Website:* www.edtoffshore.com
BP Cyprus Ltd, 6 Ayios Procopios Street, P O Box 2441, Nicosia 1521, Cyprus, *Tel:* +357 22 0239 3166, *Fax:* +357 22 0278 1272 – *Grades:* IFO180-380cSt; MGO – *Delivery Mode:* barge, pipeline, truck
ExxonMobil Marine Fuels, Mailpoint 31, ExxonMobil House, Ermyn Way, Leatherhead, Surrey KT22 8UX, United Kingdom, *Tel:* +44 1372 222 000, *Fax:* +44 1372 223 922, *Email:* marine.fuels@exxonmobil.com, *Website:* www.exxonmobil.com – *Grades:* IFO30-60cSt; MGO – *Delivery Mode:* truck
Island Oil Ltd, Island Oil Holdings Ltd, 145-149 Chr. Hadjipavlou Street, 2nd Floor Christiel Building, Limassol 3036, Cyprus, *Tel:* +357 2588 9000, *Fax:* +357 2574 5466, *Email:* bunkers@island-oil.com, *Website:* www.island-oil.com – *Grades:* IFO-180cSt; MGO; in line blending available – *Parcel Size:* no min – *Rates:* 150t/h – *Notice:* 24 hours – *Delivery Mode:* barge, truck

Waste Reception Facilities: Garbage disposal available

Towage: Two tug boats available of up to 700 hp

Repair & Maintenance: All types of minor mechanical repairs can be done in the workshops of the owners, which are very well equipped

Ship Chandlers: Rodou Charalambous & Son Ltd, P O Box 56912, Limassol 3311, Cyprus, *Tel:* +357 2533 7015, *Fax:* +357 2538 7513, *Email:* rodoucha@logosnet.cy.net

Medical Facilities: Nearest at Limassol

Airport: Larnaca Airport, 49 km

Lloyd's Agent: Orphanides & Murat Ltd, P O Box 71200, Limassol 3841, Cyprus, *Tel:* +357 2556 6099, *Fax:* +357 2556 1231, *Email:* rotacy@globalsoftmail.com, *Website:* www.orphanidesandmurat.com

DENMARK

TRISHIP A/S

Fyrtårnsvej 1, Prøvestenen
2300 Copenhagen S, Denmark

Tel: +45 39 43 39 44
Fax: +45 39 43 39 45
Email: triship@triship.dk
Web: www.triship.dk

SHIPPING AGENTS

AABENRAA

Lat 55° 2' N; Long 9° 25' E.

Admiralty Chart: 901		**Admiralty Pilot:** 18	
Time Zone: GMT +1 h		**UNCTAD Locode:** DK AAB	

Principal Facilities:

P	Q	Y	G		R		B	D	T	A	

Authority: Aabenraa Port, Mellemvej 25, DK-6200 Aabenraa, Denmark, *Tel:* +45 74 62 25 14, *Fax:* +45 74 62 31 43, *Email:* port@aabenraaport.dk, *Website:* www.aabenraaport.dk

Officials: Port Manager: Niels Kristiansen, *Email:* niels@aabenraaport.dk.

Port Security: ISPS compliant

Approach: Channel from Aabenraa Fjord to port 1000 m long with a depth of 11 m, min width 120 m. Vessels can enter by day or night

Anchorage: Anchorage can be obtained in the fjord; good holding ground

Pilotage: Available from DanPilot (Belt & Fjord Pilot), Fredericia, Tel: +45 76 20 03 20, Fax: +45 75 92 88 22, Email: littlebelt-pilot@lillebaelt.dk, Website: www.pilotage.dk

Radio Frequency: Lyngby Radio on VHF Channels 16 and 7

Tides: The tide is insignificant. Strong winds from NE to E may raise the water level approx 1.5 m. Strong winds from south-westerly direction may lower the water level approx 1 m

Traffic: 2007, 2 066 047 t of cargo handled

Maximum Vessel Dimensions: Dry cargo: 250 m loa. Tankers: 210 m loa

Working Hours: Monday-Thursday 0700-1530. Friday 0700-1500

Accommodation:

Name	Depth (m)	Remarks
Aabenraa		
Sonderjyllandskajen (Berth No.1)	11	Bulk cargo vessels of up to 250 m loa
Gammelhavn (Berth No's 2-5)	7.5	Vessels up to 180 m loa
Nyhavn (Berth No's 6-8)	6.5–9.3	See [1] below
Tanker Jetty I (Berth No.9)	11	Vessels up to 210 m loa. 6", 8" and 10" pipes for oil and molasses
Tanker Jetty II (Berth No.10)	7	Vessels up to 100 m loa. 6", 8" and 10" pipes for oil and molasses
Ro/Ro Terminal (Berth No.11)	11	Vessels up to 140 m loa. 24 reefer plugs
Sydhavn	4	Fishing Port

[1]*Nyhavn (Berth No's 6-8):* Vessels up to 200 m loa. Harbour includes a privately owned grain loader and two cement discharging plants

Mechanical Handling Equipment:

Location	Type	Capacity (t)	Qty
Aabenraa	Mobile Cranes	36	1
Aabenraa	Mobile Cranes	104	1
Aabenraa	Mobile Cranes	12	1

Bunkering: All grades available by barge or road tanker. At least 24 h advance notice is required

A/S Dan-Bunkering Ltd, Strandgade 4A, 1401 Copenhagen K, Denmark, *Tel:* +45 3345 5410, *Fax:* +45 3345 5411, *Email:* copenhagen@dan-bunkering.dk, *Website:* www.dan-bunkering.dk

Ecophoenix AB, Kungsgatan 54, 753 21 Uppsala, Sweden, *Tel:* +46 1813 1880, *Fax:* +46 1813 1881, *Email:* info@phoenixscandinavia.com

Kuwait Petroleum Corp., Banevaenget 13, 3460 Birkerod, Denmark, *Tel:* +45 7012 4545, *Fax:* +45 4599 2020, *Email:* q8@q8.dk, *Website:* www.q8.dk

Malik Supply A/S, Ved Stranden 22, DK-9000 Aalborg, Denmark, *Tel:* +45 9631 3900, *Fax:* +45 9631 3911, *Email:* info@malik.dk, *Website:* www.malik.dk

Monjasa A/S, Strevelinsvej 4, 7000 Fredericia, Denmark, *Tel:* +45 70 26 02 30, *Fax:* +45 70 26 02 33, *Email:* denmark@monjasa.com, *Website:* www.monjasa.com

OW Bunker & Trading A/S, Gasvaerksvej 48, DK-9000 Aalborg, Denmark, *Tel:* +45 98 12 72 77, *Fax:* +45 98 16 72 77, *Email:* owbunker@owbunker.dk, *Website:* www.owbunker.dk

Trumf Bunker A/S, Raadhustorvet 4, P O Box 55, 7100 Vejle, Denmark, *Tel:* +45 7642 9696, *Fax:* +45 7642 9690, *Email:* trumf@trumf-bunker.com, *Website:* www.trumf-bunker.com

Waste Reception Facilities: Oily residues, oily ballast water and garbage etc.

Towage: One tug of 450 hp is available. Large vessels may require further towage assistance on entering and leaving, and in such cases 24 h notice is required

Repair & Maintenance: Aabenraa Vaerft A/S, Kilen 40, 6200 Aabenraa, Denmark, *Tel:* +45 74 62 25 20, *Fax:* +45 74 62 34 20, *Email:* post@aabenraa-vaerft.dk, *Website:* www.aabenraa-vaerft.dk

Shipping Agents: Shipping.dk Aabenraa A/S, Gammel Havn 5, DK-6200 Aabenraa, Denmark, *Tel:* +45 74 62 77 00, *Fax:* +45 74 62 77 02, *Email:* aabenraa@shipping.dk, *Website:* www.shipping.dk

Stevedoring Companies: F.A. Carstens Shipping ApS, Skibbroen 3, P O Box 98, DK-6200 Aabenraa, Denmark, *Tel:* +45 74 62 39 00, *Fax:* +45 74 62 64 39, *Email:* carstens.shipping@mail.tele.dk

P.F. Cleemann Shipping ApS, Vikinghus, Gammelhavn 5, P O Box 89, DK-6200 Aabenraa, Denmark, *Tel:* +45 74 62 77 00, *Fax:* +45 74 62 77 02, *Email:* aabenraa@shipping.dk

E. Krag A/S, Skibbroen 16, P O Box 37, DK-6200 Aabenraa, Denmark, *Tel:* +45 74 63 10 02, *Fax:* +45 74 63 01 17, *Email:* mail@ekrag.com, *Website:* www.ekrag.com

Shipping.dk Aabenraa A/S, Gammel Havn 5, DK-6200 Aabenraa, Denmark, *Tel:* +45 74 62 77 00, *Fax:* +45 74 62 77 02, *Email:* aabenraa@shipping.dk, *Website:* www.shipping.dk

Stema Shipping A/S, Nyhavn 28, P O Box 60, DK-6200 Aabenraa, Denmark, *Tel:* +45 74 62 79 72, *Fax:* +45 74 63 03 65, *Email:* chartering@stema-shipping.dk, *Website:* www.aabenraaport.dk/stema/index.htm

Medical Facilities: Available

Airport: Vojens, 25 km

Lloyd's Agent: C. Breinholt A/S, Toldbodvej 1, P O Box 20, DK-6701 Esbjerg, Denmark, *Tel:* +45 79 18 04 11, *Fax:* +45 75 18 19 25, *Email:* mkk@breinholt.dk, *Website:* www.breinholt.dk

AALBORG

Lat 57° 2' N; Long 9° 56' E.

Admiralty Chart: 598	**Admiralty Pilot:** 18
Time Zone: GMT +1 h	**UNCTAD Locode:** DK AAL

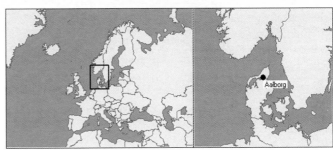

Principal Facilities:

P	Q	Y	G	C	R	L	B		A

Authority: Port of Aalborg Ltd, P O Box 8530, DK-9220 Aalborg, Denmark, *Tel:* +45 99 30 15 00, *Fax:* +45 99 30 15 15, *Email:* info@aalborghavn.dk, *Website:* www.aalborghavn.dk

Officials: Managing Director: Claus Holstein, *Tel:* +45 99 30 15 01, *Email:* ch@aalborghavn.dk.
Marketing Manager: Ole Broendum, *Tel:* +45 99 30 15 05, *Email:* ob@aalborghavn.dk.
Harbour Master: Peter J. Petersen, *Tel:* +45 99 30 15 30, *Email:* pjp@aalborghavn.dk.

Port Security: ISPS compliant

Pre-Arrival Information: Crew list and port list (last 10 ports of call). Waste notice

Approach: Entrance for deep draught vessels via the Aalborg Bugt Buoy B7, through the 12 km long and 240 m wide channel, to the Svitringen route, 15 km long and 240 m wide and then through the 7 km long and 110 m wide Egense route across Hals Barre. The 67 km long fairway from Kattegat to Aalborg has a min width of 150 m and a depth of 10.4 m NN in the artificial channel across Hals Barre and a depth of 10.1 m NN between bar and Aalborg. The max draught for vessels crossing Hals Barre is 9.3 m. The fairway from Kattegat to Aalborg is buoyed and marked by a leading light system in order to permit day and night navigation under normal circumstances. A Decca Hi-Fi system makes it possible for vessels with a special receiver to pass Hals Barre in any weather conditions
Smaller vessels with up to 3.8 m d can approach the port through the Limfjord from the N Sea, a distance of 78 nautical miles. At Thyboron and Logstor the passage is through artificial channels marked with buoys; Logstor to Aalborg can only be navigated in daylight, however

Anchorage: Anchorage can be obtained 2 miles SE of Hals Barre Lighthouse in a depth of 10.5 m or 2 nautical miles S of Buoy No.7

Pilotage: Compulsory at Hals Barre for vessels drawing more than 6 m and for tankers exceeding 1500 dwt, and for all gas tankers. Pilot boards at Hals Barre Light; pilot boat equipped with VHF Channel 16. The W entrance from Logstor to Aalborg is only navigable in daylight for vessels under 4 m d. Pilotage is also compulsory for vessels over 800 gt or with an loa of 80 m or more when passing the railway bridge at Aalborg
Pilot can be ordered from DanPilot (Great Belt), Spodsbjerg, Tel: +45 62 50 15 35, Fax: +45 62 50 15 28, Email: belt@pilotage.dk, Website: www.pilotage.dk

Radio Frequency: VHF Channels 12 and 16

Weather: In severe winters with ice there is a traffic control system operated by the Port Authority. Tugs are operating as ice-breakers in the Limfjord and port of Aalborg when necessary

Tides: Navigation conditions good. Range of tide 0.3 m; strong winds may have an effect on tidal range. Strong westerly winds may raise level to 1.3 m and easterly/southeasterly winds may set level to 0.8 m at LW and the average level 0.3 m for long periods. Currents are irregular. Density between 1017 and 1021

Traffic: 2004, 2 751 000 t of cargo handled, 46 219 TEU's

Maximum Vessel Dimensions: 101 600 dwt, 9.3 m d, 257 m loa

Working Hours: Monday to Thursday 0700-0830, 0900-1200, 1230-1530. Friday 0700-1500. Overtime possible

Accommodation:

Name	Length (m)	Depth (m)	Remarks
Central Harbour			
Quays 4030-4040	300		
Quay 4061	160	8.5	
Quays 4062-4070	500	9.8	Feedstuffs
Quays 4110-4113	933	8.5–9.5	General cargo
Quay 4120	990	9–10	Oil
North Harbour			
Quays 3012 & 3014-3016	735	9.5	
Quay 3017	99	8	
East Harbour			
Quays 8005-8006	600	9.5	Bulk terminal
Quays 8011-8012	619	8.5	Greenland trade
Quay 8013	257	8.5	Containers
Quays 8014-8016	618	8.5–9.8	Multi-purpose

Storage:

Location	Covered (m²)	Grain (t)	Cold (m³)
Aalborg	110000	161000	84000

Mechanical Handling Equipment:

Location	Type	Capacity (t)	Qty
Central Harbour	Mobile Cranes	5–10	3
North Harbour	Mobile Cranes	20	1
East Harbour	Mobile Cranes	24	3
East Harbour	Container Cranes	42–50	1

Cargo Worked: General cargo approx 20-30 t/gang/h. Suction pipes 80-120 t/h

Bunkering: Malik Supply A/S, Ved Stranden 22, DK-9000 Aalborg, Denmark, *Tel:* +45 9631 3900, *Fax:* +45 9631 3911, *Email:* info@malik.dk, *Website:* www.malik.dk
OW Bunker & Trading A/S, Gasvaerksvej 48, DK-9000 Aalborg, Denmark, *Tel:* +45 98 12 72 77, *Fax:* +45 98 16 72 77, *Email:* owbunker@owbunker.dk, *Website:* www.owbunker.dk
OW Bunker Estonia Ltd, Gasvaerksvej 48, DK-9000 Aalborg, Denmark, *Tel:* +45 98127277, *Fax:* +45 98167277, *Email:* owbunker@owbunker.dk, *Website:* www.owbunker.com
OW Bunker Klaipeda Ltd, Gasvaerksvej 48, DK-9000 Aalborg, Denmark, *Tel:* +45 9812 7277, *Fax:* +45 9816 7277, *Email:* owbunker@owbunker.dk, *Website:* www.owbunker.com
OW Icebunker Ltd, Gasvaerksvej 46-48, DK-9000 Aalborg, Denmark, *Tel:* +45 7020 4049, *Fax:* +45 7020 4051, *Email:* owi@owicebunker.com, *Website:* www.owicebunker.com
OW Riga Bunkering Ltd, Gasvaerksvej 48, DK-9000 Aalborg, Denmark, *Tel:* +45 98127277, *Fax:* +45 98167277, *Email:* owbunker@owbunker.dk, *Website:* www.owbunker.com
A/S Dan-Bunkering Ltd, Strandgade 4A, 1401 Copenhagen K, Denmark, *Tel:* +45 3345 5410, *Fax:* +45 3345 5411, *Email:* copenhagen@dan-bunkering.dk, *Website:* www.dan-bunkering.dk
Kuwait Petroleum Corp., Banevaenget 13, 3460 Birkerod, Denmark, *Tel:* +45 7012 4545, *Fax:* +45 4599 2020, *Email:* q8@q8.dk, *Website:* www.q8.dk
Malik Supply A/S, Ved Stranden 22, DK-9000 Aalborg, Denmark, *Tel:* +45 9631 3900, *Fax:* +45 9631 3911, *Email:* info@malik.dk, *Website:* www.malik.dk
Monjasa A/S, Strevelinsvej 4, 7000 Fredericia, Denmark, *Tel:* +45 70 26 02 30, *Fax:* +45 70 26 02 33, *Email:* denmark@monjasa.com, *Website:* www.monjasa.com
OW Bunker & Trading A/S, Gasvaerksvej 48, DK-9000 Aalborg, Denmark, *Tel:* +45 98 12 72 77, *Fax:* +45 98 16 72 77, *Email:* owbunker@owbunker.dk, *Website:* www.owbunker.dk
Trumf Bunker A/S, Raadhustorvet 4, P O Box 55, 7100 Vejle, Denmark, *Tel:* +45 7642 9696, *Fax:* +45 7642 9690, *Email:* trumf@trumf-bunker.com, *Website:* www.trumf-bunker.com

Waste Reception Facilities: Following types of refuse can be received: solid refuse, oleaginous refuse, sewage, residues and mixtures of noxious liquids carried in bulk

Towage: Three tugs from 580 to 2000 hp available from A/S EM.Z.Svitzer

Repair & Maintenance: The port authority owns two slipways for smaller vessels and there are several other repair workshops
Danyard Aalborg A/S, Speditorvej 1, P O Box 660, DK-9100 Aalborg, Denmark, *Tel:* +45 99 37 37 00, *Fax:* +45 99 37 37 02, *Email:* daa@navalyard.dk, *Website:* www.danyard.dk
Limfjords-Vaerftet A/S, Vestre Havn, 9000 Aalborg, Denmark, *Tel:* +45 98 12 80 44, *Fax:* +45 98 13 19 78, *Email:* info@limfjords-vaerftet.dk, *Website:* www.limfjords-vaerftet.dk One slipway for vessels up to 240 t

Ship Chandlers: Wrist Shipping A/S, Gasvaerksvej 48, DK 9000 Aalborg, Denmark, *Tel:* +45 99 31 84 84, *Fax:* +45 98 13 72 24, *Email:* shipping@wristshipping.dk, *Website:* www.wristshipping.com

Shipping Agents: Aage Christensen A/S, Strandvejen 6, P O Box 1743, DK-9100 Aalborg, Denmark, *Tel:* +45 98 13 37 55, *Fax:* +45 98 16 47 70
Janus Andersen & Co. A/S, Havnegade 15, DK-9400 Norresundby, Denmark, *Tel:* +45 98 17 14 55, *Fax:* +45 98 17 15 69, *Email:* janus-a@janus-a.dk, *Website:* www.janus-a.dk
Blue Water Shipping A/S, Groenlandshavnen, P O Box 8223, DK-9220 Aalborg, Denmark, *Tel:* +45 99 30 31 90, *Fax:* +45 99 30 30 61, *Email:* bwsaal@bws.dk, *Website:* www.bws.dk
Thor Jorgensen A/S, Osteraa 4, P O Box 1509, DK-9100 Aalborg, Denmark, *Tel:* +45 98 13 85 44, *Fax:* +45 98 13 88 45, *Email:* aal@maersk.com
K Line (Europe) Ltd, 1 Badehusvej, 9000 Aalborg, Denmark, *Tel:* +45 99 33 45 05, *Fax:* +45 99 33 45 06, *Email:* aal@kline.com, *Website:* www.klineurope.com
Scan-Shipping A/S, 1 Badehusvej, DK-9000 Aalborg, Denmark, *Tel:* +45 99 33 45 00, *Fax:* +45 99 33 45 01, *Email:* aal@scan-group.dk, *Website:* www.scan-group.com
ShipCargo, ShipCargo Ltd., Rordalsvej 27, DK-9220 Aalborg, Denmark, *Tel:* +45 70 20 08 90, *Fax:* +45 70 20 32 90, *Email:* shipcargo@shipcargo.dk, *Website:* www.shipcargo.dk
Wrist Shipping A/S, Gasvaerksvej 48, DK 9000 Aalborg, Denmark, *Tel:* +45 99 31 84 84, *Fax:* +45 98 13 72 24, *Email:* shipping@wristshipping.dk, *Website:* www.wristshipping.com

Stevedoring Companies: Arctic Container Operation A/S, Gronlandshavnen, Langerak 17, P O Box 8432, DK-9220 Aalborg, Denmark, *Tel:* +45 99 30 31 61á, *Fax:* +45 99 30 30 62á, *Email:* aco@ral.dk, *Website:* www.aco-as.dk

Surveyors: Aalborg Besigteleseskonitor ApS Survey Association Ltd, Vesteraa 4, DK 9000 Aalborg, Denmark, *Tel:* +45 98 16 60 22, *Fax:* +45 98 11 34 52, *Email:* shp@aalborgsurvey.dk, *Website:* www.aalborgsurvey.dk
Det Norske Veritas A/S, Vandmanden 36, DK-9200 Aalborg, Denmark, *Tel:* +45 99 33 17 00, *Fax:* +45 99 33 17 01, *Email:* aalborg@dnv.com, *Website:* www.dnv.com
Dwinter Marine Consultants (Carlbro) AS, Sofiendalsvej 9, DK-9200 Aalborg SV, Denmark, *Tel:* +45 98 18 65 11, *Fax:* +45 98 18 45 99, *Email:* lmc@logimatic.dk, *Website:* www.convoy.dk

Medical Facilities: Two hospitals, 0.5 km and 2 km away, one with casualty dept

Airport: Aalborg, 5 km

Railway: Public central station close to inner harbour. Cargo railway within the port area

Lloyd's Agent: Rechnitzer, Thomsen & Co. Ltd, Gasvaerksvej 46, DK-9000 Aalborg, Denmark, *Tel:* +45 98 12 44 22, *Fax:* +45 98 10 15 71, *Email:* morten.kusk@wristshipping.dk, *Website:* www.wristshipping.dk

AARHUS

Lat 56° 8' N; Long 10° 13' E.

Admiralty Chart: 2590/949	**Admiralty Pilot:** 18
Time Zone: GMT +1 h	**UNCTAD Locode:** DK AAR

Principal Facilities:

P	Q	Y	G	C	R	L	B		T	A

Authority: Port of Aarhus, Mindet 2, P O Box 130, DK-8100 Aarhus C, Denmark, *Tel:* +45 86 13 32 66, *Fax:* +45 86 12 76 62, *Email:* port@aarhus.dk, *Website:* www.aarhushavn.dk

Officials: Assistant Managing Director: Henrik Munch Jensen, *Tel:* +45 89 36 82 26, *Email:* hmj@port.aarhus.dk.
Harbour Director: Bjarne Mathiesen, *Tel:* +45 89 36 82 02, *Email:* bm@port.aarhus.dk.
Marketing Manager: Kirsten Bruun, *Tel:* +45 89 36 82 30, *Email:* kb@port.aarhus.dk.
Harbour Master: Knud Erik Moller, *Tel:* +45 89 36 82 55, *Email:* kem@port.aarhus.dk.

Port Security: ISPS compliant

Approach: Harbour entrance is marked by lights, buoys and leading lights and has a depth of 11 m at the common entrance to the North and South sections and Oil Harbour. The entrance to the East section, Bulk Terminal and Multi-purpose terminals has a depth of 14 m

Pilotage: Not compulsory. The port maintains pilots to effect piloting between the roads and the port. 24 h service. Requests for pilotage should be submitted to the Traffic Service at least 1.5 h in advance, Tel: +45 89 36 82 51, Fax: +45 86 76 02 37, Email: maritim@port.aarhus.dk

Radio Frequency: VHF Channels 16 and 12

Tides: Between +0.30 m and -0.30 m

Traffic: 2007, 12 573 000 t of cargo handled, 921 000 TEU's

Maximum Vessel Dimensions: 14 m max draft

Working Hours: Mon to Fri 0700-1630. Sat and Sun working at overtime rates

Accommodation: The port covers a land area of 226 ha and a water area of 117 ha. There are some 13.5 km of quays
Bulk facilities: Silo cap of 208 000 m3. Sixteen private grain suction plants, elevators and loading pipes. Cargo handled include feedstuffs, soya beans, salt, paper, cement, sand and gravel
Tanker facilities: Six berths in the Main Harbour, max depth 11 m; night berthing possible; water, bunkers and slop tank facilities available. Facilities for tankers at Berth No.313 in the Eastern Harbour with depth alongside of 12 m. Total tank cap of 500 000 m3

Name	Length (m)	Depth (m)	Remarks
Main Harbour			See [1] below
Basins 1 & 2		7.5	
Basins 3 & 4		10	Bulk cargo and oil handled
Basin 5		9	Ferry terminals are located in Basin 5
Container Terminal North	800	11	See [2] below
Container Terminal East	550	14	See [3] below
Eastern Harbour			See [4] below
Bulk Terminal	645	13.5	See [5] below
Multi Terminal	450	13.5	See [6] below
Tanker & Ro/ro Quay	250	12	Marshalling area of 14 000 m2

[1]*Main Harbour:* The harbour is made up of eleven basins with approx 14 km of quays
[2]*Container Terminal North:* Operated by Aarhus Stevedore Kompagni A/S, Europaplads 16, P O Box 259, DK-8100 Aarhus, Tel: +45 87 30 81 00, Fax: +45 87 30 81 01, Email: info@aask.dk, Website: www.aask.dk
Terminal area of 265 000 m2. Equipment includes five panamax cranes up to 60 t cap. Ro/ro facilities. 775 reefer points
[3]*Container Terminal East:* Operated by APM Terminals, Osthavnsvej 43, P O Box 165, DK 8100 Aarhus C, Tel: +45 89 34 88 00, Fax: +45 89 34 88 82, Email: aarapmtmkt@apmterminals.com, Website: www.apmterminals.com
Terminal area of 200 000 m2. Equipment includes three post-panamax cranes up to 90 t cap. Ro/ro facilities. 500 reefer points

[4]*Eastern Harbour:* Covers a land area of 60 ha and comprises Basins 9 and 10, quay length of 2075 m with specialised terminals

[5]*Bulk Terminal:* Covers 9.6 ha. Import quay is 430 m long with a depth alongside of 13.5 m, and there are two export quays with lengths of 125 m and 90 m. Vessels can be accommodated fully laden up to 60 000 dwt and partially laden up to 150 000 dwt Equipment on the import quay consists of two unloading cranes, each with a cap of 2500 t/h and conveyor belt system; whilst vessels at the export quays can be loaded at a rate of up to 2000 t/h. The terminal has a stockpile cap of 600 000 t and throughput cap of up to 3 million t/year

[6]*Multi Terminal:* Covers 32 ha. Two ro/ro berths with fixed ramps. Various cargoes including timber products, vehicles and transit goods

Storage:

Location	Covered (m²)	Cold (m³)
Aarhus	166000	30000

Mechanical Handling Equipment:

Location	Type	Capacity (t)	Qty
Aarhus	Mult-purp. Cranes		2
Aarhus	Mobile Cranes		1
Aarhus	Panamax	44	1
Aarhus	Post Panamax	48–90	3
Aarhus	Super Post Panamax	64–100	2
Aarhus	Quay Cranes		9

Bunkering: Supplies from quay or road tanker
Ecophoenix AB, Kungsgatan 54, 753 21 Uppsala, Sweden, *Tel:* +46 1813 1880, *Fax:* +46 1813 1881, *Email:* info@phoenixscandinavia.com
Kuwait Petroleum Corp., Banevaenget 13, 3460 Birkerod, Denmark, *Tel:* +45 7012 4545, *Fax:* +45 4599 2020, *Email:* q8@q8.dk, *Website:* www.q8.dk
Malik Supply A/S, Ved Stranden 22, DK-9000 Aalborg, Denmark, *Tel:* +45 9631 3900, *Fax:* +45 9631 3911, *Email:* info@malik.dk, *Website:* www.malik.dk
Monjasa A/S, Strevelinsvej 4, 7000 Fredericia, Denmark, *Tel:* +45 70 26 02 30, *Fax:* +45 70 26 02 33, *Email:* denmark@monjasa.com, *Website:* www.monjasa.com
OW Bunker & Trading A/S, Gasvaerksvej 48, DK-9000 Aalborg, Denmark, *Tel:* +45 98 12 72 77, *Fax:* +45 98 16 72 77, *Email:* owbunker@owbunker.dk, *Website:* www.owbunker.dk
Trumf Bunker A/S, Raadhustorvet 4, P O Box 55, 7100 Vejle, Denmark, *Tel:* +45 7642 9696, *Fax:* +45 7642 9690, *Email:* trumf@trumf-bunker.com, *Website:* www.trumf-bunker.com

Towage: Two tugs available from the Port Authority of 4750 hp and 3000 hp

Ship Chandlers: Sophus E. Johnsen & Cos Eftf. (Skibsskaarup), Hjortholmsvej 1, Lystbaadehavnen, DK 8000 Aarhus, Denmark, *Tel:* +45 86 12 26 66, *Fax:* +45 86 19 42 09, *Email:* dsc@sojus.dk, *Website:* www.lysholdt.dk

Shipping Agents: Admiral Danish Fleet, JRCC Denmark - Maritime Assistance Service Denmark, P O Box 1483, DK-8100 Aarhus C, Denmark, *Tel:* +45 89 43 30 99, *Fax:* +45 89 43 31 71, *Email:* sok@sok.dk, *Website:* www.forsvaret.dk
Aseco Container Services A/S, Balticagade 15 - Dokken, DK-8000 Aarhus, Denmark, *Tel:* +45 86 13 55 55, *Fax:* +45 86 19 68 38, *Email:* aseco@aseco.dk, *Website:* www.aseco.dk
Blue Water Shipping A/S, P O Box 50, Gamma 3, Soften, DK-8382 Aarhus, Denmark, *Tel:* +45 87 42 90 00, *Fax:* +45 87 42 90 99, *Email:* bwsaar@bws.dk, *Website:* www.bws.dk
DanShip Ltd, Kystvejen 17, P O Box 108, DK-8000 Aarhus, Denmark, *Tel:* +45 87 31 49 20, *Fax:* +45 87 31 49 21, *Email:* danship@danship.dk, *Website:* www.danship.dk
Dasena Agencies, Dasena Agencies A/S, Balticagade 15, DK-8000 Aarhus, Denmark, *Tel:* +45 86 19 22 66, *Fax:* +45 86 19 23 20, *Email:* info@dasena.dk, *Website:* www.dasena.dk
Franck & Tobiesen A/S, Havnegade 4, DK-8000 Aarhus, Denmark, *Tel:* +45 70 10 05 55, *Fax:* +45 70 20 05 75, *Email:* aar@f-t.dk, *Website:* www.f-t.dk
Greenship Denmark A/S (Aarhus), Klamsagervej 19 B, 2.sal, DK-8230 Aarhus, Denmark, *Tel:* +45   86 76 70 00, *Fax:* +45   86 76 70 01, *Email:* greenship@greenship.dk, *Website:* www.greenship.dk
Hecksher Linieagenturer A/S, Marselisborg Havnevej 56, DK-8000 Aarhus C, Denmark, *Tel:* +45 89 33 62 00, *Fax:* +45 89 33 62 01, *Email:* aar@hecksher.com, *Website:* www.hecksher.com
Chr Jensen Shipping A/S, 1 Revalgade, P O Box 81, DK-8100 Aarhus, Denmark, *Tel:* +45 33 74 75 76, *Fax:* +45 86 19 97 63, *Email:* aar@chrjensen.dk, *Website:* www.chrjensen.dk
Thor Jorgensen A/S, Maersk Terminal, Osthavnsvej 33, 8000 Aarhus, Denmark, *Tel:* +45 89 31 64 00, *Fax:* +45 89 34 86 71, *Email:* aar@maersk.com, *Website:* www.maerskline.com
K Line (Europe) Ltd, 6 Sveriges gade, 8000 Aarhus, Denmark, *Tel:* +45 86 13 53 00, *Fax:* +45 86 13 13 38, *Email:* aar@kline.dk, *Website:* www.kline.dk
Lehmann Junior A/S, Europaplads 16, DK-8100 Aarhus C, Denmark, *Tel:* +45 70 13 15 50, *Fax:* +45 35 26 70 80, *Email:* info@lehmann-junior.dk, *Website:* www.lehmann-junior.dk
Maritime Transport Agencies ApS, 56 Marselisborg Havnevej, DK-8000 Aarhus, Denmark, *Tel:* +45 86 18 48 88, *Fax:* +45 89 33 62 62, *Email:* aar@mt-a.dk, *Website:* www.mta.nu
Mediterranean Shipping Company, MSC Denmark A/S, Hveensgade 1, Shippinghuset, DK-8000 Aarhus C, Denmark, *Tel:* +45 86 20 81 80, *Fax:* +45 86 12 57 11, *Email:* info@aar.medship.dk, *Website:* www.mscgva.ch
A.P. Moller-Maersk Group, Maersk Agency Denmark, Osthavnsvej 37, P O Box 438, DK-8100 Aarhus C, Denmark, *Tel:* +45 89 34 80 00, *Fax:* +45 89 34 86 71, *Email:* dansalgen@maersk.com, *Website:* www.maerskline.com
Multi-Shipping A/S, Balticagade 15, Aarhus, Denmark, *Tel:* +45 86 13 53 00, *Fax:* +45 86 13 47 71, *Email:* multi@multishipping.dk, *Website:* www.multishipping.dk
Neptumar N.V., Kystvejen 7, DK-8000 Aarhus, Denmark, *Tel:* +45 87 31 04 80, *Fax:* +45 70 20 05 95, *Website:* www.neptumar.dk
Nordic Liner Agencies A/S, Europaplads 16, P O Box 357, DK-8100 Aarhus, Denmark, *Fax:* +45 46 90 76 01, *Email:* info@nordic-liner.dk, *Website:* www.nordic-liner.dk
Johannes Petersen A/S, Kystvejen 39, P O Box 688, DK-8100 Aarhus C, Denmark,

Tel: +45 86 12 26 88, *Fax:* +45 86 19 13 30, *Email:* agency@johannes-petersen.dk, *Website:* www.johannes-petersen.dk
Safe Shipping A/S, Balticagade 9, P O Box 5162, DK-8100 Aarhus, Denmark, *Tel:* +45 86 12 53 77, *Fax:* +45 86 13 62 63, *Email:* info@safeshipping.dk, *Website:* www.safeshipping.dk
Samskip H/f (Samband Line Ltd), Samskip A/S, Nordhavnsgade 14, P O Box 73, DK-8100 Aarhus, Denmark, *Tel:* +45 46 98 46 98, *Fax:* +45 46 98 46 80, *Email:* samskip@samskip.dk, *Website:* www.samskip.com
Scan-Shipping A/S, 6 Sveriges gade, DK-8000 Aarhus, Denmark, *Tel:* +45 86 20 44 80, *Fax:* +45 86 12 65 91, *Email:* aar@scan-group.dk, *Website:* www.scan-group.com
Seamaster A/S, Balticagade 9, P O Box 5162, DK-8100 Aarhus, Denmark, *Tel:* +45 35 44 15 33, *Fax:* +45 86 19 47 71, *Email:* obj@unilog.dk
Transocean Shipping Agency A/S, Osthavnsvej 11, DK-8100 Aarhus C, Denmark, *Tel:* +45 86 12 15 00, *Fax:* +45 86 12 11 48, *Email:* aarhus@transocean.dk, *Website:* www.transocean.dk
United Shipping Agencies A/S, Shipping Huset, Hveensgade 1, P O Box 193, DK-8100 Aarhus, Denmark, *Tel:* +45 88 83 00 00, *Fax:* +45 88 83 00 99, *Email:* info@unifeeder.com, *Website:* www.unifeeder.com

Stevedoring Companies: Aarhus Stevedore Kompagni A/S, Europaplads 16, P O Box 259, DK-8100 Aarhus C, Denmark, *Tel:* +45 87 30 81 00, *Fax:* +45 87 30 81 01, *Email:* info@aask.dk, *Website:* www.aask.dk
Franck & Tobiesen A/S, Havnegade 4, DK-8000 Aarhus, Denmark, *Tel:* +45 70 10 05 55, *Fax:* +45 70 20 05 75, *Email:* aar@f-t.dk, *Website:* www.f-t.dk
Thor Jorgensen A/S, Aarhus, Denmark, *Tel:* +45 89 31 64 00, *Fax:* +45 89 31 64 55, *Email:* aar@maersk.com

Surveyors: Aros Marine Consulting ApS, Sveriges gade 46, 8000 Aarhus, Denmark, *Tel:* +45 86 19 63 20, *Fax:* +45 86 49 63 90, *Email:* info@arosship.com, *Website:* www.arosship.com
Danish Superintending Company Ltd, Oliehavnsvej 18, DK-8000 Aarhus C, Denmark, *Tel:* +45 87 30 82 50, *Fax:* +45 87 30 82 51, *Email:* info@tally.dk, *Website:* www.tally.dk
Eurobaltic ApS, Randersvej 563, Trige, DK-8380 Aarhus, Denmark, *Tel:* +45 70 23 15 13, *Fax:* +45 70 23 15 03, *Email:* ph@euroinspections.com, *Website:* www.eurobaltic.dk

Airport: Tirstrup, 35 km

Lloyd's Agent: Eurobaltic ApS, Randersvej 563, Trige, DK-8380 Aarhus, Denmark, *Tel:* +45 70 23 15 13, *Fax:* +45 70 23 15 03, *Email:* ph@euroinspections.com, *Website:* www.eurobaltic.dk

AEROSKOBING

Lat 54° 53' N; Long 10° 25' E.

Admiralty Chart: 2532	**Admiralty Pilot:** 18
Time Zone: GMT +1 h	**UNCTAD Locode:** DK ARK

Principal Facilities:

	Y	G			B		T	A

Authority: Aeroskobing Havn, Havnen 7, DK-5970 Aeroskobing, Denmark, *Tel:* +45 62 52 12 53, *Fax:* +45 62 52 21 53, *Email:* aeroeskoebing_havn@post.tele.dk

Officials: Harbour Master: Torben Anderson.

Port Security: ISPS compliant

Pilotage: Available, Tel: +45 62 52 12 53

Radio Frequency: VHF Channels 16 and 12

Traffic: 2004, 75 000 t of cargo handled

Maximum Vessel Dimensions: 85 m loa, 4.5 m d

Working Hours: 0700-1200, 1300-1530

Accommodation:

Name	Remarks
Aeroskobing	Depth on bar 7 to 9 m. Depth in harbour 4.5 m

Mechanical Handling Equipment:

Location	Type	Qty
Aeroskobing	Mobile Cranes	1

Bunkering: Available

Medical Facilities: Hospital in the town

Airport: 9 km

Lloyd's Agent: Lars Krogius Hecksher ApS, Overodvej 5, P O Box 20, DK-2840 Holte, Denmark, *Tel:* +45 33 93 91 28, *Fax:* +45 33 93 27 90, *Email:* denmark@krogius.com, *Website:* www.krogius.com

Key to Principal Facilities:—			
A=Airport	**C**=Containers	**G**=General Cargo	**P**=Petroleum	**R**=Ro/Ro	**Y**=Dry Bulk
B=Bunkers	**D**=Dry Dock	**L**=Cruise	**Q**=Other Liquid Bulk	**T**=Towage (where available from port)	

ASNAESVAERKETS HAVN

Lat 55° 39' N; Long 11° 5' E.

Admiralty Chart: 923   **Admiralty Pilot:** 18
Time Zone: GMT +1 h   **UNCTAD Locode:** DK ASV

Principal Facilities:

Q	Y	G			B		A

Authority: DONG Energy A/S, Asnaes Power Station, Asnaesvej 16, DK-4400 Kalundborg, Denmark, *Tel:* +45 59 55 50 00, *Fax:* +45 59 55 50 04, *Email:* jeslm@dongenergy.dk, *Website:* www.dongenergy.dk

Officials: Harbour Master: Jesper Madsen.

Port Security: ISPS compliant

Approach: Depth through Kalundborg Fjord 13.5 m

Anchorage: In pos 55° 42' N; 10° 59' E, max depth 18 m

Pilotage: Compulsory for vessels over 5000 dwt. Pilot available if required from Kalundborg Pilot, *Tel:* +45 59 56 02 00, *Fax:* +45 59 56 17 00, *Email:* kalundborg@pilotage.dk

Radio Frequency: VHF Channel 16

Tides: Range of tide 0.5 m

Traffic: 2004, 1 219 000 t of cargo handled

Maximum Vessel Dimensions: 290 m loa, 13.00 m draft, 45 m beam, 175 000 dwt

Working Hours: 24 h/day

Accommodation:

Name	Length (m)	Draught (m)	Remarks
Asnaesvaerkets Havn			Harbour serves power station
Coal Pier	290	13	Coal & oil
Oil Quay	300	9.5	See [1] below
Gypsum/Coal Quay	120	9.5	Gypsum at 600 t/h & coal at 400 t/h
Ash Quay	120	7.7	Ash

[1]*Oil Quay:* One 20" and one 16" pipeline to ten shore tanks with a cap of about 480 000 m3

Mechanical Handling Equipment:

Location	Type	Capacity (t)	Qty
Coal Pier	Mult-purp. Cranes	20	2
Oil Quay	Mobile Cranes		

Cargo Worked: Discharging cap of 35 000 t/day

Bunkering: Only by barge or tank trucks, to be ordered via ship's agent

Surveyors: Core Laboratories Lda (Saybolt Division), Fyrtaarnvej 11, Proevestenen, DK-2300 Copenhagen, Denmark, *Tel:* +45 32 95 31 32, *Fax:* +45 32 95 31 34, *Email:* say_dan_cph@saybolt.dk, *Website:* www.saybolt.dk

Medical Facilities: Local hospital

Airport: Copenhagen, 99 km

Railway: Kalundborg, 5 km

Lloyd's Agent: Lars Krogius Hecksher ApS, Overodvej 5, P O Box 20, DK-2840 Holte, Denmark, *Tel:* +45 33 93 91 28, *Fax:* +45 33 93 27 90, *Email:* denmark@krogius.com, *Website:* www.krogius.com

ASSENS

Lat 55° 16' N; Long 9° 54' E.

Admiralty Chart: 2592   **Admiralty Pilot:** 18
Time Zone: GMT +1 h   **UNCTAD Locode:** DK ASN

Principal Facilities:

Q	Y	G			B	D	T	A

Authority: Assens Havn, Nordre Havnevej 19, DK-5610 Assens, Denmark, *Tel:* +45 64 71 31 65, *Fax:* +45 64 71 31 54, *Email:* assensport@mail.dk, *Website:* www.assenshavn.dk

Officials: Harbour Master: Niels Hald-Andersen.

Port Security: ISPS compliant

Pilotage: Not compulsory but recommended for vessels over 600 gt. Pilot can be ordered from DanPilot (Great Belt), Spodsbjerg, Tel: +45 62 50 15 35, Fax: +45 62 50 15 28, Email: belt@pilotage.dk, Website: www.pilotage.dk. Pilot boards in pos 55° 17.4' N; 9° 52' E

Radio Frequency: VHF Channel 16

Traffic: 2004, 129 000 t of cargo handled

Maximum Vessel Dimensions: 130 m loa, 22 m beam, 6.8 m draft

Principal Imports and Exports: Imports: Barley, Bulk grain, Fertiliser, Paper pulp, Salt, Sand, Stone chips, Sugarbeet-molasses, Wood, Wood products, Woodchips. Exports: Bagged sugar, Grain, Peas, Sugarbeet-molasses, Wooden pallets.

Working Hours: 0700-1530 on normal day

Accommodation:

Name	Length (m)	Depth (m)	Remarks
Northern Harbour			
Northern Berth	180	7	Open area of 6500 m2
Eastern Berth	170	7	Primarily used by KFK and DLG
Middle Berth	135	7	Open area of approx 2000 m2
Middle Harbour			See [1] below
Southern Harbour			See [2] below

[1]*Middle Harbour:* Depth of 5 m and primarily used as a ferry harbour for the Assens-Baagoe ferry. It is also possible to call at the S side of Middle Harbour for loading/discharging at a 125 m berth

[2]*Southern Harbour:* Depth of 4 m with a loading/discharging berth 150 m long. In immediate proximity is a storage space of approx 8000 m2. Also includes Assens Shipyard

Mechanical Handling Equipment:

Location	Type	Capacity (t)	Qty
Assens	Mobile Cranes	32	2

Bunkering: Ecophoenix AB, Kungsgatan 54, 753 21 Uppsala, Sweden, *Tel:* +46 1813 1880, *Fax:* +46 1813 1881, *Email:* info@phoenixscandinavia.com
Kuwait Petroleum Corp., Banevaenget 13, 3460 Birkerod, Denmark, *Tel:* +45 7012 4545, *Fax:* +45 4599 2020, *Email:* q8@q8.dk, *Website:* www.q8.dk
Monjasa A/S, Strevelinsvej 4, 7000 Fredericia, Denmark, *Tel:* +45 70 26 02 30, *Fax:* +45 70 26 02 33, *Email:* denmark@monjasa.com, *Website:* www.monjasa.com

Repair & Maintenance: Assens Skibsvaerft A/S, Soendre Havnevej 2A, DK-5610 Assens, Denmark, *Tel:* +45 64 71 11 34, *Fax:* +45 64 71 11 04, *Email:* asv@asyard.dk, *Website:* www.asyard.dk Two floating docks for vessels up to 80 m loa, 15.0 m beam and 1350 nrt

Shipping Agents: A.M. Fage-Pedersen Shipping ApS, 12 Ndr Havnevej, DK-5610 Assens, Denmark, *Tel:* +45 64 71 12 00, *Fax:* +45 64 71 12 55, *Email:* fageship@mail.dk

Stevedoring Companies: A.M. Fage-Pedersen Shipping ApS, 12 Ndr Havnevej, DK-5610 Assens, Denmark, *Tel:* +45 64 71 12 00, *Fax:* +45 64 71 12 55, *Email:* fageship@mail.dk

Surveyors: A.M. Fage-Pedersen Shipping ApS, 12 Ndr Havnevej, DK-5610 Assens, Denmark, *Tel:* +45 64 71 12 00, *Fax:* +45 64 71 12 55, *Email:* fageship@mail.dk

Medical Facilities: Hospital in Odense

Airport: Odense, 40 km

Railway: Odense Railway Station, 40 km

Lloyd's Agent: Lars Krogius Hecksher ApS, Overodvej 5, P O Box 20, DK-2840 Holte, Denmark, *Tel:* +45 33 93 91 28, *Fax:* +45 33 93 27 90, *Email:* denmark@krogius.com, *Website:* www.krogius.com

BANDHOLM

Lat 54° 50' N; Long 11° 29' E.

Admiralty Chart: 2597/1382/2583   **Admiralty Pilot:** 18
Time Zone: GMT +1 h   **UNCTAD Locode:** DK BDX

Principal Facilities:

P		Y	G			B		A

Authority: Knuthenborg Godskontor, Birketvej 1, DK-4941 Bandholm, Denmark, *Tel:* +45 54 78 80 89, *Fax:* +45 54 78 84 58

Port Security: ISPS compliant

Approach: Channel depth 5.8 m MWL and is marked with radar reflector buoys for night passage

Two white triangular beacons in Knuthenorg Park, when aligned, show the course from the sharp bend east of 'Hollaendergrund' to 'Havneoe'. Two similar beacons on Lindholm may be aligned to indicate the course through Bandholm channel from 'Lindholm Dyb' to the sharp bend east of 'Hollaendergrund'

The Harbour has a swinging basin of 128 m loa

Pilotage: Not compulsory but available. Pilot can be ordered from DanPilot (Great Belt), Spodsbjerg, Tel: +45 62 50 15 35, Fax: +45 62 50 15 28, Email: belt@pilotage.dk, Website: www.pilotage.dk. Pilot boards in pos 54° 56.3' N; 11° 21.6' E

Radio Frequency: VHF Channel 16

Maximum Vessel Dimensions: Approx 128 m loa, but dependent on draft

Working Hours: Monday-Thursday 0700-1530. Friday 0700-1500

Accommodation:

Name	Length (m)	Depth (m)	Remarks
Bandholm			See [1] below
West Quay	188	4.4	Grain loading rate of about 140 t/h
East Quay	277	5.8	See [2] below
North Quay	102	4.4	See [3] below

[1]*Bandholm:* Sheltered harbour with 570 m of stone quays available and easily accessible. Depth of water at entrance 5.8 m

[2]*East Quay:* Two berths handling grain, feedstuff, fertlizers, coal and woodpellets

[3]*North Quay:* Warehouse available for grain, fertiliser etc with a cap of approx 10 000 t. There is also a facility for manufacturing feedstuff, 50 000 t per year cap

Storage:

Location	Grain (t)
West Quay	20000
East Quay	46000

Mechanical Handling Equipment:

Location	Type	Qty	Remarks
Bandholm	Mobile Cranes	1	Discharge at 100-180 t/h with grab

Cargo Worked: Average daily rates: fertilisers, stones and feedstuffs about 700-1200 t

Bunkering: Oil can be delivered

Repair & Maintenance: Small deck and engine repairs possible

Shipping Agents: Alfr. Hovmand, Havnepladsen 10, DK-4941 Bandholm, Denmark, *Tel:* +45 54 76 36 11, *Fax:* +45 54 76 36 12, *Email:* alfr@hovmand.dk, *Website:* www.hovmand.dk

Medical Facilities: Available at Maribo, 8 km. Naksov Hospital, 26 km

Airport: Local airport, 20 km

Lloyd's Agent: Lars Krogius Hecksher ApS, Overodvej 5, P O Box 20, DK-2840 Holte, Denmark, *Tel:* +45 33 93 91 28, *Fax:* +45 33 93 27 90, *Email:* denmark@krogius.com, *Website:* www.krogius.com

COPENHAGEN

Lat 55° 42' N; Long 12° 37' E.

Admiralty Chart: 902	**Admiralty Pilot:** 18
Time Zone: GMT +1 h	**UNCTAD Locode:** DK CPH

Principal Facilities:

P	Q	Y	G	C	R	L	B		T	A

Authority: Copenhagen Malmo Port AB, Containervej 9, P O Box 900, DK-2100 Copenhagen, Denmark, *Tel:* +45 35 46 11 11, *Fax:* +45 35 46 11 64, *Email:* cmport@cmport.com, *Website:* www.cmport.com

Officials: Chairman: Peter Maskell.
Managing Director: Lars Karlsson, *Tel:* +45 35 46 11 01, *Email:* lars.karlsson@cmport.com.
Port Captain: Soren Andersen, *Tel:* +45 35 46 11 30, *Email:* soren.andersen@cmport.com.

Port Security: ISPS compliant

Approach: The harbour is formed by a branch of the Sound running between the islands of Amager and Sjaelland, and is divided into three parts: the N Harbour, Inner Harbour and Provesten Harbour. The Free Port is part of the N Harbour. Accessible day and night. The northern part of the N Harbour: Kalkbraenderihavnen and

Ferryport N. Depth of separate entrance channel 6.7 m. The main entrance channel is called Kronlobet, with a depth of 10 m. Entrance between the outer breakwaters 156.9 m wide. The main channel through the port from entrance to the Kvaesthusbroen has a depth of 8.5 m. As far as the Free Port there is a max depth of 10 m, to Langelinie Quay 10 m (partly 9.1 m)

Anchorage: Good anchorage can be obtained in the roadstead outside the harbour in depths up to 16.76 m

Pilotage: Upon entering or departure from the Oil Harbour and Amager Power Station Harbour the following vessels shall have a pilot on board:
1. All vessels of 1500 dwt or more
2. Tankers which have cargoes of, or which have uncleaned tanks which have last contained, a dangerous liquid chemical
3. Except other vessels of 90 m loa or less with bow propeller
Section 2. The provision does not apply to a vessel whose master has entered the Oil Harbour and Amager Power Station Harbour at least 5 times within the past 6 months in charge of that same vessel
Pilot can be ordered from DanPilot (The Sound), Copenhagen, Tel: +45 35 38 67 00, Fax: +45 35 43 10 17, Email: soundpilot@pilotage.dk, Website: www.soundpilot.dk, and boards in the following positions:
55° 45.0' N; 12° 41.0' E (Middlegrund N)
55° 31.0' N; 12° 43.0' E (Drogden)
56° 07.50' N; 12° 30.80' E (Helsingor)

Radio Frequency: Channel 12 and 16

Traffic: 2007, 18 300 000 t of cargo handled, 192 000 TEU's (includes Port of Malmo)

Accommodation: The port extends to a production area of approx 2 000 000 m2 and 3 000 000 m2 of land for future development. Total length of quay is 16.5 km with 4 ro/ro berths and there are 36 km of railway tracks. Part of the port is Denmark's only Freeport with a depth of water of 9.5 m
CMP container terminal (located in the Freeport) with 3 gantry container cranes. The terminals cover an area of 250 000 m2
Mechanical handling equipment in the Port for general cargo: 14 container trucks, 10 terminal tractors, 16 terminal trailers, 12 straddle carriers for container handling, about 80 forklift trucks (2-10 t) and 2 locomotives
The car terminal is located at Orientbassinet at the Free Port. The fenced-in terminal stores new cars tax-free until importation to Denmark or re-exportation. Adjacent to the car area at the terminal is a 32 m ro/ro berth in depth of 10 m
Bulk is handled at Nordhavnen, Sydhavnen, Osthavnen and Provestenen
Two liquid bulk terminals in depth of 12 m with a total cap of 1 000 000 m3. The terminal has test laboratories. Seven berths in depth of 12 m; night berthing possible; water and bunkers available
Large vessels passing through the bridges require tug assistance; contract charges vary according to size and distance. Heavy oils are discharged off the E coast of Amager Island in the harbour Provestenen with tanks of 1 000 000 m3 cap for inflammable liquids. Coal is also discharged at a wharf adjacent to the Amager power station by two luffing grab cranes, 7500 t total daily discharge cap, depth alongside quay 12.0 m, and in fairway to the Kongedyb 10.5 m; at the Oil Pier 12 m
Langelinie pier is the main cruise terminal in depth of 10 m. The 1 km long pier with other terminals has a cap of up to 10 cruise vessels at any one time

Name	Length (m)	Depth (m)
Provestenen		
Oil Pier (Quay 840)	69	12
Oliepirens Ostside (Quay 842)	100	12
Oliepirens Ostside (Quay 843)	105	12
Oliepirens Ostside (Quay 844)	100	12
Laehavnen (Quay 849)	65	5
Laehavnen (Quay 850)	67	5
Laehavnen (Quay 851)	65	5
Kaj I (Quay 853)	138	10.5
Kaj I (Quay 854)	105	9.1–10.5
Kaj II (Quay 855)	125	6–9.1
Kaj III (Quay 856)	88	8.5
Kaj III (Quay 857)	88	8.5
Kaj IV (Quay 858)	68	10.5
Kaj IV (Quay 859)	90	10.5
Kaj V (Quay 860)	110	10.5
Kaj V (Quay 861)	110	10.5
Refshaleoen & Margretheholmen		
Nord for Amagervaerket (Quay 825)	140	6
Amagervaerket (Quay 834)	40	12
Amagervaerket (Quay 835)	110	12
Amagervaerket (Quay 836)	110	12
Amagervaerket (Quay 837)	110	12
Amagervaerket (Quay 838)	110	12
Inderhavnen		
Havnegade (Quay 139)	67	6.9
Havnegade (Quay 140)	100	6.9
Havnegade (Quay 141)	100	6.9
Havnegade (Quay 142)	117	6.9
Havnegade (Quay 143)	120	6.9
Ostkaj (Quay 154)	111	6.9
Ostkaj (Quay 155)	125	6.9
Ostkaj (Quay 156)	125	6.9
Nordkaj (Quay 157)	45	6.2
Vestkaj (Quay 158)	95	8
Vestkaj (Quay 159)	120	8

Key to Principal Facilities:—				
A=Airport	**C**=Containers	**G**=General Cargo	**P**=Petroleum	**R**=Ro/Ro	**Y**=Dry Bulk
B=Bunkers	**D**=Dry Dock	**L**=Cruise	**Q**=Other Liquid Bulk	**T**=Towage (where available from port)

Name	Length (m)	Depth (m)
Vestkaj (Christiansholm) (Quay 642)	147	7.5
Toldboden		
Ndr. Toldbodkaj (Quay 176)	75	6.5
Ndr. Toldbodkaj (Quay 177)	75	6.5
Ndr. Toldbodkaj (Quay 178)	77	6.5
Nordkaj (Quay 179)	25	3.7
Langelinie		
Langeliniekaj (Quay 191)	100	9.1
Langeliniekaj (Quay 192)	100	9.1
Langeliniekaj (Quay 193)	100	9.1
Langeliniekaj (Quay 194)	100	9.1
Langeliniekaj (Quay 195)	100	9.1–10
Langeliniekaj (Quay 196)	100	10
Langeliniekaj (Quay 197)	100	10
Langeliniekaj (Quay 198)	100	10
Langeliniekaj (Quay 199)	131	10
Free Port		
Fortkaj (Quay 241)	70	9.5
Fortkaj (Quay 242)	70	9.5
Fortkaj (Quay 243)	125	9.5
Stubkaj (Quay 244)	123	9.5
Sundkaj (Quay 245)	150	9.5
Sundkaj (Quay 246)	150	9.5
Sundkaj (Quay 247)	135	9.5
Sundkaj (Quay 248)	180	9.5
Sundkaj (Quay 249)	63	9.5
Orientkaj (Quay 250)	65	10
Orientkaj (Quay 251)	75	10
Orientkaj (Quay 252)	50	10
Orientkaj (Quay 253)	165	10
Orientkaj (Quay 254)	165	10
Traelastkaj (Quay 255)	72	10
Traelastkaj (Quay 256)	72	7–10
Levantkaj (Quay 257)	133	7
Levantkaj (Quay 258)	130	10
Levantkaj (Quay 259)	33	10
Levantkaj (Quay 260)	135	10
Levantkaj (Quay 261)	100	10
Levantkaj (Quay 262)	100	10
Levantkaj (Quay 263)	112	10
Levantkaj (Quay 264)	100	10
Levantkaj (Quay 265)	100	10
Levantkaj (Quay 266)	98	10
Kalkbraenderihavnen		
Kalkbraenderilobskaj (Quay 400)	115	6.7
Kalkbraenderilobskaj (Quay 401)	115	6.7
Kalkbraenderilobskaj (Quay 402)	110	6.3
Kalkbraenderilobskaj (Quay 403)	75	6.3
Kalkbraenderilobskaj (Quay 404)	85	6.3
Kalkbraenderilobskaj (Quay 405)	85	6.3

Bunkering: Fuel, diesel and gas oil from all leading firms. Delivered at bunker station located just inside the main entrance to the harbour and by tankers throughout port territory and in roads

BP Marine, Islands Brygge 43, 2300 S Copenhagen, Denmark, *Tel:* +45 7211 1000, *Fax:* +45 7211 1025, *Email:* bpmarinedk@bp.com, *Website:* www.bp.com

Chevron Marine Products LLC, Regus House, Larsbjornsstraede 3, DK-1454 Copenhagen, Denmark, *Tel:* 45, *Fax:* +45 33377261, *Email:* fammd@chevron.com, *Website:* www.chevron.com

A/S Dan-Bunkering Ltd, Strandgade 4A, 1401 Copenhagen K, Denmark, *Tel:* +45 3345 5410, *Fax:* +45 3345 5411, *Email:* copenhagen@dan-bunkering.dk, *Website:* www.dan-bunkering.dk

Shell Marine Products, Naerum Hovedgade 6, Naerum, 2850 Copenhagen, Denmark, *Tel:* +45 3337 2180, *Fax:* +45 3337 2830, *Email:* smpfuelscop@shell.com, *Website:* www.shell.com

Statoil A/S, P O Box 120, DK-0900 Copenhagen, Denmark, *Tel:* +45 3342 4303, *Fax:* +45 3342 4311, *Email:* marinedk@statoil.com, *Website:* www.statoil.com

Statoil A/S, Borgmester Christiansens Gade 50, DK-2450 Copenhagen, Denmark, *Tel:* +45 7010 1101, *Fax:* +45 7010 1401, *Email:* web.dk@statoil.com, *Website:* www.statoil.com

StatoilHydro ASA, Statoil A/S, Borgmester Christiansens Gade 50, P O Box 124, 0900 Copenhagen, Denmark, *Tel:* +45 33 42 43 02, *Fax:* +45 33 42 43 11, *Email:* opsdk@statoilhydro.com, *Website:* www.statoil.com

A/S Dan-Bunkering Ltd, Strandgade 4A, 1401 Copenhagen K, Denmark, *Tel:* +45 3345 5410, *Fax:* +45 3345 5411, *Email:* copenhagen@dan-bunkering.dk, *Website:* www.dan-bunkering.dk – *Grades:* all grades – *Parcel Size:* no min/max – *Delivery Mode:* all modes

Ecophoenix AB, Kungsgatan 54, 753 21 Uppsala, Sweden, *Tel:* +46 1813 1880, *Fax:* +46 1813 1881, *Email:* info@phoenixscandinavia.com

Kuwait Petroleum Corp., Banevaenget 13, 3460 Birkerod, Denmark, *Tel:* +45 7012 4545, *Fax:* +45 4599 2020, *Email:* q8@q8.dk, *Website:* www.q8.dk

Malik Supply A/S, Ved Stranden 22, DK-9000 Aalborg, Denmark, *Tel:* +45 9631 3900, *Fax:* +45 9631 3911, *Email:* info@malik.dk, *Website:* www.malik.dk

Maritime Agency Bunker AS, Standvejen 100, DK-2900 Hellerup, Denmark, *Tel:* +45 7015 1504, *Fax:* +45 7015 0745, *Email:* marag@marag.dk, *Website:* www.marag.com – *Grades:* all grades; in line blending available – *Parcel Size:* no min/max – *Rates:* barge 400t/h, truck 60t/h – *Notice:* 24 hours – *Delivery Mode:* barge, truck

Monjasa A/S, Strevelinsvej 4, 7000 Fredericia, Denmark, *Tel:* +45 70 26 02 30, *Fax:* +45 70 26 02 33, *Email:* denmark@monjasa.com, *Website:* www.monjasa.com

OW Bunker & Trading A/S, Gasvaerksvej 48, DK-9000 Aalborg, Denmark, *Tel:* +45 98 12 72 77, *Fax:* +45 98 16 72 77, *Email:* owbunker@owbunker.dk, *Website:* www.owbunker.dk

Trumf Bunker A/S, Raadhustorvet 4, P O Box 55, 7100 Vejle, Denmark, *Tel:* +45 7642 9696, *Fax:* +45 7642 9690, *Email:* trumf@trumf-bunker.com, *Website:* www.trumf-bunker.com

Towage: Svitzer A/S, Sundkaj 9, Pakhusvej 48, DK-2100 Copenhagen O, Denmark, *Tel:* +45 39 19 39 19, *Fax:* +45 39 19 39 09, *Website:* www.svitzer.com

Ship Chandlers: Berg & Larsen A/S, Baldersbuen 29B, Hedehusene, DK 2640 Copenhagen, Denmark, *Tel:* +45 46 56 55 22, *Fax:* +45 46 56 57 11, *Email:* spares@berg-larsen.com, *Website:* www.berg-larsen.com

Dansupply A/S, Kattegatvej 39, DK 2100 Copenhagen, Denmark, *Tel:* +45 32 95 22 77, *Fax:* +45 32 95 15 77, *Email:* sales@dansupply.dk, *Website:* www.dansupply.dk

J.H. International Marine Supply ApS, Mollelodden 4, Dragor, DK 2791 Copenhagen, Denmark, *Tel:* +45 32 51 19 85, *Fax:* +45 32 51 09 30, *Email:* sales@ims-spares.dk, *Website:* www.ims-spares.dk

Olsen & Co. ApS, Dronningens Tvaergade 50, DK 1302 Copenhagen K, Denmark, *Tel:* +45 33 13 12 62, *Fax:* +45 33 12 05 80, *Email:* jho@anchorole.dk

Schierbeck Supply Services A/S, Baltikavej 10, P O Box 2528, DK-2100 Copenhagen, Denmark, *Tel:* +45 39 29 55 55, *Fax:* +45 39 29 55 66, *Email:* dsc@schierbeck.com, *Website:* www.schierbeck.com

Shipping Agents: Triship A/S, Fyrtarnsvej 1, Provestenen, DK-2300 Copenhagen, Denmark, *Tel:* +45 39 43 39 44, *Fax:* +45 39 43 39 45, *Email:* triship@triship.dk, *Website:* www.triship.dk Chief Executive Officer: Carsten Nielsen Mobile Tel: +45 28195019 Email: cn@triship.dk

ACL Ship Management AB, Transocean Shipping Agency, 53, Hoje Taastrup Boulevard, Taastrup, DK-2630 Copenhagen, Denmark, *Tel:* +45 39 40 40 11, *Fax:* +45 39 40 40 10, *Email:* klaus.kristensen@transocean.dk, *Website:* www.transocean.dk

A/S J Laurittzens Eftf, Scandiagade 15, DK-2450, Copenhagen, Denmark, *Tel:* +45 33 25 29 99, *Fax:* +45 33 25 99 47, *Email:* cc@lauri.dk, *Website:* www.lauri.dk

Aseco Container Services A/S, Sundkaj 11, DK-2100 Copenhagen, Denmark, *Tel:* +45 35 44 15 15, *Fax:* +45 35 44 15 10, *Email:* aseco@aseco.dk, *Website:* www.aseco.dk

Blue Water Shipping A/S, Ventrupparken 8 B, P O Box 315, 2670 Greve Copenhagen, Denmark, *Tel:* +45 43 66 25 66, *Fax:* +45 43 66 25 67, *Email:* bwscph@bws.dk, *Website:* www.bws.dk

CMP Agencies A/S, Fyrtarnsvej 1, DK-2300 Copenhagen S, Denmark, *Tel:* +45 39 43 39 44, *Fax:* +45 39 43 39 45, *Email:* triship@triship.dk, *Website:* www.triship.com

Columbus Shipping A/S, Ejstrupvej 12, Hvidovre, DK-2650 Copenhagen, Denmark, *Tel:* +45 39 61 94 11, *Fax:* +45 39 62 25 14, *Email:* info@columship.dk, *Website:* www.columship.dk

Danish Maritime APS, 17 Adelgade, DK 1304 Copenhagen, Denmark, *Tel:* +45 33 17 95 33, *Fax:* +45 33 17 95 30, *Email:* info@danish-maritime.dk

Dansupply A/S, Kattegatvej 39, DK 2100 Copenhagen, Denmark, *Tel:* +45 32 95 22 77, *Fax:* +45 32 95 15 77, *Email:* sales@dansupply.dk, *Website:* www.dansupply.dk

Dasena Agencies, Dasena Agencies A/S, Sundkaj 11, DK-2100 Copenhagen, Denmark, *Tel:* +45 35 43 33 00, *Fax:* +45 35 43 24 94, *Email:* info@dasena.dk, *Website:* www.dasena.dk

DFDS Tor Line AS, Sundklogsgade 11, DK-2100 Copenhagen, Denmark, *Tel:* +45 33 42 33 42, *Fax:* +45 33 42 34 69, *Email:* info@dfdstorline.com, *Website:* www.dfdstorline.com

Franck & Tobiesen A/S, Dampfaergevej 30, DK-2100 Copenhagen, Denmark, *Tel:* +45 33 13 02 55, *Fax:* +45 33 91 17 58, *Email:* nt@f-t.dk, *Website:* www.f-t.dk

Hecksher Linieagenturer A/S, Sundkaj 9, Pakhus 48, DK-2100 Copenhagen, Denmark, *Tel:* +45 39 16 81 00, *Fax:* +45 39 16 81 01, *Email:* cph@hecksher.com, *Website:* www.hecksher.com

Hellmann Worldwide Logistics, Turbinevej 11, 2730 Copenhagen, Denmark, *Tel:* +45 44 88 10 20, *Fax:* +45 44 88 10 21, *Email:* nordcons@nordcons.dk

Chr Jensen Shipping A/S, St Kongensgade 77, DK-1264 Copenhagen K, Denmark, *Tel:* +45 33 74 75 76, *Fax:* +45 33 32 22 18, *Email:* cph@chrjensen.dk, *Website:* www.chrjensen.dk

Thor Jorgensen A/S, Hoje Taastrup Boulevard 30, P O Box 131, DK-2630 Copenhagen, Denmark, *Tel:* +45 43 59 82 00, *Fax:* +45 43 52 67 77, *Email:* ctjordexpwww@maersk.com, *Website:* www.maersksealand.com

K Line (Europe) Ltd, Snorresgade 18, DK-2300 Copenhagen, Denmark, *Tel:* +45 32 95 32 42, *Fax:* +45 32 57 93 60, *Website:* www.kline.co.jp

Kalyon Shipping Nordic A/S, Sundkaj 9, P O Box 48, DK-2100 Copenhagen, Denmark, *Tel:* +45 33 37 09 00, *Fax:* +45 33 37 09 09, *Email:* jbornak@kalyon-shipping.com, *Website:* www.kalyon-shipping.com

Lehmann Junior A/S, Slotsmark 10, 2970 Hoersholm, Denmark, *Tel:* +45 70 13 15 50, *Fax:* +45 35 26 70 80, *Email:* info@lehmann-junior.dk

Maritime Transport Agencies ApS, Sundkaj 9, Pakhus 48, DK-2100 Copenhagen, Denmark, *Tel:* +45 39 16 36 80, *Fax:* +45 39 16 36 81, *Email:* cph@mt-a.dk, *Website:* www.mt-a.dk

A.P. Moller-Maersk Group, Maersk Agency Denmark, Kalvebod Brygge 43, DK-1560 Copenhagen, Denmark, *Tel:* +45 89 34 80 00, *Fax:* +45 89 34 89 91, *Email:* dansalgen@maersk.com, *Website:* www.maerskline.com

Motorships Agencies A/S, Hornemansgade 36, DK-2100 Copenhagen O, Denmark, *Tel:* +45 39 29 68 00, *Fax:* +45 39 29 75 05, *Email:* motorships@motorships.dk, *Website:* www.motorships.dk

Multi-Shipping A/S, Sundkaj 11, Pakhus 48, DK-2100 Copenhagen, Denmark, *Tel:* +45 35 44 15 55, *Fax:* +45 35 44 15 99, *Email:* multi@multishipping.dk, *Website:* www.multishipping.dk

Safe Shipping A/S, Sundkaj 11, DK-2100 Copenhagen, Denmark, *Tel:* +45 35 44 15

00, *Fax:* +45 35 44 15 70, *Email:* info@safeshipping.dk, *Website:* www.safeshipping.dk

Scan-Shipping A/S, Snorresgade 18-20, DK-2300 Copenhagen S, Denmark, *Tel:* +45 32 66 81 00, *Fax:* +45 32 57 49 00, *Email:* cph@scan-group.dk, *Website:* www.scan-group.com

Trinity Shipping Services Ltd, Redhavnsvej 15, DK-2100 Copenhagen, Denmark, *Tel:* +45 39 16 27 50, *Fax:* +45 39 16 27 60, *Email:* info.dk@iss-shipping.com, *Website:* www.trinity-shipping.dk

United Shipping Agencies A/S, Harbour House, Sundkrogsgade 21, DK-2100 Copenhagen, Denmark, *Tel:* +45 88 38 03 00, *Fax:* +45 88 38 03 49, *Email:* book-cph@unifeeder.com, *Website:* www.unifeeder.com

Stevedoring Companies: DFDS Tor Line AS, Sundklogsgade 11, DK-2100 Copenhagen, Denmark, *Tel:* +45 33 42 33 42, *Fax:* +45 33 42 34 69, *Email:* info@dfdstorline.com, *Website:* www.dfdstorline.com

Franck & Tobiesen A/S, Dampfaergevej 30, DK-2100 Copenhagen, Denmark, *Tel:* +45 33 13 02 55, *Fax:* +45 33 91 17 58, *Email:* nt@f-t.dk, *Website:* www.f-t.dk

StatoilHydro ASA, Statoil A/S, Borgmester Christiansens Gade 50, P O Box 124, 0900 Copenhagen, Denmark, *Tel:* +45 33 42 43 02, *Fax:* +45 33 42 43 11, *Email:* opsdk@statoilhydro.com, *Website:* www.statoil.com

Surveyors: ABS (Europe), Lyngby Hovedgade 98 Street K11, DK-2800 Lyngby, Denmark, *Tel:* +45 33 32 30 70, *Fax:* +45 33 32 27 70, *Email:* abscopenhagen@eagle.org, *Website:* www.eagle.org

Alpha Ship Design, Gersonvej 13, Hellerup, 2900 Copenhagen, Denmark, *Tel:* +45 39 40 04 85, *Fax:* +45 39 40 12 85, *Email:* alpha@alphashipdesign.com

Bureau Veritas, Oestbanegade 55, 2nd Floor, DK-2100 Copenhagen, Denmark, *Tel:* +45 77 31 10 00, *Fax:* +45 77 31 10 01, *Email:* info@dk.bureauveritas.com, *Website:* www.bureauveritas.com

Core Laboratories Lda (Saybolt Division), Fyrtaarnvej 11, Proevestenen, DK-2300 Copenhagen, Denmark, *Tel:* +45 32 95 31 32, *Fax:* +45 32 95 31 34, *Email:* say_dan_cph@saybolt.dk, *Website:* www.saybolt.dk

Danish Institute of Fire & Security, Jernholmen 12, Hvidovre, DK-2650 Copenhagen, Denmark, *Tel:* +45 36 34 90 00, *Fax:* +45 36 34 90 05, *Email:* dbi@dbi-net.dk, *Website:* www.dift.dk

Det Norske Veritas A/S, Tuborg Parkvej 8, 2nd Floor, DK-2900 Hellerup, Denmark, *Tel:* +45 39 45 48 00, *Fax:* +45 39 45 48 01, *Email:* copenhagen.maritime@dnv.com, *Website:* www.dnv.com

Germanischer Lloyd, Hvidovrevej 350A, DK-2650 Hvidovre, Denmark, *Tel:* +45 36 39 00 90, *Fax:* +45 36 78 11 10, *Email:* gl-copenhagen@gl-group.com, *Website:* www.gl-group.com

Knud E. Hansen A/S, Islands Brygge 41-43, DK-2300 Copenhagen S, Denmark, *Tel:* +45 32 83 13 91, *Fax:* +45 32 83 13 94, *Email:* keh@knudehansen.com, *Website:* www.knudehansen.com

Nippon Kaiji Kyokai, Bredgade 20 A, DK-1260 Copenhagen, Denmark, *Tel:* +45 35 26 32 55, *Fax:* +45 35 26 32 53, *Email:* cp@classnk.or.jp, *Website:* www.classnk.or.jp

Odegaard & Danneskiold-Samsoe A/S, 15 Titangade, DK-2200 Copenhagen, Denmark, *Tel:* +45 35 31 10 00, *Fax:* +45 35 31 10 01, *Email:* ods@lr-ods.com, *Website:* www.lr-ods.com

Registro Italiano Navale (RINA), c/o Survey Skibs & Maskininspektion Aps, Adelgade 58, 6th Floor, Copenhagen, Denmark, *Tel:* +45 33 15 45 03, *Fax:* +45 33 11 11 39, *Website:* www.rina.org

ShipTech A/S Marine Consultants, Fruebjergvej 3, P O Box 26, DK-2100 Copenhagen, Denmark, *Tel:* +45 45 76 42 10, *Fax:* +45 45 76 42 20, *Email:* shiptech@shiptech.com, *Website:* www.shiptech.com

Societe Generale de Surveillance (SGS), SGS Danmark A/S, Nitivej 10 B, Frederiksberg, DK-2000 Copenhagen, Denmark, *Tel:* +45 36 93 33 00, *Fax:* +45 36 93 33 01, *Email:* torsten.gustafson@sgs.com, *Website:* www.sgs.com

Survey Association Ltd, 60 Gammel Kongevej, 1790 Copenhagen, Denmark, *Tel:* +45 33 93 25 93, *Fax:* +45 33 55 25 31, *Email:* survey@surveyltd.dk

Airport: Kastrup International Airport

Lloyd's Agent: Lars Krogius Hecksher ApS, Overodvej 5, P O Box 20, DK-2840 Holte, Denmark, *Tel:* +45 33 93 91 28, *Fax:* +45 33 93 27 90, *Email:* denmark@krogius.com, *Website:* www.krogius.com

ELSINORE

Lat 56° 2' N; Long 12° 37' E.

Admiralty Chart: 2594	**Admiralty Pilot:** 18
Time Zone: GMT +1 h	**UNCTAD Locode:** DK HLS

Principal Facilities:

		G		L	B		T	A	

Authority: Elsinore Statshavn, Sophie Brahesgade 1A, DK-3000 Helsingor, Denmark, *Tel:* +45 49 21 05 15, *Fax:* +45 49 21 72 99, *Email:* info@helsingoerhavn.dk, *Website:* www.helsingoerhavn.dk

Officials: Port Manager: Benny Carlsen, *Email:* bca53@helsingor.dk.

Port Security: ISPS compliant

Pre-Arrival Information: 24 h notice: ETA, registry, name, call sign and ISPS details, cargo manifest, crew and passenger list

Anchorage: Available S of the port, in the roads of Elsinore, in depths of 19-25 m with sand or loose clay bottom

Pilotage: Compulsory for tankers only. Pilot can be ordered from DanPilot (The Sound), Copenhagen, *Tel:* +45 35 38 67 00, *Fax:* +45 35 43 10 17, *Email:* soundpilot@pilotage.dk, *Website:* www.soundpilot.dk. Pilot boards in pos 56° 07.5' N; 12° 30.0' E (in the vicinity of Mt Lt buoy) or further NW on request

Radio Frequency: Elsinore Harbour Office calling on VHF Channel 12

Maximum Vessel Dimensions: 145 m loa, 6.1 m draft

Working Hours: 24 h/day

Accommodation:

Name	Remarks
Elsinore	See [1] below

[1]*Elsinore:* Well sheltered harbour, easy of access even for large vessels; area approx 6.9 ha. Depth at entrance and in mid-harbour, min 7.5 m. Total length of quays 2124 m with depth alongside 5.6-6.1 m

Bunkering: A/S Dan-Bunkering Ltd, Strandgade 4A, 1401 Copenhagen K, Denmark, *Tel:* +45 3345 5410, *Fax:* +45 3345 5411, *Email:* copenhagen@dan-bunkering.dk, *Website:* www.dan-bunkering.dk

Ecophoenix AB, Kungsgatan 54, 753 21 Uppsala, Sweden, *Tel:* +46 1813 1880, *Fax:* +46 1813 1881, *Email:* info@phoenixscandinavia.com

Kuwait Petroleum Corp., Banevaenget 13, 3460 Birkerod, Denmark, *Tel:* +45 7012 4545, *Fax:* +45 4599 2020, *Email:* q8@q8.dk, *Website:* www.q8.dk

Malik Supply A/S, Ved Stranden 22, DK-9000 Aalborg, Denmark, *Tel:* +45 9631 3900, *Fax:* +45 9631 3911, *Email:* info@malik.dk, *Website:* www.malik.dk

Monjasa A/S, Strevelinsvej 4, 7000 Fredericia, Denmark, *Tel:* +45 70 26 02 30, *Fax:* +45 70 26 02 33, *Email:* denmark@monjasa.com, *Website:* www.monjasa.com

OW Bunker & Trading A/S, Gasvaerksvej 48, DK-9000 Aalborg, Denmark, *Tel:* +45 98 12 72 77, *Fax:* +45 98 16 72 77, *Email:* owbunker@owbunker.dk, *Website:* www.owbunker.dk

Trumf Bunker A/S, Raadhustorvet 4, P O Box 55, 7100 Vejle, Denmark, *Tel:* +45 7642 9696, *Fax:* +45 7642 9690, *Email:* trumf@trumf-bunker.com, *Website:* www.trumf-bunker.com

Medical Facilities: Helsingoer Sygehus, 3 km

Airport: Kastrup, 50 km

Railway: Helsingoer Station

Development: This port is to stop trading from 1st August 2008 till 1st September 2010 for construction purposes

Lloyd's Agent: Lars Krogius Hecksher ApS, Overodvej 5, P O Box 20, DK-2840 Holte, Denmark, *Tel:* +45 33 93 91 28, *Fax:* +45 33 93 27 90, *Email:* denmark@krogius.com, *Website:* www.krogius.com

ENSTEDVAERKETS HAVN

Lat 55° 1' N; Long 9° 26' E.

Admiralty Chart: 901	**Admiralty Pilot:** 18
Time Zone: GMT +1 h	**UNCTAD Locode:** DK ENS

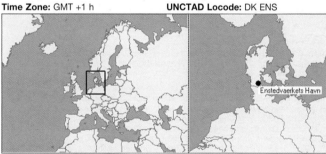

Principal Facilities:

P	Y			B		A

Authority: DONG Energy A/S, Ensted Power Station, Flensborgvej 185, DK-6200 Aabenraa, Denmark, *Tel:* +45 74 31 41 41, *Fax:* +45 76 22 19 73, *Email:* ensted@dongenergy.dk, *Website:* www.dongenergy.dk

Officials: Harbour Master: Clause Sorensen, *Tel:* +45 74 31 42 99, *Email:* clims@dongenergy.dk.

Port Security: ISPS compliant

Pilotage: Recommended from Skaw to Ensted and vice versa for vessels with a d of 13 m or more; greatest permitted d from Skaw to Ensted 17 m. Available from DanPilot (Belt & Fjord Pilot), Fredericia, *Tel:* +45 76 20 03 20, *Fax:* +45 75 92 88 22, *Email:* littlebelt-pilot@lillebaelt.dk, *Website:* www.pilotage.dk

Traffic: 2004, 4 916 000 t of cargo handled

Accommodation:

Name	Remarks
Enstedvaerkets Havn	See [1] below

[1]*Enstedvaerkets Havn:* Coal terminal in depth of 18 m for vessels up to 350 m loa. One coal unloader of 1300 t/h cap
Tanker facilities: Two berths, each for vessels up to 350 m loa; depth 18 and 15.5 m

Mechanical Handling Equipment:

Location	Type	Capacity (t)	Qty
Enstedvaerkets Havn	Mult-purp. Cranes	40	1

Bunkering: Available by barge or road tanker

Key to Principal Facilities:—			
A=Airport	**C**=Containers	**G**=General Cargo	**P**=Petroleum	**R**=Ro/Ro	**Y**=Dry Bulk
B=Bunkers	**D**=Dry Dock	**L**=Cruise	**Q**=Other Liquid Bulk	**T**=Towage (where available from port)	

A/S Dan-Bunkering Ltd, Strandgade 4A, 1401 Copenhagen K, Denmark, *Tel:* +45 3345 5410, *Fax:* +45 3345 5411, *Email:* copenhagen@dan-bunkering.dk, *Website:* www.dan-bunkering.dk

Ecophoenix AB, Kungsgatan 54, 753 21 Uppsala, Sweden, *Tel:* +46 1813 1880, *Fax:* +46 1813 1881, *Email:* info@phoenixscandinavia.com

Kuwait Petroleum Corp., Banevaenget 13, 3460 Birkerod, Denmark, *Tel:* +45 7012 4545, *Fax:* +45 4599 2020, *Email:* q8@q8.dk, *Website:* www.q8.dk

Malik Supply A/S, Ved Stranden 22, DK-9000 Aalborg, Denmark, *Tel:* +45 9631 3900, *Fax:* +45 9631 3911, *Email:* info@malik.dk, *Website:* www.malik.dk

Monjasa A/S, Strevelinsvej 4, 7000 Fredericia, Denmark, *Tel:* +45 70 26 02 30, *Fax:* +45 70 26 02 33, *Email:* denmark@monjasa.com, *Website:* www.monjasa.com

OW Bunker & Trading A/S, Gasvaerksvej 48, DK-9000 Aalborg, Denmark, *Tel:* +45 98 12 72 77, *Fax:* +45 98 16 72 77, *Email:* owbunker@owbunker.dk, *Website:* www.owbunker.dk

Trumf Bunker A/S, Raadhustorvet 4, P O Box 55, 7100 Vejle, Denmark, *Tel:* +45 7642 9696, *Fax:* +45 7642 9690, *Email:* trumf@trumf-bunker.com, *Website:* www.trumf-bunker.com

Airport: Vojens, 25 km

Lloyd's Agent: C. Breinholt A/S, Toldbodvej 1, P O Box 20, DK-6701 Esbjerg, Denmark, *Tel:* +45 79 18 04 11, *Fax:* +45 75 18 19 25, *Email:* mkk@breinholt.dk, *Website:* www.breinholt.dk

ESBJERG

Lat 55° 28' N; Long 8° 25' E.

Admiralty Chart: 420	**Admiralty Pilot:** 55
Time Zone: GMT +1 h	**UNCTAD Locode:** DK EBJ

Principal Facilities:

P Q Y G C R L B D T A

Authority: Port of Esbjerg, Hulvejen 1, P O Box 2, DK-6700 Esbjerg, Denmark, *Tel:* +45 75 12 41 44, *Fax:* +45 75 13 40 50, *Email:* adm@portesbjerg.dk, *Website:* www.portesbjerg.dk

Officials: Port Director: Ole Ingrisch, *Email:* oi@portesbjerg.dk.
Marketing Manager: Soren Clemmensen, *Email:* sc@portesbjerg.dk.
Harbour Master: Torben Jensen, *Email:* toje@portesbjerg.dk.

Port Security: ISPS compliant

Approach: By way of a dredged channel over Graadyb Bar, 200 m wide. The fairway is marked with lights and buoys. The channel depth of 10.3 m MLWS is indicated by leading lights

Anchorage: Two nautical miles W of the fairway buoy (Racon)

Pilotage: If pilot assistance is requested the pilot will board at the entrance of the dredged channel over Graadyb Bar. An advanced notice of at least 6 h must be given via Lyngby Radio. It is compulsory for tankers of 500 dwt or more to have pilot on board when navigating between the sea buoy at Graadyb Bar and the Port and vice versa. Pilot ordered from DanPilot (Belt & Fjord Pilot), Fredericia, Tel: +45 76 20 03 20, Fax: +45 75 92 88 22, Email: littlebelt-pilot@lillebaelt.dk, Website: www.pilotage.dk

Radio Frequency: Port Control listening on VHF Channel 16 and working on VHF Channels 12, 13 and 14

Tides: Under normal weather conditions the tidal range is 1.5 m. The tidal current runs at max 2-3 knots

Traffic: 2005, 4 007 000 t of cargo handled, 1 795 000 passengers

Maximum Vessel Dimensions: 250 m max loa for Australian Quay otherwise 225 m max loa, 9.15 m max d. 10.5 m max d if loa does not exceed 220 m. Also at pilot's discretion

Principal Imports and Exports: Imports: Coal, Foodstuffs, Forest products, Fuel, General cargo. Exports: , Refrigerated cargo.

Working Hours: Mon-Thurs 0700-1600. Fri 0700-1530. Overtime and weekend work can be arranged

Accommodation:

Name	Length (m)	Depth (m)	Remarks
Esbjerg			
Traffic Harbour	1200		See [1] below
Ferry Harbour	630	9.3	See [2] below
Dock Harbour	850	6.7	See [3] below
Southern & Eastern Harbour	1550		See [4] below
Australian Wharf	290	10.5	See [5] below
Taurus Wharf	380	6.3	See [6] below

[1]*Traffic Harbour:* Consists of thirteen berths and two oil jetties
Berths in depth of 10.5-11.5 m MLWS. Oil jetty 1 in depth of 10.5 m MLWS and Oil jetty 2 in depth of 7.5 m MLWS
There are two fixed ramps for ro/ro traffic. A rail mounted gantry crane of 32 t cap and a 80 t cap mobile crane are available for handling containers and general cargo.

Railtracks on the lo/lo terminal area with possibility to combine transport modes. Other commodities in this area are reefer cargo, project cargo and offshore supply and service activity
The two oil jetties handle liquid bulk commodities as well
[2]*Ferry Harbour:* Consists of 3 berths. Two fixed ramps and one adjustable ramp. Mainly ro/ro activity but also possible to handle general cargo. Rail tracks adjacent to the ro/ro terminal with possibility to combine the modes of transport
[3]*Dock Harbour:* 8 berths handling general cargo and offshore base & service activity
[4]*Southern & Eastern Harbour:* Consists of 13 berths. Englandskaj in depth of 7.6 m MLWS, otherwise rest in depth of 10.5 m MLWS
Two of the berths with adjustable ramps alongside Englandskaj, which accommodates passenger facilities
There is a fixed double ramp and rail tracks along Europakaj
A ro/ro terminal with PDI centre for new cars is located in this area; other activities are offshore supply & service activities, general cargo and forest products
[5]*Australian Wharf:* Consists of 2 berths. Two rail mounted gantry cranes handle dry bulk commodities and fossil fuels for the local power station as well
[6]*Taurus Wharf:* Consists of 5 berths mainly used for dry bulk cargo and offshore projects

Storage: Warehousing and cold storage available

Location	Grain (t)
Esbjerg	64000

Mechanical Handling Equipment:

Location	Type	Capacity (t)	Qty
Esbjerg	Mobile Cranes	160	
Esbjerg	Forklifts	55	
Australian Wharf	Mult-purp. Cranes	20	2

Cargo Worked: Grain abt 1500 t/day, general cargo abt 400 t/day, fuel abt 5000 t/day, coal 10 000 t/day

Bunkering: Delivery at berth by road tanker
Ecophoenix AB, Kungsgatan 54, 753 21 Uppsala, Sweden, *Tel:* +46 1813 1880, *Fax:* +46 1813 1881, *Email:* info@phoenixscandinavia.com
Kuwait Petroleum Corp., Banevaenget 13, 3460 Birkerod, Denmark, *Tel:* +45 7012 4545, *Fax:* +45 4599 2020, *Email:* q8@q8.dk, *Website:* www.q8.dk
Malik Supply A/S, Ved Stranden 22, DK-9000 Aalborg, Denmark, *Tel:* +45 9631 3900, *Fax:* +45 9631 3911, *Email:* info@malik.dk, *Website:* www.malik.dk
Monjasa A/S, Strevelinsvej 4, 7000 Fredericia, Denmark, *Tel:* +45 70 26 02 30, *Fax:* +45 70 26 02 33, *Email:* denmark@monjasa.com, *Website:* www.monjasa.com
OW Bunker & Trading A/S, Gasvaerksvej 48, DK-9000 Aalborg, Denmark, *Tel:* +45 98 12 72 77, *Fax:* +45 98 16 72 77, *Email:* owbunker@owbunker.dk, *Website:* www.owbunker.dk
Trumf Bunker A/S, Raadhustorvet 4, P O Box 55, 7100 Vejle, Denmark, *Tel:* +45 7642 9696, *Fax:* +45 7642 9690, *Email:* trumf@trumf-bunker.com, *Website:* www.trumf-bunker.com

Waste Reception Facilities: The port and some private companies can handle various types of waste

Towage: Two tugs available of 2500 hp and 3300 hp

Repair & Maintenance: Esbjerg Shipyard A/S, Molevej 28, DK-6700 Esbjerg, Denmark, *Tel:* +45 75 12 01 50, *Fax:* +45 75 18 01 55, *Email:* info@eds.as, *Website:* www.eds.as Docking of vessels up to 4500 t
Esma Maskinfabrik A/S, H.E. Bluhmes Vej 79, DK-6700 Esbjerg, Denmark, *Tel:* +45 75 13 81 11, *Fax:* +45 75 13 88 13, *Website:* www.esma.dk
Grumsens Maskinfabrik A/S, Morsogade 5, P O Box 1024, DK-6701 Esbjerg 1, Denmark, *Tel:* +45 75 12 54 22, *Fax:* +45 75 12 54 20, *Email:* grumsen@grumsen.dk, *Website:* www.grumsen.dk Engine repairs

Ship Chandlers: Jens Lysholdts Eftf. A/S, Fiskebrogade 8, P O Box 1080, DK-6700 Esbjerg, Denmark, *Tel:* +45 75 12 10 22, *Fax:* +45 75 12 60 96, *Email:* dsc@lysholdt.dk, *Website:* www.lysholdt.dk

Shipping Agents: Blue Water Shipping A/S, Trafikhavnskaj 11, P O Box 515, DK-6700 Esbjerg, Denmark, *Tel:* +45 79 13 41 44, *Fax:* +45 79 13 46 77, *Email:* bwsebj@bws.dk, *Website:* www.bws.dk
C. Breinholt A/S, Toldbodvej 1, P O Box 20, DK-6701 Esbjerg, Denmark, *Tel:* +45 79 18 04 11, *Fax:* +45 75 18 19 25, *Email:* mkk@breinholt.dk, *Website:* www.breinholt.dk
Dan Marine A/S, Trafikhavnskaj 19, DK-6700 Esbjerg, Denmark, *Tel:* +45 75 13 31 22, *Fax:* +45 75 13 78 77, *Email:* danmarine@danmarine.dk, *Website:* www.danmarine.dk
K Line (Europe) Ltd, Malerhusvej 1, P O Box 1077, Esbjerg, Denmark, *Tel:* +45 76 11 45 05, *Fax:* +45 76 11 45 06, *Email:* ebj@kline.dk, *Website:* www.klineurope.com
Niels Winther & Co ApS, Nordre Dokkaj 1, P O Box 21, DK-6701 Esbjerg, Denmark, *Tel:* +45 75 12 83 55, *Fax:* +45 75 12 86 17, *Email:* info@nielswinther.dk, *Website:* www.nielswinther.dk
Scan-Shipping A/S, 1 Maalerhusvej, DK-6700 Esbjerg, Denmark, *Tel:* +45 76 11 45 00, *Fax:* +45 76 11 45 01, *Email:* ebj@scan-group.dk, *Website:* www.scan-group.com

Stevedoring Companies: Blue Water Shipping A/S, Trafikhavnskaj 11, P O Box 515, DK-6700 Esbjerg, Denmark, *Tel:* +45 79 13 41 44, *Fax:* +45 79 13 46 77, *Email:* bwsebj@bws.dk, *Website:* www.bws.dk
C. Breinholt A/S, Toldbodvej 1, P O Box 20, DK-6701 Esbjerg, Denmark, *Tel:* +45 79 18 04 11, *Fax:* +45 75 18 19 25, *Email:* mkk@breinholt.dk, *Website:* www.breinholt.dk
Danbor Service A/S, Kanalen 1, DK-6700 Esbjerg, Denmark, *Tel:* +45 79 11 19 00, *Fax:* +45 79 11 19 01, *Email:* danbor@danbor.dk, *Website:* www.danbor.dk
DFDS Scandic Terminal, Dagvej 1, DK-6700 Esbjerg, Denmark, *Tel:* +45 79 17 70 00, *Fax:* +45 79 17 70 10, *Email:* hans.vejs@dfdstorline.com, *Website:* www.dfds.com
Seaport Stevedoring A/S, Amerikavej 1A, P O Box 52, DK-6701 Esbjerg, Denmark, *Tel:* +45 75 45 11 11, *Fax:* +45 75 12 57 51, *Email:* seaport@stevedoring.dk

Surveyors: Det Norske Veritas A/S, Bavnehojvej 6, DK-6700 Esbjerg, Denmark, *Tel:* +45 79 12 86 00, *Fax:* +45 79 12 86 01, *Email:* esbjerg@dnv.com, *Website:* www.dnv.com

Medical Facilities: General hospital and private clinics in the town

Airport: Esbjerg Airport, 10 km. Billund Airport, 60 km

Railway: Local railway station with connections to all parts of Europe, abt 1 km

Lloyd's Agent: C. Breinholt A/S, Toldbodvej 1, P O Box 20, DK-6701 Esbjerg, Denmark, *Tel:* +45 79 18 04 11, *Fax:* +45 75 18 19 25, *Email:* mkk@breinholt.dk, *Website:* www.breinholt.dk

FAABORG

Lat 55° 6' N; Long 10° 14' E.

Admiralty Chart: 2532/2116	**Admiralty Pilot:** 18
Time Zone: GMT +1 h	**UNCTAD Locode:** DK FAA

Principal Facilities:

			G			B		A

Authority: Faaborg Havn, Kanalvej 19, DK-5600 Faaborg, Denmark, *Tel:* +45 72 53 02 60, *Fax:* +45 62 61 16 57, *Email:* faaborghavn@faaborgmidtfyn.dk, *Website:* www.faaborghavn.dk

Officials: Harbour Master: Lasse V. Olsen, *Email:* laol@faaborgmidtfyn.dk.

Port Security: ISPS compliant

Anchorage: Faaborg Fjord in depth of 6 m

Pilotage: According to draft and tonnage; pilot must be ordered from DanPilot (Great Belt), Spodsbjerg, Tel: +45 62 50 15 35, Fax: +45 62 50 15 28, Email: belt@pilotage.dk, Website: www.pilotage.dk. Pilot boards in pos 55° 01.7' N; 10° 11.2' E

Radio Frequency: VHF Channels 16 and 12

Tides: Range of 0.25 m

Traffic: 2004, 68 000 t of cargo handled

Accommodation:

Name	Remarks
Faaborg	See [1] below

[1]*Faaborg:* Depth at entrance 4.3 m; at quays from 4.57 to 5.79 m. Two berths mainly for fishing vessels and yachts

Mechanical Handling Equipment:

Location	Type	Capacity (t)	Qty
Faaborg	Mult-purp. Cranes	5	1

Bunkering: Various oil bunkers by tank cars and barrels

Repair & Maintenance: Yard for building and repairing fishing vessels

Airport: Beldringe, 30 km

Lloyd's Agent: Lars Krogius Hecksher ApS, Overodvej 5, P O Box 20, DK-2840 Holte, Denmark, *Tel:* +45 33 93 91 28, *Fax:* +45 33 93 27 90, *Email:* denmark@krogius.com, *Website:* www.krogius.com

FAKSE LADEPLADS

Lat 55° 13' N; Long 12° 10' E.

Admiralty Chart: 2115	**Admiralty Pilot:** 18
Time Zone: GMT +1 h	**UNCTAD Locode:** DK FAK

Principal Facilities:

		Y	G			B		T	A

Authority: Port of Faxe Ltd, Hovedgaden 5, P O Box 30, DK-4654 Fakse Ladeplads, Denmark, *Tel:* +45 56 76 35 35, *Fax:* +45 56 71 86 20, *Email:* ksj@ols.dk

Officials: Harbour Master: Knud Severin Jensen.

Port Security: ISPS compliant

Approach: Narrow dredged channel, fairway approx 35 m wide, maximum draft 4.2 m

Anchorage: Anchorage can be obtained 10 nm SSW of harbour

Pilotage: Available on request to Harbour Master and recommended for vessels over 1000 dwt

Radio Frequency: VHF Channels 16 and 13

Weather: Break water and heavy swell in SE gale and storm

Traffic: 2004, 139 000 t of cargo handled

Maximum Vessel Dimensions: 85 m loa, 20 m breadth, 4.2 m draft

Principal Imports and Exports: Exports: Chalk, Grain.

Working Hours: Normal 0700-1500. 24 h service on request

Accommodation:

Name	Remarks
Fakse Ladeplads	See [1] below

[1]*Fakse Ladeplads:* Depth of water in port approx 4.8 m, depth of water in entrance approx 4.5 m

Limestone and grain handled; limestone meal conveyor max airdraft 6.0 m over normal water. Limestone meal conveyor factory 7.0 m over normal water

Three berths: Berth 1, limestone loading transporter. Berth 2, limestone meal loading bridge. Berth 3, general cargo

Storage: Several limestone and grain silos

Bunkering: Available from tank lorries

Towage: Available on request

Medical Facilities: Local hospital

Airport: Kastrup, 75 km

Railway: End railway station close to harbour

Lloyd's Agent: Lars Krogius Hecksher ApS, Overodvej 5, P O Box 20, DK-2840 Holte, Denmark, *Tel:* +45 33 93 91 28, *Fax:* +45 33 93 27 90, *Email:* denmark@krogius.com, *Website:* www.krogius.com

FAXE

alternate name, see Fakse Ladeplads

FREDERICIA

Lat 55° 33' N; Long 9° 45' E.

Admiralty Chart: 900	**Admiralty Pilot:** 18
Time Zone: GMT +1 h	**UNCTAD Locode:** DK FRC

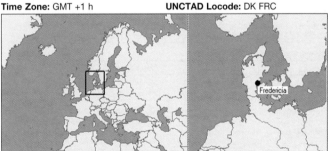

Principal Facilities:

P	Q	Y	G	C	R		B	D	T	A

Authority: Associated Danish Ports A/S, Terminal Fredericia, Vesthavnsvej 33, DK-7000 Fredericia, Denmark, *Tel:* +45 79 21 50 00, *Fax:* +45 79 21 50 05, *Email:* post@adp-as.dk, *Website:* www.adp-as.com

Officials: Chief Executive Officer: Jens Peter Peters, *Tel:* +45 79 21 50 10, *Email:* jpp@adp-as.dk.

Sales & Marketing Manager: Ole Haugsted Jorgensen, *Tel:* +45 79 21 50 35, *Email:* ohj@adp-as.dk.

Harbour Master: Bo T Nielsen, *Tel:* +45 79 21 50 21, *Email:* btn@adp-as.dk.

Port Security: ISPS compliant

Documentation: List of crew (2 copies, also in case of change of crew, a crew list should be faxed to the agent 24 h prior to arrival), tobacco/alcohol/personal effects (1 copy), inventory of duty-free goods (1 copy), tonnage certificate (1 copy), health documentation and certificates, certificates of rat control, loadline certificate, certificate of nationality, certificate of safety equipment, certificate of loading/unloading equipment, bill of lading, manifest

Anchorage: FA1 and FA2 off Treldenaes

Pilotage: Not compulsory. 24 h service from DanPilot (Belt & Fjord Pilot), Fredericia, Tel: +45 76 20 03 20, Fax: +45 75 92 88 22, Email: littlebelt-pilot@lillebaelt.dk, Website: www.pilotage.dk. Pilot boards in pos 55° 35' N; 9° 51.5' E. VHF Channel 18

Weather: W winds

Tides: 0.4 m

Traffic: 2004, 16 800 000 t of cargo handled

Maximum Vessel Dimensions: 300 m loa, 13.5 m draft

Working Hours: Monday to Thursday 0700-0830, 0900-1200, 1230-1530. Friday 0700-0830, 0900-1200, 1230-1500

Key to Principal Facilities:—				
A=Airport	**C**=Containers	**G**=General Cargo	**P**=Petroleum	**R**=Ro/Ro	**Y**=Dry Bulk
B=Bunkers	**D**=Dry Dock	**L**=Cruise	**Q**=Other Liquid Bulk	**T**=Towage (where available from port)

Accommodation:

Name	Depth (m)	Draught (m)	Remarks
Centerhavn			
Quay 21	15	13.25	See [1] below
Quay 22	15	13.25	Max 275 m loa. Dry bulk & containers
Quay 23	7.5	7.5	See [2] below
Gammel Havn			
Quay 6	7.5	7.5	
Quay 7	5.6	5.6	Dry bulk & grain
Quay 8	5.6	5.6	Quay for pilots
Quay 9	6.4	6.4	Used by Fredericia Shipping for repair & fitting
Quay 10			Used by Fredericia Shipping for repair & fitting
Skanseodde			
Quay 41		10	Oil & refined products
Quay 42	15	13	Max 275 m loa. Loading of crude oil
Kastelshavn			
Quay 1	12	12	Chemicals, acids & various liquid commodities in bulk
Quay 2	12	12	Discharge of fertilizer
Quay 3	12	12	Loading of fertilizer
Mollebugthavn			
Quay 24	9	9	See [3] below
Quay 25	10	10	See [4] below
Quay 26	13.5	13.25	See [5] below
Quay 27	12	12	See [6] below
Quay 28	10	10	Discharge of wood
Oliehavn			
Quay 20	13.5	13.5	Gasoline & diesel
Vesthavn			
Quay 12	7	7	Used by Fredericia Shipping for repair & fitting
Quay 13	7	7	See [7] below
Quay 14	9	9	Ro/ro & dry bulk
Quay 15	9	9	Max 165 m loa. Steel, general cargo & dry bulk
Quay 16	9	9	Discharge of salt
Quay 17	9	9	Ro/ro
Quay 18	10	10	Ro/ro traffic to and from Klaipeda. Ro/ro ramp

[1]*Quay 21:* Max 200 m loa. Loading of dry bulk and handling of steel & containers
[2]*Quay 23:* Max 115 m loa. Loading and discharging via hose of acid, fat, chemicals & fertilizer
[3]*Quay 24:* Max 220 m loa. Discharge of wood, steel, cars & general cargo. Ro/ro ramp
[4]*Quay 25:* Max 220 m loa. Handling of steel, wood, general cargo & cars. Ro/ro ramp
[5]*Quay 26:* Max 300 m loa. General cargo, cars, wood, steel, grain, dry bulk. Ro/ro ramp
[6]*Quay 27:* Max 300 m loa. Wood, steel, cars, general cargo & dry bulk. Ro/ro ramp
[7]*Quay 13:* Used by Fredericia Shipping for repair & fitting, also used by tugs

Mechanical Handling Equipment:

Location	Type	Capacity (t)	Qty
Fredericia	Mobile Cranes	52–100	3
Fredericia	Portal Cranes	25	7

Bunkering: Monjasa A/S, Strevelinsvej 4, 7000 Fredericia, Denmark, *Tel:* +45 70 26 02 30, *Fax:* +45 70 26 02 33, *Email:* denmark@monjasa.com, *Website:* www.monjasa.com
A/S Dan-Bunkering Ltd, Strandgade 4A, 1401 Copenhagen K, Denmark, *Tel:* +45 3345 5410, *Fax:* +45 3345 5411, *Email:* copenhagen@dan-bunkering.dk, *Website:* www.dan-bunkering.dk
Ecophoenix AB, Kungsgatan 54, 753 21 Uppsala, Sweden, *Tel:* +46 1813 1880, *Fax:* +46 1813 1881, *Email:* info@phoenixscandinavia.com
Kuwait Petroleum Corp., Banevaenget 13, 3460 Birkerod, Denmark, *Tel:* +45 7012 4545, *Fax:* +45 4599 2020, *Email:* q8@q8.dk, *Website:* www.q8.dk
Malik Supply A/S, Ved Stranden 22, DK-9000 Aalborg, Denmark, *Tel:* +45 9631 3900, *Fax:* +45 9631 3911, *Email:* info@malik.dk, *Website:* www.malik.dk
Monjasa A/S, Strevelinsvej 4, 7000 Fredericia, Denmark, *Tel:* +45 70 26 02 30, *Fax:* +45 70 26 02 33, *Email:* denmark@monjasa.com, *Website:* www.monjasa.com
OW Bunker & Trading A/S, Gasvaerksvej 48, DK-9000 Aalborg, Denmark, *Tel:* +45 98 12 72 77, *Fax:* +45 98 16 72 77, *Email:* owbunker@owbunker.dk, *Website:* www.owbunker.dk
Trumf Bunker A/S, Raadhustorvet 4, P O Box 55, 7100 Vejle, Denmark, *Tel:* +45 7642 9696, *Fax:* +45 7642 9690, *Email:* trumf@trumf-bunker.com, *Website:* www.trumf-bunker.com

Towage: One tug of 1400 hp stationed at Fredericia. Further tugs available with an advance notice of 12 h

Repair & Maintenance: Fredericia Skibsvaerft A/S, P O Box 260, DK-7000 Fredericia, Denmark, *Tel:* +45 75 92 00 00, *Fax:* +45 75 93 34 30, *Email:* fsv@fayard.dk, *Website:* www.fayard.dk Graving dock 108 m x 22 m x 5 m. Floating docks of 227.5 m x 35 m x 8 m with max 22 000 t and 165 m x 28 m x 8 m with max 12 000 t. Slipway of 70 m x 11 m x 5 m with max 1000 t

Ship Chandlers: Fredericia Ship Supply Ltd, Vesthavnsvej 2, P O Box 229, DK 7000 Fredericia, Denmark, *Tel:* +45 75 92 01 55, *Fax:* +45 75 92 02 08, *Email:* fredericia@ship-supply.dk, *Website:* www.ship-supply.dk

Shipping Agents: Fredericia Shipping A/S, Mollebugtvej 5, DK-7000 Fredericia, Denmark, *Tel:* +45 76 20 20 20, *Fax:* +45 76 20 20 21, *Email:* fs@fredericiashipping.dk, *Website:* www.fredericiashipping.dk
Monjasa A/S, Strevelinsvej 4, 7000 Fredericia, Denmark, *Tel:* +45 70 26 02 30, *Fax:* +45 70 26 02 33, *Email:* denmark@monjasa.com, *Website:* www.monjasa.com
Shipping.dk Koge A/S, Oceankaj 12, DK-7000 Fredericia, Denmark, *Tel:* +45 76 20

60 00, *Fax:* +45 76 20 60 10, *Email:* fredericia@shipping.dk, *Website:* www.shipping.dk

Surveyors: Bureau Veritas, Oldenborggade 1a, DK-7000 Fredericia, Denmark, *Tel:* +45 77 31 10 00, *Fax:* +45 77 31 12 01, *Email:* info@dk.bureauveritas.com, *Website:* www.bureauveritas.com
Det Norske Veritas A/S, Snaremosevej 186, DK-7000 Fredericia, Denmark, *Tel:* +45 76 65 67 50, *Fax:* +45 76 65 67 51, *Email:* fredericia@dnv.com, *Website:* www.dnv.com

Medical Facilities: Available

Airport: Billund, 56 km

Lloyd's Agent: Eurobaltic ApS, Randersvej 563, Trige, DK-8380 Aarhus, Denmark, *Tel:* +45 70 23 15 13, *Fax:* +45 70 23 15 03, *Email:* ph@euroinspections.com, *Website:* www.eurobaltic.dk

FREDERIKSHAVN

Lat 57° 26' N; Long 10° 33' E.

Admiralty Chart: 2107		**Admiralty Pilot:** 18
Time Zone: GMT +1 h		**UNCTAD Locode:** DK FDH

Principal Facilities:

P		Y	G		R	L	B	D	T	A

Authority: Port of Frederikshavn Ltd, Oliepieren 7, DK-9900 Frederikshavn, Denmark, *Tel:* +45 96 20 47 00, *Fax:* +45 96 20 47 11, *Email:* info@frederikshavnhavn.dk, *Website:* www.frederikshavnhavn.dk

Officials: General Manager: Preben Reinholt, *Email:* pr@frederikshavnhavn.dk.
Sales & Marketing Manager: Bo Kanstrup, *Email:* bk@frederikshavnhavn.dk.
Harbour Master: Jesper Thomsen, *Email:* jgt@frederikshavnhavn.dk.

Port Security: ISPS compliant

Approach: From the fairway buoy 1.7 nautical miles off the harbour follow the leading lights to the breakwater. The harbour is navigable day and night

Anchorage: Anchorage can be obtained 0.5 nautical miles S of Entrance Buoy in a depth of 12 m

Pilotage: Only compulsory for tankers above 1500 dwt. Available day and night. Requirements through Danpilot Skagen Tel: +45 98 44 55 66, Fax: +45 98 44 59 63, Email: danpilot@pilotage.dk

Radio Frequency: 24 h watch on VHF Channel 16. Working Channel 12

Tides: Range of tide 0.3 m

Traffic: 2006, 3 098 000 t of cargo handled, 2 500 000 passengers

Maximum Vessel Dimensions: 208 m loa, 8 m draft

Working Hours: Monday to Thursday 0700-1530. Friday 0700-1500. No work Saturday or Sunday apart from overtime

Accommodation:

Name	Remarks
Frederikshavn	See [1] below

[1]*Frederikshavn:* The harbour consists of an outer harbour with a water area of 29 ha, protected by two long stone piers and an inner harbour and fishing harbour of about 423 588 m2, in which are quays of 4800 m in all, alongside which vessels load and discharge. Safe max 7.5 m draft. Railway lines connected with the main railway system run direct to the quays. Largest vessel in harbour 60 000 dwt in ballast. Three ferry berths available
Ro/ro facilities available in the southern inner harbour at the ferry berths; ferry berth in the outer harbour; ro/ro berth in northern harbour area 120 m long and 20 m wide with safe water level of 7.0 m. Train ferry facilities for service to Gothenburg are operational
Tanker facilities: One berth; max length of vessel 200 m, max safe d 7.5 m; night berthing possible; water, bunkers and slop tank facilities available

Storage: Warehouses and also refrigerated space available

Mechanical Handling Equipment:

Location	Type	Capacity (t)
Frederikshavn	Mobile Cranes	250

Bunkering: Any kind of bunker oil supplied by boat alongside or by lorry
A/S Dan-Bunkering Ltd, Strandgade 4A, 1401 Copenhagen K, Denmark, *Tel:* +45 3345 5410, *Fax:* +45 3345 5411, *Email:* copenhagen@dan-bunkering.dk, *Website:* www.dan-bunkering.dk
Ecophoenix AB, Kungsgatan 54, 753 21 Uppsala, Sweden, *Tel:* +46 1813 1880, *Fax:* +46 1813 1881, *Email:* info@phoenixscandinavia.com
Kuwait Petroleum Corp., Banevaenget 13, 3460 Birkerod, Denmark, *Tel:* +45 7012 4545, *Fax:* +45 4599 2020, *Email:* q8@q8.dk, *Website:* www.q8.dk
Malik Supply A/S, Ved Stranden 22, DK-9000 Aalborg, Denmark, *Tel:* +45 9631 3900, *Fax:* +45 9631 3911, *Email:* info@malik.dk, *Website:* www.malik.dk
Monjasa A/S, Strevelinsvej 4, 7000 Fredericia, Denmark, *Tel:* +45 70 26 02 30, *Fax:* +45 70 26 02 33, *Email:* denmark@monjasa.com, *Website:* www.monjasa.com

OW Bunker & Trading A/S, Gasvaerksvej 48, DK-9000 Aalborg, Denmark, *Tel:* +45 98 12 72 77, *Fax:* +45 98 16 72 77, *Email:* owbunker@owbunker.dk, *Website:* www.owbunker.dk

Trumf Bunker A/S, Raadhustorvet 4, P O Box 55, 7100 Vejle, Denmark, *Tel:* +45 7642 9696, *Fax:* +45 7642 9690, *Email:* trumf@trumf-bunker.com, *Website:* www.trumf-bunker.com

Towage: Svitzer A/S, Bloden 4, 9900 Frederikshavn, Denmark, *Tel:* +45 98 42 01 90, *Fax:* +45 98 48 11 13, *Email:* svitzer.frederikshavn@mail.dk, *Website:* www.svitzerwijsmuller.com

Repair & Maintenance: Orskov Yard A/S, Havnepladsen 12, DK-9900 Frederikshavn, Denmark, *Tel:* +45 96 20 85 00, *Fax:* +45 96 20 85 85, *Email:* orskov@orskov.dk, *Website:* www.orskov.dk Two floating docks: 135 m x 21.5 m with 7500 t cap and 110 m x 20.4 m with 6500 t cap. Repair quay of 1150 m with max draught 6 m

Ship Chandlers: P. Conradsen Skibsproviantering, Langerak 83, P O Box 229, DK 9900 Frederikshavn, Denmark, *Tel:* +45 98 42 60 00, *Fax:* +45 98 43 15 15, *Email:* pc@pconrad.dk, *Website:* www.pconrad.com

Damsgaard Skibshandel A/S, Langerak 45, P O Box 289, DK 9900 Frederikshavn, Denmark, *Tel:* +45 98 42 78 79, *Fax:* +45 98 42 78 69, *Email:* damsgaard@damsgaardskibshandel.dk

Wrist Shipping A/S, Absalons Vej 22, DK 9900 Frederikshavn, Denmark, *Tel:* +45 98 41 09 77, *Fax:* +45 98 41 09 78, *Email:* wrist@wrist.dk

Shipping Agents: Frederikshavn Shipping ApS, Faergehavnsvej 31 1.sal, DK-9900 Frederikshavn, Denmark, *Tel:* +45 98 42 95 00, *Fax:* +45 98 42 62 10, *Email:* harbour@post3.tele.dk, *Website:* www.harbourservice.com

Hesselby Shipping ApS, Langerak 5, DK-9900 Frederikshavn, Denmark, *Tel:* +45 98 43 88 89, *Fax:* +45 98 43 88 82, *Email:* shipping@hesselby.dk

Nic Pedersen & Co, Umanakvej 10, P O Box 10, DK-9900 Frederikshavn, Denmark, *Tel:* +45 98 42 33 22, *Fax:* +45 98 42 19 20, *Email:* nicp@mail.dk

Wrist Shipping A/S, Absalons Vej 22, DK 9900 Frederikshavn, Denmark, *Tel:* +45 98 41 09 77, *Fax:* +45 98 41 09 78, *Email:* wrist@wrist.dk

Stevedoring Companies: Scandinavian Harbour Service ApS, Faergehavnsvej 31 1.sal, P O Box 138, DK-9900 Frederikshavn, Denmark, *Tel:* +45 98 42 95 00, *Fax:* +45 98 42 62 10, *Email:* harbour@post3.tele.dk, *Website:* www.harbourservice.com

Medical Facilities: Frederikshavn Sygehus, 3 km

Airport: Aalborg, 60 km

Railway: DSB, 500 m

Lloyd's Agent: Rechnitzer, Thomsen & Co. Ltd, Gasvaerksvej 46, DK-9000 Aalborg, Denmark, *Tel:* +45 98 12 44 22, *Fax:* +45 98 10 15 71, *Email:* morten.kusk@wristshipping.dk, *Website:* www.wristshipping.dk

FREDERIKSSUND

Lat 55° 50' N; Long 12° 3' E.

Admiralty Chart: -   **Admiralty Pilot:** 18
Time Zone: GMT +1 h   **UNCTAD Locode:** DK FDS

Principal Facilities:

Q	Y					T	

Authority: Frederikssund Havn, Teknisk Forvaltning, Heimdalsvej 6, DK-3600 Frederikssund, Denmark, *Tel:* +45 47 36 65 30, *Fax:* +45 47 36 65 90

Approach: Vessels not to exceed 5.3 m max d

Pilotage: Not compulsory but available. Pilot can be ordered from DanPilot (The Sound), Copenhagen, Tel: +45 35 38 67 00, Fax: +45 35 43 10 17, Email: soundpilot@pilotage.dk, Website: www.soundpilot.dk

Weather: W winds

Maximum Vessel Dimensions: 5.3 m d

Working Hours: 0700-1600

Accommodation:

Name	Length (m)	Depth (m)	Remarks
Frederikssund			See [1] below
South Quay	140	5.2	
East Quay			See [2] below

[1]*Frederikssund:* Harbour can be entered day and night. Krp Frederiks Bridge, about 1200 m N of Frederikssund, has a clearance of 30 m
Bulk facilities: Cargoes of coal, coke and fertilisers are handled
[2]*East Quay:* Consists of 3 berths, 140 m long and 60 m long with 5.2 m depth alongside and 80 m long with 3.8 m depth

Towage: Available

Medical Facilities: Available

Lloyd's Agent: Lars Krogius Hecksher ApS, Overodvej 5, P O Box 20, DK-2840 Holte, Denmark, *Tel:* +45 33 93 91 28, *Fax:* +45 33 93 27 90, *Email:* denmark@krogius.com, *Website:* www.krogius.com

FREDERIKSVAERK

Lat 55° 57' N; Long 12° 0' E.

Admiralty Chart: -   **Admiralty Pilot:** 18
Time Zone: GMT +1 h   **UNCTAD Locode:** DK FDV

Principal Facilities:

		Y	G			B		A

Authority: Frederiksvaerk Havn, Havnelinien 23, DK-3300 Frederiksvaerk, Denmark, *Tel:* +45 47 72 11 90, *Fax:* +45 47 72 11 90, *Email:* frvhavn@mail.dk, *Website:* www.frv-havn.dk

Officials: Harbour Master: Tom Larsen, *Email:* tom@frv-havn.dk.

Port Security: ISPS compliant

Pilotage: Not compulsory but available. Pilot can be ordered from DanPilot (The Sound), Copenhagen, Tel: +45 35 38 67 00, Fax: +45 35 43 10 17, Email: soundpilot@pilotage.dk, Website: www.soundpilot.dk

Tides: None, but with strong E winds, water level can drop by 0.5 m

Maximum Vessel Dimensions: 120 m loa, 6 m d

Working Hours: Mon-Fri 0630-2200. Sat 0630-1400. Discharging scrap/pig iron 24 h

Accommodation:

Name	Length (m)	Depth (m)	Remarks
Frederiksvaerk			
Oil Quay	90	6	Waiting berth
W Quay	250	5	For discharge of scrap & pig iron
S Loading Quay	420	6	
Coal Quay	90	5	For discharge of scrap
New Quay	400	6	See [1] below

[1]*New Quay:* A continuation of the Coal Quay. For discharge of scrap & pig iron

Mechanical Handling Equipment:

Location	Type	Capacity (t)	Qty
W Quay	Mult-purp. Cranes	5	2
S Loading Quay	Mult-purp. Cranes	24	1
New Quay	Mult-purp. Cranes	10	1

Cargo Worked: Loading 100 t/h, discharging 50-100 t/h

Bunkering: Supplied by truck

Medical Facilities: Hospital within 15 km and several doctors

Airport: Kastrup International Airport, 60 km

Lloyd's Agent: Lars Krogius Hecksher ApS, Overodvej 5, P O Box 20, DK-2840 Holte, Denmark, *Tel:* +45 33 93 91 28, *Fax:* +45 33 93 27 90, *Email:* denmark@krogius.com, *Website:* www.krogius.com

GAMMEL HAVN

harbour area, see under Fredericia

GRAASTEN

Lat 54° 55' N; Long 9° 37' E.

Admiralty Chart: -   **Admiralty Pilot:** 18
Time Zone: GMT +1 h   **UNCTAD Locode:** DK GRA

Key to Principal Facilities:—
A=Airport	**C**=Containers	**G**=General Cargo
B=Bunkers	**D**=Dry Dock	**L**=Cruise

P=Petroleum	**R**=Ro/Ro	**Y**=Dry Bulk
Q=Other Liquid Bulk	**T**=Towage (where available from port)	

Principal Facilities:

		G		B	T	A

Authority: Graasten Havn, Havnekontoret Nygade 36, DK-6300 Graasten, Denmark, *Tel:* +45 74 65 11 60, *Fax:* +45 74 65 11 60

Officials: Harbour Master: K Petersen.

Pilotage: By arrangement with Harbour Master

Radio Frequency: VHF Channels 12, 13, 16 and 19

Working Hours: 24 h

Accommodation:

Name	Length (m)	Depth (m)	Remarks
Graasten			
Quay	160	5	
Jetty	50		Berths on either side

Bunkering: Available by road tanker

Towage: One small tug available

Medical Facilities: Sonderborg, 20 km

Airport: Sonderborg, 25 km

Lloyd's Agent: C. Breinholt A/S, Toldbodvej 1, P O Box 20, DK-6701 Esbjerg, Denmark, *Tel:* +45 79 18 04 11, *Fax:* +45 75 18 19 25, *Email:* mkk@breinholt.dk, *Website:* www.breinholt.dk

GRENAA

Lat 56° 24' N; Long 10° 54' E.

Admiralty Chart: 2108	**Admiralty Pilot:** 18
Time Zone: GMT +1 h	**UNCTAD Locode:** DK GRE

Principal Facilities:

Q	Y	G	C	R		B		A

Authority: Grenaa Havn A/S, Nordhavnsvej 1, DK-8500 Grenaa, Denmark, *Tel:* +45 87 58 76 00, *Fax:* +45 86 32 43 71, *Email:* port@port-of-grenaa.com, *Website:* www.port-of-grenaa.com

Officials: Managing Director: Henning H. Laursen, *Email:* hhl@grenaahavn.dk.

Port Security: ISPS compliant

Documentation: Crew lists (2 copies), passenger lists (2 copies), crew personal effects list (1 copy), ship's bonded stores list (1 copy), stores list (1 copy), animal/pets list (1 copy), health certificate (1 copy), ship's log, last port clearance, bill of lading, cargo manifest, safety certificates

Approach: Vessels approaching should be aware of "Kalkgrunden", a limestone reef just outside harbour entrance stretching approx. 1281 m with only 1 m depth towards the E

Anchorage: N of harbour in 7-11 m depth. Holding ground is fine hard sand

Pilotage: Not compulsory except for laden tankers carrying hazardous liquid chemicals or those uncleaned from previous hazardous cargoes. These regulations do not apply to masters who have entered the harbour at least 5 times within the last six months. Pilot can be ordered from DanPilot (Great Belt), Spodsbjerg, Tel: +45 62 50 15 35, Fax: +45 62 50 15 28, Email: belt@pilotage.dk, Website: www.pilotage.dk. Pilot boards in the following positions:
Route A (transit pilotage) in pos 56° 24.0' N; 11° 05.0' E
Harbour pilot in pos 56° 26.0' N; 11° 01.0' E

Tides: Range of tide 0.3 m. Gales between N and NW can give 1.1 m HW and those between S and SE can give 1.2 m LW

Traffic: 2004, 749 000 t of cargo handled

Maximum Vessel Dimensions: 185 m loa, 9.6 m draught

Principal Imports and Exports: Imports: Containers, Fertiliser, Frozen fish, Limestone, Liquid chemicals, Logs, Molasses, Project cargo, Salt, Scrap, Wood products. Exports: Containers, Frozen meat, Grain, Liquid chemicals, Logs, Project cargo, Sand, Scrap, Wood products.

Working Hours: Mon-Tues 0700-1600. Wed-Fri 0700-1500. Evening, night shift and weekend overtime can be arranged

Accommodation: Depth at entrance 11 m, ferry harbour 7 m
Grenaa harbour is the main supply base for offshore facilities in Kattegat
Bulk facilities: Three conveyor belts, 120-300 t/h max cap. Air draught of conveyor 5 m max
Tanker facilities: Pier 140 m long in depth of 6.2 m and quay 600 m long in depth of 11 m available for fuel oil, molasses and chemicals. Storage cap of 37 000 m3

Name	Length (m)	Depth (m)	Remarks
South Harbour (Basin No.2)			
Quays 21-23	200	4.5	

Name	Length (m)	Depth (m)	Remarks
North Harbour (Basin No.3)			
Quays 31-33	210	6.5	
Quay 34	110	6.5	
Oil Pier No.35	140	6.5	
Oil Pier No.36	140	6.5	
North Harbour (Basin No.4)			
Quay 41	80	7	
Quays 42-44	308	7	
Quay 45	180	8	Ro/ro accommodation
North Harbour (Basin No.5)			
Quays 51-53	600	10	
Quay 54		11	

Storage:

Location	Open (m²)	Covered (m²)	Cold (m³)
Grenaa	1250000	21500	13500

Mechanical Handling Equipment:

Location	Type	Capacity (t)	Qty
Grenaa	Mobile Cranes	32–120	3
Grenaa	Reach Stackers	42	2

Bunkering: Ecophoenix AB, Kungsgatan 54, 753 21 Uppsala, Sweden, *Tel:* +46 1813 1880, *Fax:* +46 1813 1881, *Email:* info@phoenixscandinavia.com – *Delivery Mode:* barge, tanker
Kuwait Petroleum Corp., Banevaenget 13, 3460 Birkerod, Denmark, *Tel:* +45 7012 4545, *Fax:* +45 4599 2020, *Email:* q8@q8.dk, *Website:* www.q8.dk
Malik Supply A/S, Ved Stranden 22, DK-9000 Aalborg, Denmark, *Tel:* +45 9631 3900, *Fax:* +45 9631 3911, *Email:* info@malik.dk, *Website:* www.malik.dk – *Delivery Mode:* barge, tanker
Monjasa A/S, Strevelinsvej 4, 7000 Fredericia, Denmark, *Tel:* +45 70 26 02 30, *Fax:* +45 70 26 02 33, *Email:* denmark@monjasa.com, *Website:* www.monjasa.com – *Delivery Mode:* barge, tanker
OW Bunker & Trading A/S, Gasvaerksvej 48, DK-9000 Aalborg, Denmark, *Tel:* +45 98 12 72 77, *Fax:* +45 98 16 72 77, *Email:* owbunker@owbunker.dk, *Website:* www.owbunker.dk – *Delivery Mode:* barge, tanker
Trumf Bunker A/S, Raadhustorvet 4, P O Box 55, 7100 Vejle, Denmark, *Tel:* +45 7642 9696, *Fax:* +45 7642 9690, *Email:* trumf@trumf-bunker.com, *Website:* www.trumf-bunker.com – *Delivery Mode:* barge, tanker

Waste Reception Facilities: Reception facilities for dirty ballast, sludge, chemical waste, sewage and garbage disposal in accordance to the MARPOL convention

Repair & Maintenance: Grenaa Shipyard Ltd, Grenaa, Denmark, *Tel:* +45 86 32 18 44 Slipway for vessels up to 500 dwt

Shipping Agents: Franck & Tobiesen A/S, Neptunej 1, DK-8500 Grenaa, Denmark, *Tel:* +45 87 58 13 90, *Email:* gre@f-t.dk, *Website:* www.f-t.dk
Georg Ostergaard's Eftf, Djurslandskajen 1, DK 8500 Grenaa, Denmark, *Tel:* +45 86 32 02 44, *Fax:* +45 86 32 00 26, *Email:* agent@oestship.dk, *Website:* www.oestship.dk

Stevedoring Companies: Franck & Tobiesen A/S, Neptunej 1, DK-8500 Grenaa, Denmark, *Tel:* +45 87 58 13 90, *Email:* gre@f-t.dk, *Website:* www.f-t.dk
Georg Ostergaard's Eftf, Djurslandskajen 1, DK 8500 Grenaa, Denmark, *Tel:* +45 86 32 02 44, *Fax:* +45 86 32 00 26, *Email:* agent@oestship.dk, *Website:* www.oestship.dk
Port of Grenaa, Nordhavnsvej 1, DK-8500 Grenaa, Denmark, *Tel:* +45 87 58 76 00, *Fax:* +45 86 32 43 71, *Email:* info@grenaahavn.dk, *Website:* www.port-of-grenaa.com
Oestship, Djurslandskajen 1, 8500 Grenaa, Denmark, *Tel:* +45 86 32 02 44, *Fax:* +45 86 32 00 26, *Email:* agent@oestship.dk, *Website:* www.oestship.dk

Medical Facilities: Grenaa Central Hospital, 3.5 km

Airport: Aarhus Airport, 26 km

Railway: Grenaa, 3 km

Lloyd's Agent: Eurobaltic ApS, Randersvej 563, Trige, DK-8380 Aarhus, Denmark, *Tel:* +45 70 23 15 13, *Fax:* +45 70 23 15 03, *Email:* ph@euroinspections.com, *Website:* www.eurobaltic.dk

HADERSLEV

Lat 55° 15' N; Long 9° 30' E.

Admiralty Chart: 3465	**Admiralty Pilot:** 18
Time Zone: GMT +1 h	**UNCTAD Locode:** DK HAD

This port is no longer open to commercial shipping

Shipping Agents: Hansen JC Skibsmaegler, Honnorkajen 3, P O Box 11, DK-6100 Haderslev, Denmark, *Tel:* +45 74522404, *Fax:* +45 74525639, *Email:* jchansen@vip.cybercity.dk

HADSUND

Lat 56° 43' N; Long 10° 7' E.

Admiralty Chart: 2108	**Admiralty Pilot:** 18
Time Zone: GMT +1 h	**UNCTAD Locode:** DK HSU

This port is no longer involved in commercial trade

HANSTHOLM

Lat 57° 7' N; Long 8° 35' E.

Admiralty Chart: 1402/1422
Time Zone: GMT +1 h
Admiralty Pilot: 55
UNCTAD Locode: DK HAN

Principal Facilities:

P	Q	Y	G		R		B	D	T	A

Authority: Hanstholm Havn, Auktionsgade 39, DK-7730 Hanstholm, Denmark, *Tel:* +45 96 55 07 10, *Fax:* +45 96 55 07 20, *Email:* info@portofhanstholm.dk, *Website:* www.portofhanstholm.dk

Officials: Port Director: Hans Kjaer.
Harbour Master: Klaus Borg Hansen.

Port Security: ISPS compliant

Approach: The port is ice-free all year round. A light buoy is moored 900 m NW of the entrance. There are two leading lights, kept in line at bearing 142.6°. Entrance fairway is 9 m deep. Sand movements may cause water level to recede

Pilotage: Harbour pilots are available at Hanstholm and should be requested through Blavand radio or by VHF to the harbour watch, 8 h before ETA

Radio Frequency: VHF Channels 16 and 12, 24 h/day

Tides: Mean tidal range 0.3 m. The water level is raised in W winds by up to 1.3 m, and lowered in E winds by up to 1.5 m

Traffic: 2006, 561 000 t of cargo handled

Maximum Vessel Dimensions: The max size depends on wind, current and sea conditions. In favourable conditions max dimensions are 145 m loa, 25 m beam, 6.5 m draft

Principal Imports and Exports: Imports: Fish, Oil, Stores. Exports: Fish, Sand.

Working Hours: 24 h/day

Accommodation:

Name	Length (m)	Depth (m)	Remarks
Basin 1			
Berth 12	130	8.4	Ro/ro & general cargo
Berth 13	60	8.4	General cargo
Berth 17	221	7.5	Passenger & ro/ro ferries
Berth 18	122	9	Oil & fish
Basin 2			
Berth 23	100	7.5	Bulk, fish & stones
Berth 24	115	7.5	Fish & general cargo
Basin 3			
Berth 37	120	7.5	Fish
Berth 38	105	7.5	Fish
Berth 39	30	7.5	Fish

Storage: Warehousing and cold storage available

Mechanical Handling Equipment:

Location	Type	Capacity (t)
Hanstholm	Mobile Cranes	60
Hanstholm	Forklifts	6

Bunkering: A/S Dan-Bunkering Ltd, Strandgade 4A, 1401 Copenhagen K, Denmark, *Tel:* +45 3345 5410, *Fax:* +45 3345 5411, *Email:* copenhagen@dan-bunkering.dk, *Website:* www.dan-bunkering.dk
Ecophoenix AB, Kungsgatan 54, 753 21 Uppsala, Sweden, *Tel:* +46 1813 1880, *Fax:* +46 1813 1881, *Email:* info@phoenixscandinavia.com
Kuwait Petroleum Corp., Banevaenget 13, 3460 Birkerod, Denmark, *Tel:* +45 7012 4545, *Fax:* +45 4599 2020, *Email:* q8@q8.dk, *Website:* www.q8.dk
Malik Supply A/S, Ved Stranden 22, DK-9000 Aalborg, Denmark, *Tel:* +45 9631 3900, *Fax:* +45 9631 3911, *Email:* info@malik.dk, *Website:* www.malik.dk
Monjasa A/S, Strevelinsvej 4, 7000 Fredericia, Denmark, *Tel:* +45 70 26 02 30, *Fax:* +45 70 26 02 33, *Email:* denmark@monjasa.com, *Website:* www.monjasa.com
OW Bunker & Trading A/S, Gasvaerksvej 48, DK-9000 Aalborg, Denmark, *Tel:* +45 98 12 72 77, *Fax:* +45 98 16 72 77, *Email:* owbunker@owbunker.dk, *Website:* www.owbunker.dk
Trumf Bunker A/S, Raadhustorvet 4, P O Box 55, 7100 Vejle, Denmark, *Tel:* +45 7642 9696, *Fax:* +45 7642 9690, *Email:* trumf@trumf-bunker.com, *Website:* www.trumf-bunker.com

Towage: Hanstholm Bugserservice, Kai Lindbergsgade 59, DK-7730 Hanstholm, Denmark, *Tel:* +45 97 96 29 99, *Fax:* +45 97 96 29 97, *Email:* nj@tugdk.com, *Website:* www.tugdk.com

Repair & Maintenance: Hanstholm Ny Flytedokk A/S, Professor Lundgrens Gade 22, 7730 Hanstholm, Denmark, *Tel:* +45 97 96 27 47, *Fax:* +45 97 96 28 48, *Email:* post@hanstholm-dock.dk, *Website:* www.hanstholm-dock.dk Floating dock, length 62.5 m, width 14 m, lifting cap 1500 t

Shipping Agents: Nordshipping A/S, Auktionsgade 39, DK-7730 Hanstholm, Denmark, *Tel:* +45 97 96 22 44, *Fax:* +45 97 96 22 10, *Website:* www.nordshipping.dk

Medical Facilities: Health centre in Hanstholm, Tel: +45 97 96 19 22
Airport: Thisted Airport, 8 km
Railway: No railway to the port
Lloyd's Agent: Rechnitzer, Thomsen & Co. Ltd, Gasvaerksvej 46, DK-9000 Aalborg, Denmark, *Tel:* +45 98 12 44 22, *Fax:* +45 98 10 15 71, *Email:* morten.kusk@wristshipping.dk, *Website:* www.wristshipping.dk

HASLE

Lat 55° 11' N; Long 14° 42' E.

Admiralty Chart: 2360
Time Zone: GMT +1 h
Admiralty Pilot: 19
UNCTAD Locode: DK HSL

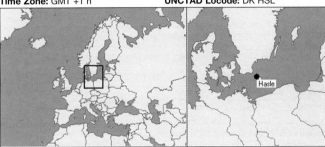

Principal Facilities:

		Y	G						A

Authority: Hasle Havn, Havnen 23, DK-3790 Hasle, Denmark, *Tel:* +45 56 96 41 82, *Fax:* +45 56 96 41 74, *Email:* thomas.steen@prk.dk, *Website:* www.hasle.dk

Officials: Managing Director: Jacob Jensen, *Email:* jacob.jensen@prk.dk.
Harbour Master: Thomas Steen.

Pilotage: Available

Radio Frequency: VHF Channels 16, 13 and 12

Maximum Vessel Dimensions: Max loa 75 m, max d 4.8 m

Accommodation:

Name	Depth (m)	Remarks
Hasle		See [1] below
Basins 1 & 2	4	
Basins 3 & 4	5	

[1]*Hasle:* Well sheltered port with depth at entrance of 5.5 m. Ramp facility of 50 t cap for bulk cargo

Airport: Ronne, 15 km

Lloyd's Agent: Lars Krogius Hecksher ApS, Overodvej 5, P O Box 20, DK-2840 Holte, Denmark, *Tel:* +45 33 93 91 28, *Fax:* +45 33 93 27 90, *Email:* denmark@krogius.com, *Website:* www.krogius.com

HELSINGOR

alternate name, see Elsinore

HIRTSHALS

Lat 57° 36' N; Long 9° 58' E.

Admiralty Chart: 1402
Time Zone: GMT +1 h
Admiralty Pilot: 55
UNCTAD Locode: DK HIR

Principal Facilities:

P		Y	G	C	R		B		T	A

Authority: Port of Hirtshals, Norgeskajen 11, P O Box 3, DK-9850 Hirtshals, Denmark, *Tel:* +45 98 94 14 22, *Fax:* +45 98 94 42 93, *Email:* hirtshalshavn@hirtshalshavn.dk, *Website:* www.hirtshalshavn.dk

Officials: Managing Director: Jens Kirketerp Jensen, *Tel:* +45 96 56 50 02, *Email:* j.jensen@hirtshalshavn.dk.
Harbour Master: Jan Bruun Pedersen, *Tel:* +45 96 56 50 03, *Email:* j.b.pedersen@hirtshalshavn.dk.

Port Security: ISPS compliant

Key to Principal Facilities:—			
A=Airport	**C**=Containers	**G**=General Cargo	**P**=Petroleum **R**=Ro/Ro **Y**=Dry Bulk
B=Bunkers	**D**=Dry Dock	**L**=Cruise	**Q**=Other Liquid Bulk **T**=Towage (where available from port)

Approach: The entrance which is from the W is protected by a 400 m long breakwater and is dredged to a depth of 8.0 m. Light-buoys are moored at both sides of the entrance. A pair of leading lights, in a line bearing 166° leads into the harbour

Pilotage: Not compulsory. Pilot service available from Harbour Office, Tel: +45 98 94 14 22, day and night

Radio Frequency: VHF Channel 16

Traffic: 2004, 1 270 000 t of cargo handled

Maximum Vessel Dimensions: Approx 140 m loa, 7.5 m max d

Working Hours: Monday and Tuesday 0700-1600. Wednesday to Friday 0700-1500. Overtime can be worked Saturday and Sunday

Accommodation:

Name	Remarks
Hirtshals	See [1] below

[1]*Hirtshals:* Harbour well protected by moles. Depth at entrance 9.5 m and 9 m in the outer harbour and along the Norgesquay. A large centre for the fishing industry

Storage: One 12 000 t cap and one 4000 t cap refrigerated warehouse with 6000 t cap bonded warehouse for frozen fish and fish products. One 500 m2 insulated warehouse for general cargo and other warehouse space for general cargo of approx 2000 t cap

Mechanical Handling Equipment:

Location	Type	Qty	Remarks
Hirtshals	Mobile Cranes	1	equipped with container spreader

Bunkering: A/S Dan-Bunkering Ltd, Strandgade 4A, 1401 Copenhagen K, Denmark, *Tel:* +45 3345 5410, *Fax:* +45 3345 5411, *Email:* copenhagen@dan-bunkering.dk, *Website:* www.dan-bunkering.dk – *Delivery Mode:* barge, truck
Ecophoenix AB, Kungsgatan 54, 753 21 Uppsala, Sweden, *Tel:* +46 1813 1880, *Fax:* +46 1813 1881, *Email:* info@phoenixscandinavia.com – *Delivery Mode:* barge, truck
Kuwait Petroleum Corp., Banevaenget 13, 3460 Birkerod, Denmark, *Tel:* +45 7012 4545, *Fax:* +45 4599 2020, *Email:* q8@q8.dk, *Website:* www.q8.dk
Malik Supply A/S, Ved Stranden 22, DK-9000 Aalborg, Denmark, *Tel:* +45 9631 3900, *Fax:* +45 9631 3911, *Email:* info@malik.dk, *Website:* www.malik.dk – *Delivery Mode:* barge, truck
Monjasa A/S, Strevlinsvej 4, 7000 Fredericia, Denmark, *Tel:* +45 70 26 02 30, *Fax:* +45 70 26 02 33, *Email:* denmark@monjasa.com, *Website:* www.monjasa.com – *Delivery Mode:* barge, truck
OW Bunker & Trading A/S, Gasvaerksvej 48, DK-9000 Aalborg, Denmark, *Tel:* +45 98 12 72 77, *Fax:* +45 98 16 72 77, *Email:* owbunker@owbunker.dk, *Website:* www.owbunker.dk – *Delivery Mode:* barge, truck
Trumf Bunker A/S, Raadhustorvet 4, P O Box 55, 7100 Vejle, Denmark, *Tel:* +45 7642 9696, *Fax:* +45 7642 9690, *Email:* trumf@trumf-bunker.com, *Website:* www.trumf-bunker.com – *Delivery Mode:* barge, truck

Waste Reception Facilities: Sludge and garbage facilities available

Towage: Available from Harbour Office

Shipping Agents: Blue Water Shipping A/S, Notkajen 2, DK-9850 Hirtshals, Denmark, *Tel:* +45 98 94 55 22, *Fax:* +45 98 94 55 20, *Email:* bwshhs@bws.dk, *Website:* www.bws.dk
Jens Berg Shipping ApS, Niels Juelsvej 14, DK-9850 Hirtshals, Denmark, *Tel:* +45 98 94 42 22, *Fax:* +45 98 94 47 36, *Email:* post@bergship.dk, *Website:* www.bergship.dk

Medical Facilities: Hospital, 16 km

Airport: Aalborg, 56 km

Railway: Hirtshals Privatbane, 2 km

Lloyd's Agent: Rechnitzer, Thomsen & Co. Ltd, Gasvaerksvej 46, DK-9000 Aalborg, Denmark, *Tel:* +45 98 12 44 22, *Fax:* +45 98 10 15 71, *Email:* morten.kusk@wristshipping.dk, *Website:* www.wristshipping.dk

HOBRO

Lat 56° 38' N; Long 9° 48' E.

Admiralty Chart: 2108	**Admiralty Pilot:** 18
Time Zone: GMT +1 h	**UNCTAD Locode:** DK HBO

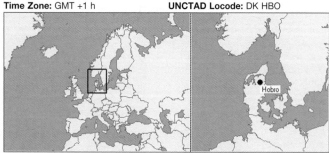

Principal Facilities:

		G		B	T	A

Authority: Hobro Havn, Ndr. Kajgade 1, DK-9500 Hobro, Denmark, *Tel:* +45 97 11 30 00, *Fax:* +45 98 51 16 38, *Email:* raadhus@mariagerfjord.dk, *Website:* www.mariagerfjord.dk

Officials: Chief Engineer: Hans Gro Hansen, *Email:* hahan@mariagerfjord.dk.

Port Security: ISPS compliant

Approach: Sand bar outside Mariagerfjord, 5.7 m d in fjord

Pilotage: Compulsory for vessels exceeding 3.5 m d and/or 1000 dwt. Pilots obtainable from DanPilot (Great Belt), Spodsbjerg, Tel: +45 62 50 15 35, Fax: +45 62

50 15 28, Email: belt@pilotage.dk, Website: www.pilotage.dk. Pilot boards in pos 56° 41.3' N; 10° 30.0' E

Traffic: 2004, 114 000 t of cargo handled

Maximum Vessel Dimensions: Approx 110 m loa, 5.1 m d

Working Hours: Mon and Tues 0700-0830, 0900-1200, 1230-1600. Wed-Fri 0700-0830, 0900-1200, 1230-1500

Accommodation:

Name	Remarks
Hobro	Depth at entrance and at quay 5.7 m; length of quay 516 m. Branch line of railway at quay

Mechanical Handling Equipment:

Location	Type	Qty
Hobro	Mult-purp. Cranes	1
Hobro	Mobile Cranes	1

Bunkering: Available by lorries

Towage: Tug boat available

Repair & Maintenance: Hobro Vaerft ApS, v/ Gunnar Brink Christensen, Skibsgade 37, DK-9500 Hobro, Denmark, *Tel:* +45 98 52 37 69, *Fax:* +45 98 51 13 90, *Email:* info@hobrovaerft.dk, *Website:* www.hobrovaerft.dk Only for small vessels

Medical Facilities: Available

Airport: Aalborg, 60 km

Lloyd's Agent: Eurobaltic ApS, Randersvej 563, Trige, DK-8380 Aarhus, Denmark, *Tel:* +45 70 23 15 13, *Fax:* +45 70 23 15 03, *Email:* ph@euroinspections.com, *Website:* www.eurobaltic.dk

HORSENS

Lat 55° 51' N; Long 9° 51' E.

Admiralty Chart: 929	**Admiralty Pilot:** 18
Time Zone: GMT +1 h	**UNCTAD Locode:** DK HOR

Principal Facilities:

P	Q	Y	G		R		B		T	A

Authority: Horsens Havn A/S, Ove Jensens Alle 35, DK-8700 Horsens, Denmark, *Tel:* +45 75 62 10 14, *Fax:* +45 75 62 14 57, *Email:* horsens.havn@horsens.dk, *Website:* www.horsenshavn.dk

Officials: Harbour Master: Peter C.H. Larsen, *Email:* pchl@horsens.dk.

Port Security: ISPS compliant

Pre-Arrival Information: Crew list, list of 10 last ports of call and garbage disposal list to be sent through ship's agent

Documentation: Crew list, crew declaration, ships declaration, cargo documents

Anchorage: S of As Hoved in a depth of 16 m

Pilotage: Available at Lillegrund from DanPilot (Belt & Fjord Pilot), Fredericia, Tel: +45 76 20 03 20, Fax: +45 75 92 88 22, Email: littlebelt-pilot@lillebaelt.dk, Website: www.pilotage.dk

Radio Frequency: Lyngby radio, call sign OXZ; Skagen radio, call sign OXP

Tides: Range of tide 0.4 m. Gales from S and SW may lower water to 1 m, N to NW winds may rise tides by 1.5 m

Traffic: 2004, 415 933 t of cargo handled

Maximum Vessel Dimensions: 160 m long, 25 m wide, 6.7 m draft

Principal Imports and Exports: Imports: Coal, Fertiliser, Foodstuffs, Grain, Iron, Oil, Timber. Exports: General cargo, Grain, Malt.

Working Hours: Mon to Thurs 0700-1530. Fri 0700-1500. No work on Sat

Accommodation:

Name	Remarks
Horsens	See [1] below

[1]*Horsens:* Depth in river and harbour 6.9 m. Length of quays 2000 m. Along the berths are modern silos and warehouses for fertilisers, grain and general cargoes. Railway alongside all quays
Bulk facilities: 20 000 m2 timber terminal

Storage: Ample warehouse and open storage facilities available

Mechanical Handling Equipment:

Location	Type	Capacity (t)	Qty
Horsens	Mobile Cranes	12–80	3

Bunkering: Light and heavy fuel available

Waste Reception Facilities: Engine slop

Towage: No tugs are stationed in the harbour, but can be ordered with 24 h notice

Repair & Maintenance: Repairing slips to lift 100 t

Stevedoring Companies: DKI Shipping ApS, Ove Jensens Alle 35, DK-8700 Horsens, Denmark, *Tel:* +45 76 26 56 00, *Fax:* +45 76 26 56 01, *Email:* mail@dki-shipping.dk

EP Spedition, Ove Jensens Alle 54, DK-8700 Horsens, Denmark, *Tel:* +45 75 61 67 66, *Fax:* +45 75 61 67 68, *Email:* ep@spedition.dk

Medical Facilities: Full facilities available

Airport: Billund, 54 km

Lloyd's Agent: Eurobaltic ApS, Randersvej 563, Trige, DK-8380 Aarhus, Denmark, *Tel:* +45 70 23 15 13, *Fax:* +45 70 23 15 03, *Email:* ph@euroinspections.com, *Website:* www.eurobaltic.dk

KALUNDBORG

Lat 55° 40' N; Long 11° 5' E.

Admiralty Chart: 923　　　　　　　　**Admiralty Pilot:** 18

Time Zone: GMT +1 h　　　　　　　**UNCTAD Locode:** DK KAL

Principal Facilities:

P	Y	G	R	B		T	

Authority: Kalundborg Havn, Baltic Plads 2, P O Box 54, DK-4400 Kalundborg, Denmark, *Tel:* +45 59 53 40 00, *Fax:* +45 59 53 40 03, *Email:* info@portofkalundborg.dk, *Website:* www.portofkalundborg.dk

Officials: Port Director: Bent Rasmussen, *Email:* br@portofkalundborg.dk.

Port Security: ISPS compliant. PFSO: Arne Rydahl, Tel: +45 59 53 40 00, Fax: +45 59 53 40 03

Pre-Arrival Information: Master's of deep-sea vessels are requested to advise their Agents of their ETA 72 h in advance, and again 24 h before ETA. For other vessels operating in Scandinavian waters, a 24 h ETA notice will be required. For coastal traffic in Danish waters, ETA is required when departing for Kalundborg. If there should be any significant change in the ETA over 2 h, additional advice is required
All vessels to inform Kalundborg Port 24 h prior to arrival of:
ship's name
IMO No.
ISSC No.
last 10 ports of call
IMDG code
waste declaration

Documentation: 1 bill of lading (if cargo), 1 crew list, 1 derat certificate or exemption, 1 load line certificate, 1 safety construction certificate, 1 safety equipment certificate, 1 safety radio certificate, 1 ship's register
Customs need a tobacco and spirit list, showing the vessel's and the crew's supply by arrival

Approach: Entrance channel: width 80 m with depth 12 m and width 100 m with depth 10 m

Anchorage: Large vessels anchor in 14.02 m of water between Roesnaes and Asnaes. Small vessels anchor between Gisselore Point and Harbour

Pilotage: Not compulsory. Pilot station situated at Kalundborg, telegram: Kalundborg Pilot, Tel: +45 59 56 02 00. Orange vessel carrying international signal flag or lights for Pilot. Contact by VHF Channels 16, 12 and 6. Pilot is taken on board at the entrance of Kalundborg Fjord
Larger vessels usually take pilot by Skaw L/V. Pilots to be ordered by ETA - telegrams to 'Danpilot, Region Skagen', at least 12 h in advance. Danpilot listening on VHF Channel 16

Radio Frequency: Office listens on VHF Channel 16 and works on Channels 12 and 13

Weather: SW to NW winds cause swell but holding ground is good

Traffic: 2004, 3 401 000 t of cargo handled

Maximum Vessel Dimensions: 235 m max loa, 32 m max beam, 11.6 m max draft

Principal Imports and Exports: Imports: Foodstuffs, Phosphate. Exports: Grain.

Working Hours: Monday to Thursday 0700-1530. Friday 0700-1500

Accommodation: Tanker facilities: Operated by Statoil A/S, Melby, Kalundborg, Tel: +45 59 57 40 00, Fax: +45 59 51 70 81. Situated 0.8 km S of Kalundborg Harbour. Finger pier with three berths, lengths range from 73.14 m to 274.31 m. Berth No.1, 12.99 m depth, 12.5 m max safe d. Berth No.2, 10.49 m depth. Berth No.3, 5 m depth. Also Berth 'E', 330 m long in depth of 15 m. Water available and night berthing possible

Name	Length (m)	Depth (m)	Remarks
West Harbour			
Quay I	250	6	
Quay II	125	6	Ramp
Quay III	80	6	
Ferries	80	6	

Name	Length (m)	Depth (m)	Remarks
East Harbour			
Quay IV	110	8	
Quay V	80	10	
Quay VI	240	10	
Quay VII	170	6	
Quay IX	280	6	
Quay X	245	7	Ramp
South Harbour			
Quay XI (Oil Berth)	170	9	
Quay XII	240	10	Ramp
Quay XIII	210	12	
Dock Harbour			
Quay XIV W	160	9	
Quay XIV E	120	5	
Quay XV	140	9.5	

Mechanical Handling Equipment:

Location	Type	Capacity (t)	Qty
Kalundborg	Mobile Cranes	25	2

Bunkering: Jorgen Schultz Shipping A/S, Vestre Havneplads 2, DK-4400 Kalundborg, Denmark, *Tel:* +45 59 57 85 00, *Fax:* +45 59 51 17 52, *Email:* schultz@schultzshipping.dk, *Website:* www.schultzshipping.com
A/S Dan-Bunkering Ltd, Strandgade 4A, 1401 Copenhagen K, Denmark, *Tel:* +45 3345 5410, *Fax:* +45 3345 5411, *Email:* copenhagen@dan-bunkering.dk, *Website:* www.dan-bunkering.dk
Ecophoenix AB, Kungsgatan 54, 753 21 Uppsala, Sweden, *Tel:* +46 1813 1880, *Fax:* +46 1813 1881, *Email:* info@phoenixscandinavia.com
Kuwait Petroleum Corp., Banevaenget 13, 3460 Birkerod, Denmark, *Tel:* +45 7012 4545, *Fax:* +45 4599 2020, *Email:* q8@q8.dk, *Website:* www.q8.dk
Malik Supply A/S, Ved Stranden 22, DK-9000 Aalborg, Denmark, *Tel:* +45 9631 3900, *Fax:* +45 9631 3911, *Email:* info@malik.dk, *Website:* www.malik.dk
Monjasa A/S, Strevelinsvej 4, 7000 Fredericia, Denmark, *Tel:* +45 70 26 02 30, *Fax:* +45 70 26 02 33, *Email:* denmark@monjasa.com, *Website:* www.monjasa.com
OW Bunker & Trading A/S, Gasvaerksvej 48, DK-9000 Aalborg, Denmark, *Tel:* +45 98 12 72 77, *Fax:* +45 98 16 72 77, *Email:* owbunker@owbunker.dk, *Website:* www.owbunker.dk
Trumf Bunker A/S, Raadhustorvet 4, P O Box 55, 7100 Vejle, Denmark, *Tel:* +45 7642 9696, *Fax:* +45 7642 9690, *Email:* trumf@trumf-bunker.com, *Website:* www.trumf-bunker.com

Waste Reception Facilities: Skip provided free of charge on pier for disposal of garbage from last sea passage. For garbage collected during stay, skips can be ordered through Agent
Mineral oil, free of chemical additives, is received free of charge. Used lube oil and slop oil (from last voyage), either in drums or up to 10 m3. by tanker truck, is also received free of charge. Contact Ship's Agent for information

Towage: Available

Repair & Maintenance: Robert Jorgensens Eftf, Kalundborg, Denmark, *Tel:* +45 59 51 13 10 Repair facilities

Ship Chandlers: Schierbeck Supply Services A/S, Vestre Havnepladsen 5B, DK 4400 Kalundborg, Denmark, *Tel:* +45 39 29 55 55, *Fax:* +45 39 29 55 66, *Email:* dsc@schierbeck.com, *Website:* www.schierbeck.com
Wrist Shipping A/S, Skibbrogade1, P O Box 68, DK 4400 Kalundborg, Denmark, *Tel:* +45 59 51 03 45, *Fax:* +45 59 51 07 51, *Email:* kalundborg@wrist.dk

Shipping Agents: Jorgen Schultz Shipping A/S, Vestre Havneplads 2, DK-4400 Kalundborg, Denmark, *Tel:* +45 59 57 85 00, *Fax:* +45 59 51 17 52, *Email:* schultz@schultzshipping.dk, *Website:* www.schultzshipping.com
Shipping.dk Kalundborg A/S, Vestre Havneplads 7, DK-4400 Kalundborg, Denmark, *Tel:* +45 70 27 44 40, *Fax:* +45 70 22 28 11, *Email:* kalundborg@shipping.dk, *Website:* www.shipping.dk
Wrist Shipping A/S, Skibbrogade1, P O Box 68, DK 4400 Kalundborg, Denmark, *Tel:* +45 59 51 03 45, *Fax:* +45 59 51 07 51, *Email:* kalundborg@wrist.dk

Stevedoring Companies: Shipping.dk Kalundborg A/S, Vestre Havneplads 7, DK-4400 Kalundborg, Denmark, *Tel:* +45 70 27 44 40, *Fax:* +45 70 22 28 11, *Email:* kalundborg@shipping.dk, *Website:* www.shipping.dk

Surveyors: Caleb Brett/Deniz Survey A.S., Dokhavnsvej 3, DK-4400 Kalundborg, Denmark, *Tel:* +45 59 51 32 23, *Fax:* +45 59 51 35 51, *Email:* opscpe.denmark@intertek.com, *Website:* www.intertek.com

Medical Facilities: Hospital and doctors available

Airport: Copenhagen (Kastrup), 130 km

Lloyd's Agent: Lars Krogius Hecksher ApS, Overodvej 5, P O Box 20, DK-2840 Holte, Denmark, *Tel:* +45 33 93 91 28, *Fax:* +45 33 93 27 90, *Email:* denmark@krogius.com, *Website:* www.krogius.com

KASTELSHAVN

harbour area, see under Fredericia

KERTEMINDE

Lat 55° 27' N; Long 10° 40' E.

Admiralty Chart: 2596　　　　　　**Admiralty Pilot:** 18

Time Zone: GMT +1 h　　　　　　**UNCTAD Locode:** DK KTD

Principal Facilities:

	Y	G		B		T	A

Authority: Kerteminde Havn, Hans Schachsvej 4, DK-5300 Kerteminde, Denmark, *Tel:* +45   65 15 15 41, *Fax:* +45   65 15 15 25, *Email:* kommune@kerteminde.dk, *Website:* www.kerteminde.dk

Officials: Harbour Master: Kent Stephensen, *Email:* kes@kerteminde.dk.

Pilotage: Not compulsory. Contact agent if pilot required

Maximum Vessel Dimensions: 80 m max loa, but longer vessels equipped with bow thruster can easily enter or leave the port by sailing backwards

Working Hours: Monday-Friday 0700-0830, 0900-1200, 1230-1600

Accommodation:

Name	Remarks
Kerteminde	Harbour 426.7 m long, 60.95 m wide. Depth at entrance 4.27 m, at quays 4.5 m

Mechanical Handling Equipment:

Location	Type	Capacity (t)	Qty
Kerteminde	Mobile Cranes	30	1

Bunkering: Oil from tank car
A/S Dan-Bunkering Ltd, Strandgade 4A, 1401 Copenhagen K, Denmark, *Tel:* +45 3345 5410, *Fax:* +45 3345 5411, *Email:* copenhagen@dan-bunkering.dk, *Website:* www.dan-bunkering.dk
Ecophoenix AB, Kungsgatan 54, 753 21 Uppsala, Sweden, *Tel:* +46 1813 1880, *Fax:* +46 1813 1881, *Email:* info@phoenixscandinavia.com
Kuwait Petroleum Corp., Banevaenget 13, 3460 Birkerod, Denmark, *Tel:* +45 7012 4545, *Fax:* +45 4599 2020, *Email:* q8@q8.dk, *Website:* www.q8.dk
Malik Supply A/S, Ved Stranden 22, DK-9000 Aalborg, Denmark, *Tel:* +45 9631 3900, *Fax:* +45 9631 3911, *Email:* info@malik.dk, *Website:* www.malik.dk
Monjasa A/S, Strevelinsvej 4, 7000 Fredericia, Denmark, *Tel:* +45 70 26 02 30, *Fax:* +45 70 26 02 33, *Email:* denmark@monjasa.com, *Website:* www.monjasa.com
OW Bunker & Trading A/S, Gasvaerksvej 48, DK-9000 Aalborg, Denmark, *Tel:* +45 98 12 72 77, *Fax:* +45   98 16 72 77, *Email:* owbunker@owbunker.dk, *Website:* www.owbunker.dk
Trumf Bunker A/S, Raadhustorvet 4, P O Box 55, 7100 Vejle, Denmark, *Tel:* +45 7642 9696, *Fax:* +45 7642 9690, *Email:* trumf@trumf-bunker.com, *Website:* www.trumf-bunker.com

Towage: Available, but not compulsory

Repair & Maintenance: Minor repairs possible

Airport: Beldringe, 35 km

Lloyd's Agent: Lars Krogius Hecksher ApS, Overodvej 5, P O Box 20, DK-2840 Holte, Denmark, *Tel:* +45   33 93 91 28, *Fax:* +45   33 93 27 90, *Email:* denmark@krogius.com, *Website:* www.krogius.com

KOBENHAVN

alternate name, see Copenhagen

KOGE

Lat 55° 27' N; Long 12° 12' E.

Admiralty Chart: 2595
Time Zone: GMT +1 h
Admiralty Pilot: 18
UNCTAD Locode: DK KOG

Principal Facilities:

P	Q	Y	G	C	R				T	

Authority: Koge Havn, Baltic Kaj 1, DK-4600 Koge, Denmark, *Tel:* +45 56 64 62 60, *Fax:* +45 56 63 74 00, *Email:* info@koegehavn.dk, *Website:* www.koegehavn.dk

Officials: Director: Thomas Elm Kampmann, *Email:* tek@stc-koege.dk.
Harbour Master: Susanne Thilqvist, *Email:* sth@koegehavn.dk.

Port Security: ISPS compliant

Pre-Arrival Information: Crew list, ISPS certificate, list with last ten ports of call and UN LOCODE and waste declaration

Documentation: Crew list, passenger list, stores, arms, health documents, bill of lading, manifest

Approach: Depth at entrance 7.0 m

Anchorage: Anchorage can be obtained 1 to 2 nautical miles E of the harbour in good holding ground

Pilotage: Compulsory for tankers. Pilot can be ordered from DanPilot (The Sound), Copenhagen, *Tel:* +45 35 38 67 00, *Fax:* +45 35 43 10 17, *Email:* soundpilot@pilotage.dk, *Website:* www.soundpilot.dk. Pilot boards in the following positions:
Vessel's approaching from the N in pos 55° 31.0' N; 12° 43.0' E (Drogden Lt)
Vessel's approaching from the S in pos 55° 27.0' N; 12° 30.0' E (Koge W)
In pos 55° 26.0' N; 12° 36.0' E (Koge E)

Radio Frequency: Coast Radio Station Lyngby Radio - OXZ VHF Channel 16. Other channels used 13 and 12

Tides: Range 0.3 m

Traffic: 2006, 1 865 000 t of cargo handled

Maximum Vessel Dimensions: Loa 160 m, max d 6.7 m

Working Hours: Monday to Thursday 0700-1530. Friday 0700-1500

Accommodation:

Name	Remarks
Koge	See [1] below

[1]*Koge:* Total length of quays is approx 2000 m with a max depth alongside of approx 7 m
Four ro/ro berths with max 175 m length, max d of 6.7 m
Tanker facilities: Pier No.11 tanker terminal. Pier No.13 bitumen terminal

Storage:

Location	Covered (m²)	Sheds / Warehouses
Koge	3600	3

Mechanical Handling Equipment:

Location	Type	Capacity (t)	Qty
Koge	Mobile Cranes	10–40	3

Waste Reception Facilities: Available by lorries

Towage: One tug available

Repair & Maintenance: Slip for vessels up to 250 dwt, only minor repairs

Shipping Agents: C.R. Holship A/S, Parketvej 1, DK-4600 Koge, Denmark, *Tel:* +45 56 63 33 77, *Email:* crship@crship.dk, *Website:* www.crship.dk
Shipping.dk Koge A/S, Havnen 12, DK-4600 Koge, Denmark, *Tel:* +45 56 65 00 06, *Fax:* +45 56 65 25 56, *Email:* koege@shipping.dk, *Website:* www.shipping.dk

Stevedoring Companies: C.R. Holship A/S, Parketvej 1, DK-4600 Koge, Denmark, *Tel:* +45 56 63 33 77, *Email:* crship@crship.dk, *Website:* www.crship.dk
Shipping.dk Koge A/S, Havnen 12, DK-4600 Koge, Denmark, *Tel:* +45 56 65 00 06, *Fax:* +45 56 65 25 56, *Email:* koege@shipping.dk, *Website:* www.shipping.dk

Medical Facilities: Hospital in the town

Railway: Koge Station, 600 m from port

Lloyd's Agent: Lars Krogius Hecksher ApS, Overodvej 5, P O Box 20, DK-2840 Holte, Denmark, *Tel:* +45   33 93 91 28, *Fax:* +45   33 93 27 90, *Email:* denmark@krogius.com, *Website:* www.krogius.com

KOLDING

Lat 55° 30' N; Long 9° 30' E.

Admiralty Chart: 900
Time Zone: GMT +1 h
Admiralty Pilot: 18
UNCTAD Locode: DK KOL

Principal Facilities:

Q	Y	G		R	L	B		T	A

Authority: Kolding Havn, Jens Holmsvej 1, DK-6000 Kolding, Denmark, *Tel:* +45 75 50 20 66, *Fax:* +45   75 50 20 58, *Email:* koldingport@kolding.dk, *Website:* www.koldingport.dk

Officials: Managing Director: Hans-Jorgen Bogeso, *Email:* hjbo@kolding.dk.
Harbour Master: Capt Kim Sandahl, *Email:* kisa@kolding.dk.

Port Security: ISPS compliant

Pre-Arrival Information: ETA/ETD must be given 1 h in advance via Agent. Vessels approaching without Pilot must make an announcement on VHF Channel 16 and 12, ten minutes before entering the buoyed channel or ten minutes before departure, giving ship's name and intentions

Documentation: Crew list (2 copies), customs list (2 copies), international tonnage certificate (1 copy), ship's documents/certificates must be valid, ISPS form sent prior to arrival (1 copy), garbage declaration sent prior to arrival (1 copy)

Approach: Well buoyed channel in depth of 7 m

Anchorage: Off Skaerbaek at the entrance to Kolding Fjord with depths up to 15 m

Pilotage: Not compulsory. Pilot ordered from DanPilot (Belt & Fjord Pilot), Fredericia, Tel: +45 76 20 03 20, Fax: +45 75 92 88 22, Email: littlebelt-pilot@lillebaelt.dk, Website: www.pilotage.dk. Vessels coming from the N take pilot off Fredericia. Vessels coming from the S take pilot off Assens. Pilots require at least 20 cm safe draft in the dredged channels (depth 7.0 m), normally 10-20 cm of high water

Radio Frequency: Kolding Harbour: VHF Channel 16 (12/13). ETA/ETD must be given to Agent min 1 h before arrival or departure. Lyngby Radio has VHF coverage throughout all Danish waters

Weather: Lasting strong NE wind may cause low water and long lasting NW'ly winds may cause high water

Traffic: 2006, 1 200 000 t of cargo handled

Maximum Vessel Dimensions: 30 000 dwt, 200 m loa, 25 m beam, 7.0 m draught

Principal Imports and Exports: Imports: Agribulk, Bitumen, Cement, Fertilizer, Fishmeal, Grain products, Iron goods, Metal ores & scrap, Paper & paper products, Timber products. Exports: Agribulk, Bagged cargoes, Scrap metal.

Working Hours: Monday-Thursday 0700-0830, 0900-1200, 1230-1530. Friday 0700-0830, 0900-1200, 1230-1500

Accommodation:

Name	Remarks
Kolding	See [1] below

[1]*Kolding:* Depth of 7 m in outer harbour and at quays; 5 to 7 m alongside quays in inner harbour. Anchorage for larger vessels 3.2 km from town, in 5.5 to 9 m. Quay 2200 m; vessels 180 m long can swing inside the harbour where turning basin is 210 m. Railways and electric light on all the quays
Major ro/ro facility between pier 7 and 8, 165 m long and 25 m wide. Minor ro/ro facilities between piers 1 and 2
Tanker facilities: Liquid heated bitumen handled at pier 9 (East)

Mechanical Handling Equipment:

Location	Type	Capacity (t)	Qty
Kolding	Mobile Cranes	4–36	6
Kolding	Portal Cranes	5–25	2

Cargo Worked: Between 150-500 t/h

Bunkering: Available through the agents by road tanker, also by small tankers alongside

Waste Reception Facilities: Galley wastes to be placed in containers. According to Danish Law the discharging of waste water and cargo wastes from cleaning of the deck, holds and tanks in the harbour and fjord is forbidden

Towage: Harbour tug/icebreaker Caspar bollard pull 7 t, to be ordered in advance via Ship's Agent or Harbour Office

Repair & Maintenance: Small repairs possible

Shipping Agents: Blue Water Shipping A/S, Birkedam 18-20, DK-6000 Kolding, Denmark, Tel: +45 76 33 85 00, Fax: +45 76 33 85 99, Email: bwskld@bws.dk, Website: www.bws.dk
Kolding Crane & Stevedoring Co., Neckelmann & Hansen, Sdr. Havnegade 7-17, Postbox 10, DK-6000 Kolding, Denmark, Tel: +45 75 52 55 22, Fax: +45 75 52 78 81, Email: info@neckha.dk, Website: www.neckha.dk

Stevedoring Companies: Kolding Crane & Stevedoring Co., Neckelmann & Hansen, Sdr. Havnegade 7-17, Postbox 10, DK-6000 Kolding, Denmark, Tel: +45 75 52 55 22, Fax: +45 75 52 78 81, Email: info@neckha.dk, Website: www.neckha.dk

Medical Facilities: Local hospital

Airport: Billund, 40 km

Railway: Kolding Station, 200 m

Lloyd's Agent: Eurobaltic ApS, Randersvej 563, Trige, DK-8380 Aarhus, Denmark, Tel: +45 70 23 15 13, Fax: +45 70 23 15 03, Email: ph@euroinspections.com, Website: www.eurobaltic.dk

KONGSDAL

Lat 56° 41' N; Long 10° 4' E.

Admiralty Chart: 2108	**Admiralty Pilot:** 18
Time Zone: GMT +1 h	**UNCTAD Locode:** DK KON

Principal Facilities:

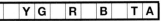

| | Y | G | | R | | B | | T | A |

Authority: Kongsdal Havn, Mariager Kommune, Teknisk Forvaltning, Fjordgade 5, DK-9550 Mariager, Denmark, Tel: +45 88 18 13 00, Fax: +45 88 18 13 97, Email: raadhus@mariagerkom.dk

Approach: Bridge at Hadsund opened during daylight; must be ordered for opening at night

Pilotage: Available from DanPilot (Great Belt), Spodsbjerg, Tel: +45 62 50 15 35, Fax: +45 62 50 15 28, Email: belt@pilotage.dk, Website: www.pilotage.dk. Pilot boards in pos 56° 41.3' N; 10° 30.0' E

Radio Frequency: VHF Channel 16

Traffic: 2004, 50 000 t of cargo handled

Maximum Vessel Dimensions: 120 m loa, 13.5 m beam, 5.1 m d

Working Hours: 0700-1600

Accommodation:

Name	Length (m)	Remarks
Kongsdal		Warehouse available for storage
Kongsdal Harbour	120	
Dania Harbour	55	
Akzo Nobel Salt	140	Tel: +45 96 68 78 88

Mechanical Handling Equipment: Cranes available upon request

Bunkering: Available by lorry

Towage: Available

Stevedoring Companies: P. Rudbeck Larsens Eftf. ApS, Daniavej 16, DK-9550 Mariager, Denmark, Tel: +45 98 58 31 88, Fax: +45 98 58 31 33, Email: rudbeck@rudbeck.com, Website: www.rudbeck.com

Airport: Aalborg

Lloyd's Agent: Eurobaltic ApS, Randersvej 563, Trige, DK-8380 Aarhus, Denmark, Tel: +45 70 23 15 13, Fax: +45 70 23 15 03, Email: ph@euroinspections.com, Website: www.eurobaltic.dk

KORSOR

Lat 55° 19' N; Long 11° 7' E.

Admiralty Chart: 2596	**Admiralty Pilot:** 18
Time Zone: GMT +1 h	**UNCTAD Locode:** DK KRR

Principal Facilities:

| | Y | G | | R | L | B | | | A |

Authority: Port of Korsoer, Amerikakajen 2, DK-4220 Korsor, Denmark, Tel: +45 58 37 00 85, Fax: +45 58 35 25 98, Email: info@korsoerhavn.dk, Website: www.korsoerhavn.dk

Officials: Port Director: Flemming Erichsen, Email: fer@korsoerhavn.dk.
Harbour Master: Jesper Kokholm, Email: jko@korsoerhavn.dk.

Port Security: ISPS compliant

Pilotage: Compulsory for all tankers and other vessels over 100 m loa passing Halsskov Bridge. Pilot can be ordered from DanPilot (Great Belt), Spodsbjerg, Tel: +45 62 50 15 35, Fax: +45 62 50 15 28, Email: belt@pilotage.dk, Website: www.pilotage.dk. Pilot boards in pos 55° 19.5' N; 11° 05.0' E (close to BY buoy)

Radio Frequency: VHF Channel 12 or 16

Maximum Vessel Dimensions: 200 m loa, 7.5 m draught

Working Hours: 24 h/day

Accommodation:

Name	Length (m)	Depth (m)
Korsor		
Amerikakajen	400	8
Inderhavn (North)	300	7
Inderhavn (South)	300	7
Cruise Ship Pier	340	8

Storage:

Location	Open (m²)	Covered (m²)
Korsor	15000	7000

Mechanical Handling Equipment: Portable conveyor belts up to 350 t/h

Location	Type	Capacity (t)	Qty
Korsor	Mobile Cranes	28	3

Key to Principal Facilities:—			
A=Airport	**C**=Containers	**G**=General Cargo	**P**=Petroleum	**R**=Ro/Ro	**Y**=Dry Bulk
B=Bunkers	**D**=Dry Dock	**L**=Cruise	**Q**=Other Liquid Bulk	**T**=Towage (where available from port)

Bunkering: A/S Dan-Bunkering Ltd, Strandgade 4A, 1401 Copenhagen K, Denmark, *Tel:* +45 3345 5410, *Fax:* +45 3345 5411, *Email:* copenhagen@dan-bunkering.dk, *Website:* www.dan-bunkering.dk
Ecophoenix AB, Kungsgatan 54, 753 21 Uppsala, Sweden, *Tel:* +46 1813 1880, *Fax:* +46 1813 1881, *Email:* info@phoenixscandinavia.com
Kuwait Petroleum Corp., Banevaenget 13, 3460 Birkerod, Denmark, *Tel:* +45 7012 4545, *Fax:* +45 4599 2020, *Email:* q8@q8.dk, *Website:* www.q8.dk
Malik Supply A/S, Ved Stranden 22, DK-9000 Aalborg, Denmark, *Tel:* +45 9631 3900, *Fax:* +45 9631 3911, *Email:* info@malik.dk, *Website:* www.malik.dk
Monjasa A/S, Strevelinsvej 4, 7000 Fredericia, Denmark, *Tel:* +45 70 26 02 30, *Fax:* +45 70 26 02 33, *Email:* denmark@monjasa.com, *Website:* www.monjasa.com
OW Bunker & Trading A/S, Gasvaerksvej 48, DK-9000 Aalborg, Denmark, *Tel:* +45 98 12 72 77, *Fax:* +45 98 16 72 77, *Email:* owbunker@owbunker.dk, *Website:* www.owbunker.dk
Trumf Bunker A/S, Raadhustorvet 4, P O Box 55, 7100 Vejle, Denmark, *Tel:* +45 7642 9696, *Fax:* +45 7642 9690, *Email:* trumf@trumf-bunker.com, *Website:* www.trumf-bunker.com

Waste Reception Facilities: Available. 24 h notice required

Towage: Can be requested

Stevedoring Companies: K.H.T., J. Poulsen Shipping A/S, Batterivej 7-9, DK-4220 Korsor, Denmark, *Tel:* +45 58 35 05 86, *Fax:* +45 58 35 05 50, *Email:* mail@jpship.dk, *Website:* www.jpship.dk

Medical Facilities: Medical centre. Hospital at Slagelse, 18 km

Airport: Kastrup/Copenhagen, 100 km

Railway: Korsor Station, 3 km

Lloyd's Agent: Lars Krogius Hecksher ApS, Overodvej 5, P O Box 20, DK-2840 Holte, Denmark, *Tel:* +45 33 93 91 28, *Fax:* +45 33 93 27 90, *Email:* denmark@krogius.com, *Website:* www.krogius.com

LEMVIG

Lat 56° 33' N; Long 8° 18' E.

Admiralty Chart: 426

Admiralty Pilot: 55

Time Zone: GMT +1 h

UNCTAD Locode: DK LVG

Principal Facilities:

			G		B	T	A

Authority: Lemvig Havn, Radhusgade 2, DK-7620 Lemvig, Denmark, *Tel:* +45 96 63 12 00, *Fax:* +45 96 63 12 30, *Email:* lemvig.kommune@lemvig.dk, *Website:* www.lemvig.dk

Officials: Harbour Master: Svend Aage Stigaard Lauridsen, *Email:* svend.aage.stigaard.lauridsen@lemvig.dk.

Port Security: ISPS compliant

Pilotage: Not compulsory but available from DanPilot (Great Belt), Spodsbjerg, Tel: +45 62 50 15 35, Fax: +45 62 50 15 28, Email: belt@pilotage.dk, Website: www.pilotage.dk

Radio Frequency: VHF Channels 16 and 13

Traffic: 2004, 62 000 t of cargo handled

Maximum Vessel Dimensions: 114 m loa, 4.16 m d

Working Hours: 8 h, overtime usually possible

Accommodation:

Name	Length (m)	Depth (m)
Lemvig		
E Harbour	121	4.11
Old Harbour	51	2.74
Fishing Harbour	210	3.05

Mechanical Handling Equipment:

Location	Type	Capacity (t)	Qty
Lemvig	Mobile Cranes	35	1

Bunkering: Oil from shore tank

Towage: One tug of 230 hp

Repair & Maintenance: Kaalund & Storgaard ApS, Lemvig, Denmark, *Tel:* +45 97 82 21 65, *Fax:* +45 97 82 26 30 Slip for fishing vessels only
Lemvig Maskin & Koleteknik ApS, Havnen 20-26, DK-7620 Lemvig, Denmark, *Tel:* +45 97 82 32 33, *Fax:* +45 97 82 32 34, *Email:* lmk@lemvigmk.dk, *Website:* www.lemvigmk.dk Repair facilities

Airport: Karup, 65 km

Lloyd's Agent: C. Breinholt A/S, Toldbodvej 1, P O Box 20, DK-6701 Esbjerg, Denmark, *Tel:* +45 79 18 04 11, *Fax:* +45 75 18 19 25, *Email:* mkk@breinholt.dk, *Website:* www.breinholt.dk

LYNGS ODDE

Lat 55° 31' N; Long 9° 45' E.

Admiralty Chart: 900

Admiralty Pilot: 18

Time Zone: GMT +1 h

UNCTAD Locode: DK LYO

Principal Facilities:

Q					B		A

Authority: Ny Nitrogen A/S, Nyhavev 73, P O Box 711, DK-7000 Fredericia, Denmark, *Tel:* +45 75 94 51 33, *Fax:* +45 75 94 51 44

Approach: Lille-Baelt is spanned by a suspension bridge between Lyngs Odde and Stavrby Skov on Funen; vertical clearance through the navigational passage of 44 m

Anchorage: Anchorage can be obtained about 1 nautical mile offshore in depths of 8-15 m and 6 nautical miles offshore in depths of 20-30 m

Pilotage: Compulsory for vessels over 500 gt. Two pilots required for vessels exceeding 170 m loa. Little Belt Pilot, Tel: +45 76 20 03 20, Fax: +45 75 92 88 22, Email: littlebelt@pilotage.dk

Radio Frequency: Available on VHF Channels 16, 13, 12, 71 & 72

Tides: Range of tide 0.4 m

Traffic: 2004, 132 000 t of cargo handled

Maximum Vessel Dimensions: 207 m loa, 11 m d

Accommodation:

Name	Length (m)	Depth (m)	Remarks
Lyngs Odde			
Quay	55	11	See [1] below

[1] *Quay:* Liquefied gas terminal. Two mooring dolphins off each end

Storage: Available

Mechanical Handling Equipment:

Location	Type
Lyngs Odde	Mobile Cranes

Bunkering: Can be brought in from Fredericia by road tanker or barge
A/S Dan-Bunkering Ltd, Strandgade 4A, 1401 Copenhagen K, Denmark, *Tel:* +45 3345 5410, *Fax:* +45 3345 5411, *Email:* copenhagen@dan-bunkering.dk, *Website:* www.dan-bunkering.dk
Ecophoenix AB, Kungsgatan 54, 753 21 Uppsala, Sweden, *Tel:* +46 1813 1880, *Fax:* +46 1813 1881, *Email:* info@phoenixscandinavia.com
Kuwait Petroleum Corp., Banevaenget 13, 3460 Birkerod, Denmark, *Tel:* +45 7012 4545, *Fax:* +45 4599 2020, *Email:* q8@q8.dk, *Website:* www.q8.dk
Malik Supply A/S, Ved Stranden 22, DK-9000 Aalborg, Denmark, *Tel:* +45 9631 3900, *Fax:* +45 9631 3911, *Email:* info@malik.dk, *Website:* www.malik.dk
Monjasa A/S, Strevelinsvej 4, 7000 Fredericia, Denmark, *Tel:* +45 70 26 02 30, *Fax:* +45 70 26 02 33, *Email:* denmark@monjasa.com, *Website:* www.monjasa.com
OW Bunker & Trading A/S, Gasvaerksvej 48, DK-9000 Aalborg, Denmark, *Tel:* +45 98 12 72 77, *Fax:* +45 98 16 72 77, *Email:* owbunker@owbunker.dk, *Website:* www.owbunker.dk
Trumf Bunker A/S, Raadhustorvet 4, P O Box 55, 7100 Vejle, Denmark, *Tel:* +45 7642 9696, *Fax:* +45 7642 9690, *Email:* trumf@trumf-bunker.com, *Website:* www.trumf-bunker.com

Repair & Maintenance: Fredericia Skibsvaerft A/S, P O Box 260, DK-7000 Fredericia, Denmark, *Tel:* +45 75 92 00 00, *Fax:* +45 75 93 34 30, *Email:* fsv@fayard.dk, *Website:* www.fayard.dk Graving dock 108 m x 22 m x 5 m. Floating docks of 227.5 m x 35 m x 8 m with max 22 000 t and 165 m x 28 m x 8 m with max 12 000 t. Slipway of 70 m x 11 m x 5 m with max 1000 t

Medical Facilities: Available at Fredericia

Airport: Billund, 50 km

Lloyd's Agent: Eurobaltic ApS, Randersvej 563, Trige, DK-8380 Aarhus, Denmark, *Tel:* +45 70 23 15 13, *Fax:* +45 70 23 15 03, *Email:* ph@euroinspections.com, *Website:* www.eurobaltic.dk

MARIAGER

Lat 56° 39' N; Long 9° 59' E.

Admiralty Chart: 613

Admiralty Pilot: 18

Time Zone: GMT +1 h

UNCTAD Locode: DK MRR

This port is no longer open to commercial shipping

Shipping Agents: P. Rudbeck Larsens Eftf. ApS, Daniavej 16, DK-9550 Mariager, Denmark, *Tel:* +45 98 58 31 88, *Fax:* +45 98 58 31 33, *Email:* rudbeck@rudbeck.com, *Website:* www.rudbeck.com

Stevedoring Companies: P. Rudbeck Larsens Eftf. ApS, Daniavej 16, DK-9550 Mariager, Denmark, *Tel:* +45 98 58 31 88, *Fax:* +45 98 58 31 33, *Email:* rudbeck@rudbeck.com, *Website:* www.rudbeck.com

MARSTAL

Lat 54° 51' N; Long 10° 31' E.

Admiralty Chart: 2116	**Admiralty Pilot:** 18
Time Zone: GMT +1 h	**UNCTAD Locode:** DK MRS

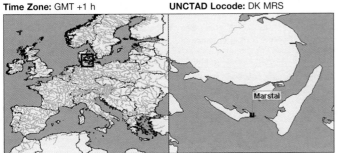

Principal Facilities:

P		Y	G		R	L	B		T	A	

Authority: Port Authority of Marstal, Marstal Harbour, Havnepladsen, DK-5960 Marstal, Denmark, *Tel:* +45 63 52 63 65, *Fax:* +45 63 52 63 66, *Email:* havn@marstal.dk

Officials: Harbour Master: Torben Lunnemann Frederiksen, *Email:* tlf@aeroekommune.dk.

Documentation: Crew list (3 copies), passenger list (3 copies), bonded stores list

Pilotage: Not compulsory, but available 24 h, Tel: +45 62 53 34 50

Radio Frequency: Port & pilot on VHF Channels 16 and 71, available 24 h

Maximum Vessel Dimensions: 115 m loa

Working Hours: Monday-Friday 0700-1530

Accommodation:

Name	Length (m)	Depth (m)	Remarks
Marstal			
Marstal Quay	518	4	See [1] below
Steamer Pier			Ferries
Steel Shipyard Pier		2.5	

[1]*Marstal Quay:* Mainly dry cargo, but can also handle tankers & passenger/cruise vessels

Bunkering: Small quantity available

Towage: Tugs are available at 24 h notice

Repair & Maintenance: Floating dock 108 m long with width 15.5 m and 3500 t cap. Two slipways of 600 t and 400 t cap
Marstal Shipyard Ltd, Havnepladsen 22, DK-5960 Marstal, Denmark, *Tel:* +45 62 53 17 28, *Fax:* +45 62 53 17 86, *Email:* info@repairyard.dk, *Website:* www.repairyard.dk

Medical Facilities: Medical assistance can be obtained at Aeroskobing, Tel: +45 62 53 10 29

Airport: Aeroskobing, 10 km

Lloyd's Agent: Lars Krogius Hecksher ApS, Overodvej 5, P O Box 20, DK-2840 Holte, Denmark, *Tel:* +45 33 93 91 28, *Fax:* +45 33 93 27 90, *Email:* denmark@krogius.com, *Website:* www.krogius.com

MASNEDSUND

see under Vordingborg

MIDDELFART

Lat 55° 30' N; Long 9° 44' E.

Admiralty Chart: 900	**Admiralty Pilot:** 18
Time Zone: GMT +1 h	**UNCTAD Locode:** DK MID

Principal Facilities:

P	Q	Y	G	C	R		B		T	A	

Authority: Associated Danish Ports A/S, Terminal Middelfart, Gl. Banegardsvej 29A, DK-5500 Middelfart, Denmark, *Tel:* +45 79 21 50 00, *Fax:* +45 79 21 50 05, *Email:* post@adp-as.dk, *Website:* www.adp-as.com

Officials: Chief Executive Officer: Jens Peter Peters, *Tel:* +45 79 21 50 10, *Email:* jpp@adp-as.dk.
Sales & Marketing Manager: Ole Haugsted Jorgensen, *Tel:* +45 79 21 50 35, *Email:* ohj@adp-as.dk.
Harbour Master: Bo T Nielsen, *Tel:* +45 79 21 50 21, *Email:* btn@adp-as.dk.

Port Security: ISPS compliant

Approach: Depth at entrance 10 m, sandy bottom

Pilotage: Not compulsory but available from DanPilot (Belt & Fjord Pilot), Fredericia, Tel: +45 76 20 03 20, Fax: +45 75 92 88 22, Email: littlebelt-pilot@lillebaelt.dk, Website: www.pilotage.dk

Radio Frequency: Fredericia Port and Little Belt Pilot on VHF Channels 18 and 16

Tides: Mean water level is 0.0 m. Average tidal range 0.3 m, extreme high water level +1.5 m, extreme low water level is -1.2 m due to strong ENE/WSW winds

Maximum Vessel Dimensions: 15 000 dwt, 9.0 m d

Working Hours: Mon-Thurs 0700-1530. Fri 0700-1500. Overtime possible

Accommodation:

Name	Length (m)	Depth (m)
Middelfart		
Quay 51	50	6.5
Quay 52	100	9

Storage: Warehousing for all kinds of cargo. No refrigerated space

Mechanical Handling Equipment:

Location	Type
Middelfart	Mobile Cranes

Cargo Worked: Bulk cargo 100-200 t/h

Bunkering: Available at short notice, delivery by truck
Bunker Holding A/S, Strandvejen 5, 5500 Middelfart, Denmark, *Tel:* +45 88 38 28 28, *Fax:* +45 88 38 28 20, *Email:* bh@bunker-holding.com, *Website:* www.bunker-holding.com
A/S Dan-Bunkering Ltd, Strandvejen 5, P O Box 71, DK-5500 Middelfart, Denmark, *Tel:* +45 64415401, *Fax:* +45 64415301, *Email:* middelfart@dan-bunkering.dk, *Website:* www.dan-bunkering.dk
A/S Dan-Bunkering Ltd, Strandvejen 5, P O Box 71, DK-5500 Middelfart, Denmark, *Tel:* +45 64415401, *Fax:* +45 64415301, *Email:* middelfart@dan-bunkering.dk, *Website:* www.dan-bunkering.dk

Towage: Available at short notice

Repair & Maintenance: Available from Fredericia

Medical Facilities: Local hospital

Airport: Bilund, 50 km

Railway: Middelfart, 2 km. Fredericia, 15 km

Lloyd's Agent: Lars Krogius Hecksher ApS, Overodvej 5, P O Box 20, DK-2840 Holte, Denmark, *Tel:* +45 33 93 91 28, *Fax:* +45 33 93 27 90, *Email:* denmark@krogius.com, *Website:* www.krogius.com

MOLLEBUGTHAVN

harbour area, see under Fredericia

NAESTVED

Lat 55° 13' N; Long 11° 45' E.

Admiralty Chart: 2118	**Admiralty Pilot:** 18
Time Zone: GMT +1 h	**UNCTAD Locode:** DK NVD

Principal Facilities:

P		Y	G			B		T	A	

Authority: Naestved Havn, Toldbodgade 4, DK-4700 Naestved, Denmark, *Tel:* +45 55 78 51 82, *Fax:* +45 55 78 51 83, *Email:* port@naestvedport.dk, *Website:* www.naestvedport.dk

Officials: Harbour Master: Jesper Moller Petersen, *Email:* jmp@naestvedport.dk.

Documentation: Crew list, passenger list, stores, arms, health documents, bills of lading, manifest

---

Key to Principal Facilities:—
A=Airport **C**=Containers **G**=General Cargo **P**=Petroleum **R**=Ro/Ro **Y**=Dry Bulk
B=Bunkers **D**=Dry Dock **L**=Cruise **Q**=Other Liquid Bulk **T**=Towage (where available from port)

Anchorage: Anchorage can only be obtained in Karrebaeksminde Roads, 1.5 nautical miles SW of the port, in a depth of 8.0 m

Pilotage: Compulsory for vessels over 55 m loa from DanPilot (Great Belt), Spodsbjerg, Tel: +45 62 50 15 35, Fax: +45 62 50 15 28, Email: belt@pilotage.dk, Website: www.pilotage.dk. Pilot boards in pos 55° 09.0' N; 11° 36.0' E

Radio Frequency: VHF Channel 16

Tides: Range 0.4 m

Traffic: 2004, 371 000 t of cargo handled

Maximum Vessel Dimensions: 3000 dwt, 118 m loa, 14.4 m beam, 5.6 m d

Principal Imports and Exports: Imports: Broken stones, Coal, Fertiliser, Foodstuff, Lumber, Oil(vegetable), Paper, Salt, Sand, Scrap, Soda. Exports: Grain/malt, Lumber, Paper, Scrap.

Working Hours: 04:00 - 23:00

Accommodation:

Name	Length (m)	Depth (m)	Remarks
Naestved			
Old West Quay	300	6	See [1] below
New West Quay	180	6	Two berths handling broken stones, malt & vegetable oil
Mellem Quay	180	6	Grain & lumber
Maglemolle Quay	360	6	Four berths handling paper & broken stones
Soda Quay	80	6	Soda

[1]*Old West Quay:* Three berths handling coal, salt, broken stones, sand, fertilisers & lumber

Storage:

Location	Open (m²)	Covered (m²)
Naestved	23800	
Old West Quay	8000	2500
New West Quay	4000	3000
Maglemolle Quay	1200	1800

Mechanical Handling Equipment:

Location	Type	Capacity (t)	Qty
Naestved	Mult-purp. Cranes	8	4
Naestved	Mobile Cranes		1
Old West Quay	Mult-purp. Cranes	4	2
New West Quay	Mobile Cranes	40	
Maglemolle Quay	Mobile Cranes	5	
Soda Quay	Mult-purp. Cranes	3	

Cargo Worked: Sand 125 t/h, grain loading 125 t/h, coal 100 t/h, gravel 125 t/h, soda 80 t/h

Bunkering: Available by road tanker

Towage: One tug of 8 t bollard pull available and recommended for vessels over 100 m length, and/or 5°2 m d

Repair & Maintenance: Minor repairs

Medical Facilities: Hospital in the town

Airport: Kastrup International Airport, 90 km

Railway: Naestved Station 2 km from port

Lloyd's Agent: Lars Krogius Hecksher ApS, Overodvej 5, P O Box 20, DK-2840 Holte, Denmark, *Tel:* +45 33 93 91 28, *Fax:* +45 33 93 27 90, *Email:* denmark@krogius.com, *Website:* www.krogius.com

NAKSKOV

Lat 54° 50' N; Long 11° 8' E.

Admiralty Chart: 2597
Time Zone: GMT +1 h
Admiralty Pilot: 18
UNCTAD Locode: DK NAK

Principal Facilities:

	Q	Y	G		R				T	

Authority: Nakskov Havn, Havnegade 2, DK-4900 Nakskov, Denmark, *Tel:* +45 54 67 73 32, *Fax:* +45 54 92 51 13, *Email:* havne@lolland.dk, *Website:* www.nakskovhavn.dk

Officials: Harbour Master: Tummas Juul.

Port Security: ISPS compliant

Pre-Arrival Information: Custom clearance carried out by ship's agent

Approach: Channel depth 6.3 m, max safe draft 5.8 m

Pilotage: Pilot to be ordered at least 4 h before arrival; DanPilot (Great Belt), Spodsbjerg, Tel: +45 62 50 15 35, Fax: +45 62 50 15 28, Email: belt@pilotage.dk, Website: www.pilotage.dk. Pilot boards in pos 54° 52.0' N; 10° 55.0' E

Radio Frequency: VHF Channels 16, 13 and 12

Traffic: 2004, 380 000 t of cargo handled

Maximum Vessel Dimensions: 183 m loa, approx 33 000 dwt, 5.8 m max draft

Principal Imports and Exports: Imports: Coal, Coke, Fertiliser, Grain, Limestone. Exports: Grain, Steel constructions, Sugar.

Working Hours: Monday to Thursday 0700-1530. Friday 0700-1500

Accommodation:

Name	Remarks
Nakskov	See [1] below

[1]*Nakskov:* Depth 6.3 m at entrance and in harbour. Lights from the roadstead to Nakskov enable vessels up to approx 33 000 dwt to go in and out by day and night throughout the year in clear weather; vessels should have good lights on board

Storage: Storage space for about 5000 t coal/coke. Private warehouse for 7000 t fertilisers plus discharging facilities for self-discharging vessels, cap 130 t/h

Location	Grain (t)
Nakskov	48000

Mechanical Handling Equipment:

Location	Type	Capacity (t)
Nakskov	Mult-purp. Cranes	100
Nakskov	Mobile Cranes	42

Cargo Worked: Loading grain, pellets and sugar, 600 to 800 t/day. Discharging grain 350 t/day, coal and limestone 800 to 1200 t/day

Waste Reception Facilities: Tank trucks for dirty ballast and small containers for garbage

Towage: Tug and icebreaker available with 24 h notice

Repair & Maintenance: Nakskov Skibs Entrepriser A/S, Skibsvaerftsvej v/dok 2, P O Box 14, DK-4900 Nakskov, Denmark, *Tel:* +45 54 95 00 95, *Fax:* +45 54 95 01 19 Two dry docks for vessels up to 33 000 dwt, 200 m long and 176 m long

Shipping Agents: Andrea Shipping ApS, Havnegade 33, P O Box 143, DK-4900 Nakskov, Denmark, *Tel:* +45 54 95 30 90, *Fax:* +45 54 95 59 00, *Email:* info@andrea-shipping.dk, *Website:* www.andrea-shipping.dk
Holger Kristiansens Succsrs. A/S, Havnegade 11, DK-4900 Nakskov, Denmark, *Tel:* +45 54 95 80 66, *Fax:* +45 54 95 71 66, *Email:* krinak@krinak.dk, *Website:* www.krinak.dk
Klaus Heun Shipping Eftf ApS, Linkopingvej 33, P O Box 209, DK-4900 Nakskov, Denmark, *Tel:* +45 54 95 00 15, *Fax:* +45 54 95 00 16, *Email:* info@heunship.dk, *Website:* www.heunship.dk

Surveyors: Klaus Heun Shipping Eftf ApS, Linkopingvej 33, P O Box 209, DK-4900 Nakskov, Denmark, *Tel:* +45 54 95 00 15, *Fax:* +45 54 95 00 16, *Email:* info@heunship.dk, *Website:* www.heunship.dk

Medical Facilities: Hospital

Railway: Lollandsbanen, connected with the port

Development: Deepening of the access channel and main outer harbour basins to 8.5 m

Lloyd's Agent: Lars Krogius Hecksher ApS, Overodvej 5, P O Box 20, DK-2840 Holte, Denmark, *Tel:* +45 33 93 91 28, *Fax:* +45 33 93 27 90, *Email:* denmark@krogius.com, *Website:* www.krogius.com

NEXO

Lat 55° 4' N; Long 15° 9' E.

Admiralty Chart: 958/2150
Time Zone: GMT +1 h
Admiralty Pilot: 19
UNCTAD Locode: DK NEX

Principal Facilities:

			G				B	D		A

Authority: Nexo Havn A/S, Havnekontoret, P O Box 90, Sdr. Hammer 2, 1, DK-3730 Nexo, Denmark, *Tel:* +45 56 49 22 50, *Fax:* +45 56 49 44 97, *Email:* info@nexohavn.dk, *Website:* www.nexohavn.dk

Officials: Director: Ivar Koefoed-Nielsen, *Email:* ikn@nexohavn.dk.

Port Security: ISPS compliant

Pilotage: Not compulsory, but available

Radio Frequency: VHF Channels 16 and 12

Tides: No tidal difference

Traffic: 2004, 28 000 t of cargo handled

Maximum Vessel Dimensions: 79 m loa, 15 m beam, max depth 5 m
Alomgside Outer Northern Pier: 110 m loa, 18 m beam, max depth 5 m

Accommodation:

Name	Remarks
Nekso	Harbour comprises six small basins. Depth of water 5 m

Mechanical Handling Equipment:

Location	Type	Capacity (t)	Qty
Nexo	Mult-purp. Cranes	8	2
Nexo	Mobile Cranes	20	1

Bunkering: Available

Repair & Maintenance: Nexo Skibs & Badebyggeri A/S, Varftsv. 8, DK-3730 Nexo, Denmark, *Tel:* +45 56 49 22 54, *Fax:* +45 56 49 26 73

Airport: Ronne, 28 km

Lloyd's Agent: Lars Krogius Hecksher ApS, Overodvej 5, P O Box 20, DK-2840 Holte, Denmark, *Tel:* +45 33 93 91 28, *Fax:* +45 33 93 27 90, *Email:* denmark@krogius.com, *Website:* www.krogius.com

NYBORG

Lat 55° 18' N; Long 10° 47' E.

Admiralty Chart: 2596/938   **Admiralty Pilot:** 18
Time Zone: GMT +1 h   **UNCTAD Locode:** DK NBG

Principal Facilities:

Q	Y	G		R		B		T	A

Authority: Associated Danish Ports A/S, Terminal Nyborg, Lindholm Havnevej 27, DK-5800 Nyborg, Denmark, *Tel:* +45 79 21 50 00, *Fax:* +45 79 21 50 05, *Email:* post@adp-as.dk, *Website:* www.adp-as.com

Officials: Chief Executive Officer: Jens Peter Peters, *Tel:* +45 79 21 50 10, *Email:* jpp@adp-as.dk.
Sales & Marketing Manager: Ole Haugsted Jorgensen, *Tel:* +45 79 21 50 35, *Email:* ohj@adp-as.dk.
Harbour Master: Bo T Nielsen, *Tel:* +45 79 21 50 21, *Email:* btn@adp-as.dk.

Port Security: ISPS compliant

Documentation: List of crew (2 copies, also in case of change of crew, a crew list should be faxed to the agent 24 h prior to arrival), tobacco/alcohol/personal effects (1 copy), inventory of duty-free goods (1 copy), tonnage certificate (1 copy), health documentation and certificates, certificates of rat control, loadline certificate, certificate of nationality, certificate of safety equipment, certificate of loading/unloading equipment, bill of lading, manifest

Approach: Depth at entrance to Avernakke 10 m and Lindholm 11 m. No obstructions

Anchorage: Outside channels and well clear of leading lights

Pilotage: Not compulsory but available from DanPilot (Great Belt), Spodsbjerg, Tel: +45 62 50 15 35, Fax: +45 62 50 15 28, Email: belt@pilotage.dk, Website: www.pilotage.dk. Pilot boards in pos 55° 16.5' N; 10° 51.5' E

Radio Frequency: VHF Channels 16 and 12 during office hours

Tides: Tidal range 0.3 m

Traffic: 2004, 464 180 t of cargo handled

Working Hours: normal hours 7am - 5pm. When required round the clock service

Accommodation:

Name	Length (m)	Depth (m)	Remarks
Nyborg			See [1] below
Avernakke		6–10	Two berths
Lindholm	750	5–11	Four berths
Quay 20		8.5	
Quay 25		11	

[1]*Nyborg:* One ro/ro terminal with depth of 5 m for vessels up to 150 m loa
Bulk facilities: One mobile conveyor with a rate of 600 t/h

Storage:

Location	Covered (m²)
Nyborg	12000
Lindholm	4000

Mechanical Handling Equipment:

Location	Type	Capacity (t)	Qty
Nyborg	Mobile Cranes	45	4

Cargo Worked: Bulk commodities about 3000 t/day

Bunkering: Oil fuel, diesel and med diesel grades at entrance to harbour. Berth for vessels of 200 m long with 10.0 m d. Delivery at 400 t/h

Towage: Available. 24 h notice required

Stevedoring Companies: Lindholm Stevedoring ApS, Lindholm Havnevej, DK-5800 Nyborg, Denmark, *Tel:* +45 63 31 07 76, *Fax:* +45 65 31 57 53
Thomas Wang A/S, Gl. Vindingevej 14, DK-5800 Nyborg, Denmark, *Tel:* +45 65 31 00 57, *Fax:* +45 65 31 00 16, *Email:* agency@wang.dk, *Website:* www.wang.dk

Medical Facilities: Local hospital

Airport: Odense, 50 km

Lloyd's Agent: Lars Krogius Hecksher ApS, Overodvej 5, P O Box 20, DK-2840 Holte, Denmark, *Tel:* +45 33 93 91 28, *Fax:* +45 33 93 27 90, *Email:* denmark@krogius.com, *Website:* www.krogius.com

NYKOBING (FALSTER)

Lat 54° 46' N; Long 11° 52' E.

Admiralty Chart: 926/944   **Admiralty Pilot:** 18
Time Zone: GMT +1 h   **UNCTAD Locode:** DK NYF

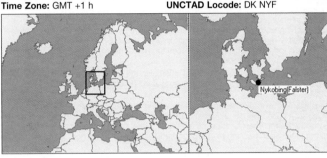

Principal Facilities:

P		Y	G				T	

Authority: Guldborgsund Havne, Fejogade 2, DK-4800 Nykobing Falster, Denmark, *Tel:* +45 54 85 05 63, *Fax:* +45 54 82 05 64, *Email:* havnen@guldborgsund.dk, *Website:* www.guldborgsundhavne.dk

Officials: Harbour Master: Viggo Engell Staberg, *Email:* vis@guldborgsund.dk.

Port Security: ISPS compliant

Approach: Vessels must pass Guldborg Bridge, located 12.8 km N of the harbour. Max breadth 25 m. Depth in channel from Guldborg is 6.4 m, max d of 5.8 m. Navigation during daylight hours only. Entrance from the south not possible

Pilotage: Not compulsory except for tankers with oil products. Pilot available from DanPilot (Great Belt), Spodsbjerg, Tel: +45 62 50 15 35, Fax: +45 62 50 15 28, Email: belt@pilotage.dk, Website: www.pilotage.dk

Traffic: 2004, 293 000 t of cargo handled

Maximum Vessel Dimensions: 5000 dwt, 129 m loa, 5.8 m d

Working Hours: Monday to Thursday 0700-1600. Friday 0700-1200

Accommodation:

Name	Remarks
Nykobing	See [1] below

[1]*Nykobing:* Harbour safe. Depth at entrance 6.2 m, width 25.9 m, depth alongside outer quay 6.2 m; depth of North Harbour 6.2 m. Railways on quays. Free local icebreaker assistance in winter

Storage:

Location	Covered (m²)
Nykobing (Falster)	1100

Mechanical Handling Equipment:

Location	Type	Capacity (t)	Qty
Nykobing (Falster)	Mobile Cranes	42	1
Nykobing (Falster)	Mobile Cranes	32	1

Towage: Tug available, 24 h notice required

Repair & Maintenance: Minor repairs on engine and hull

Shipping Agents: Holger Kristiansens Succsrs. A/S, Marina House, Femogade 4, P O Box 228, DK-4800 Nykobing Falster, Denmark, *Tel:* +45 54 82 12 02, *Fax:* +45 54 82 12 16, *Email:* krinyk@krisax.dk, *Website:* www.krinak.dk

Lloyd's Agent: Lars Krogius Hecksher ApS, Overodvej 5, P O Box 20, DK-2840 Holte, Denmark, *Tel:* +45 33 93 91 28, *Fax:* +45 33 93 27 90, *Email:* denmark@krogius.com, *Website:* www.krogius.com

NYKOBING (MORS)

Lat 56° 48' N; Long 8° 52' E.

Admiralty Chart: 427   **Admiralty Pilot:** 55
Time Zone: GMT +1 h   **UNCTAD Locode:** DK NYM

Key to Principal Facilities:—		
A=Airport	**C**=Containers	**G**=General Cargo
B=Bunkers	**D**=Dry Dock	**L**=Cruise

P=Petroleum	**R**=Ro/Ro	**Y**=Dry Bulk
Q=Other Liquid Bulk	**T**=Towage (where available from port)	

Principal Facilities:

		Y	G			B		A

Authority: Nykobing Mors Havnevesen, Morsoe Kommune, Jembanevej 7, DK-7900 Nykobing Mors, Denmark, *Tel:* +45 99 70 70 00, *Fax:* +45 99 70 72 46, *Email:* kommunen@morsoe.dk, *Website:* www.morsoe.dk

Port Security: ISPS compliant

Approach: Approaching from W through the Limfjord-Thyboron Channel in depth of 4 m. A railway bridge is situated 16 nm from Thyboron and a fixed road bridge with a vertical clearance of 26 m is situated 3 nm before Nykobing
Approaching from E through the Limfjord-Hals Bars in depth of 10 m. Two bridges in Aalborg and one bridge NE of Logstor to be passed
A 1000 m long buoyed and lighted channel dredged to 4.5 m leads NNW from Sallingsund to the harbour

Anchorage: Prohibited in the buoyed channel to the harbour and in the white sector from Glyngoere lighthouse. Otherwise good sand holding ground N and E of Orodde Point

Pilotage: Pilots obtainable from DanPilot (Great Belt), Spodsbjerg, *Tel:* +45 62 50 15 35, *Fax:* +45 62 50 15 28, Email: belt@pilotage.dk, *Website:* www.pilotage.dk. Compulsory for vessels exceeding 200 gt when passing Oddesund Bridge and compulsory when passing the Logstor dredged channel when draft is more than 3.1 m

Weather: Mostly SW'ly winds in summer and E'ly winds in winter

Traffic: 2004, 46 000 t of cargo handled

Maximum Vessel Dimensions: 120 m loa, 4.27 m max d

Working Hours: 0700-1700. Overtime can be arranged

Accommodation:

Name	Length (m)	Depth (m)	Remarks
Nykobing			See [1] below
East Pier	76	4.5	Dry cargo
South Basin	55	4.5	Consists of two berths handling dry cargo

[1]*Nykobing:* The harbour is enclosed by two stone moles and consists of a main basin dredged to a depth of 4.5 m, two smaller basins and two yacht harbours

Mechanical Handling Equipment:

Location	Type	Capacity (t)	Qty
Nykobing (Mors)	Mobile Cranes	25	1
Nykobing (Mors)	Mobile Cranes	15	1

Bunkering: Oil supplied by road tanker

Stevedoring Companies: Interfjord Spedition A/S, Hedelund 2a, DK-7870 Glyngore, Denmark, *Tel:* +45 97 73 20 00, *Fax:* +45 97 73 21 11, *Email:* info@interfjord.dk, *Website:* www.interfjord.dk

Surveyors: Aalborg Besigteleseskonitor ApS Survey Association Ltd, Vesteraa 4, DK 9000 Aalborg, Denmark, *Tel:* +45 98 16 60 22, *Fax:* +45 98 11 34 52, *Email:* shp@aalborgsurvey.dk, *Website:* www.aalborgsurvey.dk

Medical Facilities: Full hospital facilities available

Airport: Thisted Airport, 45 km. Karup, 65 km

Railway: Skive, 30 km

Lloyd's Agent: Eurobaltic ApS, Randersvej 563, Trige, DK-8380 Aarhus, Denmark, *Tel:* +45 70 23 15 13, *Fax:* +45 70 23 15 03, *Email:* ph@euroinspections.com, *Website:* www.eurobaltic.dk

ODENSE

Lat 55° 24' N; Long 10° 22' E.

Admiralty Chart: 931/2116	**Admiralty Pilot:** 18
Time Zone: GMT +1 h	**UNCTAD Locode:** DK ODE

Principal Facilities:

P		Y	G	C	R		B		T	A

Authority: Odense Havn, Londongade 1, DK-5000 Odense, Denmark, *Tel:* +45 72 28 20 00, *Fax:* +45 72 28 20 30, *Email:* info@odensehavn.dk, *Website:* www.odensehavn.dk

Officials: Port Director: Carsten Aa, *Email:* caa@odensehavn.dk.
Harbour Master: Finn Vinther, *Email:* fv@odensehavn.dk.

Port Security: ISPS compliant

Documentation: List of crew (1),passangers (1), stowaways (1), Personal effects (1), stores (1), fire arms/ammunition (1), vessels official certificates and documents

Approach: The distance from the fairway buoy to the inner port is 22.4 km. The first 16 km follows a natural channel through Odense Fjord, and the remaining 6.4 km is a canal. The passage through the fjord and canal is marked with light-buoys, leading lights and permanent structures equipped with lights. Depth of water is 7.5 m. Width at bottom 32-60 m and depth of water 11 m. No tides. Port open all year round with help of ice-breakers during the winter
The Lindoe-Terminal is situated 6 km from the entrance with width at bottom of min 60 m

Anchorage: Vessels with a d of 6 m or more should anchor about 3 miles N of Gabet in depths of 10-14 m, good holding ground. Sheltered anchorage obtainable inside Gabet in depths of 4-7.5 m

Pilotage: Inner Harbour: compulsory for all tankers carrying oil. petrol, LPG or dangerous liquid chemicals or with uncleaned tanks which have last carried such cargoes and other vessels exceeding 1500 dwt.
Lindoe-Terminal: compulsory for all tankers and other vessels exceeding 4000 dwt
Pilot available from DanPilot (Belt & Fjord Pilot), Fredericia, *Tel:* +45 76 20 03 20, *Fax:* +45 75 92 88 22, Email: littlebelt-pilot@lillebaelt.dk, *Website:* www.pilotage.dk

Radio Frequency: VHF Channels 16 and 12

Weather: Under normal conditions the port is open all year round. During the period January-March ice may occur in the fjord, but an ice-breaking tug and transisting ships will maintain an open ice-channel.

Tides: Tidal range 0.4 m. Gales from between E and SW may lower the water level by op tp 1.5 m (5) and from between W and NE may raise it by up to 1.8 m (6).

Traffic: 2004, 2 115 000 t of cargo handled

Maximum Vessel Dimensions: 6.7 m max d, part loaded 6 m max d, 160 m max loa. At Lindoe-Terminal max d is 8.4 m

Principal Imports and Exports: Imports: Cereals, Coal, Fertilizer, Foodstuffs, General cargo, Gravel, Iron, Kaolin, LPG, Paper reels, Petroleum products, Salt, Timber. Exports: Agricultural produce, Flour, General cargo, Machinery, Steel scrap.

Working Hours: Monday to Thursday 0700-1530. Friday 0700-1500

Accommodation:

Name	Length (m)	Depth (m)	Remarks
Odense			See [1] below
Lindoe-Terminal	280	11	Suitable for fully laden vessels up to 35 000 dwt

[1]*Odense:* There are three basins and a turning basin. Quays total about 4200 m, of which about 3400 m have a depth of 7.5 m
The power station for Funen is situated on the canal with its own quay (7.5 m alongside), coal cranes and one continuous unloader.
The Inner Port, which has a general depth of 7.5 m consists of three principal basins at the head of the Harbour and a number of wharves along the E and S bank of Odense Kanal with a total length of about 4 200 m
Bulk facilities: One grain loading terminal with 320 m3/h max cap
Tanker facilities: One quay; 200 and 150 m long with a depth of 7.5 m, a wooden jetty with a depth of 6 m for smaller tankers

Storage: Large open stowage places, warehouses and grain silos

Mechanical Handling Equipment:

Location	Type	Capacity (t)	Qty	Remarks
Odense	Mult-purp. Cranes	15	3	in inner harbour
Lindoe-Terminal	Mult-purp. Cranes	12–20	3	

Cargo Worked: Bulk cargo 300-500 t/h, general cargo 100-250 t/h

Bunkering: Oil and coal (loading by crane) available in adequate quantities
Kuwait Petroleum Corp., Havnegade 82, DK-5000 Odense, Denmark
A/S Dan-Bunkering Ltd, Strandgade 4A, 1401 Copenhagen K, Denmark, *Tel:* +45 3345 5410, *Fax:* +45 3345 5411, *Email:* copenhagen@dan-bunkering.dk, *Website:* www.dan-bunkering.dk
Ecophoenix AB, Kungsgatan 54, 753 21 Uppsala, Sweden, *Tel:* +46 1813 1880, *Fax:* +46 1813 1881, *Email:* info@phoenixscandinavia.com
Kuwait Petroleum Corp., Banevaenget 13, 3460 Birkerod, Denmark, *Tel:* +45 7012 4545, *Fax:* +45 4599 2020, *Email:* q8@q8.dk, *Website:* www.q8.dk
Malik Supply A/S, Ved Stranden 22, DK-9000 Aalborg, Denmark, *Tel:* +45 9631 3900, *Fax:* +45 9631 3911, *Email:* info@malik.dk, *Website:* www.malik.dk
Monjasa A/S, Strevelinsvej 4, 7000 Fredericia, Denmark, *Tel:* +45 70 26 02 30, *Fax:* +45 70 26 02 33, *Email:* denmark@monjasa.com, *Website:* www.monjasa.com
OW Bunker & Trading A/S, Gasvaerksvej 48, DK-9000 Aalborg, Denmark, *Tel:* +45 98 12 72 77, *Fax:* +45 98 16 72 77, *Email:* owbunker@owbunker.dk, *Website:* www.owbunker.dk
Trumf Bunker A/S, Raadhustorvet 4, P O Box 55, 7100 Vejle, Denmark, *Tel:* +45 7642 9696, *Fax:* +45 7642 9690, *Email:* trumf@trumf-bunker.com, *Website:* www.trumf-bunker.com

Towage: Svitzer A/S, Sundkaj 9, Pakhusvej 48, DK-2100 Copenhagen O, Denmark, *Tel:* +45 39 19 39 19, *Fax:* +45 39 19 39 09, *Website:* www.svitzer.com

Repair & Maintenance: Local workshops can undertake various kinds of repairs to boilers, machinery and electrical installations. The shipyard at Lindoe has three building docks of which the largest is suitable for vessels up to 50 000 dwt

Shipping Agents: Blue Water Shipping A/S, Emil Neckelmanns Vej 20, 5220 Odense, Denmark, *Tel:* +45 66 13 06 33, *Fax:* +45 66 14 75 70, *Email:* bwsode@bws.dk, *Website:* www.bws.dk

K Line (Europe) Ltd, Havnegade 17, P O Box 78, Odense, Denmark, *Tel:* +45 66 12 49 20, *Fax:* +45 66 12 49 25, *Email:* pla@kline.dk, *Website:* www.klineurope.com

Scan-Shipping A/S, 17 Havnegade, DK-5000 Odense, Denmark, *Tel:* +45 66 14 21 20, *Fax:* +45 66 14 21 56, *Email:* ode@scan-group.dk, *Website:* www.scan-group.com

G. Sunesen ApS, Norgekaj 62, DK-5000 Odense C, Denmark, *Tel:* +45 66 14 74 00, *Fax:* +45 65 91 31 40, *Email:* 1@sunesen.dk, *Website:* www.sunesen.dk

Stevedoring Companies: Thor Jorgensen A/S, Havnegade 4, DK-5000 Odense C, Denmark, *Tel:* +45 66 12 83 00, *Fax:* +45 66 12 81 00, *Email:* danprj@maersk.com, *Website:* www.maersksealand.com

Medical Facilities: Free pratique normally granted on arrival by boarding customs officers. Any kind of medical treatment obtainable.

Airport: Beldringe, 9 km

Lloyd's Agent: Lars Krogius Hecksher ApS, Overodvej 5, P O Box 20, DK-2840 Holte, Denmark, *Tel:* +45 33 93 91 28, *Fax:* +45 33 93 27 90, *Email:* denmark@krogius.com, *Website:* www.krogius.com

OLIEHAVN

harbour area, see under Fredericia

OREHOVED

Lat 54° 57' N; Long 11° 51' E.

Admiralty Chart: 2118/2138	**Admiralty Pilot:** 18
Time Zone: GMT +1 h	**UNCTAD Locode:** DK ORE

Principal Facilities:

	Y	G		R		B		T	A	

Authority: Guldborgsund Havne, Fejogade 2, DK-4800 Nykobing Falster, Denmark, *Tel:* +45 54 85 05 63, *Fax:* +45 54 82 05 64, *Email:* havnen@guldborgsund.dk, *Website:* www.guldborgsundhavne.dk

Officials: Harbour Master: Viggo Engell Staberg, *Email:* vis@guldborgsund.dk.

Port Security: ISPS compliant

Pilotage: Available from DanPilot (Great Belt), Spodsbjerg, Tel: +45 62 50 15 35, Fax: +45 62 50 15 28, Email: belt@pilotage.dk, Website: www.pilotage.dk

Accommodation:

Name	Remarks
Orehoved	See [1] below

[1]*Orehoved:* Depths of 7.0 m. Length of quays 160 m and 40 m. On the 40 m quay a 28 m ro/ro slip is available

Storage:

Location	Open (m²)	Covered (m²)	Sheds / Warehouses
Orehoved	3800	3600	1

Mechanical Handling Equipment:

Location	Type	Capacity (t)	Qty
Orehoved	Mobile Cranes	32	1
Orehoved	Forklifts		

Bunkering: Available

Towage: Available

Shipping Agents: Holger Kristiansens Succsrs. A/S, Marina House, Femogade 4, P O Box 228, DK-4800 Nykobing Falster, Denmark, *Tel:* +45 54 82 12 02, *Fax:* +45 54 82 12 16, *Email:* krinyk@krisax.dk, *Website:* www.krinak.dk

Airport: Kastrup International Airport, 96 km

Lloyd's Agent: Lars Krogius Hecksher ApS, Overodvej 5, P O Box 20, DK-2840 Holte, Denmark, *Tel:* +45 33 93 91 28, *Fax:* +45 33 93 27 90, *Email:* denmark@krogius.com, *Website:* www.krogius.com

RANDERS

Lat 56° 27' N; Long 10° 2' E.

Admiralty Chart: 905/2108	**Admiralty Pilot:** 18
Time Zone: GMT +1 h	**UNCTAD Locode:** DK RAN

Principal Facilities:

Q	Y	G		R		B		T	A	

Authority: Randers Havn, Kulholmsvej 1, DK-8900 Randers, Denmark, *Tel:* +45 86 42 10 57, *Fax:* +45 86 40 71 81, *Email:* randershavn@randers.dk, *Website:* www.randershavn.dk

Officials: Harbour Director: John Morgen, *Tel:* +45 89 15 15 91, *Email:* john.morgen@randers.dk.

Port Security: ISPS compliant

Pre-Arrival Information: In accordance with international regulations

Approach: An 18 nautical mile long buoyed and lighted channel, dredged to 7 m leads from Randers Fjord Light Buoy to the harbour

Anchorage: Vessels may anchor E of the fairway buoy with sandy bottom in a depth of 8 m. With strong onshore winds vessels may find a good anchorage with good holding ground approx 5 miles farther ESE close W of Tangen Shoal which breaks the sea considerably

Pilotage: Available but not compulsory from DanPilot (Great Belt), Spodsbjerg, Tel: +45 62 50 15 35, Fax: +45 62 50 15 28, Email: belt@pilotage.dk, Website: www.pilotage.dk. Pilot boards in pos 56° 37.0' N; 10° 25.0' E (near the Fairway Lt buoy)

Radio Frequency: Before entering Randers Fjord vessels must call on VHF Channel 16

Traffic: 2004, 1 148 000 t of cargo handled

Maximum Vessel Dimensions: 145 m loa, 20 m breadth, 6 m draft

Working Hours: 24 h/day

Accommodation:

Name	Length (m)	Depth (m)	Draught (m)	Remarks
Randers				See [1] below
Nordbassin	1000	7	6	See [2] below
Sydbassin	1600	6–7	5–6	See [3] below

[1]*Randers:* The harbour can accommodate vessels up to 8-10 000 dwt loaded with general or bulk cargo. One suction-pipe for discharging and three loading pipes available for loading grain. Molasses terminal, 12 500 t tanks

[2]*Nordbassin:* Consists of 22 berths handling feedstuffs, grain, coal, general cargo, wood & bulk cargo

[3]*Sydbassin:* Consists of 27 berths handling fertilizer, steel, cement, gravel, pebbles, wood, general cargo & bulk cargo

Storage:

Location	Open (m²)
Randers	3000

Mechanical Handling Equipment:

Location	Type	Capacity (t)	Qty	Remarks
Randers	Mobile Cranes	12	1	See [1] below
Randers	Mobile Cranes	5	1	

[1]*Randers:* It is possible to hire mobile cranes of 30-250 t cap from a local company

Bunkering: Coal and oil available. All major bunker firms represented

Waste Reception Facilities: Facilities available in accordance with regulations

Towage: Icebreaking tug of 900 hp available

Shipping Agents: Adolph Andersens Eftf, Kulholmsvej 2, P O Box 11, DK-8900 Randers, Denmark, *Tel:* +45 86 42 55 55, *Fax:* +45 86 42 88 82, *Email:* info@adolph-andersen.dk, *Website:* www.adolph-andersen.dk

Hassager Carl & Co., Sydhavnen, P O Box 248, DK-8900 Randers, Denmark, *Tel:* +45 86 42 05 22, *Fax:* +45 86 42 92 11, *Email:* info@adolph-andersen.dk, *Website:* www.adolph-andersen.dk

Holst Shipping A/S, Niels Brocksgade 8, 2nd Floor, DK-8900 Randers, Denmark, *Tel:* +45 86 43 44 55, *Fax:* +45 86 43 00 61, *Email:* mail@holst-shipping.com, *Website:* www.holst-shipping.com

J. L. Schultz & Co., Kulholmsvej 11, DK-8900 Randers, Denmark, *Tel:* +45 86 43 42 11, *Fax:* +45 86 41 74 41, *Email:* jls@jlschultz.dk, *Website:* www.jesveco.dk

Stevedoring Companies: Randers Stevedore ApS, Tronholmen 28B, DK-8900 Randers, Denmark, *Tel:* +45 86 42 36 38, *Fax:* +45 86 40 82 53, *Email:* sck@randersstevedore.dk, *Website:* www.randersstevedore.dk

Medical Facilities: Hospital, 2 km

Airport: Tirstrup, 45 km

Railway: Direct railway connection from the harbour to the EEC connected railway

Lloyd's Agent: Eurobaltic ApS, Randersvej 563, Trige, DK-8380 Aarhus, Denmark, *Tel:* +45 70 23 15 13, *Fax:* +45 70 23 15 03, *Email:* ph@euroinspections.com, *Website:* www.eurobaltic.dk

Key to Principal Facilities:—			
A=Airport	**C**=Containers	**G**=General Cargo	**P**=Petroleum	**R**=Ro/Ro	**Y**=Dry Bulk
B=Bunkers	**D**=Dry Dock	**L**=Cruise	**Q**=Other Liquid Bulk	**T**=Towage (where available from port)

RODBYHAVN

Lat 54° 39' N; Long 11° 21' E.

Admiralty Chart: 2364
Admiralty Pilot: 18
Time Zone: GMT +1 h
UNCTAD Locode: DK ROD

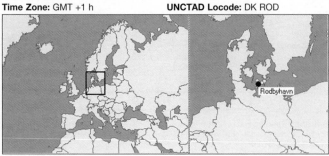

Principal Facilities:

	Y	G		B		A

Authority: Havnekontoret Scandlines A/S, Ostre Kaj 3, DK-4970 Rodbyhavn, Denmark, *Tel:* +45   54 65 71 80, *Fax:* +45   54 65 71 81, *Email:* torben.christiansen@scandlines.dk, *Website:* www.scandlines.dk

Officials: Harbour Master: Torben Christiansen.

Port Security: ISPS compliant

Pilotage: Not generally necessary, though local man can act as pilot if required. Contact Harbour Office

Radio Frequency: Call Roedby Port on VFH Channel 74 before entering the harbour

Maximum Vessel Dimensions: 80 m loa, 4.5 m draught

Principal Imports and Exports: Imports: Oil. Exports: Grain.

Working Hours: 0700-1600

Accommodation:

Name	Depth (m)	Remarks
Rodbyhavn		See [1] below
Ferry Harbour	8.5	Three berths
Traffic Harbour	4.5	See [2] below

[1]*Rodbyhavn:* Sheltered harbour with 520 m of stone quays; easily accessible. Depth of water 8.5 m at entrance, harbour average 5 m d
[2]*Traffic Harbour:* Two berths handling grain, oil & earth. East Pier and North Pier. Two grain silos with loading cap of 75-90 t/h

Storage:

Location	Cold (m³)
Rodbyhavn	3400

Mechanical Handling Equipment:

Location	Type	Capacity (t)	Qty
Traffic Harbour	Mobile Cranes	32	1

Cargo Worked: 800 t/day

Bunkering: Oil can be delivered by truck

Repair & Maintenance: Rodbyhavn Badevaerft, Rodbyhavn, Denmark, *Tel:* +45 54 60 52 06
Rodbyhavn Motor & Maskin Vaerksted, Vester Kaj 28, 4901 Rodbyhavn, Denmark, *Tel:* +45   54 60 51 52, *Fax:* +45   54 60 33 19, *Email:* rmm@pc.dk, *Website:* www.dannygroth.dk

Medical Facilities: Available at Roedby, 5 km. Hospital at Nakskov, 29 km

Airport: Maribo, 8 km

Railway: DSB, 0.5 km

Lloyd's Agent: Lars Krogius Hecksher ApS, Overodvej 5, P O Box 20, DK-2840 Holte, Denmark, *Tel:* +45   33 93 91 28, *Fax:* +45   33 93 27 90, *Email:* denmark@krogius.com, *Website:* www.krogius.com

RONNE

Lat 55° 6' N; Long 14° 42' E.

Admiralty Chart: 958
Admiralty Pilot: 19
Time Zone: GMT +1 h
UNCTAD Locode: DK RNN

Principal Facilities:

P		Y	G	C	R	L	B		T	A	

Authority: Ronne Havn A/S, Munch Petersens Vej 2, P O Box 47, DK-3700 Ronne, Denmark, *Tel:* +45   56 95 06 78, *Fax:* +45   56 95 06 31, *Email:* roennehavn@roennehavn.dk, *Website:* www.roennehavn.dk

Officials: Harbour Manager: Hans Kumler, *Email:* hk@roennehavn.dk.

Port Security: ISPS compliant

Pre-Arrival Information: 24 h notice prior ETA send message including requirements of (pilot, boatman, tug, fresh water), ISPS notification, crew list, waste notification, ship details (draft, length, gt and IMO number)

Approach: Depth in channel is 9 m

Anchorage: Anchorage can be obtained 0.6 miles W of the North Breakwater in a depth of 15-16 m. The anchorage is not safe in strong W winds

Pilotage: Not compulsory, except for tankers

Radio Frequency: Listens on channel 16, working channel 12 & 13 between 0600-2400

Weather: Port may be dangerous to approach in strong W gales

Tides: No tidal currents, but strong winds from NW through SE cause water to rise and vice versa

Traffic: 2007, 1 500 000 t of cargo handled

Maximum Vessel Dimensions: 240 m loa, 8.0 m d

Principal Imports and Exports: Imports: Agricultural products, Cement, Coal, Fish, Fuel oil, Gasoline, General cargo, Sand, Wood. Exports: Agricultural products, Fish, General cargo, Grain, Sand, Scrap metal, Stone, Wood.

Working Hours: 0700-1530

Accommodation:

Name	Length (m)	Depth (m)	Remarks
North Harbour			Consists of quays 1-10
Quays 2-5		5.5–6.5	Serve the ferry routes to Copenhagen & Ystad
Quays 6-7			Serve the passenger traffic to Sassnitz
Quay 8	40	5	Small craft
Quay 9	125	5	Used for loading/unloading general & heavy cargo
Quay 10	140	5.5–6.5	Catamaran high speed ferry
South Harbour			Consists of quays 12-25 & 31-32
Quay 12	100	7	Used solely for the purpose of unloading tankers
Quay 13	200	7	Serves the unloading of coal for Ostkraft
Quay 14	80	7	See [1] below
Quay 15	150	7	See [2] below
Quay 16	50	4	
Quay 17	120	7	Fishing vessels
Quay 18	80	4	Fishing vessels & repairs
Quay 19		4	Fishing vessels
Quay 20		4	Fishing vessels
Quay 21		4	Fishing vessels
Quay 22		7	See [3] below
Quay 23		7	Fish products & wood exported
Quay 24		4	Fishing vessels
Quay 25	55	7	Used by tug/pilot boat
Quays 31-32	240	9	Cruise vessels, ro/ro & general cargo
West Harbour			Consists of quays 26-30
Quay 26	175	7	Ferries & ro/ro
Quay 27	100	7	General & heavy cargo
Quays 28-29	265	7	See [4] below
Quay 30	90	7	General & heavy cargoes, wood

[1]*Quay 14:* Mainly used as a temporary berth for vessels waiting to be loaded with broken stone along Quay 15 and for fishing vessels
[2]*Quay 15:* Loading of broken stone with one loading system with a cap of 500 t/h
[3]*Quay 22:* Unloading of fish and loading ramp for loading of heavy cargoes from lorries (paving stones etc)
[4]*Quays 28-29:* Loading system for sand with a cap of 400 t/h and a silo and an unloading system for cement; also loading system for grain. Discharging feedstuffs

Storage:

Location	Open (m²)
Ronne	4000

Mechanical Handling Equipment:

Location	Type	Capacity (t)	Qty
Ronne	Mobile Cranes	30	1
Ronne	Mobile Cranes	60	2

Cargo Worked: Average rate of loading: macadam 500 t/h, sand loaded from silo 550 t/h
Average rate of discharging: coal 200 t/h, grain in bulk from silo 200 t/h, phosphate in bags 90 t/h

Bunkering: Available by road tanker. Bunker coal available

Towage: One tug of 900 bhp

Repair & Maintenance: Sydhavnens Motorvaerksted, Beddingsvej 2, DK-3700 Ronne, Denmark, *Tel:* +45 56 95 07 61, *Fax:* +45 56 95 05 82, *Email:* smv@mail.dk Vessels can be repaired and repainted. Slip can take vessel of max 350 dwt

Shipping Agents: Moller & Skovgaard Plum, P O Box 7, DK-3700 Ronne, Denmark, *Tel:* +45 56 95 17 00, *Fax:* +45 56 91 17 01, *Email:* info@pmsship.dk, *Website:* www.pmsship.dk

Medical Facilities: Hospital, 2 km

Airport: Bornholms Airport, 7 km

Lloyd's Agent: Lars Krogius Hecksher ApS, Overodvej 5, P O Box 20, DK-2840 Holte, Denmark, *Tel:* +45 33 93 91 28, *Fax:* +45 33 93 27 90, *Email:* denmark@krogius.com, *Website:* www.krogius.com

RUDKOBING

Lat 54° 56' N; Long 10° 43' E.

Admiralty Chart: 2597	**Admiralty Pilot:** 18
Time Zone: GMT +1 h	**UNCTAD Locode:** DK RKB

Principal Facilities:

	Y	G		B		T	A

Authority: Rudkobing Havn, Havnepladsen 9, DK-5900 Rudkobing, Denmark, *Tel:* +45 63 51 11 70, *Fax:* +45 63 51 11 71

Port Security: ISPS compliant

Documentation: Cargo manifest, crew list (2 copies), bonded stores list (2 copies)

Pilotage: Not compulsory. Pilot available upon request, which should be given 12 h prior to arrival

Radio Frequency: VHF Channels 16, 12 and 9

Traffic: 2004, 53 000 t of cargo handled

Principal Imports and Exports: Imports: Fertiliser, Foodstuffs, General cargo, Grain. Exports: General cargo, Grain.

Working Hours: Mon-Thurs 0700-1600. Fri 0700-1300. Overtime possible

Accommodation:

Name	Remarks
Rudkobing	See [1] below

[1]*Rudkobing:* Depth in dredged channel 5.0 m. Length of quayage 100.58 m. Slipways for vessels up to 100 t displacement. There is a bridge across the dredged channel with 26 m free height above water
Bulk facilities: Bulk cargo discharged by grab. Grain loaded by spout and conveyor belt

Mechanical Handling Equipment:

Location	Type	Capacity (t)	Qty
Rudkobing	Mobile Cranes	32	1

Cargo Worked: Grain spout approx 90 t/h, conveyor approx 70 t/h, grab approx 80 t/h

Bunkering: Available, delivery by truck

Waste Reception Facilities: Small amounts of garbage and dirty ballast may be removed by truck upon advanced request. No installations for reception available

Towage: Tugs available by request

Medical Facilities: Local hospital

Airport: Taasinge, 9 km

Lloyd's Agent: Lars Krogius Hecksher ApS, Overodvej 5, P O Box 20, DK-2840 Holte, Denmark, *Tel:* +45 33 93 91 28, *Fax:* +45 33 93 27 90, *Email:* denmark@krogius.com, *Website:* www.krogius.com

SKAERBAEK

Lat 55° 31' N; Long 9° 37' E.

Admiralty Chart: 900	**Admiralty Pilot:** 18
Time Zone: GMT +1 h	**UNCTAD Locode:** DK SKB

Principal Facilities:

P		G			B	T	A

Authority: DONG Energy A/S, Skaerbaek Power Station, Klippehagevej 22, DK-7000 Fredericia, Denmark, *Tel:* +45 76 22 28 00, *Fax:* +45 76 22 19 62, *Email:* skaerbaek@dongenergy.dk, *Website:* www.dongenergy.dk

Port Security: ISPS compliant

Approach: Skaerbaek is on the N side of the Kolding Fjord, within Little Belt. A dredged channel 200 m long, 49 m wide, 7 m depth leads to coal harbour and a second channel 500 m long, 80 m wide, 11.9 m depth leads to the oil berth

Anchorage: Can be obtained off Fredericia or Assens to the South. Smaller vessels can anchor at the entrance to Kolding fjord

Pilotage: Not compulsory. Local pilots from Fredericia. Pilot boards vessel at the mouth of Kolding fjord, available 24 h on VHF Channel 16. Larger vessels usually obtain pilot in the vicinity of Skaw lightvessel. Pilots to be ordered by ETA telegrams to Skaw pilot Skagen with no less than 12 h notice. Skaw pilot available on VHF Channel 16

Tides: Range of tide 1 m. Storms from the E can raise water level by 1 m above MWL and those from W-SW can lower water level by 1 m

Maximum Vessel Dimensions: Quay, max depth 6.7 m

Principal Imports and Exports: Imports: Oil.

Working Hours: Quay 0700-1500 Monday to Friday. Oil Jetty 24 h/day

Accommodation:

Name	Length (m)	Depth (m)	Remarks
Skaerbaek			
Oil Jetty		11.9	See [1] below
Coal Quay	253	7	Privately owned

[1]*Oil Jetty:* Equipped with 2 x 12" loading arms for fuel oil, 1 x 12" for diesel oil

Bunkering: Can be supplied by barge from Fredericia

Towage: Tugs available at short notice of 1400-4500 hp

Repair & Maintenance: Fredericia Shipyard: 1 hour away. Minor repairs by local staff

Medical Facilities: Good medical service. Hospitals at Kolding and Fredericia

Airport: Billund, 50 km

Railway: DSB, distance from port 15 km

Lloyd's Agent: Eurobaltic ApS, Randersvej 563, Trige, DK-8380 Aarhus, Denmark, *Tel:* +45 70 23 15 13, *Fax:* +45 70 23 15 03, *Email:* ph@euroinspections.com, *Website:* www.eurobaltic.dk

SKAGEN

Lat 57° 43' N; Long 10° 35' E.

Admiralty Chart: 2107	**Admiralty Pilot:** 55
Time Zone: GMT +1 h	**UNCTAD Locode:** DK SKA

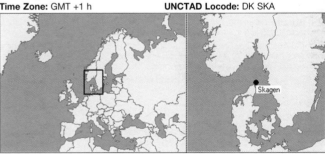

Principal Facilities:

P	Q		G		L	B		T	A

Authority: Skagen Havn, Havnevagtvej 30, DK-9990 Skagen, Denmark, *Tel:* +45 98 44 13 46, *Fax:* +45 98 45 03 38, *Email:* sh@skagenhavn.dk, *Website:* www.skagenhavn.dk

Officials: Harbour Director: Willy B. Hansen, *Tel:* +45 98 44 69 11, *Email:* wbh@skagenhavn.dk.

Port Security: ISPS compliant

Documentation: Crew list (2 copies), passenger list (2 copies), stoaways list (2 copies), tobacco/spirits/personal effects (2 copies), stores list (2 copies), arms & ammunition list (2 copies), bill of ladings (1 copy), manifests (freighted & unfreighted 1 copy of each)

Approach: Entry directly from the Kattegat through a 82 m wide entrance between the outer breakwater heads. Vessels should, when 400 m from the entrance, approach it on the leading line, indicated by two red lights, in line bearing 334°

Anchorage: Good anchorage obtainable SW of Skagen harbour in depths of 8-20 m

Pilotage: Available on a 24 h basis. Compulsory for tankers of more than 1500 dwt and for tugs with a tow greater than 150 gt or with a length exceeding 28 m. Pilot available from DanPilot (Great Belt), Spodsbjerg, Tel: +45 62 50 15 35, Fax: +45 62 50 15 28, Email: belt@pilotage.dk, Website: www.pilotage.dk

Radio Frequency: VHF Channels 16 and 12

Weather: Winds from SSW to W may create a NE running current. Winds from N to SSE may create a SW running current. The most frequent and strongest current will be running in a NE'ly direction with a speed of up to 2 knots

Tides: Normal tidal range of 0.3 m but gales from W can raise the sea level by up to 1.4 m and those from E may lower it by 0.9 m

---

Key to Principal Facilities:—

A=Airport	**C**=Containers	**G**=General Cargo	**P**=Petroleum	**R**=Ro/Ro	**Y**=Dry Bulk
B=Bunkers	**D**=Dry Dock	**L**=Cruise	**Q**=Other Liquid Bulk	**T**=Towage (where available from port)	

Traffic: 2007, 282 593 t of cargo handled

Maximum Vessel Dimensions: 130 m loa, 20 m beam, 9 m draft

Principal Imports and Exports: Imports: Fish meal, Fresh fish, General cargo, Oil. Exports: Fish produce.

Working Hours: 24 h/day

Accommodation:

Name	Depth (m)
Skagen	
East Basin No.1	6–9
East Basin No.2	7–9
Auction Basin	5–7
Middle Basin	4.5–7
West Basin	4.5–6
Pound Net Basin	3.5

Storage: Warehouses, cold storage and storage tanks for petroleum products and fish oil

Mechanical Handling Equipment:

Location	Type	Capacity (t)	Qty
Skagen	Mobile Cranes	100	1
Skagen	Mobile Cranes	20	5

Cargo Worked: 1200 t

Bunkering: A/S Dan-Bunkering Ltd, Strandgade 4A, 1401 Copenhagen K, Denmark, *Tel:* +45 3345 5410, *Fax:* +45 3345 5411, *Email:* copenhagen@dan-bunkering.dk, *Website:* www.dan-bunkering.dk – *Grades:* MDO; MGO – *Delivery Mode:* barge
Ecophoenix AB, Kungsgatan 54, 753 21 Uppsala, Sweden, *Tel:* +46 1813 1880, *Fax:* +46 1813 1881, *Email:* info@phoenixscandinavia.com – *Grades:* MDO; MGO – *Delivery Mode:* barge
Kuwait Petroleum Corp., Banevaenget 13, 3460 Birkerod, Denmark, *Tel:* +45 7012 4545, *Fax:* +45 4599 2020, *Email:* q8@q8.dk, *Website:* www.q8.dk
Malik Supply A/S, Ved Stranden 22, DK-9000 Aalborg, Denmark, *Tel:* +45 9631 3900, *Fax:* +45 9631 3911, *Email:* info@malik.dk, *Website:* www.malik.dk – *Grades:* MDO; MGO – *Delivery Mode:* barge
Monjasa A/S, Strevelinsvej 4, 7000 Fredericia, Denmark, *Tel:* +45 70 26 02 30, *Fax:* +45 70 26 02 33, *Email:* denmark@monjasa.com, *Website:* www.monjasa.com – *Grades:* MDO; MGO – *Delivery Mode:* barge
OW Bunker & Trading A/S, Gasvaerksvej 48, DK-9000 Aalborg, Denmark, *Tel:* +45 98 12 72 77, *Fax:* +45 98 16 72 77, *Email:* owbunker@owbunker.dk, *Website:* www.owbunker.dk – *Grades:* MDO; MGO – *Delivery Mode:* barge
Trumf Bunker A/S, Raadhustorvet 4, P O Box 55, 7100 Vejle, Denmark, *Tel:* +45 7642 9696, *Fax:* +45 7642 9690, *Email:* trumf@trumf-bunker.com, *Website:* www.trumf-bunker.com – *Grades:* MDO; MGO – *Delivery Mode:* barge

Waste Reception Facilities: Ships waste generated during the voyage is received without charge. Reception facilities of waste oil are also available

Towage: Two tugs of 4 t and 9.5 t bollard pull available

Repair & Maintenance: Shipyard with slips for vessels up to 1500 t displacement

Ship Chandlers: Harald Christiansens Eftf, Vestre Strandvej 6-8, P O Box 65, DK 9990 Skagen, Denmark, *Tel:* +45 98 44 13 33, *Fax:* +45 98 44 30 12, *Email:* dsc@skawsupply.dk, *Website:* www.lysholdt.dk

Shipping Agents: Saga Shipping A/S, Auktionsvej 10, P O Box 48, DK-9990 Skagen, Denmark, *Tel:* +45 98 44 33 11, *Fax:* +45 98 45 00 29, *Email:* saga@saga-shipping.dk, *Website:* www.saga-shipping.dk

Medical Facilities: Doctors and dentists available in town. Hospital in Frederikshavn, 43 km

Airport: Sindal, 50 km. Aalborg, 100 km

Railway: On Port

Lloyd's Agent: Rechnitzer, Thomsen & Co. Ltd, Gasvaerksvej 46, DK-9000 Aalborg, Denmark, *Tel:* +45 98 12 44 22, *Fax:* +45 98 10 15 71, *Email:* morten.kusk@wristshipping.dk, *Website:* www.wristshipping.dk

SKANSEODDE

harbour area, see under Fredericia

SONDERBORG

Lat 54° 55' N; Long 9° 47' E.

Admiralty Chart: 3562	**Admiralty Pilot:** 18
Time Zone: GMT +1 h	**UNCTAD Locode:** DK SGD

Principal Facilities:

P	Y	G	C		B	T	A

Authority: Sonderborg Havn, Norrebro 1, DK-6400 Sonderborg, Denmark, *Tel:* +45 74 42 27 65, *Fax:* +45 74 43 30 19, *Email:* havnen@sonderborg.dk, *Website:* www.sonderborg-kommune.dk/havn

Officials: Harbour Master: Finn Hansen, *Email:* fhan@sonderborg.dk.

Port Security: ISPS compliant

Approach: The port is divided into North and South Harbours by a lift bridge with an opening width at 30 m. N of the harbour is a bridge crossing the Alssund, with 33 m air draught and is 150 m wide

Pilotage: Not compulsory, but available

Radio Frequency: VHF Channel 16

Traffic: 2004, 67 000 t of cargo handled

Maximum Vessel Dimensions: From N, 9.5 m max d. From S through lift bridge, 6.5 m max d

Accommodation:

Name	Length (m)	Depth (m)	Remarks
Sonderborg			
North Harbour	550	6.5–7.5	
South Harbour	270		Mainly used by passenger vessels & fishing boats

Storage:

Location	Covered (m²)
North Harbour	4000

Mechanical Handling Equipment:

Location	Type	Capacity (t)	Qty
Sonderborg	Mobile Cranes	60	3

Bunkering: Available day and night

Towage: Small harbour tug available. Larger tugs available at 6 h notice

Shipping Agents: HK Samuelsen Transport A/S, Norre Havnegade 82-84, P O Box 230, DK-6400 Sonderborg, Denmark, *Tel:* +45 74 18 44 44, *Fax:* +45 74 18 44 00, *Email:* info@dk.dsv.com, *Website:* www.dsv.dk
Sven Holsoe's Eftf, Norrebro 1A, DK-6400 Sonderborg, Denmark, *Tel:* +45 74 42 35 66, *Fax:* +45 74 42 13 01, *Email:* holsoes@holsoes.dk, *Website:* www.holsoes.dk

Medical Facilities: Full hospital facilities available

Airport: Sonderborg Airport, 5 km

Railway: Sonderborg Railway Station at the port

Lloyd's Agent: C. Breinholt A/S, Toldbodvej 1, P O Box 20, DK-6701 Esbjerg, Denmark, *Tel:* +45 79 18 04 11, *Fax:* +45 75 18 19 25, *Email:* mkk@breinholt.dk, *Website:* www.breinholt.dk

STEVNS PIER

Lat 55° 19' N; Long 12° 27' E.

Admiralty Chart: -	**Admiralty Pilot:** 18
Time Zone: GMT +1 h	**UNCTAD Locode:** DK

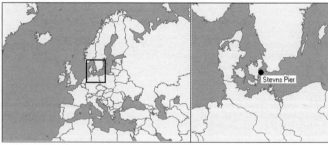

Principal Facilities:

	Y					T	A

Authority: Omya A/S, Stevns Kridtbrud, DK-4660 Store Heddinge, Denmark, *Tel:* +45 56 56 03 00, *Fax:* +45 56 56 03 01, *Email:* agency@ols.dk, *Website:* www.omya.com

Port Security: ISPS compliant

Documentation: Crew list(2 copies), Crew effects list(2 copies), stores list(1 copy). Valid de-ratting certificate, tonnage certificate as well as others required ship's documents/certificates to be presented on request. Within the period 15th December until 31st march ice breaker dues are collected

Anchorage: 0.5-1.0 mile E of the pier in depth of approx 10 m. All anchorage must be reported to Lyngby Radio

Pilotage: Compulsory for vessels over 5000 dwt and for all other vessels on first call. Pilot can be ordered from DanPilot (The Sound), Copenhagen, Tel: +45 35 38 67 00, Fax: +45 35 43 10 17, Email: soundpilot@pilotage.dk, Website: www.soundpilot.dk
Vessels coming from North, pilot boards in pos 55° 31.0' N; 12° 43.0' E (in the vicinity of Drogden Lt)
Vessels coming from South, pilot boards in pos 55° 27.0' N 12° 30.0' E (Koge W)

Radio Frequency: The master is requested to advise position to Stevns Pier 2 h before ETA on VHF Channel 16 (local radio traffic on Channel 13). The radio watch at Stevns Pier starts 2 h before vessel's notified arrival

Tides: Tidal range 0.5 m under normal weather conditions.
Information of actual weather conditions; current, wind direction, wind speed, wave height, and wave length, can be obtained directly from Stevns Pier on VHF or through the ships agent.

Maximum Vessel Dimensions: Approx 150 m loa, 25 m beam

Principal Imports and Exports: Exports: Chalk.

Working Hours: Around the clock subject to Shippers production planning.

Accommodation:

Name	Length (m)	Depth (m)	Remarks
Stevns Pier			See [1] below
Jetty	200	8	Projecting N-S at the head of the pier

[1]*Stevns Pier:* Pier projecting approx 550 m E from the coast. The loading of chalk is carried out from the stores ashore directly into the hold on conveyor belts at approx 500 t/h

Cargo Worked: 500 t/h

Waste Reception Facilities: Garbage disposal available at jetty

Towage: Tugs can be requested from Koge or Copenhagen

Airport: Kastrup International Airport, 75 km

Lloyd's Agent: Lars Krogius Hecksher ApS, Overodvej 5, P O Box 20, DK-2840 Holte, Denmark, *Tel:* +45   33 93 91 28, *Fax:* +45   33 93 27 90, *Email:* denmark@krogius.com, *Website:* www.krogius.com

STIGSNAESVAERKETS HAVN

Lat 55° 13' N; Long 11° 15' E.

Admiralty Chart: 2597
Time Zone: GMT +1 h

Admiralty Pilot: 18
UNCTAD Locode: DK STG

Principal Facilities:

P	Y			B	T	

Authority: DONG Energy A/S, Stigsnaes Power Station, Holtengardsvej 24, DK-4230 Skaelskor, Denmark, *Tel:* +45   58 16 40 00, *Fax:* +45   58 16 40 40, *Email:* olefa@dongenergy.dk, *Website:* www.dongenergy.dk

Officials: Harbour Master: Ole Fuglsbjerg, *Tel:* +45 58 16 41 57.

Port Security: ISPS compliant

Approach: Max draught permissible in channel from Skaw is 17 m bw

Anchorage: Anchorage can be obtained in Korsor Roads in pos 55° 18' N; 11° 04' E in a depth of 20 m, bottom sand

Pilotage: Pilotage is compulsory for tanker vessels above 1500 dwt. Dispensation can be granted if the captain has been in the area more than 5 times. For vessels exceeding 13 m d, pilotage is recommended to and from Skaw. Pilot ordered from DanPilot (Great Belt), Spodsbjerg, Tel: +45 62 50 15 35, Fax: +45 62 50 15 28, Email: belt@pilotage.dk, Website: www.pilotage.dk

Radio Frequency: VHF Channels 16, 13 and 12. Vessels ETA should be communicated by the Master to the Agent, 72, 48 and 24 h before arrival. Port can be contacted on VHF Channel 16, 24 h/day

Weather: Prevailing SW and NW

Tides: Practically no tide; max range 0.4 m. No tidal current but weather may change water level up to about 1.2 m and current can then be 3 knots

Traffic: 2004, 690 000 t of cargo handled

Principal Imports and Exports: Imports: Coal. Exports: Fly ash.

Working Hours: 24 h/day from Monday 0600 to Saturday 1200

Accommodation:

Name	Length (m)	Depth (m)	Draught (m)	Remarks
Oil Port				
Berth			15	See [1] below
Coal Port				
Berth			17	See [2] below
Coal Loading Berth	135	9		See [3] below
Ash Berth				See [4] below

[1]*Berth:* Two booms of 16" and 12" can be used at the same time. No dirty ballast facilities

[2]*Berth:* 290 m max loa, 45 m max beam, for vessels up to 180 000 t. Discharging by grabs. Approx 20 000 t/day of cargo handled

[3]*Coal Loading Berth:* For vessels up to 150 m loa, 19 m beam and 8.5 m d. Distance from water level to top of hatchcoaming 12.5 m. Cargo handling facilities include a

conveyor with hopper loading length at berth of 85 m with max outreach 16.5 m. Average loading rate 2000 t/h. Dumping height from conveyor belt to normal water level is 15 m

[4]*Ash Berth:* One berth for vessels of 7.5 m d, 130 m loa. Pneumatic loading from silo, average loading rate 800 m3/h

Mechanical Handling Equipment:

Location	Type	Capacity (t)	Qty
Berth	Mult-purp. Cranes	20	2

Cargo Worked: Approx 20 000 t/day

Bunkering: A/S Dan-Bunkering Ltd, Strandgade 4A, 1401 Copenhagen K, Denmark, *Tel:* +45 3345 5410, *Fax:* +45 3345 5411, *Email:* copenhagen@dan-bunkering.dk, *Website:* www.dan-bunkering.dk
Ecophoenix AB, Kungsgatan 54, 753 21 Uppsala, Sweden, *Tel:* +46 1813 1880, *Fax:* +46 1813 1881, *Email:* info@phoenixscandinavia.com
Malik Supply A/S, Ved Stranden 22, DK-9000 Aalborg, Denmark, *Tel:* +45 9631 3900, *Fax:* +45 9631 3911, *Email:* info@malik.dk, *Website:* www.malik.dk
Monjasa A/S, Strevelinsvej 4, 7000 Fredericia, Denmark, *Tel:* +45 70 26 02 30, *Fax:* +45 70 26 02 33, *Email:* denmark@monjasa.com, *Website:* www.monjasa.com
OW Bunker & Trading A/S, Gasvaerksvej 48, DK-9000 Aalborg, Denmark, *Tel:* +45 98 12 72 77, *Fax:* +45 98 16 72 77, *Email:* owbunker@owbunker.dk, *Website:* www.owbunker.dk
Trumf Bunker A/S, Raadhustorvet 4, P O Box 55, 7100 Vejle, Denmark, *Tel:* +45 7642 9696, *Fax:* +45 7642 9690, *Email:* trumf@trumf-bunker.com, *Website:* www.trumf-bunker.com

Towage: Tugs to be ordered at least 12 hrs prior to arrival

Surveyors: Caleb Brett, Intertek, Dokhavnsvej 3, Kalenborg, 4400 Stigsnaesvaerkets Havn, Denmark, *Tel:* +45 59 51 32 23, *Fax:* +45 59 51 35 51, *Email:* opscbe.denmark@intertek.com, *Website:* www.intertek.com
Saybolt Italia S.r.l., Fyrtaarnsvej 11, Copenhagen S, DK-2300 Stigsnaesvaerkets Havn, Denmark, *Tel:* +45 32 95 31 32, *Fax:* +45 32 95 31 34, *Email:* saybolt.denmark@corelab.com, *Website:* www.saybolt.com
Societe Generale de Surveillance (SGS), SGS Inspection, Stigsnaesvaerkets Havn, Denmark, *Tel:* +45 22 13 32 45, *Website:* www.sgs.com

Medical Facilities: Hospital available at Slagelse, 25 km

Lloyd's Agent: Lars Krogius Hecksher ApS, Overodvej 5, P O Box 20, DK-2840 Holte, Denmark, *Tel:* +45 33 93 91 28, *Fax:* +45 33 93 27 90, *Email:* denmark@krogius.com, *Website:* www.krogius.com

STRUER

Lat 56° 30' N; Long 8° 36' E.

Admiralty Chart: 426
Time Zone: GMT +1 h

Admiralty Pilot: 55
UNCTAD Locode: DK STR

Principal Facilities:

P	Q	Y	G	C	R		B		T	A

Authority: Holstebro-Struer Havn, Kulgade 6, DK-7600 Struer, Denmark, *Tel:* +45 97 85 02 28, *Fax:* +45 97 85 54 34, *Email:* struer@havn.dk, *Website:* www.struerhavn.dk

Officials: Harbour Master: Lars Brodersen, *Email:* lab@struer.dk.

Port Security: ISPS compliant

Approach: Depth at entrance 4.4 m, Thyboron 4.0 m, Hals 4.0 m

Pilotage: Pilot can be ordered from DanPilot (Great Belt), Spodsbjerg, Tel: +45 62 50 15 35, Fax: +45 62 50 15 28, Email: belt@pilotage.dk, Website: www.pilotage.dk

Radio Frequency: VHF Channels 16, 13 and 12

Tides: Tidal range 0.3 m

Traffic: 2004, 158 000 t of cargo handled

Maximum Vessel Dimensions: 4.0 m d, 4000 dwt, 140 m loa

Principal Imports and Exports: Imports: Fertiliser, Foodstuffs, General cargo, Grain, Oil, Pig iron. Exports: General cargo, Grain, Scrap iron, Timber.

Working Hours: 0700-1600, five days per week

Accommodation:

Name	Remarks
Struer	See [1] below

[1]*Struer:* Depth in harbour 4.4 m, 750 m of quayage. Private Wharves: 50 m of quayage Bulk facilities: Loading/discharging up to 200 t/h, by mobile cranes with grabs Tanker facilities: Statoil and Haahr operate tanker berths handling gas oil

Mechanical Handling Equipment:

Location	Type	Capacity (t)	Qty
Struer	Mobile Cranes	36	1
Struer	Mobile Cranes	16	1

Key to Principal Facilities:—				
A=Airport	**C**=Containers	**G**=General Cargo	**P**=Petroleum	**R**=Ro/Ro	**Y**=Dry Bulk
B=Bunkers	**D**=Dry Dock	**L**=Cruise	**Q**=Other Liquid Bulk	**T**=Towage (where available from port)	

Cargo Worked: 2500 t/day

Bunkering: Oil bunkering facilities

Towage: Tug boat of 350 hp available

Repair & Maintenance: Struer Skibsvaerft A/S, Ved Fjorden 2, DK-7600 Struer, Denmark, *Tel:* +45 70 22 42 32, *Fax:* +45 97 85 42 44, *Email:* dh@danhydra.dk, *Website:* www.struer-skibsvaerft.dk

Medical Facilities: Hospital within 20 km

Airport: Karup, 50 km

Lloyd's Agent: C. Breinholt A/S, Toldbodvej 1, P O Box 20, DK-6701 Esbjerg, Denmark, *Tel:* +45 79 18 04 11, *Fax:* +45 75 18 19 25, *Email:* mkk@breinholt.dk, *Website:* www.breinholt.dk

STUBBEKOBING

Lat 54° 53' N; Long 12° 2' E.

Admiralty Chart: 2138/940	**Admiralty Pilot:** 18
Time Zone: GMT +1 h	**UNCTAD Locode:** DK SBK

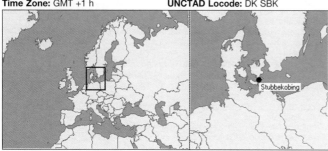

Principal Facilities:

			G				T		

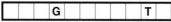

Authority: Stubbekobing Havn, Vestre Havn 3, DK-4850 Stubbekobing, Denmark, *Tel:* +45 51 74 07 09, *Email:* stubhavn@guldborgsund.dk, *Website:* www.guldborgsundhavne.dk

Officials: Harbour Master: Henrik Andersen.

Approach: Through Storstroemmen from the west and Groensund from the east

Pilotage: Not compulsory but available from DanPilot (Great Belt), Spodsbjerg, Tel: +45 62 50 15 35, Fax: +45 62 50 15 28, Email: belt@pilotage.dk, Website: www.pilotage.dk

Traffic: 2004, 87 000 t of cargo handled

Maximum Vessel Dimensions: 3000 dwt, 120 m loa, 4.8 m draft

Working Hours: Mon-Thurs 0700-1530. Fri 0700-1500

Accommodation:

Name	Remarks
Stubbekobing	Loading and discharging in western basin in a depth of 5 m

Towage: Available on request

Repair & Maintenance: Minor repairs on engine and hull

Lloyd's Agent: Lars Krogius Hecksher ApS, Overodvej 5, P O Box 20, DK-2840 Holte, Denmark, *Tel:* +45 33 93 91 28, *Fax:* +45 33 93 27 90, *Email:* denmark@krogius.com, *Website:* www.krogius.com

STUDSTRUP

Lat 56° 15' N; Long 10° 20' E.

Admiralty Chart: -	**Admiralty Pilot:** 18
Time Zone: GMT +1 h	**UNCTAD Locode:** DK SSV

Principal Facilities:

	P		Y			B		T	A	

Authority: DONG Energy A/S, Studstrup Power Station, Ny Studstrupvej 14, DK-8541 Skodstrup, Denmark, *Tel:* +45 87 49 17 00, *Fax:* +45 87 49 17 73, *Email:* poro@dongenergy.com, *Website:* www.dongenergy.dk

Officials: Harbour Master: Poul Rokkjaer.

Port Security: ISPS compliant

Approach: Entrance through Kattegat, Aarhus Bay and Kalo Vig inlet, marked by light buoys

Anchorage: Vessels can ride at anchor in larger zone outside the long channel of approx 700 m

Pilotage: Compulsory for navigation through the prohibited zone on entering Kalo Vig inlet. Pilot ordered from DanPilot (Great Belt), Spodsbjerg, Tel: +45 62 50 15 35, Fax: +45 62 50 15 28, Email: belt@pilotage.dk, Website: www.pilotage.dk

Tides: Range of tide 0.15 m. Water level may rise up to 1.25 m with W and NW winds and recede by 0.9 m with E and SE winds

Maximum Vessel Dimensions: 245 m loa, 33 m breadth, 11.0 m max draft for dry cargo vessels and 10.0 m max draft for oil tankers

Principal Imports and Exports: Imports: Coal, Oil.

Accommodation:

Name	Length (m)	Depth (m)	Remarks
Studstrupvaerket			See [1] below
Quay	495	7.7–11.3	See [2] below

[1]*Studstrupvaerket:* Privately owned harbour accessible day and night only to vessels with permission from the Power Station management
[2]*Quay:* Depth on the 405 m eastern line of the quay is 11.3 m and on the 90 m innermost line of the quay is 7.7 m. Coal is discharged by three cranes and oil is discharged by one 12'' line

Mechanical Handling Equipment:

Location	Type	Capacity (t)	Qty
Studstrup	Mobile Cranes	12	3

Bunkering: Bunker oil available by tank truck alongside quay

Towage: Not available locally but can be obtained via agent. Assistance is normally not required for vessels under 16 000 dwt

Airport: Tirstrup, 20 km

Lloyd's Agent: Eurobaltic ApS, Randersvej 563, Trige, DK-8380 Aarhus, Denmark, *Tel:* +45 70 23 15 13, *Fax:* +45 70 23 15 03, *Email:* ph@euroinspections.com, *Website:* www.eurobaltic.dk

SVANEKE

Lat 55° 8' N; Long 15° 9' E.

Admiralty Chart: 2360/2150	**Admiralty Pilot:** 19
Time Zone: GMT +1 h	**UNCTAD Locode:** DK SVA

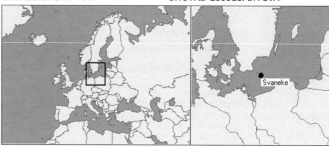

Principal Facilities:

				G						

Authority: Nexo Havn A/S, Havnekontoret, P O Box 90, Sdr. Hammer 2, 1, DK-3730 Nexo, Denmark, *Tel:* +45 56 49 22 50, *Fax:* +45 56 49 44 97, *Email:* info@nexohavn.dk, *Website:* www.nexohavn.dk

Officials: Director: Ivar Koefoed-Nielsen, *Email:* ikn@nexohavn.dk.

Port Security: ISPS compliant

Pilotage: Not available

Accommodation:

Name	Remarks
Svaneke	See [1] below

[1]*Svaneke:* Depth at entrance 4.42 m. Outside basin: width at entrance 12.19 m, depth 4.27 m, quayage 231.6 m, depth alongside 4.27 m; inner basin: width at entrance in dock gate 8.23 m, depth at quayside 3.5 m. Also one slipway available

Mechanical Handling Equipment:

Location	Type	Capacity (t)	Qty
Svaneke	Mult-purp. Cranes	3	1

Lloyd's Agent: Lars Krogius Hecksher ApS, Overodvej 5, P O Box 20, DK-2840 Holte, Denmark, *Tel:* +45 33 93 91 28, *Fax:* +45 33 93 27 90, *Email:* denmark@krogius.com, *Website:* www.krogius.com

SVENDBORG

Lat 55° 3' N; Long 10° 37' E.

Admiralty Chart: 2597	**Admiralty Pilot:** 18
Time Zone: GMT +1 h	**UNCTAD Locode:** DK SVE

Principal Facilities:

		Y	G	C	R		B		T	A

Authority: Svendborg Port Authority, Havnekontoret, Jessens Mole 11, 1st Floor, DK-5700 Svendborg, Denmark, *Tel:* +45 62 23 30 80, *Fax:* +45 62 22 06 79, *Email:* havn@svendborg.dk, *Website:* www.svendborg.dk

Officials: Harbour Master: Hans Soeby, *Email:* hans.soeby@svendborg.dk.

Port Security: ISPS compliant

Documentation: List of: crew (1), passengers (1), stowaways (1), personal effects (1), and firearms/ammunition (1). Vessels official certificates and documents

Approach: Narrow fairway, well marked by buoys and lights. Can be entered from E at Thuroe Rev or from W at Liehnskov. Vessels entering should note all side-markings change at Svendborg

Anchorage: Anchorages with good holding ground obtainable both E and W of Svendborg Sound

Pilotage: Not compulsory but obtainable through DanPilot (Great Belt), Spodsbjerg, Tel: +45 62 50 15 35, Fax: +45 62 50 15 28, Email: belt@pilotage.dk, Website: www.pilotage.dk

Radio Frequency: Lyngby Radio-OXZ. Great Belt Pilot, Tel: +45 62 50 15 35

Tides: Regular changing every 6 hrs, range 0.4 m. The current runs E and W at rates of 2-3 knots but is grately influenced by the wind and can during unsettled weather attain rates of up to 6 knots. Gales from NW will cause a W-going current and lower the sea level by up to 1.2 m and with gales from E the current will set E and the sea level raise by up to about 1.2 m

Traffic: 2004, 162 000 t of cargo handled

Maximum Vessel Dimensions: 180 m loa

Principal Imports and Exports: Imports: Cereals, Coal, Feeding stuffs, Fertilizers, Steel, Timber. Exports: Grain.

Working Hours: 0700-1600

Accommodation:

Name	Remarks
Svendborg	See [1] below

[1]*Svendborg:* Svendborg harbour which is formed by a cove with a partly artificial island in it's centre, is divided into three basins. The total quay length amounts to some 1900 m and depths alongside range between 4.3 m and 7.5 m. Depth at both E and W entrances 6.8 m. From W, bridge air restrictions 32.5 m. Two grain elevators (each of 60 t/h cap). Two large grain silos in operation

Mechanical Handling Equipment:

Location	Type	Capacity (t)	Qty
Svendborg	Mobile Cranes	32	1
Svendborg	Mobile Cranes	24	1

Bunkering: Ecophoenix AB, Kungsgatan 54, 753 21 Uppsala, Sweden, *Tel:* +46 1813 1880, *Fax:* +46 1813 1881, *Email:* info@phoenixscandinavia.com – *Misc:* coal and coke by grab
Kuwait Petroleum Corp., Banevaenget 13, 3460 Birkerod, Denmark, *Tel:* +45 7012 4545, *Fax:* +45 4599 2020, *Email:* q8@q8.dk, *Website:* www.q8.dk
Monjasa A/S, Strevelinsvej 4, 7000 Fredericia, Denmark, *Tel:* +45 70 26 02 30, *Fax:* +45 70 26 02 33, *Email:* denmark@monjasa.com, *Website:* www.monjasa.com – *Misc:* coal and coke by grab

Towage: Sufficient tugs available

Repair & Maintenance: Timber shipyard with two slipways for vessels of 100 t and 300 t displacement, and one floating dock capable to lift 1000 t

Ship Chandlers: SEA-CAT Ltd ApS, Ostre Havnevej 27, P O Box 257, DK 5700 Svendborg, Denmark, *Tel:* +45 62 21 66 62, *Fax:* +45 62 21 46 62, *Email:* mail@sea-cat.dk, *Website:* www.sea-cat.dk

Shipping Agents: Bjerrum & Jensen ApS, Gyldenbjergsvej 10, P O Box 190, DK-5700 Svendborg, Denmark, *Tel:* +45 62 21 26 00, *Fax:* +45 62 21 71 05, *Email:* broka@bjerrum-jensen.dk, *Website:* www.bjerrum-jensen.dk

Surveyors: Svendborg Marine Surveyors, Havnepladsen 3A, 3rd Floor, DK-5700 Svendborg, Denmark, *Tel:* +45 62 22 10 22, *Fax:* +45 62 22 13 68, *Email:* marine@surveyors.dk, *Website:* www.surveyors.dk

Medical Facilities: Under normal conditions pratique is granted on arrival by boarding customs officers. Medical services obtainable. Large modern hospital and private clinics

Airport: Billund International Airport, 150 km

Lloyd's Agent: Lars Krogius Hecksher ApS, Overodvej 5, P O Box 20, DK-2840 Holte, Denmark, *Tel:* +45 33 93 91 28, *Fax:* +45 33 93 27 90, *Email:* denmark@krogius.com, *Website:* www.krogius.com

THISTED

Lat 56° 57' N; Long 8° 42' E.

Admiralty Chart: 426	**Admiralty Pilot:** 55
Time Zone: GMT +1 h	**UNCTAD Locode:** DK TED

Principal Facilities:

		Y	G			B		T	A

Authority: Thisted Havn, Havnen 14, DK-7700 Thisted, Denmark, *Tel:* +45 97 91 14 00, *Fax:* +45 97 92 45 03, *Email:* thisted.havn@thisted.dk, *Website:* www.thisted.dk

Officials: Harbour Master: Lars Klemme, *Email:* lnk@thisted.dk.

Port Security: ISPS compliant

Anchorage: Available off the port in Limfjord in a depth of about 4 m

Pilotage: Compulsory for vessels with more than 3.1 m d and 150 gt in the artificial channel between Aalborg and Logstor and for vessels of 200 gt or more in passing the Oddesund Bridge. Pilot ordered from DanPilot (Great Belt), Spodsbjerg, Tel: +45 62 50 15 35, Fax: +45 62 50 15 28, Email: belt@pilotage.dk, Website: www.pilotage.dk

Traffic: 2004, 63 000 t of cargo handled

Working Hours: Monday to Friday 0700-1530. No work on Saturday and Sunday but overtime possible

Accommodation:

Name	Remarks
Thisted	See [1] below

[1]*Thisted:* Depth in the Thyboron Canal approx 3.96 m. Depth at Logstor 3.81 m. Depths in harbour range from 2.5 m to 5.6 m

Mechanical Handling Equipment:

Location	Type	Capacity (t)	Qty
Thisted	Mobile Cranes	15	1

Bunkering: Available

Towage: Available

Repair & Maintenance: Facilities for small vessels only

Airport: Thisted Airport, 15 km

Lloyd's Agent: Rechnitzer, Thomsen & Co. Ltd, Gasvaerksvej 46, DK-9000 Aalborg, Denmark, *Tel:* +45 98 12 44 22, *Fax:* +45 98 10 15 71, *Email:* morten.kusk@wristshipping.dk, *Website:* www.wristshipping.dk

VEJLE

Lat 55° 42' N; Long 9° 33' E.

Admiralty Chart: 930	**Admiralty Pilot:** 18
Time Zone: GMT +1 h	**UNCTAD Locode:** DK VEJ

Principal Facilities:

P	Q	Y	G		R		B		T	A

Authority: Vejle Havn, Sydkajen 16, DK-7100 Vejle, Denmark, *Tel:* +45 75 82 04 66, *Fax:* +45 75 83 87 54, *Email:* vejleport@vejleport.dk, *Website:* www.vejleport.dk

Officials: Managing Director: Per Kristiansen, *Email:* per@vejleport.dk.

Port Security: ISPS compliant

Approach: A deepened channel 3.0 miles long, 30 m wide, leads to sheltered harbour. There is a bridge just outside harbour entrance, across the channel, airdraft 40 m

Anchorage: Rosenvold Hage in pos 55° 40' N; 09° 48' E, depth of water 9-15 m

Pilotage: Available from DanPilot (Belt & Fjord Pilot), Fredericia, Tel: +45 76 20 03 20, Fax: +45 75 92 88 22, Email: littlebelt-pilot@lillebaelt.dk, Website: www.pilotage.dk. VHF Channel 16. Pilot boards in pos 55° 39.0' N; 9° 55.0' E

Key to Principal Facilities:—			
A=Airport	**C**=Containers	**G**=General Cargo	**P**=Petroleum	**R**=Ro/Ro	**Y**=Dry Bulk
B=Bunkers	**D**=Dry Dock	**L**=Cruise	**Q**=Other Liquid Bulk	**T**=Towage (where available from port)	

Radio Frequency: VHF Channels 16 and 12 (Mon-Thurs 0800-1500, Fri 0800-1430) or upon request

Weather: Winds from E'ly direction can cause swell in the harbour

Traffic: 2004, 879 000 t of cargo handled

Maximum Vessel Dimensions: 165 m loa, 6.8 m draught

Principal Imports and Exports: Imports: Chemicals, Coal, Fertilizers, Grain, Iron, Stones & limestone. Exports: Grain, Scrap, Steel.

Working Hours: Mon-Thurs: 0800-1500. Fri: 0800-1430

Accommodation:

Name	Remarks
Vejle	See [1] below

[1]*Vejle:* Depth at entrance 7.0 m; at docks 7.0 m; in harbour 7.0 m. Harbour basin 67.05 m wide. Quay length 1710 m
Bulk facilities: One conveyor belt at 200 t/h. Bulk by crane at 100-250 t/h depending on nature of goods
Tanker facilities: Two terminals available for chemicals with 6" and 8" pipelines

Storage: Available near or in the harbour area (private storage of nearly all kinds)

Mechanical Handling Equipment:

Location	Type	Capacity (t)	Qty
Vejle	Mobile Cranes	50	2
Vejle	Mobile Cranes	15	1

Bunkering: All kinds available by road tanker
Trumf Bunker A/S, Raadhustorvet 4, P O Box 55, 7100 Vejle, Denmark, *Tel:* +45 7642 9696, *Fax:* +45 7642 9690, *Email:* trumf@trumf-bunker.com, *Website:* www.trumf-bunker.com

Waste Reception Facilities: Garbage collected by port staff upon request; sludge by road tanker

Towage: One tug of 425 hp available on request to the harbour office. Others can be requested from other locations

Repair & Maintenance: Minor repairs possible

Shipping Agents: Lauenborg Vejle AS, Sydkajen 14, P O Box 20, DK-7100 Vejle, Denmark, *Tel:* +45 75 82 00 11, *Fax:* +45 75 82 98 39, *Email:* bsm@lauenborg.dk
Petersen Charles Vejle, Nordkajen 9, P O Box 142, DK-7100 Vejle, Denmark, *Tel:* +45 75 82 35 11, *Fax:* +45 75 82 37 61, *Email:* cpv@cpv.dk

Medical Facilities: Available at Vejle hospital

Airport: Billund Airport, 30 km

Railway: Vejle Railway Station, 500 m

Lloyd's Agent: Eurobaltic ApS, Randersvej 563, Trige, DK-8380 Aarhus, Denmark, *Tel:* +45 70 23 15 13, *Fax:* +45 70 23 15 03, *Email:* ph@euroinspections.com, *Website:* www.eurobaltic.dk

VORDINGBORG

Lat 55°·0' N; Long 11° 54' E.

Admiralty Chart: 2138

Admiralty Pilot: 18

Time Zone: GMT +1 h

UNCTAD Locode: DK VOR

Principal Facilities:

	Y	G			B		T	A

Authority: Vordingborg Havn, Sydhavnsvej 25, DK-4760 Vordingborg, Denmark, *Tel:* +45 55 37 52 54, *Fax:* +45 55 35 33 56, *Email:* tek@vordbkom.dk

Officials: Harbour Master: Hans Ove Lange.

Port Security: ISPS compliant

Approach: Depth in channel 7 m. Vessels calling Vordingborg South will require opening of Masnedsund Bridge, which carries road and rail. The bridge has a clear navigational opening width of 25 m up to a height of 18 m over waterline, then decreasing to a width of 20 m at a height of 23 m over waterline. An overhead power line spans the dredged channel approx 550 m W of the bridge, with a clearance of 36 m

Anchorage: Vordingborg Roads

Pilotage: Available from DanPilot (Great Belt), Spodsbjerg, Tel: +45 62 50 15 35, Fax: +45 62 50 15 28, Email: belt@pilotage.dk, Website: www.pilotage.dk

Radio Frequency: Port on VHF Channel 16

Tides: Range of tide 1 m in extreme weather

Traffic: 2004, 163 000 t of cargo handled

Maximum Vessel Dimensions: Approx 18 m beam, 6.3 m draft

Working Hours: Monday-Thursday 0700-1600, Friday 0700-1500

Accommodation:

Name	Length (m)	Depth (m)	Remarks
Vordingborg			See [1] below
Vordingborg West	200	7	See [2] below
Vordingborg South	460	6.5–7	See [3] below
Vordingborg North		1.7	For pleasure craft and small fishing vessels only

[1]*Vordingborg:* Vordingborg comprises three separate harbour areas; Vordingborg West: situated W of Masnedsund bridge, Vordingborg South: situated E of Masnedsund Bridge and Vordingborg Nordhavn. Berths equipped for handling grain, ore, coal and LPG carriers
[2]*Vordingborg West:* Max permitted draft of 6.3 m. Modern grain factory with conveyor loading belt at 150 t/h
[3]*Vordingborg South:* Max permitted draft of 6.3 m. Modern warehouses are available. Berths equipped for handling grain and fertilizer products with two conveyor belts at 150 t/h

Mechanical Handling Equipment:

Location	Type	Capacity (t)	Qty
Vordingborg West	Mobile Cranes	20	1
Vordingborg South	Mobile Cranes	20	1

Cargo Worked: Bulk cargo 150 t/h

Bunkering: Available by road tanker

Towage: Tugs available on request with 8 h notice

Repair & Maintenance: Most repairs, engine and equipment available. Electronic service only available from Copenhagen

Medical Facilities: Hospital available

Airport: Kastrup International Airport, 96 km

Railway: Vordingborg, 2 km

Lloyd's Agent: Lars Krogius Hecksher ApS, Overodvej 5, P O Box 20, DK-2840 Holte, Denmark, *Tel:* +45 33 93 91 28, *Fax:* +45 33 93 27 90, *Email:* denmark@krogius.com, *Website:* www.krogius.com

DJIBOUTI

DJIBOUTI

Lat 11° 32' N; Long 43° 9' E.

Admiralty Chart: 262

Admiralty Pilot: 64

Time Zone: GMT +3 h

UNCTAD Locode: DJ JIB

Principal Facilities:

P		Y	G	C	R	L	B		T	A

Authority: Port of Djibouti, P O Box 2107, Djibouti de Ville, Republic of Djibouti, *Tel:* +253 35 73 72, *Fax:* +253 35 54 76, *Email:* aboubaker.omar@dpworld.dj, *Website:* www.dpworld-djiboutiport.com

Officials: General Manager: Guido Heremans, *Email:* guido.heremans@dpworld.dj. Commercial Manager: Aboubaker Omar Hadi.

Port Security: ISPS compliant

Documentation: The following documentation should be delivered to the Authority at least 48 h prior to the vessel's arrival

Discharging vessels:
Bay plan (Container Terminal) 3 copies
Discharging list (Container Terminal) 3 copies
Hazardous & dangerous cargo declarations (Container Terminal, Statistics Central & Harbour Office) 3 copies
Passenger manifest (Harbour Office, Immigration & Statistics Central) 3 copies
Loading vessels:
Bay plan (Container Terminal) 3 copies
Loading list (Container Terminal) 3 copies
Hazardous & dangerous cargo declarations (Container Terminal, Statistics Central & Harbour Office) 3 copies
Passenger manifest (Harbour Office, Immigration & Statistics Central) 3 copies

Approach: There are three channels, of which the North passage is the one normally used by vessels

Anchorage: Good holding ground for up to 100 ocean-going vessels; min depth 7.62 m

Pilotage: Compulsory. Pilot boards in the following positions:
Djibouti Port: in the vicinity of Lt. buoy No.2 (11° 37.6' N; 43° 07.9' E)
Doraleh Oil Terminal: 11° 40.2' N; 43° 05.2' E

Radio Frequency: VHF Channels 12 and 16

Weather: Generally calm, but there are frequent gusts of westerly winds during the June-mid September monsoons

Tides: Range of tide 2.8 m

Traffic: 2007, 7 508 512 t of cargo handled, 294 902 TEU's

Maximum Vessel Dimensions: 400 m loa, 16 m draft

Principal Imports and Exports: Imports: Fertilizer, Oil products, Wheat. Exports: Beans, Coffee, Hides & skins, Sesame.

Working Hours: Port Administration: 0620-1300 Saturday to Thursday
General Cargo & Container Terminal: 24 h/day
Commercial Department/Invoice & Documentation Central: 0700-1300 and 1600-1830 Saturday to Thursday

Accommodation:

Name	Length (m)	Draught (m)	Remarks
Djibouti			See [1] below
Berth No.1	180	9.5	Container terminal
Berth No.2	220	12	Container terminal
Berth No.3	220	11	Ro/ro
Berth No.4	150	3.6	Coastal vessels & dhows
Berth No.5	230	7.2	Coastal vessels & dhows
Berth No.6A	170	7.8	Conventional cargo
Berth No.6B	93	7.8	Conventional cargo
Berth No.7	170	7.8	Conventional cargo
Berth No.8	202	9.3	Conventional cargo
Berth No.9	69.4	10	Multi-purpose berth (affected by French Navy)
Berth No.10	270	10.9	Tanker berth
Berth No.11	270	12	Tanker berth
Berth No.12	270	12	Tanker berth
Berth No.13	210	9.5	Multi-purpose & cruise berth
Berth No.14	290	12	General cargo & bulk berth
Berth No.15	107	12	General cargo & bulk berth
Doraleh			Located 8 km E of the Sea Port
Djibouti Horizon Terminal		16	See [2] below

[1]*Djibouti:* Djibouti Dry Port is located 2.1 km from the Sea Port and has a total area of 20 ha. The container storage cap is 1600 TEU's. Area of 32 000 m2 dedicated for vehicle storage. A warehouse of 6900 m2 is used for the storage of containerised cargoes
[2]*Djibouti Horizon Terminal:* Oil terminal consisting of a jetty with two berths, one for vessels up to 85 000 dwt and the other for vessels up to 30 000 dwt and storage facilities with 24 tanks of 239 650 m3 cap

Storage: Covered area of 27 200 m2, open area of 8000 m2 and yard storage of 379 610 m2

Mechanical Handling Equipment:

Location	Type	Capacity (t)	Qty
Djibouti	Container Cranes	41	2
Djibouti	Post Panamax	50	2
Djibouti	RTG's	40	10
Djibouti	Reach Stackers	42	11
Djibouti	Forklifts	2.5–48	6

Bunkering: ExxonMobil Marine Fuels, Mailpoint 31, ExxonMobil House, Ermyn Way, Leatherhead, Surrey KT22 8UX, United Kingdom, *Tel:* +44 1372 222 000, *Fax:* +44 1372 223 922, *Email:* marine.fuels@exxonmobil.com, *Website:* www.exxonmobil.com – *Grades:* 180cSt; MGO – *Delivery Mode:* truck, pipeline
Inchcape Shipping Services (ISS), Inchcape Shipping Services et Cie (Djibouti) S.A., 9-11 Rue de Geneve, P O Box 81, Djibouti de Ville, Republic of Djibouti, *Tel:* +253 35 38 44, *Fax:* +253 35 32 94, *Email:* gts.djibouti@iss-shipping.com, *Website:* www.iss-shipping.com – *Grades:* all grades – *Rates:* 300-400t/h – *Delivery Mode:* ex pipe
Shell Djibouti, BP 140, Shell Depot, Sea Port, Djibouti de Ville, Republic of Djibouti, *Tel:* +253 351 331, *Fax:* +253 353 721, *Email:* ahmed.bache@shelldj.simis.com, *Website:* www.shell.com – *Grades:* MDO; IFO; MGO – *Rates:* 10-150t/h – *Delivery Mode:* ex pipe, truck
Total France S.A., Total Marine Fuels, 51 Esplanade du General de Gaulle, F-92907 Paris la Defense Cedex 10, France, *Tel:* +33 1 4135 2755, *Fax:* +33 1 4197 0291, *Email:* marine.fuels@total.com, *Website:* www.marinefuels.total.com – *Grades:* MDO; MGO; IFO180-30cSt – *Parcel Size:* MGO 25t, IFO180 no min/max, other grades min 100t – *Notice:* 24 hours – *Delivery Mode:* ex pipe

Towage: Five tugs available of 2200-4500 hp and four mooring launches

Repair & Maintenance: Gambelli Freres, Avenue du Heron, P O Box 1917, Djibouti de Ville, Republic of Djibouti, *Tel:* +253 35 35 11, *Fax:* +253 35 61 53

Shipping Agents: Africa Shipping Ltd Sarl, 1st Floor, Palmier En Zinc Building, Place du 27 Juin, Djibouti, Republic of Djibouti, *Tel:* +253 35 90 35, *Fax:* +253 35 90 36, *Email:* info@asldjibouti.com
Chab Express Transit Services Sarl, P O Box 1996, Djibouti de Ville, Republic of Djibouti, *Tel:* +253 35 78 17, *Fax:* +253 35 65 20, *Email:* chab@intnet.dj
Diamond Shipping Services Sarl, Room No.01 - M2, Palmier En Zinc Building, Place du 27 Juin, P O Box 931, Djibouti, Republic of Djibouti, *Tel:* +253 35 89 10, *Fax:* +253 35 88 43, *Email:* diamondshipping@intnet.dj
Global Shipping Services, Avnue des Messagerie Maritime, P O Box 2666, Djibouti, Republic of Djibouti, *Tel:* +253 25 13 02, *Fax:* +253 35 04 66, *Email:* hettam@intnet.dj
Group Marill Sarl, 8 Rue Marchand, P O Box 57, Djibouti de Ville, Republic of Djibouti, *Tel:* +253 35 11 55, *Fax:* +253 35 56 23, *Email:* marill.d@intnet.dj, *Website:* www.groupe-marill.com
Gulf Agency Services - Djibouti, P O Box 1754, Rue de Bruxelles, Djibouti, Republic of Djibouti, *Tel:* +253 35 14 55, *Fax:* +253 35 77 48, *Email:* gulf.agency.services@gulfagencys.com
Inchcape Shipping Services (ISS), Inchcape Shipping Services et Cie (Djibouti) S.A., 9-11 Rue de Geneve, P O Box 81, Djibouti de Ville, Republic of Djibouti, *Tel:* +253 35 38 44, *Fax:* +253 35 32 94, *Email:* gts.djibouti@iss-shipping.com, *Website:* www.iss-shipping.com
International Maritime Shipping Services IMSS, 42 Avenue Georges Clemenceau, P O Box 1277, Djibouti de Ville, Republic of Djibouti, *Tel:* +253 35 19 88, *Fax:* +253 35 66 40, *Email:* info@imss-corp.com, *Website:* www.imss-corp.com
Compagnie Maritime et de Manutention de Djibouti, P O Box 89, Djibouti de Ville, Republic of Djibouti, *Tel:* +253 38 10 28, *Fax:* +253 35 04 66, *Email:* comad@intnet.dj
Massida Shipping Sarl, Boulevard Cheikh Osman, P O Box 661, Djibouti de Ville, Republic of Djibouti, *Tel:* +253 35 11 55, *Fax:* +253 35 55 18, *Email:* massida.shipping@intnet.dj
Mediterranean Shipping Company, MSC Djibouti, Palmier en Zinc, P O Box 2058, Djibouti, Republic of Djibouti, *Tel:* +253 35 80 18, *Fax:* +253 35 27 44, *Email:* commercial@mscjib.dj, *Website:* www.mscgva.ch

Stevedoring Companies: Afro Handling, P O Box 1966, Djibouti de Ville, Republic of Djibouti, *Tel:* +253 35 78 17, *Fax:* +253 35 65 20, *Email:* chab@intnet.dj
COMAD, Djibouti de Ville, Republic of Djibouti, *Tel:* +253 35 10 28, *Fax:* +253 35 04 66
Delta Maritime Services, P O Box 273, Boulevard Bonhoure, Djibouti de Ville, Republic of Djibouti, *Tel:* +253 35 08 40, *Fax:* +253 35 08 39, *Email:* delta@intnet.dj, *Website:* www.stm_shipping.com
Maritime Transport International, Djibouti de Ville, Republic of Djibouti, *Tel:* +253 35 14 55, *Fax:* +253 35 77 48
Okar, Djibouti de Ville, Republic of Djibouti, *Tel:* +253 35 19 29, *Fax:* +253 35 19 51
Societe Djiboutienne de Traffic Maritime, Djibouti de Ville, Republic of Djibouti, *Tel:* +253 35 23 51, *Fax:* +253 35 11 03
Trans African Stevedoring Services, Djibouti de Ville, Republic of Djibouti, *Tel:* +253 35 13 63, *Fax:* +253 35 00 86, *Email:* tats@intnet.dj

Surveyors: General Transport Services (GTS), 9/11 Rue de Geneve, P O Box 81, Djibouti de Ville, Republic of Djibouti, *Tel:* +253 353844, *Fax:* +253 353294, *Email:* gts.djibouti@iss-shipping.com, *Website:* www.iss-shipping.com

Medical Facilities: Public hospital and several clinics available

Airport: Djibouti International Airport, 7 km

Railway: Ethio-Djiboutian railway connecting 1 km from berths

Development: The port of Doraleh, located 8 km E of the Sea Port, is being developed comprising:
1) Djibouti Horizon Oil Terminal which has been completed
2) Doraleh Container Terminal with 1050 m of quay in depth of 17-20 m with six super-post-panamax cranes; expected to commence operations late 2008
3) A large industrial and commercial free zone of 600 000 m2

Lloyd's Agent: General Transport Services (GTS), 9/11 Rue de Geneve, P O Box 81, Djibouti de Ville, Republic of Djibouti, *Tel:* +253 353844, *Fax:* +253 353294, *Email:* gts.djibouti@iss-shipping.com, *Website:* www.iss-shipping.com

DOMINICA

ROSEAU

Lat 15° 17' N; Long 61° 23' W.

Admiralty Chart: 697	**Admiralty Pilot:** 71
Time Zone: GMT -4 h	**UNCTAD Locode:** DM RSU

Principal Facilities:

P	Q		G	C	R	L	B			A

Authority: Dominica Air & Sea Ports Authority, P O Box 243, Roseau, Dominica, *Tel:* +1767 448 4009, *Fax:* +1767 448 6131, *Email:* domport@cwdom.dm

Officials: General Manager: Benoit Bardouille.
Marine Manager: Eric Charles, *Tel:* +1767 448 4431 ext.121.

Key to Principal Facilities:—			
A=Airport	**C**=Containers	**G**=General Cargo	**P**=Petroleum	**R**=Ro/Ro	**Y**=Dry Bulk
B=Bunkers	**D**=Dry Dock	**L**=Cruise	**Q**=Other Liquid Bulk	**T**=Towage (where available from port)

Port Security: ISPS compliant

Pilotage: Compulsory for vessels over 100 gt. VHF 16/14, watching 0800-1600 and 2 h prior to ETA

Maximum Vessel Dimensions: At Woodbridge Bay, 43 000 gt, 8.84 m draft

Working Hours: Monday to Friday 0800-1600. Overtime, Monday to Friday 1600-2400 and 0600-0700 and Saturday 0600-1800 (50% extra). Double time, Monday to Friday 0000-0600. Saturday 1800-0600, also Sunday and Bank Holiday (100% extra)

Accommodation: Open roadstead, 27.5 to 74 m

Name	Length (m)	Depth (m)	Remarks
Roseau			
Prince Rupert's Bay	80	3.4	
Cabrits	100		Cruise ship berth with passenger reception centre
Woodbridge Bay			See [1] below

[1]*Woodbridge Bay:* Equipped for handling ex geared carriers; ro/ro ships and barges operated to end of wharf at ramp, height +3 m. Container park of 2.5 acres

Storage:

Location	Sheds / Warehouses
Woodbridge Bay	4

Mechanical Handling Equipment:

Location	Type	Capacity (t)	Qty
Roseau	Mult-purp. Cranes	55	3

Cargo Worked: 120 t/gang/day

Bunkering: Gas oil only from road tank wagon alongside pier

Shipping Agents: Archipelago Inc., P O Box 21, Goodwill Road, Roseau, Dominica, *Tel:* +1767 448 5247, *Fax:* +1767 448 5338, *Email:* archipelago@cwdom.dm
Assist Agencies, 53 Old Street, Roseau, Dominica, *Tel:* +1767 448 4544, *Fax:* +1767 448 4544, *Email:* assist_agencies@yahoo.com
Element Agencies, Woodbridge Bay, P O Box 266, Roseau, Dominica, *Tel:* +1767 448 6666, *Fax:* +1767 440 3459, *Email:* element@cwdom.dm
J.E. Nassief, P O Box 76, Roseau, Dominica, *Tel:* +1767 448 2851, *Fax:* +1767 448 5163, *Email:* jenassief@cwdom.dm
Sunrise Shipping Agency, Goodwill, P O Box 1127, Roseau, Dominica, *Tel:* +1767 448 0692, *Fax:* +1767 440 5253, *Email:* sunriseshippingdm@hotmail.com
H.H.V. Whitchurch & Co. Ltd, P O Box 771, Old Street, Roseau, Dominica, *Tel:* +1767 448 2181, *Fax:* +1767 448 5787, *Email:* insurance@whitchurch.com, *Website:* www.whitchurch.com
Wyllis Services, P O Box 443, Roseau, Dominica, *Tel:* +1767 448 3911, *Fax:* +1767 448 4528, *Email:* wyllisserv@hotmail.com

Medical Facilities: Princess Margaret Hospital at Roseau and Portsmouth Hospital

Airport: Melville Hall, 48 km

Lloyd's Agent: H.H.V. Whitchurch & Co. Ltd, P O Box 771, Old Street, Roseau, Dominica, *Tel:* +1767 448 2181, *Fax:* +1767 448 5787, *Email:* insurance@whitchurch.com, *Website:* www.whitchurch.com

DOMINICAN REPUBLIC

ANDRES

Lat 18° 26' N; Long 69° 37' W.

Admiralty Chart: 467		**Admiralty Pilot:** 70
Time Zone: GMT -4 h		**UNCTAD Locode:** DO

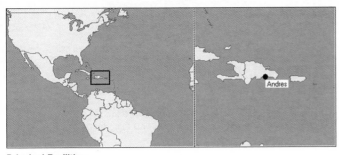

Principal Facilities:

Q						T		

Authority: AES Andres, Aurora Street No.1, Punta Caucedo Andres, Boca Chica, Dominican Republic, *Tel:* +1809 523 5160, *Fax:* +1809 523 5117, *Email:* juan.noboa@aes.com, *Website:* www.aes.com

Officials: Vice President: Angel Guastaferro, *Email:* angel.guastaferro@aes.com. Managing Director: Diego Arias, *Email:* diego.arias@aes.com. Commercial Manager: Rodolfo Cabello, *Email:* rodolfo.cabello@aes.com.

Pilotage: Compulsory and arranged through vessel's agent. Vessels should contact pilot 1 h before scheduled ETA on VHF Channel 16. Pilot boards from a tug approx 3 miles SSE of the terminal in pos 18° 21.5' N; 69° 36.5' W

Principal Imports and Exports: Imports: Fuel oil, LNG.

Accommodation:

Name	Remarks
AES Andres LNG Terminal	See [1] below

[1]*AES Andres LNG Terminal:* Comprises a T-shaped jetty with dolphins, connected to the shore by a trestle 129 m long. It has a berthing face of 125 m and is 360 m loa including dolphins with a depth alongside of 14.5 m. LNG supplied by BP

Towage: Available

Medical Facilities: Hospital in Andres but serious cases go to Santo Domingo, 29 km away

Lloyd's Agent: Frederic Schad Inc., Jose Gabriel Garcia 26, Colonial City, P O Box 941, Santo Domingo, Dominican Republic, *Tel:* +1809 689 9377, *Fax:* +1809 688 7696, *Email:* mail@fschad.com, *Website:* www.fschad.com

ARROYO BARRIL

Lat 19° 12' N; Long 69° 26' W.

Admiralty Chart: 463　　　　**Admiralty Pilot:** 70
Time Zone: GMT -4 h　　　　**UNCTAD Locode:** DO PUD

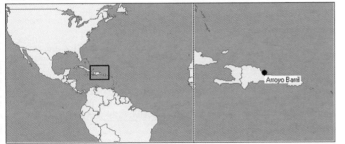

Principal Facilities:

Y	G	C		B		T	A	

Authority: Autoridad Portuaria Dominicana (APORDOM), Arroyo Barril, Dominican Republic, *Website:* www.apordom.gov.do

Documentation: Harbour Master: port clearance from last port of call, crew list (4 copies), passenger/no passenger list (4 copies), arms/no arms declaration (4 copies)
Customs: crew list (2 copies), passenger/no passenger list (2 copies), arms/no arms declaration (2 copies), personal effects list (2 copies), cargo manifests (4 copies)
Immigration: crew list (2 copies), passenger/no passenger list (2 copies)
Port Authority: cargo manifests (6 copies)
Agency: crew list (1 copy), passenger/no passenger list (1 copy), manifest if not couriered or faxed (4 copies), bills of lading if not couriered or faxed (2 copies each), crew personal effects list (1 copy), stowage plans (2 copies)
Port Doctor: deratting exemption certificate, crew list (1 copy), passenger/no passenger list (1 copy), crew vaccination list (1 copy)
Department of Agriculture: stores list (2 copies), personal effects list (2 copies), cargo manifests (2 copies)

Approach: The entrance channel is well marked with eight buoys. Sea Buoy No.2 is located at the eastern tip of Colonial Bank, or 9.6 km ESE of Punta Balandra, which has a lighthouse. Buoy No.4 is located 0.8 km S of Punta Balandra. Vessels should pass just S of Buoy No.2 with heading of 283°

Anchorage: Deep water anchorage is available at Samana Bay

Pilotage: Compulsory. Pilot boards at Punta Balandra

Radio Frequency: Pilot and Harbour Master on VHF Channel 16

Traffic: 2007, 5502 t of cargo handled

Maximum Vessel Dimensions: 198 m loa, 9.15 m draft

Working Hours: Mon-Fri 0800-1200, 1400-1800. Sat 0800-1200. Overtime available

Accommodation:

Name	Length (m)	Depth (m)	Remarks
Puerto Duarte Finger Pier	230	9.2	Located in Samana Bay See [1] below

[1]*Finger Pier:* Mostly refrigerated and dry cargo containers handled. Access ramp connecting the pier to the shore is 350 m long and 13.5 m wide

Storage:

Location	Covered (m²)	Sheds / Warehouses
Arroyo Barril	2200	1

Bunkering: Available by tank truck from Santo Domingo

Towage: None available locally but if required must come from Puerto Plata or Santo Domingo

Medical Facilities: First aid and emergency treatment only

Airport: Arroyo Barril International

Lloyd's Agent: Frederic Schad Inc., Jose Gabriel Garcia 26, Colonial City, P O Box 941, Santo Domingo, Dominican Republic, *Tel:* +1809 689 9377, *Fax:* +1809 688 7696, *Email:* mail@fschad.com, *Website:* www.fschad.com

AZUA

alternate name, see Puerto Viejo de Azua

BARAHONA

Lat 18° 12' N; Long 71° 4' W.

Admiralty Chart: 471　　　　**Admiralty Pilot:** 70
Time Zone: GMT -4 h　　　　**UNCTAD Locode:** DO BRX

Principal Facilities:

	Y	G			B		T	A

Authority: Autoridad Portuaria Dominicana (APORDOM), Barahona, Dominican Republic, *Tel:* +1809 524 5012, *Fax:* +1809 534 3663, *Website:* www.apordom.gov.do

Port Security: ISPS compliant

Documentation: Harbour Master: port clearance from last port of call, crew list (4 copies), passenger/no passenger list (4 copies), arms/no arms declaration (4 copies)
Customs: crew list (2 copies), passenger/no passenger list (2 copies), arms/no arms declaration (2 copies), personal effects list (2 copies), cargo manifests (4 copies)
Immigration: crew list (2 copies), passenger/no passenger list (2 copies)
Port Authority: cargo manifests (6 copies)
Agency: crew list (1 copy), passenger/no passenger list (1 copy), manifest if not couriered or faxed (4 copies), bills of lading if not couriered or faxed (2 copies each), crew personal effects list (1 copy), stowage plans (2 copies)
Port Doctor: deratting exemption certificate, crew list (1 copy), passenger/no passenger list (1 copy), crew vaccination list (1 copy)
Department of Agriculture: stores list (2 copies), personal effects list (2 copies), cargo manifests (2 copies)

Anchorage: Deep water anchorage available just outside the port entrance. Contact pilot for the best location

Pilotage: Compulsory. Pilot boards approx 1.5 miles outside the port. No entry or departure at night

Radio Frequency: Pilot and Harbour Master can be contacted on VHF Channel 16

Weather: Sometimes in late afternoon strong winds make docking large vessels in ballast very difficult

Traffic: 2007, 403 659 t of cargo handled

Maximum Vessel Dimensions: 600 ft loa, 100 ft beam, 27 ft draft

Principal Imports and Exports: Exports: Gypsum, Molasses, Sugar.

Working Hours: Mon-Fri 0800-1200, 1400-1800. Sat 0800-1200. Some overtime may be available

Accommodation:

Name	Length (m)	Remarks
Barahona		
Berth No.1	216	Usually occupied by Dominican Navy & fishing vessels
Berth No.2	137	Mostly used by Dominican Navy & small fishing vessels
Berth No.3	160	See [1] below

Key to Principal Facilities:—				
A=Airport	**C**=Containers	**G**=General Cargo	**P**=Petroleum	**R**=Ro/Ro	**Y**=Dry Bulk
B=Bunkers	**D**=Dry Dock	**L**=Cruise	**Q**=Other Liquid Bulk	**T**=Towage (where available from port)

Name	Length (m)	Remarks
Berth No.4	146	Used exclusively by the sugar mill for exports of sugar & blackstrap molasses

[1]Berth No.3: Used for loading gypsum in bulk. The Salt & Gypsum Mines Co. maintain a gypsum export terminal at this pier. Loading by means of a large crane which feeds a hopper and conveyor belt system, approx 400-500 t/h

Bunkering: Available by tank truck from Santo Domingo

Towage: One tug of 350 hp available, owned by local sugar mill

Repair & Maintenance: Minor repairs only

Medical Facilities: Emergency and minor medical care is available locally but more serious cases should be treated in Santo Domingo

Airport: Maria Montez International

Lloyd's Agent: Frederic Schad Inc., Jose Gabriel Garcia 26, Colonial City, P O Box 941, Santo Domingo, Dominican Republic, *Tel:* +1809 689 9377, *Fax:* +1809 688 7696, *Email:* mail@fschad.com, *Website:* www.fschad.com

BOCA CHICA

Lat 18° 26' N; Long 69° 35' W.

Admiralty Chart: 467
Time Zone: GMT -4 h

Admiralty Pilot: 70
UNCTAD Locode: DO BCC

Principal Facilities:

		G	C		B		A		

Authority: Autoridad Portuaria Dominicana (APORDOM), Boca Chica, Dominican Republic, *Tel:* +1809 523 4826, *Website:* www.apordom.gov.do

Port Security: ISPS compliant

Documentation: Harbour Master: port clearance from last port of call, crew list (4 copies), passenger/no passenger list (4 copies), arms/no arms declaration (4 copies) Customs: crew list (2 copies), passenger/no passenger list (2 copies), arms/no arms declaration (2 copies), personal effects list (2 copies), cargo manifests (4 copies) Immigration: crew list (2 copies), passenger/no passenger list (2 copies) Port Authority: cargo manifests (6 copies) Agency: crew list (1 copy), passenger/no passenger list (1 copy), manifest if not couriered or faxed (4 copies), bills of lading if not couriered or faxed (2 copies each), crew personal effects list (1 copy), stowage plans (2 copies) Port Doctor: deratting exemption certificate, crew list (1 copy), passenger/no passenger list (1 copy), crew vaccination list (1 copy) Department of Agriculture: stores list (2 copies), personal effects list (2 copies), cargo manifests (2 copies)

Anchorage: Deep water anchorage available outside the port. Contact pilot for the best location

Pilotage: Pilot can be contacted by radio telephone on 2738 mHz or VHF Channel 16. The pilot boards about 1 mile outside the first buoy. No entry or departure at night

Traffic: 2007, 239 vessels, 492 590 t of cargo handled, 20 207 TEU's

Maximum Vessel Dimensions: 140 m loa, 7.6 m draft

Working Hours: Mon-Fri 0800-1200, 1400-1800. Sat 0800-1200. Overtime available

Accommodation:

Name	Length (m)	Draught (m)
Boca Chica		
Berth No.1	140	7.6
Berth No.2	140	7.6
Berth No.3	140	7.6

Storage: A container and trailer yard and open space available for lumber

Location	Covered (m²)	Sheds / Warehouses
Boca Chica	2200	1

Mechanical Handling Equipment:

Location	Type	Capacity (t)	Remarks
Boca Chica	Shore Cranes		arranged through agents
Boca Chica	Forklifts	4.5–10	

Bunkering: Fuel and diesel oil available by tank truck from Santo Domingo, arrangements to be made in advance through agency

Repair & Maintenance: Minor repairs only

Medical Facilities: Emergency and minor medical care available locally, hospitals in Santo Domingo

Airport: Las Americas International, 6 km

Lloyd's Agent: Frederic Schad Inc., Jose Gabriel Garcia 26, Colonial City, P O Box 941, Santo Domingo, Dominican Republic, *Tel:* +1809 689 9377, *Fax:* +1809 688 7696, *Email:* mail@fschad.com, *Website:* www.fschad.com

CABO ROJO

Lat 17° 54' N; Long 71° 40' W.

Admiralty Chart: 3680
Time Zone: GMT -4 h

Admiralty Pilot: 70
UNCTAD Locode: DO CBJ

Principal Facilities:

		Y							

Authority: Ideal Dominicana S.A., Cabo Rojo, Dominican Republic

Port Security: ISPS compliant

Documentation: Harbour Master: port clearance from last port of call, crew list (4 copies), passenger/no passenger list (4 copies), arms/no arms declaration (4 copies) Customs: crew list (2 copies), passenger/no passenger list (2 copies), arms/no arms declaration (2 copies), personal effects list (2 copies), cargo manifests (4 copies) Immigration: crew list (2 copies), passenger/no passenger list (2 copies) Port Authority: cargo manifests (6 copies) Agency: crew list (1 copy), passenger/no passenger list (1 copy), manifest if not couriered or faxed (4 copies), bills of lading if not couriered or faxed (2 copies each), crew personal effects list (1 copy), stowage plans (2 copies) Port Doctor: deratting exemption certificate, crew list (1 copy), passenger/no passenger list (1 copy), crew vaccination list (1 copy) Department of Agriculture: stores list (2 copies), personal effects list (2 copies), cargo manifests (2 copies)

Anchorage: A deep water anchorage available immediately outside the port. Contact pilot for the best location

Pilotage: Compulsory. Pilot boards about 2 miles off the port. Accurate ETA is important as pilot must come from Barahona or about 2 h away by motor vehicle. No entry or departure at night

Radio Frequency: Pilot and Harbour Master can be contacted on VHF Channel 16

Maximum Vessel Dimensions: 700 ft loa, 120 ft beam, 36 ft draft

Principal Imports and Exports: Exports: Bauxite, Limestone.

Working Hours: 24 h/day

Accommodation:

Name	Length (m)	Remarks
Cabo Rojo		
Berth	100	See [1] below

[1]Berth: Privately operated by Ideal Dominicana S.A. for export of limestone & bauxite. Two mooring dolphins. Loading by conveyor belt and spout system

Cargo Worked: Approx 15 000 t/day

Medical Facilities: Only emergency and minor medical care is available locally, more serious cases should be treated in Santo Domingo

Lloyd's Agent: Frederic Schad Inc., Jose Gabriel Garcia 26, Colonial City, P O Box 941, Santo Domingo, Dominican Republic, *Tel:* +1809 689 9377, *Fax:* +1809 688 7696, *Email:* mail@fschad.com, *Website:* www.fschad.com

CAUCEDO

Lat 18° 25' N; Long 69° 37' W.

Admiralty Chart: 467
Time Zone: GMT -4 h

Admiralty Pilot: 70
UNCTAD Locode: DO CAU

Principal Facilities:

			C			B		T	A

Agencias Navieras B&R

Torre B & R, Av Abraham Lincoln 504, P O Box 1221,
Santo Domingo, Dominican Republic
Tel: +1809 562-1661   **Fax:** +1809 567-7992
Email: ops@navierasbr.com

SETIMSA

SERVICIOS TECNICOS - INDUSTRIALES Y MARITIMOS S.A.

Knowledge &
Solutions in Ports
Industrial & Ship Repair Business

- Control of the Corrosion
- Works in Confined Areas
- Specialized Welding
- Mechanics in General
- Marine Works
- Harbor Projects
- Installation and Maintenance of Cranes and RTG

PHONE: (507) 216-6024   **FAX:** (507) 216-6027
E-MAIL: info@setimsa.com

ADDRESS: Transistmica, San Vicente, Chilibre, Building #86
P.O. BOX: 0819-08221 El Dorado, PANAMA

Authority: DP World Caucedo, Zona Franca Multimodal Caucedo, Building . ADM, Suite 300, Punta Caucedo, Boca Chica, Dominican Republic, *Tel:* +1809 373 7312, *Fax:* +1809 373 7348, *Email:* william.khoury@dpworld.com, *Website:* www.caucedo.com

Officials: General Manager: Glen Hilton, *Email:* glen.hilton@dpworld.com.
Operations Manager: William Khoury, *Email:* william.khoury@dpworld.com.
Project Manager: Ricardo Alvarez, *Tel:* +1809 373 7313, *Email:* ricardo.alvarez@dpworld.com.

Port Security: 3 different security controls: DPW internal security employees. Contractor, "Security Force". Military presence
Certifications: ISPS (International Ship & Ports Security Code) certified July 2004. C-TPAT (Customs-Trade Partnership Against Terrorism) compliance. BASC (Business Anti-Smuggling Coalition) certified mid 2005. CSI (Container Security Initiative) certified 2006

Approach: Controlling depth of entrance channel 13.5 m with width of 265 m

Anchorage: Anchoring prohibited in Andres Bay (coral reef preservation area)

Pilotage: Compulsory. Vessel's should advise ETA 24 h prior to arrival, or on departure from last port if less than 24 h distant. Pilot boarding area in pos 18° 24.6' N; 69° 36.3' W

Radio Frequency: Call sign 'Caucedo Pilot Station' on VHF Channel 16 then change to VHF working channel 10 or 13

Weather: Internal weather station to control the operations. Hurricane season from June 1st to Nov 30th

Traffic: 2007, 1015 vessels, 574 441 TEU's handled

Working Hours: Vessel operations 24 h/day

Accommodation:

Name	Length (m)	Depth (m)	Remarks
Caucedo Container Terminal	640	13.5	Two berths of 300 m long. 336 reefer points

Storage: Container yard of 20 ha

Mechanical Handling Equipment:

Location	Type	Capacity (t)	Qty
Container Terminal	Post Panamax	65	5
Container Terminal	RTG's	40–65	17

Bunkering: Available

Towage: Two tugs available, one of 50 t BP and one of 65 t BP
SVITZER, Wijsmuller Hispaniola Towage Group Inc, c/o Caucedo Marine Services Ltd, Caucedo Container Terminal, Punta Caucedo, Dominican Republic, *Tel:* +1809 544 2200, *Email:* j.rannik@navierasbr.com, *Website:* www.svitzer.com

Shipping Agents: Agencias Navieras B&R, Avenida Abraham Lincoln 504, P O Box 1221, Santo Domingo, Dominican Republic, *Tel:* +1809 562 1661, *Fax:* +1809 562 3383, *Email:* ops@navierasbr.com, *Website:* www.navierasbr.com

Medical Facilities: Emergency facility 24/7 and consultations Mon-Fri 0900-1800

Airport: Las Americas International Airport

Development: End of 2006: increase TEU's cap to 960 000 with six quay cranes, 20 RTG's and 2500 additional yard TEU's
Phase 2: increase TEU's to 1 280 000 with eight quay cranes, 25 RTG's and 47 120 yard TEU's. 250 m of additional quay (total 850 m)

Phase 3: increase TEU's to 1 920 000 with twelve quay cranes, 36 RTG's and 62 720 yard TEU's. Total quay length of 1100 m
A future logistics centre of 30 hectares is due to begin at the end of 2006

Lloyd's Agent: Frederic Schad Inc., Jose Gabriel Garcia 26, Colonial City, P O Box 941, Santo Domingo, Dominican Republic, *Tel:* +1809 689 9377, *Fax:* +1809 688 7696, *Email:* mail@fschad.com, *Website:* www.fschad.com

CIUDAD TRUJILLO

alternate name, see Santo Domingo

LA ROMANA

Lat 18° 25' N; Long 68° 57' W.

Admiralty Chart: 467	**Admiralty Pilot:** 70
Time Zone: GMT -4 h	**UNCTAD Locode:** DO LRM

Principal Facilities:

Y	G	C		L		T	A

Authority: Autoridad Portuaria Dominicana (APORDOM), La Romana, Dominican Republic, *Tel:* +1809 550 7300, *Fax:* +1809 550 3342, *Website:* www.apordom.gov.do

Port Security: ISPS compliant

Documentation: Harbour Master: port clearance from last port of call, crew list (4 copies), passenger/no passenger list (4 copies), arms/no arms declaration (4 copies)
Customs: crew list (2 copies), passenger/no passenger list (2 copies), arms/no arms declaration (2 copies), personal effects list (2 copies), cargo manifests (4 copies)
Immigration: crew list (2 copies), passenger/no passenger list (2 copies)
Port Authority: cargo manifests (6 copies)
Agency: crew list (1 copy), passenger/no passenger list (1 copy), manifest if not couriered or faxed (4 copies), bills of lading if not couriered or faxed (2 copies each), crew personal effects list (1 copy), stowage plans (2 copies)
Port Doctor: deratting exemption certificate, crew list (1 copy), passenger/no passenger list (1 copy), crew vaccination list (1 copy)
Department of Agriculture: stores list (2 copies), personal effects list (2 copies), cargo manifests (2 copies)

Anchorage: The best anchorage is located W of Catalina Island in depths of 15-18 fathoms. There is no protected anchorage immediately outside the port

Pilotage: Compulsory. Pilot boards vessel about 1.5 miles from port entrance (NE of Catalina Island). No entry or sailing at night

Radio Frequency: Pilot and Harbour Master can be contacted on VHF Channel 16

Traffic: 2007, 525 633 t of cargo handled

Maximum Vessel Dimensions: 8.5 m draft

Principal Imports and Exports: Imports: Fuel, General cargo, Lumber, Steel. Exports: Molasses, Sugar.

Working Hours: Mon-Fri 0800-1200, 1400-1800. Sat 0800-1200. Sugar handled 24 h/day

Accommodation:

Name	Length (m)	Remarks
La Romana		Cruise vessels handled
West Pier	220	See [1] below
East Pier		Tender wharf

[1]*West Pier:* Sugar is loaded by conveyor belts using three spouts. Average loading rate of 400-500 t/h

Storage: The Central Romana Sugar Mill has warehouses for bulk sugar and tanks for molasses and furfural

Towage: One tug available of 620 hp

Repair & Maintenance: Minor repairs only

Medical Facilities: Full medical attention available

Airport: Casa de Campo International

Lloyd's Agent: Frederic Schad Inc., Jose Gabriel Garcia 26, Colonial City, P O Box 941, Santo Domingo, Dominican Republic, *Tel:* +1809 689 9377, *Fax:* +1809 688 7696, *Email:* mail@fschad.com, *Website:* www.fschad.com

---

Key to Principal Facilities:—
A=Airport   **C**=Containers   **G**=General Cargo   **P**=Petroleum   **R**=Ro/Ro   **Y**=Dry Bulk
B=Bunkers   **D**=Dry Dock   **L**=Cruise   **Q**=Other Liquid Bulk   **T**=Towage (where available from port)

MANZANILLO

Lat 19° 43' N; Long 71° 45' W.

Admiralty Chart: 463
Admiralty Pilot: 70
Time Zone: GMT -5 h
UNCTAD Locode: DO MAN

Principal Facilities:

			G	C		B		A	

Authority: Autoridad Portuaria Dominicana (APORDOM), Manzanillo, Dominican Republic, *Tel:* +1809 579 9557, *Fax:* +1809 579 9416, *Website:* www.apordom.gov.do

Documentation: Harbour Master: port clearance from last port of call, crew list (4 copies), passenger/no passenger list (4 copies), arms/no arms declaration (4 copies)
Customs: crew list (2 copies), passenger/no passenger list (2 copies), arms/no arms declaration (2 copies), personal effects list (2 copies), cargo manifests (4 copies)
Immigration: crew list (2 copies), passenger/no passenger list (2 copies)
Port Authority: cargo manifests (6 copies)
Agency: crew list (1 copy), passenger/no passenger list (1 copy), manifest if not couriered or faxed (4 copies), bills of lading if not couriered or faxed (2 copies each), crew personal effects list (1 copy), stowage plans (2 copies)
Port Doctor: deratting exemption certificate, crew list (1 copy), passenger/no passenger list (1 copy), crew vaccination list (1 copy)
Department of Agriculture: stores list (2 copies), personal effects list (2 copies), cargo manifests (2 copies)

Anchorage: Excellent anchorage available in Manzanillo Bay to the E of the dock in about 20 fathoms

Pilotage: Compulsory. Advance notice required as pilot has to come from Puerto Plata. No entry or departure at night

Radio Frequency: Pilot and Harbour Master can be contacted on VHF Channel 16

Traffic: 2007, 425 238 t of cargo handled, 1554 TEU's

Maximum Vessel Dimensions: 700 ft loa, 120 ft beam, 30 ft draft

Principal Imports and Exports: Exports: Fresh fruit.

Working Hours: Mon-Fri 0800-1200, 1400-1800. Sat 0800-1200. Overtime available

Accommodation:

Name	Length (m)	Remarks
Manzanillo Finger Pier	230	See [1] below

[1]*Finger Pier:* Depth at end of pier is approx 38 ft, whereas near land is only 18 ft. Mainly used for export of bananas; loading by conveyor belt

Bunkering: Available by tank truck from Santo Domingo

Medical Facilities: Emergency first aid only. Full hospitalisation in Santiago approx 100 km away

Airport: La Union International, approx 130 km

Lloyd's Agent: Frederic Schad Inc., Jose Gabriel Garcia 26, Colonial City, P O Box 941, Santo Domingo, Dominican Republic, *Tel:* +1809 689 9377, *Fax:* +1809 688 7696, *Email:* mail@fschad.com, *Website:* www.fschad.com

PALENQUE TERMINAL

Lat 18° 12' N; Long 70° 11' W.

Admiralty Chart: 471
Admiralty Pilot: 70
Time Zone: GMT -4 h
UNCTAD Locode: DO PAL

Principal Facilities:

P											

Authority: Refineria Dominicana de Petroleo S.A., P O Box 1439, Santo Domingo, Dominican Republic, *Tel:* +1809 472 9999, *Fax:* +1809 957 3566, *Email:* contacto@refidomsa.com.do, *Website:* www.refidomsa.com.do

Officials: General Manager: Alfredo Nara, *Email:* alfredo.nara@latam.shell.com.

Approach: The Pilot will explain the proposed maneuver to the Master and will receive approval before proceeding. The line of approach will depend upon the prevailing wind and current conditions and their combined effect. A good indication of their combined effect is the direction in which the hose string is lying. If the ship's length is such that the ship ends of the hoses are likely to be endangered by the propeller, the hose will be doubled back and the ship ends attached temporarily to the SBM. Once any preparation work on the hoses is complete, the service launch will attend to the mooring. The service launch will lie on the end of a long pick-up rope, the other end of which is attached to the mooring. It must be remembered that the pick-up rope is just that, a pick up rope. It is not provided for the purpose of warping the ship into the berth. The bow of the ship must be placed in the mooring position. Personnel must not be endangered by warping the ship into position on an open drum end. The Pilot must keep his attention on the operation until it is completed and most particularly on the crucial final attachment. He must not allow himself to be diverted by paperwork. The service launch requires to be well lit for night working. The SBM requires a navigational beacon. The approach should be made with the SBM slightly open on the port bow, never ahead, so that in the event of emergency the tanker can pass clear of the buoy. Great care must be taken in the approach to ensure that excessive speed is avoided in the approach. Removal of excess speed means going astern with consequent loss of control. The normal practice is to use the engines ahead only when steering is required. The ship should approach the SBM no faster than walking speed. When the bow passes the ship end of the hoses, the ship should be slowed further. By the time the pick-up rope is attached, there should be little need to drive the ship towards the SBM. The ship should arrive close to the SBM, within securing range of the ropes, stopped in the water and on a heading close to the final heading in such a way that she will not sheer across a current or across the wind

Anchorage: No anchorage allowed at the SBM

Pilotage: Compulsory and can be arranged 24 h/day. Pilot boards approx 1 mile SW of the SBM. Contact Punta Palenque pilots on VHF Channels 16 and 14

Radio Frequency: VHF Channels 14, 16 and 71

Maximum Vessel Dimensions: 820 ft loa, 48 ft draft

Principal Imports and Exports: Imports: Crude oil.

Working Hours: 24 h/day

Accommodation:

Name	Remarks
Palenque Terminal SBM	See [1] below

[1]*SBM:* Located approx 2.5 miles off Punta Palenque and used to receive reconstituted crude oil mostly from Venezuela and Mexico which is then pumped by pipeline to the refinery in Haina (Itabo)

Storage: Three floating roof tanks with total cap of 850 000 bbls

Towage: Available and compulsory

Medical Facilities: Not available except for extreme emergencies which must be taken to Santo Domingo

Airport: Las Americas International, approx 100 km. Joaquin Balaguer International, approx. 50 km

Lloyd's Agent: Frederic Schad Inc., Jose Gabriel Garcia 26, Colonial City, P O Box 941, Santo Domingo, Dominican Republic, *Tel:* +1809 689 9377, *Fax:* +1809 688 7696, *Email:* mail@fschad.com, *Website:* www.fschad.com

PUERTO DUARTE

harbour area, see under Arroyo Barril

PUERTO PLATA

Lat 19° 49' N; Long 70° 42' W.

Admiralty Chart: 463
Admiralty Pilot: 70
Time Zone: GMT -4 h
UNCTAD Locode: DO POP

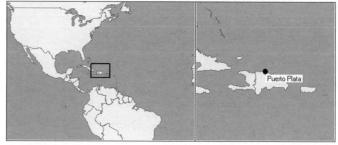

Principal Facilities:

	Y	G	C	R	L	B		T	A	

Agencias Navieras B&R

Torre B & R, Av Abraham Lincoln 504, P O Box 1221,
Santo Domingo, Dominican Republic
Tel: +1809 562-1661   **Fax:** +1809 567-7992
Email: ops@navierasbr.com

Authority: Autoridad Portuaria Dominicana (APORDOM), Puerto Plata, Dominican Republic, *Tel:* +1809 579 9557, *Fax:* +1809 568 9493, *Website:* www.apordom.gov.do

Port Security: ISPS compliant

Documentation: Harbour Master: port clearance from last port of call, crew list (4 copies), passenger/no passenger list (4 copies), arms/no arms declaration (4 copies) Customs: crew list (2 copies), passenger/no passenger list (2 copies), arms/no arms declaration (2 copies), personal effects list (2 copies), cargo manifests (4 copies) Immigration: crew list (2 copies), passenger/no passenger list (2 copies) Port Authority: cargo manifests (6 copies) Agency: crew list (1 copy), passenger/no passenger list (1 copy), manifest if not couriered or faxed (4 copies), bills of lading if not couriered or faxed (2 copies each), crew personal effects list (1 copy), stowage plans (2 copies) Port Doctor: deratting exemption certificate, crew list (1 copy), passenger/no passenger list (1 copy), crew vaccination list (1 copy) Department of Agriculture: stores list (2 copies), personal effects list (2 copies), cargo manifests (2 copies)

Anchorage: Deep water anchorage available outside the port. Contact pilot for best location. In rough weather this anchorage is frequently dangerous

Pilotage: Compulsory. Pilot boards 0.5 miles from the seabuoy. No entry or departure at night

Radio Frequency: Pilot and Harbour Master can be contacted on VHF Channel 16

Traffic: 2007, 1 557 443 t of cargo handled, 38 036 TEU's

Maximum Vessel Dimensions: 700 ft loa, 100 ft beam, 32 ft draft

Working Hours: Mon-Fri 0800-1200, 1400-1800. Sat 0800-1200. Overtime available

Accommodation:

Name	Length (m)	Remarks
Puerto Plata		
Berth No.1 (New)	300	See [1] below
Berth No.2 (New)	300	See [2] below
Berth No.3 (New)		See [3] below
Berth No.1 (Old)	110	See [4] below
Berth No.2 (Old)	110	See [5] below

[1]*Berth No.1 (New):* On the eastern side of the new finger pier. Two or more vessels may occupy this berth including cruise vessels. Storage includes a 6000 m2 cap shed managed by the Port Authority
[2]*Berth No.2 (New):* On the western side of the new finger pier. Two or more vessels may occupy this berth depending on their length including container vessels
[3]*Berth No.3 (New):* Located at the tip of the new finger pier and can accommodate vessels up to 250 ft loa
[4]*Berth No.1 (Old):* On the western side of the old finger pier. Because the pier is in poor structural condition it is only used as a lay-berth. Storage includes a small shed of approx 2000 m2 cap operated by the Port Authority
[5]*Berth No.2 (Old):* Located on the eastern side of the old finger pier. Because the pier is in poor structural condition, it is rarely used except by tankers discharging fuel and diesel oil, and as a lay-berth

Bunkering: By tank truck only from Santo Domingo
Chevron Marine Products LLC, Global Marine Products LLC, 1500 Louisiana, 4th Floor, Houston, TX 77002, United States of America, *Tel:* +1 832 8542 988, *Fax:* +1 832 8544 868, *Email:* gulfcbm@chevron.com, *Website:* www.chevron.com – *Grades:* GO – *Delivery Mode:* tank truck

Towage: One tug available of 800 hp

Repair & Maintenance: Minor repairs only

Shipping Agents: Agencias Navieras B&R, Port of Puerto Plata, Puerto Plata, Dominican Republic, *Tel:* +1809 586 1163, *Fax:* +1809 586 1104, *Email:* opspuertoplata@navierasbr.com, *Website:* www.navierasbr.com
Freship S.A., Muelle Nuevo, Puerto Plata, Dominican Republic, *Tel:* +1809 586 1320, *Fax:* +1809 586 1362, *Email:* mmedina@tropical.com, *Website:* www.tropical.com

Medical Facilities: Full medical attention available in Puerto Plata

Airport: La Union International, 20 km

Lloyd's Agent: Frederic Schad Inc., Jose Gabriel Garcia 26, Colonial City, P O Box 941, Santo Domingo, Dominican Republic, *Tel:* +1809 689 9377, *Fax:* +1809 688 7696, *Email:* mail@fschad.com, *Website:* www.fschad.com

PUERTO VIEJO DE AZUA

Lat 18° 30' N; Long 70° 40' W.

Admiralty Chart: 471   **Admiralty Pilot:** 70
Time Zone: GMT -4 h   **UNCTAD Locode:** DO PVA

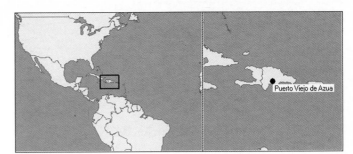

Principal Facilities:

	Q			R	B			

Authority: Autoridad Portuaria Dominicana (APORDOM), Puerto Viejo de Azua, Dominican Republic, *Tel:* +1809 248 0277, *Website:* www.apordom.gov.do

Documentation: Harbour Master: port clearance from last port of call, crew list (4 copies), passenger/no passenger list (4 copies), arms/no arms declaration (4 copies) Customs: crew list (2 copies), passenger/no passenger list (2 copies), arms/no arms declaration (2 copies), personal effects list (2 copies), cargo manifests (4 copies) Immigration: crew list (2 copies), passenger/no passenger list (2 copies) Port Authority: cargo manifests (6 copies) Agency: crew list (1 copy), passenger/no passenger list (1 copy), manifest if not couriered or faxed (4 copies), bills of lading if not couriered or faxed (2 copies each), crew personal effects list (1 copy), stowage plans (2 copies) Port Doctor: deratting exemption certificate, crew list (1 copy), passenger/no passenger list (1 copy), crew vaccination list (1 copy) Department of Agriculture: stores list (2 copies), personal effects list (2 copies), cargo manifests (2 copies)

Anchorage: Deep water anchorage available off the port

Pilotage: Compulsory. Pilot boards vessel about 0.5 mile from the seabuoy. Berthing and departure strictly during daylight hours only

Radio Frequency: Pilot and Harbour Master can be contacted on VHF Channel 16

Traffic: 2007, 175 910 t of cargo handled

Maximum Vessel Dimensions: 500 ft loa, 80 ft beam, 30 ft draft

Working Hours: Mon-Fri 0800-1200, 1400-1800. Sat 0800-1200. Overtime available

Accommodation:

Name	Length (m)	Remarks
Puerto Viejo de Azua		
Finger Pier	185	See [1] below

[1]*Finger Pier:* Almost exclusively used by LPG tankers but also has a ramp for ro/ro vessels on the W side

Bunkering: By tank truck from Santo Domingo

Medical Facilities: Emergency and minor medical care available in Azua, 15 km

Lloyd's Agent: Frederic Schad Inc., Jose Gabriel Garcia 26, Colonial City, P O Box 941, Santo Domingo, Dominican Republic, *Tel:* +1809 689 9377, *Fax:* +1809 688 7696, *Email:* mail@fschad.com, *Website:* www.fschad.com

RIO HAINA

Lat 18° 25' N; Long 70° 0' W.

Admiralty Chart: 471   **Admiralty Pilot:** 70
Time Zone: GMT -4 h   **UNCTAD Locode:** DO HAI

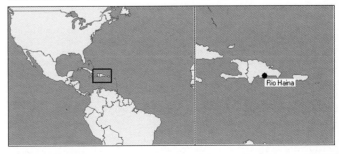

Principal Facilities:

P	Q	Y	G	C	R		B		T	A	

Authority: Autoridad Portuaria Dominicana (APORDOM), Rio Haina, Dominican Republic, *Tel:* +1809 542 8004, *Fax:* +1809 541 3774, *Website:* www.apordom.gov.do

Port Security: ISPS compliant

Documentation: Harbour Master: port clearance from last port of call, crew list (4 copies), passenger/no passenger list (4 copies), arms/no arms declaration (4 copies)
Customs: crew list (2 copies), passenger/no passenger list (2 copies), arms/no arms declaration (2 copies), personal effects list (2 copies), cargo manifests (4 copies)
Immigration: crew list (2 copies), passenger/no passenger list (2 copies)
Port Authority: cargo manifests (6 copies)
Agency: crew list (1 copy), passenger/no passenger list (1 copy), manifest if not couriered or faxed (4 copies), bills of lading if not couriered or faxed (2 copies each), crew personal effects list (1 copy), stowage plans (2 copies)
Port Doctor: deratting exemption certificate, crew list (1 copy), passenger/no passenger list (1 copy), crew vaccination list (1 copy)
Department of Agriculture: stores list (2 copies), personal effects list (2 copies), cargo manifests (2 copies)

Anchorage: It is suggested that vessels anchor off Santo Domingo as the anchorage at Rio Haina is considered unsafe and only to be used in case of emergency

Pilotage: Compulsory. The pilot boards about 1 mile from the breakwater. Night entry and sailing is restricted depending on weather conditions or vessel characteristics

Radio Frequency: Pilot and Harbour Master can be contacted on VHF Channel 16

Traffic: 2005, 9 364 942 t of cargo handled

Maximum Vessel Dimensions: 700 ft loa, 100 ft beam, 35 ft draft

Working Hours: Mon-Fri 0800-1200, 1400-1800. Sat 0800-1200. Overtime available. Sugar is usually loaded 24 h/day

Accommodation:

Name	Length (m)	Remarks
Rio Haina		
Berth No.1 West		See [1] below
Berth No.2 West		See [2] below
Berth No.3 West	181	See [3] below
Berth No.4 West	264	See [4] below

Name	Length (m)	Remarks
Berth No.5 West	194	Used by Maersk Sea-Land. Open storage available for containers
Berth No.6 West	134	See [5] below
Berth No.1 East	153	See [6] below
Berth No.2 East	185	See [7] below
Berth No.3 East	215	See [8] below
Berth No.4 East	215	See [9] below
Berth No.5 East	214	Used primarily for the handling of containers & general breakbulk cargo
Berth No.6 East	700	See [10] below
Refidomsa Cargo Buoy Moorings		See [11] below

[1]*Berth No.1 West:* Length 190 m (together with berth No.2 west). Used for loading sugar at average rate of 4000-5000 t/day and by tankers discharging fuel and/or diesel oil to shore tanks. Storage facilities include two bulk sugar warehouses with a total cap of over 150 000 t

[2]*Berth No.2 West:* Length 190 m (together with berth No.1 west). Used by liquid petroleum tankers discharging distillates to shore tanks belonging to the local refinery

[3]*Berth No.3 West:* Only 110 m can presently be used for berthing due to the state of disrepair. Presently serving as a bulk asphalt terminal with a barge as storage. Tankers dock abreast of the barge in order to discharge directly into the facility. Two sheds, each of 2100 m2 space available

[4]*Berth No.4 West:* Container vessels have preference at this dock and there is one container gantry crane available. Also used for homogeneous breakbulk cargoes. Molasses storage tanks connected by pipeline hold approx 5 000 000 gallons and are used for exporting molasses

[5]*Berth No.6 West:* Used by tankers discharging diesel fuels, lubricants & liquid paraffin to shore tanks and also by vessels discharging cement & clinker for Cementos Colon

[6]*Berth No.1 East:* Operated by Sociedad Industrial Dominicana and used to discharge feed grains and meals in bulk as well as vegetable oils and fats in bulk. Facilities include six silos, each with a cap of approx 1200 t of heavy grain. There are also six storage tanks for vegetable oils and fats with a total cap of 6000 t

[7]*Berth No.2 East:* Operated by Fertilizantes Santo Domingo (FERSAN) and used primarily for their own bulk discharging operations, exporting fertilizers in bags and also for bulk liquid chemicals. One mobile crane available

[8]*Berth No.3 East:* Used for receiving crude oil in bulk for the Falconbridge Dominicana Terminal. Also used for exporting ferronickel products on pallets, in crates and in containers

[9]*Berth No.4 East:* Used frequently by ro/ro vessels; three ramps available. Also used to discharge general breakbulk or homogeneous cargoes

[10]*Berth No.6 East:* Primarily used for handling of containers (operated by Haina International Terminal, Tel: +809 740 1025, Fax: +809 740 1029), but due to frequent congestion of other berths it is also used for bulk cargoes, steel, lumber etc. Four portainer cranes

[11]*Refidomsa Cargo Buoy Moorings:* Consists of four mooring buoys and two cargo-hose pickup buoys and used for discharging LPG and refined petroleum products to the shore installations of the Refineria Dominicana de Petroleo. Accommodates vessels up to 152.5 m long. Vessels are docked during daylight hours only

Bunkering: No heavy fuels. Standard diesel in small quantity by tank truck
Chevron Marine Products LLC, Global Marine Products LLC, 1500 Louisiana, 4th Floor, Houston, TX 77002, United States of America, *Tel:* +1 832 8542 988, *Fax:* +1 832 8544 868, *Email:* gulfcbm@chevron.com, *Website:* www.chevron.com – *Delivery Mode:* tank truck
Frederic Schad Inc., Jose Gabriel Garcia 26, Colonial City, P O Box 941, Santo Domingo, Dominican Republic, *Tel:* +1809 689 9377, *Fax:* +1809 688 7696, *Email:* mail@fschad.com, *Website:* www.fschad.com – *Delivery Mode:* truck
The Shell Company (WI) Ltd, Avenida Abraham Lincoln, Santo Domingo, Dominican Republic, *Tel:* +1809 532 0511, *Fax:* +1809 532 2002 – *Delivery Mode:* tank truck

Towage: At least two tugs are available at all times of 1200-2400 hp

Ship Chandlers: Mercantile Shipstores Dominicana S.A., Zona Franca Los Alcarrizos, Solar No.1, Menzana C, Santo Domingo, Dominican Republic, *Tel:* +1809 548 0584, *Fax:* +1809 548 0584, *Email:* rhow@mercansa.com

Shipping Agents: Agencias Navieras B&R, Avenida Abraham Lincoln 504, P O Box 1221, Santo Domingo, Dominican Republic, *Tel:* +1809 562 1661, *Fax:* +1809 562 3383, *Email:* ops@navierasbr.com, *Website:* www.navierasbr.com

Airport: Las Americas International, 25 miles

Lloyd's Agent: Frederic Schad Inc., Jose Gabriel Garcia 26, Colonial City, P O Box 941, Santo Domingo, Dominican Republic, *Tel:* +1809 689 9377, *Fax:* +1809 688 7696, *Email:* mail@fschad.com, *Website:* www.fschad.com

SAN PEDRO DE MACORIS

Lat 18° 26' N; Long 69° 18' W.

Admiralty Chart: 467		**Admiralty Pilot:** 70
Time Zone: GMT -4 h		**UNCTAD Locode:** DO SPM

Principal Facilities:

		Y	G			B		A

Authority: Autoridad Portuaria Dominicana (APORDOM), San Pedro de Macoris, Dominican Republic, *Tel:* +1809 529 2093, *Fax:* +1809 529 2069, *Website:* www.apordom.gov.do

Port Security: ISPS compliant

Documentation: Harbour Master: port clearance from last port of call, crew list (4 copies), passenger/no passenger list (4 copies), arms/no arms declaration (4 copies) Customs: crew list (2 copies), passenger/no passenger list (2 copies), arms/no arms declaration (2 copies), personal effects list (2 copies), cargo manifests (4 copies) Immigration: crew list (2 copies), passenger/no passenger list (2 copies) Port Authority: cargo manifests (6 copies) Agency: crew list (1 copy), passenger/no passenger list (1 copy), manifest if not couriered or faxed (4 copies), bills of lading if not couriered or faxed (2 copies each), crew personal effects list (1 copy), stowage plans (2 copies) Port Doctor: deratting exemption certificate, crew list (1 copy), passenger/no passenger list (1 copy), crew vaccination list (1 copy) Department of Agriculture: stores list (2 copies), personal effects list (2 copies), cargo manifests (2 copies)

Anchorage: Anchorage is about 1 mile S of the lighthouse

Pilotage: Compulsory. The pilot usually meets the vessel about 0.5 mile from seabuoy, but in case of rough weather the vessel should await 3 miles S of the buoy. No nightime arrivals or departures

Radio Frequency: Pilot and Harbour Master may be contacted on VHF Channel 16

Traffic: 2007, 1 901 419 t of cargo handled

Maximum Vessel Dimensions: 650 ft loa, 100 ft beam, 24 ft draft

Working Hours: Mon-Fri 0800-1200, 1400-1800. Sat 0800-1200. Overtime available

Accommodation:

Name	Length (m)	Remarks
San Pedro de Macoris		
Berth No.1	260	See [1] below
Berth No.2	183	See [2] below
Berth No.3	262	See [3] below

[1]*Berth No.1:* 100-150 m are occupied by a floating dry dock, Dominican naval vessels and other equipment. Used primarily to load sugar for export and also used for loading molasses in bulk and discharging bulk liquid petroleum products

[2]*Berth No.2:* Used for the export of molasses but primarily bulk clinker and coal are discharged into two hoppers by self-discharging vessels. The berth can also be used for general cargoes

[3]*Berth No.3:* Operated by FERQUIDO and primarily used for discharging bulk fertilizers & loading in bags and general cargo. There is a large warehouse for both bulk and bagged fertilizers

Bunkering: Fuel and diesel oil must be transported by tank truck from Santo Domingo

Repair & Maintenance: Minor repairs only

Medical Facilities: Local hospital

Airport: Las Americas International, 30 km

Lloyd's Agent: Frederic Schad Inc., Jose Gabriel Garcia 26, Colonial City, P O Box 941, Santo Domingo, Dominican Republic, *Tel:* +1809 689 9377, *Fax:* +1809 688 7696, *Email:* mail@fschad.com, *Website:* www.fschad.com

SANCHEZ

Lat 19° 14' N; Long 69° 36' W.

Admiralty Chart: 463	**Admiralty Pilot:** 70
Time Zone: GMT -4 h	**UNCTAD Locode:** DO SNZ

This port is no longer open to commercial shipping

SANTO DOMINGO

Lat 18° 28' N; Long 69° 52' W.

Admiralty Chart: 467	**Admiralty Pilot:** 70
Time Zone: GMT -4 h	**UNCTAD Locode:** DO SDQ

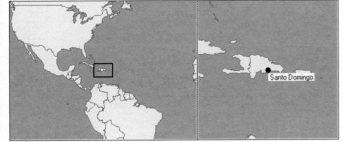

Principal Facilities:

P		Y	G	C	R	L	B	D	T	A

Authority: Autoridad Portuaria Dominicana (APORDOM), Puerto de Haina, Margen Oriental, Edificio Naviera, Piso 2, P O Box 1301, Santo Domingo, Dominican Republic, *Tel:* +1809 687 4772, *Fax:* +1809 687 2661, *Website:* www.apordom.gov.do

Officials: General Manager: Bernard Surges.

Port Security: ISPS compliant

Documentation: Harbour Master: port clearance from last port of call, crew list (4 copies), passenger/no passenger list (4 copies), arms/no arms declaration (4 copies) Customs: crew list (2 copies), passenger/no passenger list (2 copies), arms/no arms declaration (2 copies), personal effects list (2 copies), cargo manifests (4 copies) Immigration: crew list (2 copies), passenger/no passenger list (2 copies) Port Authority: cargo manifests (6 copies) Agency: crew list (1 copy), passenger/no passenger list (1 copy), manifest if not couriered or faxed (4 copies), bills of lading if not couriered or faxed (2 copies each), crew personal effects list (1 copy), stowage plans (2 copies) Port Doctor: deratting exemption certificate, crew list (1 copy), passenger/no passenger list (1 copy), crew vaccination list (1 copy) Department of Agriculture: stores list (2 copies), personal effects list (2 copies), cargo manifests (2 copies)

Anchorage: Deep water anchorage available outside the port. Contact pilot for best location

Pilotage: Compulsory. The pilot boards approx 1.5 miles outside the harbour. Limited entry and departure during nightime at pilot's discretion

Radio Frequency: Pilot and Harbour Master can be contacted on VHF Channels 16 or 12

Traffic: 2005, 311 838 t of cargo handled

Maximum Vessel Dimensions: 750 ft loa, 100 ft beam, 28 ft draft

Working Hours: Mon-Fri 0800-1200, 1400-1800. Sat 0800-1200. Overtime available

Accommodation:

Name	Length (m)	Remarks
Santo Domingo		
General Cargo Berth No.1		See [1] below
General Cargo Berth No.2		See [2] below
General Cargo Berth No.3	167	See [3] below
General Cargo Berth No's 4 & 5	290	Trailers, containers & general breakbulk cargo. Open storage available only
General Cargo Berth No.6	125	Tankers discharging petroleum products. No storage facilities available
General Cargo Berth No.7	150	Permanently occupied by a floating power plant
Don Diego Tourist Terminal	379	Cruise vessels only
Sans Souci Passenger Terminal	300	This berth is used by vessels to discharge passengers & motor vehicles from ro/ro & cruise vessels
Sans Souci Liquid Bulk Cargo Berth	300	Used exclusively for discharging liquid bulk cargoes to several tank farms located at Punta Torrecilla
Molinos del Ozama Berth		See [4] below
Pronalba Bulk Cargo Berth		See [5] below

[1]*General Cargo Berth No.1:* Berth 280 m long (together with berth No.2). Forest products, paper & general cargo are mostly discharged at this berth. Storage facilities include a shed of approx 9000 m2 cap and open storage

[2]*General Cargo Berth No.2:* Berth 280 m long (together with berth No.1). Forest products, paper & general cargo are mostly discharged at this berth. Storage facilities include a shed of approx 3360 m2 cap and limited open storage for containers

[3]*General Cargo Berth No.3:* Exclusive use of a ferry providing passenger and vehicle service to Puerto Rico. Passenger terminal

[4]*Molinos del Ozama Berth:* Private berth belonging to the local flour mill and used exclusively for bulk cargoes like wheat & corn. Silo storage for about 90 000 t of grain

[5]*Pronalba Bulk Cargo Berth:* Private installation used for discharging small dry & liquid bulk cargoes. Warehouses and tanks for approx 10 000 t of dry bulk cargoes and 5000 t of liquid bulk cargoes

Bunkering: Frederic Schad Inc., Jose Gabriel Garcia 26, Colonial City, P O Box 941, Santo Domingo, Dominican Republic, *Tel:* +1809 689 9377, *Fax:* +1809 688 7696, *Email:* mail@fschad.com, *Website:* www.fschad.com
The Shell Company (WI) Ltd, Avenida Abraham Lincoln, Santo Domingo, Dominican Republic, *Tel:* +1809 532 0511, *Fax:* +1809 532 2002
Chevron Marine Products LLC, Global Marine Products LLC, 1500 Louisiana, 4th Floor, Houston, TX 77002, United States of America, *Tel:* +1 832 8542 988, *Fax:* +1 832 8544 868, *Email:* gulfcbm@chevron.com, *Website:* www.chevron.com – *Grades:* GO – *Delivery Mode:* tank truck
Frederic Schad Inc., Jose Gabriel Garcia 26, Colonial City, P O Box 941, Santo Domingo, Dominican Republic, *Tel:* +1809 689 9377, *Fax:* +1809 688 7696, *Email:* mail@fschad.com, *Website:* www.fschad.com – *Grades:* IFO; MDO – *Delivery Mode:* barge, truck
The Shell Company (WI) Ltd, Avenida Abraham Lincoln, Santo Domingo, Dominican Republic, *Tel:* +1809 532 0511, *Fax:* +1809 532 2002 – *Grades:* IFO; MDO – *Delivery Mode:* tank truck

Towage: Compulsory. Tugs of 1200 hp and 800 hp are available. A tug of 2000 hp can be brought from Rio Haina upon request and with 36 h prior notice

Repair & Maintenance: Ciramar Shipyards International Trading Co Ltd., Jose Brea Pena No.112, Evaristo Morales, Santo Domingo, Dominican Republic, *Tel:* +1809 332 6940, *Fax:* +1809 562 7635, *Email:* ciramar@ciramar.com, *Website:* www.ciramar.com Dock No.1: 61 m x 14 m x 4.5 m with lifting cap of 960 t. Dock No.2: 155 m x 25 m x 7 m with lifting cap of 7500 t. Syncrolift of 27 m x 15.2 m x 4.3 m with lifting cap of 300 t

Ship Chandlers: Intership Supply, Urbanizacion Rivera del Caribe Kilometro 20, Autopista Las Americas, P O Box 4362, Santo Domingo, Dominican Republic, *Tel:* +1809 335 6071, *Fax:* +1809 682 9927, *Email:* intership@lycos.com
Multi-Tech Services Ltd, Avenida Mexico 61, Suite 402, Santo Domingo, Dominican Republic, *Tel:* +1809 858 8811, *Fax:* +1809 333 7449, *Email:* info@sdq-shipchandler.com, *Website:* www.sdq-shipchandler.com

Shipping Agents: Agencias Navieras B&R, Avenida Abraham Lincoln 504, P O Box 1221, Santo Domingo, Dominican Republic, *Tel:* +1809 562 1661, *Fax:* +1809 562 3383, *Email:* ops@navierasbr.com, *Website:* www.navierasbr.com
Agentes y Estibadores Portuarios S.A., Edificio Monte Mirador, Calle El Recodo 2,

Key to Principal Facilities:—			
A=Airport	**C**=Containers	**G**=General Cargo	**P**=Petroleum	**R**=Ro/Ro	**Y**=Dry Bulk
B=Bunkers	**D**=Dry Dock	**L**=Cruise	**Q**=Other Liquid Bulk	**T**=Towage (where available from port)	

Suite 401, Ensanche Bella Vista, P O Box 22205, Santo Domingo, Dominican Republic, *Tel:* +1809 535 7758, *Fax:* +1809 535 4116, *Email:* ageport@codetel.com, *Website:* www.ageport.com

OE Caribe S.A., Avenida Lope de Vega 122, Ensanche la Fe, Santo Domingo, Dominican Republic, *Tel:* +1809 334 5208, *Fax:* +1809 334 5284, *Website:* www.oceanexpress.co.uk

E.T. Heinsen C. por A., Avenida George Washington 353, Santo Domingo, Dominican Republic, *Tel:* +1809 221 6111, *Fax:* +1809 221 8686, *Email:* teddy.heinsen@etheinsen.com.do, *Website:* www.etheinsen.com.do

Frederic Schad Inc., Jose Gabriel Garcia 26, Colonial City, P O Box 941, Santo Domingo, Dominican Republic, *Tel:* +1809 689 9377, *Fax:* +1809 688 7696, *Email:* mail@fschad.com, *Website:* www.fschad.com

Maritima Dominicana S.A., Carretera Sanchez, Km 12 1/2, P O Box 1301, Santo Domingo, Dominican Republic, *Tel:* +1809 539 6000, *Fax:* +1809 539 7200, *Email:* info@mardom.com, *Website:* www.mardom.com

Mediterranean Shipping Company, MSC Dominicana S.A., Suite 504, Piso 5, Edificio Empresarial Reyna II, Avenida Pedro Henriquez Urena No.138, Ensanche La Esperilla, Santo Domingo, Dominican Republic, *Tel:* +1809 381 1006, *Fax:* +1809 381 1076, *Email:* info@mscdom.net, *Website:* www.mscgva.ch

Perez y Cia Dominicana, Avenida Mexico 66, P O Box 20319, Santo Domingo, Dominican Republic, *Tel:* +1809 689 9111, *Fax:* +1809 687 0590, *Email:* perezycia@tricom.net, *Website:* www.perezycia.com

RJ Cargo S.A., Calle Fabio Fiallo No.3, Ciudad Nueva, Santo Domingo, Dominican Republic, *Tel:* +1809 687 5047, *Fax:* +1809 688 0973, *Email:* psandoval@rjcargo.com.do, *Website:* rjcargo.com.do

Stevedoring Companies: Agencias Navieras B&R, Avenida Abraham Lincoln 504, P O Box 1221, Santo Domingo, Dominican Republic, *Tel:* +1809 562 1661, *Fax:* +1809 562 3383, *Email:* ops@navierasbr.com, *Website:* www.navierasbr.com

Maritima Dominicana S.A., Carretera Sanchez, Km 12 1/2, P O Box 1301, Santo Domingo, Dominican Republic, *Tel:* +1809 539 6000, *Fax:* +1809 539 7200, *Email:* info@mardom.com, *Website:* www.mardom.com

Perez y Cia Dominicana, Avenida Mexico 66, P O Box 20319, Santo Domingo, Dominican Republic, *Tel:* +1809 689 9111, *Fax:* +1809 687 0590, *Email:* perezycia@tricom.net, *Website:* www.perezycia.com

Surveyors: Nippon Kaiji Kyokai, P O Box 30083, San Martin, Santo Domingo, Dominican Republic, *Tel:* +1809 540 3392, *Fax:* +1809 540 3392, *Website:* www.classnk.or.jp

Medical Facilities: Local hospitals

Airport: Las Americas International, 29 km

Lloyd's Agent: Frederic Schad Inc., Jose Gabriel Garcia 26, Colonial City, P O Box 941, Santo Domingo, Dominican Republic, *Tel:* +1809 689 9377, *Fax:* +1809 688 7696, *Email:* mail@fschad.com, *Website:* www.fschad.com

ECUADOR

Ribadeneira & Abogados

Servicios Legales & Tributarios
Legal & Tax Practice

Edificio Xerox, Piso 7, Av. Amazonas N35 - 17 y Juan Pablo Sanz, Quito, ECUADOR

Office also in Guayaquil

Tel: +593 2 2455 585 / 2251 319
Fax: +593 2 2469 191 / 2435 807
Email: abogados@ralaw.com.ec

Website: www.ralaw.com.ec

BALAO TERMINAL

Lat 1° 2' N; Long 79° 44' W.

Admiralty Chart: 2799   **Admiralty Pilot:** 7
Time Zone: GMT -5 h   **UNCTAD Locode:** EC EBL

Principal Facilities:

| P | | | | | | | | | | T | A |

Authority: Superintendencia del Terminal Petrolero de Balao, P O Box 286, Esmeraldas, Ecuador, *Tel:* +593 6 272 8738, *Fax:* +593 6 272 4419, *Email:* superintendente@suinba.com, *Website:* www.suinba.com

Officials: Operations Manager: Julio Buitron.
Superintendent: Capt Javier Paredes.

Documentation: Certificates to be show at Balao: safety equipment certificate, safety construction, safety radio certificate, international oil pollution prevention, load line certificate, international tonnage certificate, minimum safe manning document, oil record book, passenger ship international certificate, insurance or other financial security in respect of civil liability for oil, pollution damage, equipments and construction's booklet
On entrance of the vessel, the following documents should be submitted to authorities: clearance from last port (1 copy), general declaration (5 copies), cargo manifest (4 copies), ship's stores declaration (4 copies), crew effects declaration (2 copies), crew list (4 copies), passenger list (4 copies), maritime declaration of health (1 copy), mail list (2 copies)

Anchorage: Anchorages available for SBM's and Tepre:
Alfa in pos 01° 01' 42" N; 79° 40' 00" W for handsize tankers
Bravo in pos 01° 01' 42" N; 79° 40' 30" W for handsize tankers
Charlie in pos 01° 01' 42" N; 79° 41' 06" W for panamax tankers
Delta in pos 01° 02' 12" N; 79° 41' 18" W for aframax tankers
Echo in pos 01° 02' 42" N; 79° 41' 30" W for aframax tankers
Foxtrox in pos 01° 02' 42" N; 79° 42' 00" W for aframax tankers
Anchorages available for OCP:
Hotel in pos 01° 02' 42" N; 79° 43' 00" W for aframax
Quebec in pos 01° 02' 42" N; 79° 43' 30" W for aframax-suezmax
Romeo in pos 01° 02' 42" N; 79° 44' 00" W for aframax-suezmax
Sierra in pos 01° 02' 42" N; 79° 44' 30" W for VLCC-suezmax
Victor in pos 01° 02' 35" N; 79° 45' 03" W for VLCC-suezmax

Pilotage: Compulsory for berthing/unberthing. Vessels should advise ETA 72 h, 24 h and 4 h prior to arrival. The pilot waiting area is located between the following geographical coordinates:
01° 02' 00"N; 79° 41' 00" W
01° 02' 00" N; 79° 41' 26" W
01° 02' 42" N; 79° 41' 30" W
01° 02' 42" N; 79° 41' 48" W

Radio Frequency: VHF Channels 16 and 14

Weather: Winds mainly SSW

Traffic: 2005, 416 vessels, 22 284 718 t of cargo handled

Maximum Vessel Dimensions: 334 m loa, 250 000 dwt, 21 m draught

Principal Imports and Exports: Imports: Diesel oil, Gasoline, Naptha. Exports: Crude oil, Fuel oil, Gasoline.

Working Hours: Mooring operations take place during daylight hours under normal weather conditions. Unmooring operations take place 24 h/day under normal weather conditions

Accommodation:

Name	Depth (m)	Draught (m)	Remarks
Sote			See [1] below
Buoy X	36.6		See [2] below
Buoy Y	36.6		See [3] below
Tepre			Import/export of refined products
CBM	16.4	12	See [4] below
OCP			Crude oil exports
Buoy C	36.6	15.2	See [5] below
Buoy P	39.2	21	See [6] below

[1]*Sote:* Crude oil loading terminal comprising two single buoy moorings
[2]*Buoy X:* SBM in pos 01° 02' 00" N; 79° 42' 09" W for vessels up to 100 000 dwt. Delivery at buoy, max 32 000 bbls/h. Vessels must provide 9 t boom to lift loading hoses
[3]*Buoy Y:* SBM in pos 01° 02' 02" N; 79° 41' 08" W for vessels up to 100 000 dwt. Delivery at buoy, max 28 000 bbls/h. Vessels must provide 5 t boom to lift loading hoses
[4]*CBM:* For vessels up to 40 000 dwt. Offshore four-buoy berth connected to shore installations at the oil refinery by submarine pipelines. Cargoes can be pumped at rates up to 800 m3/h and various hoses for the different products are available
[5]*Buoy C:* CALM in pos 01° 01' 17" N; 79° 43' 59" W for vessels up to 130 000 dwt
[6]*Buoy P:* CALM in pos 01° 01' 47" N; 79° 44' 44" W for vessels up to 250 000 dwt

Towage: Six tugs of 480 hp and one tug of 1500 hp available

Medical Facilities: Hospitals at Esmeraldas

Airport: Tachina, 25 km

Lloyd's Agent: Felvenza S.A., Cdla. Kennedy Norte Mz. 807 V.15, Guayaquil, Ecuador, *Tel:* +593 4 268 1441, *Fax:* +593 4 268 1440, *Email:* mng.director@felvenza.com, *Website:* www.felvenza.com

ESMERALDAS

Lat 0° 59' N; Long 79° 39' W.

Admiralty Chart: 2799   **Admiralty Pilot:** 7
Time Zone: GMT -5 h   **UNCTAD Locode:** EC ESM

Principal Facilities:

P		Y	G	C	R	L	B		T	A

Authority: Consortium Puerto Nuevo Milenium S.A., Av. Jaime Roldos Aguilera, Recinto Portuario, Esmeraldas, Ecuador, *Tel:* +593 6 272 1934, *Fax:* +593 6 272 8795, *Email:* cpnm@puertoesmeraldas.com.ec, *Website:* www.puertodeesmeraldas.com

Officials: President: Vinicio Gonzalez Andrade, *Email:* vgonzalez@puertoesmeraldas.com.ec.
Operations Director: Ricardo Nath, *Email:* rnath@puertoesmeraldas.com.ec.
Marketing Manager: Carmen Benitez, *Email:* cbenitez@puertoesmeraldas.com.ec.

Port Security: ISPS compliant

Documentation: General declaration (5 copies), crew list (5 copies), personel effects list (4 copies), stores list (4 copies), passenger list (4 copies), mail list (4 copies), vaccination list (1 copy)

Pilotage: Compulsory. Pilot boards vessel about 5 km N of Coquitos Point

Radio Frequency: VHF Channel 16 with Terminal Petroleo de Balao, range 60 miles Esmeraldas working and pilots on VHF Channel 6, range 20-30 miles

Tides: Max tide 3.5 m

Traffic: 2005, 186 vessels, 692 822 t of cargo handled

Principal Imports and Exports: Imports: Cement, General cargo, Gypsum, Iron bars, Petroleum products, Pipes, Rolls of wire, Vehicles. Exports: Bananas, Petroleum products, Plywood, Woodchips.

Working Hours: 0800-1200, 1300-1800, 1900-2400, 0100-0800

Accommodation:

Name	Length (m)	Depth (m)	Remarks
Esmeraldas			
Piers 2 & 3	350	11.5	See [1] below
Pier 1 (Services Pier)	105	7	General cargo & bananas for smaller vessels
Ro/ro Pier	16		

[1] *Piers 2 & 3:* Multi-purpose terminal consisting of two berths for containers, general cargo, bananas & woodchips

Storage: Main warehouse of 7200 m2 and dangerous load warehouse of 1250 m2
The port has paved storage area of 105 643 m2 for general cargo and has unpaved storage area of 108 157 m2 for the development of new projects
The container terminal has 53 843 m2 of paved yards and 46 217 m2 of ballasted yards
Storage area for bulk cargoes of 12 000 m2

Mechanical Handling Equipment: Cranes and forklifts available

Bunkering: Bominflot, Bominflot Bunkergesellschaft fur Mineralole mbH & Co. KG, Floor 6, Reconquista 1048, A1003ABV Buenos Aires, Argentina, *Tel:* +54 11 4312 0840, *Fax:* +54 11 4313 8337, *Email:* mail@bominflot.com.ar, *Website:* www.bominflot.net – *Grades:* all grades, & MDO – *Delivery Mode:* barge
Corpetrolsa S.A., Via Puntilla - Samborondon KM 1, C.C. Bocca Of. 103, Guayaquil, Ecuador, *Tel:* +593 4 2097 775, *Fax:* +593 4 2097 782, *Email:* servam@gye.satnet.net/corpetrolsa@corpetrolsa.com, *Website:* www.corpetrolsa.com
Marzam Compania Ltda, Marzam Corporation, Malecon y Calles 19, Edificio El Navio, 2do. y 3er Piso, Manta, Ecuador, *Tel:* +593 5 2626 445, *Fax:* +593 5 2624 414, *Email:* marzam@marzam-online.com, *Website:* www.marzam-online.com
Navipac S.A., Avenida Pedro J. Menendez Gilbert, s/n Frente a Solca, P O Box 522970, Guayaquil, Ecuador, *Tel:* +593 4 2293 808, *Fax:* +593 4 2296 594, *Email:* bunkers@navipac.com, *Website:* www.navipac.com – *Grades:* IFO30-380cSt; MGO; lubes – *Parcel Size:* no min/max – *Rates:* 150-400t/h – *Notice:* 72 hours – *Delivery Mode:* barge
Oceanbat S.A., Avenida Carlos Julio Arosemena, Km.1 1/2, P O Box 2386, Guayaquil, Ecuador, *Tel:* +593 4 2201226, *Fax:* +593 4 2204218, *Email:* informacion@vepamil.com.ec, *Website:* www.vepamil.com.ec – *Grades:* HFO; IFO; MGO – *Rates:* 150-180t/h – *Delivery Mode:* barge
Petro Ecuador, Alpallana E-8 86 &6 de Diciembre Avenue, P O Box 17-11-5007/5008, Quito, Ecuador, *Tel:* +593 2 226 1728, *Fax:* +593 2 256 3780, *Email:* aludena@petroecuador.com.ec – *Grades:* IFO30-380cSt; MDO; in line blending available – *Parcel Size:* 150t max – *Rates:* 150t/h – *Notice:* 72 hours – *Delivery Mode:* barge

Waste Reception Facilities: Sludge and garbage disposal

Towage: Two pusher tugs; other towage hired from Balao Terminal

Shipping Agents: Agencia Naviera Zanders, Av. Kennedy 501, Esmeraldas, Ecuador, *Tel:* +593 6 272 1145, *Fax:* +593 6 272 8769, *Email:* jzanders@zanders.com.ec, *Website:* www.zanders.com.ec
Andinave S.A., Calle Hilda Padilla No.5 y Barbissotti, Barrio Las Palmas, Esmeraldas, Ecuador, *Tel:* +593 6 271 2361, *Fax:* +593 6 272 1805, *Email:* info@andinave.com, *Website:* www.andinave.com
Cargoport, Avenue Kennedy 801, Esmeraldas, Ecuador, *Tel:* +593 6 272 2244, *Fax:* +593 6 272 8769, *Email:* jzanders@zanders.com.ec, *Website:* www.cargoport.com.ec
A.P. Moller-Maersk Group, Esmeraldas, Ecuador, *Tel:* +593 6 271 5710, *Fax:* +593 6 271 5730, *Email:* ecusalesm@maersk.com

Stevedoring Companies: Andigrain S.A., Calle Hilda Padilla No.5 y Barbissotti, Barrio Las Palmas, Esmeraldas, Ecuador, *Tel:* +593 6 272 1805, *Fax:* +593 6 272 1805, *Email:* info@andinave.com, *Website:* www.andinave.com
Cargoport, Avenue Kennedy 801, Esmeraldas, Ecuador, *Tel:* +593 6 272 2244, *Fax:* +593 6 272 8769, *Email:* jzanders@zanders.com.ec, *Website:* www.cargoport.com.ec

Medical Facilities: Public hospital and private clinic

Airport: Tachina, 50 km

Lloyd's Agent: Felvenza S.A., Cdla. Kennedy Norte Mz. 807 V.15, Guayaquil, Ecuador, *Tel:* +593 4 268 1441, *Fax:* +593 4 268 1440, *Email:* mng.director@felvenza.com, *Website:* www.felvenza.com

GUAYAQUIL

Lat 2° 17' S; Long 79° 55' W.

Admiralty Chart: 560/586	**Admiralty Pilot:** 7
Time Zone: GMT -5 h	**UNCTAD Locode:** EC GYE

Principal Facilities:

P	Q	Y	G	C		L	B	D	T	A

Key to Principal Facilities:—

A=Airport	**C**=Containers	**G**=General Cargo
B=Bunkers	**D**=Dry Dock	**L**=Cruise

P=Petroleum	**R**=Ro/Ro　　**Y**=Dry Bulk
Q=Other Liquid Bulk	**T**=Towage (where available from port)

Authority: Autoridad Portuaria de Guayaquil, Avenida 25 de Julio, P O Box 5739, Guayaquil, Ecuador, *Tel:* +593 4 248 0120, *Fax:* +593 4 248 3748, *Email:* apginfo@puertodeguayaquil.com, *Website:* www1.puertodeguayaquil.com

Officials: President: Alex Villacres Sanchez.
General Manager: Tomas Leroux Murillo.

Port Security: ISPS compliant

Approach: Channel leading into Guayaquil Harbour now only accessible at all times to vessels drawing less than 7.5 m. Vessels with deeper draught must wait for rising tide. Access channel 74 km long and 200 m wide

Pilotage: Compulsory. Pilot boards in the vicinity of the Sea Lt buoy. Vessels should advise ETA at the Sea Lt buoy (in pos 2° 44.4' S; 80° 24.7' W) via Agents 72 h in advance. Vessels should contact Data Pilot Station 8 h before arrival, Tel: +593 4 276 0312, Email: pilotdat@ees.com.ec. Guayaquil Pilots, Tel: +593 4 248 1164, Email: pilotgye@ees.com.ec

Radio Frequency: VHF Channels 16, 12 and 14

Weather: Rainy season from January to April; light SSW winds for the rest of the year

Tides: Range of tide 3.8 m

Traffic: 2007, 2063 vessels, 7 145 277 t of cargo handled, 597 622 TEU's

Maximum Vessel Dimensions: 30 000 dwt, max draft 9.6 m

Principal Imports and Exports: Imports: Cement, Machinery, Paper, Steel, Wheat. Exports: Bananas, Cocoa, Coffee, Fruit, Shrimp, Wood products.

Working Hours: 0100-0600, 0700-1200, 1300-1800, 1900-2400

Accommodation:

Name	Length (m)	Remarks
Guayaquil		See [1] below
Container Berths (1, 1A & 1B)	555	Three berths
General Cargo Berths (2-6)	925	Five berths
Bulk Cargo Berth (1D)	155	See [2] below

[1]*Guayaquil:* Container and general cargo berths operated by Contecon Guayaquil S.A. (CGSA), Avenida de La Marina, Puerto Maritimo, Guayaquil, Tel: +593 4 600 6300, Email: csc@cgsa.com.ec, Website: www.cgsa.com.ec
Container yard of 38 ha, container freight station of 1.45 ha and 200 reefer points
[2]*Bulk Cargo Berth (1D):* For solid and liquid bulk cargo. Three silos with a cap of 20 000 t, one tank for vegetable oil with cap of 240 t, three tanks for molasses with cap of 4000 m3 each and one warehouse for grain storage with an area of 5000 m2

Mechanical Handling Equipment:

Location	Type	Qty
Guayaquil	Mobile Cranes	2
Guayaquil	RTG's	8
Guayaquil	Quay Cranes	3
Guayaquil	Reach Stackers	10

Cargo Worked: 500-700 t general cargo/day

Bunkering: Corpetrolsa S.A., Via Puntilla - Samborondon KM 1, C.C. Bocca Of. 103, Guayaquil, Ecuador, *Tel:* +593 4 2097 775, *Fax:* +593 4 2097 782, *Email:* servam@gye.satnet.net/corpetrolsa@corpetrolsa.com, *Website:* www.corpetrolsa.com
Navipac S.A., Avenida Pedro J. Menendez Gilbert, s/n Frente a Solca, P O Box 522970, Guayaquil, Ecuador, *Tel:* +593 4 2293 808, *Fax:* +593 4 2296 594, *Email:* bunkers@navipac.com, *Website:* www.navipac.com
Oceanbat S.A., Avenida Carlos Julio Arosemena, Km.1 1/2, P O Box 2386,

Guayaquil, Ecuador, *Tel:* +593 4 2201226, *Fax:* +593 4 2204218, *Email:* informacion@vepamil.com.ec, *Website:* www.vepamil.com.ec
Ian Taylor y Compania S.A., Edificio Centrum Piso 12, Of.4, Avenida Francisco de Orellana y Alberto Borges, Guayaquil, Ecuador, *Fax:* +593 4 269 3301, *Email:* taylorec@taylorec.com, *Website:* www.iantaylorgroup.com
Bominflot, Bominflot Bunkergesellschaft fur Mineralole mbH & Co. KG, Floor 6, Reconquista 1048, A1003ABV Buenos Aires, Argentina, *Tel:* +54 11 4312 0840, *Fax:* +54 11 4313 8337, *Email:* mail@bominflot.com.ar, *Website:* www.bominflot.net – *Grades:* all grades & MDO – *Delivery Mode:* barge
Corpetrolsa S.A., Via Puntilla - Samborondon KM 1, C.C. Bocca Of. 103, Guayaquil, Ecuador, *Tel:* +593 4 2097 775, *Fax:* +593 4 2097 782, *Email:* servam@gye.satnet.net/corpetrolsa@corpetrolsa.com, *Website:* www.corpetrolsa.com
Marzam Compania Ltda, Marzam Corporation, Malecon y Calles 19, Edificio El Navio, 2do. y 3er Piso, Manta, Ecuador, *Tel:* +593 5 2626 445, *Fax:* +593 5 2624 414, *Email:* marzam@marzam-online.com, *Website:* www.marzam-online.com
Navipac S.A., Avenida Pedro J. Menendez Gilbert, s/n Frente a Solca, P O Box 522970, Guayaquil, Ecuador, *Tel:* +593 4 2293 808, *Fax:* +593 4 2296 594, *Email:* bunkers@navipac.com, *Website:* www.navipac.com – *Grades:* IFO30-380cSt; MGO; lubes – *Parcel Size:* no min/max – *Rates:* 150-400t/h – *Notice:* 72 hours – *Delivery Mode:* barge
Oceanbat S.A., Avenida Carlos Julio Arosemena, Km.1 1/2, P O Box 2386, Guayaquil, Ecuador, *Tel:* +593 4 2201226, *Fax:* +593 4 2204218, *Email:* informacion@vepamil.com.ec, *Website:* www.vepamil.com.ec – *Grades:* HFO; IFO; MGO – *Rates:* 150-180t/h – *Delivery Mode:* barge
Ian Taylor y Compania S.A., Edificio Centrum Piso 12, Of.4, Avenida Francisco de Orellana y Alberto Borges, Guayaquil, Ecuador, *Fax:* +593 4 269 3301, *Email:* taylorec@taylorec.com, *Website:* www.iantaylorgroup.com

Towage: Nine tugs available from 360 hp to 1250 hp
Ian Taylor y Compania S.A., Edificio Centrum Piso 12, Of.4, Avenida Francisco de Orellana y Alberto Borges, Guayaquil, Ecuador, *Fax:* +593 4 269 3301, *Email:* taylorec@taylorec.com, *Website:* www.iantaylorgroup.com

Repair & Maintenance: Astilleros Navales Ecuatorianos (ASTINAVE), Vacas Galindo y Vivero, P.O. Box 09-01-7175, Guayaquil, Ecuador, *Tel:* +593 4 244 5361, *Fax:* +593 4 244 1838, *Email:* info@astinavec.com, *Website:* www.astinavec.com Two floating dry docks, each with lifting cap of 3500 t
Sernain S.A., Cdla. 9 de Octubre Av. 2da, #208 y Calle 3era, Guayaquil, Ecuador, *Tel:* +593 4 242 1861, *Fax:* +593 4 242 0511, *Email:* comercial@sernain.com & gerencia@sernain.com, *Website:* www.sernain.com
Steamhouse International S.A., Cdla Inmaconsa Mz33 Solar 7, Km 11 1/1 via a Daule, P O Box 09-01-11142, Guayaquil, Ecuador, *Tel:* +593 4 6002160, *Fax:* +593 4 6002133, *Email:* steamhouse@telconet.net

Ship Chandlers: Apollo Marine Service S. A., Callejonno. 44 y Avenida 12 Corner, Guayaquil, Ecuador, *Tel:* +593 4 244 3600, *Fax:* +593 4 258 3290, *Email:* apolloec@telconet.net
Nordana Full Maritime Services, Guasmo Sur Coop Guayas y Quil 1 Mz 7 Sl 13, Guayaquil, Ecuador, *Tel:* +593 9401 0377 & 9617 3239, *Email:* nordana-maritime@hotmail.com
Probucam S.A., Calle I yGeneral Robles Barrio Cuba, Guayaquil, Ecuador, *Tel:* +593 4 258 4087, *Fax:* +593 4 233 8191, *Email:* info@probucam.com, *Website:* www.probucam.com
Rochem del Ecuador S.A., P O Box 09-01-5899, El oro 1301 y Guaranda, Guayaquil, Ecuador, *Tel:* +593 4 244 5733, *Fax:* +593 4 244 0154, *Email:* rochem@ecua.net.ec, *Website:* www.rochem-ec.com
South American Marine Engineering & Services, Via A Daule Km 11.5, Guayaquil, Ecuador, *Tel:* +593 4 600 2160, *Fax:* +593 4 600 2133, *Email:* southa@telconet.net
Steamhouse International S.A., Cdla Inmaconsa Mz33 Solar 7, Km 11 1/1 via a Daule, P O Box 09-01-11142, Guayaquil, Ecuador, *Tel:* +593 4 6002160, *Fax:* +593 4 6002133, *Email:* steamhouse@telconet.net
Universal Cargo S.A. - Logistics Operator, C.C Alban Borja, Edificio La Linea, 1do Piso, Oficina 9, Guayaquil, Ecuador, *Tel:* +593 4 220 5544, *Fax:* +593 4 220 3836, *Email:* gerenciaquito@universalcargoecuador.com, *Website:* www.universalcargoecuador.com

Shipping Agents: Agencia Maritima Global S.A. (Marglobal), Tulcan 809 y Hurtado, Edif San Luis, Piso 2, Guayaquil, Ecuador, *Tel:* +593 4 245 3009, *Fax:* +593 4 245 1247, *Email:* info@marglobal.com, *Website:* www.marglobal.com
Andinave S.A., Av 9 de Octubre 100 y Malecon Simon Bolivar, Edificio Previsora, Piso 29 Oficina 2901, Guayaquil, Ecuador, *Tel:* +593 4 232 5555, *Fax:* +593 4 232 5957, *Email:* info@andinave.com, *Website:* www.andinave.com
Bridge Intermodal del Ecuador S.A., Operadora del Pacifico S.A, Avenue 25 de Julio, Km 1.5 Via Puerto maritimo, Guayaquil, Ecuador, *Tel:* +593 4 248 3635, *Fax:* +593 4 248 4255, *Email:* ecuodpmng@maersk.com
CMA-CGM S.A., CMA CGM Ecuador S.A., Av 9 de Octubre 2009 y los Rios, Edificio El Marques - Piso 9, Guayaquil, Ecuador, *Tel:* +593 4 237 4502, *Fax:* +593 4 236 5626, *Email:* gql.genmbox@cma-cgm.com, *Website:* www.cma-cgm.com
Representaciones Maritimas del Ecuador S.A., Edificio Valra, piso 9, Of 1 y 2, Avenida 10 de Agosto 103 y Malecon, Guayaquil, Ecuador, *Tel:* +593 4 232 2111, *Fax:* +593 4 232 9251, *Email:* fzenck@remar.com.ec
Gemar S.A., 10 de Agosto 103 y Malecon, Valara Building, Guayaquil, Ecuador, *Tel:* +593 4 251 0651, *Fax:* +593 4 232 5111, *Email:* gemar@gemar.com.ec
Greenandes Ecuador S.A., Junin 114 y Malecon, Torres del Rio Building 5th Floor Ofc.8, Guayaquil, Ecuador, *Tel:* +593 4 230 2020, *Fax:* +593 4 230 2020, *Email:* general@greenandes.com.ec, *Website:* www.greenandes.com.ec
Inchcape Shipping Services (ISS), Cordova 1021 y Avenida 9 de Octubre, San Francisco 300 Building, Floor 19, Office 1, Guayaquil, Ecuador, *Tel:* +593 4 256 5700, *Fax:* +593 4 256 4857, *Email:* issecuador@iss-shipping.com, *Website:* www.iss-shipping.com
Investamar S.A., P O Box 5137, Guayaquil, Ecuador, *Tel:* +593 4 220 2688, *Fax:* +593 4 220 1473, *Email:* rolfbenz@investamar.com.ec
Mediterranean Shipping Company, MSC Ecuador, P O Box 10336, Centrum Building, 15th Floor Suite 1, Guayaquil, Ecuador, *Tel:* +593 4 269 3283, *Fax:* +593 4 269 3292, *Email:* mscecuador@mscecuador.com, *Website:* www.mscgva.ch
A.P. Moller-Maersk Group, Maersk del Ecuador C.A., Avenida Francisco de Orellana y Alberto Borges, Edificio Centrum, Piso 4to, Oficina 2 & 3, Guayaquil, Ecuador, *Tel:* +593 4 268 2531, *Fax:* +593 4 268 2533, *Email:* guqsalexp@maersk.com, *Website:* www.maerskline.com
Navesmar S.A., Junin 114 y Malecon, Edif Torres del Rio, piso 5, P O Box 09011226,

Guayaquil, Ecuador, *Tel:* +593 4 256 5800, *Fax:* +593 4 256 1494, *Email:* navesmar@ecua.net.ec

Surtax S.A., Miguel H. Alvivar & Victor Hugo Sicouret, Edificio Torres del Norte, Torre A, Piso 5, Oficina 506, Guayaquil, Ecuador, *Tel:* +593 4 268 7066, *Fax:* +593 4 268 7066, *Email:* makafi@depconsa.com, *Website:* www.depconsa.com

Ian Taylor y Compania S.A., Edificio Centrum Piso 12, Of.4, Avenida Francisco de Orellana y Alberto Borges, Guayaquil, Ecuador, *Fax:* +593 4 269 3301, *Email:* taylorec@taylorec.com, *Website:* www.iantaylorgroup.com

Transoceanica Cia Ltda, Malecon 1401 e Illingworth, Edifico Sudamerica, 7 Piso, P O Box 09011067, Guayaquil, Ecuador, *Tel:* +593 4 232 4360, *Fax:* +593 4 232 5528, *Email:* transoc@transoceanica.com.ec, *Website:* www.transoceanica.com.ec

Universal Cargo S.A. - Logistics Operator, C.C Alban Borja, Edificio La Linea, 1do Piso, Oficina 9, Guayaquil, Ecuador, *Tel:* +593 4 220 5544, *Fax:* +593 4 220 3836, *Email:* gerenciaquito@universalcargoecuador.com, *Website:* www.universalcargoecuador.com

Stevedoring Companies: Ian Taylor y Compania S.A., Edificio Centrum Piso 12, Of.4, Avenida Francisco de Orellana y Alberto Borges, Guayaquil, Ecuador, *Fax:* +593 4 269 3301, *Email:* taylorec@taylorec.com, *Website:* www.iantaylorgroup.com

Universal Cargo S.A. - Logistics Operator, C.C Alban Borja, Edificio La Linea, 1do Piso, Oficina 9, Guayaquil, Ecuador, *Tel:* +593 4 220 5544, *Fax:* +593 4 220 3836, *Email:* gerenciaquito@universalcargoecuador.com, *Website:* www.universalcargoecuador.com

Surveyors: ABS (Americas), Nueva Kennedy, Ciudadela Sagrada Familia, Manzana B, Villa 4, P O Box 09-01-3932, Guayaquil, Ecuador, *Tel:* +593 4 228 1811, *Fax:* +593 4 228 1841, *Email:* absguayaquil@eagle.org, *Website:* www.eagle.org

Bureau Veritas, Bureau Veritas Ecuador S.A., Av. Republica de El Salvador, N35-82 y Portugal, Edificio Twin Towers, Piso 3, P O Box 17 03 405, Quito, Ecuador, *Tel:* +593 2 227 3190, *Fax:* +593 2 225 8437, *Email:* bv.info@ec.bureauveritas.com, *Website:* www.bureauveritas.com

Det Norske Veritas A/S, 5th Floor, Office 505, Edificio Executive Center, Avenue J.T. Marengo y Ave. Joaquin Orrantia, Guayaquil, Ecuador, *Tel:* +593 4 229 2481, *Fax:* +593 4 229 2479, *Website:* www.dnv.com

Expert Shipping Services, P O Box 09-062413, Guayaquil, Ecuador, *Tel:* +593 4 238 2625, *Fax:* +593 4 238 6383, *Email:* expertshipping07@yahoo.com

Felvenza S.A., Cdla. Kennedy Norte Mz. 807 V.15, Guayaquil, Ecuador, *Tel:* +593 4 268 1441, *Fax:* +593 4 268 1440, *Email:* mng.director@felvenza.com, *Website:* www.felvenza.com

Germanischer Lloyd, Guayaquil, Ecuador, *Tel:* +593 4 229 2481, *Fax:* +593 4 229 2479, *Website:* www.gl-group.com

Medical Facilities: Available

Airport: Simon Bolivar International, 15 km

Lloyd's Agent: Felvenza S.A., Cdla. Kennedy Norte Mz. 807 V.15, Guayaquil, Ecuador, *Tel:* +593 4 268 1441, *Fax:* +593 4 268 1440, *Email:* mng.director@felvenza.com, *Website:* www.felvenza.com

LA LIBERTAD

Lat 2° 13' S; Long 80° 55' W.

Admiralty Chart: 560	**Admiralty Pilot:** 7
Time Zone: GMT -5 h	**UNCTAD Locode:** EC LLD

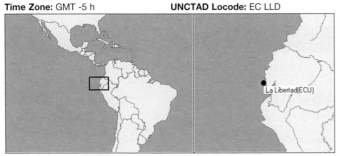

Principal Facilities:

P					B		T	

Authority: Superintendencia del Terminal Petrolero, La Libertad, Ecuador, *Tel:* +593 4 278 5785, *Fax:* +593 4 278 5873, *Email:* suinli@easynet.net.ec

Port Security: ISPS compliant

Approach: Usual anchorage for La Libertad is seaward of the mooring buoys. Anchorage also in open bay where vessels anchor in about 12.19 m of water

Pilotage: Compulsory. Pilot boards in pos 2° 00' S; 80° 64' W. ETA may be sent through Radio Naval of Guayaquil

Traffic: 2005, 168 vessels, 1 150 594 t of cargo handled

Maximum Vessel Dimensions: 43 381 dwt, 10.5 m draft, 228.7 m loa

Working Hours: 24 h/day

Accommodation:

Name	Remarks
La Libertad	See [1] below

[1]*La Libertad:* Pier for coastal vessels belonging to the Anglo-Ecuadorian Oilfields Ltd, with depths alongside from 4.88 to 6.4 m. A 14" private pipeline extends from the refinery W of La Libertad to a point 3.2 km offshore where there are four mooring buoys for tankers up to 11 m draft. Berthing is restricted to daylight hours and HT

Mechanical Handling Equipment:

Location	Type	Capacity (t)	Qty
La Libertad	Mult-purp. Cranes	15	1

Cargo Worked: Crude oil is loaded at approx 450 t/h

Bunkering: Bominflot, Bominflot Bunkergesellschaft fur Minerale mbH & Co. KG, Floor 6, Reconquista 1048, A1003ABV Buenos Aires, Argentina, *Tel:* +54 11 4312 0840, *Fax:* +54 11 4313 8337, *Email:* mail@bominflot.com.ar, *Website:* www.bominflot.net – *Grades:* all grades & MDO – *Delivery Mode:* barge

Corpetrolsa S.A., Via Puntilla - Samborondon KM 1, C.C. Bocca Of. 103, Guayaquil, Ecuador, *Tel:* +593 4 2097 775, *Fax:* +593 4 2097 782, *Email:* servam@gye.satnet.net/corpetrolsa@corpetrolsa.com, *Website:* www.corpetrolsa.com

Marzam Compania Ltda, Marzam Corporation, Malecon y Calles 19, Edificio El Navio, 2do. y 3er Piso, Manta, Ecuador, *Tel:* +593 5 2626 445, *Fax:* +593 5 2624 414, *Email:* marzam@marzam-online.com, *Website:* www.marzam-online.com

Navipac S.A., Avenida Pedro J. Menendez Gilbert, s/n Frente a Solca, P O Box 522970, Guayaquil, Ecuador, *Tel:* +593 4 2293 808, *Fax:* +593 4 2296 594, *Email:* bunkers@navipac.com, *Website:* www.navipac.com – *Grades:* IFO30-380cSt; MGO; lubes – *Parcel Size:* no min/max – *Rates:* 150-400t/h – *Notice:* 72 hours – *Delivery Mode:* barge

Oceanbat S.A., Avenida Carlos Julio Arosemena, Km.1 1/2, P O Box 2386, Guayaquil, Ecuador, *Tel:* +593 4 2201226, *Fax:* +593 4 2204218, *Email:* informacion@vepamil.com.ec, *Website:* www.vepamil.com.ec – *Grades:* HFO; IFO; MGO – *Rates:* 150-180t/h – *Delivery Mode:* barge

Petro Ecuador, Alpallana E-8 86 &6 de Diciembre Avenue, P O Box 17-11-5007/5008, Quito, Ecuador, *Tel:* +593 2 226 1728, *Fax:* +593 2 256 3780, *Email:* aludena@petroecuador.com.ec – *Grades:* MDO; IFO30-380cSt; in line blending available – *Parcel Size:* 150t max – *Rates:* 150t/h – *Notice:* 72 hours – *Delivery Mode:* barge

Towage: One tug available

Medical Facilities: Available

Lloyd's Agent: Felvenza S.A., Cdla. Kennedy Norte Mz. 807 V.15, Guayaquil, Ecuador, *Tel:* +593 4 268 1441, *Fax:* +593 4 268 1440, *Email:* mng.director@felvenza.com, *Website:* www.felvenza.com

MANTA

Lat 0° 56' S; Long 80° 43' W.

Admiralty Chart: 2799	**Admiralty Pilot:** 7
Time Zone: GMT -5 h	**UNCTAD Locode:** EC MEC

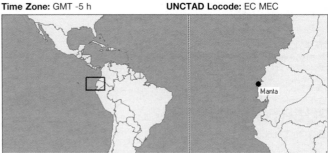

Principal Facilities:

Y	G	C	R	L	B		T	A

Authority: Autoridad Portuaria de Manta, Malecon Jaime Chavez Gutierrez, Edificio Administrativo, Manta, Ecuador, *Tel:* +593 5 262 7161, *Fax:* +593 5 262 1861, *Email:* apm1@apm.gov.ec, *Website:* www.apmanta.gov.ec

Officials: President: Lucia Fernandez Avellana de De Genna, *Email:* ldegenna@hotmail.com.
Vice President: Juan Pablo Tascon Armendaris.

Port Security: ISPS compliant

Pilotage: Compulsory for vessels over 500 gt. Pilot station 1.6 nautical mile from the breakwater light

Radio Frequency: VHF Channels 12 and 16

Tides: Range of tide 2 m

Traffic: 2005, 311 vessels, 676 358 t of cargo handled, 21 444 TEU's

Maximum Vessel Dimensions: 180 m loa, 12 000 dwt, 10 m draft

Principal Imports and Exports: Imports: Raw materials, Vegetable oil, Vehicles, Wheat. Exports: Cocoa, Coffee, Frozen fish, Processed food.

Working Hours: 24 h/day

Accommodation:

Name	Length (m)	Depth (m)	Remarks
Manta			Two ro/ro ramps
Container Terminal	1250	16	See [1] below
Deep Water Dock 1	200	11	
Deep Water Dock 2	200	11	
Deep Water Dock 3	200	11	
Deep Water Dock 4	200	11	
Fishing Dock 1	150	4.6	
Fishing Dock 2	100	5.7	
Fishing Dock 3	150	9.6	
Fishing Dock 4	40	5.1	
Fishing Dock 5	178	8.7	

[1]*Container Terminal:* Operated by Terminales Internacionales de Ecuador S.A., Edificio Fortaleza, Avenida M3 y Calle 24, Manta, Tel: +593 5 262 0300, Fax: +593 5 261 1633, Email: info@tide.com.ec, Website: www.tide.com.ec

---

Key to Principal Facilities:—				
A=Airport	**C**=Containers	**G**=General Cargo	**P**=Petroleum	**R**=Ro/Ro	**Y**=Dry Bulk
B=Bunkers	**D**=Dry Dock	**L**=Cruise	**Q**=Other Liquid Bulk	**T**=Towage (where available from port)

Mechanical Handling Equipment:

Location	Type	Capacity (t)	Qty
Manta	Mult-purp. Cranes	10–35	5

Cargo Worked: General loading: 84 t/h, liquid bulk loading 90 t/h, solid bulk loading 100 t/h, containers 15 per/h

Bunkering: Available with 72 h notice by truck or barge
Maritima de Comercio S.A. (MARDCOMSA), Avenue Malecon, calle 19, El Navio Building, Manta 5935, Ecuador, *Tel:* +593 5 2626445, *Fax:* +593 5 2624414, *Email:* mardcomsa@marzam-online.com, *Website:* www.marzam-online.com
Marzam Compania Ltda, Marzam Corporation, Malecon y Calles 19, Edificio El Navio, 2do. y 3er Piso, Manta, Ecuador, *Tel:* +593 5 2626 445, *Fax:* +593 5 2624 414, *Email:* marzam@marzam-online.com, *Website:* www.marzam-online.com
Corpetrolsa S.A., Via Puntilla - Samborondon KM 1, C.C. Bocca Of. 103, Guayaquil, Ecuador, *Tel:* +593 4 2097 775, *Fax:* +593 4 2097 782, *Email:* servam@gye.satnet.net/corpetrolsa@corpetrolsa.com, *Website:* www.corpetrolsa.com
Marzam Compania Ltda, Marzam Corporation, Malecon y Calles 19, Edificio El Navio, 2do. y 3er Piso, Manta, Ecuador, *Tel:* +593 5 2626 445, *Fax:* +593 5 2624 414, *Email:* marzam@marzam-online.com, *Website:* www.marzam-online.com
Navipac S.A., Avenida Pedro J. Menendez Gilbert, s/n Frente a Solca, P O Box 522970, Guayaquil, Ecuador, *Tel:* +593 4 2293 808, *Fax:* +593 4 2296 594, *Email:* bunkers@navipac.com, *Website:* www.navipac.com – *Grades:* IFO30-380cSt; MGO; lubes – *Parcel Size:* no min/max – *Rates:* 150-400t/h – *Notice:* 72 hours – *Delivery Mode:* barge
Oceanbat S.A., Avenida Carlos Julio Arosemena, Km.1 1/2, P O Box 2386, Guayaquil, Ecuador, *Tel:* +593 4 2201226, *Fax:* +593 4 2204218, *Email:* informacion@vepamil.com.ec, *Website:* www.vepamil.com.ec – *Grades:* HFO; IFO; MGO – *Rates:* 150-180t/h – *Delivery Mode:* barge
Xiang Shan Rongning Shipping Co. Ltd, 6th Floor, China Merchants Tower, No.118 Jian Guo Lu, Chaoyang District, Beijing 100022, People's Republic of China

Towage: Two tugs available of 1200 hp

Shipping Agents: Agencia Maritima Global S.A. (Marglobal), Avenida Malecon Jaime Chavez y Calle 19, Edificio El Navio, Manta, Ecuador, *Tel:* +593 5 262 0211, *Fax:* +593 5 262 0205, *Email:* info@mec.marglobal.com, *Website:* www.marglobal.com
BOW S.A., Malecon y Calle 17, Edificio 'Estibadores Navales' Tercer piso, Manta, Ecuador, *Tel:* +593 5 262 0103, *Fax:* +593 5 262 1091, *Email:* info@bowsa.com, *Website:* www.bowsa.com

Medical Facilities: Available

Airport: Approx 6 km from port

Lloyd's Agent: Felvenza S.A., Cdla. Kennedy Norte Mz. 807 V.15, Guayaquil, Ecuador, *Tel:* +593 4 268 1441, *Fax:* +593 4 268 1440, *Email:* mng.director@felvenza.com, *Website:* www.felvenza.com

PUERTO BOLIVAR

Lat 3° 16' S; Long 80° 0' W.

Admiralty Chart: 586	**Admiralty Pilot:** 7
Time Zone: GMT -5 h	**UNCTAD Locode:** EC PBO

Principal Facilities:

		G	C		B		T	A

Authority: Autoridad Portuaria de Puerto Bolivar, Avenida Madero Vargas via al Puerto Maritimo, Puerto Bolivar 504, Ecuador, *Tel:* +593 7 292 9999, *Fax:* +593 7 292 9634, *Email:* appb@eo.pro.ec, *Website:* www.appb.gov.ec

Officials: President: Alberto Francos.
Vice President: Victor Ricaurte.
General Manager: Byron Trujillo Erazo.

Port Security: ISPS compliant

Approach: Max channel depth of 10 m

Pilotage: Compulsory, round the clock service, ETA to be sent through Radio Naval Guayaquil 24 h before arrival. Pilot boards vessel on port side 1.6 km from the sea buoy

Radio Frequency: VHF Channel 16 monitored from 0800-1600; from 1600-0800 vessels to notify ETA 2 h in advance. VHF Channel 6 for operations

Weather: Rainy season from December to May

Tides: Range of tide, average 1.6 m

Traffic: 2005, 461 vessels, 1 427 173 t of cargo handled, 22 546 TEU's

Principal Imports and Exports: Imports: Cars, Fertiliser. Exports: Bananas.

Working Hours: 24 h/day

Accommodation:

Name	Length (m)	Depth (m)	Remarks
Puerto Bolivar			Depth at entrance 9.14 m at LW
Espigon Quay	660	7.5–9.5	Consists of four berths

Storage:

Location	Covered (m²)
Puerto Bolivar	9728

Mechanical Handling Equipment:

Location	Type	Capacity (t)	Qty
Puerto Bolivar	Mobile Cranes	15	1
Puerto Bolivar	Mobile Cranes	25	1

Cargo Worked: General cargo 60 t/h

Bunkering: Corpetrolsa S.A., Via Puntilla - Samborondon KM 1, C.C. Bocca Of. 103, Guayaquil, Ecuador, *Tel:* +593 4 2097 775, *Fax:* +593 4 2097 782, *Email:* servam@gye.satnet.net/corpetrolsa@corpetrolsa.com, *Website:* www.corpetrolsa.com
Marzam Compania Ltda, Marzam Corporation, Malecon y Calles 19, Edificio El Navio, 2do. y 3er Piso, Manta, Ecuador, *Tel:* +593 5 2626 445, *Fax:* +593 5 2624 414, *Email:* marzam@marzam-online.com, *Website:* www.marzam-online.com
Navipac S.A., Avenida Pedro J. Menendez Gilbert, s/n Frente a Solca, P O Box 522970, Guayaquil, Ecuador, *Tel:* +593 4 2293 808, *Fax:* +593 4 2296 594, *Email:* bunkers@navipac.com, *Website:* www.navipac.com – *Grades:* IFO30-380cSt; MGO; lubes – *Parcel Size:* no min/max – *Rates:* 150-400t/h – *Notice:* 72 hours – *Delivery Mode:* barge
Oceanbat S.A., Avenida Carlos Julio Arosemena, Km.1 1/2, P O Box 2386, Guayaquil, Ecuador, *Tel:* +593 4 2201226, *Fax:* +593 4 2204218, *Email:* informacion@vepamil.com.ec, *Website:* www.vepamil.com.ec – *Grades:* HFO; IFO; MGO – *Rates:* 150-180t/h – *Delivery Mode:* barge

Towage: Three tugs of 240, 340 and 1200 hp

Shipping Agents: Agencia Maritima Global S.A. (Marglobal), Autoridad Portuaria de Puerto Bolivar - Av. Bolivar Madera, Edificio Administrativo 2, Puerto Bolivar, Ecuador, *Tel:* +593 7 292 7234, *Fax:* +593 7 292 7235, *Email:* operaciones@pbo.marglobal.com, *Website:* www.marglobal.com

Medical Facilities: Available, 5 km from port

Airport: 4 km from port at Machala

Lloyd's Agent: Felvenza S.A., Cdla. Kennedy Norte Mz. 807 V.15, Guayaquil, Ecuador, *Tel:* +593 4 268 1441, *Fax:* +593 4 268 1440, *Email:* mng.director@felvenza.com, *Website:* www.felvenza.com

TEPRE TERMINAL

harbour area, see under Balao Terminal

EGYPT

ABU KIR

Lat 31° 19' N; Long 30° 3' E.

Admiralty Chart: 2681	**Admiralty Pilot:** 49
Time Zone: GMT +2 h	**UNCTAD Locode:** EG AKI

Principal Facilities:

		Y	G			B		T	A

Authority: Abu Kir Port Authority, Abu Kir, Arab Republic of Egypt, *Tel:* +20 3 562 1648, *Fax:* +20 3 562 1053, *Email:* essamkh777@yahoo.com

Officials: Harbour Master: Essam Khalifa.

Port Security: ISPS compliant

Approach: Vessels proceeding to Abu Kir Bay from a westerly direction should keep well to the N of Sultan Shoal and Culloden Reef

Anchorage: Arrival buoy in pos 31° 23' 07" N; 30° 07' 07" E. Turning buoy in pos 31° 19' 06" N; 30° 09' 09" E. Waiting area one mile NW of Nelson Island. Anchorage for large vessels can be obtained in Abu Kir Bay in a depth of 15 m

Pilotage: Pilot boards in the following positions:

Abu Kir: in the waiting area centered on pos 31° 22' 50" N; 30° 05' 00" E
Ammonia Berth: in the waiting area centered on pos 31° 21' 00" N; 30° 08' 50" E

Principal Imports and Exports: Imports: Grain. Exports: Ammonia.

Accommodation:

Name	Remarks
Abu Kir	See [1] below

[1]*Abu Kir:* Comprising five quays with a total length of 1500 m with depth alongside of 5.0 m. Large vessels unloading grain are handled in Abu Kir Bay
Grain silo converted from a bulk carrier, permanently moored at the quayside in the harbour with a cap of 45 000 t. Equipment includes conveyor belts, cranes and an automatic packaging system for cereals. Ammonia is loaded by vessels up to 160 m loa at 5000 t/day. Phosphate and fertiliser is discharged for Abu Kir Fertilizers & Chemical Industries Co. with max draft of 4.6 m

Bunkering: All grades available by barge from Suez
Macoil International S.A., Macoil Building, 103 Kallirois Street, 176 71 Athens, Greece, *Tel:* +30 210 9249 175, *Fax:* +30 210 9249 170, *Email:* macoil@otenet.gr

Towage: Available

Airport: Alexandria Airport

Lloyd's Agent: Marine Technical Services Ltd, 34 Salah El Din Street, El Laban, Alexandria, Arab Republic of Egypt, *Tel:* +20 3 494 1347, *Fax:* +20 3 391 3012, *Email:* mts-lloyds-alex@soficom.com.eg, *Website:* www.lloydsegypt.com

ABU ZENIMA

Lat 29° 2' N; Long 33° 7' E.

Admiralty Chart: 159	**Admiralty Pilot:** 64
Time Zone: GMT +2 h	**UNCTAD Locode:** EG AZA

Principal Facilities:

		Y							

Authority: Sinai Manganese Co., 1 Kasr El-Nile Street, Cairo, Arab Republic of Egypt, *Tel:* +20 2 574 0217, *Fax:* +20 2 574 0142, *Email:* info@smc-eg.com, *Website:* www.smc-eg.com

Officials: Chairman: Abou Eleyoun Ibrahim Hassan.
Commercial Manager: Sayed Hussien.

Approach: Abu Zenima Bay is entered between Ras Abu Zenima and Cairn Point and has a draft of over 18.3 m. A sand bank extends offshore about 1295 m from Ras Abu Zenima, marked by a conical buoy; on east side, edge of bank is about 185 m from pier head

Anchorage: Good anchorage may be obtained in depths of 18.3 m, sand and mud bottom

Pilotage: Master can get vessels alongside pier with assistance of Pier Master who embarks vessel

Weather: Southerly winds dangerous from November to May. Masters must haul off immediately

Maximum Vessel Dimensions: 152 m loa, 20.4 m wide, 7.62 m draft. Height from water line to top of hatch or rail should not exceed 9.75 m

Principal Imports and Exports: Exports: Ferro-manganese.

Accommodation:

Name	Length (m)	Depth (m)	Remarks
Abu Zenima			
Pier	45	10	Conveyor belt used in loading

Lloyd's Agent: Marine Technical Services Ltd, Flat 6B, 28 Cherif Street, Cairo, Arab Republic of Egypt, *Tel:* +20 2 2393 5724, *Fax:* +20 2 2393 8669, *Email:* mts-lloyds-cairo@soficom.com.eg, *Website:* www.lloydsegypt.com

ADABIYA

Lat 29° 52' N; Long 32° 28' E.

Admiralty Chart: 3214	**Admiralty Pilot:** 64
Time Zone: GMT +2 h	**UNCTAD Locode:** EG ADA

Principal Facilities:

P	Y	G	C		B		T	A

Authority: Red Sea Ports Authority, P O Box 1, Port Tewfik, Arab Republic of Egypt, *Tel:* +20 62 333 1123, *Fax:* +20 62 333 0315, *Email:* rspsite@emdb.gov.eg

Officials: Chairman: Hesham El Sersawy.
Harbour Master: Basel Bahgat.

Port Security: ISPS compliant

Pilotage: Compulsory

Radio Frequency: Vessel Traffic Information Management System (VTIMS) equipped with Inmarsat (C) established in pos 29° 51.284' N; 32° 29.050' E, Station Sign 462299912 - frequency used M.Z - sending (157.000) receiving (161.600) VHF Channel 20

Traffic: 2006, 754 vessels, 5 025 000 t of cargo handled

Maximum Vessel Dimensions: 200 m loa

Working Hours: 24 h/day

Accommodation:

Name	Length (m)	Depth (m)	Remarks
Adabiya			See [1] below
Berth No's 1 & 2	150	9.5	Military
Berth No.3	150	11	General cargo
Berth No's 4 & 5	435	12	General cargo & dry bulk
Berth No's 6, 7, 8 & 9	725	12	General cargo & tourism

[1]*Adabiya:* Operated by Egyptian Container Handling Co. (ECHCO)
Also a cement berth 100 m long with draft of 10 m and two petroleum berths, both 92 m long with draft of 9-10 m

Mechanical Handling Equipment:

Location	Type	Capacity (t)	Qty
Adabiya	Floating Cranes	8	1
Adabiya	Mult-purp. Cranes	10–70	5
Adabiya	Mobile Cranes	10	1

Cargo Worked: Bulk cargo 5000-6000 t/day, grain 100 t/h, cement 6000-8000 t/day

Bunkering: Available
Chevron Egypt S.A.E., 44 Elnadi Street, Maadi, Cairo, Arab Republic of Egypt, *Tel:* +20 2 2358 8007, *Fax:* +20 2 2358 8027, *Email:* gmpegyptb@chevron.com, *Website:* www.chevron.com
ExxonMobil Marine Fuels, Mailpoint 31, ExxonMobil House, Ermyn Way, Leatherhead, Surrey KT22 8UX, United Kingdom, *Tel:* +44 1372 222 000, *Fax:* +44 1372 223 922, *Email:* marine.fuels@exxonmobil.com, *Website:* www.exxonmobil.com
Maxcom Bunker S.p.A. u.s., Via Bartolomeo Bosco 57/7B, 16121 Genoa, Italy, *Tel:* +39 010 5605 200, *Fax:* +39 010 564 479, *Email:* bunker@maxcombunker.com, *Website:* www.maxcombunker.com
Petrolube Misr Saudi Arabian Lubricating Oil Co., P O Box 1120, 52 Lebanon Street, Mohandessen, Cairo 11511, Arab Republic of Egypt, *Tel:* +20 2 305 4670, *Fax:* +20 2 305 4811, *Email:* petrowafaa2002@hotmail.com
Shell Marketing Egypt, Corner Street 254 & 206, Degla Maadi, Cairo 11742, Arab Republic of Egypt, *Tel:* +20 2 519 8817, *Fax:* +20 2 519 8818
Solimanco Marine Services, P O Box 202, Port Said Free Zone, Port Said 42111, Arab Republic of Egypt, *Tel:* +20 66 341641, *Fax:* +20 66 232262, *Email:* mohamed1969@mail.interlink-eg.com
Tamoil Misr, 35 Abdallah Ibn Taher Street, Nasr City, Cairo 11511, Arab Republic of Egypt, *Tel:* +20 2 273 2085, *Fax:* +20 2 287 2879

Towage: Tugs available

Medical Facilities: Available

Airport: Suez, 70 km

Lloyd's Agent: Marine Technical Services Ltd, 4th Floor, Units 19 & 20, El Freepor Building, El Nahda & Palestine Streets, Port Said, Arab Republic of Egypt, *Tel:* +20 66 335 5423, *Fax:* +20 66 334 3974, *Email:* mts-lloyds-portsaid@soficom.com.eg, *Website:* www.lloydsegypt.com

AIN SUKHNA TERMINAL

Lat 29° 35' N; Long 32° 20' E.

Admiralty Chart: 2132	**Admiralty Pilot:** 64
Time Zone: GMT +2 h	**UNCTAD Locode:** EG AIS

Key to Principal Facilities:—		
A=Airport	**C**=Containers	**G**=General Cargo
B=Bunkers	**D**=Dry Dock	**L**=Cruise
P=Petroleum	**R**=Ro/Ro	**Y**=Dry Bulk
Q=Other Liquid Bulk	**T**=Towage (where available from port)	

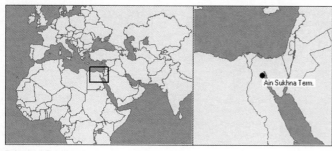

Principal Facilities:

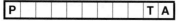

P								T	A

 Tramp Oil & Marine

Wells House, 15-17 Elmfield Road, Bromley,
Kent BR1 1LT, United Kingdom
Phone: +44 20 8315 7777   **Fax:** +44 20 8315 7788
General email: enquiries@tramp-oil.com

See listings for all global offices: **www.tramp-oil.com**

Authority: Arab Petroleum Pipelines Co. (SUMED), 431 El-Geish Avenue, Loran, Alexandria, Arab Republic of Egypt, *Tel:* +20 3 582 6711, *Fax:* +20 3 582 6713, *Email:* schedoilmove@sumed.org, *Website:* www.sumed.org

Officials: Chairman: Mahmud Nazim, *Email:* chairman@sumed.org.
Terminal Manager: Ing Abdo Saad, *Tel:* +20 3 509 0086.

Port Security: ISPS compliant

Pre-Arrival Information: To SUMED Oil Movement Attn. T. Youssef/K. Saleh Re: (72, 48 and 24 h) pre-arrival notice
Vessel name
IMO number
Flag
Port of registry
Master's name
Charterers
INMARSAT Telex. No.
INMARSAT Phone No.
INMARSAT Fax No.
Email address
Present monitoring (indicate region)
ETA Ain Sukhna
Arrival draft
Departure draft
Cargo on board (Grade A, Grade B, Grade C)
Bill of lading, bbls
Bill of lading, API
Bill of lading, date
Ships Fig., TCV bbls
Ships Fig., free water
Slops
L.O.T.
Discharge sequence (by crude type))
Discharge time (by crude type)
COW - indicate time (by crude type), stoppage time (by crude type), stoppage after discharge of bbls (by crude type)
Total time on berth
Last port of call
Next port of call
Ship security level
Master

Anchorage: Tankers anchorage waiting area in the following positions in depth of 45-58 m
A in pos 29° 29' 33" N; 32° 27' 21" E
B in pos 29° 30' 63" N; 32° 29' 48" E
C in pos 29° 33' 43" N; 32° 27' 98" E
D in pos 29° 31' 92" N; 32° 24' 39" E

Pilotage: Compulsory. Pilot boards 2 miles SE of SBM No.4. Master's of vessels proceeding to the terminal should cable their ETA's to 'SUMED' Alexandria. This cable is to be prefixed 'to be conveyed via telex 54108 or 54033 SUMED UN, operations office-oil movement'. ETA notifications to be sent (a) immediately upon sailing from loading port/s (b) in case of a change in ETA exceeding 6 h (c) 72 h, 48 h and 24 h prior to arrival

Radio Frequency: Master's are required to contact the terminal on VHF 6 h before arrival on Channels 78 and 79 if available or 16

Weather: Prevailing winds are from the NW throughout the year

Tides: Tidal range is up to a max of 7.4 ft, max rate is 0.5 knots at the surface

Traffic: 2006, 551 vessels, 128 094 641 m3 of crude oil handled

Working Hours: 24 h/day

Accommodation:

Name	Depth (m)	Draught (m)	Remarks
Ain Sukhna Terminal			See [1] below
SBM No.1	25.9	22.8	See [2] below
SBM No.2	25.9	22.8	See [3] below
SBM No.3	19.8	16.7	See [4] below
SBM No.4	40.9	31.5	See [5] below

[1]*Ain Sukhna Terminal:* Crude oil is offloaded from tankers too large to transit the Suez Canal fully laden, then pumped via the pipeline to Sidi Kerir, where tankers can load. The pipeline operates at a rate of about 6000 t/h
[2]*SBM No.1:* In pos 29° 35' 16" N; 32° 23' 35" E for tankers up to 350 000 dwt. Connected to shore by a submarine line 48" in diameter and approx 5 km long. This buoy can receive crude oil up to a max rate of 12 500 t/h
[3]*SBM No.2:* In pos 29° 34' 12" N; 32° 22' 42" E for vessels up to 350 000 dwt. Connected to shore by a submarine line 48" in diameter and approx 5 km long. This buoy can receive crude oil up to a max rate of 12 500 t/h
[4]*SBM No.3:* In pos 29° 35' 17" N; 32° 22' 16" E for vessels up to 150 000 dwt. Connected to shore by a submarine line 42" in diameter and approx 3 km long. This buoy can receive crude oil up to a max rate of 7400 t/h
[5]*SBM No.4:* In pos 29° 34' 02" N; 32° 24' 04" E for vessels up to 500 000 dwt. Connected to shore by a submarine line 52" in diameter and approx 7.5 km long. This buoy can receive crude oil up to a max rate of 12 500 t/h

Storage: Onshore facilities include 15 single-deck, floating, roof, welded steel storage tanks (103 000 m3 each), with total storage cap of 1 545 000 m3

Bunkering: Tramp Oil & Marine, World Fuel Services Corporation, 13th Floor, Portland House, Bressenden Place, London SW1E 5BH, United Kingdom, *Tel:* +44 20 7808 5000, *Fax:* +44 20 7808 5088, *Email:* pturner@wfscorp.com, *Website:* www.wfscorp.com

Towage: One tug of 3200 hp and one of 6000 hp available at all times, fully equipped for fire-fighting and anti-pollution operations. Mooring launches to assist in berthing are also available

Medical Facilities: Neither medical nor hospital facilities are provided by SUMED. In case urgent medical assistance is required the vessel should contact SUMED's harbour master by VHF radio. Private doctors and facilities are available at Suez via agents

Airport: Cairo, 120 km

Railway: Misr Railway Station, 130 km

Lloyd's Agent: Marine Technical Services Ltd, Flat 6B, 28 Cherif Street, Cairo, Arab Republic of Egypt, *Tel:* +20 2 2393 5724, *Fax:* +20 2 2393 8669, *Email:* mts-lloyds-cairo@soficom.com.eg, *Website:* www.lloydsegypt.com

ALEXANDRIA

Lat 31° 11' N; Long 29° 53' E.

Admiralty Chart: 302/3119	**Admiralty Pilot:** 49
Time Zone: GMT +2 h	**UNCTAD Locode:** EG ALY

Principal Facilities:

P	Q	Y	G	C	R	L	B	D	T	A

Tramp Oil & Marine

Wells House, 15-17 Elmfield Road, Bromley,
Kent BR1 1LT, United Kingdom
Phone: +44 20 8315 7777   **Fax:** +44 20 8315 7788
General email: enquiries@tramp-oil.com

See listings for all global offices: **www.tramp-oil.com**

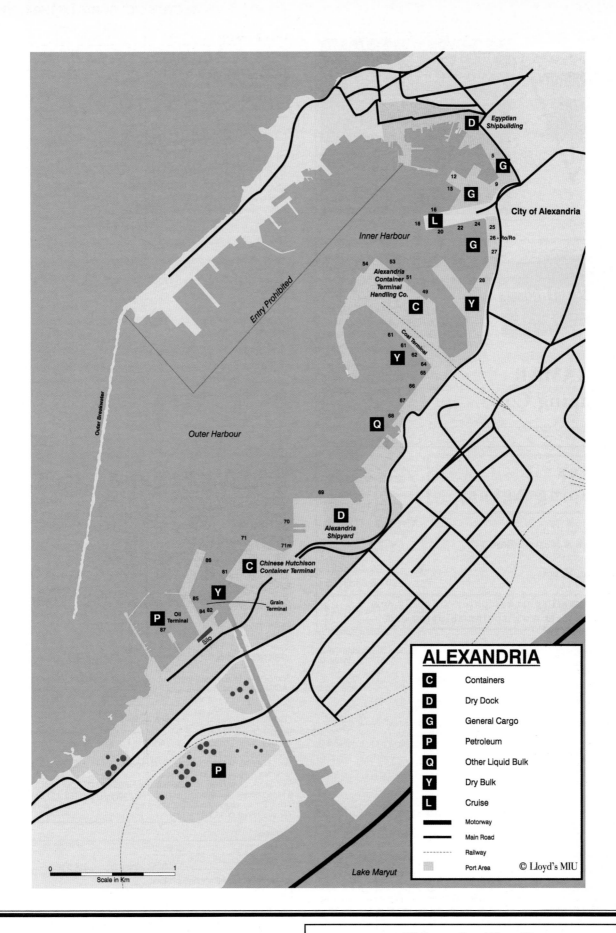

ALEXANDRIA

C	Containers
D	Dry Dock
G	General Cargo
P	Petroleum
Q	Other Liquid Bulk
Y	Dry Bulk
L	Cruise
▬▬	Motorway
▬	Main Road
- - -	Railway
░	Port Area

© Lloyd's MIU

Egyptian Shipbuilding

City of Alexandria

Inner Harbour

Alexandria Container Terminal Handling Co.

Coal Terminal

Entry Prohibited

Outer Breakwater

Outer Harbour

Alexandria Shipyard

Chinese Hutchison Container Terminal

Grain Terminal

Oil Terminal

Silo

Lake Maryut

Scale in Km

Freedom Shipping Co.

• SHIP CHANDLERS •

77 Street, Ras Elbar City
2nd Floor, Sports Club Building, Damietta, EGYPT
Tel: +20 123714752
Fax: +20 572532324
Email: freedomshipping2000@yahoo.com

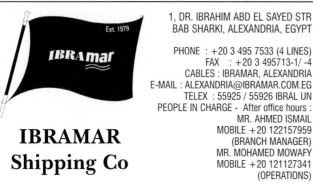
Authority: Alexandria Port Authority, 106 El Horreia Street, Alexandria, Arab Republic of Egypt, *Tel:* +20 3 480 0359, *Fax:* +20 3 486 9714, *Website:* www.alexportic.net

Port Security: ISPS compliant

Approach: Great Pass: 2 km long, 220 m width in depth of 13.7 m
Boghaz Pass: 1.6 km long, 91 m width in depth of 9.14 m

Anchorage: There are two designated waiting areas established on the north and south sides of the recommended channel in the outer harbour
Within the north waiting area the following anchorage areas have been established:
NA1 in pos 31° 10.370' N; 29° 51.055' E
NA2 in pos 31° 10.500' N; 29° 51.150' E
NA3 in pos 31° 10.620' N; 29° 51.265' E
NA4 in pos 31° 10.750' N; 29° 51.360' E
NA5 in pos 31° 10.750' N; 29° 51.155' E
NA6 in pos 31° 10.885' N; 29° 51.262' E
Within the south waiting area the following anchorage areas have been established:
SA1 in pos 31° 10.635' N; 29° 52.045' E
SA2 in pos 31° 10.760' N; 29° 52.205' E
SA3 in pos 31° 10.408' N; 29° 51.618' E
SA4 in pos 31° 10.572' N; 29° 51.762' E
SA5 in pos 31° 10.730' N; 29° 51.865' E
SA6 in pos 31° 10.860' N; 29° 52.015' E

Pilotage: Compulsory for vessels over 300 gt. Pilot boards off harbour entrance. Severe penalties for contravening regulations concerning compulsory pilotage. Waiting area at 31° 12.6' N, 29° 44.5' E with radius of 2.4 km

Radio Frequency: Call sign 'SUH' on 444.5 and 8578 kHz and VHF channel 16

Weather: Prevailing NW winds, force 2-3 in summer, 4-7 in winter

Tides: Rise of tide 0.3 m to 0.45 m

Traffic: 2006, 5033 vessels, 39 300 000 t of cargo handled, 783 300 TEU's (includes El Dekheila)

Principal Imports and Exports: Imports: Dry bulk cargo, General cargo, Liquid bulk cargo. Exports: General cargo, Oil products.

Working Hours: 24 h/day

Accommodation:

Name	Length (m)	Depth (m)	Remarks
General Cargo Berths			
Berth No.5	290	6.5	
Berth No.6	85	5.6	
Berth No.8	75	4.5	
Berth No.9	89	5.2	
Berth No.10	130	7.2	
Berth No.11	130	7.5	
Berth No.12	100	7.6	
Berth No.13	140	8.4	
Berth No.14	157	8	
Berth No.24	152	10.1	
Berth No.25	157	9.3	
Berth No.26	137	8.9	
Berth No.27	220	10.2	
Berth No.28	220	10.3	
Berth No.30	61	3.9	
Berth No.34	91	5.2	
Berth No.36	330	9.5	
Berth No.37	330	9.5	
Berth No.38	115	9.9	
Berth No.39	280	8.8	
Berth No.40	280	8.8	
Berth No.42	220	7.8	
Berth No.43	220	7.4	
Berth No.44	130	6.7	
Grain Berths			
Berth No.75	120	6.7	
Berth No.76	90	8.6	
Berth No.77	120	7.1	
Berth No.78	55	7.1	
Berth No.79	120	7.1	
Berth No.80	90	7.7	
Berth No.81	120	8.9	
Berth No.82	190	9.9	
Berth No.85	130	9.8	
Coal Berths			Four coal dischargers at rate of 7000 t/day
Berth No.60	165	8.3	
Berth No.61	345	7.5	
Berth No.62	345	8.1	
Berth No.63	345	9.8	
Berth No.64	345	10.2	
Other Bulk Berths			
Berth No.65	345	7.4	Fertilizer
Berth No.66	345	7.4	Fertilizer
Berth No.67	345	8.3	Fertilizer
Berth No.71	120	8.3	Timber
Berth No.72	90	8.7	Timber
Berth No.83	175	8.4	Timber
Berth No.71M	280	8.3	Molasses
Petroleum Berths			Situated in outer harbour for vessels up to 213 m loa
Berth No.87/1	300	10.1	
Berth No.87/2	300	10.1	
Berth No.87/3	150	10.1	
Berth No.87/4	150	10.2	
Berth No.87/5	215	10.2	
LPG/LNG Facilities			For vessels up to 125 m loa and 8.7 m draft
Container & Ro/Ro Terminal			
ACCH Container Terminal	531	14	See [1] below
AICT Container Terminal	380	12	See [2] below
Passenger Terminal Berths	698	9–10	

[1]*ACCH Container Terminal:* Operated by Alexandria Container & Cargo Handling Co., Tel: +20 3 480 0633, Fax: +20 3 486 2124, Email: alexcont@alexcont.com, Website: www.alexcont.com
Terminal area of 163 000 m2 with storage cap for 11 000 TEU's and 500 reefer points. Includes a 164 m ro/ro quay
[2]*AICT Container Terminal:* Operated by Alexandria International Container Terminals, 5 Mena Street, Kafr Abdu, Roshdy, Alexandria, Tel: +20 3 523 3312, Fax: +20 3 546 7198, Email: elsayed.may@aict.com.eg
Terminal area of 11 ha

Storage:

Location	Grain (t)
Alexandria	148000

Mechanical Handling Equipment:

Location	Type	Capacity (t)	Qty
Alexandria	Floating Cranes	70	1
Alexandria	Floating Cranes	100	1
Alexandria	Floating Cranes	120	1
ACCH Container Terminal	Panamax	32	2
ACCH Container Terminal	Post Panamax	40	1
AICT Container Terminal	Container Cranes		2
AICT Container Terminal	RTG's		5

Cargo Worked: Coal 7000 t/day, naphta 900 t/h, cotton seed oil 3500 t/day, bagged urea 3500 t/day, bagged wheat flour 1500 t/day, sulphur 1200 t/day, vegetable oil 300 t/h

Bunkering: OilTrade Ltd, El-Horia Street, Alexandria, Arab Republic of Egypt, *Tel:* +20 3 945455, *Fax:* +20 3 946466
Unimas Shipping, 1 Digla Street, Raml Station, 5th Floor, P O Box 44, Ibrahimia, Alexandria 21312, Arab Republic of Egypt, *Tel:* +20 3 486 8800, *Fax:* +20 3 487 0230, *Email:* mail@unimas.com.eg, *Website:* www.unimasegypt.com
Bominflot, Bominflot Ltd, 5-7 Ravensbourne Road, Bromley, Kent BR1 1HN, United Kingdom, *Tel:* +44 20 8315 5400, *Fax:* +44 20 8315 5429, *Email:* mail@bominflot.co.uk, *Website:* www.bominflot.net
BP Marketing Egypt, P O Box 1254, 42 Road 17, Digla, Madi, Cairo, Arab Republic of Egypt, *Tel:* +20 2 706 2345, *Fax:* +20 2 768 8075, *Email:* info@bp.com, *Website:* www.bp.com
Chevron Marine Products LLC, Chevron Products UK Ltd, 1 Westferry Circus, Canary Wharf, London E14 4HA, United Kingdom, *Tel:* +44 20 7719 4680, *Fax:* +44 20 7719 5151, *Email:* gmpukb@chevron.com, *Website:* www.chevron.com
Cockett Marine Oil Ltd, Carrick House, 36 Station Square, Petts Wood, Kent BR5 1NA, United Kingdom, *Tel:* +44 1689 883 400, *Fax:* +44 1689 877 666, *Email:* enquiries@cockett.com, *Website:* www.cockettgroup.com
ExxonMobil Marine Fuels, Mailpoint 31, ExxonMobil House, Ermyn Way, Leatherhead, Surrey KT22 8UX, United Kingdom, *Tel:* +44 1372 222 000, *Fax:* +44 1372 223 922, *Email:* marine.fuels@exxonmobil.com, *Website:* www.exxonmobil.com
Macoil International S.A., Macoil Building, 103 Kallirois Street, 176 71 Athens, Greece, *Tel:* +30 210 9249 175, *Fax:* +30 210 9249 170, *Email:* macoil@otenet.gr
Misr Petroleum Co., MISR Petroleum House, 6 Orabi Square, P O Box 228, Cairo, Arab Republic of Egypt, *Tel:* +20 2 2574 5400, *Fax:* +20 2 2574 5436, *Email:* bunker@misrpetroleum.com, *Website:* www.misrpetroleum.com
Petrolube Misr Saudi Arabian Lubricating Oil Co., P O Box 1120, 52 Lebanon Street, Mohandessen, Cairo 11511, Arab Republic of Egypt, *Tel:* +20 2 305 4670, *Fax:* +20 2 305 4811, *Email:* petrowafaa2002@hotmail.com
Societe Cooperative des Petroles (Copetrole), Cooperative Building, 94 Kasr El Eini Street, Cairo 11621, Arab Republic of Egypt, *Tel:* +20 2 2792 5221, *Fax:* +20 2 2795 6404, *Email:* co_op@link.net
Solimanco Marine Services, P O Box 202, Port Said Free Zone, Port Said 42111, Arab Republic of Egypt, *Tel:* +20 66 341641, *Fax:* +20 66 232262, *Email:* mohamed1969@mail.interlink-eg.com
Total France S.A., Total Marine Fuels, 51 Esplanade du General de Gaulle, F-92907 Paris la Defense Cedex 10, France, *Tel:* +33 1 4135 2755, *Fax:* +33 1 4197 0291, *Email:* marine.fuels@total.com, *Website:* www.marinefuels.total.com
Tramp Oil & Marine, World Fuel Services Corporation, 13th Floor, Portland House, Bressenden Place, London SW1E 5BH, United Kingdom, *Tel:* +44 20 7808 5000, *Fax:* +44 20 7808 5088, *Email:* pturner@wfscorp.com, *Website:* www.wfscorp.com – *Grades:* all grades
Unimas Shipping, 1 Digla Street, Raml Station, 5th Floor, P O Box 44, Ibrahimia, Alexandria 21312, Arab Republic of Egypt, *Tel:* +20 3 486 8800, *Fax:* +20 3 487 0230, *Email:* mail@unimas.com.eg, *Website:* www.unimasegypt.com
Universal Maritime Agency & Trading Co. Ltd (Umatco), 2444 Marisa Ct., Mississauga, Ont., Canada, *Tel:* +1 905 823 4638, *Fax:* +1 905 823 3938, *Email:* umatco@sympatico.ca
World Marine Egypt, 12 Salah Salem Street, Port Said, Arab Republic of Egypt, *Tel:* +20 66 325327, *Fax:* +20 66 326114

Towage: Compulsory for vessels over 82.3 m loa. Tugs from 1800-2500 hp available all the time
SVITZER, Wijsmuller Egypt SAE, 1st Floor, Tower No.6, Sayadila Towers, Masjed Hatem Street, Alexandria, Arab Republic of Egypt, *Tel:* +20 3 429 1618, *Fax:* +20 3 429 6168, *Email:* info@wijsmulleregypt.com, *Website:* www.svitzer.com

Repair & Maintenance: Alexandria Shipyard, Gate No.36, Kabbary, P O Box 21553, Alexandria 21553, Arab Republic of Egypt, *Tel:* +20 3 440 3090, *Fax:* +20 3 440 4672, *Email:* alexyard@soficom.com.eg, *Website:* www.soficom.com.eg/alexyard Four slipways for vessels up to 1000 dwt. Two graving docks for vessels up to 85 000 dwt. Repair quay of 1200 m
Egyptian Shiprepairs & Building Co., Elgomrok District, Port Gate No.1, Alexandria, Arab Republic of Egypt, *Tel:* +20 3 487 7415, *Fax:* +20 3 487 7417, *Email:* esrbc@esrbc.com, *Website:* www.esrbc.com Floating dock 152 m x 28 m with a lifting cap of 6000 t and three small slipways for vessels up to 600 t

Ship Chandlers: Concord Shipping Agency, 1st Floor, El Hegaz Building, Memphis Street, Port Said, Arab Republic of Egypt, *Tel:* +20 66 325 2443, *Fax:* +20 66 323 4476, *Email:* office@concordshipping.com, *Website:* www.concordshipping.com
Edwardo Marine Services Co., 22 Elnaser Street, Alexandria, Arab Republic of Egypt, *Tel:* +20 3 481 8379, *Fax:* +20 3 483 1028, *Email:* info@edwardomarine.com, *Website:* www.edwardomarine.com
The Egyptian Marine Supply & Contracting Co. SAA (CONSUP), P O Box 2025, Code No. 2157, Alexandria, Arab Republic of Egypt, *Tel:* +20 3 487 0550, *Fax:* +20 3 487 8270, *Email:* consup2000@usa.net, *Website:* www.consupegypt.com
El Dawi Sons Shipping Agency, El Saba Banat Building, 22 El Saba Banat Street, 3rd Floor, El Laban, Alexandria, Arab Republic of Egypt, *Tel:* +20 3 484 0275, *Fax:* +20 3 484 7391, *Email:* shipping@eldawisons.com, *Website:* www.eldawisons.com
El Moutaz Agency & Marine Services Co. (Zacharia), 13 Elnasr Street Elmanshia, Alexandria, Arab Republic of Egypt, *Tel:* +20 3 481 8862, *Fax:* +20 3 480 5541, *Email:* elmoutaz@dataxprs.com.eg
Freedom Shipping Co., 77 Street, Ras Elbar City, 2nd Floor, Sports Club Building, Damietta, Arab Republic of Egypt, *Tel:* +20 123714752, *Fax:* +20 572532324, *Email:* freedomshipping2000@yahoo.com
Hardy Ship Suppliers (Egypt), P O Box 197, Port Said 42511, Arab Republic of Egypt, *Tel:* +20 66 332 0850, *Fax:* +20 66 332 8194, *Email:* hardy@mosleh.com
The International Marine Services Co. (S.A.E.), 17 Dr. Ibrahim Abdelseed Street, Opposite 80 Horreya Street, Alexandria, Arab Republic of Egypt, *Tel:* +20 3 493 8747, *Fax:* +20 3 493 8746
International Shipping Enterprise S.A.E. (Intership), P O Box 281, Bani el-Abbas 8, Alexandria, Arab Republic of Egypt, *Tel:* +20 3 487 0837, *Fax:* +20 3 487 0444, *Email:* main@intershipegypt.com, *Website:* www.intershipegypt.com
Kadmar Shipping Co., 32 Saad Zaghloul Street, Alexandria 21131, Arab Republic of Egypt, *Tel:* +20 3 486 2832, *Fax:* +20 3 484 8326, *Email:* general@kadmar.com, *Website:* www.kadmar.com
Khadraco, 13 Elkobriel Kadim Street, Bab el Karasta, Alexandria 21111, Arab Republic of Egypt, *Tel:* +20 3 392 1078, *Fax:* +20 3 391 9074, *Email:* khadraco@hotmail.com
Marcos Marine Services, 19 Sidi Laloo, El-Gomrok, El-Kadim Street, Alexandria, Arab Republic of Egypt, *Tel:* +20 3 483 0510, *Fax:* +20 3 483 0878, *Email:* marcos@marcosmarine.com, *Website:* www.marcosmarine.com
Pan Marine Co, Haridy el Shazley, Haridy, 50 Omar Lotfy Street, Camp Caesar, Alexandria, Arab Republic of Egypt, *Tel:* +20 3 590 1605, *Fax:* +20 3 590 1542, *Email:* panmar@dataxprs.com.eg, *Website:* www.pan-marine.net
Rochem MariTech, 11 Sisostreis Street, Misr Insurance Building, El Attareen, Alexandria, Arab Republic of Egypt, *Tel:* +20 3 480 7878, *Fax:* +20 3 487 7551, *Email:* info@rochemeg.com, *Website:* www.rochemeg.com
Sunlight Agency, 8 Elnasr Street, El-Manshia Square, Alexandria, Arab Republic of Egypt, *Tel:* +20 3 487 5575, *Fax:* +20 3 487 5575, *Email:* sunlight@suezcanal.net, *Website:* www.sunlightagency.com

Shipping Agents: Ameaster Shipping & Trading Co. S.R.L., 20 Salah Salem Street, 6th Floor, Alexandria 21519, Arab Republic of Egypt, *Tel:* +20 3 486 1110, *Fax:* +20 3 487 0345, *Email:* info.alex@ameaster.com, *Website:* www.ameaster.com
Amon Shipping Agency, 71 El Horreia Street, Alexandria, Arab Republic of Egypt, *Tel:* +20 3 391 7045, *Fax:* +20 3 391 5650, *Email:* amon@maramon.com.eg, *Website:* www.maramon.com.eg
Arab Express Shipping Co., 59 El Horreya Street, Alexandria, Arab Republic of Egypt, *Tel:* +20 3 392 9706, *Fax:* +20 3 390 9696, *Email:* arabexpress@arabxprs.com, *Website:* www.arabxprs.com
B & G Shipping Agencies, Apartment 306, P O Box 2555, El Sarraya, 73 El Horeya Avenue, Alexandria, Arab Republic of Egypt, *Tel:* +20 3 495 0999, *Fax:* +20 3 494 6466, *Email:* general@bgshipping.com, *Website:* www.bgshipping.com
CMA-CGM S.A., CMA CGM Egypt, 55 Sultan Hussein - 1st Floor, El Azarita, Alexandria, Arab Republic of Egypt, *Tel:* +20 3 484 0170, *Fax:* +20 3 485 8943, *Email:* alx.genmbox@cma-cgm.com, *Website:* www.cma-cgm.com
Concord Shipping Agency, 1st Floor, El Hegaz Building, Memphis Street, Port Said, Arab Republic of Egypt, *Tel:* +20 66 325 2443, *Fax:* +20 66 323 4476, *Email:* office@concordshipping.com, *Website:* www.concordshipping.com
Demco Shipping & Logistics Co. SAE, 18 Sesostris Street, P O Box 227, Alexandria 21111, Arab Republic of Egypt, *Tel:* +20 3 487 4998, *Fax:* +20 3 487 7725, *Email:* demco@demcoshipping.com, *Website:* www.demcoshipping.com
Demline Egypt for Maritime Transport (Danube East Mediterranean Line), 77 Sultan Hussein Street, P O Box 1184, Alexandria 21519, Arab Republic of Egypt, *Tel:* +20 3 486 3438, *Fax:* +20 3 486 9614, *Email:* demline@globalnet.com.eg, *Website:* www.demline.com
Egyptian International Shipping Corp. (EISC), 8 Beni El Abbas Street, Azarita, P O Box 793, Alexandria, Arab Republic of Egypt, *Tel:* +20 3 486 2378, *Fax:* +20 3 487 0444, *Email:* eishipping_alex@eisgroup.com.eg, *Website:* www.eisgroup.com.eg
Egyptian Register of Shipping / International Maritime Services Co., 20 Salah Salam Street, Alexandria, Arab Republic of Egypt, *Tel:* +20 3 484 0817, *Fax:* +20 3 486 9177, *Email:* survey@egyptrs.com, *Website:* www.egyptrs.com
El Amira Shipping Agency, 1st Floor (A), 55 Sultan Hussein Street, Alexandria, Arab Republic of Egypt, *Tel:* +20 3 487 7099, *Fax:* +20 3 483 6900, *Email:* elamira@elamira.com, *Website:* www.elamira.com
Evge Egypt, Evge Shipping Agencies & Maritime Affairs SAE, 33 Safia Zaghloul Street, Alexandria 21131, Arab Republic of Egypt, *Tel:* +20 3 486 8052, *Fax:* +20 3 487 4566, *Email:* evgealex@evge-alex.com.eg, *Website:* www.evge-egypt.com
Finmar Shipping Co SAE, 3 Fernand Addah Street, El-Massalah, Ramleh Station, P O Box 1060, Alexandria, Arab Republic of Egypt, *Tel:* +20 3 486 1239, *Fax:* +20 3 484 0757, *Email:* opr-aly@finmarshipping.com, *Website:* www.finmarshipping.com
Gulf Agency Co. (Egypt) Ltd, 22 Bani El Abbassi Street, Pharanah, Bab Shark, P O Box 85, Alexandria 21111, Arab Republic of Egypt, *Tel:* +20 3 484 0256, *Fax:* +20 3 484 8480, *Email:* egypt@gacworld.com, *Website:* www.gacworld.com
Gulf Badr Group, 11 Hussein Nouh Street, Elhay Ellateeny, Alexandria 43511, Arab Republic of Egypt, *Tel:* +20 3 496 9771, *Fax:* +20 3 496 9665, *Email:* everaxd@gulfbadregypt.com, *Website:* www.gulfbadregypt.com
Ibramar Shipping Co S.A.E., Freeport Building - 5th Floor, Memphis and Nahda Street, Port Said, Arab Republic of Egypt, *Tel:* +20 66 333 9140, *Fax:* +20 66 332 4187, *Email:* portsaid@ibramar.com.eg, *Website:* www.ibramar.com
Inchcape Shipping Services (ISS), Office No.10, First Floor, Business Building, Central Road, Alexandria, Arab Republic of Egypt, *Tel:* +20 3 484 3565, *Fax:* +20 3 484 9323, *Email:* wael.azab@iss-shipping.com, *Website:* www.iss-shipping.com
International Associated Cargo Carriers (IACC), 95, 26 July Road û El Selsela Tower, Alexandria, Arab Republic of Egypt, *Tel:* +20 3 482 8428, *Fax:* +20 3 482 3793, *Email:* alex@iacc.net, *Website:* www.iacc.net
International Maritime Services Co., 20 Salah Salem, Alexandria, Arab Republic of Egypt, *Tel:* +20 3 484 0817, *Fax:* +20 3 486 9177, *Email:* agency@imsalex.com, *Website:* www.imsalex.com
International Shipping Enterprise S.A.E. (Intership), P O Box 281, Bani el-Abbas 8, Alexandria, Arab Republic of Egypt, *Tel:* +20 3 487 0837, *Fax:* +20 3 487 0444, *Email:* main@intershipegypt.com, *Website:* www.intershipegypt.com
Irano Misr Shipping Co., 6 El Horreya Avenue, Alexandria, Arab Republic of Egypt, *Tel:* +20 3 482 9295, *Fax:* +20 3 482 8608, *Email:* iranmisrco@menanet.net
Kadmar Shipping Co., 32 Saad Zaghloul Street, Alexandria 21131, Arab Republic of Egypt, *Tel:* +20 3 486 2832, *Fax:* +20 3 484 8326, *Email:* general@kadmar.com, *Website:* www.kadmar.com
Latt Trading & Shipping Co. SAE, Behind 30 Lumumba Street, El Obour Building, Shalalat, Alexandria 21131, Arab Republic of Egypt, *Tel:* +20 3 495 4795, *Fax:* +20 3 495 4794, *Email:* admin@latt.com.eg, *Website:* www.latt.com
Magic Shipping Agency, 1st Floor, Bank Misr Tower, 29 Port Said Street, Abu Qir, Alexandria, Arab Republic of Egypt, *Tel:* +20 3 562 8776, *Fax:* +20 3 562 8776, *Email:* magic_alex@magicshipping.com, *Website:* www.magicshipping.com
Mahoney Shipping & Marine Services Co., 31 Sultan Hussein Street, Ramla Station, P O Box 629, Alexandria 21519, Arab Republic of Egypt, *Tel:* +20 3 483 1000, *Fax:* +20 3 483 2000, *Email:* msms@mahoneyegypt.com, *Website:* www.mahoneyegypt.com
Marine & Engineering Services, 5 Ahmed Orabi Street, Manshi, Manshia, Alexandria, Arab Republic of Egypt, *Tel:* +20 3 484 4292, *Fax:* +20 3 484 4793, *Email:* monafahmy@mesco.com.eg, *Website:* www.mesco.com.eg
Mediterranean Shipping Company, MSC Egypt Alexandria, 55 Sultan Hussein Street, P O Box 670, Alexandria, Arab Republic of Egypt, *Tel:* +20 3 488 4000, *Fax:* +20 3 488 4001, *Email:* mscegypt@mscegypt.com, *Website:* www.mscgva.ch
Memphis Shipping Agency, 71 El Horreya Avenue, Alexandria, Arab Republic of Egypt, *Tel:* +20 3 393 7109, *Fax:* +20 3 391 9500, *Email:* commercial@memphis-eg.com, *Website:* www.memphis-eg.com

Key to Principal Facilities:—
A=Airport **C**=Containers **G**=General Cargo **P**=Petroleum **R**=Ro/Ro **Y**=Dry Bulk
B=Bunkers **D**=Dry Dock **L**=Cruise **Q**=Other Liquid Bulk **T**=Towage (where available from port)

Mideast Shipping Services, 12 Falaki Street, Alexandria, Arab Republic of Egypt, *Tel:* +20 3 482 3301, *Fax:* +20 3 487 8440, *Email:* msspts@bec.com.eg

Milmar Shipping Co., 8 Ahmed Orabi Street, Manshia, Alexandria, Arab Republic of Egypt, *Tel:* +20 3 484 3622, *Fax:* +20 3 484 3624, *Email:* milmar@milmar.com.eg

A.P. Moller-Maersk Group, Maersk Egypt S.A.E., 9 El-Batalsa Street, Al-Azarita, Alexandria 42111, Arab Republic of Egypt, *Tel:* +20 3 484 8101, *Fax:* +20 3 484 3319, *Email:* egymkt@maersk.com, *Website:* www.maerskline.com

Naggar Shipping Co., 20 Patrice Lumumba Street, Bab Sharki, P O Box 622, Alexandria 21131, Arab Republic of Egypt, *Tel:* +20 3 390 6000, *Fax:* +20 3 392 0909, *Email:* naggar@naggar.com, *Website:* www.naggar.com

National Shipping & Investment Co., 28 Tut Ankh Amoon Street, Smouha, Alexandria, Arab Republic of Egypt, *Tel:* +20 3 429 9112, *Fax:* +20 3 424 0208, *Email:* agency@national-shipping.com.eg, *Website:* www.national-shipping.com.eg

Racotis for Shipping, Behind 49 El Horreya Road, Raml Station, Alexandria, Arab Republic of Egypt, *Tel:* +20 3 392 5500, *Fax:* +20 3 391 7660, *Email:* racotis@racotis.com

RAFIMAR SAE, 9 Orabi Square, P O Box 2337, Al Manshia, Alexandria 21111, Arab Republic of Egypt, *Tel:* +20 3 484 0216, *Fax:* +20 3 484 0218, *Email:* agency@rafimar.com, *Website:* www.rafimar.com

Salamarine Egypt Co. Ltd, Behind 30 Patrice Lumumba Street, 5th Floor, Borg El Obour, Shalalat, Alexandria, Arab Republic of Egypt, *Tel:* +20 3 494 1663, *Fax:* +20 3 493 8405, *Email:* support@salamarine.com, *Website:* www.salamarine.com

Scan Arabia Shipping SAE, 19 El Pharana Street, El Shalalat, Alexandria, Arab Republic of Egypt, *Tel:* +20 3 484 3510, *Fax:* +20 3 486 9555

Sphinx Shipping Agency, El Safwa Building, 3 El Gaish & Mostafa Kamel Street, P O Box 1324, Port Said, Arab Republic of Egypt, *Tel:* +20 66 333 3891, *Fax:* +20 66 333 3895, *Email:* sphinx@sphinx-shipping.com, *Website:* www.sphinx-shipping.com

Tabadol Shipping Co, 35 Shahid Salah Moustapha Street, P O Box 25, Alexandria, Arab Republic of Egypt, *Tel:* +20 3 482 4557, *Fax:* +20 3 482 3999, *Email:* tabadol@dataxprs.com.eg

Unimas Shipping, 1 Digla Street, Raml Station, 5th Floor, P O Box 44, Ibrahimia, Alexandria 21312, Arab Republic of Egypt, *Tel:* +20 3 486 8800, *Fax:* +20 3 487 0230, *Email:* mail@unimas.com.eg, *Website:* www.unimasegypt.com

Wilhelmsen Ship Services, Barwil Egytrans Shipping Agencies SAE, 9 Hussein Hassab & Beny El-Abbasi Streets, Sultan Hussein, El-Zaher Building 2, Alexandria 21131, Arab Republic of Egypt, *Tel:* +20 3 484 3510, *Fax:* +20 3 484 9555, *Email:* barwil.alexandria@wilhelmsen.com, *Website:* www.barwilunitor.com

World Marine Corp, 29 Elnabi Danielle Street, Alexandria, Arab Republic of Egypt, *Tel:* +20 3 392 4576, *Fax:* +20 3 392 4621, *Email:* alexandria@worldmarineegypt.com.eg, *Website:* www.worldmarine.gr

Worms Alexandria Cargo Services, 47, Al Soltan Hussein Street, Al Khartoum Square, P O Box 2234, Alexandria, Arab Republic of Egypt, *Tel:* +20 3 486 5572, *Fax:* +20 3 487 6361, *Email:* wacs@wormsalx.com, *Website:* www.wormsalx.com

Stevedoring Companies: Concord Shipping Agency, 1st Floor, El Hegaz Building, Memphis Street, Port Said, Arab Republic of Egypt, *Tel:* +20 66 325 2443, *Fax:* +20 66 323 4476, *Email:* office@concordshipping.com, *Website:* www.concordshipping.com

Surveyors: Egyptian Register of Shipping / International Maritime Services Co., 20 Salah Salam Street, Alexandria, Arab Republic of Egypt, *Tel:* +20 3 484 0817, *Fax:* +20 3 486 9177, *Email:* survey@egyptrs.com, *Website:* www.egyptrs.com Managing Director: Capt M. Elsokarry

ABS (Europe), 5 Al Quiss Michael Abadir Street, Rushdy, P O Box 1717, Alexandria 21311, Arab Republic of Egypt, *Tel:* +20 3 544 4592, *Fax:* +20 3 544 4594, *Email:* absalexandria@eagle.org, *Website:* www.eagle.org

Alex Survey, 496 El Horeya Avenue, Bolkly, Alexandria, Arab Republic of Egypt, *Tel:* +20 3 583 0119, *Fax:* +20 3 582 9294, *Email:* alexsurvey@alexsurvey.com, *Website:* www.alexsurvey.com

Alexandria Maritime & Trading Center - Alexmar, 1 Hassan Alam Street, Behind Meridian Heliopolis, Misr Elgedidah, Cairo 11341, Arab Republic of Egypt, *Tel:* +20 2 2414 3681, *Fax:* +20 2 2415 1753, *Email:* alexmar@alexmar.com

Bureau Veritas, Flat 501 & 504, El Gawehara Tower, 601 El Horreya Road, Alexandria, Arab Republic of Egypt, *Tel:* +20 3 575 7510, *Fax:* +20 3 575 7515, *Email:* agel.shaban@eg.bureauveritas.com, *Website:* www.bureauveritas.com

Det Norske Veritas A/S, 1 Ibrahim Abdel-Sayed Street, Flat No.402, Bab-Sharki Quarter, Alexandria, Arab Republic of Egypt, *Tel:* +20 3 495 6718, *Fax:* +20 3 495 6719, *Email:* alexandria.office@dnv.com, *Website:* www.dnv.com

El Sharnoubygroup for Survey & Inspection, 6 Back El Nasr Street, Appartment 51/52, P O Box 323, Alexandria, Arab Republic of Egypt, *Tel:* +20 3 487 1931, *Fax:* +20 3 487 3693, *Email:* surveyors@sharnoubygroup.com, *Website:* www.sharnoubygroup.com

Germanischer Lloyd, 20 Mahmoud El Deeb Street Gleem, 2nd Floor, Alexandria, Arab Republic of Egypt, *Tel:* +20 3 584 2391, *Fax:* +20 3 584 2390, *Email:* gl-alexandria@gl-group.com, *Website:* www.gl-group.com

Global Surveyors, 6 Back El-Nasr Street, Gate No.10, 2nd Floor, Flat No.3,, P O Box 323, El Manshia, Alexandria, Arab Republic of Egypt, *Tel:* +20 3 487 1931, *Fax:* +20 3 487 3693, *Email:* surveyors@sharnobygroup.com, *Website:* www.sharnoubygroup.com

Hellenic Register of Shipping, 6 Awad Hegazy Street, Sidi Bishr, Alexandria 21411, Arab Republic of Egypt, *Tel:* +20 3 358 0700, *Fax:* +20 3 358 1773, *Email:* meconegypt@yahoo.com, *Website:* www.hrs.gr

International Shipping Bureau (ISB), Flat No.4, 1st Floor, Al Horia Mall, 23 Fawzi Moaaz Street, Smouha, Alexandria, Arab Republic of Egypt, *Tel:* +20 3 428 1888, *Fax:* +20 3 428 1888, *Email:* isbeg@gawab.com, *Website:* www.isbship.com

Korean Register of Shipping, 20 Mahmouod El Deeb Street, Gleem 2, Alexandria, Arab Republic of Egypt, *Tel:* +20 3 584 2391, *Fax:* +20 3 584 2390, *Email:* gl-alexandria@gl-group.com, *Website:* www.krs.co.kr

Marine Technical Services Ltd, 34 Salah El Din Street, El Laban, Alexandria, Arab Republic of Egypt, *Tel:* +20 3 494 1347, *Fax:* +20 3 391 3012, *Email:* mts-lloyds-alex@soficom.com.eg, *Website:* www.lloydsegypt.com

Matthews-Daniel Services (Bermuda) Ltd, Matthews-Daniel International (Egypt) Ltd, Taef Towers, Block B, Suite 441, Bhaled Ibn Walid Street, Alexandria, Arab Republic of Egypt, *Tel:* +20 3 555 1462, *Email:* mattdana@intouch.com, *Website:* www.matdan.com

Nippon Kaiji Kyokai, 4 Keneeset Debbana Street, Kism El Attarin, Alexandria, Arab Republic of Egypt, *Tel:* +20 3 486 3635, *Fax:* +20 3 484 0143, *Email:* ax@classnk.or.jp, *Website:* www.classnk.or.jp

Polish Register of Shipping, 50 El-Soufani Street, Sidi Gaber, Alexandria, Arab

Republic of Egypt, *Fax:* +20 3 543 4071, *Email:* edward.ewertowski@prs.pl, *Website:* www.prs.pl

Registro Italiano Navale (RINA), 51 Victor Amanuel Street, 4th Floor Apt. 19, Smouha, Alexandria, Arab Republic of Egypt, *Tel:* +20 3 427 5117, *Fax:* +20 3 427 5117, *Email:* assem355@hotmail.com, *Website:* www.rina.org

Societe Generale de Surveillance (SGS), SGS Egypt Ltd, 1 Youssef El Sharby Street, Alexandria, Arab Republic of Egypt, *Tel:* +20 3 545 2884, *Fax:* +20 3 545 2990, *Website:* www.sgs.com

Medical Facilities: Available

Airport: El Nozha, 10 km

Lloyd's Agent: Marine Technical Services Ltd, 34 Salah El Din Street, El Laban, Alexandria, Arab Republic of Egypt, *Tel:* +20 3 494 1347, *Fax:* +20 3 391 3012, *Email:* mts-lloyds-alex@soficom.com.eg, *Website:* www.lloydsegypt.com

DAMIETTA

Lat 31° 23' N; Long 31° 48' E.

Admiralty Chart: 2578	**Admiralty Pilot:** 49
Time Zone: GMT +2 h	**UNCTAD Locode:** EG DAM

Principal Facilities:

Q	Y	G	C	R		B		T	A

Authority: Damietta Port Authority, P O Box 13, Damietta, Arab Republic of Egypt, *Tel:* +20 57 325928 & 325940, *Fax:* +20 57 325930, *Website:* www.dam-port.com

Officials: Chairman: Rear Admiral Mohamed Ibrahim Youssef.

Port Security: ISPS compliant

Approach: Access is obtained via an entrance channel 11 km long, 15 m depth and 300 m wide reducing to 250 m wide when approaching the breakwaters. The channel is marked with 18 buoys. The outside waiting area is marked with 5 buoys. Two breakwaters, the E is 450 m long and the W is 1500 m long

Anchorage: Waiting area marked by buoys in positions: N Buoy 31° 36' 43" N, 31° 44' 58" E. W Buoy 31° 35' 41" N, 31° 44' 33" E. Middle Buoy 31° 35' 33" N, 31° 45' 20" E. E Buoy 31° 35' 25" N, 31° 46' 06" E. NE Buoy 31° 36' 30" N, 31° 46' 12" E. Depth of 18.0 m

Pilotage: Compulsory. Masters of vessels must inform Damietta Port Authority by cable 7 days before ETA, with confirmation 24 h prior

Radio Frequency: VHF Channel 14

Weather: Prevailing winds N to NW

Tides: Rise of tide 0.5 m

Traffic: 2006, 25 278 000 t of cargo handled

Maximum Vessel Dimensions: Containers: 290 m loa, 12.4 m d, 56 135 dwt. Bulk: 254 m loa, 11.5 m d, 39 537 dwt. Bulk/general cargo: 271 m loa, 12.0 m d, 65 000 dwt

Principal Imports and Exports: Imports: Cement, General cargo, Timber. Exports: Bulk cargo, Fertilizers, Fruit & vegetables.

Working Hours: 24 h/day in 3 shifts

Accommodation:

Name	Length (m)	Depth (m)	Remarks
Damietta			See [1] below
Container Berths 1-4	1050	14.5	See [2] below
General Cargo Berths 5-12	1700	12	Used for general cargo
Grain Berths 13-14	600	14.5	Used for bulk cargo (grain), vessels up to 80 000 dwt

Name	Length (m)	Depth (m)	Remarks
Multi-Purpose Berths 15-16	600	14.5	Used for multi-purpose vessels

[1]*Damietta:* Covering a surface area of about 9 km. The harbour is protected by two breakwaters, 1500 m and 450 m long. There are a total of 14 berths for ocean-going vessels. There is also 700 m of secondary berthing for small vessels in depth of 4.5 m

Spanish Egyptian Gas Company (SEGAS) liquefied natural gas (LNG) single train facility in Damietta exporting LNG to a receiving terminal at Sagunto

[2]*Container Berths 1-4:* Container terminal operated by Damietta Container & Cargo Handling Co., P O Box 11, Damietta 34511, Tel: +20 57 326746, Fax: +20 57 326745, Email: damietta@dchc.com.eg

Equipment includes six 40 t container gantry cranes and mobile cranes up to 40 t cap. Container yard of 465 000 m2

Storage: Steel storage yards of 33 000 m2, timber storage yards of 33 000 m2, western general cargo yards of 60 000 m2, eastern general cargo yards of 40 000 m2, yards between berths 8-9 of 60 000 m2, clinker storage yards of 70 000 m2 and covered warehouses of 40 000 m2

Mechanical Handling Equipment:

Location	Type	Capacity (t)	Qty	Remarks
Damietta	Mult-purp. Cranes	25	3	owned by DCHC
Damietta	Mobile Cranes	40	14	owned by DCHC
Damietta	Container Cranes	40	6	owned by DCHC
Damietta	Transtainers	15	3	owned by DCHC
Damietta	Forklifts	15	11	owned by DCHC
Damietta	Yard Tractors		30	owned by DCHC

Cargo Worked: Packed cargo 200-250 t/shift/hold, timber 200-400 t/shift/hold, equipment 200-300 t/shift/hold

Bunkering: All grades can be supplied
Bominflot, Bominflot Ltd, 5-7 Ravensbourne Road, Bromley, Kent BR1 1HN, United Kingdom, *Tel:* +44 20 8315 5400, *Fax:* +44 20 8315 5429, *Email:* mail@bominflot.co.uk, *Website:* www.bominflot.net
BP Marketing Egypt, P O Box 1254, 42 Road 17, Digla, Madi, Cairo, Arab Republic of Egypt, *Tel:* +20 2 706 2345, *Fax:* +20 2 768 8075, *Email:* info@bp.com, *Website:* www.bp.com
Chevron Marine Products LLC, Chevron Products UK Ltd, 1 Westferry Circus, Canary Wharf, London E14 4HA, United Kingdom, *Tel:* +44 20 7719 4680, *Fax:* +44 20 7719 5151, *Email:* gmpukb@chevron.com, *Website:* www.chevron.com
Cockett Marine Oil Ltd, Carrick House, 36 Station Square, Petts Wood, Kent BR5 1NA, United Kingdom, *Tel:* +44 1689 883 400, *Fax:* +44 1689 877 666, *Email:* enquiries@cockett.com, *Website:* www.cockettgroup.com
ExxonMobil Marine Fuels, Mailpoint 31, ExxonMobil House, Ermyn Way, Leatherhead, Surrey KT22 8UX, United Kingdom, *Tel:* +44 1372 222 000, *Fax:* +44 1372 223 922, *Email:* marine.fuels@exxonmobil.com, *Website:* www.exxonmobil.com
Maxcom Bunker S.p.A. u.s., Via Bartolomeo Bosco 57/7B, 16121 Genoa, Italy, *Tel:* +39 010 5605 200, *Fax:* +39 010 564 479, *Email:* bunker@maxcombunker.com, *Website:* www.maxcombunker.com
Misr Petroleum Co., MISR Petroleum House, 6 Orabi Square, P O Box 228, Cairo, Arab Republic of Egypt, *Tel:* +20 2 2574 5400, *Fax:* +20 2 2574 5436, *Email:* bunker@misrpetroleum.com, *Website:* www.misrpetroleum.com
Oil Shipping B.V., Oil Shipping B.V., Vasteland 6, 3011 BK Rotterdam, Netherlands, *Tel:* +31 10 4000 888, *Fax:* +31 10 4117 953, *Email:* rotterdambrokers@wfscorp.com, *Website:* www.wfscorp.com
Petrolube Misr Saudi Arabian Lubricating Oil Co., P O Box 1120, 52 Lebanon Street, Mohandessen, Cairo 11511, Arab Republic of Egypt, *Tel:* +20 2 305 4670, *Fax:* +20 2 305 4811, *Email:* petrowafaa2002@hotmail.com
Shell Marketing Egypt, Corner Street 254 & 206, Degla Maadi, Cairo 11742, Arab Republic of Egypt, *Tel:* +20 2 519 8817, *Fax:* +20 2 519 8818
Societe Cooperative des Petroles (Copetrole), Cooperative Building, 94 Kasr El Eini Street, Cairo 11621, Arab Republic of Egypt, *Tel:* +20 2 2792 5221, *Fax:* +20 2 2795 6404, *Email:* co_op@link.net
Solimanco Marine Services, P O Box 202, Port Said Free Zone, Port Said 42111, Arab Republic of Egypt, *Tel:* +20 66 341641, *Fax:* +20 66 232262, *Email:* mohamed1969@mail.interlink-eg.com
Total France S.A., Total Marine Fuels, 51 Esplanade du General de Gaulle, F-92907 Paris la Defense Cedex 10, France, *Tel:* +33 1 4135 2755, *Fax:* +33 1 4197 0291, *Email:* marine.fuels@total.com, *Website:* www.marinefuels.total.com
Tramp Oil & Marine, World Fuel Services Corporation, 13th Floor, Portland House, Bressenden Place, London SW1E 5BH, United Kingdom, *Tel:* +44 20 7808 5000, *Fax:* +44 20 7808 5088, *Email:* pturner@wfscorp.com, *Website:* www.wfscorp.com
Universal Maritime Agency & Trading Co. Ltd (Umatco), 2444 Marisa Ct., Mississauga, Ont., Canada, *Tel:* +1 905 823 4638, *Fax:* +1 905 823 3938, *Email:* umatco@sympatico.ca
World Marine Egypt, 12 Salah Salem Street, Port Said, Arab Republic of Egypt, *Tel:* +20 66 325327, *Fax:* +20 66 326114

Waste Reception Facilities: Anti-pollution boat of 2 x 115 hp and a shipwaste reception unit of 1 x 500 hp (700 t cap)

Towage: Five tugs available of 20-32 t bollard pull

Ship Chandlers: Edwardo Marine Services Co., P O Box 179, Port Said, Arab Republic of Egypt, *Tel:* +20 66 623 0031, *Fax:* +20 66 632 2134, *Email:* info@edwardomarine.com, *Website:* www.edwardomarine.com
The International Marine Services Co. (S.A.E.), P O Box 141, Port Said, Arab Republic of Egypt, *Tel:* +20 66 322 3601, *Fax:* +20 66 332 1925, *Email:* marinco@bec.com.eg
Lucky Dolphin Marine Services, El-Omraa Tower, El-Geish & Saphia Zaghlol Streets, P O Box 701, Port Said 42111, Arab Republic of Egypt, *Tel:* +20 66 324 4848, *Fax:* +20 66 333 3378, *Email:* info@luckydolphin.com, *Website:* www.luckydolphin.com

Shipping Agents: Ibramar Shipping Co S.A.E., Freeport Building - 5th Floor, Memphis and Nahda Street, Port Said, Arab Republic of Egypt, *Tel:* +20 66 333 9140, *Fax:* +20 66 332 4187, *Email:* portsaid@ibramar.com.eg, *Website:* www.ibramar.com
Managing Director: Omar Momen
Alexandria Maritime Services, Damietta Port Investment Building, First Upper Floor - Western Suite - Office No.233, Damietta, Arab Republic of Egypt, *Tel:* +20 57 290092, *Email:* alexmar@alexmaregypt.com, *Website:* www.alexmaregypt.com

CMA-CGM S.A., CMA CGM Egypt, Damietta Port, P O Box 11, Damietta, Arab Republic of Egypt, *Tel:* +20 57 290107, *Fax:* +20 57 290122, *Email:* dmt.mkhalil@cma-cgm.com, *Website:* www.cma-cgm.com
Concord Shipping Agency, 1st Floor, El Hegaz Building, Memphis Street, Port Said, Arab Republic of Egypt, *Tel:* +20 66 325 2443, *Fax:* +20 66 323 4476, *Email:* office@concordshipping.com, *Website:* www.concordshipping.com
Egyptian International Shipping Corp. (EISC), 3rd Floor, Damietta Container Terminal Building, Damietta, Arab Republic of Egypt, *Tel:* +20 57 373705, *Fax:* +20 57 373709, *Email:* eishipping_dam@eisgroup.com.eg, *Website:* www.eisgroup.com.eg
Finmar Shipping Co SAE, Investment Building, 1st Floor, Damietta, Arab Republic of Egypt, *Tel:* +20 57 290221, *Email:* finmar@finmarshipping.com, *Website:* www.finmarshipping.com
Gulf Agency Co. (Egypt) Ltd, 229 Investors Building, Damietta Port, Damietta, Arab Republic of Egypt, *Tel:* +20 57 291122, *Fax:* +20 57 291226, *Email:* egypt@gacworld.com, *Website:* www.gacworld.com
Gulf Badr Group, New Damietta Consultation Building, Room 307, 2 Floor, P O Box 77, Damietta 42111, Arab Republic of Egypt, *Tel:* +20 57 290009, *Fax:* +20 57 290009, *Email:* biz-dmx@gulfbadregypt.com, *Website:* www.gulfbadregypt.com
Kadmar Shipping Co., Damietta Port, The investment Building, Office 206, Damietta, Arab Republic of Egypt, *Tel:* +20 57 291777, *Fax:* +20 57 291777, *Email:* damietta@kadmar.com, *Website:* www.kadmar.com
Magic Shipping Agency, Damietta Port, 3rd Floor, Office No.33, Investment Building, Damietta, Arab Republic of Egypt, *Tel:* +20 57 290878, *Fax:* +20 57 290878, *Email:* magic_dam@magicshipping.com, *Website:* www.magicshipping.com
Mahoney Shipping & Marine Services Co., Investment Building, Office 211, 2nd Floor, Damietta, Arab Republic of Egypt, *Tel:* +20 57 290022, *Fax:* +20 57 570023, *Email:* damietta@mahoneyegypt.com, *Website:* www.mahoneyegypt.com
A.P. Moller-Maersk Group, Maersk Egypt S.A.E., Damietta Port Authority Investment Building, Damietta Port, Damietta, Arab Republic of Egypt, *Tel:* +20 57 290114/5, *Fax:* +20 57 290117, *Email:* egymkt@maersk.com, *Website:* www.maerskline.com
Naggar Shipping Co., Containers Building, Damietta Port, Damietta, Arab Republic of Egypt, *Tel:* +20 57 320727, *Fax:* +20 57 334796, *Email:* naggardai@naggar.com
Sphinx Shipping Agency, El Safwa Building, 3 El Gaish & Mostafa Kamel Street, P O Box 1324, Port Said, Arab Republic of Egypt, *Tel:* +20 66 333 3891, *Fax:* +20 66 333 3895, *Email:* sphinx@sphinx-shipping.com, *Website:* www.sphinx-shipping.com
Worms Alexandria Cargo Services, P O Box 11, Damietta 34511, Arab Republic of Egypt, *Tel:* +20 57 343650, *Fax:* +20 57 343562, *Email:* wormsdoc@dataxprs.com.eg

Stevedoring Companies: Concord Shipping Agency, 1st Floor, El Hegaz Building, Memphis Street, Port Said, Arab Republic of Egypt, *Tel:* +20 66 325 2443, *Fax:* +20 66 323 4476, *Email:* office@concordshipping.com, *Website:* www.concordshipping.com
Damietta Container & Cargo Handling Co., P O Box 11, Damietta, Arab Republic of Egypt, *Tel:* +20 57 326746, *Fax:* +20 57 326745, *Email:* damietta@dchc.com.eg

Surveyors: El Sharnoubygroup for Survey & Inspection, P O Box 90, Damietta, Arab Republic of Egypt, *Tel:* +20 57 341001, *Fax:* +20 57 341001

Medical Facilities: Hospitals at Ras el Bar, 6 km and Damietta, 8 km

Airport: Cairo International, 250 km. Alexandria International, 150 km

Railway: Damietta Railway Station, 8 km. Three railway lines serve the port

Development: New 2360 m container terminal under construction to be operated by KGL Ports International, www.kglpi.com. In the first phase the terminal will have a throughput cap of 2.5 million TEU's/year by August 2009

Lloyd's Agent: Marine Technical Services Ltd, 34 Salah El Din Street, El Laban, Alexandria, Arab Republic of Egypt, *Tel:* +20 3 494 1347, *Fax:* +20 3 391 3012, *Email:* mts-lloyds-alex@soficom.com.eg, *Website:* www.lloydsegypt.com

EAST ZEIT TERMINAL

harbour area, see under Zeit Bay Terminal

EL ALAMEIN

alternate name, see Mersa el Hamra Terminal

EL DEKHEILA

Lat 31° 7' N; Long 29° 47' E.

Admiralty Chart: 302/3119	**Admiralty Pilot:** 49
Time Zone: GMT +2 h	**UNCTAD Locode:** EG EDK

Principal Facilities:

Y	G	C	R		B		T	A

Key to Principal Facilities:—			
A=Airport	**C**=Containers	**G**=General Cargo	**P**=Petroleum	**R**=Ro/Ro	**Y**=Dry Bulk
B=Bunkers	**D**=Dry Dock	**L**=Cruise	**Q**=Other Liquid Bulk	**T**=Towage (where available from port)	

Authority: Port of El Dekheila, c/o Alexandria Port Authority, 106 El Horreia Street, Alexandria, Arab Republic of Egypt, *Tel:* +20 3 440 8395/6, *Fax:* +20 3 440 8397, *Website:* www.alexportic.net

Port Security: ISPS compliant

Approach: Access channel 3.5 km long, dredged to a depth of 20 m

Anchorage: Waiting area in position 31°13' N - 29°45' E with depths of 35-55 m. The area is very exposed and sometimes untenable in winter
Access channel is 3.5 km long and dredged to a depth of 20 m

Pilotage: Compulsory. Under supervision of the Alexandria Port Authority

Weather: Prevailing winds from W to NW, force 2-3 in summer and 4-7 in winter

Tides: Rise of tide from 0.3 m to 0.45 m

Traffic: 2006, 5033 vessels, 39 300 000 t of cargo handled, 783 300 TEU's (includes Alexandria)

Maximum Vessel Dimensions: 165 000 dwt, 20.0 m d

Principal Imports and Exports: Imports: Coal, Maize, Pallets, Scrap, Soya. Exports: Salt, Soya, Steel.

Working Hours: 24 h/day

Accommodation:

Name	Length (m)	Depth (m)	Draught (m)	Remarks
El Dekheila				
General Cargo	800	14–15		Two berths available
Ore and Bulk	600	16–20	20	See [1] below
Dry Bulk			13	See [2] below
Break Bulk			9–12	See [3] below
ACCH Container Terminal	1045	12–14		See [4] below
AICT Container Terminal	510	10–12		See [5] below

[1]*Ore and Bulk:* Mineral jetty for vessels up to 165 000 dwt
[2]*Dry Bulk:* Berth 1 has a length of 268 m for vessels up to 70 000 dwt. Berth 2 has a length of 315 m for vessels up to 160 000 dwt
[3]*Break Bulk:* Two berths with 9 m draft and a total length of 250 m. Six berths with 12 m draft and a total length of 1080 m
[4]*ACCH Container Terminal:* Owned and managed by Alexandria Container & Cargo Handling Co., Tel: +20 3 480 0633, Fax: +20 3 486 2124, Email: alexcont@alexcont.com, Website: www.alexcont.com
Terminal area of 380 000 m2 with storage cap for 15 000 TEU's and 400 reefer points
[5]*AICT Container Terminal:* Operated by Alexandria International Container Terminals, 5 Mena Street, Kafr Abdu, Roshdy, Alexandria, Tel: +20 3 523 3312, Fax: +20 3 546 7198
Terminal area of 19 ha

Storage:

Location	Open (m²)	Covered (m²)
El Dekheila	829000	14355
General Cargo	760000	14355

Mechanical Handling Equipment:

Location	Type	Capacity (t)	Qty
El Dekheila	Mult-purp. Cranes	40	2
ACCH Container Terminal	Post Panamax	45	5
AICT Container Terminal	Container Cranes		2
AICT Container Terminal	RTG's		7

Cargo Worked: Ore 35 000 t/day in two shifts. Coal 15 000 t/day in two shifts. Grains 6000-8000 t/day. Scrap 6000 t/day

Bunkering: All grades available
ExxonMobil Marine Fuels, Mailpoint 31, ExxonMobil House, Ermyn Way, Leatherhead, Surrey KT22 8UX, United Kingdom, *Tel:* +44 1372 222 000, *Fax:* +44 1372 223 922, *Email:* marine.fuels@exxonmobil.com, *Website:* www.exxonmobil.com
Macoil International S.A., Macoil Building, 103 Kallirois Street, 176 71 Athens, Greece, *Tel:* +30 210 9249 175, *Fax:* +30 210 9249 170, *Email:* macoil@otenet.gr
Misr Petroleum Co., MISR Petroleum House, 6 Orabi Square, P O Box 228, Cairo, Arab Republic of Egypt, *Tel:* +20 2 2574 5400, *Fax:* +20 2 2574 5436, *Email:* bunker@misrpetroleum.com, *Website:* www.misrpetroleum.com
Petrolube Misr Saudi Arabian Lubricating Oil Co., P O Box 1120, 52 Lebanon Street, Mohandessen, Cairo 11511, Arab Republic of Egypt, *Tel:* +20 2 305 4670, *Fax:* +20 2 305 4811, *Email:* petrowafaa2002@hotmail.com
Solimanco Marine Services, P O Box 202, Port Said Free Zone, Port Said 42111, Arab Republic of Egypt, *Tel:* +20 66 341641, *Fax:* +20 66 232262, *Email:* mohamed1969@mail.interlink-eg.com

Towage: Compulsory for vessels over 82.3 m loa. Tugs from 1800-2500 hp available all the time

Repair & Maintenance: See under Alexandria

Medical Facilities: Available

Airport: El Nozha, 20 km

Railway: Misr Railway Station, 12 km

Lloyd's Agent: Marine Technical Services Ltd, 34 Salah El Din Street, El Laban, Alexandria, Arab Republic of Egypt, *Tel:* +20 3 494 1347, *Fax:* +20 3 391 3012, *Email:* mts-lloyds-alex@soficom.com.eg, *Website:* www.lloydsegypt.com

EL TUR

Lat 28° 13' N; Long 33° 37' E.

Admiralty Chart: 2374	**Admiralty Pilot:** 64
Time Zone: GMT +2 h	**UNCTAD Locode:** EG

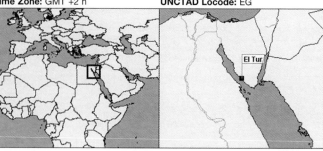

Principal Facilities:

	Y	G	C	R		B		A

Authority: Maridive Offshore Projects (S.A.E.), 10 Ahmed Yehia Street, Alexandria, Arab Republic of Egypt, *Tel:* +20 3 585 2891, *Fax:* +20 3 583 4668, *Email:* projects@mosalex.com, *Website:* www.mosalex.com

Officials: General Manager: Mostafa Ashour.
Operations Manager: Capt Mohamed Youssef.
Harbour Master: Mohamed Kamel.

Port Security: Permanent security, safety and environmental control

Pilotage: Compulsory. Vessel's should advise ETA via agent 72 h, 48 h and 24 h prior to arrival and confirm ETA at pilot station in pos 28° 13.6' N; 33° 35' E

Traffic: 2005, 665 vessels

Working Hours: 24 h/day

Accommodation:

Name	Length (m)	Depth (m)	Remarks
El Tur			Serves the offshore oil industry in the Gulf of Suez
Jetty	75	6	

Storage:

Location	Covered (m²)
El Tur	5600

Mechanical Handling Equipment:

Location	Type	Capacity (t)	Remarks
El Tur	Mult-purp. Cranes	22	See [1] below

[1]*El Tur:* Larger capacities can be arranged with 48 h notice

Bunkering: Fuel oil supplied at 20 t/h with 48 h notice

Medical Facilities: Hospitals available

Lloyd's Agent: Marine Technical Services Ltd, Flat 6B, 28 Cherif Street, Cairo, Arab Republic of Egypt, *Tel:* +20 2 2393 5724, *Fax:* +20 2 2393 8669, *Email:* mts-lloyds-cairo@soficom.com.eg, *Website:* www.lloydsegypt.com

GEISUM TERMINAL

Lat 27° 38' N; Long 33° 43' E.

Admiralty Chart: 2375	**Admiralty Pilot:** 64
Time Zone: GMT +2 h	**UNCTAD Locode:** EG GEI

Principal Facilities:

P								

Authority: The Egyptian General Petroleum Corp., Palestine Street, 4th Sector, New Maadi, Cairo, Arab Republic of Egypt, *Tel:* +20 2 353 1471, *Fax:* +20 2 377 5962, *Email:* info@egpc.com.eg

Anchorage: There is an anchorage area in pos 27° 43' 09" N, 33° 45' E

Pilotage: Compulsory. Mooring master boards at the anchorage

Radio Frequency: Continuous watch maintained on VHF Channel 16. Contact terminal 72, 48 and 24 h prior to arrival

Weather: Winds N-NW, average speed 12 knots

Tides: Range of tide 0.61 m-0.91 m

Maximum Vessel Dimensions: Min dwt 20 000 t, max dwt 150 000 t, max loa 270 m, no draft restriction

Working Hours: 24 h/day

Accommodation:

Name	Remarks
Geisum Terminal	See [1] below

[1]*Geisum Terminal:* A floating production and storage tanker Al Kahera 1, operated by Geisum Oil Co., 30 Road 276, New Maadi, (PO Box 282, Maadi), Tel: +20 352 9414/5, Fax: +20 352 9423, in a depth of 50 m. Loading is via 12'' hoses with 150 lbs ASA flanges. Vessels calling at the facility must be equipped with cranes min cap 5 t. Loading rate 2500-3500 t/h. No night berthing. There is a ballast facility available

Medical Facilities: Hospital at Hurghada

Lloyd's Agent: Marine Technical Services Ltd, Flat 6B, 28 Cherif Street, Cairo, Arab Republic of Egypt, *Tel:* +20 2 2393 5724, *Fax:* +20 2 2393 8669, *Email:* mts-lloyds-cairo@soficom.com.eg, *Website:* www.lloydsegypt.com

HAMRAWEIN

Lat 26° 15' N; Long 34° 12' E.

Admiralty Chart: 159	**Admiralty Pilot:** 64
Time Zone: GMT +2 h	**UNCTAD Locode:** EG HAM

Principal Facilities:

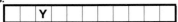

Authority: El Nasr Mining Co. (N.M.C.), El Mahamid, Edfo, Aswan, Arab Republic of Egypt, *Tel:* +20 97 711073, *Fax:* +20 97 711074, *Email:* elnasrmining@elnasrmining.com, *Website:* www.elnasrmining.com

Approach: There are sand bars

Anchorage: Anchorage in depths up to 22.2 m

Pilotage: Compulsory

Weather: Spring N winds with the occasional S wind

Maximum Vessel Dimensions: 170 m loa, 40 000 dwt

Principal Imports and Exports: Exports: Phosphate.

Working Hours: 24 h/day

Accommodation:

Name	Remarks
Hamrawein	See [1] below

[1]*Hamrawein:* Four mooring buoys. One phosphate loading quay 167 m long in depth of 14 m with draught of 9.75 m. Conveyor belt and a mechanical loader are available

Cargo Worked: 4500 t phosphate loaded daily

Medical Facilities: Central hospital at Kosseir

Lloyd's Agent: Marine Technical Services Ltd, Flat 6B, 28 Cherif Street, Cairo, Arab Republic of Egypt, *Tel:* +20 2 2393 5724, *Fax:* +20 2 2393 8669, *Email:* mts-lloyds-cairo@soficom.com.eg, *Website:* www.lloydsegypt.com

HURGHADA

Lat 27° 15' N; Long 33° 49' E.

Admiralty Chart: 3043	**Admiralty Pilot:** 64
Time Zone: GMT +2 h	**UNCTAD Locode:** EG HRG

Principal Facilities:

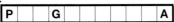

Authority: Red Sea Ports Authority, Hurghada, Arab Republic of Egypt, *Tel:* +20 65 442813, *Fax:* +20 65 442813

Approach: Gifatin Channel is entered from the N between Franken Point and the reef 1.5 km ESE, and from the S between Sha'b el-Lug and Umm Agawish el-kebir. Min depth in channel 7.3 m

Anchorage: Anchorage is obtainable in 16-18 m

Weather: Strong N winds can create a considerable sea

Maximum Vessel Dimensions: 100 m loa, 7.32 m max d

Accommodation:

Name	Length (m)	Depth (m)	Remarks
Hurghada			
North Pier			See [1] below
South Pier	15	7.3	See [2] below

[1]*Hurghada:* Tankers normally berth at the North Pier and the South Pier is connected by pipelines to the oil tanks

[2]*South Pier:* Vessels berth alongside with an anchor SE and a hawser from the stern to the hauling off buoy

Medical Facilities: Oil Company clinic available

Airport: Hurghada International

Lloyd's Agent: Marine Technical Services Ltd, 4th Floor, Units 19 & 20, El Freepor Building, El Nahda & Palestine Streets, Port Said, Arab Republic of Egypt, *Tel:* +20 66 335 5423, *Fax:* +20 66 334 3974, *Email:* mts-lloyds-portsaid@soficom.com.eg, *Website:* www.lloydsegypt.com

IDKU

Lat 31° 21' N; Long 30° 18' E.

Admiralty Chart: 2681	**Admiralty Pilot:** 49
Time Zone: GMT +2 h	**UNCTAD Locode:** EG

Principal Facilities:

Authority: Egyptian Operating Company for Natural Gas Liquefaction Projects S.A.E., 2 Port Said Street, Maadi, Cairo, Arab Republic of Egypt, *Tel:* +20 2 751 5075, *Fax:* +20 2 751 5079, *Email:* port-operations@egyptianlng.com, *Website:* www.egyptianlng.com

Officials: Port Manager: Sherif Keshk.

Approach: Approach channel 4000 m long, 230 m wide over the length of 3100 m from the seaward end and widening to 460 m over a 900 m distance towards the turning basin. It is dredged to a min depth of 14 m below CD

Anchorage: A designated waiting area is located NW of the approach channel centred on pos 31° 27.6' N; 30° 13.6' E within a 1 nautical mile radius

Pilotage: Compulsory. Vessels should advise ETA 72 h, 48 h, 24 h and 6 h prior to arrival at the pilot boarding area. Pilot boarding area in pos 31° 26.40' N; 30° 13.55' E

Radio Frequency: The port maintains watch on VHF Channels 16 and 17, and operates on VHF Channel 12

Maximum Vessel Dimensions: 300 m loa, 50 m beam, 11.7 m draft. LNG tankers of 40 000-160 000 m3 cap

Principal Imports and Exports: Exports: LNG.

Working Hours: Day time hours of operation only

Accommodation:

Name	Remarks
Idku LNG Port	See [1] below

[1]*Idku LNG Port:* Situated on approx 164 ha in Abu Qir Bay, 3 km from the town of Idku and 40 km E of Alexandria. Onshore liquefaction plant with a 2.4 km trestle style loading jetty in depth of 13 m. At the jetty head is a LNG berth comprising of a loading platform with three loading arms and one vapour return arm. Four breasting dolphins and six mooring dolphins facilitate mooring of the LNG tanker to the berth. Total storage cap of 280 000 m3 (2 x 140 000 m3 tanks)

Towage: Four tugs available of 6000 hp

Airport: Alexandria - Al Nozha

Railway: Railway available to Cairo every hour 6 am - 8 pm

Development: Production of LNG is due to start in 2005

Lloyd's Agent: Marine Technical Services Ltd, 34 Salah El Din Street, El Laban, Alexandria, Arab Republic of Egypt, *Tel:* +20 3 494 1347, *Fax:* +20 3 391 3012, *Email:* mts-lloyds-alex@soficom.com.eg, *Website:* www.lloydsegypt.com

---

Key to Principal Facilities:—

A=Airport	**C**=Containers	**G**=General Cargo
B=Bunkers	**D**=Dry Dock	**L**=Cruise

P=Petroleum	**R**=Ro/Ro	**Y**=Dry Bulk
Q=Other Liquid Bulk	**T**=Towage (where available from port)	

ISKANDARIYA

alternate name, see Alexandria

MERSA EL HAMRA TERMINAL

Lat 30° 59' N; Long 28° 52' E.

Admiralty Chart: 3326
Time Zone: GMT +2 h

Admiralty Pilot: 49
UNCTAD Locode: EG MAH

Principal Facilities:

P											

Authority: Western Desert Petroleum Co. (WEPCO), P O Box 412, Alexandria, Arab Republic of Egypt, *Tel:* +20 3 495 9203, *Fax:* +20 3 496 0963, *Email:* wepcoalex@wepcoalex.com

Officials: Operations Manager: Ing Bassiouny Mokhtar, *Tel:* +20 3 392 8214, *Email:* operationsgm@wepcoalex.com.

Port Security: ISPS compliant

Pilotage: Compulsory. Mooring master will meet vessels

Accommodation:

Name	Remarks
Mersa el Hamra Terminal	See [1] below

[1]*Mersa el Hamra Terminal:* The Mono Mooring Buoy is in an open and unsheltered roadstead located at pos 30° 58' 07" N, 28° 52' 02" E. It is 84.4 km on a bearing of 225° from Ras-el-Tin lighthouse, Alexandria and 4.8 km offshore in approx 20.1 m of water. Vessels up to 100 000 dwt can be accommodated. Two 12'' floating hoses; max loading rate 3700 t/h

Lloyd's Agent: Marine Technical Services Ltd, Flat 6B, 28 Cherif Street, Cairo, Arab Republic of Egypt, *Tel:* +20 2 2393 5724, *Fax:* +20 2 2393 8669, *Email:* mts-lloyds-cairo@soficom.com.eg, *Website:* www.lloydsegypt.com

MERSA MATRUH

Lat 31° 22' N; Long 27° 14' E.

Admiralty Chart: 3400
Time Zone: GMT +2 h

Admiralty Pilot: 49
UNCTAD Locode: EG

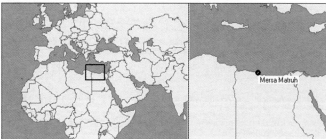

Principal Facilities:

			G	C	R					

Authority: Head of Maritime Transport Sector, Ptolemy Street, Mazarita, Alexandria, Arab Republic of Egypt, *Tel:* +20 3 484 2631, *Fax:* +20 3 484 2041, *Email:* mmt@idsc.net.eg

Accommodation:

Name	Remarks
Mersa Matruh	See [1] below

[1]*Mersa Matruh:* The existing harbour and port area is used for Naval purposes. Deepwater quays have been built providing berthing space of about 1000 m. The entrance channel and turning circle will be dredged to a depth of 9.0 m. Facilities for container handling and ro/ro vessels are to be constructed, accommodating vessels of up to 8000 dwt and 8.0 m d. Cap of the port is envisaged to be 1.2 million t/year and it is possible that it will be used as a container feeder port, serving other ports along the north African coast

Bunkering: Macoil International S.A., Macoil Building, 103 Kallirois Street, 176 71 Athens, Greece, *Tel:* +30 210 9249 175, *Fax:* +30 210 9249 170, *Email:* macoil@otenet.gr

Lloyd's Agent: Marine Technical Services Ltd, Flat 6B, 28 Cherif Street, Cairo, Arab Republic of Egypt, *Tel:* +20 2 2393 5724, *Fax:* +20 2 2393 8669, *Email:* mts-lloyds-cairo@soficom.com.eg, *Website:* www.lloydsegypt.com

MINA DUMYAT

alternate name, see Damietta

NUWEIBA

Lat 28° 58' N; Long 34° 38' E.

Admiralty Chart: 159
Time Zone: GMT +2 h

Admiralty Pilot: 64
UNCTAD Locode: EG NUW

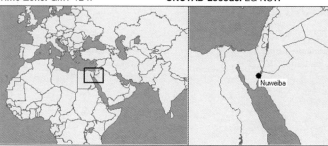

Principal Facilities:

					R		B		T	A	

Authority: Red Sea Ports Authority, Port of Nuweiba, Nuweiba, Arab Republic of Egypt, *Tel:* +20 62 520368, *Fax:* +20 62 520364

Officials: Harbour Master: Admiral Mohamed Mahmoud Aly.

Pilotage: Compulsory. Berthing and unberthing can be carried out at any time of the day

Tides: Range of tide approx 0.9 m to 1.25 m

Traffic: 2006, 1562 vessels, 644 000 t of cargo handled

Maximum Vessel Dimensions: 120 m loa, 7.32 m max d

Principal Imports and Exports: Imports: Apples, Iron ore. Exports: Ceramics, Furmtur, Iron, Vegetables.

Working Hours: 24 hours a day

Accommodation:

Name	Length (m)	Depth (m)	Remarks
Nuweiba			See [1] below
Berth No.1	94	8	Passenger ferries
Berth No.2	43	7.5	Passenger ferries
Berth No.3	120	8	General cargo

[1]*Nuweiba:* The port is private and permission to enter must be given by the ministry Maritime Transport in Alexandria

Storage:

Location	Open (m²)	Covered (m²)
Nuweiba	60000	1000

Bunkering: Bunkers supplied by trucks through Petrol Co. in Egypt

Towage: One tug of 2 x 1200 hp is available

Airport: El-Nakab Airport 100 km

Lloyd's Agent: Marine Technical Services Ltd, 4th Floor, Units 19 & 20, El Freepor Building, El Nahda & Palestine Streets, Port Said, Arab Republic of Egypt, *Tel:* +20 66 335 5423, *Fax:* +20 66 334 3974, *Email:* mts-lloyds-portsaid@soficom.com.eg, *Website:* www.lloydsegypt.com

PORT IBRAHIM

harbour area, see under Suez

PORT SAID

Lat 31° 15' N; Long 32° 18' E.

Admiralty Chart: 240/241
Time Zone: GMT +2 h

Admiralty Pilot: 49
UNCTAD Locode: EG PSD

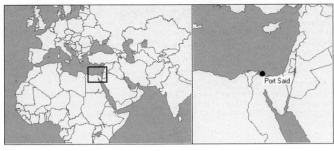

Principal Facilities:

| P | | Y | G | C | R | L | B | D | T | A |

Authority: Port Said Port Authority, Moustafa Kamel & Azmey Street, Port Said, Arab Republic of Egypt, *Tel:* +20 66 334 8270, *Fax:* +20 66 334 8262, *Email:* info@psdports.org, *Website:* www.psdports.org

Officials: Chairman: Rear Admiral Ebrahim Mohamed Seddek, *Email:* chairman@psdports.org.
Vice Chairman: Rear Admiral Magdi Attia M. El Sayed, *Email:* vicechairman@psdports.org.
Marketing: Mosad El Sharnouby.

Port Security: ISPS compliant

Documentation: Berthing application (1 copy), crew list (6 copies), passengers (6 copies), stores (3 copies), arms and ammunition (1 copy), health document (s), ISPS certificate

Approach: Ten miles before arrival at the approach buoy all vessels should contact the Suez Canal Maritime Office. Approach buoy in pos 31° 25' 30" N; 32° 22' E

Anchorage: Incoming vessels have two anchorage areas:
Northern Area: Zone 1 for vessels with draught over 42 ft and Zone 2 for vessels up to 39 ft
Southern Area: for all vessels with draught up to 42 ft

Pilotage: Compulsory for all vessels arriving, sailing or moving berth. Available 24 h/day

Radio Frequency: VHF Channel 13

Tides: Rise of tide about 0.75 m

Traffic: 2004, 3016 vessels, 10 710 000 t of cargo handled

Maximum Vessel Dimensions: 16 m draught

Principal Imports and Exports: Imports: Agricultural products, Chemicals, Metal products, Mining machinery, Transportation equipment. Exports: Cotton, Ready made garments, Rice.

Working Hours: 0600-1800. Overtime 1800-0600

Accommodation:

Name	Length (m)	Depth (m)	Draught (m)	Remarks
Port Said				See [1] below
Cheriff Basin	510		8.23	See [2] below
Abbas Quays				See [3] below
Berth No.1	250		8.23	General/bulk
Berth No.2	250		8.23	General/bulk
Berth No.3	65		8.23	Ro/ro
Arsenal Basin	300	5		See [4] below
Fishing Port		2.1–4.3		Consists of four basins
Floating Grain Plant	100		12	80 000 t grain silo has a loading/discharging cap of 7000 t/day
Container Terminal				See [5] below
Container Quay	970	14	13.2	
Ro/Ro Berth	300	11	10	
Feeder Berth	350	11	10	
Port Said East				
Suez Canal Container Terminal	1200		16.5	See [6] below

[1]*Port Said:* An artificial harbour, well sheltered by breakwaters. Depth at entrance 12.5 m, max authorised draft in harbour 10.67 m; in entrance channel and Canal 11.28 m
Bulk facilities: Floating grain discharge plant for vessels up to 11.6 m d, cap 7000 t/day. Grain silo of 80 000 t cap
There is a free zone area in the port covering some 918 698 m2
[2]*Cheriff Basin:* Three berths. General cargo & grain. Vessels drawing more than 8.23 m have to discharge cargo into lighters
[3]*Abbas Quays:* Vessels drawing more than 8.23 m have to discharge cargo into lighters
[4]*Arsenal Basin:* Used for lighters and other shallow draught vessels
[5]*Container Terminal:* Operated by Port Said Container & Cargo Handling Co., P O Box 1239, Port Said, Tel: +20 66 323 5862/4, Fax:+20 66 333 9347, Email: operation@pscchc.com, Website: www.pscchc.com
Container yard of 435 000 m2. 700 000 TEU capacity. 360 reefer points
[6]*Suez Canal Container Terminal:* Operated by Suez Canal Container Terminal (SCCT), Private Free Zone Area, Port Said East Port, P O Box 247, Port Said, Tel: +20 66 325 4960, Fax: +20 66 325 4970, Email: scct@scctportsaid.com, Website: www.scctportsaid.com
Four berths

Storage:

Location	Open (m²)	Covered (m²)	Sheds / Warehouses	Grain (t)
Port Said	32698	55050	28	80000

Mechanical Handling Equipment:

Location	Type	Capacity (t)	Qty
Port Said	Mult-purp. Cranes	3	14
Container Terminal	Mobile Cranes	80–100	2
Container Terminal	Container Cranes	45	1
Container Terminal	Container Cranes	41	2
Container Terminal	Post Panamax	40	3
Container Terminal	RTG's		8
Container Terminal	Reach Stackers		34
Container Terminal	Yard Tractors		47
Suez Canal Container Terminal	Super Post Panamax		12
Suez Canal Container Terminal	RTG's		40

Bunkering: Offshore deliveries out of Port Said harbour possible, weather permitting
Fuel, diesel and gas oil supplied by hose or tanker
Arab Unimar Shipping & Trading Co., 34 Elgomhouriah Street, Port Said, Arab Republic of Egypt, *Tel:* +20 66 237967, *Fax:* +20 66 238968
Felix Maritime Agency, 4th Floor No.7, Post Tower, Al-Gomhouria Street, Port Said, Arab Republic of Egypt, *Tel:* +20 66 333 7165, *Fax:* +20 66 334 8772, *Email:* felix@felix-eg.com, *Website:* www.felix-eg.com
Ibramar Holding Co., Ibramar Shipping Company S.A.E., 5th Floor, Freeport Building, Memphis & el Nahda Street, P O Box 460, Port Said, Arab Republic of Egypt, *Tel:* +20 66 333 9140, *Fax:* +20 66 332 4187, *Email:* portsaid@ibramar.com.eg, *Website:* www.ibramar.com
Redmar Shipping Co., El Messagria Building, 8 Palestine Street, Port Said, Arab Republic of Egypt, *Tel:* +20 66 3228 822, *Fax:* +20 66 3324 940, *Email:* operation@redmar.com.eg
Seagull Maritime Inc., Block No.3, Messagerie Building, Babel & Memphis Street, Port Said, Arab Republic of Egypt, *Tel:* +20 66 333255, *Fax:* +20 66 227962
Solimanco Marine Services, P O Box 202, Port Said Free Zone, Port Said 42111, Arab Republic of Egypt, *Tel:* +20 66 341641, *Fax:* +20 66 232262, *Email:* mohamed1969@mail.interlink-eg.com
World Marine Egypt, 12 Salah Salem Street, Port Said, Arab Republic of Egypt, *Tel:* +20 66 325327, *Fax:* +20 66 326114
Arab Unimar Shipping & Trading Co., 34 Elgomhouriah Street, Port Said, Arab Republic of Egypt, *Tel:* +20 66 237967, *Fax:* +20 66 238968
Chevron Egypt S.A.E., 44 Elnadi Street, Maadi, Cairo, Arab Republic of Egypt, *Tel:* +20 2 2358 8007, *Fax:* +20 2 2358 8027, *Email:* gmpegyptb@chevron.com, *Website:* www.chevron.com
Cockett Marine Oil Ltd, Carrick House, 36 Station Square, Petts Wood, Kent BR5 1NA, United Kingdom, *Tel:* +44 1689 883 400, *Fax:* +44 1689 877 666, *Email:* enquiries@cockett.com, *Website:* www.cockettgroup.com – *Grades:* MDO; IFO; MGO – *Parcel Size:* IFO min 15t, max 10 000t – *Delivery Mode:* barge
ExxonMobil Marine Fuels, Mailpoint 31, ExxonMobil House, Ermyn Way, Leatherhead, Surrey KT22 8UX, United Kingdom, *Tel:* +44 1372 222 000, *Fax:* +44 1372 223 922, *Email:* marine.fuels@exxonmobil.com, *Website:* www.exxonmobil.com – *Grades:* IFO30-180; MGO – *Delivery Mode:* barge
Maxcom Bunker S.p.A. u.s., Via Bartolomeo Bosco 57/7B, 16121 Genoa, Italy, *Tel:* +39 010 5605 200, *Fax:* +39 010 564 479, *Email:* bunker@maxcombunker.com, *Website:* www.maxcombunker.com
Petrolube Misr Saudi Arabian Lubricating Oil Co., P O Box 1120, 52 Lebanon Street, Mohandessen, Cairo 11511, Arab Republic of Egypt, *Tel:* +20 2 305 4670, *Fax:* +20 2 305 4811, *Email:* petrowafaa2002@hotmail.com
Shell Marketing Egypt, Corner Street 254 & 206, Degla Maadi, Cairo 11742, Arab Republic of Egypt, *Tel:* +20 2 519 8817, *Fax:* +20 2 519 8818
Societe Cooperative des Petroles (Copetrole), Cooperative Building, 94 Kasr El Eini Street, Cairo 11621, Arab Republic of Egypt, *Tel:* +20 2 2792 5221, *Fax:* +20 2 2795 6404, *Email:* co_op@link.net – *Grades:* IFO-180cSt; MDO; lubes; in line blending available – *Parcel Size:* min 15t, max 10,000t – *Rates:* 400t in summer, 300t in winter – *Notice:* 12 hours – *Delivery Mode:* wharf, barge, truck
Solimanco Marine Services, P O Box 202, Port Said Free Zone, Port Said 42111, Arab Republic of Egypt, *Tel:* +20 66 341641, *Fax:* +20 66 232262, *Email:* mohamed1969@mail.interlink-eg.com
Tamoil Misr, 35 Abdallah Ibn Taher Street, Nasr City, Cairo 11511, Arab Republic of Egypt, *Tel:* +20 2 273 2085, *Fax:* +20 2 287 2879
Unimas Shipping, 1 Digla Street, Raml Station, 5th Floor, P O Box 44, Ibrahimia, Alexandria 21312, Arab Republic of Egypt, *Tel:* +20 3 486 8800, *Fax:* +20 3 487 0230, *Email:* mail@unimas.com.eg, *Website:* www.unimasegypt.com – *Grades:* MGO and all IFO grades – *Parcel Size:* 50-800t, or as requested – *Rates:* 400t/h – *Notice:* 24 hours – *Delivery Mode:* ex wharf, barge
World Marine Egypt, 12 Salah Salem Street, Port Said, Arab Republic of Egypt, *Tel:* +20 66 325327, *Fax:* +20 66 326114 – *Grades:* MDO; FO up to 20cSt – *Parcel Size:* max 3000t – *Rates:* 500t/h – *Notice:* 24 hours – *Delivery Mode:* ex wharf, barge

Towage: Twelve tugs available

Repair & Maintenance: Port Said Engineering Works S.A.E., P O Box 170, Palestine & El Shohada Streets, Port Said, Arab Republic of Egypt, *Tel:* +20 66 324 0387, *Fax:* +20 66 324 0845
Port Said Shipyard, P O Box 42524, Port Said, Arab Republic of Egypt, *Tel:* +20 66 324 0339, *Fax:* +20 66 324 0324 Three floating docks of 25 000 t, 10 000 t and 5000 t cap. Repair quays totalling 1200 m. Floating and salvage cranes up to 500 t cap

Ship Chandlers: AC Blue Star Marine Services, P O Box 762, El Freepour Building Nahda Street, 2nd Floor, Port Said 42111, Arab Republic of Egypt, *Tel:* +20 66 324 6724, *Fax:* +20 66 324 6725, *Email:* bluestarmarine@bec.com.eg
Alhadidico Marine Services, Port Said Tower, 3rd Floor, Office No. 22, 16 Memphis Street, Borg, P O Box 734, Port Said 42511, Arab Republic of Egypt, *Tel:* +20 66 333 5958, *Fax:* +20 66 324 6434, *Email:* headoffice@elhadidico.com, *Website:* www.elhadidico.com
Billymaris Billy Mitchell Marine Services, P O Box 110, Port Said Tower, Memphis & Babil Street, Port Said, Arab Republic of Egypt, *Tel:* +20 66 333 6212, *Fax:* +20 66 333 6217, *Email:* bilymaris@bec.com.eg, *Website:* www.bilymaris.net

Key to Principal Facilities:—				
A=Airport	**C**=Containers	**G**=General Cargo	**P**=Petroleum	**R**=Ro/Ro	**Y**=Dry Bulk
B=Bunkers	**D**=Dry Dock	**L**=Cruise	**Q**=Other Liquid Bulk	**T**=Towage (where available from port)	

Castella Marine Services, 6 Hammdy & Elgish Streets, Port Said, Arab Republic of Egypt, *Tel:* +20 66 322 9975, *Fax:* +20 66 333 9792, *Email:* admin@castella-marine.com, *Website:* www.castella-marine.com

Concord Shipping Agency, 1st Floor, El Hegaz Building, Memphis Street, Port Said, Arab Republic of Egypt, *Tel:* +20 66 325 2443, *Fax:* +20 66 323 4476, *Email:* office@concordshipping.com, *Website:* www.concordshipping.com

Eastern Supply Junior, Burg El Salam Building, 23 July Street, P O Box 1088, Port Said 42111, Arab Republic of Egypt, *Tel:* +20 66 333 3775, *Fax:* +20 66 333 5700, *Email:* easternjunior@bec.com.eg

Edwardo Marine Services Co., P O Box 179, Port Said, Arab Republic of Egypt, *Tel:* +20 66 623 0031, *Fax:* +20 66 632 2134, *Email:* info@edwardomarine.com, *Website:* www.edwardomarine.com

The Egyptian Marine Supply & Contracting Co. SAA (CONSUP), P O Box 125, Port Said, Arab Republic of Egypt, *Tel:* +20 66 322 0622, *Fax:* +20 66 322 0624, *Email:* consup2003@yahoo.com

Elephant Marine Service, 19 Eltour & Akka Street, Port Said, Arab Republic of Egypt, *Tel:* +20 66 334 5131, *Fax:* +20 66 334 6158, *Email:* elephantmarine@hotmail.com, *Website:* www.elephantmarine.com

Elhadidico Marine Services, P O Box 734, Port Said 42511, Arab Republic of Egypt, *Tel:* +20 66 333 5958, *Fax:* +20 66 324 6434, *Email:* elhadidi@bec.com.eg

Hardy Ship Suppliers (Egypt), P O Box 197, Port Said 42511, Arab Republic of Egypt, *Tel:* +20 66 332 0850, *Fax:* +20 66 332 8194, *Email:* hardy@mosleh.com

The International Marine Services Co. (S.A.E.), 8 Mohamed Mamoud Street, P O Box 141, Port Said, Arab Republic of Egypt, *Tel:* +20 66 322 3601, *Fax:* +20 66 332 1925, *Email:* marinco@bec.com.eg

International Shipping Enterprise S.A.E. (Intership), P O Box 252, 38 Sultan Hussein Street, Port Said, Arab Republic of Egypt, *Tel:* +20 66 324 5001, *Fax:* +20 66 333 9818, *Email:* main@intershipegypt.com, *Website:* www.intershipegypt.com

Lucky Dolphin Marine Services, El-Omraa Tower, El-Geish & Saphia Zaghlol Streets, P O Box 701, Port Said 42111, Arab Republic of Egypt, *Tel:* +20 66 324 4848, *Fax:* +20 66 333 3378, *Email:* info@luckydolphin.com, *Website:* www.luckydolphin.com

Marcopolo Marine Services, Al Asefy Building, 5 Hafez Ibrahim & Memphis Street, Port Said 1022, Arab Republic of Egypt, *Tel:* +20 66 322 7664, *Fax:* +20 66 333 0894, *Email:* marcopolo@interlink.com.eg

Mitchell JR Shipping Agency, Elmahrousa Towers, 5 Mohamed Mahmoud & Mahmoud Sedky Street, P O Box 1217, Port Said, Arab Republic of Egypt, *Tel:* +20 66 333 8591, *Fax:* +20 66 323 5508, *Email:* adelmei@mitchellj.com.eg, *Website:* www.mitchelljr.com..eg

Mosleh Shipping Services & Co., P O Box 729, Port Said 42511, Arab Republic of Egypt, *Tel:* +20 66 333 6688, *Fax:* +20 66 332 8194, *Email:* info@mosleh.com, *Website:* www.mosleh.com

Pan Marine Co, 5 HafezIbrahim Street, Port Said, Arab Republic of Egypt, *Tel:* +20 66 590 0105, *Fax:* +20 66 590 1542, *Email:* panmar@dataxprs.com.eg

Rizco Marine Services Co., 26 Elamen Street No.3, Port Said, Arab Republic of Egypt, *Tel:* +20 66 323 6435, *Fax:* +20 66 332 5706, *Email:* rizcomarine@yahoo.com

Sharaf Maritime & Trading Corp., Sharkawy Building, P O Box 403, Port Said 42511, Arab Republic of Egypt, *Tel:* +20 66 334 8930, *Fax:* +20 66 333 7686, *Email:* sharaf@sharafcorp.com.eg, *Website:* www.sharafcorp.com.eg

Silver Sea Marine Services, P O Box 322, Port Said 42511, Arab Republic of Egypt, *Tel:* +20 66 324 5298, *Fax:* +20 66 335 7254, *Email:* silver@sedapnet.org.eg

Sinai Industrial & Marine Supplies, P O Box 924, Waha Building, El Gomhouria Street, Port Said, Arab Republic of Egypt, *Tel:* +20 66 332 7698, *Fax:* +20 66 332 1055, *Email:* sinai@bec.com.eg

Sunlight Agency, P O Box 267, 38 Mahmoud Sidky Street, Port Said, Arab Republic of Egypt, *Tel:* +20 66 322 0241, *Fax:* +20 66 332 2145, *Email:* sunlight@suezcanal.net, *Website:* www.sunlightagency.com

United Mediterranean Suppliers, El Gomhouria Street, Floor 2 Block 4, P O Box 254, Port Said 42111, Arab Republic of Egypt, *Tel:* +20 66 333 3371, *Fax:* +20 66 333 3372, *Email:* info@ums.com.eg, *Website:* www.ums.com.eg

Shipping Agents: Ameaster Shipping & Trading Co. S.R.L., 76 El Gomhoreya Street, 1st Floor, Port Said, Arab Republic of Egypt, *Tel:* +20 66 322 4863, *Fax:* +20 66 323 6025, *Email:* agency.psd@ameaster.com, *Website:* www.ameaster.com

Arab Express Shipping Co., Sonesta Trading Center, Port Said, Arab Republic of Egypt, *Tel:* +20 66 332 6711, *Fax:* +20 66 334 2198, *Email:* azmynakib@arabxprs.com, *Website:* www.arabxprs.com

Assuit Shipping Agency, 26 Palestine Street, Port Said, Arab Republic of Egypt, *Tel:* +20 66 322 2876, *Fax:* +20 66 335 1904, *Email:* info-asuit@canalshipping.net, *Website:* www.canalshipping.net

Asswan Shipping Agency, 26 Palestine Street, Port Said, Arab Republic of Egypt, *Tel:* +20 66 322 0795, *Fax:* +20 66 335 1905, *Email:* info-aswan@canalshipping.net, *Website:* www.canalshipping.net

Canal Shipping Agency Co., 26 Palestine Street, Port Said, Arab Republic of Egypt, *Tel:* +20 66 322 7500, *Fax:* +20 66 323 9896, *Email:* info@canalshipping.net, *Website:* www.canalshipping.net

CMA-CGM S.A., CMA CGM Port Said, 7 El Gomhoria Street & El Salam Street, P O Box 958, Port Said, Arab Republic of Egypt, *Tel:* +20 66 334 4349, *Fax:* +20 66 322 8896, *Email:* pts.genmbox@cma-cgm.com, *Website:* www.cma-cgm.com

Concord Shipping Agency, 1st Floor, El Hegaz Building, Memphis Street, Port Said, Arab Republic of Egypt, *Tel:* +20 66 325 2443, *Fax:* +20 66 323 4476, *Email:* office@concordshipping.com, *Website:* www.concordshipping.com

Damanhour Shipping Agency, 26 Palestine Street, Port Said, Arab Republic of Egypt, *Tel:* +20 66 322 6806, *Fax:* +20 66 335 1902, *Email:* info-dammanhor@canalshipping.net, *Website:* www.canalshipping.net

El Menia Shipping Agency, 26 Palestine Street, Port Said, Arab Republic of Egypt, *Tel:* +20 66 332 9185, *Fax:* +20 66 335 1903, *Email:* info-elmenia@canalshipping.net, *Website:* www.canalshipping.net

Fairtrans Marine Trading & Forwarding SAE, P O Box 752, Port Said 42111, Arab Republic of Egypt, *Tel:* +20 66 332 6893, *Fax:* +20 66 332 4898, *Email:* general@portsaid.fairtrans.com, *Website:* www.fairtrans.com

Farma Marine Services, Elgafareah & Elansar Streets, Port Said, Arab Republic of Egypt, *Tel:* +20 66 364 5293, *Fax:* +20 66 364 5293, *Email:* fmsshipping@yahoo.com

Felix Maritime Agency, 4th Floor No.7, Post Tower, Al-Gomhouria Street, Port Said, Arab Republic of Egypt, *Tel:* +20 66 333 7165, *Fax:* +20 66 334 8772, *Email:* felix@felix-eg.com, *Website:* www.felix-eg.com

Free Marine Shipping & Trading Co, Elnahda & Mephes Street, Freepore Building, 3rd Floor, 322-323, Port Said, Arab Republic of Egypt, *Tel:* +20 66 323 4846, *Fax:* +20 66 323 4846, *Email:* freemarine@interlink.com.eg, *Website:* www.freemarine.net

Gabmarine Shipping Agency, P O Box 1292, 21 Babel & El Gish Street, Port Said,

Arab Republic of Egypt, *Tel:* +20 66 334 2450, *Fax:* +20 66 332 2326, *Email:* gms@interlink.com.eg, *Website:* www.gabmarine.com.eg

Gulf Agency Co. (Egypt) Ltd, 3rd Floor, 13-23 July Street, Port Said, Arab Republic of Egypt, *Tel:* +20 66 324 0662, *Fax:* +20 66 333 3213, *Email:* egypt@gacworld.com, *Website:* www.gacworld.com

Gulf Badr Group, 19 Elgabarty Street, P O Box 77, Port Said 42111, Arab Republic of Egypt, *Tel:* +20 66 332 7736, *Fax:* +20 66 323 3999, *Email:* everpsd@gulfbadregypt.com, *Website:* www.gulfbadregypt.com

Ibramar Holding Co., Ibramar Shipping Company S.A.E., 5th Floor, Freeport Building, Memphis & el Nahda Street, P O Box 460, Port Said, Arab Republic of Egypt, *Tel:* +20 66 333 9140, *Fax:* +20 66 332 4187, *Email:* portsaid@ibramar.com.eg, *Website:* www.ibramar.com

Inchcape Shipping Services (ISS), Office No. 62, 6th Floor, Port Said Center Building, 23 July & Abu El Feda Street, Port Said, Arab Republic of Egypt, *Tel:* +20 66 332 7732, *Fax:* +20 66 335 1531, *Email:* mohamed.gaabary@iss-shipping.com, *Website:* www.iss-shipping.com

International Shipping Enterprise S.A.E., International Shipping Enterprise S.A.E (INTERSHIP), 38 Sultan Hussein Street, Port Said, Arab Republic of Egypt, *Tel:* +20 66 333 0368, *Fax:* +20 66 333 9818, *Email:* main@intershipegypt.com, *Website:* www.intershipegypt.com

International Shipping Enterprise S.A.E. (Intership), P O Box 252, 38 Sultan Hussein Street, Port Said, Arab Republic of Egypt, *Tel:* +20 66 324 5001, *Fax:* +20 66 333 9818, *Email:* main@intershipegypt.com, *Website:* www.intershipegypt.com

Irano Misr Shipping Co., Elnahda Building, 4th Floor, Elnahda Street, Port Said, Arab Republic of Egypt, *Tel:* +20 66 332 5892, *Fax:* +20 66 332 5893, *Email:* iranmisrco@bec.com.eg

Lucky Dolphin Marine Services, El-Omraa Tower, El-Geish & Saphia Zaghlol Streets, P O Box 701, Port Said 42111, Arab Republic of Egypt, *Tel:* +20 66 324 4848, *Fax:* +20 66 333 3378, *Email:* info@luckydolphin.com, *Website:* www.luckydolphin.com

Mahoney Shipping & Marine Services Co., Port Said, Arab Republic of Egypt, *Tel:* +20 66 324 1195, *Fax:* +20 66 333 8475, *Email:* portsaid@mahoneyegypt.com

Marine & Engineering Services, 19 El Gomhoria Street, Port Said, Arab Republic of Egypt, *Tel:* +20 66 332 2804, *Fax:* +20 66 322 6674, *Email:* info@mesco.com.eg, *Website:* www.mesco.com.eg

Mediterranean Shipping Company, Freepor Building, 4th Floor, El Nahda Street, Port Said, Arab Republic of Egypt, *Tel:* +20 66 323 0565, *Fax:* +20 66 324 4646, *Email:* psdtr@mscegypt.com

A.P. Moller-Maersk Group, Maersk Egypt S.A.E., 2 Ahmed Shawky Street, El Goumhoria Road, Port Said 43522, Arab Republic of Egypt, *Tel:* +20 66 324 4235, *Fax:* +20 66 324 4238, *Email:* egymkt@maersk.com, *Website:* www.maerskline.com

Pacific Ocean Shipping Agency, 6th Floor El-Freepor Building, El-Nahda & Memphis Street, P O Box 138, El-Shark, Port Said 42111, Arab Republic of Egypt, *Tel:* +20 66 333 3781, *Fax:* +20 66 333 3782, *Email:* info@pacificoceanshpg.com, *Website:* www.pacificoceanshpg.com

Port Said Container & Cargo Handling Company, 6th Floor, Port Said Port Authority Building, Moustafa Kamel & Azmey Street, Port Said, Arab Republic of Egypt, *Tel:* +20 66 323 7151, *Fax:* +20 66 333 9347, *Email:* info@pscchc.com, *Website:* www.pscchc.com

RAFIMAR SAE, 68 Safia Zaghloul Street, Ogeni Building, Beside Cinema El Sharq - Office 8, Port Said, Arab Republic of Egypt, *Tel:* +20 66 333 8354, *Fax:* +20 66 332 9054, *Email:* rafimar@rafimar.com, *Website:* www.rafimar.com

Sharaf Maritime & Trading Corp., Sharkawy Building, P O Box 403, Port Said 42511, Arab Republic of Egypt, *Tel:* +20 66 334 8930, *Fax:* +20 66 333 7686, *Email:* sharaf@sharafcorp.com.eg, *Website:* www.sharafcorp.com.eg

Tabadol Shipping Co, Unit 5/17, El Freeport Building, 3 El Nahda Street, Port Said, Arab Republic of Egypt, *Tel:* +20 66 334 3757, *Fax:* +20 66 334 4649, *Email:* tabadol-pst@tabadolshipping.com

United Mediterranean Suppliers, El Gomhouria Street, Floor 2 Block 4, P O Box 254, Port Said 42111, Arab Republic of Egypt, *Tel:* +20 66 333 3371, *Fax:* +20 66 333 3372, *Email:* info@ums.com.eg, *Website:* www.ums.com.eg

Wilhelmsen Ship Services, Barwil Unitor Shipping Agency, 2nd Floor, Taroub Building, 23rd of July Street, Port Said, Arab Republic of Egypt, *Tel:* +20 66 334 8891, *Fax:* +20 66 334 8892, *Email:* safwat.thabet@wilhelmsen.com, *Website:* www.wilhelmsen.com

World Marine Corp, World Marine Egypt, 52 Salah Salem Street, Selim Building, Port Said, Arab Republic of Egypt, *Tel:* +20 66 332 5327/8, *Fax:* +20 66 332 6114, *Email:* portsaid@worldmarineegypt.com.eg, *Website:* www.worldmarine.gr

Worms United Shipping Agency S.A.E., Sonesta Commercial Center, P O Box 475, Port Said 42511, Arab Republic of Egypt, *Tel:* +20 66 332 5837 & 332 8947, *Fax:* +20 66 332 5870 & 332 2640, *Email:* worms@worms-psd.com.eg, *Website:* www.worms-psd.com

Stevedoring Companies: Concord Shipping Agency, 1st Floor, El Hegaz Building, Memphis Street, Port Said, Arab Republic of Egypt, *Tel:* +20 66 325 2443, *Fax:* +20 66 323 4476, *Email:* office@concordshipping.com, *Website:* www.concordshipping.com

Ibramar Holding Co., Ibramar Shipping Company S.A.E., 5th Floor, Freeport Building, Memphis & el Nahda Street, P O Box 460, Port Said, Arab Republic of Egypt, *Tel:* +20 66 333 9140, *Fax:* +20 66 332 4187, *Email:* portsaid@ibramar.com.eg, *Website:* www.ibramar.com

Port Said Container & Cargo Handling Company, 6th Floor, Port Said Port Authority Building, Moustafa Kamel & Azmey Street, Port Said, Arab Republic of Egypt, *Tel:* +20 66 323 7151, *Fax:* +20 66 333 9347, *Email:* info@pscchc.com, *Website:* www.pscchc.com

Surveyors: ABS (Europe), Messageries Maritime Building, Block No.3, Apartment D/207, P O Box 479, Port Said 42511, Arab Republic of Egypt, *Tel:* +20 66 322 1641, *Fax:* +20 66 322 1641, *Email:* absportsaid@eagle.org

China Classification Society, 15 Kayed Bay Street, Port Said, Arab Republic of Egypt, *Tel:* +20 66 332 3633, *Fax:* +20 66 332 3633, *Email:* ccssd@ccs.org.cn, *Website:* www.ccs.org.cn

Dahroug Advocates (Egypt), 19 El Gomhouria Street, P O Box 1, Port Said 42111, Arab Republic of Egypt, *Tel:* +20 12 3545578, *Fax:* +20 66 334 9374, *Email:* dahrougadvocates@hotmail.com, *Website:* www.ship.gr/dahroug.htm

Germanischer Lloyd, Apartment No. 4, 25 El-Gabarti Street, Port Said, Arab Republic of Egypt, *Tel:* +20 66 334 3836, *Fax:* +20 66 334 3836, *Email:* gl-port.said@gl-group.com, *Website:* www.gl-group.com

Marine Technical Services Ltd, 4th Floor, Units 19 & 20, El Freepor Building, El Nahda & Palestine Streets, Port Said, Arab Republic of Egypt, *Tel:* +20 66 335 5423, *Fax:*

+20 66 334 3974, *Email:* mts-lloyds-portsaid@soficom.com.eg, *Website:* www.lloydsegypt.com

Registro Italiano Navale (RINA), Egyptian Marine & Consulting Bureau, Mamehis Street, P O Box 1000, Port Said, Arab Republic of Egypt, *Tel:* +20 66 334 6559, *Fax:* +20 66 334 6559, *Email:* emcb.pts@suezcanal.net

Medical Facilities: Hospital 200 m from port

Airport: Al Jamil Airport, 7 km

Railway: Approx 100 m from port

Development: The first 300 m berth of Phase II of the Suez Canal Container Terminal is expected to be operational by April 2010 with completion scheduled for the end of 2011 at which time SCCT will have a cap of 5.1 million TEU's and 2400 m of continuous quay with 24 super-post-panamax gantry cranes

Lloyd's Agent: Marine Technical Services Ltd, 4th Floor, Units 19 & 20, El Freepor Building, El Nahda & Palestine Streets, Port Said, Arab Republic of Egypt, *Tel:* +20 66 335 5423, *Fax:* +20 66 334 3974, *Email:* mts-lloyds-portsaid@soficom.com.eg, *Website:* www.lloydsegypt.com

PORT TEWFIK

harbour area, see under Suez

RAS BUDRAN TERMINAL

Lat 28° 56' N; Long 33° 8' E.

Admiralty Chart: 2132   **Admiralty Pilot:** 64
Time Zone: GMT +2 h   **UNCTAD Locode:** EG

Principal Facilities:

P									A

Authority: Suez Oil Co. (SUCO), 21 Ahmed Orabi Street, P O Box 2622, Cairo, Arab Republic of Egypt, *Tel:* +20 2 3346 5909, *Fax:* +20 2 3303 5434, *Email:* suco@suco-eg.com, *Website:* www.suco-eg.com

Officials: General Manager: Joe Kose, *Email:* gm@suco-eg.com.

Port Security: ISPS compliant

Documentation: All ships certificates and four crew lists and two bonded store lists

Approach: Tankers calling at the mooring must send an ETA 72, 24 and 12 h to SUCO head office including advice of any equipment required from shore and call Ras Budran 4 h prior to arrival on VHF channel 74 or 16

Anchorage: Anchorage is in pos 28° 52' 30" N, 33° 06' 54" E in depth of 40 m. It is prohibited to anchor outside this area unless special permission is obtained

Pilotage: Compulsory. Pilot will board vessel 2.5 NM SSE of the terminal

Radio Frequency: VHF channels 16 and 12 for Budran radio room and channel 74 for Marine Budran. 2638 kHz to be used from 0700-1800

Weather: Max velocity 45 knots, wind speed 20 knots, swells usually from NNW, wave heights reach 6 m

Tides: Range of tide between 0.91 and 1.22 m

Maximum Vessel Dimensions: Max dwt 250 000 t, max d 18 m, max loa 198 m

Principal Imports and Exports: Exports: Oil.

Working Hours: Berthing during daytime only. Unberthing anytime

Accommodation:

Name	Remarks
Ras Budran Terminal	See [1] below

[1]*Ras Budran Terminal:* Single buoy mooring connected to the shore by submarine pipelines. Depth at berth is 35 m. Berthing of vessels takes place during daylight hours, unberthing anytime. Vessels must be equipped with 10 t cap cranes. Loading rate 6000 t/h via 16'' hoses. Ballast facility is available
There is a service jetty, 120 m long protected by breakwaters for vessels of up to 6.5 m d

Cargo Worked: Oil loading rate 5000 t/hour - 16" hoses

Repair & Maintenance: Suez Odense Marine Service operate a floating dock length 144 m and width 22 m of 55 000 t cap supplied with gantry cranes of 150 t cap. Contact Leth Suez Transit for further information

Medical Facilities: Doctor and facilities available but no hospital

Airport: Abu Rudeis, 5 km

Lloyd's Agent: Marine Technical Services Ltd, Flat 6B, 28 Cherif Street, Cairo, Arab Republic of Egypt, *Tel:* +20 2 2393 5724, *Fax:* +20 2 2393 8669, *Email:* mts-lloyds-cairo@soficom.com.eg, *Website:* www.lloydsegypt.com

RAS EL BEHAR

harbour area, see under Zeit Bay Terminal

RAS GHARIB

Lat 28° 21' N; Long 33° 7' E.

Admiralty Chart: 2132   **Admiralty Pilot:** 64
Time Zone: GMT +2 h   **UNCTAD Locode:** EG RAG

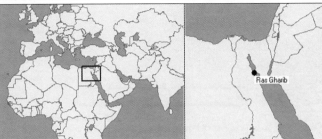

Principal Facilities:

P						B		

Authority: The Egyptian General Petroleum Corp., Palestine Street, 4th Sector, New Maadi, Cairo, Arab Republic of Egypt, *Tel:* +20 2 353 1471, *Fax:* +20 2 377 5962, *Email:* info@egpc.com.eg

Port Security: ISPS compliant

Anchorage: Vessels can safely anchor in depths of over 9.0 m

Pilotage: Compulsory, the harbour master who acts as pilot boards the vessel about 1.5 m SE of Ras Gharib

Radio Frequency: Vessel Traffic Information Management System (VTIMS) equipped with Inmarsat (C) established in pos 28° 30.915' N; 32° 29.050' E, Station Sign 462299913 - frequency used M.Z - sending (156.075) receiving (160.675) VHF Channel 61

Weather: Northerly winds of force 3-5 are experienced most of the year and occasionally short southerly gales making anchorage impossible

Maximum Vessel Dimensions: Loa 290 m, draught 16.8 m

Working Hours: 24 h/day but berthing/unberthing during daylight only

Accommodation:

Name	Depth (m)	Draught (m)	Remarks
Ras Gharib			See [1] below
Northern Pier	8.23	7.32	Vessels up to 137 m loa. Loading rate of 650 t/h
Central Pier	10.97	9.75	See [2] below
Southern Pier	23.71	16.75	See [3] below

[1]*Ras Gharib:* Tanker terminal, sheltered by a cape and a chain of reefs. Three loading piers for crude oil
The diameter of the crude oil loading lines at the three berths is 18'', 18'' and 30'' respectively
[2]*Central Pier:* Vessels up to 183 m loa. Loading rate 1200 t/h. Ballast facility is available
[3]*Southern Pier:* Vessels up to 299 m loa. Loading rate 2000 t/h. Ballast facility is available

Bunkering: Fuel oil available by barge
Chevron Egypt S.A.E., 44 Elnadi Street, Maadi, Cairo, Arab Republic of Egypt, *Tel:* +20 2 2358 8007, *Fax:* +20 2 2358 8027, *Email:* gmpegyptb@chevron.com, *Website:* www.chevron.com
ExxonMobil Marine Fuels, Mailpoint 31, ExxonMobil House, Ermyn Way, Leatherhead, Surrey KT22 8UX, United Kingdom, *Tel:* +44 1372 222 000, *Fax:* +44 1372 223 922, *Email:* marine.fuels@exxonmobil.com, *Website:* www.exxonmobil.com
Maxcom Bunker S.p.A. u.s., Via Bartolomeo Bosco 57/7B, 16121 Genoa, Italy, *Tel:* +39 010 5605 200, *Fax:* +39 010 564 479, *Email:* bunker@maxcombunker.com, *Website:* www.maxcombunker.com
Misr Petroleum Co., MISR Petroleum House, 6 Orabi Square, P O Box 228, Cairo, Arab Republic of Egypt, *Tel:* +20 2 2574 5400, *Fax:* +20 2 2574 5436, *Email:* bunker@misrpetroleum.com, *Website:* www.misrpetroleum.com
Petrolube Misr Saudi Arabian Lubricating Oil Co., P O Box 1120, 52 Lebanon Street, Mohandessen, Cairo 11511, Arab Republic of Egypt, *Tel:* +20 2 305 4670, *Fax:* +20 2 305 4811, *Email:* petrowafaa2002@hotmail.com
Shell Marketing Egypt, Corner Street 254 & 206, Degla Maadi, Cairo 11742, Arab Republic of Egypt, *Tel:* +20 2 519 8817, *Fax:* +20 2 519 8818
Solimanco Marine Services, P O Box 202, Port Said Free Zone, Port Said 42111, Arab Republic of Egypt, *Tel:* +20 66 341641, *Fax:* +20 66 232262, *Email:* mohamed1969@mail.interlink-eg.com
Tamoil Misr, 35 Abdallah Ibn Taher Street, Nasr City, Cairo 11511, Arab Republic of Egypt, *Tel:* +20 2 273 2085, *Fax:* +20 2 287 2879

Waste Reception Facilities: Oily waste reception facilities are available at sea berth No.3

Towage: Not available, but service boats are available for mooring and unmooring

Lloyd's Agent: Marine Technical Services Ltd, Flat 6B, 28 Cherif Street, Cairo, Arab Republic of Egypt, *Tel:* +20 2 2393 5724, *Fax:* +20 2 2393 8669, *Email:* mts-lloyds-cairo@soficom.com.eg, *Website:* www.lloydsegypt.com

Key to Principal Facilities:—			
A=Airport	**C**=Containers	**G**=General Cargo	**P**=Petroleum	**R**=Ro/Ro	**Y**=Dry Bulk
B=Bunkers	**D**=Dry Dock	**L**=Cruise	**Q**=Other Liquid Bulk	**T**=Towage (where available from port)	

RAS SHUKHEIR TERMINAL

Lat 28° 8' N; Long 33° 17' E.

Admiralty Chart: 2374	**Admiralty Pilot:** 64
Time Zone: GMT +2 h	**UNCTAD Locode:** EG RSH

Principal Facilities:

P							T		

Authority: The Egyptian General Petroleum Corp., Palestine Street, 4th Sector, New Maadi, Cairo, Arab Republic of Egypt, *Tel:* +20 2 353 1471, *Fax:* +20 2 377 5962, *Email:* info@egpc.com.eg

Port Security: ISPS compliant

Approach: Vessels may only approach from the E and if necessary anchor SE of the sea berth. Under no circumstances should vessels anchor N of the sea berth

Anchorage: Tankers should only anchor in the Ras Shukheir anchorage area which is defined as pos 28° 16' 25" N, 33° 33' 00" E in a depth of 66 m

Pilotage: Compulsory. Mooring master meets vessel in anchorage area

Radio Frequency: Radio room on VHF Channel 16 and pilot station on Channel 8

Weather: Winds NW-NNW, velocity 20-40 knots

Tides: Range of tide 0.61 m

Working Hours: 24 h/day

Accommodation:

Name	Depth (m)	Remarks
Ras Shukheir Terminal		See [1] below
No.1 Sea Berth	25.6	See [2] below
No.2 Sea Berth	27.4	See [3] below

[1]*Ras Shukheir Terminal:* Berthing takes place during daylight, unberthing anytime. There is a ballast facility available. Tankers must have at least 150 fathoms of anchor chain as a minimum
Vessels leaving Ras Shukheir oil terminal should time their departure to avoid impeding the navigation of vessels approaching in the southbound lane
[2]*No.1 Sea Berth:* Located approx 1707 m offshore and can accommodate vessels up to 350 m loa. Max crude oil loading rate is approx 55 000 bbls/h
[3]*No.2 Sea Berth:* Located 0.5 mile S of No.1 and can accommodate vessels up to 305 m loa. Max crude oil loading rate is 51 000 bbls/h

Cargo Worked: Loading rate 500-600 t/day

Towage: Tugs fully equipped for fire-fighting

Medical Facilities: Available

Lloyd's Agent: Marine Technical Services Ltd, Flat 6B, 28 Cherif Street, Cairo, Arab Republic of Egypt, *Tel:* +20 2 2393 5724, *Fax:* +20 2 2393 8669, *Email:* mts-lloyds-cairo@soficom.com.eg, *Website:* www.lloydsegypt.com

RAS SUDR TERMINAL

Lat 29° 35' N; Long 32° 41' E.

Admiralty Chart: 753	**Admiralty Pilot:** 64
Time Zone: GMT +2 h	**UNCTAD Locode:** EG

Principal Facilities:

P								A	

Authority: Red Sea Ports Authority, Ras Sudr Terminal, Arab Republic of Egypt

Port Security: ISPS compliant

Anchorage: Vessels may obtain anchorage in the bay, SE of the nearby cape, approx 1 mile offshore in a depth of about 13 m

Pilotage: Compulsory

Accommodation:

Name	Remarks
Ras Sudr	See [1] below

[1]*Ras Sudr:* Tanker terminal consisting of a floating offshore berth secured to two mooring buoys for vessels up to 167 m loa and 9.1 m draft. Submarine pipelines connect to shore installations. There is a small pier for service craft

Airport: Ras Sudr Airport

Lloyd's Agent: Marine Technical Services Ltd, 4th Floor, Units 19 & 20, El Freepor Building, El Nahda & Palestine Streets, Port Said, Arab Republic of Egypt, *Tel:* +20 66 335 5423, *Fax:* +20 66 334 3974, *Email:* mts-lloyds-portsaid@soficom.com.eg, *Website:* www.lloydsegypt.com

SAFAGA

Lat 26° 44' N; Long 33° 56' E.

Admiralty Chart: 3043	**Admiralty Pilot:** 64
Time Zone: GMT +2 h	**UNCTAD Locode:** EG SGA

Principal Facilities:

	Y	G		R	L	B		T	A	

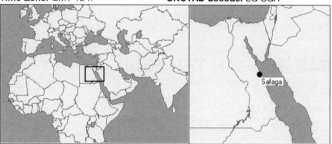

Tramp Oil & Marine

Wells House, 15-17 Elmfield Road, Bromley,
Kent BR1 1LT, United Kingdom
Phone: +44 20 8315 7777   **Fax:** +44 20 8315 7788
General email: enquiries@tramp-oil.com

See listings for all global offices: **www.tramp-oil.com**

Authority: Red Sea Ports Authority, Port of Safaga, Safaga, Arab Republic of Egypt, *Tel:* +20 65 325 6018, *Fax:* +20 65 325 3976

Officials: Harbour Master: Cdr Serrag Emara.

Port Security: ISPS compliant

Approach: Masters should endeavour to arrive at the N end of the island by sunrise, at Safaga Port by early morning; the light behind them will show up the reefs clearly. A beacon (Morewood Beacon) visible from 1.6 km is erected on the southern spit of the island. After rounding the spit, masters should keep 925 m clear of visible reefs and enter the harbour keeping the two large beacons to the N of the pier in line. Anchorage is then indicated by a small red or white flag. Safe draft through entrance 10.36 m or less

Pilotage: Compulsory with the assistance of one tug

Radio Frequency: Vessel Traffic Information Management System (VTIMS) equipped with Inmarsat (C) established in pos 26° 44.688' N; 33° 55.220' E, Station Sign 462299914 - frequency used M.Z - receiving/sending (156.55) VHF Channel 11

Weather: Wind light in the morning, gains strength during the day making tying up more difficult

Traffic: 2006, 793 vessels, 2 757 000 t of cargo handled

Maximum Vessel Dimensions: 12.7 m max draft, 290 m loa

Principal Imports and Exports: Imports: Aluminium powder, Cars, Coal, Grain. Exports: Foods, Phosphate.

Working Hours: 24 h/day

Accommodation:

Name	Length (m)	Depth (m)	Draught (m)	Remarks
Safaga				See [1] below
Berth No.1		14	11–12.7	Grain for vessels up to 290 m loa
Berth No.2	415	10	9.15	See [2] below
Berth No.3		10	9.45	See [3] below
Berth No.4	70		8.53	See [4] below
Berth No.5	420		9.75	Multi-purpose

[1]*Safaga:* There is also a coal berth for vessels up to 115 m loa with draft of 8 m and a private phosphate berth for vessels up to 260 m loa

[2]*Berth No.2:* General cargo & passengers for vessels up to 290 m loa
[3]*Berth No.3:* Aluminium for vessels up to 221 m loa. Silo of 40 000 t cap
[4]*Berth No.4:* Used for loading ground & rock phosphate

Storage:

Location	Grain (t)
Berth No.1	100000

Mechanical Handling Equipment:

Location	Type	Capacity (t)	Qty
Safaga	Mult-purp. Cranes	10	1

Cargo Worked: Grain 8000-10 000 t/day, aluminium 8000-9000 t/day, phosphate 9000-10 000 t/day, rock phosphate 1000 t/day

Bunkering: Tramp Oil & Marine, World Fuel Services Corporation, 13th Floor, Portland House, Bressenden Place, London SW1E 5BH, United Kingdom, *Tel:* +44 20 7808 5000, *Fax:* +44 20 7808 5088, *Email:* pturner@wfscorp.com, *Website:* www.wfscorp.com

Waste Reception Facilities: Garbage disposal available by truck

Towage: Two tugs of 2 x 1200 hp

Shipping Agents: Gulf Agency Co. (Egypt) Ltd, 1 Port Street, Safaga, Arab Republic of Egypt, *Tel:* +20 65 325 6510, *Fax:* +20 65 325 6511, *Email:* egypt@gacworld.com, *Website:* www.gacworld.com
Kadmar Shipping Co., El Salam Company for Transportation Building, Office 12 Front of Safaga Port, Safaga, Arab Republic of Egypt, *Tel:* +20 65 325 6635, *Fax:* +20 65 325 6635, *Email:* safaga@kadmar.com, *Website:* www.kadmar.com

Medical Facilities: Safaga hospital

Airport: Hurghada, 60 km

Lloyd's Agent: Marine Technical Services Ltd, 4th Floor, Units 19 & 20, El Freepor Building, El Nahda & Palestine Streets, Port Said, Arab Republic of Egypt, *Tel:* +20 66 335 5423, *Fax:* +20 66 334 3974, *Email:* mts-lloyds-portsaid@soficom.com.eg, *Website:* www.lloydsegypt.com

SHARM EL SHEIKH

Lat 27° 51' N; Long 34° 17' E.

Admiralty Chart: 2132	**Admiralty Pilot:** 64
Time Zone: GMT +2 h	**UNCTAD Locode:** EG SSH

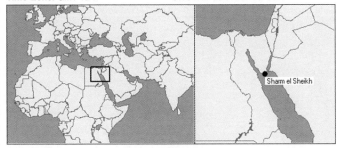

Principal Facilities:

			R	L	B		A

Authority: Red Sea Ports Authority, Port of Sharm el Sheikh, Sharm el Sheikh, Arab Republic of Egypt, *Tel:* +20 69 660557, *Fax:* +20 69 660209

Officials: Harbour Master: Capt Ibrahim El Henaway.

Approach: The approach to the bay is clear and free of dangers. The harbour is entered W of a rocky point which forms the S end of the promontory separating Sharm el Sheikh from Sharm el Moiya

Anchorage: May be obtained by small vessels in the NE corner of the bay in depth of approx 26 m, sand bottom

Pilotage: Compulsory. Pilot boards in pos 27° 50' N; 34° 17' E

Radio Frequency: VHF Channel 16

Traffic: 2006, 322 vessels

Maximum Vessel Dimensions: 30 000 dwt, 250 m loa, 9 m draft

Working Hours: 24 h/day

Accommodation:

Name	Length (m)	Depth (m)	Remarks
Sharm el Sheikh			See [1] below
Northern Berths		5	One berth 60 m long and one berth 30 m long
Western Berth	465	10	

[1]*Sharm el Sheikh:* The port is used mainly by passenger vessels and small craft

Bunkering: Available

Medical Facilities: Sharm el Sheikh hospital

Airport: Sharm el Sheikh, 20 km

Lloyd's Agent: Marine Technical Services Ltd, 4th Floor, Units 19 & 20, El Freepor Building, El Nahda & Palestine Streets, Port Said, Arab Republic of Egypt, *Tel:* +20 66 335 5423, *Fax:* +20 66 334 3974, *Email:* mts-lloyds-portsaid@soficom.com.eg, *Website:* www.lloydsegypt.com

SIDI KERIR TERMINAL

Lat 31° 6' N; Long 29° 37' E.

Admiralty Chart: 302/3325	**Admiralty Pilot:** 49
Time Zone: GMT +2 h	**UNCTAD Locode:** EG SKT

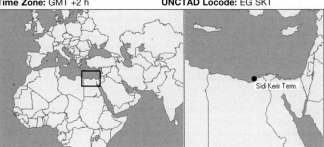

Principal Facilities:

P								T	A

Authority: Arab Petroleum Pipelines Co. (SUMED), 431 El-Geish Avenue, Loran, Alexandria, Arab Republic of Egypt, *Tel:* +20 3 582 6711, *Fax:* +20 3 582 6713, *Email:* schedoilmove@sumed.org, *Website:* www.sumed.org

Officials: Chairman: Mahmud Nazim, *Email:* chairman@sumed.org.
Terminal Manager: Ing Abdo Saad, *Tel:* +20 3 509 0086.

Port Security: ISPS compliant

Pre-Arrival Information: To SUMED Oil Movement Attn. T. Youssef/K. Saleh Re: (72, 48 and 24 h) pre-arrival notice
Vessel's name
IMO number
Flag
Port of registry
Master's name
Charterers
Shipper
INMARSAT Telex. No.
INMARSAT Phone No.
INMARSAT Fax No.
Email address
Present monitoring (indicate region)
ETA Sidi Kerir
N.O.R.T.
Vessel voyage instructions (indicate berthing instructions)
Arrival draft
Departure draft
Max trim
Cargo nomination (Grade A, Grade B, Grade C quantity H2S amount)
Ballast on board (quantity)
Type of ballast (C/S/D) to be discharged (ashore/to sea/keep on board)
Deb. sequence (before loading/simultaneous/load/deb/load) indicate quantities
Loading sequence (required flow rate)
Use of helicopter (landing/winches/none)
Last port of call
Next port of call
Ship security level
Master

Anchorage: MAP 'M17' approach To SUMED Kerir Terminal

Pilotage: Compulsory. Pilot boards 2 miles N of SBM No.1. Master's of vessels proceeding to the terminal should cable their ETA's to 'SUMED' Alexandria. This cable is to be prefixed 'to be conveyed via telex 54108 or 54033 SUMED UN, operations office-oil movement'. ETA notifications to be sent:
a) immediately upon sailing from previous port
b) in case of a change in ETA exceeding 6 h
c) 72 h, 48 h and 24 h prior to arrival

Radio Frequency: Master's are required to contact the terminal on VHF 6 h before arrival on Channels 78 and 03 if available or 16

Weather: The prevailing winds from April to September are from the N/NW but become rather more variable in direction from October to March

Tides: Tidal range is between 0.2 and 1.9 ft

Traffic: 2006, 930 vessels, 128 094 641 m3 of crude oil handled

Working Hours: 24 h/day, 7 days/week

Accommodation:

Name	Depth (m)	Draught (m)	Remarks
Sidi Kerir Terminal			See [1] below
SBM No.1	25.9	22.9	See [2] below
SBM No.2	25.9	22.9	See [3] below
SBM No.3	18.3	16.43	Laid up
SBM No.4	18.3	16.43	See [4] below
SBM No.5	18.3	16.43	See [5] below
SBM No.6	25.9	22.9	See [6] below

[1]*Sidi Kerir Terminal:* Only SBM No's 5 & 6 are equipped with deballasting sea lines leading to a water treatment system onshore
[2]*SBM No.1:* In pos 31° 06' 26" N; 29° 36' 46" E for vessels up to 350 000 dwt. Connected to shore by a submarine pipeline 48" in diameter and approx 8 km long
[3]*SBM No.2:* In pos 31° 05' 32" N; 29° 35' 38" E for vessels loading/discharging up to 350 000 dwt. Connected to shore by a submarine pipeline 48" in diameter and approx 8 km long
[4]*SBM No.4:* In pos 31° 04' 54" N; 29° 37' 39" E for vessels loading/discharging up

to 150 000 dwt. Connected to shore by a submarine pipeline 42" in diameter and approx 5 km long

5SBM No.5: In pos 31° 05' 40" N; 29° 38' 24" E for vessels up to 150 000 dwt. Connected to shore by a submarine pipeline 42" in diameter and approx 5 km long. Vessel's readiness to connect either 3 x 16" hoses if there is deballasting operation or 2 x 16" hoses if segregated ballast system on board

6SBM No.6: In pos 31° 07' 30.4" N; 29° 37' 58.3" E for vessels up to 400 000 dwt. Connected to shore by a submarine pipeline 48" in diameter and approx 8 km long. Vessel's readiness to connect either 3 x 16" hoses if there is deballasting operation or 2 x 16" hoses if segregated ballast system on board

Storage: Onshore facilities include 24 single-deck, floating, roof, welded steel storage tanks (15 tanks with a cap of 103 000 m3 each and 9 tanks with a cap of 117 000 m3 each), total storage cap of 2 610 000 m3

Bunkering: Macoil International S.A., Macoil Building, 103 Kallirois Street, 176 71 Athens, Greece, *Tel:* +30 210 9249 175, *Fax:* +30 210 9249 170, *Email:* macoil@otenet.gr

Towage: Two tugs of 2448 hp and two of 4200 hp are fully equipped for fire-fighting and anti-pollution operations

Medical Facilities: Neither medical nor hospital facilities are provided by SUMED. In case urgent medical assistance is required the vessel should contact SUMED's harbour master by VHF radio. Private doctors and facilities are available at Alexandria

Airport: Alexandria Airport, 40 km. Borg el Arab Airport, 30 km

Railway: Sidi Gaber Railway Station, 35 km. Misr Railway Station, 30 km

Development: New storage tanks of 600 000 m3 cap under construction, which, when completed will increase the storage cap to 3 200 000 m3

Lloyd's Agent: Marine Technical Services Ltd, Flat 6B, 28 Cherif Street, Cairo, Arab Republic of Egypt, *Tel:* +20 2 2393 5724, *Fax:* +20 2 2393 8669, *Email:* mts-lloyds-cairo@soficom.com.eg, *Website:* www.lloydsegypt.com

SOKHNA

Lat 29° 41' N; Long 32° 22' E.

Admiralty Chart: 2090	**Admiralty Pilot:** 64
Time Zone: GMT +2 h	**UNCTAD Locode:** EG SOK

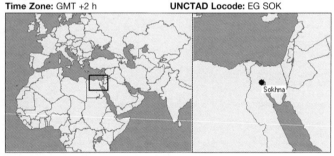

Principal Facilities:

		Y	G	C	R				

Authority: Sokhna Port Development Co., 29 Farid Street, Heliopolis, Cairo, Arab Republic of Egypt, *Tel:* +20 2 414 9944, *Fax:* +20 2 414 8877, *Email:* info@spdc.com, *Website:* www.spdc.com

Officials: Chief Executive Officer: Capt Ossama Al Sharif.
Operations Manager: Peter VanLith, *Email:* peter.vanlith@spdc.com.

Port Security: ISPS compliant

Approach: Width of access channel 350 m in depth of 17 m

Anchorage: Anchorage No.1 (S1) in pos 29° 40.93' N; 32° 27' E, 6 cable diameter
Anchorage No.2 (S2) in pos 29° 40.3' N; 32° 27' E, 6 cable diameter
Anchorage No.3 (S3) in pos 29° 39.68' N; 32° 27' E, 6 cable diameter
Anchorage No.4 (S4) in pos 29° 41.01' N; 32° 26.1' E, 5 cable diameter
Anchorage No.5 (S5) in pos 29° 40.35' N; 32° 26.01' E, 5 cable diameter
Anchorage No.6 (S6) in pos 29° 39.75' N; 32° 26.1' E, 5 cable diameter
Anchorage No.7 (S7) in pos 29° 41.67' N; 32° 26.5' E, 3 cable diameter
Anchorage No.8 (S8) in pos 29° 40.05' N; 32° 26.5' E, 3 cable diameter

Pilotage: Compulsory and available 24 h/day. Vessels should advise ETA via agent 72 h, 48 h and 24 h prior to arrival, and confirm ETA at pilot station directly. Pilot boards in pos 29° 38.78' N; 32° 24.52' E (in the vicinity of the Fairway Lt buoy)

Radio Frequency: VHF Channel 12

Traffic: 2006, 396 vessels, 300 640 TEU's handled

Maximum Vessel Dimensions: 350 m loa

Working Hours: 24 h/day

Accommodation:

Name	Length (m)	Depth (m)	Remarks
Sokhna			Sokhna Port, Tel: +20 62 371 0080, Fax: +20 62 371 0081
Container Terminal	750	17	See [1] below
General Cargo/Ro-ro Terminal	350	17	See [2] below
Fertilizer Terminal		17	See [3] below
Bulk Terminal	400	17	See [4] below
Livestock Terminal			Feedlot for 24 000 head of cattle

[1]*Container Terminal:* Operated by DP World Sokhna, Sokhna Port Development, PO Box 133, Sokhna, Tel:+20 62 371 0071, Fax: +20 62 371 0070, Email: info.sokhna@dpworld.com, Website: www.dpworld.com

Stacking area of 8000 TEU full containers, 5000 TEU empty containers, 216 reefer points, 24 parking positions for off-size containers and 28 parking positions for dangerous/hazardous containers. Railcar loading/unloading

[2]*General Cargo/Ro-ro Terminal:* One 4000 m2 general cargo warehouse, open storage area of 1 ha for general cargo and open storage area of 2 ha for ro/ro cargo

[3]*Fertilizer Terminal:* Two receiving and intake conveyors of 150 t/h each; an outtake belt conveyor equipped with two loading hoppers of 500 t/h cap. One 6800 m2 warehouse

[4]*Bulk Terminal:* For two vessels of 30 000 dwt or one vessel of 150 000 dwt. Import of scrap and DRI for the steel industry and export of cement dust and clinker in bulk

Mechanical Handling Equipment:

Location	Type	Capacity (t)	Qty	Remarks
Container Terminal	Mobile Cranes	100	4	
Container Terminal	Super Post Panamax	65	2	twin lifter
Container Terminal	RTG's	51.8	3	twin lifter
Container Terminal	Reach Stackers	42–45	11	
Container Terminal	Reach Stackers	10	2	empty handler
General Cargo/Ro-ro Terminal	Mobile Cranes	100	2	
General Cargo/Ro-ro Terminal	Forklifts	3–30	12	
Bulk Terminal	Mobile Cranes	65	2	

Towage: Available 24 h/day

Shipping Agents: Gulf Badr Group, Build No.11, 2nd Floor, Office No.3, Sokhna, Arab Republic of Egypt, *Tel:* +20 62 371 0223, *Fax:* +20 62 371 0222, *Email:* eversok@gulfbadregypt.com, *Website:* www.gulfbadregypt.com

Development: Liquid bulk terminal currently under construction and due for completion in 2008
Two super-post panamax gantries and five RTG's are on order; available beginning 2008

Lloyd's Agent: Marine Technical Services Ltd, 4th Floor, Units 19 & 20, El Freepor Building, El Nahda & Palestine Streets, Port Said, Arab Republic of Egypt, *Tel:* +20 66 335 5423, *Fax:* +20 66 334 3974, *Email:* mts-lloyds-portsaid@soficom.com.eg, *Website:* www.lloydsegypt.com

SUEZ

Lat 29° 58' N; Long 32° 33' E.

Admiralty Chart: 3214	**Admiralty Pilot:** 64
Time Zone: GMT +2 h	**UNCTAD Locode:** EG SUZ

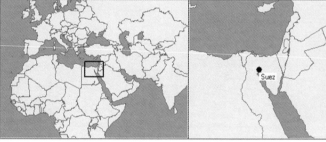

Principal Facilities:

P		Y	G	C	R		B	D	T	

Authority: Red Sea Ports Authority, P O Box 1, Port Tewfik, Arab Republic of Egypt, *Tel:* +20 62 333 1123, *Fax:* +20 62 333 0315, *Email:* rspsite@emdb.gov.eg

Officials: Chairman: Hesham El Sersawy.
Harbour Master: Basel Bahgat.

Port Security: ISPS compliant

Approach: Passage at Newport Rock and the spit buoys dredged to uniform depth of 11.28 m. Vessels with draft exceeding 11.28 m may enter harbour at high tide only, provided draft does not exceed 12.19 m

Anchorage: Vessels having a deep draft normally anchor at the outer anchorage west of the Newport Rock

Pilotage: Compulsory for entering, leaving or moving in the pilotage zone of Suez Bay, defined by an imaginary line from Ras Adabieh to Oyoun Moussa and comprising the zone to N of this line up to the entrance to the Suez Canal. Pilotage is handled by the Suez Canal Authority. Three pilot tugs. The 'Pilot Signal' must be hoisted before entering the zone. Specified anchorage sites in Suez Roads are laid down for vessels having to await pilots

No movement to or from Port Ibrahim can be effected while vessels are entering or leaving the Canal. No night movements; movements only effected from 1300 to 1630 h and passenger vessels have priority which means other vessels have very restricted berthing/unberthing times at Port Ibrahim

Weather: Bay sheltered from all points except south. During March and April a strong wind called the Khamassine blows which may close the canal and cancel movements to and from Port Ibrahim

Tides: ST rise 2.13 m, NT 1.22 m. Greatly influenced by seasons and by continuous S wind 2 or 3 days when tide rises 2.44 or 2.74 m

Traffic: 2004, 571 vessels, 715 000 t of cargo handled

Working Hours: Offices open from 0900-1400 and sometimes from 1830-2000. Dockers work round the clock in three shifts: 0800-1530 (break from noon to 1300), 1600-2230, 0000-0600

Accommodation: Tanker facilities: Seven concrete jetties for tankers of approx 18 000 dwt. Only daylight berthing permitted. Ample tank storage for bulk petroleum products. Largest vessel: 169 m loa with a loaded draft of 8.0 m

Suez New Port for loading/discharging naphtha and fuel oil. Offshore terminal for tankers with laden displacement 65 000 t max, loa 250 m max, draught 10.37 m max. Tanker to be fitted with a min of six mooring ropes and a portable gangway. Berthing/unberthing during daylight only

Name	Length (m)	Depth (m)	Remarks
Port Ibrahim			Consists of N and S Basins
North Basin	736	8.07	See [1] below
South Basin			See [2] below
Port Tewfik			See [3] below

[1]*North Basin:* Four vessels can be accommodated. However priority is given to passenger ferries and there are five lines trading to and from Jeddah and one sailing on to Aqaba. Rail connections on the quay. There is a free zone area in the port

[2]*South Basin:* The Khedivial Quay on the S Basin is 7.31 m deep at HW; berths 9, 10 and 11 are 36 m long

[3]*Port Tewfik:* Marakeb Quay accommodates passenger vessels in transit for the Suez Canal. Draft of vessels should not exceed 8.23 m; no restrictions as to size, length or beam. Application to berth at this quay must be submitted to the Suez Canal Authority in writing, stating the number of passengers on board and their anticipated movements

Storage:

Location	Covered (m²)	Sheds / Warehouses
Suez	23000	7

Mechanical Handling Equipment:

Location	Type	Capacity (t)	Qty
Suez	Floating Cranes	60	1
Suez	Mult-purp. Cranes	11–30	11
Suez	Mult-purp. Cranes	70	2
Suez	Forklifts	25	2
Suez	Forklifts	4	51

Cargo Worked: Grain 6000 t/day

Bunkering: Coal bunkers not available. Fuel, diesel and gas oil by barge.
Abu Raahil Petroleum Services Co. (ARPSCO), 1st Floor, Suez Canal Authority Building, Hud Eldars Street, Port Tawfik, Suez, Arab Republic of Egypt, *Tel:* +20 62 154 4419, *Fax:* +20 62 335 6208, *Email:* suez@arpsco.com, *Website:* www.arpsco.com
Felix Maritime Agency, Port Tawfiek, Port Said Street, Beside Green House Hotel, Suez, Arab Republic of Egypt, *Tel:* +20 62 319 1546, *Fax:* +20 62 319 9675, *Email:* flx@link.net, *Website:* www.felix-eg.com
Tramp Oil & Marine, World Fuel Services Corporation, 13th Floor, Portland House, Bressenden Place, London SW1E 5BH, United Kingdom, *Tel:* +44 20 7808 5000, *Fax:* +44 20 7808 5088, *Email:* pturner@wfscorp.com, *Website:* www.wfscorp.com

Towage: Tugs available from 1400-2400 hp

Repair & Maintenance: Port Said Engineering Works S.A.E., P O Box 170, Palestine & El Shohada Streets, Port Said, Arab Republic of Egypt, *Tel:* +20 66 324 0387, *Fax:* +20 66 324 0845
Suez Shipyard Company, 5 Shoadaa El Yemen Street, Port Tawfik, Suez, Arab Republic of Egypt, *Tel:* +20 62 322 0620, *Fax:* +20 62 322 7848, *Email:* suez_shipyard@hotmail.com, *Website:* www.suez-shipyard.com.eg Trimdock with a lifting cap of 17 000 t, pontoon length of 171 m and inside breadth of 62.3 m. Vessels up to 30 000 dwt can be docked in the conventional way and vessels up to 300 000 dwt can be accepted on the facility. Dry dock with dimensions 141 m x 21 m x 6.7 m and slipway of 250 t

Ship Chandlers: Abu Raahil Petroleum Services Co. (ARPSCO), 1st Floor, Suez Canal Authority Building, Hud Eldars Street, Port Tawfik, Suez, Arab Republic of Egypt, *Tel:* +20 62 154 4419, *Fax:* +20 62 335 6208, *Email:* suez@arpsco.com, *Website:* www.arpsco.com
American Marine Suppliers Egypt, 2 Aaqda Street, Suez, Arab Republic of Egypt, *Tel:* +20 62 335 1591, *Fax:* +20 62 322 0148, *Email:* supply@american-shipsupply.com, *Website:* www.american-shipsupply.com
Edwardo Marine Services Co., 3 El-Marwa & El-Guish Street, P O Box 163, Suez, Arab Republic of Egypt, *Tel:* +20 62 233 0429, *Fax:* +20 62 632 2134, *Email:* info@edwardomarine.com
The Egyptian Marine Supply & Contracting Co. SAA (CONSUP), P O Box 32, Suez, Arab Republic of Egypt, *Tel:* +20 62 322 0132, *Fax:* +20 62 322 4306, *Email:* consup2000@usa.net
The International Marine Services Co. (S.A.E.), 2 Al-Shouhada Street, Zaza Building, P O Box 34, Suez, Arab Republic of Egypt, *Tel:* +20 62 333 4019, *Fax:* +20 62 322 5508, *Email:* marineco@bec.com.eg
International Shipping Enterprise S.A.E. (Intership), P O Box 153, 16 Gawhar El Kaid Street, Port Tawfik, Suez, Arab Republic of Egypt, *Tel:* +20 62 333 0341, *Fax:* +20

62 333 4654, *Email:* intershipsuez@intershipegypt.com, *Website:* www.intershipegypt.com
Sinai Industrial & Marine Supplies, P O Box 15, Suez, Arab Republic of Egypt, *Tel:* +20 62 222 8144, *Fax:* +20 62 222 1541, *Email:* sinai@bec.com.eg
Sunlight Agency, P O Box 10, 5 Arafat Street, Port Tawfik, Suez, Arab Republic of Egypt, *Tel:* +20 62 332 8350, *Fax:* +20 62 322 2454, *Email:* shipping@sunlight-agency.com.eg, *Website:* www.sunlightagency.com

Shipping Agents: ABC for Shipping & Trade, 3 Port Said Street, next to Green House Hotel, Suez, Arab Republic of Egypt, *Tel:* +20 62 322 3881, *Fax:* +20 62 330 1590, *Email:* cap_badwy@yahoo.com
Ameaster Shipping & Trading Co. S.R.L., 8 El Gueish Street - 4th Floor, Port Tewfik, Arab Republic of Egypt, *Tel:* +20 62 322 3713, *Fax:* +20 62 322 1280, *Email:* info.suez@ameaster.com, *Website:* www.ameaster.com
Arab Express Shipping Co., 40 Gohar El-Kaed Street, Suez, Arab Republic of Egypt, *Tel:* +20 62 333 2521, *Fax:* +20 62 333 2520, *Website:* www.arabxprs.com
Concord Shipping Agency, 1st Floor, El Hegaz Building, Memphis Street, Port Said, Arab Republic of Egypt, *Tel:* +20 66 325 2443, *Fax:* +20 66 323 4476, *Email:* office@concordshipping.com, *Website:* www.concordshipping.com
Demco Shipping & Logistics Co. SAE, 4 El Dobat Building, Port Tawfik, Suez, Arab Republic of Egypt, *Tel:* +20 62 322 8893, *Email:* demcosuez@demcoshipping.com, *Website:* www.demcoshipping.com
Evge Egypt, 34 El Geish Street, Port Tawfik, Suez, Arab Republic of Egypt, *Tel:* +20 62 332 7397, *Fax:* +20 62 332 7397
Felix Maritime Agency, Port Tawfiek, Port Said Street, Beside Green House Hotel, Suez, Arab Republic of Egypt, *Tel:* +20 62 319 1546, *Fax:* +20 62 319 9675, *Email:* flx@link.net, *Website:* www.felix-eg.com
Finmar Shipping Co SAE, 1st Floor, Flat 3, El-Dobbat Building 5, El-Fanarat Street, Gate 9, Port Tawfik, Suez, Arab Republic of Egypt, *Tel:* +20 62 333 5490/334 3322, *Fax:* +20 62 332 3108, *Email:* antaresshipping@bec.com.eg
Gulf Agency Co. (Egypt) Ltd, 10 Gohar El Kaied Street, Port Tawfiq, Suez, Arab Republic of Egypt, *Tel:* +20 62 332 3253, *Fax:* +20 62 332 3251, *Email:* egypt@gacworld.com, *Website:* www.gacworld.com
Gulf Badr Group, 33 Elshohada Street, P O Box 129, Suez 43511, Arab Republic of Egypt, *Tel:* +20 62 333 8955, *Fax:* +20 62 333 1824, *Email:* eversuz@gulfbadregypt.com, *Website:* www.gulfbadregypt.com
Inchcape Shipping Services (ISS), 10 El Fanarat Street, Port Tawfik, Suez, Arab Republic of Egypt, *Tel:* +20 62 319 8111, *Fax:* +20 62 319 5171, *Email:* operation.suez@iss-shipping.com, *Website:* www.iss-shipping.com
International Associated Cargo Carriers (IACC), 38 Goha El Qaed Street, Suez, Arab Republic of Egypt, *Tel:* +20 62 332 8254, *Fax:* +20 62 332 8253, *Email:* iacc@iacc.net, *Website:* www.iacc.net
International Shipping Enterprise S.A.E., 16A Gohar El Kaed Street, Port Tewfik, Suez, Arab Republic of Egypt, *Tel:* +20 62 333 0341, *Fax:* +20 62 333 4564, *Email:* intershipsuez@intershipegypt.com, *Website:* www.intershipegypt.com
International Shipping Enterprise S.A.E. (Intership), P O Box 153, 16 Gawhar El Kaid Street, Port Tawfik, Suez, Arab Republic of Egypt, *Tel:* +20 62 333 0341, *Fax:* +20 62 333 4654, *Email:* intershipsuez@intershipegypt.com, *Website:* www.intershipegypt.com
Kadmar Shipping Co., 28A Al Kaed Gohar Street, Behind the Saudi Arabia Consulate, Port Tawfik, Suez, Arab Republic of Egypt, *Tel:* +20 62 334 8345, *Fax:* +20 62 332 2569, *Email:* suez@kadmar.com, *Website:* www.kadmar.com
Mediterranean Shipping Company, MSC Egypt, 46 Gohar El Kayed Street, 3rd Floor, Suez, Arab Republic of Egypt, *Tel:* +20 62 330 3987, *Fax:* +20 62 335 4945, *Email:* sueztr@mscegypt.com, *Website:* www.mscgva.ch
A.P. Moller-Maersk Group, Maersk Egypt S.A.E., 8 Mohamed Farid Street, Port Tawfik, Suez, Arab Republic of Egypt, *Tel:* +20 62 334 1423/4, *Fax:* +20 62 334 1425, *Email:* egymkt@maersk.com, *Website:* www.maerskline.com
Naggar Shipping Co., 5 Fanarat & Sawahel Street, Port Tewfik, P O Box 63, Suez 43522, Arab Republic of Egypt, *Tel:* +20 62 322 1685, *Fax:* +20 62 332 6938, *Email:* naggar@naggar.com, *Website:* www.naggar.com
RAFIMAR SAE, 8 El-Safa Street, Suez, Port Tewfik, Arab Republic of Egypt, *Tel:* +20 62 333 5995, *Fax:* +20 62 322 7814, *Email:* suez@rafimar.com, *Website:* www.rafimar.com
Scan Arabia Shipping SAE, 34 El Gueish Street, El Zahraa Building, Flat 101, Port Tewfik, Arab Republic of Egypt, *Tel:* +20 62 333 6620, *Fax:* +20 62 333 6619
Wilhelmsen Ship Services, 3 Arafat Street, El Ahlam Building, Off ElGuish Street, Port Tawfik, Suez, Arab Republic of Egypt, *Tel:* +20 62 333 6620, *Fax:* +20 62 333 6619, *Email:* barwil.egypt.operations@wilhelmsen.com, *Website:* www.barwilunitor.com

Stevedoring Companies: Concord Shipping Agency, 1st Floor, El Hegaz Building, Memphis Street, Port Said, Arab Republic of Egypt, *Tel:* +20 66 325 2443, *Fax:* +20 66 323 4476, *Email:* office@concordshipping.com, *Website:* www.concordshipping.com
Suez Mechanical Stevedoring Co., Suez, Arab Republic of Egypt, *Tel:* +20 62 326 0625, *Fax:* +20 62 322 5774

Surveyors: Bureau Veritas, Safwa Tower No.3 App. 101, Suez, Arab Republic of Egypt, *Tel:* +20 62 331 9585, *Fax:* +20 62 331 9585, *Email:* agel.shaban@eg.bureauveritas.com, *Website:* www.bureauveritas.com
Det Norske Veritas A/S, Suez, Arab Republic of Egypt, *Tel:* +20 62 322 9609, *Website:* www.dnv.com
Germanischer Lloyd, P O Box 33, Port Tawfik, Suez, Arab Republic of Egypt, *Tel:* +20 62 332 6916, *Fax:* +20 62 333 7211, *Email:* glsuez@menanet.net, *Website:* www.gl-group.com
Nippon Kaiji Kyokai, 7 El-Zaher Beibars Street, 2nd Floor, Apt.2, Port Tawfik, Suez, Arab Republic of Egypt, *Tel:* +20 62 332 6916, *Fax:* +20 62 332 6916, *Website:* www.classnk.or.jp
Registro Italiano Navale (RINA), 68 Gohar Al Kaeed Street, 3rd Floor, Suez, Arab Republic of Egypt, *Email:* suez.office@rina.org, *Website:* www.rina.org

Medical Facilities: Available

Lloyd's Agent: Marine Technical Services Ltd, 4th Floor, Units 19 & 20, El Freepor Building, El Nahda & Palestine Streets, Port Said, Arab Republic of Egypt, *Tel:* +20 66 335 5423, *Fax:* +20 66 334 3974, *Email:* mts-lloyds-portsaid@soficom.com.eg, *Website:* www.lloydsegypt.com

Key to Principal Facilities:—				
A=Airport	**C**=Containers	**G**=General Cargo	**P**=Petroleum	**R**=Ro/Ro	**Y**=Dry Bulk
B=Bunkers	**D**=Dry Dock	**L**=Cruise	**Q**=Other Liquid Bulk	**T**=Towage (where available from port)	

SUEZ CANAL

Admiralty Chart: 233   **Admiralty Pilot:** 64
Time Zone: GMT +2 h   **UNCTAD Locode:** EG
Principal Facilities:

						B	T	

Authority: Suez Canal Authority, Pilotage Building, Ismailia, Arab Republic of Egypt, *Tel:* +20 64 330000/9, *Fax:* +20 64 320784/5

Officials: Chairman: Admiral Ahmed Aly Fadel.

Pilotage: Pilotage in the canal, compulsory for ships over 300 Suez gt. A second pilot must be engaged by vessels exceeding 80 000 Suez gt. A vessel transiting the Canal will normally take on board a total of four different pilots. From the north, one from the roads into Port Said, the second from Port Said to Ismailia, the third from Ismailia to Suez and the fourth from Suez to the open sea. Vice versa for vessels from the south. The service is free for vessels passing through the Canal. Ships not transitting the Canal are subject to Pilotage dues on entering and leaving Port Said harbour, and the Authority's basins at Port Tewfik

Traffic: 2006, 18 664 vessel transits carrying 628 600 000 t of cargo

Maximum Vessel Dimensions: 190 000 dwt fully loaded; 250 000 dwt partially loaded can be accepted. Max loa, no restriction; max beam 77 m; max d 19 m. These figures vary from vessel to vessel as the Canal Authority works on the basis of breadth and draught tables
Vessels allowed to transit at a draught of over 15.2 m up to the max permitted must for the first passage effectuate a successful sea trial at the roads before entering the Canal
Vessels with beam over 61 m are allowed to transit only in calm weather, i.e. beam wind not exceeding 10 knots

Accommodation: The Suez Canal connects the Mediterranean Sea with the Red Sea. The Mediterranean entrance is at Port Said and the Red Sea entrance at Port Tewfik, Suez. The surface of the Canal is 365 m wide in some sections and 300 m in others. Navigational width between buoys is 195 m. The depth is dredged to 22.5 m
From the Mediterranean end the Canal is entered between two light buoys at the S end of Husein Basin. The main channel, 2.5 km S of the canal entrance, has been widened 45 m to the E. A new channel has been created from km 17 on the Canal to the Mediterranean Sea, giving access to vessels in and out of the Canal without passing by Port Said harbour. The Canal runs S and passes side by side with the sweet water canal, thence to Lake Timsah, which is the midway point at km 78.5. On the N shore of the lake is situated the town of Ismailia which contains the headquarters of the Canal Authority, who have a radio station for communication with vessels in transit. Ismailia is also a changing point for pilots. The Canal continues from the S end of Lake Timsah and then runs into the Great Bitter Lake and Little Bitter Lake and from there follows a course to the S entrance at Port Tewfik, which is also marked by two light buoys and vessels must pass between these when leaving or entering the Canal. It normally takes a vessel between 12 and 16 h to transit the Canal, the average time being about 14 h. Together with time spent waiting at the anchorage areas a whole day at least could be taken up to fully transit the area. The max cap of the Canal is 76 vessels/day
At certain places along the Canal additional channels have been cut and are used by the N bound convoys
In the N part of the Canal there is no perceptible tide as far as the Bitter Lakes, but in the S part the range of tide at the S end of the Little Bitter Lake is 0.2 m ST and at Port Tewfik 2.1 m ST
Berthing possibilities at km 51-61, km 76.95-81.25 and km 104-114. New areas in the Bitter Lakes have recently been established for this purpose, enabling up to sixty vessels to await the passage of other vessels
An advanced navigational control system is in operation over the full length of the Canal and approaches, with the main operations centre at Ismaila
Ships transitting the Canal are required to fulfil the following conditions:
1. The ship's loadline for tropical zones must be apparent and in compliance with the provisions of International Convention regarding loadlines
2. The ship's draft marks fore, aft and amidships will be existent on port and starboard sides
All ships have to conform to the Suez Canal Rules of Navigation and its Appendix for dangerous cargo
Regulations Concerning the "Containers"
The "containers" are closed spaces increasing the carriage capacity of the ship when situated over the main deck
They are considered as a ship's permanent equipment
It is a matter of fact that those in the cargo holds are included in the underdeck tonnage
Conditions to Consider the Container as Part of the Ship's Permanent Equipment
(1) They must belong to:

(a) the ship's owner, or
(b) the time charterer, or
(c) the container's consortium
(2) They must bear a serial number as well as the owner's name
(3) They must be registered on the ship's official documents
(4) The Captains of the containers' ships must assure to the Suez Canal Authority's Representatives all facilities concerning the measurement and number of containers, their internal capacities and the kind of cargo contained
(5) Containers ship to be considered, in ballast, if all the containers on board-those inside the cargo holds as well as those over the main deck-are empty
Computation of Tonnage of Containers' Ships
Considering the containers as part of the ship's permanent equipment the following procedure is to be adopted for the computation of tonnage:
Container vessels or lash vessels carrying containers or lashes over weather deck will be subject to the following surcharges on Suez Canal dues:
6% for vessels carrying up to three tiers of containers or lashes
8% for vessels carrying four tiers of containers or lashes
10% for vessels carrying five tiers of containers
14% for vessels carrying more than five tiers of containers
The present Regulations are subject to be revised, at any time, when deemed necessary
Regulations and Precautionary Measures Concerning the Transit of LPG, LNG or Chemicals in the Suez Canal
Regulations
(a) The Captain shall hand to the Suez Canal Authority's Officials the 'CLASSIFICATION CERTIFICATE' showing that the vessel is classed in accordance with the requirements of Article 15 of the Appendix to the 'Rules of Navigation'
(b) Cargo tanks shall be isolated either by pumprooms or by coffer dams capable of being filled with water according to Article 15, Paragraph 1
Cofferdams or pumprooms must extend from side to side of the vessel and from keel up to the main deck
Water ballast tanks or void spaces can take lieu of cofferdam
Oil bunkers are not acceptable adjacent to cargo tanks owing to the fact that leakages can occur even if the separation bulkhead is completely gas-tight and thoroughly welded
(c) It is required, both for ballast and loaded condition, that the vessel shall be able to pump out ballast water corresponding to three feet decrease in draft in case of casualties
(d) If the carrying of liquid gases or chemicals entails the keeping of a certain quantity of gases or chemicals to ensure a permanent low temperature inside the cargo tanks, the vessel will, then be considered loaded according to Article 23 of the 'Rules of Navigation'
Precautionary Measures:
(a) The transit of the vessel will be effected in day time
(b) A first class tug may be imposed for escort if the Suez Canal Authority deems it necessary, expenses of which will be charged to the vessel
(c) Date of Transit should be notified in advance
Convoy System: Three convoys daily, two from the N and one from the S
Convoy Times:
(1) From North:
First Convoy starts at 0100 h and ends at 0500 h, direct to Bitter Lakes. Max 60 vessels. Arrival time limit 1900 hours previous day
Second Convoy N2 starts at 0700 h and ends at 0900 h. This convoy is to be moored at El Ballah Western Cut. Max 15 vessels; usually 5 to 6 vessels. Arrival time limit 0300
Vessels not permitted to join the second convoy
Vessels carrying explosives; tankers in ballast (not gas free); tankers loaded with petroleum flash point -23°C; LPG and LNG; tankers carrying chemicals; vessels carrying radioactive materials
Slow or damaged ships to join this convoy
(2) From South:
One convoy only which starts at 0600 h
Conditions for vessels to join the convoys, times for registration and submission of documents (max 45 vessels):
(1) From Port Said:
First Southbound convoy N1
(a) Vessels entering the Canal directly from Sea-must:
Arrive at the waiting area at Port Said anchorage not later than 1800 h
Call the Pilot
Give full details of vessels particulars, arrival draft and cargo to the Pilot boat on arrival
It is permitted for these vessels to be registered preliminary in the Canal Authority measurement office without submitting the documents at the time of her arrival at Port Said anchorage till not later than 2030 h
Hoist Pilot Signal
(b) Vessel in Port and required to transit the Canal must adhere to the following:
Call the Pilot (by hoisting the Pilot Signal)
Having registered for transitting at the measurement office, submit documentation not later than 2030 h
Second Southbound convoy N2
Arrival time limit 0200 h
Preliminary documents can be submitted from arrival time up to 0300 h
Latest permissible time to hoist for Pilot is 0300 h
(2) From Suez:
Northbound Convoy:
Latest time permitted to arrive at the waiting area at Suez anchorage
Group A by 0100 h
Group B by 0300 h
(a) Group A consists of 3rd generation container vessels, loaded VLCC's, conventional loaded tankers, LPG and LNG carriers and heavy bulk carriers over 11.6 m d or 289.6 m length
(b) Group B consists of cargo and other vessels
Registration for both groups is within the arrival limit time
The convoy starts with 3rd generation container vessels at 0615, followed by the loaded tankers at 0700 h thence the remainder of vessels up to 1130 h
Rules: The flag of the Arab Republic of Egypt must remain on the mast during transit and in the port
Captains are responsible for all damage or accidents of whatever kind resulting from the navigation or handling of their ships by day or night. When intending to proceed through the Canal they must, at Port Said or Port Tewfik, pay dues, enter ship at

transit office, and produce papers showing tonnage measurement for Canal, names of owners, charterers, master, port of sailing and destination, quantity and nature of cargo, draft, passenger list, and list of crew
Any vessel exceeding 500 gt must, during night hours, use a searchlight approved by the Authority's Rules of Navigation

Bunkering: Available at Port Said and Suez Roads
Misr Petroleum Co., MISR Petroleum House, 6 Orabi Square, P O Box 228, Cairo, Arab Republic of Egypt, *Tel:* +20 2 2574 5400, *Fax:* +20 2 2574 5436, *Email:* bunker@misrpetroleum.com, *Website:* www.misrpetroleum.com – *Grades:* HFO; IFO; GO – *Rates:* 250-300t/h – *Delivery Mode:* barge from Suez/Alexandria, barge and pipeline for Port Said

Towage: Tugs up to 16 000 hp are available from the Suez Canal Authority
Escorting is compulsory in the following instances:
(a) Loaded vessels under 100 000 dwt will be escorted by one tug if required for technical reasons by the SCA only
(b) Loaded vessels from 100 000-150 000 dwt will be escorted by one tug
(c) Loaded vessels over 150 000 dwt will be escorted by two tugs
(d) Vessels in ballast over 200 000 dwt will be escorted by one tug
Above mentioned vessels over 13.7 m d have to prepare two polypropelene ropes 16" circumference to join the vessels stern to the tug during stopping operations. The ropes should have adequate length so as to give distance between the foreward end of the tug and the stern of the vessel of about 50 m

Repair & Maintenance: Suez Canal Shipyard have workshops, floating docks and drydocks at both Port Said and Port Tewfik

Ship Chandlers: AC Blue Star Marine Services, P O Box 762, El Freepour Building Nahda Street, 2nd Floor, Port Said 42111, Arab Republic of Egypt, *Tel:* +20 66 324 6724, *Fax:* +20 66 324 6725, *Email:* bluestarmarine@bec.com.eg

Shipping Agents: Ibramar Shipping Co S.A.E., Freeport Building - 5th Floor, Memphis and Nahda Street, Port Said, Arab Republic of Egypt, *Tel:* +20 66 333 9140, *Fax:* +20 66 332 4187, *Email:* portsaid@ibramar.com.eg, *Website:* www.ibramar.com Managing Director: Omar Momen
Sphinx Shipping Agency, El Safwa Building, 3 El Gaish & Mostafa Kamel Street, P O Box 1324, Port Said, Arab Republic of Egypt, *Tel:* +20 66 333 3891, *Fax:* +20 66 333 3895, *Email:* sphinx@sphinx-shipping.com, *Website:* www.sphinx-shipping.com Marketing Manager: Sameh Abdella

Lloyd's Agent: Marine Technical Services Ltd, 4th Floor, Units 19 & 20, El Freepor Building, El Nahda & Palestine Streets, Port Said, Arab Republic of Egypt, *Tel:* +20 66 335 5423, *Fax:* +20 66 334 3974, *Email:* mts-lloyds-portsaid@soficom.com.eg, *Website:* www.lloydsegypt.com

WADI FEIRAN TERMINAL

Lat 28° 45' N; Long 33° 12' E.

Admiralty Chart: 2132	**Admiralty Pilot:** 64
Time Zone: GMT +2 h	**UNCTAD Locode:** EG WAF

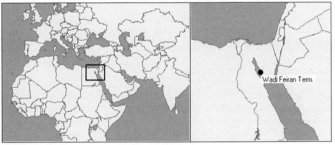

Principal Facilities:

P							

Authority: The Egyptian General Petroleum Corp., Palestine Street, 4th Sector, New Maadi, Cairo, Arab Republic of Egypt, *Tel:* +20 2 353 1471, *Fax:* +20 2 377 5962, *Email:* info@egpc.com.eg

Approach: Vessels must approach berths from a W direction, never from the N. Masters must follow the same track on their departure, to be entirely clear of shallow water

Anchorage: Anchorage can be obtained W of the conspicuous oil tanks in a depth of 31 m

Pilotage: Compulsory. Pilotage boards at outer anchorage. Mooring and unmooring operations normally take place in daylight only

Radio Frequency: VHF Channels 16 and 14

Accommodation:

Name	Length (m)	Depth (m)	Draught (m)	Remarks
Wadi Feiran Terminal				
Berth No.1	430	22.86	16.1	See [1] below
Berth No.2	430	17.68	12.2	See [2] below
Berth No.3		11	5.2	See [3] below

[1]*Berth No.1:* For tankers up to 274.32 m loa and 150 000 dwt. Loading rate is 4000 t/h through a 24" hose. Vessels are secured to mooring buoys and connected to shore pumping station by submarine pipelines
[2]*Berth No.2:* For tankers up to 244 m loa and 50 000 dwt. Loading rate is 2500 t/h through an 18" hose. Vessels are secured to mooring buoys and connected to shore pumping station by submarine pipelines
[3]*Berth No.3:* Lies 0.65 mile NW of the jetty and can accommodate tankers up to 20 000 dwt discharging only. There are three mooring buoys

Lloyd's Agent: Marine Technical Services Ltd, Flat 6B, 28 Cherif Street, Cairo, Arab Republic of Egypt, *Tel:* +20 2 2393 5724, *Fax:* +20 2 2393 8669, *Email:* mts-lloyds-cairo@soficom.com.eg, *Website:* www.lloydsegypt.com

ZAAFARANA TERMINAL

Lat 29° 11' N; Long 32° 42' E.

Admiralty Chart: 2373	**Admiralty Pilot:** 64
Time Zone: GMT +2 h	**UNCTAD Locode:** EG

Principal Facilities:

P							

Authority: Head of Maritime Transport Sector, Ptolemy Street, Mazarita, Alexandria, Arab Republic of Egypt, *Tel:* +20 3 484 2631, *Fax:* +20 3 484 2041, *Email:* mmt@idsc.net.eg

Anchorage: Anchorage for vessels waiting to berth lies about 8m S of Ras Zafarana in pos 29° 07' N 32° 40' E

Pilotage: Pilot boarding area is 11.5 miles S of the terminal and 8 miles SSE of Ras Za'farana Light

Maximum Vessel Dimensions: Loa 259 m

Accommodation:

Name	Remarks
Zaafarana Terminal	See [1] below

[1]*Zaafarana Terminal:* Consists of the FPSO 'Al Zaafarana' moored 4 cables SW of production platform HB 77-5 and connected to it by pipeline. Vessels up to 130 000 dwt drawing up to 16.7 m with a max loa of 259 m can be accommodated alongside the FPSO tanker

Lloyd's Agent: Marine Technical Services Ltd, Flat 6B, 28 Cherif Street, Cairo, Arab Republic of Egypt, *Tel:* +20 2 2393 5724, *Fax:* +20 2 2393 8669, *Email:* mts-lloyds-cairo@soficom.com.eg, *Website:* www.lloydsegypt.com

ZEIT BAY TERMINAL

Lat 27° 50' N; Long 33° 36' E.

Admiralty Chart: 2374	**Admiralty Pilot:** 64
Time Zone: GMT +2 h	**UNCTAD Locode:** EG

Principal Facilities:

P	Q						

Authority: Suez Oil Co. (SUCO), 21 Ahmed Orabi Street, P O Box 2622, Cairo, Arab Republic of Egypt, *Tel:* +20 2 3346 5909, *Fax:* +20 2 3303 5434, *Email:* suco@suco-eg.com, *Website:* www.suco-eg.com

Officials: General Manager: Joe Kose, *Email:* gm@suco-eg.com.

Port Security: ISPS compliant

Documentation: All ships certificates and four crew lists and two bonded stores lists

Approach: Tankers calling at the mooring must send an ETA 72, 24 and 12 h to SUCO head office including advice of any equipment required from shore and call radio room 4 h prior to arrival on an International Channel

Anchorage: There is a designated waiting area, a one mile circle around pos 27° 48' 30" N, 33° 37' E in depth of 25 m. It is prohibited to anchor outside this area unless special permission is obtained

Pilotage: Compulsory. Masters of vessels must contact the oil company Mooring Master VHF channel 16 or 12

Radio Frequency: VHF Channels 16, 13 and 12

Weather: Winds NNW, steady in summer, max velocity 45 knots

Tides: Range of tide between 0.91 m and 1.22 m, current 1.5 knots

Working Hours: 24 h/day

Key to Principal Facilities:—			
A=Airport	**C**=Containers	**G**=General Cargo	**P**=Petroleum	**R**=Ro/Ro	**Y**=Dry Bulk
B=Bunkers	**D**=Dry Dock	**L**=Cruise	**Q**=Other Liquid Bulk	**T**=Towage (where available from port)

Accommodation:

Name	Remarks
New East Zeit Terminal	CALM operated by Esso Suez for vessels of 35 000-130 000 dwt in depth of 30 m
Zeit Terminal (Ras el Behar)	See [1] below
LPG Berth	Operated by Suez Oil Co. for vessels up to 108 m loa in depth of 8 m

[1]*Zeit Terminal (Ras el Behar):* SBM operated by Suez Oil Co. for vessels up to 240 000 dwt with draft of 25.9 m. Berthing takes place during daylight and must be completed by 1600 hours. Loading rate is 5000 t/h through a 16'' hose. There is a ballast facility available. Vessels must be equipped with a 10 t cap crane. Ships trim not to exceed 2 m by astern

Mechanical Handling Equipment:

Location	Type	Capacity (t)	Qty
Zeit Bay Terminal	Mult-purp. Cranes	15	1

Medical Facilities: Small infirmary available in emergencies

Lloyd's Agent: Marine Technical Services Ltd, Flat 6B, 28 Cherif Street, Cairo, Arab Republic of Egypt, *Tel:* +20 2 2393 5724, *Fax:* +20 2 2393 8669, *Email:* mts-lloyds-cairo@soficom.com.eg, *Website:* www.lloydsegypt.com

EL SALVADOR

ACAJUTLA

Lat 13° 36' N; Long 89° 50' W.

Admiralty Chart: 660/1946	**Admiralty Pilot:** 8
Time Zone: GMT -6 h	**UNCTAD Locode:** SV AQJ

Principal Facilities:

P	Q	Y	G	C	R	L	B		T	A

Authority: Comision Ejecutiva Portuaria Autonoma (CEPA), Boulevard Los Heroes, Edificio Torre Roble, Metrocentro, San Salvador, El Salvador, *Tel:* +503 2452 3200,

Fax: +503 2452 4001, *Email:* francisco.portillo@cepa.gob.sv, *Website:* www.puertoacajutla.gob.sv

Officials: General Manager: Francisco Eduardo Portillo.
Public Relations Manager: Mauricio Tobar, *Email:* mauricio.tobar@cepa.gob.sv.

Pilotage: Available 24 h/day

Radio Frequency: The seaport's VHF radio service is open 24 h/day. VHF Channel 16 receives and transmits on 156.8 mHz

Tides: Average range of 1.59 m

Traffic: 2006, 629 vessels, 5 875 920 t of cargo handled, 123 329 TEU's

Maximum Vessel Dimensions: 200 m loa, 12 m draft

Principal Imports and Exports: Imports: Chemical products, Coal, Ethanol, Fertiliser, Gasoline & petroleum derivates, Iron & steel, Rice, Wheat. Exports: Coffee, Ethanol, Fruits, Molasses, Sugar.

Working Hours: Three shifts 0700-1500, 1500-2300, 2300-0700

Accommodation:

Name	Depth (m)	Draught (m)	Remarks
Acajutla			See [1] below
Breakwater Mole (Piers A & C)			See [2] below
A-1	9	8.23	Vessels up to 152 m loa
A-2	12	9.75	Vessels up to 183 m loa
C-7	14	11.89	Vessels up to 128 m loa
C-8	14	12.19	Vessels up to 128 m loa
Finger Pier (Pier B)			See [3] below
B-3	10	8.53	Vessels up to 137 m loa
B-4	12	9.45	Vessels up to 198 m loa
B-5	10	7.62	Vessels up to 137 m loa
B-6	10	8.83	Vessels up to 152 m loa
CBM	17	12.8	See [4] below

[1]*Acajutla:* Open bay. The port consists of a breakwater mole and a finger pier. One oil berth owned by RASA, the oil refinery. Length 225.5 m, 12 m draft. Berthing possible any time
[2]*Breakwater Mole (Piers A & C):* Pier A consists of two berths totalling 312.72 m. Pier C consists of two berths totalling 280 m
[3]*Finger Pier (Pier B):* Consists four berths, two inner and two outer, totalling 370 m. Equipped with a unit for loading and unloading bulk cargo with a max cap of 500 t/h for fertilizer and 400 t/h for wheat. The unit is connected to a system of belt conveyors with a cap of 500 t/h
[4]*CBM:* Located approx 1.9 km WNW of Acajutla Port and operated by El Paso Technology El Salvador S.A. de C.V. for vessels up to 60 000 dwt

Storage: Warehouses for general and containerised cargo including a covered transit warehouse of 4500 m2 at pierhead and two paved storage yards of 10 000 m2. Warehouses for bulk with a total covered space of 7540 m2 and 30 000 t cap. Also 36 000 m2 vehicles yard and 24 500 m2 general cargo yard

Location	Covered (m²)
Acajutla	34420

Mechanical Handling Equipment:

Location	Type	Capacity (t)	Qty
Acajutla	Mult-purp. Cranes	3	2
Acajutla	Mobile Cranes	60	4
Acajutla	Straddle Carriers	30	2

Cargo Worked: General 23 t/h; Grain in bulk 250 t/h; Fertilizer in bulk 200 t/h

Bunkering: Chevron Marine Products LLC, Global Marine Products LLC, 1500 Louisiana, 4th Floor, Houston, TX 77002, United States of America, *Tel:* +1 832 8542 988, *Fax:* +1 832 8544 868, *Email:* gulfcbm@chevron.com, *Website:* www.chevron.com – *Grades:* GO; FO – *Delivery Mode:* tank truck
Compania Petrolera Chevron Ltd, San Salvador, El Salvador, *Tel:* +503 2781122, *Fax:* +503 2782510 – *Grades:* DO – *Delivery Mode:* pipe
Distribuidora Shell de El Salvador S.A., Km 11.5, Carretera Al Puerto, La Libertad, San Salvador, El Salvador, *Tel:* +503 2280244, *Fax:* +503 2283145 – *Grades:* DO – *Delivery Mode:* pipe

Towage: Five tugs (2 x 250 hp, 1 x 800 hp, 1 x 1200 hp, and 1 x 1700 hp) available for docking and undocking

Repair & Maintenance: Minor repairs possible

Shipping Agents: Compania Mercantil Intercontinental S.A. de C.V. (COMISA), 79 Avenida Sur Edificio Plaza Cristal, 3ER Piso, Colonia Escalon, San Salvador, El Salvador, *Tel:* +503 2206 5400, *Fax:* +503 2206 5423, *Email:* info@comisasal.com, *Website:* www.comisasal.com
Consorcio Maritimo Salvadoreno S.A. de C.V. (CMS), Av. Las Gardenias No.4, Col. Las Mercedes, San Salvador, El Salvador, *Tel:* +503 2530 6912, *Fax:* +503 2530 6913, *Email:* administration@conmarsal.com & jvalencia@conmarsal.com, *Website:* www.conmarsal.com
Grupo Maritimo, 79 Av. Sur y Calle Cuscatlan, Local 2-11, Edif Plaza Cristal, Col. Escalon, San Salvador, El Salvador, *Tel:* +503 2206 5555, *Fax:* +503 2206 5598, *Email:* info@gmaritimo.com, *Website:* www.grupomaritimo.com
Mediterranean Shipping Company, MSC El Salvador, 83 Avenida Norte y 13 Calle Poniente #801, Colonia Escalon, San Salvador, El Salvador, *Tel:* +503 2263 2346, *Fax:* +503 2263 2160, *Email:* jjovel@msc.com.gt, *Website:* www.mscgva.ch
Terminales Portuarias S.A., Edif Administrativo, Cepu, Acajutla, El Salvador, *Tel:* +503 2452 3335, *Fax:* +503 2452 3940, *Email:* m.perez@gmaritimo.com
Remarsa-Grupo Maritimo, 79 Avenida sur y Calle Cuscatlan, Local 2-11, Edif Plaza Cristal Colonia Escalon, San Salvador, El Salvador, *Tel:* +503 2206 5555, *Fax:* +503 2206 5598, *Email:* info@gmaritimo.com, *Website:* www.grupomaritimo.com

Surveyors: Arie Van Helden S.A. de C.V., Edificio Cepa No.10, P O Box 4, Acajutla, El Salvador, *Tel:* +503 2452 3204, *Fax:* +503 2452 3513

Medical Facilities: Two clinics available. Hospital in town

Airport: San Salvador International Airport

Lloyd's Agent: Gibson & Co. Suc., 17 Calle Poniente 320, Centro de Gobierno, P O Box 242, San Salvador, El Salvador, *Tel:* +503 7887 3859, *Fax:* +503 2271 1026, *Email:* claims@gibson.com.sv, *Website:* www.gibson.com.sv

CUTUCO

Lat 13° 19' N; Long 87° 49' W.

Admiralty Chart: 1961	**Admiralty Pilot:** 8
Time Zone: GMT -6 h	**UNCTAD Locode:** SV LUN

Principal Facilities:

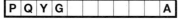

P	Q	Y	G						A

Colonia Las Mercedes
Avenida Las Gardenias No. 4
San Salvador, El Salvador, C.A.
Phones: (503) 2530-6912, (503) 2452-6532
Telefaxes: (503) 2530-6913, (503) 2414-1682
Mobiles: (503) 7150-9070, (503) 7150-9071

E-mails: administration@conmarsal.com
operations@conmarsal.com

www.conmarsal.com

Port Shipping Agents

Remarsa - Grupo Maritimo

79 Av. Sur y Calle Cuscatlan,
Local 2-11, Edif. Plaza Cristal,
Col. Escalon,
San Salvador,
EL SALVADOR

Tel: +503 2206 5555
Fax: +503 2206 5598
Email: Remarsa.sal@gmaritimo.com
info@gmaritimo.com
Web: www.grupomaritimo.com

Shipping Agents

Authority: Ferrocarriles Nacionales de El Salvador CEPA-FENADESAL, Cutuco, La Union, El Salvador, *Tel:* +503 2664 4222, *Fax:* +503 2664 4055

Approach: Depth at entrance 9.15 m. Situated in Bay of Fonseca, a good natural harbour about 6 km wide. Depth on bar 7.31 m MLW

Pilotage: Pilot available. VHF Channel 16

Tides: Strong tidal currents

Maximum Vessel Dimensions: 185 m length, 30 m breadth and 10 m draft

Principal Imports and Exports: Imports: Diesel oil, Tallow. Exports: Coffee.

Working Hours: Three shifts 0700-1100, 1300-1700, 1900-0500. Overtime payable after 1100 on Saturdays and all day Sunday

Accommodation:

Name	Length (m)	Remarks
Cutuco		The port is basically non-operational at present
Pier	168	Two berths

Storage: Six export warehouses, one of them being used for transit cargo, with an area of 2230 m2, the other five totalling an area of 20 343 m2. There is also another import warehouse owned by the Customs with an area of 3600 m2. No refrigerated space available

Shipping Agents: Consorcio Maritimo Salvadoreno S.A. de C.V. (CMS), Av. Las Gardenias No.4, Col. Las Mercedes, San Salvador, El Salvador, *Tel:* +503 2530 6912, *Fax:* +503 2530 6913, *Email:* administration@conmarsal.com & jvalencia@conmarsal.com, *Website:* www.conmarsal.com
Remarsa-Grupo Maritimo, 79 Avenida sur y Calle Cuscatlan, Local 2-11, Edif Plaza

Cristal Colonia Escalon, San Salvador, El Salvador, *Tel:* +503 2206 5555, *Fax:* +503 2206 5598, *Email:* info@gmaritimo.com, *Website:* www.grupomaritimo.com

Medical Facilities: Available

Airport: San Salvador International Airport

Development: Construction of new facilities including one terminal for containers, two for receiving and distributing grain and one for passenger traffic. During the first stage due to commence in the first quarter of 2005, a marginal wharf of 560 m long with a depth of 14 m and a terminal area of 28 ha will be constructed. Completion of the project is expected to take three years

Lloyd's Agent: Gibson & Co. Suc., 17 Calle Poniente 320, Centro de Gobierno, P O Box 242, San Salvador, El Salvador, *Tel:* +503 7887 3859, *Fax:* +503 2271 1026, *Email:* claims@gibson.com.sv, *Website:* www.gibson.com.sv

LA LIBERTAD

Lat 13° 29' N; Long 89° 19' W.

Admiralty Chart: 660	**Admiralty Pilot:** 8
Time Zone: GMT -6 h	**UNCTAD Locode:** SV LLD

This port is no longer open to commercial shipping

LA UNION

alternate name, see Cutuco

EQUATORIAL GUINEA

BATA

Lat 1° 52' N; Long 9° 46' E.

Admiralty Chart: 1322	**Admiralty Pilot:** 2
Time Zone: GMT +1 h	**UNCTAD Locode:** GQ BSG

Principal Facilities:

P		G			B		T	A

Authority: Administracion de Puertos de Guinea Ecuatorial (A.P.G.E.), Bata, Equatorial Guinea, *Tel:* +240 8 2895, *Fax:* +240 8 2874

Pilotage: Available from A.P.G.E.

Radio Frequency: VHF Channel 16

Maximum Vessel Dimensions: 19 279 dwt, 182 m loa, 8 m draft

Accommodation: A single point mooring is located approx 1 mile offshore. All grades of petroleum are pumped through a 6" pipeline connected to shore installations. The SPM is reported to be in a dilapidated state. Tankers can also discharge oil products at the New Port

Name	Remarks
Old Port	See [1] below
New Port	See [2] below

[1]*Old Port:* Open roadstead. There is a wharf constructed in three parts with a total length of 370 m, equipped with a mobile crane of 10 t cap. Vessels anchor approx 0.5 mile offshore in depths up to 7.3 m, or further out in depths of 11.9 m. Loading and discharging to lighters

[2]*New Port:* Situated S of Bata town, approx 1.6 km S of the mouth of the River Ecuco. Harbour consists of an L-shaped breakwater containing berths on each side of the shorter leg over a length of 312 m. Four general cargo vessels can be accommodated in depths of 12.0 m at the outer berths and 11.0 m at the inner. The inner berths are subject to swell and there are mooring buoys to assist with berthing. No cranes are available; loading and discharging is by ship's own gear. Anchorage can be obtained 0.5 mile W of the breakwater in a depth of 16.0 m. Berthing during daylight hours only

Mechanical Handling Equipment:

Location	Type	Capacity (t)	Qty
Old Port	Mobile Cranes	10	1

Bunkering: Bominflot, Bominflot Ltd, 5-7 Ravensbourne Road, Bromley, Kent BR1 1HN, United Kingdom, *Tel:* +44 20 8315 5400, *Fax:* +44 20 8315 5429, *Email:* mail@bominflot.co.uk, *Website:* www.bominflot.net – *Grades:* MGO

Towage: One private tug available for hire

Medical Facilities: Hospital in the town

Key to Principal Facilities:—				
A=Airport	**C**=Containers	**G**=General Cargo	**P**=Petroleum	**R**=Ro/Ro	**Y**=Dry Bulk
B=Bunkers	**D**=Dry Dock	**L**=Cruise	**Q**=Other Liquid Bulk	**T**=Towage (where available from port)

Airport: Bata, 13 km

Lloyd's Agent: Omega Marine Cameroon, Douala, Cameroon, *Email:* omega-cameroon@omega-marine.com

CEIBA TERMINAL

Lat 1° 24' N; Long 9° 13' E.

Admiralty Chart: 1888	**Admiralty Pilot:** 2
Time Zone: GMT +1 h	**UNCTAD Locode:** GQ

Principal Facilities:

P											

Authority: Hess Equatorial Guinea Inc., Ceiba House, Complejo de Bome, P O Box 834, Bata, Equatorial Guinea, *Tel:* +240   90728, *Fax:* +240   92304, *Email:* egmm@hess.com

Officials: Manager: Colin Balderson.

Pre-Arrival Information: Where the sea passage from the tanker's last port to the terminal is less than 72 h, the first ETA should be advised immediately after leaving port. Subsequent ETA's should be given 48 h and 24 h before arrival. Should the ETA change by 1 h or more following the 24 h notice, the tanker must promptly notify the terminal of the revised ETA

Pilotage: Mooring Master boards vessel 3 nautical miles N of the terminal or 3 nautical miles SW of the terminal

Radio Frequency: VHF Channel 72. Berthing and cargo operations on VHF Channel 17

Weather: Local squalls generating winds in excess of 50 knots are occasionally experienced in the area of the terminal

Maximum Vessel Dimensions: 350 000 dwt at CALM buoy with no draft restriction. 150 000 dwt at FPSO with max arrival draft of 10 m

Accommodation:

Name	Remarks
Ceiba Terminal	See [1] below

[1]*Ceiba Terminal:* Located 15 nautical miles off the coast of Equatorial Guinea in depth of approx 67 m. Consists of FPSO vessel 'Sendje Ceiba'. All crude oil loading and export operations at the terminal are carried out under the supervision of the Mooring Master. Total crude oil storage cap of 2 000 000 bbls. Berthing is normally carried out during daylight hours only and unberthing anytime. Vessel's arriving after 1500 LT will normally not be berthed until 0600 on the following day

Lloyd's Agent: Omega Marine Cameroon, Douala, Cameroon, *Email:* omega-cameroon@omega-marine.com

LUBA

Lat 3° 28' N; Long 8° 33' E.

Admiralty Chart: 1322	**Admiralty Pilot:** 2
Time Zone: GMT +1 h	**UNCTAD Locode:** GQ LUB

Principal Facilities:

		G			B		A	

Authority: Administracion de Puertos de Guinea Ecuatorial (A.P.G.E.), Luba, Equatorial Guinea

Port Security: ISPS compliant

Pilotage: Not normally necessary. If required the Rey Malabo Pilot could be summoned to Luba

Accommodation:

Name	Remarks
Luba	See [1] below

[1]*Luba:* Open roadstead. Bay is wide and able to accommodate a number of vessels. Loading and unloading by means of lighters. There is a jetty approx 122 m in length with a depth alongside of 7.3 m at the outer end. Vessels up to 6.7 m d can be accommodated

Luba Freeport has been constructed as an oil logistics centre, Fax: +240 097074, Email: info@lubafreeport.com, Website: www.lubafreeport.com

Bunkering: Bominflot, Bominflot Ltd, 5-7 Ravensbourne Road, Bromley, Kent BR1 1HN, United Kingdom, *Tel:* +44 20 8315 5400, *Fax:* +44 20 8315 5429, *Email:* mail@bominflot.co.uk, *Website:* www.bominflot.net – *Grades:* MGO

Shipping Agents: Luba Freeport, Luba, Equatorial Guinea, *Fax:* +240 097074, *Email:* info@lubafreeport.com, *Website:* www.lubafreeport.com

Airport: Malabo International Airport, 50 km

Lloyd's Agent: Omega Marine Cameroon, Douala, Cameroon, *Email:* omega-cameroon@omega-marine.com

MALABO

Lat 3° 45' N; Long 8° 47' E.

Admiralty Chart: 1322	**Admiralty Pilot:** 2
Time Zone: GMT +1 h	**UNCTAD Locode:** GQ SSG

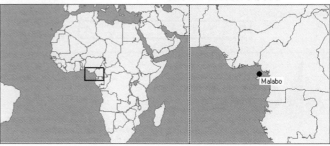

Principal Facilities:

P		Y	G			B		T	A

Authority: Administracion de Puertos de Guinea Ecuatorial (A.P.G.E.), P O Box 536, Malabo, Equatorial Guinea, *Tel:* +240 092459, *Fax:* +240 092210

Port Security: ISPS compliant

Pilotage: Available during daylight hours by local guide

Radio Frequency: VHF Channel 16

Working Hours: 0800-1500

Accommodation: Tanker facilities: A SPM located approx 2 miles offshore, midway between the New Port and Punta Europa

Name	Length (m)	Depth (m)	Remarks
Old Port			See [1] below
New Port			
Wharf	304	15	See [2] below

[1]*Old Port:* Anchorage for up to six vessels 274.3 to 731.4 m from the shore in 25.6 m of water. Entrance channel to the harbour has varying depth of 36-55 m. A pier some 27.43 m long is set at right angles to a quay 274.3 m long. Depth alongside quay up to 9.1 m. Vessels moor stern on to the pier in 16.4 m. Some moorings are reserved for Naval craft and the mail boats. Loading and unloading into barges
[2]*Wharf:* Cargoes of cement can be discharged at a rate of 2000 t/day/hatch

Storage:

Location	Covered (m²)	Sheds / Warehouses
Malabo	300	1

Mechanical Handling Equipment:

Location	Type	Capacity (t)	Qty
Malabo	Mult-purp. Cranes	45	1
Malabo	Mult-purp. Cranes	70	1
Malabo	Mult-purp. Cranes	90	2
Wharf	Mult-purp. Cranes		2
Wharf	Mobile Cranes	12	1
Wharf	Container Cranes	35	1
Wharf	Diesel Cranes	45	9
Wharf	Diesel Cranes	10	6
Wharf	Diesel Cranes	10	2

Bunkering: Bominflot, Bominflot Ltd, 5-7 Ravensbourne Road, Bromley, Kent BR1 1HN, United Kingdom, *Tel:* +44 20 8315 5400, *Fax:* +44 20 8315 5429, *Email:* mail@bominflot.co.uk, *Website:* www.bominflot.net – *Grades:* MGO

Waste Reception Facilities: Garbage disposal available

Towage: One private tug available for hire

Repair & Maintenance: Small yard for repairs to fishing vessels and small craft

Shipping Agents: Afritramp, Residencia Mary, Caracolas, Malabo, Equatorial Guinea, *Tel:* +240 098527, *Fax:* +240 091969, *Email:* dg-sdvgq@wanadoo.gq, *Website:* www.afritrampoilfield.com
MAC Guinea S.A., P O Box 982, K-4 Airport Route, Malabo, Equatorial Guinea, *Tel:* +240 090567, *Fax:* +240 090568, *Email:* general.manager@macguinea.com, *Website:* www.macguinea.com

Airport: Malabo International Airport, 8 km

Lloyd's Agent: Omega Marine Cameroon, Douala, Cameroon, *Email:* omega-cameroon@omega-marine.com

PUNTA EUROPA TERMINAL

Lat 3° 47' N; Long 8° 43' E.

Admiralty Chart: 1321   **Admiralty Pilot:** 2
Time Zone: GMT +1 h   **UNCTAD Locode:** GQ

Principal Facilities:

P	Q							T	A	

Authority: Marathon E.G. Production Ltd, P O Box 742, Malabo, Equatorial Guinea, *Tel:* +240 94283, *Fax:* +240 94284, *Email:* eqgmarinecoord@marathonoil.com

Port Security: ISPS compliant

Pre-Arrival Information: 72 h before the ETA at the Terminal, the Marine Co-ordinator will transmit the following questionnaire to the export tanker:
a) master's name on completion of loading
b) last port
c) ETA
d) expected quantity to load
e) ISPS questionnaire, to include vessels current security level, crew list, last three ports, any security incidents encountered at previous port
Notice of Readiness: upon arrival at the Terminal pilot boarding area position, the master of the tanker shall tender notice of readiness confirming that the tanker is ready to load cargo, berth or no berth. The vessel is not to tender NOR if there is any known fault or deficiency in any equipment necessary for connecting to, loading or disconnection from the nominated berth. Notwithstanding any voice communications, NOR time and date shall always be confirmed in writing
Routine Communications: the export tanker shall inform the Terminal, by Email or telephone, the vessel's ETA as follows:
a) 7 days before estimated arrival, or upon clearing at last port if there is less than 7 days steaming time before estimated arrival
b) 72 h before estimated arrival
c) 48 h before estimated arrival
d) 24 h before estimated arrival

Anchorage: No designated anchorage exists but all vessels bound for the Terminal are recommended to anchor N of Lat 3° 47' N and E of Long 8° 44' E in depth of 40 m

Pilotage: Compulsory and provided by the operating company. Pilot boarding area in pos 3° 48.4' N; 8° 43.6' E

Radio Frequency: VHF Channels 16, 73 and 74

Weather: There are two distinct seasons; the Rainy Season and the Dry Season. The Rainy Season extends from about May through to September with August being the wettest month. The Dry Season extends from December through to February. There is a Variable Season between the Wet and Dry Season when storms, known locally as 'tornadoes' may be experienced that bring high winds and torrential rain from the northeast quadrant. This squall season extends during October and from February through to May. These storms are fairly short lived but wind speeds in excess of 50 knots may be experienced

Accommodation:

Name	Depth (m)	Remarks
Punta Europa Terminal		See [1] below
Berth 1	37	See [2] below
Berth 2	37	See [3] below
Berth 3 (LNG Terminal)		In pos 3° 47.7' N; 8° 41.8' E

[1]*Punta Europa Terminal:* Consists of two conventional buoy mooring systems and an LNG export terminal. Mooring and unmooring operations are carried out during daylight hours only. No mooring or unmooring operation will normally commence later than 1600 hours local time in order to ensure completion during daylight
[2]*Berth 1:* Located approx 400 m offshore and 1100 m E of the Punta Europa lighthouse. Consists of a six-point conventional buoy-mooring berth designed to accommodate condensate (max loading rate 2300 m3/h), LPG (max loading rate 400 m3/h) and methanol (max loading rate 3500 m3/h) vessels up to 45 000 dwt and 127-210 m loa
[3]*Berth 2:* Located approx 420 m offshore and 1400 m W of the Punta Europa lighthouse. Consists of an eight-point conventional buoy-mooring berth designed to accommodate condensate (max loading rate 30 000 bbls/h), butane (max loading rate 1060 m3/h) and propane (max loading rate 2090 m3/h) vessels up to 105 000 dwt and 244 m loa

Towage: Two 60 t bollard pull tugs and one 40 t bollard pull tug

Medical Facilities: Limited emergency medical facilities are available locally in Malabo. In the event of an accident or a medical emergency the local agent should be informed and they will make arrangements to disembark the patient accordingly

Airport: Malabo International Airport

Lloyd's Agent: Omega Marine Cameroon, Douala, Cameroon, *Email:* omega-cameroon@omega-marine.com

REY MALABO

alternate name, see Malabo

SERPENTINA TERMINAL

Lat 3° 48' N; Long 8° 5' E.

Admiralty Chart: 1321   **Admiralty Pilot:** 2
Time Zone: GMT +1 h   **UNCTAD Locode:** GQ

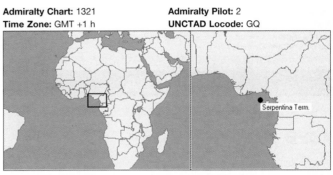

Principal Facilities:

P									

Authority: Mobil Equatorial Guinea Inc, P O Box 654, Malabo, Equatorial Guinea

Pre-Arrival Information: Vessels should send initial ETA to the Marine Super-intendents, Tel: +1 713 4319036, Fax: +1 713 4319081, Email: megi-marine@exxonmobil.com, when in receipt of orders to load at the Serpentina Terminal
Vessels should send ETA to the Marine Superintendents 72 h, 48 h, 36 h and 24 h in advance (then if the ETA changes by more than 3 h)

Anchorage: Anchorage can be obtained more than 2 miles W of FPSO Serpentina in depth of 65 m

Pilotage: Compulsory within the restricted area. Vessels must not enter the restricted area until the Mooring Master is onboard or until permission has been granted by the Mooring Master for the vessel to enter the restricted area. The Mooring Master boards in the following positions:
a) 3° 48' 00" N; 8° 02' 60" E (2 nautical miles W of FPSO Serpentina)
b) 3° 55' 00" N; 8° 06' 75" E (4 nautical miles N of the Zafiro Terminal)

Radio Frequency: VHF Channels 16 and 74

Maximum Vessel Dimensions: 350 000 dwt

Accommodation:

Name	Remarks
Serpentina Terminal	See [1] below

[1]*Serpentina Terminal:* The terminal serves the Zafiro offshore oil field which is located approx 37 miles W of Punta Europa, the NW point of Bioco. Consists of FPSO 'Serpentina' which is 363 m loa and is anchored by means of an SPM turret at the bow. The export tanker moors in tandem with the stern of the FPSO and a tug remains secured to the stern of the export tanker throughout the loading operation. Berthing during daylight hours only, unberthing at any time

Lloyd's Agent: Omega Marine Cameroon, Douala, Cameroon, *Email:* omega-cameroon@omega-marine.com

ZAFIRO TERMINAL

Lat 3° 51' N; Long 8° 7' E.

Admiralty Chart: 1321   **Admiralty Pilot:** 2
Time Zone: GMT +1 h   **UNCTAD Locode:** GQ

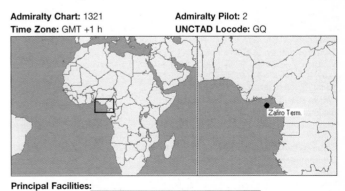

Principal Facilities:

P								T	A

Authority: Mobil Equatorial Guinea Inc, P O Box 654, Malabo, Equatorial Guinea

Port Security: ISPS compliant

Key to Principal Facilities:—				
A=Airport	**C**=Containers	**G**=General Cargo	**P**=Petroleum	**R**=Ro/Ro	**Y**=Dry Bulk
B=Bunkers	**D**=Dry Dock	**L**=Cruise	**Q**=Other Liquid Bulk	**T**=Towage (where available from port)	

Pre-Arrival Information: ETA must be sent 72 h, 48 h and 24 h in advance to Terminal Authority

Anchorage: Anchorage can be obtained approx 6 miles N of Zafiro Producer in depth of 65 m

Pilotage: Compulsory. Pilot boards 4 miles N of FPU Zafiro Producer

Maximum Vessel Dimensions: 310 000 dwt

Accommodation:

Name	Remarks
Zafiro Terminal	See [1] below

[1]*Zafiro Terminal:* The terminal serves the Zafiro offshore oil field which is located approx 37 miles W of Punta Europa, the NW point of Bioco. Consists of FPU 'Zafiro Producer', moored bow-to-bow with FSO 'Magnolia' and an SBM. The production platform 'Jade' is located roughly midway between the SBM and the two offloading vessels. Berthing during daylight hours only, unberthing at any time

Towage: Tugs are available

Airport: Malabo International Airport

Lloyd's Agent: Omega Marine Cameroon, Douala, Cameroon, *Email:* omega-cameroon@omega-marine.com

ERITREA

ASEB

alternate name, see Assab

ASSAB

Lat 13° 0' N; Long 42° 45' E.

Admiralty Chart: 1926		**Admiralty Pilot:** 64
Time Zone: GMT +3 h		**UNCTAD Locode:** ER ASA

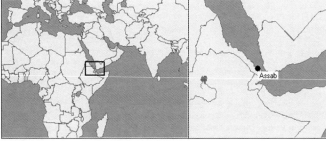

Principal Facilities:

P		Y	G	C	R		B		T	A	

Authority: Department of Maritime Transport, Assab Port Authority, P O Box 58, Assab, Eritrea, *Tel:* +291 1 660030, *Fax:* +291 1 661249

Officials: General Manager: Dawit Mengisteab.
Harbour Master: Capt Ahmed Ali.

Port Security: ISPS compliant

Pre-Arrival Information: ETA notice to be given 7 days in advance and finally 24 h before arrival

Approach: From the N vessels should keep 4.9 km from the coast SE of Ras Darma and set course to pass 3.1 km E of Sanah-Bor Islet. This course leads midway between the islet and Bosaquet shoal and when the islet bears 270°, vessels steer to pass 1.6 km on the W side of the bay until Ras Gombo light structure bears 246°. No hazards or sand bars

Anchorage: 2.4 km from North Green Light in 11-14 m depth

Pilotage: Compulsory for all vessels over 200 gt (except exempted vessels). Pilots board vessels 2.4 km NNE from breakwater and disembark at the Commercial Harbour or at the Oil Harbour. 24 h pilot service at the Commercial Harbour; for tankers 0600-1800 only. VHF Channels 16, 14 and 10

Radio Frequency: VHF Channels 16, 14 and 10

Weather: In winter winds are SSE to SSW, force 5-8, occasionally stronger and in summer winds are NW to NE, force 3

Tides: Range of tide 0.3 m to 0.6 m

Traffic: 2001, 90 486 t of cargo handled

Maximum Vessel Dimensions: 26 000 dwt, 10.3 m max draft, 210 m loa

Principal Imports and Exports: Imports: Cement, Cereals, Fertiliser, Machinery & transport. Exports: Coffee, Hides & skin, Oil seeds, Pulses.

Working Hours: Three shifts: 0700-1400, 1400-2200, 2200-0600 (break 0600-0700)

Accommodation:

Name	Length (m)	Depth (m)	Remarks
Assab			See [1] below
Berth No.1	210	10.97	Stern ramp ro/ro vessels accommodated
Berth No.2	150	10.97	
Berth No.3	135	10.06	

Name	Length (m)	Depth (m)	Remarks
Berth No.4	80	5.48	
Berth No.5	140	8.2	
Berth No.6	160	8.84	
Berth No.7	150	10.06	
Berth No.7A	115	7.5	Stern ramp ro/ro vessels accommodated

[1]*Assab:* Breakwater 711 m long gives protection to vessels in harbour. Seven berths on two jetties for ocean-going vessels
Containers are handled at the general cargo berths. Container yard covering 8.7 ha. Stern ramp ro/ro vessels can be accomodated at Berth No's 1 and 7A, max loa 145 m
Bulk facilities: Bulk cargo can be discharged at the Commercial Harbour. Bulk grain discharged by grabs and hoppers; shore cranes used for bagged grain. Vessels up to 180 m loa, 20 m beam can be accommodated
Tanker facilities: There are three terminals: Crude oil berth consisting of a CBM for tankers up to 35 000 dwt and 11.3 m d. Coastal tanker jetty with 8.0 m depth alongside for tankers up to 105 m loa. Shell tanker terminal where vessels berth heading SE with stern lines connected to two buoys, accommodating vessels up to 20 000 dwt and 8.8 m d

Storage: Six warehouses totalling 27 440 m2, four open shades totalling 22 840 m2, five asphalted open areas totalling 7554 m2, three open non-asphalted areas totalling 285 312 m2, six container stacking areas totalling 40 500 m2 and one vehicles area of 58 968 m2

Mechanical Handling Equipment:

Location	Type	Capacity (t)	Qty
Assab	Mobile Cranes	9–50	7
Assab	Shore Cranes	6–20	18
Assab	Reach Stackers	45	5
Assab	Forklifts	3–15	46

Cargo Worked: Loading: 30 t/h per hook bagged cargo. Discharging: 10-15 t/h per hook general cargo. Bulk cargo can be discharged up to 4000 t/day

Bunkering: All grades of fuel oil available by truck in unlimited quantity at rate of 300 t/h with connection at any berth
ExxonMobil Marine Fuels, Mailpoint 31, ExxonMobil House, Ermyn Way, Leatherhead, Surrey KT22 8UX, United Kingdom, *Tel:* +44 1372 222 000, *Fax:* +44 1372 223 922, *Email:* marine.fuels@exxonmobil.com, *Website:* www.exxonmobil.com – *Grades:* MGO – *Parcel Size:* available in unlimited quantity – *Rates:* 300t/h – *Delivery Mode:* ex wharf

Towage: Three tugs of 1400-2600 hp available for berthing and unberthing

Repair & Maintenance: Minor repairs from small workshops

Surveyors: BC Marine Services PLC, Assab, Eritrea, *Tel:* +291 1 661025, *Fax:* +291 1 661025, *Email:* info@bc-marine.com, *Website:* www.bc-marine.com

Medical Facilities: Hospital and doctors available

Airport: 15 km from port

Lloyd's Agent: Cargo Inspection Survey Services (CISS), 31 Kebedesh Sium Street, P O Box 906, Asmara, Eritrea, *Tel:* +291 1 120369, *Fax:* +291 1 121767, *Email:* gelatlyh@eol.com.er

MASSAWA

Lat 15° 37' N; Long 39° 29' E.

Admiralty Chart: 460		**Admiralty Pilot:** 64
Time Zone: GMT +3 h		**UNCTAD Locode:** ER MSW

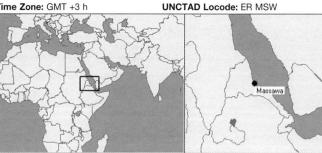

Principal Facilities:

P		Y	G	C	R		B		T	A	

Authority: Massawa Port Authority, P O Box 73, Massawa, Eritrea, *Tel:* +291 1 552493, *Fax:* +291 1 552106, *Email:* massport@tse.com.er

Officials: General Manager: Afewerki Tesfazion.
Marketing Manager: Yemane Yigzaw, *Email:* yeman50-yig@yahoo.com.
Chief Pilot: Capt Yohannes Asefaw, *Tel:* +291 1 552101.

Approach: Channel from the harbour, marked by buoys, depth 25 m, well protected by Peninsular and islands

Anchorage: Anchorage 14.63 m E of main lighthouse, N of leading light. Depth at anchorage 24.38-30.48 m and 11.89 m at entrance, no bar buoys mark the entrance

Pilotage: Compulsory for vessels of more than 100 gt. Charges according to gt

Radio Frequency: VHF Channel 16

Weather: Prevailing wind NNE, max force 4

Tides: Average range 1.2 m

Traffic: 2007, 641 816 t of cargo handled

Maximum Vessel Dimensions: 8.4 m fwd and 8.0 m aft max draft, 185 m max loa

Working Hours: 0700-1400, 1400-2200, 2200-0600

Accommodation:

Name	Length (m)	Draught (m)	Remarks
Massawa			
Berth No.1	176	5	General cargo
Berth No.2	150	7.5	General cargo
Berth No.3	137	8.7	General cargo
Berth No.4	137	8.4	General cargo
Berth No.5	137	8–12	General cargo
Berth No.6	208	12	General cargo
Salt Berth		9.6	Salt
Cement Berth		5.4	Cement
Eritro-Jordan Cement Jetty		11	Cement
Mobil Terminal	185	9	Oil terminal
AGIP Terminal	176	8.6	Oil terminal

Storage: Four warehouses with storage area of 38 445 m2, open shed of 7200 m2 and stacking area of 158 412 m2

Mechanical Handling Equipment:

Location	Type	Capacity (t)	Qty
Massawa	Mult-purp. Cranes	75	1
Massawa	Mobile Cranes	10–100	8
Massawa	Shore Cranes	5–10	5
Massawa	Forklifts	3–10	37

Cargo Worked: Loading: 30 t/h per hook bagged cargo. Discharging: 10-18 t/h per hook general cargo. Bulk cargo can be discharged up to 4000 t/day

Bunkering: ExxonMobil Marine Fuels, Mailpoint 31, ExxonMobil House, Ermyn Way, Leatherhead, Surrey KT22 8UX, United Kingdom, *Tel:* +44 1372 222 000, *Fax:* +44 1372 223 922, *Email:* marine.fuels@exxonmobil.com, *Website:* www.exxonmobil.com – *Grades:* MGO – *Delivery Mode:* ex truck

Waste Reception Facilities: Garbage disposal available

Towage: Three tugs; two of 1600 hp and one of 300 hp; also three pilot boats available for berthing and unberthing

Repair & Maintenance: Massawa Ship Repair Yard, Massawa, Eritrea, *Tel:* +291 1 552034, *Fax:* +291 1 552763 All repairs on hull and machinery; slipway for vessels up to 800 t lightweight

Shipping Agents: Eritrean Shipping & Transit Agency Services, P O Box 99, Massawa, Eritrea, *Tel:* +291 1 552733, *Fax:* +291 1 552483
Fenkel Oriental Marine Services, P O Box 178, Massawa, Eritrea, *Tel:* +291 1 552265, *Fax:* +291 1 552864

Surveyors: BC Marine Services PLC, Massawa, Eritrea, *Tel:* +291 1 551280, *Fax:* +291 1 551280, *Email:* info@bc-marine.com, *Website:* www.bc-marine.com
The Noble House Private Ltd Co., 1st Floor, No.8, Insurance Building, Massawa, Eritrea, *Tel:* +291 1 122265, *Fax:* +291 1 114008, *Email:* faidex@gemel.com.er

Medical Facilities: Hospital and doctors available

Airport: Massawa International Airport

Railway: Massawa-Ghinda

Lloyd's Agent: Cargo Inspection Survey Services (CISS), 31 Kebedesh Sium Street, P O Box 906, Asmara, Eritrea, *Tel:* +291 1 120369, *Fax:* +291 1 121767, *Email:* gelatlyh@eol.com.er

MITSIWA

alternate name, see Massawa

ESTONIA

BEKKER

Lat 59° 27' N; Long 24° 39' E.

Admiralty Chart: 2227   **Admiralty Pilot:** 20
Time Zone: GMT +2 h   **UNCTAD Locode:** EE BEK

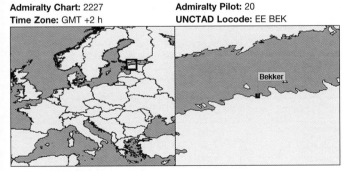

Principal Facilities:

		Y	G					

Authority: RasmusSon Ltd, Bekker Port, Kopliranna 49, 11713 Tallinn, Republic of Estonia, *Tel:* +372 6 201600, *Fax:* +372 6 201620, *Email:* bekker@bekker.ee, *Website:* www.bekker.ee

Officials: Marketing Director: Marko Jurioje.

Approach: There is a 1000 m long and 50 m wide maritime canal leading to the port, the shallowest draught of which is 8.6 m from Kronstadt zero-level

Pilotage: Compulsory. The pilot station is located at the Suurupi-2 buoy in pos 59° 37.50' N; 24° 38.00' E

Radio Frequency: VHF Channels 6 and 10

Maximum Vessel Dimensions: 140 m loa, 22 m beam, 6.5 m draught

Working Hours: 24 h/day

Accommodation:

Name	Length (m)	Draught (m)	Remarks
Bekker			
Berth No.1	170	6.5	Vessel berthing, maintenance & supplying
Berth No.2	140	5	See [1] below
Berth No.3	143	4	See [2] below
Berth No.4	200	6.5	Main berth for cargo operations

[1]*Berth No.2:* Vessel berthing, maintenance, supplying & cargo operations
[2]*Berth No.3:* Vessel berthing, maintenance, supplying & cargo operations

Storage:

Location	Open (m²)	Covered (m²)	Sheds / Warehouses
Berth No.4	19200	8873	2

Mechanical Handling Equipment:

Location	Type	Capacity (t)	Qty
Berth No.4	Mobile Cranes	40	1
Berth No.4	Portal Cranes	20	1

Lloyd's Agent: Lars Krogius Baltic Ltd, Ahtri 12, EE-10151 Tallinn, Republic of Estonia, *Tel:* +372 6 116620, *Fax:* +372 6 116685, *Email:* estonia@krogius.com, *Website:* www.krogius.com

KUNDA

Lat 59° 31' N; Long 26° 33' E.

Admiralty Chart: 2215   **Admiralty Pilot:** 19
Time Zone: GMT +2 h   **UNCTAD Locode:** EE KUN

Principal Facilities:

Q	Y	G		R		B		T	A

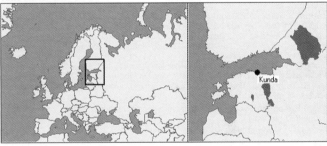

Authority: Port Kunda AS, Jaama 2, EE-44106 Kunda, Republic of Estonia, *Tel:* +372 32 29955, *Fax:* +372 32 21436, *Email:* indrek@malsco.ee

Officials: Managing Director: Tapio Aura, *Email:* tapio.aura@knc.ee.
Marketing Director: Imre Leetma, *Email:* imre.leetma@knc.ee.
Harbour Master: Eiki Orgmets, *Email:* eiki.orgmets@knc.ee.

Port Security: ISPS compliant

Documentation: Vessel particulars (1 copy), crew list (4 copies), passenger list (4 copies), stores list (3 copies), bonded stores list (3 copies), crew personal effects declaration (2 copies), cargo manifest/stowage plan (4 copies)

Approach: Channel to port is 70 m wide in depth of 10.4 m and marked by three pairs of buoys. Axis direction 342°-162° equipped with lateral system buoys and lining light beacons

Key to Principal Facilities:—				
A=Airport	**C**=Containers	**G**=General Cargo	**P**=Petroleum	**R**=Ro/Ro	**Y**=Dry Bulk
B=Bunkers	**D**=Dry Dock	**L**=Cruise	**Q**=Other Liquid Bulk	**T**=Towage (where available from port)

Anchorage: Anchorage for ocean-going vessels can be obtained in the roadstead in depths ranging between 15 m and 22 m

Pilotage: Compulsory. Pilots available round the clock

Radio Frequency: VHF Channels 14 and 16

Traffic: 2006, 413 vessels, 1 156 476 t of cargo handled

Maximum Vessel Dimensions: 150 m loa, 30 m beam, 8.5 m draught

Principal Imports and Exports: Imports: Coal, Crushed stones, Grain. Exports: Cement, Clinker, Peat, Timber logs, Wood chips.

Working Hours: Port operations 24 h/day. Port administration: Mon-Fri 0800-1700

Accommodation:

Name	Length (m)	Depth (m)	Draught (m)	Remarks
Kunda				See [1] below
Berth No.1	35	7.9	7	Max 35 m loa
Berth No.2	176	9.2	8.5	Max 150 m loa
Berth No.3	40	8.6	7.7	Max 120 m loa
Berth No.4	60	8	7.4	Max 130 m loa

[1]*Kunda:* Port of Kunda, Uus-Sadama tee 2, 44109 Kunda, Tel: +372 32 29955, Fax: +372 32 21463, Email:port.kunda@knc.ee

Storage:

Location	Open (m²)	Covered (m²)
Kunda	9700	500

Mechanical Handling Equipment:

Location	Type	Capacity (t)	Qty
Kunda	Mobile Cranes	5–8	4

Cargo Worked: Bulk 3000 t/day, other goods 1500-2000 t/day

Bunkering: Ancora AFS Shipping Estonia, Karu 11C, 10120 Tallinn, Republic of Estonia, *Tel:* +372 6 623069, *Fax:* +372 6 623070

Bominflot, AS Bominflot Estonia, Paavli 1, 33 Kopli Street, 10412 Tallinn, Republic of Estonia, *Tel:* +372 6 811 550, *Fax:* +372 6 811 551, *Email:* bunkers@bominflot.ee, *Website:* www.bominflot.net

Chevron Marine Products LLC, ul. Grodzienska 11, 80215 Gdansk, Poland, *Tel:* +48 58 5202254, *Fax:* +48 58 3412634, *Email:* kukiej@chevrontexco.com, *Website:* www.chevron.com

ExxonMobil Marine Fuels, Mailpoint 31, ExxonMobil House, Ermyn Way, Leatherhead, Surrey KT22 8UX, United Kingdom, *Tel:* +44 1372 222 000, *Fax:* +44 1372 223 922, *Email:* marine.fuels@exxonmobil.com, *Website:* www.exxonmobil.com

NT Marine AS, 6th Floor, 8 Ahtri Street, 10151 Tallinn, Republic of Estonia, *Tel:* +372 6 684 333, *Fax:* +372 6 684 330, *Email:* ntmarine@ntmarine.com, *Website:* www.ntmarine.com

Oiliken Bunkering AS, Roosikrantsi 16-2, 10119 Tallinn, Republic of Estonia, *Tel:* +372 6 314 183, *Fax:* +372 6 314 184, *Email:* bunker@oil.ee, *Website:* www.oil.ee

OW Bunker Estonia Ltd, Gasvaerksvej 48, DK-9000 Aalborg, Denmark, *Tel:* +45 98127277, *Fax:* +45 98167277, *Email:* owbunker@owbunker.dk, *Website:* www.owbunker.com

Tramp Oil & Marine, World Fuel Services Corporation, 13th Floor, Portland House, Bressenden Place, London SW1E 5BH, United Kingdom, *Tel:* +44 20 7808 5000, *Fax:* +44 20 7808 5088, *Email:* pturner@wfscorp.com, *Website:* www.wfscorp.com – *Grades:* all grades

Waste Reception Facilities: Road tankers for dirty ballast. Special containers for sludge and garbage

Towage: One tug of 2500 hp

Shipping Agents: CF & S Agents Ltd (CF&S), Uus-Sadama 2, 44106 Kunda, Republic of Estonia, *Tel:* +372 32 22305, *Fax:* +372 32 21307, *Email:* kunda@cfs.ee, *Website:* www.cfs.ee

Medical Facilities: Kunda Nordic Cement Corp medical centre, 3 km. Rakvere hospital, 25 km

Airport: Tallinn, 120 km

Railway: Kunda, 2 km

Lloyd's Agent: Lars Krogius Baltic Ltd, Ahtri 12, EE-10151 Tallinn, Republic of Estonia, *Tel:* +372 6 116620, *Fax:* +372 6 116685, *Email:* estonia@krogius.com, *Website:* www.krogius.com

MEERUSE

Lat 59° 27' N; Long 24° 40' E.

Admiralty Chart: 2227	**Admiralty Pilot:** 20
Time Zone: GMT +2 h	**UNCTAD Locode:** EE MRS

Principal Facilities:

				G						

Authority: RasmusSon Ltd, Bekker Port, Kopliranna 49, 11713 Tallinn, Republic of Estonia, *Tel:* +372 6 201600, *Fax:* +372 6 201620, *Email:* bekker@bekker.ee, *Website:* www.bekker.ee

Officials: Marketing Director: Marko Jurioje.

Port Security: ISPS compliant

Approach: There is a 500 m long and 50 m wide maritime canal leading to the port, the shallowest draught of which is 8.2 m

Pilotage: The pilot station is located at the Suurupi-2 buoy in pos 59° 37.50' N; 24° 38.00' E

Maximum Vessel Dimensions: 114 m loa, 17 m beam, 4.5 m draught

Accommodation:

Name	Length (m)	Depth (m)	Draught (m)	Remarks
Meeruse				
Berth No.1	63	1.5–4.2		
Berth No.2	70	2.7–4.2		
Berth No.3	24	2.5–3.2		
Berth No.4	70	2.5–4.7		
Berth No.5	116		5	Cargo berth
Berth No.6	50	1.6–3.4		
Berth No.7	42	.9–1.6		
Berth No.8	34	.9–3.9		
Berth No.9	62	1.7–3.5		
Berth No.10	63	1.7–3.5		
Berth No.11	175.8	3.4–8		Cargo berth

Storage:

Location	Open (m²)	Covered (m²)
Meeruse		2200
Berth No.5	7500	
Berth No.11	1500	

Lloyd's Agent: Lars Krogius Baltic Ltd, Ahtri 12, EE-10151 Tallinn, Republic of Estonia, *Tel:* +372 6 116620, *Fax:* +372 6 116685, *Email:* estonia@krogius.com, *Website:* www.krogius.com

MIIDURANNA

Lat 59° 30' N; Long 24° 49' E.

Admiralty Chart: 2227	**Admiralty Pilot:** 20
Time Zone: GMT +2 h	**UNCTAD Locode:** EE MID

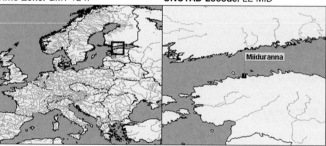

Principal Facilities:

P		Y	G			B		

Authority: Miiduranna Sadam, Haabneeme sjsk, 74001 Harjumaa, Republic of Estonia, *Tel:* +372 6 054314, *Fax:* +372 6 054316, *Email:* kapten@miidurannasadam.ee, *Website:* www.miidurannasadam.ee

Officials: Harbour Master: Viktor Palmet, *Tel:* +372 6 054312.

Pre-Arrival Information: Vessels should notify the port 72 h, 24 h and 4 h before arrival

Documentation: General declaration, cargo declaration, vessel supplies declaration, customs declaration of the crew, health declaration, crew list, passenger list, cargo manifests, bills of lading, notices on damages, general act

Pilotage: Compulsory and available 24 h/day. Request for pilot should be made via agency not later than 4 h prior to arrival at pilot station

Radio Frequency: VHF Channel 10, call sign 'Miiduranna'

Maximum Vessel Dimensions: Tankers: 195 m loa, 32 m breadth and 12.3 m draft. Dry Cargo Vessels: 110 m loa, 20 m breadth and 5.6 m draft

Working Hours: Mon-Fri 0800-2200. Overtime by agreement

Accommodation:

Name	Length (m)	Depth (m)	Draught (m)	Remarks
Miiduranna				See [1] below
Berth No.1	135	4	3.8	Cargo quay
Berth No.2	90	3	2.8	Fishing
Berth No.3	75	2.5–3	2.4	Ship repair
Berth No.4	142	3.8–5.8	3.4–5.6	Inner & outer cargo quay
Berth No.5	134	3–4		Cargo quay
Berth No.6	20	1.2–2	1.2	Small vessels
Berth No.7	56	1.2–2	1.2	Small vessels
Berth No.8	95	3.8	3.5	Cargo quay
Berth No.9	88	3.6–4	3.6	Cargo quay

Name	Length (m)	Depth (m)	Draught (m)	Remarks
Berth No.10	90	13	12.3	Oil quay with four mono-dolphins

[1]*Miiduranna:* Cargoes handled include round timber, lumber, technological shavings and oil products

Storage: Storage yards of 19 600 m2

Bunkering: Available

Waste Reception Facilities: Available

Towage: Has to be ordered if needed

Lloyd's Agent: Lars Krogius Baltic Ltd, Ahtri 12, EE-10151 Tallinn, Republic of Estonia, *Tel:* +372 6 116620, *Fax:* +372 6 116685, *Email:* estonia@krogius.com, *Website:* www.krogius.com

MUUGA

harbour area, see under Tallinn

PALDISKI

harbour area, see under Tallinn

PALJASSAARE

harbour area, see under Tallinn

PARNU

Lat 58° 23' N; Long 24° 29' E.

Admiralty Chart: 2215	**Admiralty Pilot:** 19
Time Zone: GMT +2 h	**UNCTAD Locode:** EE PAR

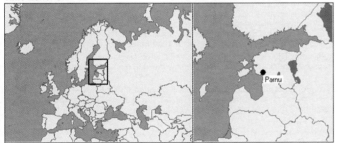

Principal Facilities:

		G		B	T	A

Tramp Oil & Marine

Wells House, 15-17 Elmfield Road, Bromley, Kent BR1 1LT, United Kingdom

Phone: +44 20 8315 7777　　**Fax:** +44 20 8315 7788

General email: enquiries@tramp-oil.com

See listings for all global offices: **www.tramp-oil.com**

Authority: Port of Parnu Authority, Emajoe 24/26, 80030 Parnu, Republic of Estonia, *Tel:* +372 44 71700, *Fax:* +372 44 71701, *Email:* sadam@transcom.ee, *Website:* www.transcom.ee

Officials: Managing Director: Matti Einmann, *Tel:* +372 44 71702, *Email:* matti.einmann@transcom.ee.
Stevedoring Manager: Vaino Raspel, *Tel:* +372 44 71732, *Email:* vaino.raspel@transcom.ee.
Harbour Master: Riho Prints, *Tel:* +372 44 71727, *Email:* riho.prints@transcom.ee.

Port Security: ISPS compliant

Approach: Approach channel is 6200 m long in depth of 6 m and 45 m wide at its narrowest point

Anchorage: Anchorage for ocean-going vessels can be obtained in the roadstead in depths ranging between 5.5 m and 8.7 m. There is an anchorage designated for foreign vessels on the E side and clear of the approach fairway

Pilotage: Compulsory and organised by the agent from the Estonian Pilot, Tel: +372 605 3888, Fax: +372 605 3881. Pilot boards in pos 58° 19' N; 24° 25' E

Radio Frequency: VHF Channels 13 and 16

Weather: Ice conditions occur in the harbour from November to April, but port remains open with help of icebreaker

Maximum Vessel Dimensions: 140 m loa, 45 m breadth

Working Hours: When required, loading of vessels and cargo delivery can take place 24 h/day

Accommodation:

Name	Length (m)	Depth (m)	Remarks
Parnu			See [1] below
AS Parnu Port			See [2] below
Quay No.1 (Floating Quay)	60	6	Round timber
Quay No.2 (General Cargo)	60	6	General cargo
Quay No.3 (Peat Berth)	78	6	Bulk cargo
Quay No.18 (City Berth)		5.8	Mooring berth
Quay No.19 (City Berth)		5	Packaged materials
Quay No.20 (City Berth)		5.5	Packaged materials
Quay No.23 (Floating Quays)		1.5–3.5	Three yachting berths. Closed in winter
Quay No.24 (Peetri Quay)	20	2.5	Pilot
AS Parnu Shipyard			See [3] below
Quay No.4 (Repair Quay)	35	4.5	Ship repair
Quay No.5 (Repair Quay)	30	4.5	Ship repair
Quay No.6 (Slipway)		6.5	
Quay No.7 (General Cargo Berth)	55	6	Round timber
Quay No.8 (Fishing Berth)	40	3.6	Fishing
Quay No.9 (Fishing Berth)	50	3.6	Fishing
Quay No.10 (General Cargo Berth)	84	6	Round timber
AS Parnu Stevedores			See [4] below
Quay No.11 (Jannsen's)	90	6	Hacked timber
Quay No.12 (Jannsen's)	100	6	Processed timber
Quay No.13 (Jannsen's)	26	4	Processed timber
AS Japs			See [5] below
Quay No.14	45	5	Fishing
Quay No.15	15	1.5–4	Fishing
Quay No.16	35	1–4	Fishing
Quay No.17	10	5	Fishing
AS Health Rehabilitation Center Viiking			See [6] below
Quay No.21 (Viiking Berth)		1.8	Pleasure craft
Environmental Inspectorate			
Quay No.22			Mooring berth rented to Alexela Oil

[1]*Parnu:* Cargoes handled include round timber, metal constructions, cement, coal, plaster, processed timber, hacked timber, sawdust, peat, briquettes, rubble, building materials, seafood, foodstuffs, cooking oil and packaged goods
[2]*AS Parnu Port:* Lootsi 6, 80012 Parnu, Tel: +372 44 71700, Fax: +372 44 71701, Email: sadam@transcom.ee
[3]*AS Parnu Shipyard:* Emajoe 22, 80030 Parnu, Tel: +372 44 41378, Fax: +372 44 33094
[4]*AS Parnu Stevedores:* Lootsi 6, 80012 Parnu, Tel: +372 44 72201, Fax: +372 44 72202, Email: sadam@transcom.ee
[5]*AS Japs:* Jannseni 36a, 80032 Parnu, Tel: +372 44 59600, Fax: +372 44 59610, Email: japs@hot.ee
[6]*AS Health Rehabilitation Center Viiking:* Sadama 4, 80012 Parnu, Tel: +372 44 31293, Fax: +372 44 31492, Email: viiking@online.ee

Storage:

Location	Covered (m²)
Parnu	4480

Mechanical Handling Equipment:

Location	Type	Capacity (t)	Qty
Parnu	Mult-purp. Cranes	5	1
Parnu	Mult-purp. Cranes	6	1

Bunkering: United Bunkering & Trading OU, Lille 4-221, EE-80010 Parnu, Republic of Estonia, *Tel:* +372 5221223, *Fax:* +372 4470560, *Email:* ubt@ubt.ee
Ancora AFS Shipping Estonia, Karu 11C, 10120 Tallinn, Republic of Estonia, *Tel:* +372 6 623069, *Fax:* +372 6 623070
Bominflot, AS Bominflot Estonia, Paavli 1, 33 Kopli Street, 10412 Tallinn, Republic of Estonia, *Tel:* +372 6 811 550, *Fax:* +372 6 811 551, *Email:* bunkers@bominflot.ee, *Website:* www.bominflot.net
Chevron Marine Products LLC, ul. Grodzienska 11, 80215 Gdansk, Poland, *Tel:* +48 58 5202254, *Fax:* +48 58 3412634, *Email:* kukiej@chevrontexco.com, *Website:* www.chevron.com
Euro Baltic Marine Services Ltd, P O Box 3717, 10508 Tallinn, Republic of Estonia, *Tel:* +372 2 641 9140, *Fax:* +372 2 641 9139
ExxonMobil Marine Fuels, Mailpoint 31, ExxonMobil House, Ermyn Way, Leatherhead, Surrey KT22 8UX, United Kingdom, *Tel:* +44 1372 222 000, *Fax:* +44 1372 223 922, *Email:* marine.fuels@exxonmobil.com, *Website:* www.exxonmobil.com
NT Marine AS, 6th Floor, 8 Ahtri Street, 10151 Tallinn, Republic of Estonia, *Tel:* +372 6 684 333, *Fax:* +372 6 684 330, *Email:* ntmarine@ntmarine.com, *Website:* www.ntmarine.com
Oiliken Bunkering AS, Roosikrantsi 16-2, 10119 Tallinn, Republic of Estonia, *Tel:* +372 6 314 183, *Fax:* +372 6 314 184, *Email:* bunker@oil.ee, *Website:* www.oil.ee
OW Bunker Estonia Ltd, Gasvaerksvej 48, DK-9000 Aalborg, Denmark, *Tel:* +45

Key to Principal Facilities:—				
A=Airport	**C**=Containers	**G**=General Cargo	**P**=Petroleum	**R**=Ro/Ro	**Y**=Dry Bulk
B=Bunkers	**D**=Dry Dock	**L**=Cruise	**Q**=Other Liquid Bulk	**T**=Towage (where available from port)	

98127277, *Fax:* +45   98167277, *Email:* owbunker@owbunker.dk, *Website:* www.owbunker.com

Tramp Oil & Marine, World Fuel Services Corporation, 13th Floor, Portland House, Bressenden Place, London SW1E 5BH, United Kingdom, *Tel:* +44 20 7808 5000, *Fax:* +44 20 7808 5088, *Email:* pturner@wfscorp.com, *Website:* www.wfscorp.com

Waste Reception Facilities: Available

Towage: Two tugs available of 1200 hp and 300 hp

Repair & Maintenance: Parnu Shipyard Ltd, Emajoe 22, 80030 Parnu, Republic of Estonia, *Tel:* +372 44 41378, *Fax:* +372 44 33094, *Email:* prnlaevatehas@hot.ee

Ship Chandlers: Deka Shipchandler Ltd, 23 B Kooli Street, 80019 Parnu, Republic of Estonia, *Tel:* +372 44 20750, *Fax:* +372 44 30837, *Email:* deka@estpak.ee

Shipping Agents: CF & S Agents Ltd (CF&S), Jannseni 28, 80010 Parnu, Republic of Estonia, *Tel:* +372 44 71500, *Fax:* +372 44 71505, *Email:* parnu@cfs.ee, *Website:* www.cfs.ee

Estonian Maritime Agency Ltd (ESTMA), Ringi Str.4, 80011 Parnu, Republic of Estonia, *Tel:* +372 44 50030, *Fax:* +372 44 50039, *Email:* agency@parnu.estma.ee, *Website:* www.estma.ee

Tallship Ltd., 33-209 J.V. Jannseni Street, 80044 Parnu, Republic of Estonia, *Tel:* +372 44 31937, *Fax:* +372 44 31844, *Email:* parnu@tallship.ee, *Website:* www.tallship.ee

Stevedoring Companies: Port of Parnu Authority, Emajoe 24/26, 80030 Parnu, Republic of Estonia, *Tel:* +372 44 71700, *Fax:* +372 44 71701, *Email:* sadam@transcom.ee, *Website:* www.transcom.ee

Medical Facilities: The City of Parnu healthcare institutions provide medical aid

Airport: Parnu Airport

Lloyd's Agent: Lars Krogius Baltic Ltd, Ahtri 12, EE-10151 Tallinn, Republic of Estonia, *Tel:* +372 6 116620, *Fax:* +372 6 116685, *Email:* estonia@krogius.com, *Website:* www.krogius.com

PYARNU

alternate name, see Parnu

ROOMASSAARE

Lat 58° 13' N; Long 22° 31' E.

Admiralty Chart: 2215	Admiralty Pilot: 19
Time Zone: GMT +2 h	UNCTAD Locode: EE ROO

Principal Facilities:

P		G				T	A

Authority: Roomassaare Harbour, Roomassaare Tee 12, 93815 Kuressaare, Republic of Estonia, *Tel:* +372 45 33619, *Fax:* +372 45 55574, *Email:* roomassaare@saarteliinid.ee, *Website:* www.saarteliinid.ee

Officials: Port Director: Renno Tammleht, *Email:* renno@saarteliinid.ee.
Finance Manager: Villu Vatsfeld, *Tel:* +372 45 30140, *Email:* villu@saarteliinid.ee.

Port Security: ISPS compliant

Documentation: Crew list (4 copies), passenger list (3 copies), cargo declaration (3 copies), crew effects declaration, ship stores

Approach: Channel to port is 1200 m wide and depth of 6 m marked by buoys, stakes and light clearing marks

Anchorage: In positions 58° 08' N; 22° 25' E and 58° 11' N; 22° 29' E

Pilotage: Compulsory

Radio Frequency: VHF Channel 16

Maximum Vessel Dimensions: 120 m loa, 5 m draft

Principal Imports and Exports: Exports: Grit, Peat, Timber.

Working Hours: 0800-1700

Accommodation:

Name	Length (m)	Depth (m)
Roomassaar		
Cargo Quay	201	5
Oil Quay	115	5

Mechanical Handling Equipment:

Location	Type	Capacity (t)	Qty
Roomassaare	Portal Cranes	10	1

Cargo Worked: 700 t/day

Towage: One tug of 165 kw

Airport: Kuressaare, 1 km

Lloyd's Agent: Lars Krogius Baltic Ltd, Ahtri 12, EE-10151 Tallinn, Republic of Estonia, *Tel:* +372 6 116620, *Fax:* +372 6 116685, *Email:* estonia@krogius.com, *Website:* www.krogius.com

SILLAMAE

Lat 59° 24' N; Long 27° 47' E.

Admiralty Chart: 2248/2264	Admiralty Pilot: 20
Time Zone: GMT +2 h	UNCTAD Locode: EE SLM

Principal Facilities:

P		Y	G		R		B		T	

Authority: Sillamae Port Authority, Suur-Karja Str. 5, 10141 Tallinn, Republic of Estonia, *Tel:* +372 6 405271, *Fax:* +372 6 405279, *Email:* silport@silport.ee, *Website:* www.silport.ee

Officials: Managing Director: Margus Vahi, *Email:* m.vahi@silport.ee.
Commercial Manager: Mihkel Uriko, *Tel:* +372 6 405274, *Email:* m.uriko@silport.ee.
Finance Manager: Monika Linkov, *Tel:* +372 6 405269, *Email:* m.linkov@silport.ee.
Marketing Manager: Andrei Birov, *Tel:* +372 6 405275, *Email:* a.birov@silport.ee.
Harbour Master: Capt Erich Moik, *Tel:* +372 6 405266, *Email:* e.moik@silport.ee.

Port Security: ISPS compliant

Documentation: Entering port the following documents must be provided prior to the beginning of loading operations, but not later than 6 h after entry. Documents must also be provided prior to departure from the port
1. General declaration
2. Crew list & list of passengers
3. Maritime declaration of health
4. Cargo declaration, declaration of vessel supplies, cargo manifests, bills of lading
5. Crew's customs declaration, general application, notifications on damages
6. Declaration of vessel food supplies and information on garbage

Approach: The sea channel is a semi-restricted single line channel classifed as a group A channel, The channel is navigable day and night with guaranteed depths of 13 m

Pilotage: Compulsory. The pilot station is located at 59° 29' N; 27° 42' E and can be contacted on VHF Channel 68 or *Tel:* +372 605 3888, 24 hours a day. 24 hours notice prior to arrival is required at the pilot station, or on departure from previous port if less than 24 hours

Radio Frequency: VHF Channel 68

Weather: All year round navigation, no ice breaking is needed in an average winter. The harbour is well sheltered from winds from W, NW and N by a 1 km long breakwater in the western part of the port. The port has a natural shelter from all the other winds by the mainland

Traffic: 2007, 1 777 659 t of cargo handled

Principal Imports and Exports: Imports: Container cargo, General cargo, Vehicles. Exports: Chemical cargo, General cargo, LPG, Metal products, Oil & petroleum products, Petro-chemical products, Scrap, Timber.

Working Hours: Monday-Friday 0800-1700

Accommodation:

Name	Length (m)	Depth (m)	Remarks
Silport			Port Office, Tel: +372 39 29102, Fax: +372 39 29153
West Quay Terminal			
A1	319	16	See [1] below
A2	319	16	See [2] below
A4	200	12	Tankers up to 30 000 dwt
A5	200	12	Tankers/drybulk up to 30 000 dwt
A6	113	12	Tankers/drybulk up to 30 000 dwt
A7	31	12	Port service vessels & vessels up to 5000 dwt

[1]*A1:* Operated by Alexela Sillamae Ltd., Kesk 2, 40231 Sillamae, Tel: +372 39 29331, Fax: +372 39 29440, Email: terminal@alexelasillamae.ee, Website: www.alexelasillamae.ee
Tankers up to 100 000 dwt

[2]*A2:* Operated by Alexela Sillamae Ltd., Kesk 2, 40231 Sillamae, Tel: +372 39 29331, Fax: +372 39 29440, Email: terminal@alexelasillamae.ee, Website: www.alexelasillamae.ee
Tankers up to 100 000 dwt

Storage: Sillamae Oil Terminal: 157 500 m3 for heavy and light oil products. SilSteve: 22 ha of outdoor and 7000 m2 of indoor storage areas for general cargo. TankChem: 55 500 m3 for different chemical products. Sillgas: 24 500 m3 for LPG

Bunkering: Available

Waste Reception Facilities: Waste treatment facilities available

Towage: Available

Shipping Agents: ATT Ltd., Kesk 2, 40231 Sillamae, Republic of Estonia, *Tel:* +372 39 29446, *Fax:* +372 39 29447, *Email:* agency@a2t.ee, *Website:* www.a2t.ee

Stevedoring Companies: AS Silsteve, Kesk 2, 40231 Sillamae, Republic of Estonia, *Tel:* +372 39 29200, *Fax:* +372 39 29207, *Email:* silsteve@silsteve.ee, *Website:* www.silsteve.ee

Medical Facilities: Available in port at Sillamae Polyclinic, Tel: 639 29190, for emergency medical care Tel: 112

Railway: A railway station of 4 tracks, each 1050 m long and 1520 mm wide (the CIS Standard) sufficient for accepting full trainloads of 66 wagons (To be expanded up to 18 tracks total incl. 4 tracks of 1500 m in length). Sillamae Oil Terminal has a combined double sided railway pier for light and heavy oil products with each side able to accommodate 44 rail tank cars

Development: Expansion of Phase 2 of Silport (for bulk and general cargo terminals) will begin in 2006. Phase 3 consisting of a container and a passenger facility will begin after the completion of Phase 2

Lloyd's Agent: Lars Krogius Baltic Ltd, Ahtri 12, EE-10151 Tallinn, Republic of Estonia, *Tel:* +372 6 116620, *Fax:* +372 6 116685, *Email:* estonia@krogius.com, *Website:* www.krogius.com

SILPORT

harbour area, see under Sillamae

TALLINN

Lat 59° 26' N; Long 24° 45' E.

Admiralty Chart: 2227

Admiralty Pilot: 20

Time Zone: GMT +2 h

UNCTAD Locode: EE TLL

Principal Facilities:

P Q Y G C R L B   T A

Lootsi 11, Tallinn 10151, Estonia
Tel: +372 6 318 151 (Office) +372 566 10138 (24 Hours)
Fax: +372 6 313 100
Email: info@pkl.ee   Web: www.pkl.ee

Towage & Salvage in Estonia, Latvia, and Finland

Authority: Port of Tallinn, 25 Sadama Street, 15051 Tallinn, Republic of Estonia, *Tel:* +372 6 318002, *Fax:* +372 6 318166, *Email:* portoftallinn@portoftallinn.com, *Website:* www.portoftallinn.com

Officials: Chairman: Ain Kaljurand, *Email:* a.kaljurand@ts.ee.
Chief Financial Officer: Marko Raid, *Tel:* +372 6 318047, *Email:* m.raid@ts.ee.
Marketing Manager: Helen Hinno, *Email:* h.hinno@ts.ee.
Harbour Master: Artur Kivistik, *Email:* a.kivistik@ts.ee.

Port Security: ISPS compliant

Pre-Arrival Information: The captain and/or agent of the vessel calling at the port should notify his planned arrival 72 h and 24 h beforehand or directly after departure from the previous port, if the duration of the voyage remains under 24 h. The written or internet forwarded advance notice should include information on the name of the vessel, expected time of arrival, country of origin, port of destination, general measures, designation and quantity of cargo, real draft and aim of entrance, data on the technical state of the vessel and health of the crew

Documentation: General declaration, notice of readiness, cargo declaration, crew list, passenger list, maritime declaration of health, ship stores declaration, crew effects declaration

Approach: Depth of Tallinn Roads ranges from 11 m to 45 m

Anchorage: Anchorage areas situated in Tallinn Bay in depths up to 30 m

Pilotage: Compulsory. Pilot should be ordered via agencies not later than 24 h prior to arrival at pilot station and then confirmed 6 h and 2 h in advance. Pilot should be ordered 4 h prior to leaving at the latest, the order shall be specified 1 h prior to leaving Pilot stations at:
(a) Suurupi (buoy 2) in pos 59° 29.4' N; 24° 33' E
(b) Tallinn (buoy 1) in pos 59° 37.5' N; 24° 38' E
(c) NE fairway of Muuga Bay in pos 59° 39' N; 25° 05.4' E
(d) NW fairway of Muuga Bay in pos 59° 39' N; 24° 44' E
(e) Four miles to NW from the gate of Paldiski South Harbour in pos 59° 23' N; 24° 00' E
(f) Three nautical miles to the north of Saaremaa Harbour in pos 58° 35' N; 22° 12' E

Radio Frequency: VHF radio station of the port works 24 h/day with the following call signs:
Old City Harbour: call sign Tallinn-Radio 5 (Port Control) on VHF Channel 14 not closer than 1 nautical mile from the port gate (North-Western mole)
Paljassaare Harbour: call sign Tallinn-Radio 32 (Port Control) on VHF Channel 11 and call sign Tallinn-Radio 5 (Port Control) on VHF Channel 14
Muuga Harbour: call sign Muuga-Radio 5 (Port Control) on VHF Channel 87
Paldiski South Harbour: call sign 'Paldiski South Harbour' on VHF Channels 9 and 16
Saaremaa Harbour: call sign Tamme Radio on VHF Channels 14 and 16

Weather: Prevailing winds from W and SW. Winds from N and NW are unfavourable for Tallinn Bay

Tides: No tides

Traffic: 2008, 29 077 000 t of cargo handled, 7 247 366 passengers

Maximum Vessel Dimensions: Old City Harbour: 320 m loa, 10.7 m draught
Muuga: 300 m loa, 18 m draught
Paljassaare: 190 m loa, 9 m draught
Paldiski South: 230 m loa, 13.5 m draught
Saaremaa: 200 m loa, 10 m draught

Principal Imports and Exports: Imports: Container cargo, Foodstuffs, Grain, Oil products, Paper, Wheeled cargo, Wood pulp. Exports: Coal, Container cargo, Fertilisers, Grain, Metals, Oil products, Paper, Peat, Timber, Wheeled cargo, Wood pulp.

Working Hours: Mon-Fri 0800-1645. Vessel traffic service and cargo handling 24 h/day including Saturday and Sunday

Accommodation:

Name	Length (m)	Depth (m)	Remarks
Old City Harbour			See [1] below
Basin No.1			
Berth 1	251.5	8.5	with ramp
Berth 3	246	7.3	With ramp
Berth 5	226	8.3	With ramp
Basin No.2			
Berth 7	242	8.2	With ramp
Berth 8	199	7	With ramp
Fitting-out Berth 9		5.2	
Berth 10	179	7.7	With ramp
Berth 11	60	7.3	
Basin No.3			
Berth 12	260	7.5	With ramp
Berth 13	164	8	With ramp
Berth 14	199	10.7	
Berth 15	188	10	
Berth 16	136	10.7	
Berth 17	183	10.7	
Admiralty Basin			
Berth 18	148	5.2	
Berth 19 (boat bridge)	83	5.2	
Berth 20 (boat bridge)	134	5.5	
Berth 21	135	5.1	With ramp
Berth 22	120	4.6	With ramp
Berth 23	212	4.4	
Vanasadam Jetty			
Berth 24	339	10.7	Cruise vessels
Berth 25	339	10.7	Cruise vessels
Muuga Harbour			See [2] below
Berth 1	205	11.4	
Berth 1A	210	14.4	
Berth 2	205	11.2	Oil transhipment
Berth 2A	80	6.6	
Fitting-out Berth 3W		5.5	
Fitting-out Berth 3O		5.5	
Berth 3	111	8.2	Oil transhipment
Berth 3A	218	13	Oil transhipment
Berth 4	278	7.5	
Berth 5	103	7.1	With ramp
Berth 6	157	9.5	
Berth 6A	183	10.9	
Berth 7	310	14.4	
Berth 8	280	14.4	
Berth 9	331	17.4	
Berth 9A	340	18	Oil transhipment
Berth 10	335	17.4	
Berth 10A	340	18	Oil transhipment
Berth 11	259	12.9	
Berth 12	175	12.4	
Berth 13	200	12.4	With ramp
Berth 14	219	12.4	Containers. Operated by Muuga CT
Berth 15	200	12.4	Containers. Operated by Muuga CT
Berth 16	198	12.4	Containers. Operated by Muuga CT

Key to Principal Facilities:—				
A=Airport	**C**=Containers	**G**=General Cargo	**P**=Petroleum	**R**=Ro/Ro	**Y**=Dry Bulk
B=Bunkers	**D**=Dry Dock	**L**=Cruise	**Q**=Other Liquid Bulk	**T**=Towage (where available from port)	

Name	Length (m)	Depth (m)	Remarks
Berth 31	210	11	Coal terminal for vessels up to 30 000 dwt
Berth 32	365	17.1	Coal terminal for vessels up to 120 000 dwt
Berth 33	198	11	Coal terminal for vessels up to 20 000 dwt
Paljassaare Harbour			See [3] below
Berth 31	100	3.4–5.4	
Berth 32	265	6.4–6.5	
Berth 33	184	8.7	
Berth 34	97	5.9–6.7	
Berth 35	400	6.4–9	
Berth 36	290	6.4	
Berth 37	90	4.5	
Berth 38	141	4.5–4.7	
Berth 39	51	4.5	
Berth 40	139	4.2–6	
Berth 41	102	6	
Paldiski South Harbour			See [4] below
Berth 1	193	12	See [5] below
Berth 2	230	12	With ramp
Berth 3	123	9	
Berth 3a	107	9	With ramp
Berth 4	163	9	With ramp
Berth 5	152	9	
Berth 6	225.5	8.8	
Berth 7	249	13.5	See [6] below
Saaremaa Harbour			See [7] below
Quay No.1	200	10	
Quay No.2	165	7	
Quay No.3	80	3–7	

[1]*Old City Harbour:* 25 Sadama Road, 15051 Tallinn, Tel: +372 6 318454, Fax: +372 6 318377, Email: vanasadam@portoftallinn.com
Passenger & cruise vessels, ro/ro cargo
[2]*Muuga Harbour:* 57 Maardu Road, 74115 Maardu, Tel: +372 6 319502, Fax: +372 6 319544, Email: muuga@portoftallinn.com
Oil & oil products, grain, fertilisers, container & ro/ro cargo, reefer cargo, timber and other bulk and general cargo
[3]*Paljassaare Harbour:* 28 Paljassaare Road, 10313 Tallinn, Tel: +372 6 100803, Fax: +372 6 100804
Timber, oil products, coal, cooking oil, reefer cargo and general cargo
[4]*Paldiski South Harbour:* 10 Rae Poik, 76806 Paldiski, Tel: +372 6 318800, Fax: +372 6 318803, Email: paldiski@portoftallinn.com
Ro/ro & PDI, metal scrap, timber, oil products, road metal, peat, other dry bulk and general cargo
[5]*Berth 1:* Operated by Alexela Terminal Ltd. Loading and storage of light oil products and oil chemicals
[6]*Berth 7:* Operated by Alexela Terminal Ltd. Loading and storage of light oil products and oil chemicals
[7]*Saaremaa Harbour:* Ninase kula, Mustjala vald, 93601 Saaremaa, Tel: +372 6 100703, Fax: +372 6 100704, Email: saaremaa@portoftallinn.com
For cruise vessels up to 200 m loa. There is also a floating quay for use by small vessels

Storage:

Location	Open (m²)	Covered (m²)	Grain (t)	Cold (m³)
Old City Harbour	95000	10400		
Muuga Harbour	670000	151000	300000	11500
Paljassaare Harbour	105000	16000		15000
Paldiski South Harbour	270000	12000		

Bunkering: A full range of bunkering fuels are available on a 24 h basis. Delivery by barge and tank trucks
Ancora AFS Shipping Estonia, Karu 11C, 10120 Tallinn, Republic of Estonia, *Tel:* +372 6 623069, *Fax:* +372 6 623070
Baltic Estonian Bunker Ltd, 46 Toostuse Street, 10416 Tallinn, Republic of Estonia, *Tel:* +372 6 464 603, *Fax:* +372 6 464 604, *Email:* beb@beb.ee, *Website:* www.beb.ee
Bominflot, AS Bominflot Estonia, Paavli 1, 33 Kopli Street, 10412 Tallinn, Republic of Estonia, *Tel:* +372 6 811 550, *Fax:* +372 6 811 551, *Email:* bunkers@bominflot.ee, *Website:* www.bominflot.net
Global Bunkering Ltd, Ranna 2, Leppneeme, Viimsi, Harjumaa, 74009 Tallinn, Republic of Estonia, *Tel:* +372 6 605 387, *Fax:* +372 6 605 388, *Email:* globalbunker@hot.ee
NT Marine AS, 6th Floor, 8 Ahtri Street, 10151 Tallinn, Republic of Estonia, *Tel:* +372 6 684 333, *Fax:* +372 6 684 330, *Email:* ntmarine@ntmarine.com, *Website:* www.ntmarine.com
Oiliken Bunkering AS, Roosikrantsi 16-2, 10119 Tallinn, Republic of Estonia, *Tel:* +372 6 314 183, *Fax:* +372 6 314 184, *Email:* bunker@oil.ee, *Website:* www.oil.ee
Vartoni Ltd, Suur-Patarei 3, 10415 Tallinn, Republic of Estonia, *Tel:* +372 6 411 166, *Fax:* +372 6 411 167, *Email:* info@vartoni.com, *Website:* www.vartoni.com
NT Marine AS, 6th Floor, 8 Ahtri Street, 10151 Tallinn, Republic of Estonia, *Tel:* +372 6 684 333, *Fax:* +372 6 684 330, *Email:* ntmarine@ntmarine.com, *Website:* www.ntmarine.com

Waste Reception Facilities: Available for bilge water and sewage 24 h/day. Chemical waste and ballast water cannot be delivered in the port

Towage: Alfons Hakans Oy Ab, Alfons Hakans OU, World Trade Centre, Ahtri 12-208, 10151 Tallinn, Republic of Estonia, *Tel:* +372 6 116190, *Fax:* +372 6 116191, *Email:* office.tallinn@alfonshakans.fi, *Website:* www.alfonshakans.fi
PKL Ltd, Lootsi Street 11, 10151 Tallinn, Republic of Estonia, *Tel:* +372 6 318151, *Fax:* +372 6 313100, *Email:* info@pkl.ee, *Website:* www.pkl.ee

Repair & Maintenance: Baltic Ship Repairers, Kopli 103, EEOO17 Tallinn, Republic of Estonia, *Tel:* +372 6 102680, *Fax:* +372 6 102999, *Email:* shipyard@bsr.ee Three floating docks: 139.5 m x 23.8 m for vessels up to 8500 t, 101 m x 22 m for vessels up to 4500 t and 153.6 m x 27.4 m for vessels up to 10 500 t

Ship Chandlers: GART-GRUPP Ltd, Port of Muuga, 5 Vilja Street, 74115 Maardu, Republic of Estonia, *Tel:* +372 6 319443, *Fax:* +372 6 319479, *Email:* gartgrupp@balticom.ee
Loigo Marine Supply Ltd, 34 A Peterburi tee, 11415 Tallinn, Republic of Estonia, *Tel:* +372 6 107701, *Fax:* +372 6 107716, *Email:* flot@loigo.ee, *www.loigo.ee*
Tridens Ltd Ship Supply Division, Port of Muuga, Hoidla tee 2, 74115 Maardu, Republic of Estonia, *Tel:* +372 6 031850, *Fax:* +372 6 031811, *Email:* dfree.order@tridens.ee, *Website:* www.tridens.ee

Shipping Agents: Approve Oy, Ravala 5, EE-10143 Tallinn, Republic of Estonia, *Tel:* +372 6 309235, *Fax:* +372 6 309236, *Email:* team@approve.ee
Aseco Container Services OU, Ahtri Street 12, 331, EE-10151 Tallinn, Republic of Estonia, *Tel:* +372 6 070847, *Fax:* +372 6 070848, *Email:* aseco@aseco.ee
Cargomasters Eesti Ou, Peterburi Road 2F, EE-11415 Tallinn, Republic of Estonia, *Tel:* +372 6 051215, *Fax:* +372 6 051216, *Email:* mkt@cargomasters.ee, *Website:* www.cargomasters.ee
CF & S Agents Ltd (CF&S), Ahtri 12, EE-10151 Tallinn, Republic of Estonia, *Tel:* +372 6 664400, *Fax:* +372 6 664444, *Email:* cfs@cfs.ee, *Website:* www.cfs.ee
CMA-CGM S.A., CMA CGM Estonia, Pirita Tee 20, EE-10127 Tallinn, Republic of Estonia, *Tel:* +372 6 660540, *Fax:* +372 6 660549, *Email:* tln.genmbox@cma-cgm.com, *Website:* www.cma-cgm.com
Dasena Agencies, World Trade Center, Ahtri 12, 10151 Tallinn, Republic of Estonia, *Tel:* +372 6 070850, *Fax:* +372 6 070854, *Email:* dasena@dasena.ee, *Website:* www.dasena.ee
Estonian Maritime Agency Ltd (ESTMA), Sadama Str.17, 10111 Tallinn, Republic of Estonia, *Tel:* +372 6 401800, *Fax:* +372 6 313560, *Email:* info@estma.ee, *Website:* www.estma.ee
Euro-Baltic Shipping Services Ltd, Kreutzwaldi Street 24A, P O Box 3717, 10508 Tallinn, Republic of Estonia, *Tel:* +372 6 419140, *Fax:* +372 6 419139, *Website:* www.ebss.ee
Inflot Shipping Agency, Tuukri 58, EE-10120 Tallinn, Republic of Estonia, *Tel:* +372 6 033183, *Fax:* +372 6 033381, *Email:* inflot@inflot.ee, *Website:* www.inflot.ee
Chr Jensen Eesti AS, Pirita Tee 20P, 10127 Tallinn, Republic of Estonia, *Tel:* +372 6 405333, *Fax:* +372 6 405335, *Email:* info@chrjensen.ee, *Website:* www.chrjensen.ee
Krogius, Lars Krogius Baltic Ltd, Ahtri 12, EE-10151 Tallinn, Republic of Estonia, *Tel:* +372 6 116620, *Fax:* +372 6 116685, *Email:* estonia@krogius.com, *Website:* www.krogius.com
Lars Krogius Baltic Ltd, Ahtri 12, EE-10151 Tallinn, Republic of Estonia, *Tel:* +372 6 116620, *Fax:* +372 6 116685, *Email:* estonia@krogius.com, *Website:* www.krogius.com
Maritime Transport & Agencies Oy, 11 Lootsi Street, 10151 Tallinn, Republic of Estonia, *Tel:* +372 6 318171, *Fax:* +372 6 318173, *Email:* mta@mta.ee, *Website:* www.mta.nu
Mediterranean Shipping Company, MSC Eesti AS, Admirali Building, 8th Floor, Ahtri 6A, 10151 Tallinn, Republic of Estonia, *Tel:* +372 6 663888, *Fax:* +372 6 663899, *Email:* info@tll.mscestonia.com, *Website:* www.mscgva.ch
Melship Eesti AS, Ravala Boulevard 6-201B, EE-0001 Tallinn, Republic of Estonia, *Tel:* +372 6 305689, *Fax:* +372 6 305686, *Email:* nnl.genmbox@cma-cgm.com
A.P. Moller-Maersk Group, Maersk Eesti AS, Jarvevana tee 9, 11314 Tallinn, Republic of Estonia, *Tel:* +372 6 799000, *Fax:* +372 6 799049, *Email:* tllsal@maersk.com, *Website:* www.maerskline.com
Nesco Agency Ltd, Tuukri 17, EE-10152 Tallinn, Republic of Estonia, *Tel:* +372 6 339400, *Fax:* +372 6 339499, *Email:* nesco@nesco.ee, *Website:* www.nesco.ee
NET Shipping Ltd Oy, Ahtri 12-77, EE-10151 Tallinn, Republic of Estonia, *Tel:* +372 6 116500, *Fax:* +372 6 116501, *Email:* anti.niit@netship.ee
John Nurminen Maritime Oy, Pirita Tee 20, EE-10127 Tallinn, Republic of Estonia, *Tel:* +372 6 054640, *Fax:* +372 6 054649, *Email:* tallinn@johnnurminen.com, *Website:* www.johnnurminen.ee
Omega Shipping Ltd, Sadama Str. 17, Office 309, EE-10111 Tallinn, Republic of Estonia, *Tel:* +372 6 277160, *Fax:* +372 6 277169, *Email:* info@omegaship.ee, *Website:* www.omegaship.ee
Pirita Marine OU, Ahtri 12-73, 10151 Tallinn, Republic of Estonia, *Tel:* +372 6 116606, *Fax:* +372 6 116609, *Email:* info@pmarine.ee, *Website:* www.pmarine.ee
Reval Logistik A.S., 4 Sadama Street, EE-10111 Tallinn, Republic of Estonia, *Tel:* +372 6 409751, *Fax:* +372 6 409786, *Email:* info@rlog.ee, *Website:* www.rlog.ee
Samskip H/f (Samband Line Ltd), 4 Sadama Street, EE-1011 Tallinn, Republic of Estonia, *Tel:* +372 6 409665, *Fax:* +372 6 409664, *Email:* tallinn@samskip.com, *Website:* www.samskip.com
Scan-Shipping Eesti A.S., Pirita tee 20, EE-10127 Tallinn, Republic of Estonia, *Tel:* +372 6 461500, *Fax:* +372 6 461510
Scanrapid Estonia Ltd, Peterburi Street 46-309, EE-11415 Tallinn, Republic of Estonia, *Tel:* +372 6 139782, *Fax:* +372 6 139820, *Email:* info@scanrapid.ee, *Website:* www.kaukohuolinta.com
Transocean Eesti AS, Ahtri 12 5th floor, P O Box 2880, EE-10151 Tallinn, Republic of Estonia, *Tel:* +372 6 116001, *Fax:* +372 6 116002, *Email:* barwil.eesti@transocean.ee, *Website:* www.transocean.ee
Tschudi & Eitzen Esco Ship Management AS, 4 Sadama Street, EE-15096 Tallinn, Republic of Estonia, *Tel:* +372 6 409711, *Fax:* +372 6 409748, *Email:* tech@edp.eml.ee

Stevedoring Companies: Alexela Terminal Ltd, Rae Poik 6, EE-76806 Paldiski, Republic of Estonia, *Tel:* +372 6 790999, *Fax:* +372 6 790998, *Email:* terminal@alexelaterminal.ee, *Website:* www.alexelaterminal.ee
Coal Terminal AS, Joe 4a, 10151 Tallinn, Republic of Estonia, *Tel:* +372 6 263652, *Fax:* +372 6 263653, *Email:* info@coalterminal.ee, *Website:* www.coalterminal.ee
Dry Bulk Terminal (DBT) Ltd, Koorma 13, EE-74115 Tallinn, Republic of Estonia, *Tel:* +372 6 319389, *Fax:* +372 6 319189, *Email:* dbt@dbtmuuga.ee, *Website:* www.dbtmuuga.ee
Estonian Metal Export Import (EMEX), Betooni 12, P O Box 2, EE-11415 Tallinn, Republic of Estonia, *Tel:* +372 6 258600, *Fax:* +372 6 012745, *Email:* firma@kuusakoski.com, *Website:* www.kuusakoski.ee
Estonian Oil Service (E.O.S.), Regati pst 1, EE-11911 Tallinn, Republic of Estonia, *Tel:* +372 6 266100, *Fax:* +372 6 313096, *Email:* info@eos.com.ee, *Website:* www.eos.com.ee
Eurodek Tallinn, Joe 3, EE-10151 Tallinn, Republic of Estonia, *Tel:* +372 6 137500, *Fax:* +372 6 137510, *Email:* eurodek@eurodek.ee, *Website:* www.eurodek.com
Eurokai, Paldiski, Republic of Estonia, *Tel:* +372 6 741118, *Fax:* +372 6 741045, *Email:* info@eurokai.ee

Galvex Estonia OU, Koorma 5, EE-74115 Maardu, Republic of Estonia, *Tel:* +372 6 056600, *Fax:* +372 6 056601, *Email:* info@galvex.net, *Website:* www.galvex.net

HTG Invest Ltd, Uus Sadama 19/13, Tallinn, Republic of Estonia, *Tel:* +372 6 318664, *Fax:* +372 6 313034, *Email:* htg@htg.tk.ee, *Website:* www.tk.ee

Muuga Container Terminal Ltd (Muuga CT), Veose 16, EE-74115 Maardu, Republic of Estonia, *Tel:* +372 6 319593, *Fax:* +372 6 319696, *Email:* muuga-ct@ct.tk.ee, *Website:* www.muuga-ct.com

Muuga Grain Terminal AS (MGT), Maardu tee 57, EE-74115 Tallinn, Republic of Estonia, *Tel:* +372 6 319232, *Fax:* +372 6 319179, *Email:* mgt@mgt.ee, *Website:* www.mgt.ee

Neste Estonia, Sopruse Street 155, EE 13417 Tallinn, Republic of Estonia, *Tel:* +372 6 319330, *Fax:* +372 6 319329, *Email:* indrek.kayu@nesteoil.com, *Website:* www.nesteoil.com

Nybit AS, 57 Maardu Street/5 Oli Street, EE-0030 Maardu, Republic of Estonia, *Tel:* +372 6 319422, *Fax:* +372 6 319423, *Email:* secretary@nybit.ee

Oiltanking, Port of Muuga, Oil Street 7, EE-74115 Tallinn, Republic of Estonia, *Tel:* +372 6 319403, *Fax:* +372 6 319406, *Email:* tallinn@oiltanking.com, *Website:* www.oiltanking.com

Pakterminal Ltd, Lasti Road 20, EE-74115 Maardu, Republic of Estonia, *Tel:* +372 6 319820, *Fax:* +372 6 319801, *Email:* pakterminal@pakterminal.ee, *Website:* www.pakterminal.ee

Petromaks Stividori AS, 9A Nylva Street, EE-10416 Tallinn, Republic of Estonia, *Tel:* +372 6 507777, *Fax:* +372 6 507700, *Email:* stividori@pmg.ee, *Website:* www.petromaks.com

Refetra Ltd, Koorma 17, EE-74102 Tallinn, Republic of Estonia, *Tel:* +372 6 319408, *Fax:* +372 6 319113, *Email:* refetra@refetra.tk.ee, *Website:* www.refetra.ee

ScanTrans AS, Nolva 13, EE-10416 Tallinn, Republic of Estonia, *Tel:* +372 6 602251, *Fax:* +372 6 602247, *Email:* strans@online.ee, *Website:* www.scantrans.ee

KS Stivideerimise AS, Paljassaare tee 28E, 10313 Tallinn, Republic of Estonia, *Tel:* +372 6 100807, *Fax:* +372 6 100990, *Email:* ks@stevedore.ee, *Website:* www.stevedore.ee

Stivis Ltd, 1 Koorma Street, EE-0030 Tallinn, Republic of Estonia, *Tel:* +372 6 319788, *Fax:* +372 6 319250, *Email:* stivis@stivis.ee, *Website:* www.stivis.ee

AS Tallink Grupp, Tartu Maantee 13, EE-10145 Tallinn, Republic of Estonia, *Tel:* +372 6 409800, *Fax:* +372 6 409810, *Email:* info@tallink.ee, *Website:* www.tallink.ee

Transcontinental OU, Tallinn, Republic of Estonia, *Tel:* +372 6 319572, *Fax:* +372 6 319489, *Email:* mtrans@online.ee

Surveyors: Bureau Veritas, Tartu Mnt 24-24b, EE 10115 Tallinn, Republic of Estonia, *Tel:* +372 6 676610, *Fax:* +372 6 676611, *Email:* tallinn@ee.bureauveritas.com, *Website:* www.bureauveritas.com

Det Norske Veritas A/S, Liivalaia 22, E-10118 Tallinn, Republic of Estonia, *Tel:* +372 6 285060, *Fax:* +372 6 285061, *Email:* tallinn.classification@dnv.com, *Website:* www.dnv.com

Germanischer Lloyd, Regati Pst. 1, Korpus 5VE, No.220/221, E-11911 Tallinn, Republic of Estonia, *Tel:* +372 6 398602, *Fax:* +372 6 398603, *Email:* gl-tallinn@gl-group.com, *Website:* www.gl-group.com

IMCS BVBA, P O Box 3011, EE-10504 Tallinn, Republic of Estonia, *Tel:* +372 6 272540, *Fax:* +372 6 272550, *Email:* info@imcs.ee, *Website:* www.imcs-group.com

Russian Maritime Register of Shipping, 58 ul Tuukri, 10120 Tallinn, Republic of Estonia, *Tel:* +372 6 684550, *Fax:* +372 6 684568, *Email:* 124rs-est@pb.uninet.ee, *Website:* www.rs-head.spb.ru

Medical Facilities: Available

Airport: Old City Harbour: Tallinn International Airport, 7 km
Muuga: Tallinn International Airport, 20 km
Paljassaare: Tallinn International Airport, 7 km
Paldiski South: Tallinn International Airport, 52 km
Saaremaa: Kuressaare Airport, 42 km

Railway: Old City Harbour: direct railway connection to the harbour, Baltic Railway Station, 3 km
Muuga: direct railway connection to the harbour, Muuga Railway Station, 1 km
Paljassaare: direct railway connection to the harbour, Baltic Railway Station, 4 km
Paldiski South: direct railway connection to the harbour, Paldiski Railway Station, 1 km

Development: Extension of the eastern part of Muuga Harbour
New quays and terminal areas in Paldiski South Harbour

Lloyd's Agent: Lars Krogius Baltic Ltd, Ahtri 12, EE-10151 Tallinn, Republic of Estonia, *Tel:* +372 6 116620, *Fax:* +372 6 116685, *Email:* estonia@krogius.com, *Website:* www.krogius.com

VENE-BALTI

Lat 59° 27' N; Long 24° 38' E.

Admiralty Chart: 2227	Admiralty Pilot: 20
Time Zone: GMT +2 h	UNCTAD Locode: EE VEB

Principal Facilities:

P		G					T	A

Authority: Vene-Balti Sadam OU, Kopli 103, 11712 Tallinn, Republic of Estonia, *Tel:* +372 6 102205, *Fax:* +372 6 102757, *Email:* port@bsr.ee, *Website:* www.portvenebalti.ee

Officials: Director: Vadim Gordunov, *Email:* v.gordunov@bsr.ee

Anchorage: There are four anchorage areas in Kopli Bay:
Anchorage Area D in depth of 10-20 m located between the following positions: 59° 27.9Æ' N; 24° 35.6' E, 59° 27.9' N; 24° 36.8' E, 59° 26.95' N; 24° 37.6' E, 59° 26.95' N; 24° 38.85' E
Anchorage Area E in depth of 31-38 m located between the following positions: 59° 29.8Æ' N; 24° 33.6' E, 59° 29.9' N; 24° 36.0' E, 59° 28.7' N; 24° 36.0' E
Anchorage Area F in depth of 15-34 m located between the following positions: 59° 34.0Æ' N; 24° 33.5' E, 59° 34.0' N; 24° 36.0' E, 59° 33.0' N; 24° 34.5' E, 59° 33.0' N; 24° 36.0' E
Anchorage Area G in depth of 30-35 m located between the following positions: 59° 29.5Æ' N; 24° 30.0' E, 59° 29.5' N; 24° 32.7' E, 59° 28.9' N; 24° 30.0' E, 59° 28.9' N; 24° 32.7' E

Pilotage: Performed by AS Eesti Loots, Tel: +372 6 053800, Fax: +372 6 053810. Pilot boards in pos 59° 29' N; 24° 33' E

Accommodation:

Name	Length (m)	Depth (m)	Draught (m)	Remarks
Vene-Balti				See [1] below
North Basin				
Berth 0	185	11.4	11	Oil terminal
Berth 1	160	9.2	8.3	Oil terminal
Berth 2	130	9.1	8.2	Oil terminal
Berth 3	100	6.7	6.2	
Berth 4	132.5	6.7	6.2	
Berth 5	132.5	6.2	5.8	
Berth 6	120	8.5	8	
Berth 7	120	8.5	8	
Berth 8	150	6	5.5	
South Basin				
Berth 9	92	8.3	7.5	
Berth 10	92	8.6	7.5	
Berth 11	92	8.6	7.5	
Berth 12	92	8.6	7.5	
Berth 13	92	8.6	7.5	
Berth 14	120	8.5	7.5	
Berth 15	120	8.5	7.5	
Berth 16	100	7.2	6.8	
Berth 17	100	7.2	6.8	
Berth 18	100	7.2	6.8	
Berth 19	100	7.7	7	
Berth 20	100	7.7	7	

[1]*Vene-Balti:* Navigational season lasts all the year round. During winter the port is serviced with the help of an icebreaker. The port has two basins (North and South) with separate entrances:
Total length of the port's 20 quays is over 2 km. Depths at the commercial quays enable berthing for dry cargo vessels with draft up to 7.5-8.0 m and for tankers with draft up to 8.3-11.0 m

Storage:

Location	Open (m²)	Covered (m²)
Vene-Balti	25000	5000

Mechanical Handling Equipment:

Location	Type	Capacity (t)
Vene-Balti	Floating Cranes	35–100
Vene-Balti	Mult-purp. Cranes	10–32

Towage: Three tractor tugs available

Stevedoring Companies: BLRT Transiit OU, Kopli 103, 11712 Tallinn, Republic of Estonia, *Tel:* +372 6 102170, *Fax:* +372 6 102822, *Email:* transiit@bsr.ee

Airport: Tallinn International Airport, 13 km

Lloyd's Agent: Lars Krogius Baltic Ltd, Ahtri 12, EE-10151 Tallinn, Republic of Estonia, *Tel:* +372 6 116620, *Fax:* +372 6 116685, *Email:* estonia@krogius.com, *Website:* www.krogius.com

FALKLAND ISLANDS

PORT STANLEY

alternate name, see Stanley Harbour

STANLEY HARBOUR

Lat 51° 41' S; Long 57° 50' W.

Admiralty Chart: 1614	Admiralty Pilot: 6
Time Zone: GMT -4 h	UNCTAD Locode: FK PSY

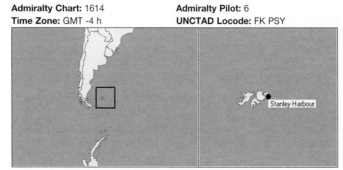

Principal Facilities:

		G	C	R	L	B		A

Authority: Fisheries Department of Falkland Islands, P O Box 598, Stanley, Falkland Islands, *Tel:* +500 27260, *Fax:* +500 27265, *Email:* jclark@fisheries.gov.fk

Officials: Harbour Master: Jonathan Clark.

Key to Principal Facilities:—			
A=Airport	**C**=Containers	**G**=General Cargo	**P**=Petroleum	**R**=Ro/Ro	**Y**=Dry Bulk
B=Bunkers	**D**=Dry Dock	**L**=Cruise	**Q**=Other Liquid Bulk	**T**=Towage (where available from port)

Port Security: PFSO: Jonathon Clark, Falklands Islands Government Marine Officer, Tel: +500 27260, Fax: +500 27265, Email: jclark@fisheries.gov.fk

Pre-Arrival Information: Every vessel entering the harbour must make an Entry Report which should give the following information:
a) vessel name
b) radio call sign
c) type of vessel (eg: trawler, jigger, reefer etc)
d) international gross registered tonnage
e) net registered tonnage
f) number of crew
g) name of local agent
h) date of entry
i) local time of entry (time of crossing the Reporting Line)
j) intentions (eg: transhipment, bunkering, anchorage, repairs, medical etc)
k) location of above intentions

Documentation: Required for customs & immigration: general declaration (1 copy), international tonnage certificate copy (1 copy), maritime declaration of health (2 copies), crew list (2 copies), passenger list (2 copies), crew & passenger embarkation/disembarkation lists (2 copies), crew effects (1 copy), ship's stores declaration including firearms & controlled medicines (1 copy), cargo manifest (1 copy), ship's fuel, oil & water arrival/departure state (1 copy)

Approach: Stanley Entrance: Proceed along Port William on a course of 266°, then through the Narrows into Stanley Harbour on a course of 186°, keeping the leading marks in line

Anchorage: Stanley Harbour vessels may anchor to the W of Navy Point at their Master's discretion. Good anchorage in 6-9 m of water. No vessel should obstruct the line of the leading lights. No vessel should anchor to the E of Navy Point without permission from the Harbour Authorities
Port William: There is a good anchorage for deep draft vessels seeking shelter from NW and NE gales. This is NNW of Navy Point with a bottom of soft mud giving good holding. Normally vessels will be allowed to anchor at the Master's own discretion in Port William, provided they do not obstruct the fairway or anchor near the line of the leading lights into Stanley Harbour

Pilotage: Not compulsory but available on request through ship's agent

Radio Frequency: Call 'FISHOPS' or 'STANLEY PORT CONTROL' on VHF Channel 16 or 10 (24 h) & HF (office hours only 0800-1630) on 4066.1 kHz

Weather: Strong westerly winds prevail, frequently gale force. The weather is extremely changeable and a careful watch on it is advised while manoeuvring or at anchor

Tides: Tidal range is a max 2 m at springs. Tidal streams in the harbour entrance (The Narrows) normally attain rates of 0.5 knots but can, under certain conditions, reach 1.5 knots or more

Principal Imports and Exports: Imports: Consumer goods, Transportation & machinery equipment. Exports: Fish, Wool.

Working Hours: Normally 0800-1630, but work can be carried out outside these hours at the request of ships

Accommodation:

Name	Length (m)	Depth (m)	Remarks
Stanley Harbour			
East Jetty	45	3.7	See [1] below
Public Jetty		3	See [2] below
Falkland Interim Port & Storage System (FIPASS)	300	6.5–7.2	See [3] below

[1]*East Jetty:* Situated on the S shore of Stanley Harbour and belongs to the Falkland Islands Company Ltd., Tel: +500 27600, Fax: +500 27603, Email: fic@horizon.co.fk
[2]*Public Jetty:* Used only for landing passengers from launches and other small craft
[3]*Falkland Interim Port & Storage System (FIPASS):* Situated to the E of the Narrows on the S shore of Stanley Harbour and consists of seven permanently moored barges providing 300 m of berthing face (including a ro/ro berth)
FIPASS Port Management services provided by Byron Mackay Port Services, Tel: +500 22636, Fax: +500 22637, Email: portservices@byronmarine.co.fk

Storage: Additional warehouse and fenced uncovered storage space available from local companies

Location	Covered (m²)	Cold (m³)
Stanley Harbour	7000	900

Mechanical Handling Equipment:

Location	Type	Capacity (t)	Qty	Remarks
Stanley Harbour	Mult-purp. Cranes	65	1	
Stanley Harbour	Forklifts	25	1	
Stanley Harbour	Yard Trailers			to transport up to 40 ft containers

Bunkering: Bunkers are available from licensed tankers in Berkeley Sound or on the centre and east berths at FIPASS with 4 days notice

Waste Reception Facilities: The Falkland Islands Co. Ltd, Crozier Place, Stanley FIQQ 1ZZ, Falkland Islands, Tel: +500 27600, Fax: +500 27603, Email: fic@horizon.co.fk, Website: www.the-falkland-islands-co.com

Repair & Maintenance: A limited range of electronic and mechanical repair services are available. Small boats may be lifted out dependent upon available crane capacity

Ship Chandlers: Seafish Chandlery, P O Box 1, Seafish House, The Chandlery Estate, Airport Road, Stanley, Falkland Islands, Tel: +500 22755, Fax: +500 22705, Email: chandlery@horizon.co.fk, Website: www.chandlery.horizon.co.fk

Shipping Agents: The Falkland Islands Co. Ltd, Crozier Place, Stanley FIQQ 1ZZ, Falkland Islands, Tel: +500 27600, Fax: +500 27603, Email: fic@horizon.co.fk, Website: www.the-falkland-islands-co.com
Stanley Services Ltd, Airport Road, P O Box 117, Stanley FIQQ 1ZZ, Falkland Islands, Tel: +500 22622, Fax: +500 22623, Email: office@stanley-services.co.fk, Website: www.stanley-services.co.fk

Sulivan Shipping Services Ltd., P O Box 159, Stanley FIQQ 1ZZ, Falkland Islands, Tel: +500 22626, Fax: +500 22625, Email: sulivan@horizon.co.fk, Website: www.sulivanshipping.com

Medical Facilities: Medical and dental services are available at the King Edward Memorial Hospital in Stanley

Airport: Mount Pleasant, 56 km. Flights to UK and Chile

Lloyd's Agent: The Falkland Islands Co. Ltd, Crozier Place, Stanley FIQQ 1ZZ, Falkland Islands, Tel: +500 27600, Fax: +500 27603, Email: fic@horizon.co.fk, Website: www.the-falkland-islands-co.com

FAROE ISLANDS

FUGLAFJORDUR
Lat 62° 15' N; Long 6° 49' W.

Admiralty Chart: 3557		**Admiralty Pilot:** 52	
Time Zone: GMT		**UNCTAD Locode:** FO FUG	

Principal Facilities:

P	Q	Y	G	C	R		B		T	A

Authority: Port of Fuglafjordur, Bakkavegur 34, FO-530 Fuglafjordur, Faroe Islands, Tel: +298 444054, Fax: +298 445154, Email: pof@online.fo

Officials: Harbour Master: Simun Jacobsen.

Port Security: ISPS compliant

Pilotage: Not compulsory but recommended for foreign vessels. Pilot boards in Fuglafjordur, Tel: + 298 444054, VHF Channel 16

Tides: Range of tide, 1.83 m ST

Principal Imports and Exports: Imports: General, Oil, Salt. Exports: Fish, Fish products.

Working Hours: Round the clock

Accommodation:

Name	Length (m)	Depth (m)
Fuglafjordur		
Quay	900	6.12

Storage: 1800 t cap

Mechanical Handling Equipment:

Location	Type	Capacity (t)
Fuglafjordur	Mobile Cranes	30

Bunkering: Available by pipelines on the oil quay

Repair & Maintenance: K.J. Hydraulik P/F Kari Johannesen, Fuglafjordur, Faroe Islands, Tel: +298 444170, Fax: +298 444265

Stevedoring Companies: P/F Havsbrun, P O Box 81, Fuglafjordur, Faroe Islands, Tel: +298 414400, Fax: +298 414401, Email: havsbrun@havsbrun.fo, Website: www.havsbrun.fo
P/F Vonin, P O Box 19, FO-530 Fuglafjordur, Faroe Islands, Tel: +298 474200, Fax: +298 474201, Email: info@vonin.com, Website: www.vonin.com

Medical Facilities: Available

Airport: Vagar, 90 km

Lloyd's Agent: Smyril Blue Water, P O Box 3296, FO-110 Torshavn, Faroe Islands, Tel: +298 309600, Fax: +298 309601, Email: cargo@smyrilbluewater.com, Website: www.smyrilbluewater.com

KLAKSVIK
Lat 62° 14' N; Long 6° 35' W.

Admiralty Chart: 3557	**Admiralty Pilot:** 52
Time Zone: GMT	**UNCTAD Locode:** FO KVI

Principal Facilities:

		G	C		L	B		A

Authority: Klaksvikar Havn, Vestara Bryggja, P O Box 26, FO-700 Klaksvik, Faroe Islands, *Tel:* +298 455101, *Fax:* +298 457340, *Email:* port@klaksvik.fo, *Website:* www.klhavn.fo

Officials: Harbour Master: Jogvan Klakkstein.

Port Security: ISPS compliant

Pre-Arrival Information: 24 h arrival notification. Also call 1 h before arrival on VHF Channel 16 or 12

Anchorage: It is possible to anchor at the entrance

Pilotage: Not compulsory but available with 12 h notice

Radio Frequency: VHF Channel 16

Tides: Range 0.8 m to 1.2 m

Maximum Vessel Dimensions: 320 m loa, 12 m draft

Principal Imports and Exports: Imports: General cargo. Exports: Fish.

Working Hours: 0800-1700

Accommodation:

Name	Length (m)	Depth (m)	Draught (m)	Remarks
Klaksvik				
West Quay	300	8.75		See [1] below
Kosin Quay	220	8–9		See [2] below
Fuel Quay	55	8		Tankers up to 6000 t
North Quay	320		12	30 m wide ro/ro ramp

[1]*West Quay:* Container vessels, general cargo vessels, cruise vessels & fishing vessels up to 160 m loa
[2]*Kosin Quay:* General cargo & fishing vessels up to 180 m loa

Storage:

Location	Open (m²)	Cold (m³)
Klaksvik	28000	12000

Mechanical Handling Equipment:

Location	Type	Capacity (t)	Qty
Klaksvik	Mobile Cranes	36	3

Bunkering: Fuel and diesel are available from Shell and Statoil at the Fuel Quay and from road tankers at all piers

Waste Reception Facilities: Waste disposal services available on request to Authority

Repair & Maintenance: Slipway with cap up to 800 t available

Shipping Agents: Faroe Ship A/S, Klaksvik, Faroe Islands, *Tel:* +298 349140, *Fax:* +298 349141, *Email:* agency@faroe-ship.fo

Medical Facilities: Modern hospital available in Klaksvik

Airport: Vagar, 90 km

Lloyd's Agent: Smyril Blue Water, P O Box 3296, FO-110 Torshavn, Faroe Islands, *Tel:* +298 309600, *Fax:* +298 309601, *Email:* cargo@smyrilbluewater.com, *Website:* www.smyrilbluewater.com

RUNAVIK

Lat 62° 6' N; Long 6° 43' W.

Admiralty Chart: 3557	**Admiralty Pilot:** 52
Time Zone: GMT	**UNCTAD Locode:** FO

Principal Facilities:

		G	C	R	L	B	D		A

Authority: Port of Runavik, Harbour Office, Fiskivinnuhavnin 3, FO-600 Saltangara, Faroe Islands, *Tel:* +298 447015, *Fax:* +298 448920, *Email:* havnarskrivstovan@runavik.fo, *Website:* www.runavik.fo

Officials: Harbour Master: Jon Nonklett.

Port Security: ISPS compliant

Anchorage: Excellent anchorage with a firm seabed in depth of 30-40 m

Pilotage: Not compulsory but available on request. Pilot station in pos 62° 03.5' N; 06° 42.5' W

Accommodation:

Name	Length (m)	Depth (m)	Remarks
Runavik			See [1] below
Kongshavn	101.7	12	Cruise berth for vessels up to 200 m loa
Glyvrar	60	6–8	Open storage area of 15 400 m2
Soldarfjordur	90	5–9	Open storage area of 19 500 m2
Skala	460	5–8	Open storage area of 15 000 m2
Oyndarfjordur	140	4–5	Open storage area of 13 700 m2
Funningsfjordur	48	5	Open storage area of 8800 m2

[1]*Runavik:* Used for the fishing industry, commercial cargo and for the oil industry in connection with the oil exploration in the Faroese subsoil

Mechanical Handling Equipment:

Location	Type	Capacity (t)	Qty
Runavik	Mobile Cranes	30–120	3

Bunkering: Bunkers can be supplied by tank lorry to any berth, by Shell and Statoil

Waste Reception Facilities: Garbage disposal facilities available

Towage: Tugs available on request

Repair & Maintenance: p/f Skala Skipasmidjan A, FO-480 Skala, Faroe Islands, *Tel:* +298 301160, *Fax:* +298 301161, *Email:* skala@faroeyard.fo, *Website:* www.faroeyard.fo 116 m long dry dock and a 1200 t cap slipway

Shipping Agents: Faroe Ship A/S, FO-620 Runavik, Faroe Islands, *Tel:* +298 349150, *Fax:* +298 349151, *Email:* info@faroeship.fo, *Website:* www.faroeship.com

Airport: Vagar Airport

Lloyd's Agent: Smyril Blue Water, P O Box 3296, FO-110 Torshavn, Faroe Islands, *Tel:* +298 309600, *Fax:* +298 309601, *Email:* cargo@smyrilbluewater.com, *Website:* www.smyrilbluewater.com

THORSHAVN

alternate name, see Torshavn

TORSHAVN

Lat 62° 0' N; Long 6° 45' W.

Admiralty Chart: 3557	**Admiralty Pilot:** 52
Time Zone: GMT	**UNCTAD Locode:** FO THO

Principal Facilities:

P		Y	G	C	R	L	B		T	A

Authority: Torshavnar Havn, Eystara Bryggja, P O Box 103, FO-100 Torshavn, Faroe Islands, *Tel:* +298 311762, *Fax:* +298 319059, *Email:* port@torshavn.fo, *Website:* www.portoftorshavn.fo

Officials: Marketing Manager: Mia Cameron, *Email:* mia@torshavn.fo.
Harbour Master: Jonsvein Lamhauge, *Email:* jonsvein@torshavn.fo.

Port Security: ISPS compliant

Pre-Arrival Information: ETA should be given to the agent or to the Harbour Office 24 h, 12 h and 2 h before arrival. The ETA should give the ship's name, loa and draught

Documentation: Passenger manifest, embarking passenger manifest, crew manifest, stores list, customs declaration (ship), customs declaration (crew), derating certificate

Approach: By either N or S end of Nolsoyarfjrodur. No sand bars. No specific hazards

Anchorage: Anchorage is available in Nolsoy Fjord, approx 3 cables from the breakwater in depth of 30-35 m

Pilotage: Pilotage is not compulsory but recommended. Pilot is taken aboard in Nolsoy Fjord, one nautical mile from the breakwater. The pilot also uses VHF Channel

Key to Principal Facilities:—

A=Airport	**C**=Containers	**G**=General Cargo	**P**=Petroleum	**R**=Ro/Ro	**Y**=Dry Bulk
B=Bunkers	**D**=Dry Dock	**L**=Cruise	**Q**=Other Liquid Bulk	**T**=Towage (where available from port)	

16 for call-up and Channel 12 as working channel. Normal working hours for the pilot are Monday to Friday from 0800 to 1700

Radio Frequency: Listening on VHF Channel 16, working on Channel 12

Tides: Range of tide 0.3 m

Traffic: 2000, 3249 commercial vessels, 387 540 t of cargo handled

Maximum Vessel Dimensions: Cruise vessel, 74136 gt, 280 loa, 8.6 draft

Principal Imports and Exports: Imports: General cargo, Oil, Salt. Exports: Fish products.

Working Hours: Normal 0800-1700

Accommodation:

Name	Length (m)	Depth (m)	Remarks
Thorshavn			Five ro/ro ramps. Container stacking area of 45 000 m2
Main E Quay	198	8.3	Ferry ramp available
East Breakwater Quay	420	5.8–8.8	Available for cruise vessels to berth
Main W Quay	198	8.1	See [1] below
Bunker Quay	60	9.3	
West Breakwater	100	8.3	
West Pier	90	8	

[1]*Main W Quay:* Storage for 7000 t of bulk salt. Tanker facilities available

Storage: 50 000 m2 of open storage is available at Sund. Storage sheds of 6000 m2 are located in the East Harbour. In addition there are 800 m2 of cold storage

Mechanical Handling Equipment:

Location	Type	Capacity (t)	Qty
Torshavn	Mobile Cranes	36	4
Torshavn	Forklifts	42	4

Bunkering: Bunkers can be supplied either at the bunker jetty (depth 9.3 m) or by tank lorry to any berth

Waste Reception Facilities: Garbage and sludge disposal available

Towage: Two tugs available of 250 hp and 730 hp

Repair & Maintenance: Torshavnar Skipasmidja p/f, J C Svabosagota 31, FO-100 Torshavn, Faroe Islands, Tel: +298 301100, Fax: +298 311156, Email: info@faroeyard.fo, Website: www.faroeyard.fo

Shipping Agents: ASPA-Marine Ltd, Heidatun 10, Argir, FO-160 Torshavn, Faroe Islands, Tel: +298 321078, Fax: +298 321076, Email: agency@aspa-marine.com
Faroe Agency P/F, Yviri vid Strond 4, P O Box 270, FO-110 Torshavn, Faroe Islands, Tel: +298 351990, Fax: +298 351991, Email: faroeagency@faroeagency.fo, Website: www.faroeagency.fo
Faroe Ship A/S, P O Box 47, Eystara Bryggja, FO-110 Torshavn, Faroe Islands, Tel: +298 349000, Fax: +298 349001, Email: agency@faroeship.fo, Website: www.faroeship.com
Johan Mortensen, Spogvavegur 57, FO-100 Torshavn, Faroe Islands, Tel: +298 213510, Fax: +298 311318, Email: johan_m@post.olivant.fo
P/f Nordic Shipping, Hoyviksvegur 61, P O Box 43, FO-110 Torshavn, Faroe Islands, Tel: +298 314980, Fax: +298 315926
P/f Smyril Line, P O Box 370, FO-110 Torshavn, Faroe Islands, Tel: +298 345941, Fax: +298 345953, Email: management@smyril-line.fo, Website: www.smyril-line.fo
SP/F Tor Shipping, Niels Finsensgota 23, P O Box 1252, FO-110 Torshavn, Faroe Islands, Tel: +298 358531, Fax: +298 358530, Email: torship@post.olivant.fo, Website: www.torship.com

Stevedoring Companies: Hf Eimskipafelag Islands, P/F Eimskip i Foroyum, Eystara Bryggia, P O Box 100, FO-110 Torshavn, Faroe Islands, Tel: +298 347000, Fax: +298 347095, Email: info@eimskip.fo, Website: www.eimskip.com
Skipagelagia Foroyar P/F, Torshavn, Faroe Islands, Tel: +298 311225, Fax: +298 310636, Email: skipafelagio@faroe-ship.fo

Surveyors: Det Norske Veritas A/S, Vestara Bryggja, FO-100 Torshavn, Faroe Islands, Tel: +298 313750, Fax: +298 317588, Email: torshavn@dnv.com, Website: www.dnv.com

Medical Facilities: Hospital in Torshavn

Airport: Vagar, 45 km

Lloyd's Agent: Smyril Blue Water, P O Box 3296, FO-110 Torshavn, Faroe Islands, Tel: +298 309600, Fax: +298 309601, Email: cargo@smyrilbluewater.com, Website: www.smyrilbluewater.com

TVOROYRI

Lat 61° 33' N; Long 6° 48' W.

Admiralty Chart: 3557	**Admiralty Pilot:** 52
Time Zone: GMT	**UNCTAD Locode:** FO TVO

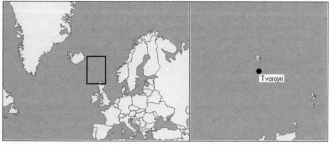

Principal Facilities:

Q	Y	G	C	R		B		T	A

Authority: Port of Tvoroyri, P O Box 20, FO-800 Tvoroyri, Faroe Islands, Tel: +298 371055, Fax: +298 371418, Email: tvhavn@post.olivant.fo, Website: www.tvoroyri.fo

Officials: Marketing Manager: Christian Jan Michelsen, Tel: +298 222 509, Email: tvhavn@post.olivant.fo.
Harbour Master: Hjalgrim Vestergard.

Port Security: ISPS compliant. PFSO: Chris Jan Michelsen

Pre-Arrival Information: ETA to be sent 24 h before arrival to agent or harbour office stating ship's name, loa and draft (fishing vessels need no notice)

Anchorage: As instructed by the Harbour Master. Depth 15 m

Pilotage: Not compulsory. When pilot required pre-arrange with agent by telegram or telephone, 2 h notice of ETA required. Pilot boat is a local fishing vessel, boarding usually takes place at harbour entrance

Radio Frequency: VHF Channels 16 and 12

Tides: Range of tide 1.22 m ST

Principal Imports and Exports: Imports: Steel. Exports: Fish products.

Working Hours: Normal 0800-1700. Overtime possible

Accommodation:

Name	Length (m)	Depth (m)	Remarks
Tvoroyri			
Quay	346	4.5–7	
Quay	89	7	
Quay	83	7	Ferries

Storage: One warehouse

Mechanical Handling Equipment:

Location	Type	Capacity (t)	Qty
Tvoroyri	Mult-purp. Cranes	16	1

Repair & Maintenance: Minor repairs only

Shipping Agents: Faroe Ship A/S, Havnarlagid 54, Tvaeroyri, FO-800 Tvoroyri, Faroe Islands, Tel: +298 349170, Fax: +298 349171, Email: zacharias@faroeship.fo, Website: www.faroeship.com

Medical Facilities: Available

Airport: Vagar, 80 km

Lloyd's Agent: Smyril Blue Water, P O Box 3296, FO-110 Torshavn, Faroe Islands, Tel: +298 309600, Fax: +298 309601, Email: cargo@smyrilbluewater.com, Website: www.smyrilbluewater.com

VAGUR

Lat 61° 28' N; Long 6° 48' W.

Admiralty Chart: 3557	**Admiralty Pilot:** 52
Time Zone: GMT	**UNCTAD Locode:** FO VAG

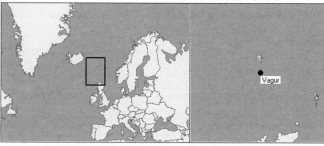

Principal Facilities:

P			G	C	R		B		T	A

Authority: Vags Kommuna, P O Box 132, FO-900 Vagur, Faroe Islands, Tel: +298 373033, Fax: +298 374110, Email: vagshavn@post.olivant.fo, Website: www.vagur.fo

Officials: Chairman: Svenning Borg, Tel: +298 373299.
Harbour Master: Hans Jacob Bech.

Port Security: ISPS compliant

Pre-Arrival Information: Port of call list etc

Approach: At entrance there are several submerged rocks out to 1.1 km from coast

Anchorage: There is anchorage in 11 to 13 m of water

Pilotage: Available via harbour office

Radio Frequency: VHF Channels 16 and 12

Weather: The whole fjord is liable to heavy ground swell in an E gale

Tides: Differences between high and low water is 1.1 m ST, 22.8 cm NT

Maximum Vessel Dimensions: 12 m max draft

Working Hours: 24 hrs

Accommodation:

Name	Length (m)	Depth (m)	Remarks
Vagur			See [1] below
Berth	52	7	
Berth	60	7	

Name	Length (m)	Depth (m)	Remarks
Berth	85	10	
Berth	70	7	
Berth	130	8	
Berth	147	8	
Berth	87	10	

[1]*Vagur:* Clearance port, located S of Tvoroyri. Good holding ground of sand and clay. Harbour basin 111.8 by 57.9 m with 4.9 m depth

Storage: Cold storage available

Mechanical Handling Equipment:

Location	Type	Capacity (t)	Qty
Vagur	Mult-purp. Cranes	15	1

Bunkering: Diesel oil available

Waste Reception Facilities: Dirty ballast and garbage disposal available

Repair & Maintenance: Bent Mortensen, Vagur, Faroe Islands, *Tel:* +298 373065, *Fax:* +298 373934
Vags Skipasmidja, Vagur, Faroe Islands, *Tel:* +298 373010, *Fax:* +298 373050

Medical Facilities: Available

Airport: Vagar

Lloyd's Agent: Smyril Blue Water, P O Box 3296, FO-110 Torshavn, Faroe Islands, *Tel:* +298 309600, *Fax:* +298 309601, *Email:* cargo@smyrilbluewater.com, *Website:* www.smyrilbluewater.com

VESTMANNA

Lat 62° 9' N; Long 7° 10' W.

Admiralty Chart: 3557   **Admiralty Pilot:** 52
Time Zone: GMT   **UNCTAD Locode:** FO VES

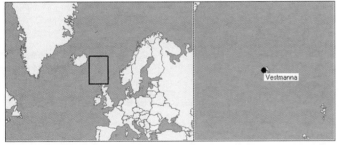

Principal Facilities:

			G					

Authority: Vestmanna Havn, P O Box 103, FO-350 Vestmanna, Faroe Islands, *Tel:* +298 424066, *Fax:* +298 424766, *Email:* vestkomm@vestkomm.fo

Port Security: ISPS compliant

Pilotage: Not compulsory

Tides: Range of tide 1.83 m ST

Working Hours: Normal hours, Mon-Fri 0800-1700

Accommodation:

Name	Remarks
Vestmanna	See [1] below

[1]*Vestmanna:* Good harbour and anchorage in 13 to 22 m of water. Two quays, 25.9 and 128.01 m long with 2.13-6.1 m and 6.1 m LW respectively. Loading and discharging by ship's gear

Repair & Maintenance: p/f Vestmanna Skipasmidja, P O Box 90, FO-350 Vestmanna, Faroe Islands, *Tel:* +298 424010, *Fax:* +298 424005, *Email:* vs@faroeyard.fo, *Website:* www.faroeyard.fo For vessels up to 700 dwt

Medical Facilities: Doctor available, Tel: +298 424003

Lloyd's Agent: Smyril Blue Water, P O Box 3296, FO-110 Torshavn, Faroe Islands, *Tel:* +298 309600, *Fax:* +298 309601, *Email:* cargo@smyrilbluewater.com, *Website:* www.smyrilbluewater.com

FIJI

LAUTOKA

Lat 17° 37' S; Long 177° 27' E.

Admiralty Chart: 1670   **Admiralty Pilot:** 61
Time Zone: GMT +12 h   **UNCTAD Locode:** FJ LTK

Principal Facilities:

P	Q	Y	G	C	R		B		T	A

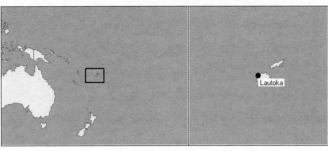
Authority: Fiji Port Corp. Ltd, P O Box 132, Lautoka, Fiji, *Tel:* +679 666 2160, *Fax:* +679 666 5799, *Email:* lavinia@fpcl.com.fj, *Website:* www.fijiports.com.fj

Officials: Harbour Master: Viliame Oioi, *Tel:* +679 666 1229.

Port Security: ISPS compliant

Anchorage: Vessels can anchor off the Lautoka berth in depths of 20 m, on good holding ground with mud bottom

Pilotage: Compulsory and provided by Ports Terminal Ltd., Tel: +679 665 1991. Pilot boards approx 26 nautical miles S of Lautoka in Navula Passage

Radio Frequency: VHF Channel 16, 24 h/day

Weather: Winds during winter S to W and during summer N to S

Tides: Neap range 0.9 m, spring range 1.3 m

Principal Imports and Exports: Imports: Bulk & bagged fertilizer, Chemical cargo, Cold storage goods, Foodstuffs, Machinery, Vehicles. Exports: Bulk sugar, Timber, Woodchips.

Working Hours: 24 h on 3 x 8 h shifts with shifts starting any time on arrival

Accommodation:

Name	Length (m)	Depth (m)	Draught (m)	Remarks
Lautoka				
Queens Wharf	295	10		See [1] below
Sugar & Woodchips Wharf	178	10.5		Handles sugar at 650 t/h and woodchips at 700 t/h
Tanker Berth		13	12	See [2] below

[1]*Queens Wharf:* General cargo. Ro/ro vessels of 20 000 dwt, 199 m loa have been berthed, starboard side to wharf
[2]*Tanker Berth:* Two 8'' hoses for loading and discharging

Storage: Warehousing available; limited refrigerated space; spaces also available for empty containers

Mechanical Handling Equipment:

Location	Type	Capacity (t)
Lautoka	Mobile Cranes	30

Bunkering: ExxonMobil Marine Fuels, 1 Harbour Front Place, 06-00 Harbour Front, Tower One, Singapore, Republic of Singapore 098633, *Tel:* +65 6885 8998, *Fax:* +65 6885 8794, *Email:* asiapac.marinefuels@exxonmobil.com, *Website:* www.exxonmobilmarinefuels.com – *Grades:* IFO80-120cSt; MGO – *Delivery Mode:* pipeline, tank truck

Towage: One tug available of 38 t bollard pull

Shipping Agents: Export Freight Services (Fiji) Ltd, P O Box 13506, Tamavua-I-Wai Road, Walu Bay, Suva, Fiji, *Tel:* +679 330 5044, *Fax:* +679 330 8293, *Email:* dhiraj@efs.com.fj, *Website:* www.efsfiji.com Manager: Dhiraj Prasad
Carpenters Shipping, P O Box 751, Lautoka, Fiji, *Tel:* +679 666 3988, *Fax:* +679 666 4896, *Email:* mgrltk.shipping@carpenters.com.fj, *Website:* www.carpship.com.fj
Neptune Shipping Agency Ltd, 3rd Level, Ra Marama House, 91 Gordon Street, Suva, Fiji, *Tel:* +679 330 4528, *Fax:* +679 330 0057, *Email:* jona@neptune.com.fj
Pacific Agencies (Fiji) Ltd, 21 Bouwala Street, P O Box 49, Lautoka, Fiji, *Tel:* +679 666 0577, *Fax:* +679 666 2985, *Email:* info@pacshipfiji.com.fj, *Website:* www.pacificagenciesfiji.com
Shipping Services (Fiji) Ltd, Lot 37/38 Service Street, Navutu Ind Subdivision, P O Box 2891, Lautoka, Fiji, *Tel:* +679 666 7677, *Fax:* +679 666 7813, *Email:* jeffrey@kitanet.net.fj
Williams & Gosling Ltd, P O Box 226, Lautoka, Fiji, *Tel:* +679 666 4090, *Fax:* +679 666 5844, *Email:* pravins@wgfiji.com.fj, *Website:* www.wgfiji.com.fj

Medical Facilities: Hospital available

Key to Principal Facilities:—				
A=Airport	**C**=Containers	**G**=General Cargo	**P**=Petroleum	**R**=Ro/Ro	**Y**=Dry Bulk
B=Bunkers	**D**=Dry Dock	**L**=Cruise	**Q**=Other Liquid Bulk	**T**=Towage (where available from port)	

Airport: Nadi International, 19 km

Lloyd's Agent: Carpenters Shipping, 22 Edinburgh Drive, Suva, Fiji, *Tel:* +679 331 2244, *Fax:* +679 330 1572, *Email:* lloydssuva.shipping@carpenters.com.fj, *Website:* www.carpship.com.fj

SUVA

Lat 18° 8' S; Long 178° 25' E.

Admiralty Chart: 1660	**Admiralty Pilot:** 61
Time Zone: GMT +12 h	**UNCTAD Locode:** FJ SUV

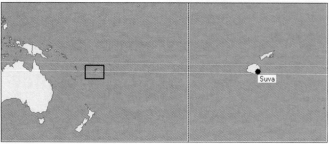

Principal Facilities:

P Q Y G C R L B   T A

EFS ═══════════ **Total Logistics At One Stop**

EXPORT FREIGHT SERVICES LTD

Suva	Lautoka
Export Freight Services	Export Freight Services
Tamavua-I-Wai Road	Shop 5, Walu Street
Walu Bay, Suva	Marine Drive, Lautoka
FIJI	FIJI
Ph: 679 330 5044	Ph: 679 664 0278
Fax: 679 330 8293	Fax: 679 664 0277
Email:info@efs.com.fj	Email:amit@efs.com.fj

N P T Shipping Agency

3rd Level, Ra Marama House, 91 Gordon St, Suva, FIJI

TEL: + 679 330 4528
FAX: + 679 330 0057
EMAIL: info@neptune.com.fj
Commercial Manager: Mr. Jona Dumaru

Operating at the ports of Lautoka and Suva

Shipping Services (Fiji) Ltd

Physical Address: 25 High Street, Toorak, Suva/Saku Lane, Marine Drive, Lautoka
Postal Address: PO Box 12671, Suva / PO Box 2891, Lautoka

TEL: (679) 330 5577/666 7677   FAX: (679) 330 1615/666 7813
EMAIL: SALFJSUV@ssfl.com.fj   WEBSITE: www.maerskline.com

We are Fiji Agents for Maersk Line and can provide agency services for both Suva and Lautoka ports

Authority: Fiji Port Corp. Ltd, P O Box 780, Suva, Fiji, *Tel:* +679 331 2700, *Fax:* +679 331 5549, *Email:* enquiries@fpcl.com.fj, *Website:* www.fijiports.com.fj

Officials: Chief Executive Officer: Capt Christopher Marshall, *Email:* chrism@fpcl.com.fj.

Port Security: ISPS compliant

Approach: Average depth of 20 m in harbour limits. No bar

Anchorage: Vessels anchoring receive anchorage position from the Port Master's office on arrival in a depth of 17 m

Pilotage: Provided by Ports Terminal Ltd and available 24 h/day. Pilot boards vessels 8 km off lower lead. VHF Channel 16

Radio Frequency: Harbour Control maintains a watch on VHF Channels 20 and 16. Working frequencies are available on channels 1-25

Weather: Prevailing winds N to NE'ly during summer and SE'ly during winter

Tides: Rise and fall: 0.9 m neap tides, 1.3 m springs

Principal Imports and Exports: Imports: Grain, Petroleum products, Raw materials, Vehicles. Exports: Groundnuts, Petroleum products, Sugar, Textiles, Timber.

Working Hours: 7 days 24 hours service availability with stevedoring commencing at any time on arrival

Accommodation:

Name	Length (m)	Depth (m)	Remarks
Suva			See [1] below
Walu Bay Wharf	183	8.8–11	
Princes Wharf	156	2.5–10	
King Wharf	495	10–12	

[1]*Suva:* The whole berth area is known as 'Kings' with three berthing faces. A container terminal with storage facilities for over 500 containers including 18 refrigerated. Ro/ro facilities at Walu Bay Wharf and Centre Kings Wharf

Storage: Space available for both dry bulk and refrigerated cargoes. Storage space for empty containers at Rokobili terminal

Mechanical Handling Equipment:

Location	Type	Capacity (t)	Qty
Suva	Forklifts	30	6

Bunkering: ExxonMobil Marine Fuels, 1 Harbour Front Place, 06-00 Harbour Front, Tower One, Singapore, Republic of Singapore 098633, *Tel:* +65 6885 8998, *Fax:* +65 6885 8794, *Email:* asiapac.marinefuels@exxonmobil.com, *Website:* www.exxonmobilmarinefuels.com – *Grades:* IFO80-120cSt; MGO – *Delivery Mode:* pipeline, tank truck

Towage: Compulsory for vessels over 3000 gt. Two tugs available
SVITZER, South Seas Towage, 1st Floor, MPL Building, 25 Eliza Street, Walu Bay, Suva, Fiji, *Tel:* +679 331 2488, *Fax:* +679 330 1762, *Website:* www.svitzer.com

Repair & Maintenance: Government slipways (1) up to 500 t; (2) up to 1000 t; (3) 200 t. Repair wharf 122 m long with 3.05 m alongside.
Industrial & Marine Engineering Ltd (IMEL), Foster Road, Walu Bay, Suva, Fiji, *Tel:* +679 331 1522 Engineers and steel boat builders fully equipped for all types of shiprepair and general engineering work. Facilities include electrical repair shop, boiler shop, machine shop and foundry

Seaman Missions: The Seamans Mission, P O Box 837, Suva, Fiji, *Tel:* +679 330 0911

Ship Chandlers: R. Chung Ship Chandlers, P O Box 997, Suva, Fiji, *Tel:* +679 992 7228, *Fax:* +679 330 9868, *Email:* rtsc@connect.com.fj

Shipping Agents: Campbell's Shipping Agency, Tofu Street, P O Box 43, Suva, Fiji, *Tel:* +679 330 6329, *Fax:* +679 330 6363, *Email:* campbellshipping@connect.com.fj
Carpenters Shipping, 22 Edinburgh Drive, Suva, Fiji, *Tel:* +679 331 2244, *Fax:* +679 330 1572, *Email:* lloydssuva.shipping@carpenters.com.fj, *Website:* www.carpship.com.fj
Export Freight Services (Fiji) Ltd, P O Box 13506, Tamavua-I-Wai Road, Walu Bay, Suva, Fiji, *Tel:* +679 330 5044, *Fax:* +679 330 8293, *Email:* dhiraj@efs.com.fj, *Website:* www.efsfiji.com
Forum Shipping Agencies (FSA), Level 2, Gohil Complex, Toorak Road, P O Box 15832, Suva, Fiji, *Tel:* +679 331 5444, *Fax:* +679 330 1127, *Email:* info@pacshipfiji.com.fj, *Website:* www.pacificagenciesfiji.com
Jaiv Clearance & Logistics, Office No.8, Natco Building, 24-26 Edinburgh Drive, P O Box 13376, Suva, Fiji, *Tel:* +679 331 5211, *Fax:* +679 331 9522, *Email:* robert@jaivfiji.com
Keith's Auto Customs Services, 15 Latita Bhindi, Vatuwqa, Suva, Fiji, *Tel:* +679 338 6008, *Fax:* +679 338 6549, *Email:* renuka@connect.com.fj
Neptune Shipping Agency Ltd, 3rd Level, Ra Marama House, 91 Gordon Street, Suva, Fiji, *Tel:* +679 330 4528, *Fax:* +679 330 0057, *Email:* jona@neptune.com.fj
Pacific Agencies (Fiji) Ltd, Corner Tourak & Suva Street, P O Box 15832, Suva, Fiji, *Tel:* +679 331 5444, *Fax:* +679 330 2754, *Email:* info@pacshipfiji.com.fj, *Website:* www.agency.adsteam.com.au
Shipping Services (Fiji) Ltd, 25 High Street, P O Box 12671, Suva, Fiji, *Tel:* +679 330 5577, *Fax:* +679 330 1615, *Email:* reception@ssfl.com.fj
Williams & Gosling Ltd, 80-82 Harris Road, P O Box 79, Suva, Fiji, *Tel:* +679 331 2633, *Fax:* +679 323 6336, *Email:* info@wgfiji.com.fj, *Website:* www.wgfiji.com.fj

Stevedoring Companies: Ports Terminal Ltd, P O Box 513, Suva, Fiji, *Tel:* +679 330 4725, *Fax:* +679 330 4769

Medical Facilities: Hospital close by

Airport: Nausori Airport, 18 km

Development: Wharf upgrading currently being done to be completed in December 2005. Full forklift container operation on wharf apron would be possible after development

Lloyd's Agent: Carpenters Shipping, 22 Edinburgh Drive, Suva, Fiji, *Tel:* +679 331 2244, *Fax:* +679 330 1572, *Email:* lloydssuva.shipping@carpenters.com.fj, *Website:* www.carpship.com.fj

FINLAND

The Finnish specialist in Maritime & Transport Law

Shipping ● Road Transport ● Aviation

Charterparty Disputes
Carriage of Goods and Passengers
Collisions
Salvage
Pollution

Sales and Purchase
CMR Claims
Insurance
Loan and Security Documentation
General Corporate and Business Law

Litigation
Commercial Disputes
Litigation
Arbitration
Arrest Proceedings
Enforcement

Aminoff & Weissenberg
Attorneys Ltd.

Kasarmikatu 44, FI-00130
Helsinki, Finland

www.jaflaw.fi

ABO

alternate name, see Turku

AJOS

alternate name, see Kemi

AKONNIEMI

harbour area, see under Varkaus

BRAHESTAD

alternate name, see Raahe

EKENAS

alternate name, see Tammisaari

HAISLAHTI

harbour area, see under Savonlinna

HAMINA

Lat 60° 31' N; Long 27° 10' E.

Admiralty Chart: 1090
Time Zone: GMT +2 h

Admiralty Pilot: 20
UNCTAD Locode: FI HMN

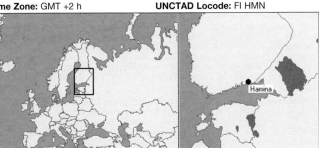

Hamina

Principal Facilities:

| P | Q | Y | G | C | R | | B | | T | |

Authority: Port of Hamina Ltd, Satamantie 4, P O Box 14, FI-49401 Hamina, Finland, *Tel:* +358 5 225 5400, *Fax:* +358 5 225 5419, *Email:* office@portofhamina.fi, *Website:* www.portofhamina.fi

Officials: Managing Director: Seppo Herrala, *Tel:* +358 5 225 5411, *Email:* seppo.herrala@portofhamina.fi.
Marketing Director: Esa Eerikainen, *Tel:* +358 5 225 5420, *Email:* esa.eerikainen@portofhamina.fi.
Harbour Master: Jouni Pukki, *Tel:* +358 5 225 5440, *Email:* jouni.pukki@portofhamina.fi.

Port Security: ISPS compliant

Documentation: Tonnage certificate, Finnish ice class certificate, tonnage and ice dues certificates (if vessel called previously), crew list (and passenger list if any on board), crews effects declaration, ship's stores declaration, cargo declaration, general declaration, fitness certificate (tankers only)

Approach: Main fairway from Orrengrund to Hamina 53 km long with 10 m max draft

Pilotage: Compulsory. Sea pilots board/disembark at the pilot station at Orrengrund. VHF Channels 13 and 16 with 24 h notice

Traffic: 2007, 5 435 112 t of cargo handled, 195 292 TEU's

Maximum Vessel Dimensions: 10 m max draft at normal water level

Working Hours: Two shifts 0600-1430 and 1430-2300. Sat 0600-1430. Overtime available

Accommodation:

Name	Length (m)	Draught (m)	Remarks
Hamina			See [1] below
Hillo	345	6.9	General & bulk cargo
Lakulahti			
L1-L2	216	8.6	General cargo
L3-L6	351	7.9	Ro/ro, general & container cargo
L7-L8	240	7.9	Ro/ro, general & container cargo
Hiirenkari			
HK1-HK2	158	7.9	General cargo
HK3	100	8.4	Ro/ro & general cargo
HK4-HK5	210	8.6	General cargo
HK6		8.6	Ro/ro cargo
Palokangas			
PK1	200	10	Ro/ro & container cargo
PK2	200	10	General & container cargo
PK3	192	10	Ro/ro & container cargo
EU0	90	10	Container cargo
EU1	185	10	Ro/ro & container cargo
EU2	190	10	Container cargo
EU3-EU4	234	10	Container cargo
Tanker Berths			
Oil Pier No.1	35	9	For vessels up to 210 m loa
Oil Pier No.2	72	10	For vessels up to 220 m loa
Oil Pier No.3	80	10	For vessels up to 250 m loa
LPG Pier	170	9	

[1]*Hamina:* Well sheltered port. Total length of quays 2800 m. Railway connections to all main quays and warehouses

Storage: Storage for china clay and urea. Open storage for coal and other bulk cargoes. In the Oil Port there are approx 500 000 m3 storage tanks for various chemicals, oil and LPG. Ten warehouses for paper of 180 000 m2. There are twelve distribution warehouses for F.S.U., total area of 70 000 m2, of which 60 000 m2 are heated

Mechanical Handling Equipment:

Location	Type	Capacity (t)	Qty	Remarks
Hamina	Mult-purp. Cranes	6	5	
Hamina	Mobile Cranes	55	4	one for container handling

Bunkering: Alongside quays by road tankers
Baltic Bunkering Ltd, Torggatan 10A, Mariehamn, Aland Islands, *Tel:* +358 18 143 00, *Fax:* +358 18 145 00, *Email:* info@balticbunkering.ax
Bunker Management Oy Ltd (BuMa), Merituulentie 424, FI-48310 Kotka, Finland, *Tel:* +358 5 2201 011, *Fax:* +358 5 2201 012, *Website:* www.bunkerman.fi
ST1 Oy, ST1 OY, P O Box 37, Purotie, FI-02211 Helsinki, Finland, *Tel:* +358 10 557 11, *Fax:* +358 9 8030 004, *Email:* matti.pentti@st1.fi, *Website:* www.st1.fi
Teboil Oy AB, Bulevardi 26, P O Box 102, FI-00120 Helsinki, Finland, *Tel:* +358 20 470 01, *Fax:* +358 20 4700 248, *Email:* bunkersales@teboil.fi, *Website:* www.teboil.fi

Waste Reception Facilities: Oily ballast, sludge and garbage disposal available

Towage: Two (or more) icebreaker tugs are available if required
Finntugs Oy, Tel: +358 5 213043, Fax: +358 5 218 4480

Ship Chandlers: Shipchandler Ivar Ek Ky, Pajamaentie 1, FI-49460 Hamina, Finland, *Tel:* +358 5 344 8579, *Fax:* +358 5 344 8645, *Email:* ivar.ek@laivanmuonitus.inet.fi

Shipping Agents: Steveco Oy, P O Box 100, FI-49401 Hamina, Finland, *Tel:* +358 5 23231, *Fax:* +358 5 232 3701, *Email:* marketing@steveco.fi, *Website:* www.steveco.fi

Stevedoring Companies: Hamina Multimodal Terminals Ky, Gerhardinvayla 4, P O Box 23, FI-49461 Hamina, Finland, *Tel:* +358 5 230 6113, *Fax:* +358 5 230 6119, *Email:* tomi.pakkanen@hmt.fi, *Website:* www.hmt.fi
Steveco Oy, P O Box 100, FI-49401 Hamina, Finland, *Tel:* +358 5 23231, *Fax:* +358 5 232 3701, *Email:* marketing@steveco.fi, *Website:* www.steveco.fi

Medical Facilities: Hamina hospital, 6 km

Airport: Helsinki International, 145 km

Lloyd's Agent: Oy Lars Krogius A/B, Vilhonvuorenkatu 11 C 8, FI-00500 Helsinki, Finland, *Tel:* +358 9 4763 6300, *Fax:* +358 9 4763 6363, *Email:* finland@krogius.com, *Website:* www.krogius.com

HANKO

Lat 59° 49' N; Long 22° 58' E.

Admiralty Chart: 3437
Time Zone: GMT +2 h

Admiralty Pilot: 20
UNCTAD Locode: FI HKO

Key to Principal Facilities:—
A=Airport
B=Bunkers
C=Containers
D=Dry Dock
G=General Cargo
L=Cruise
P=Petroleum
Q=Other Liquid Bulk
R=Ro/Ro
T=Towage (where available from port)
Y=Dry Bulk

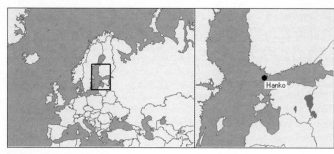

Principal Facilities:

Q	Y	G	C	R		B		T	

Authority: Port of Hanko, Western Harbour, FI-10900 Hanko, Finland, *Tel:* +358 19 220 3803, *Fax:* +358 19 220 3802, *Email:* port@hanko.fi, *Website:* www.portofhanko.fi

Officials: Port Director: Paavo O. Lyytikainen, *Tel:* +358 19 220 3801, *Email:* paavo.lyytikainen@hanko.fi.
Harbour Master: Tiina Saarinen, *Tel:* +358 19 220 3809, *Email:* tiina.saarinen@hanko.fi.

Port Security: ISPS compliant

Approach: Channel depth of 13 m

Pilotage: Compulsory, Tel: +358 (0) 20754 6151, Fax: +358 (0) 20754 6161, Email: pilotorder.south@finnpilot.fi. Pilot order form on www.pilotorder.fi. Distance from sea to port 9.6 km. Pilot boards 1.5 nautical miles ENE of Russaro or 4 nautical miles WSW of Ajax Lt. (in bad weather in Hanko roads)

Radio Frequency: Call Port on VHF Channel 12

Weather: SW winds

Traffic: 2007, 3 087 583 t of cargo handled, 47 820 TEU's

Maximum Vessel Dimensions: 250 m loa, 13 m draft

Principal Imports and Exports: Imports: Cars, Trailers. Exports: Paper, Trailers.

Working Hours: 0700-2230 in two shifts. Saturday 0700-1530

Accommodation:

Name	Length (m)	Depth (m)	Remarks
Hanko			See [1] below
Inner (Western) Harbour	1523	7.3–13	Four berths
Outer Harbour	350	7.2	Two berths

[1]*Hanko:* Two harbours, the Inner and the Outer. Both are kept open in winter by harbour icebreakers. Freeport administered by the Freeport of Finland Ltd which consists of more than 600 000 m2 of open storage space and 21 000 m2 of covered storage

Storage:

Location	Open (m2)	Covered (m2)
Hanko	250000	40000

Mechanical Handling Equipment:

Location	Type	Capacity (t)	Qty
Hanko	Mult-purp. Cranes	45	1

Bunkering: Coal and oil available by truck
Baltic Bunkering Ltd, Torggatan 10A, Mariehamn, Aland Islands, *Tel:* +358 18 143 00, *Fax:* +358 18 145 00, *Email:* info@balticbunkering.ax
Bunker Management Oy Ltd (BuMa), Merituulentie 424, FI-48310 Kotka, Finland, *Tel:* +358 5 2201 011, *Fax:* +358 5 2201 012, *Website:* www.bunkerman.fi
Shell Oy AB, Ulappasaarentie 4, FI-00980 Helsinki, Finland
ST1 Oy, ST1 OY, P O Box 37, Purotie, FI-02211 Helsinki, Finland, *Tel:* +358 10 557 11, *Fax:* +358 9 8030 004, *Email:* matti.pentti@st1.fi, *Website:* www.st1.fi
Teboil Oy AB, Bulevardi 26, P O Box 102, FI-00120 Helsinki, Finland, *Tel:* +358 20 470 01, *Fax:* +358 20 4700 248, *Email:* bunkersales@teboil.fi, *Website:* www.teboil.fi

Towage: Towboats of 2000-3000 hp available, and state ice-breakers in winter if needed

Repair & Maintenance: G-Metalli, Gunnarsstrandsv. 28, FI-10900 Hanko, Finland, *Tel:* +358 19 248 7891, *Fax:* +358 19 248 7892

Ship Chandlers: Oy Axel Liljefors Ab Ltd, P O Box 92, FI-10901 Hanko, Finland, *Tel:* +358 19 248 6495, *Fax:* +358 19 248 2301, *Email:* office@liljefors.fi

Shipping Agents: OY Hango Stevedoring AB, P O Box 26, 10901 Hanko, Finland, *Tel:* +358 19 221 9201, *Fax:* +358 19 221 9219, *Email:* office@hangostevedoring.fi, *Website:* www.hangostevedoring.fi
Victor Ek Ltd., P O Box 10, FIN-10901 Hanko, Finland, *Tel:* +358 19 266 6600, *Fax:* +358 19 248 5821, *Website:* www.victorek.fi

Stevedoring Companies: OY Hango Stevedoring AB, P O Box 26, 10901 Hanko, Finland, *Tel:* +358 19 221 9201, *Fax:* +358 19 221 9219, *Email:* office@hangostevedoring.fi, *Website:* www.hangostevedoring.fi

Medical Facilities: Available, town hospital, Tel: +358 (19) 220 3555

Airport: Helsinki International, 140 km

Railway: Hanko, 0.5 km

Lloyd's Agent: Oy Lars Krogius A/B, Vilhonvuorenkatu 11 C 8, FI-00500 Helsinki, Finland, *Tel:* +358 9 4763 6300, *Fax:* +358 9 4763 6363, *Email:* finland@krogius.com, *Website:* www.krogius.com

HELSINGFORS

alternate name, see Helsinki

HELSINKI

Lat 60° 9' N; Long 24° 56' E.

Admiralty Chart: 2224	**Admiralty Pilot:** 20
Time Zone: GMT +2 h	**UNCTAD Locode:** FI HEL

Principal Facilities:

P	Q	Y	G	C	R	L	B	D	T	A

Authority: Port of Helsinki, P O Box 800, FI-00099 Helsinki, Finland, *Tel:* +358 9 310 1621, *Fax:* +358 9 3103 3802, *Email:* port.helsinki@hel.fi, *Website:* www.portofhelsinki.fi

Officials: Managing Director: Heikki Nissinen, *Email:* heikki.nissinen@hel.fi.
Finance Director: Tauno Sieranoja, *Email:* tauno.sieranoja@hel.fi.
Operations Director: Heikki Lampinen, *Email:* heikki.lampinen@hel.fi.
Technical Director: Aarno Ahti, *Email:* aarno.ahti@hel.fi.
Harbour Master: Jukka Kallio, *Email:* jukka.t.kallio@hel.fi.

Port Security: ISPS compliant

Approach: Helsinki Lighthouse-Harmaja-West Harbour & South Harbour: The main approach to the port begins E from the Helsinki Lighthouse and proceeds towards Harmaja Island. At Harmaja Island fairway continuous towards Kustaanmiekka Strait between the islands of Suomenlinna and Vallisaari. At Kustaanmiekka the 9.5 m fairway continues to the open area known as Kruunuvuorenselka. At Kruunuvuorenselka the fairway branches off to the South Harbour (7.9-9.1 m), the cruise quay (9.3 m) and the Laajasalo Oil Terminal (9.5 m). The 9.6 m fairway also branches off S of Suomenlinna Island and proceeds to the West Harbour (8.9 m). The pilot boarding position is 2 nautical miles S of Harmaja Island. The distance from Helsinki Lighthouse to the harbours is 13 nautical miles
Helsinki Lighthouse-West Harbour (deep water fairway): This 10.8 m fairway leads from the Helsinki Lighthouse to the E of the Graskarsbadan light and then between the islands of Pihlajasaari and Melkki to the West Harbour. The pilot boarding position is 4 nautical miles N of Helsinki Lighthouse. The distance from Helsinki Lighthouse to the West Harbour is 12 nautical miles
Helsinki Lighthouse-Vuosaari Harbour: The 11.0 m fairway to Vuosaari Harbour begins 3.3 nautical miles E of Helsinki Lighthouse and continues towards Vuosaari Harbour by passing the islands of Ita-Toukki, Eestinluoto, Kuiva Hevonen and Pikku Niinisaari. The pilot boarding position is 2.7 nautical miles SSE of Eestinluoto Island. The distance from Helsinki Lighthouse to the Vuosaari Harbour is 18 nautical miles
Porkkala-Helsinki: The 9.0 m winter fairway from Porkkala to Helsinki begins 4 nautical miles W of the Porkkala Lighthouse. The fairway turns eastward at Sammaro Island towards Helsinki, along the archipelago, passing the islands of Stora Trasko, Hermanskar, Grimsholmen, Mickelskar, Brandoklacken, Kyto and Rysakari. The fairway then joins the 10.8 m fairway (leading to West Harbour) SW of Katajaluoto Island. The fairway then continues eastwards and joins the 9.6 m fairway N of Harmaja Island. The fairway then continues eastwards towards Vuosaari Harbour passing the islands of Isosaari and Villinki, and then joins the 11.0 m fairway at Kuiva Hevonen. The pilot boarding position is 4 nautical miles W of Porkkala Lighthouse. The distance from Porkkala to Suomenlinna is 25 nautical miles and from Suomenlinna to Vuosaari Harbour is 11 nautical miles
During the winter months the fairways from Helsinki Lighthouse to Harmaja and West Harbour may occasionally be closed due to ice conditions. In this case all traffic to the port of Helsinki is directed via Porkkala

Pilotage: Compulsory, Tel: +358 (0) 20754 6151, Fax: +358 (0) 20754 6161, Email: pilotorder.south@finnpilot.fi. Pilot order form on www.pilotorder.fi. Harbour pilots from the Port of Helsinki VTS Centre, Tel: +358 (0) 20448 5391, Fax: +358 (0) 204485380, Email: helsinki.vts@fma.fi. Pilot boards in the following positions:
a) Porkkala: 2.5 nautical miles SW of Sommaro. Provides pilotage for Inkoo and Kantvik
b) Harmaja: 2 nautical miles SSW of Harmaja Lt. (60° 06.30' N; 24° 58.70' E) or 60° 00.37 N; 24° 56.46 E. Provides pilotage for Helsinki and Kalkkiranta
c) Vuosaari: 60° 04.96' N; 25° 09.79' E. Provides pilotage for Vuosaari
d) Emaslo: 2 nautical miles WNW of Kalbadagrund Lt. (59° 59.10' N; 25° 36.10' E). Provides pilotage for Skoldvik(Porvoo), Tolkkinen and Kalkkiranta

Radio Frequency: Vessel traffic service on VHF Channels 71, 13 and 16

Traffic: 2007, 13 388 000 t of cargo handled, 431 406 TEU's

Principal Imports and Exports: Imports: Chemicals, Fertiliser, Grain, Liquid fuels, Minerals, Solid fuels, Unitized cargo. Exports: Forest products, Machinery & equipment, Paper.

Working Hours: 24 h/day

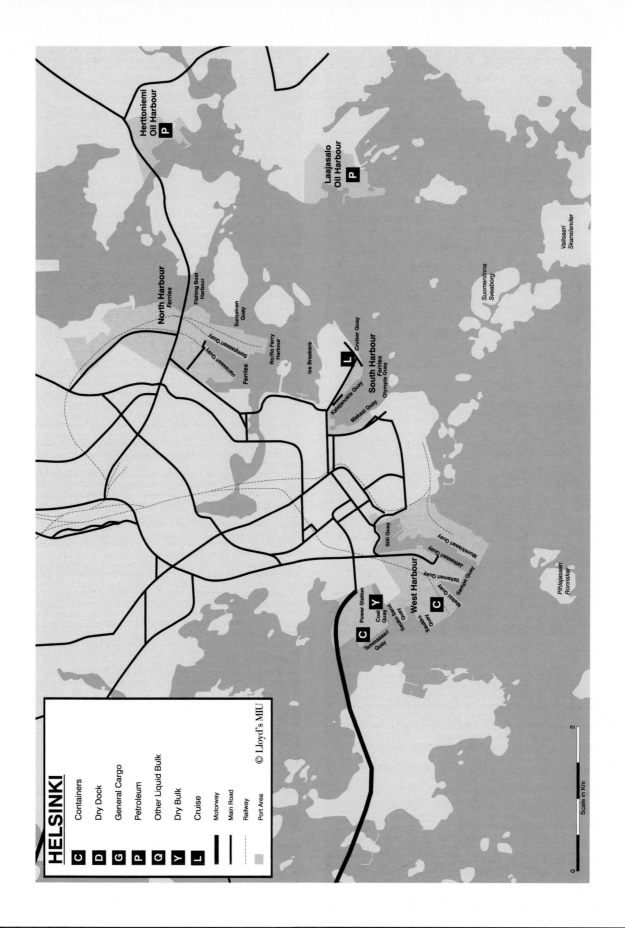

OY Seachart Ltd

P. O. Box 81, FIN-00501, Helsinki, FINLAND

Tel: +358 9 47802036   Fax: +358 9 47801651
Email: seachart@seachart.fi

Accommodation:

Name	Length (m)	Depth (m)	Remarks
Vuosaari Harbiour			See [1] below
Pier A	185	12.5	Adjustable ramp 29 m width
Pier A Extension	112	12.5	
Pier B	243	12.5	Four fixed ramps of 31.1-32.4 m width
Pier Bb	250	12.5	Ramp 20 m width
Pier C	278	12.5	See [2] below
Pier CP	250		
Pier D	749	12.5–15.5	One ramp of 30 m width
Pier E	749	12.5–15.5	
Pier F	559		
Pier G	203	12.5–15.5	Four fixed ramps of 30.4-33 m width
Pier GP1	204		Dolphin portion 94 m
Pier GP2	204		Dolphin portion 45 m
Pier H	158	12.5–15.5	
Pier I	194	15.5	
West Harbour			Passenger traffic to Tallinn
Tammasaari Quay (LTA)	135	7.6	
Jatkasaari Quay (LJ3)	150	7.5–8.2	Bridge ramp 17 m width
Jatkasaari Quay (LJ4)	200	8.8	Bridge ramp 22 m width
Jatkasaari Quay (LJ5)	195	9	Shore ramp 20.5 m width
Jatkasaari Quay (LJ6)	255	9.5	Bridge ramp 27.8 m width
Sampo Quay (LSL10)	150	6	
Valtameri Quay (LV7)	210	11	Shore ramp 22.4 m width
Melkki Quay (LMA)	200	12.1	
Melkki Quay (LMB)	200	12.1	
STX Finland Cruise Oy (LHY)		9	
Munkkisaari Quay (LHA)	196	7.8	Pneumatic grain unloader owned by State Granary
Munkkisaari Quay (LHB)	320	9	
Munkkisaari Quay (LHC)	355	9.8	
Hietalahti Quay (LKL,LJM)	170	6.5	
South Harbour			See [3] below
Olympia Quay (EO1)	150	7.5	Bridge ramp 12 m width
Olympia Quay (EO2)	220	8.8	Bridge ramp 22 m width
Makasilni Quay (EM3)	120	7.5	Pontoon ramp 11.05 m width
Makasilni Quay (EM4)	130	6.5	Shore ramp 16.5 m width
Pakkahuone Quay (EPL)	130	6	
Lubeck Quay (ELY)	75	3.8	
Kanava Quay (EKA)	85	5–5.5	
Katajanokka Quay (EK5)	120	8.8	Pontoon ramp 7.7 m width
Katajanokka Quay (EKL)	180	8.8	
Katajanokka Quay (EK6)	220	8.8	Shore ramp 24 m width
Katajanokka Quay (EK7)	220	8.8	Bridge ramp 22 m width
Cruise Quay (ERA)	200	10.3	
Cruise Quay (ERB)		9.5–10.3	Quay and dolphin 200 m
Ice-breaker Quay (EKJ)	410	5.5–8.8	
Coal Harbours			
Energy Fuel Quay	137	9.8	
Hanasaari Quay	180	8.5	
Laajasalo Oil Harbour			Import of oil products
Oy Shell AB Pier	32	9.5	
ST1 Pier	30	9.5	
Neste Oil Oyj Pier	58	9.5	

[1] *Vuosaari Harbiour:* The harbour has two 750 m container quays and 15 ro/ro berths, some of which also lend themselves to the handling of deck cargo with a crane Operators have their specific areas for cargo handling. There are three companies (Finnsteve Oy, Steveco Oy and Multi-Link Terminals Ltd) providing cargo handling and terminal services. There are two areas for thermoregulated reefer units, 400 spaces in total
It includes the Hansa Passenger Terminal, located at Gate B, which serves passenger traffic between Helsinki to Travemunde and Rostock
[2] *Pier C:* Two adjustable double ramps of 29 m width and one fixed ramp of 36.3 m width
[3] *South Harbour:* Serves passenger ferry traffic to and from Stockholm and Tallinn

Mechanical Handling Equipment:

Location	Type	Capacity (t)	Qty
Pier D	Container Cranes	40–60	5
Pier E	Container Cranes	65–90	4
Pier F	Container Cranes	40–50	1

Bunkering: Shell Oy AB, Ulappasaarentie 4, FI-00980 Helsinki, Finland
ST1 Oy, ST1 OY, P O Box 37, Purotie, FI-02211 Helsinki, Finland, *Tel:* +358 10 557 11, *Fax:* +358 9 8030 004, *Email:* matti.pentti@st1.fi, *Website:* www.st1.fi
Teboil Oy AB, Bulevardi 26, P O Box 102, FI-00120 Helsinki, Finland, *Tel:* +358 20 470 01, *Fax:* +358 20 4700 248, *Email:* bunkersales@teboil.fi, *Website:* www.teboil.fi
Baltic Bunkering Ltd, Torggatan 10A, Mariehamn, Aland Islands, *Tel:* +358 18 143 00, *Fax:* +358 18 145 00, *Email:* info@balticbunkering.ax
Bunker Management Oy Ltd (BuMa), Merituulentie 424, FI-48310 Kotka, Finland, *Tel:* +358 5 2201 011, *Fax:* +358 5 2201 012, *Website:* www.bunkerman.fi
ExxonMobil Marine Fuels, Mailpoint 31, ExxonMobil House, Ermyn Way, Leatherhead, Surrey KT22 8UX, United Kingdom, *Tel:* +44 1372 222 000, *Fax:* +44 1372 223 922, *Email:* marine.fuels@exxonmobil.com, *Website:* www.exxonmobil.com – *Grades:* MGO – *Parcel Size:* no min/max – *Notice:* 48 hours – *Delivery Mode:* truck
Shell Oy AB, Ulappasaarentie 4, FI-00980 Helsinki, Finland
ST1 Oy, ST1 OY, P O Box 37, Purotie, FI-02211 Helsinki, Finland, *Tel:* +358 10 557 11, *Fax:* +358 9 8030 004, *Email:* matti.pentti@st1.fi, *Website:* www.st1.fi
Teboil Oy AB, Bulevardi 26, P O Box 102, FI-00120 Helsinki, Finland, *Tel:* +358 20 470 01, *Fax:* +358 20 4700 248, *Email:* bunkersales@teboil.fi, *Website:* www.teboil.fi

Towage: Alfons Hakans Oy Ab, Linnankatu 36C, FI-20100 Turku, Finland, *Tel:* +358 2 515500, *Fax:* +358 2 251 5873, *Email:* office.turku@alfonshakans.fi, *Website:* www.alfonshakans.fi

Ship Chandlers: ME Group Oy (ab Mathias Eriksson), Putkitie 3, FI-00880 Helsinki, Finland, *Tel:* +358 9 758991, *Fax:* +358 9 7589 9200, *Email:* helsinki@megroup.fi, *Website:* www.megroup.fi

Shipping Agents: ACL Ship Management AB, Transocean Oy Ab, P O Box 960, Hameentie 33, 12th Floor, FI-00101 Helsinki, Finland, *Tel:* +358 9 413678, *Fax:* +358 9 413679, *Email:* sales@transocean.fi, *Website:* www.transocean.fi
CMA-CGM S.A., CMA CGM Finland, Runberginkatu 5, P O Box 1392, 00100 Helsinki, Finland, *Tel:* +358 9 685 0188, *Fax:* +358 9 6850 1860, *Website:* www.cma-cgm.com
Cosfim Oy, P O Box 373, 811 Helsinki, Finland, *Tel:* +358 9 4132 8800, *Fax:* +358 9 4132 8850, *Website:* www.cosfim.fi
Dasena Agencies, Oy Dasena Agencies Ltd, Hameentie 33, FI-00500 Helsinki, Finland, *Tel:* +358 9 681 8150, *Fax:* +358 9 6818 1520, *Email:* info@dasena.fi, *Website:* www.dasena.fi
Oy Fennoscandia Chartering AB, Tynnyrintekijankatu 2, P O Box 53, FI-00581 Helsinki, Finland, *Tel:* +358 9 642911, *Fax:* +358 9 604619, *Email:* fenscan@fenscan.fi, *Website:* www.fenscan.fi
Flagships Oy Finnish Liner Agencies AB, Georginkatu 16, P O Box 648, FI-00100 Helsinki, Finland, *Tel:* +358 9 685 0100, *Fax:* +358 9 694 7976, *Email:* flagships@flagships.fi
Oy G-Ships Finland Ltd, P O Box 26, FI-00501 Helsinki, Finland, *Tel:* +358 9 584 5315, *Fax:* +358 9 584 3288, *Email:* gships@gshipsfinland.fi, *Website:* www.cargomasters.com
Oy Loadmarine Ltd, Vilhonvuorenkuja 14 B, P O Box 81, FI-00500 Helsinki, Finland, *Tel:* +358 9 584 5312, *Fax:* +358 9 5845 3779, *Email:* management@hansaseaways.fi, *Website:* www.hansaseaways.fi
Mediterranean Shipping Company, MSC Finland Oy, Ruoholahdenkatu 21, FIN-00180 Helsinki, Finland, *Tel:* +358 9 4131 1500, *Fax:* +358 9 4131 1590, *Email:* info@hel.mscfinland.com, *Website:* www.mscgva.ch
A.P. Moller-Maersk Group, Maersk Finland Oy, Satamaradankatu 1E, P O Box 11, 00511 Helsinki, Finland, *Tel:* +358 9 425 0510, *Fax:* +358 9 4250 5120, *Email:* finsalgen@maersk.com, *Website:* www.maerskline.com
MTA-Maritime Transport & Agencies SIA, Henry Fordin Katu 5K, Helsinki, Finland, *Tel:* +358 9 4132 8200, *Fax:* +358 9 4132 8272, *Website:* www.mta.se
NET Shipping Ltd Oy, Tammasaarenkatu 1, FI-00180 Helsinki, Finland, *Tel:* +358 9 4137 9700, *Fax:* +358 9 4137 9750, *Email:* esa.hotanen@netship.fi, *Website:* www.netship.fi/index3.html
OS-Agency UAB, Hameentie 33, FI-00500 Helsinki, Finland, *Tel:* +358 9 622 0890, *Fax:* +358 9 6220 8925, *Email:* tuomas.paavolainen@os-agency.fi, *Website:* www.os-agency.com
Oy Nystroem & Co. Ab, Virkatie 1, FI-01510 Helsinki, Finland, *Tel:* +358 9 618750, *Fax:* +358 9 6187 5200, *Email:* nystrom@onystrom.fi, *Website:* www.onystrom.fi
Oy Tramp Agencies AB, Lepolantie 16A, 00660 Helsinki, Finland, *Tel:* +358 9 146 1170, *Fax:* +358 9 146 1292, *Email:* tramp@tramp.fi, *Website:* www.tramp.fi
Reval Logistics Oy, Porkkalankatu 13C, FIN-00180 Helsinki, Finland, *Tel:* +358 9 759 9430, *Fax:* +358 9 7599 4320, *Email:* finland@revallog.com, *Website:* www.revallog.com
Oy Scanbridge Shipping & Project Ab, Annankatu 10C, FI-00120 Helsinki, Finland, *Tel:* +358 9 6803 7666, *Fax:* +358 9 6803 7630
Oy Scanway Shipping Ab, 5A Itamerenkatu, FI-00180 Helsinki, Finland, *Tel:* +358 9 4150 5400, *Fax:* +358 9 4150 5495, *Email:* info@scanway-shipping.fi, *Website:* www.scan-group.com
OY Seachart Ltd, Hameentie 31A, P O Box 81, FI-00500 Helsinki, Finland, *Tel:* +358 9 4780 2036, *Fax:* +358 9 4780 1651, *Email:* seachart@seachart.fi
OY Shipco-Shipping AB, Itamerenkatu 5A, FI-00180 Helsinki, Finland, *Tel:* +358 9 4150 5460, *Fax:* +358 9 4150 5480, *Email:* hel@shipco.com, *Website:* www.shipco.com
Stella Naves Oy Ltd, Nuijamiestentie 3A, FIN-00400 Helsinki, Finland, *Tel:* +358 9 477 7910, *Fax:* +358 9 4777 9120, *Email:* helsinki@stellanaves.com, *Website:* www.stellanaves.com
Transocean Oy AB, Lintulahdenkatu 10, PL 960, FI-00101 Helsinki, Finland, *Tel:* +358 9 413678, *Fax:* +358 9 4136 7999, *Email:* info@transocean.fi, *Website:* www.transocean.fi
Tschudi Logistics Oy, Porkkalankatu 13C, 00180 Helsinki, Finland, *Tel:* +358 9 7599 4330, *Fax:* +358 9 7599 4320, *Email:* finland@tschudilogistics.com, *Website:* www.tschudilogistics.com
Unifeeder Finland Oy, Henry Fordin katu 5F, 150 Helsinki, Finland, *Tel:* +358 9 613086, *Fax:* +358 9 6130 8425, *Email:* o-hki@unifeeder.com, *Website:* www.unifeeder.com
Varova Oy, Lautatarhankatu 6, 580 Helsinki, Finland, *Tel:* +358 9 773961, *Fax:* +358 9 730074, *Email:* info@varova.fi, *Website:* www.varova.fi
Oy Victor Ek AB, Lautatarhankatu 6, FI-00580 Helsinki, Finland, *Tel:* +358 9 12511, *Fax:* +358 9 627040, *Email:* birger.stjernberg@victorek.fi, *Website:* www.victorek.com
Wilhelmsen Ship Services, Transocean OY, P O Box 960, FI-00101 Helsinki, Finland, *Tel:* +358 9 413678, *Fax:* +358 9 4136 7999, *Email:* sales@transocean.fi, *Website:* www.transocean.fi

Stevedoring Companies: Finnsteve OY AB, P O Box 225, FIN-00181 Helsinki, Finland, *Tel:* +358 105 6560, *Email:* info@finnsteve.fi, *Website:* www.finnsteve.fi
Multi-Link Terminals Ltd Oy, Tukholmankatu 2, FIN-00250 Helsinki, Finland, *Tel:* +358 20 746 0200, *Fax:* +358 20 746 0260, *Email:* mlt@mlt.fi, *Website:* www.mlt.fi
Transfennica Ltd, Etelaranta 12, P O Box 398, FI-00130 Helsinki, Finland, *Tel:* +358 9 13262, *Fax:* +358 9 652377, *Email:* info@transfennica.com, *Website:* www.transfennica.com

Surveyors: ABS (Europe), P O Box 208, FI-00121 Helsinki, Finland, *Tel:* +358 9 6129 4223, *Fax:* +358 9 6129 4251, *Email:* abshelsinki@eagle.org
Bureau Veritas, Pohjoisranta 4A, FIN-00170 Helsinki, Finland, *Tel:* +358 9 680 3530, *Fax:* +358 9 6803 5333, *Email:* helsinki@fi.bureauveritas.com, *Website:* www.bureauveritas.com
Det Norske Veritas A/S, Keilasatama 5, Espoo, 02150 Helsinki, Finland, *Tel:* +358 9 681691, *Fax:* +358 9 692 6827, *Email:* helsinki@dnv.com, *Website:* www.dnv.com
Germanischer Lloyd, Lapinrinne 1 A 10, FI-00180 Helsinki, Finland, *Tel:* +358 20 759 8920, *Fax:* +358 20 759 8921, *Email:* gl-helsinki@gl-group.com, *Website:* www.gl-group.com
Nippon Kaiji Kyokai, Ky Shiptech Kb, Ruosilantie 2B, FI-00390 Helsinki, Finland, *Tel:* +358 9 251 4110, *Fax:* +358 9 2514 1155, *Website:* www.classnk.or.jp

Registro Italiano Navale (RINA), Myyrmaentie 2b, 01600 Vantaa, Finland, *Tel:* +358 9 586 0220, *Fax:* +358 9 5860 2244, *Email:* helsinki.office@rina.org, *Website:* www.rina.org

Medical Facilities: Several hospitals near to the port

Airport: Helsinki-Vantaa, 20 km

Development: Helsinki's general cargo harbours (West and North Harbour) have moved to the new Vuosaari Harbour, 14 km E of the town centre

Lloyd's Agent: Oy Lars Krogius A/B, Vilhonvuorenkatu 11 C 8, FI-00500 Helsinki, Finland, *Tel:* +358 9 4763 6300, *Fax:* +358 9 4763 6363, *Email:* finland@krogius.com, *Website:* www.krogius.com

HERTONIEMI HARBOUR

harbour area, see under Helsinki

HIIRENKARI

harbour area, see under Hamina

HONKALAHTI

harbour area, see under Joutseno

IMATRA

Lat 61° 10' N; Long 28° 50' E.

Admiralty Chart: -	**Admiralty Pilot:** 20
Time Zone: GMT +2 h	**UNCTAD Locode:** FI IMA

Principal Facilities:

		Y	G						A

Authority: O/Y Saimaa Terminals A/B, P O Box 229, FI-53101 Lappeenranta, Finland, *Tel:* +358 20 743 2760, *Fax:* +358 20 743 2761, *Email:* auvo.muraja@saimaaterminals.fi, *Website:* www.saimaaterminals.fi

Officials: Managing Director: Auvo Muraja.

Traffic: 2001, 168 vessels, 268 000 t of cargo handled

Maximum Vessel Dimensions: 2900 dwt, 82.5 m loa, 4.35 m draft

Principal Imports and Exports: Imports: Raw timber. Exports: Paper, Steel, Timber.

Working Hours: 0600-2200

Accommodation:

Name	Remarks
Vuoksi	Three berths 80 m long with max draft 4.35 m. Terminal house of 74 000 m3

Storage:

Location	Open (m²)
Imatra	30000

Mechanical Handling Equipment:

Location	Type
Imatra	Mobile Cranes

Medical Facilities: Health centre available

Airport: Lappeenranta, 40 km

Lloyd's Agent: Oy Lars Krogius A/B, Vilhonvuorenkatu 11 C 8, FI-00500 Helsinki, Finland, *Tel:* +358 9 4763 6300, *Fax:* +358 9 4763 6363, *Email:* finland@krogius.com, *Website:* www.krogius.com

INKOO

Lat 60° 3' N; Long 24° 1' E.

Admiralty Chart: 2248	**Admiralty Pilot:** 20
Time Zone: GMT +2 h	**UNCTAD Locode:** FI INK

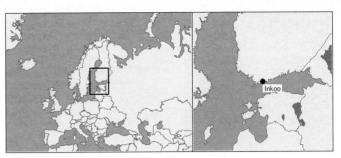

Principal Facilities:

P		Y	G			B		T	A

Authority: Inkoo Shipping OY AB, Satamatie 454, FI-10210 Inkoo, Finland, *Tel:* +358 207 631500, *Fax:* +358 207 631501, *Email:* inkooshp@inkooshipping.fi, *Website:* www.inkooshipping.fi

Officials: Managing Director: Rene Fagerstrom, *Tel:* +358 207 631502, *Email:* rene.fagerstrom@inkooshipping.fi.

Port Security: ISPS compliant

Approach: Lighted fairway 29 km long, 13 m max depth, leads from Porkkala pilot station to the port. During the winter months an icebreaker is available

Anchorage: Good anchorage area in depths of 13 m to 20 m in front of fairway leading to the port

Pilotage: Not compulsory within harbour areas. Incoming and outgoing vessels obtain pilots from Porkkala Sea Pilot Station, *Tel:* +358 9 298 4112, at 3 h notice

Traffic: 2007, 2 044 299 t of cargo handled

Maximum Vessel Dimensions: 80 000 dwt, 13 m draft

Principal Imports and Exports: Imports: Coal, Kaolin, Light clinker, Limestone. Exports: Crushed stone, Plasters on pallets.

Working Hours: Mon-Fri 0600-2200

Accommodation:

Name	Length (m)	Depth (m)	Remarks
Inkoo			The port consists of two harbours
Fortum OYJ	410	10–13	See [1] below
Inkoo Shipping OY AB	375	7.8	See [2] below

[1]*Fortum OYJ:* Tel: +358 10 454 3111
Inkoo Power plant quay, can accommodate vessels up to 80 000 dwt. Two oil discharge arms of 1500 t/h cap are available and a 20 ha coal storage yard
[2]*Inkoo Shipping OY AB:* Tel: +358 207 631500, Fax: +358 207 631501
Two berths. Harbour basin with overall length of quays 230 m and 145 m. Dry bulk storage area of 20 ha and covered storage of 17 500 m2. Discharge/loading in two shifts

Mechanical Handling Equipment:

Location	Type	Capacity (t)	Qty
Fortum OYJ	Mult-purp. Cranes	20	1
Fortum OYJ	Mult-purp. Cranes	10	3
Inkoo Shipping OY AB	Mult-purp. Cranes	10	1
Inkoo Shipping OY AB	Mobile Cranes	3	1
Inkoo Shipping OY AB	Mobile Cranes	6	1

Bunkering: Available from several firms
Baltic Bunkering Ltd, Torggatan 10A, Mariehamn, Aland Islands, *Tel:* +358 18 143 00, *Fax:* +358 18 145 00, *Email:* info@balticbunkering.ax
Bunker Management Oy Ltd (BuMa), Meriuulentie 424, FI-48310 Kotka, Finland, *Tel:* +358 5 2201 011, *Fax:* +358 5 2201 012, *Website:* www.bunkerman.fi
Shell Oy AB, Ulappasaarentie 4, FI-00980 Helsinki, Finland
ST1 Oy, ST1 OY, P O Box 37, Purotie, FI-02211 Helsinki, Finland, *Tel:* +358 10 557 11, *Fax:* +358 9 8030 004, *Email:* matti.pentti@st1.fi, *Website:* www.st1.fi
Teboil Oy AB, Bulevardi 26, P O Box 102, FI-00120 Helsinki, Finland, *Tel:* +358 20 470 01, *Fax:* +358 20 4700 248, *Email:* bunkersales@teboil.fi, *Website:* www.teboil.fi

Towage: Towing assistance can be arranged at 3 h notice (5 h notice after official hours). The towing company charges shipowners directly for assistance rendered

Shipping Agents: Inkoo Shipping OY AB, Satamatie 454, FI-10210 Inkoo, Finland, *Tel:* +358 207 631500, *Fax:* +358 207 631501, *Email:* inkooshp@inkooshipping.fi, *Website:* www.inkooshipping.fi

Stevedoring Companies: Inkoo Shipping OY AB, Satamatie 454, FI-10210 Inkoo, Finland, *Tel:* +358 207 631500, *Fax:* +358 207 631501, *Email:* inkooshp@inkooshipping.fi, *Website:* www.inkooshipping.fi

Airport: Helsinki, 70 km

Lloyd's Agent: Oy Lars Krogius A/B, Vilhonvuorenkatu 11 C 8, FI-00500 Helsinki, Finland, *Tel:* +358 9 4763 6300, *Fax:* +358 9 4763 6363, *Email:* finland@krogius.com, *Website:* www.krogius.com

JAKOBSTAD

harbour area, see under Pietarsaari

Key to Principal Facilities:—			
A=Airport	**C**=Containers	**G**=General Cargo	**P**=Petroleum	**R**=Ro/Ro	**Y**=Dry Bulk
B=Bunkers	**D**=Dry Dock	**L**=Cruise	**Q**=Other Liquid Bulk	**T**=Towage (where available from port)

JOENSUU

Lat 62° 36' N; Long 29° 45' E.

Admiralty Chart: -	**Admiralty Pilot:** 20
Time Zone: GMT +2 h	**UNCTAD Locode:** FI JOE

Principal Facilities:

		Y	G						A

Authority: Port of Joensuu, Satamatie 4, FI-80220 Joensuu, Finland, *Tel:* +358 13 267 3545, *Fax:* +358 13 267 3548, *Email:* matti.linervo@jns.fi, *Website:* www.jns.fi/satama

Officials: Harbour Master: Matti Linervo.

Port Security: ISPS compliant

Pilotage: Not compulsory but available upon request

Radio Frequency: VHF Channels 16 and 13

Traffic: 2007, 365 192 t of cargo handled

Maximum Vessel Dimensions: 82.5 m loa, 12.8 m width, 4.35 m draught

Principal Imports and Exports: Imports: Cement, Salt. Exports: Cellulose, Pellets, Poles, Sawn timber, Talc, Timber.

Working Hours: Two shifts 0700-1530, 1530-2400

Accommodation:

Name	Length (m)	Depth (m)	Remarks
Joensuu			
Ukonniemi	230	4.2–4.35	Five berths. Railway to harbour
Passenger Terminal	120	2.4	Small boat mooring facilities

Storage: Covered storage area of 1.8 ha, asphalted storage area of 2.5 ha and gravelled area of 15 ha

Location	Open (m²)	Covered (m²)
Joensuu	150000	19650

Mechanical Handling Equipment:

Location	Type	Capacity (t)
Joensuu	Mobile Cranes	36

Medical Facilities: Health centre available

Airport: Joensuu Airport, 15 km

Railway: Rail link to all berths

Lloyd's Agent: Oy Lars Krogius A/B, Vilhonvuorenkatu 11 C 8, FI-00500 Helsinki, Finland, *Tel:* +358 9 4763 6300, *Fax:* +358 9 4763 6363, *Email:* finland@krogius.com, *Website:* www.krogius.com

JOUTSENO

Lat 61° 8' N; Long 28° 29' E.

Admiralty Chart: -	**Admiralty Pilot:** 20
Time Zone: GMT +2 h	**UNCTAD Locode:** FI JOU

Principal Facilities:

		Y	G						A

Authority: O/Y Saimaa Terminals A/B, P O Box 229, FI-53101 Lappeenranta, Finland, *Tel:* +358 20 743 2760, *Fax:* +358 20 743 2761, *Email:* auvo.muraja@saimaaterminals.fi, *Website:* www.saimaaterminals.fi

Officials: Managing Director: Auvo Muraja.

Port Security: ISPS compliant

Traffic: 2001, 156 vessels, 227 000 t of cargo handled

Maximum Vessel Dimensions: 2900 dwt, 82.5 m loa, 4.35 m draft

Principal Imports and Exports: Imports: Salt. Exports: Timber.

Working Hours: 0700-1530, 1530-2300

Accommodation:

Name	Length (m)	Draught (m)	Remarks
Joutseno			
Berth	80	4.35	See [1] below
Honkalahti	80	4.35	Storage area of 3000 m2

[1]*Berth:* Operated by Metsa-Botnia O/Y, Joutseno Pulp O/Y, Tel: +358 1046 65499, Fax: +358 1046 65378
Storage area of 9000 m2

Mechanical Handling Equipment:

Location	Type
Joutseno	Mobile Cranes

Stevedoring Companies: O/Y Saimaa Terminals A/B, Joutseno, Finland, *Tel:* +358 5 544 1740, *Fax:* +358 5 544 1750

Medical Facilities: Health Centre available

Airport: Lappeenranta, 25 km

Lloyd's Agent: Oy Lars Krogius A/B, Vilhonvuorenkatu 11 C 8, FI-00500 Helsinki, Finland, *Tel:* +358 9 4763 6300, *Fax:* +358 9 4763 6363, *Email:* finland@krogius.com, *Website:* www.krogius.com

KALAJOKI

Lat 64° 15' N; Long 23° 56' E.

Admiralty Chart: -	**Admiralty Pilot:** 20
Time Zone: GMT +2 h	**UNCTAD Locode:** FI KJO

Principal Facilities:

		Y	G						

Authority: Port of Kalajoki, Satamatie 436, FIN-85180 Rahja, Finland, *Fax:* +358 8 465311, *Email:* port@kalajoki.fi, *Website:* www.portofkalajoki.fi

Officials: Port Director: Esa Anttio, *Tel:* +358 44 4691 361. Harbour Master: Aulis Aho, *Tel:* +358 44 4691 214.

Traffic: 2007, 282 826 t of cargo handled

Principal Imports and Exports: Imports: Raw materials. Exports: Grain, Plywood, Sawn timber, Scrap iron, Steel components, Wood pellets.

Accommodation:

Name	Length (m)	Depth (m)	Remarks
Kalajoki			
Quay	415	8.5	Able to berth three vessels simultaneously

Storage:

Location	Covered (m²)
Kalajoki	30000

Lloyd's Agent: Oy Lars Krogius A/B, Vilhonvuorenkatu 11 C 8, FI-00500 Helsinki, Finland, *Tel:* +358 9 4763 6300, *Fax:* +358 9 4763 6363, *Email:* finland@krogius.com, *Website:* www.krogius.com

KANTVIK

Lat 60° 5' N; Long 24° 23' E.

Admiralty Chart: 1080/2248	**Admiralty Pilot:** 20
Time Zone: GMT +2 h	**UNCTAD Locode:** FI KNT

Principal Facilities:

		Y	G			B		T	A

Authority: Finnsteve OY AB, Saukonkuja 5, FI-00180 Helsinki, Finland, *Tel:* +358 10 565 6200, *Fax:* +358 9 685 4987, *Email:* info@finnsteve.fi, *Website:* www.finnsteve.fi

Officials: Managing Director: Hans Martin, *Tel:* +358 10 565 6201, *Email:* hans.martin@finnsteve.fi. Harbour Master: Kari Alhojoki, *Tel:* +358 10 565 6521, *Email:* kari.alhojoki@finnsteve.fi.

Port Security: ISPS compliant

Approach: Four channels lead to port, the deepest of which is 9.2 m and the shallowest being 5.5 m

Anchorage: Outside Porkkala pilot station

Pilotage: Compulsory, Tel: +358 (0) 20754 6151, Fax: +358 (0) 20754 6161, Email: pilotorder.south@finnpilot.fi. Pilot order form on www.pilotorder.fi

Radio Frequency: Helsinki VTS on VHF Channel 71. Porkkala Pilot Station on VHF Channel 16

Maximum Vessel Dimensions: 180 m loa, 9.2 m draught

Principal Imports and Exports: Imports: Cement, Coal, Gypsum stone, Rape seed, Raw sugar. Exports: Metal waste & scrap, Plasterboard, Soya oil, Sugar.

Working Hours: Monday to Friday 0700-1500, 1500-2300. Saturday 0700-1500. Overtime if required

Accommodation:

Name	Length (m)	Depth (m)	Remarks
Kantvik			
South Quay	60	8.5	Gypsum stone, coal. One 20 t material handling machine
Inner Quay	50	5.5	Sugar & soya oil
North Quay	110	9.2	Raw sugar, soya beans, aluminium & coal

Storage:

Location	Open (m²)	Covered (m²)
North Quay	5000	1500

Mechanical Handling Equipment:

Location	Type	Capacity (t)	Qty	Remarks
South Quay	Mobile Cranes	20	1	See [1] below
North Quay	Mult-purp. Cranes	8	1	

[1]*South Quay:* Mantsinen material handling machine

Cargo Worked: 2560 t/day of raw sugar, 4800 t/day of coal, 4000 t/day of gypsum stone

Bunkering: ST1 Oy, ST1 OY, P O Box 37, Purotie, FI-02211 Helsinki, Finland, *Tel:* +358 10 557 11, *Fax:* +358 9 8030 004, *Email:* matti.pentti@st1.fi, *Website:* www.st1.fi
Teboil Oy AB, Bulevardi 26, P O Box 102, FI-00120 Helsinki, Finland, *Tel:* +358 20 470 01, *Fax:* +358 20 4700 248, *Email:* bunkersales@teboil.fi, *Website:* www.teboil.fi

Waste Reception Facilities: Garbage reception available

Towage: Alfons Hakans Oy Ab, Kantvik, Finland, *Tel:* +358 9 694 4531, *Fax:* +358 9 251 5873, *Email:* port.helsinki@alfonshakans.fi, *Website:* www.alfonshakans.fi

Repair & Maintenance: Kvaerner Masa-Yards (Helsinki), Munkkisaarenkatu 1, P O Box 132, FI-00151 Helsinki, Finland, *Tel:* +358 9 194 2409, *Fax:* +358 9 650051, *Email:* henrik.segercrantz@kmyh.masa-yards.fi, *Website:* www.masa-yards.fi Vessels: passenger-car ferries, LNG carriers, icebreakers and ice going ships, ships and units for the offshore oil industry, incl. Floating Storage units, Floating production Ships (hulls) and special duty supply vessels, tankers, cable ships Covered Panamax size newbuilding dock: 280.5m x 34m x9.5m

Surveyors: Vaara & Partners, Kantvik, Finland, *Tel:* +358 9 4763 6300, *Fax:* +358 9 4763 6363

Medical Facilities: Health station in Kirkkonummi, 7 km

Airport: Helsinki-Vantaa, 40 km

Railway: Kirkkonummi, 7 km

Lloyd's Agent: Oy Lars Krogius A/B, Vilhonvuorenkatu 11 C 8, FI-00500 Helsinki, Finland, *Tel:* +358 9 4763 6300, *Fax:* +358 9 4763 6363, *Email:* finland@krogius.com, *Website:* www.krogius.com

KASKINEN

Lat 62° 23' N; Long 21° 13' E.

Admiralty Chart: 2303	**Admiralty Pilot:** 20
Time Zone: GMT +2 h	**UNCTAD Locode:** FI KAS

Principal Facilities:

		Y	G			B		T	A

Authority: Port of Kaskinen, Syvasatama, FI-64260 Kaskinen, Finland, Tel: +358 40 726 5740, Fax: +358 40 220 7300, Email: portofkaskinen@kaskinen.fi, Website: www.kaskinen.fi

Officials: Port Captain: Timo Onnela, Email: timo.onnela@kaskinen.fi.

Port Security: ISPS compliant. The port areas are monitored by recording CCTV surveillance and regular guarding

Approach: The main approach channel is an 8 nautical mile long buoyed and lighted channel authorised for a draft of 9 m leading NE and N to the deep harbour. There is a turning basin 270 m in dia in the harbour waters

Pilotage: Compulsory from Vaasa pilotage area, Tel: +358 (0) 20754 6153, Fax: +358 (0) 20754 6163, Email: pilotorder.west@finnpilot.fi. Pilot order form on www.pilotorder.fi

Traffic: 2007, 1 801 746 t of cargo handled

Maximum Vessel Dimensions: 30 000 dwt, 185 m loa, 9 m draught

Principal Imports and Exports: Imports: Caustic soda, Pulpwood. Exports: Bulk products, Pulp, Sawn timber.

Working Hours: 0730-1630

Accommodation:

Name	Length (m)	Depth (m)	Remarks
Kaskinen			See [1] below
General Cargo Berths (LP1-LP5)	500	9	Five berths
Ro/ro Berth (LP6)	160	8	
Bulk Berth (LP7)	165	9	
Ro-ro/Liquid Berth (LP8)	125	9	

[1]*Kaskinen:* Sheltered from all winds. Vessels can enter day and night, there being four lighthouses

Storage: Warehouse capacity: general cargo 38 000 m2, bulk 10 000 m2, chemicals & oil 49 000 m3

Mechanical Handling Equipment:

Location	Type	Capacity (t)	Qty
Kaskinen	Mobile Cranes	100	1
Kaskinen	Mobile Cranes	110	2
Kaskinen	Mobile Cranes	65	1
Kaskinen	Mobile Cranes	90	1
Kaskinen	Forklifts	3–16	20

Bunkering: Baltic Bunkering Ltd, Torggatan 10A, Mariehamn, Aland Islands, *Tel:* +358 18 143 00, *Fax:* +358 18 145 00, *Email:* info@balticbunkering.ax
Bunker Management Oy Ltd (BuMa), Meriituulentie 424, FI-48310 Kotka, Finland, *Tel:* +358 5 2201 011, *Fax:* +358 5 2201 012, *Website:* www.bunkerman.fi
Teboil Oy AB, Bulevardi 26, P O Box 102, FI-00120 Helsinki, Finland, *Tel:* +358 20 470 01, *Fax:* +358 20 4700 248, *Email:* bunkersales@teboil.fi, *Website:* www.teboil.fi

Towage: One tug of 1350 hp available

Repair & Maintenance: Minor repairs only

Shipping Agents: OY Silva Shipping AB, Syvasatama, FI-64260 Kaskinen, Finland, *Tel:* +358 207 801800, *Fax:* +358 207 801890, *Email:* agency@silvashipping.com, *Website:* www.silvashipping.com

Medical Facilities: Hospital at Narpio, 12 km

Airport: Vaasa, 80 km

Lloyd's Agent: Oy Lars Krogius A/B, Vilhonvuorenkatu 11 C 8, FI-00500 Helsinki, Finland, *Tel:* +358 9 4763 6300, *Fax:* +358 9 4763 6363, *Email:* finland@krogius.com, *Website:* www.krogius.com

KASKO

alternate name, see Kaskinen

KELLONIEMI

harbour area, see under Kuopio

KEMI

Lat 65° 44' N; Long 24° 34' E.

Admiralty Chart: 2303	**Admiralty Pilot:** 20
Time Zone: GMT +2 h	**UNCTAD Locode:** FI KEM

Principal Facilities:

P		Y	G	C	R	L	B		T	A

Authority: Port of Kemi Authority, Ajoksentie 748, FI-94900 Kemi, Finland, Tel: +358 16 215 1600, Fax: +358 16 215 1620, Email: portofkemi@kemi.fi, Website: www.portofkemi.fi

---

Key to Principal Facilities:—		
A=Airport	**C**=Containers	**G**=General Cargo
B=Bunkers	**D**=Dry Dock	**L**=Cruise

P=Petroleum	**R**=Ro/Ro	**Y**=Dry Bulk
Q=Other Liquid Bulk	**T**=Towage (where available from port)	

Officials: Port Director: Reijo Viitala, *Tel:* +358 16 215 1623, *Email:* reijo.viitala@kemi.fi.
Project Manager: Hannu Tikkala, *Email:* hannu.tikkala@kemi.fi.

Port Security: ISPS compliant

Approach: Depth in entrance channel is 10 m

Pilotage: Compulsory from Bay of Bothnia pilotage area, Tel: +358 (0) 20754 6153, Fax: +358 (0) 20754 6163, Email: pilotorder.west@finnpilot.fi. Pilot order form on www.pilotorder.fi

Traffic: 2007, 652 vessels, 3 032 244 t of cargo handled, 10 048 TEU's

Maximum Vessel Dimensions: 220 m loa, 10 m draught

Principal Imports and Exports: Imports: Filings, Oil products, Pulp logs, Wood-chips. Exports: Dry pulp, Linerboard, Paper, Sawn wood.

Working Hours: Monday to Friday 0600-1430, 1430-2230. Saturday 0700-1530

Accommodation:

Name	Length (m)	Depth (m)	Remarks
Ajos Harbour			See [1] below
Pier 1 (SE side)	160	10	30 m wide ro/ro ramp available
Pier 1 (NW side)	190	6.7–7.7	
Pier 2	283	8.7	26 m wide ro/ro ramp available
Pier 3	186	10	Two-level ro/ro ramp
Pier 4	186	10	31 m wide ro/ro ramp available

[1]*Ajos Harbour:* Tanker facilities: One oil berth; length no limit, 10 m depth; night berthing possible; water and bunkers available. Discharging can be effected by two pipes of 30.48 cm each and one pipe of 10.16 cm for emptying the bigger pipes

Storage: Paved container handling area of 120 000 m2. Two warehouses totalling 23 000 m2

Mechanical Handling Equipment:

Location	Type	Capacity (t)	Qty	Remarks
Kemi	Mobile Cranes	25	3	
Kemi	Container Cranes	60	1	serves Piers 3 and 4

Bunkering: Bunker oil available by tank lorries or by pipeline at oil pier
Baltic Bunkering Ltd, Torggatan 10A, Mariehamn, Aland Islands, *Tel:* +358 18 143 00, *Fax:* +358 18 145 00, *Email:* info@balticbunkering.ax
Bunker Management Oy Ltd (BuMa), Merituulentie 424, FI-48310 Kotka, Finland, *Tel:* +358 5 2201 011, *Fax:* +358 5 2201 012, *Website:* www.bunkerman.fi
ExxonMobil Marine Fuels, Mailpoint 31, ExxonMobil House, Ermyn Way, Leatherhead, Surrey KT22 8UX, United Kingdom, *Tel:* +44 1372 222 000, *Fax:* +44 1372 223 922, *Email:* marine.fuels@exxonmobil.com, *Website:* www.exxonmobil.com – *Grades:* MGO – *Delivery Mode:* truck
Teboil Oy AB, Bulevardi 26, P O Box 102, FI-00120 Helsinki, Finland, *Tel:* +358 20 470 01, *Fax:* +358 20 4700 248, *Email:* bunkersales@teboil.fi, *Website:* www.teboil.fi

Waste Reception Facilities: Waste points on every quay

Towage: By agreement

Shipping Agents: Kemi Shipping Oy, Ajoksentie 708, P O Box 535, FI-94101 Kemi, Finland, *Tel:* +358 207 428200, *Fax:* +358 207 428211, *Email:* agency.kemi@kemishipping.fi, *Website:* www.kemishipping.fi

Stevedoring Companies: Kemi Shipping Oy, Ajoksentie 708, P O Box 535, FI-94101 Kemi, Finland, *Tel:* +358 207 428200, *Fax:* +358 207 428211, *Email:* agency.kemi@kemishipping.fi, *Website:* www.kemishipping.fi

Medical Facilities: Hospital in Kemi

Airport: Kemi Airport, 15 km

Railway: Railway Station in Kemi City, 10 km

Lloyd's Agent: Oy Lars Krogius A/B, Vilhonvuorenkatu 11 C 8, FI-00500 Helsinki, Finland, *Tel:* +358 9 4763 6300, *Fax:* +358 9 4763 6363, *Email:* finland@krogius.com, *Website:* www.krogius.com

KILPILAHTI

alternate name, see Skoldvik

KOKKOLA

Lat 63° 50' N; Long 23° 8' E.

Admiralty Chart: 3062	**Admiralty Pilot:** 20
Time Zone: GMT +2 h	**UNCTAD Locode:** FI KOK

Principal Facilities:

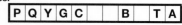

P	Q	Y	G	C			B		T	A

Authority: Port of Kokkola, Satamakatu 53, FI-67900 Kokkola, Finland, *Tel:* +358 6 824 2400, *Fax:* +358 6 824 2444, *Email:* satama@kokkola.fi, *Website:* www.port.of.kokkola.fi

Officials: Port Director: Torbjorn Witting, *Tel:* +358 6 824 2411, *Email:* torbjorn.witting@kokkola.fi.
Traffic Manager: Carita Ronnqvist, *Tel:* +358 6 824 2412, *Email:* carita.ronnqvist@kokkola.fi.

Port Security: The port is ISPS compliant. A crew list, passenger list and a list of expected visitors has to be given to the agent 24 h in advance or at latest on arrival. Advanced notification has to be given 24 h before IMDG-goods are brought into the port. When police, ambulance or fire brigade is needed contact phone number 112

Documentation: Crew list, stores list, ship's documents, manifest, bill of lading

Approach: The Yxpila harbour is approached from the NW, through a 200 m wide channel authorized for a draught of 13 m to the deep harbour, goes on as a channel with max authorized draught of 9.5 m to the general port and max draught of 8.3 m to the All Weather Terminal

Anchorage: Anchorage may be obtained 1 mile N of the breakwater in depth of 10-14 m

Pilotage: Compulsory from Kokkola pilotage area, Tel: +358 (0) 20754 6153, Fax: +358 (0) 20754 6163, Email: pilotorder.west@finnpilot.fi. Pilot order form on www.pilotorder.fi. Pilots board approx 3.5 nautical miles NNW of Tankar lighthouse

Radio Frequency: VHF Channel 16

Weather: Sometimes heavy seas by NW winds. Ice occurs between January and April and during this time icebreakers will assist only vessels with an ice class

Tides: Non-tidal

Traffic: 2008, Approx 5 600 000 t of cargo handled

Maximum Vessel Dimensions: 300 m loa, 13 m draught

Principal Imports and Exports: Imports: Alumina, Anhydrous ammonia, Containerised cargo, Limestone, Liquid chemicals, Oil, Zinc concentrate. Exports: Containerised cargo, Fertilizers, Iron ore, Iron ore pellets, Liquid chemicals, Phosphoric acid, Pyrites, Sawn timber, Zinc.

Working Hours: Municipal Harbour, Monday to Friday 0700-2400 in two shifts. Saturday 0700-1530

Accommodation:

Name	Length (m)	Draught (m)	Remarks
Kokkola-Ykspihlaja			See [1] below
Deep Quay	605	11–13	
Shore Quay (S side)	323	9.5	
All Weather Terminal (AWT)		8.3	Length 122 m basin + 124 m outside, max width 25 m, max height foremast 23.5 m
Boliden Quay	100	9.5	Discharging belt for zinc concentrate
Silverstone Quay	160	9.5	
Packhouse Quay	126	4	
Oil Quay	83	9.5	Used by vessels up to 200 m loa carrying sulphuric acid
Oil Quay	140	9.5	

[1]*Kokkola-Ykspihlaja:* The harbour is safe from all winds and open all year round. Ice class restrictions apply in Winter

Storage:

Location	Covered (m²)	Sheds / Warehouses
Kokkola	72114	13

Mechanical Handling Equipment:

Location	Type	Capacity (t)	Qty
Kokkola-Ykspihlaja	Mobile Cranes	6–60	1
Deep Quay	Shore Cranes	40	4
Shore Quay (S side)	Shore Cranes	8	2
All Weather Terminal (AWT)	Mult-purp. Cranes	50	1
Boliden Quay	Shore Cranes	10	1
Silverstone Quay	Shore Cranes	8	1

Cargo Worked: 5000 t/shift of bulk cargo, 2500 m3/shift of sawn timber

Bunkering: Baltic Bunkering Ltd, Torggatan 10A, Mariehamn, Aland Islands, *Tel:* +358 18 143 00, *Fax:* +358 18 145 00, *Email:* info@balticbunkering.ax
Bunker Management Oy Ltd (BuMa), Merituulentie 424, FI-48310 Kotka, Finland, *Tel:* +358 5 2201 011, *Fax:* +358 5 2201 012, *Website:* www.bunkerman.fi
ExxonMobil Marine Fuels, Mailpoint 31, ExxonMobil House, Ermyn Way, Leatherhead, Surrey KT22 8UX, United Kingdom, *Tel:* +44 1372 222 000, *Fax:* +44 1372 223 922, *Email:* marine.fuels@exxonmobil.com, *Website:* www.exxonmobil.com – *Grades:* MGO – *Delivery Mode:* truck
Shell Oy AB, Ulappasaarentie 4, FI-00980 Helsinki, Finland – *Delivery Mode:* truck
ST1 Oy, ST1 OY, P O Box 37, Purotie, FI-02211 Helsinki, Finland, *Tel:* +358 10 557 11, *Fax:* +358 9 8030 004, *Email:* matti.pentti@st1.fi, *Website:* www.st1.fi
Teboil Oy AB, Bulevardi 26, P O Box 102, FI-00120 Helsinki, Finland, *Tel:* +358 20 470 01, *Fax:* +358 20 4700 248, *Email:* bunkersales@teboil.fi, *Website:* www.teboil.fi – *Delivery Mode:* truck

Waste Reception Facilities: Garbage containers alongside, sludge removed by truck

Towage: Two tugs available of 4000 hp and 1400 hp from Yxpila Hinaus-Bogsering Oy Ab

Repair & Maintenance: Minor repairs available

Stevedoring Companies: O/Y M. Rauanheimo A/B, P O Box 254, 67101 Kokkola, Finland, *Tel:* +358 6 826 5300, *Fax:* +358 6 826 5320, *Email:* mrauanheimo@mrauanheimo.fi, *Website:* www.mrauanheimo.fi

Medical Facilities: Hospital in Kokkola, 4 km

Airport: Kronoby Airport, 19 km

Railway: Connections to the port

Development: Rail wagon tippler terminal inaugurated in June 2008, tips 15-18 railwagons/h. New 32 ha port area under developement

Lloyd's Agent: Oy Lars Krogius A/B, Vilhonvuorenkatu 11 C 8, FI-00500 Helsinki, Finland, *Tel:* +358 9 4763 6300, *Fax:* +358 9 4763 6363, *Email:* finland@krogius.com, *Website:* www.krogius.com

KOSULANNIEMI

harbour area, see under Varkaus

KOTKA

Lat 60° 27' N; Long 26° 56' E.

Admiralty Chart: 1090
Admiralty Pilot: 20
Time Zone: GMT +2 h
UNCTAD Locode: FI KTK

Principal Facilities:

P	Q	Y	G	C	R		B	D	T	

Authority: Port of Kotka Ltd, Laivurinkatu 7, FI-48100 Kotka, Finland, *Tel:* +358 5 234 4280, *Fax:* +358 5 218 1375, *Email:* office@portofkotka.fi, *Website:* www.portofkotka.fi

Officials: Managing Director: Kimmo Naski, *Tel:* +358 5 234 4281, *Email:* kimmo.naski@portofkotka.fi.
Technical Director: Riitta Kajatkari, *Tel:* +358 5 234 4390, *Email:* riitta.kajatkari@portofkotka.fi.
Marketing Manager: Nanna Sirola-Myllyla, *Tel:* +358 5 234 4163, *Email:* nanna.sirola@portofkotka.fi.
Traffic Manager: Markku Koskinen, *Tel:* +358 5 234 4286, *Email:* markku.koskinen@portofkotka.fi.

Port Security: ISPS compliant

Approach: Fairway to port 15.3 m deep. Port open all year round with icebreakers assisting the movements of vessels during the winter months

Pilotage: Compulsory, *Tel:* +358 (0) 20754 6152, *Fax:* +358 (0) 20754 6162, *Email:* pilotorder.east@finnpilot.fi. Pilot order form on www.pilotorder.fi
Four boarding points:
a) vessels with a max draught of 10 m are advised to use the Orrengrund 10.0 m fairway and the Orrengrund pilot boards in pos 60° 15' N; 26° 26' E
b) vessels with a max draught of 15.3 m using the Mussala fairway: Kotkan Majakka pilot boards in pos 60° 07.5' N; 26° 30' E
c) vessels with a max draught of 7.3 m from/to east: Haapasaari pilot boards in pos 60° 15' N; 27° 15' E (closed during winter)
d) vessels approaching from eastwards may take a pilot at Santio in pos 60° 27' N; 27° 42' E

Radio Frequency: Kotka VTS on VHF Channel 67, Kotka Port Operations on VHF Channel 11

Traffic: 2007, 10 278 502 t of cargo handled, 570 880 TEU's

Maximum Vessel Dimensions: 120 000 dwt, 15.3 m d, 300 m loa

Principal Imports and Exports: Imports: Chalk, China clay, Coal, General cargo, Wood. Exports: General cargo, Paper, Pulp, Sawn timber.

Working Hours: Normal working hours 0600-2200. Sat 0600-1100

Accommodation:

Name	Length (m)	Draught (m)	Remarks
Kotka			
City Terminal	962	7.7–10	Eight berths handling lo/lo and ro/ro cargo
Hietanen South	360	8.5	Three berths handling bulk cargo
Hietanen	1033	7.9–10	Six berths handling ro/ro cargo
Sunila Quay	400	6–7.9	Four berths handling bulk cargo
Kotka Container Terminal (Mussalo Area)	1436	10–12	Eight berths
Dry Bulk Terminal (Mussalo Area)	600	13.5–15.3	Four berths

Name	Length (m)	Draught (m)	Remarks
Liquid Bulk Terminal (Mussalo Area)		10–13.5	Two berths. Vopak Terminal with 34 tanks totaling 125 100 m3

Mechanical Handling Equipment:

Location	Type	Capacity (t)	Qty
City Terminal	Mult-purp. Cranes	60	1
Hietanen	Mult-purp. Cranes	40	1
Kotka Container Terminal (Mussalo Area)	Mobile Cranes		1
Kotka Container Terminal (Mussalo Area)	Container Cranes	30–40	7
Dry Bulk Terminal (Mussalo Area)	Mult-purp. Cranes	40	3
Dry Bulk Terminal (Mussalo Area)	Mult-purp. Cranes	8	1

Cargo Worked: Approx 26 000 t/day

Bunkering: Bunker Management Oy Ltd (BuMa), Merituulentie 424, FI-48310 Kotka, Finland, *Tel:* +358 5 2201 011, *Fax:* +358 5 2201 012, *Website:* www.bunkerman.fi
Baltic Bunkering Ltd, Torggatan 10A, Mariehamn, Aland Islands, *Tel:* +358 18 143 00, *Fax:* +358 18 145 00, *Email:* info@balticbunkering.ax
Bunker Management Oy Ltd (BuMa), Merituulentie 424, FI-48310 Kotka, Finland, *Tel:* +358 5 2201 011, *Fax:* +358 5 2201 012, *Website:* www.bunkerman.fi
ExxonMobil Marine Fuels, Mailpoint 31, ExxonMobil House, Ermyn Way, Leatherhead, Surrey KT22 8UX, United Kingdom, *Tel:* +44 1372 222 000, *Fax:* +44 1372 223 922, *Email:* marine.fuels@exxonmobil.com, *Website:* www.exxonmobil.com – *Grades:* MGO – *Notice:* 48 hours – *Delivery Mode:* truck
ST1 Oy, ST1 OY, P O Box 37, Purotie, FI-02211 Helsinki, Finland, *Tel:* +358 10 557 11, *Fax:* +358 9 8030 004, *Email:* matti.pentti@st1.fi, *Website:* www.st1.fi
Teboil Oy AB, Bulevardi 26, P O Box 102, FI-00120 Helsinki, Finland, *Tel:* +358 20 470 01, *Fax:* +358 20 4700 248, *Email:* bunkersales@teboil.fi, *Website:* www.teboil.fi

Waste Reception Facilities: Garbage containers on quays

Towage: Three tugs available

Ship Chandlers: Allotrans OY Ltd, Takojantie 18, FI-48220 Kotka, Finland, *Tel:* +358 5 228 4470, *Fax:* +358 5 228 4471, *Email:* info@allotrans.fi, *Website:* www.allotrans.fi
Oy Shipstores Nyman & Co Ltd., Runeberginkatu 13A, FIN-48200 Kotka, Finland, *Tel:* +358 5 212949, *Fax:* +358 5 212320, *Email:* office@shipstores-nyman.fi, *Website:* www.shipstores-nyman.fi

Shipping Agents: C & C Port Agency Finland Oy Ltd, Kirkkokatu 8A, FIN-48100 Kotka, Finland, *Tel:* +358 5 230 2270, *Fax:* +358 5 230 2279, *Email:* kotka@portagency.fi, *Website:* www.portagency.fi
Dahlbergs Agency Steveco Oy, Ruukinkatu 13, P O Box 44, FI-48101 Kotka, Finland, *Tel:* +358 5 232 3777, *Fax:* +358 5 232 3360, *Email:* agency.kotka@johndahlberg.fi, *Website:* www.steveco.fi
John Nurminen Maritime Oy, Merituulentie 424, P O Box 59, FI-48310 Kotka, Finland, *Fax:* +358 5 218 2055, *Email:* kotka.agency@johnnurminen.com, *Website:* www.johnnurminen.com
Oy Aug. Ljungqvist Ab, Kymenlaaksonkatu 2, FI-48100 Kotka, Finland, *Tel:* +358 5 230 8800, *Fax:* +358 5 218 4835, *Email:* kotka@alj.fi, *Website:* www.alj.fi
Oy Saimaa Lines Maritime Ltd, Merituulentie 424, P O Box 123, 48101 Kotka, Finland, *Tel:* +358 5 210 9240, *Fax:* +358 5 210 9240, *Email:* agency@saimaalinesmaritime.fi, *Website:* www.saimaalinesmaritime.fi
Stella Corona Oy Ltd, Merituulentie 424, 4th Floor, P O Box 264, FI-48101 Kotka, Finland, *Tel:* +358 5 210 8950, *Fax:* +358 5 210 8901, *Email:* transito@stellacorona.fi, *Website:* www.stellacompanygroup.com

Stevedoring Companies: GT-Stevedores Ltd Oy, Koulukatu 12, 48100 Kotka, Finland, *Tel:* +358 5 218 1166, *Fax:* +358 5 218 3113
RP Kuljetustekniikka Oy, Keltakalliontie 1, FIN-48770 Kotka, Finland, *Tel:* +358 5 210 8000, *Fax:* +358 5 210 8030, *Email:* sales@rpgroup.fi, *Website:* www.rpgroup.fi
Stella Stevedorica Oy Ltd, Merituulentie 424, 4th Floor, P O Box 264, FIN-48101 Kotka, Finland, *Tel:* +358 5 210 8900, *Fax:* +358 5 210 8901, *Email:* sales@stellastevedorica.com, *Website:* www.stellacompanygroup.com
Steveco Oy, Kirkkokatu 1, P O Box 44, FI-48101 Kotka, Finland, *Tel:* +358 5 23231, *Fax:* +358 5 232 3205, *Email:* marketing@steveco.fi, *Website:* www.steveco.fi

Surveyors: Saybolt Italia S.r.l., Kotka, Finland, *Tel:* +358 5 731 1311, *Fax:* +358 5 431 1350, *Website:* www.saybolt.com
Societe Generale de Surveillance (SGS), SGS Inspection Services OY, Kotka, Finland, *Tel:* +358 5 345 3355, *Fax:* +358 5 345 3366, *Website:* www.sgs.com
Oy Transitocontrol Ltd, Kotka, Finland, *Tel:* +358 5 218 1220, *Fax:* +358 5 218 4260, *Email:* transitocontrol@kolumbus.fi

Medical Facilities: Kymenlaakso Central Hospital, *Tel:* (5) 220 5111

Airport: Helsinki-Vantaa, 140 km

Railway: 1 km from Central Port

Lloyd's Agent: Oy Lars Krogius A/B, Vilhonvuorenkatu 11 C 8, FI-00500 Helsinki, Finland, *Tel:* +358 9 4763 6300, *Fax:* +358 9 4763 6363, *Email:* finland@krogius.com, *Website:* www.krogius.com

KOVERHAR

Lat 59° 52' N; Long 23° 13' E.

Admiralty Chart: 2241
Admiralty Pilot: 20
Time Zone: GMT +2 h
UNCTAD Locode: FI KVH

Key to Principal Facilities:—

A=Airport	**C**=Containers	**G**=General Cargo
B=Bunkers	**D**=Dry Dock	**L**=Cruise

P=Petroleum	**R**=Ro/Ro	**Y**=Dry Bulk
Q=Other Liquid Bulk	**T**=Towage (where available from port)	

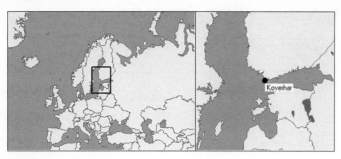

Principal Facilities:

	Y	G		B	T	

Authority: Ovako Wire Oy Ab, Koverharvagen 303, FI-10820 Lappvik, Finland, *Tel:* +358 19 221 4300, *Fax:* +358 19 221 4150, *Email:* info@ovako.com, *Website:* www.ovako.com

Port Security: ISPS compliant. PFSO: Timo Penttila, Email: timo.penttila@ovako.com

Pre-Arrival Information: ETA message required 72 h, 48 h, 24 h and 12 h prior to arrival, Fax: +358 19 244 3121, Email: agency@koverharshipping.fi

Approach: The main approach channel is 16 miles long and is authorized for a draft of 12 m as far as Koverhar roads, thence 9 m draft to the berths. Main approach channel is entered at the Ajax Light Buoy and is marked for night navigation

Anchorage: Good anchorage available 7 cables E of the harbour in depths of 14-20 m

Pilotage: Compulsory, Fax: +358 20 754 6161, Email: pilotorder.south@finnpilot.fi. Pilot boarding positions:
Hanko Inner: in pos 59° 46.87' N; 23° 00.31' E
Hanko Outer: in pos 59° 42.18' N; 23° 04.90' E

Maximum Vessel Dimensions: 190 m loa, 40 000 dwt, 25 m beam, 9 m draft

Principal Imports and Exports: Imports: Coke, Limestone, Pellets. Exports: Billets.

Working Hours: Monday to Friday 0700-2300

Accommodation:

Name	Depth (m)	Remarks
Koverhar		
Quays	9	Two quays

Mechanical Handling Equipment:

Location	Type	Capacity (t)	Qty	Remarks
Koverhar	Mult-purp. Cranes	13	3	Mobile cranes can be arranged

Cargo Worked: Loading: billets 200 t/h. Discharging: coke 500 t/h, pellets 600 t/h, limestone 600 t/h

Bunkering: Available by road truck
Baltic Bunkering Ltd, Torggatan 10A, Mariehamn, Aland Islands, *Tel:* +358 18 143 00, *Fax:* +358 18 145 00, *Email:* info@balticbunkering.ax
Bunker Management Oy Ltd (BuMa), Merituulentie 424, FI-48310 Kotka, Finland, *Tel:* +358 5 2201 011, *Fax:* +358 5 2201 012, *Website:* www.bunkerman.fi
Shell Oy AB, Ulappasaarentie 4, FI-00980 Helsinki, Finland
ST1 Oy, ST1 OY, P O Box 37, Purotie, FI-02211 Helsinki, Finland, *Tel:* +358 10 557 11, *Fax:* +358 9 8030 004, *Email:* matti.pentti@st1.fi, *Website:* www.st1.fi
Teboil Oy AB, Bulevardi 26, P O Box 102, FI-00120 Helsinki, Finland, *Tel:* +358 20 470 01, *Fax:* +358 20 4700 248, *Email:* bunkersales@teboil.fi, *Website:* www.teboil.fi

Towage: Can be arranged from Hanko

Repair & Maintenance: Minor repairs can be effected

Shipping Agents: Koverhar Shipping O/Y A/B, Koverharvagen 303, FI-10820 Lappvik, Finland, *Tel:* +358 19 221 4280, *Fax:* +358 19 244 3121, *Email:* agency@koverharshipping.fi, *Website:* www.koverharshipping.fi

Medical Facilities: Hospital and doctors available in the town

Airport: Helsinki International, 135 km, Turku, 120 km

Railway: Lappvik, 3 km

Lloyd's Agent: Oy Lars Krogius A/B, Vilhonvuorenkatu 11 C 8, FI-00500 Helsinki, Finland, *Tel:* +358 9 4763 6300, *Fax:* +358 9 4763 6363, *Email:* finland@krogius.com, *Website:* www.krogius.com

KRISTIINANKAUPUNKI

Lat 62° 16' N; Long 21° 19' E.

Admiralty Chart: 2303	**Admiralty Pilot:** 20
Time Zone: GMT +2 h	**UNCTAD Locode:** FI KRS

Principal Facilities:

P		Y	G	R			T	

Authority: Port of Kristiinankaupunki, P O Box 13, FI-64120 Kristiinankaupunki, Finland, *Tel:* +358 6 221 6200, *Fax:* +358 6 221 6285, *Email:* sven.soderlund@krs.fi, *Website:* www.krs.fi

Officials: Port Manager: Sven Soderlund.

Port Security: ISPS compliant

Approach: Approach at Haerkmeri. Depending on the ice situation the port closes in Dec/Jan and reopens at the end of April

Anchorage: Well sheltered, good anchorage with mud bottom

Pilotage: Compulsory from Vaasa pilotage area, Tel: +358 (0) 20754 6153, Fax: +358 (0) 20754 6163, Email: pilotorder.west@finnpilot.fi. Pilot order form on www.pilotorder.fi

Radio Frequency: Town equipped with UKW Station, Channel 27

Traffic: 2007, 462 097 t of cargo handled

Maximum Vessel Dimensions: Max loa 130 m, max d 5.6 m. At Coal harbour max loa approx 230 m, max d 12 m

Principal Imports and Exports: Imports: Coal, Oil. Exports: Peat moss, Sawn timber.

Working Hours: 0700-1600. Second shift possible. Non-stop discharging possible

Accommodation:

Name	Length (m)	Depth (m)	Draught (m)	Remarks
Kristinestad				See [1] below
Stone Quay	250		5.6	
Wooden Quay	75		4.57	
Coal Harbour		12		
Oil Harbour		10		See [2] below
Private Wharves				Pohjolan Voima O/Y Power Plant

[1]*Kristinestad:* Depth at entrance and in harbour 5.6 m. Fairway dredged to 6.2 m, and lights installed
[2]*Oil Harbour:* Accommodating tankers of 23 000 dwt. Discharge cap with 10" pipeline at 2500 t/h. Fresh water supply for tankers from shore installation at 30 t/h

Storage:

Location	Open (m²)	Covered (m²)
Kristiinankaupunki	305000	1500

Mechanical Handling Equipment:

Location	Type	Capacity (t)	Qty
Kristiinankaupunki	Mobile Cranes	70	3

Cargo Worked: Loading rates: sawn goods 2100 m3/shift, peat moss in bulk 6500 m3/shift

Waste Reception Facilities: Available

Towage: Available

Stevedoring Companies: AB Kristinestads Stevedoring OY, Satama, FIN-64100 Kristiinankaupunki, Finland, *Tel:* +358 6 221 1196, *Fax:* +358 6 221 1331, *Email:* infokrs@kristinestadsstevedoring.fi, *Website:* www.kristinestadsstevedoring.fi

Medical Facilities: Hospital and doctors

Lloyd's Agent: Oy Lars Krogius A/B, Vilhonvuorenkatu 11 C 8, FI-00500 Helsinki, Finland, *Tel:* +358 9 4763 6300, *Fax:* +358 9 4763 6363, *Email:* finland@krogius.com, *Website:* www.krogius.com

KRISTINESTAD

harbour area, see under Kristiinankaupunki

KUMPUSALMI

harbour area, see under Kuopio

KUOPIO

Lat 62° 51' N; Long 27° 30' E.

Admiralty Chart: -	**Admiralty Pilot:** 20
Time Zone: GMT +2 h	**UNCTAD Locode:** FI KUO

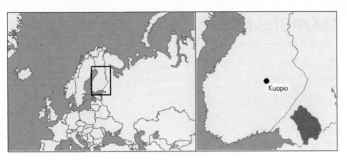

Principal Facilities:

P		Y	G					A

Authority: Harbour Office of Kuopio, Matkustajasatama, FI-70100 Kuopio, Finland, *Tel:* +358 17 185192, *Fax:* +358 17 185196, *Email:* sami.lehtonen@kuopio.fi

Officials: Port Manager: Sami Lehtonen, *Tel:* +358 17 185191.

Port Security: ISPS compliant

Pilotage: Governmental pilot to harbour

Radio Frequency: VHF Channel 16

Traffic: 2007, 145 423 t of cargo handled

Maximum Vessel Dimensions: 82.5 m loa, 12.8 m width, 4.35 m draught

Principal Imports and Exports: Imports: Raw timber, Salt. Exports: Grain, Sawn timber.

Working Hours: 24 h/day

Accommodation:

Name	Draught (m)	Remarks
Kuopio		
Kumpusalmi	4.35	See [1] below
Kelloniemi	4.35	See [2] below

[1]*Kumpusalmi:* Raw & sawn timber, salt and gravel. Room in harbour for three dry cargo vessels. Railway to harbour

[2]*Kelloniemi:* Oil harbour operated by Esso O/Y, Kelloniemi, FIN-70460 Kuopio, Tel: +358 17 364 3393
Room for one oil tanker, provided with discharge equipment

Storage: Gravel surfaced storage area of 33 661 m2. Asphalt surfaced storage area of 18 657 m2. Terminal storage of 2422 m2. Sawn timber shed of 614 m2

Mechanical Handling Equipment:

Location	Type
Kuopio	Mobile Cranes

Medical Facilities: Nearest hospital, 2 km

Airport: Rissala, 30 km

Railway: Kuopio, 4 km

Lloyd's Agent: Oy Lars Krogius A/B, Vilhonvuorenkatu 11 C 8, FI-00500 Helsinki, Finland, *Tel:* +358 9 4763 6300, *Fax:* +358 9 4763 6363, *Email:* finland@krogius.com, *Website:* www.krogius.com

LAAJASALO OIL HARBOUR

harbour area, see under Helsinki

LAKULAHTI

harbour area, see under Hamina

LAPPEENRANTA

alternate name, see Mustola

LOVIISA

Lat 60° 24' N; Long 26° 15' E.

Admiralty Chart: 1088	**Admiralty Pilot:** 20
Time Zone: GMT +2 h	**UNCTAD Locode:** FI LOV

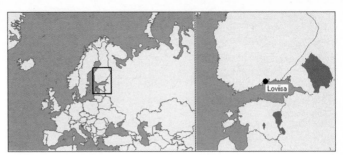

Principal Facilities:

Q	Y	G	C	R		B		T	A

Authority: Port of Loviisa, Harbour Office, FIN-07910 Valkom, Finland, *Tel:* +358 19 555731, *Fax:* +358 19 515055, *Email:* aki.marjasvaara@loviisa.fi, *Website:* www.loviisa.fi

Officials: Port Manager: Aki Marjasvaara.

Port Security: ISPS compliant

Approach: The buoyed and lighted main channel which leads from Orrengrund to the port of Loviisa is authorised for a draft of 8.5 m

Anchorage: The inner harbour affords good shelter and has depths between 4.0 to 5.0 m. The outer harbour has good holding ground in anchorages with depths of 8.5 to 13 m

Pilotage: Compulsory. Nearest pilot station, Orrengrund

Radio Frequency: VHF Channels 12 and 13

Traffic: 2007, 1 273 368 t of cargo handled

Maximum Vessel Dimensions: 8.5 m max draft

Principal Imports and Exports: Imports: Clay, Coal, Dolomite, Soda. Exports: General cargo, Grain, Paper, Plywood, Poles, Sawn wood.

Working Hours: Monday to Friday 0700-1500, 1500-2300. Saturday 0700-1510

Accommodation:

Name	Remarks
Loviisa	See [1] below

[1]*Loviisa:* Depth at entrance 8.5 m (no tide). Four quays, each with 7.3 m to 8.5 m alongside, total length of quays 755 m. Also, a small harbour, depth at entrance 4.0 m
Bulk facilities: Specialised facilities include a coal import quay 141 m long, depth alongside 8.5 m

Storage:

Location	Covered (m²)	Grain (t)
Loviisa	30674	60000

Mechanical Handling Equipment:

Location	Type	Capacity (t)	Qty
Loviisa	Mult-purp. Cranes	28	
Loviisa	Mobile Cranes		4
Loviisa	Forklifts	28	23

Bunkering: Available by road tanker

Waste Reception Facilities: Slop reception facilities available and collected by road tanker. Garbage disposal available but not compulsory. All waste can be received

Towage: Harbour tug available of 1260 hp

Repair & Maintenance: Minor repairs can be undertaken by local workshops

Shipping Agents: C & C Port Agency Finland Oy Ltd, Satamatalo, FIN-07910 Valkom, Finland, *Tel:* +358 19 515870, *Fax:* +358 19 515880, *Email:* loviisa@portagency.fi, *Website:* www.portagency.fi
Oy Aug. Ljungqvist Ab, Satamatalo, Valkon Satama, FIN-07910 Valkom, Finland, *Tel:* +358 19 515134, *Fax:* +358 19 515350, *Email:* loviisa@alj.fi, *Website:* www.alj.fi

Stevedoring Companies: Federations Stevedore in Loviisa Oy Ab, P O Box 67, FIN-07901 Loviisa, Finland, *Tel:* +358 19 517220, *Fax:* +358 19 515350, *Email:* bo.nordman@nordfed.com, *Website:* www.nordfed.com

Surveyors: Sea Load Control Ltd, Port of Loviisa, Equppatapu 5, FI-07910 Loviisa, Finland, *Tel:* +358 19 515691, *Fax:* +358 19 535319, *Email:* esa.anttio@kolumbus.fi, *Website:* www.kolumbus.fi/sea.load.control

Medical Facilities: Hospital available, 7 km

Airport: Helsinki-Vantaa, 90 km

Lloyd's Agent: Oy Lars Krogius A/B, Vilhonvuorenkatu 11 C 8, FI-00500 Helsinki, Finland, *Tel:* +358 9 4763 6300, *Fax:* +358 9 4763 6363, *Email:* finland@krogius.com, *Website:* www.krogius.com

MANTYLUOTO

Lat 61° 35' N; Long 21° 29' E.

Admiralty Chart: 3415	**Admiralty Pilot:** 20
Time Zone: GMT +2 h	**UNCTAD Locode:** FI MTL

Key to Principal Facilities:—			
A=Airport	**C**=Containers	**G**=General Cargo	**P**=Petroleum	**R**=Ro/Ro	**Y**=Dry Bulk
B=Bunkers	**D**=Dry Dock	**L**=Cruise	**Q**=Other Liquid Bulk	**T**=Towage (where available from port)	

Principal Facilities:

P		Y	G	C	R		B		T	A	

Authority: Port of Pori Authority, Merisatamantie 13, FI-28880 Pori, Finland, *Tel:* +358 2 621 2600, *Fax:* +358 2 621 2630, *Email:* info.port@pori.fi, *Website:* www.pori.fi/port

Officials: Port Director: Jaakko Nirhamo, *Tel:* +358 2 621 2601, *Email:* jaakko.nirhamo@pori.fi.
Operations Manager: Kai Heinonen, *Tel:* +358 2 621 2616, *Email:* kai.heinonen@pori.fi.
Harbour Master: Pekka Friman, *Tel:* +358 2 621 2633, *Email:* pekka.friman@pori.fi.

Port Security: ISPS compliant

Approach: Draught limitations in channels: Mantyluoto 10.0 m, Tahkoluoto Deep-water Harbour 15.3 m, Tahkoluoto Bulk Harbour and Oil Harbour, both 10.0 m

Anchorage: Anchorage can be obtained about 4 miles W of Reposaari in depths ranging from 20 m to 30 m

Pilotage: Compulsory from Rauma Sea pilotage area, Tel: +358 (0) 20754 6153, Fax: +358 (0) 20754 6163, Email: pilotorder.west@finnpilot.fi. Pilot order form on www.pilotorder.fi

Radio Frequency: VHF Channels 16, 13 and 12

Tides: No tide, but seawater level varies between 0.6 m to 1.2 m depending on wind direction and force

Traffic: 2007, 5 645 019 t of cargo handled, 39 381 TEU's

Principal Imports and Exports: Imports: Coal, Concentrates, Ore. Exports: General cargo, Timber.

Working Hours: Monday to Friday 0700-2400. Saturday 0700-1530

Accommodation:

Name	Length (m)	Depth (m)	Remarks
Pori			See [1] below
Mantyluoto	2000	10	See [2] below
Reposaari (Rafso)	250	3.6	Trawler berths
Tahkoluoto			See [3] below

[1]*Pori:* The Port of Pori Authority serves the ports of Mantyluoto, Reposaari and Tahkoluoto
[2]*Mantyluoto:* The nearest harbour for West and Central Finland. Traffic throughout the year. Icebreaker available all winter. Specialises in sawn timber, container transport & heavy lift projects
[3]*Tahkoluoto:* Located in pos 61° 38' N; 21° 23' E at the N end of Reposaari. Two harbours for bulk cargoes
Bulk Harbour: Quay length of 145 m, max d 10 m
Deepwater Harbour: Quay length of 450 m and can accommodate vessels of 120 000 dwt and 15.3 m max d. There are three luffing cranes of 30-40 t cap, one continuous loader of 1500 t/h cap and 5km of conveyors for loading and unloading with 1500-2000 t/h cap. Rail link-up with National system
Oil harbour: 105 m long with max d of 10 m. Storage of 613 700 m3

Storage: Privately owned timber shed space of 30 500 m2

Location	Covered (m²)
Mantyluoto	110500

Mechanical Handling Equipment:

Location	Type	Capacity (t)	Qty
Mantyluoto	Mult-purp. Cranes	5–200	14
Mantyluoto	Forklifts	40	

Bunkering: Available by pipeline or by road tanker
Baltic Bunkering Ltd, Torggatan 10A, Mariehamn, Aland Islands, *Tel:* +358 18 143 00, *Fax:* +358 18 145 00, *Email:* info@balticbunkering.ax
Bunker Management Oy Ltd (BuMa), Merituulentie 424, FI-48310 Kotka, Finland, *Tel:* +358 5 2201 011, *Fax:* +358 5 2201 012, *Website:* www.bunkerman.fi
Shell Oy AB, Ulappasaarentie 4, FI-00980 Helsinki, Finland
ST1 Oy, ST1 OY, P O Box 37, Purotie, FI-02211 Helsinki, Finland, *Tel:* +358 10 557 11, *Fax:* +358 9 8030 004, *Email:* matti.pentti@st1.fi, *Website:* www.st1.fi
Teboil Oy AB, Bulevardi 26, P O Box 102, FI-00120 Helsinki, Finland, *Tel:* +358 20 470 01, *Fax:* +358 20 4700 248, *Email:* bunkersales@teboil.fi, *Website:* www.teboil.fi

Waste Reception Facilities: Ekokem Oy

Towage: Five tugs available of 200-3520 hp

Repair & Maintenance: Technip Offshore Finland Oy, Pori, Finland, *Tel:* +358 2 528 2411, *Fax:* +358 2 528 2419, *Email:* tof@technip.com, *Website:* www.technip.com Repair facilities

Medical Facilities: Hospital in city of Pori

Airport: Bjorneborg, 22 km

Lloyd's Agent: Oy Lars Krogius A/B, Vilhonvuorenkatu 11 C 8, FI-00500 Helsinki, Finland, *Tel:* +358 9 4763 6300, *Fax:* +358 9 4763 6363, *Email:* finland@krogius.com, *Website:* www.krogius.com

MARIEHAMN

Lat 60° 5' N; Long 19° 55' E.

Admiralty Chart: -	**Admiralty Pilot:** 20
Time Zone: GMT +2 h	**UNCTAD Locode:** AX MHQ

Principal Facilities:

P		Y	G		R	L	B	D	T	A	

Authority: Port of Mariehamn, P O Box 5, Mariehamn, Aland Islands, *Tel:* +358 18 5310, *Fax:* +358 18 531206, *Email:* info@mariehamn.aland.fi, *Website:* www.portofmariehamn.com

Officials: Port Director: Jan Sundstrom, *Tel:* +358 18 531470, *Email:* jan.sundstrom@mariehamn.aland.fi.

Port Security: ISPS compliant

Approach: Depth of entrance to W Harbour 8.2 m. No sand bars

Anchorage: Good anchorage for small vessels can be obtained N of Grano Island in depths ranging from 9 m to 18 m

Pilotage: Compulsory from Archipelago pilotage area, Tel: +358 (0) 20754 6153, Fax: +358 (0) 20754 6163, Email: pilotorder.west@finnpilot.fi. Pilot order form on www.pilotorder.fi

Radio Frequency: Mariehamn Port, VHF Channel 16 (calling), Channel 12 (working)

Maximum Vessel Dimensions: 7.6-8.2 m draft

Working Hours: 24 h/day

Accommodation: The city has two harbours, the East and West

Name	Length (m)	Depth (m)	Remarks
East Harbour			See [1] below
West Harbour			
Berths 1 & 2	250	7.6	Cruise vessels
Berth 3	205	7.7	Ro/ro facilities available
Berth 4	156	7.8	Ro/ro facilities available
Berth 5	140	7.7	Ro/ro facilities available
Berth 6	150	8.2	See [2] below
Klintkajen	30	5	Bulk, general & timber cargoes
Power Station		6.5	

[1]*East Harbour:* East Harbour now used for small boats only; depth at entrance 3.7 m
[2]*Berth 6:* Ro/ro faclities available, mooring bollard 46 m south of quay

Mechanical Handling Equipment:

Location	Type	Capacity (t)
Mariehamn	Mobile Cranes	75

Bunkering: Available by truck

Waste Reception Facilities: Garbage disposal available

Towage: Four tugs available of 250-1850 hp
Bror Husell Chartering AB Ltd, PB 148, Elverksgatan 10, Mariehamn, Aland Islands, *Tel:* +358 18 16766, *Fax:* +358 18 12786, *Email:* info@bhc.aland.fi, *Website:* www.bhc.aland.fi

Repair & Maintenance: Algots Varv AB (Algots Shipyard), Varvsvagen, Mariehamn, Aland Islands, *Tel:* +358 18 21122, *Fax:* +358 18 22882, *Email:* info@algotshipyard.com, *Website:* www.algotshipyard.com Dry dock of 130 m x 22 m x 5.5 m. One slipway of 70 m x 145 m, max cap 7000 t. Repair quays of 50 m with max draught 5.5 m

Ship Chandlers: ME Group Oy (ab Mathias Eriksson), Dalkarbyvagen 6, P O Box 63, Mariehamn, Aland Islands, *Tel:* +358 18 22122, *Fax:* +358 18 22771, *Email:* kjell.jansson@mathis.aland.fi, *Website:* www.megroup.fi

Shipping Agents: Mariehamn Shipping Agency, Alandsvagen 66B, Mariehamn, Aland Islands, *Tel:* +358 18 12981, *Email:* masag@aland.net

Medical Facilities: Hospital

Airport: Mariehamn Airport, 4 km

Lloyd's Agent: Oy Wikestrom & Krogius AB, Huolintakatu 3, FI-20200 Turku, Finland, *Tel:* +358 2 0721 8500, *Fax:* +358 2 0721 8540, *Email:* wike.tku@wikestrom.com, *Website:* www.wikestrom.com

MUSTOLA

Lat 61° 4' N; Long 28° 18' E.

Admiralty Chart: -	**Admiralty Pilot:** 20
Time Zone: GMT +2 h	**UNCTAD Locode:** FI MUS

Principal Facilities:

		Y	G	C				A

Authority: City of Lappeenranta Port Authority, Harbour Office, Kipparinkatu 1, FI-53100 Lappeenranta, Finland, *Tel:* +358 5 616 6073, *Fax:* +358 5 616 6075, *Email:* satamalaitos@lappeenranta.fi, *Website:* www.lappeenranta.fi/mustola

Officials: Port Director: Juha Willberg, *Tel:* +358 5 616 2004, *Email:* juha.willberg@lappeenranta.fi.
Harbour Master: Jukka Nikku, *Tel:* +358 5 616 2004, *Email:* jukka.nikku@lappeenranta.fi.

Radio Frequency: VHF Channel 11

Traffic: 2005, 163 vessels, 359 240 t of cargo handled

Maximum Vessel Dimensions: 82.5 m loa, 12.8 m beam, 4.35 m draft

Principal Imports and Exports: Imports: Coal, Gypsum, Process salt, Raw timber. Exports: Peat, Sawn goods, Woodpulp.

Working Hours: 0700-2300

Accommodation:

Name	Length (m)	Draught (m)	Remarks
Mustola			
Mustola	82	4.35	See [1] below

[1]*Mustola:* Located 1 km from Mustola Lock in pos 61° 03' 4" N; 28° 20' 0" E. Consists of 7 berths. Covered storage area of 68 000 m2 and uncovered area of 50 000 m2 with warehousing of 28 000 m2. The size of the free zone area of Mustola is 32 000 m2 and 16 500 m2 of it is covered. Within the free zone area there is a container yard of 15 ha

Mechanical Handling Equipment:

Location	Type	Capacity (t)	Qty
Mustola	Mobile Cranes	150	1

Stevedoring Companies: O/Y Saimaa Terminals A/B., P O Box 229, FI-53101 Lappeenranta, Finland, *Tel:* +358 20 743 2760, *Fax:* +358 20 743 2761, *Email:* tapio.silvennoinen@saimaaterminals.fi, *Website:* www.saimaaterminals.fi

Medical Facilities: Central hospital, 5 km

Airport: Lappeenranta, 7 km

Lloyd's Agent: Oy Lars Krogius A/B, Vilhonvuorenkatu 11 C 8, FI-00500 Helsinki, Finland, *Tel:* +358 9 4763 6300, *Fax:* +358 9 4763 6363, *Email:* finland@krogius.com, *Website:* www.krogius.com

NAANTALI

Lat 60° 28' N; Long 22° 1' E.

Admiralty Chart: 3436	**Admiralty Pilot:** 20
Time Zone: GMT +2 h	**UNCTAD Locode:** FI NLI

Principal Facilities:

P	Q	Y	G		R		B	D	T	A

Authority: Port of Naantali, Harbour Office, Satamatie 13, FI-21100 Naantali, Finland, *Tel:* +358 2 437 5511, *Fax:* +358 2 435 1727, *Email:* satama@naantali.fi, *Website:* www.naantali.fi

Officials: Port Director: Yrjo Vainiala, *Email:* yrjo.vainiala@naantali.fi.
Traffic Manager: Liisa Majuri, *Tel:* +358 2 437 5515, *Email:* liisa.majuri@naantali.fi.

Port Security: ISPS compliant

Documentation: Crew list, ship's stores declaration, crew effects declaration, passenger list, international tonnage certificate

Approach: Depths in channels: Uto-Naantali 13 m and 10 m, Nyhamn-Naantali 9 m, Isokari-Naantali 10 m, Hanko-Naantali 7.3 m

Pilotage: Compulsory. Pilot channel on VHF Channel 13. Pilot comes from Uto Pilot Station. Contact Archipelago Vessel Traffic Service, Tel: +358 204 486521, Fax: +358 204 486533, VHF Channel 71

Traffic: 2007, 2176 vessels, 8 503 064 t of cargo handled

Maximum Vessel Dimensions: 70 000 dwt, 13 m draught, 250 m loa

Principal Imports and Exports: Imports: Coal, Crude oil, Ferry Traffic, Grain. Exports: Ferry Traffic, Grain, Oil Products, Scrap.

Working Hours: Mon-Fri 0600-1530, 1530-2400. Sat 0700-1530. Harbour services 24 h/day

Accommodation:

Name	Depth (m)	Remarks
Naantali		See [1] below
Main Quay (Berths 15-17)	13	
Timber Quay (Berths 23-24)	8	
Sugar Quay (Berth 25)	4.5	
Car Ferry Piers (Berths 18-20)	6–9	
Lubricating Oil Pier (Berth 22)	6	
Luonnonmaa Harbour (Berths 30-31)	7.7	

[1]*Naantali:* Total length of quays is 1320 m including four ro/ro berths and five liquid berths
Bulk facilities: Grain and coal quay 370 m long, 13 m depth. Coal elevator, two 6 t cranes and two pneumatic grain elevators
Tanker facilities: Fortum O/Y No.1 5.7 m, No.2 10 m, No.3 13 m, Lub Oil/Ferry Pier 6 m

Storage: Open storage available close to piers. Covered storage of 5700 m2 (public) and 21 300 m2 (private). Silo's of 230 000 t

Mechanical Handling Equipment:

Location	Type	Capacity (t)	Qty
Naantali	Mult-purp. Cranes	6	2
Naantali	Mobile Cranes	200	

Cargo Worked: Per working day: coal 16 000 t max, grain 2400 t. Loading/unloading tankers 12 000-43 200/24 000-108 000 t/24 h. Timber about 1000 m3, stone in blocks about 2000 t

Bunkering: All grades available
Baltic Bunkering Ltd, Torggatan 10A, Mariehamn, Aland Islands, *Tel:* +358 18 143 00, *Fax:* +358 18 145 00, *Email:* info@balticbunkering.ax
Bunker Management Oy Ltd (BuMa), Merituulentie 424, FI-48310 Kotka, Finland, *Tel:* +358 5 2201 011, *Fax:* +358 5 2201 012, *Website:* www.bunkerman.fi
ExxonMobil Marine Fuels, Mailpoint 31, ExxonMobil House, Ermyn Way, Leatherhead, Surrey KT22 8UX, United Kingdom, *Tel:* +44 1372 222 000, *Fax:* +44 1372 223 922, *Email:* marine.fuels@exxonmobil.com, *Website:* www.exxonmobil.com – *Grades:* IFO30-380cSt; MGO; MDO – *Delivery Mode:* truck
Shell Oy AB, Ulappasaarentie 4, FI-00980 Helsinki, Finland
ST1 Oy, ST1 OY, P O Box 37, Purotie, FI-02211 Helsinki, Finland, *Tel:* +358 10 557 11, *Fax:* +358 9 8030 004, *Email:* matti.pentti@st1.fi, *Website:* www.st1.fi
Teboil Oy AB, Bulevardi 26, P O Box 102, FI-00120 Helsinki, Finland, *Tel:* +358 20 470 01, *Fax:* +358 20 4700 248, *Email:* bunkersales@teboil.fi, *Website:* www.teboil.fi

Towage: Harbour ice-breaker tug. Other tugs on application from Turku

Stevedoring Companies: Stevena Oy, Satamatie 13, FIN-21100 Naantali, Finland, *Tel:* +358 2 433 8300, *Fax:* +358 2 433 8340, *Email:* stevena.info@stevena.fi, *Website:* www.stevena.fi

Medical Facilities: Advise by radio prior to arrival if medical attendance is required

Airport: Turku, 20 km

Development: The fairway will be deepened up to 15.3 m in 2008-2009

Lloyd's Agent: Oy Wikestrom & Krogius AB, Huolintakatu 3, FI-20200 Turku, Finland, *Tel:* +358 2 0721 8500, *Fax:* +358 2 0721 8540, *Email:* wike.tku@wikestrom.com, *Website:* www.wikestrom.com

NYSTAD

alternate name, see Uusikaupunki

OULU

Lat 65° 0' N; Long 25° 28' E.

Admiralty Chart: 3062	**Admiralty Pilot:** 20
Time Zone: GMT +2 h	**UNCTAD Locode:** FI OUL

Key to Principal Facilities:—		
A=Airport	**C**=Containers	**G**=General Cargo
B=Bunkers	**D**=Dry Dock	**L**=Cruise

P=Petroleum	**R**=Ro/Ro **Y**=Dry Bulk
Q=Other Liquid Bulk	**T**=Towage (where available from port)

Principal Facilities:

| P | Q | Y | G | C | R | | B | D | T | A |

Authority: Port of Oulu Authority, P O Box 23, FI-90015 Oulu, Finland, *Tel:* +358 8 5584 2753, *Fax:* +358 8 5584 2799, *Email:* kari.himanen@ouka.fi, *Website:* www.ouluport.com

Officials: Port Director: Kari Himanen.
Traffic Manager: Kuisma Ekman, *Email:* kuisma.ekman@ouka.fi.

Port Security: ISPS compliant. 24 h duty port facility security / Traffic supervisors / Vessel Services, Tel. +358 (0)8 5584 2759, GSM +358 (0)44 703 2759, Email: satamavalvojat@ouka.fi. Consignments delivered to vessels, the sender/transporter of cargo must inform the vessel representative in advance of their arrival in the port area. Herman Andersson Oy, ships agency, Tel: +358 (0)8 3150 131, Email: agency@hermanandersson.fi. All superfluous traffic in the quay areas is forbidden. Only persons performing work duties are allowed passage in the quay area. For additional information on passage permits, security regulations and new arrangements, contact Traffic Manager Kuisma Ekman, PFSO, Tel: +358 (0)8 5584 2751, Email: kuisma.ekman@ouka.fi

Approach: Two channels, depths 10 m, lead to Oulu; one via Kemi and the other via Oulu Lighthouse

Anchorage: Good anchorage can be obtained in the roadstead

Pilotage: Compulsory from Bay of Bothnia pilotage area, Tel: +358 (0) 20754 6153, Fax: +358 (0) 20754 6163, Email: pilotorder.west@finnpilot.fi. Pilot order form on www.pilotorder.fi. VHF can no longer be used to submit pilotage requests

Radio Frequency: VHF Channels 13 and 16

Weather: www.fmi.fi/weather/local.html/kunta=Oulu, www.foreca.com/eng/weather/

Traffic: 2007, 562 vessels, 3 425 040 t of cargo handled, 32 119 TEU's

Maximum Vessel Dimensions: 50 000 dwt, 200 m loa, 10 m d

Principal Imports and Exports: Imports: Chemical industrial products, Forest products, Fuel oil. Exports: Bulk cargo, Chemical industrial products, Forest products.

Working Hours: 24 h/day

Accommodation:

Name	Length (m)	Draught (m)	Remarks
Oulu			
Toppila Harbour	450	6.1	See [1] below
Vihreasaari Harbour			See [2] below
Bulk berth	150	10	
Oil berth	72	10	
Nuottasaari Harbour			Raw materials for forest industry
Chem berth			See [3] below
Main quay	320	6.4	
Oritkari Harbour			See [4] below
Main quay	343	9	
North quay	170	10	

[1]*Toppila Harbour:* Used for discharging oil and cement. All commercial traffic is due to end and be replaced by a maritime residential area
[2]*Vihreasaari Harbour:* Used to discharge oil products and dry bulk cargoes
[3]*Chem berth:* One berth 162 m long with draught of 7.5 m and one berth 75 m long in min depth of 9.5 m
[4]*Oritkari Harbour:* Cargoes handled include paper, pulp, containers and ro/ro. Three ro/ro berths, 25 m, 30 m and 40 m wide, with 7 m and 10 m d. 3.1 ha asphalted container field and 66 200 m2 of storage cap

Storage:

Location	Covered (m²)
Oulu	75000

Mechanical Handling Equipment:

Location	Type	Capacity (t)	Qty
Vihreasaari Harbour	Mult-purp. Cranes	6	1
Nuottasaari Harbour	Mult-purp. Cranes	5	1
Oritkari Harbour	Mult-purp. Cranes	50	1
Oritkari Harbour	Panamax	50	1

Bunkering: Baltic Bunkering Ltd, Torggatan 10A, Mariehamn, Aland Islands, *Tel:* +358 18 143 00, *Fax:* +358 18 145 00, *Email:* info@balticbunkering.ax
Bunker Management Oy Ltd (BuMa), Merituulentie 424, FI-48310 Kotka, Finland, *Tel:* +358 5 2201 011, *Fax:* +358 5 2201 012, *Website:* www.bunkerman.fi
Shell Oy AB, Ulappasaarentie 4, FI-00980 Helsinki, Finland
ST1 Oy, ST1 OY, P O Box 37, Purotie, FI-02211 Helsinki, Finland, *Tel:* +358 10 557 11, *Fax:* +358 9 8030 004, *Email:* matti.pentti@st1.fi, *Website:* www.st1.fi
Teboil Oy AB, Bulevardi 26, P O Box 102, FI-00120 Helsinki, Finland, *Tel:* +358 20 470 01, *Fax:* +358 20 4700 248, *Email:* bunkersales@teboil.fi, *Website:* www.teboil.fi

Waste Reception Facilities: The vessel or it's agents must contact the port supervisors to dispose of waste, tel. +358 8 5584 2759, mobile. +358 44 703 2759 or VHF phone 13 & 16

Towage: Several tug boats and a harbour ice-breaker of 3600 hp available 24 h/day

Ship Chandlers: ME Group Oy (ab Mathias Eriksson), Kansipojantie 2, FI-90520 Oulu, Finland, *Tel:* +358 8 889 8900, *Fax:* +358 8 889 8980, *Email:* oulu@megroup.fi, *Website:* www.megroup.fi

Shipping Agents: Herman Andersson OY, Poikkimaantie 12, P O Box 37, FI-90400 Oulu, Finland, *Tel:* +358 8 315 0100, *Fax:* +358 8 371743, *Email:* laivan.selvitys@storaenso.com

Stevedoring Companies: Herman Andersson OY, Poikkimaantie 12, P O Box 37, FI-90400 Oulu, Finland, *Tel:* +358 8 315 0100, *Fax:* +358 8 371743, *Email:* laivan.selvitys@storaenso.com

Surveyors: Veikko Lauriala, Oulu, Finland, *Tel:* +358 8 531 6231
Bo-Einar Wallenius, Oulu, Finland, *Tel:* +358 8 373 3980

Medical Facilities: Available at University Hospital

Airport: Oulu, 15 km

Railway: Oulu, 5 km

Lloyd's Agent: Oy Lars Krogius A/B, Vilhonvuorenkatu 11 C 8, FI-00500 Helsinki, Finland, *Tel:* +358 9 4763 6300, *Fax:* +358 9 4763 6363, *Email:* finland@krogius.com, *Website:* www.krogius.com

PALOKANGAS

harbour area, see under Hamina

PARAINEN

Lat 60° 17' N; Long 22° 18' E.

Admiralty Chart: 3437	**Admiralty Pilot:** 20
Time Zone: GMT +2 h	**UNCTAD Locode:** FI PAR

Principal Facilities:

| | | Y | | | | | B | | T | A |

Authority: Finnsementti OY, FI-21600 Parainen, Finland, *Tel:* +358 201 206205, *Fax:* +358 201 206318, *Email:* info@finnsementti.fi, *Website:* www.finnsementti.fi

Officials: Managing Director: Eero Laatio, *Email:* eero.laatio@finnsementti.fi. Harbour Master: Stig Lundqvist, *Tel:* +358 201 206350, *Email:* stig.lundqvist@finnsementti.fi.

Port Security: ISPS compliant

Pre-Arrival Information: 36 h and 24 h notice to agents

Approach: Fairway depth of 7.5 m

Anchorage: Well sheltered and safe anchorage outside harbour area

Pilotage: Compulsory

Tides: Non-tidal

Maximum Vessel Dimensions: 130 m loa, 18 m beam, 7.5 m draught, 45 m air draught

Principal Imports and Exports: Imports: Coal, Gypsum, Limestone, Stone. Exports: Cement.

Working Hours: Mon-Fri 0600-2200

Accommodation:

Name	Length (m)	Depth (m)	Remarks
Parainen			Depth at quays 5-7.5 m with total length of 800 m
Cement Quay	100	7.5	One electric belt conveyor

Mechanical Handling Equipment:

Location	Type	Capacity (t)	Qty
Parainen	Mult-purp. Cranes	150–350	1

Bunkering: Available by arrangement

Waste Reception Facilities: Waste oil collection car of 20 m3. Dry garbage reception facilities at quay

Towage: By arrangement with ship agent at Turku

Medical Facilities: Medical officer available locally

Airport: Turku, 35 km

Railway: Turku, 25 km

Lloyd's Agent: Oy Wikestrom & Krogius AB, Huolintakatu 3, FI-20200 Turku, Finland, *Tel:* +358 2 0721 8500, *Fax:* +358 2 0721 8540, *Email:* wike.tku@wikestrom.com, *Website:* www.wikestrom.com

PARGAS

alternate name, see Parainen

PATENIEMI

Lat 65° 5' N; Long 25° 24' E.

Admiralty Chart: 3062   **Admiralty Pilot:** 20
Time Zone: GMT +2 h   **UNCTAD Locode:** FI PNI
This port is no longer open to commercial shipping

PELLOS

harbour area, see under Ristiina

PIETARSAARI

Lat 63° 42' N; Long 22° 41' E.

Admiralty Chart: 2300   **Admiralty Pilot:** 20
Time Zone: GMT +2 h   **UNCTAD Locode:** FI PRS

Principal Facilities:

P		Y	G	R			T	A	

Authority: Port of Pietarsaari Authority, Laukontie 1, FI-68600 Jakobstad, Finland, *Tel:* +358 6 723 6128, *Fax:* +358 6 723 0034, *Email:* kristian.hallis@jakobstad.fi, *Website:* www.portofpietarsaari.fi

Officials: Port Director: Kristian Hallis.

Port Security: ISPS compliant

Pilotage: Compulsory from Kokkola pilotage area, Tel: +358 (0) 20754 6153, Fax: +358 (0) 20754 6163, Email: pilotorder.west@finnpilot.fi. Pilot order form on www.pilotorder.fi

Traffic: 2007, 1 783 752 t of cargo handled

Principal Imports and Exports: Imports: Fuel oil. Exports: Woodpulp.

Working Hours: Mon to Fri: 1st shift 0700-1100, 1200-1600; 2nd shift 1600-2400. Sat: one shift only 0700-1500

Accommodation:

Name	Remarks
Jakobstad	See [1] below

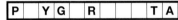

[1]*Jakobstad:* Well sheltered roadstead in 10.3 m. The port area of Jakobstad is Alholmen, about 4 km from the town. Depth at entrance 9.4 m; from roads to harbour basin 9.0 m. There are four quays, one with 5.7 m depth alongside, two with 7.4 m and one with 9.0 m. Total length of quays 660 m. Large warehouse for pulp and transit goods. Port normally open the whole winter
One oil berth operated by Neste O/Y for tankers up to 200 m loa and 9 m d
Ro/ro quay 170 m long in depth of 7.4 m

Towage: Tugs up to 1700 hp are available

Medical Facilities: Hospital and medical institutions available

Airport: Kronoby Airport, 18 km

Lloyd's Agent: Oy Lars Krogius A/B, Vilhonvuorenkatu 11 C 8, FI-00500 Helsinki, Finland, *Tel:* +358 9 4763 6300, *Fax:* +358 9 4763 6363, *Email:* finland@krogius.com, *Website:* www.krogius.com

PORI

harbour area, see under Mantyluoto

PORRKALA

alternate name, see Kantvik

PORVOO

alternate name, see Skoldvik

PUHOS

Lat 62° 6' N; Long 29° 55' E.

Admiralty Chart: -   **Admiralty Pilot:** 20
Time Zone: GMT +2 h   **UNCTAD Locode:** FI

Principal Facilities:

		Y	G						A	

Authority: Puhoksen Satama O/Y, FI-82430 Puhos, Finland, *Tel:* +358 13 682311, *Fax:* +358 13 682 3227, *Email:* mikko.lattu@puhosboard.fi

Officials: Director: Mikko Lattu.

Radio Frequency: VHF Channels 16 and 13

Traffic: 2001, 39 vessels, 80 000 t of cargo handled

Maximum Vessel Dimensions: 82.5 m loa, 12.8 m width, 4.35 m draught

Principal Imports and Exports: Exports: Particle board, Sawn timber, Wooden poles.

Working Hours: Mon-Fri 0700-1530, 1530-2300

Accommodation:

Name	Draught (m)	Remarks
Puhos		
Berth	4.35	Covered storage area of 5000 m2. Warehouse of 3200 m2

Mechanical Handling Equipment:

Location	Type
Puhos	Mobile Cranes

Airport: Joensuu Airport, 90 km

Lloyd's Agent: Oy Lars Krogius A/B, Vilhonvuorenkatu 11 C 8, FI-00500 Helsinki, Finland, *Tel:* +358 9 4763 6300, *Fax:* +358 9 4763 6363, *Email:* finland@krogius.com, *Website:* www.krogius.com

RAAHE

Lat 64° 39' N; Long 24° 24' E.

Admiralty Chart: 2301   **Admiralty Pilot:** 20
Time Zone: GMT +2 h   **UNCTAD Locode:** FI RAA

Principal Facilities:

P		Y	G	C		B		T	A	

Authority: Port of Raahe, Harbour Office, Lapaluodontie 342, FI-92180 Raahe, Finland, *Tel:* +358 8 439 3930, *Fax:* +358 8 439 3932, *Email:* port@raahe.fi, *Website:* www.portofraahe.fi

Officials: Port Director: Kaarlo Heikkinen, *Email:* kaarlo.heikkinen@raahe.fi. Secretary: Pirjo Fors, *Tel:* +358 8 439 3931, *Email:* pirjo.fors@raahe.fi.

Port Security: ISPS compliant

Approach: Channel from sea to harbours of Rautaruukki and Lapaluoto has a max depth of 8 m

Anchorage: Available outside Raahe lighthouse in 20-30 m depth. No anchoring inside breakwaters

Pilotage: Compulsory from Bay of Bothnia pilotage area, Tel: +358 (0) 20754 6153, Fax: +358 (0) 20754 6163, Email: pilotorder.west@finnpilot.fi. Pilot order form on www.pilotorder.fi

Traffic: 2007, 6 584 513 t of cargo handled

Maximum Vessel Dimensions: About 40 000 dwt, 8 m draft, approx 200 m loa at Rautaruukki and Lapaluoto

---

Key to Principal Facilities:—				
A=Airport	**C**=Containers	**G**=General Cargo	**P**=Petroleum	**R**=Ro/Ro	**Y**=Dry Bulk
B=Bunkers	**D**=Dry Dock	**L**=Cruise	**Q**=Other Liquid Bulk	**T**=Towage (where available from port)	

Principal Imports and Exports: Imports: Bulk cargo, Container cargo. Exports: , Steel products, Timber.

Working Hours: At Rautaruukki: three shifts Mon-Fri, 0600-1400, 1400-2200, 2200-0600. At Lapaluoto: Mon-Fri 0700-1430, 1430-2300

Accommodation:

Name	Length (m)	Depth (m)	Remarks
Raahe			See [1] below
Lapaluoto Quay	300	8	
Rautaruukki O/Y Quays		7–8	See [2] below

[1]*Raahe:* Max 8.0 m draft accommodating vessels up to about 20 000 dwt
[2]*Rautaruukki O/Y Quays:* Rautaruukki Steel, Harbour Office, PO Box 93, FIN-92101 Raahe, Tel: +358 8 849 3940, Fax: +358 8 849 4381, Email: martti.manelius@rautaruukki.com
Consists of two berths, 600 m long and 200 m long. Iron ore by conveyor at max discharge speed of 800 t/h

Mechanical Handling Equipment:

Location	Type	Capacity (t)	Qty
Lapaluoto Quay	Mobile Cranes	100–300	
Rautaruukki O/Y Quays	Mult-purp. Cranes	12	4
Rautaruukki O/Y Quays	Mult-purp. Cranes	60	1
Rautaruukki O/Y Quays	Mult-purp. Cranes	40	1

Bunkering: Available by road tanker
Baltic Bunkering Ltd, Torggatan 10A, Mariehamn, Aland Islands, *Tel:* +358 18 143 00, *Fax:* +358 18 145 00, *Email:* info@balticbunkering.ax
Bunker Management Oy Ltd (BuMa), Merituulentie 424, FI-48310 Kotka, Finland, *Tel:* +358 5 2201 011, *Fax:* +358 5 2201 012, *Website:* www.bunkerman.fi
Shell Oy AB, Ulappasaarentie 4, FI-00980 Helsinki, Finland
ST1 Oy, ST1 OY, P O Box 37, Purotie, FI-02211 Finland, *Tel:* +358 10 557 11, *Fax:* +358 9 8030 004, *Email:* matti.pentti@st1.fi, *Website:* www.st1.fi
Teboil Oy AB, Bulevardi 26, P O Box 102, FI-00120 Helsinki, Finland, *Tel:* +358 20 470 01, *Fax:* +358 20 4700 248, *Email:* bunkersales@teboil.fi, *Website:* www.teboil.fi

Towage: One tug of 1500 hp

Repair & Maintenance: Several experienced workshops are available

Airport: Oulu, 60 km

Lloyd's Agent: Oy Lars Krogius A/B, Vilhonvuorenkatu 11 C 8, FI-00500 Helsinki, Finland, *Tel:* +358 9 4763 6300, *Fax:* +358 9 4763 6363, *Email:* finland@krogius.com, *Website:* www.krogius.com

RAFSO

harbour area, see under Mantyluoto

RAUMA

Lat 61° 7' N; Long 21° 29' E.

Admiralty Chart: 3415

Admiralty Pilot: 20

Time Zone: GMT +2 h

UNCTAD Locode: FI RAU

Principal Facilities:

| P | Q | Y | G | C | R | | B | D | T | A |

Authority: Port Authority of Rauma, Hakunintie 19, FI-26100 Rauma, Finland, *Tel:* +358 2 834 4712, *Fax:* +358 2 822 6369, *Email:* harbour.office@portofrauma.com, *Website:* www.portofrauma.com

Officials: Port Director: Hannu Asumalahti, *Tel:* +358 2 834 4710, *Email:* hannu.asumalahti@rauma.fi.
Harbour Master: Mari Kallinen, *Tel:* +358 2 834 4709, *Email:* mari.kallinen@rauma.fi.

Port Security: ISPS compliant

Documentation: Crew list(2 copies), passenger list(2 copies), personal effects list, stores list, arms and ammunition list, deratting certificate, load line certificate, international tonnage certificate, certificate of nationality, safety equipment certificate, cargo gear certificate, certificate of ice class
Cargo documentation: dangerous cargo declarations, bills of lading manifests

Approach: Rauma Light Beacon (Racon) in pos 61° 09' N; 21° 10' E marks the point of the 8 nautical mile length Rauma main approach channel, which is authorised for a draft of 10 m and passes close N of the NW extremity of Rihtniemi Peninsula. Another approach channel, 6 nautical miles long and authorised for a draft of 7.5 m is entered NW of Kylmapihlaja Island from which it leads SE to the harbour

Anchorage: Anchorage is available at inner roads, just outside the harbour area in depths of 8-14 m, good holding in a bottom of mud. Good shelter. Also area near Rauman Majakka light house (Racon) can be used

Pilotage: Compulsory from Rauma Sea pilotage area, Tel: +358 (0) 20754 6153, Fax: +358 (0) 20754 6163, Email: pilotorder.west@finnpilot.fi. Pilot order form on www.pilotorder.fi

Radio Frequency: Turku Radio on VHF Channels 16 and 28

Traffic: 2007, 1586 vessels, 6 823 956 t of cargo handled, 168 761 TEU's

Maximum Vessel Dimensions: Tankers 180 m loa, unlimited for dry cargo vessels

Principal Imports and Exports: Imports: China clay. Exports: Chemicals, Paper, Woodpulp.

Working Hours: Mon-Fri 0700-1530, 1530-2400. Sat 0700-1530

Accommodation:

Name	Length (m)	Depth (m)	Draught (m)	Remarks
Rauma				
Central Port	415	6.2–6.4		See [1] below
Laitsaari	246	9.05	8.5	Used for export of conventional goods
Iso-Hakuni	975	7.5–11.5		
Container	160	10		
Ro/ro No.2	162	6.9		
Ro/ro No.3	130	8.3		
Ro/ro No.4	225	10		
Ro/ro No.5	187	10		
Ro/ro No.6	180	10		
Ro/ro No.7	190	10		
Inner Port				See [2] below
Chem K1	90		4.9	
Chem K2	130	6.9		
Petajas	445	11	10	See [3] below
Oil Port	200	9.15	8.5	See [4] below

[1]*Central Port:* Used for conventional traffic and includes ro/ro berth No.1, 135 m long in depth of 6.2 m
[2]*Inner Port:* Includes the chemical quays & fishing port. 46 000 m3 of storage
[3]*Petajas:* Used for bulk cargoes. Warehouses for bulk cargoes of 150 000 m3 and warehouses for unitised goods of 3200 m3
[4]*Oil Port:* Fuel oil loading rate of approx 800 t/h with 517 000 m3 of storage

Storage: Storage fields 200 000 m2. Oil harbour, storage for inflammable goods 550 000 m3

Location	Open (m2)	Covered (m2)	Sheds / Warehouses	Grain (t)
Rauma	500000	260000	40	175000

Mechanical Handling Equipment:

Location	Type	Capacity (t)	Qty
Rauma	Forklifts	1.5–20	144
Central Port	Mult-purp. Cranes	6	2
Iso-Hakuni	Mobile Cranes	8–100	3
Iso-Hakuni	Container Cranes	40	1
Iso-Hakuni	Reach Stackers	45	8
Petajas	Mult-purp. Cranes	40	1
Petajas	Mult-purp. Cranes	16	1
Petajas	Mult-purp. Cranes	45	1

Cargo Worked: 10 000-15 000 t/day

Bunkering: Baltic Bunkering Ltd, Torggatan 10A, Mariehamn, Aland Islands, *Tel:* +358 18 143 00, *Fax:* +358 18 145 00, *Email:* info@balticbunkering.ax
Bunker Management Oy Ltd (BuMa), Merituulentie 424, FI-48310 Kotka, Finland, *Tel:* +358 5 2201 011, *Fax:* +358 5 2201 012, *Website:* www.bunkerman.fi
ExxonMobil Marine Fuels, Mailpoint 31, ExxonMobil House, Ermyn Way, Leatherhead, Surrey KT22 8UX, United Kingdom, *Tel:* +44 1372 222 000, *Fax:* +44 1372 223 922, *Email:* marine.fuels@exxonmobil.com, *Website:* www.exxonmobil.com – *Grades:* IFO30-380cSt; MGO – *Notice:* 48 hours – *Delivery Mode:* truck
Shell Oy AB, Ulappasaarentie 4, FI-00980 Helsinki, Finland
ST1 Oy, ST1 OY, P O Box 37, Purotie, FI-02211 Helsinki, Finland, *Tel:* +358 10 557 11, *Fax:* +358 9 8030 004, *Email:* matti.pentti@st1.fi, *Website:* www.st1.fi
Teboil Oy AB, Bulevardi 26, P O Box 102, FI-00120 Helsinki, Finland, *Tel:* +358 20 470 01, *Fax:* +358 20 4700 248, *Email:* bunkersales@teboil.fi, *Website:* www.teboil.fi

Towage: Three tugs are available 24 h with 4 h notice required before arrival. Icebreaker tugs are also available
Alfons Hakans Oy Ab, Linnankatu 36C, FI-20100 Turku, Finland, *Tel:* +358 2 515500, *Fax:* +358 2 251 5873, *Email:* office.turku@alfonshakans.fi, *Website:* www.alfonshakans.fi

Ship Chandlers: ME Group Oy (ab Mathias Eriksson), Anderssonintie 4, FI-26100 Rauma, Finland, *Tel:* +358 2 273 0580, *Fax:* +358 2 822 1433, *Email:* rauma@megroup.fi, *Website:* www.megroup.fi

Shipping Agents: Nurminen Ship Agency, Paananvahe 4C, P O Box 203, FI-26101 Rauma, Finland, *Tel:* +358 10 545 5910, *Fax:* +358 10 545 5911, *Email:* rauma.agency@johnnurminen.com, *Website:* www.johnnurminennavis.com
OY Rauma Stevedoring Ltd, Satama, P O Box 68, FI-26100 Rauma, Finland, *Tel:* +358 2 83121, *Fax:* +358 2 831 2554, *Email:* headoffice.rst@raumasteve.fi, *Website:* www.raumastevedoring.fi

Stevedoring Companies: OY Rauma Stevedoring Ltd, Satama, P O Box 68, FI-26100 Rauma, Finland, *Tel:* +358 2 83121, *Fax:* +358 2 831 2554, *Email:* headoffice.rst@raumasteve.fi, *Website:* www.raumastevedoring.fi

Surveyors: Societe Generale de Surveillance (SGS), SGS Inspection Service of Rauma, Rauma, Finland, *Tel:* +358 2 824 1177, *Website:* www.sgs.com

Medical Facilities: Rauma Town Hospital, 3 km

Airport: Pori Airport, 50 km

Railway: Rauma, 2 km

Lloyd's Agent: Oy Lars Krogius A/B, Vilhonvuorenkatu 11 C 8, FI-00500 Helsinki, Finland, *Tel:* +358 9 4763 6300, *Fax:* +358 9 4763 6363, *Email:* finland@krogius.com, *Website:* www.krogius.com

RAUTARUUKKI

harbour area, see under Raahe

REPOSAARI

harbour area, see under Mantyluoto

RISTIINA

Lat 61° 32' N; Long 27° 25' E.

Admiralty Chart: -	**Admiralty Pilot:** 20
Time Zone: GMT +2 h	**UNCTAD Locode:** FI RIS

Principal Facilities:

			G					A

Authority: Schauman Wood O/Y, Pellos Mills, FI-52420 Pellosniemi, Finland, *Tel:* +358 204 15173, *Fax:* +358 204 15172, *Email:* nika.kekki@upm-kymmene.com

Officials: Managing Director: Nika Kekki.

Port Security: ISPS compliant

Radio Frequency: VHF Channels 16 and 13

Traffic: 2001, 35 vessels, 38 000 t of cargo handled

Maximum Vessel Dimensions: 82.5 m loa, 4.4 m d

Principal Imports and Exports: Imports: Raw timber.

Working Hours: Mon-Fri 0700-1530, 1530-2300

Accommodation:

Name	Remarks
Pellos	Room for one vessel

Storage:

Location	Open (m²)
Ristiina	5000

Mechanical Handling Equipment:

Location	Type
Pellos	Mobile Cranes

Medical Facilities: Health Centre

Airport: Mikkeli Airport, 30 km

Lloyd's Agent: Oy Lars Krogius A/B, Vilhonvuorenkatu 11 C 8, FI-00500 Helsinki, Finland, *Tel:* +358 9 4763 6300, *Fax:* +358 9 4763 6363, *Email:* finland@krogius.com, *Website:* www.krogius.com

ROYTTA

alternate name, see Tornio

SAIMAA CANAL

Admiralty Chart: -	**Admiralty Pilot:** 20
Time Zone: GMT +2 h	**UNCTAD Locode:** FI

Authority: Finnish Maritime Administration, Inland Waterways District, Itainen Kanavatie 2, FI-53420 Lappeenranta, Finland, *Tel:* +358 204 4830, *Fax:* +358 204 48310, *Email:* jukka.vaisanen@fma.fi, *Website:* www.fma.fi

Officials: Marketing Director: Seppo Virtanen, *Email:* seppo.virtanen@fma.fi.
Office Manager: Jukka Vaisanen, *Email:* jukka.vaisanen@fma.fi.

Approach: The canal can be reached from the international waters of the Gulf of Finland through an approach channel E of Someri, marked on Russian sea charts No's 1131 and 1132 and on Finnish sea charts No's 11 and 12
The channel passes Vihrevoi Island and continues by Malyj Vysotskij as the Vysotskij-Viipuri channel from which the incoming canal diverges by the S.C. Maariankivi

The distance from the international waters to Vihrevoi Island is 95 km and from there to Brusnitchnoe lock 36 km
The permissable d of the approach channel up to Malyj Vysotskij is 7.3 m and from there to Viipuri 6.5 m. The permitted passage depth in the departure channel is 4.35 m, at the MW level of -0.25 m

Pilotage: Pilotage in the Russian side between Vihrevoi and Brusnitchnoe is carried out by the Russian Pilot Service from Vyborg. All vessels must use a pilot on this channel section
Pilotage on section Brusnitchnoe-Lock to Malkia Lock is carried out by canal pilots submitted to Inland Waterways District. All vessels, excluding Finnish small vessels and floating objects less than 25 m in length, shall use a pilot when proceeding through the Canal. VHF Channel 13

Radio Frequency: VTS radio traffic: call Saimaa VTS on VHF Channel 9
Emergency radio traffic: call Saimaa VTS on VHF Channel 16
The Saimaa Canal and the Taipale Lock (in Varkaus City) and the Konnus Lock (in Leppavirta Community): call 'Name of the lock' on VHF Channel 11
Pilotage: call 'Name of pilot station' on VHF Channel 13
All vessels over 20 m loa must listen in the Saimaa Canal on VHF Channels 9 and 11 and in Lake Saimaa district on VHF Channels 9 and 16

Maximum Vessel Dimensions: 82.5 m loa, 12.6 m wide, 4.35 m draught, height of mast from the water surface 24.5 m
The d of a vessel in tw, however, must not exceed 4.5 m

Accommodation: Saimaa Vessel Traffic Centre: located next to the Malkia Lock and consists of Saimaa VTS (Saimaa Vessel Traffic Service) and the Remote-control Centre of the Saimaa Canal
The Saimaa VTS area covers the Saimaa Canal and deep-water channels (draught 4.2 m) in Lake Saimaa. The Saimaa VTS provides information services to the vessel traffic in the Lake Saimaa district and monitors in real time the movement of merchant vessels. VTS centre takes care of pilot orders for the Saimaa Canal and for Lake Saimaa. The Inland Waterways District requires that all cargo and passenger vessels navigating in the Lake Saimaa district acquire an AIS transponder
The Remote-control Centre of the Saimaa Canal can operate all the eight locks and seven movable bridges of the Canal. The Brusnitchnoe operating centre operates the first three locks from the sea and three movable bridges. In exceptional conditions during winter navigation season, locks are operated locally
The length of the Canal on the Finnish side of the border is 23.3 km and that of the part on the Russian side 19.6 km. The overall length of the Saimaa Canal being 42.9 km
The average difference in height between Lake Saimaa and the Gulf of Finland is 75.7 m. The Canal has eight locks, the heights of fall of which range between 5.54 and 12.69 m. There are waiting quays both above and below the locks
Road transports will use the seven moving bascule bridges and the six stationary bridges built across the Canal
The Canal can be used by vessels with dimensions not exceeding the following: length 82.5 m, beam 12.6 m, 4.35 m d, height of mast from water surface 24.5 m. The d of a vessel in tow, however, shall not exceed 4.5 m
Permits for navigation in the Canal may be granted upon application to vessels the dimensions of which slightly exceed the above mentioned dimensions if the vessels otherwise to their structures and properties suitable for navigation in the Canal. Additionally a special Trip Let Pass for one trip may also be granted to a vessel or an equipment carrying exceptional cargo. The permits are granted by the Inland Waterways District
The natural openwater season of the Saimaa Canal lasts on average 211 days. In mild spring and autumn seasons the openwater period lasts 255 days. Since most vessels using the Canal have been strengthened for navigation in ice, a season of navigation of almost ten months will probably be normal every year. The season begins at the beginning of April and ends at the end of January
Navigable Channels: There are three kinds of watercourses partly linked with one another in the water system of Saimaa: deepwater channels of 4.2 m on Lake Saimaa, public passages of 1.5-2.4 m and channels for floating
The main route goes from the mouth of the Canal via the town of Savonlinna to Haukivesi and bifurcates at Haukivesi via Varkaus to the towns of Kuopio and Joensuu. The most important secondary channels are those of Lappeenranta, Joutseno, Imatra, Ristiina, Siilinjarvi and Puhos (Kitee). The length of this channel network is about 813 km
The deepwater channel network of the lake area is supplemented with the 1.5-2.4 m deep boat and floating channels to Mikkeli, Iisalmi, Kaavi and Nurmes
Because the water level of the Lake Saimaa generally is above the level allowing the 4.2 m d traffic in the deepwater channels to Kuopio and Joensuu is possible under normal circumstances with 4.35 m d

Airport: Lappeenranta Airport

Railway: Lappeenranta Railway Station

Lloyd's Agent: Oy Lars Krogius A/B, Vilhonvuorenkatu 11 C 8, FI-00500 Helsinki, Finland, *Tel:* +358 9 4763 6300, *Fax:* +358 9 4763 6363, *Email:* finland@krogius.com, *Website:* www.krogius.com

SAVONLINNA

Lat 61° 54' N; Long 28° 55' E.

Admiralty Chart: -	**Admiralty Pilot:** 20
Time Zone: GMT +2 h	**UNCTAD Locode:** FI SVL

Key to Principal Facilities:—				
A=Airport	**C**=Containers	**G**=General Cargo	**P**=Petroleum	**R**=Ro/Ro	**Y**=Dry Bulk
B=Bunkers	**D**=Dry Dock	**L**=Cruise	**Q**=Other Liquid Bulk	**T**=Towage (where available from port)

Principal Facilities:

		G					A

Authority: Port of Savonlinna, Olavinkatu 27, FI-57130 Savonlinna, Finland, *Tel:* +358 15 571 4583, *Fax:* +358 15 571 4579, *Email:* jukka.vaahtoluoto@savonlinna.fi, *Website:* www.savonlinna.fi

Officials: Harbour Master: Jukka Vaahtoluoto.

Port Security: ISPS compliant

Radio Frequency: VHF Channels 16 and 13

Traffic: 2007, 33 889 t of cargo handled

Maximum Vessel Dimensions: 82.5 m loa, 4.35 m d

Working Hours: Mon-Fri 0700-1530, 1530-2300

Accommodation:

Name	Draught (m)	Remarks
Haislahti Berth	4.35	See [1] below

[1]*Berth:* Storage area of 13 000 m2, mobile cranes can be hired. Fresh water available. Rail connections

Mechanical Handling Equipment:

Location	Type
Savonlinna	Mobile Cranes

Medical Facilities: Health Centre

Airport: Savonlinna Airport, 20 km

Lloyd's Agent: Oy Lars Krogius A/B, Vilhonvuorenkatu 11 C 8, FI-00500 Helsinki, Finland, *Tel:* +358 9 4763 6300, *Fax:* +358 9 4763 6363, *Email:* finland@krogius.com, *Website:* www.krogius.com

SIILINJARVI

Lat 63° 5' N; Long 27° 40' E.

Admiralty Chart: -	**Admiralty Pilot:** 20
Time Zone: GMT +2 h	**UNCTAD Locode:** FI SII

Principal Facilities:

		Y	G					A

Authority: Kemphos OY, P O Box 20, FIN-71801 Siilinjarvi, Finland, *Tel:* +358 10 215111, *Fax:* +358 10 215 6000, *Email:* anna.nasi@yara.com, *Website:* www.kemira-growhow.com

Officials: Shipping Manager: Anna Nasi.

Port Security: ISPS compliant

Radio Frequency: VHF Channels 16 and 13

Traffic: 2001, 29 vessels, 68 000 t of cargo handled

Maximum Vessel Dimensions: 82.5 m loa, 12.6 m width, 4.35 m draught

Working Hours: Mon-Fri 0700-1530, 1530-2300

Accommodation:

Name	Remarks
Siilinjarvi	See [1] below

[1]*Siilinjarvi:* Two small quays owned by Kemira O/Y, Tel: +358 10 861215, and SP Minerals O/Y, Nilsian Kvartsi, Tel: +358 17 264 3629, Fax: +358 17 264 3600

Mechanical Handling Equipment:

Location	Type
Siilinjarvi	Mobile Cranes

Medical Facilities: Health Centre

Airport: Kuopio Airport, 20 km

Lloyd's Agent: Oy Lars Krogius A/B, Vilhonvuorenkatu 11 C 8, FI-00500 Helsinki, Finland, *Tel:* +358 9 4763 6300, *Fax:* +358 9 4763 6363, *Email:* finland@krogius.com, *Website:* www.krogius.com

SKOGBY

Lat 59° 55' N; Long 23° 19' E.

Admiralty Chart: 2241	**Admiralty Pilot:** 20
Time Zone: GMT +2 h	**UNCTAD Locode:** FI SKB

This port is no longer open to commercial shipping

SKOLDVIK

Lat 60° 18' N; Long 25° 33' E.

Admiralty Chart: 1083	**Admiralty Pilot:** 20
Time Zone: GMT +2 h	**UNCTAD Locode:** FI PRV

Principal Facilities:

P	Q				B	T	A

Authority: Neste Oil Oyj, Port of Skoldvik, Porvoo Refinery, P O Box 310, FI-06101 Porvoo, Finland, *Tel:* +358 10 45811, *Fax:* +358 10 458 1217, *Email:* skoldvik.harbour@nesteoil.com, *Website:* www.nesteoil.com

Officials: Refinery Manager: Martti Ronkainen, *Tel:* +358 10 458 2100.

Port Security: ISPS compliant

Pre-Arrival Information: The following information is requested by Neste Oil Terminal prior to arrival:
Name of ship, call sign, IMO number
Flag, port of registry, owner, contact details
Overall length and beam of the ship (summer dwt)
Gross registered tonnage, net registered tonnage, deadweight
Max draft fore during stay in port, max draft aft during stay in port
Last port of call, number and issue date of ISSC, issuing authority, ship's security level at current time, confirm ETA local time and date, next port of call
Double bottom yes/no, double hull yes/no
Mooring equipment - number, mooring equipment - material
Bow thrusters - number, bow thrusters - power, stern thrusters - number, stern thrusters - power
Last cargo, second last cargo, third last cargo
Whether loaded or in ballast, if loaded, nature of cargo, un number of cargo, name of cargo, quantity of any chemicals carried by ship, quantity of any gas carried by ship, quantity of any oil carried by ship, location, if crude oil, whether the cargo contains sour crude oil yes/no, if ballasted, type of ballast segregated/oily, quantity of ballast to be discharged ashore, estimated time of deballasting
Quantity to be loaded, requested loading rate, if several grades, preferred loading order, quantity to be discharged, requested discharging rate, if several grades, preferred discharging order
Whether the tanker is fitted with inert gas system yes/no
If fitted, gas system fully operational yes/no, the oxygen content does not exceed 8% by volume yes/no
Whether the cargo tanks have a non-flammable atmosphere yes/no, tanks arrival athmosphere
Whether crude oil wash is to be employed yes/no
Number of connections, size of connections, distance from bow to connection, position of connection above waterline, position of connection from the ship side, height from waterline to connection loaded/in ballast, number and sizes of reducers
Defects in vessel or equipment affecting discharging/loading or manouverability
If transit cargo, quantity, if transit cargo, un number, if transit cargo, name, if transit cargo, location
Has sent Neste questionnare, date
Has carried out Neste Oil vetting, date
Gas detector system is in fully operational condition yes/no
The temperature of cargo upon arrival

Pilotage: Compulsory. Pilots board at Kallbadagrund

Radio Frequency: VHF Channels 16 and 21

Maximum Vessel Dimensions: 15.3 m draft

Principal Imports and Exports: Imports: Crude oil. Exports: Chemicals, Gases, Oil products.

Working Hours: 24 h/day

Accommodation:

Name	Remarks
Skoldvik Oil Harbour	Consists of five berths (1-5) handling crude oil & petroleum products

Name	Remarks
Gas & Chemical Harbour	Consists of two berths (8 and 9) handling liquefied gases & chemicals

Bunkering: Heavy and light fuel available on request to agent
Baltic Bunkering Ltd, Torggatan 10A, Mariehamn, Aland Islands, *Tel:* +358 18 143 00, *Fax:* +358 18 145 00, *Email:* info@balticbunkering.ax
Bunker Management Oy Ltd (BuMa), Merituulentie 424, FI-48310 Kotka, Finland, *Tel:* +358 5 2201 011, *Fax:* +358 5 2201 012, *Website:* www.bunkerman.fi
ExxonMobil Marine Fuels, Mailpoint 31, ExxonMobil House, Ermyn Way, Leatherhead, Surrey KT22 8UX, United Kingdom, *Tel:* +44 1372 222 000, *Fax:* +44 1372 223 922, *Email:* marine.fuels@exxonmobil.com, *Website:* www.exxonmobil.com – *Grades:* IFO30-380cSt; MDO; MGO – *Delivery Mode:* truck
Shell Oy AB, Ulappasaarentie 4, FI-00980 Helsinki, Finland
ST1 Oy, ST1 OY, P O Box 37, Purotie, FI-02211 Helsinki, Finland, *Tel:* +358 10 557 11, *Fax:* +358 9 8030 004, *Email:* matti.pentti@st1.fi, *Website:* www.st1.fi
Teboil Oy AB, Bulevardi 26, P O Box 102, FI-00120 Helsinki, Finland, *Tel:* +358 20 470 01, *Fax:* +358 20 4700 248, *Email:* bunkersales@teboil.fi, *Website:* www.teboil.fi

Towage: Two tugs owned by Fortum

Airport: Helsinki-Vantaa, 50 km

Lloyd's Agent: Oy Lars Krogius A/B, Vilhonvuorenkatu 11 C 8, FI-00500 Helsinki, Finland, *Tel:* +358 9 4763 6300, *Fax:* +358 9 4763 6363, *Email:* finland@krogius.com, *Website:* www.krogius.com

SKURU

Lat 60° 6' N; Long 23° 33' E.

Admiralty Chart: 2241
Time Zone: GMT +2 h
Admiralty Pilot: 20
UNCTAD Locode: FI POH

Principal Facilities:

			G						A	

Authority: Celsa Steel Service Oy, Port of Skuru, FI-10410 Aminnefors, Finland, *Tel:* +358 19 22131, *Fax:* +358 19 221 3300, *Email:* info.betoniterakset@celsa-steelservice.com, *Website:* www.celsa-steelservice.com

Officials: Chief Executive Officer: Tom Isaksson, *Email:* tom.isaksson@celsa-steelservice.com.
Marketing Manager: Seppo Martikainen, *Email:* seppo.martikainen@celsa-steelservice.com.
Harbour Master: Dick Skogberg, *Email:* dick.skogberg@celsa-steelservice.com.

Port Security: ISPS compliant

Pre-Arrival Information: Timo Sjosten tel.+358 19 2214281 fax.+358 19 2443121 gsm.+358 405029502

Approach: The main approach channel is some 15 miles in length and is authorized for a draft of 12 m as far as Koverhar roads, thence some 17 miles with max 4.9 m draft to the berth at Skuru. The main approach channel is entered at the Ajax Light Buoy

Anchorage: Good anchorage available at approx pos 59° 48' N; 22° 55' E, some 12 cables S of Hanko in depths of 20 m

Pilotage: Compulsory, *Tel:* +358 (0) 20754 6151, *Fax:* +358 (0) 20754 6161, *Email:* pilotorder.south@finnpilot.fi. Pilot order form on www.pilotorder.fi. Distance from sea to port 9.6 km. Pilot boards 1.5 nautical miles ENE of Russaro or 4 nautical miles WSW of Ajax Lt. (in bad weather in Hanko roads)

Radio Frequency: VHF Channels 16 and 13

Traffic: 2005, 49 vessels, 142 000 t of cargo handled

Maximum Vessel Dimensions: 100 m loa, 16 m beam, 4.9 m draft, max air draught 28 m

Principal Imports and Exports: Imports: Steel.

Working Hours: Mon-Fri 0600-2200

Accommodation:

Name	Length (m)	Depth (m)
Skuru Quay	100	5

Mechanical Handling Equipment:

Location	Type	Capacity (t)	Qty	Remarks
Skuru	Mult-purp. Cranes	9	1	mobile cranes can be arranged

Cargo Worked: Approx 150 t/shift

Towage: Not compulsory but can be arranged from Hanko

Shipping Agents: Koverhar Shipping O/Y A/B, Koverharvagen 303, FI-10820 Lappvik, Finland, *Tel:* +358 19 221 4280, *Fax:* +358 19 244 3121, *Email:* agency@koverharshipping.fi, *Website:* www.koverharshipping.fi

Airport: Helsinki, 90 km
Railway: Karjaa, 9 km
Lloyd's Agent: Oy Lars Krogius A/B, Vilhonvuorenkatu 11 C 8, FI-00500 Helsinki, Finland, *Tel:* +358 9 4763 6300, *Fax:* +358 9 4763 6363, *Email:* finland@krogius.com, *Website:* www.krogius.com

TAHKOLUOTO

harbour area, see under Mantyluoto

TAIPALE

harbour area, see under Varkaus

TAMMISAARI

Lat 59° 59' N; Long 23° 26' E.

Admiralty Chart: 2241
Time Zone: GMT +2 h
Admiralty Pilot: 20
UNCTAD Locode: FI TAI

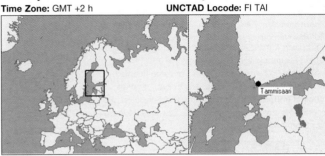

Principal Facilities:

	Y	G			B		A

Authority: Port of Tammisaari, P O Box 75, FI-10601 Tammisaari, Finland, *Tel:* +358 19 248 3231

Officials: Harbour Master: Svante Rosin.

Port Security: ISPS compliant

Pilotage: Compulsory, *Tel:* +358 204 485801, *Fax:* +358 204 458500

Radio Frequency: VHF Channels 13 and 16. Helsinki VTS on VHF Channel 67

Traffic: 2001, 7 vessels, 10 000 t of bulk cargo handled

Maximum Vessel Dimensions: 90 m loa, 4.6 m draft

Principal Imports and Exports: Imports: China clay.

Working Hours: Monday to Friday 0700-1600; lunch break 1100-1200

Accommodation:

Name	Length (m)	Draught (m)	Remarks
Tammisaari Quay	160	4.6	See [1] below

[1]*Quay:* Operated by Firma Westerlund & Co. for bulk vessels
Navigation generally begins end of April, closes end Dec. Railways: three tracks on quay

Storage: Warehouse for general cargo

Mechanical Handling Equipment:

Location	Type	Capacity (t)	Qty
Tammisaari	Mobile Cranes	60	2

Cargo Worked: Average of 1000 t/day

Bunkering: Can be arranged by agent

Repair & Maintenance: Minor repairs can be effected

Medical Facilities: Available

Airport: Helsinki, 100 km

Railway: Tammisaari, 1 km

Lloyd's Agent: Oy Lars Krogius A/B, Vilhonvuorenkatu 11 C 8, FI-00500 Helsinki, Finland, *Tel:* +358 9 4763 6300, *Fax:* +358 9 4763 6363, *Email:* finland@krogius.com, *Website:* www.krogius.com

TOLKIS

alternate name, see Tolkkinen

TOLKKINEN

Lat 60° 20' N; Long 25° 35' E.

Admiralty Chart: 2248
Time Zone: GMT +2 h
Admiralty Pilot: 20
UNCTAD Locode: FI TOK

Key to Principal Facilities:—				
A=Airport	**C**=Containers	**G**=General Cargo	**P**=Petroleum	**R**=Ro/Ro	**Y**=Dry Bulk
B=Bunkers	**D**=Dry Dock	**L**=Cruise	**Q**=Other Liquid Bulk	**T**=Towage (where available from port)	

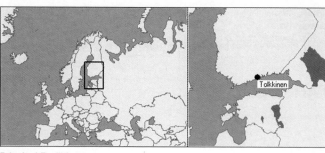

Principal Facilities:

		Y	G					T	A	

Authority: Borga Stuveri AB OY, P O Box 40, FI-06101 Borga, Finland, *Tel:* +358 19 577530, *Fax:* +358 19 577285, *Email:* borgastuveri@storaenso.com

Officials: Managing Director: Per-Erik Forsstrom, *Email:* per-erik.forsstrom@storaenso.com.

Port Security: ISPS compliant. Port Security Officer, Tel: +358 40 715 3662

Documentation: Crew effects declaration (1 copy), ship's stores declaration (1 copy), crew list (2 copies)

Approach: Depth of channel 15 m. From Oilport 7 m

Anchorage: Near Kalvo Island

Pilotage: Compulsory and to be ordered from Helsinki VTS with 6 h and 3 h notice. Pilot boards 2 miles NW of Kalbadagrund lighthouse

Radio Frequency: VHF Channels 16 and 13

Traffic: 2007, 48 vessels, 158 513 t of cargo handled

Maximum Vessel Dimensions: 160 m loa, 7 m draft

Principal Imports and Exports: Imports: Saw logs. Exports: Sawn timber.

Working Hours: Mon-Fri 0700-1600. Saw logs 24 h/day

Accommodation:

Name	Length (m)	Depth (m)
Tolkkinen		
North Quay	154	8
South Quay	63	6

Mechanical Handling Equipment:

Location	Type	Capacity (t)	Qty
Tolkkinen	Mult-purp. Cranes	5	1
Tolkkinen	Mobile Cranes	70	

Towage: Tugs available from Porvoo oil harbour at Skoldvik

Medical Facilities: Borga Hospital, 9 km

Airport: Helsinki-Vantaa, 50 km

Lloyd's Agent: Oy Lars Krogius A/B, Vilhonvuorenkatu 11 C 8, FI-00500 Helsinki, Finland, *Tel:* +358 9 4763 6300, *Fax:* +358 9 4763 6363, *Email:* finland@krogius.com, *Website:* www.krogius.com

TOPPILA

harbour area, see under Oulu

TORNIO

Lat 65° 51' N; Long 24° 9' E.

Admiralty Chart: 2302
Time Zone: GMT +2 h

Admiralty Pilot: 20
UNCTAD Locode: FI TOR

Principal Facilities:

Q	Y	G	C			B		T	A	

Authority: Port of Tornio, Outokumpu Tornio Works, Logistics Services Dept., FI-95490 Tornio, Finland, *Tel:* +358 16 4521, *Fax:* +358 16 452620, *Email:* pekka.harjuoja@outokumpu.com, *Website:* www.outokumpu.com

Officials: Harbour Master: Pekka Harjuoja, *Tel:* +358 16 452532.

Port Security: ISPS compliant

Approach: A channel 8 m deep and 90 m wide leads to the harbour

Anchorage: No anchorage within the harbour area. Only in accordance with pilot introductions

Pilotage: Compulsory from Bay of Bothnia pilotage area, Tel: +358 (0) 20754 6153, Fax: +358 (0) 20754 6163, Email: pilotorder.west@finnpilot.fi. Pilot order form on www.pilotorder.fi

Maximum Vessel Dimensions: 160 m loa

Principal Imports and Exports: Imports: Coke, Lime, Propane, Scrap. Exports: Chrome, Steel.

Working Hours: Monday to Friday 0700-1600, 1600-2400. Saturday 0700-1500

Accommodation:

Name	Length (m)	Draught (m)	Remarks
Tornio			
Quay 1			
Berth No.1	144	8	
Berth No.2	144	8	
Berth No.3	202	8	
Berth No.4	208	8	
Quay 2			
Berth No.5	151.5	8	
Berth No.6	154.1	8	
Berth No.7	150	8	Lime
Gas Quay	117	8	

Mechanical Handling Equipment:

Location	Type	Capacity (t)	Qty
Tornio	Mult-purp. Cranes	56–100	5

Bunkering: Bunker oil available
Baltic Bunkering Ltd, Torggatan 10A, Mariehamn, Aland Islands, *Tel:* +358 18 143 00, *Fax:* +358 18 145 00, *Email:* info@balticbunkering.ax
Bunker Management Oy Ltd (BuMa), Merituulentie 424, FI-48310 Kotka, Finland, *Tel:* +358 5 2201 011, *Fax:* +358 5 2201 012, *Website:* www.bunkerman.fi
Teboil Oy AB, Bulevardi 26, P O Box 102, FI-00120 Helsinki, Finland, *Tel:* +358 20 470 01, *Fax:* +358 20 4700 248, *Email:* bunkersales@teboil.fi, *Website:* www.teboil.fi

Waste Reception Facilities: Sludge oil and dry garbage

Towage: Tug to be ordered from Kemi 12 h prior to arrival

Repair & Maintenance: Only small repairs can be made at Tornio and Kemi

Stevedoring Companies: Outokumpu Shipping Oy, Roytta Harbour, P O Box 60, FIN-95400 Tornio, Finland, *Tel:* +358 16 454506, *Fax:* +358 16 454505, *Email:* stevedores.tornio@outokumpu.com

Medical Facilities: Health Centre, Tel: +358 16 432814

Airport: Kemi Airport, 25 km

Railway: Kemi, 30 km

Lloyd's Agent: Oy Lars Krogius A/B, Vilhonvuorenkatu 11 C 8, FI-00500 Helsinki, Finland, *Tel:* +358 9 4763 6300, *Fax:* +358 9 4763 6363, *Email:* finland@krogius.com, *Website:* www.krogius.com

TURKU

Lat 60° 25' N; Long 22° 13' E.

Admiralty Chart: 3436
Time Zone: GMT +2 h

Admiralty Pilot: 20
UNCTAD Locode: FI TKU

Principal Facilities:

P		Y	G	C	R	L	B	D	T	A

Authority: Port of Turku, Linnankatu 90, FI-20100 Turku, Finland, *Tel:* +358 2 267 4111, *Fax:* +358 2 267 4110, *Email:* turkuport@port.turku.fi, *Website:* www.port.turku.fi

Officials: Managing Director: Christian Ramberg, *Tel:* +358 2 267 4112, *Email:* christian.ramberg@port.turku.fi.
Harbour Master: Kari Riutta, *Tel:* +358 2 267 4123, *Email:* kari.riutta@port.turku.fi.
Marketing: Marjo Ekman, *Tel:* +358 2 267 4103, *Email:* marjo.ekman@port.turku.fi.

Port Security: ISPS compliant

Approach: The harbour is kept open all the year round, and is the safest in Finland. Four entrances: SSW entrance via Uto Fairway 10 m; WSW entrance via Nyhamn 9 m; WNW entrance via Isokari-Enskar 10 m; SSE entrance via Hanko 7.5 m. Lighthouse and pilot at each point
All fairways sheltered, well buoyed and lighted. No tide
Channel to main harbour max 10 m depth; channel to oil and chemical harbour max 9 m depth

Anchorage: Depth available at outer (Airisto) anchorage is 18-29 m

Pilotage: Compulsory on the archipelago fairways. Vessels entering call 'Turku Pilot' on VHF Channel 13, Archipelago VTS on VHF Channel 71

Harbour pilotage not compulsory as a rule. Call 'Turku Port Control' on VHF Channel 12 when passing Rajakari lighthouse and before leaving the quay

Radio Frequency: VHF Channel 12 for working within the port area

Traffic: 2007, 3 955 992 t of cargo handled, 21 982 TEU's

Maximum Vessel Dimensions: Main Harbour: max loa 250 m, max d 10 m Oil and Chemical Harbour: max loa 170 m, max d 9 m

Principal Imports and Exports: Imports: Cars, Chemicals, Metals, Oil. Exports: Diesel engines, Electronics, Forest products, Granite.

Working Hours: Monday-Friday 0630-1500, 1500-2300. Saturday 0700-1530. Overtime possible

Accommodation:

Name	Remarks
Turku	See [1] below

[1]*Turku:* Length of quays 5100 m, depths at berths range from 6.5 m to 11.0 m Full service container terminal (TCT) with container freight station and container depot in West Harbour
Several berths available for cruise vessels
Tanker facilities: Pansio Oil Harbour, one berth approx 160 m long and one berth 20 m long

Storage: Storage fields of 520 000 m2 by the Port Authority and 200 000 m2 by the Free Zone Company of Turku. Warehouses (heated and unheated) of 130 000 m2

Mechanical Handling Equipment:

Location	Type	Capacity (t)	Qty
Turku	Mult-purp. Cranes	6	4
Turku	Mult-purp. Cranes	60	1
Turku	Mult-purp. Cranes	40	1
Turku	Container Cranes	40–48	1

Bunkering: Baltic Bunkering Ltd, Torggatan 10A, Mariehamn, Aland Islands, *Tel:* +358 18 143 00, *Fax:* +358 18 145 00, *Email:* info@balticbunkering.ax
Bunker Management Oy Ltd (BuMa), Merituulentie 424, FI-48310 Kotka, Finland, *Tel:* +358 5 2201 011, *Fax:* +358 5 2201 012, *Website:* www.bunkerman.fi
ExxonMobil Marine Fuels, Mailpoint 31, ExxonMobil House, Ermyn Way, Leatherhead, Surrey KT22 8UX, United Kingdom, *Tel:* +44 1372 222 000, *Fax:* +44 1372 223 922, *Email:* marine.fuels@exxonmobil.com, *Website:* www.exxonmobil.com – *Grades:* MGO – *Notice:* 48 hours – *Delivery Mode:* truck
Shell Oy AB, Ulappasaarentie 4, FI-00980 Helsinki, Finland
ST1 Oy, ST1 OY, P O Box 37, Purotie, FI-02211 Helsinki, Finland, *Tel:* +358 10 557 11, *Fax:* +358 9 8030 004, *Email:* matti.pentti@st1.fi, *Website:* www.st1.fi
Teboil Oy AB, Bulevardi 26, P O Box 102, FI-00120 Helsinki, Finland, *Tel:* +358 20 470 01, *Fax:* +358 20 4700 248, *Email:* bunkersales@teboil.fi, *Website:* www.teboil.fi

Towage: Alfons Hakans Oy Ab, Linnankatu 36C, FI-20100 Turku, Finland, *Tel:* +358 2 515500, *Fax:* +358 2 251 5873, *Email:* office.turku@alfonshakans.fi, *Website:* www.alfonshakans.fi

Repair & Maintenance: Turku Repair Yard Ltd, P O Box 212, FI-21111 Naantali, Finland, *Tel:* +358 2 44511, *Fax:* +358 2 445 1455, *Email:* try@turkurepairyard.com, *Website:* www.turkurepairyard.com Naantali Yard: Dry dock of 255 m x 70 m x 7.4 m with lifting cap of 150 t. Floating dock of 106 m x 19 m x 6 m with lifting cap of 5000 t. Kotka Yard: Floating dock of 96 m x 16.5 m with lifting cap of 2000 t and floating dock of 127.2 m x 20.2 m x 5.1 m with lifting cap of 5 m

Ship Chandlers: Juhani Suokari Oy, Kakontie 7, FI-21420 Lieto, Finland, *Tel:* +358 2 488 6763, *Fax:* +358 2 488 6744, *Email:* j.suokari@jsoy.fi, *Website:* www.kolumbus.fi
ME Group Oy (ab Mathias Eriksson), Vitkalankatu 1, FI-20200 Turku, Finland, *Tel:* +358 2 273 0500, *Fax:* +358 2 230 5932, *Email:* turku@megroup.fi, *Website:* www.megroup.fi

Stevedoring Companies: Oy Finnsteve Ltd, P O Box 38, FI-20101 Turku, Finland, *Fax:* +358 2 230 3115, *Email:* info@finnsteve.fi, *Website:* www.finnsteve.fi
Oy Turku Stevedoring AB, Kuljetuskatu 13, FI-20200 Turku, Finland, *Tel:* +358 2 276 8500, *Fax:* +358 2 276 8501, *Email:* info@turkusteve.com, *Website:* www.turkusteve.com

Surveyors: Bureau Veritas, Linnankatu 88, FIN-20100 Turku, Finland, *Tel:* +358 2 230 2144, *Fax:* +358 2 247 4153, *Website:* www.bureauveritas.com
Det Norske Veritas A/S, Aurakatu 18, FI-20100 Turku, Finland, *Tel:* +358 2 273 7200, *Fax:* +358 2 251 7310, *Email:* turku.classification@dnv.com, *Website:* www.dnv.com
Germanischer Lloyd, Puutarhakatu 12, FI-20100 Turku, Finland, *Tel:* +358 2 250 3500, *Fax:* +358 2 250 3002, *Email:* gl-turku@gl-group.com, *Website:* www.gl-group.com
Russian Maritime Register of Shipping, Yliopistonkatu 24 B 32, FI-20100 Turku, Finland, *Tel:* +358 2 275 4200, *Fax:* +358 2 231 7282, *Email:* rs-fin@rsfin.fi, *Website:* www.rs-head.spb.ru

Medical Facilities: Fully equipped hospitals and health centres available

Airport: Turku, 11 km

Railway: Passenger railway station in the port connected with passenger ferries. Central station 3 kilometres from the main harbour

Lloyd's Agent: Oy Wikestrom & Krogius AB, Huolintakatu 3, FI-20200 Turku, Finland, *Tel:* +358 2 0721 8500, *Fax:* +358 2 0721 8540, *Email:* wike.tku@wikestrom.com, *Website:* www.wikestrom.com

UKONNIEMI

harbour area, see under Joensuu

ULEABORG

alternate name, see Oulu

UUSIKAUPUNKI

Lat 60° 48' N; Long 21° 24' E.

Admiralty Chart: 3437	**Admiralty Pilot:** 20
Time Zone: GMT +2 h	**UNCTAD Locode:** FI UKI

Principal Facilities:

Q	Y	G		R		B		T	A

Authority: Uusikaupunki Port Authority, Satamantie 9, FI-23500 Uusikaupunki, Finland, *Tel:* +358 2 8451 5299, *Fax:* +358 2 8451 5294, *Email:* esa.soini@uusikaupunki.fi, *Website:* www.portofuki.fi

Officials: Port Director: Esa Soini.

Port Security: ISPS compliant

Approach: Three channels: Hepokari 8.5 m depth, Kemira 10 m depth and Haponniemi 5 m depth. Year round navigation with ice-breakers assistance

Anchorage: Near Hepokari entrance to a port depth 8.5 m. Near Kemira port depth 10 m

Pilotage: Compulsory for foreign vessels. Govt pilots available day and night from Turku Pilot (southern fairway) and Isokari Pilot (western). VHF Channel 16 and 13

Radio Frequency: VHF Channel 13-16

Maximum Vessel Dimensions: 40 000 dwt, 10 m d, 200 m loa

Working Hours: Work day 07.00 - 15.30, but if needed all hours

Accommodation:

Name	Length (m)	Depth (m)	Draught (m)	Remarks
Uusikaupunki				See [1] below
Hepokari Harbour	450	8.5		See [2] below
Kemira	340		10	See [3] below
Private Wharves				See [4] below

[1]*Uusikaupunki:* Two fairways lead to the harbour through the sheltering archipelago; Uto-Uusikaupunki, 78 nautical miles and Isokari-Uusikaupunki, 13 nautical miles Harbour area is divided into three parts
[2]*Hepokari Harbour:* Four berths handling cars, stone, wood, animal food & steel
[3]*Kemira:* Fertilizer. Average of 400 t of cargo handled in a working day/shift
[4]*Private Wharves:* Kemira quay 340 m long, 10 m d for fertiliser. Esso quay 5 m d for distribution of LPG

Storage: Open storage is available as well as warehouses for storing agricultural bulk, other bulk or utilised cargo

Mechanical Handling Equipment:

Location	Type	Capacity (t)	Qty
Uusikaupunki	Mult-purp. Cranes	8	2
Uusikaupunki	Mobile Cranes	50	2

Cargo Worked: Bulk cargo 250 t/h

Bunkering: Baltic Bunkering Ltd, Torggatan 10A, Mariehamn, Aland Islands, *Tel:* +358 18 143 00, *Fax:* +358 18 145 00, *Email:* info@balticbunkering.ax
Bunker Management Oy Ltd (BuMa), Merituulentie 424, FI-48310 Kotka, Finland, *Tel:* +358 5 2201 011, *Fax:* +358 5 2201 012, *Website:* www.bunkerman.fi
Shell Oy AB, Ulappasaarentie 4, FI-00980 Helsinki, Finland
ST1 Oy, ST1 OY, P O Box 37, Purotie, FI-02211 Helsinki, Finland, *Tel:* +358 10 557 11, *Fax:* +358 9 8030 004, *Email:* matti.pentti@st1.fi, *Website:* www.st1.fi
Teboil Oy AB, Bulevardi 26, P O Box 102, FI-00120 Helsinki, Finland, *Tel:* +358 20 470 01, *Fax:* +358 20 4700 248, *Email:* bunkersales@teboil.fi, *Website:* www.teboil.fi

Towage: Two tugs of 1600 hp and 600 hp available

Medical Facilities: Hospital in town

Airport: Turku, 70 km

Lloyd's Agent: Oy Wikestrom & Krogius AB, Huolintakatu 3, FI-20200 Turku, Finland, *Tel:* +358 2 0721 8500, *Fax:* +358 2 0721 8540, *Email:* wike.tku@wikestrom.com, *Website:* www.wikestrom.com

VAASA

Lat 63° 6' N; Long 21° 37' E.

Admiralty Chart: 2303	**Admiralty Pilot:** 20
Time Zone: GMT +2 h	**UNCTAD Locode:** FI VAA

Key to Principal Facilities:—					
A=Airport	**C**=Containers	**G**=General Cargo	**P**=Petroleum	**R**=Ro/Ro	**Y**=Dry Bulk
B=Bunkers	**D**=Dry Dock	**L**=Cruise	**Q**=Other Liquid Bulk	**T**=Towage (where available from port)	

Principal Facilities:

P	Y	G	R	B	T	A

Authority: Port of Vaasa, P O Box 2, FI-65101 Vaasa, Finland, *Tel:* +358 6 325 4500, *Fax:* +358 6 325 4514, *Email:* port@vaasa.fi, *Website:* www.vaasa.fi/port

Officials: Port Director: Lars Holmqvist, *Email:* lars.holmqvist@vaasa.fi.

Port Security: ISPS compliant

Approach: Entrance from sea at Vaasa lighthouse in pos 63° 15' N; 20° 53' E or 63° 12' N; 20° 45' E. Length of channel to port, 24 nautical miles, 9 m depth

Pilotage: Compulsory from Vaasa pilotage area, Tel: +358 (0) 20754 6153, Fax: +358 (0) 20754 6163, Email: pilotorder.west@finnpilot.fi. Pilot order form on www.pilotorder.fi

Radio Frequency: Port listens on VHF Channels 16 and 12

Weather: Prevailing SW'ly winds. Ice occurs between January and April and during this time ice breakers assist ships with an ice class

Tides: Non-tidal

Traffic: 2007, 1 477 130 t of cargo handled

Maximum Vessel Dimensions: 200 m loa, 35 m beam, 9 m draught

Principal Imports and Exports: Imports: Coal, Fuel oil. Exports: General cargo.

Working Hours: Monday to Friday 0700-1100, 1200-1600

Accommodation: Bulk facilities: Coal pier 145 m long in depth of 9 m
Tanker facilities: One berth at Vaskiluoto 105 m long in depth of 9 m; water and bunkers available. Cap of pipelines is up to 2500 t/h

Name	Length (m)	Draught (m)	Remarks
Vaasa			
Lasse's Quay	214	9	
Coal Quay	145	9	Conveyor belt for discharge of coal at rate of 1200 t/h
Oil Quay	105	9	Three oil discharging arms at rate of 1000 t/h/product
Southern Pier	180	8.6	
Rein's Quay	240	6.8	
Passenger Harbour Quays			
Ro/ro 1	154	6.8	
Ro/ro 2	145	5.7	
Ro/ro 3	160	6.4	

Storage:

Location	Covered (m²)
Vaasa	36000

Mechanical Handling Equipment:

Location	Type	Capacity (t)	Qty
Vaasa	Mobile Cranes	140	
Lasse's Quay	Shore Cranes	5	2
Southern Pier	Shore Cranes	5	1

Bunkering: Available by truck
Baltic Bunkering Ltd, Torggatan 10A, Mariehamn, Aland Islands, *Tel:* +358 18 143 00, *Fax:* +358 18 145 00, *Email:* info@balticbunkering.ax
Bunker Management Oy Ltd (BuMa), Merituulentie 424, FI-48310 Kotka, Finland, *Tel:* +358 5 2201 011, *Fax:* +358 5 2201 012, *Website:* www.bunkerman.fi
ExxonMobil Marine Fuels, Mailpoint 31, ExxonMobil House, Ermyn Way, Leatherhead, Surrey KT22 8UX, United Kingdom, *Tel:* +44 1372 222 000, *Fax:* +44 1372 223 922, *Email:* marine.fuels@exxonmobil.com, *Website:* www.exxonmobil.com – *Grades:* MGO – *Delivery Mode:* truck
Shell Oy AB, Ulappasaarentie 4, FI-00980 Helsinki, Finland
ST1 Oy, ST1 OY, P O Box 37, Purotie, FI-02211 Helsinki, Finland, *Tel:* +358 10 557 11, *Fax:* +358 9 8030 004, *Email:* matti.pentti@st1.fi, *Website:* www.st1.fi
Teboil Oy AB, Bulevardi 26, P O Box 102, FI-00120 Helsinki, Finland, *Tel:* +358 20 470 01, *Fax:* +358 20 4700 248, *Email:* bunkersales@teboil.fi, *Website:* www.teboil.fi

Waste Reception Facilities: Waste removal facilities are available. Dirty ballast water, slops from tank washing, sludge, oil mixtures as per agreement by road tanker

Towage: Not compulsory. Harbour tugs and icebreaker available

Shipping Agents: OY Backman-Trummer AB, Teollisuuskatu 1, PL 49, FI-65101 Vaasa, Finland, *Tel:* +358 6 323 9111, *Fax:* +358 6 323 9150, *Email:* info@batru.fi, *Website:* www.backman-trummer.fi

Stevedoring Companies: Oy Blomberg Stevedoring Ab, Rahitie 1, FI-65170 Vaasa, Finland, *Tel:* +358 6 323 9202, *Email:* jea@blomberg.fi

Surveyors: Russian Maritime Register of Shipping, Vaasa, Finland, *Tel:* +358 6 327 2175, *Fax:* +358 6 327 2175, *Website:* www.rs-head.spb.ru

Medical Facilities: Hospitals and medical institutions available

Airport: About 12 km

Railway: Railway Station, 4 km

Lloyd's Agent: Oy Lars Krogius A/B, Vilhonvuorenkatu 11 C 8, FI-00500 Helsinki, Finland, *Tel:* +358 9 4763 6300, *Fax:* +358 9 4763 6363, *Email:* finland@krogius.com, *Website:* www.krogius.com

VALKOM

alternate name, see Loviisa

VARKAUS

Lat 62° 20' N; Long 27° 50' E.

Admiralty Chart: -	**Admiralty Pilot:** 20
Time Zone: GMT +2 h	**UNCTAD Locode:** FI VRK

Principal Facilities:

P	Y	G	R	B	D	T	A

Authority: Varkaus Harbour Office, P O Box 208, FI-78201 Varkaus, Finland, *Tel:* +358 17 579411, *Fax:* +358 17 579 4641, *Email:* teuvo.pitkanen@varkaus.fi

Port Security: ISPS compliant

Approach: Channel 4.35 m depth

Anchorage: Available 0.4 miles SE of Akonniemi port, 8.0 m depth

Pilotage: Fairway pilotage compulsory but harbour pilotage optional, both arranged by governmental pilots upon request

Radio Frequency: Varkaus pilot station and Taipale lock VHF Channel 16 and 13

Weather: Port open for navigation from early April through until the following January for ice strengthened vessels

Traffic: 2007, 352 332 t of cargo handled

Maximum Vessel Dimensions: 82.5 m loa, 12.6 m wide, 4.35 m draught

Principal Imports and Exports: Imports: Calcium carbonate, Coal, Pulpwood. Exports: Paper, Wood products, Woodpulp.

Working Hours: Monday to Friday, 2 shifts 0600-1400, 1400-2200. Overtime possible on Saturday and Sunday

Accommodation:

Name	Depth (m)	Remarks
Varkaus		
Taipale	4.35	See [1] below
Akonniemi	4.35	See [2] below
Kosulanniemi	4.35	See [3] below

[1]*Taipale:* Operated by City of Varkaus, Technical Office, Ahlstrominkatu 6, FIN-78100 Varkaus, Tel:+358 17 579 4616
Two general/dry bulk berths 82 m long
[2]*Akonniemi:* Operated by City of Varkaus
One oil/dry bulk berth 26.0 m long and one general cargo/dry bulk berth 50.0 m long
[3]*Kosulanniemi:* Industrial port operated by Stora Enso O/Y
Two general cargo berths 85 m and 65 m long. Covered storage area of 5000 m3, covered warehousing of 3100 m2

Storage:

Location	Open (m²)	Covered (m²)
Taipale	1500	600
Akonniemi	7000	3000

Mechanical Handling Equipment:

Location	Type	Capacity (t)
Varkaus	Mobile Cranes	130

Cargo Worked: Loading paper/woodpulp 80-110 t/h, wood products 200 m3/h. Discharging of dry bulk 100 t/h

Bunkering: Available by road tanker (6' loading/discharging swivel arm)

Towage: Several tugs available, operated by Enso O/Y

Repair & Maintenance: Minor repairs possible by several small repairers

Stevedoring Companies: Savosteve O/Y, Varkaus, Finland, *Tel:* +358 17 551 4421, *Fax:* +358 17 551 4003

Medical Facilities: District hospital in town

Airport: Varkaus Joroinen Airport, 20 km

Lloyd's Agent: Oy Lars Krogius A/B, Vilhonvuorenkatu 11 C 8, FI-00500 Helsinki, Finland, *Tel:* +358 9 4763 6300, *Fax:* +358 9 4763 6363, *Email:* finland@krogius.com, *Website:* www.krogius.com

VASA

alternate name, see Vaasa

VASKILUOTO

harbour area, see under Vaasa

VEITSILUOTO

Lat 65° 42' N; Long 24° 37' E.

Admiralty Chart: 2302
Time Zone: GMT +2 h

Admiralty Pilot: 20
UNCTAD Locode: FI

Principal Facilities:

		G	C	R		B		T	A	

Authority: Port of Kemi Authority, Ajoksentie 748, FI-94900 Kemi, Finland, *Tel:* +358 16 215 1600, *Fax:* +358 16 215 1620, *Email:* portofkemi@kemi.fi, *Website:* www.portofkemi.fi

Officials: Port Director: Reijo Viitala, *Tel:* +358 16 215 1623, *Email:* reijo.viitala@kemi.fi.
Project Manager: Hannu Tikkala, *Email:* hannu.tikkala@kemi.fi.

Port Security: There is a fence over the harbour area. The area is guarded

Approach: Vessels approach port through entrance channel, draught 7 m

Pilotage: Compulsory for vessels over 60 m loa. Pilot boards 19.2 km before Ajos. VHF Channel 16

Tides: No tide. Fluctuations of water height up to 1.5 m due to winds

Maximum Vessel Dimensions: Max draft 7 m

Principal Imports and Exports: Imports: Pigments, Timber. Exports: Board, Paper, Pulp, Sawn goods.

Working Hours: Monday to Friday 0600-1430, 1430-2230. Saturday 0700-1500

Accommodation:

Name	Remarks
Veitsiluoto	See [1] below

[1]*Veitsiluoto:* Five piers: one 135.5 m long, one 209 m long, one 230 m long and two 120 m long; depth 7 m

Mechanical Handling Equipment:

Location	Type	Capacity (t)	Qty
Veitsiluoto	Mobile Cranes		
Veitsiluoto	Container Cranes	40	1

Cargo Worked: Over 6000 t of paper or board can be loaded in 24 h

Bunkering: Available from lorries

Towage: Available on request

Repair & Maintenance: Available at Kemi

Medical Facilities: Hospital in Kemi

Airport: Kemi Airport, 15 km

Railway: Kemi Railway Station, 7 km

Lloyd's Agent: Oy Lars Krogius A/B, Vilhonvuorenkatu 11 C 8, FI-00500 Helsinki, Finland, *Tel:* +358 9 4763 6300, *Fax:* +358 9 4763 6363, *Email:* finland@krogius.com, *Website:* www.krogius.com

VUOKSI

harbour area, see under Imatra

WALKOM

alternate name, see Loviisa

YKSPIHLAJA

see under Kokkola

AJACCIO

Lat 41° 55' N; Long 8° 44' E.

Admiralty Chart: 1424
Time Zone: GMT +1 h

Admiralty Pilot: 46
UNCTAD Locode: FR AJA

Principal Facilities:

		G		R	L	B		T	A	

Authority: Chambre de Commerce et d'Industrie de Ajaccio et South Corsica (CCIACS), Quai l'Herminier, P O Box 253, F-20180 Ajaccio, Corsica, France, *Tel:* +33 4 95 51 21 80, *Fax:* +33 4 95 21 07 86, *Email:* jy.battesti@sudcorse.cci.fr, *Website:* www.sudcorse.cci.fr

Officials: Port Director: Don Paul Grimaldi.
Deputy Director: Jean Yves Battesti, *Email:* jy.battesti@sudcorse.cci.fr.
Harbour Master: Olivier Berthezene, *Email:* olivier.berthezene@equipement.gouv.fr.

Port Security: ISPS compliant

Approach: Depth at entrance about 15.24 m

Anchorage: Usually anchoring is directly opposite the port, 300 m from the disembarking area of Capucins Nord and Sud

Pilotage: Compulsory for vessels over 60 m loa and available 24 h/day. Pilot Station, Tel: +33 4 95 21 42 48, Fax: +33 4 95 21 39 28, Email: pilotajax@wanadoo.fr. VHF Channels 16 and 12. Boarding area is 0.5 nautical mile SE of Citadelle Lt Beacon in pos 41° 55.06' N; 8° 44.53' E

Radio Frequency: VHF Channel 12

Weather: Predominantly W winds

Tides: Tidal range less than 1 m

Traffic: 2006, 940 000 t of cargo handled, 1 163 000 passengers

Working Hours: 0600-2200

Accommodation:

Name	Length (m)	Depth (m)	Remarks
Ajaccio			See [1] below
Quay Gare Maritime	200	6.5	
Quay l'Herminier	90	7	
Capucins Sud Pier	156	7	
Capucins Nord Pier	176	8.2	
Trois Marie Sud Pier	96	7.5	
Trois Marie Nord Pier	146	9	

[1]*Ajaccio:* Harbour Master: Xavier Toulgouat, Tel: +33 4 95 21 68 34, Fax: +33 4 95 51 17 84

Mechanical Handling Equipment:

Location	Type	Qty
Ajaccio	Mult-purp. Cranes	1
Ajaccio	Forklifts	8

Bunkering: Fuel oil available by road tanker

Waste Reception Facilities: Containers for garbage disposal (only in closed plastic bags) on quayside

Towage: One tug available of 15 t bollard pull

Key to Principal Facilities:—			
A=Airport	**C**=Containers	**G**=General Cargo	**P**=Petroleum	**R**=Ro/Ro	**Y**=Dry Bulk
B=Bunkers	**D**=Dry Dock	**L**=Cruise	**Q**=Other Liquid Bulk	**T**=Towage (where available from port)	

Shipping Agents: Mediport Services, 1 Rue des Trois Marie, P O Box 207, F-20179 Ajaccio, Corsica, France, *Tel:* +33 4 95 51 09 89, *Fax:* +33 4 95 50 05 40, *Email:* cruise@mediportservices.com, *Website:* www.mediportservices.com

Medical Facilities: Hospital de la Misericorde, 500 m from pier

Airport: Ajaccio, 8 km

Railway: Ajaccio, 50 m

Development: Construction in progress of a new pier 260 m long in depth of 9 m; to be ready in 2006

Lloyd's Agent: Unilex Maritime S.a.r.l, Les Docks, 10 Place de la Joliette, Atrium 10.8, F-13002 Marseilles Cedex 02, France, *Tel:* +33 4 91 14 04 40, *Fax:* +33 4 91 91 54 43, *Email:* mail@unilexmaritime.com, *Website:* www.unilexmaritime.com

AMBES

Lat 45° 2' N; Long 0° 36' W.

Admiralty Chart: 3068	**Admiralty Pilot:** 22
Time Zone: GMT +1 h	**UNCTAD Locode:** FR AMS

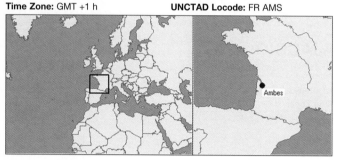

Principal Facilities:

P	Q				B	T	

Authority: Grand Port Maritime de Bordeaux, F-33810 Bec d'Ambes, France, *Tel:* +33 5 56 77 12 52, *Fax:* +33 5 56 77 04 31, *Website:* www.bordeaux-port.fr

Officials: Harbour Master: Fernandez Michel.

Port Security: ISPS compliant

Traffic: 2004, 4 031 802 t of cargo handled

Accommodation:

Name	Depth (m)	Draught (m)	Remarks
Ambes			
Berth 501	11	9.5–10	See [1] below
Berth 511-512	9.5–11	9.5–10.5	Public quay for oil tankers up to 215 m loa
Berth 515	7.5		See [2] below
Berth 517		6.5	Public quay for oil tankers up to 180 m loa
Berth 519	7	6.5	See [3] below

[1]*Berth 501:* Public quay for vessels transporting liquid ammonia and by oil tankers up to 200 m loa
[2]*Berth 515:* Private quay (COBOGAL) for vessels carrying liquefied gas up to 125 m loa
[3]*Berth 519:* Public quay for vessels up to 100 m loa. One 6 t quay crane and a conveyor belt for unloading salt

Bunkering: Available

Towage: Les Abeilles Bordeaux, Hangar 41, 14 quai Carriet, P O Box 507, F-33306 Lormont Cedex, France, *Tel:* +33 5 56 38 63 63, *Fax:* +33 5 56 38 63 69, *Email:* bordeaux@les-abeilles.com

Lloyd's Agent: Jean-Francois Chevreau, Bourse Maritime, Place Laine, F-33000 Bordeaux, France, *Tel:* +33 5 56 52 16 87, *Fax:* +33 5 56 44 67 85, *Email:* info@chevreau-lavie.fr, *Website:* www.chevreau-lavie.com

ANTIFER

harbour area, see under Le Havre

ARRIERE PORT

harbour area, see under Fecamp

BASSENS

harbour area, see under Bordeaux

BASTIA

Lat 42° 42' N; Long 9° 27' E.

Admiralty Chart: 1425	**Admiralty Pilot:** 46
Time Zone: GMT +1 h	**UNCTAD Locode:** FR BIA

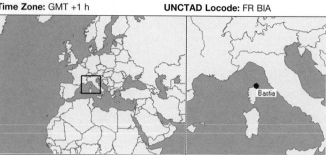

Principal Facilities:

P		G		R	L	B			A	

Authority: Capitainerie du Port de Commerce de Bastia, F-20200 Bastia, Corsica, France, *Tel:* +33 4 95 34 42 72, *Fax:* +33 4 95 34 42 88, *Email:* cap.smes.dde-2b@developpement-durable.gouv.fr, *Website:* www.bastia.port.fr

Officials: Managing Director: Antoine Breschi, *Tel:* +33 4 95 55 25 10, *Email:* a.breschi@bastia.port.fr.
Harbour Master: Gilles Bayle, *Tel:* +33 4 95 34 43 22, *Email:* gilles.bayle@developpement-durable.gouv.fr.

Pre-Arrival Information: 48 h notice including loa, breadth, max draught and Lloyd's identification number

Approach: Depth at entrance 6-12 m, on bar 6-7 m

Pilotage: Compulsory for vessels over 45 m loa, Tel: +33 4 95 31 50 95, Fax: +33 4 95 34 43 13. 24 h notice required. Boarding area 2 nautical miles off entrance

Radio Frequency: VHF Channel 12 'Bastia Port'

Tides: Max 0.6 m

Traffic: 2006, 2 161 917 passengers, 737 334 cars & caravans

Maximum Vessel Dimensions: 215 m loa, 7.5 m draught

Working Hours: 0800-1115, 1400-1715. Overtime available

Accommodation:

Name	Length (m)	Draught (m)
Bastia		
Mole Sud (P1)	157	6.7
Mole Nord (P2)	112	6.5
Quai du Fango (P3)	160	6.5
Quai de Rive (P4)	160	6.5
Quai Nord (P5)	118	5
Quai Nord Est (P6)	137	6.5
Quai Est (P7)	242	7.5
Poste 8	180	9

Storage: Warehousing and refrigerated space available

Mechanical Handling Equipment:

Location	Type	Capacity (t)	Qty
Bastia	Mult-purp. Cranes	7	2
Bastia	Forklifts		8

Cargo Worked: Ro/ro: 120 trailers/day

Bunkering: Gas oil available by truck

Repair & Maintenance: Minor repairs; no dry dock

Stevedoring Companies: Enterprise Generale de Manutention, Bastia, Corsica, France, *Tel:* +33 4 95 32 95 95, *Fax:* +33 4 95 32 90 73

Medical Facilities: Hospital, 10 minutes. Three private clinics

Airport: International Bastia Poretta, 20 km

Railway: Chemain de Fer Corse (SNCF), 1 km

Lloyd's Agent: Unilex Maritime S.a.r.l, Les Docks, 10 Place de la Joliette, Atrium 10.8, F-13002 Marseilles Cedex 02, France, *Tel:* +33 4 91 14 04 40, *Fax:* +33 4 91 91 54 43, *Email:* mail@unilexmaritime.com, *Website:* www.unilexmaritime.com

BATELLERIE

harbour area, see under Calais

BAYONNE

Lat 43° 30' N; Long 1° 29' W.

Admiralty Chart: 1175	**Admiralty Pilot:** 22
Time Zone: GMT +1 h	**UNCTAD Locode:** FR BAY

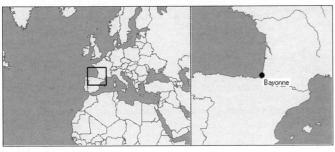

Principal Facilities:

P	Q	Y	G		L	B	D	T	A

Authority: Capitainerie du Port de Bayonne, 128 Avenue de l'Adour, F-64600 Anglet, France, *Tel:* +33 5 59 63 11 57, *Fax:* +33 5 59 42 09 43, *Email:* alain.tcheng@equipement.gouv.fr, *Website:* www.ports-basques.com

Officials: Managing Director: Pascal Agostini, *Email:* pascal.agostini@aquitaine.fr. Harbour Master: Christophe Voisin.

Port Security: ISPS compliant. The port and quays will soon be closed to the public

Documentation: Notice of arrival (c/o agent) (1 copy), inward declaration (1 copy), crew list (2 copies), report of good working order (1 copy), list of dangerous goods onboard (1 copy), personal effect list (2 copies), store list (2 copies), tonnage certificate or ships register (1 copy), health certificate (2 copies)

Approach: Pilot station at BA buoy. Vessels must contact Bayonne port and pilot station on VHF Channel 12

Anchorage: Between the following positions: 43° 33.8' N - 1° 36.3' W ; 43° 32.8' N - 1° 33.8' W ; 43° 35.7' N - 1° 31.7' W ; 43° 36.7' N - 1° 34' W
The depth is about 40 - 50 m

Pilotage: Compulsory for vessels over 60 m loa. Pilotage office is located at the Signal Tower. VHF Channel 12, Tel: +33 5 59 58 54 54, Fax: +33 5 59 58 54 59

Radio Frequency: VHF Channel 12, 24 h/day (Bayonne Port Control)

Weather: Severe gales in winter can reduce depth in the river mouth

Tides: MHWS 4.30 m, MLWS 0.80 m, MHWN 3.40 m, MLWN 1.80 m

Traffic: 2005, 3 900 000 t of cargo handled

Maximum Vessel Dimensions: 160 m loa, 25 m beam, 8.7 m draft for entry and 9.6 m draft for departure. Anything above these and each request of call will be examined carefully

Principal Imports and Exports: Imports: Chemical products, Fertilizers, Hydrocarbons, New vehicles, Refined oil products, Scrap metal, Wood logs. Exports: Crude oil, Iron, Liquid chemical products, Maize, Steel billets, Sulphur.

Working Hours: Mon - Fri: 6 am - 10 pm, Sat: 6 am - 2 pm (Dry bulk products) 24 h/day, 7 days a week (Liquid products)

Accommodation:

Name	Length (m)	Depth (m)	Draught (m)	Remarks
Tarnos Aval				See [1] below
Tarnos 1	100	10		
Tarnos 2	100	10		
Tarnos 3	100	10		
Tarnos 4	100	10		
Quai Europeen				See [2] below
Steel Works				See [3] below
M. Forgues 1 (downstream)	100	10		Import
M. Forgues 2 (upstream)	100	10		Import
Leon Tramut	105	10		Import
Delure	170	10		Export
Grain Terminal				See [4] below
Silo Maisica	240	7		
Oil Terminal				See [5] below
Saint Gobain	210	9		On four dolphins
Area Saint Bernard				See [6] below
Quai Saint Bernard	160	7		
Area Blancpignon				See [7] below
Armand Gommez	200	7		600 t/day of cargo handled
Sulphur Terminal				Operated by Total Fina Elf
Edouard Castel Quay	195	8.35		Linear shiploader for solid sulphur with a cap of 1000 t/h
Edouard Castel Dolphin	170	8.35		Pipe for loading liquid sulphur with a cap of 1000 t/h
Cruise Terminal				
Edmond Foy Quay	150	5.5		Parking area of 6000 m2 available

[1]*Tarnos Aval:* Operated by RENO, for solid bulk cargoes (fertilizers) at rate of approx 2000 t/day. Two conveyor belts running between the quayside and a fertilizer manufacturing plant. Terminal operates 24 h/day 7 days a week
[2]*Quai Europeen:* Operated by L.B.C. and RENO, liquid bulk cargoes handled at a rate of approx 3-5000 t/day. Three berths, L1 (downstream) ; L2 (in the middle) ; L3 (upstream), 330 m long 10 m d. Possibility to work two small vessels simultaneously at L1 and L3, generally large tankers are worked at L2. Two conveyor racks for sulphuric and phosphoric acid, connecting the quayside to the RENO storage. 2 x 6" diameter handling arms for chemical products, 1 x 10" diameter handling arm for crude oil, and a conveyor rack connecting the L.B.C depot. The terminal operates 24 h/day

[3]*Steel Works:* Operated by A.D.A. (Acierie de l'Atlantique), scrap iron (import) and steel billets (export) handled at a rate of approx 1000 t/day. Two cranes permitting to unload scrap iron in the storage area, 300 m x 40 m, situated 33 m from the berthing frontage. Terminal operates 24 h/day
[4]*Grain Terminal:* Operated by MAISICA; maize handled at a rate of approx 2 x 800 t/h. Two loading cranes connected to a conveyor belt running between the quayside and the silos. Storage cap of 110 000 t. Terminal operates 6 days per week, 6 am - 10 pm
[5]*Oil Terminal:* Operated by Raffinerie du Midi; handling refined oil products. A pipeline for refined hydrocarbons connecting the dock to the storage site of the Raffinerie du Midi. Storage tanks of 35 000 m3
[6]*Area Saint Bernard:* Ro/ro traffic. A floating pontoon of 800 m2 handling ships both upstream and downstream, with 30 m of gangway connecting the pontoon to the quayside able to withstand a load of up to 80 t. A 30 000 m2 parking area available for rolling stock
[7]*Area Blancpignon:* Shipboard panels, cement in bags (import) & other cargoes handled

Mechanical Handling Equipment:

Location	Type	Capacity (t)	Qty
Area Saint Bernard	Mult-purp. Cranes	30–1	
Area Saint Bernard	Mult-purp. Cranes	40–80	1
Area Blancpignon	Mobile Cranes	6	2

Cargo Worked: Bulk cargo 200-300 t/h/crane

Bunkering: Oil delivered alongside by lorries

Waste Reception Facilities: Dirty ballast can be removed by truck by private companies

Repair & Maintenance: Chantiers SAREM, 10 Avenue de l'Adour, F-64600 Anglet, France, *Tel:* +33 5 59 52 84 84, *Fax:* +33 5 59 42 00 82 Dry dock 98 m x 15 m x 5 m. Minor repairs to larger vessels can be effected

Ship Chandlers: EURL Mouesca Marine France, 82 Avenue de L'Ardour, Anglet, F-64600 Bayonne, France, *Tel:* +33 5 59 63 12 06, *Fax:* +33 5 59 63 26 47, *Email:* mouescamarinefrance@wanadoo.fr

Shipping Agents: Matrama S.A., 10 Quai de Lesseps, P O Box 734, F-64100 Bayonne, France, *Tel:* +33 5 59 44 59 70, *Fax:* +33 5 59 55 25 76, *Email:* consignation.bayonne@sea-invest.fr, *Website:* www.sea-invest.fr
Sobem, Route de la Barre, F-40220 Bayonne, France, *Tel:* +33 5 59 64 57 00, *Fax:* +33 5 59 64 57 09, *Email:* bayonne@sobem.com
Worms Services Maritimes S.A., Espace Rive Gauche, 66 Allees Marines, F-64100 Bayonne, France, *Tel:* +33 5 59 31 16 54, *Fax:* +33 5 59 31 16 34, *Email:* wsm.bayonne@bdx.worms-sm.fr, *Website:* www.worms-sm.com

Stevedoring Companies: Matrama S.A., 10 Quai de Lesseps, P O Box 734, F-64100 Bayonne, France, *Tel:* +33 5 59 44 59 70, *Fax:* +33 5 59 55 25 76, *Email:* consignation.bayonne@sea-invest.fr, *Website:* www.sea-invest.fr
Sobem, Route de la Barre, F-40220 Bayonne, France, *Tel:* +33 5 59 64 57 00, *Fax:* +33 5 59 64 57 09, *Email:* bayonne@sobem.com

Medical Facilities: Centre Hospitalier cote Basque, Tel: +33 (5) 59 44 35 35, 4 - 10 km away

Airport: Anglet Airport, Biarritz, 10 km

Railway: Gare de Bayonne, 3 km

Lloyd's Agent: Jean-Francois Chevreau, Bourse Maritime, Place Laine, F-33000 Bordeaux, France, *Tel:* +33 5 56 52 16 87, *Fax:* +33 5 56 44 67 85, *Email:* info@chevreau-lavie.fr, *Website:* www.chevreau-lavie.com

BEC D'AMBES

see under Ambes

BERRE

see under Etang de Berre

BLAINVILLE QUAY

harbour area, see under Caen

BLAYE

Lat 45° 7' N; Long 0° 38' W.

Admiralty Chart: 3068	**Admiralty Pilot:** 22
Time Zone: GMT +1 h	**UNCTAD Locode:** FR BYE

Key to Principal Facilities:—

A=Airport	**C**=Containers	**G**=General Cargo	**P**=Petroleum	**R**=Ro/Ro	**Y**=Dry Bulk
B=Bunkers	**D**=Dry Dock	**L**=Cruise	**Q**=Other Liquid Bulk	**T**=Towage (where available from port)	

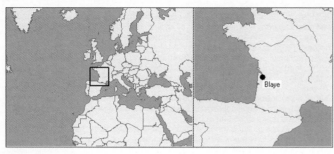

Principal Facilities:

Q	Y	G		L	B		T	A

Authority: Grand Port Maritime de Bordeaux, Blaye, France, *Tel:* +33 5 57 42 13 63, *Fax:* +33 5 57 42 28 19, *Website:* www.bordeaux-port.fr

Port Security: ISPS compliant

Traffic: 2004, 385 207 t of cargo handled

Accommodation:

Name	Length (m)	Depth (m)	Draught (m)	Remarks
Blaye				
Berth 600-601	300	10	9.5	For vessels up to 200 m loa
Berth 602 (Quay Semabla)			9–10	See [1] below
Berth 610				See [2] below

[1]*Berth 602 (Quay Semabla):* Storage for liquid bulk goods of 13 000 m3 and solid bulk goods of 90 000 t
[2]*Berth 610:* Currently being transformed so that it can receive cruise liners

Bunkering: Oil fuel available

Towage: Les Abeilles Bordeaux, Hangar 41, 14 quai Carriet, P O Box 507, F-33306 Lormont Cedex, France, *Tel:* +33 5 56 38 63 63, *Fax:* +33 5 56 38 63 69, *Email:* bordeaux@les-abeilles.com

Repair & Maintenance: Small repair shops available

Airport: Bordeaux-Merignac, 45 km

Railway: Railway tracks on the port zone linked to the mainline network

Lloyd's Agent: Jean-Francois Chevreau, Bourse Maritime, Place Laine, F-33000 Bordeaux, France, *Tel:* +33 5 56 52 16 87, *Fax:* +33 5 56 44 67 85, *Email:* info@chevreau-lavie.fr, *Website:* www.chevreau-lavie.com

BONIFACIO

Lat 41° 23' N; Long 9° 6' E.

Admiralty Chart: 1424	**Admiralty Pilot:** 46
Time Zone: GMT +1 h	**UNCTAD Locode:** FR BON

Principal Facilities:

		G		R	L	B			A

Authority: Chambre de Commerce et d'Industrie de Ajaccio et South Corsica (CCIACS), Quai l'Herminier, P O Box 253, F-20180 Ajaccio, Corsica, France, *Tel:* +33 4 95 51 21 80, *Fax:* +33 4 95 21 07 86, *Email:* jy.battesti@sudcorse.cci.fr, *Website:* www.sudcorse.cci.fr

Officials: Port Director: Don Paul Grimaldi.
Deputy Director: Jean Yves Battesti, *Email:* jy.battesti@sudcorse.cci.fr.
Harbour Master: Olivier Berthezene, *Email:* olivier.berthezene@equipement.gouv.fr.

Port Security: ISPS compliant

Anchorage: At entrance of the Bouches de Bonifacio in depth of 30-40 m

Pilotage: Compulsory for vessels over 75 m loa and available 24 h/day. Pilot station, Tel: +33 4 95 21 42 48, Fax: +33 4 95 21 39 28, Email: pilotajax@wanadoo.fr. Boarding area is 0.5 nautical mile S of Pointe de la Madonetta Lt in pos 41° 23.22' N; 9° 08.66' E

Radio Frequency: VHF Channel 12 and 16

Weather: Cross currents and very strong Mistral or Tramontana winds

Traffic: 2003, 31 822 t of cargo handled, 295 686 passengers, 90 836 vehicles

Working Hours: 0600-2200

Accommodation:

Name	Length (m)	Depth (m)
Bonifacio		
Quay 1	50	5
Quay 2	70	5
Quay d'Honneur	60	6.5

Bunkering: Available

Waste Reception Facilities: Garbage disposal by lorry

Medical Facilities: Hospital, 2 km from pier

Airport: Figari, 25 km

Lloyd's Agent: Unilex Maritime S.a.r.l, Les Docks, 10 Place de la Joliette, Atrium 10.8, F-13002 Marseilles Cedex 02, France, *Tel:* +33 4 91 14 04 40, *Fax:* +33 4 91 91 54 43, *Email:* mail@unilexmaritime.com, *Website:* www.unilexmaritime.com

BORDEAUX

Lat 44° 50' N; Long 0° 34' W.

Admiralty Chart: 3068/3069	**Admiralty Pilot:** 22
Time Zone: GMT +1 h	**UNCTAD Locode:** FR BOD

Principal Facilities:

Q	Y	G	C	R	L	B	D	T	A

Authority: Grand Port Maritime de Bordeaux, Palais de la Bourse, 3 Place Gabriel, F-33075 Bordeaux Cedex, France, *Tel:* +33 5 56 90 58 00, *Fax:* +33 5 36 90 58 77, *Email:* postoffice@bordeaux-port.fr, *Website:* www.bordeaux-port.fr

Officials: General Director: Philippe Deiss, *Email:* p-deiss@bordeaux-port.fr.
Marketing Manager: Julien Bas, *Email:* j-das@bordeaux-port.fr.
Public Relations Manager: Jean Michel Germain, *Email:* jm-germain@bordeaux-port.fr.
Harbour Master: Henri Follin, *Email:* h-follin@bordeaux-port.fr.

Port Security: ISPS compliant

Approach: The administrative area of Bordeaux Port includes the auxiliary installations at Bassens, Bec d'Ambes, Blaye, Pauillac and Le Verdon on the Garonne and the Gironde from the up-stream boundary to the sea (excluding the small ports and the bank of the Charente-Maritime), Dordogne, Bec d'Ambes to the PK26 and the outer harbour of Verdon. Entrance to the port in the Gironde is between Coubre Point and Cordouan lighthouse, via the Nouvelle Passe de l'Quest, which, over 400 m width, has min depth of 13.5 m (18.5 m at HT). The pilot buoy, called Buoy BXA, is at lat 45° 37' 04" N, long 1° 28' 36" W
Passage downstream from Bordeaux, left bank, to sea is possible for vessels drawing less than 8.5 m of water. From Bordeaux, right bank, known as Bassens, passage is possible for vessels drawing 9.5 m in min conditions. Between Blaye and the sea, passage is possible for vessels drawing 9.5 m. From Bec d'Ambes the draughts admitted are 9.5 m and 10 m. From Pauillac, passage is possible for vessels drawing 9.75 m at NT and 10.35 m at ST. Various waiting roadsteads can be utilised in the river. These are at Verdon, Richard and Suzac

Pilotage: Compulsory, Tel: +33 5 56 74 25 00, Fax: +33 5 56 74 71 18, Email: pilotage.gironde@wanado.fr; VHF Channels 12 and 14. Pilotage in the River Gironde is administered from two stations: (a) the Estuary station-Verdon to Sea and vice versa; (b) Bordeaux station-Bordeaux to Verdon and vice versa

Principal Imports and Exports: Imports: Chemical fertilisers, Mineral oil, Natural phosphates, Oil cakes. Exports: General cargo, Grain, Timber.

Working Hours: Mon-Fri 0800-1200, 1400-1800. Shiftwork possible 0700-1400, 1400-2100 or 0800-1400; 1400-2100, 1800-2220. One additional hour possible to complete operations 1800-1900 or 2100-2200 at overtime rates. Sat: shift work only 0800-1400 at overtime rates, and for special vessels such as ro/ro, containers, damaged vessels and possibly liners 1400-2100. An additional hour is possible from 1400-1500 or 2100-2200 to complete
For bulk carriers discharging at 'Quai Mineralier' at Bassens Wharf No.414 shift work every day. Saturday included, from 0700-1400, 1400-2100
For ro/ro vessels with angled stern ramp, container vessels and vessels loaded with 10 t units woodpulp bales and/or packed sawnwood accommodated at Le Verdon Ro/ro-Container Terminal at the river entrance working hours are: First shift 0800-1500, second 1600-2300, third 2400-0700 every day including Sat, Sun and holidays
Nightwork can be arranged on special occasions (shortage of berth) 2200-0540 at overtime rates provided arranged beforehand with Port Authorities and Syndicate of Shore Labourers
Sun: Work may be possible at extra charge if arranged beforehand
No work is performed on holidays

Accommodation:

Name	Remarks
Queyries	See [1] below

Name	Remarks
Bassens	
Forest Products Terminal (Berth 413)	Handling tropical timber, sawn Baltic wood & pulpwood
Phosphate Terminal (Berth 414)	Quayside conveyor belt at rate of 1000 t/h. Three silos with an overall cap of 17 000 t operated by SOFERTI
General Cargo Terminal (Berths 415-416)	See [2] below
Grain Terminal (Berth 417)	See [3] below
Ro/ro Berth (Berth 430)	See [4] below
Fertilizer & General Cargo Terminal (Berths 431-432)	See [5] below
Container Terminal (Berth 433)	Open area of 40 000 m2. 36 reefer points
Agro-Food Terminal (Berth 434)	Import of soya meal. Conveyer belt with a throughput of 1200 t/h. Three hoppers. Two weigh towers. Two sheds of 8000 m2 each
Mineral Ore Terminal (Berth 435)	See [6] below
Oilseed Terminal (Berth 436)	See [7] below
Grain Terminal (Berth 449)	Two export gantries at 14 000 t/day. Two silos of 80 000 and 150 000 t

[1]*Queyries:* Public loading jetties on the right bank extending for 250 m with depths ranging from 5 m to 6.5 m; these are specially equipped for handling timber; stone quays with 6.5 m depth alongside available here

[2]*General Cargo Terminal (Berths 415-416):* Handling quartz, kraft & sawn timber. Ship to shore self-cleaning conveyor belt. Two hoppers with a throughput of 1500 t/day. Open storage area of 36 000 m2 and a 6000 m2 shed

[3]*Grain Terminal (Berth 417):* One loading gantry of 1200 t/h cap linked to the silos by conveyor belt. Two silos of 80 000 t

[4]*Ro/ro Berth (Berth 430):* Gangway on a pontoon for embarking/disembarking live loads up to 60 t for vessels up to 135 m loa

[5]*Fertilizer & General Cargo Terminal (Berths 431-432):* Handling fertilizer, fire clay, paper pulp, kaolin & clay. Quayside shed storage of 13 000 m2 backed up by an open storage area of 21 000 m2

[6]*Mineral Ore Terminal (Berth 435):* Imports of coal, petroleum coke & cement. Conveyor belt and two hoppers provide a throughput rate of 1200 t/h. Storage area of approx 60 000 m2

[7]*Oilseed Terminal (Berth 436):* Conveyor belt at 400 t/h, suction loading for meals at 150 t/h and loading of oils at 250 m3/h. Grain silos of 67 000 m3, meals of 45 000 m3, fertilizer of 40 000 m3 and oil tanks of 16 000 m3

Mechanical Handling Equipment:

Location	Type	Capacity (t)	Qty	Remarks
Forest Products Terminal (Berth 413)	Mult-purp. Cranes	8	1	also for Berth 414
Forest Products Terminal (Berth 413)	Mult-purp. Cranes	15	3	also for Berth 414
General Cargo Terminal (Berths 415-416)	Mult-purp. Cranes	8	2	
Fertilizer & General Cargo Terminal (Berths 431-432)	Mult-purp. Cranes	8	2	
Fertilizer & General Cargo Terminal (Berths 431-432)	Mult-purp. Cranes	15	1	
Container Terminal (Berth 433)	Mult-purp. Cranes	15–25	5	also for Berths 434 and 435
Container Terminal (Berth 433)	Mobile Cranes	52	1	
Container Terminal (Berth 433)	Mobile Cranes	100	1	

Bunkering: Societe des Petroles Shell, 89 Boulevard Franklin Roosevelt, 92564 Rueil-Malmasion, F-76650 Petit Couronne, France, *Tel:* +33 2 35 67 47 03, *Fax:* +33 2 35 67 47 03

Total France S.A., Total Marine Fuels, 51 Esplanade du General de Gaulle, F-92907 Paris la Defense Cedex 10, France, *Tel:* +33 1 4135 2755, *Fax:* +33 1 4197 0291, *Email:* marine.fuels@total.com, *Website:* www.marinefuels.total.com

Towage: Les Abeilles Bordeaux, Hangar 41, 14 quai Carriet, P O Box 507, F-33306 Lormont Cedex, France, *Tel:* +33 5 56 38 63 63, *Fax:* +33 5 56 38 63 69, *Email:* bordeaux@les-abeilles.com

Repair & Maintenance: STEMA, 110 Rue Achard, F-33300 Bordeaux, France, *Tel:* +33 5 56 69 29 66, *Fax:* +33 5 56 50 32 14 Three drydocks: No.1 105 m x 15.5 m x 6.1 m, No.2 148 m x 18.3 m x 6.65 m, No.3 235 m x 32 m x 7.5 m

Ship Chandlers: R.& G. Dekytspotter Atlantic, 94 Avenue de Picot, Eysines, 33320 Bordeaux, France, *Tel:* +33 5 56 16 01 16, *Fax:* +33 5 56 57 51 23, *Email:* dksupply@dekytspotter.com

Shipping Agents: Agena Tramp, 15 Avenue de Chavailles, F-33525 Bruges, France, *Tel:* +33 5 56 43 66 30, *Fax:* +33 5 56 43 66 39, *Email:* atlantic@agenatramp.fr, *Website:* www.agenatramp.fr

CMA-CGM S.A., CMA-CGM Bordeaux, Centre Bordeaux Fret, Z.I. Bruges rue H. Delattre, F-33521 Bruges, France, *Tel:* +33 5 56 11 96 00, *Fax:* +33 5 56 11 96 31, *Email:* bod.jmallet@cma-cgm.com, *Website:* www.cma-cgm.com

K Line (Europe) Ltd, 447 Boulevard Alfred Daney, 33075 Bordeaux, France, *Tel:* +33 5 57 57 33 33, *Fax:* +33 5 56 39 91 25, *Email:* headoffice@balguerie.com, *Website:* www.balguerie.com

Leon Vincent S.A., Avenue Jean Claudeville, F-33520 Bruges, France, *Tel:* +33 5 56 69 65 65, *Fax:* +33 5 56 69 65 50, *Email:* l.vincent@anfrance.fr, *Website:* www.leonvincent.fr

Mediterranean Shipping Company, Parc d'Activites Kennedy, Bat A, 1 Avenue Rudolph Diesel, P O Box 359, Merignac, F-33694 Bordeaux, France, *Tel:* +33 5 57 92 66 00, *Fax:* +33 5 57 92 66 43, *Email:* mscbordeaux@mscfr.mscgva.ch, *Website:* www.mscgva.ch

Samab, 1 Street Richelieu, Bassens, 33530 Bordeaux, France, *Tel:* +33 5 57 77 49 50, *Fax:* +33 5 57 77 82 55, *Email:* trampbod@sea-invest.fr, *Website:* www.sea-invest.fr

Worms Services Maritimes S.A., Bureaux DuLac Batiment E15, Avenue de Chavailles, F-33525 Bordeaux, France, *Tel:* +33 5 57 19 11 60, *Fax:* +33 5 57 19 11 70, *Email:* wsmbordeaux@worms.geis.com, *Website:* www.worms-sm.com

Stevedoring Companies: Amaport, F-33530 Bassens, France, *Tel:* +33 5 56 06 07 87, *Fax:* +33 5 56 06 23 08, *Email:* amaport@wanadoo.fr

Balguerie S.A., Rue Bertrand Balguerie, F-33521 Bruges, France, *Tel:* +33 5 57 57 33 33, *Fax:* +33 5 57 57 34 34, *Email:* secretariat.bruges@balguerie.com, *Website:* www.balguerie.com

Gesvrac, Hangar G5, Quai Alfred de Vial, Bassens, France, *Tel:* +33 5 56 31 68 68, *Fax:* +33 5 56 74 70 78, *Email:* frank.humbert@sea.invest_france.com

Samab, 1 Street Richelieu, Bassens, 33530 Bordeaux, France, *Tel:* +33 5 57 77 49 50, *Fax:* +33 5 57 77 82 55, *Email:* trampbod@sea-invest.fr, *Website:* www.sea-invest.fr

Sea-Invest Bordeaux, 1 Rue Richelieu, F-33530 Bassens, France, *Tel:* +33 5 57 77 49 50, *Fax:* +33 5 57 77 82 55, *Email:* trampbod@sea-invest.fr, *Website:* www.sea-invest-sa.com

VAT, Zone Portuaire du Verdon, F-33123 Le Verdon, France, *Tel:* +33 5 56 09 64 81, *Fax:* +33 5 56 09 62 00, *Email:* jllatapie@balguerie.com

Surveyors: Jean-Francois Chevreau, Bourse Maritime, Place Laine, F-33000 Bordeaux, France, *Tel:* +33 5 56 52 16 87, *Fax:* +33 5 56 44 67 85, *Email:* info@chevreau-lavie.fr, *Website:* www.chevreau-lavie.com

Det Norske Veritas A/S, Bordeaux, France, *Tel:* +33 5 56 44 59 52, *Fax:* +33 5 56 51 25 36, *Website:* www.dnv.com

Nippon Kaiji Kyokai, Expertises Maritimes et Industrielles, 69 Rue Reinette, F-33100 Bordeaux, France, *Tel:* +33 5 56 32 32 03, *Fax:* +33 5 56 32 32 07, *Website:* www.classnk.or.jp

Airport: Bordeaux-Merignac

Railway: Quayside railway tracks and network throughout the port zone with two junctions connecting up sidings to the Bordeaux/Paris mainline and hence to the national and international network

Lloyd's Agent: Jean-Francois Chevreau, Bourse Maritime, Place Laine, F-33000 Bordeaux, France, *Tel:* +33 5 56 52 16 87, *Fax:* +33 5 56 44 67 85, *Email:* info@chevreau-lavie.fr, *Website:* www.chevreau-lavie.com

BOULOGNE

Lat 50° 44' N; Long 1° 37' E.

Admiralty Chart: 438	**Admiralty Pilot:** 28
Time Zone: GMT +1 h	**UNCTAD Locode:** FR BOL

Principal Facilities:

P	Y	G	C	R		B		T	A

Authority: Service Maritime de Boulogne, 96 Boulevard Gambetta, F-62310 Boulogne, France, *Tel:* +33 3 21 10 35 46, *Fax:* +33 3 21 87 28 79, *Email:* capboulogne@equipment.gouv.fr, *Website:* www.portboulogne.com

Officials: Marine Manager: Benoit Dufumier, *Tel:* +33 3 21 10 35 45, *Email:* benoit.dufumier@developpement-durable.gouv.fr.

Harbour Master: Philippe Reydant, *Tel:* +33 3 21 10 35 45, *Email:* philippe.reydant@developpement-durable.gouv.fr.

Port Security: ISPS compliant

Approach: Port protected by the Carnot Breakwater. Vessels whose draught exceeds 6 m are admitted according to the level of the tide

Anchorage: Available at 50° 45' N; 1° 31' E and 50° 44' N; 1° 32' 30" E. Extension possibilities in the W part of Caisson Carnot to Ophelie buoy in the S

Pilotage: Compulsory for vessels exceeding 50 m loa. When pilot boat operating, contact it by VHF Channel 12. When pilot boat in the harbour, then contact Pilot station, Tel: +33 3 21 31 36 08, Fax: +33 3 21 87 16 22

Radio Frequency: Boulogne Port Control, VHF Channel 12 or Tel: +33 3 21 31 52 43. Cross Gris Nez, VHF Channel 13 or Tel: +33 3 21 87 21 87

Weather: General NW and SW winds

Maximum Vessel Dimensions: 200 m loa, 35 000 dwt, 10.5 m d

Principal Imports and Exports: Imports: Fertiliser, Frozen goods, Newsprint, Ore, Paper, Petroleum, Wood, Woodpulp. Exports: Cement, Clinker, Flour, Lime, Scrap, Steel alloys, Sugar.

Working Hours: Quai Europe: Monday to Friday 0700-1200, 1400-1900. Saturday 0700-1200. Overtime 0600-1400, 1400-2200, 2200-0600
Quai Comilog: Monday to Friday 0600-1400, 1400-2200. Saturday 0600-1400. Overtime 2200-0600

Key to Principal Facilities:—			
A=Airport	**C**=Containers	**G**=General Cargo	**P**=Petroleum	**R**=Ro/Ro	**Y**=Dry Bulk
B=Bunkers	**D**=Dry Dock	**L**=Cruise	**Q**=Other Liquid Bulk	**T**=Towage (where available from port)

Accommodation:

Name	Length (m)	Depth (m)	Remarks
Boulogne			See [1] below
Inner Tidal Harbour			See [2] below
Darse Sarraz Bournet (Quai de l'Europe)	775	11	See [3] below
Bassin Loubet			See [4] below

[1]*Boulogne:* Ro/ro facilities: one berth (RoRo Carnot) for vessels up to 146 m loa and 28 m breadth. 55 000 m2 back-up facilities, max load on ramp 5 lorries x 35 t and on pontoon 80 t

[2]*Inner Tidal Harbour:* Consists of one berth for vessels up to 110 m loa, dredged to minus 4.5 m (plus water level according to tide), for small tankers carrying bunkers for local fishing fleets. Two ferry berths; one for passenger vessels with single ramp, one with double deck, double lane ramps, 38 t max load on each deck

[3]*Darse Sarraz Bournet (Quai de l'Europe):* For vessels up to 35 000 dwt and 200 m loa. Four rail tracks alongside quay. 63 000 m2 of covered sheds. Cement clinker silo of 42 500 t cap; rate of loading 1000-1200 t/h; work performed round the clock including Sun and holidays except May 1

[4]*Bassin Loubet:* Access lock, length 125 m, breadth 25 m, 5.5 m d (plus water level according to tide); max loa of vessels 130 m. Vessels with a length of less than 100 m can go through the lock, depending on their d, at almost any time, but vessels of 100 m up to 130 m can only go through the lock when both doors are open, ie 2 h before HW until HW. 10 000 m2 of refrigerated or insulated sheds. 15 000 m3 of cold storage on quayside

Storage: There is 55 000 m2 of warehouse storage, 8000 m2 of refrigerated storage and 111 000 m2 of open storage at the Cargo Port. There is also 28 000 m2 of open storage at the Ferry Terminal

Mechanical Handling Equipment:

Location	Type	Capacity (t)	Qty
Darse Sarraz Bournet (Quai de l'Europe)	Mult-purp. Cranes	30	2
Darse Sarraz Bournet (Quai de l'Europe)	Mult-purp. Cranes	12.5–20	2
Darse Sarraz Bournet (Quai de l'Europe)	Mult-purp. Cranes	7.5–10	2

Cargo Worked: Ore/bulk cargoes 10 000-12 000 t/day

Bunkering: Societe Maritime de Combustibles Liquides, 1 Quai de L Amiral Huguet, 62200 Boulogne, France, *Tel:* +33 3 21 30 22 37, *Fax:* +33 3 21 87 34 71
BP France S.A., Immeuble le Cervier, 12 Avenue des Beguines, Cergy-Saint-Christophe, 95866 Cergy Pontoise Cedex, France, *Tel:* +33 1 3422 4000, *Fax:* +33 1 3422 4417, *Email:* benoist.grosjean@fr.bp.com, *Website:* www.bpmarine.com – *Grades:* IFo-180; IF-380; MGO – *Parcel Size:* 25t – *Delivery Mode:* pipeline, barge, truck
Societe Maritime de Combustibles Liquides, 1 Quai de L Amiral Huguet, 62200 Boulogne, France, *Tel:* +33 3 21 30 22 37, *Fax:* +33 3 21 87 34 71
Total France S.A., Total Marine Fuels, 51 Esplanade du General de Gaulle, F-92907 Paris la Defense Cedex 10, France, *Tel:* +33 1 4135 2755, *Fax:* +33 1 4197 0291, *Email:* marine.fuels@total.com, *Website:* www.marinefuels.total.com

Towage: Societe Boulonnaise de Remorquage, 118 Boulevard Gambetta, P O Box 171, F-62203 Boulogne Cedex, France, *Tel:* +33 3 21 87 44 88, *Fax:* +33 3 21 83 94 71

Repair & Maintenance: Societe de Construction et Reparations Navales et de Mecanique (Socarenam), 2 Boulevard de Chatillon, P O Box 429, F-62206 Boulogne, France, *Tel:* +33 3 21 30 56 00, *Fax:* +33 3 21 30 53 23, *Email:* socarenam.boulogne@wanadoo.fr, *Website:* www.cscn.fr/ch_socarenam.htm Two slipways with 1500-2500 t total cap

Medical Facilities: Hospital Duchenne, Boulogne-sur-Mer, 7 km

Airport: Le Touquet, 30 km

Railway: Boulogne-sur-Mer, 4 km

Lloyd's Agent: McLarens Young France S.A, 80 Boulevard Haussmann, F-75008 Paris, France, *Tel:* +33 1 44 70 66 10, *Fax:* +33 1 43 87 40 16, *Email:* paris@mclarensyoung.com, *Website:* www.mclarensyoung.com

BOUVET

harbour area, see under St. Malo

BREST

Lat 48° 23' N; Long 4° 28' W.

Admiralty Chart: 3428	**Admiralty Pilot:** 27
Time Zone: GMT +1 h	**UNCTAD Locode:** FR BES

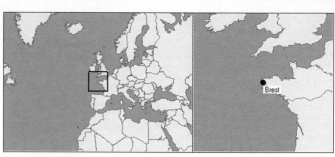

Principal Facilities:

P	Q	Y	G	C	R	L	B	D	T	A

Authority: Port de Brest, Chambre de Commerce et d'Industrie de Brest, Direction des Equipements, 1 Avenue de Kiel, F-29200 Brest, France, *Tel:* +33 2 98 46 23 60, *Fax:* +33 2 98 43 24 56, *Email:* info@brest.port.fr, *Website:* www.brest.port.fr

Officials: Harbour Master: Roland Jaouen.

Port Security: ISPS compliant

Approach: The entrance to the roadstead by the Goulet, which narrows from a width of nearly 4 km at the ocean end to 1880 m at the inner extremity. On each side of the chain of rocks (plateau des Fillettes and Roche Mengam) in the middle of the Goulet there are great depths of water never less than 20 m. Port accessible at all times and any state of tide. Min depth at entrance to Basin No.6 and repair quays, 7.48 m and at entrance to Commercial basin, 6.1 m

Anchorage: The roadstead proper extends 25 by 10 km and is deep enough at all times to accommodate vessels of 20 m max d

Pilotage: Available, Tel: +33 2 98 44 34 95, Fax: +33 2 98 43 26 58

Radio Frequency: VHF Channel 12

Traffic: 2001, 616 vessels, 2 368 397 t of cargo handled

Maximum Vessel Dimensions: 244 m loa, 77 000 dwt, 12.56 m draft

Principal Imports and Exports: Imports: Agribulk, Animal feedpellets, Bulk cement, Construction materials, Containers, Frozen cargo, Gas, Gas oil, Oil, Palm oil, Phosphates, Sand. Exports: Containers, Frozen poultry, Milk powder, Reefer cargo, Scrap metal, Seed potatoes, Soya & rapeseed oil, Vegetable oil.

Working Hours: Shift work Mon-Fri, 0600-1400, meal break 1000-1030; 1400-2200, meal break 1800-1830. Sat: Shift work 0600-1400; at 100% extra 1400-2200, 2200-0600

Accommodation:

Name	Length (m)	Depth (m)	Remarks
Brest			See [1] below
Dock 1 (West Quay)	200	6	Cruise & other goods
Dock 2 (West Quay)	110	5	Fishing
Dock 3 (Eperon Quay)	140	9	Refrigerated & other goods
Dock 5 (West Quay)	170	7	Refrigerated & other goods
Dock 5 (North Quay)	300	7	Refrigerated, wine & other goods
Dock 5 (East Quay)	300	8–10	See [2] below
Dock 6 (West Quay)	150	8	Oil terminal & molasses
Dock 6 (East Quay)	175	9	See [3] below
Dock 6 (Coaster Quay)	110	6	Cement
Dock 6 (South Quay)	230	12	See [4] below
QR2 & QR3 Berths	660	8.5–10.7	See [5] below
QR5 Berth	400	10.5–11.5	Oil & gas terminal

[1]*Brest:* Five basins or inner harbours. Railway alongside Commercial Basins. The commercial port has at high tide an area of about 41 ha of water, sheltered on the W and E by two jetties of 450 and 470 m respectively, and on the S by a breakwater of 980 m in length. The entrances at the end of the jetties are 140 and 120 m
[2]*Dock 5 (East Quay):* Refrigerated goods, reefers & containers. 60 reefer points. Agri bulk storage of 30 000 t
[3]*Dock 6 (East Quay):* Agri bulk, fertilisers & other goods. Agri bulk storage of 40 000 t. One conveyor belt at 1000 t/h
[4]*Dock 6 (South Quay):* Agri & other bulks. Agri bulk storage of 32 000 t and flat storage of 65 000 t. Two conveyor belts at 1000 t/h
[5]*QR2 & QR3 Berths:* Container & ro/ro terminal. 400 reefer points. Ro/ro linkspan with two driving lanes, width on ship side 22 m

Storage:

Location	Open (m²)	Covered (m²)	Grain (t)	Cold (m³)
Dock 2 (West Quay)		1200		
Dock 3 (Eperon Quay)				60000
Dock 5 (West Quay)				10000
Dock 5 (North Quay)	7000			36000
Dock 5 (East Quay)	8000	2500		
Dock 6 (East Quay)			160000	
QR2 & QR3 Berths	10000			

Mechanical Handling Equipment:

Location	Type	Capacity (t)	Qty
Dock 1 (West Quay)	Mobile Cranes	4	1
Dock 2 (West Quay)	Mobile Cranes	4	1
Dock 3 (Eperon Quay)	Mult-purp. Cranes	7.5	2
Dock 5 (West Quay)	Mult-purp. Cranes	6	2
Dock 5 (North Quay)	Mobile Cranes	4	
Dock 5 (East Quay)	Mult-purp. Cranes	8	2
Dock 5 (East Quay)	Mult-purp. Cranes	6	2
Dock 6 (East Quay)	Mult-purp. Cranes	8	3

Location	Type	Capacity (t)	Qty
Dock 6 (South Quay)	Mult-purp. Cranes	26	1
Dock 6 (South Quay)	Mult-purp. Cranes	8	1
Dock 6 (South Quay)	Mult-purp. Cranes	30	1
QR2 & QR3 Berths	Container Cranes	65	2

Cargo Worked: Average loading rates: potatoes in bags 600 t/day. Average discharging rates: phosphates 2500 t/day, grains 2000 t/h

Bunkering: ExxonMobil Marine Fuels, Mailpoint 31, ExxonMobil House, Ermyn Way, Leatherhead, Surrey KT22 8UX, United Kingdom, *Tel:* +44 1372 222 000, *Fax:* +44 1372 223 922, *Email:* marine.fuels@exxonmobil.com, *Website:* www.exxonmobil.com – *Delivery Mode:* truck
Societe des Petroles Shell, 89 Boulevard Franklin Roosevelt, 92564 Rueil-Malmaison, F-76650 Petit Couronne, France, *Tel:* +33 2 35 67 47 03, *Fax:* +33 2 35 67 47 03 – *Grades:* GO – *Delivery Mode:* barge, truck
Total France S.A., Total Marine Fuels, 51 Esplanade du General de Gaulle, F-92907 Paris la Defense Cedex 10, France, *Tel:* +33 1 4135 2755, *Fax:* +33 1 4197 0291, *Email:* marine.fuels@total.com, *Website:* www.marinefuels.total.com – *Grades:* IFO30-380cSt; MGO – *Misc:* own storage facilities – *Parcel Size:* no min/max – *Rates:* barge 3501 000t/h – *Notice:* 24 hours – *Delivery Mode:* barge, truck

Waste Reception Facilities: Debunkering station for dirty ballast and slops

Towage: Tugs from 1200 to 2000 hp available

Repair & Maintenance: Societe Bretonne de Reparations Navales (SOBRENA), Port de Commerce, P O Box 340, F-29273 Brest Cedex, France, *Tel:* +33 2 98 43 43 43, *Fax:* +33 2 98 44 47 22, *Email:* sobrena@sobrena.fr, *Website:* www.sobrena.com Dry dock 1 - 225 m x 27 m x 4.6 m with max cap 40 000 dwt. Dry dock 2 - 338 m x 55 m x 7 m with max cap 280 000 dwt. Dry dock 3 - 420 m x 80 m x 7 m. Two wet docks: No.1 320 m long for vessels up to 280 000 dwt and No.4 400 m long for vessels up to 550 000 dwt

Ship Chandlers: R.& G. Dekytspotter Atlantic, 11 Rue du Colonel Berthaud, ZI Portuaire, F-29200 Brest, France, *Tel:* +33 2 98 44 26 92, *Fax:* +33 2 40 92 13 69, *Email:* dksupply@dekytspotter.com
Fourniership S.A., 32 Quaide la Douane, F-29200 Brest, France, *Tel:* +33 2 98 44 36 47, *Fax:* +33 2 98 43 41 21, *Email:* fourniership@wanadoo.fr

Shipping Agents: Blue Water Shipping A/S, 18 Quai Commandant Malbert, F-29200 Brest, France, *Tel:* +33 2 98 44 90 91, *Fax:* +33 2 98 44 17 70, *Email:* brest@bws.dk, *Website:* www.bws.dk
CCI Direction des Equipments, 1 Avenue de Kiel, 29200 Brest, France, *Tel:* +33 2 98 46 23 80, *Fax:* +33 2 98 43 24 56, *Email:* info@brest.port.fr
Courtiers Maritimes Caradec Elain Morice, 38 Quai de la Douane, 29200 Brest, France, *Tel:* +33 2 98 44 49 95, *Fax:* +33 2 98 43 30 20, *Email:* brokers@wanadoo.fr
Humann & Taconet, 38 Quai de La Douane, F-33440 Brest, France, *Tel:* +33 2 98 44 49 95, *Fax:* +33 2 98 43 30 20, *Email:* broker@wandoo.fr, *Website:* www.humann-taconet.fr
Union Armoricaine de Transports, 6 Quai de la Douane, F-29283 Brest, France, *Tel:* +33 2 98 80 46 76, *Fax:* +33 2 98 44 76 66, *Email:* uniship.brest@wanadoo.fr

Stevedoring Companies: Atlantic Dock Stevedoring (ADS), 4 Rue de l'Elorn, F-29200 Brest, France, *Tel:* +33 2 98 44 59 18, *Fax:* +33 2 98 80 53 95
Blue Water Shipping A/S, 18 Quai Commandant Malbert, F-29200 Brest, France, *Tel:* +33 2 98 44 90 91, *Fax:* +33 2 98 44 17 70, *Email:* brest@bws.dk, *Website:* www.bws.dk
Manuport, 34 Quai du Cdt Malbert, F-29200 Brest, France, *Tel:* +33 2 98 43 05 50, *Fax:* +33 2 98 46 28 15, *Email:* brest@fauveder.com, *Website:* www.fauveder.com
Union Armoricaine de Transport (UAT), 6 Quai de la Douane, F-29200 Brest, France, *Tel:* +33 2 98 80 96 75, *Fax:* +33 2 98 80 34 60, *Email:* uniship.brest@uat.fr, *Website:* www.uat.fr

Surveyors: Bureau Veritas, 22 Rue Amiral Romain Desfosses, F-29604 Brest Cedex, France, *Tel:* +33 2 98 47 84 46, *Fax:* +33 2 98 47 84 57, *Email:* marc.hannetel@fr.bureauveritas.com, *Website:* www.bureauveritas.com

Medical Facilities: Hospital, Tel: +33 2 98 22 33 33

Airport: Guipavas, 10 km

Railway: 0.5 km from the port

Development: Port of Brest 2020 project

Lloyd's Agent: SNC de la Menardiere, 6 Rue Fregate la Belle Poule, P O Box 61232, F-29212 Brest Cedex 1, France, *Tel:* +33 2 98 80 32 70, *Fax:* +33 2 98 80 74 00, *Email:* expertise.de.la.menardiere@wanadoo.fr

CAEN

Lat 49° 11' N; Long 0° 21' W.

Admiralty Chart: 1349		**Admiralty Pilot:** 27	
Time Zone: GMT +1 h		**UNCTAD Locode:** FR CFR	

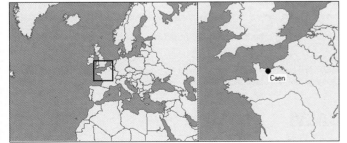

Principal Facilities:

Q	Y	G	C	R		B		T	A

Authority: Port de Commerce de Caen-Ouistreham, Bassin d'Herouville, F-14200 Herouville-Saint-Clair, France, *Tel:* +33 2 31 35 63 00, *Fax:* +33 2 31 35 63 06, *Email:* port.commerce@caen.cci.fr, *Website:* www.caen.port.fr

Officials: Port Director: Philippe Thieuw, *Email:* pthieuw@caen.cci.fr.
Harbour Master: Philippe Auzou, *Email:* philippe.auzou@equipment.gouv.fr.

Port Security: ISPS compliant

Approach: Sea channel from fairway buoy is dredged to 7 m below CD. A canal begins at Ouistreham with two locks, W lock 225 m long, 28.45 m wide and E lock 180 m long, 18 m wide. Max freshwater d in canal from Ouistreham to Herouville is 8.95 m, from Herouville to Calix is 8.6 m and from Calix to Caen is 4 m to 7 m

Pilotage: Compulsory for vessels over 50 m loa, all vessels carrying hydrocarbons or dangerous substances and vessels not equipped with VHF. Vessels must advise ETA to the pilot or Harbour Master 24 h in advance (or on departure from the previous port if the duration of the voyage is less. Caen Pilot, *Tel:* +33 2 31 97 16 81, *Fax:* +33 2 31 97 41 73. Contact on VHF Channel 16 two hours before arriving. If no answer, contact Caen Port Control on same channel. Pilot boards in pos 49° 20.00' N; 0° 14.75' W

Radio Frequency: VHF Channels 16, 74 and 68

Tides: 7.8 m MHWS, 6.5 m MHWN, 2.8 m MLWN, 1.1 m MLWS

Traffic: 2007, 3 947 708 t of cargo handled

Maximum Vessel Dimensions: 205 m loa, 23.5 m breadth, 9.0 m draft for inner port. For outer port same length and draft but no restriction on breadth

Principal Imports and Exports: Imports: African logs, Coal, Cottonseeds pellets, Fertilisers, Molasses, Phosphate, Potash, Sawn goods. Exports: Cereals, Containers, Frozen meat, Steel scrap.

Working Hours: Weekdays 0730-1200, 1400-1830

Accommodation:

Name	Length (m)	Draught (m)	Remarks
St. Peter's Dock			Exclusively used for pleasure craft
Quai de la Londe (A1)	125	3	Boating
Quai de la Londe (A4)	140	3	Cruises
Quai Caffarelli (A6)	140	3	
Quai Caffarelli (A7)	80	3	
New Dock			
Quai de Normandie (B1-B4)	375	3.8–6.1	Coal products
Quai Pt. Gaston Lamy (C1-C3)	550	6.3–7	Cruise & bulk
Quai Hyp. Lefevre (C6-C7)	150	7	
Calix Dock			
Quai de Calix (D1)	140	8.6	Heavy lifts
DPC Berth	170	8.6	Petrol
Ro/ro Berth	130	7.8	Ro/ro
Herouville Dock			
Quai Pt. Delaunay (E5-E7)	370	8.95	Sawn goods, fertiliser & timber
Mole (E2)	215	8.95	Dry bulk handled. Conveyor belt, cap 500 t/h
Blainville Quay			
Quai Pt. Henri Spriet (F1-F3)	636	9.1	Cereals, containers, scrap & general cargo
Ranville			
K1 & K2	200	5.8	
Ouistreham Ferry & Cruise Terminal			
Quai Pt. Paul Spriet (T1)	150	6	Passengers & freight. Single bridge linkspan
Quai Pt. Paul Spriet (T2)	170	7	Cruise. Double bridge linkspan and gangway

Storage:

Location	Open (m²)	Covered (m²)	Grain (t)
Quai de Calix (D1)		1845	
Quai Pt. Delaunay (E5-E7)	3700		
Blainville Quay		22350	31500
Ranville		3695	

Mechanical Handling Equipment:

Location	Type	Capacity (t)	Qty
Quai de Calix (D1)	Mult-purp. Cranes	3–6	3
Quai Pt. Delaunay (E5-E7)	Mult-purp. Cranes	6	2
Mole (E2)	Mult-purp. Cranes	10	2
Blainville Quay	Mult-purp. Cranes	10–20	3
Blainville Quay	Mult-purp. Cranes	15–26	2
Blainville Quay	Mult-purp. Cranes	45–60	1

Bunkering: BP France S.A., Immeuble le Cervier, 12 Avenue des Beguines, Cergy-Saint-Christophe, 95866 Cergy Pontoise Cedex, France, *Tel:* +33 1 3422 4000, *Fax:* +33 1 3422 4417, *Email:* benoist.grosjean@fr.bp.com, *Website:* www.bpmarine.com

Towage: Two tugs available of 1400-2200 hp

Ship Chandlers: S.G.A.E., 1110 Boulevard de Normandie, Zone du Mesnil Roux, F-76360 Barentin, France, *Tel:* +33 2 35 92 15 15, *Fax:* +33 2 35 92 50 60, *Email:* sgae@sgae.fr, *Website:* www.sgae.fr

Shipping Agents: Sogena, 58 Avenue Pierre Berthelot, P O Box 6183, F-14061 Caen Cedex 4, France, *Tel:* +33 2 31 35 44 00, *Fax:* +33 2 31 82 47 02, *Website:* www.sogena.com

Stevedoring Companies: S.C.A.C., Caen, France, *Tel:* +33 2 31 35 81 81, *Fax:* +33 2 31 35 81 85

Key to Principal Facilities:—				
A=Airport	**C**=Containers	**G**=General Cargo	**P**=Petroleum	**R**=Ro/Ro	**Y**=Dry Bulk
B=Bunkers	**D**=Dry Dock	**L**=Cruise	**Q**=Other Liquid Bulk	**T**=Towage (where available from port)	

Sogena, 58 Avenue Pierre Berthelot, P O Box 6183, F-14061 Caen Cedex 4, France, *Tel:* +33 2 31 35 44 00, *Fax:* +33 2 31 82 47 02, *Website:* www.sogena.com

Surveyors: Mr. P. Bosse, 229 Falaise Street, P O Box 6028, F-14061 Caen Cedex, France, *Tel:* +33 2 31 82 60 78, *Fax:* +33 2 31 34 01 89, *Email:* scp-bosse-fleury@wanadoo.fr
Mr. Morvan J. Bretteville, Caen, France, *Tel:* +33 2 31 90 29 97, *Fax:* +33 2 31 40 87 95

Medical Facilities: C.H.U., Tel: +33 (2) 31 06 31 06

Airport: Carpiquet Caen, 20 km

Railway: S.N.C.F., 5 km

Lloyd's Agent: Worms Services Maritimes S.A., 3 Quai du General Lawton Collins, P O Box 434, F-50104 Cherbourg, France, *Tel:* +33 2 33 43 34 02, *Fax:* +33 2 33 44 03 74, *Email:* py.laplume@leh.worms-sm.fr, *Website:* www.worms-sm.com

CALAIS

Lat 50° 57' N; Long 1° 51' E.

Admiralty Chart: 1351
Time Zone: GMT +1 h

Admiralty Pilot: 28
UNCTAD Locode: FR CQF

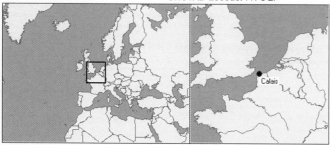

Principal Facilities:

	Y	G	C	R		B	D	T	A

Authority: Chambre de Commerce et d'Industrie de Calais, 24 Boulevard des Allies, P O Box 199, F-62104 Calais Cedex, France, *Tel:* +33 3 21 46 00 00, *Fax:* +33 3 21 46 00 99, *Email:* ccic@calais.cci.fr, *Website:* www.calais-port.com

Officials: Port Director: Patrick Fourgeaud, *Tel:* +33 3 21 46 00 04, *Email:* patrickfourgeaud@calais.cci.fr.
Communications Manager: Barron Gerard, *Tel:* +33 3 21 46 00 08, *Email:* gerard.barron@calais.cci.fr.
Marketing Manager: Anthony Petillon, *Email:* anthony.petillon@calais.cci.fr.

Port Security: ISPS compliant

Pre-Arrival Information: Vessel's should notify their ETA to Harbour Master's office 48 h in advance or on departure from previous port. ETA to be confirmed at Calais port 2h before arrival at the pilot station

Documentation: Ship pre-arrival ISPS declaration (1 copy with 24 h notice), type and amount of waste and residues (1 copy with 24 h notice), crew list (3 copies), passenger list (3 copies), stowaways list, tobacco/spirits/crew effects (3 copies), provisions list (3 copies), arms and ammunition list (3 copies), tonnage certificate (1 copy), bills of lading, freighted manifests (2 copies), unfreighted manifests (2 copies), narcotics list (3 copies)
For tankers, certificate of cargo specification and certificate of vessel's suitability to transport inflammable liquids in bulk are required

Approach: The approach channel extends 4 nautical miles W from to the entrance of Calais (depth greater than 10 m)virtually parallel to the coast. The North limit of the fairway is delimited by the East Breakwater head, CA6, CA4 and CA2 buoy
Access width of 230 m between the two breakwater heads, depth 9 m at LT and 16 m at HT. Vessel's with a large draft may only use it at slack water. For access to the wet basin Carnot, vessel's may enter from 3 h before until 2 h after high water according to their draft. Vessel's over 115 m loa may only enter (lock-gates opened) from 1.5 h before until 1 h after high tide

Anchorage: Bottom of sand and shells, providing good holding for anchoring in depths of 15-19 m, sheltered from winds from SE to WSW. Vessel's (except for tankers) less than 100 m loa may anchor between Buoys CA2 and CA4 in fine weather and wind from the south. Other vessels anchor 1.6 nautical miles to the NNE of Buoy CA4
Tanker anchorage for vessels loaded with oil is to the N of the 'Ridens de Calais'

Pilotage: Compulsory for vessels over 50 m loa in the area extending up to 3.5 nautical miles from the port entrance. Boarding of the pilot at the vicinity of buoy Calais approach. Pilot boat keeps watch on VHF Channel 17. Requests for pilots must be made through local agents or the Harbour Master's Office on VHF Channel 17, 24 h prior to arrival, and confirmed 2 h before the station, *Email:* boulognecalaispilot@wanadoo.fr

Radio Frequency: Port and pilot keep watch on VHF Channel 17

Weather: Prevailing winds W'ly and SW'ly

Tides: Mean spring range 6.3 m, mean neap range 3.9 m

Traffic: 2006, 41 500 000 t of cargo handled, 11 459 927 passengers, 1 847 197 lorries

Maximum Vessel Dimensions: Ravisse Basin (tidal): 80 000 dwt, 245 m loa, 11.5 m draft
Carnot Basin (locked): 150 m loa, 19.5 m beam, 6.4 m draft
Paul Devot Quay (tidal basin): 190 m loa, 9 m draft

Principal Imports and Exports: Imports: Coal, Forest products, General cargo, Liquid sulphur, Non-ferrous metals, Petroleum coke, Sand & sea gravel, Scrap iron, Slag, Vehicles. Exports: Bulk & refined sugar, Coal, Coke, General cargo, Submarine cables, Sulphuric acid, Vehicles.

Working Hours: Normally 0800-1200, 1400-1800. Shift work 0615-1215, 1400-2000. Sugar terminal 0615-1215, 1400-2000 and 2100-0300 or 0600-1200, 1200-1800 and 1800-2359

Accommodation:

Name	Remarks
Cross-Channel Ferry Terminal	See [1] below
Ro/Ro Berths	See [2] below
High Speed Craft - Catamaran Terminal	Located at the bottom of the basin for a Calais/Dover route for catamarans up to 100 m loa with passenger and car ramps
Ravisse Basin	See [3] below
Paul Devot Quay	See [4] below
Basin Carnot Dock	See [5] below
West Basin	See [6] below

[1]*Cross-Channel Ferry Terminal:* Five cross-channel ferry berths (No's 5-9, double decked ferry linkspans for dual loading of cars and trucks and a further provision of passenger access) for ferries up to 210 m loa and 7 m draft
[2]*Ro/Ro Berths:* Three ro/ro berths:
T1 linkspan for ro/ro vessels up to 130 m and draught of 7 m
T3 ramp for ro/ro vessels and catamarans up to 100 m and draught of 9 m
T4 linkspan for ro/ro vessels up to 180 m and draught of 9 m
[3]*Ravisse Basin:* The north side of 725 m is available for berthing with dredged depths of 12 m. Vessel's of 60 000-80 000 dwt and a max draft of 11.5 m can be accommodated
The eastern dock is available for vessels up to 245 m loa and max draft of 11.5 m. This dock is quipped for modern traffic, offering one multi-purpose berth
Equipment includes four multi-purpose cranes with cap of 600 t/h. Two loaders for bagged sugar with a cap of 70 t/h each with a storage cap of 67 000 t
This complex is also linked with the French and European motorway and rail
[4]*Paul Devot Quay:* For vessels up to 190 m loa with a max draft of 9 m including cruise vessels. Offers the nearest facilities to Calais town
Equipment includes two 15 t cranes
[5]*Basin Carnot Dock:* 1680 m of quayside in depth of 7 m for cargo vessels. Entrance through a lock, for vessels up to 150 m loa, 19.5 m beam and 6.4 m draft. Access depending on tidal conditions
Equipment includes four 12 t mobile cranes
[6]*West Basin:* Yacht tidal basin equipped with a simple lock (width 17 m), accessible at high tide. 262 berths available along the pontoons and catways. One 1 x 3 t fixed crane available on request for lifting purposes. Diesel oil and unleaded petrol can be supplied on site

Storage: Extensive open and closed storage is available if required. Carnot Basin has 25 100 m2 of warehousing

Bunkering: Most grades of fuel and diesel oil are available by road tanker and barge
BP France S.A., Immeuble le Cervier, 12 Avenue des Beguines, Cergy-Saint-Christophe, 95866 Cergy Pontoise Cedex, France, *Tel:* +33 1 3422 4000, *Fax:* +33 1 3422 4417, *Email:* benoist.grosjean@fr.bp.com, *Website:* www.bpmarine.com – *Grades:* IFO-180; IF180; MGO – *Parcel Size:* 25t – *Delivery Mode:* pipeline, barge, truck
Total France S.A., Total Marine Fuels, 51 Esplanade du General de Gaulle, F-92907 Paris la Defense Cedex 10, France, *Tel:* +33 1 4135 2755, *Fax:* +33 1 4197 0291, *Email:* marine.fuels@total.com, *Website:* www.marinefuels.total.com

Waste Reception Facilities: Two daily collection services available (except Sunday) for waste disposal. Slops disposal collection service available only by tanker trucks

Towage: Not compulsory. Two tugs available, one conventional 2250 hp and one fire-fighting 3100 hp

Repair & Maintenance: Ateliers Rogliano S.A., Cale de Radoub, F-62100 Calais, France, *Tel:* +33 3 21 96 31 14, *Fax:* +33 3 21 96 63 12, *Email:* message@roglianosa.com, *Website:* www.roglianosa.com

Ship Chandlers: S A S Ghesquiers JPG, Quai de la Loire, 62100 Calais, France, *Tel:* +33 3 21 19 66 37, *Fax:* +33 3 21 96 89 39, *Email:* contact@ghesquiers.fr

Shipping Agents: A.S.A. (Associated Shipping Agencies), 12 Boulevard des Allies, P O Box 817, F-62225 Calais Cedex, France, *Tel:* +33 3 21 96 55 03, *Email:* asa@asa-calais.com, *Website:* www.asa-calais.com
Leon Vincent S.A., Place de Suede, P O Box 851, F-62225 Calais Cedex, France, *Tel:* +33 3 21 34 44 00, *Fax:* +33 3 21 34 99 86, *Email:* calais.agence@leonvincent.fr, *Website:* www.leonvincent.fr

Surveyors: Budd Calais, P O Box 73, Site Creanor 2 routes de Bergues, 59412 Calais, France, *Tel:* +33 3 28 26 15 84, *Fax:* +33 3 28 26 13 57, *Email:* budd.calais@budd-pni.com

Medical Facilities: Extensive facilities available. Centre Hospitalier de Calais hospital in Calais

Airport: Calais-Marck, 5 km. Lille-Lesquin, 120 km. Paris-Roissy-CDG, 270 km

Railway: Calais-Ville station and Calais-Frethun station with TGV and Eurostar high speed lines services

Development: The port is finalising plans for a new outer port project called 'Calais Port 2015'. The two-phase development would largely cater for ro/ro ferry traffic and comprise seven berths (four berths at Phase 1 and three berths at Phase 2) for vessels up to 230 m loa

Lloyd's Agent: McLarens Young France S.A, 80 Boulevard Haussmann, F-75008 Paris, France, *Tel:* +33 1 44 70 66 10, *Fax:* +33 1 43 87 40 16, *Email:* paris@mclarensyoung.com, *Website:* www.mclarensyoung.com

CALVI

Lat 42° 35' N; Long 8° 48' E.

Admiralty Chart: 1425
Time Zone: GMT +1 h

Admiralty Pilot: 46
UNCTAD Locode: FR CLY

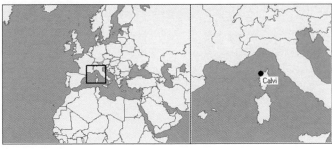

Principal Facilities:

			G		R	L	B		A

Authority: Capitainerie du Port, Quai Landry, F-20260 Calvi, France, *Tel:* +33 4 95 65 10 60, *Fax:* +33 4 95 65 15 13, *Email:* port-calvi@wanadoo.fr

Officials: Port Manager: Mariani Dernard.

Pilotage: Compulsory for vessels of 60 m loa and over and for vessels over 150 gt. Pilot provided by Haute Corse Station whose centre is at Bastia

Weather: Prevailing winds E and WNW dangerous if strong

Accommodation:

Name	Length (m)	Depth (m)	Remarks
Calvi			Depth at entrance 7.6 m
Quay	145	6.5	

Bunkering: Fuel oil available by road tanker

Medical Facilities: Antenne Medicale, 500 m

Airport: Calvi, 5 km

Lloyd's Agent: Unilex Maritime S.a.r.l, Les Docks, 10 Place de la Joliette, Atrium 10.8, F-13002 Marseilles Cedex 02, France, *Tel:* +33 4 91 14 04 40, *Fax:* +33 4 91 91 54 43, *Email:* mail@unilexmaritime.com, *Website:* www.unilexmaritime.com

CARONTE

harbour area, see under Port de Bouc

CHERBOURG

Lat 49° 38' N; Long 1° 36' W.

Admiralty Chart: 2602
Admiralty Pilot: 27
Time Zone: GMT +1 h
UNCTAD Locode: FR CER

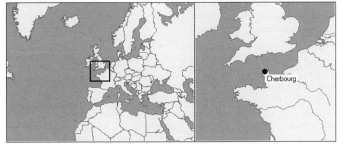

Principal Facilities:

	Y	G	C	R	L	B	D	T	A

Authority: Chambre de Commerce et d'Industrie de Cherbourg Cotentin, Hotel Atlantique, Boulevard Felix Amiot, P O Box 839, F-50108 Cherbourg Cedex, France, *Tel:* +33 2 33 23 32 25, *Fax:* +33 2 33 23 32 36, *Email:* port@cherbourg-cotentin.cci.fr, *Website:* www.port-cherbourg.com

Officials: President: Jean-Claude Camus, *Email:* jccamus@cherbourg-cotentin.cci.fr.
Director General: Jacques Trouillet, *Email:* jtrouillet@cherbourg-cotentin.cci.fr.
Port Director: Didier Aumont, *Email:* daumont@cherbourg-cotentin.cci.fr.
Commercial Director: Jacques Mesnildrey, *Tel:* +33 2 33 23 32 26, *Email:* jmesnildrey@cherbourg-cotentin.cci.fr.
Harbour Master: Florence Perouas, *Tel:* +33 2 33 20 41 25, *Email:* florence.perouas@developpement-durable.gouv.fr.

Port Security: ISPS compliant

Pilotage: Compulsory. VHF Channel 16
Deep Sea Pilotage: Services of licensed deep sea pilots for vessels bound for NW European waters including the British Isles can be arranged; pilots will board vessels off Cherbourg. Send request for this service at least 48 h in advance to either of the following
Antwerp Deep Sea Pilot Services, Antwerp, Belgium, Tel: +32 3 449 5675, Fax: +32 3 440 3541
Le Pilotage Hauturier (Deep Sea Pilots), PO Box 245, F-50108 Cherbourg, Tel: +33 2 33 20 51 23, Fax: +33 2 33 20 65 48, Email: pilotage-hauturier@wanadoo.fr
Hammond Deep Sea Pilots, Dover, United Kingdom, Tel: +44 1304 201201, after hours 203333, Fax: +44 1304 240374

Weather: Normally prevailing W winds

Tides: Average range 5 m, max 6.7 m

Traffic: 2006, 2 923 022 t of cargo handled, 777 224 passengers, 204 676 tourist cars, 97 756 freight units

Maximum Vessel Dimensions: Length no restriction, 12 m draft

Working Hours: Mon-Sat 0600-2200. Overtime on request

Accommodation:

Name	Length (m)	Depth (m)	Remarks
Cherbourg			See [1] below
Quai des Flamands	360	13	See [2] below
Quai des Mielles	400	4	See [3] below
Quai de France	600	13	See [4] below
Quai de Normandie	500	11	5 ha of storage area

[1]*Cherbourg:* Other facilities include a refrigerated warehouse, general cargo warehouses and 75 ha outdoor storage areas
Grande Rade offers many anchorage places in protected deep water (at least 11 m d at any stage of tide). Water, bunker stores and boat service with shore available
FREE TRADE ZONE: Facilities are available in an area covering 128 acres. Full port facilities and container handling equipment available
[2]*Quai des Flamands:* 50 ha of storage area fitted with railway spurs and warehouses. Purpose built facilities for the handling and storage of trade cars
[3]*Quai des Mielles:* Ro/ro linkspan (SWL 44 t) adjacent to a 30 ha industrial zone. Railroad terminal
[4]*Quai de France:* Ocean cruise terminal available with all facilities and services inside

Storage:

Location	Covered (m²)	Cold (m³)
Quai des Flamands	1260	10372

Mechanical Handling Equipment: Ro-ro/Ferry Linkspans:
Linkspan No.1 (Transatlantic Dock) single bridge linkspan, berthing 120 m, depth 6 m, cap 50 t, roadway width 3.5 m Linkspan No.2 (East of the Quai de Normandie) double bridge linkspan with two traffic lines on each bridge, berthing 190 m, depth 8 m, lower bridge roadway 6 m, load cap 280 t (special heavy goods convoy standardized D), upper bridge roadway 7 m, load cap fitted to two lanes of lorries Linkspan No.3 (Transatlantic Dock) polyvalent single bridge linkspan fitted to catamarans, depth 11 m, load cap 40 t, roadway 5 m
Linkspan No.4 (North of the Quai de Normandie) double bridge linkspan, two traffic lines on each bridge, berthing 190 m, depth 7 m, lower bridge roadway 7 m, load cap 98 t, upper bridge roadway 7 m, load cap fitted to two lanes of lorries, catamarans up to 40 m width
Linkspan No.5 (North of the Quai des Mielles) floating linkspan, roadway 3.5 m, load cap 44 t

Location	Type	Capacity (t)	Qty	Remarks
Cherbourg	Mobile Cranes	60–100	2	
Cherbourg	Reach Stackers	40	2	
Quai des Flamands	Mult-purp. Cranes	140	1	
Quai des Flamands	Mult-purp. Cranes	60–100	1	rail mounted

Bunkering: Available by barge or coastal vessel

Towage: One tug of 2300 hp, one of 1400 hp, two of 1000 hp, four of 700 hp, three of 240 hp, two of 500 hp

Repair & Maintenance: Three dry docks available, the largest being 206 m x 26 m. Syncrolift 90 m long, width 32 m with lifting cap of 4500 t. Contact Port Authority Construction Metallique de l'Ouest, 57 Rue des Fougeres, F-50110 Tourlaville, France, *Tel:* +33 2 33 44 55 06, *Fax:* +33 2 33 44 32 14, *Email:* cmo@cmo50.fr, *Website:* www.cmo-cherbourg.com
Mecagena, Cherbourg, France, *Tel:* +33 2 33 20 40 21

Ship Chandlers: S.G.A.E., 1110 Boulevard de Normandie, Zone du Mesnil Roux, F-76360 Barentin, France, *Tel:* +33 2 35 92 15 15, *Fax:* +33 2 35 92 50 60, *Email:* sgae@sgae.fr, *Website:* www.sgae.fr

Shipping Agents: Scanco, Gare Maritime, F-50100 Cherbourg, France, *Tel:* +33 2 33 44 11 11, *Fax:* +33 2 33 23 44 40, *Email:* scanco@wanadoo.fr
Worms Services Maritimes S.A., 3 Quai du General Lawton Collins, P O Box 434, F-50104 Cherbourg, France, *Tel:* +33 2 33 43 34 02, *Fax:* +33 2 33 44 03 74, *Email:* py.laplume@leh.worms-sm.fr, *Website:* www.worms-sm.com

Stevedoring Companies: Cherbourg Maritime, Zone Portuaire des Mielles, P O Box 161, F-50110 Tourlaville, France, *Tel:* +33 2 33 88 66 00, *Fax:* +33 2 33 88 66 24, *Email:* cbgmaritime@aol.com
Scanco, Gare Maritime, F-50100 Cherbourg, France, *Tel:* +33 2 33 44 11 11, *Fax:* +33 2 33 23 44 40, *Email:* scanco@wanadoo.fr
Worms Services Maritimes S.A., 3 Quai du General Lawton Collins, P O Box 434, F-50104 Cherbourg, France, *Tel:* +33 2 33 43 34 02, *Fax:* +33 2 33 44 03 74, *Email:* py.laplume@leh.worms-sm.fr, *Website:* www.worms-sm.com

Medical Facilities: Centre Hospitalier Louis Pasteur, Tel: +33 2 33 20 70 00

Airport: Maupertus International, 10 km, Tel: +33 2 33 88 57 60

Railway: Gare SNCF, Cherbourg

Lloyd's Agent: Worms Services Maritimes S.A., 3 Quai du General Lawton Collins, P O Box 434, F-50104 Cherbourg, France, *Tel:* +33 2 33 43 34 02, *Fax:* +33 2 33 44 03 74, *Email:* py.laplume@leh.worms-sm.fr, *Website:* www.worms-sm.com

COLBERT

harbour area, see under Sete

Key to Principal Facilities:—				
A=Airport	**C**=Containers	**G**=General Cargo	**P**=Petroleum	**R**=Ro/Ro	**Y**=Dry Bulk
B=Bunkers	**D**=Dry Dock	**L**=Cruise	**Q**=Other Liquid Bulk	**T**=Towage (where available from port)	

CONCARNEAU

Lat 47° 52' N; Long 3° 55' W.

Admiralty Chart: 3641	**Admiralty Pilot:** 22
Time Zone: GMT +1 h	**UNCTAD Locode:** FR COC

Concarneau

Principal Facilities:

P	Q		G						T	A	

Authority: Capitanerie du Port, Quai Est, P O Box 231, F-29182 Concarneau Cedex, France, *Tel:* +33 2 98 50 79 91, *Fax:* +33 2 98 50 85 41

Approach: Channel depth to harbour is 4 m below CD. Max length of tankers able to enter harbour during the day is 105 m, at night max length is 90 m. Max length of other vessels during the day is 115 m, and at night max length is 100 m

Anchorage: Anchorage available in roadstead outside harbour

Pilotage: Compulsory. Pilot to be ordered 24 h before arrival, Tel: +33 2 98 50 89 03 or 98 44 34 95, Fax: +33 2 98 43 26 58

Radio Frequency: VHF Channel 12

Maximum Vessel Dimensions: 115 m loa, 5.7 m max d

Working Hours: 0800-1200, 1400-1800

Accommodation:

Name	Remarks
Concarneau	See [1] below

[1]*Concarneau:* Total of 1560 m of wharves in depth of 5 m. Six 350 t slipways. 540 m long floating pontoon for yacht moorings. A 250 m long wharf is situated in the Le Moros tributary. Possible for three vessels of 100 m long to be accommodated at the same time. One petroleum quay 95 m long. Fishing and yachting port

Storage:

Location	Cold (m³)
Concarneau	80000

Mechanical Handling Equipment:

Location	Type	Capacity (t)	Qty
Concarneau	Mobile Cranes	8	6

Waste Reception Facilities: Sedimo, Concarneau, France, *Tel:* +33 2 98 56 63 59

Towage: Two tugs available; one of 300 hp and one of 450 hp

Repair & Maintenance: One 2000 t slipway which can take two 95 m long cargo vessels or four 45 m long fishing vessels, or one cargo and two fishing vessels, Tel: +33 2 98 97 07 60

Societe Concarnoise d'Atelier Mecanique, Concarneau, France, *Tel:* +33 2 98 97 02 64

Chantier Piriou Freres, Zone Industrielle du Moros, P O Box 521, 29185 Concarneau, France, *Tel:* +33 2 98 97 09 48, *Fax:* +33 2 98 97 20 36, *Email:* piriou@piriou.fr, *Website:* www.piriou.com

Surveyors: Bureau Veritas, 4 rue Penzance, F-29900 Concarneau, France, *Tel:* +33 2 98 97 10 24, *Fax:* +33 2 98 97 24 35, *Email:* pascal.foucrier@fr.bureauveritas.com, *Website:* www.bureauveritas.com

Medical Facilities: Hospital, Tel: +33 (2) 98 50 30 30

Airport: Quimper, 30 km

Railway: Rosporden, 14 km. Quimper, 25 km

Lloyd's Agent: Agence Maritime Jacquemin, 58 Avenue Perriere, F-56100 Lorient, France, *Tel:* +33 2 97 83 67 92, *Fax:* +33 2 97 37 77 31, *Email:* shiplor@wanadoo.fr

CORNIGUEL

harbour area, see under Quimper

DIEPPE

Lat 49° 56' N; Long 1° 5' E.

Admiralty Chart: 1355/2148	**Admiralty Pilot:** 28
Time Zone: GMT +1 h	**UNCTAD Locode:** FR DPE

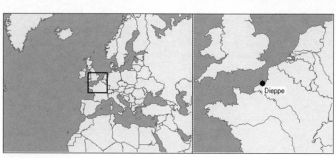

Dieppe

Principal Facilities:

Q	Y	G		R		B		T	A	

Authority: Direction Departementale de l'Equipement, Port de Dieppe, Subdivision MO3, 1 Quai du Tonkin, F-76206 Dieppe, France, *Tel:* +33 2 32 14 47 00, *Fax:* +33 2 32 14 47 13, *Email:* stmd.dde-76@equipement.gouv.fr

Officials: Harbour Master: Marc David, *Email:* marc1.david@equipement.gouv.fr.

Port Security: ISPS compliant

Pre-Arrival Information: Pre-arrival information form to be tendered 48 h before arrival through port agent
ISPS form
Garbage declaration form
Dangerous goods form (if appropriate)
Ship or agent confirmation message as per 2002/59/CE 24 h before arrival on roads

Approach: Entrance is through the NNW channel, between two pierheads 100 m wide, 400 m long and dredged to 4.5 m (indicates zero marked on French navigation charts -4 m). Fairway, slightly curved, is 400 m long, 75 m wide and dredged to -4 m

Anchorage: Anchorage possible in the vicinity of pilot buoy DI

Pilotage: Compulsory for vessels or navigating units over 50 m loa. Inbound/outbound traffic of merchant marine vessels takes place from 2 h before to 1 h after high water

Radio Frequency: VHF Channel 12

Weather: Weather forecast and spot information available at Dieppe-Port, calling on VHF Channel 12

Tides: The channel, the fore-port and the inner harbour all have depths of 7.01 m HWN and 8.84 m HWS

Maximum Vessel Dimensions: 160 m loa, 24 m breadth, 9.0 m draft

Principal Imports and Exports: Imports: Animals, Bagged cargoes, Bagged fertiliser, Bulk & refined sugar, Bulk cargo, Citrus fruit, Coke, Containerised cargoes, Crushed stone, Dry bulk, Equipment, Flour, Frozen goods, Fruit & vegetables, General cargo, Industrial equipment, Industrial sand, Iron & steel products, Iron goods, Machinery equipment, Manufactured goods, Marine dredged aggregates, Metal products, Metal waste & scrap, Sand & sea gravel, Sawn wood, Seeds, Steel bars, Timber logs, Vehicles, Zircon. Exports: Animal feedstuffs, Manufactured goods, Motor vehicles, Sand & sea gravel, Sawn wood, Timber logs, Vegetable oil, Wood.

Working Hours: 24 h/day. Overtime and nightwork possible

Accommodation:

Name	Length (m)	Remarks
New Outer Port		See [1] below
Outer Port		See [2] below
Inner Harbour		See [3] below
Tidal Basin		Three tidal docks
Duquesne Dock	350	100 m wide; reserved for fishing vessels
Canada Dock	150	See [4] below
Paris Dock	683	See [5] below

[1]*New Outer Port:* Connecting directly with the two pierheads, 400 m long, 300 m wide and dredged to 5.0 m below zero. Useful dock length of 175 m and depth 6.0 m below zero in the S is occupied by LD Lines Dieppe-Newhaven ferry service and 175 m long and depth 6.0 m below zero in the E is occupied by sand and gravel imports
[2]*Outer Port:* Connecting the New Outer Port with the fairway, 430 m long, 135 m wide and dredged to 3.5 m and 4.5 m below zero. Useful dock length of 870 m of which 450 m is occupied by the New Marina and the remainder by fishing vessels
[3]*Inner Harbour:* 250 m long, 175 m wide, dredged to 4.0 m below zero. Useful quay length 150 m, open area 3500 m2. This connects with outer port by Pollet Channel, 230 m long, 37 m wide, depth 4.0 m depth below zero, and bridged at narrowest point by swivel bridge
[4]*Canada Dock:* 100 m wide, dredged to 1 m below zero, contains two quays:
India Quay is 150 m long, dredged to 1 m below zero, fully tarred, equipped with one crane of 6-12 t cap and one mobile crane of 40 t cap
Quebec Quay is 150 m long, dredged to 2 m below zero; open storage quay surface of 10 000 m2
[5]*Paris Dock:* 106 m wide, dredged to zero, contains two quays:
Norway Quay 683 m long, with two sheds of 2170 and 2200 m2, open storage quay surface of 18 000 m2
Morocco Quay, 600 m long, shed of 16 000 m2, five conveyors. The 'Levant' shed has two conveyors and 20 000 m2 surface for fruit and citrus fruit traffic. The 'Antilles' shed for fruit traffic with cap of 3000 m2. The 'African' shed has 9000 m2 surface for vegetables and greens
Fresh water is available on both quays

Storage: Five warehouses along Morocco Quay (33 000 m2 surface), two of which are refrigerated (8000 m2 surface) and one ventilated (12 000 m2 surface). Two warehouses along Norway Quay (1600 m2 & 2200 m2 surface)

Mechanical Handling Equipment: Four railed cranes with 2 wagons of 2.2 t cap, one railed crane with 2 trolleys of 2.5 t cap, three railed hoisting cranes of 8 t cap at 25 m (6 t at 32 m & 3 t at 40 m), one mobile crane (Caillard GM900) of 40 t at 24 m and 30 t at 30 m

Cargo Worked: Per day: 4300 t container & general cargo, 160 t vegetable oil, 30 t seeds & grain, 2100 t sand & boulder, 200 t of crushed rocks

Bunkering: BP France S.A., Immeuble le Cervier, 12 Avenue des Beguines, Cergy-Saint-Christophe, 95866 Cergy Pontoise Cedex, France, *Tel:* +33 1 3422 4000, *Fax:* +33 1 3422 4417, *Email:* benoist.grosjean@fr.bp.com, *Website:* www.bpmarine.com
ExxonMobil Marine Fuels, Mailpoint 31, ExxonMobil House, Ermyn Way, Leatherhead, Surrey KT22 8UX, United Kingdom, *Tel:* +44 1372 222 000, *Fax:* +44 1372 223 922, *Email:* marine.fuels@exxonmobil.com, *Website:* www.exxonmobil.com
Total France S.A., Total Marine Fuels, 51 Esplanade du General de Gaulle, F-92907 Paris la Defense Cedex 10, France, *Tel:* +33 1 4135 2755, *Fax:* +33 1 4197 0291, *Email:* marine.fuels@total.com, *Website:* www.marinefuels.total.com

Waste Reception Facilities: Garbage disposal available after request to agent

Towage: Les Abeilles Dieppe, Hangar du Levant, Quai du Maroc, F-76200 Dieppe, France, *Tel:* +33 2 35 84 05 10, *Fax:* +33 2 35 40 19 17, *Email:* dieppe@les-abeilles.com

Repair & Maintenance: Repair firms capable of carrying out all normals repairs. One graving dock 130 m long, 18 m breadth for small vessels; one lift for 300 t vessels. Seven repair sites
ARNO Normandie Dieppe Shipyard, Rue Edouard Lavoinne, P O Box 1002, F-76205 Dieppe, France, *Tel:* +33 2 35 82 51 40, *Fax:* +33 2 35 82 54 71

Ship Chandlers: S.G.A.E., 1110 Boulevard de Normandie, Zone du Mesnil Roux, F-76360 Barentin, France, *Tel:* +33 2 35 92 15 15, *Fax:* +33 2 35 92 50 60, *Email:* sgae@sgae.fr, *Website:* www.sgae.fr

Shipping Agents: Humann & Taconet, 6 Rue Pierre Pocholle, P O Box 101, F-76203 Dieppe, France, *Tel:* +33 2 35 82 19 00, *Fax:* +33 2 35 82 93 46, *Email:* shipagency@die.humann-taconet.fr, *Website:* www.humann-taconet.fr
Leon Vincent S.A., Quai du Maroc, P O Box 79, F-76202 Dieppe Cedex, France, *Tel:* +33 2 35 06 59 00, *Fax:* +33 2 35 82 11 98, *Email:* dieppe.agence@leonvincent.fr, *Website:* www.leonvincent.fr

Surveyors: M. Bernard, Dieppe, France, *Tel:* +33 2 35 84 72 61, *Fax:* +33 2 35 06 22 76
Nippon Kaiji Kyokai, Moulin de la Source, Le Hamelet, Offranville, F-76550 Dieppe, France, *Tel:* +33 2 32 90 06 77, *Fax:* +33 2 35 82 37 40, *Website:* www.classnk.or.jp

Medical Facilities: Dieppe Hospital, Tel: +33 2 32 14 76 76

Airport: Private Airport, 4 km

Railway: Dieppe Railway Station near Duquesne Dock, Tel: +33 2 35 06 69 33

Lloyd's Agent: Humann & Taconet, 73-75 Quai de Southampton, P O Box 1395, F-76066 Le Havre Cedex, France, *Tel:* +33 2 35 19 39 86, *Fax:* +33 2 35 19 39 85, *Email:* lloydsagency-lehavre@humtac.fr, *Website:* www.humann-taconet.fr

DONGES

Lat 47° 18' N; Long 2° 4' W.

Admiralty Chart: 2985   **Admiralty Pilot:** 22
Time Zone: GMT +1 h   **UNCTAD Locode:** FR DON

Principal Facilities:

P	Q				B		T	A

Authority: Grand Port Maritime de Nantes-St.Nazaire, 18 Quai Ernest Renaud, P O Box 18609, F-44186 Nantes Cedex 4, France, *Tel:* +33 2 40 44 71 41, *Fax:* +33 2 40 44 20 01, *Email:* ser.com@nantes.port.fr, *Website:* www.nantes.port.fr

Officials: Managing Director: Francois Marendet, *Email:* f.marendet@nantes.port.fr.
Harbour Master: Capt Yves Jaouen, *Email:* y.jaouen@nantes.port.fr.

Approach: Depth in channel 12.85 m. Air draught under bridge is 60.6 m at lowest tide

Anchorage: Anchorage for vessels awaiting berth can be obtained at Charpentiers Road

Pilotage: Compulsory. Pilot boards W of Pte. de St. Gildas about 29 km off St Nazaire

Radio Frequency: VHF Channels 16 and 12

Tides: Range of tide 3.0 m to 4.5 m

Traffic: 2007, 34 004 048 t of cargo handled (includes ports of Nantes, Montoir & St. Nazaire)

Maximum Vessel Dimensions: 350 m loa, 16 m max d. Draught may vary in accordance with tide

Accommodation:

Name	Draught (m)	Remarks
Donges		See [1] below
Berth 3	7.1	
Berth 4	8.6	
Berth 5	11.6	
Arceau	10.1	
Berth 6	15.6	
Berth 7	15.6	

[1]*Donges:* Berths operated by Raffineries Elf-France, the largest berth allowing access to tankers up to 350 m loa and of 120 000 dwt fully loaded and 290 000 dwt loaded in accordance with tide, up to 16.0 m d. Four berths chiefly for discharging heavy products; five berths chiefly for loading manufactured light white products, solvents, aromatics etc. Water and bunkers available subject to tidal restrictions
The jetty is equipped with electric lighting. Ships can obtain unlimited quantities of boiler water, delivery rate 25 t/h. Fresh water available
Liquefied gas facilities at Berth No's 3 and 4, max d 9.0 m; propane 80 000 m3 storage cap

Bunkering: All kinds available

Towage: Boluda Nantes-St. Nazaire, 1 bis, boulevard de Verdun, P O Box 134, F-44603 St. Nazaire, France, *Tel:* +33 2 40 22 49 82, *Fax:* +33 2 40 22 51 93, *Email:* les-abeilles-st-nazaire@bourbon-online.com

Repair & Maintenance: Available from R 2 N shipyard at St. Nazaire

Shipping Agents: Humann & Taconet, Centre Maritime, P O Box 49, F-44480 Donges, France, *Tel:* +33 2 40 45 31 31, *Fax:* +33 2 40 45 35 35, *Email:* donges@humtac.fr, *Website:* www.humann-taconet.fr

Medical Facilities: St Nazaire Hospital and local medical office

Airport: St. Nazaire, 4 km

Lloyd's Agent: AMS Ouest, 5 Bd Vincent Gache, P O Box 36204, F-44000 Nantes, France, *Tel:* +33 2 40 41 73 84, *Fax:* +33 2 40 41 73 92, *Email:* westoffice@associated-marine-services.com

DUGUAY TROUIN

harbour area, see under St. Malo

DUNKIRK

Lat 51° 2' N; Long 2° 21' E.

Admiralty Chart: 1350   **Admiralty Pilot:** 28
Time Zone: GMT +1 h   **UNCTAD Locode:** FR DKK

Principal Facilities:

P	Q	Y	G	C	R		B	D	T	A

Authority: Grand Port Maritime de Dunkerque, Terre-Plein Guillain, P O Box 46534, F-59386 Dunkirk Cedex, France, *Tel:* +33 3 28 28 78 78, *Fax:* +33 3 28 28 78 77, *Email:* info@portdedunkerque.fr, *Website:* www.portdedunkerque.fr

Officials: President: Francois Soulet de Brugiere, *Email:* fsoulet@portdedunkerque.fr.
Commercial Director: Pierre Joly, *Tel:* +33 3 28 28 77 31, *Email:* pjoly@portdedunkerque.fr.
Harbour Master: Noel Juhere, *Tel:* +33 3 28 28 75 91, *Email:* njuhere@portdedunkerque.fr.

Port Security: ISPS compliant

Approach: Depths given below are in relation to zero on French marine charts, the mean depth of HW being +5.85 m and mean depth at LW being +4.8 m. The harbour opens on a roadstead formed by sandbanks running parallel to the coast

Anchorage: Dyck Road in pos 51° 03' N; 1° 48' E, depth 27 m to 29 m. Dunkirk Road in pos 51° 04' 30" N; 2° 23' E, depth 14 m to 16 m for vessels up to 180 m loa and short stay only

Pilotage: Dunkirk Pilots, Tel: +33 3 28 66 74 14, Fax: +33 3 28 59 01 88, Email: piloduk@wanadoo.fr
General Conditions: Pilotage is compulsory for entering or going out of port of Dunkirk, (a) in the 'inner zone' for all vessels over 50 m loa in the Eastern Port and over 70 m loa in the Western Port (b) in both the 'inner and outer zone' for vessels over 100 m loa (c) for shifting in docks when vessels are crossing a gateway and/or are assisted by tugs, and/or are entering or leaving a dry dock
Exemptions: Vessels fitted with VHF, providing they are not carrying hazardous cargoes requiring a special berth, are exempted as follows:
(i) In inner zone: under 50 m loa for Eastern Port and under 70 m loa for Western Port
(ii) In outer zone: in, under 100 m loa; out, under 100 m loa
Inner Zone: Limits: to W, a line between a point of the coast 2 miles W from the Aa's jetties and a point 2° 08' E and 51° 03' N; to E, meridian of Dunkirk lighthouse; to N, parallel of 51° 03' N, coast, 02° 20' E, parallel of 51° 04' 30"
Outer Zone: Limits: to W meridian of Calais Lighthouse; to E, meridian of lighthouse 2° 27' E; to N line three miles of LW mark; to S, Calais pilotage zone, the coast and the Dunkirk Inner Zone

Radio Frequency: Dunkirk Port Radio, continuous watch on VHF Channel 16, operations Channel 73

Traffic: 2007, 57 110 000 t of cargo handled, 197 000 TEU's

Maximum Vessel Dimensions: Eastern Port: 120 000 dwt, 14.2 m d, 289.05 m loa, 45.05 m beam. Western Port: 300 000 dwt, 20.5 m d, 350 m loa, 60 m beam

---

Key to Principal Facilities:—					
A=Airport	**C**=Containers	**G**=General Cargo	**P**=Petroleum	**R**=Ro/Ro	**Y**=Dry Bulk
B=Bunkers	**D**=Dry Dock	**L**=Cruise	**Q**=Other Liquid Bulk	**T**=Towage (where available from port)	

Principal Imports and Exports: Imports: Chemicals, Coal, Crude oil, Edible oil, General cargo, Iron ore, Metallurgical products, Sand & gravel, Textile raw materials. Exports: Cereals, Chemicals, General cargo, Metallurgical products, Petroleum products, Sugar.

Working Hours: 24 h/day, 7 days a week

Accommodation: A wide gauge canal, the Canal des Dunes, links the Eastern Port and the Western Port for barge traffic and port service craft
Waterways Connections: The waterway network has been considerably improved with the wide gauge canal from Dunkirk. This canal accommodates barges, push convoys and sea-going vessels, according to draught and air draught restrictions, up to 3000 dwt towards Lille and Valenciennes and 1350 dwt to Belgium, via the Scheldt River

Name	Length (m)	Draught (m)	Remarks
Eastern Port			See [1] below
Dock 1			
Freycinet I (Terminal Croisieres)	495.7	6.2–6.8	
Freycinet II	251.5	5.2–6.4	
Freycinet III	496.7	7.3	
Front du Mole I	187.3	5.9	
Dock 2			
Freycinet IV	430.6	7.1–7.4	
Freycinet V	630	6.9	
Front du Mole II	146	7.8	
Dock 3			
Freycinet VI	528	8.8–9.6	Four cranes of 10 t cap
Freycinet VII	517	8.5–8.8	One ro/ro ramp
Front du Mole III	114.3	8.3	
Dock 4			
Freycinet VIII	558.3	8.6	
Freycinet IX (Terminal Sucrier T.T.S.)	501	8.8–9.4	See [2] below
Dock 5			
Freycinet X	484.5	10.2–11.6	See [3] below
Freycinet XI (Sud) (Terminal Vracs Agro)	120.2	10.2	
Freycinet XI (Nord)	446.8	10.7	Two cranes of 10 t cap
Front du Mole V (Terminal CPA)		9.9–11	See [4] below
Dock 6			
Freycinet XII (Terminal Barra)	379	12.5	Four cranes of 10 t cap
Freycinet XII (Terminal Feron)	337	11.6–12.5	One crane of 10 t cap & one of 12 t cap
Freycinet XIII (Terminal Dewulf)	702	11.6–12.5	Two cranes of 40 t cap, two cranes of 10 t cap & one ro/ro ramp
Quai de Saint-Pol	160	11.6	
Raffinerie de Dunkerque			See [5] below
Bassin Maritime			
Cerealier (Silonor)	195.2	14.2	See [6] below
Quais Sollac	1630	6–14.2	Six private berths
Terminal Hanson Granulats France SA	106	6.5	
Silo Nord-Cereales	592	14	See [7] below
Central Port			
Bassin de Mardyck			
Terminal Morillon-Corvol		7.5	Sand & gravel for vessels up to 120 m loa
Total Raffinage Distribution		11.5–14.2	See [8] below
Stocknord	440	4.5–14.2	See [9] below
Quai de l'Escaut (Terminal aux Aciers Acimar)	642	11.6	One crane of 50 t cap, one of 40 t cap & one of 25 t cap
Western Port			
Avant Port			
Petrolier des Flandres		20.5	See [10] below
Ro/ro Terminal			
Quai d'Alsace	132	5.5	
Quai de Lorraine	270	6	Two berths
Quai de Ramsgate	180	7	
Container Terminal (NFTIou)			See [11] below
Quai de Flandre	1119	12.5	Five berths. Four container cranes
Quai de Lorraine	530	12.5	Two berths. Two container cranes
Terminal a Pondereux Ouest			
Berth 760	340	8	
Berth 761	280	18	
Berth 762-763		14.3	
Quai Aluminium Dunkerque	215	11.5	
Darse Aluminium Dunkerque		4	

[1]*Eastern Port:* Composed of 350 ha of wet docks behind three locks accessible by an outer harbour opened on the North Sea
De Gaulle lock: 289.05 m long, 45.05 m beam and 14.2 m draft. Watier lock: 230 m long, 32 m beam and 10.5 m draft. Trystram lock: 140 m long, 22 m beam and 8 m draft
[2]*Freycinet IX (Terminal Sucrier T.T.S.):* Operated by Trans Terminal Service, Tel: +33 3 28 63 33 15, Fax: +33 3 28 63 02 50, Email: tts@club-internet.fr
[3]*Freycinet X:* Operated by Trans Terminal Service, Tel: +33 3 28 63 33 15, Fax: +33 3 28 63 02 50, Email: tts@club-internet.fr. Three cranes of 10 t cap

[4]*Front du Mole V (Terminal CPA):* Liquid products operated by Compagnie Parisienne des Asphaltes, Tel: +33 3 28 65 92 10, Fax: +33 3 28 58 74 59
[5]*Raffinerie de Dunkerque:* Tel: +33 3 28 29 50 00, Fax: +33 3 28 29 50 29
Berth of 95 m in depth of 10.5 m for vessels up to 120 m loa and berth of 200 m in depth of 12.2 m for vessels up to 245 m loa. Hydrocarbons
[6]*Cerealier (Silonor):* Operated by Silonor, Tel: +33 3 28 24 90 10, Fax: +33 3 28 24 90 15
[7]*Silo Nord-Cereales:* Three berths operated by Nord Cereales, Tel: +33 3 28 21 50 40, Fax: +33 3 28 21 50 18, Email: sica.nord-cereales@gofornet.com
[8]*Total Raffinage Distribution:* Petroleum products for vessels of 240-275 m loa, Tel: +33 3 28 26 35 00, Fax: +33 3 28 27 22 54
[9]*Stocknord:* Petroleum products & chemicals operated by Stocknord S.A., Tel: +33 3 28 62 74 00, Fax: +33 3 28 62 74 80
[10]*Petrolier des Flandres:* For vessels up to 360 m loa. Directly linked by pipeline to the Total Fina Elf refinery
[11]*Container Terminal (NFTIou):* Operated by Nord France Terminal International (NFTI), Rue Port Ouest, F-59279 Loon Plage, Tel: +33 3 28 58 46 40, Email: helene.motte@nfti.fr, Website: www.apmterminals.com

Bunkering: BP France S.A., Immeuble le Cervier, 12 Avenue des Beguines, Cergy-Saint-Christophe, 95866 Cergy Pontoise Cedex, France, *Tel:* +33 1 3422 4000, *Fax:* +33 1 3422 4417, *Email:* benoist.grosjean@fr.bp.com, *Website:* www.bpmarine.com – Grades: IFO-180; IF-180; MGO – Parcel Size: 25t – Delivery Mode: pipeline, barge, truck
Total France S.A., Total Marine Fuels, 51 Esplanade du General de Gaulle, F-92907 Paris la Defense Cedex 10, France, *Tel:* +33 1 4135 2755, *Fax:* +33 1 4197 0291, *Email:* marine.fuels@total.com, *Website:* www.marinefuels.total.com

Towage: Societe Dunkerquoise de Remorquage et de Sauvetage, 2 Quai de Depart, P O Box 1025, F-59140 Dunkirk Cedex, France, *Tel:* +33 3 28 65 09 00, *Fax:* +33 3 28 63 92 85

Repair & Maintenance: ARNO Dunkerque S.A., Route des Docks, P O Box 2074, F-59376 Dunkirk Cedex, France, *Tel:* +33 3 28 66 48 00, *Fax:* +33 3 28 66 59 28, *Email:* arno-dunkerque@netinfo.fr, *Website:* www.arno-dk.com Six dry docks handling vessels up to 175 000 dwt

Seaman Missions: The Seamans Mission, Princess Alice House, 130 Rue de L'Ecole Maternelle, F-59140 Dunkirk, France, *Tel:* +33 3 28 59 04 36, *Fax:* +33 3 28 66 09 05, *Email:* dunkerque@mtsmail.org

Ship Chandlers: Avita SAS - FMC, Zone Eurofret, Rue de l'Europe P O 22, Port Ouest, F-59279 Craywick, France, *Tel:* +33 3 28 20 58 28, *Fax:* +33 3 28 20 58 39, *Email:* fmc@nordnet.fr

Shipping Agents: Agena Tramp, 29 rue du Gouvernement, P O Box 2510, F-59383 Dunkirk, France, *Tel:* +33 3 28 58 87 77, *Fax:* +33 3 28 58 87 55, *Email:* dunkirk@agenatramp.fr, *Website:* www.agenatramp.fr
Agence Maritime Delpierre S.A., 1 Rue Vanstabel, P O Box 4, F-59140 Dunkirk, France, *Tel:* +33 3 28 65 86 00, *Fax:* +33 3 28 66 44 22, *Email:* shipping@amdagency.com, *Website:* www.amdagency.com
Burger Port Agencies SAS, 30 Rue l'Hermitte, F-59140 Dunkirk, France, *Tel:* +33 3 28 24 58 43, *Fax:* +33 3 28 66 48 36, *Email:* dunkerque@burgergroup.fr, *Website:* www.royalburgergroup.com
CMA-CGM S.A., CMA CGM Dunkerque, Batiment des Technologies, 1er etage, 123 rte de l'Ecluse Trystram, F-59140 Dunkirk, France, *Tel:* +33 3 28 58 46 00, *Fax:* +33 3 28 58 46 30, *Email:* dnk.phaffreingue@cma-cgm.com, *Website:* www.cma-cgm.com
Dekeirel & Hardebolle, 13/34 Quai des Americains, F-59378 Dunkirk, France, *Tel:* +33 3 28 65 86 40, *Fax:* +33 3 28 63 02 83, *Email:* xdewynter@dekeirel.com, *Website:* www.dekeirel.com
Humann & Taconet, 32 Quai des Americains, F-59140 Dunkirk, France, *Tel:* +33 3 28 63 51 85, *Fax:* +33 3 28 65 17 05, *Email:* shipagency@dkq.humann-taconet.fr, *Website:* www.humann-taconet.fr
K Line (Europe) Ltd, 30/34 Quai des Americains, BP 4206, 01 Dunkirk, France, *Tel:* +33 3 28 21 05 76, *Fax:* +33 3 28 63 02 83, *Email:* keudkkall@fr.kline.com, *Website:* www.klineurope.com
Lemaire S.A.S., 30 Rue Lhermitte, 59346 Dunkirk, France, *Tel:* +33 3 28 58 77 00, *Fax:* +33 3 28 59 09 99, *Email:* agency@lemaire-dunkerque.fr
Leon Vincent S.A., Quai de Loraine, F-59279 Loon Plage, France, *Tel:* +33 3 28 28 91 70, *Fax:* +33 3 28 21 41 84, *Email:* silvester.m@lvfruit.fr, *Website:* www.leonvincent.com
Mediterranean Shipping Company, 11 Rue des Arbres, P O Box 86376, F-59377 Dunkirk Cedex 1, France, *Tel:* +33 3 28 26 32 00, *Fax:* +33 3 28 26 32 10, *Email:* mscdunkerque@mscfr.mscgva.ch, *Website:* www.mscgva.ch
Worms Services Maritimes S.A., 132 Rue de La Republique, P O Box 30054, Saint Pol On Sea, 59430 Dunkirk, France, *Tel:* +33 3 28 21 01 22, *Fax:* +33 3 28 66 23 74, *Email:* wsm.dunkerque@wanadoo.fr, *Website:* www.worms-sm.com

Surveyors: Det Norske Veritas A/S, Espace Beaumont, 28-30 rue de Beaumont, F-59140 Dunkirk, France, *Tel:* +33 3 28 66 19 10, *Fax:* +33 3 28 21 02 20, *Email:* dunkerque@dnv.com, *Website:* www.dnv.com
Germanischer Lloyd, 35 Chemin de la Distellerie, F-59380 Dunkirk, France, *Tel:* +33 3 28 62 20 41, *Fax:* +33 3 28 62 29 96, *Email:* gl-dunkirk@gl-group.com, *Website:* www.gl-group.com
Nippon Kaiji Kyokai, C. Bolender & B. Douchy 1, Rue L'Hermitte, F-59140 Dunkirk, France, *Tel:* +33 3 28 66 70 48, *Fax:* +33 3 28 66 75 94, *Website:* www.classnk.or.jp

Airport: Calais-Marck, 30 km. Lille-Lesquin, 75 km

Lloyd's Agent: McLarens Young France S.A, 80 Boulevard Haussmann, F-75008 Paris, France, *Tel:* +33 1 44 70 66 10, *Fax:* +33 1 43 87 40 16, *Email:* paris@mclarensyoung.com, *Website:* www.mclarensyoung.com

ETANG DE BERRE

Lat 43° 29' N; Long 5° 10' E.

Admiralty Chart: 155		**Admiralty Pilot:** 46	
Time Zone: GMT +1 h		**UNCTAD Locode:** FR ETB	

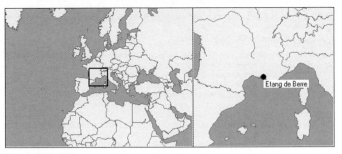

Principal Facilities:

P	Q				B	T	A

Authority: Grand Port Maritime de Marseille, Quai de la Lecque, P O Box 200, F-13110 Port de Bouc Cedex, France, *Tel:* +33 4 42 40 60 05, *Fax:* +33 4 42 40 60 40, *Email:* m.bonvalet@marseille-port.fr, *Website:* www.marseille-port.fr

Officials: Commercial Director: Monica Bonvalet, *Tel:* +33 4 91 39 43 22.
Harbour Master: Joseph Moysan, *Tel:* +33 4 91 39 41 40, *Email:* j.moysan@marseille-port.fr.

Port Security: ISPS compliant

Pre-Arrival Information: Vessel Traffic Service: The Marseilles/Fos Maritime Traffic Service (STM) is compulsory for all commercial vessels. The area of authority of the STM comprises a marine operating area and a port operating area:
(a) within the limits administered by the GPMM
(b) within the administrative limits of the installations and constructions entrusted to the GPMM
(c) within the area of jurisdiction of the GPMM
(d) in the channels and approaches to the Golfe de Fos and to the Port of Marseilles for vessels transporting hydrocarbons and dangerous substances
The Fos area lies between longitudes 4° 41.3' E (Faraman Lt) and 5° 06.5' E (Sausset-les-Pins Lt), latitude 43° 11.9' N (Le Planier Lt) and the shore, including the Canal Saint-Louis, Port-Saint-Louis-du-Rhone, the Canal de Caronte and the Etang de Berre. Fos Port Control, *Tel:* +33 4 42 40 60 60. Maritime Traffic Service Centre on VHF Channels 12 and 73. Vessels manoeuvring in the port on VHF Channels 72 and 77
Communications:
(a) communication on VHF Channel 12 and 73 must be established as early as possible between vessels and the Maritime Traffic Service (STM) Centre
(b) vessels unable to contact the STM may not cross the Cap Couronne line (43° 19.5' N)
(c) vessels on passage, manoeuvring and at anchor in any part of the area controlled by the STM must maintain a listening watch on VHF Channel 12
(d) conversations should take place in French and English using standard IMO terminology
(e) pilots can be contacted on VHF Channel 14
Vessels transporting hydrocarbons and dangerous substances must send a SURNAV message 6 h prior to entry into French territorial waters
Vessels inward-bound must contact the STM as follows:
(a) 48 h before arrival at the pilot boarding position, through the agent stating
(i) vessels name and call sign
(ii) destination and port of departure
(iii) draught
(iv) cargo
(v) loa, beam and gt
(vi) type of vessel
(vii) ETA
(b) at least 24 h before arrival stating:
(i) ETA at pilot boarding position
(ii) draught
(iii) nature and tonnage of transported dangerous substances
(iv) loa
(c) 6 h before entry into French territorial waters, vessels transporting hydrocarbons or dangerous substances must send a SURNAV message
(d) on entering the area offshore of the entrance, all vessels over 50 m loa on passage to the Golfe de Fos must report to the STM on VHF Channel 12 stating:
(i) vessels name and call sign
(ii) position
(iii) course and speed
(iv) ETA
The STM will give permission to proceed along the approach channel starting at the Fairway (Omega) Lt Buoy, and will provide information on traffic movements and weather conditions in the area
(e) the STM will advise berthing details and a time for pilot boarding, as well as any towing requirements if not already specified
(f) the STM will also advise VHF communication details as follows:
(i) at the entrance to the STM area
(ii) at the entrance to the approach channel for vessels obliged to use the channels (vessels over 1600 gt transporting hydrocarbons or dangerous substances) for Fos or Marseilles
(iii) at the entrance to the approach channel for vessels not obliged to use the channels. After identifying and authorising the vessel, the STM will instruct the vessel to proceed if the vessel is subject to an inspection by a surveyor
(g) vessels over 1600 gt transporting hydrocarbons or dangerous substances may not enter the approach channel (N of 43° 12.0' N) without the authorisation of the STM
(h) in the event of a doubtful identity, the STM will call every vessel it considers to be likely until a positive identity is obtained
Vessels in the area:
(a) all vessels must contact the STM on VHF before entering the port, getting under way or changing berths
(b) all vessels crossing (or in cases of emergency, anchoring or waiting in) the approach channel, which vessels transporting dangerous cargo are obliged to use, must inform the STM immediately
(c) all vessels wishing to anchor in the Golfe de Fos to the N of the dredged channel

must obtain prior permission from the STM. A continuous listening watch must be maintained on VHF Channel 12 while at the anchorage
(d) all vessels wishing to proceed along the Canal de Caronte or the Canal Saint-Louis must request instructions from the STM
(e) vessels transporting hydrocarbons or dangerous substances in the transhipment area of the Golfe de Fos must maintain a continuous listening watch on VHF Channel 12
(f) leisure craft must contact the Harbour Master for all movements within the port (entering, leaving or making way)
(g) vessels may only enter the dredged channel (from the Lavera Lt Buoy to the harbour basins) after checking with the STM that no other vessel has commenced passage along the channel

Approach: Access to berths is limited by the depth of the Caronte Canal, 7.32 m max draft. Port of La Mede 5.18 m d max. Port of La Pointe de Berre 6.86 m d max. The railway bridge must be opened if air draught exceeds 21 m. The bridge of Martigues can always be open. No night movements if vessel exceeds 6000 gt. Vessels exceeding 140 m must follow the currents

Anchorage: At South Berre Etang, depth of water 8 m

Pilotage: The compulsory pilotage area consists of an area N of latitude 43° 19' N between the meridians of Faramen Lt (4° 41.3' E) and Cap Couronne Lt (5° 03.3' E), including the canals, the harbour basins of the inner harbours, the Rhone as far as Arles and the Etang de Berre
Marseilles/Fos Office, *Tel:* +33 4 91 14 29 10, *Fax:* +33 4 91 56 65 79, *Email:* pilote13@nerim.fr
Golfe de Fos Pilotage, *Tel:* +33 4 42 06 21 01
VHF Channels 12 and 14
Pilotage is available 24/h day and compulsory for vessels of all categories over 50 m loa and all vessels over 70 m loa on passage to or from Darse 2 (Harbour Basin 2) Container Terminal and Darse 3 (Harbour Basin 3) berths in the Port of Fos, except for vessels transporting hydrocarbons or dangerous substances
Vessels must report ETA with at least 24 h notice (or as soon as leaving the previous port) to the Port de Bouc Harbour Master stating:
(a) loa
(b) draught (forward and aft)
(c) nature and tonnage of any dangerous cargo
Vessels must establish VHF contact with the Port de Bouc Harbour Master as early as possible
Pilot boards in the following positions:
(a) vessels transporting hydrocarbons or dangerous cargo and deep draught vessels on passage to Fos at the latitude of Cap Couronne Lt (43° 19.5' N)
(b) vessels bound for Port de Bouc, Lavera, Etang de Berre and St. Louis du Rhone between 2.5-4 nautical miles S of Lavera Lt Buoy (43° 22.6' N; 4° 58.2' E)
(c) on request between latitudes 43° 11.9' N and 43° 19.6' N
The pilotage sub-station at Port de Bouc provides pilots for Lavera, Canal de Caronte, Martigues, Etang de Berre, Fos and St. Louis du Rhone. This station comes under the authority of the Marseilles/Golfe de Fos Pilotage Office

Maximum Vessel Dimensions: 7.31 m d, 160 m loa

Accommodation:

Name	Length (m)	Draught (m)	Remarks
La Pointe de Berre			See [1] below
Berth 751	145	6	Chemical products
Berth 752	145	6.5	Petroleum products
Berth 754	125	6	Gases

[1]*La Pointe de Berre:* Operated by Societe des Petroles Shell, with three berths for refined petroleum products. They have a loading or discharge cap of 120 to 500 m3/h depending on the products

Bunkering: Available at La Pointe de Berre. By barge only at La Mede

Towage: Eight tugs available

Medical Facilities: Available at Martigues, Berre, Port de Bouc and Marignane

Airport: Marseille Provence, 15 km

Lloyd's Agent: Unilex Maritime S.a.r.l, Les Docks, 10 Place de la Joliette, Atrium 10.8, F-13002 Marseilles Cedex 02, France, *Tel:* +33 4 91 14 04 40, *Fax:* +33 4 91 91 54 43, *Email:* mail@unilexmaritime.com, *Website:* www.unilexmaritime.com

FECAMP

Lat 49° 46' N; Long 0° 22' E.

Admiralty Chart: 1354/2148	**Admiralty Pilot:** 28
Time Zone: GMT +1 h	**UNCTAD Locode:** FR FEC

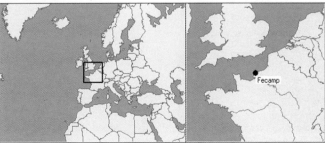

Principal Facilities:

	Y	G					A

Authority: Direction Departementale des Infrastructures Generales, 16 Grand Quai, P O Box 167, F-76404 Fecamp, France, *Tel:* +33 2 35 28 23 76, *Fax:* +33 2 35 28 75 86, *Email:* ddi-port.fecamp@cg76.fr, *Website:* www.fecamp.cci.fr

---

Key to Principal Facilities:—				
A=Airport	**C**=Containers	**G**=General Cargo	**P**=Petroleum	**R**=Ro/Ro	**Y**=Dry Bulk
B=Bunkers	**D**=Dry Dock	**L**=Cruise	**Q**=Other Liquid Bulk	**T**=Towage (where available from port)	

Officials: Harbour Master: Jerome Renier, *Email:* jrenier@fecamp-bolbec.cci.fr.

Approach: An entrance channel 220 m long by 70.1 m wide. Depth from 4.88 m NT to 6.4 m ST. About 500 m outside jetties a depth of 10.06 m at the LT

Pilotage: Compulsory for vessels over 45 m loa. Le Havre-Fecamp pilot station, Tel: +33 2 35 19 28 40, Fax: +33 2 35 43 10 91

Radio Frequency: Fecamp Harbour watching on VHF Channels 16, 12 or 9 from 3 h before to 1 h after high tide

Traffic: 2004, 347 640 t of cargo handled

Maximum Vessel Dimensions: 100 m loa (possibly 105 m loa with permission from Harbour Master), 17 m breadth, 6 m max draft NT, 7.25 m max draft ST

Principal Imports and Exports: Imports: Minerals, Salt, Sea sand, Timber. Exports: Chipboard.

Working Hours: Mon-Fri 0800-1200, 1330-1800. Overtime possible on Saturday

Accommodation:

Name	Length (m)	Depth (m)	Draught (m)	Remarks
Arriere Port				
Quai Joseph Duhamel	190	7.5		See [1] below
Bassin Freycinet				
Quai de Verdun	300	6.5–9.5	6.5	See [2] below
Quai de la Marne	300	6.5–9.5	6.5	See [3] below
Avant Port & Bassin Berigny				Marina & fishing

[1]*Quai Joseph Duhamel:* Room for one vessel of more than 80 m loa or two vessels under 80 m loa
[2]*Quai de Verdun:* Three berths including one specialised berth for minerals. Mineral storage of 1340 m2
[3]*Quai de la Marne:* Three berths including one specialised berth for oil tankers

Storage:

Location	Open (m²)	Covered (m²)	Cold (m³)
Quai Joseph Duhamel	4500	3300	
Quai de Verdun	6100	5790	
Quai de la Marne	7700	4250	2000
Avant Port & Bassin Berigny			1600

Mechanical Handling Equipment:

Location	Type	Capacity (t)	Qty
Quai de Verdun	Electric Cranes	6	2
Quai de la Marne	Mult-purp. Cranes	15	1
Quai de la Marne	Mult-purp. Cranes	12	2

Repair & Maintenance: Buquet, Fecamp, France, *Tel:* +33 2 35 28 24 53, *Fax:* +33 2 35 29 93 98
Chantier Naval Cooperative Fecamp, Quai Sadi Carnot, Fecamp, France, *Tel:* +33 2 35 10 00 66, *Fax:* +33 2 35 29 78 40

Shipping Agents: Leon Vincent S.A., Sea-invest Fecamp S.A., Chaussee Gayant, F-76400 Fecamp, France, *Tel:* +33 2 35 10 37 47, *Fax:* +33 2 35 28 61 71, *Email:* fecamp.agence@lsea-invest.fr

Stevedoring Companies: Leon Vincent S.A., Sea-invest Fecamp S.A., Chaussee Gayant, F-76400 Fecamp, France, *Tel:* +33 2 35 10 37 47, *Fax:* +33 2 35 28 61 71, *Email:* fecamp.agence@lsea-invest.fr

Medical Facilities: Fecamp hospital

Airport: Le Havre, 45 km

Railway: Railway station beside harbour area

Lloyd's Agent: Humann & Taconet, 73-75 Quai de Southampton, P O Box 1395, F-76066 Le Havre Cedex, France, *Tel:* +33 2 35 19 39 86, *Fax:* +33 2 35 19 39 85, *Email:* lloydsagency-lehavre@humtac.fr, *Website:* www.humann-taconet.fr

FOS

Lat 43° 26' N; Long 4° 54' E.

Admiralty Chart: 155		**Admiralty Pilot:** 46	
Time Zone: GMT +1 h		**UNCTAD Locode:** FR FOS	

Principal Facilities:

P	Q	Y	G	C	R		B		A

Authority: Grand Port Maritime de Marseille, Quai de la Lecque, P O Box 200, F-13110 Port de Bouc Cedex, France, *Tel:* +33 4 42 40 60 05, *Fax:* +33 4 42 40 60 40, *Email:* m.bonvalet@marseille-port.fr, *Website:* www.marseille-port.fr

Officials: Commercial Director: Monica Bonvalet, *Tel:* +33 4 91 39 43 22.

Harbour Master: Joseph Moysan, *Tel:* +33 4 91 39 41 40, *Email:* j.moysan@marseille-port.fr.

Port Security: ISPS compliant

Pre-Arrival Information: Vessel Traffic Service: The Marseilles/Fos Maritime Traffic Service (STM) is compulsory for all commercial vessels. The area of authority of the STM comprises a marine operating area and a port operating area:
(a) within the limits administered by the GPMM
(b) within the administrative limits of the installations and constructions entrusted to the GPMM
(c) within the area of jurisdiction of the GPMM
(d) in the channels and approaches to the Golfe de Fos and to the Port of Marseilles for vessels transporting hydrocarbons and dangerous substances
The Fos area lies between longitudes 4° 41.3' E (Faraman Lt) and 5° 06.5' E (Sausset-les-Pins Lt), latitude 43° 11.9' N (Le Planier Lt) and the shore, including the Canal Saint-Louis, Port-Saint-Louis-du-Rhone, the Canal de Caronte and the Etang de Berre. Fos Port Control, Tel: +33 4 42 40 60 60. Maritime Traffic Service Centre on VHF Channels 12 and 73. Vessels manoeuvring in the port on VHF Channels 72 and 77
Communications:
(a) communication on VHF Channel 12 and 73 must be established as early as possible between vessels and the Maritime Traffic Service (STM) Centre
(b) vessels unable to contact the STM may not cross the Cap Couronne line (43° 19.5' N)
(c) vessels on passage, manoeuvring and at anchor in any part of the area controlled by the STM must maintain a listening watch on VHF Channel 12
(d) conversations should take place in French and English using standard IMO terminology
(e) pilots can be contacted on VHF Channel 14
Vessels transporting hydrocarbons and dangerous substances must send a SURNAV message 6 h prior to entry into French territorial waters
Vessels inward-bound must contact the STM as follows:
(a) 48 h before arrival at the pilot boarding position, through the agent stating
(i) vessels name and call sign
(ii) destination and port of departure
(iii) draught
(iv) cargo
(v) loa, beam and gt
(vi) type of vessel
(vii) ETA
(b) at least 24 h before arrival stating:
(i) ETA at pilot boarding position
(ii) draught
(iii) nature and tonnage of transported dangerous substances
(iv) loa
(c) 6 h before entry into French territorial waters, vessels transporting hydrocarbons or dangerous substances must send a SURNAV message
(d) on entering the area offshore of the entrance, all vessels over 50 m loa on passage to the Golfe de Fos must report to the STM on VHF Channel 12 stating:
(i) vessels name and call sign
(ii) position
(iii) course and speed
(iv) ETA
The STM will give permission to proceed along the approach channel starting at the Fairway (Omega) Lt Buoy, and will provide information on traffic movements and weather conditions in the area
(e) the STM will advise berthing details and a time for pilot boarding, as well as any towing requiirements if not already specified
(f) the STM will also advise VHF communication details as follows:
(i) at the entrance to the STM area
(ii) at the entrance to the approach channel for vessels obliged to use the channels (vessels over 1600 gt transporting hydrocarbons or dangerous substances) for Fos or Marseilles
(iii) at the entrance to the approach channel for vessels not obliged to use the channels. After identifying and authorising the vessel, the STM will instruct the vessel to proceed if the vessel is subject to an inspection by a surveyor
(g) vessels over 1600 gt transporting hydrocarbons or dangerous substances may not enter the approach channel (N of 43° 12.0' N) without the authorisation of the STM
(h) in the event of a doubtful identity, the STM will call every vessel it considers to be likely until a positive identity is obtained
Vessels in the area:
(a) all vessels must contact the STM on VHF before entering the port, getting under way or changing berths
(b) all vessels crossing (or in cases of emergency, anchoring or waiting in) the approach channel, which vessels transporting dangerous cargo are obliged to use, must inform the STM immediately
(c) all vessels wishing to anchor in the Golfe de Fos to the N of the dredged channel must obtain prior permission from the STM. A continuous listening watch must be maintained on VHF Channel 12 while at the anchorage
(d) all vessels wishing to proceed along the Canal de Caronte or the Canal Saint-Louis must request instructions from the STM
(e) vessels transporting hydrocarbons or dangerous substances in the transhipment area of the Golfe de Fos must maintain a continuous listening watch on VHF Channel 12
(f) leisure craft must contact the Harbour Master for all movements within the port (entering, leaving or making way)
(g) vessels may only enter the dredged channel (from the Lavera Lt Buoy to the harbour basins) after checking with the STM that no other vessel has commenced passage along the channel

Pilotage: The compulsory pilotage area consists of an area N of latitude 43° 19' N between the meridians of Faramen Lt (4° 41.3' E) and Cap Couronne Lt (5° 03.3' E), including the canals, the harbour basins of the inner harbours, the Rhone as far as Arles and the Etang de Berre
Marseilles/Fos Office, Tel: +33 4 91 14 29 10, Fax: +33 4 91 56 65 79, Email: pilote13@nerim.fr
Golfe de Fos Pilotage, Tel: +33 4 42 06 21 01
VHF Channels 12 and 14
Pilotage is available 24/h day and compulsory for vessels of all categories over 50 m loa and all vessels over 70 m loa on passage to or from Darse 2 (Harbour Basin

2) Container Terminal and Darse 3 (Harbour Basin 3) berths in the Port of Fos, except for vessels transporting hydrocarbons or dangerous substances
Vessels must report ETA with at least 24 h notice (or as soon as leaving the previous port) to the Port de Bouc Harbour Master stating:
(a) loa
(b) draught (forward and aft)
(c) nature and tonnage of any dangerous cargo
Vessels must establish VHF contact with the Port de Bouc Harbour Master as early as possible
Pilot boards in the following positions:
(a) vessels transporting hydrocarbons or dangerous cargo and deep draught vessels on passage to Fos at the latitude of Cap Couronne Lt (43° 19.5' N)
(b) vessels bound for Port de Bouc, Lavera, Etang de Berre and St. Louis du Rhone between 2.5-4 nautical miles S of Lavera Lt Buoy (43° 22.6' N; 4° 58.2' E)
(c) on request between latitudes 43° 11.9' N and 43° 19.6' N
The pilotage sub-station at Port de Bouc provides pilots for Lavera, Canal de Caronte, Martigues, Etang de Berre, Fos and St. Louis du Rhone. This station comes under the authority of the Marseilles/Golfe de Fos Pilotage Office

Radio Frequency: Fos Port control, VHF Channel 12

Traffic: 2007, 714 304 TEU's handled

Working Hours: Shift 1 0600-1300, Shift 2 1300-2000, Shift 3 2000-0300 or 2000-0600, Shift 4 0300-0600, Shift 5 2000-2330

Accommodation: The harbour area handles bulk industrial and energy products in Dock No.1 and South Dock, chemical products and containers in Dock No.2 and metallic building, containers, general cargo and ro/ro in Dock No.3. Energy products and general cargo in South Dock
There is a total of 4000 m of quays in service of which 1260 m are privately owned; and eleven specialized berths for chemicals and energy products of which four are privately owned
The depths at the quayside berths range from 3.1 m to 22.25 m and in the tanker turning basin and access channel, the depth is 24 m
Container Terminal comprises five berths, No's 862-866 at Dock 2, Graveleau Quay. Total length 1150 m, 14.5 m draft. There are six 40 t cap gantry cranes, fifteen 40 t cap front lifters and various forklifts of 3 t to 12 t cap. Storage area covers 33 ha and the annual cap of the terminal is 400 000 TEU's. There is also a container stuffing and stripping area and one transit shed. The French Railways container terminal is equipped with two 40 t cap tracked gantries
Ro/ro facilities in the Graveleau sector: One berth (No.870) at the end of the mole between Docks 2 and 3 for sea-going barges: Max length 110 m, 6.5 m d max; three berths (No's 871-873) in Gloria Basin on the S of Brule Tabac quay, equipped with a fixed ramp. Brule Tabac quay is 650 m long with max d of 11.5 m and is equipped with one 40 t cap gantry crane, one 15 t cap crane and three 6 t cap cranes. There is a storage area of 165 ha and one shed of 9000 m2
Tanker facilities: LNG can be handled at a privately managed berth at the end of Dock 1 constituting the GDF-Suez gas tanker terminal (storage cap 150 000 m3). Crude storage cap: S.P.S.E. Terminal: 2 660 000 m3. Crau Depot: 1 910 000 m3. Esso Refinery: 800 000 m3
Refined storage cap: Fos Depot: 522 000 m3. Esso Refinery: 1 200 000 m3. LNG storage cap: 150 000 m3. The crude oil berths are connected to the S European pipeline
Deballasting station at the rear of oil jetties for treating low oil content ballast with intermediate storage basin of 80 000 m3

Name	Length (m)	Draught (m)	Remarks
Ore & Bulk Cargo Facilities			
1 W Quay (public) (Berth No's 851-853)	884		See [1] below
1 E Quay (private) (Berths 811-812)	640		See [2] below
South Dock (private) (Berth No's 821-823)	420	11.89	Three berths for the finished products of Sollac; equipped with two 50 t cap cranes
2 Eiffel (private) (Berths 859-859A)	188	4.3–5.8	Metallic building
Tanker Facilities			
Berth 800	250	13	Crude & refined petroleum for vessels up to 250 m loa
Berth 807	250	12.8	Crude & refined petroleum for vessels up to 250 m loa
Berth 801	370	20.8	Crude petroleum for vessels up to 370 m loa
Berth 802	350	17	Crude petroleum for vessels up to 350 m loa
Berth 803	420	22.25	Crude petroleum for vessels up to 414 m loa
Berth 804	420	14	Crude petroleum for vessels up to 420 m loa
DPF		3.1	Refined petroleum barges
C2 (Berth 808)	130	7	Refined petroleum for vessels up to 100 m loa
Sollac (private) (Berth 821A)	96		Refined petroleum for vessels up to 96 m loa
GDF Suez LNG Terminal (private) (Berth 830)	200	9.75	See [3] below
ARCO (private) (Berth 857)	200	11.5	See [4] below
ATOFOS (private) (Berth 858)	180	11.3	Chemical products for vessels up to 180 m loa

[1] *1 W Quay (public) (Berth No's 851-853):* Three berths for vessels up to 140 000 dwt and 300 m loa. Equipped with two unloading gantries with buckets of 20 t (2 x 800 t/h). One tracked crane with bucket of 15 t (1 x 600 t/h). Two hoppers of 70 m3. One continuous loader P+ (2200 t/h). Two conveyor belt loading gantry (2 x 1500 t/h). There is a 25 000 t alumina silo owned by Pechiney Co connected to a quayside conveyor belt and loading gantry. The terminal is accessible by Rhone river barges and the storage area of over 30 ha is connected to the rail system
[2] *1 E Quay (private) (Berths 811-812):* Operated by Sollac. Consists of two berths and equipped with two 40 t gantries, each unloading at 2000 t/h and storage cap totals 500 000 t for coal and 1.2 million t for ore

[3] *GDF Suez LNG Terminal (private) (Berth 830):* Operated by GDF Suez, Website: www.gdfsuez.com
LNG for vessels up to 180 m loa
[4] *ARCO (private) (Berth 857):* Chemical products, gas (propylene) for vessels up to 200 m loa

Bunkering: BP France S.A., Immeuble le Cervier, 12 Avenue des Beguines, Cergy-Saint-Christophe, 95866 Cergy Pontoise Cedex, France, *Tel:* +33 1 3422 4000, *Fax:* +33 1 3422 4417, *Email:* benoist.grosjean@fr.bp.com, *Website:* www.bpmarine.com – *Grades:* IFO-180; IF-180; MGO – *Parcel Size:* 25t – *Delivery Mode:* pipeline, barge, truck
ExxonMobil Marine Fuels, Mailpoint 31, ExxonMobil House, Ermyn Way, Leatherhead, Surrey KT22 8UX, United Kingdom, *Tel:* +44 1372 222 000, *Fax:* +44 1372 223 922, *Email:* marine.fuels@exxonmobil.com, *Website:* www.exxonmobil.com – *Grades:* IFO-380cSt; MGO – *Delivery Mode:* barge, pipeline
OES Ltd, 9 Avenue d'Ostende, 98000 Monte Carlo, Monaco, *Tel:* +377 93 30 81 13, *Fax:* +377 93 25 27 15
Societe des Petroles Shell, 89 Boulevard Franklin Roosevelt, 92564 Rueil-Malmasion, F-76650 Petit Couronne, France, *Tel:* +33 2 35 67 47 03, *Fax:* +33 2 35 67 47 03
Total France S.A., Total Marine Fuels, 51 Esplanade du General de Gaulle, F-92907 Paris la Defense Cedex 10, France, *Tel:* +33 1 4135 2755, *Fax:* +33 1 4197 0291, *Email:* marine.fuels@total.com, *Website:* www.marinefuels.total.com – *Grades:* IFO380-30cSt; MGO – *Misc:* own storage facilities – *Parcel Size:* no min/max – *Rates:* 300-500t/h – *Notice:* 24 hours – *Delivery Mode:* pipeline, truck, barge

Seaman Missions: The Seamans Mission, 35 Avenue Roger Salengro, F-13110 Port de Bouc, France, *Tel:* +33 4 42 06 42 87, *Fax:* +33 4 42 06 11 23, *Email:* seamenfose@netcourier.com

Ship Chandlers: International Export Agency, Z.I. Boulevard de la Merindole, F-13110 Port de Bouc, France, *Tel:* +33 4 42 40 52 82, *Fax:* +33 4 42 06 59 54, *Email:* sales.dpt@iea-shipsupply.com

Shipping Agents: Maritima del Mediterraneo S.A. (Marmedsa), Bat V Avenida J. Jacques Rousseau, 13500 Martigues, France, *Tel:* +33 4 42 81 71 60, *Fax:* +33 4 42 07 15 57, *Email:* bbegon@marmedsafr.marmedsa.com, *Website:* www.marmedsa.com Director: Bernard Begon Mobile Tel: +33 616540730 Email: bbegon@marmedsafr.marmedsa.com
Medship S.a.r.l., 59 Avenue Andre Roussin, P O Box 106, 13321 Marseilles Cedex 16, France, *Tel:* +33 4 96 17 17 00, *Fax:* +33 4 91 03 84 35, *Email:* info@marmedsafr.marmedsa.com, *Website:* www.marmedsa.com
Worms Services Maritimes S.A., 20 Quai du LaZaret, P O Box 181, F-13002 Fos, France, *Tel:* +33 4 42 48 40 00, *Fax:* +33 4 42 48 45 25, *Email:* worms@afcc.fr, *Website:* www.worms-sm.com

Surveyors: MCL Surveys (Marine Cargo & Logistics Surveys), Centre les Vallins, F-13270 Fos, France, *Tel:* +33 4 42 05 10 70, *Fax:* +33 4 42 05 52 39

Medical Facilities: Available

Airport: Marseille-Provence Airport.

Development: Fos 2XL container complex is scheduled to become operational 2010 consisting of:
a) two berths totaling 600 m and 50 ha of yard space for CMA CGM-DP World subsidiary Portsynergy
b) two berths totaling 800 m and 52 ha of yard space for Mediterranean Shipping Company
Another 8.3bn m3 per annum GDF Suez LNG terminal is scheduled to come into service in June 2009

Lloyd's Agent: Unilex Maritime S.a.r.l, Les Docks, 10 Place de la Joliette, Atrium 10.8, F-13002 Marseilles Cedex 02, France, *Tel:* +33 4 91 14 04 40, *Fax:* +33 4 91 91 54 43, *Email:* mail@unilexmaritime.com, *Website:* www.unilexmaritime.com

GENNEVILLIERS

harbour area, see under Paris

GLASSON%

harbour area, see under Etang de Berre

GRAND-COURONNE

harbour area, see under Rouen

GRANVILLE

Lat 48° 50' N; Long 1° 36' W.

Admiralty Chart: 3672		**Admiralty Pilot:** 27	
Time Zone: GMT +1 h		**UNCTAD Locode:** FR GFR	

Key to Principal Facilities:—

A=Airport	**C**=Containers	**G**=General Cargo	**P**=Petroleum	**R**=Ro/Ro	**Y**=Dry Bulk
B=Bunkers	**D**=Dry Dock	**L**=Cruise	**Q**=Other Liquid Bulk	**T**=Towage (where available from port)	

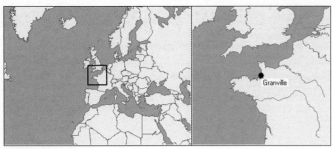

Principal Facilities:

P		Y	G					A

Authority: Le Commandant du Port, Port of Granville, Terre-Plein de l'Ecluse, F-50400 Granville, France, *Tel:* +33 2 33 91 28 28, *Fax:* +33 2 33 91 28 29

Officials: Harbour Master: Mr. Beauvilain.

Pilotage: Compulsory for vessels over 45 m in length. One pilot available; call on VHF Channel 12

Weather: Prevailing SW winds

Maximum Vessel Dimensions: 115 m loa, 18 m width, 7.0 m draft

Working Hours: 0800-1200, 1400-1800. Sat 0800-1200. Overtime possible

Accommodation:

Name	Remarks
Granville	See [1] below

[1]*Granville:* An outside port of about 13 ha protected by two breakwaters, floating basin for loading and discharging with 850 m of quay length. Depth in large basin 8 m at HWST, 6.5 m at OT, 4.5 m HWNT, 4.5 to 6 m at LT. Depth on lock's sill 4.88 to 10.36 m. Five berths, 94 to 255 m long. Also a pleasure boat harbour covering 7 ha, with a cap of 800 craft
Bulk facilities: Silo cap of 3000 m3

Storage: Warehousing cap of 7000 m3

Mechanical Handling Equipment:

Location	Type	Capacity (t)	Qty
Granville	Mobile Cranes	3	1
Granville	Electric Cranes	6	1
Granville	Electric Cranes	7	2
Granville	Electric Cranes	10	1

Cargo Worked: 3000 t/day

Airport: Breville, 16 km

Lloyd's Agent: Agence Maritime Roy s.a.r.l., 2 Chaussee des Corsaires, P O Box 179, F-35409 St. Malo, France, *Tel:* +33 2 99 56 07 21, *Fax:* +33 2 99 40 24 00, *Email:* agence-maritime-roy@wanadoo.fr

HONFLEUR

Lat 49° 25' N; Long 0° 14' E.

Admiralty Chart: 2146
Time Zone: GMT +1 h

Admiralty Pilot: 27
UNCTAD Locode: FR HON

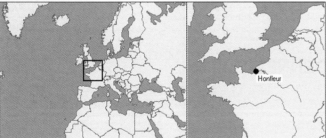

Principal Facilities:

P	Q	Y	G		L		T	A

Authority: Capitainerie de Honfleur, La Lieutenance, P O Box 80120, F-14603 Honfleur, France, *Tel:* +33 2 31 14 61 09, *Fax:* +33 2 31 14 61 09 & 31 89 42 10, *Email:* cph-honfleur@rouen.port.fr

Officials: Director: J. P. Kerangall.
Harbour Master: J. F. Quillec.

Approach: The entrance of the port is set nearly due NW by SE and perfectly sheltered from W winds. Two piers about 487.7 m long make a channel 100 m wide leading to the outer harbour where vessels may safely lie aground on soft mud

Pilotage: Under Seine Pilotage at Le Havre, Tel: +33 2 35 19 27 31

Radio Frequency: VHF Channels 73 and 17

Tides: SR 8.5 m-1 m, NR 6 m-3 m

Traffic: 2003, 493 541 t of cargo handled

Working Hours: 0700-1200, 1400-1900. Overtime can be worked from 1200-2100 for completion. No working on Sunday

Accommodation: Tanker facilities: There is a private tanker berth on the River Seine-'Miroline'. Max size of vessels about 50 000 dwt, max d about 10 m. Storage tank cap of 350 000 m3

Name	Draught (m)	Remarks
Honfleur		
River Seine	8	Four berths. 60 m-122 m long
Inner Harbour	3.5	Four berths

Storage: 30 000 m3 of open storage

Mechanical Handling Equipment:

Location	Type	Capacity (t)	Qty
Honfleur	Mult-purp. Cranes	30	2

Surveyors: Surveyfert, Zone Portuaire, Quai en Seine, F-14600 Honfleur, France, *Tel:* +33 2 31 89 71 86, *Fax:* +33 2 31 89 71 87

Medical Facilities: Hospital, Tel: +33 (2) 31 89 04 74

Airport: Saint Gatien-Deauville, 6 km

Lloyd's Agent: Humann & Taconet, 73-75 Quai de Southampton, P O Box 1395, F-76066 Le Havre Cedex, France, *Tel:* +33 2 35 19 39 86, *Fax:* +33 2 35 19 39 85, *Email:* lloydsagency-lehavre@humtac.fr, *Website:* www.humann-taconet.fr

ILE ROUSSE

Lat 42° 39' N; Long 8° 56' E.

Admiralty Chart: 1424
Time Zone: GMT +1 h

Admiralty Pilot: 46
UNCTAD Locode: FR ILR

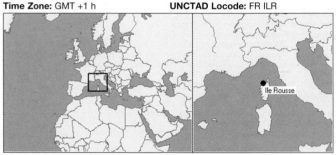

Principal Facilities:

		G	R				A

Authority: Bureau du Port de Commerce, 20220 Ile Rousse, Corsica, Italy, *Tel:* +39 95 60 00 68, *Fax:* +39 95 60 14 50

Pilotage: Compulsory for vessels of 60 m loa and over and for vessels over 150 gt. Pilot provided by Haute Corse Station whose centre is at Bastia

Working Hours: 0600-2000 (later during Summer period)

Accommodation:

Name	Length (m)	Depth (m)	Remarks
Ile Rousse			Depth at entry 9.14 m
Quay	179	4.88	

Mechanical Handling Equipment:

Location	Type	Qty
Ile Rousse	Forklifts	3

Airport: Calvi, 28 km

Lloyd's Agent: Unilex Maritime S.a.r.l, Les Docks, 10 Place de la Joliette, Atrium 10.8, F-13002 Marseilles Cedex 02, France, *Tel:* +33 4 91 14 04 40, *Fax:* +33 4 91 91 54 43, *Email:* mail@unilexmaritime.com, *Website:* www.unilexmaritime.com

JACQUES CARTIER

harbour area, see under St. Malo

LA CIOTAT

Lat 43° 10' N; Long 5° 36' E.

Admiralty Chart: 1705/2164
Time Zone: GMT +1 h

Admiralty Pilot: 46
UNCTAD Locode: FR LCT

This port is no longer open to commercial shipping

Ship Chandlers: BW Technologies, 515 Avenue de la Tramontane, Zone Athelia IV, Immeuble le Forum A31, F-13600 La Ciotat, France, *Tel:* +33 4 4298 1770, *Fax:* +33 4 4271 9705, *Email:* bwesales@bwtnet.com, *Website:* www.gasmonitors.com

LA NOUVELLE

Lat 43° 1' N; Long 3° 3' E.

Admiralty Chart: 2114
Time Zone: GMT +1 h

Admiralty Pilot: 22
UNCTAD Locode: FR

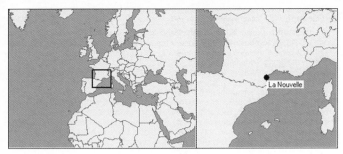

Principal Facilities:

P	Q	Y	G		R		B		T	A

Authority: Capitainerie du Port, 229 Avenue de la Mer, F-11210 Port la Nouvelle, France, *Tel:* +33 4 68 48 17 64, *Fax:* +33 4 68 40 31 42, *Email:* smnlr-cap-pln@equipement.gouv.fr

Officials: Harbour Master: Philippe Gouaut, *Email:* philippe.gouaut@equipement.gouv.fr.

Approach: Compulsory fairway for oil tankers and dangerous goods carriers

Anchorage: North area for tankers and dangerous cargo vessels in depth of 25 m South area for cargo vessels in depth of 25 m

Pilotage: Available. VHF Channel 12

Radio Frequency: Marseilles Radio, VHF Channels 24 and 26

Weather: Prevailing wind NW (Tramontane)

Maximum Vessel Dimensions: Offshore Terminal: 200 m loa, 12.0 m max d, 40 000 dwt
Berths: 145 m loa, 8.0 m max d, 22.0 m max beam

Principal Imports and Exports: Imports: Hydrocarbons. Exports: Cereals.

Working Hours: Overtime 0530-0730, 1800-2000

Accommodation:

Name	Length (m)	Depth (m)	Draught (m)	Remarks
La Nouvelle				
Tanker Terminals			8	Three berths. Max loa 145 m
Sea-Line Terminal		23		See [1] below
North Quay	210		4.5	
East Quay No.2	400		8	

[1]*Sea-Line Terminal:* Located 2.7 km NE of harbour entrance to accommodate vessels of 40 000 dwt

Storage: Three silo's

Mechanical Handling Equipment:

Location	Type	Capacity (t)	Qty
La Nouvelle	Mult-purp. Cranes	32	1
La Nouvelle	Mult-purp. Cranes	6	2
La Nouvelle	Mult-purp. Cranes	10	1

Cargo Worked: Barley in bulk approx 6000 t/day, other goods from 400-1000 t/day

Bunkering: Available by tank truck
BP France S.A., Immeuble le Cervier, 12 Avenue des Beguines, Cergy-Saint-Christophe, 95866 Cergy Pontoise Cedex, France, *Tel:* +33 1 3422 4000, *Fax:* +33 1 3422 4417, *Email:* benoist.grosjean@fr.bp.com, *Website:* www.bpmarine.com

Waste Reception Facilities: Specialized company available with trucks for all kinds of slops

Towage: Two tugs available

Ship Chandlers: EAFM, Quai Est No. 2, F-11210 La Nouvelle, France, *Tel:* +33 4 67 74 84 27, *Fax:* +33 4 67 74 40 45, *Email:* eafm-shipsupply@wanadoo.fr

Shipping Agents: Agena Tramp, 35 Rue Carnot, F-11210 La Nouvelle, France, *Tel:* +33 4 68 48 71 06, *Fax:* +33 4 68 48 71 07, *Email:* portlanouvelle@agenatramp.fr, *Website:* www.agenatramp.fr
Sud-Services, Quay Est 2, Port La Nouvelle, 11210 La Nouvelle, France, *Tel:* +33 4 68 48 38 90, *Fax:* +33 4 68 48 39 02, *Email:* sud-services@wanadoo.fr

Stevedoring Companies: Comptoir Languedocien de Transit et de Manutention, La Nouvelle, France, *Tel:* +33 4 68 48 01 02, *Fax:* +33 4 68 48 49 96, *Email:* cltm.pln@libertysurf.fr
Sud-Services, Quay Est 2, Port La Nouvelle, 11210 La Nouvelle, France, *Tel:* +33 4 68 48 38 90, *Fax:* +33 4 68 48 39 02, *Email:* sud-services@wanadoo.fr

Surveyors: Sud-Services, Quay Est 2, Port La Nouvelle, 11210 La Nouvelle, France, *Tel:* +33 4 68 48 38 90, *Fax:* +33 4 68 48 39 02, *Email:* sud-services@wanadoo.fr

Medical Facilities: Narbonne Hospital, 30 km

Airport: Perpignan, 50 km

Lloyd's Agent: Unilex Maritime S.a.r.l, Les Docks, 10 Place de la Joliette, Atrium 10.8, F-13002 Marseilles Cedex 02, France, *Tel:* +33 4 91 14 04 40, *Fax:* +33 4 91 91 54 43, *Email:* mail@unilexmaritime.com, *Website:* www.unilexmaritime.com

LA PALLICE

Lat 46° 9' N; Long 1° 13' W.

Admiralty Chart: 2743	**Admiralty Pilot:** 22
Time Zone: GMT +1 h	**UNCTAD Locode:** FR LPE

Principal Facilities:

P		Y	G	C	R	L	B	D	T	A

Authority: Grand Port Maritime de La Rochelle, P O Box 70394, F-17001 La Rochelle Cedex 1, France, *Tel:* +33 5 46 00 53 60, *Fax:* +33 5 46 43 19 28, *Email:* contact@larochelle-port.eu, *Website:* www.larochelle.port.fr

Officials: Managing Director: Jean Pierre Chalus, *Tel:* +33 5 46 00 74 98, *Email:* jp.chalus@larochelle.port.fr.
Commercial Director: Dominique Marquis, *Tel:* +33 5 46 00 53 64.
Harbour Master: Jacques Froissart, *Tel:* +33 5 46 00 56 32, *Email:* j.froissart@larochelle.fr.
Deputy Harbour Master: Pascal Courtheoux, *Tel:* +33 5 46 00 56 33, *Email:* p.courtheoux@larochelle.port.fr.

Port Security: ISPS compliant

Anchorage: Roads well sheltered from all winds from SW round to SE, afford safe anchorage. Sea-bed is hard mud

Pilotage: Compulsory for vessels exceeding 55 m loa, VHF Channel 16

Radio Frequency: Port traffic on VHF Channel 12. Distress calls on VHF Channel 16

Traffic: 2005, 1210 vessels, 6 896 479 t of cargo handled

Principal Imports and Exports: Imports: Fertiliser, Oil products, Paper, Phosphate, Sand & gravel, Timber, Woodpulp. Exports: Cereals, Frozen meat, Nitrate, Plywood.

Working Hours: 0800-1200, 1400-1800. Sat 0800-1200

Accommodation:

Name	Length (m)	Depth (m)	Draught (m)	Remarks
La Pallice				
Lock Basin				See [1] below
North Quay	565			Includes ro/ro terminal
South Quay	500			
Landing Pier				
East	540		10.5–12	
West	380		12–13	
Grain Terminal (Outer Harbour)				See [2] below
Sand & Gravel Quay (Outer Harbour)	130		9	
Oil Terminal				See [3] below
E side	300	12		For vessels up to 35 000 dwt
W side	350	16		For vessels up to 130 000 dwt
Chef de Baie	430	14		Three berths handling forest products

[1]*Lock Basin:* Approach: useful length between the doors 168.5 m, useful width 21.6 m, max draft at all tides 8.15 m and basin width 201 m. Specialised grabs for phosphates and kaolin
[2]*Grain Terminal (Outer Harbour):* Consists of two 150 m long berths dredged to 9 m and one terminal 300 m long dredged to 14 m for vessels up to 100 000 dwt. One pipeline for bulk liquid reception
[3]*Oil Terminal:* Three pipelines serving the whole oil storage area, located 2 km from the terminal at rate of 400-2000 m3/h. Total storage cap of 500 000 m3

Storage:

Location	Open (m2)	Covered (m2)	Grain (t)
La Pallice	400000	126500	
Grain Terminal (Outer Harbour)			270000
Chef de Baie			130000

Mechanical Handling Equipment:

Location	Type	Capacity (t)	Qty
Lock Basin	Mobile Cranes	63	1
Lock Basin	Electric Cranes	3–16	6
Landing Pier	Mobile Cranes	100	1
Landing Pier	Electric Cranes	3–33.5	7
Grain Terminal (Outer Harbour)	Mult-purp. Cranes		2
Chef de Baie	Mult-purp. Cranes		2
Chef de Baie	Mobile Cranes	63	1

Bunkering: Societe des Petroles Shell, 89 Boulevard Franklin Roosevelt, 92564 Rueil-Malmasion, F-76650 Petit Couronne, France, *Tel:* +33 2 35 67 47 03, *Fax:* +33 2 35 67 47 03
Total France S.A., Total Marine Fuels, 51 Esplanade du General de Gaulle, F-92907 Paris la Defense Cedex 10, France, *Tel:* +33 1 4135 2755, *Fax:* +33 1 4197 0291, *Email:* marine.fuels@total.com, *Website:* www.marinefuels.total.com

Key to Principal Facilities:—				
A=Airport	**C**=Containers	**G**=General Cargo	**P**=Petroleum	**R**=Ro/Ro	**Y**=Dry Bulk
B=Bunkers	**D**=Dry Dock	**L**=Cruise	**Q**=Other Liquid Bulk	**T**=Towage (where available from port)	

Towage: Boluda La Rochelle, Rue du Dahomey, P O Box 2031, F-17009 La Rochelle Cedex, France, *Tel:* +33 5 46 42 63 60, *Fax:* +33 5 46 42 57 95

Repair & Maintenance: Two drydocks: No.1, 179.8 m by 22.07 m; No.2, 110.94 m by 14.02 m

Ship Chandlers: R.& G. Dekytspotter Atlantic, 4 & 6 rue Montcalm, F-17000 La Pallice, France, *Tel:* +33 5 46 43 06 66, *Fax:* +33 5 46 00 04 57, *Email:* dksupply@dekytspotter.com, *Website:* www.dekytspotter.com

Shipping Agents: Agena Tramp, 134 Boulevard Emile Delmas, P O Box 2019, F-17009 La Rochelle Cedex 01, France, *Tel:* +33 5 46 35 23 65, *Fax:* +33 5 46 35 23 74, *Email:* lapallice@agenatramp.fr, *Website:* www.agenatramp.fr

Surveyors: Bureau Veritas, 3 Rue Alfred Kastler, Les Minimes, F-17044 La Rochelle, France, *Tel:* +33 5 46 50 13 70, *Fax:* +33 5 46 50 13 82, *Website:* www.bureauveritas.com

Medical Facilities: St. Louis hospital, La Rochelle

Airport: La Rochelle, 3 km

Railway: La Rochelle

Lloyd's Agent: AMS Ouest, 5 Bd Vincent Gache, P O Box 36204, F-44000 Nantes, France, *Tel:* +33 2 40 41 73 84, *Fax:* +33 2 40 41 73 92, *Email:* westoffice@associated-marine-services.com

LA ROCHELLE

Lat 46° 9' N; Long 1° 9' W.

Admiralty Chart: 2743	**Admiralty Pilot:** 22
Time Zone: GMT +1 h	**UNCTAD Locode:** FR LRH

This port is no longer open to commercial shipping

Repair & Maintenance: Shipelec, Rue de la Cote D'Ivoire, F-17000 La Rochelle, France, *Tel:* +33 5 46 56 34 67, *Fax:* +33 5 46 56 34 67, *Email:* info@shipelec.fr, *Website:* www.shipelec.fr

Shipping Agents: Comptoir General Maritime S.A., 100 Boulevard Emile Delmas, P O Box 2039, Cedex 1, F-17009 La Rochelle, France, *Tel:* +33 5 4600 6633, *Fax:* +33 5 4643 6101, *Email:* r.muratore@sdv.com
Comptoir General Maritime Varois, 100 Boulevard Emile Delmas, P O Box 2036, F-170009 La Rochelle, France, *Tel:* +33 5 46 00 66 33, *Fax:* +33 5 46 43 65 01, *Email:* lrh.shipping@sdv.com, *Website:* www.sdv.com
Comptoir General Maritime Varois, 100 Boulevard Emile Delmas, P O Box 2036, F-170009 La Rochelle, France, *Tel:* +33 5 46 00 66 33, *Fax:* +33 5 46 43 65 01, *Email:* lrh.cogemarshipping@sdv.com, *Website:* www.sdv.com
Forest Agency Service Terminal, 182 Boulevard Emile-Delmas, P O Box 2054, F-17010 La Rochelle, France, *Tel:* +33 5 4600 6180, *Fax:* +33 5 4667 7325, *Email:* fast.la-pallice@wanadoo.fr
Humann & Taconet, 112 Boulevard Emile Delmas, F-17000 La Rochelle, France, *Tel:* +33 5 46 42 83 58, *Fax:* +33 5 46 42 83 59, *Email:* lapallice@humtac.fr, *Website:* www.humann-taconet.fr
Sea Invest Shipping Agency, P O Box 2066, 1 Rue Esprinchard, 17010 La Rochelle, France, *Tel:* +33 5 46 00 48 10, *Fax:* +33 5 46 00 76 13, *Email:* tramplap@sea-invest-france.com, *Website:* www.sea-invest-sa.com

Stevedoring Companies: Comptoir General Maritime Varois, 100 Boulevard Emile Delmas, P O Box 2036, F-170009 La Rochelle, France, *Tel:* +33 5 46 43 65 01, *Email:* lrh.cogemarshipping@sdv.com, *Website:* www.sdv.com
Comptoir General Maritime Varois, 100 Boulevard Emile Delmas, P O Box 2036, F-170009 La Rochelle, France, *Tel:* +33 5 46 00 66 33, *Fax:* +33 5 46 43 65 01, *Email:* lrh.shipping@sdv.com, *Website:* www.sdv.com

LA SEYNE BREGAILLON

harbour area, see under Toulon

LAVERA

Lat 43° 23' N; Long 4° 59' E.

Admiralty Chart: 155	**Admiralty Pilot:** 46
Time Zone: GMT +1 h	**UNCTAD Locode:** FR LAV

Principal Facilities:

P	Q				B		A

Authority: Grand Port Maritime de Marseille, Quai de la Lecque, P O Box 200, F-13110 Port de Bouc Cedex, France, *Tel:* +33 4 42 40 60 05, *Fax:* +33 4 42 40 60 40, *Email:* m.bonvalet@marseille-port.fr, *Website:* www.marseille-port.fr

Officials: Commercial Director: Monica Bonvalet, *Tel:* +33 4 91 39 43 22.
Harbour Master: Joseph Moysan, *Tel:* +33 4 91 39 41 40, *Email:* j.moysan@marseille-port.fr.

Port Security: ISPS compliant

Pre-Arrival Information: Vessel Traffic Service: The Marseilles/Fos Maritime Traffic Service (STM) is compulsory for all commercial vessels. The area of authority of the STM comprises a marine operating area and a port operating area:
(a) within the limits administered by the GPMM
(b) within the administrative limits of the installations and constructions entrusted to the GPMM
(c) within the area of jurisdiction of the GPMM
(d) in the channels and approaches to the Golfe de Fos and to the Port of Marseilles for vessels transporting hydrocarbons and dangerous substances
The Fos area lies between longitudes 4° 41.3' E (Faraman Lt) and 5° 06.5' E (Sausset-les-Pins Lt), latitude 43° 11.9' N (Le Planier Lt) and the shore, including the Canal Saint-Louis, Port-Saint-Louis-du-Rhone, the Canal de Caronte and the Etang de Berre. Fos Port Control, Tel: +33 4 42 40 60 60. Maritime Traffic Service Centre on VHF Channels 12 and 73. Vessels manoeuvring in the port on VHF Channels 72 and 77
Communications:
(a) communication on VHF Channel 12 and 73 must be established as early as possible between vessels and the Maritime Traffic Service (STM) Centre
(b) vessels unable to contact the STM may not cross the Cap Couronne line (43° 19.5' N)
(c) vessels on passage, manoeuvring and at anchor in any part of the area controlled by the STM must maintain a listening watch on VHF Channel 12
(d) conversations should take place in French and English using standard IMO terminology
(e) pilots can be contacted on VHF Channel 14
Vessels transporting hydrocarbons and dangerous substances must send a SURNAV message 6 h prior to entry into French territorial waters
Vessels inward-bound must contact the STM as follows:
(a) 48 h before arrival at the pilot boarding position, through the agent stating
(i) vessels name and call sign
(ii) destination and port of departure
(iii) draught
(iv) cargo
(v) loa, beam and gt
(vi) type of vessel
(vii) ETA
(b) at least 24 h before arrival stating:
(i) ETA at pilot boarding position
(ii) draught
(iii) nature and tonnage of transported dangerous substances
(iv) loa
(c) 6 h before entry into French territorial waters, vessels transporting hydrocarbons or dangerous substances must send a SURNAV message
(d) on entering the area offshore of the entrance, all vessels over 50 m loa on passage to the Golfe de Fos must report to the STM on VHF Channel 12 stating:
(i) vessels name and call sign
(ii) position
(iii) course and speed
(iv) ETA
The STM will give permission to proceed along the approach channel starting at the Fairway (Omega) Lt Buoy, and will provide information on traffic movements and weather conditions in the area
(e) the STM will advise berthing details and a time for pilot boarding, as well as any towing requiirements if not already specified
(f) the STM will also advise VHF communication details as follows:
(i) at the entrance to the STM area
(ii) at the entrance to the approach channel for vessels obliged to use the channels (vessels over 1600 gt transporting hydrocarbons or dangerous substances) for Fos or Marseilles
(iii) at the entrance to the approach channel for vessels not obliged to use the channels. After identifying and authorising the vessel, the STM will instruct the vessel to proceed if the vessel is subject to an inspection by a surveyor
(g) vessels over 1600 gt transporting hydrocarbons or dangerous substances may not enter the approach channel (N of 43° 12.0' N) without the authorisation of the STM
(h) in the event of a doubtful identity, the STM will call every vessel it considers to be likely until a positive identity is obtained
Vessels in the area:
(a) all vessels must contact the STM on VHF before entering the port, getting under way or changing berths
(b) all vessels crossing (or in cases of emergency, anchoring or waiting in) the approach channel, which vessels transporting dangerous cargo are obliged to use, must inform the STM immediately
(c) all vessels wishing to anchor in the Golfe de Fos to the N of the dredged channel must obtain prior permission from the STM. A continuous listening watch must be maintained on VHF Channel 12 while at the anchorage
(d) all vessels wishing to proceed along the Canal de Caronte or the Canal Saint-Louis must request instructions from the STM
(e) vessels transporting hydrocarbons or dangerous substances in the transhipment area of the Golfe de Fos must maintain a continuous listening watch on VHF Channel 12
(f) leisure craft must contact the Harbour Master for all movements within the port (entering, leaving or making way)
(g) vessels may only enter the dredged channel (from the Lavera Lt Buoy to the harbour basins) after checking with the STM that no other vessel has commenced passage along the channel

Pilotage: The compulsory pilotage area consists of an area N of latitude 43° 19' N between the meridians of Faramen Lt (4° 41.3' E) and Cap Couronne Lt (5° 03.3' E), including the canals, the harbour basins of the inner harbours, the Rhone as far as Arles and the Etang de Berre
Marseilles/Fos Office, Tel: +33 4 91 14 29 10, Fax: +33 4 91 56 65 79, Email: pilote13@nerim.fr
Golfe de Fos Pilotage, Tel: +33 4 42 06 21 01
VHF Channels 12 and 14
Pilotage is available 24/h day and compulsory for vessels of all categories over 50 m loa and all vessels over 70 m loa on passage to or from Darse 2 (Harbour Basin 2) Container Terminal and Darse 3 (Harbour Basin 3) berths in the Port of Fos, except for vessels transporting hydrocarbons or dangerous substances

Vessels must report ETA with at least 24 h notice (or as soon as leaving the previous port) to the Port de Bouc Harbour Master stating:
(a) loa
(b) draught (forward and aft)
(c) nature and tonnage of any dangerous cargo
Vessels must establish VHF contact with the Port de Bouc Harbour Master as early as possible
Pilot boards in the following positions:
(a) vessels transporting hydrocarbons or dangerous cargo and deep draught vessels on passage to Fos at the latitude of Cap Couronne Lt (43° 19.5' N)
(b) vessels bound for Port de Bouc, Lavera, Etang de Berre and St. Louis du Rhone between 2.5-4 nautical miles S of Lavera Lt Buoy (43° 22.6' N; 4° 58.2' E)
(c) on request between latitudes 43° 11.9' N and 43° 19.6' N
The pilotage sub-station at Port de Bouc provides pilots for Lavera, Canal de Caronte, Martigues, Etang de Berre, Fos and St. Louis du Rhone. This station comes under the authority of the Marseilles/Golfe de Fos Pilotage Office

Maximum Vessel Dimensions: 80 000 dwt, 275 m loa, 12.8 m d

Accommodation:

Name	Draught (m)	Remarks
Lavera		See [1] below
Berth 711	9.5	Liquefied gas for vessels up to 110 m loa
Berth 712	10.1	Refined products & chemical caustic soda for vessels up to 120 m loa
Berth 714	11.3	See [2] below
Berth 721	10.8	Crude petroleum & refined products for vessels up to 230 m loa
Berth 722	11	Crude petroleum & refined products for vessels up to 230 m loa
Berth 723	11	Crude petroleum & refined products for vessels up to 230 m loa
Berth 724	11.5	Crude petroleum & refined products for vessels up to 230 m loa
Berth 725	11.6	See [3] below
Berth 726	12	Industrial fresh water & liquefied gas for vessels up to 250 m loa
Berth 727	11	Chemicals for vessels up to 200 m loa
Berth 728	10.4	Chemical products & liquefied gas for vessels up to 130 m loa
Berth 701	3.1–5.2	Refined products for vessels up to 120 m loa
Berth 705	4.6	Refined products for vessels up to 100 m loa
Berth 706	4.6	Refined products for vessels up to 100 m loa

[1]*Lavera:* Harbour for the reception of crude oil and petroleum products, liquid chemicals and gases. Depth at entrance 14.6 m. Total length of quays is 2720 m with 12.8 m max d
Each berth is equipped with articulated arms. Depending on the nature of the products (crude or refined), special pipelines connect the berths to the depots of CFR and Shell, and to the maritime terminal of the S European Pipeline and, through the latter, to the Esso refinery at Fos
Special pipelines connect the chemical berths to the depots and refineries: MAVRAC - NAPHTACHIMIE - CHLOE CHIMIE - ATOCHEM - BP CHIMIE
Special pipelines connect the gas berths to the depots and refineries: GEOGAZ - NAPHTACHIMIE
[2]*Berth 714:* Refined products, chemicals & liquefied gas for vessels up to 200 m loa
[3]*Berth 725:* Crude petroleum, refined products, industrial fresh water & liquefied gas for vessels up to 250 m loa

Bunkering: ExxonMobil Marine Fuels, Mailpoint 31, ExxonMobil House, Ermyn Way, Leatherhead, Surrey KT22 8UX, United Kingdom, *Tel:* +44 1372 222 000, *Fax:* +44 1372 223 922, *Email:* marine.fuels@exxonmobil.com, *Website:* www.exxonmobil.com – *Grades:* IFO30-380cSt; MGO; MDO – *Delivery Mode:* barge

Ship Chandlers: Ets Tilley, Nord Activites, 09 rue du Laos, F-13015 Marseilles, France, *Tel:* +33 4 91 03 17 34, *Fax:* +33 4 91 03 14 39, *Email:* tilleyco@aol.com., *Website:* www.tilley.fr
International Export Agency, Z.I. Boulevard de la Merindole, F-13110 Port de Bouc, France, *Tel:* +33 4 42 40 52 82, *Fax:* +33 4 42 06 59 54, *Email:* sales.dpt@iea-shipsupply.com

Shipping Agents: Maritima del Mediterraneo S.A. (Marmedsa), Bat V Avenida J. Jacques Rousseau, 13500 Martigues, France, *Tel:* +33 4 42 81 71 60, *Fax:* +33 4 42 07 15 57, *Email:* bbegon@marmedsafr.marmedsa.com, *Website:* www.marmedsa.com

Medical Facilities: Available at Martigues and Port de Bouc

Airport: Marseille Provence, 40 km

Lloyd's Agent: Unilex Maritime S.a.r.l, Les Docks, 10 Place de la Joliette, Atrium 10.8, F-13002 Marseilles Cedex 02, France, *Tel:* +33 4 91 14 04 40, *Fax:* +33 4 91 91 54 43, *Email:* mail@unilexmaritime.com, *Website:* www.unilexmaritime.com

LE GUILDO

Lat 48° 38' N; Long 2° 14' W.

Admiralty Chart: 2669	**Admiralty Pilot:** 27
Time Zone: GMT +1 h	**UNCTAD Locode:** FR LGU

Principal Facilities:

			G			B		A

Authority: Port Authority of Le Guildo, Chambre de Commerce et d'Indust, St. Malo, France

Pilotage: Carried out by St Malo pilots. Compulsory for vessels over 150 nrt. Rates, on application, to be paid even if not used. Captains are strictly requested to approach as near as possible the buoys of entrance of St Malo road, where they will meet the pilot boat. A notice of 12 h min of the ETA of vessels must be given by the captains (Cables: NAVAL-St Malo I & V, Telex: 730926) in order to inform the pilots in due time of the ship's position. Admittance: (in or out) in the River Arguenon. This river has no light, vessels can enter or leave during daylight tides only

Radio Frequency: Pilots on VHF Channel 12

Tides: 7.5 m to be deducted from St Malo tides table figures to obtain practicable d

Traffic: No movements reported since July 2002

Working Hours: Monday-Saturday, overtime possible

Accommodation:

Name	Remarks
Le Guildo	See [1] below

[1]*Le Guildo:* Sill depth is 6.1 m over zero on marine charts. The ground is composed of soft mud and sand and is not very stable. The beaching ground alongside the berths is considered safe. Max length of vessels is 55 m between the pp

Bunkering: Gas oil available from St Malo with 48 h notice

Repair & Maintenance: Available at St Malo

Medical Facilities: Hospital in St. Malo, 25 km

Airport: Dinard, 25 km

Lloyd's Agent: Agence Maritime Roy s.a.r.l., 2 Chaussee des Corsaires, P O Box 179, F-35409 St. Malo, France, *Tel:* +33 2 99 56 07 21, *Fax:* +33 2 99 40 24 00, *Email:* agence-maritime-roy@wanadoo.fr

LE HAVRE

Lat 49° 29' N; Long 0° 8' E.

Admiralty Chart: 2990	**Admiralty Pilot:** 27
Time Zone: GMT +1 h	**UNCTAD Locode:** FR LEH

Principal Facilities:

P	Q	Y	G	C	R	L	B	D	T	A

Authority: Grand Port Maritime du Havre, P O Box 1413, F-76067 Le Havre Cedex, France, *Tel:* +33 2 32 74 74 00, *Fax:* +33 2 32 74 74 29, *Email:* commercial-dir@havre-port.fr, *Website:* www.havre-port.net

Officials: Executive Director: Laurent Castaing, *Email:* dir.generale@havre-port.fr. Commercial Director: Pierre-Yves Collardey, *Email:* pierre-yves.collardey@havre-port.fr.
Harbour Master: Patrick Abjean, *Email:* patrick.abjean@havre-port.fr.

Port Security: ISPS compliant. Container Security Initiative (CSI) designated port

Approach: The NW channel, or harbour entrance, which is 12 km long and 300 m broad, with a depth of at least 15.5 m at LWOST, gives access to the biggest ships at any time of the tide
Four radar stations installed respectively at La Heve lighthouse, the Control Centre, the CIM Oil terminal, and the Francois 1er Central Control Terminal

Pilotage: Compulsory. Pilot station between the buoy 'Le Havre' and the first buoys of the entrance channel. VHF Channel 16

Weather: Winds W

Tides: SR 8.35 m, NR 5.8 m

Traffic: 2007, 79 400 000 t of cargo handled, 2 638 000 TEU's

Maximum Vessel Dimensions: Tankers up to 250 000 dwt in Le Havre tidal basin and tankers up to 550 000 dwt at Antifer terminal

Key to Principal Facilities:—			
A=Airport	**C**=Containers	**G**=General Cargo	**P**=Petroleum	**R**=Ro/Ro	**Y**=Dry Bulk
B=Bunkers	**D**=Dry Dock	**L**=Cruise	**Q**=Other Liquid Bulk	**T**=Towage (where available from port)	

Working Hours: According to customer requirements. 24 h/day

Accommodation: 142 berths along 28 km of quays, including 100 berths reserved for commercial calls and approx 10 berths for ship repair activities

8 oil berths in Le Havre and 2 berths in the oil terminal of Antifer accessible to large tankers up to 550 000 t, 2 ore berths for vessels up to 170 000 dwt and a multibulks centre for the trades of industrial coal and cattle food

Specialized berths for refined oil products, liquefied gas, chemicals and petrochemicals, grain and sugar in bulk or bagged, fruit and cements

7 container terminals, 2 terminals for car ferries, a site dedicated to cruise, 1 ro/ro centre for vessels carrying new vehicles, 1 combi-terminal for general cargo and container vessels, conventional trades and heavy lifts

Bulk facilities: Bulk terminal situated on Mole Central, to the seaward side of Francois 1 lock. One berth available for vessels of up to 170 000 dwt. Grain and sugar handling facilities are concentrated at the Hermann du Pasquier and Joannes Couvert quays with silo cap of 80 000 t and specialised loading and unloading installations; vessels of up to 30 000 dwt and 60 000 dwt respectively can be accommodated

Light bulk cargoes are also handled at the Quai du Rhin

A multi-purpose bulk centre, located on the south bank of the Grand Canal du Havre makes it possible to process all kinds of goods in bulk, both on export and import. The terminal has one 1200 t/h cap gantry crane and one 500 t/h cap gantry crane. Vessels up to 85 000 dwt fully laden can be accommodated and 150 000 dwt partially laden. Silo with a storage cap of 50 000 t to receive feedstuff products

Tanker facilities: Eight berths operated by the Cie Industrielle Maritime (CIM) for vessels up to 250 000 dwt. Storage cap of 4 400 000 m3. Night berthing not possible for vessels over 50 000 dwt; water and bunkers available

ANTIFER: 20 km N of Le Havre's access channel and 4 km S of the Cap d'Antifer at St Jouin-Bruneval is the port of Le Havre-Antifer, an oil terminal with two berths for tankers up to 550 000 dwt. Access channel 550 m wide: 1450 m diameter turning circle, dredged to a depth of 25 m. Port protected to the N by a breakwater 3512 m long. The oil, directly unloaded from tankers into four reservoirs with a total storage cap of 600 000 m3, is pumped to Le Havre's installations through a 26.2 km long pipeline

An LPG storage terminal is operated by the Economic Interest group NORGAL. The total storage cap is 60 000 m3 including 35 000 m3 for propane at -44°C, 5000 m3 for propane at -10°C and 20 000 m3 for butane at -10°C

One berth for 60 000 dwt tankers (Sogestrol 1) and one berth for coasters and barges (HOC/CFR)

Name	Length (m)	Draught (m)	Remarks
Container Facilities			
Atlantic Quay	800		Three berths. 25 ha area
Europe Quay	1200		See [1] below
Americas Quay	500		Two berths. 15 ha area
Asia Quay	600		Two berths. 20 ha area
Bougainville Quay	1000		See [2] below
Osaka Quay	450		Two berths. 10 ha area
Port 2000			
Terminal de France	700	14.5–16	See [3] below
Terminal Porte Oceane	700	14.5–16	See [4] below
Ro/Ro Facs			
Terminal Grande Bretagne 1			Vessels up to 165 m loa. On dolphins
Terminal d'Irlande 1			Vessels up to 160 m loa. On dolphins
Terminal d'Irlande 2			Vessels up to 160 m loa
Quai de Marseille			Vessels up to 135 m loa
Quai de la Reunion 1			Vessels up to 150 m loa
Quai du Tonkin			Vessels up to 90 m loa
Quai de Colombie			Vessels up to 80 m loa
Quai Hermann du Pasquier			Vessels up to 180 m loa
Quai de Gironde 1			Vessels up to 150 m loa
Berth Ro/ro 1			Vessels up to 110 m loa. On dolphins
Berth Ro/ro 2			Vessels up to 200 m loa. On dolphins
Quay Ro/ro 3			Vessels up to 230 m loa
2 Berths for Barges			Vessels up to 80 m loa. On dolphins
Ore & Bulk Cargo Facs			
Outer MCT 4 (Ore Berth)			Vessels up to 280 m loa
Inner MCT 4 (Ore Berth)			Vessels up to 120 m loa. Loading on barges
MCT 5 (Ore Berth)			See [5] below
MCT 6 (Ore Berth)			See [6] below
Moselle 2 (Ore Berth)			See [7] below
Moselle 3 (Ore Berth)			Vessels up to 171 m loa. Ilmenite
Cement Works (Ore Berth)			See [8] below
MTV 1 (Ore Berth)			Vessels up to 300 m loa
MTV 2 (Ore Berth)			Vessels up to 110 m loa
NHA (Ore Berth)			Vessels up to 250 m loa and 60 000 t
JCV 2 (Grain Berth)			Vessels up to 210 m loa and 60 000 dwt
HDP 3 & 4W (Grain Berth)			Vessels up to 200 m loa and 28 000 dwt
HDP 2-3 (Grain Berths)			Vessels up to 201 m loa
Quai des Arachides (Grain Berth)			Vessels up to 130 m loa and 6000 dwt
HDP 4E (Fruit Berth)			Vessels up to 200 m loa. Storage up to 150 000 cases
Gironde 5-6-7 (Fruit Berths)			Vessels up to 170 m loa. Storage up to 550 000 cases
Bresil 1 (Fruit Berth)			Vessels up to 200 m loa. Bananas
Jean Reinhart 1 (Fruit Berth)			Vessels up to 200 m loa. Fruit (air conditioned sheds)
Jean Reinhart 2 (Fruit Berth)			Vessels up to 200 m loa. Fruit (air conditioned sheds)
Jean Reinhart 3 (Fruit Berth)			Vessels up to 200 m loa. Fruit (air conditioned sheds)
Europe 1 (Fruit Berth)			Vessels up to 300 m loa. Bananas
Tanker Facs			
CIM 1 (Oil Products)			Vessels up to 175 m loa and 22 000 dwt
CIM 2 (Oil Products)			Vessels up to 198 m loa and 22 000 dwt
CIM 3 (Oil Products)			Vessels up to 242 m loa and 50 000 dwt
CIM 5 (Oil Products)			Vessels up to 230 m loa and 40 000 dwt
CIM 6 (Oil Products)			Vessels up to 260 m loa and 90 000 dwt
CIM 7 (Oil Products)			Vessels up to 278 m loa and 100 000 dwt
CIM 8 (Oil Products)			Vessels up to 320 m loa and 230 000 dwt
CIM 10 (Oil Products)			Vessels up to 350 m loa and 280 000 dwt
Antifer W (Oil Products)			Vessels up to 500 m loa and 550 000 dwt
Antifer E (Oil Products)			Vessels up to 500 m loa and 550 000 dwt
Mazeline 1 (Oil Products)			Vessels up to 350 m loa
MCT 3 (Oil Products)			Vessels up to 240 m loa
Sometran South Quay (Oil Products)			Vessels up to 80 m loa. Oil residues
Canal de Tancarville Orcher ChevronTexaco Chemical Wharf (Oil Products)			See [9] below
Canal Bossiere (Oil Products)			See [10] below
SNA (Chemical Products)			See [11] below
Sogestrol (Norgal) 1 (Chemical Products)			Vessels up to 240 m loa and 45 000 dwt
Sogestrol 3 (Chemical Products)			Vessels up to 120 m loa and 7000 dwt
Sogestrol 4 (Chemical Products)			Vessels up to 40 000 dwt
Sogestrol 5 (Chemical Products)			Vessels up to 120 m loa and 7000 dwt
Ato Chimie 1 (Chemical Products)			Vessels up to 80 m loa
Ato Chimie 2 (Chemical Products)			Vessels up to 170 m loa and 26 000 dwt
NHA (Chemical Products)			Vessels up to 182 m loa and 30 000 dwt

[1]*Europe Quay:* Four berths, two of which have easy access for rear-ramp ro/ro vessels. 45 ha area. Also a fruit storage and pallet-loading warehouse

[2]*Bougainville Quay:* Three berths. 52 ha area. One mobile floating platform for ro/ro traffic

[3]*Terminal de France:* Two 350 m long berths jointly operated by CMA CGM and Generale de Manutention Portuaire

[4]*Terminal Porte Oceane:* Two 350 m long berths jointly operated by APM Terminals and Perrigault S.A.

[5]*MCT 5 (Ore Berth):* Vessels up to 140 m loa. Loading on barges or coasters

[6]*MCT 6 (Ore Berth):* Vessels up to 300 m loa. Accessible to 150 000 t vessels; output 2400 t/h

[7]*Moselle 2 (Ore Berth):* Vessels up to 171 m loa. Dry liquid sulphur and dodecylbenzene

[8]*Cement Works (Ore Berth):* Vessels up to 200 m loa. Accessible to 25 000-30 000 t vessels

[9]*Canal de Tancarville Orcher ChevronTexaco Chemical Wharf (Oil Products):* One loading berth for vessels up to 100 m loa for refined products, one waiting berth for vessels up to 100 m loa for refined products, four berths for barges up to 80 m loa for refined products, two total solvent wharves for vessels up to 85 m loa and 60 m loa for refined products and self propelled barges respectively and Garage de Tancarville for vessels up to 80 m loa for bunkering

[10]*Canal Bossiere (Oil Products):* Jonction 1 for vessels up to 80 m loa and 4000 dwt, Jonction 2 for vessels up to 150 m loa and 12 000 dwt and Jonction 3 for vessels up to 270 m loa and 50 000 dwt

[11]*SNA (Chemical Products):* Vessels up to 180 m loa and 20 000 dwt. Liquid ammonia and urea 100-200 t/h

Storage: 5 200 000 m3 for oil products, 60 000 m3 for gaseous hydrocarbons, 360 000 m3 for chemicals, 100 000 m3 for oils and latex, 100 000 m3 for liquid fertilizers 565 000 m2 of warehouses including 42 000 m2 of air-conditioned and isothermal facility for fruit and vegetables, 87 000 m2 of warehouses for coffee and 45 000 m2 for cotton, 15 000 m3 for frozen goods and total storage cap of 460 000 t for grain

Location	Covered (m²)	Sheds / Warehouses
Atlantic Quay	10000	1
Europe Quay	21000	2
Bougainville Quay	50000	4

Mechanical Handling Equipment:

Location	Type	Capacity (t)	Qty
Le Havre	Floating Cranes	200	1
Atlantic Quay	Container Cranes	40	4
Europe Quay	Container Cranes	40	5

Location	Type	Capacity (t)	Qty
Americas Quay	Post Panamax	70	3
Asia Quay	Post Panamax	70	3
Bougainville Quay	Container Cranes		6
Osaka Quay	Post Panamax	70	2
Port 2000	Super Post Panamax		10

Bunkering: BP France S.A., Immeuble le Cervier, 12 Avenue des Beguines, Cergy-Saint-Christophe, 95866 Cergy Pontoise Cedex, France, *Tel:* +33 1 3422 4000, *Fax:* +33 1 3422 4417, *Email:* benoist.grosjean@fr.bp.com, *Website:* www.bpmarine.com – *Grades:* IFO-180; IF-180; MGO – *Parcel Size:* 25t – *Delivery Mode:* pipeline, barge, truck
ExxonMobil Marine Fuels, Mailpoint 31, ExxonMobil House, Ermyn Way, Leatherhead, Surrey KT22 8UX, United Kingdom, *Tel:* +44 1372 222 000, *Fax:* +44 1372 223 922, *Email:* marine.fuels@exxonmobil.com, *Website:* www.exxonmobil.com – *Grades:* IFO30-380cSt; MGO – *Delivery Mode:* truck, pipeline
Societe des Petroles Shell, 89 Boulevard Franklin Roosevelt, 92564 Rueil-Malmasion, F-76650 Petit Couronne, France, *Tel:* +33 2 35 67 47 03, *Fax:* +33 2 35 67 47 03 – *Delivery Mode:* truck
Total France S.A., Total Marine Fuels, 51 Esplanade du General de Gaulle, F-92907 Paris la Defense Cedex 10, France, *Tel:* +33 1 4135 2755, *Fax:* +33 1 4197 0291, *Email:* marine.fuels@total.com, *Website:* www.marinefuels.total.com – *Grades:* IFO-380cSt; MGO – *Parcel Size:* IFO-380 min 1200t/h,MGO min 25t – *Notice:* 48 hours – *Delivery Mode:* truck, pipeline

Towage: Societe Nouvelle de Remorquage du Havre, Hangen 17, Quai Johannes-Couvert, P O Box 11167, F-76063 Le Havre, France, *Tel:* +33 2 35 30 30 30, *Fax:* +33 2 35 26 17 81, *Email:* info@snrh-lehavre.com, *Website:* www.snrh-lehavre.com

Repair & Maintenance: S.I.R.E.N. Ship Repair, Route du Mole Central, P O Box 1286, F-76068 Le Havre, France, *Tel:* +33 2 35 24 72 72, *Fax:* +33 2 35 24 72 96 Floating Dock of 320 m x 54 m, max 299 000 dwt. Four drydocks, max 319 m x 38 m, max 90 000 dwt. Two repair berths
SNACH, 30 rue Jean-Jacques, P O Box 1390, F-76066 Le Havre, France, *Tel:* +33 2 35 26 64 04, *Fax:* +33 2 35 25 09 70 Repair facilities

Ship Chandlers: Logitainer S.A., Route du Mole Central, P O Box 440, F-76057 Le Havre, France, *Tel:* +33 2 35 24 78 78, *Fax:* +33 2 35 24 78 80, *Email:* lhv.contact@naxco-logistics.com, *Website:* www.naxco-logistics.com
S.G.A.E., ZI Nord, Routes des Entreprises, 76700 Gonfreville l'Orcher, France, *Tel:* +33 2 35 53 37 11, *Fax:* +33 2 35 53 96 62, *Email:* sgae.lehavre@sgae.fr, *Website:* www.sgae.fr

Shipping Agents: Agena Tramp, 156 rue Victor Hugo, P O Box 1446, F-76066 Le Havre Cedex, France, *Tel:* +33 2 35 19 72 84, *Fax:* +33 2 35 19 72 85, *Email:* seine@agenatramp.fr, *Website:* www.agenatramp.fr
Agences Maritimes Associees, Burger Port Agencies S.A.S, Centre Commerce International du Havre, Quai George V, F-76600 Le Havre, France, *Tel:* +33 2 35 19 83 00, *Fax:* +33 2 35 19 83 13, *Email:* lehavre@burgergroup.fr, *Website:* www.royalburgergroup.com
Balport, 109 Boulevard de Strasbourg, P O Box 1381, F-76066 Le Havre, France, *Tel:* +33 2 32 74 35 35, *Fax:* +33 2 32 74 35 29, *Email:* balport@balport.fr
BOSS-Blue Ocean Shipping System, Chaussee de Roselle, P O Box 252, F-76600 Le Havre, France, *Tel:* +33 2 32 72 70 50, *Fax:* +33 2 35 24 31 57, *Email:* boss.team@oceansystem.france.com
John S. Braid & Co. Ltd, Braid Logistics Europe, Parc des alizes, Voie des barges rousses, Sandouville, F-76430 Le Havre, France, *Tel:* +33 2 32 72 58 80, *Fax:* +33 2 32 72 58 88, *Email:* rbagley@braidco.com, *Website:* www.braidco.com
CLB Liner, 156 Rue Victor Hugo, P O Box 152, F-76052 Le Havre, France, *Tel:* +33 2 35 19 73 40, *Fax:* +33 2 35 19 73 41, *Email:* sales.leh@clbliner.fr, *Website:* www.clbliner.fr
CMA-CGM S.A., CMA CGM Le Havre, 1 Quai Colbert, F-76096 Le Havre Cedex, France, *Tel:* +33 2 32 74 16 00, *Fax:* +33 2 32 74 10 10, *Email:* lhv.genmbox@cma-cgm.com, *Website:* www.cma-cgm.com
CSAV Agency (France) s.a.s., World Trade Center, 182 Quai George V, F-76600 Le Havre, France, *Tel:* +33 2 35 22 28 00, *Fax:* +33 2 35 22 28 50, *Email:* www.csav.cl
Daher & Cie, Parc d'Activities Logistiques de Pont de Normandie, P O Box 720, 76060 Le Havre, France, *Tel:* +33 2 32 79 70 00, *Fax:* +33 2 32 79 70 50, *Email:* m.hauters@daher.com, *Website:* www.daher.com
Jacques Durand Viel, 73-75 Quai de Southampton, 76066 Le Havre, France, *Tel:* +33 2 35 19 39 86, *Fax:* +33 2 35 19 39 85, *Website:* www.humann-taconet.fr
Hemmer Marine Services Sarl, 112 Rue du Domaine de Pontbriand, Saint Lunaire, F-35800 Le Havre, France, *Tel:* +33 2 9916 6201, *Fax:* +33 2 9946 3976, *Email:* hemmer.marine.services@wanadoo.fr
Humann & Taconet, 73-75 Quai de Southampton, P O Box 1395, F-76066 Le Havre Cedex, France, *Tel:* +33 2 35 19 39 86, *Fax:* +33 2 35 19 39 85, *Email:* lloydsagency-lehavre@humtac.fr, *Website:* www.humann-taconet.fr
Isamar S.A., CHCI Quai George V, P O Box 86, 76050 Le Havre, France, *Tel:* +33 2 35 19 85 00, *Fax:* +33 2 35 19 85 01, *Email:* florence.maidon@fr.senatorlines.com, *Website:* www.isamar.es
K Line (Europe) Ltd, CHCI Quai George V, P O Box 108, 76050 Le Havre, France, *Tel:* +33 2 35 19 30 00, *Fax:* +33 2 35 42 12 34, *Email:* keulehsales@fr.kline.com, *Website:* www.klineurope.com
Leon Vincent S.A., Rue de Coupeauville, P O Box 38, F-76133 Le Havre, France, *Tel:* +33 2 32 92 56 00, *Fax:* +33 2 35 26 48 22, *Email:* lehavre.agence@leonvincent.fr, *Website:* www.leonvincent.fr
Logitainer S.A., Route du Mole Central, P O Box 440, F-76057 Le Havre, France, *Tel:* +33 2 35 24 78 78, *Fax:* +33 2 35 24 78 80, *Email:* lhv.contact@naxco-logistics.com, *Website:* www.naxco-logistics.com
Mediterranean Shipping Company, MSC France S.A., CHCI, Quai George V, P O Box 1339, F-76065 Le Havre Cedex, France, *Tel:* +33 2 32 74 68 00, *Fax:* +33 2 32 74 68 10, *Email:* msclehavre@mscfr.mscgva.ch, *Website:* www.mscgva.ch
Wm. H. Muller & Co., Centre de Commerce International du Havre, Quai George V, F-76600 Le Havre, France, *Tel:* +33 2 35 19 83 10, *Fax:* +33 2 35 19 83 15, *Email:* lehavre@burgergroup.fr, *Website:* www.royalburgergroup.com
Navitainer S.A., World Trade Center 182, Qua George 5th, P O Box 1337, 76065 Le Havre, France, *Tel:* +33 2 35 24 75 01, *Fax:* +33 2 35 53 15 41, *Email:* salesleh.navitainer@burgergroup.fr
Neptumar SAS, 32 Rue Pierre Brossolette, P O Box 7001X, Cedex, 76068 Le Havre,

France, *Tel:* +33 2 35 19 53 21, *Fax:* +33 2 35 19 51 82, *Email:* p.naudet@neptumarfrance.com
Royal Burger Group, Quai George V, 76600 Le Havre, France, *Tel:* +33 2 35 19 83 10, *Fax:* +33 2 35 19 83 13/4, *Email:* lehavre@burgergroup.fr, *Website:* www.burgergroup.com
Scamar, 300 Boulevard Jules Durand, P O Box 1285, 76068 Le Havre, France, *Tel:* +33 2 32 74 18 00, *Fax:* +33 2 32 74 18 10
Sogena, Quai George V, F-76056 Le Havre, France, *Tel:* +33 2 35 24 81 71, *Fax:* +33 2 35 24 15 04, *Email:* sogena.transit@sogena.com, *Website:* www.sogena.fr
Stamex, 300, Boulevard Jules Durand, 76600 Le Havre, France, *Tel:* +33 2 35 11 72 72, *Fax:* +33 2 35 53 27 58, *Email:* stamex@stamex.fr, *Website:* www.stamex.fr
Transpol, 300 Boulevard Jules Durand, P O Box 1373, 76066 Le Havre, France, *Tel:* +33 2 32 74 18 00, *Fax:* +33 2 32 74 18 08
Vopak Agencies B.V., Le Havre, France, *Tel:* +33 2 32 74 87 90, *Fax:* +33 2 32 74 87 95, *Email:* agencies.lehavre@vopak.com, *Website:* www.vopak.com
Watson Brown S.A., Centre de Commerce International du Havre, Quai George V, P O Box 728, F-76060 Le Havre, France, *Tel:* +33 2 35 19 83 00, *Fax:* +33 2 35 19 83 13, *Email:* pgallais@burgergroup.com
Worms Services Maritimes S.A., 32 Rue Pierre Brossolette, P O Box 7001X, F-76600 Le Havre, France, *Tel:* +33 2 32 10 25 79, *Fax:* +33 2 32 10 13 03, *Email:* tramping@leh.worms-sm.fr, *Website:* www.worms-sm.com
Zim Integrated Shipping Services Ltd, 35 rue du 129e Regiment d'Infanterie, F-76600 Le Havre, France, *Tel:* +33 2 32 74 95 16, *Fax:* +33 2 32 74 95 23, *Email:* gourdon.alain@fr.zim.com, *Website:* www.zim.co.il

Stevedoring Companies: Sogena, Quai George V, F-76056 Le Havre, France, *Tel:* +33 2 35 24 81 71, *Fax:* +33 2 35 24 15 04, *Email:* sogena.transit@sogena.com, *Website:* www.sogena.fr

Surveyors: Bureau Veritas, Immeuble Chais de la Transat, Avenue Lucien Corbeaux, P O Box 216, F-76053 Le Havre, France, *Tel:* +33 2 35 53 65 02, *Fax:* +33 2 35 53 65 29, *Website:* www.bureauveritas.com
Det Norske Veritas A/S, 95 Avenue Augustin Normand, F-76059 Le Havre Cedex, France, *Tel:* +33 2 35 42 26 05, *Fax:* +33 2 35 21 43 95, *Email:* lehavre@dnv.com, *Website:* www.dnv.com
Germanischer Lloyd, 73-75 Quai de Southampton, 76600 Le Havre, France, *Tel:* +33 2 35 43 42 08, *Fax:* +33 2 35 43 42 37, *Email:* gl-le.havre@gl-group.com, *Website:* www.gl-group.com
Hemmer Marine Services S.a.r.l., 61 Route d'Octcville, Sainte Adresse, F-76310 Le Havre, France, *Tel:* +33 2 35 54 32 36, *Fax:* +33 2 35 48 09 91, *Email:* hemmer.marine.services@wanadoo.fr

Medical Facilities: Hospital Le Havre (Jacques Monot), 12 km

Airport: Le Havre-Octeville

Railway: Port terminals are directly linked to the national and European rail networks

Development: The first berths in the second phase of the Port 2000 container complex will be completed in mid-2009. Completion of the six 350 m berths constituting the second phase of the facility will be staggered over the 12 months between mid-2009 and mid-2010. The first two berths will go to CMA CGM subsidiary Generale de Manutention Portuaire, which already operates two berths at Port 2000 under the name Terminal de France. A third is destined for Terminal Porte Oceane, a subsidiary of local cargo-handling group Perrigault and AP Moller's APM Terminals, which also has two berths already in operation. The remaining three berths will go to Mediterranean Shipping Co., in partnership with local company Terminaux de Normandie, also part of the Perrigault group. Following completion of the second phase of Port 2000, there will still be two more berths to construct before the facility comes up to its planned 12-berth capacity

Lloyd's Agent: Humann & Taconet, 73-75 Quai de Southampton, P O Box 1395, F-76066 Le Havre Cedex, France, *Tel:* +33 2 35 19 39 86, *Fax:* +33 2 35 19 39 85, *Email:* lloydsagency-lehavre@humtac.fr, *Website:* www.humann-taconet.fr

LE LEGUE/ST. BRIEUC

Lat 48° 32' N; Long 2° 43' W.

Admiralty Chart: 3674		**Admiralty Pilot:** 27	
Time Zone: GMT +1 h		**UNCTAD Locode:** FR SBK	

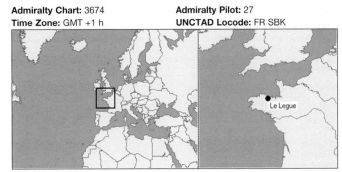

Principal Facilities:

	Y	G			B		A	

Authority: Conseil General des Cotes d'Armor, 3 Place du General de Gaulle, P O Box 2373, F-22000 St. Brieuc, France, *Tel:* +33 2 96 62 62 75, *Fax:* +33 2 96 61 48 16, *Email:* contact@cg22.fr, *Website:* www.cg22.fr

Officials: Commercial Manager: Keith Martin, *Email:* keith.martin@cotesdarmor.cci.fr.
Harbour Master: Alain Leroux, *Email:* alain.leroux@cotesdarmor.cci.fr.

Port Security: Fully trained port security officer

Pre-Arrival Information: Initial ETA should be sent 24 h prior to arrival to Ship's Agents with confirmation at 12 h and 4 h. The first message should include: vessel's name, registry, tonnage, loa, boa, max draft on arrival, preceding port, ETA fairway buoy, nature and quantity of hazardous cargo, general cargo details, any technical problems to vessel or its equipment

Documentation: Crew list, passenger list, stores list, provisions list, crew personal effects list, customs declaration, cargo manifest list, maritime declaration of health, bill of lading, stowage plan (other than bulk cargo), last port clearance, port of call list, bonded stores list, narcotics list, arms & ammunition list

The pilot, on boarding, will provide the IMO approved form for completion by Master concerning the following certificates: load line certificate, safety equipment certificate, certificate of registry, safety radio certificate, safety construction certificate, international oil pollution prevention certificate, derat or derat exemption certificate, international tonnage certificate, oil record book, seamen's books, passports & vaccination certificates

Approach: Channel from Sea Buoy (48° 34.4' N; 02° 41.1' W) is 2 nautical miles long to the port entrance, width 200 m in depth of 5.2 m above datum

Anchorage: Fairway Buoy in pos 48° 34' N; 02° 41' W in depth of 7 m

Pilotage: Cotes d'Armor Pilotage, Tel: +33 (2) 96 33 03 33, Fax: 96 33 03 33. VHF Channel 12. Pilot normally boards at Le Legue Buoy

Radio Frequency: VHF Channel 12 for Harbour Master and Pilots

Weather: Prevailing winds from the west

Tides: 12.5 m MHWS, 8.7 m MHWN, dried out at MLWN and MLWS

Traffic: 2000, 229 vessels, 300 500 t of cargo handled

Maximum Vessel Dimensions: Inner Basin: 83 m loa, 12.8 m boa, 4.8 m draft. Outer Port: 120 m loa, 5000 dwt, 5.5 m draft

Principal Imports and Exports: Imports: Animal feedstuffs, Fertilizers, General bulk products, Sawn timber. Exports: China clay (kaolin), Refractory minerals (Andoulisite), Scrap metal.

Working Hours: Mon-Fri 0800-1200, 1330-1730. Overtime rates on weekday nights only. No weekends

Accommodation:

Name	Length (m)	Depth (m)	Draught (m)	Remarks
Le Legue				See [1] below
Basin Michel Sangan (Inner Basin)				See [2] below
Berths 1-2	167	5.5	4.8	See [3] below
Berth 3	66	5.5	4.8	General cargo for vessels up to 60 m loa
Berths 4-5	178	5.5	4.8	See [4] below
Quai de la Ville Gilette				See [5] below
Berth 1	120		5	See [6] below
Terminal des Kaguerlins (Outer Port)				See [7] below
Quay Sebert 1	87		5.5	See [8] below
Quay Sebert 2	87		5.5	See [9] below

[1]*Le Legue:* Port Operating Body: Ports Concession, Chambre de Commerce et d'Industrie des Cotes d'Armor, Rue de Guernesey, P O Box 514, F-22005 Saint Brieuc, Tel: +33 2 96 78 62 15, Fax: +33 2 96 78 51 30, Internet: www.cotesdarmor.cci.fr
Director, Direction des Equipements du Patrimoine et des Achats: Alain Leroux, Email: alain.leroux@cotesdarmor.cci.fr
Harbour Master: Pierre Debois, Email: pierre.debois@equipement.gouv.fr
[2]*Basin Michel Sangan (Inner Basin):* Storage area of 1.1 ha (of which 4000 m2 is for public usage) and including 6000 m2 warehouse space and four silos, each of 600 m3 cap
[3]*Berths 1-2:* General cargo (incl. sawn timber) for vessels up to 83 m loa
[4]*Berths 4-5:* Bulk minerals and animal food for vessels up to 83 m loa
[5]*Quai de la Ville Gilette:* Open storage area of 3.8 ha (of which 3600 m2 is for public usage)
[6]*Berth 1:* NAABSA berth. Sand and scrap metal for vessels up to 90 m loa
[7]*Terminal des Kaguerlins (Outer Port):* Open storage area of 4.5 ha including three dedicated timber storage areas, a treatment plant and enclosed drying and storage shed, a highly automated mineral (china clay) warehouse of 2500 m2 and loading facility as well as storage facilities (6000 t cap) for animal feedstuffs
[8]*Quay Sebert 1:* NAABSA berth. General cargo (incl. sawn timber and fertilizers) for vessels up to 120 m loa
[9]*Quay Sebert 2:* NAABSA berth. General cargo (incl. sawn timber and china clay) for vessels up to 120 m loa

Mechanical Handling Equipment: 3 x 1.5 t bobcats, 3 x 4 t volvo frontloaders, 3 mobile band loaders at 150 t/h, bulk hoppers, rail wagon shunting truck, 2 x 50 t road weighbridges and 1 x 100 t rail weighbridge

Location	Type	Capacity (t)	Qty
Le Legue	Mobile Cranes	80	1
Le Legue	Mobile Cranes	30	3
Le Legue	Mobile Cranes	20	1
Le Legue	Forklifts	7	3
Le Legue	Forklifts	4	1

Cargo Worked: Animal feedstuffs 1800 t/day, sawn timber 2000 m3/day, kaolin 1800 t/day, refractory minerals 1800 t/day, scrap metal 1200 t/day

Bunkering: Available by road tanker with 24-48 h notice

Waste Reception Facilities: On demand

Stevedoring Companies: Corbel & Cie., Corbel Shipping Agency, Terre Plein Des Raquelins, Nouveau Port, Le Legue, 22000 St. Brieuc, France, Tel: +33 2 96 61 65 60, Fax: +33 2 96 61 74 11, Email: corbelshipping@aol.com
S.C.A.C., Quai Surcouf, F-22000 St. Brieuc, France, Tel: +33 2 96 61 69 23, Fax: +33 2 96 61 52 66

Medical Facilities: Local doctors in close proximity to port area. Hospital Le Fol, 4 km

Airport: Saint-Brieuc Armor, Tremuson, 7 km

Railway: Saint-Brieuc Station (TGV connections to Paris 3 hours), 5 km

Development: A third NAABSA berth will be in operation at the Terminal des Kaguerlins early in 2006. Also a further terminal area of 8.5 ha is planned for 2006 at this terminal
Construction on a fully enclosed deepwater port and terminal, totalling 60 ha, for vessels up to 8000 dwt, will begin in 2006 and be operational in 2009

Lloyd's Agent: Agence Maritime Roy s.a.r.l., 2 Chaussee des Corsaires, P O Box 179, F-35409 St. Malo, France, Tel: +33 2 99 56 07 21, Fax: +33 2 99 40 24 00, Email: agence-maritime-roy@wanadoo.fr

LE TREPORT

Lat 50° 4' N; Long 1° 22' E.

Admiralty Chart: 1354	**Admiralty Pilot:** 28
Time Zone: GMT +1 h	**UNCTAD Locode:** FR LTR

Principal Facilities:

	Y	G	R			T	A	

Authority: Chambre de Commerce et d'Industrie Littoral Normand-Picard, 2 Quai de la Republique, F-76470 Le Treport, France, Tel: +33 2 35 86 27 67, Fax: +33 2 35 50 22 96, Website: www.littoral-normand-picard.cci.fr/port_treport.php

Approach: Depth at entrance: NT 4 m, ST 7 m

Anchorage: At 2.5 miles, in 325° of the Green Lighthouse in depth of 9-11 m

Pilotage: Compulsory for vessels over 45 m loa

Radio Frequency: VHF Channel 12 from 4 h before HT and 4 h after HT

Weather: Winds W and SW to NW

Traffic: 2007, 300 642 t of cargo handled

Maximum Vessel Dimensions: 6300 dwt, 115 m loa, 17 m beam, 7 m draught

Principal Imports and Exports: Imports: Aggregate, Fertiliser, Phosphoric acid, Soda ash, Timber. Exports: Flints, Grain, Gravel.

Working Hours: Monday-Friday 0600-2200. Saturday 0600-1730

Accommodation:

Name	Length (m)	Remarks
Le Treport		Total of six berths for general cargo vessels and chemical tankers
North Way Dock	450	
South Way Dock	450	

Storage: Grain silo

Location	Covered (m²)	Sheds / Warehouses	Grain (t)
Le Treport	5400	3	23000

Mechanical Handling Equipment:

Location	Type	Capacity (t)	Qty
Le Treport	Mobile Cranes	3	3

Cargo Worked: Approx 4200 t/day

Towage: One tug of 500 hp available

Repair & Maintenance: Two workshops for general maintenance

Stevedoring Companies: Le Treport Shipping Stevedoring, Quai Sud, F-76470 Le Treport, France, Tel: +33 2 35 50 06 12

Medical Facilities: Hospital, 5 km

Airport: Rouen, 100 km

Railway: 500 m from port; direct connection to Paris

Lloyd's Agent: Humann & Taconet, 73-75 Quai de Southampton, P O Box 1395, F-76066 Le Havre Cedex, France, Tel: +33 2 35 19 39 86, Fax: +33 2 35 19 39 85, Email: lloydsagency-lehavre@humtac.fr, Website: www.humann-taconet.fr

LE VERDON

Lat 45° 33' N; Long 1° 5' W.

Admiralty Chart: 3058	**Admiralty Pilot:** 22
Time Zone: GMT +1 h	**UNCTAD Locode:** FR LVE

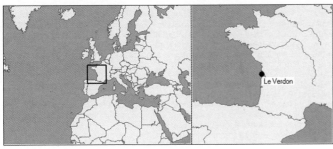

Principal Facilities:

Y	C	R	B	T	A

Authority: Grand Port Maritime de Bordeaux, Capitainerie de Port, Zone Portuaire, Route du Mole, Sur Mer, F-33123 Le Verdon, France, *Tel:* +33 5 56 09 63 91, *Fax:* +33 5 56 73 70 34, *Email:* p-deiss@bordeaux-port.fr, *Website:* www.bordeaux-port.fr

Officials: Harbour Master: Marc Bosse.

Port Security: ISPS compliant

Approach: The entrance channel is dredged to a depth of 12.7 m; vessels drawing up to 14 m may enter. Notice of ETA should be given where possible, 24 h in advance

Pilotage: Tel: +33 5 56 09 63 85, VHF Channel 14

Traffic: 2004, 231 282 t of cargo handled

Maximum Vessel Dimensions: 284 m loa

Accommodation:

Name	Length (m)	Depth (m)	Draught (m)	Remarks
Le Verdon				See [1] below
Container Terminal	600	12.5	12	See [2] below

[1]*Le Verdon:* Free Port covering 60 ha, 4000 m2 of which are in a hangar
[2]*Container Terminal:* Two berths. 80 reefer points. One ramp for quarter ramp ro/ro. One road and one rail weighbridge

Storage:

Location	Open (m²)	Covered (m²)	Sheds / Warehouses
Container Terminal	100000	12000	1

Mechanical Handling Equipment:

Location	Type	Capacity (t)	Qty
Container Terminal	Mult-purp. Cranes	15	1
Container Terminal	Container Cranes	32	1
Container Terminal	Container Cranes	40	1

Bunkering: Societe des Petroles Shell, 89 Boulevard Franklin Roosevelt, 92564 Rueil-Malmasion, F-76650 Petit Couronne, France, *Tel:* +33 2 35 67 47 03, *Fax:* +33 2 35 67 47 03
Total France S.A., Total Marine Fuels, 51 Esplanade du General de Gaulle, F-92907 Paris la Defense Cedex 10, France, *Tel:* +33 1 4135 2755, *Fax:* +33 1 4197 0291, *Email:* marine.fuels@total.com, *Website:* www.marinefuels.total.com

Airport: Bordeaux, 100 km

Railway: Quayside and port zone tracks, linked by an electric line to Bordeaux, the International Freight Centre at Bruges and the national and international rail network

Lloyd's Agent: Jean-Francois Chevreau, Bourse Maritime, Place Laine, F-33000 Bordeaux, France, *Tel:* +33 5 56 52 16 87, *Fax:* +33 5 56 44 67 85, *Email:* info@chevreau-lavie.fr, *Website:* www.chevreau-lavie.com

LIBOURNE

Lat 44° 55' N; Long 0° 14' W.

Admiralty Chart: 3068	**Admiralty Pilot:** 22
Time Zone: GMT +1 h	**UNCTAD Locode:** FR LIB

This port is no longer open to commercial shipping

LORIENT

Lat 47° 45' N; Long 3° 22' W.

Admiralty Chart: 304	**Admiralty Pilot:** 22
Time Zone: GMT +1 h	**UNCTAD Locode:** FR LRT

Principal Facilities:

P		Y	G		R	L			T	A

Authority: Port of Lorient, 3 Boulevard de la Rade, F-56100 Lorient, France, *Tel:* +33 2 97 87 76 00, *Fax:* +33 2 97 37 22 19, *Email:* lorient.port.commerce@morbihan.cci.fr, *Website:* www.lorient.port.fr

Officials: Communications Manager: Philippe Serdet, *Tel:* +33 2 97 02 40 61, *Email:* ph.serdet@morbihan.cci.fr.
Harbour Master: Capt Bernard Lepriellec, *Tel:* +33 2 97 37 11 86.

Port Security: ISPS compliant

Approach: Channel depth is 8.5 m below CD; max d 12.8 m

Anchorage: Anchorage can be obtained in pos 47° 40' N; 3° 25' W in a depth of about 20 m

Pilotage: For ships of less than 60 m length, pilotage is not compulsory. However, ships should have VHF Channel 16 or 12 and advise pilot 6 h before arrival, Tel: +33 2 97 21 46 47, Fax: +33 2 97 64 67 86

Traffic: 2007, 2 858 566 t of cargo handled

Principal Imports and Exports: Imports: Cattle feed, Petroleum products. Exports: Frozen meat, Scrap iron.

Working Hours: 0600-2200

Accommodation:

Name	Length (m)	Depth (m)	Remarks
Lorient			See [1] below
Kergroise Quay	568	9.8–10	For vessels up to 80 600 dwt
New Quay	150	9.4	Ro/ro berth, 120 t cap

[1]*Lorient:* The tanker terminal can be used to discharge bulk cargo from small coastal vessels. Ro/ro terminal for vessels up to 150 m loa and 7.8 m max d
Fishing port and yacht facilities available
Bulk facilities: Two grain elevators of 800 t/h cap. One kangaroo crane at 500 t/h. Railroad transit station
Tanker facilities: One berth 112 m long with depth alongside of 9.8 m below CD. If length from stem to manifold is more than 85 m, it is necessary to consult the Harbour Master

Storage: Private warehouses of 90 000 t total cap

Location	Grain (t)
Lorient	10000

Mechanical Handling Equipment:

Location	Type	Qty
Lorient	Mult-purp. Cranes	10
Lorient	Mobile Cranes	1

Cargo Worked: Max of 20 000 t/day

Towage: Available

Repair & Maintenance: Arenalor, Lorient, France, *Tel:* +33 2 97 88 05 00, *Fax:* +33 2 97 88 05 01 One slipway available for vessels of 60 m max length and 4.5 m max depth

Ship Chandlers: Ets Picaud, 3 & 4 Boulevard Nail, F-56100 Lorient, France, *Tel:* +33 2 97 37 39 65, *Fax:* +33 2 97 37 40 85, *Email:* ets.picaud@wanadoo.fr, *Website:* www.picaud.com
Fourniership S.A., 83 Avenue de la Perriere, F-56100 Lorient, France, *Tel:* +33 2 97 83 79 79, *Fax:* +33 2 97 83 70 67, *Email:* fournierlorient@wanadoo.fr

Shipping Agents: Blue Water Shipping A/S, 26 Bis Quai de Kergroise, F-56100 Lorient, France, *Tel:* +33 2 97 37 79 87, *Fax:* +33 2 97 37 78 90, *Email:* agency_bre@bws.dk, *Website:* www.bws.dk
Agence Maritime Jacquemin, 58 Avenue Perriere, F-56100 Lorient, France, *Tel:* +33 2 97 83 67 92, *Fax:* +33 2 97 37 77 31, *Email:* shiplor@wanadoo.fr

Surveyors: Bureau Veritas, 78 Rue Marechal Foch, F-56100 Lorient, France, *Tel:* +33 2 97 37 63 06, *Fax:* +33 2 97 21 18 97, *Website:* www.bureauveritas.com
Cabinet Clouet, 3 Rue Aplphonse Rio, P O Box 412, 56104 Lorient, France, *Tel:* +33 2 97 37 00 34, *Fax:* +33 2 97 83 43 00, *Email:* cabinet.clouet@wanadoo.fr

Medical Facilities: Hospital, 3 km from port, Tel: +33 (2) 97 64 91 11, Fax: 97 64 91 12

Airport: 10 km from port

Railway: SNCF, 3 km

Lloyd's Agent: Agence Maritime Jacquemin, 58 Avenue Perriere, F-56100 Lorient, France, *Tel:* +33 2 97 83 67 92, *Fax:* +33 2 97 37 77 31, *Email:* shiplor@wanadoo.fr

MARSEILLES

Lat 43° 20' N; Long 5° 21' E.

Admiralty Chart: 153/151	**Admiralty Pilot:** 46
Time Zone: GMT +1 h	**UNCTAD Locode:** FR MRS

Key to Principal Facilities:—					
A=Airport	**C**=Containers	**G**=General Cargo	**P**=Petroleum	**R**=Ro/Ro	**Y**=Dry Bulk
B=Bunkers	**D**=Dry Dock	**L**=Cruise	**Q**=Other Liquid Bulk	**T**=Towage (where available from port)	

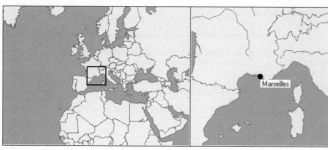

Principal Facilities:

P	Q	Y	G	C	R	L	B	D	T	A

Authority: Grand Port Maritime de Marseille, Marseille Fos Port Authority, 23 Place de la Joliette, P O Box 81965, F-13226 Marseilles Cedex 02, France, *Tel:* +33 4 91 39 40 00, *Fax:* +33 4 91 39 57 00, *Email:* gpmm@marseille-port.fr, *Website:* www.marseille-port.fr

Officials: Anne-Marie Marcialis.
President: Christian Jacques Garin, *Email:* christian.garin@marseille-port.fr.
Managing Director: Jean-Claude Terrier.
Commercial Director: Monica Bonvalet, *Tel:* +33 4 91 39 43 22, *Email:* m.bonvalet@marseille-port.fr.
Harbour Master: Joseph Moysan, *Tel:* +33 4 91 39 41 40, *Email:* j.moysan@marseille-port.fr.

Port Security: ISPS compliant. Container Security Initiative (CSI) designated port

Pre-Arrival Information: Vessel Traffic Service: The Marseilles/Fos Maritime Traffic Service (STM) is compulsory for all commercial vessels. The area of authority of the STM comprises a marine operating area and a port operating area:
(a) within the limits administered by the GPMM
(b) within the administrative limits of the installations and constructions entrusted to the GPMM
(c) within the area of jurisdiction of the GPMM
(d) in the channels and approaches to the Golfe de Fos and to the Port of Marseilles for vessels transporting hydrocarbons and dangerous substances
The Marseilles area covers the port area and the approach channels to the Port of Marseilles. Marseilles Port Control, Tel: +33 4 91 39 41 41. Maritime Traffic Service Centre on VHF Channels 12 and 73. Vessels manoeuvring in the port on VHF Channels 72 and 77
Communications:
(a) communication on VHF Channel 12 and 73 must be established as early as possible between vessels and the Maritime Traffic Service (STM) Centre
(b) vessels on passage to or from Marseilles which are likely to cross the area off the entrance to the Golfe de Fos must also contact Fos Port Control before entering
(c) vessels on passage, manoeuvring and at anchor in any part of the area controlled by the STM must maintain a listening watch on VHF Channel 12
(d) conversations should take place in French and English using standard IMO terminology
(e) pilots can be contacted on VHF Channel 08
Vessels transporting hydrocarbons and dangerous substances must send a SURNAV message 6 h prior to entry into French territorial waters
Vessels inward-bound must contact the STM as follows:
(a) 48 h before arrival at the pilot boarding position, through the agent stating
(i) vessels name and call sign
(ii) destination and port of departure
(iii) draught
(iv) cargo
(v) loa, beam and gt
(vi) type of vessel
(vii) ETA
(b) at least 24 h before arrival stating:
(i) ETA at pilot boarding position
(ii) draught
(iii) nature and tonnage of transported dangerous substances
(iv) loa
(c) 6 h before entry into French territorial waters, vessels transporting hydrocarbons or dangerous substances must send a SURNAV message
(d) on crossing the S limit of the area (43° 11.9' N), all vessels over 50 m loa on passage to Marseilles must report to the STM on VHF Channel 12 stating:
(i) vessels name and call sign
(ii) position
(iii) course and speed
(iv) ETA

The STM will give permission to proceed along the approach channel, and will provide information on traffic movements and weather conditions in the area
(e) the STM will advise berthing details and a time for pilot boarding, as well as any towing requiirements if not already specified
(f) the STM will also advise VHF communication details as follows:
(i) at the entrance to the STM area
(ii) at the entrance to the channel for vessels obliged to use the channels (vessels over 1600 gt transporting hydrocarbons or dangerous substances) for Fos or Marseilles. The STM will give permission to proceed along the approach channel
(iii) at the entrance to the channel for vessels not obliged to use the channels. After identifying and authorising the vessel, the STM will instruct the vessel to proceed if the vessel is subject to an inspection by a surveyor
(g) vessels over 1600 gt transporting hydrocarbons or dangerous substances may not enter the approach channel (N of 43° 12.0' N) without the authorisation of the STM
(h) in the event of a doubtful identity, the STM will call every vessel it considers to be likely until a positive identity is obtained
Vessels in the area: all vessels over 100 gt must contact the STM on VHF before entering the port, getting under way or changing berths. All vessels crossing (or in cases of emergency, anchoring or waiting in) the approach channel, which vessels transporting dangerous cargo are obliged to use, must inform the STM immediately

Approach: The Gulf of Marseilles is entered between Cap Couronne and Cap Croisette. The centre of the gulf is occupied by a group of islands which divide it into two parts. Approach to the port is through safe channels and guided by a series of radio beacons on the Ile de Planier and by lights and buoys

Pilotage: The compulsory pilotage area for Marseilles is limited offshore by the line joining the port of Mejean (43° 19.8' N; 5° 13.2' E), Cap Caveaux (43° 15.7' N; 5° 17.4' E) and the Ile Maire (43° 12.7' N; 5° 20.0' E). The Marseilles-Golfe de Fos pilotage station serves the area between the Pointe de l'Espiguette (43° 31' N; 3° 07' E) and Cap Camarat (43° 12' N; 6° 41' E)
L'Estaque Pilot Station (24 h), Tel: +33 4 91 46 13 73
Frioul Pilot Station (0500-2200), Tel: +33 4 91 59 01 88 & +33 4 91 59 01 89
Marseilles/Fos Office, Tel: +33 4 91 14 29 10, Fax: +33 4 91 56 65 69, Email: pilote13@nerim.fr
The L'Estaque Pilot Station maintains a VHF listening watch for both stations
Pilotage is available 24 h/day and is compulsory for vessels over 50 m loa transporting hydrocarbons or dangerous substances and for all other vessels over 70 m loa
Vessels must report their ETA to the pilotage station on VHF Channel 08 1 h in adavnce, stating the expected position for embarking pilot. ETA's transmitted with 48 h and 24 h notice will be communicated by the Harbour Master to the pilotage station
Pilot boards either at Marseilles Harbour, between 2-5 nautical miles from the N Passage or at Endoume Harbour, 1 nautical mile S of the Ile d'If (S entrance)

Traffic: 2007, 96 400 000 t of cargo handled, 1 001 957 TEU's

Working Hours: Normal time, Mon-Sat 0630-1310, 1320-2000, Intermediate shift, except on Sat 0800-1120, 1300-1620. Short night shift 2010-2330. Long night shift (non-stop) 2220-0500. Gangs employed to be either on non-stop or intermediate basis. However, on consecutive days vessels can be worked alternatively on non-stop or intermediate basis as required. Sun and holidays (to be ordered before 1200 previous working day); morning shift (non-stop) 0630-1310. Overtime hours are possible. The long night shift can neither be worked during the night Sun/Mon, nor during the night following a holiday. Oil berth for vegetable oils and tallow in bulk: uninterrupted working hours Mons 0630-Sat 1930

Accommodation: Harbour protected by a massive breakwater. Deep natural entrance; non-tidal. The extensive harbour is divided into seven basins for commercial traffic: Bassin de la Grande Joliette, Bassin d'Arenc, Bassin National, Bassin de la Pinede, Bassin du President Wilson, Bassin Leon Gourret and Bassin Mirabeau. These docks stretch along 8 km of coastline. The basins can be entered from the north or the south through two outer harbours. The approx depth of water is 20 m at the N pass and 11 m at the S pass. Total length of quays is 14 199 m. Seven waiting berths are available for ships with 3 m to 9.5 m d waiting to be assigned a commercial berth
Container & ro/ro facilities: Several quays are reserved for container traffic, notably: on Leon Gourret Mole at Cap Janet, max 14.5 m d; large ground surfaces and railways. On Mourepiane Quay in Mirabeau Basin, where a large container terminal is in operation, with quay length 920 m, 12 m d max. Container handling equipment includes three 40 t Caillard container gantry cranes, three mobile cranes of 40 t and six mobile cranes of 15 t. One transit shed: Shed 26, 8000 m2. Railways: Two quayside railway lines, two railways to the East of the dense storage area. A quayside storage area 35 m wide comprising of a working area 15 m wide equipped with two railways and a roadway for tractors and trailers, a short-term storage area 17 m wide under the rear jib of the gantries, a total of 114 000 m2 of storage areas comprising of 22 000 m2 for mixed traffic, 40 000 m2 for dense container storage, 20 000 m2 for semi-dense storage and 8000 m2 for rapid transit
There are 33 specialised ro/ro berths in operation, which permit direct loading of heavy loads into ro/ro ships. There are also numerous conventional berths that can be used for vertical loading and unloading of heavy loads, with the assistance of the Port's Atlas floating crane which has a lifting cap of 90 t
Certain ro/ro ships with stern doors can also be received at berths designed for conventional traffic. The newer types of multi-purpose ro/ro ships with angled or swivelling doors and ramps can be received at most of the Port's numerous conventional berths
Two floating pontoons with mechanically adjustable platforms enable ro/ro traffic to be handled at the majority of the remaining non-specialised berths
Bulk facilities: Minerals: Five specialised berths are available in National Basin for all types of minerals that have to be handled by bucket cranes
Two berths on Mole D, National Basin. Berth 47: Max length 135 m, 9.0 m d max; Berth 48: max length 135 m, 8.0 m d max. Storage area of 4000 m2 along the edge of the E quay. These berths are equipped with two bucket cranes permitting an annual loading or unloading cap of 250 000 t at the rate of 300 t/h berth and 150 t/h/crane
Three berths on the Seaward Breakwater: Berths 109, 110 and 111, length 151 m each with 11.6 m max d. Storage cap of 50 000 t. These berths are equipped with five bucket cranes of 7 t and facilities for storing clinker
Cereals: Berths 24 and 25, 11.0 m d. One suction conveyor
Sugar: One public berth in President Wilson Basin. Berth 20: max length 145 m, 10.5

m d max. This berth serves the Port Authority's sugar silo, located outside the port enclosure, through two covered conveyor belts
The sugar is unloaded by quayside bucket cranes into hoppers on the terrace of the quayside transit shed, and then into the silo by the conveyor belts at the rate of 250 t/h/belt. The storage cap of the silo is 24 000 t
Alumina: One public berth in President Wilson Basin. Berth 14: max length 228 m, 9.7 m d max. This berth is specialised for alumina traffic. The storage facilities comprise two quayside silos of 5250 t each, built and used by the Pechiney Co for the transit of dehydrated alumina
Wine in bulk: One public berth is available for this traffic at berth 143 and 143A
Other liquids in bulk: The Mourepiane liquid bulk depot is served by Berth 148, 220 m long, 9.5 m max d and Berth 151, 11.5 m max d. Annual unloading cap of 130 000 t. The Marseille Vrac Co, which operates these facilities, has 33 storage tanks giving a total cap of 27 000 m3. These tanks are connected to the berths by discharge pipes
Mediaco Vrac berth 143 for vessels up to 150 m loa with max d of 9.3 m, max cap 33 000 m3

Name	Remarks
Ro/ro Facilities	See [1] below
Avant Port Nord (Berth 144)	For vessels up to 193 m loa, width of inclined ramp 27.3 m and permissible draft of 10.5 m
Avant Port Nord (Berth 148)	For vessels up to 240 m loa, width of inclined ramp 24 m and permissible draft of 9.5 m
Bassin Leon Gourret (Berth 181)	No limit to loa, width of inclined ramp 25 m and permissible draft of 14 m
Bassin Mirabeau (Berth 152)	No limit to loa, width of inclined ramp 28 m and permissible draft of 11.1 m
Bassin Mirabeau (Berth 157)	No limit to loa, width of inclined ramp 24.5 m and permissible draft of 11.5 m
Bassin de la Pinede (Berth 40)	For vessels up to 167 m loa, width of inclined ramp 25.3 m and permissible draft of 9.5 m
Bassin de la Pinede (Berth 28)	For vessels up to 170 m loa, width of inclined ramp 25 m and permissible draft of 8.2 m
Bassin National (Berth 42)	For vessels up to 150 m loa, width of inclined ramp 25 m and permissible draft of 6.5 m
Bassin National (Berth 43)	For vessels up to 130 m loa, width of inclined ramp 29.9 m and permissible draft of 7.8 m
Bassin National (Berth 44)	For vessels up to 150 m loa, width of inclined ramp 24.9 m and permissible draft of 6.8 m
Bassin National (Berth 50)	For vessels up to 150 m loa, width of inclined ramp 22.3 m and permissible draft of 7.5 m
Bassin National (Berth 54)	For vessels up to 150 m loa, width of inclined ramp 18 m and permissible draft of 8.8 m
Bassin National (Berth 57)	For vessels up to 150 m loa, width of inclined ramp 31 m and permissible draft of 9 m
Bassin National (Berth 109)	No limit to loa and permissible draft of 11.6 m
Bassin d'Arenc (Berth 59)	For vessels up to 193 m loa, width of inclined ramp 30 m and permissible draft of 7.8 m
Bassin d'Arenc (Berth 60)	For vessels up to 130 m loa and permissible draft of 9 m
Bassin d'Arenc (Berth 63)	For vessels up to 150 m loa and permissible draft of 7.4 m
Bassin d'Arenc (Berth 65)	For vessels up to 150 m loa, width of inclined ramp 11 m and permissible draft of 6 m
Bassin d'Arenc (Berth 66)	For vessels up to 150 m loa, width of inclined ramp 18.4 m and permissible draft of 6.5 m
Bassin President Wilson (Berth 14)	For vessels up to 227 m loa, width of inclined ramp 17.5 m and permissible draft of 9.7 m
Bassin President Wilson (Berth 26)	For vessels up to 170 m loa, width of inclined ramp 19 m and permissible draft of 8.5 m
Bassin de la Grande Joliette (Berth 70)	No limit to loa, width of inclined ramp 40 m and permissible draft of 9.6 m
Bassin de la Grande Joliette (Berth 74)	No limit to loa, width of inclined ramp 40.4 m and permissible draft of 8.5 m
Bassin de la Grande Joliette (Berth 81)	For vessels up to 160 m loa, width of inclined ramp 15.6 m and permissible draft of 8 m
Bassin de la Grande Joliette (Berth 82)	For vessels up to 160 m loa, width of inclined ramp 17.8 m and permissible draft of 8 m
Bassin de la Grande Joliette (Berth 84)	For vessels up to 150 m loa, width of inclined ramp 19 m and permissible draft of 8 m
Bassin de la Grande Joliette (Berth 86)	For vessels up to 150 m loa, width of inclined ramp 22 m and permissible draft of 8 m
Bassin de la Grande Joliette (Berth 88)	For vessels up to 175 m loa, width of inclined ramp 28 m and permissible draft of 8 m
Bassin de la Grande Joliette (Berth 90)	For vessels up to 150 m loa, width of inclined ramp 23.4 m and permissible draft of 8 m
Bassin de la Grande Joliette (Berth 92)	For vessels up to 160 m loa, width of inclined ramp 45 m and permissible draft of 7.7 m
Bassin de la Grande Joliette (Berth 94)	For vessels up to 150 m loa, width of inclined ramp 22 m and permissible draft of 8 m
Bassin de la Grande Joliette (Berth 96)	For vessels up to 150 m loa, width of inclined ramp 16.9 m and permissible draft of 8 m

[1]*Ro/ro Facilities:* Passenger Terminals: The Grande Joliette Terminal is intended for passengers and their cars travelling on car-ferry lines to Corsica and North Africa. The North Passenger Terminal, Shed 16 in President Wilson Basin is intended for cruise ship passengers

Storage: Transit sheds total 337 000 m2, public warehouses and stores total 13 009 m2, private warehouse (coffee & cocoa) totalling 9000 m2 and public open warehouse of 3900 m2
Air conditioned transit sheds: Three public berths. Berth 54 National Basin: max length 149 m, 9.8 m d max; Berth 13 President Wilson Basin: max length 171 m, 10 m d max; Berth 152 Mirabeau Basin: max length 155 m, 11.6 m d max. These berths serve three air conditioned sheds with a total storage cap of 10 000 t: Shed 5A (National Basin) of 3772 m2 (temp +2°C); Shed 21 (Mirabeau Basin) of 19 086 m2 (temp +9° to +2°C depending on the halls); the cold store of Shed 17 (President Wilson Basin) which has an area of 3878 m2 (temp +2°C)
There are also several private cold stores close to the Port, some of them with cold rooms having a temperatures as low as -15°C

Mechanical Handling Equipment:

Location	Type	Capacity (t)	Qty
Marseilles	Floating Cranes	90	1
Marseilles	Floating Cranes	150	1
Marseilles	Mult-purp. Cranes	12	1
Marseilles	Mult-purp. Cranes	6	41
Marseilles	Mobile Cranes	15	2
Marseilles	Mobile Cranes	12	4

Bunkering: BP France S.A., Immeuble le Cervier, 12 Avenue des Beguines, Cergy-Saint-Christophe, 95866 Cergy Pontoise Cedex, France, *Tel:* +33 1 3422 4000, *Fax:* +33 1 3422 4417, *Email:* benoist.grosjean@fr.bp.com, *Website:* www.bpmarine.com – *Grades:* IFO380, 320-30cSt
ExxonMobil Marine Fuels, Mailpoint 31, ExxonMobil House, Ermyn Way, Leatherhead, Surrey KT22 8UX, United Kingdom, *Tel:* +44 1372 222 000, *Fax:* +44 1372 223 922, *Email:* marine.fuels@exxonmobil.com, *Website:* www.exxonmobil.com – *Grades:* IFO-380cSt; MGO – *Delivery Mode:* barge
Ocean Energy S.A.M., c/o Ocean Energy SAM, 57 Rue Grimaldi, Le Panorama Bloc C/D, MC 98000 Monte Carlo, Monaco, *Tel:* +377 9325 5331, *Fax:* +377 9325 5332, *Email:* oceanenergy@oceanenergy.mc, *Website:* www.oceanenergy.mc
Societe des Petroles Shell, 89 Boulevard Franklin Roosevelt, 92564 Rueil-Malmaison, F-76650 Petit Couronne, France, *Tel:* +33 2 35 67 47 03, *Fax:* +33 2 35 67 47 03 – *Grades:* IFO380-30cSt; GO – *Parcel Size:* IFO barge 100t, truck 25t – *Delivery Mode:* barge, truck
Total France S.A., Total Marine Fuels, 51 Esplanade du General de Gaulle, F-92907 Paris la Defense Cedex 10, France, *Tel:* +33 1 4135 2755, *Fax:* +33 1 4197 0291, *Email:* marine.fuels@total.com, *Website:* www.marinefuels.total.com – *Grades:* IFO380-30cSt; MGO – *Misc:* own storage facilities – *Parcel Size:* no min/max – *Rates:* 300-500t/h – *Notice:* 24 hours – *Delivery Mode:* pipeline, truck, barge

Towage: Available from two private companies. Rates on application

Repair & Maintenance: The Port Authority own ten dry docks, No.1: 171 m x 19.6 m, No.2: 137 m x 16.5 m, No.3: 99.4 m x 15.6 m, No.4: 80.1 m x 13.4 m, No.5: 121.4 m x 14.6 m, No.6: 125 m x 15.6 m, No.7: 204.6 m x 23 m, No.8: 320 m x 53 m, No.9: 250 m x 37 m, No.10: 465 m x 85 m. 28 repair berths with a total length of 4383 m
Union Naval Marseille S.A.S., Terre-Plein de Mourepiane - Porte 4, P O Box 57, F-13315 Marseilles Cedex 15, France, *Tel:* +33 4 91 03 52 00, *Fax:* +33 4 91 69 69 61, *Email:* unmarseille@unmarseille.com, *Website:* www.unmarseille.com Operate No's 8 and 9 dry docks and has access to No.10 dry dock

Seaman Missions: The Seamans Mission, 35 Avenue Roger Salengro, F-13110 Port de Bouc, France, *Tel:* +33 4 42 06 42 87, *Fax:* +33 4 42 06 11 23, *Email:* seamenfose@netcourier.com

Ship Chandlers: Cofrapex, 2 Boulevard des Bassins de Radaub, P O Box 60194, F-13474 Marseilles Cedex 2, France, *Tel:* +33 4 96 16 26 00, *Fax:* +33 4 91 02 47 62, *Email:* cofrapex@cofrapex.com, *Website:* www.cofrapex.com
EAFM, 2 Boulevard Des Bassins de Radoub, F-13002 Marseilles, France, *Tel:* +33 4 67 74 84 27, *Fax:* +33 4 67 74 40 45, *Email:* eafm-shipsupply@wanadoo.fr
Ets Tilley, Nord Activites, 09 rue du Laos, F-13015 Marseilles, France, *Tel:* +33 4 91 03 17 34, *Fax:* +33 4 91 03 14 39, *Email:* tilleyco@aol.com., *Website:* www.tilley.fr
Alexander Gaymard Supplies Co., P O Box 195, 13474 Marseilles Cedex 2, France, *Tel:* +33 4 96 16 26 00, *Fax:* +33 4 91 02 47 62, *Email:* alexander.gaymard@alexander.gaymard.com

Shipping Agents: Maritima del Mediterraneo S.A. (Marmedsa), P O Box 106, 13321 Marseilles Cedex 16, France, *Tel:* +33 4 96 17 17 00, *Fax:* +33 4 91 03 84 35, *Email:* bbegon@marmedsafr.marmedsa.com, *Website:* www.marmedsa.com Director: Bernard Begon Mobile Tel: +33 616540730 Email: bbegon@marmedsafr.marmedsa.com
Agena Tramp, 17 bis Avenue Robert Schuman, P O Box 134, F-13474 Marseilles, France, *Tel:* +33 4 91 14 48 29, *Fax:* +33 4 91 14 48 32, *Email:* med@agenatramp.fr, *Website:* www.agenatramp.fr
Amartrans, Immeuble Europrogramme, 40 Boulevard de Dunkerque, F-13002 Marseilles, France, *Tel:* +33 4 91 99 01 80, *Fax:* +33 4 91 56 24 46, *Email:* amartrans@mageos.com
CLB Liner, 30 Avenue Robert Schuman, P O Box 86, F-13472 Marseilles, France, *Fax:* +33 4 91 56 40 88, *Email:* jpmauboussin@mrs.clbliner.fr
G Feron-E de Clebsattel S.A., 10 Place de la Joliette, P O Box 35, F-13471 Marseilles, France, *Tel:* +33 4 91 39 93 95, *Fax:* +33 4 91 90 27 50
CMA-CGM S.A., CMA CGM Marseille, Immeuble Le Mirabeu, 4 Quai d'Arenc, F-13002 Marseilles Cedex, France, *Tel:* +33 4 88 91 77 00, *Fax:* +33 4 88 91 77 99, *Email:* mrs.agence@cma-cgm.com, *Website:* www.cma-cgm.com
Compagnie Marocaine de Navigation (COMANAV), 17 B Avenue Robert Schuman, 13002 Marseilles, France, *Tel:* +33 4 91 14 46 17, *Fax:* +33 4 91 14 46 19, *Website:* www.comanav.co.ma
Compagnie Meridionale de Consignation S.A., 10 Place de la Joilette, F-13002 Marseilles, France, *Tel:* +33 4 91 99 49 49, *Fax:* +33 4 91 99 49 09, *Email:* cmcf@interway.fr
Groupe Navitrans, 52 Boulevard Emmanuel Eydoux, P O Box 141, 13016 Marseilles, France, *Tel:* +33 4 91 84 13 13, *Fax:* +33 4 91 50 43 55, *Email:* navitrans@navitrans.fr, *Website:* www.navitrans.fr
Inchcape Shipping Services (ISS), 12 Bis rue Jacques de Vaucanson, ZAC Martigues Sud, F-13500 Martigues, France, *Tel:* +33 4 42 13 54 30, *Fax:* +33 4 43 13 54 34, *Email:* iss.france@iss-shipping.com, *Website:* www.iss-shipping.com
Isamar S.A., Les Docks, Atrium Feb 10.2, 10 Place de la Joliette, P O Box 13322, 13002 Marseilles, France, *Tel:* +33 4 95 09 09 03, *Fax:* +33 4 91 90 93 80, *Email:* sbouchellaleg@mrs.isamar.es, *Website:* www.isamar.es
K Line (Europe) Ltd, 10 Place de la Joliette, Atrium 10.5, Marseilles, France, *Tel:* +33 4 96 11 56 60, *Fax:* +33 4 91 91 93 18
Leon Vincent S.A., Mole Leon Gouret - Hangar 23, F-13344 Marseilles Cedex 3, France, *Tel:* +33 4 91 09 16 00, *Fax:* +33 4 91 09 16 88, *Email:* marseille.agence@lvfruit.fr, *Website:* www.leonvincent.fr
Marseille Consignation S.A., 18-20 Avenue Robert Schuman, P O Box 50087, F-13002 Marseilles, France, *Tel:* +33 4 91 91 91 34, *Fax:* +33 4 96 17 29 70, *Email:* marseilleconsignation@marscons.com
Marship Sarl, 20 Quai du Lazaret, 13002 Marseilles, France, *Tel:* +33 4 91 56 60 25, *Fax:* +33 4 91 56 60 21
Mathez Transports Internationaux, 90 Chemin du Ruisseau Mirabeau, ZONE ACTISUD, F-13016 Marseilles, France, *Tel:* +33 4 91 14 05 50, *Fax:* +33 4 91 91 44 22, *Email:* info@mathez-intl.com, *Website:* www.mathez-intl.com

Key to Principal Facilities:—
A=Airport **C**=Containers **G**=General Cargo **P**=Petroleum **R**=Ro/Ro **Y**=Dry Bulk
B=Bunkers **D**=Dry Dock **L**=Cruise **Q**=Other Liquid Bulk **T**=Towage (where available from port)

Mediterranean Shipping Company, MSC France S.A., Les Docks, Atrium 10.4, P O Box 61613, F-13567 Marseilles Cedex 02, France, *Tel:* +33 4 91 14 17 00, *Fax:* +33 4 91 14 17 10, *Email:* mscmarseille@mscfr.mscgva.ch, *Website:* www.mscgva.ch
Medship S.a.r.l., 59 Avenue Andre Roussin, P O Box 106, 13321 Marseilles Cedex 16, France, *Tel:* +33 4 96 17 17 00, *Fax:* +33 4 91 03 84 35, *Email:* info@marmedsafr.marmedsa.com, *Website:* www.marmedsa.com
Navitainer S.A., 208 Boulevard de Plombieres, Marseilles, France, *Tel:* +33 4 91 91 87 28, *Fax:* +33 4 91 91 86 74, *Email:* cmairie.navitainer@burgergroup.fr
Societe Nationale Maritime Corse Mediterranee (SNCM), 61 Boulevard des Dames, P O Box 1963, 13226 Marseilles, France, *Tel:* +33 4 91 56 32 00, *Fax:* +33 4 91 56 36 40, *Email:* info@sncm.fr, *Website:* www.sncm.fr
Universal Maritima S.a.r.l., 59 Avenue Andre Roussin, P O Box 26, F-13567 Marseilles Cedex 16, France, *Tel:* +33 4 88 57 15 00, *Fax:* +33 4 91 09 20 75, *Email:* umcustserv@umbcn.marmedsa.com, *Website:* www.universal-maritima.com
Watson Brown S.A., 10 Place de la Joliette, F-13002 Marseilles, France, *Tel:* +33 4 91 99 83 10, *Fax:* +33 4 91 56 04 31, *Email:* cmelliot@amcfrance.com
Worms Services Maritimes S.A., 8 rue Andre Allar, F-13015 Marseilles, France, *Tel:* +33 4 91 95 21 50, *Fax:* +33 4 91 50 00 57, *Email:* worms@mrs.worms-sm.fr, *Website:* www.worms-sm.com
Surveyors: ABS (Europe), Atrium 10.3, Les Docks, 10 Place de la Joliette, F-13002 Marseilles, France, *Tel:* +33 4 91 14 32 20, *Fax:* +33 4 91 90 40 58, *Email:* absmarseille@eagle.org, *Website:* www.eagle.org
Bureau Veritas, 17B Avenue Robert-Schuman, F-13235 Marseilles, France, *Tel:* +33 4 96 17 13 80, *Fax:* +33 4 91 13 23 00, *Email:* marseillemarine@fr.bureauveritas.com, *Website:* www.bureauveritas.com
Det Norske Veritas A/S, 16 Impasse Blancard, F-13007 Marseilles, France, *Tel:* +33 4 91 13 71 66, *Fax:* +33 4 91 59 15 05, *Email:* marseille@dnv.com, *Website:* www.dnv.com
Germanischer Lloyd, 511 Route de la Seds, Technopark du Griffon Batxi, F-13127 Vitrolles, France, *Tel:* +33 4 42 10 71 33, *Fax:* +33 4 42 89 91 27, *Email:* gl-marseille@gl-group.com, *Website:* www.gl-group.com
Hellenic Register of Shipping, c/o Marine Cargo & Logistics Surveys, Acropolis, 171 bis, Chemin de la Madragne Ville, F-13002 Marseilles, France, *Tel:* +33 4 95 05 15 00, *Fax:* +33 4 95 05 15 01, *Email:* mcl.surveys@wanadoo.fr, *Website:* www.hrs.gr
Nippon Kaiji Kyokai, 2 Place Sadi Carnot, F-13001 Marseilles, France, *Tel:* +33 4 91 91 69 48, *Fax:* +33 4 91 90 15 97, *Email:* ms@classnk.or.jp, *Website:* www.classnk.or.jp
Registro Italiano Navale (RINA), Technoparc du Griffon, Batiment XI, 511 Route de la Seds, Vitrolles, France, *Tel:* +33 4 42 10 71 33, *Fax:* +33 4 42 89 91 27, *Website:* www.rina.org
Airport: Marseille-Provence Airport
Lloyd's Agent: Unilex Maritime S.a.r.l, Les Docks, 10 Place de la Joliette, Atrium 10.8, F-13002 Marseilles Cedex 02, France, *Tel:* +33 4 91 14 04 40, *Fax:* +33 4 91 91 54 43, *Email:* mail@unilexmaritime.com, *Website:* www.unilexmaritime.com

MONTOIR

Lat 47° 18' N; Long 2° 8' W.

Admiralty Chart: 2985	**Admiralty Pilot:** 22
Time Zone: GMT +1 h	**UNCTAD Locode:** FR MTX

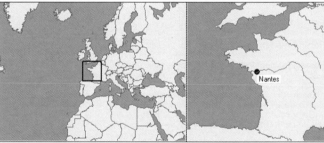

Principal Facilities:

Q	Y	G	C	R		B		T	A

Authority: Grand Port Maritime de Nantes-St.Nazaire, 18 Quai Ernest Renaud, P O Box 18609, F-44186 Nantes Cedex 4, France, *Tel:* +33 2 40 44 71 41, *Fax:* +33 2 40 44 20 01, *Email:* ser.com@nantes.port.fr, *Website:* www.nantes.port.fr
Officials: Managing Director: Francois Marendet, *Email:* f.marendet@nantes.port.fr. Harbour Master: Capt Yves Jaouen, *Email:* y.jaouen@nantes.port.fr.
Approach: Fairway dredged to 12.8 m depth LT with 300 m width. Air draught at St Nazaire bridge 60.6 m LT
Pilotage: Compulsory. Pilot boards 24 km from port. VHF Channels 16 and 12, Tel: +33 2 51 76 08 76
Traffic: 2007, 34 004 048 t of cargo handled (includes ports of Donges, Nantes & St. Nazaire)
Working Hours: Three shifts 0600-1400, 1400-2200, 2200-0600
Accommodation:

Name	Length (m)	Depth (m)	Draught (m)	Remarks
Montoir				
Agribulk Terminal	930		12.5–13.5	See [1] below
Coal Terminal	248	16		See [2] below
Container Berth	820		12.5	Three berths
Ro/ro Berth 2	200	9		
Ro/ro Berth 3	200	9		
LNG Terminal	300	12		See [3] below

[1]*Agribulk Terminal:* Two EDC's of 1200 t/h and one travelling gantry crane to load cereals of 700 t/h. Four berths handling agricultural products, cement and fertilizer

[2]*Coal Terminal:* Unloading rate of 20 000 t/day. Vessels up to 140 000 dwt can be accommodated and there is a berth for barges of 5000 dwt and 120 m loa
[3]*LNG Terminal:* Operated by GDF Suez, Website: www.gdfsuez.com
Discharging liquefied natural gas. The terminal has three storage tanks each of 125 000 m3 cap. Consists of two berths. Liquid chemical berth, 220 m max loa, 10 m max d for chemical products and molasses

Storage:

Location	Covered (m²)	Sheds / Warehouses
Container Berth	2400	1

Mechanical Handling Equipment:

Location	Type	Capacity (t)	Qty
Agribulk Terminal	Mult-purp. Cranes	30	5
Agribulk Terminal	Mult-purp. Cranes	40	1
Coal Terminal	Mult-purp. Cranes	30	2
Container Berth	Mult-purp. Cranes	45	1
Container Berth	Container Cranes	40	2
Container Berth	Container Cranes	32	1

Bunkering: Available by barge or shore line
Towage: Boluda Nantes-St. Nazaire, 1 bis, boulevard de Verdun, P O Box 134, F-44603 St. Nazaire, France, *Tel:* +33 2 40 22 49 82, *Fax:* +33 2 40 22 51 93, *Email:* les-abeilles-st-nazaire@bourbon-online.com
Repair & Maintenance: Available from R 2 N shipyard at St. Nazaire
Shipping Agents: CMA-CGM S.A., CGA Montoir, Quai de Montoir, P O Box 25, F-44550 Montoir-de-Bretagne, France, *Tel:* +33 2 40 45 85 85, *Fax:* +33 2 40 90 18 82, *Email:* mrg.genmbox@cma-cgm.com, *Website:* www.cma-cgm.com
Mediterranean Shipping Company, MSC France S.A., Rue de la Lambarde, Rond Pointe de Gron, P O Box 6, F-44550 Montoir-de-Bretagne, France, *Tel:* +33 2 51 10 58 00, *Fax:* +33 2 51 10 58 10, *Email:* mscmontoir@mscfr.mscgva.ch, *Website:* www.mscgva.ch
Medical Facilities: Available. Medical Office, Tel: +33 2 40 88 53 98. St Nazaire Hospital, Tel: +33 2 40 90 60 60
Airport: Nantes Atlantic, 60 km
Railway: St. Nazaire Railway Station, 15 km
Lloyd's Agent: AMS Ouest, 5 Bd Vincent Gache, P O Box 36204, F-44000 Nantes, France, *Tel:* +33 2 40 41 73 84, *Fax:* +33 2 40 41 73 92, *Email:* westoffice@associated-marine-services.com

NANTES

Lat 47° 12' N; Long 1° 33' W.

Admiralty Chart: 2985	**Admiralty Pilot:** 22
Time Zone: GMT +1 h	**UNCTAD Locode:** FR NTE

Principal Facilities:

P	Q	Y	G	C		L	B		T	A

Authority: Grand Port Maritime de Nantes-St.Nazaire, 18 Quai Ernest Renaud, P O Box 18609, F-44186 Nantes Cedex 4, France, *Tel:* +33 2 40 44 71 41, *Fax:* +33 2 40 44 20 01, *Email:* ser.com@nantes.port.fr, *Website:* www.nantes.port.fr
Officials: Managing Director: Francois Marendet, *Email:* f.marendet@nantes.port.fr. Harbour Master: Capt Yves Jaouen, *Email:* y.jaouen@nantes.port.fr.
Port Security: ISPS compliant
Pilotage: Compulsory for vessels over 75 m loa. VHF Channels 16 and 12, Tel: +33 2 40 69 29 00, Fax: +33 2 40 73 29 36
Radio Frequency: St. Nazaire Radio, operating frequency 1687 mHz; continuous watch on VHF Channel 16 and 12, 2182 kHz. Tide level information can be obtained on VHF Channel 73, 156.675 mHz
Tides: Range of tide 6.3 m
Traffic: 2007, 34 004 048 t of cargo handled (includes ports of Donges, Montoir & St. Nazaire)
Maximum Vessel Dimensions: 223 m loa, max d 8.5 m at lowest NT, 9.5 m at ST. Draught may be reduced according to weather conditions
Principal Imports and Exports: Imports: Phosphate, Pulp, Sugar, Wood. Exports: General cargo, Grain, Heavy lift cargo, Scrap iron.
Working Hours: 0800-1200, 1400-1800. Shifts 0500-1300, 1300-2100. No work Sat pm & Sunday
Accommodation:

Name	Length (m)	Depth (m)	Remarks
Nantes			
Quai de l'Aiguillon	180	4	Passengers

Name	Length (m)	Depth (m)	Remarks
Quai Roche Maurice	747	5.6–9.6	Bulk, molasses, grain, ammonia, casting
Emile Cormerais 1	120	5	Refined oil, spirit, situmen
Emile Cormerais 3	180	6.1	Heavy loads, bulk cargo, molasses
Quai Wilson	850	5.6–7.1	Heavy loads, bulk cargo, sugar, coal
Quai Chevire amont	300	7.6	Timber, paper, containers, sheet steel
Quai Chevire aval	154	9.1	Timber, containers, wine, sugar

Storage: 63 500 m3 for oil, 135 000 t for wine; 71 155 m2 of sheds; 23 142 m2 of private sheds; 22 000 m2 of refrigerated fruit storage

Location	Grain (t)	Cold (m³)
Nantes		16500
Quai Roche Maurice	130000	

Mechanical Handling Equipment:

Location	Type	Capacity (t)	Qty	Remarks
Nantes	Mult-purp. Cranes	60	1	heavy lift

Bunkering: Societe des Petroles Shell, 89 Boulevard Franklin Roosevelt, 92564 Rueil-Malmasion, F-76650 Petit Couronne, France, *Tel:* +33 2 35 67 47 03, *Fax:* +33 2 35 67 47 03 – *Grades:* GO – *Delivery Mode:* truck
Total France S.A., Total Marine Fuels, 51 Esplanade du General de Gaulle, F-92907 Paris la Defense Cedex 10, France, *Tel:* +33 1 4135 2755, *Fax:* +33 1 4197 0291, *Email:* marine.fuels@total.com, *Website:* www.marinefuels.total.com

Towage: Two tugs based at Nantes

Repair & Maintenance: Cernat, 11 Boulevard de Chantenay, F-44000 Nantes, France, *Tel:* +33 2 40 46 34 48 One floating dock of 92 m x 16 m, 1700 t cap with one 3 t cap crane
Reparation Navale Nazairienne (R2N), Quai des Fregates, P O Box 10323, F-44615 St. Nazaire, France, *Tel:* +33 2 40 22 94 05, *Fax:* +33 2 40 19 00 53, *Email:* contact@saint-nazaire-marine.com, *Website:* www.saint-nazaire-marine.com Four graving docks: 'Louis Joubert' 350 m x 50 m, No.1 226 m x 30 m, No.2 117 m x 11 m, No.3 159 m x 17 m

Ship Chandlers: R.& G. Dekytspotter Atlantic, 12 rue du Chene Lasse, P O Box 57, F-44801 St. Herblain Cedex, France, *Tel:* +33 2 40 92 16 05, *Fax:* +33 2 40 92 13 69, *Email:* dksupply@dekytspotter.com, *Website:* www.dekytspotter.com

Shipping Agents: Humann & Taconet, Centre Maritime, P O Box 49, F-44480 Donges, France, *Tel:* +33 2 40 45 31 31, *Fax:* +33 2 40 45 35 35, *Email:* donges@humtac.fr, *Website:* www.humann-taconet.fr
Worms Services Maritimes S.A., 9 rue Marcel Sembat, F-44100 Nantes, France, *Tel:* +33 2 40 46 24 38, *Fax:* +33 2 40 46 38 03, *Email:* worms-mttm@mttm.com, *Website:* www.worms-sm.com

Surveyors: Bureau Veritas, 8 Avenue Jacques Cartier, Atlantis, F-44800 St. Herblain Cedex, France, *Tel:* +33 2 40 92 06 89, *Fax:* +33 2 40 92 07 12, *Website:* www.bureauveritas.com
Germanischer Lloyd, 33 Quai des Antilles, F-44200 Nantes, France, *Tel:* +33 2 40 89 43 24, *Fax:* +33 2 51 72 10 41, *Email:* gl-nantes@gl-group.com, *Website:* www.gl-group.com

Airport: Nantes Atlantic, 10 km

Lloyd's Agent: AMS Ouest, 5 Bd Vincent Gache, P O Box 36204, F-44000 Nantes, France, *Tel:* +33 2 40 41 73 84, *Fax:* +33 2 40 41 73 92, *Email:* westoffice@associated-marine-services.com

NICE

Lat 43° 42' N; Long 7° 17' E.

Admiralty Chart: 149   **Admiralty Pilot:** 46
Time Zone: GMT +1 h   **UNCTAD Locode:** FR NCE

Principal Facilities:

		G	R L		A

Authority: Chambre de Commerce et d'Industrie Nice Cote d'Azur, Port de Nice, Quai Amiral Infernet, F-06300 Nice, France, *Tel:* +33 4 92 00 42 42, *Fax:* +33 4 92 00 42 10, *Email:* port.nice@cote-azur.cci.fr, *Website:* www.riviera-ports.com

Port Security: ISPS compliant

Pilotage: Compulsory for ships of over 150 nrt, Tel: +33 4 92 00 42 86, Fax: +33 4 93 89 63 87

Radio Frequency: VHF Channels 16 and 12 (24 h/day)

Traffic: 2005, 343 926 t of cargo handled, 364 632 cruise passengers

Working Hours: Overtime can be worked from 1800 to 2000 to complete a vessel

Accommodation:

Name	Length (m)	Depth (m)	Draught (m)	Remarks
Nice				Other quays are reserved for yachts
Quai Ile de Beaute	150	7.9		
Quai du Commerce	242	9		
Quai d'Entrecasteaux	75	6.5		
Quai Riboty	112	7.1		
Quai Amiral Infernet	200	8		
Dolphin Berth	150		7	

Repair & Maintenance: Minor repairs by local contractors

Airport: Nice International, 8 km

Lloyd's Agent: Unilex Maritime S.a.r.l, Les Docks, 10 Place de la Joliette, Atrium 10.8, F-13002 Marseilles Cedex 02, France, *Tel:* +33 4 91 14 04 40, *Fax:* +33 4 91 91 54 43, *Email:* mail@unilexmaritime.com, *Website:* www.unilexmaritime.com

ORSETTI

harbour area, see under Sete

PAIMBOEUF

Lat 47° 17' N; Long 2° 2' W.

Admiralty Chart: 2985   **Admiralty Pilot:** 22
Time Zone: GMT +1 h   **UNCTAD Locode:** FR PBF

The port is no lionger open to commercial shipping

PAIMPOL

Lat 48° 47' N; Long 3° 3' W.

Admiralty Chart: 3673   **Admiralty Pilot:** 27
Time Zone: GMT +1 h   **UNCTAD Locode:** FR PAI

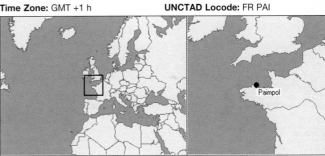

Principal Facilities:

		G		B		A

Authority: Direction Departementale de l'Equipement, Paimpol, France

Pilotage: Compulsory

Accommodation:

Name	Remarks
Paimpol	See [1] below

[1]*Paimpol:* Depth at entrance 5.18 m HSWT, 3.66 m HWNT. Wet dock 174.9 m long, 74.97 m wide; 489.8 m quayage; lock 60.04 m long, 11.89 m wide at entrance. Another wet dock 210.6 m long, 99.97 m quayage. Lock 1, length 60.04 m and breadth 11.89 m at entrance. Lock 2, 44.8 m length and 12.12 m breadth at entrance. Depth at quays 4.57 m HWST, 3.05 m HWNT. One of the docks is reserved for pleasure boats and yachts

Bunkering: Limited bunker coa; 15 000 l oil depot; gas oil by lorries

Airport: St. Brieuc, 50 km, Lannion-Servel 40 km

Lloyd's Agent: Agence Maritime Roy s.a.r.l., 2 Chaussee des Corsaires, P O Box 179, F-35409 St. Malo, France, *Tel:* +33 2 99 56 07 21, *Fax:* +33 2 99 40 24 00, *Email:* agence-maritime-roy@wanadoo.fr

PARIS

Lat 48° 52' N; Long 2° 20' E.

Admiralty Chart: 2879   **Admiralty Pilot:** 27
Time Zone: GMT +1 h   **UNCTAD Locode:** FR PAR

Key to Principal Facilities:—		
A=Airport	**C**=Containers	**G**=General Cargo
B=Bunkers	**D**=Dry Dock	**L**=Cruise
P=Petroleum	**R**=Ro/Ro	**Y**=Dry Bulk
Q=Other Liquid Bulk	**T**=Towage (where available from port)	

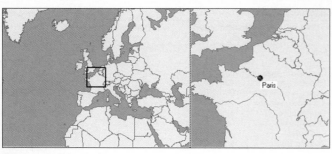

Principal Facilities:

P		Y	G	C	R		B	D		A	

Authority: Port Autonome de Paris, 2 Quai de Grenelle, F-75732 Paris Cedex, France, *Tel:* +33 1 40 58 29 29, *Fax:* +33 1 40 58 27 82, *Email:* dcom@paris-ports.fr, *Website:* www.paris-ports.fr

Officials: Chief Executive Officer: Jean-Francois Dalaise.
Managing Director: Marie-Anne Bacot.
Harbour Master: Christophe du Chatelier, *Tel:* +33 1 40 58 28 70, *Email:* christophe.duchatelier@paris-ports.fr.

Pilotage: Available from the sea to Paris and vice-versa

Traffic: 2007, 21 920 707 t of cargo handled

Accommodation:

Name	Length (m)	Draught (m)	Remarks
Paris			See [1] below
Bonneuil	3500	3	See [2] below
Gennevilliers	8000	3.5	See [3] below
Conflans-Ste-Honorine	1400	3.5	
Limay	1700	3.5	Ro/ro facilities
St-Ouen l'Aumone	200	3	
Bruyeres-sur-Oise	600	3	
Private Wharves			See [4] below

[1]*Paris:* The Port of Paris has under its control some 300 port facilities, private or public, distributed over 500 km of rivers and canals in the Ile de France Region (Seine, Oise, Marne, Yonne, Loing). 900 ha of publicly owned riverside land with 30 km of quays are used for storage and distribution. Depth of water all the year round is 4 m up to Paris-Gennevilliers with airdraft of 8.75 m. Vessels up to 120 m loa, 15.5 m beam and 3.5 m d may enter
Bulk facilities: Two 1000 t/h bucket wheels for coal unloading at Vitry and Champagne-sur-Oise power stations
[2]*Bonneuil:* Container terminal
Includes container berth operated by Paris Terminal S.A., 57 Route de L'Ile Barbiere, F-94387 Bonneuil-sur-Marne, Website: www.paris-terminal.com. Quay 110 m long in depth of 3 m
[3]*Gennevilliers:* Container terminal; ro/ro & heavy lift facilities
Includes container terminal operated by Paris Terminal S.A., Route du Bassin No.1 - CE 111, F-92631 Gennevilliers Cedex, Tel: +33 1 47 94 34 94, Fax: +33 1 47 94 33 71, Email: info@paris-terminal.com, Website: www.paris-terminal.com. Quay 500 m long in depth of 3.5 m
[4]*Private Wharves:* 220 private berths directly serving riverside industries such as power plants, silos, petroleum depots, steel and cement works etc, totalling some 50 km of quayage

Storage:

Location	Covered (m²)
Bonneuil	37000
Gennevilliers	158000
Conflans-Ste-Honorine	6000
Limay	27000

Mechanical Handling Equipment:

Location	Type	Capacity (t)	Qty
Bonneuil	Mobile Cranes	40	1
Gennevilliers	Mult-purp. Cranes	35	2
Gennevilliers	Forklifts	30	
Limay	Mult-purp. Cranes	20	3

Bunkering: One barge for fuel and water
Exaf Paris, 31/32 quia de Dion-Bouton, Puteaux Cedex, F-92811 Paris, France, *Tel:* +33 1 4696 4846, *Fax:* +33 1 4696 4079, *Email:* exaf@fr.dti.bollore.com
LQM Petroleum Services Inc., 25 Boulevard des Italiens, F-75002 Paris, France, *Tel:* +33 1 4281 0081, *Fax:* +33 1 5301 3430, *Email:* france@lqm.com, *Website:* www.lqm.com
LQM Petroleum Services Inc., 25 Boulevard des Italiens, F-75002 Paris, France, *Tel:* +33 1 4281 0081, *Fax:* +33 1 5301 3430, *Email:* france@lqm.com, *Website:* www.lqm.com

Waste Reception Facilities: Garbage and waste oil disposal facilities available

Towage: No regular tug service available; inland navigation pusher tugs may be used in case of necessity

Repair & Maintenance: Chantiers Navals d'Acheres, La Croix d'Acheres, F-78260 Paris, France, *Tel:* +33 1 39 11 02 27, *Fax:* +33 1 39 11 22 92 One 1100 t synchrolift with a 73 m x 13 m platform
Chantiers Navals de la Haute-Seine, Rue des Voeux St. Georges, F-94290 Villeneuve-le-Roi, France, *Tel:* +33 1 49 61 43 33, *Fax:* +33 1 49 61 43 30, *Email:* chs@cemex.com, *Website:* www.chantiers-chs.fr

Shipping Agents: International Maritime Agencies Ltd, 122 Avenue des Champs Elysees, F-75008 Paris, France, *Tel:* +33 1 45 63 04 19, *Fax:* +33 1 45 63 04 48

Isamar S.A., 9 Boulevard de la Madeleine, Paris, France, *Tel:* +33 1 42 61 82 04, *Fax:* +33 1 42 61 82 05, *Email:* richard.ellen@fr.senatorlines.com
Mediterranean Shipping Company, MSC France S.A., 23 Avenue de Neuilly, F-75116 Paris Cedex, France, *Tel:* +33 1 53 64 63 00, *Fax:* +33 1 53 64 63 10, *Email:* mscparis@mscfr.mscgva.ch, *Website:* www.mscgva.ch
Sagmar S.A., 3 Cite Ferembach, 75017 Paris, France, *Tel:* +33 1 44 09 47 09, *Fax:* +33 1 40 55 05 66, *Email:* sagparis@sagmar.com
Shipping Service d'Afrique, Tour Bollore, 31-32 Quai de Dion Bouton, 92811 Paris, France, *Tel:* +33 1 46 96 44 33, *Fax:* +33 1 46 96 48 07, *Email:* antoine.roquette@smtp.saga.gr
Societe Maritime Internationale, 19 Rue des Mathurins, 750009 Paris, France, *Tel:* +33 1 53 30 83 30, *Fax:* +33 1 53 30 83 49
Thomas Maritime, 3 rue du General Bertrand, F-75007 Paris, France, *Tel:* +33 1 40 56 32 32, *Fax:* +33 1 40 56 36 06, *Email:* info@thomas-maritime.fr, *Website:* www.thomas-maritime.fr
Worms Services Maritimes S.A., 48/50 Rue Notre-Dame des Victories, F-75002 Paris, France, *Tel:* +33 1 53 40 12 02, *Fax:* +33 1 53 40 12 05, *Email:* dir.generale@paris.worms-sm.fr, *Website:* www.worms-sm.com

Surveyors: Architectes Ingenieurs Associes (A.I.A.), 23 Rue de Cronstadt, 75015 Paris, France, *Tel:* +33 1 53 68 93 00, *Fax:* +33 1 53 68 93 11, *Email:* aia.paris@a-i-a.fr, *Website:* www.a-i-a.fr
Bureau Veritas, 17 Bis, Place des Reflets, La Defense 2, Paris La Defense, F-92077 Paris, France, *Tel:* +33 1 55 56 60 00, *Fax:* +33 1 42 49 52 92, *Email:* bruno.dabouis@bureauveritas.com, *Website:* www.bureauveritas.com
Det Norske Veritas A/S, Centre BFI, Tour AREVA, F-92084 Paris la Defense Cedex, France, *Tel:* +33 1 47 96 46 36, *Website:* www.dnv.com
Germanischer Lloyd, Paris, France, *Tel:* +33 1 43 87 77 01, *Fax:* +33 1 43 87 76 95, *Email:* gl-paris@gl-group.com, *Website:* www.gl-group.com
Societe Generale de Surveillance (SGS), SGS Qualitest, 191 Avenue Aristide-Briand, Cachan Cedex 01, F-94237 Paris, France, *Tel:* +33 1 41 24 88 88, *Fax:* +33 1 41 24 89 90, *Email:* fr.certification@sgs.com, *Website:* www.sgs.com

Airport: Charles de Gaulle and Orly

Lloyd's Agent: McLarens Young France S.A, 80 Boulevard Haussmann, F-75008 Paris, France, *Tel:* +33 1 44 70 66 10, *Fax:* +33 1 43 87 40 16, *Email:* paris@mclarensyoung.com, *Website:* www.mclarensyoung.com

PAUILLAC

Lat 45° 12' N; Long 0° 45' W.

Admiralty Chart: 3068		**Admiralty Pilot:** 22	
Time Zone: GMT +1 h		**UNCTAD Locode:** FR PAP	

Principal Facilities:

P						B		T	A

Authority: Grand Port Maritime de Bordeaux, Pauillac, France, *Website:* www.bordeaux-port.fr

Pilotage: Tel: +33 5 56 09 63 85

Radio Frequency: Pilotage on VHF Channel 14. Bordeaux Port Control on VHF Channel 12

Traffic: 2004, 455 693 t of cargo handled

Accommodation:

Name	Length (m)	Draught (m)	Remarks
Pauillac			
Berth 700	150	7.5	Dedicated to Airbus operations
Berth 710		10	See [1] below
Berth 711		5.5	Quay out of order

[1]*Berth 710:* Private quay (owned by Shell) for tankers up to 200 m loa

Bunkering: Available

Airport: Bordeaux-Merignac, 50 km

Railway: Linked by rail to the Bordeaux and Le Verdon railway stations

Lloyd's Agent: Jean-Francois Chevreau, Bourse Maritime, Place Laine, F-33000 Bordeaux, France, *Tel:* +33 5 56 52 16 87, *Fax:* +33 5 56 44 67 85, *Email:* info@chevreau-lavie.fr, *Website:* www.chevreau-lavie.com

PETIT COURONNE

harbour area, see under Rouen

PORT DE BOUC

Lat 43° 24' N; Long 4° 59' E.

Admiralty Chart: 155   **Admiralty Pilot:** 46
Time Zone: GMT +1 h   **UNCTAD Locode:** FR PDB

Principal Facilities:

Q	Y	G			B		T	A	

Authority: Grand Port Maritime de Marseille, Quai de la Lecque, P O Box 200, F-13110 Port de Bouc Cedex, France, *Tel:* +33 4 42 40 60 05, *Fax:* +33 4 42 40 60 40, *Email:* m.bonvalet@marseille-port.fr, *Website:* www.marseille-port.fr

Officials: Commercial Director: Monica Bonvalet, *Tel:* +33 4 91 39 43 22.
Harbour Master: Joseph Moysan, *Tel:* +33 4 91 39 41 40, *Email:* j.moysan@marseille-port.fr.

Port Security: ISPS compliant

Pre-Arrival Information: Vessel Traffic Service: The Marseilles/Fos Maritime Traffic Service (STM) is compulsory for all commercial vessels. The area of authority of the STM comprises a marine operating area and a port operating area:
(a) within the limits administered by the GPMM
(b) within the administrative limits of the installations and constructions entrusted to the GPMM
(c) within the area of jurisdiction of the GPMM
(d) in the channels and approaches to the Golfe de Fos and to the Port of Marseilles for vessels transporting hydrocarbons and dangerous substances
The Fos area lies between longitudes 4° 41.3' E (Faraman Lt) and 5° 06.5' E (Sausset-les-Pins Lt), latitude 43° 11.9' N (Le Planier Lt) and the shore, including the Canal Saint-Louis, Port-Saint-Louis-du-Rhone, the Canal de Caronte and the Etang de Berre. Fos Port Control, Tel: +33 4 42 40 60 60. Maritime Traffic Service Centre on VHF Channels 12 and 73. Vessels manoeuvring in the port on VHF Channels 72 and 77
Communications:
(a) communication on VHF Channel 12 and 73 must be established as early as possible between vessels and the Maritime Traffic Service (STM) Centre
(b) vessels unable to contact the STM may not cross the Cap Couronne line (43° 19.5' N)
(c) vessels on passage, manoeuvring and at anchor in any part of the area controlled by the STM must maintain a listening watch on VHF Channel 12
(d) conversations should take place in French and English using standard IMO terminology
(e) pilots can be contacted on VHF Channel 14
Vessels transporting hydrocarbons and dangerous substances must send a SURNAV message 6 h prior to entry into French territorial waters
Vessels inward-bound must contact the STM as follows:
(a) 48 h before arrival at the pilot boarding position, through the agent stating
(i) vessels name and call sign
(ii) destination and port of departure
(iii) draught
(iv) cargo
(v) loa, beam and gt
(vi) type of vessel
(vii) ETA
(b) at least 24 h before arrival stating:
(i) ETA at pilot boarding position
(ii) draught
(iii) nature and tonnage of transported dangerous substances
(iv) loa
(c) 6 h before entry into French territorial waters, vessels transporting hydrocarbons or dangerous substances must send a SURNAV message
(d) on entering the area offshore of the entrance, all vessels over 50 m loa on passage to the Golfe de Fos must report to the STM on VHF Channel 12 stating:
(i) vessels name and call sign
(ii) position
(iii) course and speed
(iv) ETA
The STM will give permission to proceed along the approach channel starting at the Fairway (Omega) Lt Buoy, and will provide information on traffic movements and weather conditions in the area
(e) the STM will advise berthing details and a time for pilot boarding, as well as any towing requirements if not already specified
(f) the STM will also advise VHF communication details as follows:
(i) at the entrance to the STM area
(ii) at the entrance to the approach channel for vessels obliged to use the channels (vessels over 1600 gt transporting hydrocarbons or dangerous substances) for Fos or Marseilles
(iii) at the entrance to the approach channel for vessels not obliged to use the channels. After identifying and authorising the vessel, the STM will instruct the vessel to proceed if the vessel is subject to an inspection by a surveyor
(g) vessels over 1600 gt transporting hydrocarbons or dangerous substances may not enter the approach channel (N of 43° 12.0' N) without the authorisation of the STM

(h) in the event of a doubtful identity, the STM will call every vessel it considers to be likely until a positive identity is obtained
Vessels in the area:
(a) all vessels must contact the STM on VHF before entering the port, getting under way or changing berths
(b) all vessels crossing (or in cases of emergency, anchoring or waiting in) the approach channel, which vessels transporting dangerous cargo are obliged to use, must inform the STM immediately
(c) all vessels wishing to anchor in the Golfe de Fos to the N of the dredged channel must obtain prior permission from the STM. A continuous listening watch must be maintained on VHF Channel 12 while at the anchorage
(d) all vessels wishing to proceed along the Canal de Caronte or the Canal Saint-Louis must request instructions from the STM
(e) vessels transporting hydrocarbons or dangerous substances in the transhipment area of the Golfe de Fos must maintain a continuous listening watch on VHF Channel 12
(f) leisure craft must contact the Harbour Master for all movements within the port (entering, leaving or making way)
(g) vessels may only enter the dredged channel (from the Lavera Lt Buoy to the harbour basins) after checking with the STM that no other vessel has commenced passage along the channel

Pilotage: The compulsory pilotage area consists of an area N of latitude 43° 19' N between the meridians of Faramen Lt (4° 41.3' E) and Cap Couronne Lt (5° 03.3' E), including the canals, the harbour basins of the inner harbours, the Rhone as far as Arles and the Etang de Berre.
Marseilles/Fos Office, Tel: +33 4 91 14 29 10, Fax: +33 4 91 56 65 79, Email: pilote13@nerim.fr
Golfe de Fos Pilotage, Tel: +33 4 42 06 21 01
VHF Channels 12 and 14
Pilotage is available 24/h day and compulsory for vessels of all categories over 50 m loa and all vessels over 70 m loa on passage to or from Darse 2 (Harbour Basin 2) Container Terminal and Darse 3 (Harbour Basin 3) berths in the Port of Fos, except for vessels transporting hydrocarbons or dangerous substances
Vessels must report ETA with at least 24 h notice (or as soon as leaving the previous port) to the Port de Bouc Harbour Master stating:
(a) loa
(b) draught (forward and aft)
(c) nature and tonnage of any dangerous cargo
Vessels must establish VHF contact with the Port de Bouc Harbour Master as early as possible
Pilot boards in the following positions:
(a) vessels transporting hydrocarbons or dangerous cargo and deep draught vessels on passage to Fos at the latitude of Cap Couronne Lt (43° 19.5' N)
(b) vessels bound for Port de Bouc, Lavera, Etang de Berre and St. Louis du Rhone between 2.5-4 nautical miles S of Lavera Lt Buoy (43° 22.6' N; 4° 58.2' E)
(c) on request between latitudes 43° 11.9' N and 43° 19.6' N
The pilotage sub-station at Port de Bouc provides pilots for Lavera, Canal de Caronte, Martigues, Etang de Berre, Fos and St. Louis du Rhone. This station comes under the authority of the Marseilles/Golfe de Fos Pilotage Office

Accommodation:

Name	Length (m)	Draught (m)	Remarks
Port de Bouc			
Caronte Quay (Berths 781-785)	650	7–9.14	See [1] below

[1]*Caronte Quay (Berths 781-785):* Two berths (784 and 785) handle oil seeds and oil cake, max loa 136 m, 7.2 m draft, storage cap of 10 000 t. One quayside berth for loading phosphate barges located between berth 785 and berth 780, max loa 80 m, 3.5 m d max. One berth located on the west of Berth No.781, 60 m long, 3.5 m max d, for reloading ore on to river barges
One private storage stacker with 600 m of belt conveyor, 700 t/h cap and three hopper units

Storage: Quayside transit sheds of 8200 m2 (private). Other transit sheds or warehouses of 4875 m2. Quayside ground surfaces of 16 000 m2 (private), 10 000 m2 (public). Other ground surfaces of 8000 m2 (private).

Mechanical Handling Equipment:

Location	Type	Capacity (t)	Qty
Port de Bouc	Mult-purp. Cranes	35	2

Bunkering: BP France S.A., Immeuble le Cervier, 12 Avenue des Beguines, Cergy-Saint-Christophe, 95866 Cergy Pontoise Cedex, France, *Tel:* +33 1 3422 4000, *Fax:* +33 1 3422 4417, *Email:* benoist.grosjean@fr.bp.com, *Website:* www.bpmarine.com – *Grades:* IFO380, 320-30cSt; LDO – *Parcel Size:* wharf min 500t, barge min 100t, truck min 25t – *Delivery Mode:* ex wharf, pipeline
ExxonMobil Marine Fuels, Mailpoint 31, ExxonMobil House, Ermyn Way, Leatherhead, Surrey KT22 8UX, United Kingdom, *Tel:* +44 1372 222 000, *Fax:* +44 1372 223 922, *Email:* marine.fuels@exxonmobil.com, *Website:* www.exxonmobil.com – *Grades:* IFO30-380cSt; MDO; MGO – *Delivery Mode:* barge, pipeline, truck
Ocean Energy S.A.M., c/o Ocean Energy SAM, 57 Rue Grimaldi, Le Panorama Bloc C/D, MC 98000 Monte Carlo, Monaco, *Tel:* +377 9325 5331, *Fax:* +377 9325 5332, *Email:* oceanenergy@oceanenergy.mc, *Website:* www.oceanenergy.mc
Societe des Petroles Shell, 89 Boulevard Franklin Roosevelt, 92564 Rueil-Malmaison, F-76650 Petit Couronne, France, *Tel:* +33 2 35 67 47 03, *Fax:* +33 2 35 67 47 03 – *Grades:* IFO380-30cSt; GO – *Parcel Size:* IFO barge 100t, truck 25t – *Delivery Mode:* barge, truck
Total France S.A., Total Marine Fuels, 51 Esplanade du General de Gaulle, F-92907 Paris la Defense Cedex 10, France, *Tel:* +33 1 4135 2755, *Fax:* +33 1 4197 0291, *Email:* marine.fuels@total.com, *Website:* www.marinefuels.total.com – *Grades:* IFO380-30cSt; MGO – *Misc:* own storage facilities – *Parcel Size:* no min/mix – *Rates:* 300-500t/h – *Notice:* 24 hours – *Delivery Mode:* pipeline, barge, truck

Towage: Available

Seaman Missions: The Seamans Mission, 35 Avenue Roger Salengro, F-13110 Port de Bouc, France, *Tel:* +33 4 42 06 42 87, *Fax:* +33 4 42 06 11 23, *Email:* seamenfose@netcourier.com

---

Key to Principal Facilities:—
A=Airport   **C**=Containers   **G**=General Cargo   **P**=Petroleum   **R**=Ro/Ro   **Y**=Dry Bulk
B=Bunkers   **D**=Dry Dock   **L**=Cruise   **Q**=Other Liquid Bulk   **T**=Towage (where available from port)

Ship Chandlers: International Export Agency, Z.I. Boulevard de la Merindole, F-13110 Port de Bouc, France, *Tel:* +33 4 42 40 52 82, *Fax:* +33 4 42 06 59 54, *Email:* sales.dpt@iea-shipsupply.com

Shipping Agents: Agences Maritimes Barwil Pomme, 1 Avenue Jean Moulin, P O Box 63, F-13522 Port de Bouc Cedex, France, *Tel:* +33 4 42 35 45 55, *Fax:* +33 4 42 06 48 84, *Email:* barwil.pdb.ops@wilhelmsen.com, *Website:* www.barwil.com

Medical Facilities: Available at Martigues and Port de Bouc

Airport: Marseille-Provence Airport, 45 km

Lloyd's Agent: Unilex Maritime S.a.r.l, Les Docks, 10 Place de la Joliette, Atrium 10.8, F-13002 Marseilles Cedex 02, France, *Tel:* +33 4 91 14 04 40, *Fax:* +33 4 91 91 54 43, *Email:* mail@unilexmaritime.com, *Website:* www.unilexmaritime.com

PORT JEROME

harbour area, see under Rouen

PORT VENDRES

Lat 42° 31' N; Long 3° 7' E.

Admiralty Chart: 2114	**Admiralty Pilot:** 46
Time Zone: GMT +1 h	**UNCTAD Locode:** FR POV

Principal Facilities:

Q		G		R		B		A	

Authority: Chambre de Commerce et d'Industrie, Gare Maritime, P O Box 37, F-66664 Port Vendres Cedex, France, *Tel:* +33 4 68 82 00 25, *Fax:* +33 4 68 82 54 18, *Email:* port.vendres@perpignan.cci.fr, *Website:* www.perpignan.cci.fr

Pilotage: Available, Tel: +33 4 68 40 43 50, Fax: +33 4 68 40 43 51, Email: pilonov@softel.fr. VHF Channel 16 and 12

Maximum Vessel Dimensions: 150 m loa, 7.92 m d

Accommodation:

Name	Remarks
Port Vendres	See [1] below

[1]*Port Vendres:* Sheltered harbour. Depth at entrance 16 m; at quays 6 to 8 m. Three wharves with ro/ro facilities. Tanker facilities for wine tankers only

Storage: Covered storage areas and transit and customs sheds. Refrigerated warehouses

Mechanical Handling Equipment:

Location	Type	Capacity (t)	Qty
Port Vendres	Mult-purp. Cranes	12	1

Repair & Maintenance: For small craft only

Airport: Perpignan, 30 km

Lloyd's Agent: Unilex Maritime S.a.r.l, Les Docks, 10 Place de la Joliette, Atrium 10.8, F-13002 Marseilles Cedex 02, France, *Tel:* +33 4 91 14 04 40, *Fax:* +33 4 91 91 54 43, *Email:* mail@unilexmaritime.com, *Website:* www.unilexmaritime.com

PORTO VECCHIO

Lat 41° 36' N; Long 9° 17' E.

Admiralty Chart: 1425	**Admiralty Pilot:** 46
Time Zone: GMT +1 h	**UNCTAD Locode:** FR PVO

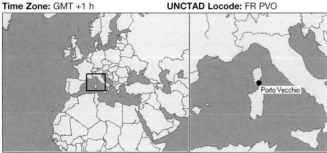

Principal Facilities:

		G		R		B		A	

Authority: Chambre de Commerce et d'Industrie de Ajaccio et South Corsica (CCIACS), Quai l'Herminier, P O Box 253, F-20180 Ajaccio, Corsica, France, *Tel:* +33 4 95 51 21 80, *Fax:* +33 4 95 21 07 86, *Email:* jy.battesti@sudcorse.cci.fr, *Website:* www.sudcorse.cci.fr

Officials: Port Director: Don Paul Grimaldi.
Deputy Director: Jean Yves Battesti, *Email:* jy.battesti@sudcorse.cci.fr.
Harbour Master: Olivier Berthezene, *Email:* olivier.berthezene@equipement.gouv.fr.

Port Security: ISPS compliant

Pilotage: Compulsory for vessels over 60 m loa and available 24 h/day. Pilot station, Tel: +33 4 95 21 42 48, Fax: +33 4 95 21 39 28, Email: pilotajax@wanadoo.fr. Boarding area is 1 nautical mile NE of Punta di a Chiappa in pos 41° 35.88' N; 9° 22.10' E

Radio Frequency: VHF Channels 12 and 16

Traffic: 2003, 197 816 t of cargo handled, 81 518 passengers, 29 553 vehicles

Accommodation:

Name	Length (m)	Depth (m)
Porto Vecchio		
Quai Duc d'Albes	140	7.5
Quai L'Herminier	90	5.8
New Pier	152	8

Bunkering: Available

Airport: Figari, 15 km

Lloyd's Agent: Unilex Maritime S.a.r.l, Les Docks, 10 Place de la Joliette, Atrium 10.8, F-13002 Marseilles Cedex 02, France, *Tel:* +33 4 91 14 04 40, *Fax:* +33 4 91 91 54 43, *Email:* mail@unilexmaritime.com, *Website:* www.unilexmaritime.com

PROPRIANO

Lat 41° 40' N; Long 8° 54' E.

Admiralty Chart: 1424	**Admiralty Pilot:** 46
Time Zone: GMT +1 h	**UNCTAD Locode:** FR PRP

Principal Facilities:

		G		R		B		A	

Authority: Chambre de Commerce et d'Industrie de Ajaccio et South Corsica (CCIACS), Quai l'Herminier, P O Box 253, F-20180 Ajaccio, Corsica, France, *Tel:* +33 4 95 51 21 80, *Fax:* +33 4 95 21 07 86, *Email:* jy.battesti@sudcorse.cci.fr, *Website:* www.sudcorse.cci.fr

Officials: Port Director: Don Paul Grimaldi.
Deputy Director: Jean Yves Battesti, *Email:* jy.battesti@sudcorse.cci.fr.
Harbour Master: Olivier Berthezene, *Email:* olivier.berthezene@equipement.gouv.fr.

Port Security: ISPS compliant

Pilotage: Compulsory for vessels over 60 m loa and available 24 h/day. Pilot station, Tel: +33 4 95 21 42 48, Fax: +33 4 95 21 39 28, Email: pilotajax@wanadoo.fr. Boarding station is 2 nautical miles W of the entrance to the port

Radio Frequency: VHF Channel 16 and 12

Traffic: 2006, 125 000 t of cargo handled, 130 000 passengers

Accommodation:

Name	Length (m)	Depth (m)
Propriano		
Old Quay	200	6.5
New Quay	156	8
Quai L'Herminier	90	7

Bunkering: Available

Airport: Ajaccio, 71 km

Lloyd's Agent: Unilex Maritime S.a.r.l, Les Docks, 10 Place de la Joliette, Atrium 10.8, F-13002 Marseilles Cedex 02, France, *Tel:* +33 4 91 14 04 40, *Fax:* +33 4 91 91 54 43, *Email:* mail@unilexmaritime.com, *Website:* www.unilexmaritime.com

QUEYRIES

harbour area, see under Bordeaux

QUIMPER

Lat 47° 58' N; Long 4° 7' W.

Admiralty Chart: -	**Admiralty Pilot:** 22
Time Zone: GMT +1 h	**UNCTAD Locode:** FR UIP

Principal Facilities:

P		G		B		A	

Authority: Conseil General du Finistere, Direction des Activities Maritimes et des Transports, 50 Rue Jean Jaures, F-29196 Quimper Cedex, France, *Tel:* +33 2 98 76 20 34, *Fax:* +33 2 98 76 21 99, *Website:* www.cg29.fr

Pilotage: Available, Tel: +33 2 98 56 32 40

Accommodation:

Name	Length (m)	Remarks
Quimper		See [1] below
Corniguel		See [2] below
Quay	226	For coasters
Quay	120	For discharging sand

[1]*Quimper:* Since the construction of two bridges over the Odet (one temporary, the other permanent) downstream from Quimper-Ville, the latter is no longer accessible to coasters
[2]*Corniguel:* Vessels of 1500 t, 78 m long, 12 m beam and 4.95 m d can enter during ST and vessels from 500 to 900 t, 72 m long, 12 m beam and 3.4 m d can enter during NT

Storage:

Location	Covered (m²)
Quimper	35000

Bunkering: Available

Surveyors: Bureau Veritas, 78 Rue Marechal Foch, F-56100 Lorient, France, *Tel:* +33 2 97 37 63 06, *Fax:* +33 2 97 21 18 97, *Website:* www.bureauveritas.com

Medical Facilities: Local hospital

Airport: 4 km

Lloyd's Agent: Agence Maritime Jacquemin, 58 Avenue Perriere, F-56100 Lorient, France, *Tel:* +33 2 97 83 67 92, *Fax:* +33 2 97 37 77 31, *Email:* shiplor@wanadoo.fr

RADICATEL

harbour area, see under Rouen

RANVILLE

harbour area, see under Caen

ROCHEFORT

Lat 45° 56' N; Long 0° 58' W.

Admiralty Chart: 2747	**Admiralty Pilot:** 22
Time Zone: GMT +1 h	**UNCTAD Locode:** FR RCO

Principal Facilities:

	Y	G				T	A

Authority: Port de Commerce de Rochefort Tonnay-Charente, P O Box 20129, F-17306 Rochefort, France, *Tel:* +33 5 46 99 58 16, *Fax:* +33 5 46 99 58 73, *Email:* info@rochefort.port.fr, *Website:* www.rochefort.port.fr

Officials: Managing Director: Francis Grimaud, *Tel:* +33 5 46 99 58 69, *Email:* f.grimaud@rochefort.cci.fr.
Harbour Master: Fabrice Brunetti, *Email:* fabrice.brunetti@cg17.fr.

Port Security: ISPS compliant

Documentation: Crew list (2 copies), crew declaration (2 copies), passengers (2 copies), stores (2 copies), manifest (1 copy), health document or certificates (1 copy), certificate of deratting (1 copy), load line certificate (1 copy), tonnage certificate (1 copy), certificate of nationality (1 copy), safety equipment certificate (1 copy), bill of lading (1 copy)

Approach: Depth at entrance 6.1 m ST and 5.01 m NT. No risk on bar, soft mud. Vessels drawing 6.1 to 7.01 m can enter River Charente (for 3 h before/after HW for vessels less than 95 m loa) and remain afloat at Soubise and in river at Rochefort at LW. Roads: 0.8 km SSW of Aix Island, well sheltered

Pilotage: Compulsory for vessels over 45 m loa. Pilot Station is located 0.5 miles SSW from Ile d'Aix lighthouse

Radio Frequency: Harbour Master's Office on VHF Channel 12. Pilot Stations on VHF Channels 16 or 74

Tides: Tidal range and flow: springs 5 m, neaps 2.4 m

Traffic: 2005, 1 012 945 t of cargo handled (includes Tonnay Charente)

Maximum Vessel Dimensions: 120 m loa and 16.5 m breadth with a max draught of 6.5 m

Working Hours: Mon-Fri 0700-1200, 1400-1800. Overtime available to 2200 and Saturday mornings

Accommodation:

Name	Length (m)	Draught (m)	Remarks
Rochefort			
Quai de l'Ecluse	120	5.7–6.5	
Quai Sud		5.7–6.5	Consists of two berths, each 110 m long
Quai Ouest		5.7–6.5	Consists of two berths, each 110 m long
Quai Bachelar		5.7–6.5	Consists of two berths, each 110 m long

Storage: Large public warehouses (8000 m2), sheds (40 000 m2), bond warehouses and general cargo sheds

Mechanical Handling Equipment:

Location	Type	Capacity (t)	Qty
Rochefort	Mobile Cranes	6–40	8

Waste Reception Facilities: Garbage disposal available via agent

Towage: Available from La Pallice at 24 h notice

Medical Facilities: Rochefort Public Hospital, Tel: +33 (5) 46 82 20 20

Airport: Rochefort, 6 km. La Rochelle, 40 km

Railway: Rochefort Railway Station, 500 m from the dock

Lloyd's Agent: Jean-Francois Chevreau, Bourse Maritime, Place Laine, F-33000 Bordeaux, France, *Tel:* +33 5 56 52 16 87, *Fax:* +33 5 56 44 67 85, *Email:* info@chevreau-lavie.fr, *Website:* www.chevreau-lavie.com

ROSCOFF

Lat 48° 43' N; Long 3° 59' W.

Admiralty Chart: 2745	**Admiralty Pilot:** 27
Time Zone: GMT +1 h	**UNCTAD Locode:** FR ROS

Principal Facilities:

		G	R	B		A	

Authority: Morlaix Chambre de Commerce et d'Industrie, Port de Roscoff-Bloscon, P O Box 43, F-29682 Roscoff Cedex, France, *Tel:* +33 2 98 61 27 85, *Fax:* +33 2 98 61 18 16, *Email:* roscoff@morlaix.cci.fr, *Website:* www.morlaix.cci.fr

Officials: Director: Jean-Pierre Addes.
Harbour Master: Philippe Le Jannou, *Tel:* +33 2 98 61 27 84, *Email:* philippe.lejannou@equipement.gouv.fr.

Port Security: ISPS compliant

Anchorage: Anchorage forbidden due to extension works (fishing harbour)

Pilotage: Compulsory. The pilot is taken E of the Isle of Batz at Astan Buoy, Tel: +33 2 98 69 73 07

Radio Frequency: Harbour Master on VHF Channels 16 and 12

Tides: Range of tide 9.6 m max

Key to Principal Facilities:—			
A=Airport	**C**=Containers	**G**=General Cargo	**P**=Petroleum	**R**=Ro/Ro	**Y**=Dry Bulk
B=Bunkers	**D**=Dry Dock	**L**=Cruise	**Q**=Other Liquid Bulk	**T**=Towage (where available from port)	

Principal Imports and Exports: Imports: Ammonia sulphate, Fertiliser, Industrial sand, Marine aggregates, Nordic wood. Exports: China clay, Seed potatoes.

Working Hours: 24 h/day

Accommodation:

Name	Length (m)	Depth (m)	Remarks
Roscoff			See [1] below
Quay Pierre Lemaire	240	7	Ferry berth
Quay No.2	90	3.5	Cargo vessels
Quay No.3	120	5	Cargo vessels

[1]*Roscoff:* Brittany Ferries, Tel: +33 2 98 29 28 00, Fax: +33 2 98 29 27 00, operate a year round service (1-3 sailings/day) between Roscoff and Plymouth and also between Roscoff and Cork (1 sailing/week) from late March to early November Irish Ferries, Tel: +33 2 98 61 17 17, Fax: +33 2 98 61 17 46, operate from Roscoff to Rosslare from late April to late September (2 sailings/week to late July and 1 sailing/week to late September)

Storage:

Location	Covered (m²)	Sheds / Warehouses
Roscoff	1200	1

Mechanical Handling Equipment:

Location	Type	Capacity (t)	Qty
Roscoff	Mobile Cranes	72	3

Bunkering: Fuel available by road tankers

Waste Reception Facilities: Galley rubbish is collected in bins on quay or directly taken away by the Harbour Authority compacting skip, depending on the amount. Industrial rubbish must be collected in special skips

Airport: Guipavas, 50 km

Railway: Roscoff, 1 km. Morlaix, 25 km

Lloyd's Agent: SNC de la Menardiere, 6 Rue Fregate la Belle Poule, P O Box 61232, F-29212 Brest Cedex 1, France, *Tel:* +33 2 98 80 32 70, *Fax:* +33 2 98 80 74 00, *Email:* expertise.de.la.menardiere@wanadoo.fr

ROUEN

Lat 49° 26' N; Long 1° 2' E.

Admiralty Chart: 2879
Time Zone: GMT +1 h

Admiralty Pilot: 27
UNCTAD Locode: FR URO

Rouen

Principal Facilities:

P Q Y G C R L B D T A

Authority: Grand Port Maritime de Rouen, 34 Boulevard de Boisguilbert, P O Box 4075, F-76022 Rouen Cedex, France, *Tel:* +33 2 35 52 54 56, *Fax:* +33 2 35 52 54 13, *Email:* harbourmaster@rouen.port.fr, *Website:* www.rouen.port.fr

Officials: General Director: Martine Bonny, *Tel:* +33 2 35 52 54 50, *Email:* dg@rouen.port.fr.
Commercial Manager: Martin Butruille, *Tel:* +33 2 35 52 54 30, *Email:* dcc@rouen.port.fr.
Harbour Master: Jean-Yves Deransi, *Tel:* +33 2 35 52 54 05, *Email:* cpr@rouen.port.fr.

Port Security: ISPS compliant

Approach: Rouen is accessible to any vessel up to 40 000 dwt fully loaded and 140 000 dwt partly loaded, 11.5 m max d HW. Suspension bridges over Seine at Tancarville and Caudebec have clearance over water under main span of 50 m. The Seine can be navigated by vessels of 9.7 to 11.7 m d up river depending on tides, ie 9.5 m all tides, 10.5 m during 50% and 11.5 m during 5% of the tides. Draught allowed is limited to 10.3 m on all tides down river, although a special technique allows vessels to proceed down river with 10.8 m d, depending on meteorological conditions. It is possible for vessels to go down river on two or three tides, mooring on buoys, and after a few hours resume their journey. This technique is possible for ships equipped with radar, usable on the river and whose speed is over 12 knots. The pilotage service publishes, each month, a list indicating days during which the descent of the river on two tides is possible. This is most important for vessels leaving Rouen with a draught over 10 m. Ships take about 6.5 h to move up the channel from the sea to Rouen

Anchorage: Anchorage can be obtained in the outer roads at La Carosse. The roads are exposed to NW and W winds

Pilotage: Compulsory. At least 12 h notice of ETA at Le Havre roads should be given, 5 h notice of ETA is compulsory

Radio Frequency: All port information is given on VHF Channel 73. Call 'Rouen Pilot' on arrival and 'Rouen Port' after entering. Ships must keep a permanent watch on VHF Channel 73 during their transit up and down the river

Traffic: 2007, 22 210 000 t of cargo handled

Principal Imports and Exports: Imports: Chemicals, Fertiliser, Forest products, Minerals, Petroleum products. Exports: Cereals, Flour, Petroleum products, Sugar.

Working Hours: Mon-Fri 0600-2200 at normal tariff; 2200-0600 with supplement

Accommodation: Tanker facilities: There is one petroleum basin at Petit Couronne with accommodation for gas carriers up to 160 m loa and 8 m d, and for inland craft. One river berth can handle tankers of 250 m loa. At Port Jerome there are seven wharves and waiting berths, capable of handling tankers up to 220 m loa and 51 000 dwt

Name	Length (m)	Depth (m)	Remarks
Saint-Gervais			
West Quay	760	9	See [1] below
River upstream (right bank)			See [2] below
River downstream (right bank)			See [3] below
River upstream (left bank)			
Elie Peninsula	600	10.5	See [4] below
Bassin aux Bois & Quai Neuf	1200	7.5–10	Eight berths. Bagged goods terminal, with 37 acre quayage
Rouen Quevilly Dock			
Rouen Quevilly			See [5] below
River downstream (left bank)			
Maprochim	220	9	Chemical products terminal: phosphate, sulphur, acids
AGQ		8.5	Reception & processing of liquid chemical products
CPA Quay	300	9–10.5	Two berths handling liquid products
Berth No.14		8	Waiting berth
Simarex Berth		10.5	See [6] below
Petit Couronne			
Petit Couronne	600	10.5	See [7] below
River downstream			
Shell		8–11	See [8] below
PAP Quay	400	8.5	Two berths handling timber & bulk
CARUE	400	11.5	See [9] below
SOGEMA	300	10–11	See [10] below
Grand-Couronne			
UCACEL MRM		11	See [11] below
SAIPOL		9.5	Storage & export vegetable oil
Grand-Couronne/Moulineaux			
Grand-Couronne/Moulineaux	900	11.5	Container terminal, with 21 acre quayage. Also a general cargo terminal
Radicatel			
Seine Container Terminal	380	10	See [12] below
Saint-Wandrille			
Saint-Wandrille	630	10	See [13] below
Port Jerome			
Port Jerome		7–11	See [14] below

[1]*West Quay:* Five berths handling containers; 13 acre storage area
[2]*River upstream (right bank):* Quay length of 2600 m consisting of 23 waiting berths in depth of 6.5-9 m
[3]*River downstream (right bank):* Fourteen berths in depth of 6.5-9 m
Storage tanks for agri-food products (vegetable oil, molasses etc.)
Skalli, semolina factory of 32 000 t vertical storage cap
Levy Silo, 27 000 t vertical storage, loading rate 460 t/h
Soufflet Silo, 57 000 t vertical storage and 113 000 t horizontal storage cap; loading rates of 650 and 400 t/h
Lecureur Silo, 40 000 t vertical storage and 75 000 t horizontal storage cap; loading rates of 500 and 1000 t/h
Waiting berths
[4]*Elie Peninsula:* Two berths. SENALIA Silos, with total of 242 000 t vertical storage cap; equipped for unloading lorries, complete trains and barges (rate 600-1200 t/h); equipment able to load 2800 t/h
[5]*Rouen Quevilly:* Two quays; one 400 m long (2 berths) in depth of 10.5 m and one forest products quay 1200 m long (6 berths) in depth of 9 m with cranes up to 25 t and nine warehouses
[6]*Simarex Berth:* Simarex Silo, 87 000 t vertical storage and 88 000 t horizontal storage cap; loading rate of 800 t/h
[7]*Petit Couronne:* Three berths. Powered export terminal for bagged goods equipped with goods wagon and truck unloading stations connected by belt conveyors to a downward conveyor
[8]*Shell:* Six berths handling petroleum & chemical products: reception storage and processing
[9]*CARUE:* Two berths. Solid bulk terminal: reception and storage
[10]*SOGEMA:* Two berths handling coal (for industrial use), fertiliser, phosphates in bulk
[11]*UCACEL MRM:* Vertical silo, 220 000 t storage cap and horizontal silo of 100 000 t storage cap with loading equipment 3000 t/h
[12]*Seine Container Terminal:* Privately owned container terminal operated by Katoen Natie Radicatel, Quai de Radicatel, F-76170 St. Jean de Folleville, Tel: +33 2 35 31 07 75, Fax: +33 2 35 31 10 88, Website: www.katoennatie.com
Four berths with 13 acre quayage
[13]*Saint-Wandrille:* Six berths with a waiting berth, reception of coils for S.L.D.
[14]*Port Jerome:* Ten berths. Reception, storage and processing of petroleum and chemical products

Storage:

Location	Open (m²)	Covered (m²)
West Quay	50000	11000

Location	Open (m²)	Covered (m²)
River upstream (right bank)		40000
River downstream (right bank)		4000
Bassin aux Bois & Quai Neuf		33000
Petit Couronne		7000
PAP Quay		6000
Grand-Couronne/Moulineaux	160000	7200
Seine Container Terminal	10000	
Saint-Wandrille		1000

Mechanical Handling Equipment:

Location	Type	Capacity (t)	Qty
West Quay	Mult-purp. Cranes	35	7
Petit Couronne	Mult-purp. Cranes	35	3
Grand-Couronne/Moulineaux	Mult-purp. Cranes	25	1
Grand-Couronne/Moulineaux	Mobile Cranes	100	1
Grand-Couronne/Moulineaux	Container Cranes	35	2

Bunkering: BP France S.A., Immeuble le Cervier, 12 Avenue des Beguines, Cergy-Saint-Christophe, 95866 Cergy Pontoise Cedex, France, *Tel:* +33 1 3422 4000, *Fax:* +33 1 3422 4417, *Email:* benoist.grosjean@fr.bp.com, *Website:* www.bpmarine.com – *Grades:* IF180-380cSt; MGO – *Parcel Size:* 25t – *Delivery Mode:* pipeline, barge, truck
Societe des Petroles Shell, 89 Boulevard Franklin Roosevelt, 92564 Rueil-Malmaion, F-76650 Petit Couronne, France, *Tel:* +33 2 35 67 47 03, *Fax:* +33 2 35 67 47 03

Towage: Sormar, 8 de Lesseps Boulevard, 9th Floor, 76000 Rouen, France, *Tel:* +33 2 35 70 03 58, *Fax:* +33 2 35 88 70 78, *Email:* lttsm@wanadoo.fr

Repair & Maintenance: Ateliers de Croisset, Rouen, France, *Tel:* +33 2 35 52 55 88 Floating dock 181 m x 25 m, lifting cap of 14 000 t; vessels up to 25 000 dwt can be accommodated

Seaman Missions: The Seamans Mission, 16 Rue Duguay Trouin, F-76000 Rouen, France, *Tel:* +33 2 35 70 71 63, *Email:* seamenrouen@wanadoo.fr

Ship Chandlers: S.G.A.E., 1110 Boulevard de Normandie, Zone du Mesnil Roux, F-76360 Barentin, France, *Tel:* +33 2 35 92 15 15, *Fax:* +33 2 35 92 50 60, *Email:* sgae@sgae.fr, *Website:* www.sgae.fr

Shipping Agents: Agena Tramp, 47 Avenue du Mont Riboudet, P O Box 4052, F-76022 Rouen, France, *Tel:* +33 2 35 19 27 85, *Fax:* +33 2 35 19 72 85, *Email:* seine@agenatramp.fr, *Website:* www.agenatramp.fr
Humann & Taconet, 22 Rue Mustel, P O Box 4013, F-76021 Rouen Cedex, France, *Tel:* +33 2 32 10 28 10, *Fax:* +33 2 32 10 28 20, *Email:* rouen@humtac.fr, *Website:* www.humann-taconet.fr
Mediterranean Shipping Company, MSC France S.A., Centre Tertiaire et Portuaire, 19 Boulevard du Midi, F-76108 Rouen Cedex, France, *Tel:* +33 2 32 81 71 00, *Fax:* +33 2 32 81 71 10, *Email:* mscrouen@mscfr.mscgva.ch, *Website:* www.mscgva.ch
Navitainer S.A., 57 Avenue de Bretagne, 76100 Rouen, France, *Tel:* +33 2 32 18 09 87, *Fax:* +33 2 35 63 14 01, *Email:* sales.navitainer@burgergroup.fr
Royal Burger Group, Imm la Bretagne, 57 Avenue de Bretagne, 76100 Rouen, France, *Tel:* +33 2 32 81 36 72, *Fax:* +33 2 35 62 58 16, *Email:* rouen@burgergroup.fr, *Website:* www.royalburgergroup.com
SAGA France, Immeuble Rouen Ocean, 3 Boulevard du Midi, P O Box 1365, 76179 Rouen, France, *Tel:* +33 2 35 58 40 40, *Fax:* +33 2 35 58 40 42, *Email:* m.canu@sagactl.com, *Website:* www.saga.fr
Sea Invest Shipping Agency, 14 Boulevard de L' Oust, P O Box 4181, F-76723 Rouen, France, *Tel:* +33 2 32 10 85 11, *Fax:* +33 2 32 10 85 16, *Email:* tramppar@sea-invest.fr, *Website:* www.sea-invest-sa.com
Vopak Agencies B.V., 8 Boulevard Ferdinand de Lesseps, F-76000 Rouen, France, *Tel:* +33 2 32 10 56 35, *Fax:* +33 2 32 10 56 40, *Email:* agencies.rouen@vopak.com, *Website:* www.vopak.com
Westerlund France S.A., 34 Boulevard du Midi, P O Box 1080, F-76173 Rouen, France, *Tel:* +33 2 35 58 17 17, *Fax:* +33 2 35 58 17 00, *Email:* westerlundfrance@westerlundgroup.com, *Website:* www.westerlundgroup.com
Worms Services Maritimes S.A., 32, rue Pierre Brossolette, Le Havre, F-76600 Rouen, France, *Tel:* +33 2 35 19 62 00, *Fax:* +33 2 72 34 01 23, *Email:* worms@rou.worms-sm.fr, *Website:* www.worms-sm.com

Airport: Rouen

Lloyd's Agent: Humann & Taconet, 73-75 Quai de Southampton, P O Box 1395, F-76066 Le Havre Cedex, France, *Tel:* +33 2 35 19 39 86, *Fax:* +33 2 35 19 39 85, *Email:* lloydsagency-lehavre@humtac.fr, *Website:* www.humann-taconet.fr

SABLES D'OLONNE

Lat 46° 30' N; Long 1° 48' W.

Admiralty Chart: 2997/2998/3638   **Admiralty Pilot:** 22

Time Zone: GMT +1 h   **UNCTAD Locode:** FR LSO

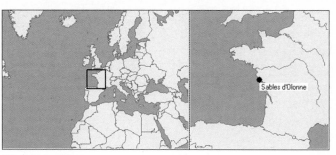

Sables d'Olonne

Principal Facilities:

Q	Y	G			B		A

Authority: Capitainerie du Port, 1 Rue Colbert, F-85100 Sables d'Olonne, France, *Tel:* +33 2 51 95 11 79, *Fax:* +33 2 51 21 40 04, *Email:* cdtport.dde85@wanadoo.fr

Officials: Harbour Master: Jean-Pierre Baret.

Port Security: ISPS compliant

Approach: The channel is more than 1000 m long and 200 m wide

Anchorage: Safe anchorage available in the waiting area defined by positions 45° 28' 18" and 45° 28' 36" N; 01° 46' 37" and 01° 47' 00" W

Pilotage: Compulsory for vessels over 50 m loa and for all vessels carrying dangerous cargo. Pilotage provided by La Loire, *Email:* pilote-major@pilots-loire.com and pilot boards in La Grande Rade bounded by lines from a position 46° 28' 90" N; 1° 50' 50" W (close S of La Petite Barge Lt buoy), passing Grande Barge Lt (46° 29' 70" N; 1° 50' 50" W) and La Peruse rock (46° 28' 52" N; 1° 45' 88" W)

Radio Frequency: Harbour Master and Pilots on VHF Channel 12

Maximum Vessel Dimensions: 110 m loa, 16 m beam

Principal Imports and Exports: Imports: Fertiliser, Liquid fertiliser, Pellets, Salt, Timber. Exports: Grain, Pellets.

Working Hours: 0700-1200, 1400-1900 Monday-Friday. No work on Saturday

Accommodation:

Name	Length (m)	Remarks
Sables d'Olonne		See [1] below
North Quay	276	Three berths (each 92 m long) for tankers & general cargo
South Quay	120	Grain. Three loading silos at rate of 300-400 t/h
East Quay	100	General cargo

[1]*Sables d'Olonne:* Wet dock: surface area of approx 4 ha comprising six mooring berths, dredged to a level of -1.5 m, for vessels up to 110 m loa and approx 16 m width

Storage:

Location	Sheds / Warehouses	Grain (t)
Sables d'Olonne South Quay	2	40000

Mechanical Handling Equipment:

Location	Type	Capacity (t)	Qty
Sables d'Olonne	Mult-purp. Cranes	40	9

Cargo Worked: Discharging on a working day: preslung bags 900-1000 t/day; timber 1800-2000 m3; bulk 1500 t. Loading: grains 300-400 t/h

Bunkering: Oil from Nantes or La Pallice by road tanker

Towage: No tugs; only pilot boat available

Stevedoring Companies: Sogam S.A., Port de Commerce, Quai Archereau, P O Box 30279, F-85107 Sables d'Olonne, France, *Tel:* +33 2 51 21 02 28, *Fax:* +33 2 51 32 88 60, *Email:* p.bauchet@sogam.sdv.com

Airport: Nantes Atlantic, 87 km

Railway: Several railway tracks provide access to the northern and southern wharves, and the warehouses

Lloyd's Agent: AMS Ouest, 5 Bd Vincent Gache, P O Box 36204, F-44000 Nantes, France, *Tel:* +33 2 40 41 73 84, *Fax:* +33 2 40 41 73 92, *Email:* westoffice@associated-marine-services.com

SAINT-GERVAIS

harbour area, see under Rouen

SAINT WANDRILLE

harbour area, see under Rouen

SETE

Lat 43° 24' N; Long 3° 42' E.

Admiralty Chart: 2114   **Admiralty Pilot:** 22

Time Zone: GMT +1 h   **UNCTAD Locode:** FR SET

Key to Principal Facilities:—				
A=Airport	**C**=Containers	**G**=General Cargo	**P**=Petroleum	**R**=Ro/Ro	**Y**=Dry Bulk
B=Bunkers	**D**=Dry Dock	**L**=Cruise	**Q**=Other Liquid Bulk	**T**=Towage (where available from port)	

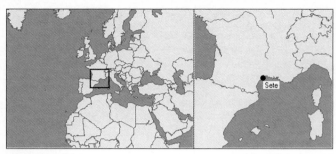

Principal Facilities:

P	Q	Y	G	C	R	L	B		T	A

Authority: Port de Sete, 2 Quai Philippe Regy, P O Box 169, F-34203 Sete, France, *Tel:* +33 4 67 46 35 01, *Fax:* +33 4 67 46 28 18, *Email:* jean-louis.catanzano@sete.cci.fr, *Website:* www.sete.port.fr

Officials: Port Director: Jean-Louis Catanzano.

Approach: Tankers must proceed through a compulsory fairway running 326° from the landing buoy in pos 43° 14' 54" N; 3° 53' 42" E

Anchorage: Anchorage can be obtained in the roadstead S of the breakwater

Pilotage: Compulsory for vessels over 55 m loa, Tel: +33 4 67 74 34 06, Fax: +33 4 67 74 89 95, Email: pilotes.sete@wanadoo.fr. Vessels should send a request for pilots and ETA 24 h in advance (between 0700-2000). Pilot boards 1-3 nautical miles S of Epi Dellon in good weather, or off the Eastern entrance during bad weather

Radio Frequency: VHF Channels 12 and 16

Traffic: 2006, 913 vessels, 3 420 413 t of cargo handled

Working Hours: 0800-1200, 1400-1800. Work on general cargo, timber and containers stops 20 min earlier; overtime possible

Accommodation: Deep water harbour well protected by a breakwater, 2.4 km long, running E-W and forming two entrances. The Eastern entrance can accommodate vessels up to 13.18 m d, whilst the Western entrance is only used for fishing boats and yachts
The northern dock, Bassin du Midi, is linked to the southern group of docks by a canal which can take vessels of 140 m loa, 20 m beam and 7 m d

Name	Length (m)	Draught (m)	Remarks
Darse 2			
I3	197	13.18	Coal & ore for bulk carriers up to 80 000 dwt, 240 m loa
I2		13.18	Dolphin berth. Loading berth for canal boats
I1		13.18	
H1 & 2		13.18	Cement terminal
Colbert			
E1	435	11	Container terminal & general cargo
E2	435	10.4	Container terminal
E3	435	10.4	Forest products
G3	342	11	Forest products
G2	342	11	See [1] below
G1		7.6	
Bassin aux Petroles			
P1	175	10.5	Tankers, oil, alcohol, molasses
P2		11	Tankers up to 40 000 dwt, refined products
Avant-Port			
Masselin	170	10.36	Bulk grain terminal
Orsetti			
D1 & 2	447	8.55	General cargo
D3	447	8.25	General cargo
B2	303	8.25	Passenger terminal
B1	303	8.25	General cargo
Nouveau Bassin			
Maroc (37)	130	7.6	Passenger terminal
Alger (36)	250	8.2	Passenger, cruise vessels
Alger (35)	250	8.2	Passenger, cruise vessels
Canal Maritime			
A5	216	4.6	Livestock, wine
A6	216	5	Wine
Orient (7-9)	301	5.5	Wine
Riquet (10)	300	5.5	Wine
Riquet (11)	300	6.4	Wine
Riquet (12)	300	6.4	Livestock; waiting berth
Maillol (27-29)	326	5.2–5.8	Waiting berths
Midi			
Sud (14)	235	7	Livestock, timber poles
Sud (15)	235	6.1	Fertiliser
Nord (16-18)	575	5.2–6.6	Ore
Nord (19-20)	575	5.8–6.3	Waiting berths
Canal Lateral			
Vauban (25)	200	3.7	Wine
Vauban (24)	200	4.6	Waiting berth
Bosq (21)	90	4.9	Wine
Sea Berth			
CBM		13.1	Tankers up to 100 000 dwt, refined products only

[1]*G2:* Fertilisers, molasses; three molasses tanks, cap 18 000 t

Storage: Cold store (-15°C) of 2500 m3; freezer centre (-25°C) of 3000 m3

Location	Covered (m²)	Sheds / Warehouses	Grain (t)
Sete	46600	14	
Masselin			21600

Mechanical Handling Equipment:

Location	Type	Capacity (t)	Qty
Sete	Floating Cranes	135	1
Sete	Mult-purp. Cranes	20	24

Bunkering: BP France S.A., Immeuble le Cervier, 12 Avenue des Beguines, Cergy-Saint-Christophe, 95866 Cergy Pontoise Cedex, France, *Tel:* +33 1 3422 4000, *Fax:* +33 1 3422 4417, *Email:* benoist.grosjean@fr.bp.com, *Website:* www.bpmarine.com – *Grades:* IF180-380cSt; MDO – *Parcel Size:* 25t – *Delivery Mode:* pipeline, barge, truck
ExxonMobil Marine Fuels, Mailpoint 31, ExxonMobil House, Ermyn Way, Leatherhead, Surrey KT22 8UX, United Kingdom, *Tel:* +44 1372 222 000, *Fax:* +44 1372 223 922, *Email:* marine.fuels@exxonmobil.com, *Website:* www.exxonmobil.com
Ocean Energy S.A.M., c/o Ocean Energy SAM, 57 Rue Grimaldi, Le Panorama Bloc C/D, MC 98000 Monte Carlo, Monaco, *Tel:* +377 9325 5331, *Fax:* +377 9325 5332, *Email:* oceanenergy@oceanenergy.mc, *Website:* www.oceanenergy.mc
Societe des Petroles Shell, 89 Boulevard Franklin Roosevelt, 92564 Rueil-Malmasion, F-76650 Petit Couronne, France, *Tel:* +33 2 35 67 47 03, *Fax:* +33 2 35 67 47 03
Total France S.A., Total Marine Fuels, 51 Esplanade du General de Gaulle, F-92907 Paris la Defense Cedex 10, France, *Tel:* +33 1 4135 2755, *Fax:* +33 1 4197 0291, *Email:* marine.fuels@total.com, *Website:* www.marinefuels.total.com

Towage: Compagnie Setoise de Remorquage et de Sauvetage, Sete, France, *Tel:* +33 4 67 74 23 56

Repair & Maintenance: Claverie Industrie, Sete, France, *Tel:* +33 4 67 48 63 52
Sonelec, E-Mar S.a.r.l, 9 Promenade JB Marty, 34200 Sete, France, *Tel:* +33 4 67 74 06 83, *Fax:* +33 4 67 46 16 96, *Email:* service.com@e-mar.fr

Shipping Agents: Agena Tramp, Gare Maritime Orsetti, Zone Portuaire, F-34200 Sete Cedex 13, France, *Tel:* +33 4 67 80 75 45, *Fax:* +33 4 67 80 75 49, *Email:* sete@agenatramp.fr, *Website:* www.agenatramp.fr
Biron S.A., 2 Quai d'Orient, P O Box 156, F-34203 Sete Cedex, France, *Tel:* +33 4 67 74 88 80, *Fax:* +33 4 67 48 39 55, *Email:* biron.sa@wanadoo.fr
CLB Liner, Gare Maritime, Orsetti Zone Portuaire, F-34200 Sete, France, *Tel:* +33 4 67 80 75 40, *Fax:* +33 4 67 80 75 49, *Email:* sete@clbliner.fr
CMA-CGM S.A., Comptoir General Maritime Seteois (CGMS), Zone Portuaire, P O Box 101, F-34200 Sete, France, *Tel:* +33 4 67 43 90 08, *Fax:* +33 4 99 04 92 30, *Email:* mrs.dmarquer@cma-cgm.com, *Website:* www.cma-cgm.com
COGEMA, ZI des Eaux Blanches, P O Box 101, F-34200 Sete, France, *Tel:* +33 4 67 46 81 81, *Fax:* +33 4 67 46 81 60, *Email:* sqf.shipping@sdv.com
Ferrari Shipping Agency, 21 Quai d'Alger, P O Box 84315, F-34204 Sete Cedex, France, *Tel:* +33 4 99 04 97 67, *Fax:* +33 4 67 18 81 34, *Email:* sete@ferrarishippingagency.com
Groupe Navitrans, Zone Portuaire, 34200 Sete, France, *Tel:* +33 4 67 48 62 20, *Fax:* +33 4 67 48 41 45, *Website:* www.navitrans.fr
Sea Invest Shipping Agency, Zone Portuaire, P O Box 17, F-34200 Sete, France, *Tel:* +33 4 67 51 63 10, *Fax:* +33 4 67 74 33 04, *Email:* trampset@sea-invest-france.com
Services Portuaires Setois (SPS), Zone Portuaire, P O Box 101, 34202 Sete, France, *Tel:* +33 4 67 46 81 81, *Fax:* +33 4 67 46 81 60, *Email:* shipping@sps.com
Sogena, Zone Portuaire Bassin Orsetti, P O Box 135, 34200 Sete, France, *Tel:* +33 4 67 18 60 45, *Fax:* +33 4 67 48 72 80, *Email:* sogena.sete@wanadoo.fr, *Website:* www.sogena.com

Stevedoring Companies: Services Portuaires Setois (SPS), Zone Portuaires, P O Box 101, 34202 Sete, France, *Tel:* +33 4 67 46 81 81, *Fax:* +33 4 67 46 81 60, *Email:* shipping@sps.com
Sogena, Zone Portuaire Bassin Orsetti, P O Box 135, 34200 Sete, France, *Tel:* +33 4 67 18 60 45, *Fax:* +33 4 67 48 72 80, *Email:* sogena.sete@wanadoo.fr, *Website:* www.sogena.com

Medical Facilities: Available, Sanitary Port Control, Tel: +33 4 67 74 32 04. Hospital, 2 km from port, Tel: +33 4 67 51 13 13

Airport: Frejorgues Airport, 28 km

Railway: SNCF, 2 km

Lloyd's Agent: Unilex Maritime S.a.r.l, Les Docks, 10 Place de la Joliette, Atrium 10.8, F-13002 Marseilles Cedex 02, France, *Tel:* +33 4 91 14 04 40, *Fax:* +33 4 91 91 54 43, *Email:* mail@unilexmaritime.com, *Website:* www.unilexmaritime.com

ST. LOUIS DU RHONE

Lat 43° 23' N; Long 4° 49' E.

Admiralty Chart: 155		**Admiralty Pilot:** 46	
Time Zone: GMT +1 h		**UNCTAD Locode:** FR PSL	

Principal Facilities:

P	Q		G		R			T	A

Authority: Grand Port Maritime de Marseille, Quai de la Lecque, P O Box 200, F-13110 Port de Bouc Cedex, France, *Tel:* +33 4 42 40 60 05, *Fax:* + 33 4 42 40 60 40, *Email:* m.bonvalet@marseille-port.fr, *Website:* www.marseille-port.fr

Officials: Commercial Director: Monica Bonvalet, *Tel:* +33 4 91 39 43 22.
Harbour Master: Joseph Moysan, *Tel:* +33 4 91 39 41 40, *Email:* j.moysan@marseille-port.fr.

Port Security: ISPS compliant

Pre-Arrival Information: Vessel Traffic Service: The Marseilles/Fos Maritime Traffic Service (STM) is compulsory for all commercial vessels. The area of authority of the STM comprises a marine operating area and a port operating area:
(a) within the limits administered by the GPMM
(b) within the administrative limits of the installations and constructions entrusted to the GPMM
(c) within the area of jurisdiction of the GPMM
(d) in the channels and approaches to the Golfe de Fos and to the Port of Marseilles for vessels transporting hydrocarbons and dangerous substances
The Fos area lies between longitudes 4° 41.3' E (Faraman Lt) and 5° 06.5' E (Sausset-les-Pins Lt), latitude 43° 11.9' N (Le Planier Lt) and the shore, including the Canal Saint-Louis, Port-Saint-Louis-du-Rhone, the Canal de Caronte and the Etang de Berre. Fos Port Control, Tel: +33 4 42 40 60 60. Maritime Traffic Service Centre on VHF Channels 12 and 73. Vessels manoeuvring in the port on VHF Channels 72 and 77
Communications:
(a) communication on VHF Channel 12 and 73 must be established as early as possible between vessels and the Maritime Traffic Service (STM) Centre
(b) vessels unable to contact the STM may not cross the Cap Couronne line (43° 19.5' N)
(c) vessels on passage, manoeuvring and at anchor in any part of the area controlled by the STM must maintain a listening watch on VHF Channel 12
(d) conversations should take place in French and English using standard IMO terminology
(e) pilots can be contacted on VHF Channel 14
Vessels transporting hydrocarbons and dangerous substances must send a SURNAV message 6 h prior to entry into French territorial waters
Vessels inward-bound must contact the STM as follows:
(a) 48 h before arrival at the pilot boarding position, through the agent stating
(i) vessels name and call sign
(ii) destination and port of departure
(iii) draught
(iv) cargo
(v) loa, beam and gt
(vi) type of vessel
(vii) ETA
(b) at least 24 h before arrival stating:
(i) ETA at pilot boarding position
(ii) draught
(iii) nature and tonnage of transported dangerous substances
(iv) loa
(c) 6 h before entry into French territorial waters, vessels transporting hydrocarbons or dangerous substances must send a SURNAV message
(d) on entering the area offshore of the entrance, all vessels over 50 m loa on passage to the Golfe de Fos must report to the STM on VHF Channel 12 stating:
(i) vessels name and call sign
(ii) position
(iii) course and speed
(iv) ETA
The STM will give permission to proceed along the approach channel starting at the Fairway (Omega) Lt Buoy, and will provide information on traffic movements and weather conditions in the area
(e) the STM will advise berthing details and a time for pilot boarding, as well as any towing requiirements if not already specified
(f) the STM will also advise VHF communication details as follows:
(i) at the entrance to the STM area
(ii) at the entrance to the approach channel for vessels obliged to use the channels (vessels over 1600 gt transporting hydrocarbons or dangerous substances) for Fos or Marseilles
(iii) at the entrance to the approach channel for vessels not obliged to use the channels. After identifying and authorising the vessel, the STM will instruct the vessel to proceed if the vessel is subject to an inspection by a surveyor
(g) vessels over 1600 gt transporting hydrocarbons or dangerous substances may not enter the approach channel (N of 43° 12.0' N) without the authorisation of the STM
(h) in the event of a doubtful identity, the STM will call every vessel it considers to be likely until a positive identity is obtained
Vessels in the area:
(a) all vessels must contact the STM on VHF before entering the port, getting under way or changing berths
(b) all vessels crossing (or in cases of emergency, anchoring or waiting in) the approach channel, which vessels transporting dangerous cargo are obliged to use, must inform the STM immediately
(c) all vessels wishing to anchor in the Golfe de Fos to the N of the dredged channel must obtain prior permission from the STM. A continuous listening watch must be maintained on VHF Channel 12 while at the anchorage
(d) all vessels wishing to proceed along the Canal de Caronte or the Canal Saint-Louis must request instructions from the STM
(e) all vessels transporting hydrocarbons or dangerous substances in the transhipment area of the Golfe de Fos must maintain a continuous listening watch on VHF Channel 12
(f) leisure craft must contact the Harbour Master for all movements within the port (entering, leaving or making way)
(g) vessels may only enter the dredged channel (from the Lavera Lt Buoy to the harbour basins) after checking with the STM that no other vessel has commenced passage along the channel

Approach: The port has access to the sea by a canal 3.0 km long and a channel 2 km long; and then with the Rhone by a sluice 132 m long and 22 m wide; the depth of water is 5.5 m at the sides and 7.0 m in the centre

Pilotage: The compulsory pilotage area consists of an area N of latitude 43° 19' N between the meridians of Faramen Lt (4° 41.3' E) and Cap Couronne Lt (5° 03.3' E),

including the canals, the harbour basins of the inner harbours, the Rhone as far as Arles and the Etang de Berre
Marseilles/Fos Office, Tel: +33 4 91 14 29 10, Fax: +33 4 91 56 65 79, Email: pilote13@nerim.fr
Golfe de Fos Pilotage, Tel: +33 4 42 06 21 01
VHF Channels 12 and 14
Pilotage is available 24/h day and compulsory for vessels of all categories over 50 m loa and all vessels over 70 m loa on passage to or from Darse 2 (Harbour Basin 2) Container Terminal and Darse 3 (Harbour Basin 3) berths in the Port of Fos, except for vessels transporting hydrocarbons or dangerous substances
Vessels must report ETA with at least 24 h notice (or as soon as leaving the previous port) to the Port de Bouc Harbour Master stating:
(a) loa
(b) draught (forward and aft)
(c) nature and tonnage of any dangerous cargo
Vessels must establish VHF contact with the Port de Bouc Harbour Master as early as possible
Pilot boards in the following positions:
(a) vessels transporting hydrocarbons or dangerous cargo and deep draught vessels on passage to Fos at the latitude of Cap Couronne Lt (43° 19.5' N)
(b) vessels bound for Port de Bouc, Lavera, Etang de Berre and St. Louis du Rhone between 2.5-4 nautical miles S of Lavera Lt Buoy (43° 22.6' N; 4° 58.2' E)
(c) on request between latitudes 43° 11.9' N and 43° 19.6' N
The pilotage sub-station at Port de Bouc provides pilots for Lavera, Canal de Caronte, Martigues, Etang de Berre, Fos and St. Louis du Rhone. This station comes under the authority of the Marseilles/Golfe de Fos Pilotage Office

Accommodation:

Name	Length (m)	Draught (m)	Remarks
St. Louis du Rhone			See [1] below
Suisse Quay (Berth 911)	130	7.5	Fishing
Suisse Quay (Berth 912)	130	7.5	Fishing
Suisse Quay (Berth 913)	200	6.8	General cargo
Tellines Quay (Berth 951)	120	7.2	Ro/ro
Tellines Quay (Berth 952)	130	7	Ro/ro, fertilisers
Tellines Quay (Berth 953)	128	7.2	Heavy loads
Tellines Quay (Berth 954)	124	7.9	Ro/ro, heavy loads
Esquineau Quay (Berth 932)	90	5.4	Salt
Frahuil Jetty (Berth 925)	120	5.5	Animal & vegetable oils
P.P.G. Jetty (Berth 916)	110	6	Refined petroleum
CREA (Berth 924)	100	3.5	Refined petroleum
Mavrac (Berth 919)	160	7.62	VCM, chemicals
Soterm (Berth 923)	110	6.2	Alcohol

[1]*St. Louis du Rhone:* Total berths 23. Total length of quays 2050 m made up of 18 berths and 5 jetties. 5 berths of less than 6 m, 17 berths of 6-8 m, 16 are public berths, 7 are private berths, two public quays (4 berths) alongside dolphins, four private jetties alongside dolphin. The draught for vessels arriving at the berths in the traditional basin, Berths 901, 908 and 909 are restricted to 6.8 m. Only berths located in the Tellines Basin and the access canal can accommodate vessels up to 7.92 m. Berths 902-907 are reserved for yachts
Four ro/ro berths available, including one for river barges, located in Tellines Dock. There is also a ro/ro berth in the St. Louis du Rhone old dock, Berth No.909, 130 m long, 6.5 m max d equipped with a 135.5 m wide ro/ro ramp

Storage: Transit sheds with a total area of 20 000 m2 and open storage space of 260 000 m2. Storage cap for animal and vegetable oils. The Frahuil jetty is 40 000 t, chemical products at Medistock jetty is 20 625 t and Goudron at Derives jetty is 8800 t

Mechanical Handling Equipment:

Location	Type
St. Louis du Rhone	Mobile Cranes

Towage: Available

Medical Facilities: Available from St. Louis du Rhone, Fos, Port de Bouc and Martigues

Airport: Marseille-Provence Airport, 80 km

Lloyd's Agent: Unilex Maritime S.a.r.l, Les Docks, 10 Place de la Joliette, Atrium 10.8, F-13002 Marseilles Cedex 02, France, *Tel:* +33 4 91 14 04 40, *Fax:* +33 4 91 91 54 43, *Email:* mail@unilexmaritime.com, *Website:* www.unilexmaritime.com

ST. MALO

Lat 48° 38' N; Long 2° 1' W.

Admiralty Chart: 2700	**Admiralty Pilot:** 27
Time Zone: GMT +1 h	**UNCTAD Locode:** FR SML

Principal Facilities:

P	Q	Y	G	C	R	L	B	D	T	A

Authority: Chambre de Commerce et d'Industrie, Port de Commerce, Outillage, 32 Bd de la Republique, F-35400 St. Malo, France, *Tel:* +33 2 99 20 51 00, *Fax:* +33 2 99 56 52 78, *Email:* ports@saint-malo.cci.fr, *Website:* www.saint-malo.cci.fr

Officials: Port Manager: Christian Fauvel, *Tel:* +33 2 99 20 64 40.
Harbour Master: Capt Bruno Lassus, *Tel:* +33 2 99 20 25 00, *Email:* bruno.lassus@equipement.gouv.fr.

Port Security: ISPS compliant

Approach: Outer Harbour protected by stone pier 574 m long

Pilotage: Compulsory for vessels over 150 nrt. Pilot Station, Tel: +33 2 99 81 61 66, Fax: +33 2 99 82 11 25. Radio: VHF Channel 12. Charges on application

Tides: St Malo has one of the largest tidal ranges in the world, therefore operators are recommended to contact the Chamber of Sworn Shipbrokers for precise information for any given period, Tel: (2) 99 20 63 00

Maximum Vessel Dimensions: Size restricted to 150 m length, 21 m beam and 9 m max d. Vessels up to 16 000 dwt have been accommodated

Working Hours: Monday-Saturday 0800-1200, 1400-1800. Overtime possible

Accommodation: Docks with 4500 m of quay, giving access to entrance locks to St Malo-St Servan wet docks. Vessels always afloat. Entrance by Main Lock: length 160 m, width 25 m, sill depth is 1.75 m over zero on marine charts. Lock regularly manned from 2.5 h before and after HW, but arrangements can be made for the admission of vessels outside these periods providing there is sufficient depth of water; although at an extra charge. There are rail connections to all quays

Name	Length (m)	Draught (m)	Remarks
Vauban			
Saint Louis	403	6–8	Three berths. Cruise vessels can be accommodated
Des Corsaires	315	9	Three berths. One ro/ro berth
Duguay Trouin			
Duguay Trouin	770	6–7.2	Seven berths
Surcouf	730	5.6–6.6	Six berths
Terre Neuve	255	4.8–5.7	Three berths
Bouvet			
Nord	536	5.7	Five berths
Ouest	105	5.7	
Du Val	285	4–5	For fishing craft only
Trichet	366	4–5	Gravel dredgers and small craft repair
Jacques Cartier			
Chateaubriand	300	8–9	Two berths. One ro/ro berth
Avant-Port			
Poste Car Ferry			See [1] below
Hydrofoils & Fast Passenger Craft			Two terminals for Channel Islands service

[1]*Poste Car Ferry:* Car Ferry Terminals: One berth ramp with depth 7 m at HIS head

Storage: 31 000 m2 of warehouses, and bonded warehouses. Phosphoric acid terminal of 11 500 t cap

Mechanical Handling Equipment:

Location	Type	Capacity (t)	Qty
St. Malo	Mobile Cranes	40	6
St. Malo	Electric Cranes	4–12	8

Bunkering: Petroles de la France (Total), P O Box 102, F-35407 St. Malo, France, *Tel:* +33 2 99 82 23 23, *Fax:* +33 2 99 82 16 83
BP France S.A., Immeuble le Cervier, 12 Avenue des Beguines, Cergy-Saint-Christophe, 95866 Cergy Pontoise Cedex, France, *Tel:* +33 1 3422 4000, *Fax:* +33 1 3422 4417, *Email:* benoist.grosjean@fr.bp.com, *Website:* www.bpmarine.com
Petroles de la France (Total), P O Box 102, F-35407 St. Malo, France, *Tel:* +33 2 99 82 23 23, *Fax:* +33 2 99 82 16 83

Towage: Three motor tugs of 600, 1360 and 1830 hp to assist ships berthing and compulsory for vessels exceeding 100 m loa

Repair & Maintenance: One dry dock for vessels up to 120 m loa, 15.5 m beam and 8 m d. A slipway to accommodate vessels up to 300 t and 45 m long is situated in the Bouvet Basin

Ship Chandlers: R.& G. Dekytspotter Atlantic, Quai de Terre Neuve, F-35400 St. Malo, France, *Tel:* +33 2 99 40 13 22, *Fax:* +33 2 40 92 13 69, *Email:* dksupply@dekytspotter.com

Shipping Agents: Societe Malouine et Granvillaise, Chaussee des Corsaires, P O Box 3, F-35401 St. Malo, France, *Tel:* +33 2 99 56 33 81, *Fax:* +33 2 99 40 12 10, *Email:* j.kerhoas@sdv.com

Stevedoring Companies: Societe Malouine et Granvillaise, Chaussee des Corsaires, P O Box 3, F-35401 St. Malo, France, *Tel:* +33 2 99 56 33 81, *Fax:* +33 2 99 40 12 10, *Email:* j.kerhoas@sdv.com

Airport: Dinard, 14 km

Railway: Gare de St. Malo, 2 km

Lloyd's Agent: Agence Maritime Roy s.a.r.l., 2 Chaussee des Corsaires, P O Box 179, F-35409 St. Malo, France, *Tel:* +33 2 99 56 07 21, *Fax:* +33 2 99 40 24 00, *Email:* agence-maritime-roy@wanadoo.fr

ST. NAZAIRE

Lat 47° 16' N; Long 2° 12' W.

Admiralty Chart: 2985	Admiralty Pilot: 22
Time Zone: GMT +1 h	UNCTAD Locode: FR SNR

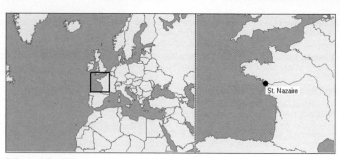

Principal Facilities:

P		Y	G	C	R		B	D	T	A

Authority: Grand Port Maritime de Nantes-St.Nazaire, 18 Quai Ernest Renaud, P O Box 18609, F-44186 Nantes Cedex 4, France, *Tel:* +33 2 40 44 71 41, *Fax:* +33 2 40 44 20 01, *Email:* ser.com@nantes.port.fr, *Website:* www.nantes.port.fr

Officials: Managing Director: Francois Marendet, *Email:* f.marendet@nantes.port.fr.
Harbour Master: Capt Yves Jaouen, *Email:* y.jaouen@nantes.port.fr.

Port Security: ISPS compliant

Approach: Access by sea channel dredged to 12.85 m depth LT from Charpentier roads to the port. Outer harbour and lock dredged to 5 m depth LT

Pilotage: Compulsory for vessels exceeding 75 m loa. VHF Channels 16 and 12, Tel: +33 (2) 51 76 08 76, Fax: 51 76 08 75

Tides: NT 2 m, ST 6 m

Traffic: 2007, 34 004 048 t of cargo handled (includes ports of Donges, Nantes & Montoir)

Maximum Vessel Dimensions: 180 m loa, 8.5 m d, 28 m breadth, South lock

Working Hours: Shifts 0600-1400, 1400-2200, normal hours 0800-1200, 1400-1800

Accommodation:

Name	Length (m)	Draught (m)	Remarks
St. Nazaire			See [1] below
Old Basin	1744	8.5	See [2] below
Penhoet Basin	2261	8.5	See [3] below

[1]*St. Nazaire:* Port is absolutely safe and well sheltered. South outer harbour entrance between pierheads 123.74 m wide. South entrance lock leads from South outer harbour to the Old Basin. Length of lock 211 m, width 30 m, depths 9 m. East entrance lock 53 m by 7.16 m HWOST
Bulk facilities: Available for soya beans, phosphate and grain
[2]*Old Basin:* Has an area of 10.5 ha and includes Joubert Dock which is 350 m x 50 m x 13.41 m HWOST
[3]*Penhoet Basin:* Has an area of 22 ha and an entrance width from Old basin of 34 m

Storage: 2300 m2 of refrigerated space

Location	Covered (m²)	Grain (t)
St. Nazaire	19000	10000

Mechanical Handling Equipment:

Location	Type	Capacity (t)	Qty	Remarks
St. Nazaire	Mult-purp. Cranes	400	1	See [1] below
St. Nazaire	Mobile Cranes	4	2	
Old Basin	Mult-purp. Cranes	14	1	At Joubert Dock
Old Basin	Mult-purp. Cranes	60	1	At Joubert Dock
Penhoet Basin	Mult-purp. Cranes	10	6	
Penhoet Basin	Mult-purp. Cranes	12	2	

[1]*St. Nazaire:* for handling of heavy industrial machinery

Bunkering: BP France S.A., Immeuble le Cervier, 12 Avenue des Beguines, Cergy-Saint-Christophe, 95866 Cergy Pontoise Cedex, France, *Tel:* +33 1 3422 4000, *Fax:* +33 1 3422 4417, *Email:* benoist.grosjean@fr.bp.com, *Website:* www.bpmarine.com
Societe des Petroles Shell, 89 Boulevard Franklin Roosevelt, 92564 Rueil-Malmaison, F-76650 Petit Couronne, France, *Tel:* +33 2 35 67 47 03, *Fax:* +33 2 35 67 47 03 – *Grades:* GO – *Delivery Mode:* truck
Total France S.A., Total Marine Fuels, 51 Esplanade du General de Gaulle, F-92907 Paris la Defense Cedex 10, France, *Tel:* +33 1 4135 2755, *Fax:* +33 1 4197 0291, *Email:* marine.fuels@total.com, *Website:* www.marinefuels.total.com

Towage: Boluda Nantes-St. Nazaire, 1 bis, boulevard de Verdun, P O Box 134, F-44603 St. Nazaire, France, *Tel:* +33 2 40 22 49 82, *Fax:* +33 2 40 22 51 93, *Email:* les-abeilles-st-nazaire@bourbon-online.com

Repair & Maintenance: Reparation Navale Nazairienne (R2N), Quai des Fregates, P O Box 10323, F-44615 St. Nazaire, France, *Tel:* +33 2 40 22 94 05, *Fax:* +33 2 40 19 00 53, *Email:* contact@saint-nazaire-marine.com, *Website:* www.saint-nazaire-marine.com Four graving docks: 'Louis Joubert' 350 m x 50 m, No.1 226 m x 30 m, No.2 117 m x 11 m, No.3 159 m x 17 m

Ship Chandlers: R.& G. Dekytspotter Atlantic, 12 rue du Chene Lasse, P O Box 57, F-44801 St. Herblain Cedex, France, *Tel:* +33 2 40 92 16 05, *Fax:* +33 2 40 92 13 69, *Email:* dksupply@dekytspotter.com, *Website:* www.dekytspotter.com

Surveyors: Det Norske Veritas A/S, Aprolis VI, 7 Rue Etoile du Matin, F-44600 St. Nazaire, France, *Tel:* +33 2 51 76 62 63, *Fax:* +33 2 51 76 62 64, *Email:* saintnazaire@dnv.com, *Website:* www.dnv.com

Medical Facilities: St. Nazaire Hospital, Tel: +33 (2) 40 90 60 60

Airport: Nantes Atlantic, 60 km

Lloyd's Agent: AMS Ouest, 5 Bd Vincent Gache, P O Box 36204, F-44000 Nantes, France, *Tel:* +33 2 40 41 73 84, *Fax:* +33 2 40 41 73 92, *Email:* westoffice@associated-marine-services.com

STRASBOURG

Lat 48° 34' N; Long 7° 42' E.

Admiralty Chart: 192/122/1406
Admiralty Pilot: 28
Time Zone: GMT +1 h
UNCTAD Locode: FR SXB

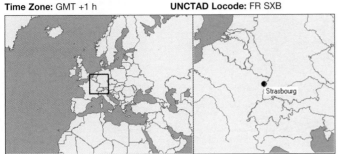

Principal Facilities:

P	Q	Y	G	C	R	L	B		T	A

Authority: Port Autonome de Strasbourg, 25 Rue de la Nuee Bleue, P O Box 407/R2, F-67010 Strasbourg Cedex, France, *Tel:* +33 3 88 21 74 74, *Fax:* +33 3 88 23 56 57, *Email:* pas@strasbourg.port.fr, *Website:* www.strasbourg.port.fr

Officials: Director: Jean-Louis Jerome, *Email:* jerome@strasbourg.port.fr.
Deputy Director: Martial Gerlinger, *Email:* m.gerlinger@strasbourg.port.fr.
Commercial Director: Jean-Marc Uhrweiller, *Email:* jm.uhrweiller@strasbourg.port.fr.

Approach: Accessible to any vessel that can navigate the Rhine. Depth of river is normally between 2.5 and 4.5 m. There are two locks, North and South, both 125 m long, 13.5 m beam. Also a bridge, air draught of 8.8 m

Pilotage: Optional. Pilot available at the port of Kehl, opposite Strasbourg

Radio Frequency: Ship to ship communications on VHF Channel 10, North Lock Channel 11, South Lock Channel 20

Traffic: 2005, 8 400 000 t of cargo handled, 183 420 TEU's

Working Hours: 0745-1145, 1345-1700

Accommodation:

Name	Remarks
Strasbourg	See [1] below

[1]*Strasbourg:* Several loading and unloading installations for cereals and fertilisers. The Plurimodal International Transport Centre (Eurofret Strasbourg) in the S part of the port covers an area of 110 ha and offers a large range of services
There are two specialised installations for reception, repair, storage and distribution of containers which is combined with transhipment equipment for heavy loads (up to 350 t)
Bulk facilities: There are mooring berths with grain aspirators, seventeen conveyor belt facilities along the river for loading gravel and hydrocarbon pumping stations in the oil dock

Storage: Storage cap: hydrocarbons 420 000 m3, cereals 500 000 t, general cargo 600 000 m2 of covered storage

Mechanical Handling Equipment:

Location	Type	Capacity (t)	Qty
Strasbourg	Floating Cranes		2
Strasbourg	Mult-purp. Cranes	2–240	25

Bunkering: Gas oil and drinking water distributed by special ships, Tel: +33 (3) 88 61 26 78

Waste Reception Facilities: Societe SITAL, Strasbourg, France, *Tel:* +33 3 88 65 68 30, *Fax:* +33 3 88 65 68 49

Towage: Three tug-boats and one pusher

Medical Facilities: Emergency, Tel: 15

Airport: Strasbourg International, 10 km

Railway: Strasbourg, approx 3 km

Lloyd's Agent: McLarens Young France S.A, 80 Boulevard Haussmann, F-75008 Paris, France, *Tel:* +33 1 44 70 66 10, *Fax:* +33 1 43 87 40 16, *Email:* paris@mclarensyoung.com, *Website:* www.mclarensyoung.com

TARNOS AVAL

harbour area, see under Bayonne

TONNAY CHARENTE

Lat 45° 57' N; Long 0° 53' W.

Admiralty Chart: 2747
Admiralty Pilot: 22
Time Zone: GMT +1 h
UNCTAD Locode: FR TON

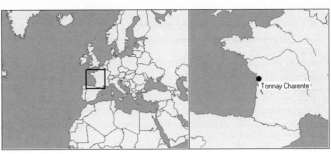

Principal Facilities:

		Y	G							A

Authority: Port de Commerce de Rochefort Tonnay-Charente, P O Box 20129, F-17306 Rochefort, France, *Tel:* +33 5 46 99 58 16, *Fax:* +33 5 46 99 58 73, *Email:* info@rochefort.port.fr, *Website:* www.rochefort.port.fr

Officials: Managing Director: Francis Grimaud, *Tel:* +33 5 46 99 58 69, *Email:* f.grimaud@rochefort.cci.fr.
Harbour Master: Fabrice Brunetti, *Email:* fabrice.brunetti@cg17.fr.

Anchorage: Available at 'Aix Island Anchorage Area'

Pilotage: Compulsory for vessels over 45 m loa

Radio Frequency: Harbour Master's Office on VHF Channel 12. Pilot Station on VHF Channels 16 or 74

Weather: Prevailing w'ly winds

Traffic: 2005, 1 012 945 t of cargo handled (includes Rochefort)

Maximum Vessel Dimensions: 120 m loa, 6.5 m draught

Working Hours: Mon-Fri 0700-1200, 1400-1800. Overtime available until 2200 and Saturday mornings

Accommodation:

Name	Length (m)	Draught (m)	Remarks
Tonnay Charente			Also three waiting berths for vessels up to 110 m loa
Jetty No.2	200	5.7–6.5	See [1] below
Silo Berth	90	6.5	See [2] below

[1]*Jetty No.2:* Two berths. Silo wharf for vessels up to 120 m loa. Cereal elevator at rate of 300 t/h
[2]*Silo Berth:* For vessels up to 120 m loa and 5500 dwt. Cereal elevator of silo (Sicatlantique) at rate of 600 t/h

Storage:

Location	Grain (t)
Tonnay Charente	20000

Mechanical Handling Equipment:

Location	Type	Capacity (t)	Qty
Tonnay Charente	Mobile Cranes	6–8	2

Airport: La Rochelle, 40 km. Rochefort, 6 km

Lloyd's Agent: Jean-Francois Chevreau, Bourse Maritime, Place Laine, F-33000 Bordeaux, France, *Tel:* +33 5 56 52 16 87, *Fax:* +33 5 56 44 67 85, *Email:* info@chevreau-lavie.fr, *Website:* www.chevreau-lavie.com

TOULON

Lat 43° 7' N; Long 5° 55' E.

Admiralty Chart: 149
Admiralty Pilot: 46
Time Zone: GMT +1 h
UNCTAD Locode: FR TLN

Principal Facilities:

	Y	G	C	R	L	B	D	T	A

Authority: Chambre de Commerce et d'Industrie du Var, Direction des Ports et Affaires Maritimes, 663 Av. de la 1ere Armee Francaise, F-83500 La Seyne-sur-Mer, France, *Tel:* +33 4 94 22 80 80, *Fax:* +33 4 94 22 80 81, *Email:* rene.bartholomei@var.cci.fr, *Website:* www.var.cci.fr

Officials: Managing Director: Bernard Stouff, *Email:* bernard.stouff@var.cci.fr.
Harbour Master: Rene Bartholomei.

Port Security: ISPS compliant. PFSO: Thierry Poirier, Tel: +33 4 94 22 89 08 or +33 6 85 61 43 03
Bay access is strictly regulated thanks to the presence of the French Navy submarine

---

Key to Principal Facilities:—
A=Airport	**C**=Containers	**G**=General Cargo
B=Bunkers	**D**=Dry Dock	**L**=Cruise

P=Petroleum	**R**=Ro/Ro	**Y**=Dry Bulk
Q=Other Liquid Bulk	**T**=Towage (where available from port)	

and aircraft carrier base located across from the port, meaning that ships entering the bay benefit from top-level security and safety

Pre-Arrival Information: Minimum notice for berth request is 24 h or before last call if transit under 24 h

Approach: The port is approached by a channel 125 m wide in depths over 12 m

Anchorage: The triangle anchorage is under control of the Navy, depth 12 m

Pilotage: Compulsory for all vessels over 45 m loa. Pilot station, Tel: +33 4 94 41 03 28, Fax: +33 4 94 41 08 85, Email: pilotes-toulon@wanadoo.fr. Pilot boards 100 m N of the semaphore station 'Cap Cepet'. VHF Channels 16 and 12

Radio Frequency: Harbour Master and Pilot's on VHF Channels 12 and 16. Cepet Navy Signal Station on VHF Channel 16

Weather: Prevailing W'ly winds

Maximum Vessel Dimensions: Toulon: max d 9.5 m. Bregaillon: max d 9.5 m

Working Hours: 24 h/day

Accommodation:

Name	Length (m)	Draught (m)	Remarks
Toulon Cote d'Azur			See [1] below
Fournel Pier	345	9.5	
Minerve Pier	176	7.5	
La Corse Pier	178	7.5	
La Seyne Bregaillon			Dedicated to freight operations
North Terminal	215	9.5	See [2] below
South Terminal	240	7	Heavy loads & barges. Storage area of 9000 m2
Marepolis	330	9.5	Mainly for cruise vessels

[1]*Toulon Cote d'Azur:* Dedicated to cruise, ferries & ro/ro traffic. Three ro/ro ramps and two passenger terminals
[2]*North Terminal:* Automobiles, ro/ro & general cargo traffic. Storage area for new cars of 50 000 m2

Storage:

Location	Open (m²)	Covered (m²)
Toulon Cote d'Azur	18300	
La Seyne Bregaillon	67000	3200

Mechanical Handling Equipment:

Location	Type	Capacity (t)	Qty
North Terminal	Mobile Cranes	26	2

Bunkering: BP France S.A., Immeuble le Cervier, 12 Avenue des Beguines, Cergy-Saint-Christophe, 95866 Cergy Pontoise Cedex, France, *Tel:* +33 1 3422 4000, *Fax:* +33 1 3422 4417, *Email:* benoist.grosjean@fr.bp.com, *Website:* www.bpmarine.com – *Grades:* IF180-360cSt; MGO – *Parcel Size:* 25t – *Delivery Mode:* pipeline, barge, truck
ExxonMobil Marine Fuels, Mailpoint 31, ExxonMobil House, Ermyn Way, Leatherhead, Surrey KT22 8UX, United Kingdom, *Tel:* +44 1372 222 000, *Fax:* +44 1372 223 922, *Email:* marine.fuels@exxonmobil.com, *Website:* www.exxonmobil.com
Ocean Energy S.A.M., c/o Ocean Energy SAM, 57 Rue Grimaldi, Le Panorama Bloc C/D, MC 98000 Monte Carlo, Monaco, *Tel:* +377 9325 5331, *Fax:* +377 9325 5332, *Email:* oceanenergy@oceanenergy.mc, *Website:* www.oceanenergy.mc
Societe des Petroles Shell, 89 Boulevard Franklin Roosevelt, 92564 Rueil-Malmasion, F-76650 Petit Couronne, France, *Tel:* +33 2 35 67 47 03, *Fax:* +33 2 35 67 47 03
Total France S.A., Total Marine Fuels, 51 Esplanade du General de Gaulle, F-92907 Paris la Defense Cedex 10, France, *Tel:* +33 1 4135 2755, *Fax:* +33 1 4197 0291, *Email:* marine.fuels@total.com, *Website:* www.marinefuels.total.com

Towage: Also several naval tugs available
Societe Nouvelle de Remorquage et de Travaux Maritimes (SNRTM), 1247 Route du Faron, F-83200 Toulon, France, *Tel:* +33 4 94 62 41 14, *Fax:* +33 4 94 09 30 34

Repair & Maintenance: Serra Freres Entreprises Maritimes, 264 Avenue Emile Fabre, F-83200 Toulon, France, *Tel:* +33 4 94 87 93 94

Ship Chandlers: Ets Pons S.A., 12 rue Etienne Pelabon, P O Box 626, F-83053 Toulon Cedex, France, *Tel:* +33 4 94 41 03 72, *Fax:* +33 4 94 36 03 98, *Email:* pons@ets-pons.fr

Shipping Agents: Comptoir General Maritime Varois, Commercial Port of Bregaillon, 663 Avenue 1ere Armee Francaise, 83500 LA Toulon, France, *Tel:* +33 4 94 94 01 09, *Fax:* +33 4 94 94 04 05, *Email:* m.bonnefoy@sdv.com, *Website:* www.sdvope.com
Imbert & Phelippeau, 552 Avenue de la Republique, F-83000 Toulon, France, *Tel:* +33 4 94 41 58 54, *Fax:* +33 4 94 41 30 74, *Email:* info@imbertetphelippeau.com, *Website:* www.imbertetphelippeau.com

Stevedoring Companies: Comptoir General Maritime Varois, Commercial Port of Bregaillon, 663 Avenue 1ere Armee Francaise, 83500 LA Toulon, France, *Tel:* +33 4 94 94 01 09, *Fax:* +33 4 94 94 04 05, *Email:* m.bonnefoy@sdv.com, *Website:* www.sdvope.com

Surveyors: Pages-Bosc-Laurain, 552 Avenue Republique, F-83000 Toulon, France, *Tel:* +33 4 94 41 16 64, *Fax:* +33 4 94 03 77 65

Medical Facilities: Several hospitals available

Airport: Toulon-Hyeres, 20 km. Marseille Provence, 80 km. Nice Cote d'Azur, 150 km

Railway: La Seyne Bregaillon commercial port is fully linked up with the European railway network, with a railway track alongside berth under travelling gantry cranes at the North Terminal

Development: Extended storage area for new cars to 100 000 m2

Lloyd's Agent: Unilex Maritime S.a.r.l, Les Docks, 10 Place de la Joliette, Atrium 10.8, F-13002 Marseilles Cedex 02, France, *Tel:* +33 4 91 14 04 40, *Fax:* +33 4 91 91 54 43, *Email:* mail@unilexmaritime.com, *Website:* www.unilexmaritime.com

TREGUIER

Lat 48° 47' N; Long 3° 14' W.

Admiralty Chart: 3672		**Admiralty Pilot:** 27
Time Zone: GMT +1 h		**UNCTAD Locode:** FR TRE

Principal Facilities:

	Y	G			B		A

Authority: Conseil General des Cotes d'Armor, 3 Place du General de Gaulle, P O Box 2373, F-22000 St. Brieuc, France, *Tel:* +33 2 96 62 62 75, *Fax:* +33 2 96 61 48 16, *Email:* contact@cg22.fr, *Website:* www.cg22.fr

Officials: Commercial Manager: Keith Martin, *Email:* keith.martin@cotesdarmor.cci.fr.
Harbour Master: Alain Leroux, *Email:* alain.leroux@cotesdarmor.cci.fr.

Pre-Arrival Information: Initial ETA should be sent 24 h prior to arrival to Ship's Agents with confirmation at 12 h and 4 h. The first message should include: vessel's name, registry, tonnage, loa, boa, max draft on arrival, preceding port, ETA fairway buoy, nature and quantity of hazardous cargo, general cargo details, any technical problems to vessel or its equipment

Documentation: Crew list, passenger list, stores list, provisions list, crew personal effects list, customs declaration, cargo manifest list, maritime declaration of health, bill of lading, stowage plan (other than bulk cargo), last port clearance, port of call list, bonded stores list, narcotics list, arms & ammunition list
The pilot, on boarding, will provide the IMO approved form for completion by Master concerning the following certificates: load line certificate, safety equipment certificate, certificate of registry, safety radio certificate, safety construction certificate, international oil pollution prevention certificate, derat or derat exemption certificate, international tonnage certificate, oil record book, seamen's books, passports & vaccination certificates

Approach: Channel from Sea Buoy (48° 54.3' N; 03° 11.2' W) is 8 nautical miles long to the port, width 300 m in depth of 7-19 m

Anchorage: Outer Anchorage in pos 48° 51' N; 03° 11' W in depth of 25-30 m La Roche Jaune on the Jaudy River in depth of 7-10 m

Pilotage: Cotes d'Armor Pilotage, Tel: +33 (2) 96 33 03 33, Fax: 96 33 03 33. VHF Channel 12. Pilot normally boards at Crublent Buoy

Radio Frequency: VHF Channel 12 for Harbour Master and Pilots

Weather: Prevailing winds from the west

Tides: 15 m MHWS, 7 m MHWN, 6 m MLWN, 3.2 m MLWS

Traffic: 2000, 74 vessels, 121 650 t of cargo handled

Maximum Vessel Dimensions: 110 m loa without bowthruster and 120 m loa with bowthruster

Principal Imports and Exports: Imports: Animal feedstuffs, Fertilizers, General bulk products, Sand, Sawn timber. Exports: Refractory minerals (Andoulisite).

Working Hours: Mon-Fri 0700-1200, 1330-1800. Overtime on weekday nights. No weekends

Accommodation:

Name	Length (m)	Remarks
Treguier		See [1] below
Cornic (Sand) Quay	75	NAABSA berth drying out at 0.5 m above datum for vessels up to 82.5 m loa
New Quay	75	Dredged to 3 m below datum for vessels up to 120 m loa
Guezennec Quay	85	NAABSA berth drying out to 4 m above datum for vessels up to 90 m loa

[1]*Treguier:* Port Operating Body: Ports Concession, Chambre de Commerce et d'Industrie des Cotes d'Armor, Rue de Guernesey, PO Box 514, F-22005 Saint Brieuc, Tel: +33 2 96 78 62 15, Fax: +33 2 96 78 51 30, Website: www.cotesdarmor.cci.fr
Director, Direction des Equipements du Patrimoine et des Achats: Alain Leroux, Email: alain.leroux@cotesdarmor.cci.fr
Port Officer: Bernard Cohan, Tel: +33 2 96 92 30 79, Fax: +33 2 96 92 30 79

Storage: Open storage area of 2.6 ha and five warehouses totalling 8000 m2

Mechanical Handling Equipment: 2 x 3 t bobcats, 2 x 7 t frontloaders, 1 mobile band loader at 250 t/h, 1 x 38 t road weighbridge

Location	Type	Capacity (t)	Qty
Treguier	Mobile Cranes	30	4
Treguier	Forklifts	7	2

Cargo Worked: Animal feedstuffs 1800 t/day, sawn timber 2000 m3/day, kaolin 1800 t/day, refractory minerals 1800 t/day, scrap metal 800 t/day, grain 1500 t/day

Bunkering: Available by road tanker with 24-48 h notice

Waste Reception Facilities: On demand

Stevedoring Companies: Coralmer, 22220 Treguier, France, *Tel:* +33 2 96 92 29 85, *Fax:* +33 2 96 92 36 06, *Email:* amo@amo-ship.com

Medical Facilities: Local doctors in close proximity to port area. Hospital Lannion, 2 km

Airport: Lannion, 15 km

Railway: Paimpol Station, 15 km

Development: A third berth of 75 m in length and linked to the Cornic and New Quays is planned, thus providing extended quay frontage and a greatly increased terminal area

Lloyd's Agent: Agence Maritime Roy s.a.r.l., 2 Chaussee des Corsaires, P O Box 179, F-35409 St. Malo, France, *Tel:* +33 2 99 56 07 21, *Fax:* +33 2 99 40 24 00, *Email:* agence-maritime-roy@wanadoo.fr

TREPORT

alternate name, see Le Treport

VANNES

Lat 47° 39' N; Long 2° 45' W.

Admiralty Chart: 2358

Time Zone: GMT +1 h

Admiralty Pilot: 22

UNCTAD Locode: FR VNE

Principal Facilities:

			G						A	

Authority: Conseil General du Morbihan, 2 rue de Saint-Tropez, P O Box 400, F-56009 Vannes, France, *Tel:* +33 2 97 54 80 00, *Fax:* +33 2 97 54 80 56, *Email:* contact@cg56.fr, *Website:* www.morbihan.fr

Officials: President: Joseph-Francois Kergueris, *Email:* josephfrancois.kergueris@cg56.fr.
Port Manager: Por Belenfant, *Email:* por.belenfant@cg56.fr.

Approach: Channel depth is 2 m below CD

Anchorage: Vessels can anchor at Meaban Buoy, Port Navalo Roads

Pilotage: Advisable. Contact pilot through Le Conquet radio operator, Tel: +33 2 98 43 63 63

Principal Imports and Exports: Imports: Sawn timber.

Working Hours: 0800-1200, 1330-1830

Accommodation:

Name	Remarks
Vannes	See [1] below

[1]*Vannes:* Total length of berths 65 m. Average depth of water within the port approx 1.5 m above zero on the marine chart. Max dimensions of ships which can enter the port on NT, 60 m loa, breadth unlimited, 3.65 m d, 700 dwt

Storage:

Location	Open (m²)
Vannes	10000

Medical Facilities: General Hospital, Tel: +33 2 97 01 41 41

Airport: Lorient, 55 km

Railway: SNCF, 3 km

Lloyd's Agent: Agence Maritime Jacquemin, 58 Avenue Perriere, F-56100 Lorient, France, *Tel:* +33 2 97 83 67 92, *Fax:* +33 2 97 37 77 31, *Email:* shiplor@wanadoo.fr

VAUBAN

harbour area, see under St. Malo

VERDON

alternate name, see Le Verdon

FRENCH GUIANA

DEGRAD DES CANNES

Lat 4° 51' N; Long 52° 16' W.

Admiralty Chart: 1033

Time Zone: GMT -3 h

Admiralty Pilot: 7A

UNCTAD Locode: GF DDC

Principal Facilities:

P	Q	Y	G	C	R	L	B		A	

Authority: Direction des Services Portuaires, Immeuble CCIG-Z.I. Degrad des Cannes, 97354 Remire, French Guiana, *Tel:* +594 29 96 60, *Fax:* +594 29 96 63, *Email:* port@guyane.cci.fr, *Website:* www.guyane.cci.fr

Approach: Access channel 18.5 km long, 80 m wide, 5.4-6.4 m depth according to variations in HW

Pilotage: Compulsory for vessels over 45 m loa. VHF Channel 16

Maximum Vessel Dimensions: 160 m loa, 5.9 m max draft

Working Hours: 0700-1600

Accommodation:

Name	Length (m)	Depth (m)	Remarks
Degrad des Cannes			See [1] below
Berth No.1	145	7-8	
Berth No.2	140	7-8	
Berth No.3	50	7-8	
Berth No.4	127		See [2] below

[1]*Degrad des Cannes:* Four berths, three on one pier. Available to receive bitumen, gas, gas oil and petroleum
[2]*Berth No.4:* There is a paved container terminal and ro/ro's are accommodated at Berth No.4, 11 m wide

Storage: Open storage of 3 ha, one bonded warehouse of 3800 m2; Rougier warehouse of 3590 m2 and other space of 41 600 m2

Mechanical Handling Equipment:

Location	Type	Capacity (t)	Qty
Degrad des Cannes	Mobile Cranes	100	2
Degrad des Cannes	Mobile Cranes	30	1
Degrad des Cannes	Mobile Cranes	15	1
Degrad des Cannes	Mobile Cranes	80	2
Degrad des Cannes	Mobile Cranes	25	2
Degrad des Cannes	Forklifts	45	

Bunkering: Chevron Marine Products LLC, Global Marine Products LLC, 1500 Louisiana, 4th Floor, Houston, TX 77002, United States of America, *Tel:* +1 832 8542 988, *Fax:* +1 832 8544 868, *Email:* gulfcbm@chevron.com, *Website:* www.chevron.com – *Grades:* GO – *Delivery Mode:* tank truck

Airport: Rochambeau, 15 km

FRENCH POLYNESIA

PAPEETE

Lat 17° 32' S; Long 149° 35' W.

Admiralty Chart: 1436

Time Zone: GMT -10 h

Admiralty Pilot: 62

UNCTAD Locode: PF PPT

Key to Principal Facilities:—				
A=Airport	**C**=Containers	**G**=General Cargo	**P**=Petroleum	**R**=Ro/Ro	**Y**=Dry Bulk
B=Bunkers	**D**=Dry Dock	**L**=Cruise	**Q**=Other Liquid Bulk	**T**=Towage (where available from port)

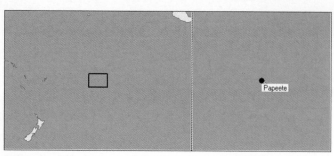

Principal Facilities:

| P | Q | | G | C | R | L | B | D | T | A |

PACIFIC

Pacific Petroleum Tahiti

Pacific Petroleum & Services, 98713 -Papeete, TAHITI, BP 20653,
Polynesie Francaise
Tel: +689 504 276   Fax: +689 504 277
Email: pmoux@pacificpetrole.com   Web: www.pacificpetrole.com
Contact: Moux Patrick

BUNKER SERVICES

Authority: Port Autonome de Papeete, P O Box 9164, Mota Uta, 98715 Papeete, French Polynesia, *Tel:* +689 505454, *Fax:* +689 421950, *Email:* commercial@portppt.pf, *Website:* www.portdepapeete.pf

Officials: General Manager: Yves Demontgolfier, *Tel:* +689 505481, *Email:* ydemontgolfier@portppt.pf.
Harbour Master: Marcel Pelletier, *Email:* mpelletier@portppt.pf.

Port Security: ISPS compliant

Documentation: Port Health: maritime declaration of health
Immigration: crew list, pax disembarking, pax in transit
Customs: manifest of cargo for discharge, provisions list, mail list, crew personal effects list, bonded stores list, ship's spare list, crew list, pax disembarking, pax in transit, animals to be unloaded, animals in transit, list of plants, complete cargo manifest
Merchant Marine Authorities: declaration of safe rules on board ship
Port Captain: entry declaration, crew list, pax disembarking, pax embarking, pax in transit, list of cargo to be loaded/unloaded/transhipped, dangerous cargo list sent prior to arrival via agent

Approach: Harbour entrance 110 m wide in max depth of 10.37 m admissible and is marked by occulting green range lights mounted on red and white striped towers which align at 149°. The barrier reef on the E side of the pass can easily be seen. Entrance to the harbour, through the barrier to the E, and shoal water to the W, is marked by lighted buoys during bad weather as there is often a heavy sea on the shoals (5 m deep)

Anchorage: Anchorage can be obtained within the harbour roads for vessels up to 180 m loa in depths of 20-25 m

Pilotage: Compulsory, Tel: +689 480454, Fax: +689 480452, Email: pilotmar@mail.pf, Website: www.pilotage.pf. The pilot service is controlled by the Pilot Station. Four pilots available. Pilot assistance is mandatory in the harbour. 24 h watch on VHF Channel 12. Vessels are requested to advise their agent giving ETA, length, width and max draft 3 days prior to arrival
For vessels over 90 m loa pilot boards in pos 17° 30.50' S; 149° 36.20' W (2 nautical miles from Toa Ta channel entrance)
For vessels under 90 m loa pilot boards in pos 17° 31.30' S; 149° 35.70' W

Radio Frequency: Nearest coastal radio is Mahina Radio-FJA. 24 h watch 500 kHz and 2182 kHz. VHF Channels 16, 26 and 27. 24 h watch on 8279 kHz (ship receives on 8803 kHz)
Harbour control and authorities are to be contacted on VHF Channel 12, 2638 kHz (USB) 1 h prior to arrival

Principal Imports and Exports: Imports: General cargo, Hydrocarbons, Vehicles. Exports: Copra, Fish, Scrap.

Working Hours: 0700-1100, 1300-1700, 1800-2200. No work undertaken from Saturday midnight until Sunday midnight

Accommodation:

Name	Length (m)	Depth (m)	Remarks
Papeete			
International Overseas Wharf	450	10.5	General cargo & containers. Container storage area of 2.7 ha
Cruise Ship Wharf	233	9.5	Passengers
Refuelling Wharf (Fare-Ute)	105	10	Petroleum
Refuelling Wharf (Motu-Uta)	79	10	Petroleum
Gas Tanker Wharf	30	7	Liquefied gas
Inter-Island Trading Wharf 1	300	6	General cargo

Name	Length (m)	Depth (m)	Remarks
Inter-Island Trading Wharf 2	150	6	General cargo
Inter-Island Trading Wharf 3	100	6	General cargo
Inter-Island Trading Wharf 4	100	6	General cargo
Inter-Island Trading Wharf 4 Bis	21	7	General cargo
Fishing Vessels Wharf	148	6	Fish
Ferries Wharf	220	6	Four berths handling passengers & cars
Fast Ferries Wharf	110	3.5	Two berths handling passengers

Storage: Private facilities only. Six bonded warehouses covering a surface area of 15 200 m2. Three of these warehouses are located alongside the International Overseas Wharf and are assigned to stevedoring companies

Mechanical Handling Equipment: Three stevedoring companies own a complete set of cranes and forklifts enabling 40' container handling

Bunkering: Shell-Polypetroles Shell S.A., P O Box 20653, Papeete, French Polynesia, *Tel:* +689 504250, *Fax:* +689 504251
Total Polynesie, P O Box 64, Papeete, French Polynesia, *Tel:* +689 420354, *Fax:* +689 431603
ExxonMobil Marine Fuels, 1 Harbour Front Place, 06-00 Harbour Front, Tower One, Singapore, Republic of Singapore 098633, *Tel:* +65 6885 8998, *Fax:* +65 6885 8794, *Email:* asiapac.marinefuels@exxonmobil.com, *Website:* www.exxonmobilmarinefuels.com – *Grades:* MGO; IFO-180cSt – *Delivery Mode:* barge, truck, pipeline
Pacific Petroleum & Services, P O Box 20653, 98713 Papeete, French Polynesia, *Tel:* +689 504262, *Fax:* +689 504263, *Email:* apontonnier@pacificpetrole.com, *Website:* www.pacificpetrole.com
Shell-Polypetroles Shell S.A., P O Box 20653, Papeete, French Polynesia, *Tel:* +689 504250, *Fax:* +689 504251 – *Delivery Mode:* barge, truck, pipeline
Total Polynesie, P O Box 64, Papeete, French Polynesia, *Tel:* +689 420354, *Fax:* +689 431603 – *Grades:* MGO; IFO-180cSt – *Parcel Size:* no min/max – *Notice:* 48 hours – *Delivery Mode:* barge, pipeline

Waste Reception Facilities: Garbage collection service available

Towage: Two harbour tugs of 400 hp and two deep sea-going tugs of 1340 hp and 3800 hp

Repair & Maintenance: D.C.N. floating dock 150 m long, 26 m wide and 6 m draft with lifting cap of 3500 t
Harbour slipway 50 m long, 12 m wide and 4 m draft with lifting cap of 800 t. Woodwork, electrical and welding repairs can be effected
Chantier Naval du Pacifique Sud, P O Box 9054, 98715 Papeete, French Polynesia, *Tel:* +689 505270, *Fax:* +689 427827, *Email:* cnps@mail.pf

Shipping Agents: Agence Maritime Internationale Tahiti, cnr Boulevard Pomare/Rue Jeanne d'Arc, P O Box 274, Papeete, French Polynesia, *Tel:* +689 428972, *Fax:* +689 432184, *Email:* amitahiti@mail.pf, *Website:* www.amitahiti.com
CMA-CGM S.A., CMA CGM Papeete, 2 Rue Wallis, P O Box 96, 98713 Papeete, French Polynesia, *Tel:* +689 545252, *Fax:* +689 436806, *Email:* ppt.genmbox@cma-cgm.com, *Website:* www.cma-cgm.com
Papeete Seairland Transports, Immeuble Franco Oceanienne, Fare-Ute, P O Box 4536, 98713 Papeete, French Polynesia, *Tel:* +689 545100, *Fax:* +689 455266, *Email:* tahiti@pst.pf
Scat Polynesie S.A., 72 Plazza Haute, P O Box 596, Papeete, French Polynesia, *Tel:* +689 455913, *Fax:* +689 455266, *Email:* scat@mail.pf
Societe Tahitienne Maritime S.A., P O Box 9170, Papeete, French Polynesia, *Tel:* +689 427805, *Fax:* +689 432416

Stevedoring Companies: J.A. Cowan et Fils, P O Box 570, 98713 Papeete, French Polynesia, *Tel:* +689 545700, *Fax:* +689 426262, *Email:* jacowan@mail.pf
Sat Nui, P O Box 470, 98713 Papeete, French Polynesia, *Tel:* +689 504800, *Fax:* +689 504801, *Email:* general@satnui.pf
Sotama-Cotada, Papeete, French Polynesia, *Tel:* +689 427805, *Fax:* +689 432416, *Email:* sotama@mail.pf

Medical Facilities: Advance notice required if medical services required aboard. Two hospitals with ambulance service are available

Airport: Faaa, 9 km

Lloyd's Agent: Compagnie Francaise Maritime de Tahiti, Immeuble Importex No.45 Fare Ute, P O Box 368, 98713 Papeete, French Polynesia, *Tel:* +689 437972, *Fax:* +689 420617, *Email:* taporo@mail.pf

GABON

CAP LOPEZ

Lat 0° 38' S; Long 8° 42' E.

Admiralty Chart: 1322	**Admiralty Pilot:** 2
Time Zone: GMT +1 h	**UNCTAD Locode:** GA CLZ

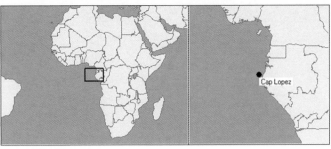

Principal Facilities:

P						B	T	A

Authority: Elf Gabon, P O Box 524, Port Gentil, Gabon, *Tel:* +241 55 63 39, *Fax:* +241 55 69 68

Anchorage: Anchorage in sandy ground 2 nautical miles, bearing 075° from the Cap Lopez lighthouse; vessels may not anchor less than 1.6 km from the berth

Pilotage: Compulsory for all manoeuvres including mooring and unmooring

Radio Frequency: Working channel VHF 72

Weather: The terminal is sheltered from SW to NW winds. Risk of tornado's mainly Feb-April

Maximum Vessel Dimensions: 340 m loa, 250 000 dwt, 20.5 m draft

Principal Imports and Exports: Exports: Crude oil.

Accommodation:

Name	Remarks
Cap Lopez	See [1] below

[1]*Cap Lopez:* Tanker Terminal: berth is located on the W side of Prince's Bay. Vessels berth portside on six dolphins; depth 25 m at MLWS. Berth consists of a loading platform 20 m x 33 m connected to land by an L-shaped pier 340 m long. Loading of crude by means of five 16'' dia arms; max loading rate 12 000 m3/h. Vessels up to 250 000 dwt can be accommodated

Bunkering: Available at berth. Contact CORELF PARIS, Fax: (1) 47 44 37 66 or Elf Oil Gabon, Tel: 552759, Fax: 551808
ExxonMobil Marine Fuels, Mailpoint 31, ExxonMobil House, Ermyn Way, Leatherhead, Surrey KT22 8UX, United Kingdom, *Tel:* +44 1372 222 000, *Fax:* +44 1372 223 922, *Email:* marine.fuels@exxonmobil.com, *Website:* www.exxonmobil.com – *Grades:* MGO – *Delivery Mode:* barge
Societe Gabonaise des Petroles Elf, P O Box 601, Libruville, Elf Gabon, Port Gentil, Gabon, *Tel:* +241 756950 – *Grades:* MGO – *Delivery Mode:* barge

Towage: Compulsory. Three tugs available; two of 3000 hp and one of 2000 hp. Tugs supply own tow rope. For berthing tankers over 150 000 dwt an additional tug or supply vessel is used

Medical Facilities: Hospital and private clinic available, 25 km

Airport: Port Gentil, 20 km

Lloyd's Agent: Omega Marine Libreville, P O Box 9720, Libreville, Gabon, *Fax:* +241 76 07 76, *Email:* omega-gabon@omega-marine.com

ETAME TERMINAL

Lat 3° 45' S; Long 10° 32' E.

Admiralty Chart: 604	**Admiralty Pilot:** 2
Time Zone: GMT +1 h	**UNCTAD Locode:** GA

Principal Facilities:

P							T	

Pre-Arrival Information: ETA should be sent on departure from last port and 72 h, 48 h and 24 h prior to arrival

Approach: When approaching from NW or SE, vessels should keep well offshore to avoid areas of offshore oil and gas activity

Anchorage: There is no designated anchorage for the terminal. In the event of a berthing delay, the decision to drift or to anchor is at the discretion of the Master

Pilotage: Compulsory and is provided by the mooring master or a local pilot. The pilot boards 2 miles ENE of the FPSO

Maximum Vessel Dimensions: 150 000 dwt

Accommodation:

Name	Remarks
Etame Marine Terminal	See [1] below

[1]*Etame Marine Terminal:* Operated by Vaalco Gabon (Etame) Inc. Offshore marine terminal for Etame oilfield producing crude oil and consists of FPSO 'Petroleo

Nautipa', moored 20 miles offshore in depth of 76 m. The loading tanker moors bow-to-bow with the FPSO at a distance of 80 m. Berthing takes place in daylight only. Total storage cap of 1 100 000 bbls

Towage: A tug will assist the berthing operation and will remain secured to the stern of the loading tanker during the loading operation

Lloyd's Agent: Omega Marine Libreville, P O Box 9720, Libreville, Gabon, *Fax:* +241 76 07 76, *Email:* omega-gabon@omega-marine.com

GAMBA TERMINAL

Lat 2° 47' S; Long 10° 0' E.

Admiralty Chart: -	**Admiralty Pilot:** 2
Time Zone: GMT +1 h	**UNCTAD Locode:** GA GAX

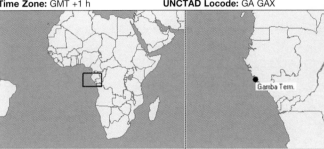

Principal Facilities:

P									

Authority: Shell Gabon, P O Box 146, Port Gentil, Gabon, *Tel:* +241 55 8465, *Fax:* +241 55 8577, *Email:* marine-department@shell.com

Officials: Marine Superintendent: C. Renton.

Port Security: ISPS compliant. The Pilot/Loading Master is the qualified Port Facility Security Officer, Tel +241 55 8465, Email: marine-department@shell.com. VHF Channel 12

Pre-Arrival Information: The following details must be sent urgently by Fax to +241 55 8577 or +31 70 303 7064 and/or by Email to marine-department@shell.com
(a) ETA (in addition ETA's required at 96, 72, 48 and 24 hrs)
(b) cargo requirements in barrels
(c) type, number and SWL of bow stoppers
(d) oil pollution certificate details
(e) last port of call
(f) owner, operator, charterer, flag, port of registry, year built
(g) sdwt, gt, nrt, loa, beam and maximum summer draft
(h) master's full name
(i) address, telephone and telex numbers of owners and operators
(j) ship's call sign
(k) USCG identifier for bills of lading if required (please confirm whether date element refers to charter party or B/L)
(l) arrival and departure drafts
(m) power voltage in pilots cabin
(n) deballast concurrent with loading, if not, deballasting time
(o) vessel inerted and IG plant fully operational
(p) name of agent in Port Gentil

Documentation: The following port papers should be prepared prior to arrival:
last port clearance (original & copy)
crew list (4 copies)
vaccination list (3 copies)
stores list including slop chest (3 copies)
personal effects declaration (3 copies)
ports visited during the last three months (3 copies)
animals & birds list (2 copies)
arms & ammunition list (2 copies)
narcotics list (2 copies)
passenger list (2 copies)
ship's particulars (2 copies)

Approach: Direct from the sea; heading dependent on the direction of the current (usually running N parallel to the coast)

Anchorage: Recommended anchorage is 2 miles NW of the SBM in a depth of 25 m

Pilotage: Compulsory for mooring and unmooring. Berthing Master boards approx 2 miles NW of SBM and berthing takes place day or night. Vessel's ETA should be sent by fax and/or email at least 4 days in advance to Marine Gamba and subsequently every 24 h

Radio Frequency: Permanent watch on VHF Channel 6 during working hours. Working channels during loading on VHF Channel 12

Weather: From October to March tornadoes can come from any direction and are always dangerous

Tides: Range of tide 1.0 m max

Maximum Vessel Dimensions: 150 000 dwt. Max arrival trim is 2.5 m by the stern with the propeller fully immersed. Max departure draft is 17.25 m

Principal Imports and Exports: Exports: Crude oil.

Working Hours: 24 h/day

Accommodation:

Name	Remarks
Gamba Terminal	See [1] below

[1]*Gamba Terminal:* SBM: depth 23.0 m, draft restriction 17.25 m, manifold height 2.75 m, under keel clearance 3.0 m for vessels up to 150 000 dwt. Loading rate, max 4600

Key to Principal Facilities:—
A=Airport	**C**=Containers	**G**=General Cargo	**P**=Petroleum	**R**=Ro/Ro	**Y**=Dry Bulk
B=Bunkers	**D**=Dry Dock	**L**=Cruise	**Q**=Other Liquid Bulk	**T**=Towage (where available from port)	

m3/h and normal 4000 m3/h. There are no facilities for discharging ballast or slops ashore therefore vessels must arrive at the terminal with clean ballast on board No crew changes are possible at this terminal; if necessary they may be arranged via the agent off Port Gentil

Lloyd's Agent: Omega Marine Libreville, P O Box 9720, Libreville, Gabon, *Fax:* +241 76 07 76, *Email:* omega-gabon@omega-marine.com

LIBREVILLE

Lat 0° 24' N; Long 9° 26' E.

Admiralty Chart: 1356	**Admiralty Pilot:** 2
Time Zone: GMT +1 h	**UNCTAD Locode:** GA LBV

Principal Facilities:

P	Q		G						A

Authority: Office des Ports et Rades du Gabon, P O Box 1051, Libreville, Gabon, *Tel:* +241 70 00 48, *Fax:* +241 70 37 35, *Email:* info@ports-gabon.com, *Website:* www.ports-gabon.com

Port Security: ISPS compliant

Approach: Max depth of channel 17 m at entrance, average 13 m

Anchorage: Vessels anchor 2 km from shore in 8.2 m with church spire and middle of customs warehouse in line-NW of base buoy

Pilotage: Not available

Tides: Range of tide 1.3 m

Maximum Vessel Dimensions: 50 m loa, 3.3 m d

Principal Imports and Exports: Imports: Fish, Vegetables.

Accommodation:

Name	Remarks
Libreville	See [1] below

[1]*Libreville:* Harbour is well sheltered. A mole providing a quay 130 m long consisting of three berths for fishing vessels and small coasters
Ocean-going vessels use facilities at Owendo

Bunkering: Total France S.A., Total Marine Fuels, 51 Esplanade du General de Gaulle, F-92907 Paris la Defense Cedex 10, France, *Tel:* +33 1 4135 2755, *Fax:* +33 1 4197 0291, *Email:* marine.fuels@total.com, *Website:* www.marinefuels.total.com

Repair & Maintenance: Atelier Navale Delmas, Libreville, Gabon, *Tel:* +241 70 09 07, *Fax:* +241 70 09 06 One slipway for vessels up to 500 t, 2.7 m d

Ship Chandlers: SAM Gabon - Daron Shipchandler, P O Box 12203, Libreville, Gabon, *Tel:* +241 44 38 10, *Fax:* +241 44 38 12, *Email:* sam-ga-lbv@daron-shipchandler.com, *Website:* www.daron-shipchandler.com

Shipping Agents: Compagnie de Manutention et Chalandage d'Owendo, Boulevard de l'Independence, P O Box 77, Libreville 2131, Gabon, *Tel:* +241 70 26 35/6
GETMA Gabon S.A., Zone Industrielle Oloumi-Owendo, P O Box 7510, Libreville, Gabon, *Tel:* +241 70 40 18, *Fax:* +241 70 34 20, *Email:* claude.barone@getma-gabon.com, *Website:* www.getma.fr
SAGA, Boulevard de l'Independence, Owendo, P O Box 72, Libreville, Gabon, *Tel:* +241 70 26 30, *Fax:* +241 70 12 07, *Email:* afritramp.lbv@ga.dti.bollore.com, *Website:* www.sagashipping.eu
Satram, Enceinte du Port d'Owendo, Libreville, Gabon, *Tel:* +241 70 41 73, *Fax:* +241 70 41 74
SDV Gabon, Zone Portuaire d'Owendo, P O Box 77, Libreville, Gabon, *Tel:* +241 70 26 35, *Fax:* +241 70 23 34/70 15 54
Socopao-Gabon S.A., Zone Portuaire d'Owendo, P O Box 72, Libreville, Gabon, *Tel:* +241 70 26 30, *Fax:* +241 70 12 07, *Email:* socopaolbv@ga.dti.bollore.com

Surveyors: Bureau Veritas, P O Box 1005, Libreville, Gabon, *Tel:* +241 74 66 81, *Fax:* +241 76 26 63, *Website:* www.bureauveritas.com

Medical Facilities: Hospitals and clinics available

Airport: Leon M'ba International, 12 km

Lloyd's Agent: Omega Marine Libreville, P O Box 9720, Libreville, Gabon, *Fax:* +241 76 07 76, *Email:* omega-gabon@omega-marine.com

LUCINA TERMINAL

Lat 3° 39' S; Long 10° 46' E.

Admiralty Chart: 604	**Admiralty Pilot:** 2
Time Zone: GMT +1 h	**UNCTAD Locode:** GA LUC

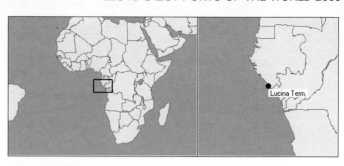

Principal Facilities:

P								T	

Authority: Perenco Gabon S.A., P O Box 780, Port Gentil, Gabon, *Tel:* +241 550642, *Fax:* +241 550647, *Email:* hmonthe@ga.perenco.com, *Website:* www.perenco.com

Officials: Manager: Daniel Kadjar.

Pre-Arrival Information: Initial ETA should be sent to Perenco S.A. via telex, fax or email at least 7 days before arrival, and subsequent confirmatory ETA messages should be passed to Perenco S.A. every 24 h

Documentation: Crew list (4 copies), passenger list (2 copies), tobacco/spirits/personal effects list (3 copies), stores list (3 copies), arms and ammunition (2 copies), last ports of call (1 copy), ports during last 3 months (3 copies), animals list (2 copies), narcotics list (2 copies), notice of readiness (1 copy)

Anchorage: Recommended anchorage is approx 2 miles NW of FSU in 35 m depth, bottom of sand and mud

Pilotage: Compulsory. All tankers using the SBM must use the Perenco S.A. pilotage service for both mooring and unmooring. Mooring Master boards approx 2 miles NW of SBM. Terminal is closed for berthing from 1500 to 0600

Radio Frequency: VHF Channel 09 (calling and working), 24 h service in French and 0600-1800 in English

Weather: From October to April there is a possibility of local tornadoes or strong winds

Principal Imports and Exports: Exports: Crude oil.

Accommodation:

Name	Remarks
Lucina Terminal	See [1] below

[1]*Lucina Terminal:* Lucina offshore development consists of 6 four pile production platforms linked by submarine pipeline to the LP-1 production platform, then to the FSU 'Banio', which itself is linked to an export SBM
The six production platforms are:
LD1 in pos 03° 41.0' S; 010° 44.3' E
LD2 in pos 03° 41.8' S; 010° 45.0' E
LD3 in pos 03° 42.5' S; 010° 46.0' E
LD4 in pos 03° 40.9' S; 010° 44.6' E
LD5 in pos 03° 42.2' S; 010° 45.8' E
LWD1 in pos 03° 41.4' S; 010° 43.7' E
Production facilities are located on four-pile platform LP1 that is connected by bridge to the adjacent platform LD1
The 85 000 dwt FSU 'Banio' is moored by means of ten anchors in pos 03° 40.0' S; 010° 45.8' E
The FSU is connected to a SBM by a 20" x 1.0 km long submarine pipeline
SBM buoy in pos 03° 39.6' S; 010° 46.2' E is 8 m in diameter and 4 m high. No draft restriction, 34 m depth, for vessels with max displacement up to 120 000 t (absolute max of 140 000 summer dwt if first port of loading). Loading rate of 2800 m3/h with max of 3000 m3/h
There are no facilities for receipt of ballast or slops ashore. Vessel's must arrive with clean ballast only, apart from contents of the slop tank

Towage: One tug (approx 4000 hp) is available and compulsory

Shipping Agents: GETMA Gabon S.A., P O Box 937, Port Gentil, Gabon, *Tel:* +241 56 12 93, *Fax:* +241 56 12 95, *Email:* stephane.barnicaud@getma-gabon.com, *Website:* www.getma.fr
SAGA, BP 518 Zi Oprag, Port Gentil, Gabon, *Tel:* +241 55 21 90, *Fax:* +241 55 56 43, *Email:* afritramp.pog@ga.dti.bollore.com, *Website:* www.sagashipping.eu

Medical Facilities: Details of any illness on board should be reported in the ETA message. No facilities are available for medical or dental treatment at the Terminal so vessels should call at Port Gentil before or after loading

Airport: From Port Gentil there are daily flights to Libreville International Airport

Lloyd's Agent: Omega Marine Libreville, P O Box 9720, Libreville, Gabon, *Fax:* +241 76 07 76, *Email:* omega-gabon@omega-marine.com

MAYUMBA

Lat 3° 23' S; Long 10° 38' E.

Admiralty Chart: 1322	**Admiralty Pilot:** 2
Time Zone: GMT +1 h	**UNCTAD Locode:** GA MYB

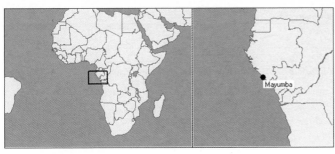

Principal Facilities:

		Y								

Authority: Office des Ports et Rades du Gabon, P O Box 1051, Libreville, Gabon, *Tel:* +241 70 00 48, *Fax:* +241 70 37 35, *Email:* info@ports-gabon.com, *Website:* www.ports-gabon.com

Port Security: ISPS compliant

Radio Frequency: There is a local telegraph office

Weather: The bay is exposed to SW winds

Maximum Vessel Dimensions: 19 511 dwt, 156.2 m loa

Principal Imports and Exports: Exports: Timber.

Accommodation:

Name	Remarks
Mayumba	See [1] below

[1]*Mayumba:* Open roadstead used for the loading of timber. Vessels anchor 1 mile WNW of the mouth of River Mayumba, 0.75 mile offshore in depth of 13-14 m

Lloyd's Agent: Omega Marine Libreville, P O Box 9720, Libreville, Gabon, *Fax:* +241 76 07 76, *Email:* omega-gabon@omega-marine.com

OGUENDJO TERMINAL

Lat 1° 27' S; Long 8° 55' E.

Admiralty Chart: 604	**Admiralty Pilot:** 2
Time Zone: GMT +1 h	**UNCTAD Locode:** GA

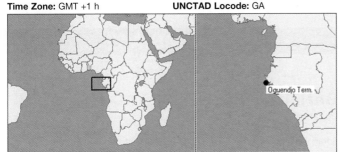

Principal Facilities:

P							T		

Authority: Perenco Gabon S.A., P O Box 780, Port Gentil, Gabon, *Tel:* +241 550642, *Fax:* +241 550647, *Email:* hmonthe@ga.perenco.com, *Website:* www.perenco.com

Officials: Manager: Daniel Kadjar.

Pre-Arrival Information: Vessels should establish radio contact with Perenco 3 days before arrival at the Terminal, and maintain such contact until just prior to arrival at the Terminal. They should send an ETA message (email) not less than 72 h prior to arrival, providing the following information:
a) ETA and name of local agent
b) estimated draft, fore and aft, upon arrival
c) type and quantity of crude oil to be loaded
d) estimated sailing draft
e) last port of call
f) whether vessel has a clean bill of health
g) distance from the bow to the centre of the vessel manifold
h) mooring equipment available on the bow
i) confirmation that hose handling gear and mooring equipment, navigation equipment, radars, steering gear and engine propulsion are in good order and conditions, that the vessel can accept one 16" dia floating hose fitted with a 150 ASA camlock coupling flange
j) whether vessel intends to load on top of existing slops and, if so, advises as to the quantity of slops in each tank on which cargo will be loaded on top
The first ETA message should also include a definate statement of the details of any equipment required from the storage vessel for connecting the floating cargo hose to the vessel's manifold. Further ETA messages should be sent when the vessel is 48 h away, confirming or giving notice of any change in the 72 h ETA, and at any other time after the 24 h ETA message when a change by more than 2 h occurs in the ETA. The 24 h ETA message should include a positive statement regarding the vessel readiness to load on arrival and the number of hours required to discharge clean ballast

Documentation: Four copies each of the following documents are required:
Crew list, deratting certificate/deratting exemption, crew customs declaration, stores list, animals list, passenger list, narcotics list, clearance from last port, arms & ammunition list, cargo manifest

The Vessel Certificates and updated Oil Record Book should also be made available to the Mooring Master and appropriate Governmental Officials

Approach: The access lane from the customary anchorage to Oguendjo Oil Terminal is an area approx 1.7 miles wide and with axis which runs from the anchorage area for approx 12 miles in a direction of 325°(T) to the Mooring Master pick-up zone which is located 2 miles S of platform 'C'

Anchorage: Vessels awaiting berth should anchor in an area between pos 1° 36' to 1° 40' S and 8° 57' to 9° 02' E and maintain constant radio watch for berthing instructions

Pilotage: Compulsory. A mooring master will board in the vicinity of pos 1° 30' S; 8° 54' E or at the anchorage area

Radio Frequency: The floating storage vessel maintains a radio watch on VHF Channel 8

Accommodation:

Name	Remarks
Oguendjo Terminal	See [1] below

[1]*Oguendjo Terminal:* The oil terminal consists of:
Production Platform 'B' in pos 01° 26' 44.5" S; 08° 57' 15" E and Production Platform 'C' in pos 01° 28' 13.5" S; 08° 54' 00" E
An offshore loading berth comprised primarily of a floating storage vessel 'Fernan Vaz', permanently moored by a 12-anchors and chains mooring system in depth of approx 28 m
A submarine pipeline which runs from Production Platform 'B' to the floating storage vessel
Vessels loading from the facility are moored from their bow to the bow of the floating storage vessel by means of a 16" braided mooring hawser. Tankers up to 170 000 dwt and 18.3 m draft can be accommodated and max loading rate is approx 48 000 bbls/h or 7600 m3/h. Berthing during daylight hours only (up to 1500 LT), unberthing at any time

Towage: One tug available which is equipped for fire-fighting; mooring boat also available

Medical Facilities: Vessel's requiring emergency medical assistance should contact the Terminal by VHF radio and supply the necessary information which will be passed on to the Vessel Agent. No medical or hospital facilities are available at the Terminal, but private doctors and hospital facilities are available at Port Gentil

Lloyd's Agent: Omega Marine Libreville, P O Box 9720, Libreville, Gabon, *Fax:* +241 76 07 76, *Email:* omega-gabon@omega-marine.com

OVENDO

alternate name, see Owendo

OWENDO

Lat 0° 17' N; Long 9° 30' E.

Admiralty Chart: 1356	**Admiralty Pilot:** 2
Time Zone: GMT +1 h	**UNCTAD Locode:** GA OWE

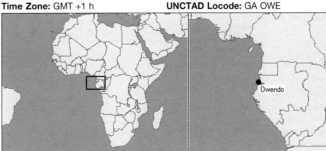

Principal Facilities:

	Y	G	C	R		B		T	A	

Authority: Office des Ports et Rades du Gabon, P O Box 1051, Libreville, Gabon, *Tel:* +241 70 00 48, *Fax:* +241 70 37 35, *Email:* info@ports-gabon.com, *Website:* www.ports-gabon.com

Port Security: ISPS compliant

Approach: Max depth of channel 17 m but average of 13 m

Pilotage: Compulsory for vessels over 500 gt. Pilot boards 1 mile off harbour. VHF Channel 16 & 12. Berthing day or night

Maximum Vessel Dimensions: Length 220 m, 9.0 m d

Principal Imports and Exports: Imports: Fish, Iron products, Manufactured goods, Rice, Wheat. Exports: Logs, Manganese ore, Timber, Uranium.

Working Hours: 0800-1200, 1400-1730. Overtime possible

Accommodation:

Name	Length (m)	Depth (m)	Remarks
Owendo			See [1] below
Quay	450	9.8	See [2] below

[1]*Owendo:* Bulk facilities: Cargoes of gypsum, sulphur and clinker as well as timber products are handled. Manganese ore terminal; loading rate of 2800 t/h
Tanker facilities: Small tankers discharge butane gas and hydrocarbons
[2]*Quay:* Operated by Gabon Port Management S.A. (Portek), Zone Portuaire d'Owendo, P O Box 1051, Libreville, Website: www.portek.com

---

Key to Principal Facilities:—			
A=Airport	**C**=Containers	**G**=General Cargo	**P**=Petroleum	**R**=Ro/Ro	**Y**=Dry Bulk
B=Bunkers	**D**=Dry Dock	**L**=Cruise	**Q**=Other Liquid Bulk	**T**=Towage (where available from port)

Three berths available. 9 ha container yard

Storage:

Location	Open (m²)	Covered (m²)
Owendo	65000	14600

Mechanical Handling Equipment:

Location	Type	Capacity (t)
Owendo	Mobile Cranes	50
Owendo	Forklifts	24

Cargo Worked: 100-800 t/day

Bunkering: Available by small tankers from Port Gentil
BP France S.A., Immeuble le Cervier, 12 Avenue des Beguines, Cergy-Saint-Christophe, 95866 Cergy Pontoise Cedex, France, *Tel:* +33 1 3422 4000, *Fax:* +33 1 3422 4417, *Email:* benoist.grosjean@fr.bp.com, *Website:* www.bpmarine.com
Societe Gabonaise des Petroles Elf, P O Box 601, Libruville, Elf Gabon, Port Gentil, Gabon, *Tel:* +241 756950
Total France S.A., Total Marine Fuels, 51 Esplanade du General de Gaulle, F-92907 Paris la Defense Cedex 10, France, *Tel:* +33 1 4135 2755, *Fax:* +33 1 4197 0291, *Email:* marine.fuels@total.com, *Website:* www.marinefuels.total.com

Towage: Compulsory for vessels over 500 gt. Tugs up to 1500 hp are available

Repair & Maintenance: Atelier Navale Delmas, Libreville, Gabon, *Tel:* +241 70 09 07, *Fax:* +241 70 09 06 One slipway for vessels up to 500 t, 2.7 m d

Medical Facilities: Hospitals and clinics available

Airport: Leon M'ba International, 28 km

Lloyd's Agent: Omega Marine Libreville, P O Box 9720, Libreville, Gabon, *Fax:* +241 76 07 76, *Email:* omega-gabon@omega-marine.com

PORT GENTIL

Lat 0° 43' S; Long 8° 47' E.

Admiralty Chart: 1322	**Admiralty Pilot:** 2
Time Zone: GMT +1 h	**UNCTAD Locode:** GA POG

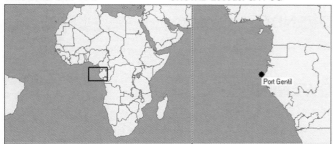

Principal Facilities:

P	Q	Y	G	C	R		B		T	A

Authority: Office des Ports et Rades du Gabon, P O Box 43, Port Gentil, Gabon, *Tel:* +241 55 38 11/2, *Fax:* +241 55 53 03

Port Security: ISPS compliant

Anchorage: In pos 0° 39' 5" S, 8° 48' 5" E in depth of 28 m

Pilotage: Compulsory day or night. VHF Channel 12. Pilot boards in pos 0° 39' 5" S, 8° 48' E

Radio Frequency: VHF Channel 12

Weather: Winds from S direction, force 2-4 during dry season June to October. Tornadoes from the E can occur during wet season from October to May

Tides: Range of tide 1.5 m

Principal Imports and Exports: Imports: General cargo. Exports: Logs, Petroleum, Plywood.

Working Hours: Two shifts per day, 0700-1700 and 1800-0600

Accommodation:

Name	Length (m)	Depth (m)	Remarks
Port Gentil			See [1] below
Quai de Commerce	375	9–11	See [2] below
Quai de Peche	285	6–7	See [3] below
Lighterage Quay	75	2.5	For harbour craft
Private Wharves			See [4] below

[1]*Port Gentil:* Deepwater port comprising three berths, capable of handling vessels up to 35 000 dwt, max d 10.5 m.
An anchorage for vessels loading hardwood is situated opposite the old port in depths of 10-15 m
Tanker facilities: Sogara Tanker Terminal in depth of 13.0 m
[2]*Quai de Commerce:* Operated by Gabon Port Management S.A. (Portek), Zone Portuaire d'Owendo, P O Box 1051, Libreville, *Website:* www.portek.com
Container vessels and ro/ro's accommodated at Commercial Pier. Containers handled by ships cranes or derricks; 10 ha container yard
[3]*Quai de Peche:* The fishing quay can also berth a cargo vessel if required, but priority is given to the fishing vessels
[4]*Private Wharves:* Shell Jetty, Elf Jetty, DPS Jetty, Halliburton Jetty and Sogara Jetty

Storage:

Location	Open (m²)	Covered (m²)
Port Gentil	20000	6000

Bunkering: Shell Gabon, P O Box 146, Port Gentil, Gabon, *Tel:* +241 55 8465, *Fax:* +241 55 8577, *Email:* marine-department@shell.com
Societe Gabonaise des Petroles Elf, P O Box 601, Libruville, Elf Gabon, Port Gentil, Gabon, *Tel:* +241 756950
ExxonMobil Marine Fuels, Mailpoint 31, ExxonMobil House, Ermyn Way, Leatherhead, Surrey KT22 8UX, United Kingdom, *Tel:* +44 1372 222 000, *Fax:* +44 1372 223 922, *Email:* marine.fuels@exxonmobil.com, *Website:* www.exxonmobil.com – *Grades:* MGO – *Delivery Mode:* truck, pipeline
Societe Gabonaise des Petroles Elf, P O Box 601, Libruville, Elf Gabon, Port Gentil, Gabon, *Tel:* +241 756950 – *Grades:* MGO – *Delivery Mode:* barge
Total France S.A., Total Marine Fuels, 51 Esplanade du General de Gaulle, F-92907 Paris la Defense Cedex 10, France, *Tel:* +33 1 4135 2755, *Fax:* +33 1 4197 0291, *Email:* marine.fuels@total.com, *Website:* www.marinefuels.total.com

Towage: Damen Marine Service Gabon S.A., SMIT Terminals, P O Box 751, Port Gentil, Gabon, *Tel:* +241 55 23 40, *Fax:* +241 55 35 48, *Email:* o.durand@smitgabon.com, *Website:* www.smit.com

Repair & Maintenance: Delmas Petroleum Services, P O Box 616, Port Gentil, Gabon, *Tel:* +241 55 23 88, *Fax:* +241 55 23 34, *Email:* pierre.meis@ga.dti.bollore.com One slip of 500 t cap
SEMTS, ZI Oprag, P O Box 428, Port Gentil, Gabon, *Tel:* +241 55 29 43, *Fax:* +241 55 06 01, *Email:* semts.pc@inet.ga One slip of 200-300 t cap

Ship Chandlers: SAM Gabon - Daron Shipchandler, P O Box 404, Port Gentil, Gabon, *Tel:* +241 55 28 60, *Fax:* +241 55 08 06, *Email:* sam-ga-pog@daron-shipchandler.com, *Website:* www.daron-shipchandler.com

Shipping Agents: Afritramp, Zone Industrielle OPRAG, P O Box 518, Port Gentil, Gabon, *Tel:* +241 55 21 90, *Fax:* +241 55 56 43, *Email:* afritramp.pog@ga.dti.bollore.com, *Website:* www.afritrampoilfield.com
GAC-GETMA, P O Box 937, Port Gentil, Gabon, *Email:* gac-getma.gabon@gacworld,com, *Website:* www.gacworld.com
SAGA, BP 518 Zi Oprag, Port Gentil, Gabon, *Tel:* +241 55 21 90, *Fax:* +241 55 56 43, *Email:* afritramp.pog@ga.dti.bollore.com, *Website:* www.sagashipping.eu

Surveyors: Bureau Veritas, P O Box 1049, Port Gentil, Gabon, *Tel:* +241 55 23 47, *Fax:* +241 56 06 89, *Email:* veritas.pog@internetgabon.com, *Website:* www.bureauveritas.com

Medical Facilities: Hospital and private clinics available

Airport: Local airport, 3 km

Lloyd's Agent: Omega Marine Libreville, P O Box 9720, Libreville, Gabon, *Fax:* +241 76 07 76, *Email:* omega-gabon@omega-marine.com

GAMBIA

BANJUL

Lat 13° 27' N; Long 16° 34' W.

Admiralty Chart: 608	**Admiralty Pilot:** 1
Time Zone: GMT	**UNCTAD Locode:** GM BJL

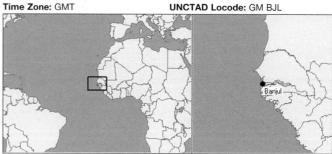

Principal Facilities:

P	Q		G	C	R	L	B		T	A

Authority: Gambia Ports Authority, P O Box 617, Banjul, The Gambia, *Tel:* +220 422 7266 & 422 9940, *Fax:* +220 422 7268, *Email:* info@gamport.gm, *Website:* www.gambiaports.com

Officials: Managing Director: Mohammed Gibba.
Deputy Managing Director: Abdourahman Bah, *Email:* abah@gamport.gm.
Harbour Master: Capt Nat Ethred Coker, *Email:* ncoker@gamport.gm.

Port Security: ISPS compliant

Approach: Max permissible draft at the entrance channel is 8.5-9.5 m. No sand bars or hazards

Anchorage: Anchorage close to wharves in depths of 14.6 m to 27.45 m

Pilotage: Compulsory for vessels entering Gambia River at No.5 Buoy; obtainable at any point on Fairway on request. ETA and draft to be communicated to Harbour Master at Banjul 48 h before estimated arrival and confirmed 12 h before arrival. Vessels arriving Monday, ETA preferably given no later than Saturday morning. Radio call sign CSG. The Pilot station has VHF facilities, calling channel 16 (156.80); working channels 12 (156.60) and 14 (156.70). Continuous listening watch kept 24 h weekdays. Listening watch on weekends if vessels are expected. Reception within a radius of 50 sea-miles. Pilot boat exhibits usual signals

Weather: Winds variable from rainy to dry seasons, SE to NW respectively and sometimes from N direction; at strongest during September and October. Dust haze common December to January

Tides: Tidal rises 1.83 m ST and 1.22 m NT

Traffic: 2005, 469 952 t of cargo handled, 25 801 TEU's

Maximum Vessel Dimensions: Max length of vessel is 182.9 m at wharves and unlimited at anchorage

Principal Imports and Exports: Exports: Cotton, Fish, Groundnuts, Hides and skins, Horticultural products, Seafoods.

Working Hours: Day shift 0800-1930. Night shift 1930-0800

Accommodation:

Name	Length (m)	Remarks
Banjul		Vegetable oil is handled by pipeline at Banjul Wharf
Old Banjul Wharf	120	The outer berth has a depth of 9.5-12 m and the inner berth has a depth of 8 m
New Banjul Wharf	300	See [1] below

[1]*New Banjul Wharf:* The outer berth can accommodate vessels with draughts of 12-14 m and the inner berth, designed for lighter vessels, has a depth of 7 m

Storage:

Location	Open (m²)	Covered (m²)
Banjul	47200	8450

Mechanical Handling Equipment:

Location	Type	Capacity (t)	Qty
Banjul	Mobile Cranes	10–20	2
Banjul	Forklifts	2.5–12	15

Cargo Worked: Up to 950 t/day general cargo, up to 2000 t/day bagged cargoes

Bunkering: Shell Marketing Gambia Ltd, Shell Installation, Dobson Street, Half Die, Banjul, The Gambia, *Tel:* +220 27434, *Fax:* +220 27992
Bominflot, Bominflot Ltd, 5-7 Ravensbourne Road, Bromley, Kent BR1 1HN, United Kingdom, *Tel:* +44 20 8315 5400, *Fax:* +44 20 8315 5429, *Email:* mail@bominflot.co.uk, *Website:* www.bominflot.net – *Grades:* IFO; MGO – *Delivery Mode:* road tanker
Shell Marketing Gambia Ltd, Shell Installation, Dobson Street, Half Die, Banjul, The Gambia, *Tel:* +220 27434, *Fax:* +220 27992

Waste Reception Facilities: Garbage disposal available on request

Towage: 1000 hp berthing tug available from Ports Authority

Repair & Maintenance: Banjul Shipyard Co. Ltd, 1 Wilberforce Street, P O Box 163, Banjul, The Gambia, *Tel:* +220 422 9275, *Fax:* +220 422 2249, *Email:* gambsyltd@qanet.gm Repairs to hull and superstructure, main and auxiliary engines and propeller and shafting. Two slipways available, one capable of handling 500 gt vessels, length 50 m, width 10 m

Shipping Agents: African Maritime Agencies, African Maritime Agencies Ltd Gambia, P O Box 185, Liberation Avenue 61, Banjul, The Gambia, *Tel:* +220 422 8618, *Fax:* +220 422 6683, *Email:* marba@gamtel.gm
Gambia Shipping Agencies Ltd, 14 Wellington Street, P O Box 257, Banjul, The Gambia, *Tel:* +220 422 7432, *Fax:* +220 422 7929, *Email:* gambiaship-x400@ponl.com
Interstate Shipping, 43 Buckle Street, Banjul, The Gambia, *Tel:* +220 422 9388, *Fax:* +220 422 9347, *Email:* interstate@gamtel.gm
Maritime Agencies (Gambia) Ltd, 61 Liberation Avenue, P O Box 185, Banjul, The Gambia, *Tel:* +220 422 8618, *Fax:* +220 422 6683, *Email:* marba@gamtel.gm, *Website:* www.maritime-agencies.com
A.P. Moller-Maersk Group, Maersk Gambia, 80 OAU Boulevard, Banjul, The Gambia, *Tel:* +220 422 4450, *Fax:* +220 422 4025, *Email:* gamordimp@maersk.com, *Website:* www.maerskline.com
Smith & Krafft (SOMICOA), Smith & Krafft (Gambia) Ltd, 36A Liberation Avenue, Banjul, The Gambia, *Tel:* +220 422 4565, *Fax:* +220 422 4566
Thocomar Gambia Ltd, 26 Ecowas Avenue, P O Box 1213, Banjul, The Gambia, *Tel:* +220 422 4211, *Fax:* +220 422 4211, *Email:* thocomar@gamtel.gm

Medical Facilities: Royal Victoria Hospital, Westfield Clinic, Kololi Clinic, Lantoro Clinic, Ndeban Clinic

Airport: Banjul International, 22 km

Lloyd's Agent: Abden Co. Ltd, P O Box 2783, Serrekunda, Banjul, The Gambia, *Tel:* +220 439 5502, *Fax:* +220 439 5142, *Email:* lloyds.banjul@qanet.gm

GEORGIA

BATUMI

Lat 41° 38' N; Long 41° 39' E.

Admiralty Chart: 3317	**Admiralty Pilot:** 24
Time Zone: GMT +3 h	**UNCTAD Locode:** GE BUS

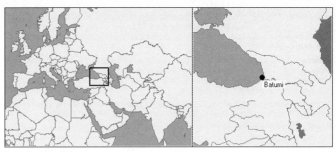

Principal Facilities:

P	Q	Y	G	R	B	T	A

Authority: Batumi Sea Trading Port Ltd, No.1 Kutaisi Street, 6003 Batumi, Adzhariya, Republic of Georgia, *Tel:* +995 222 76261, *Fax:* +995 222 76958, *Email:* bsport@batumiport.com, *Website:* www.batumiport.com

Officials: General Director: Nugzar Katamadze.

Approach: Vessels without cargo must enter port with ballast on board ensuring draught force not less than 1.5 to 1.8 m. Vessels entering or leaving port are not allowed to pass by tankers loading at the outer side of the Oil Jetty at a distance of less than 80 m

Key to Principal Facilities:—			
A=Airport	**C**=Containers	**G**=General Cargo	**P**=Petroleum	**R**=Ro/Ro	**Y**=Dry Bulk
B=Bunkers	**D**=Dry Dock	**L**=Cruise	**Q**=Other Liquid Bulk	**T**=Towage (where available from port)

Anchorage: The recommended anchorage area is located NNE of the E side of Burun-Tabiya Point in depths ranging from 15 m to 20 m. Anchorage in the inner roads can only be obtained with prior permission of the Harbour Master and at the discretion of the pilot

Pilotage: Compulsory. Pilot boards at the Reception Buoy in the outer roads, or in the inner port roads. Masters of vessels should contact the Port Authority 48 h before expected arrival and again at 24 h and confirm 4 h prior to ETA with request for pilot. 24 h service is available

Radio Frequency: Port call sign UFA. Batumi Radio: 500 & 2182 kHz (calling and working). Batumi Radio 2, Port Controller: VHF Channel 16, 156.8 mHz

Weather: Winds from the SW, W and NW can be particularly troublesome, causing a strong variable current with surge in the port. This phenomenon is known as the Tyagun, and although not frequent, usually occurs between October and May. At the time of the Tyagun, vessels are recommended to cease loading/discharging operations, vacate the berth and anchor off, or secure to mooring buoys or put to sea

Traffic: 2004, 8 181 000 t of cargo handled

Maximum Vessel Dimensions: 250 m loa & 120 000 dwt at CBM

Working Hours: Two shifts: 0800-2000, 2000-0800

Accommodation:

Name	Length (m)	Depth (m)	Draught (m)	Remarks
Oil Terminal				
Berth No.1	200	12	11.5	Max 60 000 dwt
Berth No.2	140	10.2	9.7	Max 60 000 dwt
Berth No.3	165	10.2	9.7	Max 60 000 dwt
CBM		15.5	13.5	Vessels of 185-250 m loa & 120 000 dwt See [1] below
Container Terminal				
Berth No's 4 & 5	284	12	11.5	
Dry Cargo Terminal				
Berth No.6	181	8	7.5	
Berth No.7	263	11	10.5	
Berth No.8	189	10	9.5	
Berth No.9	195	10	9.5	
Passenger Terminal				
Berth No.10	220	11.6	11.1	
Berth No.11	194	8.5	7.75	
Ferry Terminal				Railway ferry

[1]*Container Terminal:* Operated by Batumi International Container Terminal LLC (BICTL), 3F Batumi Seaport Port Building, 1 Kutaisi Street, Batumi 6003, Tel: +995 222 76269, Email: tbestenbreur@ictsi.com

Storage: Covered warehouses and concreted open storage areas are available

Mechanical Handling Equipment:

Location	Type	Capacity (t)	Qty
Dry Cargo Terminal	Portal Cranes	5–20	12

Cargo Worked: Crude petroleum 1000 t/h, diesel oil 1000 t/h, petrol 480 t/h, black oil 1400 t/h, grain in bulk 3700 t/day, ore in bulk 2000 t/day, cargo in bags & pallets from 500 t/day, cargo on slings 650 t/day, bags in bulk 450 t/day, general cargo (design) 700 t/day, cargo in boxes 400 t/day, wood 500 t/day

Bunkering: Available at the oil berths and also by barge

Towage: Compulsory for berthing and unberthing

Repair & Maintenance: Only minor repairs can be effected

Ship Chandlers: Scorpio Ship Supply, 4 Khulo Street, 384500 Batumi, Adzhariya, Republic of Georgia, *Tel:* +995 222 77426, *Fax:* +995 222 77426, *Email:* info@scorpiosupply.com, *Website:* www.scorpiosupply.com

Shipping Agents: Albatros Shipping & Forwarding Ltd, 57 Agmashenebeli Street, 4400 Poti, Republic of Georgia, *Tel:* +995 393 70482, *Fax:* +995 393 29014, *Email:* albpoti@mail.ru
Geoinspect Ltd, 59 King Pharnavaz Street, 6010 Batumi, Adzhariya, Republic of Georgia, *Tel:* +995 222 31293, *Fax:* +995 222 31291, *Email:* info@geoinspect.ge, *Website:* www.geoinspect.ge
Georgian Navigation Co Ltd., 31 Kutaisi Street, 6000 Batumi, Adzhariya, Republic of Georgia, *Tel:* +995 9315 8218, *Fax:* +995 2227 6993, *Email:* crew_geonav@yahoo.com & geonaw@gmail.com
Inter Maritime Agency Co.Ltd, 2/9 Z.Gorgiladze Street, 6010 Batumi, Adzhariya, Republic of Georgia, *Tel:* +995 222 76250, *Fax:* +995 222 76251, *Email:* inter@inter-agency.com, *Website:* www.inter-agency.com
TeRo Co. Ltd Shipping & Forwarding Agency, 4 Shavsheti Street, 6017 Batumi, Adzhariya, Republic of Georgia, *Tel:* +995 222 76771, *Fax:* +995 222 76770, *Email:* batumi@teroagency.com, *Website:* www.teroagency.com
Wilhelmsen Ship Services, Barwil Georgia Ltd, 5 Kutaisi Street, 6013 Batumi, Adzhariya, Republic of Georgia, *Tel:* +995 222 76710, *Fax:* +995 222 76711, *Email:* agency@barwilbatumi.ge, *Website:* www.barwil.com

Surveyors: Geoinspect Ltd, 59 King Pharnavaz Street, 6010 Batumi, Adzhariya, Republic of Georgia, *Tel:* +995 222 31293, *Fax:* +995 222 31291, *Email:* info@geoinspect.ge, *Website:* www.geoinspect.ge
Geomar Co. Ltd, Office 13, Floor 32 Gogebashvili Street, 6003 Batumi, Adzhariya, Republic of Georgia, *Tel:* +995 222 76201, *Fax:* +995 222 76202, *Email:* info@geomar.ge, *Website:* www.geomar.ge
Nippon Kaiji Kyokai, Batumi, Adzhariya, Republic of Georgia, *Tel:* +995 222 25344, *Website:* www.classnk.or.jp
Russian Maritime Register of Shipping, 20 ul. Gogebashvili, 384517 Batumi, Adzhariya, Republic of Georgia, *Tel:* +995 222 76522, *Fax:* +995 222 76664, *Email:* 181rs_grz@gol.ge, *Website:* www.rs-head.spb.ru

Medical Facilities: There is a hospital in the town

Airport: Poti Airport, 60km

Lloyd's Agent: Vitsan Interservices Ltd, Gogerasevili Street 32/14, Batumi, Adzhariya, Republic of Georgia, *Tel:* +995 222 76153, *Fax:* +995 222 76153, *Email:* ofis@vitsanbatumi.com, *Website:* www.vitsan.com.tr

KULEVI TERMINAL

Lat 42° 17' N; Long 41° 38' E.

Admiralty Chart: 3317	**Admiralty Pilot:** 24
Time Zone: GMT +3 h	**UNCTAD Locode:** GE

Principal Facilities:

P							T	

Approach: The terminal is approached from the open sea via a dredged channel 2.4 miles long, 210 m wide and 12 m depth

Anchorage: Vessels anchor at anchorage area No.200 off Poti in pos 42° 11.3' N; 41° 36.8' E

Pilotage: Compulsory. Vessel's should advise ETA via agents. Pilot boards 1.5 nautical miles NW of the Fairway Lt Buoy in pos 42° 18' 20" N; 41° 34' 00" E. Berthing is carried out during daylight hours only

Maximum Vessel Dimensions: 244 m loa, 105 000 dwt, 15 m draught

Accommodation:

Name	Length (m)	Depth (m)	Remarks
Kulevi Terminal			See [1] below
Berth No.1	290	17.1	
Berth No.2	230	13.6	
Berth No.3	60	5.5	

[1]*Kulevi Terminal:* The terminal consists of three tanker loading berths and several storage tanks for oil and oil products supplied by railway from Azerbaijan, Turkmenistan and Kazakhstan

Towage: Four tugs are provided to assist in turning the vessel and berthing

Lloyd's Agent: Vitsan Interservices Ltd, Gogerasevili Street 32/14, Batumi, Adzhariya, Republic of Georgia, *Tel:* +995 222 76153, *Fax:* +995 222 76153, *Email:* ofis@vitsanbatumi.com, *Website:* www.vitsan.com.tr

POTI

Lat 42° 9' N; Long 41° 39' E.

Admiralty Chart: 3317	**Admiralty Pilot:** 24
Time Zone: GMT +3 h	**UNCTAD Locode:** GE PTI

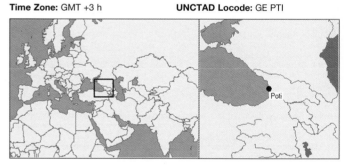

Principal Facilities:

P	Q	Y	G	C	R			T	A

Geoinspect Ltd

59 King Pharnavaz Street,
6010 Batumi, Georgia
Tel: +995 223 31293   Fax: +995 222 31291
Mobile: +995 99 55 1998
Email: info@geoinspect.ge

Surveyors

Poti Cargoservice Ltd

47/4 Agmashenebeli Str, Poti 440, Georgia

Tel: +995 393 25853
Fax: +995 393 24184
Email: psc@access.sanet.ge

Managing Director: Mr. Alexander Gurtovoy

shipping agents

Authority: Poti Sea Port Ltd, 52 David Agmashenebeli Street, 4401 Poti, Republic of Georgia, *Tel:* +995   393 20660, *Fax:* +995   393 20688, *Email:* contact@potiseaport.com, *Website:* www.potiseaport.com

Officials: General Director: Lasha Akhaladze, *Email:* lakhaladze@potiseaport.com. Marketing Manager: Zviad Chkhartishvili, *Email:* marketing@potiseaport.com. Harbour Master: Vakhtang Tavberidze.

Port Security: ISPS compliant

Documentation: Upon arrival, the Master has to hand over to a representative of the local shipping agency the following documents (filled in with full accordance of the IMO requirements) duly signed by the vessel's administration for further examination by:
Boarding Port of Call Officials:
(1) Ship's register
(2) Measurement certificate
(3) Load line (or International Load Line Examination Certificate)
(4) Passenger Ship Safety Certificate
(5) International Certificate on Civil Liability for Oil Pollution Damage (for vessels carrying more than 2000 t of oil)
Health Authorities:
(1) Ship's Health Certificate
(2) Depart Certificate
(3) International Certificate of Vaccination
(4) Maritime Sanitary Declaration
Customs Officials:
(1) General Declaration
(2) Cargo Declaration

LOGOS LIMITED

322/14, Agmashenebeli Str,
Poti 400, GEORGIA

TEL: +995 393 28334
FAX: +995 393 42824
EMAIL: logos777@gol.ge
& logosagent@gol.ge

Director: Mr. Irakli Goginava

Shipping Agents

(3) Ship's crew personal Effects Declaration
(4) Crew List
(5) Passenger List
The Master has to declare to the customs and the port through shipping agency:
(1) Cargo manifest, Bill of Loading, cargo Plan, packing list and other documents for the cargoes carried by the vessel
(2) Other ship's documents on request
Cargo Documentation:
(1) Bill if Loading
(2) Cargo Manifest
(3) Cargo Plan
(4) Certificate of Origin
(5) Packing List
(6) Phytosanitary Certificate

Anchorage: Vessels can find anchorage with good holding ground in depths of 10-30 m in the roadstead, at a distance 1.3 nautical miles NW and 1.1 nautical mile W of the head of the western moll, in anchorage No's 421 and 422. In outer port which is protected by New North, and western Molls, and by Western Breakwater. Safe anchorage for deep draft vessels, except in periods when swell, a strong variable current with surge occurs, with winds from NW, W and SW. The roads are open to winds blowing from the sea. Therefore, in the event of stormy weather, vessels are recommended to leave anchorage in the outer roads for the sea

Pilotage: Compulsory. Pilot boards vessel in the outer roads 0.5 nautical mile from the Poti lightbuoy in pos 42° 09' N; 41° 38' E. The Harbour Master's office will give the master of the vessel appropriate instructions if the pilot is able to disembark in the outer due to stormy weather or heavy seas

Radio Frequency: VHF Channel 16 for communication between port and vessels

Weather: Prevailing winds W and E

Tides: Max range 60 cm in winter months

Traffic: 2007, 7 734 000 t of cargo handled, 184 792 TEU's

Maximum Vessel Dimensions: 280 m loa, 90 000 dwt, 12.5 m draft

Principal Imports and Exports: Imports: Coal, Equipment, Flour, Oil products, Wheat. Exports: Citrus, Manganese, Scrap, Timber.

Working Hours: 24 h/day

Accommodation:

Name	Length (m)	Depth (m)	Remarks
Poti			See [1] below
Berth No.1	200	12.5	Liquid cargo
Berth No.2	183	12.5	Ferry terminal
Berth No.3	215	8.5	General & bulk cargo
Berth No.4	154	8.5	General & bulk cargo
Berth No.5	173	8.5	General & bulk cargo
Berth No.6	212	9.75	General & bulk cargo
Berth No.7	211	8.25	Container terminal
Berth No.8	215	9.75	General & bulk cargo
Berth No.9	220	8	General & bulk cargo
Berth No.10	264	8	General & bulk cargo
Berth No.11	71	8	General & bulk cargo
Berth No.12	250	6.1	Ro/ro & passenger terminal
Berth No.13	97	6.5	Ro/ro & passenger terminal
Berth No.14	250	8.4	Grain & General cargo
Berth No.15			Not working

[1]*Poti:* The port consists of an outer roadstead and an inner harbour. The inner harbor, which is protected by breakwaters, consists of three basins approached by a channel. The length of entrance channel is 1900 m and the width 100 m. The total area of basins is 643 400 m2

Storage:

Location	Open (m²)	Covered (m²)
Berth No.1	1600	
Berth No.2	10200	
Berth No.4	4700	
Berth No.5	11350	
Berth No.6	7231	
Berth No.7	16248	
Berth No.8	6210	
Berth No.9	3200	
Berth No.10	3100	9831

Mechanical Handling Equipment:

Location	Type	Capacity (t)	Qty
Berth No.2	Portal Cranes	16–32	2
Berth No.3	Portal Cranes	16–32	5
Berth No.4	Portal Cranes	16–32	3
Berth No.5	Portal Cranes	16–32	3
Berth No.6	Portal Cranes	16–32	2
Berth No.7	Portal Cranes	40	2
Berth No.8	Portal Cranes	16–32	3
Berth No.9	Portal Cranes	5–6	3
Berth No.10	Portal Cranes	5–20	4

Waste Reception Facilities: Garbage disposal is available and should be ordered through agents

Towage: Three tugs available

Repair & Maintenance: Minor repairs only

Ship Chandlers: Atlas Co. Ltd. Shipping & Forwarding Agency, 150/32 Chavcha-vadze Street, 4400 GEO Poti, Republic of Georgia, *Tel:* +995 393 78800, *Fax:* +995 393 78800, *Email:* atlas@gol.ge Managing Director: Vyacheslav Boldyrev

Shipping Agents: Ahlers & Partners, Stalin Embarkment 30/82, 384691 Poti, Republic of Georgia, *Tel:* +995 393 70732, *Fax:* +995 393 70731, *Email:* info@poti.ahlers.com, *Website:* www.ahlers.com

Key to Principal Facilities:—				
A=Airport	**C**=Containers	**G**=General Cargo	**P**=Petroleum	**R**=Ro/Ro **Y**=Dry Bulk
B=Bunkers	**D**=Dry Dock	**L**=Cruise	**Q**=Other Liquid Bulk	**T**=Towage (where available from port)

Albatros Shipping & Forwarding Ltd, 57 Agmashenebeli Street, 4400 Poti, Republic of Georgia, *Tel:* +995 393 70482, *Fax:* +995 393 29014, *Email:* albpoti@mail.ru

Argo Shipping Agency Ltd, 24/44 Stalin Embankment, 384691 Poti, Republic of Georgia, *Tel:* +995 393 20787, *Fax:* +995 393 20788, *Email:* argoship@iberiapak.ge, *Website:* www.georgia.net.ge

Astro Poti, Stalin Embankment 30/82, 384691 Poti, Republic of Georgia, *Tel:* +995 393 20699, *Fax:* +995 393 24497, *Email:* astrosp@iberiapac.ge, *Website:* www.astrosweb.com

Cautrexpoti Ltd, 28/80 Stalin Embankment, 384690 Poti, Republic of Georgia, *Tel:* +995 393 22106, *Fax:* +995 393 22103

CMA-CGM S.A., CMA CGM Georgia, 1 Kokaia Alley, Poti, Republic of Georgia, *Tel:* +995 393 28436, *Fax:* +995 393 21278, *Website:* www.cma-cgm.com

Logos Ltd., 22/14 Agmashenebeli Street, 4400 Poti, Republic of Georgia, *Tel:* +995 393 28334, *Fax:* +995 393 42824, *Email:* logos777@gol.ge

Maritime Transport & Agencies AB, Gegidze Street 17/1, Poti, Republic of Georgia, *Tel:* +995 393 29059, *Fax:* +995 393 29059, *Email:* merab.kuchukhidze@mta.ge, *Website:* www.mta.nu

Metrol International Ltd, Apartment 24, 24 St. Avenue April 9th, 384691 Poti, Republic of Georgia, *Tel:* +995 393 20626, *Fax:* +995 393 20626

A.P. Moller-Maersk Group, Maersk Georgia LLC, 12 Larnaka Street, 384690 Poti, Republic of Georgia, *Tel:* +995 322 44870, *Fax:* +995 322 44875, *Email:* ptiopt@maersk.com, *Website:* www.maerskline.com

Pace Shipping Agency Ltd, 15/39 Gegidzes Street, 384691 Poti, Republic of Georgia, *Tel:* +995 393 70501, *Fax:* +995 393 70502, *Email:* pace-shipping@pace.ge, *Website:* www.pacetransport.com

Poti Cargoservice Ltd., 47/4 Agmashenebeli Street, 4400 Poti, Republic of Georgia, *Tel:* +995 393 25853, *Fax:* +995 393 24184, *Email:* pcs@access.sanet.ge

Potivneshtrans Ltd, ul Gegidze 19, 384691 Poti, Republic of Georgia, *Tel:* +995 393 70092/3, *Fax:* +995 393 70091, *Email:* pvt@gol.ge

Sisamtrans llc, 37 David Agmashenebeli Street, Poti, Republic of Georgia, *Tel:* +995 393 25550, *Fax:* +995 393 25550, *Email:* sisam.poti@access.sanet.ge

Sofmar Shipping Agency, 30/39 9th April Street, 4401 Poti, Republic of Georgia, *Tel:* +995 393 20265, *Fax:* +995 393 20267, *Email:* sofmar@gol.ge, *Website:* www.sofmar.ge

TeRo Co. Ltd Shipping & Forwarding Agency, 1 Liepaya Street, 4400 Poti, Republic of Georgia, *Tel:* +995 393 70431, *Fax:* +995 393 70433, *Email:* ops@teropoti.com, *Website:* www.teroagency.com

T&M Ltd, Building No.8, 5 Lipei Street, Poti, Republic of Georgia, *Tel:* +995 393 42030, *Fax:* +995 393 75536, *Email:* tmpoti@access.sanet.ge

Wilhelmsen Ship Services, Barwil Georgia Ltd, 3 Tabidze Street, 4403 Poti, Republic of Georgia, *Tel:* +995 393 71681, *Fax:* +995 393 71686, *Email:* barwil@barwilpti.com.ge, *Website:* www.barwilpti.com.ge

Surveyors: Argo Shipping Agency Ltd, 24/44 Stalin Embankment, 384691 Poti, Republic of Georgia, *Tel:* +995 393 20787, *Fax:* +995 393 20788, *Email:* argoship@iberiapak.ge, *Website:* www.georgia.net.ge

Cargo Inspections Group (CIG), Agmashtenebeli Str.14, Poti, Republic of Georgia, *Tel:* +995 393 20860, *Fax:* +995 393 28055, *Email:* georgia@cargoinspections.cpm, *Website:* www.cargoinspections.com

Geoinspect Ltd, 10 David Agmashenebeli Street, Poti, Republic of Georgia, *Tel:* +995 955 97505, *Fax:* +995 222 31291, *Email:* info@geoinspect.ge, *Website:* www.geoinspect.ge

Medical Facilities: Medical assistance, if required, is available through agents, including vaccination and inoculation as well as dispensary and hospital treatment

Airport: Poti, 3 km

Development: The depth of the entrance channel and some of the berths will increase to 13 m

Lloyd's Agent: Vitsan Interservices Ltd, Gogerasevili Street 32/14, Batumi, Adzhariya, Republic of Georgia, *Tel:* +995 222 76153, *Fax:* +995 222 76153, *Email:* ofis@vitsanbatumi.com, *Website:* www.vitsan.com.tr

SUKHUMI

Lat 43° 10' N; Long 41° 2' E.

Admiralty Chart: 3313	Admiralty Pilot: 24
Time Zone: GMT +3 h	UNCTAD Locode: GE SUI

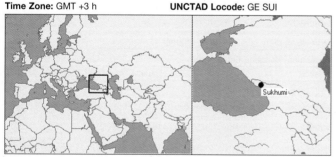

Principal Facilities:

P		G		L B		A

Authority: Port of Sukhumi Authority, Rustaveli ul.66, 389400 Sukhumi, Republic of Georgia, *Tel:* +995 88122 28202, 23403 & 23400

Anchorage: Anchorage can be obtained in the outer roads E of the port, off the mouth of the Besleta River in depths ranging between 12 m to 50 m; holding ground mud. Vessels at anchor can sometimes be troubled by SW winds from seaward and also by land winds

Pilotage: Compulsory for foreign flag vessels. Pilot boards at the outer roads. Navigation is permitted at any time of the day or night

Radio Frequency: Port call sign UFF. Sukhumi Radio: 500, 454 & 2182 kHz (calling); 500, 450 & 2182 kHz (working). Sukhumi Radio 1, Port Controller: VHF Channel 16, 156.8 mHz; VHF Channel 9, 156.45 mHz

Maximum Vessel Dimensions: 180 m loa, 7.6 m d. Passenger vessels can be accommodated up to 190 m loa

Accommodation:

Name	Depth (m)	Remarks
Sukhumi		Facilities exist for tankers and cruise ships visit the port
Cargo Pier	2.4–6	Cargoes handled include mineral building materials
Passenger Piers		See [1] below

[1]*Passenger Piers:* Two berths. The main passenger pier has a depth alongside of 7.8 m and there is a passenger terminal

Storage: Enclosed warehouses are available

Mechanical Handling Equipment:

Location	Type	Capacity (t)	Qty
Sukhumi	Mult-purp. Cranes	12	1
Sukhumi	Mobile Cranes	5	

Bunkering: Fuel oil can be supplied by lighter

Medical Facilities: There are two hospitals in the town

Airport: Sukhumi Airport

Lloyd's Agent: Vitsan Interservices Ltd, Gogerasevili Street 32/14, Batumi, Adzhariya, Republic of Georgia, *Tel:* +995 222 76153, *Fax:* +995 222 76153, *Email:* ofis@vitsanbatumi.com, *Website:* www.vitsan.com.tr

SUPSA TERMINAL

Lat 42° 1' N; Long 41° 43' E.

Admiralty Chart: 3313/3317	Admiralty Pilot: 24
Time Zone: GMT +3 h	UNCTAD Locode: GE

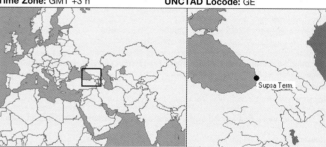

Principal Facilities:

P									

Authority: Georgian Pipeline Company, 38 Saburtalo Street, Tbilisi, Republic of Georgia, *Tel:* +995 32 699600, *Fax:* +995 32 941184, *Email:* badzgarm@bp.com

Port Security: ISPS compliant

Anchorage: Two anchorages available in pos 42° 02' 05" N; 41° 41' 27" E and 42° 02' 58" N; 41° 40' 39" E

Pilotage: Compulsory. Two loading master's board vessel 3 nautical miles W of SPM via a service launch 'Tamari'

Radio Frequency: Supsa Marine on VHF Channels 16 and 07. Marine and loading operation will be carried out on VHF Channel 49

Maximum Vessel Dimensions: 240-290 m loa, 33-50 m beam, 60 000-164 000 dwt, max draft 17.5 m, max loaded displacement 199 000 t

Accommodation:

Name	Remarks
Supsa Terminal	See [1] below

[1]*Supsa Terminal:* Marine Terminal, Tel: +995 293 76771, Fax: +995 293 76775 Oil delivered by pipeline from Baku to Supsa. Consists of a SPM in depth of 50 m. Vessels moored during daylight hours only. Loading rate from SPM to export tanker is 1000-6000 m3/h

Supsa Storage Terminal is located 3 km inshore from the pipeline manifold and consists of four storage tanks, each with a cap of 39 500 m3

Shipping Agents: TeRo Co. Ltd Shipping & Forwarding Agency, Sup'sa, Republic of Georgia, *Email:* ops@terosupsa.com, *Website:* www.teroagency.com

Lloyd's Agent: Vitsan Interservices Ltd, Gogerasevili Street 32/14, Batumi, Adzhariya, Republic of Georgia, *Tel:* +995 222 76153, *Fax:* +995 222 76153, *Email:* ofis@vitsanbatumi.com, *Website:* www.vitsan.com.tr

GERMANY

BAYER TERMINAL

harbour area, see under Brunsbuttel

BOLLHORNKAI

harbour area, see under Kiel

BRAKE

Lat 53° 20' N; Long 8° 29' E.

Admiralty Chart: 3406
Time Zone: GMT +1 h

Admiralty Pilot: 55
UNCTAD Locode: DE BKE

Principal Facilities:

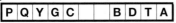

| P | Q | Y | G | C | | B | D | T | A |

Tramp Oil & Marine

Wells House, 15-17 Elmfield Road, Bromley,
Kent BR1 1LT, United Kingdom
Phone: +44 20 8315 7777   **Fax:** +44 20 8315 7788
General email: enquiries@tramp-oil.com

See listings for all global offices: **www.tramp-oil.com**

Authority: Niedersachsen Ports GmbH & Co. KG, Port of Brake, P O Box 1262, 26912 Brake, Germany, Tel: +49 4401 925-0, Fax: +49 4401 3272, Email: brake@nports.de, Website: www.brake-port.de

Officials: Harbour Master: Heiko Uflacker, Email: huflacker@nports.de.

Port Security: ISPS compliant

Approach: The lower Weser has a channel depth of 9.15 m MSLW. Sea-going vessels with 11.9 m max draught can reach the port installations by making use of the tide

Pilotage: Compulsory for vessels over 1000 gt. Available at Bremen or Bremerhaven

Radio Frequency: Brake lock radio. VHF Channel 10

Tides: Tidal range is 3.8 m

Traffic: 2007, 6 432 000 t of cargo handled

Maximum Vessel Dimensions: 275 m loa, 12.2 m draught

Working Hours: 0600-1400, 1400-2200, 2200-0600. Sun 0600-1200, 1200-1800, 1800-2400, 2400-0600

Accommodation: Situated on the west bank of the Lower Weser, 47 nautical miles from the open North Sea between Bremerhaven and Bremen

Name	Length (m)	Depth (m)	Remarks
South Pier - Agri Terminal			
Seagoing Section	410	12.8	See [1] below
River Shipping Section	122	6	See [2] below
North Pier - Bulk Terminal			
Pier	940	11.5–12.8	See [3] below
North Pier - Sulphur Terminal			
Pier	220	9.8	See [4] below
Fat Refinery Terminal			
Pier	166	8.1	See [5] below
Inner Harbour			See [6] below
East Quay No.1 Berth	72		Berths for four deep-sea trawlers handling fish
East Quay No.2 Berth	116		Interim moorings for river and coastal shipping
South East Quay No.1 Berth	180		See [7] below
South East Quay No.2 Berth	40		Bunkerage berth
South East Quay No.3 Berth	50		Berths for fifteen pleasure craft
West Quay No.1 Berth	30		Berths for fifteen pleasure craft
West Quay No.2 Berth	90		See [8] below
West Quay No.3 Berth	110		See [9] below
West Quay No.4 Berth	118		Interim moorings for river and coastal vessels
Canal Harbour - West Quay	197		See [10] below
Canal Harbour - East Quay No.1 Berth	35		Berths for fifteen pleasure craft
Canal Harbour - East Quay No.2 Berth	55		Fireboats and pontoons
Canal Harbour - East Quay No.3 Berth	95		Dolphin moorings

[1]*Seagoing Section:* Operated by J. Muller Agri Terminal GmbH & Co KG, P O Box 1354, 26913 Brake, Tel: +49 4401 914-0, Fax: +49 4401 914229, Email: agri@mueller.de, Website: www.jmueller.de
Two berths for vessels up to 200 m loa or one berth for vessels up to 275 m loa handling grain and feedstuffs. Two grain/feed grab hoists with a total discharging volume of 1400 t/h, three ship chargers with a total performance of 1800 t/h and four wagon/truck loading/discharging stations with a total throughput cap of 2400 t/h. Silos and warehouses with a storage cap of 330 000 t
[2]*River Shipping Section:* Operated by J. Muller Agri Terminal Co Ltd
Handling grains and feed. One grain/feed ship charger with a loading cap of 600 t/h
[3]*Pier:* Operated by J. Muller Breakbulk Terminal GmbH & Co KG, P O Box 1355, 26913 Brake, Tel: +49 4401 914-3, Fax: +49 4401 914419, Email: bbt@jmueller.de, Website: www.jmueller.de
Two berths for vessels up to 200 m loa or one berth for vessels up to 275 m loa handling forest products, iron & steel, containers, project and general cargo. Equipment includes three slewing and luffing cranes with lifting cap of 25 t and two loading bridges with lifting cap of 88 t. Covered storage area of 113 410 m2 and open storage area of 62 960 m2
[4]*Pier:* Operated by NEAG - North German Natural Gas Processing Company Ltd
Handling liquid and solid sulphur. One ship charger with cap 1000 m3/h, one conveyor system 550 m long with cap 1000 m3/h and one liquid sulphur transfer terminal with cap 450 t/h
[5]*Pier:* Private quay with cargo handling facilities for vegetable and animal oils, fats, mineral oils and molasses with discharging cap of approx 1500 t/h
[6]*Inner Harbour:* For inland waterways vessels and coasters up to 2500 dwt as well as LASH barges. Protected by a sea lock of 95 m x 16 m
[7]*South East Quay No.1 Berth:* Operated by J. Muller Breakbulk Terminal GmbH & Co KG
Handling iron & steel, machinery components, forest products and miscellaneous general goods. One luffing and slewing crane with lifting cap of 32 t. Covered storage area of 2555 m2 and open storage area of 2555 m2
[8]*West Quay No.2 Berth:* Interim moorings for lash lighters, river and coastal vessels
[9]*West Quay No.3 Berth:* Operated by North Cape Minerals Co Ltd
Handling chemicals. One mobile crane with lifting cap of 11 t
[10]*Canal Harbour - West Quay:* Operated by BVU Handels Co Ltd
Handling building materials. One track crane with lifting cap of 6 t and open storage area of 950 m2

Storage: Breakbulk Logistics Centre (BLC) with roofed area of 95 000 m2 and 53 000 m2 of open space

Bunkering: Drinking and boiler water available on application to the agent
BMT Bremer Mineraoel Transport GmbH & Co. KG, Konsul-Smidt Street 8 Floor, 28217 Bremen, Germany, Tel: +49 421 3391710, Fax: +49 421 3391741, Email: info@bmt-bremen.com
Bominflot, Bominflot Bunkergesellschaft fur Mineralole mbH & Co. KG, Grosse Baeckerstrasse 11, 20095 Hamburg, Germany, Tel: +49 40 350 930, Fax: +49 40 3509 3116, Email: mail@bominflot.de, Website: www.bominflot.net
B.O.T. Broring Oil Trading GmbH, B.O.T. Broering Oil Trading GmbH, Carl Ronning-strasse 9, 28195 Bremen, Germany, Tel: +49 421 170 091, Fax: +49 421 170 093, Email: home@b-o-t.info, Website: www.broering.info
Deutsche BP AG, Max Born Strasse 2, 22761 Hamburg, Germany, Tel: +49 40 639 4628, Fax: +49 40 6395 4670, Email: rudi.schrader@de.bp.com, Website: www.bp.com
ExxonMobil Marine Fuels, Mailpoint 31, ExxonMobil House, Ermyn Way, Leather-head, Surrey KT22 8UX, United Kingdom, Tel: +44 1372 222 000, Fax: +44 1372 223 922, Email: marine.fuels@exxonmobil.com, Website: www.exxonmobil.com
Friedrich G. Frommann, Wallgraben 47, 21073 Hamburg, Germany, Tel: +49 40 7662 680, Fax: +49 40 7662 6818, Email: frommann@fgfshell.de, Website: www.fgfshell.de
Germany Transport & Logistics GmbH, Buchtstrasse 4, 22087 Hamburg, Germany, Tel: +49 40 64225 7070, Fax: +49 40 64225 7075, Email: info@gtl-hamburg.de
Hans Rinck Bunkering Service, P O Box 226, 21637 Horneburg, Germany, Tel: +49 4163 814 10, Fax: +49 4163 814 122, Email: mail@hans-rinck.com, Website: www.hans-rinck.com
Maxcom Bunker S.p.A. u.s., Maxcom Energy S.p.A., Eckerkamp 7a, 22391 Ham-burg, Germany, Tel: +49 40 417568, Fax: +49 40 417563, Email: maxcom@ehmcke.com, Website: www.maxcom.it
Tramp Oil & Marine, World Fuel Services Corporation, 13th Floor, Portland House, Bressenden Place, London SW1E 5BH, United Kingdom, Tel: +44 20 7808 5000, Fax: +44 20 7808 5088, Email: pturner@wfscorp.com, Website: www.wfscorp.com – Delivery Mode: barge

Towage: Schlepperburo Bremen, Geo-Plate Strasse 1, 27568 Bremen, Germany, Tel: +49 421 348 8180, Fax: +49 421 487450, Email: info@bugsier.de, Website: www.bugsier.de

Shipping Agents: JAL Schiffahrt und Logistic Service, Lindenstrasse 17, 26919 Brake, Germany, Tel: +49 4401 936548, Fax: +49 4401 936551, Email: jal.brake@t-online.de, Website: www.jal-shipping.de

Medical Facilities: St Bernhard Hospital, Brake, Tel: +49 4401 1050

Airport: Bremen, 45 km

Lloyd's Agent: Reck & Co. GmbH, Herrlichkeit 5, 28199 Bremen, Germany, Tel: +49 421 59834-0, Fax: +49 421 598 3450, Email: mail@reck.de, Website: www.reck.de

Key to Principal Facilities:—			
A=Airport	C=Containers	G=General Cargo	P=Petroleum	R=Ro/Ro	Y=Dry Bulk
B=Bunkers	D=Dry Dock	L=Cruise	Q=Other Liquid Bulk	T=Towage (where available from port)	

BREMEN

Lat 53° 6' N; Long 8° 45' E.

Admiralty Chart: 3407	**Admiralty Pilot:** 55
Time Zone: GMT +1 h	**UNCTAD Locode:** DE BRE

Principal Facilities:

P	Q	Y	G	C	R	L	B		T	A

Tramp Oil & Marine

Wells House, 15-17 Elmfield Road, Bromley,
Kent BR1 1LT, United Kingdom
Phone: +44 20 8315 7777   **Fax:** +44 20 8315 7788
General email: enquiries@tramp-oil.com

See listings for all global offices: **www.tramp-oil.com**

Authority: Hansestadt Bremisches Hafenamt, Hafenkaptiaen Uberseetor 20, 28217 Bremen, Germany, *Tel:* +49 421 361 8504, *Fax:* +49 421 361 8387, *Email:* bremenport@hbh.bremen.de, *Website:* www.bremen-ports.de

Officials: Harbour Master: Capt Andreas Mai, *Tel:* +49 421 361 8271, *Email:* andreasmai@hbh.bremen.de.

Port Security: ISPS compliant

Pre-Arrival Information: All vessels are obliged to report their ship data, details of security measures according to SOLAS XI-2 and details of waste disposal information to Port Authority by electronic message latest 12 h before arrival. The electronic message may be executed directly in the port community system or alternatively sending a fax (via local agent or directly) to the Bremen Ship Reporting Service, where the data is keyed in against a service fee. For details and further information see www.bremen-ports.de, especially ships-arrival-form and waste-notification-form

Approach: The river fairway is lit; radar advice (VTS) and pilots available. A water depth of 14.0 m is available as far as Geeste River mouth, a depth of 13.0-11.9 m is available between Geeste River mouth and Nordenham/Brake and a depth of 9.0 m is available between Brake and Bremen. Vessels above loa of 190 m or a draft over 7.6 m are restricted by tide

Anchorage: Anchorage with enough swinging space is available on the river at 'Hohe Weg Reede' approx 15 nautical miles N of Bremerhaven and for smaller vessels up to 120 m loa at 'Blexen Reede' SW of River Geeste

Pilotage: River Weser pilotage area is divided into two districts. Sea pilots (Weser II/Jade) and river pilots (Weser I) are available. For ports S of Bremerhaven changeover of pilots takes place off Bremerhaven, usually in vicinity of River Geeste mouth

Pilotage is compulsory for all oil, gas and chemical tankers, nuclear powered ships and all sea-going vessels with a length overall of 90 m or more or a beam overall of 13 m and more

Under normal weather conditions the pilot vessel is cruising 5 nautical miles N of Wangerooge Lighthouse at buoys Weser 3/Jade 2. In rough weather the pilot vessel will be found at the inside position near light buoys 17 and 19 at 'Hohe Weg'

The following vessels have to take the pilot at Light Vessel 'German Bight' when inbound:

tankers with loa of 130 m and more or boa of 21 m and more
bulk vessels with loa of 250 m and more or boa of 40 m and more or a draft of more than 13.5 m
all other vessels with loa of 350 m and more or boa of 45 m and more
Request for pilotage sent to: Weser/Jade Pilot Bremerhaven, via VHF Channel 6 or Tel: +49 471 944242, Fax: +49 471 944 2439, Email: dispo@weserjadepilot.de
When taking a pilot at German Bight Light Vessel 24 h notice is required. 12 h notice is required when taking the pilot at the boarding position near Racon buoy Weser3/Jade2

Following particulars to be transmitted:
vessel's name
overall length, largest width, current draft in fresh water (in metres)
ETA at German Bight light vesselboarding position
port of destination
Corrected ETA messages should be sent one hour prior to arrival by VHF Channel 6 or 16 to Weser Pilot vessel
Pilots can also be ordered to the port of sailing at any North Sea or English Channel port 24 h prior to sailing

In case helicopter transfer of the pilot is required, the request should be sent 24 h in advance to the pilot station by stating in addition to the above information whether a marked winching area or a landing area is provided and indicating as to where this area is located

An updated ETA message should be sent to the pilot station 6 h in advance, while the exact time of arrival has to be transmitted about 2 h in advance

Short-term requests for helicopter transfer of pilots will be honoured, but in these cases no guarantee will be given that the transfer is performed at the time desired

Radio Frequency: Bremen Port Radio on VHF Channel 3 for harbour traffic control. Oslebshausen Lock Radio on VHF Channel 12 for lock traffic only

Weather: Prevailing winds SE'ly to W'ly with average speed 7-16 kn. Basins normally ice free; ice occurs only under extreme frost

Tides: Tidal range is approx 4.1 m at normal tide, with tidal currents of 2.5-3.5 knots

Traffic: 2007, 69 212 000 t of cargo handled, 4 912 177 TEU's (includes Bremerhaven)

Working Hours: 24 h/day

Accommodation: The port is divided into the Hemelinger Hafen, Europahafen, Neustaedter Hafen, Holz-und Fabrikhafen, Gertreidehafen, Werfthafen, Kap Horn Hafen, Klocknerhafen, Car Terminal and the Industriehafen area. The Industriehafen is protected by Oslebshausen lock, the other parts of the port are open to the tide Inland Transport: Railways to all parts of Germany and Central Europe. Inland shipping to the Rhine via the Unterweser-Kusten-Kanal, the Dortmund-Ems-Kanal, or the Mittellandkanal-Dortmund-Ems-Kanal. To the Elbe via the Mittelweser-Mittellandkanal. Truck transport to everywhere in Europe

Name	Length (m)	Depth (m)	Remarks
R Weser Berths			
Europahafen	2690	6.4–8.5	
Holz-und Fabrikhafen	2280	6.2–10.5	
Getreidehafen	725	4–11.5	
Werfthafen	1360	6.2–7.2	
Kap Horn Hafen	250	9	
Neustaedter Hafen	2600	10.5–11.5	Ro/ro facilities available
Hohentorshafen	420	3–5.5	
Mittelsburener Hafen	1800	11.5	
Car Terminal		5.5–8.5	Lengths of 320 m and 200 m
Weserhafen Hemelingen	3050	3.5	Three docks for barges & small sea-going vessels only See [1] below
Industriehafen			
Hafen A	550	8.6–10.2	
Hafen E	450	8.8–10.2	
Hafen F	280	5–9.7	
Kohlenhafen	900	9.8–10.2	
Kalihafen	500	9.8–10.2	
Huttenhafen	960	8–10.2	
Olhafen Quay	190	5–9.7	

[1]*Industriehafen:* An artificial basin, entry to which is through the Oslebshausen lock

Bunkering: BMT Bremer Mineraoel Transport GmbH & Co. KG, Konsul-Smidt Street 8 Floor, 28217 Bremen, Germany, *Tel:* +49 421 3391710, *Fax:* +49 421 3391741, *Email:* info@bmt-bremen.com

B.O.T. Broring Oil Trading GmbH, B.O.T. Broering Oil Trading GmbH, Carl Ronningstrasse 9, 28195 Bremen, Germany, *Tel:* +49 421 170 091, *Fax:* +49 421 170 093, *Email:* home@b-o-t.info, *Website:* www.broering.info

Bremer Mineraloel Transport GmbH & Co KG (BMT), Speicher 1, Uberseestadt, Konsul-Smidt-Strasse 8F, 28217 Bremen, Germany, *Tel:* +49 421 3391 710, *Fax:* +49 421 3391 741, *Email:* info@bmt-bremen.com

United Fuel Services GmbH & Co KG, Schuesselkorb 17/18, D-28195 Bremen, Germany, *Tel:* +49 421 8357 600, *Fax:* +49 421 8357 6099, *Email:* bunkers@ufuels.com, *Website:* www.ufuels.com

BMT Bremer Mineraoel Transport GmbH & Co. KG, Konsul-Smidt Street 8 Floor, 28217 Bremen, Germany, *Tel:* +49 421 3391710, *Fax:* +49 421 3391741, *Email:* info@bmt-bremen.com

Bominflot, Bominflot Bunkergesellschaft fur Mineralole mbH & Co. KG, Grosse Baeckerstrasse 11, 20095 Hamburg, Germany, *Tel:* +49 40 350 930, *Fax:* +49 40 3509 3116, *Email:* mail@bominflot.de, *Website:* www.bominflot.net

B.O.T. Broring Oil Trading GmbH, B.O.T. Broering Oil Trading GmbH, Carl Ronningstrasse 9, 28195 Bremen, Germany, *Tel:* +49 421 170 091, *Fax:* +49 421 170 093, *Email:* home@b-o-t.info, *Website:* www.broering.info

Deutsche BP AG, Max Born Strasse 2, 22761 Hamburg, Germany, *Tel:* +49 40 639 4628, *Fax:* +49 40 6395 4670, *Email:* rudi.schrader@de.bp.com, *Website:* www.bp.com

ExxonMobil Marine Fuels, Mailpoint 31, ExxonMobil House, Ermyn Way, Leatherhead, Surrey KT22 8UX, United Kingdom, *Tel:* +44 1372 222 000, *Fax:* +44 1372 223 922, *Email:* marine.fuels@exxonmobil.com, *Website:* www.exxonmobil.com

Friedrich G. Frommann GmbH, Wallgraben 47, 21073 Hamburg, Germany, *Tel:* +49 40 7662 680, *Fax:* +49 40 7662 6818, *Email:* frommann@fgfshell.de, *Website:* www.fgfshell.de

Germany Transport & Logistics GmbH, Buchtstrasse 4, 22087 Hamburg, Germany, *Tel:* +49 40 64225 7070, *Fax:* +49 40 64225 7075, *Email:* info@gtl-hamburg.de

Hans Rinck Bunkering Service, P O Box 226, 21637 Horneburg, Germany, *Tel:* +49 4163 814 10, *Fax:* +49 4163 814 122, *Email:* mail@hans-rinck.com, *Website:* www.hans-rinck.com

Maxcom Bunker S.p.A. u.s., Maxcom Energy S.p.A., Eckerkamp 7a, 22391 Hamburg, Germany, *Tel:* +49 40 417568, *Fax:* +49 40 417563, *Email:* maxcom@ehmcke.com, *Website:* www.maxcom.it

Tramp Oil & Marine, World Fuel Services Corporation, 13th Floor, Portland House, Bressenden Place, London SW1E 5BH, United Kingdom, *Tel:* +44 20 7808 5000, *Fax:* +44 20 7808 5088, *Email:* pturner@wfscorp.com, *Website:* www.wfscorp.com – *Grades:* all grades

Waste Reception Facilities: Dirty ballast can be discharged into barges or road tankers supplied by private operators. Clean ballast can also be discharged Barges or road tankers for reception of slops, oily waste, etc. are available.
Garbage Removal: A waste notification specifying the amount of all types of waste on board and indicating also the
intended disposal has to be effected 24 h before arrival.

According to local regulations garbage of any kind accumulated during the vessel's stay has to
be disposed prior to sailing. For normal household waste receptacles will be placed on board upon arrival. The number of receptacles supplied is dependent on vessel's size and number of crew. Receptacles are collected prior to sailing. Charges will be collected automatically with harbour dues.
Apart from household waste other types of waste require different receptacles which can be ordered via agents from private operators

Towage: A sufficient number of tugs at 2200 hp are available. Towage is not compulsory

Repair & Maintenance: Several smaller shipyards
Fr. Lurssen Werft GmbH & Co. KG, Zum Alten Speicher 11, 28759 Bremen, Germany, *Tel:* +49 421 660 4334, *Fax:* +49 421 660 4395, *Email:* info@luerssen.de, *Website:* www.luerssen.de Three slipways with caps up to 540 t, 1200 t and 2000 t

Ship Chandlers: H. Albert GmbH, Doventorsdeich 17/21, 28195 Bremen, Germany, *Tel:* +49 421 30404-0, *Fax:* +49 421 304 0444, *Email:* info@albert-gmbh.de, *Website:* www.albert-gmbh.de
Interbrew Export & Licenses GmbH & Co. KG, P O Box 107307, 28073 Bremen, Germany, *Tel:* +49 421 5094-0, *Fax:* +49 421 509 4346, *Email:* service@becks.de
Intermarine Service & Handels GmbH, Speicherhof 207, 28217 Bremen, Germany, *Tel:* +49 421 393040, *Fax:* +49 421 393010, *Email:* info@intermarine-bremen.de
Karagiannidis & Sons GmbH, P O Box 150549, 28095 Bremen, Germany, *Tel:* +49 421 27741-0, *Fax:* +49 421 277 4119, *Email:* info@karagiannidis.com, *Website:* www.karagiannidis.com
Karpa Trading GmbH, Schwachhauser Heerstrasse 68, 28209 Bremen, Germany, *Tel:* +49 421 168 2360, *Fax:* +49 421 168 2635, *Email:* tkara@karpa-trading.com
Uwe Kloska GmbH, Pillauer Strasse 15, 28217 Bremen, Germany, *Tel:* +49 421 618020, *Fax:* +49 421 618 0220, *Email:* mail@kloska-bremen.de, *Website:* www.kloska.com
Seekarte Kapitan A. Dammeyer, Korffsdeich 3, 28217 Bremen, Germany, *Tel:* +49 421 395051, *Fax:* +49 421 396 2235, *Email:* seekarte@seekarte.de, *Website:* www.seekarte.de
TBSG Versorgung + Logistik GmbH, Reiherstrasse 229, 28239 Bremen, Germany, *Tel:* +49 421 399550, *Fax:* +49 421 399 5521, *Email:* info@tbsg.de, *Website:* www.tbsg.de

Shipping Agents: Allmaritim Schiffahrtskontor GmbH, Jupiterstrasse 4, Stuhr, 28816 Bremen, Germany, *Tel:* +49 421 565 9919, *Fax:* +49 421 257 3986, *Email:* info@allmaritim.de, *Website:* www.allmaritim.de
CMA-CGM S.A., CMA-CGM (Deutschland) GmbH, Obernstrasse 52-54, Hansehof, 28195 Bremen, Germany, *Tel:* +49 421 165660, *Fax:* +49 421 165 6610, *Email:* bre.genmbox@cma-cgm.com, *Website:* www.cma-cgm.com
Karl Geuther GmbH & Co., Martinistrasse 58, 28195 Bremen, Germany, *Tel:* +49 421 17600, *Fax:* +49 421 176 0302, *Email:* geuther@bre.geuther.com, *Website:* www.geuther.com
H. Glahr & Co. GmbH, Schlachte 31, P O Box 105467, 28054 Bremen, Germany, *Tel:* +49 421 17640, *Fax:* +49 421 176 4205, *Email:* shipping@glahr.de, *Website:* www.glahr.de
Paul Gunther Schiffsmakler GmbH & Co. KG, Kohlhokerstrasse 29, 28203 Bremen, Germany, *Tel:* +49 421 16250, *Fax:* +49 421 162 5251, *Email:* info@pagunt.com, *Website:* www.pagunt.com
Hanseatic Shipping & Chartering GmbH, Langenstrasse 44, 28195 Bremen, Germany, *Tel:* +49 421 302 9170, *Fax:* +49 421 302 9178, *Email:* ts@hsc-stuhr.de
A Hartrodt International, Competence Center North/South America, Lloydstrasse 4, 28217 Bremen, Germany, *Tel:* +49 421 36380, *Fax:* +49 421 363 8262, *Email:* ah_bre@bremen.hartrodt.com, *Website:* www.hartrodt.de
Nicolaus Haye & Co. (GmbH & Co.), P O Box 105049, 28050 Bremen, Germany, *Tel:* +49 421 17650, *Fax:* +49 421 176 5212
Incotrans GmbH Linienagentur, Carl-Zeiss Strasse 34, Stuhr, 28816 Bremen, Germany, *Tel:* +49 421 328 8300, *Fax:* +49 421 328 8304, *Email:* info@incotrans.com, *Website:* www.incotrans.com
Mann Lines Ltd, Mann Lines GmbH, Birkenstrasse 15, 28195 Bremen, Germany, *Tel:* +49 421 163850, *Fax:* +49 421 163 8520, *Email:* service@mannlines.de, *Website:* www.mannlines.ee
Mediterranean Shipping Company, MSC Germany GmbH, Hafenstrasse 55, 28217 Bremen, Germany, *Tel:* +49 421 308040, *Fax:* +49 421 12773, *Email:* bremen@mscgermany.com, *Website:* www.mscgermany.com
A.P. Moller-Maersk Group, Maersk Deutschland A/S & Co.KG, Hanseatenhof 6, 28195 Bremen, Germany, *Tel:* +49 421 30840, *Fax:* +49 421 308 4103, *Email:* bresal@maersk.com, *Website:* www.maerskline.com
Neptun Schiffahrts-Agentur GmbH, Langenstrasse 44, 28195 Bremen, Germany, *Tel:* +49 421 176 3263, *Fax:* +49 421 176 3271, *Email:* neptun@neptun-agency.com, *Website:* www.neptunship.de
D. Oltmann Agency Services GmbH & Co. KG, P O Box 102727, 28027 Bremen, Germany, *Tel:* +49 421 360 6243, *Fax:* +49 421 360 6333, *Email:* info@oltmann-agency.com, *Website:* www.oltmann.com
Hugo Trumpy GmbH, CarlZeiss Strasse 34, 28816 Bremen, Germany, *Tel:* +49 421 337580, *Fax:* +49 421 337 5810, *Email:* ht@hugotrumpy.de
Ultra Schiffahrt GmbH, Altenwall 2-5, 28195 Bremen, Germany, *Tel:* +49 421 528 5847, *Fax:* +49 421 528 5867, *Email:* info@ultrashipping.de, *Website:* www.ultrashipping.de
Unimar Linienagentur GmbH, Altenwall 21, 28195 Bremen, Germany, *Tel:* +49 421 16250, *Fax:* +49 421 162 5251, *Email:* tamke@neptumar.de, *Website:* www.neptumar.de
Van Ommeren Hamburg GmbH, Van Ommeren GmbH, Altenwall 2-5, 28195 Bremen, Germany, *Tel:* +49 421 36810, *Fax:* +49 421 368 1235, *Email:* liner.bremen@vanommeren.de, *Website:* www.royalburgergroup.com
Wiking Transtainer Systems GmbH, Martinistrasse 50, D-28195 Bremen, Germany, *Tel:* +49 421 176 0440, *Fax:* +49 421 176 0371, *Email:* wiking@bre.wiking-ship.de
Zim Integrated Shipping Services Ltd, Tiefer 4, P O Box 103024, 28195 Bremen, Germany, *Tel:* +49 421 363080, *Fax:* +49 421 363 0866, *Email:* agency@msbre.com, *Website:* www.shipagent.de

Surveyors: Bureau Veritas, Hillmannplatz 11, 28195 Bremen, Germany, *Tel:* +49 421 169 1951, *Fax:* +49 421 169 1953, *Email:* ger_hbr@de.bureauveritas.com, *Website:* www.bureauveritas.com
Capt. H.J. Moeller & Partner, Expert Bureau Capt. H.J. Moeller & Partner, Old Faehrweg 8, 27568 Bremerhaven, Germany, *Tel:* +49 471 946090, *Fax:* +49 471 946 0999, *Email:* office@moeller-expert.com, *Website:* www.moeller-expert.com

Airport: Bremen, approx 5 km
Railway: Bremen, approx 5 km
Lloyd's Agent: Reck & Co. GmbH, Herrlichkeit 5, 28199 Bremen, Germany, *Tel:* +49 421 59834-0, *Fax:* +49 421 598 3450, *Email:* mail@reck.de, *Website:* www.reck.de

BREMERHAVEN

Lat 53° 33' N; Long 8° 35' E.

Admiralty Chart: 3621	**Admiralty Pilot:** 55
Time Zone: GMT +1 h	**UNCTAD Locode:** DE BRV

Principal Facilities:

P		Y	G	C	R	L	B	D	T	A

Tramp Oil & Marine

Wells House, 15-17 Elmfield Road, Bromley, Kent BR1 1LT, United Kingdom
Phone: +44 20 8315 7777 **Fax:** +44 20 8315 7788
General email: enquiries@tramp-oil.com

See listings for all global offices: **www.tramp-oil.com**

Authority: Hansestadt Bremisches Hafenamt, Steubenstrasse 7a, 27568 Bremerhaven, Germany, *Tel:* +49 471 5961 3417, *Fax:* +49 471 5961 3423, *Email:* bremerhaven-port@hbh.bremen.de, *Website:* www.bremen-ports.de

Officials: Harbour Master: Capt Andreas Mai, *Email:* andreas-mai@hbh.bremen.de.

Port Security: ISPS compliant. Container Security Initiative (CSI) designated port

Documentation: Crew list (4 copies), passenger list (3 copies), stowaways (2 copies), tobacco/spirits/personal effects (2 copies), stores (2 copies), arms & ammunition (2 copies), health documents or certificate (1 copy), certificate of deratting (1 copy), load line certificate (1 copy), tonnage certificate (1 copy), certificate of nationality (1 copy), safety equipment certificate (1 copy), cargo gear certificate (1 copy), bills of lading copy (1 copy), manifests freighted/unfreighted (1 copy), dangerous cargo manifest (3 copies), tanker check list (1 copy for river pilot), IOPP certificate incl. supplements (1 copy), oil record book (1 copy), drinking water certificate (1 copy only for German vessels)

Approach: The river fairway is lighted. A water depth of 14 m is available as far as Geeste River mouth. Radar advice (VTS) and pilots available. Panamax vessels drawing above 12.8 m and post-panamax vessels drawing above 12.7 m are restricted by tide

Anchorage: Anchorage with enough swinging space is available on the river at 'Hohe Weg Reede', approx 15 nautical miles N of Bremerhaven and for smaller vessels up to 120 m loa at 'Blexen Reede', SW of River Geeste

Pilotage: River Weser pilotage area is divided into two districts: Sea pilots (Weser II / Jade) and river pilots (Weser I)
For ports S of Bremerhaven changeover of pilots takes place off Bremerhaven, usually in the vicinity of River Geeste mouth
River Weser pilotage: compulsory for all loaded oil, gas and chemical tankers and for all sea-going vessels with a length overall of 90 m or more or a beam overall of 13 m or more. Under normal weather conditions the pilot vessel is cruising 5 nautical miles N of Wangerooge lighthouse at buoys Weser3/Jade2. In rough weather the pilot vessel will be found at the inside position near light buoys 17 and 19 at 'Hohe Weg Roads'
The following vessels have to take the pilot at Light Vessel "German Bight" when inbound: tankers with an loa of 150 m and over or a beam of 23 m and over, bulk vessels with an loa of 250 m and over or a beam of 40 m and over or a draft of more than 13.5 m, all other vessels with an loa of 350 m and over or a beam of 45 m and over
Requests for ordering a pilot on arrival to Weser/Jade Pilot Bremerhaven via VHF Channel 6 or Tel: +49 471 944242, Fax: +49 471 944 2439, Email: dispo@weserjadepilot.de. When taking a pilot at German Bight light vessel a 24 h notice is required and a 12 h notice is required when taking a pilot at the boarding position near Racon buoy Weser3/Jade2. Corrected ETA messages should be sent 3 h and 1 h prior to arrival by VHF Channel 6 or 16 to Weser Pilot vessel
For berthing/unberthing in Bremerhaven docking pilots board vessels at 'Stromkaje' (Container Terminal). For vessels bound for 'Fischereihafen' docking pilots board near River Geeste mouth. Pilotage is compulsory for oil, gas or chemical carriers over

60 m loa or 10 m in breadth and for all other sea-going vessels of more than 90 m loa and/or 13 m in breadth. Service available 24 h/day and requests should be made 2 h prior to arrival, however 1 h before arrival or departure via Harbour Master's Office, Tel: +49 471 5961 3417/8 or via Bremerhaven Port Radio on VHF Channel 12
Ordering procedure on departure for Sea Pilots: request for pilot shall be sent to the pilot station not later than 2 h prior to sailing by stating as well the sailing draft in freshwater in metres. For vessel departures between 1900-0800 the pilot has to be ordered by 1700 at the latest

Radio Frequency: Bremerhaven Port Radio on VHF Channel 12, Bremerhaven North Lock Radio on VHF Channel 10 and Fischereihafen Lock Radio on VHF Channel 10

Tides: Range of tide approx 3.8 m at normal tide with tidal currents of 2.5-3.5 knots

Traffic: 2007, 69 212 000 t of cargo handled, 4 912 177 TEU's (includes Bremen)

Maximum Vessel Dimensions: Container terminal approx 400 m loa, Uberseehafen 335 m loa and Fischereihafen 220 m loa. The max dimensions do not necessarily apply to all berths, quays or areas within the port

Working Hours: Mon-Fri: early shift 0600-1400, day shift 0730-1530, late shift 1430-2230, night shift 2230-0600
Sat: early shift 0600-1400, day shift 0730-1530, late shift 1430-2030, night shift 2030-0230
Sun & holidays: 1st shift 0600-1200, 2nd shift 1200-1800, 3rd shift 1800-2400, 4th shift 2400-0600
In urgent cases and to finish a vessel, overtime can be worked but must be ordered in advance before end of shift

Accommodation: Main port activities are the handling of containers, automobiles, fish, fruits and passengers
The port is divided into the Uberseehafen area and the Fischereihafen area. Except for two berths along R Weser (container, passenger and part of the fruit terminal) the port is protected by locks
Lock Dimensions: Nordschleuse - 372 m long, 45 m width of gate in depth of 11 m LW. Kaiserschleuse - 223 m long, 27.25 m width of gate in depth of 6.8 m LW

Name	Length (m)	Depth (m)	Remarks
Uberseehafen			See [1] below
Columbus Quay	1020	9–11	Passenger & fruit terminal
Stromkaje	4900	12–15	See [2] below
Car Terminal		10.5	Kaiserhafen II & III, Nordhafen, Osthafen
Fruit Terminal		9–11	Verbindungshafen
Oil Terminal		9–11	Verbindungshafen
Kaiserhafen I		8.5–10.5	
Fischereihafen			See [3] below

[1]*Uberseehafen:* Berths along River Weser: Columbus Quay and Stromkaje
Berths behind locks: Nordhafen, Osthafen, Verbindungshafen, Kaiserhafen I, Kaiserhafen II and Kaiserhafen III

[2]*Stromkaje:* Container terminal operators:
Eurogate Container Terminal Bremerhaven GmbH., Senator-Borttscheller-Strasse 1, 27568 Bremerhaven, Tel: +49 471 142502, Fax: +49 471 1425 4300, Email: ctb@eurogate.eu, Website: www.eurogate.eu
Quay length of 3040 m with nine main berths and three short sea berths. Terminal area of 2 017 000 m2 and equipment includes 32 container cranes (including 17 super-post-panamax and 12 post-panamax)
MSC Gate Bremerhaven GmbH & Co. KG, Senator-Borttscheller-Strasse 1, 27568 Bremerhaven, Tel: +49 471 926 6868, Fax: +49 471 302 0753, Email: info-mscgate@mscgate.de, Website: www.mscgate.de
Quay length of 600 m (2 berths) with 5 container cranes (including 3 for post-panamax vessels)
North Sea Terminal Bremerhaven GmbH & Co., Senator-Borttscheller-Strasse 6, D-27568 Bremerhaven, Tel: +49 471 944 6400, Fax: +49 471 944 6429, Email: sekretariat@ntb.eu, Website: www.ntb.eu
Quay length of 1100 m (3 berths) with 10 super-post-panamax cranes and one 70 t mobile harbour crane

[3]*Fischereihafen:* Situated South of River Geeste. Divided into five basins (Handelshafen, Fischereihafen I, Fischereihafen II, Luneorthafen and Labradorhafen), enclosed by locks. Water depth of 5-7.5 m handling fish, timber, gravel, foodstuffs and cars

Mechanical Handling Equipment: Floating cranes with a cap up to 600 t are available. Mobile cranes with different lifting caps can also be hired

Location	Type	Capacity (t)	Qty
Columbus Quay	Electric Cranes	4–8	7
Stromkaje	Container Cranes	75–103	27

Bunkering: All grades of oil available from different suppliers, usually by barge
BMT Bremer Mineraoel Transport GmbH & Co. KG, Konsul-Smidt Street 8 Floor, 28217 Bremen, Germany, Tel: +49 421 3391710, Fax: +49 421 3391741, Email: info@bmt-bremen.com
Bominflot, Bominflot Bunkergesellschaft fur Mineralole mbH & Co. KG, Grosse Baeckerstrasse 11, 20095 Hamburg, Germany, Tel: +49 40 350 930, Fax: +49 40 3509 3116, Email: mail@bominflot.de, Website: www.bominflot.net
B.O.T. Broring Oil Trading GmbH, B.O.T. Broering Oil Trading GmbH, Carl Ronningstrasse 9, 28195 Bremen, Germany, Tel: +49 421 170 091, Fax: +49 421 170 093, Email: home@b-o-t.info, Website: www.broering.info
Deutsche BP AG, Max Born Strasse 2, 22761 Hamburg, Germany, Tel: +49 40 639 4628, Fax: +49 40 6395 4670, Email: rudi.schrader@de.bp.com, Website: www.bp.com
ExxonMobil Marine Fuels, Mailpoint 31, ExxonMobil House, Ermyn Way, Leatherhead, Surrey KT22 8UX, United Kingdom, Tel: +44 1372 222 000, Fax: +44 1372 223 922, Email: marine.fuels@exxonmobil.com, Website: www.exxonmobil.com
Friedrich G. Frommann GmbH, Wallgraben 47, 21073 Hamburg, Germany, Tel: +49 40 7662 680, Fax: +49 40 7662 6818, Email: frommann@fgfshell.de, Website: www.fgfshell.de
Germany Transport & Logistics GmbH, Buchtstrasse 4, 22087 Hamburg, Germany, Tel: +49 40 64225 7070, Fax: +49 40 64225 7075, Email: info@gtl-hamburg.de
Hans Rinck Bunkering Service, P O Box 226, 21637 Horneburg, Germany, Tel: +49 4163 814 10, Fax: +49 4163 814 122, Email: mail@hans-rinck.com, Website: www.hans-rinck.com

Maxcom Bunker S.p.A. u.s., Maxcom Energy S.p.A., Eckerkamp 7a, 22391 Hamburg, Germany, Tel: +49 40 417568, Fax: +49 40 417563, Email: maxcom@ehmcke.com, Website: www.maxcom.it
Tramp Oil & Marine, World Fuel Services Corporation, 13th Floor, Portland House, Bressenden Place, London SW1E 5BH, United Kingdom, Tel: +44 20 7808 5000, Fax: +44 20 7808 5088, Email: pturner@wfscorp.com, Website: www.wfscorp.com – Delivery Mode: barge

Waste Reception Facilities: No fixed ballast reception facilities available ashore, but dirty ballast can be discharged into barges or road tankers supplied by private operators. Clean ballast can be discharged
Garbage Removal: A waste notification specifying the amount of all types of waste on board and indicating also the
intended disposal has to be effected 24 h before arrival.
According to local regulations garbage of any kind accumulated during the vessel's stay has to be disposed prior to sailing. For normal household waste receptacles will be placed on board upon arrival. The number of receptacles supplied is dependent on vessel's size and number of crew. Receptacles are collected prior to sailing. Charges will be collected automatically with harbour dues.
Apart from household waste other types of waste require different receptacles which can be ordered via agents from private operators

Towage: Sufficient number of tugs available day and night

Repair & Maintenance: Bremerhavener Dock GmbH, Dockstrasse 19, 27572 Bremerhaven, Germany, Tel: +49 471 799710, Fax: +49 471 799718, Email: info@bredo.de, Website: www.bredo.de Three floating docks up to 50 000 dwt. Repair quay of 200 m with max draught 8 m
Lloyd Werft Bremerhaven GmbH, Bruckenstrasse 25, 27568 Bremerhaven, Germany, Tel: +49 471 4780, Fax: +49 471 478610, Email: info@lloydwerft.com, Website: www.lloydwerft.com Two dry docks: 222 m x 26 m x 10 m and 335 m x 35 m x 11.5 m. Two floating docks: 286 m x 38 m x 94 m and 146 m x 21 m x 6.5 m. Two repair quays of 400 m and 200 m with max draught 10.5 m
Rickmers Lloyd Dockbetrieb GmbH & Co. KG, P O Box 120454, 27568 Bremerhaven, Germany, Tel: +49 471 48010, Fax: +49 471 480140, Email: rickmers-lloyd@lloydwerft.com, Website: www.lloydwerft.com One floating dock of 7200 t lifting cap for vessels up to 156 loa, 20.5 m breadth and 6.5 m draft

Ship Chandlers: Hans Heidorn Shipping Services GmbH, Immenhofweg, 27612 Stotel-Loxstedt, Germany, Tel: +49 471 941 3794, Fax: +49 471 941 3793, Email: heidorn-shipping@hans-heidorn.de
Uwe Kloska GmbH, Riedemannstrasse 30, 27572 Bremerhaven, Germany, Tel: +49 471 932200, Fax: +49 471 932 2040, Email: mail@kloska-bremerhaven.de, Website: www.kloska-bremerhaven.de
Rolf Lubbe Hebe- und Zurrsysteme, P O Box 29 02 13, 27532 Bremerhaven, Germany, Tel: +49 471 96290-0, Fax: +49 471 961 2003, Email: info@rolf-luebbe.de, Website: www.rolf-luebbe.de
Odin Schiffsausrustung GmbH, Unter der Rampe 5, 27572 Bremerhaven, Germany, Tel: +49 471 979400, Fax: +49 471 71200, Email: odinsar@aol.com, Website: www.odinsar.de
Weser Shipstores GmbH, Weserstrasse 159, 27578 Bremerhaven, Germany, Tel: +49 471 49042, Fax: +49 471 416258, Email: weser-shipstores@t-online.de, Website: www.weser-shipstores.de

Shipping Agents: K Line (Europe) Ltd, Gatehouse 2 5th Floor, Bremerhaven, Germany, Tel: +49 471 944590, Fax: +49 471 414604, Email: keubrvall@de.kline.com
A.P. Moller-Maersk Group, Maersk Deutschland A/S & Co.KG, Terminal Office, Gatehouse 5, 27568 Bremerhaven, Germany, Tel: +49 471 1428 6611, Fax: +49 471 1428 6690, Email: geropsmng@maersk.com, Website: www.maerskline.com
D. Oltmann Agency Services GmbH & Co. KG, P O Box 310264, 27538 Bremerhaven, Germany, Tel: +49 471 944 6020, Fax: +49 471 944 6060, Email: info@oltmann-agency.com, Website: www.oltmann.com
Sartori & Berger, Geo-Plate Strasse 1, 27568 Bremerhaven, Germany, Tel: +49 471 941 3093, Fax: +49 471 941 3095, Email: bremerhaven@sartori-berger.de, Website: www.sartori-berger.de

Surveyors: Germanischer Lloyd, Geo-Plate-Str. 1, 27568 Bremerhaven, Germany, Tel: +49 471 92449-0, Fax: +49 471 924 4930, Email: gl-bremerhaven@gl-group.com, Website: www.gl-group.com
Capt. H.J. Moeller & Partner, Expert Bureau Capt. H.J. Moeller & Partner, Old Faehrweg 8, 27568 Bremerhaven, Germany, Tel: +49 471 946090, Fax: +49 471 946 0999, Email: office@moeller-expert.com, Website: www.moeller-expert.com

Medical Facilities: Port health and quarantine station at Bremerhaven with all kinds of medical services available. Requests via VHF Channel 12 Bremerhaven Port Radio. Port doctor is available, vaccination service on request

Airport: Bremen, 62 km

Railway: Central Station, 8 km

Development: Container Terminal (CT) 4 project consists of four new berths for mega-container vessels, the first of which was inaugurated in October 2006. The last berth is due to go into operation in April 2008. All will be operated by North Sea Terminal Bremerhaven (NTB)

Lloyd's Agent: Reck & Co. GmbH, Herrlichkeit 5, 28199 Bremen, Germany, Tel: +49 421 59834-0, Fax: +49 421 598 3450, Email: mail@reck.de, Website: www.reck.de

BRUNSBUTTEL

Lat 53° 54' N; Long 9° 8' E.

Admiralty Chart: 2469	**Admiralty Pilot:** 55	
Time Zone: GMT +1 h	**UNCTAD Locode:** DE BRB	

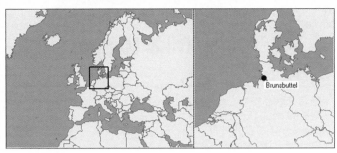

Principal Facilities:

P	Q	Y	G	C		L	B		T	A

Tramp Oil & Marine

Wells House, 15-17 Elmfield Road, Bromley,
Kent BR1 1LT, United Kingdom
Phone: +44 20 8315 7777   **Fax:** +44 20 8315 7788
General email: enquiries@tramp-oil.com

See listings for all global offices: **www.tramp-oil.com**

Authority: Hafengesellschaft Brunsbuttel mbH, Elbehafen, 25541 Brunsbuttel, Germany, *Tel:* +49 4852 884-0, *Fax:* +49 4852 88426, *Email:* info@elbehafen.de, *Website:* www.elbehafen.de

Officials: Managing Director: Hans Helmut Schramm, *Tel:* +49 4852 88415, *Email:* h-h.schramm@elbehafen.de.
Marketing Manager: Norbert Feis, *Tel:* +49 4852 88419, *Email:* n.feis@elbehafen.de.
Port Captain: Capt Lars Sell, *Tel:* +49 4852 88448, *Email:* l.sell@elbehafen.de.

Port Security: ISPS compliant

Anchorage: Neufeld Reede: approx 3 miles from Brunsbuttel with max allowed d of 9.5 m
South Reede: off Brunsbuttel for vessels up to 120 m loa with max allowed d of 10.0 m

Pilotage: Elbe River pilots, VHF Channel 8 or 16. Kiel Canal pilots, VHF Channel 9 or 13. Tankers exceeding 130 m loa and/or 21 m breadth which are in laden condition and/or not gas free are obliged to take the pilot at the German Bight lightfloat. Tankers up to 220 m loa and/or 32 m breadth which are in ballast and gas free can take the pilot at the Elbe-1 pilot station. Bulkers exceeding 220 m loa and/or 32 m breadth are obliged to take the pilot at the German Bight lightfloat

Radio Frequency: Traffic information can be obtained from Revierzentrale Cuxhaven on VHF Channel 71 and Revierzentrale Brunsbuttel on VHF Channel 68

Traffic: 2003, 8 064 377 t of cargo handled

Maximum Vessel Dimensions: 350 m loa, 55 m width, 13.8 m draft (oil pier), 14.8 m draft (dry cargo pier), 4.7 m draft (inner basin for smaller vessels)

Working Hours: Offices: Mon-Fri 0800-1630. Tankers: round the clock. Bulk and other cargo: Mon-Fri 0700-1600

Accommodation:

Name	Length (m)	Draught (m)	Remarks
Elbeharbour			See [1] below
Tanker Berth		13.8	See [2] below
Bulk Terminal	550	14.8	Pilot boards at Elbe I light vessel
Gas Terminal		13.8	See [3] below
Oil Harbour			See [4] below
Ostermoor Harbour			Situated at the northern part of the Kiel Canal at km 5,65
Heavy Fuel Oil Berth			See [5] below
Bulk Berth			See [6] below
LPG Berth			Handling ammonia, with 60 000 m3 of storage
Elf Union Terminal			See [7] below
Bayer Terminal			See [8] below

[1]*Elbeharbour:* Containers can be discharged, loaded and stored at Elbeharbour terminal. Container storage cap of 2000 TEU's. 500 TEU dangerous goods area
[2]*Tanker Berth:* Handling crude oil. Also a shore installation with one 30" pipeline. No loading possible, discharging cap of 10 000 m3/h. Bunker fuel and diesel oil available by barge or lorry. Fresh water available
[3]*Gas Terminal:* Fully refrigerated 18 000 m3 liquefied propane shore storage tank. The cargo quantity onboard vessel may not exceed 15 000 m3 or 6000 m3 for a single tank. Fresh water available
[4]*Oil Harbour:* Situated at the northern part of the Kiel Canal at km 3,55
Two T-shaped jetties available, draft depending on beam, but 10.4 m max draft, freshwater, 235 m max loa, 27 m max beam. Also three small jetties for barges and coasters only
[5]*Heavy Fuel Oil Berth:* Draft depending on beam, but 10.4 m max draft freshwater, 235 m max loa, 32.5 m max beam. Bunker fuel and diesel oil available by barge, or at Brunsbuttel inner harbour bunker stations. Fresh water available

[6]*Bulk Berth:* Handling bagged and bulk urea. Storage cap of 85 000 t. Airdraft limited to 45 m
[7]*Elf Union Terminal:* Situated inside of the Kiel Canal. Two T-shaped berths, d depending on beam, but 10.4 m max d freshwater, 235 m max loa. One T-shaped berth and one continuous pier, d depending on beam, but 9.5 m max d freshwater, 235 m max loa, 32.5 m max beam. Max distance bow or stern to C/M limited to 115 m. Bunker fuel, diesel oil and fresh water available
[8]*Bayer Terminal:* Situated inside of the Kiel Canal. One T-shaped berth, 6.5 m max d freshwater, handling caustic soda, aniline oil, formaldehyde and sulphuric acid

Storage:

Location	Open (m²)	Covered (m²)
Brunsbuttel	483900	27900

Mechanical Handling Equipment:

Location	Type	Capacity (t)	Qty
Brunsbuttel	Mult-purp. Cranes	12–120	5
Brunsbuttel	Reach Stackers	45	2
Brunsbuttel	Forklifts	30	7

Cargo Worked: At Elbeharbour: coal 10 000-25 000 t/day, clinkers 12 000 t/day, fertilizers 5000 t/day

Bunkering: Total Bitumen Deutschland GmbH, Industriegebiet Sud, 25541 Brunsbuttel, Germany, *Tel:* +49 4852 888 260, *Fax:* +49 4852 888 263, *Email:* infobunker@total.de, *Website:* www.total.de
Bominflot, Bominflot Bunkergesellschaft fur Mineralole mbH & Co. KG, Grosse Baeckerstrasse 11, 20095 Hamburg, Germany, *Tel:* +49 40 350 930, *Fax:* +49 40 3509 3116, *Email:* mail@bominflot.de, *Website:* www.bominflot.net
B.O.T. Broring Oil Trading GmbH, B.O.T. Broering Oil Trading GmbH, Carl Ronningstrasse 9, 28195 Bremen, Germany, *Tel:* +49 421 170 091, *Fax:* +49 421 170 093, *Email:* home@b-o-t.info, *Website:* www.broering.info
Deutsche BP AG, Max Born Strasse 2, 22761 Hamburg, Germany, *Tel:* +49 40 639 4628, *Fax:* +49 40 6395 4670, *Email:* rudi.schrader@de.bp.com, *Website:* www.bp.com
Deutsche Calpam GmbH, Grosse Elbstrasse 141 a, 22767 Hamburg, Germany, *Tel:* +49 40 3068 620, *Fax:* +49 40 3068 6216, *Email:* bunkers@calpam.de, *Website:* www.calpam.de
ExxonMobil Marine Fuels, Mailpoint 31, ExxonMobil House, Ermyn Way, Leatherhead, Surrey KT22 8UX, United Kingdom, *Tel:* +44 1372 222 000, *Fax:* +44 1372 223 922, *Email:* marine.fuels@exxonmobil.com, *Website:* www.exxonmobil.com
Friedrich G. Frommann GmbH, Wallgraben 47, 21073 Hamburg, Germany, *Tel:* +49 40 7662 680, *Fax:* +49 40 7662 6818, *Email:* frommann@fgfshell.de, *Website:* www.fgfshell.de
Germany Transport & Logistics GmbH, Buchtstrasse 4, 22087 Hamburg, Germany, *Tel:* +49 40 64225 7070, *Fax:* +49 40 64225 7075, *Email:* info@gtl-hamburg.de
Hans Rinck Bunkering Service, P O Box 226, 21637 Horneburg, Germany, *Tel:* +49 4163 814 10, *Fax:* +49 4163 814 122, *Email:* mail@hans-rinck.com, *Website:* www.hans-rinck.com
Maxcom Bunker S.p.A. u.s., Maxcom Energy S.p.A., Eckerkamp 7a, 22391 Hamburg, Germany, *Tel:* +49 40 417568, *Fax:* +49 40 417563, *Email:* maxcom@ehmcke.com, *Website:* www.maxcom.it
Total Bitumen Deutschland GmbH, Industriegebiet Sud, 25541 Brunsbuttel, Germany, *Tel:* +49 4852 888 260, *Fax:* +49 4852 888 263, *Email:* infobunker@total.de, *Website:* www.total.de
Tramp Oil & Marine, World Fuel Services Corporation, 13th Floor, Portland House, Bressenden Place, London SW1E 5BH, United Kingdom, *Tel:* +44 20 7808 5000, *Fax:* +44 20 7808 5088, *Email:* pturner@wfscorp.com, *Website:* www.wfscorp.com
Tramp Oil & Marine, Tramp Oil Germany GmbH & Co. KG, (a World Fuel Services Company), Bremer Str.2, 28816 Stuhr, Germany, *Tel:* +49 421 165 610, *Fax:* +49 421 1656 161, *Email:* bunkers.bremen@wfscorp.com, *Website:* www.wfscorp.com
Heinrich Wegener & Sohn Bunkergesellschaft mbH, Focksweg 34, 21129 Hamburg, Germany, *Tel:* +49 40 7421 9010, *Fax:* +49 40 7421 2635, *Email:* general@wegener-bunker.de, *Website:* www.wegener-bunker.de

Waste Reception Facilities: Sludge/engine slops can be discharged into barges or road trucks. Garbage disposal can be given ashore into containers

Towage: Five tugs of 10-32.2 t bollard pull
Hans Schramm & Sohn GmbH & Co. KG, Am Sudufer, 25541 Brunsbuttel, Germany, *Tel:* +49 4852 83010, *Fax:* +49 4852 830123, *Email:* info@hans-schramm.de, *Website:* www.hans-schramm.de

Repair & Maintenance: Barthels & Luders GmbH, Schleswiger Strasse 2, Brunsbuttel, Germany, *Tel:* +49 4852 8870, *Fax:* +49 4852 88786

Shipping Agents: Cargo-Service Hanse-Tally- Kontor GmbH, Elbehafen, 25541 Brunsbuttel, Germany, *Tel:* +49 4852 87077, *Fax:* +49 4852 87107, *Email:* info@cargo-service-htk.de, *Website:* www.cargo-service-htk.de
Sartori & Berger, Schleuseninsel, 25541 Brunsbuttel, Germany, *Tel:* +49 4852 8890, *Fax:* +49 4852 88935, *Email:* brunsbuettel@sartori-berger.de, *Website:* www.sartori-berger.de
UCA United Canal Agency GmbH, Schleuse, Brunsbuttel, Germany, *Tel:* +49 4852 83090, *Fax:* +49 4852 830920, *Email:* ucabb@kiel-canal.de, *Website:* www.kiel-canal.de

Stevedoring Companies: Sartori & Berger, Schleuseninsel, 25541 Brunsbuttel, Germany, *Tel:* +49 4852 8890, *Fax:* +49 4852 88935, *Email:* brunsbuettel@sartori-berger.de, *Website:* www.sartori-berger.de

Medical Facilities: Hospital, doctors and dentists available

Airport: Hamburg Airport, 90 km

Railway: Itzehoe, 40 km. 9 km of port-owned rail tracks

Lloyd's Agent: Reck & Co. GmbH, Wikinghaus, Schopenstehl 22, D-20095 Hamburg, Germany, *Tel:* +49 40 2789 6375, *Fax:* +49 40 2780 6418, *Email:* hamburg@reck.de, *Website:* www.reck.de

---

Key to Principal Facilities:—				
A=Airport	**C**=Containers	**G**=General Cargo	**P**=Petroleum	**R**=Ro/Ro	**Y**=Dry Bulk
B=Bunkers	**D**=Dry Dock	**L**=Cruise	**Q**=Other Liquid Bulk	**T**=Towage (where available from port)	

BUSUM

Lat 54° 7' N; Long 8° 51' E.

Admiralty Chart: 1875/3767

Time Zone: GMT +1 h

Admiralty Pilot: 55

UNCTAD Locode: DE BUM

Principal Facilities:

		G	R	B	T	

Authority: Amt fur landliche Raume Husum, Hafenamt Busum, Am Fischereihafen 7, 25761 Busum, Germany, *Tel:* +49 4834 3607, *Fax:* +49 4834 936383, *Email:* rainer.wallhof@lkn.landsh.de

Officials: Harbour Master: Rainer Wallhof.

Port Security: ISPS compliant

Pre-Arrival Information: 24 h notice of ETA to be given by vessel's agent

Documentation: Crew list (1 copy), provisions and bonded stores list (1 copy), personal effects list (1 copy), health certificate (1 copy)

Approach: Through fairway 'Suderpiep' marked by buoys. Distance from fairway buoy to Busum port is 16 nautical miles. The channel into the port is marked by leading lights (Iso white, 4 sec) bearing 355.1°

Anchorage: Anchorage can be obtained in the roadstead to the S of the port entrance

Pilotage: Not compulsory but recommended. To obtain pilot contact vessel agent at least 12 h prior to arrival at 'Elbe 1'

Radio Frequency: Busum Port Radio on VHF Channel 11

Tides: Mean tide level of 3.5 m

Maximum Vessel Dimensions: 120 m loa, 20 m breadth

Principal Imports and Exports: Imports: Fertilizer. Exports: Grain.

Working Hours: Port operations 24 h/day

Accommodation:

Name	Length (m)	Depth (m)	Remarks
Busum			See [1] below
Basin I	160		Completely dry at LW
Basin II	420	2	
Basin III	500	3.5	
Basin IV			Pleasure craft jetty with 100 berths

[1]*Busum:* The port comprises four basins. The principal berths for commercial vessels are situated in Basins II and III. The inner harbour is closed by a flood barrier when water level reaches more than 0.3 m above normal HW

Bunkering: Fuel oil and lubricating oil available

Towage: Tugs are available from Cuxhaven if required

Repair & Maintenance: Repairs possible. Ship lift for vessels up to 400 t and 50 m loa

Medical Facilities: Hospital in Heide, 20 km

Lloyd's Agent: Reck & Co. GmbH, Wikinghaus, Schopenstehl 22, D-20095 Hamburg, Germany, *Tel:* +49 40 2789 6375, *Fax:* +49 40 2780 6418, *Email:* hamburg@reck.de, *Website:* www.reck.de

BUTZFLETH

Lat 53° 39' N; Long 9° 31' E.

Admiralty Chart: 3625

Time Zone: GMT +1 h

Admiralty Pilot: 55

UNCTAD Locode: DE BUZ

Principal Facilities:

	Q	Y	G			B		T	A

Authority: Butzfleth Port Authority, Aussenstelle, Butzfleth, 21683 Stade, Germany, *Tel:* +49 4146 93810, *Fax:* +49 4146 938119, *Email:* kwildfuehr@nports.de, *Website:* www.nports.de

Officials: Port Captain: Knud Wildfuehr, *Tel:* +49 4721 500151.

Port Security: ISPS compliant

Approach: Elbe River Fairway has 13 m depth at NN below chart zero. Tidal range: 2.95 m. Current 3-5 knots

Anchorage: A deep water anchorage for deep draft vessels, very large crude carriers (VLCC's) and ultra large crude carriers (ULCC's) lies S of the light-vessel Deutsche Bucht, approx pos lat 54° 05' N; long 07° 27' E

In the vicinity of Elbe 1 light-vessel (8 km inside) for large and deep-going vessels, N of red radarline, approx pos lat 54° 01' N; long 08° 15' E, depth of water about 14 to 21 m below chart zero

Neuwerk Roads, approx pos lat 53° 58' N; long 08° 30' E, depth of water about 8 to 16 m below chart zero

Medem Roads, approx pos lat 53° 51.5' N; long 08° 46.5' E, depth of water about 6 to 12 m below chart zero

Neufeld roads, approx pos lat 53° 51.7' N; long 09° 00' E, depth of water about 9 to 10 m below chart zero

NE Roads, off Brunsbuttel, permission only for one tide, approx pos lat 53° 55' N; long 09° 12' E, depth of water about 13 to 14 m below chart zero

Freiburg Roads, approx pos lat 53° 50.6' N; long 09° 19.5' E, depth of water up to about 13 m below chart zero

There are further anchorages for small vessels at S anchorage off Brunsbuttel, Grauerort and Twielenfleth Roads

The bottom at all these anchorages consists of sand and mud

Pilotage: Pilotcutter stationed off Elbe I light vessel. VHF Channels 13 and 16. River pilots are also docking pilots

Traffic: 2003, 4 333 800 t of cargo handled

Maximum Vessel Dimensions: 80 000 dwt, 13.5 m d at the Elbe Pier Terminal. Vessels of over 300 m loa or 45 m beam are limited to 12.5 m d on arrival at Elbe 1 Lightvessel

Accommodation:

Name	Length (m)	Depth (m)	Remarks
Butzfleth			
Elbe Pier Terminal	325	15	See [1] below
Elbclearing Terminal			See [2] below
Dow Deutschland Inc Terminal			See [3] below
Northwest Quay			See [4] below

[1]*Elbe Pier Terminal:* Aluminium Oxide Stade GmbH operate the Elbe Pier Terminal. Bauxite is discharged at a rate of 800 t/h. Petrocoke at 400 t/h

[2]*Elbclearing Terminal:* North Jetty handles bulk cargo and special cargoes, such as coke, form slags, drums, timber, steel etc. Length of jetty 80 m; vessels of up to 5000 dwt, 7 m d can be accommodated. 20 000 m2 of open storage. Elbclearing offer a variety of port services, including stevedoring, cleaning of ship's holds, mooring personal, towage, motor boat service on the river and ship's supply

[3]*Dow Deutschland Inc Terminal:* The inner handles ethylene, propylene, propylenedichloridea as imports. Exports include propyleneoxyde and ethylenedichloride. Vessels limited to 155 m x 25 m x 9 m d at Berth No.1; 200 m x 33 m x 9 m d at Berth No.3. The outer berths handle the export of perchlorothylene, propyleneglycol, carbon tetrachloride and soda-lye, accommodating vessels up to 65 000 dwt, 13.5 m d, depth alongside Berth No. 2 about 15 m below chart zero

[4]*Northwest Quay:* Bulk & special cargoes such as minerals,slags, fertiliser & general cargo. Vessels limited to 148 m x 20 m x 7 m d. One 25 t crane

Storage: Open storage only, except at Aluminium plant where dry bauxite is stored under cover

Cargo Worked: General cargo and containers are handled by Messrs Elbclearing, located directly on the installation. Lorries and trucks are available for forwarding

Bunkering: Bominflot, Bominflot Bunkergesellschaft fur Mineralole mbH & Co. KG, Grosse Baeckerstrasse 11, 20095 Hamburg, Germany, *Tel:* +49 40 350 930, *Fax:* +49 40 3509 3116, *Email:* mail@bominflot.de, *Website:* www.bominflot.net

B.O.T. Broering Oil Trading GmbH, B.O.T. Broering Oil Trading GmbH, Carl Ronningstrasse 9, 28195 Bremen, Germany, *Tel:* +49 421 170 091, *Fax:* +49 421 170 093, *Email:* home@b-o-t.info, *Website:* www.broering.info

Deutsche BP AG, Max Born Strasse 2, 22761 Hamburg, Germany, *Tel:* +49 40 639 4628, *Fax:* +49 40 6395 4670, *Email:* rudi.schrader@de.bp.com, *Website:* www.bp.com

Deutsche Calpam GmbH, Grosse Elbstrasse 141 a, 22767 Hamburg, Germany, *Tel:* +49 40 3068 620, *Fax:* +49 40 3068 6216, *Email:* bunkers@calpam.de, *Website:* www.calpam.de

ExxonMobil Marine Fuels, Mailpoint 31, ExxonMobil House, Ermyn Way, Leatherhead, Surrey KT22 8UX, United Kingdom, *Tel:* +44 1372 222 000, *Fax:* +44 1372 223 922, *Email:* marine.fuels@exxonmobil.com, *Website:* www.exxonmobil.com

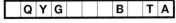

Friedrich G. Frommann GmbH, Wallgraben 47, 21073 Hamburg, Germany, *Tel:* +49 40 7662 680, *Fax:* +49 40 7662 6818, *Email:* frommann@fgfshell.de, *Website:* www.fgfshell.de

Germany Transport & Logistics GmbH, Buchtstrasse 4, 22087 Hamburg, Germany, *Tel:* +49 40 64225 7070, *Fax:* +49 40 64225 7075, *Email:* info@gtl-hamburg.de

Hans Rinck Bunkering Service, P O Box 226, 21637 Horneburg, Germany, *Tel:* +49 4163 814 10, *Fax:* +49 4163 814 122, *Email:* mail@hans-rinck.com, *Website:* www.hans-rinck.com

Maxcom Bunker S.p.A. u.s., Maxcom Energy S.p.A., Eckerkamp 7a, 22391 Hamburg, Germany, *Tel:* +49 40 417568, *Fax:* +49 40 417563, *Email:* maxcom@ehmcke.com, *Website:* www.maxcom.it

Ostsee Mineralol-Bunker GmbH, Thomas-Mann-Strasse 20, 18055 Rostock, Germany, *Tel:* +49 381 2522 30, *Fax:* +49 381 2522 316/26, *Email:* info@ostsee-bunker.de

Tramp Oil & Marine, World Fuel Services Corporation, 13th Floor, Portland House, Bressenden Place, London SW1E 5BH, United Kingdom, *Tel:* +44 20 7808 5000, *Fax:* +44 20 7808 5088, *Email:* pturner@wfscorp.com, *Website:* www.wfscorp.com

Heinrich Wegener & Sohn Bunkergesellschaft mbH, Focksweg 34, 21129 Hamburg, Germany, *Tel:* +49 40 7421 9010, *Fax:* +49 40 7421 2635, *Email:* general@wegener-bunker.de, *Website:* www.wegener-bunker.de

Towage: For the Aluminium Co: towage to be ordered from Brunsbuttel or Hamburg via agents. Four tugs compulsory for mooring. For DOW Deutschland Inc: at the outer berth it is left to the Master's and Pilot's discretion to accept tug assistance for mooring or unmooring, for reportable cargo vessels exceeding 110 m loa and 5000 gt are obliged to take tug assistance; at the inner berth two tugs, each of a min 600 hp are compulsory for mooring, one tug for unmooring. A tug of 1760 hp is stationed at the jetty 24 h daily (VHF Channel 16) for assistance and fire fighting

Repair & Maintenance: Possible by repair gangs from Hamburg. Floating crane of 15 t cap and mobile crane of 50 t cap available for repairs on jetty

Shipping Agents: Herbert C. Meyer GmbH & Co. KG, P O Box 1628, 21656 Stade, Germany, *Tel:* +49 4146 1001, *Fax:* +49 4146 1004, *Email:* info@meyership.de, *Website:* www.meyership.de

Medical Facilities: Hospital, doctors and dentists available. Seamen's Mission near the port, Tel: +49 (4146) 1233

Airport: Hamburg Airport, 70 km

Lloyd's Agent: Reck & Co. GmbH, Wikinghaus, Schopenstehl 22, D-20095 Hamburg, Germany, *Tel:* +49 40 2789 6375, *Fax:* +49 40 2780 6418, *Email:* hamburg@reck.de, *Website:* www.reck.de

COLOGNE

Lat 50° 56' N; Long 7° 0' E.

Admiralty Chart: -	**Admiralty Pilot:** 28
Time Zone: GMT +1 h	**UNCTAD Locode:** DE CGN

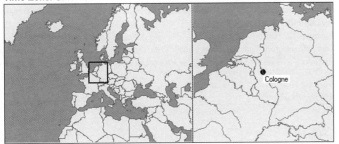

Principal Facilities:

	Y	G	C	R	L	B		A

Authority: Hafen und Guterverkehr Koln AG (HGK), Harry-Blum-Platz 2, 50678 Cologne, Germany, *Tel:* +49 221 390 0, *Fax:* +49 221 390 1343, *Email:* hgkpresse@hgk.de, *Website:* www.hgk.de

Officials: Marketing Manager: Dr Rolf Bender, *Email:* bender@hgk.de.

Port Security: ISPS compliant

Working Hours: Mon-Fri 0800-1600. Godorf on Sat 0600-1200. Overtime possible on arrangement

Accommodation:

Name	Remarks
Cologne	See [1] below
Deutz	Water area of 104 200 m2 and fairway breadth of 22 m
Niehl I	See [2] below
Niehl II (Olhafen)	See [3] below
Godorf	See [4] below

[1]*Cologne:* Ranging from 670 to 699 km up the Rhine. There are four basins for transit and storage of general and bulk cargo of about 72 510 m2 served by slewing cranes of 50 t cap and loading bridges of 35 t cap. All wharves are equipped with rails

[2]*Niehl I:* Water area of 420 000 m2 and fairway breadth of 90 m. Two container terminals with four loading bridges of 30 t and 35 t cap for containers and bulk cargo

[3]*Niehl II (Olhafen):* Water area of 75 300 m2 and fairway breadth of 53 m. Specially equipped for loading and discharging tankers

[4]*Godorf:* Water area of 119 600 m2 and fairway breadth of 70 m. Specially equipped for loading and discharging tankers with oil or gas

Storage:

Location	Open (m2)	Covered (m2)
Cologne	680000	161600
Niehl I		16000

Mechanical Handling Equipment:

Location	Type	Capacity (t)	Qty
Cologne	Mult-purp. Cranes	50	27

Bunkering: All kinds of fuel supplied from shore station or bunkering boats. Coal, water and provisions also available

Repair & Maintenance: Several building and repair yards

Shipping Agents: CTS-Container Terminal GmbH, P O Box 680187, 50704 Cologne, Germany, *Tel:* +49 221 752 0820, *Fax:* +49 221 752 0840, *Email:* info@cts.container-terminal.de, *Website:* www.cts.container-terminal.de

Airport: Koln, 20 km

Railway: Hafen und Guterverkehr Koln AG: direct lines to Rotterdam, Antwerp and Basel

Lloyd's Agent: Joras Euro-Survey GmbH & Co. KG, Muelheimer Strasse 208, D-47057 Duisburg, Germany, *Tel:* +49 203 378000, *Fax:* +49 203 378 8888, *Email:* survey@joras.com, *Website:* www.joras.com

CUXHAVEN

Lat 53° 52' N; Long 8° 42' E.

Admiralty Chart: 3619	**Admiralty Pilot:** 55
Time Zone: GMT +1 h	**UNCTAD Locode:** DE CUX

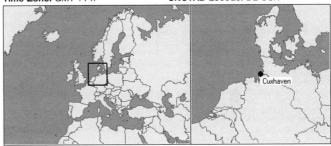

Principal Facilities:

Y	G	C	R	L	B	D	T

Authority: Niedersachsen Ports GmbH & Co. KG, Port of Cuxhaven, Am Schleusenpriel 2, 27472 Cuxhaven, Germany, *Tel:* +49 4721 500-0, *Fax:* +49 4721 500100, *Email:* cuxhaven@nports.de, *Website:* www.cuxhaven-port.de

Officials: Harbour Master: Thomas Christiansen, *Tel:* +49 4721 500150, *Email:* tchristiansen@nports.de.

Port Security: ISPS compliant

Approach: Channel depth at MHW is 17.6 m and at MLW is 14.6 m

Anchorage: Aussenelbe Reede (Outer-Elbe-Roads), N of buoy 'Elbe' (River Elbe approach buoy)
Neuwerk Reede (Roads) between buoys 13 and 17 and S of these buoys
Medem Reede (Roads) between buoys 32a and 34 and E of these buoys

Pilotage: Lotsenbruederschaft Elbe, Hamburg, Tel: +49 40 824075, Fax: +49 40 8227 8175. Pilot station situated in Alten Hafen

Radio Frequency: VHF Channel 69 provides information on the harbour situation, takes requests from harbour pilots and provides information on berths

Tides: Tidal range 3 m with current up to 7 knots

Traffic: 2006, 2 031 925 t of cargo handled, 68 354 TEU's

Maximum Vessel Dimensions: 350 m loa, 14 m draught

Principal Imports and Exports: Imports: Fertilizers, Fish & fish products, General cargo, Gravel, Ro/ro, Sand & stones, Steel. Exports: General cargo, Gravel, Ro/ro, Sand & stones.

Working Hours: 24 h/day except Public Holiday's

Accommodation: Located on the south side of the Elbe estuary opposite the entrance to the Kiel Canal

Key to Principal Facilities:—			
A=Airport	**C**=Containers	**G**=General Cargo	**P**=Petroleum **R**=Ro/Ro **Y**=Dry Bulk
B=Bunkers	**D**=Dry Dock	**L**=Cruise	**Q**=Other Liquid Bulk **T**=Towage (where available from port)

Name	Length (m)	Depth (m)	Remarks
CuxPort			See [1] below
Europakai Berth No.1	180	13.5	Ro/ro
Europakai Berth No.2	200	13.5	Ro/ro
Europakai Berth No.3		15.8	Ro/ro, general cargo & bulk cargo
Humberkai	110	7	Steel
Amerikahafen			See [2] below
Lentzkai	255	7	Cold store of 8000 t
Neuer Lentzkai	180	7	Stones
Steubenhoft	400	14	See [3] below
Neuer Fischereihafen			See [4] below
Alter Fischereihafen			See [5] below
Alter Hafen			See [6] below
Fahrhafen			See [7] below
Jachthafen			Basin for approx 270 yachts

[1]*CuxPort:* Operated by CuxPort GmbH, Neufelder Schanze 4, 27472 Cuxhaven, Tel: +49 4721 748-0, Fax: +49 4721 748122, Email: info@cuxport.de, Website: www.cuxport.de
Multi-purpose terminal with total area of 42 ha of which 14.3 ha are operational. Consists of three berths (Europakai) at R. Elbe and one berth (Humberkai). Two large ro/ro ramps, station for general cargo (of which 6000 m2 is sheltered) and one roofed warehouse of 10 000 m2
[2]*Amerikahafen:* Multi-purpose harbour with quays for transhipment and ship's equipment for vessels carrying general cargo and for small bulk carriers
[3]*Steubenhoft:* Operated by Cruise & Ferry Cuxhaven GmbH, Neue Industriestrasse 14, 27472 Cuxhaven, Tel: +49 4721 600621, Email: info@cruise-cuxhaven.de, Website: www.cruise-cuxhaven.de
Passenger & cruise vessels. Ro/ro link span bridge
[4]*Neuer Fischereihafen:* Multi-purpose harbour with quays for transhipment and supply of trawlers and luggers, offshore supply vessels and bulk cargo transhipment (fertilizer etc). Vessels enter and exit any time through sea lock 190 m long, 24 m wide and depth of 9 m below the mean set of tide
[5]*Alter Fischereihafen:* Multi-purpose harbour with quays for fitting out fishing cutters. Fish processing and factories
[6]*Alter Hafen:* Harbour for small tankers, tugs and berths for ships of port authority in depth of 4.5 m
[7]*Fahrhafen:* Multi-purpose terminal with 300 m of quay directly at the R. Elbe for passengers, dispatching of motor vehicles and cargo. Two ro/ro linkspans. Storage area of approx 60 000 m2

Storage: Dockside sheds of 14 000 m2, warehouses of 5000 m2, three refrigerated sheds, open storage for bulk cargo of 59 000 m2 and paved open storage area for general cargo of 210 000 m2

Mechanical Handling Equipment:

Location	Type	Capacity (t)	Qty
Cuxhaven	Floating Cranes		2
Cuxhaven	Mult-purp. Cranes	60	14
Cuxhaven	Mobile Cranes		13

Bunkering: B.O.T. Broring Oil Trading GmbH, Baudirektor Hahn Strasse 2, 27472 Cuxhaven, Germany, Tel: +49 4721 745 70, Fax: +49 4721 757 77, Email: home@broering.info, Website: www.broering.info
Bominflot, Bominflot Bunkergesellschaft fur Mineralole mbH & Co. KG, Grosse Baeckerstrasse 11, 20095 Hamburg, Germany, Tel: +49 40 350 930, Fax: +49 40 3509 3116, Email: mail@bominflot.de, Website: www.bominflot.net
B.O.T. Broring Oil Trading GmbH, B.O.T. Broering Oil Trading GmbH, Carl Ronningstrasse 9, 28195 Bremen, Germany, Tel: +49 421 170 091, Fax: +49 421 170 093, Email: home@b-o-t.info, Website: www.broering.info
Deutsche BP AG, Max Born Strasse 2, 22761 Hamburg, Germany, Tel: +49 40 639 4628, Fax: +49 40 6395 4670, Email: rudi.schrader@de.bp.com, Website: www.bp.com
Deutsche Calpam GmbH, Grosse Elbstrasse 141 a, 22767 Hamburg, Germany, Tel: +49 40 3068 620, Fax: +49 40 3068 6216, Email: bunkers@calpam.de, Website: www.calpam.de
ExxonMobil Marine Fuels, Mailpoint 31, ExxonMobil House, Ermyn Way, Leatherhead, Surrey KT22 8UX, United Kingdom, Tel: +44 1372 222 000, Fax: +44 1372 223 922, Email: marine.fuels@exxonmobil.com, Website: www.exxonmobil.com
Friedrich G. Frommann, Wallgraben 47, 21073 Hamburg, Germany, Tel: +49 40 7662 680, Fax: +49 40 7662 6818, Email: frommann@fgfshell.de, Website: www.fgfshell.de
Germany Transport & Logistics GmbH, Buchtstrasse 4, 22087 Hamburg, Germany, Tel: +49 40 64225 7070, Fax: +49 40 64225 7075, Email: info@gtl-hamburg.de
Hans Rinck Bunkering Service, P O Box 226, 21637 Horneburg, Germany, Tel: +49 4163 814 10, Fax: +49 4163 814 122, Email: mail@hans-rinck.com, Website: www.hans-rinck.com
Maxcom Bunker S.p.A. u.s., Maxcom Energy S.p.A., Eckerkamp 7a, 22391 Hamburg, Germany, Tel: +49 40 417568, Fax: +49 40 417563, Email: maxcom@ehmcke.com, Website: www.maxcom.it
Ostsee Mineralol-Bunker GmbH, Thomas-Mann-Strasse 20, 18055 Rostock, Germany, Tel: +49 381 2522 30, Fax: +49 381 2522 316/26, Email: info@ostsee-bunker.de
Tramp Oil & Marine, World Fuel Services Corporation, 13th Floor, Portland House, Bressenden Place, London SW1E 5BH, United Kingdom, Tel: +44 20 7808 5000, Fax: +44 20 7808 5088, Email: pturner@wfscorp.com, Website: www.wfscorp.com
Heinrich Wegener & Sohn Bunkergesellschaft mbH, Focksweg 34, 21129 Hamburg, Germany, Tel: +49 40 7421 9010, Fax: +49 40 7421 2635, Email: general@wegener-bunker.de, Website: www.wegener-bunker.de

Towage: Bugsier- Reederei- und Bergungsgesellschaft mbH & Co KG, Johannisbollwerk 10, P O Box 112273, 20459 Hamburg, Germany, Tel: +49 40 311110, Fax: +49 40 313693, Email: info@bugsier.de, Website: www.bugsier.de
Otto Wulf GmbH & Co. Tauch und Bergungsunternehmen, Helgolander Strasse 10, 27472 Cuxhaven, Germany, Tel: +49 4721 7166 0, Fax: +49 4721 716633, Email: info@wulf-tow.com, Website: www.seatowage.com

Repair & Maintenance: Mutzelfeldtwerft GmbH, Woltmannstrasse 2, P O Box 480, 27472 Cuxhaven, Germany, Tel: +49 4721 60120, Fax: +49 4721 601212, Email:

info@muetzelfeldtwerft.de, Website: www.muetzelfeldtwerft.de One floating dock of 140 m x 25 m for vessels up to 15 000 dwt
Ship Chandlers: Wilhelm Gafers GmbH, Neue Reihe 5, 27472 Cuxhaven, Germany, Tel: +49 4721 33015, Fax: +49 4721 33841, Email: wgaefers@t-online.de
Shipping Agents: Peter Hein GmbH, P O Box 327, 27453 Cuxhaven, Germany, Tel: +49 4721 57130, Fax: +49 4721 37765, Email: peter-hein-gmbh@freenet.de
Surveyors: IMCS BVBA, Vogelsand 56, 27476 Cuxhaven, Germany, Tel: +49 4721 681010, Fax: +49 4721 681011, Email: imcsge@t-online.de, Website: www.imcs-group.com
Airport: Hamburg-Fuhlsbuttel, 140 km. Bremen, 110 km
Lloyd's Agent: Reck & Co. GmbH, Wikinghaus, Schopenstehl 22, D-20095 Hamburg, Germany, Tel: +49 40 2789 6375, Fax: +49 40 2780 6418, Email: hamburg@reck.de, Website: www.reck.de

DUISBURG

Lat 51° 26' N; Long 6° 45' E.

Admiralty Chart: -	**Admiralty Pilot:** 28
Time Zone: GMT +1 h	**UNCTAD Locode:** DE DUI

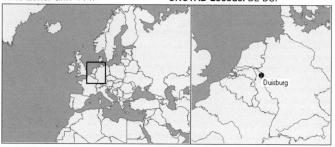

Principal Facilities:

P	Q		G	C	R		B		T	A

Authority: Duisburger Hafen AG, Alte Ruhrorter Strasse 42-52, 47119 Duisburg, Germany, Tel: +49 203 8030, Fax: +49 203 803430, Email: mail@duisport.de, Website: www.duisport.de
Officials: Chief Executive Officer: Erich Staake, Tel: +49 203 803330, Email: erich.staake@duisport.de.
Marketing Manager: Sabine Liedmeier, Tel: +49 203 803 2226, Email: sabine.liedmeier@duisport.de.
Harbour Master: Dirk Scheel, Tel: +49 203 803 4240, Email: dirk.scheel@duisport.de.
Port Security: ISPS compliant
Pilotage: No harbour pilots. Ordinary pilotage not compulsory but available
Radio Frequency: Duisburg Port Radio, VHF Channel 13
Maximum Vessel Dimensions: Inland waterways craft of any size; seagoing ships according to channel conditions of R Rhine
Working Hours: 0730-1800
Accommodation:

Name	Length (m)	Remarks
Duisburg		See [1] below
DeCeTe Duisburger Container Terminal GmbH	900	See [2] below
Rhein-Ruhr Terminal GmbH	235	See [3] below
DUSS Terminal Duisburg mbH		See [4] below
RAG Hafenumschlag Ruhrort GmbH		See [5] below
DIT Duisburg Intermodal Terminal GmbH		See [6] below
D3T Duisburg Trimodal Terminal	350	Area of 37 500 m2 for handling up to 75 000 containers/year

[1]*Duisburg:* Water level at Ruhrort +0.4 m, except interior port E of km 3.5 where there is no change. Average water level is 4.5 m. The port comprises twenty two docks, covering a water area of 180 ha. 40 km of quay and bank, including 17 km for transhipment. Storehouses with approx 370 000 m2 storage space. Inland transport: the River Rhine and its tributaries and West German canals, railways and road transport in all directions and pipelines
Freight Traffic Centre Duisburg: Logistics centres for compilation and distribution of all kinds of general cargo
Special service (PCD Packing) offered at handling site for heavy and bulky goods
[2]*DeCeTe Duisburger Container Terminal GmbH:* Alte Ruhrorter Strasse 20, 47119 Duisburg Tel: +49 203 809060, Fax: +49 203 809 0634, Email: info@decete.de, Website: www.decete.de
Unitised cargo & containers. Ro/ro facilities. Surface area 16 ha. Equipment includes four gantry cranes (50 t), four reach stackers (42 t) and four forklifts (8 t). 20 reefer points
[3]*Rhein-Ruhr Terminal GmbH:* Moerserstrasse 66, D-47059 Duisburg, Tel: +49 203 31856-0, Fax: +49 203 318 5622, Email: info@rrt.container-terminal.de, Website: www.rrt.de
53 000 m2 outside storage area
[4]*DUSS Terminal Duisburg mbH:* Alte Ruhrorter Strasse 11, D-47119 Duisburg, Tel: +49 203 809 0540, Fax: +49 203 809 0566, Email: duisburg@duss-terminal.de, Website: www.duss-terminal.de
Intermodal terminal

[5]*RAG Hafenumschlag Ruhrort GmbH:* Tel: +49 203 45000-0, Fax: +49 203 450 0062
Imported coal terminal. Area of 85 000 m2 with crane facilities
[6]*DIT Duisburg Intermodal Terminal GmbH:* Gaterweg 201, D-47229 Duisburg, Tel: +49 2065 499-0, Fax: +49 2065 499291, Email: zentrale@dit-duisburg.de, Website: www.dit-duisburg.de
The traffic zones, intermediate and permanent storage area, rail tracks and berths cover a total area of 130 000 m2

Mechanical Handling Equipment:

Location	Type	Capacity (t)	Qty
DeCeTe Duisburger Container Terminal GmbH	Container Cranes	50	4
Rhein-Ruhr Terminal GmbH	Container Cranes	48	1
DUSS Terminal Duisburg mbH	Container Cranes	50	3
DIT Duisburg Intermodal Terminal GmbH	Container Cranes	55	2
D3T Duisburg Trimodal Terminal	Container Cranes	40	1

Bunkering: Tank stores for the storage of mineral oil and chemicals with a cap of 1 000 000 m3, ten bunker boats
WGL Tankschiffahrt GmbH, Dr.-Hammacher-Strasse 49, 47119 Duisburg, Germany, *Tel:* +49 203 5794-111, *Fax:* +49 203 5794-199, *Email:* info@wgl-tankschiffahrt.de, *Website:* www.wgl-tankschiffahrt.de

Towage: Available

Repair & Maintenance: Dockyards, factories and ship repairing plants with slips up to 110 m length for inland waterways craft and sea-going ships

Ship Chandlers: RMS Schiffahrtskontor GmbH, P O Box 130752, 47118 Duisburg, Germany, *Tel:* +49 203 8040, *Fax:* +49 203 804460, *Email:* rms-team@rheinmaas.de, *Website:* www.rheinmaas.de

Stevedoring Companies: PCD Packing Centre Duisburg GmbH, Alte Ruhrorter Str. 14, 47119 Duisburg, Germany, *Tel:* +49 203 809450, *Fax:* +49 203 809 4599, *Email:* info@packing-center.de, *Website:* www.packing-center.de

Airport: Dusseldorf, 35 km

Railway: Deutsche Bahn AB; direct access from the port

Lloyd's Agent: Joras Euro-Survey GmbH & Co. KG, Muelheimer Strasse 208, D-47057 Duisburg, Germany, *Tel:* +49 203 378000, *Fax:* +49 203 378 8888, *Email:* survey@joras.com, *Website:* www.joras.com

ECKERNFORDE

Lat 54° 28' N; Long 9° 51' E.

Admiralty Chart: 2116   **Admiralty Pilot:** 18
Time Zone: GMT +1 h   **UNCTAD Locode:** DE ECK

Principal Facilities:

	Y	G		B		A

Authority: Stadtwerke Eckernforde GmbH, Bornbrook 1, 24340 Eckernforde, Germany, *Tel:* +49 4351 9050, *Fax:* +49 4351 905199, *Email:* info@stadtwerke-eckernfoerde.de, *Website:* www.stadtwerke-eckernfoerde.de

Officials: General Manager: Dietmar Steffens, *Tel:* +49 4351 905110, *Email:* d.steffens@stadtwerke-eckernfoerde.de.

Port Security: ISPS compliant. PFSO: Dirk Bock, Tel: +49 4351 905332, Email: d.bock@stadtwerke-eckernfoerde.de

Documentation: Vessel particulars (1 copy), crew list (1 copy), passenger list (1 copy), crew personal effects declaration (1 copy), vaccination list (1 copy), cargo manifest/stowage plan (1 copy)

Anchorage: Good anchorage in the roads between bearing E to SE by W, 1-1.5 miles from the port in depth of 18-21 m. Anchorage not allowed in harbour area

Pilotage: Not compulsory. Nearest pilot station: Kiel Light Tower

Radio Frequency: VHF Channels 10 (Harbour Master) and 14 (Pilots)

Tides: None. E winds can raise water level by 1.5 m

Maximum Vessel Dimensions: In outer harbour up to 5 m draft; in inner harbour up to 3 m draft

Accommodation:

Name	Depth (m)	Remarks
Eckernforde		
Outer Harbour	5–5.5	Protected from E gales by pier of 60 m length
Inner Harbour	2–3.5	See [1] below

[1]*Inner Harbour:* Three large grain silos. Mobile crane discharging cap up to 200 t/h, loading by conveyor belts up to 100 t/h

Bunkering: Diesel oil available

Medical Facilities: Doctor and hospitals available

Airport: Kiel-Holtenau, 30 km

Railway: Approx 10 mins from port

Lloyd's Agent: Reck & Co. GmbH, Wikinghaus, Schopenstehl 22, D-20095 Hamburg, Germany, *Tel:* +49 40 2789 6375, *Fax:* +49 40 2780 6418, *Email:* hamburg@reck.de, *Website:* www.reck.de

ELBEHARBOUR

harbour area, see under Brunsbuttel

ELSFLETH

Lat 53° 14' N; Long 8° 28' E.

Admiralty Chart: 3406/3407   **Admiralty Pilot:** 55
Time Zone: GMT +1 h   **UNCTAD Locode:** DE ELS
This port is no longer open to commercial shipping

EMDEN

Lat 53° 21' N; Long 7° 11' E.

Admiralty Chart: 3632   **Admiralty Pilot:** 55
Time Zone: GMT +1 h   **UNCTAD Locode:** DE EME

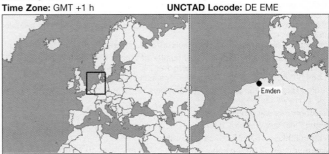

Principal Facilities:

P	Q	Y	G	C	R		B	D	T	A

Authority: Niedersachsen Ports GmbH & Co. KG, Port of Emden, P O Box 2044, 26700 Emden, Germany, *Tel:* +49 4921 897-0, *Fax:* +49 4921 897137, *Email:* emden@nports.de, *Website:* www.emden-port.de

Officials: Managing Director: Berend Snippe, *Tel:* +49 4921 897100, *Email:* bsnippe@nports.de.
Head of Marketing & Sales: Friedrich Voss, *Tel:* +49 4921 897118, *Email:* fvoss@nports.de.
Harbour Master: Frank Herbig, *Tel:* +49 4921 897120, *Email:* fherbig@nports.de.

Port Security: ISPS compliant

Approach: Navigation in the approaches does not impose any length restrictions, whereas draughts are limited to 13.7 m from sea to Dukegat lightening area, 13.4 m from lightening area to sea, 10.7 m from lightening area to Emden Port and 10.4 m from Emden Port to lightening area. These draughts are subject to wind and weather conditions
Traffic Schemes: Vessel Traffic Service: Description: This system is mandatory for all vessels over 40 m loa and all vessels carrying dangerous cargoes
Call: Ems Traffic
Fax: Traffic Centre Emden (+49 4921 802387)
Tel: Ems Traffic (+49 4921 802381)
Telex: 27939
Frequency: VHF Channels 15, 16, 18, 20, 21
Procedure:
1) Vessels bound for Die Ems should inform Traffic Centre Emden, in writing, 24 h before ETA or on departure from last port
2) Vessels should report vessel's name, position, dimensions and destination to Ems Traffic immediately before navigating in Die Ems as follows:
    (a) Inward bound on VHF Channel 18
    (b) Outward bound on locally designated VHF Channels
    (c) Inward and outward bound (Gandersum to Papenburg) on VHF Channel 15
3) Vessels should report to Ems Traffic on the appropriate VHF Channel when passing the Reporting Points below and immediately on entering and leaving a harbour, berth or anchorage on the Ems
4) Vessels should also report on the appropriate VHF Channel when they wish to use one of the following roadsteads:
    (a) Emden Roads on VHF Channel 21
    (b) Dry cargo unloading roads in Alte Ems on VHF Channel 18
    (c) Alte Ems Tanker Roads on VHF Channel 18
    (d) Gas Tanker Roads on VHF Channel 20
Reporting Points: Vessels should inform Ems Traffic of vessel's name, call sign, position, speed and time of passing the following:
1 (a) Lightbuoy No.H1 (Hubertgat) on VHF Channel 18
or (b) Lightbuoy No.1 (Westerems) on VHF Channel 18
or (c) Riffgat lightbuoy on VHF Channel 18
or (d) Osterems lightbuoy on VHF Channel 18

Key to Principal Facilities:—			
A=Airport	**C**=Containers	**G**=General Cargo	**P**=Petroleum **R**=Ro/Ro **Y**=Dry Bulk
B=Bunkers	**D**=Dry Dock	**L**=Cruise	**Q**=Other Liquid Bulk **T**=Towage (where available from port)

2 (a) Buoy No.A5/H15 (Hubertgat/Alte Ems, inward bound only) on VHF Channel 18
or (b) Lightbuoy No.13 (Westerems, inward bound only) on VHF Channel 18
3 Lightbuoy No.35 (outward bound only for the Alte Ems/Hubertgat) on VHF Channel 18
4 Lightbuoy No.41 on VHF Channel 20
5 Lightbuoy No.65 (at same time inward bound, report for Emden) on VHF Channel 21
6 Gandersum on VHF Channel 15
7 Papenburg on VHF Channel 15
Vessels should maintain continuous listening watch on the appropriate VHF Channels as follows:
1) Lightbuoy No.1 to lightbuoy No.35 (Westerems/Randzelgat) on VHF Channel 18
2) Lightbuoy H1 to buoy No.A5/H15 (Hubertgat) on VHF Channel 18
3) Buoy No.A5/H15 to lightbuoy No.35 (Alte Ems) on VHF Channel 18
4) Lightbuoy No.35 to buoy No.57/Oterdum-Reede on VHF Channel 20
5) Buoy No.57/Oterdum-Reede to lightbuoy No.86 on VHF Channel 21
6) Lightbuoy No.86 to Papenburg on VHF Channel 15
Radar and Information Service:
Radar Advice: Provided on request or if instructed by the VTS Centre (in German or English) on the appropriate VHF Channel for areas 'a-c' below. The request should include vessel's name, call sign and position. The service is provided as follows:
1) When visibility is less than 2000 m
2) When pilot vessel is in a sheltered position
3) When lightbuoys are withdrawn due to ice
4) When required by traffic situation or when requested by a vessel
   (a) Borkum Radar Station on VHF Channel 18 in area lightbuoy No.1 to lightbuoy No.35
   (b) Knock Radar Station on VHF Channel 20 in area lightbuoy No.35 to lightbuoy No.57
   (c) Wybelsum Radar Station on VHF Channel 21 in area lightbuoy No.57 to Emden harbour entrance
Information Broadcasts: Ems Traffic broadcasts every hour + 50 on VHF Channels 15, 18, 20 and 21 (and on VHF Channel 15 for Papenburg to Gandersum and Leda) (in German). The broadcast includes the following:
1) Information relevant to the safe passage through the VTS area
2) General fairway and traffic situation (eg. local storm warnings, weather messages, visibility and ice reports when appropriate, casualties, dredging operations and pilot information)
Restrictions: Depth restriction on vessels up to 10.7 m draft for normal HW conditions
Pilotage: Compulsory. Pilot normally boards off Wester Ems Light Buoy in pos 53° 37' N; 6° 20' E. Tankers and gas tankers over 130 m loa and 21 m beam pick up pilot in pos 53° 59' N; 6° 21' E. Pilot vessel operates on VHF Channels 12 and 16
Radio Frequency: Ems Traffic, VHF Channels 18, 20 and 21. Emden Port/Locks on VHF Channel 13
Weather: Easterly winds sometimes create lower water levels
Tides: Tidal range approx 3.2 m
Traffic: 2005, 5 463 119 t of cargo handled
Maximum Vessel Dimensions: 8.5 m draught (at any time), 10.7 m draught (max for access)
Principal Imports and Exports: Imports: Building materials, Containers, Forest products, LPG, Motor vehicles, Slurry chalk. Exports: Containers, General & project cargo, Motor vehicles.
Working Hours: Usual working times Monday - Saturday
1st shift: 06.00 hours till 14.00 hours
2nd shift: 14.00 hours till 22.00 hours
at requirement:
3rd shift: 22.00 hours till 06.00 hours
Partial dayshift: 08.00 hours till 16.00 hours
Day preceding a Holiday
06.00 hours till 12.00 hours with possibility of 2 hours overtime for completion
Sundays and Holidays
Overtime possible on request
Accommodation: The port is divided into two sections: The Outer Harbour and Emskai, tidal berths/basins at the River Ems and the Inner Harbour, a non-tidal area which is separated from the River Ems by two locks:
Great Sealock: 260 m long and 40 m wide, restricting vessels size to 240 m loa and 33 m beam. Upon special permission a slight increase to 250 m loa and 35 m beam may be possible
Nesserlander Lock: 110 m long and 22 m wide (lockgates 14 m wide), restricting vessels size to 90 m loa and 12 m beam

Name	Length (m)	Depth (m)	Draught (m)	Remarks
Outer Harbour (Aussenhafen)				Consists of the river berth 'Emskai' and the basin 'Outer Harbour'
Emskai			8.5	See [1] below
VW Berth	500	10	9.5	See [2] below
Granary	200	8.5		See [3] below
Freier Platz	500	8.5		See [4] below
New Inner Harbour (Neuer Binnenhafen)				See [5] below
Nordkai	475	11.5		See [6] below
Sudkai	932	10–11.9		See [7] below
Binnenschiffsbecken (N side)	190	8.5		Handling of cars
EVAG-Terminal 1				See [8] below
Inner Harbour (Binnenhafen)				See [9] below
West Side				See [10] below
Olhafen		10.5		See [11] below
Industriehafen South	850	9.7		General cargo
Industriehafen North	380	5		No cargo handled at present

Name	Length (m)	Depth (m)	Draught (m)	Remarks
Industriehafen Shipyard Quay	460	9		Supply & repair of vessels. Shipyard cranes available
Stichkanal				See [12] below
Borssumer Hafen		5		See [13] below

[1]*Emskai:* Situated in the deep water of the Ems. Berthing length of 272 m plus a further 175 m with dolphins; handling general cargo, forest products, vehicles, containers, construction materials etc. Ro/ro-stern-and quarter ramp, 64 000 m2 of open storage
[2]*VW Berth:* Situated in the south for handling automobiles with 374 000 m2 of open storage, paved area and warehousing. Loading rate of 1500 vehicles/day
[3]*Granary:* Situated in the Outer Harbour, handling all kinds of grain products and feedstuff and equipped with two shore elevators. Discharging/loading cap is 5000 t/day for heavy grain and 3000 t/day for soya
[4]*Freier Platz:* Situated in the Outer Harbour, handling all kinds of general cargo. North of the berth is a hydraulic ro/ro-stern ramp
[5]*New Inner Harbour (Neuer Binnenhafen):* Non-tidal harbour entered by the sea locks, handling motor vehicles, containers & other general cargo and dry bulk cargoes
[6]*Nordkai:* Divided into two parts:
Western (Container Terminal): length 250 m, storage space of 48 500 m2. Equipment includes one container bridge of 53/70 t, one mobile container crane of 40/80 t, four van carriers, two 40 t reach stackers (5 high), forklifts, tug masters and trailers
Eastern (General Cargo Berth): length 225 m and equipped with two 15 t cranes. There is 3900 m2 covered storage, 13 000 m2 of paved area and 32 000 m2 unpaved area for cargo storage
[7]*Sudkai:* Equipped with two 15 t and one 40 t cap cranes. There is 20 000 m2 of paved area, 120 000 m2 of bulk cargo storage and 4000 m2 covered storage. Discharging cap of coal is 24 000 t/day and coal loading cap is 10 000 t/day
[8]*EVAG-Terminal 1:* No.1 (north) in depth of 9 m and No.2 (south) in depth of 10 m. Car terminal of 174 000 m2. Two ro/ro stern ramps available
[9]*Inner Harbour (Binnenhafen):* Consists of several basins/berths. Non-tidal harbour entered by the sea locks, handling slurry chalk, building materials, general cargo, containers, LPG and ship yard
[10]*West Side:* In depths of 9.5 m, 7 m and 5 m. Consists of several basins/berths. In the south is a building material berth 200 m long on dolphins and a shipyard. In the north is a general cargo and ro/ro berth
[11]*Olhafen:* Three tanker berths, one in the south at the LPG Terminal and two in the north at the Slurry Chalk Terminal (one for sea-going and one for inland tankers)
LPG Terminal: 255 m long handling butane and propane. There are two storage tanks of 4000 m3 and nine storage tanks at the tank farm of 23 000 m3 cap. Discharge rate of 500 m3/h and loading rate of 200 m3/h. Extensive storage cap of approx 60 000 m3 for oil products, which is partly being used
Slurry Chalk Terminal: one berth 160 m loa. Average handling rate up to 300 t/h with several storage tanks of 35 000 m3
[12]*Stichkanal:* West side: 570 m long in depth of 7 m. Supply and repair of vessels. Shipyard cranes available
East side: 480 m long plus 220 m on dolphins in depth of 7 m. Handling all kinds of dry bulk. Three cranes of 10-35 t cap
[13]*Borssumer Hafen:* For small ships handling building materials

Bunkering: International Bunkering GmbH, Schweckendieckplatz 4, P O Box 1732, 26697 Emden, Germany, *Tel:* +49 4921 927440, *Fax:* +49 4921 827430, *Email:* info@interbunker.de, *Website:* www.interbunker.de
Weert Ihnen Gmbh & Co. KG, Schweckendieplatz 4, 26721 Emden, Germany, *Tel:* +49 4921 927 50, *Fax:* +49 4921 927 430, *Email:* weert-ihnen@t-online.de, *Website:* www.weertihnen.de
International Bunkering GmbH, Schweckendieckplatz 4, P O Box 1732, 26697 Emden, Germany, *Tel:* +49 4921 927440, *Fax:* +49 4921 827430, *Email:* info@interbunker.de, *Website:* www.interbunker.de

Towage: Various tugs always available of 1000 hp to 2500 hp
Emder Schlepp-Betrieb GmbH, Am Delft 6-7, 26721 Emden, Germany, *Tel:* +49 4921 97640, *Fax:* +49 4921 976444, *Email:* info@esb-tow.de, *Website:* www.esb-tow.de

Repair & Maintenance: Siept van Brethorst, P O Box 1238, 26692 Emden, Germany, *Tel:* +49 4921 20128, *Fax:* +49 4921 32803, *Email:* s.v.brethorst@t-online.de, *Website:* www.van-brethorst.de Minor repairs
Cassens Schiffswerft und Maschinenfabrik GmbH, II Hafeneinschnitt, P O Box 2442, 26704 Emden, Germany, *Tel:* +49 4921 8270, *Fax:* +49 4921 827226, *Email:* info@cassens-werft.de, *Website:* www.cassens-werft.de Floating dock No.1 92 m x 14.8 m with lifting cap 1800 t. Floating dock No.2 116.4 m x 21.3 m with lifting cap 5000 t
Nordseewerke GmbH, P O Box 2351, Zum Zungenkai, 26725 Emden, Germany, *Tel:* +49 4921 85-0, *Fax:* +49 4921 31327, *Email:* nordseewerke@thyssenkrupp.com, *Website:* www.nordseewerke.com Graving dock No.1 218 m x 30 m for vessels up to 55 000 dwt. Floating dock No.3 176.5 m x 27 m with lifting cap of 9500 t. Floating dock No.4 136.2 m x 17 m with lifting cap of 4000 t

Seaman Missions: The Seamans Mission, Am Seemannsheim 1, 26723 Emden, Germany, *Tel:* +49 4921 92080, *Fax:* +49 4921 20839, *Email:* info@seemannsheim-emden.de

Ship Chandlers: Emder Schiffsausrustungs GmbH, P O Box 1442, Zu Den Hafenbecken 7-9, 26694 Emden, Germany, *Tel:* +49 4921 80090, *Fax:* +49 4921 27607, *Email:* esg@emder.de, *Website:* www.emder.de

Shipping Agents: Anker-Schiffahrts-GmbH, Am Flugeldeish 30, Emden, Germany, *Tel:* +49 4921 19250, *Fax:* +49 4921 925400, *Email:* info-emden@anker-leschaco.com, *Website:* www.anker-leschaco.com
Emder Verkehrsgesellschaft AG, Schweekendieckplatz 1, 26721 Emden, Germany, *Tel:* +49 4921 8950, *Fax:* +49 4921 895 5150, *Email:* info@evag.com, *Website:* www.evag.com
Ems Ports Agency & Stevedoring Beteiligungs GmbH & Co. KG, Terminal Nordkai Emden, Zum Nordkai 42, 26725 Emden, Germany, *Tel:* +49 4921 99908, *Fax:* +49 4921 99908, *Email:* info@epas-emden.de, *Website:* www.epas-emden.de
Sartori & Berger, An Derpromenade, Am Alten Binnenhafen 10, 26721 Emden, Germany, *Tel:* +49 4921 994621, *Fax:* +49 4921 994623, *Email:* emden@sartori-berger.de, *Website:* www.sartori-berger.de

Stevedoring Companies: Ems Ports Agency & Stevedoring Beteiligungs GmbH & Co. KG, Terminal Nordkai Emden, Zum Nordkai 42, 26725 Emden, Germany, *Tel:* +49

4921 99908, *Fax:* +49 4921 99908, *Email:* info@epas-emden.de, *Website:* www.epas-emden.de

Surveyors: Germanischer Lloyd, Schweckendieckplatz 3, 26721 Emden, Germany, *Tel:* +49 4921 97710, *Fax:* +49 4921 977120, *Email:* gl-emden@gl-group.com, *Website:* www.gl-group.com

Airport: Local airport at Emden. Nearest international airport at Bremen, 150 km

Lloyd's Agent: Reck & Co. GmbH, Herrlichkeit 5, 28199 Bremen, Germany, *Tel:* +49 421 59834-0, *Fax:* +49 421 598 3450, *Email:* mail@reck.de, *Website:* www.reck.de

FAHRHAFEN

harbour area, see under Cuxhaven

FLENSBURG

Lat 54° 48' N; Long 9° 26' E.

Admiralty Chart: 919/3562   **Admiralty Pilot:** 18
Time Zone: GMT +1 h   **UNCTAD Locode:** DE FLF

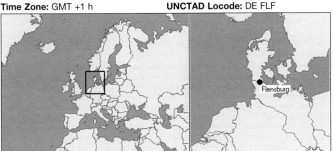

Principal Facilities:

	Y	G		B	T	

Authority: Flensburger Hafen GmbH, Am Industriehafen 7, 24937 Flensburg, Germany, *Tel:* +49 461 487 1300, *Fax:* +49 461 487 1974, *Email:* hafenbehoerde@flensburg.de, *Website:* www.flensburgerhafen.de

Officials: Managing Director: Frank Partik, *Tel:* +49 461 487 1505, *Email:* frank.partik@flensburgerhafen.de.
Harbour Master: F. Petry, *Tel:* +49 461 487 1301.

Port Security: ISPS compliant

Documentation: Crew list (2 copies), passenger list (2 copies), stores list (2 copies), EG cargo lists, bills of lading, general declaration, ship's certificates

Approach: No hazards if following the leading lights on the fairway

Anchorage: Just outside the entrance, NE of Mittelgrund and W of Kielseng leading lights in depth of 10-17 m
The other possible anchorage is at lightbuoy Flensburger Foerde in depth of 22 m

Pilotage: Compulsory in Flensburg Fjord for tankers of every size and dry cargo vessels with a length of 90 m and breadth of 13 m and over. Pilot boards at lightbuoy No.2 Flensburger Foerde, Tel: +49 431 362858. Give notice at least 5h before arriving at the lightbuoy and before leaving port

Traffic: 2003, 323 vessels, 573 737 t of cargo handled

Maximum Vessel Dimensions: Max d 8.5 m

Principal Imports and Exports: Imports: Coal, Fertiliser, Foodstuffs, Stone chips, Woodpulp. Exports: General cargo, Grain.

Working Hours: Mon to Thurs 0700-1600. Fri 0700-1300. Dec 24 and 31, 0700-1200. No work is possible on General Holidays

Accommodation:

Name	Length (m)	Depth (m)	Remarks
Flensburg			See [1] below
Powerstation Quay	150	8.5	
Harnis Quay		6–7	One berth 470 m long and one 240 m long
Schiffbruck Quay	220	5–6.5	
Innen Quay	260	5	Passenger vessels
Ballast Quay	140	5	Passenger vessels
Nordertor Quay		5	One berth 56 m long and one 67 m long

[1]*Flensburg:* Total port area covers 119 ha
Bulk facilities: Three elevators for grain and feedstuff, discharging 120 t/h, loading 170 t/h; one elevator for coal discharging

Storage:

Location	Open (m²)	Covered (m²)	Sheds / Warehouses	Grain (t)
Flensburg	4700	7100	5	83750

Mechanical Handling Equipment:

Location	Type	Capacity (t)	Qty
Flensburg	Mult-purp. Cranes	3–7	6

Bunkering: One bunkering station delivering diesel oil to small boats/craft only. Delivery by trucks. Fuel oil from Kiel, Rendsburg or Brunsbuttel. Bunkering services arranged through ship's agent

Waste Reception Facilities: Available for bilge water, sludge, sewage and garbage

Towage: Tugs available subject to 7 h notice via agent

Medical Facilities: Available

Airport: Hamburg Fuhlsbuttel, 160 km, Sonderborg, Denmark, 30 km

Lloyd's Agent: Reck & Co. GmbH, Wikinghaus, Schopenstehl 22, D-20095 Hamburg, Germany, *Tel:* +49 40 2789 6375, *Fax:* +49 40 2780 6418, *Email:* hamburg@reck.de, *Website:* www.reck.de

FRANKFURT

Lat 50° 7' N; Long 8° 40' E.

Admiralty Chart: -   **Admiralty Pilot:** -
Time Zone: GMT +1 h   **UNCTAD Locode:** DE FRA

Principal Facilities:

Q	Y	G	C		B		A

Authority: Hafen Frankfurt Managementgesellschaft mbH, Lindleystrasse 14, 60314 Frankfurt, Germany, *Tel:* +49 69 2123 6037, *Fax:* +49 69 2124 0617, *Email:* info@hfm-frankfurt.de, *Website:* www.hafen-frankfurt.de

Officials: Port Director: Bernd Fuenkner, *Tel:* +49 69 2123 5025, *Email:* bernd.fuenkner@hfm-frankfurt.de.
Managing Director: Ralf Karpa, *Email:* ralf.karpa@hfm-frankfurt.de.
Communications Manager: Ulrich Lang, *Tel:* +49 69 2123 5191, *Email:* ulrich.lang@hfm-frankfurt.de.

Approach: Channel depth of 3.2 m

Principal Imports and Exports: Imports: General cargo. Exports: .

Accommodation:

Name	Length (m)	Depth (m)	Remarks
Frankfurt			See [1] below
West Harbour	1100	2.7–2.9	See [2] below
East Harbour	8130	2.7–2.9	See [3] below

[1]*Frankfurt:* Vessels up to 6000 t may use the harbours. General facilities include private cranes. Special transhipment plants. Belt railway, 56 km of track. Tanks for mineral oils of 120 000 m3 cap. Container terminal covering an area of 30 000 m2
[2]*West Harbour:* River harbour Gutleuthof, 47 600 m2 of water area. Mainly used for loading and discharging manufactured goods etc
[3]*East Harbour:* Four basins with total of 226 600 m2 water area. Wharf for loading and storing of commercial goods, stores for staple goods and transhipment areas for coal, iron, steel, construction materials, sand, gravel and scrap. Industrial harbour, petroleum harbour

Storage:

Location	Grain (t)
Frankfurt	70000

Mechanical Handling Equipment:

Location	Type	Capacity (t)	Qty
Frankfurt	Container Cranes	35	1

Bunkering: Coal at shore stations; oil by bunker boat

Shipping Agents: CMA-CGM S.A., CMA CGM (Deutschland) GmbH, Schillstrasse 4, Frankfurt, 63067 Offenbach am Main, Germany, *Tel:* +49 69 800 8120, *Fax:* +49 69 8008 1299, *Email:* fra.genmbox@cma-cgm.com, *Website:* www.cma-cgm.com
DSA Deutsche Shiffahrts-Agentur GmbH & Co., Arndtstrasse 55, 60325 Frankfurt, Germany, *Tel:* +49 69 756 1260, *Fax:* +49 69 7561 2633, *Email:* contact-dsafrankfurt@rantzau.de, *Website:* www.rantzau.de
A.P. Moller-Maersk Group, Maersk Deutschland GmbH (Frankfurt), Cargo City Sud, Gebaude 537D, 60549 Frankfurt, Germany, *Tel:* +49 69 669859-0, *Fax:* +49 69 6698 5911, *Email:* frmsal@maersk.com, *Website:* www.maerskline.com

Airport: Frankfurt Rhein-Main, 12 km

Lloyd's Agent: Friedrich Hartmann vorm. J. Kerschgens, 2 Beethovenstrasse, D-68165 Mannheim, Germany, *Tel:* +49 621 423090, *Fax:* +49 621 416354, *Email:* hartmann@hartmann-expert.de, *Website:* www.hartmann-expert.de

GLUCKSTADT

Lat 53° 47' N; Long 9° 25' E.

Admiralty Chart: 3625   **Admiralty Pilot:** 55
Time Zone: GMT +1 h   **UNCTAD Locode:** DE GLU

Key to Principal Facilities:—			
A=Airport	**C**=Containers	**G**=General Cargo	**P**=Petroleum	**R**=Ro/Ro	**Y**=Dry Bulk
B=Bunkers	**D**=Dry Dock	**L**=Cruise	**Q**=Other Liquid Bulk	**T**=Towage (where available from port)	

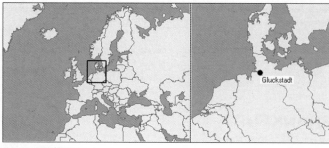

Principal Facilities:

	Y	G	C		B		A

Authority: Hafengesellschaft Gluckstadt mbH & Co. KG, Aussenhafen Sud, 25348 Gluckstadt, Germany, *Tel:* +49 4124 91230, *Fax:* +49 4124 912323, *Email:* info@hafen-glueckstadt.de, *Website:* www.hafen-glueckstadt.de

Officials: Port Manager: Sabine Meyer, *Email:* s.meyer@hafen-glueckstadt.de.

Port Security: ISPS compliant

Anchorage: River Elbe, between bouys 76 & 78

Pilotage: Harbour pilot available, but not compulsory

Tides: Average tidal range of 2.8 m

Maximum Vessel Dimensions: 150 m loa, 18 m breadth, 6 m draft (at high tide)

Working Hours: Mon-Fri 0700-1600, overtime can be arranged

Accommodation:

Name	Remarks
Aussehafen-Sued	See [1] below

[1]*Aussehafen-Sued:* Operated by Hafengesellschaft Gluckstadt mbH & Co KG, Tel: +49 4124 91230, Fax: +49 4124 912323
Container, general & bulk cargo handled

Storage:

Location	Open (m²)	Covered (m²)	Sheds / Warehouses
Gluckstadt	20000	4100	3

Mechanical Handling Equipment:

Location	Type	Capacity (t)	Qty
Gluckstadt	Mult-purp. Cranes	45	1

Bunkering: Available

Repair & Maintenance: Available

Airport: Hamburg Airport, 60 km

Railway: Gluckstadt station 1 km

Lloyd's Agent: Reck & Co. GmbH, Wikinghaus, Schopenstehl 22, D-20095 Hamburg, Germany, *Tel:* +49 40 2789 6375, *Fax:* +49 40 2780 6418, *Email:* hamburg@reck.de, *Website:* www.reck.de

HAMBURG

Lat 53° 32' N; Long 9° 59' E.

Admiralty Chart: 3268	**Admiralty Pilot:** 55
Time Zone: GMT +1 h	**UNCTAD Locode:** DE HAM

Principal Facilities:

P	Q	Y	G	C	R	L	B	D	T	A

Authority: Hamburg Port Authority, Neuer Wandrahm 4, 20457 Hamburg, Germany, *Tel:* +49 40 42847 2301, *Fax:* +49 40 42847 2588, *Email:* info@hpa.hamburg.de, *Website:* www.hamburg-port-authority.de

Officials: Managing Director: Jens Meier, *Email:* jens.meier@hpa.hamburg.de.
Marketing Manager: Brita Schemmann, *Tel:* +49 40 42847 3023, *Email:* brita.schemmann@hpa.hamburg.de.
Harbour Master: Capt Joerg Pollmann, *Tel:* +49 40 42847 2571, *Email:* joerg.pollmann@hpa.hamburg.de.

Port Security: ISPS compliant. Container Security Initiative (CSI) designated port

Documentation: Crew list (6 copies), passenger list (6 copies), provisions lists and stores lists (2 copies), dangerous cargo lists (3 copies), health certificates, general cargo declaration, ship's register, oil liability certificate for more than 2000 t of oil

Approach: Depth in approaches 16.3 m HW. Entering with max d should be arranged with Elbe river and harbour pilots. Depths in port up to 15.3 m LW, except Hansa-Port where it is 15.6 m. The bottom in approaches and harbour basins is soft sand and mud-no rocks-so that there is no imminent danger of severe damage to ships. An open tidal port, Hamburg has no locks; ships may approach and leave the port at any time without delay

Pilotage: Compulsory on the River Elbe and in Hamburg port area for tankers and other vessels over 90 m loa, 13 m breadth. The river and port pilots are supplied by a private organisation. River pilots are under the supervision of the Directorate of Waterways; harbour pilots are under the supervision of the port authority. 65 harbour pilots

Radio Frequency: Hamburg Radio operates continuously on VHF Channels 16 and 27. A coordinated chain of 22 land based radar stations covers the Elbe fairway from 4 miles W of Elbe lightbuoy to well into the port of Hamburg
Radar monitoring assistance is available on request when the visibility drops below 3000 m and/or if particular situations arise. Periodical situation reports are broadcasted in German and English. While the vessel is underway within the port limits, it has to adhere to the reporting point system on VHF Channel 74. Port Authority can be contacted 24 h on VHF Channel 14 'Hamburg Port Traffic'

Tides: Under normal meteorological conditions the mean tidal range is approx 3.5 m. Deep draught vessels can arrive at high tide and discharge immediately in order to remain afloat at low tide

Traffic: 2007, 140 400 000 t of cargo handled, 9 889 792 TEU's

Working Hours: Mon-Fri 0650-1500, 1500-2310, 2310-0650. Sat 0700-1300, 1300-1900, 1900-0100, 0100-0700. Sun & Holidays 0700-1300, 1300-1900, 1900-0100, 0100-0700
No work on New Year's Day, Easter Sunday, Whit Sunday, May 1 and Christmas Day except in urgent cases such as bunkering, passenger ships and ships damaged at sea. Days preceding these holidays worked 0700-1230. In urgent cases and to finish loading or discharging, overtime can be worked

Accommodation: Total area of the port: 7399 ha; of water surface 3068 ha. Ships are handled at quay and dolphin berths. 31 harbour basins with 41 km of quay-walls and additional dolphin berths can accommodate about 320 sea-going ships at once. There are many specialised terminals handling a wide range of cargoes throughout the port complex. In addition there are 27 basins with 35 km of quay-walls and various dolphin berths for rivercraft. Basins for rivercraft surround those for sea-going ships and are inter-connected by small channels. Barges can thus reach all transhipment places without disturbing sea-going traffic. Similarly a dense network of port rail-tracks (total length, 427 km) and roads connects all quay berths and storage plants with the main lines of the German and Central-European traffic system. Two and three-rail tracks and wide shed platforms with truck-approaches alongside sheds facilitate direct loading from wagon or truck into sea-going ships and vv. Normal truck-traffic is handled on wide roads on the shore side of sheds
Cruise vessel facilities at Ueberseebrucke in depth of 10.5 m, at Grasbrook in depth of 10.0 m and at Fahrschiffterminal (Edgar Engelhardt Kai) in depth of 8.6 m
Tanker facilities: Vessels up to 110 000 dwt can be accommodated. Water and bunkering at all berths. The total capacity of tank storage units is 5 366 000 m3, plus special tank storage of 120 000 m3 for edible oils, chemicals etc. There is a large oil refinery situated in Hamburg

Name	Length (m)	Depth (m)	Draught (m)	Remarks
Free Port				See [1] below
Container, General Cargo & Ro/ro Terminals				See [2] below
Burchardkai Container Terminal	2850	16.5		See [3] below
TCT Tollerort Container Terminal	995	15.2		See [4] below
Altenwerder Container Terminal	1400	16.7		See [5] below
Eurogate Container Terminal				See [6] below
Berth No.1	380	15.5		
Berth No.2				Under construction
Berth No.3				Under construction
Berth No.4	130	12.8		
Berth No.5	335	15.1		
Berth No.6	329	15.1		
Berth No.7	330	15.1		
Berth No.7a	230	15.1		
Buss Hansa Terminal	840	12.5		See [7] below
Buss Kuhwerder Terminal	1150	11.5		See [8] below
Buss Ross Terminal	230	10		See [9] below
O'Swaldkai Terminal	1050	9.6–11.6		See [10] below
Sud-West Terminal	1500	8.9–11.6		See [11] below
Wallmann Terminal (Reiherstieg)	640	13		See [12] below
Eichholtz Terminal	440	14		See [13] below
Ore & Bulk Cargo Terminals				
Hansaport Bulk Terminal				See [14] below
Midgard Terminal Harburg 2	426	9.4–10.9		Comprising approx 13 ha. Ore, concentrates, stones etc
HEW Wedel	320	12.65		Coal only for electricity works
Kali-Transport Terminal	500	11.4		See [15] below
IHSW Terminal	420		12.5	See [16] below

Name	Length (m)	Depth (m)	Draught (m)	Remarks
Cellpap Terminal Hamburg Umschlags-und Transport GmbH with Shed 25/26, Grasbrook & Dradenau	1350	7.6–11.6		Specializing in handling forest products (paper, pulp and kraftliner); also general cargo, heavy lift, iron and steel and containers. One ro/ro berth
FA. Louis Hagel GmbH & Co.	300	7.6–11.1		See [17] below
Hamburg-Kuhwerder/Johannes Stroeh KG		8.4		Grain. For vessels up to 200 m loa; 2 fixed elevators at 800 t/h
Getreide Terminal		12.4		See [18] below
Silo P. Kruse Terminal		12.6		See [19] below
Neuhof Terminal		12.4		See [20] below
Tanker Terminals				
Kohlfleethafen/Bominflot			10.5	Two berths
Petroleumhafen			11.9	Eight berths
Kattwyk/Oiltanking			13.3	
Kattwyk/Shell			13.3	Two berths
Blumensandhafen/Oiltanking			13.3	
Neuhof/VOPAK Dupeg Terminal			12.3	See [21] below
Jetty 1			7.5	See [22] below
Jetty 2			12.5	See [23] below
Jetty 3			10.5	See [24] below
Jetty 4			11.5	See [25] below
Neuhof/BP Schmierstoff			13.3	
Harburg IV/Holborn			12	Five berths
Oiltanking Moorburg			12.7	
Schluisgrovehafen/Haltermann			11.5	

[1]*Free Port:* The Free Port of Hamburg, with some 1600 ha of land, forms the heart of the universal Port of Hamburg. It includes virtually all general cargo warehouses with a total storage area of 713 000 m2. Extensive facilities of all kinds for short or long term storage of merchandise are situated inside or outside the so called 'warehouse city'. The Free Port offers cargo-handling facilities for containers and other specialist traffic, ie sugar and forest products

Generally, non-Community goods may be transported on transit or stored in transit sheds within the Free Port without being subject to the export authorisation procedures

Within the Free Port there are hardly any restrictions of any kind through customs formalities for shipping and goods traffic: incoming ships may begin discharging without waiting for customs examination. Goods can be transported, traded, stored for any length of time and in unlimited quantitites, inspected, sampled and undergo warehouse handling, ie repacking, refilling, splitting etc without customs formalities. Forwarding from warehouse or shed to the ship within the Free Port area is not subject to customs formalities. This offers considerable advantages to importers and exporters. Only when the goods leave the Free Port are they presented for customs clearance at one of the six customs offices

[2]*Container, General Cargo & Ro/ro Terminals:* There are also two ro/ro berths at HHLA-Forstprodukten-Terminal Dradenau, one ro/ro berth at 'Auto-Terminal-Hamburg' Rethe, one ro/ro berth at Altona-Ausrustungskai for DFDS Hamburg-Harwich ferry. Further ro/ro plants at sheds 74 and 81

[3]*Burchardkai Container Terminal:* Operated by HHLA Container-Terminal Burchardkai GmbH (CTB), Container Terminal Burchardkai, D-21129 Hamburg, Tel: +49 40 3088-1, Fax: +49 40 3088 2622, Email: ctb@hhla.de, Website: www.hhla.de
Ten berths available for container and ro/ro vessels. Terminal area of 160 ha with one berth for ro/ro vessels

[4]*TCT Tollerort Container Terminal:* Operated by HHLA Container Terminal Tollerort GmbH (CTT), Am Vulkanhafen 30, D-20457 Hamburg, Tel: +49 40 74001-0, Fax: +49 40 7401 1100, Email: seevogel@hhla.de, Website: www.hhla.de
Terminal area of 40 ha with four berths available. Container repair workshop on the terminal

[5]*Altenwerder Container Terminal:* Operated by HHLA Container-Terminal Altenwerder GmbH (CTA), Am Ballinkai 1, D-21129 Hamburg, Tel: +49 40 53309-0, Fax: +49 40 53309 2129, Email: cta@hhla.de, Website: www.hhla.de
Terminal area of 80 ha with four berths. 1050 reefer points

[6]*Eurogate Container Terminal:* Operated by Eurogate Container Terminal Hamburg GmbH, Kurt-Eckelmann-Str.1, D-21129, Hamburg, Tel: +49 40 7405-0, Fax: +49 40 7405 2479, Email: ct-hamburg@eurogate.de, Website: www.eurogate.de
Eurocargo Container Freight Station & Warehouse Co Ltd., Tel: +49 40 7405 2232, Fax: +49 40 7405 2550, Email: eurocargo@eurogate.de, adjacent to the Eurogate marine terminal, comprises approx 10 ha with 48 000 m2 shed space. In addition, Eurogate disposes of 360 000 m2 at the land terminal in Altenwerder West, 2 km away from the marine terminal, which is used by ReMain Repair & Maintenance of Containers Co Ltd and Oceangate Distribution. ReMain operates workshop facilities with an annual repair cap of 35 000 containers and Oceangate operates sprinkler protected and partly heated sheds of 35 000 m2 and storage cap for 17 000 TEU's
[7]*Buss Hansa Terminal:* Operated by Buss Hansa GmbH, Am Travehafen/Schuppen 80-82, D-20457 Hamburg, Tel: +49 40 75193-0, Fax: +49 40 75193 3100, Email: info@buss-ports.de, Website: www.buss-ports.de
Total terminal area of 185 000 m2 with three berths available
[8]*Buss Kuhwerder Terminal:* Operated by Buss Umschlagsgesellschaft Kuhwerder mbH, Nehlsstrasse 55, D-20457 Hamburg, Tel: +49 40 3198 1219, Fax: +49 40 3198 2000, Email: kuhwerder-terminal@buss-group.de, Website: www.buss-ports.de
Terminal area of 208 000 m2. Seven berths
[9]*Buss Ross Terminal:* Operated by Buss Ross Terminal GmbH & Co KG, Am Travehafen/Schuppen 80-82, D-20457 Hamburg, Tel: +49 40 75193-0, Email: info@buss-ports.de, Website: www.buss-ports.de
Terminal area of 50 000 m2
[10]*O'Swaldkai Terminal:* Operated by UNIKAI Lagerei & Speditionsges mbH,

Sachsenbrucke/Schuppen 48, D-20457 Hamburg, Tel: +49 40 7200 2100, Fax: +49 40 7200 2101, Email: info@unikai.de, Website: www.unikai.de
Three berths (each 350 m long) for ro/ro vessels. Integrated fruit handling terminal in front of sheds 44-46 and a multi-purpose terminal in front of shed 48 with a further 200 000 m2 of container storage/ro-ro area
[11]*Sud-West Terminal:* Operated by C. Steinweg (Sud-West-Terminal) GmbH & Co KG, Am Kamerunkai 5, D-20457 Hamburg, Tel: +49 40 78950-0, Fax: +49 40 7895 0193, Email: hamburg@de.steinweg.com, Website: www.csteinweg.com
Comprising approx 20 ha, six berths available with one berth for ro/ro vessels
[12]*Wallmann Terminal (Reiherstieg):* Operated by Wallmann & Co. (GmbH & Co.), Pollhornweg 31-39, D-21107 Hamburg, Tel: +49 40 75207-0, Fax: +49 40 7520 7203, Email: mail@wallmann-hamburg.de, Website: www.wallmann-hamburg.de
Three berths. Warehouses and open storage areas available
[13]*Eichholtz Terminal:* Operated by Eichholtz GmbH, Rossweg 20, D-20457 Hamburg, Tel: +49 40 741 3900-0, Fax: +49 40 7413 90021, Email: info@eichholtz.de, Website: www.eichholtz.de
13 300 storage places for containers (TEU) full and empty. 165 000 m2 of storage area including 100 000 m2 of open area. Equipment for cleaning green coffee, seeds and nuts. 20 000 m3 of refrigerated warehousing
[14]*Hansaport Bulk Terminal:* Operated by Hansaport Hafenbetriebsgesellschaft mbH, Am Sandauhafen 20, D-21129 Hamburg, Tel: +49 40 74003-0, Fax: +49 40 7400 3222, Email: info@hansaport.de, Website: www.hansaport.de
Iron ore, coal, stones etc. At the discharging section of the terminal, there is 760 m of quay length with 15.6 m depth at MLW. The max draught is 15.1 m for vessels up to 330 m loa or 45 m breadth; for vessels exceeding this there are additional restrictions, contact Oberhafenamt Hamburg. The average discharge rate for iron is 35 000 t/day and for coal 20 000 t/day with storage cap of 2 000 000 t for iron ore and 1 000 000 t for coal. The loading section of the terminal has a quay length of 290 m with depth of 9.0 m at MLW. There is one loading appliance for iron ore at 1500 t/h and for coal at 1000 t/h. This terminal is equipped with a modern rail loading station where up to 30 000 t/day of bulk cargo can be loaded into rail cars
[15]*Kali-Transport Terminal:* Operated by Kali-Transport Gesellschaft GmbH, Blumensand 27, D-21107 Hamburg, Tel: +49 40 75275-0, Fax: +49 40 7527 5122, Email: kalitransport@k-plus-s.com, Website: www.kali-transport.com
Fertilizers, potash etc. Three conveyors with a max cap of 20 000 t/day. One loader for bags, two discharging bridges and covered storage for 285 000 t
[16]*IHSW Terminal:* Ore, scrap, slags, billets and wire rod for import and export for ISPAT Hamburger Stahlwerke GmbH
[17]*FA. Louis Hagel GmbH & Co.:* Two berths handling bulk fertiliser. One conveyor with cap of 800 t/h
[18]*Getreide Terminal:* Operated by G.T.H. Getreide Terminal Hamburg GmbH & Co. KG, Eversween 11, D-21107 Hamburg, Tel: +49 40 75106-0, Fax: +49 40 7510 6133, Email: zentrale@getreide-terminal.de
Transshipment & warehousing of grain, oilseeds and green coffee
[19]*Silo P. Kruse Terminal:* Operated by Silo P. Kruse Betriebs-GmbH & Co.KG, Blumensand 31-33, D-21107 Hamburg, Tel: +49 40 75206-0, Fax: +49 40 7520 6206, Email: info@silo-p-kruse.de, Website: www.silo-p-kruse.com
Grain. For vessels up to 272 m loa; 3 elevators discharging at 1150 t/h
[20]*Neuhof Terminal:* Operated by Neuhof Hafengesellschaft mbH, Kohlbrandstrasse 3, D-21107 Hamburg, Tel: +49 40 752527-0, Fax: +49 40 752 2512, Email: info@neuhof-hafen.de, Website: www.neuhof-hafen.de
Grain. For vessels up to 280 m loa. Two pneumatic unloaders and one mechanical unloader. Silo cap of approx 180 000 t
[21]*Neuhof/VOPAK Dupeg Terminal:* Operated by Vopak Dupeg Terminal Hamburg GmbH, Rethedamm 15, D-21107 Hamburg, Tel: +49 40 75196-0, Fax: +49 40 7519 6332, Website: hamburg.vopak.com
Four jetties for vessels & barges. 285 tanks with cap of 700 900 m3
[22]*Jetty 1:* For vessels up to 160 m loa and 18 000 dwt. Bunker fuels & gas oil
[23]*Jetty 2:* For vessels up to 255 m loa and 85 000 dwt. Heavy fuels, gasoil, paraffins, latex & vegoils
[24]*Jetty 3:* For vessels up to 230 m loa (325 m loa in ballast) and 200 000 dwt. Heavy fuels, gasoil & gasoline
[25]*Jetty 4:* For vessels up to 235 m loa and 55 000 dwt. Heavy fuels, gasoil, gasoline, naphtha, components, biofuels, lube oils, vegoils, chemical products & fatty alkohols

Mechanical Handling Equipment: 52 quay cranes up to 25 t lifting cap, 33 quay cranes up to 45 t lifting cap and four quay cranes with more than 46 t lifting cap. Four mobile cranes up to 70 t cap, 42 container gantries (16 post-panamax), 15 transtainers, more than 120 VAN/straddle carriers/reachstackers

Location	Type	Capacity (t)	Qty
Burchardkai Container Terminal	Container Cranes		7
Burchardkai Container Terminal	Post Panamax		13
TCT Tollerort Container Terminal	Post Panamax		7
Altenwerder Container Terminal	Container Cranes		2
Altenwerder Container Terminal	Post Panamax		13
Eurogate Container Terminal	Container Cranes		2
Eurogate Container Terminal	Post Panamax	68	19
Buss Hansa Terminal	Mobile Cranes	104	3
Buss Hansa Terminal	Container Cranes	50	2
Buss Kuhwerder Terminal	Mult-purp. Cranes	40–45	2
Buss Kuhwerder Terminal	Mult-purp. Cranes	8	2
Buss Kuhwerder Terminal	Mobile Cranes	140	1
Buss Ross Terminal	Mobile Cranes	104	1
O'Swaldkai Terminal	Mobile Cranes	104	1
O'Swaldkai Terminal	Container Cranes		1
Sud-West Terminal	Mult-purp. Cranes	8–45	14

Key to Principal Facilities:—			
A=Airport	**C**=Containers	**G**=General Cargo	**P**=Petroleum	**R**=Ro/Ro	**Y**=Dry Bulk
B=Bunkers	**D**=Dry Dock	**L**=Cruise	**Q**=Other Liquid Bulk	**T**=Towage (where available from port)	

Location	Type	Capacity (t)	Qty
Wallmann Terminal (Reiherstieg)	Mobile Cranes	140	1
Wallmann Terminal (Reiherstieg)	Quay Cranes	45	
Eichholtz Terminal	Reach Stackers	45	2
Eichholtz Terminal	Forklifts	3–16	55
Midgard Terminal Harburg 2	Mult-purp. Cranes		4
HEW Wedel	Mult-purp. Cranes		3
IHSW Terminal	Mult-purp. Cranes		2
Cellpap Terminal Hamburg Umschlags-und Transport GmbH with Shed 25/26, Grasbrook & Dradenau	Mult-purp. Cranes	104	6

Bunkering: Reinhold Bange (GmbH & Co.), Bei dem Neuen Krahn 2, 20457 Hamburg, Germany, *Tel:* +49 40 3760 5101, *Fax:* +49 40 3760 5140, *Email:* info@bange-hamburg.de, *Website:* www.bange-hamburg.de
Bominflot, Bominflot Bunkergesellschaft fur Mineralole mbH & Co. KG, Grosse Baeckerstrasse 11, 20095 Hamburg, Germany, *Tel:* +49 40 350 930, *Fax:* +49 40 3509 3116, *Email:* mail@bominflot.de, *Website:* www.bominflot.net
Deutsche BP AG, Max Born Strasse 2, 22761 Hamburg, Germany, *Tel:* +49 40 639 4628, *Fax:* +49 40 6395 4670, *Email:* rudi.schrader@de.bp.com, *Website:* www.bp.com
Deutsche Calpam GmbH, Grosse Elbstrasse 141 a, 22767 Hamburg, Germany, *Tel:* +49 40 3068 620, *Fax:* +49 40 3068 6216, *Email:* bunkers@calpam.de, *Website:* www.calpam.de
Frachtcontor Junge & Co., Frachtcontor Junge & Co. GmbH, Ballindamm 17, 20095 Hamburg, Germany, *Tel:* +49 40 300 00, *Fax:* +49 40 3000 338, *Email:* info@frachtcontor.de, *Website:* www.frachtcontor.com
Friedrich G. Frommann GmbH, Wallgraben 47, 21073 Hamburg, Germany, *Tel:* +49 40 7662 680, *Fax:* +49 40 7662 6818, *Email:* frommann@fgfshell.de, *Website:* www.fgfshell.de
GEFO Gesellschaft fur Oeltransporte mbH, Kurze Muehren 2, P O Box 102345, 20095 Hamburg, Germany, *Tel:* +49 40 3010 5125, *Fax:* +49 40 3010 5161, *Email:* bunkers.1@gefo.com, *Website:* www.gefo.com
Germany Transport & Logistics GmbH, Buchtstrasse 4, 22087 Hamburg, Germany, *Tel:* +49 40 64225 7070, *Fax:* +49 40 64225 7075, *Email:* info@gtl-hamburg.de
IBT Bunkering & Trading GmbH, Raboisen 32, 20095 Hamburg, Germany, *Tel:* +49 40 2201 191, *Fax:* +49 40 2295 030, *Email:* info@ibtbunker.com, *Website:* www.ibtbunker.com
Maxcom Bunker S.p.A. u.s., Maxcom Energy S.p.A., Eckerkamp 7a, 22391 Hamburg, Germany, *Tel:* +49 40 417568, *Fax:* +49 40 417563, *Email:* maxcom@ehmcke.com, *Website:* www.maxcom.it
Nordic Shipping GmbH, Poststrasse 14-16, 20354 Hamburg, Germany, *Tel:* +49 40 3552 000, *Fax:* +49 40 3552 0035, *Email:* bunkers@nordicshipping.de, *Website:* www.nordicshipping.de
Petrol Bunkering & Trading Germany GmbH, Lohe 43 F, 22397 Hamburg, Germany, *Tel:* +49 40 66 99 75 07, *Fax:* +49 40 66 99 75 10, *Email:* petrolbunkering@aol.com
United Bunker GmbH Oil Trading & Services, Tankweg 1, 21129 Hamburg, Germany, *Tel:* +49 40 3339 940, *Fax:* +49 40 3339 9420, *Email:* united.bunker@t-online.de
Heinrich Wegener & Sohn Bunkergesellschaft mbH, Focksweg 34, 21129 Hamburg, Germany, *Tel:* +49 40 7421 9010, *Fax:* +49 40 7421 2635, *Email:* general@wegener-bunker.de, *Website:* www.wegener-bunker.de
Wendland-Elektro, Eschelsweg 4, 22767 Hamburg, Germany, *Tel:* +49 40 317 8990, *Fax:* +49 40 3178 9999, *Email:* wendland-elektro@t-online.de, *Website:* www.wendland-elektro.de

Waste Reception Facilities: All services available

Towage: A harbour fleet of 25 tugs for large vessels, 30 small tugs for rivercraft, 191 launches and 500 lighters (covered and uncovered) connect ships in midstream with storage plants and may themselves be used for storage when required. 4 floating cranes with lifting cap up to 1000 t-partly self-propelled

Repair & Maintenance: Barthels & Luders GmbH, Norderelbstrasse 15, 20457 Hamburg, Germany, *Tel:* +49 40 311880, *Fax:* +49 40 3118 8700, *Email:* service@barthels-lueders.com, *Website:* www.barthels-lueders.com
Blohm + Voss GmbH, Hermann Blohm Strasse 3, P O Box 100720, 20005 Hamburg, Germany, *Tel:* +49 40 3119 8000, *Fax:* +49 40 3119 3333, *Email:* info@thyssenkrupp.com, *Website:* www.thyssenkrupp.com Three floating docks: No.6 162.5 m x 24.5 m x 8 m for vessels up to 18 000 dwt, No.10 287.5 m x 44.2 m x 10.2 m for vessels up to 130 000 dwt, No.11 320 m x 52 m x 10.8 m for vessels up to 250 000 dwt. Elbe 17 graving dock 351.2 m x 59.2 m x 9.5 m for vessels up to 320 000 dwt
Theodor Buschmann Schiffswerft GmbH & Co., Reiherstiegdeich 53, P O Box 930224, 21107 Hamburg, Germany, *Tel:* +49 40 751 9830, *Fax:* +49 40 751 8324, *Email:* info@werft-thbuschmann.de, *Website:* www.buschmann-werft.com Facilities include three slipways up to 55 m length and 1000 t lifting cap
Gall & Seitz GmbH, Vogelreth 2-4, Freihafen, 20457 Hamburg, Germany, *Tel:* +49 40 7801 8411, *Fax:* +49 40 7801 8419, *Email:* shiprepair@gall-seitz.com, *Website:* www.gall-seitz.com Repair and overhaul of main and auxiliary engines
Norderwerft GmbH & Co KG, Ellerholzdamm 13, D-20457 Hamburg, Germany, *Tel:* +49 40 31100-0, *Website:* www.norderwerft.de
Turbo-Technik Reparatur-Werft GmbH & Co, Alstertwiete 5, D-20099 Hamburg, Germany, *Tel:* +49 40 280 1055, *Fax:* +49 40 280 3396, *Email:* hamburg@turbotechnik.com, *Website:* www.turbotechnik.com Wet docking for vessels up to 250 000 t. Dry docks: Navy dry dock available on request at Wilhelmshaven. Repair quays of 315 m with max draught 11 m (at Wilhelmshaven)

Ship Chandlers: Albatros Schiffsausrnstungs & Aussenhandels GmbH, Reiherdamm 44, 20457 Hamburg, Germany, *Tel:* +49 40 335034, *Fax:* +49 40 330405, *Email:* info@albatros.de
Wilhelm Albers GmbH & Co. KG, Bilstrae 217, 20539 Hamburg, Germany, *Tel:* +49 40 8197 8560, *Fax:* +49 40 8219 78585, *Email:* info@wilhelm-albers-hamburg.de, *Website:* www.wilhelm-albers-hamburg.de
Baste & Lange GmbH, Am Genter Ufer 4a, 21129 Hamburg, Germany, *Tel:* +49 40 781109-0, *Fax:* +49 40 7811 0990, *Email:* service@bastelange.com, *Website:* www.bastelange.com
C.L. Becker GmbH, Suderstrasse 129, 20537 Hamburg, Germany, *Tel:* +49 40 250 0750, *Fax:* +49 40 250 3578, *Email:* info@clbecker.de, *Website:* www.clbecker.de
Beisser Gebruder GmbH, Ellerholzdamm 46, 20457 Hamburg, Germany, *Tel:* +49 40 365892, *Fax:* +49 40 367466, *Email:* info@beissergebrueder.de
Burchard Redelstorff GmbH, Wendenstrasse 195, 20537 Hamburg, Germany, *Tel:* +49 40 250 2709, *Fax:* +49 40 250 3248, *Email:* mail@redelstorff.de, *Website:* www.redelstorff.de
Canel & Sohn GmbH & Co., Grossmannstrasse 8, 20539 Hamburg, Germany, *Tel:* +49 40 780970-0, *Fax:* +49 40 782950, *Email:* mail@canel.de
Holger Classen GmbH & Co. KG, Alsterdorfer Strasse 234, 22297 Hamburg, Germany, *Tel:* +49 40 511280, *Fax:* +49 40 5112 8111, *Email:* info@holger-clasen.de, *Website:* www.holger-clasen.de
CMR-AUTRONIC GmbH, Poppenbutteler Bogen 82, 22399 Hamburg, Germany, *Tel:* +49 40 4840 2331, *Fax:* +49 40 4840 2337, *Email:* mail@cmr-autronic.de, *Website:* www.cmr-autronic.de
Cosalt GmbH, Winsbergring 8, 22525 Hamburg, Germany, *Tel:* +49 40 675 0960, *Fax:* +49 40 6750 9611, *Email:* info@cosalt.de, *Website:* www.cosalt.de
J.J. Darboven International GmbH, Pinkertweg 13, 22113 Hamburg, Germany, *Tel:* +49 40 7333 5120, *Fax:* +49 40 7333 5134, *Email:* international@darboven.com, *Website:* www.darboven.com
De Mora Industry & Ship Spare Parts, Ohechaussee 112, 22848 Norderstedt, Germany, *Tel:* +49 40 3861 1680, *Fax:* +49 40 3861 1682, *Email:* info@demora.de, *Website:* www.demora.de
Draeger Safety AG & Co. KGaA, Albert-Schweitzer-Ring 22, 22045 Hamburg, Germany, *Tel:* +49 40 668670, *Fax:* +49 40 6686 7150, *Email:* vertrieb.nord@draeger.com, *Website:* www.draeger-safety.com
East Wind Schiffs- und Werftbedarf Import-Export GmbH, Bei dem Neuen Krahn 2, 20457 Hamburg, Germany, *Tel:* +49 40 78850-0, *Fax:* +49 40 788 5025, *Email:* service@east-wind.de, *Website:* www.east-wind.de
Elbtrade Im- und Export GmbH, Stubbenhuk 10, 20459 Hamburg, Germany, *Tel:* +49 40 373726, *Fax:* +49 40 373728, *Email:* hamburg@elbtrade.de, *Website:* www.elbtrade.de
Georg Fischers Schiffsschmiede, Obenhauptstrasse 1B, 22335 Hamburg, Germany, *Tel:* +49 40 391671/2, *Fax:* +49 40 395997, *Email:* info@german-mooring-systems.com, *Website:* www.german-mooring-systems.com
GMS General Marine Spares Im- und Export GmbH, P O Box 1263, Kroegerskoppel 3, 24548 Henstedt-Ulzburg, Germany, *Tel:* +49 40 419 3906-0, *Fax:* +49 40 4193 90625, *Email:* gmsgmbhgermany@aol.com
Hanse Nautic GmbH Bade & Hornig Eckardt & Messtorff, P O Box 112045, 20420 Hamburg, Germany, *Tel:* +49 40 374 8110, *Fax:* +49 40 37481144, *Email:* info@hansenautic.com, *Website:* www.hansenautic.com
Hansheng Marine Service Center GmbH, Jostweg 3, 22339 Hamburg, Germany, *Tel:* +49 40 5272 1600, *Fax:* +49 40 5272 1618, *Email:* hansheng@t-online.de
Hans Heidorn Shipping Services GmbH, Neuhoefer Brueckenstrasse 8, 21107 Hamburg, Germany, *Tel:* +49 40 369 8080, *Fax:* +49 40 3698 08350, *Email:* heidorn-shipping@hans-heidorn.de, *Website:* www.hans-heidorn.de
Gebr. Heinemann, P O Box 11 14 69, 20414 Hamburg, Germany, *Tel:* +49 40 301020, *Fax:* +49 40 3010 2116, *Email:* info@gebr-heinemann.de, *Website:* www.gebr-heinemann.de
Hellenic Shipstores GmbH, Buchheisterstrasse 6, 20457 Hamburg, Germany, *Tel:* +49 40 3178 4223, *Fax:* +49 40 319 4841, *Email:* info@rump-kg.de, *Website:* www.rump-kg.de
Walter Hering, P O Box 740368, 22093 Hamburg, Germany, *Tel:* +49 40 736172-0, *Fax:* +49 40 7361 7261, *Email:* Seil-Hering@t-online.de
Hoff Ship Service GmbH, Friesenweg 1, 20457 Hamburg, Germany, *Tel:* +49 40 309788-0, *Fax:* +49 40 3097 8840, *Email:* info@hoffship.de
Holsten-Brauerei AG, Holstenstrasse 224, 22765 Hamburg, Germany, *Tel:* +49 40 3810 1622, *Fax:* +49 40 3810 1240, *Email:* kj.nens@holsten.de
HTH - Marine-Technik Handelsgesellschaft mbH, Grevenweg 72, 20537 Hamburg, Germany, *Tel:* +49 40 370903-0, *Fax:* +49 40 3709 0333, *Email:* hth@hth-mt.de, *Website:* www.hth-mt.de
HTS - Hamburger Technik Service GmbH, Ausschlaeger Billdeich 32, 20539 Hamburg, Germany, *Tel:* +49 40 317830-0, *Fax:* +49 40 316851, *Email:* hts@hts-hamburg.de, *Website:* www.hts-hamburg.de
Hygrapha GmbH & Co. KG, Liebigstrasse 67, 22113 Hamburg, Germany, *Tel:* +49 40 731053-0, *Fax:* +49 40 7310 5310, *Email:* hygrapha@hygrapha.com, *Website:* www.hygrapha.com
Kanapee Marine Trading GmbH, Hainzholz 55, 22453 Hamburg, Germany, *Tel:* +49 40 555 8740, *Fax:* +49 40 5558 7410, *Email:* Kanapeemar@aol.com
Emil Kritzky GmbH Schiffsausrustung, Kamerunweg 3, 20457 Hamburg, Germany, *Tel:* +49 40 788130, *Fax:* +49 40 788 1327, *Email:* kritzky@kritzky.com, *Website:* www.kritzky.com
Mares Shipping GmbH, Bei dem Neuen Krahn 2, 20457 Hamburg, Germany, *Tel:* +49 40 374 7840, *Fax:* +49 40 3747 8446, *Email:* ga@mares.de, *Website:* www.mares.de
Mares Shipping GmbH, Bei dem Neuen Krahn 2, 20457 Hamburg, Germany, *Tel:* +49 40 374 7840, *Fax:* +49 40 3747 8446, *Email:* sales@mares.de, *Website:* www.mares.de
Marine Shipstores D. Medri GmbH, Ellerholzdamm 2-5, 20457 Hamburg, Germany, *Tel:* +49 40 317831-0, *Fax:* +49 40 317 5913, *Email:* wave@medri.de
Marine Supply Handels Gesellschaft mbH, Friesenweg 4, 22763 Hamburg, Germany, *Tel:* +49 40 880 7634, *Fax:* +49 40 880 7002, *Email:* info@scantrading.de, *Website:* www.scantrading.de
Mariport Im- & Export GmbH, Waidmannstr 12 b, 22769 Hamburg, Germany, *Tel:* +49 40 781716, *Fax:* +49 40 787600, *Email:* info@mariport.de, *Website:* www.mariport.de
Martechnic GmbH, Adlerhorst 4, 22459 Hamburg, Germany, *Tel:* +49 40 853 1280, *Fax:* +49 40 8531 2816, *Email:* info@martechnic.com, *Website:* www.martechnic.com
Herbert Metzendorff & Co., Hohe-Schaar Street 47, 21107 Hamburg, Germany, *Tel:* +49 40 756 0590, *Fax:* +49 40 759562, *Email:* hmetzendorff-hh@t-online.de, *Website:* www.metzendorff-co.com
Moller & Bottger GmbH, Buschwerder Winkel 1, 21107 Hamburg, Germany, *Tel:* +49 40 851718-0, *Fax:* +49 40 8517 1885, *Email:* mbpool@mb-ship-service.de, *Website:* www.moeboe.de
Neptun Schiffsausrustung Gerhard van der Linde OHG, Ubersee-Zentrum Hamburg, Schumacherwerder, 20457 Hamburg, Germany, *Tel:* +49 40 370908-0, *Fax:* +49 40 3709 0811, *Email:* info@neptun-shipstores.de, *Website:* www.neptun-shipstores.de

Nera GmbH, Muehlenstieg 5, 22041 Hamburg, Germany, *Tel:* +49 40 682770, *Fax:* +49 40 6827 7135, *Email:* nera.hh@nera.no, *Website:* www.e-sl.de

J. H. Peters & Bey GmbH, Schnackenburgallee 151, 22525 Hamburg, Germany, *Tel:* +49 40 547 6000, *Fax:* +49 40 5476 0076, *Email:* mail@peters-bey.com, *Website:* www.peters-bey.com

Pfeifer Seil- und Hebetechnik GmbH, Bullenhuser Damm 53, 20539 Hamburg, Germany, *Tel:* +49 40 780463-0, *Fax:* +49 40 787013, *Email:* psh-hamburg@Pfeifer.de, *Website:* www.pfeifer.de

Pickenpack & von Riegen GmbH, P O Box 110623, 20406 Hamburg, Germany, *Tel:* +49 40 31800-0, *Fax:* +49 40 3180 0180, *Email:* info@schaar-niemeyer.com, *Website:* www.schaar-niemeyer.com

Hans-Ulrich Pillekamp GmbH, Admiralitatstrasse 58, 20459 Hamburg, Germany, *Tel:* +49 40 367535, *Fax:* +49 40 363814, *Email:* pillekamp-gmbh@t-online.de, *Website:* www.pillekamp.de

Promarine GmbH, Tarpenring 4, 22419 Hamburg, Germany, *Tel:* +49 40 5393 3690, *Fax:* +49 40 5393 3699, *Email:* info@promarine-hamburg.de, *Website:* www.pro-marine-hamburg.de

Wilh. Richers GmbH & Co., P O Box 110623, 20406 Hamburg, Germany, *Tel:* +49 40 781102-0, *Fax:* +49 40 7811 02280, *Email:* office@wilh-richers.de, *Website:* www.wilh-richers.de

A. Riva GmbH, Magdeburger Street 5-7, 20457 Hamburg, Germany, *Tel:* +49 40 334156, *Fax:* +49 40 334174/5, *Email:* biskupek@ssc.de

Wilhelm Rump KG (GmbH & Co.), Buchheisterstrasse 6, 20457 Hamburg, Germany, *Tel:* +49 40 317842-0, *Fax:* +49 40 319 4841, *Email:* info@rump-kg.com, *Website:* www.rump-kg.com

Friedrich Sanger GmbH, Magdeburger Street 5-7, 20457 Hamburg, Germany, *Tel:* +49 40 33410, *Fax:* +49 40 334174/5, *Email:* fs@ssc.de

Scantrading Schiffstechnik GmbH, Friesenweg 4, 22763 Hamburg, Germany, *Tel:* +49 40 880 4022/4, *Fax:* +49 40 880 7002, *Email:* info@scantrading.de, *Website:* www.scantrading.de

Schaar & Niemeyer (GmbH & Co.) KG, P. O. Box 110623, 20406 Hamburg, Germany, *Tel:* +49 40 318000, *Fax:* +49 40 3180 0180, *Email:* info@schaar-niemeyer.com, *Website:* www.schaar-niemeyer.com

Rudolf Seldis (GmbH & Co.) KG, Martin-Luther-Strasse 20, 20459 Hamburg, Germany, *Tel:* +49 40 374949-0, *Fax:* +49 40 365178, *Email:* seldis@seldis.de

Richard Sump GmbH, Afrika Street 1, 20457 Hamburg, Germany, *Tel:* +49 40 780 9480, *Fax:* +49 40 7809 4820, *Email:* info@sump.de, *Website:* www.sump.de

Louis Taxt GmbH & Co., Neuhoefer Brueckenstrasse 8, 21107 Hamburg, Germany, *Tel:* +49 40 713901-0, *Fax:* +49 40 713901-280, *Email:* info@Louis-Taxt.com

Wendland-Elektro, Eschelsweg 4, 22767 Hamburg, Germany, *Tel:* +49 40 317 8990, *Fax:* +49 40 3178 9999, *Email:* wendland-elektro@t-online.de, *Website:* www.wendland-elektro.de

Carl Wolf, Beckedorf Bogen 25, 21218 Hamburg, Germany, *Tel:* +49 40 338948, *Fax:* +49 40 338637, *Email:* info@carl-wolf-elektro.de

Shipping Agents: Abou Merhi Lines S.A.L., Nehlstrasse/Schuppen 71b, 20457 Hamburg, Germany, *Tel:* +49 40 3178 5066, *Fax:* +49 40 3178 5093, *Email:* abou-merhi-hamburg@t-online.de, *Website:* www.aboumerhilines.com

Ahlmann-Zerssen GmbH & Co KG, Pollhornweg 25, 21107 Hamburg, Germany, *Tel:* +49 40 7527 0537, *Fax:* +49 40 7527 0531, *Email:* hamburg@ahlmann-zerssen.de, *Website:* www.ahlmann-zerssen.de

Balkan & Black Sea Shipping Co., 42a Kanalstrasse, 22085 Hamburg, Germany, *Tel:* +49 40 227 0120, *Fax:* +49 40 227 9726, *Email:* info@bbss-ham.de, *Website:* www.bbss-ham.de

Reinhold Bange (GmbH & Co.), Bei dem Neuen Krahn 2, 20457 Hamburg, Germany, *Tel:* +49 40 3760 5101, *Fax:* +49 40 3760 5140, *Email:* info@bange-hamburg.de, *Website:* www.bange-hamburg.de

BEL Schiffahrts- und Speditionsges m.b.H., Obenhauptstrasse 13, 22335 Hamburg, Germany, *Tel:* +49 40 378 5040, *Fax:* +49 40 3785 0455, *Email:* bel-ham@t-online.de

CMA-CGM S.A., CMA CGM (Deutschland) GmbH, Neuer Dovenhof, Brandstwiete 1, 20457 Hamburg, Germany, *Tel:* +49 40 235300, *Fax:* +49 40 2353 0100, *Email:* hbg.genmbox@cma-cgm.com, *Website:* www.cma-cgm.com

CSAV Group Agencies (Germany) GmbH, Am Sandtorkai 74, 20457 Hamburg, Germany, *Tel:* +49 40 37649-0, *Fax:* +49 40 37649-299, *Email:* shipping@csavagenciy-de.com

DSA Deutsche Shiffahrts-Agentur GmbH & Co., Palmaille 45, 22767 Hamburg, Germany, *Tel:* +49 40 3801 6392, *Fax:* +49 40 3801 6255, *Email:* contact-dalsa@rantzau.de, *Website:* www.rantzau.de

Hf Eimskipafelag Islands, Eimskip Transport GmbH, Brandsende 6, 20095 Hamburg, Germany, *Tel:* +49 40 323 3300, *Fax:* +49 40 3233 3060, *Email:* info@eimskip.de, *Website:* www.eimskip.is

Ernst Glassel GmbH & Co KG, Alter Wall 67-69, 20457 Hamburg, Germany, *Tel:* +49 40 376070, *Fax:* +49 40 3760 7447, *Email:* gla@glaessel.de, *Website:* www.glaessel.de

GMT Shipping Line Ltd, GMT BS Africa Line GmbH, Grosse Bleichen 8, 4th Floor, 20354 Hamburg, Germany, *Tel:* +49 40 8090 6450, *Fax:* +49 40 8090 6455, *Email:* commercial@gmtbs-shipping.com, *Website:* www.gmtshipping.com

A Hartrodt International, Hogerdamm 35, P O Box 10 29 29, 20020 Hamburg, Germany, *Tel:* +49 40 239 0314, *Fax:* +49 40 239 0253, *Email:* ah_ham@hartrodt.com, *Website:* www.hartrodt.com

Ibramar Schiffahrts GmbH, Raboisen 16, 20095 Hamburg, Germany, *Tel:* +49 40 300 8660, *Fax:* +49 40 3008 6699, *Email:* agency@ibramar.com, *Website:* www.ibramar.com

Incotrans GmbH Linienagentur, Kleine Reichenstrasse 1, Reichenhof, 20457 Hamburg, Germany, *Tel:* +49 40 309 6480, *Fax:* +49 40 3096 4888, *Email:* agency@incotrans.com, *Website:* www.incotrans.com

MacAndrews & Co Ltd, Neuer Dovenhof, Brandstwiete 1, 20457 Hamburg, Germany, *Tel:* +49 40 689 8890, *Fax:* +49 40 6898 8910, *Email:* bschmidtke@macandrews.com, *Website:* www.macandrews.com

Mediterranean Shipping Company, MSC Germany GmbH, Willy Brandt Strasse 49, 20457 Hamburg, Germany, *Tel:* +49 40 30295-0, *Fax:* +49 40 330236, *Email:* hamburg@mscgermany.com, *Website:* www.mscgermany.com

A.P. Moller-Maersk Group, Maersk Deutschland A/S & Co.KG, Am Sandtorkai 70-73, 20457 Hamburg, Germany, *Tel:* +49 40 235210, *Fax:* +49 40 2352 1671, *Website:* www.maerskline.com

Neptun Schiffahrts-Agentur GmbH, Alter Wall 67 - 69, 20459 Hamburg, Germany, *Tel:* +49 40 3764 9425, *Fax:* +49 40 3764 9426, *Email:* agency@neptunship.de, *Website:* www.neptunship.de

Samskip H/f (Samband Line Ltd), Samskip GmbH, Rodingsmarkt 29, 20459 Hamburg, Germany, *Tel:* +49 40 361 4160, *Fax:* +49 40 374 3474, *Email:* hamburg@samskip.de, *Website:* www.samskip.com

Sartori & Berger, Mattenwiete 6, 20457 Hamburg, Germany, *Tel:* +49 40 325 7960, *Fax:* +49 40 3257 9625, *Email:* hamburg@sartori-berger.de, *Website:* www.sartori-berger.de

Wilhelm Tietjen Befrachtungsges. mbH, Grosse Elbstrasse 131, 22767 Hamburg, Germany, *Tel:* +49 40 381171, *Fax:* +49 40 380 0087, *Email:* info@tietjen-online.de, *Website:* www.tietjen-online.de

Transnaval Schiffahrtsges mbH & Co., Neuer Wall 52, 20354 Hamburg, Germany, *Tel:* +49 40 309 5210, *Fax:* +49 40 3095 2116, *Email:* hamburg@btl-feerders.com, *Website:* www.schoeller-holdings.com/btl.htm

Ultra Schiffahrt GmbH, Neustaedter Neuer Weg 2, 20459 Hamburg, Germany, *Tel:* +49 40 369 8520, *Fax:* +49 40 3698 5261, *Email:* w.ulrich@ultrashipping.de, *Website:* www.ultrashipping.de

Surveyors: ABS (Europe), Roedingsmarkt 26, 20459 Hamburg, Germany, *Tel:* +49 40 378 5870, *Fax:* +49 40 3785 8787, *Email:* abshamburg@eagle.org, *Website:* www.eagle.org

Bureau Veritas, Veritaskai 1, 21079 Hamburg, Germany, *Tel:* +49 40 2362 5600, *Fax:* +49 40 2362 5620, *Email:* info@de.bureauveritas.com, *Website:* www.bureauveritas.com

China Classification Society, Koenigstrasse 28, 22767 Hamburg, Germany, *Tel:* +49 40 386 0890, *Fax:* +49 40 3860 8918, *Email:* ccshb@ccs.org.cn, *Website:* www.ccs.org.cn

Det Norske Veritas A/S, Bei den Muhren 1, 20457 Hamburg, Germany, *Tel:* +49 40 890 5900, *Fax:* +49 40 8905 9030, *Email:* hamburg@dnv.com, *Website:* www.dnv.com

Hellenic Register of Shipping, c/o Arnold Peters Shipping Agency, P O Box 110742, 20407 Hamburg, Germany, *Tel:* +49 40 309 7150, *Fax:* +49 40 3097 1539, *Email:* peters.shipping.hamburg@t-online.de, *Website:* www.hrs.gr

Korean Register of Shipping, Emkendorfstrasse 42A, 22605 Hamburg, Germany, *Tel:* +49 40 8891 3791, *Fax:* +49 40 8891 3792, *Email:* kr-hmb@krs.co.kr, *Website:* www.krs.co.kr

Nippon Kaiji Kyokai, Spaldingstrasse 77a, 20097 Hamburg, Germany, *Tel:* +49 40 233032, *Fax:* +49 40 230863, *Email:* hb@classnk.or.jp, *Website:* www.classnk.or.jp

Airport: Hamburg Airport, 12 km

Railway: Hamburg-Hauptbahnhof (Main Station), approx 1 mile from port Hamburg-Altona, approx 1 mile from port

Lloyd's Agent: Reck & Co. GmbH, Wikinghaus, Schopenstehl 22, D-20095 Hamburg, Germany, *Tel:* +49 40 2789 6375, *Fax:* +49 40 2780 6418, *Email:* hamburg@reck.de, *Website:* www.reck.de

HEILIGENHAFEN

Lat 54° 22' N; Long 10° 59' E.

Admiralty Chart: 2364	**Admiralty Pilot:** 18
Time Zone: GMT +1 h	**UNCTAD Locode:** DE HHF

Principal Facilities:

		Y	G			B		

Authority: Heiligenhafener Verkehrsbetriebe GmbH & Co. KG, Am Jachthafen 4a, 23774 Heiligenhafen, Germany, *Tel:* +49 4362 900435, *Fax:* +49 4362 900436, *Email:* s.schwarck@hvbkg.de, *Website:* www.hvbkg.de

Officials: General Manager: Manfred Wohnrade, *Email:* m.wohnrade@hvbkg.de. Harbour Master: Sven Schwarck.

Port Security: ISPS compliant

Approach: Dredged entrance channel approx 1800 m long, 35 m wide and 5 m deep. It is marked by red fairway buoys and green fairway buoys with light reflecting colour bands spaced 50 m apart. Depth in channel and inner harbour, 4.5 m with normal water conditions

Anchorage: Good holding ground outside channel entrance, sheltered from all winds

Pilotage: Compulsory for vessels of more than 90 m loa, pilot available on VHF Channel 14 or from port authority. Vessels of more than 90 m loa and 4.3 m d are obliged to report to port authority prior to entering approach channels, *Tel:* +49 4502 71117

Radio Frequency: VHF Channel 14 from 0800-1600

Weather: Normal conditions, mostly W'ly winds

Maximum Vessel Dimensions: 120 m loa, 4.8 m draft

Working Hours: 0800-1600

Accommodation:

Name	Length (m)	Depth (m)	Remarks
Heiligenhafen			See [1] below
Quay	260	4.5-5	See [2] below

[1]*Heiligenhafen:* Yachting harbour between town and harbour, cap of 1000 craft

---

A=Airport	**C**=Containers	**G**=General Cargo	**P**=Petroleum	**R**=Ro/Ro	**Y**=Dry Bulk
B=Bunkers	**D**=Dry Dock	**L**=Cruise	**Q**=Other Liquid Bulk	**T**=Towage (where available from port)	

Key to Principal Facilities:—

²*Quay:* Vessels with cargoes of 300 t and over should advise Agents or Harbour Master, leaving ample time to ensure effective berthing. Four grain storage silo's

Storage:

Location	Grain (t)
Quay	30000

Mechanical Handling Equipment:

Location	Type	Capacity (t)	Qty
Heiligenhafen	Mult-purp. Cranes	2	1

Bunkering: Limited supplies of bunker oil available alongside quay. Bunkering services can be arranged

Repair & Maintenance: Two yards undertake minor repairs and may carry out engine overhauls

Medical Facilities: Hospital available in the city

Airport: Hamburg, 140 km

Railway: Oldenburg, 10 km

Lloyd's Agent: Reck & Co. GmbH, Wikinghaus, Schopenstehl 22, D-20095 Hamburg, Germany, *Tel:* +49 40 2789 6375, *Fax:* +49 40 2780 6418, *Email:* hamburg@reck.de, *Website:* www.reck.de

HUSUM

Lat 54° 28' N; Long 9° 2' E.

Admiralty Chart: 3767
Time Zone: GMT +1 h
Admiralty Pilot: 55
UNCTAD Locode: DE HUS

Principal Facilities:

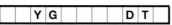

Y G | D T

Authority: Amt fur Landiche Raume Husum, Hafenbehorde, Am Aussenhafen, 25813 Husum, Germany, *Tel:* +49 4841 661317, *Fax:* +49 4841 661321, *Email:* hafen.husum@lkn.landsh.de

Officials: Managing Director: Carl L. Ahrens, *Email:* carl.ahrens@lkn.landsh.de. Port Captain: Hermut Goetze, *Tel:* +49 4841 661313.

Port Security: ISPS compliant

Approach: Over the Mittelhever, Heverstrom and Husumer Au Channel well buoyed and marked with lighted beacons for night navigation

Pilotage: Not compulsory, but advisable when using port for the first time. Pilot goes out to meet vessel before Husum. Two pilots available. Call Harbour Office, Husum, 24 h before arrival at Fairway buoy, Tel: +49 4841 667217. If pilots are available they will board depending on wind and weather conditions in the Mittlehever, within or outside bar; pilots can also board during passage through Kiel-Kanal

Radio Frequency: Husum Port on VHF Channel 11

Weather: Prevailing winds from SW to NW

Tides: At low tide shallowest water levels at the bar of the Mittelhever are approx 5.6 m and in Heverstrom approx 3.1 m. Average tide levels approx 3 to 3.5 m

Maximum Vessel Dimensions: 120 m loa, 18 m width and 4 m draft max Vessels over 70 m loa may be faced with manoeuvreing difficulties; vessels with a width of 9 to 13 m and/or 3.4 to 3.8 m draft must notify Husum Port (VHF Channel 11) with their ETA; vessels over 13 m width and/or 3.8 to 4 m draft require an entry permit from the port authority

Accommodation:

Name	Remarks
Husum	See ¹ below
Outer Harbour	See ² below
Inner Harbour	See ³ below

¹*Husum:* Harbour bottom soft silt; uneven bottom so vessels must take care at LW. A lifting railway bridge divides the harbour into an outer and inner section. Vessels requiring passage to give two long signals to the bridge keeper in the signals box. Bridge will be raised if necessary
²*Outer Harbour:* 4 m deep at average HW. 180 m quay at silo to the NE of the harbour. 280 m quay in front of fishing harbour
³*Inner Harbour:* Dry at LW. Quay 480 m serviceable length; vessels of 3 m draft can reach harbour at average HW

Storage: For grain, fodder and fertilisers 100 000 t; five grain silos, each 1200 t cap; one open storage area in the N part of port

Mechanical Handling Equipment:

Location	Type	Capacity (t)	Qty
Outer Harbour	Mult-purp. Cranes	9	2

Towage: Husum shipyard tug

Repair & Maintenance: Husumer Dock und Reparatur GmbH & Co. KG, Roedemis-Hallig, D-25813 Husum, Germany, *Tel:* +49 4841 6300, *Fax:* +49 4841 63081, *Email:* info@husumer-dock.de, *Website:* www.husumer-dock.de

Airport: Hamburg-Fuhlsbuttel, about 150 km

Lloyd's Agent: Reck & Co. GmbH, Wikinghaus, Schopenstehl 22, D-20095 Hamburg, Germany, *Tel:* +49 40 2789 6375, *Fax:* +49 40 2780 6418, *Email:* hamburg@reck.de, *Website:* www.reck.de

ITZEHOE

Lat 53° 56' N; Long 9° 31' E.

Admiralty Chart: 3625
Time Zone: GMT +1 h
Admiralty Pilot: 55
UNCTAD Locode: DE ITZ

Principal Facilities:

Y G | B D | A

Authority: Stadtwerke Itzehoe GmbH, Gasstrasse 18, 25524 Itzehoe, Germany, *Tel:* +49 4821 7740, *Fax:* +49 4821 774117, *Email:* info@stadtwerke-itzehoe.de, *Website:* www.stadtwerke-itzehoe.de

Port Security: ISPS compliant

Approach: Vessels can enter the port at HW only

Pilotage: Pilots available at Gluckstadt

Radio Frequency: VHF Channel 16

Tides: Tidal range 2.2 m

Maximum Vessel Dimensions: 1700 max dwt, 80 m loa, 3.8 m d

Working Hours: Mon-Thurs 0700-1200, 1300-1600. Fri 0700-1200, 1300-1430

Accommodation:

Name	Length (m)	Depth (m)
Itzehoe		
Town Harbour Quay	420	1.9–4

Storage:

Location	Grain (t)
Town Harbour Quay	35000

Mechanical Handling Equipment:

Location	Type	Capacity (t)	Qty
Itzehoe	Mult-purp. Cranes	3	1
Itzehoe	Mult-purp. Cranes	6	1
Town Harbour Quay	Mult-purp. Cranes	6	2

Cargo Worked: Up to 150 t/h

Bunkering: Available from road tanker

Repair & Maintenance: Peters Schiffbau GmbH, Am Hafen 6, 25599 Wewelsfleth, Germany, *Tel:* +49 4829 710, *Fax:* +49 4829 71290, *Email:* info@peters-schiffbau.de, *Website:* www.peters-ag.de

Medical Facilities: Local hospital

Airport: Hamburg Airport, 60 km

Lloyd's Agent: Reck & Co. GmbH, Wikinghaus, Schopenstehl 22, D-20095 Hamburg, Germany, *Tel:* +49 40 2789 6375, *Fax:* +49 40 2780 6418, *Email:* hamburg@reck.de, *Website:* www.reck.de

JACHTHAFEN

harbour area, see under Cuxhaven

KAPPELN

Lat 54° 40' N; Long 9° 56' E.

Admiralty Chart: -
Time Zone: GMT +1 h
Admiralty Pilot: -
UNCTAD Locode: DE KAP

Principal Facilities:

		Y	G			B			A	

Authority: Shipbroker Artur Koch, Dehnthof 21, 24937 Kappeln, Germany, *Tel:* +49 4642 2354, *Fax:* +49 461 807600, *Email:* info@cjbw.de, *Website:* www.cjbw.de

Officials: General Manager: Jurgen Jensen, *Email:* j.jensen@t-online.de.
Harbour Master: Norbert Bierlein, *Tel:* +49 4642 3156.

Port Security: ISPS compliant

Pilotage: Compulsory for vessels of more than 75 m loa or 3.8 m d or 13.0 m breadth. Pilot enters at Kiel Light Tower

Working Hours: Mon to Fri 0700-1800. Sat 0700-1200

Accommodation:

Name	Draught (m)	Remarks
Kappeln		See [1] below
N Harbour	4.5	See [2] below
S Harbour	4.5	See [3] below

[1]*Kappeln:* Depth of water between gateway Schleimunde and Kappeln 4.5 m at normal water level. Distance between Schleimunde and Kappeln about 6.5 km
[2]*N Harbour:* Grain loading/discharging rate is 65 t/h. For vessels max length 120 m, max beam 13 m
[3]*S Harbour:* Grain loading rate is 60-100 t/h. For vessels max length 120 m, max beam 13 m. Passage width of the swing bridge is 22.5 m

Storage:

Location	Grain (t)
N Harbour	4500
S Harbour	4000

Mechanical Handling Equipment:

Location	Type	Capacity (t)	Qty
S Harbour	Mobile Cranes	3	1

Bunkering: Bunkering services can be arranged at S Harbour and N Harbour

Airport: Flensburg, 50 km

Lloyd's Agent: Reck & Co. GmbH, Wikinghaus, Schopenstehl 22, D-20095 Hamburg, Germany, *Tel:* +49 40 2789 6375, *Fax:* +49 40 2780 6418, *Email:* hamburg@reck.de, *Website:* www.reck.de

KARLSRUHE

Lat 49° 3' N; Long 8° 20' E.

Admiralty Chart: -	**Admiralty Pilot:** 28
Time Zone: GMT +1 h	**UNCTAD Locode:** DE KAE

Principal Facilities:

	P	Q		G	C	R				

Authority: Rheinhafen Karlsruhe, Karlsruher Versorgungs-Verkehrs-und Hafen GmbH, Geschaftsbereich Rheinhafen, Werftstr. 2, 76189 Karlsruhe, Germany, *Tel:* +49 721 599 7400, *Fax:* +49 721 599 7409, *Email:* rhhka@rheinhafen.de, *Website:* www.rheinhafen.de

Officials: Chief Executive Officer: Alexander Schwarzer, *Email:* schwarzer@rheinhafen.de.
Marketing Manager: Hilde Brand, *Tel:* +49 721 599 7420, *Email:* hildebrand@rheinhafen.de.
Harbour Master: Pernt Ertel, *Email:* ertel@rheinhafen.de.

Traffic: 2005, 2 756 954 t of cargo handled at Rhine Port and 3 708 525 t of cargo handled at Oil Port

Working Hours: Mon-Fri 0700-1700

Accommodation:

Name	Remarks
Karlsruhe	
Rhine Port	See [1] below
Oil Port	See [2] below

[1]*Rhine Port:* Covering 300 ha with 72 ha (six docks) water area. Equipment includes 20 loading bridges of 4-11 t, 5 electrical cranes of 4-15 t and 1 container crane of 50 t
[2]*Oil Port:* Covering 43 ha with 35 ha water area. Tank storage of 4 802 000 m3. Eleven loading facilities for mineral oil and one loading facility for liquid gas

Storage:

Location	Open (m²)	Covered (m²)	Grain (t)
Rhine Port	600000	215000	14000

Shipping Agents: KALAG Lagerhaus-und Speditionsges mbH, Werftstrasse 12, 76189 Karlsruhe, Germany, *Tel:* +49 721 5963 0, *Fax:* +49 721 596 3303, *Email:* walter.burger@wincanton.eu, *Website:* www.wincanton.eu

Lloyd's Agent: Friedrich Hartmann vorm. J. Kerschgens, 2 Beethovenstrasse, D-68165 Mannheim, Germany, *Tel:* +49 621 423090, *Fax:* +49 621 416354, *Email:* hartmann@hartmann-expert.de, *Website:* www.hartmann-expert.de

KEHL

Lat 48° 35' N; Long 7° 50' E.

Admiralty Chart: -	**Admiralty Pilot:** -
Time Zone: GMT +1 h	**UNCTAD Locode:** DE KEH

Principal Facilities:

	P		Y	G	C	R				A	

Authority: Hafenverwaltung Kehl, Hafenstrasse 19, 77694 Kehl, Germany, *Tel:* +49 7851 897-0, *Fax:* +49 7851 89766, *Email:* info@hafen-kehl.de, *Website:* www.hafen-kehl.de

Officials: Port Director: Dr Karlheinz Hillenbrand, *Tel:* +49 7851 89722, *Email:* dr.hillenbrand@hafen-kehl.de.
Harbour Master: John M. Clausen, *Tel:* +49 7851 89731, *Email:* j.clausen@hafen-kehl.de.

Traffic: 2004, 3 600 000 t of cargo handled

Working Hours: Mon-Fri 0700-1600

Accommodation:

Name	Remarks
Kehl	See [1] below

[1]*Kehl:* The harbour is located in the slack water area of the Freistett/Gambsheim dam and accommodates all vessels which can navigate R Rhine. The depth of water remains constant at approx 6 m in the harbour
Tanker facilities: Three unloading facilities for petroleum of all types
One transhipment facility for container and relay traffic with a lifting cap of 42.5 t

Storage: Container storage space of 15 400 m2

Location	Open (m²)	Covered (m²)
Kehl	230000	36000

Mechanical Handling Equipment:

Location	Type	Capacity (t)	Qty
Kehl	Mult-purp. Cranes	100	30

Repair & Maintenance: Schiffswerft Karcher, Graudenzer Strasse 41, 77694 Kehl, Germany, *Tel:* +49 7851 2765 Repair facilities

Medical Facilities: Kehl District hospital, 2 km

Airport: Strasbourg International, 20 km

Railway: 42 km of rail on harbour territory with access to DB (Germany) and SNCF (France)

Lloyd's Agent: Friedrich Hartmann vorm. J. Kerschgens, 2 Beethovenstrasse, D-68165 Mannheim, Germany, *Tel:* +49 621 423090, *Fax:* +49 621 416354, *Email:* hartmann@hartmann-expert.de, *Website:* www.hartmann-expert.de

Key to Principal Facilities:—					
A=Airport	**C**=Containers	**G**=General Cargo	**P**=Petroleum	**R**=Ro/Ro	**Y**=Dry Bulk
B=Bunkers	**D**=Dry Dock	**L**=Cruise	**Q**=Other Liquid Bulk	**T**=Towage (where available from port)	

KIEL
Lat 54° 19' N; Long 10° 8' E.

Admiralty Chart: 2344	**Admiralty Pilot:** 18
Time Zone: GMT +1 h	**UNCTAD Locode:** DE KEL

Principal Facilities:

P		Y	G	C	R	L	B	D	T	A

Tramp Oil & Marine

Wells House, 15-17 Elmfield Road, Bromley,
Kent BR1 1LT, United Kingdom
Phone: +44 20 8315 7777   **Fax:** +44 20 8315 7788
General email: enquiries@tramp-oil.com

See listings for all global offices: **www.tramp-oil.com**

Authority: Seehafen Kiel GmbH & Co. KG, Bollhornkai 1, 24103 Kiel, Germany, *Tel:* +49 431 982 2142, *Fax:* +49 431 982 4441, *Email:* marketing@port-of-kiel.de, *Website:* www.port-of-kiel.de

Officials: Managing Director: Dirk Claus, *Tel:* +49 431 982 2100, *Email:* direktion@port-of-kiel.de.
Marketing Director: Heinz Bachmann, *Tel:* +49 431 982 2101.
Harbour Master: Juergen Melzer, *Tel:* +49 431 901 1073, *Email:* hafenamt@kiel.de.
Marketing: Anne Stubing.

Port Security: ISPS compliant. Restricted terminal areas, secure fencing and gates, controlled access to port facilities, monitoring of port facilities, lighting at piers and terminals, supervising of ship supply within restricted areas, ID-check of all persons entering the restricted areas, observation of shore and waterside areas, security inspections/screening at clearance points of:
a) vehicles
b) persons entering the security zone
c) hand luggage
d) luggage
24 h patrol and gate security provided by trained guards, emergency and evacuation plans and procedures, certified security personnel according to DIN EN ISO 9001

Documentation: Passenger manifest (2 copies), disembarking passenger manifest (2 copies), embarking passenger manifest (2 copies), crew manifest (2 copies), stores list (1 copy), customs ship declaration (1 copy), customs crew declaration (1 copy), customs passenger declaration (1 copy)

Approach: Located at the inner end of the Kieler Forde, sheltered on the seaward side by the narrow Kiel Canal. An excellent, tideless, natural harbour, almost invariably free from ice. Connected to the Elbe and the N Sea through the Kiel Canal. Depth at entrance and on bar 16 m, max d allowed 9.5 m

Anchorage: Off Kiel Lighthouse in pos 54° 31' N; 10° 18' E in depth of 11 m
In Heikendorf Roads in pos 54° 22.2' N; 11° 11.3' E in depth of 10 m
In Holtenau Roads in pos 54° 22.5' N; 10° 10' E in depth of 12 m

Pilotage: Charges for pilotage on the Kiel Forde from Outer Pilot Station to Kiel Harbour and Holtenau Canal terminal locks and vv, incorporate Pilotage Fees (Lotsgebuhr) and Pilotage Dues (Lotsgeld). Apply for complete new tariff from ship's agents

Radio Frequency: Kiel Port Radio, VHF Channel 16 and 11

Traffic: 2007, 5 303 288 t of cargo handled

Principal Imports and Exports: Imports: Forest products, Milk products, Textile products. Exports: Beverages, Cars, Frozen goods, Grain, Milk products.

Working Hours: Mon-Fri 0700-1600 (meal 0830-0900, 1200-1230). Sat 0700-1300. Overtime can be arranged and should be announced the day before. At Ostuferhafen: on principle 24 h/day, depending on schedules or agreements

Accommodation:

Name	Remarks
Bollhornkai	See [1] below
Schwedenkai	See [2] below
Scheerhafen	See [3] below
Sartorikai	Quay length of 210 m in depth of 5.8 m
Nordhafen	See [4] below
Ostuferhafen	See [5] below

Name	Remarks
Norwegenkai	See [6] below
Ostseekai	See [7] below

[1]*Bollhornkai:* North quay 270 m long in depth of 9 m. Two ro/ro piers. Rail connection and cargo handling of intermodal traffic
South quay 245 m long in depth of 8.2 m. One ro/ro pier. Rail connection and cargo handling of intermodal traffic

[2]*Schwedenkai:* Quay length of 180 m in depth of 8.2 m. Traffic area of 11 000 m2. One ro/ro pier and ferry terminal with a cap of 2500 passengers

[3]*Scheerhafen:* S of Kiel Canal entrance. The N Pier, 8000 m2 free storing accommodation, offering facilities for handling and transhipment of bulk cargo and commodities of any kind and quantity. Quayage 300 m with depth 9.5 m; covered shed space of 1400 m2 cap. In the basin between the N and S pier a privately owned tanker jetty of 155 m length is available, fuel depots of 36 000 m3

[4]*Nordhafen:* Quay length of 1100 m in depth of 9.5 m. Forest products, ro/ro, general cargo & grain. Silo's of 77 000 t

[5]*Ostuferhafen:* Quay length of 1700 m in depth of up to 13 m. Includes seven ro/ro berths. Rail connection and cargo handling for intermodal traffic. Silo's of 120 000 t

[6]*Norwegenkai:* Quay length of 300 m in depth of 10 m. Two ro/ro piers. Rail connection and cargo handling for intermodal traffic. Ferry terminal with cap of 2500 passengers

[7]*Ostseekai:* Quay length of 600 m in depth of 10 m. Traffic area of 10 000 sq m. Two berths. Terminal with a cap of some 3000 passengers

Storage:

Location	Open (m²)	Covered (m²)
Bollhornkai	26000	
Scheerhafen	8000	1400
Sartorikai	2500	
Nordhafen	15550	28530
Ostuferhafen	207000	25000
Norwegenkai	40000	
Ostseekai	10000	

Mechanical Handling Equipment:

Location	Type	Capacity (t)	Qty	Remarks
Bollhornkai	Mult-purp. Cranes	24	2	At north quay
Ostuferhafen	Mult-purp. Cranes	40–45	1	At berth 1

Bunkering: BMT Bremer Mineraoel Transport GmbH & Co. KG, Konsul-Smidt Street 8 Floor, 28217 Bremen, Germany, *Tel:* +49 421 3391710, *Fax:* +49 421 3391741, *Email:* info@bmt-bremen.com
Bominflot, Bominflot Bunkergesellschaft fur Mineralole mbH & Co. KG, Grosse Baeckerstrasse 11, 20095 Hamburg, Germany, *Tel:* +49 40 350 930, *Fax:* +49 40 3509 3116, *Email:* mail@bominflot.de, *Website:* www.bominflot.net
Deutsche BP AG, Max Born Strasse 2, 22761 Hamburg, Germany, *Tel:* +49 40 639 4628, *Fax:* +49 40 6395 4670, *Email:* rudi.schrader@de.bp.com, *Website:* www.bp.com
ExxonMobil Marine Fuels, Mailpoint 31, ExxonMobil House, Ermyn Way, Leatherhead, Surrey KT22 8UX, United Kingdom, *Tel:* +44 1372 222 000, *Fax:* +44 1372 223 922, *Email:* marine.fuels@exxonmobil.com, *Website:* www.exxonmobil.com
Germany Transport & Logistics GmbH, Buchtstrasse 4, 22087 Hamburg, Germany, *Tel:* +49 40 64225 7070, *Fax:* +49 40 64225 7075, *Email:* info@gtl-hamburg.de
Hans Rinck Bunkering Service, P O Box 226, 21637 Horneburg, Germany, *Tel:* +49 4163 814 10, *Fax:* +49 4163 814 122, *Email:* mail@hans-rinck.com, *Website:* www.hans-rinck.com
Ostsee Mineralol-Bunker GmbH, Thomas-Mann-Strasse 20, 18055 Rostock, Germany, *Tel:* +49 381 2522 30, *Fax:* +49 381 2522 316/26, *Email:* info@ostsee-bunker.de
Total Bitumen Deutschland GmbH, Industriegebiet Sud, 25541 Brunsbuttel, Germany, *Tel:* +49 4852 888 260, *Fax:* +49 4852 888 263, *Email:* infobunker@total.de, *Website:* www.total.de
Tramp Oil & Marine, World Fuel Services Corporation, 13th Floor, Portland House, Bressenden Place, London SW1E 5BH, United Kingdom, *Tel:* +44 20 7808 5000, *Fax:* +44 20 7808 5088, *Email:* pturner@wfscorp.com, *Website:* www.wfscorp.com

Waste Reception Facilities: Sewage water reception facilities available at Bollhorn wharf and Ostuferhafen at jetty. Garbage disposal to be arranged in advance with local agent or port administration

Towage: Schlepp und Fahrgesellschaft Kiel mbH, 4 Kaistrabe 51, 24114 Kiel, Germany, *Tel:* +49 431 594 1261, *Fax:* +49 431 594 1286, *Email:* andreas@sfk-kiel.de, *Website:* www.sfk-kiel.de

Repair & Maintenance: Lindenau GmbH, Schiffswerft & Maschinenfabrik, Skagerrakufer 10, 24159 Kiel, Germany, *Tel:* +49 431 3993 0, *Fax:* +49 431 393062, *Email:* info@lindenau-shipyard.de, *Website:* www.lindenau-shipyard.de Newbuilding facilities:- 1 berth 185m x 33m max. vessel capacity 40,000dwt. Designer & builder of cargo, chemical, gas carriers, double hull tankers, seismic research, drilling accommodation modules, passenger ships, multipurpose, special container vessels. Repair facilities:- pre-fabrication quays; no.1 40m x 14m, no.2 60m x 14m. Floating docks; no.1 85m x 12.64m x 3.6m max. 1,500dwt; no.2 165m x 25.4m x 6.5m max. 10,000dwt. Repair quays; total length 750m, max. vessel length 210m & draught 7m. Works; ballast water and tank cleaning, Specialised work, conversions and lengthenings. Other work undertaken, development and design.

Ship Chandlers: Cosalt GmbH, Eckernforder Strasse 163, 24116 Kiel, Germany, *Tel:* +49 431 543 73, *Fax:* +49 431 548 921, *Email:* info.kiel@cosalt.de, *Website:* www.cosalt.de
Nautischer Dienst Kapt. Stegmann, P O Box 8070, 24154 Kiel, Germany, *Tel:* +49 431 331772, *Fax:* +49 431 331761, *Email:* naudi@t-online.de, *Website:* www.naudi.de
Hermann Tiessen Schiffsausrustungs GmbH & Co. KG, Tiessenkai 9, 24259 Kiel, Germany, *Tel:* +49 431 361223, *Fax:* +49 431 363223, *Email:* order@tiessen-holtenau.de
Transit-team Schiffsausrustung Gerberding GmbH, Schleuseninsel 37, 24159 Kiel, Germany, *Tel:* +49 431 30808/9, *Fax:* +49 431 335485, *Email:* ttkiel@aol.com
Zerssen & Citti Ship Service GmbH, Maklerstrasse 11-14, 24159 Kiel, Germany, *Tel:*

+49 431 3017-0, *Fax:* +49 431 301 7264, *Email:* shipsupply@zerssen-citti.de, *Website:* www.zerssen-citti.de

Shipping Agents: Ahlmann-Zerssen GmbH & Co KG, Uferstrasse 65, Silo Kiel-Nordhafen, 24106 Kiel, Germany, *Tel:* +49 431 389 0444, *Fax:* +49 431 389 0477, *Email:* kiel@ahlmann-zerssen.de, *Website:* www.ahlmann-zerssen.de
Karl Grammerstorf Kiel-Kanal GmbH, Schleuse, 24159 Kiel, Germany, *Tel:* +49 431 339350, *Fax:* +49 431 339 3534
NSA Schiffahrt und Transport GmbH, Ostuferhafen 15, 24149 Kiel, Germany, *Tel:* +49 431 209 9374, *Fax:* +49 431 209 9652, *Email:* agency-kiel@nsa-kiel.de, *Website:* www.nsa-fracht.de
Sartori & Berger, P O Box 3807, Wall 47-51, 24103 Kiel, Germany, *Tel:* +49 431 9810, *Fax:* +49 431 96108, *Email:* info@sartori-berger.de, *Website:* www.sartori-berger.de
UCA United Canal Agency GmbH, Maklerstrasse 11-14, D-24159 Kiel, Germany, *Tel:* +49 431 301070, *Fax:* +49 431 305 3385, *Email:* ucaki@kiel-canal.de, *Website:* www.kiel-canal.de

Stevedoring Companies: Baltic Terminal Kiel International GmbH, Ostuferhafen 22, 24149 Kiel, Germany, *Tel:* +49 431 209 4100, *Fax:* +49 431 209 4101, *Email:* info@btki-kiel.com, *Website:* www.btki-kiel.com
Sartori & Berger, P O Box 3807, Wall 47-51, 24103 Kiel, Germany, *Tel:* +49 431 9810, *Fax:* +49 431 96108, *Email:* info@sartori-berger.de, *Website:* www.sartori-berger.de

Surveyors: Germanischer Lloyd, Sophienblatt 1, 24103 Kiel, Germany, *Tel:* +49 431 675066, *Fax:* +49 431 673235, *Email:* gl-kiel@gl-group.com, *Website:* www.gl-group.com
Nippon Kaiji Kyokai, Kiel, Germany, *Tel:* +49 431 675066, *Fax:* +49 431 673235, *Website:* www.classnk.or.jp

Medical Facilities: Available, but advance notice to agents recommended if medical assistance required

Airport: Kiel-Holtenau

Railway: Main railway station, 0.5 km; own railway operation company

Lloyd's Agent: Reck & Co. GmbH, Wikinghaus, Schopenstehl 22, D-20095 Hamburg, Germany, *Tel:* +49 40 2789 6375, *Fax:* +49 40 2780 6418, *Email:* hamburg@reck.de, *Website:* www.reck.de

KIEL CANAL

Admiralty Chart: 2469   **Admiralty Pilot:** 18
Time Zone: GMT +1 h   **UNCTAD Locode:** DE

Authority: Wasser-und Schiffahrtsamt Kiel-Holtenau, Schleuseninsel 2, 24159 Kiel, Germany, *Tel:* +49 431 3603-0, *Fax:* +49 431 360 3414, *Email:* wsa-kiel-holtenau@wsv.bund.de, *Website:* www.wsa-kiel.wsv.de

Port Security: ISPS compliant

Pre-Arrival Information: The operator of any vessel bound for the internal waters of the Federal Republic of Germany and carrying dangerous or polluting goods, whether in bulk or in packaged form, shall forward, by facsimile or by electronic data transmission, the following particulars to the Central Reporting Point (Zentrale Meldestelle), Am Alten Hafen 2, 27472 Cuxhaven, Fax: +49 4721 567393 or 567394 - on such vessel's departure from a port located outside the European Union, provided that the vessel's first port of call, or her first mooring or anchoring site, will be located in the Federal Republic of Germany, or when the intention is to pass through the Kiel Canal:
(a) Name, call sign, IMO identification number if available and type of vessel
(b) Flag of vessel
(c) Length, beam and draught of the vessel in metres
(d) Port of destination
(e) ETA and ETD at the port
(f) Intended route
(g) Correct technical names of the dangerous or polluting goods, the appropriate United Nations numbers (UN numbers) where available, the Classes in accordance with the IMDG, IBC and IGC Codes and, if applicable, the vessel class according to the INF Code, the quantities of such goods and their location on board and, if in portable tanks or freight containers, the tank or container identification number(s)
(h) Confirmation that a list or manifest or appropriate loading plan, giving details of the dangerous or polluting goods carried and of their location on the vessel, is kept on the navigating bridge or in the vessel's operation centre
(i) Number of persons on board

Documentation: Before entering the Kiel Canal (not later than leaving the locks) the masters of vessels are obliged to give following declarations to the canal authorities through their agents
Documentation required for passage through the Kiel Canal (Section 43(1) Navigable Waterways Ordinance)
Documentation required to be presented, respectively submitted, when reporting in for passage through the Kiel Canal:
(a) An application form completed and signed by the master
(b) Certificate of Tonnage Measurement, respectively, Gauging Certificate
(c) In the case of a vessel carrying 'certain dangerous goods' in terms of Section 2 (1) (Item 16) SeeSchStrO: A form, completed and signed by the master, giving details of the cargo
(d) In the case of a vessel other than described in the preceding item: Cargo documentation and other documentation as required
(e) A vessel exempted from compulsory pilotage shall carry on board both the exemption certificate and a documentary proof of the identity of such certificate's holder and shall present these

Anchorage: Holtenau-Reede Road: This Road can be used only by vessels who are waiting for admission into the next free locks, or for a berth in the Port of Kiel to be accessible, or for the weather to improve. However, this regulation shall not apply to vessels wishing to enter, repectively leave, the ports, berthing and mooring sites at Kiel-Holtenau and Kiel-Friedrichsort nor to pleasure craft

Pilotage: Compulsory between Kiel lighthouse and Holtenau for vessels of 90 m loa or 13 m beam and more as well as for all chemical, gas and oil tankers
Canal pilot compulsory for vessels exceeding 45 m loa, 9.5 m beam and 3.1 m draft or 55 m loa, 8.5 m beam and 3.1 m draft, and for all vessels carrying dangerous cargo as well as composite units being towed other than those within the description of

particularly dangerous composite; units being towed are up to 40 m loa, 10 m beam and 3.1 m draft
Canal pilots are stationed at Holtenau, at Rusterbergen by Rendsburg, and at Brunsbuttel
Also in Kiel Canal helmsmen are compulsory for vessels exceeding 100 m loa, 15.5 m beam and 6.1 m draft or 115 m loa, 14 m beam and 6.1 m draft or tankers carrying certain dangerous goods

Radio Frequency: Kiel Traffic on VHF Channel 22
Kiel Canal locks: Kiel Canal 1, VHF Channel 13 (Brunsbuttel locks). Kiel Canal 4, VHF Channel 12 (Kiel-Holtenau locks)
Traffic Control Stations: Kiel Canal 2, VHF Channel 02 (between Brunsbuttel and Breiholz). Kiel Canal 3, VHF Channel 03 (between Breiholz and Kiel-Holtenau)
Ship-to-ship on VHF Channel 73

Traffic: 2005, 42 552 vessels transitted the Canal carrying 88 186 330 t of cargo

Maximum Vessel Dimensions: Permitted max measurements Kiel-Holtenau 'Aussenhafen': 85 m loa, 13 m beam, 4.5 m draft at normal water level (only 3 ships lying side by side with an utmost extension of 28 m)
Permitted max measurements Kiel-Holtenau 'Binnenhafen': 85 m loa, 13 m beam (only 2 ships lying side by side)
Permitted max measurements Brunsbuttel 'Segelschiffsdalben': 100 m loa, 16 m beam, 6.5 m draft (only 2 ships lying side by side)
Permitted max measurements Brunsbuttel 'Bahnhofsdalben': 140 m loa, 19 m beam, 8 m draft (only 2 ships lying side by side)
Permitted max measurements Brunsbuttel 'Sudkai': vessels up to 3500 gt meaning 100 m loa, 16 m beam, 4.0-6.5 m draft (only 2 ships lying side by side)
The max dimensions for vessels transiting the canal are: 235 m loa, 32.5 m beam, 40 m air draft. The water draft varies from 7 m (23') for vessels of max dimensions to 9.5 m (31'02") for vessels of 160 m loa and 27 m beam

Accommodation:

Name	Remarks
Kiel Canal	See [1] below

[1]*Kiel Canal:* The Kiel Canal connects the North Sea with the Baltic thus avoiding the dangerous route via the Skaw and through the Danish Sound and Belts. It starts from the mouth of the Elbe at Brunsbuttel and reaches the Baltic at Kiel-Holtenau near the port of Kiel. The canal is 98.7 km long with width varying between 102 m and 214 m, and has two double set of locks at each end
The average time of transit is between seven and eight hours, including lock time at both Brunsbuttel and Kiel. The max speed allowed on the waterway is 8.1 knots but for vessels with dimensions of traffic group 6 or d exceeding 8.5 m max speed allowed is 6.5 knots

Shipping Agents: UCA United Canal Agency GmbH, Maklerstrasse 11-14, D-24159 Kiel, Germany, *Tel:* +49 431 301070, *Fax:* +49 431 305 3385, *Email:* ucaki@kiel-canal.de, *Website:* www.kiel-canal.de

Airport: Kiel-Holtenau, 2 km. Hamburg-Fuhlsbuettel, 85 km

Lloyd's Agent: Reck & Co. GmbH, Wikinghaus, Schopenstehl 22, D-20095 Hamburg, Germany, *Tel:* +49 40 2789 6375, *Fax:* +49 40 2780 6418, *Email:* hamburg@reck.de, *Website:* www.reck.de

KOLN

alternate name, see Cologne

KREFELD

Lat 51° 20' N; Long 6° 34' E.

Admiralty Chart: -   **Admiralty Pilot:** -
Time Zone: GMT +1 h   **UNCTAD Locode:** DE KRE

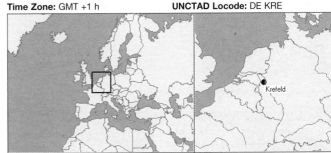

Principal Facilities:

P	Q	Y	G					A

Authority: Hafen und Bahnbetriebe der Stadt Krefeld, Oberstrasse 13, 47829 Krefeld, Germany, *Tel:* +49 2151 4927 0, *Fax:* +49 2151 492750, *Email:* hafen-und-bahnbetriebe@krefeld.de, *Website:* www.hafen-und-bahnbetriebe.krefeld.de

Officials: Managing Director: Elisabeth Lehnen.
Harbour Master: Engelbert Brzezina, *Tel:* +49 2151 571144.

Port Security: ISPS compliant

Accommodation:

Name	Remarks
Krefeld	See [1] below

[1]*Krefeld:* Depth at entrance 4 m at MLW. Seven grain elevators (four pneumatic), 12 pressure installations, six chutes, ten loading tubes, seven granaries. Six public warehouses and nine private

---

Key to Principal Facilities:—				
A=Airport	**C**=Containers	**G**=General Cargo	**P**=Petroleum	**R**=Ro/Ro	**Y**=Dry Bulk
B=Bunkers	**D**=Dry Dock	**L**=Cruise	**Q**=Other Liquid Bulk	**T**=Towage (where available from port)	

Storage:

Location	Covered (m²)	Grain (t)
Krefeld	131500	125000

Mechanical Handling Equipment:

Location	Type	Capacity (t)	Qty
Krefeld	Mult-purp. Cranes	200	11

Airport: Dusseldorf, 26 km

Lloyd's Agent: Joras Euro-Survey GmbH & Co. KG, Muelheimer Strasse 208, D-47057 Duisburg, Germany, *Tel:* +49 203 378000, *Fax:* +49 203 378 8888, *Email:* survey@joras.com, *Website:* www.joras.com

LABOE

Lat 54° 24' N; Long 10° 13' E.

Admiralty Chart: 2113/2341	**Admiralty Pilot:** 18
Time Zone: GMT +1 h	**UNCTAD Locode:** DE LAB

Principal Facilities:

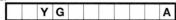

	Y	G					A

Authority: Laboe Harbour, Gemeinde Laboe, Reventloustr. 20, 24235 Laboe, Germany, *Tel:* +49 4343 4271 0, *Fax:* +49 4343 1628, *Email:* hafenmeister@laboe.de, *Website:* www.laboe.de

Officials: Harbour Master: Michael Schafer.

Radio Frequency: Laboe Port Channel 69

Accommodation:

Name	Remarks
Laboe	See [1] below

[1]*Laboe:* Harbour protected by mole. Entrance channel 23 m wide, 4.0 m deep. Two berths, one of 80 m and one of 55 m length. A basin for smaller craft of up to 2.5 m d is able to berth 330 boats including yachts
The port is used mainly by fishing vessels and yachts, little commercial traffic

Mechanical Handling Equipment:

Location	Type	Capacity (t)
Laboe	Mult-purp. Cranes	20

Waste Reception Facilities: Available

Repair & Maintenance: Slip for vessels up to 400 t

Airport: Kiel-Holtenau, 35 km

Lloyd's Agent: Reck & Co. GmbH, Wikinghaus, Schopenstehl 22, D-20095 Hamburg, Germany, *Tel:* +49 40 2789 6375, *Fax:* +49 40 2780 6418, *Email:* hamburg@reck.de, *Website:* www.reck.de

LEER

Lat 53° 13' N; Long 7° 27' E.

Admiralty Chart: 3509/3761	**Admiralty Pilot:** 55
Time Zone: GMT +1 h	**UNCTAD Locode:** DE LEE

Principal Facilities:

	Y	G			B		T	A

Authority: Stadtwerke Leer GmbH, Schleusenweg 16, 26789 Leer, Germany, *Tel:* +49 491 92770 0, *Fax:* +49 491 927 7010, *Email:* info@stadtwerke-leer.de, *Website:* www.stadtwerke-leer.de

Officials: Managing Director: Dr Thomas Helmke, *Email:* thomas.helmke@leer.de.

Port Security: ISPS compliant

Approach: Depth in river from Emden to Leer 5.7 m. Lock is 192 m long, 26 m broad, 7 m deep

Pilotage: Pilot boat by Westerems (Borkum) VHF Channels 9 and 16. Pilot station at Emden for Emden to Leer, VHF Channel 12

Radio Frequency: Emden Traffic on VHF Channel 15

Weather: Water level can sink around 1 m in high E winds

Traffic: 2005, 668 121 t of cargo handled

Working Hours: Mon-Fri 0600-1800. Sat 0600-1300

Accommodation:

Name	Length (m)	Depth (m)	Remarks
Leer			See [1] below
Piers	3100	6	

[1]*Leer:* The port can be accessed around the clock via the 26 m wide and 192 m long Leer Sea Lock
Cargoes handled include iron & scrap, fats & oils, construction materials & crushed stones, fertilisers, animal feed, fuels, mineral oils, salts and grain

Storage:

Location	Open (m²)	Covered (m²)	Grain (t)
Leer	85000	27000	30000

Mechanical Handling Equipment:

Location	Type	Capacity (t)	Qty
Leer	Floating Cranes	8–10	2
Leer	Mult-purp. Cranes	18	2
Leer	Mobile Cranes	150	1
Leer	Mobile Cranes	10	2

Bunkering: Supplies of oil and bunkers from bunker boat 'Leda'
Carl Buttner Mineraloel GmbH, Industriestrasse 13-15, 26789 Leer, Germany, *Tel:* +49 491 9278 721, *Fax:* +49 491 9278 725, *Email:* info@carl-buettner.de, *Website:* www.carl-buettner.de

Towage: One small tug for assistance. Larger tugs can be ordered from Emden

Repair & Maintenance: Minor repairs only

Medical Facilities: Available

Airport: Bremen, 120 km. Regional airport at Leer-Papenburg

Railway: Leer, 1 km

Lloyd's Agent: Reck & Co. GmbH, Herrlichkeit 5, 28199 Bremen, Germany, *Tel:* +49 421 59834-0, *Fax:* +49 421 598 3450, *Email:* mail@reck.de, *Website:* www.reck.de

LUBECK

Lat 53° 52' N; Long 10° 40' E.

Admiralty Chart: 2364	**Admiralty Pilot:** 55
Time Zone: GMT +1 h	**UNCTAD Locode:** DE LBC

Principal Facilities:

	Y	G	C	R	L	B		T	A

Authority: Lubecker Hafen-Gesellschaft mbH, Zum Hafenplatz 1, 23570 Lubeck, Germany, *Tel:* +49 4502 807-0, *Fax:* +49 4502 807 9999, *Email:* lhg.info@lhg-online.de, *Website:* www.lhg-online.de

Officials: Managing Director: Hans-Gerd Gielessen.
Business Development Manager: Falk Ohlig, *Tel:* +49 4502 807 5111, *Email:* falk.ohlig@lhg-online.de.
Harbour Master: Henning Redlich, *Email:* henning.redlich@luebeck.dlrg.de.

Port Security: ISPS compliant

Approach: About 20 km upstream from the mouth of the Trave River. Depth from buoy A up to Travemunde 10 m, and from there to Lubeck is a depth of 9.5 m

Anchorage: Travemunde roads in depth of 16 m

Pilotage: Compulsory for vessels over 60 m loa or 10 m boa. Pilot Station on VHF Channels 13 and 67 continuously (call Trave-Traffic). Boarding area 1 mile NE of the entrance, near anchorage area

Radio Frequency: VHF Channels 13 and 67

Weather: Prevailing w'ly winds

Traffic: 2007, 29 359 034 t of cargo handled

Maximum Vessel Dimensions: 8.7 m draught at River Trave to Lubeck

Principal Imports and Exports: Imports: Technical products, Wood products. Exports: Cars, Machinery, Technical products, Wood products.

Working Hours: 24 h/day

Accommodation:

Name	Length (m)	Depth (m)	Remarks
Lubeck			
Nordlandkai	1550	9.5	See [1] below
Konstinkai	1108	9.5	See [2] below
Schlutup	230	8.5	See [3] below
Travemunde			
Skandinavienkai	1852	9.5	See [4] below

[1]*Nordlandkai:* Multi-purpose terminal consisting of five berths for paper & forest products, trucks, trailers, export cars & containers
[2]*Konstinkai:* Multi-purpose terminal for ro/ro, forest products & project cargoes
[3]*Schlutup:* Forest products, lorries, trailers, containers & combined transport
[4]*Skandinavienkai:* Nine ro/ro berths (two for loading/discharging railcars, three equipped with upper deck ramps and two equipped with pontoons)
Accompanied lorries, trailers, containers, new and second-hand export cars, railcars, combined transport units & dangerous goods

Storage: Konstinkai: shed capacity of 23 500 m2 (+ 7300 m2 additional roof capacity)
Nordlandkai: shed capacity of 140 000 m2 (+ 22 000 m2 additional roof capacity)
Schlutup: shed capacity of 65 000 m2

Mechanical Handling Equipment:

Location	Type	Capacity (t)	Qty
Nordlandkai	Mobile Cranes	100	1
Konstinkai	Quay Cranes	45	1
Schlutup	Reach Stackers		1
Skandinavienkai	Reach Stackers		1

Bunkering: Gas oil and water available by barge. Full bunkering services available
Frachtcontor Junge & Co., Manfred Schroder, Fabrikstrasse 12-20, 23568 Lubeck, Germany, *Tel:* +49 451 619640, *Fax:* +49 451 692 6292, *Email:* info@Schroeder-schiffsmakler.de
North Sea Petroleum GmbH, Pleskowstrasse 2, 23564 Lubeck, Germany, *Tel:* +49 451 791 061, *Fax:* +49 451 798 078, *Email:* nsphl@t-online.de
ExxonMobil Marine Fuels, Mailpoint 31, ExxonMobil House, Ermyn Way, Leatherhead, Surrey KT22 8UX, United Kingdom, *Tel:* +44 1372 222 000, *Fax:* +44 1372 223 922, *Email:* marine.fuels@exxonmobil.com – *Website:* www.exxonmobil.com – *Grades:* MGO – *Delivery Mode:* barge, truck, pipeline
North Sea Petroleum GmbH, Pleskowstrasse 2, 23564 Lubeck, Germany, *Tel:* +49 451 791 061, *Fax:* +49 451 798 078, *Email:* nsphl@t-online.de – *Grades:* all grades – *Delivery Mode:* barge, truck
Ostsee Mineralol-Bunker GmbH, Thomas-Mann-Strasse 20, 18055 Rostock, Germany, *Tel:* +49 381 2522 30, *Fax:* +49 381 2522 316/26, *Email:* info@ostsee-bunker.de

Towage: J. Johannsen & Sohn Seeschlepp und Transport GmbH, Einsiedelstrasse 47, 23554 Lubeck, Germany, *Tel:* +49 451 408810, *Fax:* +49 451 404777, *Email:* johannsen-schlepper@arcor.de, *Website:* www.luebeck-logistik.de/johannsen/

Ship Chandlers: Draeger Safety AG & Co. KGaA, Revalstrasse 1, 23560 Lubeck, Germany, *Tel:* +49 451 8820, *Fax:* +49 451 882 2080, *Email:* info@draeger.com, *Website:* www.draeger.com

Shipping Agents: F.H. Bertling AB, F.H. Bertling Schiffahrtskontor GmbH & Co. KG, Grosse Altefare 23, P O Box 1182, 23501 Lubeck, Germany, *Tel:* +49 451 799020, *Fax:* +49 451 799 0270, *Email:* sybille@bertling.de, *Website:* www.bertling.de
Frachtcontor Junge & Co., Manfred Schroder, Fabrikstrasse 12-20, 23568 Lubeck, Germany, *Tel:* +49 451 619640, *Fax:* +49 451 692 6292, *Email:* info@Schroeder-schiffsmakler.de
Hans Lehmann KG, Seelandstrasse 15, 23569 Lubeck, Germany, *Tel:* +49 451 39001-0, *Fax:* +49 451 390001-39, *Email:* info@hans-lehmann.de, *Website:* www.hans-lehmann.de
Hans Lehmann KG, Seelandstrasse 15, 23569 Lubeck, Germany, *Tel:* +49 451 39001-0, *Fax:* +49 451 390001-39, *Email:* lehmann@hans-lehmann.de, *Website:* www.hans-lehmann.de
Mediterranean Shipping Company, MSC Germany GmbH, Grosse Altefare 23, P O Box 1182, 23552 Lubeck, Germany, *Tel:* +49 451 98980-0, *Fax:* +49 451 989 8075, *Email:* luebeck@mscgermany.com, *Website:* www.mscgermany.com
Sartori & Berger, Fabrikstrasse 12-20, 23568 Lubeck, Germany, *Tel:* +49 451 619 6412, *Fax:* +49 451 692 6292, *Email:* luebeck@sartori-berger.de, *Website:* www.sartori-berger.de
Transfennica Ltd, Seelandstrasse 31, 23569 Lubeck, Germany, *Tel:* +49 451 484850, *Fax:* +49 451 484 8521, *Email:* info.germany@transfennica.fi, *Website:* www.transfennica.com

Surveyors: Nippon Kaiji Kyokai, Lubeck, Germany, *Tel:* +49 451 396 8328, *Fax:* +49 451 396 8343, *Website:* www.classnk.or.jp
Orbis Marine Consult, Fabrikstrasse 41, 23568 Lubeck, Germany, *Tel:* +49 451 611 6111, *Fax:* +49 451 611 6116, *Email:* mail@orbismarine.com, *Website:* www.orbismarine.com

Medical Facilities: Available

Airport: Hamburg Airport, 60 km. Lubeck-Blankensee, 10 km

Lloyd's Agent: Reck & Co. GmbH, Wikinghaus, Schopenstehl 22, D-20095 Hamburg, Germany, *Tel:* +49 40 2789 6375, *Fax:* +49 40 2780 6418, *Email:* hamburg@reck.de, *Website:* www.reck.de

LUDWIGSHAFEN AM RHEIN

Lat 49° 28' N; Long 8° 27' E.

Admiralty Chart: -
Admiralty Pilot: -
Time Zone: GMT +1 h
UNCTAD Locode: DE LUH

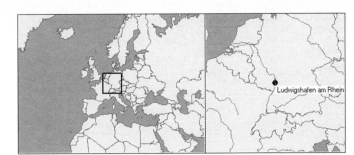

Principal Facilities:

P	Q	Y	G	C					

Authority: Hafenbetriebe Ludwigshafen am Rhein GmbH, P O Box 210624, 67006 Ludwigshafen, Germany, *Tel:* +49 621 5984 0, *Fax:* +49 621 598 4135, *Email:* info@hafenbetriebe-ludwigshafen.de, *Website:* www.hafenbetriebe-ludwigshafen.de

Officials: Managing Director: Franz Reindl.
Harbour Master: Dirk Beutel.

Traffic: 2007, 7 941 510 t of cargo handled

Accommodation:

Name	Remarks
Ludwigshafen am Rhein	See [1] below

[1]*Ludwigshafen am Rhein:* The port handles chemical products, mineral oil and oil products, mineral rock, gravel, cement, general cargo and recycling materials. There is a total quayage of 14 500 m

Storage: Tank storage of 140 000 m3 is available

Location	Open (m²)	Covered (m²)	Grain (t)
Ludwigshafen am Rhein	468005	73288	31000

Mechanical Handling Equipment:

Location	Type	Capacity (t)	Qty
Ludwigshafen am Rhein	Mult-purp. Cranes	5–25	12
Ludwigshafen am Rhein	Container Cranes	50	3

Railway: 14.5 km

Lloyd's Agent: Friedrich Hartmann vorm. J. Kerschgens, 2 Beethovenstrasse, D-68165 Mannheim, Germany, *Tel:* +49 621 423090, *Fax:* +49 621 416354, *Email:* hartmann@hartmann-expert.de, *Website:* www.hartmann-expert.de

MANNHEIM

Lat 49° 29' N; Long 8° 28' E.

Admiralty Chart: -
Admiralty Pilot: 28
Time Zone: GMT +1 h
UNCTAD Locode: DE MHG

Principal Facilities:

P	Q	Y	G	C	R		B		T	A

Authority: Staatliche Rhein-Neckar-Hafengesellschaft Mannheim mbH, Rheinvorlandstr 5, 68159 Mannheim, Germany, *Tel:* +49 621 292 2991, *Fax:* +49 621 292 3167, *Email:* info@hafen-mannheim.de, *Website:* www.hafen-mannheim.de

Officials: Port Director: Roland Horner.
Harbour Master: Wilhelm Muessig, *Email:* muessigw@hafen-mannheim.de.

Pilotage: Pilots have their own telephone lines

Radio Frequency: International Rhine Radio via VHF Channel 11, call Mannheim Port

Traffic: 2007, 8 346 029 t of cargo handled

Maximum Vessel Dimensions: 135 m loa

Working Hours: Cargo normally worked 0600-1800

Accommodation:

Name	Remarks
Mannheim	See [1] below

[1]*Mannheim:* Four harbours, consisting of Commercial Docks, Rheinau Docks, Old Rhine Docks and Industrial Docks, all totalling 14 docks
Safe berth for two-cone ships at Old Rhine Docks (oil dock). Safe berth at Commercial Docks (eight power outlets available) according to ISPS Code

Key to Principal Facilities:—		
A=Airport	**C**=Containers	**G**=General Cargo
B=Bunkers	**D**=Dry Dock	**L**=Cruise

P=Petroleum	**R**=Ro/Ro	**Y**=Dry Bulk
Q=Other Liquid Bulk	**T**=Towage (where available from port)	

Loading berth for (private) cars at Rhine-km 425.60 to 425.71 near Kurt Schumacher Bridge
Ro/ro terminal at Rheinau Docks. Discharge facility for liquefied gas at the Commercial Docks

Storage:

Location	Open (m²)	Covered (m²)	Grain (t)
Mannheim	2259873	1187190	303064

Mechanical Handling Equipment: 111 transhipment and crane bridges, 54 gantry cranes, 22 heavy lift cranes of 150 t cap, 64 mobile cranes and 248 other lifting units

Towage: Available

Repair & Maintenance: Deutz AG, Carl-Benz-Strasse 5, P O Box 102263, 68167 Mannheim, Germany, *Tel:* +49 621 750090, *Fax:* +49 621 750 0933 Engines built 234/Y, 604B, 628, 632, 440, 645, 640, medium and high speed marine diesel engines, ranging from 10 kW to 7,250 kW (13.6 to 9,860 hp) for marine propulsion and auxiliary use Other work undertaken Gas engines (spark ignition and dual-fuel); total energy sets and plants; gen sets and total energy sets with industrial gas turbines

Shipping Agents: CMA-CGM S.A., CMA CGM (Deutschland) GmbH, Rheinvorlandstrasse 5, 68159 Mannheim, Germany, *Tel:* +49 621 9763 3700, *Fax:* +49 621 9763 3710, *Email:* mhg.bvogel@cma-cgm.com, *Website:* www.cma-cgm.com
Rhenania Intermodal Transport GmbH, Antwerpener Street 24, 68219 Mannheim, Germany, *Tel:* +49 621 804 8374, *Fax:* +49 621 804 8242, *Email:* info@wincanton.eu, *Website:* www.wincanton.eu

Stevedoring Companies: Rhenus AG & Co. KG, Landzungen Street 17, 68159 Mannheim, Germany, *Tel:* +49 621 2999-0, *Fax:* +49 621 299 9212, *Email:* info.mannheim@de.rhenus.com, *Website:* www.rhenus.com

Medical Facilities: University clinic and hospitals available

Airport: Mannheim-Neuostheim, 4 km

Railway: Mannheim Central Station, 1 km

Lloyd's Agent: Friedrich Hartmann vorm. J. Kerschgens, 2 Beethovenstrasse, D-68165 Mannheim, Germany, *Tel:* +49 621 423090, *Fax:* +49 621 416354, *Email:* hartmann@hartmann-expert.de, *Website:* www.hartmann-expert.de

NEUSS/DUSSELDORF

Lat 51° 12' N; Long 6° 42' E.

Admiralty Chart: -	**Admiralty Pilot:** -
Time Zone: GMT +1 h	**UNCTAD Locode:** DE NSS

Principal Facilities:

P		Y	G	C	R			T	A

Authority: Neuss Duesseldorfer Haefen GmbH & Co. KG., Hammer Landstrasse 3, 41460 Neuss, Germany, *Tel:* +49 2131 5323 0, *Fax:* +49 2131 532 3105, *Email:* info@nd-haefen.de, *Website:* www.nd-haefen.de

Officials: Managing Director: Ulrich Gross, *Tel:* +49 2131 532 3101, *Email:* ugross@nd-haefen.de.
Marketing Manager: Thomas Duttchen, *Tel:* +49 2131 532 3200, *Email:* tduettchen@nd-haefen.de.
Harbour Master: Jan Sonke Eckel, *Tel:* +49 2131 532 3350, *Email:* jeckel@nd-haefen.de.

Port Security: ISPS compliant

Traffic: 2004, 8 475 000 t of cargo handled, 167 000 TEU's

Accommodation:

Name	Length (m)	Remarks
Neuss/Duesseldorfer Haefen		See [1] below
Rail-Road Terminal		See [2] below
Container Terminal	260	See [3] below

[1]*Neuss/Duesseldorfer Haefen:* Consists of 31 cargo handling and transhipment facilities with total harbour area covering 550 ha and total shore length of 29 km. Open and covered storage facilities
[2]*Rail-Road Terminal:* Operated by Neuss Trimodal GmbH, Tilsiter Str. 13A, 41460 Neuss, Tel: +49 2131 718 9110, Fax: +49 2131 718 9115, Email: nhm-gmbh@t-online.de
Cargo handling & transhipment facility covering an area of approx 80 000 m2. Five reach stackers for mobile container handling
[3]*Container Terminal:* Operated by Neuss Trimodal GmbH, Tel: +49 2131 15570, Fax: +49 2131 155722, Email: info.neuss@rhenania.com
Terminal area covering 35 000 m2

Storage:

Location	Covered (m²)	Grain (t)
Neuss/Duesseldorfer Haefen	250000	300000

Mechanical Handling Equipment:

Location	Type	Capacity (t)	Qty
Neuss/Duesseldorfer Haefen	Mult-purp. Cranes	35	28
Container Terminal	Container Cranes	35	2

Towage: Available by municipal tugs

Airport: Duesseldorf, 10 km. Moenchengladbach, 25 km

Railway: Neuss, 1 km. Duesseldorf, 7 km

Lloyd's Agent: Joras Euro-Survey GmbH & Co. KG, Muelheimer Strasse 208, D-47057 Duisburg, Germany, *Tel:* +49 203 378000, *Fax:* +49 203 378 8888, *Email:* survey@joras.com, *Website:* www.joras.com

NORD-OSTSEE KANAL

alternate name, see Kiel Canal

NORDENHAM

Lat 53° 29' N; Long 8° 29' E.

Admiralty Chart: 3621	**Admiralty Pilot:** 55
Time Zone: GMT +1 h	**UNCTAD Locode:** DE NHA

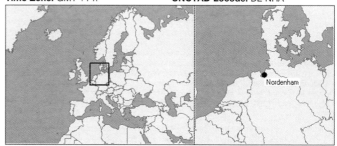

Principal Facilities:

Q	Y	G	C	R		B		T	A

Tramp Oil & Marine

Wells House, 15-17 Elmfield Road, Bromley, Kent BR1 1LT, United Kingdom
Phone: +44 20 8315 7777 **Fax:** +44 20 8315 7788
General email: enquiries@tramp-oil.com

See listings for all global offices: **www.tramp-oil.com**

Authority: Rhenus Midgard GmbH, Midgardstrasse 50, P O Box 1452 & 1453, 26954 Nordenham, Germany, *Tel:* +49 4731 810, *Fax:* +49 4731 81243, *Email:* info.nordenham@de.rhenus.com, *Website:* www.rhenus.com

Officials: Harbour Master: Werner Janssen, *Email:* werner.janssen@de.rhenus.com.

Port Security: ISPS compliant

Documentation: Crew list (4 copies), crew effects list (2 copies), bonded stores list (1 copy), maritime declaration of health (1 copy)

Approach: Depth at entrance 11 m at LWT. No bar. No locks

Anchorage: Off 'Weserpilot' and for vessels up to 120 m loa at Blexen Roadstead off Bremerhaven, 9 m depth

Pilotage: Compulsory for vessels exceeding 90 m loa and/or 13 m beam. Pilots available 24 h

Radio Frequency: VHF Channel 16

Weather: Prevailing W'ly winds

Tides: Range of tide 3.8 m

Traffic: 2005, 5 739 864 t of cargo handled

Maximum Vessel Dimensions: 270 m loa, 175 000 dwt, 13.4 m draft

Principal Imports and Exports: Imports: Bulk cargo, Wood. Exports: General cargo.

Working Hours: 0600-1400, 1400-2200, 2200-0600. Sat 0600-1400. Overtime possible against extra costs

Accommodation:

Name	Length (m)	Draught (m)	Remarks
Nordenham			
Rhenus Midgard AG & Co. KG			
Nordenham Terminal	1090	13.4	See [1] below
Blexen Terminal	600	12.1	See [2] below
Metaleurop Weser GmbH	230	8	See [3] below
Kronos Titan	200		See [4] below
Mobil Oil AG & Weser Tanklager-Gesellschaft mbH			For storage of mineral oils. Truck and barge transport links

[1]*Nordenham Terminal:* Bulk cargo for vessels up to 175 000 dwt. Open storage area of 132 000 m2 and warehouses of 12 500 m2

[2]*Blexen Terminal:* 600 m long including dolphins for vessels up to 125 000 dwt. Open storage area of 25 000 m2 and warehouses of 48 000 m2

[3]*Metaleurop Weser GmbH:* Johannastrasse 2, 26954 Nordenham, Tel: +49 4731 3611, Website: www.metaleurop.fr

Ore, zinc, lead and sulphuric acid. Storage cap for ore of 50 000 t, for metal blocks of 10 000 t and for sulphuric acid of 5000 m3. Railway, truck and barge transport links

[4]*Kronos Titan:* Production of titandioxyde. Railway, truck and barge transport links

Mechanical Handling Equipment:

Location	Type	Capacity (t)	Qty	Remarks
Rhenus Midgard AG & Co. KG	Mult-purp. Cranes	65	1	at Nordenham Terminal
Rhenus Midgard AG & Co. KG	Mult-purp. Cranes	36	3	at Nordenham Terminal
Metaleurop Weser GmbH	Mult-purp. Cranes	5	1	
Metaleurop Weser GmbH	Mult-purp. Cranes	10	1	

Cargo Worked: Midgard terminal: bulk cargoes 30 000 t/day, others vary according to type of cargo and size of vessel

Bunkering: BMT Bremer Mineraoel Transport GmbH & Co. KG, Konsul-Smidt Street 8 Floor, 28217 Bremen, Germany, *Tel:* +49 421 3391710, *Fax:* +49 421 3391741, *Email:* info@bmt-bremen.com

Bominflot, Bominflot Bunkergesellschaft fur Mineralole mbH & Co. KG, Grosse Baeckerstrasse 11, 20095 Hamburg, Germany, *Tel:* +49 40 350 930, *Fax:* +49 40 3509 3116, *Email:* mail@bominflot.de, *Website:* www.bominflot.net

B.O.T. Broring Oil Trading GmbH, B.O.T. Broering Oil Trading GmbH, Carl Ronning-strasse 9, 28195 Bremen, Germany, *Tel:* +49 421 170 091, *Fax:* +49 421 170 093, *Email:* home@b-o-t.info, *Website:* www.broering.info

Deutsche BP AG, Max Born Strasse 2, 22761 Hamburg, Germany, *Tel:* +49 40 639 4628, *Fax:* +49 40 6395 4670, *Email:* rudi.schrader@de.bp.com, *Website:* www.bp.com

ExxonMobil Marine Fuels, Mailpoint 31, ExxonMobil House, Ermyn Way, Leather-head, Surrey KT22 8UX, United Kingdom, *Tel:* +44 1372 222 000, *Fax:* +44 1372 223 922, *Email:* marine.fuels@exxonmobil.com, *Website:* www.exxonmobil.com

Friedrich G. Frommann GmbH, Wallgraben 47, 21073 Hamburg, Germany, *Tel:* +49 40 7662 680, *Fax:* +49 40 7662 6818, *Email:* frommann@fgfshell.de, *Website:* www.fgfshell.de

Germany Transport & Logistics GmbH, Buchtstrasse 4, 22087 Hamburg, Germany, *Tel:* +49 40 64225 7070, *Fax:* +49 40 64225 7075, *Email:* info@gtl-hamburg.de

Hans Rinck Bunkering Service, P O Box 226, 21637 Horneburg, Germany, *Tel:* +49 4163 814 10, *Fax:* +49 4163 814 122, *Email:* mail@hans-rinck.com, *Website:* www.hans-rinck.com

Maxcom Bunker S.p.A. u.s., Maxcom Energy S.p.A., Eckerkamp 7a, 22391 Hamburg, Germany, *Tel:* +49 40 417568, *Fax:* +49 40 417563, *Email:* maxcom@ehmcke.com, *Website:* www.maxcom.it

Tramp Oil & Marine, World Fuel Services Corporation, 13th Floor, Portland House, Bressenden Place, London SW1E 5BH, United Kingdom, *Tel:* +44 20 7808 5000, *Fax:* +44 20 7808 5088, *Email:* pturner@wfscorp.com, *Website:* www.wfscorp.com

Waste Reception Facilities: Stuhrenberg Transporte Nordenham, Nordenham, Germany, *Tel:* +49 4731 96900, *Fax:* +49 4731 3010

Towage: Arbeitsgemeinschaft Weser Schleppdienst, Geo Plate Street No 1, 27568 Nordenham, Germany, *Tel:* +49 471 487422, *Fax:* +49 471 487448, *Email:* info@bugsier.de, *Website:* www.bugsier.de

Repair & Maintenance: Seggermann & Heine Anlagenbau GmbH (SEM), Neptun-strasse 8, 26954 Nordenham, Germany, *Tel:* +49 4731 9383 0, *Fax:* +49 4731 938363, *Email:* info@sem-anlagenbau.de Minor repairs

Shipping Agents: Rhenus Midgard GmbH, Midgardstrasse 50, P O Box 1452 & 1453, 26954 Nordenham, Germany, *Tel:* +49 4731 810, *Fax:* +49 4731 81243, *Email:* info.nordenham@de.rhenus.com, *Website:* www.rhenus.com

Stevedoring Companies: Rhenus Midgard GmbH, Midgardstrasse 50, P O Box 1452 & 1453, 26954 Nordenham, Germany, *Tel:* +49 4731 810, *Fax:* +49 4731 81243, *Email:* info.nordenham@de.rhenus.com, *Website:* www.rhenus.com

Surveyors: Capt. H.J. Moeller & Partner, Expert Bureau Capt. H.J. Moeller & Partner, Old Faehrweg 8, 27568 Bremerhaven, Germany, *Tel:* +49 471 946090, *Fax:* +49 471 946 0999, *Email:* office@moeller-expert.com, *Website:* www.moeller-expert.com

Schiffsbesichtiger in Bremen und Bremerhaven, Segelmacher strasse 1, 28777 Bremen, Germany, *Tel:* +49 421 389 2710, *Fax:* +49 421 389 2711, *Email:* info@schiffsbesichtiger.de, *Website:* www.schiffsbesichtiger.de

Medical Facilities: Doctors and hospital available

Airport: Bremen, 70 km

Railway: Nordenham, 1 km

Lloyd's Agent: Reck & Co. GmbH, Herrlichkeit 5, 28199 Bremen, Germany, *Tel:* +49 421 59834-0, *Fax:* +49 421 598 3450, *Email:* mail@reck.de, *Website:* www.reck.de

NORWEGENKAI

harbour area, see under Kiel

OLDENBURG

Lat 53° 9' N; Long 8° 14' E.

Admiralty Chart: 3406/3407		**Admiralty Pilot:** 55	
Time Zone: GMT +1 h		**UNCTAD Locode:** DE OLO	

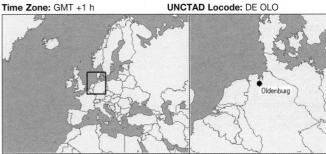

Principal Facilities:

P		Y	G			B		T	A

Authority: Niedersachsen Ports GmbH & Co. KG, Port of Oldenburg, Amt fur Wirtschaftsforderung, Industriestrasse 1, 26105 Oldenburg, Germany, *Tel:* +49 441 235 2259, *Fax:* +49 441 235 3130, *Email:* hafen@stadt-oldenburg.de, *Website:* www.oldenburg.de

Officials: Harbour Master: Gerd Hinkelmann.

Port Security: ISPS compliant

Documentation: Crew lists (2 copies), Passenger lists (2 copies), Personal effects (2 copies), Medical certificate (1 copy), Tonnage certificate (1 copy), Derating certificate (1copy), Bill of Ladings (1 copy)

Pilotage: Not compulsory

Radio Frequency: VHF Channel 73

Weather: Mainly NW winds

Tides: Up to 2.6 m

Traffic: 2005, 1 329 416 t of cargo handled

Maximum Vessel Dimensions: 3000 gt, 4 m draft

Principal Imports and Exports: Imports: Cereals, Fertiliser, Foodstuffs, Gravel, Sand, Stones. Exports: Foodstuffs, Scrap.

Working Hours: 0700-1600. Other times upon request

Accommodation: The total water surface of the port covers 51 500 m2 and the total usable quay length is 1900 m

Name	Length (m)	Remarks
Industriehafen		
Rhein-Umschlag Quay	510	See [1] below
OHU Handels Quay (Quay Dalbenstrasse)	195	See [2] below
RCG Quay (Quay Dalbenstrasse)	145	
North Quay		
RCG Quay	255	See [3] below
East Port		See [4] below

[1]*Rhein-Umschlag Quay:* Private facilities operated by Rhein-Umschlag GmbH & Co KG, Rheinstrasse 35, 26135 Oldenburg, Tel: +49 441 21009-0, Fax: +49 441 210 0910, Email: zentrale@rhein-umschlag.de, Website: www.rhein-umschlag.de

Handling mainly building materials; silo of 2200 t cap, gravel store of 1500 t cap, cement works and mixing works for road construction materials. Two loading bridges, one of 10 t cap at 63 m outreach and one of 12.5 t cap at 63 m outreach. Warehouse storage cap of 12 000 t for bulk materials. Open storage of 120 000 t

[2]*OHU Handels Quay (Quay Dalbenstrasse):* Quay OHU Handels und Umschlagsge-sellschaft mbH, Dalbenstrasse 17, 26135 Oldenburg, Tel: +49 441 26999, Fax: +49 441 9507 9321

Handling mainly building materials. Warehouse storage cap of 30 000 t for bulk materials

[3]*RCG Quay:* Raiffeisen Central-Genossenschaft Nordwest (RCG).

A dust-free movable discharging bridge, 100 t/h cap, one bridge for heavy grain, 150 t/h cap, concentrated feed works. Mineral oil tank storage of 6000 m2. 275 m alternate discharge place

[4]*East Port:* Municipal Port: Usable quay length of 520 m

Vereinigte Transport-Beton-Werke GmbH & Co., gravel storage of 8000 t cap and cement works; luffing jib crane of 6 t cap at 20 m outreach

Rhein-Umschlag GmbH & Co KG, open air storage areas of 9600 m2, two storage fillers

Tholen GmbH & Co KG, open air storage area of 7760 m2, gravel and sand storage boxes; one crane of 5 t cap

OHU Handels und Umschlagsgesellschaft m.b.H., grain and feedstuff storage hall with a cap of 22 000 t; one crane of 5 t cap

Storage:

Location	Open (m2)	Covered (m2)	Grain (t)
OHU Handels Quay (Quay Dalbenstrasse)	45000		

Location	Open (m²)	Covered (m²)	Grain (t)
RCG Quay (Quay Dalbenstrasse)	20000	1750	6500
RCG Quay		8940	50000

Mechanical Handling Equipment:

Location	Type	Capacity (t)	Qty
Rhein-Umschlag Quay	Mult-purp. Cranes	5	1
OHU Handels Quay (Quay Dalbenstrasse)	Mult-purp. Cranes	35	1
RCG Quay (Quay Dalbenstrasse)	Mult-purp. Cranes	6	2

Bunkering: On request by bunker boat from Bremen

Waste Reception Facilities: Discharge of sludge into tank trucks according to Marpol is possible. Inquiry must be given to Harbour Master

Towage: Tugs available from Elsfleth

Airport: Bremen, 45 km

Railway: Own railway at Quay Dalbenstrasse with direct connection to German DB

Lloyd's Agent: Reck & Co. GmbH, Herrlichkeit 5, 28199 Bremen, Germany, *Tel:* +49 421 59834-0, *Fax:* +49 421 598 3450, *Email:* mail@reck.de, *Website:* www.reck.de

OSTERMOOR

harbour area, see under Brunsbuttel

PAPENBURG

Lat 53° 5' N; Long 7° 23' E.

Admiralty Chart: 3632
Time Zone: GMT +1 h

Admiralty Pilot: 55
UNCTAD Locode: DE PAP

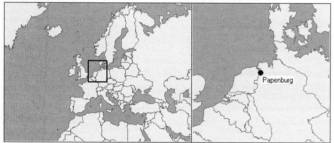

Principal Facilities:

P		Y	G			B	D	T	

Authority: Niedersachsen Ports GmbH & Co. KG, Stadt Papenburg, Wirtschaftsforderung, Hauptkanal rechts 68-69, 26871 Papenburg, Germany, *Tel:* +49 4961 82226, *Fax:* +49 4961 82315, *Email:* info@papenburg.de, *Website:* www.papenburg.de

Officials: Marketing Manager: Winfried Nehe, *Email:* winfried.nehe@papenburg.de. Harbour Master: Rudolf Schepers, *Tel:* +49 4961 946712, *Email:* hafen@papenburg.de.

Port Security: ISPS compliant

Approach: Depth in channel 6 m

Anchorage: Anchorage can be obtained at Emden roads in a depth of 5 m or at Dukegat Roads in a depth of 10 m

Pilotage: Compulsory. Available from Emden Pilot Station

Radio Frequency: Papenburg Lock Radio, VHF Channel 13

Weather: Mostly SW winds

Tides: Range of tide 2.5-3.5 m

Traffic: 2005, 946 720 t of cargo handled

Principal Imports and Exports: Imports: Dung, Fodder, Grain, Peat, Stone, Timber. Exports: Fodder, Peat, Timber.

Working Hours: Harbour 0700-1200, 1230-1630. Lock 24 h/day

Accommodation:

Name	Length (m)	Depth (m)	Remarks
Papenburg			See [1] below
Deverhafen	980	5	Operated by Schulte & Bruns. Timber & fertilizer
Industriehafen Nord	450	6	See [2] below
Industriehafen Sud	1070	6	Operated by Schulte & Bruns. Stone
Sielkanal	560	6	Operated by Schulte & Bruns. Peat moss

[1]*Papenburg:* Vessels up to 5.5 m draft can reach the port via a lock of 26 m breadth and 200 m length

[2]*Industriehafen Nord:* Operated by Schulte & Bruns, Ems-Mill. Wood chips, peat moss, stone, food

Storage:

Location	Open (m²)	Covered (m²)
Papenburg	202000	33850

Mechanical Handling Equipment:

Location	Type	Capacity (t)	Qty
Deverhafen	Mult-purp. Cranes	3–6	4
Industriehafen Nord	Mult-purp. Cranes	5–15	2
Industriehafen Sud	Mult-purp. Cranes	5–36	3

Bunkering: MDO/IFO by barge from C. Buttner, Esso - H. Bunte by truck, Shell - C. Buttner by truck, Aral - W. Ritzerfeld by truck

Waste Reception Facilities: Available by mobile trucks

Towage: One tug of 600 hp available. Ships with draft over 5.5 m must take a tug boat to pass the lock

Shipping Agents: BERA GmbH & Co KG, Seeschleusenstrasse 1, 26871 Papenburg, Germany, *Tel:* +49 4961 66690, *Fax:* +49 4961 666 9183, *Email:* info@bera-papenburg.de, *Website:* www.bera-papenburg.de
Schulte & Bruns GmbH & Co KG, Deverhafen - Dockerhaus, 26871 Papenburg, Germany, *Tel:* +49 4961 806-0, *Fax:* +49 4961 806116, *Email:* schulte-bruns@schulte-bruns.de, *Website:* www.schulte-bruns.de

Stevedoring Companies: Schulte & Bruns GmbH & Co KG, Deverhafen - Dockerhaus, 26871 Papenburg, Germany, *Tel:* +49 4961 806-0, *Fax:* +49 4961 806116, *Email:* schulte-bruns@schulte-bruns.de, *Website:* www.schulte-bruns.de

Medical Facilities: Marienhospital, Papenburg, Tel: +49 4961 930

Airport: Bremen, 120 km

Railway: Papenburg Station, 2.5 km

Lloyd's Agent: Reck & Co. GmbH, Herrlichkeit 5, 28199 Bremen, Germany, *Tel:* +49 421 59834-0, *Fax:* +49 421 598 3450, *Email:* mail@reck.de, *Website:* www.reck.de

PASSAU

Lat 48° 35' N; Long 13° 28' E.

Admiralty Chart: -
Time Zone: GMT +1 h

Admiralty Pilot: -
UNCTAD Locode: DE PAS

Principal Facilities:

	Y	G		R				

Authority: Port of Regensburg, Linzer Strasse 6, 93055 Regensburg, Germany, *Tel:* +49 941 79597 0, *Fax:* +49 941 79597 40, *Email:* regensburg@bayernhafen.de, *Website:* www.bayernhafen.de

Officials: Port Director: Dr Dirk Rosencrantz, *Email:* d.rosencrantz@bayernhafen.de.

Accommodation:

Name	Length (m)	Remarks
Passau		
Passau Racklau	200	
Passau Schalding		See [1] below

[1]*Passau Schalding:* Operated by Donau-Lloyd-Mat GmbH, Industriestr. 14c, 94036 Passau, Tel: +49 851 98985-0, Fax: +49 851 98551
Ro/ro ramp for cars and trucks

Mechanical Handling Equipment:

Location	Type	Capacity (t)	Qty
Passau Racklau	Mobile Cranes	40	1

Railway: 112 m length of rail siding

Lloyd's Agent: Friedrich Hartmann vorm. J. Kerschgens, 2 Beethovenstrasse, D-68165 Mannheim, Germany, *Tel:* +49 621 423090, *Fax:* +49 621 416354, *Email:* hartmann@hartmann-expert.de, *Website:* www.hartmann-expert.de

REGENSBURG

Lat 49° 1' N; Long 12° 7' E.

Admiralty Chart: -
Time Zone: GMT +1 h

Admiralty Pilot: -
UNCTAD Locode: DE REG

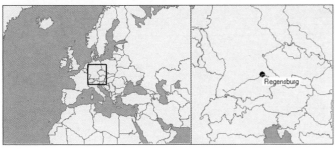

Principal Facilities:

		Y	G	C	R		B			

Authority: Port of Regensburg, Linzer Strasse 6, 93055 Regensburg, Germany, *Tel:* +49 941 79597 0, *Fax:* +49 941 79597 40, *Email:* regensburg@bayernhafen.de, *Website:* www.bayernhafen.de

Officials: Managing Director: Joachim Zimmermann, *Tel:* +49 941 795 0411, *Email:* j.zimmermann@bayernhafen.de.
Port Master: Uwe Raschke, *Tel:* +49 941 795 9724, *Email:* hvr.hafenmeister@bayernhafen.de.
Administrative Assistant: Andrea Hilger, *Tel:* +49 941 795 9711, *Email:* a.hilger@bayernhafen.de.

Traffic: 2007, 2 278 000 t of ship traffic handled out of a total of 7 321 000 t

Accommodation:

Name	Remarks
Regensburg	See [1] below

[1]*Regensburg:* Total port area of 1 620 000 m2 consisting of the Danube Wharf, Western Port and Eastern Port
5200 m of wharfage including one ro/ro facility, one rolling road terminal, one container terminal, four mineral oil pumping facilities and one heavy cargo platform

Storage: Silos of 108 000 m3, oil tanks of 81 000 m3 and cold storage of 52 000 m3

Location	Open (m²)	Covered (m²)
Regensburg	185000	133000

Mechanical Handling Equipment:

Location	Type	Capacity (t)	Qty
Regensburg	Mult-purp. Cranes	100	15

Bunkering: Available

Waste Reception Facilities: Disposal of bilge water, oily water, oil waste, remains of liquid fuel or liquids endangering water can be done with the bilge oil separator 7

Lloyd's Agent: Friedrich Hartmann vorm. J. Kerschgens, 2 Beethovenstrasse, D-68165 Mannheim, Germany, *Tel:* +49 621 423090, *Fax:* +49 621 416354, *Email:* hartmann@hartmann-expert.de, *Website:* www.hartmann-expert.de

RENDSBURG

Lat 54° 19' N; Long 9° 40' E.

Admiralty Chart: 2469	**Admiralty Pilot:** 55
Time Zone: GMT +1 h	**UNCTAD Locode:** DE REN

Principal Facilities:

		Y	G	C	R			B	D	T	A

Authority: Kreishafenamt Rendsburg, Am Kreishafen 4, 24768 Rendsburg, Germany, *Tel:* +49 4331 140712, *Fax:* +49 4331 5336, *Email:* info@kreishafen-rd.de, *Website:* www.wfg-rd.de/kreishafen

Officials: Managing Director: Dr Gerald Gehrtz, *Tel:* +49 4331 131120, *Email:* info@wfg-rd.de.
Harbour Master: Hans-Joachim Kobrock, *Tel:* +49 4331 14070.

Port Security: ISPS compliant

Approach: On Kiel Canal and R Eider. Railway junction and nodal point for the traffic of the N

Pilotage: Compulsory. Fees are included in Canal tariff. Kiel Canal pilotage

Traffic: 2001, 542 vessels, 382 626 t of cargo handled

Maximum Vessel Dimensions: At Kreishafen max loa is 165 m. At Obereiderhafen max loa is 120 m

Principal Imports and Exports: Imports: Animal feedpellets, Coal, Fertiliser, Pig iron, Stones. Exports: Fertiliser, Grain, Wood, Wood chips.

Working Hours: Monday-Thursday 0600-2100. Friday 0600-1930. Saturday 0600-1200 as overtime

Accommodation:

Name	Depth (m)	Remarks
Rendsburg		
Kreishafen	7.1–8.8	
Obereiderhafen	4.5	
Private Wharves		See [1] below

[1]*Private Wharves:* Ahlmann-Kai (also Agency, Tel: +49 4331 137777, Fax: +49 4331 137744)
Depth about 4.5 m, length about 470 m

Storage: Warehouse for fertilizer, no refrigerated space

Mechanical Handling Equipment:

Location	Type	Capacity (t)	Qty
Kreishafen	Mult-purp. Cranes	5–18	5
Obereiderhafen	Mult-purp. Cranes	3	1

Bunkering: Diesel oil can be delivered by road tanker

Waste Reception Facilities: Disposal of dirty ballast, sludge and garbage possible by truck

Towage: Two tugs of 450 hp and one of 750 hp owned by HDW-Nobiskrug. One tug of 450 hp owned by small states shipyard. Tugs can also be arranged from Kiel or Brunsbuttel when above are not available

Repair & Maintenance: HDW Nobiskrug GmbH & Co. KG, P O Box 1 60, 24757 Rendsburg, Germany, *Tel:* +49 4331 2070, *Fax:* +49 4331 207117, *Email:* hnk@hdw-nobiskrug.de, *Website:* www.hdw-nobiskrug.de Two dry docks: Dry dock I of 151.75 m x 22.4 m x 5.8 m, Dry dock II of 193 m x 31.6 m x 6.3 m; for vessels up to 30 000 dwt
Kroeger Werft GmbH & Co. KG, Huettenstrasse 25, Schacht-Audorf, 24790 Rendsburg, Germany, *Tel:* +49 4331 9510, *Fax:* +49 4331 951145, *Email:* info@luerssen-rendsburg.de, *Website:* www.luerssen.de Floating dock of 120 m x 22 m, draft 5.5 m, lifting cap of 4000 t. Quays of 300 m with max draught 6 m

Shipping Agents: Ahlmann-Zerssen GmbH & Co KG, Am Kreishafen 14, 24768 Rendsburg, Germany, *Tel:* +49 4331 137777, *Fax:* +49 4331 137744, *Email:* info@ahlmann-zerssen.de, *Website:* www.ahlmann-zerssen.de

Medical Facilities: Hospital and several doctors

Airport: Hamburg Airport, 100 km

Railway: Station approx 1 km from port

Lloyd's Agent: Reck & Co. GmbH, Wikinghaus, Schopenstehl 22, D-20095 Hamburg, Germany, *Tel:* +49 40 2789 6375, *Fax:* +49 40 2780 6418, *Email:* hamburg@reck.de, *Website:* www.reck.de

ROSTOCK

Lat 54° 5' N; Long 12° 8' E.

Admiralty Chart: 2370	**Admiralty Pilot:** 18
Time Zone: GMT +1 h	**UNCTAD Locode:** DE RSK

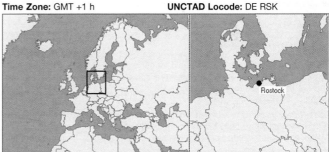

Principal Facilities:

P	Q	Y	G	C	R	L	B	D	T	A

Authority: Hafen-und Seemannsamt Rostock, P O Box 481046, 18132 Rostock, Germany, *Tel:* +49 381 381 8710, *Fax:* +49 381 381 8735, *Email:* port.authority@rostock.de, *Website:* www.rostock-port.de

Key to Principal Facilities:—			
A=Airport	**C**=Containers	**G**=General Cargo	
B=Bunkers	**D**=Dry Dock	**L**=Cruise	
P=Petroleum	**R**=Ro/Ro	**Y**=Dry Bulk	
Q=Other Liquid Bulk	**T**=Towage (where available from port)		

Rostocker Zementumschlag

Rostock Shipping Agency

Please contact us:

RZU GmbH
Ost-West-Str. 12
D-18147 Rostock
Fon: +49 (0) 3 81-6 73 00-13
Fax: +49 (0) 3 81-6 73 00-44
E-Mail: info@rzu-gmbh.de

✓ stevedoring with own quay/shore equipment/ stock

✓ shipping agency at all german baltic ports

✓ forwarding agency

Officials: Corporate Affairs Manager: Christian Hardt, *Email:* c.hardt@rostock-port.de.
Harbour Master: Gisbert Ruhnke, *Email:* gisbert.ruhnke@rostock.de.

Port Security: ISPS compliant

Documentation: Customs: cargo manifest, ship stores list, crew effect list
Immigration: crew list, passport or seamen's book
Port Health Authority: maritime declaration of health, derat certificate
Port Authority: international tonnage certificate 1969

Approach: River Warnow is approached from the Bay of Mecklenburg through a buoyed and lighted fairway channel, 5 nautical miles long in depth of 14.5 m, leading to Warnemunde and a sea channel leading to Seehafen Rostock

Anchorage: In the roads, 4-6 nautical miles NW of Warnemunde, there are two recommended anchorages in depths of 13-17 m, bottom of mud and sand. They are unsheltered from W, N and NE winds. Anchorage No.1 is for general vessels and Anchorage No.2 is for tankers, vessels with dangerous cargo and for bunkering

Pilotage: Compulsory for tankers (oil, chemical, gas), for vessels in an area N of Berth No.60 of 100 m loa or 15 m breadth or 7.5 m draft and over and for vessels in an area S of Berth No.60 of 60 m loa or 10 m breadth or 5 m draft and over
Pilotage exemption is possible in an area N of Berth No.60 for vessels up to 120 m loa, 10 m breadth and 8 m draft
The pilot station is situated in Warnemunde. Pilots are available 24 h/day and pilot station monitors on VHF Channel 14, call sign 'Warnemunde Pilot'. Message to be sent 3 h before arrival at pilot position stating name of ship, call sign, loa, breadth, gt, draught, port of call and ETA to boarding position
Pilot boards in pos 54° 12.5' N; 12° 02.4' E for vessels with a draft up to 6.5 m, 54° 14.5' N; 12° 02.3' E for vessels with a draft over 6.5 m and 54° 17.0' N; 12° 00.0' E for vessels with a draft over 11.58 m
The pilotage company is Lotsenbruderschaft "WIROST", Tel: +49 381 206 0380, Fax: +49 381 206 0301, Email: info@rostockpilot.de

Radio Frequency: Warnemunde Traffic: VHF Channel 73. Warnemunde Pilot: VHF Channel 14. Rostock Port: VHF Channel 10

Weather: Prevailing W'ly winds

Tides: Tide is imperceptible but strong winds from S directions may lower and gales from N directions may raise the water level up to +/- 1.5 m

Traffic: 2006, 26 600 000 t of cargo handled

Maximum Vessel Dimensions: 250 m loa, 40 m beam, 13 m draft but vessels exceeding 230 m loa, 36 m beam and/or draught 12 m are requested to obtain permission from Waterway and Shipping Board

Principal Imports and Exports: Imports: Ammonia, Building materials, Coal, Crude oil, Fruit, Ore, Paper, Steel. Exports: Grain, Pulpwood, Scrap.

Working Hours: Mon-Fri 0530-1330, 1330-2130. Overtime possible on special request 2130-0530 at extra cost
Sat 0530-1330. Overtime possible on special request 1330-0530 Mon at extra cost

Accommodation:

Name	Draught (m)	Remarks
Seehafen Rostock		See [1] below
Oil Harbour		
Berth 1	4.57	
Berth 2	4.22	
Berth 3	13	
Berth 4	11.58	
Berth 5	11.58	
Berth 6	13	
Basin C		
Berth 12	10.36	Fertilizers
Berth 16	10.36	Grain
Berth 17	13	Grain
Berth 18	13	Grain
Basin B		
Berth 21	9.45	Cement, stones
Berth 22	10.06	Stones

Name	Draught (m)	Remarks
Berth 23	10.06	Coal, ore
Berth 24	13	Coal, ore
Berth 30	7.32	Cement
Berth 31	9.45	Sugar terminal
Berth 32	9.75	Cement
Berth 33	9.75	General cargo
Berth 34	9.75	General cargo
Berth 35	10.06	General cargo
Berth 36	9.45	Wood
Berth 37	9.45	Wood
Basin A		
Berth 41	9.75	General cargo
Berth 42	9.75	Steel
Berth 43	9.75	Steel
Berth 44	10.36	Scrap
Berth 45	10.36	Scrap
Berth 46	10.36	General cargo
Berth 50	8.68	Closed
Berth 51	9.75	Closed
Berth 52	9.75	Closed
Berth 53	9.75	Ferry (Superfast)
Berth 54	10.36	Ferry (Silja Line)
Berth 55	9	
Warnow Quay		
Berth 60	10.36	Paper
Berth 61	10.36	Paper
Berth 62	7.92	Ro/ro
Berth 63	9.45	Ro/ro
Berth 64	8.1	Ferry (Scandlines)
Berth 65	8.1	Ferry (TT-Line)
Berth 66	9.45	Ferry (TT-Line)
Berth 67	9	Ferry (Scandlines)
Rostocker Fischereihafen		See [2] below
Berth 1	5.49	
Berth 2	5.18	
Berth 3	5.18	
Berth 4	5.18	
Berth 5	5.49	
Berth 6	5.49	
Berth 7	5.49	
Berth 8	5.49	
Berth 9	5.18	
Berth 10	5.18	
Berth 11	5.18	
Berth 18	5.49	
Berth 19	7.92	
Berth 20	7.92	
Berth 21	7.92	
Berth 22	7.92	
Berth 23	7.92	
Berth 24	7.92	
Berth 25	7.92	
Berth 26	7.92	
Stadthafen (Old City Port)		See [3] below
Berth 71	3.96	
Berth 72	4.57	
Berth 73	4.57	
Berth 74	4.57	
Berth 75	4.57	
Berth 78	3.66	
Berth 79	6.4	
Berth 80	6.4	
Berth 81	6.4	
Berth 82	6.1	
Berth 83	6.1	
Berth 83E	5.49	
Berth 83S	4.01	
Berth 84	4.57	
Berth 85	4.57	
Berth 86	4.57	
Berth 87	4.57	
Berth 88	4.57	
Berth 89	5.03	
Berth 90	5.03	
Berth 91	5.03	
Berth 92	4.57	
Berth 93	1.98	
Berth 94	1.98	
Warnemunde		See [4] below
Berth P1	6.55	
Berth P2	6.55	
Berth P3	6.55	
Berth P4	6.55	
Berth P5	6.55	
Berth P6	6.55	
Berth P7	8.38	
Berth P8	8.38	
Metallaufbereitung (MAB)		See [5] below
Berth 1	5.79	
Berth 2	5.79	
Berth 3	5.79	
Berth 4	5.79	
Hydro Agri (Chemical Harbour)		Operated by Hydro Agri Rostock GmbH, PO Box 102021, 18004 Rostock
Berth 07	8.45	For gas tankers (ammonia)

Name	Draught (m)	Remarks
Musing Kai		See [6] below
Berth 01	3.9	
Berth 02	5.8	
Berth 03	5.8	
Berth 04	5.8	

[1]*Seehafen Rostock:* Port Operators:
Hafen-Entwicklungsgesellschaft Rostock mbH, PO Box 481240, 18134 Rostock, Tel: +49 381 350 4000, Fax: +49 381 350 4005, Email: info@rostock-port.de - port development company

Seehafen Rostock Umschlagsgesellschaft mbH, PO Box 481009, 18132 Rostock, Tel: +49 381 66620, Fax: +49 381 666 2105, Email: atzmon@portofrostock.de - cargo handling company

Oil Harbour (GOR), Oewerwischenweg 1, 18146 Rostock, Tel: +49 381 648100, Fax: +49 381 648250, Email: goer-gmbh@t-online.de - cargo handling company

[2]*Rostocker Fischereihafen:* Operated by Rostocker Fischereihafen GmbH, Fischerweg 408, 18069 Rostock, Tel: +49 381 811 2317, Fax: +49 381 811 2728, Email: info@rfh.de, Website: www.rfh.de
Handles a wide range of goods including bulk, refrigerated & general cargoes

[3]*Stadthafen (Old City Port):* Operated by Hafen-und Seemannsamt Rostock, PO Box 481046, 18132 Rostock, Tel: +49 381 381 8710, Fax: +49 381 381 8735, Email: port.authority@rostock.de
No cargo handling takes place. The quays are used for medium-sized passenger vessels, river craft and local traffic as well as yachts

[4]*Warnemunde:* Operated by Hafen-Entwicklungsgesellschaft Rostock mbH, PO Box 481240, 18134 Rostock, Tel: +49 381 350 4000, Fax: +49 381 350 4005, Email: info@rostock-port.de
Passenger vessels

[5]*Metallaufbereitung (MAB):* Operated by INTERSEROH-Metallaufbereitung Rostock GmbH, PO Box 102087, 18003 Rostock, Tel: +49 381 809060, Fax: +49 381 809 0624, Email: mabrostock@t-online.de
Handling of bulk cargoes

[6]*Musing Kai:* Operated by Anton Musing GmbH & Co KG, Industriestrasse 14, 18069 Rostock, Tel: +49 381 655655, Fax: +49 381 655656
Used entirely for handling bulk cargoes

Storage:

Location	Open (m²)	Covered (m²)	Grain (t)	Cold (m³)
Seehafen Rostock	1020000	170000	400000	7000

Mechanical Handling Equipment:

Location	Type	Capacity (t)
Seehafen Rostock	Shore Cranes	3.2–63

Bunkering: Frachtcontor Junge & Co., Frachtcontor Junge & Co. GmbH, P O Box 481218, 18134 Rostock, Germany, *Tel:* +49 381 350 5982, *Fax:* +49 381 350 5985, *Email:* agency.hro@frachtcontor.de, *Website:* www.frachtcontor.de

Ostsee Mineralol-Bunker GmbH, Thomas-Mann-Strasse 20, 18055 Rostock, Germany, *Tel:* +49 381 2522 30, *Fax:* +49 381 2522 316/26, *Email:* info@ostsee-bunker.de

Singer Ol & Technik GmbH, Oll-Daniel Weg 5, 18069 Rostock, Germany, *Tel:* +49 381 86510, *Fax:* +49 381 8651 024, *Email:* singer.oel@t-online.de, *Website:* www.singer-oel.de

Bominflot, Bominflot Bunkergesellschaft fur Mineralole mbH & Co. KG, Grosse Baeckerstrasse 11, 20095 Hamburg, Germany, *Tel:* +49 40 350 930, *Fax:* +49 40 3509 3116, *Email:* mail@bominflot.de, *Website:* www.bominflot.net

Hans Rinck Bunkering Service, P O Box 226, 21637 Horneburg, Germany, *Tel:* +49 4163 814 10, *Fax:* +49 4163 814 122, *Email:* mail@hans-rinck.com, *Website:* www.hans-rinck.com

Ostsee Mineralol-Bunker GmbH, Thomas-Mann-Strasse 20, 18055 Rostock, Germany, *Tel:* +49 381 2522 30, *Fax:* +49 381 2522 316/26, *Email:* info@ostsee-bunker.de

Tramp Oil & Marine, World Fuel Services Corporation, 13th Floor, Portland House, Bressenden Place, London SW1E 5BH, United Kingdom, *Tel:* +44 20 7808 5000, *Fax:* +44 20 7808 5088, *Email:* pturner@wfscorp.com, *Website:* www.wfscorp.com

Waste Reception Facilities: Garbage removal available on request. Facilities available for receipt of dirty ballast water

Towage: Tugs available up to 3000 hp

Repair & Maintenance: Neptun Werft GmbH, Werftallee 13, 18119 Rostock, Germany, *Tel:* +49 381 384 1002, *Fax:* +49 381 384 1011, *Email:* info@neptunwerft.de, *Website:* www.neptun-stahlbau.de Floating dock 210 m x 37 m with lifting cap 23 000 t. Repair quay 240 m with max draught 6 m

Ship Chandlers: ROFIA GmbH, Zum Kuhlhaus 5, 18069 Rostock, Germany, *Tel:* +49 381 811 2805, *Fax:* +49 381 811 2482, *Email:* office@rofia.com, *Website:* www.rofia.com

Schiffsversorgung Rostock GmbH, Goedeke-Michels-Street 1b, 18147 Rostock, Germany, *Tel:* +49 381 670490, *Fax:* +49 381 670 4999, *Email:* mail@svr.de, *Website:* www.svr.com

Scan-Mot Schiffstechnik GmbH, Fischerweg 408, 18069 Rostock, Germany, *Tel:* +49 381 811 3375, *Fax:* +49 381 811 3379, *Email:* scan-mot-ralf-lubach@gmx.de, *Website:* www.scan-mot.com

Nautischer Dienst Kapt. Stegmann, P O Box 481203, 18134 Rostock-Uberseehafen, Germany, *Tel:* +49 381 670 0570, *Fax:* +49 381 670 0571, *Email:* naudi.rostock@web.de, *Website:* www.naudi.de

Shipping Agents: Ahlmann-Zerssen GmbH & Co KG, Ost-West-Strasse 5, 18147 Rostock, Germany, *Tel:* +49 381 673 3333, *Fax:* +49 381 673 3344, *Email:* rostock@rostock.ahlmann-zerssen.de, *Website:* www.ahlmann-zerssen.de

Baltimar Schiffahrt & Transport GmbH, Zum Olhafen 7, 18147 Rostock, Germany, *Tel:* +49 381 350 4420, *Fax:* +49 381 350 4425, *Email:* agency@baltimar.de, *Website:* www.baltimar.de

Baume + Greinert Schiffahrts-und Agentur GmbH, P O Box 481131, 18133 Rostock, Germany, *Tel:* +49 381 350 4680, *Fax:* +49 381 350 4685, *Email:* baeume-greinert@t-online.de, *Website:* www.baeume-schiffahrt.de

Frachtcontor Junge & Co., Frachtcontor Junge & Co. GmbH, P O Box 481218, 18134 Rostock, Germany, *Tel:* +49 381 350 5982, *Fax:* +49 381 350 5985, *Email:* agency.hro@frachtcontor.de, *Website:* www.frachtcontor.de

NSA Schiffahrt und Transport GmbH, Am Skandinavienkai 14, 18147 Rostock, Germany, *Tel:* +49 381 350 4920/1, *Fax:* +49 381 350 4925, *Email:* schneider.nsa-rostock@t-online.de

H C Roever Maritime Agency (Weser) GmbH, Zum Oelhafen 7, 18147 Rostock, Germany, *Tel:* +49 381 670 0972, *Fax:* +49 381 670 0974, *Email:* rostock@hcroever.de

Rostocker Zementumschlagsgesellschaft mbH, Ost-West Strasse 12, 18147 Rostock, Germany, *Tel:* +49 381 673 0013, *Fax:* +49 381 673 0044, *Email:* ott@mibau.de

Sartori & Berger, Ost-West-Strasse 5, 18147 Rostock, Germany, *Tel:* +49 381 670890, *Fax:* +49 381 670 8910, *Email:* rostock@sartori-berger.de, *Website:* www.sartori-berger.de

Schiffsmaklerei Shipping & Chartering GmbH, Ost-West-Strasse 12, 18147 Rostock, Germany, *Tel:* +49 381 673060, *Fax:* +49 381 673 0620, *Email:* office@sm-shipping.de, *Website:* www.sm-shipping.de

SK Schiffahrtskontor GmbH, Neuer Markt 17, 18055 Rostock, Germany, *Tel:* +49 381 403150, *Fax:* +49 381 403 1510, *Email:* info@sk-schiffahrtskontor.de, *Website:* www.sk-schiffahrtskontor.de

Stevedoring Companies: Rostocker Zementumschlagsgesellschaft mbH, Ost-West Strasse 12, 18147 Rostock, Germany, *Tel:* +49 381 673 0013, *Fax:* +49 381 673 0044, *Email:* ott@mibau.de

Surveyors: Det Norske Veritas A/S, Rostock, Germany, *Tel:* +49 381 700 6492, *Fax:* +49 381 700 6493, *Website:* www.dnv.com

Germanischer Lloyd, Doberaner Str. 44-47, 18057 Rostock, Germany, *Tel:* +49 381 492880, *Fax:* +49 381 492 8830, *Email:* gl-rostock@gl-group.com, *Website:* www.gl-group.com

Russian Maritime Register of Shipping, Fischerweg 408, 18069 Rostock, Germany, *Tel:* +49 381 811 2950, *Fax:* +49 381 811 2952, *Website:* www.rs-head.spb.ru

TTS Automation AS, Langestrasse 1A, 18055 Rostock, Germany, *Tel:* +49 381 458 2101, *Fax:* +49 381 458 2100

Medical Facilities: All medical services available in the town of Rostock

Airport: Rostock-Laage, 40 km

Railway: Deutsche Bahn AG, directly connected to the port

Lloyd's Agent: Reck & Co. GmbH, P O Box 42 04 25, D-12099 Berlin, Germany, *Tel:* +49 30 745 9033, *Fax:* +49 30 8049 6422, *Email:* berlin@reck.de, *Website:* www.reck.de

SASSNITZ

Lat 54° 31' N; Long 13° 38' E.

Admiralty Chart: 2365		**Admiralty Pilot:** 18	
Time Zone: GMT +1 h		**UNCTAD Locode:** DE SAS	

Principal Facilities:

Y	G	C	R	L			

Authority: Fahrhafen Sassnitz GmbH, 18546 Sassnitz, Germany, *Tel:* +49 38392 550, *Fax:* +49 38392 55240, *Email:* info@faehrhafen-sassnitz.de, *Website:* www.faehrhafen-sassnitz.de

Officials: Managing Director: Harm Sievers, *Tel:* +49 38392 55210, *Email:* sievers@faehrhafen-sassnitz.de.
Marketing Manager: Detlef Unger, *Tel:* +49 38392 55205, *Email:* unger@faehrhafen-sassnitz.de.
Harbour Master: Karl-Heinz Vuytech, *Tel:* +49 38392 55312, *Email:* hafenamt@sassnitz.de.

Port Security: ISPS compliant

Approach: Open sea approach

Pilotage: Not compulsory

Radio Frequency: Sassnitz Port on VHF Channel 15

Accommodation:

Name	Length (m)	Depth (m)	Draught (m)	Remarks
Sassnitz				See [1] below
Berth No.2	110	7	6.4	Ro/ro & conventional cargo
Berth No.3	190	7	6.4	Ro/ro & conventional cargo
Berth No.4	220	10	8.5	Ro/ro with broad gauge track access
Berth No.5	220	10	8.5	Ro/ro with broad gauge track access
Berth No.6	250	10.5	9.5	See [2] below
Berth No.7	250	10.5	9.5	See [3] below
Berth No.8	190	10.5	9.5	See [4] below
Berth No.11	167	10.5	9.5	Conventional cargo

Key to Principal Facilities:—				
A=Airport	**C**=Containers	**G**=General Cargo	**P**=Petroleum	**R**=Ro/Ro	**Y**=Dry Bulk
B=Bunkers	**D**=Dry Dock	**L**=Cruise	**Q**=Other Liquid Bulk	**T**=Towage (where available from port)	

Name	Length (m)	Depth (m)	Draught (m)	Remarks
Northern Mole Berth	250	10.5	9.5	Conventional cargo

[1]*Sassnitz:* Ferry services to: Trelleborg, Sweden (5 times a day); Ronne, Denmark (up to twice a day); St. Petersburg, Russia (twice a week); Klaipeda, Lithuania (3 times a week)
[2]*Berth No.6:* Ro/ro passengers with normal gauge track access
[3]*Berth No.7:* Ro/ro passengers with normal gauge track access
[4]*Berth No.8:* Operated by Sea Terminal Sassnitz GmbH & Co KG, 18546 Sassnitz/Neu-Mukran, Tel: +49 38392 55373, Fax: +49 38392 55372, Email: hj.zentner@sea-terminal-sassnitz.de, Website: www.sea-terminal-sassnitz.de Ro/ro & conventional cargo with track access

Storage: Warehouses of 5700 m2, open air (surfaced) of 30 000 m2, open air (unsurfaced) of 100 000 m2, traffic area (surfaced) of 50 000 m2, marshalling area of 25 000 m2 and parking (surfaced) of 14 000 m2

Mechanical Handling Equipment:

Location	Type	Capacity (t)	Qty	Remarks
Sassnitz	Mult-purp. Cranes	10	1	at berths 4 & 5
Sassnitz	Mobile Cranes	104	1	at berth 8
Sassnitz	Portal Cranes	32	2	
Sassnitz	Forklifts	3–7	6	
Sassnitz	Yard Tractors		3	

Bunkering: Frachtcontor Junge & Co., Frachtcontor Junge & Co. GmbH, 18546 Sassnitz, Germany, *Tel:* +49 38392 55390, *Fax:* +49 38392 55405, *Email:* agency.sas@frachtcontor.de, *Website:* www.frachtcontor.de

Shipping Agents: Ahlmann-Zerssen GmbH & Co KG, Fahrhafen Sassnitz, 18546 Sassnitz, Germany, *Tel:* +49 38392 55366, *Fax:* +49 38392 55365, *Email:* sassnitz@ahlmann-zerssen.de, *Website:* www.ahlmann-zerssen.de
Frachtcontor Junge & Co., Frachtcontor Junge & Co. GmbH, 18546 Sassnitz, Germany, *Tel:* +49 38392 55390, *Fax:* +49 38392 55405, *Email:* agency.sas@frachtcontor.de, *Website:* www.frachtcontor.de

Lloyd's Agent: Reck & Co. GmbH, P O Box 42 04 25, D-12099 Berlin, Germany, *Tel:* +49 30 745 9033, *Fax:* +49 30 8049 6422, *Email:* berlin@reck.de, *Website:* www.reck.de

SCHEERHAFEN

harbour area, see under Kiel

SCHWEDENKAI

harbour area, see under Kiel

STRALSUND

Lat 54° 19' N; Long 13° 6' E.

Admiralty Chart: 2365
Time Zone: GMT +1 h
Admiralty Pilot: 18
UNCTAD Locode: DE STL

Principal Facilities:

		Y	G		L		D	T	A	

Authority: Seehafen Stralsund GmbH, Hafenstrasse 20, 18439 Stralsund, Germany, *Tel:* +49 3831 2542 0, *Fax:* +49 3831 254297, *Email:* info@seehafen-stralsund.de, *Website:* www.seehafen-stralsund.de

Officials: Managing Director: Wolfgang Ostenberg, *Tel:* +49 3831 254212, *Email:* ostenberg@seehafen-stralsund.de.
Marketing Manager: Soren Jurrat, *Tel:* +49 3831 254221, *Email:* jurrat@seehafen-stralsund.de.
Operations Manager: Axel Breede, *Tel:* +49 3831 254215, *Email:* breede@seehafen-stralsund.de.
Harbour Master: Ingolf Traeger, *Tel:* +49 3831 260130, *Email:* hafenamt@stralsund.de.

Port Security: ISPS compliant

Pre-Arrival Information: ETA message should include: vessel's name, call sign, IMO number, flag state, gt, draft, last port of call, next port of call, notification of ship-generated waste

Documentation: Crew list (2 copies), passenger list (2 copies), stores list, cargo documents, ship's certificates

Approach: Eastern entrance via Thiessow (Landtief), max draught 6.6 m. N entrance from Gellen, max draught 3.7 m

Eastern entrance (via Thiessow) is through a bridge and a tug is compulsory for vessels exceeding 1000 gt, 90 m loa and/or 13 m breadth

Anchorage: Altefaehr Roads in pos 54° 19.31' N; 13° 07.1' E in depth of 7 m (north fairway)
Drigge Roads in pos 54° 16.9' N; 13° 08.0' E in depth of 12 m (east fairway)

Pilotage: From E entrance: compulsory for vessels over 85 m loa and/or 13 m breadth. From N entrance: compulsory for vessels over 60 m loa and/or 10 m breadth. Contact Stralsund pilot on VHF Channels 14 and 16 24 h/day

Radio Frequency: Stralsund radio on VHF Channel 11. Stralsund traffic (traffic control centre) on VHF Channel 67

Weather: Prevailing NW and E'ly winds

Tides: Non-tidal

Maximum Vessel Dimensions: Max loa 130 m, max breadth 22 m, max draft 6.6 m

Principal Imports and Exports: Imports: Building materials, Bulk & bagged fertiliser, Coal, Cold storage goods, Limestone, Metals, Timber. Exports: Grain, Gypsum, Metal & metal products, Rape seed, Scrap, Steel sheets, Timber.

Working Hours: Mon-Fri 0600-2300. Sat 0600-1400. Sat from 1400 to Mon 0600, night-shift and holidays work possible at overtime rates

Accommodation:

Name	Remarks
Stralsund	See [1] below

[1]*Stralsund:* Length of quay 2800 m (25 berths) with depth alongside of 7.5 m. Direct transhipment into river barges can be effected. Harbour kept open in winter by icebreaker
City Port (Berths 1-9) used by cruise vessels, traditional vessels and authority vessels
Northern Port (Berths 10-16) handles cargo such as gypsum, agrarian goods, scrap, wood, metals, cold storage goods, building materials and coal
Southern Port (Berths 17-22) handles transhipment cargo such as sheet metals, steel, agrarian goods and building materials
Frankenhafen (Berhs 34-36) handles building materials and timber

Storage:

Location	Open (m²)	Covered (m²)	Grain (t)	Cold (m³)
Stralsund	55000	3000	30000	3000

Mechanical Handling Equipment:

Location	Type	Capacity (t)	Qty	Remarks
Stralsund	Shore Cranes	20	8	
Stralsund	Diesel Cranes	0–20	3	available in all areas
Stralsund	Forklifts	0–4	4	

Towage: Three tugs available
BBB Schlepp und Hafendienst GmbH, Neue Badenstrasse, 18439 Stralsund, Germany, *Tel:* +49 3831 297020, *Fax:* +49 3831 297031

Repair & Maintenance: Volkswerft Stralsund GmbH, An der Werft 5, 18439 Stralsund, Germany, *Tel:* +49 3831 660, *Fax:* +49 3831 663202, *Email:* contact@volkswerft.de, *Website:* www.volkswerft.de Maintenance and inspections. Ship conversion and lengthening. Repairs of all types. Usage of all facilities like ship lift to heave ships up to panamax size

Shipping Agents: Ahlmann-Zerssen GmbH & Co KG, Hafenstrasse 20, 18439 Stralsund, Germany, *Tel:* +49 3831 703930, *Fax:* +49 3831 703932, *Email:* stralsund@ahlmann-zerssen.de, *Website:* www.ahlmann-zerssen.de
Schiffsmaklerei Shipping & Chartering GmbH, Hafenstrasse 20, 18439 Stralsund, Germany, *Tel:* +49 3831 280600, *Fax:* +49 3831 280603, *Email:* sm-stralsund@t-online.de, *Website:* www.sm-shipping.de

Stevedoring Companies: Seehafen Stralsund GmbH, Hafenstrasse 20, 18439 Stralsund, Germany, *Tel:* +49 3831 2542 0, *Fax:* +49 3831 254297, *Email:* info@seehafen-stralsund.de, *Website:* www.seehafen-stralsund.de

Surveyors: Germanischer Lloyd, Philipp-Julius-Weg 1, 18437 Stralsund, Germany, *Tel:* +49 3831 47340, *Fax:* +49 3831 473412, *Email:* gl-stralsund@gl-group.com, *Website:* www.gl-group.com
Nippon Kaiji Kyokai, Stralsund, Germany, *Tel:* +49 3831 47340, *Fax:* +49 3831 473412, *Website:* www.classnk.or.jp

Medical Facilities: Hospital and doctors available in the town

Airport: Ostseeflughafen Stralsund, 25 km

Railway: Railways inside the port close to the berths. Stralsund Central Railway Station, 2 km

Lloyd's Agent: Reck & Co. GmbH, P O Box 42 04 25, D-12099 Berlin, Germany, *Tel:* +49 30 745 9033, *Fax:* +49 30 8049 6422, *Email:* berlin@reck.de, *Website:* www.reck.de

TRAVEMUNDE

harbour area, see under Lubeck

UTERSEN

Lat 53° 40' N; Long 9° 39' E.

Admiralty Chart: 3266
Time Zone: GMT +1 h
Admiralty Pilot: 55
UNCTAD Locode: DE UET

This port is no longer open to commercial shipping

WARNEMUNDE

harbour area, see under Rostock

WILHELMSHAVEN

Lat 53° 31' N; Long 8° 9' E.

Admiralty Chart: 3618	**Admiralty Pilot:** 55
Time Zone: GMT +1 h	**UNCTAD Locode:** DE WVN

Principal Facilities:

P Q Y G C R   B D T A

Tramp Oil & Marine

Wells House, 15-17 Elmfield Road, Bromley,
Kent BR1 1LT, United Kingdom
Phone: +44 20 8315 7777   **Fax:** +44 20 8315 7788
General email: enquiries@tramp-oil.com

See listings for all global offices: **www.tramp-oil.com**

Authority: Niedersachsen Ports GmbH & Co. KG, Port of Wilhelmshaven, Neckarstrasse 10, 26360 Wilhelmshaven, Germany, *Tel:* +49 4421 4800-0, *Fax:* +49 4421 480 0599, *Email:* wilhelmshaven@nports.de, *Website:* www.wilhelmshaven-port.de

Officials: Managing Director: Martin Janssen, *Email:* mjanssen@nports.de.
Harbour Master: Lutz Wilhelm, *Email:* lwilhelm@nports.de.

Port Security: ISPS compliant

Approach: Distance from the Jade estuary to Hooksiel is 36 km, from the lightship "GB" to Hooksiel is 77 km
Distance from the Jade estuary to the "Alter Vorhafen" is 53 km, from the lightship "GB" to the Alter Vorhafen is 94 km
The fairway is 300 m wide and up to 18.5 m below CD and leads to the NWO Jetty (Nord-West-Olleitungsgesellschaft). Under normal channel conditions and with at least average tidal bore, the approach can accommodate vessels of up to 350 m loa, 52 m beam with incoming draft of 20 m and outgoing draft of 19 m
Vessels exceeding these limits require special permission to be applied for in advance from the Port Authority

Anchorage: 1) Deep water anchorage for large vessels SW of "German Bight" lightship
2) Anchorage for large and deep sea vessels SE of light buoy "3/Jade 2"
3) Schillig tanker roads for vessels with IMDG class 2 and 3 cargoes and a max draft of 13.5 m, a max length of 350 m and a max displacement of 250 000 dwt
4) Schillig roads for all non-tanker vessels up to 14 m draft and 260 m loa
5) Quarantine anchorage for all vessels falling under quarantine with up to 12 m draft and 180 m loa
6) Explosives anchorage for vessels carrying volatile substances (IMGD subclasses 1.3 and 1.4)
7) North Tanker roads for vessels carrying IMDG class 2 and 3 cargoes with a max draft of 12 m and 230 m loa
8) South Tanker roads for tankers in ballast with a max draft of 13 m and 260 m loa
9) Wilhelmshaven anchorage for all vessels other than tankers, ships under quarantine or carrying explosives; for all vessels waiting for the lock

Pilotage: Advance notice for pilot boarding at Weser light-vessel is required 12 h prior to ETA and for pilot boarding at German Bight light-vessel, 24 h prior to ETA

Radio Frequency: Wilhelmshaven Port on VHF Channel 11. Coastal radio station, VHF Channels 16 and 20. Wilhelmshaven Lock Radio, working on VHF Channel 13 during official service hours
Jade Radar Chain is continuously on service and offers shore based radar assistance and various information concerning traffic movements, tidal and weather conditions, dredging activities etc, call sign Jade-Traffic, VHF Channels 20 and 63; situation reports are transmitted every half hour

Weather: Strong winds from the W can be expected from October to April

Tides: Mean rise of tide 3.6 m

Traffic: 2006, 43 107 000 t of cargo handled

Maximum Vessel Dimensions: 350 m loa, 20 m draft, 260 000 dwt. Vessels exceeding these limits need an official permit of navigation from the waterway authority

Principal Imports and Exports: Imports: Chemicals, Crude oil, Fertiliser, Salt, Sand, Timber. Exports: Caustic soda, Crude oil products.

Working Hours: 24 h/day at specialised terminals, otherwise differs from berth to berth

Accommodation: One sea lock at the southern end of the Neuer Vorhafen with two basins fitted with sliding lock-gates; each 350 m long and 57 m wide. The outer sill is 11.46 m below CD, the inner sill lies 14.75 m below average harbour water level

Name	Length (m)	Depth (m)	Remarks
Inner Port			
Hannoverkai (Nordhafen)	315	11	2-3 berths according to ship size
Luneburgkai (Nordhafen)	275	11	2-3 berths according to ship size
Braunschweigkai (Nordhafen)	270	12	2-3 berths according to ship size
Ausrustungshafen		6.5	See [1] below
Nordwestkai (Verbindungshafen)	150	7	1-2 berths, one ro/ro facility
Sudwestkai (Verbindungshafen)	320	10	2-3 berths according to ship size, 6000 m2 of cold storage
Nord-Gazelle-Brucke & Bontekai (Grosser Hafen)	500	8	
Handelshafen	980	4.8–6	See [2] below
Kanalhafen	600	5	
Outer Port			See [3] below
Alter Vorhafen (Helgolandkai/Wangeroogkai)	365	3.6	See [4] below
Flut-und Pontonhafen		3	See [5] below
ICI Tanker Jetty (Voslapper Groden)		9	See [6] below
Wilhelmshavener Raffineriegesellschaft mbH (WRG) Tanker Jetty			See [7] below
Jetty 1		17.5	
Jetty 1A		12	
Jetty 2		7.5	
Jetty 3		7.5	
Niedersachsenbrucke Bulk Terminal			See [8] below
Inner	300	12	
Outer	300	15	
Nord-West Oelleitung (NWO) Tanker Jetty		16–20.8	See [9] below

[1]*Ausrustungshafen:* Three berths including two lay-up berths at dolphins for vessels up to 20 000 dwt
[2]*Handelshafen:* Ship's silos with a total of 720 m3 cap, 5000 m2 covered area, open storage for 70 000 t of bulk cargo and 12 000 m2 stockyard area
[3]*Outer Port:* There is also a Navy Base within the port area. Communication by water with the interior is provided for by the Ems-Jade-Kanal linking Wilhelmshaven and Emden, admitting small craft only
[4]*Alter Vorhafen (Helgolandkai/Wangeroogkai):* Passenger services. Consists of 6 berths. 5 600 m2 of quay area and 9 000 m2 parking and stock yard area available
[5]*Flut-und Pontonhafen:* Quay length of approx 730 m of which 230 m at pontoons (12 t capacity). There are several berths, number dependant on the size of the vessel and 2 slipways for smaller boats and sports craft. Limited storage space. Ample stockyard area is available in the immediate vicinity (in the Alter Vorhafen)
[6]*ICI Tanker Jetty (Voslapper Groden):* For vessels up to 12 000 dwt and 137 m loa. Berth 2 for ethylene only and Berth 3 for VCM and ECM and their residues only. Storage cap: ethylene 7700 m3, ECM 16 000 m3 and VCM 11 000 m3
[7]*Wilhelmshavener Raffineriegesellschaft mbH (WRG) Tanker Jetty:* Two berths at an offshore jetty and two berths at a shore jetty. Loading gantries for crude oil and derivatives. Storage tank of 1 300 000 m3
[8]*Niedersachsenbrucke Bulk Terminal:* Operated by Midgard AG & Co, and accommodates vessels up to 190 000 dwt. Coal and chemicals (caustic soda solution) are handled at the berth, one 32 t gantry crane, 35 m outreach, one conveyor fed outloading boom, 1000 t/h cap and a conveyor belt to a power station
[9]*Nord-West Oelleitung (NWO) Tanker Jetty:* Berth No's 1 and 2, 18.59 m max d, Berth No.4, 20.12 m max d. Day and night berthing. Pipelines linking the terminal with refineries in Hamburg and the Ruhr area

Storage:

Location	Open (m²)	Covered (m²)
Hannoverkai (Nordhafen)	4000	
Luneburgkai (Nordhafen)	8000	7000
Braunschweigkai (Nordhafen)	10000	
Nordwestkai (Verbindungshafen)	13000	5000
Sudwestkai (Verbindungshafen)	30000	

Mechanical Handling Equipment:

Location	Type	Capacity (t)	Qty	Remarks
Wilhelmshaven	Floating Cranes	100	1	
Luneburgkai (Nordhafen)	Mult-purp. Cranes	18	2	
Braunschweigkai (Nordhafen)	Mobile Cranes	100	1	
Sudwestkai (Verbindungshafen)	Mobile Cranes	35	1	

Key to Principal Facilities:—				
A=Airport	**C**=Containers	**G**=General Cargo	**P**=Petroleum	**R**=Ro/Ro	**Y**=Dry Bulk
B=Bunkers	**D**=Dry Dock	**L**=Cruise	**Q**=Other Liquid Bulk	**T**=Towage (where available from port)	

Location	Type	Capacity (t)	Qty	Remarks
Handelshafen	Mult-purp. Cranes	15	1	
Handelshafen	Portal Cranes	20	1	for scrap iron

Bunkering: Fuel and gas oil available

BMT Bremer Mineraoel Transport GmbH & Co. KG, Konsul-Smidt Street 8 Floor, 28217 Bremen, Germany, *Tel:* +49 421 3391710, *Fax:* +49 421 3391741, *Email:* info@bmt-bremen.com

Bominflot, Bominflot Bunkergesellschaft fur Mineralole mbH & Co. KG, Grosse Baeckerstrasse 11, 20095 Hamburg, Germany, *Tel:* +49 40 350 930, *Fax:* +49 40 3509 3116, *Email:* mail@bominflot.de, *Website:* www.bominflot.net

B.O.T. Broring Oil Trading GmbH, B.O.T. Broering Oil Trading GmbH, Carl Ronning-strasse 9, 28195 Bremen, Germany, *Tel:* +49 421 170 091, *Fax:* +49 421 170 093, *Email:* home@b-o-t.info, *Website:* www.broering.info

ExxonMobil Marine Fuels, Mailpoint 31, ExxonMobil House, Ermyn Way, Leather-head, Surrey KT22 8UX, United Kingdom, *Tel:* +44 1372 222 000, *Fax:* +44 1372 223 922, *Email:* marine.fuels@exxonmobil.com, *Website:* www.exxonmobil.com

Hans Rinck Bunkering Service, P O Box 226, 21637 Horneburg, Germany, *Tel:* +49 4163 814 10, *Fax:* +49 4163 814 122, *Email:* mail@hans-rinck.com, *Website:* www.hans-rinck.com

Tramp Oil & Marine, World Fuel Services Corporation, 13th Floor, Portland House, Bressenden Place, London SW1E 5BH, United Kingdom, *Tel:* +44 20 7808 5000, *Fax:* +44 20 7808 5088, *Email:* pturner@wfscorp.com, *Website:* www.wfscorp.com

Waste Reception Facilities: Refuse skips are available on request in all parts of the harbour for general and household garbage and is free of charge, *Email:* marpol@nhajw.niedersachsen.de

Towage: Four tugs always available at the port, extra tugs can be arranged on request

Schleppgemeinschaft Wilhelmshaven, Neuer Vorhafen, 26384 Wilhelmshaven, Germany, *Tel:* +49 4421 41210, *Email:* info@bugsier.de, *Website:* www.bugsier.de

Repair & Maintenance: Hannoverkai Navitek GmbH, Navitek GmbH, Schiffsrepar-aturen und technische Beratung, Hafeninsel, 26382 Wilhelmshaven, Germany, *Tel:* +49 4421 430 1000, *Fax:* +49 4421 430 1029, *Email:* info@navitek.de, *Website:* www.navitek.de

Neue Jadewerft GmbH, Hannoversche Strasse 10, 26384 Wilhelmshaven, Germany, *Tel:* +49 4421 399 0, *Fax:* +49 4421 399100, *Email:* njw@neue-jadewerft.com, *Website:* www.neue-jadewerft.com Floating dock 150 m x 26.2 m x 12 m for max 8000 t. Slipway 80 m long for max 1800 t. Wet docking up to 300 000 t and 300 m length

Turbo-Technik Reparatur-Werft GmbH & Co, Hannoversche Strasse 11, D-26384 Wilhelmshaven, Germany, *Tel:* +49 4421 30780, *Fax:* +49 4421 305086, *Email:* info@turbotechnik.com, *Website:* www.turbotechnik.com Boiler manufacturing, maintenance, repairs, retubing. Diesel engine overhauls and repairs. Propeller, shaft seals. Turbo charger repairs. Ship repairs. Steam turbine repairs. Voyage repairs. Spare part reconditioning and service. Electrical repairs and rewind.

Ship Chandlers: Schiffsausrustung Wilhelmshaven Niederl. der Emder GmbH, P O Box 24 53, 26389 Wilhelmshaven, Germany, *Tel:* +49 4421 9800-0, *Fax:* +49 4421 980015, *Email:* saw@emder.de, *Website:* www.emder.de

Shipping Agents: Aug. Bolten Wm. Miller's Nachfolger (GmbH & Co.) KG, Allmers-strasse 24, 26386 Wilhelmshaven, Germany, *Tel:* +49 4421 507777, *Fax:* +49 4421 507775, *Email:* bolten.wilhelmshaven@aug-bolten.de, *Website:* www.aug-bolten.de

Rhenus Midgard GmbH, Luneburger Strasse 6, 26384 Wilhelmshaven, Germany, *Tel:* +49 4421 9360, *Fax:* +49 4421 936125, *Email:* agency.wilhelmshaven@de.rhenus.com, *Website:* www.rhenus.com

Neptun Schiffahrts-Agentur GmbH, Luisenstrasse 5, P O Box 2054, 26360 Wilhelm-shaven, Germany, *Tel:* +49 4421 15100, *Fax:* +49 4421 151015, *Email:* agency@neptunship.de, *Website:* www.neptunship.de

Sartori & Berger, Gokerstrasse 79a, 26384 Wilhelmshaven, Germany, *Tel:* +49 4421 93100, *Fax:* +49 4421 931040, *Email:* wilhelmshaven@sartori-berger.de, *Website:* www.sartori-berger.de

Surveyors: Societe Generale de Surveillance (SGS), SGS Controll-co GmbH, Wilhelmshaven, Germany, *Tel:* +49 4421 55973, *Fax:* +49 4421 56172, *Website:* www.sgs.com

Medical Facilities: Three hospitals within 10 km, one of which has a helicopter rescue base

Airport: Local airport for small aircraft and helicopters only. Nearest international airport at Bremen. Linked to Wilhelmshaven-Oldenburg rail rout 120 km

Development: Construction of JadeWeserPort Container Terminal featuring a terminal area of 120 ha with 1725 m of quay in depth of 18 m, to be operated by Eurogate Container Terminal Wilhelmshaven, and expected to be operational in 2011

Lloyd's Agent: Reck & Co. GmbH, Herrlichkeit 5, 28199 Bremen, Germany, *Tel:* +49 421 59834-0, *Fax:* +49 421 598 3450, *Email:* mail@reck.de, *Website:* www.reck.de

WISMAR

Lat 53° 53' N; Long 11° 27' E.

Admiralty Chart: 2359 **Admiralty Pilot:** 18
Time Zone: GMT +1 h **UNCTAD Locode:** DE WIS

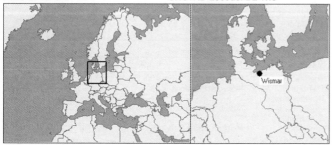

Principal Facilities:

P	Q	Y	G	C	R		B	D	T	A

Authority: Seehafen Wismar GmbH, Kopenhagener Strasse, Hafenhaus, 23966 Wismar, Germany, *Tel:* +49 3841 452 0, *Fax:* +49 3841 452304, *Email:* info@hafen-wismar.de, *Website:* www.hafen-wismar.de

Officials: Managing Director: Michael Kremp, *Tel:* +49 3841 452300, *Email:* mkremp@hafen-wismar.de.
Public Relations Manager: Sigrun Smeilus, *Tel:* +49 3841 452311, *Email:* ssmeilus@hafen-wismar.de.
Harbour Master: Harald Forst, *Tel:* +49 3841 452343, *Email:* hafenamt@wismar.de.

Port Security: ISPS compliant

Documentation: Health declaration, crew lists (3 copies), passenger lists (3 copies), bonded stores list, crew personal effects list, cargo documents, ship's certificates On arrival Master to complete Master's Declaration and Master's Report

Approach: Bay sheltered from all winds. Fairway from outer roads (fairway buoy Wismar) to harbour entrance is about 26 km long, well marked with buoys and landmarks. IALA 'A' buoy marking system

Anchorage: Outer Roads (N of Hannibal Shoal) in depths of 10-16.8 m with bottom of sand and stones in the following positions: 54° 06' 40" N; 11° 20' 60" E, 54° 06' 40" N; 11° 25' 40" E, 54° 04' 90" N; 11° 25' 40" E, 54° 04' 90" N; 11° 20' 60" E Inner Roads in depths of 6-9 m with bottom of sand and stones in the following positions: 53° 59' 80" N; 11° 20' 60" E, 53° 59' 50" N; 11° 21' 70" E, 53° 59' 03" N; 11° 21' 70" N; 53° 58' 30" N; 11° 21' 00" E, 53° 58' 50" N; 11° 20' 70" E

Pilotage: Compulsory for commercial vessels over 90 m loa and 13 m boa or draught over 5 m. 4 h notice required. Wismar pilots, VHF 24 h, meet vessels day and night near Wismar light buoy

Radio Frequency: Wismar Traffic on VHF Channel 12, Wismar Port on VHF Channel 11, Rugen Radio keep a constant watch on VHF Channel 16, Timmendorf VHF Channel 14

Weather: Prevailing westerly winds

Tides: Max/min +1.2 m/-1.2 m

Traffic: 2007, 1615 vessels, 4 140 000 t of cargo handled

Maximum Vessel Dimensions: 200 m loa, 28 m beam, 8.23 m draft (permission for draft of 8.5 m is possible)

Working Hours: Mon-Fri 0600-2200. Sat 0600-1400. Overtime if required

Accommodation:

Name	Length (m)	Draught (m)	Remarks
Wismar			
Berth 1	120	8.23	Liquid chemicals
Berth 2	180	6.7	Pulp/sawn logs (self loaders)
Berth 3	146	8.23	Sawn timber, pulp logs, sawn logs
Berth 4	147	8.23	General/bulk cargoes
Berth 5	118	8.23	General/bulk cargoes, grain
Berth 6	135	8.23	General/bulk cargoes
Berth 7	143	8.23	Potash, fertilisers, salt, chemicals
Berth 8	135	8.23	Potash, fertilisers, salt
Berth 9	128	8.23	Ro/ro cargoes
Berth 10	192	8.23	See [1] below
Berth 11	180	8.23	See [2] below
Berth 12	134	8.23	See [3] below
Berth 13	204	8.23	General/bulk cargoes, metals, scrap
Berth 14	202	8.23	General/bulk cargoes, metals, scrap
Berth 15	177	8.23	General/bulk cargoes, metals, scrap
Berth 16	149	6.7	Waiting berth at dolphins
Berth 17	149	6.1	Waiting berth at dolphins
Berth 18	181	8.23	Passenger vessels
Berth 19	156	7.56	Berths for tourism
Berth 20	142	7.62	Sailing boats
Berth 21	106	5.8	Berths for tourism

[1]*Berth 10:* General/bulk cargoes, metals, sawn timber, sawn logs, peat moss
[2]*Berth 11:* General/bulk cargoes, metals, sawn timber, sawn logs, peat moss
[3]*Berth 12:* General/bulk cargoes, metals, sawn timber, sawn logs, peat moss

Storage: Halls for weather and environmentally sensitive bulk cargoes of 60 000 t

Location	Open (m²)	Covered (m²)
Wismar	85000	19300

Mechanical Handling Equipment:

Location	Type	Capacity (t)
Wismar	Mult-purp. Cranes	45
Wismar	Forklifts	1.5–45

Bunkering: Diesel oil and fuel oil available by tank-cars only
Germany Transport & Logistics GmbH, Buchtstrasse 4, 22087 Hamburg, Germany, *Tel:* +49 40 64225 7070, *Fax:* +49 40 64225 7075, *Email:* info@gtl-hamburg.de
IBT Bunkering & Trading GmbH, Raboisen 32, 20095 Hamburg, Germany, *Tel:* +49 40 2201 191, *Fax:* +49 40 2295 030, *Email:* info@ibtbunker.com, *Website:* www.ibtbunker.com
Tramp Oil & Marine, World Fuel Services Corporation, 13th Floor, Portland House, Bressenden Place, London SW1E 5BH, United Kingdom, *Tel:* +44 20 7808 5000, *Fax:* +44 20 7808 5088, *Email:* pturner@wfscorp.com, *Website:* www.wfscorp.com

Waste Reception Facilities: Disposal of oily residues is possible via agent

Towage: One tug of 750 hp available; further capacity on demand

Shipping Agents: Ahlmann-Zerssen GmbH & Co KG, Kopenhagener Strasse, Hafenhaus, 23966 Wismar, Germany, *Tel:* +49 3841 210033, *Fax:* +49 3841 200219, *Email:* wismar@ahlmann-zerssen.de, *Website:* www.ahlmann-zerssen.de

Surveyors: Nippon Kaiji Kyokai, Wismar, Germany, *Tel:* +49 3841 704609, *Fax:* +49 3841 704604, *Website:* www.classnk.or.jp

Medical Facilities: Local hospital and harbour doctor

Airport: Lubeck-Blankensee, 50 km. Rostock-Laage, 80 km. Hamburg, 120 km

Railway: Loading and unloading facilities; 20 km harbour-own track network

Lloyd's Agent: Reck & Co. GmbH, P O Box 42 04 25, D-12099 Berlin, Germany, *Tel:* +49 30 745 9033, *Fax:* +49 30 8049 6422, *Email:* berlin@reck.de, *Website:* www.reck.de

WOLGAST

Lat 54° 3' N; Long 13° 47' E.

Admiralty Chart: 2150	**Admiralty Pilot:** 19
Time Zone: GMT +1 h	**UNCTAD Locode:** DE WOL

Principal Facilities:

Q	Y	G			B	D		A

Authority: Wolgaster Hafengesellschaft mbH, Peenestrasse 1, 17438 Wolgast, Germany, *Tel:* +49 3836 201703, *Fax:* +49 3836 201705, *Email:* wolgast-hafen@t-online.de, *Website:* www.wolgast-port.de

Officials: Managing Director: Hellmut Heinz.
Harbour Master: Helmut Gerhardt, *Tel:* +49 3836 251137, *Email:* helmut.gerhardt@wolgast.de.

Port Security: ISPS compliant

Anchorage: Landtief Reede, Osttief Reede and Ruden Reede

Pilotage: Pilot station at Stralsund

Radio Frequency: Wolgast Traffic on VHF Channel 9 and Wolgast Port on VHF Channel 15

Traffic: 2001, 527 vessels

Maximum Vessel Dimensions: 150 m loa, 24 m breadth, 5.7 m draft

Principal Imports and Exports: Imports: Agribulk, Agribulk commodities, Animal feed, Building materials, Fertiliser, General cargo, Stone. Exports: Bulk cargo, General cargo, Grain, Liquid products, Wood & timber manufactures.

Working Hours: Mon-Fri 0600-2200 or as required

Accommodation:

Name	Length (m)	Depth (m)	Draught (m)	Remarks
Wolgast				
Stadthafen	650	6	5.7	Seven berths (8-14)
Sudhafen	900	6	5.7	Six berths (1-6)

Storage:

Location	Open (m²)	Covered (m²)	Sheds / Warehouses	Grain (t)
Stadthafen	10000	5150	2	21500
Sudhafen	8000		1	25000

Mechanical Handling Equipment:

Location	Type	Qty
Wolgast	Mobile Cranes	8

Location	Type	Qty
Wolgast	Portal Cranes	2

Bunkering: Available

Repair & Maintenance: Peene-Werft GmbH, Schiffbauerdamm 1, P O Box 1164, 17438 Wolgast, Germany, *Tel:* +49 3836 250501, *Fax:* +49 3836 250153, *Email:* info.pw@peene-werft.de, *Website:* www.peene-werft.de

Shipping Agents: Ahlmann-Zerssen GmbH & Co KG, Schusterstrasse 1, 17438 Wolgast, Germany, *Tel:* +49 3836 237233, *Fax:* +49 3836 237235, *Email:* wolgast@ahlmann-zerssen.de, *Website:* www.ahlmann-zerssen.de

Medical Facilities: Hospital in Wolgast, 1000 m

Airport: Heringsdorf, 35 km

Railway: Wolgast, 300 m

Lloyd's Agent: Reck & Co. GmbH, P O Box 42 04 25, D-12099 Berlin, Germany, *Tel:* +49 30 745 9033, *Fax:* +49 30 8049 6422, *Email:* berlin@reck.de, *Website:* www.reck.de

GHANA

TAKORADI

Lat 4° 53' N; Long 1° 45' W.

Admiralty Chart: 3102	**Admiralty Pilot:** 1
Time Zone: GMT	**UNCTAD Locode:** GH TKD

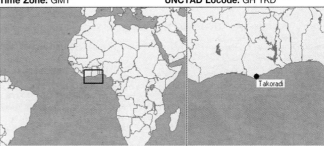

Principal Facilities:

P		Y	G	C	R		B		T	

Authority: Ghana Ports & Harbours Authority, P O Box 708, Takoradi, Ghana, *Tel:* +233 31 24073, *Fax:* +233 31 22814, *Email:* takoradi@ghanaports.net, *Website:* www.ghanaports.gov.gh

Officials: Port Director: Nestor P. Galley.
Marketing Manager: George Bredu.
Harbour Master: Capt Frederick Adjaben, *Email:* fadjaben@yahoo.com.

Port Security: ISPS compliant

Approach: Apart from the 'Takoradi Reef' S of the main breakwater, approach is free from hazards and sand bars. Channel depth at entrance approx 11.5 m

Anchorage: At Takoradi Bay in depth of 11 m plus

Pilotage: Compulsory. Boarding ground NE by six cables. 24 h service

Radio Frequency: VHF Channels 14 and 16

Weather: Generally calm but occasional easterly squalls from April to June

Tides: Semi-diurnal. Tidal range approx 1.0 m

Traffic: 2006, 610 vessels, 4 719 000 t of cargo handled

Maximum Vessel Dimensions: 185.9 m loa; 10.97 m d aft, 10.36 m d fwd

Principal Imports and Exports: Imports: Break-bulk cargoes, Clinker, Containerised cargoes, Industrial raw materials, Petroleum products, Wheat. Exports: Agricultural produce, Bauxite, Cocoa, Containerised cargoes, Forest products, Manganese.

Working Hours: 0730-1230, 1400-1700; overtime for vessels discharging/loading on request. Port runs two shifts from 0730-1930 and 1930-0730 with 30 mins break for meals. Extra hours considered as overtime payable at double rate

Accommodation:

Name	Depth (m)	Remarks
Takoradi		See ¹ below
Wharves 2-4	9	See ² below
Wharves 5-6	10	
Buoy 1	10.6	
Buoy 3	11	
Buoy 4	9.5	
Buoy 5	8.6	
Buoys 6-8	8	
Private Wharves		Oil wharf & manganese wharf

¹*Takoradi:* Bulk facilities: Bauxite terminal and specialised manganese ore wharf; loading rate of about 300 t/h at both facilities
Tanker facilities: One berth operated by Shell Co of Ghana; length of 175.2 m, 8.84 m d; no night berthing; water and bunkers available
²*Wharves 2-4:* Ro/ro berth with ramp at W end of No.2 wharf for medium sized vessels drawing about 7.5 m. Vessels drawing between 7.5 and 8.6 m are accommodated at No.4 wharf

---

Key to Principal Facilities:—

A=Airport	**C**=Containers	**G**=General Cargo
B=Bunkers	**D**=Dry Dock	**L**=Cruise

P=Petroleum	**R**=Ro/Ro	**Y**=Dry Bulk
Q=Other Liquid Bulk	**T**=Towage (where available from port)	

Storage: Six transit sheds, cap 12 500 t; two sawn timber sheds, cap 3000 t; nineteen cocoa sheds, cap 50 000 t; one cargo platform for containers with open storage area of 5000 t; 100 reefer points

Mechanical Handling Equipment:

Location	Type	Capacity (t)	Qty
Takoradi	Mobile Cranes	14–90	4
Takoradi	Reach Stackers	10–45	9
Takoradi	Forklifts	3–28	82

Bunkering: Bominflot, Bominflot Ltd, 5-7 Ravensbourne Road, Bromley, Kent BR1 1HN, United Kingdom, *Tel:* +44 20 8315 5400, *Fax:* +44 20 8315 5429, *Email:* mail@bominflot.co.uk, *Website:* www.bominflot.net – *Grades:* IFO; MGO
ExxonMobil Marine Fuels, Mailpoint 31, ExxonMobil House, Ermyn Way, Leatherhead, Surrey KT22 8UX, United Kingdom, *Tel:* +44 1372 222 000, *Fax:* +44 1372 223 922, *Email:* marine.fuels@exxonmobil.com, *Website:* www.exxonmobil.com – *Grades:* MGO – *Delivery Mode:* truck
Fianoo Ship Chandler, P O Box 210, Takoradi, Ghana, *Tel:* +233 20 811 8027, *Fax:* +233 20 23006, *Email:* supmark@africaonline.com.gh
Jed Tech Ltd., P O Box 14801, No.79B Virkam Estates, Baatsonaa, Spintex Road, Accra 14801, Ghana, *Tel:* +233 21 20813 5742, *Fax:* +233 21 81 5765, *Email:* booms52@yahoo.com

Towage: Compulsory. Tugs available up to 5000 hp from Port Authority

Repair & Maintenance: A small drydock used only for fishing vessels and a 500 t cap patent slip are owned by Ghana Ports & Harbours Authority

Shipping Agents: Afritramp, 13/13 New Manful Road, P O Box 0712, Market Circle, Takoradi, Ghana, *Tel:* +233 31 20987, *Fax:* +233 31 22454, *Email:* afritramp.ghana@gh.dti.bollore.com, *Website:* www.afritrampoilfield.com
Antrak Group (GH) Ltd, Harbour Business Area, No 13/13 Amanful Road, Opposite Ghana House, Takoradi, Ghana, *Tel:* +233 31 22779, *Fax:* +233 31 22454, *Email:* adwowa.baiden@gh-antrak.com
Cross Ocean Agencies Ltd, GPHA Shed 4 Top, Takoradi Port, Takoradi, Ghana, *Tel:* +233 31 20530, *Fax:* +233 31 20530, *Email:* crossoceantdi@ghana.com, *Website:* www.crossocean.com.gh
Deseret West Agencies, P O Box ME 1185, Takoradi, Ghana, *Fax:* +233 31 25245, *Email:* aas@yahoo.com
Gusapa Agencies Ltd, Swanzy House, Axim Road, P O Box 178, Takoradi, Ghana, *Tel:* +233 31 22727, *Fax:* +233 31 24727
Mediterranean Shipping Company, MSCA (Ghana) Ltd, Dock Road, P O Box 27, Takoradi, Ghana, *Tel:* +233 31 22562, *Fax:* +233 31 23372, *Email:* info.takoradi@mscgh.mscgva.ch, *Website:* www.mscgva.ch
A.P. Moller-Maersk Group, Maersk Ghana Ltd, Chapel Hill, off Axim Road, P O Box 839, Takoradi, Ghana, *Tel:* +233 31 21120, *Fax:* +233 31 21110, *Email:* tkdord@maersk.com, *Website:* www.maerskline.com
Panalpina (Ghana) Ltd, 36 Nzema Road, Harbour Area, Takoradi, Ghana, *Tel:* +233 31 23659, *Fax:* +233 31 23631, *Email:* patakoradi@tkd.panmail.com
Paramount Investment Ghana Ltd, P O Box 113, Takoradi, Ghana, *Tel:* +233 31 21668, *Fax:* +233 31 24586
Saga-Ghana Ltd, Harbour Area, P O Box 268, Takoradi, Ghana, *Tel:* +233 31 22911/2/3, *Fax:* +233 31 24747
Supermaritime Benin S.A., P O Box 1154, Scoa Building, Harbour Road, Takoradi, Ghana, *Tel:* +233 31 24262/23767, *Fax:* +233 31 23006, *Email:* supmartk@africaonline.com.gh

Stevedoring Companies: Atlantic Port Services Ltd, Axim Road, Harbour Area, P O Box 76, Takoradi, Ghana, *Tel:* +233 31 22019, *Fax:* +233 31 24818, *Email:* info@atlanticportservices.com, *Website:* www.atlanticportservices.com
Dashwood Shipping Agencies Ltd, P O Box 2966, Takoradi, Ghana, *Tel:* +233 31 32384, *Fax:* +233 31 32384
Odart Stevedoring Co Ltd, P O Box AX295, Takoradi, Ghana, *Tel:* +233 31 25486, *Fax:* +233 31 25486, *Email:* info@odartstevedore.com, *Website:* www.odartstevedore.com
Speedline Stevedoring Services Ltd, P O Box 374, Takoradi, Ghana, *Tel:* +233 31 30196, *Fax:* +233 31 30195

Medical Facilities: Well equipped port clinic, also hospitals in Takoradi and Sekondi

Railway: Ghana Railway Corporation, located 100 m from port

Lloyd's Agent: Ghana Inspections Ltd, TFS Building 3rd Floor, Room 405, Community 1, Tema, Ghana, *Tel:* +233 22 205523, *Fax:* +233 22 204356, *Email:* its@gil-its.com, *Website:* www.gil-its.com

TEMA

Lat 5° 37' N; Long 0° 0' E.

Admiralty Chart: 1380/3432		**Admiralty Pilot:** 1
Time Zone: GMT		**UNCTAD Locode:** GH TEM

Principal Facilities:

P		Y	G	C	R		B	D	T	A	

Authority: Ghana Ports & Harbours Authority, P O Box 150, Tema, Ghana, *Tel:* +233 22 202631, *Fax:* +233 22 202812, *Email:* headquarters@ghanaports.net, *Website:* www.ghanaports.gov.gh

Officials: Director General: Ben Owusu Mensah, *Email:* dg@ghanaports.com.
Port Director: Gordon Anim, *Email:* ganim@ghanaports.net.
Marketing Manager: Alice Torkonoo, *Email:* atorkornoo@ghanaports.net.

Port Security: ISPS compliant

Documentation: Port Health: maritime declaration of health, valid certificates for cholera and yellow fever, derat certificate, crew list (1 copy), passenger list (1 copy)
Immigration: crew list (1 copy), passenger list (1 copy), ports of call list (1 copy)
Customs: manifest (2 copies), dangerous cargo list, crew list (1 copy), passenger list (1 copy), ports of call list (1 copy), port clearance issued by customs at last port of call

Approach: 125 m wide, 12.5 m deep access channel

Anchorage: Safe anchorage is available 0.75-2 miles from ENE to SW off main entrance in depth of 30.6 m with good holding ground

Pilotage: Compulsory. Arrivals 0600-1800. Departures 0600-2300 except for Valco and Oil berth, departures 0600-1800

Radio Frequency: 24 h watch on VHF Channels 14 and 16. Channel 16 is the national listening channel and Channel 14 is the port working channel

Weather: SW squalls during the whole year except for July and August

Tides: Range of tide 1.92 m; HW 2.01 m, LW 0.09 m

Traffic: 2006, 7 678 000 t of cargo handled, 425 409 TEU's

Maximum Vessel Dimensions: 244 m loa, 9.7 m draft

Principal Imports and Exports: Imports: Alumina, Cereals, Clinker, Crude oil, Petroleum products, Sugar, Vehicles. Exports: Aluminium, Chemicals, Cocoa products, Coffee, Food products, Fruit & vegetables, Sawn timber.

Working Hours: 0730-1230, 1400-1700. Overtime may be worked for loading/discharging operations up to 2000 with an additional two hours' work if vessel is to sail immediately. Weekend: overtime at double rates

Accommodation:

Name	Depth (m)	Remarks
Tema		See [1] below
Berth 1	11.5	Max 183 m loa
Berth 2	11.5	Max 183 m loa
Berth 3		Max 183 m loa
Berth 4	9	Max 183 m loa
Berth 5	9	Max 183 m loa
Berth 6	8	Max 183 m loa
Berth 7	8	Max 183 m loa
Berth 8	8	Max 183 m loa
Berth 9	8	Max 183 m loa
Berth 10	8	Max 183 m loa
Berth 11	8	Max 183 m loa
Berth 12	8	Max 183 m loa
Oil Berth	9.6	Max 244 m loa
Valco Berth	9.6	Max 175 m loa

[1]*Tema:* Circular turning basin of 225 m radius in depth of 11.5 m. Containers handled at the general cargo berths. Container yard area of 4460 m2. Also specialised container handling facilities available at Berth 12 and the adjacent landside area with two 35 t multi-purpose cranes together with a container freight station, a container parking area and reefer points

Storage:

Location	Open (m²)	Covered (m²)
Tema	97200	53270

Mechanical Handling Equipment:

Location	Type	Capacity (t)	Qty
Tema	Mult-purp. Cranes	35	2
Tema	Mobile Cranes	19	1
Tema	Mobile Cranes	6	2
Tema	Mobile Cranes	3	1
Berth 1	Mult-purp. Cranes	5	1
Berth 1	Mult-purp. Cranes	3	3
Berth 2	Mult-purp. Cranes	3	3
Berth 2	Mult-purp. Cranes	5	1
Berth 4	Mult-purp. Cranes	3	3
Berth 4	Mult-purp. Cranes	5	1
Berth 5	Mult-purp. Cranes	5	1
Berth 5	Mult-purp. Cranes	3	3

Bunkering: No coal bunkers available
City Marine Services, P O Box BT 442, City Marine Services, Community2, Tema, Ghana, *Tel:* +233 22 201949, *Fax:* +233 22 201949, *Email:* citymarineservice@yahoo.com
Inter Maritime Services Ltd, 2nd Floor, Obuowe Building, Inner Fishing Harbour, Tema Fishing Harbour, Accra, Ghana, *Tel:* +233 22 208 437, *Fax:* +233 22 215 759, *Email:* intermaritime@yahoo.com, *Website:* www.intermaritimeghana.com
Tramp Oil & Marine, World Fuel Services Corporation, 13th Floor, Portland House, Bressenden Place, London SW1E 5BH, United Kingdom, *Tel:* +44 20 7808 5000, *Fax:* +44 20 7808 5088, *Email:* pturner@wfscorp.com, *Website:* www.wfscorp.com – *Grades:* all grades

Towage: Six tugs available of 1320-2200 hp

Repair & Maintenance: There is a small dry dock 53.03 m in length and 14.02 m wide at the gate. Also two slipways, one of 150 t and one of 12 t
PSC Tema Shipyard Ltd, Harbour Road, P O Box 454, Tema, Ghana, *Tel:* +233 22 202641, *Fax:* +233 22 202123 Two dry docks: No.1 277 m x 45 m x 6 m for vessels up to 100 000 dwt. No.2 106 m x 13 m x 5 m for vessels up to 10 000 dwt. Quays 368 m long with max draught 6 m

Ship Chandlers: Sekpo Enterprise, 2nd Floor, Soli Building, Tema Inner Fishing Harbour, P O Box 1244, Tema, Ghana, *Tel:* +233 22 203519, *Fax:* +233 22 202984, *Email:* sekpo@africaonline.com.gh, *Website:* www.sekpo.com Manager: Cornelius K Sekpodome
Allport Ghana Ltd, P O Box PMB, Tema, Ghana, *Tel:* +233 22 203995, *Fax:* +233 22 203996, *Email:* info@allportghana.com, *Website:* www.allportghana.com
Benya Shipping S.A., P O Box 2573, Tema, Ghana, *Tel:* +233 22 202846, *Fax:* +233 22 204796, *Email:* ekabenyaship@yahoo.com
City Marine Services, P O Box BT 442, City Marine Services, Community2, Tema, Ghana, *Tel:* +233 22 201949, *Fax:* +233 22 201949, *Email:* citymarineservice@yahoo.com
Cone Freight Logistics (Gh) Ltd, TFS Building, Suite 102, Comm 1, P O Box 968, Tema, Ghana, *Tel:* +233 22 204687, *Fax:* +233 22 216845, *Email:* conefreight@yahoo.com
Felixwalters Agencies Ghana Limited, Torman Street Fishing Road, Kaas Fisheries Building, P O Box 1819, Tema, Ghana, *Tel:* +233 22 200176, *Fax:* +233 22 200177, *Email:* felixwalters_ghanauk@yahoo.co.uk
Jebril Ghia Limited, Box DTD HSE Plot 3, Tema Community 11, Near the Presby Church, Tema, Ghana, *Tel:* +233 22 311009, *Fax:* +233 22 311008, *Email:* jebrilghialtd@yahoo.com
Joemar Shipping & Investment Company Ltd, Joemar House, Near internal Revenue Service, Community Four, P O Box 167, Tema, Ghana, *Tel:* +233 22 214079, *Fax:* +233 22 212519, *Email:* marfo@joemarshipping.net
Sealane Shipping & Trading Company Limited, 2nd Floor, Room 308 Community Four, Thorky House, P O Box 93, Tema, Ghana, *Tel:* +233 22 207074, *Fax:* +233 22 200470, *Email:* sealane@ghana.com

Shipping Agents: ACVEG Shipping & Trading Co. Ltd, GPHA Civil Workshop Railway, Opposite Graphic Corporation, P O Box SC 123, Tema, Ghana, *Tel:* +233 22 212322, *Fax:* +233 22 215120, *Email:* info@acvegshipping.com, *Website:* www.acvegshipping.net
Afimexco Ghana Ltd, Ghana Commercial Bank Building, near Meridian, 3rd Floor Room 317, and P O Box CO1610, Tema, Ghana, *Tel:* +233 22 201065, *Fax:* +233 22 201066, *Email:* ceo@afimexcogroupe.com
Afritramp, Scanship/Afritramp, Mensah Utreh Road, Commercial Warehouse Area, P O Box 64, Tema, Ghana, *Tel:* +233 22 212030, *Fax:* +233 22 212499, *Email:* afritramp.ghana@gh.dti.bollore.com, *Website:* www.afritrampoilfield.com
Air-Sea Service Gh. Ltd, West Coast Dyeing Industry Heavy Ind. Area, Tema, Ghana, *Tel:* +233 22 304399, *Fax:* +233 22 302601, *Email:* airseagh@yahoo.com
Allport Ghana Ltd, P O Box PMB, Tema, Ghana, *Tel:* +233 22 203995, *Fax:* +233 22 203996, *Email:* info@allportghana.com, *Website:* www.allportghana.com
Alraine Shipping Agencies Ltd, P O Box 587, Tema, Ghana, *Tel:* +233 22 202651, *Fax:* +233 22 202571
Antrak Group (GH) Ltd, P O Box 148, Tema, Ghana, *Tel:* +233 22 202068, *Fax:* +233 22 202268, *Email:* jean-pierre.david@gh-antrak.com
Carloking Services, 101/103 Vertical Court, P O Box 11344, Tema, Ghana, *Tel:* +233 22 204554, *Fax:* +233 22 201395, *Email:* mac@carloking.com, *Website:* www.carloking.com
City Marine Services, P O Box BT 442, City Marine Services, Community2, Tema, Ghana, *Tel:* +233 22 201949, *Fax:* +233 22 201949, *Email:* citymarineservice@yahoo.com
Cone Freight Logistics (Gh) Ltd, TFS Building, Suite 102, Comm 1, P O Box 968, Tema, Ghana, *Tel:* +233 22 204687, *Fax:* +233 22 216845, *Email:* conefreight@yahoo.com
Consolidated Shipping Agencies Ltd, Tema Main Harbour, Commercial Warehouse Area, Tema, Ghana, *Tel:* +233 22 204016, *Fax:* +233 22 204017, *Website:* www.conshiponline.com
Cross Ocean Agencies Ltd, Room 204/205, 2nd Floor, Ecobank Premises, Meridian Road, P O Box CO1914, Tema, Ghana, *Tel:* +233 22 212359, *Fax:* +233 22 212357, *Email:* coal@crossocean.com.gh, *Website:* www.crossocean.com.gh
Daddo Maritime Services Ltd, 4th Floor, Tema Central Mall Building, Nestle-Sanyo Road, Tema, Ghana, *Email:* dms.operations@daddogroup.com, *Website:* www.daddogroup.com
Dei Shipping Trading Company Limited, Greenwich Tower, 1st Floor, P O Box CS8511, Tema, Ghana, *Tel:* +233 22 206107, *Fax:* +233 22 204519, *Email:* deiship@africaonline.com.gh
Dolphin Shipping Services Ltd, Manna House, 3rd Floor, Inner Fishing Harbour, P O Box CO 986, Tema, Ghana, *Tel:* +233 22 204292, *Fax:* +233 22 202984, *Email:* dolphin@africaonline.com.gh, *Website:* www.dolphinships.com
Ebamas International Freight Services, P M B Co 95, P O Box 18, Community 1, Tema, Ghana, *Fax:* +233 22 214994, *Email:* ebamas2000@yahoo.com
Faithwings Ventures Co. Ltd, Agency Block, Room 4A, Main Harbour, P O Box CS 8581, Tema, Ghana, *Tel:* +233 22 204075, *Email:* faithfvcl@yahoo.co.uk
Felixwalters Agencies Ghana Limited, Torman Street Fishing Road, Kaas Fisheries Building, P O Box 1819, Tema, Ghana, *Tel:* +233 22 200176, *Fax:* +233 22 200177, *Email:* felixwalters_ghanauk@yahoo.co.uk
Flying Eagle Shipping Ltd, Torman Str, Fishing Harbor Road, Kaas Fishing Biding, Prudential Bank, P O Box CO 1819, Tema, Ghana, *Tel:* +233 22 200176, *Fax:* +233 22 296862, *Email:* sales@flyingeagleshipping.com, *Website:* www.flyingeagleshipping.com
Goshmelo Shipping & Trading Co. Ltd, P O Box TT-575, New Town, Tema, Ghana, *Tel:* +233 22 212387, *Fax:* +233 22 212387, *Email:* info@goshmeloghana.com, *Website:* www.goshmeloghana.com
Hellmann Worldwide Logistics, Asafoatse Kotei Building, Tema, Ghana, *Tel:* +233 22 202097, *Fax:* +233 22 214994, *Email:* info-gh@gh.hellmann.net, *Website:* www.hellmann.net
Hull Blyth Group, African Steamship Hull Blyth Ghana Ltd, Seatec House, 38 Akosombo Road, P O Box 214, Tema, Ghana, *Tel:* +233 22 300894/5, *Fax:* +233 22 300898, *Email:* hbenquiries@hull-blyth.com, *Website:* www.hull-blyth.com
Inter-Continental Shipp. Ltd, P O Box 1621, Tema, Ghana, *Tel:* +233 22 202905, *Fax:* +233 22 202059
International Shipping Agency Ghana Ltd, P O Box 2478, Tema, Ghana, *Tel:* +233 22 210675, *Fax:* +233 22 210680, *Email:* seeman.amir@isag-tem.com
Jetlinks Shipping Ltd, Comm 9, P O Box CE 11478, Tema, Ghana, *Tel:* +233 22 310190, *Fax:* +233 22 310890, *Email:* jetlinksshipping@yahoo.com
Joemar Shipping & Investment Company Ltd, Joemar House, Near internal Revenue Service, Community Four, P O Box 167, Tema, Ghana, *Tel:* +233 22 214079, *Fax:* +233 22 212519, *Email:* marfo@joemarshipping.net
Judah Shipping Co. Ltd, Opposite Apostolic Church and Adjacent to Guiness Depot, Community 5, P O Box CT 895, Tema Comm. 5, Accra, Ghana, *Tel:* +233 22 204324, *Fax:* +233 22 214800, *Email:* judah_shipping@yahoo.co.uk
Khuda Services Gh. Ltd, Greenwich Tower, Room 4, Tema, Ghana, *Tel:* +233 22 210756, *Fax:* +233 22 206157, *Email:* labaran@aol.com, *Website:* www.khudaservices.com
Liner Agencies & Trading (Ghana) Ltd, P O Box 214, Tema, Ghana, *Tel:* +233 22 202173, *Fax:* +233 22 202989
Map Shipping Co Ltd, 4th Floor, Getma House, Fishing Habour Road, Tema, Ghana, *Tel:* +233 22 211919, *Fax:* +233 22 205384, *Email:* mapship@africaonline.com.gh, *Website:* www.mapship.com
Maritime Agencies (West Africa) Ltd, P O Box B339, Tema, Ghana, *Tel:* +233 22 712471, *Fax:* +233 22 202370, *Email:* ama@ama-shipping.com
Matapee Agency Ltd, P O Box 1614, Tema, Ghana, *Tel:* +233 22 202093, *Fax:* +233 22 213511, *Email:* matapee2006@yahoo.co.uk
McDan Shipping Company Ltd, Room 6 1st Floor, GIFF Secretariat, Opposite Meridian Hotel, Tema Harbour Area, Tema, Ghana, *Tel:* +233 22 210146, *Fax:* +233 22 216495, *Email:* dan@mcdanshipping.net, *Website:* www.mcdanshipping.net
Mediterranean Shipping Company, MSCA (Ghana) Ltd, James Ahiadome Complex, Meridian Street, P O Box CO 3010, Tema, Ghana, *Tel:* +233 22 211839, *Fax:* +233 22 200424, *Email:* info.tema@mscgh.mscgva.ch, *Website:* www.mscgva.ch
A.P. Moller-Maersk Group, Maersk Ghana Ltd, Obourwe Building, Torman Road, Fishing Harbour Area, P O Box 8800, Tema, Ghana, *Tel:* +233 22 206740, *Fax:* +233 22 202048, *Email:* tmaordimp@maersk.com, *Website:* www.maerskline.com
Navigators International Ltd, Long-Room, behind CEPS Building, P O Box Ce 11669, Tema, Ghana, *Tel:* +233 22 203299, *Fax:* +233 22 293303, *Email:* navigators@ghana.com, *Website:* www.navigatorsinternational.com
Noble Shipping Ag. Ltd, Ground Floor, Black Start Line Building, P O Box 6990, Tema, Ghana, *Tel:* +233 22 206651, *Fax:* +233 22 206651, *Email:* nobleshipping@yahoo.com
Ovimex International Ghana Ltd, Sonturk Building, Comm 2, P O Box 1957, Tema, Ghana, *Tel:* +233 22 201587, *Email:* ovimex@africaonline.com.gh
Panalpina (Ghana) Ltd, P O Box 132, Tema, Ghana, *Tel:* +233 22 204899/204223, *Fax:* +233 22 206694, *Email:* info.tema@panalpina.com, *Website:* www.panalpina.com
Paramount Investment Ghana Ltd, Community One, P O Box 807, Tema, Ghana, *Tel:* +233 22 206527, *Fax:* +233 22 204778, *Email:* benbaisie@hotmail.com
Premier Handlers Ltd, Commercial 2, Shopping Center Area, P O Box BT 662, Tema, Ghana, *Tel:* +233 22 201136, *Fax:* +233 22 214849, *Email:* appiah-albert@yahoo.com
Ro-Ro Services (Ghana) Ltd, P O Box 148, Tema, Ghana, *Tel:* +233 22 206586, *Fax:* +233 22 202268
Saga-Ghana Ltd, P O Box 215, Tema, Ghana, *Tel:* +233 22 204031/5, *Fax:* +233 22 204035, *Email:* sagatema@africaonline.com.gh
Santa Shipping Agency, Former Talk of the Town Hotel, Comm. 2, P O Box1836, Tema, Ghana, *Tel:* +233 22 205540, *Fax:* +233 22 205161, *Email:* santaflo@yahoo.com
Scanship (Ghana) Ltd, Mensah Utreh Road, P O Box 64, Tema, Ghana, *Tel:* +233 22 202651, *Fax:* +233 22 712932, *Email:* scan@scanship-gh.com
Sealane Shipping & Trading Company Limited, 2nd Floor, Room 308 Community Four, Thorky House, P O Box 93, Tema, Ghana, *Tel:* +233 22 207074, *Fax:* +233 22 200470, *Email:* sealane@ghana.com
Societe Inter-Continentale d'Affrements et d'Agence Maritime (SICAAM S.A.), Sicaam-GH Ltd, Ampenebea House, Community 9, Tema, Ghana, *Tel:* +233 22 306421, *Fax:* +233 22 306309, *Email:* sicamship@africaonline.com.gh
Super Shipping Services Ltd, P O Box KIA 9270, Accra, Ghana, *Tel:* +233 22 206050, *Fax:* +233 22 205791, *Email:* supershipping7@yahoo.com
Supermaritime Benin S.A., P O Box 151, Industrial Area Community 1, New Town, Tema, Ghana, *Tel:* +233 22 202874, *Fax:* +233 22 206777, *Email:* opsghana@supermaritime.net, *Website:* www.supermaritime.com
Teamwork Freight Services, TFS Building, Tema Town Center, Commercial 1, P O

Key to Principal Facilities:—
A=Airport C=Containers G=General Cargo P=Petroleum R=Ro/Ro Y=Dry Bulk
B=Bunkers D=Dry Dock L=Cruise Q=Other Liquid Bulk T=Towage (where available from port)

Box CO 2078, Tema, Ghana, *Tel:* +233 22 206364, *Fax:* +233 22 202074, *Email:* teamwork@africaonline.com.gh

Trans Global Shipping Limited, 134 Commercial Warehouse Area, Main Harbour, Near Shell Building, P O Box AN 3108, Tema, Ghana, *Tel:* +233 22 202222, *Fax:* +233 22 206568, *Email:* trans@transglobalgh.com, *Website:* www.transglobalgh.com

Vano Trading Co. Ltd, 3rd Floor Commercial Bank, P O Box AS467 Ashaiman, Tema, Ghana, *Fax:* +233 22 252027, *Email:* vanotrad@yahoo.com

Walina Ghana Ltd, Bits & Pieces Building, Comm 1, P O Box CT712, Tema, Ghana, *Tel:* +233 22 212023, *Fax:* +233 22 216421

Stevedoring Companies: Allport Ghana Ltd, P O Box PMB, Tema, Ghana, *Tel:* +233 22 203995, *Fax:* +233 22 203996, *Email:* info@allportghana.com, *Website:* www.allportghana.com

Atlantic Port Services Ltd, P O Box 360, Tema, Ghana, *Tel:* +233 22 204271, *Fax:* +233 22 204272, *Email:* apstema@ighmail.com, *Website:* www.atlanticportservices.com

Dashwood Shipping Agencies Ltd, P O Box 797, Tema, Ghana, *Tel:* +233 22 208604, *Fax:* +233 22 208605

Golden Gate Services Ltd, Bits & Pieces Building, Comm 1, P O Box CT712, Accra, Tema, Ghana, *Tel:* +233 22 201000, *Fax:* +233 22 216421, *Email:* goldgate@ghana.com

Map Shipping Co Ltd, 4th Floor, Getma House, Fishing Habour Road, Tema, Ghana, *Tel:* +233 22 211919, *Fax:* +233 22 205384, *Email:* mapship@africaonline.com.gh, *Website:* www.mapship.com

McDan Shipping Company Ltd, Room 6 1st Floor, GIFF Secretariat, Opposite Meridian Hotel, Tema Harbour Area, Tema, Ghana, *Tel:* +233 22 210146, *Fax:* +233 22 216495, *Email:* dan@mcdanshipping.net, *Website:* www.mcdanshipping.net

Odart Stevedoring Co Ltd, 3rd Floor Oceanic Building, Fishing Harbour Road, Tema, Ghana, *Tel:* +233 22 216300, *Fax:* +233 22 210662, *Email:* info@odartstevedore.com, *Website:* www.odartstevedore.com

Speedline Stevedoring Services Ltd, P O Box CO1453, Merskline Building, Comm 1, Tema, Ghana, *Tel:* +233 22 213126, *Fax:* +233 22 204219, *Email:* speedlinestevedoring@hotmail.com

Surveyors: Allport Ghana Ltd, P O Box PMB, Tema, Ghana, *Tel:* +233 22 203995, *Fax:* +233 22 203996, *Email:* info@allportghana.com, *Website:* www.allportghana.com

Bureau Veritas, c/o Wiltex Ltd, P O Box 623, Tema, Ghana, *Tel:* +233 22 202183, *Fax:* +233 22 206540, *Website:* www.bureauveritas.com

Det Norske Veritas A/S, Room SF7, Second Floor, Evergreen House, Community 4, Tema, Ghana, *Tel:* +233 22 215912, *Fax:* +233 22 215911, *Website:* www.dnv.com

Ghana Inspections Ltd, TFS Building 3rd Floor, Room 405, Community 1, Tema, Ghana, *Tel:* +233 22 205523, *Fax:* +233 22 204356, *Email:* its@gil-its.com, *Website:* www.gil-its.com

Nippon Kaiji Kyokai, Greenwich Maritime Company Ltd, Inner Fishing Harbour, 1st Floor, Kaleawo Ice Plant, P O Box 8493, Tema, Ghana, *Tel:* +233 22 206572, *Fax:* +233 22 203543, *Website:* www.classnk.or.jp

Omega Marine Ghana Ltd, House No. RP 11-011 Community, 11 P O Box CE 12185, Tema, Ghana, *Tel:* +233 22 301205, *Fax:* +233 22 301199, *Website:* www.omega-marine.com

Wiltex Ltd, P O Box 623, Tema, Ghana, *Tel:* +233 22 202183, *Fax:* +233 22 206540, *Email:* wiltex@4u.com.gh, *Website:* www.wiltexghana.com

Medical Facilities: Port clinic available but serious cases are referred to the General Hospital

Airport: Kotoka International Airport, 28 km

Development: Berths 1 and 2 are being extended to provide a dedicated container terminal with 570 m of quay capable of handling two 250 m long container vessels simultaneously

Lloyd's Agent: Ghana Inspections Ltd, TFS Building 3rd Floor, Room 405, Community 1, Tema, Ghana, *Tel:* +233 22 205523, *Fax:* +233 22 204356, *Email:* its@gil-its.com, *Website:* www.gil-its.com

GIBRALTAR

GIBRALTAR

Lat 36° 8' N; Long 5° 21' W.

Admiralty Chart: 144/145	**Admiralty Pilot:** 67
Time Zone: GMT +1 h	**UNCTAD Locode:** GI GIB

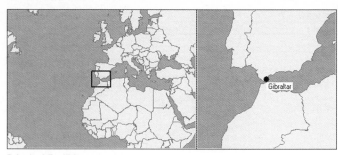

Principal Facilities:

P		G	C	R	L	B	D	T	A

PUERTO Y BAHÍA
General Ship Supplier

Poligono Ind. Tres Caminos, C / La Dorada s/n
11510 Puerto Real, Cadiz, SPAIN

TEL: +34 956 282 807 / 750   FAX: +34 956 250 454
EMAIL: commercial@puertoybahia.com
WEB: www.puertoybahia.com

**General Ship Suppliers • Ship Management
Ship Repairs • Transportation and Product Care**

PO Box 638,
Units 1, 2 and 3
Air Transit Shed,
Gibraltar Airport,
Gibraltar

Tel: Tel: + 350 20048879   **Fax:** + 350 20045589
Email: shipping@redwood.gi   **Website**: www.redwood.gi

ISO 9001 CERTIFIED ORGANISATION

• FREIGHT FORWARDING •
PORT SERVICES • REMOVALS

Authority: Gibraltar Port Authority, Port Office, North Mole, Gibraltar, Gibraltar, *Tel:* +350 77254, *Fax:* +350 51513, *Email:* ceo.gpa@gibtelecom.net, *Website:* www.gibraltarport.com

Officials: Chief Executive: Capt Peter Hall.
Marketing: Tony Davis, *Email:* davis@gibtelecom.gi.

Port Security: ISPS compliant. Access is restricted to pass-holders. There are two security barriers and cruise passengers must also proceed through airline-style security when reboarding their ship via the Cruise Terminal

Pre-Arrival Information: To comply with ISPS, all vessels arriving at Gibraltar must submit a security declaration providing information such as the last ten ports the vessel has visited prior to calling at Gibraltar, as well as other relevant security information. Vessels must also comply with an EU Directive and supply details of what waste it is carrying and whether it intends to discharge this waste at Gibraltar - if not, it must also satisfy the Gibraltar Port Authority that it has sufficient capacity to hold its waste until its designated port of discharge

Anchorage: The Bay of Gibraltar. Eastside for vessls awaiting orders

Pilotage: Compulsory

Radio Frequency: VHF Channels 12 and 16 for port. VHF Channel 71 for agents, bunker barges etc

Tides: Range of tide 1 m

Traffic: 2007, 8351 vessels of which 5640 called for bunkers, 227 cruise vessels carrying 275 993 passengers

Maximum Vessel Dimensions: 420 m loa and 9.2 m draft for vessels alongside. There are no restrictions for ship's anchoring in the Bay of Gibraltar

Working Hours: Mon-Fri 0800-1200, 1300-1700. Night shift 1700-2200. Weekends and holidays are workable 0800-1900 at overtime rates

Accommodation:

Name	Remarks
Gibraltar	See [1] below

[1]*Gibraltar:* Western Arm: the outer side is 490 m long accepting vessels up to 9.6 m draft, the inner side is 450 m long with max of 8 m draft. Height of quay above LLW 3.35 m and at HHW 2.13 m. Vessels of deeper d can be accommodated on half-tide basis according to tidal rise
Tanker facilities: Eleven oil berths with lengths 100 m to 486.6 m, 7.31 to 9.75 m d. Night berthing, water and bunkering at all berths, slop tank facilities at two. Slop barge available
Vessels can anchor in the bay in 15 to 50 fm, the only danger in entering being the Pearl Rock with 2.44 m water on it
One container berth, but containers can be handled at other berths. Ro/ro possible but no specialized berth at present

Mechanical Handling Equipment:

Location	Type	Capacity (t)	Qty
Gibraltar	Mult-purp. Cranes	120	4

Bunkering: Quick bunkering day or night from alongside and anchorage berths. Vessels arriving at night must give prior notice before 1600 h on the day of arrival. Vessels calling for bunkers only are exempt from port dues
Aegean Bunkering (Gib) Ltd, Suite 2, Block 4, Water Gardens, Gibraltar, Gibraltar, *Tel:* +350 200 50245, *Fax:* +350 200 45421, *Email:* mail@aegeangib.gi, *Website:* www.ampni.com
Bunkers (Gibraltar) Limited, Suite 621 cd, Europort, Gibraltar, Gibraltar, *Tel:* +350 200 74743, *Fax:* +350 200 77270, *Email:* sales@bunkersgibraltar.com, *Website:* www.bunkersgibraltar.com
Compania Espanola de Petroleos S.A. (CEPSA), Europort Building 7, P O Box 51,

Gibraltar, Gibraltar, *Tel:* +350 200 76170, *Fax:* +350 200 46277, *Email:* enquiries@gibunco.com, *Website:* www.gibunco.com
Gibraltar Underwater Contractors Ltd (GIBUNCO), Building 7, 2nd Floor, Europort, P O Box 51, Gibraltar, Gibraltar, *Tel:* +350 200 70454, *Fax:* +350 200 76195, *Email:* enquiries@gibunco.com, *Website:* www.gibunco.com
Maritima del Estrecho S.A., Suite 13, Water Gardens 2, Waterport, Gibraltar, Gibraltar, *Tel:* +350 200 76697, *Fax:* +350 200 42839, *Email:* maritima@maritima.gi, *Website:* www.maritima.com
A. Mateos & Sons Ltd, 299 Main Street, P O Box 139, Gibraltar, Gibraltar, *Tel:* +350 200 71241, *Fax:* +350 200 73781, *Email:* agency@mateos.gi, *Website:* www.mateos-gibraltar.com
Peninsula Petroleum Ltd, Europort Building 7, 2nd Floor, P O Box 51, Gibraltar, Gibraltar, *Tel:* +350 200 52641, *Fax:* +350 200 47816, *Email:* bunkers@peninsulapetroleum.com, *Website:* www.peninsulapetroleum.com
Rock Maritime Services Ltd, Suite 5 2nd Floor, Leon House, 1 Secretarys Lane, Gibraltar, Gibraltar, *Tel:* +350 200 79974, *Fax:* +350 200 79975, *Email:* rms@rms.gi, *Website:* www.rms.gi
Shell Co. of Gibraltar Ltd, P O Box 231, Shell House, Line Wall Road, Gibraltar, Gibraltar, *Tel:* +350 200 48200, *Fax:* +350 200 70517, *Email:* corporate-scgl-gibraltar-g@shell.com, *Website:* www.shell.gi
Shell Co. of Gibraltar Ltd, P O Box 231, Western Arm, North Mole, Gibraltar, Gibraltar, *Tel:* +350 200 48215, *Fax:* +350 200 70517, *Email:* corporate-scgl-gibraltar-g@shell.com, *Website:* www.shell.gi
Tarik Shipagents & Bunkering Services Ltd, Unit 3 Block 4, Watergardens, Waterport, P O Box 479, Gibraltar, Gibraltar, *Tel:* +350 200 72836, *Fax:* +350 200 72861, *Email:* info@tarik.gi, *Website:* www.tarik.gi
Tarik Shipping Ltd, Unit 3, Block 4, Water Gardens, Waterport, P O Box 479, Gibraltar, Gibraltar, *Tel:* +350 200 72836, *Fax:* +350 200 72861, *Email:* all@tarik.gi, *Website:* www.tarik.gi
Vemaoil Co. Ltd, Commercial Unit N-30, Suite 2, Ragged Staff Wharf, Queensway Quay, Gibraltar, Gibraltar, *Tel:* +350 200 40984, *Fax:* +350 200 74240, *Email:* vemaoil@gibnet.gi, *Website:* www.vemaoil.com
Aegean Bunkering (Gib) Ltd, Suite 2, Block 4, Water Gardens, Gibraltar, Gibraltar, *Tel:* +350 200 50245, *Fax:* +350 200 45421, *Email:* mail@aegeangib.gi, *Website:* www.ampni.com
Bunkers (Gibraltar) Limited, Suite 621 cd, Europort, Gibraltar, Gibraltar, *Tel:* +350 200 74743, *Fax:* +350 200 77270, *Email:* sales@bunkersgibraltar.com, *Website:* www.bunkersgibraltar.com
Compania Espanola de Petroleos S.A. (CEPSA), Europort Building 7, P O Box 51, Gibraltar, Gibraltar, *Tel:* +350 200 76170, *Fax:* +350 200 46277, *Email:* enquiries@gibunco.com, *Website:* www.gibunco.com
Chevron Marine Products LLC, Chevron Products UK Ltd, 1 Westferry Circus, Canary Wharf, London E14 4HA, United Kingdom, *Tel:* +44 20 7719 4680, *Fax:* +44 20 7719 5151, *Email:* gmpukb@chevron.com, *Website:* www.chevron.com
Maritima del Estrecho S.A., Suite 13, Water Gardens, Waterport, Gibraltar, Gibraltar, *Tel:* +350 200 76697, *Fax:* +350 200 42839, *Email:* maritima@maritima.gi, *Website:* www.maritima.com
ExxonMobil Marine Fuels, Mailpoint 31, ExxonMobil House, Ermyn Way, Leatherhead, Surrey KT22 8UX, United Kingdom, *Tel:* +44 1372 222 000, *Fax:* +44 1372 223 922, *Email:* marine.fuels@exxonmobil.com, *Website:* www.exxonmobil.com
Compania Logistica de Hidrocarburos S.A. (CLH S.A.), Calle Mendez Alvaro 44, 28045 Madrid, Spain, *Tel:* +34 91 7746000, *Fax:* +34 91 7746000, *Email:* info@clh.es, *Website:* www.clh.es
A. Mateos & Sons Ltd, 299 Main Street, P O Box 139, Gibraltar, Gibraltar, *Tel:* +350 200 71241, *Fax:* +350 200 73781, *Email:* agency@mateos.gi, *Website:* www.mateos-gibraltar.com
Peninsula Petroleum Ltd, 3rd Floor, 68 Pall Mall, London SW1Y 5ES, United Kingdom, *Tel:* +44 20 7766 3999, *Fax:* +44 20 7930 9096, *Email:* bunkers@peninsulapetroleum.com, *Website:* www.peninsulapetroleum.com
Petrolifera Ducar S.L., Factoria San Amoro, P O Box 28, Ceuta, Spain, *Tel:* +34 56 511700, *Fax:* +34 56 517544
RYTTSA Bunker (Repsol - YPF Trading & Transporte S.A.), Paseo de la Castellana 278-280, 28046 Madrid, Spain, *Tel:* +34 91 3488 000, *Fax:* +34 91 3487 529, *Email:* bunkerspain@repsolypf.com, *Website:* www.ryttsabunker.com
Rock Maritime Services Ltd, Suite 5 2nd Floor, Leon House, 1 Secretarys Lane, Gibraltar, Gibraltar, *Tel:* +350 200 79974, *Fax:* +350 200 79975, *Email:* rms@rms.gi, *Website:* www.rms.gi
Tarik Shipping Ltd, Unit 3, Block 4, Water Gardens, Waterport, P O Box 479, Gibraltar, Gibraltar, *Tel:* +350 200 72836, *Fax:* +350 200 72861, *Email:* all@tarik.gi, *Website:* www.tarik.gi
Tramp Oil & Marine, World Fuel Services Corporation, 13th Floor, Portland House, Bressenden Place, London SW1E 5BH, United Kingdom, *Tel:* +44 20 7808 5000, *Fax:* +44 20 7808 5088, *Email:* pturner@wfscorp.com, *Website:* www.wfscorp.com
Trust Marine Enterprises Co. Ltd, 141 Filonos Street, 185 36 Piraeus, Greece, *Tel:* +30 210 4180083, *Fax:* +30 210 4136213
Vemaoil Co. Ltd, Commercial Unit N-30, Suite 2, Ragged Staff Wharf, Queensway Quay, Gibraltar, Gibraltar, *Tel:* +350 200 40984, *Fax:* +350 200 74240, *Email:* vemaoil@gibnet.gi, *Website:* www.vemaoil.com

Towage: T.P. Towage Co. Ltd, P O Box 801, Gibraltar, Gibraltar, *Tel:* +350 200 41912, *Fax:* +350 200 43050, *Email:* tp.towage@gibtelecom.net, *Website:* www.tptowage.com

Repair & Maintenance: Fenmar Ltd, Unit 8, 12 Berth North Mole, The Port, P O Box 1433, Gibraltar, Gibraltar, *Tel:* +350 200 45098, *Fax:* +350 200 45098, *Email:* agency@fenmar.gi, *Website:* www.fenmar.gi
John M. Piris & Sons Ltd, 33 Main Street, Suite 4, Gibraltar, Gibraltar, *Tel:* +350 200 73171, *Fax:* +350 200 44370, *Email:* pirelec@gibnet.gi
SERVELEC Spain - Solano Enterprises S.L., C/Araba 8, Lonja Baracaldo, 48901 Vizcaya, Spain, *Tel:* +34 94 438 1150, *Fax:* +34 94 418 0331, *Email:* info@servelec.com, *Website:* www.servelec.com
Straits Overseas Ltd, 65 Harbour Deck, New Harbours, Gibraltar, Gibraltar, *Tel:* +350 200 76452, *Fax:* +350 200 76452, *Email:* straits@gibnet.gi

Seaman Missions: The Seamans Mission, The Flying Angel Club, North Mole, Gibraltar, Gibraltar, *Tel:* +350 200 41799

Ship Chandlers: Albatros Shipping S.L., Avenida Aguamarina, Alm 1, 11203 Algeciras, Spain, *Tel:* +34 956 635381, *Fax:* +34 956 662267, *Email:* office@albatros-shipping.com, *Website:* www.albatros-shipping.com
James Molinary Ltd, 40/42 Irish Town, Gibraltar, Gibraltar, *Tel:* +350 200 78881, *Fax:* +350 200 75334, *Email:* jamesmol@gibnet.gi, *Website:* www.molinary.com

---

Key to Principal Facilities:—
A=Airport   **C**=Containers   **G**=General Cargo   **P**=Petroleum   **R**=Ro/Ro   **Y**=Dry Bulk
B=Bunkers   **D**=Dry Dock   **L**=Cruise   **Q**=Other Liquid Bulk   **T**=Towage (where available from port)

Provimar S.A., Industrial Park Unit 6, North Mole, P O Box 779, Gibraltar, Gibraltar, *Tel:* +350 200 46265, *Fax:* +350 200 51657, *Email:* gibraltar@provimar.es

Puerto y Bahia S.L., Poligono Tres Caminos, Calle La Dorada s/n, Puerto Real, 11510 Cadiz, Spain, *Tel:* +34 956 282807, *Fax:* +34 956 250454, *Email:* spain@puertoybahia.com, *Website:* www.puerto-y-bahia.com

Tarik Shipagents & Bunkering Services Ltd, Unit 3 Block 4, Watergardens, Waterport, P O Box 479, Gibraltar, Gibraltar, *Tel:* +350 200 72836, *Fax:* +350 200 72861, *Email:* info@tarik.gi, *Website:* www.tarik.gi

Shipping Agents: M.H. Bland & Co. Ltd, Cloister Building, 6/8 Market Lane, P O Box 554, Gibraltar, Gibraltar, *Tel:* +350 200 75009, *Fax:* +350 200 71608, *Email:* agency.gibraltar@mhbland.com, *Website:* www.mhbland.com

Clifton Ship Agency, Suite 52, Victoria House, 26 Main Street, Gibraltar, Gibraltar, *Tel:* +350 200 76761, *Fax:* +350 200 73888, *Email:* agency@clifton.gi

Cotran (Gibraltar) Ltd, 2B Garrison House, Gavino's Court, Gibraltar, Gibraltar, *Tel:* +350 200 46801, *Fax:* +350 200 46110

Fenmar Ltd, Unit 8, 12 Berth North Mole, The Port, P O Box 1433, Gibraltar, Gibraltar, *Tel:* +350 200 45098, *Fax:* +350 200 45098, *Email:* agency@fenmar.gi, *Website:* www.fenmar.gi

Gibunco Marine Co. Ltd, No.4 Jetty North Mole, P O Box 51, Gibraltar, Gibraltar, *Tel:* +350 200 42994, *Fax:* +350 200 47814, *Email:* enquiries@gibunco.com, *Website:* www.gibunco.com

Global Agency Company, Suite 21B Don House, 30/38 Main Street, P O Box 490, Gibraltar, Gibraltar, *Tel:* +350 200 51777, *Fax:* +350 200 51779, *Email:* operations@gacgibraltar.com, *Website:* www.gacgibraltar.com

Inchcape Shipping Services (ISS), Inchcape Shipping Services (Gibraltar) Ltd, 4th Floor, Leon House, 1 Secretary's Lane, P O Box 194, Gibraltar, Gibraltar, *Tel:* +350 200 79294, *Fax:* +350 200 75959, *Email:* iss.gibraltar@iss-shipping.com, *Website:* www.iss-shipping.com

Lucas Imossi Shipping Ltd, 47 Irish Town, P O Box 167, Gibraltar, Gibraltar, *Tel:* +350 200 73500, *Fax:* +350 200 73550, *Email:* enquiries@imossi.gib.gi, *Website:* www.imossishipping.gi

Marine Service Shipping, Suite 204, Neptune House, Marina Bay, Gibraltar, Gibraltar, *Tel:* +350 200 73606, *Fax:* +350 200 76562, *Email:* admin@marine-service.gi

Maritima del Estrecho S.A., Suite 13, Water Gardens 2, Waterport, Gibraltar, Gibraltar, *Tel:* +350 200 76697, *Fax:* +350 200 42839, *Email:* maritima@maritima.gi, *Website:* www.maritima.com

Redwood International Ltd, Units 1,2 & 3 Air Transit Shed, Gibraltar Airport, Gibraltar, Gibraltar, *Email:* kenneth@redwood.gi, *Website:* www.redwood.gi

Rock Maritime Services, Suite 5, 2nd Floor, Leon House, 1 Secretary Lane, Gibraltar, Gibraltar, *Tel:* +350 200 79974, *Fax:* +350 200 79975, *Email:* rms@rms.gi, *Website:* www.rms.gi

Smith Imossi & Co. Ltd, 47 Irish Town, P O Box 185, Gibraltar, Gibraltar, *Tel:* +350 200 78353, *Fax:* +350 200 72514, *Email:* info@smith-imossi.gi, *Website:* www.smithimossi.com

Sorek Shipping Gibraltar Ltd, Haven Court, 5 Library Ramp, P O Box 489, Gibraltar, Gibraltar, *Tel:* +350 200 79129, *Fax:* +350 200 72673, *Email:* legal@sorekgib.com, *Website:* www.sorekgib.com

Tarik Shipping Ltd, Unit 3, Block 4, Water Gardens, Waterport, P O Box 479, Gibraltar, Gibraltar, *Tel:* +350 200 72836, *Fax:* +350 200 72861, *Email:* all@tarik.gi, *Website:* www.tarik.gi

Turner & Co (Gibraltar) Ltd, 65/67 Irish Town, P O Box 109, Gibraltar, Gibraltar, *Tel:* +350 200 78305, *Fax:* +350 200 72006, *Email:* turner@gibtelecom.net

Wilhelmsen Ship Services, Suite 22, Block 6, Watergardens, P O Box 624, Gibraltar, Gibraltar, *Tel:* +350 200 70541, *Fax:* +350 200 70927, *Email:* wss.gibraltar@wilhelmsen.com, *Website:* www.barwilunitor.com

Wilhelmsen Ship Services, Suite 22, Block 6, Watergardens, P O Box 624, Gibraltar, Gibraltar, *Tel:* +350 200 70666, *Fax:* +350 200 70927, *Email:* wss.gibraltar@wilhelmsen.com, *Website:* www.barwilunitor.com

Surveyors: Hellenic Register of Shipping, c/o Sorek Services Limited, P O Box 489, Haven Court, 5 Library Ramp, Gibraltar, Gibraltar, *Tel:* +350 200 71987, *Fax:* +350 200 72673, *Email:* sorek@gibnynex.gi, *Website:* www.hrs.gr

Medical Facilities: Port doctor available 24 h/day. Medical facilities at St. Bernards Hospital

Airport: 1 km from port

Lloyd's Agent: Smith Imossi & Co. Ltd, 47 Irish Town, P O Box 185, Gibraltar, Gibraltar, *Tel:* +350 200 78353, *Fax:* +350 200 72514, *Email:* info@smith-imossi.gi, *Website:* www.smithimossi.com

GREECE

ACHLADI

Lat 38° 53' N; Long 22° 49' E.

Admiralty Chart: 1571	**Admiralty Pilot:** 48
Time Zone: GMT +2 h	**UNCTAD Locode:** GR ACL

Principal Facilities:

		Y	G			B		

Authority: Stylis Harbour Authority, 353 00 Stylis, Greece, *Tel:* +30 22380 22329, *Fax:* +30 22380 22329

Port Security: ISPS compliant

Pilotage: Not compulsory but available from Volos

Radio Frequency: VHF Channel 12

Weather: Port affected only by SE winds

Working Hours: 24 h

Accommodation:

Name	Length (m)	Depth (m)	Remarks
Achladi			See [1] below
Berth	200	18.3	

[1]*Achladi:* Port operated by Agroinvest S.A. for the loading and discharge of animal food and grain etc

Storage:

Location	Grain (t)
Achladi	120000

Mechanical Handling Equipment:

Location	Type	Capacity (t)	Qty
Achladi	Mult-purp. Cranes	5	1

Cargo Worked: 400 t/h

Bunkering: Available by road tanker

Airport: Athens, 250 km

Lloyd's Agent: International Insurance Services E.P.E., 117 Notara Street, 185 35 Piraeus, Greece, *Tel:* +30 210 428 4080, *Fax:* +30 210 428 4405, *Email:* grlloyds@otenet.gr

ADHAMAS

harbour area, see under Milos Island

AGIOI THEODOROI

Lat 37° 55' N; Long 23° 5' E.

Admiralty Chart: 1598	**Admiralty Pilot:** 48
Time Zone: GMT +2 h	**UNCTAD Locode:** GR AGT

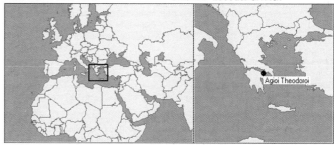

Principal Facilities:

P	Q					B		T	A

Authority: Motor Oil (Hellas) Refineries S.A., P O Box 23, 201 00 Corinth, Greece, *Tel:* +30 27410 486022, *Fax:* +30 27410 48255, *Email:* motoroil.refinery@moh.gr, *Website:* www.moh.gr

Officials: Managing Director: John Kosmadakis.
Harbour Master: John Trakakis.

Anchorage: Good anchorage area 0.8 km from outer jetty in 36.5 m to 48.8 m of water, with sandy bottom

Pilotage: Compulsory. Pilot boards vessel approx 1.5 km SSE of outer jetty. Terminal listening 24 h on VHF Channel 14

Radio Frequency: VHF Channel 14

Maximum Vessel Dimensions: 323 114 dwt, 346.2 m loa

Working Hours: Continuous

Accommodation:

Name	Depth (m)	Remarks
Agioi Theodoroi		
Main Outer Jetty Tanker Berth	22	See [1] below
Finger Pier		See [2] below

[1]*Main Outer Jetty Tanker Berth:* Situated at the head of a T-shaped pier which projects 300 m SSE from the shore. The berth can accommodate tankers up to 400 000 dwt and has a max loading/discharge rate of 15 000 t/h

[2]*Finger Pier:* Projects each side of the main pier, providing on the W side two berths with 12 m to 13 m depth for vessels up to 50 000 dwt and on the E side two berths

with 7 m to 8 m depth for coastal tankers. Night berthing possible, but caution should be exercised

Bunkering: Aegean Marine Petroleum S.A., 42 Hatzikiriakou Avenue, 185 38 Piraeus, Greece, *Tel:* +30 210 4586 000, *Fax:* +30 210 4586 245, *Email:* marinefuels@ampni.com, *Website:* www.ampni.com

Aegean Petroleum (UK) Ltd, 207 Coppergate House, 16 Brune Street, London E1 7NJ, United Kingdom, *Tel:* +44 20 7953 7990, *Fax:* +44 20 7953 7856, *Email:* piraeusbunkers@aegeanpetroleum.co.uk

Alpha Petroleum S.A., 7 Spirou Miliou Street, 124 62 Piraeus, Greece, *Tel:* +30 210 557 7405, *Fax:* +30 210 557 7302

Baluco S.A., 182 Androutsou & Bouboulinas Streets, 185 35 Piraeus, Greece, *Tel:* +30 210 4190 562, *Fax:* +30 210 4190 566, *Email:* bunkers@baluco.com, *Website:* www.baluco.com

BP Greece Ltd, 43 Iroon Polytechniou Avenue, 185 35 Piraeus, Greece, *Tel:* +30 210 422 4615, *Fax:* +30 210 422 4669

Brilliant Maritime Services Ltd, 170 Ipsilantou Street, 185 35 Piraeus, Greece, *Tel:* +30 210 4101 280, *Fax:* +30 210 4101 285, *Email:* sales@bmsbunkers.com, *Website:* www.bmsbunkers.com

Chevron Marine Products LLC, 4 Possidonos Avenue, Kallithea, 176 74 Piraeus, Greece, *Tel:* +30 210 9473 000, *Fax:* +30 210 9480 062, *Email:* gmpgreb@chevron.com, *Website:* www.chevron.com

Eko Abee (Hellenic Fuels and Lubricants), 3rd Floor, 87 Akti Miaouli, 185 38 Piraeus, Greece, *Tel:* +30 210 4290 920, *Fax:* +30 210 4290 958, *Email:* eko@eko.gr, *Website:* www.eko.gr

Energy Net Ltd, 18 Davaki Street, Pefki, 151 21 Athens, Greece, *Tel:* +30 210 6144 400, *Fax:* +30 210 6144 494, *Email:* enet@otenet.gr

Gram Marine S.A., 9 Afentouli Street, 185 36 Piraeus, Greece, *Tel:* +30 210 4287 935, *Fax:* +30 210 4287 934, *Email:* grammarine@ath.forthnet.gr

Interoil Trading S.A., 32 Zosimadon Street, 185 31 Piraeus, Greece, *Tel:* +30 210 422 5941, *Fax:* +30 210 413 7051, *Email:* interoil@otenet.gr

Mamidoil-Jetoil S.A., 227-229 Kifissias Avenue, Kifissia, 145 61 Athens, Greece, *Tel:* +30 210 8763100, *Fax:* +30 210 8055955, *Email:* info@jetoil.gr, *Website:* www.jetoil.gr

Martechnic Bunkering Ltd, Martechnic Bunkering Ltd, 15 Aristidou Street, 185 31 Piraeus, Greece, *Tel:* +30 210 4227 267, *Fax:* +30 210 4227 271, *Email:* martbunk@otenet.gr

Mediterranean Bunker Services S.A., 3 Irodotou Street, 185 38 Piraeus, Greece, *Tel:* +30 210 4297 440, *Fax:* +30 210 4297 443, *Email:* mbsisid@otenet.gr

Motor Oil (Hellas) Corinth Refineries S.A., 12A Irodou Attikou Street, Maroussi, 15124 Athens, Greece, *Tel:* +30 210 8094 000, *Fax:* +30 210 8094 444, *Email:* info@moh.gr, *Website:* www.moh.gr

OW Bunker Malta Ltd, A. Laskou 12 & Akti Themistokleous 20, Freattyda Square, 185 36 Piraeus, Greece, *Tel:* +30 210 4284 455, *Fax:* +30 210 4284 459, *Email:* piraeus@owbunker.com, *Website:* www.owbunker.com

Seka S.A., 53-55 Akti Miaouli, 185 36 Piraeus, Greece, *Tel:* +30 210 4293 160, *Fax:* +30 210 4293 745, *Email:* seka@seka.gr, *Website:* www.seka.gr – *Grades:* IFO380-180cSt; MDO; MGO – *Notice:* 48 hours – *Delivery Mode:* barge

Sekavin S.A., 53-55 Akti Miaouli, 185 36 Piraeus, Greece, *Tel:* +30 210 4293 160/71, *Fax:* +30 210 4293 345, *Email:* sekavinsales@ath.forthnet.gr, *Website:* www.sekavin.gr

Shell Company (Hellas) Ltd, 2 Eleftheriou Venizelou Avenue, Kallithea, 176 76 Athens, Greece, *Tel:* +30 210 929 5911, *Fax:* +30 210 929 5378

Shipoil Ltd, 99 Kolokotroni Street, 185 35 Piraeus, Greece, *Tel:* +30 210 4221 373, *Fax:* +30 210 4223 916, *Email:* shipoil@otenet.gr

United Petroleum International S.A., 9 Filellinon Street, 185 36 Piraeus, Greece, *Tel:* +30 210 429 4396, *Fax:* +30 210 429 4735, *Email:* upi@itel.gr

Towage: Compulsory. Five tugs available

Shipping Agents: Mylaki Shipping Agency Ltd, 43 Iroon Polytechniou Avenue, 185 35 Piraeus, Greece, *Tel:* +30 210 422 3355, *Fax:* +30 210 422 3356, *Email:* mylaki@otenet.gr, *Website:* www.mylaki-shipping.gr

Medical Facilities: Hospitals in Corinth and Piraeus

Airport: Athens Airport, 85 km

Railway: Corinth-Athens, approx 45 km

Lloyd's Agent: International Insurance Services E.P.E., 117 Notara Street, 185 35 Piraeus, Greece, *Tel:* +30 210 428 4080, *Fax:* +30 210 428 4405, *Email:* grlloyds@otenet.gr

AKHLADHI

alternate name, see Achladi

ALEXANDROUPOLIS

Lat 40° 51' N; Long 25° 57' E.

Admiralty Chart: 1636

Time Zone: GMT +2 h

Admiralty Pilot: 48

UNCTAD Locode: GR AXD

Principal Facilities:

P	Y	G	R	B	T	A

Authority: Alexandroupolis Port Authority S.A., 2 Botsari Street, 681 00 Alexandroupolis, Greece, *Tel:* +30 25510 26468, *Fax:* +30 25510 21430, *Email:* alex@yen.gr

Officials: Harbour Master: Eustathios Papachristou.

Approach: Port entry can be very difficult with strong S or SW winds. Masters must keep watch for fishing boats

Anchorage: Clear anchorage and good holding ground to drop anchor 0.5-1 mile S of the entrance in a depth of 8-10 m. Entrance 180 m wide

Pilotage: Independent pilots serve the port and are available from Neptun Independent Pilot Service, *Tel:* +30 2551 031015, *Fax:* +30 2551 020449. Pilot boards vessel 0.5 mile S of the entrance in daylight hours only

Radio Frequency: VHF Channel 12 for Port Authority and Pilots

Weather: Strong S or SW winds can sometimes stop work in the port

Maximum Vessel Dimensions: 180 m loa, 6.5 m d

Principal Imports and Exports: Imports: Soft wheat, Timber. Exports: Grain.

Working Hours: Mon-Fri 0730-1530

Accommodation:

Name	Length (m)	Draught (m)	Remarks
Alexandroupolis			See [1] below
Wharf A (Berths 1-3)	255	6.5	Grain
Wharf B (Berths 4-5)	150	6.5	Bagged cargo
Wharf C (Berths 6-7)	250	6.5	Grain. Loading silo with loading rate 600 t/h
Wharf D (Berths 8-9)	150	5.5	General cargo. Storage available only at these berths

[1]*Alexandroupolis:* Private oil terminal for discharging only, approx 1.5 miles E of the port with max d of 6.5 m

Mechanical Handling Equipment:

Location	Type	Capacity (t)
Alexandroupolis	Mobile Cranes	50

Cargo Worked: General and bagged cargo 100 t/gang/day, timber 120 m3/gang/day, grain 2000-3000 t/day

Bunkering: Gas oil available by road tanker

Towage: Two tugs available of 500 hp and 700 hp. Compulsory for vessels over 1000 gt

Repair & Maintenance: Minor repairs only can be carried out

Shipping Agents: Karavetis Shipping Agency, 1B Kountouriotou Street, 681 00 Alexandroupolis, Greece, *Tel:* +30 25510 37074, *Fax:* +30 25510 37073, *Email:* agency@karavetis.com, *Website:* www.karavetis.com

Mylaki Shipping Agency Ltd, 6 Markou Botsari Street, Agioi Theodoroi, 681 00 Alexandroupolis, Greece, *Tel:* +30 25510 33935, *Fax:* +30 25510 33936, *Email:* mylaki@otenet.gr, *Website:* www.mylaki-shipping.gr

Surveyors: Hellenic Register of Shipping, 49 Kon/nou Palaiologou Street, 681 00 Alexandroupolis, Greece, *Tel:* +30 25510 33547, *Fax:* +30 25510 33547, *Email:* kurkulis@otenet.gr, *Website:* www.hrs.gr

Medical Facilities: Fully equipped general hospital at Alexandroupolis

Airport: 5 km from port

Railway: Railway Station, 200 m

Lloyd's Agent: International Insurance Services E.P.E., 117 Notara Street, 185 35 Piraeus, Greece, *Tel:* +30 210 428 4080, *Fax:* +30 210 428 4405, *Email:* grlloyds@otenet.gr

ALIVERI

Lat 38° 23' N; Long 24° 3' E.

Admiralty Chart: 1571

Time Zone: GMT +2 h

Admiralty Pilot: 48

UNCTAD Locode: GR ALV

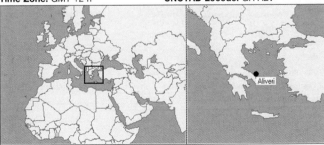

Principal Facilities:

P		Y	G				T	

Authority: Port Authority of Aliveri, Karavos, 345 00 Aliveri, Greece, *Tel:* +30 22230 22318, *Fax:* +30 22230 23633, *Email:* aliveri@yen.gr

Officials: Harbour Master: Anastasios Merzanidis.

Port Security: ISPS compliant

Anchorage: Anchorage can be obtained in Aliveri Bay in depths of 27 m to 29 m; good holding ground

Pilotage: Compulsory for vessels bound for Milaki. Pilot boards 1 mile SW of the cement factory berth. Call pilot boat on VHF Channel 14, working Channel 12

Key to Principal Facilities:—
A=Airport **C**=Containers **G**=General Cargo **P**=Petroleum **R**=Ro/Ro **Y**=Dry Bulk
B=Bunkers **D**=Dry Dock **L**=Cruise **Q**=Other Liquid Bulk **T**=Towage (where available from port)

Maximum Vessel Dimensions: Aliveri: 122 050 dwt, 261.2 m loa. Milaki: 153 265 dwt, 274.3 m loa

Accommodation:

Name	Length (m)	Remarks
Aliveri		
Aliveri		See [1] below
Milaki Pier	350	See [2] below

[1]*Aliveri:* The small harbour of Aliveri, alternatively known as Karavos, serves the town of Aliverion 1.6 km inland. It is protected from the S by a breakwater and has depths of 4 m to over 5 m in parts. Town Quay can accommodate vessels of up to 5 m d and there are other berths for small craft
Aliverion Power Station is located near the E side of the head of the bay. The berth is protected by a breakwater 366 m long with a depth of 9 m along the N side
Facilities at Aliveri for tankers supplying oil to the power station; vessels secure to two mooring buoys, submarine pipeline to the shore
[2]*Milaki Pier:* Cement factory located near the SE corner of the bay. The N side of the pier is used for unloading cargoes of coal and slag by a gantry grab crane, depths alongside range from 14.9 m at the shore end to 18 m at the seaward end; the S side is used for loading cement by a pipeline facility and depths alongside range from 13 m to 23 m

Towage: A tug is available to assist with berthing. Additional tugs can be brought in from Chalkis if required

Shipping Agents: Karavos Marine Services, Karavos Harbour, 345 00 Aliveri, Greece, *Tel:* +30 22230 29784, *Fax:* +30 22230 29786, *Email:* kms13@otenet.gr

Medical Facilities: Small hospital in Aliverion town

Airport: Athens International, approximately 140 km

Lloyd's Agent: International Insurance Services E.P.E., 117 Notara Street, 185 35 Piraeus, Greece, *Tel:* +30 210 428 4080, *Fax:* +30 210 428 4405, *Email:* grlloyds@otenet.gr

ARGOSTOLI

Lat 38° 12' N; Long 20° 29' E.

Admiralty Chart: 203	**Admiralty Pilot:** 47
Time Zone: GMT +2 h	**UNCTAD Locode:** GR ARM

Principal Facilities:

		Y	G					A	

Authority: Argostoli Port Police, Ioanni Metaxa 9, 281 00 Argostoli, Kefallonia, Greece, *Tel:* +30 26710 22224, *Fax:* +30 26710 22202, *Email:* kefa@yen.gr

Officials: Harbour Master: Mazis Antonios.

Port Security: ISPS compliant

Pilotage: Not available

Radio Frequency: VHF Channel 12

Maximum Vessel Dimensions: 150 m loa, 5 m draft

Principal Imports and Exports: Imports: Bricks, Marble chips, Tiles. Exports: Putty.

Working Hours: 24 h/day

Accommodation:

Name	Remarks
Argostoli	See [1] below

[1]*Argostoli:* Situated in Livadi Bay on the S coast of Cephalonia Island. Harbour exposed to NE winds. Depth at quayside 4-7 m

Storage:

Location	Open (m²)
Argostoli	7500

Towage: Kipriotis Bros, Argostoli, Kefallonia, Greece, *Tel:* +30 26710 23773

Surveyors: Hellenic Register of Shipping, 7 Tsigante Street, 281 00 Argostoli, Kefallonia, Greece, *Tel:* +30 26710 26924, *Fax:* +30 26710 26925, *Email:* seamus@otenet.gr, *Website:* www.hrs.gr

Medical Facilities: Hospital, 2 km

Airport: Cephalonia Airport, approx 10 km

Lloyd's Agent: International Insurance Services E.P.E., 117 Notara Street, 185 35 Piraeus, Greece, *Tel:* +30 210 428 4080, *Fax:* +30 210 428 4405, *Email:* grlloyds@otenet.gr

ASPROPYRGOS

Lat 38° 1' N; Long 23° 35' E.

Admiralty Chart: 1513	**Admiralty Pilot:** 48
Time Zone: GMT +2 h	**UNCTAD Locode:** GR ASS

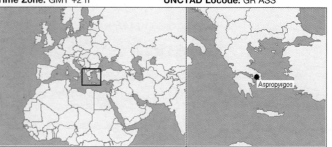

Principal Facilities:

P	Q					B		T	A

Authority: Hellenic Petroleum S.A., Aspropyrgos Industrial Installations, 17th km National Road, Athens-Corinth, P O Box 1085, 193 00 Aspropyrgos, Greece, *Tel:* +30 210 553 3000, *Fax:* +30 210 553 9298-9, *Email:* info@hellenic-petroleum.gr, *Website:* www.hellenic-petroleum.gr

Officials: Chairman: Efthymios Christodoulou, *Email:* echristodoulou@hellenic-petroleum.gr.
Managing Director: John Costopoulos, *Email:* jcostopoulos@hellenic-petroleum.gr.
Sales Director: George Dimogiorgas, *Tel:* +30 210 553 6131, *Email:* gdimogiorgas@hellenic-petroleum.gr.
Marketing Manager: Apostolos Rizakos, *Email:* arizakos@hellenic-petroleum.gr.

Port Security: ISPS compliant

Pre-Arrival Information: To be sent to agent 72, 48 and 24 h prior to arrival. Vessel's over 150 m loa, wishing to transit the Strait of Salamis at night must ask permission from Piraeus Central Harbour Office or Elefsis Harbour Office at least 6 h in advance and no later than 2200 h

Approach: Two approach channels lead to the Gulf of Eleusis. The W entrance, Poros Megaron is dredged to 7.9 m over a bottom width of 180 m and is used by vessels up to 183 m loa. The SE entrance through the Strait of Salamis is dredged to a depth of 10.89 m over a width of 240 m. Both channels are buoyed and lighted but there are some restrictions concerning night navigation in the E channel. Max speed 6 knots

Anchorage: For vessels proceeding to Aspropyrgos Terminals there are two anchorage areas I and II for large vessels, 1 and 3 miles respectively WSW of Piraeus harbour breakwater. Anchorage may also be obtained in Ormos Keratsiniou, off Peramas oil piers

Pilotage: Compulsory for vessels over 150 gt. Piraeus pilot boards one mile off the breakwater. VHF Channel 12

Radio Frequency: Athina Radio (SVA), VHF Channel 15

Weather: During winter prevailing winds are North. Remaining seasons are variable

Tides: Tidal range approx 0.45 m

Maximum Vessel Dimensions: 60 000 dwt, 220 m loa, 10.8 m draft

Principal Imports and Exports: Imports: Crude oil. Exports: Refined oil.

Working Hours: 24 h/day

Accommodation:

Name	Depth (m)	Remarks
Aspropyrgos		
Oil Jetty	11.8	See [1] below
Oil Jetty	7.2	See [2] below
LPG Berth	7.2	See [3] below

[1]*Oil Jetty:* Extends 170 m W from the shore, near the refinery. Eastern berth is equipped with three 8" dia mechanical operating arms for crude oil and oil products. Western berth is equipped with four 8" dia mechanical operating arms for oil products
[2]*Oil Jetty:* For small tankers up to 100 m loa and 5000 dwt. The 2 berths are equipped with 6" hoses for shipment of refined products
[3]*LPG Berth:* Situated midway between the two oil jetties for vessels up to 115 m loa for loading LPG and refined products

Cargo Worked: Crude oil max 50 000-55 000 t, oil products max 30 000-35 000 t and LPG-propylene max 5000 t, all depending on ship's draught

Bunkering: Available except at LPG pier
Aegean Marine Petroleum S.A., 42 Hatzikiriakou Avenue, 185 38 Piraeus, Greece, *Tel:* +30 210 4586 000, *Fax:* +30 210 4586 245, *Email:* marinefuels@ampni.com, *Website:* www.ampni.com
Aegean Petroleum (UK) Ltd, 207 Coppergate House, 16 Brune Street, London E1 7NJ, United Kingdom, *Tel:* +44 20 7953 7990, *Fax:* +44 20 7953 7856, *Email:* piraeusbunkers@aegeanpetroleum.co.uk
Alpha Petroleum S.A., 7 Spirou Miliou Street, 124 62 Piraeus, Greece, *Tel:* +30 210 557 7405, *Fax:* +30 210 557 7302
Baluco S.A., 182 Androutsou & Bouboulinas Streets, 185 35 Piraeus, Greece, *Tel:* +30 210 4190 562, *Fax:* +30 210 4190 566, *Email:* bunkers@baluco.com, *Website:* www.baluco.com
BP Greece Ltd, 43 Iroon Polytechniou Avenue, 185 35 Piraeus, Greece, *Tel:* +30 210 422 4615, *Fax:* +30 210 422 4669
Brilliant Maritime Services Ltd, 170 Ipsilantou Street, 185 35 Piraeus, Greece, *Tel:* +30 210 4101 280, *Fax:* +30 210 4101 285, *Email:* sales@bmsbunkers.com, *Website:* www.bmsbunkers.com
Chevron Marine Products LLC, 4 Possidonos Avenue, Kallithea, 176 74 Piraeus,

Greece, *Tel:* +30 210 9473 000, *Fax:* +30 210 9480 062, *Email:* gmpgreb@chevron.com, *Website:* www.chevron.com

Eko Abee (Hellenic Fuels and Lubricants), 3rd Floor, 87 Akti Miaouli, 185 38 Piraeus, Greece, *Tel:* +30 210 4290 920, *Fax:* +30 210 4290 958, *Email:* eko@eko.gr, *Website:* www.eko.gr

Energy Net Ltd, 18 Davaki Street, Pefki, 151 21 Athens, Greece, *Tel:* +30 210 6144 400, *Fax:* +30 210 6144 494, *Email:* enet@otenet.gr

Gram Marine S.A., 9 Afentouli Street, 185 36 Piraeus, Greece, *Tel:* +30 210 4287 935, *Fax:* +30 210 4287 934, *Email:* grammarine@ath.forthnet.gr

Interoil Trading S.A., 32 Zosimadon Street, 185 31 Piraeus, Greece, *Tel:* +30 210 422 5941, *Fax:* +30 210 413 7051, *Email:* interoil@otenet.gr

Mamidoil-Jetoil S.A., 227-229 Kifissias Avenue, Kifissia, 145 61 Athens, Greece, *Tel:* +30 210 8763100, *Fax:* +30 210 8055955, *Email:* info@jetoil.gr, *Website:* www.jetoil.gr

Martechnic Bunkering Ltd, Martechnic Bunkering Ltd, 15 Aristidou Street, 185 31 Piraeus, Greece, *Tel:* +30 210 4227 267, *Fax:* +30 210 4227 271, *Email:* martbunk@otenet.gr

Mediterranean Bunker Services S.A., 3 Irodotou Street, 185 38 Piraeus, Greece, *Tel:* +30 210 4297 440, *Fax:* +30 210 4297 443, *Email:* mbsisid@otenet.gr

Motor Oil (Hellas) Corinth Refineries S.A., 12A Irodou Attikou Street, Maroussi, 15124 Athens, Greece, *Tel:* +30 210 8094 000, *Fax:* +30 210 8094 444, *Email:* info@moh.gr, *Website:* www.moh.gr

OW Bunker Malta Ltd, A. Laskou 12 & Akti Themistokleous 20, Freattyda Square, 185 36 Piraeus, Greece, *Tel:* +30 210 4284 455, *Fax:* +30 210 4284 459, *Email:* piraeus@owbunker.com, *Website:* www.owbunker.com

Sekavin S.A., 53-55 Akti Miaouli, 185 36 Piraeus, Greece, *Tel:* +30 210 4293 160/71, *Fax:* +30 210 4293 345, *Email:* sekavinsales@ath.forthnet.gr, *Website:* www.sekavin.gr

Shell Company (Hellas) Ltd, 2 Eleftheriou Venizelou Avenue, Kallithea, 176 76 Athens, Greece, *Tel:* +30 210 929 5911, *Fax:* +30 210 929 5378

Shipoil Ltd, 99 Kolokotroni Street, 185 35 Piraeus, Greece, *Tel:* +30 210 4221 373, *Fax:* +30 210 4223 916, *Email:* shipoil@otenet.gr

United Petroleum International S.A., 9 Filellinon Street, 185 36 Piraeus, Greece, *Tel:* +30 210 429 4396, *Fax:* +30 210 429 4735, *Email:* upi@itel.gr

Towage: Compulsory. Tugs normally meet vessel at the entrance of the Eleusis channel

Medical Facilities: First aid facilities available. Full hospital facilities available in Eleusis, 10 km away

Airport: El. Venizelos International Airport at Spata, 50 km

Lloyd's Agent: International Insurance Services E.P.E., 117 Notara Street, 185 35 Piraeus, Greece, *Tel:* +30 210 428 4080, *Fax:* +30 210 428 4405, *Email:* grlloyds@otenet.gr

ASTAKOS-PLATIYALI

Lat 38° 28' N; Long 21° 6' E.

Admiralty Chart: 2402	**Admiralty Pilot:** 47
Time Zone: GMT +2 h	**UNCTAD Locode:** GR AST

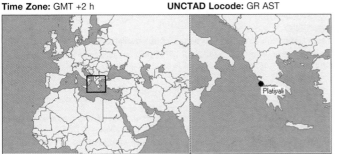

Principal Facilities:

Q	Y	G	C	R		B	D		A

Authority: AKARPORT S.A., 18-20 Amaroussiou Halandriou Street, 151 25 Amaroussion, Greece, *Tel:* +30 210 619 4020, *Fax:* +30 210 619 4010, *Email:* info@akarport.com, *Website:* www.akarport.com

Officials: Managing Director: Basil G. Koutsis.

Port Security: Control tower, security gate, fence monitor, port security, water front patrol, security detectors

Documentation: Application, document of acceptance

Approach: Free and safe approach

Anchorage: The port area is a natural safe anchorage able to offer safe shelter to all kinds and sizes of ships. May be obtained in the bay in depths of 18 to 22 m, good holding, mud

Pilotage: Compulsory (through Agency) and available 24 h. Pilot board distance: 2 miles

Radio Frequency: VHF Channel 16 (distress) and VHF Channel 12 (safety)

Weather: The port and the anchorage is safe

Traffic: 2002, 150 vessels, 1 650 000 t of cargo handled

Maximum Vessel Dimensions: 150 000 dwt fully loaded

Principal Imports and Exports: Imports: Cereals, Containers, Fertilizers. Exports: Trailers.

Working Hours: 24 h/day

Accommodation:

Name	Draught (m)	Remarks
Astakos Platiyali		See [1] below
Container Terminal	11–14.5	See [2] below
General & Bulk Cargo	8–12.5	See [3] below
Ro/Ro & Car Terminal	8–12.5	Terminal area of 200 000 m2

[1]*Astakos Platiyali:* Port Office: Tel: +30 26310 22600, Fax: +30 26310 27526, Email: akaragnt@otenet.gr
Depth at entrance about 18.29 m, depth of 8-16 m alongside the quays. Anchorage in 16.4 to 40.1 m. Total seafront quay-wall length is 2300 m

[2]*Container Terminal:* Terminal area of 162 000 m2 with 3137 ground slots. Equipment includes three post-panamax gantry cranes and two mobile cranes

[3]*General & Bulk Cargo:* Terminal area of 350 000 m2. Equipment includes two mobile cranes

Storage: Open storage for containers, cars and metals. Three warehouses of 30 000 m2. Three tanks

Mechanical Handling Equipment:

Location	Type	Capacity (t)	Qty
Astakos-Platiyali	Mult-purp. Cranes	15	4
Astakos-Platiyali	Mobile Cranes		14
Astakos-Platiyali	Container Cranes	50–60	3
Astakos-Platiyali	Forklifts		24

Bunkering: Small quantities in barrels

Waste Reception Facilities: Available for all types of disposals

Repair & Maintenance: Minor repairs undertaken

Stevedoring Companies: Akarport S.A., 18-20 Amaroussiou Halandriou str, 151 25 Athens, Greece, *Tel:* +30 210 619 4020, *Fax:* +30 210 619 4010, *Email:* info@akarport.com, *Website:* www.akarport.com

Medical Facilities: Hospital 19 km from port

Airport: Akiton Airport, 35 km

Lloyd's Agent: International Insurance Services E.P.E., 117 Notara Street, 185 35 Piraeus, Greece, *Tel:* +30 210 428 4080, *Fax:* +30 210 428 4405, *Email:* grlloyds@otenet.gr

AYIA MARINA

Lat 38° 53' N; Long 22° 35' E.

Admiralty Chart: 1571	**Admiralty Pilot:** 48
Time Zone: GMT +2 h	**UNCTAD Locode:** GR AGM

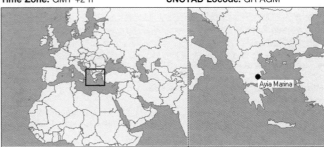

Principal Facilities:

		Y					

Authority: Stylis Harbour Authority, 353 00 Stylis, Greece, *Tel:* +30 22380 22329, *Fax:* +30 22380 22329

Port Security: ISPS compliant

Pilotage: Not available

Working Hours: 0800-2200

Accommodation:

Name	Remarks
Ayia Marina	See [1] below

[1]*Ayia Marina:* Open port, owned and operated by Metalia Voxitou Elefsinos A.E. (Skalistiris Enterprises S.A.), consisting only of poles and vessels must drop anchor when berthing. Vessels up to 9.1 m d can be accommodated for loading bauxite and chrome ore which come from the mines of Mount Parnassos and Mount Iti. Loading is effected by an electric elevator at approx 1000 t/day. Surrounding waters are clear with good holding ground with a max depth of 23.8 m

Cargo Worked: 300 t/h

Medical Facilities: Medical centre at Stylis

Lloyd's Agent: International Insurance Services E.P.E., 117 Notara Street, 185 35 Piraeus, Greece, *Tel:* +30 210 428 4080, *Fax:* +30 210 428 4405, *Email:* grlloyds@otenet.gr

AYIAS ANNAS BAY

harbour area, see under Mykonos

Key to Principal Facilities:—				
A=Airport	**C**=Containers	**G**=General Cargo	**P**=Petroleum	**R**=Ro/Ro	**Y**=Dry Bulk
B=Bunkers	**D**=Dry Dock	**L**=Cruise	**Q**=Other Liquid Bulk	**T**=Towage (where available from port)

AYIOS NIKOLAOS (CRETE)

Lat 35° 11' N; Long 25° 43' E.

Admiralty Chart: 1707	**Admiralty Pilot:** 48
Time Zone: GMT +2 h	**UNCTAD Locode:** GR ANI

Principal Facilities:

		Y	G			L	B			A	

Authority: Agios Nikolaos Port Authority, Harbour Office, 21 Akti Koundourou, 721 00 Ayios Nikolaos, Crete, Greece, *Tel:* +30 28410 90108, *Fax:* +30 28410 82733, *Website:* www.yen.gr

Officials: Harbour Master: Zaxarias Papoutsakis.

Port Security: ISPS compliant

Approach: Vessels up to 20 000 dwt can approach without difficulty

Anchorage: Vessels up to 400 000 dwt can anchor in the Bay of Mirabello

Pilotage: Not compulsory

Radio Frequency: VHF Channels 12 and 19

Weather: The port is open to the N winds, and protected by the islet Ayioi Pantes

Maximum Vessel Dimensions: 130 m loa

Working Hours: 0700-1500

Accommodation:

Name	Length (m)	Depth (m)	Remarks
Ayios Nikolaos			See [1] below
NE Pier	140	8.53	
W Pier	70	8.53	
SW Pier	62	8.53	
New Dock	140	9	Used by cruisers

[1]*Ayios Nikolaos:* No loading or unloading facilities; vessels use own gear. The inner old harbour is only used for fishing boats. Max depth 2 m

Cargo Worked: Approx 400 t/day general cargo and approx 150-200 t of bulk cargo

Bunkering: Available in small quantities at the piers by road tanker

Surveyors: Hellenic Register of Shipping, Almyros, 741 00 Ayios Nikolaos, Crete, Greece, *Tel:* +30 28410 24093, *Fax:* +30 28410 24093, *Email:* atsali@otenet.gr, *Website:* www.hrs.gr

Medical Facilities: General hospital available

Airport: Iraklion Airport, 67 km

Lloyd's Agent: International Insurance Services E.P.E., 117 Notara Street, 185 35 Piraeus, Greece, *Tel:* +30 210 428 4080, *Fax:* +30 210 428 4405, *Email:* grlloyds@otenet.gr

CATACOLO

alternate name, see Katakolon

CHALKIS

Lat 38° 27' N; Long 23° 36' E.

Admiralty Chart: 1554	**Admiralty Pilot:** 48
Time Zone: GMT +2 h	**UNCTAD Locode:** GR QKG

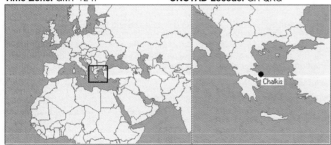

Principal Facilities:

	Q	Y	G		R		B		T		

Authority: Chalkis Central Port Authority, 2 Athinon Street, 341 00 Chalkis, Greece, *Tel:* +30 22210 28888, *Fax:* +30 22210 88888, *Email:* halk@yen.gr

Officials: Harbour Master: Christos Zafiriou.

Port Security: ISPS compliant

Approach: Depth in southern approach channel limits dimensions of vessel to 170 m loa, 6.1 m d and in the northern channel to 95 m loa, 5.5 m d. Max air draught at the new bridge is 34.2 m

Anchorage: Anchorage can be obtained at Bourtziou Anchorage in pos 38° 23' N, 23° 38.5' E in depth of 12 m

Pilotage: Compulsory for all foreign vessels and for Greek vessels trading in Greece over 1000 gt. Pilot boards 1-1.5 miles SSE of Avlis Lighthouse for vessels approaching from the south side and 1 mile N of red and green light buoys to the N of Evripos bridge for vessels approaching from the north. Application for pilot should be made through vessels agent or to the Harbour Master's Office by VHF Channel 12 at least 24 h prior to ETA

Radio Frequency: No local radio station. All messages should be passed through Athens Radio on VHF Channel 16. Harbour Master's Office keeps continuous watch on VHF Channel 12

Tides: Strong sea currents can be experienced every 6 h

Maximum Vessel Dimensions: 160 m loa, max d 6.1 m

Principal Imports and Exports: Imports: Fertiliser, Iron coils, Timber. Exports: Cement, General cargo, Iron pipes.

Working Hours: Summer 0700-1500. Winter 0800-1600

Accommodation:

Name	Length (m)	Remarks
Chalkis		
South Harbour	582	See [1] below
North Harbour		Small wharves for local passenger vessels & small craft
Private Wharves		See [2] below

[1]*South Harbour:* 240 m has a depth alongside of 6.4 m, 152 m with a depth of 5.8 m and 190 m with a depth of 5.2 m
[2]*Private Wharves:* Chalkis Cement Co Factory, Interchem Hellas, Shelman Co Factory and Socia Hellas

Mechanical Handling Equipment:

Location	Type	Capacity (t)	Qty
Chalkis	Mult-purp. Cranes	40	2
Chalkis	Mobile Cranes	70	

Cargo Worked: Iron rolls 1000 t/h, cement bags 1500 t/day

Bunkering: Available by small ship tanker and by trucks
Aegean Petroleum (UK) Ltd, 207 Coppergate House, 16 Brune Street, London E1 7NJ, United Kingdom, *Tel:* +44 20 7953 7990, *Fax:* +44 20 7953 7856, *Email:* piraeusbunkers@aegeanpetroleum.co.uk
Alpha Petroleum S.A., 7 Spirou Miliou Street, 124 62 Piraeus, Greece, *Tel:* +30 210 557 7405, *Fax:* +30 210 557 7302
BP Greece Ltd, 43 Iroon Polytechniou Avenue, 185 35 Piraeus, Greece, *Tel:* +30 210 422 4615, *Fax:* +30 210 422 4669
Mamidoil-Jetoil S.A., 227-229 Kifissias Avenue, Kifissia, 145 61 Athens, Greece, *Tel:* +30 210 8763100, *Fax:* +30 210 8055955, *Email:* info@jetoil.gr, *Website:* www.jetoil.gr

Waste Reception Facilities: Garbage disposal available

Towage: Compulsory for berthing or unberthing vessels over 1000 gt. It is also compulsory for vessels over 120 m loa to have a tug follow the vessel from the south pilot anchorage up to the South Harbour. Four tugs up to 1000 hp available

Repair & Maintenance: Chalkis Shipyards S.A., P O Box 19237, Chalkis, Greece, *Tel:* +30 22210 31502, *Fax:* +30 22210 32009, *Email:* info@chalkis-shipyards.gr, *Website:* www.chalkis-shipyards.gr Two floating docks, one 195 m x 33.5 m x 3.9 m with a lifting cap of 15 000 t for vessels up to 48 000 dwt and the other 151.0 m x 31.0 m x 4.25 m with a lifting cap of 7500 t for vessels up to 20 000 dwt

Shipping Agents: Bourji Shipping Agencies, 6 Evripou Street, 341 00 Chalkis, Greece, *Tel:* +30 22210 74909, *Fax:* +30 22210 61471, *Email:* mail@bourji.gr, *Website:* www.bourji.gr
Mylaki Shipping Agency Ltd, 10-12 Voudouri Avenue, 341 00 Chalkis, Greece, *Tel:* +30 22210 74810, *Fax:* +30 22210 76760, *Email:* mylaki@otenet.gr, *Website:* www.mylaki-shipping.gr
N.Boukos-B.Demetriou Shipping Agencies, 14-16 K.Karamanli Street, 341 00 Chalkis, Greece, *Tel:* +30 22210 22231, *Fax:* +30 22210 86044, *Email:* evianave@otenet.gr
Span Hellas, Kotsou 9, P O Box 31, GR-341 00 Chalkis, Greece, *Tel:* +30 22210 81230, *Fax:* +30 22210 22272

Surveyors: Hellenic Register of Shipping, 5 Tsirigoti & Ifigenias Corner, 341 00 Chalkis, Greece, *Tel:* +30 22210 87669, *Fax:* +30 22210 87669, *Email:* ktzela@tee.gr, *Website:* www.hrs.gr

Medical Facilities: General hospital available

Airport: Athens International, 105 km

Railway: Station, 500 m from port

Lloyd's Agent: International Insurance Services E.P.E., 117 Notara Street, 185 35 Piraeus, Greece, *Tel:* +30 210 428 4080, *Fax:* +30 210 428 4405, *Email:* grlloyds@otenet.gr

CHIOS

Lat 38° 23' N; Long 26° 9' E.

Admiralty Chart: 1625	**Admiralty Pilot:** 48
Time Zone: GMT +2 h	**UNCTAD Locode:** GR JKH

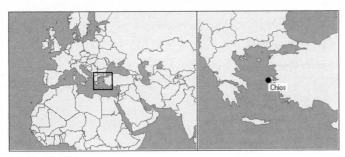

Principal Facilities:

P		Y	G						A

Authority: Central Port Authority of Chios, Neorion 2, Prokymaia, 821 00 Chios, Greece, *Tel:* +30 22710 44433/4, *Fax:* +30 22710 44432, *Email:* chio@yen.gr

Officials: Harbour Master: Charalambos Bournias, *Email:* bourniash@panafonet.gr.

Documentation: Crew list, stores list, crew declaration, cargo manifest, passenger list

Anchorage: Anchorage area is 0.5 to 1 nautical mile NE from north breakwater

Pilotage: Not compulsory for foreign vessels in contact with agents or Central Port Authority of Chios

Radio Frequency: VHF Channels 16 and 12

Tides: Chios Harbour 0.5 m at HW

Maximum Vessel Dimensions: 160 m loa, 7.0 m draft

Principal Imports and Exports: Imports: Cement, Steel, Timber. Exports: Fish, Lemons, Mastic gum.

Working Hours: Mon-Fri 0730-1400

Accommodation:

Name	Length (m)	Draught (m)	Remarks
Chios			
North Quay	210	7	Used by coasters & passenger vessels

Mechanical Handling Equipment:

Location	Type	Capacity (t)
Chios	Mobile Cranes	10–25

Repair & Maintenance: Minor hull and engine repairs available

Surveyors: Hellenic Register of Shipping, 14 Rodokanaki Street, 821 00 Chios, Greece, *Tel:* +30 22710 42743, *Fax:* +30 22710 42743, *Email:* kutsurad@otenet.gr, *Website:* www.hrs.gr

Medical Facilities: Two private clinics and government hospital in Chios town

Airport: Chios Airport, 3 km

Lloyd's Agent: International Insurance Services E.P.E., 117 Notara Street, 185 35 Piraeus, Greece, *Tel:* +30 210 428 4080, *Fax:* +30 210 428 4405, *Email:* grlloyds@otenet.gr

CORFU

Lat 39° 37' N; Long 19° 57' E.

Admiralty Chart: 206	**Admiralty Pilot:** 47
Time Zone: GMT +2 h	**UNCTAD Locode:** GR CFU

Principal Facilities:

P	Q	Y	G		R	L	B		T	A

Authority: Corfu Port Authority S.A., Xenofontos Stratigoy 2, 491 00 Corfu, Greece, *Tel:* +30 26610 32655 & 40002, *Fax:* +30 26610 39918, *Email:* kerk@yen.gr

Officials: Harbour Master: George Alasakis.

Approach: Entrance depth 32.9 m. Any size vessel may enter. Safe inner port for small vessels. The harbour lies between the Island of Vido and the town, where any depth of water up to 27.4 m is to be found

Anchorage: Safe anchorage in the area between Vido Island and Corfu, depth 30 m. During strong N and NW winds safe anchorage in the roadstead at Garitsa Bay, 0.8 km from the shore, where depths are in excess of 20 m. Anchorage in the new harbour is unsatisfactory when NW winds blow due to mud bottom. It is forbidden to approach Lazareto Islet

Pilotage: Compulsory. Vessels ETA should be given to Port Authority 48 h and 24 h before arrival. Vessels should await pilot in pos 39° 38' N; 19° 57' E, nearest to the coast of Ptychia Island, Vido and Corfu, dependent on weather conditions

Radio Frequency: VHF Channels 12 and 13

Weather: During summer strong NW winds and in winter S or SE winds render work alongside ship difficult. Harbour protected from all other winds

Tides: Range of tide 0.6 m max

Maximum Vessel Dimensions: Max draught 7.54 m

Principal Imports and Exports: Imports: Sand, Stones. Exports: Olive oil.

Working Hours: 0800-1400, 1400-1700, overtime 1700-1900

Accommodation:

Name	Remarks
Corfu	See [1] below
Private Wharves	BP and Petrogaz have their own tanker terminals

[1]*Corfu:* Quay approx 1300 m with 7.3 m depth. Max d 7 m, dependent on weather conditions. Anchorage for vessels carrying inflammable liquid or explosives is between Lazareto Islet and NW of Breakwater Point
Bulk facilities: Three silos for the discharge of bulk grain are situated at Mandouki

Bunkering: Aegean Petroleum (UK) Ltd, 207 Coppergate House, 16 Brune Street, London E1 7NJ, United Kingdom, *Tel:* +44 20 7953 7990, *Fax:* +44 20 7953 7856, *Email:* piraeusbunkers@aegeanpetroleum.co.uk

Waste Reception Facilities: Garbage collected by trucks

Towage: Two tugs available, one of 1000 hp and one of 1350 hp

Repair & Maintenance: Michael Avgerinos, Corfu, Greece, *Tel:* +30 26610 32036 Spyros Sgouropoulos, Corfu, Greece, *Tel:* +30 26610 30333 Minor repairs

Surveyors: Hellenic Register of Shipping, 3rd Parodos Elefth. Venizelou 4, Neo Limani, 491 00 Corfu, Greece, *Tel:* +30 26610 44180, *Fax:* +30 26610 22933, *Email:* skour@tee.gr, *Website:* www.hrs.gr

Medical Facilities: Clinics available

Airport: 2.5 km from port

Lloyd's Agent: International Insurance Services E.P.E., 117 Notara Street, 185 35 Piraeus, Greece, *Tel:* +30 210 428 4080, *Fax:* +30 210 428 4405, *Email:* grlloyds@otenet.gr

DRAPETZONA

see under Piraeus

ELEFSIS

alternate name, see Eleusis

ELEUSIS

Lat 38° 2' N; Long 23° 30' E.

Admiralty Chart: 1598	**Admiralty Pilot:** 48
Time Zone: GMT +2 h	**UNCTAD Locode:** GR EEU

Principal Facilities:

P	Q	Y	G			B		T	A

Authority: Eleusis Port Authority S.A., 10 Kanellopoulou Street, 192 00 Eleusis, Greece, *Tel:* +30 210 554 3504, *Fax:* +30 210 554 7980

Port Security: ISPS compliant

Pilotage: Vessels bound to E take a pilot at the station in Piraeus roads. Passage between Perama and the Salamis Strait is normally prohibited (the island is a military zone). Agents must have advance notice of the ship's ETA and a permit must be obtained for the trip. Passage is only permitted during daylight

Weather: Prevailing winds S, SE and SW

Working Hours: 0800-1200, 1300-1700

Accommodation:

Name	Remarks
Eleusis	See [1] below

[1]*Eleusis:* Vessels with up to 3.66 m d can enter the old port. E of the old port and at a distance of 300 m approx, there is a quay 300 m long and 80 m wide. For the first 145 m of the quay, vessels with up to 7.31 m d can be berthed and for the remainder, vessels of 10 m d can berth. The distance between the old and the new harbour is 345 m, depth 7.31 m. The port has a labour force of about 150 men, although more may be recruited if required. The output per hour of each gang is between 8 and 14 t, depending on the type of cargo being worked. For timber the output rises to 10 m3.

Key to Principal Facilities:—				
A=Airport	**C**=Containers	**G**=General Cargo	**P**=Petroleum	**R**=Ro/Ro	**Y**=Dry Bulk
B=Bunkers	**D**=Dry Dock	**L**=Cruise	**Q**=Other Liquid Bulk	**T**=Towage (where available from port)

Bulk facilities: Chalibourgik S.A. own a 180 m long quay, 15 m wide with 9.14 m alongside; equipped with four 10 t cranes. Eleusis Bauxite Mines S.A. own an ideal anchorage with buoys for loading. The former company assists with unloading ore and the latter with loading bauxite

Tanker facilities: Petrola Hellas S.A. Refinery is situated 2.7 km W of the main port. There are three piers. No.1 is 247 m long and 14.2 m wide; No.2 is 511 m long and 31 m wide; No.3 is 369 m long and 30 m wide. At either side of the piers vessels of up to 9.75 m d can be berthed

Mobil Oil pier, situated at Skaramanga, in pos 38° 01' 21" N, 23° 35' 35" E, opposite Koumoundourou Lake. Length of pier 550 m with 13 m depth alongside

Hellenic Aspropyrgos Refinery S.A. has a quay 93 m long, 12.7 m wide and 8.53 m deep and also an ore pier 700 m long, 30 m wide and 12.19 m deep

Mamidakis quay, 40 m long, 5 m wide with 8.2 m d

Texaco S.A. has a quay 90 m long, 6 m wide and 4.88 m deep

Petrogas S.A., situated 6 km E of the main port, has a quay 58 m long, 5 m wide and 4.88 m deep

Supplies of fuel, provisions and water are available

Bunkering: Supplies of fuel are from land installations and floating tanks

Aegean Marine Petroleum S.A., 42 Hatzikiriakou Avenue, 185 38 Piraeus, Greece, Tel: +30 210 4586 000, Fax: +30 210 4586 245, Email: marinefuels@ampni.com, Website: www.ampni.com

Aegean Petroleum (UK) Ltd, 207 Coppergate House, 16 Brune Street, London E1 7NJ, United Kingdom, Tel: +44 20 7953 7990, Fax: +44 20 7953 7856, Email: piraeusbunkers@aegeanpetroleum.co.uk

Alpha Petroleum S.A., 7 Spirou Miliou Street, 124 62 Piraeus, Greece, Tel: +30 210 557 7405, Fax: +30 210 557 7302

Baluco S.A., 182 Androutsou & Bouboulinas Streets, 185 35 Piraeus, Greece, Tel: +30 210 4190 562, Fax: +30 210 4190 566, Email: bunkers@baluco.com, Website: www.baluco.com

BP Greece Ltd, 43 Iroon Polytechniou Avenue, 185 35 Piraeus, Greece, Tel: +30 210 422 4615, Fax: +30 210 422 4669

Brilliant Maritime Services Ltd, 170 Ipsilantou Street, 185 35 Piraeus, Greece, Tel: +30 210 4101 280, Fax: +30 210 4101 285, Email: sales@bmsbunkers.com, Website: www.bmsbunkers.com

Chevron Marine Products LLC, 4 Possidonos Avenue, Kallithea, 176 74 Piraeus, Greece, Tel: +30 210 9473 000, Fax: +30 210 9480 062, Email: gmpgreb@chevron.com, Website: www.chevron.com

Eko Abee (Hellenic Fuels and Lubricants), 3rd Floor, 87 Akti Miaouli, 185 38 Piraeus, Greece, Tel: +30 210 4290 920, Fax: +30 210 4290 958, Email: eko@eko.gr, Website: www.eko.gr

Energy Net Ltd, 18 Davaki Street, Pefki, 151 21 Athens, Greece, Tel: +30 210 6144 400, Fax: +30 210 6144 494, Email: enet@otenet.gr

Gram Marine S.A., 9 Afentouli Street, 185 36 Piraeus, Greece, Tel: +30 210 4287 935, Fax: +30 210 4287 934, Email: grammarine@ath.forthnet.gr

Interoil Trading S.A., 32 Zosimadon Street, 185 31 Piraeus, Greece, Tel: +30 210 422 5941, Fax: +30 210 413 7051, Email: interoil@otenet.gr

Mamidoil-Jetoil S.A., 227-229 Kifissias Avenue, Kifissia, 145 61 Athens, Greece, Tel: +30 210 8763100, Fax: +30 210 8055955, Email: info@jetoil.gr, Website: www.jetoil.gr

Martechnic Bunkering Ltd, Martechnic Bunkering Ltd, 15 Aristidou Street, 185 31 Piraeus, Greece, Tel: +30 210 4227 267, Fax: +30 210 4227 271, Email: martbunk@otenet.gr

Mediterranean Bunker Services S.A., 3 Irodotou Street, 185 38 Piraeus, Greece, Tel: +30 210 4297 440, Fax: +30 210 4297 443, Email: mbsisid@otenet.gr

Motor Oil (Hellas) Corinth Refineries S.A., 12A Irodou Attikou Street, Maroussi, 15124 Athens, Greece, Tel: +30 210 8094 000, Fax: +30 210 8094 444, Email: info@moh.gr, Website: www.moh.gr

OW Bunker Malta Ltd, A. Laskou 12 & Akti Themistokleous 20, Freattyda Square, 185 36 Piraeus, Greece, Tel: +30 210 4284 455, Fax: +30 210 4284 459, Email: piraeus@owbunker.com, Website: www.owbunker.com

Petrotrade Management S.A., 63 Dragatsaniou Street, 185 45 Piraeus, Greece, Tel: +30 210 408 0100, Fax: +30 210 408 0108 – Grades: all grades; lubes – Rates: 300-400t/h – Delivery Mode: barge

Sekavin S.A., 53-55 Akti Miaouli, 185 36 Piraeus, Greece, Tel: +30 210 4293 160/71, Fax: +30 210 4293 345, Email: sekavinsales@ath.forthnet.gr, Website: www.sekavin.gr

Shell Company (Hellas) Ltd, 2 Eleftheriou Venizelou Avenue, Kallithea, 176 76 Athens, Greece, Tel: +30 210 929 5911, Fax: +30 210 929 5378

Shipoil Ltd, 99 Kolokotroni Street, 185 35 Piraeus, Greece, Tel: +30 210 4221 373, Fax: +30 210 4223 916, Email: shipoil@otenet.gr

United Petroleum International S.A., 9 Filellinon Street, 185 36 Piraeus, Greece, Tel: +30 210 429 4396, Fax: +30 210 429 4735, Email: upi@itel.gr

Towage: Compulsory for vessels up to 120 m (day) and 75 m (night) for passing the Salamis Straits

Repair & Maintenance: Elefsis Shipbuilding and Industrial Enterprises S.A., 192 00 Eleusis, Greece, Tel: +30 210 553 5111, Fax: +30 210 554 6016, Email: cm@mail.elefsis-shipyards.gr, Website: www.elefsis-shipyards.gr Three floating docks: No.1 162 m x 24 m with max cap 22 000 dwt and lifting cap 7500 t, No.2 227 m x 35 m with max cap 70 000 dwt and lifting cap 18 000 t, No.3 252 m x 41 m with max cap 120 000 dwt and lifting cap 30 000 t

Shipping Agents: Elefsis Shipping Agency, 29 Kanellopoulou Street, 192 00 Eleusis, Greece, Tel: +30 210 554 1665, Fax: +30 210 554 9264, Email: info@elefshipagent.com, Website: www.elefshipagent.com

Mylaki Shipping Agency Ltd, 1 Karaiskaki Street, 192 00 Eleusis, Greece, Tel: +30 210 556 1654, Fax: +30 210 556 1655, Email: mylaki@otenet.gr, Website: www.mylaki-shipping.gr

Transmar Shipping Agents, 6th Floor, 131 Praxitelous, 18532 Piraeus, Greece, Tel: +30 210 422 4824, Fax: +30 210 422 3756, Email: agency@transmar.gr, Website: www.transmar.gr

Airport: Athens Airport, 12 km

Lloyd's Agent: International Insurance Services E.P.E., 117 Notara Street, 185 35 Piraeus, Greece, Tel: +30 210 428 4080, Fax: +30 210 428 4405, Email: grlloyds@otenet.gr

GYTHION

Lat 36° 45' N; Long 22° 34' E.

Admiralty Chart: 1683	**Admiralty Pilot:** 48
Time Zone: GMT +2 h	**UNCTAD Locode:** GR GYT

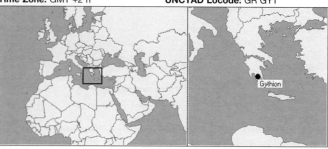

Principal Facilities:

			G						

Authority: Gythion Port Authority, Tzanetaki Tzani Street, 232 00 Gythion, Greece, Tel: +30 27330 22262, Fax: +30 27330 22262, Email: renage@in.gr

Officials: Harbour Master: George Kalianos.

Approach: No hazards, sand bottom, depths from 5 m to 6 m

Anchorage: Anchorage can be obtained about 300-400 m off the port in a depth of 20 m

Pilotage: Not available

Radio Frequency: VHF Channel 12 (port authority) and VHF Channel 6 (agency)

Weather: N and S winds

Maximum Vessel Dimensions: 130 m max loa, 6.5 m max d

Principal Imports and Exports: Imports: Bricks, Manure. Exports: Citrus, Kernel oil, Olive oil.

Working Hours: 0800-1200, 1330-1730. Continuation available

Accommodation:

Name	Remarks
Gythion	See [1] below

[1]Gythion: Harbour protected from S winds by the island of Kranai which is connected to the mainland by a short causeway. A jetty extends 110 m, with a depth of 7 m. No cranes, vessel's use own gear

Mechanical Handling Equipment:

Location	Type	Capacity (t)	Qty
Gythion	Mult-purp. Cranes	40	1

Cargo Worked: Up to 400 t/day with two gangs

Medical Facilities: Sparta Hospital, 40 km from port and a health centre in Gythion Port

Airport: Kalamata, 120 km. Athens, 320 km

Railway: Kalamata, 120 km. Tripolis, 90 km

Lloyd's Agent: International Insurance Services E.P.E., 117 Notara Street, 185 35 Piraeus, Greece, Tel: +30 210 428 4080, Fax: +30 210 428 4405, Email: grlloyds@otenet.gr

HALKIS

alternate name, see Chalkis

HERAKLION

alternate name, see Iraklion

IGOUMENITSA

Lat 39° 32' N; Long 20° 13' E.

Admiralty Chart: 2408	**Admiralty Pilot:** 47
Time Zone: GMT +2 h	**UNCTAD Locode:** GR IGO

Principal Facilities:

P	Y	G		R		B		T	A

Authority: Igoumenitsa Port Authority S.A., New Port of Igoumenitsa, Central Passenger Station, 461 00 Igoumenitsa, Greece, *Tel:* +30 26650 22235 & 22240, *Fax:* +30 26650 26122, *Email:* olig@olig.gr, *Website:* www.olig.gr

Officials: Managing Director: Nikolaos Kotsios, *Tel:* +30 26650 99300/3.

Port Security: ISPS compliant

Approach: The entrance to the port is formed by a channel 1850 m long, 100 m wide and 7.9 m depth. There are four light buoys across the channel

Radio Frequency: VHF Channel 12

Tides: Range 0.5 m

Maximum Vessel Dimensions: 6688 dwt, 152.6 m loa

Working Hours: 24 h/day

Accommodation:

Name	Remarks
Igoumenitsa	See [1] below

[1]*Igoumenitsa:* Provides mooring services to the liners and all the necessary port services to passengers and vehicles. The port is predominantly a passenger port, connecting Igoumenitsa with the Northern Ionian Islands (Corfu & Paxi), Patras and in Italy (Brindisi, Bari, Ancona, Venice & Trieste)
The New Port of Igoumenitsa is located in the southern side of the land harbour area, near Ladohori Village. It occupies a total land area of 210 acres. There are five places for mooring ro/ro vessels and twelve piers with the capability to moor seven ships simultaneously
On the northern side of the new port is Igoumenitsa's old port which is used for domestic purposes

Cargo Worked: 100 t/day

Bunkering: Marine diesel oil can be obtained

Towage: Two tugs available

Shipping Agents: Balkans Service Trailors S.A., New Port - Igoumenitsa, 461 00 Igoumenitsa, Greece, *Fax:* +30 26650 21235, *Email:* lefkaditis@bst.gr, *Website:* www.bst.gr

Medical Facilities: Medical Centre at Igoumenitsa and a hospital at Filiata, 30 km from Igoumenitsa

Airport: Ioannina, 95 km

Lloyd's Agent: International Insurance Services E.P.E., 117 Notara Street, 185 35 Piraeus, Greece, *Tel:* +30 210 428 4080, *Fax:* +30 210 428 4405, *Email:* grlloyds@otenet.gr

IRAKLION

Lat 35° 16' N; Long 25° 10' E.

Admiralty Chart: 1707	**Admiralty Pilot:** 48
Time Zone: GMT +2 h	**UNCTAD Locode:** GR NAI

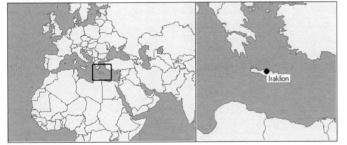

Principal Facilities:

P	Q	Y	G	C	R	L	B		T	A

Authority: Heraklion Port Authority S.A., P O Box 1068, 711 10 Iraklion, Crete, Greece, *Tel:* +30 2810 338116, *Fax:* +30 2810 226110, *Email:* info@portheraklion.gr, *Website:* www.portheraklion.gr

Officials: President: Manolis Ntabakis.
Chief Executive Officer: George Milakis.

Port Security: ISPS compliant

Documentation: 4 cargo manifests, 6 crew lists (1 to port police, 1 to customs office & 4 to immigration office), 7 passenger lists (1 to port police, 1 to customs office & 5 to immigration office), declaration of crew's personal effects (1 copy), list of stores and provisions (duty free shop list, bar list), maritime declaration of health, vaccination certificates

Approach: Information on VHF Channel 12. Port Authority and Pilot arrange the approach. Advance notice of ETA should be passed to Port Authority and Agents

Anchorage: Anchorage E of port entrance is forbidden owing to numerous underwater cables. In good weather conditions anchorage is to be found 0.75 mile N of North Breakwater with Venetian Castle bearing 180°. In bad weather conditions best anchorage position is approx 3 nautical miles to the W of the North Breakwater and 1,5 nautical miles from the coast at Linoperamata Bay. Depth of water requires a big scope of anchor chain. Also in bad weather conditions good anchorage is Bay of St. George in Dia

Pilotage: Compulsory for all foreign vessels and arranged through agent. Pilot, *Tel:* +30 281 022 6326. Contact may be made with pilot station on VHF Channel 12 during daylight. The pilotage area extends 0.5-1 mile NE of breakwater. Pilot boat is wooden and 12 m long with a black hull and white deckhouse. It is equipped with VHF which

has a range of 50 miles. In bad weather vessels should proceed close to the port entrance for boarding

Radio Frequency: Harbour Police maintain a 24 h watch on VHF Channel 12

Weather: Frequent winds from N to NW

Tides: Usual rise and fall of tide 1 ft

Traffic: 2002, 3320 vessels, 3 100 000 t of cargo handled, 15 500 TEU's, 1 900 000 passengers

Maximum Vessel Dimensions: Length and beam no limit. Max draught 14.5 m

Working Hours: Monday-Friday 0700-1430. 24 h working is possible, 7 days a week

Accommodation:

Name	Length (m)	Depth (m)	Remarks
Iraklion			See [1] below
Old Venetian Port	700	1.8–3.66	See [2] below
Pier I	386	10	
Pier II	482	10	Passenger terminal of 2500 m2
Pier III	959	9.5–12.5	
Pier IV	851	13–14	Container terminal
Pier V	380	10–12	Dangerous goods pier

[1]*Iraklion:* Passenger Port (Piers I & II) and Commercial Port (Piers III, IV & V): protected by a long breakwater with a length of approx 2390 m. The entrance is 250 m wide. Vessels can berth alongside the North Breakwater (sometimes used by cruise vessels) which has depths alongside up to 15 m. Inland area of 455 000 m2 and a water area of 827 000 m2
Tanker Facilities: only small tankers discharge in Heraklion Port and Linoperamata Bay. At Heraklion tankers discharging liquid fuel are required to berth at East Breakwater (fuel pier), Pier V and Pier III
[2]*Old Venetian Port:* Vessels up to 300 t can enter the port, the entrance to which is very narrow (50 m). Used as a marina for fishing vessels, small craft and yachts

Storage: Covered and open storage available

Mechanical Handling Equipment:

Location	Type	Capacity (t)	Qty	Remarks
Iraklion	Mult-purp. Cranes	12.5	2	for bulk & general cargo
Iraklion	Mult-purp. Cranes	40	1	for containers
Iraklion	Mult-purp. Cranes	6.3	4	for general cargo
Iraklion	Mobile Cranes	80	1	
Iraklion	Mobile Cranes	100	1	
Iraklion	Reach Stackers	40	1	
Iraklion	Reach Stackers	50	2	

Cargo Worked: 20 TEU's/h/gang. Other cargo 200 t/h/gang

Bunkering: In Passenger and Commercial Port bunkers are available ex-berth by truck. Also, in the entrance of the Venetian Port, there is an underground fuel tank for fishing vessels and yachts
Aegean Petroleum (UK) Ltd, 207 Coppergate House, 16 Brune Street, London E1 7NJ, United Kingdom, *Tel:* +44 20 7953 7990, *Fax:* +44 20 7953 7856, *Email:* piraeusbunkers@aegeanpetroleum.co.uk
Mamidoil-Jetoil S.A., 227-229 Kifissias Avenue, Kifissia, 145 61 Athens, Greece, *Tel:* +30 210 8763100, *Fax:* +30 210 8055955, *Email:* info@jetoil.gr, *Website:* www.jetoil.gr
Seka S.A., 53-55 Akti Miaouli, 185 36 Piraeus, Greece, *Tel:* +30 210 4293 160, *Fax:* +30 210 4293 745, *Email:* seka@seka.gr, *Website:* www.seka.gr

Towage: One tug of 1400 hp and two tugs of 1100 hp. Compulsory for foreign vessels over 1000 gt berthing and unberthing. Also there is a fire-fighting tug

Repair & Maintenance: Minor repairs available by machine shops. No facilities for deck repair

Shipping Agents: GMJ Adamis & Sons, 23-25 August Street, 712 02 Iraklion, Crete, Greece, *Tel:* +30 2810 246202, *Fax:* +30 2810 224717
Candia Trust Ltd., 25th August & 2 Zotou Street, 712 02 Iraklion, Crete, Greece, *Tel:* +30 2810 282322, *Fax:* +30 2810 223511, *Email:* info@candiatrust.gr, *Website:* www.candiatrust.gr
A.P. Corpis & Co. Ltd, 2 Mitsotaki Street, 712 02 Iraklion, Crete, Greece, *Tel:* +30 2810 282551, *Fax:* +30 2810 242925, *Email:* hermla@maersk.com
Maravelias & Co Ltd, Candia Trust Ltd, 2 Zotou & 25th August Streets, GR-71202 Iraklion, Crete, Greece, *Tel:* +30 2810 282559, *Fax:* +30 2810 223511, *Email:* info@candiatrust.gr, *Website:* www.candiatrust.gr
Scandinavian Near East Agency S.A., 32,25th of August Str, GR-71202 Iraklion, Crete, Greece, *Tel:* +30 2810 283860, *Fax:* +30 2810 284860, *Email:* info@echamaraki.gr, *Website:* www.echamaraki.gr
Kyriakos J Tsainis Shipping Agency, 25th August & Koroneou Street 10, P O Box 1116, GR-71202 Iraklion, Crete, Greece, *Tel:* +30 2810 222326, *Fax:* +30 2810 226260, *Email:* tsainis@her.forthnet.gr

Surveyors: Hellenic Register of Shipping, 31 25th August Street, 712 02 Iraklion, Crete, Greece, *Tel:* +30 2810 346390, *Fax:* +30 2810 346210, *Website:* www.hrs.gr

Medical Facilities: Advance notice should be passed to Agents if medical attention is required. Clinics and medical treatment available in the town

Airport: Heraklion International Airport, 4 km

Development: In the future Pier V will be used as a dangerous goods handling pier and ship repair zone, equipped with bunkering and slops facilities

Lloyd's Agent: International Insurance Services E.P.E., 117 Notara Street, 185 35 Piraeus, Greece, *Tel:* +30 210 428 4080, *Fax:* +30 210 428 4405, *Email:* grlloyds@otenet.gr

Key to Principal Facilities:—				
A=Airport	**C**=Containers	**G**=General Cargo	**P**=Petroleum	**R**=Ro/Ro	**Y**=Dry Bulk
B=Bunkers	**D**=Dry Dock	**L**=Cruise	**Q**=Other Liquid Bulk	**T**=Towage (where available from port)	

ITEA

Lat 38° 26' N; Long 22° 25' E.

Admiralty Chart: 2405	**Admiralty Pilot:** 47
Time Zone: GMT +2 h	**UNCTAD Locode:** GR ITA

Principal Facilities:

	Y	G		R		B		

Authority: Port Authority of Itea, 332 00 Itea, Greece, *Tel:* +30 22650 32319 & 35220, *Fax:* +30 22650 34888

Officials: Harbour Master: Christos Psarris.

Port Security: ISPS compliant

Approach: Average depth of channel is 10.4 m; no hazards

Anchorage: Anchorage can be obtained inside the harbour in the vicinity of the pier head in depths ranging from 8 m to 10 m

Pilotage: Compulsory. Pilot boards 0.6 nautical mile SE of the Itea Pier in pos 38° 25.8' N; 22° 25.3' E. Masters of vessels should advise ETA at least 24 h prior to arrival. In the event of bad weather, vessels should enter harbour without pilot and anchor using both anchors

Radio Frequency: VHF Channel 12

Principal Imports and Exports: Exports: Bauxite.

Working Hours: Monday-Thursday 0800-1200, 1300-1700 (winter); 0800-1200, 1400-1800 (summer). Friday work finishes 1 h earlier. Saturday 0800-1300. Bauxite loading is carried out round the clock

Accommodation:

Name	Length (m)	Remarks
Itea		See [1] below
Pier	120	See [2] below
Parnassos		See [3] below

[1]*Itea:* An anchorage area suitable for laid-up vessels occupies most of the W part of the harbour, with depths up to 18.3 m

[2]*Pier:* Depths alongside on the W side ranging from 6.5 m to 7.2 m, and on the E side from 6.5 m to 7.5 m; depth at pierhead is 7.4 m. Vessels up to 130 m loa can be accommodated on the W side and up to 83 m loa on the E side. Loading and unloading is carried out by ship's own gear. There is a passenger and car ferry service to Aiyion on the other side of the Gulf of Corinth

[3]*Parnassos:* Private installation for the loading of bauxite by conveyor located at Parnassos. Vessels up to 40 000 dwt, max loaded draught 10.4 m can be accommodated

Bunkering: Available in limited quantities
Aegean Marine Petroleum S.A., 42 Hatzikiriakou Avenue, 185 38 Piraeus, Greece, *Tel:* +30 210 4586 000, *Fax:* +30 210 4586 245, *Email:* marinefuels@ampni.com, *Website:* www.ampni.com
Aegean Petroleum (UK) Ltd, 207 Coppergate House, 16 Brune Street, London E1 7NJ, United Kingdom, *Tel:* +44 20 7953 7990, *Fax:* +44 20 7953 7856, *Email:* piraeusbunkers@aegeanpetroleum.co.uk
Alpha Petroleum S.A., 7 Spirou Miliou Street, 124 62 Piraeus, Greece, *Tel:* +30 210 557 7405, *Fax:* +30 210 557 7302
Baluco S.A., 182 Androutsou & Bouboulinas Streets, 185 35 Piraeus, Greece, *Tel:* +30 210 4190 562, *Fax:* +30 210 4190 566, *Email:* bunkers@baluco.com, *Website:* www.baluco.com
BP Greece Ltd, 43 Iroon Polytechniou Avenue, 185 35 Piraeus, Greece, *Tel:* +30 210 422 4615, *Fax:* +30 210 422 4669
Brilliant Maritime Services Ltd, 170 Ipsilantou Street, 185 35 Piraeus, Greece, *Tel:* +30 210 4101 280, *Fax:* +30 210 4101 285, *Email:* sales@bmsbunkers.com, *Website:* www.bmsbunkers.com
Chevron Marine Products LLC, 4 Possidonos Avenue, Kallithea, 176 74 Piraeus, Greece, *Tel:* +30 210 9473 000, *Fax:* +30 210 9480 062, *Email:* gmpgreb@chevron.com, *Website:* www.chevron.com
Eko Abee (Hellenic Fuels and Lubricants), 3rd Floor, 87 Akti Miaouli, 185 38 Piraeus, Greece, *Tel:* +30 210 4290 920, *Fax:* +30 210 4290 958, *Email:* eko@eko.gr, *Website:* www.eko.gr
Energy Net Ltd, 18 Davaki Street, Pefki, 151 21 Athens, Greece, *Tel:* +30 210 6144 400, *Fax:* +30 210 6144 494, *Email:* enet@otenet.gr
Gram Marine S.A., 9 Afentouli Street, 185 36 Piraeus, Greece, *Tel:* +30 210 4287 935, *Fax:* +30 210 4287 934, *Email:* grammarine@ath.forthnet.gr
Interoil Trading S.A., 32 Zosimadon Street, 185 31 Piraeus, Greece, *Tel:* +30 210 422 5941, *Fax:* +30 210 413 7051, *Email:* interoil@otenet.gr
Mamidoil-Jetoil S.A., 227-229 Kifissias Avenue, Kifissia, 145 61 Athens, Greece, *Tel:* +30 210 8763100, *Fax:* +30 210 8055955, *Email:* info@jetoil.gr, *Website:* www.jetoil.gr
Martechnic Bunkering Ltd, Martechnic Bunkering Ltd, 15 Aristidou Street, 185 31 Piraeus, Greece, *Tel:* +30 210 4227 267, *Fax:* +30 210 4227 271, *Email:* martbunk@otenet.gr
Mediterranean Bunker Services S.A., 3 Irodotou Street, 185 38 Piraeus, Greece, *Tel:* +30 210 4297 440, *Fax:* +30 210 4297 443, *Email:* mbsisid@otenet.gr

Motor Oil (Hellas) Corinth Refineries S.A., 12A Irodou Attikou Street, Maroussi, 15124 Athens, Greece, *Tel:* +30 210 8094 000, *Fax:* +30 210 8094 444, *Email:* info@moh.gr, *Website:* www.moh.gr
OW Bunker Malta Ltd, A. Laskou 12 & Akti Themistokleous 20, Freattyda Square, 185 36 Piraeus, Greece, *Tel:* +30 210 4284 455, *Fax:* +30 210 4284 459, *Email:* piraeus@owbunker.com, *Website:* www.owbunker.com
Sekavin S.A., 53-55 Akti Miaouli, 185 36 Piraeus, Greece, *Tel:* +30 210 4293 160/71, *Fax:* +30 210 4293 345, *Email:* sekavinsales@ath.forthnet.gr, *Website:* www.sekavin.gr
Shell Company (Hellas) Ltd, 2 Eleftheriou Venizelou Avenue, Kallithea, 176 76 Athens, Greece, *Tel:* +30 210 929 5911, *Fax:* +30 210 929 5378
Shipoil Ltd, 99 Kolokotroni Street, 185 35 Piraeus, Greece, *Tel:* +30 210 4221 373, *Fax:* +30 210 4223 916, *Email:* shipoil@otenet.gr
United Petroleum International S.A., 9 Filellinon Street, 185 36 Piraeus, Greece, *Tel:* +30 210 429 4396, *Fax:* +30 210 429 4735, *Email:* upi@itel.gr

Shipping Agents: Scandinavian Near East Agency S.A., 61 Akti Posidonos, GR-33200 Itea, Greece, *Tel:* +30 22650 32314

Medical Facilities: Hospital at Anfissa, 13 km

Airport: Athens, 202 km

Lloyd's Agent: International Insurance Services E.P.E., 117 Notara Street, 185 35 Piraeus, Greece, *Tel:* +30 210 428 4080, *Fax:* +30 210 428 4405, *Email:* grlloyds@otenet.gr

KALAMAKI

Lat 37° 55' N; Long 23° 5' E.

Admiralty Chart: 1600	**Admiralty Pilot:** 48
Time Zone: GMT +2 h	**UNCTAD Locode:** GR KLM

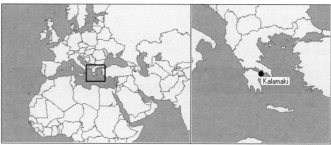

Principal Facilities:

P		Y	G			B		T	A

Authority: Isthmia Port Authority, Isthmia, 200 10 Corinth, Greece, *Tel:* +30 27410 37555, *Fax:* +30 27410 37777, *Email:* isth@mail.yen.gr

Officials: Harbour Master: Ioannis Bakoulas.

Port Security: ISPS compliant

Pilotage: Pilot available

Radio Frequency: VHF Channels 16 and 11

Maximum Vessel Dimensions: 72 000 dwt, 227 m loa, 12.35 m d

Working Hours: 24 h

Accommodation:

Name	Length (m)	Draught (m)	Remarks
Kalamaki			
Soya Mills Berth	64	11.9	See [1] below

[1]*Soya Mills Berth:* Berthing face of 64 m, together with mooring bollards and a depth alongside in excess of 12 m. The bulk handling facility consists of a fixed tower equipped with two suction pipes, which can operate together up to 250 t/h, for the discharging of soya beans. Vessel has to shift from hatch to hatch. A dolphin berth is situated close to the main jetty and is used for the discharge of logs

Bunkering: Available by barge

Towage: Tugs can be arranged from the Corinth Canal if required

Medical Facilities: General hospital at Corinthos

Airport: Athens Airport

Railway: Kalamaki, 1 km

Lloyd's Agent: International Insurance Services E.P.E., 117 Notara Street, 185 35 Piraeus, Greece, *Tel:* +30 210 428 4080, *Fax:* +30 210 428 4405, *Email:* grlloyds@otenet.gr

KALAMATA

Lat 37° 0' N; Long 22° 7' E.

Admiralty Chart: 2404	**Admiralty Pilot:** 47
Time Zone: GMT +2 h	**UNCTAD Locode:** GR KLX

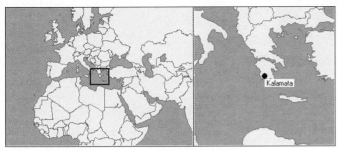

Principal Facilities:

	P		Y	G	C	R		B			A	

Authority: Port Authority of Kalamata, Port Office, Custom House Square, 241 01 Kalamata, Greece, *Tel:* +30 27210 22218, *Fax:* +30 27210 96220, *Email:* kala@yen.gr

Officials: Harbour Master: Salvanos Aristotelis.

Anchorage: Anchorage can be obtained SE of the port at Almyros in a depth of 20 m

Pilotage: Compulsory. VHF Channel 12

Weather: Moderate NW winds during summer

Maximum Vessel Dimensions: 20 000 dwt, 175 m loa, 9 m d

Principal Imports and Exports: Exports: Currants, Figs, Olive oil, Olives.

Working Hours: 0800-1200, 1330-1700 and overtime 1800-2100

Accommodation:

Name	Remarks
Kalamata	See [1] below

[1]*Kalamata:* Harbour is formed by a mole running alongside the shore for 300 m, ending in a breakwater 920 m long which is then surrounded by another breakwater, 400 m long. Depth at entrance 10 m; width 180 m. Vessels drawing up to 9 m can enter port. Depth at quays 7.15 m to 9 m. A container quay is available. There is also one privately owned silo for grain

Storage: One warehouse of 3000 m3

Mechanical Handling Equipment:

Location	Type	Capacity (t)	Qty
Kalamata	Mult-purp. Cranes	150	1

Cargo Worked: 72 t/hatch/day, two gangs only

Bunkering: Aegean Petroleum (UK) Ltd, 207 Coppergate House, 16 Brune Street, London E1 7NJ, United Kingdom, *Tel:* +44 20 7953 7990, *Fax:* +44 20 7953 7856, *Email:* piraeusbunkers@aegeanpetroleum.co.uk
Alpha Petroleum S.A., 7 Spirou Miliou Street, 124 62 Piraeus, Greece, *Tel:* +30 210 557 7405, *Fax:* +30 210 557 7302
Mamidoil-Jetoil S.A., 227-229 Kifissias Avenue, Kifissia, 145 61 Athens, Greece, *Tel:* +30 210 8763100, *Fax:* +30 210 8055955, *Email:* info@jetoil.gr, *Website:* www.jetoil.gr
Petrotrade Management S.A., 63 Dragatsaniou Street, 185 45 Piraeus, Greece, *Tel:* +30 210 408 0100, *Fax:* +30 210 408 0108 – *Grades:* all grades; lubes – *Rates:* 300-400t/h – *Delivery Mode:* barge, truck

Repair & Maintenance: Kakalikas Brothers, Kalamata, Greece, *Tel:* +30 27210 89578 Repair facilities

Ship Chandlers: Patapios Spy. Karabetsos, 173 Navarino Street, 24100 Kalamata, Greece, *Tel:* +30 27210 29677, *Fax:* +30 27210 26038

Shipping Agents: G. Andreas Zervakis Ltd, Navrinou 17, 241 00 Kalamata, Greece, *Tel:* +30 27210 82161, *Fax:* +30 27210 86717, *Email:* gzer@otenet.gr
G. Bouchalis Steamship Agency, 13 Likourgou, 241 00 Kalamata, Greece, *Tel:* +30 27210 97974, *Fax:* +30 27210 94134, *Email:* bouchali@otenet.gr

Surveyors: Hellenic Register of Shipping, 1 Hydras Street, 241 00 Kalamata, Greece, *Tel:* +30 27210 98913, *Fax:* +30 27210 98913, *Email:* kvrio@tee.gr, *Website:* www.hrs.gr

Medical Facilities: Available

Airport: Kalamata Airport, 5 km

Lloyd's Agent: International Insurance Services E.P.E., 117 Notara Street, 185 35 Piraeus, Greece, *Tel:* +30 210 428 4080, *Fax:* +30 210 428 4405, *Email:* grlloyds@otenet.gr

KALI LIMENES

Lat 34° 56' N; Long 24° 50' E.

Admiralty Chart: 1707
Time Zone: GMT +2 h
Admiralty Pilot: 48
UNCTAD Locode: GR KLL

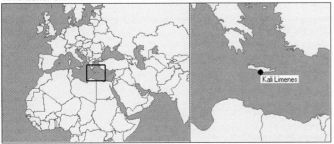

Principal Facilities:

						B		T	A	

Authority: Seka S.A., 53-55 Akti Miaouli, 185 36 Piraeus, Greece, *Tel:* +30 210 4293 160, *Fax:* +30 210 4293 745, *Email:* seka@seka.gr, *Website:* www.seka.gr

Officials: Chief Executive Officer: Antonis Theoharis, *Tel:* +30 210 4293 160, *Email:* atheoharis@seka.gr.
General Manager: Dimitris Stathogiannopoulos, *Tel:* +30 210 4294 557, *Email:* dstathogiannopoulos@seka.gr.
Port Manager: Pablos Mattheakis, *Tel:* +30 210 4293 160, *Email:* seka_kl@otenet.gr.
Sales Manager: Tasos Anastasoulis, *Tel:* +30 210 4293 160, *Email:* tanastasoulis@seka.gr

Port Security: ISPS compliant

Approach: Entrance to the bay is free from obstructions and depth is 14.07 m to 30.48 m

Pilotage: Compulsory. VHF Channels 14 and 16

Tides: Max range 0.61 m

Working Hours: 24 h/day

Accommodation:

Name	Remarks
Kali Limenes	See [1] below

[1]*Kali Limenes:* Well protected bay taking vessels up to 12.8 m d. Bunker deliveries are made from three piers. Two vessels (one handy size and one liberty size) can be supplied simultaneously. There are jetties capable of taking vessels alongside for bunkering only. Vessels should notify their ETA and bunker and other requirements to SEKA at least 48 h in advance. Crew changes are effected through Iraklion and undertaken by SEKA

Bunkering: Aegean Petroleum (UK) Ltd, 207 Coppergate House, 16 Brune Street, London E1 7NJ, United Kingdom, *Tel:* +44 20 7953 7990, *Fax:* +44 20 7953 7856, *Email:* piraeusbunkers@aegeanpetroleum.co.uk
Mamidoil-Jetoil S.A., 227-229 Kifissias Avenue, Kifissia, 145 61 Athens, Greece, *Tel:* +30 210 8763100, *Fax:* +30 210 8055955, *Email:* info@jetoil.gr, *Website:* www.jetoil.gr
Seka S.A., 53-55 Akti Miaouli, 185 36 Piraeus, Greece, *Tel:* +30 210 4293 160, *Fax:* +30 210 4293 745, *Email:* seka@seka.gr, *Website:* www.seka.gr
Trust Marine Enterprises Co. Ltd, 141 Filonos Street, 185 36 Piraeus, Greece, *Tel:* +30 210 4180083, *Fax:* +30 210 4136213 – *Grades:* IFO301-180cSt; MGO – *Parcel Size:* MGO min 30t; IFO min 100t – *Rates:* FO 800t/h; MGO 200t/h – *Delivery Mode:* ex wharf

Towage: One tug is available of 730 hp

Repair & Maintenance: Minor repairs available through local agents. 48 h notice required

Medical Facilities: Available

Airport: Iraklion Airport, 80 km

Lloyd's Agent: International Insurance Services E.P.E., 117 Notara Street, 185 35 Piraeus, Greece, *Tel:* +30 210 428 4080, *Fax:* +30 210 428 4405, *Email:* grlloyds@otenet.gr

KALYMNOS

Lat 36° 57' N; Long 26° 59' E.

Admiralty Chart: 1531/1532
Time Zone: GMT +2 h
Admiralty Pilot: 48
UNCTAD Locode: GR KMI

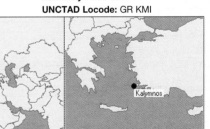

Principal Facilities:

			G		R					

Authority: Port Authority of Kalymnos, St Nikolas, 852 00 Kalymnos, Greece, *Tel:* +30 22430 29304, *Fax:* +30 22430 50137, *Email:* kalylx@yahoo.gr

Officials: Harbour Master: George Chasanidis.

Pilotage: Not available

Accommodation:

Name	Length (m)	Depth (m)	Remarks
Kalymnos			See [1] below
Quay	140	7	
Quay	135	7	
Quay	60	5	

[1]*Kalymnos:* Harbour consists of three main quays. Three further quays on the W side of the harbour are used for smaller vessels and have total length of 200 m and depth 5 m. In continuation of these smaller quays there are old quays undergoing reconstruction to provide a further 200 m of berthing space. Fishing vessels use a 100 m long quay on the N side. Small warehouses for storage are available. No cranes

---

Key to Principal Facilities:—					
A=Airport	**C**=Containers	**G**=General Cargo	**P**=Petroleum	**R**=Ro/Ro	**Y**=Dry Bulk
B=Bunkers	**D**=Dry Dock	**L**=Cruise	**Q**=Other Liquid Bulk	**T**=Towage (where available from port)	

Repair & Maintenance: Minor repairs only for small boats

Surveyors: Hellenic Register of Shipping, P O Box 47, 852 00 Kalymnos, Greece, *Tel:* +30 22430 59280, *Fax:* +30 22430 59282, *Email:* psaroba@otenet.gr, *Website:* www.hrs.gr

Lloyd's Agent: International Insurance Services E.P.E., 117 Notara Street, 185 35 Piraeus, Greece, *Tel:* +30 210 428 4080, *Fax:* +30 210 428 4405, *Email:* grlloyds@otenet.gr

KANABA

harbour area, see under Milos Island

KARAVOS

see under Aliveri

KARLOVASSI

harbour area, see under Samos

KATAKOLON

Lat 37° 39' N; Long 21° 20' E.

Admiralty Chart: 2404	**Admiralty Pilot:** 47
Time Zone: GMT +2 h	**UNCTAD Locode:** GR KAK

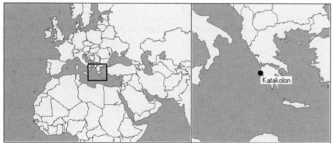

Principal Facilities:

		Y	G			B		T	

Authority: Katakolon Port Authority, Harbour Office, 270 67 Katakolon, Greece, *Tel:* +30 26210 41206, *Fax:* +30 26210 42160, *Email:* limenkat@operamail.com

Officials: Harbour Master: Andreas Daras.

Pilotage: Private pilot available. VHF Channels 16 and 12

Working Hours: 0700-1200 and 1400-1700 (summer), 0800-1200 and 1300-1700 (winter)

Accommodation:

Name	Remarks
Katakolon	See [1] below

[1]*Katakolon:* Length of piers up to 200 m, depths at LW in inner harbour 8 m. Elevator available for discharging cargo

Bunkering: Available by truck

Towage: One salvage tug stationed at port

Repair & Maintenance: Minor repairs only

Shipping Agents: Elefsis Shipping Agency, Katakolon Port, 270 67 Katakolon, Greece, *Tel:* +30 26210 42184, *Fax:* +30 26210 42186, *Email:* info@elefshipagent.com, *Website:* www.elefshipagent.com

Airport: Athens, 320 km

Lloyd's Agent: International Insurance Services E.P.E., 117 Notara Street, 185 35 Piraeus, Greece, *Tel:* +30 210 428 4080, *Fax:* +30 210 428 4405, *Email:* grlloyds@otenet.gr

KAVALA

Lat 40° 55' N; Long 24° 25' E.

Admiralty Chart: 1687	**Admiralty Pilot:** 48
Time Zone: GMT +2 h	**UNCTAD Locode:** GR KVA

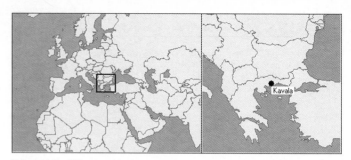

Principal Facilities:

P	Q	Y	G		R		B		T	A

Authority: Kavala Port Authority S.A., Averof 1, 651 10 Kavala, Greece, *Tel:* +30 2510 223716 & 224967, *Fax:* +30 2510 223628, *Email:* olkavala@otenet.gr, *Website:* www.portkavala.gr

Officials: Chief Executive: Nikolaos Panagiotopoulos, *Tel:* +30 2510 223282. Harbour Master: George Zaglavaras.

Port Security: ISPS compliant

Approach: Good approach with depths of 19 m to 23 m off the entrance. Depth at entrance 13.5 m

Anchorage: Anchorage can be obtained 0.8 km SW of the entrance

Pilotage: Compulsory. Pilot boards 0.8 km off entrance. VHF Channel 12

Maximum Vessel Dimensions: 190 m loa, 11.5 m draught

Principal Imports and Exports: Imports: Fertiliser, Timber, Woodpulp. Exports: Corn, Paper, Pellets, Sugar, Tobacco, Wheat.

Working Hours: Summer: Monday-Friday 0700-1430, Saturday 0700-0930. Winter: Monday-Friday 0730-1500, Saturday 0730-1000

Accommodation:

Name	Remarks
Kavala	
Commercial Port (Nea Karvali)	See [1] below
Passenger Port	See [2] below
Prinos Oil Terminal	See [3] below

[1]*Commercial Port (Nea Karvali):* Protected by western breakwater 400 m long in depth of 12 m. Can accommodate two vessels of 190 m loa and 11.5 m draught as well as a ro/ro vessel
[2]*Passenger Port:* Protected by breakwaters 1950 m long in depth of 4-10 m. The windward pier is 560 m long and the lee one is 230 m long
[3]*Prinos Oil Terminal:* In pos 40° 55' 56" N; 24° 31' 22" E. Sea berth consisting of open sea mooring buoys located in the Gulf of Kavala between Thassos Island and the mainland. Min water depth is approx 25 m

Mechanical Handling Equipment:

Location	Type	Capacity (t)	Qty
Commercial Port (Nea Karvali)	Mult-purp. Cranes	12–100	4
Commercial Port (Nea Karvali)	Forklifts	2.5–4	10
Commercial Port (Nea Karvali)	Forklifts	35	2

Bunkering: Only diesel oil of the Greek State Distilleries is supplied, but not in large quantities. Delivery by truck
Aegean Petroleum (UK) Ltd, 207 Coppergate House, 16 Brune Street, London E1 7NJ, United Kingdom, *Tel:* +44 20 7953 7990, *Fax:* +44 20 7953 7856, *Email:* piraeusbunkers@aegeanpetroleum.co.uk
Alpha Petroleum S.A., 7 Spirou Miliou Street, 124 62 Piraeus, Greece, *Tel:* +30 210 557 7405, *Fax:* +30 210 557 7302
Eko Abee (Hellenic Fuels and Lubricants), 3rd Floor, 87 Akti Miaouli, 185 38 Piraeus, Greece, *Tel:* +30 210 4290 920, *Fax:* +30 210 4290 958, *Email:* eko@eko.gr, *Website:* www.eko.gr

Towage: Two tugs of 400 and 800 hp available

Repair & Maintenance: Only minor engine repairs can be effected

Ship Chandlers: Jola Supplies, 13 Androu, 652 01 Kavala, Greece, *Tel:* +30 2510 838815, *Fax:* +30 2510 836323, *Email:* lagoudis@mail.gr

Shipping Agents: Scandinavian Near East Agency S.A., 3 Kassandrou Street, GR-65403 Kavala, Greece, *Tel:* +30 2510 223457, *Fax:* +30 2510 224177, *Email:* symeonag@otenet.gr

Medical Facilities: Two hospitals available

Airport: Kavalla Airport, 35 km

Development: 1050 m of breakwater to be added to the existing 400 m at the Commercial Port

Lloyd's Agent: International Insurance Services E.P.E., 117 Notara Street, 185 35 Piraeus, Greece, *Tel:* +30 210 428 4080, *Fax:* +30 210 428 4405, *Email:* grlloyds@otenet.gr

KERKIRA

alternate name, see Corfu

KHALKIS

alternate name, see Chalkis

KHIOS

alternate name, see Chios

KOS

Lat 36° 53' N; Long 27° 19' E.

Admiralty Chart: 1055
Time Zone: GMT +2 h

Admiralty Pilot: 48
UNCTAD Locode: GR KGS

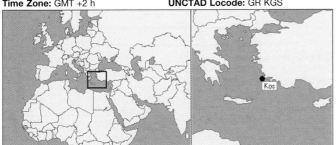

Principal Facilities:

P		G	R				A	

Authority: Port Authority of Kos, 25 Akti Kountouriotis, 853 00 Kos, Kos Island, Greece, *Tel:* +30 22420 26594, *Fax:* +30 22420 24185, *Email:* kos@yen.gr

Officials: Harbour Master: Georgios Seferiadis.

Pilotage: Not available

Accommodation:

Name	Remarks
Kos	See [1] below

[1]*Kos:* Harbour consists of five quays: one 140 m long with depth alongside of 8 m, one 70 m long with depth of 6 m, two quays 78 m and 94 m long, both with depth of 4.5 m and a quay 120 m long with depth of 3.5 m. Small warehouses for storage are available. No cranes

Airport: Situated near Antimahia Village, 26 km

Lloyd's Agent: International Insurance Services E.P.E., 117 Notara Street, 185 35 Piraeus, Greece, *Tel:* +30 210 428 4080, *Fax:* +30 210 428 4405, *Email:* grlloyds@otenet.gr

KYMASSI

Lat 38° 49' N; Long 23° 31' E.

Admiralty Chart: 1085
Time Zone: GMT +2 h

Admiralty Pilot: 48
UNCTAD Locode: GR KYM

Principal Facilities:

P		Y	G						

Authority: Harbour Authority of Mandoudhi, 340 04 Mandoudhi, Greece, *Tel:* +30 22270 22020

Officials: Harbour Master: Gerasimos Axarlis.

Approach: The best approach to the berth is close to the N side of the bay. No hazards

Anchorage: Anchorage can be obtained in Kymassi Bay in a depth of 32 m; sandy bottom

Pilotage: Available during daylight hours only. Masters of vessels should request services of pilot 24 h prior to arrival. Pilot boards approx 900 m NE of the jetty. Night berthing is not allowed

Radio Frequency: VHF Channel 12

Weather: Winds normally N to NW and NE. Winds from between N and SE can set up a swell in the bay, making the berths untenable

Maximum Vessel Dimensions: 22 000 dwt, 8.23 m d, max loa 170 m

Working Hours: 24 h/day for bulk cargoes

Accommodation:

Name	Remarks
Kymassi	See [1] below

[1]*Kymassi:* One berth for the loading of magnesite. Y-shaped concrete jetty with two mooring buoys, depth alongside 10.7 m; vessels of up to 8.23 m d can be accommodated. Conveyor system equipped with adjustable spout. There is also an anchor/buoy berth within the bay, in a depth of approx 30 m, where loading is carried out from lighters

Mechanical Handling Equipment:

Location	Type	Capacity (t)	Qty
Kymassi	Mult-purp. Cranes	60	2

Cargo Worked: Bagged cargo 1200 t/h, palletised cargo 1000 t/h, bulk cargo loading 500 t/h, discharging 1200 t/h

Medical Facilities: Medical centre available

Lloyd's Agent: International Insurance Services E.P.E., 117 Notara Street, 185 35 Piraeus, Greece, *Tel:* +30 210 428 4080, *Fax:* +30 210 428 4405, *Email:* grlloyds@otenet.gr

LAMIA

alternate name, see Stylis

LAURIUM

Lat 37° 42' N; Long 24° 4' E.

Admiralty Chart: 1571
Time Zone: GMT +2 h

Admiralty Pilot: 48
UNCTAD Locode: GR LAV

Principal Facilities:

P	Q	Y	G			B		T	A

Authority: Lavrion Port Authority S.A., Cote A. Papandreou, 195 00 Lavrion, Greece, *Tel:* +30 22920 27711, *Fax:* +30 22920 25769, *Email:* info@oll.gr, *Website:* www.oll.gr

Officials: Managing Director: John Bakalis.
Harbour Master: Christos Zisimatos.

Port Security: ISPS compliant

Approach: Sandbank in N approach at NW point of Mocronisos Island. In S approach a rocky bank about eight cables from Cape Fonias. Another bank in N entrance of port about 230 m E of white light with a depth of 5.5 m

Anchorage: Anchorage for most size vessels at 900 m distance from white light, Akra Ergastiria, 35 m depth, sandy bottom

Pilotage: Compulsory. VHF Channels 12 and 16. Pilot boards 1-5 miles from port depending on dimensions and draught of vessel

Radio Frequency: VHF Channel 12

Tides: Max range of tide 0.35 m

Maximum Vessel Dimensions: 140 m loa, 6.1 m d, 10 000 dwt

Working Hours: 24 h/day

Key to Principal Facilities:—				
A=Airport	**C**=Containers	**G**=General Cargo	**P**=Petroleum	**R**=Ro/Ro	**Y**=Dry Bulk
B=Bunkers	**D**=Dry Dock	**L**=Cruise	**Q**=Other Liquid Bulk	**T**=Towage (where available from port)	

Accommodation:

Name	Length (m)	Depth (m)	Remarks
Laurium			See [1] below
Pier		5–6	100 m and 80 m length berths
Pier	120	7	

[1]*Laurium:* One pier owned by D.O.W. Chemical, 5.5 m depth; tankers mooring on four buoys using one anchor
One pier owned by Electricity Company, 14 m depth; tankers mooring only stern line using both anchors with max chains

Mechanical Handling Equipment:

Location	Type	Capacity (t)
Laurium	Mobile Cranes	18

Cargo Worked: Bulk cargo 300 t/gang/day, bagged cargo 150 t/gang/day

Bunkering: Available by road tanker in small quantities
Aegean Marine Petroleum S.A., 42 Hatzikiriakou Avenue, 185 38 Piraeus, Greece, *Tel:* +30 210 4586 000, *Fax:* +30 210 4586 245, *Email:* marinefuels@ampni.com, *Website:* www.ampni.com
Aegean Petroleum (UK) Ltd, 207 Coppergate House, 16 Brune Street, London E1 7NJ, United Kingdom, *Tel:* +44 20 7953 7990, *Fax:* +44 20 7953 7856, *Email:* piraeusbunkers@aegeanpetroleum.co.uk
Alpha Petroleum S.A., 7 Spirou Miliou Street, 124 62 Piraeus, Greece, *Tel:* +30 210 557 7405, *Fax:* +30 210 557 7302
Baluco S.A., 182 Androutsou & Bouboulinas Streets, 185 35 Piraeus, Greece, *Tel:* +30 210 4190 562, *Fax:* +30 210 4190 566, *Email:* bunkers@baluco.com, *Website:* www.baluco.com
BP Greece Ltd, 43 Iroon Polytechniou Avenue, 185 35 Piraeus, Greece, *Tel:* +30 210 422 4615, *Fax:* +30 210 422 4669
Brilliant Maritime Services Ltd, 170 Ipsilantou Street, 185 35 Piraeus, Greece, *Tel:* +30 210 4101 280, *Fax:* +30 210 4101 285, *Email:* sales@bmsbunkers.com, *Website:* www.bmsbunkers.com
Chevron Marine Products LLC, 4 Possidonos Avenue, Kallithea, 176 74 Piraeus, Greece, *Tel:* +30 210 9473 000, *Fax:* +30 210 9480 062, *Email:* gmpgreb@chevron.com, *Website:* www.chevron.com
Eko Abee (Hellenic Fuels and Lubricants), 3rd Floor, 87 Akti Miaouli, 185 38 Piraeus, Greece, *Tel:* +30 210 4290 920, *Fax:* +30 210 4290 958, *Email:* eko@eko.gr, *Website:* www.eko.gr
Energy Net Ltd, 18 Davaki Street, Pefki, 151 21 Athens, Greece, *Tel:* +30 210 6144 400, *Fax:* +30 210 6144 494, *Email:* enet@otenet.gr
Gram Marine S.A., 9 Afentouli Street, 185 36 Piraeus, Greece, *Tel:* +30 210 4287 935, *Fax:* +30 210 4287 934, *Email:* grammarine@ath.forthnet.gr
Interoil Trading S.A., 32 Zosimadon Street, 185 31 Piraeus, Greece, *Tel:* +30 210 422 5941, *Fax:* +30 210 413 7051, *Email:* interoil@otenet.gr
Mamidoil-Jetoil S.A., 227-229 Kifissias Avenue, Kifissia, 145 61 Athens, Greece, *Tel:* +30 210 8763100, *Fax:* +30 210 8055955, *Email:* info@jetoil.gr, *Website:* www.jetoil.gr
Martechnic Bunkering Ltd, Martechnic Bunkering Ltd, 15 Aristidou Street, 185 31 Piraeus, Greece, *Tel:* +30 210 4227 267, *Fax:* +30 210 4227 271, *Email:* martbunk@otenet.gr
Mediterranean Bunker Services S.A., 3 Irodotou Street, 185 38 Piraeus, Greece, *Tel:* +30 210 4297 440, *Fax:* +30 210 4297 443, *Email:* mbsisid@otenet.gr
Motor Oil (Hellas) Corinth Refineries S.A., 12A Irodou Attikou Street, Maroussi, 15124 Athens, Greece, *Tel:* +30 210 8094 000, *Fax:* +30 210 8094 444, *Email:* info@moh.gr, *Website:* www.moh.gr
OW Bunker Malta Ltd, A. Laskou 12 & Akti Themistokleous 20, Freattyda Square, 185 36 Piraeus, Greece, *Tel:* +30 210 4284 455, *Fax:* +30 210 4284 459, *Email:* piraeus@owbunker.com, *Website:* www.owbunker.com
Sekavin S.A., 53-55 Akti Miaouli, 185 36 Piraeus, Greece, *Tel:* +30 210 4293 160/71, *Fax:* +30 210 4293 345, *Email:* sekavinsales@ath.forthnet.gr, *Website:* www.sekavin.gr
Shell Company (Hellas) Ltd, 2 Eleftheriou Venizelou Avenue, Kallithea, 176 76 Athens, Greece, *Tel:* +30 210 929 5911, *Fax:* +30 210 929 5378
Shipoil Ltd, 99 Kolokotroni Street, 185 35 Piraeus, Greece, *Tel:* +30 210 4221 373, *Fax:* +30 210 4223 916, *Email:* shipoil@otenet.gr
United Petroleum International S.A., 9 Filellinon Street, 185 36 Piraeus, Greece, *Tel:* +30 210 429 4396, *Fax:* +30 210 429 4735, *Email:* upi@itel.gr

Towage: Available from Piraeus, depending on size of vessel and weather conditions

Repair & Maintenance: Minor repairs available

Shipping Agents: Transmar Shipping Co. S.A., 6 Kountouriotou Street, 185 35 Lavrion, Greece, *Tel:* +30 22920 27388, *Fax:* +30 22920 27388, *Email:* agency@transmar.gr, *Website:* www.transmar.gr

Medical Facilities: Available at Public Health Centre and Athens Hospitals

Airport: Athens Airport, 45 km

Lloyd's Agent: International Insurance Services E.P.E., 117 Notara Street, 185 35 Piraeus, Greece, *Tel:* +30 210 428 4080, *Fax:* +30 210 428 4405, *Email:* grlloyds@otenet.gr

LAVRION

alternate name, see Laurium

LEROS

Admiralty Chart: 1531/1532	**Admiralty Pilot:** 48
Time Zone: GMT +2 h	**UNCTAD Locode:** GR LRS

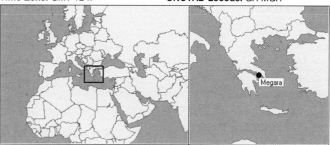

Principal Facilities:

		G						A

Authority: Port Authority of Leros, 854 01 Leros Island, Greece, *Tel:* +30 22470 22334, *Fax:* +30 22470 22334, *Email:* leros@mail.yen.gr

Officials: Harbour Master: Ioannis Litras.

Pilotage: Not available

Accommodation:

Name	Length (m)	Depth (m)	Remarks
Leros			
Port Lakki	80	8	
Ayia Marina			See [1] below

[1]*Ayia Marina:* Two quays in harbour, one 60 m long with depth alongside of 7 m and one 70 m long with 5 m depth

Storage:

Location	Sheds / Warehouses
Port Lakki	1

Airport: Partheni, 10 km

Lloyd's Agent: International Insurance Services E.P.E., 117 Notara Street, 185 35 Piraeus, Greece, *Tel:* +30 210 428 4080, *Fax:* +30 210 428 4405, *Email:* grlloyds@otenet.gr

MEGARA

Lat 37° 58' N; Long 23° 24' E.

Admiralty Chart: 1598	**Admiralty Pilot:** 48
Time Zone: GMT +2 h	**UNCTAD Locode:** GR MGR

Principal Facilities:

P						B		T	A	

Authority: Eleusis Port Authority, 10 Kanellopoulou Street, 192 00 Eleusis, Greece, *Tel:* +30 210 554 3504, *Fax:* +30 210 554 7980

Approach: From the passage between the E end of Revithousa Island and Cape Karas, the pier is approached on a NW course

Anchorage: SW of N Pachi Island in depth of approx 30 fathoms

Pilotage: Compulsory. Pilot boards SW of N Pachi Island only during daylight hours

Radio Frequency: Athina Radio (SVA), VHF Channel 16

Tides: Tidal range approx 0.3 m

Maximum Vessel Dimensions: 75 000 dwt, 12.0 m d

Principal Imports and Exports: Imports: Gas oil.

Working Hours: 24 h/day

Accommodation:

Name	Remarks
Megara	See [1] below

[1]*Megara:* Pier projecting 205 m from shore with berthing head 63 m long in depth of 12.8 m. The pier is equipped with fender tails. Vessels discharge cargoes by three 8" dia flexible hoses

Bunkering: Aegean Marine Petroleum S.A., 42 Hatzikiriakou Avenue, 185 38 Piraeus, Greece, *Tel:* +30 210 4586 000, *Fax:* +30 210 4586 245, *Email:* marinefuels@ampni.com, *Website:* www.ampni.com
Aegean Petroleum (UK) Ltd, 207 Coppergate House, 16 Brune Street, London E1 7NJ, United Kingdom, *Tel:* +44 20 7953 7990, *Fax:* +44 20 7953 7856, *Email:* piraeusbunkers@aegeanpetroleum.co.uk
Alpha Petroleum S.A., 7 Spirou Miliou Street, 124 62 Piraeus, Greece, *Tel:* +30 210 557 7405, *Fax:* +30 210 557 7302
Baluco S.A., 182 Androutsou & Bouboulinas Streets, 185 35 Piraeus, Greece, *Tel:* +30 210 4190 562, *Fax:* +30 210 4190 566, *Email:* bunkers@baluco.com, *Website:* www.baluco.com
BP Greece Ltd, 43 Iroon Polytechniou Avenue, 185 35 Piraeus, Greece, *Tel:* +30 210 422 4615, *Fax:* +30 210 422 4669
Brilliant Maritime Services Ltd, 170 Ipsilantou Street, 185 35 Piraeus, Greece, *Tel:* +30 210 4101 280, *Fax:* +30 210 4101 285, *Email:* sales@bmsbunkers.com, *Website:* www.bmsbunkers.com
Chevron Marine Products LLC, 4 Possidonos Avenue, Kallithea, 176 74 Piraeus, Greece, *Tel:* +30 210 9473 000, *Fax:* +30 210 9480 062, *Email:* gmpgreb@chevron.com, *Website:* www.chevron.com
Eko Abee (Hellenic Fuels and Lubricants), 3rd Floor, 87 Akti Miaouli, 185 38 Piraeus, Greece, *Tel:* +30 210 4290 920, *Fax:* +30 210 4290 958, *Email:* eko@eko.gr, *Website:* www.eko.gr
Energy Net Ltd, 18 Davaki Street, Pefki, 151 21 Athens, Greece, *Tel:* +30 210 6144 400, *Fax:* +30 210 6144 494, *Email:* enet@otenet.gr
Gram Marine S.A., 9 Afentouli Street, 185 36 Piraeus, Greece, *Tel:* +30 210 4287 935, *Fax:* +30 210 4287 934, *Email:* grammarine@ath.forthnet.gr
Interoil Trading S.A., 32 Zosimadon Street, 185 31 Piraeus, Greece, *Tel:* +30 210 422 5941, *Fax:* +30 210 413 7051, *Email:* interoil@otenet.gr
Mamidoil-Jetoil S.A., 227-229 Kifissias Avenue, Kifissia, 145 61 Athens, Greece, *Tel:* +30 210 8763100, *Fax:* +30 210 8055955, *Email:* info@jetoil.gr, *Website:* www.jetoil.gr
Martechnic Bunkering Ltd, Martechnic Bunkering Ltd, 15 Aristidou Street, 185 31 Piraeus, Greece, *Tel:* +30 210 4227 267, *Fax:* +30 210 4227 271, *Email:* martbunk@otenet.gr
Mediterranean Bunker Services S.A., 3 Irodotou Street, 185 38 Piraeus, Greece, *Tel:* +30 210 4297 440, *Fax:* +30 210 4297 443, *Email:* mbsisid@otenet.gr
Motor Oil (Hellas) Corinth Refineries S.A., 12A Irodou Attikou Street, Maroussi, 15124 Athens, Greece, *Tel:* +30 210 8094 000, *Fax:* +30 210 8094 444, *Email:* info@moh.gr, *Website:* www.moh.gr
OW Bunker Malta Ltd, A. Laskou 12 & Akti Themistokleous 20, Freattyda Square, 185 36 Piraeus, Greece, *Tel:* +30 210 4284 455, *Fax:* +30 210 4284 459, *Email:* piraeus@owbunker.com, *Website:* www.owbunker.com
Sekavin S.A., 53-55 Akti Miaouli, 185 36 Piraeus, Greece, *Tel:* +30 210 4293 160/71, *Fax:* +30 210 4293 345, *Email:* sekavinsales@ath.forthnet.gr, *Website:* www.sekavin.gr
Shell Company (Hellas) Ltd, 2 Eleftheriou Venizelou Avenue, Kallithea, 176 76 Athens, Greece, *Tel:* +30 210 929 5911, *Fax:* +30 210 929 5378
Shipoil Ltd, 99 Kolokotroni Street, 185 35 Piraeus, Greece, *Tel:* +30 210 4221 373, *Fax:* +30 210 4223 916, *Email:* shipoil@otenet.gr
United Petroleum International S.A., 9 Filellinon Street, 185 36 Piraeus, Greece, *Tel:* +30 210 429 4396, *Fax:* +30 210 429 4735, *Email:* upi@itel.gr

Towage: Compulsory

Medical Facilities: Available at Megara Town, 7 km

Airport: Athens Airport, 60 km

Lloyd's Agent: International Insurance Services E.P.E., 117 Notara Street, 185 35 Piraeus, Greece, *Tel:* +30 210 428 4080, *Fax:* +30 210 428 4405, *Email:* grlloyds@otenet.gr

MESOLONGION

Lat 38° 22' N; Long 21° 25' E.

Admiralty Chart: 1676
Admiralty Pilot: 47
Time Zone: GMT +2 h
UNCTAD Locode: GR MEL

Principal Facilities:

		G	R				

Authority: Port Authority of Mesolongion, 302 00 Mesolongion, Greece, *Tel:* +30 26310 51121, *Fax:* +30 26310 51121

Approach: Depth in channel 5.49 m, width 40 m

Anchorage: Vessels may obtain anchorage approx 0.5 nautical miles off the landing pier in depth of 15-20 m

Pilotage: Private pilot available

Radio Frequency: VHF Channel 12-18

Maximum Vessel Dimensions: Any vessel with d up to 5.49 m

Principal Imports and Exports: Imports: General cargo, Timber. Exports: Animal feed, Salt.

Working Hours: Mon-Sat 0730-1500

Accommodation:

Name	Remarks
Mesolongion	Total length of piers 570 m with max depth alongside of 10.7 m

Medical Facilities: Hospital in the town, 2 km from port

Lloyd's Agent: International Insurance Services E.P.E., 117 Notara Street, 185 35 Piraeus, Greece, *Tel:* +30 210 428 4080, *Fax:* +30 210 428 4405, *Email:* grlloyds@otenet.gr

MILAKI

harbour area, see under Aliveri

MILOS ISLAND

Admiralty Chart: 1037
Admiralty Pilot: 48
Time Zone: GMT +2 h
UNCTAD Locode: GR MLO

Principal Facilities:

		Y	G	R				A

Authority: Milos Port Authority, 848 01 Milos, Greece, *Tel:* +30 22870 22101, *Fax:* +30 22870 22100, *Email:* milos@yen.gr

Officials: Harbour Master: Lt Hametis Iantelis.

Port Security: ISPS compliant

Pilotage: Not available

Radio Frequency: VHF Channel 12

Accommodation:

Name	Remarks
Milos Island	Three main berthing areas for commercial vessels
Adhamas	See [1] below
Voudia Bay	See [2] below
Kanaba	See [3] below

[1]*Adhamas:* In pos 36° 43.5' N; 24° 26.7' E. For vessels up to approx 125 m loa handling primarily fruit and passenger vessels
[2]*Voudia Bay:* In pos 36° 45.0' N; 24° 32.2' E. For cargo vessels and tankers up to approx 112 m loa handling primarily fuel oil and perlite. Storage available for fuel oil
[3]*Kanaba:* In pos 36° 42.6' N; 24° 27.6' E. For cargo vessels and tankers up to approx 106 m loa handling primarily water, fuel oil and perlite. Storage available for fuel oil

Medical Facilities: There is a medical centre at Plaka Village, 15 mins from Adhamas and Kanaba, and 25 mins from Voudia Bay

Airport: 3.5 km from Adhamas, 1.5 km from Kanaba and 7.5 km from Voudia Bay

Lloyd's Agent: International Insurance Services E.P.E., 117 Notara Street, 185 35 Piraeus, Greece, *Tel:* +30 210 428 4080, *Fax:* +30 210 428 4405, *Email:* grlloyds@otenet.gr

MITILINI

alternate name, see Mytilene

MYKONOS

Lat 37° 27' N; Long 25° 20' E.

Admiralty Chart: 1538
Admiralty Pilot: 48
Time Zone: GMT +2 h
UNCTAD Locode: GR JMK

Key to Principal Facilities:—					
A=Airport	**C**=Containers	**G**=General Cargo	**P**=Petroleum	**R**=Ro/Ro	**Y**=Dry Bulk
B=Bunkers	**D**=Dry Dock	**L**=Cruise	**Q**=Other Liquid Bulk	**T**=Towage (where available from port)	

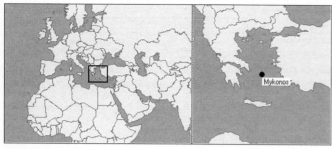

Principal Facilities:

	Y	G		L			A	

Authority: Port Authority of Mykonos, 846 00 Mykonos, Greece, *Tel:* +30 22890 22218, *Fax:* +30 22890 27825, *Email:* myko@yen.gr

Officials: Harbour Master: Pablos Tiftikidis.

Port Security: ISPS compliant

Pilotage: Not compulsory

Radio Frequency: VHF Channel 12

Maximum Vessel Dimensions: 150 m loa, 6.2 m d

Working Hours: 24 h/day

Accommodation:

Name	Remarks
Mykonos	
Mykonos Harbour	See [1] below
Ayias Annas Bay	See [2] below

[1]*Mykonos Harbour:* Situated on the W side of the island. Vessels can berth alongside the Northern Breakwater in a depth of approx 10.1 m. The W end of this breakwater is reserved for ferries. There is a quay 150 m long inside the harbour used for small craft

[2]*Ayias Annas Bay:* Situated on the SE coast of the island. There is a small pier with four mooring buoys located on the NE side of the bay, for the loading of baryte ore. Vessels of about 22 000 dwt can be accommodated. Loading rates up to 5000 t/day. The loading of vessels is considered unsafe during prevailing SW to W winds. Anchorage may be obtained in the bay in depths ranging from 16.5 m to 18.3 m

Bunkering: Marine diesel oil is available by road tanker

Medical Facilities: Medical centre at Mykonos

Airport: Mykonos Airport, 3 km

Lloyd's Agent: International Insurance Services E.P.E., 117 Notara Street, 185 35 Piraeus, Greece, *Tel:* +30 210 428 4080, *Fax:* +30 210 428 4405, *Email:* grlloyds@otenet.gr

MYTILENE

Lat 39° 6' N; Long 26° 33' E.

Admiralty Chart: 1675	**Admiralty Pilot:** 48
Time Zone: GMT +2 h	**UNCTAD Locode:** GR MJT

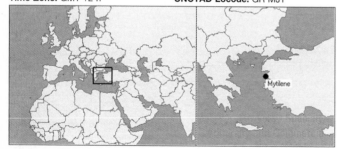

Principal Facilities:

	Q	Y	G		R		B			A	

Authority: Port Authority of Mytilene, 75 Kountouriotis P. Street, 811 00 Mytilene, Greece, *Tel:* +30 22510 24115, *Fax:* +30 22510 47888, *Email:* mitl@yen.gr

Officials: Harbour Master: Apostolos Mikromastoras.

Documentation: Quarantine: maritime declaration of health, valid derat certificate, international vaccination certificates
Customs: crew effects declaration (2 copies), ship's stores declaration (2 copies), bonded goods declaration (2 copies), crew list (2 copies)
Immigration: crew list, passenger list
Port Authority: crew list, passenger list, ship's certificates or memorandum, ship's documents

Anchorage: Available off the outer port in depths of approx 18 m

Pilotage: Not compulsory but can be obtained if required. Entry is not allowed after sunset

Radio Frequency: VHF Channels 12 and 16

Weather: S and N winds during winter, N and NE winds during summer, all force 4-8

Working Hours: 0730-1430

Accommodation:

Name	Length (m)	Draught (m)	Remarks
Mytilene			See [1] below
Inner Port	120	5.6	
Old Dock	264	9	
New Dock	190	8.5	
Commercial Port		5.6	Berths 200 m long & 100 m long

[1]*Mytilene:* Tanker facilities: At Geras Bay (Eko-Mamidakis), Tel: +30 2251 091009 and at Pamfila (BP), Tel: +30 2251 031253

Bunkering: Supplied by tanker trucks only at the New Dock of Outer Port with advance notice

Towage: Not available. Tugs can be brought in from Piraeus if necessary

Repair & Maintenance: Local machine shops undertake very minor repairs

Surveyors: Hellenic Register of Shipping, 27 Mitropoleos Street, 811 00 Mytilene, Greece, *Tel:* +30 22510 29908, *Fax:* +30 22510 45162, *Email:* geodynam@otenet.gr, *Website:* www.hrs.gr

Medical Facilities: Hospital and dental facilities are available. Vaccination cards required

Airport: Mytilene Airport, 8 km

Lloyd's Agent: International Insurance Services E.P.E., 117 Notara Street, 185 35 Piraeus, Greece, *Tel:* +30 210 428 4080, *Fax:* +30 210 428 4405, *Email:* grlloyds@otenet.gr

NAUPLIA

Lat 37° 34' N; Long 22° 48' E.

Admiralty Chart: 1683	**Admiralty Pilot:** 48
Time Zone: GMT +2 h	**UNCTAD Locode:** GR NPL

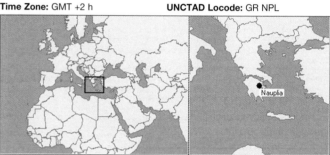

Principal Facilities:

			G						

Authority: Nauplia Port Authority, 5 Kotsonopoulou Street, 211 00 Nauplia, Greece, *Tel:* +30 27520 22974, *Fax:* +30 27520 27022, *Email:* nafp@yen.gr

Officials: Harbour Master: Panagiotis Lazopoulos.

Pilotage: Local pilot available

Radio Frequency: Available on VHF Channel 12

Principal Imports and Exports: Imports: Boxboards, Fertiliser. Exports: Lemons, Oranges.

Working Hours: 0700-1400. Sat 0700-1200. Overtime 1530-1830

Accommodation:

Name	Length (m)	Draught (m)
Nauplia		
Pier	300	5.5
Pier	200	5.5
Pier	80	5.5

Cargo Worked: 100 t/gang/day

Medical Facilities: State Hospital

Lloyd's Agent: International Insurance Services E.P.E., 117 Notara Street, 185 35 Piraeus, Greece, *Tel:* +30 210 428 4080, *Fax:* +30 210 428 4405, *Email:* grlloyds@otenet.gr

NAVPLION

alternate name, see Nauplia

NEA KARVALI

alternate name, see Kavala

NEA MOUDHANIA

Lat 40° 14' N; Long 23° 17' E.

Admiralty Chart: 1085　　　　　**Admiralty Pilot:** 48
Time Zone: GMT +2 h　　　　　**UNCTAD Locode:** GR NMA

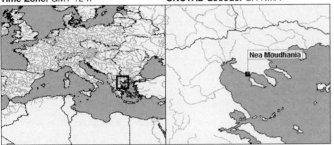

Principal Facilities:

		Y					T	A	

Authority: Port Police Control, 632 00 Nea Moudhania, Greece, *Tel:* +30 23730 21172, *Fax:* +30 23730 23680

Officials: Harbour Master: Evangelos Vetsikas.

Accommodation:

Name	Length (m)	Depth (m)	Remarks
Nea Moudhania Pier	230	5.6–10.5	See [1] below

[1]*Pier:* Used for export of magnesite ore by Grecian Magnesite S.A.

Towage: One tug boat

Airport: Thessaloniki, 65 km

Lloyd's Agent: International Insurance Services E.P.E., 117 Notara Street, 185 35 Piraeus, Greece, *Tel:* +30 210 428 4080, *Fax:* +30 210 428 4405, *Email:* grlloyds@otenet.gr

PACHI

Lat 37° 58' N; Long 23° 22' E.

Admiralty Chart: 1513　　　　　**Admiralty Pilot:** 48
Time Zone: GMT +2 h　　　　　**UNCTAD Locode:** GR

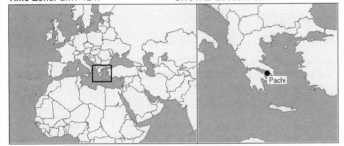

Principal Facilities:

P						B		T	A

Authority: Eleusis Port Authority, 10 Kanellopoulou Street, 192 00 Eleusis, Greece, *Tel:* +30 210 554 3504, *Fax:* +30 210 554 7980

Port Security: ISPS compliant

Anchorage: SW of N Pachi Island in depth of approx 30 fathoms

Pilotage: Compulsory. Pilot boards SW of N Pachi Island

Radio Frequency: Athina Radio (SVA), VHF Channel 16

Maximum Vessel Dimensions: 600 000 dwt, 29 m d

Principal Imports and Exports: Imports: Crude oil.

Working Hours: 24 h/day

Accommodation:

Name	Remarks
Pachi	See [1] below

[1]*Pachi:* Crude oil discharging terminal consisting of a T-shaped pier projecting 100 m S from the shore with a berthing face 130 m long with a depth of 31 m at the head of the pier. One berth, equipped with four unloading arms of 16" dia and able to accommodate vessels from 20 000 dwt to 600 000 dwt and 29 m d

Bunkering: Aegean Marine Petroleum S.A., 42 Hatzikiriakou Avenue, 185 38 Piraeus, Greece, *Tel:* +30 210 4586 000, *Fax:* +30 210 4586 245, *Email:* marinefuels@ampni.com, *Website:* www.ampni.com
Aegean Petroleum (UK) Ltd, 207 Coppergate House, 16 Brune Street, London E1 7NJ, United Kingdom, *Tel:* +44 20 7953 7990, *Fax:* +44 20 7953 7856, *Email:* piraeusbunkers@aegeanpetroleum.co.uk
Alpha Petroleum S.A., 7 Spirou Miliou Street, 124 62 Piraeus, Greece, *Tel:* +30 210 557 7405, *Fax:* +30 210 557 7302
Baluco S.A., 182 Androutsou & Bouboulinas Streets, 185 35 Piraeus, Greece, *Tel:* +30 210 4190 562, *Fax:* +30 210 4190 566, *Email:* bunkers@baluco.com, *Website:* www.baluco.com
BP Greece Ltd, 43 Iroon Polytechniou Avenue, 185 35 Piraeus, Greece, *Tel:* +30 210 422 4615, *Fax:* +30 210 422 4669
Brilliant Maritime Services Ltd, 170 Ipsilantou Street, 185 35 Piraeus, Greece, *Tel:* +30 210 4101 280, *Fax:* +30 210 4101 285, *Email:* sales@bmsbunkers.com, *Website:* www.bmsbunkers.com
Chevron Marine Products LLC, 4 Possidonos Avenue, Kallithea, 176 74 Piraeus, Greece, *Tel:* +30 210 9473 000, *Fax:* +30 210 9480 062, *Email:* gmpgreb@chevron.com, *Website:* www.chevron.com
Eko Abee (Hellenic Fuels and Lubricants), 3rd Floor, 87 Akti Miaouli, 185 38 Piraeus, Greece, *Tel:* +30 210 4290 920, *Fax:* +30 210 4290 958, *Email:* eko@eko.gr, *Website:* www.eko.gr
Energy Net Ltd, 18 Davaki Street, Pefki, 151 21 Athens, Greece, *Tel:* +30 210 6144 400, *Fax:* +30 210 6144 494, *Email:* enet@otenet.gr
Gram Marine S.A., 9 Afentouli Street, 185 36 Piraeus, Greece, *Tel:* +30 210 4287 935, *Fax:* +30 210 4287 934, *Email:* grammarine@ath.forthnet.gr
Interoil Trading S.A., 32 Zosimadon Street, 185 31 Piraeus, Greece, *Tel:* +30 210 422 5941, *Fax:* +30 210 413 7051, *Email:* interoil@otenet.gr
Mamidoil-Jetoil S.A., 227-229 Kifissias Avenue, Kifissia, 145 61 Athens, Greece, *Tel:* +30 210 8763100, *Fax:* +30 210 8055955, *Email:* info@jetoil.gr, *Website:* www.jetoil.gr
Martechnic Bunkering Ltd, Martechnic Bunkering Ltd, 15 Aristidou Street, 185 31 Piraeus, Greece, *Tel:* +30 210 4227 267, *Fax:* +30 210 4227 271, *Email:* martbunk@otenet.gr
Mediterranean Bunker Services S.A., 3 Irodotou Street, 185 38 Piraeus, Greece, *Tel:* +30 210 4297 440, *Fax:* +30 210 4297 443, *Email:* mbsisid@otenet.gr
Motor Oil (Hellas) Corinth Refineries S.A., 12A Irodou Attikou Street, Maroussi, 15124 Athens, Greece, *Tel:* +30 210 8094 000, *Fax:* +30 210 8094 444, *Email:* info@moh.gr, *Website:* www.moh.gr
OW Bunker Malta Ltd, A. Laskou 12 & Akti Themistokleous 20, Freattyda Square, 185 36 Piraeus, Greece, *Tel:* +30 210 4284 455, *Fax:* +30 210 4284 459, *Email:* piraeus@owbunker.com, *Website:* www.owbunker.com
Sekavin S.A., 53-55 Akti Miaouli, 185 36 Piraeus, Greece, *Tel:* +30 210 4293 160/71, *Fax:* +30 210 4293 345, *Email:* sekavinsales@ath.forthnet.gr, *Website:* www.sekavin.gr
Shell Company (Hellas) Ltd, 2 Eleftheriou Venizelou Avenue, Kallithea, 176 76 Athens, Greece, *Tel:* +30 210 929 5911, *Fax:* +30 210 929 5378
Shipoil Ltd, 99 Kolokotroni Street, 185 35 Piraeus, Greece, *Tel:* +30 210 4221 373, *Fax:* +30 210 4223 916, *Email:* shipoil@otenet.gr
United Petroleum International S.A., 9 Filellinon Street, 185 36 Piraeus, Greece, *Tel:* +30 210 429 4396, *Fax:* +30 210 429 4735, *Email:* upi@itel.gr

Towage: Compulsory

Medical Facilities: Available at Megara Town and Eleusis

Airport: Athens Airport, 60 km

Lloyd's Agent: International Insurance Services E.P.E., 117 Notara Street, 185 35 Piraeus, Greece, *Tel:* +30 210 428 4080, *Fax:* +30 210 428 4405, *Email:* grlloyds@otenet.gr

PAKHI

alternate name, see Pachi

PARNASSOS

harbour area, see under Itea

PATMOS

Lat 37° 18' N; Long 26° 35' E.

Admiralty Chart: 1056　　　　　**Admiralty Pilot:** 48
Time Zone: GMT +2 h　　　　　**UNCTAD Locode:** GR PMS

Principal Facilities:

				G					

Authority: Patmos Port Authority, 855 00 Patmos, Greece, *Tel:* +30 22470 31231, *Fax:* +30 22470 34131

Officials: Port Master: Konstantinos Kastrinakis.

Port Security: Hellenic Coast Guard, Tel: +30 22470 31231

Pre-Arrival Information: Hellenic coast guard, Tel; +30 22470 31231

Documentation: Customs Service, Tel; +30 22470 31312

Anchorage: Aspri & Kambos

Pilotage: Not available

Key to Principal Facilities:—
A=Airport　　　　**C**=Containers　　　　**G**=General Cargo　　　　**P**=Petroleum　　　　**R**=Ro/Ro　　　　**Y**=Dry Bulk
B=Bunkers　　　　**D**=Dry Dock　　　　**L**=Cruise　　　　**Q**=Other Liquid Bulk　　　　**T**=Towage (where available from port)

Radio Frequency: VHF channel 12 & Olympia radio channel 16

Weather: Winter: strong S-SE winds, rain, high humidity. Summer: Strong N-NW winds, high humidity

Working Hours: 24 hrs

Accommodation:

Name	Length (m)	Depth (m)	Remarks
Patmos			
Quay No.1	196	8	No warehouses or cranes
Quay No.2			

Repair & Maintenance: Minor repairs only for small boats

Medical Facilities: Small clinic near the port, Tel; +30 22470 31211

Airport: The Island is soon to be connected to Piraeus with small hydroplanes

Development: Construction of a tourist port accommodating vessels of up to 20 m will begin in the last quarter of 2006

Lloyd's Agent: International Insurance Services E.P.E., 117 Notara Street, 185 35 Piraeus, Greece, *Tel:* +30 210 428 4080, *Fax:* +30 210 428 4405, *Email:* grlloyds@otenet.gr

PATRAS

Lat 38° 15' N; Long 21° 44' E.

Admiralty Chart: 1676	**Admiralty Pilot:** 47	
Time Zone: GMT +2 h	**UNCTAD Locode:** GR GPA	

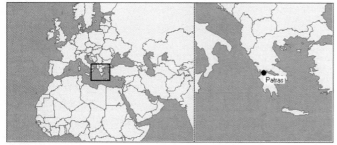

Principal Facilities:

P	Q	Y	G	C	R		B		T	

Authority: Patras Port Authority S.A., Patras Harbour Office, Othonos Amalias 85, 261 10 Patras, Greece, *Tel:* +30 2610 362648, *Fax:* +30 2610 341450, *Email:* info@patrasport.gr, *Website:* www.patrasport.gr

Officials: Managing Director: Sotiris Mammasis, *Email:* manager@patrasport.gr. Harbour Master: Apostolos Liourdis, *Tel:* +30 2610 341002.

Port Security: ISPS compliant

Approach: There are two entrances to the harbour, N entrance and S entrance. One green and one red flashing lights indicate the N entrance of the harbour, one red flashing buoy marks the S entrance

Pilotage: Compulsory for all foreign merchant vessels and Greek vessels over 1300 gt. Pilot boards in pos 38° 15.47' N; 21° 42.73' E (1 nautical mile from harbour entrance). Pilotage not available at night except in emergency. Pilot station and pilot launch equipped with VHF Channel 12

Tides: Tidal range 0.96 m max

Working Hours: Tues, Thurs and Fri 0800-1200, 1330-1730. Mon and Wed 0800-1200, 1330-1630. Sat 0800-1100

Accommodation:

Name	Length (m)	Depth (m)	Remarks
Patras			See ¹ below
Dock 1 (Gounari Pier)	130	9	
Dock 2 (Gounari Pier)	120	9	
Docks 3-4	340	14	
Docks 5-6 (Agiou Nikolaou Mole)	200	9	
Docks 7-8 (Agiou Nikolaou Mole)	200	9	
Dock 9	120	9	
Dock 10	300	9	
Dock 11 (Astiggos Pier)	160	9	
Dock 12 (Astiggos Pier)	70	14	
Dock 13 (Astiggos Pier)	120	14	
Docks 14-15	375	14	
Dock 16 (North Pier)	220	14	
Dock 17 (North Pier)	80	14	
Dock 18 (North Pier)	120	9	

¹*Patras:* The port is connected with ferry-boat lines with ports in Italy and Albania, the Ionian Islands and the port of Igoumenitsa

Storage:

Location	Open (m²)	Covered (m²)
Patras	80000	8000

Mechanical Handling Equipment:

Location	Type	Capacity (t)	Qty
Patras	Mult-purp. Cranes	18–110	5
Patras	Reach Stackers	30.5	1
Patras	Forklifts	2.5–16	17

Bunkering: Small tanker available supplying bunkers at Patras Roads
Aegean Petroleum (UK) Ltd, 207 Coppergate House, 16 Brune Street, London E1 7NJ, United Kingdom, *Tel:* +44 20 7953 7990, *Fax:* +44 20 7953 7856, *Email:* piraeusbunkers@aegeanpetroleum.co.uk
Alpha Petroleum S.A., 7 Spirou Miliou Street, 124 62 Piraeus, Greece, *Tel:* +30 210 557 7405, *Fax:* +30 210 557 7302
BP Greece Ltd, 43 Iroon Polytechniou Avenue, 185 35 Piraeus, Greece, *Tel:* +30 210 422 4615, *Fax:* +30 210 422 4669
Chevron Marine Products LLC, 4 Possidonos Avenue, Kallithea, 176 74 Piraeus, Greece, *Tel:* +30 210 9473 000, *Fax:* +30 210 9480 062, *Email:* gmpgreb@chevron.com, *Website:* www.chevron.com
Eko Abee (Hellenic Fuels and Lubricants), 3rd Floor, 87 Akti Miaouli, 185 38 Piraeus, Greece, *Tel:* +30 210 4290 920, *Fax:* +30 210 4290 958, *Email:* eko@eko.gr, *Website:* www.eko.gr
Shell Company (Hellas) Ltd, 2 Eleftheriou Venizelou Avenue, Kallithea, 176 76 Athens, Greece, *Tel:* +30 210 929 5911, *Fax:* +30 210 929 5378

Towage: Three private tugs available

Repair & Maintenance: Minor repairs available

Shipping Agents: Mertikas Shipping & Travel Agency, Iroon Politechniou & Pente Pigadion 2, 264 41 Patras, Greece, *Tel:* +30 2610 428750, *Fax:* +30 2610 432164, *Email:* info@mertikas.gr, *Website:* www.mertikas.gr
Mylaki Shipping Agency Ltd, Navmahias Ellis 1, 264 41 Patras, Greece, *Tel:* +30 2610 427029, *Fax:* +30 2610 434297, *Email:* igglesis@pat.orthnet.gr, *Website:* www.mylaki-shipping.gr
Scandinavian Near East Agency S.A., 62 Othnos & Amalias, P O Box 1012, 26221 Patras, Greece, *Tel:* +30 2610 271702, *Fax:* +30 2610 223020, *Email:* cacouris@otenet.gr, *Website:* www.cacouris.gr

Surveyors: Hellenic Register of Shipping, 29 Samou Street, 260 00 Patras, Greece, *Tel:* +30 2610 226233, *Fax:* +30 2610 226233, *Email:* aziguras@otenet.gr, *Website:* www.hrs.gr

Medical Facilities: Hospitals and various clinics

Lloyd's Agent: International Insurance Services E.P.E., 117 Notara Street, 185 35 Piraeus, Greece, *Tel:* +30 210 428 4080, *Fax:* +30 210 428 4405, *Email:* grlloyds@otenet.gr

PILOS

alternate name, see Pylos

PIRAEUS

Lat 37° 56' N; Long 23° 38' E.

Admiralty Chart: 1596	**Admiralty Pilot:** 48	
Time Zone: GMT +2 h	**UNCTAD Locode:** GR PIR	

Principal Facilities:

P	Q	Y	G	C	R	L	B	D	T	A

131, Praxitelous Str. (6th floor)
18532 Piraeus, GREECE

Tel: +30 210 4224824 (5 lines)
Fax: +30 210 4223756
Mob:+30 6936 918018
E-mail: agency@transmar.gr

BRANCH OFFICE
Kountouriotou 6, Lavrion-GREECE
Tel/Fax: +30 22920-27388

Authority: Piraeus Port Authority S.A., 10 Akti Miaouli, 185 38 Piraeus, Greece, *Tel:* +30 210 455 0229, *Fax:* +30 210 455 0310, *Email:* olp@apopsinet.gr, *Website:* www.olp.gr

Officials: President: Dionysios Bechrakis, *Tel:* +30 210 455 0282, *Email:* olp-president@olp.gr.
Chief Executive Officer: Nikolaos Anastassopoulos, *Tel:* +30 210 451 2250, *Email:* anastassopoulosn@olp.gr.
Marketing Manager: Ioanna Karles, *Tel:* +30 210 451 2250.
Harbour Master: Pouliakas Apostolos, *Tel:* +30 210 451 1129, *Email:* apostolos.pouliakas@yahoo.gr.

Port Security: ISPS compliant. Container Security Initiative (CSI) designated port

Pilotage: Compulsory for all foreign vessels and Greek vessels over 500 gt. Pilot boards in following positions:
a) Vessels proceeding to harbours and port installations E of Nisos Salamina, or entering Kolpos Elevsinas via Steno Navstathmou Navigation Channel in pos 37° 56' N; 23° 36' 05" E
b) Vessels proceeding to harbours and port installations W of Nisos Salamina, or entering Kolpos Elevsinas via Poros Megaron in pos 37° 56' N; 23° 22' E

Traffic: 2007, 20 121 916 t of cargo handled, 1 373 138 TEU's

Working Hours: Loading/unloading round the clock

Accommodation:

Name	Length (m)	Depth (m)	Remarks
Central Passenger Port			See [1] below
Commercial Port			
Container Terminal	2774		See [2] below
Pier I		11.5–12	See [3] below
Pier II		14–16	See [4] below
Car Terminals	1400		See [5] below
General & Conventional Cargo Terminal			See [6] below
Tourist Harbour			See [7] below

[1]*Central Passenger Port:* Protected by two breakwaters at entrance; orientation from NE to SW; total water surface of about 1 100 000 m2. Depths of water varying from 6 to 12 m alongside the quays and up to 27 m natural depth in the middle
The part of the port dedicated to domestic traffic comprises 6500 m of quays and four terminals for domestic passenger traffic. For cruise traffic there are quays totalling 2500 m and two passenger terminals
[2]*Container Terminal:* Situated at Neo Ikonion. Total area of 900 000 m2. Storage area of 626 000 m2. Container freight station of 19 200 m2
[3]*Pier I:* The total length of the dock is 763 m, of which 300 m on the eastern side, 178 m on the southern front and 285 m on the western side
[4]*Pier II:* The total length of the dock is 2011 m, of which 790 m on the eastern side, 520 m on the southern front and 701 m on the western side
[5]*Car Terminals:* Three car terminals as follows:
At the Sector G1, which is located in Drapetsona and occupies land area of approx 74 000 m2 with storage cap of 7500 PVU's
At the Sector G2, which is located in Keratsini and occupies land area of approx 20 700 m2 with storage cap of 2500 PVU's
At Karvounoskala in Keratsini, occupying approx 70 000 m2 of storage area
[6]*General & Conventional Cargo Terminal:* Handling and storage of conventional cargo is carried out through the facilities of Hercules Port, at Keratsini. The mechanical equipment used for the loading and unloading of conventional cargo includes electric cranes, mobile cranes, forklifts and tractors of various types. For the storage of conventional cargo the necessary warehouses are available in the port
Handling of liquid cargo, especially oil and by-products takes place at a dedicated location leased to 3rd party in New Ikonion, while nearby private tanks are also available on demand
[7]*Tourist Harbour:* (Under the jurisdiction of the Greek National Tourist Organization) Small Harbour of Zea (Freattys): Situated to E of main port. Circular length of quays 2200 m; water surface about 230 000 m2, depths up to 4.5 and 8 m (Freattys). Used as an anchorage place for small pleasure boats, as well as reception port. Outside this harbour, at Freattys Bay, there are two sea-walls of 440 and 165 m length, forming a small harbour to accommodate tourist and larger vessels
Small Harbour of Mounichia (Mikcolimano): E of main port, following above. Circular length of 800 m; water surface of about 57 000 m2, depths up to 5 m. Harbour walls 150 and 60 m length, quay walls 700 m length, depth up to 2 m. Used as anchorage place for pleasure boats and as nautical sport centre. A 65 m long wharf where Dragon type boats may dock
Phaleron Bay: A large bay extending to E of main port. Circular length of shore of about 3000 m. Depth ranges from 1 to 25 m. Used in cases of emergency for anchorage of large liners; also for anchorage of warships. Small harbour available with piers of 725 m total length and 2.5 m depth for berthing pleasure craft

Mechanical Handling Equipment:

Location	Type	Qty
Container Terminal	Container Cranes	6
Container Terminal	Post Panamax	8
Container Terminal	Straddle Carriers	64

Bunkering: Aegean Marine Petroleum S.A., 42 Hatzikiriakou Avenue, 185 38 Piraeus, Greece, *Tel:* +30 210 4586 000, *Fax:* +30 210 4586 245, *Email:* marinefuels@ampni.com, *Website:* www.ampni.com
Alpha Petroleum S.A., 7 Spirou Miliou Street, 124 62 Piraeus, Greece, *Tel:* +30 210 557 7405, *Fax:* +30 210 557 7302
Amoil International Ltd, Arvanitis Building, 116 Kolokotroni Street, 185 35 Piraeus, Greece, *Tel:* +30 210 4284 273, *Fax:* +30 210 4283 560, *Email:* amoil@team.net.gr, *Website:* www.amoil.net
Azoil Ltd, 20 Smirnis Street, 2nd Floor, Glyfada, 16562 Athens, Greece, *Tel:* +30 210 4280 040, *Fax:* +30 210 4599 926, *Email:* azoil@otenet.gr, *Website:* www.azoil.eu
Balkan & Black Sea Shipping Co., Balkan & Black Sea Shipping Co. (Hellas) Ltd, Papadopoulos Building (Oppodamias Square), Ethnikis Antistaseos and D. Gounari 39-41, P O Box 80111, 185 31 Piraeus, Greece, *Tel:* +30 210 4222 301, *Fax:* +30 210 4111 364, *Email:* bbsshellas@bbsshellas.gr, *Website:* www.navbul.com
BP Greece Ltd, 1st Floor, 89 Akti Miaouli, 185 38 Piraeus, Greece, *Tel:* +30 210 4595 810, *Fax:* +30 210 4595 869, *Email:* anna.sourka@bp.com, *Website:* www.bp.com
Brilliant Maritime Services Ltd, 170 Ipsilantou Street, 185 35 Piraeus, Greece, *Tel:* +30 210 4101 280, *Fax:* +30 210 4101 285, *Email:* sales@bmsbunkers.com, *Website:* www.bmsbunkers.com
Chevron Marine Products Hellas S.A., Chevron Marine Products Hellas S.A., 4 Posidonos Avenue, Kallithea, 176 74 Piraeus, Greece, *Tel:* +30 210 9473 000, *Fax:* +30 210 9480 645, *Email:* dlfammgre@chevron.com, *Website:* www.chevron.com
Chevron Marine Products LLC, 4 Possidonos Avenue, Kallithea, 176 74 Piraeus, Greece, *Tel:* +30 210 9473 000, *Fax:* +30 210 9480 062, *Email:* gmpgreb@chevron.com, *Website:* www.chevron.com
Daphnis Marine Enterprises, 81 Akti Miaouli, 185 38 Piraeus, Greece, *Tel:* 30 210, *Fax:* +30 210 453 9068
Delship Agencies, 5 Bouboulinas Street, 185 35 Piraeus, Greece, *Tel:* +30 210 413 5498, *Fax:* +30 210 412 7867, *Email:* agency@delshipagencies.com, *Website:* www.delship.gr
Dynamic Petroleum S.A., 2nd Floor, 7 Zoodochou Pigis Street, 185 38 Piraeus, Greece, *Tel:* +30 210 4082 590, *Fax:* +30 210 4082 595, *Email:* bunkers@dynamicpetroleum.gr, *Website:* www.dynamicpetroleum.gr
Eko Abee (Hellenic Fuels and Lubricants), 3rd Floor, 87 Akti Miaouli, 185 38 Piraeus, Greece, *Tel:* +30 210 4290 920, *Fax:* +30 210 4290 958, *Email:* eko@eko.gr, *Website:* www.eko.gr
Eteka S.A., 2 Tripoleos Street, Neo Ikonio, Perama, 188 63 Piraeus, Greece, *Tel:* +30 210 4009030, *Fax:* +30 210 4287505, *Email:* etekaoil@otenet.gr
Express Energy Inc., 3 Iassonos Street, 185 37 Piraeus, Greece, *Tel:* +30 210 4287 107, *Fax:* +30 210 4287 106, *Email:* exenergy@hol.gr, *Website:* www.expressenergy.gr
Gram Marine S.A., 9 Afentouli Street, 185 36 Piraeus, Greece, *Tel:* +30 210 4287 935, *Fax:* +30 210 4287 934, *Email:* grammarine@ath.forthnet.gr
Hellenic Register of Shipping, 23 Akti Miaouli, 185 35 Piraeus, Greece, *Tel:* +30 210 422 1900, *Fax:* +30 210 422 1913, *Email:* hrs@hrs.gr, *Website:* www.hrs.gr
IMS Oil Trading Ltd, 6-8 Aitolikou Street, 185 45 Piraeus, Greece, *Tel:* +30 210 4588 100, *Fax:* +30 210 4140 888, *Email:* imsoil@otenet.gr
Interaccess Marine Corp., 59 Iroon Polytechniou Avenue, 185 35 Piraeus, Greece, *Tel:* +30 210 4280 136, *Fax:* +30 210 4536 744, *Email:* enquiries@interaccessbunkering.com
Interbunkering Ltd, 6 Skouze Street, 185 36 Piraeus, Greece, *Tel:* +30 210 429 2517 21, *Fax:* +30 210 429 3025
International Shipping Enterprise S.A.E., 59 Akti Miaouli, 185 36 Piraeus, Greece, *Tel:* +30 210 429 3293, *Fax:* +30 210 429 3381, *Email:* harrier@harrier.gr, *Website:* www.harrier.gr
Ionian Oil and Trading S.A., 67 Akti Miaouli Street, 185 37 Piraeus, Greece, *Tel:* +30 210 4280 771, *Fax:* +30 210 4280 024, *Email:* costalos@hol.gr
Mamidoil-Jetoil S.A., Jetoil Bunkering, 16 Defteras Merarchias Street, 185 35 Piraeus, Greece, *Tel:* +30 210 4284122-4, *Fax:* +30 210 4281356, *Email:* bunkering@jetoil.gr, *Website:* www.jetoil.gr
Marine Fuels Ltd, 116 Kolokotroni Street, 185 35 Piraeus, Greece, *Tel:* +30 210 4511 750, *Fax:* +30 210 4511 780, *Email:* bunkers@marinefuels.gr
Martechnic Bunkering Ltd, Martechnic Bunkering Ltd, 15 Aristidou Street, 185 31 Piraeus, Greece, *Tel:* +30 210 4227 267, *Fax:* +30 210 4227 271, *Email:* martbunk@otenet.gr
Mediterranean Bunker Services S.A., 3 Irodotou Street, 185 38 Piraeus, Greece, *Tel:* +30 210 4297 440, *Fax:* +30 210 4297 443, *Email:* mbsisid@otenet.gr
Millennium Oil Ltd, 31 Leosthenous Street, 185 35 Piraeus, Greece, *Tel:* +30 210 4529 794, *Fax:* +30 210 4524 023, *Email:* milloil@otenet.gr
Nurius Oil & Trading Ltd, 1 Kanari Street, 185 37 Piraeus, Greece, *Tel:* +30 210 459 8802, *Fax:* +30 210 459 8806, *Email:* lubs@nurius.gr
Ocean Energy (Hellas) Ltd, 9 Filellinon Street, Floor 4, Office No. 5, 185 36 Piraeus, Greece, *Tel:* +30 210 4292 781, *Fax:* +30 210 4292 165, *Email:* greece@oceanenergy.mc, *Website:* www.oceanenergy.mc
Oils Overseas S.A., 35-39 Akti Miaouli, 185 35 Piraeus, Greece, *Tel:* +30 210 4292 340, *Fax:* +30 210 4292 656, *Email:* bunkers@oils.gr, *Website:* www.oils.gr
OW Bunker Malta Ltd, A. Laskou 12 & Akti Themistokleous 20, Freattyda Square, 185 36 Piraeus, Greece, *Tel:* +30 210 4284 455, *Fax:* +30 210 4284 459, *Email:* piraeus@owbunker.com, *Website:* www.owbunker.com
Peninsula Petroleum Ltd, 3 Irodotou Street, 185 38 Piraeus, Greece, *Tel:* +30 210 4287 800, *Fax:* +30 210 4287 802, *Email:* bunkers@peninsulapetroleum.com, *Website:* www.peninsulapetroleum.com
Petco Fuels SA, 153 Kolokotroni Street, 185 36 Piraeus, Greece, *Tel:* +30 210 4286 233, *Fax:* +30 210 4286 209, *Email:* petcogr@otenet.gr
Petrogres Services Ltd, Petrogres Trading Ltd., 10 Spyrou Trikoupi Street, 185 38 Piraeus, Greece, *Tel:* +30 210 4595 500, *Fax:* +30 210 4595 555, *Email:* lubes@leone.gr
Petrotrade Management S.A., 63 Dragatsaniou Street, 185 45 Piraeus, Greece, *Tel:* +30 210 408 0100, *Fax:* +30 210 408 0108
Phaedra Maritime S.A., 24 Akti Posidonos Street, 185 31 Piraeus, Greece, *Tel:* +30 210 4120 396, *Fax:* +30 210 4175 750, *Email:* phaedram@ath.forthnet.gr

---

Key to Principal Facilities:—				
A=Airport	**C**=Containers	**G**=General Cargo	**P**=Petroleum	**R**=Ro/Ro	**Y**=Dry Bulk
B=Bunkers	**D**=Dry Dock	**L**=Cruise	**Q**=Other Liquid Bulk	**T**=Towage (where available from port)

Seagull Maritime Inc., Seagull Maritime House, 8 Economou & Thoukididou Streets, 185 38 Piraeus, Greece, *Tel:* +30 210 428 4530, *Fax:* +30 210 428 4535
Seka S.A., 53-55 Akti Miaouli, 185 36 Piraeus, Greece, *Tel:* +30 210 4293 160, *Fax:* +30 210 4293 745, *Email:* seka@seka.gr, *Website:* www.seka.gr
Sekavin S.A., 53-55 Akti Miaouli, 185 36 Piraeus, Greece, *Tel:* +30 210 4293 160/71, *Fax:* +30 210 4293 345, *Email:* sekavinsales@ath.forthnet.gr, *Website:* www.sekavin.gr
Shell Marine Products, 3 Irodotou Street, 185 38 Piraeus, Greece, *Tel:* +30 210 4596 915, *Fax:* +30 210 4596 950, *Email:* jenny.tsambarli@shell.com, *Website:* www.shell.com
Shipoil Ltd, 99 Kolokotroni Street, 185 35 Piraeus, Greece, *Tel:* +30 210 4221 373, *Fax:* +30 210 4223 916, *Email:* shipoil@otenet.gr
Star Bunkers S.A., 82 Kolokotroni Street, 185 35 Piraeus, Greece, *Tel:* +30 210 413 2260, *Fax:* +30 210 413 2225
Termoil S.A., 2 Afendouli Street, 185 36 Piraeus, Greece, *Tel:* +30 210 429 2992, *Fax:* +30 210 429 2995, *Email:* bunkers@termoil.gr, *Website:* www.termoil.gr
Tradmar International S.A., 19 Merarchias Street, 185 35 Piraeus, Greece, *Tel:* +30 210 4296 140, *Fax:* +30 210 4296 311, *Email:* charter@tradmar.gr, *Website:* www.tradmar.gr
Tradoil Overseas S.A., 108 Kolokotroni Street, 185 35 Piraeus, Greece
Transmarine Shipping & Trading Ltd, 164 Karaiskou Street, 185 36 Piraeus, Greece, *Tel:* +30 210 4286 850, *Fax:* +30 210 4286 851, *Email:* info@transmarine.gr, *Website:* www.transmarine.gr
Trust Marine Enterprises Co. Ltd, 141 Filonos Street, 185 36 Piraeus, Greece, *Tel:* +30 210 4180083, *Fax:* +30 210 4136213
United Petroleum International S.A., 9 Filellinon Street, 185 36 Piraeus, Greece, *Tel:* +30 210 429 4396, *Fax:* +30 210 429 4735, *Email:* upi@itel.gr
Vestoil Ltd, 5th Floor Vestalco Building, 15 Agiou Spyridonos Street, 185 35 Piraeus, Greece, *Tel:* +30 210 4226 202, *Fax:* +30 210 4221 342, *Email:* vest@hol.gr, *Website:* www.vestoil.com
Vestoil Trading & Shipping S.A., Vestalco Building, 15 Agiou Spyridonos Street, 185 35 Piraeus, Greece, *Tel:* +30 210 4226 202, *Fax:* +30 210 4221 342, *Email:* vest@hol.gr, *Website:* www.vestoil.com
Eko Abee (Hellenic Fuels and Lubricants), 3rd Floor, 87 Akti Miaouli, 185 38 Piraeus, Greece, *Tel:* +30 210 4290 920, *Fax:* +30 210 4290 958, *Email:* eko@eko.gr, *Website:* www.eko.gr
International Shipping Enterprise S.A.E., 59 Akti Miaouli, 185 36 Piraeus, Greece, *Tel:* +30 210 429 3293, *Fax:* +30 210 429 3381, *Email:* harrier@harrier.gr, *Website:* www.harrier.gr
Interaccess Marine Corp., 59 Iroon Polytechniou Avenue, 185 35 Piraeus, Greece, *Tel:* +30 210 4280 136, *Fax:* +30 210 4536 744, *Email:* enquiries@interaccessbunkering.com
Mamidoil-Jetoil S.A., Jetoil Bunkering, 16 Defteras Merarchias Street, 185 35 Piraeus, Greece, *Tel:* +30 210 4284122-4, *Fax:* +30 210 4281356, *Email:* bunkering@jetoil.gr, *Website:* www.jetoil.gr
Power Oil S.A., 396 Maria Kiouri Street, Neo Ikonio, 188 63 Perama, Greece, *Tel:* +30 210 4000315, *Fax:* +30 210 4000689, *Email:* poweroil@otenet.gr

Towage: Private towage companies

Repair & Maintenance: Elefsis Shipbuilding and Industrial Enterprises S.A., 192 00 Eleusis, Greece, *Tel:* +30 210 553 5111, *Fax:* +30 210 554 6016, *Email:* cm@mail.elefsis-shipyards.gr, *Website:* www.elefsis-shipyards.gr Chairman: Nicholas Tavoularis Three floating docks: No.1 162 m x 24 m with max cap 22 000 dwt and lifting cap 7500 t, No.2 227 m x 35 m with max cap 70 000 dwt and lifting cap 18 000 t, No.3 252 m x 41 m with max cap 120 000 dwt and lifting cap 30 000 t
There are two dry docks accommodating ships up to 10 000 t
Two floating docks at Perama Coast of 4000 and 15 000 t cap respectively. One is of 114 m length and the other of 202 m length
Carell S.A., 541A, Gr. Lambraki Street, Keratsini, 187 57 Piraeus, Greece, *Tel:* +30 210 400 4401, *Fax:* +30 210 400 7511, *Email:* carell@hol.gr, *Website:* www.carell.gr Can accommodate vessels up to 200 m loa and 30 m breadth by hiring any one of the four state docks
Navinco Ltd., 12 Filellinon Street, 185 36 Piraeus, Greece, *Tel:* +30 210 418 3371, *Fax:* +30 210 452 5724, *Email:* info@navinco.gr, *Website:* www.navinco.gr Ship repairs including steel, piping, boiler, machinery etc. works, as well as dry-dockings and on-board repairs with flying squads

Ship Chandlers: Aenos Transit S.A., 3 Konstantinoupoleos & Retsina Street, 18540 Piraeus, Greece, *Fax:* +30 210 413 1223, *Email:* aenostr@otenet.gr
Aronis Tranzit Ltd, 14 Moutsopoulou Street, Kaminia, 18540 Piraeus, Greece, *Tel:* +30 210 417 7895, *Fax:* +30 210 413 1376, *Email:* info@aronis-transit.gr, *Website:* www.aronis-transit.gr
J.& D. Athanassiadis S.A., 78 Kastoros Street, 18545 Piraeus, Greece, *Tel:* +30 210 461 6936, *Fax:* +30 210 462 8325, *Email:* jdsupplies@shipstores.gr
Atpac Maritime Agencies Inc., P O Box 80024, 18510 Piraeus, Greece, *Tel:* +30 210 428 5977, *Fax:* +30 210 428 6175, *Email:* atpac@hol.gr
Castellana Marine & Trading Ltd, Vrilission 15, Chalandri, 152 34 Athens, Greece, *Tel:* +30 210 608 4822, *Fax:* +30 210 608 4823, *Email:* castella@otenet.gr
Cool Ships Supplies S.A., 64 Dragatsaniou Street, 18545 Piraeus, Greece, *Tel:* +30 210 406 1170, *Fax:* +30 210 406 1177, *Email:* cool_supplies@ath.forthnet.gr, *Website:* www.coolshipsupplies.gr
Cosmos Tranzit Ltd, 1 Tompazi Street, 185 37 Piraeus, Greece, *Tel:* +30 210 428 7262, *Fax:* +30 210 428 7263, *Email:* cosmos97@hol.gr
Cyber Trade Ltd, P O Box 80670, 18510 Piraeus, Greece, *Tel:* +30 210 428 8008, *Fax:* +30 210 428 8010, *Email:* cyber-pl@otenet.gr
Destel Shipping Agencies Ltd, 1st Floor, 23 Aristidou Street, 185 31 Piraeus, Greece, *Tel:* +30 210 4171818, *Fax:* +30 210 4171812, *Email:* destel@otenet.gr, *Website:* www.destel.gr
Diro-Madouvalos Brothers S.A., Marias Kiouri 328, 18863 Perama, Greece, *Tel:* +30 210 400 9370, *Fax:* +30 210 400 9559, *Email:* diro-sa@otenet.gr, *Website:* www.diro.gr
Efodiastiki S.A., 49 Doganis Street, 18546 Piraeus, Greece, *Tel:* +30 210 463 7120, *Fax:* +30 210 463 7075, *Email:* efodia@hol.gr, *Website:* www.efodiastiki.gr
Elliniki Trofodotiki EPE, Haidariou 25-27, 18543 Piraeus, Greece, *Fax:* +30 210 421 2057, *Email:* blueseamar@internet.gr
Environmental Protection Engineering S.A., 24 Dervenakion Street, 18545 Piraeus, Greece, *Tel:* +30 210 406 0000, *Fax:* +30 210 461 7423, *Email:* epe@epe.gr, *Website:* www.epe.gr
Euro-Trust S.A., Hatzianesti Street 30, Ag. Ioannis Rentis, 18233 Piraeus, Greece, *Tel:* +30 210 490 3771, *Fax:* +30 210 490 3158, *Email:* eutrust@otenet.gr
Glaros Hellas, 15 Pentagion Street, Skaramangas, 124 61 Athens, Greece, *Tel:* +30 210 558 2410, *Fax:* +30 210 558 2415, *Email:* glaros@hol.gr, *Website:* www.glaros.gr
Global Marine Service Inc., 98B Filonos Street, 18536 Piraeus, Greece, *Tel:* +30 210 428 7910, *Fax:* +30 210 418 3895, *Email:* gms@ath.forthnet.gr
Hardy Marine Services, 73 Akti Miaouli Street, 18537 Piraeus, Greece, *Tel:* +30 210 453 1133, *Fax:* +30 210 452 0972, *Email:* hardymar@hol.gr
Iason Ltd, 25th Martiou 115 Street, 18755 Piraeus, Greece, *Tel:* +30 210 400 9503, *Fax:* +30 210 400 9582, *Email:* iasonltd@otenet.gr
International Ship Stores Supplies Ltd, 26 Asklipiou Street, 18545 Piraeus, Greece, *Tel:* +30 210 412 0966, *Fax:* +30 210 412 0023, *Email:* isss@hol.gr
George Isaakidis Ltd, 34 Socratous Street, 18648 Piraeus, Greece, *Tel:* +30 210 461 0722, *Fax:* +30 210 462 7390, *Email:* isaakid@otenet.gr
D. Koronakis Industry S. A., 56 Gravias Street, 18545 Piraeus, Greece, *Tel:* +30 210 406 0600, *Fax:* +30 210 461 2548, *Email:* koronakis@koronakis.gr, *Website:* www.koronakis.gr
D. Lampropoulos S.A., 68 Mavromihali Street, 18545 Piraeus, Greece, *Tel:* +30 210 417 8525, *Fax:* +30 210 413 2659, *Email:* sales@dlampropoulos.gr, *Website:* www.dlampropoulos.gr
Them. Lymberopoulos Evep S.A., 30 Rodopis & Egaleo Street, 18545 Piraeus, Greece, *Tel:* +30 210 462 0554, *Fax:* +30 210 462 2498, *Email:* lymberop@otenet.gr
Mantarakis Group S.A., 11 Skouze Street, 185 35 Piraeus, Greece, *Tel:* +30 210 459 9705, *Fax:* +30 210 459 9706, *Email:* sales@mangrp.gr, *Website:* www.mangrp.gr
Mavrikos Imports S.A., 7 Naxou Street, 185 41 Piraeus, Greece, *Tel:* +30 210 481 3064, *Fax:* +30 210 483 1453, *Email:* mavrikos@otenet.gr, *Website:* www.mavrikosimports.gr
Meridian S.A., 120 Athinon Avenue, 10442 Athens, Greece, *Tel:* +30 210 515 4742, *Fax:* +30 210 515 4744, *Email:* ggeorgak@meridiandf.gr
MIB International Ltd, 16 Dodekanisoy Street, 185 41 Piraeus, Greece, *Tel:* +30 210 481 5324/5, *Fax:* +30 210 482 5748, *Email:* info@mibint.com, *Website:* www.mibint.com
Okeanos Ship Suppliers, 4 Parnassidos & Kerkyras Street, 18541 Piraeus, Greece, *Tel:* +30 210 483 7161, *Fax:* +30 210 483 7110, *Email:* okeanos@okeanos.gr, *Website:* www.okeanos.gr
Panousopoulos Dimitrios 'Filindra', 2D. Pouri Street, 18535 Piraeus, Greece, *Tel:* +30 210 412 2744, *Fax:* +30 210 411 3246, *Email:* filindra@mail.otenet.gr
Pilion Hellas Ltd, 17 Salaminos Street, 18545 Piraeus, Greece, *Tel:* +30 210 461 4921, *Fax:* +30 210 463 6933, *Email:* pilionsa@otenet.gr
Pilot Marine Supplies, 11 Kitheronos Street, 18540 Piraeus, Greece, *Tel:* +30 210 422 6591, *Fax:* +30 210 422 6594, *Email:* pilot95@otenet.gr
Pleiades Hellas S.A., 73A Chris Smirnis, Piraeus, Greece, *Tel:* +30 210 413 6066, *Fax:* +30 210 413 7288, *Email:* phellas@otenet.gr
Polymarine - Polychronopoulos S.A., 24 Dervenakion Street, 18545 Piraeus, Greece, *Tel:* +30 210 406 0000, *Fax:* +30 210 462 1669, *Email:* poly@epe.gr, *Website:* www.polymarine.gr
Poseidon Marine Supplies, 6-8 Almiridos, 185 40 Piraeus, Greece, *Tel:* +30 210 422 5930, *Fax:* +30 210 411 0991, *Email:* info@poseidonms.com, *Website:* www.poseidonms.com
Royal Ship Suppliers Gerasimos Kyriakatos & Co., 123 Notara Street, 18536 Piraeus, Greece, *Tel:* +30 210 451 4486, *Fax:* +30 210 452 4237, *Email:* royal@ath.forthnet.gr
Shipping Tobacco Trading S.A., 11 Sachtouri Street, 185 36 Piraeus, Greece, *Tel:* +30 210 452 3180, *Fax:* +30 210 418 4884, *Email:* nke1@tellas.gr
Syrmatoschinotechnici K.& A. Synodinos & Co., 10 P Vlahakou Street, 185 45 Piraeus, Greece, *Tel:* +30 210 417 0709, *Fax:* +30 210 417 7722, *Email:* info@cargogear.gr, *Website:* www.synodinos.gr
Unimarine Services Ltd / Uniservice Mediterranean S.A., 35 Hadjikyriakou Avenue, 18538 Piraeus, Greece, *Tel:* +30 210 453 8417, *Fax:* +30 210 428 2668, *Email:* info@unimarine.gr, *Website:* www.unimarine.gr
Vita Ships Supplies, 60 Filinos Street, 185 35 Piraeus, Greece, *Tel:* +30 210 411 9358, *Fax:* +30 210 413 3287, *Email:* vitalis@otenet.gr
Zervoudakis Marine Supplies Ltd, 31 Milou Street, 185 45 Piraeus, Greece, *Tel:* +30 210 462 3700, *Fax:* +30 210 462 7900, *Email:* zerv@otenet.gr, *Website:* www.zervoudakis.gr

Shipping Agents: Adamis Shipping Agencies Ltd, 3rd Floor, Akti Miaouli & 2 Kantharou Street, 185 37 Piraeus, Greece, *Tel:* +30 210 4284180, *Fax:* +30 210 4284186, *Email:* info@adamis.com.gr, *Website:* www.adamis.com.gr
Alshic Holdings S.A., 9 Afentouli Street, 185 36 Piraeus, Greece, *Tel:* +30 210 428 8223, *Fax:* +30 210 428 8283, *Email:* stem@alshic-bunkers.com, *Website:* www.alshic-bunkers.com
Astra Shipping Agency, 5 Akti Miaouli, GR-18535 Piraeus, Greece, *Tel:* +30 210 422 5560, *Fax:* +30 210 422 5573, *Email:* astra@franpo.gr
Athlomar Shipping & Trading Co. Ltd, 141 Filonos Street, 185 36 Piraeus, Greece, *Tel:* +30 210 429 4114, *Fax:* +30 210 429 3897
BFK Trade & Shipping Co. Ltd, 96 Iroon Polytechniou Avenue, GR-185 36 Piraeus, Greece, *Tel:* +30 210 428 3715, *Fax:* +30 210 428 3718, *Email:* management@bfk.gr, *Website:* www.bfkshipping.com
Callitsis Shipping Agencies Ltd, Callitsis Building, 56 Filonos Street, 185 35 Piraeus, Greece, *Tel:* +30 210 410 1331, *Fax:* +30 210 410 1339, *Email:* info@callitsisagency.gr, *Website:* www.callitsisagency.gr
Candia Co. S.A., 7 Platonos Street, GR-18535 Piraeus, Greece, *Tel:* +30 210 411 0011, *Fax:* +30 210 417 2629
Felix Cauchi & Son Shipping & Transport SA, 26 Skouze Street, 185 35 Piraeus, Greece, *Tel:* +30 210 428 4300, *Fax:* +30 210 428 4345
CMA-CGM S.A., CMA CGM Greece, 85 Akti Miaouli Street & 2 Flessa Street, 185 38 Piraeus, Greece, *Tel:* +30 210 429 0011, *Fax:* +30 210 429 0091, *Email:* pir.genmbox@cma-cgm.com, *Website:* www.cma-cgm.com
N. Cotzias (Agencies) Co. Ltd, 7-9 Akti Miaouli, 185 35 Piraeus, Greece, *Tel:* +30 210 422 2660, *Fax:* +30 210 422 2678, *Email:* cotzias@cotzias.gr, *Website:* www.cotzias.gr
Romilos J. Davelopoulos Co., 2 Iasonos Street & Akti Miaouli, GR-18537 Piraeus, Greece, *Tel:* +30 210 452 1784, *Fax:* +30 210 454 2897, *Email:* info@davelopoulos.gr, *Website:* www.davelopoulos.gr
Dealmar Shipping Management S.A., 6th Floor, 27-31 Hatzikyriakou Avenue, 185 38 Piraeus, Greece, *Tel:* +30 210 428 3115/7, *Fax:* +30 210 428 3118, *Email:* dsm@dsm.gr
Delship Agencies, 5 Bouboulinas Street, 185 35 Piraeus, Greece, *Tel:* +30 210 413 5498, *Fax:* +30 210 412 7867, *Email:* agency@delshipagencies.com, *Website:* www.delship.gr

European Maritime Agency Ltd, 93 Akti Miaouli, 18538 Piraeus, Greece, *Tel:* +30 210 429 1580/82, *Fax:* +30 210 429 1583
Frangopulos & Co. S.A., 5 Akti Miaouli Street, 185 35 Piraeus, Greece, *Tel:* +30 210 422 5560, *Fax:* +30 210 422 5573, *Email:* pontzst@franpo.gr, *Website:* www.franpo.gr
GAC Shipping S.A., 3 Konstantinou Paleologou Street, 185 35 Piraeus, Greece, *Tel:* +30 210 414 0400, *Fax:* +30 210 414 0477, *Email:* agency.gr@gacworld.com, *Website:* www.gacworld.com
Gemma Shipping Agency Ltd, 33 Akti Miaouli, 18535 Piraeus, Greece, *Tel:* +30 210 429 3681, *Fax:* +30 210 429 3633
Global Maritime Agency S.A., 10 Skouze & 121 Filonos Streets, GR-18536 Piraeus, Greece, *Tel:* +30 210 428 3783, *Fax:* +30 210 428 3793, *Email:* info@glomar.gr, *Website:* www.glomar.gr
Hardy Marine Services, 73 Akti Miaouli Street, 18537 Piraeus, Greece, *Tel:* +30 210 453 1133, *Fax:* +30 210 452 0972, *Email:* hardymar@hol.gr
Hellenic Shipping Agencies Ltd, 63 Dragatsaniou street, 18545 Piraeus, Greece, *Tel:* +30 210 408 0110, *Fax:* +30 210 461 2923, *Email:* info@hellenicshipping.gr, *Website:* www.hellenicshipping.gr
Inchcape Shipping Services (ISS), 55 Polydefkous Street, 185 45 Piraeus, Greece, *Tel:* +30 210 414 6600, *Fax:* +30 210 422 4908, *Email:* piraeusops@iss-shipping.com, *Website:* www.iss-shipping.com
Interforex Shipping Agency Ltd, 4-6 Bouboulinas Street, 18755 Piraeus, Greece, *Tel:* +30 210 432 8380, *Fax:* +30 210 432 8262
International Shipping Enterprise S.A.E., 59 Akti Miaouli, 185 36 Piraeus, Greece, *Tel:* +30 210 429 3293, *Fax:* +30 210 429 3381, *Email:* harrier@harrier.gr, *Website:* www.harrier.gr
Itra Shipping Co. Ltd, 38 Akti Possidonos, 185 31 Piraeus, Greece, *Tel:* +30 210 411 8311, *Fax:* +30 210 411 7767, *Email:* itra@hol.gr
Kouridakis Stavros Ltd, 15 Aristidou Street, 185 31 Piraeus, Greece, *Tel:* +30 210 417 7942, *Fax:* +30 210 411 2469, *Email:* chkour@ath.forthnet.gr, *Website:* www.kouridakis-shipagent.gr
Marico (Piraeus) Shipping Transport & Agency S.A., 4 Akti Tryfonos Moutsopoulou Street, 185 35 Piraeus, Greece, *Tel:* +30 210 429 7384/93, *Fax:* +30 210 429 6017
Medcargo D Theodorikas Shipping S.A., Akti Poseidonos 12, GR-18531 Piraeus, Greece, *Tel:* +30 210 417 9470, *Fax:* +30 210 417 9422, *Email:* medcargo@otenet.gr
Mediterranean Shipping Company, MSC Greece S.A., 12 Akti Poseidonos Street, 5th Floor, 185 31 Piraeus, Greece, *Tel:* +30 210 414 5500, *Fax:* +30 210 422 6669, *Email:* generic@mscgr.mscgva.ch, *Website:* www.mscgva.ch
Medtrans Ltd, 51 Akti Miaouli Street, GR-185 36 Piraeus, Greece, *Tel:* +30 210 429 3860, *Fax:* +30 210 458 5555, *Email:* info@medtrans.gr, *Website:* www.medtrans.gr
Metalock do Brasil Ltda, S.S.R.S. Ltd, 95 Kolokotroni Street, 5th Floor, 185 35 Piraeus, Greece, *Tel:* +30 210 422 1956, *Fax:* +30 210 422 4328, *Email:* ssrs@otenet.gr, *Website:* www.ssrs-ltd.com
Minamar Chartering & Management Co. Ltd, 81 Akti Miaouli Street, Stoa Lumu, 185 38 Piraeus, Greece, *Tel:* +30 210 452 4267, *Fax:* +30 210 452 4651, *Email:* minamar@otenet.gr
A.P. Moller-Maersk Group, Maersk Hellas S.A ., 193-195 Sygrou Avenue, 171 21 Piraeus, Greece, *Tel:* +30 210 947 3200, *Fax:* +30 210 940 0717, *Email:* pircusexp@maersk.com, *Website:* www.maerskline.com
Mylaki Shipping Agency Ltd, 43 Iroon Polytechniou Avenue, 185 35 Piraeus, Greece, *Tel:* +30 210 422 3355, *Fax:* +30 210 422 3356, *Email:* mylaki@otenet.gr, *Website:* www.mylaki-shipping.gr
Paco Shipping Services Network S.A., City Plaza, Suite 321, 85 Vouliagmenia Avenue, Glyfada, Athens, Greece, *Tel:* +30 210 964 6370, *Fax:* +30 210 964 6371
Roussos Bros. Ltd, 14 Botsari Street, 185 38 Piraeus, Greece, *Tel:* +30 210 452 4953, *Fax:* +30 210 452 2019, *Email:* agency@roussosbros.gr, *Website:* www.roussosbros.gr
Sarlis & Angelopulos (Agency) Ltd, 85 Akti Miaouli, 185 38 Piraeus, Greece, *Tel:* +30 210 429 1600, *Fax:* +30 210 429 1632, *Email:* sarlis@net.gr, *Website:* www.sarlis.gr
Sealink Trading & Shipping S.A., 85 Akti Miaouli,, 6th Floor, GR-18538 Piraeus, Greece, *Tel:* +30 210 429 0932, *Fax:* +30 210 429 1382, *Email:* server@sealink.gr
Sekavar S.A., 53-55 Akti Miaouli Street, 185 36 Piraeus, Greece, *Tel:* +30 210 429 3165, *Fax:* +30 210 429 3718, *Email:* sekavar@ath.forthnet.gr, *Website:* www.sekavar.gr
Spanos Maritime & Trading Co. Ltd, 9 Filellinon Street, 185 36 Piraeus, Greece, *Tel:* +30 210 429 4738, *Fax:* +30 210 429 4893, *Email:* spanmar@spanosmaritime.gr, *Website:* www.spanosmaritime.gr
Termoil S.A., 2 Afendouli Street, 185 36 Piraeus, Greece, *Tel:* +30 210 429 2992, *Fax:* +30 210 429 2995, *Email:* bunkers@termoil.gr, *Website:* www.termoil.gr
Transmar Shipping Co. S.A., 6th Floor, 131 Praxitelous Street, 185 32 Piraeus, Greece, *Tel:* +30 210 422 4824, *Fax:* +30 210 422 3756, *Email:* transmar@transmar.gr, *Website:* www.transmar.gr
Unistar Shipping Ltd, Piraeus Container Terminal Sebo Ikoniou, Piraeus, Greece, *Tel:* +30 210 432 5915, *Fax:* +30 210 435 5915, *Email:* uship@otenet.gr
Velikar Enterprises Ltd, Filellinon Street 45, 185 36 Piraeus, Greece, *Tel:* +30 210 452 2417, *Fax:* +30 210 452 2417, *Email:* info@velikar.com, *Website:* www.velikar.com
Venieris & Co. Shipping Ltd, 2 Navarinou Street, 18531 Piraeus, Greece, *Tel:* +30 210 422 6808, *Fax:* +30 210 422 6818, *Email:* piraeus-info@venieris.gr, *Website:* www.venieris.gr
Vernicos Shipping Group, 35-39 Akti Miaouli Street, P O Box 80421, 185 10 Piraeus, Greece, *Tel:* +30 210 429 2211, *Fax:* +30 210 429 2210, *Email:* nivercos@hols.gr, *Website:* www.vernicos.gr
Wilhelmsen Ship Services, Barwil Hellas Ltd Shipping Agencies, 2 Iasonos Street, 185 37 Piraeus, Greece, *Tel:* +30 210 452 1784, *Fax:* +30 210 428 7398, *Email:* barwil.piraeus@wilhelmsen.com, *Website:* www.barwilunitor.com

Stevedoring Companies: Germa Shipping & Stevedoring Co., 27-31 Hatzikyriakou Street, 185 38 Piraeus, Greece, *Tel:* +30 210 453 0200, *Fax:* +30 210 453 1689, *Email:* germaco@otenet.gr, *Website:* www.germashipping.com

Surveyors: Euro Maritime Consultants Ltd, 11 2as Merarchias Street, 185 35 Piraeus, Greece, *Tel:* +30 210 422 0048, *Fax:* +30 210 411 8383, *Email:* euromc@ath.forthnet.gr Managing Director: Yiannis Romanidis
ABS (Europe), Floor 3A, 6 Skouze Street, P O Box 80139, 185 36 Piraeus, Greece, *Tel:* +30 210 429 3215, *Fax:* +30 210 429 3659, *Email:* abspiraeus@eagle.org, *Website:* www.eagle.org
Alpha Marine Services Ltd, 26 Skouze Street, 5th Floor, 185 36 Piraeus, Greece, *Tel:* +30 210 451 8717, *Fax:* +30 210 428 3253, *Email:* info@alphamarine.gr, *Website:* www.alphamarine.gr
Associated Marine Enterprises Ltd, 3rd Floor, 99 Akti Miaouli, 185 38 Piraeus, Greece, *Tel:* +30 210 429 0155, *Fax:* +30 210 429 0057
Bureau Veritas, 23 Etolikou Street, 185 45 Piraeus, Greece, *Tel:* +30 210 406 3000, *Fax:* +30 210 406 3063, *Email:* office@gr.bureauveritas.com, *Website:* www.bureauveritas.com
China Classification Society, Skouze 26, 185 36 Piraeus, Greece, *Tel:* +30 210 452 0065, *Fax:* +30 210 428 1420, *Email:* ccsyd@ccs.org.cn, *Website:* www.ccs.org.cn
Container & Cargo Services Inc., 5-7 Kanari, 185 37 Piraeus, Greece, *Tel:* 30 210, *Fax:* +30 210 428 4005
P.A. Costouros & Associates, 31-33 D. Gounari Street, 185 31 Piraeus, Greece, *Tel:* +30 210 422 3320, *Fax:* +30 210 422 3321, *Email:* costouro@hol.gr
Cyprus Bureau of Shipping, 14 Skouze, 185 36 Piraeus, Greece, *Tel:* +30 210 452 2321, *Fax:* +30 210 452 2330, *Email:* cbs@otenet.gr, *Website:* www.cbs.com.cy
Det Norske Veritas A/S, 26-28 Akti Kondyli, 185 45 Piraeus, Greece, *Tel:* +30 210 410 0200, *Fax:* +30 210 422 0621, *Email:* pirmar@dnv.com, *Website:* www.dnv.com
Elkco Marine Consultants (GR) Ltd, 79 Akti Miaouli & 1 Kanai Street, 185 37 Piraeus, Greece, *Tel:* +30 210 452 8200, *Fax:* +30 210 452 6260, *Email:* elkcogr@hol.gr, *Website:* www.elkco.gr
Evdemon and Partners S.A, 14 Skouze Street, 185 36 Piraeus, Greece, *Tel:* +30 210 418 1514, *Fax:* +30 210 451 9431, *Email:* evdemon@hol.gr, *Website:* www.evdemon.gr
Ferriby Marine, Ferriby Marine (Greece), 40-44 Tompazi, 185 37 Piraeus, Greece, *Tel:* +30 210 453 7030, *Fax:* +30 210 451 0094, *Email:* tsamis_m@otenet.gr, *Website:* www.ferriby-marine.com
Francis & Arnold (Hellas), 145 Kolokotroni Street, 185 36 Piraeus, Greece, *Tel:* +30 210 453 5567, *Fax:* +30 210 428 2768, *Email:* fran@hol.gr
Germanischer Lloyd, 85 Akti Miaouli, 185 38 Piraeus, Greece, *Tel:* +30 210 429 0373, *Fax:* +30 210 429 0357, *Email:* gl-piraeus@gl-group.com, *Website:* www.gl-group.com
Hellas Marine Services Ltd, 116 Kolokotroni Street, 185 35 Piraeus, Greece, *Tel:* +30 210 451 3400, *Fax:* +30 210 418 1266, *Email:* hellasmarine@hellasmarine.gr, *Website:* www.hellasmarine.gr
Hellenic Register of Shipping, 23 Akti Miaouli, 185 35 Piraeus, Greece, *Tel:* +30 210 422 1900, *Fax:* +30 210 422 1913, *Email:* hrs@hrs.gr, *Website:* www.hrs.gr
International Marine Technical Services Ltd, 98B Filonos Street, 185 36 Piraeus, Greece, *Tel:* +30 210 452 6438, *Fax:* +30 210 418 0060
International Register of Shipping (BSS), 10 ANT. 1st Floor, Ampatielou Street, 185 36 Piraeus, Greece, *Tel:* +30 210 429 3837, *Fax:* +30 210 429 3502, *Email:* isbgr@otenet.gr, *Website:* www.intlreg.com
International Shipping Bureau (ISB), 10 ANT., 1st Floor, Ampatielou Street, 185 36 Piraeus, Greece, *Tel:* +30 210 429 3837, *Fax:* +30 210 429 3502, *Email:* info@isb.gr, *Website:* www.isbship.com
Intership Maritime Inc., 22 Kolokotroni Street, 185 36 Piraeus, Greece, *Tel:* +30 210 428 7370, *Fax:* +30 210 428 7372, *Email:* contact@intership.gr, *Website:* www.intership.gr
Kalimbassieris Maritime Co Ltd, 65 Akti Miaouli, 185 36 Piraeus, Greece, *Tel:* +30 210 429 4444, *Fax:* +30 210 429 4443, *Email:* pir.consult@kalimbassieris.com, *Website:* www.kalimbassieris.com
Kaminco (Overseas) Inc., 11 Nirvana, 166 73 Piraeus, Greece, *Tel:* +30 210 452 8240, *Fax:* +30 210 429 4887, *Email:* administration@kaminco.com, *Website:* www.kaminco.com
Kappa Marine Consultants Ltd, 37A Filellinon Street, 185 36 Piraeus, Greece, *Tel:* +30 210 428 4400, *Fax:* +30 210 428 4442, *Email:* kappaltd@otenet.gr
Korean Register of Shipping, 2 Kantharou Street, 185 37 Piraeus, Greece, *Tel:* +30 210 428 6736, *Fax:* +30 210 428 6728, *Email:* kr-pru@krs.co.kr, *Website:* www.krs.co.kr
Macrymichalos Brothers S.A., 139 Elftheriou Venizelou Avenue, Nea Erythrea, 146 71 Athens, Greece, *Tel:* +30 210 935 0285, *Fax:* +30 210 935 2028, *Email:* info@macbros-ltd.com, *Website:* www.macbros-ltd.com
Malliaroudakis Maritime Consultancy Ltd, 17 Tsamadou Street, 185 31 Piraeus, Greece, *Tel:* +30 210 422 0303, *Fax:* +30 210 413 7161, *Email:* mmc@otenet.gr
Marine Training & Safety Consultants Ltd, 2 Efplias Street, 185 37 Piraeus, Greece, *Tel:* +30 210 428 0740, *Fax:* +30 210 418 2917, *Email:* aleontop@ath.forthnet.gr
Marinecare Ltd, 98 Filimos Street, 185 36 Piraeus, Greece, *Tel:* +30 210 428 0130, *Fax:* +30 210 453 8420
Anthony Al. Mattheou & Associates, 17-19 Akti Miaouli, 185 35 Piraeus, Greece, *Tel:* +30 210 411 7707, *Fax:* +30 210 422 1880, *Email:* mattheou@otenet.gr
Mentor Marine Consultants, 4-6 Efplias Street, 185 37 Piraeus, Greece, *Tel:* +30 210 418 6002, *Fax:* +30 210 418 6004, *Email:* mentcons@hol.gr
National Shipping Adjuster Inc., 9 Sotiros Street, 185 35 Piraeus, Greece, *Tel:* +30 210 427 4087/8, *Fax:* +30 210 427 4086
Nichol Marine Services Ltd, 144 Notara Street, 185 36 Piraeus, Greece, *Tel:* +30 210 4292862, *Fax:* +30 210 428 6751, *Email:* nichol@otenet.gr
Nippon Kaiji Kyokai, Possidonos Av. & 1-3 Pindou Street, Moschato, 183 44 Piraeus, Greece, *Tel:* +30 210 483 2404, *Fax:* +30 210 483 2405, *Email:* pr@classnk.or.jp, *Website:* www.classnk.or.jp
Oceanking Maritime Inc, 31 Bouboulinas Street, 185 35 Piraeus, Greece, *Tel:* +30 210 429 6774, *Fax:* +30 210 429 6820, *Email:* info@oceanking.gr, *Website:* www.oceanking.gr
Overseas Maritime Consultants E.P.E., 57 Notara Street, 185 35 Piraeus, Greece, *Tel:* +30 210 422 2736, *Fax:* +30 210 422 2737, *Email:* comms@overseasmaritime.com, *Website:* www.overseasmaritime.com
Overseas Maritime (Hellas) Ltd, 72 Kolokotroni Street, 185 35 Piraeus, Greece, *Tel:* +30 210 422 2730, *Fax:* +30 210 422 2737, *Email:* comms@overseasmaritime.com, *Website:* www.overseasmaritime.com
Panamanian Services S.A., 25 Agiou Spiridonos Street, 185 35 Piraeus, Greece, *Tel:* +30 210 422 6569, *Fax:* +30 210 411 5367, *Email:* shipping@panservices.gr
Polish Register of Shipping, 5-7 Agiou Nikolaou Street, 185 37 Piraeus, Greece, *Tel:* +30 210 452 8320, *Fax:* +30 210 418 5845, *Email:* piraeus@prs.pl, *Website:* www.prs.pl
Registro Italiano Navale (RINA), 47-49 Akti Miaouli, 185 36 Piraeus, Greece, *Tel:* +30 210 429 2144, *Fax:* +30 210 429 2950, *Email:* piraeus.office@rina.org, *Website:* www.rina.org
Russian Maritime Register of Shipping, 128 Alkiviadou & Sotiros Dios Street, 185 35 Piraeus, Greece, *Tel:* +30 210 412 1177, *Fax:* +30 210 412 8708, *Email:* rshellas@otenet.gr, *Website:* www.rs-head.spb.ru
Shiptech Ltd, 9 Efplias Street, 185 37 Piraeus, Greece, *Tel:* +30 210 453 3763, *Fax:* +30 210 453 4645, *Email:* info@shiptech.gr, *Website:* www.shiptech.gr

Key to Principal Facilities:—
A=Airport **C**=Containers **G**=General Cargo **P**=Petroleum **R**=Ro/Ro **Y**=Dry Bulk
B=Bunkers **D**=Dry Dock **L**=Cruise **Q**=Other Liquid Bulk **T**=Towage (where available from port)

S.V.L. & Associates S.A., 21-23 Leosthenous Street, 185 36 Piraeus, Greece, *Tel:* +30 210 428 3969, *Fax:* +30 210 428 0219

Transport Counsellors International Ltd, 26 Skouze Street, 185 36 Piraeus, Greece, *Tel:* +30 210 428 4030/1, *Fax:* +30 210 428 4021, *Email:* tci@hol.gr, *Website:* www.tci.gr

C.N. Zachopoulos & Associates Ltd, 1 Charilaou Trikoupi Street, 185 36 Piraeus, Greece, *Tel:* +30 210 453 1165, *Fax:* +30 210 418 3126, *Email:* info@zacho.gr, *Website:* www.zacho.gr

Zouppas & Co. Ltd, 95 Kolokotroni Street, 185 35 Piraeus, Greece, *Tel:* +30 210 422 1554, *Fax:* +30 210 413 0138

Medical Facilities: Two public hospitals in Piraeus

Airport: Athens Airport, 14 km

Development: Extension of Pier 1 at the container terminal together with new machinery and equipment, scheduled to be completed 2009

Cosco Pacific is set to operate two piers at Piraeus port. The company will lease and operate Pier 2 and construct Pier 3 at the Piraeus Port Container Terminal. It has agreed to upgrade Pier 2 by 2014 and complete the construction of Pier 3 by 2015 to bring the capacity of the terminal up to 3.7 m TEU's

Lloyd's Agent: International Insurance Services E.P.E., 117 Notara Street, 185 35 Piraeus, Greece, *Tel:* +30 210 428 4080, *Fax:* +30 210 428 4405, *Email:* grlloyds@otenet.gr

PORT LAKKI

harbour area, see under Leros

PREVEZA

Lat 38° 57' N; Long 20° 45' E.

Admiralty Chart: 2405	**Admiralty Pilot:** 48
Time Zone: GMT +2 h	**UNCTAD Locode:** GR PVK

Principal Facilities:

P		Y	G			B		A

Authority: Port Authority of Preveza, 6 Spilliadou Street, 481 00 Preveza, Greece, *Tel:* +30 26820 22226, *Fax:* +30 26820 28854, *Email:* preb@yen.gr

Officials: Commercial Manager: Apostolos Tasis.
Harbour Master: Politis Panagiotis.

Port Security: ISPS compliant

Approach: Depth in channel of 8.85 m

Pilotage: Available privately

Radio Frequency: Port police on VHF Channel 12

Maximum Vessel Dimensions: 165 m loa

Working Hours: Sunday-Friday 0730-1430, overtime 1500-2000. Saturday 0730-1230

Accommodation:

Name	Depth (m)	Remarks
Preveza		
New Piers	11–13	250 m long and 100 m long
Old Piers		110 m long, 6-12 m depth and 100 m long, 4-9 m depth

Mechanical Handling Equipment:

Location	Type	Capacity (t)	Qty
Preveza	Mult-purp. Cranes	45	1

Cargo Worked: 100-200 t/gang. 200 t/gang for preslung cargo

Bunkering: Available by road tanker

Medical Facilities: Available

Airport: Aktion, 5 km

Lloyd's Agent: International Insurance Services E.P.E., 117 Notara Street, 185 35 Piraeus, Greece, *Tel:* +30 210 428 4080, *Fax:* +30 210 428 4405, *Email:* grlloyds@otenet.gr

PRINOS

harbour area, see under Kavala

PYLOS

Lat 36° 55' N; Long 21° 42' E.

Admiralty Chart: 2404	**Admiralty Pilot:** 47
Time Zone: GMT +2 h	**UNCTAD Locode:** GR PYL

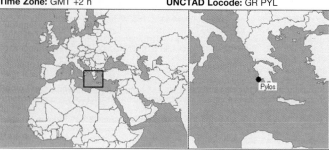

Principal Facilities:

			G			B		

Authority: Port Authority of Pylos, Harbour Office, Paralia, 240 01 Pylos, Greece, *Tel:* +30 27230 22225, *Fax:* +30 27230 22007, *Email:* pylos@mail.yen.gr

Officials: Harbour Master: Charalabos Mouzakis.

Documentation: Crew list, registry, safety equipment

Anchorage: Good anchorage for vessels of any size at Navarino Bay

Pilotage: Compulsory

Radio Frequency: VHF Channel 12

Weather: Strong SSE to SSW winds give a large swell and it is dangerous to enter port

Tides: Range of tide 0.3 m

Traffic: 2 vessels per day

Working Hours: 0800-1200, 1330-1730. Overtime can be worked 1800-2100

Accommodation:

Name	Length (m)	Depth (m)	Remarks
Pylos			Open port. Harbour only suitable for small vessels
Pier	100	10	Able to accept vessels up to 40 m loa

Mechanical Handling Equipment:

Location	Type	Capacity (t)	Qty
Pylos	Mult-purp. Cranes	25	1
Pylos	Mult-purp. Cranes	30	1

Cargo Worked: 72 t/hatch/day

Bunkering: Available by road tanker
Petrotrade Management S.A., 63 Dragatsaniou Street, 185 45 Piraeus, Greece, *Tel:* +30 210 408 0100, *Fax:* +30 210 408 0108 – *Grades:* all grades; lubes – *Rates:* 300-400t/h – *Delivery Mode:* barge, truck
Trust Marine Enterprises Co. Ltd, 141 Filonos Street, 185 36 Piraeus, Greece, *Tel:* +30 210 4180083, *Fax:* +30 210 4136213 – *Grades:* MGO; lubes – *Parcel Size:* min 25t, max 250t – *Notice:* 48 hours – *Delivery Mode:* barge, truck

Waste Reception Facilities: Pylos Municipality

Towage: Not available

Shipping Agents: G. Andreas Zervakis Ltd, Psamadou Street, 241 01 Pylos, Greece, *Tel:* +30 27230 22244, *Fax:* +30 27230 22896, *Email:* contact@zervakisltd.gr, *Website:* www.zervakisltd.gr

Medical Facilities: Public hospital available

Airport: Athens Airport, 360 km

Lloyd's Agent: International Insurance Services E.P.E., 117 Notara Street, 185 35 Piraeus, Greece, *Tel:* +30 210 428 4080, *Fax:* +30 210 428 4405, *Email:* grlloyds@otenet.gr

RETHIMNON

Lat 35° 22' N; Long 24° 28' E.

Admiralty Chart: 1707	**Admiralty Pilot:** 48
Time Zone: GMT +2 h	**UNCTAD Locode:** GR RET

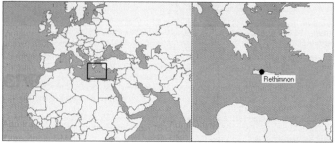

Principal Facilities:

		G		B		A

Authority: Port Authority of Rethimnon, 49 Nearchou Street, 741 00 Rethimnon, Crete, Greece, *Tel:* +30 28310 22276, *Fax:* +30 28310 55150, *Email:* reth@yen.gr

Officials: Harbour Master: Antonios Orfanos.

Approach: Depth at entrance to port 9-10 m

Anchorage: Anchorage 1.5 miles NNE of port in depth of 30 m

Pilotage: Not available

Radio Frequency: VHF Channel 12

Tides: Tides of 0.1 m

Maximum Vessel Dimensions: 150 m loa

Working Hours: 0730-1500

Accommodation:

Name	Remarks
Rethimnon	Depth at port 6-10 m. Loading and unloading using vessel's own gear or private cranes

Storage: Customs warehouses of 2000 m2 and private warehouses

Cargo Worked: 900 t/day

Bunkering: Available by road tanker

Medical Facilities: Hospital available

Airport: Iraklion Airport, 75 km

Lloyd's Agent: International Insurance Services E.P.E., 117 Notara Street, 185 35 Piraeus, Greece, *Tel:* +30 210 428 4080, *Fax:* +30 210 428 4405, *Email:* grlloyds@otenet.gr

REVITHOUSA TERMINAL

Lat 37° 57' N; Long 23° 24' E.

Admiralty Chart: 1513	**Admiralty Pilot:** 48
Time Zone: GMT +2 h	**UNCTAD Locode:** GR REV

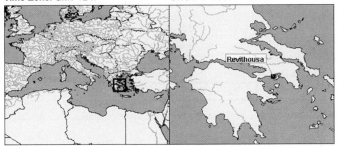

Principal Facilities:

	Q								

Authority: Public Gas Corp. of Greece (DEPA) S.A., Marinou Antuypa 92, 141 21 Athens, Greece, *Tel:* +30 210 270 1000, *Fax:* +30 210 270 1010, *Email:* pr@depa.gr, *Website:* www.depa.gr

Officials: Marketing: Kiriaki Karakitsou, *Tel:* +30 210 679 3642, *Email:* k.karakitsou@depa.gr.

Pre-Arrival Information: ETA to be given 72 h, 48 h, 24 h and 12 h via the vessel's agent

Anchorage: Located 1.5 miles W of Nisos Pakhi

Pilotage: Compulsory and available 24 h. Final advice on arrival should be given to Piraeus pilot station at least 6 h prior to arrival. Pilot boards 2 miles SSW of the terminal

Maximum Vessel Dimensions: 290 m loa, 11 m draught

Accommodation:

Name	Remarks
Revithousa Terminal	See [1] below

[1]*Revithousa Terminal:* Terminal Station, Tel: +30 210 550 8299, Fax: +30 210 550 8201
Single jetty with a sheet-piled face used by tankers discharging LNG from Algeria into two storage tanks totaling 130 000 m3

Towage: Tugs are compulsory and available from Piraeus

Lloyd's Agent: International Insurance Services E.P.E., 117 Notara Street, 185 35 Piraeus, Greece, *Tel:* +30 210 428 4080, *Fax:* +30 210 428 4405, *Email:* grlloyds@otenet.gr

RHODES

Lat 36° 26' N; Long 28° 13' E.

Admiralty Chart: 1532	**Admiralty Pilot:** 48
Time Zone: GMT +2 h	**UNCTAD Locode:** GR RHO

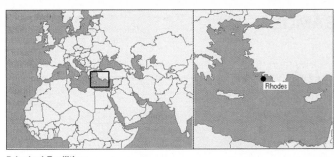

Principal Facilities:

		G	R	L	B		T	A

Authority: Central Port Authority of Rhodes, 1 Eleftherias Square, Mandraki, 851 00 Rhodes, Greece, *Tel:* +30 22410 28666, *Fax:* +30 22410 27365, *Email:* rodo@yen.gr

Port Security: ISPS compliant

Documentation: Crew list (4 copies), ship's declaration, crew declaration, ammunition list, animal list, master's declaration, list of certificates, vaccination list

Approach: No special hazards

Anchorage: Available 0.75 nautical mile E of the breakwater in depth of more than 50 m

Pilotage: Compulsory for both Greek and foreign vessels over 500 gt and also compulsory for Greek vessels under 500 gt which come from a foreign port

Radio Frequency: VHF Channel 12 (Port Authority and pilot service)

Weather: Prevailing SE winds November-February. Prevailing NW and W winds March-October

Tides: Usual rise 30-40 cm

Maximum Vessel Dimensions: 300 m loa, 60 000 dwt, 10 m draft

Principal Imports and Exports: Imports: General cargo. Exports: .

Working Hours: 0800-1500

Accommodation:

Name	Length (m)	Depth (m)	Remarks
Rhodes			See [1] below
Commercial Harbour		7–10	
East Pier	375		
West Pier	350		
140 Dock	140		
Accandia Harbour			See [2] below
Mandraki			See [3] below

[1]*Rhodes:* Consists of three harbours: the Commercial, the Accandia and the Mandraki harbour
[2]*Accandia Harbour:* Two moles, one 60 m long, 6 m deep and another 285 m long, 6.6 m deep; both used by cruise ships and not by cargo vessels
[3]*Mandraki:* The Perimetric quay is 720 m long. Electricity, water and gas oil available, 5 m draft max. Used by small boats, especially yachts

Storage: Warehouses at Commercial quay, but no refrigerated space

Mechanical Handling Equipment: Multi-purpose cranes and forklifts available

Bunkering: Aegean Petroleum (UK) Ltd, 207 Coppergate House, 16 Brune Street, London E1 7NJ, United Kingdom, *Tel:* +44 20 7953 7990, *Fax:* +44 20 7953 7856, *Email:* piraeusbunkers@aegeanpetroleum.co.uk

Waste Reception Facilities: Slops and garbage disposal facilities

Towage: Three port tugs

Ship Chandlers: Olympic Meat, Georgioy Seferi 82, Rhodes, Greece, *Tel:* +30 22410 69191, *Fax:* +30 22410 69191, *Email:* stamatise@yahoo.com

Shipping Agents: D.E. Demetriades & Co. Ltd, 3 Pavlou Mela Street, P O Box 47, GR 85100 Rhodes, Greece, *Tel:* +30 22410 27306, *Fax:* +30 22410 22615, *Email:* dimitcom@otenet.gr
Roditis Shipping Agency, 6 Sofokoli Venizelou Street, 85100 Rhodes, Greece, *Tel:* +30 22410 37101, *Fax:* +30 22410 37401, *Email:* info@roditisyachting.gr, *Website:* www.roditisyachting.gr

Surveyors: Hellenic Register of Shipping, 60 Australias Street, 851 00 Rhodes, Greece, *Tel:* +30 22410 33678, *Fax:* +30 22410 33678, *Email:* ghalkitis@hotmail.com, *Website:* www.hrs.com

Medical Facilities: Hospital, 5 km

Airport: Diagoras, 15 km

Development: Construction of new wharf in Accandia Harbour

Lloyd's Agent: International Insurance Services E.P.E., 117 Notara Street, 185 35 Piraeus, Greece, *Tel:* +30 210 428 4080, *Fax:* +30 210 428 4405, *Email:* grlloyds@otenet.gr

RODAS

alternate name, see Rhodes

SALONICA

alternate name, see Thessaloniki

Key to Principal Facilities:—				
A=Airport	**C**=Containers	**G**=General Cargo	**P**=Petroleum	**R**=Ro/Ro	**Y**=Dry Bulk
B=Bunkers	**D**=Dry Dock	**L**=Cruise	**Q**=Other Liquid Bulk	**T**=Towage (where available from port)	

SAMOS

Lat 37° 44' N; Long 26° 58' E.

Admiralty Chart: 1526   **Admiralty Pilot:** 48
Time Zone: GMT +2 h   **UNCTAD Locode:** GR SMI

Principal Facilities:

P		G	R				A

Authority: Port Authority of Samos, 1 Sofouli Them. Street, 831 00 Samos, Greece, *Tel:* +30 22730 27318, *Fax:* +30 22730 88800, *Email:* samo@yen.gr

Officials: Harbour Master: Stylianos Partsafas, *Tel:* +30 22730 27890.

Pilotage: Not available

Radio Frequency: VHF Channel 12. Radio Ellas, Channels 16 and 7

Principal Imports and Exports: Imports: Hides. Exports: Tobacco, Wine.

Accommodation:

Name	Length (m)	Depth (m)	Remarks
Samos			
Samos Harbour	111	7–8.8	Length of breakwater 174 m. No warehousing or cranes
Malagari Jetty	28	3.8	Lying directly opposite Samos Harbour
Karlovassi		6.5	Breakwater length 517 m
Marathocampos		6.5	Breakwater length 290 m

Shipping Agents: Dimitris Kasmirlis, 15 Th. Sofoulis Street, 831 00 Samos, Greece, *Tel:* +30 22730 88882, *Fax:* +30 22730 88855, *Email:* 889@rhenia.gr

Surveyors: Hellenic Register of Shipping, Lekka, 831 00 Samos, Greece, *Tel:* +30 22730 34639, *Fax:* +30 22730 33695, *Website:* www.hrs.gr

Medical Facilities: Samos Hospital

Airport: Samos, 16 km

Lloyd's Agent: Dimitris Kasmirlis, 15 Th. Sofoulis Street, 831 00 Samos, Greece, *Tel:* +30 22730 88882, *Fax:* +30 22730 88855, *Email:* 889@rhenia.gr

SKARAMANGA

see under Eleusis

STYLIS

Lat 38° 54' N; Long 22° 37' E.

Admiralty Chart: 1571   **Admiralty Pilot:** 48
Time Zone: GMT +2 h   **UNCTAD Locode:** GR SYS

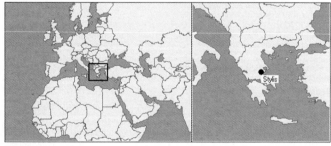

Principal Facilities:

		G			B		

Authority: Stylis Harbour Authority, 353 00 Stylis, Greece, *Tel:* +30 22380 22329, *Fax:* +30 22380 22329

Approach: Channel 1000 m long in depth of 5.5 m

Pilotage: Not available

Radio Frequency: VHF Channel 12

Weather: Prevailing winds of N, NE, NW and SW

Principal Imports and Exports: Imports: Fertiliser, Paper, Timber. Exports: Olive oil, Olives.

Working Hours: 0800-1500

Accommodation:

Name	Length (m)	Depth (m)	
Stylis			
Berth	210	6	
Berth	100	6	

Mechanical Handling Equipment:

Location	Type	Remarks
Stylis	Mobile Cranes	Mobile cranes can be hired locally

Cargo Worked: 100-200 t/day

Bunkering: Available by road tanker

Airport: Athens, 225 km

Railway: Station, 500 m from port

Lloyd's Agent: International Insurance Services E.P.E., 117 Notara Street, 185 35 Piraeus, Greece, *Tel:* +30 210 428 4080, *Fax:* +30 210 428 4405, *Email:* grlloyds@otenet.gr

SUDA BAY

Lat 35° 29' N; Long 24° 3' E.

Admiralty Chart: 1706   **Admiralty Pilot:** 48
Time Zone: GMT +2 h   **UNCTAD Locode:** GR SUD

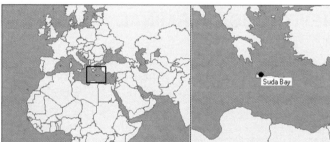

Principal Facilities:

Q	G					A

Authority: Suda Bay Port Authority Station, Suda Bay, Greece, *Tel:* +30 28120 89240, *Fax:* +30 28120 89884

Port Security: ISPS compliant

Pilotage: Compulsory

Radio Frequency: Souda Bay Port Authority on VHF Channel 12 and Souda Port Control (naval base) on VHF Channel 16

Working Hours: Mon-Fri 0800-1600

Accommodation:

Name	Length (m)	Draught (m)
Suda Bay		
Pier	150	7–12

Storage:

Location	Covered (m²)	Sheds / Warehouses
Suda Bay	750	1

Mechanical Handling Equipment:

Location	Type	Capacity (t)	Qty
Suda Bay	Mult-purp. Cranes	90	1

Medical Facilities: One naval hospital and one civilian hospital

Airport: Chania International, 20 km

Lloyd's Agent: International Insurance Services E.P.E., 117 Notara Street, 185 35 Piraeus, Greece, *Tel:* +30 210 428 4080, *Fax:* +30 210 428 4405, *Email:* grlloyds@otenet.gr

SYROS

Lat 37° 26' N; Long 24° 57' E.

Admiralty Chart: 1538   **Admiralty Pilot:** 48
Time Zone: GMT +2 h   **UNCTAD Locode:** GR JSY

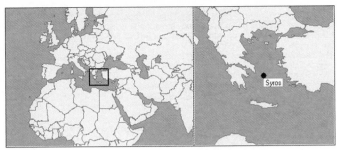

Principal Facilities:

	Y	G			B	D	T	A

Authority: Syros Port Authority, Platia Laikis Kiriarchias, 841 00 Syros, Greece, *Tel:* +30 22810 82690, *Fax:* +30 22810 82633, *Email:* syro@yen.gr

Port Security: ISPS compliant

Documentation: Crew list (4 copies), passenger list (2 copies), deratting certificate, loadline certificate, tonnage certificate, certificate of nationality, safety equipment certificate, cargo gear certificate

Approach: Approaches to the port are free of hazards

Anchorage: Vessels are not permitted to anchor within the port

Pilotage: Compulsory

Radio Frequency: Syros Port Control on VHF Channel 12

Weather: Prevailing winds NW to N to NE

Maximum Vessel Dimensions: 75 000 dwt, 6.9 m draft

Principal Imports and Exports: Imports: Building materials, Timber. Exports: Fresh vegetables.

Working Hours: 0800-1600. Overtime available

Accommodation:

Name	Length (m)	Draught (m)	Remarks
Syros			See [1] below
Telonio	117	6.9	
Passenger Berths 1 & 2	140	5.8	

[1]*Syros:* Harbour protected by breakwater 378 m long. Depth at entrance 30 m

Mechanical Handling Equipment:

Location	Type	Capacity (t)	Qty
Syros	Mobile Cranes	10	2

Cargo Worked: Approx 500 t/day

Bunkering: Aegean Petroleum (UK) Ltd, 207 Coppergate House, 16 Brune Street, London E1 7NJ, United Kingdom, *Tel:* +44 20 7953 7990, *Fax:* +44 20 7953 7856, *Email:* piraeusbunkers@aegeanpetroleum.co.uk
Sekavin S.A., 53-55 Akti Miaouli, 185 36 Piraeus, Greece, *Tel:* +30 210 4293 160/71, *Fax:* +30 210 4293 345, *Email:* sekavinsales@ath.forthnet.gr, *Website:* www.sekavin.gr – *Grades:* IFO -180cSt; MDO; MGO – *Notice:* 24 hours – *Delivery Mode:* pipe
Trust Marine Enterprises Co. Ltd, 141 Filonos Street, 185 36 Piraeus, Greece, *Tel:* +30 210 4180083, *Fax:* +30 210 4136213 – *Grades:* IFO30-180cSt; MGO – *Parcel Size:* MGO min 30t, IFO min 100t, no max – *Rates:* IFO 500-700t/h – *Notice:* 48 hours – *Delivery Mode:* ex wharf

Towage: Four tugs available from Neorion Shipyard

Repair & Maintenance: Neorion New S.A. Syros Shipyards, 1 Neoriou Street, 841 00 Hermoupolis, Syros, Greece, *Tel:* +30 22810 96000, *Fax:* +30 22810 82008, *Email:* sec@neorion-shipyards.gr, *Website:* www.neorion-holdings.gr Two floating docks; 230 m x 35 m for vessels up to 75 000 dwt and 195 m x 33.5 m for vessels up to 40 000 dwt. Quay space totaling 1100 m; served by 1 x 40 t, 1 x 20 t and 3 x 25 t traveling jib cranes, enable vessels up to 150 000 dwt. to be repaired afloat

Medical Facilities: General hospital available

Airport: Syros Airport, 4 km

Lloyd's Agent: International Insurance Services E.P.E., 117 Notara Street, 185 35 Piraeus, Greece, *Tel:* +30 210 428 4080, *Fax:* +30 210 428 4405, *Email:* grlloyds@otenet.gr

THESSALONIKI

Lat 40° 38' N; Long 22° 55' E.

Admiralty Chart: 2070	**Admiralty Pilot:** 48
Time Zone: GMT +2 h	**UNCTAD Locode:** GR SKG

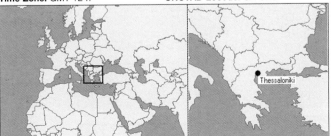

Principal Facilities:

P	Q	Y	G	C	R		B	D	T	A

Authority: Thessaloniki Port Authority S.A., P O Box 10467, 541 10 Thessaloniki, Greece, *Tel:* +30 2310 593 202, *Fax:* +30 2310 510 500, *Email:* secretariat@thpa.gr, *Website:* www.thpa.gr

Officials: Chairman: Lazaros Kanavouras, *Tel:* +30 2310 593 202, *Email:* lkanavouras@thpa.gr.
Chief Executive Officer: Ioannis Tsaras, *Tel:* +30 2310 593 202, *Email:* itsaras@thpa.gr.
Marketing: Miltiadis Arvanitidis, *Tel:* +30 2310 593 202.

Port Security: ISPS compliant

Approach: Entrance to bay 16 km from the town. Breakwater 1000 m long, shelters the main part of the harbour. E entrance to harbour inside breakwater 183 m wide; W entrance 152 m wide
NB: Inflammable or dangerous cargo is handled according to law

Anchorage: Anchorage can be obtained in the roads about 300-500 m off the breakwater in depths ranging from 11 m to 14 m

Pilotage: Compulsory for vessels exceeding 1000 gt. Vessels are boarded in roads from 0630 until sunset and entrance to the port at night is at the pilot's discretion. Pilot Station has installed VHF facilities: Channel 12, range 16-24 km

Tides: Max range of tide 0.7 m

Traffic: 2007, 2987 vessels, 18 827 651 t of cargo handled, 447 211 TEU's, 143 051 passengers

Maximum Vessel Dimensions: 74 000 gt, 290 m loa, 22 m draught

Principal Imports and Exports: Imports: Cereals, Coal, Containers, Crude oil, Fertilizers, Ores & scrap, Refined oil products, Steel Products. Exports: Containers, General cargo, Processed steel products, Refined oil products.

Working Hours: Mon-Fri 0730-1430, 1500-2200. Saturday 0800-1300. Overtime available at all times
Container terminal: 0800-1530, 1600-2230, 2400-0730

Accommodation:

Name	Length (m)	Depth (m)	Remarks
Thessaloniki			See [1] below
Pier No.1	750	5.5–8	Land area of 29 000 m2
Pier No.2	800	8–10	Land area of 34 000 m2
Pier No.3	800	10	Land area of 28 000 m2
Pier No.4	1020	10–12	Land area of 53 000 m2
Pier No.5	1115	10–12	Land area of 59 000 m2
Pier No.6	1375	12	See [2] below
EKO Sea Berth			See [3] below
EKO Islet Berth			See [4] below
Mamidakis Sea Berth			See [5] below
Old Jet Oil Sea Berth			See [6] below
New Jet Oil Sea Berth			See [7] below

[1]*Thessaloniki:* On the W side of the main commercial port are the oil installations for anchoring and berthing tankers with submarine pipelines for unloading crude oil and refined products and loading fuel oil and refined products
Two containership berths (500 m), depth 12 m, area of 180 000 m2 with four container gantry cranes (two post-panamax) and one rail-mounted transtainer. Also three ro/ro ramps, one of 52 m and two of 30 m with depths of 12 m
[2]*Pier No.6:* Land area of 350 000 m2. Includes container berths totaling 595 m
[3]*EKO Sea Berth:* Crude oil discharged here for EKO refinery and loading fuel oil. Sea berth designed for vessels of 95 000 dwt. Distance from buoys to stern buoys 500 m. Sea berth safety draft of 12.8 m for vessels up to 258 m loa
[4]*EKO Islet Berth:* For loading refined products and discharging liquefied gas. Inshore safety draft of 8.8 m for vessels up to 6000 dwt and 150 m loa. Offshore safety draft of 9.75 m for vessels up to 22 000 dwt and 170 m loa
[5]*Mamidakis Sea Berth:* For discharging crude oil and refined products to installation. Sea berth safety draft of 12.0 m. Tankers anchor and moor on buoys astern
[6]*Old Jet Oil Sea Berth:* For discharging refined products to installation. Sea berth safety draft of 9.89 m. Tankers anchor and moor on buoys astern
[7]*New Jet Oil Sea Berth:* For discharging crude oil to installation. Sea berth safety draft of 14.16 m. Tankers anchor and moor on buoys astern

Storage:

Location	Open (m2)	Covered (m2)	Grain (t)
Thessaloniki	500000	85000	20000

Mechanical Handling Equipment:

Location	Type	Capacity (t)	Qty
Thessaloniki	Floating Cranes	60	1
Thessaloniki	Mult-purp. Cranes	150	1
Thessaloniki	Mobile Cranes	150	2
Thessaloniki	Mobile Cranes	30	10
Thessaloniki	Container Cranes	40	1
Thessaloniki	Container Cranes	45	1
Thessaloniki	Post Panamax	50	2
Thessaloniki	Electric Cranes	3–45	44
Thessaloniki	Transtainers	50	1
Thessaloniki	Straddle Carriers		17
Thessaloniki	Forklifts	25	138
Thessaloniki	Yard Tractors		4

Bunkering: Tankers berthed at EKO Terminal for loading/discharging can be supplied with bunkers. Small quantities can also be supplied at roads. For cargo vessels bunkers can be supplied alongside the piers by trucks

Balkan & Black Sea Shipping Co., Balkan & Black Sea Shipping Company (Hellas) Limited, 51 Polytechniou Street, 546 25 Thessaloniki, Greece, *Tel:* +30 2310 524020, *Fax:* +30 2310 539081, *Email:* bbssthes@hol.gr, *Website:* www.navbul.com

Cyclon Hellas S.A., 90 26th Octovriou Street, Porto Centre, 546 27 Thessaloniki, Greece, *Tel:* +30 231 0523 998, *Fax:* +30 231 0523 799, *Email:* nnikoletopoulos@cyclon.gr, *Website:* www.cyclon.gr

Aegean Petroleum (UK) Ltd, 207 Coppergate House, 16 Brune Street, London E1 7NJ, United Kingdom, *Tel:* +44 20 7953 7990, *Fax:* +44 20 7953 7856, *Email:* piraeusbunkers@aegeanpetroleum.co.uk

Alpha Petroleum S.A., 7 Spirou Miliou Street, 124 62 Piraeus, Greece, *Tel:* +30 210 557 7405, *Fax:* +30 210 557 7302

Eko Abee (Hellenic Fuels and Lubricants), 3rd Floor, 87 Akti Miaouli, 185 38 Piraeus, Greece, *Tel:* +30 210 4290 920, *Fax:* +30 210 4290 958, *Email:* eko@eko.gr, *Website:* www.eko.gr

Petrotrade Management S.A., 63 Dragatsaniou Street, 185 45 Piraeus, Greece, *Tel:* +30 210 408 0100, *Fax:* +30 210 408 0108 – *Grades:* all grades; lubes – *Rates:* 300-400t/h – *Delivery Mode:* barge, truck

Trust Marine Enterprises Co. Ltd, 141 Filonos Street, 185 36 Piraeus, Greece, *Tel:* +30 210 4180083, *Fax:* +30 210 4136213 – *Grades:* MGO; lubes – *Parcel Size:* min 25t – *Notice:* 48 hours – *Delivery Mode:* truck

Towage: Eleven tugs available of 480-3168 hp. All tugs have radio telephone and VHF Channel 8

Gigilinis Salvage & Towage, 13 N. Kountouriotou Street, 546 25 Thessaloniki, Greece, *Tel:* +30 2310 530017, *Fax:* +30 2310 540646, *Email:* gigilinis.tugs@axiom.gr, *Website:* www.gigilinis.gr

Repair & Maintenance: Repairs afloat only. The drydock cap is restricted to coasters of up to 850 dwt

Ship Chandlers: Cosmatos Brothers Co., 5 J. Koletti Street, 54627 Thessaloniki, Greece, *Tel:* +30 2310 528262, *Fax:* +30 2310 540436, *Email:* cosmatos@otenet.gr

E.& A. Papageorgiou S.A. (Volos Ship Suppliers), Volos Ship Suppliers, Port of Thessaloniki, Warehouse No.14, 541 10 Thessaloniki, Greece, *Tel:* +30 2310 544213, *Fax:* +30 2310 544235, *Email:* sales@volossuppliers.gr, *Website:* www.volossuppliers.gr

Zak Shipstores Co., Warehouse No.15, Port of Thessaloniki, 541 10 Thessaloniki, Greece, *Tel:* +30 2310 593586, *Fax:* +30 2310 517188, *Email:* info@zakshipstores.gr, *Website:* www.zakshipstores.gr

Shipping Agents: Balkan & Black Sea Shipping Co., Balkan & Black Sea Shipping Company (Hellas) Limited, 51 Polytechniou Street, 546 25 Thessaloniki, Greece, *Tel:* +30 2310 524020, *Fax:* +30 2310 539081, *Email:* bbssthes@hol.gr, *Website:* www.navbul.com

CMA-CGM S.A., CMA CGM Greece, 7 Karatassou Street, 546 26 Thessaloniki, Greece, *Tel:* +30 2310 567478, *Fax:* +30 2310 550709, *Email:* skg.genmbox@cma-cgm.com, *Website:* www.cma-cgm.com

J.E. Cosmatos & Co., 5 I.Koletti Street, 546 27 Thessaloniki, Greece, *Tel:* +30 2310 550950/4, *Fax:* +30 2310 540435, *Email:* agency@cosmatos.gr, *Website:* www.cosmatos.gr

Romilos J. Davelopoulos Co., 19 N. Kountouriotou Street, GR-54625 Thessaloniki, Greece, *Tel:* +30 2310 530050, *Fax:* +30 2310 540096, *Email:* davelopoulos@the.forthnet.gr, *Website:* www.davelopoulos.gr

Economou International Shipping Agencies Ltd, 42, 26th October St, Thessaloniki, Greece, *Tel:* +30 2310 502907, *Fax:* +30 2310 566974, *Email:* mflerianou@economou.gr

GAC Shipping S.A., 11 Kountouriotou Street, 546 25 Thessaloniki, Greece, *Tel:* +30 2310 516395, *Fax:* +30 2310 516972, *Email:* greece@gacworld.com, *Website:* www.gacworld.com

Global Maritime Agency S.A., 25 Katouni street, GR-54625 Thessaloniki, Greece, *Tel:* +30 2310 566580, *Fax:* +30 2310 566649, *Email:* infosal@glomar.gr, *Website:* www.glomar.gr

Hellastir Maritime SA, 26th October Street, GR-54627 Thessaloniki, Greece, *Tel:* +30 2310 532858, *Fax:* +30 2310 532808, *Website:* www.zim.co.il

Hellenic Shipping Agencies Ltd, 42, 26th October str, 546 27 Thessaloniki, Greece, *Tel:* +30 2310 545212, *Fax:* +30 2310 542219, *Email:* doc.import@hellenicshipping.gr, *Website:* www.hellenicshipping.gr

Medcargo D Theodorikas Shipping S.A., 26th October Street 42, GR-54627 Thessaloniki, Greece, *Tel:* +30 2310 553876, *Fax:* +30 2310 553878, *Email:* mcsskg@otenet.gr

Mediterranean Shipping Company, MSC Greece S.A., Commercial and Business Center Limani, 43 26th October Street - 5th Floor, 546 27 Thessaloniki, Greece, *Tel:* +30 2310 507600, *Fax:* +30 2310 507680, *Email:* generic@mscskg.gr, *Website:* www.mscgva.ch

A.P. Moller-Maersk Group, Maersk Hellas S.A., Atrina Center 38-40, 26th Oktrovriou Street, 546 27 Thessaloniki, Greece, *Tel:* +30 2310 555080, *Fax:* +30 2310 557080, *Email:* slktrm@maersk.com, *Website:* www.maerskline.com

Mylaki Shipping Agency Ltd, 8 Eleftheriou Venizelou Street, 546 24 Thessaloniki, Greece, *Tel:* +30 2310 283375, *Fax:* +30 2310 223932, *Email:* mylaki@otenet.gr, *Website:* www.mylaki-shipping.gr

Nautilus II Cia Nav. S.A., 13 N. Kountouriotou Street, P O Box 19886, 546 25 Thessaloniki, Greece, *Tel:* +30 2310 530017, *Fax:* +30 2310 540646, *Email:* gigilinis.shpn@axiom.gr

Pamar Shipping Co Ltd., 4 Katouni Street, 546 25 Thessaloniki, Greece, *Tel:* +30 2310 511609, *Fax:* +30 2310 525581, *Email:* info@pamar.gr, *Website:* www.pamar.gr

S.B.S. Samothrakitis Shipping Ltd, 3 Katouni Street, 546 25 Thessaloniki, Greece, *Tel:* +30 2310 535277, *Fax:* +30 2310 523107, *Email:* kostassamothrakitis@sbsshipping.gr, *Website:* www.sbsshipping.gr

Unistar Shipping Ltd, 12 Kastritsiou, Thessaloniki, Greece, *Tel:* +30 2310 278807, *Fax:* +30 2310 278806, *Email:* the@unistar.gr

Wilhelmsen Ship Services, Barwil Hellas Ltd Shipping Agencies, 19 N. Kountouriotou Street, P O Box 10845, 541 10 Thessaloniki, Greece, *Tel:* +30 2310 530050, *Fax:* +30 2310 540096, *Email:* barwil.thessaloniki@wilhelmsen.com, *Website:* www.barwilunitor.com

Surveyors: Hellenic Register of Shipping, 2 Fassianou & Kountouriotou, 546 25 Thessaloniki, Greece, *Tel:* +30 2310 544762, *Fax:* +30 2310 544763, *Email:* hrs-thes@otenet.gr, *Website:* www.hrs.gr

Medical Facilities: Hospital, 4 km

Airport: 16 km

Railway: Thessaloniki, 1 km. All quays are connected to the European network

Lloyd's Agent: International Insurance Services E.P.E., 117 Notara Street, 185 35 Piraeus, Greece, *Tel:* +30 210 428 4080, *Fax:* +30 210 428 4405, *Email:* grlloyds@otenet.gr

VATHI

Lat 38° 22' N; Long 20° 44' E.

Admiralty Chart: 203	**Admiralty Pilot:** 47
Time Zone: GMT +2 h	**UNCTAD Locode:** GR VAT

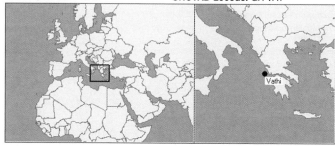

Principal Facilities:

		G	R	B		

Authority: Vathi Harbour Office, Ithaca, 283 00 Vathi, Greece, *Tel:* +30 26740 32909, *Fax:* +30 26740 32629, *Email:* bakajohn@otenet.gr

Officials: Harbour Master: Andreas Bakayannis.

Pilotage: A pilot can be made available on request

Radio Frequency: VHF Channels 16 and 12

Weather: Harbour is safe and well sheltered, but small craft are not protected from NW and NE winds

Principal Imports and Exports: Exports: Olive oil.

Working Hours: 0700-1500 for cargo vessels

Accommodation:

Name	Remarks
Vathi	See [1] below

[1]*Vathi:* Two small piers with depths alongside from 3.5 m to 7.9 m. Discharging by ship's gear. Passenger and ro/ro ferry pier with depth alongside of 11 m

Bunkering: Small quantities of gas oil available from road tanker

Medical Facilities: Hospital available

Lloyd's Agent: International Insurance Services E.P.E., 117 Notara Street, 185 35 Piraeus, Greece, *Tel:* +30 210 428 4080, *Fax:* +30 210 428 4405, *Email:* grlloyds@otenet.gr

VOLOS

Lat 39° 21' N; Long 22° 57' E.

Admiralty Chart: 1571	**Admiralty Pilot:** 48
Time Zone: GMT +2 h	**UNCTAD Locode:** GR VOL

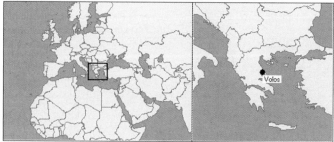

Principal Facilities:

P		Y	G	C	R		B		T	A

Authority: Volos Port Authority S.A., Kentriki Provlita, 382 21 Volos, Greece, *Tel:* +30 24210 29633, *Fax:* +30 24210 31115, *Email:* admin@port-volos.gr, *Website:* www.port-volos.gr

Officials: Managing Director: Alexis Valassas.
Harbour Master: Dimitris Tsikogias.

Port Security: ISPS compliant

Documentation: Cargo manifest (1 set), one copy of bill of lading, crew lists (6 copies), stores list (3 copies), crew effects declaration (3 copies)

Approach: Depth at entrance and bar 10.06 m; depth in harbour 10.67 m. Max safe draft of 9.76 m

Anchorage: Anchorage can be obtained approx 1 mile off the breakwater in depths over 12.2 m

Pilotage: Compulsory. Pilot boards 1 mile off the port

Radio Frequency: VHF Channels 16 and 12. Volos Pilot Channel 6

Weather: Port is safe and well protected. SW wind seldom affects port area

Maximum Vessel Dimensions: 35 000 dwt, 200 m loa, 9.8 m d

Principal Imports and Exports: Imports: Cotton, Fertiliser, Grain, Scrap iron, Steel products, Timber. Exports: Agricultural products, Cement, Cotton in bales, Flour, Iron rods, Wheat.

Working Hours: Two shifts 0730-1400, 1400-2100

Accommodation:

Name	Depth (m)	Remarks
Volos		See [1] below
Pier 1	8.23	Rail connections with the national system
Pier 2	9.76	Rail connections with the national system
Pier 3	9.76	

[1]*Volos:* The quays extend for a total of approx 2500 m including the grain silo jetty. There are three piers
Bulk facilities: Silos Pier, located on the W side of the port. E side of pier 475 m long, W side 367 m, head 153 m, depth alongside at LW of 11 m, channel depth at LW of 12 m, turning basin at LW of 11 m. Max permissible height from waterline to top of hatch coaming 20 m. There is an open stockpile area for 50 000 t
Tanker facilities: BP and Shell terminals. 11.58 m d, length 152.39 to 213.35 m

Storage:

Location	Open (m²)	Covered (m²)	Grain (t)
Volos	190000	8000	15000

Mechanical Handling Equipment:

Location	Type	Capacity (t)	Qty
Volos	Mobile Cranes	140	5
Volos	Electric Cranes	40	9
Volos	Forklifts	15	13

Cargo Worked: 120-250 t per gang depending on commodity

Bunkering: Aegean Petroleum (UK) Ltd, 207 Coppergate House, 16 Brune Street, London E1 7NJ, United Kingdom, *Tel:* +44 20 7953 7990, *Fax:* +44 20 7953 7856, *Email:* piraeusbunkers@aegeanpetroleum.co.uk
Alpha Petroleum S.A., 7 Spirou Miliou Street, 124 62 Piraeus, Greece, *Tel:* +30 210 557 7405, *Fax:* +30 210 557 7302
Petrotrade Management S.A., 63 Dragatsaniou Street, 185 45 Piraeus, Greece, *Tel:* +30 210 408 0100, *Fax:* +30 210 408 0108 – *Grades:* all grades; lubes – *Rates:* 300-400t/h – *Delivery Mode:* barge, truck
Trust Marine Enterprises Co. Ltd, 141 Filonos Street, 185 36 Piraeus, Greece, *Tel:* +30 210 4180083, *Fax:* +30 210 4136213 – *Grades:* MGO38-180cSt – *Notice:* 48 hours – *Delivery Mode:* truck, barge

Waste Reception Facilities: For slops and oily bilge water, removal by tankers. Garbage is collected daily by a private enterprise

Towage: Compulsory for vessels over 1000 gt. Five tugs available of 400 hp to 1050 hp

Repair & Maintenance: Euromechaniki, Adelphi Emmanouil 6, 38335 Volos, Greece, *Tel:* +30 24210 61959, *Fax:* +30 24210 61959, *Email:* vkoutsiaris@yahoo.com

Ship Chandlers: E.& A. Papageorgiou S.A. (Volos Ship Suppliers), 99 Mitropoltou Grigoriou, 383 34 Volos, Greece, *Tel:* +30 24210 28295, *Fax:* +30 24210 22936, *Email:* info@volossuppliers.gr, *Website:* www.volossuppliers.gr

Shipping Agents: Flokas Shipping - Volos, Hatziargiri 1, 383 33 Volos, Greece, *Tel:* +30 24210 24351, *Fax:* +30 24210 26349, *Email:* flokas@otenet.gr
Mylaki Shipping Agency Ltd, 32 Argonafton Street, 382 21 Volos, Greece, *Tel:* +30 24210 23496, *Fax:* +30 24210 39361, *Email:* mylaki@otenet.gr, *Website:* www.mylaki-shipping.gr
Scandinavian Near East Agency S.A., 2nd Floor, 32 Argonafton, GR-38221 Volos, Greece, *Tel:* +30 24210 23460, *Fax:* +30 24210 37117

Surveyors: Hellenic Register of Shipping, 2 Solonos Street, 383 33 Volos, Greece, *Tel:* +30 24210 29241, *Fax:* +30 24210 29241, *Website:* www.hrs.gr

Medical Facilities: Available

Airport: Anchialos Airport, 25 km

Lloyd's Agent: International Insurance Services E.P.E., 117 Notara Street, 185 35 Piraeus, Greece, *Tel:* +30 210 428 4080, *Fax:* +30 210 428 4405, *Email:* grlloyds@otenet.gr

VOUDIA BAY

harbour area, see under Milos Island

YALI

Lat 36° 39' N; Long 27° 7' E.

Admiralty Chart: 1531	Admiralty Pilot: 48
Time Zone: GMT +2 h	UNCTAD Locode: GR YLI

Principal Facilities:

		Y					T	A	

Authority: Lava Mining & Quarrying Co., 49-51 Sofocli Venizelou Street, 141 23 Lycovrissi, Greece, *Tel:* +30 210 289 8372, *Fax:* +30 210 281 7778, *Email:* lava@aget.gr, *Website:* www.lava.gr

Officials: Manager: Eleftherios Fedros.
Marketing Manager: Chris Kavafkis.

Port Security: ISPS compliant

Documentation: Crew list (5 copies), passenger list (2 copies), ship stores declaration list (2 copies), crew personal effects (2 copies), health declaration list (2 copies), narcotics list (2 copies), ship's certificates, bills of lading or authorisation from Master to Agency for signing bill of lading

Anchorage: Safe anchorage in the roads (36° 39' N; 27° 09' 03" +) or bearing from loading installation (PYLON) 330° distance 7 cables, except in strong southerly winds. With strong southerly winds safe anchorage is NW of Kos Island

Pilotage: Mooring Master available from Piraeus and boards at the anchorage

Radio Frequency: Yali Quarry on VHF Channel 6 and Harbour Master on VHF Channel 12

Weather: No mooring when strong S-SE winds

Maximum Vessel Dimensions: 195 m loa, 24 m beam, 32 ft draft
Max airdraft from sea level up to deck line 12.5 m
Max airdraft from sea level up to hatch coaming 15 m

Principal Imports and Exports: Exports: Pumice stone.

Accommodation:

Name	Remarks
Yali Terminal	See [1] below

[1]*Yali Terminal:* One berth for ocean-going vessels near to the pumice quarry, with nine mooring buoys, capable of accepting vessels up to 195 m loa and 32 ft max draft. Pumice stone is loaded by aerial chute-conveyor belt, fed from the shore by conveyor belts at a rate of 300-1000 t/h. During loading operations vessels have to be shifted from hatch to hatch

Cargo Worked: 700-1000 t/day depending on cargo quality

Towage: One tug available at Yali Terminal

Shipping Agents: Mylaki Shipping Agency Ltd, 43 Iroon Polytechniou Avenue, 185 35 Piraeus, Greece, *Tel:* +30 210 422 3355, *Fax:* +30 210 422 3356, *Email:* mylaki@otenet.gr, *Website:* www.mylaki-shipping.gr

Medical Facilities: Nearest medical and hospital facilities are at the Island of Kos, 8 miles N of Yali

Airport: Kos, 15 km

Lloyd's Agent: International Insurance Services E.P.E., 117 Notara Street, 185 35 Piraeus, Greece, *Tel:* +30 210 428 4080, *Fax:* +30 210 428 4405, *Email:* grlloyds@otenet.gr

YERAKINI

Lat 40° 16' N; Long 23° 26' E.

Admiralty Chart: 1085	Admiralty Pilot: 48
Time Zone: GMT +2 h	UNCTAD Locode: GR YER

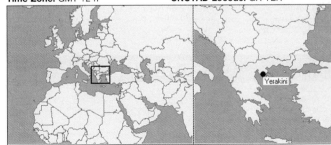

Principal Facilities:

		Y	G			B		A	

Key to Principal Facilities:—					
A=Airport	**C**=Containers	**G**=General Cargo	**P**=Petroleum	**R**=Ro/Ro	**Y**=Dry Bulk
B=Bunkers	**D**=Dry Dock	**L**=Cruise	**Q**=Other Liquid Bulk	**T**=Towage (where available from port)	

Authority: Grecian Magnesite S.A., Yerakini, Chalkidiki, 631 00 Polygyros, Greece, *Tel:* +30 23710 51251, *Fax:* +30 23710 51011, *Email:* magmine@otenet.gr, *Website:* www.grecianmagnesite.com

Officials: Sales & Marketing Manager: Minnas Halaris, *Tel:* +30 210 724 0446.

Pilotage: Compulsory. Pilot is embarked at Thessaloniki

Accommodation:

Name	Remarks
Yerakini	See [1] below

[1]*Yerakini:* Port operated by mining company. Magnesite ore mine is 2 km inland. There is a pier 41.6 m long with depths ranging from 1.3 m to 2.8 m. Vessels moor offshore at a buoy to the SW of the pier in a depth of 7.3 m. Magnesite ore is loaded from lighters. Stormy weather from the S can hinder loading operations

Cargo Worked: 500-1500 t/day

Bunkering: Can be taken from the pier to vessel with lighters

Airport: Thessaloniki, 80 km

Lloyd's Agent: International Insurance Services E.P.E., 117 Notara Street, 185 35 Piraeus, Greece, *Tel:* +30 210 428 4080, *Fax:* +30 210 428 4405, *Email:* grlloyds@otenet.gr

YITHION

alternate name, see Gythion

ZAKINTHOS

alternate name, see Zante

ZANTE

Lat 37° 47' N; Long 20° 54' E.

Admiralty Chart: 2404	**Admiralty Pilot:** 47
Time Zone: GMT +2 h	**UNCTAD Locode:** GR ZNT

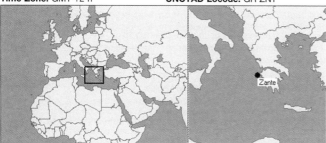

Principal Facilities:

			G		B		A	

Authority: Harbour of Zante, Provlita Agiou, 291 00 Zante, Greece, *Tel:* +30 26950 28117, *Fax:* +30 26950 48370

Radio Frequency: VHF Channel 12

Maximum Vessel Dimensions: 100 m loa, 5 m d

Accommodation:

Name	Remarks
Zante	See [1] below

[1]*Zante:* Depth 5.49 m alongside of mole. Depth 7.4 to 8.4 m off end of mole. Depth in harbour less and variable 6.1 to 6.4 m. Ships may anchor in from 18.3 to 22 m at a distance of 460 to 914 m from the town, sheltering themselves behind a mole or jetty when the wind is from the NE. 2.44 m d max near warehouse. No lighters available

Bunkering: Limited quantities available

Medical Facilities: General hospital

Airport: Landing strip 3 km from port

Lloyd's Agent: International Insurance Services E.P.E., 117 Notara Street, 185 35 Piraeus, Greece, *Tel:* +30 210 428 4080, *Fax:* +30 210 428 4405, *Email:* grlloyds@otenet.gr

GREENLAND

AASIAAT

Lat 68° 43' N; Long 52° 53' W.

Admiralty Chart: -	**Admiralty Pilot:** 12
Time Zone: GMT -3 h	**UNCTAD Locode:** GL JEG

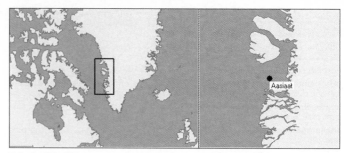

Principal Facilities:

		G	C			B		T	

Authority: Royal Arctic Line A/S, P O Box 219, DK-3950 Aasiaat, Greenland, *Tel:* +299 89 20 33, *Fax:* +299 89 21 32, *Email:* hra@ral.gl, *Website:* www.ral.gl

Officials: Port Captain: Hans Rafaelsen.

Port Security: ISPS compliant

Approach: Depth at entrance is 54 m

Anchorage: Anchorage can be obtained in the roadstead, but advice from the Harbour Authority is recommended, as the area is open to winds and has poor holding ground

Pilotage: Not compulsory, but advisable. Harbour official acts as pilot. Request for services must be advised at least 24 h prior to arrival

Radio Frequency: Aasiaat Radio Station, call sign OYR

Weather: Ice conditions usually occur from mid December to early May and can attain a thickness of 0.6 m. Ice floes can enter the port area after break up and hinder navigation. Polar darkness from December 2 to January 11 and midnight sun from May 22 to July 23

Tides: Max height of HT is 3.1 m, LW 1.5 m

Principal Imports and Exports: Exports: Frozen fish, Prawns.

Accommodation:

Name	Length (m)	Depth (m)	Remarks
Aasiaat			See [1] below
Atlantic Quay	110	8.1	Vessels up to 136 m loa, 6.2 m d can be accommodated
Minor Quay	70	6.5	
Fishing Quay	25	7.4	Situated 2.5 km E of the harbour

[1]*Aasiaat:* Anchorage and mooring berth available in the roadstead in a depth of 30 m. A mooring berth is located in the harbour for vessels not exceeding 61 m loa in a depth of 13 m

Mechanical Handling Equipment:

Location	Type	Capacity (t)	Qty
Aasiaat	Mobile Cranes	5	1
Aasiaat	Forklifts		

Bunkering: Limited supplies of light marine diesel can be obtained

Towage: Launches assist with berthing

Repair & Maintenance: Minor repairs are usually possible. Slipway for small vessels up to 250 t

Medical Facilities: There is a hospital in the settlement

Lloyd's Agent: Blue Water Shipping A/S, Blue Water Greenland AS, Industrivj 22, P O Box 1380, 3900 Nuuk, Greenland, *Tel:* +299 32 54 10, *Fax:* +299 32 54 11, *Email:* bwgnuuk@bws.dk, *Website:* www.bws.dk

AMMASSALIK

Lat 65° 35' N; Long 37° 30' W.

Admiralty Chart: -	**Admiralty Pilot:** 12
Time Zone: GMT -3 h	**UNCTAD Locode:** GL AGM

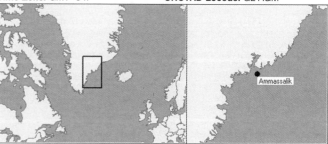

Principal Facilities:

		G			B		T	

Authority: Royal Arctic Line A/S, Talittarpimmut B-180, DK-3913 Tasiilaq, Greenland, *Tel:* +299 98 11 33, *Fax:* +299 98 11 36

Officials: Port Captain: Jorgen Pedersen.

Port Security: ISPS compliant

Approach: Deep and narrow entrance channel to almost landlocked harbour

Anchorage: Anchorage can be obtained in a depth of about 20 m

Radio Frequency: Ammassalik Radio, call sign OZL

Accommodation:

Name	Length (m)	Depth (m)	Remarks
Ammassalik			There are also mooring berths
Kong Oscars Havn	30	8.7	

Bunkering: Fuel oil is available

Towage: Launches assist with berthing

Repair & Maintenance: Minor repairs can be effected

Medical Facilities: Hospital available

Lloyd's Agent: Blue Water Shipping A/S, Blue Water Greenland AS, Industrivj 22, P O Box 1380, 3900 Nuuk, Greenland, *Tel:* +299 32 54 10, *Fax:* +299 32 54 11, *Email:* bwgnuuk@bws.dk, *Website:* www.bws.dk

ANGMAGSSALIK

alternate name, see Ammassalik

CHRISTIANSHAAB

alternate name, see Qasigiannguit

EGEDESMINDE

alternate name, see Aasiaat

FAERINGEHAVN

alternate name, see Kangerluarsoruseq

FREDERIKSHAAB

alternate name, see Paamiut

GODHAVN

alternate name, see Qeqertarsuaq

GODTHAAB

alternate name, see Nuuk

GRONNEDAL

alternate name, see Kangilinnguit

HOLSTEINSBORG

alternate name, see Sisimiut

ILULISSAT

Lat 69° 13' N; Long 51° 6' W.

Admiralty Chart: -	**Admiralty Pilot:** 12
Time Zone: GMT -3 h	**UNCTAD Locode:** GL JAV

Principal Facilities:

		G	C		B		A

Authority: Royal Arctic Line A/S, P O Box 400, DK-3952 Ilulissat, Greenland, *Tel:* +299 94 35 33, *Fax:* +299 94 45 32, *Email:* kag@ral.gl, *Website:* www.ral.gl

Officials: Port Captain: Karl Geisler.

Port Security: ISPS compliant

Approach: Permission to enter the harbour must be obtained from the Port Authority prior to approach

Anchorage: Anchorage can be obtained off the harbour in the bay in depths ranging from 20 m to 40 m; good holding ground

Pilotage: Recommended for larger vessels. Requests for pilot should be made to the Port Authority together with ETA information

Weather: Prevailing E and NE winds, becoming strong during the autumn. Ice conditions occur during the winter. Discharge of ice from Jakobshavn Isfjord, or the effect of spring tides on the icebergs can cause a local phenomenon known as 'Kanele', which causes a heavy swell without any warning, lasting for about six minutes. The water in the Inner Harbour can become violently disturbed. Polar darkness from December 1 to June 12 and midnight sun from May 21 to July 24

Tides: MHWST 2.8 m, MHWNT 1.6 m. Max HT is 3.3 m

Accommodation:

Name	Length (m)	Depth (m)	Remarks
Outer harbour			
Atlantic Quay	110	8	Warehousing is available
Inner harbour			See [1] below

[1]*Inner harbour:* Depths of 5.5 m to 6 m. One mooring berth on which vessels are secured stern on. Quay for fishing vessels with a berthing length of 40 m, depth alongside of 5 m. There is an inlet at the head of the harbour navigable by small craft up to 23 m beam. Special precautions are necessary for vessels secured at certain berths in the harbour during the 'Kanele'

Mechanical Handling Equipment:

Location	Type	Capacity (t)
Ilulissat	Mobile Cranes	5
Ilulissat	Forklifts	

Bunkering: Limited supplies of light marine diesel can be obtained

Repair & Maintenance: Boatyard for small craft with slipway; lifting cap up to 40 t

Medical Facilities: Small hospital in the town

Airport: Jakobshavn Airport, 10 km

Lloyd's Agent: Blue Water Shipping A/S, Blue Water Greenland AS, Industrivj 22, P O Box 1380, 3900 Nuuk, Greenland, *Tel:* +299 32 54 10, *Fax:* +299 32 54 11, *Email:* bwgnuuk@bws.dk, *Website:* www.bws.dk

JAKOBSHAVN

alternate name, see Ilulissat

JULIANEHAAB

alternate name, see Qaqortoq

KANGERLUARSORUSEQ

Lat 63° 42' N; Long 51° 33' W.

Admiralty Chart: -	**Admiralty Pilot:** 12
Time Zone: GMT -3 h	**UNCTAD Locode:** GL FHN

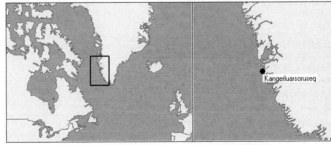

Principal Facilities:

P		G			B	T	A

Authority: Kangerluarsoruseq Port Authority, Port Office, Kangerluarsoruseq, Greenland

Port Security: ISPS compliant

Anchorage: Anchorage for large vessels can be obtained almost anywhere in the fjord in depths ranging from 18 m to 64 m

Pilotage: Not compulsory, but advisable. Pilot should be ordered at least 12 h prior to arrival

Weather: Prevailing N winds. Ice-free virtually all the year round

---

Key to Principal Facilities:—			
A=Airport	**C**=Containers	**G**=General Cargo	**P**=Petroleum	**R**=Ro/Ro	**Y**=Dry Bulk
B=Bunkers	**D**=Dry Dock	**L**=Cruise	**Q**=Other Liquid Bulk	**T**=Towage (where available from port)	

Tides: Max height of HT 4 m, LW 2 m

Accommodation:

Name	Length (m)	Depth (m)	Remarks
Kangerluarsoruseq			See [1] below
Wharf	225	5	
Nordafar Quay	250	4.7–7	Presently under repair

[1]*Kangerluarsoruseq:* Fishing vessels are much in evidence in the harbour during the summer. There is a fish processing plant at Nordafar on the N side of the fjord Tanker facilities: Facilities of Polaroil at Sydhavnen on the S side of the fjord. Vessels of about 26 000 dwt, up to 180 m loa and 12.2 m d can be accommodated

Mechanical Handling Equipment:

Location	Type	Capacity (t)	Qty
Kangerluarsoruseq	Mobile Cranes	3	1
Kangerluarsoruseq	Forklifts		

Bunkering: Fuel and diesel oil available. Bunker station of Polaroil open all year, but closed during the night between 2200-0600

Towage: A salvage tug is on station from April to November

Repair & Maintenance: Minor repairs can be effected from May to November. There is a slipway for small craft

Medical Facilities: A nursing station is available during the summer

Airport: Nuuk, 56 km

Lloyd's Agent: Blue Water Shipping A/S, Blue Water Greenland AS, Industrivj 22, P O Box 1380, 3900 Nuuk, Greenland, *Tel:* +299 32 54 10, *Fax:* +299 32 54 11, *Email:* bwgnuuk@bws.dk, *Website:* www.bws.dk

KANGERLUSSUAQ

Lat 66° 58' N; Long 50° 57' W.

Admiralty Chart: -	**Admiralty Pilot:** 12
Time Zone: GMT -3 h	**UNCTAD Locode:** GL SFJ

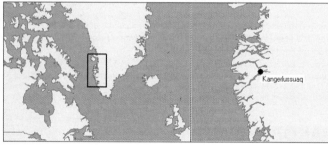

Principal Facilities:

P		G			B		A

Authority: Pilersuisoq A/S, P O Box 1011, 3910 Kangerlussuaq, Greenland, *Tel:* +299 84 17 08

Approach: The entrance to Kangerlussuaq is located between Qeqertasugssuk Island and Simiutaq Island. The fjord extends in a NE direction for a distance of about 100 miles. Depths in the fairway at the entrance vary from 37 m to 110 m, but further into the fjord, much greater depths are to be found, ranging from 165 m to over 365 m in places

Anchorage: Various anchorage areas are available along the length of the fjord. At the head of the fjord by the harbour, anchorage can be obtained 0.8 km E of Brennan Point in a depth of 70 m or 3 miles E of Brennan Point in a depth of 40 m; good holding grounds, but bottom slopes steeply. The advice of the Harbour Master should be sought before anchoring

Pilotage: No authorized pilot. Chief of Port Operations assists berthing

Radio Frequency: VHF Channel 16, 2716 kHz. ETA should be reported 24 h prior to arrival

Weather: Strong winds may be experienced from E and SE direction. Ice conditions occur during the winter months; the fjord is usually completely frozen over from about 30 miles within the entrance, making entry for vessels impossible from January to June. Midnight sun from June 15 to July 1

Tides: MHWST 3 m, MHWNT 1.6 m. Max HT is 3.6 m

Maximum Vessel Dimensions: 11 000 dwt for mooring

Accommodation:

Name	Remarks
Kangerlussuaq	See [1] below

[1]*Kangerlussuaq:* Harbour for ocean-going vessels is located at the head of the fjord at Camp Lloyd. The port is mainly used to supply a United States defence area base. Wharf can accommodate vessels up to 54 m loa and 3.6 m d. Mooring buoys and anchor berths for larger vessels. Landing craft and lighters are available. American supply ships have preference in mooring at all berths
Tanker facilities: Mooring berth for tankers about 700 m SSE of Emmons Point, 300 m in length between buoys in depths ranging from 10.5 m to 14.6 m. Two submerged oil pipelines to shore

Storage: Limited storage space available

Mechanical Handling Equipment:

Location	Type	Capacity (t)
Kangerlussuaq	Mult-purp. Cranes	60

Bunkering: Available with heavy fuel trucks shipside

Medical Facilities: Limited facilities available

Airport: Sondre Stromfjord Airport

Lloyd's Agent: Blue Water Shipping A/S, Blue Water Greenland AS, Industrivj 22, P O Box 1380, 3900 Nuuk, Greenland, *Tel:* +299 32 54 10, *Fax:* +299 32 54 11, *Email:* bwgnuuk@bws.dk, *Website:* www.bws.dk

KANGILINNGUIT

Lat 61° 12' N; Long 48° 6' W.

Admiralty Chart: 276	**Admiralty Pilot:** 12
Time Zone: GMT -3 h	**UNCTAD Locode:** GL JGR

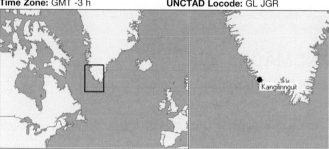

Principal Facilities:

		G		B		

Authority: Island Commander Greenland, DK-3930 Kangilinnguit, Greenland, *Tel:* +299 691911, *Fax:* +299 691949, *Email:* iscomgl@glk.gl, *Website:* www.glk.gl

Officials: Harbour Master: Kim Haick, *Email:* dv@glk.gl.

Port Security: ISPS compliant

Approach: Permission to enter Arsuk Fjord must be obtained from the Naval Radio Station at Gronnedal immediately prior to entry. The fjord is deep and virtually free from dangers

Anchorage: Kungnat Bugten in pos 61° 11' N; 48° 23.5' W is recommended

Pilotage: Naval Base render pilotage if necessary

Radio Frequency: Naval Radio Station, call sign OVC; 24 h watch on VHF Channels 12 or 16

Weather: Winds are predominant from S and SE direction. Ice conditions usually occur in the outer fjord from December to April. The berth is untenable during strong winds funnelled down the valley and vessels must leave the berth at such time

Accommodation:

Name	Length (m)	Depth (m)	Remarks
Kangilinnguit			There is a Naval base in the harbour
Pier	90	10	See [1] below

[1]*Pier:* Only suitable for small vessels. The berth is untenable during strong winds funnelled down the valley and vessels must leave the berth at such time

Bunkering: Supplies of marine diesel fuel are available

Medical Facilities: Small hospital at the Naval Base

Lloyd's Agent: Blue Water Shipping A/S, Blue Water Greenland AS, Industrivj 22, P O Box 1380, 3900 Nuuk, Greenland, *Tel:* +299 32 54 10, *Fax:* +299 32 54 11, *Email:* bwgnuuk@bws.dk, *Website:* www.bws.dk

MANIITSOQ

Lat 65° 25' N; Long 52° 54' W.

Admiralty Chart: -	**Admiralty Pilot:** 12
Time Zone: GMT -3 h	**UNCTAD Locode:** GL JSU

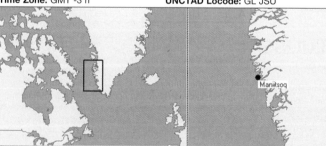

Principal Facilities:

		G	C		B		T	

Authority: Royal Arctic Line A/S, P O Box 288, DK-3912 Maniitsoq, Greenland, *Tel:* +299 81 36 33, *Fax:* +299 81 38 32, *Email:* pbi@ral.gl, *Website:* www.ral.gl

Officials: Port Captain: Pavia Biilmann, *Tel:* +299 81 79 43.

Port Security: ISPS compliant

Approach: Depth at entrance 30 m

Anchorage: Anchorage can be obtained in the roadstead 1 mile E of the harbour in depths ranging from 13 m to 29 m

Pilotage: Not compulsory, but recommended. Available by arrangement with the Harbour Authority. Pilot will board between Faltings Skaer and the harbour entrance

Radio Frequency: Maniitsoq Radio, VHF extension from Nuuk, call sign OXI

Weather: Strong S to SW winds can cause a heavy sea and a swell in the harbour, making manoeuvring difficult. Harbour sheltered from N and NW winds. Ice conditions occur from December to April, but does not cause much hindrance to navigation, as the ice easily breaks up

Tides: MHWST 4.2 m, MHWNT 2 m. Max HT is 4.8 m

Accommodation:

Name	Length (m)	Depth (m)	Remarks
Maniitsoq			See [1] below
Atlantic Quay	60	8	See [2] below
Quay	157	3.5	For fishing vessels
Fishing pier	60	5–6.5	

[1]*Maniitsoq:* Larger vessels can discharge/load at anchorage berths in a depth of about 27 m. Lighters are available
[2]*Atlantic Quay:* Vessels of 100 m loa and 6 m d can be accommodated. Container handling equipment to 30 t

Storage: Warehousing is available

Mechanical Handling Equipment:

Location	Type	Capacity (t)
Maniitsoq	Mobile Cranes	5
Maniitsoq	Forklifts	

Bunkering: Fuel oil is available at Atlantic Quay

Towage: Launches assist with berthing

Repair & Maintenance: Minor repairs possible. Slipway for small vessels up to 225 t

Medical Facilities: Hospital in the town

Lloyd's Agent: Blue Water Shipping A/S, Blue Water Greenland AS, Industrivj 22, P O Box 1380, 3900 Nuuk, Greenland, *Tel:* +299 32 54 10, *Fax:* +299 32 54 11, *Email:* bwgnuuk@bws.dk, *Website:* www.bws.dk

NANORTALIK

Lat 60° 8' N; Long 45° 15' W.

Admiralty Chart: -　　　　　**Admiralty Pilot:** 12
Time Zone: GMT -3 h　　　　**UNCTAD Locode:** GL JNN

Principal Facilities:

P		G	C		B	T	

Authority: Royal Arctic Line A/S, P O Box 129, DK-3922 Nanortalik, Greenland, *Tel:* +299 61 34 33, *Fax:* +299 61 34 32, *Email:* uvp@ral.gl, *Website:* www.ral.gl

Officials: Port Director: Uvdloriaq Petersen.

Port Security: ISPS compliant

Anchorage: Anchorage can be obtained in the harbour only with permission from the Harbour Authority, or in Qagssit Bay, 3 miles NE of Nanortalik in depths ranging from 40 m to 50 m

Pilotage: Can be arranged with the Harbour Authority through Qaqortoq Radio

Radio Frequency: Nanortalik Radio, call sign OXF, VHF extension from Qaqortoq

Weather: Strong gusty winds off the mountains can be experienced. Ice conditions occur during the winter months and can be a hindrance to navigation from early January to the end of July. Southerly winds can cause ice to block the harbour entrance

Accommodation:

Name	Remarks
Nanortalik	See [1] below

[1]*Nanortalik:* Harbour has general depths ranging from 10 m to 30 m. Alongside berth for cargo vessels of up to 40 m loa and 4 m d. Mooring berths are provided in the middle of the harbour for larger vessels in depths of 20 m. Vessels of 100 m loa and 6 m d can be accommodated. Quay for cargo and fishing vessels 30 m long in depth of 7.0 m at LW
Tanker facilities: Facilities at fuel installation in a depth of 10 m; vessels secure stern on

Mechanical Handling Equipment: Container handling equipment to 30 t

Location	Type	Capacity (t)
Nanortalik	Mobile Cranes	5

Bunkering: Limited supplies of light marine diesel can be obtained

Towage: Launches assist with berthing

Repair & Maintenance: Minor repairs can be effected

Medical Facilities: Hospital in the town

Lloyd's Agent: Blue Water Shipping A/S, Blue Water Greenland AS, Industrivj 22, P O Box 1380, 3900 Nuuk, Greenland, *Tel:* +299 32 54 10, *Fax:* +299 32 54 11, *Email:* bwgnuuk@bws.dk, *Website:* www.bws.dk

NARSAQ

Lat 60° 54' N; Long 45° 59' W.

Admiralty Chart: -　　　　　**Admiralty Pilot:** 12
Time Zone: GMT -3 h　　　　**UNCTAD Locode:** GL JNS

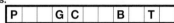

Principal Facilities:

P		G	C		B		T	

Authority: Royal Arctic Line A/S, P O Box 125, DK-3921 Narsaq, Greenland, *Tel:* +299 66 16 33, *Fax:* +299 66 16 32, *Email:* fil@ral.gl, *Website:* www.ral.gl

Officials: Harbour Master: Finn Lindberg.

Port Security: ISPS compliant

Anchorage: Anchorage can be obtained in the bay to the SE of Narssaq in a depth of 30 m, but the holding ground is poor and area is exposed to SE winds. Better anchorage areas are available in Narssaq Sound or off Qaqortoq

Pilotage: Available by arrangement through Qaqortoq

Radio Frequency: Narsaq Radio, call sign OXF, VHF extension from Qaqortoq

Weather: Ice conditions may occur during the winter; although ice floes can hamper navigation from January to early August. Only ice-strengthened vessels will be accepted at the port during this period

Tides: MHWST 3 m

Accommodation: Tanker facilities: An anchor berth for tankers is located S of the main quay on the W side of East Harbour, at which vessels secure stern on

Name	Length (m)	Depth (m)	Draught (m)	Remarks
East Harbour				See [1] below
Main quay	60	8.3		
Fishing quay			4	Situated on the N side of the harbour
West Harbour				See [2] below

[1]*East Harbour:* Provides berths for ocean-going vessels, either at mooring berths or alongside. Vessels of up to 135 m loa, 6.5 m d can be accommodated
[2]*West Harbour:* In Narsaq Cove, is suitable for small vessels only

Mechanical Handling Equipment: Container handling equipment to 30 t

Location	Type	Capacity (t)
Narsaq	Mobile Cranes	5
Narsaq	Forklifts	

Bunkering: Limited supplies of light marine diesel can be obtained

Towage: Launches are available to assist with berthing

Medical Facilities: Services are available.

Lloyd's Agent: Blue Water Shipping A/S, Blue Water Greenland AS, Industrivj 22, P O Box 1380, 3900 Nuuk, Greenland, *Tel:* +299 32 54 10, *Fax:* +299 32 54 11, *Email:* bwgnuuk@bws.dk, *Website:* www.bws.dk

NARSARSUAQ

Lat 61° 9' N; Long 45° 26' W.

Admiralty Chart: -　　　　　**Admiralty Pilot:** 12
Time Zone: GMT -3 h　　　　**UNCTAD Locode:** GL UAK

Key to Principal Facilities:—			
A=Airport	**C**=Containers	**G**=General Cargo	**P**=Petroleum　　**R**=Ro/Ro　　**Y**=Dry Bulk
B=Bunkers	**D**=Dry Dock	**L**=Cruise	**Q**=Other Liquid Bulk　**T**=Towage (where available from port)

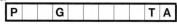

Principal Facilities:

P		G					T	A

Authority: Pilersuisoq A/S, P O Box 503, Narsarsuaq, Greenland, *Tel:* +299 49 77 18

Port Security: ISPS compliant

Anchorage: Anchorage can be obtained at the head of Narssarssuaq Reach in depths ranging from 18 m to 29 m

Pilotage: Not available. Masters of vessels should inform the official at the observation base of their ETA well in advance of arrival. Day and night navigation

Radio Frequency: VHF through Qaqortoq Radio, call sign OXF

Weather: Strong winds reaching storm force can blow from the SE. Ice conditions occur in winter; thickness of ice can reach 1 m. Ice floes can be hazardous on break up of winter ice

Tides: MHWST 3 m, MHWNT 1.6 m. Max HT is 3.6 m

Accommodation:

Name	Remarks
Narsarsuaq	See [1] below

[1]*Narsarsuaq:* Quay extends from shore, 140 m in length; depths alongside range from 6 m to 11 m on the W side and 5 m to 8 m on the E side. Vessels of 130 m loa and 8 m d can be accommodated
Tanker facilities: Tankers can berth on the main quay; pipelines for receiving supplies of fuel and oil

Mechanical Handling Equipment:

Location	Type	Capacity (t)
Narsarsuaq	Mobile Cranes	4
Narsarsuaq	Forklifts	

Towage: Launches are available to assist with berthing

Airport: Narsarsuaq Airport

Lloyd's Agent: Blue Water Shipping A/S, Blue Water Greenland AS, Industrivj 22, P O Box 1380, 3900 Nuuk, Greenland, *Tel:* +299 32 54 10, *Fax:* +299 32 54 11, *Email:* bwgnuuk@bws.dk, *Website:* www.bws.dk

NARSSAQ

alternate name, see Narsaq

NARSSARSSUAQ

alternate name, see Narsarsuaq

NUUK

Lat 64° 10' N; Long 51° 44' W.

Admiralty Chart: - **Admiralty Pilot:** 12
Time Zone: GMT -3 h **UNCTAD Locode:** GL GOH

Principal Facilities:

P	Q		G	C		L	B		T	A

Authority: Royal Arctic Line A/S, P O Box 1059, DK-3900 Nuuk, Greenland, *Tel:* +299 34 91 00, *Fax:* +299 32 24 50, *Email:* ral@ral.gl, *Website:* www.ral.gl

Officials: General Manager: Taatsiannguaq Olsen, *Tel:* +299 34 92 01, *Email:* tol@ral.gl.

Port Security: ISPS compliant

Approach: Depth at entrance 19 m

Anchorage: Anchorage can be obtained in Malene Bight in depths of 15 m to 19 m, or in the roadstead in a depth of 45 m

Pilotage: Not compulsory but available. Port Manager can act as pilot. Pilotage can be arranged through the Port Authority during normal working hours. 24 h notice of ETA should be given

Radio Frequency: Nuuk Radio Station, call sign OXI

Weather: Winds mainly from S and SW direction. Ice rarely forms locally, but floating ice drifts into the harbour usually between May and July can hinder navigation

Tides: Max height of HT is 5.1 m, LW 2.1 m

Working Hours: Mon-Fri 0800-1600, outside these hours if necessary

Accommodation:

Name	Length (m)	Depth (m)	Remarks
Nuuk			See [1] below
Atlantic Quay	170	4.6–7	See [2] below
New Atlantic Quay	100	10	
Schooner Quay	52	4.7–5	
Cutter Quay	205	2.6–3.6	For fishing vessels
Sand Berth	30	5	

[1]*Nuuk:* Depth in the harbour ranges from 10 m to 17 m. There are several mooring buoys in the harbour and other small quays for fishing vessels
Tanker facilities: There is a tanker facility for tankers up to 30 000 dwt near to the tank and gas farm and shore installations on the W side of the harbour. Vessels secure stern on. Connections by pipeline. Another berth for tankers of 30 000 dwt is located in the N part of the inner harbour with a depth alongside of 12.6 m
[2]*Atlantic Quay:* Vessels up to 135 m loa and 7 m d can be accommodated

Storage: Refrigerated storage available and warehousing

Mechanical Handling Equipment: Container handling equipment up to 35 t

Location	Type	Capacity (t)
Atlantic Quay	Mobile Cranes	5
Atlantic Quay	Forklifts	

Bunkering: Available

Towage: Launches are available to assist with berthing

Repair & Maintenance: Slipway for vessels up to 1860 t

Shipping Agents: Blue Water Shipping A/S, Blue Water Greenland AS, Industrivj 22, P O Box 1380, 3900 Nuuk, Greenland, *Tel:* +299 32 54 10, *Fax:* +299 32 54 11, *Email:* bwgnuuk@bws.dk, *Website:* www.bws.dk
Royal Arctic Line A/S, P O Box 1629, Aqqusinersuaq 52, GR-3900 Nuuk, Greenland, *Tel:* +299 34 91 00, *Fax:* +299 32 33 32, *Email:* ras@ral.dk, *Website:* www.ral.gl

Surveyors: Det Norske Veritas A/S, Augo Lyngip Aqqutaa 8, P O Box 440, DK-3900 Nuuk, Greenland, *Tel:* +299 32 33 08, *Fax:* +299 32 49 08, *Email:* nuuk@dnv.com, *Website:* www.dnv.com

Medical Facilities: There is a hospital in the town

Airport: Nuuk Airport, 10 km

Lloyd's Agent: Blue Water Shipping A/S, Blue Water Greenland AS, Industrivj 22, P O Box 1380, 3900 Nuuk, Greenland, *Tel:* +299 32 54 10, *Fax:* +299 32 54 11, *Email:* bwgnuuk@bws.dk, *Website:* www.bws.dk

PAAMIUT

Lat 62° 0' N; Long 49° 40' W.

Admiralty Chart: - **Admiralty Pilot:** 12
Time Zone: GMT -3 h **UNCTAD Locode:** GL JFR

Principal Facilities:

P		G	C			B		T	

Authority: Royal Arctic Line A/S, P O Box 515, DK-3940 Paamiut, Greenland, *Tel:* +299 68 16 33, *Fax:* +299 68 16 32, *Email:* nlo@ral.gl, *Website:* www.ral.gl

Officials: Port Captain: Niels Lorentzen, *Email:* nlo@ral.gl.

Port Security: ISPS compliant

Approach: Depth at entrance 17-20 m

Anchorage: Anchorage can be obtained in the roadstead E of Skarvo in depths ranging from 18 m to 20 m; holding ground is not good and the area is exposed to SW winds

Pilotage: Not compulsory, but advisable. Local representative acts as pilot and will board vessel off Satuarssugssuaq if required

Radio Frequency: Paamiut Radio, call sign OXF, VHF extension from Qaqortoq

Weather: Ice conditions can occur during the winter, forming locally between December and March, although the ice frequently breaks up. Access can be difficult between April and August when drifting pack ice and icebergs can hinder navigation. Considerable fog is experienced in summer

Tides: Average height of HT is 3.8 m, LW 2 m

Accommodation:

Name	Length (m)	Depth (m)	Remarks
Paamiut			See [1] below
Atlantic Quay	90	7–8.6	See [2] below

[1]*Paamiut:* Depths in the harbour range from 11 m to 15 m. There is a wharf for fishing vessels in the S part of the harbour, 106 m long with depths alongside of 3.5 m to 7 m and also a smaller wharf for fishing vessels in the N part of the harbour, 63 m long and 3.5 m depth. Lighters are available

Tanker facilities: Small wharf on the S side of the harbour with a depth alongside of 5 m
²*Atlantic Quay:* Vessels up to 100 m loa and 6 m d can be accommodated

Mechanical Handling Equipment: Container handling equipment up to 30 t

Location	Type	Capacity (t)
Paamiut	Mobile Cranes	5
Paamiut	Forklifts	

Bunkering: Diesel oil and gas oil is available at the fuel installation

Towage: Launches are available to assist with berthing

Repair & Maintenance: Minor repairs can be effected. Slipway for small vessels up to 250 t

Medical Facilities: There is a hospital in the settlement

Lloyd's Agent: Blue Water Shipping A/S, Blue Water Greenland AS, Industrivj 22, P O Box 1380, 3900 Nuuk, Greenland, *Tel:* +299 32 54 10, *Fax:* +299 32 54 11, *Email:* bwgnuuk@bws.dk, *Website:* www.bws.dk

PITUFFIK

Lat 76° 33' N; Long 68° 52' W.

Admiralty Chart: -	**Admiralty Pilot:** 12
Time Zone: GMT -4 h	**UNCTAD Locode:** GL THU

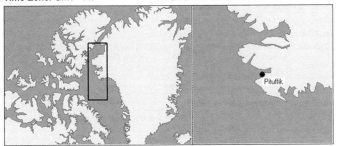

Principal Facilities:

	P		G				T		

Authority: Thule Air Base, United States Government, Ministry of Defence, Pituffik, Greenland

Approach: Permission to enter North Star Bay must be obtained from the US Base Authority

Pilotage: Not available. US Harbour Service assists vessels to berth. ETA should be sent well in advance to the US Base Authority and also to the officials at Dundas Radio Station

Accommodation:

Name	Remarks
Pituffik	See ¹ below

¹*Pituffik:* The port is operated by the United States Harbour Services; the whole of the bay is under their jurisdiction, forming part of a US defence area. A pier 305 m long is located at the end of a causeway and has a max depth alongside of 9.4 m. Vessels up to 130 m loa and 7 m d can be accommodated. Anchorages and mooring berths are also available in the bay in depths ranging from 13 m to 18 m; good holding ground. Lighter berths are situated near to the causeway. US icebreakers are available during severe ice conditions
Tanker facilities: Mooring berth with three buoys for tankers discharging fuel oil. There are six oil storage tanks

Mechanical Handling Equipment:

Location	Type
Pituffik	Mobile Cranes
Pituffik	Forklifts

Bunkering: Not readily available, but can sometimes be obtained from tankers in the vicinity

Towage: Launches are available to assist with berthing

Repair & Maintenance: Minor repairs can be effected. Divers are available

Medical Facilities: Hospital at the US Air Force Base

Lloyd's Agent: Blue Water Shipping A/S, Blue Water Greenland AS, Industrivj 22, P O Box 1380, 3900 Nuuk, Greenland, *Tel:* +299 32 54 10, *Fax:* +299 32 54 11, *Email:* bwgnuuk@bws.dk, *Website:* www.bws.dk

QAANAAQ

Lat 77° 28' N; Long 69° 13' W.

Admiralty Chart: -	**Admiralty Pilot:** 12
Time Zone: GMT -4 h	**UNCTAD Locode:** GL NAQ

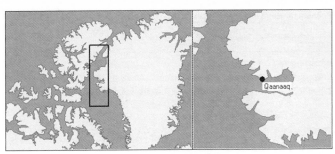

Principal Facilities:

				G							

Authority: KNI Pilersuisoq AS, GR-3971 Qaanaaq, Greenland, *Tel:* +299 50044, *Fax:* +299 50144

Approach: Depths in approach channels off the settlement range from 6.1 m to 7 m

Weather: Calm conditions usually prevail during the navigation period; fog can be frequent. Strong winds can be experienced from the E and SE. Ice conditions occur, with winter ice forming quickly during October, attaining a thickness of 1.8 m. Break up commences during May, but large ice floes remain until the end of July. Polar darkness from November 1 to February 10 and midnight sun from April 23 to August 20

Tides: MHWST 3 m, MHWNT 1.7 m. Max HT is 3.4 m

Accommodation:

Name	Remarks
Qaanaaq	See ¹ below

¹*Qaanaaq:* Anchorage and mooring berths approx 550 m offshore in a depth of 15 m; good holding ground. Cargo unloaded by lighters and landed on the beach at the settlement. Vessels of about 80 m loa and up to a max of 6 m d are normally handled

Medical Facilities: There is a hospital at the settlement

Lloyd's Agent: Blue Water Shipping A/S, Blue Water Greenland AS, Industrivj 22, P O Box 1380, 3900 Nuuk, Greenland, *Tel:* +299 32 54 10, *Fax:* +299 32 54 11, *Email:* bwgnuuk@bws.dk, *Website:* www.bws.dk

QAQORTOQ

Lat 60° 43' N; Long 46° 2' W.

Admiralty Chart: -	**Admiralty Pilot:** 12
Time Zone: GMT -3 h	**UNCTAD Locode:** GL JJU

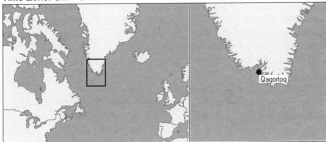

Principal Facilities:

				G	C			B		T	

Authority: Royal Arctic Line A/S, P O Box 508, DK-3920 Qaqortoq, Greenland, *Tel:* +299 64 16 33, *Fax:* +299 64 16 32, *Email:* eti@ral.gl, *Website:* www.ral.gl

Officials: Port Captain: Efraim Tittusen.

Port Security: ISPS compliant

Approach: Depth at entrance 15 m

Anchorage: Anchorage can be obtained in the outer harbour. Large vessels can anchor in a bay 1.5 miles NNE of Julianehaab

Pilotage: Not compulsory, but recommended. Available by arrangement with the Harbour Manager. Pilot will normally board off Akia

Radio Frequency: Qaqortoq coastal radio station, call sign OXF. VHF R/T facility available

Weather: W winds can cause heavy swell in the harbour as well as NW and WNW winds. Ice conditions occur from late March to mid August when pack ice can completely fill the harbour

Tides: Max height of HT is 3.2 m, LW 1.4 m

Accommodation:

Name	Length (m)	Depth (m)	Remarks
Qaqortoq			See ¹ below
Atlantic Quay	100	6.8	Vessels of 100 m loa and 6 m d can be accommodated

¹*Qaqortoq:* Harbour protected by a breakwater 145 m long. There is another quay, also 60 m long for smaller vessels, plus smaller quays and jetties. An anchorage berth is located in the outer harbour in a depth of 29 m. Lighters are available

Storage: Warehousing is available

Key to Principal Facilities:—				
A=Airport	**C**=Containers	**G**=General Cargo	**P**=Petroleum	**R**=Ro/Ro	**Y**=Dry Bulk
B=Bunkers	**D**=Dry Dock	**L**=Cruise	**Q**=Other Liquid Bulk	**T**=Towage (where available from port)	

Mechanical Handling Equipment: Container handling equipment up to 30 t

Location	Type	Capacity (t)	Qty
Qaqortoq	Mult-purp. Cranes	30	1

Bunkering: Light marine diesel fuel is available, Tel: 638180

Towage: Launches are available to assist with berthing

Repair & Maintenance: Minor repairs can be effected. Slipway for small vessels up to 250 t. There is a 35 t cap crane at the repair berth

Medical Facilities: Hoapital in the town.

Lloyd's Agent: Blue Water Shipping A/S, Blue Water Greenland AS, Industrivj 22, P O Box 1380, 3900 Nuuk, Greenland, *Tel:* +299 32 54 10, *Fax:* +299 32 54 11, *Email:* bwgnuuk@bws.dk, *Website:* www.bws.dk

QASIGIANNGUIT

Lat 68° 49' N; Long 51° 11' W.

Admiralty Chart: -	**Admiralty Pilot:** 12
Time Zone: GMT -3 h	**UNCTAD Locode:** GL JCH

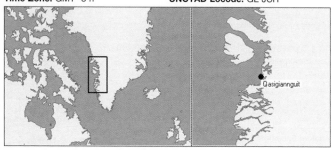

Principal Facilities:

	P		G	C				T	

Authority: Royal Arctic Line A/S, P O Box 149, DK-3951 Qasigiannguit, Greenland, *Tel:* +299 91 10 33, *Fax:* +299 91 10 32, *Email:* hgr@ral.gl, *Website:* www.ral.gl

Officials: Port Captain: Hans Gronvold.
Harbour Master: John Rasmussen.

Port Security: ISPS compliant

Approach: Depth in approach channels exceed 100 m

Anchorage: Anchorage can be obtained in the outer and inner harbours in depths ranging from 20 m to 100 m and 10 m to 20 m respectively

Pilotage: An unlicensed pilot is usually available

Radio Frequency: VHF Channels 16, 13 and 12

Weather: Strong E winds with gusts from the mountains can render the anchorage areas unsafe; vessels must be prepared to put to sea. Ice conditions occur during the winter months and drifting ice can be encountered off the port during early summer after the break up. Fog is also frequent during this period. Polar darkness from early December to mid June and midnight sun from late April to late July

Accommodation:

Name	Length (m)	Depth (m)	Remarks
Qasigiannguit			
Atlantic Quay	40	8	See [1] below

[1]*Qasigiannguit:* Mooring berth in the Inner Harbour near to Atlantic Quay in a depth of 13 m. Vessels of 135 m loa and 7.4 m d can be accommodated. There is a jetty 75 m long with a depth of 4 m for smaller vessels and boat moorings for small craft are available at the head of the Inner Harbour in depths of 1.4 m to 3.7 m
Tanker facilities: Facilities at fuel installation; jetty 10 m long with depth alongside of 3.5 m; vessels secure stern on
Lighters are available

Mechanical Handling Equipment: Container handling equipment up to 30 t

Location	Type	Capacity (t)	Qty
Qasigiannguit	Reach Stackers	30–40	1
Qasigiannguit	Forklifts		

Towage: Launches are available to assist with berthing

Medical Facilities: Hospital available

Lloyd's Agent: Blue Water Shipping A/S, Blue Water Greenland AS, Industrivj 22, P O Box 1380, 3900 Nuuk, Greenland, *Tel:* +299 32 54 10, *Fax:* +299 32 54 11, *Email:* bwgnuuk@bws.dk, *Website:* www.bws.dk

QEQERTARSUAQ

Lat 69° 15' N; Long 53° 33' W.

Admiralty Chart: -	**Admiralty Pilot:** 12
Time Zone: GMT -3 h	**UNCTAD Locode:** GL JGO

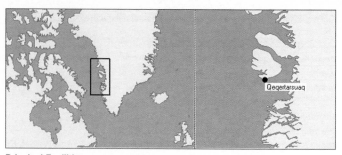

Principal Facilities:

			G			B		

Authority: KNI Pilersuisoq AS, Holten MYllerip Aqq 3c, GR-3953 Qeqertarsuaq, Greenland, *Tel:* +299 47244, *Fax:* +299 47103

Approach: Depths in channels in excess of 183 m

Anchorage: Anchorage can be obtained in the middle of the Outer Harbour in a depth of 37 m

Pilotage: Unlicensed pilots are available. Boarding point will be arranged with Port Authority. ETA to be advised through Qeqertarsuaq Radio

Weather: Ice conditions occur in the harbour during late November or December and can reach a thickness of 1 m, and seldom break up until May. Polar darkness from November 25 to January 15 and midnight sun from May 19 to July 26

Tides: Max height of HT 2.9 m, LW 1.4 m

Accommodation:

Name	Remarks
Qeqertarsuaq	See [1] below

[1]*Qeqertarsuaq:* Inner Harbour formed by bay with depths of about 6.82 m; vessels of up to 80 m loa, 6 m d can be moored. There are two small quays with depths alongside of 5 m and a small jetty, and also mooring buoys for small craft. Quay for fishing vessels 15 m long with depth 7 m at LW. Larger vessels of about 100 m loa and 6.5 m d can be accommodated in the Outer Harbour

Mechanical Handling Equipment:

Location	Type	Capacity (t)
Qeqertarsuaq	Mobile Cranes	5

Bunkering: Limited supplies of light marine diesel can be obtained

Medical Facilities: Hospital and doctors available

Lloyd's Agent: Blue Water Shipping A/S, Blue Water Greenland AS, Industrivj 22, P O Box 1380, 3900 Nuuk, Greenland, *Tel:* +299 32 54 10, *Fax:* +299 32 54 11, *Email:* bwgnuuk@bws.dk, *Website:* www.bws.dk

SISIMIUT

Lat 66° 57' N; Long 53° 41' W.

Admiralty Chart: -	**Admiralty Pilot:** 12
Time Zone: GMT -3 h	**UNCTAD Locode:** GL JHS

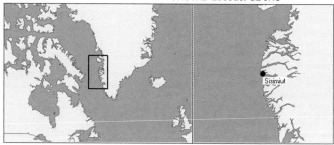

Principal Facilities:

	Q		C				T	A	

Authority: Royal Arctic Line A/S, P O Box 450, DK-3911 Sisimiut, Greenland, *Tel:* +299 86 59 33, *Fax:* +299 86 57 32, *Email:* hfe@ral.gl, *Website:* www.ral.gl

Officials: Port Captain: Hans Fencker.

Port Security: ISPS compliant

Approach: Depth at entrance 28 m

Anchorage: No.1: in pos 66° 56' 45" N; 53° 41' 50" W in depth of 40-43 m
No.2: in pos 66° 56' 49" N; 53° 40' 50" W in depth of 40-43 m
Anchorage is forbidden in pos 66° 56' 37" N; 53° 41' 22" W

Pilotage: Available through Harbour Authority if required; 36 h notice of ETA should be given. Pilot will board off Jakobs Skaer, or in the Outer Harbour. Day or night navigation

Radio Frequency: VHF Channels 16 (distress, safety & calling) and 12 (port operations)

Weather: Strong W to SW winds can create a swell in the Outer Harbour, which if reach gale force, can render the harbour unsafe. Ice conditions occur from early January to end of April in the harbour, and can hinder navigation

Tides: Max height of HT is 4.4 m, LW 2 m

Accommodation: Facilities exist at fuel installations near to the mooring berths

Name	Length (m)	Depth (m)	Remarks
Outer Harbour			See [1] below
Atlantic Quay	60	8–12	See [2] below
Offshore Quay	25	6–8	
Schooner Quay	15	7	
Inner Harbour			See [3] below
Industry Pier	51	9.5	Located on the W side of entrance

[1]*Outer Harbour:* Mooring berths are available for larger vessels, cargo transfer by lighters

[2]*Atlantic Quay:* Discharging/loading with ship's own gear. Vessels of 180 m loa can be accommodated

[3]*Inner Harbour:* Entrance off the SE corner of the Outer Harbour. Various quays used mainly by fishing vessels with depths alongside ranging from 0.5 m to 5 m

Storage: Warehousing is available at Atlantic Quay

Mechanical Handling Equipment:

Location	Type	Capacity (t)	Qty
Atlantic Quay	Mobile Cranes	40	1
Atlantic Quay	Reach Stackers		1
Atlantic Quay	Forklifts	3.5	10

Towage: Launches are available to assist with berthing

Repair & Maintenance: Minor repairs possible. Slipway for small vessels up to 250 t

Shipping Agents: Blue Water Shipping A/S, Blue Water Greenland A/S, Muunup Aqq, P O Box 250, GR 3911 Sisimiut, Greenland, *Tel:* +299 86 63 65, *Fax:* +299 86 44 70, *Email:* sisimiut@bws.dk, *Website:* www.bws.dk

Stevedoring Companies: Blue Water Shipping A/S, Blue Water Greenland A/S, Muunup Aqq, P O Box 250, GR 3911 Sisimiut, Greenland, *Tel:* +299 86 63 65, *Fax:* +299 86 44 70, *Email:* sisimiut@bws.dk, *Website:* www.bws.dk
Pisiffik A/S, P O Box 1012, 3911 Sisimiut, Greenland, *Tel:* +299 86 41 41, *Fax:* +299 86 52 41, *Email:* nan@pisiffik.gl, *Website:* www.pisiffik.gl

Surveyors: Bureau Veritas, c/o B. Larsen, Televej 2, DK-3911 Sisimiut, Greenland, *Tel:* +299 86 42 60, *Fax:* +299 86 53 26, *Website:* www.bureauveritas.com

Medical Facilities: Hospital in the town, Tel: +299 86 42 11, Fax: 86 45 33

Airport: Sisimiut Airport, Tel: +299 86 51 99

Lloyd's Agent: Blue Water Shipping A/S, Blue Water Greenland AS, Industrivj 22, P O Box 1380, 3900 Nuuk, Greenland, *Tel:* +299 32 54 10, *Fax:* +299 32 54 11, *Email:* bwgnuuk@bws.dk, *Website:* www.bws.dk

SONDRE STROMFJORD

alternate name, see Kangerlussuaq

SUKKERTOPPEN

alternate name, see Maniitsoq

TASIILOQ

alternate name, see Ammassalik

THULE

alternate name, see Qaanaaq

UMANAK

alternate name, see Uummannaq

UPERNAVIK

Lat 72° 47' N; Long 56° 9' W.

Admiralty Chart: -   **Admiralty Pilot:** 12

Time Zone: GMT -3 h   **UNCTAD Locode:** GL JUV

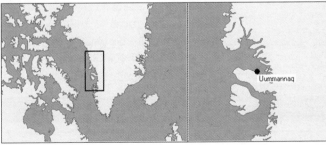

Principal Facilities:

P		G							

Authority: Royal Arctic Line A/S, Umiarsualiviup Aqq. B-745, DK-3962 Upernavik, Greenland, *Tel:* +299 96 20 33, *Fax:* +299 96 20 34, *Email:* jle@ral.gl, *Website:* www.ral.gl

Officials: Port Captain: Jakob Lennert.

Port Security: ISPS compliant

Anchorage: Anchorage can be obtained off the S end of Upernavik Island in depths ranging from 30 m to 40 m

Pilotage: An unlicensed pilot is available by arrangement with the Harbour Authority through Upernavik Radio. Pilot normally boards 1 mile off harbour entrance. Day and night navigation

Weather: Winds predominant from N and SW direction in summer. Ice conditions occur from November to early June, causing the harbour to freeze over; ice can attain a thickness of 0.6 m. Fog is common when the ice breaks up. Polar darkness from early November to early February and midnight sun from mid May to early August

Tides: 2.0 m MHWST, 1.3 m MHWNT

Accommodation:

Name	Length (m)	Depth (m)	Remarks
Upernavik			See [1] below
Schooner Quay	15	4.2	

[1]*Upernavik:* Mooring berths located in a bay for vessels of 75 m loa and 5 m d. Vessels discharge cargo into lighters. Quay for fishing vessels 8 m long in depth of 1.5 m at LW

Tanker facilities: Facilities at fuel installation on the S side of the harbour; vessels secure stern on

Mechanical Handling Equipment:

Location	Type
Upernavik	Forklifts

Medical Facilities: Hospital available

Lloyd's Agent: Blue Water Shipping A/S, Blue Water Greenland AS, Industrivj 22, P O Box 1380, 3900 Nuuk, Greenland, *Tel:* +299 32 54 10, *Fax:* +299 32 54 11, *Email:* bwgnuuk@bws.dk, *Website:* www.bws.dk

UUMMANNAQ

Lat 70° 41' N; Long 52° 8' W.

Admiralty Chart: -   **Admiralty Pilot:** 12

Time Zone: GMT -3 h   **UNCTAD Locode:** GL UMD

Principal Facilities:

		G						T	

Authority: Royal Arctic Line A/S, P O Box 205, DK-3961 Uummannaq, Greenland, *Tel:* +299 95 12 33, *Fax:* +299 95 15 35, *Email:* jtr@ral.gl, *Website:* www.ral.gl

Officials: Port Captain: Jens Trolle.

Port Security: ISPS compliant

Anchorage: Anchorage can be obtained off the harbour entrance

Pilotage: An unlicensed pilot is available by arrangement with the Harbour Authority and his services are recommended. Pilot normally boards off the harbour entrance. Small vessels can enter the port day or night, but larger vessels are usually advised to navigate during daylight hours only

Weather: Ice conditions occur from November to late June, causing the harbour to freeze over. After the ice breaks up, drifting ice remains in the area for as long as a month, causing a hindrance to navigation. Polar darkness from late November to late January and midnight sun from mid May to end of July

Tides: MHWST 2 m, MHWNT 1.3 m. Max HT is 2.3 m

Key to Principal Facilities:—					
A=Airport	**C**=Containers	**G**=General Cargo	**P**=Petroleum	**R**=Ro/Ro	**Y**=Dry Bulk
B=Bunkers	**D**=Dry Dock	**L**=Cruise	**Q**=Other Liquid Bulk	**T**=Towage (where available from port)	

Accommodation:

Name	Remarks
Uummannaq	See [1] below

[1]*Uummannaq:* Harbour located at the head of a cove; mooring berths for ocean-going vessels in a depth of about 12 m, discharge to lighters. Vessels of 80 m loa and 6 m d can be accommodated. There is a quay 16 m long for small vessels with a depth alongside of 4.2 m and the lighterage wharf is 32 m long with a max depth of 2.5 m. Small craft can also berth at this wharf

Storage: Warehousing is available

Mechanical Handling Equipment:

Location	Type	Capacity (t)	Qty
Uummannaq	Mult-purp. Cranes	3	1
Uummannaq	Mobile Cranes	10	1
Uummannaq	Forklifts		

Towage: Launches are available to assist with berthing

Repair & Maintenance: Minor repairs can be effected. There is a patent slip with a lifting cap of 40 t

Medical Facilities: Hospital available

Lloyd's Agent: Blue Water Shipping A/S, Blue Water Greenland AS, Industrivj 22, P O Box 1380, 3900 Nuuk, Greenland, *Tel:* +299 32 54 10, *Fax:* +299 32 54 11, *Email:* bwgnuuk@bws.dk, *Website:* www.bws.dk

GRENADA

ST. GEORGE'S

Lat 12° 2' N; Long 61° 44' W.

Admiralty Chart: 799	**Admiralty Pilot:** 71
Time Zone: GMT -4 h	**UNCTAD Locode:** GD STG

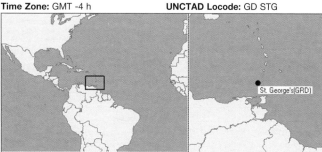

St. George's(GRD)

Principal Facilities:

P	Q	Y	G	C		L	B			A

Authority: Grenada Ports Authority, P O Box 494, Carenage, St. George's, Grenada, *Tel:* +1473 440 3013, *Fax:* +1473 440 3418, *Email:* grenport@spiceisle.com

Officials: General Manager: Ambrose Phillip.
Port Manager: Ian Evans.
Administration: Edward Lord, *Tel:* +1473 440 3694.

Port Security: ISPS compliant. Security is provided by a contingent of the Grenada Police Force

Documentation: Crew lists (4 copies), international declaration of health, crew declaration, clearance from last port, ship stores list, passenger list (2 copies), arrival report (to be filled out on arrival on a supplied form)

Approach: Min channel depth is 19.5 m almost up to the pier. The channel curves to the N with shoaling water on both sides and is well marked by buoys and ranges

Anchorage: Anchorage in pos 12° 03' 12" N; 61° 45' 48" W

Pilotage: Compulsory for vessels over 200 gt, VHF Channel 16, call sign J3YB. 24 h notice to be given. Pilot boards NE of Annas Shoal

Radio Frequency: Port Control on VHF Channel 16, call sign J3YA

Weather: Wind varies from N to E for most of the year with occasional light wind from the W during July to September

Tides: 0.61 m rise and fall

Traffic: 2005, 582 116 t of cargo handled

Maximum Vessel Dimensions: Max draft 8.54 m, single screw vessel 183 m loa which may be increased

Principal Imports and Exports: Imports: Construction materials, Food, Light manufactured goods. Exports: Bananas, Cocoa, Spices.

Working Hours: 0700-1200, 1300-1800, 1900-2300

Accommodation:

Name	Length (m)	Depth (m)	Remarks
St. George's			
Commercial Berth	335	9.1	Cargo vessels
Melville Street Cruise Terminal	375	9.8–10.5	North and South berth

Storage: Three transit sheds on wharf, two 30.48 m by 30.48 m and one high duty goods warehouse, 18.29 by 22.86 m

Mechanical Handling Equipment: All loading and discharging are done by ship's own gear. The port operates two reach stackers of 40 t cap each, twenty forklifts with cap of 3-5 t and five tractor trailers. A vacuum pump and hopper are used to discharge grain

Bunkering: Sol EC Ltd, Grand Mall, P O Box 72, St. George's, Grenada, *Tel:* +1473 4403 066, *Fax:* +1473 4404 112, *Email:* info@solpetroleum.com, *Website:* www.solpetroleum.com
ExxonMobil Marine Fuels, Suite 900, One Alhambra Plaza, Coral Gables, FL 33134, United States of America, *Tel:* +1 305 459 6358, *Fax:* +1 305 459 6412, *Email:* emmf@exxonmobil.com, *Website:* www.exxonmobilmarinefuels.com – *Grades:* GO – *Delivery Mode:* truck
Sol EC Ltd, Grand Mall, P O Box 72, St. George's, Grenada, *Tel:* +1473 4403 066, *Fax:* +1473 4404 112, *Email:* info@solpetroleum.com, *Website:* www.solpetroleum.com

Repair & Maintenance: Grenada Yacht Services Ltd, St. George's, Grenada, *Tel:* +1473 440 2508, *Fax:* +1473 440 4109 Minor repairs
Spice Island Marine Services Ltd, P O Box 449, True Blue, St. George's, Grenada, *Tel:* +1473 444 4342, *Fax:* +1473 444 2816, *Email:* simsco@spiceisle.com, *Website:* www.spiceislandmarine.com Minor repairs

Ship Chandlers: W.E. Julien & Co. Ltd, P O Box 76, The Carenage, St. George's, Grenada, *Tel:* +1473 440 2046, *Fax:* +1473 440 2301, *Email:* w.e.julien@caribsurf.com

Shipping Agents: Jonas Browne & Hubbard (Grenada) Ltd, The Carenage, P O Box 25, St. George's, Grenada, *Tel:* +1473 440 2087, *Fax:* +1473 440 4008, *Email:* hubbards@spiceisle.com
George F. Huggins & Co. (Grenada) Ltd, Grand E'Tang Road, P O Box 46, Carenage, St. George's, Grenada, *Tel:* +1473 440 2032, *Fax:* +1473 440 4129, *Email:* hugship@spiceisle.com, *Website:* www.hugginsgrenada.com
W.E. Julien & Co. Ltd, P O Box 76, The Carenage, St. George's, Grenada, *Tel:* +1473 440 2046, *Fax:* +1473 440 2301, *Email:* w.e.julien@caribsurf.com
Meyer Agencies Ltd, Admiral's Level, Somers Wharf, 14 Water Street, St. George's GE BX, Grenada, *Tel:* +1473 297 2303, *Fax:* +1473 292 1583, *Email:* jevonb@meyer.bm
Paddy's Shipping, P O Box 225, Carenage, St. George's, Grenada, *Tel:* +1473 440 3261, *Fax:* +1473 407 1888, *Email:* paddysshipping@yahoo.com
Port Said Trading, P O Box 753, St. George's, Grenada, *Tel:* +1473 440 2614, *Fax:* +1473 440 2604, *Email:* magua@caribsurf.com
St. Louis Service, The Carenage, P O Box 311, St. George's, Grenada, *Tel:* +1473 440 2921, *Fax:* +1473 440 6620, *Email:* stlouisservices@caribsurf.com
Star Agency (Grenada) Ltd, Hillsborough Street, P O Box 2, St. George's, Grenada, *Tel:* +1473 440 2064, *Fax:* +1473 440 4171, *Email:* stargnd@caribsurf.com
Tradship International Ltd, Tyrell Street, St. George's, Grenada, *Tel:* +1473 440 4466, *Fax:* +1473 440 4262

Medical Facilities: General hospital available and private hospitals and clinics

Airport: Point Salines International Airport, 6.5 miles

Lloyd's Agent: Jonas Browne & Hubbard (Grenada) Ltd, The Carenage, P O Box 25, St. George's, Grenada, *Tel:* +1473 440 2087, *Fax:* +1473 440 4008, *Email:* hubbards@spiceisle.com

GUADELOUPE

BASSE TERRE

Lat 16° 2' N; Long 61° 45' W.

Admiralty Chart: 491
Admiralty Pilot: 71
Time Zone: GMT -4 h
UNCTAD Locode: GP BBR

Principal Facilities:

		G	C	R	L	B		A	

Authority: Port Autonome de la Guadeloupe, Quai Ferdinand de Lesseps, P O Box 485, Pointe a Pitre Cedex 97165, Guadeloupe, *Tel:* +590 590 68 61 70, *Fax:* +590 590 68 61 71, *Email:* v-tarer@port-guadeloupe.com, *Website:* www.port-guadeloupe.com

Officials: General Manager: Yves Simon, *Tel:* +590 590 68 62 10, *Email:* y-simon@port-guadeloupe.com.
Public Relations Manager: Viviane Tarer, *Tel:* +590 590 68 62 33.
Harbour Master: Bernard Legall, *Tel:* +590 68 63 20, *Mobile Tel:* +590 558 517, *Email:* b-legall@port-guadeloupe.com.

Port Security: ISPS compliant. Watch re-enforced when cruise vessel is berthing. Passenger control by XR

Pre-Arrival Information: Authorities require 24 h notice of the vessel's arrival

Approach: The port is open to the sea and is an open roads port

Anchorage: On an 18 fathom bank N of the pier, 2 cables from the shore

Pilotage: Compulsory for vessels over 120 m loa (entry) and over 160 m loa (entry and leaving). There is no pilot station in Basse Terre and pilot has to come from Pointe a Pitre, therefore when arriving call 'Basse Terre Port Control' on VHF Channel 16 or 12 and the Port Officer will issue you with instructions. Vessels must wait for the pilot approx 1 mile from the pier. Pilot usually comes on board on the port side

Radio Frequency: Port Authority on VHF Channel 16 and 12

Weather: Fair except during hurricane season. Dominant wind from SW

Tides: Max range of tide 0.50 m

Traffic: 2005, 43 350 t of cargo handled

Maximum Vessel Dimensions: 220 m loa

Working Hours: 0700-1100, 1300-1700. Extension possible

Accommodation:

Name	Length (m)	Depth (m)	Remarks
Basse Terre Quay	210	9.5	See [1] below

[1]*Quay:* Extension to the South of 40 m with three dolphins. Extension to the North of 30 m with a ro/ro berth. In the North Basin there is a vedette quay 40 m long in depth of 2.5 m and a ro/ro berth 48 m long in depth of 5.5-8 m. 2 ha of container stacking with 96 reefer plugs

Storage:

Location	Covered (m²)	Sheds / Warehouses
Basse Terre	1500	1

Mechanical Handling Equipment:

Location	Type	Capacity (t)	Qty
Basse Terre	Mobile Cranes	35	1

Cargo Worked: Approx 10 t/h

Bunkering: Gas oil delivered by tank truck alongside at the berth (arranged by agent)

Waste Reception Facilities: Waste by skip alongside the berth (arranged by agent). Slops by tank truck alongside the berth (arranged by agent)

Towage: One tug available from Pointe a Pitre

Shipping Agents: SARL Manupro, 9 Rue Christophe Colombo, P O Box 18, Basse Terre 97101, Guadeloupe, *Tel:* +590 590 81 16 16, *Fax:* +590 590 81 22 87

Medical Facilities: Doctor and hospital available

Airport: 60 km

Lloyd's Agent: Jean Pierre Porry, Immeuble du Port, 8 Avenue Francois Mitterand, 97200 Fort de France, Martinique, *Tel:* +596 596 63 73 45, *Fax:* +596 596 60 07 54, *Email:* contact@agencesporry.fr

GUSTAVIA

Lat 17° 55' N; Long 62° 50' W.

Admiralty Chart: 2079
Admiralty Pilot: 71
Time Zone: GMT -4 h
UNCTAD Locode: GP GUS

Principal Facilities:

		Y	G	C	R	L			A

Authority: Port of Gustavia, P O Box 695, St. Barthelemy 97133, Guadeloupe, *Tel:* +590 590 27 66 97, *Fax:* +590 590 27 81 54, *Email:* port.de.gustavia@wanadoo.fr

Officials: Port Director: Bruno Greaux.

Port Security: Port Security Officer: Ernest Brin. Assistant Port Security Officer: Frederic Blanchard

Pre-Arrival Information: Cargo vessels or Agents need to inform the port of their arrival 48 h before by Fax: +590 27 81 54

Approach: W Channel has depths ranging from 7.3 m to 12.8 m

Anchorage: Anchorage can be obtained off the harbour in depths of 7-12 m

Pilotage: Available on request through the Port Captain. VHF Channel 16/12

Weather: Weather information is posted at the office every day

Tides: Non-tidal

Maximum Vessel Dimensions: 130 m loa, 5.0 m draft

Principal Imports and Exports: Imports: Automobiles, Aviation fuel, Bagged cement, Bulk cargo, Commercial goods by containers, Construction materials, Containerised general cargoes, Diesel oil, Gasoline, Sand & gravel.

Working Hours: Mon-Fri 0600-1800. Sat 0600-1200

Accommodation:

Name	Length (m)	Draught (m)	Remarks
Gustavia Public Wharf	80	5.5	See [1] below Ro/ro & containers

[1]*Gustavia:* The harbour basin has general depths ranging from 5 m to 6 m. Vessels discharge/load using ship's own gear. There is a marina with berthing facilities for about 200 yachts. The port is regularly visited by cruise vessels

Medical Facilities: Hospital in the town

Airport: St. Jean Airport

Lloyd's Agent: Jean Pierre Porry, Immeuble du Port, 8 Avenue Francois Mitterand, 97200 Fort de France, Martinique, *Tel:* +596 596 63 73 45, *Fax:* +596 596 60 07 54, *Email:* contact@agencesporry.fr

MARIGOT

Lat 18° 4' N; Long 63° 6' W.

Admiralty Chart: 2079
Admiralty Pilot: 71
Time Zone: GMT -4 h
UNCTAD Locode: GP MSB

Principal Facilities:

		G	C	R				A	

Authority: Port of Marigot, Regie Municiple du Port, P O Box 3218, Galis Bay, Marigot, St. Martin Cedex 97067, Guadeloupe, *Tel:* +590 590 87 59 06, *Fax:* +590 590 87 87 77, *Email:* marigotport@wanadoo.fr

Officials: Port Director: Alberic Ellis.

Documentation: Crew list (2 copies), passenger list (2 copies), personal effects list, health declaration, manifests - freighted and unfreighted, last port clearance, stores list

Approach: Channel depth of 7 m

Radio Frequency: VHF Channels 16 and 13

Key to Principal Facilities:—			
A=Airport	**C**=Containers	**G**=General Cargo	**P**=Petroleum	**R**=Ro/Ro	**Y**=Dry Bulk
B=Bunkers	**D**=Dry Dock	**L**=Cruise	**Q**=Other Liquid Bulk	**T**=Towage (where available from port)	

Tides: Range of 1-2 m

Maximum Vessel Dimensions: Max loa 120 m, max draft 6 m

Principal Imports and Exports: Imports: Breakbulk cargo, Containerised cargo. Exports: Aggregates, Scrap metals.

Working Hours: 0700-1700

Accommodation:

Name	Length (m)	Depth (m)	Remarks
Marigot			See [1] below
Galis Bay Principal Quay	100	6	
Galis Bay Annexe Quay	100	5	

[1]Marigot: Container storage space of 10 000 m2. Ro/ro berth of 38 m

Storage:

Location	Open (m²)
Marigot	20000

Mechanical Handling Equipment:

Location	Type	Capacity (t)	Qty
Marigot	Mobile Cranes	200	1

Waste Reception Facilities: Special container disposal for garbage

Medical Facilities: General hospital situated in the town

Airport: Princess Juliana, 5 km

Lloyd's Agent: Jean Pierre Porry, Immeuble du Port, 8 Avenue Francois Mitterand, 97200 Fort de France, Martinique, *Tel:* +596 596 63 73 45, *Fax:* +596 596 60 07 54, *Email:* contact@agencesporry.fr

POINTE A PITRE

Lat 16° 13' N; Long 61° 32' W.

Admiralty Chart: 804

Time Zone: GMT -4 h

Admiralty Pilot: 71

UNCTAD Locode: GP PTP

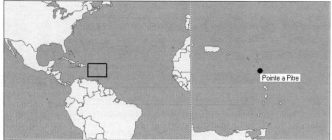

Principal Facilities:

P		Y	G	C	R	L	B			A	

Authority: Port Autonome de la Guadeloupe, Quai Ferdinand de Lesseps, P O Box 485, Pointe a Pitre Cedex 97165, Guadeloupe, *Tel:* +590 590 68 61 70, *Fax:* +590 590 68 61 71, *Email:* v-tarer@port-guadeloupe.com, *Website:* www.port-guadeloupe.com

Officials: General Manager: Yves Simon, *Tel:* +590 590 68 62 10, *Email:* y-simon@port-guadeloupe.com.
Public Relations Manager: Viviane Tarer, *Tel:* +590 590 68 62 33.
Harbour Master: Bernard Legall, *Tel:* +590 68 63 20, *Mobile Tel:* +590 558 517, *Email:* b-legall@port-guadeloupe.com.

Approach: Accessible to deep draft vessels, the access channel has been dredged to 11 m

Pilotage: Compulsory for vessels over 50 m loa

Radio Frequency: VHF Channel 12

Weather: Cyclone season July to November; ESE winds from force five to a max of force seven. W current outside harbour, no current inside

Tides: No tide so vessels can enter port at any time

Traffic: 2007, 3 435 967 t of cargo handled, 168 839 TEU's

Principal Imports and Exports: Imports: Construction materials, Consumption goods. Exports: Bananas, Rum, Sugar.

Working Hours: 0700-1100, 1300-1700 except for Container Terminal which works 24 h

Accommodation:

Name	Length (m)	Depth (m)	Remarks
Pointe a Pitre			
Quay No.1	151	7.5	Max length of vessel 165 m
Quay No.2	180	9	Max length of vessel 260 m
Quay No's 3 & 4	278	9	
Quay No's 5 & 6	323	8.8	
Quay No's 7 & 8	306	8.3	
Quay No.9		7.7	Mineral quay. Max length of vessel 182 m
Quay No.10		7.5	Oil & gas quay. Max length of vessel 125 m
Quay No.11A	150	8.3	Sugar & rum quay. Max length of vessel 135 m

Name	Length (m)	Depth (m)	Remarks
Quay No.11B	150	8.8	Grain quay. Max length of vessel 175 m
Quay No.12	188	11	
Quay No.13	160	11	
Quay No.14	240	11	Container terminal. Max length of vessel 240 m

Storage:

Location	Covered (m²)	Sheds / Warehouses
Quay No.14	3000	1

Mechanical Handling Equipment:

Location	Type	Capacity (t)	Qty
Quay No.14	Mult-purp. Cranes	40	3

Bunkering: Chevron Marine Products LLC, Global Marine Products LLC, 1500 Louisiana, 4th Floor, Houston, TX 77002, United States of America, *Tel:* +1 832 8542 988, *Fax:* +1 832 8544 868, *Email:* gulfcbm@chevron.com, *Website:* www.chevron.com
Elf, c/o Bamex, Acajou Lamentin, Fort de France, Martinique, *Tel:* +596 596 503756, *Fax:* +596 596 505763
Ocean Energy S.A.M., c/o Ocean Energy SAM, 57 Rue Grimaldi, Le Panorama Bloc C/D, MC 98000 Monte Carlo, Monaco, *Tel:* +377 9325 5331, *Fax:* +377 9325 5332, *Email:* oceanenergy@oceanenergy.mc, *Website:* www.oceanenergy.mc
SAP Texaco, Term Jarry, Baie Mahault 97122, Guadeloupe, *Tel:* +590 590 266194
Shell des Antilles et de la Guyane Francaises, Immeuble Sodega, Route de L Aeroport, Abymes 97139, Guadeloupe, *Tel:* +590 590 828735, *Fax:* +590 590 828735
Total France S.A., Total Marine Fuels, 51 Esplanade du General de Gaulle, F-92907 Paris la Defense Cedex 10, France, *Tel:* +33 1 4135 2755, *Fax:* +33 1 4197 0291, *Email:* marine.fuels@total.com, *Website:* www.marinefuels.total.com

Ship Chandlers: TCS The Caribbean Supplier, Hangar No.44, Port Autonome de Guadeloupe, P O Box 15, Pointe a Pitre, Grande Terre 97003, Guadeloupe, *Tel:* +590 590 21 55 75, *Fax:* +590 590 21 24 87, *Email:* tcs.guad@caribsup.com

Shipping Agents: A.P. Moller-Maersk Group, Maersk France S.A., Immeuble le Caducee, ZAC de Houelebourg Sud II Jarry, Pointe a Pitre, Grande Terre 97122, Guadeloupe, *Tel:* +590 590 38 20 40, *Fax:* +590 590 38 20 49, *Email:* ptpmla@maersk.com, *Website:* www.maerskline.com
SGCM, 8 Rue de Le Chapelle, 97122 Baie Mahault, P O Box 2360, Pointe a Pitre, Grande Terre 97001, Guadeloupe, *Tel:* +590 590 38 05 55, *Fax:* +590 590 26 95 39, *Email:* bernard.aubery@sgcm.fr
Somacotra S.A., P O Box 291, Pointe a Pitre Cedex 97175, Guadeloupe, *Tel:* +590 590 91 59 26, *Fax:* +590 590 91 40 57, *Email:* somacotra@wanadoo.fr
Transcaraibes S.A., P O Box 114, Pointe a Pitre, Grande Terre 97163, Guadeloupe, *Tel:* +590 590 26 63 27, *Fax:* +590 590 26 67 49, *Email:* transcaraibes.gpe@wanadoo.fr

Stevedoring Companies: Generale de Manutention Guadeloupeenne, 8 Rue de la Chapelle, P O Box 2360, Jarry, Guadeloupe, *Tel:* +590 590 38 05 55, *Fax:* +590 590 26 95 39
G.I.E. Cabre, Pointe a Pitre, Grande Terre, Guadeloupe, *Tel:* +590 590 81 16 16, *Fax:* +590 590 81 22 87
S.G.C.M., Pointe a Pitre, Grande Terre, Guadeloupe, *Tel:* +590 590 26 96 92, *Fax:* +590 590 26 95 39
Societe de Cordination des Transports, Pointe a Pitre, Grande Terre, Guadeloupe, *Tel:* +590 590 26 64 74, *Fax:* +590 590 26 64 73
Somacotra S.A., P O Box 291, Pointe a Pitre Cedex 97175, Guadeloupe, *Tel:* +590 590 91 59 26, *Fax:* +590 590 91 40 57, *Email:* somacotra@wanadoo.fr
Transcaraibe, Pointe a Pitre, Grande Terre, Guadeloupe, *Tel:* +590 590 26 63 27, *Fax:* +590 590 26 67 49

Surveyors: Caruel, Pointe a Pitre, Grande Terre, Guadeloupe, *Tel:* +590 590 82 01 16, *Fax:* +590 590 91 35 08

Medical Facilities: General Hospital near port

Airport: Le Raizet Airport, 5 km

Lloyd's Agent: Jean Pierre Porry, Immeuble du Port, 8 Avenue Francois Mitterand, 97200 Fort de France, Martinique, *Tel:* +596 596 63 73 45, *Fax:* +596 596 60 07 54, *Email:* contact@agencesporry.fr

ST. BARTHELEMY

see under Gustavia

GUAM

APRA

Lat 13° 27' N; Long 144° 37' E.

Admiralty Chart: 1109

Time Zone: GMT +10 h

Admiralty Pilot: 60

UNCTAD Locode: GU APR

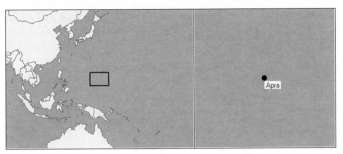

Principal Facilities:

P		G	C	R	L			A

Authority: Port Authority of Guam, 1026 Cabras Highway, Suite 201, Piti 96915, Guam, *Tel:* +1 671 477 5931/472, *Fax:* +1 671 477 4445, *Email:* webmaster@portofguam.com, *Website:* www.portofguam.com

Officials: Chairman: Jose D. Leon Guerrero.
General Manager: Kenneth Tagawa.
Harbour Master: Frank G. Santos, *Email:* fgsantos@portofguam.com.

Port Security: ISPS compliant

Pre-Arrival Information: Vessels must submit notice of arrival 96 h prior to US Coast Guard and Harbour Control

Approach: The draft of the channel is 12-30 metres. Vessels approaching the harbour must pass through Alpha Hotel Point, where a pilot shall board and thereafter shall keep the entrance leading lights aligned. When entering, pass buoys no 1&2 and line ship up on range 083. Entrance is 700' wide and 130 to 140 feet deep. There are no obstacles within the channel.

Anchorage: There are six anchorage positions within the harbour, two are general, two are military and two are navy
General anchorage positions:
13 27'22"N 144 37'57"E in depth of 42.8 m
13 27'31"N 144 38'33"E in depth of 34.3 m
Explosive anchorage positions:
13 26'55"N 144 37'52"E in depth of 43.4 m
13 27'39"N 144 38'12"N in depth of 38.9 m
Navy anchorage positions:
13 26'58"N 144 38'49"E in depth of 36.4 m
13 26'53"N 144 38'18"E in depth of 27 m

Pilotage: Pilotage is required for all vessels over 500 gt and all vessels upon first entry to the port. Pilots are licensed by U.S. Coast Guard and Port Authority. Pilotage is avilable 24 h from private operators and should be requested at least 24 h prior to arrival. Pilot normally boards at Alpha Hotel Point, located 2 nautical miles W of the harbour entrance

Radio Frequency: 24 h watch on VHF Channels 16, 13 and 12 (156.6, 156.65 and 156.8 mHz), call sign WRV 574

Weather: Typhoon season from June to January. Winds ENE for 70% of the year, average 6-7 knots

Tides: Range of tide: springs 0.79 m, neaps 0.64 m

Traffic: 2007, 1281 vessels, 2 068 775 t of cargo handled, 99 630 TEU's

Maximum Vessel Dimensions: Cargo vessels should not exceed 11 m draught if going to Foxtrot 4, 5 and 6. Vessels at Foxtrot 3 should not exceed 10 m or 182.8 m loa

Working Hours: 0700-1900 and 1900-0700 with an hour break at 1200 and 2400

Accommodation:

Name	Length (m)	Depth (m)	Draught (m)	Remarks
Apra				See [1] below
Delta (Navy)	202	13.95		
Echo (Navy)	227	13		
Foxtrot 1	167	21.3	16.16	See [2] below
Foxtrot 2	200	7.6		Minor ship repair/fisheries
Foxtrot 3	228	10.36		See [3] below
Foxtrot 4, 5 & 6	599	10.34–11.6		See [4] below
Golf	135	15.2		See [5] below
Hotel	152	10.3		Passenger & general cargo

[1]*Apra:* Depth in inner harbour of 9.75 m. Commercial Port in Outer Harbour
[2]*Foxtrot 1:* Shell Guam Inc., PO Box 3190, Agana, Tel: + 1671 477 4348, operate this pier capable of berthing vessels up to 135 000 dwt
[3]*Foxtrot 3:* General cargo, passenger vessels & fishing vessels
[4]*Foxtrot 4, 5 & 6:* General cargo & container. Can accommodate two full container vessels or three smaller breakbulk and container vessels. Container storage area of 26.5 acres with 180 reefer points
[5]*Golf:* Operated by Mobil Oil Guam Inc., Tel: +1671 472 3300
Used for refined products

Storage: 26.5 acre open container storage yard. Two warehouses at 86 000 sq ft. 180 reefer slots

Location	Covered (m²)	Sheds / Warehouses
Apra	30096	2

Mechanical Handling Equipment:

Location	Type	Capacity (t)	Qty
Foxtrot 4, 5 & 6	Mobile Cranes	150	1
Foxtrot 4, 5 & 6	Container Cranes	40	2
Foxtrot 4, 5 & 6	RTG's	40	2

Cargo Worked: Breakbulk 50 t/h (4 hooks), ro/ro 150 units/h, 32 TEU's/h

Bunkering: ExxonMobil Marine Fuels, Mailpoint 31, ExxonMobil House, Ermyn Way, Leatherhead, Surrey KT22 8UX, United Kingdom, *Tel:* +44 1372 222 000, *Fax:* +44 1372 223 922, *Email:* marine.fuels@exxonmobil.com, *Website:* www.exxonmobil.com – *Grades:* MGO – *Delivery Mode:* truck

Waste Reception Facilities: MARPOL ship garbage disposal available from Pacific Environmental Resources, Inc. Regular garbage disposal is available from many private contractors. No facilities for ballast, sludge or chemical waste.

Towage: Cabras Marine Corp., Suite 114, 1026 Cabras Highway, Piti 96915, Guam, *Tel:* +1 671 477 7345, *Fax:* +1 671 477 6206, *Email:* cabmar@ite.net, *Website:* www.cabrasmarine.com

Repair & Maintenance: Cabras Marine Corp., Suite 114, 1026 Cabras Highway, Piti 96915, Guam, *Tel:* +1 671 477 7345, *Fax:* +1 671 477 6206, *Email:* cabmar@ite.net, *Website:* www.cabrasmarine.com
Casamar Guam Inc., 178 Industrial Avenue, Agana, Guam, *Tel:* +1 671 472 1468, *Fax:* +1 671 477 4800, *Email:* casamar@kuentos.guam.net, *Website:* www.casamarintl.com
Xenotechnics, Guam, Guam, *Tel:* +1 671 339 5258, *Fax:* +1 671 339 4198 Two dry docks

Shipping Agents: Ambyth Shipping & Trading Inc., 1026 Cabras Highway, Suite 205, Piti 96925, Guam, *Tel:* +1 671 477 7250, *Fax:* +1 671 472 1264, *Email:* ops@ambyth.guam.net, *Website:* www.ambyth.com
Inchcape Shipping Services (ISS), Inchcape Shipping Services (Guam) LLC, 1026 Cabras Highway, Suite 116, PAG Building, Piti 96915, Guam, *Tel:* +1 671 477 5921/3, *Fax:* +1 671 477 5924, *Email:* iss.guam@iss-shipping.com, *Website:* www.iss-shipping.com
Marianas Steamship Agencies Inc., Commercial Port Apra Harbor, P O Box 3219, Agana, Guam, *Tel:* +1 671 472 8584, *Fax:* +1 671 472 8585, *Email:* marsteam@msa-guam.com, *Website:* www.msa-guam.com
Norton Lilly International Inc., 1052 Cabras Highway, Suite 101, Piti 96915, Guam, *Tel:* +1 671 475 4654, *Fax:* +1 671 475 4653, *Email:* guam-ops@nortonlilly.com, *Website:* www.nortonlilly.com

Medical Facilities: Guam Memorial Hospital, Tamuning, Guam.
U.S.Naval Hospital, Agana Heights, Guam
Several smaller clinics throughout the island.

Airport: Guam International, 19 km

Lloyd's Agent: Ocean Surveys and Management Co., 4224 Waialae Avenue, No.485, Honolulu, HI 96816, United States of America, *Tel:* +1 808 525 5000, *Fax:* +1 808 525 5020, *Email:* osm@oceansurveys.net

GUATEMALA

PUERTO BARRIOS

Lat 15° 43' N; Long 88° 35' W.

Admiralty Chart: 2988	**Admiralty Pilot:** 69A
Time Zone: GMT -6 h	**UNCTAD Locode:** GT PBR

Principal Facilities:

P		Y	G	C	R			T	A

Authority: Terminal Portuaria Puerto Barrios, 9a. Calle 1a. y 2a. Avenue Terminal Portuaria, Puerto Barrios, Guatemala, *Tel:* +502 7920 1500, *Fax:* +502 7920 1548, *Website:* www.puertobarriosonline.com

Port Security: ISPS compliant

Approach: Approach is from the North, passing through Amatique Bay. Depth in channel 11 m

Anchorage: In Santo Tomas Bay, depth to 6 fathoms. Good anchorage SW of the pier in 9.5 m of water

Pilotage: Compulsory, pilot boards 2 miles off Puerto Barrios from a small unmarked launch. If awaiting pilot vessel may anchor about 3 miles north of Puerto Barrios keeping port entrance clear. VHF Channel 16

Tides: Tidal range is less than 0.3 m

Traffic: 2006, 1 818 900 t of cargo handled, 236 003 TEU's

Principal Imports and Exports: Imports: Fertilizer, Paper, Petroleum, Steel. Exports: Bananas, Coffee, Melons.

Working Hours: 0700-1200, 1200-1700. After 1700 operations can continue if necessary

Accommodation:

Name	Depth (m)	Remarks
Puerto Barrios		See [1] below

Key to Principal Facilities:—

A=Airport	**C**=Containers	**G**=General Cargo	**P**=Petroleum	**R**=Ro/Ro	**Y**=Dry Bulk
B=Bunkers	**D**=Dry Dock	**L**=Cruise	**Q**=Other Liquid Bulk	**T**=Towage (where available from port)	

Name	Depth (m)	Remarks
Finger Pier		See [2] below
South Wharf	8–9.5	See [3] below
North Wharf	7–7.5	See [4] below

[1]*Puerto Barrios:* Operated by Compania Bananera Independiente de Guatemala S.A., *Tel:* +502 7948 2240, *Fax:* +502 7948 2291

[2]*Finger Pier:* Consists of two wharves with 304.8 m each side. Container and ro/ro yard. Sideloaders used. Containers discharged using ship's own gear. Four banana loading conveyors

[3]*South Wharf:* On south side approach to pierhead. One outer berth with 7m depth and one inner berth of 4.88 m. Tankers dock astern to the S end of the pier using two anchors. A floating hose is used for discharging

[4]*North Wharf:* Outer berth (outer end) has a depth of 8.22 m, inner end berth has a depth of 7.62 m and inner berth also has a depth of 7.62 m

Storage: Available for general cargo, containers and automobiles

Towage: Three tugs available

Shipping Agents: Presersa, Cerro Brujo Rura Al Atlantico, Km 292, Puerto Barrios 18001, Guatemala, *Tel:* +502 7884 3018, *Fax:* +502 7884 3013, *Email:* presersa@terra.com.gt

Stevedoring Companies: Alomar S.A., 9a. Calle y 3a. Avenida, Puerto Barrios, Guatemala, *Tel:* +502 7948 7788
Servicios Portuarios Aldana S.A. (SERPA), 10a. Calle 1a. y 2a. Avenidas, Puerto Barrios, Guatemala, *Tel:* +502 7948 0032, *Email:* serpa1@yupimail.com

Airport: Puerto Barrios Airport, 2 km

Railway: The railway has access to the port facilities

Lloyd's Agent: G.W.F. Franklin S.A., 8 Avenida 14-10, Zona 10, Guatemala City 01010, Guatemala, *Tel:* +502 5554 0554, *Fax:* +502 2366 7303, *Email:* mail@franklin.com.gt, *Website:* www.franklin.com.gt

PUERTO QUETZAL

Lat 13° 55' N; Long 90° 47' W.

Admiralty Chart: 659/1946	**Admiralty Pilot:** 8	
Time Zone: GMT -6 h	**UNCTAD Locode:** GT PRQ	

Principal Facilities:

Q	Y	G	C	R	L	B		T	A

Authority: Empresa Portuaria Quetzal, Empresa Portuaria Quetzal, Kilometro 102, Autopista Puerto Quetzal, Escuintla, P O Box (502) 77201111,, Puerto Quetzal 01001 206A, Guatemala, *Tel:* +502 7881 2917, *Fax:* +502 7881 2304, *Email:* mercadeo@puerto-quetzal.com, *Website:* www.puerto-quetzal.com

Officials: General Manager: Jose Eduardo Garrido Valdez, *Tel:* +502 23611370, *Email:* edugarri@gmail.com.
Manager: Jose Pinto Gordon, *Tel:* +502 56300151, *Email:* gmendez@puerto-quetzal.com.
Marketing: Helga Veronica Morh Giron, *Tel:* +502 77201111 ext. 511, *Email:* atencionalcliente@puerto-quetzal.com.

Port Security: ISPS compliant

Approach: Access channel width of 210 m between the pierheads of the breakwaters and 340 m at the entrance of the docks in depth of 12 m. The east breakwater has a length of 307 m and the west one has a length of 1140 m

Anchorage: Four anchorage areas available in depth of 10.9 m

Pilotage: Compulsory. Vessels should advise ETA via agent 12 h prior to arrival. Pilot boards within a circle of radius 1.5 nautical miles centred on pos 13° 54.95' N; 90° 47.05' W

Radio Frequency: VHF Channel 16

Tides: Max range of tide is 1.83 m

Traffic: 2006, 1239 vessels, 7 170 100 t of cargo handled, 262 434 TEU's

Maximum Vessel Dimensions: Max draft 10.5 m

Principal Imports and Exports: Imports: Corn, Fertiliser, General cargo, Iron, Wheat. Exports: Coffee, Cotton, Latex, Sugar.

Working Hours: 0700-1430, 1430-2130, 2130-0700

Accommodation:

Name	Length (m)	Depth (m)	Remarks
Puerto Quetzal			
Commercial Wharf	810	10.9	See [1] below
South Wharf	170	5	For the berthing of smaller vessels
Coal Terminal		12	One pier formed by four dolphins

[1]*Commercial Wharf:* Two berths for general cargo, two berths for general solid & liquid cargo and one multi-purpose ramp

Storage: Container yard of 51 700 m2, general load yard of 8800 m2, ro/ro area of 2133 m2 and vehicles yard of 16 400 m2

Location	Open (m²)	Covered (m²)
Puerto Quetzal	62213	13600

Mechanical Handling Equipment:

Location	Type	Capacity (t)	Qty
Puerto Quetzal	Mult-purp. Cranes	32	1
Puerto Quetzal	Mobile Cranes	28	2
Puerto Quetzal	Forklifts	14	14

Bunkering: Chevron Marine Products LLC, Global Marine Products LLC, 1500 Louisiana, 4th Floor, Houston, TX 77002, United States of America, *Tel:* +1 832 8542 988, *Fax:* +1 832 8544 868, *Email:* gulfcbm@chevron.com, *Website:* www.chevron.com – *Grades:* GO; FO – *Delivery Mode:* tank truck
Shell Guatemala S.A., 24 Avenida 35-81, Zona 12, Guatemala City 01012, Guatemala, *Tel:* +502 22761944, *Fax:* +502 22760963 – *Grades:* FO – *Delivery Mode:* truck

Towage: Four tugs available of 960-3508 hp (three private)

Repair & Maintenance: Minor repairs can be carried out

Shipping Agents: Comercial Maritima S.A., Edif de Servicios Auxiliares, Modulo 207, Puerto Quetzal, Guatemala, *Tel:* +502 7881 1527, *Fax:* +502 7881 1527
Compania Internacional de Representaciones S.A. (COIRSA), Avenida Reforma 8-60, Zona 9 Edificio Galerias Reforma Torre II, Officina 706, Guatemala City 01009, Guatemala, *Tel:* +502 2334 5002, *Fax:* +502 2334 7958, *Email:* cjmendez@terra.com.gt
Presersa, Autopista Puerto Quetzal, KM 97.5, Puerto Quetzal, Guatemala, *Tel:* +502 7884 3018, *Fax:* +502 7884 3013, *Email:* agemarpresersa@disagro.com, *Website:* www.disagro.com
Transmares S.A., Office 103-104, Complejo Portuatio Quetzal, Puerto Quetzal 1485, Guatemala, *Tel:* +502 7881 2813, *Fax:* +502 7881 1732, *Email:* operations.pq@transmares.net, *Website:* www.transmares.org

Medical Facilities: Nearest hospital in Escuintla, 52 km. Doctors available in port

Airport: 8 km

Lloyd's Agent: G.W.F. Franklin S.A., 8 Avenida 14-10, Zona 10, Guatemala City 01010, Guatemala, *Tel:* +502 5554 0554, *Fax:* +502 2366 7303, *Email:* mail@franklin.com.gt, *Website:* www.franklin.com.gt

SANTO TOMAS DE CASTILLA

Lat 15° 41' N; Long 88° 36' W.

Admiralty Chart: 2988	**Admiralty Pilot:** 69A	
Time Zone: GMT -6 h	**UNCTAD Locode:** GT STC	

Principal Facilities:

P	Q	Y	G	C	R	L	B		T	A

Authority: Empresa Portuaria Nacional Santo Tomas de Castilla (EMPORNAC), Santo Tomas de Castilla 18001, Guatemala, *Tel:* +502 7948 3060, *Fax:* +502 7948 3288, *Email:* turismo@santotomasport.com.gt, *Website:* www.santotomasport.com.gt

Officials: General Director: Escuardo Vargas, *Email:* escuardovargas@yahoo.com.
Harbour Master: Escuardo Nufio.

Port Security: ISPS compliant

Approach: Channel depth of 11 m

Anchorage: Vessels with a draft of less than 7.62 m can anchor in the Inner Bay. Bottom is soft grey mud

Pilotage: Compulsory. Pilot can be obtained on VHF Channel 16 and boards vessel 4.9 km off the pier

Weather: Trade winds, May to October

Tides: Range of tide 0.4 m

Traffic: 2006, 4 623 400 t of cargo handled, 336 816 TEU's

Working Hours: 0600-1400, 1400-2100, 2100-0600

Accommodation:

Name	Length (m)	Remarks
Santo Tomas de Castilla		Marginal wharf totalling 914.56 m consisting of six dock berths
Dock No.1	152.4	Passengers, general cargo & military vessels
Dock No.2	152.4	Ro/ro, passengers, general cargo & military vessels
Dock No.3	152.4	Ro/ro, containers & liquid bulk

Name	Length (m)	Remarks
Dock No.4	152.4	Ro/ro, containers, conventional & multi-purpose cargo
Dock No.5	152.4	Ro/ro, containers, conventional, multi-purpose & refrigerated cargo
Dock No.6	152.4	Liquid bulk, containers & multi-purpose cargo

Storage: Ample open storage available for containers

Location	Covered (m²)	Sheds / Warehouses
Santo Tomas de Castilla	39470	8

Mechanical Handling Equipment:

Location	Type	Capacity (t)	Qty	Remarks
Santo Tomas de Castilla	Mult-purp. Cranes	140	1	private
Santo Tomas de Castilla	Mobile Cranes	10–130	3	

Bunkering: Shell Guatemala S.A., 24 Avenida 35-81, Zona 12, Guatemala City 01012, Guatemala, *Tel:* +502 22761944, *Fax:* +502 22760963 – *Grades:* FO – *Delivery Mode:* truck

Towage: Compulsory. Four tugs available; one of 2720 hp, one of 1600 hp, one of 1500 hp and one of 450 hp

Repair & Maintenance: Rudy Barrera, Santo Tomas de Castilla, Guatemala, *Tel:* +502 7948 0847, *Fax:* +502 7948 0581

Shipping Agents: Comercial Maritima S.A., Calle de la Marina 17, Santo Tomas de Castilla, Guatemala, *Tel:* +502 7881 1527, *Fax:* +502 7948 3089
Compania Internacional de Representaciones S.A. (COIRSA), Avenida Reforma 8-60, Zona 9 Edificio Galerias Reforma Torre II, Officina 706, Guatemala City 01009, Guatemala, *Tel:* +502 2334 5002, *Fax:* +502 2334 7958, *Email:* cjmendez@terra.com.gt
Danmar S.A., 15 Calle 3-20, Zona 10, Centro Ejecutivo, Officina 201, Guatemala City, Guatemala, *Tel:* +502 2329 6000, *Fax:* +502 2329 6001, *Email:* info@danmar.com.gt, *Website:* www.danmar.com.gt
A.P. Moller-Maersk Group, Maersk Guatemala S.A., Calle Principal, Frente al Parque Belga, Santo Tomas de Castilla, Guatemala, *Tel:* +502 7948 3217, *Fax:* +502 7948 3109, *Email:* sdctrmmng@maersk.com, *Website:* www.maerskline.com
Transmares S.A., ZOLIC, Modulo 10, Santo Tomas de Castilla, Guatemala, *Tel:* +502 7948 3134, *Fax:* +502 7948 3216, *Email:* operations.stc@transmares.net, *Website:* www.transmares.org

Medical Facilities: Hospital available

Airport: Puerto Barrios, 8 km

Lloyd's Agent: G.W.F. Franklin S.A., 8 Avenida 14-10, Zona 10, Guatemala City 01010, Guatemala, *Tel:* +502 5554 0554, *Fax:* +502 2366 7303, *Email:* mail@franklin.com.gt, *Website:* www.franklin.com.gt

GUINEA

CONAKRY

Lat 9° 30' N; Long 13° 42' W.

Admiralty Chart: 412/601

Admiralty Pilot: 1

Time Zone: GMT

UNCTAD Locode: GN CKY

Principal Facilities:

P	Y	G	C	R		B		T	A	

Authority: Port Autonome de Conakry, P O Box 805, Conakry, Guinea, *Tel:* +224 3041 4564, *Fax:* +224 3041 2604, *Email:* pac@biasy.net

Officials: General Manager: Almamy Kabele Camara.

Port Security: ISPS compliant

Approach: Port entered through channel in south fairway 3.2 miles long with width 150 m and dredged to 9.5 m. Nine buoys are positioned along the channel towards the entrance of the port which is entirely protected by a dyke

Anchorage: Anchorage in outer and inner roads, depth of water 13.0 m

Pilotage: Compulsory for all vessels over 20 m long entering or leaving at any time during the day or night. Pilot boards at Conakry Buoy just off Kassa Island in pos 9° 27' 3" N, 13° 44' 05" W

Radio Frequency: VHF Channel 16. Conakry Radio 2182 kHz and 2586 kHz

Tides: Range of tide 0.5 m to 3.0 m

Traffic: 2003, 5 280 528 t of cargo handled

Maximum Vessel Dimensions: 30 000 dwt

Working Hours: 1st Shift 0800-1800, 2nd Shift 2000-0600. Overtime on Sat, Sun and Holidays, 1st Shift 0800-1800, 2nd Shift 2000-0600

Accommodation:

Name	Length (m)	Depth (m)	Remarks
Conakry			See ¹ below
Berth 0-1	350	10	Alumina friguia
Berth 2-5	480	8–8.5	Commercial piers
Berth 6	155	7	Barge landing
Berth 7	160	8	Fish jetty
Berth 8-9	300	11	Bauxite
Berth 10	190	10	Oil jetty
Container Berth	269	10.5	Container terminal. Stripping shed of 1600 m2

¹*Conakry:* The port covers an area of 48 ha, 10 of which are used for handling of general cargo and 8 for container handling. 28 reefer points at the commercial port and 60 reefer points at the container terminal

Storage: Three warehouses totalling 9000 m2 privately managed by port users. Further shed space totalling 4000 m2 available. Cold storage facilities available

Mechanical Handling Equipment: Mobile cranes and forklifts run and owned by private companies handle units up to 50 t

Bunkering: ExxonMobil Marine Fuels, Mailpoint 31, ExxonMobil House, Ermyn Way, Leatherhead, Surrey KT22 8UX, United Kingdom, *Tel:* +44 1372 222 000, *Fax:* +44 1372 223 922, *Email:* marine.fuels@exxonmobil.com, *Website:* www.exxonmobil.com – *Grades:* MGO – *Delivery Mode:* truck

Towage: Compulsory. Two tugs up to 1600 hp are available

Repair & Maintenance: One floating dock of 700 t lifting cap located at the inner port boundary

Shipping Agents: AMA-GETMA S.A., Cite Chemin de Fer, Immeuble Kassa, P O Box 1648, Conakry, Guinea, *Tel:* +224 3045 4730, *Fax:* +224 3041 4273, *Email:* shipping@getmaguinee.com.gn
Geodis Overseas, c/o Sogimac, P O Box 63, Conakry, Guinea, *Tel:* +224 3041 1072, *Fax:* +224 3041 1628
A.P. Moller-Maersk Group, Maersk Guinea S.A., Immeuble Maersk, Almamya, Commune de Kaloum, Conakry 1166, Guinea, *Tel:* +224 3045 5565, *Fax:* +224 3045 5570, *Email:* ckyordmng@maersk.com, *Website:* www.maerskline.com
SAGA France, P O Box 3177, Ex Cite Chemin de Fer, Avenue du Port, Immeuble, Conakry, Guinea, *Tel:* +224 3041 2457, *Fax:* +224 3041 2025
SDV Guinee, P O Box 2011, Conakry, Guinea, *Tel:* +224 3044 4392, *Fax:* +224 3041 4789
SOAEM Guinae, Imm Zaidan, Boulevard du Commerce, P O Box 3177, Conakry, Guinea, *Tel:* +224 3041 2457, *Fax:* +224 3044 2025, *Email:* jean-jacques.corneille@smtp.saga.fr
Societe Guineene de Consignation Maritime et de Manutention, 10 Avenue de la Gare, P O Box 3115, Conakry, Guinea, *Tel:* +224 3044 4485, *Fax:* +224 3041 4594
Socopao Guinee, P O Box 3339, Conakry 1, Guinea, *Tel:* +224 3041 2994, *Fax:* +224 3041 3764, *Email:* socship@sotelgui.net.gn

Stevedoring Companies: AMA-GETMA S.A., Cite Chemin de Fer, Immeuble Kassa, P O Box 1648, Conakry, Guinea, *Tel:* +224 3045 4730, *Fax:* +224 3041 4273, *Email:* shipping@getmaguinee.com.gn

Surveyors: Compagnie des Experts Maritimes de Guinee, Cite des Chemin de Fer, Immeuble Kindia, 2nd Floor, Conakry, Guinea, *Tel:* +224 3041 3861, *Fax:* +224 3041 5080, *Email:* cemgui@sotelgui.net.gn

Medical Facilities: Available

Airport: Conakry Gbessia, 15 km

Lloyd's Agent: Omega Marine Guinea, P O Box 6213, Conakry, Guinea, *Tel:* +224 6033 1942, *Email:* omega-guinea@omega-marine.com

KAKANDE

former name, see Kamsar

KAMSAR

Lat 10° 39' N; Long 14° 37' W.

Admiralty Chart: 1562

Admiralty Pilot: 1

Time Zone: GMT

UNCTAD Locode: GN KMR

Principal Facilities:

P		Y	G					T	A

Key to Principal Facilities:—				
A=Airport	**C**=Containers	**G**=General Cargo	**P**=Petroleum	**R**=Ro/Ro	**Y**=Dry Bulk
B=Bunkers	**D**=Dry Dock	**L**=Cruise	**Q**=Other Liquid Bulk	**T**=Towage (where available from port)	

Authority: Direction du Port, CBG-Port Kamsar, P O Box 523, Conakry, Guinea, *Email:* aliou.thiam@cbg-guinee.com

Officials: Director: Aliou Thiam.
Harbour Master: Capt Karim Diallo.

Port Security: ISPS compliant

Documentation: Narcotics Lists (2), Vaccination List (1), Crew Lists (6), Passenger Lists (6), Crew Declaration (Personal Effects) List (1), Stores List (1), Last Ports of Call Lists (6), Manifests of Cargo (12), Copies of Bills of Loading (2)

Approach: The channel from the mouth of Rio Nunez to the bauxite loading wharf at Kamsar is 17 km long and has a min width of 120 m and consists of nineteen light buoys. The outer channel, starting from buoy 1 and 2 up to buoys 8 and 9 has a depth of 9-12 m below reference datum level and the inner channel from buoys 8 and 9 to the bauxite loading wharf is dredged to 8.25 and 8.5 m below reference datum level. The turning basin for inbound vessels is dredged to a min of 7.75 m below reference datum level and extends westward, 360 m from the bauxite loading wharf

Pilotage: Compulsory for all vessels over 45.75 m loa and for vessels under 45.75 m loa on their first call. Pilots may be contacted on VHF Channel 16

Accommodation:

Name	Length (m)	Depth (m)	Remarks
Kamsar			
Bauxite Loading Wharf	274	13.5	See [1] below
General Cargo Quays			See [2] below

[1]*Bauxite Loading Wharf:* Attached to the mobile self loader is a chicksan-arm with an 8'' connection for the discharging of petroleum products. Loading rate for bauxite is 4000 t/h; discharge rate for petroleum is 450 t/h at 100 lb/in2 back pressure at ship's pumps. Storage facilities ashore are one 7000 m3 and three 10 000 m3 bunker 'C' tanks, three 3000 m3 diesel oil tanks and two 1400 m3 gasoline tanks
[2]*General Cargo Quays:* At the entrance to the Dougoufissa Creek for vessels up to 100 m long, max 6.0 m d. One of these wharves is equipped with a heavy lift crane/derrick, swl 110 t. These vessels will be aground at LW as there is only 3.5 m alongside at LLW. For loading or discharging at anchor for general cargo vessels there is one 200 t barge available

Towage: Two tugs available; one of 2896 bhp and one of 2850 bhp. There is also a mooring boat available

Medical Facilities: Hospital available only in emergencies

Airport: Boke Airport, 55 km

Lloyd's Agent: Omega Marine Guinea, P O Box 6213, Conakry, Guinea, *Tel:* +224 6033 1942, *Email:* omega-guinea@omega-marine.com

GUINEA-BISSAU

BISSAU

Lat 11° 51' N; Long 15° 35' W.

Admiralty Chart: 1724
Time Zone: GMT -1 h

Admiralty Pilot: 1
UNCTAD Locode: GW OXB

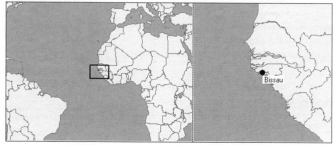

Principal Facilities:

P		Y	G	C					A

Authority: Administracao dos Portos da Guinea-Bissau, Av. 3 de Agosto, P O Box 693, Bissau, Guinea-Bissau, *Tel:* +245 320 4110, *Fax:* +245 320 4114

Officials: Managing Director: Pedro Tipote.
Harbour Master: Cdr Carlos Vaz Cunha.

Documentation: Entrance declaration
Clearance from the last port of call
List of the crew members effects and/or all passengers on board, either in transit or disembarking in Bissau
Provisions list
List of passengers baggage
List of cargo to be disembarked in Bissau
List of cargo (inside sealed envelope)
Cargo manifest

Anchorage: Between Bissau and Ilheu do Rei

Pilotage: Compulsory. Vessels take on pilot at Caio Island, which is approx 50 miles. To call the pilot send request via Agent to the port's Maritime Service, Tel: +245 21 31 40, 24 h before with ETA at Caio Island. Pilot boat available

Radio Frequency: VHF Channel 16

Tides: 4-5 m max

Principal Imports and Exports: Imports: Cement, General cargo. Exports: Fish, Groundnuts, Palm kernels, Timber, Vegetable oil.

Working Hours: 1st shift 0730-1500, 2nd shift 1500-2300, 3rd shift 2300-0700
Accommodation:

Name	Length (m)	Depth (m)	Remarks
Bissau			See [1] below
Commercial Wharf	260	9–10	See [2] below
Old Commercial Wharf	140	4–5	'T' shape wharf for fishing vessels
Dicol Wharf (Oil Terminal)	140	11	See [3] below
Pindjiguiti Wharf	132		Coastal & local traffic

[1]*Bissau:* Roadstead opposite port, between mainland and Ilheu do Rei, well sheltered and safe
[2]*Commercial Wharf:* 'T' shape wharf able to receive two medium vessels simultaneously or one big vessel
[3]*Dicol Wharf (Oil Terminal):* 2.5 km from the main port. 'T' shape wharf for vessels up to 20 000 t

Storage: Container park of over 20 000 m2

Location	Open (m2)	Covered (m2)	Sheds / Warehouses
Bissau	50000	7815	8

Mechanical Handling Equipment:

Location	Type	Capacity (t)	Qty
Bissau	Mobile Cranes	35	1

Shipping Agents: Agemar Bissau, Rua Antonio N'Bana No.17, P O Box 1103, Bissau, Guinea-Bissau, *Tel:* +245 320 2959, *Fax:* +245 320 2962, *Email:* agemaroxb@hotmail.com
Empresa Nacional de Agencias e Transportes Maritimos, Rua Guerra Mendes 4-4a, P O Box 244, Bissau, Guinea-Bissau, *Tel:* +245 321 2675, *Fax:* +245 321 3023
Star Shipping Bissau Lda, Rue Guere Mendes, Bissau Velho, Bissau, Guinea-Bissau, *Tel:* +245 320 6538, *Fax:* +245 320 6537
Transmar Services, Rua N 4-3, P O Box 401, Bissau, Guinea-Bissau, *Tel:* +245 320 2462, *Fax:* +245 320 2478

Airport: Osvaldo Vieira, 7 km

Lloyd's Agent: H.P. Rosa, 14 Rua No. 7, P O Box 41, Bissau, Guinea-Bissau, *Tel:* +245 320 2383, *Fax:* +245 320 1364, *Email:* hprosa@eguitel.com

GUYANA

EVERTON

harbour area, see under New Amsterdam

GEORGETOWN

Lat 6° 49' N; Long 58° 11' W.

Admiralty Chart: 519/533
Time Zone: GMT -4 h

Admiralty Pilot: 7A
UNCTAD Locode: GY GEO

Principal Facilities:

P		Y	G	C		L	B	D	T	A

Authority: Maritime Administration Department, Ministry of Public Works Building, Fort Street, Kingston, Georgetown, Guyana, *Tel:* +592 225 7330, *Fax:* +592 226 9581, *Email:* marad@networksgy.com

Officials: Director General: Ivor B. English.
Port Director: Taig B. Kalicharran, *Tel:* +592 226 7842, *Email:* taigk@yahoo.com.

Port Security: ISPS compliant

Approach: Channel 70 m wide in depth of 5 m

Anchorage: There are five anchorages in depths of 5.5-6.7. Bottom is soft mud and provides good holding ground

Pilotage: Compulsory. Pilots are picked up and dropped in an area within the sectored radius of 925 m and centre of Demerara Light from 350° through 360° to 080°

Radio Frequency: VHF Channel 16

Weather: NE trade winds

Tides: 2.9 m MHWS, 2.23 m MHWN, 0.34 m MLWS, 1.04 m MLWN

Principal Imports and Exports: Imports: Food products, Fuel, Lubricants, Manufactured goods, Vehicles. Exports: Alcohol, Bauxite, Rice, Sugar, Timber.

Working Hours: Mon-Thurs 0800-1630, Fri 0800-1530

Accommodation:

Name	Length (m)	Depth (m)	Remarks
Georgetown			See [1] below
Guyana Fertilisers Ltd	110	1.1–3	See [2] below
Muneshwers Ltd	166	5.2–6.1	See [3] below
DIDCO Trading Co Ltd	150		See [4] below
John Fernandes Ltd	202	5.3–6.1	See [5] below
Demerara Shipping Ltd	109	3.8–4.7	See [6] below
Guyana National Industrial Co Ltd	233	3.2–5	See [7] below
Guyana National Shipping Corp	274	4.1–6.9	See [8] below
Demerara Sugar Terminal	127	5.8–8.8	See [9] below

[1]*Georgetown:* Containers can be handled at all major general cargo wharves but vessels own gear must be used
Bulk facilities: Timber mills with timber loading facilities and shrimp-freezing depots.
Flour mill with two suction hoses discharged wheat in bulk at approx 60 t/h per hose
Demerara Distillers Ltd loads bulk alcohol at rate of approx 100 000 l/h
Tanker facilities: Oil storage terminals owned by Shell, ChevronTexaco, Esso and Guyana Oil Co. Ltd, are situated on the east bank of the river
[2]*Guyana Fertilisers Ltd:* 15-16 Holmes Street, Georgetown, Tel: +592 225 8544, Fax: +592 227 1260
Discharge bulk fertiliser into bags at rate of approx 65 t/h and loads fertiliser at rate of approx 30 t/h
[3]*Muneshwers Ltd:* 45-47 Water Street, Georgetown, Tel: +592 226 7859, Fax: +592 226 1031, Email: muneshwers.ltd@networksgy.com
Equipment includes one 30 t crane and one 80 t crane
[4]*DIDCO Trading Co Ltd:* 1 Public Road, Ruimveldt, Georgetown, Tel: +592 225 2475, Fax: +592 225 2316, Email: didcoships@telsnetgy.net, Website: www.didcokfc.com
Equipment includes 5 t and one 40 t cap cranes
[5]*John Fernandes Ltd:* 24 Water Street, Georgetown, Tel: +592 227 3344, Fax: +592 226 1881, Email: sales@jf-ltd.com, Website: www.jf-ltd.com
Equipment includes two cranes up to 100 t cap
[6]*Demerara Shipping Ltd:* 8-12 Water & Schumaker Street, Werk-en-Rust, Georgetown, Tel: +592 227 3411, Fax: +592 225 9512, Email: demship_karen@solutions2000.net
Equipment includes one 30 t crane
[7]*Guyana National Industrial Co Ltd:* 1-9 Lombard Street, Charlestown, Georgetown, Tel: +592 225 5398, Fax: +592 226 0432, Email: gnicoperations@futurenetgy.com
Equipment includes two 30 t cranes
[8]*Guyana National Shipping Corp:* 5-9 Lombard Street, La Penitence, Georgetown, Tel: +592 226 1840, Fax.: +592 225 0849, Email: gnsc@guyana.net.gy, Website: www.gnsc.com
Equipment includes two 32-40 t cap cranes
[9]*Demerara Sugar Terminal:* Ramp Road, River View, Ruimveldt, Georgetown, Tel: +592 226 4343, Fax: +592 226 6104, Email: raymondf@guysuco.com, Website: guysuco.com
Loads ocean-going vessels with raw bulk sugar through two travelling, retractable booms and telescopic chutes at the rate of 500 t/h

Bunkering: No coal
Guyana Oil Co. Ltd, 166 Waterloo Street, North Cummingsburg, Georgetown, Guyana, *Tel:* +592 2272 040, *Fax:* +592 2265 345, *Email:* guyoil@gol.net.gy
Shell Antilles (Guyana) Ltd, Lot BB Rome, Georgetown, Guyana, *Tel:* +592 2 66667, *Fax:* +592 2 72249, *Website:* www.bunkerworld.com 12.8.05
Texaco West Indies Ltd, Providence, East Bank, Georgetown, Guyana, *Tel:* +592 56666, *Fax:* +592 662783
Guyana Oil Co. Ltd, 166 Waterloo Street, North Cummingsburg, Georgetown, Guyana, *Tel:* +592 2272 040, *Fax:* +592 2265 345, *Email:* guyoil@gol.net.gy

Towage: Tugs available from private companies

Repair & Maintenance: Guyana National Engineering Corp. Ltd, 2-9 Lombard Street, Georgetown, Guyana, *Tel:* +592 226 3290, *Fax:* +592 225 8625 Dry dock: length 63.7 m, on blocks 61.87 m, breadth bottom 12.6 m, at entrance 8.46 m, depth on sill at HWOST 2.89 m. Hull and engine repairs carried out on large vessels lying at anchor

Shipping Agents: C & V Caribbean Shipping Ltd., 110 Laluni Street, Queenstown, Georgetown, Guyana, *Tel:* +592 227 1245, *Fax:* +592 227 3346, *Email:* richard@cvshipping.com, *Website:* www.cvshipping.com
Delmur Co., 365 Omai Street, Prashad Nagar, Georgetown, Guyana, *Tel:* +592 227 4099, *Fax:* +592 227 3977, *Email:* delmur@telsnetgy.net
Demerara Shipping Co. Ltd, 8-12 Water & Schumaker Streets, Werk-en-Rust, Georgetown, Guyana, *Tel:* +592 226 4455, *Fax:* +592 225 9512, *Email:* demship_sales@solutions2000.net
John Fernandes Ltd., 24 Water Street, P O Box 10211, Georgetown, Guyana, *Tel:*

+592 227 3344, *Fax:* +592 226 1881, *Email:* chris@jf-ltd.com, *Website:* www.jf-ltd.com
Guyana Freight Services Inc., 214 Almond Street, Queenstown, Georgetown, Guyana, *Tel:* +592 225 7186, *Fax:* +592 225 7261, *Email:* gfsioperations@guyanafreight.com
Guyana National Industrial Co. Ltd, 5-9 Lombard Street, P O Box 10988, Georgetown, Guyana, *Tel:* +592 226 1732, *Fax:* +592 225 3815, *Email:* simone@gnsc.com, *Website:* www.gnsc.com
Guyana National Shipping Corp. Ltd, 5-9 Lombard Street, Georgetown, Guyana, *Tel:* +592 226 8896, *Fax:* +592 225 3815, *Email:* e.o@solutions2000.net, *Website:* www.gnsc.com
Laparkan Trading (Guyana) Co Ltd., 2-9 Lombard Street, Charlestown, Georgetown, Guyana, *Tel:* +592 227 3560, *Fax:* +592 227 6808, *Email:* oscar.phillips@laparkan.com, *Website:* www.laparkan.com
N.M. Services Ltd., Lot 5 Ruimveldt, Georgetown, Guyana, *Tel:* +592 225 8557, *Fax:* +592 225 7676, *Email:* operations@webworksgy.com, *Website:* www.nmslgy.com
R & M Shipping Agency, Lot 10 Ixora Avenue, Eccles, East Bank Demerara, Georgetown, Guyana, *Tel:* +592 618 9005, *Fax:* +592 233 3723, *Email:* rm_shippinggy@yahoo.com
Tropical Shipping, 1-9 Lombard Street, Charlestown, Georgetown, Guyana, *Tel:* +592 227 7203, *Fax:* +592 227 7202, *Email:* geo.mnrg@guyana.net.gy, *Website:* www.tropical.com

Stevedoring Companies: John Fernandes Ltd, 24 Water Street, P O Box 10211, Georgetown, Guyana, *Tel:* +592 227 3344, *Fax:* +592 226 1881, *Email:* chris@jf-ltd.com, *Website:* www.jf-ltd.com
Guyana National Industrial Co. Ltd, 5-9 Lombard Street, P O Box 10988, Georgetown, Guyana, *Tel:* +592 226 1732, *Fax:* +592 225 3815, *Email:* simone@gnsc.com, *Website:* www.gnsc.com

Surveyors: Guyana National Shipping Corp. Ltd, 5-9 Lombard Street, Georgetown, Guyana, *Tel:* +592 226 8896, *Fax:* +592 225 3815, *Email:* e.o@solutions2000.net, *Website:* www.gnsc.com

Medical Facilities: There is a public hospital along with several other private ones

Airport: Timehri, 47 km

Lloyd's Agent: Guyana National Shipping Corp. Ltd, 5-9 Lombard Street, Georgetown, Guyana, *Tel:* +592 226 8896, *Fax:* +592 225 3815, *Email:* e.o@solutions2000.net, *Website:* www.gnsc.com

NEW AMSTERDAM

Lat 6° 15' N; Long 57° 31' W.

Admiralty Chart: 2784	**Admiralty Pilot:** 7A
Time Zone: GMT -4 h	**UNCTAD Locode:** GY NAM

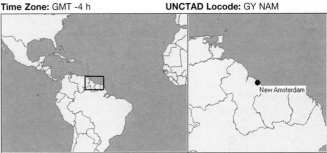

Principal Facilities:

P		Y	G			B			

Authority: Maritime Administration Department, Ministry of Public Works Building, Fort Street, Kingston, Georgetown, Guyana, *Tel:* +592 225 7330, *Fax:* +592 226 9581, *Email:* marad@networksgy.com

Officials: Director General: Ivor B. English.
Port Director: Taig B. Kalicharran, *Tel:* +592 226 7842, *Email:* taigk@yahoo.com.

Port Security: ISPS compliant

Approach: Vessels cross the Berbice Bar drawing 8.2 m. It is composed of fairly hard mud. Due to changing depths in ship channel the Harbour Master will advise the min depth for any particular period

Anchorage: Off Crab Island in depths of 5 m and also off Heathburn

Pilotage: Compulsory. Pilot boards at Georgetown Station. Rates on application

Radio Frequency: Demerara Radio 8RB on 2182 and 300 kcs. Georgetown Lighthouse: VHF Channel 16

Weather: NE trade winds

Principal Imports and Exports: Imports: Fuel. Exports: Bauxite, Molasses, Sugar.

Accommodation: Tanker facilities: Guyana Oil Co. at Heathburn and Shell Oil Co. at Providence, both with a depth of 4.88 m to 5.49 m LW

Name	Remarks
New Amsterdam	See [1] below
Everton	See [2] below

[1]*New Amsterdam:* Vessels can discharge/load at anchorage in the river in depths ranging from 3 m MLWS to 5.8 m MHWS by lighters
[2]*Everton:* Situated further upstream on the Berbice river, ocean-going vessels loading bauxite are handled at the facilities of Berbice Mining Enterprises Ltd. Wharf 61 m long with a min depth alongside of 5.8 m MLWS

Bunkering: Guyana Oil Co. Ltd, 166 Waterloo Street, North Cummingsburg, Georgetown, Guyana, *Tel:* +592 2272 040, *Fax:* +592 2265 345, *Email:* guyoil@gol.net.gy
Texaco West Indies Ltd, Providence, East Bank, Georgetown, Guyana, *Tel:* +592 56666, *Fax:* +592 662783

Medical Facilities: A public hospital and private doctors are available

Lloyd's Agent: Guyana National Shipping Corp. Ltd, 5-9 Lombard Street, Georgetown, Guyana, *Tel:* +592 226 8896, *Fax:* +592 225 3815, *Email:* e.o@solutions2000.net, *Website:* www.gnsc.com

HAITI

CAP HAITIEN

Lat 19° 46' N; Long 72° 12' W.

Admiralty Chart: 465	Admiralty Pilot: 70
Time Zone: GMT -5 h	UNCTAD Locode: HT CAP

Principal Facilities:

		G	C	R		B		A

Authority: Autorite Portuaire Nationale, Rue 18, Boulevard du Front-de-Mer, Cap Haitien, Haiti, *Tel:* +509 2262 2100, *Fax:* +509 2262 9100, *Email:* apncap@apn.gouv.ht, *Website:* www.apn.gouv.ht

Port Security: ISPS compliant

Pre-Arrival Information: Pre-arrival form filled out & all manifests should be communicated through port agents to the port authority 48 h before vessel arrival

Approach: Western channel: one mile long in depth of 10-15 m, well marked by navigation aids
Eastern channel: marked by a beacon runway light

Anchorage: Broad swinging and anchoring basin in depths of 11-18 m

Pilotage: Compulsory and available 24 h/day

Radio Frequency: VHF Channels 16 or 12

Weather: Winds mainly from NE direction

Principal Imports and Exports: Imports: General cargo. Exports: Canned fruit & juices, Cocoa, Coffee, Sand & gravel, Sisal.

Working Hours: Monday to Friday 0700-1600. Saturday 0700-1200. Overtime on request

Accommodation:

Name	Length (m)	Draught (m)	Remarks
Cap Haitien			
Cruise Ship Terminal	176	10.5	Seven bollards
Commercial Vessel Quay	250	9.5	See [1] below
Coastal Shipping Quay	100	3.5	Open air space of 0.5 ha
Marina	100	2.4	

[1]*Commercial Vessel Quay:* Specially prepared area for handling containers, together with sufficient power points for refrigerated containers. Full flood lighting has been provided to enable the facilities to operate throughout the night. Ro/ro ramp is available

Storage: Covered storage of 2210 m2 and open storage of 72 000 m2 (45 000 m2 being reserved for containers)

Bunkering: Limited quantities available by road tanker and also by tank barge

Shipping Agents: Cap Shipping S.A., P O Box 30, Cap Haitien, Haiti, *Tel:* +509 2262 0501, *Fax:* +509 2262 0008

Medical Facilities: Available at Govt. hospital

Airport: Cap Haitien International Airport, 6.5 km

Lloyd's Agent: Ets. J.B. Vital S.A., P O Box 87, Angle Rues Bonne Foi & Courbe, Port au Prince Ht 6110, Haiti, *Tel:* +509 2221 4065, *Fax:* +509 2223 1323, *Email:* etsjbvitalsa@msn.com

MIRAGOANE

Lat 18° 28' N; Long 73° 6' W.

Admiralty Chart: 466	Admiralty Pilot: 70
Time Zone: GMT -5 h	UNCTAD Locode: HT MIR

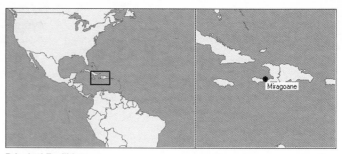

Principal Facilities:

		Y	G					A

Authority: Authorite Portuaire Nationale, Rue du Bord de Mer, Miragoane, Haiti, *Tel:* +509 2403 1684

Approach: Least depth in fairway is 13.7 m

Anchorage: Anchorage can be obtained in Miragoane Bay in depths ranging from 14.6 m to 18.3 m. Limited anchorage can also be obtained in the inner harbour in depths up to 12.8 m

Pilotage: Available only upon ship's agent request in or out

Accommodation:

Name	Remarks
Miragoane	See [1] below

[1]*Miragoane:* Limited port facilities. Vessels must discharge with ship's own gear. A concrete 35 m long pier accommodating vessels up to 10 000 t has been built by the Reynolds Co for the shipment of bauxite in bulk, depth alongside of 10.7 m

Medical Facilities: Hospital in the town

Airport: Port au Prince International Airport, 82Km

Lloyd's Agent: Ets. J.B. Vital S.A., P O Box 87, Angle Rues Bonne Foi & Courbe, Port au Prince Ht 6110, Haiti, *Tel:* +509 2221 4065, *Fax:* +509 2223 1323, *Email:* etsjbvitalsa@msn.com

PORT AU PRINCE

Lat 18° 33' N; Long 72° 20' W.

Admiralty Chart: 466	Admiralty Pilot: 70
Time Zone: GMT -5 h	UNCTAD Locode: HT PAP

Principal Facilities:

P	Q	Y	G	C	R	L	B	D	T	A

Authority: Autorite Portuaire Nationale, P O Box 616, Port au Prince HT 6110, Haiti, *Tel:* +509 2223 2440, *Fax:* +509 2221 3479, *Email:* apnpap@apn.gouv.ht, *Website:* www.apn.gouv.ht

Port Security: ISPS compliant

Documentation: A pre-arrival form is available to be filled out by port agents. Cargo manifests should be sent with the form

Approach: Depth at entrance, min 15.24 m

Anchorage: Eleven anchoring buoys in the following positions:
Buoy A in pos 18° 33' 13.1" N; 72° 22' 43.1" W
Buoy B in pos 18° 33' 19" N; 72° 23' 07.7" W
Buoy C in pos 18° 33' 24.6" N; 72° 23' 31.5" W
Buoy D in pos 18° 33' 52.4" N; 72° 22' 57" W
Buoy E in pos 18° 33' 58.1" N; 72° 23' 20.6" W
Buoy F in pos 18° 34' 04.1" N; 72° 23' 45" W
Buoy H in pos 18° 34' 09.1" N; 72° 24' 09.2" W
Buoy J in pos 18° 34' 27" N; 72° 23' 23" W
Buoy K in pos 18° 34' 44" N; 72° 23' 57" W
Buoy L in pos 18° 34' 42" N; 72° 22' 45" W
Buoy Q in pos 18° 34' 16.4" N; 72° 22' 55" W

Pilotage: Compulsory for vessels of 800 gt and over

Radio Frequency: VHF Channels 12 or 16

Tides: Tidal range of 38-45 cm

Traffic: 2000/01, 821 vessels, 2 166 403 t of cargo handled

Maximum Vessel Dimensions: 205 m loa, 8.8 m draft

Principal Imports and Exports: Imports: Agricultural products, Aid cargoes, Automobiles, Bagged cargoes, Bagged cement, Bagged raw & refined sugar, Break-bulk cargoes, Bulk & bagged grain, Caustic soda, Clinker, Fuel oil, General cargo, Industrial raw materials, Iron & steel, Machinery & transport equipment, Soyabean, Soyabean oil, Sugar, Wheat, Wood & timber manufactures. Exports: Canned fruit, Cocoa, Coffee, Fish, Fresh fruit, Manufactured products, Scrap metal, Sisal.

Working Hours: Monday to Friday 0700-1600. Saturday 0700-1200. Overtime on request

Accommodation:

Name	Length (m)	Depth (m)	Remarks
Port au Prince			
Main Terminal	1250	8–10	See [1] below
Private Quays			See [2] below

[1]*Main Terminal:* Seven berths available. Two ro/ro ramps; one cruise ship terminal of 500 m long. Container warehousing space of 84 972 m2, covered storage space of 11 240 m2 and open storage space of 10 060 m2

[2]*Private Quays:* Varreux Terminal: operated by SONTRAM, PO Box 1310, Port au Prince, Tel: +509 2510 7063, Fax: +509 2513 5069, Email: sontram@compa.net. Consisting of four berths in depth of 9 m
Lafiteau Quay: in depth of 9 m
Fond Mombin Quay: in depth of 8 m
Shell Terminal: in depth of 10-18 m for import of oil products, cap of 6 699 000 gallons
Le Ciment du Sud Quay: 120 m long in depth of 12 m. One ro/ro ramp. Pipelines for cement and oil. One crane of 50 t cap and forklifts up to 5 t cap

Storage:

Location	Covered (m²)	Sheds / Warehouses
Port au Prince	11238	2

Mechanical Handling Equipment:

Location	Type	Capacity (t)	Qty
Main Terminal	Mult-purp. Cranes	150	1
Main Terminal	Container Cranes	30	1
Main Terminal	Forklifts	33	32

Bunkering: The Shell Company (WI) Ltd, Delmas 17-19, Route del Delmas, Port au Prince, Haiti, *Tel:* +509 161600, *Fax:* +509 161243
Chevron Marine Products LLC, Global Marine Products LLC, 1500 Louisiana, 4th Floor, Houston, TX 77002, United States of America, *Tel:* +1 832 8542 988, *Fax:* +1 832 8544 868, *Email:* gulfcbm@chevron.com, *Website:* www.chevron.com – *Grades:* GO – *Delivery Mode:* tank truck
The Shell Company (WI) Ltd, Delmas 17-19, Route del Delmas, Port au Prince, Haiti, *Tel:* +509 161600, *Fax:* +509 161243 – *Delivery Mode:* tanker truck
Texaco Caribbean Inc., Delmas, Casier 867, Port au Prince, Haiti, *Tel:* +509 146 1971 – *Delivery Mode:* tanker truck

Towage: Three tugs of 800-1100 hp are available

Ship Chandlers: A.I Shipping International, Apartment No.1, Sonadim Building, Angle Boulevard, Toussaint Louverture & Patrice Lumumba, Port au Prince, Haiti, *Tel:* +509 2250 6911, *Fax:* +509 2250 8815, *Email:* info@aishippingintl.com, *Website:* www.aishippingintl.com

Shipping Agents: Agemar S.A., Boulevard de la Saline, P O Box 1077, Port au Prince, Haiti, *Tel:* +509 2222 2600, *Fax:* +509 2222 2615, *Email:* agemar@agemar.com
A.I Shipping International, Apartment No.1, Sonadim Building, Angle Boulevard, Toussaint Louverture & Patrice Lumumba, Port au Prince, Haiti, *Tel:* +509 2250 6911, *Fax:* +509 2250 8815, *Email:* info@aishippingintl.com, *Website:* www.aishippingintl.com
Chatelain Cargo Services, 42 Route de l' Aeroport, P O Box 1056, Port au Prince, Haiti, *Tel:* +509 2250 1651, *Fax:* +509 2250 1398, *Email:* pvc@chatelaincargo.com, *Website:* www.chatelaincargo.com
Enmarcolda S.A., Bas de Delmas, P O Box 603, Port au Prince, Haiti, *Tel:* +509 2223 1312, *Fax:* +509 2222 1515, *Email:* dadesky@dadesky.com
Antoine Hogarth S.A., Rue Assad 1, Turgeau, P O Box 1255, Port au Prince, Haiti, *Tel:* +509 2244 5880, *Fax:* +509 2244 5880, *Email:* anthogarth@acn2.net
Madsen Export Import S.A., 35 Avenue Marie-Jeane, P O Box 1334, Port au Prince, Haiti, *Tel:* +509 2222 0028, *Fax:* +509 2223 2551
Mediterranean Shipping Company, MSC Haiti, Rue Pie Xii - #13, Bicentenaire, Port au Prince, Haiti, *Tel:* +509 2510 7103, *Email:* info@msc-haiti.com, *Website:* www.mscgva.ch
Reginald Villard Agent Maritime (RVAM), Suite 8, 2nd Floor, 37 Avenue Marie Jeanne, Bicentennaire, P O Box 19104, Port au Prince 6110, Haiti, *Tel:* +509 2224 3068, *Fax:* +509 2224 3063, *Email:* operations@rvamhaiti.com, *Website:* www.rvamhaiti.com
Agencies Maritimes Reunies S.A., 13 Rue Bonne F01, P O Box 1097, Port au Prince, Haiti, *Tel:* +509 2222 4361, *Fax:* +509 2222 2341
R. Sassine Co. S.A., Boulevard de la Saline, P O Box 645, Port au Prince, Haiti, *Tel:* +509 2222 2600, *Fax:* +509 2222 2316, *Email:* rsassine@rsassine.com
Termerair S.A., Boulevard de la Saline, P O Box 603, Port au Prince, Haiti, *Tel:* +509 2223 1212, *Fax:* +509 2222 1515
Ets. J.B. Vital S.A., P O Box 87, Angle Rues Bonne Foi & Courbe, Port au Prince Ht 6110, Haiti, *Tel:* +509 2221 4065, *Fax:* +509 2223 1323, *Email:* etsjbvitalsa@msn.com

Stevedoring Companies: Agences Maritimes Reunies S.A., Port au Prince, Haiti, *Tel:* +509 2222 4361, *Fax:* +509 2222 2341, *Email:* agemar@agemar.com
Reginald Villard Agent Maritime (RVAM), Suite 8, 2nd Floor, 37 Avenue Marie Jeanne, Bicentennaire, P O Box 19104, Port au Prince 6110, Haiti, *Tel:* +509 2224 3068, *Fax:* +509 2224 3063, *Email:* operations@rvamhaiti.com, *Website:* www.rvamhaiti.com
R. Sassine Co. S.A., Boulevard de la Saline, P O Box 645, Port au Prince, Haiti, *Tel:* +509 2222 2600, *Fax:* +509 2222 2316, *Email:* rsassine@rsassine.com

Medical Facilities: All services available

Airport: Port au Prince International Airport, 5 km

Lloyd's Agent: Ets. J.B. Vital S.A., P O Box 87, Angle Rues Bonne Foi & Courbe, Port au Prince Ht 6110, Haiti, *Tel:* +509 2221 4065, *Fax:* +509 2223 1323, *Email:* etsjbvitalsa@msn.com

HONDURAS

HENECAN

alternate name, see San Lorenzo

LA CEIBA

Lat 15° 47' N; Long 86° 45' W.

Admiralty Chart: 513	**Admiralty Pilot:** 69A
Time Zone: GMT -6 h	**UNCTAD Locode:** HN LCE

Principal Facilities:

		G					A

Authority: Empresa Nacional Portuaria, La Ceiba, Honduras, *Tel:* +504 441 9445, *Fax:* +504 441 9445, *Email:* mercadeo@enp.hn, *Website:* www.enp.hn

Officials: Port Superintendent: Ramon Armando Guzman Montoya.

Anchorage: Anchorage in stream in depths of 8.4-9.2 m

Pilotage: Available on request

Radio Frequency: VHF Channel 16

Tides: Range of tide 0.3 m

Maximum Vessel Dimensions: 10 000 dwt, 8.0 m draft, 159 m loa

Principal Imports and Exports: Imports: Animal oil, Chemical products, Fertiliser. Exports: Citric, Lumber.

Working Hours: 24 h/day

Accommodation:

Name	Length (m)	Depth (m)	Apron Width (m)	Remarks
La Ceiba				See [1] below
Pier	426	5.17–7.3	17	Extending at right angles from beach
Private Wharves				See [2] below

[1]*La Ceiba:* The port is at present closed for international traffic
[2]*Private Wharves:* Pier for coastal traffic 200 m long and 4.5 m deep, with access through an artificial channel

Storage:

Location	Covered (m²)	Sheds / Warehouses
La Ceiba	1886	1

Cargo Worked: 15 t/day

Medical Facilities: Available

Airport: Goloson International, 8 km

Railway: Ferrocarril Nacional has an installation on the wharf

Lloyd's Agent: Agencia Guzman y Cia S.A. de C.V., 2 Avenue, 6/7 Calle Este, Bo El Centro, P O Box 13, Puerto Cortes 21301, Honduras, *Tel:* +504 665 0287, *Fax:* +504 665 0753, *Email:* linaguzman@agenciaguzman.com

OMOA

harbour area, see under Puerto Cortes

PUERTO CASTILLA

Lat 16° 1' N; Long 86° 3' W.

Admiralty Chart: 513	**Admiralty Pilot:** 60A
Time Zone: GMT -6 h	**UNCTAD Locode:** HN PCA

Key to Principal Facilities:—					
A=Airport	**C**=Containers	**G**=General Cargo	**P**=Petroleum	**R**=Ro/Ro	**Y**=Dry Bulk
B=Bunkers	**D**=Dry Dock	**L**=Cruise	**Q**=Other Liquid Bulk	**T**=Towage (where available from port)	

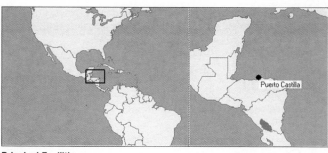

Principal Facilities:

Q		G	C	R				A

Authority: Empresa Nacional Portuaria, Puerto Castilla, Colon, Honduras, *Tel:* +504 429 8013, *Fax:* +504 429 8013, *Email:* mercadeo@enp.hn, *Website:* www.enp.hn

Officials: Port Superintendent: Luis Carlos Ulloa Mencia.

Port Security: ISPS compliant

Anchorage: 0.5-1 nautical mile S of the pier in depths of 33 m

Pilotage: Compulsory for vessels over 300 gt. Pilot must be ordered 24 h in advance

Radio Frequency: VHF Channel 16

Weather: Safe in NE and S winds but dangerous during NNW or W winds

Tides: Range of tide 0.3 m

Traffic: 2006, 834 842 t of cargo handled, 85 714 TEU's

Maximum Vessel Dimensions: 50 000 gt, 206 m loa, 10 m draft

Principal Imports and Exports: Imports: Fertiliser, General cargo. Exports: Bananas, Citric, Lumber.

Working Hours: Mon-Thurs 0700-1600. Fri 0700-1500. Port is open 24 h

Accommodation: Tanker facilities: Two tanks for diesel of 12 000 bbls cap each, two tanks for gasoline of 50 000 bbls cap each, two tanks for palm oil of 20 000 bbls cap each, two tanks for bunkers of 20 000 bbls cap each, two tanks for asphalt of 20 000 bbls cap each and one fresh water tank of 500 000 gallons

Name	Length (m)	Depth (m)
Puerto Castilla		
Pier	225	9–11

Storage:

Location	Open (m²)	Covered (m²)	Sheds / Warehouses
Puerto Castilla	68000	6000	2

Mechanical Handling Equipment:

Location	Type	Capacity (t)	Qty
Puerto Castilla	Mult-purp. Cranes	25	1
Puerto Castilla	Mult-purp. Cranes	22	1
Puerto Castilla	Forklifts	7	

Cargo Worked: 1480 t/day

Medical Facilities: Available

Airport: Trujillo Airport, 14 km

Lloyd's Agent: Agencia Guzman y Cia S.A. de C.V., 2 Avenue, 6/7 Calle Este, Bo El Centro, P O Box 13, Puerto Cortes 21301, Honduras, *Tel:* +504 665 0287, *Fax:* +504 665 0753, *Email:* linaguzman@agenciaguzman.com

PUERTO CORTES

Lat 15° 50' N; Long 87° 56' W.

Admiralty Chart: 2988	**Admiralty Pilot:** 69A
Time Zone: GMT -6 h	**UNCTAD Locode:** HN PCR

Principal Facilities:

P	Q	Y	G	C	R	L	B		T	A

Authority: Empresa Nacional Portuaria, Barrio El Centro, 1st Avenue, 1st Street, Puerto Cortes, Honduras, *Tel:* +504 665 0110, *Fax:* +504 665 1402, *Email:* gerencia@enp.hn, *Website:* www.enp.hn

Officials: General Manager: Roberto Babun Sikaffi, *Tel:* +504 665 0987.
Port Superintendent: Oscar Orlando Delgado, *Tel:* +504 665 0192, *Email:* odelgado@enp.hn.
Marketing: Karla Margarita Carrasco Johnson, *Tel:* +504 665 1423, *Email:* mercadeo@enp.hn.

Port Security: ISPS compliant. Container Security Initiative (CSI) designated port

Pre-Arrival Information: Vessels should forward ETA to ship agent 72 h prior to arrival

Approach: North Channel 1200 m long, 400 m wide in depth of 14 m. Well marked with a white light and red and green buoys

Anchorage: Anchorage must be at least 5 cables S of the berths and channel entrance. Depths of 9-16 m in the bay

Pilotage: Compulsory for vessels over 300 gt

Radio Frequency: VHF Channels 16 and 06

Weather: Prevailing NE'ly and SE'ly winds

Tides: 0.3 m MHWN, 0.15 m MLWN

Traffic: 2006, 7 396 849 t of cargo handled, 507 946 TEU's

Maximum Vessel Dimensions: Dry cargo vessels up to 9 m draft. Tankers up to 50 000 gt and 11 m draft

Principal Imports and Exports: Imports: Chemicals, Corn, Electric & electronic supplies, Fertilizers, Fuel, Oats, Oil, Steel. Exports: Bananas, Cantaloupes, Citrics, Coffee, Lumber, Minerals, Seafood, Textiles.

Working Hours: 0700-1200, 1300-1700, 1800-2330, 2400-0600

Accommodation:

Name	Length (m)	Depth (m)	Remarks
Puerto Cortes			
Pier No.1	46	13	Petroleum & derivates
Pier No.1A	70	11	Molasses & chemicals
Pier No.3	198	11	General cargo & bananas
Pier No.4	325	10.5	General cargo, lo/lo & ro/ro
Pier No.5	476	10.5	General cargo, lo/lo & ro/ro
Omoa Terminal	150	8	See [1] below

[1] *Omoa Terminal:* LPG. Underwater pipeline connecting to shore terminal. Mooring in daylight only. 24 h unloading

Storage:

Location	Open (m²)	Covered (m²)	Sheds / Warehouses
Puerto Cortes	32000	14300	3

Mechanical Handling Equipment:

Location	Type	Capacity (t)	Qty
Puerto Cortes	Mult-purp. Cranes	45	2
Puerto Cortes	Mobile Cranes	45	7

Cargo Worked: Breakbulk 176 t/shift, grain 640 t/shift, lumber 640 t/shift, bananas 180 t/shift

Bunkering: Chevron Marine Products LLC, Global Marine Products LLC, 1500 Louisiana, 4th Floor, Houston, TX 77002, United States of America, *Tel:* +1 832 8542 988, *Fax:* +1 832 8544 868, *Email:* gulfcbm@chevron.com, *Website:* www.chevron.com – *Grades:* GO – *Delivery Mode:* tank truck
Texaco Caribbean Inc., P O Box 112, San Pedro Sula, Honduras, *Tel:* +504 530097 – *Grades:* GO; IFO180-240cSt – *Parcel Size:* min 200t – *Notice:* 72 hours – *Delivery Mode:* pipeline, truck, wharf

Waste Reception Facilities: No collection services available for waste and garbage disposal, however agents can arrange waste reception with private contractors

Towage: Three tugs available. Two tugs compulsory for vessels over 10 000 gt

Repair & Maintenance: Minor repairs only by agent in advance

Shipping Agents: A.P. Moller-Maersk Group, Maersk Honduras, Puerto Cortes Terminal, Contiguo al Cuerpo de Bomberos, Puerto Cortes, Honduras, *Tel:* +504 665 1206, *Fax:* +504 665 1028, *Email:* hondocexp@maersk.com, *Website:* www.maerskline.com
Operadores Navieros S.A., 2-3 Avenida 2 Calle, Plaza Commercial ENG, Gegunda Nivel CS, Puerto Cortes, Honduras, *Tel:* +504 665 4334, *Fax:* +504 665 4337, *Email:* lmoncada@gmihon.com

Stevedoring Companies: Operadores Navieros S.A., 2-3 Avenida 2 Calle, Plaza Commercial ENG, Gegunda Nivel CS, Puerto Cortes, Honduras, *Tel:* +504 665 4334, *Fax:* +504 665 4337, *Email:* lmoncada@gmihon.com

Medical Facilities: Private clinics and a public hospital in the city

Airport: Ramon Villeda Morales International, approx 60 km

Railway: Ferrocarril Nacional de Honduras is in the port

Lloyd's Agent: Agencia Guzman y Cia S.A. de C.V., 2 Avenue, 6/7 Calle Este, Bo El Centro, P O Box 13, Puerto Cortes 21301, Honduras, *Tel:* +504 665 0287, *Fax:* +504 665 0753, *Email:* linaguzman@agenciaguzman.com

SAN LORENZO

Lat 13° 25' N; Long 87° 27' W.

Admiralty Chart: 1961	**Admiralty Pilot:** 8
Time Zone: GMT -6 h	**UNCTAD Locode:** HN SLO

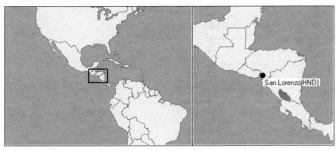

Principal Facilities:

| P | Q | Y | G | C | R | | | T | |

Authority: Empresa Nacional Portuaria, P O Box 32, San Lorenzo, Honduras, *Tel:* +504 781 5142, *Fax:* +504 781 5127, *Email:* supciasanlo@enp.hn, *Website:* www.enp.hn

Officials: General Manager: Roberto Babun.
Port Superintendent: Luis Carlos Rivera Pineda.
Harbour Master: Jose Humberto Maldonado.

Approach: Vessels should not attempt to cross the bar without a pilot. The bar at the channel entrance lies about 4.83 km SE of Isla del Tigre. The channel has been well marked with positioned buoys that include the DGPS system. The length of the channel is 32 km, width 122 m and min depth of 8.53 m. Due to silting the depth of the access channel is 7.31 m at MLW

Anchorage: Anchorages are designated about 0.6 km and 1.61 km SSW of the pier in depth of 9.4 m

Pilotage: Compulsory and should be ordered through local agent. Vessel's should call pilot vessel on VHF Channel 16 1 h before arrival at the Sea Lt. Buoy
Pilot boards in pos 13° 11.00' N; 87° 35.50' W

Radio Frequency: VHF Channel 16

Weather: Winds from the N do not affect port working

Tides: Range of tide 3.0-3.65 m

Traffic: 2006, 920 324 t of cargo handled

Principal Imports and Exports: Imports: Fertiliser, General cargo, Petroleum products. Exports: Coffee, Cotton, Sugar.

Working Hours: Mon-Thurs 0700-1600. Fri 0700-1500

Accommodation:

Name	Length (m)	Depth (m)	Remarks
San Lorenzo			One T shaped concrete pier has four berths
Berth No.1	157	9.8–10.6	
Berth No.2	139	9.1–10	
Berth No.3	116	6.7	
Berth No.4	134	6.7	

Storage: 1200 m2 open warehouse for lumber, 2400 m2 warehouse for general cargo, 1800 m2 open warehouse for cotton, 3100 m2 warehouse for sugar, open non-paved storage of 29 000 m2, open paved storage of 10 000 m2, one tank for molasses with cap of 100 000 gallons

Mechanical Handling Equipment:

Location	Type	Capacity (t)	Qty
San Lorenzo	Mult-purp. Cranes	30	1
San Lorenzo	Mult-purp. Cranes	60	1
San Lorenzo	Forklifts		7

Cargo Worked: Sugar 1000 t/day, cotton 22.7 t/gang/h, lumber 30 t/gang/h

Towage: Available

Stevedoring Companies: Operadores Navieros S.A., 2-3 Avenida 2 Calle, Plaza Commercial ENG, Gegunda Nivel CS, Puerto Cortes, Honduras, *Tel:* +504 665 4334, *Fax:* +504 665 4337, *Email:* lmoncada@gmihon.com

Medical Facilities: Available

Lloyd's Agent: Agencia Guzman y Cia S.A. de C.V., 2 Avenue, 6/7 Calle Este, Bo El Centro, P O Box 13, Puerto Cortes 21301, Honduras, *Tel:* +504 665 0287, *Fax:* +504 665 0753, *Email:* linaguzman@agenciaguzman.com

ICELAND

AKRANES

Lat 64° 19' N; Long 22° 5' W.

Admiralty Chart: 2734	**Admiralty Pilot:** 11
Time Zone: GMT	**UNCTAD Locode:** IS AKR

Principal Facilities:

| | Y | G | | | B | | T | A |

Authority: Associated Icelandic Ports, Faxabraut 1, IS-300 Akranes, Iceland, *Tel:* +354 431 1361, *Fax:* +354 431 2626, *Email:* hofnin@faxaports.is, *Website:* www.faxaports.is

Officials: Port Director: Gisli Gislason.
Marketing Director: Agust Agustson.
Harbour Master: Thorvaldur Gudmundsson, *Tel:* +354 525 8931, *Email:* valdi@faxaports.is.

Port Security: ISPS compliant

Documentation: Vessels arriving from countries outside the Schengen convention must submit their crew list to the Icelandic coastguard 24 h prior to arrival

Approach: Shoals and rocks are covered by Akranes and Krossvik light structures

Anchorage: Anchorage can be obtained in depths ranging from 14.5 m to 16.5 m; good holding ground

Pilotage: Compulsory for all foreign vessels. Pilot boards off lightbuoy No.11 in pos 64° 17' 36" N; 22° 07' 30" W

Radio Frequency: Reykjavik Radio, VHF Channel 16; port working VHF Channel 14

Weather: Strong onshore winds from the W and SW can force vessels to vacate berths in very rough sea

Traffic: 2006, 100 047 t of cargo handled

Maximum Vessel Dimensions: 8824 dwt, 7.9 m d, 137 m loa

Principal Imports and Exports: Imports: Industrial Goods. Exports: Cement, Fishmeal, Fishoil, Frozen Fish.

Working Hours: 0800-1700 or by agreement

Accommodation:

Name	Length (m)	Depth (m)	Draught (m)	Remarks
Akranes				See [1] below
Main Pier (Under reconstruction)	290	8.5–10	9.5	One berth of 160 m and one berth of 130 m

[1] *Akranes:* Depth at harbour entrance is approx 10 m. There is a pier serving a cement factory and also a sheltered harbour for fishing vessels

Storage: No harbour storage available

Mechanical Handling Equipment:

Location	Type	Capacity (t)	Qty	Remarks
Akranes	Mult-purp. Cranes	2	2	For general cargo
Akranes	Mobile Cranes	90		

Cargo Worked: 600-1000 t/day

Bunkering: ExxonMobil Marine Fuels, Mailpoint 31, ExxonMobil House, Ermyn Way, Leatherhead, Surrey KT22 8UX, United Kingdom, *Tel:* +44 1372 222 000, *Fax:* +44 1372 223 922, *Email:* marine.fuels@exxonmobil.com, *Website:* www.exxonmobil.com – *Grades:* IF40; MGO – *Delivery Mode:* truck

Waste Reception Facilities: Containers for waste are available

Towage: Available

Repair & Maintenance: Skipasmidastod Thorgeir & Ellert h/f, Bakkatuni 26, IS-300 Akranes, Iceland, *Tel:* +354 430 2000, *Fax:* +354 430 2001, *Email:* sales@skaginn.is, *Website:* www.skaginn.is Syncrolift for vessels up to 500 t

Shipping Agents: Hf Eimskipafelag Islands, Dalbraut 6, IS-300 Akranes, Iceland, *Tel:* +354 431 1500, *Fax:* +354 431 1612, *Email:* trukkur@aknet.is

Medical Facilities: Local hospital available

Airport: Keflavik International Airport, 99 km

Lloyd's Agent: Konnun ehf, Hesthals 6-8, 110 Reykjavik, Iceland, *Tel:* +354 570 9240, *Fax:* +354 570 9004, *Email:* konnun@frumherji.is, *Website:* www.frumherji.is/konnun

AKUREYRI

Lat 65° 41' N; Long 18° 3' W.

Admiralty Chart: 2899/2955	**Admiralty Pilot:** 11
Time Zone: GMT	**UNCTAD Locode:** IS AKU

Key to Principal Facilities:—
A=Airport   **C**=Containers   **G**=General Cargo   **P**=Petroleum   **R**=Ro/Ro   **Y**=Dry Bulk
B=Bunkers   **D**=Dry Dock   **L**=Cruise   **Q**=Other Liquid Bulk   **T**=Towage (where available from port)

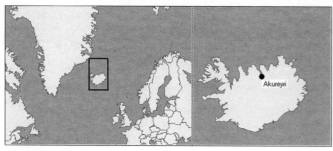

Principal Facilities:

P		Y	G	C		L	B	D	T	A	

Authority: Port Authority of Akureyri, Fiskitangi, IS-600 Akureyri, Iceland, *Tel:* +354 460 4200, *Fax:* +354 460 4209, *Email:* port@port.is, *Website:* www.port.is

Officials: Port Director: Hordur Blondal, *Tel:* +354 460 4201, *Email:* hordur@port.is. Marketing Manager: Petur Olafsson, *Tel:* +354 460 4202, *Email:* petur@port.is.

Port Security: ISPS compliant

Documentation: Vessels arriving from countries outside the Schengen convention must submit their crew list to the Icelandic coastguard 24 h prior to arrival

Approach: Oddeyri provides a natural shelter and an excellent anchorage. Entrance to the harbour has a width of 800 m and a depth of 47 m

Anchorage: Pollurinn, depth 25 m

Pilotage: Compulsory for vessels over 100 m loa and available 24 h/day. For other vessels not compulsory but available by arrangement with Harbour Master, Tel: +354 460 4200. Pilot station located in pos 65° 43' N; 18° 06' W, three nautical miles from the anchorage and pier

Radio Frequency: VHF Channels 12 and 16

Tides: Range of tide 1.7 m

Traffic: 2006, 772 vessels, 146 304 t of cargo handled

Maximum Vessel Dimensions: Up to 300 m loa

Principal Imports and Exports: Imports: Cattle feed, General cargo. Exports: Fishmeal, Fishoil, Frozen fish.

Working Hours: 0800-1600 but there ia a 24 h service, Tel: +354 460 4200

Accommodation:

Name	Length (m)	Depth (m)	Remarks
Akureyri			See [1] below
Krossanes (Berth No.1)	130	6.5–9	See [2] below
Sandgerdisbot (Berth No.2)		2.5	Boat harbour, fish landing
Flotkvi (Berth No.3)			Floating dock of 5000 t
Slippkantur (Berth No.4)	275	6–7	Ship repairs, asphalt tank
Austurbakki (Berth No.5)	170	7	Fish landing
Togarabryggja (Berth No.6)	67	6.5	Fish landing & general cargo
Togarabryggja (Berth No.7)	110	6.5	Fish landing & general cargo
Isbryggja (Berth No.8)	65	6.5	Ice
Londunarkantur (Berth No.9)	75	6	Fish landing
Tangabryggja (Berth No.11)	170	8–11	General cargo, cattle feed & cruise vessels
Oddeyrarbryggja (Berth No.12)	140	9	General cargo & cruise vessels
Torfunefsbryggja & Torfunef (Berth No.13)		3–5.5	Torfunefsbryggja for small cruise vessels, tenders etc. Torfunef for tenders
Pollurinn (Berth No.14)		25–35	Anchorage
Vesturbakki (Berth No.15)	190	9	Fishing harbour

[1]*Akureyri:* Natural, well-protected harbour formed by Oddeyri peninsula and the end of the fiord
[2]*Krossanes (Berth No.1):* One berth 80 m long in depth of 9 m for oil, fish oil, meal and cement. One berth 50 m long in depth of 6 m for capelin and herring landing

Mechanical Handling Equipment:

Location	Type	Capacity (t)	Qty
Akureyri	Mobile Cranes	40	3

Bunkering: Available with delivery by truck
ExxonMobil Marine Fuels, Mailpoint 31, ExxonMobil House, Ermyn Way, Leatherhead, Surrey KT22 8UX, United Kingdom, *Tel:* +44 1372 222 000, *Fax:* +44 1372 223 922, *Email:* marine.fuels@exxonmobil.com, *Website:* www.exxonmobil.com – *Grades:* IF40; MGO – *Delivery Mode:* truck

Waste Reception Facilities: Garbage service available by truck

Towage: One tug of 242 hp and one of 800 hp available

Repair & Maintenance: Slippurinn Akureyri ehf, Naustatanga 2, 600 Akureyri, Iceland, *Tel:* +354 460 7600, *Fax:* +354 460 7601, *Email:* slipp@slipp.is, *Website:* www.slipp.is Slipway 85 m x 15.4 m with lifting cap 2000 t. Floating Dock 116.4 m x 23.3 m with lifting cap 5000 t. Repair quay of 300 m

Shipping Agents: Hf Eimskipafelag Islands, Oddeyrarskali vid Strandgotu, IS-600 Akureyri, Iceland, *Tel:* +354 460 7100, *Fax:* +354 460 7117, *Email:* info@eimskip.is, *Website:* www.eimskip.com

Medical Facilities: Full hospital facilities available

Airport: Akureyri Airport, 5 km

Lloyd's Agent: Konnun ehf, Hesthals 6-8, 110 Reykjavik, Iceland, *Tel:* +354 570 9240, *Fax:* +354 570 9004, *Email:* konnun@frumherji.is, *Website:* www.frumherji.is/konnun

BOLUNGARVIK

Lat 66° 10' N; Long 23° 14' W.

Admiralty Chart: 2976	**Admiralty Pilot:** 11
Time Zone: GMT	**UNCTAD Locode:** IS BOL

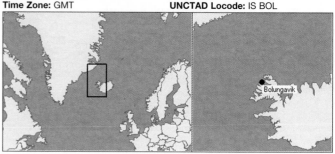

Principal Facilities:

			G							A	

Authority: Bolungarvikurhofn, Adalstraeti 12, IS-415 Bolungarvik, Iceland, *Tel:* +354 450 7000, *Fax:* +354 450 7009, *Email:* hafnarvog@bolungarvik.is, *Website:* www.bolungarvik.is

Officials: Harbour Master: Grimur Atlason, *Email:* grimur@bolungarvik.is.

Documentation: Vessels arriving from countries outside the Schengen convention must submit their crew list to the Icelandic coastguard 24 h prior to arrival

Pilotage: Available from Isafjordur

Accommodation:

Name	Length (m)	Depth (m)
Bolungavik		
Brimbrjotur	200	6.7–7
Grundargadur	120	7

Medical Facilities: Small hospital and a doctor is available

Airport: Isafjordur, 30 km

Lloyd's Agent: Konnun ehf, Hesthals 6-8, 110 Reykjavik, Iceland, *Tel:* +354 570 9240, *Fax:* +354 570 9004, *Email:* konnun@frumherji.is, *Website:* www.frumherji.is/konnun

BUDAREYRI

harbour area, see under Eskifjordur

BUDIR

harbour area, see under Faskrudhsfjordur

DALVIK

Lat 65° 58' N; Long 18° 31' W.

Admiralty Chart: 2899	**Admiralty Pilot:** 11
Time Zone: GMT	**UNCTAD Locode:** IS DAL

Principal Facilities:

			G							A	

Authority: Dalvikurbyggd-Hafnasjodur, Radhusinu, IS-620 Dalvik, Iceland, *Tel:* +354 466 1373, *Fax:* +354 466 1063, *Email:* sij@dalvik.is, *Website:* www.dalvik.is

Officials: Harbour Master: Svanfridur Jonasdottir, *Tel:* +354 460 4902.

Port Security: ISPS compliant

Documentation: Vessels arriving from countries outside the Schengen convention must submit their crew list to the Icelandic coastguard 24 h prior to arrival

Accommodation:

Name	Remarks
Dalvik	See [1] below

[1]*Dalvik:* Trading Station. Harbour protected by two breakwaters, entrance 45 m wide

with a depth of 5 m. Depths at berths range from 2 m to 6 m. Anchorage can be obtained in the bay in depths of 22 m to 26 m

Shipping Agents: Hf Eimskipafelag Islands, P O Box 55, IS-620 Dalvik, Iceland, *Tel:* +354 466 1800, *Fax:* +354 466 1804, *Email:* mrh@eimskip.is, *Website:* www.eimskip.com

Medical Facilities: A doctor is available. Nearest hospital is at Akureyri, 32 km

Airport: Akureyri, 45 km

Lloyd's Agent: Konnun ehf, Hesthals 6-8, 110 Reykjavik, Iceland, *Tel:* +354 570 9240, *Fax:* +354 570 9004, *Email:* konnun@frumherji.is, *Website:* www.frumherji.is/konnun

DJUPIVOGUR

Lat 64° 40' N; Long 14° 15' W.

Admiralty Chart: 2901	**Admiralty Pilot:** 11
Time Zone: GMT	**UNCTAD Locode:** IS DJU

Principal Facilities:

			G		L			

Authority: Port of Djupivogur, Bakki 1, IS-765 Djupivogur, Iceland, *Tel:* +354 478 8869, *Fax:* +354 478 8188, *Email:* hofn@djupivogur.is, *Website:* www.djupivogur.is

Officials: Harbour Master: Stefan Gudmundsson.

Port Security: ISPS compliant

Documentation: Vessels arriving from countries outside the Schengen convention must submit their crew list to the Icelandic coastguard 24 h prior to arrival

Approach: Narrow approach to harbour and limited swinging area

Anchorage: Anchorage can be obtained in the outer roadstead in depths ranging from 13 m to 15 m

Pilotage: Available and recommended to enter port

Accommodation:

Name	Remarks
Djupivogur	See [1] below

[1]*Djupivogur:* Trading Station. Quay 60 m long with depths alongside up to 5.5 m. There is a small jetty with a depth alongside of 3 m. The inner anchorage can accommodate vessels up to 55 m loa in depths ranging from 3.7 m to 5.5 m Vessels of up to 3500 dwt have been reported

Medical Facilities: A doctor is available

Lloyd's Agent: Konnun ehf, Hesthals 6-8, 110 Reykjavik, Iceland, *Tel:* +354 570 9240, *Fax:* +354 570 9004, *Email:* konnun@frumherji.is, *Website:* www.frumherji.is/konnun

ESKIFJORDUR

Lat 65° 5' N; Long 13° 59' W.

Admiralty Chart: 2902	**Admiralty Pilot:** 11
Time Zone: GMT	**UNCTAD Locode:** IS ESK

Principal Facilities:

			G	C				A	

Authority: Fjardabyggd Port Authority, Port of Eskifjordur, Strandgotu 49, IS-735 Eskifjordur, Iceland, *Tel:* +354 476 1199, *Fax:* +354 476 1597, *Email:* ehofn@fjardabyggd.is, *Website:* www.fjardabyggd.is

Officials: Port Manager: Kristofer Ragnarsson, *Email:* kristofer.ragnarsson@fjardabyggd.is.

Port Security: ISPS compliant

Documentation: Vessels arriving from countries outside the Schengen convention must submit their crew list to the Icelandic coastguard 24 h prior to arrival

Approach: No navigational difficulties are present in Reydarfjordur

Anchorage: Anchorage can be obtained in depths 50 m to 60 m in middle of the fjord

Pilotage: Available

Radio Frequency: VHF Channel 12

Weather: Sudden strong squalls can descend from the mountains. Polar ice can be experienced during the winter at the anchorages

Maximum Vessel Dimensions: 4450 dwt, 120 m loa, 7-8 m d

Principal Imports and Exports: Exports: Fish products.

Accommodation:

Name	Length (m)	Depth (m)	Remarks
Eskifjordur			See [1] below
Hraofrystibryggja Pier	100	5–6.3	
Braeoslubryggja Pier	55		
Hafnarbryggja		6.2–8.9	See [2] below
Budareyri			See [3] below

[1]*Eskifjordur:* 500 m2 container yard. There are also other berths for smaller fishing vessels
[2]*Hafnarbryggja:* A berthing face of 70 m on the W side and 100 m on the N side
[3]*Budareyri:* Trading Station located near the head of Reydarfjordur. Two piers, one of which is 152 m long with a depth at the head of 5.8 m; the other has a berthing face of 46 m with a depth alongside also of 5.8 m

Storage: Available

Mechanical Handling Equipment:

Location	Type	Capacity (t)	Qty
Eskifjordur	Mult-purp. Cranes	4	1

Cargo Worked: 10-100 t/h

Waste Reception Facilities: Garbage containers on each wharf and a tank for sludge

Shipping Agents: Hf Eimskipafelag Islands, Strandgotu 18, IS-735 Eskifjordur, Iceland, *Tel:* +354 476 1800, *Fax:* +354 476 1809, *Email:* esk@eimskip.is, *Website:* www.eimskip.com

Medical Facilities: A modern hospital and doctors are available

Airport: Egilsstaoaflugvollur, 70 km

Lloyd's Agent: Konnun ehf, Hesthals 6-8, 110 Reykjavik, Iceland, *Tel:* +354 570 9240, *Fax:* +354 570 9004, *Email:* konnun@frumherji.is, *Website:* www.frumherji.is/konnun

FASKRUDHSFJORDUR

Admiralty Chart: 2901	**Admiralty Pilot:** 11
Time Zone: GMT	**UNCTAD Locode:** IS FAS

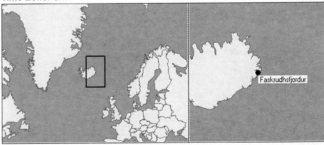

Principal Facilities:

	P		G			B		A	

Authority: Hafnarsjodur Budahrepps, Hafnargata 27, IS-750 Faskrudsfjordur, Iceland, *Tel:* +354 475 1323, *Fax:* +354 475 1459, *Email:* hofnfas@austurbyggd.is

Port Security: ISPS compliant

Documentation: Vessels arriving from countries outside the Schengen convention must submit their crew list to the Icelandic coastguard 24 h prior to arrival

Anchorage: Deep anchorage available in the fjord in depths ranging from 15 m to 50 m; steep shelving bottom. Better anchorage can be obtained off Budir

Tides: Range of tide 1.8 m

Maximum Vessel Dimensions: 6500 dwt, 123 m loa, 8.9 m d

Accommodation:

Name	Length (m)	Depth (m)	Remarks
Budir			See [1] below
Jetty	80	7.6	
Faskrudsfjordur			
Fiokeyri jetty	110	7	
Hafskipabryggja jetty	60	9	

[1]*Budir:* Important fishing port and Trading Station located near the head of Faskrudsfjordur. Five jetties about 25 m in length with depths alongside of 4.6 m. There are also other berths for smaller fishing vessels

Bunkering: Fuel oil and diesel oil are available from hoses at jetty

Waste Reception Facilities: Garbage disposal available

Key to Principal Facilities:—				
A=Airport	**C**=Containers	**G**=General Cargo	**P**=Petroleum	**R**=Ro/Ro	**Y**=Dry Bulk
B=Bunkers	**D**=Dry Dock	**L**=Cruise	**Q**=Other Liquid Bulk	**T**=Towage (where available from port)	

Repair & Maintenance: Repairs to small craft only can be effected; slipway for vessels up to 50 t

Medical Facilities: Hospital at Budir and doctors are available

Airport: Egilsstadir, 80 km

Lloyd's Agent: Konnun ehf, Hesthals 6-8, 110 Reykjavik, Iceland, *Tel:* +354 570 9240, *Fax:* +354 570 9004, *Email:* konnun@frumherji.is, *Website:* www.frumherji.is/konnun

GRENIVIK

Lat 65° 57' N; Long 18° 12' W.

Admiralty Chart: 2899 **Admiralty Pilot:** 11
Time Zone: GMT **UNCTAD Locode:** IS GRE

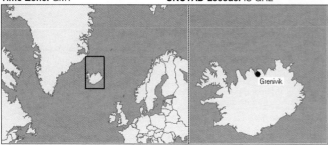

Principal Facilities:

			G							A	

Authority: Port Authority of Akureyri, Fiskitangi, IS-600 Akureyri, Iceland, *Tel:* +354 460 4200, *Fax:* +354 460 4209, *Email:* port@port.is, *Website:* www.port.is

Officials: Port Director: Hordur Blondal, *Tel:* +354 460 4201, *Email:* hordur@port.is. Marketing Manager: Petur Olafsson, *Tel:* +354 460 4202, *Email:* petur@port.is.

Documentation: Vessels arriving from countries outside the Schengen convention must submit their crew list to the Icelandic coastguard 24 h prior to arrival

Maximum Vessel Dimensions: 6.0 m max draft

Accommodation:

Name	Remarks
Grenivik	Jetty 140 m long

Mechanical Handling Equipment:

Location	Type	Qty
Grenivik	Mult-purp. Cranes	1

Repair & Maintenance: Velsmidjan Vik h.f., Grenivik, Iceland, *Tel:* +354 463 3216, *Fax:* +354 463 3246

Airport: Akureyri, 45 km

Lloyd's Agent: Konnun ehf, Hesthals 6-8, 110 Reykjavik, Iceland, *Tel:* +354 570 9240, *Fax:* +354 570 9004, *Email:* konnun@frumherji.is, *Website:* www.frumherji.is/konnun

GRINDAVIK

Lat 63° 50' N; Long 22° 26' W.

Admiralty Chart: 2734 **Admiralty Pilot:** 11
Time Zone: GMT **UNCTAD Locode:** IS GRI

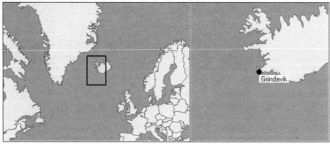

Principal Facilities:

			G					A	

Authority: Grindavikurhofn AB, Vikurbraut 62, 240 Grindavik, Iceland, *Tel:* +354 426 8046, *Fax:* +354 426 7435, *Email:* ghofn@grindavik.is, *Website:* www.grindavik.is

Officials: Harbour Master: Sverrir Vilbergsson, *Email:* sverrir@grindavik.is.

Port Security: ISPS compliant

Documentation: Vessels arriving from countries outside the Schengen convention must submit their crew list to the Icelandic coastguard 24 h prior to arrival

Approach: Channel 35-70 m wide in min depth of 7 m leads directly to the harbour

Anchorage: Anchorage can be obtained in the nearby bay of Jarngerdarstadvik in a depth of 7 m. The anchorage can become untenable during winds from SE to SW

Pilotage: Available

Radio Frequency: VHF Channel 14

Maximum Vessel Dimensions: 4552 dwt, 90 m loa

Accommodation:

Name	Remarks
Grindavik	Depths at quays in the harbour range from 3.2 m to 7.5 m

Waste Reception Facilities: Garbage disposal available

Repair & Maintenance: Machine and electrical repairs

Medical Facilities: Available

Airport: Keflavik, 25 km

Lloyd's Agent: Konnun ehf, Hesthals 6-8, 110 Reykjavik, Iceland, *Tel:* +354 570 9240, *Fax:* +354 570 9004, *Email:* konnun@frumherji.is, *Website:* www.frumherji.is/konnun

GRUNDARFJORDUR

Lat 64° 55' N; Long 23° 13' W.

Admiralty Chart: 2976 **Admiralty Pilot:** 11
Time Zone: GMT **UNCTAD Locode:** IS GRF

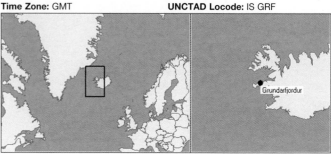

Principal Facilities:

	P		Y	G	C		L				

Authority: Port of Grundarfjordur, Grundargata 30, IS-350 Grundarfjordur, Iceland, *Tel:* +354 430 8500, *Fax:* +354 430 8501, *Email:* port@grundarfjordur.is, *Website:* www.grundarfjordur.is

Officials: Harbour Master: Hafsteinn Gardarsson, *Tel:* +354 438 6705.

Port Security: ISPS compliant

Documentation: Vessels arriving from countries outside the Schengen convention must submit their crew list to the Icelandic coastguard 24 h prior to arrival

Anchorage: Good anchorage 0.6 nautical mile from tender dock in pos 64° 55.8' N; 23° 14' W

Pilotage: Available. Pilot station 7 nautical miles from pier in pos 65° 02' N; 23° 26' W

Radio Frequency: VHF Channel 12

Weather: Heavy squalls from the hills can occur during S and SW winds

Tides: Tidal range of 4 m

Maximum Vessel Dimensions: Vessels alongside: 170 m loa with 6.5 m max draught at LT. Bigger vessels at anchorage with 14 m max draught at LT

Principal Imports and Exports: Imports: Bulk cargo, Frozen fish, Frozen seafoods, Gas oil. Exports: Frozen seafoods.

Working Hours: 24 h/day

Accommodation:

Name	Length (m)	Depth (m)	Remarks
Grundarfjordur			See [1] below
Nordurgardur Pier	230	6.5	
Midgardur Pier	80	6	

[1]*Grundarfjordur:* Two piers suitable for medium-sized vessels. Anchorage for vessels loading/discharging can be obtained in depths of about 14 m

Storage: Good facilities for salt and frozen goods

Mechanical Handling Equipment: Crane and container loading/offloading service

Bunkering: ExxonMobil Marine Fuels, Mailpoint 31, ExxonMobil House, Ermyn Way, Leatherhead, Surrey KT22 8UX, United Kingdom, *Tel:* +44 1372 222 000, *Fax:* +44 1372 223 922, *Email:* marine.fuels@exxonmobil.com, *Website:* www.exxonmobil.com – *Grades:* IF40; MGO – *Delivery Mode:* truck

Shipping Agents: Hf Eimskipafelag Islands, Grundarfjordur, Iceland, *Tel:* +354 438 1800, *Fax:* +354 438 1010, *Email:* asgeir@ragnarogasgeir.is, *Website:* www.eimskip.com

Medical Facilities: Local medical clinic 500 m from pier

Airport: Closest international airport, 2.5 h from port

Lloyd's Agent: Konnun ehf, Hesthals 6-8, 110 Reykjavik, Iceland, *Tel:* +354 570 9240, *Fax:* +354 570 9004, *Email:* konnun@frumherji.is, *Website:* www.frumherji.is/konnun

GRUNDARTANGI

Lat 64° 21' N; Long 21° 47' W.

Admiralty Chart: 2734 **Admiralty Pilot:** 11
Time Zone: GMT **UNCTAD Locode:** IS GRT

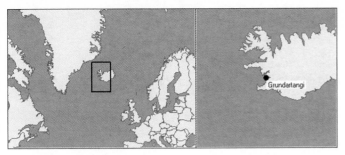

Principal Facilities:

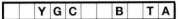

	Y	G	C		B		T	A

Authority: Associated Icelandic Ports, Port of Grundartangi, Grundartangi, Skilamannahreppur, IS-301 Akranes, Iceland, *Tel:* +354 894 5818, *Fax:* +354 433 8820, *Email:* hofnin@faxaports.is, *Website:* www.faxaports.is

Officials: Port Director: Gisli Gislason.
Marketing Director: Agust Agustson.
Harbour Master: Thorvaldur Gudmundsson, *Tel:* +354 525 8931, *Email:* valdi@faxaports.is.

Port Security: ISPS compliant

Documentation: Cargo manifest, crew & passenger list, crew customs declaration, stores list, customs clearance from last port

Approach: Depths in the fairway to the fjord range from 24-44 m

Anchorage: Anchorage can be obtained at Mariuhofn in pos 64° 20' 8" N; 21° 41' 8" W in depths ranging from 16.5 m to 19.5 m MLWS; good holding ground

Pilotage: Akranes Pilot on VHF Channel 14, Tel: +354 431 1361, Fax: +354 431 2626, Email: akhofn@akranes.is. Pilot boards in pos 64° 17' N; 22° 07' W

Radio Frequency: Pilot station, pilot vessel, harbour master and tugs on VHF Channel 14. Coastguard on VHF Channel 16

Weather: Prevailing wind direction is NE to SE. The harbour is always ice free

Tides: Max range of tide 4.5 m. Average spring tide 3.9 m, neap tide 1.5 m

Traffic: 2006, 1 012 106 t of cargo handled

Principal Imports and Exports: Imports: Raw materials. Exports: Aluminium, Ferrosilicon.

Working Hours: Monday to Friday 0730-1530. Overtime can be arranged

Accommodation:

Name	Length (m)	Depth (m)	Remarks
Grundartangi			See [1] below
Berth A	120	8	See [2] below
Berth B	250	13	See [3] below

[1]*Grundartangi:* Two factories mainly use the port. An Aluminium Smelter and a Ferro Silicon Plant
[2]*Berth A:* Used by Ferro Silicon Plant. 300 m long conveyor belt from hopper on the berth up to the plant. Unloading cap of 10 t with grab and 12 t with hook. Discharge rates of 300-450 t/h
[3]*Berth B:* General use. Suction unloader and container handling

Bunkering: Supplied by barge or tank lorries

Waste Reception Facilities: Garbage collection is available, to be arranged by agent

Towage: Use of tugs is not compulsory. Available from Akranes, Harnarfjordur and Reykjavik

Repair & Maintenance: Minor repairs available

Stevedoring Companies: Klafi ehf, Tel: +354 433 8850, Fax: 433 8820, Email: klafi@aknet.is
Kiafi ehf, 301 Grundartangi, Iceland, *Tel:* +354 433 8850, *Fax:* +354 433 8820, *Email:* klafi@klafi.is

Surveyors: Det Norske Veritas A/S, Reykjavik, Iceland, *Tel:* +354 551 4150, *Fax:* +354 561 5150, *Email:* reykjavik@dnv.com, *Website:* www.dnv.com
Konnun ehf, Hesthals 6-8, 110 Reykjavik, Iceland, *Tel:* +354 570 9240, *Fax:* +354 570 9004, *Email:* konnun@frumherji.is, *Website:* www.frumherji.is/konnun

Medical Facilities: All health and medical services available. Hospital at Akranes, 20 km

Airport: Keflavik Airport, 80 km

Lloyd's Agent: Konnun ehf, Hesthals 6-8, 110 Reykjavik, Iceland, *Tel:* +354 570 9240, *Fax:* +354 570 9004, *Email:* konnun@frumherji.is, *Website:* www.frumherji.is/konnun

HAFNARFJORDUR

Lat 64° 4' N; Long 21° 55' W.

Admiralty Chart: 2902	**Admiralty Pilot:** 11
Time Zone: GMT	**UNCTAD Locode:** IS HAF

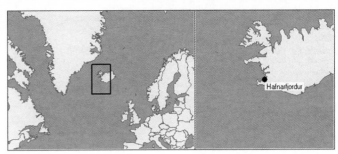

Principal Facilities:

P		Y	G	C		L	B	D	T	A

Authority: Hafnarfjordur Port Authority, Oseyrarbraut 4, IS-220 Hafnarfjordur, Iceland, *Tel:* +354 414 2300, *Fax:* +354 414 2301, *Email:* port@hafnarfjordur.is, *Website:* www.hafnarfjardarhofn.is

Officials: Port Director: Mar Sveinbjornsson, *Email:* mar@hafnarfjordur.is.
Harbour Master: Capt Kristinn Aadnegard, *Email:* kristinn.a@hafnarfjordur.is.

Port Security: ISPS compliant

Documentation: Cargo manifest, crew and passenger list, crew declaration to customs, stores list, custom clearance from last port

Approach: Vessels of, or exceeding 7 m draft approaching Hafnarfjordur and Straumsvik are warned that shoals exist in pos 64° 04' 48" N; 22° 08' 48" W, or 1.5 miles in 260° direction from the Valhusagrunn buoy

Anchorage: For vessels awaiting pilots anchorage can be obtained 1 mile SE of the outer buoy

Pilotage: Compulsory for foreign vessels. Pilot usually boards 1 mile SSE of the outer buoy (Valhusagrunn, red). Smaller vessels and Master's familiar with the port can proceed to the inner buoy (Helgasker, green)

Radio Frequency: VHF Channel 14

Weather: See under www.vedur.is

Tides: Range up to 4.5 m. Average spring tide 3.9 m, neaps 1.5 m

Maximum Vessel Dimensions: Max draft for tankers arriving is 9.5 m. Max draft for other vessels is 10 m

Principal Imports and Exports: Imports: Asphalt, Bulk cargo, Containerised cargo, Fuel, Salt, Steel, Timber. Exports: Fish products, General cargo, Scrap metal.

Working Hours: Monday to Friday 0800-1700. Overtime can be arranged

Accommodation:

Name	Length (m)	Depth (m)	Apron Width (m)	Remarks
Hafnarfjordur				See [1] below
Hvaleyrar Quay	200	8		Bulk cargoes
Hvaleyrar II	200	10		
North Quay	245	6–6.5		General cargo & unloading fish
South Quay	430	6–8		General & bulk cargoes
Finger Pier	70	5.5–6.5	10	Used mainly for unloading fish & asphalt
Oseyrar Pier	130	2.5–6	25	Mainly used for fishing vessels

[1]*Hafnarfjordur:* Inner harbour is enclosed by breakwater Hvaleyrargardur: entrance 200 m wide in depth of 11 m with bottom of soft clay. The new harbour is situated between S breakwater and Hvaleyrargardur
Tanker facilities: Oil Pier, inside the head of S breakwater in depth of 8.5 m

Storage:

Location	Covered (m²)	Grain (t)
South Quay	55000	14000

Mechanical Handling Equipment:

Location	Type
Hafnarfjordur	Mobile Cranes

Bunkering: Gara ehf, Baejarhrauni 2, IS-220 Hafnarfjordur, Iceland, *Tel:* +354 581 1688, *Fax:* +354 581 1685, *Email:* gara@centrum.is
ExxonMobil Marine Fuels, Mailpoint 31, ExxonMobil House, Ermyn Way, Leatherhead, Surrey KT22 8UX, United Kingdom, *Tel:* +44 1372 222 000, *Fax:* +44 1372 223 922, *Email:* marine.fuels@exxonmobil.com, *Website:* www.exxonmobil.com – *Grades:* IF40; MGO – *Delivery Mode:* truck

Waste Reception Facilities: Garbage and waste oil disposal, collection service available. Contact ship's agent

Towage: Two tugs of 15 t and 4 t bollard pull. Further tugs available

Repair & Maintenance: VOOV ehf, Hafnarfjordur, Iceland, *Tel:* +354 555 4199, *Fax:* +354 555 1421, *Email:* voov@centrum.is Two floating docks with lifting cap of 2750 t and 13 500 t

Ship Chandlers: Markus Lifenet Ltd, Breidvangur 30, 220 Hafnarfjordur, Iceland, *Tel:* +354 565 1375, *Fax:* +354 565 1376, *Email:* pthp@simnet.is, *Website:* www.markuslifenet.com

Shipping Agents: Hf Eimskipafelag Islands, vid Oseyrarbraut, IS-220 Hafnarfjordur, Iceland, *Tel:* +354 525 7900, *Fax:* +354 525 7909, *Email:* sif@eimskip.is, *Website:* www.eimskip.com
Gara ehf, Baejarhrauni 2, IS-220 Hafnarfjordur, Iceland, *Tel:* +354 581 1688, *Fax:* +354 581 1685, *Email:* gara@centrum.is

Key to Principal Facilities:—			
A=Airport	**C**=Containers	**G**=General Cargo	**P**=Petroleum	**R**=Ro/Ro	**Y**=Dry Bulk
B=Bunkers	**D**=Dry Dock	**L**=Cruise	**Q**=Other Liquid Bulk	**T**=Towage (where available from port)	

Stevedoring Companies: Hf Eimskipafelag Islands, vid Oseyrarbraut, IS-220 Hafnarfjordur, Iceland, *Tel:* +354 525 7900, *Fax:* +354 525 7909, *Email:* sif@eimskip.is, *Website:* www.eimskip.com

Surveyors: Det Norske Veritas A/S, Fjardargata 13-15, IS-220 Hafnarfjordur, Iceland, *Tel:* +354 551 4150, *Fax:* +354 561 5150, *Email:* reykjavik@dnv.com, *Website:* www.dnv.com

Medical Facilities: 24 h emergency service, Tel: 112. National Hospital, 9 km

Airport: Reykjavik Airport, 10 km. Keflavik Airport, 35 km

Lloyd's Agent: Konnun ehf, Hesthals 6-8, 110 Reykjavik, Iceland, *Tel:* +354 570 9240, *Fax:* +354 570 9004, *Email:* konnun@frumherji.is, *Website:* www.frumherji.is/konnun

HOFN

see under Hornafjordur

HORNAFJORDUR

Admiralty Chart: 1535	**Admiralty Pilot:** 11
Time Zone: GMT	**UNCTAD Locode:** IS HFN

Principal Facilities:

Q	Y	G	C		B	D	T	A

Authority: Hofns Major, Sturlaugur Porsteinsson, Hafnarbraut 27, P O Box 132, IS-780 Hornafjordur, Iceland, *Tel:* +354 478 1222 & 1474, *Fax:* +354 478 1922 & 2074, *Email:* hofnin@hornafjordur.is

Officials: Manager: Sigfus Hardarson.

Port Security: ISPS compliant

Documentation: Vessels arriving from countries outside the Schengen convention must submit their crew list to the Icelandic coastguard 24 h prior to arrival

Approach: Difficult entry to the fjord on account of strong tidal streams and shifting sandbanks. Entry is best effected during slack water. The channel to Hofn has a least depth of 4.0 m and is narrow over the first part; the second part has a least depth of 4.0 m

Anchorage: Anchorage may be obtained in pos 64° 13' 40" N, 15° 04' 00" W, 3-4 miles E of harbour entrance

Pilotage: Available and strongly recommended

Radio Frequency: VHF Channels 12 and 16

Tides: MLT 4.8 m, MHT 6.2 m

Maximum Vessel Dimensions: 3800 dwt, 90-100 m loa, 6.0 m d

Accommodation:

Name	Length (m)	Depth (m)	Remarks
Hornafjordur			
Alaugarey E	45	5.5	
Alaugarey S	72	6	
Osland	50	6.3	
Krossey	120	5.5–6.3	
Iskantur	40	6.3	
Mikligardur		6	
Trebryggja	90	4–5	
Braedslubryggja	77	6–6.3	Consists of two berths

Storage: Warehousing and refrigerated space available

Mechanical Handling Equipment:

Location	Type
Hornafjordur	Mult-purp. Cranes

Bunkering: With a hose placed on the wharves

Waste Reception Facilities: Available

Towage: Available

Repair & Maintenance: Velsmidja Hornafjardar, Hornafjordur, Iceland, *Tel:* +354 478 1340, *Fax:* +354 478 2145 Repair facilities

Shipping Agents: Hf Eimskipafelag Islands, Hornafjordur, Iceland, *Tel:* +354 478 1577, *Fax:* +354 478 1997, *Email:* hp-synir@eldhorn.is, *Website:* www.eimskip.com

Medical Facilities: Available

Airport: Arnanesflugvollur, 7 km

Lloyd's Agent: Konnun ehf, Hesthals 6-8, 110 Reykjavik, Iceland, *Tel:* +354 570 9240, *Fax:* +354 570 9004, *Email:* konnun@frumherji.is, *Website:* www.frumherji.is/konnun

HUSAVIK

Lat 66° 3' N; Long 17° 22' W.

Admiralty Chart: 2900	**Admiralty Pilot:** 11
Time Zone: GMT	**UNCTAD Locode:** IS HUS

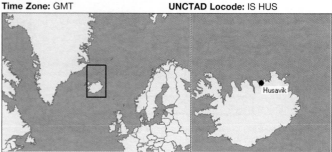

Principal Facilities:

P		G	C		L	B		A

Authority: Husavik Hofn, IS-640 Husavik, Iceland, *Tel:* +354 464 1575, *Fax:* +354 464 2275, *Email:* port@husavik.is

Officials: Harbour Master: Einar Njalsson.

Port Security: ISPS compliant

Documentation: Vessels arriving from countries outside the Schengen convention must submit their crew list to the Icelandic coastguard 24 h prior to arrival

Anchorage: Anchorage can be obtained outside the main harbour in depths ranging from 40 m to 80 m

Pilotage: No registered pilot, but if required Tel: +354 464 1575 or 1196

Traffic: 1997, 167 vessels, 66 690 t of cargo handled

Accommodation:

Name	Remarks
Husavik	See [1] below

[1] *Husavik:* The harbour has berths for vessels up to 5000-6000 gt. Max depth 6.8 m Container storage of 5000 m2 and cranes are available

Storage: Warehousing and refrigeration space available

Mechanical Handling Equipment:

Location	Type
Husavik	Mobile Cranes

Cargo Worked: 500-700 t/day

Bunkering: ExxonMobil Marine Fuels, Mailpoint 31, ExxonMobil House, Ermyn Way, Leatherhead, Surrey KT22 8UX, United Kingdom, *Tel:* +44 1372 222 000, *Fax:* +44 1372 223 922, *Email:* marine.fuels@exxonmobil.com, *Website:* www.exxonmobil.com – *Grades:* IF40; MGO – *Delivery Mode:* truck

Repair & Maintenance: Grimur h.f., Husavik, Iceland, *Tel:* +354 464 1055, *Fax:* +354 464 2355 Repair facilities

Shipping Agents: Hf Eimskipafelag Islands, IS-640 Husavik, Iceland, *Tel:* +354 464 1020, *Fax:* +354 464 1006, *Email:* sah@nett.is, *Website:* www.eimskip.com

Medical Facilities: Hospital and doctors available at all hours

Airport: Adaldalsflugvollur, 12 km

Lloyd's Agent: Konnun ehf, Hesthals 6-8, 110 Reykjavik, Iceland, *Tel:* +354 570 9240, *Fax:* +354 570 9004, *Email:* konnun@frumherji.is, *Website:* www.frumherji.is/konnun

HVAMMSTANGI

Lat 65° 24' N; Long 20° 57' W.

Admiralty Chart: 2899	**Admiralty Pilot:** 11
Time Zone: GMT	**UNCTAD Locode:** IS HVM

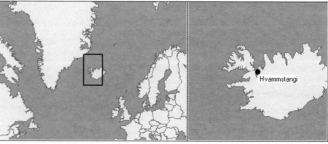

Principal Facilities:

			G			B			

Authority: Hvammstangahreppur, Klapparstig 4, IS-530 Hvammstangi, Iceland, *Tel:* +354 5 451 2753, *Fax:* +354 5 451 2307, *Email:* hofn@hunathing.is, *Website:* www.hunathing.is

Officials: Harbour Master: Petur Arnarson.

Documentation: Vessels arriving from countries outside the Schengen convention must submit their crew list to the Icelandic coastguard 24 h prior to arrival

Approach: Channel depth over 6.0 m

Pilotage: Not available

Maximum Vessel Dimensions: 80 m loa, 5.5 m d

Accommodation:

Name	Length (m)	Depth (m)
Hvammstangi Nordurbryggja	70	6

Bunkering: Hose on wharf, by tank truck
ExxonMobil Marine Fuels, Mailpoint 31, ExxonMobil House, Ermyn Way, Leatherhead, Surrey KT22 8UX, United Kingdom, *Tel:* +44 1372 222 000, *Fax:* +44 1372 223 922, *Email:* marine.fuels@exxonmobil.com, *Website:* www.exxonmobil.com – *Grades:* IF40; MGO – *Delivery Mode:* truck

Repair & Maintenance: Minor repairs only

Shipping Agents: Hf Eimskipafelag Islands, Hvammstangi, Iceland, *Tel:* +354 451 2370, *Fax:* +354 451 2354, *Website:* www.eimskip.com

Medical Facilities: Available

Lloyd's Agent: Konnun ehf, Hesthals 6-8, 110 Reykjavik, Iceland, *Tel:* +354 570 9240, *Fax:* +354 570 9004, *Email:* konnun@frumherji.is, *Website:* www.frumherji.is/konnun

ISAFJORDUR

Lat 66° 5' N; Long 23° 6' W.

Admiralty Chart: 2976	**Admiralty Pilot:** 11
Time Zone: GMT	**UNCTAD Locode:** IS ISA

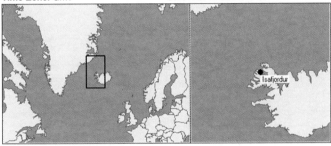

Principal Facilities:

P		G	C		L	B		T	A	

Authority: Port of Isafjordur, Harbour Building, IS-400 Isafjordur, Iceland, *Tel:* +354 456 3295, *Fax:* +354 456 4523, *Email:* hafnarstjori@isafjordur.is, *Website:* www.isafjordur.is/port

Officials: Harbour Master: Gudmundur M. Kristjansson.

Port Security: ISPS compliant

Approach: Narrow channel to Asgeirsbakki

Anchorage: Anchorage can be obtained in depths ranging from 12 m to 14 m

Pilotage: Compulsory. Pilot station in pos 66° 06' 42" N; 23° 04' 06" W

Radio Frequency: Radio station call sign TFZ, 2182 kHz, VHF Channel 16. Harbour service working on VHF Channel 12

Weather: Polar ice can prevent navigation during the early part of the year

Tides: STHW 2.5 m, STLW 0.1 m, NTHW 2.1 m, NTLW 0.3 m

Maximum Vessel Dimensions: 30 000 gt, 200 m loa, 7.5 m draft

Principal Imports and Exports: Imports: General cargo, Oil. Exports: Fish.

Working Hours: 24 h/day if needed

Accommodation:

Name	Length (m)	Depth (m)	Remarks
Isafjordur			Landlocked harbour
Asgeirsbakki Wharf	260	5–8	See [1] below
Sundahofn	55	4	See [2] below
Sundabakki	220	7–8	See [3] below

[1]*Asgeirsbakki Wharf:* Tanker facilities available for vessels up to 3000 gt with a depth of 5-6 m alongside
[2]*Sundahofn:* Tanker facilities available with a berthing length of 12 m and a depth of 4 m
[3]*Sundabakki:* Vessels up to 30 000 gt can be accommodated with a draft of 7.5 m. General cargo & containers

Storage: Two warehouses are available

Mechanical Handling Equipment:

Location	Type	Capacity (t)	Qty
Isafjordur	Mult-purp. Cranes	2	5
Isafjordur	Mobile Cranes	40	1

Bunkering: ExxonMobil Marine Fuels, Mailpoint 31, ExxonMobil House, Ermyn Way, Leatherhead, Surrey KT22 8UX, United Kingdom, *Tel:* +44 1372 222 000, *Fax:* +44 1372 223 922, *Email:* marine.fuels@exxonmobil.com, *Website:* www.exxonmobil.com – *Grades:* IF40; MGO – *Delivery Mode:* truck

Waste Reception Facilities: Garbage containers on every wharf. Waste reception for dirty ballast, sludge and chemical waste

Towage: One small tug of 26 gt available

Repair & Maintenance: Skipasmidastodin, Sudurtangi 6, 400 Isafjordur, Iceland, *Tel:* +354 456 3899, *Fax:* +354 456 4471, *Email:* skipas@snerpa.is Slipway for vessels up to 600 gt
Velsmidsan Prymur H.F., Isafjordur, Iceland, *Tel:* +354 456 3711, *Fax:* +354 456 4701 Slipway for vessels up to 600 gt

Shipping Agents: Hf Eimskipafelag Islands, Eyrarskala vid Sundahofn, IS-400 Isafjordur, Iceland, *Tel:* +354 450 5100, *Fax:* +354 450 5109, *Email:* jph@eimskip.is, *Website:* www.eimskip.com

Medical Facilities: Hospital in the town and doctors are available

Airport: Isafjardarflugvollur, 8 km

Lloyd's Agent: Konnun ehf, Hesthals 6-8, 110 Reykjavik, Iceland, *Tel:* +354 570 9240, *Fax:* +354 570 9004, *Email:* konnun@frumherji.is, *Website:* www.frumherji.is/konnun

KEFLAVIK

Lat 64° 0' N; Long 22° 33' W.

Admiralty Chart: 2734	**Admiralty Pilot:** 11
Time Zone: GMT	**UNCTAD Locode:** IS KEF

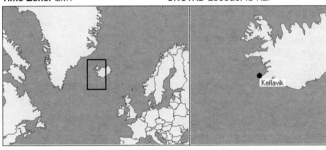

Principal Facilities:

		G		L	B		T	A	

Authority: Port of Keflavik, Vikurbraut 11, IS-230 Keflavik, Iceland, *Tel:* +354 421 4099, *Fax:* +354 421 2666, *Email:* hass@hass.is, *Website:* www.hass.is

Officials: Managing Director: Petur Johannsson, *Email:* petur@hass.is.

Port Security: ISPS compliant. Harbour area is marked by a fence

Documentation: Vessels arriving from countries outside the Schengen convention must submit their crew list to the Icelandic coastguard 24 h prior to arrival

Approach: Entrance is easy at all times

Anchorage: Anchorage can be obtained outside the harbour in a depth of 27 m; good holding ground

Pilotage: Compulsory for vessels over 100 gt. Pilot available day and night, is reached via Reykjavik radio and boards vessel one mile outside Vatnsnes

Radio Frequency: VHF Channel 12

Tides: Range of tide 4.8 m

Maximum Vessel Dimensions: 180 m loa

Working Hours: Office hours 0800-1700. Standby duty 24 h

Accommodation:

Name	Length (m)	Draught (m)	Remarks
Keflavik Quay	165	7–13	See [1] below

[1]*Keflavik:* Floating dock available for cruise vessels and shorter quays for small vessels

Mechanical Handling Equipment:

Location	Type
Keflavik	Mult-purp. Cranes

Bunkering: Fuel oil available from hose and truck
ExxonMobil Marine Fuels, Mailpoint 31, ExxonMobil House, Ermyn Way, Leatherhead, Surrey KT22 8UX, United Kingdom, *Tel:* +44 1372 222 000, *Fax:* +44 1372 223 922, *Email:* marine.fuels@exxonmobil.com, *Website:* www.exxonmobil.com – *Grades:* IF40; MGO – *Delivery Mode:* truck

Towage: Can be arranged

Repair & Maintenance: Minor repairs only

Airport: Keflavik International Airport, 6 km

Lloyd's Agent: Konnun ehf, Hesthals 6-8, 110 Reykjavik, Iceland, *Tel:* +354 570 9240, *Fax:* +354 570 9004, *Email:* konnun@frumherji.is, *Website:* www.frumherji.is/konnun

NESKAUPSTADUR

Lat 65° 9' N; Long 13° 41' W.

Admiralty Chart: 2901	**Admiralty Pilot:** 11
Time Zone: GMT	**UNCTAD Locode:** IS NES

Key to Principal Facilities:—		
A=Airport	**C**=Containers	**G**=General Cargo
B=Bunkers	**D**=Dry Dock	**L**=Cruise
P=Petroleum	**R**=Ro/Ro	**Y**=Dry Bulk
Q=Other Liquid Bulk	**T**=Towage (where available from port)	

Principal Facilities:

P		G	C		L	B		A

Authority: Fjardabyggd Port Authority, Port of Neskaupstadur, Egilsbraut 1, IS-740 Neskaupstadur, Iceland, *Tel:* +354 477 1333, *Fax:* +354 477 1440, *Email:* nhofn@fjardabyggd.is, *Website:* www.fjardabyggd.is

Officials: Port Director: Steinthor Petursson, *Email:* steinthor.petursson@fjardabyggd.is.

Port Security: ISPS compliant

Documentation: Vessels arriving from countries outside the Schengen convention must submit their crew list to the Icelandic coastguard 24 h prior to arrival

Approach: Clear approach in mid fjord

Anchorage: Anchorage can be obtained anywhere in the fjord in depths of about 35 m

Pilotage: Compulsory for vessels over 100 m loa and all vessels carrying dangerous cargoes. Pilot station is in pos 65° 09.5' N; 13° 39.0' W

Radio Frequency: Nesradio, call sign TFM, 2182 kHz. VHF Channel 16 (calling), working Channels 23, 25, 26 and 27

Weather: Heavy squalls can descend from the mountains

Tides: Range of tide 1.5 m

Maximum Vessel Dimensions: 150 m loa, 7000 dwt

Principal Imports and Exports: Exports: Fish products.

Accommodation:

Name	Length (m)	Depth (m)	Remarks
Neskaupstadur			
Village Harbour Pier	70	7–8	Warehouse available
Main Industrial Harbour	570	7–8	Fishmeal & fish processing plant nearby

Bunkering: Diesel and fuel oil is available by pipeline and road tanker ExxonMobil Marine Fuels, Mailpoint 31, ExxonMobil House, Ermyn Way, Leatherhead, Surrey KT22 8UX, United Kingdom, *Tel:* +44 1372 222 000, *Fax:* +44 1372 223 922, *Email:* marine.fuels@exxonmobil.com – *Website:* www.exxonmobil.com – *Grades:* IF40; MGO – *Delivery Mode:* truck

Towage: Available

Repair & Maintenance: Minor repairs can be effected. Slipway for vessels up to 600 t

Shipping Agents: Hf Eimskipafelag Islands, Egilsbraut 6, IS-740 Neskaupstadur, Iceland, *Tel:* +354 477 1190, *Fax:* +354 477 1090, *Email:* ibd@eimskip.is, *Website:* www.eimskip.com

Medical Facilities: Neskaupstadur District Hospital

Airport: Local airport, 500 m

Lloyd's Agent: Konnun ehf, Hesthals 6-8, 110 Reykjavik, Iceland, *Tel:* +354 570 9240, *Fax:* +354 570 9004, *Email:* konnun@frumherji.is, *Website:* www.frumherji.is/konnun

NORDFJORDUR

alternate name, see Neskaupstadur

REYKJAVIK

Lat 64° 8' N; Long 21° 56' W.

Admiralty Chart: 2734/2735	**Admiralty Pilot:** 11
Time Zone: GMT	**UNCTAD Locode:** IS REY

Principal Facilities:

P	Q	Y	G	C		L	B		T	A

Authority: Associated Icelandic Ports, Tryggvagata 17, IS-101 Reykjavik, Iceland, *Tel:* +354 525 8900, *Fax:* +354 525 8990, *Email:* hofnin@faxaports.is, *Website:* www.faxaports.is

Officials: Port Director: Gisli Gislason, *Tel:* +354 525 8910, *Email:* gislig@faxaports.is.
Marketing Director: Agust Agustson, *Tel:* +354 525 8904, *Email:* agag@faxaports.is.
Harbour Master: Thorvaldur Gudmundsson, *Tel:* +354 525 8931, *Email:* valdi@faxaports.is.

Port Security: ISPS compliant

Documentation: Vessels arriving from countries outside the Schengen convention must submit their crew list to the Icelandic coastguard 24 h prior to arrival

Approach: The approach to the harbour is unrestricted and ice free all the year round

Anchorage: Good anchorage in roads for bigger vessels at Kollafjordur 2.4 km N of Engey lighthouse. Anchorage prohibited in neighbourhood of entrance

Pilotage: Compulsory. Vessels must notify Harbour Office 24 h before ETA. For pilot at least three hours before ETA through VHF Channel 12. Pilot boards and is dropped off at Lightbuoy No.7

Radio Frequency: VHF Channel 12 and Channel 17 working frequency

Weather: Prevailing winds from SE and E, but strong gales may be expected from N and NE. The harbour is easily accessible under severe weather conditions

Tides: 0.22 m MLWST, 2.13 m MW, 3.99 m MHWST, 2.98 m MHWNT, 1.32 m MLWNT

Traffic: 2006, 2 182 724 t of cargo handled, 74 cruise vessels

Maximum Vessel Dimensions: 50 000 dwt, 8.0 m draft, 240 m loa

Principal Imports and Exports: Imports: Building materials, Consumer goods, Grain, Petroleum products. Exports: Fish, Fish products.

Working Hours: Normally 8 h or two shifts of 8 h

Accommodation: Container & ro/ro facilities: Two terminals in Sunda Harbour, equipped with a container gantry crane of 32.5 t cap and a floating linkspan for ro/ro vessels at the Eimskip 24 ha terminal. The Samband Line 10 ha terminal is operated with mobile cranes. Container handling in both terminals is by front lift trucks
Tanker facilities: Terminal at Orfirisey for petroleum products accommodating tankers up to 45 000 dwt with depth of 12 m at moorings. Berth for coastal tankers at Eyjargardur-Orfirisey Terminal

Name	Length (m)	Depth (m)	Remarks
Reykjavik			See [1] below
Sunda Harbour			See [2] below
Vatnagardar	780	8.3	See [3] below
Kleppsvik	550	7–8	See [4] below
Grafarvogur		4.5	See [5] below
Eidsvik			See [6] below
Skarfabakki	450	12	Cargo & cruise vessels

[1]*Reykjavik:* Old Harbour: Protected by two moles, leaving an entrance of 100 m width. The harbour is mainly a fishing harbour where coastal and passenger traffic is also served. Quayage of about 2900 m, of which 600 m is for smaller fishing craft. Depth at entrance is 7 m MLWST. Larger vessels preferably berthed at HW. Depths at quays 6-8 m MLWST. Bottom is sand and mud
[2]*Sunda Harbour:* Entrance to harbour not restricted and depth of water is more than 8 m MLWST
[3]*Vatnagardar:* Containerised cargo is handled. A special quay for grain
[4]*Kleppsvik:* Approach channel 50 m wide, dredged to 7 m MLWST. Containerised cargo is handled
[5]*Grafarvogur:* Approach channel dredged to 4 m MLWST. Harbour is used for the discharging and storing of cement, gravel and asphalt for industries in the vicinity
[6]*Eidsvik:* A deep water quay for the State Fertilizer Plant is situated at Eidsvik

Storage: There are also bonded warehouses

Location	Covered (m²)	Cold (m³)
Reykjavik	50000	3000

Mechanical Handling Equipment:

Location	Type	Capacity (t)	Qty
Reykjavik	Mobile Cranes	100	20

Cargo Worked: 2500 t/day

Bunkering: Gas and fuel oil available
Oiluverzlun Islands HF, Sundagardar 2, IS-104 Reykjavik, Iceland, *Tel:* +354 5151 000, *Fax:* +354 5151 010, *Email:* olis@olis.is, *Website:* www.olis.is
Olis Iceland Oil, Sundagardar 2, 104 Reykjavik, Iceland, *Tel:* +354 5151 000, *Fax:* +354 5151 210, *Email:* olis@olis.is, *Website:* www.olis.is
Skeljungur HF, Skeljungur HF, P O Box 8740, 128 Reykjavik, Iceland, *Tel:* +354 5603 800, *Fax:* +354 5603 888, *Email:* thorsteinn@shell.com, *Website:* www.shell.com
Skeljungur HF, Holmaslod 8, IS-101 Reykjavik, Iceland, *Tel:* +354 4443 000, *Fax:* +354 4443 001, *Email:* skeljungur@skeljungur.is, *Website:* www.skeljungur.is
ExxonMobil Marine Fuels, Mailpoint 31, ExxonMobil House, Ermyn Way, Leatherhead, Surrey KT22 8UX, United Kingdom, *Tel:* +44 1372 222 000, *Fax:* +44 1372 223 922, *Email:* marine.fuels@exxonmobil.com, *Website:* www.exxonmobil.com – *Grades:* IF40; MGO – *Delivery Mode:* truck
Gara ehf, Baejarhrauni 2, IS-220 Hafnarfjordur, Iceland, *Tel:* +354 581 1688, *Fax:* +354 581 1685, *Email:* gara@centrum.is
Oiluverzlun Islands HF, Sundagardar 2, IS-104 Reykjavik, Iceland, *Tel:* +354 5151 000, *Fax:* +354 5151 010, *Email:* olis@olis.is, *Website:* www.olis.is
OW Icebunker Ltd, Gasvaerksvej 46-48, DK-9000 Aalborg, Denmark, *Tel:* +45 7020 4049, *Fax:* +45 7020 4051, *Email:* owi@owicebunker.com, *Website:* www.owicebunker.com – *Grades:* GO; IFO-30cSt – *Parcel Size:* no min, max – *Rates:* barge 60t/h, truck 30t/h – *Notice:* 48 hours – *Delivery Mode:* barge, truck

Skeljungur HF, Holmaslod 8, IS-101 Reykjavik, Iceland, *Tel:* +354 4443 000, *Fax:* +354 4443 001, *Email:* skeljungur@skeljungur.is, *Website:* www.skeljungur.is

Towage: Two 10 t bollard pull, one 17 t bollard pull and one 39.5 t bollard pull tugs are available. Rates according to size of vessel and time

Repair & Maintenance: Gjorvi h.f., Grandagardur 18, 101 Reykjavik, Iceland, *Tel:* +354 552 8922, *Fax:* +354 562 1740, *Email:* gjorvi@media.is
Landssmidjan h.f., Solvholsgotu 13, Reykjavik, Iceland, *Tel:* +354 552 0680, *Fax:* +354 551 9199
Stalsmidjan ehf., Myrargata 10-12, P O Box 940, IS-121 Reykjavik, Iceland, *Tel:* +354 552 4400, *Fax:* +354 552 5504, *Email:* stalsmidjan@stalsmidjan.is, *Website:* www.stalsmidjan.is

Shipping Agents: Hf Eimskipafelag Islands, Korngoraum 2, IS-104 Reykjavik, Iceland, *Tel:* +354 5257000, *Fax:* +354 5257709, *Email:* eimskip@eimskip.is, *Website:* www.eimskip.com
S.F. Gudjonsson Gunnar, Harbour Building, Tryggvagotu, P O Box 290, IS-121 Reykjavik, Iceland, *Tel:* +354 562 9200, *Fax:* +354 562 3116, *Email:* ggship@vortex.is
MS Armann Shipbrokers, P O Box 290, Reykjavik, Iceland, *Tel:* +354 562 9200, *Fax:* +354 562 3116, *Email:* armann@vortex.is
Nesskip H/f, Nesskip's House, Austurstrond 1, P O Box 176, IS-170 Seltjarnarnes, Iceland, *Tel:* +354 563 9900, *Fax:* +354 563 9919, *Email:* nesskip@nesskip.is, *Website:* www.nesskip.is
Samskip H/f (Samband Line Ltd), Kjalarvogur, IS-104 Reykjavik, Iceland, *Tel:* +354 458 8000, *Fax:* +354 458 8100, *Email:* samskip@samskip.is, *Website:* www.samskip.com

Stevedoring Companies: Hf Eimskipafelag Islands, Korngoraum 2, IS-104 Reykjavik, Iceland, *Tel:* +354 5257000, *Fax:* +354 5257709, *Email:* eimskip@eimskip.is, *Website:* www.eimskip.com
Londun hf., Kjalarvogi 21, P O Box 1517, IS-121 Reykjavik, Iceland, *Tel:* +354 552 9844, *Fax:* +354 562 9844, *Email:* londun@londun.is, *Website:* www.londun.is
Samskip H/f (Samband Line Ltd), Kjalarvogur, IS-104 Reykjavik, Iceland, *Tel:* +354 458 8000, *Fax:* +354 458 8100, *Email:* samskip@samskip.is, *Website:* www.samskip.com

Surveyors: Bureau Veritas, c/o Gudfinnur G. Johnsen, Eskkiihlid 6, IS-105 Reykjavik, Iceland, *Tel:* +354 553 3313, *Fax:* +354 553 3313, *Email:* isl_rjv@is.bureauveritas.com, *Website:* www.bureauveritas.com
Det Norske Veritas A/S, Fjardargata 13-15, IS-220 Hafnarfjordur, Iceland, *Tel:* +354 551 4150, *Fax:* +354 561 5150, *Email:* reykjavik@dnv.com, *Website:* www.dnv.com
Germanischer Lloyd, Hafnarhvoll, Tryggvagata 11, IS-101 Reykjavik, Iceland, *Tel:* +354 552 2851, *Fax:* +354 562 2878, *Email:* gl-reykjavik@gl-group.com, *Website:* www.gl-group.com
E. Hermannsson, Klettagardar 11, P O Box 814, IS-121 Reykjavik, Iceland, *Tel:* +354 568 3100, *Fax:* +354 568 3075, *Email:* einarhe@centrum.is
Konnun ehf, Hesthals 6-8, 110 Reykjavik, Iceland, *Tel:* +354 570 9240, *Fax:* +354 570 9004, *Email:* konnun@frumherji.is, *Website:* www.frumherji.is/konnun
Nippon Kaiji Kyokai, P O Box 814, IS-121 Reykjavik, Iceland, *Tel:* +354 568 3100, *Fax:* +354 568 3075, *Website:* www.classnk.or.jp

Airport: Reykjavik Airport, 2 km

Lloyd's Agent: Konnun ehf, Hesthals 6-8, 110 Reykjavik, Iceland, *Tel:* +354 570 9240, *Fax:* +354 570 9004, *Email:* konnun@frumherji.is, *Website:* www.frumherji.is/konnun

SEYDHISFJORDUR

Lat 65° 15' N; Long 13° 55' W.

Admiralty Chart: 2901	**Admiralty Pilot:** 11
Time Zone: GMT	**UNCTAD Locode:** IS SEY

Principal Facilities:

P		G	C	R	L	B		A	

Authority: Port of Seydisfjordur, Hafnargata 44, IS-710 Seydisfjordur, Iceland, *Tel:* +354 472 1424, *Fax:* +354 472 1574, *Email:* port@sfk.is, *Website:* www.sfk.is/hofnin

Officials: Harbour Master: Olafur Hr. Sigurdusson, *Tel:* +354 472 2300, *Email:* oli@sfk.is.

Port Security: ISPS compliant. Port Security Officer: Johann P. Hansson

Documentation: Vessels arriving from countries outside the Schengen convention must submit their crew list to the Icelandic coastguard 24 h prior to arrival

Pilotage: Available on request

Radio Frequency: Harbour on VHF Channel 12 and Nesradio on VHF Channel 16

Tides: LW 0.12 m, HW 1.71 m

Principal Imports and Exports: Imports: Commercial goods, Oil, Salt. Exports: Fish products.

Working Hours: 0800-1700

Accommodation:

Name	Length (m)	Depth (m)	Remarks
Seydhisfjordur			The port has three privately owned tanker terminals
Fjardarhofn	150	6.5	There is one main container and ro/ro terminal
Engros	65	6.5	
Baejarbryggja	45	6.5	
Fiskvinnslubryggja	60	6.5	

Storage: Privately owned refrigerated space

Mechanical Handling Equipment:

Location	Type	Capacity (t)	Qty
Seydisfjordur	Mult-purp. Cranes	35	1
Seydisfjordur	Mult-purp. Cranes	25	1

Bunkering: Loading by hoses, tank trucks or direct from storage tanks

Waste Reception Facilities: Garbage containers on all main terminals. Dirty ballast and sludge disposal available on request

Repair & Maintenance: Stalstjornur ehf, Fjardargotu, 710 Seydisfjordur, Iceland, *Tel:* +354 472 1300, *Fax:* +354 472 1404, *Email:* saevar@stal.is, *Website:* www.stal.is

Shipping Agents: Hf Eimskipafelag Islands, Fjardargotu 8, IS-710 Seydisfjordur, Iceland, *Tel:* +354 472 1600, *Fax:* +354 472 1660, *Email:* info@eimskip.is, *Website:* www.eimskip.com

Medical Facilities: Hospital available

Airport: Egilstadaflugvollur, 30 km

Lloyd's Agent: Konnun ehf, Hesthals 6-8, 110 Reykjavik, Iceland, *Tel:* +354 570 9240, *Fax:* +354 570 9004, *Email:* konnun@frumherji.is, *Website:* www.frumherji.is/konnun

SIGLUFJORDUR

Lat 66° 12' N; Long 18° 52' W.

Admiralty Chart: 2899	**Admiralty Pilot:** 11
Time Zone: GMT	**UNCTAD Locode:** IS SIG

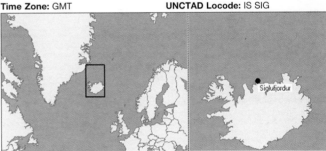

Principal Facilities:

		G		B	T	A	

Authority: Captain of the Port, Havegur 58, IS-580 Siglufjordur, Iceland, *Tel:* +354 464 9177, *Fax:* +354 464 9179, *Email:* shs@siglo.is

Officials: Harbour Master: Sigurdur Sigurdsson.

Port Security: ISPS compliant

Documentation: Vessels arriving from countries outside the Schengen convention must submit their crew list to the Icelandic coastguard 24 h prior to arrival

Anchorage: Anchorage can be obtained E of the harbour in depths ranging from 25 m to 30 m with good holding ground. Gales from the N cause heavy seas, so vessels may seek anchorage in small bay SW of Siglunes

Pilotage: Available. Pilot meets vessel about 400 m from harbour entrance

Radio Frequency: Siglufjordur Radio, call sign TFX, 2182 kHz. VHF Channels 16, 24, 26 and 27

Maximum Vessel Dimensions: Approx 120 m loa

Principal Imports and Exports: Exports: Seafood.

Working Hours: 0700-1200, 1300-1700. Overtime can be arranged

Accommodation:

Name	Length (m)	Depth (m)	Remarks
Siglufjordur			See [1] below
Hafnargardur	125	6	Situated on the S side of the N mole
Londunarbryggja Quay	100	7	
Baejarbryggjan (Town Quay)	100	6	
Togarabryggja Quay	60	6	
Ingvarsbryggja Quay	65	7	

[1] *Siglufjordur:* There are several piers and wharves inside the N mole, four quays being used by larger vessels have depths up to 7 m at LW

Bunkering: Fuel available in general grades only

Towage: Available

Repair & Maintenance: Moderate sized vessels can be repaired. Diver available

Shipping Agents: Hf Eimskipafelag Islands, Tjarnargata 14, IS-580 Siglufjordur, Iceland, *Tel:* +354 467 1129, *Fax:* +354 467 1239, *Email:* tormod@simnet.is, *Website:* www.eimskip.com

Key to Principal Facilities:—			
A=Airport	**C**=Containers	**G**=General Cargo	**P**=Petroleum	**R**=Ro/Ro	**Y**=Dry Bulk
B=Bunkers	**D**=Dry Dock	**L**=Cruise	**Q**=Other Liquid Bulk	**T**=Towage (where available from port)	

Medical Facilities: A hospital is available

Airport: Akureyri Airport, 64km

Lloyd's Agent: Konnun ehf, Hesthals 6-8, 110 Reykjavik, Iceland, *Tel:* +354 570 9240, *Fax:* +354 570 9004, *Email:* konnun@frumherji.is, *Website:* www.frumherji.is/konnun

STODHVARFJORDUR

Lat 64° 50' N; Long 13° 50' W.

Admiralty Chart: 2901	**Admiralty Pilot:** 11
Time Zone: GMT	**UNCTAD Locode:** IS STD

Principal Facilities:

			G					A	

Authority: Stodvarhreppur, Skolabraut 10, IS-755 Stodvarfjordur, Iceland, *Tel:* +354 475 8967, *Fax:* +354 475 8967

Port Security: ISPS compliant

Documentation: Vessels arriving from countries outside the Schengen convention must submit their crew list to the Icelandic coastguard 24 h prior to arrival

Pilotage: Available with advance notice

Maximum Vessel Dimensions: 7 m max d

Working Hours: 24 h if needed

Accommodation:

Name	Length (m)	Depth (m)
Stodhvarfjordur		
Pier	85	7

Medical Facilities: Available

Airport: Egilsstaoaflugvollur, 100 km

Lloyd's Agent: Konnun ehf, Hesthals 6-8, 110 Reykjavik, Iceland, *Tel:* +354 570 9240, *Fax:* +354 570 9004, *Email:* konnun@frumherji.is, *Website:* www.frumherji.is/konnun

STRAUMSVIK

Lat 64° 3' N; Long 22° 3' W.

Admiralty Chart: 2735	**Admiralty Pilot:** 11
Time Zone: GMT	**UNCTAD Locode:** IS STR

Principal Facilities:

	Q	Y	G			B		A	

Authority: Hafnarfjordur Port Authority, Oseyrarbraut 4, IS-220 Hafnarfjordur, Iceland, *Tel:* +354 414 2300, *Fax:* +354 414 2301, *Email:* port@hafnarfjordur.is, *Website:* www.hafnarfjardarhofn.is

Officials: Port Director: Mar Sveinbjornsson, *Email:* mar@hafnarfjordur.is. Harbour Master: Capt Kristinn Aadnegard, *Email:* kristinn.a@hafnarfjordur.is.

Port Security: ISPS compliant

Documentation: Vessels arriving from countries outside the Schengen convention must submit their crew list to the Icelandic coastguard 24 h prior to arrival

Approach: Vessels of, or exceeding 7 m draft approaching Hafnarfjordur and Straumsvik are warned that shoals exist in pos 64° 04' 48" N; 22° 08' 48" W, or 1.5 miles in 260° direction from the Valhusagrunn buoy

Anchorage: For vessels awaiting pilots anchorage can be obtained 1 mile SE of the outer buoy

Pilotage: Compulsory for foreign vessels. Pilot usually boards 1 mile SSE of the outer buoy (Valhusagrunn, red). Smaller vessels and Master's familiar with the port can proceed to the inner buoy (Helgasker, green)

Radio Frequency: VHF Channel 14

Weather: See under www.vedur.is

Tides: Tidal range 4.5 m

Maximum Vessel Dimensions: Max draft 11.7 m

Principal Imports and Exports: Imports: Alumina, Liquefied gas. Exports: Aluminium.

Working Hours: Alumina 24 h, general cargo in two shifts

Accommodation:

Name	Length (m)	Depth (m)	Remarks
Straumsvik			See [1] below
Berth A	220	12	Aluminium factory & LPG vessels
Berth B	100	10	General & bulk cargo

[1]*Straumsvik:* Entrance is shelterd by a 300 m breakwater. The entrance channel is 160 m wide in depth of 10 m

Storage: Dry storages 3500 m2, 15 000 m3

Mechanical Handling Equipment:

Location	Type	Capacity (t)
Straumsvik	Mobile Cranes	300

Bunkering: Oil available by barge

Waste Reception Facilities: Collection service for waste oil and garbage disposal arranged by ship's agent

Medical Facilities: 24 h emergency service, Tel: 112. National Hospital, 9 km

Airport: Reykjavik Airport, 15 km

Lloyd's Agent: Konnun ehf, Hesthals 6-8, 110 Reykjavik, Iceland, *Tel:* +354 570 9240, *Fax:* +354 570 9004, *Email:* konnun@frumherji.is, *Website:* www.frumherji.is/konnun

SUNDA HARBOUR

harbour area, see under Reykjavik

THORLAKSHOFN

Lat 63° 51' N; Long 21° 20' W.

Admiralty Chart: 2733	**Admiralty Pilot:** 11
Time Zone: GMT	**UNCTAD Locode:** IS THH

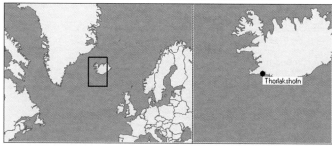

Principal Facilities:

		G			B		A	

Authority: Thorlakshofn Port Authority, Port Office, IS-815 Thorlakshofn, Iceland, *Tel:* +354 483 3659, *Fax:* +354 483 3528, *Email:* hofn@olfus.is, *Website:* www.olfus.is

Officials: Harbour Master: Kristin Son.

Port Security: ISPS compliant

Accommodation:

Name	Remarks
Thorlakshofn	See [1] below

[1]*Thorlakshofn:* Small harbour with a depth of 6 m at the entrance, primarily used for fishing vessels. Anchorage for commercial vessels may be obtained off the harbour in depths ranging from 11 m to 15 m; good holding ground
Vessels of up to 6800 dwt have been reported

Bunkering: ExxonMobil Marine Fuels, Mailpoint 31, ExxonMobil House, Ermyn Way, Leatherhead, Surrey KT22 8UX, United Kingdom, *Tel:* +44 1372 222 000, *Fax:* +44 1372 223 922, *Email:* marine.fuels@exxonmobil.com, *Website:* www.exxonmobil.com – *Grades:* IF40; MGO – *Delivery Mode:* truck

Airport: Reykjavik Airport, 40 km

Lloyd's Agent: Konnun ehf, Hesthals 6-8, 110 Reykjavik, Iceland, *Tel:* +354 570 9240, *Fax:* +354 570 9004, *Email:* konnun@frumherji.is, *Website:* www.frumherji.is/konnun

THORSHOFN

Lat 66° 12' N; Long 15° 20' W.

Admiralty Chart: 2900　　　　**Admiralty Pilot:** 11
Time Zone: GMT　　　　　　　**UNCTAD Locode:** IS THO

Principal Facilities:

		G					

Authority: Langaneshafnir, Langanesvegur 2, IS-680 Thorshofn, Iceland, *Tel:* +354 862 5198, *Fax:* +354 468 1323, *Email:* bjorn@langanesbyggd.is, *Website:* www.langanesbyggd.is

Officials: Manager: Bjorn Ingimarsson, *Tel:* +354 468 1220.
Harbour Master: Steinn Karlsson, *Email:* hofn@langanesbyggd.is.

Port Security: ISPS compliant

Documentation: Vessels arriving from countries outside the Schengen convention must submit their crew list to the Icelandic coastguard 24 h prior to arrival

Pilotage: Available

Accommodation:

Name	Remarks
Thorshofn	See [1] below

[1]*Thorshofn:* Trading Station. Harbour has depths ranging from 3.3 m to 5 m. Anchorage for commercial vessels may be obtained in a depth of about 10 m; good holding ground
Vessels of up to 5900 dwt have been reported

Repair & Maintenance: Minor repairs to small craft only can be effected

Medical Facilities: Hospital available

Lloyd's Agent: Konnun ehf, Hesthals 6-8, 110 Reykjavik, Iceland, *Tel:* +354 570 9240, *Fax:* +354 570 9004, *Email:* konnun@frumherji.is, *Website:* www.frumherji.is/konnun

VESTMANNAEYJAR

Lat 63° 26' N; Long 20° 16' W.

Admiralty Chart: 2733/2902　　**Admiralty Pilot:** 11
Time Zone: GMT　　　　　　　**UNCTAD Locode:** IS VES

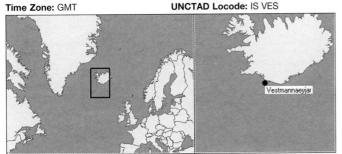

Principal Facilities:

P	Y	G	C		L	B		T	A

Authority: Hafnarstjorn Vestmannaeyja, Skildingavegur 5, 900 Vestmannaeyjar, Iceland, *Tel:* +354 481 1192, *Fax:* +354 481 3115, *Email:* omk@vestmannaeyjar.is, *Website:* www.vestmannaeyjar.is

Officials: Harbour Master: Olafur M. Kristinsson.

Port Security: ISPS compliant. Three port facilities: Binnabryggja-Skai, Fridarhafnarbryggja and Nausthamar

Documentation: Vessels arriving from countries outside the Schengen convention must submit their crew list to the Icelandic coastguard 24 h prior to arrival

Approach: A tortuous channel with high cliffs on the N side and lava flow on the S, leads into the harbour
Depth at entrance between breakwaters is 9 m and at approach to quays is 8 m

Anchorage: Anchorage about 2 km from entrance to harbour and on the N side of the island, depth 28 m to 34 m. Good holding ground

Pilotage: Compulsory. Pilot available 24 h. ETA to be advised by radio with 24 h notice. The pilot station is normally E of the harbour entrance but in SE gales it is N of Heimaey

Radio Frequency: Vestmannaeyjar Radio, call sign TFV, 2182 kHz and VHF Channel 16. Vestmannaeyjar Harbour on VHF Channel 12

Tides: HW and LW occur 43 min earlier than Reykjavik. Spring rise 3 m MLWS, neap rise 2 m MLWS

Maximum Vessel Dimensions: 160 m loa

Principal Imports and Exports: Imports: Goods connected to fishing industry. Exports: Fish products.

Working Hours: Mon-Fri 0800-1700

Accommodation:

Name	Length (m)	Depth (m)	Remarks
Vestmannaeyjar			
Binnabryggja	127	8	Containers
Skai	90	7	Containers
Fridarhofn	210	8	Fish products
Eidi	150	8	
Nausthamar	150	8	Dry bulk & cruise vessels

Storage: Available

Bunkering: Diesel and marine oil available. Loading from quay
ExxonMobil Marine Fuels, Mailpoint 31, ExxonMobil House, Ermyn Way, Leatherhead, Surrey KT22 8UX, United Kingdom, *Tel:* +44 1372 222 000, *Fax:* +44 1372 223 922, *Email:* marine.fuels@exxonmobil.com, *Website:* www.exxonmobil.com – *Grades:* IF40; MGO – *Delivery Mode:* truck

Waste Reception Facilities: Garbage disposal available

Towage: Harbour/sea-going tug of 1000 hp

Repair & Maintenance: Skipalyftan H/f, Vestmannaeyjar, Iceland, *Tel:* +354 488 3550, *Fax:* +354 481 1493

Shipping Agents: Hf Eimskipafelag Islands, Eimskip Vestmannaeyjar, Botni, Frioarhofn, IS-900 Vestmannaeyjar, Iceland, *Tel:* +354 481 3500, *Fax:* +354 481 3501, *Email:* vem@eimskip.is, *Website:* www.eimskip.com

Stevedoring Companies: Hf Eimskipafelag Islands, Eimskip Vestmannaeyjar, Botni, Frioarhofn, IS-900 Vestmannaeyjar, Iceland, *Tel:* +354 481 3500, *Fax:* +354 481 3501, *Email:* vem@eimskip.is, *Website:* www.eimskip.com
Londunarthjonustan, Vestmannaeyjar, Iceland, *Tel:* +354 852 2581

Medical Facilities: Hospital available

Airport: Vestmannaeyjar Airport

Lloyd's Agent: Konnun ehf, Hesthals 6-8, 110 Reykjavik, Iceland, *Tel:* +354 570 9240, *Fax:* +354 570 9004, *Email:* konnun@frumherji.is, *Website:* www.frumherji.is/konnun

VOPNAFJORDUR

Lat 65° 45' N; Long 14° 49' W.

Admiralty Chart: 2900　　　　**Admiralty Pilot:** 11
Time Zone: GMT　　　　　　　**UNCTAD Locode:** IS VPN

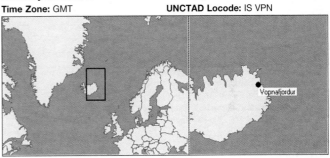

Principal Facilities:

			G					A

Authority: Vopnafjardarhofn, Hamrahlid 15, 690 Vopnafjordur, Iceland, *Tel:* +354 473 1299, *Fax:* +354 473 1559, *Email:* hofn@vopnafjardarhreppur.is, *Website:* www.vopnafjardarhreppur.is

Officials: Harbour Master: Bjorgvin Hreinsson.

Port Security: ISPS compliant

Documentation: Vessels arriving from countries outside the Schengen convention must submit their crew list to the Icelandic coastguard 24 h prior to arrival

Approach: Clear approach to port in mid fjord, irregular depths

Pilotage: Available

Weather: Heavy squalls can descend from the mountains, particularly affecting the S shore of the fjord during southerly winds. Polar ice can be hazardous in the harbour during the end of the winter period

Maximum Vessel Dimensions: 4552 dwt, 95.6 m loa

Accommodation:

Name	Depth (m)	Remarks
Vopnafjordur		See [1] below
Jetty	5.5	
Jetty	6.6	
Jetty	4.3	

[1]*Vopnafjordur:* Trading Station. Harbour with limited accommodation for vessels of up to 3 m d. There are also some small quays

Medical Facilities: Small hospital and a doctor is available

Airport: Egilsstadir Airport, 58 km

Key to Principal Facilities:—			
A=Airport	**C**=Containers	**G**=General Cargo	**P**=Petroleum	**R**=Ro/Ro	**Y**=Dry Bulk
B=Bunkers	**D**=Dry Dock	**L**=Cruise	**Q**=Other Liquid Bulk	**T**=Towage (where available from port)	

Lloyd's Agent: Konnun ehf, Hesthals 6-8, 110 Reykjavik, Iceland, *Tel:* +354 570 9240, *Fax:* +354 570 9004, *Email:* konnun@frumherji.is, *Website:* www.frumherji.is/konnun

INDIA

BALLARD PIER

harbour area, see under Mumbai

BEDI

Lat 22° 33' N; Long 70° 2' E.

Admiralty Chart: 43/673
Time Zone: GMT +5.5 h

Admiralty Pilot: 38
UNCTAD Locode: IN BED

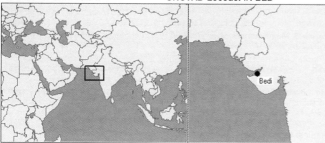

Principal Facilities:

		Y	G			B		T	A	

Authority: Gujarat Maritime Board, Bedi Port, Jamnagar, Gujarat, India 361 009, *Tel:* +91 288 275 5106, *Website:* www.gmbports.org

Officials: Port Officer: Capt Sudhir Chaddha.

Port Security: ISPS compliant

Documentation: Crew list (6 copies), stores list (3 copies), personal property declaration (3 copies), last port clearance, cargo manifest, bills of lading, light dues receipt

Approach: Channel from anchorage to dock basin is 9 km long and dries over low water

Pilotage: Not compulsory. Local guides available on request between Pirotan lighthouse and Rozi anchorage

Radio Frequency: Bedi Radio, call sign VUK 5, frequency 500 kc/s. VHF available keeping watch on Channel 16 between 0900-1200, 1500-2000

Weather: Strong winds and heavy swell likely in the afternoons during the monsoon season, May 15 to September 14

Tides: Range of tide ST 1.89 m to 5.94 m, NT 1.04 m to 5.39 m

Principal Imports and Exports: Imports: Dates, Fertilizer, Vegetable oil. Exports: Agricultural products, Oil Cakes, Salt.

Working Hours: 24 h/day

Accommodation:

Name	Remarks
Bedi	See [1] below

[1]*Bedi:* All weather tidal lighterage port. Anchorage is 7 miles from Bedi port and 4 miles from Rozi port, which is part of Bedi. Vessels work cargo in the anchorage zone in a radius of 2 nautical miles NNE of Kalvan Light; depths range from 8 m to 15 m
At Bedi, a basin 304.8 m by 76.19 m for unloading and loading barges, sailing vessels etc. Five quays of total length 2075 m. Additional loading quays at Rozi near mouth of Bedi Creek totalling 366 m with road connections, storage space, cranes and water
The facilities at Bedi and Rozi ports provide a total of 26 loading points for barges. Numerous barges available (port and private) with cap of 100-500 t
Fourteen export vessels and three import vessels are permitted to work at a time during non-monsoon period (Oct 11-Jne 9) and ten export vessels and three import vessels are permitted to work at a time during monsoon period (Jne 10-Oct 10)

Storage: Bedi: Transit sheds of 8830 m2, covered storage of 14 600 m2 and open storage of 17 520 m2. Rozi: Transit sheds of 3710 m2, covered storage of 12 760 m2 and open storage of 14 223 m2

Mechanical Handling Equipment:

Location	Type	Capacity (t)	Qty
Bedi	Mobile Cranes	12.5	5

Cargo Worked: Export cargo 750 t/day, Import cargo 1000 t/day. These rates can be enhanced by using private barges, for which prior permission has to be obtained from the Port Authority

Bunkering: M/S Global Fuels & Lubricants Inc., 11-12 Mangal Society, 76C Rafi Ahmed Kidwai Road, King Circle, Mumbai, Maharashtra, India 400 019, *Tel:* +91 22 2374 5987, *Fax:* +91 22 2409 1627, *Email:* globalfuels@vsnl.com, *Website:* www.bunkerindia.com – *Delivery Mode:* barge
Indian Oil Corp. Ltd, Indian Oil Bhavan Head Office, G9 Ali Yavar Jung Marg, Bandra (East), Mumbai, Maharashtra, India 400051, *Tel:* +91 22 2644 7368, *Fax:* +91 22 2642 2434, *Email:* partha_datta@indianoil.co.in, *Website:* www.indianoil.co.in – *Delivery Mode:* barge

Towage: Four tugs available up to 1600 bhp

Repair & Maintenance: Minor repairs undertaken locally by Harshad Engineering Works and Shree Venkatesh Engineering Works

Shipping Agents: Barbados Maritime Agencies Private Ltd, 103, 1st Floor Cams Corner, Bedi Port Road, Jamnagar, Gujarat, India 361002, *Tel:* +91 288 267 3982, *Fax:* +91 288 266 3982, *Email:* barbados@sancharnet.in, *Website:* www.barbados.co.in

Stevedoring Companies: Chowgule Brothers Private Ltd, Chowgule House, 403 Mormugao Harbour, Mormugao, Goa, India 403 803, *Tel:* +91 832 252 5144, *Fax:* +91 832 252 1011, *Email:* info.cb@chowgule.co.in, *Website:* www.chowgulebros.com

Medical Facilities: Available in local hospital

Airport: Jamnagar, 11 km

Railway: Jamnagar Station, 7 km

Lloyd's Agent: Wilson Surveyors and Adjusters Private Ltd, Golden Arcade, II Floor, Room No.209, Plot No.141/142, Sector 8, Gandhidam, Kutch, Gujarat, India 370 201, *Tel:* +91 2836 238333, *Fax:* +91 2836 238333, *Email:* kandla@wilsur.com, *Website:* www.wilsur.com

BELEKERI

Lat 14° 42' N; Long 74° 15' E.

Admiralty Chart: 3464
Time Zone: GMT +5.5 h

Admiralty Pilot: 38
UNCTAD Locode: IN BLK

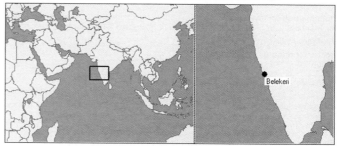

Principal Facilities:

		Y	G							

Authority: Port Conservator, Port Office, Belekeri, Karnataka, India, *Tel:* +91 8382 21342

Pilotage: Not compulsory. Available on request to Port Officer at Karwar

Principal Imports and Exports: Exports: Iron ore, Manganese ore.

Working Hours: Regular office hours from 1000-1730. Overtime extra. Ore loading 24 h/day

Accommodation:

Name	Remarks
Belekeri	See [1] below

[1]*Belekeri:* The anchorage for shallow draught vessels in open roadstead is at Kukra Island, bearing 080° (T), distance 2.4 km in depths of 8.23-8.84 m. Anchorage for deep draught vessels is also at Kukra Island, bearing 080° (T), distance 4 km in depths of 10.6-11.28 m. Two wharves for general cargo with depths alongside of 5 m and 3 m. Shipping operations are suspended during SW Monsoon, May 16-September 15
Iron and manganese ore loaded by lighters to vessels at anchorage. Quay for lighters equipped with two mechanical ore loaders connected to a conveyor belt. Open storage area to hold 1 million t of ore.
No vessels handled from April 1993 onwards as no sufficient draft available for loading barges at jetty on account of no dredging was carried out

Cargo Worked: Loading rate for iron and manganese ore is 3000-4000 t/day

Repair & Maintenance: Marine Electrical Agencies, Karwar, Karnataka, India, *Tel:* +91 8382 26847 Minor repairs

Stevedoring Companies: Chowgule Brothers Private Ltd, Chowgule House, 403 Mormugao Harbour, Mormugao, Goa, India 403 803, *Tel:* +91 832 252 5144, *Fax:* +91 832 252 1011, *Email:* info.cb@chowgule.co.in, *Website:* www.chowgulebros.com

Medical Facilities: Government hospital at Ankola

Lloyd's Agent: Wilson Surveyors and Adjusters Private Ltd, C-204 Remi Bizcourt, Veera Desai Road, Andheri West, Mumbai, Maharashtra, India 400 053, *Tel:* +91 22 6696 3606, *Fax:* +91 22 6696 3669, *Email:* mumbai@wilsur.com, *Website:* www.wilsur.com

BEYPORE

Lat 11° 10' N; Long 75° 48' E.

Admiralty Chart: 3461
Time Zone: GMT +5.5 h

Admiralty Pilot: 38
UNCTAD Locode: IN BEY

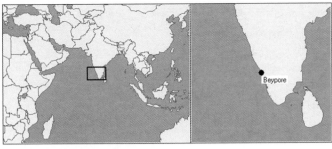

Principal Facilities:

P		Y	G			B		T	A

Authority: The Port Officer, P O Box 1108, Port Office, Beach Road, Kozhikode, Kerala, India 673 015, *Tel:* +91 495 241 4863, *Fax:* +91 495 241 4863

Pre-Arrival Information: ETA messages to be sent by Master/Agent 24 h prior to arrival. The message should contain the arrival date/time

Documentation: Crew personal effects list, last port clearance, certificate of registry, load line certificate, safety radio certificate, safety equipment certificate, cargo manifest, crew list, port & light dues receipt, passenger list

Anchorage: Safe anchorage can be obtained in depth of 7-10 m between Beypore Light House bearing 090°(T) and 045°(T)

Pilotage: Not necessary for outer roads, but compulsory for entering the harbour

Radio Frequency: Messages are normally passed through Cochin Radio (VWN), Bombay Radio (VWB) and Madras Radio (VWM) addressed to Port Authorities and Agents. VHF communication facility available on channel 16

Tides: Approx 1.5 m spring

Maximum Vessel Dimensions: Any size vessel can be operated at anchorage but at the wharf draft is restricted to 3.2 m

Working Hours: 0800-1800

Accommodation:

Name	Length (m)	Depth (m)	Remarks
Beypore Wharf	152	3.5	See [1] below

[1]*Beypore:* Open roadstead. Vessels should anchor about 2.4 km WSW of flagstaff in mud bottom. Cargoes handled include general cargo, petroleum products in barrels, bauxite, dry bulk cargo, cement, timber, tiles, bricks, granite etc

Storage: Two godowns of 600 t cap

Mechanical Handling Equipment:

Location	Type	Capacity (t)	Qty
Wharf	Shore Cranes	3	5

Bunkering: Fuel is available and supplied in tanker lorries on advance request

Waste Reception Facilities: Can be arranged through Agents

Towage: Two tugs available on request

Repair & Maintenance: Minor repairs only can be carried out

Medical Facilities: There is a government medical college hospital and a general hospital in the city

Airport: Calicut Airport, 28 km

Railway: Calicut Railway Station, 8 km

Lloyd's Agent: Peirce Leslie India Ltd, Peirce Leslie Surveyours and Assessors Ltd., Bristow Road, Willingdon Island, Kochi, Kerala, India 682 003, *Tel:* +91 484 266 8362, *Fax:* +91 484 266 8394, *Email:* plsacok@sify.com, *Website:* www.plsurvey.in

BHARATHI DOCK

harbour area, see under Chennai

BHAVNAGAR

Lat 21° 45' N; Long 72° 14' E.

Admiralty Chart: 3460	**Admiralty Pilot:** 38
Time Zone: GMT +5.5 h	**UNCTAD Locode:** IN BHU

Principal Facilities:

		Y	G			B		T	A

Authority: Gujarat Maritime Board, Port of Bhavnagar, Nava Bandar, Bhavnagar, Gujarat, India 364 005, *Tel:* +91 278 221 0221, *Fax:* +91 278 221 1026, *Website:* www.gmbports.org

Officials: Port Officer: Capt G G Pandey.

Anchorage: The anchorage is in the vicinity of pos 21° 41' 30" N; 72° 16' 36" E where vessels up to 12 m draft are worked with no dimensional restrictions in a depth of 21 m LW

Pilotage: Compulsory. Pilot station 4.5 miles NNE of Piram Island Lighthouse

Radio Frequency: VHF Channel 16 W/T 500 kHz (calling), 488.5 kHz (working)

Tides: Rise of tide 12.04 m MHWS, 10.18 m MHWN, 8.31 m MLWS, 3.52 m MLWN; current up to 6 knots

Principal Imports and Exports: Imports: Building materials, Coal & coke, Fertilizer, Rock phosphate, Scrap iron, Sulphur, Timber, Wood. Exports: Clay, Oil cakes, Onions, Rape seed, Salt, Scrap.

Working Hours: 0800-1200, 1300-1700. Overtime 1800-2200, 2300-0300

Accommodation:

Name	Length (m)	Remarks
Bhavnagar		See [1] below
Concrete Jetty	270	See [2] below

[1]*Bhavnagar:* Operations take place throughout the year at anchorage and jetty. There are five dumb barges available with a total cap of 1400 t and three self-propelled barges, two each of 500 t and one of 250 t

[2]*Concrete Jetty:* Situated inside the Lock Gate, which has a 21.94 m wide entrance allowing vessels of 19.8 m max width and 143.8 m length to enter with permissible draft of 4 m; jetty can accommodate two vessels

Storage: Storage space in port transit sheds of 16 491 m3. Ample open storage areas available for bulk cargoes. Further godown space available in the Old Port area. No refrigerated space available

Mechanical Handling Equipment:

Location	Type	Capacity (t)	Qty
Bhavnagar	Mult-purp. Cranes	5	5
Bhavnagar	Mobile Cranes	5	3

Cargo Worked: Loading and unloading at anchorage at an average rate of 600-1200 t/day. Loading rate for bagged cargo and salt 1000-1200 t/day

Bunkering: Small quantities of fuel can be supplied by tankers at alongside berths and by drums to vessels at the anchorage through cargo barge

Towage: Three tugs with a cap of 277-1700 bhp are available

Ship Chandlers: Alang Shipping Services Private Ltd, 45 Madhav Darshan Complex, Waghawadi Road, Bhavnagar, Gujarat, India 364001, *Tel:* +91 278 300 1875, *Fax:* +91 278 300 1876, *Email:* alang@alangship.com, *Website:* www.alangship.com
Samrat Marine, 225 Madhav Darshan, Waghawadi Road, Bhavnagar, Gujarat, India 364001, *Tel:* +91 278 252 0597, *Fax:* +91 278 251 0892, *Email:* samrat@sancharonline.net/samratmarine@indiatimes.com
Unique Marine & Machinery Private Ltd, 422/D Royal Complex, Hajurpayga Road, Bhavnagar, Gujarat, India 364001, *Tel:* +91 278 645 1911, *Fax:* +91 278 252 5283, *Email:* sales@ummship.com, *Website:* www.ummship.com

Shipping Agents: Agrawal Shipping Private Ltd, 334 Madhav Darshan, Waghawadi Road, Bhavnagar, Gujarat, India 360001, *Tel:* +91 278 241 1261, *Fax:* +91 278 243 1368, *Email:* sanjay@agrawalship.com, *Website:* www.agrawalship.com
Alang Shipping Services Private Ltd, 45 Madhav Darshan Complex, Waghawadi Road, Bhavnagar, Gujarat, India 364001, *Tel:* +91 278 300 1875, *Fax:* +91 278 300 1876, *Email:* alang@alangship.com, *Website:* www.alangship.com
Ashit Shipping Co., 1st Floor, AshihJyot Complex, Sanskarmandal Chowk, Atabhai Road, Bhavnagar, Gujarat, India 364002, *Tel:* +91 278 256 4052, *Fax:* +91 278 256 4051, *Email:* ashitad1@sancharnet.in, *Website:* www.ashitshipping.com
J.M. Baxi & Co, 404/405 - 4th Floor, Prithvi Complex, Kala Nala, Bhavnagar, Gujarat, India 364 001, *Tel:* +91 278 251 6757, *Fax:* +91 278 300 4244, *Email:* bhavngr@jmbaxi.com, *Website:* www.jmbaxi.com
Hind Shipping Agencies, City Centre Complex B-210 2nd Floor, Kalanala, Bhuvan Circle, Opp State Bank of Saurashtra, Bhavnagar, Gujarat, India 384002, *Tel:* +91 278 242 0127, *Fax:* +91 278 242 8966, *Email:* hindshipad1@sanchar-net.com
Interocean Shipping (India) Pvt Ltd., Flat No.208-211, Madhav Darshan, Waghawadi Road, Bhavnagar, Gujarat, India 364 001, *Tel:* +91 278 242 1610, *Fax:* +91 278 242 1611, *Email:* bhavnagar@interoceangroup.com, *Website:* www.interoceangroup.com

Surveyors: J.B. Boda Surveyors Private Ltd, 2nd Floor, 303 Silver Point, Opposite Rotary Hall, Ghogha Circle, Bhavnagar, Gujarat, India 364 002, *Tel:* +91 278 220 9481, *Fax:* +91 278 220 8335, *Email:* jbbbhv@jbbodamail.com, *Website:* www.jbboda.net
Unique Marine & Machinery Private Ltd, 422/D Royal Complex, Hajurpayga Road, Bhavnagar, Gujarat, India 364001, *Tel:* +91 278 645 1911, *Fax:* +91 278 252 5283, *Email:* sales@ummship.com, *Website:* www.ummship.com

Medical Facilities: Government and private hospitals in Bhavnagar City, 13 km

Airport: Bhavnagar Airport, 7 km

Railway: Bhavnagar Terminus Station, 12 km

Lloyd's Agent: Wilson Surveyors and Adjusters Private Ltd, Golden Arcade, II Floor, Room No.209, Plot No.141/142, Sector 8, Gandhidam, Kutch, Gujarat, India 370 201, *Tel:* +91 2836 238333, *Fax:* +91 2836 238333, *Email:* kandla@wilsur.com, *Website:* www.wilsur.com

BOMBAY

former name, see Mumbai

Key to Principal Facilities:—

A=Airport	**C**=Containers	**G**=General Cargo	**P**=Petroleum	**R**=Ro/Ro	**Y**=Dry Bulk
B=Bunkers	**D**=Dry Dock	**L**=Cruise	**Q**=Other Liquid Bulk	**T**=Towage (where available from port)	

CALCUTTA

former name, see Kolkata

CALINGAPATNAM

former name, see Kalingapatnam

CHENNAI

Lat 13° 5' N; Long 80° 17' E.

Admiralty Chart: 574
Admiralty Pilot: 21
Time Zone: GMT +5.5 h
UNCTAD Locode: IN MAA

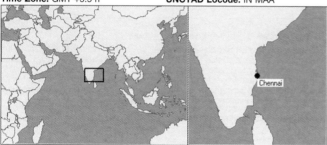

Principal Facilities:

P	Q	Y	G	C	R	L	B		T	A	

Authority: Chennai Port Trust, Rajaji Salai, Chennai, Tamil Nadu, India 600 001, *Tel:* +91 44 2536 2201, *Fax:* +91 44 2536 1228, *Email:* apro@chennaiport.gov.in, *Website:* www.chennaiport.gov.in

Officials: Capt P P Mokashi.
Chairman: N Chandrasekaran.
Chairman: K Suresh, *Email:* cpt@chennaiport.com.
Controller: S Chelladurai.
Deputy Conservator: Capt M.K. Sinha, *Email:* dc@chennaiport.com.
Finance Director / Manager: L Rabindra Ganapathy.
Manager: K Dhikpathy.
Traffic Manager: P. Venkateswarlu, *Email:* tm@chennaiport.com.
Chief Marine Superintendent: V Ranganathan.
Chief Engineer: V Meenakshi Sundaram.
Harbour Master: S Abraham.
Harbour Master: Capt A Arokiaswamy.
Secretary: K Ramachandra Rao.
Secretary: K. P. Ramanathan, *Email:* sccy@chennaiport.com.

Port Security: ISPS compliant

Approach: The approach channel to the port has two sections: (a) the entrance channel within the protection of Outer Arm (b) the outer channel beyond the protection of Outer Arm
The entrance channel is approx 7 km long with width gradually increasing from 244 m to 410 m at the bent portion, then maintains a constant width of 305 m. The depth of outer channel is 19.2 m below CD and inner channel is 18.6 m below CD

Anchorage: Situated NE of the harbour in depth of 8-9 fathoms. The holding ground is good with coarse sandy bottom. There is no limitation to the number of vessels that can be anchored

Pilotage: Compulsory for all movements inside harbour. ETA is required at least 48 h prior to arrival, when agents will contact the Port Authority for berthing arrangements. Boarding areas: Approx 2 km NE of breakwater for vessels up to 230 m loa and approx 8 km NE of breakwater for vessels over 230 m loa

Radio Frequency: Continuous watch on VHF Channel 16 is maintained by the signal station at North Quay. VHF Channels 14 and 12 are reserved for pilotage operations and VHF Channel 10 is available for communications with vessels

Weather: Occasional bad weather from October to January

Tides: Max tidal height 1.3 m. Range at ST 1.0 m and at NT 0.4 m

Traffic: 2007/08, 57 154 000 t of cargo handled, 1 128 000 TEU's

Maximum Vessel Dimensions: 151 439 dwt, 275 m loa, max d 16.2 m

Principal Imports and Exports: Imports: Chemicals, Iron ore, Oil, Paper reels, Pharmaceuticals, Scrap, Sugar, Woodpulp. Exports: Garments, Granite, Leather goods, Manganese ore.

Working Hours: 1st Shift 0600-1400, 2nd Shift 1400-2200, 3rd Shift 2200-0600

Accommodation:

Name	Length (m)	Draught (m)	Remarks
Dr. Ambedkar Dock			
North Quay	198	8.53	
West Quay 1	170	10.5	
West Quay 2	170	12	
West Quay 3	170	12	
West Quay 4	170	11	
Centre Berth	170	12	
South Quay 1	246	9.5	
South Quay 2	179	9.5	
South Quay 3	254	9.14	
East Quay (Centre)	372	12	

Name	Length (m)	Draught (m)	Remarks
East Quay (South)	372	9	
Naval Berth	200	10.7	
Chennai Container Terminal			See [1] below
Berth No.1	200	13.4	For vessels up to 177.8 m loa
Berth No.2	200	13.4	For vessels up to 177.8 m loa
Berth No.3	200	13.4	For vessels up to 177.8 m loa
Berth No.4	285	13.4	For vessels up to 177.8 m loa
Bharathi Dock			See [2] below
Bharathi Dock 1	339	14.6	Oil berth for vessels up to 274.3 m loa & 100 000 dwt
Bharathi Dock 2	274	16.5	See [3] below
Bharathi Dock 3	304	16.5	Oil berth for vessels up to 274.3 m loa & 140 000 dwt
Jawahar Dock			
Jawahar Dock 1	218	10.4	See [4] below
Jawahar Dock 2	218	10.4	See [5] below
Jawahar Dock 3	218	10.4	See [6] below
Jawahar Dock 4	218	11	See [7] below
Jawahar Dock 5	218	11	See [8] below
Jawahar Dock 6	218	11	Bulk, breakbulk & fertilisers for vessels up to 193 m loa
Moorings			
Mooring 3		10.66	For vessels up to 152.8 m loa

[1]*Chennai Container Terminal:* Chennai Container Terminal Pvt. Ltd., Chennai Port Trust Administrative Building, Ground Floor, No.1 Rajaji Salai, Chennai 600 001, Tel: +91 44 2590 9798, Fax: +91 44 2590 0485, Website: www.dpworld.com/chennai
[2]*Bharathi Dock:* Two tanker berths (No's 1 & 3) at Bharathi Dock. Five marine loading arms are connected via pipelines to the Madras refineries and other petroleum installations; average handling rate for crude oil is 3000 t/h and for petroleum products is 1000 t/h. The berth can also be used for transhipment of crude from large to smaller tankers
[3]*Bharathi Dock 2:* Iron ore berth for vessels up to 274.3 m loa & 150 000 dwt. Two shiploaders, each of 4000 t/h cap
[4]*Jawahar Dock 1:* Leased to Ege Seramik (Malaysia) Sdn Bhd and T. Arumaidurai & Co. Bulk & breakbulk for vessels up to 193 m loa. Transit shed
[5]*Jawahar Dock 2:* Bulk, breakbulk, phosphoric acid & molasses berth for vessels up to 193 m loa
[6]*Jawahar Dock 3:* Bulk & breakbulk berth for vessels up to 193 m loa. Transit shed
[7]*Jawahar Dock 4:* Bulk, breakbulk, phosphoric acid & molasses for vessels up to 193 m loa
[8]*Jawahar Dock 5:* Leased to ACT India Ltd. Bulk & breakbulk berth for vessels up to 193 m loa. Transit shed

Storage: Twelve warehouses with total area of 65 686 m2, twelve transit sheds with total area of 47 841 m2 and a covered area for FCI of 43 450 m2. Two container freight stations totalling 12 400 m2. Open storage area of 325 000 m2 and container parking yard of 81 000 m2

Mechanical Handling Equipment:

Location	Type	Capacity (t)	Qty
West Quay 1	Shore Cranes	10	1
West Quay 2	Shore Cranes	15	1
West Quay 3	Shore Cranes	10	1
West Quay 4	Shore Cranes	10	1
Centre Berth	Shore Cranes	15	1
South Quay 1	Shore Cranes	50	1
South Quay 1	Shore Cranes	10	3
South Quay 2	Shore Cranes	10	2
South Quay 3	Shore Cranes	15	2
Chennai Container Terminal	Container Cranes		7
Chennai Container Terminal	RTG's		24
Jawahar Dock 1	Shore Cranes	10	1
Jawahar Dock 2	Shore Cranes	20	1
Jawahar Dock 3	Shore Cranes	10	3
Jawahar Dock 4	Shore Cranes	20	1
Jawahar Dock 6	Shore Cranes	20	1

Cargo Worked: Grains, bulk and bagged 1800 t/day. Fertilizer/raw material 1200 t/day. Coal 15 000 t/day. General cargo 550 t/day. Crude oil 4000-7000 t/h. Oil products 700-1000 t/h. Ore 8000 t/h

Bunkering: Asean International Ltd, P O Box 7860, Block Z Suite 42/43, Saif Zone, Sharjah, United Arab Emirates, *Tel:* +971 6 557 0083, *Fax:* +971 6 557 0085
Bharat Petroleum Corp. Ltd, 4th Floor, Old Admin Building, Mahul, Chembur, Mumbai, Maharashtra, India 400 074, *Tel:* +91 22 2554 3493, *Fax:* +91 22 2554 0621, *Email:* josecm@bharatpetroleum.in, *Website:* www.baratpetroleum.in
Bominflot, Bominoil Private Ltd, 504 Maker Chambers V, 221 Nariman Point, Mumbai, Maharashtra, India 400 021, *Tel:* +91 22 2281 7133, *Fax:* +91 22 2281 7145, *Email:* bominoil@vsnl.com, *Website:* www.bominflot.net
Cockett Marine Oil Ltd, Carrick House, 36 Station Square, Petts Wood, Kent BR5 1NA, United Kingdom, *Tel:* +44 1689 883 400, *Fax:* +44 1689 877 666, *Email:* enquiries@cockett.com, *Website:* www.cockettgroup.com – *Grades:* MDO; FO; IFO – *Delivery Mode:* pipeline
M/S Global Fuels & Lubricants Inc., 11-12 Mangal Society, 76C Rafi Ahmed Kidwai Road, King Circle, Mumbai, Maharashtra, India 400 019, *Tel:* +91 22 2374 5987, *Fax:* +91 22 2409 1627, *Email:* globalfuels@vsnl.com, *Website:* www.bunkerindia.com
Indian Oil Corp. Ltd, Indian Oil Bhavan Head Office, G9 Ali Yavar Jung Marg, Bandra (East), Mumbai, Maharashtra, India 400051, *Tel:* +91 22 2644 7368, *Fax:* +91 22 2642 2434, *Email:* partha_datta@indianoil.co.in, *Website:* www.indianoil.co.in – *Grades:* FO; MDO; HDO – *Delivery Mode:* pipeline

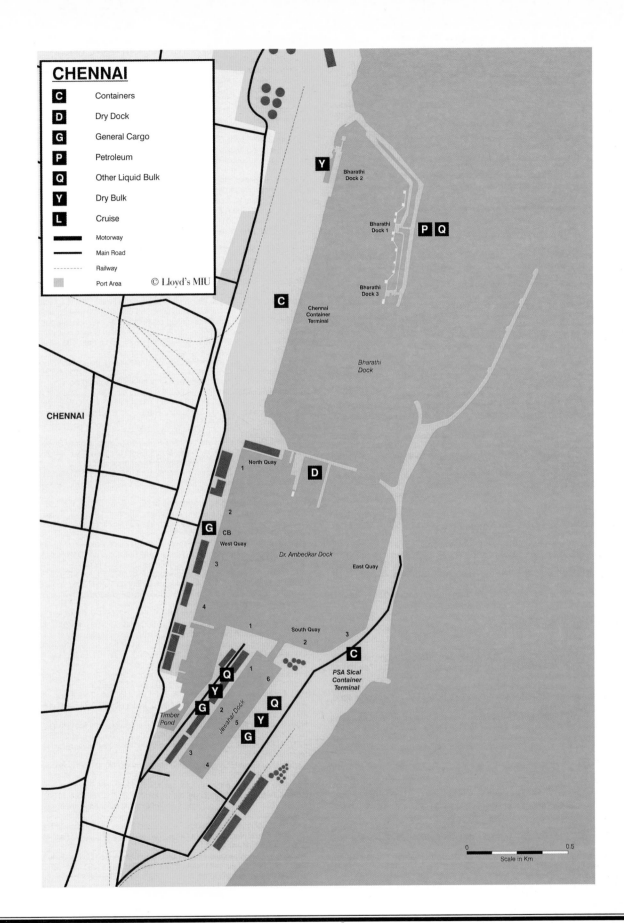

CHENNAI

C	Containers
D	Dry Dock
G	General Cargo
P	Petroleum
Q	Other Liquid Bulk
Y	Dry Bulk
L	Cruise
	Motorway
	Main Road
	Railway
	Port Area

© Lloyd's MIU

Bharathi Dock 2

Bharathi Dock 1

P **Q**

Bharathi Dock 3

Chennai Container Terminal

Bharathi Dock

CHENNAI

North Quay

D

G CB
West Quay

Dr. Ambedkar Dock

East Quay

South Quay

PSA Sical Container Terminal

C

Q
Y
G

Q
Y
G

Jawahar Dock

Timber Pond

Scale in Km

0   0.5

Chennai School of Ship Management

**37/39 Perambur High Road,
Chennai - 600012,
Tamil Nadu
India**

Email: deepsea6@rediffmail.com
Web: www.cssmmarine.com

**Tel: +91 44 6456 2752
Fax: +91 44 2451 4927**

CSSM
Since 1998

Waste Reception Facilities: Available for oily ballast and sludge

Towage: Six tugs are available with bollard pull ranging from 12 t to 31 t

Repair & Maintenance: All deck and engine repairs which do not require dry-docking of vessels are carried out by established workshops. There is a boat basin to effect minor repairs to the ports floating craft. This is being remodelled to shelter larger craft
Chidambaram Shipcare Private Ltd, 38 Second Line Beach, Chennai, Tamil Nadu, India 600 001, *Tel:* +91 44 2522 0304, *Fax:* +91 44 2522 0080, *Email:* headoffice@shipcare.in, *Website:* www.shipcare.in

Ship Chandlers: Navigator Ship Supply, 15 Moore Street, Suite No.105, 1st Floor Rattan Complex, Tarrys, Chennai, Tamil Nadu, India, *Tel:* +91 44 2524 7886, *Fax:* +91 44 2522 7797, *Email:* navship@vsnl.net Chief Operating Officer: Mohammed Saud
Admiral Marine Services Private Ltd, New No. 23 Moore Street, Chennai, Tamil Nadu, India 600 001, *Tel:* +91 44 4216 0050, *Fax:* +91 44 4216 0052, *Email:* enquiries@admiralmarine.com, *Website:* www.admiralmarine.com
Chennai Marine Trading Private Ltd, 8-13 Sivan Koil Tank Street, Villivakkam, Chennai, Tamil Nadu, India 600 049, *Tel:* +91 44 4355 4335/6, *Fax:* +91 44 4355 4318/9, *Email:* chennaimarine@vsnl.net/chennaimar@eth.net
Chidambaram Shipcare Private Ltd, 38 Second Line Beach, Chennai, Tamil Nadu, India 600 001, *Tel:* +91 44 2522 0304, *Fax:* +91 44 2522 0080, *Email:* headoffice@shipcare.in, *Website:* www.shipcare.in
Fairdeal International, 240/2 Thambu Chetty Street, 2nd Floor, Chennai, Tamil Nadu, India 600 001, *Tel:* +91 44 2524 4492, *Fax:* +91 44 2524 4877, *Email:* fairin@md3.vsnl.net.in, *Website:* www.fairdeal-international.com
Fairmacs Shipstores Private Limited, 87 Moore Street, Chennai, Tamil Nadu, India 600 001, *Tel:* +91 44 2523 1383, *Fax:* +91 44 2522 7404, *Email:* vivek-bond@fairmacs.com, *Website:* www.fairmacs.com
Globe Maritime, 18 Kitabath Khan Street, Ellis Road, Mount Road, Chennai, Tamil Nadu, India 600 002, *Tel:* +91 44 2858 8224, *Fax:* +91 44 2858 3658, *Email:* globemaritime@eth.net, *Website:* www.globemaritime.com
The Liberty Marine Syndicate Private Ltd, Office No.184, 3rd Floor, Thambu Chetty Street, Chennai, Tamil Nadu, India 600 001, *Tel:* +91 44 2521 4412, *Fax:* +91 44 2521 4413, *Email:* chennai@libertyshipping.com, *Website:* www.libertyshipping.com
Madras Hardtools Private Ltd, No 1 Perianna Maistry Street, P O Box 1687, Chennai, Tamil Nadu, India 600 001, *Tel:* +91 44 2522 2922, *Fax:* +91 44 2522 2088, *Email:* info@madrashardtools.com, *Website:* www.madrashardtools.com
Maritime Overseas Corp., 11 Singapore Plaza, 164 Linghi Chetty Street, P O Box 1816, Chennai, Tamil Nadu, India 600 001, *Tel:* +91 44 2534 1944, *Fax:* +91 44 2535 8953, *Email:* mocmi@md4.vsnl.net.in
A.S. Moloobhoy & Sons, Old No.48, New No.91, 1st Floor, East Madha Church Street, Royapuram, Chennai, Tamil Nadu, India 600 013, *Tel:* +91 44 2598 0471, *Fax:* +91 44 2598 0462, *Email:* chennai@asmoloobhoy.com, *Website:* www.asmoloobhoy.com
Poseidon Shipstores (India), #108-109 Triplicane High Road, Suit Nos. 7-10, "Hameedia Complex", Chennai, Tamil Nadu, India 600 005, *Tel:* +91 44 4215 7788, *Fax:* +91 44 2841 6694, *Email:* info@poseidonshipstores.com, *Website:* www.poseidonshipstores.com
S. Ramasubban & Co., SR Enclave, 84/2 (New 60) Moore Street, Chennai, Tamil Nadu, India 600 001, *Tel:* +91 44 2522 8916, *Fax:* +91 44 2524 4997, *Email:* src@md3.vsnl.net.in, *Website:* www.ramasubban.com
Seatraffic, New No.4 (30) Errabalu Street, 2nd Floor, Chennai, Tamil Nadu, India 600 001, *Tel:* +91 44 2522 8135, *Fax:* +91 44 2522 8403, *Email:* seatraffic@eth.net
SF Marine Private Ltd, 110 East Madha Church Street, Royapuram, Chennai, Tamil Nadu, India 600 013, *Tel:* +91 44 5569 1352/2590 4275, *Fax:* +91 44 2590 4283, *Email:* sfmarine@md3.vsnl.net.in
Spence & Co., 220 N.S.C. Bose Road, Chennai, Tamil Nadu, India 600 001, *Tel:* +91 44 2538 5859, *Fax:* +91 44 2536 3145, *Email:* spence@eth.net

Shipping Agents: Access India Shipping Agencies Private Ltd, 223-225 Linghi Chetty Street, Chennai, Tamil Nadu, India 600001, *Tel:* +91 44 2529 8304, *Fax:* +91 44 2521 8303, *Email:* access_shipping@vsnl.net, *Website:* www.accessshipping.com
Albatross Shipping Pvt. Ltd, Transworld House, No.2, Ground Floor, 9th Lane, Dr.Radha Krishnan Salai, Mylapore, Chennai, Tamil Nadu, India 600 004, *Tel:* +91 44 4200 9868, *Fax:* +91 44 4200 9876, *Email:* shiv@alba.co.in
Arebee Star Maritime Agencies Private Ltd, SM Plaza, 2nd Floor, 45 Armenian Street, Chennai, Tamil Nadu, India 600001, *Tel:* +91 44 2523 1571, *Fax:* +91 44 2524 4360, *Email:* arebee@md2.vsnl.net.in
AS Shipping Agencies Private Ltd, 113 Armenian Street, Chennai, Tamil Nadu, India 600001, *Tel:* +91 44 2534 2261, *Fax:* +91 44 2534 2208
Aspinwall & Co. Ltd, 48 Rajaji Salai, Chennai, Tamil Nadu, India 600 001, *Tel:* +91 44 2522 5901, *Fax:* +91 44 2522 0696, *Email:* maa.mng@aspinwallgroup.com, *Website:* www.aspinwallgroup.com
J.M. Baxi & Co, 3rd Floor Clive Battery Complex 4 & 4A, Rajaji Salai, Chennai, Tamil Nadu, India 600 001, *Tel:* +91 44 2521 2036, *Fax:* +91 44 2524 3813, *Email:* chennai@jmbaxi.com, *Website:* www.jmbaxi.com
Boxtrans Shipping Agencies Pvt Ltd, Clive Battery Comples 4 & 4A, Rajaji Salai, Chennai, Tamil Nadu, India 600001, *Tel:* +91 44 2523 4121, *Fax:* +91 44 2522 9282, *Email:* chennai@boxtransindia.com, *Website:* www.boxtransindia.com
Chakiat Agencies Private Ltd, 2nd Floor, 40 Rajaji Salai, P O Box 1880, Chennai, Tamil Nadu, India 600 001, *Tel:* +91 44 2522 3241, *Fax:* +91 44 2522 5634, *Email:* chakiat@md3.vsnl.net.in, *Website:* www.chakiat.co.in
Choice Intermodal Services, 2nd Floor, 165 Lotus Court, Thambu Chetty Street, Chennai, Tamil Nadu, India 600 001, *Tel:* +91 44 2527 9191, *Fax:* +91 44 2527 9190, *Email:* choicemd@md2.vsnl.net.in
Chowgule Brothers Private Ltd, P O Box 1694, Linghi Chetty Street, Chennai, Tamil Nadu, India 600001, *Tel:* +91 44 2534 1131, *Fax:* +91 44 2534 0137, *Email:* chennai.cb@chowgule.co.in
Contfreight Shipping Agency India Private Ltd, 2nd Floor, Nafees Manzil 112/1 Broadway, Chennai, Tamil Nadu, India 600108, *Tel:* +91 44 2521 9344, *Fax:* +91 44 2521 0997, *Email:* vinod@hsms.sinwa.hanjin.com
CSAV Group Agencies (India) Pvt Ltd, Unit 3C, 3rd Floor, Heavitree No. 47, Spur Tank Road, Chetpet, Chennai, Tamil Nadu, India 600031, *Tel:* +91 44 4355 5181, *Fax:* +91 44 4355 5187, *Email:* info@csavagencies-india.com, *Website:* www.csavagencies-india.com
Emirates Shipping Agencies (India) Private Ltd, GJ Plaz 1st Floor, 358 Lloyds Road, Gopalapuram, Chennai, Tamil Nadu, India 600086, *Tel:* +91 44 4393 1000, *Fax:* +91 44 4393 1001, *Email:* k.jerald@in.emiratesline.com
Everett (India) Private Ltd, 1st Floor, 105 (OLD NO. 51), Armenian Street, Chennai, Tamil Nadu, India 600 001, *Tel:* +91 44 2535 4910, *Fax:* +91 44 2535 4863, *Email:* admin-chennai@everett.co.in, *Website:* www.everett.co.in
Evergreen India Private Ltd, Century Centre 2nd Floor 75 TTK Road, Alwarpet, Chennai, Tamil Nadu, India 600018, *Tel:* +91 44 3984 9700, *Fax:* +91 44 3984 9998, *Email:* cenbiz@evergreen-shipping.co.in, *Website:* www.evergreen-marine.com
Fairmacs Shipping & Transport Services Private Ltd, 31 Moore Street, Chennai, Tamil Nadu, India 600 001, *Tel:* +91 44 2523 1383, *Fax:* +91 44 2522 6941, *Email:* corpadmin@draftcargo.com, *Website:* www.fairmacs.com
Forbes Patvolk (A Division of Forbes Gokak Ltd), The Catholic Centre, 108 Armenian Street, P O Box 45, Chennai, Tamil Nadu, India 600001, *Tel:* +91 44 2538 2521, *Fax:* +91 44 2538 7164, *Email:* patship@vsnl.com, *Website:* www.forbespatvolk.com
GAC Shipping (India) Pvt Ltd, P O Box 1804, Chennai, Tamil Nadu, India 600 001, *Tel:* +91 44 2522 1588, *Fax:* +91 44 2523 3074, *Email:* chennai@gacworld.com, *Website:* www.gacworld.com
German Express Shipping Agency (I) Private Ltd, 88 Rajaji Salai, Chennai, Tamil Nadu, India 600001, *Tel:* +91 44 2533 0771, *Fax:* +91 44 2533 0784, *Email:* chennai@gesaindia.com
Greenways Shipping Agencies Private Ltd, 113 Armenian Street, Chennai, Tamil Nadu, India 600001, *Tel:* +91 44 2534 2261, *Fax:* +91 44 2534 2891, *Email:* sp@shippingline.com
A Hartrodt International, 15 S M Plaza, 93 Armenian Street, Chennai, Tamil Nadu, India 600 001, *Tel:* +91 44 2523 2119, *Fax:* +91 44 2523 0286, *Email:* linksmadras@eth.net, *Website:* www.hartrodt.com
IAL Shipping Agencies (Mumbai) Private Ltd, 631/A, MS Towers, Poonamallee High Road, Aminjikarai, Chennai, Tamil Nadu, India 600029, *Tel:* +91 44 6677 9000, *Fax:* +91 44 6677 9050, *Email:* ialc@ial.com, *Website:* www.ial.com
International Clearing & Shipping Agency, 2nd Floor, 325 Linghi Chetty Streer, P O Box 1257, Chennai, Tamil Nadu, India 600 001, *Tel:* +91 44 2534 2351, *Fax:* +91 44 2534 0288, *Email:* icsa@icsagroup.com, *Website:* www.icsagroup.com
Interocean Shipping Agency, 255 Angappa Naicken Street, Husaina Manzil, Chennai, Tamil Nadu, India 600 001, *Tel:* +91 44 2534 2500, *Fax:* +91 44 2534 0053, *Email:* inship@vsnl.com, *Website:* www.interocean.org.in
Interocean Shipping (India) Pvt Ltd., 3 Jaffar Syrang Street, First Floor, Chennai, Tamil Nadu, India 600 001, *Tel:* +91 44 2523 2340, *Fax:* +91 44 2524 4217, *Email:* interocean2@vsnl.com, *Website:* www.interoceangroup.com
K Steamship Agencies Private Ltd, 4 Second Line Beach, Chennai, Tamil Nadu, India 600001, *Tel:* +91 44 2522 2831, *Fax:* +91 44 2522 8970, *Website:* www.kline.co.jp
Kinship Services (India) Private Ltd, 2nd Floor, 166 Thambu Chetty Street, Chennai, Tamil Nadu, India 600 001, *Tel:* +91 44 2535 4702, *Fax:* +91 44 2534 3043, *Email:* liteship@md2.vsnl.net.in, *Website:* www.kinshipping.com
Macoline Shipping Private Ltd, 3rd Floor, 157 Linghi Chetty Street, Chennai, Tamil Nadu, India 600001, *Tel:* +91 44 2533 2218, *Fax:* +91 44 2553 2189, *Email:* macnels@md4.vsnl.net.in, *Website:* www.macnels.com.sg
Marine Container Services (I) Private Ltd, 18 Swami Sivananda Salai, Chepauk, Chennai, Tamil Nadu, India 600005, *Tel:* +91 44 2536 5636, *Fax:* +91 44 2538 9197, *Email:* ymlmaa@vsnl.com
Mediterranean Shipping Company, MSC Agency (India) Pvt Ltd, No.3, 3rd Floor, Salzburg Square, 107 Harrington Road, Chetpet, Chennai, Tamil Nadu, India 600 031, *Tel:* +91 44 4225 2900, *Fax:* +91 44 4284 9886, *Email:* chennai@mscindia.com, *Website:* www.mscindia.com
Merchant Shipping Services Private Ltd, 4th Floor, Salzburg Square, 107 Harrington Road, Chetpet, Chennai, Tamil Nadu, India 600031, *Tel:* +91 44 2821 8576/8578, *Fax:* +91 44 2821 8574, *Email:* merschn@merchantshpg.com
A.P. Moller-Maersk Group, Maersk India Pvt Ltd, Door No's 25/26 Prince Towers, 1st Floor, College Road, Nungambakkam, Chennai, Tamil Nadu, India 600 006, *Tel:* +91 44 6678 9500, *Fax:* +91 44 6678 9555, *Email:* maaordcus@maersk.com, *Website:* www.maerskline.com
Peirce Leslie Surveyor's & Assessors Ltd, 37 Dr PV Cherian Crescent, Egmore, Chennai, Chennai, Tamil Nadu, India 600 008, *Tel:* +91 44 2827 1158, *Fax:* +91 44 2824 2357, *Email:* plint@vsnl.net.in, *Website:* www.plsurvey.in
Pen Shipping Agencies Private Ltd, 4-4A Rajaji Salai, 5th Floor, Clive Battery Complex, Chennai, Tamil Nadu, India 600001, *Tel:* +91 44 2524 9350/9354, *Fax:* +91 44 2524 9358, *Email:* chennai@tpnindia.com
Premier Shipping Agency, 235/112 Angappa Street, 3rd Floor, Chennai, Tamil Nadu, India, *Tel:* +91 44 2522 9614, *Fax:* +91 44 2522 9959
Red Eagle Maritime Services (I) Pvt Ltd, No. 94, 2nd Floor, Armenian Centre, Armenian Street, Chennai, Tamil Nadu, India 600001, *Tel:* +91 44 2522 0637, *Fax:* +91 44 2522 0682, *Email:* redeagle@vsnl.net
Ruth Shipping Agencies Pvt Ltd, Sea View Tower, 1st Floor Phase-II, 12/9 Krishnan Koil Street, Chennai, Tamil Nadu, India 600001, *Tel:* +91 44 2526 2281, *Fax:* +91 44 4216 4066, *Email:* chn@ruthshipping.com, *Website:* www.ruthshipping.com
Samrat Shipping & Transport Systems Private Ltd, 5th Floor, Rowther Chambers, 53/55 Rajaji Street, Chennai, Tamil Nadu, India 600001, *Tel:* +91 44 2523 0243, *Fax:* +91 44 2523 0245
Samsara Shipping (Private) Ltd, No.1, 4th Floor, Salzburg Square, 107 Harrington Road, Chetpet, Chennai, Tamil Nadu, India 600 031, *Tel:* +91 44 2836 3019, *Fax:* +91 44 2836 2827, *Email:* chennai@samsarashipping.com, *Website:* www.samsarashipping.com
Sea Tech Services Ltd, Kakani Tower, 2nd Floor, 15/15 Khader Nawaz Khan Road, Chennai, Tamil Nadu, India 600006, *Tel:* +91 44 2822 0718, *Fax:* +91 44 2822 0716, *Email:* stslmad@attmail.com
Seahorse Ship Agencies Private Ltd, 4 Krishnan Koil Street, Chennai, Tamil Nadu, India 600001, *Tel:* +91 44 2524 4509, *Fax:* +91 44 2522 3838, *Email:* ssamaa@seahorsegroup.co.in
Seaworld Shipping & Logistics Private Ltd, Rowther Chambers, 2nd Floor, 53/55 Rajaji Salai, Chennai, Tamil Nadu, India 600001, *Tel:* +91 44 2522 7730, *Fax:* +91 44 2522 7710, *Email:* jagadeesan@cni.seaworldship.com, *Website:* www.seaworldship.com
Sentrans Maritime Private Ltd, 3rd Floor, 139 Angappa Naicken Street, Chennai, Tamil Nadu, India 600001, *Tel:* +91 44 2524 5133/4, *Fax:* +91 44 2522 8509, *Email:* sentransmadras@vsnl.com
South India Corp (Agencies) Ltd, Leelavathi Building, 69 Armenian Street, P O Box 113, Chennai, Tamil Nadu, India 600001, *Tel:* +91 44 2522 0723, *Fax:* +91 44 2522 2258, *Email:* shpcheopr@vsnl.net
Southern Shipping Corp Private Ltd, 100/1, Dr Dhakrishnan Salat, Mylapore, Chennai, Tamil Nadu, India 600 004, *Tel:* +91 44 2847 5717, *Fax:* +91 44 2847 5709, *Email:* souship@giosmdo1.vsdl.net.in
United Liner Agencies of India Private Ltd, 4th Floor, Clive Battery Complex, Chennai,

Tamil Nadu, India 600001, *Tel:* +91 44 2524 9351, *Fax:* +91 44 2524 9358, *Email:* chennai@ulaindia.com, *Website:* www.ulaindia.com
Unitrans Shipping & Trading Co., 2nd Floor, 163/81 Thambu Chetty Street, Chennai, Tamil Nadu, India 600001, *Tel:* +91 44 2522 1565, *Fax:* +91 44 2522 7283, *Email:* unitrans@md4.vsnl.net.in
Volkart Fleming Shipping & Services Ltd, Catholic Centre Annexe, 64 Armenian Street, P O Box 45, Chennai, Tamil Nadu, India 600001, *Tel:* +91 44 2538 2551, *Fax:* +91 44 2538 3484, *Email:* admin@patvolkchennai.com

Stevedoring Companies: Chowgule Brothers Private Ltd, P O Box 1694, Linghi Chetty Street, Chennai, Tamil Nadu, India 600001, *Tel:* +91 44 2534 1131, *Fax:* +91 44 2534 0137, *Email:* chennai.cb@chowgule.co.in
Kinship Services (India) Private Ltd, 2nd Floor, 166 Thambu Chetty Street, Chennai, Tamil Nadu, India 600 001, *Tel:* +91 44 2534 3043, *Email:* liteship@md2.vsnl.net.in, *Website:* www.kinshipping.com

Surveyors: J.B. Boda Surveyors Private Ltd, M. L. M. Building No.9, Wallajah Road, Chennai, Tamil Nadu, India 600 002, *Tel:* +91 44 2852 1342, *Fax:* +91 44 2852 5265, *Email:* jbbodachennai@jbbodamail.com, *Website:* www.jbboda.net
Bureau Veritas, 'Park Circle', 1st Floor, 20 Moores Road, Nungambakkam, Chennai, Tamil Nadu, India 600 006, *Tel:* +91 44 4226 4500, *Fax:* +91 44 4226 4510, *Email:* bv.chennai@in.bureauveritas.com, *Website:* www.bureauveritas.com
Chowgule Brothers Private Ltd, P O Box 1694, Linghi Chetty Street, Chennai, Tamil Nadu, India 600001, *Tel:* +91 44 2534 1131, *Fax:* +91 44 2534 0137, *Email:* chennai.cb@chowgule.co.in
Det Norske Veritas A/S, No.3/10/2 McNichols Road, Chetpet, Chennai, Tamil Nadu, India 600 031, *Tel:* +91 44 2836 3357/2836 3070/71, *Fax:* +91 44 2836 2906, *Email:* chennai@dnv.com, *Website:* www.dnv.com
Germanischer Lloyd, Chennai, Tamil Nadu, India, *Tel:* +91 44 2432 0335, *Fax:* +91 44 2432 8186, *Email:* gl-chennai@gl-group.com, *Website:* www.gl-group.com
Indian Register of Shipping, 3 Raja Annamalai Building, 3rd Floor, 19 Marshall's Road, Chennai, Tamil Nadu, India 600 008, *Tel:* +91 44 2855 4615, *Fax:* +91 44 2855 3439, *Email:* chennai@irclass.org, *Website:* www.irclass.org
Metcalfe & Hodgkinson Private Ltd, Chennai, Tamil Nadu, India, *Tel:* +91 44 2522 2711, *Fax:* +91 44 2525 0390, *Email:* chennai@metcalfeindia.com, *Website:* www.metcalfeindia.com
Nippon Kaiji Kyokai, 1F, 98-99 Luz Church Road, Mylapore, Chennai, Tamil Nadu, India 600 004, *Tel:* +91 44 2499 8270, *Fax:* +91 44 2499 8270, *Email:* md@classnk.or.jp, *Website:* www.classnk.or.jp
Sunama Experts Private Ltd, 1st Floor, 266 Poonamallee High Road, Aminjikarai, Chennai, Tamil Nadu, India 600 029, *Tel:* +91 44 2522 3969, *Fax:* +91 44 2644 6187, *Email:* deltamds.hub@smy.sprintrpg.ems.vsnl.net

Medical Facilities: The Port Trust maintains an ultra-modern main hospital and two dispensaries

Airport: Chennai International, 19 km

Railway: Indian Railways (Southern Region), 1 km

Development: PSA-Sical is to develop a second container terminal at the port

Lloyd's Agent: Wilson Surveyors and Adjusters Private Ltd, TMB Mansion, 3rd Floor, 739 Anna Salai, Chennai, Tamil Nadu, India 600 002, *Tel:* +91 44 2852 2811, *Fax:* +91 44 2852 3349, *Email:* chennai@wilsur.com, *Website:* www.wilsur.com

COCHIN

former name, see Kochi

COLACHEL

Lat 8° 10' N; Long 77° 15' E.

Admiralty Chart: 1586
Admiralty Pilot: 38
Time Zone: GMT +5.5 h
UNCTAD Locode: IN COL
This port is to be developed and is expected to be completed in phases by 2011

CUDDALORE

Lat 11° 42' N; Long 79° 46' E.

Admiralty Chart: 575
Admiralty Pilot: 21
Time Zone: GMT +5.5 h
UNCTAD Locode: IN CDL

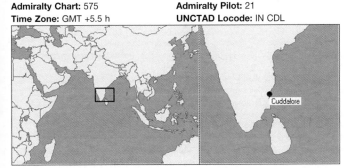

Principal Facilities:

		Y	G				T	

Authority: The Port Officer, Tamil Nadu Port Department, Marine House, Beach Road, Devanam Pattinam, Cuddalore, Tamil Nadu, India 607 002, *Tel:* +91 4142 338025

Radio Frequency: VHF Channels 16 and 11
Tides: Range of tide 0.75 m ST, 0.15 m NT

Principal Imports and Exports: Imports: Fertilizer, Flourspar, Propylene gas. Exports: Tapioca starch.

Working Hours: 0600-1800

Accommodation:

Name	Remarks
Cuddalore	See [1] below

[1]*Cuddalore:* Open roadstead. Vessels anchor in 5-7 fathoms of water, one mile with Cuddalore Lighthouse bearing 265° to 295°. Shore berths for lighters transferring cargo to or from vessels at anchorage. Total length of wharfage with platform 1033 m, total length of jetties 460 m, depths alongside of 1.8 m at MLWST. Cargo is handled by lighters with carrying cap of 15-20 t each

Storage: 30 000 t cap of privately owned warehousing space, no refrigerated space. Open stacking area of 60 acres

Mechanical Handling Equipment:

Location	Type	Capacity (t)	Qty
Cuddalore	Mobile Cranes	10	1

Cargo Worked: Approx 800 t/day

Towage: Two tugs available for towing lighters

Medical Facilities: Available

Lloyd's Agent: Wilson Surveyors and Adjusters Private Ltd, TMB Mansion, 3rd Floor, 739 Anna Salai, Chennai, Tamil Nadu, India 600 002, *Tel:* +91 44 2852 2811, *Fax:* +91 44 2852 3349, *Email:* chennai@wilsur.com, *Website:* www.wilsur.com

DAHEJ

Lat 21° 43' N; Long 72° 35' E.

Admiralty Chart: 1486
Admiralty Pilot: 38
Time Zone: GMT +5.5 h
UNCTAD Locode: IN DAH

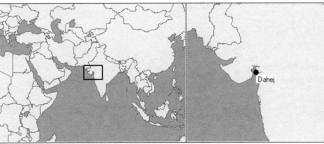

Principal Facilities:

P	Q						T	

Authority: Gujarat Chemical Port Terminal Co. Ltd (GCPTCL), 2nd Floor, Gunjan Tower, Subhanpura, Vadodara, Gujarat State, India 390 023, *Tel:* +91 265 228 5000, *Fax:* +91 265 228 2367, *Email:* corporate@gcptcl.com, *Website:* www.gcptcl.com

Officials: Managing Director: Sandesh K. Anand.
Marketing Manager: Amit Datta.

Port Security: ISPS compliant

Pre-Arrival Information: The following arrival parameters are required to be given in ETA notices for berthing vessels at the company's jetty:
a) length overall
b) PBL on arrival
c) free board on arrival
d) draft on arrival
e) trim

Approach: Through Grant Channel or Malacca Banks

Anchorage: Available 1.5 nautical miles W of the jetty

Pilotage: Available

Radio Frequency: Port Control on VHF Channel 16

Weather: Prevailing SW winds during March to October and NE winds during November to February

Tides: HW 10.8 m. LW 0.3 m

Traffic: 2005/06, 148 vessels, 1 134 924 t of cargo handled

Maximum Vessel Dimensions: 215 m loa, 40 000 dwt

Accommodation:

Name	Length (m)	Depth (m)	Draught (m)	Remarks
Dahej				
GCPTCL Jetty	241	16–18	12	See [1] below
Petronet LNG Terminal				See [2] below
Reliance Dahej Marine Terminal	126			Tanker terminal

[1]*GCPTCL Jetty:* Site Office: Tel: +91 2641 256004/5, Fax: +91 2641 256048, Email: site@gcptcl.com
Oil, petroleum products & chemicals handled. Four breasting dolphins, four mooring dolphins and four fenders. 311 300 m3 of storage for liquid and gaseous chemicals
[2]*Petronet LNG Terminal:* Operated by Petronet LNG Ltd., GIDC Industrial Estate, Plot No.7/A, Dahej 392 130, Tel: +91 2641 257249, Fax: +91 2641 257252, Website: www.petronetlng.com
LNG imported from Ras Laffan Liquefied Natural Gas Co Ltd (RasGas). 2.4 km long

---

Key to Principal Facilities:—

A=Airport	**C**=Containers	**G**=General Cargo	**P**=Petroleum	**R**=Ro/Ro	**Y**=Dry Bulk
B=Bunkers	**D**=Dry Dock	**L**=Cruise	**Q**=Other Liquid Bulk	**T**=Towage (where available from port)	

jetty. Unloading platform at Jetty head with unloading arms etc. Two LNG tanks of 160 000 m3 gas storage cap

Towage: Available for berthing/unberthing

Stevedoring Companies: Chowgule Brothers Private Ltd, Chowgule House, 403 Mormugao Harbour, Mormugao, Goa, India 403 803, *Tel:* +91 832 252 5144, *Fax:* +91 832 252 1011, *Email:* info.cb@chowgule.co.in, *Website:* www.chowgulebros.com

Medical Facilities: Available

Airport: Vadodara, approx 130 km

Railway: Bharuch Railway Station, approx 50 km

Development: Construction of a bulk terminal operated by Adani Petronet (Dahej) Pvt Ltd for imports/exports of coal, steel and fertilizers

Lloyd's Agent: Wilson Surveyors and Adjusters Private Ltd, Golden Arcade, II Floor, Room No.209, Plot No.141/142, Sector 8, Gandhidam, Kutch, Gujarat, India 370 201, *Tel:* +91 2836 238333, *Fax:* +91 2836 238333, *Email:* kandla@wilsur.com, *Website:* www.wilsur.com

DHAMRA

Lat 20° 47' N; Long 86° 54' E.

Admiralty Chart: 814   **Admiralty Pilot:** 21
Time Zone: GMT +5.5 h   **UNCTAD Locode:** IN

Currently under construction and expected to become operational in 2010. The project will initially have two berths totaling 700 m with a draught of 18 m focusing on bulk cargoes like steel

DR. AMBEDKAR DOCK

harbour area, see under Chennai

ENNORE

Lat 13° 14' N; Long 80° 20' E.

Admiralty Chart: -   **Admiralty Pilot:** 21
Time Zone: GMT +5.5 h   **UNCTAD Locode:** IN ENR

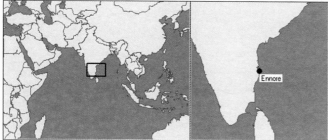

Principal Facilities:

		Y					T	A	

Authority: Ennore Port Ltd, No.23, First Floor, P.T. Lee Chengalvaraya Naicker Maaligai, Rajaji Salai, Chennai, Tamil Nadu, India 600 001, *Tel:* +91 44 2525 1666, *Fax:* +91 44 2525 1665, *Email:* info@epl.gov.in, *Website:* www.ennoreport.gov.in

Officials: Managing Director: Sellakannu Velumani.

Port Security: ISPS compliant

Approach: The entrance channel is 3775 m long, 250 m wide and dredged to a depth of 16 m
The south breakwater is 1070 m long and the north breakwater is 3080 m long

Pilotage: Compulsory. Pilot boards in the following positions:
1 cable S of the Fairway Lt. buoy in pos 13° 12' 92" N; 80° 22' 40" E
In pos 13° 14' 08" N; 80° 23' 03" E (waiting area)
In pos 13° 13' N; 80° 22' E (waiting area for Ennore minor port)

Radio Frequency: VHF Channels 16 and 74

Traffic: 2007/08, 11 563 000 t of cargo handled

Maximum Vessel Dimensions: 77 000 dwt

Accommodation:

Name	Remarks
Ennore	See [1] below

[1]*Ennore:* The 220 ha wide harbour basin is dredged to a depth of 15 m and at present consists of two 280 m long coal berths accommodating 65 000 dwt and 77 000 dwt vessels
Loading of iron ore takes place at the inner anchorage, fed by barges loading at the jetty

Towage: Three tugs of 40 t bollard pull

Airport: Chennai Airport, 24 km

Development: A 360 m multi liquid cargo jetty is due to be completed August 2008
A 360 m coal jetty is due to be completed August 2010
A 560 m iron ore jetty is due to be completed August 2010

Lloyd's Agent: Wilson Surveyors and Adjusters Private Ltd, TMB Mansion, 3rd Floor, 739 Anna Salai, Chennai, Tamil Nadu, India 600 002, *Tel:* +91 44 2852 2811, *Fax:* +91 44 2852 3349, *Email:* chennai@wilsur.com, *Website:* www.wilsur.com

GANGAVARAM

Lat 17° 37' N; Long 83° 14' E.

Admiralty Chart: -   **Admiralty Pilot:** 21
Time Zone: GMT +5.5 h   **UNCTAD Locode:** IN

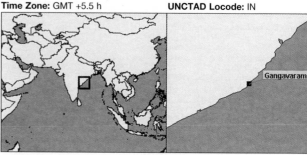

Authority: Gangavaram Port Ltd., Hansa Crest, 1st Floor Plot No.62, Road No.1, Jubilee Hills, Hyderabad, Andhra Pradesh, India 500 033, *Tel:* +91 40 4434 9999, *Fax:* +91 40 4434 9990, *Email:* port@gangavaram.com, *Website:* www.gangavaram.com

Accommodation:

Name	Remarks
Gangavaram	Situated 15 km S of Visakhapatnam Port

Development: Phase 1 development of this port includes the construction of five berths (one iron ore berth, one coal berth and three multi-purpose berths) in depth of 21 m
Equipment includes a fully mechanised coal handling system for vessels up to 200 000 dwt, a fully mechanised iron ore loading system for vessels up to 200 000 dwt and modern harbour mobile cranes for other bulk and break bulk cargoes
Commercial operations are likely to commence August 2008

Lloyd's Agent: Wilson Surveyors and Adjusters Private Ltd, Fatima Building 2nd Floor, 23-13-28 Thompson Street, Visakhapatnam, Andhira Pradesh, India 530 001, *Tel:* +91 891 272 5611, *Fax:* +91 891 272 5655, *Email:* vizag@wilsur.com, *Website:* www.wilsur.com

GOA

alternate name, see Mormugao

HALDIA

Lat 22° 1' N; Long 88° 5' E.

Admiralty Chart: 136   **Admiralty Pilot:** 21
Time Zone: GMT +5.5 h   **UNCTAD Locode:** IN HAL

Principal Facilities:

P	Q	Y	G	C		B		T	

Authority: Kolkata Port Trust, Haldia Dock Complex, Jawahar Tower Annexe, Haldia Township, Haldia, Midnapore, West Bengal, India 721 607, *Tel:* +91 3224 263100, *Fax:* +91 3224 252135, *Website:* www.kolkataporttrust.gov.in

Approach: The channel to Haldia can at present accept vessels up to a depth of 9.5 m

Pilotage: Available. VHF Channel 16

Radio Frequency: Call sign VWST, VHF Channel 16

Weather: SW and NE monsoon winds. Average wind during SW monsoon is 15-20 knots

Tides: Range of tide 2-5 m

Traffic: 2007/08, 43 541 000 t of cargo handled, 128 000 TEU's

Maximum Vessel Dimensions: 150 000 dwt, 237.9 m loa

Principal Imports and Exports: Imports: Coking coal, Containers, Crude oil, Fertilizer, Liquid cargo, Raw materials. Exports: Coal, Containerised cargo.

Working Hours: Three shifts 0600-1400, 1400-2200, 2200-0600

Accommodation:

Name	Length (m)	Depth (m)	Remarks
Haldia			See [1] below
Berth No.1 (Satish Samanta Oil Jetty)	91		For tankers up to 237.9 m loa & approx 90 000 dwt

Name	Length (m)	Depth (m)	Remarks
Berth No.2 (2nd Oil Jetty)			For tankers up to 150 000 dwt
Berth No.3	337		See [2] below
Berth No.4			See [3] below
Berth No.4A			See [4] below
Berth No.5	243		See [5] below
Berth No's 6 & 7	234		See [6] below
Berth No.8			See [7] below
Berth No.9	220	13.7	Containers
Berth No.10	220	11.5	Containers
Berth No.11	260	11.5	Dry bulk & containerised cargo
Berth No.12	220		See [8] below

[1]*Haldia:* Dock system consists of eleven berths served by one lock entrance with three electrically operated caisson type gates with a clear length of 300.4 m between outer and inner gates, further sub-divisible into chambers of 93 m and 199.6 m, depending on ship length. Lock barrel width 39.65 m and depth 10.37 m below lowest low water. Ships having max length 231.71 m and 33.54 m beam can negotiate. Lead-in-jetty 335.5 m in length facilitates manoeuvring. Turning basin of 549 m diameter and depth available in dock of 13.72 m

[2]*Berth No.3:* Berthing face 197 m in length and 17.08 m wide. Two ship loaders having travel of 179.5 m. Can accommodate vessels up to 231.71 m. Two entirely independent 3000 t/h handling systems on same berthing face, operable jointly or singly. Each loading circuit provided with 1500 t/h wagon tippler; 3000 t/h stockpile conveyor serving a 300 000 t cap stockpiling area, two bucket wheel type rail mounted stacker-cum-reclaimers each having stacking cap of 1500 t/h, average reclaiming cap of 1250 t/h, one 7500 t cap bunker and one rail mounted shuttle boom type shiploader. The conveyor system carries coal from tipplers to stockyard for storage. Ship loaders, rail mounted and shuttle boom type, have rating cap of 3000 t/h each. This berth can also handle oil tankers

[3]*Berth No.4:* Capable of loading conventional ships and bulk of 2000 t/h, two wagon tipplers of cap 1500 t/h each; two stock yards with total cap of 175 000 t; two stacker reclaimers, each stacking cap of 1500 t/h and reclaiming cap of 1000 t/h; two ship loaders, cap of 1500 t/h each with mechanical trimmers

[4]*Berth No.4A:* For handling dry bulk cargo, mainly imported coking coal for Steel Authority of India Ltd. Two ship unloaders, two stacker reclaimers and automatic wagon loading and conveyor systems

[5]*Berth No.5:* Rapid mechanical discharge of rock phosphate, potash and sulphur, capable of handling bulk carriers of the 60 000 dwt class at rate of 6000 to 8000 t/day. Mechanised transit shed with storage cap of 30 000 t. Berthing face 178.7 m and width 20.1 m

[6]*Berth No's 6 & 7:* Bulk and breakbulk cargoes as well as facilities for pipeline discharge of liquid bulk cargoes

[7]*Berth No.8:* Mainly used for handling coking coal. General and other dry bulk cargo also handled

[8]*Berth No.12:* Under construction to handle breakbulk and container cargo

Bunkering: The Liberty Marine Syndicate Private Ltd, 22 Durgachak, Block A, Haldia, India 721 602, *Tel:* +91 3224 273630, *Fax:* +91 3224 274660, *Email:* logistics@libertyshipping.com, *Website:* www.libertyshipping.com
Asean International Ltd, P O Box 7860, Block Z Suite 42/43, Saif Zone, Sharjah, United Arab Emirates, *Tel:* +971 6 557 0083, *Fax:* +971 6 557 0085
Bharat Petroleum Corp. Ltd, 4th Floor, Old Admin Building, Mahul, Chembur, Mumbai, Maharashtra, India 400 074, *Tel:* +91 22 2554 3493, *Fax:* +91 22 2554 0621, *Email:* josecm@bharatpetroleum.in, *Website:* www.baratpetroleum.in
Bominflot, Bominoil Private Ltd, 504 Maker Chambers V, 221 Nariman Point, Mumbai, Maharashtra, India 400 021, *Tel:* +91 22 2281 7133, *Fax:* +91 22 2281 7145, *Email:* bominoil@vsnl.com, *Website:* www.bominflot.net
Cockett Marine Oil Ltd, Carrick House, 36 Station Square, Petts Wood, Kent BR5 1NA, United Kingdom, *Tel:* +44 1689 883 400, *Fax:* +44 1689 877 666, *Email:* enquiries@cockett.com, *Website:* www.cockettgroup.com – *Grades:* IFI; MDO; MGO – *Parcel Size:* min IFO 50t, min MDO/MGO 10t – *Delivery Mode:* barge, road tank wagon, pipeline
M/S Global Fuels & Lubricants Inc., 11-12 Mangal Society, 76C Rafi Ahmed Kidwai Road, King Circle, Mumbai, Maharashtra, India 400 019, *Tel:* +91 22 2374 5987, *Fax:* +91 22 2409 1627, *Email:* globalfuels@vsnl.com, *Website:* www.bunkerindia.com
Indian Oil Corp. Ltd, Indian Oil Bhavan Head Office, G9 Ali Yavar Jung Marg, Bandra (East), Mumbai, Maharashtra, India 400051, *Tel:* +91 22 2644 7368, *Fax:* +91 22 2642 2434, *Email:* partha_datta@indianoil.co.in, *Website:* www.indianoil.co.in – *Grades:* GO; DO; IFO – *Parcel Size:* min 10t – *Rates:* 30t/h – *Notice:* 48-72 hours – *Delivery Mode:* barge, pipeline, truck
Laxmi Marine, Plot No 119, Ward 6, Industrial Area, Bharat Nagar, Gandhidham, Gujarat, India 370 201, *Tel:* +91 2836 237 209, *Fax:* +91 2836 237 211, *Email:* info@laxmimarine.com, *Website:* www.laxmimarine.com

Towage: Five tugs are available

Ship Chandlers: The Liberty Marine Syndicate Private Ltd, 22 Durgachak, Block A, Haldia, India 721 602, *Tel:* +91 3224 273630, *Fax:* +91 3224 274660, *Email:* logistics@libertyshipping.com, *Website:* www.libertyshipping.com

Shipping Agents: Five Star Logistics Private Ltd, Ranchik, Purba Medinipur, Haldia, India 721 602, *Tel:* +91 3224 252415, *Fax:* +91 3224 252308, *Email:* marketing@fivestarorex.com, *Website:* www.fivestarorex.com
GAC Shipping (India) Pvt Ltd, Block A, Plot No.27, First Floor, Durgachak, Haldia, India 721 602, *Tel:* +91 3224 276079, *Fax:* +91 3224 276007, *Email:* shipping.haldia@gacworld.com, *Website:* www.gacworld.com
Interocean Shipping (India) Pvt Ltd., Chiranjivpur CPT Camp, Room No.2, Block L1, Haldia, India 721 604, *Tel:* +91 3224 252615, *Fax:* +91 3224 252614, *Email:* haldia@interoceangroup.com, *Website:* www.interoceangroup.com
Merchant Shipping Services Private Ltd, Room No.7 Block B, Chiranjibpur Camp, Chiranjibpur, Haldia, India 721604, *Tel:* +91 3224 253811, *Fax:* +91 3224 253812, *Email:* mershal@merchantshpg.com, *Website:* www.merchantshpg.com
Samsara Shipping (Private) Ltd, Dock Zone, Block - B, Chiranjibpur Camp, Room No. 7, Haldia, India 721 604, *Tel:* +91 3224 253812, *Fax:* +91 3224 253812, *Email:* haldia@samsarashipping.com, *Website:* www.samsarashipping.com
Seatrans Marine Private Limited, 2nd Floor, India Hotel Extn. Building, Medinipur (EST), Khanjanchak, Durgachak, Haldia, India 721602, *Tel:* +91 3224 275724, *Fax:*

+91 3224 278217, *Email:* seatrans.haldia@seatrans.co.in, *Website:* www.seatrans.co.in

Stevedoring Companies: Five Star Logistics Private Ltd, Ranchik, Purba Medinipur, Haldia, India 721 602, *Tel:* +91 3224 252415, *Fax:* +91 3224 252308, *Email:* marketing@fivestarorex.com, *Website:* www.fivestarorex.com

Surveyors: J.B. Boda Surveyors Private Ltd, Room No.93 Haldia Oil Jetty, Haldia, India 721 604, *Tel:* +91 3224 252286, *Fax:* +91 3224 252286, *Email:* jbbhld@jbbodamail.com, *Website:* www.jbboda.net
Metcalfe & Hodgkinson Private Ltd, Haldia, India, *Tel:* +91 3224 277376, *Fax:* +91 3224 277376, *Email:* haldia@metcalfeindia.com, *Website:* www.metcalfeindia.com

Medical Facilities: There is a hospital in the Haldia Dock complex with moderate facilities. Modern hospitals available at Calcutta

Railway: Haldia Railway station, 2 km

Lloyd's Agent: Wilson Surveyors and Adjusters Private Ltd, Suite No.806, 8th Floor, O M Towers, 32 Chowringhee Road, Kolkata, West Bengal, India 700 071, *Tel:* +91 33 2217 5800, *Fax:* +91 33 2217 5797, *Email:* kolkata@wilsur.com, *Website:* www.wilsur.com

HAZIRA

Lat 21° 6' N; Long 72° 39' E.

Admiralty Chart: 3465   **Admiralty Pilot:** 38
Time Zone: GMT +5.5 h   **UNCTAD Locode:** IN

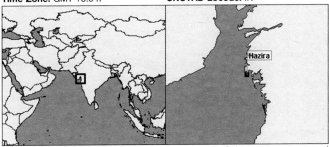

Principal Facilities:

Q						T

Authority: Hazira Port Private Ltd, 101-103 Abhjeet II, Mithakali Circle, Ahmedabad, India 380 006, *Tel:* +91 79 3001 1100, *Website:* www.porthazira.com

Officials: Port Manager: Jan Teertstra, *Tel:* +91 261 305 1155.

Port Security: ISPS compliant. PFSO: Sunil Kumar Kakar, Email: hlpl-haz-pfso@shell.com

Pre-Arrival Information: 1) The following pre-arrival messages should to be sent both to Hazira Port Control and the LNG Terminal. Messages should also be copied to the ship's agent
First Standard Message:
a) name, IMO no, flag and port of registry, Gt/nrt/sdwt
b) ship's telephone number, fax number, email id
c) master's name, nationality; number and nationality of crew members
d) loa, max beam and max depth
e) arrival draft and displacement
f) departure draft and displacement (Marpol Annex 1 reg 13 (2) a & b Refers). In any case trim shall be not more than 3.0 m
g) load port, last port (with dates of departure) and next port. Last 3 ports and 3 cargoes
h) cargo on board - grade, B/L quantity, temp and pressure
i) confirm vessel has a valid 'Oil Pollution Indemnity Certificate'
j) name and address of P & I club and their local representative
k) confirm all navigational equipments (As per SOLAS ch V reg 19), propulsion units, and other deck and engine machinery operational - notify deficiencies if any
l) name, telephone/fax numbers of the owners
m) ports touched in last 30 days - for quarantine purposes
n) status of ISPS certificate and security level at which ship is currently operating
o) name last 10 ports of call where interface with port or ship took place
p) the security level at which ship operated at any previous port where it conducted a ship or port interface during last 10 calls at port facilities
q) any special or additional security measures that were taken by the ship in any previous port where it has conducted a ship/port interface during last 10 calls at port facilities
r) confirmation that appropriate ship security procedures were maintained during any ship to ship activity during last 10 calls at port facilities
s) any other security related information to ensure safety and security persons, port facilities, ships and other property
t) does vessel comply with ISM code. Validity of ISM DOC/SOC and issuing authority During voyage: If the ETA deviates more than 12 h from that initially advised on departure and/or there are any changes to DD, EE or FF then port and terminal must be advised
2) 72 h before arrival:
ship's name and call sign
update ETA
3) 48 h before arrival:
ship's name and call sign
ETA and arrival draft
estimated cargo tank temperatures and tank pressure
confirm the following have been tested and/or are fully operational:
navigation, mooring, safety & engine systems
cargo system & boil off control systems
gas detection systems

Key to Principal Facilities:—				
A=Airport	**C**=Containers	**G**=General Cargo	**P**=Petroleum	**R**=Ro/Ro	**Y**=Dry Bulk
B=Bunkers	**D**=Dry Dock	**L**=Cruise	**Q**=Other Liquid Bulk	**T**=Towage (where available from port)	

ESD system, alarms and interlocks
cargo tank high level alarms
high & low pressure alarms
remotely operated valves
cargo lines are free of oxygen
no tank leakages
If the ETA changes by more than 6 hours following the issue of the 96 hour message and before sending the 24 hour message then the revised ETA must be advised to the Port
4) 24 h before arrival:
ship's name and call sign
confirm ETA
send pratique message via ship's agent
if the ETA changes by more than 6 h following the issue of the 96 h message and before sending the 24 h message then the revised ETA must be advised to the port
5) 12 h before arrival:
ship's name and call sign
confirm ETA

Documentation: The following documents are required by shore authorities upon arrival for clearance of the vessel:
1) Customs Authority:
original last port clearance
maritime declaration of health (3 copies)
vaccination list (3 copies)
voyage memo (ports called in last 30 days or last 10 ports of call) with arrival and departure dates and security levels (3 copies)
bills of lading, cargo manifest and transit cargo if any (1 copy)
ist of ships stores including bonded stores and deck stores (3 copies)
personal effects declaration with crew currency (3 copies)
ships currency declaration (3 copies)
nil lists (If there are no passengers, stowaways, animals, arms, ammunitions) (3 copies)
list of narcotic medicines (3 copies)
crew list (name, rank, nationality, passport number, seamen book number, date of and place of embarkation) (7 copies)
following statutory certificates (2 copies each):
a) ship registry certificate
b) ISPS certificate
c) international load line certificate
d) cargo ship safety equipment certificate
e) cargo ship radio certificate
f) cargo ship safety construction certificate
g) international oil pollution certificate
h) deratting exemption certificate
2) Quarantine Authority: At Hazira the customs-boarding officer usually gives quarantine (free pratique) but if the vessel is coming from yellow fever area, Port Health Officer from Kandla will board the vessel
Following set of documents are required anyway:
crew list 1 copy)
maritime declaration of health (1 copy)
vaccination list (1 copy)
deratting certificate (1 copy)
3) Immigration Authority: Custom Authorities are clearing the vessel on behalf of Immigration. For sign on and sign off of Foreign Nationals 48 h notice with confirmed air ticket is required. Ship's Agent will have to get landing permission from the local police. For Indian Nationals this is not applicable
Documents required in case of crew change (Foreign or Indian Nationals):
crew list (1 copy)
personal effects declaration (1 copy)
sign on/sign off crew passport (1 copy)
4.　Port Authority (Hazira Port Private Limited):
Following documents required by Port Authority:
bill of lading, cargo manifest, transit cargo list (1 copy)
crew list (1 copy)
Following statutory certificates (1 copy each):
a) ship registry certificate
b) ISPS certificate
c) international load line certificate
d) cargo ship safety equipment certificate
e) cargo ship radio certificate
f) cargo ship safety construction certificate
g) international oil pollution certificate
h) derating exemption certificate
The following documents are required by the Hazira LNG terminal for cargo clearance:
sale and ourchase agreement or detailed contracts
commercial Invoice
original bill of lading
certificate of origin
certificate of quality
certificate of quantity
load port ullage report (pre and post loading)
last 3 documents will require signature of independent surveyor
Other documents will be prepared and given by importer in consultation with CHA

Approach: An entrance channel connects the port with the deep water of the Sutherland Channel. The dredged depth of -12 m CD allows for arrival and departure of LNG carriers up to a draft of 11.5 m. The straight approach channel has a clear width of 400 m at the seaside tapering off to a width of 300 m between the breakwaters to allow unobstructed easy entrance/departure of ships. The orientation of the approach channel is heading 070-250°N. Breakwaters provide protection from the SW monsoon waves and swells and for the currents parallel to the coastline Turning basin with a radius of 300 m for the manoeuvring of tug-assisted LNG Carriers during berthing and unberthing

Anchorage: The recommended anchorage is located approx 11 miles SW of the harbour, outside the Magdalla Port Limits, where the sea bottom is sand and is of good holding ground. Anchoring is prohibited within port limits, unless the anchor is used temporarily to support vessel maneuvering or in case of an emergency. An alternative anchorage is located just outside of the Hazira port limits in the Sutherland

Channel Tanker Anchorage where depth is more than 20 m and the sea bottom is sand and is of good holding ground. Spring tidal currents however are very strong and in excess of 4.5 knots. The Magdalla Port controls this anchorage, which lies within the Magdalla port limits, and free use of this anchorage must be agreed with Magdalla Port Control

Pilotage: Compulsory. Pilot boards in pos 20° 54' N; 72° 35' E (S of General Lighterage Area)

Radio Frequency: Hazira Port Control listens on VHF Channels 16 and 69

Maximum Vessel Dimensions: LNG vessels: 145 000 m3, 295 m loa, 50 m beam, 11.5 m draft

Accommodation:

Name	Depth (m)	Remarks
Hazira		
LNG Berth	13	See [1] below

[1]*LNG Berth:* Four breasting and five mooring dolphins accommodating LNG carriers with a cap of 75 000-145 000 m3. Unloading platform fitted with three unloading arms (two liquid and one vapour) 16" LVL ANSI 150. Liquid arms flow rate of 5000 m3/h for each arm

Storage: Two LNG storage tanks, each with a cap of 160 000 m3

Towage: Four tugs of 60 t bollard pull each

Shipping Agents: J.M. Baxi & Co, Ramsa Tower, Mezzanine Floor, Office No.03/04/05, Near Adajan Circle, Rander Road, Surat, India 395 009, *Tel:* +91 261 269 2790, *Fax:* +91 261 268 6302, *Email:* surat@jmbaxi.com, *Website:* www.jmbaxi.com
Interocean Shipping (India) Pvt Ltd., B-10 903 Indralok Complex, Opposite Lakeview Garden, Surat-Dumas Road, Piplod, Surat, India 395 007, *Tel:* +91 261 222 3578, *Fax:* +91 261 221 0825, *Email:* surat@interoceangroup.com, *Website:* www.interoceangroup.com

Surveyors: J.B. Boda Surveyors Private Ltd, Maker Bhavan No.1, Sir Vithaldas Thackersey Marg, Mumbai, Maharashtra, India 400 020, *Tel:* +91 22 2262 4517, *Fax:* +91 22 2262 3747, *Email:* jbbodamumbai@vsnl.com, *Website:* www.jbboda.net

Medical Facilities: Doctor available at the Terminal's clinic. In cases where more extensive medical treatment is required there is a hospital located in Surat

Railway: The nearest rail head exists at Kawas, approx 16 km. Mumbai-Delhi railway line, 43 km

Development: Construction of bulk and/or container terminals expected to commence in 2008
PSA International is developing a container terminal consisting of two berths with a draft of 12.5 m and is scheduled to be operational in 2009

Lloyd's Agent: Wilson Surveyors and Adjusters Private Ltd, Golden Arcade, II Floor, Room No.209, Plot No.141/142, Sector 8, Gandhidam, Kutch, Gujarat, India 370 201, *Tel:* +91 2836 238333, *Fax:* +91 2836 238333, *Email:* kandla@wilsur.com, *Website:* www.wilsur.com

INDIRA DOCK

harbour area, see under Mumbai

JAFRABAD

Lat 20° 52' N; Long 71° 22' E.

Admiralty Chart: 1979	**Admiralty Pilot:** 38
Time Zone: GMT +5.5 h	**UNCTAD Locode:** IN JBD

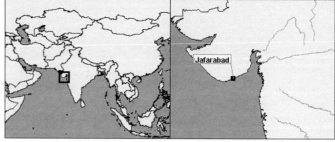

Principal Facilities:

	Y	G			B		A

Authority: Gujarat Maritime Board, Port of Jafrabad, Jafrabad, Gujarat, India, *Tel:* +91 2794 245152, *Fax:* +91 2794 245165, *Website:* www.gmbports.org

Officials: Port Officer: C. M. Rathod.

Approach: A channel about 40 m wide leads across the bar to a basin 300 m in diameter which surrounds the L-shaped jetty

Anchorage: In fine weather anchorage can be obtained 2.5 km from shore at a depth of 14 m

Pilotage: Not compulsory, pilotage information can be obtained from the port officer

Tides: Mean spring range about 1.9 m, mean neap range about 0.7 m

Principal Imports and Exports: Imports: Coal, Coke. Exports: Clinker, Roof Tiles, Salt.

Accommodation:

Name	Length (m)	Draught (m)	Remarks
Jafarabad			
Clinker Jetty	211	5	See [1] below

[1]*Clinker Jetty:* Operated by L & T Cement Plants. Clinker is loaded on their own conyeyor belt at a rate of 300 mt per hour

Storage: There are seven warehouses available with an area of 1310 m2 with a storage capacity of 2500 mt. Sufficient open space is also available

Bunkering: Private bunkering and ship stores are available

Shipping Agents: Chowgule Brothers Private Ltd, Dhorania, Giriraj Chowck, P O Box 12, Jafrabad, Gujarat, India 365 540, *Tel:* +91 2794 245144, *Fax:* +91 2794 245527, *Email:* jafrabad.cb@choqgule.co.in

Stevedoring Companies: Chowgule Brothers Private Ltd, Dhorania, Giriraj Chowck, P O Box 12, Jafrabad, Gujarat, India 365 540, *Tel:* +91 2794 245144, *Fax:* +91 2794 245527, *Email:* jafrabad.cb@choqgule.co.in

Surveyors: Chowgule Brothers Private Ltd, Dhorania, Giriraj Chowck, P O Box 12, Jafrabad, Gujarat, India 365 540, *Tel:* +91 2794 245144, *Fax:* +91 2794 245527, *Email:* jafrabad.cb@choqgule.co.in

Airport: Bhavnagar

Lloyd's Agent: Wilson Surveyors and Adjusters Private Ltd, Golden Arcade, II Floor, Room No.209, Plot No.141/142, Sector 8, Gandhidam, Kutch, Gujarat, India 370 201, *Tel:* +91 2836 238333, *Fax:* +91 2836 238333, *Email:* kandla@wilsur.com, *Website:* www.wilsur.com

JAMNAGAR TERMINAL

Lat 22° 34' N; Long 69° 47' E.

Admiralty Chart: 699/43		**Admiralty Pilot:** 38	
Time Zone: GMT +5.5 h		**UNCTAD Locode:** IN JGA	

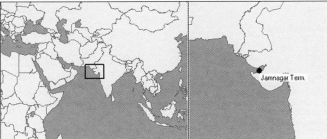
Jamnagar Term.

Principal Facilities:

P	Q						T	A

Authority: Reliance Ports & Terminals Pvt Ltd (RPTL), Village Meghpar, Taluka, Lalpur, Jamnagar, Gujarat, India 361 280, *Tel:* +91 288 231 3186, *Fax:* +91 288 231 3198, *Email:* port_operation@ril.com

Officials: Operations Manager: Sunil Pradhan, *Email:* sunil_y_pradhan@ril.com. Port Officer: Capt Raman Kumar.

Port Security: ISPS compliant. Equipped with two high-speed security boats. Communication regarding security is through the Port Operation Centre on VHF Channel 71 and/or Tel: +91 288 231 2600, Email: port_operation@ril.com, pfso_jamnagar@ril.com and vankala.rao@zmail.ril.com. Pre-arrival notification of secruity (PANS) is required to be sent with 72 h notice

Pre-Arrival Information: Vessels are required to inform Reliance Jamnagar Marine Terminal by fax or email of their ETA at the Pilot Boarding Area 72 h, with confirmation 48 h, 24 h and 12 h prior to their arrival in the prescribed standard pre-arrival format

Documentation: Crew lists (6 copies), vessel stores list (4 copies), vessel property list (4 copies), crew personal effects declaration (4 copies), ship currency list (4 copies), crew currency list (4 copies), arms & ammunition list (4 copies), passenger list (4 copies), animal list (4 copies), maritime declaration of health (2 copies), list of last ports of call (2 copies), crew vaccination list (2 copies), last port clearance (original and 2 copies)

Approach: Approach to Reliance Jamnagar Marine Terminal is marked by a fairway buoy in pos 22° 32.02' N; 69° 45.32' E. SPM1 is fitted with RACON 'R' in pos 22° 34' 19.22" N; 69° 47' 11.60" W. SPM3 is fitted with RACON 'O' in pos 22° 36' 33" N; 69° 49' 56" E. Caution should be exercised when navigating in this area due to the proximity of the SPM's

Anchorage: VLCC Anchorage:
22° 39.00' N; 69° 53.45' E
22° 41.80' N; 69° 58.30' E
22° 37.35' N; 69° 53.45' E
22° 40.15' N; 69° 58.30' E
Chemical & Gas Anchorage Area (Temporary Area):
22° 31.0' N; 69° 46.7' E
22° 30.0' N; 69° 46.7' E
22° 30.0' N; 69° 44.8' E
22° 31.0' N; 69° 44.8' E
Lighterage & Transhipment Area (Temporary Area):
22° 34.0' N; 69° 44.8' E
22° 34.6' N; 69° 46.0' E
22° 31.0' N; 69° 46.0' E
22° 31.0' N; 69° 44.8' E
Product SPM Anchorage:
22° 37.35' N; 69° 53.45' E
22° 40.15' N; 69° 58.30' E

22° 36.20' N; 69° 53.45' E
22° 38.95' N; 69° 58.30' E

Pilotage: Compulsory for all vessels using the terminal. Contact Reliance Port Control on VHF Channels 16 or 71
Pilot boarding area for tanker berths in pos 22° 32.4' N; 69° 46.7' E and for SPM's in pos 22° 36' N; 69° 47' E

Radio Frequency: VHF Channels 16 and 71

Weather: Monsoon: May 1st to September 30th

Tides: The vertical spring tidal range is approx 6.5 m

Maximum Vessel Dimensions: At three crude discharge SPM's: 345 m loa, 350 000 dwt, 22.5 m draft
At two product SPM's: 300 m loa, 150 000 dwt, 18.5 m draft
At four berths of jetty: 252 m loa, 120 000 dwt, 14.5 m draft

Principal Imports and Exports: Imports: Crude oil, Fuel oil. Exports: Gas oil, Jet fuel, LPG, Motor spirit, Naptha.

Working Hours: 24 h/day

Accommodation:

Name	Depth (m)	Draught (m)	Remarks
Jamnagar Terminal			See [1] below
SPM No.1	32	22.5	See [2] below
SPM No.2	30	22.5	See [3] below
SPM No.3	32	22.5	See [4] below
SPM No.4	25	18.5	See [5] below
SPM No.5	25	18.5	See [6] below
Berth A		12.5	See [7] below
Berth B		13.5	See [8] below
Berth C		13.5	See [9] below
Berth D		14.5	See [10] below

[1]*Jamnagar Terminal:* Consists of five offshore SPM's, located approx 15 km offshore, and connected to the Marine Tank Farm via 48" and 30" subsea pipelines and four onshore berths, located between Goos and Munde reefs
[2]*SPM No.1:* In pos 22° 34' 19.22" N; 69° 47' 11.60" E, for vessels of 20 000-350 000 dwt & 345 m loa
[3]*SPM No.2:* In pos 22° 35' 29.99" N; 69° 48' 30.01" E, for vessels of 20 000-350 000 dwt and 345 m loa
[4]*SPM No.3:* In pos 22° 36' 33" N; 69° 49' 56" E, for vessels of 20 000-350 000 dwt & 345 m loa
[5]*SPM No.4:* In pos 22° 35' 22" N; 69° 51' 52" E, for vessels of 20 000-150 000 dwt & 300 m loa
[6]*SPM No.5:* In pos 22° 34' 43" N; 69° 50' 07" E, for vessels of 20 000-150 000 dwt & 300 m loa
[7]*Berth A:* For vessels of 105-195 m loa (fair weather & monsoon)
[8]*Berth B:* For vessels of 108.5-228 m loa (fair weather & monsoon)
[9]*Berth C:* For vessels of 160-246 m loa (fair weather) & 160-228 m loa (monsoon)
[10]*Berth D:* For vessels of 160-252 m loa (fair weather) & 160-246 m loa (monsoon)

Storage: Captive terminal tending to the needs of the Reliance refinery at Jamnagar. No third party storage is available

Bunkering: Not available at the terminal but may be arranged through Agents at the anchorage only
Asean International Ltd, P O Box 7860, Block Z Suite 42/43, Saif Zone, Sharjah, United Arab Emirates, *Tel:* +971 6 557 0083, *Fax:* +971 6 557 0085
Bapu's Shipping Agency, Plot No 32, Sector 9, Near Central Bank Of India, Gandhidham, Gujarat, India 370 201, *Tel:* +91 2836 222 002, *Fax:* +91 2836 236 036, *Email:* info@shipsupplier.biz, *Website:* www.shipsupplier.biz
Bharat Fuels, Off No.38, C.L. Sharma Shopping Complex, Sector 8, Near Oslo Cinema, Gandhidham, Gujarat, India 370201, *Tel:* +91 2836 227 627, *Fax:* +91 2836 225 925, *Email:* bharatpetro_gim@sancharnet.in/bharatpetro@indiatimes.com, *Website:* www.bharatpetroleum.in
Bharat Petroleum Corp. Ltd, 4th Floor, Old Admin Building, Mahul, Chembur, Mumbai, Maharashtra, India 400 074, *Tel:* +91 22 2554 3493, *Fax:* +91 22 2554 0621, *Email:* josecm@bharatpetroleum.in, *Website:* www.baratpetroleum.in
Bominflot, Bominoil Private Ltd, 504 Maker Chambers V, 221 Nariman Point, Mumbai, Maharashtra, India 400 021, *Tel:* +91 22 2281 7133, *Fax:* +91 22 2281 7145, *Email:* bominoil@vsnl.com, *Website:* www.bominflot.net
M/S Global Fuels & Lubricants Inc., 11-12 Mangal Society, 76C Rafi Ahmed Kidwai Road, King Circle, Mumbai, Maharashtra, India 400 019, *Tel:* +91 22 2374 5987, *Fax:* +91 22 2409 1627, *Email:* globalfuels@vsnl.com, *Website:* www.bunkerindia.com
Gujarat Marine Private Ltd, Manali Chambers, Plot No. 306, Sector 1/A, Gandhidham, Gujarat, India 370 201, *Tel:* +91 2836 222 518, *Fax:* +91 2836 239 057, *Email:* bunker@gujmar.com, *Website:* www.gujmar.com
Hindustan Petroleum Corp. Ltd, Hindustan Bhawan, Vallabhdas Marg, Mumbai, Maharashtra, India 400 038, *Tel:* +91 22 2226 0079 – *Grades:* MDO; IFO180cSt – *Parcel Size:* min barge 150t, no max – *Rates:* 50-100t/h – *Notice:* 48-72 hours – *Delivery Mode:* barge, truck
Indian Oil Corp. Ltd, Indian Oil Bhavan Head Office, G9 Ali Yavar Jung Marg, Bandra (East), Mumbai, Maharashtra, India 400051, *Tel:* +91 22 2644 7368, *Fax:* +91 22 2642 2434, *Email:* partha_datta@indianoil.co.in, *Website:* www.indianoil.co.in
Jaisu Shipping Co. Private Ltd, Kewalramani House, Dinshaw Building Road, Near Custom House, New Kandla, Kandla, India 370 210, *Tel:* +91 2836 270 428, *Fax:* +91 2836 270 650, *Email:* jaisu_shipping@yahoo.com/mail@jaisu.in, *Website:* www.jaisu.in – *Grades:* IFO80-180cSt; MDO; MGO; lubes; in line blending available – *Misc:* own storage facilities – *Parcel Size:* min 10t, max 2900t – *Rates:* 100-500t/h – *Notice:* 12 hours – *Delivery Mode:* barge, pipeline, truck
Laxmi Marine, Plot No 119, Ward 6, Industrial Area, Bharat Nagar, Gandhidham, Gujarat, India 370 201, *Tel:* +91 2836 237 209, *Fax:* +91 2836 237 211, *Email:* info@laxmimarine.com, *Website:* www.laxmimarine.com
Link Enterprises, Plot 44, Sector 9/A, Morabia Commercial Centre, P O Box 248, Gandhidham, Gujarat, India 370 201, *Tel:* +91 2836 230 107, *Fax:* +91 2836 231 285, *Email:* info@asiaship.com
Mithi Overseas Private Ltd, Plot No.265/12-B, Bajaj Chambers, Near Shiv Cinema, Gandhidham, Gujarat, India 370 201, *Tel:* +91 2836 235417, *Fax:* +91 2836 235417, *Email:* mithioverseas@yahoo.com
Umamarine, Sector 1/A, Plot No 310, Gandhidham, Gujarat, India 370 201, *Tel:* +91

Key to Principal Facilities:—

A=Airport	**C**=Containers	**G**=General Cargo	**P**=Petroleum	**R**=Ro/Ro	**Y**=Dry Bulk
B=Bunkers	**D**=Dry Dock	**L**=Cruise	**Q**=Other Liquid Bulk	**T**=Towage (where available from port)

2836 221465, *Fax:* +91 2836 232830, *Email:* info@umamarine.com, *Website:* www.umamarine.com

Waste Reception Facilities: Garbage reception facilities are available at each berth on the jetty

Towage: Compulsory. Six tugs available of 3200-5000 hp

Ship Chandlers: Inayat Moosa & Co., Avani Apartment, Opposite Poultry Farm, Saru Section Road, Jamnagar, Gujarat, India 361002, *Tel:* +91 288 255 2079, *Fax:* +91 288 254 0121, *Email:* info@inayatmoosa.com, *Website:* www.inayatmoosa.com

Shipping Agents: J.M. Baxi & Co, Jalpari, Pratap Palace Road, Jamnagar, Gujarat, India 361 008, *Tel:* +91 288 267 4028, *Fax:* +91 288 255 5817, *Email:* jamngr@jmbaxi.com, *Website:* www.jmbaxi.com
Chowgule Brothers Private Ltd, Moon Appartments, 2nd Floor Pandit Nehru Road, Jamnagar, Gujarat, India 361 008, *Tel:* +91 288 255 3761, *Fax:* +91 288 255 3571, *Email:* jamnagar.cb@chowgule.co.in
GAC Shipping (India) Pvt Ltd, Zaver Chambers, Office 2, 4th Floor, Pandit Nehru Marg, Jamnagar, Gujarat, India 361 008, *Tel:* +91 288 255 2844, *Fax:* +91 288 255 8011, *Email:* jamnagar@gacworld.com, *Website:* www.gacworld.com
Samsara Shipping (Private) Ltd, 2nd F Floor, Milestone Apartment, Opposite Custon House Office, Pandit Nehru Marg, Panchvati, Jamnagar, Gujarat, India 361002, *Tel:* +91 288 266 0440/1, *Fax:* +91 288 255 1855, *Email:* samsjamnagar@samsarashipping.com, *Website:* www.samsarashipping.com

Stevedoring Companies: Chowgule Brothers Private Ltd, Moon Appartments, 2nd Floor Pandit Nehru Road, Jamnagar, Gujarat, India 361 008, *Tel:* +91 288 255 3761, *Fax:* +91 288 255 3571, *Email:* jamnagar.cb@chowgule.co.in

Surveyors: Chowgule Brothers Private Ltd, Moon Appartments, 2nd Floor Pandit Nehru Road, Jamnagar, Gujarat, India 361 008, *Tel:* +91 288 255 3761, *Fax:* +91 288 255 3571, *Email:* jamnagar.cb@chowgule.co.in

Medical Facilities: Available through agent at Jamnagar City. Limited emergency medical treatment is available at the terminal

Airport: Situated 25 km from the terminal with daily flights available to Mumbai

Railway: Situated 30 km from the terminal and well connected to other parts of India

Lloyd's Agent: Wilson Surveyors and Adjusters Private Ltd, Golden Arcade, II Floor, Room No.209, Plot No.141/142, Sector 8, Gandhidam, Kutch, Gujarat, India 370 201, *Tel:* +91 2836 238333, *Fax:* +91 2836 238333, *Email:* kandla@wilsur.com, *Website:* www.wilsur.com

JAWAHAR DOCK

harbour area, see under Chennai

JAWAHAR DWEEP

harbour area, see under Mumbai

JAWAHARLAL NEHRU

Lat 18° 56' N; Long 72° 51' E.

Admiralty Chart: 2627	**Admiralty Pilot:** 38
Time Zone: GMT +5.5 h	**UNCTAD Locode:** IN NSA

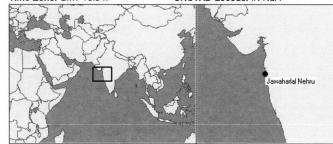

Jawaharlal Nehru

Principal Facilities:

P	Y		C	R		B		T	A

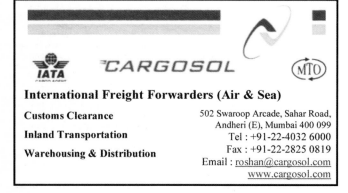

Authority: Jawaharlal Nehru Port Trust, Administration Building, Sheva, Navi Mumbai, Maharashtra, India 400 707, *Tel:* +91 22 2724 2290, *Fax:* +91 22 2724 2642, *Email:* skkaul@jnport.com, *Website:* www.jnport.gov.in

Officials: Chairman: Syed Shahzad Hussain, *Email:* chairman@jnport.com.
Deputy Conservator: Capt Jitendra Mishra, *Tel:* +91 22 2724 2301, *Email:* jmishra@jnport.com.
Secretary: Shiben Kaul, *Tel:* +91 22 2724 2233.

Port Security: ISPS compliant. PFSO: Capt. B.S. Kumar, Tel: +91 22 2724 2334, Fax: +91 22 2724 4170, Email: bskumar@jnport.com

Approach: Main approach as for Mumbai, then through a separately dredged channel running South of Elephanta Island known as JNP Channel, which has a min dredged depth of 11 m CD

Pilotage: Compulsory for vessels over 100 grt. Pilots board vessels at the pilot boarding ground in pos 18° 51.5' N; 72° 49.5' E

Radio Frequency: Continuous watch maintained by the Port Signal Station on VHF Channels 16 and 13. Call sign: Jawahar Port

Traffic: 2007/08, 55 756 000 t of cargo handled, 4 060 000 TEU's

Maximum Vessel Dimensions: 100 000 grt, 250 m loa, 12.5 m draft

Working Hours: 1st Shift 0700-1500, 2nd Shift 1500-2330, 3rd Shift 2300-0730

Accommodation:

Name	Length (m)	Depth (m)	Draught (m)	Remarks
Jawaharlal Nehru Port Container Terminal				See [1] below
CB01		13.5	12	See [2] below
CB02		13.5	12	See [3] below
CB03		13.5	12	See [4] below
Nhava Sheva International Container Terminal				See [5] below
CB04-05	600	13.5	12	
Gateway Terminal (India) Pvt. Ltd.				See [6] below
Quay	712	13.5	12	Containers
Jawaharlal Nehru BPCL Liquid Cargo Jetty				See [7] below
LB01	250		12–12.5	
LB02	180		10	
Crude Oil Facility				See [8] below

[1] *Jawaharlal Nehru Port Container Terminal:* Three berths with total quay length of 680 m. Container yard of 35 ha with an additional paved area of 180 000 m2 with 280 reefer points
Capacity 1.1 million TEU's per annum
[2] *CB01:* Can accommodate three vessels up to 200 m loa
[3] *CB02:* Can accommodate three vessels up to 200 m loa
[4] *CB03:* Can accommodate three vessels up to 200 m loa
[5] *Nhava Sheva International Container Terminal:* Operated by Nhava Sheva International Container Pvt Ltd., Operation Center, Container Gate, Sheva, Navi Mumbai 400 707, Tel: +91 22 2724 3500, Fax: +91 22 2724 3527, Email: info@nsict.co.in, Website: www.nsict.co.in
Ground slots for 4212 TEU's. 672 reefer points
Capacity 1.2 million TEU's per annum
[6] *Gateway Terminal (India) Pvt. Ltd.:* Operated by AP Moller Group, GTI House, Jawaharlal Nehru Port, Sheva, Navi Mumbai 400 707, Tel: +91 22 6681 1000, Fax: +91 22 2724 1235, Email: projects@gatewayterminals.com, Website: www.gatewayterminals.com
Capacity 1.3 million TEU's per annum
[7] *Jawaharlal Nehru BPCL Liquid Cargo Jetty:* 300 m jetty. Bunkering and portable water facilities at both liquid cargo berths
Capacity 5.5 million t per annum
[8] *Crude Oil Facility:* For despatch of crude oil from ONGC's Western Oil Field. Two 16" dia loading arms with cap of 6500 kl/h

Mechanical Handling Equipment:

Location	Type	Capacity (t)	Qty
Jawaharlal Nehru Port Container Terminal	Post Panamax	40	6
Jawaharlal Nehru Port Container Terminal	Super Post Panamax		2
Jawaharlal Nehru Port Container Terminal	RTG's		18
Jawaharlal Nehru Port Container Terminal	Reach Stackers		11
Nhava Sheva International Container Terminal	Post Panamax	40	4
Nhava Sheva International Container Terminal	Super Post Panamax	40	3
Nhava Sheva International Container Terminal	RTG's		29
Nhava Sheva International Container Terminal	Reach Stackers		3
Gateway Terminal (India) Pvt. Ltd.	Post Panamax		8

Cargo Worked: Bulk: approx 4000 t/day
Container: 50 moves/h/crane

Bunkering: Pipeline for supplying oil and LDO at all JNP berths. Bunkers provided by prior arrangement, Tel: (2157) 487/8

Towage: Compulsory for all vessels berthing at the port. Three tugs available of 30 t bollard pull

Shipping Agents: Cargosol, 502 Swaroop Arcade, Oppo. Adarsh Industrial Estate, Sahar Road, Andheri (E), Mumbai, Maharashtra, India 400 093, Tel: +91 22 4032 6000, Fax: +91 22 2825 0819, Email: roshan@cargosol.com
CSAV Group Agencies (India) Pvt Ltd, 2nd Floor Port User's Building, Jawaharlal Nehru, India, Tel: +91 22 5610 8103/4, Fax: +91 22 2724 0262, Email: hhedge@csavagencies-india.com
GAC Shipping (India) Pvt Ltd, B-38/2, Sector III, JNPT Township, Near Township Telephone Exchange, Nhava Sheva, India 400 707, Tel: +91 22 2747 0776, Fax: +91 22 2747 0778, Email: jnpt@gacworld.com, Website: www.gacworld.com
Samsara Shipping (Private) Ltd, Unit No.602 & 603, 6th Floor, 'Anchorage', The Ship Agents Premises Co-Operative Society Ltd, Plot No.2, Sector-11, Dronagiri Node, (Opp. JNPT Town Ship Gate), Navi Mumbai, Maharashtra, India 400 707, Tel: +91 22 2724 3103, Fax: +91 22 2724 3111, Email: comm-jnptsams@samsarashipping.com, Website: www.samsarashipping.com

Medical Facilities: Available 7 km from port, at Port Hospital

Airport: Chatrapati Shivaji International Airport, Sahar, Mumbai, 65 km

Railway: Mumbai Chatrapati Shivaji Terminus, approx 70 km

Development: Adding a fourth container terminal by 2012 on reclaimed land
Dredging a channel to allow fully laden post-panamax ships to berth at the port
Purchasing additional container cranes at the port's existing three terminals

Lloyd's Agent: Wilson Surveyors and Adjusters Private Ltd, C-204 Remi Bizcourt, Veera Desai Road, Andheri West, Mumbai, Maharashtra, India 400 053, Tel: +91 22 6696 3606, Fax: +91 22 6696 3669, Email: mumbai@wilsur.com, Website: www.wilsur.com

KAKINADA

Lat 17° 0' N; Long 82° 17' E.

Admiralty Chart: 575	**Admiralty Pilot:** 21
Time Zone: GMT +5.5 h	**UNCTAD Locode:** IN KAK

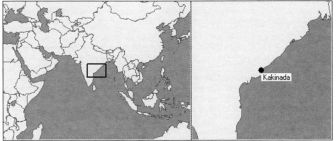

Principal Facilities:

P	Y	G	C		B		T	A

Authority: Kakinada Seaports Ltd, 2nd Floor, Port Administrative Building, Beach Road, Kakinada, Andhra Pradesh, India 533 007, Tel: +91 884 236 5089, Fax: +91 884 238 5402, Email: mailkkd@kakinadaseaports.in, Website: www.kakinadaseaports.in

Officials: Director: Karnati Venkateswara Rao, Email: kvrao@kakinadaseaports.in.
Assistant General Manager: Murli Krishna, Email: mkt@kakinadaseaports.in.
Marine Manager: Capt Jacob Satyaraju, Email: capt@kakinadaseaports.in.

Port Security: ISPS compliant

Documentation: Standard pre-arrival information collected by the agents and furnished to the deep water port

Approach: Approach channel in depth of 12.5 m

Anchorage: 1 nautical mile NE of Fairway Buoy for vessels calling at deep water port

Pilotage: Pilot not required for the anchorage but compulsory for vessels going to the deep water port with 72 h notice prior to ETA

Radio Frequency: Anchorage Port on VHF Channels 16 and 12. Deep Water Port on VHF Channels 16 and 14

Weather: NE monsoon October to December. SW monsoon June to August

Tides: MHWS 1.5 m, MHWN 1.1 m, MLWN 0.6 m, MLWS 0.2 m

Traffic: 2007/08, approx 12 600 000 t of cargo handled

Maximum Vessel Dimensions: 190 m loa, 32.4 m beam, 11.5 m draft at HT

Principal Imports and Exports: Imports: Acid, Ammonia, Coal, Edible oil, Oil & petroleum products. Exports: Iron ore.

Working Hours: Loading/unloading round the clock

Accommodation:

Name	Remarks
Kakinada	See [1] below

[1]*Kakinada*: Open roadstead. Good anchorage off Vakalapudi Lighthouse, distance 2 to 3.5 miles on bearing 280°-320°(T), depths ranging from 7 m to 12 m. Holding ground of sand and mud. Unloading into steel barges using ship's gear
There are 16 RCC wharf walls beside thirty three finger jetties. Depths alongside of 2.5 m. Mechanised steel barges with a cap of up to 250 dwt are in operation
The deep water port has a 910 m long wharf consisting of:
a) four multi-purpose berths
b) two finger jetties (90 m x 40 m) consisting of four berths for offshore supply vessels
Ship-to-ship crude transhipments carried out off deep water port
Alumina mechanised loading facility in operation

Storage:

Location	Covered (m²)	Sheds / Warehouses
Kakinada	15600	5

Mechanical Handling Equipment:

Location	Type	Capacity (t)	Qty	Remarks
Kakinada	Floating Cranes	50	1	at Anchorage Port
Kakinada	Mobile Cranes	100	1	See [1] below
Kakinada	Mobile Cranes	20	1	at Deep Water Port
Kakinada	Mobile Cranes	35	1	at Deep Water Port
Kakinada	Shore Cranes	40	4	See [2] below
Kakinada	Forklifts	2-3	9	at Deep Water Port

[1]*Kakinada*: Liebherr LMH 400 at Deep Water Port
[2]*Kakinada*: Liebherr 40 x 29.5M FCC cranes at Deep Water Port

Bunkering: Quantities up to 15 t can be supplied in drums. At deep water port bunkers for MDO are arranged through agents with 2-3 days advance notice
Aditya Marine M/S, 41-1-35, Nagaratnam Building Upstairs, Rangainaidu Street, Kakinada, Andhra Pradesh, India 533 007, Tel: +91 884 236 6717, Fax: +91 884 236 6716, Email: adioil@rediffmail.com
Aditya Marine M/S, 41-1-35, Nagaratnam Building Upstairs, Rangainaidu Street, Kakinada, Andhra Pradesh, India 533 007, Tel: +91 884 236 6717, Fax: +91 884 236 6716, Email: adioil@rediffmail.com
Asean International Ltd, P O Box 7860, Block Z Suite 42/43, Saif Zone, Sharjah, United Arab Emirates, Tel: +971 6 557 0083, Fax: +971 6 557 0085
Bharat Petroleum Corp. Ltd, 4th Floor, Old Admin Building, Mahul, Chembur, Mumbai, Maharashtra, India 400 074, Tel: +91 22 2554 3493, Fax: +91 22 2554 0621, Email: josecm@bharatpetroleum.in, Website: www.baratpetroleum.in
Bominflot, Bominoil Private Ltd, 504 Maker Chambers V, 221 Nariman Point, Mumbai, Maharashtra, India 400 021, Tel: +91 22 2281 7133, Fax: +91 22 2281 7145, Email: bominoil@vsnl.com, Website: www.bominflot.net
M/S Global Fuels & Lubricants Inc., 11-12 Mangal Society, 76C Rafi Ahmed Kidwai Road, King Circle, Mumbai, Maharashtra, India 400 019, Tel: +91 22 2374 5987, Fax: +91 22 2409 1627, Email: globalfuels@vsnl.com, Website: www.bunkerindia.com

Towage: Four tugs of 22-50 t bollard pull

Ship Chandlers: Aditya Marine M/S, 41-1-35, Nagaratnam Building Upstairs, Rangainaidu Street, Kakinada, Andhra Pradesh, India 533 007, Tel: +91 884 236 6717, Fax: +91 884 236 6716, Email: adioil@rediffmail.com

Shipping Agents: J.M. Baxi & Co, 1st Floor - East Block - Parvathi Towers, Military Road, Near Dairy Farm Centre, Kakinada, Andhra Pradesh, India 533 007, Tel: +91 884 236 3785, Fax: +91 884 236 1208, Email: kakinada@jmbaxi.com, Website: www.jmbaxi.com
GAC Shipping (India) Pvt Ltd, Plot 13, 1st Floor, 3-20-2A Ramamohanraja Nagar, Pallamaraju Nagar Main Road, Kakinada, Andhra Pradesh, India 533 003, Tel: +91 884 236 1744, Fax: +91 884 238 4127, Email: kakinada@gacworld.com, Website: www.gacworld.com
G.R. Enterprises, Pallam Raju Nagar, Road No.3, Kakinada, Andhra Pradesh, India 530003, Tel: +91 884 236 9084, Fax: +91 884 236 9083, Email: gprc_kkd@sol.net.in
Inchcape Shipping Services (ISS), Inchcape Shipping Services Pvt Ltd, Plot No.9, Road No.1, Pallamraju Nagar, Kakinada, Andhra Pradesh, India 533 003, Tel: +91 884 234 1500, Fax: +91 884 234 1500, Email: youriss.india@iss-shipping.com, Website: www.iss-shipping.com
Interocean Shipping (India) Pvt Ltd., Door No.16-23-61/A2, Pallam Raju Nagar, Kakinada, Andhra Pradesh, India 533 001, Tel: +91 884 235 2045, Fax: +91 884 235 2044, Email: kakinada@interoceangroup.com, Website: www.interoceangroup.com
Merchant Shipping Services Private Ltd, Plot 10 Sagar Jyoti Complex, Diary Farm Centre, Kakinada, Andhra Pradesh, India 533007, Tel: +91 884 234 6244, Fax: +91

Key to Principal Facilities:—

A=Airport	**C**=Containers	**G**=General Cargo
B=Bunkers	**D**=Dry Dock	**L**=Cruise

P=Petroleum	**R**=Ro/Ro
Q=Other Liquid Bulk	**T**=Towage (where available from port)

Y=Dry Bulk

884 234 6244, *Email:* samskakinada@samsarashipping.com, *Website:* www.merchantshpg.com
Samsara Shipping (Private) Ltd, Plot No.10, Sagar Jyoti Complex, Ground Floor, Dairy Farm Centre, Kakinada, Andhra Pradesh, India 533 007, *Tel:* +91 884 234 6244, *Fax:* +91 884 234 6244, *Email:* samskakinada@samsarashipping.com, *Website:* www.samsarashipping.com

Stevedoring Companies: G.R. Enterprises, Pallam Raju Nagar, Road No.3, Kakinada, Andhra Pradesh, India 530003, *Tel:* +91 884 236 9084, *Fax:* +91 884 236 9083, *Email:* gprc_kkd@sol.net.in

Surveyors: J.B. Boda Surveyors Private Ltd, D. No.16-23-3/3A, Parvati Niwas Pallam Raju Nagar, Road No.1, Kakinada, Andhra Pradesh, India 533 007, *Tel:* +91 884 237 5350, *Fax:* +91 884 236 7043, *Email:* jbbkkd@jbbodamail.com, *Website:* www.jbboda.net
Metcalfe & Hodgkinson Private Ltd, Kakinada, Andhra Pradesh, India, *Tel:* +91 884 237 8249, *Fax:* +91 884 237 8249, *Email:* kakinada@metcalfeindia.com, *Website:* www.metcalfeindia.com

Medical Facilities: Government hospital in town and a number of private hospitals available

Airport: Rajahmundry Airport, 80 km. Visakhapatnam Airport, 165 km

Railway: At Kakinada and Samalkot stations

Lloyd's Agent: Wilson Surveyors and Adjusters Private Ltd, TMB Mansion, 3rd Floor, 739 Anna Salai, Chennai, Tamil Nadu, India 600 002, *Tel:* +91 44 2852 2811, *Fax:* +91 44 2852 3349, *Email:* chennai@wilsur.com, *Website:* www.wilsur.com

KALINGAPATNAM

Lat 18° 20' N; Long 84° 8' E.

Admiralty Chart: -	**Admiralty Pilot:** -
Time Zone: GMT +5.5 h	**UNCTAD Locode:** IN CAP

Principal Facilities:

			G						

Authority: Port Conservator, Kalingapatnam, Andhra Pradesh, India

Working Hours: 0800-1200, 1300-1700

Accommodation:

Name	Remarks
Kalingapatnam	See [1] below

[1]*Kalingapatnam:* Open roadstead available for ships of any size. Anchorage 0.8 km from shore. All cargo is shipped by lighters of 2 t cap, of which there are about 40 available. Nearest major port, Visakhapatnam

Medical Facilities: Available

Lloyd's Agent: Wilson Surveyors and Adjusters Private Ltd, Fatima Building 2nd Floor, 23-13-28 Thompson Street, Visakhapatnam, Andhira Pradesh, India 530 001, *Tel:* +91 891 272 5611, *Fax:* +91 891 272 5655, *Email:* vizag@wilsur.com, *Website:* www.wilsur.com

KANDLA

Lat 23° 2' N; Long 70° 13' E.

Admiralty Chart: 3466	**Admiralty Pilot:** 38
Time Zone: GMT +5.5 h	**UNCTAD Locode:** IN IXY

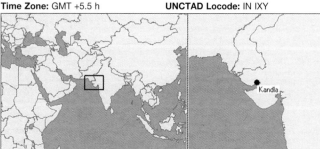

Principal Facilities:

P	Q	Y	G	C			B	D	T	A

Authority: Kandla Port Trust, Business Development Cell, P O Box 50, Administrative Building, Gandhidham, Kutch, Gujarat, India 370 201, *Tel:* +91 2836 238055, *Fax:* +91 2836 239055, *Email:* bdc@kandlaport.com, *Website:* www.kandlaport.gov.in

Officials: Business Development Manager: Sanjay Bhaty.
Harbour Master: Capt Ravi Chabra.

Port Security: ISPS compliant

Documentation: Last port clearance, crew list, ship's certificates, manifest, light dues receipts

Approach: The approach channel from fairway buoy to harbour is 2.4 km long with a sand bar which is dredged continually. The present depth at the bar is 4.3 m CD. The entrance channel is marked with light-buoys and beacons and has a width of 183 m. Vessels up to 225.55 m loa can generally negotiate the channel at HW neap tides, draught up to 8.14 m. Vessels with draught up to 9.45 m are frequently permitted and occasionally up to max 10.06 to 10.36 m. Night navigation of port is possible at certain times. A statement showing the max permissible draft allowed to ships entering or leaving Kandla port for each day is issued by the Deputy Conservator quarterly

Pilotage: Compulsory. The pilot boards incoming vessels and disembarks from outgoing vessels in the vicinity of Outer Tuna Buoy in pos 22° 50.7' N; 70° 7.1' E and assists in piloting vessel to and from her assigned berth and also in berthing and unberthing vessels

Radio Frequency: VHF Channel 16

Weather: SW monsoons from June-September; wind velocity September-March 13 km, April-August 25 km

Tides: 3.9 m at NT and 5.88 m at ST

Traffic: 2007/08, 64 893 000 t of cargo handled, 167 000 TEU's

Maximum Vessel Dimensions: 240 m loa, 55 000 dwt, 10.7 m draft

Principal Imports and Exports: Imports: Edible oil, Fertilizer, General cargo, Grain, Iron and steel, Metal & metal products, Oils, Sugar, Sulphur. Exports: Food grains, Iron, Molasses, Salt, Steel.

Working Hours: First shift 0000-0800, second shift 0800-1600, third shift 1600-2400

Accommodation:

Name	Remarks
Kandla	See [1] below

[1]*Kandla:* Natural and well protected harbour consisting of eleven dry cargo berths and six oil jetties connected to installations with pipelines of various sizes
One deep draft mooring and four cargo moorings in the Inner Harbour area for stream handling. Loading/unloading facilities for barges
Container terminal with one berth (No.11) operated by ABG Kandla Container Terminal Ltd. Berth No.12 is under construction
Nine weighbridges including four of 40 t cap, one of 50 t cap, one of 60 t cap, one of 80 t cap and two private weighbridges of 40 t & 20 t cap respectively

Storage: Four transit sheds with 30 000 t storing cap, three temporary transit sheds with 6050 t cap; two transit sheds with 3000 t cap at Bunder area, four double-storey warehouses each of 15 000 t cap for bagged cargoes; a 5000 t warehouse owned by Central Warehousing Corp in the cargo jetty area. Eight godowns with total cap of 40 000 t. Separate sheds for dangerous and inflammable goods. One bonded warehouse with 1000 t cap. Open storage yards available in transit area and rental area served by railway lines; total area for rental purposes is 339 610 m2 of which 193 110 m2 has asphalt surface. Two tanks for storing vegetable oil with 400 t total cap and various privately owned storage tanks for edible oil and chemicals

Mechanical Handling Equipment:

Location	Type	Capacity (t)	Qty
Kandla	Mult-purp. Cranes	12–16	4
Kandla	Mult-purp. Cranes	3–6	12
Kandla	Mobile Cranes	70	2
Kandla	Container Cranes		2
Kandla	RTG's		2

Cargo Worked: 185 t/gang/shift, 6264 t/shift/day

Bunkering: Jaisu Shipping Co. Private Ltd, Kewalramani House, Dinshaw Building Road, Near Custom House, New Kandla, Kandla, India 370 210, *Tel:* +91 2836 270 428, *Fax:* +91 2836 270 650, *Email:* jaisu_shipping@yahoo.com/mail@jaisu.in, *Website:* www.jaisu.in
Asean International Ltd, P O Box 7860, Block Z Suite 42/43, Saif Zone, Sharjah, United Arab Emirates, *Tel:* +971 6 557 0083, *Fax:* +971 6 557 0085
Bapu's Shipping Agency, Plot No 32, Sector 9, Near Central Bank Of India, Gandhidham, Gujarat, India 370 201, *Tel:* +91 2836 222 002, *Fax:* +91 2836 236 036, *Email:* info@shipsupplier.biz, *Website:* www.shipsupplier.biz
Bharat Fuels, Off No.38, C.L. Sharma Shopping Complex, Sector 8, Near Oslo Cinema, Gandhidham, Gujarat, India 370201, *Tel:* +91 2836 227 627, *Fax:* +91 2836 225 925, *Email:* bharatpetro_gim@sancharnet.in/bharatpetro@indiatimes.com, *Website:* www.bharatpetroleum.in
Bharat Petroleum Corp. Ltd, 4th Floor, Old Admin Building, Mahul, Chembur, Mumbai, Maharashtra, India 400 074, *Tel:* +91 22 2554 3493, *Fax:* +91 22 2554 0621, *Email:* josecm@bharatpetroleum.in, *Website:* www.baratpetroleum.in
Bominflot, Bominoil Private Ltd, 504 Maker Chambers V, 221 Nariman Point, Mumbai, Maharashtra, India 400 021, *Tel:* +91 22 2281 7133, *Fax:* +91 22 2281 7145, *Email:* bominoil@vsnl.com, *Website:* www.bominflot.net
Cockett Marine Oil Ltd, Carrick House, 36 Station Square, Petts Wood, Kent BR5 1NA, United Kingdom, *Tel:* +44 1689 883 400, *Fax:* +44 1689 877 666, *Email:* enquiries@cockett.com, *Website:* www.cockettgroup.com
M/S Global Fuels & Lubricants Inc., 11-12 Mangal Society, 76C Rafi Ahmed Kidwai Road, King Circle, Mumbai, Maharashtra, India 400 019, *Tel:* +91 22 2374 5987, *Fax:* +91 22 2409 1627, *Email:* globalfuels@vsnl.com, *Website:* www.bunkerindia.com
Gujarat Marine Private Ltd, Manali Chambers, Plot No. 306, Sector 1/A, Gandhidham, Gujarat, India 370 201, *Tel:* +91 2836 222 518, *Fax:* +91 2836 239 057, *Email:* bunker@gujmar.com, *Website:* www.gujmar.com
Hindustan Petroleum Corp. Ltd, Hindustan Bhawan, Vallabhdas Marg, Mumbai, Maharashtra, India 400 038, *Tel:* +91 22 2226 0079
Indian Oil Corp. Ltd, Indian Oil Bhavan Head Office, G9 Ali Yavar Jung Marg, Bandra (East), Mumbai, Maharashtra, India 400051, *Tel:* +91 22 2644 7368, *Fax:* +91 22 2642 2434, *Email:* partha_datta@indianoil.co.in, *Website:* www.indianoil.co.in
Jaisu Shipping Co. Private Ltd, Kewalramani House, Dinshaw Building Road, Near Custom House, New Kandla, Kandla, India 370 210, *Tel:* +91 2836 270 428, *Fax:* +91

2836 270 650, *Email:* jaisu_shipping@yahoo.com/mail@jaisu.in, *Website:* www.jaisu.in

Laxmi Marine, Plot No 119, Ward 6, Industrial Area, Bharat Nagar, Gandhidham, Gujarat, India 370 201, *Tel:* +91 2836 237 209, *Fax:* +91 2836 237 211, *Email:* info@laxmimarine.com, *Website:* www.laxmimarine.com

Link Enterprises, Plot 44, Sector 9/A, Morabia Commercial Centre, P O Box 248, Gandhidham, Gujarat, India 370 201, *Tel:* +91 2836 230 107, *Fax:* +91 2836 231 285, *Email:* info@asiaship.com

Mithi Overseas Private Ltd, Plot No.265/12-B, Bajaj Chambers, Near Shiv Cinema, Gandhidham, Gujarat, India 370 201, *Tel:* +91 2836 235417, *Fax:* +91 2836 235417, *Email:* mithioverseas@yahoo.com

Umamarine, Sector 1/A, Plot No 310, Gandhidham, Gujarat, India 370 201, *Tel:* +91 2836 221465, *Fax:* +91 2836 232830, *Email:* info@umamarine.com, *Website:* www.umamarine.com

Towage: Five tugs up to 50 t bollard pull are available

Repair & Maintenance: Floating dry dock for vessels of up to 100 m in length, 15 m beam, 2700 dwt. Repair workshop available. Various local companies are engaged in repair work

Ship Chandlers: Inayat Moosa & Co., 103 Golden Archade, 1st Floor, Section 8, Oslo Road, Gandhidham, Gujarat, India 370201, *Tel:* +91 2836 229244, *Fax:* +91 2836 229196, *Email:* info@inayatmoosa.com, *Website:* www.inayatmoosa.com

Kandla Marine Works, DBZ South 13, Gandhidham Kutch, Kandla, India 370201, *Tel:* +91 2836 220165, *Fax:* +91 2836 236724, *Email:* kandlamarineworks@yahoo.co.in/kandlamarineworks@gipl.net

A.S. Moloobhoy & Sons, Anchor House, Shivkripa Building, Plot 135, Sector 1-A, Behind Royal Laxmi Furniture, Kandla, India 370 201, *Tel:* +91 2836 396543, *Fax:* +91 2836 225060, *Email:* kandla@asmoloobhoy.com, *Website:* www.asmoloobhoy.com

Sabari Marine Enterprises, Plots 12 & 13, Ward No 10 BC, Opposite IFFCO Colony, Gandhidham, Gujarat, India 370 201, *Tel:* +91 2836 228266, *Fax:* +91 2836 227637, *Email:* sabari_marine@d2visp.com, *Website:* www.sabarimarine.com

Uma Marine, Sector 1/A, Plot No. 310, Gandhidham, Kandla, India 370 201, *Tel:* +91 2836 221465, *Fax:* +91 2836 232830, *Email:* info@umamarine.com, *Website:* www.umamarine.com

Shipping Agents: Albatross Shipping Pvt. Ltd, Plot No.334, Ward 12-B, Aashirvad Complex, Near Punjab National Bank, Gandhidham-Kachch, Kandla, India 370201, *Tel:* +91 2836 236828, *Fax:* +91 2836 232413, *Email:* n.santwani@alba.co.in

Ambica Maritime Ltd, Plot 2, National Highway, Kasez Post Office, Near PSL, Gandhidham, Gujarat, India 370 230, *Fax:* +91 2836 252447, *Email:* operations@ambicamaritime.com, *Website:* www.ambicamaritime.com

Arebee Star Maritime Agencies Private Ltd, DBZ-S/1321, Gandhidham (Kutch), Kandla, India 370210, *Tel:* +91 2836 235832, *Fax:* +91 2836 235831, *Email:* arebeeknd@icenet.net

J.M. Baxi & Co, Seva Sadan II, Kandla, India 370 210, *Tel:* +91 2836 270630, *Fax:* +91 2836 270646, *Email:* kdla@jmbaxi.com, *Website:* www.jmbaxi.com

CMA-CGM S.A., CMA CGM Global (India) Pvt Ltd, ICICI Building, Room No.202, 2nd Floor, Plot No.41, Ward 12B, Gandhidham, Kandla, India 370 201, *Tel:* +91 2836 230026, *Fax:* +91 2836 234541, *Email:* knd.genmbox@cma-cgm.com, *Website:* www.cma-cgm.com

Contfreight Shipping Agency India Private Ltd, 3rd Floor, Chetna Chambers, Plot 387 Sector 9, Gandhidham, Kandla, India 370201, *Tel:* +91 2836 234779, *Fax:* +91 2836 233615, *Email:* ixyba@csaindia.com

Darabshaw B. Cursetjee's Sons (Gujarat) Private Ltd, Clearing Agents Building, Kandla Port, Kutch, Kandla, India 370210, *Tel:* +91 2836 270263, *Fax:* +91 2836 270631, *Email:* dbc@gipl.com

GAC Shipping (India) Pvt Ltd, P O Box 225, Gujarat, India 370 201, *Tel:* +91 2836 231427, *Fax:* +91 2836 231429, *Email:* kandla@gacworld.com, *Website:* www.gacworld.com

Greenways Shipping Agencies Private Ltd, Room 203, Maritime House, Sector 9, Plot 5, Gandhidham, Kandla, India 370201, *Fax:* +91 2836 223079, *Email:* kandla@gwsbombay.com

Interocean Shipping (India) Pvt Ltd., Plot No.72, Ward 10/A, Opposite IFFCO Colony Main Gate, Gandhidham, Gujarat, India 370 201, *Tel:* +91 2836 232501, *Fax:* +91 2836 232579, *Email:* gandhidham@interoceangroup.com, *Website:* www.interoceangroup.com

Samrat Shipping & Transport Systems Private Ltd, 104 Maritime House, Plot 45, Sec 9, Gandidham, Kandla, India 370201, *Tel:* +91 2836 231286, *Fax:* +91 2836 228890

Samsara Shipping (Private) Ltd, Room No.402, 4th Floor, Plot No.1, Seva Sadan II, Kandla, India 370 210, *Tel:* +91 2836 270323, *Fax:* +91 2836 270741, *Email:* commkdl@samsarashipping.com, *Website:* www.samsarashipping.com

Stevedoring Companies: Darabshaw B. Cursetjee's Sons (Gujarat) Private Ltd, Clearing Agents Building, Kandla Port, Kutch, Kandla, India 370210, *Tel:* +91 2836 270263, *Fax:* +91 2836 270631, *Email:* dbc@gipl.com

Kandla Stevedores Association, Kandla, India, *Tel:* +91 2836 270416

Surveyors: J.B. Boda Surveyors Private Ltd, Bungalow No.16, Sector No.4, Gandhidham, Gujarat, India 370 201, *Tel:* +91 2836 231801, *Fax:* +91 2836 228321, *Email:* jbbkdl@jbbodamail.com, *Website:* www.jbboda.net

Indian Register of Shipping, Plot No. 455, Ward 12 C, Lilasha Nagar, Gandhidham, Gujarat, India 370 201, *Tel:* +91 2836 238623, *Fax:* +91 2836 233695, *Email:* kandla@irclass.org, *Website:* www.irclass.org

Metcalfe & Hodgkinson Private Ltd, Gandhidham, Gujarat, India, *Tel:* +91 2836 227140, *Fax:* +91 2836 231629, *Email:* gandhidham@metcalfeindia.com, *Website:* www.metcalfeindia.com

Medical Facilities: Port Trust Hospital and private hospitals within port limits. Port health officers also available

Airport: Bhuj Airport, 72 km

Railway: Gandhidham Railway Station, 15 km

Development: A two year project is underway widening and deepening over 27 km of the navigational channel for the port to accommodate VLCC's. The dredging work will increase the available draught from 11.5 m to 13.5 m and is expected to be completed by end 2008

Lloyd's Agent: Wilson Surveyors and Adjusters Private Ltd, Golden Arcade, II Floor, Room No.209, Plot No.141/142, Sector 8, Gandhidam, Kutch, Gujarat, India 370 201, *Tel:* +91 2836 238333, *Fax:* +91 2836 238333, *Email:* kandla@wilsur.com, *Website:* www.wilsur.com

KARWAR

Lat 14° 49' N; Long 74° 6' E.

Admiralty Chart: 3464	**Admiralty Pilot:** 38
Time Zone: GMT +5.5 h	**UNCTAD Locode:** IN KRW

Principal Facilities:

P	Y	G			B	T	A

Authority: Karwar Port Office, Port Officer, Karwar Port, Karwar, Karnataka, India 581 302, *Tel:* +91 8382 221342, *Fax:* +91 8382 221488, *Email:* directorate@sancharnet.in, *Website:* www.karnatakaports.in

Officials: Port Officer: Capt C. Swamy, *Email:* portoffkwr@bsnl.in.

Approach: Inner Approach Channel and Diversion Channel 122 m wide, 10.1 m depth, indicated by transit markers. Outer Approach Channel 10.6 m depth

Pilotage: Compulsory. The Port Officer renders pilotage service

Radio Frequency: VHF Channels 16, 12 and 10

Weather: Shipping operations at anchorage only are suspended during SW Monsoon, May 26 to August 31

Maximum Vessel Dimensions: Max loa 182 m, max draft 7.5 m

Principal Imports and Exports: Imports: Fertilizer, Industrial salt, Rock phosphate, Timber logs. Exports: Granite stone, Hydrochloric acid, Iron ore, Manganese ore, Marine products, Molasses, Phosphoric acid, Sulphuric acid.

Working Hours: Regular office hours 1000-1730. Overtime extra

Accommodation:

Name	Remarks
Karwar	See [1] below

[1]*Karwar:* Open roadstead. The anchorage for shallow draft vessels is with the Port Signal Station bearing 120° (T), distance 1 to 2 miles in about 7.31 m to 8.53 m of water. Anchorage for deep-draft vessels is with the Signal Station bearing 099° (T), distance three miles in depths of 11.58 m to 12.8 m. Salt, rock phosphate and fertiliser unloaded by barges at rate of 600 t/day

Two berths available for unloading of salt, rock phosphate and general cargo. No.1, length 122 m with d of 7.0 m. No.2, length 172 m with d of 7.0 m. No shore cranes available

Storage: Within the port area there are three transit sheds, one of 150 m x 24 m and two of 40 m x 18 m. Outside the port area, approx 1 km from the wharf there is a transit shed 120 m x 24 m. Two steel tanks for storage of molasses with total cap of approx 15 000 t

Mechanical Handling Equipment:

Location	Type	Capacity (t)	Qty
Karwar	Mult-purp. Cranes	10	1

Cargo Worked: 1000-1500 t/day

Bunkering: Available at wharf by pump

Towage: A tug of 12 t bollard pull is available

Ship Chandlers: Ocean Marine Supplies, Old Port Office, Opposite Karwar Port, Baithakal, Karwar, Karnataka, India, *Tel:* +91 8382 225792, *Email:* omships@sancharnet.in

Shipping Agents: J.M. Baxi & Co, Shree Datta Prasad Complex - Gr. Floor, Dr. Pikle Road, Karwar, Karnataka, India 581 301, *Tel:* +91 8382 221731, *Fax:* +91 8382 220675, *Email:* karwar@jmbaxi.com, *Website:* www.jmbaxi.com

Samsara Shipping (Private) Ltd, H.No.542/3, 2nd Floor, Pats Korner, Dr. Kamalkar Road, Karwar, Karnataka, India 581 301, *Tel:* +91 8382 226692, *Fax:* +91 8382 226692, *Email:* merskarwar@merchantshpg.com, *Website:* www.samsarashipping.com

Stevedoring Companies: Chowgule Brothers Private Ltd, Chowgule House, 403 Mormugao Harbour, Mormugao, Goa, India 403 803, *Tel:* +91 832 252 5144, *Fax:* +91 832 252 1011, *Email:* info.cb@chowgule.co.in, *Website:* www.chowgulebros.com

Medical Facilities: Government hospital about 1.5 km from port and private hospitals

Airport: Dabolim Airport, 90 km

Railway: Karwar, approx 6 km

Lloyd's Agent: Peirce Leslie India Ltd, Peirce Leslie Surveyours and Assessors Ltd., Bristow Road, Willingdon Island, Kochi, Kerala, India 682 003, *Tel:* +91 484 266 8362, *Fax:* +91 484 266 8394, *Email:* plsacok@sify.com, *Website:* www.plsurvey.in

KOCHI

Lat 9° 58' N; Long 76° 14' E.

Admiralty Chart: 65	**Admiralty Pilot:** 38
Time Zone: GMT +5.5 h	**UNCTAD Locode:** IN COK

Key to Principal Facilities:—				
A=Airport	**C**=Containers	**G**=General Cargo	**P**=Petroleum	**R**=Ro/Ro	**Y**=Dry Bulk
B=Bunkers	**D**=Dry Dock	**L**=Cruise	**Q**=Other Liquid Bulk	**T**=Towage (where available from port)

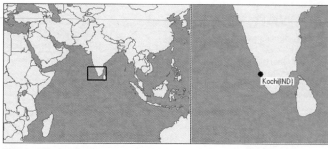

Principal Facilities:

P Q Y G C R L B D T A

Authority: Cochin Port Trust, Willingdon Island, Kochi, Kerala, India 682 009, Tel: +91 484 266 6871, Fax: +91 484 266 8163, Email: mail@cochinport.com, Website: www.cochinport.com

Officials: Chairman: Narayana Ramachandran, Email: chairman@cochinport.com.
Traffic Manager: Damodar Nayak, Email: tm@cochinport.com.
Harbour Master: Capt Joseph J. Alapatt.
Secretary: Cyril C. George, Email: secretary@cochinport.com.

Port Security: ISPS compliant

Documentation: Original vessel documents, last port clearance, crew list (2 copies), deck cargo certificate (1 copy), arrival passenger list (1 copy), bonded stores list, currency declaration, general stores list

Approach: The approach channel up to the Cochin Gut is approx 1000 m long with a designed width of 200 m and a maintained dredged depth of 13.8 m

Anchorage: Anchorage can be obtained approx 4 nm NW of the Fairway Buoy in a depth of 12 m to 15 m; good holding ground

Pilotage: Compulsory and available 24 h. Pilot station 0.5 mile W of Fairway Buoy

Radio Frequency: Kochi Port Control Station maintains continuous watch on VHF Channel 16

Weather: The predominant wind direction during the monsoon period i.e. from June to September, is W to SW. During the non-monsoon periods, the predominant wind direction is from NE during the morning and W during the evening

Tides: MHHWL 0.9 m, MLHWL 0.8 m, MSL 0.6 m, MHLWL 0.6 m, MLLWL 0.3 m

Traffic: 2007/08, 15 810 000 t of cargo handled, 254 000 TEU's

Maximum Vessel Dimensions: 250 m loa, 115 000 dwt, 12.5 m draft

Principal Imports and Exports: Imports: Cement, Clinker, Coal, Crude oil, Food grains, Iron & steel, Iron scrap, Machinery, Newsprint, Raw cashew, Rock sulphate, Sulphur, Wheat. Exports: Cashews, Coffee, Coir products, Machinery, Marine products, Spices, Tea, Textiles.

Working Hours: 24 h/day

Accommodation:

Name	Length (m)	Draught (m)	Remarks
Kochi			
Kochi Oil Terminal	250	12.5	POL & crude oil
South Tanker Berth	170	9.14	POL
North Tanker Berth	213	9.14	POL
Fertilizer Berth (Q10)	207	10.7	Sulphur, rock phosphate & phosphoric acid
North Coal Berth	105	9.14	Under reconstruction to a berth 127 m long
South Coal Berth	170	9.14	Liquid bulk
Ernakulam Wharf (Q5-Q6)	345	10	General cargo
Mattancherry Wharf (Q1-Q4)	670	9.14	General cargo
Container Terminal (Q7-Q9)	573	12.5	See [1] below
Boat Train Pier (BTP)	200	9.14	General cargo & liquid bulk
Ship-To-Ship (STS) Transfer Operation			See [2] below

[1]*Container Terminal (Q7-Q9):* Operated by India Gateway Terminal Private Ltd (IGTPL), P O Box 525, Subramanian Road, Willingdon Island, Kochi 682 003, Tel: +91 484 408 0282, Fax: +91 484 408 0250, Email: frank.carter@dpworld.com
[2]*Ship-To-Ship (STS) Transfer Operation:* Located at outer roads and centred in pos 10° 03.5' N; 76° 04.5' E for loading and unloading of liquid bulk cargo and gas

Storage:

Location	Open (m²)	Covered (m²)
Kochi	10000	59722

Mechanical Handling Equipment:

Location	Type	Capacity (t)	Qty
Kochi	Mult-purp. Cranes	35.5	9
Kochi	Mobile Cranes		2
Container Terminal (Q7-Q9)	Panamax	60	2
Container Terminal (Q7-Q9)	RTG's		5
Container Terminal (Q7-Q9)	Reach Stackers		5

Bunkering: Asean International Ltd, P O Box 7860, Block Z Suite 42/43, Saif Zone, Sharjah, United Arab Emirates, Tel: +971 6 557 0083, Fax: +971 6 557 0085
Bharat Petroleum Corp. Ltd, 4th Floor, Old Admin Building, Mahul, Chembur,

Mumbai, Maharashtra, India 400 074, Tel: +91 22 2554 3493, Fax: +91 22 2554 0621, Email: josecm@bharatpetroleum.in, Website: www.baratpetroleum.in
Bominflot, Bominoil Private Ltd, 504 Maker Chambers V, 221 Nariman Point, Mumbai, Maharashtra, India 400 021, Tel: +91 22 2281 7133, Fax: +91 22 2281 7145, Email: bominoil@vsnl.com, Website: www.bominflot.net
Cockett Marine Oil Ltd, Carrick House, 36 Station Square, Petts Wood, Kent BR5 1NA, United Kingdom, Tel: +44 1689 883 400, Fax: +44 1689 877 666, Email: enquiries@cockett.com, Website: www.cockettgroup.com – Grades: IFO; MDO; MGO – Parcel Size: min IFO 50t, min MDO/MGO 10t – Delivery Mode: barge, road tank wagon, pipeline
M/S Global Fuels & Lubricants Inc., 11-12 Mangal Society, 76C Rafi Ahmed Kidwai Road, King Circle, Mumbai, Maharashtra, India 400 019, Tel: +91 22 2374 5987, Fax: +91 22 2409 1627, Email: globalfuels@vsnl.com, Website: www.bunkerindia.com
Indian Oil Corp. Ltd, Indian Oil Bhavan Head Office, G9 Ali Yavar Jung Marg, Bandra (East), Mumbai, Maharashtra, India 400051, Tel: +91 22 2644 7368, Fax: +91 22 2642 2434, Email: partha_datta@indianoil.co.in, Website: www.indianoil.co.in – Grades: FO; GO; MDO – Parcel Size: max 2000t – Rates: 80-100t/h – Notice: 24-48 hours – Delivery Mode: wharf
Laxmi Marine, Plot No 119, Ward 6, Industrial Area, Bharat Nagar, Gandhidham, Gujarat, India 370 201, Tel: +91 2836 237 209, Fax: +91 2836 237 211, Email: info@laxmimarine.com, Website: www.laxmimarine.com
Olympic Marine Co., P O Box 5009, Fujairah, United Arab Emirates, Tel: +971 9 224726, Fax: +971 9 226491, Email: olympic@olympgroup.com

Waste Reception Facilities: Private agencies available

Towage: Four tugs available

Repair & Maintenance: Cochin Shipyard Ltd, Business Development Division, Administrative Building, Perumanoor, P O Box 1653, Kochi, Kerala, India 682 015, Tel: +91 484 236 0678, Fax: +91 484 237 0897, Email: info@cochinshipyard.com, Website: www.cochinshipyard.com

Ship Chandlers: P.N. Bhaskaran Sons, V/234 Catholic Syrian Bank Building, Mattancherry, Kochi, Kerala, India 682 002, Tel: +91 484 228 6044, Email: pnbsons@md4.vsnl.net.in
Chennai Marine Trading Private Ltd, 54-93 Ward No.27, Palakkappilly House, Perumanoor, Kochi, Kerala, India 682 015, Tel: +91 484 325 9556, Fax: +91 484 266 5553, Email: chennaimarine@vsnl.net
Minar Enterprises, Door No.24/487, 1st Floor, Nima Cold Storage Building, G.V. Ayyar Road, Willingdon Island, Kochi, Kerala, India 682 003, Tel: +91 484 301 7881, Fax: +91 484 301 7880, Email: mail@minarenterprises.com, Website: www.minarenterprises.com
A.S. Moloobhoy & Sons, Anchor House, H.B - 60, 2nd Cross Road, Panampillay Nagar, Ernakulam, Kochi, Kerala, India 682 036, Tel: +91 484 232 2557, Fax: +91 484 232 2559, Email: kochi@asmoloobhoy.com, Website: www.asmoloobhoy.com
John Philips & Co., 10/63 Post Office Box No.1, Fort Kochi, Kochi, Kerala, India 682 001, Tel: +91 484 266 8972, Fax: +91 484 266 8658, Email: johnphilips@eth.net, Website: www.johnphilipsandco.com

Shipping Agents: Albatross Shipping Pvt. Ltd, Transworld House, 5th Cross Road, Willingdon Island, Kochi, Kerala, India 682003, Tel: +91 484 266 8537, Fax: +91 484 266 8505, Email: maidas@alba.co.in
Aspinwall & Co. Ltd, P O Box 560, Subramaniam Road, Willingdon Island, Kochi, Kerala, India 682003, Tel: +91 484 266 6267, Fax: +91 484 266 6890, Email: cok.gen@aspinwallgroup.com, Website: www.aspinwallgroup.com
J.M. Baxi & Co, No.XXIV/1566 Subramanian Road, Willingdon Island, Kochi, Kerala, India 682 003, Tel: +91 484 266 7474, Fax: +91 484 266 8489, Email: cochin@jmbaxi.com, Website: www.jmbaxi.com
Chakiat Agencies Private Ltd, Chakiat House, Subramanian Road, Willingdon Island, P O Box 525, Kochi, Kerala, India 682 003, Tel: +91 484 266 8300, Fax: +91 484 266 8085, Email: p_narayan@chakiat.net, Website: www.chakiat.co.in
Choice Intermodal Services, Door No:24/1374, Voltas Compound, Willingdon Island, Kochi, Kerala, India 682 003, Tel: +91 484 266 6141, Fax: +91 484 266 8327, Email: choice@vsnl.com
CMA-CGM S.A., CMA CGM (East & South) India Pvt Ltd, Transworld House, 1st Floor, 5th Cross Road, Willingdon Island, Kochi, Kerala, India 682 003, Tel: +91 484 401 7100, Fax: +91 484 401 7107, Email: coh.genmbox@cma-cgm.com, Website: www.cma-cgm.com
Contfreight Shipping Agency India Private Ltd, First Floor, Teepeeyem Centre, Naval Road, Willingdon Island, Kochi, Kerala, India 682003, Tel: +91 484 266 6797, Fax: +91 484 266 6081, Email: mjmathew@csaindia.com
CSAV Group Agencies (India) Pvt Ltd, Nilhat House, Bristow Road, Willingdon Island, Kochi, Kerala, India 682 003, Tel: +91 484 404 5041, Fax: +91 484 404 5047, Email: rmathachan@csavagencies-india.com, Website: www.csavagencies-india.com
Darragh Smail & Co. (India) Private Ltd, P O Box 522, Willingdon Island, Kochi, Kerala, India 682003, Tel: +91 484 266 7461/2, Fax: +91 484 266 8263, Email: darragh@md2.vsnl.net.in
Evergreen India Private Ltd, Door CC 39/6720, B & B1 Bab Towers, 2nd Floor Mahatma Gandhi Road, Kochi, Kerala, India 682015, Tel: +91 484 398 3999, Fax: +91 484 398 3998, Email: cokbiz@evergreen-shipping.co.in, Website: www.evergreen-line.com
Forbes Patvolk (A Division of Forbes Gokak Ltd), Indira Gandhi Road, Willingdon Island, P O Box 556, Kochi, Kerala, India 682003, Tel: +91 484 266 6621/2, Fax: +91 484 266 8025, Email: cokgenmail@forbespatvolk.com, Website: www.forbespatvolk.com
GAC Shipping (India) Pvt Ltd, GAC House Subramanian Road, P O Box 515, Kochi, Kerala, India 682 003, Tel: +91 484 266 8372, Fax: +91 484 266 8388, Email: india@gacworld.com, Website: www.gacworld.com
William Goodacre & Sons (India) Ltd, Marar Road, Willingdon Island, P O Box 557, Kochi, Kerala, India 682003, Tel: +91 484 266 6172, Fax: +91 484 266 8499, Email: goodacre@satyam.net.in
Greenways Shipping Agencies Private Ltd, 1st & 2nd Floors Nima House, Building 24, 1391 Ventraraman Road, P O Box 595, Kochi, Kerala, India 682003, Tel: +91 484 266 6634, Fax: +91 484 266 8219, Email: cochin@gwsbombay.com
IAL Shipping Agencies (Mumbai) Private Ltd, 4B 4th Floor, Darragh Smail Centre, 5th Cross Road, Willingdon Island, Kochi, Kerala, India 400074, Tel: +91 484 266 6228, Fax: +91 484 266 6701, Email: kbk@ial.com, Website: www.ial.com
International Clearing & Shipping Agency, XXIV /1437 Teepeyam House, Britow Road, Willingdon Island, Kochi, Kerala, India 682 003, Tel: +91 484 266 9970, Fax: +91 484 266 9974, Email: maa_biju@icsagroup.com, Website: www.icsagroup.com
Interocean Shipping (India) Pvt Ltd., Interocean House, Lakshadeep Quarters Road,

Kochi, Kerala, India 682 029, *Tel:* +91 484 266 7708, *Fax:* +91 484 266 7604, *Email:* kochi@interoceangroup.com, *Website:* www.interoceangroup.com
Kinship Services (India) Private Ltd, Kinship House, Plot No.1 & 6, Cat IV, Door No. CC24/492, Marar Road, Kochi, Kerala, India 682 003, *Tel:* +91 484 266 9256, *Fax:* +91 484 266 8004, *Email:* kinship@vsnl.com, *Website:* www.kinshipping.com
Marine Container Services (I) Private Ltd, Nonsuch Tea Est Building 24/502, GV Ayyar Road, Wilingdon Island, Kochi, Kerala, India 682 003, *Tel:* +91 484 266 8459, *Fax:* +91 484 266 8252, *Email:* mscch@seahorsegroup.co.in
Mediterranean Shipping Company, MSC Agency (India) Pvt Ltd, 1st Floor B, Darragh Smail Centre, XXIV/1469 A, 5th Cross Road, Willington Island, Kochi, Kerala, India 682 003, *Tel:* +91 484 266 9483, *Fax:* +91 484 266 9485, *Email:* jnelluvely@mscindia.com, *Website:* www.mscindia.com
Merchant Shipping Services Private Ltd, Darragh Smail Centre, 1st Floor, 5th Cross Road, Willington Island, Kochi, Kerala, India 682003, *Tel:* +91 484 266 9836, *Fax:* +91 484 266 9838, *Email:* merscok@merchantshpg.com
A.P. Moller-Maersk Group, Maersk India Pvt Ltd, Amalgam House, 24/1604, Plot No.9, Bristow Road, Willington Island, Kochi, Kerala, India 682 003, *Tel:* +91 484 398 3500, *Fax:* +91 484 398 3535, *Email:* cokordcus@maersk.com, *Website:* www.maerskline.com
NLS Agency (India) Private Ltd, Transworld House, Opposite Darragh Small Centre, 5th Cross Road, Wellington Island, Kochi, Kerala, India 682003, *Tel:* +91 484 266 7599, *Fax:* +91 484 266 6276, *Email:* krishnan@nlsd.co.in, *Website:* www.nlsd.co.in
OSA Shipping Private Ltd, Cochin Chamber Annexe, Bristow Road, Willingdon Island, Kochi, Kerala, India 682003, *Tel:* +91 484 266 6585, *Fax:* +91 484 266 8353, *Email:* kdmadan@vsnl.com
Samrat Shipping & Transport Systems Private Ltd, Building 24/1289, Venkatraman Road, Kochi, Kerala, India 682003, *Tel:* +91 484 266 8368/6, *Fax:* +91 484 266 6746
Samsara Shipping (Private) Ltd, 2nd Floor, Darragh Smail Centre, 5th Cross Road, Willington Island, Kochi, Kerala, India 682 003, *Tel:* +91 484 266 6026, *Fax:* +91 484 266 9838, *Email:* cochin@samsarashipping.com, *Website:* www.samsarashipping.com
Seaworld Shipping & Logistics Private Ltd, Plot 27B, Handicrafts Building, 1st Floor, Indira Gandhi Road, Willingdon Island, Kochi, Kerala, India 682 003, *Tel:* +91 484 266 9952, *Fax:* +91 484 266 9951, *Website:* www.seaworldship.com
AV Thomas & Co. Ltd, Bristow Road, P O Box 520, Willingdon Island, Kochi, Kerala, India 682003, *Tel:* +91 484 266 6323, *Fax:* +91 484 266 8493, *Email:* avtcok@satyam.net.in, *Website:* www.avtlogistics.com
Trans Asian Shipping Services (P) Ltd, Ground Floor, BBTC Building, Subramannium Road, Kochi, Kerala, India 682-003, *Tel:* +91 484 2669095, *Fax:* +91 484 2669088, *Email:* amm@tassgroup.com, *Website:* www.tassgroup.com
United Trade Links (Shipping & Trading), Airlinks House, Venketraman Road, Willingdon Island, Kochi, Kerala, India 682003, *Tel:* +91 484 266 6887, *Fax:* +91 484 266 6889, *Email:* utl@spectrum.ncl.in
Wilhelmsen Ship Services, Barwil Forbes Shipping Services Ltd, Indira Gandhi Road Opposite SBI, P O Box 556, Willingdon Island, Kochi, Kerala, India 682003, *Tel:* +91 484 266 8022, *Fax:* +91 484 266 8025, *Email:* barwil.mumbai@barwil.com, *Website:* www.barwil.com

Stevedoring Companies: Aspinwall & Co. Ltd, P O Box 560, Subramaniam Road, Willingdon Island, Kochi, Kerala, India 682003, *Tel:* +91 484 266 6267, *Fax:* +91 484 266 6890, *Email:* cok.gen@aspinwallgroup.com, *Website:* www.aspinwallgroup.com
Kinship Services (India) Private Ltd, Kinship House, Plot No.1 & 6, Cat IV, Door No. CC24/492, Marar Road, Kochi, Kerala, India 682 003, *Tel:* +91 484 266 9256, *Fax:* +91 484 266 8004, *Email:* kinship@vsnl.com, *Website:* www.kinshipping.com
Poovath Paree & Co., Poovath Paree & Sons, Subramaniam Road, Kochi, Kerala, India 682003, *Tel:* +91 484 266 6589, *Fax:* +91 484 266 7019, *Email:* sadiqpoovath@satyam.net.in

Surveyors: J.B. Boda Surveyors Private Ltd, Coastal Building, 1st Floor, Milne Road, Willingdon Island, Kochi, Kerala, India 682 003, *Tel:* +91 484 266 6234, *Fax:* +91 484 266 6824, *Email:* jbbkochi@jbbodamail.com, *Website:* www.jbboda.net
Indian Register of Shipping, Marhaba Complex, 1st Floor, Opposite St. Thomas Girls High School, Pandit Karuppan Road, Perumanoor, Kochi, Kerala, India 682 015, *Tel:* +91 484 266 5726, *Fax:* +91 484 266 4580, *Email:* kochi@irclass.org, *Website:* www.irclass.org
Nippon Kaiji Kyokai, 11A Amrit Retreat, Vivek Nagar, K.P. Vallon Road, Kadavanthara, Kochi, Kerala, India, *Tel:* +91 484 231 2499, *Fax:* +91 484 231 2499, *Website:* www.classnk.or.jp

Medical Facilities: Cochin Port Trust Hospital, 1 km. Tel: +91 484 266 6402. Other facilities available in the city

Airport: Kochi International Airport, 42 km

Railway: Kochi Terminus, 1 km

Development: DP World Cochin is constructing an International Container Transshipment Terminal at Vallarpadam. Start up of operations in Phase 1A of the project is expected to take place no later than in the 1st quarter of 2009. The first phase of development involves the building of 600 m of quay, an on-dock railhead serviced by rail-mounted gantry cranes, 30 ha of yard space and the acquisition of six super post-panamax cranes. All container activity will migrate from the existing terminal to the new one when it is finished

Lloyd's Agent: Peirce Leslie India Ltd, Peirce Leslie Surveyours and Assessors Ltd., Bristow Road, Willingdon Island, Kochi, Kerala, India 682 003, *Tel:* +91 484 266 8362, *Fax:* +91 484 266 8394, *Email:* plsacok@sify.com, *Website:* www.plsurvey.in

KOLKATA

Lat 22° 35' N; Long 88° 21' E.

Admiralty Chart: 135   **Admiralty Pilot:** 21

Time Zone: GMT +5.5 h   **UNCTAD Locode:** IN CCU

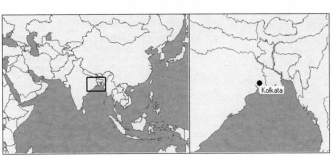

Principal Facilities:

P		Y	G	C			B	D	T	A

Authority: Kolkata Port Trust, 15 Strand Road, Kolkata, West Bengal, India 700 001, *Tel:* +91 33 2230 3451, *Fax:* +91 33 2230 4901, *Email:* portofcalcutta@portofcalcutta.com, *Website:* www.kolkataporttrust.gov.in

Officials: Chairman: Dr Anup Kumar Chanda, *Tel:* +91 33 2230 5370, *Email:* chairman@portofcalcutta.com.
Terminal Manager: Gautam Gupta, *Tel:* +91 33 2439 4940, *Email:* kodsmktg@gmail.com.
Traffic Manager: Utpal Sinha, *Tel:* +91 33 2439 2926, *Email:* kodsmktg@gmail.com.
Harbour Master: Capt Kondal Rao Dadi, *Tel:* +91 33 2439 1730, *Email:* dkrao54@hotmail.com.
Secretary: Satyabrata Das, *Tel:* +91 33 2230 6349, *Email:* sbdas@portofcalcutta.com

Port Security: ISPS compliant

Approach: The approach channel to the port, 130 km in length, presents some navigational hazards. Vessels have to negotiate several sand bars and sharp bends. There are over 120 channel buoys of which 82 are lighted; and about 500 river marks of which 140 are lighted. Since the sand bars are subject to seasonal, and at times, sudden fluctuations, the depth and alignment of the navigational channel requires a heavy dredging commitment round the clock and for most days of the year. A forecast of monthly drafts is published by the Port Authorities about two months ahead, and owners are advised to obtain prior information before arrival. Powerful despatch vessels cum tugs and lighting launches are maintained. There are two lighthouses in the lower reaches of the River Hooghly, one at Saugor Island and the other at Dariapur

Anchorage: Available in the River Hooghly at Saugor Roads, Haldia, Kalpi, Diamond Harbour, Royapur, Ulubaria and Garden Reach

Pilotage: Compulsory. Commences at Eastern Channel Light Vessel. Owing to the state of the bars in the upper reaches during neap tides, inward vessels, deeply laden, may be neaped at Sandheads at any time of the year. This takes place most frequently during the months of December to May inclusive. Drafts vary from 6.1 to 7.92 m according to the seasons of the year. Pilot vessel call sign VWST, VHF Channel 16

Tides: Bore tides of varying severity occur throughout the year, the equinoctial ones being most dangerous. Ships are frequently held at Sandheads, at the mouth of the river (205 km from port) during these tides. Drafts of vessels lying in the river are also then restricted to 5.49 m for vessels between 122 m and 152.5 m and 4.88 m for shorter vessels (both freshwater draft), vessels over 152.5 m are usually not allowed to remain in the river during bore tides

Traffic: 2007/08, 13 741 000 t of cargo handled, 297 000 TEU's

Maximum Vessel Dimensions: 65 000 dwt, 230 m loa, 32.2 m beam, 8.5 m max draft

Principal Imports and Exports: Imports: Agricultural products, Coal, Fertilisers, Petroleum products, Vegetable oil, Wooden logs. Exports: Aluminium, Jute products, Steel, Textiles.

Working Hours: 1st Shift 0630-1030, 1130-1530. 2nd Shift 1530-1900, 1930-2230. 3rd Shift 2230-0200, 0230-0630

Accommodation:

Name	Length (m)	Depth (m)	Remarks
Kidderpore Dock 1			
Berth No.1	133		General cargo
Berth No.2			Repair berth
Berth No.3	128	6.5	General cargo & containers
Berth No.4	136		General cargo
Berth No.5	229		General cargo
Berth No.6	118	7.6	General cargo & containers
Berth No.7			
Berth No.8	128		General cargo
Berth No.9	108		General cargo & fertiliser
Berth No.10	161		General cargo
Berth No.11	151		General cargo, passenger terminal
Berth No.12	143		General cargo
Kidderpore Dock 2			See [1] below
Netaji Subhas Dock			
Berth No.1	200		General cargo, containers & heavy lift
Berth No.2	187		General cargo
Berth No.3	183		General cargo & cement
Berth No.4	181	7.6	General cargo & containers
Berth No.5	182	6.5	General cargo & containers
Berth No.7	192	7.8	Containers
Berth No.8	225	8	Containers
Berth No.12	152		Petroleum. Dolphin berth for oil tankers
Berth No.13	174		General cargo
Berth No.14	174		General cargo

Name	Length (m)	Depth (m)	Remarks
Budge Budge			Six petroleum wharves
Berth No.1	189		Petroleum, vegetable oil & other liquid cargoes
Berth No.2	102		Petroleum, vegetable oil & other liquid cargoes
Berth No.3	163		Petroleum, vegetable oil & other liquid cargoes
Berth No.5	189		Petroleum, vegetable oil & other liquid cargoes
Berth No.7	189		Petroleum, vegetable oil & other liquid cargoes
Berth No.8	189		Petroleum, vegetable oil & other liquid cargoes

[1]*Kidderpore Dock 2*: Dock 2 has length 1372.5 m, width 122 m and designed depth of 9.15 m. Eight general cargo berths served by single and double-storey sheds and two coal berths with wagon tippler and conveyor belt system. Two lay-up berths and two buoy berths. Ten level luffing full portal electric quay cranes of 3 t cap; four back roof cranes of 1.75 t cap each; two yard cranes of 1.75 t cap and 11 lifts of 2 t cap. Eight yard cranes varying between 6 to 30 t cap. 16 electric lifts of 1.18 t cap and 22 electric lifts of 1.63 t cap. Mechanical coal loading plant with wagon tipplers, conveyor belt system and two travelling loaders. There is also a mechanical grain handling plant. The coal loading plant is to be decommissioned and the entire coal traffic will be handled at Haldia in the near future

Storage:

Location	Open (m²)	Covered (m²)
Berth No.1	2565	3345
Berth No.2	2693	
Berth No.3	3887	
Berth No.4	9098	3344
Berth No.5	4128	6689
Berth No.6	11849	3345
Berth No.7	4374	
Berth No.8	4647	3344
Berth No.9	3812	3345
Berth No.10	5683	3345
Berth No.11	1604	3344
Berth No.12	5699	3344
Berth No.1	6000	
Berth No.2	3831	11757
Berth No.3	3600	11758
Berth No.4	3400	11758
Berth No.5	11000	6000
Berth No.7	50000	9000
Berth No.12		1872
Berth No.13	1278	10093
Berth No.14	2555	15235

Mechanical Handling Equipment:

Location	Type	Capacity (t)	Qty
Berth No.1	Shore Cranes		4
Berth No.3	Shore Cranes		1
Berth No.4	Shore Cranes		2
Berth No.5	Shore Cranes		3
Berth No.6	Shore Cranes		3
Berth No.7	Shore Cranes		3
Berth No.8	Shore Cranes		3
Berth No.10	Shore Cranes		3
Berth No.11	Shore Cranes		2
Berth No.12	Shore Cranes		2
Berth No.1	Shore Cranes	200	1
Berth No.3	Mult-purp. Cranes	3	1
Berth No.5	Shore Cranes	5	2
Berth No.7	Shore Cranes	3	5
Berth No.13	Mult-purp. Cranes	3	3

Bunkering: Bunkering coal supplied at Kidderpore Docks, Garden Reach jetties and in stream
The Liberty Marine Syndicate Private Ltd, Sagar Trade Cube, 104 S. P. Mukherjee Road, Kolkata, West Bengal, India 700 026, *Tel:* +91 33 2455 0046, *Fax:* +91 33 2455 1586, *Email:* accounts@libertyshipping.com, *Website:* www.libertyshipping.com
Yogi Seaways Private Ltd, 34 Netaji Subhas Road, Kolkata, West Bengal, India 700 001, *Tel:* +91 33 2242 1672, *Fax:* +91 33 2242 1697, *Email:* hmco@vsnl.com
Asean International Ltd, P O Box 7860, Block Z Suite 42/43, Saif Zone, Sharjah, United Arab Emirates, *Tel:* +971 6 557 0083, *Fax:* +971 6 557 0085
Bharat Petroleum Corp. Ltd, 4th Floor, Old Admin Building, Mahul, Chembur, Mumbai, Maharashtra, India 400 074, *Tel:* +91 22 2554 3493, *Fax:* +91 22 2554 0621, *Email:* josecm@bharatpetroleum.in, *Website:* www.baratpetroleum.in
Bominflot, Bominoil Private Ltd, 504 Maker Chambers V, 221 Nariman Point, Mumbai, Maharashtra, India 400 021, *Tel:* +91 22 2281 7133, *Fax:* +91 22 2281 7145, *Email:* bominoil@vsnl.com, *Website:* www.bominflot.net
Cockett Marine Oil Ltd, Carrick House, 36 Station Square, Petts Wood, Kent BR5 1NA, United Kingdom, *Tel:* +44 1689 883 400, *Fax:* +44 1689 877 666, *Email:* enquiries@cockett.com, *Website:* www.cockettgroup.com – *Grades:* IFO180cSt; DO – *Parcel Size:* min IFO 50t, min DO 10t – *Delivery Mode:* barge, road tank wagon, pipeline
M/S Global Fuels & Lubricants Inc., 11-12 Mangal Society, 76C Rafi Ahmed Kidwai Road, King Circle, Mumbai, Maharashtra, India 400 019, *Tel:* +91 22 2374 5987, *Fax:* +91 22 2409 1627, *Email:* globalfuels@vsnl.com, *Website:* www.bunkerindia.com
Indian Oil Corp. Ltd, Indian Oil Bhavan Head Office, G9 Ali Yavar Jung Marg, Bandra (East), Mumbai, Maharashtra, India 400051, *Tel:* +91 22 2644 7368, *Fax:* +91 22 2642 2434, *Email:* partha_datta@indianoil.co.in, *Website:* www.indianoil.co.in – *Grades:* GO; DO; IFO180cSt – *Parcel Size:* min 10t – *Rates:* 30t/h – *Notice:* 48-72 hours – *Delivery Mode:* barge, pipeline, truck

Laxmi Marine, Plot No 119, Ward 6, Industrial Area, Bharat Nagar, Gandhidham, Gujarat, India 370 201, *Tel:* +91 2836 237 209, *Fax:* +91 2836 237 211, *Email:* info@laxmimarine.com, *Website:* www.laxmimarine.com

Towage: Eleven tugs are available

Repair & Maintenance: Garden Reach Shipbuilders & Engineers Ltd (GRSE), 43-46 Garden Reach Road, Kolkata, West Bengal, India 700 024, *Tel:* +91 33 2469 8117, *Fax:* +91 33 2469 8114, *Email:* cadgrse@cal3.vsnl.net.in, *Website:* www.grse.nic.in Finger jetty 185 m x 12 m. Basin No.1 193 m x 43 m x 7 m. Basin No.2 229 m x 50 m x 7 m. Two public docks used, lengths 152 m & 137 m (property of Kolkata Port Trust). Slipways: No.1 90 m x 77 m cap 1000 t, No.2 55 m x 44 m cap 50 t. Wet basin 109 m x 24 m x 5 m covered non tidal wet basin
Hooghly Dock & Port Engineers Ltd., Nazirgrunge Works, Danesh Shaik Lane, Howrah, Kolkata, West Bengal, India, *Tel:* +91 33 2668 4746, *Fax:* +91 33 2688 6406, *Email:* hdpelnw@satyam.net.in, *Website:* www.hooghlydock.gov.in One dry dock of 94 m x 13.3 m x 5 m

Ship Chandlers: Bombay Marine Traders, 6B Dr. Suresh Sarkar Road, Kolkata, West Bengal, India 700 014, *Tel:* +91 33 2284 7139, *Fax:* +91 33 2237 4997, *Email:* subir@cal.vsnl.net.in
Chennai Marine Trading Private Ltd, 31/2/1A Kabithirtha Sarani, Watgunge, Kidderpore, Kolkata, West Bengal, India 700 023, *Tel:* +91 33 2459 9941, *Fax:* +91 33 2459 9691, *Email:* chennaimarine@vsnl.net
The Liberty Marine Syndicate Private Ltd, Sagar Trade Cube, 104 S. P. Mukherjee Road, Kolkata, West Bengal, India 700 026, *Tel:* +91 33 2455 0046, *Fax:* +91 33 2455 1586, *Email:* accounts@libertyshipping.com, *Website:* www.libertyshipping.com
Maritime Overseas Corp., 40 Dr. Sudhir Basu Road, Kolkata, West Bengal, India 700 023, *Tel:* +91 33 2449 4168, *Fax:* +91 33 2449 3397/2982, *Email:* venuseng@vsnl.net
A.S. Moloobhoy & Sons, 49/5/2D Karl Marx Sarani, Beside Bhukailash Maidan Kidderpore, Kolkata, West Bengal, India 700 023, *Tel:* +91 33 2459 4747, *Fax:* +91 33 2459 9874, *Email:* kolkata@asmoloobhoy.com, *Website:* www.asmoloobhoy.com
NCGB Marine Private Ltd, 3A St. George Terrace, Hastings, Kolkata, West Bengal, India 700 022, *Tel:* +91 33 2234 4080, *Fax:* +91 33 2223 0199, *Email:* ncgbcal@vsnl.com
West Bengal Trading Corp., 9 Clive Row, Kolkata, West Bengal, India 700 001, *Tel:* +91 33 2242 6433, *Fax:* +91 33 2242 3638, *Email:* wbtcship@vsnl.net, *Website:* www.wbtcship.com

Shipping Agents: Albatross Shipping Pvt. Ltd, 9th Floor Om Towers, No. 32 Chowringhee Road, Kolkata, West Bengal, India 700071, *Tel:* +91 33 2288 4026, *Fax:* +91 33 2288 3569, *Email:* sattanathan.k@alba.co.in
Arebee Star Maritime Agencies Private Ltd, 6th Floor, Rear Building, 12/1 Lindsay Street, Kolkata, West Bengal, India 700087, *Tel:* +91 33 2244 6984/8303, *Fax:* +91 33 2244 8283, *Email:* arebecal@cal.vsnl.net.in
Balailal Mookerjee & Co. Private Ltd, Wardley House, 25 Swallow Lane, Kolkata, West Bengal, India 700001, *Tel:* +91 33 2230 8181, *Fax:* +91 33 2230 9639, *Email:* balailal@vsnl.com
J.M. Baxi & Co, Mukherjee House - 4th Floor, 17 Brabourne Road, Kolkata, West Bengal, India 700 001, *Tel:* +91 33 2242 4211, *Fax:* +91 33 2242 3676, *Email:* calagent@jmbaxi.com, *Website:* www.jmbaxi.com
Capstan Shipping & Estates Private Ltd, Lansdown Court, Flat 17, 5B Sarat Bose Road, Kolkata, West Bengal, India 700020, *Tel:* +91 33 2282 4476, *Fax:* +91 33 2282 3878, *Email:* capstan@vsnl.com
CMA-CGM S.A., CMA CGM (East & South) India Pvt Ltd, OM Tower, 10th Floor, Flat 1001, 33 Chowringhee Road, Kolkata, West Bengal, India 700 071, *Tel:* +91 33 4006 0833, *Fax:* +91 33 4006 0840, *Email:* cta.genmbox@cma-cgm.com, *Website:* www.cma-cgm.com
Contfreight Shipping Agency India Private Ltd, 3rd Floor, Binoy Bhawan, 27-B Camac Street, Kolkata, West Bengal, India 700016, *Tel:* +91 33 2240 5960, *Fax:* +91 33 2240 8344, *Email:* pinaki@hanjin.com
Emirates Shipping Agencies (India) Private Ltd, Diamond Chambers Block 1&2, 6th Floor, Flat O, Chowringhee Lane, Kolkata, West Bengal, India 700016, *Tel:* +91 33 4002 6400, *Fax:* +91 33 4002 6401, *Email:* archita.roy@in.emiratesline.com, *Website:* www.emiratesline.com
Everett (India) Private Ltd, 4 Government Place North, Kolkata, West Bengal, India 700 001, *Tel:* +91 33 2248 6295/7, *Fax:* +91 33 2248 9583, *Email:* operation@everett.co.in, *Website:* www.everett.co.in
Evergreen India Private Ltd, 5th Floor Block A Jindal Towers, 21/1A/3 Darga Road, Kolkata, West Bengal, India 70017, *Tel:* +91 33 3982 9999, *Fax:* +91 33 3984 9998, *Email:* ccumgt@evergreen-shipping.co.in, *Website:* www.@evergreen-marine.com
Five Star Logistics Private Ltd, 2nd Floor, Lesley House, 19/A Jawaharlal Nehru Road, Kolkata, West Bengal, India 700 087, *Tel:* +91 33 2217 1040, *Fax:* +91 33 2217 1040, *Email:* marketing@fivestarorex.com, *Website:* www.fivestarorex.com
Forbes Patvolk (A Division of Forbes Gokak Ltd), Royal Insurance Building, 5&7 Netaji Subhas Road, P O Box 71, Kolkata, West Bengal, India 700001, *Tel:* +91 33 2248 4442/45, *Fax:* +91 33 2248 4406, *Email:* patvolk@cal.vsnl.net.in
GAC Shipping (India) Pvt Ltd, 238-B, 4th Floor, A.J.C. Bose Road, Kolkata, West Bengal, India 700 020, *Tel:* +91 33 4003 4500, *Fax:* +91 33 2287 2979, *Email:* kolkata@gacworld.cm, *Website:* www.gacworld.com
Greenways Shipping Agencies Private Ltd, 1A/B, 1st Floor, Rawdon Chambers, 11A Rawdon Street, Kolkata, West Bengal, India 700017, *Tel:* +91 33 2247 4960, *Fax:* +91 33 2247 0328, *Email:* greenway@vsnl.com
International Clearing & Shipping Agency, 230A Chitrakoot Building, Flat No.53, A.J.C. Bose Road, Kolkata, West Bengal, India 700 016, *Tel:* +91 33 4007 6403, *Fax:* +91 33 4007 6405, *Email:* cal_prabhat@icsagroup.com, *Website:* www.icsagroup.com
Interocean Shipping (India) Pvt Ltd., Flat No.10A, Poddar Point, 113 Park Street, Kolkata, West Bengal, India 700 016, *Tel:* +91 33 2229 7019, *Fax:* +91 33 2245 7387, *Email:* inter_ocean@vsnl.com, *Website:* www.interoceangroup.com
Macoline Shipping Private Ltd, 507, Krishna Building, 5th Floor, 224, A.J.C. Bose Road, Kolkata, West Bengal, India 700017, *Tel:* +91 33 2281 4446, *Fax:* +91 33 2281 4448, *Email:* macoline@cal3.vsnl.net.in, *Website:* www.macnels.com.sg
Marine Container Services (I) Private Ltd, 2nd Floor, 7C Kiron Shankar Roy Road, Kolkata, West Bengal, India 700001, *Tel:* +91 33 2248 1856, *Fax:* +91 33 2248 6506, *Email:* mcscal@seahorsegroup.co.in
Merchant Shipping Services Private Ltd, 9th Floor, Bells House, 21, Camac Street, Kolkata, West Bengal, India 700016, *Tel:* +91 33 2282 1470, *Fax:* +91 33 2283 5827, *Email:* commcal@samsarashippping.com, *Website:* www.merchantshpg.com
A.P. Moller-Maersk Group, Maersk India Pvt Ltd, 401-402 A/B Jasmine Tower, 31 Shakespeare Sarani, Kolkata, West Bengal, India 700 017, *Tel:* +91 33 6610 1600, *Fax:* +91 33 6610 1699, *Email:* ccusal@maersk.com, *Website:* www.maerskline.com

Oasis Shipping Private Ltd, 21 Camac Street, Bells House, 9th Floor, Kolkata, West Bengal, India 700 016, *Tel:* +91 33 2282 0857, *Fax:* +91 33 2282 3168, *Email:* commcal@oasisshipping.com

Purba Bharati Shipping Agency Private Ltd, 1st Floor, 8 Strand Road, Kolkata, West Bengal, India 700001, *Tel:* +91 33 2210 2327, *Fax:* +91 33 2248 1460, *Email:* purbasa@vsnl.net

Samrat Shipping & Transport Systems Private Ltd, Shree Manjari, 1st Floor, Block 7, 1/1 Camac Street, Kolkata, West Bengal, India 700016, *Tel:* +91 33 2220 9495/7/8, *Fax:* +91 33 2249 5648

Samsara Shipping (Private) Ltd, 9th Floor, 21 Camac Street, Kolkata, West Bengal, India 700 071, *Tel:* +91 33 2282 6659, *Fax:* +91 33 2282 3168, *Email:* commcal@samsarashipping.com, *Website:* www.samsarashipping.com

Seabridge Maritime Agencies Private Ltd, 4th & 6th Floors, 418 & 612 Krishna Building, 224 AJC Bose Road, Kolkata, West Bengal, India 700017, *Tel:* +91 33 2280 2644, *Fax:* +91 33 2240 5666, *Email:* cscal@sbmapl.com

Seahorse Ship Agencies Private Ltd, 7-c Kiron Shankar Roy Road, Kolkata, West Bengal, India 700001, *Tel:* +91 33 2220 7477, *Fax:* +91 33 2228 1396

Seatrans Marine Private Limited, 209 A, 2nd Floor, Unit No.46, "Karnani Estate", J.C. Bose Road, Kolkata, West Bengal, India 700 017, *Tel:* +91 33 3022 9256, *Fax:* +91 33 3022 8256, *Email:* seatrans@seatrans.co.in, *Website:* www.seatrans.co.in

Seaworld Shipping & Logistics Private Ltd, 4G, Crescent Tower, 4th Floor, 229 AJC Bose, Kolkata, West Bengal, India 700020, *Tel:* +91 33 2287 3310, *Fax:* +91 33 2287 3317, *Email:* seaworldship@vsnl.com, *Website:* www.seaworldship.com

Sentrans Maritime Private Ltd, 2nd Floor, 9B Wood Street, Kolkata, West Bengal, India 700016, *Tel:* +91 33 2247 4586/0094, *Fax:* +91 33 2247 9828, *Email:* sentrans@sentrans.com, *Website:* www.sentrans.com

Tata NYK Transport Systems Ltd, Constantia,, 8th Floor, 11 Dr. U. N. Brahmachari Street, Kolkata, West Bengal, India 700017, *Tel:* +91 33 3021 9191, *Fax:* +91 33 3021 9110/9150, *Email:* ccu_gen@sg.nykline.com, *Website:* www.nykline.com

Transindia Shipping & Logistics Pvt Ltd, Unit 4G, Crescent Tower,4th Floor, 229 A.J.C. Bose Road, Kolkata, West Bengal, India 700 020, *Tel:* +91 33 2287 3310, *Fax:* +91 33 2287 3317, *Email:* rajannair@cal.seaworldship.com, *Website:* www.seaworldship.com

United Liner Agencies of India Private Ltd, 4th Floor, Meekerjee House, 17 Brabourne Road, Kolkata, West Bengal, India 700001, *Tel:* +91 33 2242 1880, *Fax:* +91 33 2242 3676, *Email:* calcutta@ulaindia.com

Yogi Seaways Private Ltd, 34 Netaji Subhas Road, Kolkata, West Bengal, India 700 001, *Tel:* +91 33 2242 1672, *Fax:* +91 33 2242 1697, *Email:* hmco@vsnl.com

Stevedoring Companies: Five Star Logistics Private Ltd, 2nd Floor, Lesley House, 19/A Jawaharlal Nehru Road, Kolkata, West Bengal, India 700 087, *Tel:* +91 33 2217 1040, *Fax:* +91 33 2217 1040, *Email:* marketing@fivestarorex.com, *Website:* www.fivestarorex.com

Surveyors: J.B. Boda Surveyors Private Ltd, 4th Floor, Metro Tower 1, Ho-Chi-Minh Sarani, Kolkata, West Bengal, India 700 071, *Tel:* +91 33 2288 1335, *Fax:* +91 33 2288 7157, *Email:* jbbcal@jbbodamail.com, *Website:* www.jbboda.net

Det Norske Veritas A/S, P-108, Block F, New Alipore, Kolkata, West Bengal, India 700 053, *Tel:* +91 33 2478 9002, *Fax:* +91 33 2478 6680, *Website:* www.dnv.com

Germanischer Lloyd, Flat 3B, Merlin Villa, 3rd Floor, 88A Hazra Road, Kolkata, West Bengal, India 700 026, *Tel:* +91 33 2476 6212, *Fax:* +91 33 2485 3404, *Website:* www.gl-group.com

Indian Register of Shipping, 21 Hemanta Basu Sarani, Kolkata, West Bengal, India 700 001, *Tel:* +91 33 2248 2570, *Fax:* +91 33 2248 3237, *Email:* calcutta@irclass.org, *Website:* www.irclass.org

Nippon Kaiji Kyokai, 96 Kankulia Road, Block 1, Flat 5, Kolkata, West Bengal, India 700 029, *Tel:* +91 33 2461 0136, *Fax:* +91 33 2461 0199, *Website:* www.classnk.or.jp

Season Ship Management & Maritime Services, I/1 Baghajatin Regent Estate, Kolkata, West Bengal, India 700 092, *Tel:* +91 33 2483 6782, *Fax:* +91 33 2483 2197, *Email:* seasonship@yahoo.co.uk

Medical Facilities: Modern hospitals available in the town

Airport: Dum Dum Airport, 19 km

Development: Construction of berth No.13 a multi-purpose cargo berth is soon to begin, it will have a back up area of 15 000 m2

Lloyd's Agent: Wilson Surveyors and Adjusters Private Ltd, Suite No.806, 8th Floor, O M Towers, 32 Chowringhee Road, Kolkata, West Bengal, India 700 071, *Tel:* +91 33 2217 5800, *Fax:* +91 33 2217 5797, *Email:* kolkata@wilsur.com, *Website:* www.wilsur.com

KRISHNAPATNAM

Lat 14° 18' N; Long 80° 5' E.

Admiralty Chart: -	**Admiralty Pilot:** 21
Time Zone: GMT +5.5 h	**UNCTAD Locode:** IN KRI

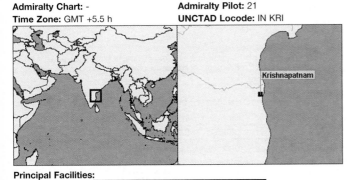

Principal Facilities:

		Y	G								

Authority: Krishnapatnam Port Co Ltd., P O Bag No..1, Muthukur, Nellore, India 524 344, *Tel:* +91 861 237 7046, *Fax:* +91 861 237 7041, *Email:* mkpadia@krishnapatnamport.com, *Website:* www.krishnapatnam.com

Officials: Chief Executive Officer: M.K. Padia.

Weather: During June-September the wind blows from SW. During the remaining period it blows NE-NNE

Tides: The mean tidal variation is of the order of 0.7 m at spring tides and 0.3 m at neap tides

Working Hours: 24 h/day

Accommodation:

Name	Length (m)	Draught (m)	Remarks
Krishnapatnam			
Berths	1200	15.6	See [1] below

[1]*Berths:* Four berths in all (each 300 m long); two to handle coal and one each for iron ore and general cargo

Mechanical Handling Equipment: Equipped with state-of-the-art ship unloaders and ship loaders. The machinery can unload 3000 t/h and load 1500 t/h. There are also two mobile cranes, stackers, reclaimers and conveyers

Airport: Chennai and Tirupati

Development: The port is being developed to handle vessels up to 200 000 dwt. On completion of the third and final phase of expansion and development, Krishnapatnam port will have a total of 41 berths with quay length of 12.5 km and a draught of 19 m

Lloyd's Agent: Wilson Surveyors and Adjusters Private Ltd, TMB Mansion, 3rd Floor, 739 Anna Salai, Chennai, Tamil Nadu, India 600 002, *Tel:* +91 44 2852 2811, *Fax:* +91 44 2852 3349, *Email:* chennai@wilsur.com, *Website:* www.wilsur.com

KULPI

Lat 22° 6' N; Long 88° 13' E.

Admiralty Chart: 136	**Admiralty Pilot:** 21
Time Zone: GMT +5.5 h	**UNCTAD Locode:** IN

This port is currently under construction with the first phase having a 450 m quay and a handling capacity of 650 000 TEU's. The development will also include a special economic zone

MACHILIPATNAM

Lat 16° 10' N; Long 81° 12' E.

Admiralty Chart: 2061	**Admiralty Pilot:** 21
Time Zone: GMT +5.5 h	**UNCTAD Locode:** IN MAP

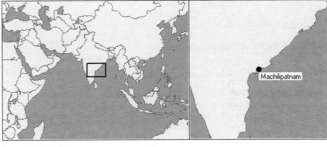

Principal Facilities:

			G					T	A

Authority: The Port Officer, Machilipatnam Port, Machilipatnam, Andhra Pradesh, India 521 003, *Tel:* +91 8671 2334

Radio Frequency: VHF Channels 16 and 12

Principal Imports and Exports: Imports: Bulk & bagged fertilizer. Exports: General cargo, Iron ore, Ricebran.

Accommodation:

Name	Remarks
Machilipatnam	See [1] below

[1]*Machilipatnam:* Open roadstead. Depths of about 9.5 m are obtained with good holding ground in a position with the lighthouse (painted black and white) bearing 270°, from lighthouse 9 km. There is a sand bar with a depth variation of 1 to 2 m which can be crossed by lighters at HT into a dredged channel of max d 2.5 m. Shore facilities have been provided at the new port area for loading and unloading cargo lighters, about 1.5 miles E of the old port

Storage: Two cargo sheds of 9000 t are available

Towage: One tug of 150 hp and two launches of 40 hp available for towage

Medical Facilities: Government hospital available. Private nursing homes with efficient physicians and surgeons also available. Agent arranges medical aid on advance information

Airport: Gannavaram, 64 km

Development: Maytas Infra Pvt Ltd (MIPL) is to develop the port

Lloyd's Agent: Wilson Surveyors and Adjusters Private Ltd, TMB Mansion, 3rd Floor, 739 Anna Salai, Chennai, Tamil Nadu, India 600 002, *Tel:* +91 44 2852 2811, *Fax:* +91 44 2852 3349, *Email:* chennai@wilsur.com, *Website:* www.wilsur.com

Key to Principal Facilities:—			
A=Airport	**C**=Containers	**G**=General Cargo	**P**=Petroleum	**R**=Ro/Ro	**Y**=Dry Bulk
B=Bunkers	**D**=Dry Dock	**L**=Cruise	**Q**=Other Liquid Bulk	**T**=Towage (where available from port)	

MADRAS

former name, see Chennai

MAGDALLA

Lat 21° 8' N; Long 72° 44' E.

Admiralty Chart: 1486 **Admiralty Pilot:** 38
Time Zone: GMT +5.5 h **UNCTAD Locode:** IN MDA

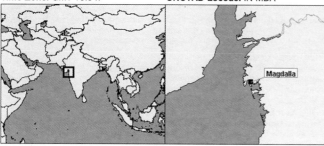

Principal Facilities:

	Q	Y	G				D	T	A	

Authority: Gujarat Maritime Board, Port of Magdalla, Makai Bridge, Nanpura, Surat, India 395003, *Tel:* +91 261 247 4825, *Fax:* +91 261 247 5645, *Website:* www.gmbports.org

Officials: Port Officer: Capt B R Pathak.

Anchorage: Tanker and bulk carrier lighterage operations takes place 10 nm SW of Magdalla Port in deep water as nominated by the Port officer. The available draft is 10-15 m

Pilotage: Not compulsory

Principal Imports and Exports: Imports: Building Materials, Butane, Clinker, Ethylene, Fertilizers, Foodgrains, Iron ore, Machinery, Sponge Iron. Exports: Cotton Seeds, Fruits, General Cargo, Sponge Iron.

Accommodation:

Name	Length (m)	Depth (m)
Magdalla		
Jetty No.1	210.8	21
Jetty No.2	143.5	

Storage: Four warehouses with an area of 2814 m2 and six open areas covering 17 000 m2

Mechanical Handling Equipment:

Location	Type	Capacity (t)	Qty
Magdalla	Mobile Cranes	18.5	1

Towage: One twin screw tug of 470 bhp

Repair & Maintenance: One drydock 155 m x 30 m for vessels up to 12 000 dwt ABG Shipping Ltd, Near Magdala Port, Dumas Road, Surat, India 395 007, *Tel:* +91 261 272 5191, *Fax:* +91 261 272 6481, *Website:* www.abgindia.com

Airport: 4 km

Lloyd's Agent: Wilson Surveyors and Adjusters Private Ltd, Golden Arcade, II Floor, Room No.209, Plot No.141/142, Sector 8, Gandhidam, Kutch, Gujarat, India 370 201, *Tel:* +91 2836 238333, *Fax:* +91 2836 238333, *Email:* kandla@wilsur.com, *Website:* www.wilsur.com

MALPE

Lat 13° 21' N; Long 74° 42' E.

Admiralty Chart: 1564 **Admiralty Pilot:** 38
Time Zone: GMT +5.5 h **UNCTAD Locode:** IN MAL

Principal Facilities:

		G					A	

Authority: Deputy Port Conservator, Port Office, Malpe, Karnataka, India 576 118, *Tel:* +91 8252 537592

Approach: Port well protected by granite islands between two of which is a wide channel 7.62 m deep. The channel between the two breakwaters maintains a depth of 4.5 m LWOST

Anchorage: Approx 800 m NW of Daria Bahadur Ghar Island in depth of 6 m

Pilotage: Unlicensed pilots take sailing vessels in and out in high tide. The services of the Port Officer at Coondapoor, who is a licensed pilot can be obtained if required

Radio Frequency: VHF Channel 16

Weather: Generally fair except during SW monsoon from mid May to mid September

Tides: Max tidal range 2 m. During monsoon season sea swell reaches 1.5 m

Principal Imports and Exports: Imports: Bentonite lumps, Cement, Salt, Soda ash, Wheat. Exports: Bricks, Silica sand.

Working Hours: 1000-1730

Accommodation:

Name	Remarks
Malpe	See [1] below

[1]*Malpe:* Open roadstead. Anchorage in 9.15 m about 1.6 mile WNW of lighthouse. One RCC Passenger Jetty in depth of 3.7 m and one wooden jetty in depth of 3.0 m

Storage: A cargo shed is available

Cargo Worked: 300 t/day

Medical Facilities: Government hospital at Udipi

Airport: Bajpe, 68 km

Railway: Indrali, 7 km

Lloyd's Agent: Peirce Leslie India Ltd, Peirce Leslie Surveyours and Assessors Ltd., Bristow Road, Willingdon Island, Kochi, Kerala, India 682 003, *Tel:* +91 484 266 8362, *Fax:* +91 484 266 8394, *Email:* plsacok@sify.com, *Website:* www.plsurvey.in

MANDVI

Lat 22° 49' N; Long 69° 21' E.

Admiralty Chart: 43 **Admiralty Pilot:** 38
Time Zone: GMT +5.5 h **UNCTAD Locode:** IN MDV

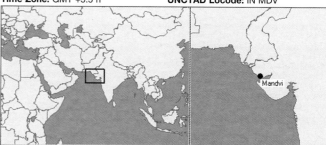

Principal Facilities:

		Y				B		T	A	

Authority: Gujarat Maritime Board, Port of Mandvi, Mandvi, Gujarat, India 370 465, *Tel:* +91 2834 223033, *Fax:* +91 2834 230033, *Email:* bogmbmandvi@kut.gov.in, *Website:* www.gmbports.org

Officials: Port Officer: Hukum Chand Patidar.

Anchorage: Approx 2 km S of Albert Edward Breakwater with Ravalpir Lt. bearing 0.63° in depth of 10 m

Radio Frequency: VHF Channel 16

Tides: 4.1 m MHWS, 3.6 m MHWN, 1.7 m MLWS, 1.0 m MLWN

Principal Imports and Exports: Imports: Building materials, Dates, Fertilizer, General cargo. Exports: Bentonite, Clay, Cotton seeds, General cargo, Oil cakes, Salt.

Working Hours: 0800-1200, 1400-1800, 2000-0400. Overtime available with permission of Port Authority

Accommodation:

Name	Remarks
Mandvi	See [1] below

[1]*Mandvi:* Open roadstead. Cargo handled in stream at the anchorage. Barges and local sailing vessels work cargo from a jetty 245 m long, but only at HW as the creek is completely dry at LW; movements of lighterage craft restricted to about 2 h before and 2 h after HW

Storage:

Location	Open (m2)	Covered (m2)	Sheds / Warehouses
Mandvi	20000	618	4

Cargo Worked: Approx 1000-1200 t/day for bulk cargoes

Bunkering: Available by bunker barge from Kandla as and when required

Towage: One tug available of 277 bhp

Medical Facilities: Good hospital facilities and private clinics available

Airport: Bhuj Airport, 60 km

Lloyd's Agent: Wilson Surveyors and Adjusters Private Ltd, Golden Arcade, II Floor, Room No.209, Plot No.141/142, Sector 8, Gandhidam, Kutch, Gujarat, India 370 201, *Tel:* +91 2836 238333, *Fax:* +91 2836 238333, *Email:* kandla@wilsur.com, *Website:* www.wilsur.com

MANGALORE

see under New Mangalore

MASULIPATAM

alternate name, see Machilipatnam

MORMUGAO

Lat 15° 25' N; Long 73° 48' E.

Admiralty Chart: 492
Time Zone: GMT +5.5 h

Admiralty Pilot: 38
UNCTAD Locode: IN MRM

Mormugao

Principal Facilities:

P	Q	Y	G	C	R	L	B	D	T	A

Authority: Mormugao Port Trust, Administrative Office, Headland Sada, Mormugao, Goa, India 403 804, *Tel:* +91 832 252 1150, *Fax:* +91 832 252 1155, *Email:* mgpt@sancharnet.in, *Website:* www.mptgoa.com

Officials: Chairman: Praveen Agarwal, *Email:* chmgpt@sancharnet.in.
Deputy Conservator: Capt Sharad S. Karnad, *Email:* sharad.karnad@mptgoa.com.
Traffic Manager: Nagappan Vaiyapuri.

Port Security: ISPS compliant

Pre-Arrival Information: ETA should be sent through the agent before 48 hrs. and then 24 hrs. prior to the arrival of the vessel. When the vessel is within the VHF range (at least 2 hrs before arrival) it has to give updated ETA to Port signal station Call sign "Goa Port"

Documentation: The following items must be signed by the master after arrival at the Port and the documents are placed at the disposal of the Port:
1. Ships papers
2. certificate of Registry
3. Derat certificate
4. Safety Equipment certificate
5. Load Line certificate
6. Radio Telegraphy certificate
7. Indian light dues
The following documents are also required:
1. Passenger List, 10 copies
2. Crew list, 10 copies
3. Last Port Clearance
4. Bill of Landing,(in case of imports),3 copies
5. Stores list, 3 copies
6. Personal property list, 3 copies

Approach: There is no separate fairway buoy; the entrance to the channel is marked by green and red buoys, situated approx. 3.6 nm W of the breakwater at a depth of 14.4 m below LWS. The approach channel is marked by lighted buoys. The length of the channel is 4 nm, width 250 m and depth 14.4 m below LWS

Anchorage: There are anchorages available E of the breakwater for vessels with max draft of 5.8 m. W of the breakwater there are anchorages 2-5 nautical miles from the breakwater lighthouse for vessels of any size and draft
Vessels awaiting a pilot can anchor 2.5 nautical miles W of the breakwater light in depths of 12.5 m. Vessels with deeper draft can anchor approx 4 nautical miles W of the breakwater light in depths of 16.5 m. Deep laden vessels should await high tide

Pilotage: Compulsory and available 24 h with prior notice to the Harbour Master. Vessels are boarded approx 1 nautical mile off the W of the breakwater close to the entrance channel. For pilotage services vessels should call the signal station as soon as possible when the vessel is within VHF range, Fax: +91 834 251 2216. During SW monsoons only daytime pilotage is available

Radio Frequency: 24 h continuous monitoring by Port Signal Station on VHF Channel 16 (call sign 'Goa Port'). Working channels 10, 11, 12 & 14

Weather: Two distinct seasons; fair season from October to May and the SW monsoon from June to September. Normal wind force varies between force 4 to 7 during monsoon season. Cyclonic storms up to 120 km/h may strike during the monsoon season

Tides: Range of tide 1.8 m MHHW, 2.4 m MHHWST, 0.15 m MLLW, 0.08 m MLLWST. The strength of the current either at flood or ebb does not generally exceed 1 knot. Waves or swell during the fair season rarely exceed 2 m in the open sea, the direction being mainly towards W and NW; during the monsoons the waves or swell can reach 4 m, mainly from the SW

Traffic: 2007/08, 35 128 000 t of cargo handled

Maximum Vessel Dimensions: 335 m loa, 275 000 dwt, 14 m draft

Principal Imports and Exports: Imports: Bulk liquids, Chemicals, Coal, Coke, Fertilizer, General cargo, Iron and steel, Limestones, Machinery, Petroleum. Exports: Alumina, Frozen shrimp, Iron ore, Manganese ore, Oil cakes.

Working Hours: First shift 0730-1500 with half-hour break 1230-1300. Second shift 1500-2300 with half-hour break 2030-2100. Third shift 2300-0700 with half-hour break 0330-0400
Berthing and unberthing can be carried out throughout 24 h without any overtime charge

Accommodation:

Name	Length (m)	Draught (m)	Remarks
Mormugao			See [1] below
Berth No.5A	210	11–11.7	Coal/coke for vessels up to 190 m loa
Berth No.6A	240	12–14	Coal/coke for vessels up to 225 m loa
Berth No.7	100	3.5	Pellets, coke etc for vessels up to 100 m loa
Berth No.8	298	11–12.5	Liquid bulk for vessels up to 260 m loa
Berth No.9	357.5	12–14	See [2] below
Berth No.10	250	10–11.4	See [3] below
Berth No.11	270	11.8–12.5	See [4] below

[1]*Mormugao:* Harbour has accommodation for vessels alongside quay wall protected from force of SW monsoon by a breakwater 522.4 m long, quay wall 939.4 m long runs at right angles to the breakwater
There are three mooring dolphins for iron ore, other ores and general cargoes with four transhippers, each with an average loading cap of approx 15 000 t/day
[2]*Berth No.9:* Iron ore for vessels up to 335 m loa, 50 m beam and air draft of 19.5 m. Equipment includes eight barge unloaders at 750 t/h each, one continuous barge unloader at 1250 t/h, three stackers at 3250 t/h each, two reclaimers at 4000 t/h each and two shiploaders at 4000 t/h each
[3]*Berth No.10:* General cargo & container berth for vessels up to 225 m loa
[4]*Berth No.11:* General cargo & container berth for vessels up to 225 m loa

Storage: General Cargo: covered storage (owned by the port) consists of seven sheds totalling 27 082 m2 with storage cap of 51 483 t and covered storage (owned by Central Warehousing Corp and Food Corp of India) consists of four sheds totalling 14 480 m2 with storage cap of 22 216 m2. Open storage for containers of 16 000 m2 with storage cap of 48 000 t and open storage for other cargo of 309 389 m2 with storage cap of 688 167 t
Liquid Cargo: POL products have 25 tanks with cap of 192 611 kls, phosphoric acid have 3 tanks with cap of 22 500 kls, furnace oil, caustic soda, molasses etc have 13 tanks with cap of 38 395 klls, other liquid products have 2 tanks with cap of 10 000 t and ammonia has 1 tank with cap of 5000 t

Mechanical Handling Equipment:

Location	Type	Capacity (t)	Qty
Mormugao	Mobile Cranes	18	1
Mormugao	Reach Stackers	40	1
Mormugao	Forklifts	3–5	9

Cargo Worked: General cargo 1200 t/day, coal and coke 1500 t/day, iron ore by MOHP 45 000 t/day for vessels over 60 000 dwt and 30 000 t/day for vessels less than 60 000 dwt, import of petroleum products 5000 t/day

Bunkering: Vessels in stream have to hire a private bunkering barge, available in port, to receive bunkers
Asean International Ltd, P O Box 7860, Block Z Suite 42/43, Saif Zone, Sharjah, United Arab Emirates, *Tel:* +971 6 557 0083, *Fax:* +971 6 557 0085
Bharat Petroleum Corp. Ltd, 4th Floor, Old Admin Building, Mahul, Chembur, Mumbai, Maharashtra, India 400 074, *Tel:* +91 22 2554 3493, *Fax:* +91 22 2554 0621, *Email:* josecm@bharatpetroleum.in, *Website:* www.baratpetroleum.in
Bominflot, Bominoil Private Ltd, 504 Maker Chambers V, 221 Nariman Point, Mumbai, Maharashtra, India 400 021, *Tel:* +91 22 2281 7133, *Fax:* +91 22 2281 7145, *Email:* bominoil@vsnl.com, *Website:* www.bominflot.net
Cockett Marine Oil Ltd, Carrick House, 36 Station Square, Petts Wood, Kent BR5 1NA, United Kingdom, *Tel:* +44 1689 883 400, *Fax:* +44 1689 877 666, *Email:* enquiries@cockett.com, *Website:* www.cockettgroup.com – *Grades:* IFO; MDO; MGO – *Parcel Size:* min IFO 50t, min MDO/MGO 10t – *Delivery Mode:* barge, road tank wagon, pipeline
Hindustan Petroleum Corp. Ltd, Hindustan Bhawan, Vallabhdas Marg, Mumbai, Maharashtra, India 400 038, *Tel:* +91 22 2226 0079 – *Grades:* MDO; IFO180cSt – *Parcel Size:* min barge 150t, no max – *Rates:* 50-100t/h – *Notice:* 48-72 hours – *Delivery Mode:* barge, truck
Indian Oil Corp. Ltd, Indian Oil Bhavan Head Office, G9 Ali Yavar Jung Marg, Bandra (East), Mumbai, Maharashtra, India 400051, *Tel:* +91 22 2644 7368, *Fax:* +91 22 2642 2434, *Email:* partha_datta@indianoil.co.in, *Website:* www.indianoil.co.in
Olympic Marine Co., P O Box 5009, Fujairah, United Arab Emirates, *Tel:* +971 9 224726, *Fax:* +971 9 226491, *Email:* olympic@olympgroup.com

Towage: Four tugs available; one of 30 t bollard pull and three of 45 t bollard pull

Repair & Maintenance: Goa Shipyard Ltd, Vasco-da-Gama, Goa, India 403 802, *Tel:* +91 832 251 2152, *Fax:* +91 832 251 3870, *Email:* contactus@goashipyard.com, *Website:* www.goashipyard.co.in Quays of 180 m with max draught 4 m
Western India Shipyard Limited, P O Box 21, Mormugao Harbour, Mormugao, Goa, India 403 803, *Tel:* +91 832 252 0252, *Fax:* +91 832 252 0258, *Email:* wislcomm@sancharnet.in, *Website:* www.westinshp.com Floating dock of 230 m x 34 m with lifting cap of 20 000 t. Graving dock of 62 m x 16 m

Ship Chandlers: George & Sons Marine Suppliers, Shop No.6, 2nd Floor, Apna Bazar Building, Vasco-da-Gama, Goa, India, *Tel:* +91 832 251 8144, *Fax:* +91 832 251 1044, *Email:* georgeshipchandlers@lycos.com

Shipping Agents: Aspinwall & Co. Ltd, 3rd Floor Chase International, Fr Joseph Vaz Road, Vasco-da-Gama, Goa, India 403 802, *Tel:* +91 832 251 0910, *Fax:* +91 832 251 1006, *Email:* goa.mng@aspinwallgroup.com, *Website:* www.aspinwallgroup.com
J.M. Baxi & Co, Colaco Building, Swatantrya Path, Vasco-da-Gama, Goa, India 403 802, *Tel:* +91 832 251 2583, *Fax:* +91 832 251 3917, *Email:* mgoa@jmbaxi.com, *Website:* www.jmbaxi.com

Key to Principal Facilities:—				
A=Airport	**C**=Containers	**G**=General Cargo	**P**=Petroleum	**R**=Ro/Ro	**Y**=Dry Bulk
B=Bunkers	**D**=Dry Dock	**L**=Cruise	**Q**=Other Liquid Bulk	**T**=Towage (where available from port)	

Chowgule Brothers Private Ltd, Chowgule House, 403 Mormugao Harbour, Mormugao, Goa, India 403 803, *Tel:* +91 832 252 5144, *Fax:* +91 832 252 1011, *Email:* info.cb@chowgule.co.in, *Website:* www.chowgulebros.com

CMA-CGM S.A., CMA CGM Global (India) Pvt Ltd, Chase International, 1st Floor, Vasco Da Gama, Goa, India 403 802, *Tel:* +91 832 251 4923, *Fax:* +91 832 250 1934, *Email:* vdg.genmbox@cma-cgm.com, *Website:* www.cma-cgm.com

GAC Shipping (India) Pvt Ltd, F-1 4th Floor Karma Paes Avenue, P O Box 115, FL Gomes Road, Vasco-da-Gama, Goa, India 403 802, *Tel:* +91 832 250 0188, *Fax:* +91 832 250 0190, *Email:* goa@gacworld.com, *Website:* www.gacworld.com

Inchcape Shipping Services (ISS), Inchcape Shipping Services Private Ltd, TFO-01, Chase International Building, Vasco-da-Gama, Goa, India 403 802, *Tel:* +91 832 251 1358, *Fax:* +91 832 251 1358, *Email:* youriss.india@iss-shipping.com, *Website:* www.iss-shipping.com

Interocean Shipping (India) Pvt Ltd., A-1, 5th Floor, Filomena Figueiredo Complex, Swatantra Path, Vasco-da-Gama, Goa, India 403 802, *Tel:* +91 832 250 1216, *Fax:* +91 832 251 0772, *Email:* goa@interoceangroup.com, *Website:* www.interoceangroup.com

Machado & Sons Agents & Stevedores Private Ltd, Q-9/10 Tilak Commercial Complex, 2nd Floor, F.L. Gomes Road, P O Box 719, Vasco-da-Gama, Goa, India 403 802, *Tel:* +91 832 251 2444, *Fax:* +91 832 250 1659, *Email:* machado@sancharnet.in

Samsara Shipping (Private) Ltd, Karma Empress, Q-2, 5th Floor, Near Kadamba Bus Stand, Mormugao, Goa, India 403 802, *Tel:* +91 832 250 1838, *Fax:* +91 832 251 3123, *Email:* samsgoa@samsarashipping.com, *Website:* www.samsarashipping.com

Stevedoring Companies: Agencia Commercial Maritima, P O Box 22, Swatantra Path, Vasco-da-Gama, Goa, India 403 802, *Tel:* +91 832 251 3934, *Fax:* +91 832 251 3480, *Email:* acm_goa@sancharnet.in

Agencia Ultramarina Private Ltd, P O Box 42, Vasco-da-Gama, Goa, India 403 802, *Tel:* +91 832 251 2397, *Fax:* +91 832 251 8939, *Email:* aupl@sancharnet.in

J.M. Baxi & Co, Colaco Building, Swatantrya Path, Vasco-da-Gama, Goa, India 403 802, *Tel:* +91 832 251 2583, *Fax:* +91 832 251 3917, *Email:* mgoa@jmbaxi.com, *Website:* www.jmbaxi.com

Elesbao Pereira & Sons, P O Box 106, Vasco-da-Gama, Goa, India 403 802, *Tel:* +91 832 251 1727, *Fax:* +91 832 251 3036, *Email:* epson_goa@sancharnet.in

Machado & Sons Agents & Stevedores Private Ltd, Q-9/10 Tilak Commercial Complex, 2nd Floor, F.L. Gomes Road, P O Box 719, Vasco-da-Gama, Goa, India 403 802, *Tel:* +91 832 251 2444, *Fax:* +91 832 250 1659, *Email:* machado@sancharnet.in

Menezes & Sons, 11-16 Ground Floor, Vishwambhar Building, Mormugao, Goa, India, *Tel:* +91 832 251 0913

Mormugao Stevedores Association, P O Box 22, Swatantra Path, Vasco-da-Gama, Goa, India 403 802, *Tel:* +91 832 251 3934, *Fax:* +91 832 251 3480

Surveyors: J.B. Boda Surveyors Private Ltd, F.X. Tower, 1st Floor, Opposite M.P.T. Institute, Swatantra Path, Mormugao, Goa, India 403 802, *Tel:* +91 832 251 2902, *Fax:* +91 832 251 2609, *Email:* jbbgoa@jbbodamail.com, *Website:* www.jbboda.net

Bureau Veritas, 4 Lakshjyothi Complex, 2nd Floor, Near KTC Bus Stand, Mundvel, Vasco-da-Gama, Goa, India 403 802, *Tel:* +91 832 251 2955, *Fax:* +91 832 251 6299, *Email:* bv.goa@in.bureauveritas.com, *Website:* www.bureauveritas.com

Captain V. Pereira, Mormugao, Goa, India, *Tel:* +91 832 251 3175

Scansea Marine, Mormugao, Goa, India, *Email:* scansea@hotmail.com, *Website:* www.scanseamarine.com

Seascan Services, Mormugao, Goa, India, *Tel:* +91 832 251 3515

Societe Generale de Surveillance (SGS), SGS India Private Ltd, Above State Bank of India, P O Box 101, 3rd Floor Satyabhama Joshi Building, Vasco Da Gama, Mormugao, Goa, India 403802, *Tel:* +91 832 251 3031, *Fax:* +91 832 251 3428, *Email:* dilip.rege@sgs.com, *Website:* www.sgs.com

Tata Marine Agencies (Division of Tata Tea Limited), Tata Tea Ltd, Mormugao, Goa, India, *Tel:* +91 832 251 2324

Tecnomar Marine Surveyors, 2nd Floor, Laxmi Chambers, Mormugao, Goa, India 403 803, *Tel:* +91 832 252 2349, *Fax:* +91 832 252 2348, *Email:* tecnomar@vsnl.net

Wilson & Co. Ltd, A1, Dharmanand Kosambi Building, Swatantha Path, P O Box 98, Mormugao, Goa, India 403 802, *Tel:* +91 832 251 2324, *Fax:* +91 832 251 1049, *Email:* wilsonco@sancharnet.in, *Website:* www.wilsur.com

Medical Facilities: Available at Mormugao Port Hospital

Airport: Dabolim Airport, 8 km

Railway: Southern Central Railway, 4 km

Lloyd's Agent: Wilson Surveyors and Adjusters Private Ltd, C-204 Remi Bizcourt, Veera Desai Road, Andheri West, Mumbai, Maharashtra, India 400 053, *Tel:* +91 22 6696 3606, *Fax:* +91 22 6696 3669, *Email:* mumbai@wilsur.com, *Website:* www.wilsur.com

MUMBAI

Lat 18° 54' N; Long 72° 49' E.

Admiralty Chart: 2621/2624	**Admiralty Pilot:** 38
Time Zone: GMT +5.5 h	**UNCTAD Locode:** IN BOM

Principal Facilities:

P	Q	Y	G	C	R	L	B	D	T	A

Authority: Mumbai Port Trust, Administrative Offices Building, Shoorji Vallabhdas Marg, Ballard Estate, Mumbai, Maharashtra, India 400 001, *Tel:* +91 22 6656 5656, *Fax:* +91 22 2261 1011, *Email:* mbpt@vsnl.com, *Website:* www.mumbaiport.gov.in

Officials: Chairman: Rahul Asthana, *Tel:* +91 22 6656 4011, *Email:* chairman@mbptmail.com.

Business Development Manager: Sham Sundar Hariharprasad Tiwari, *Tel:* +91 22 6656 4417, *Email:* bdc@mbptmail.com.

Traffic Manager: V. Ranganath, *Tel:* +91 22 6656 4051, *Email:* tm@mbptmail.com.

Chief Engineer: U.M. Suryavanshi, *Email:* ce@mbptmail.com.

Harbour Master: Vijay Pereira, *Tel:* +91 22 6656 4022, *Email:* hm@mbptmail.com.

Port Security: ISPS compliant

Approach: The approach to Mumbai harbour is very safe; there are two lighthouses called Prongs and Kanhoji Angre (Kennery Lighthouse) which give good guidance to navigators. Channel depths (Main Channel) is 10.0 m CD and Indira Dock Channel is 7.0 m CD

Anchorage: There are many inner anchorages in the harbours, max depth being 9.6 m CD. They are safe with bottom of mud and good holding ground

Pilotage: Compulsory and supplied by launches. The boarding area is just eastward of SE Prongs buoy. Pilots are supplied through a control station manned around the clock and keeping watch on VHF Channels 12 and 16. The Prongs Lighthouse is manned and keeps watch on VHF Channels 12 and 16 and guides the vessels into harbour if required

Weather: From mid-May to mid-September the SW monsoon is quite severe and strong gusty SW winds are experienced

Tides: Average tidal range is 3.8 m in Mumbai harbour

Traffic: 2007/08, 57 039 000 t of cargo handled, 118 000 TEU's

Maximum Vessel Dimensions: Indira Docks 9.14 m draft, tankers docking at Jawahar Island 12.24 m draft and undocking of crude oil tankers 12.85 m draft

Principal Imports and Exports: Imports: Bulk sulphur, Chemicals, Iron & steel, Machinery, Paper reels, Petroleum crude & products, Pulses, Rock phosphate. Exports: Iron & steel, Oil cakes, Petroleum crude & products, Rice, Sanitary wares, Sugar, Tubes.

Working Hours: 1st shift 0800-1700, 2nd shift 1700-2330, 3rd shift 2330-0600

Accommodation: Besides the wet docks, there are, along the harbour front, a number of 'Bunders' which are open wharves and basins where the traffic carried by the sailing vessels is handled. These Bunders have extensive facilities for loading, unloading and storing the cargo and have an aggregate quayage of 12 500 m

Container freight stations: 60 180 m2 covered and 214 773 m2 open

Linkspan at New Ferry Wharf to handle ro/ro vessels

Tanker facilities: Marine Oil Terminal at Butcher Island provides four berths and is connected to oil refineries by submarine pipelines. The terminal can take tankers up

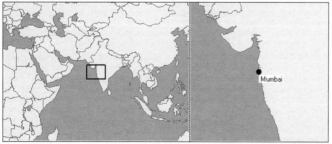

to 70 000 dwt and 244 m long, and approx 9.75 m draft dependent on tides. Min depth in approach channel is 10.8 m with a min depth alongside of 14.3 m. Vessels of 300 m loa, 125 000 dwt displacement and 12.7 m draft can be accommodated. The max draft figure may vary during neap tides and monsoons. The berth is connected to the shore by a jetty 1.4 km in length and is equipped with five marine loading arms for rapid transfer of crude oil and products, pipelines for oil bunkers and deballasting facilities

One berth at Pir Pau Oil Pier where tankers up to 170.7 m length with 6.4 m draft are handled

LPG/butane tankers up to 170.6 m can berth at Pir Pau Pier. Normally this berth is allotted for 48 h only and draft permitted is restricted. Presently the berth has 6.2 m depth CD

A new pier at Pir Pau for handling liquid chemicals and petroleum products including LPG for vessels up to 35 000 dwt, approx 200 m loa with a draft of approx 10.5-12 m

Name	Length (m)	Draught (m)	Remarks
Indira Dock			
Berth No.1	180	8.84–9.14	Container
Berth No.2	158	8.84–9.14	Container
Berth No.3	158	8.84–9.14	Container
Berth No.4	158	8.84–9.14	Container
Berth No.5	158	8.84–9.14	Container
Berth No.6	158	8.84–9.14	Multi-purpose
Berth No.7	152	8.84–9.14	Multi-purpose
Berth No.8	152	8.84–9.14	Multi-purpose
Berth No.9	152	8.84–9.14	General cargo & tanker
Berth No.10	152	8.84–9.14	Multi-purpose
Berth No.11	152	8.84–9.14	Multi-purpose
Berth No.12	152	8.84–9.14	Multi-purpose
Berth No.12A	180	8.84–9.14	Multi-purpose
Berth No.12B	180	8.84–9.14	Multi-purpose
Berth No.13	158	8.84–9.14	General & bulk
Berth No.13A	180	8.84–9.14	Multi-purpose
Berth No.13B	180	8.84–9.14	Multi-purpose
Berth No.14	158	8.84–9.14	General & bulk
Berth No.15	158	8.84–9.14	General & bulk
Berth No.16	158	8.84–9.14	Multi-purpose
Berth No.17	158	8.84–9.14	Multi-purpose
Berth No.18	183	7.5	Multi-purpose
Berth No.19	168	7.5	Multi-purpose
Berth No.20	168	7.5	Multi-purpose
Berth No.21	168	7.5	Multi-purpose
Berth No.22	168	7	Ship repairs
Berth No.23	122	7	Ship repairs
Jetty End	130	8.84–9.14	Heavy lifts
Victoria Dock			
Berth No.1	122	6.7	Multi-purpose
Berth No.2	122	6.7	Multi-purpose
Berth No.3	122	6.7	Multi-purpose
Berth No.4	122	6.7	Multi-purpose
Berth No.5	122	6.7	Multi-purpose
Berth No.6	122	6.7	Multi-purpose
Berth No.7	122	6.7	Multi-purpose
Berth No.8	122	6.7	Multi-purpose
Berth No.9	152	6.7	Multi-purpose
Berth No.10	152	6.7	Multi-purpose
Berth No.11	152	6.7	Multi-purpose
Berth No.12	100	6.7	Multi-purpose
Berth No.13	100	6.7	Multi-purpose
Berth No.14	100	6.7	Multi-purpose
Berth No.15	138	6.7	Holding berth for tugs & launches
Prince's Dock			
Berth A	138	6.1–6.4	Multi-purpose
Berth B	138	6.1–6.4	Multi-purpose
Berth C	140	6.1–6.4	Multi-purpose
Berth D	140	6.1–6.4	Multi-purpose
Berth F	140	6.1–6.4	Multi-purpose
Berth G	100	6.1–6.4	Multi-purpose
Berths K, L & M	431	6.1–6.4	Ship repairs
Berths N & O	212	6.1–6.4	Multi-purpose
Berths P & Q	212	6.1–6.4	Multi-purpose
Jetty End	75	6.1–6.4	Ship repairs
Jawahar Dweep			
JD-1	244	11.6	Petroleum/chemicals
JD-2	244	11	Petroleum/chemicals
JD-3	244	11.6	Petroleum/chemicals
JD-4	493	14.3	Petroleum/chemicals
Pir Pau			
Old Jetty	174	9.7	Petroleum/chemicals
New Jetty	197	12	Petroleum/chemicals
Ballard Pier			
Ballard Pier Extention	232	10	Passenger/container
Ballard Pier Station	244	9.5	Container
New Ferry Wharf			
Ferry Jetty	312	3.2	Passengers
Ferry Berths	249	3.2	Ferries

Storage: No refrigerated space in the docks but sufficient covered and open accommodation is available

Cargo Worked: General cargo approx 1061 t/day. Container 3287 t/day. Dry bulk cargo 1170 t/day

Bunkering: Bharat Petroleum Corp. Ltd, 4th Floor, Old Admin Building, Mahul, Chembur, Mumbai, Maharashtra, India 400 074, Tel: +91 22 2554 3493, Fax: +91 22 2554 0621, Email: josecm@bharatpetroleum.in, Website: www.baratpetroleum.in
Blue Light Star Marine Services Private Ltd, Marine House, Ground Floor, Suite No-

H, 93 Dr. Maheshwari Road, Sandhurst Road, Mumbai, Maharashtra, India 400 009, Tel: +91 22 2371 0583, Fax: +91 22 2371 0243, Email: blsmspl@vsnl.com
Bominflot, Bominoil Private Ltd, 504 Maker Chambers V, 221 Nariman Point, Mumbai, Maharashtra, India 400 021, Tel: +91 22 2281 7133, Fax: +91 22 2281 7145, Email: bominoil@vsnl.com, Website: www.bominflot.net
Hindustan Petroleum Corp. Ltd, Hindustan Bhawan, Vallabhdas Marg, Mumbai, Maharashtra, India 400 038, Tel: +91 22 2226 0079
Indian Oil Corp. Ltd, Indian Oil Bhavan Head Office, G9 Ali Yavar Jung Marg, Bandra (East), Mumbai, Maharashtra, India 400051, Tel: +91 22 2644 7368, Fax: +91 22 2642 2434, Email: partha_datta@indianoil.co.in, Website: www.indianoil.co.in
M/S Global Fuels & Lubricants Inc., 11-12 Mangal Society, 76C Rafi Ahmed Kidwai Road, King Circle, Mumbai, Maharashtra, India 400 019, Tel: +91 22 2374 5987, Fax: +91 22 2409 1627, Email: globalfuels@vsnl.com, Website: www.bunkerindia.com
Raj Shipping Agencies Ltd, Banaji Mansion, 17 Banaji Street, Fort Mumbai, Mumbai, Maharashtra, India 400 023, Tel: +91 22 2204 7272, Fax: +91 22 2287 3986, Email: rajship@vsnl.com, Website: www.rajshipping.com
Solidarity Corp., 34 Juhu Shopping Centre, Gulmohar Cross 9th Road, Juhu Scheme, Mumbai, Maharashtra, India 400 049, Tel: +91 22 623 3548, Fax: +91 22 623 9464, Email: solicorp@vsnl.com
Vinergy International Private Limited (Bunkers India), A Block South Wing, 1st Floor, Shiv Sagar Estate, Dr Annie Besant Road, Worli, Mumbai, Maharashtra, India 400 018, Tel: +91 22 6653 7222, Fax: +91 22 6653 7225, Email: bunkers@vinergy.in, Website: www.vinergy.in
Blue Light Star Marine Services Private Ltd, Marine House, Ground Floor, Suite No-H, 93 Dr. Maheshwari Road, Sandhurst Road, Mumbai, Maharashtra, India 400 009, Tel: +91 22 2371 0583, Fax: +91 22 2371 0243, Email: blsmspl@vsnl.com
Raj Shipping Agencies Ltd, Banaji Mansion, 17 Banaji Street, Fort Mumbai, Mumbai, Maharashtra, India 400 023, Tel: +91 22 2204 7272, Fax: +91 22 2287 3986, Email: rajship@vsnl.com, Website: www.rajshipping.com

Waste Reception Facilities: Dirty ballast can be discharged into reception facilities tank at JD Island. Sludge normally not permitted and chemical waste depending on type and category may be disposed of. Garbage facility normally arranged by vessel's agents

Towage: Amit Shipmanagement Private Ltd, 408 Veena Chambers, Clive Road, Mumbai, Maharashtra, India 400 009, Tel: +91 22 2377 6824, Fax: +91 22 2373 6600, Email: amitship@vsnl.com
SVITZER, SVITZER India Pvt Ltd, B-307, Galleria, Hiranandani Gardens, Powai, Mumbai, Maharashtra, India 400 076, Tel: +91 22 2570 1963/4, Fax: +91 22 2570 1965, Email: wijsmuller@eth.net, Website: www.svitzer.com

Repair & Maintenance: ABG Shipyard Ltd, 5th Floor, Bhupati Chambers, Opera House, 13 Mathew Road, Mumbai, Maharashtra, India 400 004, Tel: +91 22 6656 3000, Fax: +91 22 2364 9236, Email: info@abgindia.com, Website: www.abgindia.com Two dry docks: 155 m x 30 m x 7 m and 125 m x 22 m x 5 m

Ship Chandlers: Admiral Marine Services Private Ltd, 15/18 Al-Karim Manzil, Palton Road, Mumbai, Maharashtra, India 400 001, Tel: +91 22 2261 9850, Fax: +91 22 2261 9132, Email: enquiries@admiralmarine.com, Website: www.admiralmarine.com
Atlas Marine Supply, 408 Sharda Chamber No. 1, 4th Floor, 31 Keshavji Naik Road, Mumbai, Maharashtra, India 400 009, Tel: +91 22 2374 6563, Fax: +91 22 2370 0353, Email: wwat@bom8.vsnl.net.in
Blue Light Star Marine Services Private Ltd, Marine House, Ground Floor, Suite No-H, 93 Dr. Maheshwari Road, Sandhurst Road, Mumbai, Maharashtra, India 400 009, Tel: +91 22 2371 0583, Fax: +91 22 2371 0243, Email: blsmspl@vsnl.com
C.& C. Marine Combine, 25 Bank Street, Mumbai, Maharashtra, India 400 001, Tel: +91 22 2266 0525, Fax: +91 22 2267 0896, Email: ccmarine@bom5.vsnl.net.in, Website: www.ccmarine.in
Cawasji Behramji & Co., 166 Sassoon Dock, Colaba, Mumbai, Maharashtra, India 400 005, Tel: +91 22 2218 7307, Fax: +91 22 2218 2991, Email: tssindia@vsnl.com
Chennai Marine Trading Private Ltd, 413 Loha Bhavan, 4th Floor, 93 P.D Mello Road, Carnac Bunder, Mumbai, Maharashtra, India 400 009, Tel: +91 22 3240 2497/ 2348 1475, Fax: +91 22 6639 0169, Email: chennaimarine@vsnl.net
Continental Chandlers, P O Box 1350, Mumbai, Maharashtra, India 400 001, Tel: +91 22 2265 7913, Fax: +91 22 2266 1509, Email: continental@chandlersindia.com, Website: www.continentalchandlers.com
Elite Traders, 90B Mohammed Ali Road, Mumbai, Maharashtra, India 400 003, Tel: +91 22 2341 2868, Fax: +91 22 2341 2976, Email: elite1@mtnl.in
Industrial Hardware Stores, 172-4 Abdul Rehman Street, Mumbai, Maharashtra, India 400 003, Tel: +91 22 2370 5824, Fax: +91 22 2370 5823, Email: seafarer@vsnl.com
International Marine Ship Stores Suppliers, Navratan Building, Room 313, 3rd Floor, 69 - P'D Mello Road, Carnac Bunder, Mumbai, Maharashtra, India 400 009, Tel: +91 22 2344 0057, Fax: +91 22 2343 9719, Email: intmar@vsnl.com
Laxmi Enterprise, 42/43 Lakdi Bunder Road, Darukhana, Mazagaon, Mumbai, Maharashtra, India 400 010, Tel: +91 22 2374 2583, Fax: +91 22 2374 2584, Email: laxmient@bom2.vsnl.net.in, Website: www.aeromarineindia.com
The Liberty Marine Syndicate Private Ltd, Lok Centre, Marol Maroshi Road, Andheri (E), Mumbai, Maharashtra, India 400 059, Tel: +91 22 2852 7711, Fax: +91 22 2852 7755, Email: libertygroup@vsnl.com, Website: www.libertyshipping.com
Marine Offshore Supply, 284 Nagdevi Street, Mumbai, Maharashtra, India 400 003, Tel: +91 22 2345 2616, Fax: +91 22 2345 0002, Email: marine@bom5.vsnl.net.in
Maritime Overseas Corp., Suite 120, 4th Floor, Development Bank Building, Crawford Market Branch, Mumbai, Maharashtra, India 400 001, Tel: +91 22 2261 3894, Fax: +91 22 2263 4930, Email: united@hathway.com
Mercury International, 207 Sant Tukaram Road, Iron Market, Masjid Bunder, Mumbai, Maharashtra, India 400 009, Tel: +91 22 6633 3121, Fax: +91 22 2378 1802, Email: ship.mercury@gmail.com
Mercury Marine Suppliers, 3rd Floor, Room No 40/41 Tarvotti Bhavan, 203 P. D'Mello Road, Fort, Mumbai, Maharashtra, India 400 001, Tel: +91 22 2265 9421, Fax: +91 22 2262 3406, Email: contact@mercurymarinesuppliers.com, Website: www.mercurymarinesuppliers.com
M.M. Shipping / Mumbai Marine Suppliers, 7/10 Botawala Building, Office No.8, 1st Floor Horniman Circle, Fort, Mumbai, Maharashtra, India 400 001, Tel: +91 22 2340 2430, Fax: +91 22 2340 2429, Email: mmarine@vsnl.net, Website: www.mmschandlers.com
A.S. Moloobhoy & Sons, Anchor House, Plot No.58, 1st Magazine Cross Street, Darukhana, Mazagon, Mumbai, Maharashtra, India 400 010, Tel: +91 22 2372 4911, Fax: +91 22 2374 2678, Email: admin@asmoloobhoy.com, Website: www.asmoloobhoy.com
Moosajee Jeevajee Ent. Pvt Ltd, 449/451 Katha Bazar, Mandvi, Mumbai, Mahara-

shtra, India 400 009, *Tel:* +91 22 2342330, *Fax:* +91 22 23443766, *Email:* moosajee@vsnl.com, *Website:* www.shipsuppliers.com
Ocean Marine International, 1st Floor Unity Co-op Housing Society Ltd., 188 Sheriff Devji Street, Mumbai, Maharashtra, India 400 003, *Tel:* +91 22 2343 4216, *Fax:* +91 22 2344 9900, *Email:* empire@bom8.vsnl.net.in/oceanmarineintl@gmail.com
Rasesh Shipping Services, 1 Rex Chambers, Ground Floor, Wallchand Hirachand Marg, Ballard Estate, Mumbai, Maharashtra, India 400 001, *Tel:* +91 22 2269 1602, *Fax:* +91 22 2269 1605, *Email:* raseshshipping@hotmail.com, *Website:* www.raseshshipping.com
M/s Royal Marine Co., 6 Rex Chambers, Ground Floor, W H Marg, Opposite Red Gate, Indira Dock, Mumbai, Maharashtra, India 400 001, *Tel:* +91 22 2261 4581, *Fax:* +91 22 2261 7486, *Email:* royalmarine@halanigroup.com, *Website:* www.halanigroup.com
SAIF Marine, 220 Vyapar Bhavan, 49 P D'Mello Road, Mumbai, Maharashtra, India 400 009, *Tel:* +91 22 2374 0620, *Fax:* +91 22 2377 1803, *Email:* saifmarine@yahoo.com
Siganporia Brothers, P O Box 324, Mumbai, Maharashtra, India 400 001, *Tel:* +91 22 2344 2718, *Fax:* +91 22 2343 4719, *Email:* siganporia@vsnl.com
Spence & Co., Suite No.417, 115 L.M.Tilak Marg, Opposite Crawford Market, Mumbai, Maharashtra, India 400 003, *Tel:* +91 22 2340 0603, *Fax:* +91 22 2341 5658, *Email:* spenceco@vsnl.net
The Star Incandescent Light Co., 6 Kerawalla Building, 61 Mangaldas Road, Lohar Chaw, Mumbai, Maharashtra, India 400 002, *Tel:* +91 22 2208 7807, *Fax:* +91 22 2208 4560, *Email:* stilco@india.com
Western Marine Traders, Stall No.229 / 230, 1st Lane, Inside Crawford Market, Mumbai, Maharashtra, India 400 001, *Tel:* +91 22 2344 0316, *Fax:* +91 22 2341 1167, *Email:* western_marine_traders@yahoo.com
World Wide Offshore & Ship Supply Co., 408 Sarda Chamber No. 1, 4th Floor, 31 Keshavji Naik Road, Mumbai, Maharashtra, India 400 009, *Tel:* +91 22 2374 6563, *Fax:* +91 22 2370 0353, *Email:* wwat@bom8.vsnl.net.in

Shipping Agents: Albatross Shipping Pvt. Ltd, 3rd Floor Gettmala Building II, Near Shah Industrial Estate, Off Deonar Village Road, Govandi, Mumbai, Maharashtra, India 400088, *Tel:* +91 22 6768 1500, *Fax:* +91 22 6797 8354, *Email:* admin@alba.co.in, *Website:* www.balajiship.com
Ambica Maritime Ltd, Eucharistic Congress Building 3, Convent Street, Colaba, Mumbai, Maharashtra, India 400 039, *Tel:* +91 22 2284 3035, *Fax:* +91 22 2288 5401, *Website:* www.ambicamaritime.com
Arebee Star Maritime Agencies Private Ltd, Imperial Chambers, 3rd Floor Wilson Road, Ballard Est, P O Box 1170, Mumbai, Maharashtra, India 400001, *Tel:* +91 22 2261 1403, *Fax:* +91 22 2261 7735, *Email:* arebee@bom2.vsnl.net.in, *Website:* www.arebeestar.com
Aspinwall & Co. Ltd, Door No. 307, "Shree Nandham",, A-Wing, 3rd Floor,, Plot No.59, Sector-11, C.B.D Belapur (East), Navi-Mumbai, Mumbai, Maharashtra, India 400 018, *Tel:* +91 22 2756 6447, *Fax:* +91 22 6795 5668, *Email:* bom.mng@aspinwallgroup.com, *Website:* www.aspinwallgroup.com
Astec Brasil Ltda, c/o Faredeal Shipping Agencies (Mumbai) Private Ltd, Oberoi Garden Estates, C/1114, 1115, 1st Floor, Off Saki Vihar Road, Chandvli, Andheri (East), Mumbai, Maharashtra, India 400 072, *Tel:* +91 22 6675 4160, *Fax:* +91 22 6675 4165, *Email:* vivek@faredealshipping.com, *Website:* www.astecbrasil.com.br
Atlantic Shipping Agencies Pvt Ltd, Suite 23, MI Estate, DS Marg, Worli, Mumbai, Maharashtra, India 400 018, *Tel:* +91 22 6667 7351, *Fax:* +91 22 2496 5215, *Email:* atlantic@atlanticshpg.com, *Website:* www.atlanticshpg.com
Atlantic Shipping Private Ltd, 124-B Mittal Court, 224 Nariman Point, Mumbai, Maharashtra, India 400021, *Tel:* +91 22 2285 4939, *Fax:* +91 22 2202 5718, *Email:* atlantic@atlanticshpg.com, *Website:* www.atlanticshpg.com
Axis Shipping Agency Private Ltd, 2nd Floor, Kulkami Patil Bhavan, 14 Murzban Road, Mumbai, Maharashtra, India 400001, *Tel:* +91 22 6636 5252, *Fax:* +91 22 6636 5272, *Email:* axis@ckb-india.com, *Website:* www.ckb-india.com
J.M. Baxi & Co, 16 Bank Street, Fort, P O Box 731, Mumbai, Maharashtra, India 400 001, *Tel:* +91 22 2266 3871, *Fax:* +91 22 2265 4638, *Email:* corp@jmbaxi.com, *Website:* www.jmbaxi.com
Beacon Maritime Carriers Private Ltd, Landsdowne House, 3rd Floor, 18 Mahakavi Bhushan Marg, Mumbai, Maharashtra, India 400039, *Tel:* +91 22 2284 5115, *Fax:* +91 22 2284 1805
Bernhard Schulte Shipmanagement (India) Private Ltd, 401 Olympia Hiranandani Gardens, Powai, Mumbai, Maharashtra, India 400 076, *Tel:* +91 22 5697 1588, *Fax:* +91 22 5697 1558, *Email:* eurasia.mumbai@eurasiagroup.com, *Website:* www.eurasiagroup.com
Boxtrans Shipping Agencies Pvt Ltd, 29 NGN Vaidya Marg, Fort, Mumbai, Maharashtra, India 400001, *Tel:* +91 22 2266 4227, *Fax:* +91 22 2266 1512, *Email:* cis@jmbaxi.com
Chowgule Brothers Private Ltd, P O Box 1770, Malhotra House, 3rd Floor opposite GPO, Mumbai, Maharashtra, India 400 001, *Tel:* +91 22 2267 5579, *Fax:* +91 22 2261 0659, *Email:* mumbai.cb@chowgule.co.in
CMA-CGM S.A., CMA CGM Global (India) Pvt Ltd, Hamilton House, 8 J.N. Heredia Marg, Ballard Estate, Mumbai, Maharashtra, India 400 038, *Tel:* +91 22 3988 8999, *Fax:* +91 22 3981 0990, *Email:* mby.genmbox@cma-cgm.com, *Website:* www.cma-cgm.com
Container Marine Agencies Private Ltd, 2nd & 3rd Floor Rupam,, 239 P D'Mello Road, Rupam, Mumbai, Maharashtra, India 400001, *Tel:* +91 22 2264 2412, *Fax:* +91 22 2261 2832, *Email:* mum.genmbox@cma-cgm.com
Container Movement (Bombay) Transport Private Ltd, 25-26 Vaswani Mansion, 120 Dinsha Vachha Road, Churchgate, Mumbai, Maharashtra, India 400020, *Tel:* +91 22 6658 2222, *Fax:* +91 22 2287 3400, *Email:* contactus.mum@cmtindia.com
Crescent Shipping Agency (India) Ltd, New Geetmala Building, 2nd Floor, Near Shah Industrial Estate, Govandi (E), Mumbai, Maharashtra, India 400 088, *Tel:* +91 22 6798 5400, *Fax:* +91 22 6798 5454, *Email:* crescent@csa.co.in, *Website:* www.crescent.co.in
CSAV Group Agencies (India) Pvt Ltd, Technopolis Knowledge Park, Ground Floor, Unit 6 & 7, Mahakali Caves Road, Andheri (East), Mumbai, Maharashtra, India 400093, *Tel:* +91 22 4050 9000, *Fax:* +91 22 2687 6147, *Email:* info@csavagencies-india.com, *Website:* www.csavagencies-india.com
DBC Freight International, 3rd Floor, Wakefield House, Sprott Road, Ballard Estate, Mumbai, Maharashtra, India 400038, *Tel:* +91 22 2262 3506/7, *Fax:* +91 22 2262 2014/16
Depe Global Shipping Agencies Private Ltd, Suite 7/9, 1st Floor, Elphinston House, 17 Murzban Road, Mumbai, Maharashtra, India 400001, *Tel:* +91 22 2204 0714, *Fax:* +91 22 2204 2227
Diamond Maritime Agency Private Ltd, 101/102 Technopolis Knowledge Park, Mahakalu Caves Road, Chakala, Andheri E, Mumbai, Maharashtra, India 400093, *Tel:* +91 22 6679 0673, *Fax:* +91 22 6696 5162
Eastern Steamships Private Ltd, 4th Floor, Landsdowne House, 18 Mahakavi Bhushan Marg, Mumbai, Maharashtra, India 400039, *Tel:* +91 22 2202 0263/4, *Fax:* +91 22 2202 7890
Emirates Shipping Agencies (India) Private Ltd, Unit 101, C Wing, Business Square, 151 Andheri-Kurla Road, Opposite Apple Heritage, Chakala, Mumbai, Maharashtra, India 400093, *Tel:* +91 22 4036 6000, *Fax:* +91 22 4036 6006, *Email:* roop.kumar@in.emiratesline.com, *Website:* www.emiratesline.com
Everett (India) Private Ltd, G2/G3, Silverline, CHS, J.B.Nagar, S.B. Marg, Andheri (East), Mumbai, Maharashtra, India 400 059, *Tel:* +91 22 2835 3934, *Fax:* +91 22 2838 5610, *Email:* admin-mumbai@everett.co.in, *Website:* www.everett.co.in
Evergreen India Private Ltd, Marathon Nextgen Innova A, G-01, opposite Peninsula Corporate Park, Mumbai, Maharashtra, India 400013, *Tel:* +91 22 3984 9999, *Fax:* +91 22 3984 9998, *Email:* biz@evergreen-shipping.co.in, *Website:* www.evergreen-marine.com
Forbes Patvolk (A Division of Forbes Gokak Ltd), Forbes Building, Charanjit Rai Marg., Mumbai, Maharashtra, India 400001, *Tel:* +91 22 2200 8081, *Fax:* +91 22 2203 1639, *Email:* trchandran@vsnl.net
Freight Connection India Pvt Ltd, Cambatta Building, 4th Floor MK Road, opposite Churchgate Station, Mumbai, Maharashtra, India 400020, *Tel:* +91 22 5631 5235, *Fax:* +91 22 5631 5245, *Email:* fcipl1@vsnl.com, *Website:* www.fcipl.com
GAC Shipping (India) Pvt Ltd, P O Box 226, Mumbai, Maharashtra, India 400 001, *Tel:* +91 22 4030 7800, *Fax:* +91 22 4030 7900, *Email:* mumbai@gacworld.com, *Website:* www.gacworld.com
Gokul Maritime Private Ltd, 1st Floor Rm 13/14, Ashok Chamber Dana Bunder D R Marg, Mumbai, Maharashtra, India 400 009, *Tel:* +91 22 6631 4541, *Fax:* +91 22 6631 4544, *Email:* gokul_shipping@yahoo.com
Golden Globe Lines Private Ltd, 24 Calicut Street, Ballard Est, Mumbai, Maharashtra, India 400001, *Tel:* +91 22 2267 6100, *Fax:* +91 22 2269 2435
Greenways Shipping Agencies Private Ltd, 1st Floor, Suite 7/9, Elphinstone House, 17 Murzban Road, Mumbai, Maharashtra, India 400001, *Tel:* +91 22 2207 0714/5, *Fax:* +91 22 2207 2227/5996, *Email:* bombay@gwsbombay.com
A Hartrodt International, Corporate Headquarters, Union Co-op Insurance Building, 23 Sir P.M.Road, Mumbai, Maharashtra, India 400 001, *Tel:* +91 22 4036 1818, *Fax:* +91 22 2204 4802, *Email:* hartrodtindia@vsnl.net, *Website:* www.hartrodt.com
High Tide Ship Management Private Ltd, 4/308 Kamdhenu, Lokhandwala Andheri (W), Mumbai, Maharashtra, India 400 053, *Tel:* +91 22 2637 5346/9, *Fax:* +91 22 2637 5346, *Email:* info@hightideship.com, *Website:* www.hightideship.com
Hind Shipping Agencies, 201 Janmabhoomi Chambers, 29 Walchang Hirachand Marg, Ballard Est, Mumbai, Maharashtra, India 400038, *Tel:* +91 22 2234 8041, *Fax:* +91 22 2261 0842, *Email:* hindship@bom7.vsnl.net.in
IAL Shipping Agencies (Mumbai) Private Ltd, 6th Floor Kalpataru Court, C Gidwani Road, behind RK Studio, Chembur, Mumbai, Maharashtra, India 400074, *Tel:* +91 22 2550 9000/9036, *Fax:* +91 22 2595 2626, *Email:* ialm@ialbom.com, *Website:* www.ial.com
Inchcape Shipping Services (ISS), Inchcape Shipping Services India Pvt. Ltd, 308 Monarch Plaza, Sector 11, CBD Belapur, Navi Mumbai, Maharashtra, India 400 614, *Tel:* +91 22 6789 4800, *Fax:* +91 22 2757 1864, *Email:* youriss.india@iss-shipping.com, *Website:* www.iss-shipping.com
Indian Maritime Enterprises Private Ltd, 4th Foor, 206 EMCA Streer, 289 Sahid Bagat Singh Road, Mumbai, Maharashtra, India 400001, *Tel:* +91 22 2226 4877, *Fax:* +91 22 2261 2676
Interocean Shipping (India) Pvt Ltd., 506 Embassy Centre, 207 Nariman Point, Mumbai, Maharashtra, India 400 021, *Tel:* +91 22 2284 1166, *Fax:* +91 22 2287 3874, *Email:* mumbai@interoceangroup.com, *Website:* www.interoceangroup.com
K Steamship Agencies Private Ltd, 16 Bank Street, P O Box 731, Fort, Mumbai, Maharashtra, India 400001, *Tel:* +91 22 2266 3871, *Fax:* +91 22 2266 2908, *Email:* mail.mum@jmbaxi.com, *Website:* www.jmbaxi.com
Macoline Shipping Private Ltd, 5th Floor, Orient House, Adi Marzban Path, Mangalore Street, Ballard Est, Mumbai, Maharashtra, India 400038, *Tel:* +91 22 5635 6793, *Fax:* +91 22 5635 6799, *Email:* macnels@vsnl.net
Maltrans Shipping Agencies (I) Private Ltd, 3rd Floor, Panthaky House, 8 Maruti Cross Lane, Mumbai, Maharashtra, India 400001, *Tel:* +91 22 2267 9660, *Fax:* +91 22 2267 9661
Marine Container Services (I) Private Ltd, Anchorage Building, 6th Floor Sector 11, Dronagiri Node, Mumbai, Maharashtra, India 400707, *Tel:* +91 22 2724 2169, *Fax:* +91 22 2724 2158, *Email:* mcsnsa@seahorsegroup.co.in
Marine Transport Co. Private Ltd, New Kamani Chambers, Adi Marazban Path, Ballard Est, Mumbai, Maharashtra, India 400038, *Tel:* +91 22 2261 4094, *Fax:* +91 22 2261 1657
Maritime Services Private Ltd, 301-303 Emca House, 3rd Floor, 289 Sahid Bhagat Singh Road, Mumbai, Maharashtra, India 400001, *Tel:* +91 22 4093 5555/2262 1181, *Fax:* +91 22 2262 0579, *Email:* mspl@msplindia.net
Mediterranean Shipping Company, 3rd Floor Vakils House, 18 Sprott Road, Ballard Estate, Mumbai, Maharashtra, India, *Tel:* +91 22 6637 8000, *Fax:* +91 22 6637 8191, *Email:* comm@mscindia.com, *Website:* www.mscindia.com
Meecon Private Ltd, Nirmal 21st Floor, Nariman Point, Mumbai, Maharashtra, India 400021, *Tel:* +91 22 2202 7381, *Fax:* +91 22 2202 5663, *Email:* tmsanghavi@vsnl.com
Merchant Shipping Services Private Ltd, 102 Technopolis Knowledge Park, Mahakali Caves Road, Chakal, Mumbai, Maharashtra, India 400093, *Tel:* +91 22 5696 5000, *Fax:* +91 22 5696 5181, *Email:* com-mum@merchantshpg.com, *Website:* www.merchantshpg.com
Meridian Shipping Agency Private Ltd, Geetmala Building, Near Shah Industrial Estate, Govandi (East), Mumbai, Maharashtra, India 400 088, *Tel:* +91 22 6755 5000, *Fax:* +91 22 6755 5050, *Email:* info@msaship.co.in, *Website:* www.msaship.co.in
A.P. Moller-Maersk Group, Maersk India Pvt Ltd, CG House, 11th Floor, Dr Annie Besant Road, Prabhadevi, Mumbai, Maharashtra, India 400 025, *Tel:* +91 22 2433 7878, *Fax:* +91 22 2433 7898, *Email:* indmktgen@maersk.com, *Website:* www.maerskline.com
Multiport Marine Services Private Ltd, 65-68 Mahendra Chambers, 2nd Floor, 134-136 Dr. DN Road, Mumbai, Maharashtra, India 400001, *Tel:* +91 22 2207 5689, *Fax:* +91 22 2207 7096
Natvar Parikh Industries Ltd, 2nd Floor, Asian Bulding, R Kamamni Marg, Ballard Estate, Mumbai, Maharashtra, India 400 009, *Tel:* +91 22 5655 3600, *Fax:* +91 22 5635 2457, *Email:* npil@bom3.vsnl.net.in, *Website:* www.npil.net
NLS Agency (India) Private Ltd, Shrikant Chambers B-Wing, 3rd Floor next to RK

Studio, Mumbai, Maharashtra, India 400071, *Tel:* +91 22 2520 1141, *Fax:* +91 22 2520 1140, *Email:* csdesk.mum@nlsd.co.in, *Website:* www.nlsd.co.in
Oasis Shipping Private Ltd, 101/102 Technopolis Knowledge Park, Mahakali Caves Road, Chakala, Andheri, Mumbai, Maharashtra, India 400093, *Tel:* +91 22 6696 5040, *Fax:* +91 22 6696 5059, *Email:* comm@oasisshipping.com, *Website:* www.oasisshipping.com
Oceanic Shipping Agency Private Ltd, Darabshaw House, Shoorji Vallabhdas Marg, Ballard Estate, Mumbai, Maharashtra, India 400038, *Tel:* +91 22 2261 4107/4109, *Fax:* +91 22 2261 6385
Omega Shipping Private Ltd, Ground Floor, Hansraj Damodar Trust Building, 12/14 Goa Street, Ballard Estate, Mumbai, Maharashtra, India 400038, *Tel:* +91 22 2265 0558, *Fax:* +91 22 2265 7855, *Email:* sm@omegaship.com
Orient Ship Agency Private Ltd, Ground Floor, Udyog Bhavan, Walchand Hirachand Marg, Ballard Estate, P O Box 1390, Mumbai, Maharashtra, India 400038, *Tel:* +91 22 2265 1433, *Fax:* +91 22 6636 0584, *Email:* jalal_admin@osapl.com
Parekh Marine Agencies Private Ltd, Wakefield House, 1st Floor, Sprott Road, Ballard Estate, Mumbai, Maharashtra, India 400038, *Tel:* +91 22 6634 4444, *Fax:* +91 22 2265 2003, *Email:* agency@pmapl.com, *Website:* www.parekhgroup.in
Peirce Leslie Surveyor's & Assessors Ltd, 1st Floor, 4 Neelkanth Udyog Bhavan, Sakinaka Junction, Andheri (East), Mumbai, Maharashtra, India 400072, *Tel:* +91 22 2857 8935/6, *Fax:* +91 22 2857 8938, *Email:* plfsmum@satyam.net.in
Pen Shipping Agencies Private Ltd, 29 Bank Street, Fort, Mumbai, Maharashtra, India 400 001, *Tel:* +91 22 2266 3543, *Fax:* +91 22 2266 1512, *Email:* cis@jmbaxi.com, *Website:* www.jmbaxi.com
POL India Agencies Ltd, Bharat Insurance Building, 15a, Horniman Circle, Mumbai, Maharashtra, India 400001, *Tel:* +91 22 2266 1411/1413, *Fax:* +91 22 2266 4756, *Email:* pial97@vsnl.com, *Website:* www.polindia.com
Prudential Shipping Agencies Private Ltd, 55A/63A Walchand Hirachand Marg, Mumbai, Maharashtra, India 400001, *Tel:* +91 22 2269 2787, *Fax:* +91 22 2265 2841, *Email:* prudential@mastergroups.com, *Website:* www.mastergroups.com
Sai Shipping Co. Private Ltd, 2nd Floor, 201, 1112A Embassy Centre, Nariman Point, Mumbai, Maharashtra, India 400 021, *Tel:* +91 22 2285 2061, *Fax:* +91 22 2287 5178, *Email:* agency@saiship.com
Samrat Shipping & Transport Systems Private Ltd, 16 Jolly Maker Chamber, II Nariman Point, Mumbai, Maharashtra, India 400021, *Tel:* +91 22 2202 2326/2021, *Fax:* +91 22 2202 5798, *Email:* mail@samrat.com, *Website:* www.samrat.com
Samsara Shipping (Private) Ltd, 106/107 Technopolis Knowledge Park, Mahakali Caves Road, Chakala, Andheri (E), Mumbai, Maharashtra, India 400 093, *Tel:* +91 22 6677 5000, *Fax:* +91 22 6677 5050, *Email:* cntrmktg@samsaragroup.com, *Website:* www.samsarashipping.com
Sea Tech Services Ltd, Grants Building Annex, Colaba, 19A Arthur Bunder Road, Mumbai, Maharashtra, India 400005, *Tel:* +91 22 2285 0905/0868, *Fax:* +91 22 2285 0807
Seabridge Maritime Agencies Private Ltd, 109 Bajaj Bhavan, Nariman Point, Mumbai, Maharashtra, India 400021, *Tel:* +91 22 2285 5007, *Fax:* +91 22 2202 5982, *Email:* idmrg@giasmd01.vsnl.net.in
Seahorse Ship Agencies Private Ltd, 30/32 Adi Marzban Street, Ballard Est, Mumbai, Maharashtra, India 400001, *Tel:* +91 22 2269 1837, *Fax:* +91 22 2269 1272
Seaworld Shipping & Logistics Private Ltd, NCL Building, 8th Floor, Bandra Kurla Complex, Bandra East, Mumbai, Maharashtra, India 400051, *Tel:* +91 22 6698 8888, *Fax:* +91 22 6698 8820, *Email:* seaworldship@vsnl.com, *Website:* www.seaworldship.com
Star Freight Private Ltd, 103 Paras Apartment, Prathana Samaj Road, Vile Parle (East), Mumbai, Maharashtra, India 400 057, *Tel:* +91 22 2612 3268, *Fax:* +91 22 2612 4572, *Email:* starfreight@jsbindia.com, *Website:* www.jbscargoindia.com
Sun Logistics, Orient House, Ground Floor, Adi Marzban Path, Ballard Estate, Mumbai, Maharashtra, India 400038, *Tel:* +91 22 6633 3888, *Fax:* +91 22 2261 1144, *Email:* office@sunlogistics.co.in, *Website:* www.sunlogistics.co.in
Sunrich Shipmanagement Private Ltd, 124-B Mittal Court, 224 Nariman Point, Mumbai, Maharashtra, India 400021, *Tel:* +91 22 2285 4939, *Fax:* +91 22 2202 5718, *Email:* asl@bom3.vsnl.net.in, *Website:* www.sunrichgroup.com
Supreme Maritime Agencies Private Ltd, 2nd Floor, 65/68 Mahendra Chambers, 134/136 Dr DN Road, Mumbai, Maharashtra, India 400001, *Tel:* +91 22 2207 5689, *Fax:* +91 22 2207 7096
Tata NYK Transport Systems Ltd, NEVILLE HOUSE,, 1ST FLOOR, J.N.HEREDIA MARG BALLARD ESTATE, Mumbai, Maharashtra, India 400001, *Tel:* +91 22 6658 5353, *Fax:* +91 22 6658 5344, *Email:* tntsbom@vsnl.com, *Website:* www.nykline.com
Transindia Shipping & Logistics Pvt Ltd, NCL Building, 8th Floor Bandra Kurla Complex, Bandra East, Mumbai, Maharashtra, India 400051, *Tel:* +91 22 6698 8888, *Fax:* +91 22 6698 8820, *Email:* seaworldship@vsnl.com, *Website:* www.seaworldship.com
Transocean Shipping Agency Private Ltd, 7 Kumpta Street, Ballard Est, Mumbai, Maharashtra, India 400038, *Tel:* +91 22 2269 8340, *Fax:* +91 22 2262 0711
Transworld Shipping Services (I) Private Ltd, 11/14 Kalpaturu Court, C. Gidwani Road, 289 Shahid Bhagat Singh Road, Chembur, Mumbai, Maharashtra, India 400 074, *Tel:* +91 22 6797 8000, *Fax:* +91 22 2520 2036, *Email:* ramaswamy@twss.co.in, *Website:* www.transworldindia.com
Trident Shipping Agencies Private Ltd, Cumbatta Building, 5th Floor, J Tata Road, Mumbai, Maharashtra, India 400020, *Tel:* +91 22 2204 2369, *Fax:* +91 22 2204 3572
United Arab Shipping Agencies Company, 11/14 Kalpaturu Court, C Gidwani Road, Chembur, Mumbai, Maharashtra, India 40074, *Tel:* +91 22 5597 8000, *Fax:* +91 22 2520 2036, *Email:* ray@twss.co.in, *Website:* www.uasc.com.kw
United Liner Agencies of India Private Ltd, Dubash House, 15 JN Heredia Marg, Ballard Estate, Mumbai, Maharashtra, India, *Tel:* +91 22 2267 5101, *Fax:* +91 22 2269 2720, *Email:* kmganapathy@ulaindia.com
Venkatesh Karriers Ltd, United India Building, 2nd floor, Sir PM Road, Fort, Mumbai, Maharashtra, India 400 001, *Tel:* +91 22 6665 8300/01, *Fax:* +91 22 6665 8391, *Email:* operations@vklagency.com
Volkart Fleming Shipping & Services Ltd, Volkart Building, 4th Floor, 19 JN Heredia Marg, Ballard Estate, Mumbai, Maharashtra, India 400001, *Tel:* +91 22 2262 1831, *Fax:* +91 22 2262 1837
Wilhelmsen Ship Services, Barwil Forbes Shipping Services Ltd, 113 Mittal Court, 'A' Wing 11th Floor, Nariman Point, Mumbai, Maharashtra, India 400021, *Tel:* +91 22 2264 0140, *Fax:* +91 22 2287 3767, *Email:* barwil.mumbai@barwil.com, *Website:* www.barwil.com
Yang Ming Marine Transport Corp., World Trade Center, Center 1, 13th Floor, Cuffee Parade, Mumbai, Maharashtra, India, *Tel:* +91 22 6622 1111, *Fax:* +91 22 6622 1100, *Website:* www.yml.in

Stevedoring Companies: J.M. Baxi & Co, 16 Bank Street, Fort, P O Box 731, Mumbai, Maharashtra, India 400 001, *Tel:* +91 22 2266 3871, *Fax:* +91 22 2265 4638, *Email:* corp@jmbaxi.com, *Website:* www.jmbaxi.com
Chowgule Brothers Private Ltd, P O Box 1770, Malhotra House, 3rd Floor opposite GPO, Mumbai, Maharashtra, India 400 001, *Tel:* +91 22 2267 5579, *Fax:* +91 22 2261 0659, *Email:* mumbai.cb@chowgule.co.in
Flaminco Services Proprietary Ltd, Nanabhoy Building No.5, Sitladevi Temple Road, Mahim (W), Mumbai, Maharashtra, India 400 016, *Fax:* +91 22 2444 4613, *Email:* flamaar.fipl@gems.vsnl.net.in
Inmartech, Kamanwala Chambers No.5 B, 3rd Floor, P.M.Road, Mumbai, Maharashtra, India 400 001, *Tel:* +91 22 2266 0252, *Fax:* +91 22 2266 4097, *Email:* inmartec@vsnl.com
Sahi Oretrans (Private) Ltd, 30 Western India House, 3rd Floor, Sir P.M. Road, Mumbai, Maharashtra, India 400 001, *Tel:* +91 22 4033 5454, *Fax:* +91 22 4033 5432, *Email:* sot@vsnl.com, *Website:* www.sahioretrans.com
Sai Shipping Co. Private Ltd, 2nd Floor, 201, 1112A Embassy Centre, Nariman Point, Mumbai, Maharashtra, India 400 021, *Tel:* +91 22 2285 2061, *Fax:* +91 22 2287 5178, *Email:* agency@saiship.com
Vinsons, Emca House No.47, 4th Floor Shahid Bhagat Singh, Road No.289, Mumbai, Maharashtra, India 400 001, *Tel:* +91 22 2261 2903, *Fax:* +91 22 2261 6848, *Email:* vinsons@bom3.vsnl.net.in

Surveyors: ABS (Pacific), 3rd Floor, City Ice Building, 298 Perin Nariman Street, Mumbai, Maharashtra, India 400 001, *Tel:* +91 22 2266 0199, *Fax:* +91 22 2266 1510, *Email:* absmumbai@eagle.org, *Website:* www.eagle.org
Dr. Amin, Dr. Superintendents & Surveyors Private Ltd, 6th Floor, Aban House, 25 Ropewalk Lane, Mumbai, Maharashtra, India 400 023, *Tel:* +91 22 2285 5065/6, *Fax:* +91 22 2285 5489, *Email:* amin.bom@gems.vsnl.net.in
J. Basheer & Associates Surveyors Private Ltd, 12-A Khatau Building, Alkesh Dinesh Modi Marg, Fort, Mumbai, Maharashtra, India 400 001, *Tel:* +91 22 2263 0019, *Fax:* +91 22 2263 1090, *Email:* mail@jbplsurveyors.com, *Website:* www.jbplsurveyors.com
J.B. Boda Surveyors Private Ltd, Maker Bhavan No.1, Sir Vithaldas Thackersey Marg, Mumbai, Maharashtra, India 400 020, *Tel:* +91 22 2262 4517, *Fax:* +91 22 2262 3747, *Email:* jbbodamumbai@vsnl.com, *Website:* www.jbboda.net
Bureau Veritas, 6th Floor, Marwah Centre, Krishanlal Marwah Marg, Opp Ansa Industrial Estate, Off Saki Vihar Road, Andheri East, Mumbai, Maharashtra, India 400 072, *Tel:* +91 22 6695 6300, *Fax:* +91 22 6695 6310, *Email:* infobvindia@in.bureauveritas.com, *Website:* www.bureauveritas.com
Chowgule Brothers Private Ltd, P O Box 1770, Malhotra House, 3rd Floor opposite GPO, Mumbai, Maharashtra, India 400 001, *Tel:* +91 22 2267 5579, *Fax:* +91 22 2261 0659, *Email:* mumbai.cb@chowgule.co.in
P.L. D'Abreo, 101 Bella Villa, 54 St. Andrew Road, Bandra, Mumbai, Maharashtra, India 400050, *Tel:* +91 22 2643 0082, *Fax:* +91 22 2645 8343, *Email:* louise_d_souza@yahoo.com
Deep Sea Diving Private Ltd, 11, K Building, 24 Walchand Hirachand Marg, Ballard Estate, Mumbai, Maharashtra, India 400 001, *Tel:* +91 22 2261 5113, *Fax:* +91 22 2261 5169, *Email:* captnd@deepseadive.com, *Website:* www.deepseadive.com
Det Norske Veritas A/S, B 42/168 Sundar Nagar, Kalina Santacruz East, Mumbai, Maharashtra, India 400 098, *Tel:* +91 22 2666 9800, *Fax:* +91 22 2665 1412, *Email:* mumbai-sio@dnv.com, *Website:* www.dnv.com
Ericson & Richards, Kamani Chamber, 32 R. Kamani Marg, Ballard Estate, Fort, Mumbai, Maharashtra, India 400 001, *Tel:* +91 22 2269 3844, *Fax:* +91 22 2261 3596, *Email:* erichard@mtnl.net.in, *Website:* www.ericsonandrichards.com
Germanischer Lloyd, 412-A Embassy Centre, Nariman Point, Mumbai, Maharashtra, India 400 021, *Tel:* +91 22 2282 6808, *Fax:* +91 22 2282 6810, *Email:* gl-mumbai@gl-group.com, *Website:* www.gl-group.com
i-maritime Consultancy Private Limited, 206 Hermes Atrium, Plot No.57, Sector 11, Central Business District, Belapur, Mumbai, Maharashtra, India 400 614, *Tel:* +91 22 2757 7834, *Fax:* +91 22 2757 9612, *Email:* consult@imaritime.com, *Website:* www.imaritime.com
Indian Register of Shipping, 72 Maker Towers, 7th Floor, Cuffe Parade, Mumbai, Maharashtra, India 400 005, *Tel:* +91 22 2218 6376, *Fax:* +91 22 2218 1241, *Email:* mumbai@irclass.org, *Website:* www.irclass.org
Integral Marine Consultants Sdn Bhd, 14/15 Hansraj Damodar Trust Building, 12/14 Goa Street, Ballard Estate, Mumbai, Maharashtra, India 400 038, *Tel:* +91 22 2265 9891, *Fax:* +91 22 2266 5376
Intertek Caleb Brett, Unit No. D1 Udyog Sadan No.3, M.I.D.C. Central Road, Andheri East, Mumbai, Maharashtra, India 400 093, *Tel:* +91 22 2824 4767, *Fax:* +91 22 2824 4768, *Email:* operation.mumbai@intertek.com, *Website:* www.intertek.com
Korean Register of Shipping, Germanischer Lloyds, 412 A Embassy Centre, Nariman Point, Mumbai, Maharashtra, India 400 021, *Tel:* +91 22 2282 6808, *Fax:* +91 22 2230 1055, *Email:* gl-mumbai@gl-group.com, *Website:* www.gl-group.com
Meecon Private Ltd, 21st Floor, Nirmal Building, Nariman Point, Mumbai, Maharashtra, India 400 021, *Tel:* +91 22 2202 7381, *Fax:* +91 22 2202 5663, *Email:* meecon@hathway.com, *Website:* www.imcnet.org/home/meecon
Metcalfe & Hodgkinson Private Ltd, Mumbai, Maharashtra, India, *Tel:* +91 22 2261 2526, *Fax:* +91 22 2261 5053, *Email:* mumbai@metcalfeindia.com, *Website:* www.metcalfeindia.com
Narichanis Consultancy & Agency (Private) Ltd, 59 Lakhsmi Insurance Building, 22 Sir P.M. Road, Mumbai, Maharashtra, India 400 001, *Tel:* +91 22 2265 2685, *Fax:* +91 22 2266 3950, *Email:* admiralty@bom5.vsnl.net.in
Nilachal Shipping Private Ltd, 14-15 Hansraj Damodar Trust Building, 12-14 Goa Street, Ballard Estate, Mumbai, Maharashtra, India 400-038, *Tel:* +91 22 2265 9891, *Fax:* +91 22 2266 5376, *Email:* nilachal@bom3.vsnl.net.in
Nippon Kaiji Kyokai, 1402 Maker Chambers V, Nariman Point, Mumbai, Maharashtra, India 400 021, *Tel:* +91 22 2204 8524, *Fax:* +91 22 6632 4095, *Email:* by@classnk.or.jp, *Website:* www.classnk.or.jp
Registro Italiano Navale (RINA), 607/608 B Wing - Everest Chambers, Marol, Andheri-Kurla Road, Andheri (East), Mumbai, Maharashtra, India 400059, *Tel:* +91 22 2851 5862, *Fax:* +91 22 2852 5139, *Email:* bombay.office@rina.org, *Website:* www.rina.org
Sai Shipping Co. Private Ltd, 2nd Floor, 201, 1112A Embassy Centre, Nariman Point, Mumbai, Maharashtra, India 400 021, *Tel:* +91 22 2285 2061, *Fax:* +91 22 2287 5178, *Email:* agency@saiship.com
Saigal Seatrade Private Ltd, B-2-02 Neelam Centre, Hind Cycle Road, Worli, Mumbai, Maharashtra, India 400 030, *Tel:* +91 22 2491 0505, *Fax:* +91 22 2491 0512, *Email:* seatrade@vsnl.com, *Website:* www.saigalseatrade.com
Societe Generale de Surveillance (SGS), SGS India Ltd, SGS House, Naoroji

Key to Principal Facilities:—
A=Airport **C**=Containers **G**=General Cargo **P**=Petroleum **R**=Ro/Ro **Y**=Dry Bulk
B=Bunkers **D**=Dry Dock **L**=Cruise **Q**=Other Liquid Bulk **T**=Towage (where available from port)

Purdoomji Road, Colaba, Mumbai, Maharashtra, India 400 001, *Tel:* +91 22 2202 5183, *Fax:* +91 22 2283 6623, *Website:* www.sgs.com

Tata Marine Agencies (Division of Tata Tea Limited), New Excelsior Building, 4th Floor, Amrit Keshav Nayak Marg., P O Box 73, Mumbai, Maharashtra, India 400 001, *Tel:* +91 22 2201 7760, *Fax:* +91 22 2201 7646, *Email:* llds@tatateamum.ms.gw.wiprobt.ems.vsnl.

Wilhelmsen Marine Consultants, 31/32 Apple Heritage, Plot 54-C, Sir Mathurdas Vasanji Road, Andheri (E), Mumbai, Maharashtra, India 400 093, *Tel:* +91 22 2687 3210, *Fax:* +91 22 2687 0977, *Email:* bmc.india@barbership.com, *Website:* www.barbership.com

Medical Facilities: A number of hospitals in the city

Airport: Sahar Airport, 32 km

Railway: The Port of Mumbai owns and operates it's own railway which is connected to the broad guage maine lines of the Central and Western Railway at it's interchange railway yard at Wadala. The railway runs about 10 km of straight route between Ballard Pier and Wadala and has an extensive network of track about 100 km. It serves the Docks as well as the important installations and factories on the Port Trust estates

Development: Gammon India will operate and manage the existing container terminal for an initial 5 years and also develop and manage the new offshore container terminal consisting of two berths which is scheduled to be operational by December 2010

Lloyd's Agent: Wilson Surveyors and Adjusters Private Ltd, C-204 Remi Bizcourt, Veera Desai Road, Andheri West, Mumbai, Maharashtra, India 400 053, *Tel:* +91 22 6696 3606, *Fax:* +91 22 6696 3669, *Email:* mumbai@wilsur.com, *Website:* www.wilsur.com

MUNDRA

Lat 22° 49' N; Long 69° 42' E.

Admiralty Chart: 43/670
Time Zone: GMT +5.5 h

Admiralty Pilot: 38
UNCTAD Locode: IN MUN

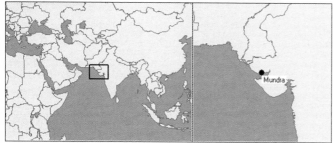

Principal Facilities:

P	Q	Y	G	C		B		T	A	

Authority: Mundra Port & SEZ Ltd., P O Box 1, Navinal Island, Mundra (Kutch), Gujarat, India 370 421, *Tel:* +91 2838 289248, *Fax:* +91 2838 289200, *Email:* mktg@mundraport.com, *Website:* www.mundraport.com

Officials: Chief Executive Officer: Capt Sandeep Mehta.
Managing Director: Gautam Adani.
Harbour Master: Capt Mohan Joshi, *Tel:* +91 2838 289201, *Email:* mohan.joshi@mundraport.com.

Port Security: ISPS compliant

Documentation: Certificate of registry (1 copy), safety equipment certificate (1 copy), safety radio telegraphy certificate (1 copy), safety construction certificate (1 copy), IOPP certificate (1 copy), safe manning certificate (1 copy), load line certificate (1 copy), tonnage certificates (2 copies), certificate of entry (1 copy), cargo gear certificates (1 copy), crew lists (4 copies), passenger lists (4 copies), stowaway lists (4 copies), crew effects lists (4 copies), bonded stores lists (4 copies), ship stores lists (4 copies), arms/ammunition lists (4 copies), bill of lading (1 copy), cargo manifest (1 copy freighted), cargo manifest (1 copy unfreighted), foreign currency declarations (4 copies), narcotics lists (4 copies), health declaration (1 copy), derat certificate (1 copy), clearance form last port (1 copy)

Approach: Berths 1 and 3 have an open approach from sea with depths not less than 15 m. Berths 2 and 4 are on the inshore side of the 'T' shaped jetty and have approach depths of 10-15 m

Anchorage: Available in pos 22° 41.00' N; 69° 43.45' E

Pilotage: Vessels should send their ETA 7 days, 5 days, 3 days, 48 h and 24 h prior to arrival. Pilot boards in pos 22° 42' 55" N; 69° 42' 50" E (port) and 22° 38' 85" N; 69° 39' 20" E (SPM)

Radio Frequency: VHF Channels 16 and 73

Weather: Generally dry weather. SW'ly winds April-September gusting up to 22 knots. NE'ly winds September-April

Tides: Semi-diurnal and run up to 3.5 knots at springs and 2 knots at neaps

Traffic: 2006/07, 19 700 000 t of cargo handled

Maximum Vessel Dimensions: 250 m loa, 18.5 m draft

Principal Imports and Exports: Imports: Coal, Fertilizers, Petro-chemicals, Scrap, Steel plates, Vegetable oils. Exports: Bauxite, Bentonite, Rice, Steel pipes, Wheat.

Working Hours: 24 h/day

Accommodation:

Name	Length (m)	Depth (m)	Draught (m)	Remarks
Mundra				Port-based special economic zone (SEZ)
Berth No.1	250	15		See [1] below

Name	Length (m)	Depth (m)	Draught (m)	Remarks
Berth No.2	180	12		See [2] below
Berth No.3	200	13.5		See [3] below
Berth No.4	180	12		See [4] below
Barge Berth				See [5] below
Mundra International Container Terminal	632		18.5	See [6] below
SPM		32		See [7] below

[1]*Berth No.1:* Dry & liquid bulk cargo for vessels up to 275 m loa
[2]*Berth No.2:* Liquid bulk cargo for vessels up to 183 m loa
[3]*Berth No.3:* Dry & liquid bulk cargo for vessels up to 225 m loa
[4]*Berth No.4:* Dry & liquid bulk cargo for vessels up to 225 m loa
[5]*Barge Berth:* For harbour craft mooring up to 73 m loa
[6]*Mundra International Container Terminal:* Mundra International Container Terminal, New Mundra Port, Navinal Island, Mundra 370 421, Tel: +91 2838 288269, Fax: +91 2838 288278, Email: krishnadas@mict.poports.co.in
Consists of two berths. 240 reefer points. 25 ha container yard
[7]*SPM:* Situated approx 9 km from the port in pos 22° 40.65' N; 69° 39.28' E for VLCC's up to 360 000 dwt. Max flow rate of 8000 m3/h

Storage: 81 liquid cargo storage tanks totalling 338 260 kl

Location	Open (m²)	Covered (m²)
Mundra	759801	137080

Mechanical Handling Equipment:

Location	Type	Capacity (t)	Qty
Mundra	Mobile Cranes		2
Mundra International Container Terminal	Post Panamax	40	2
Mundra International Container Terminal	Super Post Panamax	40	2
Mundra International Container Terminal	RTG's	40	12
Mundra International Container Terminal	Reach Stackers	40	4

Bunkering: Available by road tankers with advance notice

Waste Reception Facilities: Available on a chargeable basis with prior notice

Towage: Six tugs available of 15-56 t bollard pull

Repair & Maintenance: Small repair facility is available

Shipping Agents: GAC Shipping (India) Pvt Ltd, No.14, 1st Floor - Super Bazaar 1, 175/3, Adani Port Road, Mundra (Kutch), Gujarat, India 370 415, *Tel:* +91 2838 231427, *Fax:* +91 2838 231429, *Email:* mundra@gacworld.com, *Website:* www.gacworld.com
Samsara Shipping (Private) Ltd, 1st Floor, Users Building, MICT CFS, Adani Port, Mundra (Kutch), Gujarat, India 370 421, *Tel:* +91 2838 570309, *Fax:* +91 2838 226922, *Email:* opnsmum@samsarashipping.com, *Website:* www.samsarashipping.com

Stevedoring Companies: Chowgule Brothers Private Ltd, Chowgule House, 403 Mormugao Harbour, Mormugao, Goa, India 403 803, *Tel:* +91 832 252 5144, *Fax:* +91 832 252 1011, *Email:* info.cb@chowgule.co.in, *Website:* www.chowgulebros.com

Medical Facilities: Port has health centre on premises with primary medical facilities. Hospital situated in Mundra Town, 18 km

Airport: Bhuj Airport, approx 73 km

Railway: Bhuj, approx 70 km. Gandhidham, 65 km

Development: A bulk terminal 451.5 m long in depth of 18.5 m will be built seaward side of the Container Terminal
NYK Line and Wallenius Wilhelmsen Lines have signed a deal to set up a dedicated auto terminal

Lloyd's Agent: Wilson Surveyors and Adjusters Private Ltd, Golden Arcade, II Floor, Room No.209, Plot No.141/142, Sector 8, Gandhidam, Kutch, Gujarat, India 370 201, *Tel:* +91 2836 238333, *Fax:* +91 2836 238333, *Email:* kandla@wilsur.com, *Website:* www.wilsur.com

NAGAPATTINAM

Lat 10° 46' N; Long 79° 51' E.

Admiralty Chart: 575
Time Zone: GMT +5.5 h

Admiralty Pilot: 21
UNCTAD Locode: IN NPT

Principal Facilities:

			G						

Authority: Nagapattinam Port, Port Office, P O Box 6, Nagapattinam, Tamil Nadu, India 611 001, *Tel:* +91 4365 242255, *Fax:* +91 4365 242363, *Email:* roseanbarasan@yahoo.co.in

Officials: Port Officer: Capt Mariaraj Anbarasan.

Pilotage: Vessels should send ETA at least 48 h in advance to local agent. Pilot boards in pos 10° 48.8' N; 79° 53.4' E

Radio Frequency: Port Radio Station on VHF Channels 16 and 14. Available 0600-1000 and 1500-1900 (except Saturdays, Sundays and other Govt holidays)

Weather: Monsoon season Oct 16 to Dec 31

Principal Imports and Exports: Imports: Fertilizer, Food grains. Exports: Chillies, General cargo, Onions, Textiles.

Working Hours: 0600-1800

Accommodation:

Name	Remarks
Nagapattinam	See [1] below

[1]*Nagapattinam:* Open roadstead. Vessels anchor according to draft and prevailing weather conditions. In fine weather, good anchorage in depths of 7-14 m with lighthouse bearing 281° to 255°. Port only capable of handling launches and lighters at wharf of 645 m length

Storage: Eleven cargo sheds of approx 17 500 t cap. No refrigerated space

Mechanical Handling Equipment:

Location	Type	Capacity (t)	Qty
Nagapattinam	Mobile Cranes	4	1

Cargo Worked: 750-1000 t/day depending on type of cargo

Towage: One motor launch of 66 hp belonging to the Port Dept for lighterage purposes

Medical Facilities: Available

Railway: Nagapattinam, 1 km

Lloyd's Agent: Wilson Surveyors and Adjusters Private Ltd, TMB Mansion, 3rd Floor, 739 Anna Salai, Chennai, Tamil Nadu, India 600 002, *Tel:* +91 44 2852 2811, *Fax:* +91 44 2852 3349, *Email:* chennai@wilsur.com, *Website:* www.wilsur.com

NAVLAKHI

Lat 22° 58' N; Long 70° 27' E.

Admiralty Chart: 670/682/699	**Admiralty Pilot:** 38
Time Zone: GMT +5.5 h	**UNCTAD Locode:** IN NAV

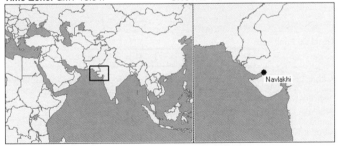

Principal Facilities:

		Y	G				T		

Authority: Gujarat Maritime Board, Port of Navlakhi, Navlakhi, Gujarat, India 363 680, *Tel:* +91 2829 220435, *Fax:* +91 2829 232470, *Website:* www.gmbports.org

Port Security: ISPS compliant

Approach: Vessels pass Tuna Buoy, which is located about 24 km from the shore and is traditionally the boarding point for pilot

Pilotage: Not compulsory but an experienced pilot can be made available by Port Authority. Pilot normally boards in outer anchorage in pos 22° 44' N; 70° 05' E. No nightime pilotage

Radio Frequency: Radio messages should be via Kandla or Mumbai Radio Station. VHF Channel 16 for ship to shore communication is provided

Tides: Range of tide ST 0.37 m to 7.21 m, NT 2.14 m to 6.16 m

Principal Imports and Exports: Imports: Fertilizer, Fluorspar. Exports: Rice, Salt, Soyabean meal.

Working Hours: 0800-1200, 1300-1700. Overtime can be worked by arrangement

Accommodation:

Name	Length (m)	Remarks
Navlakhi		See [1] below
Versamedi	244	For lighters
Sui	305	For lighters

[1]*Navlakhi:* Open roadstead. The all weather anchorage is 32 km from Tuna Buoy and is marked by light buoys. Anchorage is approx 2.4 km from the cargo area, allowing two vessels to be worked, depth 8.9 m. Vessels do not work during monsoon. Cargo is handled in two creeks, Versamedi and Sui

Storage: There are 15 godowns with 17 960 m2 of covered area and cap of 21 000 t, open space is available. Transit shed of 6500 m2. No refrigerated space

Mechanical Handling Equipment:

Location	Type	Capacity (t)	Qty
Navlakhi	Mult-purp. Cranes	3	2

Location	Type	Capacity (t)	Qty
Navlakhi	Mult-purp. Cranes	5	2
Navlakhi	Mobile Cranes	12	3

Towage: Four tugs of 191-382 hp available for lighterage purposes

Repair & Maintenance: Port workshop for minor repairs only

Shipping Agents: J.M. Baxi & Co, Port Guest House, Navlakhi, Gujarat, India 363 680, *Tel:* +91 2829 289283, *Fax:* +91 2829 241708, *Email:* navalakhi@jmbaxi.com, *Website:* www.jmbaxi.com

Stevedoring Companies: Chowgule Brothers Private Ltd, Chowgule House, 403 Mormugao Harbour, Mormugao, Goa, India 403 803, *Tel:* +91 832 252 5144, *Fax:* +91 832 252 1011, *Email:* info.cb@chowgule.co.in, *Website:* www.chowgulebros.com

Medical Facilities: Small dispensary at the port. Hospital at Morvi, 45 km

Lloyd's Agent: Wilson Surveyors and Adjusters Private Ltd, Golden Arcade, II Floor, Room No.209, Plot No.141/142, Sector 8, Gandhidam, Kutch, Gujarat, India 370 201, *Tel:* +91 2836 238333, *Fax:* +91 2836 238333, *Email:* kandla@wilsur.com, *Website:* www.wilsur.com

NEW MANGALORE

Lat 12° 55' N; Long 74° 48' E.

Admiralty Chart: 3461	**Admiralty Pilot:** 38
Time Zone: GMT +5.5 h	**UNCTAD Locode:** IN NML

Principal Facilities:

P	Q	Y	G	C	R		B		T	A

Authority: New Mangalore Port Trust, Panambur, Mangalore, Karnataka, India 575 010, *Tel:* +91 824 240 7341, *Fax:* +91 824 240 8390, *Email:* nmptchairman@sify.com, *Website:* www.newmangalore-port.com

Officials: Chairman: Ponnusamy Tamilvanan, *Tel:* +91 824 240 7300.
Deputy Chairman: Muduvathi Bhaskarachar, *Tel:* +91 824 240 7315, *Email:* dychairman@sancharnet.in.
Traffic Manager: Sunkari Gopalakrishna, *Tel:* +91 824 240 7440, *Email:* gopaltrafficmanager@yahoo.com.
Harbour Master: Capt Radhey Raman Tripathi, *Tel:* +91 824 240 7419.

Port Security: ISPS compliant

Documentation: IMO declaration (2 copies), general declaration (2 copies), IMO crew list (2 copies), IMO passenger list (2 copies), maritime declaration of health (2 copies), ship movement details, ship officers details
Certificates to be produced: ship registry, safety radio certificate, safety equipment certificate, international load line, international oil pollution certificate
Also following information to be given: P&I club address and validity, class certificate validity, safety manning certificate validity, cargo gear annual survey date

Approach: Channel length of 7500 m, width 245 m with depth in outer channel of 15.4 m and in inner channel of 15.1 m with max permissible draft of 14 m. Turning basin of 570 m diameter

Anchorage: Anchorage can be obtained in pos 12° 54' 78" N; 74° 44' 46" E in depth of 18-20 m

Pilotage: Compulsory and available 24 h. Pilot station is located 0.5 mile off fairway buoy in pos 12° 54' 55" N; 74° 45' 24" E

Radio Frequency: Mangalore Radio, call sign VWL, 500 kcs

Weather: SW monsoon from June to September

Tides: HHWS 1.68 m CD, MHHW 1.48 m CD, MLHW 1.26 m CD, MSL 0.95 m CD, MLLW 0.26 m CD, LLWS 0.03 m CD

Traffic: 2007/08, 36 019 000 t of cargo handled

Maximum Vessel Dimensions: 245 m loa, 90 000 dwt, 14 m draft

Principal Imports and Exports: Imports: Finished fertilizers, Green Peas, Liquid ammonia, Phosphoric acid, POL products, Scrap, Sulphur, Timber logs, Wheat, Woodpulp, Yellow Peas. Exports: Granite, Molasses, Plywood, POL products, Stones.

Working Hours: Three shifts 0600-1400, 1400-2200, 2200-0600

Accommodation:

Name	Length (m)	Draught (m)	Remarks
New Mangalore			
Berth No.1	125	7	General cargo for vessels up to 4000 dwt
Berth No.2	198	10.5	General cargo for vessels up to 30 000 dwt
Berth No.3	198	10.5	General cargo for vessels up to 30 000 dwt
Berth No.4	198	9.5	See [1] below
Berth No.5	198	9.5	General cargo & bulk cement for vessels up to 30 000 dwt

Name	Length (m)	Draught (m)	Remarks
Berth No.6	198	9.5	General cargo for vessels up to 30 000 dwt
Berth No.7	198	9.5	General cargo for vessels up to 30 000 dwt
Berth No.8	300	13	Iron ore for vessels up to 60 000 dwt
Berth No.9	330	10.5	POL/LPG for vessels up to 45 000 dwt
Berth No.10	320	14	Crude oil/POL for vessels up to 85 000 dwt
Berth No.11	320	14	POL products for vessels up to 85 000 dwt
Berth No.12	320	12.5	Liquid cargo tankers up to 50 000 dwt
Virtual Jetty		9.13	POL for vessels up to 35 000 dwt
Berth No.14	350	14	General cargo for vessels up to 90 000 dwt

[1]*Berth No.4:* General cargo & liquid ammonia for vessels up to 30 000 dwt

Storage: Three transit sheds of 5574 m2, 4380 m2 and 4920 m2
Two overflow sheds of 4380 m2 each
Two warehouses owned by Port Trust of 2190 m2 each, four warehouses owned by CWC of 2190 m2 each, three private warehouses of 2190 m2 each and one workshop godown of 2400 m2
Open storage of approx 38 000 m2

Mechanical Handling Equipment:

Location	Type	Capacity (t)	Qty
New Mangalore	Mobile Cranes	10–75	3
New Mangalore	Electric Cranes	10	3
New Mangalore	Forklifts	3–10	7

Bunkering: Asean International Ltd, P O Box 7860, Block Z Suite 42/43, Saif Zone, Sharjah, United Arab Emirates, *Tel:* +971 6 557 0083, *Fax:* +971 6 557 0085 – *Delivery Mode:* pipeline, road tanker
Bharat Petroleum Corp. Ltd, 4th Floor, Old Admin Building, Mahul, Chembur, Mumbai, Maharashtra, India 400 074, *Tel:* +91 22 2554 3493, *Fax:* +91 22 2554 0621, *Email:* josecm@bharatpetroleum.in, *Website:* www.baratpetroleum.in – *Delivery Mode:* pipeline, road tanker
Bominflot, Bominoil Private Ltd, 504 Maker Chambers V, 221 Nariman Point, Mumbai, Maharashtra, India 400 021, *Tel:* +91 22 2281 7133, *Fax:* +91 22 2281 7145, *Email:* bominoil@vsnl.com, *Website:* www.bominflot.net – *Delivery Mode:* pipeline, road tanker
Cockett Marine Oil Ltd, Carrick House, 36 Station Square, Petts Wood, Kent BR5 1NA, United Kingdom, *Tel:* +44 1689 883 400, *Fax:* +44 1689 877 666, *Email:* enquiries@cockett.com, *Website:* www.cockettgroup.com – *Grades:* FO; IFO; MDO; MGO – *Parcel Size:* min IFO 50t, min MDO/MGO 10t; – *Delivery Mode:* barge
M/S Global Fuels & Lubricants Inc., 11-12 Mangal Society, 76C Rafi Ahmed Kidwai Road, King Circle, Mumbai, Maharashtra, India 400 019, *Tel:* +91 22 2374 5987, *Fax:* +91 22 2409 1627, *Email:* globalfuels@vsnl.com, *Website:* www.bunkerindia.com – *Delivery Mode:* pipeline, road tanker
Indian Oil Corp. Ltd, Indian Oil Bhavan Head Office, G9 Ali Yavar Jung Marg, Bandra (East), Mumbai, Maharashtra, India 400051, *Tel:* +91 22 2644 7368, *Fax:* +91 22 2642 2434, *Email:* partha_datta@indianoil.co.in, *Website:* www.indianoil.co.in – *Delivery Mode:* pipeline, road tanker
Olympic Marine Co., P O Box 5009, Fujairah, United Arab Emirates, *Tel:* +971 9 224726, *Fax:* +971 9 226491, *Email:* olympic@olympgroup.com – *Delivery Mode:* pipeline, road tanker

Waste Reception Facilities: 500 m3 cap tank available to collect dirty ballast

Towage: Five tugs available of 22.5-45 t bollard pull

Repair & Maintenance: Ramakrishna Shiprepairing Private Ltd, 4th Mile, Kulur, Mangalore, Karnataka, India 575 013, *Tel:* +91 824 245 9131, *Fax:* +91 824 245 4510, *Email:* rkspl@dataone.in, *Website:* www.rkshiprepair.com
Viva Engineering, Mangalore, Karnataka, India, *Tel:* +91 824 240 8512

Ship Chandlers: Admiral Marine Services Private Ltd, 20/18/1115 Rossario Church Cross Road, Mangalore, Karnataka, India 575 001, *Tel:* +91 824 241 0499, *Fax:* +91 824 241 0499, *Email:* enquiries@admiralmarine.com, *Website:* www.admiralmarine.com
Ocean Marine Supplies, First Floor, Plaza Complex (Regency), Bendoorwell Circle, Mangalore, Karnataka, India 575 002, *Tel:* +91 824 525 4444, *Fax:* +91 824 525 2222, *Email:* contact@oceanmarinesupplies.com, *Website:* www.oceanmarinesupplies.com

Shipping Agents: Aspinwall & Co. Ltd, P O Box 901, Kulshekhar, Mangalore, Karnataka, India 575 005, *Tel:* +91 824 221 1415, *Fax:* +91 824 221 1498, *Email:* mlr.mng@aspinwallgroup.com, *Website:* www.aspinwallgroup.com
J.M. Baxi & Co, Sadhoo Complex - 1st Floor - NH 17, Bangra Kulur, Mangalore, Karnataka, India 575 013, *Tel:* +91 824 245 8015, *Fax:* +91 824 245 8379, *Email:* mngr@jmbaxi.com, *Website:* www.jmbaxi.com
Chowgule Brothers Private Ltd, Door No.1/17/1198/19, N.J.Arcade 2nd Floor, Ladyhill, Kuloor Ferry Road, Mangalore, Karnataka, India 575 006, *Tel:* +91 824 428 1628, *Fax:* +91 824 245 5479, *Email:* mangalore.cb@chowgule.co.in
CMA-CGM S.A., CMA CGM Global (India) Pvt Ltd, Commerce Centre, 2nd Floor, Kulur-Kavoor Road, Kulur, Mangalore, Karnataka, India 575 013, *Tel:* +91 824 245 2722, *Fax:* +91 824 245 2711, *Email:* mgr.genmbox@cma-cgm.com, *Website:* www.cma-cgm.com
GAC Shipping (India) Pvt Ltd, ABCO Trade Centre (4th floor), Kottara Chowki, Mangalore, Karnataka, India 575 006, *Tel:* +91 824 245 0425, *Fax:* +91 824 245 0427, *Email:* mangalore@gacworld.com, *Website:* www.gacworld.com
Interocean Shipping (India) Pvt Ltd., 203 Veekay Towers, Kulur Ferry Road, Kulur, Mangalore, Karnataka, India, *Tel:* +91 824 245 2131, *Fax:* +91 824 245 2141, *Email:* mangalore@interoceangroup.com, *Website:* www.interoceangroup.com
Samsara Shipping (Private) Ltd, Commerce Centre, Kulur Kavour Road, Mangalore, Karnataka, India 575 013, *Tel:* +91 824 245 1065, *Fax:* +91 824 245 1067, *Email:* samsmlr@samsarashipping.com, *Website:* www.samsarashipping.com

Stevedoring Companies: Aspinwall & Co., P O Box 901, Kulshekhar, Mangalore, Karnataka, India 575 005, *Tel:* +91 824 221 1415, *Fax:* +91 824 221 1498, *Email:* mlr.mng@aspinwallgroup.com
Chowgule Brothers Private Ltd, Door No.1/17/1198/19, N.J.Arcade 2nd Floor, Ladyhill, Kuloor Ferry Road, Mangalore, Karnataka, India 575 006, *Tel:* +91 824 428 1628, *Fax:* +91 824 245 5479, *Email:* mangalore.cb@chowgule.co.in
Evergreen Suppliers, 5th Floor, Ramabhavan Complex, Kodialbail, Mangalore, Karnataka, India 575 003, *Tel:* +91 824 244 0450, *Fax:* +91 824 244 1243, *Email:* evergreensuppliers@airtelbroadband.in
Hassain Haji & Co., Katadeeja Court, Near Old Municipal office, Bandur, Mangalore, Karnataka, India 575 001, *Tel:* +91 824 242 0737, *Fax:* +91 824 242 0456, *Email:* hasanaji@airtel.broadband.in, *Website:* www.hassanhaji.com

Surveyors: J.B. Boda Surveyors Private Ltd, 101 Veekay Towers, 1st Floor, Kulur Ferry Road, Kulur, Mangalore, Karnataka, India 575 013, *Tel:* +91 824 245 8913, *Fax:* +91 824 245 8922, *Email:* jbbmng@jbbodamail.com, *Website:* www.jbboda.net
Chowgule Brothers Private Ltd, Door No.1/17/1198/19, N.J.Arcade 2nd Floor, Ladyhill, Kuloor Ferry Road, Mangalore, Karnataka, India 575 006, *Tel:* +91 824 428 1628, *Fax:* +91 824 245 5479, *Email:* mangalore.cb@chowgule.co.in

Medical Facilities: New Mangalore Port Trust Hospital, 2 km

Airport: Bajpe, 18 km

Railway: The port is served by a broad guage railway line and is well connected with Mangalore, Kerala State and Chennai

Lloyd's Agent: Peirce Leslie India Ltd, Peirce Leslie Surveyours and Assessors Ltd., Bristow Road, Willingdon Island, Kochi, Kerala, India 682 003, *Tel:* +91 484 266 8362, *Fax:* +91 484 266 8394, *Email:* plsacok@sify.com, *Website:* www.plsurvey.in

NEW TUTICORIN

Lat 8° 45' N; Long 78° 13' E.

Admiralty Chart: 3581	**Admiralty Pilot:** 38
Time Zone: GMT +5.5 h	**UNCTAD Locode:** IN TUT

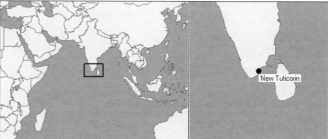

Principal Facilities:

P		Y	G	C		L	B		T	A

Authority: Tuticorin Port Trust, Bharathi Nagar, Tuticorin, Tamil Nadu, India 628 004, *Tel:* +91 461 235 2313, *Fax:* +91 461 235 2385, *Email:* info@tuticorinport.gov.in, *Website:* www.tuticorinport.gov.in

Officials: Chairman: G. J. Rao, *Email:* chairman@tuticorinport.gov.in.
Deputy Conservator: Capt John Mani, *Email:* capt_john_mani@yahoo.co.in.
Harbour Master: Capt Vasu Venkatramaniya.

Port Security: ISPS compliant

Documentation: Original vessel documents, last port clearance, bonded stores list, currency declaration, general stores list, crew list

Approach: Approach channel 2.4 km long and 183 m wide with permissable draft of 10.7 m and depth of 12.5 m

Pilotage: Compulsory at Zone A and available 24 h for dry bulk, breakbulk and container vessels but for tankers, only available during daytime. Not compulsory at Zone B anchorage

Radio Frequency: VHF Channnels 16 and 12

Tides: Tidal range of 1.0 m

Traffic: 2007/08, 21 480 000 t of cargo handled, 450 000 TEU's

Maximum Vessel Dimensions: 229 m loa, 10.7 m draft

Principal Imports and Exports: Imports: Coal, Fertilizer, Granite, Raw cashew, Timber logs. Exports: Cement, Construction materials, General cargo, Granite, Salt, Sugar.

Working Hours: 0600-1400, 1400-2200, 2200-0600 (three shifts)

Accommodation:

Name	Remarks
New Tuticorin	See [1] below

[1]*New Tuticorin:* An artificial harbour with rubble-mound breakwaters 4103 m and 3888 m in length providing a sheltered basin of 388 ha. Width at entrance 152 m. Main wharf of 877 m with four berths, two of which are 192 m long and two 168 m long. Two additional berths, each 168 m long with draft of 8.24-10.7 m. Also there are two shallow berths with draft of 5.85 m for small vessels
Tuticorin Container Terminal (TCT), operated by PSA-Sical Terminals Ltd., Tuticorin Container Terminal Building, Berth No.7, Harbour Estate, Tuticorin 628 004, Tel: +91 461 235 4001, Fax: +91 461 235 2260, Email: ttn_psasical@sancharnet.in: 370 m long with draft of 10.7 m and equipped with two 40 t post-panamax cranes and four RTG's. 900 ground slots and 84 reefer points
Cruise facilities: Vessels up to 100 m loa with a draft of 4.8 m are accommodated at the Finger Jetty. Other tourist vessels are accommodated in the other conventional berths
Bulk facilities: Two coal jetties of 225 m loa and 10.7 m draft available. Discharge of coal is carried out by vessel's own gear to the shore reception system consisting of

hoppers and conveyors. Part discharge of coal by vessels over 10.7 m draft is also carried out by lighterage operation by self-propelled barges at anchorage

Tanker facilities: There is a mooring berth at the N breakwater for oil products, 228 m long with draft of 10.7 m

Storage: Two transit sheds each of 5400 m2, three warehouses totalling 15 550 m2 and a fumigation chamber of 739 m2. Open storage available within the port limits for stacking different types of cargo

Location	Open (m²)
New Tuticorin	72000

Mechanical Handling Equipment:

Location	Type	Capacity (t)	Qty
New Tuticorin	Mult-purp. Cranes	3–10	10
New Tuticorin	Mobile Cranes	75	
New Tuticorin	Post Panamax	40	3
New Tuticorin	RTG's		4

Cargo Worked: Approx 2725 t/day

Bunkering: Cashwell Agencies, 58 V.O.C. Market, Tuticorin, Tamil Nadu, India 628 001, *Tel:* +91 461 2338 863, *Fax:* +91 461 2326 311, *Email:* cashwell@md4.vsnl.net.in, *Website:* www.cashwellagencies.com
Cockett Marine Oil Ltd, Carrick House, 36 Station Square, Petts Wood, Kent BR5 1NA, United Kingdom, *Tel:* +44 1689 883 400, *Fax:* +44 1689 877 666, *Email:* enquiries@cockett.com, *Website:* www.cockettgroup.com – *Grades:* IFO; MDO; MGO – *Parcel Size:* min IFO 50t, min MDO/MGO 10t – *Delivery Mode:* barge, road tank wagon, pipeline

Waste Reception Facilities: Through private companies and arranged by ship's agents

Towage: Four 30 t bollard pull and three 10 t bollard pull tugs

Ship Chandlers: Admiral Marine Services Private Ltd, 21C/1A WGC Road, Tuticorin, Tamil Nadu, India 628 001, *Tel:* +91 461 232 6083, *Fax:* +91 461 232 6083, *Email:* enquiries@admiralmarine.com, *Website:* www.admiralmarine.com

Shipping Agents: Macsons Shipping Agencies Pvt Ltd., Ceeyem Building, 18D South Raja Street, Tuticorin, Tamil Nadu, India 628 001, *Tel:* +91 461 230 1444, *Fax:* +91 461 233 9777, *Email:* info@macsonshipping.com, *Website:* www.macsonshipping.com Director: Roshan A. Miranda
Albatross Shipping Pvt. Ltd, Plot no 19-B, 1st Floor, World Trade Avenue, Transfield House, Tuticorin, Tamil Nadu, India 628004, *Tel:* +91 461 235 3102, *Fax:* +91 461 235 2452, *Email:* kantha@alba.co.in
Aspinwall & Co. Ltd, 11A World Trade Avenue, Harbour Estate, Tuticorin, Tamil Nadu, India 682 004, *Tel:* +91 461 235 3744, *Fax:* +91 461 235 3635, *Email:* tut.mng@aspinwallgroup.com, *Website:* www.aspinwallgroup.com
J.M. Baxi & Co, 54 Beach Road, Tuticorin, Tamil Nadu, India 628 001, *Tel:* +91 461 232 1937, *Fax:* +91 461 232 0830, *Email:* tuti@jmbaxi.com, *Website:* www.jmbaxi.com
CMA-CGM S.A., CMA CGM (East & South) India Pvt Ltd, Transworld House, Plot No 19-B, World Trade Avenue, Tuticorin, Tamil Nadu, India 628 004, *Tel:* +91 461 400 3000, *Fax:* +91 461 400 3009, *Email:* tti.genmbox@cma-cgm.com, *Website:* www.cma-cgm.com
CSAV Group Agencies (India) Pvt Ltd, A/142nd Floor TSAA Building, World Trade Avenue, Harbour Est., Tuticorin, Tamil Nadu, India, *Tel:* +91 461 235 3540/1, *Fax:* +91 461 235 3675, *Email:* bkravi@csavagencies-india.com
GAC Shipping (India) Pvt Ltd, 4/143, C.G.E. Colony, Tiruchendur Road, Levinjipuram, Tuticorin, Tamil Nadu, India 628 003, *Tel:* +91 461 237 5361, *Fax:* +91 461 237 7462, *Email:* tuticorin@gacworld.com, *Website:* www.gacworld.com
Interocean Shipping (India) Pvt Ltd., 6L Sivanthakulam, 1st Street, Tuticorin, Tamil Nadu, India 628 008, *Tel:* +91 461 237 5695, *Fax:* +91 461 237 5685, *Email:* tuticorin@interoceangroup.com, *Website:* www.interoceangroup.com
A.P. Moller-Maersk Group, Maersk India Pvt. Ltd, No.185 & 186 Palayamkottai Road (West), Tuticorin, Tamil Nadu, India 628 004, *Tel:* +91 461 231 1999, *Fax:* +91 461 231 1082, *Email:* tutordcus@maersk.com, *Website:* www.maerskline.com
Samsara Shipping (Private) Ltd, TSA Building, 1st Floor, 5-A, World Trade Avenue, Harbour Estate, Tuticorin, Tamil Nadu, India 628 004, *Tel:* +91 461 235 4154, *Fax:* +91 461 235 4163, *Email:* samstut@samsarashipping.com, *Website:* www.samsarashipping.com

Stevedoring Companies: Aspinwall & Co. Ltd, 11A World Trade Avenue, Harbour Estate, Tuticorin, Tamil Nadu, India 682 004, *Tel:* +91 461 235 3744, *Fax:* +91 461 235 3635, *Email:* tut.mng@aspinwallgroup.com, *Website:* www.aspinwallgroup.com
J.M. Baxi & Co, 54 Beach Road, Tuticorin, Tamil Nadu, India 628 001, *Tel:* +91 461 232 1937, *Fax:* +91 461 232 0830, *Email:* tuti@jmbaxi.com, *Website:* www.jmbaxi.com
Pearl Shipping Agencies, 4-58A CGE Colony, 5th Street, Tuticorin, Tamil Nadu, India 628 008, *Tel:* +91 461 237 8001, *Fax:* +91 461 237 8008, *Email:* pearl@md2.vsnl.net.in, *Website:* www.pearlship.com

Surveyors: J.B. Boda Surveyors Private Ltd, 52 Beach Road, Tuticorin, Tamil Nadu, India 628 001, *Tel:* +91 461 232 1928, *Fax:* +91 461 232 2580, *Email:* jbbttn@jbbodamail.com, *Website:* www.jbboda.net
Nippon Kaiji Kyokai, 16 Emperor Street, Tuticorin, Tamil Nadu, India 628 001, *Tel:* +91 461 232 3995, *Fax:* +91 461 232 3995, *Email:* sureshtmathew@gmail.com, *Website:* www.classnk.or.jp

Medical Facilities: Port Hospital, 4 km

Airport: Tuticorin, 25 km

Railway: Southern Railway, approx 10 km

Lloyd's Agent: Peirce Leslie India Ltd, Peirce Leslie Surveyours and Assessors Ltd., Bristow Road, Willingdon Island, Kochi, Kerala, India 682 003, *Tel:* +91 484 266 8362, *Fax:* +91 484 266 8394, *Email:* plsacok@sify.com, *Website:* www.plsurvey.in

NHAVA SHEVA

harbour area, see under Jawaharlal Nehru

OKHA

alternate name, see Port Okha

PANAJI

Lat 15° 29' N; Long 73° 49' E.

Admiralty Chart: 492	**Admiralty Pilot:** 38
Time Zone: GMT +5.5 h	**UNCTAD Locode:** IN PAN

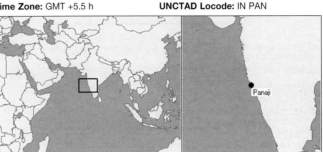

Principal Facilities:

		G					T	A

Authority: Captain of Ports Department, Panaji, Goa, India 403 001, *Tel:* +91 832 225070

Port Security: ISPS compliant

Documentation: Stores list (5 copies), crew personal effects list (5 copies), last port clearance, crew list (8 copies), certificate of registry, load line certificate, safety radio certificate, safety equipment certificate

Approach: Sand bars, depth 3.4 m

Anchorage: Anchorage is located in pos 15° 28.57' N; 73° 46.91' E

Radio Frequency: Harbour control on VHF Channel 16 and coastguard on VHF Channels 8 & 16

Weather: The afternoon wind blows predominantly from the sector between south west and north west through out the year. The main wind speed varies from 5 to 10 knots with maximum occuring during the monsoon period from Jun to Sep

Tides: Tidal range of 2.3 m MHWS, 2.06 m MHWN, 0.37 m MLWN, 0.00 m MLWS

Maximum Vessel Dimensions: 70-80 m loa, 3.2 m draft

Principal Imports and Exports: Imports: Coal, Iron ore, Kerosene, Lime, Pig iron. Exports: Cotton, Salt, Seeds.

Working Hours: 0930-1745

Accommodation:

Name	Length (m)	Depth (m)
Panaji		
Steamer Jetty	92	4.3

Towage: One tug of 470 hp and 4 t bp to be requested via the port captain

Shipping Agents: Machado & Sons Agents & Stevedores Private Ltd, Q-9/10 Tilak Commercial Complex, 2nd Floor, F.L. Gomes Road, P O Box 719, Vasco-da-Gama, Goa, India 403 802, *Tel:* +91 832 251 2444, *Fax:* +91 832 250 1659, *Email:* machado@sancharnet.in

Medical Facilities: There is a local hospital

Airport: Dabolim Airport, 27 km

Lloyd's Agent: Wilson Surveyors and Adjusters Private Ltd, C-204 Remi Bizcourt, Veera Desai Road, Andheri West, Mumbai, Maharashtra, India 400 053, *Tel:* +91 22 6696 3606, *Fax:* +91 22 6696 3669, *Email:* mumbai@wilsur.com, *Website:* www.wilsur.com

PANJIM

alternate name, see Panaji

PARADIP

Lat 20° 16' N; Long 86° 41' E.

Admiralty Chart: 538	**Admiralty Pilot:** 21
Time Zone: GMT +5.5 h	**UNCTAD Locode:** IN PRT

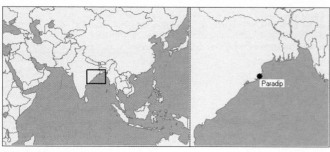

Principal Facilities:

P		Y	G	C			B	D	T	

Authority: Paradip Port Trust, District Jagatsinghpur, Paradip, Orissa, India 754 142, *Tel:* +91 6722 222046, *Fax:* +91 6722 222256, *Email:* ppt@ori.nic.in, *Website:* www.paradipport.gov.in

Officials: Chairman: Kaveti Raghuramaiah, *Email:* chmppt@paradipport.gov.in.
Deputy Conservator: Capt Gouri Prasad Biswal, *Tel:* +91 6722 222025, *Email:* deputyconservator_ppt@email.com.
Traffic Manager: Saroj Misra.
Harbour Master: Atul Kumar Mohapatra, *Tel:* +91 6722 222012, *Email:* harbourmaster_ppt@email.com.

Port Security: ISPS compliant

Pre-Arrival Information: Vessel's inbound should send ETA at least 24 h in advance. Messages should include the following:
a) name of vessel
b) last port of call
c) ETA
d) gt, loa, beam, draught, dwt & speed
e) dangerous cargo
f) type & quantity of cargo
g) name of local agent

Documentation: Crew list (8 copies), ship's stores list Form IV (3copies), crew private property list Form V) including foreign currency declaration (3 copies), currency declaration (3 copies), passenger list (3 copies), cargo manifest (3 copies), 'no opium' certificate (3 copies), survey bottom cargo manifest (3 copies), deck cargo certificate (3 copies), hazardous cargo certificate (3 copies), arrival of pets abroad (3 copies), declaration for 'no monkeys on board' (3 copies)
The Master should deposit the following documents with the Port Authority through the agents (originals):
Ship's registration, international load line certificate, safety radio certificate, light dues certificate, safety equipment certificate, international ship security certificate, last port clearance, international health certificate, ship sanitation control certificate, last 3 ports certificate, cavities certificate, ballast certificate, vaccination certificate, arms & ammunition certificate, safety construction certificate, international tonnage certificate, ballast water reporting form
All vessels discharging ballast water in the port are required to complete a ballast water reporting form and send it to the Harbour Master/Chief Officer for onward transmission to the Director General of Shipping

Approach: Approach is from the open sea. There is a Fairway Buoy in pos 20° 14.55' N; 086° 42.9' E, approx 2 nautical miles from the breakwater. The approach channel, with a dredged depth of 13 m, has a length of 2020 m and width of 190 m and is connected to an entrance channel, length 500 m, width 160 m, depth 13 m. The port has a large turning basin 520 m in diameter, also dredged to a depth of 13 m

Anchorage: Tanker anchorage in pos 20° 11.5' N; 086° 45.0' E (the limits of this anchorage are covered by a circle, radius 0.75 nautical mile from its centre)
General anchorage in pos 20° 11.5' N; 086° 42' E (the limits of this anchorage are covered by a circle, radius 0.75 nautical mile from its centre)
VLCC-I Anchorage in pos 20° 00' N; 086° 41' E (radius of 1.5 nautical miles)
VLCC-II Anchorage in pos 20° 07.5' N; 086° 46.5' E (radius of 1.5 nautical miles)

Pilotage: Pilotage is compulsory for all vessels of more than 200 gt and is available 24 h/day. Notice of ETA must be sent to the Harbour Master/Traffic Master or agent 24 h prior to arrival in the roads. The pilot normally boards 2 nautical miles SE of harbour entrance (20° 14.6' N; 086° 42.8' E)

Radio Frequency: VHF Channels 12 & 16

Weather: The port experiences both SW monsoon (winds 35-42 km/h) from June to September and NE monsoon (winds 18-24 km/h) from November to February

Tides: MHWS 2.58 m, MLWS 0.71 m, MHWN 2.02 m, MLWN 1.32 m

Traffic: 2007/08, 1636 vessels, 42 440 000 t of cargo handled

Maximum Vessel Dimensions: 75 000 dwt, 260 m loa, 13 m draught

Principal Imports and Exports: Imports: Coal, Fertiliser, Hardcoke, Phosphoric acid, POL. Exports: Chrome ore, Food products, Iron ore, Steel coils, Thermal coal.

Working Hours: Normally 0600-1400, 1400-2200, 2200-0600

Accommodation:

Name	Length (m)	Draught (m)	Remarks
Paradip			
Iron Ore Berth	155	12.5–13	See [1] below
Coal Berths (CB-1 & CB-2)	520	13	See [2] below
East Quay No.1	260	11	See [3] below
East Quay No.2	260	11	See [4] below
East Quay No.3	230	12	See [5] below
Central Quay	755	12.5	See [6] below
Multi-Purpose Cargo Berth	250	12.5	See [7] below
South Quay	265	12	See [8] below
Fertiliser Berth (FB1)	252	12.5	Max 230 m loa, max 65 000 dwt
Fertiliser Berth (FB2)	230	12.5	Max 230 m loa, max 65 000 dwt

Name	Length (m)	Draught (m)	Remarks
Oil Jetty	290	14	Oil products. Max 230 m loa, max 65 000 dwt
SPM			See [9] below

[1]*Iron Ore Berth:* Max 260 m loa, max 60 000-75 000 dwt. Rated cap of 2500 t/h. Two rotary type wagon tippers rated at 2500 t/h and three bucket wheel reclaimers (2 x 1250 t/h and 1 x 2000 t/h). Open yard cap of 650 000 t
This berth can be used for bulk loading/unloading of other ores by ship's own gear, or transhipment of petroleum products when there is no iron ore vessel for loading
[2]*Coal Berths (CB-1 & CB-2):* Max 260 m loa, max 60 000-75 000 dwt. Two 4000 t/h reclaimers and two 4000 t/h stackers
[3]*East Quay No.1:* Max 260 m loa, max 40 000 dwt. Loading/unloading bulk cargo
[4]*East Quay No.2:* Max 260 m loa, max 40 000 dwt. Loading/unloading bulk cargo
[5]*East Quay No.3:* Max 230 m loa, max 60 000 dwt. Loading/unloading bulk cargo
[6]*Central Quay:* Three berths handling fertiliser, steel & scrap. Max 230 m loa, max 65 000 dwt
[7]*Multi-Purpose Cargo Berth:* General/break bulk cargo. Max 190 m loa, max 45 000 dwt
[8]*South Quay:* General/break bulk cargo. Max 230 m loa, max 65 000 dwt
[9]*SPM:* In pos 20° 04.42' N; 86° 41.31' E for unloading of crude oil from VLCC's

Storage: Four transit sheds on general cargo berths totalling 16 060 m2 with total cap of 30 000 t. Warehouses with a total area of 7711 m2 are also available. Over 15 000 000 m2 of open stacking area is available. A 500 TEU container yard with 15 reefer points and rail link

Mechanical Handling Equipment:

Location	Type	Capacity (t)	Qty
Paradip	Quay Cranes	13.2–75	10
Paradip	Forklifts	3	2

Bunkering: Bunkering facilities are available via road tanker
The Liberty Marine Syndicate Private Ltd, 22 Madhuban Market Complex, Paradip, Orissa, India 754 142, *Tel:* +91 6722 222009, *Fax:* +91 6722 222086, *Email:* paradip@libertyshipping.com, *Website:* www.libertyshipping.com
Asean International Ltd, P O Box 7860, Block Z Suite 42/43, Saif Zone, Sharjah, United Arab Emirates, *Tel:* +971 6 557 0083, *Fax:* +971 6 557 0085
Bharat Petroleum Corp. Ltd, 4th Floor, Old Admin Building, Mahul, Chembur, Mumbai, Maharashtra, India 400 074, *Tel:* +91 22 2554 3493, *Fax:* +91 22 2554 0621, *Email:* josecm@bharatpetroleum.in, *Website:* www.baratpetroleum.in
Bominflot, Bominoil Private Ltd, 504 Maker Chambers V, 221 Nariman Point, Mumbai, Maharashtra, India 400 021, *Tel:* +91 22 2281 7133, *Fax:* +91 22 2281 7145, *Email:* bominoil@vsnl.com, *Website:* www.bominflot.net
Cockett Marine Oil Ltd, Carrick House, 36 Station Square, Petts Wood, Kent BR5 1NA, United Kingdom, *Tel:* +44 1689 883 400, *Fax:* +44 1689 877 666, *Email:* enquiries@cockett.com, *Website:* www.cockettgroup.com – *Grades:* IFO; MDO; MGO – *Parcel Size:* min IFO 50t, min MDO/MGO 10t – *Delivery Mode:* barge, road tank wagon, pipeline
M/S Global Fuels & Lubricants Inc., 11-12 Mangal Society, 76C Rafi Ahmed Kidwai Road, King Circle, Mumbai, Maharashtra, India 400 019, *Tel:* +91 22 2374 5987, *Fax:* +91 22 2409 1627, *Email:* globalfuels@vsnl.com, *Website:* www.bunkerindia.com
The Liberty Marine Syndicate Private Ltd, 22 Madhuban Market Complex, Paradip, Orissa, India 754 142, *Tel:* +91 6722 222009, *Fax:* +91 6722 222086, *Email:* paradip@libertyshipping.com, *Website:* www.libertyshipping.com

Waste Reception Facilities: Garbage collection can be arranged via agents

Towage: Five tugs are available (2 x 30, 1 x 40, 2 x 50 t bollard pull), all fitted with foam fire fighting capabilities

Repair & Maintenance: Dry dock of 75 m x 15 m x 6 m for vessels up to 60 m loa

Ship Chandlers: Admiral Marine Services Private Ltd, 26 Madhuban Market Complex, Paradip, Orissa, India 754 142, *Tel:* +91 6722 222684, *Email:* enquiries@admiralmarine.com, *Website:* www.admiralmarine.com
The Liberty Marine Syndicate Private Ltd, 22 Madhuban Market Complex, Paradip, Orissa, India 754 142, *Tel:* +91 6722 222009, *Fax:* +91 6722 222086, *Email:* paradip@libertyshipping.com, *Website:* www.libertyshipping.com

Shipping Agents: J.M. Baxi & Co, 48 Badapadia - Thakur Lane, Opposite Bus Stand, Paradip, Orissa, India 754 142, *Tel:* +91 6722 222052, *Fax:* +91 6722 222308, *Email:* paradp@jmbaxi.com, *Website:* www.jmbaxi.com
E.C. Bose & Co., 60 Madhuban Market Complex, District Jagatsinghbur, Paradip, Orissa, India 754 142, *Tel:* +91 6722 222145, *Fax:* +91 6722 222745, *Email:* ecbpdp@sancharnet.in, *Website:* ecboseplc.com
Everett (India) Private Ltd, Suite No.2, 1st Floor, Trade Centre, Paradip, Orissa, India 754 142, *Tel:* +91 6722 220969, *Fax:* +91 6722 220969, *Email:* everett-paradip@everett.co.in, *Website:* www.everett.co.in
Forbes Patvolk (A Division of Forbes Gokak Ltd), Suite 11, Trade Centre, Paradip, Orissa, India 754 142, *Tel:* +91 6722 222180, *Fax:* +91 6722 222580, *Email:* patvolkpdp@sify.com, *Website:* www.forbespatvolk.com
GAC Shipping (India) Pvt Ltd, HIG 32, Gaurav Vihar, Madhuban, Paradip Port, Paradip, Orissa, India 754 142, *Tel:* +91 6722 221974, *Fax:* +91 6722 221975, *Email:* paradip@gacworld.com, *Website:* www.gacworld.com
G.R. Enterprises, G P R & Co., P O Box 64, MC-22, Madhuban Area, Paradip, Orissa, India 754142, *Tel:* +91 6722 222218, *Fax:* +91 6722 222372, *Email:* gprcpdp@bsnl.in
Interocean Shipping (India) Pvt Ltd., H.I.G - 36, OSHB Complex, Gaurav Vihar, Jagannath Marg, Paradip, Orissa, India 754 142, *Tel:* +91 6722 220239, *Fax:* +91 6722 220259, *Email:* paradip@interoceangroup.com, *Website:* www.interoceangroup.com
Merchant Shipping Services Private Ltd, MB-129, Madhuban Jagatsinghpur, Paradip, Orissa, India 754142, *Tel:* +91 6722 222581, *Fax:* +91 6722 221057, *Email:* merspdp@merchantshpg.com
Samsara Shipping (Private) Ltd, MB-129, Madhuban, Jagatsinghpur, Paradip, Orissa, India 754 142, *Tel:* +91 6722 222581, *Fax:* +91 6722 221057, *Email:* samspdp@samsarashipping.com, *Website:* www.samsarashipping.com
Seatrans Marine Private Limited, Room 202, 2nd Floor, OBC Building, Bank Street, Jagatsinghpur, Paradip, Orissa, India 754142, *Tel:* +91 6722 222219, *Fax:* +91 6722 223080, *Email:* operation@seatrans.co.in, *Website:* www.seatrans.co.in

Stevedoring Companies: E.C. Bose & Co., 60 Madhuban Market Complex, District Jagatsinghbur, Paradip, Orissa, India 754 142, *Tel:* +91 6722 222145, *Fax:* +91 6722 222745, *Email:* ecbpdp@sancharnet.in, *Website:* ecboseplc.com

G.R. Enterprises, G P R & Co., P O Box 64, MC-22, Madhuban Area, Paradip, Orissa, India 754142, *Tel:* +91 6722 222218, *Fax:* +91 6722 222372, *Email:* gprcpdp@bsnl.in

Karam Chand Thapar & Bros (CS) Ltd, 53 Madhuban Market Complex, Paradip, Orissa, India 754 142, *Tel:* +91 6722 222402, *Fax:* +91 6722 222503, *Email:* lionchopra@yahoo.com, *Website:* www.kctcoalsales.com

L.M. Hati & Co., Paradip, Orissa, India 754 142, *Tel:* +91 6722 222331, *Fax:* +91 6722 222828

Orissa Stevedores Ltd, 'V' Point, East Paradip, Jagatsinghpur, Paradip, Orissa, India 754 142, *Tel:* +91 6722 222134, *Fax:* +91 6722 222787, *Email:* oslpdp@sify.com

Surveyors: J.B. Boda Surveyors Private Ltd, Plot No.187, Jayadeva Sadan Chaack, Paradip, Orissa, India 754 142, *Tel:* +91 6722 223862, *Fax:* +91 6722 222320, *Email:* jbbpdp@jbbodamail.com, *Website:* www.jbboda.net

Seascan Services, Sea Marine Surveyor (Utkal), 45 Madhuvan Market Complex, Paradip, Orissa, India 754 142, *Tel:* +91 6722 222899, *Fax:* +91 6722 220604, *Email:* seamarine@sancharnet.in

Medical Facilities: A 62 bed hospital is available at the port

Airport: Bhubaneswar, 120 km

Railway: The port is connected with broad gauge Railway System (double track) of the East Coast Railway

Development: Dredging has begun on deepening of the approach channel from 12.8 m to 18.7 m and entrance channel and the turning circle from 12.8 m to 17.1 m, handling vessels up to 125 000 dwt (draught available for vessels will be 16.0 m)

Plans to enhance the draught at existing docks to 14 m, to accommodate Panamax vessels and to extend the existing iron ore berth from 155 m to 205 m to be completed with dredging project above

There are also plans to build two bulk berths at the port for Capesize Bulk Carriers, one for exports of iron ore and the other for imports of coking coal, after dredging of the channel is completed. Both berths will have a capacity for 16 m draught and 125 000 dwt vessels. There are also plans to install two 20 t shore cranes

Lloyd's Agent: Wilson Surveyors and Adjusters Private Ltd, Fatima Building 2nd Floor, 23-13-28 Thompson Street, Visakhapatnam, Andhira Pradesh, India 530 001, *Tel:* +91 891 272 5611, *Fax:* +91 891 272 5655, *Email:* vizag@wilsur.com, *Website:* www.wilsur.com

PIPAVAV

Lat 20° 59' N; Long 71° 34' E.

| **Admiralty Chart:** 1474/1486 | **Admiralty Pilot:** 38 |
| **Time Zone:** GMT +5.5 h | **UNCTAD Locode:** IN PAV |

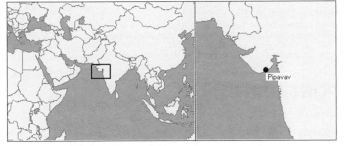

Principal Facilities:

| P | Q | Y | G | C | | | | A |

Authority: Gujarat Pipavav Port Limited (GPPL), CG House, 1st Floor, Dr. Annie Besant Road, Worli, Mumbai, Maharashtra, India 400 030, *Tel:* +91 22 2438 3301, *Fax:* +91 22 2438 3332, *Email:* feedback@portofpipavav.com, *Website:* www.pipavav.com

Officials: Chief Operating Officer: Ravi Gaitonde.
Managing Director: Philip Littlejohn.
Marketing Manager: Umang Khosla, *Email:* ukhosla@portofpipavav.com.
Harbour Master: Capt Ashok Gole, *Email:* harbourmaster@portofpipavav.com

Port Security: ISPS compliant. Manned by Port Security round the clock. It has an approved Port Facilty Security Plan. SOC No. DGS/SOC/029

Pre-Arrival Information: ETA notice (7 days, 5 days, 3 days, 48 h & 24 h), loa, breadth, draft (arrival & departure), last & next port of call, ISPS compliance, all trading certificates & if free pratique required, then radio message

Approach: All weather deep channel 300 m wide with average depth of 12.5 m. The port is protected from the swell of SW monsoons by a natural breakwater formed by Shiyal Bet and Savai Bet Islands

Anchorage: Vessels to anchor as advised by Port Control
A1; 20° 52' 7'' N 71° 30' 7'' E
A2; 20° 52' 7'' N 71° 31' 5'' E
B1; 20° 53' 0'' N 71° 32' 3'' E
B2; 20° 53' 0'' N 71° 32' 9'' E
B3; 20° 52' 7'' N 71° 33' 6'' E
B4; 20° 53' 3'' N 71° 33' 6'' E

Pilotage: Compulsory. Pilot boards at anchorage in pos 20° 53' N; 71° 30.2' E

Radio Frequency: VHF Channels 16 and 71

Weather: December-February: NE winds up to 20 knots. June-August (monsoon): SW swells 2-3 m and winds up to 30 knots

Tides: Average tidal range, Spring 3.5 m and Neap 2 m

Traffic: 2007, 16 650 000 t of bulk cargo handled, 192 017 TEU's

Maximum Vessel Dimensions: Max 300 m loa, Max draft 12.5 m on a tide of 2 m

Principal Imports and Exports: Imports: Coal, Containers, Iron Ore, LPG, Machinery, Urea. Exports: Cement, Clinker, Containers, Dry Fish, Food Grain, Machinery, Raw Cotton, Salt, Scrap, Soda Ash, Steel, Stone, Wood Pulp.

Working Hours: 24 h/day, Port holidays; January 26, August 15 and October 2

Accommodation:

Name	Length (m)	Draught (m)	Remarks
Pipavav			See [1] below
Dry Cargo Berths	1055	12.5	See [2] below
LPG/Liquid Cargo Berth	65	12.5	

[1]*Pipavav:* Port Office, Tel: +91 2794 286001, Fax: +91 2794 286044

[2]*Dry Cargo Berths:* 325 m dedicated for bulk and break-bulk cargo and 730 m dedicated for container handling

Storage: Seven warehouses of 600 m2 each and two warehouses of 3600 m2 and 3120 m2 respectively are located in the immediate stackyard behind the dry cargo berths. Six additional warehouses of 6600 m2 each are located in the warehousing zone, 1.5 km from the jetties

Open storage for bulk cargoes of 200 000 m2 and container storage of 104 000 m2 with 420 reefer points

Mechanical Handling Equipment:

Location	Type	Capacity (t)	Qty	Remarks
Pipavav	Mobile Cranes	75	6	2 x 20 t, 2 x 30 t, 2 x 75 t
Pipavav	Panamax		3	
Pipavav	Post Panamax		3	
Pipavav	RTG's		18	
Pipavav	Quay Cranes	40	3	
Pipavav	Shore Cranes	26	2	bulk
Pipavav	Harbour Cranes	100	1	container & bulk
Pipavav	Reach Stackers	45	5	
Pipavav	Forklifts	3	6	
Pipavav	Yard Trailers	35	40	30 container & 10 bulk

Towage: Two tugs, 42 t bhp and 35 t bhp

Repair & Maintenance: Pipavav Shipyard Ltd, Pipavav Port, Post Ucchaiya, Via-Rajula, District Amreli, Gujarat, India 365 560, *Tel:* +91 2794 286200, *Fax:* +91 2794 286373, *Email:* contact@pipavavshipyard.com, *Website:* www.pipavavshipyard.com

Shipping Agents: J.M. Baxi & Co, Room No.24 - 2nd Floor - Port Users Complex, Port of Pipavav, Pipavav, India 365 560, *Tel:* +91 2794 286092, *Fax:* +91 2794 286335, *Email:* pipavav@jmbaxi.com, *Website:* www.jmbaxi.com

Stevedoring Companies: Chowgule Brothers Private Ltd, Chowgule House, 403 Mormugao Harbour, Mormugao, Goa, India 403 803, *Tel:* +91 832 252 5144, *Fax:* +91 832 252 1011, *Email:* info.cb@chowgule.co.in, *Website:* www.chowgulebros.com

Medical Facilities: Port dispensary manned by one qualified doctor

Airport: Diu 90 km. Bhavnagar 140 km. Rajkot 230 km

Railway: On dock rail facility. Dedicated container and bulk rail sidings inside the port. Connected to all major North West India ICDs with weekly train services. Capable of handling double stacked container trains. Connected to the broad gauge rail network of Indian Railways

Development: The harbour is to be dredged to 14.5 m and is expected to be completed by mid-2009

Lloyd's Agent: Wilson Surveyors and Adjusters Private Ltd, C-204 Remi Bizcourt, Veera Desai Road, Andheri West, Mumbai, Maharashtra, India 400 053, *Tel:* +91 22 6696 3606, *Fax:* +91 22 6696 3669, *Email:* mumbai@wilsur.com, *Website:* www.wilsur.com

PIR PAU

harbour area, see under Mumbai

PORBANDAR

Lat 21° 36' N; Long 69° 36' E.

| **Admiralty Chart:** 3460 | **Admiralty Pilot:** 38 |
| **Time Zone:** GMT +5.5 h | **UNCTAD Locode:** IN PBD |

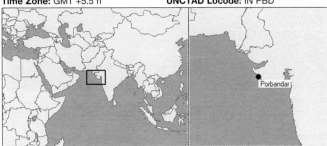

Principal Facilities:

| | Q | Y | G | | | B | | T | A |

Authority: Gujarat Maritime Board, Port of Porbandar, 21 Vagheswari Plot, Opposite Vishal Port Colony, Porbandar, Gujarat, India 360 575, *Tel:* +91 286 224 2408, *Fax:* +91 286 224 4013, *Email:* popbr1@rediffmail.com, *Website:* www.gmbports.org

Key to Principal Facilities:—			
A=Airport	**C**=Containers	**G**=General Cargo	**P**=Petroleum	**R**=Ro/Ro	**Y**=Dry Bulk
B=Bunkers	**D**=Dry Dock	**L**=Cruise	**Q**=Other Liquid Bulk	**T**=Towage (where available from port)

Officials: Port Officer: Mahendra Kumar Mohanty.

Port Security: ISPS compliant

Approach: The harbour is well protected by a 2625 m long breakwater extending from the shore up to a depth of 12.0 m

Anchorage: Outside the breakwater there is an ample deep water area where vessels can safely anchor and cargo can be worked by lighters in good weather with no draught restriction. During monsoon season working is impossible due to rough weather

Pilotage: Compulsory. Pilots available during daytime only, from sunrise to sunset. Vessels requiring pilot should anchor 0.5 km S of the breakwater

Weather: Heavy swells during monsoon season May 15 to September 15

Tides: Range of tide approx 2.7 m. Current does not exceed 1 knot in fair weather

Principal Imports and Exports: Imports: Coal, Fertilizer, LPG. Exports: Agricultural products, Bauxite, Building Materials, Cement, Clinker, Cotton, Fruits, Groundnuts, Oil cakes, Reefer cargo.

Working Hours: 0800-1200, 1300-1700, 1800-2200, 2300-0300. Normal working at berth 0800-2200. Round the clock in the anchorage

Accommodation:

Name	Length (m)	Depth (m)	Remarks
Porbandar			
Jetty	385	9.75	Vessels up to 200 m loa, 8.5 m draft can berth alongside

Storage: Private refrigerated space. Ample area for storage of bulk cargo is available

Location	Covered (m²)
Porbandar	20080

Mechanical Handling Equipment:

Location	Type	Capacity (t)	Qty
Porbandar	Mult-purp. Cranes	16	1
Porbandar	Mult-purp. Cranes	75	1
Porbandar	Mult-purp. Cranes	12.5	1

Cargo Worked: 35-40 t/h/gang

Bunkering: M/S Global Fuels & Lubricants Inc., 11-12 Mangal Society, 76C Rafi Ahmed Kidwai Road, King Circle, Mumbai, Maharashtra, India 400 019, *Tel:* +91 22 2374 5987, *Fax:* +91 22 2409 1627, *Email:* globalfuels@vsnl.com, *Website:* www.bunkerindia.com – *Delivery Mode:* road tanker

Towage: Five tugs available

Shipping Agents: J.M. Baxi & Co, Sisodia Mansion, Gopnath Plot 25, Porbandar, Gujarat, India 360 575, *Tel:* +91 286 224 5401, *Fax:* +91 286 224 5401, *Email:* porb@jmbaxi.com, *Website:* www.jmbaxi.com

Stevedoring Companies: Chowgule Brothers Private Ltd, Chowgule House, 403 Mormugao Harbour, Mormugao, Goa, India 403 803, *Tel:* +91 832 252 5144, *Fax:* +91 832 252 1011, *Email:* info.cb@chowgule.co.in, *Website:* www.chowgulebros.com

Surveyors: J.B. Boda Surveyors Private Ltd, Mahalaxmi Mandir Mahatma Gandhi Road, Porbandar, Gujarat, India 360 575, *Tel:* +91 286 224 5782, *Fax:* +91 286 224 5782, *Email:* jbbpbr@jbbodamail.com, *Website:* www.jbboda.net

Medical Facilities: Available

Airport: Local airport, 4.8 km

Railway: 2 km from port

Lloyd's Agent: Wilson Surveyors and Adjusters Private Ltd, Golden Arcade, II Floor, Room No.209, Plot No.141/142, Sector 8, Gandhidam, Kutch, Gujarat, India 370 201, *Tel:* +91 2836 238333, *Fax:* +91 2836 238333, *Email:* kandla@wilsur.com, *Website:* www.wilsur.com

PORT BLAIR

Lat 11° 40' N; Long 92° 43' E.

Admiralty Chart: 514

Admiralty Pilot: 21

Time Zone: GMT +5.5 h

UNCTAD Locode: IN IXZ

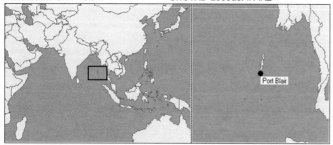

Principal Facilities:

P		Y	G	C	R		B	D		A	

Authority: The Chief Port Administrator, Port Management Board, Andaman & Nicobar Islands, Port Blair, South Andaman Island, India 744 101, *Tel:* +91 3192 233679, *Fax:* +91 3192 233675, *Email:* cpapmb@and.nic.in, *Website:* www.and.nic.in/harbour.htm

Officials: Port Administrator: Ananth Chandra Bose, *Email:* ananthbose@hotmail.com.

Harbour Master: Ashwini Kumar, *Tel:* +91 3192 237804.

Port Security: ISPS compliant

Approach: Approach depths vary from 20-60 m

Pilotage: Compulsory

Radio Frequency: VHF Channel 16 (156.80 mHz). During the day 0700-1900, 6220 kHz. During the night 1900-0700, 3632.5 kHz

Tides: Tidal range up to 2 m

Maximum Vessel Dimensions: 300 m loa, 8.0 m max d

Working Hours: 24 h

Accommodation:

Name	Length (m)	Depth (m)
Port Blair		
Haddo I	180	8
Haddo II	225	8
Haddo III	150	8
Haddo IV	135	8
Chatham	220	8
Hope Town	100	8
Phoneix Bay Jetties	130	5

Storage: Ample warehouses at wharves and ample space for containers including refrigerated containers

Mechanical Handling Equipment: Haddo Wharves: 25 t and 6 t wharf crane, 10 t and 25 t mobile crane, forklifts of 3-25 t cap
Chatham Wharf: 6 t wharf crane and 3 t forklift
Hope Town: 6 t wharf crane

Cargo Worked: 500 t/gang/shift (8 h shift)

Bunkering: M/S Global Fuels & Lubricants Inc., 11-12 Mangal Society, 76C Rafi Ahmed Kidwai Road, King Circle, Mumbai, Maharashtra, India 400 019, *Tel:* +91 22 2374 5987, *Fax:* +91 22 2409 1627, *Email:* globalfuels@vsnl.com, *Website:* www.bunkerindia.com – *Delivery Mode:* pipeline

Waste Reception Facilities: Garbage disposal available

Repair & Maintenance: Dry docks and slipways available

Ship Chandlers: A.S. Moloobhoy & Sons, 106/2 J.N. Road, Delanipur, Near Palika Palace Hotel, Port Blair, South Andaman Island, India 744 102, *Tel:* +91 3192 240510, *Email:* portblair@asmoloobhoy.com, *Website:* www.asmoloobhoy.com

Shipping Agents: J.M. Baxi & Co, Port Blair, South Andaman Island, India, *Tel:* +91 3192 243235, *Email:* blair@jmbaxi.com, *Website:* www.jmbaxi.com

Surveyors: Indian Register of Shipping, Middle Point, Near ICT Computers, Andaman and Nicobar Island, Port Blair, South Andaman Island, India 744 101, *Tel:* +91 3192 244498, *Fax:* +91 3192 244498, *Email:* pblirsblair@sancharnet.in, *Website:* www.irclass.org

Medical Facilities: Local hospital available

Airport: Port Blair, 5 km

Lloyd's Agent: Wilson Surveyors and Adjusters Private Ltd, Suite No.806, 8th Floor, O M Towers, 32 Chowringhee Road, Kolkata, West Bengal, India 700 071, *Tel:* +91 33 2217 5800, *Fax:* +91 33 2217 5797, *Email:* kolkata@wilsur.com, *Website:* www.wilsur.com

PORT OKHA

Lat 22° 28' N; Long 69° 5' E.

Admiralty Chart: 673

Admiralty Pilot: 38

Time Zone: GMT +5.5 h

UNCTAD Locode: IN OKH

Principal Facilities:

P		Y	G			B	T	

Authority: Gujarat Maritime Board, Port of Okha, Okha, Gujarat, India 361 350, *Tel:* +91 2892 262001, *Fax:* +91 2892 262002, *Website:* www.gmbports.org

Officials: Port Officer: Capt R. K. Raman.

Port Security: ISPS compliant

Approach: Vessels have to pass through a dredged channel where drafts vary daily between 7.31 and 8.23 m. Owing to the extreme narrow entrance channel max breadth of vessels is restricted to 30 m

Pilotage: Compulsory. Pilot boards 0.4 nautical mile N of No.1 port hand Lt buoy in pos 22° 30' 67" N; 69° 05' 20" E. Pilotage during daylight hours only

Radio Frequency: VHF Channel 16

Tides: 3.5 m MHWS, 3.0 m MHWN, 1.2 m MLWS, 0.4 m MLWN

Principal Imports and Exports: Imports: Coal, Coke, Fertilizer, Mineral oil, Refined petroleum products, Sulphur, Wheat. Exports: Bauxite, Cement clinker, Salt, Soda ash, Soyabean meal.

Working Hours: 0800-1200, 1300-1700, 1800-2200, 2300-0300

Accommodation:

Name	Draught (m)	Remarks
Port Okha		See [1] below
Dry Cargo Berth	8.53	Dry cargo vessels and tankers up to 158 m loa can be accommodated
Sayaji Pier (East)	8.53	For vessels up to 180 m loa
Sayaji Pier (West)	6.5	For vessels up to 110 m loa

[1]*Port Okha:* Anchorage at roadstead about 1 mile from the shore, 190° from Samiyani Lighthouse; no restrictions to size and draft. Operations performed by private barges day and night from a 304.8 m wharf wall on the shore, except during monsoon period from May 15 to September 14 when daylight hours only are normally worked, depending on weather

Storage:

Location	Open (m²)	Covered (m²)	Sheds / Warehouses
Port Okha	59030	26110	18

Mechanical Handling Equipment:

Location	Type	Capacity (t)	Qty
Port Okha	Mult-purp. Cranes	16	1
Port Okha	Mult-purp. Cranes	12.5	2

Cargo Worked: Dry cargo 150-200 t/gang/day. 700-800 t/gang/day if vessel uses own grabbing gear

Bunkering: Bharat Fuels, Off No.38, C.L. Sharma Shopping Complex, Sector 8, Near Oslo Cinema, Gandhidham, Gujarat, India 370201, *Tel:* +91 2836 227 627, *Fax:* +91 2836 225 925, *Email:* bharatpetro_gim@sancharnet.in/bharatpetro@indiatimes.com, *Website:* www.bharatpetroleum.in – *Delivery Mode:* pipeline, road tanker
Bharat Petroleum Corp. Ltd, 4th Floor, Old Admin Building, Mahul, Chembur, Mumbai, Maharashtra, India 400 074, *Tel:* +91 22 2554 3493, *Fax:* +91 22 2554 0621, *Email:* josecm@bharatpetroleum.in, *Website:* www.baratpetroleum.in – *Delivery Mode:* pipeline, road tanker
Bominflot, Bominoil Private Ltd, 504 Maker Chambers V, 221 Nariman Point, Mumbai, Maharashtra, India 400 021, *Tel:* +91 22 2281 7133, *Fax:* +91 22 2281 7145, *Email:* bominoil@vsnl.com, *Website:* www.bominflot.net – *Delivery Mode:* pipeline, road tanker
Cockett Marine Oil Ltd, Carrick House, 36 Station Square, Petts Wood, Kent BR5 1NA, United Kingdom, *Tel:* +44 1689 883 400, *Fax:* +44 1689 877 666, *Email:* enquiries@cockett.com, *Website:* www.cockettgroup.com – *Grades:* IFO; MDO; MGO – *Parcel Size:* min IFO 50t, min MDO/MGO 10t – *Delivery Mode:* road tank wagon, pipeline
Indian Oil Corp. Ltd, Indian Oil Bhavan Head Office, G9 Ali Yavar Jung Marg, Bandra (East), Mumbai, Maharashtra, India 400051, *Tel:* +91 22 2644 7368, *Fax:* +91 22 2642 2434, *Email:* partha_datta@indianoil.co.in, *Website:* www.indianoil.co.in – *Delivery Mode:* pipeline, road tanker
Link Enterprises, Plot 44, Sector 9/A, Morabia Commercial Centre, P O Box 248, Gandhidham, Gujarat, India 370 201, *Tel:* +91 2836 230 107, *Fax:* +91 2836 231 285, *Email:* info@asiaship.com – *Delivery Mode:* pipeline, road tanker
Zee Shipping Co. Private Ltd, 101 Shreeji Vihar, Bedi Bundar Road, Jamnagar, Gujarat, India 361002, *Tel:* +91 288 2757 011, *Fax:* +91 288 2757 044, *Email:* zeeship@zeeship.com – *Delivery Mode:* pipeline, road tanker

Towage: Two tugs of 382 bhp, one tug of 1600 bhp and one tug of 3400 bhp

Repair & Maintenance: Minor repairs can be carried out in emergencies

Shipping Agents: J.M. Baxi & Co, J. Bhatia Bidg, Navi Nagari, Okha, Gujarat, India 361 350, *Tel:* +91 2892 262022, *Fax:* +91 2892 262082, *Email:* okha@jmbaxi.com, *Website:* www.jmbaxi.com

Stevedoring Companies: Chowgule Brothers Private Ltd, Chowgule House, 403 Mormugao Harbour, Mormugao, Goa, India 403 803, *Tel:* +91 832 252 5144, *Fax:* +91 832 252 1011, *Email:* info.cb@chowgule.co.in, *Website:* www.chowgulebros.com

Medical Facilities: Small Government dispensary at Port Okha. Well equipped private hospital for specialised treatment 11 km from port

Airport: Jamnagar, 180 km

Lloyd's Agent: Wilson Surveyors and Adjusters Private Ltd, Golden Arcade, II Floor, Room No.209, Plot No.141/142, Sector 8, Gandhidam, Kutch, Gujarat, India 370 201, *Tel:* +91 2836 238333, *Fax:* +91 2836 238333, *Email:* kandla@wilsur.com, *Website:* www.wilsur.com

PUDUCHERRY

Lat 11° 56' N; Long 79° 50' E.

Admiralty Chart: 575	**Admiralty Pilot:** 21
Time Zone: GMT +5.5 h	**UNCTAD Locode:** IN PNY

Principal Facilities:

		Y	G				T	

Authority: Govt. of Puducherry, Ports Department, No.1 Rue Dumas, Pondicherry, Tamil Nadu, India 605 001, *Tel:* +91 413 233 7114, *Fax:* +91 413 233 8092, *Email:* port@pon.nic.in, *Website:* port.puducherry.gov.in

Officials: Director: S. Manohar.

Port Security: ISPS compliant

Pilotage: Assistance provided if required

Traffic: 2005/06, 42 vessels, 96 213 t of cargo handled

Principal Imports and Exports: Imports: Fluorspar. Exports: Cement.

Accommodation:

Name	Length (m)	Draught (m)	Remarks
Puducherry			See [1] below
New Port			
Cargo Quay	150	2.5	Four transit sheds, each with a storage cap of 3500 t
Old Port			
RCC Pier	286	4.5–6	See [2] below

[1]*Puducherry:* Open roadstead anchorage port suitable for lighterage operations during February to September
[2]*RCC Pier:* Working head of 102 m long. Seven transit sheds with a total storage cap of 12 750 t

Mechanical Handling Equipment:

Location	Type	Capacity (t)	Qty
Puducherry	Mobile Cranes	5–10	1

Cargo Worked: Max 2000 t/day with one vessel

Towage: One small towing launch available capable of towing 200 t

Repair & Maintenance: Minor repairs can be carried out. One slipway for vessels of 30 m x 8 m weighing up to 150 t

Shipping Agents: J.M. Baxi & Co, 62 Beach Road, Pondicherry, Tamil Nadu, India 605 001, *Tel:* +91 413 233 9565, *Fax:* +91 413 222 0405, *Email:* pondicherry@jmbaxi.com, *Website:* www.jmbaxi.com

Medical Facilities: Available

Lloyd's Agent: Wilson Surveyors and Adjusters Private Ltd, TMB Mansion, 3rd Floor, 739 Anna Salai, Chennai, Tamil Nadu, India 600 002, *Tel:* +91 44 2852 2811, *Fax:* +91 44 2852 3349, *Email:* chennai@wilsur.com, *Website:* www.wilsur.com

RATNAGIRI

Lat 16° 59' N; Long 73° 17' E.

Admiralty Chart: 3460	**Admiralty Pilot:** 38
Time Zone: GMT +5.5 h	**UNCTAD Locode:** IN RTC

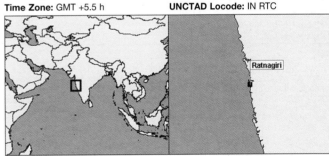

Principal Facilities:

	Q	Y						

Authority: Maharashtra Maritime Board, Ratnagiri Regional Port Office, Mandvi, Maharashtra, India 415 612, *Tel:* +91 95235 222 2160, *Website:* www.mmbmumbai.com

Port Security: ISPS compliant

Accommodation:

Name	Length (m)	Draught (m)	Remarks
Ganeshgule			
Berth	129	5	Cement clinker
Finolex Jetty			See [1] below

[1]*Finolex Jetty:* Operated by Finolex Industries Ltd., Ranpar Pawas Road, P O Box 11, Ratnagiri 415612, Tel: +91 2352 38027, Fax: +91 2352 38045, Email: fil@finolexind.com, Website: www.finolex.com
Import of feedstock for manufacture of PVC as well as for import of LPG

Lloyd's Agent: Wilson Surveyors and Adjusters Private Ltd, C-204 Remi Bizcourt, Veera Desai Road, Andheri West, Mumbai, Maharashtra, India 400 053, *Tel:* +91 22 6696 3606, *Fax:* +91 22 6696 3669, *Email:* mumbai@wilsur.com, *Website:* www.wilsur.com

ROZI

see under Bedi

Key to Principal Facilities:—				
A=Airport	**C**=Containers	**G**=General Cargo	**P**=Petroleum	**R**=Ro/Ro	**Y**=Dry Bulk
B=Bunkers	**D**=Dry Dock	**L**=Cruise	**Q**=Other Liquid Bulk	**T**=Towage (where available from port)

SALAYA

Lat 22° 18' N; Long 69° 35' E.

Admiralty Chart: 673   **Admiralty Pilot:** 38
Time Zone: GMT +5.5 h   **UNCTAD Locode:** IN SAL
This port is no longer open to commercial shipping

SIKKA

Lat 22° 26' N; Long 69° 50' E.

Admiralty Chart: 699   **Admiralty Pilot:** 38
Time Zone: GMT +5.5 h   **UNCTAD Locode:** IN SIK

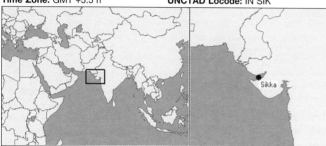

Principal Facilities:

P	Q	Y			B		T	A

Authority: Gujarat Maritime Board, Bedi Port, Jamnagar, Gujarat, India 361 009, *Tel:* +91 288 423763, *Website:* www.gmbports.org

Documentation: Crew list (6 copies), stores list (3 copies), personal property declaration (3 copies), last port clearance, cargo manifest, bills of lading, light dues receipt

Approach: Deep water channel from off Port Okha to Sikka well marked by light buoys, min depth 23 m

Pilotage: Compulsory for vessels carrying phosphoric acid or liquid ammonia. Pilot boards in pos 22° 30' N; 69° 46' E two hours before HW, during daylight hours only. Vessels should report to Bedi Port Radio

Weather: During monsoon period May 15 to September 14 weather is rough with strong wind and moderate to rough seas

Tides: 5.36 m MHWS, 0.7 m MLWS, 1.74 m MLWN, 3.04 m MSL

Principal Imports and Exports: Imports: Coal, Crude oil, Liquid ammonia, Machinery, Phosphoric acid, Propylene. Exports: Cement, Clinker, Salt.

Working Hours: 24 h/day

Accommodation:

Name	Remarks
Sikka	See [1] below

[1]*Sikka:* All weather intermediate anchorage port. Natural harbour with sheltered anchorage 4 km offshore. The channel is safely navigable throughout the year
Lighter fleet at Bedi brought to Sikka for handling coal and salt; other cargo of cement and clinker worked by Digvijay Cement Co Ltd with their own fleet and labour
A 48.8 m long jetty for vessels up to 165 m loa and 8 m draft handles phosphoric acid and liquid ammonia for the Gujarat State Fertilizers Co Ltd DAP plant at Motikhavdi
Oil operations take place at Jamnagar Terminal

Bunkering: Asean International Ltd, P O Box 7860, Block Z Suite 42/43, Saif Zone, Sharjah, United Arab Emirates, *Tel:* +971 6 557 0083, *Fax:* +971 6 557 0085
Bapu's Shipping Agency, Plot No 32, Sector 9, Near Central Bank Of India, Gandhidham, Gujarat, India 370 201, *Tel:* +91 2836 222 002, *Fax:* +91 2836 236 036, *Email:* info@shipsupplier.biz, *Website:* www.shipsupplier.biz
Bharat Fuels, Off No.38, C.L. Sharma Shopping Complex, Sector 8, Near Oslo Cinema, Gandhidham, Gujarat, India 370201, *Tel:* +91 2836 227 627, *Fax:* +91 2836 225 925, *Email:* bharatpetro_gim@sancharnet.in/bharatpetro@indiatimes.com, *Website:* www.bharatpetroleum.in
Bharat Petroleum Corp. Ltd, 4th Floor, Old Admin Building, Mahul, Chembur, Mumbai, Maharashtra, India 400 074, *Tel:* +91 22 2554 3493, *Fax:* +91 22 2554 0621, *Email:* josecm@bharatpetroleum.in, *Website:* www.baratpetroleum.in
Bominflot, Bominoil Private Ltd, 504 Maker Chambers V, 221 Nariman Point, Mumbai, Maharashtra, India 400 021, *Tel:* +91 22 2281 7133, *Fax:* +91 22 2281 7145, *Email:* bominoil@vsnl.com, *Website:* www.bominflot.net
M/S Global Fuels & Lubricants Inc., 11-12 Mangal Society, 76C Rafi Ahmed Kidwai Road, King Circle, Mumbai, Maharashtra, India 400 019, *Tel:* +91 22 2374 5987, *Fax:* +91 22 2409 1627, *Email:* globalfuels@vsnl.com, *Website:* www.bunkerindia.com
Gujarat Marine Private Ltd, Manali Chambers, Plot No. 306, Sector 1/A, Gandhidham, Gujarat, India 370 201, *Tel:* +91 2836 222 518, *Fax:* +91 2836 239 057, *Email:* bunker@gujmar.com, *Website:* www.gujmar.com
Hindustan Petroleum Corp. Ltd, Hindustan Bhawan, Vallabhdas Marg, Mumbai, Maharashtra, India 400 038, *Tel:* +91 22 2226 0079 – *Grades:* MDO; IFO180cSt – *Parcel Size:* min barge 150t, no max – *Rates:* 50-100t/h – *Notice:* 48-72 hours – *Delivery Mode:* barge, truck
Indian Oil Corp. Ltd, Indian Oil Bhavan Head Office, G9 Ali Yavar Jung Marg, Bandra (East), Mumbai, Maharashtra, India 400051, *Tel:* +91 22 2644 7368, *Fax:* +91 22 2642 2434, *Email:* partha_datta@indianoil.co.in, *Website:* www.indianoil.co.in – *Delivery Mode:* barge
Jaisu Shipping Co. Private Ltd, Kewalramani House, Dinshaw Building Road, Near Custom House, New Kandla, Kandla, India 370 210, *Tel:* +91 2836 270 428, *Fax:* +91 2836 270 650, *Email:* jaisu_shipping@yahoo.com/mail@jaisu.in, *Website:* www.jaisu.in – *Grades:* IFO80-180cSt; MDO; MGO; lubes; in line blending available

– *Misc:* own storage facilities – *Parcel Size:* min 10t, max 2900t – *Rates:* 100-500t/h – *Notice:* 12 hours – *Delivery Mode:* barge, pipeline, truck
Laxmi Marine, Plot No 119, Ward 6, Industrial Area, Bharat Nagar, Gandhidham, Gujarat, India 370 201, *Tel:* +91 2836 237 209, *Fax:* +91 2836 237 211, *Email:* info@laxmimarine.com, *Website:* www.laxmimarine.com
Link Enterprises, Plot 44, Sector 9/A, Morabia Commercial Centre, P O Box 248, Gandhidham, Gujarat, India 370 201, *Tel:* +91 2836 230 107, *Fax:* +91 2836 231 285, *Email:* info@asiaship.com
Mithi Overseas Private Ltd, Plot No.265/12-B, Bajaj Chambers, Near Shiv Cinema, Gandhidham, Gujarat, India 370 201, *Tel:* +91 2836 235417, *Fax:* +91 2836 235417, *Email:* mithioverseas@yahoo.com
Umamarine, Sector 1/A, Plot No 310, Gandhidham, Gujarat, India 370 201, *Tel:* +91 2836 221465, *Fax:* +91 2836 232830, *Email:* info@umamarine.com, *Website:* www.umamarine.com

Towage: Required

Medical Facilities: Available at Jamnagar

Airport: Jamnagar, 25 km

Railway: Jamnagar Station, 40 km

Lloyd's Agent: Wilson Surveyors and Adjusters Private Ltd, Golden Arcade, II Floor, Room No.209, Plot No.141/142, Sector 8, Gandhidam, Kutch, Gujarat, India 370 201, *Tel:* +91 2836 238333, *Fax:* +91 2836 238333, *Email:* kandla@wilsur.com, *Website:* www.wilsur.com

THALASSERY

Lat 11° 45' N; Long 75° 28' E.

Admiralty Chart: 1564/1565   **Admiralty Pilot:** 38
Time Zone: GMT +5.5 h   **UNCTAD Locode:** IN TEL

Principal Facilities:

			G						

Authority: The Port Officer, P O Box 1108, Port Office, Beach Road, Kozhikode, Kerala, India 673 015, *Tel:* +91 495 241 4863, *Fax:* +91 495 241 4863

Weather: Uncertain May to September

Tides: ST rise 1.52 m, NT 0.99 m

Working Hours: 1000-1700

Accommodation:

Name	Remarks
Thalacherry	Open roadstead. Anchorage in 9 m, soft mud, about 2.4 km from shore

Storage: Two godowns of 150 m2

Railway: Talassery Railway Station, 1 km

Lloyd's Agent: Peirce Leslie India Ltd, Peirce Leslie Surveyours and Assessors Ltd., Bristow Road, Willingdon Island, Kochi, Kerala, India 682 003, *Tel:* +91 484 266 8362, *Fax:* +91 484 266 8394, *Email:* plsacok@sify.com, *Website:* www.plsurvey.in

TUTICORIN

see under New Tuticorin

VADINAR TERMINAL

Lat 22° 30' N; Long 69° 42' E.

Admiralty Chart: 699   **Admiralty Pilot:** 38
Time Zone: GMT +5.5 h   **UNCTAD Locode:** IN VAD

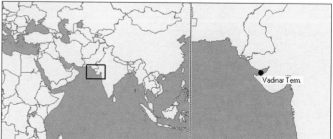

Principal Facilities:

P							T	A

Authority: Kandla Port Trust, Offshore Oil Terminal, Vadinar, Jamnagar, Gujarat, India 361 010, *Tel:* +91 2833 256749, *Fax:* +91 2833 256540, *Email:* com@kandlaport.com, *Website:* www.kandlaport.gov.in

Officials: Operations Manager: Dr G. S. Rao.

Documentation: Stores list (6 copies), crew list (6 copies), personal property declaration (6 copies), last port clearance, cargo manifest, bills of lading, light dues receipt

Approach: Deep water channel from off Port Okha to Vadinar well marked by light buoys in min depth of 23 m

Anchorage: Tankers normally anchor 2.5 to 3 miles NNW from SBM's in a depth of 35 m

Pilotage: Compulsory. Pilot boards in pos 22° 33' N; 69° 38' E. VHF Channels 12 and 16. Master to confirm in advance to Port Authorities and Agents: Vessel has on board cargo or cargo plus ballast equal to at least 70% of summer dwt; vessel has copy of Gulf of Kutch charts; all navigational equipment is in good working order

Tides: Range of tide 3 m to 4 m

Traffic: 2005/06, 20 490 000 t of crude oil handled

Accommodation:

Name	Length (m)	Draught (m)	Remarks
Vadinar Terminal			
SBM's		22	See [1] below
Product Jetty	150		See [2] below

[1]*SBM's:* Three SBM's capable of berthing VLCC's up to 300 000 dwt. Crude oil discharged through submarine pipelines to shore
[2]*Product Jetty:* Approx 5 km from the mooring buoys for berthing of tugs, barges, launches etc

Storage: Ten storage tanks of 75 000 kl cap each

Mechanical Handling Equipment:

Location	Type	Capacity (t)	Qty
Product Jetty	Mobile Cranes	3	1

Towage: One tug of 40 t bollard pull is available

Airport: Jamnagar, 55 km

Railway: Jamnagar, 70 km

Lloyd's Agent: Wilson Surveyors and Adjusters Private Ltd, Golden Arcade, II Floor, Room No.209, Plot No.141/142, Sector 8, Gandhidam, Kutch, Gujarat, India 370 201, *Tel:* +91 2836 238333, *Fax:* +91 2836 238333, *Email:* kandla@wilsur.com, *Website:* www.wilsur.com

VERAVAL

Lat 20° 54' N; Long 70° 22' E.

Admiralty Chart: 3460	**Admiralty Pilot:** 38
Time Zone: GMT +5.5 h	**UNCTAD Locode:** IN VVA

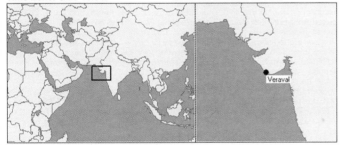

Principal Facilities:

		Y	G				T	A

Authority: Gujarat Maritime Board, Port of Veraval, Bundar Road, Veraval, Gujarat, India 362 265, *Tel:* +91 2876 220001, *Fax:* +91 2876 243138, *Email:* povrl@sancharnet.in, *Website:* www.gmbports.org

Officials: Port Officer: Rajeshkumar N. Damor.

Approach: Veraval Light, exhibited on coast, height 33.5 m, 15 second flash timing; range of visibility 26 miles

Radio Frequency: VHF Channels 11, 12, 13 and 14 for communication between ship and shore

Tides: 2.1 m MHWS, 1.8 m MHWN, 1.1 m MLWS, 0.56 MLWN

Maximum Vessel Dimensions: 203 m loa, 9.5 m draft, 23 339 gt

Principal Imports and Exports: Imports: Coal & coke, Fertilizers, Food grains, Pig iron, Wood pulp. Exports: Cement, Fish, Lime powder, Limestone, Oil cakes, Onions, Soda ash.

Working Hours: 0800-1200, 1300-1700, 1800-2200, 2300-0300

Accommodation:

Name	Remarks
Veraval	See [1] below

[1]*Veraval:* Open roadstead. Fair weather intermediate anchorage port, closed to shipping during monsoon period May 15 to September 15. Anchorage is 2 km from port in depths up to 14.07 m and handling vessels up to 35 000 t. Vessels load and discharge by barges working to the two deepwater basins inside the port with six wharf walls of 22.05 m and loading ramps for the barges. Direct berthing facility for barges up to 3000 dwt. There is a separate fishing harbour. Port linked with the National Rail system

Storage:

Location	Open (m²)	Covered (m²)
Veraval	33305	16746

Mechanical Handling Equipment:

Location	Type	Capacity (t)	Qty
Veraval	Mult-purp. Cranes	12.5–16	1
Veraval	Mobile Cranes	12	3

Towage: Four tugs available of 218-414 bhp

Repair & Maintenance: Minor repairs only

Shipping Agents: J.M. Baxi & Co, Bunder Road, Veraval, Gujarat, India 362 265, *Tel:* +91 2876 221954, *Email:* veraval@jmbaxi.com, *Website:* www.jmbaxi.com
CSAV Group Agencies (India) Pvt Ltd, Bungalow 3, opposite Rameshwar, Kamnath Society Bhalpara Road, Gujrat, Veraval, Gujarat, India, *Tel:* +91 2876 233188/232952, *Fax:* +91 2876 233199, *Email:* ssarveypalli@csavagencies-india.com
Samsara Shipping (Private) Ltd, Office No.111, 1st Floor, Rameshwar Building, Prabhas Patan Road, City Survey Block 'G', Survey No.29, Veraval, Gujarat, India, *Tel:* +91 2876 645264, *Email:* samsveraval@samsarashipping.com, *Website:* www.samsarashipping.com

Surveyors: J.B. Boda Surveyors Private Ltd, Nilkanth Complex, 2nd Floor Nava Patel Wada, Satta Bazar, Veraval, Gujarat, India 362 265, *Tel:* +91 2876 221759, *Fax:* +91 2876 242003, *Email:* jbbvrl@jbbodamail.com, *Website:* www.jbboda.net

Medical Facilities: Municipal hospital and private practitioners

Airport: Keshod, 45 km

Lloyd's Agent: Wilson Surveyors and Adjusters Private Ltd, Golden Arcade, II Floor, Room No.209, Plot No.141/142, Sector 8, Gandhidam, Kutch, Gujarat, India 370 201, *Tel:* +91 2836 238333, *Fax:* +91 2836 238333, *Email:* kandla@wilsur.com, *Website:* www.wilsur.com

VISAKHAPATNAM

Lat 17° 42' N; Long 83° 18' E.

Admiralty Chart: 239	**Admiralty Pilot:** 21
Time Zone: GMT +5.5 h	**UNCTAD Locode:** IN VTZ

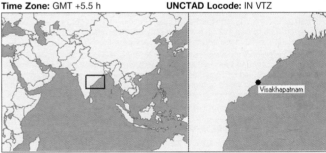

Principal Facilities:

P	Q	Y	G	C			B	D	T	A

Authority: Visakhapatnam Port Trust, Port Diagonal Road, Harbour Approach, Visakhapatnam, Andhira Pradesh, India 530 035, *Tel:* +91 891 256 4841/7, *Fax:* +91 891 256 5023, *Email:* info@vizagport.com, *Website:* www.vizagport.com

Officials: Chairman: K Rathna Kishore, *Tel:* +91 891 256 2758.
Deputy Chairman: Sri J Mohana Rao.
Company Secretary: D Naresh Kumar.
Deputy Conservator: Capt S. S. Tripathi.
Operations Manager: M Ragiya.
Shipping Manager: K. S.D. Dathu Raju.
Accounts: K V Gupta.
Harbour Master: Capt S. Mathur.

Port Security: ISPS compliant

Key to Principal Facilities:—			
A=Airport	**C**=Containers	**G**=General Cargo	**P**=Petroleum	**R**=Ro/Ro	**Y**=Dry Bulk
B=Bunkers	**D**=Dry Dock	**L**=Cruise	**Q**=Other Liquid Bulk	**T**=Towage (where available from port)

BUNKER SUPPLIERS

41-1-35 Rangainaidu Street,
Kakinada, 533007, (A.P.)
INDIA

TEL: +91-884-2366717 / 2366718
FAX: +91-884-2366716
EMAIL: adioil@rediffmail.com / adifuels@rediffmail.com
RAMBABU   Mobile: +91 9848257582

We can service at Visakhapatnam & Kakinada Ports. (A.P) India

Documentation: Crew list (8 copies), passenger list (8 copies), stowaways (8 copies), personal effects list (3 copies), stores list (3 copies), arms & ammunition list (3 copies), health documents or certificates (1 copy), certificate of deratting (1 copy), load line certificate (1 copy), ship's register (1 copy), certificate of nationality (1 copy), safety equipment certificate (1 copy), cargo gear certificate (1 copy), bill of ladings (2 copies), manifests (2 copies), clearance from last port (1 copy)

Approach: The port is entered between two detached breakwaters leaving a 240 m wide and 16.5 m deep entrance. The maritime traffic within the harbour limits is controlled from two co-operating signal stations: No.1 signal station at the middle of the East Breakwater and No.2 signal station on Ross Hill on the N side of the entrance to the inner harbour

Anchorage: Waiting vessels should anchor 1.5 miles E of Dolphin's Nose Lighthouse in depth of 22 m. Anchors should be buoyed. Pilotage is compulsory. Minimum of two tugs will assist vessels and in the case of iron ore vessels, three/four tugs are used for berthing at Outer Harbour. Ship's with loa up to 195 m, beam of 30.48 m and draft up to 9.14 m can be berthed in Inner Harbour at all stages of tide and ship's draft up to 10.06 m and 193.55 m loa are allowed on a minimum rising tide of 0.91 m. Vessels up to 183 m loa and 9.16 m draft are permitted during night periods

Pilotage: Compulsory for vessels over 100 gt entering, leaving or shifting berth in the harbour. Pilots board vessels in the anchorage approx 5 cables SE of the entrance. The pilot ladder should be rigged on the starboard side. Pilots are ordered from the Deputy Conservator, Visakhapatnam Port Trust, Tel: +91 891 256 5042 or VHF Channel 16 (Port Control)

Radio Frequency: Port Control on VHF Channel 16

Weather: Heavy rainfall is experienced during the SW monsoon (July/August) and the NE monsoon (October/November)

Tides: 1.5 m MHWS, 1.1 m MHWN, 0.6 m MLWN

Traffic: 2007/08, 64 597 000 t of cargo handled, 71 000 TEU's

Maximum Vessel Dimensions: Outer Harbour: 150 000 dwt, 280 m loa, 50 m beam, 17-17.3 m draft. Inner Harbour: 40 000 dwt, 225 m loa, 9.14-10.7 m draft

Principal Imports and Exports: Imports: Coal, Edible oil, Fertilizers, Limestone, Liquid ammonia, Petroleum, Petroleum products, Phosphoric acid, Zinc concentrates. Exports: Chrome ore, Iron ore, Manganese ore, Steel products.

Working Hours: Around the clock. Three shifts 0630-1430, 1500-2130, 2200-0430

Accommodation: Fisheries Harbour with protected water basin of 24 ha with a draft of 7.5 m and quay length of 1624 m caters for 56 trawlers and 300 mechanised boats

Name	Length (m)	Draught (m)	Remarks
Inner Harbour			
East Quay 1	167.6	10.06	See [1] below
East Quay 2	167.6	10.06	See [2] below
East Quay 3	167.6	10.06	See [3] below
East Quay 4	231	10.06	See [4] below
East Quay 5	167.6	10.06	See [5] below
East Quay 6	182.9	10.21	See [6] below
East Quay 7	255	10.21	Loading/unloading of all cargoes
East Quay 8	255	10.21	
East Quay 9	255	10.21	
West Quay 1	212	10.21	See [7] below
West Quay 2	226.7	10.21	See [8] below
West Quay 3	201.1	10.21	See [9] below
West Quay 4	243	10.21	
West Quay 5	241.7	10.21	See [10] below
Fertiliser Berth	173.1	10.06	See [11] below
RE WQ-1	170	8	
Oil Refinery Berth 1	183	10.06	See [12] below
Oil Refinery Berth 2	183	9.75	See [13] below
Outer Harbour			
Oil Berth 1	270	16.5	Loading of iron ore
Oil Berth 2	270	16.5	Loading of iron ore
Oil Mooring	250	15	See [14] below
Container Terminal	449	14.9	See [15] below

Name	Length (m)	Draught (m)	Remarks
General Cargo Berth	356	14.5	General cargo & bulk coking coal
Offshore Tanker Terminal	408	17	Crude handled by pipeline
LPG Berth	370.9	13	

[1]*East Quay 1:* Priority for manganese & other ores. Ore is brought alongside vessels in dumpers loaded by shore cranes with net slings

[2]*East Quay 2:* Fertilisers & general cargo. Served by BG lines on either side. Shore cranes available

[3]*East Quay 3:* Priority for foodgrains & general cargo. Served by BG lines on either side. Shore cranes available

[4]*East Quay 4:* General cargo, heavy lifts, iron & steel and fertilisers. Alongside transit shed attached. Served by BG lines on either side. Shore cranes available

[5]*East Quay 5:* Sulphur, rock phosphate & iron and steel. Adjacent open area for stacking. Opposite this berth is a shed with all sides open available. Shore cranes available

[6]*East Quay 6:* General cargo & fertilisers. Alongside transit shed attached. Served by BG lines on either side. Shore cranes available

[7]*West Quay 1:* Edible oil & general cargo. Priority for coking coal. Adjacent open area used for stacking bulk cargoes

[8]*West Quay 2:* General cargo. Priority for coking coal. Adjacent open area served by BG lines on either side

[9]*West Quay 3:* Priority for coking coal. Adjacent open area served by BG lines for coking coal. No shore cranes

[10]*West Quay 5:* Thermal coal, alumina & caustic soda. Adjacent open area with single BG line. No shore cranes. NALCO installed conveyor for loading alumina

[11]*Fertiliser Berth:* Sulphur & rock phosphate. Discharged by grab into hopper and conveyed into a silo by conveyor belt. Fertiliser discharge is also allowed subject to berth availability

[12]*Oil Refinery Berth 1:* Import of crude oil and export of petroleum products & bunkering. Bunkers and oil are handled by pipeline. LPG vessels also handled

[13]*Oil Refinery Berth 2:* Import of crude oil and export of petroleum products & bunkering. Bunkers and oil are handled by pipeline

[14]*Oil Mooring:* Transhipment of POL mainly from bigger to smaller tankers

[15]*Container Terminal:* Operated by Visakha Container Terminal Pvt. Ltd., Manganese House, 1st Floor, Harbour Road, Visakhapatnam 530 001, Tel: +91 891 250 2164, Fax: +91 891 272 1981, Email: sm@vctpl.com, Website: www.vctpl.com

Storage: Ample open storage space available. There are five transit sheds alongside the quay wall totalling 30 959 m2 with 52 600 t cargo cap. Iron ore storage area of 85 000 m2. Limited refrigerated storage available

Mechanical Handling Equipment:

Location	Type	Capacity (t)	Qty
Visakhapatnam	Floating Cranes		2
Visakhapatnam	Mobile Cranes	100	2
Visakhapatnam	RTG's	42	2
Visakhapatnam	Electric Cranes	10–20	23
Visakhapatnam	Forklifts	3–12	15

Cargo Worked: Iron ore 2500 t/h, fertilisers 1500 t/h, rock phosphate and sulphur 2700-3000 t/day, steel cargoes 1500-1700 t/day

Bunkering: Coal available
Aditya Marine M/S, 41-1-35, Nagaratnam Building Upstairs, Rangainaidu Street, Kakinada, Andhra Pradesh, India 533 007, *Tel:* +91 884 236 6717, *Fax:* +91 884 236 6716, *Email:* adioil@rediffmail.com
Asean International Ltd, P O Box 7860, Block Z Suite 42/43, Saif Zone, Sharjah, United Arab Emirates, *Tel:* +971 6 557 0083, *Fax:* +971 6 557 0085
Bharat Petroleum Corp. Ltd, 4th Floor, Old Admin Building, Mahul, Chembur, Mumbai, Maharashtra, India 400 074, *Tel:* +91 22 2554 3493, *Fax:* +91 22 2554 0621, *Email:* josecm@bharatpetroleum.in, *Website:* www.baratpetroleum.in
Bominflot, Bominoil Private Ltd, 504 Maker Chambers V, 221 Nariman Point, Mumbai, Maharashtra, India 400 021, *Tel:* +91 22 2281 7133, *Fax:* +91 22 2281 7145, *Email:* bominoil@vsnl.com, *Website:* www.bominflot.net
Cockett Marine Oil Ltd, Carrick House, 36 Station Square, Petts Wood, Kent BR5 1NA, United Kingdom, *Tel:* +44 1689 883 400, *Fax:* +44 1689 877 666, *Email:* enquiries@cockett.com, *Website:* www.cockettgroup.com – *Grades:* IFO; MDO; MGO – *Parcel Size:* min IFO 50t, min MDO/MGO 10t – *Delivery Mode:* barge, road tank wagon, pipeline
M/S Global Fuels & Lubricants Inc., 11-12 Mangal Society, 76C Rafi Ahmed Kidwai Road, King Circle, Mumbai, Maharashtra, India 400 019, *Tel:* +91 22 2374 5987, *Fax:* +91 22 2409 1627, *Email:* globalfuels@vsnl.com, *Website:* www.bunkerindia.com

Waste Reception Facilities: Garbage removal on request with 72 h notice

Towage: Several tugs operate in the harbour. A minimum of two tugs assist vessels and in the case of iron ore vessels three or four are used for berthing at Outer Harbour

Repair & Maintenance: The port also has a dry dock with 137.2 m in length, 18.4 m in breadth and 5.6 m in depth for port craft and small ships. Repairs can be effected by a number of local companies
Hindustan Shipyard Ltd, Gandhigram, Visakhapatnam, Andhira Pradesh, India 530 005, *Tel:* +91 891 257 8450, *Fax:* +91 891 257 7502, *Email:* hsl@hslvizag.com, *Website:* www.hsl.nic.in Dry dock of 244 m x 38 m x 11 m, max cap 70 000 dwt. Repair quays in Wet Basin, lengths 226 m and 168 m with max draught 10 m
Sri Venkateswara Engineering, 9-19-23/2 Kameshwara Nilayam, C.M.B. Compound, Visakhapatnam, Andhira Pradesh, India 530 003, *Tel:* +91 891 664 9618, *Fax:* +91 891 664 9618, *Email:* srivenengg@gmail.com

Ship Chandlers: Admiral Marine Services Private Ltd, 23-35-1 Plot No.203A, Marine Enclave, Main Road, Visakhapatnam, Andhira Pradesh, India 530 001, *Tel:* +91 891 256 6735, *Fax:* +91 891 256 2325, *Email:* enquiries@admiralmarine.com, *Website:* www.admiralmarine.com
Chennai Marine Trading Private Ltd, Door No. 43-8-2/2, T.S.N. Colony, Opposite Kamala Nehru School, Visakhapatnam, Andhira Pradesh, India 530 016, *Tel:* +91 891 274 5691, *Fax:* +91 891 274 5479, *Email:* chennaimarine@vsnl.net
Dolphin Safety Services, 26-8-66, Raja Ram Mahon Roy Road, Visakhapatnam, Andhira Pradesh, India 530 001, *Tel:* +91 891 256 8941, *Fax:* +91 891 252 6406, *Email:* dssvizag@yahoo.com
Maritime Overseas Corp., 26-8-119 Raja Rammohan Roy Road, Visakhapatnam,

Andhira Pradesh, India 530001, *Tel:* +91 891 255 6140, *Fax:* +91 891 256 3601, *Email:* eccvizag@hotmail.com
Mohsin Brothers (Division of Mohsin Enterprises (Private) Ltd), Harbour Road, Visakhapatnam, Andhira Pradesh, India 530 001, *Tel:* +91 891 256 7700, *Fax:* +91 891 256 1448, *Email:* mohsinbrothers@iqara.net, *Website:* www.mohsingroup.com
A.S. Moloobhoy & Sons, New Anchor House, Door No.24-4-8, Harbour Approach Road, Visakhapatnam, Andhira Pradesh, India 530 001, *Tel:* +91 891 256 6590, *Fax:* +91 891 256 8416, *Email:* vizag@asmoloobhoy.com, *Website:* www.asmoloobhoy.com
Sri Sai Marine Supplier, Sri Sai Marine Supplier & Chandling, Plot No.114, Sector-4, Visakhapatnam, Andhira Pradesh, India 530017, *Tel:* +91 891 255 2980, *Fax:* +91 891 255 2980, *Email:* psvathi@sancharnet.in, *Website:* www.saimarine.com

Shipping Agents: Esskay Shipping (P) Ltd, Esskay House, Door No.25-40-40, Gagulavari Street, Visakhapatnam, Andhira Pradesh, India 530 001, *Tel:* +91 891 256 8403, *Fax:* +91 891 256 5133, *Email:* info@esskayshipping.com, *Website:* www.esskayshipping.com Vice President: G.V.V.S.N Varma Mobile Tel: +91 9848097004
Aspinwall & Co. Ltd, 201 Venu Regency Plaza, Waltair Main Road, Visakhapatnam, Andhira Pradesh, India 530 003, *Tel:* +91 891 256 8287, *Fax:* +91 891 556 6367, *Email:* vhp.mng@aspinwallgroup.com, *Website:* www.aspinwallgroup.com
J.M. Baxi & Co, Manganese House - 1st Floor, Harbour Road, Visakhapatnam, Andhira Pradesh, India 530 001, *Tel:* +91 891 250 2840, *Fax:* +91 891 256 1416, *Email:* vizag@jmbaxi.com, *Website:* www.jmbaxi.com
E.C. Bose & Co., Thompson Street, Visakhapatnam, Andhira Pradesh, India 520 001, *Tel:* +91 891 256 5849, *Fax:* +91 891 256 9164, *Website:* ecboseplc.com
Bothra Group Companies, 28-2-47 Daspalla Centre, 1st Floor, Suryabagh, Visakhapatnam, Andhira Pradesh, India 530 020, *Tel:* +91 891 256 9208, *Fax:* +91 891 256 9326, *Email:* info@bothragroup.com, *Website:* www.bothragroup.com
Chakiat Agencies Private Ltd, Door No: 11-9-43/1, Plot No: MIG 43, Dasapalla Hills, Visakhapatnam, Andhira Pradesh, India 530 003, *Tel:* +91 891 270 6601, *Fax:* +91 891 256 2735, *Email:* chakiatvsh@sify.com, *Website:* www.chakiat.co.in
Everett (India) Private Ltd, F-9, Marine Towers, 25-9-14/12, Rajavari Street, Visakhapatnam, Andhira Pradesh, India 530 001, *Tel:* +91 891 252 5650, *Fax:* +91 891 256 6676, *Email:* mgreddy@everett.co.in, *Website:* www.everett.co.in
Forbes Patvolk (A Division of Forbes Gokak Ltd), 7-8-22/2 (5), Harbour Park Road, Amulya Enclave, 2nd Floor, Visakhapatnam, Andhira Pradesh, India 530020, *Tel:* +91 891 256 6362, *Fax:* +91 891 256 6384, *Email:* kv@forbespatvolk.com, *Website:* www.forbespatvolk.com
GAC Shipping (India) Pvt Ltd, 101 & 102 Marine Enclave, Ground Floor, 23-25-1 Main Road, Visakhapatnam, Andhira Pradesh, India 530 001, *Tel:* +91 891 273 7701, *Fax:* +91 891 273 7688, *Email:* vizag@gacworld.com, *Website:* www.gacworld.com
G.R. Enterprises, Daspalla Hills No.3, Visakhapatnam, Andhira Pradesh, India, *Tel:* +91 891 256 1192, *Fax:* +91 891 256 6489, *Email:* grevizag@yahoo.com
Interocean Shipping (India) Pvt Ltd., IV/1 Sunrise Apartments, Beach Road, Pandu Ranga Puram, Visakhapatnam, Andhira Pradesh, India 530 003, *Tel:* +91 891 252 6747, *Fax:* +91 891 252 6748, *Email:* vizag@interoceangroup.com, *Website:* www.interoceangroup.com
K. Ramabrahmam & Sons Private Ltd, Port Area, Harbour Approach Road, Visakhapatnam, Andhira Pradesh, India 530035, *Tel:* +91 891 256 3011, *Fax:* +91 891 256 5975, *Email:* krsvizag@sify.com
K.V. Unni Krishnan Roy & Chatterjee Co. Private Ltd, Roychatt Building, 25-12-36 Godeyvari Street, Andhra Pradesh, Visakhapatnam, Andhira Pradesh, India 530 001, *Tel:* +91 891 250 8323, *Fax:* +91 891 252 5881, *Email:* roynchatt@yahoo.com, *Website:* www.roynchatt.com
K.V. Unni Krishnan Roy & Chatterjee Co. Private Ltd, Roychatt Building, 25-12-36 Godeyvari Street, Andhra Pradesh, Visakhapatnam, Andhira Pradesh, India 530 001, *Tel:* +91 891 250 4860, *Fax:* +91 891 252 5881, *Email:* roynchatt@yahoo.com, *Website:* www.roynchatt.com
K.V. Unni Krishnan Roy & Chatterjee Co. Private Ltd, Roychatt Building, 25-12-36 Godeyvari Street, Andhra Pradesh, Visakhapatnam, Andhira Pradesh, India 530 001, *Tel:* +91 891 250 8323, *Fax:* +91 891 252 5881, *Email:* oper@roynchatt.com, *Website:* www.roynchatt.com
K.V. Unni Krishnan Roy & Chatterjee Co. Private Ltd, Roychatt Building, 25-12-36 Godeyvari Street, Andhra Pradesh, Visakhapatnam, Andhira Pradesh, India 530 001, *Tel:* +91 891 250 4860, *Fax:* +91 891 252 5881, *Email:* oper@roynchatt.com, *Website:* www.roynchatt.com
Merchant Shipping Services Private Ltd, 30-15-190, 3rd Floor, Founta Plaza, Daba Gardens, Visakhapatnam, Andhira Pradesh, India 530020, *Tel:* +91 891 252 5805, *Fax:* +91 891 252 5743, *Email:* mersvizag@merchantshpg.com, *Website:* www.merchantshpg.com
Monship Agency Services, Marine Towers, Block 2, 25-9-14/9 Godavari Ward, Andhra Pradesh, Visakhapatnam, Andhira Pradesh, India 530001, *Tel:* +91 891 256 6994, *Fax:* +91 891 256 0037, *Email:* monship@bsnl.in, *Website:* www.monson.com.au
Riteways Private. Ltd, Port View, Andhra Pradesh, Visakhapatnam, Andhira Pradesh, India 530035, *Tel:* +91 891 256 3011, *Fax:* +91 891 256 5975, *Email:* krsons@vsnl.com, *Website:* www.krsons.com
Samsara Shipping (Private) Ltd, Founta Plaza, 30-15-190, 3rd Floor, Daba Garden, Visakhapatnam, Andhira Pradesh, India 530 020, *Tel:* +91 891 252 5805, *Fax:* +91 891 252 5743, *Email:* samsvizag@samsarashipping.com, *Website:* www.samsarashipping.com
Seatrans Marine Private Limited, 2nd Floor, D. No.25-12-7/1, Godevari Street, Shri Dhana Lakshmi Arcade, Visakhapatnam, Andhira Pradesh, India 530 001, *Email:* seatrans@seatrans.co.in, *Website:* www.seatrans.co.in
Tata NYK Transport Systems Ltd, 2nd & 3rd Floors, Fatima Building, 23-13-28 Thompson Street, Visakhapatnam, Andhira Pradesh, India 530001, *Tel:* +91 891 250 2626, *Fax:* +91 891 256 0578

Stevedoring Companies: Balailal Mukherjee, Balailal Mookerjee & Co Pvt Ltd, 22-31-21 Mookerjee House Vision, Beach Road, Andhra Pradesh, Visakhapatnam, Andhira Pradesh, India 530001, *Tel:* +91 891 256 3026, *Fax:* +91 891 256 2716, *Email:* vizag@balailal.com
H.K. Banerjee & Co., 10-1-33 Waltair Uplands, Visakhapatnam, Andhira Pradesh, India, *Tel:* +91 891 257 7106
E.C. Bose & Co., Thompson Street, Visakhapatnam, Andhira Pradesh, India 520 001, *Tel:* +91 891 256 5849, *Fax:* +91 891 256 9164, *Website:* ecboseplc.com
Esskay Shipping (P) Ltd, Esskay House, Door No.25-40-40, Gagulavari Street, Visakhapatnam, Andhira Pradesh, India 530 001, *Tel:* +91 891 256 8403, *Fax:* +91 891 256 5133, *Email:* info@esskayshipping.com, *Website:* www.esskayshipping.com
G.R. Enterprises, Daspalla Hills No.3, Visakhapatnam, Andhira Pradesh, India, *Tel:* +91 891 256 1192, *Fax:* +91 891 256 6489, *Email:* grevizag@yahoo.com
K.V. Unni Krishnan Roy & Chatterjee Co. Private Ltd, Roychatt Building, 25-12-36 Godeyvari Street, Andhra Pradesh, Visakhapatnam, Andhira Pradesh, India 530 001, *Tel:* +91 891 250 4860, *Fax:* +91 891 252 5881, *Email:* roynchatt@yahoo.com, *Website:* www.roynchatt.com
K.V. Unni Krishnan Roy & Chatterjee Co. Private Ltd, Roychatt Building, 25-12-36 Godeyvari Street, Andhra Pradesh, Visakhapatnam, Andhira Pradesh, India 530 001, *Tel:* +91 891 250 8323, *Fax:* +91 891 252 5881, *Email:* oper@roynchatt.com, *Website:* www.roynchatt.com
K.V. Unni Krishnan Roy & Chatterjee Co. Private Ltd, Roychatt Building, 25-12-36 Godeyvari Street, Andhra Pradesh, Visakhapatnam, Andhira Pradesh, India 530 001, *Tel:* +91 891 250 8323, *Fax:* +91 891 252 5881, *Email:* roynchatt@yahoo.com, *Website:* www.roynchatt.com
K.V. Unni Krishnan Roy & Chatterjee Co. Private Ltd, Roychatt Building, 25-12-36 Godeyvari Street, Andhra Pradesh, Visakhapatnam, Andhira Pradesh, India 530 001, *Tel:* +91 891 250 4860, *Fax:* +91 891 252 5881, *Email:* oper@roynchatt.com, *Website:* www.roynchatt.com
Prathyusha Associates, 25-40-12, Gangulvan Street, Near Lakshmi Talkies, Andhra Pradesh, Visakhapatnam, Andhira Pradesh, India 530 001, *Tel:* +91 891 254 9788, *Fax:* +91 891 254 9095, *Email:* prathyushag@eth.net, *Website:* www.prathyushagroup.com
Rao & Reddy, 23-23-2 Beach Road, Visakhapatnam, Andhira Pradesh, India 530 001, *Tel:* +91 891 256 5310, *Fax:* +91 891 256 0077, *Email:* vdrandco@sancharnet.in
Riteways Private. Ltd, Port View, Andhra Pradesh, Visakhapatnam, Andhira Pradesh, India 530035, *Tel:* +91 891 256 3011, *Fax:* +91 891 256 5975, *Email:* krsons@vsnl.com, *Website:* www.krsons.com
Seaways Shipping Ltd, Door 10-1-31, 3 Floor, Signature Tower, CBM Compound, Andhra Pradesh, Visakhapatnam, Andhira Pradesh, India 530 003, *Tel:* +91 891 256 1538, *Fax:* +91 891 256 0579, *Email:* vizag@seawaysindia.com, *Website:* www.seawaysindia.com
South India Corp. (Agencies) Ltd, Sical Logistics Limited, Marine Towers 1, P O Box 18, 25-9-14 Rajavari Street, Visakhapatnam, Andhira Pradesh, India 530 001, *Tel:* +91 891 256 2446, *Fax:* +91 891 256 0379, *Email:* shpviz@sify.com/shpvizag@sical.com, *Website:* www.sical.com
V. Dhana Reddy & Co., Door number 23-23-2, 2nd Floor Thompson Street, Visakhapatnam, Andhira Pradesh, India 530 001, *Tel:* +91 891 256 5310, *Fax:* +91 891 256 0077, *Email:* vdrandco@sancharnet.in
V.B.C. Exports Ltd, Plot No.23, 24 & 25, Fishing Harbour, Visakhapatnam, Andhira Pradesh, India 530 001, *Tel:* +91 891 255 8950

Surveyors: J.B. Boda Surveyors Private Ltd, Bhagwan Bhavan 26-3-10/2, G.S.N. Sastry Road Near Municipal Stadium, Visakhapatnam, Andhira Pradesh, India 530 001, *Tel:* +91 891 250 2165, *Fax:* +91 891 256 1505, *Email:* jbbvzn@jbbodamail.com, *Website:* www.jbboda.net
Ericson & Richards, Gordon Woodroffe Building, Port Area, Visakhapatnam, Andhira Pradesh, India 530 035, *Tel:* +91 891 250 2688, *Fax:* +91 891 256 7285, *Email:* vizag@ericsonandrichards.com, *Website:* www.ericsonandrichards.com
Indian Register of Shipping, D.No.7-18-1 Kirlampudi Layout, Waltair Uplands, Visakhapatnam, Andhira Pradesh, India 530 017, *Tel:* +91 891 270 4319, *Fax:* +91 891 275 4662, *Email:* vizag@irclass.org, *Website:* www.irclass.org
Metcalfe & Hodgkinson Private Ltd, Visakhapatnam, Andhira Pradesh, India, *Tel:* +91 891 250 8466, *Fax:* +91 891 255 9929, *Email:* visakhapatnam@metcalfeindia.com, *Website:* www.metcalfeindia.com
Peters & Prasad Associates, 25-9-14/17, Marine Towers, Block No.2, Godavari Ward, Visakhapatnam, Andhira Pradesh, India 530 001, *Tel:* +91 891 256 8328, *Fax:* +91 891 256 9381, *Email:* quality@pnpassoc.com
Pinnacle Marine Services Private Ltd, 71-52-10, 1st Floor, K.R. & Sons Building, Opposite Port Main Gate, Visakhapatnam, Andhira Pradesh, India 530 035, *Tel:* +91 891 652 2655, *Fax:* +91 891 256 7820, *Email:* survey@pinnaclemarine.co.in
Sevenseas Services Private Ltd, 25-12-40, Godeyvari Street, Visakhapatnam, Andhira Pradesh, India 530001, *Tel:* +91 891 256 4795, *Fax:* +91 891 253 7252, *Email:* pmr_seveen@hotmail.com
Societe Generale de Surveillance (SGS), SGS (India) Private Ltd, 24-1-30, 1st Floor, Haroon Manzil, Thomson Street, Visakhapatnam, Andhira Pradesh, India 530 000, *Tel:* +91 891 256 6964, *Fax:* +91 891 256 6298, *Website:* www.sgs.com
Wilson & Co. Ltd, Wilson Surveyors and Adjusters Pvt. Ltd, Thompson Street, Visakhapatnam, Andhira Pradesh, India 530001, *Tel:* +91 891 272 5611, *Fax:* +91 891 272 5655, *Email:* vizag@wilsur.com, *Website:* www.wilsur.com

Medical Facilities: Port hospital, approx 6 km

Airport: Visakhapatnam Airport, 14 km

Development: Approval has been given for the construction of three 14 m draught berths at the inner harbour (West Quay 6 for multi-purpose cargo, West Quay 8 for alumina and East Quay 10 for liquid chemicals)

Lloyd's Agent: Wilson Surveyors and Adjusters Private Ltd, Fatima Building 2nd Floor, 23-13-28 Thompson Street, Visakhapatnam, Andhira Pradesh, India 530 001, *Tel:* +91 891 272 5611, *Fax:* +91 891 272 5655, *Email:* vizag@wilsur.com, *Website:* www.wilsur.com

VIZAG

alternate name, see Visakhapatnam

Key to Principal Facilities:—
A=Airport **C**=Containers **G**=General Cargo **P**=Petroleum **R**=Ro/Ro **Y**=Dry Bulk
B=Bunkers **D**=Dry Dock **L**=Cruise **Q**=Other Liquid Bulk **T**=Towage (where available from port)

INDONESIA

AMAMAPARE

Lat 4° 49' S; Long 136° 58' E.

Admiralty Chart: 3527	**Admiralty Pilot:** 35
Time Zone: GMT +9 h	**UNCTAD Locode:** ID AMA

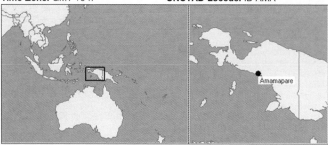

Principal Facilities:

	Y			B		T	A	

Authority: Port of Amamapare, Jalan Pelabuhan, Amamapare, Irian Jaya, Indonesia, *Tel:* +62 967 34018

Port Security: ISPS compliant

Approach: Approach channel is 19 km long in a depth of 7.0 m

Anchorage: Sheltered anchorage can be obtained in the river in depths of 27 m

Pilotage: Available during daytime only

Radio Frequency: VHF Channels 12 and 16

Tides: Range of tide 1.5 m

Maximum Vessel Dimensions: 20 000 dwt, 190 m loa

Working Hours: 0800-1200, 1300-1700

Accommodation:

Name	Length (m)	Depth (m)	Remarks
Amamapare			See [1] below
Jetty	70	11	

[1]*Amamapare:* Amamapare is the port facility for the Freeport Indonesia project. From Amamapare, Freeport Indonesia ships 2.5 million t of copper concentrate each year to smelters around the world. Facilities at the port complex include three 45 000 t concentrate storage barns, a 195 megawatt coal-fired power plant, a cargo dock and other usual port facilities such as Indonesian Customs offices, a dry dock and spillway, marine maintenance facilities, a dormitory for 400 workers, sewerage treatment plant, warehouses, a water plant and a fish purchasing dock

Mechanical Handling Equipment:

Location	Type	Capacity (t)	Qty
Amamapare	Floating Cranes	100	1

Bunkering: Fuel and diesel oil available and supplied by barge at cap of 200 t/day

Towage: Two tugs available of 500 hp

Medical Facilities: Clinic medical centre

Airport: Tamika Airport, 45 km

Lloyd's Agent: P.T. Carsurin, Sarana Penjaminan Building, 7th Floor, Jl Angkasa Block B-9 Kav 6, Kemayoran, Jakarta 10720, Jawa, Indonesia, *Tel:* +62 21 654 0425, *Fax:* +62 21 654 0418, *Email:* lloyds@carsurin.com, *Website:* www.carsurin.com

AMBON

Lat 3° 42' S; Long 128° 10' E.

Admiralty Chart: 2791	**Admiralty Pilot:** 35
Time Zone: GMT +8 h	**UNCTAD Locode:** ID AMQ

Principal Facilities:

P		G	C	R		B		T	A	

Authority: PT (Persero) Pelabuhan Indonesia IV, Port of Ambon, Jalan Yos Sudarso No.1, Ambon 97126, Ambon Island, Indonesia, *Tel:* +62 911 353457

Port Security: ISPS compliant

Documentation: Passenger list (14 copies), crew list (7 copies), custom document (2 copies), health document (2 copies), cargo manifest (7 copies), bills of lading (7 copies), ship's papers (5 copies), sailing permit

Approach: Channel 15 miles long with width 1-4 miles in depth of 20 m. There are no hazards or sand bars

Anchorage: Available in pos 3° 41' 55" S, 128° 10' 25" E in depths of 9-20 m

Pilotage: Compulsory. Request for pilot by calling Ambon Pilot Station on VHF Channel 12

Radio Frequency: VHF Channels 16, 14, 12, 20 and 22

Weather: W winds November-January, E winds May-August

Traffic: 1999, 91 070 t of cargo handled

Maximum Vessel Dimensions: 39 512 dwt, 200 m loa, 9.2 m d

Principal Imports and Exports: Imports: Cement in bags, Spare parts, White rice. Exports: Cocoa beans, Frozen shrimp, Frozen tuna, Nutmeg, Plywood.

Working Hours: Vessel operations 24 h/day

Accommodation:

Name	Length (m)	Depth (m)	Remarks
Ambon			
Yos Soedarso Wharf	451	9–11	Passenger terminal of 800 m2
Siwabessy Wharf	87	9	
Slamet Riyadi Wharf	100	4.5	Two berths available
Private Wharves			See [1] below

[1]*Private Wharves:* Operated by Perum Perikani, 114 m wooden jetty
Maprodin Ltd., 35 m wooden jetty
Lipi Wharf, 40 m wooden jetty
Nusantara Fishery Ltd

Storage:

Location	Covered (m2)
Ambon	3050

Mechanical Handling Equipment:

Location	Type	Capacity (t)	Qty
Ambon	Mobile Cranes	35	1
Ambon	Mobile Cranes	25	1
Ambon	Forklifts	5	8

Bunkering: PT Pertamina, Jalan Jos Sudarso 32-34, P O Box 265, Tanjung Priok, Jawa, Indonesia, *Tel:* +62 21 430 1086, *Fax:* +62 21 430 1562 – *Grades:* DO; MDO; IFO100-300cSt – *Parcel Size:* no min/max – *Rates:* 100-150t/h – *Notice:* 48 hours – *Delivery Mode:* barge, pipeline

Towage: One tug of 800 hp

Repair & Maintenance: PT Dok & Perkapalan Waiame, Jl. Dr. JB. Sitanala Tanah Lapang Kecil, Ambon 97115, Ambon Island, Indonesia, *Tel:* +62 911 341771, *Fax:* +62 911 341730

Shipping Agents: P.T. (PELNI) Pelayaran Nasional Indonesia, Jl DI Panjaitan No.19, Ambon, Ambon Island, Indonesia, *Tel:* +62 911 342328, *Fax:* +62 911 342328, *Email:* agencies@pelni.co.id, *Website:* www.pelni.co.id

Surveyors: P.T. Biro Klasifikasi Indonesia, Jalan Raya Pelabuhan, Pelabuhan Complex, Ambon 97216, Ambon Island, Indonesia, *Tel:* +62 911 355036, *Fax:* +62 911 352745, *Email:* bkiab@klasifikasiindonesia.com, *Website:* www.klasifikasiindonesia.com

Medical Facilities: Harbour Medical Hospital, Tel: +62 (911) 353595

Airport: Pattimura Airport, 7 miles

Lloyd's Agent: P.T. Carsurin, Sarana Penjaminan Building, 7th Floor, Jl Angkasa Block B-9 Kav 6, Kemayoran, Jakarta 10720, Jawa, Indonesia, *Tel:* +62 21 654 0425, *Fax:* +62 21 654 0418, *Email:* lloyds@carsurin.com, *Website:* www.carsurin.com

AMPENAN

alternate name, see Lembar

ANOA TERMINAL

Lat 5° 13' N; Long 105° 36' E.

Admiralty Chart: -	**Admiralty Pilot:** -
Time Zone: GMT +7 h	**UNCTAD Locode:** ID

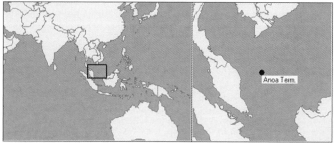

Principal Facilities:

P												

Authority: Premier Oil Natuna Sea BV, Plaza City View, 4th Floor, Jalan Kemang Timur No.22, Jakarta 12510, Jawa, Indonesia, *Tel:* +62 21 718 2001, *Fax:* +62 21 718 2010, *Email:* anoa_pic@premier-oil.com

Officials: Manager: James Chu.
Marine Superintendent: Arif Santoso, *Email:* arifsantoso@premier-oil.com.
Marine Superintendent: A J Nikijuluw, *Email:* jimmynikijuluw@premier-oil.com.

Port Security: ISPS compliant

Anchorage: Located in pos 5° 12' N; 105° 38' E where mooring master boards vessel

Pilotage: Compulsory

Radio Frequency: VHF Channels 16 and 71

Accommodation:

Name	Remarks
Anoa Terminal	See [1] below

[1]*Anoa Terminal:* Consists of FPSO 'Anoa Natuna' which is connected by pipeline to a production platform situated 1 nautical mile NW of the FPSO. The FPSO can receive vessels from 50 000-160 000 dwt and there is no draft limitation

Lloyd's Agent: P.T. Carsurin, Sarana Penjaminan Building, 7th Floor, Jl Angkasa Block B-9 Kav 6, Kemayoran, Jakarta 10720, Jawa, Indonesia, *Tel:* +62 21 654 0425, *Fax:* +62 21 654 0418, *Email:* lloyds@carsurin.com, *Website:* www.carsurin.com

ARJUNA TERMINAL

Lat 5° 53' S; Long 107° 45' E.

Admiralty Chart: 1066/1653	**Admiralty Pilot:** 36
Time Zone: GMT +7 h	**UNCTAD Locode:** ID AJN

Principal Facilities:

P	Q											

Authority: Atlantic Richfield Indonesia Inc., Landmark Center Tower B, Jl. Jenderal Sudirman Kav. 70A, P O Box 1063, Jakarta 12910, Jawa, Indonesia, *Tel:* +62 21 737474

Pre-Arrival Information: Vessels must provide an arrival letter to Kepulauan Seribu Harbour Administration 2 days before arrival stating:
Name of vessel
Flag
Size/measurement
Principal/general agent
ETA
Last port & next port
Activity plan

Pilotage: Compulsory. Vessels will normally be berthed during daylight hours. Mooring master boards in the anchorage area in pos 5° 50' S; 107° 47' E

Radio Frequency: VHF/FM Radio Telephone: International and marine calling and safety Channel 16, frequency 156.8 mHz

Maximum Vessel Dimensions: 250 000 dwt, 350.2 m loa, 30 m draft

Working Hours: 24 h/day weather permitting

Accommodation:

Name	Length (m)	Depth (m)	Remarks
Arjuna Terminal			
SBM 1 (Storage barge 'Arco Arjuna')	142	40	In pos 5° 54' 15'' S; 107° 44' 22''E
SBM 2 (Export for loading buoy No.2)	260	40	In pos 5° 53' 19'' S; 107° 45' 18''E
SBM 3 (Storage barge 'Cempaka Nusantara')	275	40	In pos 5° 54' 11'' S; 107° 43' 45''E
SBM 4 (Export for loading buoy No.4)	325	40	In pos 5° 53' 29'' S; 107° 43' 20''E
SBM 5 (Storage barge 'Arjuna Sakti')	140	17.2	For LNG vessels up to 42 000 dwt. In pos 5° 53' 10'' S; 107° 44' 13''E
SBM 6 (Export for loading buoy No.6)			In pos 5° 52' 19'' S; 107° 45' 18''E
SBM 7 (Citra Ayu)	325		In pos 5° 46' 02'' S; 107° 04' 14''E
SBM 8		33.5	
SBM 9		33.5	

Cargo Worked: 35 000 bbls/h pumping cap of crude oil

Lloyd's Agent: P.T. Carsurin, Sarana Penjaminan Building, 7th Floor, Jl Angkasa Block B-9 Kav 6, Kemayoran, Jakarta 10720, Jawa, Indonesia, *Tel:* +62 21 654 0425, *Fax:* +62 21 654 0418, *Email:* lloyds@carsurin.com, *Website:* www.carsurin.com

ARUN

alternate name, see Blang Lancang

BAGAN ASAHAN

harbour area, see under Teluk Nibung

BALIKPAPAN

Lat 1° 16' S; Long 116° 49' E.

Admiralty Chart: 2639	**Admiralty Pilot:** 34
Time Zone: GMT +8 h	**UNCTAD Locode:** ID BPN

Principal Facilities:

P	Y	G	C			B		T	A			

Authority: PT (Persero) Pelabuhan Indonesia IV, Port of Balikpapan, Jalan Yos Sudarso No.30, Balikpapan 76101, Borneo, Indonesia, *Tel:* +62 542 531223, *Fax:* +62 542 531227

Port Security: ISPS compliant

Documentation: Passenger list (14 copies), crew list (7 copies), custom document (2 copies), health document (2 copies), cargo manifest (7 copies), bills of lading (7 copies), ship's papers (5 copies), sailing permit

Approach: ETA should be telegraphed 48 h in advance to radio PKN, stating deepest draft requirements etc. Depth at entrance and/or on bar 7.31 m LWST, 10.06 m HWST

Pilotage: Compulsory. Application for sea and harbour pilots made via Balikpapan pilot radio station on VHF channel 12. Pilot boards in pos 1° 21' S; 116° 55' E. Vessels should order at least 4 h prior to arrival

Radio Frequency: VHF Channel 16

Traffic: 1999, 433 178 t of cargo handled

Maximum Vessel Dimensions: 88 034 dwt, 242.9 m loa

Working Hours: Vessel operations 24 h/day

Accommodation: Bulk facilities: coal terminal operated by PT Dermaga Perkasapratama situated on a 33 ha area in Teluk Tebang for vessels of 15 000-80 000 dwt. Length of wharf 235 m and two mooring dolphins 276.5 m apart in depth of 15.0 m LWD. One shiploader, max rate of 2800 t/h

Name	Depth (m)	Remarks
Dry Cargo Berths		
No.6 Jetty	12	Max 35 000 dwt & 213 m loa
No.7 Jetty	12	Max 35 000 dwt & 213 m loa
No.7A Jetty	10	Max 10 000 dwt & 120 m loa
Tanker Berths		
No.1 Wharf	9.5	Max 20 000 dwt & 165 m loa
No.2 Wharf	10	Max 36 000 dwt & 195 m loa
No.3 Wharf	12	Max 20 000 dwt & 165 m loa
No.4 Jetty	12	Max 36 000 dwt & 195 m loa
No.5 Jetty	11	Max 36 000 dwt & 185 m loa
No.5A Jetty (Inner)	5	Max 5000 dwt & 110 m loa
No.5B Jetty (Outer)	13	Max 35 000 dwt & 190 m loa
No.5C Jetty (Outer)	12.6	Max 35 000 dwt & 190 m loa

Storage: Waterfront storage of 3599 m2

Mechanical Handling Equipment:

Location	Type	Capacity (t)	Qty
Balikpapan	Mobile Cranes	25	1
Balikpapan	Mobile Cranes	35	1
Balikpapan	Forklifts	2–5	5

Bunkering: C.V. Bahtera Camar, Jalan Lagoa Terusan Bl No.4, Jakarta 14270, Jawa, Indonesia, *Tel:* +62 21 435 3209, *Fax:* +62 21 430 6048
Buana Jaya C.V., jalan Sungai Kapuas No.15, Jakarta 14270, Jawa, Indonesia, *Tel:* +62 21 44835302, *Fax:* +62 21 44835302
Kartika Jasa Karya P.T., Jalan Perak Timur 564/A1, Surabaya 60165, Jawa, Indonesia, *Tel:* +62 31 3293 459, *Fax:* +62 31 3294 736, *Email:* kemusuk@rad.net.id
PT Pertamina, Jalan Jos Sudarso 32-34, P O Box 265, Tanjung Priok, Jawa, Indonesia, *Tel:* +62 21 430 1086, *Fax:* +62 21 430 1562 – *Grades:* DO; MFO; IFO100-

---

Key to Principal Facilities:—

A=Airport	**C**=Containers	**G**=General Cargo
B=Bunkers	**D**=Dry Dock	**L**=Cruise

P=Petroleum	**R**=Ro/Ro	**Y**=Dry Bulk
Q=Other Liquid Bulk	**T**=Towage (where available from port)	

300cSt – *Misc:* no lubes available – *Parcel Size:* no min/max – *Rates:* 100-150t/h – *Notice:* 48 hours – *Delivery Mode:* barge, pipeline

Towage: Three tugs available up to 2400 hp

Repair & Maintenance: For minor repairs vessels can use the assistance of PT Pertamina

Shipping Agents: P.T. Bahana Utama Line, Balikpapan, Borneo, Indonesia, *Tel:* +62 542 396815, *Fax:* +62 542 419445, *Email:* balikpapan@bahana-line.com, *Website:* www.bahana-line.com

Surveyors: P.T. Biro Klasifikasi Indonesia, Jalan M.T. Haryono No.8, Ring Road, Balikpapan 76114, Borneo, Indonesia, *Tel:* +62 542 876433, *Fax:* +62 542 876645, *Email:* bkibp@klasifikasiindonesia.com, *Website:* www.klasifikasiindonesia.com Nippon Kaiji Kyokai, BRI Building 7th Floor 707, Jl. Jendera Sudirman 37, Balikpapan, Borneo, Indonesia, *Tel:* +62 542 396142, *Fax:* +62 542 396143, *Website:* www.classnk.or.jp

Medical Facilities: Hospital facilities available

Airport: Sepinggan Airport, 12 km

Lloyd's Agent: P.T. Carsurin, Sarana Penjaminan Building, 7th Floor, Jl Angkasa Block B-9 Kav 6, Kemayoran, Jakarta 10720, Jawa, Indonesia, *Tel:* +62 21 654 0425, *Fax:* +62 21 654 0418, *Email:* lloyds@carsurin.com, *Website:* www.carsurin.com

BALONGAN TERMINAL

Lat 6° 16' S; Long 108° 27' E.

Admiralty Chart: 1066/1653A	**Admiralty Pilot:** 36
Time Zone: GMT +7 h	**UNCTAD Locode:** ID BAL

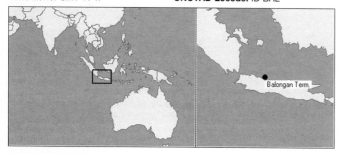

Principal Facilities:

P							T	A

Authority: PN Pertamina PKK UP VI Balongan, Jl. Raya Balongan Indramayu, Balongan, Jawa, Indonesia, *Tel:* +62 234 28232 & 28997, *Fax:* +62 234 28629 & 28183

Approach: Vessels should anchor 3 miles N of lighted buoy to await berthing instructions in pos 6° 13' 13" S, 108° 47' 00" E in depth of 7 m

Pilotage: Compulsory. Request for pilotage to be made 3 h before arrival or departure

Radio Frequency: Balongan Radio Station, call sign PKQ-2. VHF Channel 16

Maximum Vessel Dimensions: Crude oil: 150 000 dwt, 290 m loa, 20 m draft

Principal Imports and Exports: Exports: Crude oil.

Working Hours: Continuous

Accommodation:

Name	Depth (m)	Remarks
Balongan Terminal		
Single Buoy Mooring	22	See [1] below
Conventional Buoy Mooring	9	To accommodate tankers up to 6500 dwt

[1]*Single Buoy Mooring:* For crude oil export to accommodate tankers up to 150 000 dwt and 20 m draft. Pipelines run in a 230° direction from the SBM to the shore at Balongan

Towage: Five tugs available of 1200-3000 hp

Airport: Penggung, 40 km

Lloyd's Agent: P.T. Carsurin, Sarana Penjaminan Building, 7th Floor, Jl Angkasa Block B-9 Kav 6, Kemayoran, Jakarta 10720, Jawa, Indonesia, *Tel:* +62 21 654 0425, *Fax:* +62 21 654 0418, *Email:* lloyds@carsurin.com, *Website:* www.carsurin.com

BANJARMASIN

Lat 3° 20' S; Long 114° 35' E.

Admiralty Chart: 3015	**Admiralty Pilot:** 34
Time Zone: GMT +8 h	**UNCTAD Locode:** ID BDJ

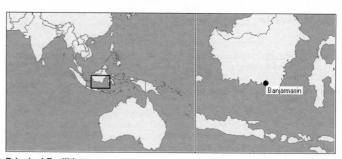

Principal Facilities:

P	Y	G	C		B		T	A

Authority: P.T. (Persero) Pelabuhan Indonesia III, Cabang Banjarmasin, Jl. Barito Hilir No.6, Banjarmasin 70117, Borneo, Indonesia, *Tel:* +62 511 53670, *Fax:* +62 511 52552

Officials: General Manager: H. Hairillah.

Port Security: ISPS compliant

Approach: Depth at bar 3.2 m LWS. A canal named 'Alur Barito' between Martapura/Barito river for outgoing vessels is in operation

Anchorage: The anchorage area is in pos 3° 40' 00" S; 114° 25' 12" E in depth of 14 m

Pilotage: Compulsory and available 24 h. Pilot boards at anchorage area at outer buoy

Radio Frequency: Banjarmasin Coastal Radio Station, call sign PKG, VHF Channel 16. Pilot channel 12

Tides: Lowest 1.6 m LWS. Highest 2.9 m LWS

Traffic: 2002, 746 ocean-going vessels and 7552 inter-island vessels

Principal Imports and Exports: Imports: Chemicals, Spare parts. Exports: Coal, Plywood, Rubber, Sugar.

Working Hours: Mon-Fri 0800-1700

Accommodation:

Name	Length (m)	Depth (m)	Remarks
Banjarmasin			See [1] below
Martapura Baru Harbour	425	5	Used for inter-insular cargoes
Trisakti Harbour	510	9	See [2] below

[1]*Banjarmasin:* Pertamina owns an oil wharf 20 m long provided with a fixed crane of 25 t max cap. Transhipment of coal is by loading from barges to bulk carriers at an anchorage 15 nautical miles off the Barito river entrance channel. Loading is either by ship's gear or by three floating transhipment cranes which can load vessels up to 200 000 dwt at up to 30 000 t/day

[2]*Trisakti Harbour:* Used for import-export cargoes and is situated on the Barito River

Storage:

Location	Open (m²)	Covered (m²)	Sheds / Warehouses
Martapura Baru Harbour	4800	2000	2
Trisakti Harbour	2635	8450	2

Mechanical Handling Equipment: Two gantry cranes of 25 t cap, four forklifts of 2-7 t cap, two super stackers of 40 t cap, two top loaders of 36 t cap and two transtainers

Cargo Worked: Breakbulk cargo (foreign) 15 t/gang/h & 294 t/ship/day, breakbulk cargo (domestic) 20 t/gang/h & 447 t/ship/day, bagged cargo 275 t/ship/day

Bunkering: PT Pertamina, Jalan Jos Sudarso 32-34, P O Box 265, Tanjung Priok, Jawa, Indonesia, *Tel:* +62 21 430 1086, *Fax:* +62 21 430 1562 – *Grades:* DO; MDO; IFO100-300cSt – *Parcel Size:* no min/max – *Rates:* 100-150t/h – *Notice:* 48 hours – *Delivery Mode:* barge, pipeline

Towage: One tug available of 800 hp

Repair & Maintenance: Minor repairs only by workshops

Shipping Agents: P.T. Bahana Utama Line, Jl Yos Sudarso 9F, Kalimantan Selatan, Banjarmasin, Borneo, Indonesia, *Tel:* +62 511 52165, *Fax:* +62 511 67852, *Email:* banjarmasin@bahana-line.com, *Website:* www.bahana-line.com
P.T. Bumi Laut Shipping Corp., Jl Cempaka VIII, 18 RT 09, Banjarmasin 70112, Borneo, Indonesia, *Tel:* +62 511 69938, *Fax:* +62 511 69938
P.T. (PELNI) Pelayaran Nasional Indonesia, Jl Laks RE Martadinata No.10, Banjarmasin, Borneo, Indonesia, *Tel:* +62 511 53077, *Fax:* +62 511 66171, *Email:* agencies@pelni.co.id, *Website:* www.pelni.co.id
PT Perusahaan Pelayaran Samudera Gesuri Lloyd, Jl Mayjen Sutoyo S 178, Banjarmasin, Borneo, Indonesia, *Tel:* +62 511 21434, *Fax:* +62 511 21434
PT Perusahaan Pelayaran Samudera Trikora Lloyd, Jalan RE Martadinata 10, Banjarmasin 70112, Borneo, Indonesia, *Tel:* +62 511 63336, *Fax:* +62 511 66171

Stevedoring Companies: PBM Bamara Surya, Banjarmasin, Borneo, Indonesia, *Tel:* +62 511 52431
PBM Banjar Jaya Samudera, Banjarmasin, Borneo, Indonesia, *Tel:* +62 511 66014
PBM Intan Giri Arta, Banjarmasin, Borneo, Indonesia, *Tel:* +62 511 66072
PBM Karya Berkah Lestari, Banjarmasin, Borneo, Indonesia, *Tel:* +62 511 52384
PBM Lambang Jaya Barito, Banjarmasin, Borneo, Indonesia, *Tel:* +62 511 51741
PBM Putra Jaya Gempita, Banjarmasin, Borneo, Indonesia, *Tel:* +62 511 50047
PBM Sarana Bandar Nasional, Banjarmasin, Borneo, Indonesia, *Tel:* +62 511 53171
PBM Sari Bintang Terang, Banjarmasin, Borneo, Indonesia, *Tel:* +62 511 68034

Surveyors: P.T. Biro Klasifikasi Indonesia, Skip Lama No.19, Banjarmasin 70112, Borneo, Indonesia, *Tel:* +62 511 50175, *Fax:* +62 511 50175, *Email:* bkibj@klasifikasiindonesia.com, *Website:* www.klasifikasiindonesia.com
Nippon Kaiji Kyokai, Banjarmasin, Borneo, Indonesia, *Tel:* +62 511 50175, *Fax:* +62 511 50175, *Website:* www.classnk.or.jp

Medical Facilities: Sari Mulia Hospital, Ulin Hospital, Dr. Suharso Hospital and Suaka Insan Hospital

Airport: Syamsuddin Noor, 26 km

Development: Basirih Terminal with wharf 100 m x 20 m. Basirih Port is being developed to replace the Martapura Port, which is to be used by motor sailing boats New independently operated container terminal to be built S side of Trisakti, 240 m long with 72 000 m2 of container yard

Lloyd's Agent: P.T. Carsurin, Sarana Penjaminan Building, 7th Floor, Jl Angkasa Block B-9 Kav 6, Kemayoran, Jakarta 10720, Jawa, Indonesia, *Tel:* +62 21 654 0425, *Fax:* +62 21 654 0418, *Email:* lloyds@carsurin.com, *Website:* www.carsurin.com

BANTEN

Lat 6° 1' S; Long 105° 58' E.

Admiralty Chart: 918	**Admiralty Pilot:** 36
Time Zone: GMT +7 h	**UNCTAD Locode:** ID BTN

Principal Facilities:

P		Y	G	C				T		

Authority: PT (Persero) Pelabuhan Indonesia II, Port of Banten, Jalan Raya Pelabuhan No.1, Ciwandan 42166, Banten, Indonesia, *Tel:* +62 254 601418, *Fax:* +62 254 601419, *Website:* www.bantenport.co.id

Port Security: ISPS compliant

Approach: Channel depth of 15 m LWS

Pilotage: Pilot from Jakarta. Vessels must inform agent/port authority of arrival 72 h in advance

Radio Frequency: Cigading radio, call sign PKZ 34

Working Hours: 0800-1600, 1600-2400, 0000-0800

Accommodation:

Name	Length (m)	Draught (m)	Remarks
Banten			
Multi-Purpose Berth	202	15	See [1] below
General Cargo Berth	122		For vessels up to 20 000 dwt

[1]*Multi-Purpose Berth:* Operated by Portek Systems. Container & bulk cargoes. Weighbridge facilities

Mechanical Handling Equipment:

Location	Type	Qty
Multi-Purpose Berth	Panamax	2
Multi-Purpose Berth	RTG's	2
Multi-Purpose Berth	Straddle Carriers	24

Towage: Seven tug boats and three pilot tugs

Medical Facilities: Cilegon State Hospital, 10 km. Krakatau Steel Hospital, 6 km

Railway: Government railway at Merak, approx 20 km

Lloyd's Agent: P.T. Carsurin, Sarana Penjaminan Building, 7th Floor, Jl Angkasa Block B-9 Kav 6, Kemayoran, Jakarta 10720, Jawa, Indonesia, *Tel:* +62 21 654 0425, *Fax:* +62 21 654 0418, *Email:* lloyds@carsurin.com, *Website:* www.carsurin.com

BEKAPAI TERMINAL

Lat 1° 0' S; Long 117° 30' E.

Admiralty Chart: 3030	**Admiralty Pilot:** 34
Time Zone: GMT +8 h	**UNCTAD Locode:** ID BEK

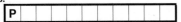

Principal Facilities:

P										

Authority: Bekapai Terminal Authority, Port Office, Balikpapan, Borneo, Indonesia

Pilotage: Compulsory. Mooring master boards at anchorage. 72, 48 and 24 h notice of arrival required

Maximum Vessel Dimensions: 60 000 dwt, 213.3 m loa

Accommodation:

Name	Remarks
Bekapai Terminal	See [1] below

[1]*Bekapai Terminal:* Anchorage in pos 00° 59' S, 117° 27' E in depth of 33.5 m. Berthing at oil storage barge Waipiti at any stage of tide in daylight only. Vessels may leave port day or night

Lloyd's Agent: P.T. Carsurin, Sarana Penjaminan Building, 7th Floor, Jl Angkasa Block B-9 Kav 6, Kemayoran, Jakarta 10720, Jawa, Indonesia, *Tel:* +62 21 654 0425, *Fax:* +62 21 654 0418, *Email:* lloyds@carsurin.com, *Website:* www.carsurin.com

BELAWAN

Lat 3° 48' N; Long 98° 43' E.

Admiralty Chart: 3584	**Admiralty Pilot:** 44
Time Zone: GMT +7 h	**UNCTAD Locode:** ID BLW

Principal Facilities:

P		Y	G	C			B	D	T	A

Authority: PT (Persero) Pelabuhan Indonesia I, Port of Belawan, Jalan Sumatera No.1, Belawan 20411, Sumatra, Indonesia, *Tel:* +62 61 694 1919, *Fax:* +62 61 694 1300, *Email:* belawan@inaport1.co.id, *Website:* belawan.inaport1.co.id

Port Security: ISPS compliant

Approach: Channel 11 nautical miles long, width 100 m in depth of 10 m

Anchorage: Outer Anchorage in pos 3° 58' 10" N, 98° 47' 48" E, NE of No.2 light buoy at the pilot boarding position

Pilotage: Compulsory for vessels over 150 gt. Pilot can be contacted on VHF Channel 12 and must be ordered by agent at least 6 h prior to arrival. Pilotage is available 24 h/day

Radio Frequency: Jakarta Radio, call sign 'PKX', working hours are 0000-0400 on 8.542 kHz and 0000-1200 on 8.752 kHz

Tides: Range of tide 2.5 m

Traffic: 2006, 13 851 790 t of cargo handled

Maximum Vessel Dimensions: 22 594 gt, 225 m loa, 7.5 m draft

Principal Imports and Exports: Imports: Fertiliser, Garlic, Iron, Soya bean meal. Exports: Palm oil, Plywood, Pulp, Rubber, Vegetables.

Working Hours: 24 h/day

Accommodation:

Name	Length (m)	Depth (m)	Remarks
Belawan			
Belawan Lama	602	6	General cargo
Ujung Baru	1660	9	General cargo. Max vessel 200 m loa
Citra 201-203	625	7	General cargo
Container Terminal (International)	500	10.5	See [1] below
Container Terminal (Domestic)	350	10.5	Container yard of 30 669 m2
Citra Oil Jetty	75	9	Tankers
Passenger & Cruise Ship Berth	150	9	
Ferry Berth	115	7	
Private Wharves			See [2] below

[1]*Container Terminal (International):* International and domestic container terminals operated by Belawan Container Terminal, Tel: +62 61 694 0032, Fax: +62 61 694 1942, Email: info@utpkbelawan.co.id
Container yard of 94 600 m2. 96 reefer points. Three 40 t gantry cranes and seven 40 t transtainers

[2]*Private Wharves:* PLTU Wharves 100 m long. PT Semen Andalas Indonesia Jetty 75 m long. PT Tjipta Rimba Djaya 150 m long. Pertamina Jetty 75 m long

Storage:

Location	Open (m²)	Covered (m²)	Sheds / Warehouses
Belawan Lama	23325	5372	6
Ujung Baru	15885	31508	10
Citra 201-203	28730	16800	3
Container Terminal (International)		10400	2

Key to Principal Facilities:—

A=Airport	**C**=Containers	**G**=General Cargo	**P**=Petroleum	**R**=Ro/Ro	**Y**=Dry Bulk
B=Bunkers	**D**=Dry Dock	**L**=Cruise	**Q**=Other Liquid Bulk	**T**=Towage (where available from port)	

Mechanical Handling Equipment:

Location	Type	Capacity (t)	Qty
Belawan	Floating Cranes	40	1
Belawan	Mobile Cranes	10–40	4
Belawan	Forklifts	5–25	8

Cargo Worked: General cargo 20 t/h, liquid cargo 200 t/h, dry cargo 200 t/h

Bunkering: C.V. Bahtera Camar, Jalan Lagoa Terusan Bl No.4, Jakarta 14270, Jawa, Indonesia, *Tel:* +62 21 435 3209, *Fax:* +62 21 430 6048
PT Pertamina, Jalan Jos Sudarso 32-34, P O Box 265, Tanjung Priok, Jawa, Indonesia, *Tel:* +62 21 430 1086, *Fax:* +62 21 430 1562 – *Grades:* DO; MDO; IFO100-300cst – *Parcel Size:* no min/max – *Rates:* 100-150t/h – *Notice:* 48 hours – *Delivery Mode:* barge, pipeline, truck
C.V. Purba Jaya, Jalan Edam II No. 5, Tanjung Priok, Jakarta 14310, Jawa, Indonesia, *Tel:* +62 21 4393 1240, *Fax:* +62 21 4393 0792, *Email:* pijar@indo.net.id

Towage: Five tugs available of 1600-2400 hp

Repair & Maintenance: Minor repairs only. Drydock available for coasters only

Shipping Agents: Arpeni Pratama Ocean Line, P.T. Perusahaan Pelayaran Samudera Khusus (APOL), Jl Deli 7A, Belawan 20411, Sumatra, Indonesia, *Tel:* +62 61 694 1939, *Fax:* +62 61 694 1939, *Email:* operations1@apolmdn.com
P.T. Bumi Laut Shipping Corp., Jl Asahan 5, Belawan 20441, Sumatra, Indonesia, *Tel:* +62 61 664 2586, *Fax:* +62 61 664 3515
P.T. Inter Oceanindo Logistikama, Mandiri Building 6th Floor, Belawan, Sumatra, Indonesia, *Tel:* +62 61 451 8596, *Fax:* +62 61 456 4259
Jardine Shipping Services, Jalan Karo No.20, Belawan, Sumatra, Indonesia, *Tel:* +62 61 694 4871, *Fax:* +62 61 694 4046, *Email:* victorsr@indoset.new.id, *Website:* www.jardine-shipping.com
PT Perusahaan Pelayaran Samudera Gesuri Lloyd, 3rd Floor, Jl Ujung Baru, Terminal Penumpang, Belawan, Sumatra, Indonesia, *Fax:* +62 61 664 1068

Stevedoring Companies: Usaha Bongka Muat PT (Persero), Pelabuhan Indonesia I, Belawan, Sumatra, Indonesia, *Tel:* +62 61 696 3289, *Fax:* +62 61 694 1300

Surveyors: P.T. Superintending Company of Indonesia (SUCOFINDO), Jalan Anggada No.1, Belawan, Sumatra, Indonesia, *Tel:* +62 61 694 4984, *Fax:* +62 61 694 4983, *Email:* sciblw@indosat.net.id, *Website:* www.sucofindo.co.id

Medical Facilities: Belawan Bahagia Hospital, Tel: (61) 640120 & 641927

Airport: Polonia Airport, 30 km

Lloyd's Agent: P.T. Carsurin, Sarana Penjaminan Building, 7th Floor, Jl Angkasa Block B-9 Kav 6, Kemayoran, Jakarta 10720, Jawa, Indonesia, *Tel:* +62 21 654 0425, *Fax:* +62 21 654 0418, *Email:* lloyds@carsurin.com, *Website:* www.carsurin.com

BENGKALIS

Lat 1° 28' N; Long 102° 6' E.

Admiralty Chart: 3933/3947	**Admiralty Pilot:** 44
Time Zone: GMT +7 h	**UNCTAD Locode:** ID BKI

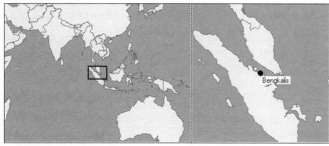

Principal Facilities:

		G							

Authority: PT (Persero) Pelabuhan Indonesia I, Port of Bengkalis, Jalan Sudirman, Bengkalis 28712, Sumatera, Indonesia, *Tel:* +62 766 21267, *Fax:* +62 766 21267

Port Security: ISPS compliant

Anchorage: 200-300 m off pier in 9-11 m of water. Mud bottom

Accommodation:

Name	Length (m)	Depth (m)	Remarks
Bengkalis			Passenger terminal of 60 m2
Multi-Purpose Berth	73	5	For vessels up to 750 dwt
Ferry Terminal	30	4.5	For vessels up to 300 dwt

Storage:

Location	Open (m²)	Covered (m²)	Sheds / Warehouses
Bengkalis	1731	11200	2

Repair & Maintenance: Minor repairs possible. Slipway for vessels up to 80 gt

Lloyd's Agent: P.T. Carsurin, Sarana Penjaminan Building, 7th Floor, Jl Angkasa Block B-9 Kav 6, Kemayoran, Jakarta 10720, Jawa, Indonesia, *Tel:* +62 21 654 0425, *Fax:* +62 21 654 0418, *Email:* lloyds@carsurin.com, *Website:* www.carsurin.com

BENGKULU

Lat 3° 47' S; Long 102° 15' E.

Admiralty Chart: 2965	**Admiralty Pilot:** 36
Time Zone: GMT +7 h	**UNCTAD Locode:** ID BKS

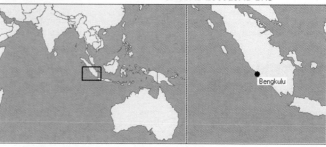

Principal Facilities:

P		Y	G			B		T	

Authority: PT (Persero) Pelabuhan Indonesia II, Port of Bengkulu, Pelabuhan Pulau Baai, Bengkulu 38216, Sumatera, Indonesia, *Tel:* +62 736 51409, *Email:* blkipc2@bengkulu.wasantara.net.id

Port Security: ISPS compliant

Approach: Entrance Channel 800 m long and 400 m wide. Breakwater 395 m long on the right side and 937 m long on the left side

Anchorage: In pos 3° 52' 14" S, 102° 17' 10" E in depth of 12 m

Pilotage: Available 24 h, VHF Channel 12

Radio Frequency: 6215 kHz and 2182 kHz

Maximum Vessel Dimensions: 30 000 dwt, 160 m loa, 10 m depth

Working Hours: 0800-1600, 1600-2400, 2400-0800

Accommodation:

Name	Length (m)	Depth (m)
Bengkulu		
Pulau Baai Wharf	165	10

Storage:

Location	Open (m²)	Covered (m²)
Pulau Baai Wharf	2220	2450

Mechanical Handling Equipment:

Location	Type	Capacity (t)	Qty
Bengkulu	Mobile Cranes	4	1
Bengkulu	Mobile Cranes	25	1
Bengkulu	Forklifts	3	4

Cargo Worked: General cargo 18 t/gang/h, bulk cargo 25 t/gang/h, bag cargo 48 t/gang/h

Bunkering: Mobile tank oil

Towage: One tug of 1160 hp

Shipping Agents: P.T. (PELNI) Pelayaran Nasional Indonesia, Jl Siti Khatijah No.10, Bengkulu, Sumatera, Indonesia, *Tel:* +62 736 21013, *Fax:* +62 736 21029, *Email:* agencies@pelni.co.id, *Website:* www.pelni.co.id

Medical Facilities: Port Health Centre

Lloyd's Agent: P.T. Carsurin, Sarana Penjaminan Building, 7th Floor, Jl Angkasa Block B-9 Kav 6, Kemayoran, Jakarta 10720, Jawa, Indonesia, *Tel:* +62 21 654 0425, *Fax:* +62 21 654 0418, *Email:* lloyds@carsurin.com, *Website:* www.carsurin.com

BENOA

Lat 8° 45' S; Long 115° 15' E.

Admiralty Chart: 946	**Admiralty Pilot:** 34
Time Zone: GMT +8 h	**UNCTAD Locode:** ID BOA

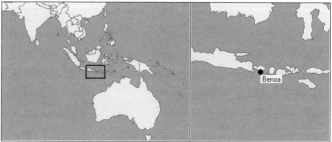

Principal Facilities:

P		G		L		A

Authority: Port of Benoa, Jln. Raya Pelabuhan Benoa, Benoa, Bali Island, Indonesia, *Tel:* +62 361 720560, *Fax:* +62 361 723351, *Email:* plb3bna@denpasar.wasantara.net.id

Approach: Reefs on both sides of Benoa channel, and beacons and buoys should not be depended on. Great caution should be exercised when navigating the channel. Channel depth 9.0 m

Anchorage: Two designated anchorage areas, North and South, with depths ranging from 25 m to 39 m and 21 m to 46 m respectively

Pilotage: Compulsory. Pilot boards close off entrance channel in daylight hours only. Customs and health officials board vessels inside harbour

Radio Frequency: Benoa Radio, call sign 'PKD', VHF Channels 16, 14, 13, 12 and 22. Frequencies 500 kHz, 6491.5 kHz, 2182 kHz, 6215.5 kHz

Maximum Vessel Dimensions: 172 m loa, 7.8 m d, 10 000 dwt

Principal Imports and Exports: Exports: Garments, Tuna fish.

Working Hours: 24 h/day

Accommodation:

Name	Length (m)	Depth (m)	Remarks
Benoa			Passenger terminal, cap 600 people
Cargo Jetty I	206	6	General cargo
Cargo Jetty II	290	9	Passengers
Local Jetty	150	5	Fish
P.T. PSB Jetty	60	5.5	Fish
Pertamina Jetty	46	6	Fuel oil
P.T. BBS Marina	120	5	Passenger (yacht)
P.T. BCN Jetty	30	5	Passenger (catamaran)
P.T. Mabuan Intan Express Jetty	40	5	Passenger (catamaran)

Storage: Four warehouses of 2136 m2 and two open storage areas of 6400 m3

Cargo Worked: 20 t/h/shift

Shipping Agents: P.T. (PELNI) Pelayaran Nasional Indonesia, Benoa, Bali Island, Indonesia, *Tel:* +62 361 723483, *Fax:* +62 361 720962, *Email:* agencies@pelni.co.id, *Website:* www.pelni.co.id

Medical Facilities: Port Health Department available

Airport: Ngurah Rai International Airport, 10 km

Development: Benoa to be developed into a dedicated container port with bulk and general cargo being moved to Celukan Bawang

Lloyd's Agent: P.T. Carsurin, Sarana Penjaminan Building, 7th Floor, Jl Angkasa Block B-9 Kav 6, Kemayoran, Jakarta 10720, Jawa, Indonesia, *Tel:* +62 21 654 0425, *Fax:* +62 21 654 0418, *Email:* lloyds@carsurin.com, *Website:* www.carsurin.com

BIAK

Lat 1° 10' S; Long 136° 4' E.

Admiralty Chart: 3249		**Admiralty Pilot:** 35	
Time Zone: GMT +9 h		**UNCTAD Locode:** ID BIK	

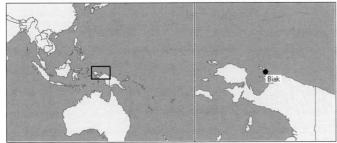

Principal Facilities:

P		Y	G	C		B		A

Authority: PT (Persero) Pelabuhan Indonesia IV, Port of Biak, Jalan Jend. Sudirman No.51, Biak, Irian Jaya, Indonesia, *Tel:* +62 981 21812, *Fax:* +62 981 21135, *Email:* pelindo4@biak.wasantara.net.id

Documentation: Passenger list (2 copies), crew list (2 copies), custom document (4 copies), health document (3 copies), cargo manifest (2 copies), bills of lading (2 copies), ship's papers (2 copies), sailing permit

Approach: Channel width 100-150 m in depth of 15-20 m

Anchorage: In pos 1° 12' 00" S; 136° 06' 00" E in depth of 25 m

Pilotage: Compulsory. Two pilots available, 24 h

Radio Frequency: Biak radio, call sign PKY2. VHF Channels 16 for pilot and 12 for radio station

Traffic: 1999, 125 956 t of cargo handled

Maximum Vessel Dimensions: 40 000 dwt, 200 m loa, 12.0 m d

Principal Imports and Exports: Imports: Spare parts. Exports: Moulding wood, Plywood.

Working Hours: 0800-1200, 1300-1700, 1900-2400, 0100-0600

Accommodation:

Name	Length (m)	Depth (m)
Biak		
Concrete Wharf	202	12
Pertamina Wharf	57	11

Name	Length (m)	Depth (m)
MTI Wharf	40	14

Storage: Storage area of 4600 m2. Container terminal area of 3390 m2

Cargo Worked: General cargo 480 t/gang/day. Bulk cargo 600 t/gang/day

Bunkering: PT Pertamina, Jalan Jos Sudarso 32-34, P O Box 265, Tanjung Priok, Jawa, Indonesia, *Tel:* +62 21 430 1086, *Fax:* +62 21 430 1562 – *Grades:* DO; MDO; IFO100-300cSt – *Parcel Size:* no min/max – *Rates:* 100-150t/h – *Notice:* 48 hours – *Delivery Mode:* barge, pipeline

Shipping Agents: P.T. (PELNI) Pelayaran Nasional Indonesia, Jl Jend Sudirman No.37, Biak, Irian Jaya, Indonesia, *Tel:* +62 981 23255, *Fax:* +62 981 22225, *Email:* agencies@pelni.co.id, *Website:* www.pelni.co.id

Airport: Frank Kaisiepo, 3 km

Lloyd's Agent: P.T. Carsurin, Sarana Penjaminan Building, 7th Floor, Jl Angkasa Block B-9 Kav 6, Kemayoran, Jakarta 10720, Jawa, Indonesia, *Tel:* +62 21 654 0425, *Fax:* +62 21 654 0418, *Email:* lloyds@carsurin.com, *Website:* www.carsurin.com

BIMA

Lat 8° 25' S; Long 118° 43' E.

Admiralty Chart: 895		**Admiralty Pilot:** 34	
Time Zone: GMT +8 h		**UNCTAD Locode:** ID BMU	

This port is no longer open to commercial shipping

BIMA TERMINAL

Lat 5° 45' S; Long 107° 5' E.

		Admiralty Pilot: 36	
Time Zone: GMT +7 h		**UNCTAD Locode:** ID BMT	

This terminal is no longer operational

BITUNG

Lat 1° 26' N; Long 125° 11' E.

Admiralty Chart: 2638		**Admiralty Pilot:** 34	
Time Zone: GMT +8 h		**UNCTAD Locode:** ID BIT	

Principal Facilities:

P		G	C	R		B		T	A

Authority: PT (Persero) Pelabuhan Indonesia IV, Port of Bitung, Jalan DS Sumolang, Bitung, Sulawesi, Indonesia, *Tel:* +62 438 21380, *Fax:* +62 438 21196, *Email:* pelindo4@manado.wasantara.net.id

Port Security: ISPS compliant

Documentation: Passenger list (5 copies), crew list (4 copies), custom document (2 copies), health document (2 copies), cargo manifest (7 copies), bills of lading (7 copies), ship's papers (5 copies), sailing permit

Approach: No sand bars, channel depth 40 m LWS

Pilotage: Compulsory. Call Bitung Pilot Station on VHF Channel 12

Radio Frequency: Radio station, call sign PKM

Weather: SW winds from September-March, NW winds from April-August

Tides: Tidal range 1.15 m

Traffic: 1999, 1 298 462 t of cargo handled

Working Hours: Monday to Thursday 0800-1200, 1300-1700, 1900-2200. Friday 0800-1100, 1300-1700, 1900-2200. Saturday 0800-1200, 1300-1700, 1900-2200. 24 h can be worked on request

Accommodation:

Name	Length (m)	Depth (m)	Draught (m)	Remarks
Bitung				See [1] below
Samudera Quay	605	15		See [2] below
Nusantara Harbour	502	6		
IKD Quay	146		6	
Privatre Wharves				See [3] below

[1]*Bitung:* Small quay 60 m long for local vessels. A passenger hall of 1098 m2
[2]*Samudera Quay:* Min draft of 9 m along the eastern side and 5 m along the western side
[3]*Privatre Wharves:* Six privately owned facilities; PT Pertamina, PT Union Pacific

---

Key to Principal Facilities:—				
A=Airport	**C**=Containers	**G**=General Cargo	**P**=Petroleum	**R**=Ro/Ro	**Y**=Dry Bulk
B=Bunkers	**D**=Dry Dock	**L**=Cruise	**Q**=Other Liquid Bulk	**T**=Towage (where available from port)	

Foods, PT Sinar Pure Foods International, PT Estadha Pesca, PT Megah Galaxy and PT Deho

Storage: Three storage areas along the wharf totalling 10 049 m2 and one warehouse behind of 4320 m2. Open storage of 12 000 m2. Privately owned warehouses outside the port boundaries totalling 22 540 m2

Mechanical Handling Equipment:

Location	Type	Capacity (t)	Qty
Bitung	Mobile Cranes	25	1
Bitung	Mobile Cranes	100	1
Bitung	Forklifts	5	6

Cargo Worked: 15 t/h/gang

Bunkering: Bunker station. Fuel oil may be obtained by tanker wagons alongside wharf

Towage: One tug available of 1160 hp and one of 960 hp

Repair & Maintenance: P.T. Iki Shipbuilding, Bitung, Sulawesi, Indonesia, *Tel:* +62 438 21440, *Fax:* +62 438 21450 Minor repairs
P.T. Surya, Bitung, Sulawesi, Indonesia, *Tel:* +62 438 21363 Minor repairs

Shipping Agents: P.T. Bahana Utama Line, Bitung, Sulawesi, Indonesia, *Tel:* +62 438 36049, *Fax:* +62 438 36049, *Email:* bitung@bahana-line.com, *Website:* www.bahana-line.com

Surveyors: P.T. Biro Klasifikasi Indonesia, Jalan DS Sumolang No.1, Pos Pelabuhan, Bitung 95522, Sulawesi, Indonesia, *Tel:* +62 438 21129, *Fax:* +62 438 21282, *Email:* bkibt@klasifikasiindonesia.com, *Website:* www.klasifikasiindonesia.com
Nippon Kaiji Kyokai, Bitung, Sulawesi, Indonesia, *Tel:* +62 438 21129, *Fax:* +62 438 21282, *Website:* www.classnk.or.jp

Medical Facilities: Barunawati Hospital, 1 km

Airport: Sam Ratulangi Airport, 25 km

Lloyd's Agent: P.T. Carsurin, Sarana Penjaminan Building, 7th Floor, Jl Angkasa Block B-9 Kav 6, Kemayoran, Jakarta 10720, Jawa, Indonesia, *Tel:* +62 21 654 0425, *Fax:* +62 21 654 0418, *Email:* lloyds@carsurin.com, *Website:* www.carsurin.com

BLANG LANCANG

Lat 5° 15' N; Long 97° 4' E.

Admiralty Chart: 3574	**Admiralty Pilot:** 44
Time Zone: GMT +7 h	**UNCTAD Locode:** ID BLL

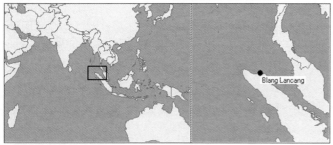

Principal Facilities:

P	Q	G		B		A

Authority: Pertamina PKK Blang Lancang, P O Box 22, Lhokseumawe, Sumatera, Indonesia, *Tel:* +62 645 21566 ext 2151, *Fax:* +62 645 21922 & 41312

Approach: There are no navigational hazards in the approaches, channel depth 14 m

Anchorage: LNG & LPG carriers in pos 5° 15' 15" N; 97° 07' 45" E in depth of 60 m. Crude oil carriers in pos 5° 15' 15" N; 97° 05' 25" E in depth of 60 m

Pilotage: Compulsory. Pilots board vessels at the anchorage or in the vicinity of the Sea Buoy. For oil tankers mooring during daytime only and unmooring 24 h. For LNG & LPG tankers 24 h berthing and unberthing

Radio Frequency: Lhokseumawe Radio (PKB-20) & Harbour Master: VHF Channel 16. Pertamina Blang Lancang, Ship's Agency & Pilot: VHF Channel 9

Maximum Vessel Dimensions: LNG dock: 70 000 dwt, 13 m d, loa 300 m. LPG dock: 65 000 dwt, 13 m d, loa 255 m. MBM: 100 000 dwt, loa 275 m. SPM: 280 000 dwt. Cargo dock: loa 150 m, 6 m d

Working Hours: 24 h

Accommodation:

Name	Length (m)	Depth (m)	Remarks
Blang Lancang			
LNG North	760	14	LNG cargo
LNG South	760	14	LNG cargo
LPG	260	14	LPG cargo
Cargo Dock	300	6	Materials for Pertamina project
MBM	275	30	Condensate (light crude oil). Consists of nine buoys
SBM		30	Condensate

Storage: Available for Pertamina materials only

Mechanical Handling Equipment:

Location	Type	Capacity (t)
Blang Lancang	Mult-purp. Cranes	150

Bunkering: C.V. Bahtera Camar, Jalan Lagoa Terusan Bl No.4, Jakarta 14270, Jawa, Indonesia, *Tel:* +62 21 435 3209, *Fax:* +62 21 430 6048
PT Pertamina, Jalan Jos Sudarso 32-34, P O Box 265, Tanjung Priok, Jawa, Indonesia, *Tel:* +62 21 430 1086, *Fax:* +62 21 430 1562 – *Grades:* DO; MDO; IFO100-300cSt – *Parcel Size:* no min/max – *Rates:* 100-150t/h – *Notice:* 48 hours – *Delivery Mode:* barge, pipeline
C.V. Purba Jaya, Jalan Edam II No. 5, Tanjung Priok, Jakarta 14310, Jawa, Indonesia, *Tel:* +62 21 4393 1240, *Fax:* +62 21 4393 0792, *Email:* pijar@indo.net.id

Medical Facilities: Available

Airport: Malikussaleh, 27 km

Lloyd's Agent: P.T. Carsurin, Sarana Penjaminan Building, 7th Floor, Jl Angkasa Block B-9 Kav 6, Kemayoran, Jakarta 10720, Jawa, Indonesia, *Tel:* +62 21 654 0425, *Fax:* +62 21 654 0418, *Email:* lloyds@carsurin.com, *Website:* www.carsurin.com

BONTANG

Lat 0° 6' N; Long 117° 29' E.

Admiralty Chart: 3040	**Admiralty Pilot:** 34
Time Zone: GMT +8 h	**UNCTAD Locode:** ID BXT

Principal Facilities:

Q	G				T	A

Authority: PT Badak NGL Co., Jalan Cendrawasih No.1, Bontang 75324, Kalimantan, Indonesia, *Tel:* +62 548 21133, *Fax:* +62 548 21605, *Email:* abdulhalim@badaklng.co.id, *Website:* www.badaklng.co.id

Officials: Operations Manager: Suyatmo Achmad, *Tel:* +62 548 552954, *Email:* suyatmoachmad@badaklng.co.id.
Head of Marine Services: Abdul Halim, *Tel:* +62 548 551226.

Port Security: ISPS compliant

Approach: Channel 9 miles long, width 300 m in depth of 14 m MLWS. Turning basin at Docks 1, 2 & 3 with diameter of 750 m in depth of 14 m MLWS

Anchorage: Anchorage for LNG/LPG vessels can be obtained in pos 0° 00' 40" S; 117° 37' 30" E in a depth of 50 m
Anchorage for general cargo vessels can be obtained in pos 0° 02' 15" S; 117° 35' 20" E in a depth of 25 m

Pilotage: Compulsory for vessels of 150 gt and over. Request for pilot should be submitted at least 6 h prior to vessel arriving at the pilotage waters limit at the outer bar and for outgoing vessels 6 h prior to ETD. Vessel requesting a pilot at daylight should display the international code G flag. Pilot boarding at Buoy No.1

Radio Frequency: VHF Channel 16 (safety and calling), Channels 12 and 9 (working) Coastal Radio Station: Bontang Radio (call sign PKN 7)

Maximum Vessel Dimensions: 77 358 dwt, 290 m loa

Working Hours: Monday to Thursday 0700-1200, 1300-1600. Friday 0700-1130, 1330-1700. Overtime is worked to handle LNG/LPG tankers and also other vessels if required

Accommodation:

Name	Length (m)	Depth (m)	Draught (m)	Remarks
Bontang				
Dock 1	425	14	12.6	LNG only for vessels up to 290 m loa
Dock 2	467	14	12.6	See [1] below
Dock 3			12.6	See [2] below
General Cargo Jetty				General cargo vessels

[1]*Dock 2:* LNG & LPG for vessels up to 290 m loa
[2]*Dock 3:* Under construction for LNG & LPG vessels up to 290 m loa

Storage: Five LNG storage tanks with total cap of 508 768 m3. Four LPG storage tanks with total cap of 160 000 m3

Mechanical Handling Equipment:

Location	Type	Capacity (t)	Qty
Bontang	Mult-purp. Cranes	125	1

Cargo Worked: 125 000 m3 LNG per 14 h shift, general cargo 133 t/shift

Bunkering: PT Pertamina, Pertamina Tongkang, Area Pelsus Pertamina PKK, PT Badak, Timur, Bontang 75324, Kalimantan, Indonesia, *Tel:* +62 548 551 575/261 82, *Fax:* +62 548 551 573/271 90, *Email:* ptkbontang@hotmail.com, *Website:* www.pertaminatongkang.co.id

Towage: Four tugs of 4200 hp are available; also three mooring boats

Shipping Agents: P.T. Bahana Utama Line, Bontang, Kalimantan, Indonesia, *Tel:* +62 548 41332, *Fax:* +62 548 41907, *Email:* bontang@bahana-line.com, *Website:* www.bahana-line.com
Jardine Shipping Services, Jalan Pelabuhan No.22, Rt 39/Rw 15, Bontang 75321,

Kalimantan, Indonesia, *Tel:* +62 548 25368, *Fax:* +62 548 25368, *Email:* jttssmd@samarinda.org, *Website:* www.jardine-shipping.com

Surveyors: P.T. Pertamina Tongkang, Bontang, Kalimantan, Indonesia, *Tel:* +62 548 26281, *Fax:* +62 548 23918

Medical Facilities: PT Badak NGL Co hospital

Airport: Bontang Airport, 2 km

Lloyd's Agent: P.T. Carsurin, Sarana Penjaminan Building, 7th Floor, JI Angkasa Block B-9 Kav 6, Kemayoran, Jakarta 10720, Jawa, Indonesia, *Tel:* +62 21 654 0425, *Fax:* +62 21 654 0418, *Email:* lloyds@carsurin.com, *Website:* www.carsurin.com

BOOM BARU

harbour area, see under Palembang

BULA

Lat 3° 5' S; Long 130° 29' E.

Admiralty Chart: 3242	**Admiralty Pilot:** 35
Time Zone: GMT +8 h	**UNCTAD Locode:** ID BUA

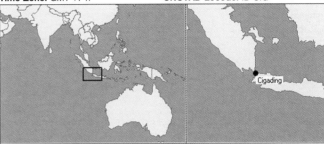

Principal Facilities:

P						T		

Authority: Citic Seram Energy Ltd., P O Box 1097 JKS, Jakarta 12010, Jawa, Indonesia, *Tel:* +62 21 766 2840, *Fax:* +62 21 766 2845, *Email:* contact@citicseram.com, *Website:* www.kufpec.com

Officials: President: Tan Zhong Fu.

Anchorage: The designated anchorage area is located in pos 3° 05' 12" S; 130° 30' E in depth of 70 m

Pilotage: Pilot boards in pos 3° 05' S; 130° 32' E

Radio Frequency: Listening on VHF Channel 16 and working on VHF Channel 9

Maximum Vessel Dimensions: 85 000 dwt

Accommodation:

Name	Depth (m)	Remarks
Bula Petroleum Terminal	17	Crude oil export. T-jetty with three cargo lines and hose handling crane

Towage: One available at the terminal. Larger tankers require two tugs, which means one has to come from Ambon

Lloyd's Agent: P.T. Carsurin, Sarana Penjaminan Building, 7th Floor, JI Angkasa Block B-9 Kav 6, Kemayoran, Jakarta 10720, Jawa, Indonesia, *Tel:* +62 21 654 0425, *Fax:* +62 21 654 0418, *Email:* lloyds@carsurin.com, *Website:* www.carsurin.com

CELUKAN BAWANG

Lat 8° 11' S; Long 114° 50' E.

Admiralty Chart: 946	**Admiralty Pilot:** 34
Time Zone: GMT +8 h	**UNCTAD Locode:** ID CEB

Principal Facilities:

			G					A	

Authority: Port Administrator, Jalan Pelabuhan Celukan Bawang No.35, Singaraja, Celukan Bawang, Bali Island, Indonesia, *Tel:* +62 362 92333, *Fax:* +62 362 92893, *Email:* plb3cbw@singaraja.wasantara.net.id

Approach: Length of approach channel 800 m with width 150 m in depth of between 17 m to 30 m. Band of coral exists approx 100 m from the wharves

Radio Frequency: 156 and 158 mHz

Weather: Dry season June-October. Rainy season November-May

Tides: Range of tide between 1.5-2 m

Working Hours: Normal 7 h day

Accommodation:

Name	Length (m)	Remarks
Celukan Bawang Wharf	58	Harbour is sheltered from E and W winds Vessels up to 5000 dwt, 99 m loa and 7 m draft. There are two sheds of 810 m2

Cargo Worked: 8 t/gang/h

Medical Facilities: Hospital available

Airport: Ngurahrai Airport, 100 km

Lloyd's Agent: P.T. Carsurin, Sarana Penjaminan Building, 7th Floor, JI Angkasa Block B-9 Kav 6, Kemayoran, Jakarta 10720, Jawa, Indonesia, *Tel:* +62 21 654 0425, *Fax:* +62 21 654 0418, *Email:* lloyds@carsurin.com, *Website:* www.carsurin.com

CIGADING

Lat 6° 1' S; Long 105° 57' E.

Admiralty Chart: 918	**Admiralty Pilot:** 36
Time Zone: GMT +7 h	**UNCTAD Locode:** ID CIG

Principal Facilities:

	Y	G			B	T	

Authority: PT Krakatau Bandar Samudera, Port of Cigading, JI. May Jend. S. Parman Km 13, Cigading 42447, Jawa, Indonesia, *Tel:* +62 254 311121, *Fax:* +62 254 311178, *Email:* komersial@cigadingport.com, *Website:* www.cigadingport.com

Officials: President: Kuswanto Atmosumarto, *Email:* kuswanto@cigadingport.com. Marketing Director: Zamhari Hamid, *Email:* zamhari@cigadingport.com.

Approach: The port should be approached from a position about 0.8 km S of Tanjung Leneng

Anchorage: Anchorage area 1.4 km NW of the jetties in 24 m of water

Pilotage: Compulsory. Window schedule should be communicated 1 month in advance then ETA should be communicated 7 days, 3 days and 1 day in advance. Night berthing available

Radio Frequency: Jetty Master radio station. VHF Channel 16, call sign 'Papa Charlie'

Weather: Monsoon season in December, January and February. Winds mostly SE to NE

Tides: Max tidal range 1 m

Traffic: 2003, 6 653 000 t of cargo handled

Maximum Vessel Dimensions: 150 000 dwt

Working Hours: 24 h/day

Accommodation:

Name	Length (m)	Depth (m)
Outer Jetties		
Jetty No.1	150	13
Jetty No.2	150	14
Jetty No.3	270	16
Jetty No.4	285	20
Jetty No.5	240	14
Inner Jetties		
Jetty No.1	121	10
Jetty No.2	122	12
Jetty No.3	142	14
Jetty No.4	143	14

Storage: Open storage available together with five sheds for storing grain, one of 1746 m2, two of 3900 m2, one of 7260 m2 and one of 6510 m2

Mechanical Handling Equipment: Four ship unloader cranes, one multi-purpose crane and one shiploader crane

Cargo Worked: Iron ore 30 000 t/day, coal 15 000 t/day, corn 15 000 t/day, soybean 15 000 t/day, soybean meal 10 000 t/day, gypsum 8000 t/day, sugar 8000 t/day

Bunkering: Ardila Insan Sejahtera P.T., Jalan Mantang No.2, Tanjung Priok, Jakarta, Jawa, Indonesia, *Tel:* +62 21 874 5147, *Fax:* +62 21 874 5324

C.V. Bahtera Camar, Jalan Lagoa Terusan BI No.4, Jakarta 14270, Jawa, Indonesia, *Tel:* +62 21 435 3209, *Fax:* +62 21 430 6048

Buana Jaya C.V., jalan Sungai Kapuas No.15, Jakarta 14270, Jawa, Indonesia, *Tel:* +62 21 44835302, *Fax:* +62 21 44835302

Key to Principal Facilities:—			
A=Airport	**C**=Containers	**G**=General Cargo	**P**=Petroleum	**R**=Ro/Ro	**Y**=Dry Bulk
B=Bunkers	**D**=Dry Dock	**L**=Cruise	**Q**=Other Liquid Bulk	**T**=Towage (where available from port)	

Kartika Jasa Karya P.T., Jalan Perak Timur 564/A1, Surabaya 60165, Jawa, Indonesia, *Tel:* +62 31 3293 459, *Fax:* +62 31 3294 736, *Email:* kemusuk@rad.net.id
PT Antraco Nusa Bhakti, Jln. Demak 407, Surabaya, Surabaya 6000, Jawa, Indonesia, *Tel:* +62 31 3524065, *Fax:* +62 31 805 1067, *Email:* info@talokomarine.com, *Website:* www.talokomarine.com
PT Pertamina, Jalan Jos Sudarso 32-34, P O Box 265, Tanjung Priok, Jawa, Indonesia, *Tel:* +62 21 430 1086, *Fax:* +62 21 430 1562 – *Grades:* DO; MDO; IFO100-300cSt – *Parcel Size:* no min/max – *Rates:* 100-150t/h – *Notice:* 48 hours – *Delivery Mode:* barge, pipeline
C.V. Purba Jaya, Jalan Edam II No. 5, Tanjung Priok, Jakarta 14310, Jawa, Indonesia, *Tel:* +62 21 4393 1240, *Fax:* +62 21 4393 0792, *Email:* pijar@indo.net.id

Waste Reception Facilities: The pumping out of dirty ballast, sludge, chemical waste and garbage disposal is prohibited

Towage: Tug assistance is compulsory

Surveyors: P.T. Biro Klasifikasi Indonesia, Jl. Gerem Raya No.1, Pulo Merak Km.5, Cilegon 42438, Jawa, Indonesia, *Tel:* +62 254 391775, *Fax:* +62 254 391776, *Email:* bkicg@klasifikasiindonesia.com, *Website:* www.klasifikasiindonesia.com

Medical Facilities: Available

Airport: Cengkareng International Airport, approx 130 km

Lloyd's Agent: P.T. Carsurin, Sarana Penjaminan Building, 7th Floor, Jl Angkasa Block B-9 Kav 6, Kemayoran, Jakarta 10720, Jawa, Indonesia, *Tel:* +62 21 654 0425, *Fax:* +62 21 654 0418, *Email:* lloyds@carsurin.com, *Website:* www.carsurin.com

CILACAP

Lat 7° 44' S; Long 109° 0' E.

Admiralty Chart: 912

Admiralty Pilot: 34

Time Zone: GMT +7 h

UNCTAD Locode: ID CXP

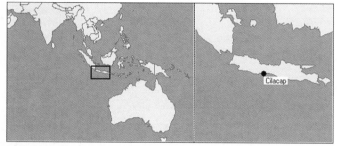

Principal Facilities:

| P | Q | Y | G | | | B | | T | A | |

Authority: P.T. (Persero) Pelabuhan Indonesia III, Cabang Tanjung Intan, Jalan Laut Jawa, Cilacap 53213, Jawa, Indonesia, *Tel:* +62 282 34651/2, *Fax:* +62 282 34653, *Email:* plb3clp@cilacap.wasantara.net.id, *Website:* www.tgintan.pp3.co.id

Approach: Channel width of 200 m from outer bar to Crude Island Berth (CIB). Inside channel width to Area 60 of 80 m. Channel depths, outer bar to CIB jetty 14.5 m LWS; CIB to Area 70, including Sand Irons jetty 12.0 m LWS; Area 70 to Cargo wharf 9.0 m LWS; Cargo wharf to Area 60 6.0 m LWS

Anchorage: Safe anchorage in inner roads, depth 9 m and outer roads, depth 12 m, during west monsoon only

Pilotage: Compulsory for vessels over 150 gt. Pilot station located in the S end of Jalan Yos Sudarso, Cilacap and is available 24 h/day

Radio Frequency: VHF Channels 16, 14 and 12. Frequencies 156.6 mHz and 156.8 mHz

Weather: Rainy season October to December, winds W to N in west monsoon; variable season January to April; dry season April to October, winds E to SE

Tides: Range of tide approx 1 m. High swell of around 2 m occurs with E wind

Working Hours: 24 h/day in three shifts. 0800-1600, 1600-2400, 2400-0800

Accommodation:

Name	Length (m)	Depth (m)	Remarks
Tanjung Intan			
Berth I	120	9	
Berth II	124	9	
Berth III	50	8.9	
Berth IV	71	7.5	
Berth VI	120	9	
Pertamina Tanker Jetties			See ¹ below
PT Pusri Jetty		7	
Pasir Besi Berth (PT Aneka Tambang)		11	
PT Semen Cibinong Berths			See ² below

¹*Pertamina Tanker Jetties:* Crude Island Berth (2 jetties), 17 m depth LWS
Area 70 (3 jetties), 13 m depth LWS
Area 60 (3 jetties), 7 m depth LWS
PDN Jetty, 7 m depth LWS
²*PT Semen Cibinong Berths:* Karang Talun Plant Site (Berth 1), depth 4 m LWS
Karang Talun Plant Site (Berth 2), depth 3.5 m LWS
Wijayapura, depth 3.9 m LWS
Nusakambangan, depth 4 m LWS

Storage: Transit shed of 3500 m2 with 7350 t cap. Warehouses of 3600 m2 with 7560 t cap

Mechanical Handling Equipment:

Location	Type	Capacity (t)	Qty
Cilacap	Mobile Cranes	15	1
Cilacap	Forklifts	10	

Cargo Worked: General cargo 21 t/gang/h, bulk cargo 27 t/gang/h, bagged cargo 15 t/gang/h

Bunkering: Buana Jaya C.V., jalan Sungai Kapuas No.15, Jakarta 14270, Jawa, Indonesia, *Tel:* +62 21 44835302, *Fax:* +62 21 44835302
Kartika Jasa Karya P.T., Jalan Perak Timur 564/A1, Surabaya 60165, Jawa, Indonesia, *Tel:* +62 31 3293 459, *Fax:* +62 31 3294 736, *Email:* kemusuk@rad.net.id
PT Pertamina, Jalan Jos Sudarso 32-34, P O Box 265, Tanjung Priok, Jawa, Indonesia, *Tel:* +62 21 430 1086, *Fax:* +62 21 430 1562 – *Grades:* DO; MDO; IFO100-300cSt – *Parcel Size:* no min/max – *Rates:* 100-150t/h – *Notice:* 48 hours – *Delivery Mode:* barge, pipeline
C.V. Purba Jaya, Jalan Edam II No. 5, Tanjung Priok, Jakarta 14310, Jawa, Indonesia, *Tel:* +62 21 4393 1240, *Fax:* +62 21 4393 0792, *Email:* pijar@indo.net.id

Towage: One tug available of 2800 hp

Repair & Maintenance: Minor repairs only. No docking facilities

Shipping Agents: PT Perusahaan Pelayaran Samudera Gesuri Lloyd, Cilacap, Jawa, Indonesia, *Tel:* +62 282 34998

Medical Facilities: Pertamina hospital, port health service and public health services

Airport: Tunggul Wulung Airport, 15 km

Railway: 1 km from port

Lloyd's Agent: P.T. Carsurin, Sarana Penjaminan Building, 7th Floor, Jl Angkasa Block B-9 Kav 6, Kemayoran, Jakarta 10720, Jawa, Indonesia, *Tel:* +62 21 654 0425, *Fax:* +62 21 654 0418, *Email:* lloyds@carsurin.com, *Website:* www.carsurin.com

CINTA TERMINAL

Lat 5° 27' S; Long 106° 14' E.

Admiralty Chart: 2056

Admiralty Pilot: 36

Time Zone: GMT +7 h

UNCTAD Locode: ID CIN

Principal Facilities:

| P | | | | | | | | T | A | |

Authority: CNOOC SES Ltd., Jakarta Stock Exchange Building, Tower 1, 6th-9th Floor, Jl. Sudirman Kav 52, Jakarta 12190, Jawa, Indonesia, *Tel:* +62 21 515 9095, *Fax:* +62 21 515 9080, *Email:* maruto_wisnuadji@cnooc.co.id

Pre-Arrival Information: Vessels must provide an arrival letter to Kepulauan Seribu Harbour Administration 2 days before arrival stating:
Name of vessel
Flag
Size/measurement
Principal/general agent
ETA
Last port & next port
Activity plan

Pilotage: Compulsory. 24 h service. Pilot boards vessel at the anchorage area in pos 5° 25' 25" S; 106° 12' 09" E

Radio Frequency: VHF Channel 16, Cinta Port Radio call sign '6ZFT'

Maximum Vessel Dimensions: 175 000 dwt, 325 m loa, 31.5 m draft

Working Hours: 24 h/day, weather permitting

Accommodation:

Name	Remarks
Cinta Terminal	See ¹ below

¹*Cinta Terminal:* Storage barge 'Cinta Natomas', 141 000 dwt, moored permanently to a SBM in pos 5° 25' 40" S, 106° 14' 42" E
Second storage SBM in pos 5° 27' 03" S, 106° 13' 00" E
First export SBM in pos 5° 25' 25" S, 106° 14' 29" E handling tankers from 20 000 dwt to 175 000 dwt. There are two 12" diameter hoses and the average loading rate is 16 000 bbls/h
Tankers berth in daylight hours only and unberth on a 24 h basis. Permanently fixed oil-producing platforms are located in the terminal area
SBM Asoka Nusantara in pos 5° 26' 23" S; 106° 13' 45" E

Cargo Worked: 15 000 bbls/h

Towage: Two 750 hp tugs for berthing

Medical Facilities: Available at Pabelokan Island, about 5 miles SW from Cinta Terminal

Airport: Sokarno-Hatta, 96 km

Lloyd's Agent: P.T. Carsurin, Sarana Penjaminan Building, 7th Floor, Jl Angkasa Block B-9 Kav 6, Kemayoran, Jakarta 10720, Jawa, Indonesia, *Tel:* +62 21 654 0425, *Fax:* +62 21 654 0418, *Email:* lloyds@carsurin.com, *Website:* www.carsurin.com

CIREBON

Lat 6° 41' S; Long 108° 33' E.

Admiralty Chart: 918	**Admiralty Pilot:** 36
Time Zone: GMT +7 h	**UNCTAD Locode:** ID CBN

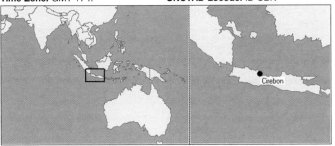

Principal Facilities:

Y	G	C		B	D	T	A

Authority: PT (Persero) Pelabuhan Indonesia II, Port Of Cirebon, Jalan Perniagaan No.4, Cirebon 45112, Jawa, Indonesia, *Tel:* +62 231 204241, *Fax:* +62 231 203201, *Email:* gmcrb@cirebonport.com, *Website:* www.cirebonport.co.id

Officials: General Manager: Putera Mulya Ismail.

Port Security: ISPS compliant

Approach: Channel depth of 7 m LWS. Harbour accessible to vessels up to 7.0 m max draft

Pilotage: Available. ETA should be informed through ship's agent 24 h prior to arrival Compulsory pilotage in the following areas:
(a) 6° 40' 00" S; 108° 37' 40" E
(b) 6° 44' 30" S; 108° 37' 40" E
(c) 6° 44' 30" S; 108° 35' 40" E
(d) 6° 40' 00" S; 108° 33' 10" E

Radio Frequency: Coastal radio station, call sign 'PKZ.2' on VHF Channels 16, 10 and 14

Weather: Normal dry season April to September. Rainy season October to March

Tides: HHWS 1.27 m, average HWS 0.89 m, average LWN 0.3 m

Traffic: 2003, 1779 vessels, 1 730 361 t of cargo handled

Maximum Vessel Dimensions: 140 m loa, 6000 dwt, 7 m draft. Vessels with draft over 7 m can be handled in the anchorage area, 5-10 km offshore

Working Hours: Port operations: Monday-Thursday 0800-1200, 1300-1700; Friday 0800-1200, 1300-1630; Saturday 0800-1400. Three shift system also worked: 0800-1600, 1600-2400, 0000-0800

Accommodation: Facilities at the port include container stacking facilities, a coal terminal, an asphalt terminal and CPO tankfarms
Container yard of 4000 m2

Name	Length (m)	Depth (m)
Muarajati I Basin		
Muarajati I	275	7
Muarajati III	80	7
Port I Basin		
Samadikun	67	3.5
Perniagaan I	11	3.5
Perniagaan II	11	3.5
Perniagaan III	11	3.5
Perniagaan IV	11	3.5
Suryat Sumantri I	11	3.5
Suryat Sumantri II	11	3.5
Suryat Sumantri III	23.5	3.5
Suryat Sumantri IV	11	3.5
Suryat Sumantri V	11	3.5
Port II Basin		
Muarajati II	248	5.5
Linggarjati I	131	4.5
Linggarjati II	40	4.5
Pelita I	30	4
Pelita III	30	4
Sailing Basin		
Sailing Vessel Berth	150	2

Storage:

Location	Open (m²)	Covered (m²)
Cirebon	14120	16159

Mechanical Handling Equipment:

Location	Type	Qty
Cirebon	Mobile Cranes	2

Bunkering: Available by road tanker with prior arrangement through ship's agent

Waste Reception Facilities: Regular garbage disposal carried out by Port Cooperative

Towage: Two tugs available of 800 hp and 1700 hp

Repair & Maintenance: Two graving docks of 1000 dwt cap and 4000 dwt cap available
P.T. Dok Kodja Bahari, Jalan Bali 5, Pelabuhan, Cirebon 45112, Jawa, Indonesia, *Tel:* +62 231 202418, *Fax:* +62 231 211809, *Email:* dkb-crb@indo.net.id, *Website:* www.kodjabahari.com Minor repairs

Shipping Agents: P.T. Bahana Utama Line, Cirebon, Jawa, Indonesia, *Tel:* +62 231 210518, *Fax:* +62 231 210518, *Email:* cirebon@bahana-line.com, *Website:* www.bahana-line.com
P.T. Djakarta Lloyd (PERSERO), Jalan Ambon 1, Pelabuhan, Cirebon, Jawa, Indonesia, *Tel:* +62 231 204805, *Fax:* +62 231 204805, *Email:* dlloydmail@dlloyd.co.id, *Website:* www.dlloyd.co.id
P.T. (PELNI) Pelayaran Nasional Indonesia, Jl Perniagaan No.14, Cirebon, Jawa, Indonesia, *Tel:* +62 231 233524, *Fax:* +62 231 203353, *Email:* agencies@pelni.co.id, *Website:* www.pelni.co.id
PT Perusahaan Pelayaran Samudera Trikora Lloyd, Jalan Ciremai Raya 4, Perumnas Cirebon, Cirebon 45142, Jawa, Indonesia, *Tel:* +62 231 208552, *Fax:* +62 231 208552

Surveyors: P.T. Biro Klasifikasi Indonesia, Jl. Tuparev Km.3, Cirebon 45153, Jawa, Indonesia, *Tel:* +62 231 205266, *Fax:* +62 231 205266, *Email:* bkicn@klasifikasiindonesia.com, *Website:* www.klasifikasiindonesia.com
Nippon Kaiji Kyokai, Cirebon, Jawa, Indonesia, *Tel:* +62 231 205266, *Fax:* +62 231 205266, *Website:* www.classnk.or.jp

Medical Facilities: Port hospital nearby. General hospital, 5 km

Airport: Penggung, 10 km

Railway: Cirebon Railway Station, 3 km

Lloyd's Agent: P.T. Carsurin, Sarana Penjaminan Building, 7th Floor, Jl Angkasa Block B-9 Kav 6, Kemayoran, Jakarta 10720, Jawa, Indonesia, *Tel:* +62 21 654 0425, *Fax:* +62 21 654 0418, *Email:* lloyds@carsurin.com, *Website:* www.carsurin.com

DABO

Lat 0° 30' S; Long 104° 34' E.

Admiralty Chart: 1789	**Admiralty Pilot:** 36
Time Zone: GMT +7 h	**UNCTAD Locode:** ID DAS

This port is no longer open to commercial shipping

DUMAI

Lat 1° 41' N; Long 101° 27' E.

Admiralty Chart: 3933	**Admiralty Pilot:** 44
Time Zone: GMT +7 h	**UNCTAD Locode:** ID DUM

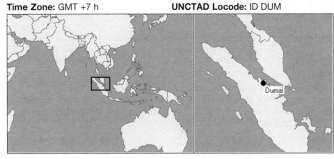

Principal Facilities:

P		Y	G		B		T	A

Authority: PT (Persero) Pelabuhan Indonesia I, Port of Dumai, Jln. Datuk Laksamana, Dumai 28814, Sumatera, Indonesia, *Tel:* +62 765 31469, *Fax:* +62 765 31768, *Email:* port1dmi@dumai.wasantara.net.id, *Website:* dumai.inaport1.co.id

Officials: General Manager: Rosihan Anwar.

Port Security: ISPS compliant

Documentation: Data of ship (ship tonnage, ship particulars, ship condition etc) 1 copy
Data of cargo (manifest, stowage plan, dangerous & cargo list etc) 1 copy

Approach: The Bengkalis and Rupat Strait Channels have been dredged to a depth of 16 m

Anchorage: Min depth of water in anchorage is 13-14 m with good holding on a clay bottom

Pilotage: Harbour pilots available

Radio Frequency: VHF Channels 12 and 16

Weather: The dominant wind direction is S from May to October and N to E from November to April

Traffic: 2003, 6163 vessels

Working Hours: 24 h/day

Accommodation:

Name	Length (m)	Depth (m)	Remarks
Multi-Purpose Berths			Owned by Port of Dumai
Dermaga Lama	348	9	General cargo
Dermaga Baru (Multi-Purpose)	400	10	Dry, liquid cargo and general cargo
Pandu	34	6	Pilot boats
Tunda	80	9	Tug boats
Trestel for Cruise	109.5	1.5	Passenger terminal
Pelra	75	3	
Tanker Terminals			See [1] below
DP-1	360	16.1	See [2] below

Key to Principal Facilities:—			
A=Airport	**C**=Containers	**G**=General Cargo	**P**=Petroleum	**R**=Ro/Ro	**Y**=Dry Bulk
B=Bunkers	**D**=Dry Dock	**L**=Cruise	**Q**=Other Liquid Bulk	**T**=Towage (where available from port)	

Name	Length (m)	Depth (m)	Remarks
DP-2	200	13.1	Ado, kero, prem & napta for vessels of 5000-10 000 dwt
DP-3	260	13.9	See [3] below
DP-4	300	15	Coke for vessels of 10 000-25 000 dwt
DP-5	260	16	See [4] below
DP-6	115	15	LPG for vessels of 1000-3000 dwt
Wharf I	368	18.5	Crude oil for vessels up to 150 000 dwt
Wharf II	434	17.9	Crude oil for vessels up to 150 000 dwt
Wharf III	356	17.9	Crude oil for vessels up to 100 000 dwt
Wharf IV	306	15.5	Crude oil for vessels up to 55 000 dwt

[1]*Tanker Terminals:* DP1-6 owned by Pertamina and Wharves I-IV owned by Caltex
[2]*DP-1:* Ado, kero, prem, LSWR & napta for vessels of 10 000-100 000 dwt
[3]*DP-3:* Ado, kero, prem, super 98, avtur & JP-5 for vessels of 5000-35 000 dwt
[4]*DP-5:* Ado, kero, prem, avtur, super 98 & LPG for vessels of 5000-35 000 dwt

Storage: Open storage of 3000 m2 (cap 7200 t), covered storage of 16 030 m2 (cap 17 560 t), yard storage of 14 293 m2 (cap 24 148 t)

Mechanical Handling Equipment:

Location	Type	Capacity (t)	Qty
Dumai	Mobile Cranes	40	1
Dumai	Mobile Cranes	35	1
Dumai	Forklifts	5	2
Dumai	Forklifts	3	1

Bunkering: Buana Jaya C.V., jalan Sungai Kapuas No.15, Jakarta 14270, Jawa, Indonesia, *Tel:* +62 21 44835302, *Fax:* +62 21 44835302
PT Pertamina, Jalan Jos Sudarso 32-34, P O Box 265, Tanjung Priok, Jawa, Indonesia, *Tel:* +62 21 430 1086, *Fax:* +62 21 430 1562 – *Grades:* DO; MDO; IFO100-300cSt – *Parcel Size:* no min/max – *Rates:* 100-150t/h – *Notice:* 48 hours – *Delivery Mode:* barge, pipeline

Towage: One 3500 hp, three 3200 hp and two 2400 hp tugs available

Repair & Maintenance: P.T. Patra Dock, Dumai, Sumatera, Indonesia, *Tel:* +62 765 31094, *Fax:* +62 765 31631, *Email:* patradock@yahoo.com Floating dock 31 m wide for vessels up to 20 000 dwt

Surveyors: P.T. Biro Klasifikasi Indonesia, Jl. Sungai Rokan No.96, Dumai 28814, Sumatera, Indonesia, *Tel:* +62 765 32574, *Fax:* +62 765 31364, *Email:* bkidm@klasifikasiindonesia.com, *Website:* www.klasifikasiindonesia.com
Nippon Kaiji Kyokai, Dumai, Sumatera, Indonesia, *Tel:* +62 765 32574, *Fax:* +62 765 31364, *Website:* www.classnk.or.jp

Medical Facilities: Available in port. Putri Tujuh Hospital, approx 500 m from port

Airport: Pinang Kampai Airport, owned by Pertamina

Lloyd's Agent: P.T. Carsurin, Sarana Penjaminan Building, 7th Floor, Jl Angkasa Block B-9 Kav 6, Kemayoran, Jakarta 10720, Jawa, Indonesia, *Tel:* +62 21 654 0425, *Fax:* +62 21 654 0418, *Email:* lloyds@carsurin.com, *Website:* www.carsurin.com

FAK FAK

Lat 2° 56' S; Long 132° 18' E.

Admiralty Chart: 3743	**Admiralty Pilot:** 35
Time Zone: GMT +9 h	**UNCTAD Locode:** ID FKQ

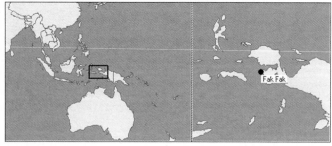

Principal Facilities:

			G						A

Authority: PT (Persero) Pelabuhan Indonesia IV, Port of Fak Fak, Jalan Izak Tellusa No.5, Fak Fak 98611, Irian Jaya, Indonesia, *Tel:* +62 956 22607, *Fax:* +62 956 22606

Documentation: Passenger list (5 copies), crew list (4 copies), custom document (2 copies), health document (2 copies), cargo manifest (7 copies), bills of lading (7 copies), ship's papers (5 copies), sailing permit

Pilotage: Compulsory

Radio Frequency: VHF Channel 16

Traffic: 1999, 37 487 t of cargo handled

Maximum Vessel Dimensions: Max draft 6 m

Working Hours: 18 h/day

Accommodation:

Name	Length (m)	Apron Width (m)
Fak Fak		
Fak Fak Pier	100	12
Pertamina Pier	15	5

Storage:

Location	Covered (m²)	Sheds / Warehouses
Fak Fak	600	1

Mechanical Handling Equipment:

Location	Type	Capacity (t)	Qty
Fak Fak	Forklifts	3	1

Medical Facilities: Hospital facilities or port doctor available

Airport: Torea Airport, 11 km

Lloyd's Agent: P.T. Carsurin, Sarana Penjaminan Building, 7th Floor, Jl Angkasa Block B-9 Kav 6, Kemayoran, Jakarta 10720, Jawa, Indonesia, *Tel:* +62 21 654 0425, *Fax:* +62 21 654 0418, *Email:* lloyds@carsurin.com, *Website:* www.carsurin.com

GILIMANUK

Lat 8° 10' S; Long 114° 26' E.

Admiralty Chart: 3726	**Admiralty Pilot:** 34
Time Zone: GMT +8 h	**UNCTAD Locode:** ID GIL

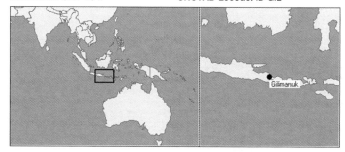

Principal Facilities:

			G	R					

Authority: Port Administrator, Jalan Br. Jineng Agung, Gilimanuk 82253, Bali Island, Indonesia, *Tel:* +62 365 61014, *Fax:* +62 365 61259

Approach: Light buoy established at a rock 0.8 km N of the port

Anchorage: Available 40 m offshore in depth of 30 m

Weather: Strong winds and rough seas can be experienced from June to September

Tides: Range of tide 0.3 m to 2.9 m

Maximum Vessel Dimensions: 539 dwt, 47.9 m loa, 3.5 m draft

Accommodation:

Name	Remarks
Gilimanuk	See [1] below

[1]*Gilimanuk:* Its sole function is to act as the terminal of the ferry-boat service operated by the State Railways which connects the overland communication from Bali to Java at Gilimanuk. Terminal provided with two wooden floating bridges 60 m in length

Storage:

Location	Covered (m²)	Sheds / Warehouses
Gilimanuk	1200	4

Medical Facilities: Hospital available

Airport: Ngurah Rai Tuban, approx 160 km

Lloyd's Agent: P.T. Carsurin, Sarana Penjaminan Building, 7th Floor, Jl Angkasa Block B-9 Kav 6, Kemayoran, Jakarta 10720, Jawa, Indonesia, *Tel:* +62 21 654 0425, *Fax:* +62 21 654 0418, *Email:* lloyds@carsurin.com, *Website:* www.carsurin.com

GORONTALO

Lat 0° 30' N; Long 123° 3' E.

Admiralty Chart: 3240	**Admiralty Pilot:** 34
Time Zone: GMT +8 h	**UNCTAD Locode:** ID GTO

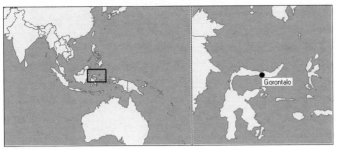

Principal Facilities:

P		G					A

Authority: PT (Persero) Pelabuhan Indonesia IV, Port of Gorontalo, Jalan Mayor Dullah No.176, Gorontalo 96100, Sulawesi Utara, Indonesia, *Tel:* +62 435 21216, *Fax:* +62 435 24808, *Email:* pelindo4@gorontalo.wasantara.net.id

Port Security: ISPS compliant

Documentation: Passenger list (5 copies), crew list (4 copies), custom document (2 copies), health document (2 copies), cargo manifest (7 copies), bills of lading (7 copies), ship's papers (5 copies), sailing permit

Weather: W winds from September-March, E winds from April-August

Tides: Tidal range 1.1 m

Traffic: 1999, 219 325 t of cargo handled

Maximum Vessel Dimensions: 5000 dwt, 106 m loa, 10 m draft

Working Hours: 0800-1200, 1300-2100. 24 h can be worked on request

Accommodation:

Name	Remarks
Gorontalo	See [1] below

[1]*Gorontalo:* Anchorage in roads. Loading and discharging from barges and lighters. Two quays, 75 m length and 10 m depth, and 59 m length and 7 m depth. Passenger hall of 550 m2

Storage:

Location	Sheds / Warehouses
Gorontalo	2

Cargo Worked: 550 t per working day

Repair & Maintenance: Minor facilities available

Shipping Agents: P.T. (PELNI) Pelayaran Nasional Indonesia, Jl 23 Januari No.31, Gorontalo, Sulawesi Utara, Indonesia, *Tel:* +62 435 21089, *Fax:* +62 435 21145, *Email:* agencies@pelni.co.id, *Website:* www.pelni.co.id

Medical Facilities: Dr. Aloei Sabu Hospital, approx 2 km

Airport: Jalaluddin Airport, 40 km

Lloyd's Agent: P.T. Carsurin, Sarana Penjaminan Building, 7th Floor, Jl Angkasa Block B-9 Kav 6, Kemayoran, Jakarta 10720, Jawa, Indonesia, *Tel:* +62 21 654 0425, *Fax:* +62 21 654 0418, *Email:* lloyds@carsurin.com, *Website:* www.carsurin.com

GRESIK

Lat 7° 9' S; Long 112° 39' E.

Admiralty Chart: 945/921	**Admiralty Pilot:** 34
Time Zone: GMT +7 h	**UNCTAD Locode:** ID GRE

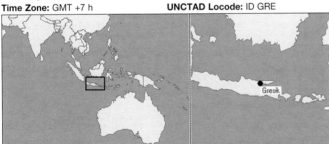

Principal Facilities:

P	Q	Y	G				A

Authority: Port of Gresik, Jalan Yos Sudarso No.1, Gresik, Jawa, Indonesia, *Tel:* +62 31 398 1941, *Fax:* +62 31 398 2735

Port Security: ISPS compliant

Documentation: Ship's certificate, sailing permit, log book etc

Approach: Depth in channel is 10.0 m, width 90 m

Anchorage: Anchorage can be obtained off the port in pos 7° 09' 00" S; 112° 39' 00" E; sandy bottom

Pilotage: Compulsory. Pilot normally boards at Karang Jamuang Station at the outer entrance of the port of Surabaya

Radio Frequency: Gresik Coastal Radio Station, equipment frequencies: 4055 kHz and 5316 kHz for fixed station and 6224 kHz for mobile station. VHF Channel 16

Weather: Dry season June-October. Rainy season November-May

Tides: Range of tide about 2.5 m

Maximum Vessel Dimensions: 55 596 dwt, 218.4 m loa, 10.0 m draft

Principal Imports and Exports: Imports: Ethelhexanol, Oxylin, Phosphate rock, Phosphoric acid, Sulphur. Exports: Cement, Gypsum, Oil products, Plywood, Sawn timber.

Working Hours: Three shifts 0700-1500, 1500-2300, 2300-0700

Accommodation:

Name	Length (m)	Depth (m)	Remarks
Gresik			See [1] below
Petrokimia Wharf	620	12–14	Facilities for product tankers and chemical tankers
PT Cement Wharf	290	9–12	
PLTU/PLTG Wharf	300	11	

[1]*Gresik:* Three small public jetties with a total length of 575 m and depth of water alongside of 3 m LWS. A floating log-pound with depth of 1.5 m is in use by two plywood companies

Storage:

Location	Covered (m²)	Sheds / Warehouses
Gresik	1400	2

Mechanical Handling Equipment:

Location	Type	Qty	Remarks
Petrokimia Wharf	Mult-purp. Cranes	2	load cap about 500 t/h

Cargo Worked: 150 t/shift

Bunkering: Only available by barge at Surabaya Anchorage
Aditya Aryaprawira Corp., Wisma Mitra Sunter 01-02, Sunter Boulevard Block C-1, Jalan Yos Sudarso Kav 89, Jakarta 14350, Jawa, Indonesia, *Tel:* +62 21 6514732, *Fax:* +62 21 6514731, *Email:* info@adityacorp.com, *Website:* www.adityacorp.com
C.V. Bahtera Camar, Jalan Lagoa Terusan Bl No.4, Jakarta 14270, Jawa, Indonesia, *Tel:* +62 21 435 3209, *Fax:* +62 21 430 6048
Buana Jaya C.V., jalan Sungai Kapuas No.15, Jakarta 14270, Jawa, Indonesia, *Tel:* +62 21 44835302, *Fax:* +62 21 44835302
Kartika Jasa Karya P.T., Jalan Perak Timur 564/A1, Surabaya 60165, Jawa, Indonesia, *Tel:* +62 31 3293 459, *Fax:* +62 31 3294 736, *Email:* kemusuk@rad.net.id
PT Antraco Nusa Bhakti, Jln. Demak 407, Surabaya, Surabaya 6000, Jawa, Indonesia, *Tel:* +62 31 3524065, *Fax:* +62 31 805 1067, *Email:* info@talokomarine.com, *Website:* www.talokomarine.com
PT Pertamina, Jalan Jos Sudarso 32-34, P O Box 265, Tanjung Priok, Jawa, Indonesia, *Tel:* +62 21 430 1086, *Fax:* +62 21 430 1562 – *Grades:* DO; MDO; IFO100-300cSt – *Parcel Size:* no min/max – *Rates:* 100-150t/h – *Notice:* 48 hours – *Delivery Mode:* barge, pipeline
C.V. Purba Jaya, Jalan Edam II No. 5, Tanjung Priok, Jakarta 14310, Jawa, Indonesia, *Tel:* +62 21 4393 1240, *Fax:* +62 21 4393 0792, *Email:* pijar@indo.net.id

Medical Facilities: Small clinic located in port area. Hospitals at Surabaya City

Airport: Juanda Airport, Surabaya, 40 km

Railway: Pasar Turi Station, 17 km

Lloyd's Agent: P.T. Carsurin, Sarana Penjaminan Building, 7th Floor, Jl Angkasa Block B-9 Kav 6, Kemayoran, Jakarta 10720, Jawa, Indonesia, *Tel:* +62 21 654 0425, *Fax:* +62 21 654 0418, *Email:* lloyds@carsurin.com, *Website:* www.carsurin.com

GUNUNG SITOLI

Lat 1° 17' N; Long 97° 37' E.

Admiralty Chart: 400	**Admiralty Pilot:** 44
Time Zone: GMT +7 h	**UNCTAD Locode:** ID GNS

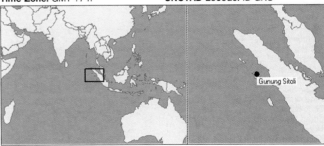

Principal Facilities:

		G	R			A

Authority: PT (Persero) Pelabuhan Indonesia I, Port of Gunung Sitoli, Jalan Kol. Yos Sudarso, Gunung Sitoli 22812, Nias Island, Sumatera, Indonesia, *Tel:* +62 639 21662, *Fax:* +62 639 21662

Approach: Harbour sheltered from westerly and south-westerly winds, but exposed to northerly and south-easterly winds which can cause a considerable swell, channel depth 12 m

Anchorage: Anchorage in depth of 30-36 m LWS, approx 450 m from the berth. Mud bottom

Tides: HW 1.2 m, LW 0.4 m

Working Hours: 24 h

Accommodation:

Name	Remarks
Gunung Sitoli	See [1] below

Key to Principal Facilities:—					
A=Airport	**C**=Containers	**G**=General Cargo	**P**=Petroleum	**R**=Ro/Ro	**Y**=Dry Bulk
B=Bunkers	**D**=Dry Dock	**L**=Cruise	**Q**=Other Liquid Bulk	**T**=Towage (where available from port)	

[1]Gunung Sitoli: As a result of a recent earthquake in this region it has been reported that the wharf was totally demolished

Storage:

Location	Open (m²)	Covered (m²)
Gunung Sitoli	1480	960

Cargo Worked: 144 t/shift/day

Medical Facilities: General hospital

Airport: Binaka, 22 km

Lloyd's Agent: P.T. Carsurin, Sarana Penjaminan Building, 7th Floor, Jl Angkasa Block B-9 Kav 6, Kemayoran, Jakarta 10720, Jawa, Indonesia, *Tel:* +62 21 654 0425, *Fax:* +62 21 654 0418, *Email:* lloyds@carsurin.com, *Website:* www.carsurin.com

JAKARTA

Lat 6° 6' S; Long 106° 52' E.

Admiralty Chart: 923/933	**Admiralty Pilot:** 36
Time Zone: GMT +7 h	**UNCTAD Locode:** ID JKT

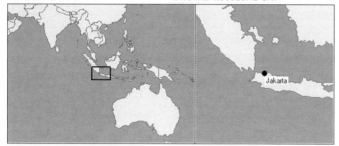

Principal Facilities:

P	Q	Y	G	C	R		B	D	T	A

Authority: Tanjung Priok Port Authority, Jalan Raya Pelabuhan No.9, Tanjung Priok 14310, Jawa, Indonesia, *Tel:* +62 21 436 7305, *Fax:* +62 21 437 2933, *Website:* www.priokport.co.id

Port Security: ISPS compliant

Approach: Length of channel 8000 m, width 250-350 m, depth of 11-12 m LWS

Pilotage: Compulsory. Pilots available 24 h. Vessels must inform Port Authority of arrival 24 h in advance

Radio Frequency: Tanjung Priok Radio, call sign PKZ6, VHF Channel 16, frequency 156.8 mHz and VHF Channel 69, frequency 156.475 mHz

Tides: High water 1.5 m LWS, low water 0.5 m LWS

Traffic: 2006, 3 280 000 TEU's handled

Maximum Vessel Dimensions: Basin I: 225 m loa. Basin II: 195 m loa. Basin III: 220 m loa. Nusantara Basin: 80 m loa

Working Hours: 24 h/day, three shifts

Accommodation:

Name	Length (m)	Depth (m)	Draught (m)	Remarks
Jakarta				See [1] below
Inter-Island Wharves	3254	5–6		
Ocean-Going Wharves	3138	5–11		
Jakarta International Container Terminal				See [2] below
Terminal 1	1710		11–14	See [3] below
Terminal 2	510		8.6	See [4] below
Terminal 009	400	8.5		See [5] below
Scrap Iron Terminal	200	12		
Dry Bulk Wharves	187	12		
Liquid Terminal	180	12		
Oil Jetty	100	12		

[1]Jakarta: Harbour protected by breakwater and unaffected by tide
Bulk facilities: Coal berth and fertilizer berth, both 150 m long with 7-9 m depth alongside in Basin II. Grain berth 140 m long, 9-10 m depth in Basin III. Bogasari Flour Mills Berth 162 m long, 12 m depth; three conveyors
Tanker facilities: There are four berths in the Mineral Oil Harbour, each 25 m long with 10 m depth. Tankers of 198 m loa and 8.84 m d can be accommodated. Vessels must always berth heading north, and must turn in the harbour to come alongside quay stern first. Night berthing possible. Water and bunkers available. DKP Berth, 276 m long, depth alongside 10 m for chemicals
[2]Jakarta International Container Terminal: Joint venture between Hutchison Port Holdings and PT (Persero) Pelabuhan Indonesia II, Jalan Sulawesi Ujung No.1, Tanjung Priok, Jakarta 14310, Tel: +62 21 4390 5111, Fax: +62 21 4390 2446, Website: www.jict.co.id
[3]Terminal 1: Container yard area of 36.9 ha. 260 reefer points
[4]Terminal 2: Container yard area of 9.2 ha. 68 reefer points
[5]Terminal 009: Container terminal operated by P.T. Serbaguna Terminal, Tel: +62 21 4390 3186, Fax: +62 21 4390 3186, Email: terminals@portek.com
Two berths. Container yard of 8 ha with reefer facilities

Storage: Numerous Port Authority and privately owned transit sheds and warehouses available. Transit sheds totalling 245 412 m2, warehouses of 7945 m2

Location	Open (m²)
Jakarta	384784

Mechanical Handling Equipment:

Location	Type	Capacity (t)	Qty	Remarks
Jakarta	Floating Cranes	30–200	4	
Jakarta	Mult-purp. Cranes	3	3	
Jakarta	Mobile Cranes	40		
Jakarta International Container Terminal	Container Cranes		18	14 at Terminal 1 and 4 at Terminal 2
Jakarta International Container Terminal	RTG's		51	40 at Terminal 1 and 11 at Terminal 2
Terminal 009	Panamax		4	
Terminal 009	RTG's		11	

Cargo Worked: 30 500 t/day, 160 t/gang/day

Bunkering: Aditya Aryaprawira Corp., Wisma Mitra Sunter 01-02, Sunter Boulevard Block C-1, Jalan Yos Sudarso Kav 89, Jakarta 14350, Jawa, Indonesia, *Tel:* +62 21 6514732, *Fax:* +62 21 6514731, *Email:* info@adityacorp.com, *Website:* www.adityacorp.com
Anroven Andalan C.V., Jalan Raya Boulevard No.8, Kelapa Gading, Jakarta 14250, Jawa, Indonesia, *Tel:* +62 21 4584 4015, *Fax:* +62 21 4584 4012
Ardila Insan Sejahtera P.T., Jalan Mantang No.2, Tanjung Priok, Jakarta, Jawa, Indonesia, *Tel:* +62 21 874 5147, *Fax:* +62 21 874 5324
Buana Jaya C.V., jalan Sungai Kapuas No.15, Jakarta 14270, Jawa, Indonesia, *Tel:* +62 21 44835302, *Fax:* +62 21 44835302
C.V. Purba Jaya, Jalan Edam II No. 5, Tanjung Priok, Jakarta 14310, Jawa, Indonesia, *Tel:* +62 21 4393 1240, *Fax:* +62 21 4393 0792, *Email:* pijar@indo.net.id
Aditya Aryaprawira Corp., Wisma Mitra Sunter 01-02, Sunter Boulevard Block C-1, Jalan Yos Sudarso Kav 89, Jakarta 14350, Jawa, Indonesia, *Tel:* +62 21 6514732, *Fax:* +62 21 6514731, *Email:* info@adityacorp.com, *Website:* www.adityacorp.com
Ardila Insan Sejahtera P.T., Jln. Mantang No.2, Tanjung Priok, Jakarta, Jawa, Indonesia, *Tel:* +62 21 874 5147, *Fax:* +62 21 874 5324
C.V. Bahtera Camar, Jalan Lagoa Terusan BI No.4, Jakarta 14270, Jawa, Indonesia, *Tel:* +62 21 435 3209, *Fax:* +62 21 430 6048
Buana Jaya C.V., jalan Sungai Kapuas No.15, Jakarta 14270, Jawa, Indonesia, *Tel:* +62 21 44835302, *Fax:* +62 21 44835302
Kartika Jasa Karya P.T., Jalan Perak Timur 564/A1, Surabaya 60165, Jawa, Indonesia, *Tel:* +62 31 3293 459, *Fax:* +62 31 3294 736, *Email:* kemusuk@rad.net.id
PT Antraco Nusa Bhakti, Jln. Demak 407, Surabaya, Surabaya 6000, Jawa, Indonesia, *Tel:* +62 31 3524065, *Fax:* +62 31 805 1067, *Email:* info@talokomarine.com, *Website:* www.talokomarine.com
PT Pertamina, Jalan Jos Sudarso 32-34, P O Box 265, Tanjung Priok, Jawa, Indonesia, *Tel:* +62 21 430 1086, *Fax:* +62 21 430 1562 – *Grades:* DO; MDO; IFO100-300cSt – *Parcel Size:* no min/max – *Rates:* 100-150t/h – *Notice:* 48 hours – *Delivery Mode:* barge, pipeline
C.V. Purba Jaya, Jalan Edam II No. 5, Tanjung Priok, Jakarta 14310, Jawa, Indonesia, *Tel:* +62 21 4393 1240, *Fax:* +62 21 4393 0792, *Email:* pijar@indo.net.id

Towage: Eleven tugs available from 800 to 2500 hp. Towage compulsory for vessels exceeding 80 m loa
SVITZER, PT Aquaria Shipping Ltd, Beltway Office Park, Building C û 6th Floor Suite 604, Jl TB Simatupang No.41, Jakarta 12550, Jawa, Indonesia, *Tel:* +62 21 781 1781, *Fax:* +62 21 781 1783, *Email:* info@aquariashipping.co.id, *Website:* www.svitzer.com

Repair & Maintenance: P.T. Dok & Perkapalan Kodja Bahari, Jalan Sindang Laut No. 101 Cilincing, Jakarta, Jawa, Indonesia, *Tel:* +62 21 430 2228/32, *Fax:* +62 21 430 3039 Seven floating docks, the largest being 175 m x 29 m with lifting cap of 12 000 t. Two dry docks of 120 m x 22 m for vessels up to 8000 dwt and 112 m x 22 m for vessels up to 5000 dwt

Ship Chandlers: PT Aloratama Indah, Jalan Edam I No.39, Tanjung Priok, Jakarta 14310, Jawa, Indonesia, *Tel:* +62 21 435 6824, *Fax:* +62 21 4393 1141, *Email:* alorind@dnet.net.id
C.V. Indah Raya, No.21 Jalan Gunung Sahari, Jakarta 10720, Jawa, Indonesia, *Tel:* +62 21 600 6131, *Fax:* +62 21 628 4055, *Email:* inkasea@cbn.net.id
C.V. Karya Candra Jaya, Jalan Johar No.29, Jakarta 14270, Jawa, Indonesia, *Tel:* +62 21 435 3049, *Fax:* +62 21 4393 3795, *Email:* kcj@cbn.net.id
PT Perusahaan Pelayaran Samudera Trikora Lloyd, 4th Floor, Graha Satria 1&2, Jalan RS Fatmawati 5, Jakarta 12430, Jawa, Indonesia, *Tel:* +62 21 7591 5381, *Fax:* +62 21 7591 5385, *Email:* tkldir@cbn.net.id, *Website:* www.boedihardjogroup.com
C.V. Purba Jaya, Jalan Edam II No. 5, Tanjung Priok, Jakarta 14310, Jawa, Indonesia, *Tel:* +62 21 4393 1240, *Fax:* +62 21 4393 0792, *Email:* pijar@indo.net.id
P.T. Pelayaran Taruna Cipta Kencana, Jalan Mayjen Suprapto, Komplek Graha Cempaka Mas Blok E/26, Jakarta 10640, Jawa, Indonesia, *Tel:* +62 21 426 7068, *Fax:* +62 21 426 7072, *Email:* tcksmg@tck.co.id
Tunas Mawar Jaya C.V., Jalan Mundu No. 59 Block L, Tanjung Priok, Jakarta 14270, Jawa, Indonesia, *Tel:* +62 21 4393 3281, *Fax:* +62 21 430 0351, *Email:* pt_tmj@indo.net.id

Shipping Agents: P.T. Ahlers Thoeng Indonesia, Mayapada Tower, 7th Floor, Suite 7-02, Jakarta 12920, Jawa, Indonesia, *Tel:* +62 21 525 3389, *Fax:* +62 21 522 8815, *Email:* ahlers@cbn.net.id, *Website:* www.ahlersthoeng.com
Amas International Lines, Pulomas Satu, Tower 2 / 2-07, Jalan Jend. A. Yani No. 2, Jakarta 13210, Jawa, Indonesia, *Tel:* +62 21 475 7860, *Fax:* +62 21 475 7947, *Email:* ops@amas.co.id, *Website:* www.amas.co.id
P.T. Andal Lautan Niaga, 6th Floor, Graha Mustika Ratu, Jl Gatot Suroto Kav 74-75, Jakarta 12870, Jawa, Indonesia, *Tel:* +62 21 830 6564, *Fax:* +62 21 830 6709, *Email:* henri@pacific.net.id
P.T. Andal Segara Harapan, 6th Floor, Graha Mustika Ratu, Jalan Gatot Suroto Kav 74-75, Jakarta 12870, Jawa, Indonesia, *Tel:* +62 21 830 6555, *Fax:* +62 21 837 4805, *Email:* aatex@cbn.net.id
Andhika GAC, PT. Andhika GAC, Graha Surya Internusa, Suite 1201, 8 Jalan HR Rasuna Said Kav X-0, Jakarta 12950, Jawa, Indonesia, *Tel:* +62 21 522 7230, *Fax:*

+62 21 522 7231, *Email:* shipping.indonesia@gacworld.com, *Website:* www.gacworld.com

Arpeni Pratama Ocean Line, P.T. Perusahaan Pelayaran Samudera Khusus (APOL), Jalan Yos Sudarso No.47A, Jakarta 14320, Jawa, Indonesia, *Tel:* +62 21 435 3941, *Fax:* +62 21 435 8425, *Email:* kacab_tjp@apol.co.id, *Website:* www.apol.co.id

P.T. Awards Shipping Agency Indonesia, Sarana Penjaminan, 8th Floor, Jl Angkasa Kav 6, Jakarta, Jawa, Indonesia, *Tel:* +62 21 654 2081, *Fax:* +62 21 654 2082, *Website:* www.awards.com.hk

P.T. Bahana Utama Line, Pulomas Build.IV Lt.2 Room 9-10, Jl. Jend. A. Yani No.2, Jakarta 13210, Jawa, Indonesia, *Tel:* +62 21 489 3316, *Fax:* +62 21 489 7082, *Email:* jakartabr@bahana-line.com, *Website:* www.bahana-line.com

P.T. Baruna Shipping Line, Jalan Re Martadinata, Ancol, Jakarta, Jawa, Indonesia, *Tel:* +62 21 691 9066, *Fax:* +62 21 691 9069, *Email:* info@barunaline.com

Ben Line Agencies Ltd, Wisma Budi, 3rd Floor, Suite 304, Jalan HR Rasuna Said Kav, C-6, Jakarta 12940, Indonesia, *Tel:* +62 21 527 3290, *Fax:* +62 21 527 3291, *Email:* jkt-genmbox@benline.co.id, *Website:* www.benlineagencies.com

P.T. Bhumi Daerah Express, Jl Kopi 2C, Jakarta 11230, Jawa, Indonesia, *Tel:* +62 21 690 0492, *Fax:* +62 21 692 8565

P.T. Bumi Laut Shipping Corp., Harmoni Plaza, Block J 5-7, Jalan Suryopranoto 2, Jakarta 10130, Jawa, Indonesia, *Tel:* +62 21 633 0668, *Fax:* +62 21 633 0742/4, *Email:* iqan@blg.co.id

P.T. Djakarta Lloyd (PERSERO), Djakarta Lloyd Building, Jalan Senen Raya 44, Jakarta 10410, Jawa, Indonesia, *Tel:* +62 21 345 6208, *Fax:* +62 21 384 0255, *Email:* dlloydmail@dlloyd.co.id, *Website:* www.dlloyd.co.id

P.T. Freight Liner Indonesia, Jl Kunir 32,, Blok A8, Jakarta 11110, Jawa, Indonesia, *Tel:* +62 21 690 8107, *Fax:* +62 21 690 0718

P.T. Garbantara Citra Buana, Fortune Building, 3rd Floor, Jl Mampang Prapatan Raya No 96, Jakarta, Jawa, Indonesia, *Tel:* +62 21 798 9036, *Fax:* +62 21 798 9036

P.T. Harpul Hoegh Lines, Suite 202 South Tower, Kuningan Plaza, Jl HR Rasuna Said, Kav V11-14, Jakarta 12940, Jawa, Indonesia, *Tel:* +62 21 520 0972, *Fax:* +62 21 525 1017, *Email:* hphlind@indosat.net.id, *Website:* www.harpership.com.sg

P.T. Harta Hariman, Menara Era, 7th Floor, Jl Senen Raya Kav, Jakarta 10410, Jawa, Indonesia, *Tel:* +62 21 386 2820, *Fax:* +62 21 386 2850

Inchcape Shipping Services (ISS), ISS-Equinox PT, Globe Building Jl. Buncit Raya Kav. 31-33, P O Box 12740, Jakarta, Jawa, Indonesia, *Tel:* +62 21 7918 7006, *Fax:* +62 21 7918 7097, *Email:* agency@ppequinox.com, *Website:* www.iss-shipping.com

Karunia Manning & Crew Management, Jl Swasembada Barat VIII No.42, Jakarta 14220, Jawa, Indonesia, *Tel:* +62 21 435 4264, *Fax:* +62 21 430 4359, *Email:* sudirman@karunia.co.id, *Website:* www.karunia.co.id

P.T. Karunia Tirta Buana, Blok 17, Perkantoran Cempaka Putih Permai, Jl Let Jend Suprapto 10, Jakarta 10510, Jawa, Indonesia, *Tel:* +62 21 420 4272, *Fax:* +62 21 420 4274

P.T. Layar Sentosa Shipping Corp., Jalan Majapahit 34 30-32, Jakarta 10160, Jawa, Indonesia, *Tel:* +62 21 385 4781, *Fax:* +62 21 231 0281, *Email:* salesjkt@larsen.co.id

A.P. Moller-Maersk Group, Maersk Line, Menara Batavia 15th Floor, Jl. K. H. Mas Mansyur Kav. 126, Jakarta 10220, Jawa, Indonesia, *Tel:* +62 21 3006 5555, *Fax:* +62 21 574 5234, *Website:* www.maerskline.com

P.T. Newship Nusabersama, 4th Floor, Jl Tanah Abang III/14, Jakarta 10160, Jawa, Indonesia, *Tel:* +62 21 350 4980, *Fax:* +62 21 350 0631, *Email:* mgmt@jkt.newship.co.id

Oldendorff Indotrans Indonesia, 21st Floor, Mid Plaza 2 Building, Jl Jend Sudirman Kav 10-11, Jakarta 10220, Jawa, Indonesia, *Tel:* +62 21 570 0588, *Fax:* +62 21 571 9968, *Email:* pt_oi@oldendorff.co.id

P.T. Pelayaran Wang Jaya Samudera, Kompleks Marina Tama, Jl Gunung Sahari Raya, 2 Blok G, 12B, Jakarta 14430, Jawa, Indonesia, *Tel:* +62 21 645 4668, *Fax:* +62 21 645 4669, *Email:* export@wangjaya.com, *Website:* www.wangjaya.com

P.T. Perusahaan Pelayaran Kalimantan, 40 Kebon Bawang V, P O Box 1092, Jakarta 14010, Jawa, Indonesia, *Tel:* +62 21 435 0422/5931, *Fax:* +62 21 435 5933/5934

P.T. Pilindo Megah Selatan, Graha Atrium Building, 9th Floor, Suite 901Jl, Senen Raya, Jakarta, Jawa, Indonesia, *Tel:* +62 21 345 8660, *Fax:* +62 21 345 8628

P.T. Samudera Pacific Maju, Jl Muara Karang Raya 163/5, Jakarta 14450, Jawa, Indonesia, *Tel:* +62 21 660 3301, *Fax:* +62 21 669 7047, *Email:* contact@spm.co.id, *Website:* www.spm.co.id

P.T. Pelayaran Samudera Selatan, Jl KH Zainul Arifin 41 A/B, Jakarta 10130, Jawa, Indonesia, *Tel:* +62 21 632 3084/3077, *Fax:* +62 21 632 2826, *Email:* pilrep@indo.net.id

P.T. Samudera Shipping Services, 1st Floor, Samudera Indonesia Building, Jalan Letjen S. Parman, Kav. 35, Jakarta, Jawa, Indonesia, *Tel:* +62 21 534 4887, *Fax:* +62 21 530 7894

P.T. Pelayaran Taruna Cipta Kencana, Jalan Mayjen Suprapto, Komplek Graha Cempaka Mas Blok E/26, Jakarta 10640, Jawa, Indonesia, *Tel:* +62 21 426 7068, *Fax:* +62 21 426 7072, *Email:* tcksmg@tck.co.id

Wallem Shipping Agencies Limited, Jl Majapahit 30A, Jakarta, Jawa, Indonesia, *Tel:* +62 21 380 6369, *Fax:* +62 21 351 9264, *Email:* infoships@wallemsentosa.co.id, *Website:* www.wallem.com

Surveyors: ABS (Pacific), Gedung Perkantoran Bidakara, Room 2003, 20th Floor, J1 Jend. Gatot Subroto Kav. 71-73, Jakarta 12870, Jawa, Indonesia, *Tel:* +62 21 8379 3067, *Fax:* +62 21 8379 3072, *Email:* absjakarta@eagle.org

Bureau Veritas, Setiabudi 2 Building, 5th Floor, Suite 506-507, Jl. H.R. Rasuna Said, Kav.62 Kuningan, Jakarta 12920, Jawa, Indonesia, *Tel:* +62 21 521 0393, *Fax:* +62 21 521 0806, *Email:* office.jakarta@bureauveritas.com, *Website:* www.bureauveritas.com

Det Norske Veritas A/S, Granadi Building 11th Floor (North Wing), Jl. H.R. Rasuna Said Kav.X-1 No.8-9, Jakarta 12950, Jawa, Indonesia, *Tel:* +62 21 252 6233, *Fax:* +62 21 252 1756, *Website:* www.dnv.com

Germanischer Lloyd, Wisma Barito Pacific Tower B, 3rd Floor, Jl. Letjend S. Parman Kav 62-63, Jakarta 11410, Jawa, Indonesia, *Tel:* +62 21 5367 9201, *Fax:* +62 21 5367 9177, *Email:* gl-jakarta@gl-group.com, *Website:* www.gl-goup.com

Integral Marine Consultants Sdn Bhd, Jl. Parang Tritis IV, 10 Ancol Barat, Jakarta 14430, Jawa, Indonesia, *Tel:* +62 21 690 9520, *Fax:* +62 21 690 9694, *Email:* gimk@uninet.net.id

Matthews-Daniel Services (Bermuda) Ltd, Matthews-Daniel PT (PT Menara Dirgatama Ind), C/o Gedung Cawang Kencana, 6th Floor Room 601, Jl May Jend Sutoyo, Kav 22, Jakarta 13630, Jawa, Indonesia, *Tel:* +62 21 800 0602, *Fax:* +62 21 801 1341, *Website:* www.matdan.com

Nippon Kaiji Kyokai, Menara Cakrawala, 17th Floor, Jalan Thamrin 9, Jakarta 10340, Jawa, Indonesia, *Tel:* +62 21 314 2138, *Fax:* +62 21 310 2012, *Email:* jk@classnk.or.jp, *Website:* www.classnk.or.jp

Societe Generale de Surveillance (SGS), P.T. Superintending Co of Indonesia, 4th Floor, Graha Sucofindo, Jl. Raya Pasar Minggu Kav 34, Jakarta 12780, Jawa, Indonesia, *Tel:* +62 21 798 3666, *Fax:* +62 21 798 3888, *Website:* www.sgs.com

Medical Facilities: Available in the port area. Hospital in Jakarta town

Airport: Sukarno-Hatta International Airport, 25 km

Development: Work has begun on the new 15 berth Jakarta New Port which will include container, multipurpose and automotive terminals, as well as being able to handle naval vessels. It is being built by Indonesian and Japanese Companies comprising of 15 berths, 300 metres long, with a draught of 16 metres.The port is to be built in five phases over six years. The breakwater will be built in the first phase by December 2005, with the automotive terminal second in 2006

Lloyd's Agent: P.T. Carsurin, Sarana Penjaminan Building, 7th Floor, Jl Angkasa Block B-9 Kav 6, Kemayoran, Jakarta 10720, Jawa, Indonesia, *Tel:* +62 21 654 0425, *Fax:* +62 21 654 0418, *Email:* lloyds@carsurin.com, *Website:* www.carsurin.com

JAMBI

Lat 1° 35' S; Long 103° 37' E.

Admiralty Chart: 1788	**Admiralty Pilot:** 36
Time Zone: GMT +7 h	**UNCTAD Locode:** ID DJB

Principal Facilities:

P		Y	G	C				A

Authority: PT (Persero) Pelabuhan Indonesia II, Port of Jambi, Jalan Pelabuhan Talang Duku, Jambi 36251, Sumatra, Indonesia, *Tel:* +62 741 35071, *Fax:* +62 741 35064

Port Security: ISPS compliant

Approach: Depth on outer bar 5.5 m at HW and 3.5 m at LW. Distance from outer bar to Telok Majelis (pilot station) is 10 miles and from Telok Majelis to Jambi is 75 miles. Channel width of 80 m in depth of 3.5 m LWS

Anchorage: The following positions for vessels waiting to load/discharge at the outer bar:
A: 0° 54' 03" S; 103° 47' 50" E
B: 0° 54' 03" S; 103° 48' 20" E
C: 0° 54' 33" S; 103° 47' 50" E
D: 0° 54' 33" S; 103° 48' 20" E
Position area for vessels awaiting pilot is 0° 54' 20" S; 103° 47' 10" E
All in depths of 9 m

Pilotage: Compulsory. Pilot station at Telok Majelis in pos 1° 03' 42" S; 103° 48' 22" E

Radio Frequency: Coastal Radio Station, Jambi Port Radio, call sign 'PKC3', working frequencies 1100 and 8799 kHz. Pilot station on VHF Channels 12 and 14

Tides: Difference between high water and low water levels is 3.5 m

Principal Imports and Exports: Imports: Asphalt, General cargo, Machinery. Exports: Palm oil, Plywood, Rubber (pallets), Sawn timber.

Working Hours: Mon-Thurs 0800-1600. Fri 0800-1300. Sat 0800-1400. 24 h working available if needed

Accommodation:

Name	Remarks
Jambi	See [1] below
Private Wharves	Sabak Indah wharves for chemicals and Ayong Susana wharves for general cargo

[1]*Jambi:* Two floating pontoon jetties (Ferrocement I and II), each 66.8 m long in depth of 5 m
Tanker facilities: Kasang oil wharf 32 m long, owned by Pertamina, 7 miles upstream from Jambi Port

Mechanical Handling Equipment:

Location	Type	Capacity (t)	Qty
Jambi	Mobile Cranes	15	1
Jambi	Mobile Cranes	50	1
Jambi	Forklifts	10	2

Repair & Maintenance: P.T. Sijenjang Raya Dock Yard, Jambi, Sumatra, Indonesia, *Tel:* +62 741 20318, *Fax:* +62 741 31051 Repair facilities

Shipping Agents: PT Panurjwan, 32 Kolonel Polisi M Taher, Talang Banjar, Jambi, Sumatra, Indonesia, *Tel:* +62 741 31184, *Fax:* +62 741 34378

Stevedoring Companies: Usha Terminal Cabang Pelabuhan Jambi, Jambi, Sumatra, Indonesia, *Tel:* +62 741 35068, *Fax:* +62 741 53323

Medical Facilities: Port Health Clinic and Public Hospital

Airport: Sultan Thaha, 15 km

Lloyd's Agent: P.T. Carsurin, Sarana Penjaminan Building, 7th Floor, Jl Angkasa Block B-9 Kav 6, Kemayoran, Jakarta 10720, Jawa, Indonesia, *Tel:* +62 21 654 0425, *Fax:* +62 21 654 0418, *Email:* lloyds@carsurin.com, *Website:* www.carsurin.com

JAYAPURA

Lat 2° 32' S; Long 140° 43' E.

Admiralty Chart: 3250	**Admiralty Pilot:** 35
Time Zone: GMT +9 h	**UNCTAD Locode:** ID DJJ

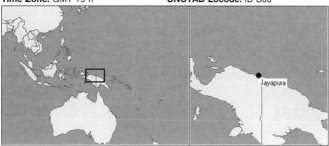

Principal Facilities:

P		G	C	R		B			A	

Authority: PT (Persero) Pelabuhan Indonesia IV, Port of Jayapura, Jalan Koti II/21, Jayapura 99221, Irian Jaya, Indonesia, *Tel:* +62 967 533330, *Fax:* +62 967 532741

Documentation: Passenger list (14 copies), crew list (7 copies), custom document (2 copies), health document (2 copies), cargo manifest (7 copies), bills of lading (7 copies), ship's papers (5 copies), sailing permit

Approach: Channel 1.5 nautical miles long, breadth 500 m, depth 50 m LWS

Pilotage: Compulsory, 24 h working. Two pilots available

Radio Frequency: Jayapura Coastal Radio Station: Call sign PNK. Frequency 12682.5 kHz, 17074.4 kHz, 8802.6 kHz

Traffic: 1999, 295 443 t of cargo handled

Maximum Vessel Dimensions: 10 000 dwt, 150 m loa, 10 m draft

Working Hours: 0800-1200, 1300-1700, 1900-2400, 0000-0500

Accommodation: Tanker facilities: Pertamina oil jetty 120 m long in depth of 20 m

Name	Length (m)	Depth (m)
Jayapura		
Main Berth	132	11
APO Berth	33	8
New Berth	82	12

Storage: One godown of 2200 m2

Mechanical Handling Equipment:

Location	Type	Capacity (t)	Qty
Jayapura	Mobile Cranes	25	1
Jayapura	Forklifts	3	4

Bunkering: PT Pertamina, Jalan Jos Sudarso 32-34, P O Box 265, Tanjung Priok, Jawa, Indonesia, *Tel:* +62 21 430 1086, *Fax:* +62 21 430 1562 – *Grades:* DO; MDO; IFO100-300cSt – *Rates:* 300t per day – *Delivery Mode:* tanker truck

Shipping Agents: P.T. (PELNI) Pelayaran Nasional Indonesia, Jl Argapura No.15, Jayapura 99222, Irian Jaya, Indonesia, *Tel:* +62 967 536931, *Fax:* +62 967 533370, *Email:* agencies@pelni.co.id, *Website:* www.pelni.co.id

Medical Facilities: Jayapura Hospital

Airport: Sentani Airport, 38 km

Lloyd's Agent: P.T. Carsurin, Sarana Penjaminan Building, 7th Floor, Jl Angkasa Block B-9 Kav 6, Kemayoran, Jakarta 10720, Jawa, Indonesia, *Tel:* +62 21 654 0425, *Fax:* +62 21 654 0418, *Email:* lloyds@carsurin.com, *Website:* www.carsurin.com

KALIANGET

Lat 7° 4' S; Long 113° 59' E.

Admiralty Chart: 945	**Admiralty Pilot:** 34
Time Zone: GMT +7 h	**UNCTAD Locode:** ID KAT

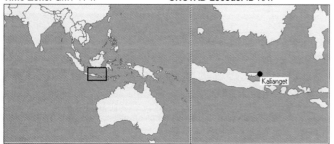

Principal Facilities:

		G		R				A	

Authority: Harbour Office, 6 Jalan Pelabuhan, Kalianget 69471, Madura Island, Indonesia, *Tel:* +62 328 661926, *Fax:* +62 328 662447, *Email:* portina3@rad.net.id, *Website:* www.pp3.co.id

Approach: Depth of channel 4-5 m

Pilotage: Available

Radio Frequency: Kalianget Coastal Radio Station, VHF Channels 16, 14, 13 and 12. Frequencies 2192, 6215 and 5316 mHz

Weather: Dry season June-October. Rainy season November-May

Maximum Vessel Dimensions: 80 m loa, 2500 dwt, 3 m max draft

Working Hours: 0700-1400, 1500-2100

Accommodation:

Name	Length (m)	Remarks
Kalianget		
Wharf	80	Owned by the Port Authority
Wharf	96	Operated by Perum Garam with warehouse

Cargo Worked: 12 t/gang/h

Repair & Maintenance: Minor repairs available from PT Prima Daya Samudera, Jl. Hayam Wuruk, Kalianget

Medical Facilities: Port health centre available

Airport: Trunojoyo Airport, 4 km

Lloyd's Agent: P.T. Carsurin, Sarana Penjaminan Building, 7th Floor, Jl Angkasa Block B-9 Kav 6, Kemayoran, Jakarta 10720, Jawa, Indonesia, *Tel:* +62 21 654 0425, *Fax:* +62 21 654 0418, *Email:* lloyds@carsurin.com, *Website:* www.carsurin.com

KASIM TERMINAL

Lat 1° 18' S; Long 131° 1' E.

Admiralty Chart: 1420	**Admiralty Pilot:** 35
Time Zone: GMT +9 h	**UNCTAD Locode:** ID KAS

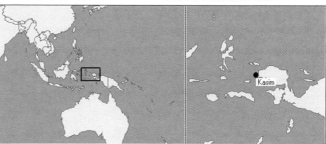

Principal Facilities:

P								T	A	

Authority: Petro-China International (Bermuda) Ltd., Kasim Marine Terminal, Sorong, Irian Jaya, Indonesia, *Email:* kasim@petrochina.co.id

Port Security: ISPS compliant

Approach: Channel 30 miles long, 360 m wide in a depth of 16.5 m

Anchorage: In pos 0° 53' 00" S; 131° 01' 14" E in depth of 40 m

Pilotage: Compulsory. Three pilots available and two pilot boats of 450 hp

Radio Frequency: VHF Channel 16

Tides: Max tide 1.2 m

Maximum Vessel Dimensions: 135 000 dwt, 274 m loa, 14.5 m draft

Principal Imports and Exports: Exports: Crude oil.

Accommodation:

Name	Remarks
Kasim Marine Terminal	
Tanker Berth	See [1] below

[1]*Tanker Berth:* Tanker berth with four breasting dolphins and a loading platform with max draft alongside of 14.5 m. Crude oil is loaded through 2 x 16" chicksan loading arms at max rate of 30 000 bbls/h

Towage: Two tugs of 4000 hp

Medical Facilities: Doctor and clinic available

Airport: Jefman, 19 km

Lloyd's Agent: P.T. Carsurin, Sarana Penjaminan Building, 7th Floor, Jl Angkasa Block B-9 Kav 6, Kemayoran, Jakarta 10720, Jawa, Indonesia, *Tel:* +62 21 654 0425, *Fax:* +62 21 654 0418, *Email:* lloyds@carsurin.com, *Website:* www.carsurin.com

KENDARI

Lat 3° 58' S; Long 122° 35' E.

Admiralty Chart: 3616	**Admiralty Pilot:** 34
Time Zone: GMT +8 h	**UNCTAD Locode:** ID KDI

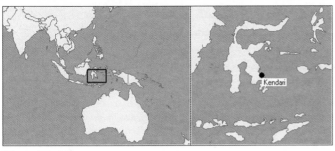

Principal Facilities:

P		G	C		B		A

Authority: PT (Persero) Pelabuhan Indonesia IV, Port of Kendari, Jalan Konggoasa No.1, Kendari 93127, Sulawesi Tenggara, Indonesia, *Tel:* +62 401 321087, *Fax:* +62 401 321976, *Email:* pelindo4@kendari.wasantara.net.id, *Website:* www.kendariport.freetzi.com

Documentation: Passenger list (6 copies), crew list (4 copies), custom document (2 copies), health document (2 copies), cargo manifest (5 copies), bills of lading (5 copies), ship's papers (5 copies), sailing permit

Approach: Navigation channel 2.16 mile long, 150 m width in depth of 10-30 m, bottom of sand and clay

Pilotage: Compulsory. Two pilot boats available

Radio Frequency: Kendari Coastal Radio Station: call sign PKF3 operates 12 h on VHF Channel 16

Traffic: 2007, 667 537 t of cargo handled

Maximum Vessel Dimensions: Max draft 9 m

Working Hours: 24 h/day

Accommodation:

Name	Length (m)	Remarks
Kendari		
Nusantara Pier	270	
Pertamina Jetty	120	Tankers
Cargo Pier	110	

Storage: Two container yards, one of 2968 m2 and one of 2380 m2

Location	Covered (m²)	Sheds / Warehouses
Kendari	1000	1

Mechanical Handling Equipment:

Location	Type	Capacity (t)	Qty
Kendari	Mobile Cranes	15	1
Kendari	Forklifts	3	2

Bunkering: PT Pertamina, Jalan Jos Sudarso 32-34, P O Box 265, Tanjung Priok, Jawa, Indonesia, *Tel:* +62 21 430 1086, *Fax:* +62 21 430 1562 – *Grades:* DO; MDO; IFO100-300cSt – *Parcel Size:* no min/max – *Rates:* 100-150t/h – *Notice:* 48 hours – *Delivery Mode:* barge, pipeline

Shipping Agents: P.T. (PELNI) Pelayaran Nasional Indonesia, Jl Laki Dende No.10, Kendari, Sulawesi Tenggara, Indonesia, *Tel:* +62 401 321915, *Fax:* +62 401 322156, *Email:* agencies@pelni.co.id, *Website:* www.pelni.co.id

Surveyors: P.T. Biro Klasifikasi Indonesia, Jl. Bunga Matahari No.64, Kema Raya, Kendari 93121, Sulawesi Tenggara, Indonesia, *Tel:* +62 401 321622, *Fax:* +62 401 322847, *Email:* bkikd@klasifikasiindonesia.com, *Website:* www.klasifikasiindonesia.com

Medical Facilities: Hospital facilities or port doctor available

Airport: Wolter Monginsidi Airport, 25 km

Lloyd's Agent: P.T. Carsurin, Sarana Penjaminan Building, 7th Floor, Jl Angkasa Block B-9 Kav 6, Kemayoran, Jakarta 10720, Jawa, Indonesia, *Tel:* +62 21 654 0425, *Fax:* +62 21 654 0418, *Email:* lloyds@carsurin.com, *Website:* www.carsurin.com

KIJANG

Lat 0° 51' N; Long 104° 37' E.

Admiralty Chart: 3937	**Admiralty Pilot:** 36
Time Zone: GMT +7 h	**UNCTAD Locode:** ID KID

Principal Facilities:

		Y	G						A

Authority: Port of Kijang, Jl. Hang Jebat No.29, Kijang, Bintan Island, Indonesia, *Tel:* +62 21177

Port Security: ISPS compliant

Approach: Channel depths 10-24 m. Vessels must manoeuvre cautiously

Pilotage: Compulsory to use harbour pilot

Tides: Max 1.9 m, min 0.2 m

Accommodation:

Name	Length (m)	Depth (m)	Remarks
Kijang			
Sea Communication Wharf	50	9	See [1] below
PT Aneka Tambang Wharf	135	11	Used for loading bauxite
PT Korindo Abadi Wharf	200	8	See [2] below
PT Wirah Indah Kencana Wharf		7	Used for loading granite by tug or barge

[1]*Sea Communication Wharf:* Used for loading and unloading of goods and embarkation and disembarkation of passengers
[2]*PT Korindo Abadi Wharf:* Used for loading plywoods and unloading spare parts. Warehousing of 14 m x 190 m and 14 m x 230 m

Mechanical Handling Equipment:

Location	Type	Capacity (t)
PT Korindo Abadi Wharf	Mult-purp. Cranes	50

Cargo Worked: Bauxite: loading by escalator 300 t/h. Plywood: loading by crane 100 m3/h. General cargo: loading by crane 15 t/h

Medical Facilities: PT Aneka Tambang hospital, 1 km

Airport: Kijang, 12 km

Lloyd's Agent: P.T. Carsurin, Sarana Penjaminan Building, 7th Floor, Jl Angkasa Block B-9 Kav 6, Kemayoran, Jakarta 10720, Jawa, Indonesia, *Tel:* +62 21 654 0425, *Fax:* +62 21 654 0418, *Email:* lloyds@carsurin.com, *Website:* www.carsurin.com

KRUENG GEUKUEH

see under Lhokseumawe

KUALA KAPUAS

Lat 3° 0' S; Long 114° 22' E.

Admiralty Chart: 1066	**Admiralty Pilot:** 36
Time Zone: GMT +8 h	**UNCTAD Locode:** ID KKA

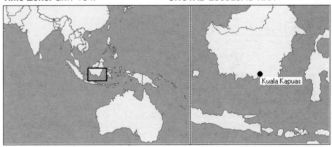

Principal Facilities:

			G						

Authority: P.T. (Persero) Pelabuhan Indonesia III, Kuala Kapuas, South Kalimantan, Indonesia, *Tel:* +62 513 21101

Documentation: 2 x 24 h health book, ship's certificate, sailing permit, crew list, passports, officer certificate

Pilotage: Compulsory

Radio Frequency: VHF Channel 12

Accommodation:

Name	Length (m)	Depth (m)
Kuala Kapuas		
Wooden Jetty	100	2–6

Lloyd's Agent: P.T. Carsurin, Sarana Penjaminan Building, 7th Floor, Jl Angkasa Block B-9 Kav 6, Kemayoran, Jakarta 10720, Jawa, Indonesia, *Tel:* +62 21 654 0425, *Fax:* +62 21 654 0418, *Email:* lloyds@carsurin.com, *Website:* www.carsurin.com

KUPANG

Lat 10° 10' S; Long 123° 34' E.

Admiralty Chart: 3296	**Admiralty Pilot:** 34
Time Zone: GMT +8 h	**UNCTAD Locode:** ID KOE

Key to Principal Facilities:—				
A=Airport	**C**=Containers	**G**=General Cargo	**P**=Petroleum	**R**=Ro/Ro	**Y**=Dry Bulk
B=Bunkers	**D**=Dry Dock	**L**=Cruise	**Q**=Other Liquid Cargo	**T**=Towage (where available from port)

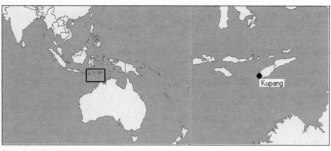

Principal Facilities:

P		Y	G		R		B		T	A

Authority: Port Administrator, Jalan Yos Sudarso No.23, Kupang, Timor, Indonesia, *Tel:* +62 391 821790

Approach: Channel depths approx 50 m. Shallow water marked by buoy in pos 10° 12' 29" S; 123° 30' 41" E

Anchorage: Anchorage can be obtained in pos 10° 11' 52" S; 123° 30' 45" E in depths ranging from 50 m to 90 m

Pilotage: Masters must request pilot 3 h before vessel is due alongside

Radio Frequency: Kupang Radio, call sign PKK. Calling frequency 500 kc/s; working frequency 430 kc/s. VHF Channel 16 (156.8 mHz), Channel 14 (156.7 mHz), Channel 12 (156.6 mHz)

Weather: Strong winds and rough seas can be experienced from December to February

Tides: Range of tide 2.4 m

Maximum Vessel Dimensions: 169 m loa, 10 000 dwt, 9 m draft

Principal Imports and Exports: Imports: Asphalt, Coal, Gypsum. Exports: Cattle, Coffee, Sandalwood.

Working Hours: Normal 0800-1600. 24 h when required. No work Sundays and other holidays

Accommodation:

Name	Length (m)	Depth (m)	Remarks
Kupang			See [1] below
Tenau Wharf	223	9	
Passenger Pier	94	5.5	
Kupang Wharf	28		Equipped for cattle shipments

[1]*Kupang:* One tanker berth, average discharging rate of 300 t/h. Small tank farm on shore

Storage:

Location	Open (m²)	Covered (m²)	Sheds / Warehouses
Kupang	15000	2500	2

Mechanical Handling Equipment:

Location	Type	Capacity (t)	Qty
Kupang	Mobile Cranes	25	1
Kupang	Mobile Cranes	15	1
Kupang	Forklifts	5	1

Cargo Worked: 300 t/day/shift. General cargo 12 t/gang/h, bagged cargo 19 t/gang/h, bulk cargo 89 t/gang/h

Bunkering: PT Pertamina, Jalan Jos Sudarso 32-34, P O Box 265, Tanjung Priok, Jawa, Indonesia, *Tel:* +62 21 430 1086, *Fax:* +62 21 430 1562 – *Grades:* DO; MDO; IFO100-300cSt – *Parcel Size:* no min/max – *Rates:* 20-30t/h – *Notice:* 48 hours – *Delivery Mode:* pipeline

Towage: Small tugs available of 150 hp

Medical Facilities: Hospital at Tenau Port

Airport: El Tari Airport, approx 19 km

Lloyd's Agent: P.T. Carsurin, Sarana Penjaminan Building, 7th Floor, Jl Angkasa Block B-9 Kav 6, Kemayoran, Jakarta 10720, Jawa, Indonesia, *Tel:* +62 21 654 0425, *Fax:* +62 21 654 0418, *Email:* lloyds@carsurin.com, *Website:* www.carsurin.com

LALANG TERMINAL

Lat 1° 11' N; Long 102° 13' E.

Admiralty Chart: 3947
Time Zone: GMT +7 h

Admiralty Pilot: 44
UNCTAD Locode: ID LAT

Principal Facilities:

P									T	

Authority: Kondur Petroleum S.A., Menara Global, 10th Floor, Jalan Gatot Subroto Kav. 27, Jakarta 12950, Jawa, Indonesia, *Tel:* +62 21 5270606, *Fax:* +62 21 5270101, *Website:* www.kondur.co.id

Port Security: ISPS compliant

Anchorage: Anchorage is 3.2 km N of the terminal in a depth of 21 m. There is a restricted area 6.5 km long and 3.25 km wide centred on the terminal

Pilotage: Compulsory. Pilot boards approx 2 nautical miles N of Fairway Lt. Buoy in pos 1° 54.2' N; 101° 51.5' E

Radio Frequency: VHF Channel 16

Tides: The flood tide bears S at a rate of 4.5 knots and the ebb to the N at 3 knots

Accommodation:

Name	Remarks
Lalang Terminal	See [1] below

[1]*Lalang Terminal:* A 138 000 dwt storage barge (Ladinda) moored to a platform and connected by underwater pipeline to an area abreast of Layang 12.87 km S. Berthing is carried out in daylight and vessels with a draft exceeding 16.75 m leave at HT

Towage: Two tugs of 3600 hp

Lloyd's Agent: P.T. Carsurin, Sarana Penjaminan Building, 7th Floor, Jl Angkasa Block B-9 Kav 6, Kemayoran, Jakarta 10720, Jawa, Indonesia, *Tel:* +62 21 654 0425, *Fax:* +62 21 654 0418, *Email:* lloyds@carsurin.com, *Website:* www.carsurin.com

LANGSA TERMINAL

Lat 5° 19' N; Long 98° 3' E.

Admiralty Chart: 1353
Time Zone: GMT +7 h

Admiralty Pilot: 44
UNCTAD Locode: ID

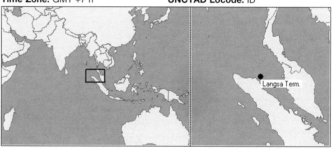

Principal Facilities:

P										

Authority: Matrix Oil NL, 7th Floor Suite 703-704, Jl. Sultan Iskanda Muda, Blok V-TA, Jakarta 12310, Jawa, Indonesia, *Tel:* +62 21 7590 5656, *Fax:* +62 21 7590 5666

Port Security: ISPS compliant

Pilotage: Compulsory

Radio Frequency: The terminal maintains a continuous watch on VHF Channel 16

Maximum Vessel Dimensions: 30 000-80 000 dwt, no draft limitation

Working Hours: 24 h/day

Accommodation:

Name	Remarks
Langsa Terminal	See [1] below

[1]*Langsa Terminal:* Consists of the 33 000 dwt FPSO 'MV8 Langsa Venture' moored in depth of 100 m with storing cap of 230 000 bbls. Export tankers normally berth during daylight hours only. Transfer to export tanker is through a 10" floating hose

Lloyd's Agent: P.T. Carsurin, Sarana Penjaminan Building, 7th Floor, Jl Angkasa Block B-9 Kav 6, Kemayoran, Jakarta 10720, Jawa, Indonesia, *Tel:* +62 21 654 0425, *Fax:* +62 21 654 0418, *Email:* lloyds@carsurin.com, *Website:* www.carsurin.com

LAWE-LAWE TERMINAL

Lat 1° 27' S; Long 116° 45' E.

Admiralty Chart: 3014
Time Zone: GMT +8 h

Admiralty Pilot: 34
UNCTAD Locode: ID LLA

Principal Facilities:

P									

Authority: Union Oil Company of Indonesia, Ratu Plaza Building, 7th Floor, Jl. Jend. Sudirman, P O Box 264 JKT, Jakarta, Jawa, Indonesia, *Tel:* +62 21 712509

Anchorage: The anchorage in a depth of 30 m is 1° 26' S; 116° 47' E

Pilotage: Compulsory. The mooring master boards the vessel at the anchorage. ETA to be advised 72, 48 and 24 h in advance

Radio Frequency: Lawe-Lawe radio call sign PKN 28. VHF Channel 16

Maximum Vessel Dimensions: 136 586 dwt, 276.4 m loa

Accommodation:

Name	Remarks
Lawe-Lawe Terminal	See [1] below

[1]*Lawe-Lawe Terminal:* A SBM 9.25 km offshore in a depth of 26 m. Tankers must be equipped with a derrick for hose lifting. Loading rate 20 000 bbls/h

Medical Facilities: First aid only

Lloyd's Agent: P.T. Carsurin, Sarana Penjaminan Building, 7th Floor, Jl Angkasa Block B-9 Kav 6, Kemayoran, Jakarta 10720, Jawa, Indonesia, *Tel:* +62 21 654 0425, *Fax:* +62 21 654 0418, *Email:* lloyds@carsurin.com, *Website:* www.carsurin.com

LEMBAR

Lat 8° 34' S; Long 116° 4' E.

Admiralty Chart: 946	**Admiralty Pilot:** 34
Time Zone: GMT +8 h	**UNCTAD Locode:** ID

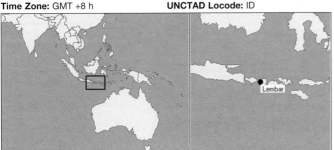

Principal Facilities:

P	Y	G		B		A

Authority: Port Administrator, Jalan Raya Pelabuhan, Lembar 83364, Lombok, Indonesia, *Tel:* +62 370 681187, *Fax:* +62 370 681019

Officials: Harbour Master: Lilik Hariwanto.

Anchorage: Anchorage available 50 m offshore in depth of 30 m

Pilotage: Available if required. At least 24 h advance notice must be given

Radio Frequency: Lembar Radio, call sign PKD3, 438 and 500 kHz

Weather: Strong winds and rough seas can be experienced from March to June

Maximum Vessel Dimensions: 115 m loa, 5000 dwt, 6.9 m draft

Working Hours: Normal 0800-1600. 24 h when required. No work Sundays and other holidays

Accommodation:

Name	Remarks
Lembar	See [1] below

[1]*Lembar:* Total wharf length of 228 m. Large vessels can be worked at the anchorage in a depth of 16 m. There are two lighters available of 40 t cap each

Storage:

Location	Open (m²)	Covered (m²)	Sheds / Warehouses
Lembar	12750	720	1

Mechanical Handling Equipment:

Location	Type	Capacity (t)	Qty
Lembar	Forklifts	3	1

Cargo Worked: 300 t/day/shift, bulk cargo 16 t/gang/h, bagged cargo 25 t/gang/h, general cargo 18 t/gang/h

Bunkering: Available

Medical Facilities: Hospital available at Lembar

Airport: Seleparang Airport, 30 km

Lloyd's Agent: P.T. Carsurin, Sarana Penjaminan Building, 7th Floor, Jl Angkasa Block B-9 Kav 6, Kemayoran, Jakarta 10720, Jawa, Indonesia, *Tel:* +62 21 654 0425, *Fax:* +62 21 654 0418, *Email:* lloyds@carsurin.com, *Website:* www.carsurin.com

LHOKNGA

Lat 5° 27' N; Long 95° 14' E.

Admiralty Chart: 2917/2777	**Admiralty Pilot:** 44
Time Zone: GMT +7 h	**UNCTAD Locode:** ID LHK

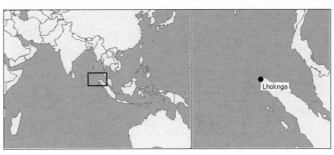

Principal Facilities:

	Y		B	T	

Authority: PT Semen Andalas Indonesia, Jl. Meulalboh Km 17, Lhoknga 23523, Banda Aceh, Indonesia, *Tel:* +62 651 770015, *Fax:* +62 651 770019

Anchorage: Vessels anchor in pos 5° 28' 20" N; 95° 12' 40" E in depth of 20 m and over

Pilotage: Compulsory. Pilot boarding station is located in pos 5° 27' 30" N; 95° 12' 30" E

Radio Frequency: VHF Channel 12

Maximum Vessel Dimensions: Max loa 150 m, max d 9.1 m

Accommodation:

Name	Length (m)	Depth (m)
Lhoknga Wharf	120	9

Mechanical Handling Equipment:

Location	Type	Capacity (t)	Qty
Lhoknga	Mult-purp. Cranes	5	1

Bunkering: Available

Towage: One tug of 730 hp

Medical Facilities: Doctor and clinic available

Lloyd's Agent: P.T. Carsurin, Sarana Penjaminan Building, 7th Floor, Jl Angkasa Block B-9 Kav 6, Kemayoran, Jakarta 10720, Jawa, Indonesia, *Tel:* +62 21 654 0425, *Fax:* +62 21 654 0418, *Email:* lloyds@carsurin.com, *Website:* www.carsurin.com

LHOKSEUMAWE

Lat 5° 10' N; Long 97° 9' E.

Admiralty Chart: 2777/3584	**Admiralty Pilot:** 44
Time Zone: GMT +7 h	**UNCTAD Locode:** ID LSW

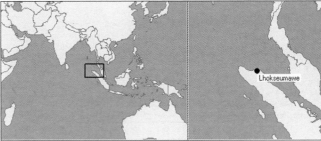

Principal Facilities:

Q	Y	G		R		B		T	A

Authority: PT (Persero) Pelabuhan Indonesia I, Port of Lhokseumawe, Jalan Pelabuhan Umum, Krueng Guekeuh, Lhokseumawe 24354, Sumatera, Indonesia, *Tel:* +62 645 56373, *Fax:* +62 645 56022

Officials: General Manager: M. Rumawi.

Port Security: Coast Guard and Police

Documentation: Cargo manifest, bill of lading, crew list, crew documentation, vessel documentation

Approach: There are no navigational hazards in the approaches. Channel depths in Lhokseumawe Old Harbour 11 m and in Krueng Geukueh fertilizer & public harbour 10 m

Anchorage: Lhokseumawe Old Harbour (for general cargo and tugs/barges): in pos 5° 10' 32" N; 97° 09' 20" E in depth of 9-11 m
Krueng Geukueh Harbour (fertilizer and general cargo): in pos 5° 16' 00" N; 97° 01' 40" E in depth of 25-40 m

Pilotage: Compulsory. Pilot boards vessel at the anchorage. Berthing/unberthing during the day only

Radio Frequency: Lhokseumawe Radio (PKB-20) & Harbour Master: VHF Channel 16. Lhokseumawe Port Control, Pilot & Ship Agents: VHF Channel 12

Maximum Vessel Dimensions: 190 m loa, 20 000 dwt, 9 m draft

Working Hours: 24 h/day

Key to Principal Facilities:—				
A=Airport	**C**=Containers	**G**=General Cargo	**P**=Petroleum	**R**=Ro/Ro	**Y**=Dry Bulk
B=Bunkers	**D**=Dry Dock	**L**=Cruise	**Q**=Other Liquid Bulk	**T**=Towage (where available from port)

Accommodation:

Name	Length (m)	Depth (m)	Remarks
Lhokseumawe			Passenger terminal of 290 m2
Multi-Purpose Berth	267	10	For vessels up to 20 000 dwt
Liquid Bulk Berth	80	6	For vessels up to 5000 dwt
Ro/Ro Berth	165	6	For vessels up to 5000 dwt

Storage:

Location	Open (m²)	Covered (m²)	Sheds / Warehouses
Lhokseumawe	20158	2600	1

Mechanical Handling Equipment:

Location	Type	Capacity (t)	Qty
Lhokseumawe	Mobile Cranes	25	1
Lhokseumawe	Mobile Cranes	10	1
Lhokseumawe	Forklifts	3	2
Lhokseumawe	Forklifts	5	1

Cargo Worked: 18 t/gang/h for general cargo, 45 t/gang/h for bagged cargo

Bunkering: Available by truck

Waste Reception Facilities: Garbage disposal available

Towage: Two tugs available

Repair & Maintenance: Not available

Shipping Agents: P.T. (PELNI) Pelayaran Nasional Indonesia, Jl Merdeka No.27, Lhokseumawe, Sumatera, Indonesia, *Tel:* +62 645 43454, *Fax:* +62 645 43458, *Email:* agencies@pelni.co.id, *Website:* www.pelni.co.id

Medical Facilities: Available

Airport: Malikussaleh, 18 km

Lloyd's Agent: P.T. Carsurin, Sarana Penjaminan Building, 7th Floor, Jl Angkasa Block B-9 Kav 6, Kemayoran, Jakarta 10720, Jawa, Indonesia, *Tel:* +62 21 654 0425, *Fax:* +62 21 654 0418, *Email:* lloyds@carsurin.com, *Website:* www.carsurin.com

MACASSAR

alternate name, see Makassar

MAKASSAR

Lat 5° 8' S; Long 119° 24' E.

Admiralty Chart: 2638
Time Zone: GMT +8 h
Admiralty Pilot: 34
UNCTAD Locode: ID MAK

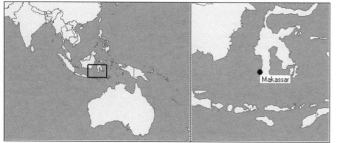

Principal Facilities:

P	Q	Y	G	C	R		B		T	A

Authority: PT (Persero) Pelabuhan Indonesia IV, Port of Makassar, Jalan Soekarno 1, Makassar 90173, Sulawesi, Indonesia, *Tel:* +62 411 316549, *Fax:* +62 411 313513, *Email:* portmks@indosat.net.id

Port Security: ISPS compliant

Documentation: Passenger list (5 copies), crew list (4 copies), custom document (2 copies), health document (2 copies), cargo manifest (7 copies), bills of lading (7 copies), ship's papers (5 copies), sailing permit

Approach: Entrance channel is 2 nautical miles long, width 150 m in depth of 16 m

Anchorage: Vessels anchor and await pilot in pos 5° 07' 25" S; 119° 24' 02" E

Pilotage: Compulsory. Notice for ETA and request for pilot must be made 4 h in advance by calling Makassar Coast Radio Station on VHF Channel 12

Radio Frequency: Makassar Radio (call sign PKF). VHF Channel 16

Tides: Range of tide 1.4 m

Traffic: 2005, 9 681 802 t of cargo handled, 244 199 TEU's

Principal Imports and Exports: Imports: Heavy industrial equipment, Wheat. Exports: Cocoa, Molasses, Pallets, Plywood, Rice.

Working Hours: Vessel operations 24 h

Accommodation:

Name	Length (m)	Depth (m)	Remarks
Makassar			
Soekarno Quay	1360	9	Conventional cargo
Cement	100		
Flour	142		

Name	Length (m)	Depth (m)	Remarks
General	968		
Passenger	150		
Hatta (Makassar) Container Terminal	850	11	See ¹ below
Hatta Multi-Purpose Terminal	410	12	Five berths for general & bagged cargo etc
Hasanuddin Quay	214	5	Two berths for ro/ro, general cargo etc
Paotere (Traditional Port)	532	5	General, bulk & unitised cargo
Berdikari Sari Utama Flour Mills	142	9	Wheat, flour
Packing Plan Cement	100	9	Cement
Passenger Quay	150	9	Passengers
UPPDN Pertamina	250	9	Two berths for oil

¹*Hatta (Makassar) Container Terminal:* Six berths operated by PT Makassar Terminal Services (MTS), 7B Jalan Botolempangan, Makassar, Tel: +62 411 331774, Fax: +62 411 332808, Email: rcruz@ictsi.com, Website: www.ictsi.com
Terminal area of 12 ha, container yard area of 11.4 ha and container freight station of 0.4 ha. 36 reefer points

Storage:

Location	Open (m²)	Covered (m²)	Sheds / Warehouses
Soekarno Quay	74051	19200	5
Paotere (Traditional Port)	14762		

Mechanical Handling Equipment:

Location	Type	Capacity (t)	Qty
Makassar	Mult-purp. Cranes	40	5
Makassar	Mobile Cranes	25	1
Makassar	Mobile Cranes	15	1
Makassar	Mobile Cranes	40	1
Makassar	Container Cranes	40	2
Makassar	Forklifts	15	14
Hatta (Makassar) Container Terminal	Container Cranes		4
Hatta (Makassar) Container Terminal	Transtainers		8
Hatta (Makassar) Container Terminal	Reach Stackers		2
Hatta (Makassar) Container Terminal	Forklifts		10

Bunkering: Bunkering can only be done alongside Sukarno Quay and Oil Jetty of Pertamina
Aditya Aryaprawira Corp., Wisma Mitra Sunter 01-02, Sunter Boulevard Block C-1, Jalan Yos Sudarso Kav 89, Jakarta 14350, Jawa, Indonesia, *Tel:* +62 21 6514732, *Fax:* +62 21 6514731, *Email:* info@adityacorp.com, *Website:* www.adityacorp.com
C.V. Bahtera Camar, Jalan Lagoa Terusan Bl No.4, Jakarta 14270, Jawa, Indonesia, *Tel:* +62 21 435 3209, *Fax:* +62 21 430 6048
Buana Jaya C.V., jalan Sungai Kapuas No.15, Jakarta 14270, Jawa, Indonesia, *Tel:* +62 21 44835302, *Fax:* +62 21 44835302
Kartika Jasa Karya P.T., Jalan Perak Timur 564/A1, Surabaya 60165, Jawa, Indonesia, *Tel:* +62 31 3293 459, *Fax:* +62 31 3294 736, *Email:* kemusuk@rad.net.id
PT Pertamina, Jalan Jos Sudarso 32-34, P O Box 265, Tanjung Priok, Jawa, Indonesia, *Tel:* +62 21 430 1086, *Fax:* +62 21 430 1562 – *Grades:* DO; MDO; IFO100-300cSt – *Parcel Size:* no min/max – *Rates:* 100-150t/h – *Notice:* 48 hours – *Delivery Mode:* barge, pipeline
C.V. Purba Jaya, Jalan Edam II No. 5, Tanjung Priok, Jakarta 14310, Jawa, Indonesia, *Tel:* +62 21 4393 1240, *Fax:* +62 21 4393 0792, *Email:* pijar@indo.net.id

Waste Reception Facilities: Only garbage disposal available

Towage: Three tugs available of 800-1500 hp

Repair & Maintenance: PT Industri Kapal Indonesia (Persero), Jln. Galangan Kapal, P O Box 1196, Makassar 90211, Sulawesi, Indonesia, *Tel:* +62 411 448653, *Fax:* +62 411 448658, *Email:* ptiki@ptiki.com, *Website:* www.ptiki.com Engine repairs

Shipping Agents: P.T. Bahana Utama Line, Makassar, Sulawesi, Indonesia, *Tel:* +62 411 852329, *Fax:* +62 411 835186, *Email:* makassar@bahana-line.com, *Website:* www.bahana-line.com
P.T. Layar Sentosa Shipping Corp., Jl Tentara Pelajar 68, Ujung Pandang, Makassar 90173, Sulawesi, Indonesia, *Tel:* +62 411 311988, *Fax:* +62 411 311988
P.T. Mandiri Abadi Santosa, Jl Nusantara 26, Makassar, Sulawesi, Indonesia, *Tel:* +62 411 332211, *Fax:* +62 411 314477, *Email:* budi.hartono@meratusline.com, *Website:* www.meratusline.com
P.T. (PELNI) Pelayaran Nasional Indonesia, Jl Jend Sudirman No.38, Makassar, Sulawesi, Indonesia, *Tel:* +62 411 331395, *Fax:* +62 411 317964, *Email:* agencies@pelni.co.id, *Website:* www.pelni.co.id
PT Perusahaan Pelayaran Samudera Trikora Lloyd, 1E, Jalan Bacan, Makassar 9000, Sulawesi, Indonesia, *Tel:* +62 411 318464, *Fax:* +62 411 313359

Surveyors: P.T. Biro Klasifikasi Indonesia, Jl. Sungai Cerekang No.28, Makassar 90115, Sulawesi, Indonesia, *Tel:* +62 411 311993, *Fax:* +62 411 315460, *Email:* bkims@klasifikasiindonesia.com, *Website:* www.klasifikasiindonesia.com
Nippon Kaiji Kyokai, Makassar, Sulawesi, Indonesia, *Tel:* +62 411 311993, *Fax:* +62 411 315460, *Website:* www.classnk.or.jp
P.T. Superintending Company of Indonesia (SUCOFINDO), Jln Uripmohardjo No. 90, P O Box 1022, Makassar, Sulawesi, Indonesia, *Tel:* +62 411 451890, *Fax:* +62 411 451796, *Email:* andarias@sucofindo.co.id, *Website:* www.sucofindo.co.id

Medical Facilities: Port health centre, Tel: +62 (411) 323610

Airport: Hasanuddin Airport, 21 km

Lloyd's Agent: P.T. Carsurin, Sarana Penjaminan Building, 7th Floor, Jl Angkasa Block B-9 Kav 6, Kemayoran, Jakarta 10720, Jawa, Indonesia, *Tel:* +62 21 654 0425, *Fax:* +62 21 654 0418, *Email:* lloyds@carsurin.com, *Website:* www.carsurin.com

MANADO

Lat 1° 30' N; Long 124° 50' E.

Admiralty Chart: 2637	**Admiralty Pilot:** 34
Time Zone: GMT +8 h	**UNCTAD Locode:** ID MDC

This port is no longer open to commercial shipping

Repair & Maintenance: P.T. Surya, Jalan Doktor Sam Ratulangi II 86, Manado, Sulawesi, Indonesia, *Tel:* +62 431 851847, *Fax:* +62 431 851413, *Email:* pelsur@sby.dnet-net.id

Shipping Agents: P.T. Djakarta Lloyd (PERSERO), Wisma Taurus, Jalan Raya Tomohon 69, Manado 95361, Sulawesi, Indonesia, *Tel:* +62 431 824422, *Fax:* +62 431 824422, *Email:* dlmb@manadoi.wasantara.net.id

PT Tempura Emas-PR Sarijasa Transutama, 13 Jl Hasannuddin, Manado, Sulawesi, Indonesia, *Tel:* +62 431 850133, *Fax:* +62 431 850136

MANOKWARI

Lat 0° 52' S; Long 134° 5' E.

Admiralty Chart: 1416	**Admiralty Pilot:** 35
Time Zone: GMT +9 h	**UNCTAD Locode:** ID MKW

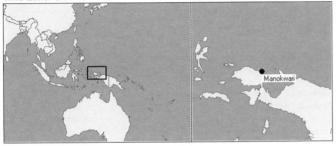

Principal Facilities:

		P		G	R				A

Authority: PT (Persero) Pelabuhan Indonesia IV, Port of Manokwari, Jalan Banjarmasin No.3, Manokwari, Irian Jaya, Indonesia, *Tel:* +62 986 211334, *Fax:* +62 986 211837, *Email:* pelindo4@manokwari.wasantara.net.id

Documentation: Passenger list (12 copies), crew list (7 copies), custom document (2 copies), health document (2 copies), cargo manifest (7 copies), bills of lading (7 copies), ship's papers (5 copies), sailing permit

Approach: No hazards or sand bars. Channel depth of 25 m LWS

Pilotage: Compulsory, 24 h. Three pilots available

Radio Frequency: Manokwari coastal radio station, call sign PKY3 (mobile) and BAT3 (fixed)

Traffic: 1999, 92 915 t of cargo handled

Maximum Vessel Dimensions: 7000 dwt, 150 m loa, 9.6 m d

Working Hours: 0800-1200, 1300-1800, 2000-2400, 0100-0600

Accommodation:

Name	Length (m)	Depth (m)
Manokwari		
Pier A	73	5
Pier B	90	10
Pertamina Oil Jetty	15	8

Storage:

Location	Open (m²)	Covered (m²)
Manokwari	2450	1762

Mechanical Handling Equipment:

Location	Type	Capacity (t)	Qty
Manokwari	Mobile Cranes	4	1
Manokwari	Forklifts	3	2

Cargo Worked: General cargo 350 t/day, bulk and bag cargo 400 t/day, liquid cargo 360 t/day

Shipping Agents: P.T. (PELNI) Pelayaran Nasional Indonesia, Jl Siliwangi No.24, Manokwari, Irian Jaya, Indonesia, *Tel:* +62 986 215165, *Fax:* +62 986 215168, *Email:* agencies@pelni.co.id, *Website:* www.pelni.co.id

Medical Facilities: Manokwari General Hospital

Airport: Rendani Airport, 8 km

Lloyd's Agent: P.T. Carsurin, Sarana Penjaminan Building, 7th Floor, Jl Angkasa Block B-9 Kav 6, Kemayoran, Jakarta 10720, Jawa, Indonesia, *Tel:* +62 21 654 0425, *Fax:* +62 21 654 0418, *Email:* lloyds@carsurin.com, *Website:* www.carsurin.com

MAUMERE

Lat 8° 36' S; Long 122° 13' E.

Admiralty Chart: 1697	**Admiralty Pilot:** 34
Time Zone: GMT +9 h	**UNCTAD Locode:** ID MOF

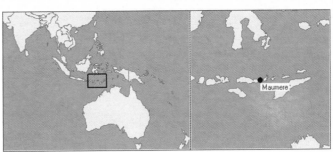

Principal Facilities:

			G			B		T	A

Authority: Port Administrator, Jalan Pelabuhan No.3, Maumere, Flores, Indonesia, *Tel:* +62 382 54618

Anchorage: Anchorage 100 m offshore in depth of 30 m

Radio Frequency: 5316 and 5165 kHz

Weather: Strong winds and rough seas can be experienced from June to September

Tides: Range of tide 1.42 m

Working Hours: Normal 0800-1600. 24 h when required. No work on Sundays and other holidays

Accommodation:

Name	Remarks
Maumere	See [1] below

[1]*Maumere:* One public pier 60 m long, 10 m wide, depth of 6 m one side and 8 m the other. Berth No.1 can accommodate vessels up to 450 dwt, 45 m loa, 4 m depth; Berth No.2, 3500 dwt, 70 m loa, 7 m depth. Lighters available with cap up to 4 t. Port used only for domestic traffic

Storage:

Location	Covered (m²)	Sheds / Warehouses
Maumere	3150	2

Mechanical Handling Equipment:

Location	Type	Capacity (t)	Qty
Maumere	Forklifts	7	2

Cargo Worked: 200 t/day/shift, 15 t/gang/h of general cargo, 20 t/gang/h bagged cargo

Bunkering: Available by road tanker

Towage: Small tugs available of 140 hp

Medical Facilities: Public hospital about 3 km from port

Airport: Waioti Airport, approx 6 km

Lloyd's Agent: P.T. Carsurin, Sarana Penjaminan Building, 7th Floor, Jl Angkasa Block B-9 Kav 6, Kemayoran, Jakarta 10720, Jawa, Indonesia, *Tel:* +62 21 654 0425, *Fax:* +62 21 654 0418, *Email:* lloyds@carsurin.com, *Website:* www.carsurin.com

MEKAR PUTIH

Lat 4° 1' S; Long 116° 2' E.

Admiralty Chart: 3017	**Admiralty Pilot:** 34
Time Zone: GMT +8 h	**UNCTAD Locode:** ID

Principal Facilities:

	Y								

Authority: PT Indonesia Bulk Terminal, Jl. HR Rasuna Said, Blok X-5, Kav. 1-2, Menara Karya, 23rd Floor, Jakarta 12920, Jawa, Indonesia, *Tel:* +62 21 522 9250, *Fax:* +62 21 522 4341, *Email:* marketing@ibt.co.id, *Website:* ptibt.com

Pre-Arrival Information: Vessel's should send their ETA 14, 7, 5, 3, 2 and 1 day prior to arrival

Documentation: On arrival vessels are required to produce the following certificates and documents which will remain with the Harbour Master until the vessel is cleared:
Nationality Certificate
Seaworthiness certificate
Measurement certificate
Derat certificate
International Loadline certificate
Safety Equipment certificate
Safety Radio and Radiotelephony certificate
Certificate of approval
Health Book
Vaccination certificates
Last port clearance
Subsciption of Light and Harbour dues and Wharfage
Crew and Passenger lists
Ship's articles
Crew passports

Anchorage: The designated anchorage is 2.5 miles W of the jetty in pos 4° 01' S; 115° 59' E in depth of 20 m

Pilotage: Compulsory and available 24 h/day. Pilot normally boards in the vicinity of the anchorage

Radio Frequency: VHF Channel 12

Key to Principal Facilities:—				
A=Airport	**C**=Containers	**G**=General Cargo	**P**=Petroleum	**R**=Ro/Ro	**Y**=Dry Bulk
B=Bunkers	**D**=Dry Dock	**L**=Cruise	**Q**=Other Liquid Bulk	**T**=Towage (where available from port)

Weather: Prevailing winds are SW between November and April and SE between June and September

Tides: Max range is 2.1 m

Maximum Vessel Dimensions: 20 000-80 000 dwt, 230 m loa, 36 m breadth, 14.5 m draught

Principal Imports and Exports: Exports: Coal.

Working Hours: 24 h/day

Accommodation:

Name	Length (m)	Depth (m)	Remarks
South Pulau Laut Coal Terminal			See [1] below
Export Jetty	288	14.5–16.5	See [2] below

[1]*South Pulau Laut Coal Terminal:* Mekar Putih Office: Pulau Laut Barat, Kalimantan Selatan 72153, Tel: +62 518 38800, Fax: +62 518 38822, Email: controlroom@ibt.co.id
The coal is mined at Tutupan, in South Kalimantan and shipped by barge to the terminal
[2]*Export Jetty:* Five berthing dolphins and two mooring dolphins. Served by two coal shiploaders at max loading rate of 3000 t/h

Towage: Two 40 t bollard pull tugs available

Shipping Agents: Arpeni Pratama Ocean Line, P.T. Perusahaan Pelayaran Samudera Khusus (APOL), Jl Brig Jend H Hasan Basri 117, Semayap-Pulau laut Utara, Kotabaru 72117, Indonesia, *Tel:* +62 518 24614/5, *Fax:* +62 518 23393, *Email:* kacab_ktb@apol.co.id, *Website:* www.apol.co.id
P.T. Bahana Utama Line, Jl. H.Hasan Basri 106B, Semayap, Kotabaru, Indonesia, *Tel:* +62 518 23113, *Fax:* +62 518 23113, *Email:* kotabaru@bahana-line.com, *Website:* bahana-line.com

Medical Facilities: Limited medical assistance. The nearest hospital is at Banjarmasin

Airport: Banjarmasin

Lloyd's Agent: P.T. Carsurin, Sarana Penjaminan Building, 7th Floor, Jl Angkasa Block B-9 Kav 6, Kemayoran, Jakarta 10720, Jawa, Indonesia, *Tel:* +62 21 654 0425, *Fax:* +62 21 654 0418, *Email:* lloyds@carsurin.com, *Website:* www.carsurin.com

MENENG

Lat 8° 7' S; Long 114° 23' E.

Admiralty Chart: 946	**Admiralty Pilot:** 34
Time Zone: GMT +7 h	**UNCTAD Locode:** ID

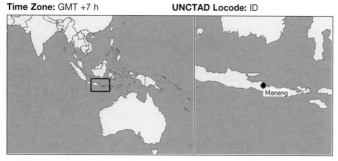

Principal Facilities:

P		G			B	T	

Authority: Port Administrator, Meneng, Jawa, Indonesia

Pilotage: Compulsory for vessels exceeding 5000 gt. 48 h notice required

Accommodation:

Name	Remarks
Meneng	See [1] below

[1]*Meneng:* Draft alongside quay 12.2 m. Max loa 152.4 m, 200 m east of quay, depth 7.3 m; berth length 110 m

Storage: One transit godown 20 by 50 m2 owned by Port Administration. Two 2nd line godowns 10 000 t cap, owned by PT Jakarta Lloyd Banyuwangi Branch

Location	Open (m²)
Meneng	10000

Mechanical Handling Equipment:

Location	Type	Capacity (t)	Qty
Meneng	Mult-purp. Cranes	15	1
Meneng	Forklifts	2	1

Bunkering: PT Pertamina, Jalan Jos Sudarso 32-34, P O Box 265, Tanjung Priok, Jawa, Indonesia, *Tel:* +62 21 430 1086, *Fax:* +62 21 430 1562 – *Grades:* DO; MDO; IFO100-300cSt – *Parcel Size:* no min/max – *Rates:* 100-150t/h – *Notice:* 48 hours – *Delivery Mode:* barge, pipeline

Towage: Two 80 hp tugs available

Lloyd's Agent: P.T. Carsurin, Sarana Penjaminan Building, 7th Floor, Jl Angkasa Block B-9 Kav 6, Kemayoran, Jakarta 10720, Jawa, Indonesia, *Tel:* +62 21 654 0425, *Fax:* +62 21 654 0418, *Email:* lloyds@carsurin.com, *Website:* www.carsurin.com

MERAK

Lat 5° 56' S; Long 105° 58' E.

Admiralty Chart: 918	**Admiralty Pilot:** 36
Time Zone: GMT +7 h	**UNCTAD Locode:** ID MRK

Principal Facilities:

P	Q	Y	G	C			B		

Authority: P.T. Santa Fe-Pomeroy (Indonesia), Jalan Pulorida Km 2.5, Tanjung Sekong, Merak, Jawa, Indonesia, *Tel:* +62 254 571408/10, *Fax:* +62 254 571189 & 571403, *Email:* sfmerak@indosat.net.id

Officials: Harbour Master: Mr Sudiono.

Anchorage: Can be obtained 0.5 m from berths

Pilotage: Available

Radio Frequency: Merak coastal radio station on VHF Channel 16 during daylight hours only

Tides: Min 0.3 m, max 0.9 m

Maximum Vessel Dimensions: 20 000 dwt, 174 m loa, 11 m draught

Working Hours: O700-1500, 1500-2300 & 2300-0700 (by request only)

Accommodation:

Name	Remarks
Merak	See [1] below

[1]*Merak:* Consists of two jetties and two berths in depth of 5.4 m
Also chemical jetty (PT Polychem Lindo) 136 m long in depth of 13 m for vessels up to 174 m loa and 11 m draught

Storage: Open storage available and warehouses

Mechanical Handling Equipment:

Location	Type	Capacity (t)	Qty
Merak	Mult-purp. Cranes		4
Merak	Mult-purp. Cranes	50	3
Merak	Forklifts	6	7
Merak	Yard Trailers	25	7

Bunkering: PT Pertamina, Jalan Jos Sudarso 32-34, P O Box 265, Tanjung Priok, Jawa, Indonesia, *Tel:* +62 21 430 1086, *Fax:* +62 21 430 1562 – *Grades:* DO; MDO; IFO100-300cSt – *Parcel Size:* no min/max – *Rates:* 100-150t/h – *Notice:* 48 hours – *Delivery Mode:* barge, pipeline

Shipping Agents: Jardine Shipping Services, Jalan Mess Baruna No.3A, Gerem Raya, Merak, Jawa, Indonesia, *Tel:* +62 254 570277, *Fax:* +62 254 570278, *Email:* bmmrk@indosat.net.id, *Website:* www.jardine-shipping.com

Stevedoring Companies: PT Merak Jaya Asri, Merak, Jawa, Indonesia, *Tel:* +62 254 391341, *Fax:* +62 254 392596
PT Peteka Karya Samudera, Merak, Jawa, Indonesia, *Tel:* +62 254 571625, *Fax:* +62 254 571617

Surveyors: P.T. Superintending Company of Indonesia (SUCOFINDO), Merak, Jawa, Indonesia, *Tel:* +62 254 386444, *Fax:* +62 254 386450

Medical Facilities: Public health centre, 3 km

Railway: Merak Station, 2.5 km

Lloyd's Agent: P.T. Carsurin, Sarana Penjaminan Building, 7th Floor, Jl Angkasa Block B-9 Kav 6, Kemayoran, Jakarta 10720, Jawa, Indonesia, *Tel:* +62 21 654 0425, *Fax:* +62 21 654 0418, *Email:* lloyds@carsurin.com, *Website:* www.carsurin.com

MERAUKE

Lat 8° 28' S; Long 140° 23' E.

Admiralty Chart: 3528	**Admiralty Pilot:** 35
Time Zone: GMT +9 h	**UNCTAD Locode:** ID MKQ

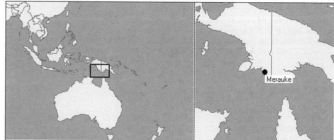

Principal Facilities:

			G					A

Authority: PT (Persero) Pelabuhan Indonesia IV, Port of Merauke, Jalan Yos Sudarso No.9, Merauke 49613, Irian Jaya, Indonesia, *Tel:* +62 971 321884, *Fax:* +62 971 321884

Documentation: Passenger list (6 copies), crew list (4 copies), custom document (2 copies), health document (1 copy), cargo manifest (4 copies), bills of lading (7 copies), ship's papers (5 copies), sailing permit

Pilotage: Compulsory

Radio Frequency: Merauke Coastal Radio Station: call sign PKY5 operates 12 h on VHF Channel 16

Traffic: 1999, 151 144 t of cargo handled

Maximum Vessel Dimensions: Max draft 6 m

Working Hours: 24 h/day

Accommodation:

Name	Length (m)	Apron Width (m)	Remarks
Merauke			
Concrete Piers			See [1] below
Wood Pier	45	4	
Pertamina Jetty	70	5	

[1]*Concrete Piers:* One berth 74 m long with width of 12 m and one berth 84 m long with width of 15 m

Storage:

Location	Covered (m²)	Sheds / Warehouses
Merauke	640	1

Mechanical Handling Equipment:

Location	Type	Capacity (t)	Qty
Merauke	Forklifts	2	1

Bunkering: PT Pertamina, Jalan Jos Sudarso 32-34, P O Box 265, Tanjung Priok, Jawa, Indonesia, *Tel:* +62 21 430 1086, *Fax:* +62 21 430 1562 – *Grades:* DO; MDO; IFO100-300cSt – *Parcel Size:* no min/max – *Rates:* 100-150t/h – *Notice:* 48 hours – *Delivery Mode:* barge, pipeline
C.V. Purba Jaya, Jalan Edam II No. 5, Tanjung Priok, Jakarta 14310, Jawa, Indonesia, *Tel:* +62 21 4393 1240, *Fax:* +62 21 4393 0792, *Email:* pijar@indo.net.id

Shipping Agents: P.T. (PELNI) Pelayaran Nasional Indonesia, Jl Sabang No.318, Merauke, Irian Jaya, Indonesia, *Tel:* +62 971 321628, *Fax:* +62 971 325631, *Email:* agencies@pelni.co.id, *Website:* www.pelni.co.id

Medical Facilities: Hospital facilities or port doctor available

Airport: Mopah Airport, 6 km

Lloyd's Agent: P.T. Carsurin, Sarana Penjaminan Building, 7th Floor, Jl Angkasa Block B-9 Kav 6, Kemayoran, Jakarta 10720, Jawa, Indonesia, *Tel:* +62 21 654 0425, *Fax:* +62 21 654 0418, *Email:* lloyds@carsurin.com, *Website:* www.carsurin.com

MISOOL TERMINAL

Lat 1° 33' S; Long 130° 31' E.

Admiralty Chart: 3242	**Admiralty Pilot:** 35
Time Zone: GMT +9 h	**UNCTAD Locode:** ID

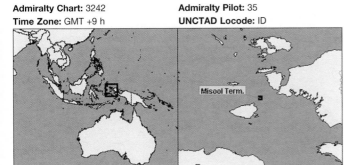

Principal Facilities:

P										

Authority: JOB Pertamina-Petrochina Salawati, Patra Office Tower 15th Floor, Jl. Gatot Subroto Kav. 32-33, Jakarta 12950, Jawa, Indonesia, *Tel:* +62 21 5296 3220, *Fax:* +62 21 5296 3432, *Website:* www.jobpertamina-petrochina.com

Pre-Arrival Information: Vessels should send ETA to the terminal on departure from their last port of call and 72 h, 48 h and 24 h prior to arrival. Any subsequent change to ETA of more than 2 h should be advised accordingly
The initial message should contain the following information:
a) vessel's name and call sign
b) cargo requirements
c) de-ballast time
d) max loading rate
e) arrival draught (fore and aft)
f) last port of call
g) confirmation that vessel has clear bill of health
h) if there is any sickness onboard give all available information as to the possible type of sickness

i) distance in feet from the bow to the vessel's loading manifold
j) confirmation that the minimum standards of acceptance have been complied with

Anchorage: The designated tanker anchorage area is of 1 nautical mile radius centred on pos 1° 33' 50" S; 130° 34' 30" E

Pilotage: Compulsory within the terminal area. Pilot boards in the anchorage area or at a point advised by the Mooring Master or Terminal Superintendent

Radio Frequency: VHF Channels 16 and 71

Maximum Vessel Dimensions: 20 000-85 000 dwt

Accommodation:

Name	Remarks
Misool Marine Terminal	See [1] below

[1]*Misool Marine Terminal:* Consists of FPSO Brotojoyo. Crude oil average loading rate of 18 000 bbls/h via 1 x 12 " hose. Berthing carried out during daylight hours only; unberthing any time

Towage: Two tugs available

Lloyd's Agent: P.T. Carsurin, Sarana Penjaminan Building, 7th Floor, Jl Angkasa Block B-9 Kav 6, Kemayoran, Jakarta 10720, Jawa, Indonesia, *Tel:* +62 21 654 0425, *Fax:* +62 21 654 0418, *Email:* lloyds@carsurin.com, *Website:* www.carsurin.com

MUARAJATI

harbour area, see under Cirebon

NORTH PULAU LAUT COAL TERMINAL

see under Tanjung Pemancingan

OYONG TERMINAL

Lat 7° 18' S; Long 113° 22' E.

Admiralty Chart: 945	**Admiralty Pilot:** 34
Time Zone: GMT +8 h	**UNCTAD Locode:** ID

Principal Facilities:

P										

Authority: Santos (Sampang) Pty Ltd., Level 4, Ratu Plaza Office Tower, Jalan Jendral Sudirman Kav 9, Jakarta 10270, Jawa, Indonesia, *Tel:* +62 21 2750 2750, *Fax:* +62 21 720 4503, *Website:* www.santos.com

Port Security: ISPS compliant

Pre-Arrival Information: The offtake tanker should forward ETA 72 h, 48 h, 24 h and 12 h prior to arrival to Santos

Documentation: Bill of lading (1 copy), crew list (4 copies), derat certificate (1 copy), last port clearance certificate (1 copy), load line certificate (1 copy), maritime declaration of health (4 copies), registry certificate (1 copy), safety construction certificate (1 copy), safety equipment certificate (1 copy), safety telegraphy/radio certificate (1 copy), tonnage certificate (1 copy)

Pilotage: Compulsory. Mooring master boards vessel prior to berthing

Radio Frequency: The terminal listens on VHF Channel 16 and works on VHF Channel 17

Maximum Vessel Dimensions: 30 000-140 000 dwt

Principal Imports and Exports: Exports: Crude oil.

Accommodation:

Name	Remarks
Oyong Terminal	See [1] below

[1]*Oyong Terminal:* Consists of FSO 'Shanghai' in depth of 45 m with crude oil storage cap of 373 000 bbls. Mooring operations undertaken during daylight hours 0600-1630; unmooring throughout 24 h

Medical Facilities: None available

Lloyd's Agent: P.T. Carsurin, Sarana Penjaminan Building, 7th Floor, Jl Angkasa Block B-9 Kav 6, Kemayoran, Jakarta 10720, Jawa, Indonesia, *Tel:* +62 21 654 0425, *Fax:* +62 21 654 0418, *Email:* lloyds@carsurin.com, *Website:* www.carsurin.com

PADANG

alternate name, see Teluk Bayur

PALEMBANG

Lat 2° 59' S; Long 104° 46' E.

Admiralty Chart: 3476	**Admiralty Pilot:** 36
Time Zone: GMT +7 h	**UNCTAD Locode:** ID PLM

Key to Principal Facilities:—			
A=Airport	**C**=Containers	**G**=General Cargo	**P**=Petroleum	**R**=Ro/Ro	**Y**=Dry Bulk
B=Bunkers	**D**=Dry Dock	**L**=Cruise	**Q**=Other Liquid Bulk	**T**=Towage (where available from port)	

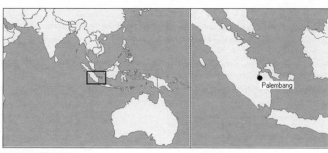

Principal Facilities:

P	Q	Y	G	C			B	D	T	A

Authority: PT (Persero) Pelabuhan Indonesia II, Port of Palembang, Jalan Belinyu No.1, Boom Baru, Palembang 30115, Sumatra, Indonesia, *Tel:* +62 711 710611, *Fax:* +62 711 711758, *Email:* datin@palembangport.com, *Website:* www.palembangport.com

Port Security: ISPS compliant

Approach: Channel is 100 km long and 120 m wide with max depth 6.5 m LWS, bottom is sandy and muddy

Pilotage: Compulsory. Ship's agent should inform pilot division of ETA 24 h in advance

Radio Frequency: VHF Channels 12, 14 and 16

Tides: Range 3 m to 3.5 m

Traffic: 2004, 4030 vessels, 11 750 415 t of cargo handled

Maximum Vessel Dimensions: 181 m loa

Principal Imports and Exports: Imports: Fertiliser, General cargo, Rice, Salt, Sugar, Wheat. Exports: Ammonia, Coal, Crude palm oil, Non crude oil, Rubber, Wood products.

Accommodation:

Name	Length (m)	Depth (m)	Remarks
Boom Baru			
Conventional Wharf	475	7	
Container Wharf	265	9	Container storage of 47 100 m2
Berthing Dolphin (12 unit)	7.8	5	
Sungai Lais			
Sailing Vessel Wharf	280	3	

Storage:

Location	Open (m²)	Covered (m²)
Boom Baru	8173	9785
Sungai Lais	16700	230

Mechanical Handling Equipment:

Location	Type	Capacity (t)	Qty
Palembang	Mobile Cranes	35	4

Bunkering: PT Pertamina, Jalan Jos Sudarso 32-34, P O Box 265, Tanjung Priok, Jawa, Indonesia, *Tel:* +62 21 430 1086, *Fax:* +62 21 430 1562 – *Grades:* DO; MDO; IFO100-300cSt – *Parcel Size:* no min/max – *Rates:* 100-150t/h – *Notice:* 48 hours – *Delivery Mode:* barge, pipeline

Towage: Three tugs of 1700-1800 hp

Repair & Maintenance: P.T. Intan Sengkunyit, Jalan Intan Sei Selincah 2, Palembang 30119, Sumatra, Indonesia, *Tel:* +62 711 712523, *Fax:* +62 711 711017

Shipping Agents: P.T. Pelayaran Samudera Admiral Lines, Palembang, Sumatra, Indonesia, *Tel:* +62 711 356933
P.T. Bahana Utama Line, Jl. AKBP.Cek Agus 1344-F, Kenten Raya, Palembang 30114, Sumatra, Indonesia, *Tel:* +62 711 369920, *Fax:* +62 711 364451, *Email:* palembang@bahana-line.com, *Website:* www.bahana-line.com
P.T. Bintika Bangunusa, Jalan R E Martadinata, 17-18 2 Llir, Palembang 30118, Sumatra, Indonesia, *Tel:* +62 711 716381, *Fax:* +62 711 716379, *Email:* bbnplm@palembang.wasantara.co.id, *Website:* www.bbngroup.org
P.T. Bumi Laut Shipping Corp., Jl Veteran 188, Palembang 30126, Sumatra, Indonesia, *Tel:* +62 711 312638, *Fax:* +62 711 322113, *Email:* mra-plbg@telkom.net
P.T. Djakarta Lloyd (PERSERO), P O Box 0148, Palembang, Sumatra, Indonesia, *Tel:* +62 711 313609, *Fax:* +62 711 313209, *Email:* diplg@mdp.net
P.T. Jayakusuma Perdana Lines, Jl RE Martadinata 24, Palembang 30118, Sumatra, Indonesia, *Tel:* +62 711 720145, *Fax:* +62 711 720147, *Email:* bcddkt@jpldkt.co.id
P.T. Layar Sentosa Shipping Corp., Jl Veteran 188, Palembang 30126, Sumatra, Indonesia, *Tel:* +62 711 312638, *Fax:* +62 711 312638, *Email:* mra-plbg@telkom.net
P.T. Mandiri Abadi Santosa, Jl R Sukamto 1335B, Palembang, Sumatra, Indonesia, *Tel:* +62 711 811763, *Fax:* +62 711 811763
P.T. Newship Nusabersama, Jl Mayor Memet Sastrawijaya, 20 Boombaru, Palembang, Sumatra, Indonesia, *Tel:* +62 711 720123, *Fax:* +62 711 720121, *Email:* palembangccni@plm.newship.co.id
PT Panurjwan, 773 Jenderal Sudirman, Palembang 30126, Sumatra, Indonesia, *Tel:* +62 711 313616, *Fax:* +62 711 311288
PT Perusahaan Pelayaran Samudera Gesuri Lloyd, Jl Kol Atmo 593-A, Palembang, Sumatra, Indonesia, *Tel:* +62 711 311012
PT Perusahaan Pelayaran Samudera Trikora Lloyd, Jalan Veteran 246, Palembang 30120, Sumatra, Indonesia, *Tel:* +62 711 310708, *Fax:* +62 711 313671

Surveyors: P.T. Biro Klasifikasi Indonesia, Jl. Perintis Kemerdekaan 5 Ilir, Palembang 30115, Sumatra, Indonesia, *Tel:* +62 711 713171, *Fax:* +62 711 713173, *Email:* bkipb@klasifikasiindonesia.com, *Website:* www.klasifikasiindonesia.com
P.T. Superintending Company of Indonesia (SUCOFINDO), Jalan Jendal Sudirman No. 774, P O Box 1045, Palembang 30129, Sumatra, Indonesia, *Tel:* +62 711 312990,

Fax: +62 711 313835, *Email:* posma@sucofindo.co.id, *Website:* www.sucofindo.co.id

Medical Facilities: Port Health Centre

Airport: Sultan Badaruddin II Airport, 12 km

Lloyd's Agent: P.T. Carsurin, Sarana Penjaminan Building, 7th Floor, Jl Angkasa Block B-9 Kav 6, Kemayoran, Jakarta 10720, Jawa, Indonesia, *Tel:* +62 21 654 0425, *Fax:* +62 21 654 0418, *Email:* lloyds@carsurin.com, *Website:* www.carsurin.com

PANARUKAN

Lat 7° 42' S; Long 113° 56' E.

Admiralty Chart: 946	**Admiralty Pilot:** 34
Time Zone: GMT +7 h	**UNCTAD Locode:** ID PRN

Principal Facilities:

		G				T	

Authority: Port Administrator, Jalan Raya Pelabuhan, Panarukan, Jawa, Indonesia, *Tel:* +62 338 67248

Radio Frequency: VHF Channels 12, 13 and 14 (15.660 mHz)

Weather: Dry season June-October. Rainy season November-May

Working Hours: Monday to Thursday 0700-1400. Friday 0700-1300. Stevedoring, same as above. Overtime is usually possible

Accommodation:

Name	Remarks
Panarukan	See [1] below

[1]*Panarukan:* Anchorage in open roadstead. Cargo is loaded and discharged into lighters of which there are thirteen with total cap 1000 t. At least 48 h notice of arrival must be given and 24 h notice of number of stevedoring gangs, materials, dunnage etc (Sundays and holidays discounted)

Towage: Three tugs available

Lloyd's Agent: P.T. Carsurin, Sarana Penjaminan Building, 7th Floor, Jl Angkasa Block B-9 Kav 6, Kemayoran, Jakarta 10720, Jawa, Indonesia, *Tel:* +62 21 654 0425, *Fax:* +62 21 654 0418, *Email:* lloyds@carsurin.com, *Website:* www.carsurin.com

PANGKALAN SUSU

Lat 4° 7' N; Long 98° 12' E.

Admiralty Chart: 3574/1353	**Admiralty Pilot:** 44
Time Zone: GMT +7 h	**UNCTAD Locode:** ID PKS

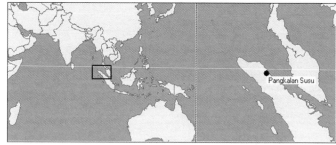

Principal Facilities:

P	Q		G			B	T	

Authority: PT (Persero) Pelabuhan Indonesia I, Port of Pangkalan Susu, Jalan Pelabuhan No.3, Pangkalan Susu, Sumatera, Indonesia, *Tel:* +62 620 51018

Approach: Hazards between outer bar/buoy No.1 to buoy No.3, depth 3.7 m LWS and also submerged wreck in pos bearing 2.24°, 0.8 miles from buoy No.4

Anchorage: For tankers awaiting pilot in pos 4° 16' 00" N; 98° 25' 00" E. For cargo vessels awaiting pilot in pos 4° 16' 00" N; 98° 22' 00" E. For cargo vessels loading plywood and sawn timber in pos 4° 16' 00" N; 98° 22' 28" E

Pilotage: 24 h service at HW

Radio Frequency: VHF Channels 12, 14 and 16

Maximum Vessel Dimensions: For tankers loading crude oil at SBM max 50 000 gt

Working Hours: 24 h

Accommodation:

Name	Length (m)	Depth (m)	Remarks
Pangkalan Susu			
Jetty A/B	200	4.5	
Jetty C/D	201	4.7	
Single Mooring Buoy			In pos 4° 13' 00" N; 98° 24' 00" E
Private Jetty	60	4.5	

Mechanical Handling Equipment:

Location	Type	Capacity (t)	Qty	Remarks
Pangkalan Susu	Mobile Cranes	30	1	owned by Pertamina

Bunkering: C.V. Bahtera Camar, Jalan Lagoa Terusan Bl No.4, Jakarta 14270, Jawa, Indonesia, *Tel:* +62 21 435 3209, *Fax:* +62 21 430 6048
PT Pertamina, Jalan Jos Sudarso 32-34, P O Box 265, Tanjung Priok, Jawa, Indonesia, *Tel:* +62 21 430 1086, *Fax:* +62 21 430 1562 – *Grades:* DO; MDO; IFO100-300cSt – *Parcel Size:* no min/max – *Rates:* 100-150t/h – *Notice:* 48 hours – *Delivery Mode:* barge, pipeline
C.V. Purba Jaya, Jalan Edam II No. 5, Tanjung Priok, Jakarta 14310, Jawa, Indonesia, *Tel:* +62 21 4393 1240, *Fax:* +62 21 4393 0792, *Email:* pijar@indo.net.id

Towage: Four tugs available; one of 1700 hp and three of 300 hp

Repair & Maintenance: P.T. Dock Pertamina, Pangkalan Susu, Sumatera, Indonesia

Medical Facilities: Pertamina hospital

Railway: Medan Station, approx 100 km

Lloyd's Agent: P.T. Carsurin, Sarana Penjaminan Building, 7th Floor, Jl Angkasa Block B-9 Kav 6, Kemayoran, Jakarta 10720, Jawa, Indonesia, *Tel:* +62 21 654 0425, *Fax:* +62 21 654 0418, *Email:* lloyds@carsurin.com, *Website:* www.carsurin.com

PANGKALBALAM

Lat 2° 6' S; Long 106° 10' E.

Admiralty Chart: 1788	**Admiralty Pilot:** 36
Time Zone: GMT +7 h	**UNCTAD Locode:** ID PGX

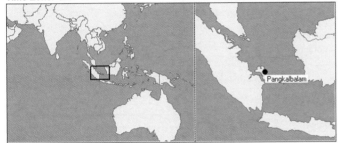

Principal Facilities:

P		GC		B		TA

Authority: PT (Persero) Pelabuhan Indonesia II, Port of Pangkal Balam, Jalan Yos Sudarso No.1, Pangkalpinang 33114, Bangka Island, Indonesia, *Tel:* +62 717 421737, *Email:* pbalam@ppinang.wasantara.net.id

Port Security: ISPS compliant

Anchorage: Anchorage can be obtained about 100 m from the wharf in a depth of 8 m at LWS

Radio Frequency: Coastal radio station, call sign PKC 5

Weather: Winds from W during April to October, SE from November to March

Tides: Range of tide about 2 m

Maximum Vessel Dimensions: 1500 dwt, 5 m d, 70 m loa

Working Hours: 0800-1200, 1300-1600, 1800-2200

Accommodation:

Name	Length (m)	Depth (m)
Pangkalbalam		
Wharf	188	5
PN Pertamina Oil Jetty	24	

Storage:

Location	Open (m²)	Covered (m²)	Sheds / Warehouses
Pangkalbalam	4820	1305	2

Mechanical Handling Equipment:

Location	Type	Capacity (t)	Qty
Pangkalbalam	Mobile Cranes	15	3
Pangkalbalam	Forklifts	2	

Cargo Worked: 820 t/day

Bunkering: Available by pipeline on berth

Towage: Four privately owned tugs available up to 350 hp

Repair & Maintenance: Slipway with cap up to 500 dwt. Repairs can be effected by various local companies

Medical Facilities: Available

Airport: Pangkal Pinang Airport, 10 km

Lloyd's Agent: P.T. Carsurin, Sarana Penjaminan Building, 7th Floor, Jl Angkasa Block B-9 Kav 6, Kemayoran, Jakarta 10720, Jawa, Indonesia, *Tel:* +62 21 654 0425, *Fax:* +62 21 654 0418, *Email:* lloyds@carsurin.com, *Website:* www.carsurin.com

PANJANG

Lat 5° 28' S; Long 105° 20' E.

Admiralty Chart: 2965	**Admiralty Pilot:** 36
Time Zone: GMT +7 h	**UNCTAD Locode:** ID PNJ

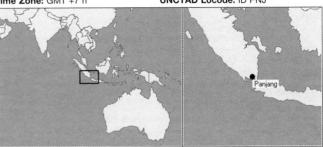

Principal Facilities:

P		YGCR		BDTA

Authority: PT (Persero) Pelabuhan Indonesia II, Port of Panjang, Jalan Yos Sudarso No.334, Panjang 35241, Sumatra, Indonesia, *Tel:* +62 721 31149, *Email:* pjgipc2@lampung.wasantara.net.id

Port Security: ISPS compliant

Approach: Natural breakwater of sand and coral fortified by an extension of the coastal reef on the NE side of the head of Teluk Lampung. The entrance which has a min depth of 12-15 m over a width of 3-4 cables lies on the N side, the harbour is completely sheltered

Anchorage: Four anchorage areas for vessels awaiting pilot: (a) 5° 28' 20" S, 105° 17' 00" E (b) 5° 28' 20" S, 105° 17' 40" E (c) 5° 29' 30" S, 105° 17' 00" E (d) 5° 29' 30" S, 105° 17' 40" E

Pilotage: Compulsory. Invisible reef embraces harbour basin, hence use of pilot in entering and leaving port is compulsory. VHF Channels 12 and 14

Radio Frequency: Coastal radio station, call sign 'PKC4', frequencies 6523, 43966, 430 and 500 k/cs

Maximum Vessel Dimensions: 40 000 dwt, 200 m loa, 10.5 m d

Working Hours: 0800-1600, 1600-2400, 2400-0800

Accommodation:

Name	Length (m)	Depth (m)	Remarks
Public Wharves			
Concrete Wharf A	172	8.5	
Concrete Wharf B	210	6.5	
Concrete Wharf C	140	4.5	
Concrete Wharf D1	200	10	
Concrete Wharf D2	200	10.5	
Concrete Wharf D3	87	12	
Private Wharves			
Pertamina Oil Jetty (2 units)		5.5	
SBM-Pertamina	150	8	
PT Perkebunan X - Palm oil jetty	38	7	
PT Andatu Lestari Wharf	75	8	
Tarahan Wharf	174	17	See [1] below

[1]*Tarahan Wharf:* Operated by PT Tambang Batubara Bukit Asam, Tel: +62 721 31545, Fax: +62 721 31577, Website: www.ptbukitasam.com
Coal terminal with stockpile cap of 60 000 t

Storage: Container freight station of 6000 m2

Location	Open (m²)	Covered (m²)
Panjang	24793	13382

Mechanical Handling Equipment:

Location	Type	Capacity (t)	Qty
Panjang	Mobile Cranes	15	2

Bunkering: PT Pertamina, Jalan Jos Sudarso 32-34, P O Box 265, Tanjung Priok, Jawa, Indonesia, *Tel:* +62 21 430 1086, *Fax:* +62 21 430 1562 – *Grades:* DO – *Notice:* 48 hours – *Delivery Mode:* truck

Waste Reception Facilities: Garbage disposal available

Towage: Three tugs available of 978, 1160 and 1700 hp

Repair & Maintenance: P.T. Noatu, Panjang, Sumatra, Indonesia, *Tel:* +62 721 31728, *Fax:* +62 721 31729 Minor repairs

Shipping Agents: P.T. Pelayaran Samudera Admiral Lines, Panjang, Sumatra, Indonesia, *Tel:* +62 721 31279, *Fax:* +62 721 31722, *Email:* admiral@uninet.net.id
P.T. Bahana Utama Line, Jl Yos Sudarso 49/10, Bandar Lampung, Panjang 35241, Sumatra, Indonesia, *Tel:* +62 721 342272, *Fax:* +62 721 31699, *Email:* bulpjg@indo.net.id, *Website:* www.bahana-line.com
P.T. Djakarta Lloyd (PERSERO), Jalan Sumatera Pelabuhan Panjang, Bandar

Key to Principal Facilities:—			
A=Airport	**C**=Containers	**G**=General Cargo	**P**=Petroleum **R**=Ro/Ro **Y**=Dry Bulk
B=Bunkers	**D**=Dry Dock	**L**=Cruise	**Q**=Other Liquid Cargo **T**=Towage (where available from port)

Lampung, Panjang 35421, Sumatra, Indonesia, *Tel:* +62 721 31439, *Fax:* +62 721 31458

PT Panurjwan, Jl Sumatra 14, Panjang 35241, Sumatra, Indonesia, *Tel:* +62 721 31247, *Fax:* +62 721 31161

P.T. (PELNI) Pelayaran Nasional Indonesia, Jl Sumatera No.70, Panjang, Sumatra, Indonesia, *Tel:* +62 721 31732, *Fax:* +62 721 31441, *Email:* agencies@pelni.co.id, *Website:* www.pelni.co.id

PT Perusahaan Pelayaran Samudera Trikora Lloyd, 1 Jalan Sulawesi, Bandar Lampung, Panjang 35241, Sumatra, Indonesia, *Tel:* +62 721 31414, *Fax:* +62 721 31188

Medical Facilities: Abdul Muluk general hospital

Airport: Branti Airport, 35 km

Railway: Perum Kereta Api-Tanjung Karang Station, abt 10 km

Lloyd's Agent: P.T. Carsurin, Sarana Penjaminan Building, 7th Floor, Jl Angkasa Block B-9 Kav 6, Kemayoran, Jakarta 10720, Jawa, Indonesia, *Tel:* +62 21 654 0425, *Fax:* +62 21 654 0418, *Email:* lloyds@carsurin.com, *Website:* www.carsurin.com

PANTOLOAN

Lat 0° 42' S; Long 119° 50' E.

Admiralty Chart: 2638	**Admiralty Pilot:** 34
Time Zone: GMT +8 h	**UNCTAD Locode:** ID PTL

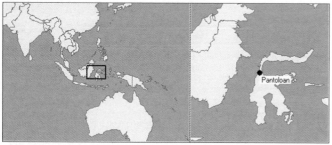

Principal Facilities:

P		G	C	R		B		T	A

Authority: PT (Persero) Pelabuhan Indonesia IV, Port of Pantoloan, Jalan Kompleks Pelabuhan No.23, Pantoloan 94352, Sulawesi Tengah, Indonesia, *Tel:* +62 451 91815, *Fax:* +62 451 91081, *Email:* pelindo4@palu.wasantara.net.id

Documentation: Passenger list (12 copies), crew list (6 copies), custom document (2 copies), health document (2 copies), cargo manifest (6 copies), bills of lading (6 copies), ship's papers (5 copies), sailing permit

Anchorage: Anchorage can be obtained in pos 0° 42' 35" S; 119° 51' 28" E in depths ranging from 15 m to 30 m

Pilotage: Compulsory. Two pilots and one pilot boat

Radio Frequency: Coastal radio station, call sign 'PKM9', frequency 2182 kHz

Tides: Tidal range max 1.3 m

Traffic: 1999, 489 212 t of cargo handled

Maximum Vessel Dimensions: 20 000 dwt, 160 m loa, 10 m draft

Principal Imports and Exports: Imports: Asphalt, Heavy industrial equipment. Exports: Cocoa beans, Plywood.

Working Hours: 0800-1200, 1300-1700, 1900-2200

Accommodation:

Name	Length (m)	Depth (m)	Remarks
Pantoloan			
Concrete Wharf	250	7–12	Passenger terminal with cap for 500 persons
Pertamina Oil Wharf	50	7–8	At Loli Oge, for vessels up to 10 000 dwt

Storage:

Location	Open (m²)	Covered (m²)	Sheds / Warehouses
Pantoloan	2500	2000	2

Mechanical Handling Equipment:

Location	Type	Capacity (t)	Qty
Pantoloan	Mult-purp. Cranes	25	1
Pantoloan	Forklifts	2	7

Cargo Worked: 600 t to 750 t/day

Bunkering: PT Pertamina, Jalan Jos Sudarso 32-34, P O Box 265, Tanjung Priok, Jawa, Indonesia, *Tel:* +62 21 430 1086, *Fax:* +62 21 430 1562 – *Grades:* DO; MDO; IFO100-300cSt – *Parcel Size:* no min/max – *Rates:* 100-150t/h – *Notice:* 48 hours – *Delivery Mode:* barge, pipeline

Towage: One tug of 800 hp

Medical Facilities: Port medical service

Airport: Mutiara Airport, 28 km

Lloyd's Agent: P.T. Carsurin, Sarana Penjaminan Building, 7th Floor, Jl Angkasa Block B-9 Kav 6, Kemayoran, Jakarta 10720, Jawa, Indonesia, *Tel:* +62 21 654 0425, *Fax:* +62 21 654 0418, *Email:* lloyds@carsurin.com, *Website:* www.carsurin.com

PARE PARE

Lat 4° 0' S; Long 119° 37' E.

Admiralty Chart: 2638	**Admiralty Pilot:** 34
Time Zone: GMT +8 h	**UNCTAD Locode:** ID PAP

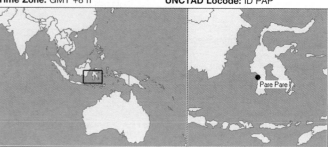

Principal Facilities:

P		G		R		B			

Authority: PT (Persero) Pelabuhan Indonesia IV, Port of Pare Pare, Jalan Andi. Cammi Komplek Pelabuhan, Pare Pare 91111, Sulawesi Selatan, Indonesia, *Tel:* +62 421 21069, *Fax:* +62 421 24071

Documentation: Passenger list (10 copies), crew list (7 copies), custom document (2 copies), health document (2 copies), cargo manifest (7 copies), bills of lading (7 copies), ship's papers (5 copies), sailing permit

Approach: Channel depth of 18.0 m

Pilotage: Compulsory and available from 0600-1900

Radio Frequency: VHF Channels 12, 16 and 26

Weather: W winds January-June, E winds July-December

Tides: Tidal range 1.6 m

Traffic: 1999, 305 029 t of cargo handled

Maximum Vessel Dimensions: 12 000 dwt, 160 m loa, 10.0 m draft

Principal Imports and Exports: Imports: Cement in bags. Exports: Cocoa beans, White rice.

Working Hours: 0700-1200, 1300-1700, 1800-2200

Accommodation:

Name	Length (m)	Depth (m)
Pare Pare		
Nusantara Pier	235	9–14
Pertamina Jetty	70	

Storage:

Location	Covered (m²)	Sheds / Warehouses
Pare Pare	1216	2

Mechanical Handling Equipment:

Location	Type	Capacity (t)	Qty
Pare Pare	Forklifts	10	4

Cargo Worked: General cargo 500 t/day, bulk cargo 700 t/day

Bunkering: PT Pertamina, Jalan Jos Sudarso 32-34, P O Box 265, Tanjung Priok, Jawa, Indonesia, *Tel:* +62 21 430 1086, *Fax:* +62 21 430 1562 – *Grades:* DO; MDO; IFO100-300cSt – *Parcel Size:* no min/max – *Rates:* 100-150t/h – *Notice:* 48 hours – *Delivery Mode:* barge, pipeline

Medical Facilities: General hospital available

Airport: Hasanuddin Airport, 155 km

Lloyd's Agent: P.T. Carsurin, Sarana Penjaminan Building, 7th Floor, Jl Angkasa Block B-9 Kav 6, Kemayoran, Jakarta 10720, Jawa, Indonesia, *Tel:* +62 21 654 0425, *Fax:* +62 21 654 0418, *Email:* lloyds@carsurin.com, *Website:* www.carsurin.com

PEKANBARU

Lat 0° 33' N; Long 101° 27' E.

Admiralty Chart: -	**Admiralty Pilot:** -
Time Zone: GMT +7 h	**UNCTAD Locode:** ID PKU

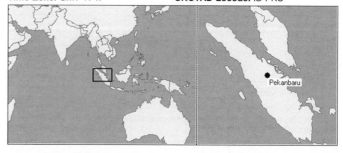

Principal Facilities:

P		G	C				A

Authority: PT (Persero) Pelabuhan Indonesia I, Port of Pekanbaru, Jalan Saleh Abbas No.3, Pekanbaru 28152, Sumatra, Indonesia, *Tel:* +62 761 22826, *Fax:* +62 761 33711, *Email:* pkuport@yahoo.com, *Website:* pekanbaru.inaport1.co.id

Officials: General Manager: Muhammad Rumawi.

Port Security: ISPS compliant

Pilotage: Pilot station at Siak Sri Indapura

Radio Frequency: VHF Channels 12, 14 and 16

Working Hours: 0800-2400. Round the clock if necessary

Accommodation:

Name	Length (m)	Depth (m)	Remarks
Pekanbaru			See [1] below
Pekanbaru	282	3.5–5	For vessels up to 1000 dwt
Perawang	80	5–7	

[1]*Pekanbaru:* Cargoes handled include pulp, palm oil, plywood and paper. Passenger terminal of 225 m2

Storage:

Location	Open (m²)	Covered (m²)
Pekanbaru	5215	1920

Mechanical Handling Equipment:

Location	Type	Capacity (t)	Qty
Pekanbaru	Mobile Cranes	5	1
Pekanbaru	Forklifts	5	3

Repair & Maintenance: C.V. Lancang Kuning, Pekanbaru, Sumatra, Indonesia Minor repairs only

Surveyors: P.T. Biro Klasifikasi Indonesia, Jl. Ikhlas No.1/E, Labuhan Baru, Pekanbaru 28291, Sumatra, Indonesia, *Tel:* +62 761 65861, *Fax:* +62 761 65861, *Email:* bkipu@klasifikasiindonesia.com, *Website:* www.klasifikasiindonesia.com

Medical Facilities: Hospital, 1 km

Airport: Simpang Tiga, 6 km

Lloyd's Agent: P.T. Carsurin, Sarana Penjaminan Building, 7th Floor, Jl Angkasa Block B-9 Kav 6, Kemayoran, Jakarta 10720, Jawa, Indonesia, *Tel:* +62 21 654 0425, *Fax:* +62 21 654 0418, *Email:* lloyds@carsurin.com, *Website:* www.carsurin.com

PEMANGKAT

Lat 1° 8' N; Long 108° 55' E.

Admiralty Chart: 3720
Time Zone: GMT +8 h

Admiralty Pilot: 36
UNCTAD Locode: ID PEM

This port is no longer open to commercial shipping

PERAWANG

harbour area, see under Pekanbaru

PONTIANAK

Lat 0° 1' S; Long 109° 21' E.

Admiralty Chart: 3721
Time Zone: GMT +8 h

Admiralty Pilot: 36
UNCTAD Locode: ID PNK

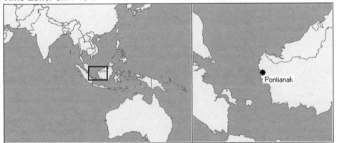

Principal Facilities:

		G	C		B		A

Authority: PT (Persero) Pelabuhan Indonesia II, Port of Pontianak, Jalan Pakasih No.11, Pontianak 78113, Borneo, Indonesia, *Tel:* +62 561 732181, *Fax:* +62 561 732612, *Email:* ptkipc2@pontianak.wasantara.net.id

Port Security: ISPS compliant

Approach: Ocean-going vessels approaching port are advised to navigate into rivermouth at Muara Jungkat and then along channel 16.8 nautical miles in length, 50-80 m wide and 5 m depth at LWST

Anchorage: At river mouth at Muara Jungkat in depth of 10 m

Pilotage: Compulsory. Pilots on 24 h service. Lumber carriers for Telok Ayer (lat 0° 38' S; long 109° 17' E) must take pilot and other officials on board at entrance of Kapuas Kecil in pos 0° 06' N; 108° 03' E

Weather: During September to December anchorage at the river mouth at Jungkat is unsafe

Tides: July-September max 1.5 m LWS, November-June max 1.8 m LWS

Principal Imports and Exports: Exports: Frozen shrimp, Sawn plywood, Sawn timber, White pepper.

Working Hours: 0800-1600

Accommodation:

Name	Depth (m)	Remarks
Pontianak		Total berthing length of 736 m
Berth No's 2-5	5	
Berth No.1	2.5	

Storage: Four waterfront warehouses of 8800 m2. Salt storage of 334 m2

Location	Open (m²)
Pontianak	22150

Mechanical Handling Equipment:

Location	Type	Capacity (t)	Qty
Pontianak	Mult-purp. Cranes	25	1
Pontianak	Forklifts	5	8

Cargo Worked: General cargo 12.7 t/gang/h, sawn timber 20 t/gang/h

Bunkering: PT Pertamina, Jalan Jos Sudarso 32-34, P O Box 265, Tanjung Priok, Jawa, Indonesia, *Tel:* +62 21 430 1086, *Fax:* +62 21 430 1562 – *Grades:* DO; MDO; IFO100-300cSt – *Parcel Size:* no min/max – *Rates:* 100-150t/h – *Notice:* 48 hours – *Delivery Mode:* barge, pipeline

Repair & Maintenance: Minor repairs effected by local dockyard. Slipway is accessible to vessels up to 200 gt

Shipping Agents: Arpeni Pratama Ocean Line, P.T. Perusahaan Pelayaran Samudera Khusus (APOL), Jl Gajah Mada 20, Pontianak 78121, Borneo, Indonesia, *Tel:* +62 561 734572/735883, *Fax:* +62 561 739661, *Email:* arpeni-ptk@ptk.centrin.net.id
P.T. Bahana Utama Line, Pontianak, Borneo, Indonesia, *Tel:* +62 561 767544, *Fax:* +62 561 739429, *Email:* pontianak@bahana-line.com, *Website:* www.bahana-line.com
PT Panurjwan, Jl Pattimura 211, Kalimantan Barat, Pontianak 78117, Borneo, Indonesia, *Tel:* +62 561 738390, *Fax:* +62 561 760035
P.T. (PELNI) Pelayaran Nasional Indonesia, Jl S Abdulrahman No.12, Pontianak, Borneo, Indonesia, *Tel:* +62 561 748124, *Fax:* +62 561 748131, *Email:* agencies@pelni.co.id, *Website:* www.pelni.co.id
PT Pelayaran Samudera Intan Permata, Jl Pattimura Komp, Block B,1-8-10 Pattimura Indah, Pontianak 78117, Borneo, Indonesia, *Tel:* +62 561 734960, *Fax:* +62 561 739345, *Email:* intanship@pte.centrin.net.id

Surveyors: P.T. Biro Klasifikasi Indonesia, Jl. Gusti Hamzah No.211, Pontianak 78116, Borneo, Indonesia, *Tel:* +62 561 739579, *Fax:* +62 561 739579, *Email:* bkipk@klasifikasiindonesia.com, *Website:* www.klasifikasiindonesia.com
Nippon Kaiji Kyokai, Pontianak, Borneo, Indonesia, *Tel:* +62 561 739579, *Fax:* +62 561 739579, *Website:* www.classnk.or.jp

Medical Facilities: A general hospital is available at Sungai Jawi, Sungai Raya and Siantan

Airport: Supadio Airport, 18 km

Lloyd's Agent: P.T. Carsurin, Sarana Penjaminan Building, 7th Floor, Jl Angkasa Block B-9 Kav 6, Kemayoran, Jakarta 10720, Jawa, Indonesia, *Tel:* +62 21 654 0425, *Fax:* +62 21 654 0418, *Email:* lloyds@carsurin.com, *Website:* www.carsurin.com

PROBOLINGGO

Lat 7° 43' S; Long 113° 13' E.

Admiralty Chart: 946
Time Zone: GMT +7 h

Admiralty Pilot: 34
UNCTAD Locode: ID PRO

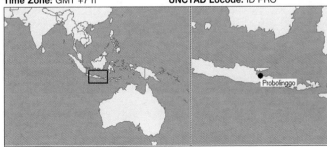

Principal Facilities:

P	Q	Y	G				T	A

Authority: Administrasi Pelabuhan Probolinggo, Jalan Tg. Tembaga Timur, Probolinggo, Jawa, Indonesia, *Tel:* +62 335 421685

Port Security: ISPS compliant

Documentation: Ship's certificates, sailing permit, log book etc

Approach: Depth in channel 3 m

Anchorage: Anchorage can be obtained 0.6 miles NE of breakwater in pos 7° 42' 45" S; 113° 13' 07" E during the wet season and 0.8 miles NW of breakwater in pos 7° 42' 45" S; 113° 12' 55" E during the dry season; depth of water 15 m

Key to Principal Facilities:—				
A=Airport	**C**=Containers	**G**=General Cargo	**P**=Petroleum	**R**=Ro/Ro	**Y**=Dry Bulk
B=Bunkers	**D**=Dry Dock	**L**=Cruise	**Q**=Other Liquid Bulk	**T**=Towage (where available from port)	

Pilotage: Available up to 500 dwt

Radio Frequency: Call sign 8AD6. 2182 kHz, 6215.5 kHz and 6218.8 kHz

Weather: Prevailing W wind December to March and prevailing NE wind September to November causes rough seas

Tides: 3 m HT, 1.2 m LT

Maximum Vessel Dimensions: 35 000 dwt at anchorage

Principal Imports and Exports: Imports: Methanol. Exports: Cattle fodder, Plywood, Tapioca chips.

Working Hours: 24 h for discharging/loading. 0700-1400 for officials

Accommodation:

Name	Remarks
Probolinggo	See [1] below

[1]*Probolinggo:* Open roadstead. Preferred anchorage, lighthouse SE-SSE distance about 1.5 km. Depth alongside pier 1-2 m. Barges and lighters available, max cap 400 t. Vessels up to 35 000 dwt can be handled at the anchorage and coasters up to 500 t can be berthed in port

Storage:

Location	Open (m²)	Covered (m²)
Probolinggo	7880	33518

Mechanical Handling Equipment:

Location	Type	Capacity (t)	Qty
Probolinggo	Mult-purp. Cranes	40	2
Probolinggo	Mobile Cranes	25	1
Probolinggo	Forklifts	5	19

Cargo Worked: Fodder 900 t/day, logs 2000 m3/day, general cargo 500 t/day

Towage: Six tugs available, max of 1800 hp

Shipping Agents: Arpeni Pratama Ocean Line, P.T. Perusahaan Pelayaran Samudera Khusus (APOL), Jalan K.H. Mansyur 19, Probolinggo 67219, Jawa, Indonesia, *Tel:* +62 335 426635, *Fax:* +62 335 434796, *Email:* kacab_sby@apol.co.id
P.T. (PELNI) Pelayaran Nasional Indonesia, Jl Tembaga Timur, Probolinggo 21202, Jawa, Indonesia, *Tel:* +62 335 428119, *Fax:* +62 335 421802, *Email:* agencies@pelni.co.id, *Website:* www.pelni.co.id

Medical Facilities: Port clinic and public hospital

Airport: Juanda Airport, 60 km

Railway: Probolinggo, 2 km

Lloyd's Agent: P.T. Carsurin, Sarana Penjaminan Building, 7th Floor, Jl Angkasa Block B-9 Kav 6, Kemayoran, Jakarta 10720, Jawa, Indonesia, *Tel:* +62 21 654 0425, *Fax:* +62 21 654 0418, *Email:* lloyds@carsurin.com, *Website:* www.carsurin.com

PROINTAL

Lat 5° 57' S; Long 106° 0' E.

Admiralty Chart: 2056

Admiralty Pilot: 36

Time Zone: GMT +7 h

UNCTAD Locode: ID PNT

This port is no longer open to commercial shipping

PULANG PISAU

Lat 2° 45' S; Long 114° 15' E.

Admiralty Chart: 3029/941B

Admiralty Pilot: 34

Time Zone: GMT +8 h

UNCTAD Locode: ID PPS

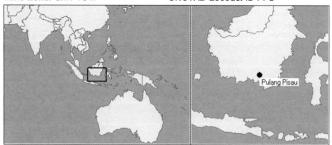

Principal Facilities:

			G			B			

Authority: P.T. (Persero) Pelabuhan Indonesia III, Jl. Samudera No.1, Pulang Pisau 73561, Kalimantan Tengah, Indonesia, *Tel:* +62 513 61145, *Fax:* +62 513 61197

Documentation: 2 x 24 h health book, ship's certificate, sailing permit, crew list, passports, officer certificate

Pilotage: Compulsory

Radio Frequency: VHF Channel 12

Tides: 4 m LWS, 12 m HHW

Maximum Vessel Dimensions: 100 m loa, 6000 dwt

Working Hours: 6 days/week

Accommodation:

Name	Length (m)
Pulang Pisau Wooden Jetty	90

Storage: Warehouse and open storage available

Bunkering: Available

Lloyd's Agent: P.T. Carsurin, Sarana Penjaminan Building, 7th Floor, Jl Angkasa Block B-9 Kav 6, Kemayoran, Jakarta 10720, Jawa, Indonesia, *Tel:* +62 21 654 0425, *Fax:* +62 21 654 0418, *Email:* lloyds@carsurin.com, *Website:* www.carsurin.com

PULAU BUNYU

Lat 3° 25' N; Long 117° 57' E.

Admiralty Chart: 1852

Admiralty Pilot: 34

Time Zone: GMT +8 h

UNCTAD Locode: ID PBJ

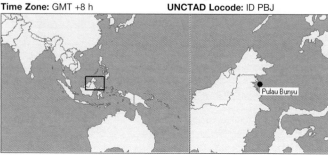

Principal Facilities:

P							T	

Authority: Pertamina Dak Kalimantan, Pulau Bunyu Port Administrator, Balikpapan, Borneo, Indonesia, *Tel:* +62 542 21453, *Fax:* +62 542 22638

Anchorage: Outer anchorage in pos 3° 26.15' N; 117° 50' E. Inner anchorage in pos 3° 28' N; 117° 59' E

Pilotage: Compulsory pilotage by sea and harbour pilot. Berthing and unberthing to CBM during daylight hours only

Radio Frequency: Port radio on VHF Channels 16 and 19 for ship to shore communication

Maximum Vessel Dimensions: 35 000 dwt at CBM, 30 000 dwt at Methanol Jetty, 3000 dwt at Cargo Jetty

Principal Imports and Exports: Exports: Crude oil.

Accommodation:

Name	Length (m)	Depth (m)	Remarks
Bunyu Terminal Pertamina CBM		11	Crude oil handled by vessels up to 35 000 dwt
Methanol Jetty	265	11	
Cargo Jetty	105	5.5	

Towage: One tug available from Tarakan

Medical Facilities: Available in emergencies only

Lloyd's Agent: P.T. Carsurin, Sarana Penjaminan Building, 7th Floor, Jl Angkasa Block B-9 Kav 6, Kemayoran, Jakarta 10720, Jawa, Indonesia, *Tel:* +62 21 654 0425, *Fax:* +62 21 654 0418, *Email:* lloyds@carsurin.com, *Website:* www.carsurin.com

PULAU SAMBU

Lat 1° 9' N; Long 103° 54' E.

Admiralty Chart: 3937

Admiralty Pilot: 36

Time Zone: GMT +7 h

UNCTAD Locode: ID PSS

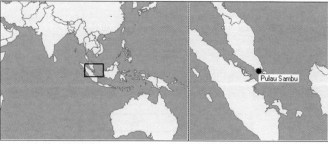

Principal Facilities:

P		G			B		

Authority: PN Pertamina, Pulau Sambu 29411, Sumatera, Indonesia, *Tel:* +62 778 310059

Pilotage: Compulsory

Radio Frequency: Sekupang Radio, call sign 'PKJ20'. VHF Channel 26, daytime only

Maximum Vessel Dimensions: 225 m loa, 10.5 m d

Working Hours: Monday to Saturday (except Friday) 0700-1400. Friday 0700-1130

Accommodation:

Name	Length (m)	Depth (m)	Remarks
Pulau Sambu			See [1] below
No.5 Cargo Wharf	19	2.6	
No.6 Cargo Wharf (Government Pier)	27	3	
No.1 Oil Wharf	110	9	
No.3 Oil Wharf	105	8.5	

[1]*Pulau Sambu:* Owned and operated by PN Pertamina. Depth at entrance 16 m, S entrance 14 m. Depth in harbour 12 m

Mechanical Handling Equipment:

Location	Type	Capacity (t)	Qty
Pulau Sambu	Mobile Cranes	10	1

Bunkering: PT Pertamina, Jalan Jos Sudarso 32-34, P O Box 265, Tanjung Priok, Jawa, Indonesia, *Tel:* +62 21 430 1086, *Fax:* +62 21 430 1562 – *Grades:* DO; MDO; IFO100-300cSt – *Parcel Size:* no min/max – *Rates:* 100-150t/h – *Notice:* 48 hours – *Delivery Mode:* barge, pipeline

Medical Facilities: Pertamina clinic

Lloyd's Agent: P.T. Carsurin, Sarana Penjaminan Building, 7th Floor, Jl Angkasa Block B-9 Kav 6, Kemayoran, Jakarta 10720, Jawa, Indonesia, *Tel:* +62 21 654 0425, *Fax:* +62 21 654 0418, *Email:* lloyds@carsurin.com, *Website:* www.carsurin.com

SABANG

Lat 5° 53' N; Long 95° 19' E.

Admiralty Chart: 2917

Admiralty Pilot: 34

Time Zone: GMT +7 h

UNCTAD Locode: ID SBG

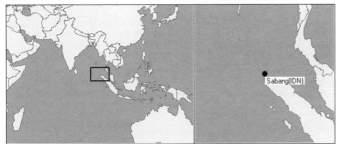

Principal Facilities:

			G							

Authority: PT (Persero) Pelabuhan Indonesia I, Port of Sabang, Jalan Perdagangan No.17, Sabang, Sumatera, Indonesia, *Tel:* +62 652 21208

Port Security: ISPS compliant

Approach: Entrance gate from northerly direction to Sabang Bay in pos 5° 00' N, 95° 20' E. Pulau Klah light buoy acts as a guide to vessels berthing at Sabang. Channel depth of 15-30 m

Anchorage: Anchorage in Sabang Bay in depth of approx 9.0 m LWS

Radio Frequency: Call sign PKA, 438 kHz and 500 kHz, working hours 0100-1600

Maximum Vessel Dimensions: 5000 dwt, 150 m loa, 8.0 m d

Working Hours: 24 h/day

Accommodation:

Name	Length (m)	Depth (m)
Sabang		
Passenger Berth	32	8.2
General Cargo Berth	280	7.5

Storage: Six transit sheds, each 2500 t cap. No refrigerated space

Cargo Worked: 160 t/day

Repair & Maintenance: One floating dock, lifting cap 1500 t, owned and operated by the Navy

Medical Facilities: General hospital

Lloyd's Agent: P.T. Carsurin, Sarana Penjaminan Building, 7th Floor, Jl Angkasa Block B-9 Kav 6, Kemayoran, Jakarta 10720, Jawa, Indonesia, *Tel:* +62 21 654 0425, *Fax:* +62 21 654 0418, *Email:* lloyds@carsurin.com, *Website:* www.carsurin.com

SAMARINDA

Lat 0° 30' S; Long 117° 9' E.

Admiralty Chart: 3731

Admiralty Pilot: 34

Time Zone: GMT +8 h

UNCTAD Locode: ID SRI

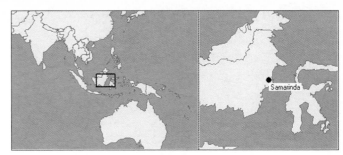

Principal Facilities:

P		Y	G	C				T	A

Authority: PT (Persero) Pelabuhan Indonesia IV, Port of Samarinda, Jalan Niaga Timur No.130, Samarinda, Tarakan 75112, Kalimantan Timur, Indonesia, *Tel:* +62 541 741092, *Fax:* +62 541 741092, *Email:* pelindos@samarinda.wasantara.net.id

Documentation: Passenger list (14 copies), crew list (7 copies), custom document (3 copies), health document (3 copies), cargo manifest (7 copies), bills of lading (7 copies), ship's papers (5 copies), sailing permit

Approach: Channel depth of 6 m MLWS

Pilotage: Compulsory

Radio Frequency: VHF Channels 12 and 16

Traffic: 1999, 1 037 997 t of cargo handled

Working Hours: Vessel operations 24 h/day

Accommodation:

Name	Remarks
Samarinda	See [1] below

[1]*Samarinda:* Three concrete wharves of lengths 555 m, 100 m and 112 m with depth alongside of 5-7 m LWS

Storage:

Location	Open (m²)	Covered (m²)
Samarinda	34320	4400

Mechanical Handling Equipment:

Location	Type	Capacity (t)	Qty
Samarinda	Floating Cranes	1	100
Samarinda	Mobile Cranes	25	1
Samarinda	Mobile Cranes	15	1
Samarinda	Forklifts	5	4

Cargo Worked: General cargo 18 t/gang/h, bagged cargo 21 t/gang/h

Towage: One tug of 800 hp and one of 240 hp

Repair & Maintenance: P.T. Kaltim Shipyard, Samarinda, Borneo, Indonesia, *Tel:* +62 541 732420

Shipping Agents: Arpeni Pratama Ocean Line, P.T. Perusahaan Pelayaran Samudera Khusus (APOL), Jalan Gajah Mada No.102, Samarinda 75122, Borneo, Indonesia, *Tel:* +62 541 742131, *Fax:* +62 541 731306, *Email:* apolsmd@samarinda.org, *Website:* www.apol.co.id
P.T. Bahana Utama Line, Samarinda, Borneo, Indonesia, *Tel:* +62 541 742692, *Fax:* +62 541 732765, *Email:* samarinda@bahana-line.com, *Website:* www.bahana-line.com
Jardine Shipping Services, Jalan K S Tubun No 53, Kalimantan, Samarinda 75123, Borneo, Indonesia, *Tel:* +62 541 738943, *Fax:* +62 541 271011, *Email:* jttssmd@samarinda.org, *Website:* www.jardine-shipping.com
P.T. (PELNI) Pelayaran Nasional Indonesia, Jl Yos Sudarso No.76, Samarinda, Borneo, Indonesia, *Tel:* +62 541 205323, *Fax:* +62 541 205323, *Email:* agencies@pelni.co.id, *Website:* www.pelni.co.id

Surveyors: P.T. Biro Klasifikasi Indonesia, Jl. Manggis No.40, Samarinda, Borneo, Indonesia, *Tel:* +62 541 734475, *Fax:* +62 541 734475, *Email:* bkisd@klasifikasiindonesia.com, *Website:* www.klasifikasiindonesia.com

Medical Facilities: Hospital facilities available

Airport: Samarinda Airport, 6 km

Lloyd's Agent: P.T. Carsurin, Sarana Penjaminan Building, 7th Floor, Jl Angkasa Block B-9 Kav 6, Kemayoran, Jakarta 10720, Jawa, Indonesia, *Tel:* +62 21 654 0425, *Fax:* +62 21 654 0418, *Email:* lloyds@carsurin.com, *Website:* www.carsurin.com

SAMBAS

Lat 1° 22' N; Long 109° 18' E.

Admiralty Chart: 3720

Admiralty Pilot: 36

Time Zone: GMT +8 h

UNCTAD Locode: ID SBS

This port is no longer open to commercial shipping

SAMPIT

Lat 2° 59' S; Long 113° 3' E.

Admiralty Chart: 3161

Admiralty Pilot: 34

Time Zone: GMT +8 h

UNCTAD Locode: ID SMQ

Key to Principal Facilities:—				
A=Airport	**C**=Containers	**G**=General Cargo	**P**=Petroleum	**R**=Ro/Ro	**Y**=Dry Bulk
B=Bunkers	**D**=Dry Dock	**L**=Cruise	**Q**=Other Liquid Bulk	**T**=Towage (where available from port)	

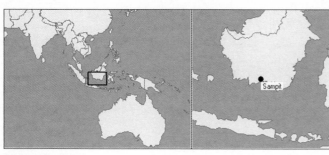

Principal Facilities:

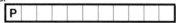

			G						A	

Authority: P.T. (Persero) Pelabuhan Indonesia III, Jalan Usman Harun No.2, Sampit 74322, Central Kalimantan, Indonesia, Tel: +62 531 21055, Fax: +62 531 21123

Documentation: Health book, ship's certificate, sailing permit, crew list, passports, officer certificate

Approach: Port is approx 665 miles from Mentaya Estuary

Pilotage: Compulsory

Radio Frequency: VHF Channel 12

Tides: 5.5 m LWS

Maximum Vessel Dimensions: 6000 dwt

Working Hours: 0700-1100, 1200-1600

Accommodation:

Name	Length (m)
Sampit Concrete Wharf	316

Storage: Stacking area of 4500 m2

Mechanical Handling Equipment:

Location	Type	Capacity (t)	Qty
Sampit	Mult-purp. Cranes	40	1
Sampit	Forklifts	5	1

Shipping Agents: P.T. (PELNI) Pelayaran Nasional Indonesia, Jl Usman Harun No.55, Sampit, Central Kalimantan, Indonesia, Tel: +62 531 22006, Fax: +62 531 24502, Email: agencies@pelni.co.id, Website: www.pelni.co.id

Airport: H. Asan Airport

Lloyd's Agent: P.T. Carsurin, Sarana Penjaminan Building, 7th Floor, Jl Angkasa Block B-9 Kav 6, Kemayoran, Jakarta 10720, Jawa, Indonesia, Tel: +62 21 654 0425, Fax: +62 21 654 0418, Email: lloyds@carsurin.com, Website: www.carsurin.com

SANGATTA TERMINAL

Lat 0° 25' N; Long 117° 35' E.

Admiralty Chart: 3022	**Admiralty Pilot:** 34
Time Zone: GMT +8 h	**UNCTAD Locode:** ID

Principal Facilities:

P									

Authority: Port Authority of Tanjung Bara Coal Terminal, P6 Building, Tan Jung Bara, Sangatta 75611, Indonesia, Tel: +62 549 525088, Fax: +62 549 525146, Email: pudinaung.lawrence@kpc.co.id, Website: www.kpc.co.id

Officials: Lawrence Pudinaung, Email: pudinaung.lawrence@kpc.co.id. General Manager: Herlan Siagian.

Port Security: ISPS compliant

Anchorage: For vessels awaiting berth the anchorage is located in pos 0° 18' 58" N, 117° 37' 35" E

Pilotage: Mooring master available

Radio Frequency: Sangatta Radio, call sign PKN-4 on VHF

Maximum Vessel Dimensions: 36 500 dwt, 220 m loa, 21 m d

Accommodation:

Name	Remarks
Sangatta Terminal	See [1] below

[1]Sangatta Terminal: CBM (4 buoys) in depth of 21.0 m. Crude oil is loaded at rate of 8570 bbls/h through two 12'' hoses

Lloyd's Agent: P.T. Carsurin, Sarana Penjaminan Building, 7th Floor, Jl Angkasa Block B-9 Kav 6, Kemayoran, Jakarta 10720, Jawa, Indonesia, Tel: +62 21 654 0425, Fax: +62 21 654 0418, Email: lloyds@carsurin.com, Website: www.carsurin.com

SANTAN TERMINAL

Lat 0° 7' S; Long 117° 32' E.

Admiralty Chart: 3040	**Admiralty Pilot:** 34
Time Zone: GMT +8 h	**UNCTAD Locode:** ID SAT

Principal Facilities:

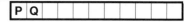

P	Q									

Authority: Chevron Indonesia Co., P O Box 276, Pasir Ridge, Balikpapan 76102, Borneo, Indonesia, Tel: +62 542 548100, Fax: +62 542 548210, Email: stnmmaster@chevron.com

Port Security: ISPS compliant

Pre-Arrival Information: 72 h prior to arrival at the Terminal, tankers should advise the Company of their ETA and other information requested in "details of cable/facsimile" in this section by a facsimile sent via Radio Room in Santan Terminal. They should also confirm or amend it when they are 48 h and again when 24 h distant from the Terminal

The following information should be included in the cables/facsimiles:

1. Name of vessel, call sign and summer deadweight
2. ETA in GMT and date (local time is GMT + 8 hours)
3. Cargo requirements
4. Tanker draft on arrival
5. If there is any sickness aboard or clean bill of health
6. Last port of call
7. Any hull, bulkhead, valve or pipeline leaks on tanker which could affect loading or cause pollution
8. Ship's length overall in meters
9. Tanker freeboard loaded and empty
10. Distance from bow to loading manifold in meters
11. Length of the flat hull (parallel middle body) in meters (gas tanker only)
12. Flange dimensions of tanker manifold connection if not to ANSI series 300 (gas tanker only)
13. Bow chain stopper available on board (crude tanker only)

Approach: Channel 1.6 km wide with a depth of 50 m

Anchorage: Anchorage can be obtained between 3.5 and 7 miles SE of Tanjung Santan approx 2.5 miles E of the SBM

Pilotage: Pilotage by the Mooring Master is compulsory and available for berthing 0600-1800 LT. Night berthing is available subject to the approval of the Harbour Master. Pilot boards in pos 0° 05.5' S; 117° 34.0' E (in the anchorage area)

Radio Frequency: VHF radio in use for the terminal and/or pilots. Pilot information should contact "Santan Control" on VHF Channel 16 and the working frequency of Santan Control is on VHF Channel 9

Maximum Vessel Dimensions: SBM: 18 000-125 000 dwt. LPG Jetty: 60-110 m loa

Working Hours: 24 h/day

Accommodation:

Name	Depth (m)	Draught (m)	Remarks
Santan Terminal			
Single Buoy Mooring	28	20	See [1] below
LPG Jetty	11.5	7.5	See [2] below

[1]Single Buoy Mooring: In pos 0° 6' 18.6" S; 117° 32' 18.8" E. Loading of crude and condensate. Tanker must be equipped with a hose lifting derrick at the port side manifold, with a min lifting cap of 15 t SWL. Manifold connection size is 12". Tankers must be able to terminate its flanges to 12" of ANSI 150 series
[2]LPG Jetty: In pos 0° 5' 25.7" S; 117° 30' 44.2" E. Loading of LPG. Cargo carrying cap not less than 500 t and not more than 3000 t. Freeboard when empty not more than 7 m

Lloyd's Agent: P.T. Carsurin, Sarana Penjaminan Building, 7th Floor, Jl Angkasa Block B-9 Kav 6, Kemayoran, Jakarta 10720, Jawa, Indonesia, Tel: +62 21 654 0425, Fax: +62 21 654 0418, Email: lloyds@carsurin.com, Website: www.carsurin.com

SEMANGKA BAY TERMINAL

Lat 5° 35' S; Long 104° 37' E.

Admiralty Chart: 2965	**Admiralty Pilot:** 36
Time Zone: GMT +7 h	**UNCTAD Locode:** ID SMB

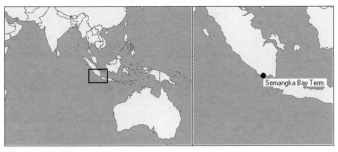

Principal Facilities:

P						T	

Authority: Semangka Bay Port Authority, Harbour Masters Office, Kota Agung Public Pier, Kota Agung, Sumatra, Indonesia

Anchorage: Anchorage available within the following positions in depths of 32-90 m
5° 32' S; 104° 36' E
5° 32' S; 104° 39' E
5° 36' S; 104° 36' E
5° 36' S; 104° 39' E

Pilotage: Compulsory. Pilot normally boards from a tug at the anchorage or 2 miles from FSO if berthing on arrival

Radio Frequency: Kota Agung Radio can be contacted on VHF Channels 16 and 9

Maximum Vessel Dimensions: Max dwt 390 000 t, max draft 22 m, max loa 370 m

Working Hours: 24 h/day

Accommodation:

Name	Remarks
Semangka Bay Terminal	See [1] below

[1]*Semangka Bay Terminal:* Consists of floating storage offloading tanker 'Thai Resource' anchored 2.2 miles inside Teluk Semangka Bay. Berthing during daylight hours only. Gas oil and kerosene discharged by tankers to FSO at max rate of 4000 m3/h

Towage: Two 3500 hp tugs available

Medical Facilities: Available at Bandar Lampung, 100 km

Lloyd's Agent: P.T. Carsurin, Sarana Penjaminan Building, 7th Floor, Jl Angkasa Block B-9 Kav 6, Kemayoran, Jakarta 10720, Jawa, Indonesia, *Tel:* +62 21 654 0425, *Fax:* +62 21 654 0418, *Email:* lloyds@carsurin.com, *Website:* www.carsurin.com

SEMARANG

Lat 6° 58' S; Long 110° 25' E.

Admiralty Chart: 918	**Admiralty Pilot:** 36
Time Zone: GMT +7 h	**UNCTAD Locode:** ID SRG

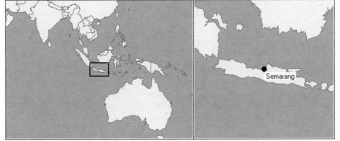

Principal Facilities:

P	Q	Y	G	C		L	B		T	A

Authority: Port Administration of Tanjung Emas, Jalan Coaster No.10, Semarang, Jawa, Indonesia, *Tel:* +62 24 354 5721, *Fax:* +62 24 354 5892, *Email:* tgemas@idola.net.id

Port Security: ISPS compliant

Approach: Navigation channel in depth of 10 m

Anchorage: In pos 6° 53' S, 110° 23.50' E in depth of 13.0 m LWS

Pilotage: Compulsory to enter inner harbour. Pilots available 24 h/day. VHF Channel 12, Tel: +62 24 545112 & 545725

Radio Frequency: Coastal radio station (Semarang Radio) PKR. Frequencies 500 kHz and 2282 kHz. VHF Channel 16

Weather: From November to March port affected by W monsoon

Tides: Range of tide 1.64 m

Maximum Vessel Dimensions: 240 m loa, 9.0 m draft

Principal Imports and Exports: Imports: Raw cotton, Raw materials, Steel scrap. Exports: Furniture, Garments, Molasses, Particle board, Plywood, Seafood, Textiles.

Working Hours: 24 h/day in three shifts

Accommodation:

Name	Length (m)	Depth (m)	Remarks
Semarang			See [1] below
Ocean Wharf	605	9	
Domestic Wharf	320	5-6	
KBT Wharf	500	3	

[1]*Semarang:* Three toploaders of 30.5 t cap, spreaders of 40 t cap and various other gear available for container handling. Container freight station of 6000 m2. Passenger terminal of 4530 m2

Storage:

Location	Open (m²)	Covered (m²)
Semarang	113846	44390

Mechanical Handling Equipment:

Location	Type	Capacity (t)	Qty
Semarang	Mult-purp. Cranes	40	3
Semarang	Forklifts	10	

Bunkering: C.V. Bahtera Camar, Jalan Lagoa Terusan Bl No.4, Jakarta 14270, Jawa, Indonesia, *Tel:* +62 21 435 3209, *Fax:* +62 21 430 6048
Buana Jaya C.V., jalan Sungai Kapuas No.15, Jakarta 14270, Jawa, Indonesia, *Tel:* +62 21 44835302, *Fax:* +62 21 44835302
Kartika Jasa Karya P.T., Jalan Perak Timur 564/A1, Surabaya 60165, Jawa, Indonesia, *Tel:* +62 31 3293 459, *Fax:* +62 31 3294 736, *Email:* kemusuk@rad.net.id
PT Antraco Nusa Bhakti, Jln. Demak 407, Surabaya, Surabaya 6000, Jawa, Indonesia, *Tel:* +62 31 3524065, *Fax:* +62 31 805 1067, *Email:* info@talokomarine.com, *Website:* www.talokomarine.com
PT Pertamina, Jalan Jos Sudarso 32-34, P O Box 265, Tanjung Priok, Jawa, Indonesia, *Tel:* +62 21 430 1086, *Fax:* +62 21 430 1562 – *Grades:* DO; MDO; IFO100-300cSt – *Parcel Size:* no min/max – *Rates:* DO 650t per day, MDO/IFO 3300t per day – *Notice:* 48 hours – *Delivery Mode:* barge, pipeline
C.V. Purba Jaya, Jalan Edam II No. 5, Tanjung Priok, Jakarta 14310, Jawa, Indonesia, *Tel:* +62 21 4393 1240, *Fax:* +62 21 4393 0792, *Email:* pijar@indo.net.id

Towage: Three tugs of 800 hp, 870 hp and 1500 hp

Repair & Maintenance: P.T. Jasa Wahana Tirta Samudera, Semarang, Jawa, Indonesia, *Tel:* +62 24 354 9567
P.T. Koja Bahari, Semarang, Jawa, Indonesia, *Tel:* +62 24 354 0232

Shipping Agents: P.T. Ahlers Thoeng Indonesia, Suite 502, 5th Floor, Wisma HSBC, 135 Jl Gajah Mada, Semarang 050134, Jawa, Indonesia, *Tel:* +62 24 844 3048, *Fax:* +62 24 844 3051/8221, *Email:* semarang@ahlersthoeng.com
P.T. Andal Lautan Niaga, 52 Puri Anjosmoro Blok 61, Semarang 50144, Jawa, Indonesia, *Tel:* +62 24 761 7676, *Fax:* +62 24 761 8783, *Email:* dhadis@smg.bit.net.id
Arpeni Pratama Ocean Line, P.T. Perusahaan Pelayaran Samudera Khusus (APOL), Wisma HSBC, 4th Floor, Suite 405, Jl Gajah Mada 135, Semarang 50134, Jawa, Indonesia, *Tel:* +62 24 845 4326/8, *Fax:* +62 24 845 4329, *Email:* arpeni_smg@apol.co.id
P.T. Awards Shipping Agency Indonesia, Ruko Semarang Indah Block D, Xi/1B Madukoro Raya, Semarang, Jawa, Indonesia, *Tel:* +62 24 761 4708, *Fax:* +62 24 760 5527, *Email:* gilda@awardsindo.com
P.T. Bahana Utama Line, Kompleks Semarang Indah Blok, 3 Maduko Raya, Semarang 50144, Jawa, Indonesia, *Tel:* +62 24 762 3585, *Fax:* +62 24 762 3585, *Email:* semarang@bahana-line.com, *Website:* www.bahana-line.com
P.T. Bhum Mulia Prima, 19 Jl MH Thamrin, Semarang 50134, Jawa, Indonesia, *Tel:* +62 24 355 3383, *Fax:* +62 24 354 5466, *Email:* rclsrg@rclgroup.com
Jardine Shipping Services, Jl Puri Anjasmoro, Block F1, No 3A, Semarang 50144, Jawa, Indonesia, *Tel:* +62 24 761 9401, *Fax:* +62 24 761 9405, *Email:* bmjtssmr@indosat.net.id, *Website:* www.jardine-shipping.com
P.T. Layar Sentosa Shipping Corp., Jl Usman Jantin 20/V-V 3rd Floor, Perkantoran Tanjung Mas, Semarang 50241, Jawa, Indonesia, *Tel:* +62 24 354 4123, *Fax:* +62 24 355 5569, *Email:* larsensmg@larsen.co.id
A.P. Moller-Maersk Group, Maersk Line, HSBC Building, 4th Floor, Jl. Gajah Mada No.135, Semarang 50241, Jawa, Indonesia, *Tel:* +62 24 845 1500, *Fax:* +62 24 845 1505, *Email:* semcusgen@maersk.com, *Website:* www.maerskline.com
P.T. (PELNI) Pelayaran Nasional Indonesia, Jl Mpu Tantular No.25-27, Semarang, Jawa, Indonesia, *Tel:* +62 24 354 6723, *Fax:* +62 24 355 5156, *Email:* agencies@pelni.co.id, *Website:* www.pelni.co.id
PT Perusahaan Pelayaran Samudera Trikora Lloyd, Komplek Pelabuhan, Tanjung Emas, Jalan Usman Janatin 14V, Semarang 20129, Jawa, Indonesia, *Tel:* +62 24 351 2681, *Fax:* +62 24 351 2682
Wilhelmsen Ship Services, Barwil Tirta Samudera, Jalan Sembodro 2C No.153, Pondok Indraprasta, Kelurahan Pelombokan, Semarang 50171, Jawa, Indonesia, *Tel:* +62 24 355 1423/5/6, *Fax:* +62 24 356 1356, *Email:* barwil.semarang.ops@barwil.com, *Website:* www.barwil.com
P.T. Zhonghai Indo Shipping, Jl Puri Anjosmoro Blok G1 38, Semarang 50144, Jawa, Indonesia, *Tel:* +62 24 761 8000, *Fax:* +62 24 761 8061, *Email:* aryono@srg.gpi-g.com

Medical Facilities: Port health centre clinic

Airport: Ahmad Yani Airport, 10 km

Railway: Tawang Station, 2 km

Lloyd's Agent: P.T. Carsurin, Sarana Penjaminan Building, 7th Floor, Jl Angkasa Block B-9 Kav 6, Kemayoran, Jakarta 10720, Jawa, Indonesia, *Tel:* +62 21 654 0425, *Fax:* +62 21 654 0418, *Email:* lloyds@carsurin.com, *Website:* www.carsurin.com

SENIPAH TERMINAL

Lat 1° 3' S; Long 117° 13' E.

Admiralty Chart: 2639/2636/941B	**Admiralty Pilot:** 34
Time Zone: GMT +8 h	**UNCTAD Locode:** ID SPH

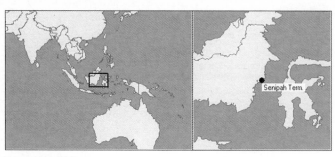

Principal Facilities:

P								T	A	

Authority: Total E&P Indonesie, Kuningan Plaza, Menara Utara, Jl. HR. Rasuna Said Kav. C 11-14, P O Box 1010, Jakarta 10010, Jawa, Indonesia, *Tel:* +62 21 252 2690, *Fax:* +62 21 252 0814, *Email:* eddy.yusuf@total.com

Pre-Arrival Information: Vessels ETA should be advised 72 h, 48 h, 24 h and 3 h before arrival

Documentation: Port Health Officer:
a) smallpox vaccination certificate
b) certificate of inoculation against any contagious disease
Customs, Immigration & Harbour Master:
a) crew list
b) cargo manifest for transit cargo
c) declaration of personel belongings
d) ship's store list
e) bonded stores list
f) narcotics list
g) ammunition list
h) inventory list
i) foreign exchange list
j) passport or seamans book
Certificates of Vessel:
a) certificate of registry
b) international tonnage certificate
c) classification of certificate
d) international load line certificate
e) safety equipment certificate
f) safety construction certificate
g) safety radio telegraphy certificate
h) certificate of insurance oil pollution
i) international oil pollution prevention
j) port state control
k) life raft certificate
l) derating or exemption derating certificate
m) indonesia health book
n) last port clearance
o) safe manning certificate
p) document of compliance
q) safety management certificate
r) fire extinguisher certificate

Pilotage: Compulsory. Mooring master boards in pos 1° 05' 29" S; 117° 15' 01" E (3 miles SE of SBM)

Radio Frequency: Senipah Radio call sign 'PKN-22' on VHF Channel 9

Weather: Winds from July to October in S'ly direction generally 15-20 knots and from November to June winds are variable generally 5-10 knots

Maximum Vessel Dimensions: 125 000 dwt at SBM

Accommodation:

Name	Depth (m)	Remarks
Senipah Terminal		
SBM	28	See [1] below
Jetty	3.5	For vessels up to 500 dwt

[1]*SBM:* Single Buoy Mooring (SBM) for export of crude oil for tankers of 33 000-125 000 dwt, is marked by quick flashing yellow light at seaward end of a pipeline that extends 9.2 km SE from a position on the shore about 5 km SW of Senipah village. Loading is from two submarine pipelines of 26'' dia. Max loading rate of 19 000 bbls/h. Mooring takes place only in daylight

Towage: One tug and two mooring boats available

Medical Facilities: Emergency cases only

Airport: Sepinggan Airport, 70 km

Lloyd's Agent: P.T. Carsurin, Sarana Penjaminan Building, 7th Floor, Jl Angkasa Block B-9 Kav 6, Kemayoran, Jakarta 10720, Jawa, Indonesia, *Tel:* +62 21 654 0425, *Fax:* +62 21 654 0418, *Email:* lloyds@carsurin.com, *Website:* www.carsurin.com

SIBOLGA

Lat 1° 44' N; Long 98° 46' E.

Admiralty Chart: 400	**Admiralty Pilot:** 35
Time Zone: GMT +7 h	**UNCTAD Locode:** ID SLG

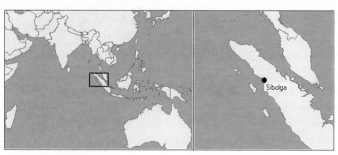

Principal Facilities:

P		G	R				A	

Authority: PT (Persero) Pelabuhan Indonesia I, Port of Sibolga, Jalan Horas Pelabuhan, Baru Sambas, Sibolga 22532, Sumatera, Indonesia, *Tel:* +62 631 22875, *Fax:* +62 631 22875

Approach: Channel depth of 9-12 m LWS

Anchorage: Two miles from the wharf in depths of 15-20 m

Tides: 0.7-1.1 m

Working Hours: Mon-Fri 0800-1600. Sat 0800-1200

Accommodation:

Name	Length (m)	Depth (m)	Remarks
Sibolga			Passenger terminal of 304 m2
Multi-Purpose Berth	209	2.6–6.5	For vessels up to 5000 dwt
Ferry Terminal	35	5	For vessels up to 1000 dwt

Storage:

Location	Open (m²)	Covered (m²)	Sheds / Warehouses
Sibolga	1783	2900	2

Mechanical Handling Equipment:

Location	Type	Capacity (t)	Qty
Sibolga	Forklifts	3	2
Sibolga	Forklifts	5	1

Cargo Worked: 13 t/gang/h

Waste Reception Facilities: Garbage disposal available

Shipping Agents: P.T. (PELNI) Pelayaran Nasional Indonesia, Jl Patuan Anggi No.39, Sibolga, Sumatera, Indonesia, *Tel:* +62 631 22291, *Fax:* +62 631 22927, *Email:* agencies@pelni.co.id, *Website:* www.pelni.co.id

Medical Facilities: Public hospital

Airport: Pinang Sori, 27 km

Lloyd's Agent: P.T. Carsurin, Sarana Penjaminan Building, 7th Floor, Jl Angkasa Block B-9 Kav 6, Kemayoran, Jakarta 10720, Jawa, Indonesia, *Tel:* +62 21 654 0425, *Fax:* +62 21 654 0418, *Email:* lloyds@carsurin.com, *Website:* www.carsurin.com

SINGKAWANG

Lat 0° 55' N; Long 108° 58' E.

Admiralty Chart: 3720	**Admiralty Pilot:** 36
Time Zone: GMT +8 h	**UNCTAD Locode:** ID SKW

This port is no longer open to commercial shipping

SORONG

Lat 0° 53' S; Long 131° 14' E.

Admiralty Chart: 1420	**Admiralty Pilot:** 35
Time Zone: GMT +9 h	**UNCTAD Locode:** ID SOQ

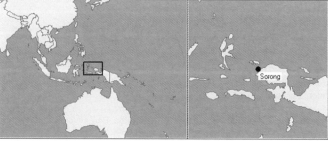

Principal Facilities:

P		G	C	R		B		T	A	

Authority: PT (Persero) Pelabuhan Indonesia IV, Port of Sorong, Jalan Jend. Ahmad Yani No.13, Sorong 98413, Irian Jaya, Indonesia, *Tel:* +62 951 323875, *Fax:* +62 951 323805

Documentation: Passenger list (5 copies), crew list (4 copies), custom document (2 copies), health document (2 copies), cargo manifest (7 copies), bills of lading (7 copies), ship's papers (5 copies), sailing permit

Approach: Outer Bars Channel in depth of 28 m. Entrance Channel in depth of 20 m

Anchorage: In pos 0° 53' 24" S, 131° 14' 24" E in depth of 20 m

Pilotage: Compulsory. Four pilots and one pilot boat of 250 hp available

Radio Frequency: VHF Channel 16, 20 and 26

Tides: Tidal range 1.8 m

Traffic: 1999, 240 482 t of cargo handled

Maximum Vessel Dimensions: 20 000 dwt, 170 m loa, 8.0 m d

Principal Imports and Exports: Exports: Crude oil, Plywood, Shrimp, Tuna fish.

Working Hours: 0800-1200, 1300-1800, 2000-2400, 0100-0600

Accommodation:

Name	Length (m)	Depth (m)
Sorong		
Sorong Wharf	280	10
Dg Minyak	125	15
Oil Jetty	60	8

Storage:

Location	Covered (m²)
Sorong	1950

Mechanical Handling Equipment:

Location	Type	Capacity (t)	Qty
Sorong	Mobile Cranes	25	1
Sorong	Forklifts	3	4

Cargo Worked: 750 t to 1000 t/day for general cargo, 900 t to 1250 t/day for bulk cargo

Bunkering: PT Pertamina, Jalan Jos Sudarso 32-34, P O Box 265, Tanjung Priok, Jawa, Indonesia, *Tel:* +62 21 430 1086, *Fax:* +62 21 430 1562 – *Grades:* DO; MDO; IFO100-300cSt; lubes – *Parcel Size:* no min/max – *Rates:* 100-150t/h – *Notice:* 48 hours – *Delivery Mode:* barge, pipeline

Towage: Two tugs of 1500 hp available from Pertamina

Repair & Maintenance: Pertamina Dok Karim, Kasim, Indonesia, *Tel:* +62 951 321721 Floating dock of 200 t lifting cap
Usaha Mina Dock, Sorong, Irian Jaya, Indonesia, *Tel:* +62 951 323697

Shipping Agents: P.T. (PELNI) Pelayaran Nasional Indonesia, Jl Jend A Yani Kompleks Pelabuhan, Sorong, Irian Jaya, Indonesia, *Tel:* +62 951 321716, *Fax:* +62 951 323873, *Email:* agencies@pelni.co.id, *Website:* www.pelni.co.id

Surveyors: P.T. Biro Klasifikasi Indonesia, Jl. Jend. Sudirman No.104, Sorong 98414, Irian Jaya, Indonesia, *Tel:* +62 951 322600, *Fax:* +62 951 323870, *Email:* bkisr@klasifikasiindonesia.com, *Website:* www.klasifikasiindonesia.com

Medical Facilities: Public hospital and Pertamina clinic

Airport: Jeffman Airport, 11 km

Lloyd's Agent: P.T. Carsurin, Sarana Penjaminan Building, 7th Floor, Jl Angkasa Block B-9 Kav 6, Kemayoran, Jakarta 10720, Jawa, Indonesia, *Tel:* +62 21 654 0425, *Fax:* +62 21 654 0418, *Email:* lloyds@carsurin.com, *Website:* www.carsurin.com

SOUTH PULAU LAUT COAL TERMINAL

see under Mekar Putih

SUNGAI KOLAK

former name, see Kijang

SUNGAI LAIS

harbour area, see under Palembang

SUNGEI PAKNING

Lat 1° 22' N; Long 102° 11' E.

Admiralty Chart: 3947	**Admiralty Pilot:** 44
Time Zone: GMT +7 h	**UNCTAD Locode:** ID SEQ

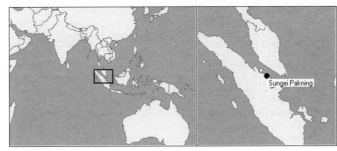

Principal Facilities:

P		G			B		T	A

Authority: PT (Persero) Pelabuhan Indonesia I, Port of Sungei Pakning, Jl. Kol Yos Sudarso No.2, Sungei Pakning, Sumatera, Indonesia, *Tel:* +62 766 91121, *Fax:* +62 766 91023

Approach: In 16 m depth

Pilotage: Compulsory. Pilots meet vessels at anchorage. 24 h service available

Radio Frequency: VHF Channels 12, 16 and 9

Tides: 1.4 m LWS, 3.3 m HT

Maximum Vessel Dimensions: 84 000 dwt, 225 m loa, 13.7 m d

Working Hours: Monday-Thursday 0730-1430. Friday 0730-1130. Saturday 0730-1300

Accommodation:

Name	Remarks
Sungei Pakning	See ¹ below

¹*Sungei Pakning:* Crude oil installation operated and owned by Pertamina Oil. Wharf capable of berthing one 85 000 t tanker or two 50 000 t tankers simultaneously located 548.6 m offshore. Wharf has central loading platform 54.86 m long, 12.19 m wide. Flanking mooring platforms are connected to central platform by walkways, bridges 31.7 m in length.
There is a Government Wharf available for small craft

Bunkering: Buana Jaya C.V., jalan Sungai Kapuas No.15, Jakarta 14270, Jawa, Indonesia, *Tel:* +62 21 44835302, *Fax:* +62 21 44835302
PT Pertamina, Jalan Jos Sudarso 32-34, P O Box 265, Tanjung Priok, Jawa, Indonesia, *Tel:* +62 21 430 1086, *Fax:* +62 21 430 1562 – *Grades:* DO; MDO; IFO100-300cSt – *Parcel Size:* no min/max – *Rates:* 100-150t/h – *Notice:* 48 hours – *Delivery Mode:* barge, pipeline

Towage: Three tug boats from Pertamina

Medical Facilities: Available in emergencies only

Airport: 5 km

Lloyd's Agent: P.T. Carsurin, Sarana Penjaminan Building, 7th Floor, Jl Angkasa Block B-9 Kav 6, Kemayoran, Jakarta 10720, Jawa, Indonesia, *Tel:* +62 21 654 0425, *Fax:* +62 21 654 0418, *Email:* lloyds@carsurin.com, *Website:* www.carsurin.com

SURABAYA

Lat 7° 12' S; Long 112° 44' E.

Admiralty Chart: 975	**Admiralty Pilot:** 34
Time Zone: GMT +7 h	**UNCTAD Locode:** ID SUB

Principal Facilities:

P	Q	Y	G	C	R		B		T	A

Authority: Port of Tanjung Perak, Jl. Tanjung Perak Timur 620, Surabaya 60165, Jawa, Indonesia, *Tel:* +62 31 329 1992, *Fax:* +62 31 329 3994, *Email:* timasti@perakport.co.id, *Website:* www.perakport.co.id

Officials: General Manager: Achmad Barota, *Tel:* +62 31 329 3994.
Commercial Manager: Iputu Ariawan, *Tel:* +62 31 329 1257.

Port Security: ISPS compliant

Approach: West Navigation Channel 25 nautical miles long, 100 m wide with a depth of 9.7 m at LWS, marked with 24 buoys. East Navigation Channel 22.5 nautical miles long, 100 m wide with depth of 2.5 m LWS, marked with 8 buoys

Anchorage: Zone A for vessels less than 100 m loa bounded by a line joining the following positions: 07° 11' 35" S; 112° 43' 37" E, 07° 11' 30" S; 112° 42' 50" E, 07° 11' 16" S; 112° 43' 37" E, 07° 10' 51" S; 112° 42' 50" E
Zone B for vessels of 100-150 m loa bounded by a line joining the following positions: 07° 11' 30" S; 112° 42' 50" E, 07° 11' 21" S; 112° 41' 32" E, 07° 10' 34" S; 112° 41' 32" E, 07° 10' 51" S; 112° 42' 50" E
Zone C for vessels over 150 m loa bounded by a line joining the following positions:

Key to Principal Facilities:—				
A=Airport	**C**=Containers	**G**=General Cargo	**P**=Petroleum	**R**=Ro/Ro	**Y**=Dry Bulk
B=Bunkers	**D**=Dry Dock	**L**=Cruise	**Q**=Other Liquid Bulk	**T**=Towage (where available from port)

07° 10' 21" S; 112° 41' 32" E, 07° 10' 34" S; 112° 41' 32" E, 07° 10' 00" S; 112° 40' 40" E, 07° 10' 00" S; 112° 40' 56" E

Pilotage: Compulsory. Pilot boards at Karang Jamuang Station, situated at the outer entrance to the port. Request for pilot through shipping agents 10 h prior to entry and at least 8 h prior to departure. Pilot VHF Channels 6, 8, 12 and 16

Radio Frequency: Radio Station call signal PKD operating on frquencies 500 kHz, 2182 kHz, 6215.5 kHz, 8461 kHz, 8796.4 kHz, 12704.5 kHz and 16861.7 kHz. VHF Channels 16, 12, 14, 20, 22, 26 and 28

Tides: Range of tide 2.2 m

Maximum Vessel Dimensions: 210 m loa, 9.55 m max draft

Working Hours: Monday to Thurdsay 0700-1500. Friday 0700-1100, 1300-1430

Accommodation:

Name	Length (m)	Depth (m)	Remarks
Surabaya			See [1] below
Jamrud Utara	1200	9.2	Ocean-going
Jamrud Barat	210	8	Inter-island
Jamrud Selatan	800	8	Inter-island
Perak	140	7	
Berlian Timur	785	9	Ocean-going
Berlian Barat	700	9.5	Ocean-going
Nilam Timur	860	9	Bulk & liquid cargo
Mirah Terminal	640	7	Inter-island
Intan Terminal	100	4	Oil discharge
Kalimas Terminal	2270	2	Sailing vessels & ferry boats
International Container Wharf	1000	10.5	See [2] below
Domestic Container Wharf	450	7.5	See [3] below

[1]*Surabaya:* Tanker facilities: Two berths at Semampir Jetty operated by PN Pertamina 170.7 m in length, draft 9.45 m and 10.97 m. Water and bunkers available. One berth 16 m long, 8 m deep, operated at Nilam Utara by PN Pertamina
[2]*International Container Wharf:* Operated by Terminal Petikemas Surabaya (TPS), Jl. Tanjung Mutiara 1, Surabaya 60177, Tel: +62 31 328 3265, Fax: +62 31 329 1628, Website: www.tps.co.id
Area of 29 ha with cap for 30 000 TEU's and 250 reefer points. Container freight station stacking area of 10 000 m2 and 6500 m2 for dangerous/special goods
[3]*Domestic Container Wharf:* Operated by Terminal Petikemas Surabaya (TPS), Jl. Tanjung Mutiara 1, Surabaya 60177, Tel: +62 31 328 3265, Fax: +62 31 329 1628, Website: www.tps.co.id
Area of 9 ha with cap for 9000 TEU's

Storage:

Location	Open (m²)	Covered (m²)	Sheds / Warehouses
Jamrud Utara	1912	22391	7
Jamrud Selatan	5677	23495	7
Perak		6718	2
Berlian Timur		8780	2
Berlian Barat	19500	9166	2
Nilam Timur	14125	18235	4
Mirah Terminal	15965	13700	4
Kalimas Terminal	3200	6714	4

Mechanical Handling Equipment: Container Wharves operated by TPS: eleven container cranes, twenty three RTG's and three reach stackers

Bunkering: Kartika Jasa Karya P.T., Jalan Perak Timur 564/A1, Surabaya 60165, Jawa, Indonesia, *Tel:* +62 31 3293 459, *Fax:* +62 31 3294 736, *Email:* kemusuk@rad.net.id
PT Antraco Nusa Bhakti, Jln. Demak 407, Surabaya, Surabaya 6000, Jawa, Indonesia, *Tel:* +62 31 3524065, *Fax:* +62 31 805 1067, *Email:* info@talokomarine.com, *Website:* www.talokomarine.com
Aditya Aryaprawira Corp., Wisma Mitra Sunter 01-02, Sunter Boulevard Block C-1, Jalan Yos Sudarso Kav 89, Jakarta 14350, Jawa, Indonesia, *Tel:* +62 21 6514732, *Fax:* +62 21 6514731, *Email:* info@adityacorp.com, *Website:* www.adityacorp.com
C.V. Bahtera Camar, Jalan Lagoa Terusan BI No.4, Jakarta 14270, Jawa, Indonesia, *Tel:* +62 21 435 3209, *Fax:* +62 21 430 6048
Buana Jaya C.V., jalan Sungai Kapuas No.15, Jakarta 14270, Jawa, Indonesia, *Tel:* +62 21 44835302, *Fax:* +62 21 44835302
Kartika Jasa Karya P.T., Jalan Perak Timur 564/A1, Surabaya 60165, Jawa, Indonesia, *Tel:* +62 31 3293 459, *Fax:* +62 31 3294 736, *Email:* kemusuk@rad.net.id
PT Antraco Nusa Bhakti, Jln. Demak 407, Surabaya, Surabaya 6000, Jawa, Indonesia, *Tel:* +62 31 3524065, *Fax:* +62 31 805 1067, *Email:* info@talokomarine.com, *Website:* www.talokomarine.com
PT Pertamina, Jalan Jos Sudarso 32-34, P O Box 265, Tanjung Priok, Jawa, Indonesia, *Tel:* +62 21 430 1086, *Fax:* +62 21 430 1562 – *Grades:* DO; MDO; IFO100-300cSt – *Parcel Size:* no min/max – *Rates:* 100-150t/h – *Notice:* 48 hours – *Delivery Mode:* barge, pipeline
C.V. Purba Jaya, Jalan Edam II No. 5, Tanjung Priok, Jakarta 14310, Jawa, Indonesia, *Tel:* +62 21 4393 1240, *Fax:* +62 21 4393 0792, *Email:* pijar@indo.net.id

Towage: Nine tugs are available of 800-2400 hp

Ship Chandlers: C.V. Karya Candra Jaya, Jalan Simorejo GG XII No. 2, Surabaya 60181, Jawa, Indonesia, *Tel:* +62 31 535 8202, *Fax:* +62 31 535 8202, *Email:* kcj@cbn.net.id
C.V. Ora et Labora, Jalan Bulak Rukem Tomor 2J No. 5, Surabaya, Jawa, Indonesia, *Tel:* +62 31 381 1523, *Fax:* +62 31 389 8114, *Email:* oeltony@sby.dnet.net.id
P.T. Santosa Cipta Karya, Gili IV, 17 Surabaya, Surabaya 60162, Jawa, Indonesia, *Tel:* +62 31 352 5399, *Fax:* +62 31 355 2545, *Email:* sc-karya@indo.net.id
C.V. Surya Baharl Sejabtera, JL Teluk Wede No.8, Surabaya 60165, Jawa, Indonesia, *Tel:* +62 31 328 1781, *Fax:* +62 31 328 1712, *Email:* adrw_sbs@sby.dnet.net.id

Shipping Agents: P.T. Pelayaran Samudera Admiral Lines, Surabaya, Jawa, Indonesia, *Tel:* +62 31 329 3001
P.T. Ahlers Thoeng Indonesia, Suite 2E, 10th Floor, Wisma Dharmala, 101-103 Jl Panglima Sudirman, Surabaya 60271, Jawa, Indonesia, *Tel:* +62 31 549 1295, *Fax:* +62 31 532 7984, *Email:* ahlersti@indosat.net.id
Arpeni Pratama Ocean Line, P.T. Perusahaan Pelayaran Samudera Khusus (APOL),

Jalan Perak Timur 138, Surabaya, Jawa, Indonesia, *Tel:* +62 31 356 7055/6, *Fax:* +62 31 356 8046/9, *Email:* domi@apol.co.id
P.T. Awards Shipping Agency Indonesia, Jl Teluk Kumai 109, Surabaya 60165, Jawa, Indonesia, *Tel:* +62 31 328 6565, *Fax:* +62 31 328 6566, *Email:* alex@awardsindo.com
P.T. Bahana Utama Line, Jl Perak Timur 134, Surabaya 60614, Jawa, Indonesia, *Tel:* +62 31 353 4315, *Fax:* +62 31 353 4112, *Email:* surabaya@bahana-line.com, *Website:* www.bahana-line.com
Ben Line Agencies Ltd, 6th Floor, Medan Pemuda Building, Jalan Premuda No. 27-31, Surabaya, Jawa, Indonesia, *Tel:* +62 31 548 1500, *Fax:* +62 31 548 0040, *Email:* sby-genmbox@benline.co.id, *Website:* www.benlineagencies.com
P.T. Bhum Mulia Prima, Gedung Yosindo, Ground Floor, Jl Rajawali 84, Surabaya 60164, Jawa, Indonesia, *Tel:* +62 31 356 0088, *Fax:* +62 31 356 0098/9, *Email:* rclssub@rclgroup.com
P.T. Bumi Laut Shipping Corp., Jl Perak Timur 522, Surabaya 60165, Jawa, Indonesia, *Tel:* +62 31 329 5105, *Fax:* +62 31 329 3103
P.T. Djakarta Lloyd (PERSERO), Jalan Prapat Kurung Utara 2, Surabaya 1042, Jawa, Indonesia, *Tel:* +62 31 329 3219, *Fax:* +62 31 329 1635, *Email:* dlsby@indosat.net.id
P.T. Garbantara Citra Buana, 428 Jl Perak Timur, Surabaya, Jawa, Indonesia, *Tel:* +62 31 329 2130, *Fax:* +62 31 329 1397, *Website:* www.garbantara.com
P.T. Harta Hariman, Jl Perak Timur 536, Surabaya, Jawa, Indonesia, *Tel:* +62 31 329 5308, *Fax:* +62 31 329 4106
P.T. Intrajasa Madaya, 3rd Floor, Daya Sinar Mas Building, Jalan Rajawali 14, Surabaya 60175, Jawa, Indonesia, *Tel:* +62 31 354 8066, *Fax:* +62 31 357 7137, *Email:* info@sub-mscid.com
P.T. Jangkar Pacific, Jl Kalianget 100, Surabaya 60165, Jawa, Indonesia, *Tel:* +62 31 329 4680, *Fax:* +62 31 329 4692/3, *Email:* mail@sub.jangkarpacific.com
Jardine Shipping Services, Kompleks pengampon square, Jl.Semut Baru No. C-03, Surabaya 60172, Jawa, Indonesia, *Tel:* +62 31 355 1555, *Fax:* +62 31 357 5799, *Email:* cs02@sub.jardine-shipping.co.id, *Website:* www.jardine-shipping.com
P.T. Layar Sentosa Shipping Corp., Jl Perak Timur 524, Janjung Perak, Surabaya 60165, Jawa, Indonesia, *Tel:* +62 31 329 9281/9284, *Fax:* +62 31 329 9285, *Email:* larsensby@larsen.co.id
A.P. Moller-Maersk Group, Maersk Line, Wisma BII, 12th Floor, Jl. Pemuda No.60-70, Surabaya 50134, Jawa, Indonesia, *Tel:* +62 31 548 0606, *Fax:* +62 31 548 0638, *Email:* subcus@maersk.com, *Website:* www.maerskline.com
PT Perusahaan Pelayaran Samudera Trikora Lloyd, 2 Jalan Teluk Lampung, Tanjung Perak, Surabaya 60165, Jawa, Indonesia, *Tel:* +62 31 329 1020, *Fax:* +62 31 329 5571
Wilhelmsen Ship Services, Barwil Unitor Ships Service, Perwira Building 2nd Floor, Jalan Perak Timur 144, Surabaya 60164, Jawa, Indonesia, *Tel:* +62 31 354 7999, *Fax:* +62 31 354 7991, *Email:* barwil.surabaya.ops@wilhelmsen.com, *Website:* www.wilhelmsen.com
P.T. Zhonghai Indo Shipping, Jl Perak Timur 280, Surabaya 60165, Jawa, Indonesia, *Tel:* +62 31 328 3440, *Fax:* +62 31 328 3441, *Email:* info@sub.zhonghai.net

Stevedoring Companies: P.T. Mentari Sejati Perkasa, Jalan Perak Barat No.231, Surabaya 60165, Jawa, Indonesia, *Tel:* +62 31 329 2727, *Fax:* +62 31 329 5211, *Email:* msp@ptmsp.com, *Website:* www.ptmsp.com

Surveyors: P.T. Biro Klasifikasi Indonesia, Jl. Kalianget No.14, Surabaya 60165, Jawa, Indonesia, *Tel:* +62 31 329 5448, *Fax:* +62 31 329 4520, *Email:* bkisb@klasifikasiindonesia.com, *Website:* www.klasifikasiindonesia.com
Bureau Veritas, Graha Pena 12th Floor, Suite 1204, Jl. A. Yani No.88, Surabaya, Jawa, Indonesia, *Tel:* +62 31 829 4570, *Fax:* +62 31 829 4571, *Website:* www.bureauveritas.com
Nippon Kaiji Kyokai, Plaza BRI 8th Floor, Suite 804, Jl. Basuki Rahmad 122, Surabaya, Jawa, Indonesia, *Tel:* +62 31 532 2266, *Fax:* +62 31 532 2244, *Email:* sb@classnk.or.jp, *Website:* www.classnk.or.jp
P.T. Superintending Company of Indonesia (SUCOFINDO), Jalan Kalibutuh No.215, P O Box 1030, Surabaya 60175, Jawa, Indonesia, *Tel:* +62 31 546 9123, *Fax:* +62 31 546 9144, *Email:* soedarno@sucofindo.co.id, *Website:* www.sucofindo.co.id

Medical Facilities: Port Hospital, Tel: +62 (31) 329 4801

Airport: Juanda Airport, Surabaya, 25 km

Railway: Pasar Turi Station, 4 km. Semut Station, 6 km. Gubeng Station, 9 km

Lloyd's Agent: P.T. Carsurin, Sarana Penjaminan Building, 7th Floor, Jl Angkasa Block B-9 Kav 6, Kemayoran, Jakarta 10720, Jawa, Indonesia, *Tel:* +62 21 654 0425, *Fax:* +62 21 654 0418, *Email:* lloyds@carsurin.com, *Website:* www.carsurin.com

TANJUNG BARA

Lat 0° 32' N; Long 117° 38' E.

Admiralty Chart: 3022	**Admiralty Pilot:** 34
Time Zone: GMT +8 h	**UNCTAD Locode:** ID TBA

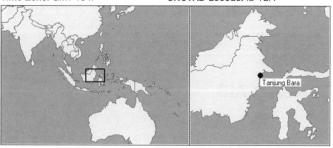

Principal Facilities:

	Y	G					T	A	

Authority: PT Kaltim Prima Coal, P O Box 620, Balikpapan, Borneo, Indonesia, *Tel:* +62 549 521402, *Fax:* +62 549 521780, *Email:* augustinus.sagala@kpc.co.id, *Website:* www.kpc.co.id

Officials: Terminal Manager: Augustinus Sagala, Tel: +62 549 525277.

Port Security: While Tanjung Bara Coal Terminal (TBCT) is a safe and secure port there have been incidents of unexpected persons climbing on board the vessel at the anchorage

Pre-Arrival Information: 1) Vessel must have complied with ISPS code and have sent their CoC prior to arrival at Tanjung Bara
2) Vessel must communicate their ETA directly to the company 72 h, 48 h and 24 h prior to arrival
3) The following questionnaire must be completed:
(a) Arrival draft
(b) Estimated metric tonnage to load
(c) Estimated departure draft
(d) Is all navigation, propulsion steering and other equipment require for the safe entry into and departure from the port
(e) Is all ballast water clean, requirements amount and duration of ballast water discharge
(f) Have all bending moment and stress calculation been calculated
(g) Ore/oil and OBO vessels state last three cargoes
(h) Maximum air draft on arrival including hatches opened where appropriate

Approach: Channel depths in North Channel 20-80 m, in South Channel 20-100 m

Anchorage: Cape/Panamax size vessels: Point A in pos 00° 31' 18" N; 117° 41' 06" E in depth of 45 m. Point B in pos 00° 32' 00" N; 117° 41' 29" E in depth of 40 m. Point C in pos 00° 31' 42" N; 117° 40' 36" E in depth of 30 m
Handy size vessels: Point D in pos 00° 30' 48" N; 117° 39' 00" E in depth of 15-20 m. Point E in pos 00° 31' 06" N; 117° 39' 30" E in depth of 15-20 m
Domestic vessels: Point F in pos 00° 30' 04" N; 117° 38' 48" E in depth of 15-20 m

Pilotage: Compulsory. North boarding in pos 00° 33' 00" N; 117° 47' 00" E and South boarding in pos 00° 31' 00" N; 117° 45' 00" E

Radio Frequency: VHF Channels 16, 12 and 14

Weather: Predominantly NE wind between Jan-June and SE between July-Dec, generally below 12 knots

Tides: Range of tide 2.5 m at ST

Traffic: 2002, 17 600 000 t of coal exported

Maximum Vessel Dimensions: 310 m loa, 50 m beam, 210 000 dwt

Principal Imports and Exports: Imports: Ammonium nitrate, General cargo, Heavy equipment. Exports: Coal.

Working Hours: 24 h/day

Accommodation:

Name	Length (m)	Depth (m)	Draught (m)	Remarks
Tanjung Bara				
Wharf 1	85	4		Small craft
Wharf 2	90	6		General cargo vessels up to 115 m loa
Wharf 3	350	18	17.25	See [1] below
Private Wharves				See [2] below

[1]*Wharf 3:* Concrete coal loading wharf with four breasting dolphins. 400 m long from dolphin to dolphin. Vessels must maintain 0.75 m underkeel clearance during loading. Two shiploaders, both rated at 4200 t/h. Stockpile cap of 1 200 000 t
[2]*Private Wharves:* Berth 10 m long in depth of 2 m LWS for pleasure craft

Storage: Port warehouse and storage only for Kaltim Prima Coal cargoes

Mechanical Handling Equipment:

Location	Type	Capacity (t)	Qty
Tanjung Bara	Mobile Cranes	10	1
Tanjung Bara	Mobile Cranes	150	1
Tanjung Bara	Mobile Cranes	15	1
Tanjung Bara	Mobile Cranes	50	2

Cargo Worked: Coal 4700 t/h, general cargo 1500 t/day

Towage: Two tugs of 40 t bollard pull

Medical Facilities: Clinic operated by the company with doctor on 24 h standby

Airport: Tanjung Bara, 4 km

Lloyd's Agent: P.T. Carsurin, Sarana Penjaminan Building, 7th Floor, Jl Angkasa Block B-9 Kav 6, Kemayoran, Jakarta 10720, Jawa, Indonesia, *Tel:* +62 21 654 0425, *Fax:* +62 21 654 0418, *Email:* lloyds@carsurin.com, *Website:* www.carsurin.com

TANJUNG EMAS

alternate name, see Semarang

TANJUNG INTAN

harbour area, see under Cilacap

TANJUNG PANDAN

Lat 2° 45' S; Long 107° 38' E.

Admiralty Chart: 1788
Time Zone: GMT +7 h

Admiralty Pilot: 36
UNCTAD Locode: ID TJQ

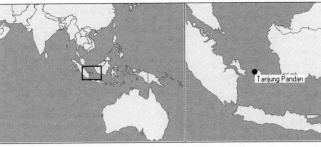

Principal Facilities:

		G					T	A

Authority: PT (Persero) Pelabuhan Indonesia II, Port of Tanjung Pandan, Jalan Pelabuhan No.1, Tanjung Pandan 33411, Sumatera, Indonesia, *Tel:* +62 719 21049, *Fax:* +62 719 21885, *Email:* tpandan@ppinang.wasantara.net.id

Port Security: ISPS compliant

Approach: Channel depths 3 m LWS and 5.5 m HWS

Anchorage: Vessels of moderate size can obtain anchorage at approx pos 2° 43' 10" S; 107° 33' 40" E. This anchorage however is unsafe during NW monsoon where vessels can anchor near Pulau Sebongkok at approx pos 2° 51' 30" S; 107° 30' 20" E

Pilotage: Local pilot can be obtained

Radio Frequency: VHF channel 16 (calling), VHF Channel 12 (working)

Weather: NW monsoon prevails from November to March, wind direction N to W. SE monsoon prevails from April to September, wind direction S to E

Maximum Vessel Dimensions: 2000 dwt, 5.3 m max d, 65 m max loa

Principal Imports and Exports: Imports: Construction equipment, General cargo. Exports: Kaolin clay.

Working Hours: 24 h/day

Accommodation:

Name	Length (m)	Depth (m)
Tanjung Pandan Wharf	304	2.8–5.3

Mechanical Handling Equipment:

Location	Type	Capacity (t)	Qty
Tanjung Pandan	Mobile Cranes	5	2

Cargo Worked: About 480 t/day

Towage: Two tugs of 300 and 700 bhp

Medical Facilities: Port health centre

Airport: Buluh Tumbang, 15 km

Lloyd's Agent: P.T. Carsurin, Sarana Penjaminan Building, 7th Floor, Jl Angkasa Block B-9 Kav 6, Kemayoran, Jakarta 10720, Jawa, Indonesia, *Tel:* +62 21 654 0425, *Fax:* +62 21 654 0418, *Email:* lloyds@carsurin.com, *Website:* www.carsurin.com

TANJUNG PEMANCINGAN

Lat 3° 12' S; Long 116° 17' E.

Admiralty Chart: 3017
Time Zone: GMT +8 h
Principal Facilities:

Admiralty Pilot: 34
UNCTAD Locode: ID TPN

		Y						

Authority: PT Arutmin Indonesia, Wisma Bakrie 2, Level 10, Jalan H.R. Rasuna Said Kav. B-2, Jakarta 12920, Jawa, Indonesia, *Tel:* +62 21 5794 5678, *Fax:* +62 21 5798 7126, *Email:* marketing@arutmin.com, *Website:* www.arutmin.com

Anchorage: Alpha Anchorage is situated in the NE channel in pos 3° 12.4' S; 116° 19.6' E in depth of 10-17 m
Bravo Anchorage is situated approx 0.5 miles W of the berth in pos 3° 11.8' S; 116° 16.7' E in depth of 10-17 m

Pilotage: Compulsory and available 24 h/day. Pilot boards vessel at anchorage in the NE channel 2 h before slack water

Radio Frequency: VHF Channel 14

Tides: 2.8 m MHWS, 2.0 m MHWN

Maximum Vessel Dimensions: 320 m loa, 150 000 dwt

Principal Imports and Exports: Exports: Coal.

Working Hours: 24 h/day

Accommodation:

Name	Length (m)	Depth (m)	Remarks
North Pulau Laut Coal Terminal			See [1] below
Berth	275	18	

[1]*North Pulau Laut Coal Terminal:* Senakin barges carrying coal travel 45 km to NPLCT, while Satui, Mulia, Asam-asam and Batulicin barges carrying coal travel 130 km to NPLCT
This port is designed to receive four barges simultaneously. Coal is moved by mechanised conveyors. A rail-mounted coal-loader which travels the length of the

vessel allows ocean-going vessels to remain stationary during loading at rate of approx 2000 t/h

Towage: Five tugs available of 33-50 t bollard pull

Medical Facilities: Small medical centre on site. Hospital in Kotabaru

Lloyd's Agent: P.T. Carsurin, Sarana Penjaminan Building, 7th Floor, Jl Angkasa Block B-9 Kav 6, Kemayoran, Jakarta 10720, Jawa, Indonesia, *Tel:* +62 21 654 0425, *Fax:* +62 21 654 0418, *Email:* lloyds@carsurin.com, *Website:* www.carsurin.com

TANJUNG PERAK

alternate name, see Surabaya

TANJUNG PRIOK

alternate name, see Jakarta

TANJUNG SEKONG

Lat 5° 55' S; Long 106° 0' E.

Admiralty Chart: 2056
Admiralty Pilot: 36
Time Zone: GMT +7 h
UNCTAD Locode: ID TSE

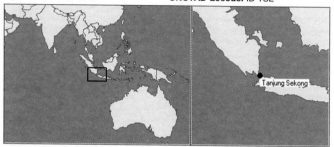

Principal Facilities:

P	Q		G			B			

Authority: P.T. Santa Fe-Pomeroy Indonesia, Jalan Pulorida Km. 2.5, Tanjung Sekong, Merak, Jawa, Indonesia, *Tel:* +62 254 71408/10, *Fax:* +62 254 71189 & 71403, *Email:* sfmerak@indosat.net.id

Officials: President: R. A.D. Wright.

Approach: There are no navigation lights

Anchorage: Anchorage can be obtained approx 0.5 km from the berths

Pilotage: Available

Radio Frequency: Merak coastal radio station. VHF Channel 16, daylight hours only

Tides: Min 0.3 m, max 0.9 m

Maximum Vessel Dimensions: 2000 dwt, 90 m loa, 4.5 m draft

Principal Imports and Exports: Imports: Baryte, Bentonite ore.

Working Hours: 24 h upon prior request

Accommodation:

Name	Remarks
Tanjung Sekong	Consists of two jetties and two berths with depth alongside of 5.4 m

Storage: Ten warehouses of 1530 m2 cap each

Location	Covered (m²)	Sheds / Warehouses
Tanjung Sekong	15300	10

Mechanical Handling Equipment:

Location	Type	Capacity (t)	Qty
Tanjung Sekong	Mult-purp. Cranes	45	5

Cargo Worked: 500 t/day

Bunkering: Available

Stevedoring Companies: PT Merak Jaya Asri, Merak, Jawa, Indonesia, *Tel:* +62 254 391341, *Fax:* +62 254 392596
PT Peteka Karya Samudera, Merak, Jawa, Indonesia, *Tel:* +62 254 571625, *Fax:* +62 254 571617

Surveyors: P.T. Sucofindo, Tanjung Sekong, Indonesia, *Tel:* +62 254 386444, *Fax:* +62 254 386450

Medical Facilities: Available

Railway: Merak Railway Station, 3 km

Lloyd's Agent: P.T. Carsurin, Sarana Penjaminan Building, 7th Floor, Jl Angkasa Block B-9 Kav 6, Kemayoran, Jakarta 10720, Jawa, Indonesia, *Tel:* +62 21 654 0425, *Fax:* +62 21 654 0418, *Email:* lloyds@carsurin.com, *Website:* www.carsurin.com

TANJUNG UBAN

Lat 1° 4' N; Long 104° 13' E.

Admiralty Chart: 3937
Admiralty Pilot: 36
Time Zone: GMT +7 h
UNCTAD Locode: ID TAN

Principal Facilities:

P	Q		G			B			

Authority: PT (Persero) Pelabuhan Indonesia I, Port of Tanjung Uban, Jl. Akasia No.1, Tanjung Uban, Indonesia, *Tel:* +62 771 81215

Port Security: ISPS compliant

Pilotage: Compulsory for vessels over 70 gt. North entrance boarding point in pos 1° 15.17' N; 104° 12.00' E and south entrance boarding point in pos 1° 02.92' N; 104° 12.00' E

Radio Frequency: Coastal radio station: Tanjung Uban Radio, call sign PKJ-5

Accommodation:

Name	Depth (m)	Remarks
Tanjung Uban		
No.1 Jetty	17.4	For vessels up to 240 m loa
No.2 Jetty (Oil)	11.7	For vessels up to 210 m loa
No.2 Jetty (LPG)	11.7	For vessels up to 115 m loa
No.3 Jetty (Barge)	6.4	For vessels up to 48 m loa
No.4 Jetty	11.4	For vessels up to 160 m loa
No.5 Jetty		For vessels up to 185 m loa

Storage: Storage tanks available for oil products

Bunkering: PT Pertamina, Jalan Jos Sudarso 32-34, P O Box 265, Tanjung Priok, Jawa, Indonesia, *Tel:* +62 21 430 1086, *Fax:* +62 21 430 1562 – *Grades:* DO; MDO; IFO100-300cSt – *Parcel Size:* max 500t per vessel, subject to official approval – *Rates:* 100-150t/h – *Notice:* 48 hours – *Delivery Mode:* barge, pipeline

Repair & Maintenance: Minor repairs possible. Nearest drydock, Singapore

Lloyd's Agent: P.T. Carsurin, Sarana Penjaminan Building, 7th Floor, Jl Angkasa Block B-9 Kav 6, Kemayoran, Jakarta 10720, Jawa, Indonesia, *Tel:* +62 21 654 0425, *Fax:* +62 21 654 0418, *Email:* lloyds@carsurin.com, *Website:* www.carsurin.com

TANJUNG WANGI

Lat 8° 12' S; Long 114° 23' E.

Admiralty Chart: 946
Admiralty Pilot: 34
Time Zone: GMT +7 h
UNCTAD Locode: ID BJU

This port is no longer open to commercial shipping

Shipping Agents: P.T. Djakarta Lloyd (PERSERO), P O Box 107, Tanjung Wangi 68451, Jawa, Indonesia, *Tel:* +62 333 510 464, *Fax:* +62 333 510 958, *Email:* dlloyd_bwi@telkom.net

TAPAKTUAN

Lat 3° 16' N; Long 97° 12' E.

Admiralty Chart: 2948
Admiralty Pilot: 44
Time Zone: GMT +7 h
UNCTAD Locode: ID TPK

This port is no longer open to commercial shipping

TARAKAN

Lat 3° 17' N; Long 117° 36' E.

Admiralty Chart: 2639
Admiralty Pilot: 34
Time Zone: GMT +8 h
UNCTAD Locode: ID TRK

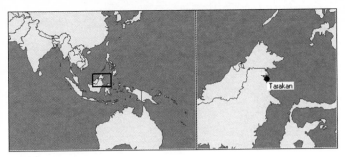

Principal Facilities:

P		Y	G			B		A

Authority: PT (Persero) Pelabuhan Indonesia IV, Port of Tarakan, Jalan Yos Sudarso No.9, Tarakan 77126, Kalimantan Timur, Indonesia, *Tel:* +62 551 21527, *Fax:* +62 551 21528, *Email:* pelindos@tarakan.wasantara.net.id

Officials: Manager: Muhammed Mimkaimbav.

Port Security: ISPS compliant

Documentation: Passenger list (5 copies), crew list (5 copies), custom document (5 copies), health document (5 copies), cargo manifest (5 copies), bills of lading (5 copies), ship's papers (1 copy), sailing permit

Pilotage: Compulsory. VHF Channel 12

Radio Frequency: Tarakan Radio, call sign PKO, frequencies 487.5 kHz, 8445 kHz and 6337 kHz

Traffic: 1999, 349 296 t of cargo handled

Maximum Vessel Dimensions: Max loa 225 m, max draft 9 m

Principal Imports and Exports: Exports: Frozen shrimp, Plywood, Sawn timber, Woodchips.

Working Hours: 0730-1600

Accommodation:

Name	Length (m)	Depth (m)	Remarks
Tarakan			
Public Wharf	250	8–9	
CBM	225	9	For crude oil in pos 3° 17' 00'' N; 117° 38' 12'' E

Storage:

Location	Open (m²)	Covered (m²)
Tarakan	3224	1700

Mechanical Handling Equipment:

Location	Type	Capacity (t)	Qty	Remarks
Tarakan	Mobile Cranes	25	1	from private company

Cargo Worked: General cargo 30 t/h/gang, logs 40 m3/h/gang

Bunkering: C.V. Bahtera Camar, Jalan Lagoa Terusan BI No.4, Jakarta 14270, Jawa, Indonesia, *Tel:* +62 21 435 3209, *Fax:* +62 21 430 6048
Buana Jaya C.V., jalan Sungai Kapuas No.15, Jakarta 14270, Jawa, Indonesia, *Tel:* +62 21 44835302, *Fax:* +62 21 44835302
Kartika Jasa Karya P.T., Jalan Perak Timur 564/A1, Surabaya 60165, Jawa, Indonesia, *Tel:* +62 31 3293 459, *Fax:* +62 31 3294 736, *Email:* kemusuk@rad.net.id
PT Pertamina, Jalan Jos Sudarso 32-34, P O Box 265, Tanjung Priok, Jawa, Indonesia, *Tel:* +62 21 430 1086, *Fax:* +62 21 430 1562 – *Grades:* DO; MDO; IFO100-300cSt – *Parcel Size:* no min/max – *Rates:* 100-150t/h – *Notice:* 48 hours – *Delivery Mode:* barge, pipeline

Shipping Agents: P.T. Djakarta Lloyd (PERSERO), Jalan Yos Sudarso I 3-4, Tarakan, Kalimantan Timur, Indonesia, *Tel:* +62 551 21547, *Fax:* +62 551 22403
P.T. (PELNI) Pelayaran Nasional Indonesia, Jl Yos Sudaraso No.10, Tarakan, Kalimantan Timur, Indonesia, *Tel:* +62 551 21529, *Fax:* +62 551 21529, *Email:* agencies@pelni.co.id, *Website:* www.pelni.co.id

Medical Facilities: Public and Navy hospital

Airport: Juata Airport, 3 km

Lloyd's Agent: P.T. Carsurin, Sarana Penjaminan Building, 7th Floor, Jl Angkasa Block B-9 Kav 6, Kemayoran, Jakarta 10720, Jawa, Indonesia, *Tel:* +62 21 654 0425, *Fax:* +62 21 654 0418, *Email:* lloyds@carsurin.com, *Website:* www.carsurin.com

TEGAL

Lat 6° 51' S; Long 109° 8' E.

Admiralty Chart: 918	**Admiralty Pilot:** 36
Time Zone: GMT +7 h	**UNCTAD Locode:** ID TEG

Principal Facilities:

			G			B	T	

Authority: PT Pelabuhan III Cabang Tegal, Jl. R.E. Martadinata No.9, Tegal, Jawa, Indonesia, *Tel:* +62 283 53369 & 51488

Anchorage: 2-3 miles from the coast in depths of 10-12 m

Pilotage: Available

Radio Frequency: VHF Channel 16, frequency 5316 & 10226 mHz

Tides: Range of tide 0.95 m

Maximum Vessel Dimensions: Max loa 150 m, max draft 10.0 m in the roads, max dwt 26 000

Principal Imports and Exports: Exports: Molasses.

Working Hours: Mon-Fri 0800-1600. Sat 0800-1300

Accommodation:

Name	Length (m)	Depth (m)
Tegal		
Coaster Wharf	450	4.3

Storage:

Location	Open (m²)	Covered (m²)
Tegal	2800	840

Mechanical Handling Equipment:

Location	Type	Capacity (t)	Qty
Tegal	Mult-purp. Cranes	25	1

Bunkering: PT Pertamina, Jalan Jos Sudarso 32-34, P O Box 265, Tanjung Priok, Jawa, Indonesia, *Tel:* +62 21 430 1086, *Fax:* +62 21 430 1562 – *Grades:* DO; MDO; IFO100-300cSt – *Parcel Size:* no min/max – *Rates:* 100-150t/h – *Notice:* 48 hours – *Delivery Mode:* barge, pipeline

Towage: Three tugs of 200 hp

Medical Facilities: Naval facilities available in Tegal town

Railway: Tegal station, 1.5 km

Lloyd's Agent: P.T. Carsurin, Sarana Penjaminan Building, 7th Floor, Jl Angkasa Block B-9 Kav 6, Kemayoran, Jakarta 10720, Jawa, Indonesia, *Tel:* +62 21 654 0425, *Fax:* +62 21 654 0418, *Email:* lloyds@carsurin.com, *Website:* www.carsurin.com

TELANAIPURA

alternate name, see Jambi

TELUK BAYUR

Lat 1° 0' S; Long 100° 21' E.

Admiralty Chart: 2965	**Admiralty Pilot:** 34
Time Zone: GMT +7 h	**UNCTAD Locode:** ID PDG

Principal Facilities:

P		Y	G	C			B		T	A

Authority: PT (Persero) Pelabuhan Indonesia II, Port of Teluk Bayur, Jalan Semarang No.3, Teluk Bayur 25217, Sumatera, Indonesia, *Tel:* +62 751 61646, *Fax:* +62 751 61169, *Website:* www.telukbayurport.com

Approach: The port basin is characterised by sand/mud channel of 30.89 ha in depth of 9-12 m

Pilotage: Compulsory. Pilotage service provided 24 h/day

Radio Frequency: Port radio, call sign 'PKP2', VHF Channels 10, 16 and 20

Key to Principal Facilities:—					
A=Airport	**C**=Containers	**G**=General Cargo	**P**=Petroleum	**R**=Ro/Ro	**Y**=Dry Bulk
B=Bunkers	**D**=Dry Dock	**L**=Cruise	**Q**=Other Liquid Bulk	**T**=Towage (where available from port)	

Weather: Rainy season November to March with max speed of west monsoon approx 15-25 knots

Tides: MLWS 0.1 m, MHWS 1.94 m

Traffic: 2005, 3000 vessels, 8 983 564 t of cargo handled, 34 349 TEU's

Working Hours: 0800-1200, 1300-1600, 1600-2400, 2400-0800

Accommodation:

Name	Length (m)	Remarks
Teluk Bayur		See [1] below
Coventional	740	
Container	222	
Dedicated	583	
Oil Jetty	20	

[1]*Teluk Bayur:* Cargoes handled include coal, cement, crude oil, fertiliser, rubber and crude palm oil. Passenger terminal area of 1608 m2

Storage: Ample storage facilities for coal, cement, containers, fertiliser, fuel gas, crude palm oil and bulk asphalt

Mechanical Handling Equipment:

Location	Type	Capacity (t)	Qty
Teluk Bayur	Mobile Cranes	25	1
Teluk Bayur	Forklifts	2–5	22

Cargo Worked: Coal 800-1000 t/h, cement in bags 50-80 t/h, cement in bulk 200-400 t/h

Bunkering: C.V. Bahtera Camar, Jalan Lagoa Terusan BI No.4, Jakarta 14270, Jawa, Indonesia, *Tel:* +62 21 435 3209, *Fax:* +62 21 430 6048 – *Delivery Mode:* truck
Buana Jaya C.V., jalan Sungai Kapuas No.15, Jakarta 14270, Jawa, Indonesia, *Tel:* +62 21 44835302, *Fax:* +62 21 44835302 – *Delivery Mode:* truck
Kartika Jasa Karya P.T., Jalan Perak Timur 564/A1, Surabaya 60165, Jawa, Indonesia, *Tel:* +62 31 3293 459, *Fax:* +62 31 3294 736, *Email:* kemusuk@rad.net.id – *Delivery Mode:* truck
PT Pertamina, Jalan Jos Sudarso 32-34, P O Box 265, Tanjung Priok, Jawa, Indonesia, *Tel:* +62 21 430 1086, *Fax:* +62 21 430 1562 – *Grades:* DO; MDO; IFO100-300cSt – *Parcel Size:* no min/max – *Rates:* 100-150t/h – *Notice:* 48 hours – *Delivery Mode:* truck

Towage: Three tugs available

Stevedoring Companies: P.T. Angsindo Jaya Pratama, Jl. TG Priok No.36, Teluk Bayur, Sumatera, Indonesia, *Tel:* +62 751 61575
P.T. Anugrah Bahari Sakti, Jl. TG Priok No.2, Teluk Bayur, Sumatera, Indonesia, *Tel:* +62 751 61900
P.T. Bachtera Adhiguna, Jl. TG Priok No.38, Teluk Bayur, Sumatera, Indonesia, *Tel:* +62 751 61636
P.T. Bomala Sapta Krida, Teluk Bayur, Sumatera, Indonesia, *Tel:* +62 751 61644
P.T. Harapan Budi Mandiri, Teluk Bayur, Sumatera, Indonesia, *Tel:* +62 751 61567
P.T. Rintis Prasetya Stevedoring, Teluk Bayur, Sumatera, Indonesia, *Tel:* +62 751 62660
P.T. S.B.N., Jl. TG Priok No.14, Teluk Bayur, Sumatera, Indonesia, *Tel:* +62 751 61624
P.T. Sumber Jaya Rona Samudra, Teluk Bayur, Sumatera, Indonesia, *Tel:* +62 751 61530
P.T. Varuna Tirta Prakasya, Jl. TG Priok No.28, Teluk Bayur, Sumatera, Indonesia, *Tel:* +62 751 61510

Surveyors: P.T. Biro Klasifikasi Indonesia, Teluk Bayur, Sumatera, Indonesia, *Tel:* +62 751 61553, *Fax:* +62 751 31831
Nippon Kaiji Kyokai, Teluk Bayur, Sumatera, Indonesia, *Tel:* +62 751 61553, *Fax:* +62 751 33442, *Website:* www.classnk.or.jp

Medical Facilities: Available at the port

Airport: Tabing Airport, 18 km

Lloyd's Agent: P.T. Carsurin, Sarana Penjaminan Building, 7th Floor, Jl Angkasa Block B-9 Kav 6, Kemayoran, Jakarta 10720, Jawa, Indonesia, *Tel:* +62 21 654 0425, *Fax:* +62 21 654 0418, *Email:* lloyds@carsurin.com, *Website:* www.carsurin.com

TELUK NIBUNG

Lat 3° 0' N; Long 99° 49' E.

Admiralty Chart: 3945	**Admiralty Pilot:** 44
Time Zone: GMT +7 h	**UNCTAD Locode:** ID TJB

Principal Facilities:

			G					A	

Authority: PT (Persero) Pelabuhan Indonesia I, Port of Teluk Nibung, Jalan Pelabuhan Teluk Nibung, Tanjung Balai, Asahan 21351, Sumatera, Indonesia, *Tel:* +62 623 92022, *Fax:* +62 623 95083

Approach: Channel to Teluk Nibung is 8 miles long with width of 25-50 m

Radio Frequency: SSB 5295.5 kHz

Tides: Range of tide 1.5 m

Working Hours: 0800-1600

Accommodation:

Name	Length (m)	Depth (m)	Remarks
Teluk Nibung			Passenger terminal of 120 m2
Multi-Purpose Berth	199	3	For vessels up to 500 dwt
Bagan Asahan			Passenger terminal of 525 m2
Multi-Purpose Berth	140	6	For vessels up to 1000 dwt

Storage:

Location	Open (m²)	Covered (m²)
Teluk Nibung	8125	3820

Cargo Worked: General cargo 18 t/gang/h

Medical Facilities: Public hospital belongs to the local government

Airport: Polonia Airport, 80 km

Railway: Tanjung Balai Asahan Station, 8 km

Lloyd's Agent: P.T. Carsurin, Sarana Penjaminan Building, 7th Floor, Jl Angkasa Block B-9 Kav 6, Kemayoran, Jakarta 10720, Jawa, Indonesia, *Tel:* +62 21 654 0425, *Fax:* +62 21 654 0418, *Email:* lloyds@carsurin.com, *Website:* www.carsurin.com

TELUK SEMANGKA

alternate name, see Semangka Bay Terminal

TERNATE

Admiralty Chart: 2786	**Admiralty Pilot:** 35
Time Zone: GMT +8 h	**UNCTAD Locode:** ID TTE

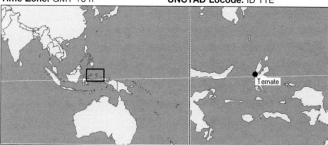

Principal Facilities:

P		G	C				T	A

Authority: PT (Persero) Pelabuhan Indonesia IV, Port of Ternate, Jalan Jend. Ahmad Yani Complex Pelabuhan, Ternate 97714, Maluku, Indonesia, *Tel:* +62 921 21129, *Fax:* +62 921 21206

Port Security: ISPS compliant

Documentation: Passenger list (14 copies), crew list (7 copies), custom document (2 copies), health document (2 copies), cargo manifest (7 copies), bills of lading (7 copies), ship's papers (5 copies), sailing permit

Pilotage: Compulsory. Government pilot available

Radio Frequency: VHF Channels 12, 13, 14 and 15

Traffic: 1999, 197 382 t of cargo handled

Maximum Vessel Dimensions: 10 000 dwt, 100 m loa, 7 m max draft

Working Hours: 0800-2300. 24 h can be worked on request

Accommodation:

Name	Length (m)	Depth (m)	Remarks
Ternate			See [1] below
Achmad Yani Wharf	248	7.6	

[1]*Ternate:* There is also a wooden jetty with a depth of 1 m for sailing vessels

Storage:

Location	Open (m²)	Covered (m²)	Sheds / Warehouses
Ternate	1800	1932	3

Mechanical Handling Equipment:

Location	Type	Capacity (t)	Qty
Ternate	Mult-purp. Cranes	25	1
Ternate	Forklifts	3	2
Ternate	Forklifts	2	2

Towage: One tug available upon request

Shipping Agents: P.T. (PELNI) Pelayaran Nasional Indonesia, Jl Jend A Yani Kompleks Pelabuhan, Ternate, Maluku, Indonesia, *Tel:* +62 921 21434, *Fax:* +62 921 21276, *Email:* agencies@pelni.co.id, *Website:* www.pelni.co.id

Medical Facilities: Government Hospital

Airport: Sultan Babullah Airport, 4 km

Lloyd's Agent: P.T. Carsurin, Sarana Penjaminan Building, 7th Floor, Jl Angkasa Block B-9 Kav 6, Kemayoran, Jakarta 10720, Jawa, Indonesia, *Tel:* +62 21 654 0425, *Fax:* +62 21 654 0418, *Email:* lloyds@carsurin.com, *Website:* www.carsurin.com

IRAN

TUBAN

Lat 6° 46' S; Long 111° 57' E.

Admiralty Chart: 3731

Admiralty Pilot: 34

Time Zone: GMT +7 h

UNCTAD Locode: ID TBN

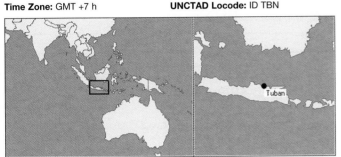

Principal Facilities:

P													

Anchorage: VLCC Anchorage: bounded by the following co-ordinates
06° 38' 00" S; 111° 57' 00" E
06° 39' 10" S; 111° 57' 00" E
06° 39' 10" S; 111° 58' 00" E
06° 39' 00" S; 111° 58' 00" E
Export Vessel Anchorage: bounded by the following co-ordinates
06° 38' 00" S; 111° 56' 00" E
06° 39' 10" S; 111° 56' 00" E
06° 39' 10" S; 111° 56' 90" E
06° 38' 00" S; 111° 56' 90" E
General Purpose Anchorage: all lighterage operations for handling of petrochemical liquid cargo products must be conducted at this anchorage which is bounded by the following co-ordinates
06° 38' 00" S; 111° 56' 00" E
06° 39' 10" S; 111° 56' 00" E
06° 39' 10" S; 111° 58' 00" E
06° 39' 00" S; 111° 58' 00" E

Pilotage: Compulsory for both terminals. At the Petrochemical Complex the pilot boards either in pos 6° 38' 42" S; 111° 56' 00" E or at the anchorage and for Tuban Marine Terminal the pilot boards either at the anchorage (a circle area of 1 nautical mile radius centred on pos 6° 39' 00" S; 112° 09' 37" E) or at a position agreed between the vessel and the Mooring Master

Radio Frequency: VHF Channel 16

Accommodation:

Name	Depth (m)	Draught (m)	Remarks
Tanjung Awar Awar			See [1] below
Berth No.3	13.5	9.8	For vessels up to 91-140 m loa & 10 000 dwt
Berth No.4	13.5	10.6	For vessels up to 76-187 m loa & 40 000 dwt
Berth No.5	13.5	10.6	For vessels up to 76-187 m loa & 40 000 dwt
Tuban Marine Terminal			See [2] below

[1]*Tanjung Awar Awar:* Operated by Trans Pacific Petrochemical Indotama (TPP) Petrochemical complex
[2]*Tuban Marine Terminal:* Operated by JOB Pertamina-Petrochina, *Website:* www.jobpertamina-petrochina.com
In pos 06° 44' S; 112° 09' E. Consists of FSO 'Cinta Natomas'. The mooring system can accept export tankers of 20 000-140 000 dwt and the max loading rate is 20 000 bbls/h. Berthing during daylight hours only, unberthing at any time

Lloyd's Agent: P.T. Carsurin, Sarana Penjaminan Building, 7th Floor, Jl Angkasa Block B-9 Kav 6, Kemayoran, Jakarta 10720, Jawa, Indonesia, *Tel:* +62 21 654 0425, *Fax:* +62 21 654 0418, *Email:* lloyds@carsurin.com, *Website:* www.carsurin.com

UJUNG PANDANG

alternate name, see Makassar

ABADAN

Lat 30° 20' N; Long 48° 17' E.

Admiralty Chart: 3844

Admiralty Pilot: 63

Time Zone: GMT +3.5 h

UNCTAD Locode: IR ABD

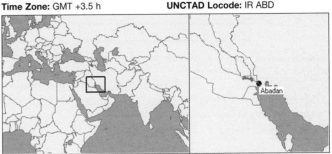

Principal Facilities:

		G	C	R		B		T	A	

Authority: Abadan Port, Edare Bandar Va Kashtirani, Abadan 63168-1-1164, Iran, *Tel:* +98 631 222 8916, *Fax:* +98 631 222 6033, *Email:* minaei@khomeiniport.com, *Website:* www.khomeiniport.com/abadan

Port Security: ISPS compliant

Documentation: Valid classification and registration certificates, copies of B/L's, cargo manifest, stowage plan for vessels importing cargo

Approach: Channel restricted to vessels up to 3500 dwt and 4.2 m d

Pilotage: Compulsory. Pilot boards from cutter patrolling a few kilometres from the entrance of the Rooka Channel

Radio Frequency: VHF Channel 16

Accommodation:

Name	Remarks
Abadan	Four general cargo jetties and one passenger jetty

Storage: Available

Bunkering: N.I.B.C. Iranian Oil Co., National Iranian Tanker Co. (N.I.T.C), 67 Shahid Atefy Street, Africa Avenue, Tehran 1917797163, Iran, *Tel:* +98 21 2222 2465, *Fax:* +98 21 2201 3392, *Email:* connserb@nitc.co.ir, *Website:* www.nitc.co.ir – *Grades:* FO; DO – *Rates:* 200t/h

Waste Reception Facilities: Garbage collection service available

Towage: Available

Repair & Maintenance: Minor repairs only

Shipping Agents: GAC Shipping FZCO, Dubai Airport Free Zone, P O Box 54593, Dubai, United Arab Emirates, *Tel:* +971 4 299 0021, *Fax:* +971 4 299 0030, *Email:* gacfzco.dubai@gacworld.com, *Website:* www.gacworld.com Operations Manager: Thomas M. Jayabhai Mobile Tel: +971 50 6520677
Iran Gulf Shipping Services, Iran Gulf Building, 42 Babak Markazi, Africa Expressway, Tehran 19177, Iran, *Tel:* +98 21 8887 9050, *Fax:* +98 21 8879 9107, *Email:* operations@irgulf.net, *Website:* www.irangulf.com

Medical Facilities: Available

Airport: Abadan, 25 km

Railway: Regular rail service is available at Khorramshahr, 30 km

Lloyd's Agent: Iran Marine Services Co., Ayatollah Taleghani Boulevard, Across to Shohada Library, 3rd Floor Etemadi Building, Bandar Abbas, Iran, *Tel:* +98 761 222 6904, *Fax:* +98 761 222 0160, *Email:* imsba@ims-ir.com, *Website:* www.ims-ir.com

AMIRABAD

Lat 36° 51' N; Long 53° 19' E.

UNCTAD Locode: IR

New port consisting of approx 1000 ha area is being constructed in the Caspian Sea

ASALUYEH TERMINAL

Lat 27° 31' N; Long 52° 32' E.

Admiralty Chart: -

Admiralty Pilot: 63

Time Zone: GMT +3.5 h

UNCTAD Locode: IR ASA

Key to Principal Facilities:—				
A=Airport	**C**=Containers	**G**=General Cargo	**P**=Petroleum	**R**=Ro/Ro	**Y**=Dry Bulk
B=Bunkers	**D**=Dry Dock	**L**=Cruise	**Q**=Other Liquid Bulk	**T**=Towage (where available from port)

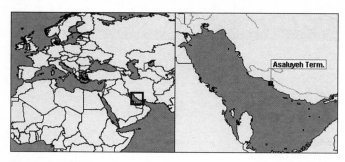

Principal Facilities:

P									

Authority: National Iranian Oil Terminals Co., 88 Hodjat Souri Street, Pasdaran Avenue, Tehran, Iran, *Tel:* +98 21 22592 4001, *Email:* admin@nioc-otc.com, *Website:* www.nioc-otc.com

Port Security: ISPS compliant

Principal Imports and Exports: Exports: Condensate.

Accommodation:

Name	Remarks
South Pars Terminal	See [1] below

[1]*South Pars Terminal:* Consists of a SPM exporting condensate for vessels up to 250 000 dwt, located at 7640 m from Total refinery and 30" pipeline carries the condensate from the shore to SPM

Shipping Agents: GAC Shipping FZCO, Dubai Airport Free Zone, P O Box 54593, Dubai, United Arab Emirates, *Tel:* +971 4 299 0021, *Fax:* +971 4 299 0030, *Email:* gacfzco.dubai@gacworld.com, *Website:* www.gacworld.com Operations Manager: Thomas M. Jayabhai Mobile Tel: +971 50 6520677
Chabahar Shipping Services Logistics Co., No. 254 Africa Express Way, Tehran 15867, Iran, *Tel:* +98 21 8865 0805, *Fax:* +98 21 8865 0817, *Email:* info@cssir.com, *Website:* www.cssir.com
Iran Gulf Shipping Services, Iran Gulf Building, 42 Babak Markazi, Africa Expressway, Tehran 19177, Iran, *Tel:* +98 21 8887 9050, *Fax:* +98 21 8879 9107, *Email:* operations@irgulf.net, *Website:* www.irangulf.com
Seawaves Shipping Services Co. Ltd, 9 Lida Street, North Vanak Square, Vali Asr Avenue, P O Box 15875, Tehran 1873, Iran, *Tel:* +98 21 8877 0571, *Fax:* +98 21 8877 4361, *Email:* operations@seawaves-shipping.net, *Website:* www.seawaves-shipping.com

Lloyd's Agent: Iran Marine Services Co., Ayatollah Taleghani Boulevard, Across to Shohada Library, 3rd Floor Etemadi Building, Bandar Abbas, Iran, *Tel:* +98 761 222 6904, *Fax:* +98 761 222 0160, *Email:* imsba@ims-ir.com, *Website:* www.ims-ir.com

BAHREGAN

see under Ras Bahregan Terminal

BANDAR ABBAS

Lat 27° 8' N; Long 56° 12' E.

Admiralty Chart: 3599	**Admiralty Pilot:** 63
Time Zone: GMT +3.5 h	**UNCTAD Locode:** IR BND

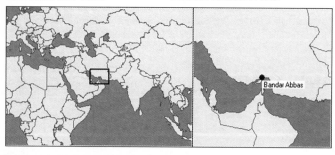

Principal Facilities:

P	Q	Y	G	C	R		B	D	T	A

Authority: Bandar Abbas Port Authority, Shahid Rajaei Port Complex, P O Box 79171-83797, Bandar Abbas, Iran, *Tel:* +98 761 556 3966, *Fax:* +98 761 556 4056, *Email:* mail.info@bpa.ir, *Website:* www.bpa.ir

Officials: Managing Director: Mohammad Reza Ashkriz, *Email:* ashkriz@bpa.ir.

Port Security: ISPS compliant

Approach: The approach channel is 6400 m long, 400-450 m wide in depth of 11-13 m. The fairway buoy is located in pos 27° 4.34' N; 56° 9.35' E. The channel comprises two green buoys and three red buoys

Anchorage: Commercial anchorages within the following coordinates:
27° 05.4' N; 56° 12.6' E
27° 01.9' N; 56° 12.6' E
27° 05.4' N; 56° 17.9' E
27° 01.9' N; 56° 17.9' E
Military anchorages within the following coordinates:
27° 06.40' N; 56° 10.00' E
27° 06.40' N; 56° 11.75' E
27° 05.50' N; 56° 10.00' E
27° 05.50' N; 56° 11.75' E

Pilotage: Compulsory. The traffic control tower at the fairway buoy coordinates pilotage on VHF Channel 13 around-the-clock

Radio Frequency: VHF Channels 16, 19, 21 and 25

Weather: With the exception of about 2 months during the winter, the air is generally wet and humid, but with little rainfall. Temperature seldom falls below 10°C in winter, and seldom exceeds 40°C in summer
Prevailing winds variable 45-50 knots northerly

Traffic: 2007, 1 722 513 TEU's handled

Principal Imports and Exports: Imports: General cargo, Grain, Iron, Rice, Soda, Wheat. Exports: Almonds, Bitumen, Clinker, Dates, Dried fruits, Steel slabs.

Working Hours: 0700-0500. Direct loading 24 h/day

Accommodation:

Name	Length (m)	Draught (m)	Remarks
Bandar Shahid Rejaie			
Berth No.1	210	11.2	Oil for vessels up to 190 m loa
Berth No.2	210	11.5	Oil for vessels up to 220 m loa
Berth No.3	200	10.2	Vegetable oil & general cargo for vessels up to 200 m loa
Berth No.4	200	12	Containers for vessels up to 290 m loa
Berth No.5	200	12.5	Containers for vessels up to 290 m loa
Berth No.6	200	12.5	Containers for vessels up to 290 m loa
Berth No.7	200	12.5	Containers for vessels up to 290 m loa
Berth No.8	200	11.7	Containers for vessels up to 290 m loa
Berth No.9	200	4.5	Containers for vessels up to 140 m loa
Berth No.10	200	10.5	General cargo for vessels up to 290 m loa
Berth No.11	200	10.5	General cargo for vessels up to 290 m loa

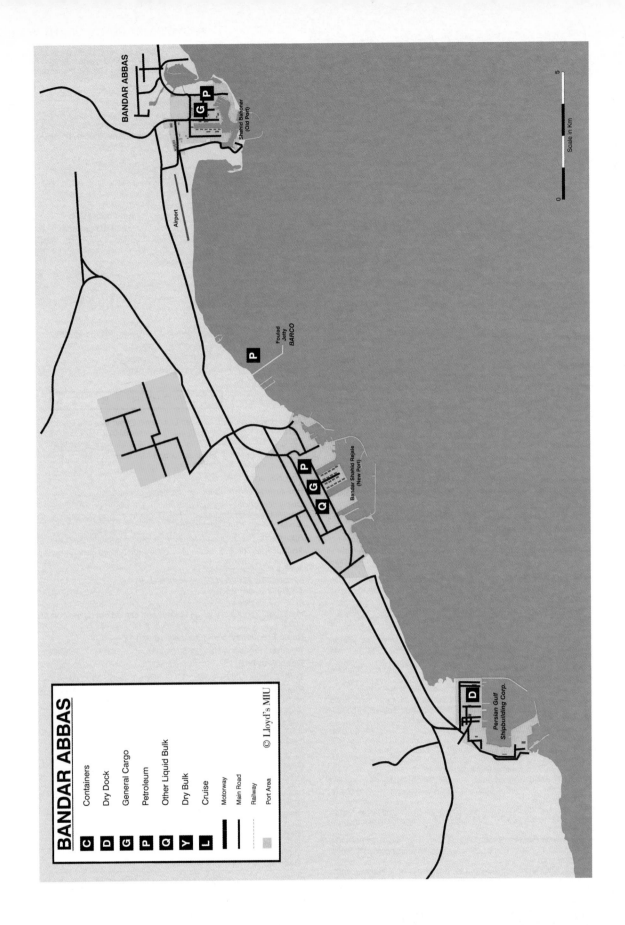

BANDAR ABBAS

BANDAR ABBAS

Shahid Bahonar
(Old Port)

Airport

Fouled
Jetty
BARCO

Bandar Shahid Rejaie
(New Port)

Persian Gulf
Shipbuilding Corp.

Scale in Km

© Lloyd's MIU

C	Containers
D	Dry Dock
G	General Cargo
P	Petroleum
Q	Other Liquid Bulk
Y	Dry Bulk
L	Cruise

Motorway
Main Road
Railway
Port Area

GULF AGENCY CO FZCO

Dubai Airport Free Zone, P.O. Box 54593
Dubai, United Arab Emirates
TEL: +971 4 299002
FAX: +971 4 2990030
EMAIL: iran@gacworld.com
WEB: www.gacworld.com

Name	Length (m)	Draught (m)	Remarks
Berth No.12	200	10.5	General cargo for vessels up to 290 m loa
Berth No.13	200	10.5	General cargo for vessels up to 290 m loa
Berth No.14	200	10.5	General cargo for vessels up to 290 m loa
Berth No.15	200	12.5	Bulk cargo for vessels up to 290 m loa
Berth No.16	200	12.5	Bulk cargo for vessels up to 290 m loa
Berth No.17	200	12.5	Bulk cargo for vessels up to 290 m loa
Berth No.18	200	12.5	Bulk cargo for vessels up to 290 m loa
Berth No.19	200	10.5	General cargo for vessels up to 290 m loa
Berth No.20	200	10.5	General cargo for vessels up to 290 m loa
Berth No.21	200	10.5	General cargo for vessels up to 290 m loa
Berth No.22	200	10.5	General cargo for vessels up to 290 m loa
Berth No.23	200	10.5	Vegetable oil & general cargo for vessels up to 290 m loa
Berth No.24	200	10.2	General cargo for vessels up to 190 m loa

Bunkering: Available by barge
Iran Marine Services Co., Ayatollah Taleghani Boulevard, Across to Shohada Library, 3rd Floor Etemadi Building, Bandar Abbas, Iran, *Tel:* +98 761 222 6904, *Fax:* +98 761 222 0160, *Email:* imsba@ims-ir.com, *Website:* www.ims-ir.com
Seawaves Shipping Services Co. Ltd, Bandar Abbas, Iran, *Tel:* +98 761 555 6204, *Fax:* +98 761 555 4689, *Email:* b.abbas@seawaves-shipping.com, *Website:* www.seawaves-shipping.com

Towage: Six tugs available (three with fire-fighting equipment)

Ship Chandlers: IRISL Marine Services & Engineering Co. (Imseng Co.), P O Box 79145-3387, Bandar Abbas, Iran, *Tel:* +98 761 556 1305, *Fax:* +98 761 556 0937, *Email:* branch-ba@imsengco.com, *Website:* www.imsengco.com

Shipping Agents: GAC Shipping FZCO, Dubai Airport Free Zone, P O Box 54593, Dubai, United Arab Emirates, *Tel:* +971 4 299 0021, *Fax:* +971 4 299 0030, *Email:* gacfzco.dubai@gacworld.com, *Website:* www.gacworld.com Operations Manager: Thomas M. Jayabhai Mobile Tel: +971 50 6520677
Anis Trading & Shipping Services Co. Ltd, Irani Building Eskeleh, Saheli Avenue, Bushire, Iran, *Tel:* +98 9121255469 & 9191255469, *Fax:* +98 771 252 5433 & 252 5156, *Email:* abolqasem@iranigroup.ir & iranigroup@iranigroup.ir, *Website:* www.iranigroup.ir
Chabahar Shipping Services Logistics Co., No. 254 Africa Express Way, Tehran 15867, Iran, *Tel:* +98 21 8865 0805, *Fax:* +98 21 8865 0817, *Email:* info@cssir.com, *Website:* www.cssir.com
Iran Gulf Shipping Services, Iran Gulf Building, 42 Babak Markazi, Africa Expressway, Tehran 19177, Iran, *Tel:* +98 21 8887 9050, *Fax:* +98 21 8879 9107, *Email:* operations@irgulf.net, *Website:* www.irangulf.com
Jahan Darya Zamin Shipping AG, Bolvar Imam Yadbood Square, Askari Building 6, Bandar Abbas, Iran, *Tel:* +98 761 223 2413, *Fax:* +98 761 223 2412, *Email:* behnja@jahandarya.com
Jet Marine Services, 2nd Floor Kameli Building, Imam Khomeini Avenue, Bandar Abbas, Iran, *Tel:* +98 761 223 0585, *Fax:* +98 761 223 0823, *Email:* bandarabbas@jms-group.biz
A.P. Moller-Maersk Group, Maersk Iran A.S., 2nd Floor PTB Terminal, Shaheed Rajaee Container Terminal, Bandar Abbas, Iran, *Tel:* +98 761 555 5523, *Fax:* +98 761 556 4009, *Email:* irnopstrm@maersk.com, *Website:* www.maerskline.com
Fanus E. Sahel Co. Ltd, Suite 19, 4th Floor Panahi Building, Moradi Crossroads, Seyed Jamaludeen Avenue, Bandar Abbas 79188-9-3868, Iran, *Tel:* +98 761 224 0442, *Fax:* +98 761 224 0443, *Email:* fanus_bnd@parsonline.net
Sea Glow Shipping Agency LLC, Zarouge Bandar Building, 2nd Floor, Jahan Allex (Ex. Dr. Ibrahimi), Parastoo Alley, Jahanbar Crossway, Bandar Abbas, Iran, *Tel:* +98 761 555 7774, *Fax:* +98 761 556 1903, *Email:* seaglow@seaglowiran.com
Sea Hope Shipping Services Co. Ltd, Bandar Abbas, Iran, *Tel:* +98 761 223 2460, *Fax:* +98 761 223 2467, *Email:* behnam@seahopeiran.com
Sea Mystries Shipping Co, Bandar Abbas, Iran, *Tel:* +98 761 555 1325, *Fax:* +98 761 555 4307, *Email:* info@seamystriesshipping.com, *Website:* www.seamystriesshipping.com
Seas Ark S.A., 2nd Floor, Khateeb Building, Imam Khomaini Avenue, Bandar Abbas, Iran, *Tel:* +98 761 224 0411, *Fax:* +98 761 224 8362, *Email:* seasark@myway.com, *Website:* www.seasark.com
Seawaves Shipping Services Co. Ltd, Bandar Abbas, Iran, *Tel:* +98 761 555 6204, *Fax:* +98 761 555 4689, *Email:* b.abbas@seawaves-shipping.com, *Website:* www.seawaves-shipping.com
Seven Seas Shipping & Shipping Services Co. Ltd, 3rd Floor, No.6 Homa Central Airline Building, Before Yadbood Square, Imam Khomeine Avenue, Bandar Abbas 79177-47739, Iran, *Tel:* +98 761 224 0489, *Fax:* +98 761 222 3343, *Email:* general@sevenseasir.com
South Shipping Line (Iran), Boulevard Imam Khomeini, Sorou Area, Bandar Abbas, Iran, *Tel:* +98 761 555 2000, *Fax:* +98 761 555 3004

Stevedoring Companies: Seawaves Shipping Services Co. Ltd, Bandar Abbas, Iran, *Tel:* +98 761 555 6204, *Fax:* +98 761 555 4689, *Email:* b.abbas@seawaves-shipping.com, *Website:* www.seawaves-shipping.com

Surveyors: Det Norske Veritas A/S, No.25 5th Floor, West Block, Iran Air Building, P O Box 79145-3963, Bandar Abbas, Iran, *Tel:* +98 761 333 2472, *Fax:* +98 761 334 2265, *Email:* thr@dnv.com, *Website:* www.dnv.com
Seawaves Shipping Services Co. Ltd, Bandar Abbas, Iran, *Tel:* +98 761 555 6204, *Fax:* +98 761 555 4689, *Email:* b.abbas@seawaves-shipping.com, *Website:* www.seawaves-shipping.com

Airport: Bandar Abbas International Airport, 40 km

Railway: Railway connections to the port, linking to the Iranian rail network and the establishment of a cross border rail connection in the northeast that joins up with the Central Asian rail system

Development: A second container terminal with two berths is scheduled to open with a 850 m quay in depth of 17 m

Lloyd's Agent: Iran Marine Services Co., Ayatollah Taleghani Boulevard, Across to Shohada Library, 3rd Floor Etemadi Building, Bandar Abbas, Iran, *Tel:* +98 761 222 6904, *Fax:* +98 761 222 0160, *Email:* imsba@ims-ir.com, *Website:* www.ims-ir.com

BANDAR ANZALI

Lat 37° 26' N; Long 49° 29' E.

Admiralty Chart: -	**Admiralty Pilot:** -
Time Zone: GMT +3.5 h	**UNCTAD Locode:** IR BAZ

Principal Facilities:

P		Y	G	C	R		B		T	A

Authority: Anzali Port Special Economic Zone, Mostafa Khomeini Street, P O Box 43156-77171, Bandar Anzali, Iran, *Tel:* +98 181 322 4009, *Fax:* +98 181 322 3903/322 7988, *Email:* anzaliport@anzaliport.ir, *Website:* www.anzaliport.ir

Officials: Managing Director: Farhad Montaser Kohsari.
Harbour Master: Mahmood Mirnabili.

Port Security: ISPS compliant

Pre-Arrival Information: On the basis of FAL form

Documentation: Principal documents are based on FAL forms:
crew list, general declaration, passenger list, cargo declaration, ship's store declaration, crew's effect declaration

Approach: The approach to the port is a channel dredged to 6 m

Anchorage: There is only one exposed anchorage defined by the following points in a depth of 20 m:
37° 29.7' N; 49° 25.1' E
37° 30.6' N; 49° 25.7' E
37° 30.1' N; 49° 28.1' E
37° 29.2' N; 49° 27.6' E

Pilotage: Compulsory for all vessels and carried out by the port authority. Two pilot boats

Radio Frequency: VHF Channels 16 and 12

Weather: Prevailing NE and SW winds

Tides: Non-tidal

Traffic: 2005, 1062 vessels, 3 417 282 t of cargo handled

Principal Imports and Exports: Imports: Asbestos, Forest products, Machinery parts, Steel. Exports: Automobiles, Foodstuffs, Fruit.

Working Hours: 0700-2100. Overtime available

Accommodation:

Name	Length (m)	Draught (m)
Bandar Anzali		
Berth No.1	67.5	5.5
Berth No.2	118	5.5
Berth No.3	118	5.5
Berth No.4	118	5.5
Berth No.5	145	5.5
Berth No.6	155	5.5
Berth No.7	155	5.5
Berth No.8	155	5.5
Berth No.9	155	5.5
Berth No.10	185	5.5

Storage: 49.8 ha of open storage and 22 709 m2 of warehousing available. 2000 t cap silo

Mechanical Handling Equipment:

Location	Type	Qty	Remarks
Bandar Anzali	Mult-purp. Cranes	55	See [1] below
Bandar Anzali	Transtainers	1	
Bandar Anzali	Reach Stackers	2	

[1]*Bandar Anzali:* Twenty five of less than 30 t cap, fourteen of 30-100 t cap, one super heavy crane of 100 t cap, two 100 t cap gottwald cranes, ten rail cranes and three grove cranes

Bunkering: Supplied by private companies
Seawaves Shipping Services Co. Ltd, Bandar Anzali, Iran, *Tel:* +98 181 322 4425, *Fax:* +98 181 322 4425, *Website:* www.seawaves-shipping.com

Towage: Four tugs up to 1500 hp available

Shipping Agents: GAC Shipping FZCO, Dubai Airport Free Zone, P O Box 54593, Dubai, United Arab Emirates, *Tel:* +971 4 299 0021, *Fax:* +971 4 299 0030, *Email:* gacfzco.dubai@gacworld.com, *Website:* www.gacworld.com Operations Manager: Thomas M. Jayabhai Mobile Tel: +971 50 6520677
Iran Gulf Shipping Services, Iran Gulf Building, 42 Babak Markazi, Africa Expressway, Tehran 19177, Iran, *Tel:* +98 21 8887 9050, *Fax:* +98 21 8879 9107, *Email:* operations@irgulf.net, *Website:* www.irangulf.com
Khazar Sea Shipping Lines, Tohid Square, End of Mostafa Khomeini Street, P O Box 43145, Bandar Anzali, Iran, *Tel:* +98 181 322 3801, *Fax:* +98 181 322 4744, *Email:* m.d@khazarshipping.com, *Website:* www.khazarshipping.com
Seas Ark S.A., No.23 Najafour Street, Bayandor Avenue, Gomrok Square, Gahzian, Bandar Anzali, Iran, *Tel:* +98 181 322 4638, *Fax:* +98 181 322 4638, *Email:* info@seasark.com, *Website:* www.seasark.com
Seawaves Shipping Services Co. Ltd, Bandar Anzali, Iran, *Tel:* +98 181 322 4425, *Fax:* +98 181 322 4425, *Website:* www.seawaves-shipping.com

Stevedoring Companies: Kaveh Marine & Port Services, Bandar Anzali, Iran, *Tel:* +98 181 322 3457, *Fax:* +98 181 322 3981, *Email:* anzali@kavehco.com, *Website:* www.kavehco.com
Seawaves Shipping Services Co. Ltd, Bandar Anzali, Iran, *Tel:* +98 181 322 4425, *Fax:* +98 181 322 4425, *Website:* www.seawaves-shipping.com

Surveyors: Seawaves Shipping Services Co. Ltd, Bandar Anzali, Iran, *Tel:* +98 181 322 4425, *Fax:* +98 181 322 4425, *Website:* www.seawaves-shipping.com

Medical Facilities: Medical centre situated in the port

Airport: Rasht, 40 km

Railway: Railway is under construction

Lloyd's Agent: Irano-German Insurance Services (Private Co. Ltd), Avenue Bozorg-mehr No.62, 3rd Floor, Tehran 14168-44984, Iran, *Tel:* +98 21 6646 8495, *Fax:* +98 21 6640 2277, *Email:* igis@parsonline.net, *Website:* www.igis-surveyor.com

BANDAR IMAM KHOMEINI

Lat 30° 25' N; Long 49° 4' E.

Admiralty Chart: 1269	**Admiralty Pilot:** 63
Time Zone: GMT +3.5 h	**UNCTAD Locode:** IR BKM

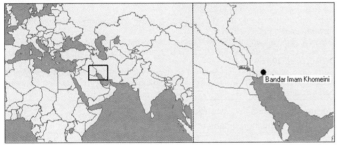

Principal Facilities:

P	Q	Y	G	C	R		B		T	A	

DTS
DARYADAR TABAN SHIPPING

SHIPPING AGENCY AT BIK & BND
NO.150 - DR. MOFATEH AVE - TEHRAN-IRAN
TEL: (009821) 88829988 - 88845661
FAX: (009821) 88307313
EMAIL: ali@daryadar.com /dtss@dpi.net.ir

FANUS-E-SAHEL Co. LTD.

(LICENSED SHIPPING AGENCY)

No 19, 4th Floor, Panahi Building, Moradi Crossroads
Syed Jamaledin Asad Abdi Street
Bandar Abbas 79188-9-3868, IRAN

Tel: +98 21 88 96 3049 / 88 96 9814
Fax: +98 21 88 96 5419
Email: fanus@parsonline.net

Authority: Imam Khomeini Port Complex, P O Box 159, Bandar Imam Khomeini, Iran, *Tel:* +98 652 252 2050, *Fax:* +98 652 252 2317, *Email:* marketing@khomeiniport.com, *Website:* www.khomeiniport.com

Officials: Director General: Jalil Eslami, *Tel:* +98 652 252 2020, *Email:* eslami@khomeiniport.com.
Marketing Manager: Mohammad Ali Eazi, *Tel:* +98 652 252 2025.
Harbour Master: Amin Mousafour, *Tel:* +98 652 252 2462, *Email:* moosapour2002@yahoo.com.

Port Security: ISPS compliant

Documentation: Quarantine Officer: crew list, marine declaration of health, list of ports of call, crew vacccination cards
Customs Officer: crew list, stores list, crew declaration, cargo manifest
Port Authority: last port, port clearance, crew list, stores list, passenger list
Agents: bills of lading, cargo manifest, stowage plan, freight manifest (for vessels discharging cargo)

Approach: The 72 km, 250-700 m width and 12 m CD/15 m MSL approach channel is navigable for two ocean-going vessels at the same time

Anchorage: Outer anchorage at Khor Musa light vessel (position has to be obtained from Bandar Imam Khomeini Port Control). Inner anchorage (position will be given by Bandar Imam Khomeini Port Control)

Pilotage: Compulsory. Application for pilot to be made 24 h in advance of vessels arrival at Khoormosa pilot station through Bandar Imam Khomeini port radio - EQN 500 kHz

Radio Frequency: Bandar Imam Khomeini port radio EQN 500 kHz. Port control on VHF Channels 13 and 16

Traffic: 2006, 29 166 000 t of cargo handled

Maximum Vessel Dimensions: Vessels of 12.5 m draft can enter the port at any time. Higher drafts depending on state of tide

Principal Imports and Exports: Imports: Flour, General cargo, Grain, Iron ore, Rice. Exports: Clinker, Steel slabs.

Working Hours: Sat-Wed 24 h/day. Thurs-Fri 0700-2100 (overtime applicable)

Accommodation:

Name	Length (m)	Depth (m)	Remarks
Bandar Imam Khomeini			See [1] below
Container Berths	1037	11–14	Five berths. Max 100 000 dwt
Mineral Berths	405	12	Two berths. Max 60 000 dwt
Grain Berths	1908	11.5–12.5	Nine berths. Max 60 000 dwt
General Cargo Berths	3288	10–12	Eighteen berths. Max 45 000 dwt
Liquid Berth	182.5	11–12.5	One berth. Max 45 000 dwt
Cereal Berths	480	11–13	See [2] below

[1]*Bandar Imam Khomeini:* Cargo Terminal No.1: This terminal has three sheds with an area of 12 600 m2 and yards with 140 000 m2. As it is possible to handle different kinds of cargo at this terminal, most of the cargo handling operation is done here. It has been divided into two parts, the area for the storage of general cargo and the area for storage of separate heavy items for industrial establishments
Cargo Terminal No.2: This terminal has three sheds with an area of 27 000 m2 and yards with 87 500 m2. The terminal has been allocated for general cargo and break bulk
Cargo Terminal No.3: This terminal has three sheds with an area of 27 000 m2 and yards with 111 000 m2. The terminal has been allocated for general cargo and break bulk
Export Terminal: This terminal has two sheds with an area of 18 000 m2 and yards with 105 000 m2. It is used for the export of non-oil products such as metal products, building materials, plastic materials and mineral materials
Industrial Concentrates Terminal: For iron ore and aluminium concentrate. The terminal can accommodate two ships simultaneously and is connected to the trans-country railway network
Container Terminal: Special cranes for handling containers. Capacity of 20 000 TEU's
Grain Terminal: Transit silo with 70 000 t capacity which, if the capacities of open warehouses are also added, this capacity will reach 170 000 t. The grain suction towers are capable to give services simultaneously to five bulk grain carriers with a draft of 13 m and daily discharge of 50 000 t of different kinds of grain
[2]*Cereal Berths:* Two berths. Max 70 000 dwt. Six pneumatic ship unloaders, each with a handling cap of 280 t/h

Storage:

Location	Open (m²)	Covered (m²)	Grain (t)
Bandar Imam Khomeini	2000000	300000	70000

Mechanical Handling Equipment:

Location	Type	Capacity (t)	Qty
Bandar Imam Khomeini	Mult-purp. Cranes	15–220	58
Bandar Imam Khomeini	Container Cranes	40	2
Bandar Imam Khomeini	Transtainers	40	3
Bandar Imam Khomeini	Reach Stackers	45	4
Bandar Imam Khomeini	Forklifts	3–40	84

Bunkering: Available by barge
Seawaves Shipping Services Co. Ltd, Bandar Imam Khomeini, Iran, *Tel:* +98 652 233 8492, *Fax:* +98 652 233 4757, *Email:* bik@seawaves-shipping.com, *Website:* www.seawaves-shipping.com

Towage: Nine tugs available of 1200-4400 hp

Key to Principal Facilities:—			
A=Airport	**C**=Containers	**G**=General Cargo	**P**=Petroleum	**R**=Ro/Ro	**Y**=Dry Bulk
B=Bunkers	**D**=Dry Dock	**L**=Cruise	**Q**=Other Liquid Bulk	**T**=Towage (where available from port)	

Ship Chandlers: IRISL Marine Services & Engineering Co. (Imseng Co.), Sarbandar, Bandar Imam Khomeini, Iran, *Tel:* +98 652 222 5220, *Fax:* +98 652 222 5219, *Email:* Imsengco-bk@irisl.net

Shipping Agents: GAC Shipping FZCO, Dubai Airport Free Zone, P O Box 54593, Dubai, United Arab Emirates, *Tel:* +971 4 299 0021, *Fax:* +971 4 299 0030, *Email:* gacfzco.dubai@gacworld.com, *Website:* www.gacworld.com Operations Manager: Thomas M. Jayabhai Mobile Tel: +971 50 6520677
Chabahar Shipping Services Logistics Co., No. 254 Africa Express Way, Tehran 15867, Iran, *Tel:* +98 21 8865 0805, *Fax:* +98 21 8865 0817, *Email:* info@cssir.com, *Website:* www.cssir.com
Daryadar Taban Shipping Service Co., 238 Mofateh Avenue, Tehran 1584863716, Iran, *Tel:* +98 21 8882 9988, *Fax:* +98 21 88830 7313, *Email:* dtss@dpi.net.ir
Iran Gulf Shipping Services, Iran Gulf Building, 42 Babak Markazi, Africa Expressway, Tehran 19177, Iran, *Tel:* +98 21 8887 9050, *Fax:* +98 21 8879 9107, *Email:* operations@irgulf.net, *Website:* www.irangulf.com
Fanus E. Sahel Co. Ltd, 10th Floor, Leon Building, Dr. Fatemi Square, Tehran 14316, Iran, *Tel:* +98 21 8896 9814, *Fax:* +98 21 8896 5419, *Email:* fanus@parsonline.net
Seawaves Shipping Services Co. Ltd, Bandar Imam Khomeini, Iran, *Tel:* +98 652 233 8492, *Fax:* +98 652 233 4757, *Email:* bik@seawaves-shipping.com, *Website:* www.seawaves-shipping.com

Stevedoring Companies: Kaveh Marine & Port Services, Bandar Imam Khomeini, Iran, *Tel:* +98 652 252 2925, *Fax:* +98 652 252 2926, *Email:* bik@kavehco.com, *Website:* www.kavehco.com
Seawaves Shipping Services Co. Ltd, Bandar Imam Khomeini, Iran, *Tel:* +98 652 233 8492, *Fax:* +98 652 233 4757, *Email:* bik@seawaves-shipping.com, *Website:* www.seawaves-shipping.com

Surveyors: Seawaves Shipping Services Co. Ltd, Bandar Imam Khomeini, Iran, *Tel:* +98 652 233 8492, *Fax:* +98 652 233 4757, *Email:* bik@seawaves-shipping.com, *Website:* www.seawaves-shipping.com

Medical Facilities: Available

Airport: 20 km

Railway: The port has 27 km of railway track inside its operational area and is linked to the railway network of the country

Development: A 10 ha private container terminal is currently under construction, this will include 9000 m2 of warehouse space and is due to become operational by early 2007

Lloyd's Agent: Iran Marine Services Co., Ayatollah Taleghani Boulevard, Across to Shohada Library, 3rd Floor Etemadi Building, Bandar Abbas, Iran, *Tel:* +98 761 222 6904, *Fax:* +98 761 222 0160, *Email:* imsba@ims-ir.com, *Website:* www.ims-ir.com

BANDAR MAHSHAHR

Lat 30° 28' N; Long 49° 11' E.

Admiralty Chart: 1269	**Admiralty Pilot:** 63
Time Zone: GMT +3.5 h	**UNCTAD Locode:** IR BMR

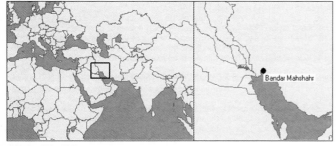

Principal Facilities:

P	Q	Y	G	C	R		B		T	A

Authority: National Iranian Oil Terminals Co., 88 Hodjat Souri Street, Pasdaran Avenue, Tehran, Iran, *Tel:* +98 21 22592 4001, *Email:* admin@nioc-otc.com, *Website:* www.nioc-otc.com

Port Security: ISPS compliant

Documentation: Quarantine Officer: crew list, marine declaration of health, list of ports of call, crew vacccination cards
Customs Officer: crew list, stores list, crew declaration, cargo manifest
Port Authority: last port, port clearance, crew list, stores list, passenger list
Agents: bills of lading, cargo manifest, stowage plan, freight manifest (for vessels discharging cargo)

Approach: Vessels bound for Bandar Mahshahr are required to anchor at inner anchorage at Bandar Imam Khomeini in order to obtain pratique before proceeding further. With the cooperation between Bandar Mahshahr port control and Bandar Imam Khomeini port control, an oil company berthing master will board incoming vessels at inner anchorage and then proceed to Bandar Mahshahr, a distance of approx 11.2 km

Anchorage: Outer anchorage at Khor Musa light vessel (position has to be obtained from Bandar Imam Khomeini Port Control). Inner anchorage (position will be given by Bandar Imam Khomeini Port Control)

Pilotage: Pilotage from inner anchorage to Bandar Mahshahr controlled and carried out by National Iranian Oil Co. Applied for through Bandar Imam Khomeini port control VHF Channel 16-13

Radio Frequency: Bandar Imam Khomeini port radio EQN 500 kHz, telex: 612051 BDHR IR. Continuous watch on 500 kHz to be maintained at all time while navigating in Khor Musa waterway

Weather: Possibility of strong NW winds accompanied by thick dust, especially from June to August. Fresh SE winds accompanied by squalls common in winter from November to March. Sufficient ballast must be retained on board to allow safe manoeuvring during prevailing weather conditions

Tides: Max tidal range 3.5 m

Working Hours: 24 h/day

Accommodation:

Name	Depth (m)	Remarks
Bandar Mahshahr		See [1] below
Jetty No.1	13.41	See [2] below
Jetty No.2	11.73	See [3] below
Jetty No.3	11.89	See [4] below
Jetty No.4	11.28	See [5] below
Jetty No.5	11.89	See [6] below
Jetty No.6	13.25	See [7] below
LNG Plant		2 x 16'' loading arms

[1]*Bandar Mahshahr:* S limit of Port of Mahshahr is at Beacon No.4, approx 1.3 km S from No.6 Jetty. No anchorages at Port of Mahshahr or Mahshahr Roadstead. Inward bound vessels must anchor at N side of Khor Musa Channel, W of Bandar Khomeini and await arrival of Oil Company Berthing Master
Incoming vessels met by tugs in the channel, about 1.6 km below Port limits. Two tugs used for berthing and unberthing according to state of tide etc. Vessels arriving on flood tide turned off the jetties by one tug and berthed starboard side to jetty with two tugs. Vessels arriving on ebb tide berth port side to jetty using two tugs. Loading procedure: after vessel has berthed, Oil Company Official will board to confirm loading procedure etc. On discharge of ballast, tank lids should be left open for inspection. Oil ballast handling facilities have been constructed. Jetties 1, 2, 5 and 6 are equipped for this purpose and can handle 2000 t/h of oily water and 200 t/h of oily slops.
Radio Station: Oil Company has a coastal station at Abadan Terminal with call sign of EQZ and VHF Radio Telephone
LNG Plant, for preparation of refrigerated propane, butane and pentane (latter loaded at jetties 1-4) for export. Jetty No.6 is equipped with two loading and vapour return arms for this purpose
[2]*Jetty No.1:* Max cap 35 000 dwt (subject to overall length not exceeding 237.7 m and the rise of tide on bar). 6 x 10'' & 1 x 8'' loading arms. Approx distance between loading units 268 m
[3]*Jetty No.2:* Max cap 45 000 dwt. 6 x 10'' & 1 x 8'' loading arms. Approx distance between loading units 256 m
[4]*Jetty No.3:* Max cap 50 000 dwt. 3 x 10'' & 1 x 8'' loading arms. Approx distance between loading units 259 m
[5]*Jetty No.4:* Max cap 40 000 dwt. 3 x 10'' & 1 x 8'' loading arms. Approx distance between loading units 292.5 m
[6]*Jetty No.5:* Max cap 55 000 dwt (subject to overall length not exceeding 237.7 m and the rise of tide on bar). 5 x 10'' & 1 x 8'' loading arms. Approx distance between loading units 422 m
[7]*Jetty No.6:* Max cap 60 000 dwt (subject to overall length not exceeding 237.7 m and the rise of tide on bar). 4 x 10'' & 1 x 8'' loading arms. Approx distance between loading units 422 m

Storage: Shore storage is available for petroleum products

Mechanical Handling Equipment:

Location	Type	Capacity (t)
Bandar Mahshahr	Mult-purp. Cranes	10

Bunkering: Bunkering is possible directly from the jetty subject to availability

Towage: Available

Repair & Maintenance: Iranmash, NIOC Abadan Refinery

Shipping Agents: GAC Shipping FZCO, Dubai Airport Free Zone, P O Box 54593, Dubai, United Arab Emirates, *Tel:* +971 4 299 0021, *Fax:* +971 4 299 0030, *Email:* gacfzco.dubai@gacworld.com, *Website:* www.gacworld.com Operations Manager: Thomas M. Jayabhai Mobile Tel: +971 50 6520677
Iran Gulf Shipping Services, Iran Gulf Building, 42 Babak Markazi, Africa Expressway, Tehran 19177, Iran, *Tel:* +98 21 8887 9050, *Fax:* +98 21 8879 9107, *Email:* operations@irgulf.net, *Website:* www.irangulf.com

Medical Facilities: Available

Airport: Mahshahr Airport

Railway: Regular rail service is available at Khorramshahr, 150 km

Lloyd's Agent: Iran Marine Services Co., Ayatollah Taleghani Boulevard, Across to Shohada Library, 3rd Floor Etemadi Building, Bandar Abbas, Iran, *Tel:* +98 761 222 6904, *Fax:* +98 761 222 0160, *Email:* imsba@ims-ir.com, *Website:* www.ims-ir.com

BANDAR SHAHID BEHESTI

harbour area, see under Chah Bahar

BANDAR SHAHID REJAIE

harbour area, see under Bandar Abbas

BUSHIRE

Lat 28° 59' N; Long 50° 50' E.

Admiralty Chart: 27	**Admiralty Pilot:** 63
Time Zone: GMT +3.5 h	**UNCTAD Locode:** IR BUZ

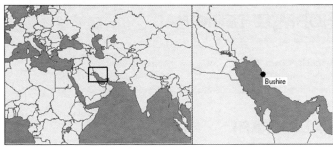

Principal Facilities:

Q	Y	G		B		T	A

ANIS TRADING & SHIPPING SERVICES CO. LTD

Irani Building Eskeleh, Saheli Avenue, Persian Gulf, Bushire, IRAN
Tel: +98 9121 255 469   Fax: +98 7712 525 433
Email: iranigroup@iranigroup.ir & abolqasem@iranigroup.ir
Web: www.iranigroup.ir
Managing Director: Mr. Abol Qasem Irami

SHIPPING AGENTS

FANUS-E-SAHEL Co. LTD.
(LICENSED SHIPPING AGENCY)

No 19, 4th Floor, Panahi Building, Moradi Crossroads
Syed Jamaledin Asad Abdi Street
Bandar Abbas 79188-9-3868, IRAN

Tel: +98 21 88 96 3049 / 88 96 9814
Fax: +98 21 88 96 5419
Email: fanus@parsonline.net

Authority: Ports & Shipping Organisation, PSO Building, South Didar Street, Shahid Haghani Highway, Vanak Square, Tehran, Iran, *Tel:* +98 21 849 31, *Fax:* +98 21 8651 191, *Email:* mahmoodi@pso.ir, *Website:* www.pso.ir

Officials: Marketing Director: Ramazan Ali Mahmoodi, *Email:* mahmoodi@pso.ir.

Port Security: ISPS compliant

Documentation: Valid classification and registration certificates, copies of B/L's, cargo manifest, stowage plan for vessels importing cargoes

Approach: Vessels up to 8.6 m d and 200 m loa can enter the dredged channel

Anchorage: In the outer port, anchorage may be obtained in approx pos 28° 57.3' N; 50° 43.2' E
The outer anchorage, NW of the entrance to the dredged channel, is used by vessels waiting to enter Khowr-E Soltani, or whose draft will not permit them to enter the inner anchorage; this anchorage is exposed

Pilotage: Compulsory. Vessels should anchor at the outer buoy and await a pilot. The pilot boards in the outer anchorage, approx 1.25 nautical miles from the entrance channel

Radio Frequency: VHF Channel 16 and 6

Weather: Prevailing NW winds

Working Hours: Sat-Wed 24 h/day. Thurs-Fri 0700-2100 (overtime applicable)

Accommodation:

Name	Length (m)	Depth (m)	Remarks
Bushire			
General Cargo	416	7.3–8	Max 25 000-30 000 dwt. Three berths
Dolphin		5.8	
Barges	280	3	Max 2000 dwt
Private	300	1.8	Max 1000 dwt. Three berths
Chemical		4	Max 4000 dwt

Storage:

Location	Open (m²)	Covered (m²)
Bushire	443000	30312

Mechanical Handling Equipment:

Location	Type	Capacity (t)	Qty
Bushire	Mult-purp. Cranes	40	1
Bushire	Mult-purp. Cranes	27	5
Bushire	Mult-purp. Cranes	60	1
Bushire	Mult-purp. Cranes	16	7
Bushire	Mult-purp. Cranes	35	2
Bushire	Forklifts	13	2
Bushire	Forklifts	10	4
Bushire	Forklifts	15	2
Bushire	Forklifts	5	23

Bunkering: Seawaves Shipping Services Co. Ltd, Bushire, Iran, *Tel:* +98 771 353 8483, *Fax:* +98 771 353 8773, *Email:* bushehr@seawaves-shipping.com, *Website:* www.seawaves-shipping.com
Iran Marine Services Co., IMS Building, 151 Mirdamad Boulevard, Tehran 19116, Iran, *Tel:* +98 21 2222 2249, *Fax:* +98 21 2222 3380, *Email:* info@imsiran.com, *Website:* www.imsiran.com – *Delivery Mode:* barge
N.I.B.C. Iranian Oil Co., National Iranian Tanker Co. (N.I.T.C), 67 Shahid Atefy Street, Africa Avenue, Tehran 1917797163, Iran, *Tel:* +98 21 2222 2465, *Fax:* +98 21 2201 3392, *Email:* connserb@nitc.co.ir, *Website:* www.nitc.co.ir – *Delivery Mode:* barge

Towage: A variety of tugs available up to 1200 hp

Repair & Maintenance: Effected by Imico, no dry dock available

Ship Chandlers: Morvarid Cian, 2nd Floor, Ghanbary Building, Shohada Street, Bushire, Iran, *Tel:* +98 771 252 5669, *Fax:* +98 771 252 6760, *Email:* mlsc@jhaligonline.net

Shipping Agents: GAC Shipping FZCO, Dubai Airport Free Zone, P O Box 54593, Dubai, United Arab Emirates, *Tel:* +971 4 299 0021, *Fax:* +971 4 299 0030, *Email:* gacfzco.dubai@gacworld.com, *Website:* www.gacworld.com Operations Manager: Thomas M. Jayabhai Mobile Tel: +971 50 6520677
Anis Trading & Shipping Services Co. Ltd, Irani Building Eskeleh, Saheli Avenue, Bushire, Iran, *Tel:* +98 9121255469 & 9191255469, *Fax:* +98 771 252 5433 & 252 5156, *Email:* abolqasem@iranigroup.ir & iranigroup@iranigroup.ir, *Website:* www.iranigroup.ir
Chabahar Shipping Services Logistics Co., No. 254 Africa Express Way, Tehran 15867, Iran, *Tel:* +98 21 8865 0805, *Fax:* +98 21 8865 0817, *Email:* info@cssir.com, *Website:* www.cssir.com
Iran Gulf Shipping Services, Iran Gulf Building, 42 Babak Markazi, Africa Expressway, Tehran 19177, Iran, *Tel:* +98 21 8887 9050, *Fax:* +98 21 8879 9107, *Email:* operations@irgulf.net, *Website:* www.irangulf.com
Fanus E. Sahel Co. Ltd, 10th Floor, Leon Building, Dr. Fatemi Square, Tehran 14316, Iran, *Tel:* +98 21 8896 9814, *Fax:* +98 21 8896 5419, *Email:* fanus@parsonline.net
Sea Mystries Shipping Co, Bushire, Iran, *Tel:* +98 771 252 6706, *Fax:* +98 771 252 6478, *Email:* info@seamystriesshipping.com, *Website:* www.seamystriesshipping.com
Seas Ark S.A., Mehr Bandar Co. PJS, Mehaban Building, 149 Saheli Street, P O Box 1188, Bushire, Iran, *Tel:* +98 771 252 2412, *Fax:* +98 771 252 2184, *Email:* info@mehrbandar.com, *Website:* www.seasark.com
Seawaves Shipping Services Co. Ltd, Bushire, Iran, *Tel:* +98 771 353 8483, *Fax:* +98 771 353 8773, *Email:* bushehr@seawaves-shipping.com, *Website:* www.seawaves-shipping.com

Stevedoring Companies: Seas Ark S.A., Mehr Bandar Co. PJS, Mehaban Building, 149 Saheli Street, P O Box 1188, Bushire, Iran, *Tel:* +98 771 252 2412, *Fax:* +98 771 252 2184, *Email:* info@mehrbandar.com, *Website:* www.seasark.com
Seawaves Shipping Services Co. Ltd, Bushire, Iran, *Tel:* +98 771 353 8483, *Fax:* +98 771 353 8773, *Email:* bushehr@seawaves-shipping.com, *Website:* www.seawaves-shipping.com

Surveyors: Seawaves Shipping Services Co. Ltd, Bushire, Iran, *Tel:* +98 771 353 8483, *Fax:* +98 771 353 8773, *Email:* bushehr@seawaves-shipping.com, *Website:* www.seawaves-shipping.com

Medical Facilities: Available

Airport: 3 km

Lloyd's Agent: Iran Marine Services Co., Ayatollah Taleghani Boulevard, Across to Shohada Library, 3rd Floor Etemadi Building, Bandar Abbas, Iran, *Tel:* +98 761 222 6904, *Fax:* +98 761 222 0160, *Email:* imsba@ims-ir.com, *Website:* www.ims-ir.com

CHAH BAHAR

Lat 25° 20' N; Long 60° 32' E.

Admiralty Chart: 2851	**Admiralty Pilot:** 63
Time Zone: GMT +3.5 h	**UNCTAD Locode:** IR ZBR

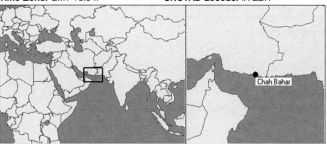

Principal Facilities:

	Y	G	C		B		T	A

Authority: Ports & Shipping Organisation, PSO Building, South Didar Street, Shahid Haghani Highway, Vanak Square, Tehran, Iran, *Tel:* +98 21 849 31, *Fax:* +98 21 8651 191, *Email:* mahmoodi@pso.ir, *Website:* www.pso.ir

Key to Principal Facilities:—			
A=Airport	**C**=Containers	**G**=General Cargo	**P**=Petroleum	**R**=Ro/Ro	**Y**=Dry Bulk
B=Bunkers	**D**=Dry Dock	**L**=Cruise	**Q**=Other Liquid Bulk	**T**=Towage (where available from port)	

Officials: Marketing Director: Ramazan Ali Mahmoodi, *Email:* mahmoodi@pso.ir.

Port Security: ISPS compliant

Approach: The south side of Chah Bahar Bay is bordered by a reef and foul ground extending up to 3 cables offshore

The Bay is entered between Damagheh-ye Chah Bahar and Damagheh-ye Puzim. The bay opens up to a width of 10 miles and is 9 m deep. For the first 4 miles within the entrance points the shores are steep and rocky and at the head, low and sandy backed by swamp and saltpans extending into a large low plain. Tidal streams are weak. Currents that exist depend on the prevailing wind

A light-buoy (in pos 25° 15' N; 60° 30' E) is moored about 3 miles SE of Damagheh-ye Puzim and about 6.5 cables SSE of an obstruction with a depth of 16 m over it

Anchorage: The anchorage area occupies the central area of the bay outside the 10 m depth contour. The chartered depth of the anchorages is 10.2 m and the holding ground is described as soft mud

The anchorage area is used for vessels discharging into barges using ship's gear. The anchorage coordinates are 25° 22' N; 60° 30' E, 25° 18' N; 60° 30' E and 25° 18' N; 60° 33' E

Small vessels may obtain anchorage in Bandar-e Chah Bahar in a depth of 7 m, sand, about 1 mile NNW of Damagheh-ye Chah Bahar; local craft anchor in depths of less than 4 m about half a mile off the town

During the SW monsoon, when a heavy SSE swell is rolling into the bay, sheltered anchorage with no swell may be obtained near the W side of Chah Bahar Bay, 3.5 miles E of Konarak - this anchorage also affords good shelter during a Shamal (NW wind)

Pilotage: Compulsory. Pilots embark in the anchorage area inside the bay

Principal Imports and Exports: Imports: Containers, Dry cargo, Fertiliser, General cargo, Grain, Liquid cargo. Exports: Containers, Fertiliser, General cargo, Grain.

Working Hours: Normally 0700-2000 with overtime available. No work on Friday

Accommodation:

Name	Length (m)	Draught (m)	Remarks
Shahid Beheshti			
Jetty No.1	150	8.3	General cargo & containers for vessels up to 25 000 dwt
Jetty No.2	150	8.3	Tankers for vessels up to 25 000 dwt
Jetty No.3	150	9	General cargo & containers for vessels up to 25 000 dwt
Jetty No.4	150	9	General cargo & containers for vessels up to 25 000 dwt
Kalantari			
Jetty No.1		3	Cargo motor launches & coastguard vessels
Jetty No.2		4	Motor launches & barges
Jetty No.3		4	Motor launches & barges
Jetty No.4		5	Tugs & barges under 5000 dwt
Jetty No.5	175	10.3	General cargo & containers for vessels up to 40 000 dwt

Storage:

Location	Open (m²)	Covered (m²)	Sheds / Warehouses
Shahid Beheshti	350000	18000	2
Kalantari	7000	4000	2

Mechanical Handling Equipment: 60 tractors/trailers, 10 grabs of 3-5 t cap, 1 toplift, 8 grain unloading funnels and 6 pneumatic ship unloaders

Location	Type	Capacity (t)	Qty
Shahid Beheshti	Mobile Cranes	25–60	8
Shahid Beheshti	Forklifts	3–35	17

Bunkering: Available by road tankers

Towage: Three tugs available up to 3200 hp

Repair & Maintenance: There are no shipyards or repair facilities available

Shipping Agents: GAC Shipping FZCO, Dubai Airport Free Zone, P O Box 54593, Dubai, United Arab Emirates, *Tel:* +971 4 299 0021, *Fax:* +971 4 299 0030, *Email:* gacfzco.dubai@gacworld.com, *Website:* www.gacworld.com Operations Manager: Thomas M. Jayabhai Mobile Tel: +971 50 6520677
Iran Gulf Shipping Services, Iran Gulf Building, 42 Babak Markazi, Africa Expressway, Tehran 19177, Iran, *Tel:* +98 21 8887 9050, *Fax:* +98 21 8879 9107, *Email:* operations@irgulf.net, *Website:* www.irangulf.com

Airport: 45 km

Lloyd's Agent: Iran Marine Services Co., Ayatollah Taleghani Boulevard, Across to Shohada Library, 3rd Floor Etemadi Building, Bandar Abbas, Iran, *Tel:* +98 761 222 6904, *Fax:* +98 761 222 0160, *Email:* imsba@ims-ir.com, *Website:* www.ims-ir.com

CYRUS TERMINAL

alternate name, see Soroosh Terminal

ENZELI

alternate name, see Bandar Anzali

HORMUZ TERMINAL

Lat 26° 50' N; Long 56° 44' E.

Admiralty Chart: 3172	**Admiralty Pilot:** 63
Time Zone: GMT +3.5 h	**UNCTAD Locode:** IR HOR

This terminal is no longer operational

KALANTARI

harbour area, see under Chah Bahar

KHARG ISLAND

Lat 29° 14' N; Long 50° 19' E.

Admiralty Chart: 11	**Admiralty Pilot:** 63
Time Zone: GMT +3.5 h	**UNCTAD Locode:** IR KHK

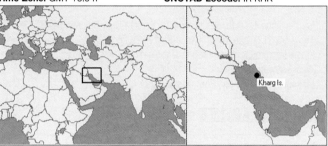

Principal Facilities:

P	Q					B		T	A

Authority: National Iranian Oil Terminals Co., 88 Hodjat Souri Street, Pasdaran Avenue, Tehran, Iran, *Tel:* +98 21 22592 4001, *Email:* admin@nioc-otc.com, *Website:* www.nioc-otc.com

Port Security: ISPS compliant

Pre-Arrival Information: Master's should signal their ETA at Kharg Terminal about 72 h before arrival and confirm, correcting ETA if necessary, 48 h and 24 h before arrival. When confirming ETA, any expected delays for repairs or other reasons, prior to berthing, should also be included in the standard message
Tankers calling at Kharg Island are requested to telex the following information 72 h prior to their arrival and repeat 48 h before arrival, through their agents:
ETA at Kharg Island
Cargo requirements and supplier
If loading two grades, indicate sequence of loading
Arrival and departure drafts, forw'd and aft
Deballasting time before loading
Height of manifold above sea level when vessel is ready to load
Loading rate
Summer deadweight and arrival displacement
Length overall and distance from bow to center of manifold
Condition of derricks or cranes port and starboard
Condition of accommodation ladder port and starboard
Mooring wires must be connected to a min of 10 m nylon tails
Three reducers of 16" x 12" to be available on board
International nrt plus grt
Vessel's registration and IMO number
Master's name and nationality and number of crew
Radio free pratique by quarantine message addressed to Port Health Kharg
There are oil pollution patrol by launch and helicopter around Kharg. Ensure clean ballast and pipelines, no oily discharge from any source is allowed
All cargo tank openings must be closed whilst tugs are alongside
Port safety regulations rigorously enforced
Cable anchoring time and position
Report departure time from Kharg anchorage on VHF Channel 12. Terminal is operating on VHF Channels 16, 12 and 77
Intership VHF traffic to be clear of Channels 10, 12, 14 and 77 whilst at anchorage and alongside
Bunkering is available at Kharg (marine fuel only)
EDP is available, vessel using EDP to cable ships figures within 12 h
Ensure that all exhaust uptakes are closed before berthing to prevent funnel sparking alongside
Propeller turning alongside berth to keep to minimum and be strictly watched
Vessels should have sufficient ballast onboard and stern trim of not more than 4 m for safe berthing maneuvering
Pilot boarding arrangements by means of pilot ladder and accommodation ladder
Is inert gas system operating with 02 content of below 8%
Is ship equipped with sufficient enclosed type fairleads suitable for ship-to-ship operation
Fire wires of sufficient length and adequate strength must be available for use
Local time is GMT +3.5 h for the period from 21st September to 21st March and GMT +4.5 h from 21st March to 21st September
Kharg Terminal telex numbers are 612007 & 612169 NMKG IR. Fax: +98 772 282 2982
ISM Certificate issuance/expiry date
Name approved type of bow fittings for SPM Moorings
Ship terminal final information exchange by VHF

Approach: Vessels approaching Kharg from the south should keep at least 4 km to the east of the Island. Vessels approaching from the north should keep to the west of the island (outside the restricted area)

Anchorage: Area A (Anchorage for Sea Island Jetty):
A1 29° 10.0' N; 50° 20.0' E
A2 29° 10.0' N; 50° 22.8' E
A3 29° 08.2' N; 50° 20.0' E
A4 29° 08.2' N; 50° 22.8' E
Area B (Anchorage for Dangerous Goods):
B1 29° 10.0' N; 50° 24.0' E
B2 29° 10.0' N; 50° 26.3' E
B3 29° 08.2' N; 50° 24.0' E
B4 29° 08.2' N; 50° 26.3' E
Area C (Anchorage for T Jetty):
C1 29° 13.5' N; 50° 24.0' E
C2 29° 13.5' N; 50° 27.3' E
C3 29° 11.0' N; 50° 24.0' E
C4 29° 11.0' N; 50° 17.3' E
Area D (Anchorage for Ship to Ship oil transhipment):
D1 29° 15.4' N; 50° 23.3' E
D2 29° 15.4' N; 50° 25.4' E
D3 29° 13.9' N; 50° 23.3' E
D4 29° 13.9' N; 50° 25.4' E

Pilotage: Compulsory

Radio Frequency: Initial contact should be made on VHF Channel 16 and then transfer to VHF Channel 12 for port operations

Weather: The oil loading jetty, being on the eastern side of the Island, is sheltered from the prevailing NW'ly winds, but exposed to the SE. The sea island berths are exposed to NW'ly and S'ly winds and swell, and are more frequently affected by unfavorable weather

Tides: Tide is mainly diurnal with mean range between LLW and HHW of 1.4 m, and an extreme range of 2.4 m. Chart Datum is 1.22 m below MSL. The tidal streams run approx parallel to the line of the Oil Loading Jetty with a max rate of about 1.25 knots

Principal Imports and Exports: Exports: Crude oil.

Working Hours: 24 h/day

Accommodation: In addition to the Oil Company's installations within the harbour limits, there is also a Sea Loading Oil Terminal and a Small Craft Harbour belonging to the IOOC, who also have oil installations on Kharg Island and offshore, to the SE of the Island. A combined LPG and Sulphur Loading Berth exists on the SE corner of Kharg Island

Name	Depth (m)	Remarks
Eastern Jetty (T Jetty)		See [1] below
Berth No.3 (outer)	21.3	Max 275 000 dwt. Three 16'' and two 12'' loading arms
Berth No.5 (outer)	21.3	Max 275 000 dwt. Three 16'' and two 12'' loading arms
Berth No.6 (inner)	20.4	Max 100 000 dwt. Three 16'' and two 12'' loading arms
Berth No.7 (outer)	18.3	Max 175 000 dwt. Three 16'' and two 12'' loading arms
Berth No.9 (outer)	17.4	Max 175 000 dwt. Three 16'' and two 12'' loading arms
Berth No.10 (inner)	17.7	Max 90 000 dwt. Five 12'' loading arms
Western Jetty (Sea Island)		Loading rates of up to 150 000 bbls/h
Berth No.11 (outer)	32	Max 500 000 dwt. Six 16'' loading arms
Berth No.12 (inner)	29.5	Max 300 000 dwt. Four 16'' and two 12'' loading arms
Berth No.15 (outer)	31	Max 500 000 dwt. Six 16'' loading arms

[1]*Eastern Jetty (T Jetty):* Loading rates of up to 54 000 bbls/h. All berths are fitted with chiksan hydraulic loading units for crude oil and bunker delivery

Bunkering: Bunkering facilities are installed at T Jetty and Sea Island berths and may be loaded up to a max rate of 1000 t/h. Bunkering normally commences before loading cargo
Seawaves Shipping Services Co. Ltd, Kharg Island, Iran, *Tel:* +98 77228 22311, *Fax:* +98 77228 22759, *Email:* kharg@seawaves-shipping.com, *Website:* www.seawaves-shipping.com
Iran Marine Services Co., IMS Building, 151 Mirdamad Boulevard, Tehran 19116, Iran, *Tel:* +98 21 2222 2249, *Fax:* +98 21 2222 3380, *Email:* info@imsiran.com, *Website:* www.imsiran.com
N.I.B.C. Iranian Oil Co., National Iranian Tanker Co. (N.I.T.C), 67 Shahid Atefy Street, Africa Avenue, Tehran 1917797163, Iran, *Tel:* +98 21 2222 2465, *Fax:* +98 21 2201 3392, *Email:* connserb@nitc.co.ir, *Website:* www.nitc.co.ir

Waste Reception Facilities: The dumping overside of garbage and refuse is prohibited in the harbour area. The local PSO have a garbage boat service, which is available upon request

Towage: A combination of privately and chartered tugs are available for operation. All tugs can be mobilized for fire fighting if required

Shipping Agents: GAC Shipping FZCO, Dubai Airport Free Zone, P O Box 54593, Dubai, United Arab Emirates, *Tel:* +971 4 299 0021, *Fax:* +971 4 299 0030, *Email:* gacfzco.dubai@gacworld.com, *Website:* www.gacworld.com Operations Manager: Thomas M. Jayabhai Mobile Tel: +971 50 6520677
Iran Gulf Shipping Services, Iran Gulf Building, 42 Babak Markazi, Africa Expressway, Tehran 19177, Iran, *Tel:* +98 21 8887 9050, *Fax:* +98 21 8879 9107, *Email:* operations@irgulf.net, *Website:* www.irangulf.com
Sea Mystries Shipping Co, Kharg Island, Iran, *Tel:* +98 77228 23418, *Fax:* +98 77228 22396, *Email:* info@seamystriesshipping.com, *Website:* www.seamystriesshipping.com
Seawaves Shipping Services Co. Ltd, Kharg Island, Iran, *Tel:* +98 77228 22311, *Fax:*

+98 77228 22759, *Email:* kharg@seawaves-shipping.com, *Website:* www.seawaves-shipping.com

Stevedoring Companies: Seawaves Shipping Services Co. Ltd, Kharg Island, Iran, *Tel:* +98 77228 22311, *Fax:* +98 77228 22759, *Email:* kharg@seawaves-shipping.com, *Website:* www.seawaves-shipping.com

Surveyors: Seawaves Shipping Services Co. Ltd, Kharg Island, Iran, *Tel:* +98 77228 22311, *Fax:* +98 77228 22759, *Email:* kharg@seawaves-shipping.com, *Website:* www.seawaves-shipping.com

Medical Facilities: There is a small hospital with clinic on Kharg Island for medical treatment to a certain extent. More serious cases may have to be sent by air to the mainland

Airport: Khark Airport

Lloyd's Agent: Iran Marine Services Co., Ayatollah Taleghani Boulevard, Across to Shohada Library, 3rd Floor Etemadi Building, Bandar Abbas, Iran, *Tel:* +98 761 222 6904, *Fax:* +98 761 222 0160, *Email:* imsba@ims-ir.com, *Website:* www.ims-ir.com

KHORRAMSHAHR

Lat 30° 20' N; Long 48° 10' E.

Admiralty Chart: 3845	**Admiralty Pilot:** 63
Time Zone: GMT +3.5 h	**UNCTAD Locode:** IR KHO

Principal Facilities:

Y	G	C		B		T	A

Authority: Khorramshahr Port Office, Khorramshahr, Iran, *Tel:* +98 632 422 4096, *Fax:* +98 632 422 2237, *Email:* ghanavati_khport@yahoo.com, *Website:* www.khport.ir

Officials: Manager: Gholamreza Ghanavati.
Harbour Master: Alireza Khojasteh, *Email:* akhojasteh@yahoo.com.

Port Security: ISPS compliant

Documentation: All valid classification and registration certificates

Approach: Owing to the Iran-Iraq war the channel is restricted to small vessels and barges. ETA at outer bar should be advised 72 h in advance to 'Port and Shipping Organisation' Khorramshahr Port Control

Anchorage: Anchorage for small vessels in the vicinity of Hartah Point in pos 30° 23' N; 48° 11' E

Pilotage: Compulsory for all vessels who should send ETA 24 h prior to arrival at Kafka Lt. buoy (29° 50.21' N; 48° 46.52' E) where pilot boards

Radio Frequency: VHF Channel 16

Tides: Tidal range 3.4 m

Maximum Vessel Dimensions: 20 000 dwt

Principal Imports and Exports: Imports: Electronic products, Furniture. Exports: Construction materials, Minerals, Steel products.

Working Hours: 12 h/day (can be extended when necessary)

Accommodation:

Name	Length (m)	Draught (m)	Remarks
Khorramshahr			
Berth No.1	126	6	General cargo
Berth No's 2-4	860	9	General cargo
Berth No's 5-9	180	6	Containers
Berth No.10 (chahar post - quay)	180	6	General cargo
Berth No.11 (chahar post - quay)	180	6	General cargo
Berth No.12 (chahar post - quay)	180	6	General cargo
Berth No.13 (chahar post - quay)	180	6	General cargo
Berth No.14	260	3	
Berth No.15	100	5	Passengers

Storage:

Location	Open (m²)	Covered (m²)
Khorramshahr	341827	125600

Mechanical Handling Equipment: Seventeen light cranes up to 30 t cap, six heavy duty cranes of 30-100 t cap, two super heavy duty cranes up to 100 t cap, two gadwall cranes of 100 t cap, four rail cranes and seven reach stackers

Bunkering: Available

Towage: Four tugs available up to 1500 hp

Shipping Agents: GAC Shipping FZCO, Dubai Airport Free Zone, P O Box 54593, Dubai, United Arab Emirates, *Tel:* +971 4 299 0021, *Fax:* +971 4 299 0030, *Email:*

Key to Principal Facilities:—				
A=Airport	**C**=Containers	**G**=General Cargo	**P**=Petroleum	**R**=Ro/Ro	**Y**=Dry Bulk
B=Bunkers	**D**=Dry Dock	**L**=Cruise	**Q**=Other Liquid Bulk	**T**=Towage (where available from port)	

gacfzco.dubai@gacworld.com, *Website:* www.gacworld.com Operations Manager: Thomas M. Jayabhai Mobile Tel: +971 50 6520677

Iran Gulf Shipping Services, Iran Gulf Building, 42 Babak Markazi, Africa Expressway, Tehran 19177, Iran, *Tel:* +98 21 8887 9050, *Fax:* +98 21 8879 9107, *Email:* operations@irgulf.net, *Website:* www.irangulf.com

Sea Mystries Shipping Co, Khorramshahr, Iran, *Tel:* +98 632 422 0791, *Fax:* +98 632 422 9432, *Email:* info@seamystriesshipping.com, *Website:* www.seamystriesshipping.com

Stevedoring Companies: Kaveh Marine & Port Services, Khorramshahr, Iran, *Tel:* +98 632 422 8228, *Fax:* +98 632 422 9129, *Email:* khorramshahr@kavehco.com, *Website:* www.kavehco.com

Medical Facilities: Available

Airport: Abadan, 15 km

Railway: Regular rail services available

Development: Six new berths have become operational with a total length of 864 m and average draught of 9 m

Lloyd's Agent: Iran Marine Services Co., Ayatollah Taleghani Boulevard, Across to Shohada Library, 3rd Floor Etemadi Building, Bandar Abbas, Iran, *Tel:* +98 761 222 6904, *Fax:* +98 761 222 0160, *Email:* imsba@ims-ir.com, *Website:* www.ims-ir.com

KISH ISLAND

Lat 26° 33' N; Long 54° 2' E.

| **Admiralty Chart:** 2887 | **Admiralty Pilot:** 63 |
| **Time Zone:** GMT +3.5 h | **UNCTAD Locode:** IR KIH |

Principal Facilities:

			G								

Radio Frequency: VHF Channel 16

Accommodation:

Name	Remarks
Kish Island	Consists of one jetty 600 m long which can handle three small vessels simultaneously

Mechanical Handling Equipment: Cranes and forklifts available

Shipping Agents: GAC Shipping FZCO, Dubai Airport Free Zone, P O Box 54593, Dubai, United Arab Emirates, *Tel:* +971 4 299 0021, *Fax:* +971 4 299 0030, *Email:* gacfzco.dubai@gacworld.com, *Website:* www.gacworld.com Operations Manager: Thomas M. Jayabhai Mobile Tel: +971 50 6520677

Lloyd's Agent: Iran Marine Services Co., Ayatollah Taleghani Boulevard, Across to Shohada Library, 3rd Floor Etemadi Building, Bandar Abbas, Iran, *Tel:* +98 761 222 6904, *Fax:* +98 761 222 0160, *Email:* imsba@ims-ir.com, *Website:* www.ims-ir.com

LAVAN ISLAND

Lat 26° 47' N; Long 53° 20' E.

| **Admiralty Chart:** 3409 | **Admiralty Pilot:** 63 |
| **Time Zone:** GMT +3.5 h | **UNCTAD Locode:** IR LVP |

Principal Facilities:

P						B		A

Authority: Iranian Offshore Oil Co. (IOOC), 339 Shahid Beheshti Avenue, Tehran, Iran, *Tel:* +98 21 8871 4102, *Fax:* +98 21 8871 7420

Port Security: ISPS compliant

Pre-Arrival Information: Vessels should send ETA 96 h and 48 h in advance by Fax: +98 21 871 6345 (Production & Planning and Export Co-ordination, attention Lavan Marine)

Documentation: Crew and passenger list (5 copies), stores list (2 copies), bonded stores list (2 copies), clear bill of health from last port (1 copy), bills of lading (4 copies), manifests (6 copies)

Approach: Vessels should approach from the S which is open and free of dangers

Anchorage: Anchorage is E of the Oil Loading Dock at 53° 22' E

Pilotage: Compulsory for all vessels. Vessels should await the Berthing Master 2 nautical miles SE of the Oil Loading Terminal

Radio Frequency: VHF Channel 12

Weather: Prevailing NE and SW winds

Tides: Mean range of 1.06 m, extreme range of 1.67 m and an extreme height of 2.13 m above CD

Working Hours: 24 h/day

Accommodation:

Name	Depth (m)	Remarks
Lavan Island		Two-berth jetty available with an overall length of 378 m
No.1 Outer Berth	20	See [1] below
No.2 Inner Berth	18	See [2] below
SBM	56	See [3] below

[1]*No.1 Outer Berth:* Max 225 000 dwt. Export of crude oil. Four 26" loading arms can transfer oil to tankers at rate of 52 000 bbls/h

[2]*No.2 Inner Berth:* Max 70 000 dwt. Export of refined products of the Lavan Refining Complex including gas oil, oil and furnace oil. One 16" loading arm and one 8" loading arm transfers oil products to tankers at rate of 500 t/h

[3]*SBM:* In pos 26° 45.6' N; 53° 20.8' E. Max 300 000 dwt. Loading rate of 40 000-50 000 bbls/h. Berthing during daylight hours only with unberthing 24 h/day. Vessels must be equipped with a 16" floating pipe

Storage: Only shore tank storage facilities for import and export of petroleum product fuel and crude oil

Bunkering: Iran Marine Services Co., IMS Building, 151 Mirdamad Boulevard, Tehran 19116, Iran, *Tel:* +98 21 2222 2249, *Fax:* +98 21 2222 3380, *Email:* info@imsiran.com, *Website:* www.imsiran.com

N.I.B.C. Iranian Oil Co., National Iranian Tanker Co. (N.I.T.C), 67 Shahid Atefy Street, Africa Avenue, Tehran 1917797163, Iran, *Tel:* +98 21 2222 2465, *Fax:* +98 21 2201 3392, *Email:* connserb@nitc.co.ir, *Website:* www.nitc.co.ir – *Grades:* FO; GO

Shipping Agents: GAC Shipping FZCO, Dubai Airport Free Zone, P O Box 54593, Dubai, United Arab Emirates, *Tel:* +971 4 299 0021, *Fax:* +971 4 299 0030, *Email:* gacfzco.dubai@gacworld.com, *Website:* www.gacworld.com Operations Manager: Thomas M. Jayabhai Mobile Tel: +971 50 6520677

Iran Gulf Shipping Services, Iran Gulf Building, 42 Babak Markazi, Africa Expressway, Tehran 19177, Iran, *Tel:* +98 21 8887 9050, *Fax:* +98 21 8879 9107, *Email:* operations@irgulf.net, *Website:* www.irangulf.com

Medical Facilities: The company operates a small clinic on the island for emergencies only

Airport: Lavan Airport

Lloyd's Agent: Iran Marine Services Co., Ayatollah Taleghani Boulevard, Across to Shohada Library, 3rd Floor Etemadi Building, Bandar Abbas, Iran, *Tel:* +98 761 222 6904, *Fax:* +98 761 222 0160, *Email:* imsba@ims-ir.com, *Website:* www.ims-ir.com

NOVSHEHR

alternate name, see Now Shahr

NOW SHAHR

Lat 36° 38' N; Long 51° 30' E.

| **Admiralty Chart:** - | **Admiralty Pilot:** - |
| **Time Zone:** GMT +3.5 h | **UNCTAD Locode:** IR NSH |

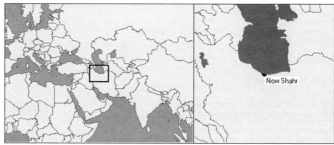

Now Shahr

Principal Facilities:

P	Q	Y	G	C	R		B		T	A

Authority: Golestan & Mazandaran Provinces Port & Shipping, Ferdosi Street, Now Shahr, Iran, *Tel:* +98 191 323 3031, *Fax:* +98 191 325 0982, *Email:* pouryazdan@nowshahrport.ir, *Website:* www.nowshahrport.ir

Officials: Director General: Seyed Nabi Saidpour.

Port Security: ISPS compliant

Documentation: Bills of lading, cargo manifest, stowage plan, crew list, valid classification and registration certificates

Approach: The dredged channel 200 m wide in depth of 6 m accommodates vessels up to 4000 dwt

Anchorage: Available in following positions:
36° 42' N; 51° 32' E in depth of 20 m
36° 42' N; 51° 34' E in depth of 20 m
36° 40' N; 51° 34' E in depth of 30 m
36° 40' N; 51° 32' E in depth of 30 m

Pilotage: Compulsory. Pilot boards at anchorage

Radio Frequency: VHF Channel 16 (calling) and 13, 14 & 15 (working)

Principal Imports and Exports: Imports: Chemical products, General cargo, Oil products. Exports: Fruit & vegetables.

Working Hours: 0650-1345, 1345-2045

Accommodation:

Name	Length (m)	Depth (m)	Remarks
Now Shahr			
East Wharf	300	5	Two berths for general cargo
West Wharf	360	4.5–5	Two berths for general cargo
Oil Berth	150	5	Dolphin berth
Ro/ro Berth	12	5	

Storage:

Location	Open (m²)	Covered (m²)	Sheds / Warehouses
Now Shahr	125362	27412	7

Mechanical Handling Equipment:

Location	Type	Qty
Now Shahr	Mult-purp. Cranes	24
Now Shahr	Forklifts	27

Bunkering: Available

Towage: Tugs available up to 1000 hp

Shipping Agents: Iran Gulf Shipping Services, Iran Gulf Building, 42 Babak Markazi, Africa Expressway, Tehran 19177, Iran, *Tel:* +98 21 8887 9050, *Fax:* +98 21 8879 9107, *Email:* operations@irgulf.net, *Website:* www.irangulf.com

Surveyors: Iran Group of Surveyors (IGS), No.4, 21st Street, Sanaii Street, Ostad Motahari Avenue, Tehran 15866, Iran, *Tel:* +98 21 8882 4072, *Fax:* +98 21 8882 4076, *Email:* info@igs-iran.com, *Website:* www.igs-iran.com
Rah Avaran Inspection Co., 151 Mirdamad Boulevard, Tehran, Iran, *Tel:* +98 21 8808 8071, *Fax:* +98 21 8808 8591

Medical Facilities: Available

Airport: Now Shahr, 3 km

Lloyd's Agent: Irano-German Insurance Services (Private Co. Ltd), Avenue Bozorgmehr No.62, 3rd Floor, Tehran 14168-44984, Iran, *Tel:* +98 21 6646 8495, *Fax:* +98 21 6640 2277, *Email:* igis@parsonline.net, *Website:* www.igis-surveyor.com

QESHM ISLAND

Admiralty Chart: 2887
Admiralty Pilot: 63
Time Zone: GMT +3.5 h
UNCTAD Locode: IR QSH

Principal Facilities:

Q	Y	G		R					

Accommodation:

Name	Remarks
Kaveh	See [1] below
Bahman	See [2] below
Fajr Jetty	See [3] below
Dargahan	See [4] below

[1]*Kaveh:* Located in the N of Qeshm Island near the Northern Industrial Zone. The port provides services for vessels up to 100 000 dwt handling general cargo and bulk & liquid materials. The jetty consists of a 230 m access bridge and 290 m of quay with a 19 m depth and a 14 m depth at LW in the north and south fronts of the jetty respectively
[2]*Bahman:* Located in the eastern section of the island and is one of the most important ports for the transport of cargo and passengers. It is adjoined by several service facilities in an area of 24 ha. The length of the jetty is 170 m
[3]*Fajr Jetty:* This jetty has a length of 520 m and is located at kilometer marker 4 of the Qeshm Dargahan highway. Its main purpose is to serve commuters from the mainland and the loading and unloading of construction materials
[4]*Dargahan:* Located in the N of Qeshm Island. The ports function is to serve Dargahan and nearby villages as a general cargo and passenger terminal. The jetty area is 7000 m2, having a 90 m length quay wall with a depth of 6.2 m at LT. The jetty has east and west facing ramps serving a variety of SBM's located offshore. The jetty can accommodate general cargo vessels of 3000-4000 dwt

Shipping Agents: GAC Shipping FZCO, Dubai Airport Free Zone, P O Box 54593, Dubai, United Arab Emirates, *Tel:* +971 4 299 0021, *Fax:* +971 4 299 0030, *Email:* gacfzco.dubai@gacworld.com, *Website:* www.gacworld.com Operations Manager: Thomas M. Jayabhai Mobile Tel: +971 50 6520677

Lloyd's Agent: Iran Marine Services Co., Ayatollah Taleghani Boulevard, Across to Shohada Library, 3rd Floor Etemadi Building, Bandar Abbas, Iran, *Tel:* +98 761 222 6904, *Fax:* +98 761 222 0160, *Email:* imsba@ims-ir.com, *Website:* www.ims-ir.com

RAS BAHREGAN TERMINAL

Lat 29° 47' N; Long 50° 11' E.

Admiralty Chart: 2884
Admiralty Pilot: 63
Time Zone: GMT +3.5 h
UNCTAD Locode: IR RBA

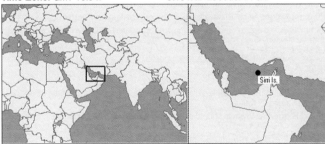
Ras Bahregan Term.

Principal Facilities:

P								T	

Authority: Iranian Offshore Oil Co. (IOOC), 339 Shahid Beheshti Avenue, Tehran, Iran, *Tel:* +98 21 8871 4102, *Fax:* +98 21 8871 7420

Pre-Arrival Information: Vessels should send ETA 96 h and 48 h in advance by Fax: +98 21 871 6345 (Production & Planning and Export Co-ordination, attention Bahregan Marine)

Documentation: All valid classification and registration certificates, crew list (5 copies), last port clearance (original + 2 copies), radio classification certificate, nett tonnage certificate, maritime declaration of health (3 copies), voyage list, vaccination list, crew personnal effects declaration, stores list

Approach: Vessels should wait for berthing master approx 2 miles off the SBM

Anchorage: Anchorage may be obtained by tankers awaiting mooring master, 2 nautical miles SW of SBM

Pilotage: Compulsory for all vessels. Vessels should await the Berthing Master 2 nautical miles S of the Oil Loading Terminal

Radio Frequency: VHF Channel 11

Weather: Prevailing NW and SE winds

Working Hours: 24 h/day, 7 days a week

Accommodation:

Name	Remarks
Ras Bahregan	See [1] below

[1]*Ras Bahregan:* One single buoy mooring. Anchorage suggested is about 1.6 km from this. Tankers accommodated up to 250 000 dwt, min depth 24 m. Loading rate is approx 6000 t/h

Towage: Two tugs available of 450-2500 hp

Shipping Agents: Iran Gulf Shipping Services, Iran Gulf Building, 42 Babak Markazi, Africa Expressway, Tehran 19177, Iran, *Tel:* +98 21 8887 9050, *Fax:* +98 21 8879 9107, *Email:* operations@irgulf.net, *Website:* www.irangulf.com

Lloyd's Agent: Iran Marine Services Co., Ayatollah Taleghani Boulevard, Across to Shohada Library, 3rd Floor Etemadi Building, Bandar Abbas, Iran, *Tel:* +98 761 222 6904, *Fax:* +98 761 222 0160, *Email:* imsba@ims-ir.com, *Website:* www.ims-ir.com

SHAHID BEHESHTI

alternate name, see Chah Bahar

SIRRI ISLAND

Lat 25° 54' N; Long 54° 33' E.

Admiralty Chart: 3409
Admiralty Pilot: 63
Time Zone: GMT +3.5 h
UNCTAD Locode: IR SXI

Sirri Is.

Principal Facilities:

P								T	A

Authority: Iranian Offshore Oil Co. (IOOC), 339 Shahid Beheshti Avenue, Tehran, Iran, *Tel:* +98 21 8871 4102, *Fax:* +98 21 8871 7420

Port Security: ISPS compliant

Pre-Arrival Information: Vessels should send ETA 96 h and 48 h in advance by Fax: +98 21 871 6345 (Production & Planning and Export Co-ordination, attention Sirri Marine)

Documentation: All valid classification and registration certificates, crew list (5 copies), last port clearance (original + 2 copies), radio classification certificate, nett tonnage certificate, maritime declaration of health (3 copies), voyage list, vaccination list, crew personnal effects declaration, stores list

---

Key to Principal Facilities:—
A=Airport   **C**=Containers   **G**=General Cargo   **P**=Petroleum   **R**=Ro/Ro   **Y**=Dry Bulk
B=Bunkers   **D**=Dry Dock   **L**=Cruise   **Q**=Other Liquid Bulk   **T**=Towage (where available from port)

Anchorage: Anchorage area is situated 2 nautical miles E of the loading dock. Vessels should keep clear of a runway and pipeline in the anchorage area
Prohibited Anchorage: entry into area bounded by lines joining the following positions, and anchorage in it, is prohibited, (a) 25° 55' N; 54° 33.1' E (b) 25° 55' N; 54° 34.6' E (c) 25° 52' N; 54° 34.6' E (d) 25° 52' N; 54° 31.1' E

Pilotage: Compulsory for all vessels. Pilot boards in pos 25° 52.20' N; 54° 24.40' E

Radio Frequency: VHF Channel 16

Tides: Range of tide 1.0-1.5 m. Tidal streams run strongly at the loading platform making berthing difficult at times

Principal Imports and Exports: Exports: Crude oil.

Working Hours: 24 h/day

Accommodation:

Name	Remarks
Sirri Island	See [1] below

[1]Sirri Island: Crude oil loading jetty accommodating tankers up to 350 000 dwt. It has four loading arms, each capable of transferring up to 25 000 bbls/h

Towage: Two tugs of 4000 hp are available

Shipping Agents: GAC Shipping FZCO, Dubai Airport Free Zone, P O Box 54593, Dubai, United Arab Emirates, Tel: +971 4 299 0021, Fax: +971 4 299 0030, Email: gacfzco.dubai@gacworld.com, Website: www.gacworld.com Operations Manager: Thomas M. Jayabhai Mobile Tel: +971 50 6520677
Iran Gulf Shipping Services, Iran Gulf Building, 42 Babak Markazi, Africa Expressway, Tehran 19177, Iran, Tel: +98 21 8887 9050, Fax: +98 21 8879 9107, Email: operations@irgulf.net, Website: www.irangulf.com

Medical Facilities: Available in emergencies

Airport: Sirri Island Airport

Lloyd's Agent: Iran Marine Services Co., Ayatollah Taleghani Boulevard, Across to Shohada Library, 3rd Floor Etemadi Building, Bandar Abbas, Iran, Tel: +98 761 222 6904, Fax: +98 761 222 0160, Email: imsba@ims-ir.com, Website: www.ims-ir.com

SOROOSH TERMINAL

Lat 29° 2' N; Long 49° 28' E.

Admiralty Chart: 2882/2884
Admiralty Pilot: 63
Time Zone: GMT +3.5 h
UNCTAD Locode: IR CYT

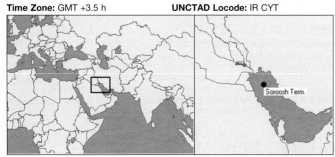
Soroosh Term.

Principal Facilities:

P							T	

Authority: Iranian Offshore Oil Co. (IOOC), 339 Shahid Beheshti Avenue, Tehran, Iran, Tel: +98 21 8871 4102, Fax: +98 21 8871 7420

Port Security: ISPS compliant

Pre-Arrival Information: Vessels must send pre-arrival information to the Terminal at least 7 days prior to accepted date range or ETA, whichever is earlier. Henceforth vessels should send ETA 96 h and 48 h in advance by Fax: +98 21 871 6345 (Production & Planning and Export Co-ordination, attention Bahregan Marine). ETA should also be advised to the Terminal 72 h, 48 h and 24 h prior to arrival

Documentation: All valid classification and registration certificates

Anchorage: The designated anchorage area is situated SE of the FSU and bounded by the following co-ordinates:
28° 58' N; 49° 29' E
28° 58' N; 49° 31' E
29° 00' N; 49° 29' E
29° 00' N; 49° 31' E

Pilotage: Compulsory for all vessels. Berthing Master boards 2 nautical miles SE of the Oil Loading Terminal

Radio Frequency: Vessels should commence calling on VHF Channel 12, 4 h before arrival

Weather: Prevailing NW and SE winds

Tides: Tidal range 1.8-2.4 m

Working Hours: 24 h/day

Accommodation:

Name	Remarks
Soroosh Terminal	See [1] below

[1]Soroosh Terminal: There are six steel mooring buoys. Safest approach from the SE. Buoys are not lighted. Max cap 300 000 dwt. Vessels loaded by submarine pipeline and one hose at one loading berth in approx 42.67 m of water. The FSU 'Soorena' is moored in pos 29° 01' N; 49° 27' E

Towage: Tugs available

Shipping Agents: GAC Shipping FZCO, Dubai Airport Free Zone, P O Box 54593, Dubai, United Arab Emirates, Tel: +971 4 299 0021, Fax: +971 4 299 0030, Email:

gacfzco.dubai@gacworld.com, Website: www.gacworld.com Operations Manager: Thomas M. Jayabhai Mobile Tel: +971 50 6520677
Iran Gulf Shipping Services, Iran Gulf Building, 42 Babak Markazi, Africa Expressway, Tehran 19177, Iran, Tel: +98 21 8887 9050, Fax: +98 21 8879 9107, Email: operations@irgulf.net, Website: www.irangulf.com

Lloyd's Agent: Iran Marine Services Co., Ayatollah Taleghani Boulevard, Across to Shohada Library, 3rd Floor Etemadi Building, Bandar Abbas, Iran, Tel: +98 761 222 6904, Fax: +98 761 222 0160, Email: imsba@ims-ir.com, Website: www.ims-ir.com

SOUTH PARS TERMINAL

harbour area, see under Asaluyeh Terminal

IRAQ

AL BASRA TERMINAL

Lat 29° 41' N; Long 48° 48' E.

Admiralty Chart: 1265
Admiralty Pilot: 63
Time Zone: GMT +3 h
UNCTAD Locode: IQ MAB

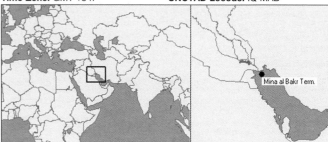
Mina al Bakr Term.

Principal Facilities:

P						B	T	

Authority: State Oil Marketing Organisation, Ministry of Oil Building, Baghdad, Iraq, Email: dg@iraqports.com

Pre-Arrival Information: Vessels should send ETA to the Terminal 72 h, 48 h and 24 h prior to arrival stating the following information:
a) vessel's name and call sign
b) port of registry
c) flag
d) IMO number and official number
e) nrt and gt
f) loa and beam
g) master's name
h) crew list
i) destination
j) purpose of voyage
k) ISPS level
l) ISSG number

Approach: There is a warning zone extending 3000 m from the outer edge of the terminal structure, in all directions, creating a racetrack shape 7030 m long by 6107 m wide, oriented northwest to southeast, centred on the terminal
There is an exclusion zone extending 2000 m from the outer edges of the terminal structure in all directions. Only tankers and support vessels authorized by terminal operators or Coalition Maritime Security Forces are allowed to enter the exclusion zone

Pilotage: Compulsory for all vessels over 15.85 m draft. Vessels must contact the Maritime Security Forces (MSF) on VHF Channel 16 within a 5 nautical mile radius of the Checkpoint (29° 35' 00" N; 48° 53' 00" E). Vessels should also contact the Terminal on VHF Channel 16, 5 h before arrival at the Fairway Light Buoy
Pilot boards in pos 29° 20' 00" N; 49° 03' 00" E (in the vicinity of the Fairway Light Buoy)

Radio Frequency: VHF Channels 12 and 16

Tides: Max tidal range of 3.2 m

Maximum Vessel Dimensions: 365 m loa, 350 000 dwt, 21 m departure draft

Accommodation:

Name	Remarks
Al Basra Terminal	See [1] below

[1]Al Basra Terminal: Operated by South Oil Company of Basrah
Supplied by a 48" undersea pipeline from the southernmost tip of the Al Faw Peninsula, the terminal has four berths (No's 1 and 3 on the east side and no's 2 and 4 on the west side) capable of handling very large carrier type vessels and offloading 300 000-400 000 bbls/day to each berth

Bunkering: Available

Towage: Three tugs of 4500 hp each are always available for berthing and unberthing

Lloyd's Agent: Inchcape Shipping Services (ISS), Business Center, Port Administration Building, Umm Qasr New Port, Umm Qasr, Iraq, Tel: +964 40 761516, Fax: +964 40 761516, Email: inchcape.ummqasr@iss-shipping.com, Website: www.iss-shipping.com

AL FAW

alternate name, see Fao

FAO

Lat 29° 59' N; Long 48° 28' E.

Admiralty Chart: 3842/3843   **Admiralty Pilot:** 63
Time Zone: GMT +3 h   **UNCTAD Locode:** IQ FAO
This port is no longer open to commercial shipping

KHOR AL AMAYA TERMINAL

Lat 29° 47' N; Long 48° 48' E.

Admiralty Chart: 1265/135   **Admiralty Pilot:** 63
Time Zone: GMT +3 h   **UNCTAD Locode:** IQ KHA

Principal Facilities:

P							T		

Authority: State Oil Marketing Organisation, Ministry of Oil Building, Baghdad, Iraq, *Email:* dg@iraqports.com

Pre-Arrival Information: Vessels should send ETA to the Terminal 72 h, 48 h and 24 h prior to arrival stating the following information:
a) vessel's name and call sign
b) port of registry
c) flag
d) IMO number and official number
e) nrt and gt
f) loa and beam
g) master's name
h) crew list
i) destination
j) purpose of voyage
k) ISPS level
l) ISSG number

Approach: There is a warning zone extending 3000 m from the outer edge of the terminal structure, in all directions, creating a racetrack shape 6990 m long by 6107 m wide, oriented northwest to southeast, centred on the terminal
There is an exclusion zone extending 2000 m from the outer edges of the terminal structure in all directions. Only tankers and support vessels authorized by terminal operators or Coalition Maritime Security Forces are allowed to enter the exclusion zone

Pilotage: Compulsory for all vessels. Vessels must contact the Maritime Security Forces (MSF) on VHF Channel 16 within a 5 nautical mile radius of the Checkpoint (29° 35' 00" N; 48° 53' 00" E)
Pilot boards in pos 29° 20' 00" N; 49° 03' 00" E

Radio Frequency: VHF Channels 16 and 12

Accommodation:

Name	Remarks
Khor al Amaya Terminal	See [1] below

[1]*Khor al Amaya Terminal:* Operated by South Oil Company of Basrah
Berth No's 7 and 8 are now operating. The two rehabilitated berths have a total loading cap of 200 000-300 000 bbls/day. The sailing draught is 17 m

Towage: Three sea-going tugs of about 4000 hp each are always available for berthing and unberthing

Lloyd's Agent: Inchcape Shipping Services (ISS), Business Center, Port Administration Building, Umm Qasr New Port, Umm Qasr, Iraq, *Tel:* +964 40 761516, *Fax:* +964 40 761516, *Email:* inchcape.ummqasr@iss-shipping.com, *Website:* www.iss-shipping.com

KHOR AL ZUBAIR

harbour area, see under Umm Qasr

MINA AL BAKR TERMINAL

former name, see Al Basra Terminal

UMM QASR

Lat 30° 2' N; Long 47° 57' E.

Admiralty Chart: 1228/1235   **Admiralty Pilot:** 63
Time Zone: GMT +3 h   **UNCTAD Locode:** IQ UQR

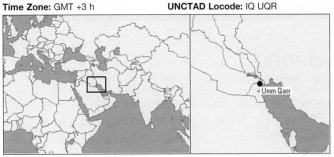

Principal Facilities:

Y	G	C	R		B		T	A

Authority: Iraq Port Authority, Umm Qasr, Iraq, *Email:* ummqasrport@iraqports.com, *Website:* www.iraqports.com

Pre-Arrival Information: Vessels bound for Umm Qasr or Khor al Zubair carrying commercial or humanitarian cargo should contact Umm Qasr Port on VHF Channels 16 or 12 for the latest details concerning navigation in the Khawr Abd Allah. Vessels should pass their ETA 48 h, 24 h and 12 h prior to arrival and should also report inward-bound and outward-bound when passing buoys 23 and 24

Approach: The port is situated at the S end of the Khor Zubair where it joins the Khor Abdullah. The sea approach to Umm Qasr is some 103 km in length along the Khor Abdullah, commencing in deep waters off the Persian Gulf near the mouth of the Shatt al Arab

Pilotage: Compulsory. Sea pilots board near the Al Bakr Terminal in pos 29° 41' N; 48° 48' E and No.2 Lt Buoy. Harbour pilots board in the vicinity of No.36 Buoy in pos 30° 00.04' N; 47° 58.00' E

Radio Frequency: River Pilots on VHF Channels 16 and 14. Harbour Pilots and Port Radio on VHF Channels 16 and 12

Weather: SW and NE monsoons

Accommodation:

Name	Remarks
Umm Qasr	See [1] below
Khor al Zubair	See [2] below

[1]*Umm Qasr:* Commercial operations have restarted with all 21 berths open to shipping. Types of cargo handled at the port include rice, wheat, flour, vegetable oil, sugar, cement, and ro/ro and container cargoes
[2]*Khor al Zubair:* Email: khuralzubarport@iraqports.com. Located approx 8 km N of Umm Qasr and can be reached via a 10 km long channel with min depth of 10 m that can take a Panamax size vessel of 240 m loa. The port comprises twelve berths totaling 3000 m. Berths 1-8 are used for dry cargo and containers and Berths 9-12 are used for oil/wet cargo. Part of Berth 7 and all of Berth 8 have been dredged to a depth of 11 m. There are no container gantry cranes and all container vessels need to be geared to facilitate cargo discharge. The container yard has a stacking cap of up to 10 000 TEU's. The port has access to mobile shore cranes for break bulk cargo handling. There are silos behind Berths 4-7 plus a conveyor system for fertiliser export

Bunkering: Monjasa A/S, Strevelinsvej 4, 7000 Fredericia, Denmark, *Tel:* +45 70 26 02 30, *Fax:* +45 70 26 02 33, *Email:* denmark@monjasa.com, *Website:* www.monjasa.com

Towage: Two harbour tugs are presently operational

Shipping Agents: Inchcape Shipping Services (ISS), Business Center, Port Administration Building, Umm Qasr New Port, Umm Qasr, Iraq, *Tel:* +964 40 761516, *Fax:* +964 40 761516, *Email:* inchcape.ummqasr@iss-shipping.com, *Website:* www.iss-shipping.com

Surveyors: Middle East Shipping Surveys Co., P O Box 2415, Aqaba 77110, Jordan, *Tel:* +962 3 201 6590, *Fax:* +962 3 201 6592, *Email:* midsurveys@index.com.jo Manager: Ali Al-Aqrabawi

Airport: Basrah Airport

Key to Principal Facilities:—				
A=Airport	**C**=Containers	**G**=General Cargo	**P**=Petroleum	**R**=Ro/Ro	**Y**=Dry Bulk
B=Bunkers	**D**=Dry Dock	**L**=Cruise	**Q**=Other Liquid Bulk	**T**=Towage (where available from port)	

Lloyd's Agent: Inchcape Shipping Services (ISS), Business Center, Port Administration Building, Umm Qasr New Port, Umm Qasr, Iraq, *Tel:* +964 40 761516, *Fax:* +964 40 761516, *Email:* inchcape.ummqasr@iss-shipping.com, *Website:* www.iss-shipping.com

ISRAEL

ASHDOD

Lat 31° 49' N; Long 34° 38' E.

Admiralty Chart: 1591	**Admiralty Pilot:** 49
Time Zone: GMT +2 h	**UNCTAD Locode:** IL ASH

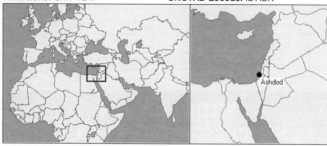

Principal Facilities:

| | Y | G | C | R | L | B | | T | A |

CARMEL INTERNATIONAL SHIPPING SERVICES LTD.

Carmel International Shipping Services (1992) Ltd

51 Hameginim Avenue, PO Box 1472, Haifa, 31014 Israel

Tel: +972 4 8545454   Fax: +972 4 8515886

Email: charter@carmelship.co.il
Website: www.carmelship.co.il

ASHDOD * HAIFA * EILAT

AGENCY * SHIPS' OPERATION * CHARTERING * BROKERAGE

PERCO SEAS LTD.

Sole Representatives of "Seafreight Shipping Ltd." - London
CONVENTIONAL, CONTAINER, BULK, CRUISE VESSELS, TANKERS
E-mail: percosea@netvision.net.il
Web: www.perco-seas.com

HAIFA HEAD OFFICE:	ASHDOD BRANCH:	EILAT BRANCH:
19, Ben Gurion Avenue	5 Hatayelet St.	Port Area
POB 9158	Tel: +972-52-3213883	Tel: +972-52-3783960
Tel: +972-4-8535111	Fax: +972-3-7252718	Fax: +972-3-7252718
Fax: +972-4-8535353		

Authority: Israel Ports Development & Assets Co., Ashdod Port Co. Ltd, P O Box 9001, 77191 Ashdod, Israel, *Tel:* +972 8 851 7600, *Fax:* +972 8 851 7641, *Email:* sharong@ashdodport.co.il, *Website:* www.ashdodport.co.il

Officials: Chief Executive Officer: Shuki Sagis, *Email:* shukis@ashdodport.co.il. Marketing Manager: Sharon Gilat. Operations Manager: Denny Elyssi, *Email:* dennye@ashdodport.co.il.

Port Security: ISPS compliant. Container Security Initiative (CSI) designated port

Pre-Arrival Information: All vessels bound for Israeli ports are required to transmit a 'IMOT Report' when 100 nautical miles off the Israeli coast. This report must be sent to the Israeli Navy by Fax: +972 3 606 4567 or Email: shipping@idf.gov.il. The Israeli Navy will confirm receipt by Inmarsat C
The report should state the following information:
a) vessel's name (and previous name)
b) call sign
c) flag and port of registry
d) IMO number
e) MMSI
f) satellite telephone and telex numbers
g) year of build
h) gt
i) type of vessel and cargo on board

j) number of crew and passengers
k) agents name, telephone and fax
l) name of owner and operator
m) is vessel holding a valid ISPS certificate
n) security level on board (1, 2 or 3)
o) last and previous port, date of departure
p) port of destination
q) position, course and speed
r) ETA
s) crew list (including name, rank, nationality, residence (country and city), age, gender, seniority in company, date of signing-on passport and SB number
All vessels should report to the Israeli Navy on VHF Channel 16 when 25 nautical miles off the Israeli coast stating vessel's name and call sign, present position, course and speed and ETA

Anchorage: Anchorage area W of the port in depth of 22-29 m

Pilotage: Compulsory

Radio Frequency: Port Control: VHF Channels 12, 14, 16 and 17

Weather: Strong S-SW winds which may be dust laden occur during the winter months. Storms can be expected from December to March and are normally worse during January

Tides: Negligable

Traffic: 2007, 16 232 000 t of cargo handled, 808 700 TEU's

Working Hours: Sunday-Thursday: 0630-1430, 1500-2230, 2230-0530. Friday: 0630-1 h before Saturday entrance. Saturday: 2230-0530

Accommodation:

Name	Length (m)	Depth (m)	Remarks
Ashdod			
Pier 1	775	10	General cargo
Pier 3	624	10.5	General cargo
Pier 5	480	13.8	General cargo
Pier 7	485	12	Containers
Pier 9	438	13.8	Containers & general cargo
Pier 21	850	14	General cargo
Pier 23	600	15.5	Containers

Storage: Storage areas for containers, chilled cargoes, grain, sulphur, coal and vehicles. Bonded warehouses. Tank farm for the storage and supply of fuels

Mechanical Handling Equipment:

Location	Type	Qty
Ashdod	RTG's	24
Ashdod	Portal Cranes	25
Ashdod	Forklifts	123

Bunkering: United Petroleum Export Co. Ltd (UNEX), P O Box 1548, 5 Pal Yam Avenue, 33095 Haifa, Israel, *Tel:* +972 4 8678 291, *Fax:* +972 4 8678 290, *Email:* webmail@unex.co.il – *Grades:* HFO; IFO; MGO – *Notice:* 24 hours – *Delivery Mode:* barge, pipeline, truck

Waste Reception Facilities: Sludge and garbage disposal facilities available

Towage: Five sea-going tugs with fire fighting and salvage equipment; two of 30 t bollard pull, one of 35 t bollard pull and one with 45 t bollard pull

Repair & Maintenance: Workshops for minor repairs

Ship Chandlers: Layam Co. Ltd, P O Box 4048, Ashdod, Israel, *Tel:* +972 8 852 1330, *Fax:* +972 8 856 3104, *Email:* rachel_p@layam.com
Sakal Brothers Ltd, Warehouse No.301, Ashdod, Israel, *Tel:* +972 8 856 4628, *Fax:* +972 8 856 3749, *Email:* Amir-p@sakal.co.il

Shipping Agents: Dynamic Shipping Services, 3 Khayat Street, P O Box 33193, 31331 Haifa, Israel, *Tel:* +972 4 864 5745, *Fax:* +972 4 866 0361, *Email:* agency@dynamic-shipping.com, *Website:* www.dynamic-shipping.com General Manager: Zimi Cohen Email: zimi@dynamic-shipping.com
Allalouf & Co. Shipping Ltd, Rear Port Area, 3rd Floor, P O Box 4081, 31007 Ashdod, Israel, *Tel:* +972 8 851 3333, *Fax:* +972 8 852 1165, *Email:* avigelber@allalouf.com, *Website:* www.allalouf.com
Ardo Shipping Ltd, Offices Center Building 1, Port Area, P O Box 4018, 77140 Ashdod, Israel, *Tel:* +972 8 852 5226/9, *Fax:* +972 8 856 0943
Carmel International Shipping Services (1992) Ltd, 3 Habosem Street, P O Box 4020, 77140 Ashdod, Israel, *Tel:* +972 8 852 4811, *Fax:* +972 8 852 2719, *Email:* carmlash@carmelship.co.il
China Shipping (Israel) Agency Co Ltd, Zim Building Floor 1, 77140 Ashdod, Israel, *Tel:* +972 8 853 8866, *Fax:* +972 8 853 8877, *Email:* liluz@csisrael.com, *Website:* www.csisrael.com
Conmart Ltd, Offices Building, Room 423, P O Box 4102, 77140 Ashdod, Israel, *Tel:* +972 8 856 1255, *Fax:* +972 8 856 4193, *Email:* ashdod@conmart.co.il, *Website:* www.conmart.co.il
Coral Maritime Services Ltd, P O Box 4071, 77140 Ashdod, Israel, *Tel:* +972 8 852 0998, *Fax:* +972 8 852 0984, *Email:* ashdod@coral-maritime.co.il, *Website:* www.coral-maritime.co.il
M Dizengoff & Co. Ltd, P O Box 4005, 77140 Ashdod, Israel, *Tel:* +972 8 851 1341, *Fax:* +972 8 851 2308, *Email:* man@dizman-ash.zim.il
Gold Line Shipping Ltd, Oref Hanamal, 4th Floor, Ashdod, Israel, *Tel:* +972 8 852 8514, *Fax:* +972 8 853 0070, *Email:* levi@goldline-gls.com
Israel Scandinavian Maritime Agency Ltd, P O Box 4060, 77110 Ashdod, Israel, *Tel:* +972 8 856 0253, *Fax:* +972 8 856 0538, *Email:* commercial@israscan.co.il, *Website:* www.israscan.co.il
Mano Maritime Ltd, Mol Ha'Ir Building, Room 118, 11 Hamada Street, North Industrial Area P O Box 4043, 77140 Ashdod, Israel, *Tel:* +972 8 852 4011, *Fax:* +972 8 852 4820, *Email:* manoash@mano.co.il, *Website:* www.mano.co.il
Mediterranean Shipping Company, MSC (Israel) Ltd, Building No.3, Gate 3, 3rd Floor, Ha Bosem Street, P O Box 4039, 77104 Ashdod, Israel, *Tel:* +972 8 851 1200, *Fax:* +972 8 856 3945, *Email:* infoash@mscisr.com, *Website:* www.mscgva.ch
Mercury Shipping Agency Ltd, 3 Habosem Street, P O Box 12521, 77610 Ashdod, Israel, *Tel:* +972 8 856 0888, *Fax:* +972 8 856 0550
A.P. Moller-Maersk Group, Maersk Israel Ltd, 3 Habosem Street, 77610 Ashdod,

Israel, *Tel:* +972 8 862 8000, *Fax:* +972 8 862 8009, *Email:* asdmng@maersk.com, *Website:* www.maerskline.com
MSC Israel Ltd, Room 218/21, Building 2, Port Area, P O Box 4039, 77140 Ashdod, Israel, *Tel:* +972 8 856 4044, *Fax:* +972 8 856 3945, *Email:* infoashd@mayron.co.il
Packer Shipping Ltd, Ashdod rear Port Area, Ashdod, Israel, *Tel:* +972 8 853 4762, *Fax:* +972 8 856 0966, *Email:* ashdod@packer-shipping.co.il
Perco Seas Ltd, 5 Hatayelet Road, Ashdod, Israel, *Tel:* +972 4 853 5111, *Fax:* +972 4 853 5353, *Email:* percosea@netvision.net.il, *Website:* www.perco-seas.com
A. Rosenfeld Shipping Ltd, Agents Building 2, Suite 102, P O Box 4098, 77100 Ashdod, Israel, *Tel:* +972 8 853 1211, *Fax:* +972 8 853 1213, *Email:* ashdodport@rosenfeld.net, *Website:* www.rosenfeld.net
Seagull Maritime Ltd, 2nd Building, Port Area, Ashdod, Israel, *Tel:* +972 8 866 6537, *Email:* plan@seagull-maritime.com
Tiran Shipping Agencies 1997 Ltd, 3 Habosen Street, Building 3, 3rd Floor, Ashdod, Israel, *Tel:* +972 8 863 3133, *Fax:* +972 8 852 9912, *Email:* tiran_hfa@tiran.co.il, *Website:* www.tiran.co.il

Surveyors: Carmel International Shipping Services (1992) Ltd, 3 Habosem Street, P O Box 4020, 77140 Ashdod, Israel, *Tel:* +972 8 852 4811, *Fax:* +972 8 852 2719, *Email:* carmlash@carmelship.co.il
Galram Surveyors and Adjusters Ltd, P O Box 4094, Ashdod Port, 77140 Ashdod, Israel, *Tel:* +972 8 856 1634, *Fax:* +972 8 853 1325, *Email:* galram@galram.com, *Website:* www.galram.com

Medical Facilities: Hospital, 20 km from town

Airport: Ben Gurion International Airport, 30 km

Lloyd's Agent: Galram Surveyors and Adjusters Ltd, P O Box 4094, Ashdod Port, 77140 Ashdod, Israel, *Tel:* +972 8 856 1634, *Fax:* +972 8 853 1325, *Email:* galram@galram.com, *Website:* www.galram.com

ASHKELON

Lat 31° 38' N; Long 34° 31' E.

Admiralty Chart: 1591	**Admiralty Pilot:** 49
Time Zone: GMT +2 h	**UNCTAD Locode:** IL AKL

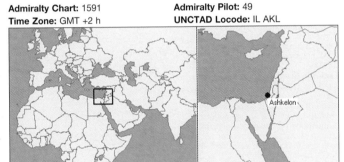

Principal Facilities:

P	Q						A

Authority: Ashkelon Terminal Eilat-Ashkelon Pipeline Co. Ltd, P O Box 801, 78101 Ashkelon, Israel, *Tel:* +972 8 674 0601, *Fax:* +972 8 674 0659, *Email:* eapc@eapc.co.il, *Website:* www.eapc.co.il

Officials: Shipping Manager: Yoram Neeman, *Tel:* +972 8 674 0634, *Email:* yoram@eapc.co.il.

Port Security: ISPS compliant

Pre-Arrival Information: All vessels bound for Israeli ports are required to transmit a 'IMOT Report' when 100 nautical miles off the Israeli coast. This report must be sent to the Israeli Navy by Fax: +972 3 606 4567 or Email: shipping@idf.gov.il. The Israeli Navy will confirm receipt by Inmarsat C
The report should state the following information:
a) vessel's name (and previous name)
b) call sign
c) flag and port of registry
d) IMO number
e) MMSI
f) satellite telephone and telex numbers
g) year of build
h) gt
i) type of vessel and cargo on board
j) number of crew and passengers
k) agents name, telephone and fax
l) name of owner and operator
m) is vessel holding a valid ISPS certificate
n) security level on board (1, 2 or 3)
o) last and previous port, date of departure
p) port of destination
q) position, course and speed
r) ETA
s) crew list (including name, rank, nationality, residence (country and city), age, gender, seniority in company, date of signing-on passport and SB number
All vessels should report to the Israeli Navy on VHF Channel 16 when 25 nautical miles off the Israeli coast stating vessel's name and call sign, present position, course and speed and ETA

Anchorage: If required anchorage can be obtained in the following positions:
31° 40.63' N; 34° 29.44' E
31° 40.05' N; 34° 28.98' E
31° 39.48' N; 34° 28.50' E
The recommended anchorage for coal carriers is in pos 31° 38.90' N; 34° 28.09' E

Pilotage: Compulsory. The terminal pilot will board the vessel at the boarding point located at the intersection of 31° 40' N; 34° 29' E or at the anchorage

Radio Frequency: VHF Channels 16, 13 and 21 USA

Traffic: 2000, 302 tankers

Maximum Vessel Dimensions: 250 000 dwt, 335.2 m loa, 22 m d

Principal Imports and Exports: Imports: Coal, Crude oil, Crude oil products, Gas oil, Gasoline, Jet fuel, LPG. Exports: Crude oil.

Working Hours: 24 h/day. SPM mooring in daylight only, unberthing 24 h/day. Multi-Buoy Berth berthing/unberthing daylight only

Accommodation:

Name	Length (m)	Depth (m)	Draught (m)	Remarks
Ashkelon				See [1] below
Berth No.1 (Multibuoy)		22	17.5	See [2] below
Berth No.2 (Multibuoy)		19	14.5	See [3] below
SPM Berth No.3		31		See [4] below
SPM Berth No.4		31		See [5] below
LPG Berth		14	8.5	See [6] below
Coal Jetty	283.6	22.5	18	See [7] below

[1]*Ashkelon:* Operated by Eilat Ashkelon Pipeline Co. Tanker terminal for loading and discharging crude oil, tankfarm receives oil from either a 42" diameter pipeline from Eilat or from tankers discharging. Oil loading facilities consist of two multi-buoy moorings at Berth No's 1 and 2 and two mono-buoy moorings at Berth No's 3 and 4, each connected to the shore by submarine pipelines
[2]*Berth No.1 (Multibuoy):* In pos 31° 40.15' N; 34° 31.00' E. Distillates for tankers of 20 000-80 000 dwt
[3]*Berth No.2 (Multibuoy):* In pos 31° 39.6' N; 34° 31.2' E. Fuel oil for tankers of 20 000-80 000 dwt. Tankfarm with two tanks, each of 57 000 m3 nominal cap
[4]*SPM Berth No.3:* In pos 31° 39.42' N; 34° 29.83' E. For VLCC's up to 300 000 dwt. Loading/discharge rate 6500 m3/h. Facilities for disposal of dirty ballast
[5]*SPM Berth No.4:* In pos 31° 38.75' N; 34° 28.30' E. For VLCC's up to 300 000 dwt. Loading/discharge rate 6500 m3/h. Facilities for disposal of dirty ballast
[6]*LPG Berth:* In pos 31° 39' N; 34° 31.2' E. For tankers up to 10 000 dwt discharging at rate up to 200 t/h
[7]*Coal Jetty:* Serving the Israel Electric Company's Rutenberg power station. Coal carriers up to 200 000 dwt are unloaded at this jetty by means of two gantry grab cranes at a rate of 1800 t/h each

Bunkering: United Petroleum Export Co. Ltd (UNEX), P O Box 1548, 5 Pal Yam Avenue, 33095 Haifa, Israel, *Tel:* +972 4 8678 291, *Fax:* +972 4 8678 290, *Email:* webmail@unex.co.il – *Grades:* HFO; IFO; MGO – *Delivery Mode:* barge, pipeline, truck

Ship Chandlers: Layam Co. Ltd, P O Box 4048, Ashdod, Israel, *Tel:* +972 8 852 1330, *Fax:* +972 8 856 3104, *Email:* rachel_p@layam.com
Maurice A. Raphael Ltd, P O Box 118, 31 000 Haifa, Israel, *Tel:* +972 4 866 7103, *Fax:* +972 4 866 3427, *Email:* mraphael@netvision.net.il
Sakal Brothers Ltd, Warehouse No.301, Ashdod, Israel, *Tel:* +972 8 856 4628, *Fax:* +972 8 856 3749, *Email:* Amir-p@sakal.co.il

Medical Facilities: Hospital 4 km away

Airport: Ben Gurion International Airport, 50 km

Railway: From Ashkelon to North Israel

Development: Upgrading Berth No's 1 & 2 for product tankers

Lloyd's Agent: Galram Surveyors and Adjusters Ltd, P O Box 4094, Ashdod Port, 77140 Ashdod, Israel, *Tel:* +972 8 856 1634, *Fax:* +972 8 853 1325, *Email:* galram@galram.com, *Website:* www.galram.com

EILAT

Lat 29° 33' N; Long 34° 57' E.

Admiralty Chart: 801	**Admiralty Pilot:** 64
Time Zone: GMT +2 h	**UNCTAD Locode:** IL ETH

Principal Facilities:

P		Y	G	C	R		B		T	A

Authority: Israel Ports Development & Assets Co., Eilat Port Co. Ltd, P O Box 37, 88100 Eilat, Israel, *Tel:* +972 8 635 8332, *Fax:* +972 8 635 8300, *Email:* saars@eilatport.co.il, *Website:* www.israports.co.il

Officials: Manager: Dr Moshe Naveh.
Port Manager: Moshe Midz.
Harbour Master: Capt Guy Gilron, *Email:* guyg@eilatport.co.il.
Marketing: Saar Shapira, *Email:* saars@eilatport.co.il.

Port Security: ISPS compliant

Pre-Arrival Information: All vessels bound for Israeli ports are required to transmit a 'IMOT Report' when 100 nautical miles off the Israeli coast. This report must be sent to the Israeli Navy by Fax: +972 3 606 4567 or Email: shipping@idf.gov.il. The Israeli Navy will confirm receipt by Inmarsat C
The report should state the following information:

Key to Principal Facilities:—					
A=Airport	**C**=Containers	**G**=General Cargo	**P**=Petroleum	**R**=Ro/Ro	**Y**=Dry Bulk
B=Bunkers	**D**=Dry Dock	**L**=Cruise	**Q**=Other Liquid Bulk	**T**=Towage (where available from port)	

a) vessel's name (and previous name)
b) call sign
c) flag and port of registry
d) IMO number
e) MMSI
f) satellite telephone and telex numbers
g) year of build
h) gt
i) type of vessel and cargo on board
j) number of crew and passengers
k) agents name, telephone and fax
l) name of owner and operator
m) is vessel holding a valid ISPS certificate
n) security level on board (1, 2 or 3)
o) last and previous port, date of departure
p) port of destination
q) position, course and speed
r) ETA
s) crew list (including name, rank, nationality, residence (country and city), age, gender, seniority in company, date of signing-on passport and SB number
All vessels should report to the Israeli Navy on VHF Channel 16 when 25 nautical miles off the Israeli coast stating vessel's name and call sign, present position, course and speed and ETA

Anchorage: There are nine designated anchorage positions off the port in depths ranging from 30 m to 100 m:
1) 29° 32' 49" N; 34° 57' 64" E
2) 29° 32' 37" N; 34° 57' 97" E
3) 29° 32' 37" N; 34° 57' 34" E
4) 29° 32' 17" N; 34° 57' 70" E
5) 29° 32' 06" N; 34° 58' 04" E
6) 29° 32' 22" N; 34° 57' 02" E
7) 29° 30' 02" N; 34° 57' 29" E
8) 29° 31' 82" N; 34° 57' 65" E
9) 29° 31' 69" N; 34° 58' 06" E

Pilotage: Compulsory. Pilot station for dry cargo vessels in pos 29° 31.2' N; 34° 56.4' E. Pilot station for tankers in pos 29° 29.5' N; 34° 55.1' E

Radio Frequency: VHF Channel 14 for dry cargo vessels, Channel 13 for tankers and Channel 11 for small craft

Weather: Mostly N and NE prevailing winds, occasional southerly gales during winter

Tides: Range of 1.35 m at spring tides

Traffic: 2007, 2 535 000 t of cargo handled

Working Hours: Winter: 0600-1400, 1530-2300, Fridays 0600-1300, 1400-2000. Summer: 0530-1330, 1600-2300, Fridays 0530-1230, 1400-2000

Accommodation:

Name	Length (m)	Depth (m)	Draught (m)	Remarks
Eilat				See [1] below
Berth No's 1-3	528	13	12–12.1	General, bulk & container cargo
Shallow Berth	202	6	5.5	
Eilat Oil Terminal				See [2] below
No.1 Jetty		16	15	See [3] below
No.2 Jetty		30	27	See [4] below

[1]*Eilat:* Container facilities: Container handling area of 28 000 m2 with storage for 2200 containers
Bulk facilities: Three sheds with total storage cap of 170 000 t for potash and phosphates; loading by belt conveyor, cap approx 800 t/h
FREE PORT ZONE: Facilities available covering an area of 50 acres with warehousing and open storage available, Tel: +972 8 635 8332, Fax: +972 8 635 8300
[2]*Eilat Oil Terminal:* Operated by Eilat-Ashkelon Pipeline Co Ltd., P O Box 1, 88000 Eilat, Tel: +972 8 637 6171, Fax: +972 8 632 6308, Email: marudi@eapc.co.il, Website: www.eapc.co.il
[3]*No.1 Jetty:* For vessels up to 100 000 dwt with max discharge rate of 10 000 m3/h
[4]*No.2 Jetty:* For vessels up to 500 000 dwt with max discharge rate of 20 000 m3/h

Storage:

Location	Open (m²)	Covered (m²)
Eilat	30000	25000

Mechanical Handling Equipment:

Location	Type	Capacity (t)	Qty
Eilat	Mult-purp. Cranes	25–50	6
Eilat	Mobile Cranes	80	1
Eilat	Mobile Cranes	14	4
Eilat	Transtainers	50	3
Eilat	Forklifts	36	3

Cargo Worked: Bulk 600 t/h, containers 12-15 units/gang/h, steel products 580 t/shift, vehicles either by crane, 150 units/shift or driven off, 500 cars/shift, pre-slung bags 450 t/shift

Bunkering: United Petroleum Export Co. Ltd (UNEX), P O Box 1548, 5 Pal Yam Avenue, 33095 Haifa, Israel, *Tel:* +972 4 8678 291, *Fax:* +972 4 8678 290, *Email:* webmail@unex.co.il – *Grades:* HFO; IFO; MGO – *Delivery Mode:* road tanker

Towage: Two sea-going tugs of 3000 hp available

Repair & Maintenance: Minor repairs can be performed

Shipping Agents: M Dizengoff & Co. Ltd, New Port, P O Box 11, 88100 Eilat, Israel, *Tel:* +972 8 636 3113, *Fax:* +972 8 637 5669, *Email:* man@dizman-eth.zim.co.il

Medical Facilities: Yosseftal Hospital, 5 km

Airport: Eilat, 4 km

Lloyd's Agent: Galram Surveyors and Adjusters Ltd, P O Box 4094, Ashdod Port, 77140 Ashdod, Israel, *Tel:* +972 8 856 1634, *Fax:* +972 8 853 1325, *Email:* galram@galram.com, *Website:* www.galram.com

HADERA

Lat 32° 28' N; Long 34° 53' E.

Admiralty Chart: 1591	**Admiralty Pilot:** 49
Time Zone: GMT +2 h	**UNCTAD Locode:** IL HAD

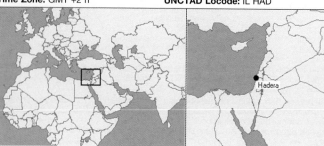

Principal Facilities:

P	Y			B		T	A

Authority: Port of Hadera, P O Box 314, 38102 Hadera, Israel, *Tel:* +972 4 624 4200, *Fax:* +972 4 624 4220, *Email:* aharonw@mot.gov.il

Officials: Port Manager: Aharon Weissman.
Harbour Master: Capt Meir Inbal, *Email:* inbalm@mot.gov.il.

Port Security: ISPS compliant

Pre-Arrival Information: All vessels bound for Israeli ports are required to transmit a 'IMOT Report' when 100 nautical miles off the Israeli coast. This report must be sent to the Israeli Navy by Fax: +972 3 606 4567 or Email: shipping@idf.gov.il. The Israeli Navy will confirm receipt by Inmarsat C
The report should state the following information:
a) vessel's name (and previous name)
b) call sign
c) flag and port of registry
d) IMO number
e) MMSI
f) satellite telephone and telex numbers
g) year of build
h) gt
i) type of vessel and cargo on board
j) number of crew and passengers
k) agents name, telephone and fax
l) name of owner and operator
m) is vessel holding a valid ISPS certificate
n) security level on board (1, 2 or 3)
o) last and previous port, date of departure
p) port of destination
q) position, course and speed
r) ETA
s) crew list (including name, rank, nationality, residence (country and city), age, gender, seniority in company, date of signing-on passport and SB number
All vessels should report to the Israeli Navy on VHF Channel 16 when 25 nautical miles off the Israeli coast stating vessel's name and call sign, present position, course and speed and ETA

Approach: All approaches to the port from seaward are clear of any dangers or obstructions

Anchorage: Anchorage can be obtained 1.3 nautical miles NNW of the jetty in a depth of 25-30 m

Pilotage: Compulsory for all vessels berthing and unberthing. Pilot boards at a point, bearing 350°T, 1.3 nautical miles from the coal pier

Radio Frequency: VHF Channels 16 and 10

Weather: During winter months a heavy swell can be experienced. Vessels may have to vacate berth as the jetty is completely exposed

Maximum Vessel Dimensions: 225 000 dwt, 48 m beam, 18 m draft

Working Hours: 24 h/day. No cargo discharge on Saturdays and Holidays

Accommodation:

Name	Remarks
Hadera	See [1] below

[1]*Hadera:* Coal unloading terminal serving a power station of the Electric Corporation. A jetty extends 1.8 km offshore with a berthing face at the end of about 300 m, depth alongside 20.5 m min, capable of receiving vessels up to 225 000 dwt. Bulk coal is discharged for the adjacent power station by two 35 t gantry cranes, each with a 1200 t/h cap and one 40 t gantry crane with a 1500 t/h cap. Two belt conveyor systems with 3000 t/h cap and 4500 t/h cap are fitted
A small craft harbour for tugs and boats is situated near to the root of the jetty
Tanker facilities: Mooring buoys for tankers up to 70 000 dwt are located approx 0.5 nautical mile N of the jetty in depth of 18 m

Mechanical Handling Equipment:

Location	Type	Capacity (t)	Qty
Hadera	Mult-purp. Cranes	35	2
Hadera	Mult-purp. Cranes	40	1

Cargo Worked: Average 40 000 t/day

Bunkering: United Petroleum Export Co. Ltd (UNEX), P O Box 1548, 5 Pal Yam Avenue, 33095 Haifa, Israel, *Tel:* +972 4 8678 291, *Fax:* +972 4 8678 290, *Email:* webmail@unex.co.il – *Grades:* HFO; IFO; MGO – *Delivery Mode:* barge, pipeline, truck

Waste Reception Facilities: A 35 m3 tank for oily bilge/residues available at jetty. Garbage disposal also available

Towage: Two tugs of 55 t bollard pull

Medical Facilities: Government hospital in the town

Airport: Ben Gurion International Airport, 50 km

Lloyd's Agent: Galram Surveyors and Adjusters Ltd, P O Box 4094, Ashdod Port, 77140 Ashdod, Israel, *Tel:* +972 8 856 1634, *Fax:* +972 8 853 1325, *Email:* galram@galram.com, *Website:* www.galram.com

HAIFA

Lat 32° 49' N; Long 35° 0' E.

Admiralty Chart: 1585	**Admiralty Pilot:** 49	
Time Zone: GMT +2 h	**UNCTAD Locode:** IL HFA	

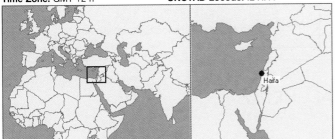

Principal Facilities:

P Q Y G C R L B D T A

CARMEL INTERNATIONAL SHIPPING SERVICES LTD.

Carmel International Shipping Services (1992) Ltd

51 Hameginim Avenue, PO Box 1472, Haifa, 31014 Israel

Tel: +972 4 8545454 Fax: +972 4 8515886

Email: charter@carmelship.co.il
Website: www.carmelship.co.il

Authority: Israel Ports Development & Assets Co., Haifa Port Co. Ltd, P O Box 33539, 31334 Haifa, Israel, *Tel:* +972 4 851 8255, *Fax:* +972 4 867 8687, *Website:* www.haifaport.org.il

Port Security: ISPS compliant. Container Security Initiative (CSI) designated port

Pre-Arrival Information: All vessels bound for Israeli ports are required to transmit a 'IMOT Report' when 100 nautical miles off the Israeli coast. This report must be sent to the Israeli Navy by Fax: +972 3 606 4567 or Email: shipping@idf.gov.il. The Israeli Navy will confirm receipt by Inmarsat C

The report should state the following information:
a) vessel's name (and previous name)
b) call sign
c) flag and port of registry
d) IMO number
e) MMSI
f) satellite telephone and telex numbers
g) year of build
h) gt
i) type of vessel and cargo on board
j) number of crew and passengers
k) agents name, telephone and fax
l) name of owner and operator
m) is vessel holding a valid ISPS certificate
n) security level on board (1, 2 or 3)
o) last and previous port, date of departure
p) port of destination
q) position, course and speed
r) ETA
s) crew list (including name, rank, nationality, residence (country and city), age, gender, seniority in company, date of signing-on passport and SB number

All vessels should report to the Israeli Navy on VHF Channel 16 when 25 nautical miles off the Israeli coast stating vessel's name and call sign, present position, course and speed and ETA

Pilotage: Compulsory. 24 h service. Vessels boarded by pilot seaward of main breakwater

Radio Frequency: Port Signal Station, 24 h service. VHF Channels 16, 14 and 12

Weather: Haifa Bay provides good anchorage protected from all winds, though occasional SW gales may make it difficult for ships in light condition to stay at anchor in roadstead

Traffic: 2007, 21 457 000 t of cargo handled, 1 149 000 TEU's

Maximum Vessel Dimensions: 130 529 dwt, 272 m loa; max d 13.5 m

Working Hours: Administration 0730-1600. Cargo handling: Three shifts 0630-1430, 1500-2200, 2200-0430

Accommodation:

Name	Length (m)	Depth (m)	Remarks
Haifa			See [1] below
Western Terminal	411	10.5	See [2] below
Eastern Terminal	950	12–13.5	
Grain Berth		13.5	See [3] below

[1]*Haifa:* Port is enclosed by main breakwater 2826 m long on the N and lee breakwater 765 m long to the E. Entrance between the two is 183 m wide. Inside the main basin the oil dock and general cargo dock are situated

Kishon Harbour: To E of main harbour around the lower reaches of the Kishon rivulet, lies the Kishon Harbour which is enclosed by two breakwaters 600 m and 350 m long respectively; entrance channel is 80 m wide. The harbour itself is limited to vessels of 9.5 m d

Deepwater Wharves: Total length of wharves in main port and Kishon Zone is 4500 m with alongside depth of up to 13.5 m

Chemicals and edible oils in bulk are unloaded or loaded, stored and distributed by Chemical Terminal of Haifa Port in the Kishon Harbour. Tankers of up to 20 000 dwt can be accommodated. Max 8.5 m d. Throughout rates, per net pumping h; unloading up to 600 t, loading up to 400 t. Storage cap of 45 000 m2

Tanker facilities: Jetty for handling refined fuels and bunkers. Up to two tankers can be accommodated at the jetty at one time, draft up to 10.4 m

An additional Chemical Terminal area serves chemical tankers. Two berths; W Quay, length 123 m and E Quay, length 207 m. Depth at quays 8.5 m

FREE PORT ZONE: Facilities available covering an area of 75 acres with storage of 112 000 ft2, Tel: +972 3 512 1956, Fax: +972 3 562 0902

[2]*Western Terminal:* Various container handling gear. Ro/ro facilities available, depth 8 m

[3]*Grain Berth:* Owned and operated by Dagon Batey-Mamguroth Le-Israel Ltd, for discharge, handling and distribution of grain and seeds. The berth is able to accommodate vessels of 66 000 dwt. Three mobile elevators on the main wharf discharge cargo from vessels on to a concrete quay bridge 281 m long. This bridge is connected to the silo by two other bridges of 180 m and 153.5 m length. Four belt conveyors, two of 250 t/h and two of 600 t/h transport the grain from the quay to the silo. For loading, one of the 250 t/h cap conveyors can be reversed. Nominal discharge cap of all three elevators is 1800 t/h. The silo is equipped for cleaning, dust extraction, ventilation and fumigation of grain

Storage: For transit storage of general cargo there are, in the Main Port, ten sheds totalling 53 000 m2 floor space, and in the Kishon Zone seven sheds totalling 25 000 m2

Open stacking areas near wharves totalling 195 000 m2 for timber, iron, steel and cars

Location	Grain (t)
Grain Berth	100000

Mechanical Handling Equipment:

Location	Type	Capacity (t)	Qty
Haifa	Mult-purp. Cranes	35	19
Western Terminal	Container Cranes	35	2
Eastern Terminal	Container Cranes	35	8
Eastern Terminal	Portal Cranes	32	2

Bunkering: United Petroleum Export Co. Ltd (UNEX), P O Box 1548, 5 Pal Yam Avenue, 33095 Haifa, Israel, *Tel:* +972 4 8678 291, *Fax:* +972 4 8678 290, *Email:* webmail@unex.co.il

United Petroleum Export Co. Ltd (UNEX), P O Box 1548, 5 Pal Yam Avenue, 33095 Haifa, Israel, *Tel:* +972 4 8678 291, *Fax:* +972 4 8678 290, *Email:* webmail@unex.co.il – *Grades:* HFO; IFO; MGO – *Delivery Mode:* barge, pipeline, truck

Towage: Four sea-going tugs with fire fighting and salvage equipment; three with 30 t bollard pull and one with 35 t bollard pull

Repair & Maintenance: Israel Shipyards Ltd, P O Box 10630, 26118 Haifa, Israel, *Tel:* +972 4 846 0246, *Fax:* +972 4 841 8744, *Email:* marketing@israel-shipyards.com, *Website:* www.israel-shipyards.com Floating dock with lifting cap of 20 000 t. Repair quay of 900 m with max draught 14 m

Ship Chandlers: Layam Co. Ltd, P O Box 1312, Haifa, Israel, *Tel:* +972 4 860 5612, *Fax:* +972 4 862 8368, *Email:* rachel_p@layam.com
Maurice A. Raphael Ltd, P O Box 118, 31 000 Haifa, Israel, *Tel:* +972 4 866 7103, *Fax:* +972 4 866 3427, *Email:* mraphael@netvision.net.il
James Richardson Proprietary Ltd, 8th Hanamal Street, P O Box 34144, 31 340 Haifa, Israel, *Tel:* +972 4 864 5585, *Fax:* +972 4 864 5737, *Email:* info@j-r.co.il, *Website:* www.dutyfree.co.il
Sakal Brothers Ltd, P O Box 33760, Haifa, Israel, *Tel:* +972 4 866 6650, *Fax:* +972 4 867 3693, *Email:* dror-a@sakal.co.il

Shipping Agents: Dynamic Shipping Services, 3 Khayat Street, P O Box 33193, 31331 Haifa, Israel, *Tel:* +972 4 864 5745, *Fax:* +972 4 866 0361, *Email:* agency@dynamic-shipping.com, *Website:* www.dynamic-shipping.com General Manager: Zimi Cohen Email: zimi@dynamic-shipping.com
Allalouf & Co. Shipping Ltd, 40 Hanamal Street, P O Box 337752, 31007 Haifa, Israel, *Tel:* +972 4 861 1811, *Fax:* +972 4 867 0530, *Email:* saidnader@allalouf.com, *Website:* www.allalouf.com
Ardo Shipping Ltd, Levant House, 1 Shaar Palmer Street, P O Box 33086, 31330 Haifa, Israel, *Tel:* +972 4 867 3173, *Fax:* +972 4 864 5866, *Website:* www.ardoship.co.il
Carmel International Shipping Services (1992) Ltd, 51 Hameginim Avenue, P O Box 1472, 31014 Haifa, Israel, *Tel:* +972 4 854 5454, *Fax:* +972 4 851 5886, *Email:* charter@carmelship.co.il, *Website:* www.carmelship.co.il
China Shipping (Israel) Agency Co Ltd, 5 Pal Yam Avenue, Floor 8, 33095 Haifa, Israel, *Tel:* +972 4 864 5502, *Fax:* +972 4 864 5542, *Email:* aangel@csisrael.com, *Website:* www.csisrael.com
Conmart Ltd, Conmart House, 54 Hameginim Boulevard, P O Box 2576, 31025 Haifa, Israel, *Tel:* +972 4 855 8558, *Fax:* +972 4 851 5555/7020, *Email:* haifa@conmart.co.il, *Website:* www.conmart.co.il
Coral Maritime Services Ltd, 1 Nathanson Street, 31336 Haifa, Israel, *Tel:* +972 4 867

Key to Principal Facilities:—					
A=Airport	**C**=Containers	**G**=General Cargo	**P**=Petroleum	**R**=Ro/Ro	**Y**=Dry Bulk
B=Bunkers	**D**=Dry Dock	**L**=Cruise	**Q**=Other Liquid Bulk	**T**=Towage (where available from port)	

1266, *Fax:* +972 4 866 7374, *Email:* coral@coral-maritime.co.il, *Website:* www.coral-maritime.co.il

M Dizengoff & Co. Ltd, 2 Pal-Yam Street, City Windows, Oren Building, 33095 Haifa, Israel, *Tel:* +972 4 867 3715, *Fax:* +972 4 867 8796, *Email:* mail@dizrep.co.il, *Website:* www.m-dizengoff.co.il

Gadot Yam Chemical Shipping Ltd, 102 Haazmaout Road, 33411 Haifa, Israel, *Tel:* +972 4 853 5216, *Fax:* +972 4 853 8260, *Email:* gyhaifa@gadot-yam.com, *Website:* www.gadot.com

Gold Line Shipping Ltd, 16 Habankim Street, 31330 Haifa, Israel, *Tel:* +972 4 856 2222, *Fax:* +972 4 852 5545, *Email:* info@goldline-gls.com, *Website:* www.goldline-gls.com

Israel Scandinavian Maritime Agency Ltd, Khayat Square 2, P O Box 33557, 31334 Haifa, Israel, *Tel:* +972 4 864 3162, *Fax:* +972 4 866 4902, *Email:* commercial@israscan.co.il, *Website:* www.israscan.co.il

Kamor Shipping Services Ltd, 53 Haatzmauth Street, P O Box 33331, 31332 Haifa, Israel, *Tel:* +972 4 868 1000, *Fax:* +972 4 868 1010, *Email:* kamor@kamor.co.il, *Website:* www.kamor.co.il

Mano Maritime Ltd, 2 Pal-Yam Avenue, P O Box 1400, 33031 Haifa, Israel, *Tel:* +972 4 860 6677, *Fax:* +972 4 866 1666, *Email:* main@mano.co.il, *Website:* www.mano.co.il

Mediterranean Shipping Company, MSC (Israel) Ltd, 157 Yaffo Street, P O Box 34004, 31339 Haifa, Israel, *Tel:* +972 4 854 9000, *Fax:* +972 4 851 0161, *Email:* infohfa@mscisr.com, *Website:* www.mscgva.ch

Mercury Shipping Agency Ltd, 2 pal Yam Boulevard, P O Box 1261, 33095 Haifa, Israel, *Tel:* +972 4 866 6673, *Fax:* +972 4 866 6674, *Email:* hfamng@maersk.com

A.P. Moller-Maersk Group, Maersk Israel Ltd, 2 Pal-Yam Avenue, Brosh Building, 33095 Haifa, Israel, *Tel:* +972 4 861 9000, *Fax:* +972 4 861 9011, *Email:* hfasal@maersk.com, *Website:* www.maerskline.com

MSC Israel Ltd, 157 Jaffe Road, Amot Building, 31339 Haifa, Israel, *Tel:* +972 4 851 1744, *Fax:* +972 4 851 0161, *Email:* infohfa@mscisr.com

Oriental Shipping Ltd, 37 Hameginim Street, P O Box 33933, 31330 Haifa, Israel, *Tel:* +972 4 850 7070, *Fax:* +972 4 850 7080, *Email:* info@osl.co.il

Packer Shipping Ltd, 3 Palmer's Gate, P O Box 34060, 31339 Haifa, Israel, *Tel:* +972 4 867 6690, *Fax:* +972 4 867 1448, *Email:* agency@packer-shipping.co.il

Perco Seas Ltd, 19 Ben Gurian Avenue, P O Box 9158, 31090 Haifa, Israel, *Tel:* +972 4 853 5111, *Fax:* +972 4 853 5353, *Email:* percosea@netvision.net.il, *Website:* www.perco-seas.com

A. Rosenfeld Shipping Ltd, P O Box 74, 104 Ha'atzmaut Road, 31000 Haifa, Israel, *Tel:* +972 4 861 3613, *Fax:* +972 4 853 7002, *Email:* haifa@rosenfeld.net, *Website:* www.rosenfeld.net

Seagull Maritime Ltd, 39/41 Hameginim Avenue, P O Box 33628, Haifa, Israel, *Tel:* +972 4 862 3111, *Fax:* +972 4 862 5333, *Email:* info@seagull-mariitme.com, *Website:* www.seagull-maritime.com

ST & T. Sea Transport & Trading, P O Box 7040, 31070 Haifa, Israel, *Tel:* +972 4 834 1002, *Fax:* +972 4 834 1003, *Email:* agency@seatransport.co.il, *Website:* www.seatransport.co.il

Tanker Services Ltd, 5 Palyam Avenue, 31000 Haifa, Israel, *Tel:* +972 4 862 3202, *Fax:* +972 4 862 2845, *Email:* tankers@tankers.co.il

Tiran Shipping Agencies 1997 Ltd, 44-46 Jaffa Street, 31331 Haifa, Israel, *Tel:* +972 4 850 9000, *Fax:* +972 4 855 6888, *Email:* tiran_hfa@tiran.co.il, *Website:* www.tiran.co.il

Stevedoring Companies: Gadot Yam Chemical Shipping Ltd, 102 Haazmaout Road, 33411 Haifa, Israel, *Tel:* +972 4 853 5216, *Fax:* +972 4 853 8260, *Email:* gyhaifa@gadot-yam.com, *Website:* www.gadot.com

Surveyors: Carmel International Shipping Services (1992) Ltd, 51 Hameginim Avenue, P O Box 1472, 31014 Haifa, Israel, *Tel:* +972 4 854 5454, *Fax:* +972 4 851 5886, *Email:* charter@carmelship.co.il, *Website:* www.carmelship.co.il

Det Norske Veritas A/S, 18 Ovadia Street, 34563 Haifa, Israel, *Tel:* +972 4 833 9106, *Fax:* +972 4 833 9102, *Website:* www.dnv.com

ECSL Engineering Consultants & Surveyors Ltd, P O Box 1999, 74 Sea Road, 31000 Haifa, Israel, *Tel:* +972 4 837 0234, *Fax:* +972 4 838 6551, *Email:* ecsl@netvision.net.il

Galram Surveyors and Adjusters Ltd, P O Box 379, 7 Pal-Yam Avenue, Zim Building, Room 315, 31000 Haifa, Israel, *Tel:* +972 4 866 7383, *Fax:* +972 4 866 7382, *Email:* haifa@galram-surveys.co.il, *Website:* www.galram.com

Hellenic Register of Shipping, c/o Eltek Shipping A. Elharar, Shaar Palmer 1, Office No.513A, 33031 Haifa, Israel, *Tel:* +972 4 862 6215, *Fax:* +972 4 867 7676, *Email:* eltek@netvision.net.il, *Website:* www.hrs.gr

Y. Hollander Marine Surveying Co. Ltd, 3 Habankim Street, P O Box 33375, 31333 Haifa, Israel, *Tel:* +972 4 852 4819, *Fax:* +972 4 852 3889

Israel Kirstein Corp Ltd, 74 Sea Road, Mount Carmel, P O Box No.1478, 34746 Haifa, Israel, *Tel:* +972 4 838 1652, *Fax:* +972 4 838 6551, *Email:* ikcl@netvision.net.il

Nippon Kaiji Kyokai, P O Box 1999, 31000 Haifa, Israel, *Tel:* +972 4 837 0234, *Fax:* +972 4 838 6551, *Website:* www.classnk.or.jp

Perco Seas Ltd, 19 Ben Gurian Avenue, P O Box 9158, 31090 Haifa, Israel, *Tel:* +972 4 853 5111, *Fax:* +972 4 853 5353, *Email:* percosea@netvision.net.il, *Website:* www.perco-seas.com

Polish Register of Shipping, c/o Engineering Consultants & Surveyors Ltd (ECSL), 74 Sea Road, Mount Carmel, P O Box 1999, 31000 Haifa, Israel, *Tel:* +972 4 838 8412, *Fax:* +972 4 838 6551, *Email:* ecsl@netvision.net.il, *Website:* www.prs.pl

Airport: Ben Gurion International Airport

Lloyd's Agent: Galram Surveyors and Adjusters Ltd, P O Box 4094, Ashdod Port, 77140 Ashdod, Israel, *Tel:* +972 8 856 1634, *Fax:* +972 8 853 1325, *Email:* galram@galram.com, *Website:* www.galram.com

ALGHERO

Lat 40° 34' N; Long 8° 19' E.

Admiralty Chart: 1202	**Admiralty Pilot:** 45
Time Zone: GMT +1 h	**UNCTAD Locode:** IT AHO

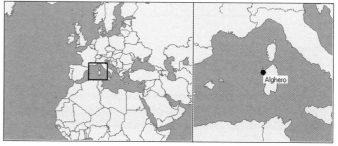

Principal Facilities:

		G		B		A

Authority: Ufficio Circondariale Marittimo di Alghero, Via Eleonora D'Arborea 2, I-07041 Alghero, Italy, *Tel:* +39 079 953174, *Fax:* +39 079 984606, *Email:* alghero@guardiacostiera.it, *Website:* www.alghero.guardiacostiera.it

Officials: Harbour Master: Emilio Del Santo.

Port Security: ISPS compliant

Anchorage: Good bay anchorage in summer in approx 21 m, sandy bottom and varec to approx 1400 m, W from the islet of Maddalena; in about 12.80 m, sandy and varec bottom, to approx 400 m E of Torre Lazzaretto

Pilotage: Not compulsory

Radio Frequency: VHF Channel 16

Working Hours: 0800-1200, 1300-1700

Accommodation:

Name	Remarks
Alghero	See [1] below

[1]*Alghero:* Entrance to port flanked to the S by a breakwater dam equipped with a white intermittent light and to the N by a shoal shown by a red buoy. At Banchina Sanita, small vessels can be accommodated in a depth of 4.0 m. Owing to lack of depth only small boats can be accommodated at other quays; there is a dock for small boats in the northern part of the port

Bunkering: Available. Three automatic distributors for gasoline

Towage: Not compulsory

Repair & Maintenance: Available. Six re-fitting yards for wooden vessels

Shipping Agents: Agenzie Marittime Sarde S.r.l., 27 Via Vittorio Emanuele, I-07041 Alghero, Italy, *Tel:* +39 079 979005, *Fax:* +39 079 977236, *Email:* marittimesarde@amsitaly.com, *Website:* www.amsitaly.com

Airport: Alghero Airport, 9 km

Lloyd's Agent: Gastaldi International S.r.l., Mura di Santa Chiara 1, I-16128 Genoa, Italy, *Tel:* +39 010 530931, *Fax:* +39 010 530 9343, *Email:* info@gastaldi-int.it, *Website:* www.gastaldi-int.it

ANCONA

Lat 43° 37' N; Long 13° 30' E.

Admiralty Chart: 1444	**Admiralty Pilot:** 47
Time Zone: GMT +1 h	**UNCTAD Locode:** IT AOI

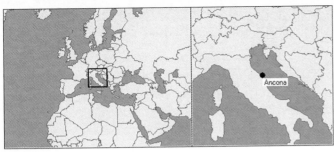

Principal Facilities:

P		Y	G	C	R		B		T	A

Authority: Autorita Portuale di Ancona, Molo S. Maria, I-60121 Ancona, Italy, *Tel:* +39 071 207891, *Fax:* +39 071 207 8940, *Email:* info@autoritaportuale.ancona.it, *Website:* www.autoritaportuale.ancona.it

Officials: President: Giovanni Montanari, *Tel:* +39 071 207 8923, *Email:* segreteria@autoritaportuale.ancona.it.
General Secretary: Tito Vespasiani, *Tel:* +39 071 207 8924, *Email:* t.vespasiani@autoritaportuale.ancona.it.
Marketing Manager: Stefano Sargenti, *Tel:* +39 071 207 8928, *Email:* s.sargenti@autoritaportuale.ancona.it.

Port Security: ISPS compliant

Pilotage: Compulsory for vessels over 500 gt; VHF Channel 12, Tel: +390 071 54297. Pilot boards vessel 0.8 km NNE of port

Tides: Minimal

Traffic: 2007, 9 157 428 t of cargo handled, 106 604 TEU's

Maximum Vessel Dimensions: 230 m loa, 11.15 m d, no breadth restriction

Principal Imports and Exports: Imports: Cement, Cereals, Coal, Metals. Exports: Furniture, Textile products.

Working Hours: 24 h/day

Accommodation:

Name	Length (m)	Depth (m)	Remarks
Ancona			
Dock 1 (Molo Clementino)	290	11	See [1] below
Dock 2 (Molo L. Rizzo)	190	11	See [2] below
Dock 3 (Molo L. Rizzo)	120	11	One hydraulic mobile crane of 20/40 t at Docks 3-4
Dock 4 (Molo L. Rizzo)	200	11	
Dock 5 (Darsena S. Primano)	100	11	
Dock 6 (Darsena S. Primano)	100	11	
Dock 7 (Calata Guasco)	200	11	
Dock 8 (Molo Wojtyla)	130	11	
Dock 9 (Molo Wojtyla)	130	11	
Dock 10 (Calata N. Sauro)	135	11	
Dock 11 (Molo S. Maria)	130	11	
Dock 12 (Molo S. Maria)	80	11	
Dock 13 (Molo S. Maria)	160	11	
Dock 14 (Calata Repubblica)	185	11	
Dock 15 (Molo XXX Settembre)	220	11	Two stationary cranes of 10/20 t
Dock 16 (Molo XXX Settembre)	150	8	
Dock 17 (Calata Da Chio)	235	8	
Dock 18 (Molo Sud)	130	8	
Dock 19 (Molo Sud)	140	12.5	Ten pneumatic grain elevators at Docks 19/22
Dock 20 (Molo Sud)	150	12.5	
Dock 21 (Molo Sud)	150	12.5	
Dock 22 (Molo Sud)	200	12.5	
Dock 23 (Nuova Darsena)	270	11	See [3] below
Dock 24 (Nuova Darsena)	150	11	
Dock 25 (Nuova Darsena)	260	11	Three stationary cranes of 20/35 t
Falconara Oil Jetty			See [4] below

[1]*Dock 1 (Molo Clementino):* Two stationary cranes of 8/16 t and two stationary cranes of 10/20 t
[2]*Dock 2 (Molo L. Rizzo):* One unloading bridge crane of 8 t and one unloading bridge crane of 12 t
[3]*Dock 23 (Nuova Darsena):* Two portainers of 42 t and one hydraulic mobile crane of 100 t at Docks 23/25
[4]*Oil Jetty:* Refinery of the Anonima Petroli Italiana of Rome (API) which has three types of mooring
Pier 1385 m long with three berths in depth of 5-8.5 m for loading/unloading of finished and unfinished products
Man-made island (3.6 km from the coast) in depth of 12.5 m used for unloading crude oil as well as unloading/unloading of finished and unfinished oils
Two berths on breasting dolphins can handle vessels of 60 000-95 000 dwt
SPM (16 km from coast) in depth of 30 m for unloading crude oil for vessels up to 400 000 dwt

Bunkering: Adriano & Armando Montevecchi S.N.C, Via Cialdini 57, P O Box 382, 60122 Ancona, Italy, *Tel:* +39 071 501011, *Fax:* +39 071 56752, *Email:* montevecchi.an@archibugi.com, *Website:* www.archibugi.com
AGIP Petroli S.p.A., ENI, Via Laurentina 449, 00142 Rome, Italy, *Tel:* +39 06 59881, *Fax:* +39 06 5988 5700, *Email:* gioacchino.costa@eni.it, *Website:* www.eni.it

Alma Petroli S.p.A., Via Di Roma 67, 48100 Ravenna, Italy, *Tel:* +39 0544 343 17, *Fax:* +39 0544 371 69, *Email:* info@almapetroli.com, *Website:* www.almapetroli.com
ExxonMobil Marine Fuels, Mailpoint 31, ExxonMobil House, Ermyn Way, Leatherhead, Surrey KT22 8UX, United Kingdom, *Tel:* +44 1372 222 000, *Fax:* +44 1372 223 922, *Email:* marine.fuels@exxonmobil.com, *Website:* www.exxonmobil.com – *Grades:* MGO; IFO40cSt; lubes – *Parcel Size:* min truck 12t – *Rates:* 200-300t/h – *Notice:* 24 hours – *Delivery Mode:* barge, truck
Marodi Service SAS, Via Decorati Al Valor Civile 80, 30173 Venice, Italy, *Tel:* +39 041 538 2143, *Fax:* +39 041 922841, *Email:* marodi@marodi.it, *Website:* www.marodi.it

Towage: Not compulsory. Tugs available from 1200-5000 hp

Repair & Maintenance: Construzioni Riparazioni Navali, Ancona, Italy, *Tel:* +39 071 204866
Cantiere Navale Tommasi, Via Enrico Mattei 14, P O Box 370, 60125 Ancona, Italy, *Tel:* +39 071 204302, *Fax:* +39 071 202473, *Email:* info@tugbuilder.com, *Website:* www.tugbuilder.com

Ship Chandlers: Provvedinavi S.r.l., Via Fornaci Comunali 33, 60125 Ancona, Italy, *Tel:* +39 071 201206, *Fax:* +39 071 206489, *Email:* aldo.magistrelli@it201206.191.it

Shipping Agents: Alessandro Archibugi & Figlio S.r.l., Via Cialdini 57, I-60122 Ancona, Italy, *Tel:* +39 071 501011, *Fax:* +39 071 56752, *Email:* archibugi.an@archibugi.com, *Website:* www.archibugi.com
Frittelli Maritime Group S.p.A., Lungomare Vanvitelli 18, 60121 Ancona, Italy, *Tel:* +39 071 227 0421, *Fax:* +39 071 227 0500, *Email:* info@fritellimaritime.it, *Website:* www.frittelli.it
G&G Mauro Srl, Via Loggia 4/6, I-60121 Ancona, Italy, *Tel:* +39 071 204090, *Fax:* +39 071 202618, *Email:* info@marittimamauro.it, *Website:* www.marittimamauro.it
Maritime Agency Srl, Via XXIX Settembre 10, 60100 Ancona, Italy, *Tel:* +39 071 204915, *Fax:* +39 071 202296
Maritransport Srl, Via XXIX Settembre 2/0, I-60122 Ancona, Italy, *Tel:* +39 071 204275, *Fax:* +39 071 203435, *Email:* maritransport@fastnet.it
Marittima Ravennate S.p.A., Lungomare Vanvitelli 18, I-60100 Ancona, Italy, *Tel:* +39 071 207 0902, *Fax:* +39 071 207 0902, *Email:* mail@marittimaravennate.com, *Website:* www.marittimaravennate.com
Adriano & Armando Montevecchi S.N.C, Via Cialdini 57, P O Box 382, 60122 Ancona, Italy, *Tel:* +39 071 501011, *Fax:* +39 071 56752, *Email:* montevecchi.an@archibugi.com, *Website:* www.archibugi.com

Stevedoring Companies: Maritransport Srl, Via XXIX Settembre 2/0, I-60122 Ancona, Italy, *Tel:* +39 071 204275, *Fax:* +39 071 203435, *Email:* maritransport@fastnet.it

Surveyors: Marittima Ravennate S.p.A., Lungomare Vanvitelli 18, I-60100 Ancona, Italy, *Tel:* +39 071 207 0902, *Fax:* +39 071 207 0902, *Email:* mail@marittimaravennate.com, *Website:* www.marittimaravennate.com
Nippon Kaiji Kyokai, Ancona, Italy, *Tel:* +39 071 202204, *Fax:* +39 071 203182, *Website:* www.classnk.or.jp
Registro Italiano Navale (RINA), Via Marsala 8, Ancona, Italy, *Tel:* +39 071 202204, *Fax:* +39 071 203182, *Email:* ancona.office@rina.org, *Website:* www.rina.org
Se.Co.Mar. - Marine & Cargo Surveyors, 150/B Via Primo Maggio, 60131 Ancona, Italy, *Tel:* +39 071 286 8083, *Fax:* +39 071 250 9914, *Email:* info@secomar.net, *Website:* www.secomar.net

Airport: Falconara, 14 km

Railway: Passenger station inside the port. All docks covered by tracks

Lloyd's Agent: Radonicich Insurance Services S.r.l., Via F. Orsini 6/A, Marghera, 30175 Venice, Italy, *Tel:* +39 041 538 2103, *Fax:* +39 041 926108, *Email:* radinsur@portofvenice.net

ANZIO

Lat 41° 27' N; Long 12° 38' E.

Admiralty Chart: 906	**Admiralty Pilot:** 47
Time Zone: GMT +1 h	**UNCTAD Locode:** IT ANZ

Principal Facilities:

		G		B		A

Authority: Ufficio Circondariale Marittimo di Anzio, Via Riviera Zanardelli 58, I-00042 Anzio, Italy, *Tel:* +39 06 984 4525, *Fax:* +39 06 984 6235, *Email:* circomare.anzio@libero.it

Pilotage: Compulsory

Working Hours: Mon-Fri 0700-1900

Accommodation:

Name	Remarks
Anzio	See [1] below

[1]*Anzio:* Depth at harbour entrance 4.5 m. Four quays with 4.5 m alongside at Molo Innocenziano for commercial operations

Bunkering: AGIP Petroli S.p.A., ENI, Via Laurentina 449, 00142 Rome, Italy, *Tel:* +39 06 59881, *Fax:* +39 06 5988 5700, *Email:* gioacchino.costa@eni.it, *Website:* www.eni.it

---

Key to Principal Facilities:			
A=Airport	**C**=Containers	**G**=General Cargo	**P**=Petroleum	**R**=Ro/Ro	**Y**=Dry Bulk
B=Bunkers	**D**=Dry Dock	**L**=Cruise	**Q**=Other Liquid Qas	**T**=Towage (where available from port)	

Airport: Fiumicino Airport, 60 km

Lloyd's Agent: Gastaldi International S.r.l., Via San Godenzo 187, I-00189 Rome, Italy, *Tel:* +39 06 331 1737, *Fax:* +39 06 331 1708, *Email:* rome@gastaldi-int.com, *Website:* www.gastaldi-int.it

ARBATAX

Lat 39° 56' N; Long 9° 42' E.

Admiralty Chart: 1210	**Admiralty Pilot:** 46
Time Zone: GMT +1 h	**UNCTAD Locode:** IT ATX

Principal Facilities:

Authority: Ufficio Circondariale Marittimo di Arbatax, Via Tirreno 1/A, I-08041 Arbatax, Sardinia, Italy, *Tel:* +39 0782 667093, *Fax:* +39 0782 667093, *Email:* arbatax@guardiacostiera.it, *Website:* www.arbatax.guardiacostiera.it

Officials: Harbour Master: Antonio Frigo.

Port Security: ISPS compliant

Anchorage: Anchorage can be obtained 1.5 miles off the port in depths ranging from 15 m to 30 m; good holding ground
Punto A: in pos 39° 57.2' N; 09° 42.7' E
Punto B: in pos 39° 58.1' N; 09° 41.8' E
Punto C: in pos 39° 58.1' N; 09° 42.8' E
Punto D: in pos 39° 57.2' N; 09° 42.7' E

Pilotage: Not compulsory but available. Entry to the port is available during day or night. Pilot boards to the N of the Eastern Breakwater (Molo di Levante) at a distance of 2/3 miles

Radio Frequency: VHF Channels 16 and 12

Weather: Prevailing winds NW-W-SE

Maximum Vessel Dimensions: 240 m loa, 7.6 m draft

Principal Imports and Exports: Imports: Metal. Exports: Gravel.

Working Hours: Normal 0800-1200, 1300-1700. Extra shifts available on request

Accommodation:

Name	Length (m)	Depth (m)	Remarks
Arbatax			See [1] below
Banchina di Ponente	420	7–8	
Banchina di Riva	228	7–7.3	
Banchina Sud	440	7	
Banchina Centrale	68	4	
Banchina di Levante	192	9–10	

[1]*Arbatax:* Two platforms for containers. Seven trucks and three tractors for ro/ro

Mechanical Handling Equipment:

Location	Type	Capacity (t)	Qty
Arbatax	Mobile Cranes	40	1

Cargo Worked: Approx 1000-1200 t/day

Bunkering: Available by road tanker from Sarroch Refinery, 200 km

Waste Reception Facilities: Garbage disposal available

Towage: One tug of 1200 hp available

Repair & Maintenance: Mulas Paolo Shipyard, Arbatax, Sardinia, Italy, *Tel:* +39 0782 667625
Valdes Shipyard, Arbatax, Sardinia, Italy, *Tel:* +39 0782 624214

Surveyors: Dogana Secondaria di Arbatax, Arbatax, Sardinia, Italy, *Tel:* +39 0782 667071

Medical Facilities: First aid station at Tortoli, 2 km. Hospital at Lanusei, 30 km

Airport: 5 km (only available in summer)

Lloyd's Agent: Gastaldi International S.r.l., Mura di Santa Chiara 1, I-16128 Genoa, Italy, *Tel:* +39 010 530931, *Fax:* +39 010 530 9343, *Email:* info@gastaldi-int.it, *Website:* www.gastaldi-int.it

AUGUSTA

Lat 37° 12' N; Long 15° 13' E.

Admiralty Chart: 966/973	**Admiralty Pilot:** 45
Time Zone: GMT +1 h	**UNCTAD Locode:** IT AUG

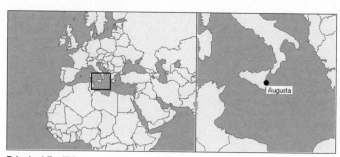

Principal Facilities:

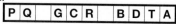

Authority: Compamare Augusta, Capitaneria di Porto Guardia Costiera, Via dei Cantieri, I-96011 Augusta, Italy, *Tel:* +39 0931 978922, *Fax:* +39 0931 978009, *Email:* augusta@guardiacostiera.it, *Website:* www.harbours.net/augusta

Officials: Harbour Master: Gian-Carlo Russo.

Port Security: ISPS compliant

Approach: Harbour is well sheltered from E and SE by breakwaters; it is safely approached day and night through E entrance, max d in roads 21.6 m. Vessels proceeding to SELM Piers inside the breakwaters must enter roads via the E entrance. Operations possible at any hour, weather permitting, but Harbour Master entitled to prohibit berthing at jetties if dangerous to vessels

Pilotage: Compulsory for vessels over 500 gt with advance notice. Augusta Bay Pilots, Tel: +39 0931 974652 & 976166. VHF Channel 12, 24 h service

Radio Frequency: VHF Channels 16 and 9

Weather: Strong SE and E winds occur occasionally in winter

Tides: Very slight with a variation of less than 0.61 m

Maximum Vessel Dimensions: 550 000 dwt

Principal Imports and Exports: Imports: Crude oil, LPG. Exports: Fuels.

Working Hours: 24 h/day

Accommodation:

Name	Draught (m)	Remarks
Augusta		See [1] below
Berth No.1 (North)	11.5	See [2] below
Berth No.1 (South)	8.15	See [3] below
Berth No.2	8.8	See [4] below
Berth No.3 (South)	5.7	Operated by Sasol Italy SpA Vessels up to 3500 dwt & 90 m loa
Berth No.6 (Strbd)	4.9	See [5] below
Berth No.7 (Strbd)	10.67	See [6] below
Berth No.8 (Port)	10.7	See [7] below
Berth No.9 (Strbd)	7.92	See [8] below
Berth No.10 (Strbd)	15.54	See [9] below
Berth No.11 (Port)	16.46	See [10] below
Berth No.12 (Port)	8.53	See [11] below
Berth No.13	7	See [12] below
Berth No.14	7	See [13] below
Berth No.17 (Strbd)	4.5	Operated by Agip SpA Priolo Vessels up to 1000 dwt & 70 m loa
Berth No.18 (Strbd)	7.4	Operated by Agip SpA Priolo Vessels up to 6000 dwt & 120 m loa
Berth No.19 (Strbd)	12.8	See [14] below
Berth No.20 (Strbd)	22.4	See [15] below
Berth No.21 (Strbd)	22.4	See [16] below
Berth No.22 (Port)	14	See [17] below
Berth No.23 (Port)	7.5	Operated by Agip SpA Priolo Vessels up to 6000 dwt & 120 m loa
Berth No.24 (Port)	3.6	Operated by Agip SpA Priolo Vessels up to 1000 dwt & 70 m loa
Berth No.25 (Strbd)	14	See [18] below
Berth No.26 (Port)	14	See [19] below
Berth No.27 (Stern)	11.4	See [20] below
Berth No.33 (Strbd)	6.5	Operated by Enichem Priolo Vessels up to 4000 dwt & 95 m loa
Berth No.34 (Strbd)	8.6	See [21] below
Berth No.35 (Port)	10	See [22] below
Berth No.36	3.7	Operated by Enichem Priolo Vessels up to 1000 dwt

[1]*Augusta:* Berths 4-5 are operated by the military and berths 15-16 by NATO navy. Berths 33-36 are situated outside the port breakwater. Ro/ro terminal in the new Commercial Harbour for vessels up to 10.8 m d

[2]*Berth No.1 (North):* Operated by Sasol Italy SpA
Vessels up to 50 000 dwt & 210 m loa

[3]*Berth No.1 (South):* Operated by Sasol Italy SpA
Vessels up to 50 000 dwt & 210 m loa

[4]*Berth No.2:* Operated by Maxcom Petroli SpA
Bunker storage for vessels up to 50 000 dwt

[5]*Berth No.6 (Strbd):* Operated by Esso Italiana Srl Augusta
Vessels of 550-2500 dwt & 60-95 m loa. Clean, dirty, asphalt & LPG

[6]*Berth No.7 (Strbd):* Operated by Esso Italiana Srl Augusta
Vessels of 1000-10 000 dwt & 60-160 m loa. Clean, dirty & asphalt

[7]*Berth No.8 (Port):* Operated by Esso Italiana Srl Augusta
Vessels of 1000-38 000 dwt & 60-250 m loa. Clean, dirty & asphalt

[8]*Berth No.9 (Strbd):* Operated by Esso Italiana Srl Augusta
Vessels of 1000-10 000 dwt & 60-143 m loa. Clean, dirty, lubes & toluene

[9]*Berth No.10 (Strbd):* Operated by Esso Italiana Srl Augusta
Vessels of 3000-90 000 dwt & 70-277 m loa. Crude, clean, dirty & lubes

[10]*Berth No.11 (Port):* Operated by Esso Italiana Srl Augusta
Vessels of 14 000-140 000 dwt & 153-297 m loa. Crude, clean & dirty

[11]*Berth No.12 (Port):* Operated by Esso Italiana Srl Augusta
Vessels of 1000-12 000 dwt & 65-150 m loa. Clean, dirty & lubes

[12]*Berth No.13:* Operated by Cementerie Unicem SpA
Vessels up to 5000 dwt & 110 m loa

[13]*Berth No.14:* Operated by Cementerie Unicem SpA
Vessels up to 4000 dwt & 100 m loa

[14]*Berth No.19 (Strbd):* Operated by Agip SpA Priolo
Vessels up to 48 000 dwt & 220 m loa

[15]*Berth No.20 (Strbd):* Operated by Agip SpA Priolo
Vessels up to 250 000 dwt & 350 m loa

[16]*Berth No.21 (Strbd):* Operated by Agip SpA Priolo
Vessels up to 375 000 dwt & 380 m loa

[17]*Berth No.22 (Port):* Operated by Agip SpA Priolo
Vessels up to 48 000 dwt & 220 m loa

[18]*Berth No.25 (Strbd):* Operated by Agip SpA Priolo
Vessels up to 70 000 dwt & 250 m loa

[19]*Berth No.26 (Port):* Operated by Agip SpA Priolo
Vessels up to 35 000 dwt & 205 m loa

[20]*Berth No.27 (Stern):* Operated by Agip SpA Priolo
Vessels up to 26 000 dwt & 200 m loa

[21]*Berth No.34 (Strbd):* Operated by Enichem Priolo
Vessels up to 10 000 dwt & 160 m loa

[22]*Berth No.35 (Port):* Operated by Enichem Priolo
Vessels up to 12 000 dwt & 160 m loa

Bunkering: Bella Giovanni Shipping & Trading S.r.l., Via X Ottobre, 89, 96011 Augusta, Italy, *Tel:* +39 0931 978733, *Fax:* +39 0931 209820, *Email:* gbella@gbella.it, *Website:* www.gbella.it

Italnoli S.r.l., Via Marina di Ponente 71, 96011 Augusta, Italy, *Tel:* +39 0931 522006, *Fax:* +39 0931 975276, *Email:* augusta@italnoli.it, *Website:* www.italnoli.it

OilTrader Ltd, Asian Di Fasulo Antonio & Co SAS, Via Principe Umberto 456, 96011 Augusta, Italy, *Tel:* +39 0931 978800, *Fax:* +39 0931 976030, *Email:* asiansas@alice.it, *Website:* www.asianfasulo.it

AGIP Petroli S.p.A., ENI, Via Laurentina 449, 00142 Rome, Italy, *Tel:* +39 06 59881, *Fax:* +39 06 5988 5700, *Email:* gioacchino.costa@eni.it, *Website:* www.eni.it – *Grades:* GO; IFO-180cSt – *Parcel Size:* min GO 50t, min FO 150t – *Delivery Mode:* barge

ExxonMobil Marine Fuels, Mailpoint 31, ExxonMobil House, Ermyn Way, Leatherhead, Surrey KT22 8UX, United Kingdom, *Tel:* +44 1372 222 000, *Fax:* +44 1372 223 922, *Email:* marine.fuels@exxonmobil.com, *Website:* www.exxonmobil.com – *Grades:* IF180-380, MGO – *Misc:* own storage facilities – *Parcel Size:* min MGO 35t; min FO 175t – *Rates:* 600-800t/h – *Notice:* 48 hours – *Delivery Mode:* barge

Gori Petrol Group, V. Cristoforo Colombo 1, San Gregorio di Catania, 95027 Catania, Sicily, Italy, *Tel:* +39 095 492 386, *Fax:* +39 095 7122 710, *Email:* info@goripetrolgroup.191.it

Marodi Service SAS, Via Decorati Al Valor Civile 80, 30173 Venice, Italy, *Tel:* +39 041 538 2143, *Fax:* +39 041 922841, *Email:* marodi@marodi.it, *Website:* www.marodi.it

Maxcom Bunker S.p.A. u.s., Via Bartolomeo Bosco 57/7B, 16121 Genoa, Italy, *Tel:* +39 010 5605 200, *Fax:* +39 010 564 479, *Email:* bunker@maxcombunker.com, *Website:* www.maxcombunker.com – *Grades:* all grades – *Parcel Size:* no min/max – *Rates:* 500t/h – *Notice:* 12-24 hours – *Delivery Mode:* barge

Nautilus Oil Co. S.r.l., Via Emerico Amari 8, 90139 Palermo, Sicily, Italy, *Tel:* +39 091 582244, *Fax:* +39 091 612 2196, *Email:* nautoil@libero.it

Towage: Compulsory. Fifteen tugs up to 5000 hp available

Repair & Maintenance: Cantiere E.Noe S.p.A., Molo Darsena, I-96011 Augusta, Italy, *Tel:* +39 0931 521779, *Fax:* +39 0931 975811, *Email:* mail@cantierenoe.it, *Website:* www.cantierenoe.it Floating dock (Kimek 8500): 155 m x 32.5 m with lifting cap of 8500 t

Ship Chandlers: Intermediterranean Marine Suppliers S.r.l., Via Principe Umberto 343/345, I-96011 Augusta, Italy, *Tel:* +39 0931 976800, *Fax:* +39 0931 978033, *Email:* info@intermediterranean.it

Mellina Agosta S.r.l., C.da Balate km.1 S.P. 1, 96011 Augusta, Italy, *Tel:* +39 0931 512663, *Fax:* +39 0931 512840, *Email:* mellinaaug@mellinaagosta.191.it, *Website:* www.mellinaagosta.it

Promar S.r.l., Via Darsena 12, I-96011 Augusta, Italy, *Tel:* +39 0931 522879, *Fax:* +39 0931 521893, *Email:* promar@promar-srl.com, *Website:* www.promar-srl.com

Shipping Agents: CSA S.p.A., Via X Ottobre, 96011 Augusta, Italy, *Tel:* +39 0931 521093, *Fax:* +39 0931 977493, *Email:* shipservice.au@csaspa.com, *Website:* www.csaspa.com

Inchcape Shipping Services (ISS), ISS-Augusta Srl, Piazza della Rotonda 16, I-96011 Augusta, Italy, *Tel:* +39 0931 977992, *Fax:* +39 0931 971061, *Email:* iss.augusta@iss-shipping.com, *Website:* www.iss-shipping.com

Italnoli S.r.l., Via Marina di Ponente 71, 96011 Augusta, Italy, *Tel:* +39 0931 522006, *Fax:* +39 0931 975276, *Email:* augusta@italnoli.it, *Website:* www.italnoli.it

Medistar Shipping Agency S.r.l., Via Marina Di Ponente 71/B, I-96011 Augusta, Italy, *Tel:* +39 0931 522888, *Fax:* +39 0931 522850, *Email:* augusta@medistarshipping.com, *Website:* www.medistarshipping.com

Wilhelmsen Ship Services, Barwil Si Marittima S.r.l., Via Capitaneria 32, 96011 Augusta, Italy, *Tel:* +39 0931 971064, *Fax:* +39 0931 971198, *Email:* barwil.augusta@barwil.com, *Website:* www.barwil.com

Surveyors: Nippon Kaiji Kyokai, Augusta, Italy, *Tel:* +39 0931 511499, *Fax:* +39 0931 511496, *Website:* www.classnk.or.jp

Registro Italiano Navale (RINA), Lungomare Rossini 30, Augusta, Italy, *Tel:* +39 0931 511499, *Fax:* +39 0931 511496, *Email:* augusta.office@rina.org, *Website:* www.rina.org

Medical Facilities: Augusta hospital, Tel: +39 (0931) 983555

Airport: Catania International Airport, 40 km

Railway: Augusta Railway Station, 1 km

Lloyd's Agent: Tagliavia & Capanna Srl, Via Emerico Amari 8, I-90139 Palermo, Sicily, Italy, *Tel:* +39 091 587377, *Fax:* +39 091 322435, *Email:* info@tagliaviacapanna.it

BAGNOLI

Lat 40° 48' N; Long 14° 10' E.

Admiralty Chart: 916	**Admiralty Pilot:** 46
Time Zone: GMT +1 h	**UNCTAD Locode:** IT BLN

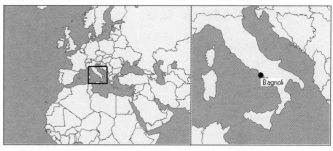

Principal Facilities:

	Y	G			B		A

Authority: Capitaneria di Porto di Napoli, Sezione Staccata di Bagnoli, Via Coroglio 10, I-80124 Naples, Italy, *Tel:* +39 081 723 2272

Pilotage: Bagnoli Pilot is on watch from 0600 to 0600. VHF radio Channels 9 and 12; otherwise use flag or Morse/sound 'G' letter. When in port vessels must give pilots one hour's notice for any service required

Weather: Bagnoli is mainly exposed to SW winds. In the event of bad weather vessels should shift to anchorage in the Baia roads, a sheltered, naturally bay about 4.8 km from Bagnoli. Anchorage depths in this area extend from 20 m to 45 m. Anchorage is allowed in the alignment from the lighthouse of Nisida Island to the lighthouse of Capo Miseno

Tides: There is a tidal range of about 30 cm

Maximum Vessel Dimensions: 80 000 dwt, 12.56 m d max

Accommodation:

Name	Length (m)	Draught (m)	Remarks
Bagnoli			See [1] below
Italsider (North)	647	10.9–12.6	See [2] below
Italsider (South)	384	9	See [3] below
Federconsorzi	245	5.1	See [4] below

[1]*Bagnoli:* Anchorage depth in the Bagnoli roads is from 15 to 30 m, sandy bottom
[2]*Italsider (North):* Ore & coal discharging. Two turnable gantry cranes and conveyor belts (cap 32 t). Ore discharge rate 1100 t/h. Coal discharge rate 900 t/h. Air draught 30 m
[3]*Italsider (South):* Loading pier. Four turntable cranes and rails. Air draught 25 m
[4]*Federconsorzi:* Discharging phosphates and pyrites. One fixed gantry crane and aerial ropeway. Rate 450 t/8 h shift

Bunkering: All grades available ex barge only. Oil companies require 48 h notice prior to delivery

AGIP Petroli S.p.A., ENI, Via Laurentina 449, 00142 Rome, Italy, *Tel:* +39 06 59881, *Fax:* +39 06 5988 5700, *Email:* gioacchino.costa@eni.it, *Website:* www.eni.it

Chevron Marine Products LLC, Piazza Della Vittoria 12/14, 16121 Genoa, Italy, *Tel:* +39 010 5451 611, *Fax:* +39 010 566 762, *Email:* dlfammita@chevron.com, *Website:* www.chevron.com

ExxonMobil Marine Fuels, Mailpoint 31, ExxonMobil House, Ermyn Way, Leatherhead, Surrey KT22 8UX, United Kingdom, *Tel:* +44 1372 222 000, *Fax:* +44 1372 223 922, *Email:* marine.fuels@exxonmobil.com, *Website:* www.exxonmobil.com – *Grades:* MGO; lubes – *Misc:* own storage facilities – *Parcel Size:* min 12t – *Notice:* 24 hours – *Delivery Mode:* truck

Towage: Tugs have to be ordered from Naples

Medical Facilities: Hospital and private facilities in Naples

Airport: Capodichino, 8 km

Lloyd's Agent: Gastaldi International S.r.l., Mura di Santa Chiara 1, I-16128 Genoa, Italy, *Tel:* +39 010 530931, *Fax:* +39 010 530 9343, *Email:* info@gastaldi-int.it, *Website:* www.gastaldi-int.it

Key to Principal Facilities:—				
A=Airport	**C**=Containers	**G**=General Cargo	**P**=Petroleum	**R**=Ro/Ro	**Y**=Dry Bulk
B=Bunkers	**D**=Dry Dock	**L**=Cruise	**Q**=Other Liquid Cargo	**T**=Towage (where available from port)

BARI

Lat 41° 8' N; Long 16° 53' E.

Admiralty Chart: 140
Time Zone: GMT +1 h
Admiralty Pilot: 47
UNCTAD Locode: IT BRI

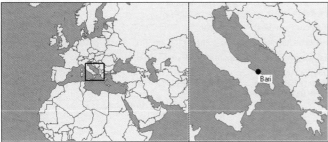

Principal Facilities:

P		Y	G	C	R	L	B		T	A

P. Lorusso & Co. S.r.l.

133 via Piccinni, Bari 70122 Italy

TEL: +39 080 521 2840
FAX: +39 080 521 8229
EMAIL: osurol@interbusiness.it
WEB: www.agenzialorusso.com

SHIPPING AGENTS

AGENCY SINCE 1848
TITI SHIPPING

TEL: +39-0831-523514
FAX: +39-0831-521036
EMAIL: info@titishipping.it
WEB: www.titishipping.it

PORTS OF BRINDISI AND BARI

Authority: Autorita Portuale di Bari, Piazzale Cristoforo Colombo 1, I-70122 Bari, Italy, *Tel:* +39 080 578 8511, *Fax:* +39 080 524 5449, *Email:* apbari@porto.bari.it, *Website:* www.porto.bari.it

Officials: President: Francesco P. Mariani, *Tel:* +39 080 578 8502, *Email:* segreteria@porto.bari.it.
General Secretary: Mario Sommariva, *Email:* segretario.generale@porto.bari.it.
Harbour Master: Salvatore Giuffre, *Tel:* +39 080 521 6860.
Marketing: Guiseppe Nisio, *Tel:* +39 080 578 8506, *Email:* nisio@porto.bari.it.

Port Security: ISPS compliant

Pilotage: Compulsory for vessels over 500 gt, Tel/Fax: +39 080 521 1507, Email: corpopilotibari@hotmail.com. VHF Channel 16 and 12

Tides: Tidal range of 0.3-0.4 m

Traffic: 2007, 5 554 796 t of cargo handled, 64 000 TEU's

Maximum Vessel Dimensions: 300 m loa, 12 m draft

Accommodation:

Name	Remarks
Bari	See [1] below

[1]Bari: Really two ports, the old and the new, the former being the fishing port. New port protected by two breakwaters, Nuovo Molo Foraneo and Molo S Cataldo Entrance about 350 m wide and depths average 11 to 11.5 m. In strong N wind, ships should manoeuvre outside port to arrive at the entrance with stem in SE direction Operational docks: 1350 m long with depths 5.1-11.2 m for all commercial operations, 175 m long with depth 9.15 m reserved for grain silo operations, 560 m long with depths 3-7.3 m for passenger and car ferries, 380 m long with depths 5.49-5.79 m for livestock carriers and 830 m long with depths 9.4-14.3 m for oil tankers
Bulk facilities: Two grain discharge suction pipes, rate approx 100 t/h each
Single or double track rail connections to all docks

Storage: Bonded warehouse with 5000 m2 covered area and cement storage of 3000 t

---

Location	Grain (t)
Bari	25000

Mechanical Handling Equipment:

Location	Type	Capacity (t)
Bari	Mult-purp. Cranes	150

Bunkering: Barion S.r.l., 14 Corso A de Tullio, 70122 Bari, Italy, Tel: +39 080 523 5020, *Fax:* +39 080 524 6810, *Email:* info@barion.it, *Website:* www.barion.it
AGIP Petroli S.p.A., ENI, Via Laurentina 449, 00142 Rome, Italy, Tel: +39 06 59881, *Fax:* +39 06 5988 5700, *Email:* gioacchino.costa@eni.it, *Website:* www.eni.it – *Grades:* GO – *Parcel Size:* min 25t – *Delivery Mode:* truck
Basile Petroli S.p.A., S.S. 172 Per Martina Franca, C. Da Carmin 6900, P O Box 6 Succ., 74100 Taranto, Italy, *Tel:* +39 099 4723 332, *Fax:* +39 099 4723 361, *Email:* bunkerdept@basilepetroli.it, *Website:* www.basilepetroli.it

Towage: Three tugs available
Rimorchiatori Napoletani S.r.l., Molo Foraneo Banchina No.8, 70122 Bari, Italy, *Tel:* +39 080 521 9342, *Fax:* +39 080 523 2511, *Email:* oper.bari@rimnap.it, *Website:* www.rimnap.it

Ship Chandlers: Cianciola-Montanari Shipchandlers della Work System S.r.l., Banchina 13/14, I-70122 Bari, Italy, *Tel:* +39 080 523 5260, *Fax:* +39 080 521 2730, *Email:* cianbari@tin.it
Provveditorie Marittime del Mediterraneo S.r.l. (PROMED), Strada Provinciale Bari, Modugno 83/d, I-70026 Bari, Italy, *Tel:* +39 080 536 7124, *Fax:* +39 080 536 7125, *Email:* promed@promedshipsupply.it, *Website:* www.promedshipsupply.it

Shipping Agents: Barion S.r.l., 14 Corso A de Tullio, 70122 Bari, Italy, *Tel:* +39 080 523 5020, *Fax:* +39 080 524 6810, *Email:* info@barion.it, *Website:* www.barion.it
DG Cargo S.r.l., Via Principe Amedeo 212, I-70122 Bari, Italy, *Tel:* +39 080 524 0264, *Fax:* +39 080 524 0281, *Email:* info@dgcargo.it, *Website:* www.dgcargo.it
Nicola Girone S.r.l., Via Massaua 1/E, 70123 Bari, Italy, *Tel:* +39 080 534 1736, *Fax:* +39 080 534 1786, *Email:* gironeba@tin.it, *Website:* www.nicolagirone.com
Longo Shipbrokers S.r.l., Via Cairoli 27, I-70122 Bari, Italy, *Tel:* +39 080 524 2166, *Fax:* +39 080 523 5497, *Email:* agency@longoshipbrokers.com, *Website:* www.longoshipbrokers.com
P. Lorusso & Co. S.r.l., 133 Via Piccinni, I-70122 Bari, Italy, *Tel:* +39 080 521 2840, *Fax:* +39 080 521 8229, *Email:* vdbdirezione@agenzialorusso.it, *Website:* www.agenzialorusso.it
Poseidone S.r.l., Piazza Massari 36, Bari, Italy, *Tel:* +39 080 573 9698, *Fax:* +39 080 572 7928, *Email:* poseidone@poseidone.it, *Website:* www.poseidone.it

Surveyors: Agema International Bari-Milan, Via Diomede Fresa 2, 70126 Bari, Italy, *Tel:* +39 080 546 1691, *Fax:* +39 080 546 1695, *Email:* agemainternational@virgilio.it
Agema International Bari-Milan, Via Diomede Fresa 2, 70126 Bari, Italy, *Tel:* +39 080 546 1691, *Fax:* +39 080 546 1695, *Email:* agemainternational@alice.it
Det Norske Veritas A/S, Via Junipero Serra 19, I-70126 Bari, Italy, *Tel:* +39 080 548 6905, *Fax:* +39 080 548 6906, *Email:* bari@dnv.com, *Website:* www.dnv.com
Registro Italiano Navale (RINA), 33 Piazza Aldo Moro, I-70122 Bari, Italy, *Tel:* +39 080 524 2268, *Fax:* +39 080 524 2438, *Email:* bari.office@rina.org, *Website:* www.rina.org

Airport: Bari-Palese Airport, 7 km

Railway: Single or double track rail connections to all docks

Lloyd's Agent: P. Lorusso & Co. S.r.l., 133 Via Piccinni, I-70122 Bari, Italy, *Tel:* +39 080 521 2840, *Fax:* +39 080 521 8229, *Email:* vdbdirezione@agenzialorusso.it, *Website:* www.agenzialorusso.it

BARLETTA

Lat 41° 19' N; Long 16° 16' E.

Admiralty Chart: 1443
Time Zone: GMT +1 h
Admiralty Pilot: 47
UNCTAD Locode: IT BLT

Principal Facilities:

P		Y	G			B		T	A

Authority: Capitaneria di Porto di Barletta, Via Cristoforo Colombo 45, I-70051 Barletta, Italy, *Tel:* +39 0883 531020, *Fax:* +39 0883 533400, *Email:* barletta@guardiacostiera.it

Officials: Harbour Master: Cosimo Roberto Carbonara.

Port Security: ISPS compliant

Pilotage: Compulsory for vessels over 500 gt. Pilot boards one nautical mile N of the breakwater. VHF Channel 12

Radio Frequency: VHF Channel 06 for ship communications and VHF Channel 16 for SOS

Maximum Vessel Dimensions: 120 m loa, 6.6 m draft

Working Hours: Mon-Sat 0900-1200

Accommodation:

Name	Remarks
Barletta	See [1] below

[1]*Barletta:* Vessels lie alongside breakwater. Max depth at entrance 8.53 m; at quay No's 4, 5, 6, 7 and 8, about 8.23 to 8.53 m; No's 9 and 10, about 8.53 m; No's 11 and 12, 9.14 m. Railway connected with harbour

Storage:

Location	Grain (t)
Barletta	25000

Bunkering: Available by road trucks

Towage: One tug available

Repair & Maintenance: Available only for small wooden ships

Ship Chandlers: Cianciola-Montanari Shipchandlers della Work System S.r.l., Via Colombo 36, I-70051 Barletta, Italy, *Tel:* +39 0883 523 5260, *Fax:* +39 0883 521 2730, *Email:* cianbari@tin.it

Medical Facilities: Available

Airport: Palese, 50 km

Lloyd's Agent: P. Lorusso & Co. S.r.l., 133 Via Piccinni, I-70122 Bari, Italy, *Tel:* +39 080 521 2840, *Fax:* +39 080 521 8229, *Email:* vdbdirezione@agenzialorusso.it, *Website:* www.agenzialorusso.it

BRINDISI

Lat 40° 39' N; Long 17° 59' E.

Admiralty Chart: 1418	**Admiralty Pilot:** 47
Time Zone: GMT +1 h	**UNCTAD Locode:** IT BDS

Principal Facilities:

P	Q	Y	G	C	R		B		T	A

AGENCY SINCE 1848

TITI *SHIPPING*

Vico de Lubelli, 8
72100 Brindisi, ITALY

TEL: +39-0831-523514
FAX: +39-0831-521036
EMAIL: info@titishipping.it
WEB: www.titishipping.it

Authority: Autorita Portuale di Brindisi, Piazza Vittorio Emanuele II 7, I-72100 Brindisi, Italy, *Tel:* +39 0831 562649, *Fax:* +39 0831 562225, *Email:* info@porto.brindisi.it, *Website:* www.porto.br.it

Officials: President: Giuseppe Giurgola, *Email:* presidente@porto.brindisi.it. General Secretary: Nicola Del Nobile, *Email:* segretario@porto.brindisi.it.

Port Security: ISPS compliant

Pilotage: Compulsory. VHF Channel 12

Radio Frequency: VHF Channels 16 and 11

Traffic: 2006, 10 497 701 t of cargo handled

Working Hours: 24 h/day

Accommodation:

Name	Length (m)	Depth (m)	Remarks
Brindisi			See [1] below
Costa Morena Riva	300	8.5	
Costa Morena Diga	500	12	
Pontile Enichem	200	10	

[1]*Brindisi:* Container facilities operated by Brindisi Terminal Italia SpA, Tel: +39 0831 558119, Fax: +39 0831 540651, Email: info@brindisiterminal.com, Website: www.brindisiterminal.com

Mechanical Handling Equipment:

Location	Type	Capacity (t)	Qty
Brindisi	Floating Cranes	70	1
Brindisi	Mobile Cranes	40	1
Brindisi	Mobile Cranes	15	1

Bunkering: Titi Shipping S.r.l., Vico de Lubelli 8, 72100 Brindisi, Italy, *Tel:* +39 0831 523514, *Fax:* +39 0831 521036, *Email:* survey@titishipping.it, *Website:* www.titishipping.it
AGIP Petroli S.p.A., ENI, Via Laurentina 449, 00142 Rome, Italy, *Tel:* +39 06 59881, *Fax:* +39 06 5988 5700, *Email:* gioacchino.costa@eni.it, *Website:* www.eni.it – *Grades:* GO – *Parcel Size:* min 25t – *Delivery Mode:* truck
Basile Petroli S.p.A., S.S. 172 Per Martina Franca, C. Da Carmin 6900, P O Box 6 Succ., 74100 Taranto, Italy, *Tel:* +39 099 4723 332, *Fax:* +39 099 4723 361, *Email:* bunkerdept@basilepetroli.it, *Website:* www.basilepetroli.it

Towage: Available

Ship Chandlers: Cianciola-Montanari Shipchandlers della Work System S.r.l., Via Regina Giovanna di Bulgaria 5, I-72100 Brindisi, Italy, *Tel:* +39 0831 562417, *Fax:* +39 0831 590253, *Email:* cianbari@tin.it

Shipping Agents: Angela Gioia S.r.l., Via del Mare 6, I-72100 Brindisi, Italy, *Tel:* +39 0831 562824, *Fax:* +39 0831 562785, *Email:* info@angelagioiasrl.com, *Website:* www.angelagioiasrl.com
Barion S.r.l., Corso G Garibaldi 53, Brindisi, Italy, *Tel:* +39 0831 525810, *Fax:* +39 0831 529488, *Email:* barion@mail.futura.it
CSA S.p.A., Via F. Consiglio 59, I-72100 Brindisi, Italy, *Tel:* +39 0831 521218, *Fax:* +39 0831 561759, *Email:* shipservice.br@csaspa.com, *Website:* www.csaspa.com
LOG-MED S.r.l., Corso Garibaldi 27, I-72100 Brindisi, Italy, *Tel:* +39 0831 560563, *Fax:* +39 0831 590191
Poseidone S.r.l., Viale Regina Margherita 50, I-72100 Brindisi, Italy, *Tel:* +39 0831 524872, *Fax:* +39 0831 564025, *Email:* poseidone@poseidone.it, *Website:* www.poseidone.it
Servizi Portuali Generali S.r.l., Via Giordano Bruno 24, I-72100 Brindisi, Italy, *Tel:* +39 0831 560340, *Fax:* +39 0831 561692, *Email:* spg@spgbrindisi.it, *Website:* www.spgbrindisi.it
Titi Shipping S.r.l., Vico de Lubelli 8, 72100 Brindisi, Italy, *Tel:* +39 0831 523514, *Fax:* +39 0831 521036, *Email:* survey@titishipping.it, *Website:* www.titishipping.it
Zaccaria & Co. Srl, 27 Corso Garibaldi, I-72100 Brindisi, Italy, *Tel:* +39 0831 521045, *Fax:* +39 0831 528193, *Email:* zacmar@tin.it, *Website:* www.zaccariashipping.com

Surveyors: Hellenic Register of Shipping, c/o Lonoce S.r.l., Corso Garibaldi 6, I-72100 Brindisi, Italy, *Tel:* +39 0831 562602, *Fax:* +39 0831 590454, *Email:* lonsrl@tin.it, *Website:* www.hrs.gr
Lonoce S.r.l., Corso Garibaldi 6, 72100 Brindisi, Italy, *Tel:* +39 0831 562602, *Fax:* +39 0831 590454, *Email:* lonsrl@tin.it

Airport: International airport 4 km from town

Development: Construction of a LNG terminal in the Capo Bianco area

Lloyd's Agent: P. Lorusso & Co. S.r.l., 133 Via Piccinni, I-70122 Bari, Italy, *Tel:* +39 080 521 2840, *Fax:* +39 080 521 8229, *Email:* vdbdirezione@agenzialorusso.it, *Website:* www.agenzialorusso.it

CAGLIARI

Lat 39° 12' N; Long 9° 5' E.

Admiralty Chart: 1208	**Admiralty Pilot:** 46
Time Zone: GMT +1 h	**UNCTAD Locode:** IT CAG

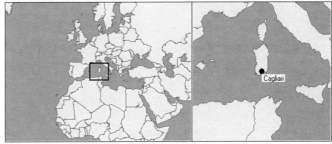

Principal Facilities:

P	Q	Y	G	C	R	L	B		T	A

Authority: Autorita Portuale di Cagliari, Molo Sanita Porto di Cagliari, I-09123 Cagliari, Sardinia, Italy, *Tel:* +39 070 679531, *Fax:* +39 070 6795 3345, *Email:* autorita.portuale@tiscali.it, *Website:* www.porto.cagliari.it

Officials: President: Paolo Fadda, *Email:* paolo.fadda@porto.cagliari.it. General Secretary: Antonio Conti, *Email:* amconti@porto.cagliari.it. Marketing Manager: Valeria Mangiarotti, *Email:* valeria.mangiarotti@porto.cagliari.it. Harbour Master: Capt Domenico De Michele, *Tel:* +39 070 651518.

Port Security: ISPS compliant

Approach: Channel depth 13 m

Pilotage: Compulsory for vessels over 500 gt within one mile from outer breakwater, Tel: +39 070 652929. VHF Channel 12

Traffic: 2007, 35 261 756 t of cargo handled, 547 336 TEU's

Working Hours: 0800-1200, 1400-1800 in summer. 0800-1200, 1300-1700 in winter. Saturday overtime 0700-1300

Accommodation:

Name	Length (m)	Depth (m)	Remarks
Cagliari			See [1] below
Banchina Ichnusa	68	7.3	Passenger ships & small craft
Molo Capitaneria	128	6.4	Passenger ships & small craft
Calata Darsena	227	2.1–5.1	Passenger ships & small craft

Key to Principal Facilities:—			
A=Airport	**C**=Containers	**G**=General Cargo	**P**=Petroleum	**R**=Ro/Ro	**Y**=Dry Bulk
B=Bunkers	**D**=Dry Dock	**L**=Cruise	**Q**=Other Liquid Bulk	**T**=Towage (where available from port)	

Name	Length (m)	Depth (m)	Remarks
Pontile Dogana	124	3–3.9	Passenger ships & small craft
Pontile Sanita	60	5.1	Passenger ships & small craft
Calata Azuni	117	5.1–6.1	Passenger ships & small craft
Calata di Ponente	93	7.9–8.8	Passenger ships & small craft
Calata Sant' Agostino	285	7.9	Bulk and/or general cargo
Molo Sabaudo (inner)	325	7.9	Bulk and/or general cargo
Molo Sabaudo (outer)	327	8.2	See [2] below
Molo Rinascita (inner)	400	8.8	Bulk and/or general cargo. Wheat silo
Molo Rinascita (outer)	400	8.8	Bulk and/or general cargo
Molo di Levante	350	9.7	Bulk and/or general cargo
Private Wharves			See [3] below

[1]*Cagliari:* Harbour formed by two breakwaters opening toward SW. Depth at entrance 8.38 m

Cagliari International Container Terminal (CICT), 09124 Cagliari, Tel: +39 070 25051, Fax: +39 070 250 5291, Email: infocict@contshipitalia.com, Website: www.cict.it, featuring a 1520 m long pier in depth of 14 m and a 325 000 m2 area fitted with seven post-panamax gantry cranes and two mobile cranes

Tanker facilities: Available at the military Wharf, Molo di Levante. Tankers with oil and chemical cargoes are not allowed to discharge at the commercial port

[2]*Molo Sabaudo (outer):* Bulk and/or general cargo. Conveyor belt for bags containing cereals, max beam 13 m

[3]*Private Wharves:* Chemical terminal 6.4 km from the port on the W coast of the gulf of Cagliari; max safe d 6.0 m

Mechanical Handling Equipment:

Location	Type	Capacity (t)	Qty	Remarks
Cagliari	Mult-purp. Cranes	32		
Cagliari	Mobile Cranes	100	1	private

Bunkering: AGIP Petroli S.p.A., ENI, Via Laurentina 449, 00142 Rome, Italy, *Tel:* +39 06 59881, *Fax:* +39 06 5988 5700, *Email:* gioacchino.costa@eni.it, *Website:* www.eni.it – *Grades:* GO – *Misc:* no night service – *Parcel Size:* min 25t – *Delivery Mode:* truck

Towage: One tug available of 1700 hp. Four tugs available on request from Sarroch

Ship Chandlers: Cianciola Sardegna S.r.l., Via T. Congiu 5, Elmas, 09034 Cagliari, Sardinia, Italy, *Tel:* +39 070 241192, *Fax:* +39 070 211 0302, *Email:* ship-chandler@cianciola.com, *Website:* www.cianciola.com
Italfornavi S.r.l., Viale Elmas 204 KM 3,350, 09034 Elmas, Cagliari, Sardinia, Italy, *Tel:* +39 070 240061, *Fax:* +39 070 240428, *Email:* italfornavi@italfornavi.com

Shipping Agents: Agenzia Marittima Cincotta S.r.l., Via Sa Perdixedda 18B, P O Box 10, I-09123 Cagliari, Sardinia, Italy, *Tel:* +39 070 605 0204, *Email:* cagliari@cincotta.com, *Website:* www.cincottashipping.com
Carimar S.r.l., Building A, Via Riva di Tonente s/n, I-09123 Cagliari, Sardinia, Italy, *Tel:* +39 070 684441, *Fax:* +39 070 682157, *Email:* info@carimar.it, *Website:* www.carimar.it
Efispau S.r.l., Viale A. Diaz 29, I-09125 Cagliari, Sardinia, Italy, *Tel:* +39 070 655665, *Fax:* +39 070 668113, *Email:* efispau@efispau.com, *Website:* www.efispau.com
Enrico Pernis Shipping Agency Ltd, Representative Office, Viale A.Diaz 29, 7th Floor, P O Box 273, Cagliari, Sardinia, Italy, *Tel:* +39 070 60401, *Fax:* +39 070 660034, *Email:* cagliari@pernis.com, *Website:* www.pernis.com
LCA S.r.l., Via Sa Perdixedda nr 18/B, Cagliari, Sardinia, Italy, *Tel:* +39 070 640 5267, *Fax:* +39 070 640 2601, *Email:* p.bianchi@lca.col.it
Plaisant & Co. Ship Agency S.r.l., Via Roma 121, I-09124 Cagliari, Sardinia, Italy, *Tel:* +39 070 668208, *Fax:* +39 070 659924, *Email:* plaisant.cagliari@plaisant.it, *Website:* www.plaisant.it
Pons Ltd Shipping Agency & Logistics, Via Concezione 3, I-09124 Cagliari, Sardinia, Italy, *Tel:* +39 070 661371, *Fax:* +39 070 653677, *Email:* info@ponsltd.com, *Website:* www.ponsltd.com
Sarda Marittima S.r.l., Via Roma 47, 09124 Cagliari, Sardinia, Italy, *Tel:* +39 070 667941, *Fax:* +39 070 670495, *Email:* sarmasrl@hotmail.com

Surveyors: Bureau Veritas, Viale La Playa 7 Romagnoli 6, I-09100 Cagliari, Sardinia, Italy, *Tel:* +39 070 667620, *Fax:* +39 070 666728, *Website:* www.bureauveritas.com
Nippon Kaiji Kyokai, Cagliari, Sardinia, Italy, *Tel:* +39 070 651331, *Fax:* +39 070 662787, *Website:* www.classnk.or.jp
Pons Ltd Shipping Agency & Logistics, Via Concezione 3, I-09124 Cagliari, Sardinia, Italy, *Tel:* +39 070 661371, *Fax:* +39 070 653677, *Email:* info@ponsltd.com, *Website:* www.ponsltd.com
Registro Italiano Navale (RINA), Via Barone Rossi 29, Cagliari, Sardinia, Italy, *Tel:* +39 070 651331, *Fax:* +39 070 662787, *Email:* cagliari.office@rina.org, *Website:* www.rina.org

Medical Facilities: Available

Airport: About 10 km from the port

Lloyd's Agent: Gastaldi International S.r.l., Mura di Santa Chiara 1, I-16128 Genoa, Italy, *Tel:* +39 010 530931, *Fax:* +39 010 530 9343, *Email:* info@gastaldi-int.it, *Website:* www.gastaldi-int.it

CASTELLAMMARE DI STABIA

Lat 40° 41' N; Long 14° 28' E.

Admiralty Chart: 916	**Admiralty Pilot:** 46
Time Zone: GMT +1 h	**UNCTAD Locode:** IT CAS

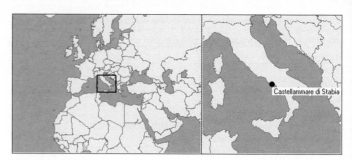

Principal Facilities:

			G	R	B		A

Authority: Capitaneria di Porto di Castellammare di Stabia, Piazzale Incrociatore S. Giorgio 4, I-80053 Castellammare di Stabia, Italy, *Tel:* +39 081 871 1086, *Fax:* +39 081 871 0078, *Email:* castellammaredistabia@guardiacostiera.it

Officials: Harbour Master: Mario Valente.

Port Security: ISPS compliant

Pilotage: Compulsory for vessels over 500 gt. Pilot boards in pos 40° 42.60' N; 14° 27.35' E

Radio Frequency: Harbour Master on VHF Channel 16

Maximum Vessel Dimensions: Length 130 to 150 m, breadth 18 to 20 m, d at bow mooring 8.23 m

Working Hours: 0800-1200, 1300-1700, 1700-2400

Accommodation:

Name	Length (m)	Depth (m)	Remarks
Castellammare di Stabia			See [1] below
Molo Sottoflutto	162	4	
Banchina Fontana	320	4	
Banchina Marinella	260	4	
Pontile Silos	120	7	See [2] below
Banchina Mare Morto	213	2.3	Fishing vessels

[1]*Castellammare di Stabia:* Depth at entrance 16 m. Depth at quays from 4 to 7 m
[2]*Pontile Silos:* Three elevators for discharging cereals and salt, rates of 30 t/h

Bunkering: By tank truck only for gasoline and naphtha

Towage: Available from Naples if required

Repair & Maintenance: Fincantieri-Cantieri Navali Italiani S.p.A. Castellammare di Stabia, Piazza Amendola 5, 80053 Castellammare di Stabia, Italy, *Tel:* +39 081 871 4522, *Fax:* +39 081 871 4403

Airport: Capodichino, 30 km

Lloyd's Agent: Gastaldi International S.r.l., Mura di Santa Chiara 1, I-16128 Genoa, Italy, *Tel:* +39 010 530931, *Fax:* +39 010 530 9343, *Email:* info@gastaldi-int.it, *Website:* www.gastaldi-int.it

CATANIA

Lat 37° 31' N; Long 15° 6' E.

Admiralty Chart: 992	**Admiralty Pilot:** 45
Time Zone: GMT +1 h	**UNCTAD Locode:** IT CTA

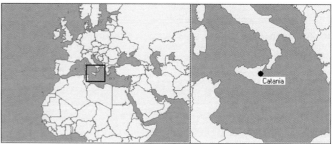

Principal Facilities:

P		Y	G	C	R		B		T	A

Authority: Autorita Portuale di Catania, Piazzale Circumetnea 2, I-95131 Catania, Sicily, Italy, *Tel:* +39 095 535888, *Fax:* +39 095 535888, *Website:* www.porto.catania.it

Port Security: ISPS compliant

Approach: A large harbour, capable of accommodating the largest ships. Depth at entrance 11.28 m approx

Pilotage: Compulsory, Tel: +39 095 531906

Traffic: 2003, 4 127 195 t of cargo handled

Working Hours: Mon to Fri 0800-1200 and 1300-1700; for completion only 1700-1900 at extra 25%. Shift hours: Mon to Fri, 1st shift 0700-1330; 2nd shift 1330-2000 at extra 27.50%; Sat, 1st shift 0700-1300 at extra 27.50%. 2nd shift 1330-2000 at extra 40%; Sun 1st and 2nd shifts at extra 77.50%

Accommodation:

Name	Length (m)	Depth (m)	Remarks
Catania			See [1] below
Berths 1 & 2	361	7.92	See [2] below
Berths 4 & 5			For small vessels, in the Porto Peschereccio
Berth 6	154	8.99	See [3] below
Berth 7	130	8.84	
Berth 8	140	8.84	
Berth 9	130	5.49–8.53	
Berths 10 & 11	307	8.84	
Berth 12 (Molo Centrale)	120	9.14	Head of the harbour's central quay
Berth 13	182	8.99	
Berth 14	169	8.53–8.84	
Berths 15 & 16	114	5.79–6.1	
Berths 17-20			See [4] below
Berth 21 (Molo di Levante)	111	6.25	
Berth 22	60	4.88–6.1	
Berth 22B	120	4.88	

[1]*Catania:* Marangolo Container Terminal available with storage for 1000 TEU's. One mobile crane for loading and discharging 20 and 40 ft containers of up to 30 t. Two straddle carriers of up to 40 t cap. Two forklift trucks of up to 12 t cap. Four berths for ro/ro ships

[2]*Berths 1 & 2:* On the Molo Mezzogiorno (lateral mole at entrance to harbour). Tankers can be discharged here at rate of 400 t/h

[3]*Berth 6:* Petrol and commercial berth on W side of harbour. Six privately owned silos including one of 22 000 t cap. Discharging rate 500 t/day

[4]*Berths 17-20:* 142, 137, 135, 156, 170 m with 6.7 to 7.31 m, 5.49 to 6.1 m and 6.55 m respectively

Mechanical Handling Equipment:

Location	Type	Capacity (t)	Qty
Catania	Mobile Cranes	5	3
Catania	Mobile Cranes	2	2

Bunkering: Gori Petrol Group, V. Cristoforo Colombo 1, San Gregorio di Catania, 95027 Catania, Sicily, Italy, *Tel:* +39 095 492 386, *Fax:* +39 095 7122 710, *Email:* info@goripetrolgroup.191.it
AGIP Petroli S.p.A., ENI, Via Laurentina 449, 00142 Rome, Italy, *Tel:* +39 06 59881, *Fax:* +39 06 5988 5700, *Email:* gioacchino.costa@eni.it, *Website:* www.eni.it – *Grades:* GO; IFO180cSt – *Parcel Size:* min GO 50t, min FO 150t – *Rates:* 200-250t/h – *Delivery Mode:* barge
ExxonMobil Marine Fuels, Mailpoint 31, ExxonMobil House, Ermyn Way, Leatherhead, Surrey KT22 8UX, United Kingdom, *Tel:* +44 1372 222 000, *Fax:* +44 1372 223 922, *Email:* marine.fuels@exxonmobil.com, *Website:* www.exxonmobil.com – *Grades:* MGO; IFO; in line blending available – *Misc:* own storage facilities – *Parcel Size:* min MGO 35t, min IFO 175t – *Rates:* 600-800t/h – *Notice:* 48 hours – *Delivery Mode:* barge
Gori Petrol Group, V. Cristoforo Colombo 1, San Gregorio di Catania, 95027 Catania, Sicily, Italy, *Tel:* +39 095 492 386, *Fax:* +39 095 7122 710, *Email:* info@goripetrolgroup.191.it
Marodi Service SAS, Via Decorati Al Valor Civile 80, 30173 Venice, Italy, *Tel:* +39 041 538 2143, *Fax:* +39 041 922841, *Email:* marodi@marodi.it, *Website:* www.marodi.it
Maxcom Bunker S.p.A. u.s., Via Bartolomeo Bosco 57/7B, 16121 Genoa, Italy, *Tel:* +39 010 5605 200, *Fax:* +39 010 564 479, *Email:* bunker@maxcombunker.com, *Website:* www.maxcombunker.com – *Grades:* all grades – *Parcel Size:* no min/max – *Rates:* 500t/h – *Notice:* 12-24 hours – *Delivery Mode:* barge
Nautilus Oil Co. S.r.l., Via Emerico Amari 8, 90139 Palermo, Sicily, Italy, *Tel:* +39 091 582244, *Fax:* +39 091 612 2196, *Email:* nautoil@libero.it

Towage: Compulsory for tankers over 2000 gt

Repair & Maintenance: Minor repairs handled by two firms

Ship Chandlers: Fratelli Sciotto, Via Gravina 13, I-95131 Catania, Sicily, Italy, *Tel:* +39 095 531395, *Fax:* +39 095 531556, *Email:* fsciotto@augol.it
Mellina Agosta S.r.l., Via Dusmet 131, 95131 Catania, Sicily, Italy, *Tel:* +39 095 310203, *Fax:* +39 095 326580, *Email:* mellinact@mellinaagosta.191.it, *Website:* www.mellinaagosta.it

Shipping Agents: CSA S.p.A., Via Antonino di San Giuliano, I-95131 Catania, Sicily, Italy, *Tel:* +39 095 746 2164, *Fax:* +39 095 535494, *Email:* shipservice.ct@csaspa.com, *Website:* www.csaspa.com
Europea Servizi Terminalistici Srl, Molo Sporgente Centrale, I-95131 Catania, Sicily, Italy, *Tel:* +39 095 533102, *Fax:* +39 095 747 7545, *Email:* a.pandolfo@esterminal.com, *Website:* www.esterminal.com
Fratelli Bonanno S.r.l., Via Anzalone 7, 95131 Catania, Sicily, Italy, *Tel:* +39 095 310629, *Fax:* +39 095 314469, *Email:* bonann@tin.it
Marangolo S.r.l., Zona Industriale, 8A Strada 20/24, 95121 Catania, Sicily, Italy, *Tel:* +39 095 713 9141, *Fax:* +39 095 713 9142, *Email:* administrator@marangolo.it, *Website:* www.marangolo.it

Stevedoring Companies: Marangolo S.r.l., Zona Industriale, 8A Strada 20/24, 95121 Catania, Sicily, Italy, *Tel:* +39 095 713 9141, *Fax:* +39 095 713 9142, *Email:* administrator@marangolo.it, *Website:* www.marangolo.it

Surveyors: Det Norske Veritas A/S, Via A. de Gasperi 187, I-95127 Catania, Sicily, Italy, *Tel:* +39 095 370020, *Fax:* +39 095 372871, *Email:* catania@dnv.com, *Website:* www.dnv.com
Nippon Kaiji Kyokai, Catania, Sicily, Italy, *Tel:* +39 095 325826, *Fax:* +39 095 325826, *Website:* www.classnk.or.jp

Airport: Fontanarossa, 5 km

Lloyd's Agent: Tagliavia & Capanna Srl, Via Emerico Amari 8, I-90139 Palermo, Sicily, Italy, *Tel:* +39 091 587377, *Fax:* +39 091 322435, *Email:* info@tagliaviacapanna.it

CHIOGGIA

Lat 45° 13' N; Long 12° 17' E.

Admiralty Chart: 1473/1483	**Admiralty Pilot:** 47
Time Zone: GMT +1 h	**UNCTAD Locode:** IT CHI

Principal Facilities:

	Y	G		R		B		T	A

Authority: Capitaneria di Porto di Chioggia, Piazza S. Croce 1290, I-30015 Chioggia, Italy, *Tel:* +39 041 550 8211, *Fax:* +39 041 550 8204, *Email:* aspo@portodichioggia.it, *Website:* www.portodichioggia.it

Port Security: ISPS compliant

Approach: Entrance is narrow and current strong. Depth at entrance 8.38 m

Pilotage: Compulsory for vessels over 500 gt. Available on application to Port Captain on VHF Channel 14

Weather: Main winds, SE and NE. Some fog in winter

Tides: Two HW and two LW each day; about 1 m above datum

Maximum Vessel Dimensions: 150 m loa, 6.3 m d, 10 000 gt

Working Hours: Mon to Fri 0800-1200, 1400-1800. Sat 0700-1330

Accommodation:

Name	Length (m)	Depth (m)	Draught (m)	Remarks
Chioggia				See [1] below
New Quay of Canal Lombardo Esterno	650	6.3		
Banchina Marittima	460	4.8		
Canal Lombardo Interno	120	4.7		
Val da Rio	1500		5.5	See [2] below

[1]*Chioggia:* Anchorage for ships lightening on barges (Lat 45° 12' 48" N; long 12° 20' 00" E), over 10.67 m in depth. Depth at entrance 8.38 m. Depth in outer port up to 10.67 m
Special quay for ro/ro; length 60 m, depth 6.3 m

[2]*Val da Rio:* Dry cargoes only, vessels up to 140 m loa, 100 000 m2 of open storage, 10 000 m of covered storage

Storage: Mocomar Srl for covered storage. No refrigerated facilities

Location
Val da Rio

Mechanical Handling Equipment:

Location	Type	Capacity (t)	Qty
Chioggia	Mobile Cranes	150	20

Bunkering: ExxonMobil Marine Fuels, Mailpoint 31, ExxonMobil House, Ermyn Way, Leatherhead, Surrey KT22 8UX, United Kingdom, *Tel:* +44 1372 222 000, *Fax:* +44 1372 223 922, *Email:* marine.fuels@exxonmobil.com, *Website:* www.exxonmobil.com – *Grades:* MGO; IFO40-380cSt; lubes; in line blending available – *Parcel Size:* no min – *Rates:* 200-300t/h – *Notice:* 24 hours – *Delivery Mode:* barge
Marodi Service SAS, Via Decorati Al Valor Civile 80, 30173 Venice, Italy, *Tel:* +39 041 538 2143, *Fax:* +39 041 922841, *Email:* marodi@marodi.it, *Website:* www.marodi.it – *Grades:* all grades
Maxcom Bunker S.p.A. u.s., Via Bartolomeo Bosco 57/7B, 16121 Genoa, Italy, *Tel:* +39 010 5605 200, *Fax:* +39 010 564 479, *Email:* bunker@maxcombunker.com, *Website:* www.maxcombunker.com – *Grades:* MGO; IFO40-380cSt – *Misc:* own storage facilities – *Parcel Size:* max 1000t – *Rates:* 500-600t/h – *Notice:* 12-24 hours – *Delivery Mode:* barge

Towage: One tug available but others obtainable from Venice. The port is divided into two zones: Zone A between breakwaters head at the entrance to port and Buoys Camp S Felice; Zone B between Buoys Camp S Felice and all quays enclosing Buoys Camp Canal Perognolo

Repair & Maintenance: Catozzo Luigi, Chioggia, Italy, *Tel:* +39 041 406627 Hull and machinery workshop. No dry dock

Ship Chandlers: Omega S.r.l., Via Saloni 59, I-30015 Chioggia VE, Italy, *Tel:* +39 041 401029, *Fax:* +39 041 403031, *Email:* omega_chioggia@hotmail.com

Medical Facilities: Hospital

Airport: Venice, 59 km

Lloyd's Agent: Radonicich Insurance Services S.r.l., Via F. Orsini 6/A, Marghera, 30175 Venice, Italy, *Tel:* +39 041 538 2103, *Fax:* +39 041 926108, *Email:* radinsur@portofvenice.net

Key to Principal Facilities:—		
A=Airport	**C**=Containers	**G**=General Cargo
B=Bunkers	**D**=Dry Dock	**L**=Cruise

P=Petroleum	**R**=Ro/Ro	**Y**=Dry Bulk
Q=Other Liquid Bulk	**T**=Towage (where available from port)	

CIRO MARINA

Lat 39° 22' N; Long 17° 8' E.

Admiralty Chart: -	**Admiralty Pilot:** 45
Time Zone: GMT +1 h	**UNCTAD Locode:** IT

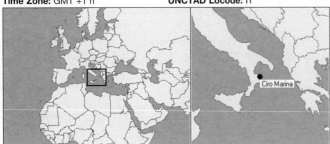

Principal Facilities:

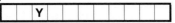

				Y								

Authority: Capitaneria di Porto di Ciro Marina, Via del Porto, I-88072 Ciro Marina, Italy, *Tel:* +39 0962 36328, *Fax:* +39 0962 371472

Officials: Harbour Master: Antonio Lavia.

Port Security: ISPS compliant

Pilotage: Available from Crotone Pilot Station

Radio Frequency: VHF Channels 16 and 14

Accommodation:

Name	Remarks
Ciro Marina	See [1] below

[1]*Ciro Marina:* Dolphin berth for the loading of mineral salt in a depth of 14.5 m. Jetty carrying the loading belt is about 300 m long. Loading rate up to 2000 t/h. Vessel has to move along berth to load all hatches. Vessels of 14 000 dwt can be accommodated. The port is exposed to winds from WSW through N to ESE and a swell can be experienced

Lloyd's Agent: Tagliavia & Capanna Srl, Via Emerico Amari 8, I-90139 Palermo, Sicily, Italy, *Tel:* +39 091 587377, *Fax:* +39 091 322435, *Email:* info@tagliaviacapanna.it

CIVITAVECCHIA

Lat 42° 5' N; Long 11° 47' E.

Admiralty Chart: 907	**Admiralty Pilot:** 46
Time Zone: GMT +1 h	**UNCTAD Locode:** IT CVV

Principal Facilities:

P		Y	G	C	R	L	B		T	A	

Authority: Autorita Portuale di Civitavecchia, Piazza Imperatore Traiano, I-00053 Civitavecchia, Italy, *Tel:* +39 0766 366201, *Fax:* +39 0766 366243, *Email:* civitavecchia@portidiroma.it, *Website:* www.portodicivitavecchia.it

Officials: Marketing Manager: Giovanni Marinucci, *Email:* marinucci@portodicivitavecchia.it.

Port Security: ISPS compliant

Approach: Harbour is protected to W and S by sea walls running NNW, so that surf is much reduced in the port entrance area. The port is safe for vessels during the whole year and is accessible, weather permitting, day and night

Pilotage: Compulsory for vessels over 500 gt in, out and/or shifting. VHF Channel 14

Maximum Vessel Dimensions: 50 000 max dwt, 223.5 m max loa, 35 m max beam, 10.5 m max d

Working Hours: Office: Mon to Thurs, 0800-1400, 1500-1830, Fri to Sat, 0800-1400. Labourers: Mon to Sun, 0600-1230, 1230-1900, 1900-0300

Accommodation:

Name	Length (m)	Depth (m)	Remarks
Civitavecchia			See [1] below
Pier 1	86	7.9	
Pier 2	184	8.7	
Pier 3	192	6.1	
Piers 4 & 5			See [2] below
Pier 6	178	6.16	
Pier 7	228	8.54	
Pier 8	243	9.5	See [3] below
Pier 9	133	7.3	See [4] below
Piers 10 & 11	474	8.7	
Piers 12 & 13			See [5] below
Pier 14	186	10.5	
Pier 15	133	5.49	For ro/ro vessels only with stockage area of 25 500 m2
Pier 16	208	12	See [6] below
Pier 18	310	11.37	Ro/ro & lo/lo vessels
Pier 19	139	10.45	
Pier 20	249	10.77	Ro/ro & lo/lo vessels

[1]*Civitavecchia:* Darsena Romana used by mooring barges or small craft. Other five piers are used by ferry/mailboats for services between Civitavecchia and Sardinia, transporting passengers, cars, rail trucks and cargoes. Several movable grabs are available. Railway connections at most quays. Loading and discharging are normally carried out direct from railway wagons or road trucks into ship's holds or vice versa Tanker facilities: Tankers can be loaded/discharged only at the Darsena Deol, composed of two jetties, 310 m long, 10.5 m d and 250 m long, 10.2 m d
[2]*Piers 4 & 5:* North berth 87 m long in depth of 5.49 m and South berth 103.9 m long in depth of 6.5 m
[3]*Pier 8:* Equipped with two suckers for the discharge of grain cargoes. Ore and bulk coal cargoes can be discharged at an average rate of 6000 t/day
[4]*Pier 9:* Connected by a pipe system to the cement silos which have a cap of approx 5000 t
[5]*Piers 12 & 13:* Used for cruise vessels only. One berth 238 m long in depth of 8.53 m, one berth 150 m long in depth of 8 m, one berth 130 m long in depth of 8 m, one berth 260 m long in depth of 8 m and one berth 370 m long in depth of 10 m
[6]*Pier 16:* For ro/ro & lo/lo vessels with stockage area of 13 500 m2 and stacking area of 11 800 m2

Storage: Two bonded warehouses available for general cargo. No refrigerated space available

Location	Grain (t)
Pier 8	40000

Mechanical Handling Equipment:

Location	Type	Capacity (t)	Qty
Civitavecchia	Mult-purp. Cranes	25	13
Civitavecchia	Mobile Cranes	22	6
Pier 7	Mult-purp. Cranes	6	2
Pier 16	Mult-purp. Cranes	40	2

Bunkering: Storage of liquid fuels, diesel oils, gas and gas oil exceeds 200 000 t AGIP Petroli S.p.A., ENI, Via Laurentina 449, 00142 Rome, Italy, *Tel:* +39 06 59881, *Fax:* +39 06 5988 5700, *Email:* gioacchino.costa@eni.it, *Website:* www.eni.it – *Grades:* GO; IFO-180cSt – *Parcel Size:* min 50t – *Delivery Mode:* barge
ExxonMobil Marine Fuels, Mailpoint 31, ExxonMobil House, Ermyn Way, Leatherhead, Surrey KT22 8UX, United Kingdom, *Tel:* +44 1372 222 000, *Fax:* +44 1372 223 922, *Email:* marine.fuels@exxonmobil.com, *Website:* www.exxonmobil.com – *Grades:* MGO; IFO-180cSt; lubes – *Misc:* own storage facilities – *Parcel Size:* min MGO 35t, min IFO 180t – *Delivery Mode:* barge
Gori Petrol Group, V. Cristoforo Colombo 1, San Gregorio di Catania, 95027 Catania, Sicily, Italy, *Tel:* +39 095 492 386, *Fax:* +39 095 7122 710, *Email:* info@goripetrolgroup.191.it

Towage: Six tugs from 1200 to 3380 hp available

Repair & Maintenance: Metallurgica S.r.l., Civitavecchia, Italy, *Tel:* +39 0766 23228 Minor repairs carried out and salvage services available. Two slipways available for vessels up to 300 gt

Ship Chandlers: Mediterranea Marittima di Navigazione e Servizi S.p.A., Calata Laurenti 20, 00053 Civitavecchia, Italy, *Tel:* +39 0766 581151, *Fax:* +39 0766 31111, *Email:* mediterranea@mediterranea.com, *Website:* www.mediterranea.com
Pro. Nav. Shipsupply S.r.l., Via Luigi Cadorna 13, 00053 Civitavecchia, Italy, *Tel:* +39 0766 21705, *Fax:* +39 0766 371580, *Email:* pronav@centumcellae.it, *Website:* www.pronavshipsupply.com

Shipping Agents: Ant. Bellettieri & Co. S.r.l., Largo Plebiscito 23, I-00053 Civitavecchia, Italy, *Tel:* +39 0766 5861, *Fax:* +39 0766 586206, *Email:* bellettieri@bellettieri.it, *Website:* www.bellettieri.it
CSA S.p.A., Via Sottoportici del Consolato, Civitavecchia, Italy, *Tel:* +39 0766 580066, *Fax:* +39 0766 580068, *Email:* shipservice.cv@csaspa.com, *Website:* www.csaspa.com
Spedimar S.r.l., Piazzale degli Eroi 1/5, 00053 Civitavecchia, Italy, *Tel:* +39 0766 23248, *Fax:* +39 0766 21904, *Email:* spedimar@tin.it, *Website:* www.spedimar.com

Surveyors: Nippon Kaiji Kyokai, Via C.Battisti 25, I-00053 Civitavecchia, Italy, *Tel:* +39 0766 20267, *Fax:* +39 0766 32330, *Email:* sales@marinepanservice.com
Registro Italiano Navale (RINA), Largo Cavour 6/2, Civitavecchia, Italy, *Tel:* +39 0766 23923, *Fax:* +39 0766 371252, *Email:* roma.office@rina.org, *Website:* www.rina.org

Medical Facilities: Ambulance available. Also a hospital and clinic available in town

Airport: Fiumicino Airport, 50 km

Development: Rome Cruise Terminal, formed by Carnival, Royal Caribbean and MSC, is due to start construction of a state-of-the-art terminal in 2006. The port authority is also doubling berthing space for passenger ships in the inner port to 3 km

Lloyd's Agent: Gastaldi International S.r.l., Via San Godenzo 187, I-00189 Rome, Italy, *Tel:* +39 06 331 1737, *Fax:* +39 06 331 1708, *Email:* rome@gastaldi-int.com, *Website:* www.gastaldi-int.it

CROTONE

Lat 39° 5' N; Long 17° 8' E.

Admiralty Chart: 140 **Admiralty Pilot:** 46
Time Zone: GMT +1 h **UNCTAD Locode:** IT CRV

Principal Facilities:

P	Q	Y	G			B		T	

Authority: Capitaneria di Porto di Crotone, Via del Molo Porto Nuovo, I-88900 Crotone, Italy, *Tel:* +39 0962 20721, *Fax:* +39 0962 902094

Port Security: ISPS compliant

Approach: Entrance to Porto Nuovo is from a sheltered road with easy access, about 182.8 m wide and 8.54 m d

Pilotage: Compulsory for all vessels over 500 gt and for tankers of any size. Rates for each inward and outward pilotage, for anchorage, movement from/to one part of the roadstead or from one quay or jetty to another, on application

Working Hours: Mon to Fri 0700-1200, 1300-1630. Sat 0700-1300 but subject to surcharge of 27.5%. Between 0600-0700 and 1700-2000 surcharge of 25% payable on stevedoring tariffs. Details on application of alternative shift working hours for stevedores

Accommodation:

Name	Length (m)	Draught (m)	Remarks
Crotone			See [1] below
Molo Giunti	298	8.54	See [2] below
Molo Foraneo	426		See [3] below
Molo di Riva	304	8.54	See [4] below

[1]*Crotone:* The port is sheltered by a 3657 m long breakwater and is divided into two parts, Porto Vecchio (S side of harbour) and Porto Nuovo (N side). The former is well sheltered but only usable by vessels with max length of 60.95 m and approx 3.96 to 4.27 m d. It has mooring to banchina Foranes, banchina Nord, banchina W and Molo Pennelo. Tidal range 0.46 m
The Porto Nuovo is larger and fitted with berths for vessels of up to 30 000 dwt, max length 198 m and 8.54 m d
Three quays at Porto Nuovo for operating vessels: Molo Giunti (N side), Molo Foraneo (E side) and Molo Riva (W side)

[2]*Molo Giunti:* 124.96 m is used for the discharging of phosphates in bulk by Montedison silos (total cap 8000 t): fitted with two redlers average daily rate approx 4000 t. Also used for the discharging and sometimes for the loading of chemical products by Montedison shore pipelines. Other 124.96 m used for the discharging of bulk cargoes by Montedison crane, also for the discharging and sometimes for the loading of chemical products by Montedison shore pipelines

[3]*Molo Foraneo:* First 198.1 m from the entrance, with 7.62 to 8.23 m d is used for the discharging of fuel oil, gas oil and petrol by Victoria shore pipelines on the N side, and for the discharging of bulk cargoes by Montedison shore crane
The other 228.6 m with a d alongside decreasing from 7.62 to 5.49 m is used for the berthing of the tugs on duty in the port

[4]*Molo di Riva:* Fitted with a mobile mechanical conveyor, belonging to Montedison, for the loading of tripolyphosphate in bags. Also fitted with a mobile crane belonging to Soc Min Met Pertusola, for the discharging and loading of bulk cargoes and for the loading of bulk cargoes and zinc in ignots

Mechanical Handling Equipment:

Location	Type	Capacity (t)	Qty
Molo Giunti	Mult-purp. Cranes	8	1
Molo Foraneo	Mult-purp. Cranes	8	1
Molo di Riva	Mult-purp. Cranes		2

Bunkering: Fratelli Tricoli & Co. S.r.l., Via Cristoforo Colombo 193, 88900 Crotone, Italy, *Tel:* +39 0962 21422, *Fax:* +39 0962 27639, *Email:* fratellitricoli@fratellitricoli.191.it, *Website:* www.fratellitricoli.it
Fratelli Tricoli & Co. S.r.l., Via Cristoforo Colombo 193, 88900 Crotone, Italy, *Tel:* +39 0962 21422, *Fax:* +39 0962 27639, *Email:* fratellitricoli@fratellitricoli.191.it, *Website:* www.fratellitricoli.it – *Grades:* GO; IFO – *Delivery Mode:* tank

Towage: Compulsory for vessels over 2500 gt and for vessels of over 1600 gt carrying dangerous cargoes. Service provided by Societa Rimorchiatori Calabresi

Shipping Agents: CSA S.p.A., Via Marinella 12, I-88900 Crotone, Italy, *Tel:* +39 0962 27901, *Fax:* +39 0962 27909, *Email:* shipservice.kr@csaspa.com, *Website:* www.csaspa.com
Fratelli Tricoli & Co. S.r.l., Via Cristoforo Colombo 193, 88900 Crotone, Italy, *Tel:* +39 0962 21422, *Fax:* +39 0962 27639, *Email:* fratellitricoli@fratellitricoli.191.it, *Website:* www.fratellitricoli.it
INGEMAR S.r.l., Via C. Colombo 199, I-88900 Crotone, Italy, *Tel:* +39 0962 25165, *Fax:* +39 0962 26591, *Email:* ingemar@ingemaragency.it

Medical Facilities: Three hospitals

Airport: Lametia Terme, 110 km

Lloyd's Agent: Tagliavia & Capanna Srl, Via Emerico Amari 8, I-90139 Palermo, Sicily, Italy, *Tel:* +39 091 587377, *Fax:* +39 091 322435, *Email:* info@tagliaviacapanna.it

ENICHEM PIERS

harbour area, see under Sarroch

FALCONARA

harbour area, see under Ancona

FIUMICINO

Lat 41° 46' N; Long 12° 14' E.

Admiralty Chart: 906 **Admiralty Pilot:** 46
Time Zone: GMT +1 h **UNCTAD Locode:** IT FCO

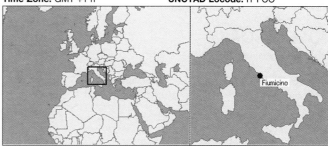

Principal Facilities:

P		G			B		T	A

Authority: Autorita Portuale di Fiumicino, Via del Pesce del Volante, I-00054 Fiumicino, Italy, *Tel:* +39 06 6504 7931, *Email:* fiumicino@portidiroma.it, *Website:* www.port-of-rome.org

Officials: Harbour Master: Rear Admiral Francesco Mulas.

Port Security: ISPS compliant

Anchorage: For vessels over 30 000 gt:
F1 in pos 41° 48.3' N; 12° 06.6' E
F2 in pos 41° 47.5' N; 12° 07.4' E
F3 in pos 41° 46.5' N; 12° 07.4' E
For vessels up to 30 000 gt:
F4 in pos 41° 43.0' N; 12° 09.8' E
F5 in pos 41° 42.4' N; 12° 10.6' E
F6 in pos 41° 42.0' N; 12° 11.5' E

Pilotage: Compulsory for mooring/unmooring at tanker's terminals and for small vessels and fast ferries in the channel port. Pilot office, Tel: +39 06 650 5091

Radio Frequency: VHF Channel 16

Tides: Max range approx 0.4 m

Maximum Vessel Dimensions: 296 m loa, 200 000 dwt, 15.2 m draft

Principal Imports and Exports: Imports: Crude oil. Exports: Clean petroleum products.

Working Hours: Mooring only: sunrise until 2 h before sunset at 'R2' and until 3 h before sunset at 'R1'. Unmooring takes place at any time. Platforms are operational 24 h

Accommodation:

Name	Length (m)	Depth (m)	Draught (m)	Remarks
Fiumicino				See [1] below
Port Channel South Quay	200	3.3	3	
R1		23	15.54	See [2] below
R2		19.5	13.72	See [3] below

[1]*Fiumicino:* Situated at the entrance of the Tiber River from the sea
There are two sea lines connected to the Raffineria di Roma on shore. Anchorage positions are approx 1.6 km S of Platform 'R2' for large tankers and 3.2 km S of Platform 'R1' for smaller tankers. SW winds sometimes create problems for vessels operating at the platforms

[2]*R1:* SPM located in pos 41° 45' 01" N; 12° 09' 03" E for tankers of 30 000-290 000 dwt but a max displacement of 200 000 t is allowed. Used for discharging crude oil. An oil pollution craft on stand-by is compulsory for tankers discharging/loading. A tug, made fast at the stern of tankers, is compulsory for all vessels moored. Tug assistance is compulsory for all crude oil vessels mooring

[3]*R2:* SPM located in pos 41° 44' 06" N; 12° 10' 01" E for tankers of 10 000-150 000 dwt but a max displacement of 130 000 t is allowed. Used for loading/unloading black and white products. An oil pollution craft on stand-by is compulsory for tankers discharging/loading. A tug, made fast at the stern of tankers, is compulsory for all vessels moored. Tug assistance is compulsory for all vessels

Bunkering: Italnoli S.r.l., Viale della Pesca 18, I-00054 Fiumicino, Italy, *Tel:* +39 06 650 6148, *Fax:* +39 06 650 6205, *Email:* operations@italnoli.it, *Website:* www.italnoli.it
AGIP Petroli S.p.A., ENI, Via Laurentina 449, 00142 Rome, Italy, *Tel:* +39 06 59881,

---

Key to Principal Facilities:—			
A=Airport	**C**=Containers	**G**=General Cargo	**P**=Petroleum	**R**=Ro/Ro	**Y**=Dry Bulk
B=Bunkers	**D**=Dry Dock	**L**=Cruise	**Q**=Other Liquid Bulk	**T**=Towage (where available from port)

Fax: +39 06 5988 5700, *Email:* gioacchino.costa@eni.it, *Website:* www.eni.it – *Grades:* GO – *Delivery Mode:* tank truck

Waste Reception Facilities: Only available for garbage. At Sea Terminals garbage is collected daily by barge

Towage: Servizi Marittimi e Portuali S.r.l. (SEMARPO), Via Torre Clementina 224, 00054 Fiumicino, Italy, *Tel:* +39 06 650 7795, *Fax:* +39 06 650 5883

Repair & Maintenance: Not available locally, nearest location is Civitavecchia

Shipping Agents: Italnoli S.r.l., Viale della Pesca 18, I-00054 Fiumicino, Italy, *Tel:* +39 06 650 6148, *Fax:* +39 06 650 6205, *Email:* operations@italnoli.it, *Website:* www.italnoli.it

Surveyors: Gastaldi International S.r.l., Via San Godenzo 187, I-00189 Rome, Italy, *Tel:* +39 06 331 1737, *Fax:* +39 06 331 1708, *Email:* rome@gastaldi-int.com, *Website:* www.gastaldi-int.it

Medical Facilities: Local sanitary office and hospital at Lido di Roma, 8 km

Airport: Fiumicino International Airport, 4 km

Development: New commercial port for fishing vessels and small cargo vessels. Work to start in the middle of 2005

Lloyd's Agent: Gastaldi International S.r.l., Mura di Santa Chiara 1, I-16128 Genoa, Italy, *Tel:* +39 010 530931, *Fax:* +39 010 530 9343, *Email:* info@gastaldi-int.it, *Website:* www.gastaldi-int.it

FOLLONICA

Lat 42° 55' N; Long 10° 45' E.

Admiralty Chart: -	**Admiralty Pilot:** 46
Time Zone: GMT +1 h	**UNCTAD Locode:** IT FOL

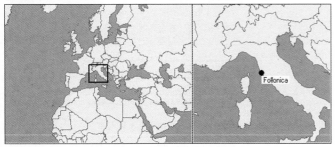

Principal Facilities:

P	Q	Y	G					T	A	

Authority: Capitaneria di Porto di Follonica, Piazza del Popolo 1, I-58022 Follonica, Italy, *Tel:* +39 0566 45240, *Fax:* +39 0566 45240, *Email:* follonica@guardiacostiera.it

Officials: Harbour Master: Luigi Morrone.

Approach: Entrance 0.8 km from head of new pier, depth 10 m

Anchorage: Available in pos 42° 53' 05" N; 10° 45' 00" E

Pilotage: Compulsory for vessels over 500 gt and available from Piombino

Radio Frequency: Piombino on VHF Channel 12

Tides: Range of tide 0.4 to 0.6 m every 12 h

Maximum Vessel Dimensions: 140 m loa, 6.55 m draft at wharf

Principal Imports and Exports: Imports: Sulphuric acid. Exports: .

Working Hours: 24 h/day

Accommodation:

Name	Draught (m)	Remarks
Follonica		
Solmine Wharf	6.55	See [1] below

[1]*Solmine Wharf:* Private wharf with pipeline for loading sulphuric acid. Ships up to 5500 t may also load cast iron ashes at this pier

Towage: Obtainable from the port of Piombino, 16 km (daytime service only)

Medical Facilities: Hospital at Massa Marittima, 21 km

Airport: Pisa, 100 km

Lloyd's Agent: Gastaldi International S.r.l., Mura di Santa Chiara 1, I-16128 Genoa, Italy, *Tel:* +39 010 530931, *Fax:* +39 010 530 9343, *Email:* info@gastaldi-int.it, *Website:* www.gastaldi-int.it

FORMIA

Lat 41° 15' N; Long 13° 36' E.

Admiralty Chart: 906	**Admiralty Pilot:** 48
Time Zone: GMT +1 h	**UNCTAD Locode:** IT FOM

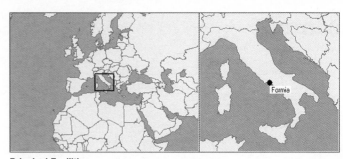

Principal Facilities:

	Y	G		R		B			

Authority: Capitaneria di Porto di Formia, Piazzale Amerigo Vespucci 7, I-04023 Formia, Italy, *Tel:* +39 0771 21552, *Fax:* +39 0771 21552, *Email:* locamare_formia@libero.it

Officials: Harbour Master: Marco Vigliotti, *Email:* marcovigliotti@libero.it.

Anchorage: Anchorage may be obtained off the port in a depth of 13 m

Pilotage: Not compulsory, but advisable

Accommodation:

Name	Length (m)	Depth (m)	Draught (m)	Remarks
Formia				See [1] below
Main Quay	130	4–6	5.2	On inner arm of the breakwater

[1]*Formia:* Harbour protected by a breakwater 560 m long. Depths of 6-7 m in the centre of the harbour. A mooring is available for vessels up to 100 m loa, max d 6.3 m off the quay. There is further quayage on a mole, depth 3-4 m, used by fishing vessels

Mechanical Handling Equipment:

Location	Type	Qty	Remarks
Formia	Mobile Cranes	3	for general cargo

Bunkering: Fuel oil is available

Medical Facilities: Hospital in the town

Lloyd's Agent: Gastaldi International S.r.l., Mura di Santa Chiara 1, I-16128 Genoa, Italy, *Tel:* +39 010 530931, *Fax:* +39 010 530 9343, *Email:* info@gastaldi-int.it, *Website:* www.gastaldi-int.it

FORO ITALICA

harbour area, see under Siracusa

GAETA

Lat 41° 13' N; Long 13° 34' E.

Admiralty Chart: 906	**Admiralty Pilot:** 46
Time Zone: GMT +1 h	**UNCTAD Locode:** IT GAE

Principal Facilities:

P		Y	G		R		B	D	T	A

Authority: Autorita Portuale di Gaeta, Lungomare Caboto, I-04024 Gaeta, Italy, *Tel:* +39 0771 471096, *Fax:* +39 0771 712664, *Email:* gaeta@portidiroma.it, *Website:* www.port-of-rome.org

Officials: Safety Director / Manager: Guido Guinderi, *Email:* guinderi@portidiroma.it.

Port Security: ISPS compliant

Anchorage: Anchorages can be found outside compulsory pilotage area in depths of 16-44 m

Pilotage: Compulsory for vessels over 499 gt. Pilot boards about 2 miles off Punta Stendardo; docking performed during daylight with certain exceptions for favourable weather conditions; undocking usually until midnight. VHF Channel 12. Rates on application

Radio Frequency: Harbour Authorities: VHF Channel 16. Pilot information: VHF Channel 12

Tides: Negligible; tidal range of below approx 0.3 m

Principal Imports and Exports: Imports: Aluminium, China clay, Clay, Coke, Fertiliser, Frozen fish, Fruit, Iron & steel reels, Phosphate, Sand, Sulphate, Wood, Woodpulp. Exports: Cement, Marble stone.

Working Hours: 0800-1200, 1300-1700. Extra time may be worked 0700-1330, 1330-2000

Accommodation:

Name	Length (m)	Depth (m)	Remarks
Gaeta			
Banchina Commerciale		7.2	See [1] below
Banchina Caboto	100	5	Used only by passenger vessels
Pontile Petroli	200	15	See [2] below

[1]*Banchina Commerciale:* At base berth (Banchina di Riva) 130 m long but operating for only 100 m and other berth 240 m long
[2]*Pontile Petroli:* Two vessels are capable of mooring at the same time on N and S side

Mechanical Handling Equipment:

Location	Type	Capacity (t)	Qty
Gaeta	Mobile Cranes	35	2
Gaeta	Mobile Cranes	40	1
Gaeta	Mobile Cranes	80	1
Gaeta	Mobile Cranes	20	3

Waste Reception Facilities: Dirty ballast, sludge, garbage disposal and chemical waste (except noxious and toxic) facilities are available from Se. Ma. Ter Srl, Tel: +39 0771 466027, Fax: +39 0771 466037

Towage: Two tugs available. Compulsory for vessels of 100 m loa and over, or during bad weather
Rimorchiatori Napoletani S.r.l., Via Duomo 30, 04024 Gaeta, Italy, Tel: +39 0771 460614, Fax: +39 0771 466352, Email: oper.gaeta@rimnap.it, Website: www.rimnap.it

Repair & Maintenance: Sa. Ri. Co. Mar S.r.l., Gaeta, Italy, Tel: +39 0771 662781, Fax: +39 0771 464424

Shipping Agents: Europa S.r.l., Lungomare Caboto 154, 04024 Gaeta, Italy, Tel: +39 0771 712292, Fax: +39 0771 712694, Email: europa@europasrl.com, Website: www.europasrl.com
Italnoli S.r.l., Lungomare Caboto 344, I-04024 Gaeta, Italy, Tel: +39 0771 712352, Fax: +39 0771 712354, Email: gaeta@italnoli.it, Website: www.italnoli.it
Agenzia Marittima Lellimar di Luigi Lelli, Largo Albani 3/4, 04024 Gaeta, Italy, Tel: +39 0771 461750, Fax: +39 0771 464055, Email: lellimar@lellimar.it, Website: www.lellimar.it
Spedimar S.r.l., Lungomare Caboto 74, 04024 Gaeta, Italy, Tel: +39 0771 470178, Fax: +39 0771 470995, Email: spedimar@tin.it, Website: www.spedimar.com

Surveyors: Nippon Kaiji Kyokai, Gaeta, Italy, Tel: +39 0771 712291, Fax: +39 0771 712694, Website: www.classnk.or.jp
Registro Italiano Navale (RINA), c/o Agenzia Marittima Europa Srl, Lungomare Caboto 154, Gaeta, Italy, Tel: +39 0771 712292, Fax: +39 0771 712694, Email: europa@dimensione.com, Website: www.rina.org

Medical Facilities: Local doctors and hospital available

Airport: Capodichino, 96 km

Lloyd's Agent: Gastaldi International S.r.l., Mura di Santa Chiara 1, I-16128 Genoa, Italy, Tel: +39 010 530931, Fax: +39 010 530 9343, Email: info@gastaldi-int.it, Website: www.gastaldi-int.it

GALLIPOLI

Lat 40° 3' N; Long 18° 0' E.

Admiralty Chart: 140	**Admiralty Pilot:** 45
Time Zone: GMT +1 h	**UNCTAD Locode:** IT GAL

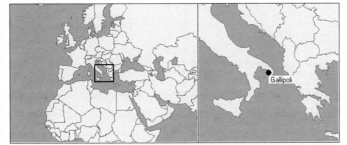

Principal Facilities:

		G		B	T	A

Authority: Capitaneria di Porto di Gallipoli, Lungomare Marconi 1, I-73014 Gallipoli, Italy, Tel: +39 0833 266862, Fax: +39 0833 264023

Port Security: ISPS compliant

Approach: The port of Gallipoli is situated on the E side of the Gulf of Taranto on an island linked with the mainland by a bridge, and is perfectly safe except at the entrance, where there is a blind rock 'Rafo' towards the N, at about 400 m from the lighthouse situated on the north of the new quay. A white light marks the rock. Depth at entrance 10 m

Pilotage: Available. VHF Channel 16

Maximum Vessel Dimensions: 10 000 dwt, 10.0 m d, 150 m loa, 18.2 m beam

Working Hours: Mon-Fri 0700-1500

Accommodation:

Name	Length (m)	Depth (m)
Gallipoli		
Foraneo Quay	200	7.8
Tramontana Quay	300	10.5
Molo Sottoflutto Quay	110	7
Banchina di Riva Quay	145	5
Ferrovia Quay	100	6
Lido Quay	80	7

Mechanical Handling Equipment:

Location	Type	Remarks
Gallipoli	Mult-purp. Cranes	Private

Bunkering: Nuova an pa di Vicenzo Barba, Via Porto Canneto, 73014 Gallipoli, Italy, Tel: +39 083 3261356, Fax: +39 083 326 1032
Nuova an pa di Vicenzo Barba, Via Porto Canneto, 73014 Gallipoli, Italy, Tel: +39 083 3261356, Fax: +39 083 326 1032 – Delivery Mode: road tanker

Towage: Compulsory for vessels exceeding 120 m loa. Tugs available from other ports

Repair & Maintenance: Minor repairs available

Medical Facilities: Available

Airport: Brindisi, 85 km

Lloyd's Agent: P. Lorusso & Co. S.r.l., 133 Via Piccinni, I-70122 Bari, Italy, Tel: +39 080 521 2840, Fax: +39 080 521 8229, Email: vdbdirezione@agenzialorusso.it, Website: www.agenzialorusso.it

GELA

Lat 37° 4' N; Long 14° 15' E.

Admiralty Chart: 965	**Admiralty Pilot:** 45
Time Zone: GMT +1 h	**UNCTAD Locode:** IT GEA

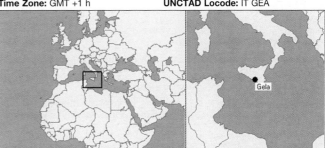

Principal Facilities:

P	Q	Y	G			B		T	A

Authority: Ufficio Circondariale Marittimo di Gela, Viale Fererico II di Svevia 156, I-93012 Gela, Sicily, Italy, Tel: +39 0933 917755, Fax: +39 0933 911524, Email: gela@guardiacostiera.it

Officials: Harbour Master: Raffaele Macauda.

Port Security: ISPS compliant

Anchorage: Anchorage A: for vessels under 2000 gt bounded by the following positions 37° 01.90' N; 14° 15.62' E, 37° 02.48' N; 14° 16.11' E, 37° 02.57' N; 14° 15.81' E, 37° 02.06' N; 14° 15.39' E
Anchorage B: for vessels under 2000 gt bounded by the following positions 37° 02.16' N; 14° 15.12' E, 37° 02.52' N; 14° 15.42' E, 37° 02.74' N; 14° 14.92' E, 37° 02.38' N; 14° 14.70' E
Anchorage C: for vessels over 5000 gt bounded by the following positions 37° 02.38' N; 14° 14.58' E, 37° 03.22' N; 14° 14.80' E, 37° 03.40' N; 14° 13.43' E, 37° 02.54' N; 14° 13.68' E
Anchorage D: for vessels over 5000 gt bounded by the following positions 37° 00.96' N; 14° 14.04' E, 37° 01.67' N; 14° 14.50' E, 37° 02.12' N; 14° 14.38' E, 37° 02.26' N; 14° 13.53' E, 37° 01.17' N; 14° 13.28' E
Anchorage E: for vessels over 30 000 gt bounded by the following positions 36° 59.78' N; 14° 14.16' E, 37° 00.33' N; 14° 14.59' E, 37° 00.56' N; 14° 13.80' E, 37° 00.56' N; 14° 13.27' E, 36° 59.78' N; 14° 13.27' E
Anchorage F: for vessels under 5000 gt bounded by the following positions 37° 00.51' N; 14° 15.03' E, 37° 01.06' N; 14° 15.50' E, 37° 01.20' N; 14° 15.30' E, 37° 00.80' N; 14° 14.89' E, 37° 00.58' N; 14° 14.75' E

Pilotage: Compulsory for all vessels over 500 gt. VHF Channels 16 and 12

Maximum Vessel Dimensions: 9.3 m d at breakwater berths

Working Hours: 0800-1200, 1300-1700

Accommodation:

Name	Length (m)	Depth (m)	Draught (m)	Remarks
Gela				See [1] below
ANIC Co				See [2] below
Breakwater Berths				
No.1	180	9.3	7.3	See [3] below
No.2	250	9.3	7.3	See [4] below
No.3	130		7.3	See [5] below
No.4	180	9.3	7.3	See [6] below
No.5	70		7.3	See [7] below
No.6	120		8.5	See [8] below
Iron Pier	350		6.1	See [9] below

Key to Principal Facilities:—

A=Airport	**C**=Containers	**G**=General Cargo
B=Bunkers	**D**=Dry Dock	**L**=Cruise
P=Petroleum	**R**=Ro/Ro	**Y**=Dry Bulk
Q=Other Liquid Bulk	**T**=Towage (where available from port)	

[1]*Gela:* A jetty about 2800 m long extends seawards to the SW from the vicinity of the ANIC Company's Chemico-Petroleum plant, and has two berths (E and W) at the head, each of which are of 180 m length. Two dry cargo vessels of up to 41 000 displacement t may be moored there, 9.6 m d (E side) and 8.52 m d (W side). The Jetty is protected by a curving breakwater of 1200 m length, equipped for handling petroleum products

[2]*ANIC Co:* 34" sealine operates at approx 2200 m S of the breakwater for the discharging of crude oil and fuel oil. Vessels of up to 80 000 dwt and of not more than 12.8 m d may be moored there

[3]*No.1:* loading and discharging black products, loading liquid chemicals, premium gasoline and gasoil, max 88 500 dwt

[4]*No.2:* loading and discharging black products, loading liquid chemicals, premium gasoline and gasoil, max 88 500 dwt

[5]*No.3:* loading fuels, gasoil, gasolines and discharging naphtha

[6]*No.4:* loading fuels, gasoil, gasolines, kerosene and discharging naphtha

[7]*No.5:* loading LPG, solvents and loading/discharging liquid chemicals and premium gasoline

[8]*No.6:* loading LPG, solvents and loading/discharging liquid chemicals and premium gasoline

[9]*Iron Pier:* Operated by ANIC; two berths N and S, equipped for loading/discharging liquid chemicals and solvents; can take vessels up to 100 m long

Mechanical Handling Equipment:

Location	Type	Qty	Remarks
Gela	Mult-purp. Cranes	2	grabs for discharging bulk cargo only
Gela	Mobile Cranes		to load goods in bags

Bunkering: AGIP Petroli S.p.A., ENI, Via Laurentina 449, 00142 Rome, Italy, *Tel:* +39 06 59881, *Fax:* +39 06 5988 5700, *Email:* gioacchino.costa@eni.it, *Website:* www.eni.it – *Grades:* GO – *Parcel Size:* max 200t – *Notice:* 48 hours – *Delivery Mode:* truck
Asta Carburanti di Asta Salvatore, Sede: via Dei Roveri 11, 11 - 97013 Comiso, Sicily, Italy, *Tel:* +39 0932 798682, *Fax:* +39 0932 798682, *Email:* asta.carburanti@tin.it – *Grades:* GO; IFO – *Parcel Size:* max 200t – *Notice:* 48 hours – *Delivery Mode:* truck
Gori Petrol Group, V. Cristoforo Colombo 1, San Gregorio di Catania, 95027 Catania, Sicily, Italy, *Tel:* +39 095 492 386, *Fax:* +39 095 7122 710, *Email:* info@goripetrolgroup.191.it – *Grades:* GO; IFO – *Parcel Size:* max 200t – *Notice:* 48 hours – *Delivery Mode:* truck

Towage: Two 1000 hp, one 1600 hp and one 1950 hp tugs available. Regular service hours from 0800-1700

Repair & Maintenance: Very small shop available for repairs

Shipping Agents: CSA S.p.A., Via Cardano 16, I-93012 Gela, Sicily, Italy, *Tel:* +39 0933 937390, *Fax:* +39 0933 835348, *Email:* shipservice.gela@csaspa.com, *Website:* www.csaspa.com
Euroimpianti Italia S.r.l., Via Ettore Romagnoli, I-93012 Gela, Sicily, Italy, *Tel:* +39 0933 933699, *Fax:* +39 0933 937022, *Website:* www.fasulo.it/euroimpianti
Fasulo Marco Italia, Via XXIV Maggio 68/70, 93012 Gela, Sicily, Italy, *Tel:* +39 0933 901106, *Fax:* +39 0933 902248, *Email:* info@fasulomarco.it, *Website:* www.fasulomarco.com
Fasulo Marco Italia, Via XXIV Maggio 68/70, 93012 Gela, Sicily, Italy, *Tel:* +39 0933 901106, *Fax:* +39 0933 902248, *Email:* shipsagents@fasulomarco.com, *Website:* www.fasulomarco.com

Airport: Catania, 100 km, Palermo, 240 km

Lloyd's Agent: Tagliavia & Capanna Srl, Via Emerico Amari 8, I-90139 Palermo, Sicily, Italy, *Tel:* +39 091 587377, *Fax:* +39 091 322435, *Email:* info@tagliaviacapanna.it

GENOA

Lat 44° 25' N; Long 8° 55' E.

Admiralty Chart: 354/55/56   **Admiralty Pilot:** 46

Time Zone: GMT +1 h   **UNCTAD Locode:** IT GOA

Principal Facilities:

P	Q	Y	G	C	R	L	B	D	T	A

Authority: Autorita Portuale di Genova, Palazzo San Giorgio, Via della Mercanzia 2, I-16123 Genoa, Italy, *Tel:* +39 010 241 2625, *Fax:* +39 010 241 2309, *Email:* info@porto.genova.it, *Website:* www.porto.genova.it

Officials: President: Luigi Merlo, *Email:* appres@porto.genova.it.
General Secretary: Giambattista D'Aste, *Email:* g.daste@porto.genova.it.
Harbour Master: Ferdinando Lolli, *Tel:* +39 010 277 7356, *Email:* segram@cpgenova.it.

Port Security: ISPS compliant. Container Security Initiative (CSI) designated port

Approach: No hazards or sand bars in outer port. Channel depths vary from 12 m to 19 m. At the end of the channel, close to the container terminal, there are two sand and mud banks, min depth 10.2 m
There are three designated entrances to the port, each with its own associated traffic separation scheme and reporting point:
1) East Entrance: for vessels using this entrance a traffic separation zone 100 m wide has been established between 44° 20.2' N; 8° 58.6' E and 44° 23.4' N; 8° 56.9' E
2) Multedo Entrance-Porto Petroli: for vessels using this entrance a traffic separation zone 100 m wide has been established between 44° 21.7' N; 8° 46.3' E, 44° 24.4' N; 8° 47.7' E and 44° 24.8' N; 8° 48.2' E
3) Voltri-Pra Entrance: for vessels using this entrance a traffic separation zone 100 m wide has been established between 44° 22.9' N; 8° 42.9' E and 44° 25.1' N; 8° 45.9' E

Anchorage: Available off breakwater, port authority specifies area according to size of vessel

Pilotage: Compulsory for vessels over 500 gt and available 24 h/day. Carried out by the Pilot Corps, *Tel:* +39 010 246 1003, *Fax:* +39 010 246 1114. VHF Channels 16, 12 and 10
Pilot boards at Eastern entrance in pos 44° 22.50' N; 8° 57.00' E, Voltri entrance in pos 44° 24.50' N; 8° 45.00' E and for Multedo Oil Harbour in pos 44° 23.52' N; 8° 47.00' E

Radio Frequency: VHF Channel 12 for Commercial Port, VHF Channel 10 for Oil Port

Tides: Range of tide 0.34 m ST, 0.24 m NT

Traffic: 2007, 58 650 389 t of cargo handled, 1 855 026 TEU's

Working Hours: 0630-1300, 1300-1930, 1930-0100

Accommodation:

Name	Length (m)	Draught (m)	Remarks
Container Terminals			
Messina Terminal	760	9–11	See [1] below
Southern European Container Hub (SECH)	526	14	See [2] below
Voltri Terminal Europa (VTE)	1400	15	See [3] below
Multipurpose Terminal SpA	2252	9–11	See [4] below
General Cargo Terminals			
Genoa Terminal SpA	1800	11	See [5] below
Grimaldi Ro/ro Terminal	426	9	See [6] below
Centro Smistamento Merci (CSM)			See [7] below
Terminal Frutta Genova Srl	700	10	See [8] below
Genova Cold Terminal Srl			See [9] below
FO.RE.ST Terminal	193	11	See [10] below
Bulk Terminals			
SAAR Depositi Portuali SpA	110	14	See [11] below
Terminal Rinfuse Genova SpA	1862	9–11.5	See [12] below
Silomar SpA			See [13] below
Tirreno Silos Srl			See [14] below
Transacomar SaS			See [15] below
Passenger Terminals			
Cruise Terminals			See [16] below
Ferry Terminals			See [17] below
Oil Terminals			
Multedo Oil Terminal			See [18] below

[1]*Messina Terminal:* Operated by Ignazio Messina & C. SpA, Via Lungomare Canepa, I-16149 Genoa Tel: +39 010 60391, Fax: +39 010 603 9445, Email: secr@messinaline.it, Website: www.messinaline.it
Containers & ro/ro. Total area of 166 000 m2 and covered area of 18 000 m2
[2]*Southern European Container Hub (SECH):* Managed by Terminal Contenitori Porto di Genova SpA, Calata Sanita - Palazzina Uffici, I-16126 Genoa, Tel: +39 010 64831, Fax: +39 010 648 3146, Email: terminal.contenitori@sech.it, Website: www.sech.it
Containers. Total area of 174 000 m2, stacking cap of 13 000 TEU's and 144 reefer points
[3]*Voltri Terminal Europa (VTE):* Tel: +39 010 699 6515, Fax: +39 010 699 6528, Email: info.mkng@vte.it, Website: www.vte.it

Containers, cars & ro/ro. Total area of 1 200 000 m2, 9600 ground slots and 530 reefer points. On-terminal rail link to the Milan line

[4]*Multipurpose Terminal SpA:* Tel: +39 010 241 3355, Fax: +39 010 241 3261
Containers & general cargo

[5]*Genoa Terminal SpA:* Operated by Genoa Terminal SpA, Tel: +39 010 60301, Fax: +39 010 462594, Email: gt@genoaterminal.it
General cargo, containers, forest products & steel. Total area of 202 995 m2

[6]*Grimaldi Ro/ro Terminal:* Tel: +39 010 550 9279, Fax: +39 010 246 3470
Containers, general cargo & ro/ro. Total area of 23 061 m2

[7]*Centro Smistamento Merci (CSM):* Tel: +39 010 65711, Fax: +39 010 657 1207, Email: csmamm@tin.it
Groupage centre. Total area of 45 000 m2 including 18 000 m2 of covered warehousing

[8]*Terminal Frutta Genova Srl:* Ponta Somalia Levante, I-16149 Genoa, Tel: +39 010 602 5200, Fax: +39 010 602 5215, Email: segreteria@clerici.com, Website: www.terminalfrutta.com
Fruit terminal. Total area of 70 000 m2. Fourteen cold storage rooms available and 90 reefer plugs

[9]*Genova Cold Terminal Srl:* Operated by Clerici Logistics Group, Tel: +39 010 60251, Fax: +39 010 602 5210, Website: www.clerici.com
Cold store equipped with shelves and has three autonomous rooms with stacking cap of 1600 t on a 1500 m2 tract of land

[10]*FO.RE.ST Terminal:* Tel: +39 010 415341, Fax: +39 010 645 4728
Forest products. Total area of 16 500 m2

[11]*SAAR Depositi Portuali SpA:* Ponte Paleocapa, I-16126 Genoa, Tel: +39 010 254801, Fax: +39 010 255919, Email: info@saardp.com, Website: www.saardp.com
Vegetable & animal oils. Total area of 15 912 m2. Four unloading extensions. Storage cap of 80 000 m3

[12]*Terminal Rinfuse Genova SpA:* Tel: +39 010 248 8620, Fax: +39 010 248 0056
Solid bulk. Total area of 162 719 m2

[13]*Silomar SpA:* Ponte Etiopia, I-16149 Genoa, Tel: +39 010 415303, Fax: +39 010 646 9794, Email: direzione@silomar.it, Website: www.silomar.it
Liquid chemical bulk. Total area of 13 091 m2
Berthing facilities: Etiopia East, 210 m long with draught of 9 m. Etiopia Head, 145 m long with draught of 10 m. Etiopia West, 180 m long with draught of 10 m. Calata Massaua, 130 m long with draught of 7 m

[14]*Tirreno Silos Srl:* Tel: +39 010 416495, Fax: +39 010 460062
Liquid food bulk. Sixty six tanks provide total storage cap of 12 000 m3
Berthing facilities: Calata Ignazio Inglese, 85 m long with draught of 8 m. Ponte Etiopia Levante, 210 m long with draught of 10.5 m

[15]*Transacomar SaS:* Tel: +39 010 460285, Fax: +39 010 645 7337
Liquid food bulk. Total area of 3947 m2. Twelve stainless steel tanks and 164 epox tanks totalling 13 000 m3
Berthing facilities: Calata Mogadiscio, 110 m long with draught of 9 m. Ponte Somalia Head, 170 m long with draught of 8.3 m

[16]*Cruise Terminals:* Operated by Stazioni Marittime SpA, Ponte dei Mille, I-16126 Genoa, Tel: +39 010 241 2534, Fax: +39 010 241 2647, Email: mail@stazionimarittimegenova.com, Website: www.stazionimarittimegenova.com
Two cruise terminals:
Ponte dei Mille (three berths)
Ponte Andrea Doria (two berths) covers 9400 m2 over two levels

[17]*Ferry Terminals:* Operated by Stazioni Marittime SpA, Ponte dei Mille, I-16126 Genoa, Tel: +39 010 241 2534, Fax: +39 010 241 2647, Email: mail@stazionimarittimegenova.com, Website: www.stazionimarittimegenova.com
Three ferry terminals:
Ponte Caracciolo (one berth)
Ponte Colombo (four berths)
Ponte Assereto (five berths)

[18]*Multedo Oil Terminal:* Operated by Porto Petroli di Genova SpA, Tel: +39 010 861 5574, Fax: +39 010 861 5599, Email: info@portopetroli.com, Website: www.portopetroli.com
The port terminal covers an area of 342 000 m2 (126 139 m2 excluding the water surface). It consists of a quay with a working length of approx 400 m, and four jetties perpendicular to the coast: Alpha, Beta, Gamma and Delta. The facility also has a mooring buoy and an offshore platform for unloading operations. This platform, called the Island, is 1.5 miles from the coast and has a depth of 50 m. It is connected to the terminal by a 120 cm dia underwater pipeline which allows the handling of oil tankers up to 500 000 dwt

Storage:

Location	Open (m2)	Covered (m2)	Grain (t)
Genoa	323950	379988	110000

Mechanical Handling Equipment:

Location	Type	Capacity (t)	Qty
Genoa	Floating Cranes	275	6
Messina Terminal	Container Cranes	45	3
Messina Terminal	Reach Stackers		4
Messina Terminal	Forklifts	16–42	30
Southern European Container Hub (SECH)	Post Panamax	45	4
Southern European Container Hub (SECH)	Super Post Panamax	60	1
Southern European Container Hub (SECH)	Reach Stackers		15
Voltri Terminal Europa (VTE)	Post Panamax	40–50	10
Voltri Terminal Europa (VTE)	RTG's	35–45	23
Voltri Terminal Europa (VTE)	Reach Stackers		22
Multipurpose Terminal SpA	Mobile Cranes		1

Location	Type	Capacity (t)	Qty
Multipurpose Terminal SpA	Container Cranes		1
Genoa Terminal SpA	Mult-purp. Cranes		8
Genoa Terminal SpA	Forklifts	2.5–25	40
Grimaldi Ro/ro Terminal	Reach Stackers		2
Grimaldi Ro/ro Terminal	Forklifts	6–42	22
Centro Smistamento Merci (CSM)	Forklifts	2.5–32	14
Terminal Frutta Genova Srl	Mult-purp. Cranes	3–9	6
Terminal Frutta Genova Srl	Forklifts		40
Genova Cold Terminal Srl	Mult-purp. Cranes	6	3
FO.RE.ST Terminal	Forklifts	7	10
Terminal Rinfuse Genova SpA	Mult-purp. Cranes	12–20	7

Bunkering: Alpha Trading S.p.A., Via Brigata Liguria 3/19, 16121 Genoa, Italy, *Tel:* +39 010 5472 200, *Fax:* +39 010 5472 209, *Email:* bunkers@alphatrading.it, *Website:* www.alphatrading.it

Burke & Novi Shipping S.r.l., P O Box 981, Via Domenica Fiasella No. 4/14, 16121 Genoa, Italy, *Tel:* +39 010 549 21, *Fax:* +39 010 543 342, *Email:* tankers@burkenovi.com, *Website:* www.burkenovi.com

Agenzia Marittima Cambiaso & Risso Srl, Viale IV Novembre 6/78, 16121 Genoa, Italy, *Tel:* +39 010 571 01, *Fax:* +39 010 589 359, *Email:* info@crgroup.it, *Website:* www.cambiasorisso.com

Chevron Marine Products LLC, Piazza Della Vittoria 12/14, 16121 Genoa, Italy, *Tel:* +39 010 5451 611, *Fax:* +39 010 566 762, *Email:* dlfammita@chevron.com, *Website:* www.chevron.com

Fratelli Cosulich Bunkers (S) Pte Ltd, Ponte Morosini 41, 16126 Genoa GE, Italy, *Tel:* +39 010 2715 280, *Fax:* +39 010 2715 480, *Email:* bunker@cosulich.it, *Website:* www.cosulich.it

Gestarma S.r.l., Via Boccardo 1/128, I-16121 Genoa, Italy, *Tel:* +39 010 553 5154, *Fax:* +39 010 553 1117, *Email:* info@gestarma.it, *Website:* www.gestarma.com

Maxcom Bunker S.p.A. u.s., Via Bartolomeo Bosco 57/7B, 16121 Genoa, Italy, *Tel:* +39 010 5605 200, *Fax:* +39 010 564 479, *Email:* bunker@maxcombunker.com, *Website:* www.maxcombunker.com

Shell Italia Marine, Plazza della Vittoria 14/7, 16121 Genoa, Italy, *Tel:* +39 010 566 444, *Fax:* +39 010 562 773, *Email:* giorgio.barabino@shell.com, *Website:* www.shell.com/marine

Getoil S.r.l., Getoil S.r.l., Via Buonarroti 14, 20145 Milan, Italy, *Tel:* +39 02 468 851, *Fax:* +39 02 4692 760, *Email:* getoil@getoil.it/commerciale@getoil.it

Towage: Rimorchiatori Riuniti S.p.A., 4th Floor, Via Ponte Reale 2, 16124 Genoa, Italy, *Tel:* +39 010 24981, *Fax:* +39 010 249 8200, *Email:* info@rimorchiatori.it, *Website:* www.rimorchiatori.it

Repair & Maintenance: 40 workshops. Six drydocks: No.1, 170.5 m x 24.7 m x 8.2 m; No.2, 208.9 m x 17.9 m x 7.6 m; No.3, 257.7 m x 37.8 m x 10.4 m; No.4, 280.3 m x 39.9 m x 12.5 m; No.5, 250.1 m x 37.8 m x 8.8 m; Darsena, 60.1 m x 21.3 m x 6.1 m

Campanella Officine Meccaniche Navali S.r.l., Calata Gadda, 16126 Genoa, Italy, *Tel:* +39 010 208961, *Fax:* +39 010 200694

Ente Bacini S.r.l., Via al Molo Giano, I-16128 Genoa, Italy, *Tel:* +39 010 246 1184, *Fax:* +39 010 246 1202, *Email:* mail@entebacinigenova.it, *Website:* www.entebacinigenova.it

Fincantieri-Cantieri Navali Italiani S.p.A. Genoa, via Cipro 11, 16154 Genoa, Italy, *Tel:* +39 010 59951, *Fax:* +39 010 599 5379

T. Mariotti S.p.A., Via dei Pescatori, Molo Cagni, 16128 Genoa, Italy, *Tel:* +39 010 24081, *Fax:* +39 010 240824, *Email:* info@mariottiyard.it, *Website:* www.mariottiyard.it

OMSA, Genoa, Italy, *Tel:* +39 010 202651

Scarsi GB S.r.l., Calata Boccardo, 16126 Genoa, Italy, *Tel:* +39 010 246 1146, *Fax:* +39 010 275 8016 Engine repairs

Ship Chandlers: Ditta Cavo Luigi di Cavo Carlo, Via Milano 71, I-16126 Genoa, Italy, *Tel:* +39 010 246 2124, *Fax:* +39 010 252698, *Email:* admin@cavo.net, *Website:* www.cavo.net Owner: Carlo Cavo

AL.MA - Alimentari Marittimi S.p.A., Palazzo Nuova Darsena, Via de Marini 60, I-16149 Genoa, Italy, *Tel:* +39 010 248 5011, *Fax:* +39 010 275 8084, *Email:* info@almacatering.com, *Website:* www.almacatering.com

Canepa & Campi S.r.l., Via Gramsci 4-6, Sant'olcese, 16010 Genoa, Italy, *Tel:* +39 010 726 1006, *Fax:* +39 010 717 0020, *Email:* rcampi@canepaecampi.com, *Website:* www.canepaecampi.com

De Gregori & Ronco S.r.l., Via Milano 73A, 16126 Genoa, Italy, *Tel:* +39 010 251 8545, *Fax:* +39 010 251 8561, *Email:* dgronco@tin.it

Eurosupply S.p.A., Via Rivarolo 53 A, I-16161 Genoa, Italy, *Tel:* +39 010 749 9190, *Fax:* +39 010 726 1614, *Email:* info@eurosupply.it, *Website:* www.eurosupply.it

Giacomo Farina & Figli S.A.s., Via di Francia 28N, I-16149 Genoa, Italy, *Tel:* +39 010 418399, *Fax:* +39 010 642 4174, *Email:* info@giacomofarina.com, *Website:* www.giacomofarina.com

Frugone S.A.s., Via Milano 75 B (ex Coop Negro), I-16126 Genoa, Italy, *Tel:* +39 010 261119, *Fax:* +39 010 255445, *Email:* info@frugomar.it, *Website:* www.frugomar.it

Gecom S.r.l., Via Scarsellini 83, I-16149 Genoa, Italy, *Tel:* +39 010 644 4726, *Fax:* +39 010 644 4815, *Email:* gecom@gecomsrl.it, *Website:* www.gecomsrl.it

I.CO S.r.l., Via M. Fanti 100R, I-16149 Genoa, Italy, *Tel:* +39 010 465055, *Fax:* +39 010 417500, *Email:* ico@icotools.com, *Website:* www.icotools.com

I.F.N. S.r.l., Via Sampierdarena 6 B/R, I-16149 Genoa, Italy, *Tel:* +39 010 418722, *Fax:* +39 010 645 4878, *Email:* ifnsrl@tiscali.it

Italian Scandinavian Ship Supply Ltd, Ponte Colombo, I-16126 Genoa, Italy, *Tel:* +39 010 246 8868, *Fax:* +39 010 246 8964, *Email:* itasca@italianscandinavian.it

Jonassohn S.r.l., Via Inferiore Rocca dei Corvi 10, I-16161 Genoa, Italy, *Tel:* +39 010 741 1456, *Fax:* +39 010 741 5116, *Email:* info@jonassohn.it, *Website:* www.jonassohn.it

La Naval Provveditoria S.r.l., Via Gramsci 11/1, I-16126 Genoa, Italy, *Tel:* +39 010 246 9381, *Fax:* +39 010 247 7609, *Email:* sales@lanavalprovveditoria.it, *Website:* www.lanavalprovveditoria.it

Ligabue Catering SLL, Ponte Etiopia, I-16149 Genoa, Italy, *Tel:* +39 010 642 1611, *Fax:* +39 010 642 1666, *Email:* mauro.conte@ligabue.it

Marine Consultant & Services S.r.l., Calata Zingari, I-16126 Genoa, Italy, *Tel:* +39 010 252061, *Fax:* +39 010 252075, *Email:* info@marineconsultantservices.com, *Website:* www.marineconsultantservices.com

Marine Stores S.r.l., Ponte Caracciolo, I-16126 Genoa, Italy, *Tel:* +39 010 27500, *Fax:* +39 010 275 0099, *Email:* marinestores@marinestores.it

Mercandino S.r.l., Via Balleydier 15, I-16149 Genoa, Italy, *Tel:* +39 010 246 3452, *Fax:* +39 010 255338, *Email:* info@mercandino.it, *Website:* www.mercandino.it

Monti & Barabino S.p.A., Via Buranello 85R, I-16149 Genoa, Italy, *Tel:* +39 010 413341, *Fax:* +39 010 414281, *Email:* info@montiebarabino.it, *Website:* www.montiebarabino.it

Provveditoria Marittima Ligure Angelo Novelli S.r.l., Via De Marini 60, I-16149 Genoa, Italy, *Tel:* +39 010 267743/4, *Fax:* +39 010 246 3356, *Email:* info@pmlangelonovelli.it

Scoccimarro S.p.A. - Servizi Marittimi e Aerei, Via de Marini 60, I-16149 Genoa, Italy, *Tel:* +39 010 235871, *Fax:* +39 010 235 8724, *Email:* info@scoccimarro.it, *Website:* www.scoccimarro.it

Sirito & C S.r.l., Via de Marini 60, I-16149 Genoa, Italy, *Tel:* +39 010 246 4810, *Fax:* +39 010 246 4841, *Email:* sirito@vermar.it

Tec Container S.r.l., Via Fieschi 1/7, I-16121 Genoa, Italy, *Tel:* +39 010 542523, *Fax:* +39 010 553 1142, *Email:* teccontainer@teccontainer.it, *Website:* www.teccontainer.it

Tiberio Corte S.p.A., Via de Marini 60, I-16149 Genoa, Italy, *Tel:* +39 010 24861, *Fax:* +39 010 248 6300, *Email:* info@tiberiocorte.com, *Website:* www.tiberiocorte.com

Ver. Mar S.r.l., Via de Marini 60, I-16149 Genoa, Italy, *Tel:* +39 010 246 4810, *Fax:* +39 010 246 4841, *Email:* vermar@vermar.it

Zernavi - Servizi Marittimi S.r.l., Palazzina Ponte, Caracciolo, I-16126 Genoa, Italy, *Tel:* +39 010 25361, *Fax:* +39 010 253 6327, *Email:* info@zerbonecatering.it, *Website:* www.zerbonecatering.it

Shipping Agents: Adriatic Shipping Co. S.r.l., Via di Francia 28, 16149 Genoa, Italy, *Tel:* +39 010 605 2265, *Fax:* +39 010 644 4381

AEM-Agenzie Europee Maritime S.r.l., Via Ceccardi 1/9, I-16121, Genoa, Italy, *Tel:* +39 010 576701, *Fax:* +39 010 576 1421, *Email:* dir@aemitalia.com, *Website:* www.aemitalia.com

Asco Italia S.r.l., Piazza della Vittoria 11/8, I-16121 Genoa, Italy, *Tel:* +39 010 591038/9, *Fax:* +39 010 591043, *Email:* jshmal@tin.it

Roberto Bucci Ltd, Cia A Diaz 1/10, 16129 Genoa, Italy, *Tel:* +39 010 566687, *Fax:* +39 010 587913, *Email:* buccige@tin.it, *Website:* www.bucci.it

Bulk Service Lines Agencies SrL, Via Corsica 21/4, 16128 Genoa, Italy, *Tel:* +39 010 553 0381, *Fax:* +39 010 553 0366, *Email:* commercial@bslagencies.it, *Website:* www.bslagencies.it

C.& F. Italia S.r.l., Palazzina Arti Marinaresche VTE, I-16158 Genoa, Italy, *Tel:* +39 010 613 3054, *Fax:* +39 010 691418, *Email:* depoli.a@candf.it

Thos Carr & Son S.r.l., Via Roma 2, I-16121 Genoa, Italy, *Tel:* +39 010 270 9400, *Fax:* +39 010 270 9449, *Email:* info@thoscarr.it, *Website:* www.thoscarr.it

Cemar Agency Network, Via XX Settembre 2/10, I-16121 Genoa, Italy, *Tel:* +39 010 589595, *Fax:* +39 010 589593, *Email:* agency@cemar.it, *Website:* www.cemar.it

CMA-CGM S.A., Via Corsica 19/3, I-16128 Genoa, Italy, *Tel:* +39 010 59671, *Fax:* +39 010 596 7272, *Email:* gen.genmbox@cma-cgm.com, *Website:* www.cma-cgm.com

Fratelli Cosulich Bunkers (S) Pte Ltd, Ponte Morosini 41, I-16126 Genoa GE, Italy, *Tel:* +39 010 2715 280, *Fax:* +39 010 2715 480, *Email:* bunker@cosulich.it, *Website:* www.cosulich.it

CSA S.p.A., Via Pedemonte 16, I-16100 Genoa, Italy, *Tel:* +39 010 65441, *Fax:* +39 010 659 1433, *Email:* csa.genova@csaspa.com, *Website:* www.csaspa.com

Deep Sea Agencies S.r.l., Via San Siro 10, I-16124 Genoa, Italy, *Tel:* +39 010 24941, *Fax:* +39 010 249 4247, *Email:* htgoa@hugotrumpy.it, *Website:* www.hugotrumpy.com

Eurochartering S.r.l., Via E Raggio 3/9, I-16124 Genoa, Italy, *Tel:* +39 010 254 1082, *Fax:* +39 010 247 1024, *Email:* eurofix@eurochartering.it

Evergreen Shipping Agency (Italy), Via Dante 2, Interno 80, 16121 Genoa, Italy, *Tel:* +39 010 531311, *Fax:* +39 010 531 3130, *Email:* gna@evergreen-shipping.it, *Website:* www.evergreen-italy.it

Express S.r.l., Torre del Distripark, 4th Floor, Int. 10, Voltri Terminal Europa, I-16158 Genoa, Italy, *Tel:* +39 010 613 0053, *Fax:* +39 010 612 1752, *Email:* info@expressge.com, *Website:* www.express-srl.com

Finseas S.r.l., Shipping Agency Division, Piazza Galeazzo Alessi 1, I-16128 Genoa, Italy, *Tel:* +39 010 53611, *Fax:* +39 010 585811, *Email:* finsea@finsea.it, *Website:* www.finsea.it

Francesco Parisi SAGL, Francesco Parisi S.p.A., Piazza Brignole 3/2, P O Box 872, I-16122 Genoa, Italy, *Tel:* +39 010 57521, *Fax:* +39 010 575 2290, *Email:* goadir@francescoparisi.com, *Website:* www.francescoparisi.com

Freeship S.r.l., Via XX Settembre 19/5, I-16121 Genoa, Italy, *Tel:* +39 010 592207, *Fax:* +39 010 542431, *Email:* info@freeship.it, *Website:* www.freeship.it

Gastaldi & C. S.p.A., Mura di Santa Chiara 1, I-16128 Genoa, Italy, *Tel:* +39 010 599 9731, *Fax:* +39 010 599 9276, *Email:* bunker.gc@gastaldi.it, *Website:* www.gastaldi.it

Gestarma S.r.l., Via Boccardo 1/128, I-16121 Genoa, Italy, *Tel:* +39 010 553 5154, *Fax:* +39 010 553 1117, *Email:* info@gestarma.it, *Website:* www.gestarma.com

Greensisam S.p.A., 2 Via Dante, I-16129 Genoa, Italy, *Tel:* +39 010 553 2059, *Fax:* +39 010 532399, *Email:* gsigna@sisam.it

A Hartrodt International, A. Hartrodt Italiana S.r.l., Piazza Scuole Pie 7, I-16123 Genoa, Italy, *Tel:* +39 010 24971, *Fax:* +39 010 249 7233, *Email:* ahgoa@hartrodt.it, *Website:* www.hartrodt.it

Intermare S.p.A., Corso Paganini 39/2, I-16125 Genoa, Italy, *Tel:* +39 010 24951, *Fax:* +39 010 211663, *Email:* info@intermare.com, *Website:* www.intermare.com

Intersea S.p.A., Piazza Galeazzo Alessi 1, 16128 Genoa, Italy, *Tel:* +39 010 536 1210, *Fax:* +39 010 536 1324, *Email:* inter.sea@finsea.it, *Website:* www.finsea.it

Magdi S.r.l., Piazza de Ferrari 4, I-16121 Genoa, Italy, *Tel:* +39 010 251 0463, *Fax:* +39 010 247 4599, *Email:* magdi@aleph.it

Mar-Int S.r.l., Via Casaregis 43/13, I-16129 Genoa, Italy, *Tel:* +39 010 315576, *Fax:* +39 010 317724, *Email:* shipping@marint.it

Marsano & Tirreno, Via Garibaldi 12, 16124 Genoa, Italy, *Tel:* +39 010 270 9310, *Fax:* +39 010 270 9479, *Email:* info@marsanoetirreno.it, *Website:* www.marsanoetirreno.it

Medmar S.p.A., Via Corsica 2/14, I-16128 Genoa, Italy, *Tel:* +39 010 596531, *Fax:* +39 010 596 3460, *Email:* medmar@finsea.it, *Website:* www.finsea.it

A.P. Moller-Maersk Group, Maersk Italia SpA, Via Magazzini del Cotone 17, I-16128 Genoa, Italy, *Tel:* +39 010 20961, *Fax:* +39 010 209 6236, *Website:* www.maerskline.com

Sama S.r.l., Via Romana di Voltri 28, I-16158 Genoa, Italy, *Tel:* +39 010 613 2277, *Fax:* +39 010 612 1549, *Email:* sama@split.it

Paolo Scerni S.p.A., Via XII Ottobre 2n, 16121 Genoa, Italy, *Tel:* +39 010 534 3239, *Fax:* +39 010 534 3237, *Email:* info@grupposcerni.it, *Website:* www.grupposcerni.it

Stevedoring Companies: Paolo Scerni S.p.A., Via XII Ottobre 2n, 16121 Genoa, Italy, *Tel:* +39 010 534 3239, *Fax:* +39 010 534 3237, *Email:* info@grupposcerni.it, *Website:* www.grupposcerni.it

Surveyors: ABS (Europe), ABS Italy S.r.l., Edificio Millo 2nd Floor, Via al Porto Antico, 16128 Genoa, Italy, *Tel:* +39 010 254921, *Fax:* +39 010 254 9225, *Email:* absgenoa@eagle.org

Bureau Veritas, Via XX Settembre 14, I-16121 Genoa, Italy, *Tel:* +39 010 586564, *Fax:* +39 010 543368, *Email:* marina.genoa.it@bureauveritas.com, *Website:* www.bureauveritas.com

Cargo Inspectors Group S.r.l., Via Bombrini 11/5, I-16149 Genoa, Italy, *Tel:* +39 010 642 2332, *Fax:* +39 010 642 2329, *Email:* cig@cargogroup.it, *Website:* www.cargogroup.it

Det Norske Veritas A/S, Piazza R. Rossetti 5, I-16129 Genoa, Italy, *Tel:* +39 010 587492, *Fax:* +39 010 565680, *Website:* www.dnv.com

Germanischer Lloyd, Piazza Borgo Pila 40, Torre A Int.43, Corte Lambruschini, I-16129 Genoa, Italy, *Tel:* +39 010 595 9777, *Fax:* +39 010 576 1933, *Email:* gl-genoa@gl-group.com, *Website:* www.gl-group.com

Nippon Kaiji Kyokai, Via Roma 2/31, I-16121 Genoa, Italy, *Tel:* +39 010 585001, *Fax:* +39 010 585003, *Email:* ge@classnk.or.jp, *Website:* www.classnk.or.jp

Registro Italiano Navale (RINA), Pizza della Vittoria 11/A-2, 16121 Genoa, Italy, *Tel:* +39 010 572971, *Fax:* +39 010 572 9729, *Email:* genova.office@rina.org, *Website:* www.rina.org

Saybolt Italia S.r.l., Via Pra No 5-1, 16157 Genoa, Italy, *Tel:* +39 010 697 4795, *Fax:* +39 010 697 4805, *Email:* saybolt.genova@corelab.com, *Website:* www.saybolt.com

Studio Tecnico Navale Ansaldo, Via Cairoli 1/4, 16124 Genoa, Italy, *Tel:* +39 010 247 5038, *Fax:* +39 010 247 5020, *Email:* segreteria@stnansaldo.it, *Website:* www.stnansaldo.it

Medical Facilities: All kinds of medical facilities available

Airport: Cristoforo Colombo

Railway: Porta Principe near the entrance of commercial port

Development: New container terminal at Calata Bertolo to be constructed with work due to begin 2008 consisting of 620 m of berth with draught up to 18 m

Lloyd's Agent: Gastaldi International S.r.l., Mura di Santa Chiara 1, I-16128 Genoa, Italy, *Tel:* +39 010 530931, *Fax:* +39 010 530 9343, *Email:* info@gastaldi-int.it, *Website:* www.gastaldi-int.it

GIOIA TAURO

Lat 38° 26' N; Long 15° 54' E.

Admiralty Chart: 1019	**Admiralty Pilot:** 45
Time Zone: GMT +1 h	**UNCTAD Locode:** IT GIT

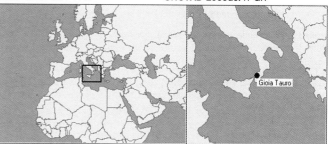

Principal Facilities:

			C	R			T	

Authority: Autorita Portuale Gioia Tauro, Contrada Lamia, I-89013 Gioia Tauro, Reggio Calabria, Italy, *Tel:* +39 0966 504688, *Fax:* +39 0966 505438, *Email:* info@portodigioiatauro.it, *Website:* www.portodigioiatauro.it

Officials: President: Giuseppe Guacci.

Port Security: ISPS compliant. Container Security Initiative (CSI) designated port

Approach: Port entrance 250 m wide with d of 20 m. South turning basin dia of 750 m with draft 15 m. North turning basin dia of 350 m with draft 12.5 m

Pilotage: Compulsory

Traffic: 2007, 3 444 337 TEU's handled

Accommodation:

Name	Length (m)	Draught (m)	Remarks
Gioia Tauro			See [1] below
Lo/Lo Terminal (Pier East)	3011	13.5–15.5	
Ro/Ro Terminal (Pier North)	200	13.5–15.5	

[1]*Gioia Tauro:* Operated by Medcenter Container Terminal SpA, Area Porto c/o Terminal Contenitori, I-89013 Gioia Tauro, *Tel:* +39 0966 7141, *Fax:* +39 0966 765486

Mechanical Handling Equipment:

Location	Type	Qty
Gioia Tauro	Mobile Cranes	3
Gioia Tauro	Quay Cranes	22
Gioia Tauro	Straddle Carriers	80
Gioia Tauro	Reach Stackers	9

Towage: Con Tug S.r.l., Porto Terminal Contenitori, Palazzina 1, 89013 Gioia Tauro, Reggio Calabria, Italy, *Tel:* +39 0966 714241, *Fax:* +39 0966 714240, *Email:* contugsrl@contug.it

Shipping Agents: Medmar S.p.A., Area Portuale di Gioia Tauro, 89026 Gioia Tauro, Reggio Calabria, Italy, *Tel:* +39 0966 761510, *Fax:* +39 0966 761509, *Email:* operat@saimaregit.it, *Website:* www.saimaregit.it

Development: Lo/lo berth to be increased by 350 m with draft of 17 m

Lloyd's Agent: Tagliavia & Capanna Srl, Via Emerico Amari 8, I-90139 Palermo, Sicily, Italy, *Tel:* +39 091 587377, *Fax:* +39 091 322435, *Email:* info@tagliaviacapanna.it

GRANILI DOCK

harbour area, see under Naples

IMPERIA

Lat 43° 53' N; Long 8° 2' E.

Admiralty Chart: 351
Time Zone: GMT +1 h

Admiralty Pilot: 46
UNCTAD Locode: IT IMP

Principal Facilities:

Q		G|C		B		A

Authority: Capitaneria di Porto di Imperia, Via Scarincio 17, I-18100 Imperia, Italy, *Tel:* +39 0183 666333, *Fax:* +39 0183 652224, *Email:* imperia@guardiacostiera.it

Officials: Harbour Master: Gianpaolo Conti.

Port Security: ISPS compliant

Approach: Depth in channel 9 m, no bar

Pilotage: Compulsory for vessels over 500 t. Pilot boards in pos 43° 52' N; 8° 03.5' E

Radio Frequency: Imperia Pilot Station, VHF Channel 16

Weather: Porto Maurizio basin open to E winds, Oneglia basin open to W winds

Tides: Rise of tide 0.3 m

Maximum Vessel Dimensions: 10 000 dwt, 160 m loa, 8 m d

Principal Imports and Exports: Imports: Machinery, Oil, Woodpulp. Exports: Machinery, Vegetable oil.

Working Hours: Mon to Fri 0800-1200, 1400-1800, Saturday 0600-1230

Accommodation:

Name	Length (m)	Depth (m)	Remarks
Imperia			Two basins situated one mile apart
Porto Maurizio	180	7	See [1] below
Oneglia	230	8.5	See [2] below

[1]*Porto Maurizio:* Facilities for storing vegetable oil in tanks, 9000 t cap
[2]*Oneglia:* Facilities for storing vegetable oil in tanks, 1600 t cap

Storage:

Location	Covered (m²)
Imperia	300

Mechanical Handling Equipment:

Location	Type	Capacity (t)	Qty
Imperia	Forklifts	30	2
Porto Maurizio	Mobile Cranes	140	
Oneglia	Mult-purp. Cranes	23	4
Oneglia	Mobile Cranes	40	2

Cargo Worked: Approx 100 t/gang of general cargo

Bunkering: AGIP Petroli S.p.A., ENI, Via Laurentina 449, 00142 Rome, Italy, *Tel:* +39 06 59881, *Fax:* +39 06 5988 5700, *Email:* gioacchino.costa@eni.it, *Website:* www.eni.it – *Grades:* GO – *Parcel Size:* min 25t – *Notice:* 36 hours – *Delivery Mode:* truck
Alpha Trading S.p.A., Via Brigata Liguria 3/19, 16121 Genoa, Italy, *Tel:* +39 010 5472 200, *Fax:* +39 010 5472 209, *Email:* bunkers@alphatrading.it, *Website:* www.alphatrading.it – *Grades:* GO; IFO30/40cSt – *Parcel Size:* no min – *Notice:* 36 hours – *Delivery Mode:* truck

Towage: Not available. Tugs from Savona with 12 h notice

Repair & Maintenance: Available locally for small craft

Medical Facilities: Ospedale Civile di Imperia

Airport: Villanova d'Albenga, 30 km

Lloyd's Agent: Gastaldi International S.r.l., Mura di Santa Chiara 1, I-16128 Genoa, Italy, *Tel:* +39 010 530931, *Fax:* +39 010 530 9343, *Email:* info@gastaldi-int.it, *Website:* www.gastaldi-int.it

LA MADDALENA

Lat 41° 13' N; Long 9° 24' E.

Admiralty Chart: 1212
Time Zone: GMT +1 h

Admiralty Pilot: 46
UNCTAD Locode: IT MDA

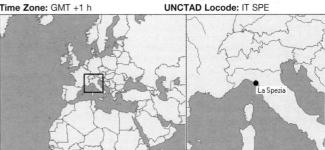

Principal Facilities:

		G			B|D|T	

Authority: Capitaneria di Porto di La Maddalena, Piazza S. Boin 3, I-07024 La Maddalena, Sardinia, Italy, *Tel:* +39 0789 737095, *Fax:* +39 0789 739131

Anchorage: Anchorage in the roadstead, with mooring buoys for small vessels

Pilotage: Not available

Radio Frequency: VHF Channel 16

Tides: Range of tide 0.34 m

Maximum Vessel Dimensions: 6324 dwt, 112.8 m loa

Accommodation:

Name	Length (m)	Depth (m)	Remarks
La Maddalena			
Cala Gavetta	450	6.4	Used mainly for small craft & coasters
Pontile Poste			With only shallow water and used by the Palau ferry
Banchina Commerciale			
New	154		E of Cala Gavetta and used for cargo operations
Old	280	6.5	Just W of Pontile Poste and used by ferries

Mechanical Handling Equipment:

Location	Type	Capacity (t)
La Maddalena	Mult-purp. Cranes	20

Bunkering: AGIP Petroli S.p.A., ENI, Via Laurentina 449, 00142 Rome, Italy, *Tel:* +39 06 59881, *Fax:* +39 06 5988 5700, *Email:* gioacchino.costa@eni.it, *Website:* www.eni.it

Towage: Naval tugs available

Repair & Maintenance: Floating dock for vessels up to 400 t

Medical Facilities: There is a naval hospital

Lloyd's Agent: Gastaldi International S.r.l., Mura di Santa Chiara 1, I-16128 Genoa, Italy, *Tel:* +39 010 530931, *Fax:* +39 010 530 9343, *Email:* info@gastaldi-int.it, *Website:* www.gastaldi-int.it

LA SPEZIA

Lat 44° 6' N; Long 9° 49' E.

Admiralty Chart: 118
Time Zone: GMT +1 h

Admiralty Pilot: 46
UNCTAD Locode: IT SPE

Principal Facilities:

P|Q|Y|G|C|R		B|D|T|A

Authority: La Spezia Port Authority, Via del Molo 1, I-19126 La Spezia, Italy, *Tel:* +39 0187 546320, *Fax:* +39 0187 599664, *Email:* info@porto.laspezia.it, *Website:* www.portolaspezia.it

Key to Principal Facilities:—				
A=Airport	**C**=Containers	**G**=General Cargo	**P**=Petroleum	**R**=Ro/Ro	**Y**=Dry Bulk
B=Bunkers	**D**=Dry Dock	**L**=Cruise	**Q**=Other Liquid Bulk	**T**=Towage (where available from port)	

Officials: President: Cirillo Orlandi, *Tel:* +39 0187 546316, *Email:* cirillo.orlandi@porto.laspezia.it.
General Secretary: Franco Pomo, *Tel:* +39 0187 546314, *Email:* franco.pomo@porto.laspezia.it.
Marketing Manager: Sergio Somaglia, *Tel:* +39 0187 546316, *Email:* sergio.somaglia@porto.laspezia.it.
Harbour Master: Vittorio Alessandro, *Tel:* +39 0187 258101, *Email:* laspezia@guardiacostiera.it.

Port Security: ISPS compliant. Container Security Initiative (CSI) designated port

Pilotage: Compulsory. Pilot Station is in the approach of Torre Scuola. VHF Channel 14 available

Radio Frequency: VHF Channels 16, 14, and 12. Channel 9 port information service

Tides: Range of tide 0.3 m

Traffic: 2006, 19 292 000 t of cargo handled, 1 136 664 TEU's

Working Hours: 24 h/day

Accommodation:

Name	Length (m)	Depth (m)	Draught (m)	Remarks
La Spezia				See [1] below
Paita Wharf	550	11–13		See [2] below
Malaspina Wharf	200	8–10		See [3] below
Garibaldi Pier	900	9–12		See [4] below
Artom Wharf	300	10–11		See [5] below
Fornelli Pier	1138	13–13.5		See [6] below
Angelo Ravano Terminal	265			See [7] below
Terminal del Golfo				See [8] below
Main Quay	160	12		See [9] below
Secondary Quay	150	8–11		See [10] below
Enel Terminal	250		12–13	See [11] below
Panigaglia Terminal	500	10–11		See [12] below
S. Stefano Intermodal Centre				See [13] below

[1]*La Spezia:* The port is located inside a 1300 ha gulf area, protected by a 2200 m breakwater

[2]*Paita Wharf:* Multi-purpose and ro/ro area managed by Speter (Tel: +39 0187 526711), Compagnia Lavoratori Portuali (Tel: +39 0187 764711), Rolcim and Mazzi Magazzini
Yard area of 110 000 m2. Equipment includes three quay cranes up to 35 t cap. Dry bulk silos of 12 000 m3 cap, cement silos of 4200 t cap. Three rail tracks

[3]*Malaspina Wharf:* Multi-purpose and ro/ro area managed by Compagnia Lavoratori Portuali, Piazza G. B. Paita 1, I-19124 La Spezia, Tel: +39 0187 764711, Fax: +39 0187 764748
Yard area of 8000 m2. Storage area of 72 000 m2, covered warehousing storage of 2500 m2. Two rail tracks

[4]*Garibaldi Pier:* Expansion works in progress for an additional yard area of 50 000 m2. Multi-purpose and ro/ro area managed by Speter, Compagnia Lavoratori Portuali, Terminal Riuniti, Monfer and Sepor. This pier is used on both sides which are equipped with fenders. Yard area of 60 000 m2. Equipment includes two quay cranes up to 12 t cap and three mobile cranes up to 100 t cap. Covered warehousing of 4000 m2, uncovered of 5000 m2, cereal silos of 30 000 t cap and cement silos of 5500 t cap. Three rail tracks

[5]*Artom Wharf:* Multi-purpose area managed by La Spezia Container Terminal (Contship) and Compagnia Lavoratori Portuali
Yard area of 40 000 m2. Equipment includes four quay cranes up to 25 t cap and mobile cranes up to 100 t cap

[6]*Fornelli Pier:* Lo/lo container terminal managed by La Spezia Container Terminal (Contship Italia group), Tel: +39 0187 5551, Fax: +39 0187 555419, Website: www.contshipitalia.com
Total yard area (Fornelli & Ravano) of 285 000 m2, dedicated to yard 69 000 m2, yard cap 21 700 TEU's. Equipment includes eight post-panamax cranes, eight RMG's, three RTG's, one mobile crane and twenty front handlers. 400 reefer points. Five rail tracks
Gate facilities: 6 truck lanes and 2 railway gates are available for through checking

[7]*Angelo Ravano Terminal:* Lo/lo container terminal managed by La Spezia Container Terminal (Contship Italia group) and the container freight station Terrestre Marittima, Tel: +39 0187 5551
Dredging works are now in progress. Yard area of 70 000 m2. Covered warehousing storage of 2500 m2. Equipment includes two RTG's. Three rail tracks

[8]*Terminal del Golfo:* Lo/lo & ro/ro container terminal operated by Terminal del Golfo SpA (Tarros group), Tel: +39 0187 599 2115, Fax: +39 0187 599 2117, Email: operativo@terminaldelgolfo.com, Website: www.terminaldelgolfo.com
Yard area of 40 000 m2

[9]*Main Quay:* Available for lo/lo & ro/ro operations. Equipped with a 35 t portal crane

[10]*Secondary Quay:* Can accommodate a lo/lo vessel or three vessels working as ro/ro. Equipment includes two mobile cranes

[11]*Enel Terminal:* Coal and oil products terminal managed by Enel SpA, Tel: +39 0187 501189
Yard area of 30 000 m2. Equipment includes two quay side cranes. Coal discharged at 1000 t/h cap

[12]*Panigaglia Terminal:* LPG terminal managed by GNL Italia (ENI group), located on the W side of the Gulf of La Spezia
Yard area of 45 000 m2. Liquid gas discharge cap of over 2 500 000 t/year

[13]*S. Stefano Intermodal Centre:* La Spezia Port Authority is carrying out an important project for the development of rail transport from/to the port with the realisation of an intermodal platform in S. Stefano Magra nearby the port. Special equipment will be dedicated to rail waggons loading operations. This way, the port will be directly linked with the Interporto of Parma through a shuttle service with 36-52 TEUs trains (1200-1600 t). This project will also reduce rail handling costs as well by developing infrastructural facilities and logistics activities reaching the area of Verona/Brennero

Storage: Bonded warehouse facilities available at Paita, Malaspina and Garibaldi Piers as well as at the Angelo Ravano Terminal

Mechanical Handling Equipment:

Location	Type	Capacity (t)	Qty
La Spezia	Quay Cranes	100	31

Bunkering: Dalmare S.p.A., Via Castelli 6, 57122 Leghorn, Italy, *Tel:* +39 0586 437 111, *Fax:* +39 0586 437 112, *Email:* info@dalesio.it, *Website:* www.dalesio.it

Waste Reception Facilities: All waste facilities are available (dirty ballast, sludge, chemical waste & garbage disposal)

Towage: Rimorchiatori Riuniti Spezzini-Imprese Marittime e Salvataggi S.r.l., Viale Italia 13, 19124 La Spezia, Italy, *Tel:* +39 0187 735062, *Fax:* +39 0187 20994, *Email:* rimspez@rimspez.it

Repair & Maintenance: Gestione Bacini La Spezia S.p.A., Viale San Bartolomeo 446, Muggiano, 19139 La Spezia, Italy, *Tel:* +39 0187 560778, *Fax:* +39 0187 543550
Six dry docks up to 200 m long. One floating dock with lifting cap of 40 000 t for vessels up to 246 m long, 39 m wide and 100 000 dwt
San Marco Shipping S.r.l., Viale S. Bartolomeo 362, 19100 La Spezia, Italy, *Tel:* +39 0187 544111, *Fax:* +39 0187 524181

Ship Chandlers: Marine Consultant & Services S.r.l., Piazza G. Garibaldi 19, I-19122 La Spezia, Italy, *Tel:* +39 0187 254011, *Fax:* +39 0187 254038, *Email:* info@marineconsultantservices.com, *Website:* www.marineconsultantservices.com
Natali Alessandro & C S.n.c., Via Parma 17/P, I-19125 La Spezia, Italy, *Tel:* +39 0187 516896, *Fax:* +39 0187 515253, *Email:* info@natalicompany.com, *Website:* www.natalicompany.com
Pedrotec S.r.l., Via delle Pianazze 150A, I-19136 La Spezia, Italy, *Tel:* +39 0187 98491, *Fax:* +39 0187 984204, *Email:* info@pedrotec.com, *Website:* www.pedrotec.com

Shipping Agents: Agenzia Marittima Astengo Giuseppe, Viale Italia 33, 17100 La Spezia, Italy, *Tel:* +39 0187 739623, *Fax:* +39 0187 754793, *Email:* shipagentastengo@tin.it
CSA S.p.A., Via San Bartolomeo 20, I-19126 La Spezia, Italy, *Tel:* +39 0187 53671, *Fax:* +39 0187 536 7291, *Email:* optlaspezia@csaspa.com, *Website:* www.csaspa.com
Ernesto Laviosa S.r.l., Viale S.Bartolomeo 109, 19126 La Spezia, Italy, *Tel:* +39 0187 770565, *Fax:* +39 0187 734981, *Email:* ships@col.it
Greensisam S.p.A., 2 Via Valdilocchi, 19100 La Spezia, Italy, *Tel:* +39 0187 524777, *Fax:* +39 0187 520582, *Email:* gsigna@sisam.it
Hector Alinghieri S.r.l., Via Crispi 39, 19124 La Spezia, Italy, *Tel:* +39 0187 770160, *Fax:* +39 0187 732332, *Email:* ships@hector.it
Agenzia Marittima Le Navi S.p.A., Viale San Bartolomeo 20, I-19126 La Spezia, Italy, *Tel:* +39 0187 5701, *Fax:* +39 0187 570858, *Email:* lenavi_itspe@msclenavi.it, *Website:* www.msclenavi.it
MAGNANI S.r.l., Corso Nazionale 5, I-19126 La Spezia, Italy, *Tel:* +39 0187 506285, *Fax:* +39 0187 506205, *Email:* magnani@porto.laspezia.it
Medmar S.p.A., Via XXIV Maggio 26, 19100 La Spezia, Italy, *Tel:* +39 0187 777147, *Fax:* +39 0187 257045, *Email:* medlsp@finsea.it
Agenzia Marittima Transmar S.r.l., Viale Bartholomeo 20, I-19126 La Spezia, Italy, *Tel:* +39 0187 5511, *Fax:* +39 0187 551301, *Email:* transmar@transmar.it
Agenzie Marittime Unite S.r.l., Viale Italia 33, P O Box 69, I-19100 La Spezia, Italy, *Tel:* +39 0187 764553, *Fax:* +39 0187 734009, *Email:* valeriaferrari@darioperioli.it

Surveyors: Nippon Kaiji Kyokai, La Spezia, Italy, *Tel:* +39 0187 511149, *Fax:* +39 0187 509779, *Website:* www.classnk.or.jp
Registro Italiano Navale (RINA), Via G. Costantini 16/6, La Spezia, Italy, *Tel:* +39 0187 511149, *Fax:* +39 0187 509779, *Email:* laspezia.office@rina.org, *Website:* www.rina.org

Medical Facilities: Available

Airport: Pisa International Airport, 80 km. Genoa International Airport, 110 km

Railway: The port areas are fully rail connected

Lloyd's Agent: Gastaldi International S.r.l., Mura di Santa Chiara 1, I-16128 Genoa, Italy, *Tel:* +39 010 530931, *Fax:* +39 010 530 9343, *Email:* info@gastaldi-int.it, *Website:* www.gastaldi-int.it

LAMPEDUSA

Lat 35° 30' N; Long 12° 36' E.

Admiralty Chart: 193	**Admiralty Pilot:** 45
Time Zone: GMT +1 h	**UNCTAD Locode:** IT LMP

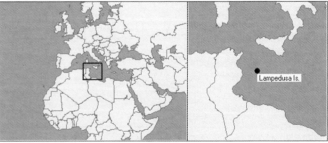

Principal Facilities:

Q	G			B		A

Authority: Ufficio Locale Marittimo di Lampedusa, Piazza Castello No.18, I-92010 Lampedusa, Sicily, Italy, *Tel:* +39 0922 970141, *Fax:* +39 0922 970141, *Email:* lampedusa@guardiacostiera.it, *Website:* www.lampedusa.guardiacostiera.it

Officials: Harbour Master: Achille Selleri.

Anchorage: Anchorage can be obtained off the harbour in depths of 15 m. Good holding ground

Pilotage: Provided by a local company

Radio Frequency: VHF Channel 16 from 0800-2000

Maximum Vessel Dimensions: 2420 dwt, 113.3 m loa

Accommodation:

Name	Length (m)	Depth (m)	Remarks
Lampedusa			The harbour is divided into three bays
Cala Palma			Mainly used for small craft
Cala Salina			Mainly used for small craft
Cala Guitgia	860	5	Equipped to accommodate tankers

Bunkering: Naphtha available on Cala Salina quay

Shipping Agents: Agenzia Marittima Strazzera di Sebastiano, Angelo & C snc, Lungomare Luigi Rizzo, sn, 92010 Lampedusa, Sicily, Italy, *Tel:* +39 0922 970003, *Fax:* +39 0922 970809, *Email:* info@agemarstrazzera.it, *Website:* www.agemarstrazzera.it

Airport: Lampedusa

Lloyd's Agent: Tagliavia & Capanna Srl, Via Emerico Amari 8, I-90139 Palermo, Sicily, Italy, *Tel:* +39 091 587377, *Fax:* +39 091 322435, *Email:* info@tagliaviacapanna.it

LEGHORN

Lat 43° 33' N; Long 10° 18' E.

Admiralty Chart: 119		**Admiralty Pilot:** 46	
Time Zone: GMT +1 h		**UNCTAD Locode:** IT LIV	

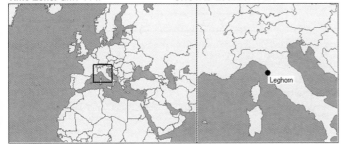

Principal Facilities:

P	Q	Y	G	C	R	L	B	D	T	A

Authority: Autorita Portuale di Livorno, Palazzo Rosciano, Scali Rosciano 6, I-57123 Leghorn, Italy, *Tel:* +39 0586 249411, *Fax:* +39 0586 249514, *Email:* info@porto.livorno.it, *Website:* www.portauthority.li.it

Officials: President: Roberto Piccini, *Tel:* +39 0586 249417, *Email:* presidenza@portauthority.li.it.
General Secretary: Giorgio Gionfriddo, *Tel:* +39 0586 249415, *Email:* gionfriddo@porto.livorno.it.
Marketing Manager: Gabriele Gargiulo.

Port Security: ISPS compliant. Container Security Initiative (CSI) designated port

Approach: N entrance for small craft only. S entrance, first part between the S extremity of the Diga Curvilinea and the W extremity of the Diga della Vegliaia, depth 10 m; second part between the S extremity of the Diga Curvilinea and the lighthouse rock, depth from 10 to 10.2 m. Entrance of the Porto Mediceo, depth not uniform. Dredging to 9 m in progress. Depth of the outer harbour from 5.8 to 10 m

Anchorage: Indicated by Avvisatore Maritimo (VHF Channel 10, 156.50 mHz) for cargo and passenger ships

Pilotage: Compulsory for vessels over 500 gt. Corpo Piloti del Porto, Tel +39 0586 897045

Radio Frequency: Livorno Radio: VHF Channel 16 (156.80 mHz); Avvisatore Marittimo: VHF Channel 10 (156.50 mHz)

Traffic: 2006, 28 630 566 t of cargo handled, 657 592 TEU's

Working Hours: 0800-1200, 1400-1800. Overtime can be arranged as follows: 1200-1400, 1800-2000 for completion only. Double shift 0700-1300, 1330-2000 against 25% extra. Night shift 2000-0230 (summer) or 2000-0030 (winter). Saturday, work performed only in double shift at overtime rates

Accommodation:

Name	Length (m)	Draught (m)	Remarks
Leghorn			See [1] below
Darsena Toscana Terminal	1600	13	See [2] below
Darsena Toscana East Bank Terminal	300		See [3] below
Seal Terminal			See [4] below
Paduletta Terminal			See [5] below
LTM Terminal	1300		See [6] below
Lorenzini Terminal			See [7] below
Giolfo & Calcagno Terminal	80		See [8] below
Sintermar Terminal	562		See [9] below
Doc Livorno Terminal	190		See [10] below
D'Alesio Terminal	240		See [11] below
AGIP Gas Terminal	210		See [12] below
Livorno Forest Terminal	94		See [13] below
Leonardo da Vinci Terminal	167		See [14] below
Bartoli Terminal	210		See [15] below

Name	Length (m)	Draught (m)	Remarks
Tozzi Terminal			See [16] below
Porto Commerciale Terminal	760		See [17] below
Silos del Tirreno Terminal	200		See [18] below
Marchi Terminal			See [19] below
Figli di Nado Neri Terminal			See [20] below
Calata Orlando Terminal	450	10	See [21] below
Dole Terminal			See [22] below
Porto di Livorno 2000 Terminal	1500		See [23] below
Novoil Terminal	134		See [24] below
Carbochimica Terminal	113		See [25] below
Grandi Molini Italiani SpA Terminal	134		See [26] below
Labromare Faro Verde Terminal	180		See [27] below

[1]*Leghorn:* 11 000 m of quays with 95 berths for vessels up to 13 m draught

[2]*Darsena Toscana Terminal:* Tel: +39 0586 258111, Fax: +39 0586 258240, Email: tdt@tdt.it, Website: www.contshipitalia.com
Container terminal with 180 000 m2 of storage yards, a 49 500 m2 railway terminal, 10 000 m2 for reefer containers with 60 reefer points

[3]*Darsena Toscana East Bank Terminal:* Tel: +39 0586 841800, Fax: +39 0586 841804, Email: cilp@gruppocpl.it
Multi-purpose public terminal

[4]*Seal Terminal:* Tel: +39 0586 841630, Fax: +39 0586 841635, Email: seal@gruppocpl.it
Specialised area for the storage and disposal of toxic and non-toxic waste and asbestos treatment. Surface area of 25 000 m2

[5]*Paduletta Terminal:* Tel: +39 0586 841800, Fax: +39 0586 841804, Email: cilp@gruppocpl.it
Multi-purpose terminal for cars, forest products, iron & steel and plant engineering. Eight warehouses with total cap of 170 000 m3

[6]*LTM Terminal:* Tel: +39 0586 444488, Fax: +39 0586 440378
General cargo & ro/ro traffic

[7]*Lorenzini Terminal:* Tel: +39 0586 207111, Fax: +39 0586 405199, Email: logri@etrurianet.it
Containers, ro/ro, general cargo & plant engineering. Covered area of 3638 m2

[8]*Giolfo & Calcagno Terminal:* Tel: +39 0586 424001, Fax: +39 0586 420148, Email: gcalcagno@libero.it
Handling & storage of frozen cargo. Covered storage of 13 359 m2

[9]*Sintermar Terminal:* Via Leonardo da Vinci 41, I-57123 Leghorn, Tel: +39 0586 44671, Fax: +39 0586 401147, Email: sintdir@tin.it, Email: segreteria@sintermar.it, Website: www.sintermar.it
Container terminal (three berths) with 250 reefer points. Container storage area of 110 000 m2 and warehouse of 3000 m2

[10]*Doc Livorno Terminal:* Tel: +39 0586 424279, Fax: +39 0586 422249, Email: docliv@tin.it
Chemical products, solvents & vegetable oils. 65 tanks with total storage cap of 100 000 m3. This terminal also runs the latex (natural rubber) depot, which offers 21 tanks for a total cap of 3700 m3

[11]*D'Alesio Terminal:* Tel: +39 0586 442911, Fax: +39 0586 429653, Email: g.dalesio@tin.it
Liquid bulk handling & storage. 43 tanks with total storage cap of 190 000 m3

[12]*AGIP Gas Terminal:* Tel: +39 0586 946111, Fax: +39 0586 946213, Email: pierpaolo.terenzoni@agippetroli.eni.it
Handling & storage of liquid propane gas. Storage cap of 45 000 m3

[13]*Livorno Forest Terminal:* Tel: +39 0586 890133, Fax: +39 0586 895000
Handling & storage of paper and forest products

[14]*Leonardo da Vinci Terminal:* Tel: +39 0586 841620, Fax: +39 0586 841618, Email: cilp@gruppocpl.it
Specialises in new car traffic

[15]*Bartoli Terminal:* Tel: +39 0586 400599, Fax: +39 0586 427270, Email: ikbartol@tin.it
Handling copper & non-ferrous metals

[16]*Tozzi Terminal:* Tel: +39 0586 890128, Fax: +39 0586 883049
Handling of paper, forest products & containers. Covered area of 2403 m2

[17]*Porto Commerciale Terminal:* Tel: +39 0586 841754, Fax: +39 0586 841711, Email: cilp@gruppocpl.it
Multi-purpose terminal specialising in the handling of containers and forest products. Two 100 000 m3 warehouses

[18]*Silos del Tirreno Terminal:* Tel: +39 0586 880411, Fax: +39 0586 880222
Handling and temporary storage of cereals, flour, legumes & oil seeds. Private bonded warehouse

[19]*Marchi Terminal:* Tel: +39 0586 250111, Fax: +39 0586 250243, Email: fanfani@gfanfani.com
Handling and storage of paper and forest products

[20]*Figli di Nado Neri Terminal:* Tel: +39 0586 895174, Fax: +39 0586 888421, Email: s.sabaz@nerilivorno.it
Comprises Scotto Terminal and Magnale Terminal handling, storing and distributing paper and forest products

[21]*Calata Orlando Terminal:* Tel: +39 0586 829266, Fax: +39 0586 828218, Email: tco@iol.it
Specialising in dry bulk cargo

[22]*Dole Terminal:* Tel: +39 0586 827611, Fax: +39 0586 827699
Handling and temperature controlled storage of fresh fruit & vegetables. Three cold storage units. 100 reefer points

[23]*Porto di Livorno 2000 Terminal:* Tel: +39 0586 892207, Fax: +39 0586 892209, Email: info@portolivorno2000.it, Website: www.portolivorno2000.it
Passenger traffic with berths for cruise vessels & ferries

[24]*Novoil Terminal:* Tel: +39 0586 429801, Fax: +39 0586 429393
Specialises in unloading oleiferous seeds, the storage of solid bulk & the storage of vegetables in bonded warehouses

[25]*Carbochimica Terminal:* Tel: +39 0586 424106, Fax: +39 0586 424342, Email: carbolivorno.comm@tin.it
Distillation of coal tar, furnace oil, naphtalene oil and creosote and pitch production for the steel, aluminium & fettling industries

Key to Principal Facilities:—							
A=Airport	**C**=Containers		**G**=General Cargo		**P**=Petroleum	**R**=Ro/Ro	**Y**=Dry Bulk
B=Bunkers	**D**=Dry Dock		**L**=Cruise		**Q**=Other Liquid Bulk	**T**=Towage (where available from port)	

[26]*Grandi Molini Italiani SpA Terminal:* Tel: +39 0586 251711, Fax: +39 0586 251727, Email: gmispali@grandimolini.it
Handling of cereals
[27]*Labromare Faro Verde Terminal:* Fax: +39 0586 409748, Email: labromare@lam.it
Anti sea & land pollution and solid & liquid waste disposal

Mechanical Handling Equipment:

Location	Type	Capacity (t)	Qty
Darsena Toscana Terminal	Container Cranes		4
Darsena Toscana Terminal	Post Panamax		2
Darsena Toscana Terminal	RTG's		5
Darsena Toscana Terminal	Forklifts		40
Sintermar Terminal	Container Cranes		3
Sintermar Terminal	Transtainers		4
Sintermar Terminal	Reach Stackers		12
Tozzi Terminal	Forklifts		12
Tozzi Terminal	Yard Trailers		100
Porto Commerciale Terminal	Mult-purp. Cranes	8–30	6
Porto Commerciale Terminal	Container Cranes		2

Bunkering: Coal at Cappellini Basin
Dalmare S.p.A., Via Castelli 6, 57122 Leghorn, Italy, *Tel:* +39 0586 437 111, *Fax:* +39 0586 437 112, *Email:* info@dalesio.it, *Website:* www.dalesio.it

Towage: Tugs available of 700-3000 bhp

Repair & Maintenance: Cantieri Navali Fratelli Orlando S.c.r.l., 92 Piazza Mazzini, 57123 Leghorn, Italy, *Tel:* +39 0586 827811, *Fax:* +39 0586 827890, *Email:* orlando@portnet.it Two dry docks available, lengths 350 m and 137 m, width 56 m and 17.5 m respectively. Vessels up to 300 000 dwt can be accommodated

Ship Chandlers: Ligabue Catering SLL, Via Salvatore Orlando 28, 51722 Leghorn, Italy, *Tel:* +39 0586 439411, *Fax:* +39 0586 439420, *Email:* fedele.silvestri@ligabue.it, *Website:* www.ligabue.it
Marine Consultant & Services S.r.l., Via San Carlo 10, I-57126 Leghorn, Italy, *Tel:* +39 0586 211452, *Fax:* +39 0586 211452, *Email:* Info@marineconsultantservices.com, *Website:* www.marineconsultantservices.com
George Menaboni S.r.l., P O Box 162, I-57123 Leghorn, Italy, *Tel:* +39 0586 426122, *Fax:* +39 0586 426880, *Email:* george@sysnet.it, *Website:* www.menaboni.com
Sosema S.r.l., Via dell'Ecologia 7, I-57122 Leghorn, Italy, *Tel:* +39 0586 426131, *Fax:* +39 0586 409921, *Email:* info@sosema.it, *Website:* www.sosema.it
Tubino S.r.l., Via Chiabrera 36/38, 57121 Leghorn, Italy, *Tel:* +39 0586 426397, *Fax:* +39 0586 449770, *Email:* tubino@tubinosrl.it, *Website:* www.tubinosrl.com

Shipping Agents: AEM-Agenzie Europee Maritime S.r.l., Via Fiume 71, I- 57123, Leghorn, Italy, *Tel:* +39 0586 895500, *Fax:* +39 0586 895504, *Website:* www.aemitalia.com
Cesare Fremura S.r.l., Piazza Cavour 12, P O Box 346, I-57100 Leghorn, Italy, *Tel:* +39 0586 846111, *Fax:* +39 0586 846255, *Email:* hq@fremuragroup.com, *Website:* www.fremuragroup.com
CMA-CGM S.A., CMA CGM Italy Srl, Via Varese 12, I-57122 Leghorn, Italy, *Tel:* +39 0586 263311, *Fax:* +39 0586 263399, *Email:* liv.genmbox@cma-cgm.com, *Website:* www.cma-cgm.com
Comesmar Livorno, Via Varese 8, 57122 Leghorn, Italy, *Tel:* +39 0586 830110, *Fax:* +39 0586 830170, *Email:* r.priami@comesmar.it
Fratelli Cosulich Bunkers (S) Pte Ltd, Via Leonardo Vinci 5, 57100 Leghorn, Italy, *Tel:* +39 0586 444407, *Fax:* +39 0586 443629, *Email:* agency@li.cosulich.it, *Website:* www.cosulich.it
CSA S.p.A., Via Piave 6, I-57123 Leghorn, Italy, *Tel:* +39 0586 82631, *Fax:* +39 0586 882455, *Email:* csa.livorno@csaspa.com, *Website:* www.csaspa.com
G. Fanfani & C. S.r.l., Via del Marzocco 25, I-57123 Leghorn, Italy, *Tel:* +39 0586 250111, *Fax:* +39 0586 250243, *Email:* fanfani@gfanfani.com, *Website:* www.gfanfani.com
Gastaldi & C. S.p.A., 11 Scali degli Isolotti, 57123 Leghorn, Italy, *Tel:* +39 0586 274411, *Fax:* +39 0586 274460, *Email:* livorno.gc@gastaldi.it, *Website:* www.gastaldi.it
LV Ghianda S.r.l., Via Vittorio Veneto 24, P O Box 70, 57100 Leghorn, Italy, *Tel:* +39 0586 826835, *Fax:* +39 0586 826821, *Email:* lvghianda@lvghianda.it
Giorgio Gragnani S.r.l., Via della Cateratte 82, I-57122 Leghorn, Italy, *Tel:* +39 0586 236511, *Fax:* +39 0586 236500, *Email:* info@gragnani.it, *Website:* www.gragnani.it
Greensisam S.p.A., Scali Cerere 9, 57122 Leghorn, Italy, *Tel:* +39 0586 413111, *Fax:* +39 0586 413235, *Email:* biz@evergreen-shipping.it, *Website:* www.shipmentlink.com/it
Meditalia Marittima Italiana S.r.l., Via Montegrappa 15, scala 1, 57123 Leghorn, Italy, *Tel:* +39 0586 893174, *Fax:* +39 0586 885235, *Email:* info@meditaliaweb.com, *Website:* www.meditaliaweb.com
A.P. Moller-Maersk Group, Maersk Italia SpA, Via Borra, I-57123 Leghorn, Italy, *Tel:* +39 0586 823606, *Fax:* +39 0586 823609, *Email:* livsalmng@maersk.com, *Website:* www.maerskline.com
G. Panessa & C. S.r.l., Scali del Corso 11, Livorno, I-57123 Leghorn, Italy, *Tel:* +39 0586 270111, *Fax:* +39 0586 270225, *Email:* info@g-panessa-co.it, *Website:* www.g-panessa-co.it
Hugo Trumpy S.p.A., Viale Italia 183, Leghorn, Italy, *Tel:* +39 0586 502074, *Fax:* +39 0586 260044, *Email:* htleg@htleg.it

Surveyors: Fratelli Cosulich Bunkers (S) Pte Ltd, Via Leonardo Vinci 5, 57100 Leghorn, Italy, *Tel:* +39 0586 444407, *Fax:* +39 0586 443629, *Email:* agency@li.cosulich.it, *Website:* www.cosulich.it
Nippon Kaiji Kyokai, Leghorn, Italy, *Tel:* +39 0586 893567, *Fax:* +39 0586 890005, *Website:* www.classnk.or.jp
Registro Italiano Navale (RINA), Via Grande 143, Leghorn, Italy, *Tel:* +39 0586 202011, *Fax:* +39 0586 202020, *Email:* livorno.office@rina.org, *Website:* www.rina.org
Sauro Spadoni, P O Box 706, Via delle Cateratte, 57122 Leghorn, Italy, *Tel:* +39 0586 887568, *Fax:* +39 0586 891174, *Email:* info@saurospadoni.it

Medical Facilities: Doctor and ambulance available

Airport: San Giusto Airport, 18 km

Railway: Two railway stations with 60 km of track within the customs boundary

Development: Rhodia Italia Terminal with a 142 m quay is currently being built

Lloyd's Agent: Ditta Vincenzo Capanna S.a.S., Via Claudio Cogorano 25, P O Box 286, I-57123 Leghorn, Italy, *Tel:* +39 0586 894132, *Fax:* +39 0586 885332, *Email:* capanna@capanna.it, *Website:* www.capanna.it

LICATA

Lat 37° 6' N; Long 13° 56' E.

Admiralty Chart: 965	**Admiralty Pilot:** 45
Time Zone: GMT +1 h	**UNCTAD Locode:** IT LIC

Principal Facilities:

		Y	G			B		T	

Authority: Ufficio Circondariale Marittimo di Licata, Via Libotti 9, I-92027 Licata, Sicily, Italy, *Tel:* +39 0922 774113, *Fax:* +39 0922 774113, *Email:* licata@guardiacostiera.it

Officials: Harbour Master: Capt Fabio Critrolo.

Port Security: ISPS compliant

Pilotage: Compulsory, Tel & Fax: +39 0933 939303. Pilots communicate with vessel on VHF Channel 12

Radio Frequency: Port Authority on VHF Channel 16

Maximum Vessel Dimensions: 160 m loa, 6 m draft, 5000 dwt

Principal Imports and Exports: Imports: Cement, Fertiliser, Iron, Wine, Wood. Exports: Agricultural products.

Working Hours: 24 h/day

Accommodation:

Name	Remarks
Licata	See [1] below

[1]*Licata:* One wharf 190 m long with 6 m draft for commercial cargoes. Another wharf 230 m long, used mainly by fishing vessels

Mechanical Handling Equipment:

Location	Type	Capacity (t)	Qty
Licata	Mult-purp. Cranes	13	1
Licata	Mult-purp. Cranes	20	1
Licata	Mult-purp. Cranes	30	2
Licata	Mult-purp. Cranes	10	1

Bunkering: Available
AGIP Petroli S.p.A., ENI, Via Laurentina 449, 00142 Rome, Italy, *Tel:* +39 06 59881, *Fax:* +39 06 5988 5700, *Email:* gioacchino.costa@eni.it, *Website:* www.eni.it – *Grades:* GO – *Delivery Mode:* truck
Asta Carburanti di Asta Salvatore, Sede: via Dei Roveri 11, 11 - 97013 Comiso, Sicily, Italy, *Tel:* +39 0932 798682, *Fax:* +39 0932 798682, *Email:* asta.carburanti@tin.it
Gori Petrol Group, V. Cristoforo Colombo 1, San Gregorio di Catania, 95027 Catania, Sicily, Italy, *Tel:* +39 095 492 386, *Fax:* +39 095 7122 710, *Email:* info@goripetrolgroup.191.it

Repair & Maintenance: Minor repairs only

Stevedoring Companies: Compagnia Portuale 'Monte Ecnomo' S.C.A.R.L., Piazza Regolo Attilio 36, I-92027 Licata, Sicily, Italy, *Tel:* +39 0922 774882

Surveyors: Nippon Kaiji Kyokai, Licata, Sicily, Italy, *Tel:* +39 0922 773016, *Fax:* +39 0922 773016, *Website:* www.classnk.or.jp
Registro Italiano Navale (RINA), c/o Agenzia Marittima Cigna Srl, Piazza A. Regolo 26, Licata, Sicily, Italy, *Tel:* +39 0922 773016, *Fax:* +39 0922 773016, *Website:* www.rina.org

Medical Facilities: Doctor available

Railway: Nearest railway, 1 km

Lloyd's Agent: Tagliavia & Capanna Srl, Via Emerico Amari 8, I-90139 Palermo, Sicily, Italy, *Tel:* +39 091 587377, *Fax:* +39 091 322435, *Email:* info@tagliaviacapanna.it

LIPARI

Lat 38° 28' N; Long 14° 57' E.

Admiralty Chart: 172	**Admiralty Pilot:** 46
Time Zone: GMT +1 h	**UNCTAD Locode:** IT LIP

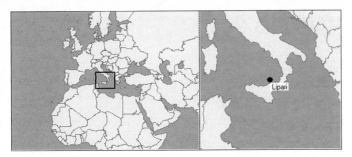

Principal Facilities:

	G		B	

Authority: Capitaneria di Porto di Lipari, Via F. Crispi 125, I-98055 Lipari, Sicily, Italy, *Tel:* +39 090 981 1320, *Fax:* +39 090 981 1320, *Email:* lipari@guardiacostiera.it, *Website:* www.lipari.guardiacostiera.it

Officials: Harbour Master: Luca Politi, *Email:* politiluca@hotmail.com.

Port Security: ISPS compliant

Anchorage: Anchorage can be obtained in Lipari roadstead in depths between 29 m to 40 m or off Porticello with local knowledge

Pilotage: Compulsory for vessels over 500 gt. Local pilots operate a 24 h service, *Tel:* +39 090 981 2211 & 981 1548, VHF Channel 16

Radio Frequency: VHF Channel 16, from 0800-2000

Maximum Vessel Dimensions: 4570 dwt, 119.2 m loa

Accommodation:

Name	Length (m)	Depth (m)	Remarks
Lipari			
Rifugio Pignataro	250	2–5	Capable of berthing medium tonnage vessels
Sottomonastero	110	2–5	
Porticello	274	14	See [1] below

[1]*Porticello:* There are mooring buoys in the vicinity. This facility is used for the loading of pumice by conveyor

Bunkering: Eolian Bunker, Via Francesco Crispi, 98055 Lipari, Sicily, Italy, *Tel:* +39 090 9812 335, *Fax:* +39 090 9811 961, *Email:* info@eolianbunker.com
AGIP Petroli S.p.A., ENI, Via Laurentina 449, 00142 Rome, Italy, *Tel:* +39 06 59881, *Fax:* +39 06 5988 5700, *Email:* gioacchino.costa@eni.it, *Website:* www.eni.it – *Grades:* GO; IFO; lubes
Eolian Bunker, Via Francesco Crispi, 98055 Lipari, Sicily, Italy, *Tel:* +39 090 9812 335, *Fax:* +39 090 9811 961, *Email:* info@eolianbunker.com – *Grades:* GO; IFO; lubes

Shipping Agents: Destefano Speciale & C., Bachina Sottomonastero, 98040 Lipari, Sicily, Italy, *Tel:* +39 090 674300, *Fax:* +39 090 678 1341, *Email:* ops@speciagt.it, *Website:* www.destefanospeciale.it

Medical Facilities: Hospital at Lipari

Lloyd's Agent: Tagliavia & Capanna Srl, Via Emerico Amari 8, I-90139 Palermo, Sicily, Italy, *Tel:* +39 091 587377, *Fax:* +39 091 322435, *Email:* info@tagliaviacapanna.it

LIVORNO

alternate name, see Leghorn

LUSID PIER

harbour area, see under Piombino

MAGONA PIER

harbour area, see under Piombino

MANFREDONIA

Lat 41° 37' N; Long 15° 55' E.

Admiralty Chart: 1443   **Admiralty Pilot:** 47

Time Zone: GMT +1 h   **UNCTAD Locode:** IT MFR

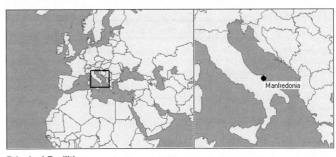

Principal Facilities:

P	Q	G		B	T	A

Authority: Capitaneria di Porto di Manfredonia, Piazza Marconi 27, I-71043 Manfredonia, Italy, *Tel:* +39 0884 583871, *Fax:* +39 0884 587388, *Email:* manfredonia@guardiacostiera.it, *Website:* www.manfredonia.guardiacostiera.it

Officials: Harbour Master: Capt Giuseppe Sciarrone.

Port Security: ISPS compliant

Approach: Old Commercial Port: Depth of water at harbour entrance is approx 7.5 m. New Industrial Port: Depth of water at harbour entrance is approx 10.0 m

Anchorage: In pos 41° 37' 00" N; 15° 55' 00" E (max d 7.0 m). In pos 41° 37' 00" N; 15° 56' 30" E (max d 8.5 m). In pos 41° 36' 30" N; 15° 57' 00" E (max d 10.0 m)

Pilotage: Compulsory for vessels over 500 gt. Service carried out by two pilots, 24 h service

Radio Frequency: VHF Channel 12

Maximum Vessel Dimensions: 35 000 dwt, max d 9.9 m, no restrictions for loa

Working Hours: Mon-Sat 0700-1300, 1300-1900

Accommodation:

Name	Length (m)	Draught (m)	Remarks
New Industrial Port			
A1	300	9.9	Bulk grain
A2	250	9.9	Bulk grain
A3	265	9.9	General cargo
A4	265	9.9	General cargo
A5	315	9.9	Chemical/gas oil
AU	150	6.8	Chemical/gas oil
Old Commercial Port			
Pier No.1	150	7	General cargo
Pier No.2	150	7	General cargo
Pier No.3	150	7	General cargo
Pier No.6	80	6.7	Passengers

Mechanical Handling Equipment:

Location	Type	Capacity (t)	Qty
New Industrial Port	Mult-purp. Cranes	25	2
Old Commercial Port	Mult-purp. Cranes	6	2
Old Commercial Port	Mobile Cranes	50	1

Bunkering: Available by road tanker with 24 h notice

Waste Reception Facilities: All services carried out by the 'Ecolmare Gargano'

Towage: Two tugs are available of 1300-1800 hp

Repair & Maintenance: Officine Elettromeccaniche Mondelli, Manfredonia, Italy, *Tel:* +39 0884 581151 Repair facilities

Ship Chandlers: Cianciola-Montanari Shipchandlers della Work System S.r.l., Mol Ponente, I-71043 Manfredonia, Italy, *Tel:* +39 0884 533046, *Fax:* +39 0884 533046, *Email:* cianbari@tin.it

Airport: Foggia, 48 km

Lloyd's Agent: P. Lorusso & Co. S.r.l., 133 Via Piccinni, I-70122 Bari, Italy, *Tel:* +39 080 521 2840, *Fax:* +39 080 521 8229, *Email:* vdbdirezione@agenzialorusso.it, *Website:* www.agenzialorusso.it

MARINA DI CARRARA

Lat 44° 2' N; Long 10° 2' E.

Admiralty Chart: 118   **Admiralty Pilot:** 46

Time Zone: GMT +1 h   **UNCTAD Locode:** IT MDC

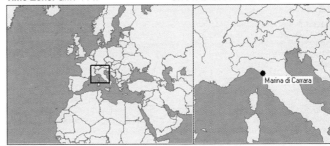

Key to Principal Facilities:—				
A=Airport	**C**=Containers	**G**=General Cargo	**P**=Petroleum	**R**=Ro/Ro	**Y**=Dry Bulk
B=Bunkers	**D**=Dry Dock	**L**=Cruise	**Q**=Other Liquid Bulk	**T**=Towage (where available from port)

Principal Facilities:

	Y	G	C	R		B		T	A	

Authority: Autorita Portuale di Marina di Carrara, Viale G. da Verrazzzano, Varco Portuale di Levante, I-54036 Marina di Carrara, Italy, *Tel:* +39 0585 787205, *Fax:* +39 0585 788346, *Email:* info@portauthoritymdc.ms.it, *Website:* www.portofcarrara.it

Officials: President: Luigi Guccinelli, *Email:* guccinelli@portauthoritymdc.ms.it. General Secretary: Luigi Bosi, *Email:* bosi@portauthoritymdc.ms.it.

Port Security: ISPS compliant

Approach: Depth at entrance 10 m, depth at bar 10 m and depths at wharves 9.3-10 m

Anchorage: Anchorage area available in depth of 11-13 m with a one mile radius centred at 1.5 miles from the red light of the port in a direction of 210°

Pilotage: Compulsory for vessels over 500 gt, Tel: +39 0585 633315, Fax: +39 0585 633321, Email: pilcar@tin.it

Radio Frequency: Pilot Station on VHF Channel 12. Harbour Master on VHF Channel 16

Tides: Medium tide 15 cm

Traffic: 2003, 3 060 021 t of cargo handled

Maximum Vessel Dimensions: 220 m loa, 35 000 dwt, 10 m draft

Principal Imports and Exports: Imports: Coils, Stone, Woodpulp. Exports: Marble, Pipes.

Working Hours: 0730-1200, 1330-1730 or 0700-1330, 1330-2000, 2000-0230

Accommodation:

Name	Length (m)	Draught (m)	Remarks
Marina di Carrara			See [1] below
Fiorillo Quay	440	9	
Taliercio Quay	440	10	
Chiesa Quay	390	10	
Buscaiol Quay	300	7	

[1]*Marina di Carrara:* The port also has an intermodal transport centre, 500 m away with a total surface area of 200 000 m2 with 10 000 m2 of covered warehousing

Storage:

Location	Covered (m²)
Marina di Carrara	15000

Mechanical Handling Equipment:

Location	Type	Capacity (t)	Qty
Marina di Carrara	Mobile Cranes	70–100	12
Marina di Carrara	Forklifts	3–40	117

Bunkering: AGIP Petroli S.p.A., ENI, Via Laurentina 449, 00142 Rome, Italy, *Tel:* +39 06 59881, *Fax:* +39 06 5988 5700, *Email:* gioacchino.costa@eni.it, *Website:* www.eni.it – *Grades:* GO; IFO – *Delivery Mode:* barge. truck
Alpha Trading S.p.A., Via Brigata Liguria 3/19, 16121 Genoa, Italy, *Tel:* +39 010 5472 200, *Fax:* +39 010 5472 209, *Email:* bunkers@alphatrading.it, *Website:* www.alphatrading.it – *Grades:* GO; IFO; in line blending available – *Parcel Size:* no min – *Rates:* 75-300t/h – *Delivery Mode:* barge, truck
ExxonMobil Marine Fuels, Mailpoint 31, ExxonMobil House, Ermyn Way, Leatherhead, Surrey KT22 8UX, United Kingdom, *Tel:* +44 1372 222 000, *Fax:* +44 1372 223 922, *Email:* marine.fuels@exxonmobil.com, *Website:* www.exxonmobil.com
Getoil S.r.l., Getoil S.r.l., Via Buonarroti 14, 20145 Milan, Italy, *Tel:* +39 02 468 851, *Fax:* +39 02 4692 760, *Email:* getoil@getoil.it/commerciale@getoil.it
Gori Petrol Group, V. Cristoforo Colombo 1, San Gregorio di Catania, 95027 Catania, Sicily, Italy, *Tel:* +39 095 492 386, *Fax:* +39 095 7122 710, *Email:* info@goripetrolgroup.191.it
New Energy Srl, Bunker Department, Via Menini 5, 55049 Viareggio, Italy, *Tel:* +39 0584 383923, *Fax:* +39 0584 389101

Waste Reception Facilities: Garbage and sludge service

Towage: Two tugs available of 2067-2200 hp. Another tug of 1700 hp is available on request

Ship Chandlers: Marine Consultant & Services S.r.l., Via F. Cavallotti 28/A, I-54036 Marina di Carrara, Italy, *Tel:* +39 0585 787676, *Fax:* +39 0585 787676, *Email:* supply@marineconsultantservices.com, *Website:* www.marineconsultantservices.com

Shipping Agents: BM Shipping Group S.p.A., Viale Giovanni da Verrazzano 5, P O Box 88, 54036 Marina di Carrara, Italy, *Tel:* +39 0585 771205, *Fax:* +39 0585 630422, *Email:* info@bmshipping.com, *Website:* www.bmshipping.com
Vittorio Bogazzi & Figli S.p.A., Via Cadorna 49/A, 54036 Marina di Carrara, Italy, *Tel:* +39 0585 631665, *Fax:* +39 0585 631649, *Email:* info@bogazzi.it, *Website:* www.bogazzi.it
SeaGull Shipping Co. Ltd, 1 bis, via Capitan Fiorillo, 54036 Marina di Carrara, Italy, *Tel:* +39 0585 784626, *Fax:* +39 0585 774364, *Email:* seagullshipping@seagullshipping.191.com, *Website:* www.seagull-shipping.com

Stevedoring Companies: BM Shipping Group S.p.A., Viale Giovanni da Verrazzano 5, P O Box 88, 54036 Marina di Carrara, Italy, *Tel:* +39 0585 771205, *Fax:* +39 0585 630422, *Email:* info@bmshipping.com, *Website:* www.bmshipping.com
Porto di Carrara S.p.A., Marina di Carrara, Italy, *Tel:* +39 0585 784430, *Fax:* +39 0585 784413

Medical Facilities: Hospitals available 5 km and 8 km from port

Airport: Pisa, 50 km

Railway: Railway connection inside the port area

Lloyd's Agent: Ditta Vincenzo Capanna S.a.S., Via Claudio Cogorano 25, P O Box 286, I-57123 Leghorn, Italy, *Tel:* +39 0586 894132, *Fax:* +39 0586 885332, *Email:* capanna@capanna.it, *Website:* www.capanna.it

MARSALA

Lat 37° 47' N; Long 12° 26' E.

Admiralty Chart: 964	**Admiralty Pilot:** 45
Time Zone: GMT +1 h	**UNCTAD Locode:** IT MRA

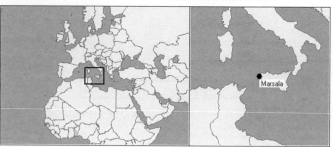

Principal Facilities:

P	Q	Y	G			B		A	

Authority: Ufficio Circondariale Marittimo di Marsala, Piazza Piemonte e Lombardo 38, I-91025 Marsala, Sicily, Italy, *Tel:* +39 0923 951184, *Fax:* +39 0923 951030, *Email:* marsala@guardiacostiera.it, *Website:* www.harbours.net/marsala

Officials: Harbour Master: Scrima Maurizio.

Port Security: ISPS compliant

Approach: Port entrance approx 200 m wide. Vessels of high draught must beware of zones of sand which are formed by high winds. The port is exposed to high winds which occur in all seasons except summer

Pilotage: Compulsory for vessels exceeding 500 gt. Performed by Corporazione Piloti Trapani/Marsala

Radio Frequency: VHF Channel 16

Tides: Range of tide 0.35 m although occasionally reaching 1 m

Maximum Vessel Dimensions: 140 m loa, 5.6 m d

Principal Imports and Exports: Imports: Wood. Exports: Wine.

Working Hours: 0800-1200, 1300-1700. Sat 0800-1200

Accommodation:

Name	Draught (m)	Remarks
Marsala		A large and spacious harbour
Martello Pier	4.5	
Centrale Pier	5.5	
Curvilinea Pier	5.2	
Colombo Pier	6.5	
Molo Levanto	5.4	
Prolungamento Curvilinea	5.2	

Mechanical Handling Equipment:

Location	Type	Capacity (t)	Qty
Marsala	Mult-purp. Cranes	20	1
Marsala	Mult-purp. Cranes	10	1

Cargo Worked: 3000 t of wine per day through pipeline

Bunkering: AGIP Petroli S.p.A., ENI, Via Laurentina 449, 00142 Rome, Italy, *Tel:* +39 06 59881, *Fax:* +39 06 5988 5700, *Email:* gioacchino.costa@eni.it, *Website:* www.eni.it – *Grades:* GO; IFO – *Notice:* 24-48 hours – *Delivery Mode:* road tanker

Towage: Somat S.r.l., Via Spalti 83, 91100 Trapani, Sicily, Italy, *Tel:* +39 0923 29445, *Fax:* +39 0923 27711, *Email:* somat@libero.it

Repair & Maintenance: Available for vessels up to 100 gt

Shipping Agents: Medimare S.n.c., Piazza Piemonte e Lombardo 36/C, Marsala, Sicily, Italy, *Tel:* +39 0923 711743, *Fax:* +39 0923 718745, *Email:* info@medimare.com, *Website:* www.medimare.com
Ignazio Zichittella SAS Agency, 63 Via Mario Nuccio, I-91025 Marsala, Sicily, Italy, *Tel:* +39 0923 714000, *Fax:* +39 0923 956833, *Email:* zicmar@tin.it, *Website:* www.zichittella.it

Airport: Birgi, 20 km

Lloyd's Agent: Tagliavia & Capanna Srl, Via Emerico Amari 8, I-90139 Palermo, Sicily, Italy, *Tel:* +39 091 587377, *Fax:* +39 091 322435, *Email:* info@tagliaviacapanna.it

MAZARA DEL VALLO

Lat 37° 39' N; Long 12° 34' E.

Admiralty Chart: 964	**Admiralty Pilot:** 45
Time Zone: GMT +1 h	**UNCTAD Locode:** IT MAZ

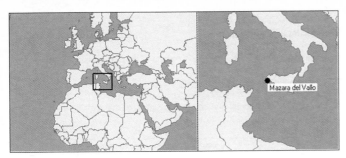

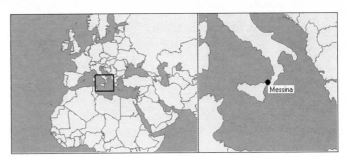

Principal Facilities:

Q	G		B		A

Authority: Capitaneria di Porto di Mazara del Vallo, Lungomare Fata Morgana, I-91026 Mazara del Vallo, Sicily, Italy, *Tel:* +39 0923 946471, *Fax:* +39 0923 941020, *Email:* mazaradelvallo@guardiacostiera.it, *Website:* www.guardiacostiera.it/mazaradelvallo

Officials: Harbour Master: Giuseppe Sarchese.

Approach: Mainly a fishing harbour formed by estuary of River Mazaro, average width 60 m. Expanse of water between rocks and jetty and river estuary proper form the outer harbour, of which eastern portion is not navigable owing to the rocky S Vito Bar with depth 1 m gradually decreasing towards the Saint's statue. Depth at the new port is 5.6 m, with 4 m max d in the port channel. There are sand banks inside the port which are signified

Pilotage: Compulsory for vessels exceeding 500 gt

Radio Frequency: VHF Channel 16

Tides: Tide 0.3 m, current inconsiderable

Maximum Vessel Dimensions: 120 m loa, 5.6 m d

Principal Imports and Exports: Imports: Cement. Exports: Wine.

Working Hours: 0800-1200, 1300-1700, overtime 1700-1900

Accommodation:

Name	Length (m)	Remarks
Mazaro River		
Levante Berth	190	Only operative for 76 m
Caito Quay	340	
New Port		
Berth 1 (N side)	170	
Berth 2 (S side)	150	
Berth 2 (N side)	150	
Banchina de Riva	110	

Storage: Silos for wine and privately owned fish storage of 4000 m3

Mechanical Handling Equipment:

Location	Type	Capacity (t)	Remarks
Mazara del Vallo	Mult-purp. Cranes	25	private

Cargo Worked: 1000 t of wine per day

Bunkering: AGIP Petroli S.p.A., ENI, Via Laurentina 449, 00142 Rome, Italy, *Tel:* +39 06 59881, *Fax:* +39 06 5988 5700, *Email:* gioacchino.costa@eni.it, *Website:* www.eni.it – *Grades:* GO; IFO – *Notice:* 24-48 hours – *Delivery Mode:* road tanker

Towage: Vessels coming into Mazara usually contact Palermo or Trapani radio stations

Repair & Maintenance: Three shipbuilding and repairing yards for vessels up to 800 t, Tel: +39 0923 941307 & 942845

Shipping Agents: Medimare S.n.c., Via Nino Bixio 26/A, 91026 Mazara del Vallo, Sicily, Italy, *Tel:* +39 0923 946011, *Fax:* +39 0923 946227, *Email:* info@medimare.com, *Website:* www.medimare.com

Surveyors: Nippon Kaiji Kyokai, Mazara del Vallo, Sicily, Italy, *Tel:* +39 0923 942178, *Website:* www.classnk.or.jp
Registro Italiano Navale (RINA), c/o Medimare S.r.l., Via Nino Bixio 26, I-91026 Mazara del Vallo, Sicily, Italy, *Tel:* +39 0923 946011, *Fax:* +39 0923 946227, *Email:* info@medimare.com, *Website:* www.rina.org

Airport: Birgi, 30 km

Lloyd's Agent: Tagliavia & Capanna Srl, Via Emerico Amari 8, I-90139 Palermo, Sicily, Italy, *Tel:* +39 091 587377, *Fax:* +39 091 322435, *Email:* info@tagliaviacapanna.it

MELILLI

harbour area, see under Santa Panagia

MESSINA

Lat 38° 11' N; Long 15° 33' E.

Admiralty Chart: 992

Admiralty Pilot: 45

Time Zone: GMT +1 h

UNCTAD Locode: IT MSN

Principal Facilities:

	Y	G		R	L	B	D	T	A

Authority: Autorita Portuale di Messina, Via V. Emanuele II 27, I-98122 Messina, Sicily, Italy, *Tel:* +39 090 679991 & 770127, *Fax:* +39 090 710120, *Email:* segreteria@porto.messina.it, *Website:* www.porto.messina.it

Officials: President: Vincenzo Garofalo, *Email:* garofalo@porto.messina.it.
Marketing Manager: Cristiana Laura.
Harbour Master: Renato Citraro, *Email:* citraro@porto.messina.it.

Port Security: ISPS compliant

Approach: Width of entrance 45.71 m, depth 8.23 to 8.84 m

Pilotage: Compulsory for vessels over 15 000 t. Embarking of pilots takes place leeward. Pilot can be contacted via VHF Channels 12 and 16

Radio Frequency: VHF Channel 16

Weather: This port is secure in any weather conditions

Working Hours: Mon to Fri 0800-1200, 1300-1700. Work in double shifts can be arranged from first day of loading/discharging
Sat 0800-1400 against 25% increase for completion only if prior notice given
Holidays: For completion only work at overtime rates can be arranged if prior notice given. Work on the abolished general holidays is against 100% extra

Accommodation:

Name	Length (m)	Draught (m)
Messina		
Vespri Quay	102	6.5
Colapesce Quay	295	9–11
1 Settembre Quay	224	9–10.5
Marconi Quay	183	10
Peloro Quay	151	9
Rizzo Quay	200	9
Norimberga SW Quay	165	8
Norimberga Head Quay	98	7.5
Norimberga NE Quay	137	7
Egeo Quay	165	6

Mechanical Handling Equipment:

Location	Type	Qty
Messina	Mult-purp. Cranes	5

Bunkering: Available by pipeline at the Colapesce and 1 Settembre Quay; at other quays by road tanker
AGIP Petroli S.p.A., ENI, Via Laurentina 449, 00142 Rome, Italy, *Tel:* +39 06 59881, *Fax:* +39 06 5988 5700, *Email:* gioacchino.costa@eni.it, *Website:* www.eni.it – *Grades:* GO – *Parcel Size:* min 25t – *Delivery Mode:* truck
Gori Petrol Group, V. Cristoforo Colombo 1, San Gregorio di Catania, 95027 Catania, Sicily, Italy, *Tel:* +39 095 492 386, *Fax:* +39 095 7122 710, *Email:* info@goripetrolgroup.191.it
Luise International & Co., 15 Via G. Melisurgo, 80133 Naples, Italy, *Tel:* +39 081 552 8670, *Fax:* +39 081 552 7368, *Email:* luise@luise.com

Towage: Two tugs available of 4000 hp and 1500 hp

Repair & Maintenance: Cassaro, Messina, Sicily, Italy, *Tel:* +39 090 47551
Rodriquez Cantieri Navale S.p.A., Via San Raineri 22, 98122 Messina, Sicily, Italy, *Tel:* +39 090 77651, *Fax:* +39 090 675294, *Email:* marketing@rodriquez.it, *Website:* www.rodriquez.it
SMEB-Cantieri Navali S.p.A., Via S.Raineri, P O Box 25, I-98122 Messina, Sicily, Italy, *Tel:* +39 090 640 3200, *Fax:* +39 090 774585, *Email:* smeb@eniware.it, *Website:* www.smeb.it

Shipping Agents: Destefano Speciale & C., Via 1 Settembre 84, 98122 Messina, Sicily, Italy, *Tel:* +39 090 774044, *Fax:* +39 090 678 1341, *Email:* ops@speciagt.it, *Website:* www.destefanospeciale.it

Surveyors: Registro Italiano Navale (RINA), Via Alessio Valore 21, Isolato 301 Bis, Messina, Sicily, Italy, *Tel:* +39 090 675421, *Fax:* +39 090 717973, *Email:* messina.office@rina.org, *Website:* www.rina.org

Airport: Reggio Calabria, 12 km

Lloyd's Agent: Tagliavia & Capanna Srl, Via Emerico Amari 8, I-90139 Palermo, Sicily, Italy, *Tel:* +39 091 587377, *Fax:* +39 091 322435, *Email:* info@tagliaviacapanna.it

MILAZZO

Lat 38° 13' N; Long 15° 15' E.

Admiralty Chart: 805

Admiralty Pilot: 45

Time Zone: GMT +1 h

UNCTAD Locode: IT MLZ

Key to Principal Facilities:—				
A=Airport	**C**=Containers	**G**=General Cargo	**P**=Petroleum	**R**=Ro/Ro	**Y**=Dry Bulk
B=Bunkers	**D**=Dry Dock	**L**=Cruise	**Q**=Other Liquid Bulk	**T**=Towage (where available from port)

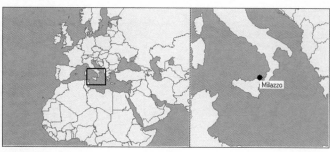

Principal Facilities:

P	Q		G		R		B		T	

Authority: Capitaneria di Porto di Milazzo, Via Molo Marullo, I-98057 Milazzo, Sicily, Italy, *Tel:* +39 090 922 3109, *Fax:* +39 090 922 2612, *Email:* milazzo@guardiacostiera.it, *Website:* www.harbours.net/milazzo

Officials: Harbour Master: Massimo Tomei.

Port Security: ISPS compliant

Radio Frequency: Pilots on VHF Channel 12

Maximum Vessel Dimensions: 300 000 dwt

Accommodation:

Name	Length (m)	Draught (m)	Remarks
Milazzo			
Mediterranea Refinery Pier No.1	480		Tankers
Mediterranea Refinery Pier No.2	631		Tankers
Foraneo Quay	430	6–12	
Marullo Quay	340	6–7	
Luigi Rizzo Quay	210	7–9	
Eolie Pier		5–8	North side 75 m long and south side 65 m long
XX Luglio Quay	550	8–12	

Storage: Some private warehouses on the quay are available

Mechanical Handling Equipment:

Location	Type	Capacity (t)	Qty	Remarks
Milazzo	Mult-purp. Cranes	20	1	private

Bunkering: AGIP Petroli S.p.A., ENI, Via Laurentina 449, 00142 Rome, Italy, *Tel:* +39 06 59881, *Fax:* +39 06 5988 5700, *Email:* gioacchino.costa@eni.it, *Website:* www.eni.it – *Grades:* GO – *Parcel Size:* min 25t – *Delivery Mode:* truck

Towage: Compulsory for tankers over 3000 gt. Four tugs available; two of 2500 hp and two of 1800 hp

Repair & Maintenance: Small repair shops

Ship Chandlers: Eolian Marine Suppliers S.n.c., Via Massimiliano Regis 6, I-98057 Milazzo, Sicily, Italy, *Tel:* +39 090 928 3376, *Fax:* +39 090 928 6763, *Email:* eolmar@tin.it

Shipping Agents: Destefano Speciale & C., Via del Sole 32, 98057 Milazzo, Sicily, Italy, *Tel:* +39 090 928 1521, *Fax:* +39 090 678 1341, *Email:* milazzo@speciagt.it, *Website:* www.destefanospeciale.it
Inchcape Shipping Services (ISS), Via Dei Mille 46, I-98057 Milazzo, Sicily, Italy, *Tel:* +39 090 922 3463, *Fax:* +39 090 250 9962, *Email:* iss.milazzo@iss-shipping.com, *Website:* www.iss-shipping.com
Italnoli S.r.l., Via M. Regis 6, I-98057 Milazzo, Sicily, Italy, *Tel:* +39 090 928 2176, *Fax:* +39 090 928 2256, *Email:* milazzo@italnoli.it, *Website:* www.italnoli.it

Lloyd's Agent: Tagliavia & Capanna Srl, Via Emerico Amari 8, I-90139 Palermo, Sicily, Italy, *Tel:* +39 091 587377, *Fax:* +39 091 322435, *Email:* info@tagliaviacapanna.it

MOLFETTA

Lat 41° 13' N; Long 16° 38' E.

Admiralty Chart: -	**Admiralty Pilot:** 47
Time Zone: GMT +1 h	**UNCTAD Locode:** IT MOL

Principal Facilities:

	Y		G			B		A	

Authority: Capitaneria di Porto di Molfetta, Banchina Seminario, I-70056 Molfetta, Italy, *Tel:* +39 080 397 1076, *Fax:* +39 080 397 1727, *Email:* molfetta@guardiacostiera.it

Officials: Harbour Master: Luigi Leotta.

Port Security: ISPS compliant

Anchorage: In sand and mud 10-12 m d

Pilotage: Available. Service from Bari-Molfetta Pilots Corporation on VHF Channel 12

Radio Frequency: VHF Channel 16

Weather: Principal winds from N/NE

Maximum Vessel Dimensions: 160 m loa, 7 m d, 20 000 dwt

Working Hours: 0800-1200, 1300-1700

Accommodation:

Name	Length (m)	Draught (m)	Remarks
Molfetta			See [1] below
Berth 1	160	7	
Berth 2	130	7.2	
Berth 3	115	6.2	

[1]*Molfetta:* The port, formed by a mole and stone dyke is sheltered from all winds except the W

Mechanical Handling Equipment:

Location	Type	Capacity (t)	Qty
Molfetta	Mult-purp. Cranes	70	4

Cargo Worked: Bulk 2000 t/day, bags 600 t/day, iron 1200 t/day

Bunkering: By truck

Towage: No tugs available. From Barletta and Bari if required

Medical Facilities: Available

Airport: Palese, 20 km

Lloyd's Agent: P. Lorusso & Co. S.r.l., 133 Via Piccinni, I-70122 Bari, Italy, *Tel:* +39 080 521 2840, *Fax:* +39 080 521 8229, *Email:* vdbdirezione@agenzialorusso.it, *Website:* www.agenzialorusso.it

MONFALCONE

Lat 45° 47' N; Long 13° 33' E.

Admiralty Chart: 1471	**Admiralty Pilot:** 47
Time Zone: GMT +1 h	**UNCTAD Locode:** IT MNF

Principal Facilities:

P		Y	G	C	R		B		T	A

Authority: Azienda Speciale per il Porto di Monfalcone, Via Terme Romane 5, I-34074 Monfalcone, Italy, *Tel:* +39 0481 414097, *Fax:* +39 0481 414099, *Email:* info@monfalconeport.it, *Website:* www.monfalconeport.it

Officials: General Manager: Sergio Signore.
Harbour Master: Giuseppe Romano, *Tel:* +39 0481 496611.

Port Security: ISPS compliant

Approach: The access channel is 4500 m long, 166 m wide in depth of 11.7 m

Anchorage: Vessels anchor approx 4.9 km from port entrance between Duino and Sistiana, which provides good shelter in approx 12 m depth

Pilotage: Compulsory for vessels exceeding 500 gt. Pilot boards vessel 1.6 km from port entrance and is available daylight hours only. VHF Channel 14

Radio Frequency: Communication through Trieste Radio. Port Control on VHF Channel 16

Weather: Dominant winds are from ENE (Bora) and from S (Scirocco)

Tides: Range of tide 0.5-1.5 m

Traffic: 2007, 4 411 900 t of cargo handled

Working Hours: Two shifts 0730-1400, 1400-2030

Accommodation:

Name	Length (m)	Draught (m)	Remarks
Monfalcone			See [1] below
Portorosega Wharf	1000	9.5	Nine berths
De Franceschi Wharf	120	10	See [2] below
Endesa Wharf	330		See [3] below

[1]*Monfalcone:* Harbour Master's Office: Viale Cosulich 24, Tel: +39 0481 712111, Email: cpmflamm@libero.it
[2]*De Franceschi Wharf:* One berth handling grain. Two mobile cranes with a max cap of 250 t/h. Silos available of 70 000 t cap
[3]*Endesa Wharf:* Two berths for unloading coal and fuel oil for power station, for vessels of 180 m max loa. Vessels berth and depart in daylight hours only

Storage: Public Depots & Warehouses:

Azienda Speciale per il Porto di Monfalcone della Camera di Commercio, Industria, Artigianato ed Agricoltura di Gorizia: an area of 150 000 m2, customs warehouses of 16 000 m2 and over 12 000 m2 of movable sheds located next to the quay
Consorzio per lo Sviluppo Industriale del Comune di Monfalcone: a 75 000 m2 multi-purpose open air yard under customs control. A 106 000 m2 open air yard used as a depot
Private Warehouses (in port area or nearby):
Mar/Ter Spedizioni SpA: 45 000 m2 of customs warehouses and open space of 40 000 m2
C.I.T.A. Srl: 4100 m2 of nationalised cargo warehouse space and open space of 35 000 m2
Friuldocks Srl: customs warehouse of 4700 m2
Ocean Sped Srl: customs warehouse of approx 10 000 m2 and open space of 28 000 m2
Francesco Parisi Group SpA: customs warehouses of 10 620 m2 and open space of 24 700 m2
De Franceschi SpA Monfalcone: Silos with storage cap of 70 000 t for grains and by-products
Zenith C Srl: open space of approx 7500 m2
In the port area there are three 1000 t cap silos receiving/delivering bulk cement of Baumit Italia SpA in Pordenone, and two silos with a storage cap of approx 3500 t each for cement and solid bulk of the firm Friulcem SpA

Mechanical Handling Equipment:

Location	Type	Capacity (t)	Qty
Monfalcone	Mult-purp. Cranes	45	6
Monfalcone	Mobile Cranes	25	7

Cargo Worked: Cars 1200 units/day, china clay 3000 t/day, coal 3000 t/day, containers 400 TEU's/day, cotton 500 t/day, grains in bulk 4000 t/day, iron fods in bundles 3000 t/day, iron ingots 3000 t/day, iron scrap 3000 t/day, timber logs 3000 t/day, timber sawn in bundles 1500 t/day, timber small logs wired 4000 t/day, timber small logs 1500 t/day, woodpulp 12 000 t/day

Bunkering: Available by barge from Trieste
AGIP Petroli S.p.A., ENI, Via Laurentina 449, 00142 Rome, Italy, *Tel:* +39 06 59881, *Fax:* +39 06 5988 5700, *Email:* gioacchino.costa@eni.it, *Website:* www.eni.it – *Grades:* GO; IFO – *Delivery Mode:* barge, truck subject to enquiry
Marodi Service SAS, Via Decorati Al Valor Civile 80, 30173 Venice, Italy, *Tel:* +39 041 538 2143, *Fax:* +39 041 922841, *Email:* marodi@marodi.it, *Website:* www.marodi.it
Maxcom Bunker S.p.A. u.s., Via Bartolomeo Bosco 57/7B, 16121 Genoa, Italy, *Tel:* +39 010 5605 200, *Fax:* +39 010 564 479, *Email:* bunker@maxcombunker.com, *Website:* www.maxcombunker.com

Repair & Maintenance: Minor repairs only

Shipping Agents: Agenzia Marittima Adriacostanzi S.r.l., Via delle Vigne 28, I-34074 Monfalcone, Italy, *Tel:* +39 0481 798073, *Fax:* +39 0481 46811, *Email:* info@adriacostanzi.it, *Website:* www.adriacostanzi.it
CSA S.p.A., Via Terme Romane 5, I-34121 Monfalcone, Italy, *Tel:* +39 0481 411423, *Fax:* +39 0481 410861, *Email:* shipservice.ts@csaspa.com, *Website:* www.csaspa.com
Francesco Parisi SAGL, Francesco Parisi S.p.A., Via delle Terme Romane 5, I-34074 Monfalcone, Italy, *Tel:* +39 0481 40539, *Fax:* +39 0481 798876, *Email:* monfalcone@francescoparisi.com, *Website:* www.francescoparisi.com
Friultrans S.r.l., Via Terme Romane 5, I-34074 Monfalcone, Italy, *Tel:* +39 0481 410570, *Fax:* +39 0481 795601, *Email:* monfalcone@friultrans.com, *Website:* www.friultrans.com
Inchcape Shipping Services (ISS), Via Terme Romane 5, I-34074 Monfalcone, Italy, *Tel:* +39 0481 410604, *Fax:* +39 0481 410861, *Email:* monfalcone@iss-tositti.it, *Website:* www.iss-shipping.com
Marlines S.r.l., Via Terme Romane 5, I-34074 Monfalcone, Italy, *Tel:* +39 0481 410213, *Fax:* +39 0481 410235, *Email:* marlines@marlines.it, *Website:* www.marlines.it
Samer & Co. Shipping Ltd, Via Terme Romane 5, I-34074 Monfalcone, Italy, *Tel:* +39 0481 411423, *Fax:* +39 0481 410861, *Email:* samer.monfalcone@samer.com, *Website:* www.samer.com
Tomaso Prioglio International S.p.A., Via Terme Romane 5, I-34074 Monfalcone, Italy, *Tel:* +39 0481 672 8111, *Fax:* +39 0481 40533, *Email:* prioglio@tomasopriogliointernational.com, *Website:* www.tomasoprioglio.it
Wilhelmsen Ship Services, Via Terme Romane 05, 34074 Monfalcone, Italy, *Tel:* +39 0481 412660, *Fax:* +39 0481 412707, *Email:* tsl@mar-ter.it

Medical Facilities: Hospital with full medical facilities available

Airport: Ronchi Airport, 5 km

Railway: The Trieste-Venice/Udine-Tarvisio rail connection is very close to the port

Development: Construction of a new 660 m long wharf
Dredging of the access channel to the port up to 13 m

Lloyd's Agent: Samer & Co. Shipping Ltd, Piazza dell 'Unita d'Italia 7, I-34121 Trieste, Italy, *Tel:* +39 040 670 2711, *Fax:* +39 040 6702 7300, *Email:* samer@samer.com, *Website:* www.samer.com

MONOPOLI

Lat 40° 57' N; Long 17° 18' E.

Admiralty Chart: -

Admiralty Pilot: 47

Time Zone: GMT +1 h

UNCTAD Locode: IT MNP

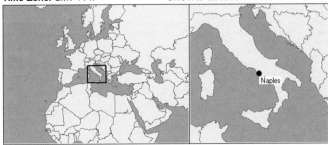

Principal Facilities:

Q	Y	G		R		B		A

Authority: Ufficio Circondariale Marittimo di Monopoli, Largo Fontanelle 12/A, I-70043 Monopoli, Italy, *Tel:* +39 080 930 3105, *Fax:* +39 080 937 9509, *Email:* monopoli@guardiacostiera.it, *Website:* www.guardiacostiera.it/monopoli

Officials: Harbour Master: Gianluca Massaro.

Port Security: ISPS compliant

Approach: Depth at entrance 11 m

Anchorage: Two points of anchorage available for vessels in depth of approx 25 m
40° 58.4' N; 017° 18.5' E
40° 56.9' N; 017° 20.4' E

Pilotage: Compulsory for vessels over 400 gt

Radio Frequency: Available on VHF Channel 16 (calling)

Maximum Vessel Dimensions: 110 m loa, 6.7 m draft

Working Hours: 0600-1200, 1300-1900 or 0800-1200, 1300-1700

Accommodation:

Name	Length (m)	Depth (m)	Remarks
Monopoli			
Banchina Solfatara Est (No.1)		6.4–6.7	For vessels up to 110 m loa
Banchina Solfatara NW (No.2)		5.5–5.7	For vessels up to 90 m loa
Punta del Tonno		5.5	For vessels up to 70 m loa
Molo Margherita	180	1–4.5	For fishing boats

Mechanical Handling Equipment:

Location	Type	Capacity (t)	Qty
Monopoli	Mult-purp. Cranes	40	1
Monopoli	Mult-purp. Cranes	32	1
Monopoli	Mult-purp. Cranes	50	1
Monopoli	Mult-purp. Cranes	25	1
Monopoli	Forklifts		2

Bunkering: Bunkers for vessels is available by tank cars, while bunkers for fishing boats is possible only by petrol pumps located on Solfatara Pier

Repair & Maintenance: Maellaro Paolo & C. S.n.c., Monopoli, Italy, *Tel:* +39 080 930 3138 Engineer and mechanical repairs
Navalcantieri Monopoli Ltd, Monopoli, Italy, *Tel:* +39 080 930 1339 Repairs for small wooden vessels
Muolo & Leoci, Monopoli, Italy, *Tel:* +39 080 930 3046 Mechanical repairs

Shipping Agents: Dormio Luciana Srl, Via C Colombo 37, P O Box 122, I-70043 Monopoli, Italy, *Tel:* +39 080 930 3188, *Fax:* +39 080 930 3189, *Email:* info@dormio.it, *Website:* www.dormio.it

Medical Facilities: Hospital available

Airport: Palese, 50 km

Railway: Monopoli Station, 500 m

Lloyd's Agent: P. Lorusso & Co. S.r.l., 133 Via Piccinni, I-70122 Bari, Italy, *Tel:* +39 080 521 2840, *Fax:* +39 080 521 8229, *Email:* vdbdirezione@agenzialorusso.it, *Website:* www.agenzialorusso.it

NAPLES

Lat 40° 50' N; Long 14° 16' E.

Admiralty Chart: 915

Admiralty Pilot: 46

Time Zone: GMT +1 h

UNCTAD Locode: IT NAP

Principal Facilities:

P	Q	Y	G	C	R	L	B	D	T	A

Key to Principal Facilities:—					
A=Airport	C=Containers	G=General Cargo	P=Petroleum	R=Ro/Ro	Y=Dry Bulk
B=Bunkers	D=Dry Dock	L=Cruise	Q=Other Liquid Bulk	T=Towage (where available from port)	

Authority: Autorita Portuale di Napoli, Consorzio Autonomo del Porto, Piazzale Pisacane, I-80133 Naples, Italy, *Tel:* +39 081 228 3402, *Fax:* +39 081 206888, *Email:* info@porto.napoli.it, *Website:* www.porto.napoli.it

Officials: General Secretary: Dr Pietro Capogreco, *Email:* p.capogreco@porto.napoli.it.

Port Security: ISPS compliant. Container Security Initiative (CSI) designated port

Approach: Approaches to the Gulf of Naples are free of navigational dangers. Ships approaching Naples from the N are cautioned to avoid the Procida Canal, between Procida Island and Cape Miseno (1.5 miles wide) in view of the heavy traffic usually met in this area and other navgation hazards. Passing well clear West of Ischia Island is recommended. Caution is necessary because numerous fishing boats are likely to be encountered in the area, especially at night and in the early morning

The main entrance to Naples lies between the extremities of Diga Duca degli Abruzzi and Molo San Vincenzo on the SW, and the extremity of Antemurale Thaon de Revel on the NE, and leads into Avamporto Ammiraglio Francesco Caracciolo which, with numerous basins, forms the W part of the harbour

The two breakwaters Duca degli Abruzzi and Foranea afford two entrances, E and W, 250 m and 280 m wide respectively, the latter the most commonly used. Molo San Vincenzo (length 1,475 m), houses a lighthouse visible for 32 km. All sea entrances and pier heads indicated by fixed lights

The E entrance to Naples, which lies between the head of Molo di Progresso and Diga Foranea Emanuele Filiberto Duca d'Aosta, is approached by a channel in which a depth of about 14 m is maintained by dredging, entered 8 cables SSE of the head of Molo di Progresso, and marked on each side by light-buoys; this depth is maintained through Avamporto di Levante as far as the W side of Molo di Progresso. Entry by the E entrance is difficult with SE winds

Vessels bound for the W part of the harbour should enter and leave through Bocca Principale. Vessels of not more than 12 m draught bound for the E part of the harbour may use either entrance; vessels of greater draught must use the E entrance, at reduced speed

Anchorage: Anchorage A1 for vessels not carrying dangerous goods centered on pos 40° 49' 70" N; 14° 15' 56" E (radius 250 m)

Anchorage A2 for vessels not carrying dangerous goods centered on pos 40° 49' 68" N; 14° 16' 08" E (radius 250 m)

Anchorage A3 for vessels not carrying dangerous goods centered on pos 40° 49' 40" N; 14° 15' 56" E (radius 250 m)

Anchorage A4 for vessels carrying dangerous goods centered on pos 40° 49' 33" N; 14° 16' 06" E (radius 350 m)

Anchorage A5 for vessels carrying dangerous goods centered on pos 40° 49' 10" N; 14° 15' 31" E (radius 350 m)

Anchorage B1 for tankers carrying or have carried dangerous liquid products centered on pos 40° 48' 53" N; 14° 19' 25" E (radius 250 m)

Anchorage B2 for tankers carrying or have carried dangerous liquid products centered on pos 40° 48' 20" N; 14° 19' 47" E (radius 350 m)

Anchorage B3 for tankers carrying or have carried dangerous liquid products centered on pos 40° 48' 33" N; 14° 18' 93" E (radius 250 m)

Anchorage C1 for vessels not carrying dangerous goods centered on pos 40° 49' 40" N; 14° 17' 58" E (radius 250 m)

Anchorage C2 for vessels carrying dangerous goods excluding tankers centered on pos 40° 49' 13" N; 14° 17' 66" E (radius 250 m)

Anchorage C3 for vessels carrying dangerous goods including tankers centered on pos 40° 48' 85" N; 14° 17' 73" E (radius 250 m)

Pilotage: Compulsory for vessels over 500 gt, Tel: +39 081 563 4045, Fax: +39 081 563 4089. Pilots board one mile S of the harbour entrances. Tankers are not given clearance after dark, but all other vessels may enter/leave with a pilot at all times

Traffic: 2007, 21 500 000 t of cargo handled, 460 812 TEU's

Principal Imports and Exports: Imports: Chemicals, Coal, Crude oil, Fertiliser, Fish, Foodstuffs, Grain, Iron and steel, Minerals, Oil derivatives, Timber. Exports: Building materials, Chemicals, Foodstuffs, Fruit and vegetables, Iron and steel.

Working Hours: Working hours 0800-1200 and 1300-1700 (Monday to Friday) 24h available 0800-1430, 1430-2100, 2100-0230, 0230-0800

Accommodation: A natural harbour situated on the northern shore in the Gulf of Naples

The port covers an area of 1 336 000 m2 and is divided into three zones, the first for passenger traffic, the second for cargo and passengers and the third, on the extreme easterly end, is the container and oil section

Mooring buoys are available along the Molo San Vincenzo and two more near the central part of the Foranea breakwater

In addition there is a naval dockyard and arsenal

The harbour, protected by the breakwaters - Molo San Vincenzo, Diga Duca degli Abruzzi, Antemurale Thaon de Revel, Diga Foranea Emanuela Filiberto Duca d'Aosta and Molo del Progresso affords good shelter. The bottom is mud with good holding ground

The W part of Porto di Napoli comprises Avamporto Ammiraglio Francesco Carraciolo and, on its W and N sides, Bacino Angioino, Bacino del Piliero, Darsena Bacini and Darsena Armando Diaz

Banchina del Molo San Vincenzo, on the N side of Molo San Vincenzo, is reserved for Italian naval vessels; the quay is fringed by a narrow bank on which the depths are less than 9 m

Comprises all berths between the Pontile Duchessa d'Aosta to Vittorio Emanuele pier. The free port is available for loading, unloading, manipulation, transhipment etc free of customs

Name	Length (m)	Draught (m)	Remarks
Naples			
Molo San Vincenzo		5.19	Naval vessels only
Basin Angioino			
Berth No's 1-4 (Calata Beverello)	180	4–7.5	Used by passenger ferries. Services to Capri, Ischia & Procida
Berth No.5 (Molo Angioino)	195	8.5	See [1] below
Berth No's 6-7 (Molo Angioino)	300	9.77	See [2] below
Berth No.8 (Molo Angioino)	137	8.5	Four berths for Mediterranean style mooring

Name	Length (m)	Draught (m)	Remarks
Basin del Piliero			
Berth No.9 (Molo Angioino Levante)		10.68	See [3] below
Berth No.10 (Molo Angioino Levante)		10.68	See [4] below
Berth No.11 (Molo Angioino Levante)		9.77	See [5] below
Calata Piliero	290	7–8.9	Three berths handling bulk, general cargo & ro/ro
Calata Porta di Massa	290	7–9.14	Three berths handling bulk & general cargo
Molo Immacolatella Vecchia		6.1–8.54	Used for administration purposes and tug berthing. Consists of five berths
Molo Carlo Pisacane Ponente	240	10.06	Two berths handling timber
Molo Carlo Pisacane Levante	261	8.23	Two berths handling oil & fats
Calata Villa del Popolo Ponente	170	6.6	
Pontile Silos Ponente	110	9.75–10.97	Cereals
Pontile Silos Levante	110	9.75–10.97	Cereals
Calata Villa del Popolo Levante	185	7.9	Silo of 42 000 t cap
Molo Carmine Ponente	380	7.92	Two berths handling bulk & general cargo
Molo Martello		9.16	See [6] below
Bacini Dock			
Molo del Carmine Levante	330	8.2	Consists of two berths
Bacino No.1		5.25	Dock of 115.42 m x 16.2 m. Repairs
Bacino No.2		7	See [7] below
Molo Cesario Console Ponente	210	8.5	
Bacini/A. Diaz Docks			Consists of three berths
A. Diaz Dock			
Molo Cesario Console Levante	370	8.5	Consists of two berths
Calata Della Marinella	610	8.9	Consists of three berths
Vittorio Emanuele II Ponente	400	6.9	Consists of two berths
Vittorio Emanuele II	350		See [8] below
Vittorio Veneto Dock			
Vittorio Emanuele II Levante	365	9.49	Two berths handling timber & wood pulp
Calata Vittorio Veneto	210	7.62–9.14	Oils, fats & chemical products
Flavia Gioia Ponente	248	10.06	See [9] below
Nuovo Basin			
Flavio Gioia	102	6.6	
Molo Bausan	160	6.5	
Granili Dock			
Flavio Gioia Levante	248	10.06	Two berths handling timber, steel coils & bananas
Calata Granili	180	9.75	Bulk minerals, general cargo & phosphates
Molo Bausan Ponente	250	13.5	See [10] below
Pollena Dock			
Molo Bausan Levante	270	13.5	Consists of two berths
Calata Pollena	154	11	
Calata Vigliena Ponente	110	8	
Pellegrino Dock		5.5	Consists of two berths
Calata Vigliena Levante	75	8.75	
Vigliena Ponente	250	9.15	See [11] below
Vigliena	100	6–9.44	Three berths handling petroleum
Petroli Dock			
Vigliena Levante	320	10.67–11.28	Three berths handling crude oil & petroleum products
Calata Petroli	280	7.31–8.23	Two berths handling chemicals & gas
Molo Progresso Ponente	340	13.11–13.42	Two berths handling crude oil, fuel oil & LPG

[1]*Berth No.5 (Molo Angioino):* Passenger terminal, three mobile passenger gangways. Ro/ro facilities available

[2]*Berth No's 6-7 (Molo Angioino):* Passenger terminal, four mobile passenger gangways, 12 passenger and freight lifting units and a heliport

[3]*Berth No.9 (Molo Angioino Levante):* Passenger Terminal, five mobile passenger gangways. Total quay length of 412 m for berths 9, 10 & 11

[4]*Berth No.10 (Molo Angioino Levante):* Passenger terminal, five mobile passenger gangways. Total quay length of 412 m for berths 9, 10 & 11

[5]*Berth No.11 (Molo Angioino Levante):* Passenger terminal, five mobile passenger gangways. Total quay length of 412 m for berths 9, 10 & 11

[6]*Molo Martello:* Area being demolished and reconstructed. Four floating docks

[7]*Bacino No.2:* Dock of 206.16 m x 22 m for vessels up to 202.5 m x 20.2 m. Repairs

[8]*Vittorio Emanuele II:* Landing stage at jetty head. Five Mediterranean style mooring berths

[9]*Flavia Gioia Ponente:* Two berths handling timber, steel coils, bananas & containers. Terminal Flavia Gioia to become the second container terminal operator using 13 000 m2 of quay

[10]*Molo Bausan Ponente:* Two berths handling containers. Container park of 300 000 m2 for the Bausan Quay. 125 reefer points. Terminal managed by Conateco

[11]*Vigliena Ponente:* Two berths handling petroleum products. Max draught 8.99 m for loading and 9.14 m for discharge

Storage: Large number of sheds and warehouses, bonded stores, cold rooms, silos and tanks at the relevant berths

Mechanical Handling Equipment:

Location	Type	Capacity (t)	Qty	Remarks
Naples	Floating Cranes	60	1	
Naples	Floating Cranes	100	1	
Naples	Mult-purp. Cranes	40	67	
Naples	Mobile Cranes	100	1	
Calata Piliero	Mult-purp. Cranes	6	4	
Calata Porta di Massa	Mult-purp. Cranes	6	4	
Calata Porta di Massa	Mult-purp. Cranes	15	2	
Molo Carlo Pisacane Ponente	Mult-purp. Cranes	6	2	
Molo Carlo Pisacane Ponente	Mult-purp. Cranes	15	4	
Molo Carlo Pisacane Levante	Mult-purp. Cranes	12	1	
Molo Carlo Pisacane Levante	Mult-purp. Cranes	3	1	
Calata Villa del Popolo Ponente	Mult-purp. Cranes	3	1	
Calata Villa del Popolo Levante	Mult-purp. Cranes	3	1	
Molo Carmine Ponente	Mult-purp. Cranes	3	4	
Molo Carmine Ponente	Mult-purp. Cranes	6	1	
Bacino No.1	Mult-purp. Cranes	5	2	
Bacino No.2	Mult-purp. Cranes	10	1	
Molo Cesario Console Levante	Mult-purp. Cranes	40	1	
Molo Cesario Console Levante	Mult-purp. Cranes	15	1	
Molo Cesario Console Levante	Mult-purp. Cranes	6	1	
Calata Della Marinella	Mult-purp. Cranes	3	1	
Vittorio Emanuele II Ponente	Mult-purp. Cranes	3	2	
Vittorio Emanuele II Levante	Mult-purp. Cranes	3	4	
Calata Vittorio Veneto	Mult-purp. Cranes	12	1	
Calata Vittorio Veneto	Mult-purp. Cranes	6	3	
Flavia Gioia Ponente	Mult-purp. Cranes	12	2	
Flavia Gioia Ponente	Mult-purp. Cranes	45	1	
Flavia Gioia Ponente	Mult-purp. Cranes	15	1	
Flavio Gioia Levante	Mult-purp. Cranes	15	3	
Flavio Gioia Levante	Mult-purp. Cranes	6	2	
Flavio Gioia Levante	Mult-purp. Cranes	40	1	
Calata Granili	Mult-purp. Cranes	6	2	
Calata Granili	Mult-purp. Cranes	12	4	
Molo Bausan Ponente	Mult-purp. Cranes	50	4	portainer gantries
Molo Bausan Ponente	Mobile Cranes	100	1	

Bunkering: FATEG, FATEG S.r.l, Via Medina 40, 80133 Naples, Italy, *Tel:* +39 081 5800 157, *Fax:* +39 081 5800 156, *Email:* fateg@fateg.it

Nuova Bunker S.r.l., Via le Croci, 18 Prima Traversa, Monte di Procida, 80070 Naples, Italy, *Tel:* +39 081 868 3615, *Fax:* +39 081 868 3614

Polaris Srl, Via Alcide de Gasperi, no.55, 80133 Naples, Italy, *Tel:* +39 081 4202 350, *Fax:* +39 081 7041 522, *Email:* polaris@gruppopolaris.com, *Website:* www.gruppopolaris.com

Trader S.a.s., Via de Gasperi 55, 80133 Naples, Italy, *Tel:* +39 081 5521 730, *Fax:* +39 081 5514 252, *Email:* trader@traderbunker.it

DB Traderoil Srl, Via A De Gasperi 55, 80133 Naples, Italy, *Tel:* +39 081 7901 966, *Fax:* +39 081 5514 905, *Email:* dbtraderoil@dbtraderoil.it

AGIP Petroli S.p.A., ENI, Via Laurentina 449, 00142 Rome, Italy, *Tel:* +39 06 59881, *Fax:* +39 06 5988 5700, *Email:* gioacchino.costa@eni.it, *Website:* www.eni.it

Chevron Marine Products LLC, Piazza Della Vittoria 12/14, 16121 Genoa, Italy, *Tel:* +39 010 5451 611, *Fax:* +39 010 566 762, *Email:* dlfammita@chevron.com, *Website:* www.chevron.com

ExxonMobil Marine Fuels, Mailpoint 31, ExxonMobil House, Ermyn Way, Leatherhead, Surrey KT22 8UX, United Kingdom, *Tel:* +44 1372 222 000, *Fax:* +44 1372 223 922, *Email:* marine.fuels@exxonmobil.com, *Website:* www.exxonmobil.com – *Grades:* MGO; lubes – *Misc:* own storage facilities – *Parcel Size:* min 12t – *Notice:* 24 hours – *Delivery Mode:* truck

Kuwait Petroleum Italia S.p.A., Viale dell'Oceano Indiano 13, 00144 Rome, Italy, *Tel:* +39 06 5208 8568, *Fax:* +39 06 5208 8857, *Email:* ascioli@q8.it, *Website:* www.q8.it – *Grades:* GO; IFO – *Parcel Size:* min GO 20t, min IFO180 100t, min IFO380 300t – *Notice:* 24 hours – *Delivery Mode:* barge, pipeline subject to enquiry

Nuova Bunker S.r.l., Via le Croci, 18 Prima Traversa, Monte di Procida, 80070 Naples, Italy, *Tel:* +39 081 868 3615, *Fax:* +39 081 868 3614 – *Grades:* MGO; FO

DB Traderoil Srl, Via A De Gasperi 55, 80133 Naples, Italy, *Tel:* +39 081 7901 966, *Fax:* +39 081 5514 905, *Email:* dbtraderoil@dbtraderoil.it

Towage: Twenty nine tugs available

Rimorchiatori Napoletani S.r.l., Pontile Vittorio Emanuele II, 80133 Naples, Italy, *Tel:* +39 081 563 5055, *Fax:* +39 081 285030, *Email:* oper.napoli@rimnap.it, *Website:* www.rimnap.it

Repair & Maintenance: Giovanni Carrino Figli, Calata Pollena, (Zona S. Erasmo), 80133 Naples, Italy, *Tel:* +39 081 752 4601, *Fax:* +39 081 752 0945, *Email:* paulocarrino@carrino.it, *Website:* www.carrino.it Three dry docks: one of 335 m x 40

m, one of 202 m x 21 m and one of 115 m x 16 m. One floating dock of 233 m x 37 m

La Nuova Meccanica Navale S.p.A., Via Marina dei Gigli 29, I-80146 Naples, Italy, *Tel:* +39 081 559 1110, *Fax:* +39 081 752 4277, *Email:* nmn@nmn.it, *Website:* www.nmn.it

Cantieri del Mediterraneo S.p.A., Via Marinella, Varco 6, 80133 Naples, Italy, *Tel:* +39 081 785 8111, *Fax:* +39 081 785 8232, *Email:* info@cantieridelmediterraneo.com, *Website:* www.cantieridelmediterraneo.com Three dry docks of 115 m x 16 m x 5.6 m, max 5000 dwt, 206 m x 21 m x 7 m, max 15 000 dwt and 335 m x 40 m x 11.4 m, max 80 000 dwt. Floating dock 227 m x 35 m x 7 m with lifting cap of 25 000 t. Repair quays of 3900 m in total with max draught 9 m

G.& R. Salvatori, Calata Villa del Popolo, I-80133 Naples, Italy, *Tel:* +39 081 262166, *Fax:* +39 081 201374, *Email:* mapshyrd@tin.it All types of ship repair using public dry docks for vessels to 330 m loa

Ship Chandlers: Cimmino General Supply S.r.l., Calata Porta di Massa 2/A, I-80133 Naples, Italy, *Tel:* +39 081 781 0040, *Fax:* +39 081 790 4689, *Email:* info@cimminosupply.it, *Website:* www.cimminosupply.it Managing Director: Giovanni Cimmino

General Shipchandler S.r.l. Hermes, Stazione Marittima Fabbr.40 - 42, I-80133 Naples, Italy, *Tel:* +39 081 552 0683, *Fax:* +39 081 551 8972, *Email:* teamwork@tin.it

Luise Catering S.r.l., Calata Porta Massa, I-80133 Naples, Italy, *Tel:* +39 081 552 7812, *Fax:* +39 081 552 7819, *Email:* luisecatering@tiscalinet.it

Provveditorie Marittime del Mediterraneo S.r.l. (PROMED), Immacolatella Vecchia, Porto di Napoli, I-80134 Naples, Italy, *Tel:* +39 081 552 7482, *Fax:* +39 081 552 7455, *Email:* promed@promedshipsupply.it

Servizi Catering G.V. S.r.l., Calata Porta Massa, I-80133 Naples, Italy, *Tel:* +39 081 551 3076, *Fax:* +39 081 552 4998, *Email:* servizicatering@hotmail.com

Sicomar S.r.l. (Incomar Sud S.A.s.), Via Nominale 18, I-80146 Naples, Italy, *Tel:* +39 081 752 2799, *Fax:* +39 081 752 7401, *Email:* info@incomarsud.com

Shipping Agents: Agenzia Tripcovich S.r.l., Via Melisurgo 4, I-80133 Naples, Italy, *Tel:* +39 081 551 7072, *Fax:* +39 081 551 8667, *Email:* info@marimed.it, *Website:* www.tripcovich.com

COMAG S.r.l., Via Melisurgo 15, I-80133 Naples, Italy, *Tel:* +39 081 551 4966, *Fax:* +39 081 552 2216, *Email:* nap.dmuca@cma-cgm.com

CSA S.p.A., Via Melisurgo 4, I-80100 Naples, Italy, *Tel:* +39 081 790 4411, *Fax:* +39 081 551 6240, *Email:* csa.napoli@csaspa.com, *Website:* www.csaspa.com

Express S.r.l., Via Cervantes 55/27, Naples, Italy, *Tel:* +39 081 420 1811, *Fax:* +39 081 420 1829, *Email:* pasquale.cerullo@expressna.com

Gastaldi & C. S.p.A., Piazza Matteotti 7, 80133 Naples, Italy, *Tel:* +39 081 420 6511, *Fax:* +39 081 420 6520, *Email:* napoli.gc@gastaldi.it, *Website:* www.gastaldi.it

Hamal S.r.l., Via del Fiumicello 7, 80142 Naples, Italy, *Tel:* +39 081 553 1515, *Fax:* +39 081 553 1519, *Email:* kitnap@klineitalia.it, *Website:* www.klineitalia.it

Agenzia Marittima Le Navi S.p.A., 84 Piazza Municipio, Int 3, I-80133 Naples, Italy, *Tel:* +39 081 428 8801, *Fax:* +39 081 428 8862, *Email:* lenavi_itmil@lenav.mcgva.ch

Marinter-Shipping Agency S.r.l., Via Melisurgo 4, 80133 Naples, Italy, *Tel:* +39 081 551 9786, *Fax:* +39 081 551 9786, *Email:* marinter@fin.it

A.P. Moller-Maersk Group, Maersk Italia SpA, Via Fiumicello 7 - 10th Floor, I-80142 Naples, Italy, *Tel:* +39 081 563 9711, *Fax:* +39 081 563 6218, *Website:* www.maerskline.com

Giulio Morelli S.p.A., Via A de Gasperi 55, 80133 Naples, Italy, *Tel:* +39 081 552 5308, *Fax:* +39 081 551 5498, *Email:* morelli@portnet.it

Agenzia Marittima Tirreno Sud S.A.S., Piazza Municipio 84, I-80133 Naples, Italy, *Tel:* +39 081 552 6133, *Fax:* +39 081 552 1315, *Email:* export.itnap@cnshipping.it

Surveyors: Bureau Veritas, Via Santa Brigida 39, I-80133 Naples, Italy, *Tel:* +39 081 497 1511, *Fax:* +39 081 252 8262, *Email:* napoli@it.bureauveritas.com, *Website:* www.bureauveritas.com

Det Norske Veritas A/S, Via Cervantes 64, I-80133 Naples, Italy, *Tel:* +39 081 552 1454, *Fax:* +39 081 552 5198, *Website:* www.dnv.com

Nippon Kaiji Kyokai, Naples, Italy, *Tel:* +39 081 552 5863, *Fax:* +39 081 552 0846, *Website:* www.classnk.or.jp

Registro Italiano Navale (RINA), Piazza Municipio 84, Naples, Italy, *Tel:* +39 081 542 3911, *Fax:* +39 081 542 3947, *Email:* napoli.office@rina.org, *Website:* www.rina.org

SMC Ship Management & Consultancy, Via Belvedere 1, Sant'Agnello, 80065 Naples, Italy, *Tel:* +39 081 808 3928, *Fax:* +39 081 808 3928, *Email:* info@smc.na.it, *Website:* www.smc.na.it

Airport: Naples (Capodichino) Airport, 4 km

Railway: Rail terminal adjacent to docks. The harbour railway serves all quays and links up to a shunting yard. Naples has a Trans European railway terminal

Lloyd's Agent: Gastaldi International S.r.l., Via A. Depretis 19, I-80133 Naples, Italy, *Tel:* +39 081 552 5561, *Fax:* +39 081 551 1270, *Email:* naples@gastaldi-int.com, *Website:* www.gastaldi-int.it

NAPOLI

alternate name, see Naples

OLBIA

Lat 40° 55' N; Long 9° 34' E.

Admiralty Chart: 1210		**Admiralty Pilot:** 46	
Time Zone: GMT +1 h		**UNCTAD Locode:** IT OLB	

Key to Principal Facilities:—
A=Airport	**C**=Containers	**G**=General Cargo	**P**=Petroleum	**R**=Ro/Ro	**Y**=Dry Bulk		
B=Bunkers	**D**=Dry Dock	**L**=Cruise	**Q**=Other Liquid Bulk	**T**=Towage (where available from port)			

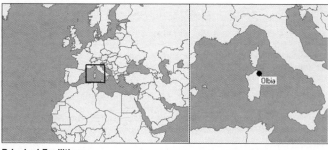

Principal Facilities:

		G	R	L	B		T	A	

Authority: Autorita Portuale di Olbia e Golfo Aranci, Stazione Marittima Isola Bianca, I-07026 Olbia, Sardinia, Italy, *Tel:* +39 0789 204179, *Fax:* +39 0789 209026, *Email:* ap.olbiagolfoaranci@tiscali.it, *Website:* www.olbiagolfoaranci.it

Officials: President: Dr Paolo Piro.

Port Security: ISPS compliant

Pilotage: Compulsory for vessels over 500 gt. Pilot boards 1 mile E of Isola Bocca Lighthouse. Corpo dei Piloti, Tel: +39 0789 22274, Fax: +39 0789 22274. VHF Channel 16, 24 h service

Radio Frequency: Porto Cervo Radio Station, Tel: +39 (0789) 92576, VHF Channel 16

Tides: Range of tide 30 cm

Maximum Vessel Dimensions: 214 m loa

Working Hours: 24 h/day

Accommodation:

Name	Length (m)	Depth (m)	Remarks
Isola Bianca			Ro/ro & cruise vessels
Jetty No.1	175	9	
Jetty No.2 (Jetty Head)		9	
Jetty No.3	175	9	
Jetty No.4	205	9	
Jetty No.5 (Jetty Head)		9	
Jetty No.6 (Jetty Head)		9	
Jetty No.7	175	9	
Jetty No.8	170	9	
Industrial Harbour			Ro/ro & cargo vessels
North	253	8	
South	180	8	

Mechanical Handling Equipment:

Location	Type	Capacity (t)	Qty
Olbia	Mult-purp. Cranes	25	6

Bunkering: Only available by tank truck

Towage: One tug of 2000 hp available

Repair & Maintenance: Shipyards available in the town

Shipping Agents: Agenzie Marittime Sarde S.r.l., Via Boccherini 48, I-07026 Olbia, Sardinia, Italy, *Tel:* +39 0789 26169, *Fax:* +39 0789 26199, *Email:* amsolbia@tiscali.it, *Website:* www.amsitaly.com

Surveyors: Nippon Kaiji Kyokai, Olbia, Sardinia, Italy, *Tel:* +39 0789 25221, *Fax:* +39 0789 25221, *Website:* www.classnk.or.jp
Registro Italiano Navale (RINA), Via Briosco 19, Olbia, Sardinia, Italy, *Tel:* +39 0789 50600, *Fax:* +39 0789 57469, *Email:* olbia.office@rina.org, *Website:* www.rina.org

Medical Facilities: Hospital available in the town

Airport: Costa Smeralda, 3 km

Railway: Olbia Station

Lloyd's Agent: Gastaldi International S.r.l., Mura di Santa Chiara 1, I-16128 Genoa, Italy, *Tel:* +39 010 530931, *Fax:* +39 010 530 9343, *Email:* info@gastaldi-int.it, *Website:* www.gastaldi-int.it

ORISTANO

Lat 39° 52' N; Long 8° 33' E.

Admiralty Chart: 1205	**Admiralty Pilot:** 46
Time Zone: GMT +1 h	**UNCTAD Locode:** IT QOS

Principal Facilities:

P	Q	Y	G	C	R			T	A	

Authority: Capitanerie di Porto di Oristano, Porto Industriale di Oristano, 09170 Oristano, Sardinia, Italy, *Tel:* +39 0783 72262, *Fax:* +39 0783 72262, *Email:* oristano@guardiacostiera.it, *Website:* www.oristano.guardiacostiera.it

Officials: Harbour Master: Francesco Calia.

Port Security: ISPS compliant

Approach: Channel depths of 13.5 m

Pilotage: Compulsory for vessels over 500 gt within one mile from the outer breakwater, Tel: +39 0783 290779. VHF Channel 12. Mooring and unmooring operations allowed only during daylight hours

Weather: A swell is experienced inside harbour during strong W winds

Tides: Range of tide 0.35 m

Maximum Vessel Dimensions: 60 000 dwt, 12.3 m d, 300 m loa

Working Hours: 0800-1200, 1300-1700. Saturday overtime 0600-1230. Shift work 0600-1400, 1400-2200

Accommodation: Tanker facilities: 130 m max loa, 7 m max d. Liquid chemical berth, length 48 m

Name	Length (m)	Depth (m)	Remarks
Outer Harbour			See [1] below
Inner Harbour			Used by industrial traffic
Molo Sottoflutto	120	9.2	Private berth of Enichem Fibre SpA
Banchina Sottoflutto	306	10.4	
Banchina Est	407	10.4	
Banchina Nord	500	11.3	
Banchina Martini	250	11.3	See [2] below
Banchina S.S.B.	169	10.4	See [3] below
Banchina SIMEC	170	9	Private berth of Semolerie Sassaresi
Pontile V.I.C.	40	6.4	
Pontile Sipsa	20	6.1	

[1]*Outer Harbour:* Protected on N side and S and SW sides by two moles and handles general cargo
[2]*Banchina Martini:* Private berth of Silos e Mangimi Martini for discharging cereals with suction pipes
[3]*Banchina S.S.B.:* Private berth of the Mi. Chi. Sa Company equipped with a conveyor

Mechanical Handling Equipment:

Location	Type	Capacity (t)	Qty	Remarks
Oristano	Mult-purp. Cranes	120		
Oristano	Mobile Cranes	6	1	private, for bulk cargoes

Towage: One tug of 700 hp available. Other tugs from Cagliari if required

Shipping Agents: Efispau S.r.l., Via D. Petri 9a, I-09170 Oristano, Sardinia, Italy, *Tel:* +39 0783 78454, *Fax:* +39 0783 71584, *Email:* efispau.or@efispau.com, *Website:* www.efispau.com

Medical Facilities: Available

Airport: Elmas Cagliari, 90 km

Lloyd's Agent: Gastaldi International S.r.l., Mura di Santa Chiara 1, I-16128 Genoa, Italy, *Tel:* +39 010 530931, *Fax:* +39 010 530 9343, *Email:* info@gastaldi-int.it, *Website:* www.gastaldi-int.it

ORTONA

Lat 42° 21' N; Long 14° 24' E.

Admiralty Chart: 1443	**Admiralty Pilot:** 47
Time Zone: GMT +1 h	**UNCTAD Locode:** IT OTN

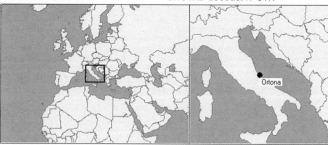

Principal Facilities:

P		Y	G		R		B			A	

Authority: Capitaneria di Porto di Ortona, Via Cervana 8, I-66026 Ortona, Italy, *Tel:* +39 085 906 3290, *Fax:* +39 085 906 1461, *Email:* ortona@guardiacostiera.it, *Website:* www.ortona.guardiacostiera.it

Officials: Harbour Master: Giuseppe Fama, *Email:* fama@guardiacostiera.it. Deputy Harbour Master: Angelo Capuzzimato.

Approach: Entrance channel dredged to a depth of 7.5 m

Pilotage: Compulsory in poor visibility and sea conditions and recommended at all times for larger vessels

Weather: Strong E winds affect water in the harbour and are dangerous; not so heavy when from SE direction

Maximum Vessel Dimensions: 200 m loa, 6.5 m draft

Accommodation:

Name	Length (m)	Draught (m)	Remarks
Ortona			
North New Quay	457	7.1	55 000 m2 storage area
Hammer Quay	130	5.7	
Shore Quay	236	5.7	24 000 m2 storage area
Shore New Quay	260	5.7	25 000 m2 storage area
Commercial Quay	200	5.7	

Mechanical Handling Equipment:

Location	Type
Ortona	Mobile Cranes

Bunkering: AGIP Petroli S.p.A., ENI, Via Laurentina 449, 00142 Rome, Italy, *Tel:* +39 06 59881, *Fax:* +39 06 5988 5700, *Email:* gioacchino.costa@eni.it, *Website:* www.eni.it – *Delivery Mode:* road tanker

Shipping Agents: Alessandro Archibugi & Figlio S.r.l., Via Porto 64/68, I-66028 Ortona, Italy, *Tel:* +39 085 906 4178, *Fax:* +39 085 906 7358, *Email:* archibugi.an@archibugi.com, *Website:* www.archibugi.com
Fiore S.r.l., Via Cervana, I-66026 Ortona, Italy, *Tel:* +39 085 906 6900, *Fax:* +39 085 906 2886, *Email:* info@fioreortona.com, *Website:* www.fioreortona.com
Fratino G. & Figli S.r.l., Via Porto 34, I-66026 Ortona, Italy, *Tel:* +39 085 906 3855, *Fax:* +39 085 906 4186, *Email:* nfratin@tin.it, *Website:* www.fratino.com

Stevedoring Companies: Fiore S.r.l., Via Cervana, I-66026 Ortona, Italy, *Tel:* +39 085 906 6900, *Fax:* +39 085 906 2886, *Email:* info@fioreortona.com, *Website:* www.fioreortona.com

Surveyors: Registro Italiano Navale (RINA), Via Cervana 1 - Zona Porto, Ortona, Italy, *Tel:* +39 085 906 8359, *Fax:* +39 085 906 8979, *Website:* www.rina.org

Airport: Pescara, 17 km

Lloyd's Agent: Radonicich Insurance Services S.r.l., Via F. Orsini 6/A, Marghera, 30175 Venice, Italy, *Tel:* +39 041 538 2103, *Fax:* +39 041 926108, *Email:* radinsur@portofvenice.net

OTRANTO

Lat 40° 9' N; Long 18° 30' E.

Admiralty Chart: -	**Admiralty Pilot:** 47
Time Zone: GMT +1 h	**UNCTAD Locode:** IT OTO

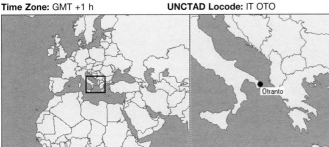

Principal Facilities:

		G		B		A

Authority: Capitaneria di Porto di Otranto, Via del Porto, I-73028 Otranto, Italy, *Tel:* +39 0836 801073, *Fax:* +39 0836 801073, *Email:* otranto@guardiacostiera.it, *Website:* www.guardiacostiera.it/otranto

Officials: Harbour Master: Giancarlo Salvemini.

Port Security: ISPS compliant

Anchorage: Good holding ground in a depth of 6 m to 7 m

Pilotage: Available

Radio Frequency: VHF Channel 16, from 0800-2000

Maximum Vessel Dimensions: 5300 dwt, 102.0 m loa

Working Hours: Mon-Fri 0700-1200, 1300-1700

Accommodation:

Name	Length (m)	Depth (m)	Remarks
Otranto			See [1] below
Molo S. Nicola	260	6–7	See [2] below

[1]*Otranto:* There are also 210 m of commercial quay but only a small part of this is used due to shallow water
[2]*Molo S. Nicola:* Used by vessels working pumice, phosphates & fertilizers

Mechanical Handling Equipment:

Location	Type	Capacity (t)	Qty
Otranto	Mult-purp. Cranes	7	1

Bunkering: AGIP Petroli S.p.A., ENI, Via Laurentina 449, 00142 Rome, Italy, *Tel:* +39 06 59881, *Fax:* +39 06 5988 5700, *Email:* gioacchino.costa@eni.it, *Website:* www.eni.it – *Grades:* GO

Airport: Brindisi, 87 km

Lloyd's Agent: P. Lorusso & Co. S.r.l., 133 Via Piccinni, I-70122 Bari, Italy, *Tel:* +39 080 521 2840, *Fax:* +39 080 521 8229, *Email:* vdbdirezione@agenzialorusso.it, *Website:* www.agenzialorusso.it

---

PALERMO

Lat 38° 7' N; Long 13° 21' E.

Admiralty Chart: 963	**Admiralty Pilot:** 45
Time Zone: GMT +1 h	**UNCTAD Locode:** IT PMO

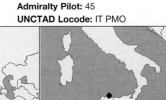

Principal Facilities:

P	Q	Y	G	C	R	L	B	D	T	A

Agenzia Maritima Luigi Cestelli S.r.l.

Via Enrico Amari 8, I-90139, Palermo, Sicily, ITALY
TEL: +39 091 611 8266   FAX: +39 091 611 8819
EMAIL: luigipmo@tin.it

Chairman/Owner - Mr. Luigi Cestelli

Shipping Agents in Palermo and Trapani

Authority: Autorita Portuale di Palermo, Via Piano dell'Ucciardone 4, I-90139 Palermo, Sicily, Italy, *Tel:* +39 091 627 7111, *Fax:* +39 091 637 4291, *Email:* autport@autport.pa.it, *Website:* www.autport.pa.it

Officials: President: Antonino Bevilacqua, *Email:* presidenza@autport.pa.it.
Marketing Manager: Daniela Mezzatesta, *Email:* promotion@autport.pa.it.
Operations Manager: Renato Coroneo, *Email:* renatocoroneo@neomedia.it.
Harbour Master: Admiral Ferdinando Lavaggi, *Email:* palermo@guardiacostiera.it.

Port Security: ISPS compliant

Approach: The entrance has an approach depth of 15.24-18.3 m

Anchorage: Open anchorage can be obtained off the harbour in good holding ground. The holding ground inside the harbour is poor. Anchorage can be obtained anywhere between Punta del Corsaro and the village of Aspra in depths of 16-18 m, good holding ground. Prohibited anchorage: Anchoring within 5 cables of the submarine cable is prohibited. From a position onshore close E of the terminal, the submarine cable is laid NNE and then curves ENE passing 1.75 nm N of Capo Mongerbino. The cable terminates at Santa Agata di Militello

Pilotage: Compulsory for vessels over 500 gt. Pilot boards in pos 38° 07' 67" N; 13° 24' 03" E. The pilot station listens on VHF Channel 12 (156.600 mHz)

Radio Frequency: The harbour office is constantly listening 24 h/day on VHF Channel 16

Weather: Well sheltered from all winds

Tides: There is a tidal range of 0.6 m

Traffic: 2007, 6 600 000 t of cargo handled

Principal Imports and Exports: Imports: Coal, Grain, Steel plate. Exports: Wine.

Working Hours: Monday to Friday 0800-1200, 1300-1700. For completion 1700-1900. Night shift 2000-2400, 0100-0500 on overtime rates

Accommodation:

Name	Length (m)	Depth (m)	Draught (m)	Remarks
Palermo				See [1] below
Quattroventi Quay	345	9–15	7.4	Containers
Puntone Quay	400	14	13.4	Containers
S. Lucia Pier - East Side	50	10	9.4	
S. Lucia Pier - South Side	275	8–10	7.4–9.4	
S. Lucia Pier - North Side	200	12		
Marinai d'Italia - Quay 1	115	11	10.4	
Piave Pier - North Side	326	12	11.4	See [2] below
Piave Pier - East Side	85	12	11.4	
Piave Pier - South Side	326	12	11.4	Three quay cranes
Marinai d'Italia - Quay 2	110	11		

Key to Principal Facilities:—

A=Airport	**C**=Containers	**G**=General Cargo
B=Bunkers	**D**=Dry Dock	**L**=Cruise
P=Petroleum	**R**=Ro/Ro	**Y**=Dry Bulk
Q=Other Liquid Bulk	**T**=Towage (where available from port)	

Name	Length (m)	Depth (m)	Draught (m)	Remarks
V. Veneto Pier - North Side	326	12	11.4	
V. Veneto Pier - East Side	65	12	11.4	
V. Veneto Pier - South Side	326	8–12	7.4	
Marinai d'Italia - Quay 3	115	8	7.4	
Sammuzzo Quay	350	8–12	7.4	
Trapezoidale Mole - East Side	300	9–15		Ro/ro & multi-purpose quay

[1]*Palermo:* Oil products can be discharged at the following terminals in roadstead: AGIP for vessels up to 185 m loa, 32 ft draft and 50 000 dwt at rate of 400-800 t/h and ESSO for vessels up to 49 ft draft at rate of 600-700 t/h
[2]*Piave Pier - North Side:* Silo for cereals at Piave Pier, cap 29 100 t with discharge rate 250 t/h

Storage:

Location	Open (m²)	Grain (t)	Cold (m³)
Palermo	58000	29100	3000

Cargo Worked: General 800 t/day, coal 1000 t/gang/day. Handling equipment at silos capable of unloading grain at 250 t/h

Bunkering: AGIP Petroli S.p.A., ENI, Via Laurentina 449, 00142 Rome, Italy, *Tel:* +39 06 59881, *Fax:* +39 06 5988 5700, *Email:* gioacchino.costa@eni.it, *Website:* www.eni.it
Gori Petrol Group, V. Cristoforo Colombo 1, San Gregorio di Catania, 95027 Catania, Sicily, Italy, *Tel:* +39 095 492 386, *Fax:* +39 095 7122 710, *Email:* info@goripetrolgroup.191.it
Luise International & Co., 15 Via G. Melisurgo, 80133 Naples, Italy, *Tel:* +39 081 552 8670, *Fax:* +39 081 552 7368, *Email:* luise@luise.com

Towage: Two tugs of 3370 hp and 1200 hp; a further two tugs of 2000 hp and 1200 hp are available with advance notice

Repair & Maintenance: Fincantieri-Cantieri Navali Italiani S.p.A. Palermo, Stabilimento di Palermo, Via dei Cantieri 75, 90142 Palermo, Sicily, Italy, *Tel:* +39 091 620 6111, *Fax:* +39 091 547228 Two graving docks and two floating docks, together with a machine shop

Ship Chandlers: General Marine Suppliers S.n.c., Via Ruggero Loria 14, I-90142 Palermo, Sicily, Italy, *Tel:* +39 091 546311, *Fax:* +39 091 361460, *Email:* gemasu@tiscalinet.it

Shipping Agents: Agenzia Maritima Luigi Cestelli S.r.l., Via Enrico Amari 8, I-90139 Palermo, Sicily, Italy, *Tel:* +39 091 611 8266, *Fax:* +39 091 611 8819, *Email:* luigipmo@tin.it
Europea Servizi Terminalistici Srl, Via E. Giafar, Scalo Ferroviario Brancaccio, 90124 Palermo, Sicily, Italy, *Tel:* +39 091 630 6005, *Fax:* +39 091 630 4028, *Email:* a.pandolfo@esterminal.com, *Website:* www.esterminal.com
Placido Mancuso & Figli S.N.C., Via Roma 386, 90139 Palermo, Sicily, Italy, *Tel:* +39 091 588661, *Fax:* +39 091 585155, *Email:* mancuso.palermo@infcom.it
Tagliavia & Co S.r.l., Via Cavour 117, 90133 Palermo, Sicily, Italy, *Tel:* +39 091 582533, *Fax:* +39 091 380 4901, *Email:* info@tagliavia.it, *Website:* www.tagliavia.it

Surveyors: Det Norske Veritas A/S, Palermo, Sicily, Italy, *Tel:* +39 091 586811, *Fax:* +39 091 332695, *Website:* www.dnv.com
Nippon Kaiji Kyokai, Palermo, Sicily, Italy, *Tel:* +39 091 582572, *Fax:* +39 091 328061, *Website:* www.classnk.or.jp
Registro Italiano Navale (RINA), Via Francesco Crispi 248, Palermo, Sicily, Italy, *Tel:* +39 091 743 9511, *Fax:* +39 091 743 9536, *Email:* palermo.office@rina.org, *Website:* www.rina.org

Medical Facilities: Medical assistance for crew members is ensured through vessel's agent

Airport: Punta Raisi Airport, 25 km

Lloyd's Agent: Tagliavia & Capanna Srl, Via Emerico Amari 8, I-90139 Palermo, Sicily, Italy, *Tel:* +39 091 587377, *Fax:* +39 091 322435, *Email:* info@tagliaviacapanna.it

PESARO

Lat 43° 55' N; Long 12° 54' E.

Admiralty Chart: -
Admiralty Pilot: 47
Time Zone: GMT +1 h
UNCTAD Locode: IT PES

Principal Facilities:

P		Y	G				B		A

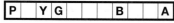

Authority: Capitaneria di Porto di Pesaro, Calata Caio Duilio 47, I-61100 Pesaro, Italy, *Tel:* +39 0721 400016/7, *Fax:* +39 0721 400016, *Email:* pesaro@guardiacostiera.it, *Website:* www.pesaro.guardiacostiera.it

Officials: Harbour Master: Aurelio Caligiore, *Email:* caligiore_aurelio@hotmail.com.

Port Security: ISPS compliant

Approach: Entrance canal immediately S of the mouth of the River Foglia, depth of water abt 4.5 m

Pilotage: Available

Working Hours: 0800-1200, 1400-1700

Accommodation:

Name	Remarks
Pesaro	See [1] below

[1]*Pesaro:* Total length of operative docks 530 m with depth alongside approx 4 m Tanker facilities: Tankers up to 4000 dwt can discharge at a jetty connected to storage facilities of 119 000 m3. Hydrocarbon traffic is approx 60 000 t annually

Mechanical Handling Equipment:

Location	Type
Pesaro	Mobile Cranes
Pesaro	Forklifts

Cargo Worked: Silos, loading/discharging cap 40 t/h

Bunkering: Fuel can be supplied by trucks, in barrels. Any category

Repair & Maintenance: Slip for vessels up to 1000 gt

Airport: Rimini Airport, 40 km

Lloyd's Agent: Radonicich Insurance Services S.r.l., Via F. Orsini 6/A, Marghera, 30175 Venice, Italy, *Tel:* +39 041 538 2103, *Fax:* +39 041 926108, *Email:* radinsur@portofvenice.net

PESCARA

Lat 42° 27' N; Long 14° 13' E.

Admiralty Chart: 200
Admiralty Pilot: 47
Time Zone: GMT +1 h
UNCTAD Locode: IT PSR

Principal Facilities:

		G			B		A

Authority: Capitaneria di Porto di Pescara, Piazza della Marina 1, I-65100 Pescara, Italy, *Tel:* +39 085 694040, *Fax:* +39 085 451 0117, *Email:* pescara@guardiacostiera.it, *Website:* www.guardiacostiera.it/pescara

Officials: Harbour Master: Meli Giuseppe.
Deputy Harbour Master: Antonio Basile.

Port Security: ISPS compliant

Pilotage: Not compulsory. Berthing during daylight hours only

Maximum Vessel Dimensions: 5.2 m draft

Accommodation:

Name	Remarks
Pescara	See [1] below

[1]*Pescara:* Depth at entrance to harbour approx 6.0 m. Total length of berthing space for commercial operations is nearly 500 m with depth alongside of approx 5.0 m. Berths are equipped with cranes. Facilities for fishing vessels on the North Quay. Mooring assistance compulsory for all vessels over 500 gt

Bunkering: Available by road tanker

Repair & Maintenance: Minor repairs

Surveyors: Nippon Kaiji Kyokai, Pescara, Italy, *Tel:* +39 085 65710, *Fax:* +39 085 694969, *Website:* www.classnk.or.jp
Registro Italiano Navale (RINA), Piazza Duca d'Aosta 31, Pescara, Italy, *Tel:* +39 085 27547, *Fax:* +39 085 33159, *Email:* pescara.office@rina.org, *Website:* www.rina.org

Airport: Pescara

Lloyd's Agent: Radonicich Insurance Services S.r.l., Via F. Orsini 6/A, Marghera, 30175 Venice, Italy, *Tel:* +39 041 538 2103, *Fax:* +39 041 926108, *Email:* radinsur@portofvenice.net

PIOMBINO

Lat 42° 56' N; Long 10° 33' E.

Admiralty Chart: 131
Admiralty Pilot: 46
Time Zone: GMT +1 h
UNCTAD Locode: IT PIO

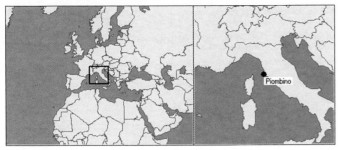

Principal Facilities:

P	Y	G		R		B		T	A

Authority: Autorita Portuale di Piombino, Piazzale Premuda 6/a, I-57025 Piombino, Italy, *Tel:* +39 0565 229210, *Fax:* +39 0565 229229, *Email:* info@porto.piombino.li.it, *Website:* www.porto.piombino.li.it

Officials: President: Luciano Guerrieri, *Email:* lguerrieri@porto.piombino.li.it. General Secretary: Paola Mancuso, *Email:* pmancuso@porto.piombino.li.it. Marketing Manager: Giampiero Costagli, *Email:* gcostagli@porto.piombino.li.it. Harbour Master: Massimiliano Mezzani, *Tel:* +39 0565 221000.

Port Security: ISPS compliant

Anchorage: Anchorage 'A' for vessels with max 7 m draft bounded by the following positions:
42° 56.46' N; 10° 34.02' E
42° 56.66' N; 10° 35.32' E
42° 56.46' N; 10° 35.52' E
42° 55.66' N; 10° 34.42' E
Anchorage 'B' for tankers arriving from and leaving for Torre del Sale bounded by the following positions:
42° 55.96' N; 10° 37.02' E
42° 55.96' N; 10° 38.02' E
42° 55.46' N; 10° 38.02' E
42° 55.46' N; 10° 37.02' E
Circular anchorage areas for vessels over 7 m draft centred on the following positions:
42° 54.161' N; 10° 34.776' E
42° 53.561' N; 10° 35.366' E
42° 53.511' N; 10° 36.366' E
42° 53.961' N; 10° 37.216' E
42° 54.761' N; 10° 37.316' E
A circular area for the lighterage of dry bulk goods is centred on position 42° 54.461' N; 10° 36.016' E

Pilotage: Compulsory and available 24 h/day from Piloti dei Porto di Piombino, Tel: +39 0565 225535, Fax: +39 0565 225535, Email: pilotipiombino@tin.it. Pilot boarding area is 1 mile ESE from the south breakwater but bulk carriers are generally boarded 2 miles SE of the entrance, especially in bad weather. Four licensed pilots

Radio Frequency: Harbour Master on VHF Channels 16 and 13. Pilot Station on VHF Channel 12. Agencies on VHF Channels 12 and 10

Weather: S and SE gales cause heavy swell conditions inside the harbour

Tides: Max range of 30 cm

Traffic: 2005, 8 286 271 t of cargo handled

Maximum Vessel Dimensions: 260 m loa, 11.89 m draft

Principal Imports and Exports: Imports: Coal, Fertiliser, Iron ore, Zinc. Exports: Steel products.

Working Hours: 24 h/day

Accommodation:

Name	Length (m)	Draught (m)	Remarks
Lusid Pier			See [1] below
Piers 1-3	470	9.15	
Pier 4	270	11.89	
Magona Pier			See [2] below
North	155	7	
South	104	7	
Trieste Wharf	160	7	
Passenger Piers			For ferries to/from Elba, Corsica & Sardinia
Dente Nord	85	6.5	
Elba Wharf	75	6	
Batteria Wharf	300	6	

[1]*Lusid Pier:* Discharging iron ore & coals and loading various steel products
[2]*Magona Pier:* Discharging hot rolled coils and loading galvanized steel products

Storage:

Location	Covered (m²)	Sheds / Warehouses
Piombino	5400	3

Mechanical Handling Equipment: Two overhead travelling cranes, five self-moving cranes, three break boom cranes, one oscillating crane, one bulk solids unloader, twenty six high lift trucks, two hydraulic buckets, two hoppers, twenty one trailers and seven wheeled loaders

Bunkering: Dalmare S.p.A., Via Castelli 6, 57122 Leghorn, Italy, *Tel:* +39 0586 437 111, *Fax:* +39 0586 437 112, *Email:* info@dalesio.it, *Website:* www.dalesio.it

Towage: Available

Medical Facilities: Town hospital, 1 km

Airport: Pisa, 90 km

Railway: Railway station in harbour

Lloyd's Agent: Ditta Vincenzo Capanna S.a.S., Via Claudio Cogorano 25, P O Box 286, I-57123 Leghorn, Italy, *Tel:* +39 0586 894132, *Fax:* +39 0586 885332, *Email:* capanna@capanna.it, *Website:* www.capanna.it

POLLENA DOCK

harbour area, see under Naples

PORTICI

Lat 40° 48' N; Long 14° 20' E.

Admiralty Chart: -	**Admiralty Pilot:** 46
Time Zone: GMT +1 h	**UNCTAD Locode:** IT PTC

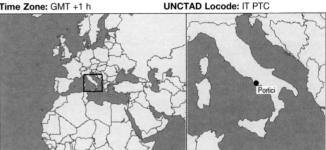

Principal Facilities:

		G		B		A

Authority: Capitaneria di Porto di Portici, I-80055 Portici, Italy, *Tel:* +39 081 776 7827

Anchorage: Anchorage can be obtained in the port roadstead in depths of about 15 m; exposed to S winds

Pilotage: Compulsory for vessels over 500 gt

Radio Frequency: VHF Channel 16

Accommodation:

Name	Length (m)	Depth (m)	Remarks
Portici			See [1] below
Berth 1	115	7.5	
Berth 2	115	7.5	
Berth 3	78	6	

[1]*Portici:* Harbour protected by breakwaters; depth at entrance and in the harbour is 8 m and in proximity to the quays up to 7.5 m. Three commercial quays. No shore cranes, vessels discharge/load using ship's own gear

Bunkering: Limited quantities of fuel oil are available

Towage: Tugs available from Naples if required

Repair & Maintenance: A small slipway is available; minor repairs can be effected

Airport: Capodichino, 16 km

Lloyd's Agent: Gastaldi International S.r.l., Mura di Santa Chiara 1, I-16128 Genoa, Italy, *Tel:* +39 010 530931, *Fax:* +39 010 530 9343, *Email:* info@gastaldi-int.it, *Website:* www.gastaldi-int.it

PORTO EMPEDOCLE

Lat 37° 17' N; Long 13° 32' E.

Admiralty Chart: 965	**Admiralty Pilot:** 45
Time Zone: GMT +1 h	**UNCTAD Locode:** IT PEM

Principal Facilities:

	Y	G		R		B		T	A

Authority: Capitaneria di Porto di Porto Empedocle, Via Gioeni 55, I-92014 Porto Empedocle, Sicily, Italy, *Tel:* +39 0922 636640, *Fax:* +39 0922 535747, *Email:* portoempedocle@guardiacostiera.it

Officials: Harbour Master: Maurizio Trogu.

Port Security: ISPS compliant

Anchorage: Good anchorage in the roadstead, 1000 m off W Pier with the light bearing 333 deg; mud bottom

---

Key to Principal Facilities:—				
A=Airport	**C**=Containers	**G**=General Cargo	**P**=Petroleum	**R**=Ro/Ro	**Y**=Dry Bulk
B=Bunkers	**D**=Dry Dock	**L**=Cruise	**Q**=Other Liquid Bulk	**T**=Towage (where available from port)

Pilotage: Compulsory for all vessels over 500 gt. Pilots provide look-out service from tower near the head of the Crispi Pier; no prior notice required

Maximum Vessel Dimensions: 132 285 dwt, 276.5 m loa

Accommodation:

Name	Length (m)	Depth (m)	Remarks
Porto Empedocle			See [1] below
New E Pier	500		See [2] below
Quay	600	8.5–11.5	

[1]*Porto Empedocle:* The port is formed by two outer breakwaters and an inner seawall dividing the old port from the outport. Operating depth at both basins 7 m. There are in all 550 m of quay

[2]*New E Pier:* Equipped with a conveyor belt for loading rocksalt, the cap of which is 380 t/h and two conveyors for bagged cargo (50 t/h) or for bulk cargo (100 t/h)

Mechanical Handling Equipment:

Location	Type	Capacity (t)	Qty
New E Pier	Mobile Cranes	20	3
Quay	Mult-purp. Cranes	10	1

Bunkering: AGIP Petroli S.p.A., ENI, Via Laurentina 449, 00142 Rome, Italy, *Tel:* +39 06 59881, *Fax:* +39 06 5988 5700, *Email:* gioacchino.costa@eni.it, *Website:* www.eni.it – *Grades:* GO – *Rates:* 30t/h – *Delivery Mode:* truck
Asta Carburanti di Asta Salvatore, Sede: via Dei Roveri 11, 11 - 97013 Comiso, Sicily, Italy, *Tel:* +39 0932 798682, *Fax:* +39 0932 798682, *Email:* asta.carburanti@tin.it
Gori Petrol Group, V. Cristoforo Colombo 1, San Gregorio di Catania, 95027 Catania, Sicily, Italy, *Tel:* +39 095 492 386, *Fax:* +39 095 7122 710, *Email:* info@goripetrolgroup.191.it

Towage: One tug of 2000 hp

Repair & Maintenance: Minor repairs only

Surveyors: Nippon Kaiji Kyokai, Porto Empedocle, Sicily, Italy, *Tel:* +39 0922 637576, *Website:* www.classnk.or.jp

Airport: Catania, 180 km, Palermo, 150 km

Lloyd's Agent: Tagliavia & Capanna Srl, Via Emerico Amari 8, I-90139 Palermo, Sicily, Italy, *Tel:* +39 091 587377, *Fax:* +39 091 322435, *Email:* info@tagliaviacapanna.it

PORTO FOXI

alternate name, see Sarroch

PORTO MARGHERA

see under Venice

PORTO NOGARO

Lat 45° 47' N; Long 13° 13' E.

Admiralty Chart: 1471	**Admiralty Pilot:** 47
Time Zone: GMT +1 h	**UNCTAD Locode:** IT PNG

Principal Facilities:

	Y	G	C			T	A

Authority: Della Zona Dell'Aussa Corno, Port of Porto Nogaro, Via Pradamano 2, I-33100 Udine, Italy, *Tel:* +39 0432 520581, *Fax:* +39 0432 520782, *Email:* info@aussacorno.it, *Website:* www.aussacorno.it

Officials: General Manager: Marzio Serena.
Harbour Master: Pierluigi Milella.

Port Security: ISPS compliant

Approach: From Porto Buso, pos 45° 42' 30" N; 13° 15' 6" E, between the islands of Porto Buso and San Andrea, through a lagoon canal 5 nautical miles long, depth 7.5 m and average width 100 m; thence a river canal, Fiume Corno, 4 nautical miles long, depth 6.5 m and average width 40 m; three turning basins

Pilotage: Compulsory. Pilot boat will approach vessels 1 mile from breakwater on request. VHF Channel 12
High tension electricity cables cross the canal and no vessels of 36.5 m above water line are allowed. Entry during daylight hours only

Weather: www.osmer.fvg.it

Tides: The max difference between high and low tide is 70 cm

Traffic: 2006, 1 230 000 t of cargo handled

Maximum Vessel Dimensions: 180 m loa, 22 m breadth, 7 m draft

Principal Imports and Exports: Imports: Dry bulk cargo, Iron & steel, Mineral sands, Urea. Exports: Bagged cargoes, Steel products, Wood & timber manufactures.

Working Hours: Monday to Friday 0800-1900. Saturday 0800-1200. Overtime can be worked on Saturdays and Sundays

Accommodation:

Name	Length (m)	Depth (m)	Remarks
Porto Nogaro			
Porto Vecchio Quay	420	7.5	Surface area of 34 000 m2
Margreth Quay	840	7.5	Surface area of 331 000 m2

Storage:

Location	Open (m²)
Porto Vecchio Quay	17000
Margreth Quay	61300

Mechanical Handling Equipment: Cranes capable of moving up to 250 t and forklifts for all commercial activities

Airport: Ronchi dei Legionari Airport, 25 km

Railway: Direct rail link to San Giorgio di Nogaro station

Lloyd's Agent: Samer & Co. Shipping Ltd, Piazza dell 'Unita d'Italia 7, I-34121 Trieste, Italy, *Tel:* +39 040 670 2711, *Fax:* +39 040 6702 7300, *Email:* samer@samer.com, *Website:* www.samer.com

PORTO SANTO STEFANO

Lat 42° 27' N; Long 11° 7' E.

Admiralty Chart: 131	**Admiralty Pilot:** 46
Time Zone: GMT +1 h	**UNCTAD Locode:** IT PSS

Principal Facilities:

P		Y	G			B	T

Authority: Ufficio Circondariale Marittimo di Porto Santo Stefano, Via G. Civinini 2, I-58019 Porto Santo Stefano, Italy, *Tel:* +39 0564 812529, *Fax:* +39 0564 813325, *Email:* portosantostefano@guardiacostiera.it, *Website:* www.portosantostefano.guardiacostiera.it

Officials: Harbour Master: Maurizio Tattoli.

Pilotage: Compulsory for vessels over 500 gt. Pilots obtainable through vessel's agent or through Port Authority

Working Hours: 0600-1230, 1230-1900 for dry cargo vessels

Accommodation:

Name	Remarks
Porto Santo Stefano	Remaining quays for fishing vessels & yachts
Banchina Toscana	See [1] below
Pontile del Valle	See [2] below

[1]*Banchina Toscana:* Phosphates & fertilisers in bulk and bagged are loaded/unloaded with depths alongside of 7.0 m for vessels of 90 m loa, 6.5 m for vessels of 100 m loa and 6 m for vessels of 110 m loa. During the summer this quay is used yachts
[2]*Pontile del Valle:* Only small passenger vessels & hydrofoils (in regular service to nearest islands), are allowed to moor

Mechanical Handling Equipment:

Location	Type	Qty
Banchina Toscana	Mult-purp. Cranes	1

Bunkering: Available by tanker truck (to dry cargo ships). Not available at tanker wharf

Towage: Tugs from Leghorn when ordered, 48 h notice required. For tankers, employment of two tugboats with fire extinguisher compulsory. Tugboats must remain alongside during whole operation of unloading. Also used for mooring/unmooring operations of tankers

Repair & Maintenance: Several small repair firms

Airport: Flumicino, 150 km

Lloyd's Agent: Gastaldi International S.r.l., Mura di Santa Chiara 1, I-16128 Genoa, Italy, *Tel:* +39 010 530931, *Fax:* +39 010 530 9343, *Email:* info@gastaldi-int.it, *Website:* www.gastaldi-int.it

PORTO TORRES

Lat 40° 50' N; Long 8° 22' E.

Admiralty Chart: 1202	**Admiralty Pilot:** 46
Time Zone: GMT +1 h	**UNCTAD Locode:** IT PTO

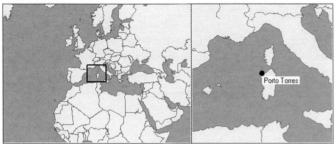

Principal Facilities:

P	Q	Y	G	C	R		B		T	A

Authority: Capitaneria di Porto di Porto Torres, Via del Mare, I-07046 Porto Torres, Sardinia, Italy, *Tel:* +39 079 502258/9, *Fax:* +39 079 502090, *Email:* portotorres@guardiacostiera.it

Officials: Harbour Master: Filippo Marini.
Harbour Master: Giuseppe Bonelli.

Port Security: ISPS compliant

Pilotage: Compulsory for ships over 500 gt. VHF Channel 12, Tel: +39 079 514936 & 510672

Maximum Vessel Dimensions: At Civic port: 8 m max d. At ENICHEM port: 14.5 m max d. No length restrictions

Working Hours: 0800-1200, 1330-1730. At ENICHEM port: 0700-2200 continuous

Accommodation: Tanker facilities: Eight berths, 13.41 m d max. Slop tank facilities available after agreement with receivers

Name	Depth (m)	Remarks
Porto Torres		
Civic Port	7–9	
A.S.I.	12–15	Container & ro/ro facilities available
Enichem Port	12–15	Conveyor belt
Private Wharves		Tanker & dry cargo berths operated by Enichem SpA

Mechanical Handling Equipment:

Location	Type	Capacity (t)	Qty
Porto Torres	Mobile Cranes	25	1
A.S.I.	Mult-purp. Cranes	25	2
Enichem Port	Mult-purp. Cranes	10	3

Bunkering: AGIP Petroli S.p.A., ENI, Via Laurentina 449, 00142 Rome, Italy, *Tel:* +39 06 59881, *Fax:* +39 06 5988 5700, *Email:* gioacchino.costa@eni.it, *Website:* www.eni.it – *Grades:* GO – *Parcel Size:* min 25t – *Delivery Mode:* truck
ExxonMobil Marine Fuels, Mailpoint 31, ExxonMobil House, Ermyn Way, Leatherhead, Surrey KT22 8UX, United Kingdom, *Tel:* +44 1372 222 000, *Fax:* +44 1372 223 922, *Email:* marine.fuels@exxonmobil.com, *Website:* www.exxonmobil.com – *Grades:* MGO; lubes – *Misc:* own storage facilities – *Parcel Size:* min 12t – *Notice:* 36 hours – *Delivery Mode:* truck

Towage: Three tugs of 4410 hp, 3000 hp and 2000 hp available

Repair & Maintenance: Sardil S.r.l., SS. 131 KM.234, Porto Torres, Sardinia, Italy, *Tel:* +39 079 501647, *Fax:* +39 079 512300 Minor repairs

Shipping Agents: Agenzie Marittime Sarde S.r.l., Corso Vittorio Emanuel 44, 07046 Porto Torres, Sardinia, Italy, *Tel:* +39 079 517020, *Fax:* +39 079 516 7149, *Email:* marittimesarde@tiscali.it, *Website:* www.amsitaly.com Manager: Luciano Laureanti
Agenzia Marittima Cincotta S.r.l., Piazza Garibaldi 1, I-07046 Porto Torres, Sardinia, Italy, *Tel:* +39 079 501040, *Fax:* +39 079 667775, *Email:* portotorres@cincotta.com, *Website:* www.cincotta.com
Plaisant & Co. Ship Agency S.r.l., Via Josto 36, I-07046 Porto Torres, Sardinia, Italy, *Tel:* +39 079 514562, *Fax:* +39 079 508233, *Email:* plaisant.portotorres@plaisant.it, *Website:* www.plaisant.it

Medical Facilities: Sassari hospital, 19 km

Airport: Alghero-Fertilia, 30 km

Lloyd's Agent: Gastaldi International S.r.l., Mura di Santa Chiara 1, I-16128 Genoa, Italy, *Tel:* +39 010 530931, *Fax:* +39 010 530 9343, *Email:* info@gastaldi-int.it, *Website:* www.gastaldi-int.it

PORTO VESME

Lat 39° 12' N; Long 8° 24' E.

Admiralty Chart: 1202	**Admiralty Pilot:** 46
Time Zone: GMT +1 h	**UNCTAD Locode:** IT PVE

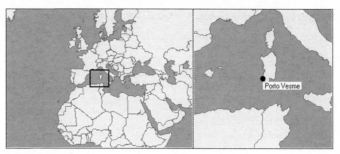

Principal Facilities:

P	Q	Y	G		R		B		T	A

Authority: Ufficio Locale Marittimo di Porto Vesme, Via Molo Centrale Portovesme, I-09010 Portoscuso, Italy, *Tel:* +39 0781 509114, *Fax:* +39 0781 509114

Officials: Harbour Master: Federico Mazza.

Port Security: ISPS compliant

Documentation: Stores list, crew effects declaration, crew list, narcotic list, maritime declaration of health, cargo manifest

Approach: Medium size and deep draft vessels with draught more than 5.2 m have to approach the harbour through the North Channel and generally await pilot in P1 Anchorage (also pilot boarding position) in pos 39° 13.8' N; 8° 19' E
Small size vessels (draught up to 5.2 m) can cross South Channel and south pilot boarding pos in 39° 07.6' N; 8° 22' E

Anchorage: P1 in pos 39° 13.8' N; 8° 19' E, depth 40 m
P2 in pos 39° 12.9' N; 8° 18' E, depth 40 m
P3 in pos 39° 07.5' N; 8° 21' E, depth 10 m
P4 in pos 39° 07.8' N; 8° 22.3' E, depth 7 m
P5 in pos 39° 04.8' N; 8° 19.2' E, depth 35 m
S3 in pos 38° 59.6' N; 8° 28.5' E, depth 20 m
S4 in pos 38° 59.6' N; 8° 30' E, depth 26 m

Pilotage: Compulsory for all vessels over 500 gt and for vessels that intend to drop anchor in the inner road

Radio Frequency: Harbour Master on VHF Channel 16 (0800-2000). Pilot station on VHF Channel 12. Porto Vesme harbour tug on VHF Channel 12/16

Weather: Should NW gales occur while vessels are riding in P1 or P2 anchorage waiting berths, the Master's usually weigh anchor and lie up either in the Gulf of Palmas (S3 or S4) or on the S side of the Island of San Pietro (P5). From these anchorages vessels can subsequently either pick up the pilot and proceed directly to Portovesme or proceed again to P1 and P2 anchorages when the weather has improved

Tides: Max range 30 cm

Traffic: 2002, 5 457 140 t of cargo handled

Maximum Vessel Dimensions: 92 000 dwt, 12 m draught

Principal Imports and Exports: Imports: Bauxite ore, Caustic soda, Coal, Coke, Fuel oil, Lead & zinc concentrates, Petcoke. Exports: Alumina hydrate, Aluminium billets, Aluminium T bars, Gypsum, Lead & zinc ingots in bundles, Sandy alumina, Sulphuric acid.

Working Hours: Daybreak till sunset (berthing/unberthing allowed only in daylight)

Accommodation:

Name	Length (m)	Draught (m)	Remarks
Porto Vesme			
Commercial Pier	280	8.23	Public pier with two berths (No's 2 & 3)
ENEL Pier	180	8.39	See [1] below
Eurallumina Wharf		12	See [2] below
Portovesme Pier	40	8.5	See [3] below

[1]*ENEL Pier:* Private facility (Berth 7) operated by ENEL SpA. Conveyor belts for coal and petroleum coke and pipeline for fuel oil
[2]*Eurallumina Wharf:* Private facility with two berths (No.10 250 m long & No.11 200 m long) operated by Eurallumina SpA. Conveyor belts for bauxite and alumina and pipeline for caustic soda
[3]*Portovesme Pier:* Private facility (Berth 12) operated by Portovesme Srl for loading of sulphuric acid by pipeline

Mechanical Handling Equipment:

Location	Type	Capacity (t)	Qty
Commercial Pier	Mobile Cranes	20	5

Bunkering: Available by lorry from Cagliari
AGIP Petroli S.p.A., ENI, Via Laurentina 449, 00142 Rome, Italy, *Tel:* +39 06 59881, *Fax:* +39 06 5988 5700, *Email:* gioacchino.costa@eni.it, *Website:* www.eni.it – *Grades:* GO – *Parcel Size:* min 25t – *Delivery Mode:* truck

Waste Reception Facilities: Facilities for garbage (food waste). Sludge oil can be discharged into a lorry that comes from Cagliari if requested

Towage: Rimorchiatori Sardi S.p.A., Moby S.p.A., Molo Capitaneria, 09125 Cagliari, Sardinia, Italy, *Tel:* +39 070 60561, *Fax:* +39 070 654041, *Email:* info@rimorchiatorisardi.it, *Website:* www.rimorchiatorisardi.com

Repair & Maintenance: A.I.C.O.M., Porto Vesme, Sardinia, Italy, *Tel:* +39 0781 509000
So.Co. Mar Sarde, Porto Vesme, Sardinia, Italy, *Tel:* +39 0781 508355
S.T.S. Srl, Porto Vesme, Sardinia, Italy, *Tel:* +39 0781 508801

Shipping Agents: Plaisant & Co. Ship Agency S.r.l., Molo Centrale, I-09010 Porto Vesme, Sardinia, Italy, *Tel:* +39 0781 508130, *Fax:* +39 0781 508186, *Email:* plaisant.portovesme@plaisant.it, *Website:* www.plaisant.it

---

Key to Principal Facilities:—				
A=Airport	**C**=Containers	**G**=General Cargo	**P**=Petroleum	**R**=Ro/Ro	**Y**=Dry Bulk
B=Bunkers	**D**=Dry Dock	**L**=Cruise	**Q**=Other Liquid Bulk	**T**=Towage (where available from port)	

Stevedoring Companies: Lavoratori Portuali S.r.l., Porto Vesme, Sardinia, Italy, *Tel:* +39 0781 509709
Sardagru S.r.l., Porto Vesme, Sardinia, Italy, *Tel:* +39 0781 509346, *Fax:* +39 0781 509346, *Email:* sardagru@tiscalinet.it, *Website:* www.sardagru.it

Surveyors: GLP Surveys, Porto Vesme, Sardinia, Italy, *Tel:* +39 0781 509768
Societe Generale de Surveillance (SGS), SGS Alfalab, Porto Vesme, Sardinia, Italy, *Tel:* +39 0781 508841, *Fax:* +39 0781 509768, *Website:* www.sgs.com

Medical Facilities: Not available in port. Sirai Hospital, approx 20 km

Airport: Elmas Cagliari, 90 km

Railway: Carbonia, approx 22 km

Development: Construction of a 400 m ore quay in the SE area of the port is expected to be completed by the middle of 2005 and fully operational by the end of 2005 beginning of 2006.
Extension of approx 70 m to the Commercial Pier

Lloyd's Agent: Gastaldi International S.r.l., Mura di Santa Chiara 1, I-16128 Genoa, Italy, *Tel:* +39 010 530931, *Fax:* +39 010 530 9343, *Email:* info@gastaldi-int.it, *Website:* www.gastaldi-int.it

PORTOFERRAIO

Lat 42° 49' N; Long 10° 20' E.

Admiralty Chart: 131	**Admiralty Pilot:** 46
Time Zone: GMT +1 h	**UNCTAD Locode:** IT PFE

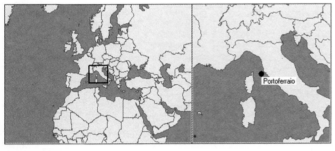

Principal Facilities:

		Y	G		L	B		A	

Authority: Capitaneria di Porto di Portoferraio, Calata Buccari 10, I-57037 Portoferraio, Elba, Italy, *Tel:* +39 0565 914000, *Fax:* +39 0565 918598, *Email:* portoferraio@guardiacostiera.it, *Website:* www.guardiacostiera.it/portoferraio

Officials: Harbour Master: Nerio Busdraghi.

Port Security: ISPS compliant

Approach: Vessels using the approach channel must pass starboard to starboard

Anchorage: Anchorage can be obtained in Zone B, SE of Punta del Torrione (42° 48.6' N; 10° 19.8' E) in depths of 9-25 m

Pilotage: Compulsory and available 24 h/day for vessels over 500 gt

Accommodation:

Name	Length (m)	Draught (m)	Remarks
Portoferraio			
Alto Fondale	115	7.5	Ferries & cruise vessels
Molo Massimo Nord	75	4	Ferries
Molo Massimo Sud	75	4	Ferries
Pontile No.3 Nord	128	7	Ferries & cruise vessels
Pontile No.3 Sud	128	8	Ferries & cruise vessels
Pontile No.1 Nord	470	9.5	
Pontile No.1 Sud	270	11.89	
Calata Depositi	115	5	Fishing vessels & small cruise vessels

Bunkering: Gas oil available by tank truck

Airport: Campo Elba, 15 km

Lloyd's Agent: Ditta Vincenzo Capanna S.a.S., Via Claudio Cogorano 25, P O Box 286, I-57123 Leghorn, Italy, *Tel:* +39 0586 894132, *Fax:* +39 0586 885332, *Email:* capanna@capanna.it, *Website:* www.capanna.it

POZZUOLI

Lat 40° 49' N; Long 14° 7' E.

Admiralty Chart: 916	**Admiralty Pilot:** 46
Time Zone: GMT +1 h	**UNCTAD Locode:** IT POZ

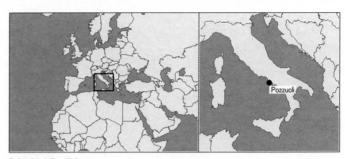

Principal Facilities:

P		G			B		A	

Authority: Capitaneria di Porto di Pozzuoli, Largo San Paolo, I-80078 Pozzuoli, Italy, *Tel:* +39 081 526 1160, *Fax:* +39 081 526 5022, *Email:* pozzuoli@guardiacostiera.it, *Website:* www.guardiacostiera.it/pozzuoli

Officials: Harbour Master: Sergio Castellano.

Port Security: ISPS compliant

Anchorage: In good weather vessels over 50 m loa may obtain anchorage about 4 cables WSW of Molo Caligliano Head and vessels under 50 m loa about 2.5 cables NW of Molo Caligliano Head

Pilotage: Compulsory for vessels over 500 gt. Pilot boards in the following positions:
a) 1 nautical mile E of Molo di Sopratutto (large vessels)
b) 0.5 nautical mile E of Molo di Sopratutto (small vessels)

Accommodation:

Name	Length (m)	Depth (m)	Remarks
Pozzuoli			See [1] below
Molo Caligoliano	280	6.2–8.15	
Emporio Quay West	132	3–5	
Emporio Quay North	150	4–5	
Pontile Pirelli	445		Privately owned berth
Banchina Villa		4	Used for ferries

[1]*Pozzuoli:* Good, well-sheltered anchorage in 9.1 to 14.6 m
Tanker Terminals: Two oil berths, lengths: 228 m, 7.62 m d. Night berthing possible. Water and bunkers available

Mechanical Handling Equipment:

Location	Type	Capacity (t)	Qty
Pozzuoli	Mobile Cranes	60	2
Pozzuoli	Mobile Cranes	15	2

Bunkering: From Naples by barge. By truck barge if small quantity to be supplied

Towage: Tugs available from Naples if required

Repair & Maintenance: For small ships up to 500 t at Baia

Airport: Capodichino, 12 km

Lloyd's Agent: Gastaldi International S.r.l., Mura di Santa Chiara 1, I-16128 Genoa, Italy, *Tel:* +39 010 530931, *Fax:* +39 010 530 9343, *Email:* info@gastaldi-int.it, *Website:* www.gastaldi-int.it

PRIOLO

see under Augusta

PUNTO FRANCO

harbour area, see under Trieste

RAVENNA

Lat 44° 28' N; Long 12° 14' E.

Admiralty Chart: 1445/1467	**Admiralty Pilot:** 47
Time Zone: GMT +1 h	**UNCTAD Locode:** IT RAN

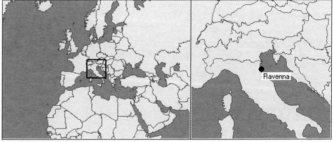

Principal Facilities:

P	Q	Y	G	C	R		B	D	T	A	

Authority: Autorita Portuale di Ravenna, Via Antico Squero 31, I-48100 Ravenna, Italy, *Tel:* +39 0544 608811, *Fax:* +39 0544 608888, *Email:* info@port.ravenna.it, *Website:* www.port.ravenna.it

Officials: President: Giuseppe Parrello, *Email:* giuseppe.parrello@port.ravenna.it. General Secretary: Fabio Maletti, *Email:* fabio.maletti@port.ravenna.it. Marketing Manager: Luca Antonellini, *Email:* luca.antonellini@port.ravenna.it. Harbour Master: Tiberio Piattelli, *Email:* cpravenna@linknet.it.

Port Security: ISPS compliant

Documentation: For Maritime Authority:
Ship safety certificates, four crew lists (2 for arrivals and 2 for departures), four passenger lists (2 for arrivals and 2 for departures)
For Customs:
Crew list (1 copy), passenger list (1 copy), cargo manifest, bills of lading, provision list (1 copy), stores list (1 copy), customs declaration of each crew member (1 copy)
For Maritime Health:
Crew list (1 copy), passenger list (1 copy), derat certificate or exemption, maritime health declaration
For Police:
Crew list (2 copies), passenger list (2 copies), all passports must be checked

Approach: Vessels should use caution when approaching and anchoring at the port as production platforms, well structures, submerged pipelines and cables exist in the area

Anchorage: Anchorage is prohibited in proximity of submarine pipelines and cables. Vessels waiting for a berth may anchor at a distance of more than 1.5 miles from the outer breakwater head according to their draft and subject to weather conditions

Pilotage: Compulsory and available 24 h/day. Contact 'Ravenna Pilot Station' on VHF Channel 12 (frequency 156.600 mHz), Tel: +39 0544 530204, Fax: +39 0544 530453, Email: operativo@piloti.ra.it, Website: www.piloti.ra.it

Radio Frequency: Harbour Master on VHF Channel 16. Port services, pilotage, moormen and tug services on VHF Channel 12. Port informer (in contact with ship agents 0630-2200) on VHF Channel 9. Mercantile trade on VHF Channels 25, 26 and 27

Weather: The prevailing winds are from NW, winds from NE (Bora) and SE are less frequent but they may reach gale force. Fog may occur during wintertime, mainly from September to March

Tides: Mean spring range 0.52 m and the tide variation is 0.91 m max

Traffic: 2007, 26 304 507 t of cargo handled, 206 580 TEU's

Maximum Vessel Dimensions: 261 m loa, 33 m breadth, 9.45 m draft

Principal Imports and Exports: Imports: Cereals, Chemicals, Clay, Fertiliser, LPG, Petroleum, Steel coils. Exports: Fertiliser, LPG, Machinery, Steel pipes.

Working Hours: 24 h/day

Accommodation:

Name	Length (m)	Depth (m)	Draught (m)	Remarks
Ravenna				See [1] below
Adriatank Srl	100		5.18	See [2] below
Agip Petroli	660		9.14	See [3] below
Alma Petroli SpA	230		9.14	See [4] below
Colacem	256		6.71	See [5] below
Consorzio Agrario di Ravenna Scrl	186	5.5		See [6] below
De.co.ra Srl	90		5.18	See [7] below
Docks Cereali SpA	636		9.45	See [8] below
Docks E.C.S. Srl			5.18	See [9] below
Enel SpA	270		7.62	See [10] below
Enel SpA- Terminale Marino	360		11.5	Five oil storage tanks totalling 173 000 m3
Polimeri Europa SpA	400		8.53	See [11] below
Bunge Italia SpA	311		8.53	See [12] below
Eurodocks Srl	545		9.45	See [13] below
Fassa Srl	185		5.18	See [14] below
Fosfitalia SpA	175		8.53	See [15] below
Frigoterminal del Porto di Ravenna SpA	240		9.45	See [16] below
Yara Italia SpA	500		8.53	See [17] below
I.F.A. Srl	280		9.45	See [18] below
Italterminal Srl	270		6.71	See [19] below
Lloyd Ravenna SpA	253		9.45	See [20] below
Marcegaglia SpA	355		9.45	See [21] below
Na.Dep. Srl	250		6.71	See [22] below
Nadep Ovest Srl	170		6.71	See [23] below
P.I.R. SpA Divisione Magazzini Generali	170		8.53	See [24] below
P.I.R. SpA - Petra	660		9.14	See [25] below
Riparbelli & C. Srl			5.18	See [26] below
S.A.P.I.R. SpA	1340		9.45	See [27] below
Setramar SpA	615		9.45	See [28] below
Soco SpA	245		6.5	See [29] below
Terminal Container Ravenna (TCR)	670		9.45	See [30] below
T&C Srl (Cruise & Ferry Terminal)	440	10.5		See [31] below
Largo Trattaroli Lato Fantuzzi	427	10.5		
Banchina Pubblica (BP)	2121	5.5		

[1]*Ravenna:* The entrance to the port is protected by two outer breakwaters, each 2.5 km long, allowing vessels to enter the port in any weather. The port area covers 2080 ha including 1500 ha already urbanized or being urbanized and 580 ha of water

surface. On the whole the port has over 12 km of quays for port operations. Water depth in the harbour is 11.5 m

[2]*Adriatank Srl:* Via d'Alaggio 119, I-48100 Ravenna, Tel: +39 0544 420354, Fax: +39 0544 423935, Email: adriatank@gruppopir.com, Website: www.gruppopir.com
Liquid chemicals & food storage. 23 chemical storage tanks totalling 28 500 m3 and 21 foodstuff storage tanks totalling 17 000 m3

[3]*Agip Petroli:* Tel: +39 0544 34317, Fax: +39 0544 37169, Email: info@almapetroli.com
Consists of 11 berths. Supply and transport centre for oil products with 14 oil storage tanks totalling 1 490 000 m3

[4]*Alma Petroli SpA:* Tel: +39 0544 696411, Fax: +39 0544 696410, Email: raffineria@almapetroli.com, Website: www.almapetroli.com
Refining of heavy crude oil. Storage yards of 4300 m2 and five oil storage tanks totalling 61 000 m3

[5]*Colacem:* Tel: +39 0544 430351, Fax: +39 0544 435372, Email: info@colacem.it, Website: www.colacem.it
Terminal operates in the field of the unloading and storage of cement and of other aggregates for the construction industry. Situated at the entrance of the port of Ravenna, the plant is provided of 2 silos for cement and a plant for the storage of bulk goods

[6]*Consorzio Agrario di Ravenna Scrl:* Tel: +39 0544 542111, Fax: +39 0544 213171, Website: www.consorzioagrarioravenna.it
Consists of two berths. Warehouses for loading/unloading and storing of primary products for the zootechnical field, both bulk and bagged products. Bulk storage of 39 400 m3 and silos of 5100 m3

[7]*De.co.ra Srl:* Tel: +39 0544 452854, Fax: +39 0544 451393, Email: decora@gruppopir.com
Storage and handling of bulk liquid petro-chemicals with 14 oil storage tanks totalling 17 000 m3

[8]*Docks Cereali SpA:* Via Classicana 59, I-48100 Ravenna, Tel: +39 0544 436206, Fax: +39 0544 436650, Email: info@dockscereali.it
Consists of seven berths. Loading, unloading and storage of bulk and bagged cereals, flours, fertilisers and foodstuffs. Two 750 t/h gantry cranes. Bulk storage of 285 000 m3, silos of 125 000 m3 and storage yards of 40 000 m2

[9]*Docks E.C.S. Srl:* Tel: +39 0544 591054, Fax: +39 0544 591056, Email: docksecs@libero.it
Storing and handling fertilizers, raw materials and various goods. One crane of 150 t cap. General cargo storage of 10 000 m2, bulk storage of 48 000 m3, silos of 6000 m3 and storage yards of 50 000 m2

[10]*Enel SpA:* Tel: +39 0544 298380, Fax: +39 0544 298389
Unloading combustible oil. Six oil storage tanks totalling 173 000 m3

[11]*Polimeri Europa SpA:* Tel: +39 0544 513111, Fax: +39 0544 513611
Consists of two berths. Pier equipped for loading of fertilisers as well as bulk and bagged goods. There is also a pier fitted for the loading and unloading of hydro-carbons, liquid products and LPG. 22 oil storage tanks totalling 62 000 m3 and 46 chemical storage tanks totalling 86 000 m3

[12]*Bunge Italia SpA:* Tel: +39 0544 537711, Fax: +39 0544 538519
Consists of two berths. The capacity of the crushing plant is 1600 t/day for soybeans or 1200 t/day for sunseeds, while the refining capacity is 400-450 t/day. Bulk storage space of 113 000 m3, silos of 211 000 m3 and 60 foodstuff storage tanks totalling 33 000 m3

[13]*Eurodocks Srl:* Via Classicana 49, I-48100 Ravenna, Tel: +39 0544 436863, Fax: +39 0544 436869, Email: eurodocks@eurodocks.it, Website: www.eurodocks.it
Consists of two berths. Loading, unloading and storage operations of various goods including bulk products, general cargo, containers, iron & steel products, machinery and timber. One 750 t/h gantry crane. General cargo storage of 24 000 m2, bulk storage of 175 000 m3 and storage yards of 80 000 m2

[14]*Fassa Srl:* Fax: +39 0544 688965, Email: fassaravenna@tin.it
Bulk storage of 8000 m3

[15]*Fosfitalia SpA:* Via Baiona 135, I-48100 Ravenna, Tel: +39 0544 451777, Website: www.fosfitalia.it
Production and trade of chemical, zootechnical and agricultural products. General cargo storage of 1500 m2, silos of 1300 m3 and three chemical oil storage tanks of 5000 m3

[16]*Frigoterminal del Porto di Ravenna SpA:* Tel: +39 0544 289711, Fax: +39 0544 289901
Consists of two berths. Refrigeration sector plant handling various commodities including fruit and vegetable products, frozen and deep frozen. The terminal has direct rail connection to the warehouses and quay. General cargo storage of 5000 m2 and storage yard for containers & vehicles of 7500 m2

[17]*Yara Italia SpA:* Tel: +39 0544 513976, Fax: +39 0544 513218
Two berths handling fertilisers. General cargo storage of 45 000 m2, bulk storage of 240 000 m3, silos of 10 000 m3 and storage yards of 20 000 m2

[18]*I.F.A. Srl:* Tel: +39 0544 458201, Fax: +39 0544 456599, Email: info@ifasrl.it
Consists of two berths. Three cranes of 40-60 t cap. General storage of 30 000 m2, bulk storage of 200 000 m3 and storage yard of 60 000 m2

[19]*Italterminal Srl:* Tel: +39 0544 436511, Fax: +39 0544 436552, Email: italterminal@italterminal.it
Extends over an area of 70 000 m2 (of which 22 000 m2 covered warehouses). Equipped with all kind of services for unloading/loading with 2 mobile cranes with a lifting capacity of 63 t and 40 t and hoppers. Italterminal bonded warehouse and licensed VAT deposit, can unload and store any dry bulk cargo including dangerous goods and, thanks to 8 bagging/paletizing equipment it can blend/package up to 3000 t of fertilizers daily

[20]*Lloyd Ravenna SpA:* Tel: +39 0544 436303, Fax: +39 0544 435072, Email: setramar@setramar.it, Website: www.setramar.it
Two berths handling and storage of cereals, grains, coal, ores, fertilisers and inert products. Two 500 t/h gantry cranes. Bulk storage of 248 000 m3 and storage yards of 110 000 m2

[21]*Marcegaglia SpA:* Tel: +39 0544 516611, Fax: +39 0544 453487, Email: info@gruppomarcegaglia.com
Consists of two berths. Loading, discharging and storage of steel products. Three 35 t/h cranes. General cargo storage of 30 000 m2 and storage yards of 100 000 m2

[22]*Na.Dep. Srl:* Tel: +39 0544 436355, Fax: +39 0544 436056, Email: info@nadep.it, Website: www.nadep.it
Six berths handling and storage of general cargo (also one ro/ro berth). Two 32 t/h cranes, one 250 t/h gantry crane and one portainer. General cargo storage of 29 000 m2, bulk storage of 300 000 m3 and storage yards of 50 000 m2. Also storage yard of 50 000 m2 for vehicles and containers

---

Key to Principal Facilities:—				
A=Airport	**C**=Containers	**G**=General Cargo	**P**=Petroleum	**R**=Ro/Ro	**Y**=Dry Bulk
B=Bunkers	**D**=Dry Dock	**L**=Cruise	**Q**=Other Liquid Bulk	**T**=Towage (where available from port)	

[23]*Nadep Ovest Srl:* Tel: +39 0544 487081, Fax: +39 0544 435034, Email: nadepovesta@ravimm.it, Website: www.ravimm.it
Terminal operator specialising in loading and unloading of raw materials and goods in bulk, pallets, big bags, iron and steel pipes, wood and timber. It has a bonded storehouse with a warehouse for goods transformation and storage of goods and with large uncovered areas close to the port terminal
[24]*P.I.R. SpA Divisione Magazzini Generali:* Tel: +39 0544 696611, Fax: +39 0544 538581, Email: magazzinigenerali@gruppopir.com, Website: www.gruppopir.com
General cargo storage of 11 500 m2, bulk storage of 35 000 m3, storage yard of 60 000 m2 and 1 foodstuff storage tank of 1400 m3
[25]*P.I.R. SpA - Petra:* Tel: +39 0544 434311, Fax: +39 0544 436582, Email: petra-ra@gruppopir.com, Website: www.gruppopir.com
Two berths handling chemical, petrochemical & other liquid bulk products. 26 oil storage tanks totalling 92 000 m3 and 57 chemical storage tanks totalling 79 000 m3
[26]*Riparbelli & C. Srl:* Tel: +39 0544 452859, Fax: +39 0544 453361, Email: uriparb@tin.it
Import, export and storage of general cargo, fertilisers, dry goods & cement. One crane of 125 t cap and one gantry crane of 100 t/h. Bulk storage of 96 000 m3 and silos of 8500 m3
[27]*S.A.P.I.R. SpA:* Tel: +39 0544 289711, Fax: +39 0544 289901, Email: segreteria@sapir.it, Website: www.sapir.it
Seventeen berths handling general cargo, containers & non-flammable liquids. Three ro/ro berths. Ten cranes of 16-60 t cap and four portainers. General cargo storage of 23 550 m2, bulk storage of 135 000 m3, storage yards of 150 000 m2 and storage yard for containers and vehicles of 300 000 m2. 4 chemical storage tanks totalling 10 000 m3 and 18 foodstuff storage tanks totalling 18 000 m3
[28]*Setramar SpA:* Tel: +39 0544 435711, Fax: +39 0544 435001, Email: setramar@setramar.it, Website: www.setramar.it
Seven berths handling non-flammable bulk products, dry bulk products, timber, general cargo & containers. Two ro/ro berths. One crane of 100 t cap and four gantry cranes at 350 t/h. General cargo storage of 12 400 m2, bulk storage of 178 500 m3, silos of 13 600 m3, storage yards of 210 000 m2 for general cargo & solid bulks and 96 000 m2 for containers & vehicles
[29]*Soco SpA:* Tel: +39 0544 436303, Fax: +39 0544 435001, Website: www.setramar.it
Private bonded warehouse with a handling capacity of 1 000 000 t/year; extends over an area of 145 000 m2 (of which 68 000 m2 storeroom). It provides unloading, loading, storage services and ancillary handling operations with specialization in bulk cargo such as fertilizers, minerals, inerts and general cargo
[30]*Terminal Container Ravenna (TCR):* Tel: +39 0544 434411, Fax: +39 0544 434239, Email: segreteria@tcravenna.com, Website: www.tcravenna.com
Extending over an area of approx 300 000 m2, dedicated to lo/lo and ro/ro vessels. Loading and unloading operations carried out by 4 paceco gantry cranes. In the yard there are 4 RMG's and 18 reach stackers for handling road and rail carriers
[31]*T&C Srl (Cruise & Ferry Terminal):* One ro/ro berth and one cruise-ship berth. Occupies overall an area of 125 000 m2. The future Cruise Passenger Terminal at Porto Corsini is currently under construction and to be completed in 2010

Bunkering: Alma Petroli S.p.A., Via Di Roma 67, 48100 Ravenna, Italy, *Tel:* +39 0544 343 17, *Fax:* +39 0544 371 69, *Email:* info@almapetroli.com, *Website:* www.almapetroli.com
Petrokan S.p.A., Via Trieste 143, P O Box 213, 48100 Ravenna, Italy, *Tel:* +39 0544 608 211, *Fax:* +39 0544 420 364, *Email:* chartering@navenna.it
AGIP Petroli S.p.A., ENI, Via Laurentina 449, 00142 Rome, Italy, *Tel:* +39 06 59881, *Fax:* +39 06 5988 5700, *Email:* gioacchino.costa@eni.it, *Website:* www.eni.it – *Grades:* GO; IFO30-180cSt – *Parcel Size:* min 25t – *Delivery Mode:* barge, truck
Alma Petroli S.p.A., Via Di Roma 67, 48100 Ravenna, Italy, *Tel:* +39 0544 343 17, *Fax:* +39 0544 371 69, *Email:* info@almapetroli.com, *Website:* www.almapetroli.com
Cockett Marine Oil Ltd, Carrick House, 36 Station Square, Petts Wood, Kent BR5 1NA, United Kingdom, *Tel:* +44 1689 883 400, *Fax:* +44 1689 877 666, *Email:* enquiries@cockett.com, *Website:* www.cockettgroup.com
ExxonMobil Marine Fuels, Mailpoint 31, ExxonMobil House, Ermyn Way, Leatherhead, Surrey KT22 8UX, United Kingdom, *Tel:* +44 1372 222 000, *Fax:* +44 1372 223 922, *Email:* marine.fuels@exxonmobil.com, *Website:* www.exxonmobil.com – *Grades:* MGO; IFO40cst; lubes – *Parcel Size:* min truck 12t – *Rates:* 200-300t/h – *Notice:* 24 hours – *Delivery Mode:* barge, truck
Marodi Service SAS, Via Decorati Al Valor Civile 80, 30173 Venice, Italy, *Tel:* +39 041 538 2143, *Fax:* +39 041 922841, *Email:* marodi@marodi.it, *Website:* www.marodi.it
Petrokan S.p.A., Via Trieste 143, P O Box 213, 48100 Ravenna, Italy, *Tel:* +39 0544 608 211, *Fax:* +39 0544 420 364, *Email:* chartering@navenna.it

Waste Reception Facilities: Secomar S.p.A., Via del Marchesato 35, 48023 Marina di Ravenna, Italy, *Tel:* +39 0544 530534, *Fax:* +39 0544 550419, *Email:* secomar@libero.it
SIMAP S.r.l., Ravenna, Italy, *Tel:* +39 0544 423048, *Fax:* +39 0544 423054, *Email:* simap@tin.it

Towage: Societa Esercizio Rimorchi e Salvataggi (S.E.R.S.) S.r.l., Via di Roma 47, 48100 Ravenna, Italy, *Tel:* +39 0544 39719, *Fax:* +39 0544 33594, *Email:* info@sers.it, *Website:* www.sers.it

Repair & Maintenance: Cantieri Ravenna S.r.l., Via 13 Marzo 1987 N.3, Porto Industriale S. Vitale, 48100 Ravenna, Italy, *Tel:* +39 0544 289511, *Fax:* +39 0544 436608, *Email:* mbox@cantieriravenna.it
Cosmi S.p.A., Via Teodorico 7, 48100 Ravenna, Italy, *Tel:* +39 0544 605111, *Fax:* +39 0544 605922, *Email:* cosmispa@gruppocosmi.com, *Website:* www.gruppocosmi.com
Rosetti Marino S.p.A., Via Trieste 230, 48100 Ravenna, Italy, *Tel:* +39 0544 518111, *Fax:* +39 0544 518188, *Email:* rosetti@rosetti.it, *Website:* www.rosetti.it

Ship Chandlers: Barbagelata Adriatica S.r.l., Via Burchiella 35, I-48100 Ravenna, Italy, *Tel:* +39 0544 436421, *Fax:* +39 0544 436054, *Email:* ravenna@barbagelatasupply.com
Cianciola-Montanari Shipchandlers della Work System S.r.l., Via Classicana 93, I-48100 Ravenna, Italy, *Tel:* +39 0544 436320, *Fax:* +39 0544 436267, *Email:* info@montanariravenna.it
Ligabue Catering SLL, Via D'Alaggio 89, I-48100 Ravenna, Italy, *Tel:* +39 0544 590303, *Fax:* +39 0544 590311, *Email:* stefano.dimaggio@ligabue.it
Neptune S.r.l., Via Zara 28, I-48100 Ravenna, Italy, *Tel:* +39 0544 590588, *Fax:* +39 0544 590580, *Email:* info@neptune.it, *Website:* www.neptune.it
Provveditoria Marittima Sonino S.r.l., Via Pag 37, I-48100 Ravenna, Italy, *Tel:* +39 0544 420333, *Fax:* +39 0544 423866
Sea Trade Services S.r.l., Via Darsena 4, I-48100 Ravenna, Italy, *Tel:* +39 0544

426911, *Fax:* +39 0544 426969, *Email:* info@seatradeservices.com, *Website:* www.seatradeservices.com

Shipping Agents: Agmar S.r.l., Via Magazzini Anteriori 27, I-48100 Ravenna, Italy, *Tel:* +39 0544 422733, *Fax:* +39 0544 421588, *Email:* agmar@agmarravenna.it, *Website:* www.agmarravenna.it
Alessandro Archibugi & Figlio S.r.l., Via Magazzini Anteriori 27, I-48100 Ravenna, Italy, *Tel:* +39 0544 422682, *Fax:* +39 0544 423930, *Email:* archibugi@tin.it, *Website:* www.archibugi.com
Casadei & Ghinassi S.r.l., Via Teodorico 7, I-48100 Ravenna, Italy, *Tel:* +39 0544 688043, *Fax:* +39 0544 450903, *Email:* agency-dept@casadei-ghinassi.it, *Website:* www.casadei-ghinassi.it
CMA-CGM S.A., CMA-CGM Italy Srl, Via S. Allende 54, I-48100 Ravenna, Italy, *Tel:* +39 0544 466501, *Fax:* +39 0544 466520, *Website:* www.cma-cgm.com
Corship S.p.A., Via Teodorico 15, I-48100 Ravenna, Italy, *Tel:* +39 0544 451538, *Fax:* +39 0544 451703, *Email:* corship@corshipspa.com, *Website:* www.corshipspa.com
Fratelli Cosulich Bunkers (S) Pte Ltd, Via Teodorico 15, 48100 Ravenna, Italy, *Tel:* +39 0544 685111, *Fax:* +39 0544 685150, *Email:* dbellini@ra.cosulich.it, *Website:* www.cosulich.it
CSA S.p.A., Via Teodorico 15, Ravenna, Italy, *Tel:* +39 0544 451538, *Fax:* +39 0544 471703, *Email:* shipservice.ra@csaspa.com, *Website:* www.csaspa.com
Fiore S.r.l., Via Magazzini Anteriori 51, I-48100 Ravenna, Italy, *Tel:* +39 0544 598511, *Fax:* +39 0544 423414, *Email:* fiore@fioreravenna.it, *Website:* www.fioreravenna.it
Inter Marine Shipping S.r.l., Via Zampeschi 20, I-48100 Ravenna, Italy, *Tel:* +39 0544 600211, *Fax:* +39 0544 600299, *Email:* ims@ims-ravenna.it, *Website:* www.ims-ravenna.it
Italteam Shipping S.r.l., Via Baiona 53, I-48100 Ravenna, Italy, *Tel:* +39 0544 456202, *Fax:* +39 0544 456264, *Email:* italteam@italteam-shipping.it, *Website:* www.italteam-shipping.it
Marino Giada S.r.l., Via Magazzini Posteriori 53, I-48100 Ravenna, Italy, *Tel:* +39 0544 422585, *Fax:* +39 0544 420505, *Email:* shipagency@marinogiada.com, *Website:* www.marinogiada.com
Societa Mediterranea di Navigazione S.r.l., Piazza Caduti Sul Lavoro 3, 48100 Ravenna, Italy, *Tel:* +39 0544 598911, *Fax:* +39 0544 423799, *Email:* mediterranea@mediterraneanav.it, *Website:* www.mediterraneanav.it
Navenna S.r.l., Via Trieste 143, 48100 Ravenna, Italy, *Tel:* +39 0544 420430, *Fax:* +39 0544 420364, *Email:* navenna@navenna.it
Ravenna Cargo & Ships Assistance Organization S.r.l., Via Magazzini Anteriori/Traversa Sud 30, I-48100 Ravenna, Italy, *Tel:* +39 0544 590209, *Fax:* +39 0544 590229, *Email:* racargo@tin.it, *Website:* www.ravennacargo.it
Santi Shipping Services S.r.l., Via Alberoni 14, 48100 Ravenna, Italy, *Tel:* +39 0544 216099, *Fax:* +39 0544 217492, *Email:* santishipping@yahoo.it
Scotto Shipping Agency S.r.l., Via Trieste 90/A, I-48100 Ravenna, Italy, *Tel:* +39 0544 591575, *Fax:* +39 0544 598259, *Email:* scottoshipping@virgilio.it
Seaways S.r.l., Via Aquileia 5, I-48100 Ravenna, Italy, *Tel:* +39 0544 599311, *Fax:* +39 0544 420410, *Email:* seaways@linknet.it
Sitris Adriatica S.r.l., Via Magazzini Anteriori 47, I-48100 Ravenna, Italy, *Tel:* +39 0544 422448, *Fax:* +39 0544 422669, *Email:* sitris@sitris.com, *Website:* www.sitris.com
Spedra S.p.A., Via Classicana 99, I-48100 Ravenna, Italy, *Tel:* +39 0544 436401, *Fax:* +39 0544 436316, *Email:* spedra@setramar.it, *Website:* www.setramar.it
Raffaele Turchi & C. s.a.s., Via Alberoni 31, I-48100 Ravenna, Italy, *Tel:* +39 0544 212417, *Fax:* +39 0544 217579, *Email:* turchiship@raffaeleturchi.it, *Website:* www.raffaeleturchi.it
Viamar S.r.l., Via Darsena 15, I-48100 Ravenna, Italy, *Tel:* +39 0544 456611, *Fax:* +39 0544 456612, *Email:* info@viamar.ravenna.it, *Website:* www.viamar.ravenna.it

Stevedoring Companies: Compagnia Portuale S.r.l., Ravenna, Italy, *Tel:* +39 0544 452863, *Fax:* +39 0544 451190, *Email:* posta@compagniaportuale.ravenna.it

Surveyors: Bureau Veritas, Viale Vincenzo Randi 68/A, I-48100 Ravenna, Italy, *Tel:* +39 0544 270423, *Fax:* +39 0544 278584, *Website:* www.bureauveritas.com
Nippon Kaiji Kyokai, Ravenna, Italy, *Tel:* +39 0544 422591, *Fax:* +39 0544 422512, *Website:* www.classnk.or.jp
Registro Italiano Navale (RINA), Via Candiano 27, Ravenna, Italy, *Tel:* +39 0544 422591, *Fax:* +39 0544 422512, *Email:* ravenna.office@rina.org, *Website:* www.rina.org

Medical Facilities: Santa Maria delle Croci Hospital

Airport: Forli Airport, 30 km. Rimini Airport, 60 km. Bologna Airport, 80 km

Railway: Railway connection is available in all terminals

Lloyd's Agent: Radonicich Insurance Services S.r.l., Via F. Orsini 6/A, Marghera, 30175 Venice, Italy, *Tel:* +39 041 538 2103, *Fax:* +39 041 926108, *Email:* radinsur@portofvenice.net

REGGIO DI CALABRIA

Lat 38° 7' N; Long 15° 39' E.

Admiralty Chart: 992	Admiralty Pilot: 45
Time Zone: GMT +1 h	UNCTAD Locode: IT REG

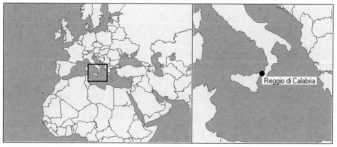

Principal Facilities:

			G	R	B		A

Authority: Capitaneria di Porto di Reggio di Calabria, Via Ambito Porto, I-89100 Reggio di Calabria, Italy, *Tel:* +39 0965 650090, *Fax:* +39 0965 656333, *Email:* reggiocalabria@guardiacostiera.it, *Website:* www.guardiacostiera.it/reggiocalabria

Officials: Harbour Master: Virgilio Muriana, *Tel:* +39 0965 656268.

Approach: Depth at entrance 10 m. No natural hazard

Anchorage: Rada Pentimele, 0.5 miles from the 'Molo Foraneo,' depth 20 m

Pilotage: Compulsory for vessels over 500 gt and available 24 h. VHF Channels 16 and 12, 24 h/day. Pilot boards 0.5 nautical miles NW of the port entrance

Radio Frequency: Port authority, VHF Channel 16

Weather: Prevailing N-NW winds

Tides: Range of tide 0.2 m

Maximum Vessel Dimensions: 50 000 dwt, 11 m d, 200 m loa

Working Hours: Not less than 12 h/day except on Saturday and Sunday

Accommodation:

Name	Length (m)	Depth (m)	Remarks
Reggio di Calabria			Harbour area of 18 acres
Banchina Margottini	120	10	
Banchina Levante	280	11.5	
Banchina Levante Nuova	410	12	
Banchina Ponente Tratto No.1	30	7.5	
Banchina Ponente Tratto No.2	400	12	
Yacht Marina			See [1] below

[1]*Yacht Marina:* For vessels up to 12 m loa, together with hydrofoil wharves on the left side of the Margottini berth

Storage:

Location	Sheds / Warehouses
Reggio di Calabria	3

Mechanical Handling Equipment:

Location	Type	Capacity (t)	Qty
Reggio di Calabria	Mobile Cranes	52	1

Cargo Worked: Refrigerated 100 t/day, coal 3000 t every six working hours

Bunkering: Fuel oil available. Tanker storage facilities from Arico available at Banchina di Ponente wharf

Towage: Not available at Reggio Calabria. If required, tug boats may be requested at nearby harbour of Messina

Medical Facilities: Ospedali Riuniti Hospital, 1 km

Airport: Tito Minniti, 4 km

Lloyd's Agent: Tagliavia & Capanna Srl, Via Emerico Amari 8, I-90139 Palermo, Sicily, Italy, *Tel:* +39 091 587377, *Fax:* +39 091 322435, *Email:* info@tagliaviacapanna.it

SALERNO

Lat 40° 40' N; Long 14° 44' E.

Admiralty Chart: 907	**Admiralty Pilot:** 46
Time Zone: GMT +1 h	**UNCTAD Locode:** IT SAL

Principal Facilities:

		G	C	R		B		T	A	

Authority: Autorita Portuale di Salerno, Via Andrea Sabatini 8, I-84121 Salerno, Italy, *Tel:* +39 089 258 8111, *Fax:* +39 089 251450, *Email:* info@porto.salerno.it, *Website:* www.portosalerno.it

Officials: President: Fulvio Bonavitacola, *Email:* autoritaportuale@porto.salerno.it. Harbour Master: Vincenzo De Luca, *Tel:* +39 089 258 7910. Secretary: Federica Navas, *Email:* f.navas@porto.salerno.it.

Port Security: ISPS compliant

Approach: Channel to port has a depth of 13.5 m

Anchorage: Anchorage A for vessels less than 150 t in pos 40° 39' N; 14° 44.7' E
Anchorage B for vessels less than 150 t in pos 40° 38.9' N; 14° 45.4' E
Anchorage C for vessels over 150 t in pos 40° 38.6' N; 14° 44.2' E
Anchorage D for vessels over 150 t in pos 40° 35.5' N; 14° 44.9' E

Pilotage: Compulsory for vessels of over 500 gt

Radio Frequency: VHF Channels 14 (pilot) and 16 (emergency, harbour master) 24 h/day

Traffic: 2007, 2856 vessels, 10 893 386 t of cargo handled, 385 306 TEU's

Working Hours: Mon-Sat: 24 h/day in four shifts

Accommodation:

Name	Length (m)	Draught (m)	Remarks
Salerno			See [1] below
Manfredi Quay	360		On Eastern Breakwater
Berth 1		8.8	
Berth 2			Used only by small vessels
Berth 3			Used only by small vessels
East Mole	380	9–10.5	See [2] below
Ligea Quay	250	8.5	See [3] below
Main Mole		9–10.5	
Eastern Trapezio	380		Berths 13, 14 & 15 (container terminal)
Head Trapezio	130		Berth 16 (containers)
Westen Trapezio	380		Berths 17, 18 & 19 (containers & fruit)
Banchina Rossa Quay	226	8.5	See [4] below
Banchina Sottoflutto Quay	365	9.5–10	See [5] below

[1]*Salerno:* Two breakwaters (the Eastern 1790 m and the Western 1180 m) protect the port from all winds. Width of port entrance 260 m. Port consists of a basin, formed by three moles (Eastern, Main, Western), enclosed by a water area of approx 800 000 m2

[2]*East Mole:* Terminal for timber, scrap iron, metallurgical products and various goods

[3]*Ligea Quay:* Berths 11 & 12 between East and Main Moles. Terminal for timber and various goods

[4]*Banchina Rossa Quay:* Berths 20 & 21 between Main Mole and Western Breakwater. Ro/ro terminal

[5]*Banchina Sottoflutto Quay:* Berths 22, 23, 24 & 25 on Western Breakwater. Ro/ro & ro/pax terminal

Mechanical Handling Equipment:

Location	Type	Capacity (t)	Qty
Salerno	Mult-purp. Cranes		18
Salerno	Transtainers	40	1
Salerno	Forklifts		

Bunkering: Kuwait Petroleum Italia S.p.A., Viale dell'Oceano Indiano 13, 00144 Rome, Italy, *Tel:* +39 06 5208 8568, *Fax:* +39 06 5208 8857, *Email:* ascioli@q8.it, *Website:* www.q8.it – Grades: GO; FO – *Parcel Size:* min GO 20t, min IFO180 100t, min IFO380 300t – *Notice:* 48 hours – *Delivery Mode:* barge, truck
Marodi Service SAS, Via Decorati Al Valor Civile 80, 30173 Venice, Italy, *Tel:* +39 041 538 2143, *Fax:* +39 041 922841, *Email:* marodi@marodi.it, *Website:* www.marodi.it

Waste Reception Facilities: Trirena, Salerno, Italy, *Tel:* +39 089 253437, *Fax:* +39 089 237867

Towage: Three tugs available of 1200 hp, 2000 hp and 2200 hp

Repair & Maintenance: Only small repairs can be performed by local workshop

Shipping Agents: Michele Autuori S.r.l., Piazza Umberto I, I-84121 Salerno, Italy, *Tel:* +39 089 230311, *Fax:* +39 089 253101, *Email:* autuori@autuori.it, *Website:* www.autuori.it General Manager: Antonia Autuori *Email:* autuori@autuori.it
Societa Meridionale Trasporti Cantalamessa, Via A Sabatini N 7, 84124 Salerno, Italy, *Tel:* +39 089 220215, *Fax:* +39 089 222146, *Email:* tito.smt@tin.it
COMAG S.r.l., Via Ligea 38, 84121 Salerno, Italy, *Tel:* +39 089 253108, *Fax:* +39 089 258 4911, *Email:* andolfi@tin.it, *Website:* www.francescoandolfi.it
Gallozzi Shipping Ltd, via Porto 122, 84134 Salerno, Italy, *Tel:* +39 089 226318, *Fax:* +39 089 258 2528, *Email:* marketing@gsl.gallozzi.com, *Website:* www.gallozzi.com
Star Agenzia Maritima S.r.l., Via Porto 122, Salerno, Italy, *Tel:* +39 089 254344/6, *Fax:* +39 089 233684

Stevedoring Companies: Amoruso Giuseppe S.p.A., Piazza Umberto 1, I-84121 Salerno, Italy, *Tel:* +39 089 258 1411, *Fax:* +39 089 241208, *Email:* commerciale@amoruso.it, *Website:* www.gruppo-amoruso.it
Cargo Service S.r.l., Salerno, Italy, *Tel:* +39 089 227376, *Fax:* +39 089 254025
Impresa Compagnia Portuale S.r.l., Via Molo Manfredi 32, I-84100 Salerno, Italy, *Tel:* +39 089 226815
Magazzini Generali Salerno S.r.l., Via Molo Manfredi 1, I-84100 Salerno, Italy, *Tel:* +39 089 252418, *Fax:* +39 089 253339, *Email:* magazzinigeneralisa@libero.it
Michele Autuori S.r.l., Piazza Umberto I, I-84121 Salerno, Italy, *Tel:* +39 089 230311, *Fax:* +39 089 253101, *Email:* autuori@autuori.it, *Website:* www.autuori.it
Salerno Auto Terminal (SAT), I-84121 Salerno, Italy, *Tel:* +39 089 253202, *Fax:* +39 089 253344
Salerno Container Terminal S.p.A., Via Sorgente Camillo 98, I-84125 Salerno, Italy, *Tel:* +39 089 727711, *Fax:* +39 089 727760
Terminal Frutta S.r.l., Molo Trapezio, I-84100 Salerno, Italy, *Tel:* +39 089 256411, *Fax:* +39 089 256340, *Email:* rognoni@clerici.com
Vitale Luigi & C. Sas, Via Porto 122, I-84100 Salerno, Italy, *Tel:* +39 089 226665

Surveyors: Nippon Kaiji Kyokai, Piazze F. Alario 1, I-84121 Salerno, Italy, *Tel:* +39 089 225985, *Fax:* +39 089 239434, *Email:* info@studiodellacorte.it, *Website:* www.studiodellacorte.it
Registro Italiano Navale (RINA), c/o Agenzia Marittima Della Corte & C. Srl, Piazza F. Alario 1, Salerno, Italy, *Tel:* +39 089 225985, *Fax:* +39 089 239434, *Website:* www.rina.org

Medical Facilities: San Leonardo Hospital, *Tel:* +39 (089) 671111

Airport: Capodichino, 54 km

Development: Salerno Port Authority has worked out plans for a new port which includes a container terminal with a max cap of 2.5-3 million TEU's, to be built 2 km from the shoreline. The new rectangular island will have a natural depth of 19-20 m and excellent motorway and railway links

Lloyd's Agent: Gastaldi International S.r.l., Via A. Depretis 19, I-80133 Naples, Italy, *Tel:* +39 081 552 5561, *Fax:* +39 081 551 1270, *Email:* naples@gastaldi-int.com, *Website:* www.gastaldi-int.it

Key to Principal Facilities:—			
A=Airport	**C**=Containers	**G**=General Cargo	**P**=Petroleum **R**=Ro/Ro **Y**=Dry Bulk
B=Bunkers	**D**=Dry Dock	**L**=Cruise	**Q**=Other Liquid Bulk **T**=Towage (where available from port)

SAN BENEDETTO DEL TRONTO

Lat 42° 57' N; Long 13° 53' E.

Admiralty Chart: 220
Admiralty Pilot: 47
Time Zone: GMT +1 h
UNCTAD Locode: IT SDB

Principal Facilities:

	P		G							

Authority: Capitaneria di Porto San Benedetto del Tronto, Viale Marinai d'Italia 14, I-63039 San Benedetto del Tronto, Italy, *Tel:* +39 0735 592744, *Fax:* +39 0735 594094, *Email:* compamaresbt@libero.it

Pilotage: Compulsory, by local company, Tel: +39 0735 69137 & 60301. Vessels can only leave/enter in favourable weather conditions due to shallow water

Radio Frequency: VHF Channel 16, 0800-2000

Accommodation:

Name	Remarks
San Benedetto del Tronto	See [1] below

[1]*San Benedetto del Tronto:* Harbour is formed by two moles, the northern (Molo Nord) and southern (Molo Sud). Depth at entrance is approx 5.0 m and ranges from 3.5 m to 5 m in the northern part of the harbour, the southern part being a shoal. There is a further mole 250 m long attached to the root of the quayed N Mole with a depth alongside of 3 m. Vessels with d up to 4 m can berth at quays when free from fishing boats. A pier 200 m long for yachts has been completed, 3.5-4 m d

Mechanical Handling Equipment:

Location	Type	Capacity (t)	Qty
San Benedetto del Tronto	Mult-purp. Cranes	40	1

Repair & Maintenance: Drydock for vessels up to 200 t, workshop for minor repairs

Shipping Agents: Alessandro Archibugi & Figlio S.r.l., Viale C. Colombo 72, I-63039 San Benedetto del Tronto, Italy, *Tel:* +39 0735 593519, *Fax:* +39 0735 593565, *Website:* www.archibugi.com

Lloyd's Agent: Radonicich Insurance Services S.r.l., Via F. Orsini 6/A, Marghera, 30175 Venice, Italy, *Tel:* +39 041 538 2103, *Fax:* +39 041 926108, *Email:* radinsur@portofvenice.net

SAN REMO

Lat 43° 49' N; Long 7° 47' E.

Admiralty Chart: 351
Admiralty Pilot: 46
Time Zone: GMT +1 h
UNCTAD Locode: IT SRE

Principal Facilities:

		G			B		A

Authority: Ufficio Circondariale Marittimo di San Remo, Corso N. Sauro 22, I-18038 San Remo, Italy, *Tel:* +39 0184 505531, *Fax:* +39 0184 509968, *Email:* sanremo@guardiacostiera.it, *Website:* www.sanremo.guardiacostiera.it

Officials: Harbour Master: Tenente di Vascello.

Radio Frequency: Available on VHF Channel 9 & 16

Maximum Vessel Dimensions: Length 100 m, 4 m d

Accommodation:

Name	Length (m)	Depth (m)	Remarks
San Remo Quay	100	4	See [1] below Loading is by hand

[1]*San Remo:* No natural hazards. Harbour open to E winds. Depth at entrance 5.4 to

6.4 m. Although considered a commercial port, few commercial operations take place. Quays almost fully used for tourist and fishing

Mechanical Handling Equipment:

Location	Type	Capacity (t)	Qty	Remarks
San Remo	Mobile Cranes	35	1	with 12 h notice

Bunkering: AGIP Petroli S.p.A., ENI, Via Laurentina 449, 00142 Rome, Italy, *Tel:* +39 06 59881, *Fax:* +39 06 5988 5700, *Email:* gioacchino.costa@eni.it, *Website:* www.eni.it – *Grades:* GO; IFO

Repair & Maintenance: Repairs to wooden vessels undertaken by local shipwrights. Slipways available. Shipyard available and one floating dock capable of taking 160 t

Medical Facilities: Hospital (10 km)

Airport: Albenga, 60 km

Lloyd's Agent: Gastaldi International S.r.l., Mura di Santa Chiara 1, I-16128 Genoa, Italy, *Tel:* +39 010 530931, *Fax:* +39 010 530 9343, *Email:* info@gastaldi-int.it, *Website:* www.gastaldi-int.it

SANT' ANTIOCO

Lat 39° 2' N; Long 8° 26' E.

Admiralty Chart: 1207
Admiralty Pilot: -
Time Zone: GMT +1 h
UNCTAD Locode: IT SAT

Principal Facilities:

		Y	G			B			A

Authority: Capitaneria di Porto di Sant' Antioco, Localita Ponti, I-09017 Sant' Antioco, Sardinia, Italy, *Tel:* +39 0781 840815, *Fax:* +39 0781 83071, *Email:* santantioco@guardiacostiera.it, *Website:* www.guardiacostiera.it/santantioco

Officials: Harbour Master: Marco Patrick Mincio.

Port Security: ISPS compliant

Approach: The access channel is 1 km long, 80 m wide and 5.6-5.8 m deep

Pilotage: Compulsory only for vessels over 500 gt within 0.5 mile from outermost buoys, Tel: +39 0781 83008, Fax: +39 0781 83881. VHF Channel 12

Working Hours: Mon-Fri 0800-1200, 1300-1700

Accommodation:

Name	Length (m)	Draught (m)
Sant' Antioco		
Banchina Sardamag	100	6
Banchina di Ponente	390	6
Banchina di Testata	230	6
Banchina di Levante	325	6
Banchina Sanita	100	6

Mechanical Handling Equipment:

Location	Type	Capacity (t)
Sant' Antioco	Mobile Cranes	10

Bunkering: On the quay with 30 t tanker lorries

Towage: No tugs available, but if required from Porto Vesme

Repair & Maintenance: Minor repairs only

Airport: Elmas Cagliari, 80 km

Lloyd's Agent: Gastaldi International S.r.l., Mura di Santa Chiara 1, I-16128 Genoa, Italy, *Tel:* +39 010 530931, *Fax:* +39 010 530 9343, *Email:* info@gastaldi-int.it, *Website:* www.gastaldi-int.it

SANTA PANAGIA

Lat 37° 7' N; Long 15° 16' E.

Admiralty Chart: 1941
Admiralty Pilot: 45
Time Zone: GMT +1 h
UNCTAD Locode: IT SPA

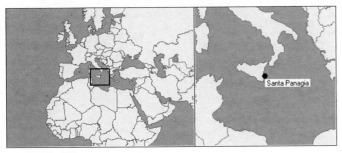

Principal Facilities:

P	Q					B	T	A

Authority: Industria Siciliana Asfalti Bitumi (ISAB), Santa Panagia, Italy

Pre-Arrival Information: The Ship's Master of an Italian flag vessel must inform the Siracusa Harbour Master-Sez. Staccata Santa Panagia, at least 36 h before ETA in the Bay of Santa Panagia

The Ship's Master of non-Italian flagged vessels must inform the Siracusa Harbour Master-Sez. Staccata Santa Panagia, at least 72 h before ETA in the Bay of Santa Panagia

The above required infomation, in case where the sailing time from the previous port is less than 72 h (or 36 h for Italian-flagged vessels) the message is to be sent to the Port Authority before leaving the previous port

Approach: Free of navigational dangers

Anchorage: Anchorage for large vessels awaiting berths at the oil terminal can be obtained in the following zones:

Corridor A: (for vessels of 25 000-50 000 gt) lies between the seaward port limit and a line parallel with it 6 cables NE

Corridor B: (for vessels exceeding 50 000 gt) lies between the outer limit of Corridor A and a line parallel with it a further 5 cables NE

Corridor C: (for vessels less than 25 000 gt) lies inshore between the seaward port limit and the remainder of Baia di Santa Panagia, but clear of prohibited areas

Pilotage: Compulsory in Baia di Santa Panagia. For all inbound vessels this applies from 1.5 miles E of the port seaward limits line. For all outbound vessels pilotage is compulsory out to a position 1 mile E of the port seaward limits line. The pilot will board large vessels approaching from the S off Porto di Siracusa, and about 1 mile N of Capo Santa Panagia for vessels approaching from N. A second pilot is recommended for vessels of 60 000 gt and above. Vessels berth during daytime only, umberthing at any time

Weather: Bay open to NNE and ESE winds; NE gales quite frequent from October to April

Accommodation:

Name	Length (m)	Depth (m)	Remarks
Melilli			See [1] below
Platform 1			
Berth 5	330	25	See [2] below
Berth 6	370	26	See [3] below
Platform 2			
Berth 1	220	18	See [4] below
Berth 2	200	13	See [5] below
Platform 3			
Berth 7	100	6	See [6] below

[1]*Melilli:* One 1300 m finger pier fitted with three platforms providing five berths. Berthing only during the day; unmooring day or night, crew or passengers may not walk through terminal. Boat service between ship and shore operates 24 h/day (VHF Channel 9)

All berths provided with one 28" pipeline for dirty ballast and slops which must be discharged to shore tanks (two of 45 000 m3 cap). Berths provided with shore gangway. Crude washing permitted if agents have obtained authorisation. Nitrogen for cleaning

[2]*Berth 5:* For crude oil, fuels and clean products for vessels up to 250 000 dwt
[3]*Berth 6:* For crude oil, fuels and clean products for vessels up to 400 000 dwt
[4]*Berth 1:* For crude oil, butane and clean products for vessels up to 45 000 dwt
[5]*Berth 2:* For crude oil and clean products for vessels up to 30 000 dwt
[6]*Berth 7:* For coastal tankers up to 5000 dwt and LPG carriers up to 3000 dwt

Bunkering: AGIP Petroli S.p.A., ENI, Via Laurentina 449, 00142 Rome, Italy, *Tel:* +39 06 59881, *Fax:* +39 06 5988 5700, *Email:* gioacchino.costa@eni.it, *Website:* www.eni.it – *Grades:* GO; IFO180cSt – *Parcel Size:* min GO 50t, min IFO 150t – *Delivery Mode:* barge
ExxonMobil Marine Fuels, Mailpoint 31, ExxonMobil House, Ermyn Way, Leatherhead, Surrey KT22 8UX, United Kingdom, *Tel:* +44 1372 222 000, *Fax:* +44 1372 223 922, *Email:* marine.fuels@exxonmobil.com, *Website:* www.exxonmobil.com – *Grades:* MGO; IFO; in line blending available – *Misc:* own storage facilities – *Parcel Size:* min MGO 35t, min IFO 175t – *Rates:* 600-800t/h – *Notice:* 48 hours – *Delivery Mode:* barge
Gori Petrol Group, V. Cristoforo Colombo 1, San Gregorio di Catania, 95027 Catania, Sicily, Italy, *Tel:* +39 095 492 386, *Fax:* +39 095 7122 710, *Email:* info@goripetrolgroup.191.it
Marodi Service SAS, Via Decorati Al Valor Civile 80, 30173 Venice, Italy, *Tel:* +39 041 538 2143, *Fax:* +39 041 922841, *Email:* marodi@marodi.it, *Website:* www.marodi.it
Maxcom Bunker S.p.A. u.s., Via Bartolomeo Bosco 57/7B, 16121 Genoa, Italy, *Tel:* +39 010 5605 200, *Fax:* +39 010 564 479, *Email:* bunker@maxcombunker.com, *Website:* www.maxcombunker.com – *Grades:* all grades – *Parcel Size:* no min/max – *Rates:* 500t/h – *Notice:* 12-24 hours – *Delivery Mode:* barge
Nautilus Oil Co. S.r.l., Via Emerico Amari 8, 90139 Palermo, Sicily, Italy, *Tel:* +39 091 582244, *Fax:* +39 091 612 2196, *Email:* nautoil@libero.it

Towage: Nine tugs from 1000 to 3300 hp

Repair & Maintenance: Minor repairs and maintenance

Airport: Catania, 56 km

Lloyd's Agent: Tagliavia & Capanna Srl, Via Emerico Amari 8, I-90139 Palermo, Sicily, Italy, *Tel:* +39 091 587377, *Fax:* +39 091 322435, *Email:* info@tagliaviacapanna.it

SARAS SEA TERMINAL

harbour area, see under Sarroch

SARROCH

Lat 39° 5' N; Long 9° 0' E.

Admiralty Chart: 1208	**Admiralty Pilot:** 46
Time Zone: GMT +1 h	**UNCTAD Locode:** IT PFX

Principal Facilities:

P	Q		G				T	A

Authority: Capitaneria di Porto di Sarroch, 09018 Sarroch, Sardinia, Italy, *Tel:* +39 070 900057, *Fax:* +39 070 900193, *Email:* seziomare@tiscali.it

Officials: Harbour Master: Massimo Carta.

Port Security: ISPS compliant

Anchorage: The following anchorage areas are available: G1, 39° 05' N, 9° 05' E, for vessels exceeding 12.8 m d. G2, 39° 04' 27" N, 9° 03' 30" E, for vessels less than 12.8 m d. G3, 39° 06' 18" N, 9° 02' 54" E, for vessels less than 5000 gt. G4, 39° 03' 12" N, 9° 06' E, for large vessels of 250 000 dwt

Pilotage: Compulsory for vessels over 500 gt, Tel: +39 070 900006 & 900187. VHF Channel 9; call sign 'Sarroch Pilot'

Weather: Heavy seas with easterly winds

Maximum Vessel Dimensions: 20.72 m draft, 300 000 dwt, 360 m loa

Accommodation:

Name	Draught (m)	Remarks
Saras Sea Terminal		
Pier 1	12.04	See [1] below
Pier 2	10.97	See [2] below
Pier 3	11.43	Oils, jet fuel, gas oils & gasoline for vessels up to 65 000 dwt
Pier 4	11.58	Oils, jet fuel, gas oils & gasoline for vessels up to 50 000 dwt
Pier 5	10.67	See [3] below
Pier 6	6.1	Oils, gasoline, gas oils & MTBE for vessels up to 2000 dwt
Pier 7	9.45	Oils, jet fuel, gas oils, gasoline & LPG for vessels up to 15 000 dwt
Pier 9	6.7	LPG, oils, gas oils, gasoline, jet fuel & MTBE for vessels up to 4000 dwt
Pier 10	6.1	LPG, oils, gas oils, gasoline & jet fuel for vessels up to 4000 dwt
Island 1	20.72	Crude & fuel oils for vessels up to 300 000 dwt
Island 2	17.37	Crude & fuel oils for vessels up to 160 000 dwt
Enichem Piers		
Pier A1	10	Chemical products for vessels up to 18 000 dwt
Pier A2	7	Chemical products for vessels up to 6000 dwt

[1]*Pier 1:* Crude oils, fuel oils, gas oils, jet fuel & gasoline for vessels up to 40 000 dwt
[2]*Pier 2:* Crude oils, fuel oils, gas oils, jet fuel & gasoline for vessels up to 33 000 dwt
[3]*Pier 5:* Oils, gas oils, jet fuel, gasoline, MTBE & LPG for vessels up to 8000 dwt

Towage: Four 4500 hp tugs always on call

Repair & Maintenance: There are good workshops for shiprepair works

Shipping Agents: Inchcape Shipping Services (ISS), ISS-Tositti Sardinia Srl, Via Liguria 4, I-09018 Sarroch, Sardinia, Italy, *Tel:* +39 070 903030, *Fax:* +39 070 903043, *Email:* sardinia@iss-tositti.it, *Website:* www.iss-shipping.com
Medistar Shipping Agency S.r.l., Via Sardegna 16, I-09018 Sarroch, Sardinia, Italy, *Tel:* +39 070 906080, *Fax:* +39 070 906082, *Email:* star@starsardinia.it, *Website:* www.starsardinia.it
Pons Ltd Shipping Agency & Logistics, Via Al Mare Porto Foxi, Sarroch, Sardinia, Italy, *Tel:* +39 070 661371, *Fax:* +39 070 653677, *Email:* info@ponsltd.com, *Website:* www.ponsltd.com

Medical Facilities: Hospitals available at Cagliari, 34 km

Airport: Elmas Cagliari, 43 km

Key to Principal Facilities:—				
A=Airport	**C**=Containers	**G**=General Cargo	**P**=Petroleum	**R**=Ro/Ro	**Y**=Dry Bulk
B=Bunkers	**D**=Dry Dock	**L**=Cruise	**Q**=Other Liquid Bulk	**T**=Towage (where available from port)	

Lloyd's Agent: Gastaldi International S.r.l., Mura di Santa Chiara 1, I-16128 Genoa, Italy, *Tel:* +39 010 530931, *Fax:* +39 010 530 9343, *Email:* info@gastaldi-int.it, *Website:* www.gastaldi-int.it

SAVONA

Lat 44° 18' N; Long 8° 29' E.

Admiralty Chart: 350	**Admiralty Pilot:** 46
Time Zone: GMT +1 h	**UNCTAD Locode:** IT SVN

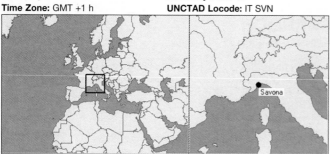

Principal Facilities:

P	Q	Y	G	C	R	L	B		T	A

Authority: Autorita Portuale di Savona, Via Gramsci 14, I-17100 Savona, Italy, *Tel:* +39 019 85541, *Fax:* +39 019 827399, *Email:* authority@porto.sv.it, *Website:* www.porto.sv.it

Officials: President: Cristoforo Canavese, *Email:* canavese@porto.sv.it.
General Secretary: Emma Mazzitelli, *Email:* mazzitelli@porto.sv.it.
Marketing: Alberto Pozzobon, *Email:* pozzobon@porto.sv.it.

Port Security: ISPS compliant

Documentation: Crew list, store list, port list, cargo manifest, declaration of health, vaccination list, narcotic list, declaration (no arms/ammunitions)

Approach: Entrance through two breakwaters, Vecchio Molo Frangiflutti, 220 m and Molo Sottoflutto, 180 m. Entrance width 240 m, depth on channel 10.35 m. Entrance to Darsena Alto Fondale through two breakwaters, Vecchio Molo Frangiflutti, S side and Molo Frangiflutti, entrance width 250 m, depths of 14 m

Anchorage: Safe anchorage can be obtained in Savona roads in a depth of 25 m; recommended area 330° W of the breakwater

Pilotage: Compulsory for foreign vessels

Radio Frequency: Savona Port Control, VHF Channel 13

Weather: Entrances open to E winds

Traffic: 2006, 16 502 000 t of cargo handled, 231 489 TEU's

Principal Imports and Exports: Imports: Cereals, Petroleum, Steel, Woodpulp. Exports: Machinery, Steel, Vehicles.

Working Hours: Monday to Saturday 0630-1930

Accommodation: No bar. 10.35 m d max in channel. The harbour consists of 29 quays, numbered 1 to 26 and 31 to 33, of which 16 only are normally used for berthing of operative vessels
Quays 18-25 are used for tourist and fishing purposes and small craft, 4.5 m max d
Quays 17-26 are inoperative and only used for vessels repairs
Reefer Terminal Quay at Vado Ligure roads, loading and discharge plant for refrigerated cargoes, max loa of vessels 200 m, 9.12 m max d, equipped with four conveyors which load and discharge cargo directly on to and from trucks. Shed cap of 15 000 m2
Container & ro/ro facilities: Molo delle Casse, open area for container storage of 40 000 m2 equipped with mobile stacking cranes. Porto Vado South quay 470 m long with max d of 12.0 m, two cranes of 45 t cap and container storage area of 25 000 m2. Also accommodation for 2000 vehicles near to Quay 10
Bulk facilities: Savona silos quay No.16a discharging cereals and derivates. Quay length 130 m, 10.3 m max d. If Quay No.16 is free, part of this can be used, allowing bulk vessels of 200 m loa to berth. Silo cap of 68 829 m3 equipped with four suckers, max rate 440 t/h. Funivie Alto Tirreno Quay discharging coal, minerals and derivates, 140 m quay length, 220 m max loa, 9.12 m max d, although vessels of 9.7 m d, 200 m loa can berth, keeping 2 m away from quay and grounding on muddy bottom. Discharging performed by four grab elevators conveyed to storehouse, rate 800 t/h. St. Raphael Pier in Vado Ligure roads, South side discharging coal, grain and derivates, 12.45 m max d, 220 m max loa, 30 m max breadth, discharge performed by two 15 t grab elevators, rate 15 000 t/day. North Side, loading coal and derivates, 9.12 m max d, 200 m max loa, 22 m max breadth, loading performed by one pneumatic tower, max rate 140 t/h. Pier is served by rubber belt conveyors. Ferruzzi Grain silos, near St. Raphael Pier, 53 000 m3 cap
Tanker facilities: Facilities in Vado Ligure roads for discharge only: Erg Pier, 435 m long, 8.9 m d, discharge rate 600 m3/h; Industria Italiana Petroli Pier, 420 m long, 8.82 m d, discharge rate 1000 m3/h; AGIP Pier, 700 m long, 11.56 m d, discharge rate 1000 m3/h. On the left side of this pier is Montedison berth, 6.9 m d for tankers discharging sulphuric acid; Esso Pier, 345 m long, 9.12 m d, discharging rate 400 m3/h. Also at this pier is a lubricating oil discharge berth, 7.3 m d, discharging rate 300 m3/h; Sarpom Terminal, conventional buoy mooring consisting of seven buoys with submarine pipelines from vessels to shore tanks, 35 m depth, accommodating tankers over 50 000 dwt and up to 250 000 dwt, discharging rate 11 000 t/h

Name	Length (m)	Draught (m)	Remarks
Savona			
Quay 1	120	7	Automobiles
Quays 2-3	220	7.5	General cargo & forest products
Quays 8-10	340	8.6	Cruise
Quay 13	120	7.4	General bulk

Name	Length (m)	Draught (m)	Remarks
Quay 14	120	7.4	General bulk
Quay 15	150	8.5	Steel products
Quay 16	150	8.5	Steel products
Quay 31	200	15.5	General cargo & forest products
Quay 32	200	15.5	General cargo & forest products
Quay 33	200	15.5	Automobiles
Vado Ligure Reefer Terminal			At roads, 3 miles W of Savona
PVS	150	10	
PVN	200	9	

Mechanical Handling Equipment:

Location	Type	Capacity (t)	Qty
Savona	Mobile Cranes	35–45	7
Quays 8-10	Mult-purp. Cranes	20	2

Cargo Worked: Steel products 2500 t/shift, general bulk 800 t//shift, cars 300/shift, general cargo 250 t/shift, woodpulp 3000 t/shift, paper rolls 1500 t/shift, lumber 1000 t/shift

Bunkering: National Fueling S.r.l., Via Luigi Corsi, 6/1, 17100 Savona, Italy, *Tel:* +39 019 809 386, *Fax:* +39 019 8489 173, *Email:* info@nationalfueling.com, *Website:* www.nationalfueling.com
Rossmare International SAS, Piazza Leon Pancaldo No.1, 17100 Savona, Italy, *Tel:* +39 019 821 177, *Fax:* +39 019 853 073, *Email:* info@rossmare.com, *Website:* www.rossmare.com
AGIP Petroli S.p.A., ENI, Via Laurentina 449, 00142 Rome, Italy, *Tel:* +39 06 59881, *Fax:* +39 06 5988 5700, *Email:* gioacchino.costa@eni.it, *Website:* www.eni.it – *Grades:* GO; IFO – *Delivery Mode:* barge, truck
Alpha Trading S.p.A., Via Brigata Liguria 3/19, 16121 Genoa, Italy, *Tel:* +39 010 5472 200, *Fax:* +39 010 5472 209, *Email:* bunkers@alphatrading.it, *Website:* www.alphatrading.it – *Grades:* GO; IFO; in line blending available – *Parcel Size:* no min – *Rates:* 75-300t/h – *Delivery Mode:* barge, truck
Chevron Marine Products LLC, Piazza Della Vittoria 12/14, 16121 Genoa, Italy, *Tel:* +39 010 5451 611, *Fax:* +39 010 566 762, *Email:* dlfammita@chevron.com, *Website:* www.chevron.com
ExxonMobil Marine Fuels, Mailpoint 31, ExxonMobil House, Ermyn Way, Leatherhead, Surrey KT22 8UX, United Kingdom, *Tel:* +44 1372 222 000, *Fax:* +44 1372 223 922, *Email:* marine.fuels@exxonmobil.com, *Website:* www.exxonmobil.com – *Grades:* IF30-380 cSt; MGO, MDO – *Misc:* own storage facilities – *Parcel Size:* no min/max – *Rates:* 400-600t/h – *Notice:* 12 hours – *Delivery Mode:* barge, truck
Getoil S.r.l., Getoil S.r.l., Via Buonarroti 14, 20145 Milan, Italy, *Tel:* +39 02 468 851, *Fax:* +39 02 4692 760, *Email:* getoil@getoil.it/commerciale@getoil.it
Gori Petrol Group, V. Cristoforo Colombo 1, San Gregorio di Catania, 95027 Catania, Sicily, Italy, *Tel:* +39 095 492 386, *Fax:* +39 095 7122 710, *Email:* info@goripetrolgroup.191.it
Luise International & Co., 15 Via G. Melisurgo, 80133 Naples, Italy, *Tel:* +39 081 552 8670, *Fax:* +39 081 552 7368, *Email:* luise@luise.com
Marodi Service SAS, Via Decorati Al Valor Civile 80, 30173 Venice, Italy, *Tel:* +39 041 538 2143, *Fax:* +39 041 922841, *Email:* marodi@marodi.it, *Website:* www.marodi.it
Maxcom Bunker S.p.A. u.s., Via Bartolomeo Bosco 57/7B, 16121 Genoa, Italy, *Tel:* +39 010 5605 200, *Fax:* +39 010 564 479, *Email:* bunker@maxcombunker.com, *Website:* www.maxcombunker.com – *Grades:* MGO; IFO – *Parcel Size:* no min IFO/MGO, max 1000t – *Rates:* 500-600t/h – *Notice:* 24 hours – *Delivery Mode:* barge, pipeline, truck
Shell Italia Marine, Piazza della Vittoria 14/7, 16121 Genoa, Italy, *Tel:* +39 010 566 444, *Fax:* +39 010 562 773, *Email:* giorgio.barabino@shell.com, *Website:* www.shell.com/marine

Towage: Societa Carmelo Noli fu Giovanni S.r.l., Piazza P. Rebagliati 3, 17100 Savona, Italy, *Tel:* +39 019 821118, *Fax:* +39 019 821254, *Email:* info@carmelonoli.it

Repair & Maintenance: Cantieri Sparano S.N.C., Via Molo delle Casse, I-17100 Savona, Italy, *Tel:* +39 019 821348, *Fax:* +39 019 821347, *Email:* cantierisparano@cantieriasparano.191.it
Parodi S.r.l., Via del Molo 9R, I-17100 Savona, Italy, *Tel:* +39 019 821158, *Fax:* +39 019 821159, *Email:* parodisrl@libero.it

Ship Chandlers: Francesco Baglietto & Figlio S.A.s., Via Piave 33, I-17047 Vado Ligure, Italy, *Tel:* +39 019 886400, *Fax:* +39 019 886444, *Email:* f.baglietto@libero.it, *Website:* www.francescobagliettoefiglio.com
La Naval Provveditoria S.r.l., Via Chiodo 6/r, 17100 Savona, Italy, *Tel:* +39 019 822715, *Fax:* +39 019 821299, *Email:* info@lanavalprovveditoria.it, *Website:* www.lanavalprovveditoria.it

Shipping Agents: Agenzia Marittima Saidelli S.r.l., Via Santorre di Santarosa 2/5, P O Box 234, 1-17100 Savona, Italy, *Tel:* +39 019 823916, *Fax:* +39 019 800655, *Email:* sailor@saidelli.com
Inchcape Shipping Services (ISS), ISS-Tositti Savona Srl, Via Gramsci 14/12, I-17100 Savona, Italy, *Tel:* +39 019 450 0652, *Fax:* +39 019 450 0655, *Email:* savona@iss-tositti.it, *Website:* www.iss-shipping.com
Medmar S.p.A., Via A Gramsci 14/12, 17100 Savona, Italy, *Tel:* +39 019 848 5722, *Fax:* +39 019 833 5303, *Email:* medsvn@finsea.it, *Website:* www.finsea.it

Stevedoring Companies: MUST S.p.A., Paleocapa 6/2, I-17100 Savona, Italy, *Tel:* +39 019 84131, *Fax:* +39 019 812112, *Email:* must@campostano.com
Reefer Terminal, Banchina Raffaello Orsero - Porto Vado, I-17028 Savona, Italy, *Tel:* +39 019 28911, *Fax:* +39 019 289 1560, *Email:* info@reefer.it
Savona Terminal Auto, Via Gramsci 8/3, I-17100 Savona, Italy, *Tel:* +39 019 821375, *Fax:* +39 019 821147, *Email:* agenzia.sv@marittimaspedizioni.it
Savona Terminals, Piazza Rebagliati 1/6, I-17100 Savona, Italy, *Tel:* +39 019 800899, *Fax:* +39 019 813652, *Email:* savona.terminals@campostano.com, *Website:* www.campostano.com

Surveyors: Registro Italiano Navale (RINA), Via Mondovi 1 & 2, Savona, Italy, *Tel:* +39 019 848 5139, *Fax:* +39 019 848 6734, *Email:* savona.office@rina.org, *Website:* www.rina.org

Medical Facilities: San Paolo hospital

Airport: Genoa, 40 km

Railway: Savona Mongrifone, 1.5 km

Development: Construction of a new box terminal to be operated by APM Terminals. The new terminal is anticipated to have 700 m of berth with depths up to 20 m, backed by 25 ha of yard space. It is expected to become fully operational in 2012

Lloyd's Agent: Gastaldi International S.r.l., Mura di Santa Chiara 1, I-16128 Genoa, Italy, *Tel:* +39 010 530931, *Fax:* +39 010 530 9343, *Email:* info@gastaldi-int.it, *Website:* www.gastaldi-int.it

SCALO LEGNAMI

harbour area, see under Trieste

SIRACUSA

Lat 37° 3' N; Long 15° 18' E.

Admiralty Chart: 966/973	**Admiralty Pilot:** 45
Time Zone: GMT +1 h	**UNCTAD Locode:** IT SIR

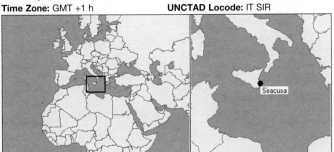

Principal Facilities:

		Y	G			B		T	A	

Authority: Capitaneria di Porto di Siracusa, Piazza IV Novembre, I-96100 Siracusa, Sicily, Italy, *Tel:* +39 0931 481011, *Fax:* +39 0931 69260, *Email:* siracusa@guardiacostiera.it, *Website:* www.harbours.net/siracusa

Officials: Harbour Master: Antonino Munafo.

Port Security: ISPS compliant

Approach: No hazards or sand bars. Width of entrance 1200 m, depth of entrance 20 to 25 m

Pilotage: Available. VHF Channel 14 (24 h service)

Radio Frequency: Port Authority contacted on VHF Channels 16 and 9

Weather: Winds W and SW

Tides: Range of tide approx 0.61 m

Working Hours: Winter 0700-1200, 1300-1630. Summer 0700-1200, 1400-1700 Sat 0700-1330 (27.5% increase in rates). No work on Sun or holidays

Accommodation:

Name	Length (m)
S. Antonio Docks	
Berth 1 (W side)	220
Berth 2 (S side)	145
Berth 3 (E side)	210
Berth 4 (Maritime Station)	194
Berth 5 (N side)	135
Berth 6 (S side)	225
Berth 7 (Mazzini)	170
Zanagora Dock	
Berth 9 (W side)	
Berth 10 (S side)	72
Foro Italico	
Berth 11A	96
Berth 11B	88
Berth 11C	185

Mechanical Handling Equipment:

Location	Type
Siracusa	Mult-purp. Cranes
Siracusa	Forklifts

Bunkering: AGIP Petroli S.p.A., ENI, Via Laurentina 449, 00142 Rome, Italy, *Tel:* +39 06 59881, *Fax:* +39 06 5988 5700, *Email:* gioacchino.costa@eni.it, *Website:* www.eni.it – *Grades:* GO; IFO180cSt – *Parcel Size:* min GO 50t, min IFO 150t – *Delivery Mode:* barge
ExxonMobil Marine Fuels, Mailpoint 31, ExxonMobil House, Ermyn Way, Leatherhead, Surrey KT22 8UX, United Kingdom, *Tel:* +44 1372 222 000, *Fax:* +44 1372 223 922, *Email:* marine.fuels@exxonmobil.com, *Website:* www.exxonmobil.com – *Grades:* MGO; IFO; in line blending available – *Misc:* own storage facilities – *Parcel Size:* min MGO 35t, min IFO 175t – *Rates:* 600-800t/h – *Notice:* 48 hours – *Delivery Mode:* barge
Gori Petrol Group, V. Cristoforo Colombo 1, San Gregorio di Catania, 95027 Catania, Sicily, Italy, *Tel:* +39 095 492 386, *Fax:* +39 095 7122 710, *Email:* info@goripetrolgroup.191.it
Marodi Service SAS, Via Decorati Al Valor Civile 80, 30173 Venice, Italy, *Tel:* +39 041 538 2143, *Fax:* +39 041 922841, *Email:* marodi@marodi.it, *Website:* www.marodi.it
Maxcom Bunker S.p.A. u.s., Via Bartolomeo Bosco 57/7B, 16121 Genoa, Italy, *Tel:*

+39 010 5605 200, *Fax:* +39 010 564 479, *Email:* bunker@maxcombunker.com, *Website:* www.maxcombunker.com – *Grades:* all grades – *Parcel Size:* no min/max – *Rates:* 500t/h – *Notice:* 12-24 hours – *Delivery Mode:* barge
Nautilus Oil Co. S.r.l., Via Emerico Amari 8, 90139 Palermo, Sicily, Italy, *Tel:* +39 091 582244, *Fax:* +39 091 612 2196, *Email:* nautoil@libero.it

Towage: One 2000 hp tug always available; other tugs available

Repair & Maintenance: Officina ORTO, Siracusa, Sicily, Italy, *Tel:* +39 0931 65006

Ship Chandlers: Golino & Rizza S n c, Via Tripoli 42, I-96100 Syracuse, Sicily, Italy, *Tel:* +39 0931 69300, *Fax:* +39 0931 60333, *Email:* golinorizza@virgilio.it

Shipping Agents: Medistar Shipping Agency S.r.l., Via Torino 2, Citta' Giardino, I-96010 Siracusa, Sicily, Italy, *Tel:* +39 0931 745333, *Fax:* +39 0931 745334, *Email:* agency@medistarshipping.com, *Website:* www.medistarshipping.com

Medical Facilities: Available

Airport: Catania, 60 km

Lloyd's Agent: Tagliavia & Capanna Srl, Via Emerico Amari 8, I-90139 Palermo, Sicily, Italy, *Tel:* +39 091 587377, *Fax:* +39 091 322435, *Email:* info@tagliaviacapanna.it

SYRACUSE

alternate name, see Siracusa

TALAMONE

Lat 42° 33' N; Long 11° 8' E.

Admiralty Chart: -	**Admiralty Pilot:** 46
Time Zone: GMT +1 h	**UNCTAD Locode:** IT TAL

Principal Facilities:

				G						

Authority: Ufficio Locale Marittimo di Talamone, Via della Marina 3, I-58010 Talamone, Italy, *Tel:* +39 0564 887003, *Fax:* +39 0564 887003, *Email:* talamone@guardiacostiera.it

Officials: Harbour Master: Fabrizio Marchitelli.

Port Security: ISPS compliant

Pilotage: Available from Porto Santo Stefano

Traffic: 2001, 13 vessels, 947 t of cargo handled

Maximum Vessel Dimensions: 180 m loa, 15 000 dwt (at roads)

Working Hours: 0700-1900

Accommodation:

Name	Remarks
Talamone	See [1] below

[1]Talamone: Accessible only through small channel. Three small piers of 50, 60 and 60 m respectively, only used rarely for loading and unloading general cargo on small coasters. The port is an important loading place for explosives and arms. Vessels anchor in the roads and load on to two small barges, which are towed alongside by a tug. Smaller vessels of up to 1000 dwt, anchor about 300 m from pier head in depth of 7 to 8 m of water. Loading by means of barges from the above pier. Ship's gear to be used. Normal loading time: daylight; rate of loading approx 150 t/day. Vessels over 1000 t approx have to drop anchor at about 400 m from pier head in 9 to 10 m of water. Barges are loaded at a small shore pier, opposite harbour

Towage: Obtainable from Leghorn

Airport: Flumicino, 160 km

Lloyd's Agent: Gastaldi International S.r.l., Mura di Santa Chiara 1, I-16128 Genoa, Italy, *Tel:* +39 010 530931, *Fax:* +39 010 530 9343, *Email:* info@gastaldi-int.it, *Website:* www.gastaldi-int.it

TARANTO

Lat 40° 27' N; Long 17° 12' E.

	Admiralty Pilot: 45
Time Zone: GMT +1 h	**UNCTAD Locode:** IT TAR

Key to Principal Facilities:—				
A=Airport	**C**=Containers	**G**=General Cargo	**P**=Petroleum	**R**=Ro/Ro	**Y**=Dry Bulk
B=Bunkers	**D**=Dry Dock	**L**=Cruise	**Q**=Other Liquid Bulk	**T**=Towage (where available from port)

Port of TARANTO

In the heart of the Mediterranean

The Port of Taranto, Italy's second-largest cargo handling port, has an ideal location in the heart of the Mediterranean, close to international shipping routes between the Suez Canal and Gibraltar. Thanks to its modern, state-of-the-art container terminal, with fast access to the national road and rail networks and a wide range of deepsea and shortsea liner services, Taranto is a perfect hub for intermodal services throughout Europe and between Europe and the rest of the world.

- World-class container handling and transhipment services
- Excellent choice of regular mainline and feedership calls
- New investment in purpose-built logistics and distribution parks right next to the port
- New purpose-built quays for ro-ro and ferry services
- First-rate inland transport services by road and rail to all parts of Italy and Europe
- Choice of international airports within local region

www.port.taranto.it

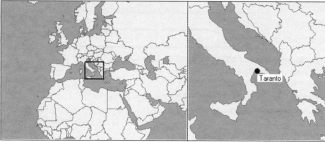

Principal Facilities:

| P | | Y | G | C | R | | B | | T | A |

Authority: Autorita Portuale di Taranto, P O Box Aperta Succursale 2, 74100 Taranto, Italy, *Tel:* +39 099 471 1611, *Fax:* +39 099 460 0476, *Email:* authority@port.taranto.it, *Website:* www.port.taranto.it

Officials: President: Michele Conte.
General Sales Manager: Dr Francesco Benincasa, *Email:* franco.benincasa@port.taranto.it.
Harbour Master: Dibi Tonto, *Email:* taranto@guardiacostiera.it.

Port Security: ISPS compliant

Approach: No hazards in Gulf of Taranto. However, large draught vessels should be wary of deep shoal, which is signalled by a lightbuoy in pos 40° 25' 18" N; 17° 11' 00" E
Mar Grande is a wide bay allowing easy approach and manoeuvring. It is bounded by two breakwaters which reinforce the natural protection offered by promontories and islets. The main harbour entrance is 1400 m wide. An access channel with 25.0 m depth leads from the middle of Mar Grande to the berths of Pier 4. Ships are piloted along specific routes to their moorings. Three offshore breakwaters protect the complex of piers inside Mar Grande. West Pier and Multipurpose Pier, which lie outside Mar Grande, are protected by a large offshore breakwater

Anchorage: Safe anchorage can be obtained in Mar Grande road in depths ranging from 16 m to 44 m

Pilotage: Compulsory for vessels over 500 gt. Pilotage service is provided by Corpo dei Piloti del Porto

Radio Frequency: VHF Channel 11 for maritime information. VHF Channel 12 for pilots, tugs and harbour master. VHF Channel 14 for service. VHF Channel 16 for emergency

Weather: Currents outside sheltered bays are rather weak; influenced by winds and following E-W direction

Tides: Tidal range rarely exceeds 40 cm

Traffic: 2006, 49 434 294 t of cargo handled, 892 303 TEU's

Maximum Vessel Dimensions: No limits on length and breadth. Max draught is 25.0 m at Pier 4

Principal Imports and Exports: Imports: Coal, Containerised cargo, Crude oil, Fertiliser, Iron ore, Tuna. Exports: Cement, Containerised cargo, Oil products, Pig iron, Steel pipes, Steel products.

Working Hours: 24 h/day

Accommodation:

Name	Length (m)	Draught (m)	Remarks
Taranto			See [1] below
Quay 1	240	8.5	See [2] below
Pier 1 (East Side)	320	9.5	See [3] below
Pier 1 (West Side)	330	12.5	See [4] below
Pier 1 (Head)	130	8	Mixed cargo for vessels up to 2000 dwt
Quay 2	290	12.5	See [5] below
Pier 2 (East Side)	515	16	See [6] below
Pier 2 (Head)	143	10.5–16	See [7] below
Pier 2 (West Side)	550	10.5	See [8] below
Quay 3	230	12.5	See [9] below
Pier 3 (East Side)	615	12.5	See [10] below
Pier 3 (Head)	200	12.5	See [11] below
Pier 3 (West Side)	630	12.5	See [12] below
Quay 4	300	12.5	See [13] below
Pier 4 (East Side)	167	12.5	See [14] below
Pier 4 (West Side)	434	25	See [15] below
Pier 4 (Head)	72	25	See [16] below
Oil Jetty		11	See [17] below
Buoy Mooring		22	See [18] below
Pier 5 (West Side)	1200	12.5	See [19] below
Multi-Purpose Pier (Taranto Container Terminal)	2000	14.5	See [20] below

[1]*Taranto:* AGIP Petroli S.p.A. has a concession to operate a 560 m long jetty, with 1120 m of berthage, used for loading and discharging refined oil products and by-products. The AGIP refinery is supplied with raw materials by tankers of up to 300 000 dwt. These vessels can be accommodated at single buoy moorings within the bay of Mar Grande. A submarine pipeline allows direct transhipment of crude oil from ship to processing plant
[2]*Quay 1:* Mixed cargo & ro/ro for vessels up to 20 000 dwt. Operating area of 1800 m2
[3]*Pier 1 (East Side):* Mixed cargo for vessels up to 25 000 dwt. Operating area of 1600 m2

[4]*Pier 1 (West Side):* Mixed cargo for vessels up to 25 000 dwt. Operating area of 13 000 m2

[5]*Quay 2:* Mixed cargo for vessels up to 22 000 dwt. Operating area of 30 000 m2

[6]*Pier 2 (East Side):* Discharge of iron ore for vessels up to 100 000 dwt. Concessionaire ILVA SpA. Operating area of 9000 m2

[7]*Pier 2 (Head):* Fuel & tar for vessels up to 40 000 dwt. Concessionaire ILVA SpA

[8]*Pier 2 (West Side):* Iron & steel products for vessels up to 40 000 dwt. Concessionaire ILVA SpA. Operating area of 10 600 m2

[9]*Quay 3:* Scrap, iron & slag for vessels up to 12 000 dwt. Concessionaire ILVA SpA. Operating area of 4000 m2

[10]*Pier 3 (East Side):* Iron & steel products for vessels up to 45 000 dwt. Concessionaire ILVA SpA. Operating area of 10 800 m2

[11]*Pier 3 (Head):* Fuel & tar for vessels up to 30 000 dwt. Concessionaire ILVA SpA. Operating area of 13 400 m2

[12]*Pier 3 (West Side):* Finished steel products for vessels up to 45 000 dwt. Concessionaire ILVA SpA. Operating area of 12 200 m2

[13]*Quay 4:* Cement loading/unloading for vessels up to 12 000 dwt. Concessionaire ILVA SpA and CEMENTIR SpA

[14]*Pier 4 (East Side):* Cement loading for vessels up to 6000 dwt. Concessionaire CEMENTIR SpA

[15]*Pier 4 (West Side):* Discharge of iron ore & coal for vessels up to 300 000 dwt. Concessionaire ILVA SpA

[16]*Pier 4 (Head):* Bitumen loading for vessels up to 2000 dwt. Concessionaire ILVA SpA

[17]*Oil Jetty:* Length 560 m + 560 m. Loading of refined oil products and discharge of crude oil for vessels up to 20 000 dwt. Concessionaire ENI SpA

[18]*Buoy Mooring:* Discharge of crude oil for vessels up to 300 000 dwt. Concessionaire ENI SpA

[19]*Pier 5 (West Side):* Iron & steel products for vessels up to 45 000 dwt. Concessionaire ILVA SpA. Operating area of 631 300 m2

[20]*Multi-Purpose Pier (Taranto Container Terminal):* Operated by Taranto Container Terminal SpA, S.S. 106 - Molo Polisettoriale, I-74100 Taranto, Tel: +39 099 462 2111, Fax: +39 099 476 4744, Email: tct@tct-it.com, Website: www.tct-it.com Container yard area of 1 000 000 m2

Mechanical Handling Equipment: Quays 1 & 2 and Pier 1 (East and West Side): mobile cranes up to 80 t cap for general cargo
ILVA Piers: six grab cranes of 42-63 t cap discharging raw materials, four grab cranes of 30 t/h handling scrap, one continuous unloader for minerals and coal of 7200 t/h, one continuous loader for blast furnace slag of 1100 t/h, twelve units for steel products of 32-63 t/h and four conveyors which link the port with raw materials stockpiles (two of 3600 t/h for minerals, one of 7200 t/h for minerals and one of 1100 t/h for slag)
Container Terminal: eight super post-panamax cranes of 45 t cap, twenty two RTG's of 40.6 t cap, three reach stackers, one mobile harbour crane of 100 t cap, five side loaders and fifty prime movers

Bunkering: Basile Petroli S.p.A., S.S. 172 Per Martina Franca, C. Da Carmin 6900, P O Box 6 Succ., 74100 Taranto, Italy, *Tel:* +39 099 4723 332, *Fax:* +39 099 4723 361, *Email:* bunkerdept@basilepetroli.it, *Website:* www.basilepetroli.it
AGIP Petroli S.p.A., ENI, Via Laurentina 449, 00142 Rome, Italy, *Tel:* +39 06 59881, *Fax:* +39 06 5988 5700, *Email:* gioacchino.costa@eni.it, *Website:* www.eni.it
Basile Petroli S.p.A., S.S. 172 Per Martina Franca, C. Da Carmin 6900, P O Box 6 Succ., 74100 Taranto, Italy, *Tel:* +39 099 4723 332, *Fax:* +39 099 4723 361, *Email:* bunkerdept@basilepetroli.it, *Website:* www.basilepetroli.it

Waste Reception Facilities: Disposal possible by barge. Tankers operating at AGIP refinery pier can dispose of dirty ballast directly to shore facilities

Towage: Compulsory for vessels over 20 000 gt, but at petroleum piers over 2000 gt
Rimorchiatori Napoletani S.r.l., Corso Vittorio Emanuele II 17, 74100 Taranto, Italy, *Tel:* +39 099 470 7522, *Fax:* +39 099 471 4474, *Email:* oper.taranto@rimnap.it, *Website:* www.rimnap.it

Repair & Maintenance: Cantiere Navale Vernaglione S.r.l., Taranto, Italy, *Tel:* +39 099 471 1056
Cantiere Navalmeccanico E.Stanisci S.r.l., SS 106 Jonica Km 109, I-74100 Taranto, Italy, *Tel:* +39 099 475 1721, *Fax:* +39 099 475 1704
Cantieri Italia, Taranto, Italy, *Tel:* +39 099 372186
Ferplast S.r.l., Taranto, Italy, *Tel:* +39 099 471 8112

Ship Chandlers: Brin Mar Marine Service, Via Costantinopoli 71, 74100 Taranto, Italy, *Tel:* +39 099 470 9137, *Fax:* +39 099 470 9137, *Email:* info@brinmar@it
Cianciola-Montanari Shipchandlers della Work System S.r.l., Lato Sud Porto Mercantile, I-74100 Taranto, Italy, *Tel:* +39 099 471 4081, *Fax:* +39 099 470 6954, *Email:* cianbari@tin.it

Shipping Agents: Anchor Shipping Agents S.p.A., Corso due Mari 33, 74100 Taranto, Italy, *Tel:* +39 099 453 5432, *Fax:* +39 099 452 8008, *Email:* anchorship.ta@campostano.com
Antemar S.r.l., Via Pupino 117, 74100 Taranto, Italy, *Tel:* +39 099 453 5147, *Fax:* +39 099 455 1092, *Email:* antemar@libero.it
Ausiello S.r.l., Corso Umberto 49, 74100 Taranto, Italy, *Tel:* +39 099 459 0461, *Fax:* +39 099 453 4624, *Email:* ausiello@interfree.it
Carmed S.r.l., P O Box 401, 74100 Taranto, Italy, *Tel:* +39 099 476 4047, *Fax:* +39 099 476 4111, *Email:* pcippone@carmed.it
CSA S.p.A., Piazza Kennedy 8, I-74100 Taranto, Italy, *Tel:* +39 099 453 5678, *Fax:* +39 099 459 6637, *Email:* generalhub@csaspa.com, *Website:* www.csaspa.com
Dott Vincenzo Caffio S.r.l., Corso Vittorio Emanuele II 3, 74100 Taranto, Italy, *Tel:* +39 099 471 6666, *Fax:* +39 099 471 6095, *Email:* agmar.carrio@planio.it
Evergreen Shipping Agency (Italy), Molo Polisettoriale SS 106, 74100 Taranto, Italy, *Tel:* +39 099 476 4753, *Fax:* +39 099 476 1661, *Email:* tra@evergreen-shipping.it, *Website:* www.evergreen-italy.it
Nicola Girone S.r.l., 17 Corso Vittorio Emanuele II, 74100 Taranto, Italy, *Tel:* +39 099 471 3768, *Fax:* +39 099 471 3832, *Email:* gironeta@tin.it, *Website:* www.nicolagirone.com
GM Trading & Chartering, Via Anfiteatro 13, 74100 Taranto, Italy, *Tel:* +39 099 453 7525, *Fax:* +39 099 459 4533, *Email:* operations@gmshipping.it, *Website:* www.gmshipping.it
Intramar S.A., S.S. 106 Molo Polisettoriale, P O Box 555, 74100 Taranto, Italy, *Tel:* +39 099 476 4721, *Fax:* +39 099 476 1668, *Email:* intramar@intramar.it, *Website:* www.intramar.it

Pignatelli Marzo E Danese S.r.l., Cosro V Emanuele 2,, 74100 Taranto, Italy, *Tel:* +39 099 471 6698, *Fax:* +39 099 470 9576, *Email:* agency@shipagents.it
Valentino Gennarini S.r.l., 31 Corso Vittorio Emanuele II, I-74100 Taranto, Italy, *Tel:* +39 099 470 7484, *Fax:* +39 099 471 4682, *Email:* agency@gennarini.net, *Website:* www.gennarini.net

Stevedoring Companies: Impresa Portuale Italcave, Strada Provinciale Taranto-Statte Km.3, 74100 Taranto, Italy, *Tel:* +39 099 471 8222, *Fax:* +39 099 470 7543, *Email:* italcave@italcave.it, *Website:* www.italcave.it
Impresa Portuale 'Neptunia', Molo S. Nicolicchio Porto Mercantile, I-74100 Taranto, Italy, *Tel:* +39 099 471 1088, *Fax:* +39 099 471 1089, *Email:* neptunia@impresaneptunia.it, *Website:* www.impresaneptunia.it
Impresa Portuale Peyrani Sud S.p.A., Via Solito 69, I-74100 Taranto, Italy, *Tel:* +39 099 471 4261, *Fax:* +39 099 470 6842, *Email:* elpiano@peyranisud.191.it

Surveyors: Registro Italiano Navale (RINA), Via Anfiteatro 88, Taranto, Italy, *Tel:* +39 099 453 3081, *Fax:* +39 099 452 9041, *Email:* taranto.office@rina.org, *Website:* www.rina.org

Medical Facilities: Available

Airport: Brindisi, 75 km. Bari, 90 km. There is also Grottaglie Airport, approx 20 km from the port

Railway: The port is is directly linked to the national railroad net. There are daily container train services connecting the port with intermodal terminals at Ancona, Bologna, Nola and Civitavecchia

Lloyd's Agent: P. Lorusso & Co. S.r.l., 133 Via Piccinni, I-70122 Bari, Italy, *Tel:* +39 080 521 2840, *Fax:* +39 080 521 8229, *Email:* vdbdirezione@agenzialorusso.it, *Website:* www.agenzialorusso.it

TORRE ANNUNZIATA

Lat 40° 45' N; Long 14° 26' E.

Admiralty Chart: 916	**Admiralty Pilot:** 46
Time Zone: GMT +1 h	**UNCTAD Locode:** IT TOA

Principal Facilities:

	Y	G			B		T	A

Authority: Ufficio Circondariale Marittimo di Torre Annunziata, Largo Crocelle 1, I-80058 Torre Annunziata, Italy, *Tel:* +39 081 861 1855, *Fax:* +39 081 862 2978, *Email:* torreannunziata@guardiacostiera.it, *Website:* www.guardiacostiera.it/torreannunziata

Officials: Harbour Master: Gennaro Fusco.

Port Security: ISPS compliant

Documentation: Vessels for discharging wheat, barley and maize compulsory authorisation for the carriage of grain in bulk as per SOLAS 74 adopted by Resolution MSC 23 (59)
Vessels for discharging mono ethylene glycol compulsory copies of COF or ICOF, IOPP, CLC also vessels will be inspected by port chemist before berthing for granting gas free certificate

Approach: Banchina Levante, Banchina Ponente and Banchina Crocelle 8.54 m d and 8.8 m at high tide

Pilotage: Compulsory for vessels over 500 gt. Entry during daylight hours only for vessels exceeding 80 m loa

Radio Frequency: VFH Channels 15 & 16

Weather: Winds SW and SE

Traffic: 2000, 65 commercial vessels, 293 000 t of cargo handled

Maximum Vessel Dimensions: No restrictions, 8.8 d at high tide

Working Hours: 0800 - 1700 Monday to Friday

Accommodation:

Name	Length (m)	Depth (m)	Draught (m)	Remarks
Torre Annunziata				
SO.LA.CE.N. SpA	250	8.53		Wheat, maize & barley
I.SE.CO.L.D. SpA			8.54	See [1] below

[1]*I.SE.CO.L.D. SpA:* Two berths handling mono ethylene glycol. Storage of 15 000 t

Storage:

Location	Grain (t)
SO.LA.CE.N. SpA	70000

Mechanical Handling Equipment:

Location	Type	Capacity (t)	Qty
SO.LA.CE.N. SpA	Mult-purp. Cranes	20	1
SO.LA.CE.N. SpA	Mobile Cranes	10	1

Bunkering: By barge from Naples

Waste Reception Facilities: Garbage collection (galley, cabin) made by local company
Inside port facilities for dirty ballast, sludge etc

Towage: No tugs available in harbour. If required can be sent from Naples Rimorchiatori Napoletani S.r.l., Torre Annunziata, Italy, *Tel:* +39 081 552 7695

Repair & Maintenance: If necessary from Naples

Medical Facilities: Hospital 2 km away

Airport: Capodichino, 30 km

Railway: Torre Annunziata Centrale, 2 km

Lloyd's Agent: Gastaldi International S.r.l., Mura di Santa Chiara 1, I-16128 Genoa, Italy, *Tel:* +39 010 530931, *Fax:* +39 010 530 9343, *Email:* info@gastaldi-int.it, *Website:* www.gastaldi-int.it

TRAPANI

Lat 38° 2' N; Long 12° 31' E.

Admiralty Chart: 964   **Admiralty Pilot:** 45
Time Zone: GMT +1 h   **UNCTAD Locode:** IT TPS

Principal Facilities:

| Q | | G | C | R | | B | D | T | A |

Cantiere Navale di Trapani S.p.A.

Via Bacino - Zona Isolella, Trapani, Sicily 91100, ITALY

Tel: +39 0923 27866   Fax: +39 0923 21143
Email: cnt@cantierenavalespa.it
Website: www.cantierenavalespa.it

Agenzia Maritima Luigi Cestelli S.r.l.

Via Enrico Amari 8, I-90139, Palermo, Sicily, ITALY
TEL: +39 091 611 8266   FAX: +39 091 611 8819
EMAIL: luigipmo@tin.it

Chairman/Owner - Mr. Luigi Cestelli

Shipping Agents in Palermo and Trapani

Authority: Consorzio dei Porto di Trapani, Molo Sanita, Stazione Marittima, I-91100 Trapani, Sicily, Italy, *Tel:* +39 0923 871622, *Fax:* +39 0923 871622, *Email:* consorzioportotrapani@tin.it, *Website:* www.portotrapani.it

Officials: President: Capt Francesco Bosco.
Harbour Master: Capt Giuseppe Impallomeni.

Approach: Series of rocks from Torre Ligny to N, shallow to W of Torre Nubia

Anchorage: Four anchorage areas, three reserved for general use and one reserved for vessels carrying dangerous goods and waste material

Pilotage: Compulsory for vessels over 500 gt. Pilot boards 4 cables W of the harbour entrance

Radio Frequency: VHF Channels 16 and 12

Traffic: 2003, 2 074 121 t of cargo handled, 12 912 TEU's

Maximum Vessel Dimensions: 200 m loa, 35 000 dwt, 8.3 m draft

Principal Imports and Exports: Imports: General cargo. Exports: Marble, Salt, Wine.

Working Hours: Mon-Fri 0800-1200, 1300-1700. Sat 0800-1200

Accommodation:

Name	Length (m)	Depth (m)	Remarks
Trapani			
Sanita Wharf E	110	8	Local passenger ferries
Sanita Wharf W	100	6.5	Local passenger ferries
Garibaldi Quay	145	8.5	Tunisia & Sardinia ferries
Dogana Quay	177	4.5	Passengers
Marinella Quay	306	3.5	
Sommergibile Quay	110	5	Works in progress
Isolella South Quay	120	8	Ship repair
Isolella North Quay	190	8	Containers
Isolella West Quay	70	8	Vessels to Egadi Islands
Ronciglio Quay	303	7	Ro/ro cargo
Sporgente Ronciglio East	220	8.3	Alcohol terminal & ro/ro cargo
Sporgente Ronciglio West	140	7	Ro/ro cargo

Storage: Only open storage available

Mechanical Handling Equipment:

Location	Type	Capacity (t)	Qty
Trapani	Mult-purp. Cranes	180–200	2
Trapani	Portal Cranes		1
Trapani	Reach Stackers	42	1
Trapani	Forklifts	40	4
Trapani	Forklifts	5	8

Bunkering: By tanker lorries. Small quantities obtainable from the three service stations at the Marinella Quay

Waste Reception Facilities: Somat, 83 Via Spalti, I-91100 Trapani, Sicily, Italy, *Tel:* +39 0923 29445, *Fax:* +39 0923 27711, *Email:* somat@libero.it

Towage: Somat S.r.l., Via Spalti 83, 91100 Trapani, Sicily, Italy, *Tel:* +39 0923 29445, *Fax:* +39 0923 27711, *Email:* somat@libero.it

Repair & Maintenance: Cantiere Navale di Trapani S.p.A., Via Bacino - Zona Isolella, 91100 Trapani, Sicily, Italy, *Tel:* +39 0923 27866, *Fax:* +39 0923 21143, *Email:* cnt@cantierenavalespa.it, *Website:* www.cantierenavalespa.it Two floating docks, one of 122.4 m x 21.6 m x 6 m with lifting cap of 5000 t and one of 115.6 m x 23.7 m x 6 m with lifting cap of 4000 t. Repair quay 240 m long with max draught 8.5 m

Ship Chandlers: General Marine Suppliers S.n.c., Via Francesco Crispi 20, I-91100 Trapani, Sicily, Italy, *Tel:* +39 0923 692 7229, *Fax:* +39 0923 361460, *Email:* gemasu@tiscalinet.it

Shipping Agents: Agenzia Maritima Luigi Cestelli S.r.l., Via Enrico Amari 8, I-90139 Palermo, Sicily, Italy, *Tel:* +39 091 611 8266, *Fax:* +39 091 611 8819, *Email:* luigipmo@tin.it
SCS, Riccardo Sanges & Co., via Eurialo 7, 91100 Trapani, Sicily, Italy, *Tel:* +39 0923 27563, *Fax:* +39 0923 22654, *Email:* p.adamo@riccardosanges.it, *Website:* www.riccardosanges.it
Trident S.r.l., Via Eurialo 7, I-91100 Trapani, Sicily, Italy, *Tel:* +39 0923 27081, *Fax:* +39 0923 22655

Stevedoring Companies: SCS, Riccardo Sanges & Co., via Eurialo 7, 91100 Trapani, Sicily, Italy, *Tel:* +39 0923 27563, *Fax:* +39 0923 22654, *Email:* p.adamo@riccardosanges.it, *Website:* www.riccardosanges.it

Surveyors: Nippon Kaiji Kyokai, Trapani, Sicily, Italy, *Tel:* +39 0923 21255, *Fax:* +39 0923 24947, *Website:* www.classnk.or.jp
Registro Italiano Navale (RINA), c/o Riccardo Sanges & C., Via Eurialo 7, Trapani, Sicily, Italy, *Tel:* +39 0923 21655, *Fax:* +39 0923 22654, *Website:* www.rina.org

Medical Facilities: Hospital S. Antonio, 4 km

Airport: Birgi, 16 km

Railway: Trapani Railway, 2 km

Development: 80 m extension to the Isolella North Berth

Lloyd's Agent: Tagliavia & Capanna Srl, Via Emerico Amari 8, I-90139 Palermo, Sicily, Italy, *Tel:* +39 091 587377, *Fax:* +39 091 322435, *Email:* info@tagliaviacapanna.it

TRIESTE

Lat 45° 39' N; Long 13° 48' E.

Admiralty Chart: 1473   **Admiralty Pilot:** 47
Time Zone: GMT +1 h   **UNCTAD Locode:** IT TRS

Principal Facilities:

| P | Q | Y | G | C | R | L | B | D | T | A |

Authority: Autorita Portuale di Trieste, Via Von Bruck 3, I-34143 Trieste, Italy, *Tel:* +39 040 6731, *Fax:* +39 040 673 2406, *Email:* info@porto.trieste.it, *Website:* www.porto.trieste.it

Officials: President: Claudio Boniciolli, *Tel:* +39 040 673 2200.

General Secretary: Martino Conticelli, *Tel:* +39 040 673 2200, *Email:* mconticelli@porto.trieste.it.

Port Security: ISPS compliant

Pre-Arrival Information: Vessel's should send ETA 48 h in advance to agent. Changes of ETA of more than 1 h should also be notified to the agent. Vessel's should send ISPS pre-arrival form and garbage form 24 h in advance to the agent. Tug assistance is compulsory for tankers over 3000 gt

Approach: Northern Channel is used by vessels approaching or leaving the Old Free Port, Maritime Station, New Free Port, Shipyard, Timber Terminal and Steelworks Southern Channel is used by tankers, vessels approaching or leaving the industrial canal and vessels that cannot enter the Northern Channel for draught or traffic reasons

Anchorage: Zone A reserved for tankers
Zone B reserved for tankers and vessels carrying dangerous cargo
Zone C reserved for other vessels

Pilotage: Compulsory for vessels over 500 gt. Contact pilot on VHF Channel 14

Radio Frequency: VHF Channel 14 (pilots and mooring services), VHF Channel 11 (routine traffic), VHF Channel 10 (towage), VHF Channel 71 (services)

Weather: Frequent ENE winds, particularly in winter

Tides: Max tidal range is approx 0.85 m

Traffic: 2007, 46 267 801 t of cargo handled, 265 863 TEU's

Maximum Vessel Dimensions: No limit on length or breadth. Max draft 18 m

Working Hours: 24 h/day

Accommodation: The Port of Trieste covers a total area of 2 304 000 m2 and is characterised by five Free Port Zones: Old Free Zone, New Free Zone, Timber Terminal Free Zone, Mineral Oil Free Zone and Industrial Free Zone, which cover a total area of 1 765 000 m2. In these zones, the discharging, loading, transhipment, warehousing and general handling of goods and materials are free of Customs duties The commercial port is formed by three free zones: Punto Franco Vecchio (Old Free Area), Punto Franco Nuovo (New Free Area) and Scalo Legnami (Timber Terminal)

Name	Length (m)	Draught (m)	Remarks
Punto Franco Vecchio (Old Free Area)			
Livestock Terminal			See [1] below
Berth No.3	109	6.08	
Berth No.4	115	6.08	
Berth No.5	168	5.18	
Adria Terminal			See [2] below
Berth No.12	239	11.89	
Berth No.13	239	11.89	
Berth No.14	196	8.84	
Ro/ro Ferry I & II Ramps			Ro/ro/ferry terminal for traffic with Albania
Berth No.15	160	5.79	
Berth No.22	149	5.79	
Pier III Terminal			General cargo & harbour service
Berth No.17	105	6.68	
Berth No.18	105	5.49	
Berth No.19	76	3.03	
Berth No.20	105	6.4	
Pier IV Terminal			
Berth No.24	134	5.49	
Berth No.25	85	4.27	
Berth No.26	154	6.4	
Stazione Marittima Terminal			Passenger terminal for cruise vessels & ferries
Berth No.29	210	9.3	
Berth No.30	240	7.9	
Punto Franco Nuovo (New Free Area)			
Riva Traiana Terminal			See [3] below
Berth No.31	255	12.16	
Berth No.31a	325	12.19	
Pier V Terminal			See [4] below
Berth No.32	90	9.45	
Berth No.33	235	9.45	
Berth No.34	165	4.88	
Berth No.35	200	8.84	
Berth No.36	166	9.14	
General Cargo Terminal			See [5] below
Berth No.37	180	8.53	
Berth No.38	180	8.53	
Pier VI Terminal			See [6] below
Berth No.39	165	9.75	
Berth No.40	194	10.06	
Berth No.41	167	7.31	
Berth No.42	192	9.14	
Berth No.43	185	9.14	
Cereals Terminal			See [7] below
Berth No.44	155	9.5	
Berth No.45	154	9.45	
Riva 71 - Cap 69/71			General cargo & ro/ro
Berth No.46	160	7.69	
Berth No.47	200	7.69	
Ferry Terminal - Mooring 57			Operated by Anek Lines, for traffic with Greece
Berth No.57	360	13.1	
Pier VII Container Terminal			See [8] below
Berth No.49	177	12.77	
Berth No.50	200	15.85	
Berth No.51	273	16.76	
Berth No.52	111	17.98	
Berth No.53	190	16.76	

Name	Length (m)	Draught (m)	Remarks
Berth No.54	190	14.93	
Berth No.55	163	14.93	
Coal Terminal			See [9] below
Berth No.52	395	17.37	
Scalo Legnami (Timber Terminal)			98 600 m2 of covered storage and 104 000 m2 of uncovered storage
Berth A	85	10	
Berth A1	120	10	
Berth B	150	11.58	
Industrial Port & Oil Harbour			
Steel Products Terminal			See [10] below
Berth A.F.S.	350	12.8	
Petrol Terminal			See [11] below
Berth No.1	450	16.46	
Berth No.2	450	16.46	
Berth No.3	450	16.46	
Berth No.4	450	16.46	
Oils Terminal			Combustible oils and gas oil unloading
San Sabbo 1	216	9.75	
San Sabbo 2	176	10.36	
Cement Terminal			Cement production and export
Italcementi	200	7.92	
Industrial Products Terminal			Industrial machinery production and export
Ortolan Mare	260	8.51	
Industrial Products II Terminal			Marine engine shipments
Grandi Motori	150	7.92	
Chemical Products Terminal			Methanol
Alder	50	6.99	
Frozen Products Terminal			Frozen fish unloading
Frigomar	145	7.62	
Oil Terminal			Gas oil and fuel unloading
Silone	141	6.4	
Silone Testata	200	10.36	

[1] *Livestock Terminal:* Operated by T.P. Service Srl, Tel: +39 040 672 8111, Fax: +39 040 672 8200, for transit of live animals
[2] *Adria Terminal:* Operated by Compagnia Portuale di Monfalcone, Tel: +39 0481 410417
Multi-purpose facility with 70 000 m2 of open storage area and warehouses of 20 000 m2. Equipped with three cranes of 16 t cap and two cranes of 30 t cap
[3] *Riva Traiana Terminal:* Ro/ro/ferry terminal with a 35 000 m2 storage yard, which is currently being extended to 90 000 m2
[4] *Pier V Terminal:* General cargo traffic. It includes 25 000 m2 of warehousing, other storage areas, food and liquid bulk silos and a yard for the storage, refurbishing and stuffing of containers
The fresh fruit terminal, operated by Terminal Frutta Trieste Srl, Tel: +39 040 311571, Fax: +39 040 311871, Email: info@tft.it, is equipped with refrigerated air plants for the conservation of fruit with total covered area of 25 000 m2
[5] *General Cargo Terminal:* Includes warehouse No's 55 and 58. Overall covered storage area of 12 000 m2 and a yard of 3000 m2 for the stacking, stuffing and unstuffing of containers
[6] *Pier VI Terminal:* Operated by Francesco Parisi SpA, Via Miramare 5, I-34135 Trieste, Tel: +39 040 419 3111, Fax: +39 040 44263, Email: trsinfo@francescoparisi.com, Website: www.francescoparisi.com
Multi-purpose terminal with 48 000 m2 of warehousing and 30 000 m2 of uncovered areas. Equipped with seven quay cranes of 8 t cap
[7] *Cereals Terminal:* Operated by Trieste Terminal Cereali Srl, Tel: +39 040 302928, Fax: +39 040 301287, Email: ttc@ttcereali.it
Equipped with 46 000 t cap silos, a mill for the processing of the finished product, a depot for the storage of goods, a pneumatic aspirator with a cap of 600 t/h and an automatic plant for the finished product loading with a cap of 2000 bags/h
[8] *Pier VII Container Terminal:* Operated by Trieste Marine Terminal SpA, Molo VII, Punto Franco Nuovo, I-34123 Trieste Tel: +39 040 318 6444, Fax: +39 040 318 6445, Email: info@trieste-marine-terminal.com, Website: www.trieste-marine-terminal.com
Covers a total area of 400 000 m2 and is equipped with seven post-panamax cranes and five reach stackers
[9] *Coal Terminal:* Coal drain plug for North Adriatic thermoelectric power plants
[10] *Steel Products Terminal:* Specializing in steel commerce and iron & steel production
[11] *Petrol Terminal:* Main wharf with two parallel branchs and moorings for supply ships. Max 250 000 t connected to the tanks yard with four pipelines by 42"

Bunkering: The port has 145 000 m3 of storage for fuel. Bunkering is carried out mainly by barges
Giuliana Bunkeraggi S.P.A., Via Lazzaretto Vecchio 9, 34123 Trieste, Italy, *Tel:* +39 040 303 808, *Fax:* +39 040 304 273, *Email:* giulianabunker@yahoo.it
AGIP Petroli S.p.A., ENI, Via Laurentina 449, 00142 Rome, Italy, *Tel:* +39 06 59881, *Fax:* +39 06 5988 5700, *Email:* gioacchino.costa@eni.it, *Website:* www.eni.it – *Grades:* GO; IFO – *Parcel Size:* no min/max – *Delivery Mode:* barge, pipeline
Giuliana Bunkeraggi S.p.A., Via Lazzaretto Vecchio 9, 34123 Trieste, Italy, *Tel:* +39 040 303 808, *Fax:* +39 040 304 273, *Email:* giulianabunker@yahoo.it
Marodi Service SAS, Via Decorati Al Valor Civile 80, 30173 Venice, Italy, *Tel:* +39 041 538 2143, *Fax:* +39 041 922841, *Email:* marodi@marodi.it, *Website:* www.marodi.it
Maxcom Bunker S.p.A. u.s., Via Bartolomeo Bosco 57/7B, 16121 Genoa, Italy, *Tel:* +39 010 5605 200, *Fax:* +39 010 564 479, *Email:* bunker@maxcombunker.com, *Website:* www.maxcombunker.com

Waste Reception Facilities: Available by a private company

Towage: Tripmare S.r.l., Via Felice Veniziani 1, 34124 Trieste, Italy, *Tel:* +39 040 308376, *Fax:* +39 040 309297, *Email:* tripmare@spin.it

---

Key to Principal Facilities:—

A=Airport	**C**=Containers	**G**=General Cargo
B=Bunkers	**D**=Dry Dock	**L**=Cruise

P=Petroleum	**R**=Ro/Ro	**Y**=Dry Bulk
Q=Other Liquid Bulk	**T**=Towage (where available from port)	

Ship Chandlers: Alberti S.r.l., P O Box 592, Punto Franco Vecchio 2 A, I-34100 Trieste, Italy, *Tel:* +39 040 778 5811, *Fax:* +39 040 778 5850, *Email:* alberti@alberti.it, *Website:* www.alberti.it

Barbagelata Adriatica S.r.l., Molo Bersaglieri 42, I-34124 Trieste, Italy, *Tel:* +39 040 300707, *Fax:* +39 040 311074, *Email:* trieste@barbagelatasupply.com

Domar S.r.l., Via dello Scalo Legnami 3 -3b, 34146 Trieste, Italy, *Tel:* +39 040 383238, *Fax:* +39 040 302101, *Email:* domar@domarsrl.it, *Website:* www.domarsrl.it

R S S.r.l., Strada di Monti d'Oro 12/1, 34147 Trieste, Italy, *Tel:* +39 040 282 0050, *Fax:* +39 040 282 0051, *Email:* info@rs-seaservice.com, *Website:* www.rs-seaservice.com

Shipping Agents: Agenzia Marittima Adriacostanzi S.r.l., Via Luigi Einaudi 3, I-34121 Trieste, Italy, *Tel:* +39 040 367646, *Fax:* +39 040 368706, *Email:* info@adriacostanzi.it, *Website:* www.adriacostanzi.it

Agenzia Marittima Alto Adriatico S.r.l., Via Flavia 60/1, I-34148 Trieste, Italy, *Tel:* +39 040 812711, *Fax:* +39 040 826682, *Email:* operativo@amaa.it, *Website:* www.amaa.it

Alessandro Billitz & Succ. S.r.l., Via Geppa 4, I-34132 Trieste, Italy, *Tel:* +39 040 37911, *Fax:* +39 040 361819, *Email:* info@billitztrieste.com, *Website:* www.billitztrieste.com

CMA-CGM S.A., CMA CGM Italy Srl, Via Valdirivio 6, I-34121 Trieste, Italy, *Tel:* +39 040 766276, *Fax:* +39 040 348 0578, *Email:* ste.genmbox@cma-cgm.com, *Website:* www.cma-cgm.com

Fratelli Cosulich Bunkers (S) Pte Ltd, Via Dante 5, 34122 Trieste, Italy, *Tel:* +39 040 679 7111, *Fax:* +39 040 679 7777, *Email:* info@ts.cosulich.it, *Website:* www.cosulich.it

Evergreen Shipping Agency (Italy), Passeggio S Andrea 4, I-34123 Trieste, Italy, *Tel:* +39 040 347 6231, *Fax:* +39 040 347 6228, *Email:* trs@evergreen-shipping.it, *Website:* www.evergreen-italy.it

Francesco Parisi SAGL, Francesco Parisi S.p.A., Viale Miramare 5, P O Box 577, 34135 Trieste, Italy, *Tel:* +39 040 419 3111, *Fax:* +39 040 44263, *Email:* trsinfo@francescoparisi.com, *Website:* www.francescoparisi.com

Greensisam S.p.A., Evergreen Shipping Agency (Italy) S.p.A., Passeggio Saintandrea No 4, I-34123 Trieste, Italy, *Tel:* +39 040 347 6231, *Fax:* +39 040 347 6228, *Email:* trs@evergreen-shipping.it

Inchcape Shipping Services (ISS), Piazza Dell'Unita' D' Italia 7, I-34121 Trieste, Italy, *Tel:* +39 040 6702 7375, *Fax:* +39 040 6702 7377, *Email:* trieste@iss-tositti.it, *Website:* www.iss-shipping.com

Italmar S.r.l., Passeggio S Andrea 4, I-34123 Trieste, Italy, *Tel:* +39 040 318 0300, *Fax:* +39 040 318 0388, *Email:* headoffice@italiamarittima.it, *Website:* www.italiamarittima.it

Agenzia Marittima Mediterranea S.r.l., Via Milano 4/1, I-34132 Trieste, Italy, *Tel:* +39 040 679 8711, *Fax:* +39 040 370328, *Email:* lenavi_ittrs@msclenavi.it, *Website:* www.msclenavi.it

Medmar S.p.A., Via Economou 1, 34123 Trieste, Italy, *Tel:* +39 040 312444, *Fax:* +39 040 322 0825, *Email:* medtrs@finsea.it

Navimar S.r.l., P. O. Box 464, 460407 Trieste, Italy, *Tel:* +39 040 365442, *Fax:* +39 040 365445, *Email:* info@navimar.it, *Website:* www.navimar.it

Samer & Co. Shipping Ltd, Piazza dell 'Unita d'Italia 7, I-34121 Trieste, Italy, *Tel:* +39 040 670 2711, *Fax:* +39 040 6702 7300, *Email:* samer@samer.com, *Website:* www.samer.com

Trimar S.r.l., Via Santa Caterina da Siena 7, I-34122 Trieste, Italy, *Tel:* +39 040 362535, *Fax:* +39 040 361981, *Email:* agency@trimar.it, *Website:* www.trimar.it

Wetzler S.r.l., Via C. Ghega 1, I-34132 Trieste, Italy, *Tel:* +39 040 770 7721, *Fax:* +39 040 368896, *Email:* info@wetzler.it, *Website:* www.wetzler.it

Wilhelmsen Ship Services, Riva Grumula 2, 34123 Trieste, Italy, *Tel:* +39 040 318 2111, *Fax:* +39 040 318 2177, *Email:* info@martinoli.com

Surveyors: Bureau Veritas, Via Della Geppa 9 - II piano, P O Box 550, I-34132 Trieste, Italy, *Tel:* +39 040 064 1590, *Fax:* +39 040 064 1618, *Email:* marine.trieste@it.bureauveritas.com, *Website:* www.bureauveritas.com

G.R. Dicovi & Associates, Via Cerreto 7/2, 34136 Trieste, Italy, *Tel:* +39 040 421718, *Fax:* +39 040 421718, *Email:* grdicovi@tin.it

Hellenic Register of Shipping, c/o Studio Ingegneria Navale Dott. Ing. C. Cosmidis, Vile 20 Settembre, 3, I-30125 Trieste, Italy, *Tel:* +39 040 639176, *Fax:* +39 040 633793, *Email:* cosnav.engineering@tin.it, *Website:* www.hrs.gr

Nippon Kaiji Kyokai, Trieste, Italy, *Tel:* +39 040 413666, *Fax:* +39 040 417536, *Website:* www.classnk.or.jp

Registro Italiano Navale (RINA), Viale Miramare 9, Trieste, Italy, *Tel:* +39 040 419 4911, *Fax:* +39 040 419 4922, *Email:* trieste.office@rina.org, *Website:* www.rina.org

Sim Co. VR, Via Genova 21, 34121 Trieste, Italy, *Tel:* +39 040 347 8167, *Fax:* +39 040 347 4294, *Email:* info@simcovr.it, *Website:* www.simcovr.it

Technifrance, Navaltecno, Via Mazzini 13, 34121 Trieste, Italy, *Tel:* +39 040 368524, *Fax:* +39 040 368572, *Website:* www.technifrance.com

Airport: Ronchi dei Legionari, 38 km

Railway: 70 km of track serving all quays, and fully connected to the Italian and European networks

Lloyd's Agent: Samer & Co. Shipping Ltd, Piazza dell 'Unita d'Italia 7, I-34121 Trieste, Italy, *Tel:* +39 040 670 2711, *Fax:* +39 040 6702 7300, *Email:* samer@samer.com, *Website:* www.samer.com

VADA

Lat 43° 21' N; Long 10° 27' E.

Admiralty Chart: 131	**Admiralty Pilot:** 46
Time Zone: GMT +1 h	**UNCTAD Locode:** IT VDA

Principal Facilities:

Q	G							

Authority: Capitaneria di Porto di Vada, I-57018 Vada, Italy, *Tel:* +39 0586 788121, *Fax:* +39 0586 788121, *Email:* vada@guardiacostiera.it

Officials: Harbour Master: Vincenzo Ferraro.

Port Security: ISPS compliant

Anchorage: One mile from shore in a depth of 22 m

Maximum Vessel Dimensions: 13 125 dwt, 141.8 m loa

Principal Imports and Exports: Imports: Coal, Raw materials. Exports: Petrochemical products, Sodium products.

Accommodation:

Name	Remarks
Vada	See [1] below

[1]*Vada:* Two piers, one used by LPG carriers extends 1.8 km from the shore with a berthing depth of 11 m. The smaller pier 140 m long is able to berth two vessels with a draft of 3.4 m. Several mooring buoys are located near the pierhead

Lloyd's Agent: Ditta Vincenzo Capanna S.a.S., Via Claudio Cogorano 25, P O Box 286, I-57123 Leghorn, Italy, *Tel:* +39 0586 894132, *Fax:* +39 0586 885332, *Email:* capanna@capanna.it, *Website:* www.capanna.it

VADO LIGURE

harbour area, see under Savona

VASTO

Lat 42° 6' N; Long 14° 43' E.

Admiralty Chart: -	**Admiralty Pilot:** 47
Time Zone: GMT +1 h	**UNCTAD Locode:** IT VSO

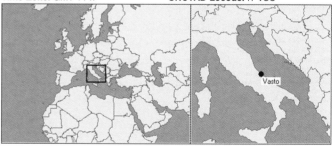

Principal Facilities:

P		Y	G			B		

Authority: Capitaneria di Porto di Vasto, Via Pennaluce 27, Loc. Punta Penna, I-66054 Vasto, Italy, *Tel:* +39 0873 310340, *Fax:* +39 0873 310322, *Email:* vasto@guardiacostiera.it

Officials: Harbour Master: Ivan Savarese.

Port Security: ISPS compliant

Pilotage: Compulsory for vessels over 500 gt and 60 m loa. Pilot boards 1 nautical mile NE of Punta Penna Lighthouse

Radio Frequency: Vessels must contact the Harbour Master on VHF Channel 16

Accommodation:

Name	Length (m)	Depth (m)	Remarks
Vasto			See [1] below
Banchina Ponente	270	6	
Banchina di Riva	300	5.3	

[1]*Vasto:* The harbour is formed by two moles, Molo di Levante 457 m long and Molo di Ponente 548 m long. Depth at entrance approx 7.5 m

Mechanical Handling Equipment:

Location	Type
Banchina Ponente	Mobile Cranes
Banchina di Riva	Mobile Cranes

Bunkering: Available by road tanker

Lloyd's Agent: Radonicich Insurance Services S.r.l., Via F. Orsini 6/A, Marghera, 30175 Venice, Italy, *Tel:* +39 041 538 2103, *Fax:* +39 041 926108, *Email:* radinsur@portofvenice.net

VENEZIA

alternate name, see Venice

VENICE

Lat 45° 26' N; Long 12° 20' E.

Admiralty Chart: 1442/1483
Time Zone: GMT +1 h

Admiralty Pilot: 47
UNCTAD Locode: IT VCE

Principal Facilities:

```
P Q Y G C R L B D T A
```

Authority: Autorita Portuale di Venezia, Zattere 1401, P O Box 745, I-30123 Venice, Italy, *Tel:* +39 041 533 4111, *Fax:* +39 041 533 4254, *Email:* apv@porto.venezia.it, *Website:* www.port.venice.it

Officials: President: Paolo Costa, *Email:* paolo.costa@porto.venezia.it.
General Secretary: Franco Sensini, *Tel:* +39 041 533 4225, *Email:* franco.sensini@port.venice.it.
Marketing Director: Capt Antonio Revedin, *Tel:* +39 041 533 4284, *Email:* antonio.revedin@port.venice.it.
Harbour Master: Admiral Gabriele Calcagno, *Tel:* +39 041 240 5711.

Port Security: ISPS compliant

Documentation: Crew list (4 copies), cargo manifest (2 copies), stores list (2 copies), light dues receipt of payment

Approach: The port of Venice which also includes Porto Marghera is situated in the lagoon area between Lido Port entrance and the port entrance of Malamocco and embraces all the canals leading from the entrances to the dry docks. Venice Marittima Commercial Docks, Porto Marghera and S Leonardo Terminal (crude oil). The Malamocco-Porto Marghera canal already serving S Leonardo Terminal with a 13.7 m d, has been dredged from S Leonardo to Porto Marghera to 9.0 m d for vessels with max 25 m beam, 8.85 m d for vessels with 25-27 m beam and 8.7 m d for vessels with 27-30 m beam. Vessels over 30 m the max draft allowed to be agreed with Harbour Masters Office

Anchorage: Available 5 miles N of Porto di Lido entrance in average depth of 17 m

Pilotage: Compulsory and available from Corporazione Piloti Estuario Veneto, *Tel:* +39 041 220 7011, *Fax:* +39 041 731313

Radio Frequency: VHF Channel 13 (Pilot Station)

Weather: Prevailing N winds during the winter months, E winds in the summer. There are eight days of dense fog per year on average

Tides: The average rise of tide within the lagoon is 0.5 m, 0.7 m MST, 0.3 m MNT

Traffic: 2007, 30 194 845 t of cargo handled, 329 510 TEU's

Principal Imports and Exports: Imports: Chemicals, Coal, Crude oil, Grain, Steel products. Exports: Project cargo, Steel products, Wheat flour.

Working Hours: Monday to Friday 0800-1200, 1300-1700. Saturday 0800-1430

Accommodation:

Name	Length (m)	Depth (m)	Remarks
Venice			
Terminal Intermodale Venezia Srl (TIV)	1925	10	See [1] below

Name	Length (m)	Depth (m)	Remarks
Terminal Molo B Srl (TMB)	2363	11	See [2] below
Terminal Rinfuse Marghera Srl (TRM)	255	10	See [3] below
Pagnan SpA	297	11	See [4] below
Silos Granari del Veneto	185	9	See [5] below
Centro Intermodale Adriatico SpA (CIA)	178	9	See [6] below
Multi Service Srl	606	10	See [7] below
Venezia Terminal Passeggeri SpA			See [8] below

[1]*Terminal Intermodale Venezia Srl (TIV):* Porto Commerciale Marghera Molo A, I-30175 Marghera, Tel: +39 041 533 4651, Fax: +39 041 533 4443, Email: tiv.info@tiv.it, Website: www.tiv.it
Consists of four berths (Veneto, Trento, Bolzano & Lombardia) handling containers, scrap iron, project cargo, forest products, marble blocks & steel products
[2]*Terminal Molo B Srl (TMB):* Tel: +39 041 533 4484, Fax: +39 041 533 4577
Consists of four berths (Aosta, Piemonte, Romagna & Emilia) handling cereals, meals, coal & bulk liquids. Grain silo of 135 000 t cap
[3]*Terminal Rinfuse Marghera Srl (TRM):* Via delle Industrie 52, I-30175 Marghera, Tel: +39 041 251 7111, Fax: +39 041 251 7100, Email: info@trm.venezia.it, Website: www.trm.venezia.it
Consists of two berths (1N & 2N) handling coal, coke, ore & silver sand. Grain silo of 10 000 t cap
[4]*Pagnan SpA:* Consists of two berths (1S & 2S) handling agricultural products in bulk. Silo of 120 000 t cap
[5]*Silos Granari del Veneto:* Consists of one berth (1W) handling wheat in bulk & bagged wheat flour. Silo of 26 000 t cap
[6]*Centro Intermodale Adriatico SpA (CIA):* Tel: +39 041 259 1100, Fax: +39 041 259 1220, Email: cia@portofvenice.net
Consists of one berth (Cia W) handling bulk cargo, steel products & fertilizer. Silo of 42 500 t cap
[7]*Multi Service Srl:* Consists of two berths (Friuli & Cadore) handling agricultural products, steel products & scrap iron. Two mobile and one quayside crane
[8]*Venezia Terminal Passeggeri SpA:* Fabbricato 248, Marittima, I-30135 Venice, Tel: +39 041 240 3000, Fax: +39 041 240 3091, Email: vtp@vtp.it, Website: www.vtp.it
Operates in the Marittima and S. Basilio areas with total quay length of 3039 m (six piers and twelve berths)
The Ferry Terminal 123 assists ferries for the Eastern Mediterranean area
The San Basilio Terminal accommodates medium-size cruise ships, mega-yachts and high speed hydrofoils
Cruise Terminals 103, 107/108 and 117 in the Marittima area are multi-purpose facilities which, additionally to their original purpose, are utilised for hosting meetings, conventions and fairs

Bunkering: Marodi Service SAS, Via Decorati Al Valor Civile 80, 30173 Venice, Italy, *Tel:* +39 041 538 2143, *Fax:* +39 041 922841, *Email:* marodi@marodi.it, *Website:* www.marodi.it
AGIP Petroli S.p.A., ENI, Via Laurentina 449, 00142 Rome, Italy, *Tel:* +39 06 59881, *Fax:* +39 06 5988 5700, *Email:* gioacchino.costa@eni.it, *Website:* www.eni.it
Esso Italiano S.p.A., Via dei Petroli, 30010 Venice, Italy, *Tel:* +39 041 531 5595
ExxonMobil Marine Fuels, Mailpoint 31, ExxonMobil House, Ermyn Way, Leatherhead, Surrey KT22 8UX, United Kingdom, *Tel:* +44 1372 222 000, *Fax:* +44 1372 223 922, *Email:* marine.fuels@exxonmobil.com, *Website:* www.exxonmobil.com – *Grades:* IF180-380 cSt; MGO – *Misc:* own storage facilities – *Parcel Size:* no min – *Rates:* 200-300t/h – *Notice:* 24 hours – *Delivery Mode:* barge, truck
Marodi Service SAS, Via Decorati Al Valor Civile 80, 30173 Venice, Italy, *Tel:* +39 041 538 2143, *Fax:* +39 041 922841, *Email:* marodi@marodi.it, *Website:* www.marodi.it – *Grades:* all grades
Maxcom Bunker S.p.A. u.s., Via Bartolomeo Bosco 57/7B, 16121 Genoa, Italy, *Tel:* +39 010 5605 200, *Fax:* +39 010 564 479, *Email:* bunker@maxcombunker.com, *Website:* www.maxcombunker.com – *Grades:* MGO; IFO40-380cSt – *Misc:* own storage facilities – *Parcel Size:* max 1000t – *Notice:* 12-24 hours – *Delivery Mode:* barge

Waste Reception Facilities: Specialised firms available for waste disposal

Towage: Rimorchiatori Riuniti Panfido & Co. S.r.l., Riva degli Schiavoni 4164, 30122 Venice, Italy, *Tel:* +39 041 520 4422, *Fax:* +39 041 522 3561, *Email:* cmv@rrpanfido.it

Repair & Maintenance: Venice Drydocks, Castello 2737/F, 30122 Venice, Italy, *Tel:* +39 041 798511, *Fax:* +39 041 277 6457, *Email:* cav@cav-venezia.it Three dry docks available for vessels up to 75 000 t, 20 000 t and 3000 t dwt; also 550 m of repair berths

Ship Chandlers: Barbagelata Adriatica S.r.l., Via Elettricita 20, I-30175 Venice, Italy, *Tel:* +39 041 921033, *Fax:* +39 041 926273, *Email:* venezia@barbagelatasupply.com
Ligabue Catering SLL, Piazzale Roma 499, I-30135 Venice, Italy, *Tel:* +39 041 270 5611, *Fax:* +39 041 270 5661, *Email:* ligabue@ligabue.it, *Website:* www.ligabue.it
Provveditoria Marittima Sonino S.r.l., Punto Franco Dorsoduro 1826/A, I-30123 Venice, Italy, *Tel:* +39 041 520 0111, *Fax:* +39 041 520 0313, *Email:* sonino@portofvenice.net, *Website:* www.sonino.net

Shipping Agents: Bassani S.p.A., San Basilio - Santa Marta - Fabbricato 17, I-30123 Venice, Italy, *Tel:* +39 041 522 7244, *Fax:* +39 041 523 0336, *Email:* shipping@bassani.it, *Website:* www.bassani.it
Cattaruzza Shipping & Co. S.r.l., Via dell'Atomo 8/6, I-30175 Venice, Italy, *Tel:* +39 041 921620, *Fax:* +39 041 538 3145, *Email:* agency@cattaruzza.com, *Website:* www.cattaruzza.com
CMA-CGM S.A., CMA CGM Italy Srl, Via A Volta 2, I-30175 Venice, Italy, *Tel:* +39 041 369 7111, *Fax:* +39 041 3697 1205, *Email:* svz.genmbox@cma-cgm.com, *Website:* www.cma-cgm.com
Fratelli Cosulich Bunkers (S) Pte Ltd, Via Banchina dell'Azoto 15/A, Marghera, 30175 Venice, Italy, *Tel:* +39 041 509 8011, *Fax:* +39 041 509 8025, *Email:* info@ve.cosulich.it, *Website:* www.cosulich.it
Duodo & Co. S.n.c., Via delle Macchine 49, I-30175 Marghera, Italy, *Tel:* +39 041 291 1911, *Fax:* +39 041 291 1930, *Email:* duodo@duodo.com, *Website:* www.duodo.com
Elmar Shipping Agency, Straniero Francesco Viale San Marco 90/B, I-30173 Mestre, Italy, *Tel:* +39 041 504 0527, *Fax:* +39 041 504 0929, *Email:* agency@elmarshipping.com, *Website:* www.elmarshipping.com
Greensisam S.p.A., Evergreen Shipping Agency (Italy) S.p.A., 9 Via Dell Elettricita, I-

30175 Venice, Italy, *Tel:* +39 041 538 1288, *Fax:* +39 041 538 1308, *Email:* vns@evergreen-shipping.it

Inchcape Shipping Services (ISS), ISS-Tositti Srl, Santa Marta Punto Franco, Fabbricato 17, I-30123 Venice, Italy, *Tel:* +39 041 271 2647, *Fax:* +39 041 271 2648, *Email:* venezia@iss-tositti.it, *Website:* www.iss-shipping.com

Marittima Ravennate S.p.A., Via D. Manin 43, Mestre, 30174 Venice, Italy, *Tel:* +39 041 504 0827, *Fax:* +39 041 505 8246, *Email:* mail@marittimaravennate.com, *Website:* www.marittimaravennate.com

Marodi Service SAS, Via Decorati Al Valor Civile 80, 30173 Venice, Italy, *Tel:* +39 041 538 2143, *Fax:* +39 041 922841, *Email:* marodi@marodi.it, *Website:* www.marodi.it

Medmar S.p.A., S Marta, Porto Franco Fabbricato 17, 30123 Venice, Italy, *Tel:* +39 041 271 2658, *Fax:* +39 041 271 2522, *Email:* medmarcom@vegaservice.net, *Website:* www.finsea.it

Servizi Portuali Adriatico S.r.l., Via Jacopo Salamonio 3/6, I-30175 Marghera, Italy, *Tel:* +39 041 538 3136, *Fax:* +39 041 538 3145, *Email:* info@spashippingagency.com, *Website:* www.spashippingagency.com

Traspedi SNC, Dorsoduro 1826, 30123 Venice, Italy, *Tel:* +39 041 521 0733, *Fax:* +39 041 541 0631, *Email:* traspedi@tin.it

Wilhelmsen Ship Services, San Basilio I, Santa Marta, Fabbricato 17, 30123 Venice, Italy, *Tel:* +39 041 272 7860, *Fax:* +39 041 523 0336, *Email:* shipping@bassani.it, *Website:* www.bassani.it

Surveyors: Studio Sandro Cedolini, Venice, Italy, *Tel:* +39 041 538 3150, *Fax:* +39 041 538 4070

Hellenic Register of Shipping, c/o Udicer/Nautitest S.a.s., Via Riviera del Brenta 12, Fiesso d'Artico, I-30032 Venice, Italy, *Tel:* +39 041 516 1880, *Fax:* +39 041 516 9478, *Email:* udicer@iol.it, *Website:* www.hrs.gr

Marine Surveys S.r.l., Venice, Italy, *Tel:* +39 041 528 6023, *Fax:* +39 041 528 6023

Radonicich Insurance Services S.r.l., Via F. Orsini 6/A, Marghera, 30175 Venice, Italy, *Tel:* +39 041 538 2103, *Fax:* +39 041 926108, *Email:* radinsur@portofvenice.net

Studio Tecnico Navale Giorgett, Cannaregio 3837/a, 30100 Venice, Italy, *Tel:* +39 041 698544, *Fax:* +39 041 698951, *Email:* stng@stng.it

Medical Facilities: Umberto Primo General Hospital, 2 km

Airport: Marco Polo International Airport, 15 km

Railway: State Railway SpA, 2 km

Lloyd's Agent: Radonicich Insurance Services S.r.l., Via F. Orsini 6/A, Marghera, 30175 Venice, Italy, *Tel:* +39 041 538 2103, *Fax:* +39 041 926108, *Email:* radinsur@portofvenice.net

VITTORIO VENETO DOCK

harbour area, see under Naples

ZANAGORA DOCK

harbour area, see under Siracusa

IVORY COAST

ABIDJAN

Lat 5° 18' N; Long 4° 0' W.

Admiralty Chart: 3101/3103

Admiralty Pilot: 1

Time Zone: GMT

UNCTAD Locode: CI ABJ

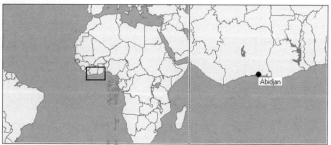

Principal Facilities:

| P | Q | Y | G | C | R | | B | D | T | A |

Authority: Port Autonome d'Abidjan, P O Box V85, Abidjan, Ivory Coast, *Tel:* +225 2123 8000, *Fax:* +225 2123 8080, *Email:* info@paa-ci.org, *Website:* www.paa-ci.org

Officials: General Manager: Marcel Gossio.
Harbour Master: Fally Tia Paul.

Port Security: ISPS compliant

Approach: Depth at entrance 13.5 m. Depth on bar 13.5 m. Max draft allowed is 10.37 m for inward vessels and 10.67 m for outward vessels

Anchorage: Eighteen mooring berths

Pilotage: Compulsory and 24 h/day for vessels of more than 150 nrt. VHF Channels 16, 12 and 13

Traffic: 2006, 18 656 000 t of cargo handled

Maximum Vessel Dimensions: 260 m loa, 12.5 m depth

Principal Imports and Exports: Exports: Cocoa nibs, Coffee beans, Cotton in fibre, Processed timber.

Working Hours: Administration: Mon to Fri 0730-1200, 1430-1730. Other hours in overtime. Port Services: 24 h/day

Accommodation:

Name	Remarks
Abidjan	See [1] below

[1]*Abidjan:* Also serves the landlocked states of Mali (by truck only), Burkina Faso and Niger (both by rail and/or truck)
Twenty eight quay berths totalling 4.6 km including several specialized berths for fertilizers, phosphates, hydrocarbons and oil. Also some terminals for containers, timber and fruit and veg
Container & ro/ro facilities: five berths (No's 21-25) stretching over 800 m for container handling. Berth No.22 in depth of 11.5 m. Berths 23-24 in depth of 12.5 m. Berth No.25 in depth of 12.5 m is equipped with a ro/ro ramp. Equipment at the terminal includes three 40 t container gantry cranes; 25 ha of paved yards
Bulk facilities:Discharge of grain by elevators and belt conveyors at Berth No.1. Palm oil loaded at Berth No.16. Facilities also for handling wine in bulk
There is also a fishing port 1050 m long equipped with quayside amenities like water, electricity and gas oil
All the quays are connected to the road and rail network

Storage:

Location	Open (m²)	Covered (m²)
Abidjan	378678	142826

Mechanical Handling Equipment:

Location	Type	Capacity (t)	Qty
Abidjan	Mobile Cranes		
Abidjan	Container Cranes	40	3

Cargo Worked: A min of 500 t of cargo/day must be worked on the quayside; vessels handling less than this or lying idle during overtime periods may be required to shift berth at their own expense in favour of vessels wishing to work over 500 t of cargo

Bunkering: Fuel, diesel, gas oil and lubes available by barge at inner anchorage, and by bunker tanker on roads off Abidjan

Shell Cote d'Ivoire, Rue des Petroliers, Abidjan, Ivory Coast, *Tel:* +225 369 366, *Fax:* +225 358 499

Societe Ivoirienne de Raffinage, P O Box 1269, Abidjan 01, Ivory Coast, *Tel:* +225 237 126, *Fax:* +225 232 856

Societe Ivoirienne (SITRAM), P O Box 1546, Rue de Petroliers, Abidjan, Ivory Coast, *Tel:* +225 369 200

Addax Bunkering Services, c/o Addax BV, 12 Rue Michel-Servet, P O Box 404, 1211 Geneva 12, Switzerland, *Tel:* +41 22 702 9040, *Fax:* +41 22 702 9100, *Email:* abs@aogltd.com – *Grades:* MDO; MGO; HFO; IFO

Bominflot, Bominflot Ltd, 5-7 Ravensbourne Road, Bromley, Kent BR1 1HN, United Kingdom, *Tel:* +44 20 8315 5400, *Fax:* +44 20 8315 5429, *Email:* mail@bominflot.co.uk, *Website:* www.bominflot.net – *Grades:* MDO; MGO; HFO; IFO

BP France S.A., Immeuble le Cervier, 12 Avenue des Beguines, Cergy-Saint-Christophe, 95866 Cergy Pontoise Cedex, France, *Tel:* +33 1 3422 4000, *Fax:* +33 1 3422 4417, *Email:* benoist.grosjean@fr.bp.com, *Website:* www.bpmarine.com – *Grades:* MDO; MGO; HFO; IFO

ExxonMobil Marine Fuels, Mailpoint 31, ExxonMobil House, Ermyn Way, Leatherhead, Surrey KT22 8UX, United Kingdom, *Tel:* +44 1372 222 000, *Fax:* +44 1372 223 922, *Email:* marine.fuels@exxonmobil.com, *Website:* www.exxonmobil.com – *Grades:* IF180; MGO – *Delivery Mode:* barge, pipeline

Shell Cote d'Ivoire, Rue des Petroliers, Abidjan, Ivory Coast, *Tel:* +225 369 366, *Fax:* +225 358 499 – *Grades:* MDO; MGO; HFO; IFO

Societe Ivoirienne de Raffinage, P O Box 1269, Abidjan 01, Ivory Coast, *Tel:* +225 237 126, *Fax:* +225 232 856 – *Grades:* MDO; MGO; HFO; IFO

Societe Ivoirienne (SITRAM), P O Box 1546, Rue de Petroliers, Abidjan, Ivory Coast, *Tel:* +225 369 200 – *Grades:* MDO; MGO; HFO; IFO

Total France S.A., Total Marine Fuels, 51 Esplanade du General de Gaulle, F-92907 Paris la Defense Cedex 10, France, *Tel:* +33 1 4135 2755, *Fax:* +33 1 4197 0291, *Email:* marine.fuels@total.com, *Website:* www.marinefuels.total.com – *Grades:* MDO; MGO; HFO; IFO

Towage: Ivoirienne de Remorquage et de Sauvetage (IRES), Station Capitainerie du Port 01, P O Box 38, Abidjan 01, Ivory Coast, *Tel:* +225 2124 0189, *Fax:* +225 2124 1627

Repair & Maintenance: Compagnie Abidjanaise de Reparations Navales et de Travaux Industriels (CARENA), P O Box 453, Abidjan, Ivory Coast, *Tel:* +225 2022 2227, *Fax:* +225 2021 6056, *Email:* carena@carena-ci.com, *Website:* www.carena-ci.com

Ship Chandlers: Benya Shipping S.A., P O Box 220, Abidjan 05, Ivory Coast, *Tel:* +225 2124 1686, *Fax:* +225 2124 1933, *Email:* ekabenya@globeaccess.net
CIAM, 15 P O Box 593, Abidjan 15, Ivory Coast, *Tel:* +225 2127 5343, *Fax:* +225 2127 5349, *Email:* ciam@ciam-ci.com
Kumasan Ship Services, 16 P O Box 1871, Abidjan 16, Ivory Coast, *Tel:* +225 2135 5574, *Fax:* +225 2135 8436, *Email:* kumasan@aviso.ci
SERAMAR, P O Box 23, 23 Treion Ville, Abidjan 784, Ivory Coast, *Tel:* +225 2124 6659, *Fax:* +225 2124 6659, *Email:* infoseramar@yahoo.fr

Shipping Agents: AMICI-International Maritime Agency of Cote d'Ivoire, Km 1 Boulevard de Marseille 16, P O Box 643, Abidjan 16, Ivory Coast, *Tel:* +225 2135 2850, *Fax:* +225 2135 2853, *Email:* amicisn.abj@afnet.net
Benya Shipping S.A., P O Box 220, Abidjan 05, Ivory Coast, *Tel:* +225 2124 1686, *Fax:* +225 2124 1933, *Email:* ekabenya@globeaccess.net
GETMA Ivory Coast S.A., Boulevard de Vridi 18, P O Box 3298, Abidjan 18, Ivory Coast, *Tel:* +225 2175 5165, *Fax:* +225 2175 5160, *Email:* p.pilarczyk@getma-ci.com, *Website:* www.getma.fr
Hull Blyth Group, Hull Blyth Cote d'Ivoire Ltd, P O Box 1569, Abidjan 01, Ivory Coast, *Tel:* +225 2121 8600, *Fax:* +225 2125 0504, *Email:* commercial@hull-blyth.com, *Website:* www.hull-blyth.com
Mediterranean Shipping Company, MSC Cote d'Ivoirie, Treichville Zone Portuaire, Rue des Gallions, Abidjan, Ivory Coast, *Tel:* +225 2175 6666, *Fax:* +225 2175 6660, *Email:* info@mscci.mscgva.ch, *Website:* www.mscgva.ch
A.P. Moller-Maersk Group, Maersk Cote d'Ivorie S.A., Boulevard de Vridi, Zone Portuaire, P O Box 6939, Abidjan, Ivory Coast, *Tel:* +225 2121 9100, *Fax:* +225 2121 9110, *Website:* www.maerskline.com
SDV Cote d'Ivoire, Avenue Christiani Treichville, P O Box 4082, Abidjan 01, Ivory Coast, *Tel:* +225 2122 0420, *Fax:* +225 2122 0790, *Email:* sdvabj-dept.commercial@ci.dti.bollore.com
Socopao-Cote d'Ivoire S.A., Boulevard De Vridi, Concession Ex Hino, P O Box 1297, Abidjan 01, Ivory Coast, *Tel:* +225 2124 4654, *Fax:* +225 2124 2130, *Email:* socapao@aviso.ci
Supermaritime Benin S.A., Treichville Zone 2, Locaux ex-Bracodi, Abidjan, Ivory Coast, *Tel:* +225 2175 4666, *Fax:* +225 2175 4370, *Email:* supmarci@aviso.ci, *Website:* www.supermaritime.com

Stevedoring Companies: Benya Shipping S.A., P O Box 220, Abidjan 05, Ivory Coast, *Tel:* +225 2124 1686, *Fax:* +225 2124 1933, *Email:* ekabenya@globeaccess.net
GETMA Ivory Coast S.A., Boulevard de Vridi 18, P O Box 3298, Abidjan 18, Ivory Coast, *Tel:* +225 2175 5165, *Fax:* +225 2175 5160, *Email:* p.pilarczyk@getma-ci.com, *Website:* www.getma.fr

Surveyors: Bureau Veritas, P O Box 1453, Abidjan, Ivory Coast, *Tel:* +225 2031 2500, *Fax:* +225 2022 7715, *Website:* www.bureauveritas.com
Camis-CI, P O Box 2122, Abidjan, Ivory Coast, *Tel:* +225 2124 4714, *Fax:* +225 2124 4718, *Email:* t.massiot@camis-ci.com
Control Union CI, P O Box 2655, Abidjan 01, Ivory Coast, *Tel:* +225 2127 0555, *Fax:* +225 2127 0491, *Email:* controlunion@aviso.ci
Nippon Kaiji Kyokai, P O Box 1033, Abidjan, Ivory Coast, *Tel:* +225 2021 2015, *Fax:* +225 2022 5188, *Website:* www.classnk.or.jp
Omega Marine Cote d'Ivoire, P O Box 2997, Treichville, Zone 2 A Boulevard de Marseille, Abidjan, Ivory Coast, *Tel:* +225 2135 5216, *Fax:* +225 2135 7804, *Email:* omega-ivorycoast@omega-marine.com, *Website:* www.omega-marine.com

Airport: Abidjan/Felix Houphouet-Boigny, 8 km

Lloyd's Agent: Omega Marine Cote d'Ivoire, P O Box 2997, Treichville, Zone 2 A Boulevard de Marseille, Abidjan, Ivory Coast, *Tel:* +225 2135 5216, *Fax:* +225 2135 7804, *Email:* omega-ivorycoast@omega-marine.com, *Website:* www.omega-marine.com

BAOBAB TERMINAL

Lat 4° 58' N; Long 4° 33' W.

Admiralty Chart: 3101/3103	**Admiralty Pilot:** 1
Time Zone: GMT	**UNCTAD Locode:** CI

Principal Facilities:

P										

Pre-Arrival Information: ETA should be sent at least 7 days prior to arrival and thence 72 h, 48 h and 24 h in advance to the terminal and to the Abidjan Port Authority

Anchorage: The designated anchorage is a circular area of radius 1 mile centred on pos 5° 04.1' N; 4° 23.4' W

Pilotage: Compulsory. Vessel's are boarded by the Mooring Master approx 2 nautical miles from the terminal

Radio Frequency: VHF Channel 74

Maximum Vessel Dimensions: 60 000 dwt, max bow to manifold distance 172 m

Accommodation:

Name	Remarks
Baobab Marine Terminal	See [1] below

[1]*Baobab Marine Terminal:* Operated by MODEC International LLC. Consists of FPSO 'Baobab Ivoirien MV10', turret-moored in a depth of 970 m, approx 13 miles offshore and 38 miles WSW of Abidjan. Berthing operations, weather permitting, are conducted during daylight hours only; unberthing is permitted at any time. Vessels are moored in tandem, bow to stern, and loading is by means of a floating hose arrangement between the FPSO and the tanker. Storage cap of 2 000 000 bbls

Lloyd's Agent: Omega Marine Cote d'Ivoire, P O Box 2997, Treichville, Zone 2 A Boulevard de Marseille, Abidjan, Ivory Coast, *Tel:* +225 2135 5216, *Fax:* +225 2135 7804, *Email:* omega-ivorycoast@omega-marine.com, *Website:* www.omega-marine.com

SAN PEDRO

Lat 4° 44' N; Long 6° 37' W.

Admiralty Chart: 3099	**Admiralty Pilot:** 1
Time Zone: GMT	**UNCTAD Locode:** CI SPY

Principal Facilities:

Q	Y	G	C	R			T	A

Authority: Port Autonome de San Pedro, P O Box 339/340, San Pedro, Ivory Coast, *Tel:* +225 3471 7200, *Fax:* +225 3471 7215, *Email:* direction@sanpedro-portci.com, *Website:* www.sanpedro-portci.com

Officials: Managing Director: Desire Dallo, *Email:* dallo@sanpedro-portci.com. Commercial Director: Guy Manouan, *Email:* gmanouan@sanpedro-portci.com. Harbour Master: Noe Pierre, *Email:* pnoe@pasp.ci.

Port Security: ISPS compliant

Approach: Approach channel 650 m long, 150 m wide in depth of 13.5 m. The port is protected by the 145 m Eastern Pier and 65 m Western Pier

Anchorage: Anchorage area 1 mile around entrance buoy in depth of 10.4 m

Pilotage: Compulsory. Three pilots available. VHF Channels 12 and 16

Tides: Range of tide 1.5 m

Traffic: 2005, 1 001 991 t of cargo handled, 49 271 TEU's

Maximum Vessel Dimensions: 25 000 dwt, loa 220 m, 9.8 m d

Principal Imports and Exports: Imports: Clinker, Fertiliser, Fish, Gypsum, Rice. Exports: Citrus fruit, Coffee, Cotton, Palm oil, Sugar, Timber.

Working Hours: Mon to Fri 0730-1200, 1430-1800. Sat 0730-1200

Accommodation:

Name	Length (m)	Depth (m)	Remarks
San Pedro			See [1] below
South Quay	155	9	
West Quay	581	11	
Service Quay	104	4	
Cement Berth	200	11	
Timber Quay	160	4	

[1]*San Pedro:* There are also five SBM's for loading timber varying from 100-200 m with depth of 11.0 m

Storage:

Location	Covered (m²)	Sheds / Warehouses
San Pedro	13800	3

Towage: Compulsory. One tug available up to 1300 hp

Shipping Agents: AMICI-International Maritime Agency of Cote d'Ivoire, P O Box 1839, San Pedro, Ivory Coast, *Tel:* +225 3471 4743, *Fax:* +225 3471 4742, *Email:* amici.spy@aviso.ci, *Website:* www.amici-shipping.com
Geodis Overseas Cote d'Ivoire, BP 541, Entree Principale du Port de San Pedro, San Pedro, Ivory Coast, *Tel:* +225 3471 2164, *Fax:* +225 3431 6205, *Email:* shipping.shp@geodis.ci, *Website:* www.geodis.ci
GETMA Ivory Coast S.A., San Pedro, Ivory Coast, *Tel:* +225 3471 1348, *Fax:* +225 3471 2985, *Email:* spedro@getma.ci, *Website:* www.getma.fr

Key to Principal Facilities:—				
A=Airport	**C**=Containers	**G**=General Cargo	**P**=Petroleum	**R**=Ro/Ro	**Y**=Dry Bulk
B=Bunkers	**D**=Dry Dock	**L**=Cruise	**Q**=Other Liquid Bulk	**T**=Towage (where available from port)	

A.P. Moller-Maersk Group, Maersk Cote d'Ivorie S.A., Zone Portuaire, P O Box 2091, San Pedro, Ivory Coast, *Tel:* +225 3471 4514, *Fax:* +225 3471 1301, *Email:* sp0sal@maersk.com, *Website:* www.maerskline.com

SDV Cote d'Ivoire, Avenue d'Italie, BP 369, San Pedro, Ivory Coast, *Tel:* +225 3471 1589, *Fax:* +225 3471 1567, *Email:* sdv-spy@aviso.ci

Sivom Shipping, P O Box 217, San Pedro, Ivory Coast, *Tel:* +225 3471 2060, *Fax:* +225 3471 2700, *Email:* poolshipping@sivomspy.ci

Socopao-Cote d'Ivoire S.A., Boulevard du Port, P O Box 363, San Pedro, Ivory Coast, *Tel:* +225 3471 1589, *Fax:* +225 3471 1567, *Email:* sdv-spy@aviso.ci

Supermaritime Benin S.A., 01 BP 1744, San Pedro, Ivory Coast, *Tel:* +225 3471 8645, *Fax:* +225 3471 8645, *Email:* supmarci@aviso.ci

Airport: 7 km from port

Lloyd's Agent: Omega Marine Cote d'Ivoire, P O Box 2997, Treichville, Zone 2 A Boulevard de Marseille, Abidjan, Ivory Coast, *Tel:* +225 2135 5216, *Fax:* +225 2135 7804, *Email:* omega-ivorycoast@omega-marine.com, *Website:* www.omega-marine.com

JAMAICA

KINGSTON

Lat 17° 59' N; Long 76° 49' W.

Admiralty Chart: 454	**Admiralty Pilot:** 70
Time Zone: GMT -5 h	**UNCTAD Locode:** JM KIN

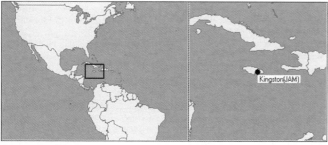

Kingston[JAM]

Principal Facilities:

P		Y	G	C	R	L	B	D	T	A

Authority: Port Authority of Jamaica, 15-17 Duke Street, Kingston, Jamaica, *Tel:* +1876 922 0290/8, *Fax:* +1876 924 9437, *Email:* paj@portjam.com, *Website:* www.portjam.com

Officials: Chief Executive Officer: Noel A. Hylton, *Email:* nhylton@portjam.com. Vice President: Rosalie Donaldson, *Email:* rdonaldson@portjam.com. Harbour Master: Capt Hopeton Delisser, *Email:* hdelisser@portjam.com.

Port Security: ISPS compliant. Container Security Initiative (CSI) designated port

Approach: East Channel is approx 220 m wide in depth of 17.7 m
Ship Channel in depth of 13.7 m

Pilotage: Compulsory, *Tel:* +1 876 922 5749

Radio Frequency: Kingston Radio on VHF Channel 16 and Pilotage on VHF Channel 11
Kingston Radio call sign '6YI' keeps continuous watch and operates 24 h/day

Traffic: 2007, 2653 vessels, 17 795 135 t of cargo handled

Maximum Vessel Dimensions: 320 m loa, 13 m draft

Working Hours: Weekdays, Sundays and holidays 0700-1400, 1400-2100, 2100-0600. Saturdays 0700-1400

Accommodation:

Name	Length (m)	Depth (m)	Draught (m)	Remarks
Public Wharves				See [1] below
Berth No.1	160	7.62	6.72	
Berth No.2	182.8	9.14	8.25	
Berth No.3	182.8	10.06	9.16	
Berth No.4	182.8	10.36	9.47	
Berth No.5	182.8	10.06	9.16	
Berth No.6	182.8	9.75	8.86	
Berth No.7	182.8	10.06	9.16	
Berth No's 8 & 9		15		See [2] below
North Container Terminal (Port Bustamante)	413	15.2		Two berths. 47 ha of yard space for stacking containers
South Container Terminal (Gordon Cay)	1220	14		Four berths. 82 ha (25 ha unpaved) of container storage space
Private Wharves				
Esso Standard Dry Cargo Pier				See [3] below
Caribbean Cement Co Pier	152		8.4	Loading of cement and discharge of coal
Shell Co Pier			9.1	See [4] below
Jamaica Gypsum Pier			8.5	See [5] below

Name	Length (m)	Depth (m)	Draught (m)	Remarks
Wherry Wharf			6.7	See [6] below
Rapid Sheffield Wharf			6.7	See [7] below
Texaco Caribbean Pier			7.5	See [8] below

[1]*Public Wharves:* Multi-purpose terminal handling ro/ro, lo/lo, container, general break bulk and bulk shipping services, operated by Kingston Wharves Ltd.,Third Street, New Port West, Kingston, Tel: +1876 923 9211, Fax: +1876 923 5361, Email: kingstonwharves@kwljm.com, Website: www.kingstonwharves.com.jm. A continuous quay nearly 1600 m long provides nine deepwater berths. The 25 ha terminal offers 22 ha of open storage with 30 000 m2 of covered warehousing and cold storage. The company also has 53 000 m2 of secure off-dock storage for motor vehicles
North and South Container Terminals operated by APM Terminals (Jamaica) Ltd., P O Box 1122, GPO Kingston, Port Bustamante, Tel: +1876 923 5141, Fax: +1876 923 6678
[2]*Berth No's 8 & 9:* Being rebuilt and expanded to handle container vessels
[3]*Esso Standard Dry Cargo Pier:* Import of petroleum products and bulk fertiliser for vessels up to 113 m loa and 5.8 m draft
[4]*Shell Co Pier:* Bulk cargo terminal predominantly used by Jamaica Flour Mills for vessels up to 183 m loa
[5]*Jamaica Gypsum Pier:* Handling gypsum, limestone and other aggregates for vessels up to 172 m loa
[6]*Wherry Wharf:* At Newport East is used for import and export of lumber, corn and animal feed for vessels up to 107 m loa
[7]*Rapid Sheffield Wharf:* At Newport East and used as a sufferance wharf for the import of lumber for vessels up to 107 m loa
[8]*Texaco Caribbean Pier:* Import of petroleum products and chemicals for tankers up to 167 m loa. Also used for bunkering vessels

Mechanical Handling Equipment:

Location	Type	Capacity (t)	Qty	Remarks
Public Wharves	Mobile Cranes		3	available for hire
North Container Terminal (Port Bustamante)	Super Post Panamax	65	4	
South Container Terminal (Gordon Cay)	Post Panamax	40	5	
South Container Terminal (Gordon Cay)	Super Post Panamax	65	4	

Bunkering: Lannaman & Morris (Shipping) Ltd, 2 Seventh Avenue, Newport West, P O Box 1012, Kingston 15, Jamaica, *Tel:* +1876 923 4811, *Fax:* +1876 923 9091, *Email:* mgt@lannaman.com, *Website:* www.lannaman.com
Petrojam Ltd, 96 Marcus Garvey Drive, P O Box 241, Kingston 15, Jamaica, *Tel:* +1876 9238 611, *Fax:* +1876 923 5698, *Email:* mah@petrojam.com, *Website:* www.petrojambunkering.com
Petroleum Corp. of Jamaica, 36 Trafalgar Road, Kingston 10, Jamaica, *Tel:* +1876 9295 380, *Fax:* +1876 9292 409, *Email:* ica@pcj.com, *Website:* www.pcj.com
The Shell Company (WI) Ltd, Cool Petroleum and Gas Products Ltd, 236 Windward Road, Rockfort, Kingston, Jamaica, *Tel:* +1876 9287 300, *Fax:* +1876 9286 045, *Email:* winston.ormsby@coolcorp.com, *Website:* www.coolcorp.com
Chevron Marine Products LLC, Global Marine Products LLC, 1500 Louisiana, 4th Floor, Houston, TX 77002, United States of America, *Tel:* +1 832 8542 988, *Fax:* +1 832 8544 868, *Email:* gulfcbm@chevron.com, *Website:* www.chevron.com – *Grades:* IFO120-380cSt; MGO – *Delivery Mode:* barge, tank truck
ExxonMobil Marine Fuels, Suite 900, One Alhambra Plaza, Coral Gables, FL 33134, United States of America, *Tel:* +1 305 459 6358, *Fax:* +1 305 459 6412, *Email:* emmf@exxonmobil.com, *Website:* www.exxonmobilmarinefuels.com
Petrojam Ltd, 96 Marcus Garvey Drive, P O Box 241, Kingston 15, Jamaica, *Tel:* +1876 9238 611, *Fax:* +1876 923 5698, *Email:* mah@petrojam.com, *Website:* www.petrojambunkering.com – *Grades:* MGO; IFO – *Delivery Mode:* wharf, barge, pipeline
The Shell Company (WI) Ltd, Cool Petroleum and Gas Products Ltd, 236 Windward Road, Rockfort, Kingston, Jamaica, *Tel:* +1876 9287 300, *Fax:* +1876 9286 045, *Email:* winston.ormsby@coolcorp.com, *Website:* www.coolcorp.com – *Misc:* no pipeline facilities – *Notice:* 24 hours – *Delivery Mode:* truck

Towage: Two tugs of 4000 hp are available

Repair & Maintenance: There are dry dock facilities for small vessels and fishing boats. Light repairs either alongside one of the regular piers or out at an anchorage Berry's Marine Services Ltd, 92a Hagley Park Road, Kingston, Jamaica, *Tel:* +1876 933 6783

Ship Chandlers: Universal Meats, 48 Constant Spring Road, Kingston 10, Jamaica, *Tel:* +1876 968 4450, *Fax:* +1876 968 4457, *Email:* unimeat@cwjamaica.com

Shipping Agents: AAA Cargo, 78 Slipe Road, Region 5, Kingston, Jamaica, *Tel:* +1876 926 1832, *Fax:* +1876 926 1832, *Email:* cargo2007@cwjamaica.com
A.E. Parnell & Co. Ltd, 40 Second Street, Newport west, P O Box 98, Kingston 13, Jamaica, *Tel:* +1876 923 8728, *Fax:* +1876 923 5077, *Email:* admin@aeparnell.com, *Website:* www.aeparnell.com
A.J. Barned & Sons, 28 Third Street, Newport West, Kingston 13, Jamaica, *Tel:* +1876 923 6773, *Fax:* +1876 923 4720, *Email:* praisewarrior1@hotmail.com
Carib Star Shipping Ltd, 4 Fourth Avenue, Newport West, Kingston, Jamaica, *Tel:* +1876 923 4900, *Fax:* +1876 923 8527, *Email:* caribstar@caribstar-jm.com, *Website:* www.caribstar-jm.com
Caribbean Freight Handlers, 67-69 First Street, Newport West, Kingston 13, Jamaica, *Tel:* +1876 764 9979, *Fax:* +1876 764 9985, *Email:* info@caribbeanfreighthandlers.com, *Website:* www.caribbeanfreighthandlers.com
Champion Customs Brokers Ltd, 1 Gretna Green Avenue, Kingston 11, Jamaica, *Tel:* +1876 823 1484, *Fax:* +1876 923 6264, *Email:* championcustoms@cwjamaica.com
CMA-CGM S.A., CMA CGM Jamaica Ltd, Kingport Building Third Street, Newport West, Kingston 13, P O Box 86, Kingston, Jamaica, *Tel:* +1876 923 0843, *Fax:* +1876 923 9407, *Email:* jam.genmbox@cma-cgm.com, *Website:* www.cma-cgm.com
Door to Door International Services, 14-15 First Street, Unit 19 Newport West,

Kingston 13, Jamaica, *Tel:* +1876 937 1641, *Fax:* +1876 901 7574, *Email:* info@doortodoorrja.com
Fag.Mor Agency Ltd, 8 Kensington Avenue, Kingston, Jamaica, *Tel:* +1876 922 7820, *Fax:* +1876 922 0043, *Email:* mutty@cwjamaica.com, *Website:* www.fmacustomsbroker.com
R.S. Gamble (1998) Ltd, 40 Second Street, Newport West, Kingston 11, Jamaica, *Tel:* +1876 757 5168, *Fax:* +1876 937 1441, *Email:* admin@rsgamble.com
Grace Kennedy & Co. (Shipping) Ltd, Kingport Building, Third Street, Newport West, P O Box 86, Kingston, Jamaica, *Tel:* +1876 923 8581, *Fax:* +1876 923 6536, *Email:* rachel.mathews@gkco.com, *Website:* www.graceshipping.net
Green Cove Maritime (Jamaica) Ltd, 4 Fourth Avenue, Newport West, Kingston 13, Jamaica, *Tel:* +1876 923 0400/2, *Fax:* +1876 923 0420, *Email:* gcmjamaica@cwjamaica.com
Irie Customs Broker Ltd, Kingston, Jamaica, *Tel:* +1876 937 7015, *Fax:* +1876 901 7741, *Email:* cbaj470@cwjamaica.com
Jamaica Freight & Shipping Co. Ltd, 80-82 Second Street, Port Bustamante, P O Box 167, Kingston 13, Jamaica, *Tel:* +1876 923 9271, *Fax:* +1876 923 4091, *Email:* jfs@jashipco.com, *Website:* www.jashipco.com
Kent Shipping (Jamaica) Ltd, 2 Seventh Avenue, Kingston 15, Jamaica, *Tel:* +1876 937 0244, *Fax:* +1876 937 1937, *Email:* mgt@lannaman.com
Lannaman & Morris (Shipping) Ltd, 2 Seventh Avenue, Newport West, P O Box 1012, Kingston 15, Jamaica, *Tel:* +1876 923 4811, *Fax:* +1876 923 9091, *Email:* mgt@lannaman.com, *Website:* www.lannaman.com
Lasocean Agencies Ltd, 75 First Street, Newport West, P O Box 515, Kingston 13, Jamaica, *Tel:* +1876 923 6421, *Fax:* +1876 923 6130, *Email:* lasocean@cwjamaica.com
H Macaulay Orrett Ltd, Third Street, Newport West, P O Box 203, Kingston 11, Jamaica, *Tel:* +1876 923 5451/5458, *Fax:* +1876 923 5459
Perez y Cia (Jamaica) Ltd, 6-12 Newport Boulevard, Kingston 13, Jamaica, *Tel:* +1876 901 4833, *Fax:* +1876 757 7737, *Email:* cdonaldson@perezyciaja.com, *Website:* www.perezycia.com
Royale Ocean Shipping Co. Ltd, Newport Centre Building, 6 Newport Boulevard, Kingston, Jamaica, *Tel:* +1876 757 9227, *Fax:* +1876 757 9221, *Email:* operations@royaleoceanshipping.com, *Website:* www.royaleoceanshipping.com
Shipmanagement Services Ltd, Jamaica Fruit & Shipping Co. Ltd, P O Box 167, Port Bustamante, Kingston 13, Jamaica, *Tel:* +1876 923 9271, *Fax:* +1876 923 4091, *Email:* jfs@jashipco.com, *Website:* www.jashipco.com

Stevedoring Companies: A.E. Parnell & Co. Ltd, 40 Second Street, Newport west, P O Box 98, Kingston 13, Jamaica, *Tel:* +1876 923 8728, *Fax:* +1876 923 5077, *Email:* admin@aeparnell.com, *Website:* www.aeparnell.com
Jamaica Freight & Shipping Co. Ltd, 80-82 Second Street, Port Bustamante, P O Box 167, Kingston 13, Jamaica, *Tel:* +1876 923 9271, *Fax:* +1876 923 4091, *Email:* jfs@jashipco.com, *Website:* www.jashipco.com
Kingston Wharves Ltd (KWL), Kingport Building, Third Street, Newport West, Port Bustamante, P O Box 260, Kingston 13, Jamaica, *Tel:* +1876 923 9211, *Fax:* +1876 923 5361, *Email:* kingstonwharves@kwljm.com, *Website:* www.kingstonwharves.com.jm
Lannaman & Morris (Shipping) Ltd, 2 Seventh Avenue, Newport West, P O Box 1012, Kingston 15, Jamaica, *Tel:* +1876 923 4811, *Fax:* +1876 923 9091, *Email:* mgt@lannaman.com, *Website:* www.lannaman.com
Shipmanagement Services Ltd, Jamaica Fruit & Shipping Co. Ltd, P O Box 167, Port Bustamante, Kingston 13, Jamaica, *Tel:* +1876 923 9271, *Fax:* +1876 923 4091, *Email:* jfs@jashipco.com, *Website:* www.jashipco.com
Shipping Services (Stev) Ltd, 80-82 Second Street Port Bustamante, P O Box 167, Kingston 13, Jamaica, *Tel:* +1876 923 9271, *Fax:* +1876 937 6815, *Email:* michael.bernard@jashipco.com
Terminal Services Ltd, Kingston, Jamaica, *Tel:* +1876 923 5482, *Fax:* +1876 923 0018
Universal Freight Handlers Ltd, 76 Marcus Garvey Drive, Kingston, Jamaica, *Tel:* +1876 923 6674, *Fax:* +1876 923 4798, *Email:* info@uhfl.com, *Website:* www.uhfl.com
Western Freight Services Ltd, Kingston, Jamaica, *Tel:* +1876 979 8446, *Fax:* +1876 979 8556
Xars Equipment & Trucking Co. Ltd, 126-132 Second Street, Newport West, P O Box 1813, Kingston 8, Jamaica, *Tel:* +1876 923 7589, *Fax:* +1876 923 6050, *Email:* xars@cwjamaica.com, *Website:* www.xarstrucking.com

Surveyors: BMT Murray Fenton Ltd, 24 Trafalgar Road, Kingston 10, Jamaica, *Tel:* +1876 960 4465, *Fax:* +1876 920 4965, *Email:* carinco@infochan.com
Caribbean Inspection Co. Ltd, 24 Trafalgar Road, Kingston 10, Jamaica, *Tel:* +1876 929 6673, *Fax:* +1876 929 4965
R.S. Gamble (1998) Ltd, 40 Second Street, Newport West, Kingston 11, Jamaica, *Tel:* +1876 757 5168, *Fax:* +1876 937 1441, *Email:* admin@rsgamble.com
Lannaman & Morris (Shipping) Ltd, 2 Seventh Avenue, Newport West, P O Box 1012, Kingston 15, Jamaica, *Tel:* +1876 923 4811, *Fax:* +1876 923 9091, *Email:* mgt@lannaman.com, *Website:* www.lannaman.com
Panama Maritime Group, Office No.43, 44 Hemingway Crescent, Kingston 20, Jamaica, *Tel:* +1876 934 8518, *Fax:* +1876 934 8522, *Email:* ericarmenteros@yahoo.com
Shipowners' P & I Services Ltd, Kingston, Jamaica, *Tel:* +1876 923 9271, *Fax:* +1876 923 4091

Medical Facilities: Full range of services available

Airport: Norman Manley International, 19 km

Development: Construction of West Container Terminal, 475 m long in depth of 15 m with 65 ha of yard space; scheduled to be completed 2008

Lloyd's Agent: R.S. Gamble (1998) Ltd, 40 Second Street, Newport West, Kingston 11, Jamaica, *Tel:* +1876 757 5168, *Fax:* +1876 937 1441, *Email:* admin@rsgamble.com

MONTEGO BAY

Lat 18° 27' N; Long 77° 56' W.

Admiralty Chart: 464		**Admiralty Pilot:** 70
Time Zone: GMT -5 h		**UNCTAD Locode:** JM MBJ

Key to Principal Facilities:—			
A=Airport	**C**=Containers	**G**=General Cargo	**P**=Petroleum	**R**=Ro/Ro	**Y**=Dry Bulk
B=Bunkers	**D**=Dry Dock	**L**=Cruise	**Q**=Other Liquid Bulk	**T**=Towage (where available from port)

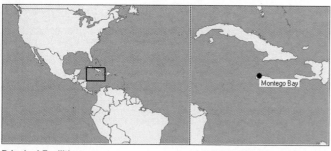

Principal Facilities:

P		G	C	R	L	B		A

Authority: Port Authority of Jamaica, 15-17 Duke Street, Kingston, Jamaica, *Tel:* +1876 922 0290/8, *Fax:* +1876 924 9437, *Email:* paj@portjam.com, *Website:* www.portjam.com

Officials: Chief Executive Officer: Noel A. Hylton, *Email:* nhylton@portjam.com.
Vice President: Rosalie Donaldson, *Email:* rdonaldson@portjam.com.
Harbour Master: Capt Hopeton Delisser, *Email:* hdelisser@portjam.com.

Port Security: ISPS compliant

Approach: Channel marks in line 20° 48' 02", 487.6 m turning basin with 10.4 m min depth of water. Entry day and night. No current in harbour

Anchorage: Anchorage can be obtained in the roadstead about 0.5 miles from the shore in depths ranging from 9.1 m to 11 m or in depths 12.8 m to 14.6 m at harbour. Designated anchorage 'A' may be reserved in advance through Harbour Master at Kingston

Pilotage: Compulsory. Pilots available from Kingston

Weather: Winds, NE

Traffic: 2007, 715 773 t of cargo handled, 154 cruise vessels

Maximum Vessel Dimensions: 268 m loa

Accommodation:

Name	Draught (m)	Remarks
Montego Bay		See [1] below
Berth 2	9.1	See [2] below
Berth 3	6.2	Operated by Port Handlers Ltd for vessels up to 160 m loa
Berth 4	5.9	Operated by Port Handlers Ltd for vessels up to 160 m loa
Berths 5 & 6 (cruise vessels)	9.6	For two vessels up to 198 m loa or one vessel up to 268 m loa

[1]*Montego Bay:* Berths 2, 3 & 4 are reached through a 457 m channel, 121.9 m wide dredged to a min of 10.36 m draft
Tanker facilities: One berth available with 9.1 m draft. Slop discharge facilities available
[2]*Berth 2:* Operated by Port Handlers Ltd., 14 Montego Freeport Shopping Centre, P O Box 302, Montego Bay, Tel: +1876 979 8815, Fax: +1876 979 8552, for vessels up to 213 m loa

Storage:

Location	Covered (m²)	Cold (m³)
Montego Bay	2139	2335

Bunkering: All grades (viscosities) available from Shell, Esso and ChevronTexaco in limited quantities. At least four days' notice required. No bunker 'C'
Chevron Marine Products LLC, Global Marine Products LLC, 1500 Louisiana, 4th Floor, Houston, TX 77002, United States of America, *Tel:* +1 832 8542 988, *Fax:* +1

832 8544 868, *Email:* gulfcbm@chevron.com, *Website:* www.chevron.com – *Grades:* IFO120-380cSt; MGO – *Delivery Mode:* tank truck

Repair & Maintenance: Minor repairs can be effected alongside

Shipping Agents: Grace Kennedy & Co. (Shipping) Ltd, Shop 25, Freeport Shopping Centre, Montego Bay, Jamaica, *Tel:* +1876 979 8077, *Fax:* +1876 979 8078
Lannaman & Morris (Shipping) Ltd, No. 26, Montego Bay Freeport, P O Box 431, Montego Bay, Jamaica, *Tel:* +1876 684 9890, *Fax:* +1876 684 9889, *Email:* mgt@lannaman.com, *Website:* www.lannaman.com
Maritime & Transport Services Ltd, Unit 35, Catherine Hall, Trade Centre, Montego Bay, Jamaica, *Tel:* +1876 979 7252, *Fax:* +1876 971 3759, *Email:* jammla@maersk.com
Royale Ocean Shipping Co. Ltd, Newport Centre Building, 6 Newport Boulevard, Kingston, Jamaica, *Tel:* +1876 757 9227, *Fax:* +1876 757 9221, *Email:* operations@royaleoceanshipping.com, *Website:* www.royaleoceanshipping.com
Swaby's Shipping & Freighting Company Ltd, 4 East Street, P O Box 1010, Montego Bay, Jamaica, *Tel:* +1876 952 1210, *Fax:* +1876 979 5441, *Email:* bevram50@yahoo.com
Western Shipping Agency Ltd, 18 North Street, P O Box 1479, Montego Bay, Jamaica, *Tel:* +1876 952 4271, *Fax:* +1876 952 7191, *Email:* westship@cwjamaica.com

Stevedoring Companies: Lannaman & Morris (Shipping) Ltd, No. 26, Montego Bay Freeport, P O Box 431, Montego Bay, Jamaica, *Tel:* +1876 684 9890, *Fax:* +1876 684 9889, *Email:* mgt@lannaman.com, *Website:* www.lannaman.com

Surveyors: Lannaman & Morris (Shipping) Ltd, No. 26, Montego Bay Freeport, P O Box 431, Montego Bay, Jamaica, *Tel:* +1876 684 9890, *Fax:* +1876 684 9889, *Email:* mgt@lannaman.com, *Website:* www.lannaman.com

Medical Facilities: Available at Cornwall Regional Hospital

Airport: Sangster's International Airport

Lloyd's Agent: R.S. Gamble (1998) Ltd, 40 Second Street, Newport West, Kingston 11, Jamaica, *Tel:* +1876 757 5168, *Fax:* +1876 937 1441, *Email:* admin@rsgamble.com

OCHO RIOS

Lat 18° 24' N; Long 77° 6' W.

Admiralty Chart: 464	**Admiralty Pilot:** 70
Time Zone: GMT -5 h	**UNCTAD Locode:** JM OCJ

Principal Facilities:

		Y	G		L	B		A

Authority: Port Authority of Jamaica, 15-17 Duke Street, Kingston, Jamaica, *Tel:* +1876 922 0290/8, *Fax:* +1876 924 9437, *Email:* paj@portjam.com, *Website:* www.portjam.com

Officials: Chief Executive Officer: Noel A. Hylton, *Email:* nhylton@portjam.com.
Vice President: Rosalie Donaldson, *Email:* rdonaldson@portjam.com.
Harbour Master: Capt Hopeton Delisser, *Email:* hdelisser@portjam.com.

Port Security: ISPS compliant

Pilotage: Compulsory. Order by radio to Port Superintendent 24 h before arrival. Made available from Kingston

Traffic: 2007, 275 cruise vessels

Maximum Vessel Dimensions: 274 m loa, 12.19 m draft

Accommodation:

Name	Length (m)	Draught (m)	Remarks
Ocho Rios			
Cruise Ship Berth 1		9	For vessels up to 222 m loa
Cruise Ship Berth 2		9.75	For vessels up to 274 m loa
Reynolds Jamaica Mines Wharf	274.3	12.2	Mainly used for export of bulk sugar. Storage cap of 20 000 t

Bunkering: Only possible if special arrangements are made with at least 4 days notice
Lannaman & Morris (Shipping) Ltd, Ocho Rios Pier, P O Box 201, Ocho Rios, Jamaica, *Tel:* +1876 974 2253, *Fax:* +1876 974 2744, *Email:* lnmochorios@cwjamaica.com, *Website:* www.lannaman.com

Repair & Maintenance: Only minor repairs possible

Shipping Agents: Lannaman & Morris (Shipping) Ltd, Ocho Rios Pier, P O Box 201, Ocho Rios, Jamaica, *Tel:* +1876 974 2253, *Fax:* +1876 974 2744, *Email:* lnmochorios@cwjamaica.com, *Website:* www.lannaman.com

Surveyors: Lannaman & Morris (Shipping) Ltd, Ocho Rios Pier, P O Box 201, Ocho Rios, Jamaica, *Tel:* +1876 974 2253, *Fax:* +1876 974 2744, *Email:* lnmochorios@cwjamaica.com, *Website:* www.lannaman.com

Airport: Montego Bay or Kingston

Lloyd's Agent: R.S. Gamble (1998) Ltd, 40 Second Street, Newport West, Kingston 11, Jamaica, *Tel:* +1876 757 5168, *Fax:* +1876 937 1441, *Email:* admin@rsgamble.com

PORT ANTONIO

Lat 18° 11' N; Long 76° 27' W.

Admiralty Chart: 458	Admiralty Pilot: 70
Time Zone: GMT -5 h	UNCTAD Locode: JM POT

Principal Facilities:

		G		L	B		A	

Authority: Port Authority of Jamaica, 15-17 Duke Street, Kingston, Jamaica, *Tel:* +1876 922 0290/8, *Fax:* +1876 924 9437, *Email:* paj@portjam.com, *Website:* www.portjam.com

Officials: Chief Executive Officer: Noel A. Hylton, *Email:* nhylton@portjam.com.
Vice President: Rosalie Donaldson, *Email:* rdonaldson@portjam.com.
Harbour Master: Capt Hopeton Delisser, *Email:* hdelisser@portjam.com.

Port Security: ISPS compliant

Anchorage: Anchorage in E harbour for vessels up to 152 m loa and draft of 7.9 m. In W harbour for vessels up to 167 m loa and draft of 7.9 m

Pilotage: Compulsory. Made available from Kingston

Traffic: 2004, 38 cargo vessels & 9 cruise vessels, 36 196 t of cargo handled & 3484 cruise passengers

Maximum Vessel Dimensions: 167 m loa, 8.7 m draft

Accommodation:

Name	Draught (m)	Remarks
Port Antonio		
Ken Wright Cruiseship Pier	8.7	For vessels up to 167 m loa
Boundbrook Wharf	7.9	For vessels up to 167 m loa

Bunkering: All grades of fuel available

Stevedoring Companies: Shipping Services (Stev) Ltd, 80-82 Second Street Port Bustamante, P O Box 167, Kingston 13, Jamaica, *Tel:* +1876 923 9271, *Fax:* +1876 937 6815, *Email:* michael.bernard@jashipco.com

Airport: Spring Garden, 9.6 km

Lloyd's Agent: R.S. Gamble (1998) Ltd, 40 Second Street, Newport West, Kingston 11, Jamaica, *Tel:* +1876 757 5168, *Fax:* +1876 937 1441, *Email:* admin@rsgamble.com

PORT BUSTAMANTE

see under Kingston

PORT ESQUIVEL

Lat 17° 53' N; Long 77° 7' W.

Admiralty Chart: 257	Admiralty Pilot: 70
Time Zone: GMT -5 h	UNCTAD Locode: JM PEV

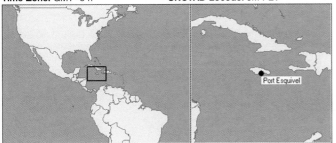

Principal Facilities:

	Y	G			B		A	

Authority: Port Authority of Jamaica, 15-17 Duke Street, Kingston, Jamaica, *Tel:* +1876 922 0290/8, *Fax:* +1876 924 9437, *Email:* paj@portjam.com, *Website:* www.portjam.com

Officials: Chief Executive Officer: Noel A. Hylton, *Email:* nhylton@portjam.com.

Vice President: Rosalie Donaldson, *Email:* rdonaldson@portjam.com.
Harbour Master: Capt Hopeton Delisser, *Email:* hdelisser@portjam.com.

Port Security: ISPS compliant

Approach: Vessels proceed through a dredged channel approx 1 mile long with a min depth of 12 m

Pilotage: Compulsory. Pilot should be ordered by radio to local agent 48 h in advance from Kingston

Traffic: 2005, 2 608 821 t of cargo handled

Accommodation:

Name		Remarks
Port Esquivel		See [1] below

[1]*Port Esquivel:* Port built for Alumina Jamaica Ltd. The wharf, situated in a basin at the inner end of the channel, for vessels up to 198 m long with a max draft of 11 m. This wharf is used mainly in the export of bulk alumina. Conveyors take alumina to storage and feed to loading tower. The port is able to unload 35 560 t of alumina in a turn around time of 38 h. Also a cargo pier able to accommodate vessels up to 67 m loa and 4.9 m draft

Storage: Open storage area

Bunkering: Bunker 'C' fuel and fresh water available at rates of 155 long t and 150 short t/h respectively
Chevron Marine Products LLC, Global Marine Products LLC, 1500 Louisiana, 4th Floor, Houston, TX 77002, United States of America, *Tel:* +1 832 8542 988, *Fax:* +1 832 8544 868, *Email:* gulfcbm@chevron.com, *Website:* www.chevron.com – *Grades:* IFO120-380cSt; MGO – *Delivery Mode:* barge, tank truck
ExxonMobil Marine Fuels, Suite 900, One Alhambra Plaza, Coral Gables, FL 33134, United States of America, *Tel:* +1 305 459 6358, *Fax:* +1 305 459 6412, *Email:* emmf@exxonmobil.com, *Website:* www.exxonmobilmarinefuels.com
Petrojam Ltd, 96 Marcus Garvey Drive, P O Box 241, Kingston 15, Jamaica, *Tel:* +1876 9238 611, *Fax:* +1876 923 5698, *Email:* mah@petrojam.com, *Website:* www.petrojambunkering.com – *Grades:* IFO; MGO – *Delivery Mode:* barge
The Shell Company (WI) Ltd, Cool Petroleum and Gas Products Ltd, 236 Windward Road, Rockfort, Kingston, Jamaica, *Tel:* +1876 9287 300, *Fax:* +1876 9286 045, *Email:* winston.ormsby@coolcorp.com, *Website:* www.coolcorp.com – *Notice:* 24 hours – *Delivery Mode:* truck

Repair & Maintenance: Well equipped machine shop available for welding and minor ship repairs

Stevedoring Companies: Shipping Services (Stev) Ltd, 80-82 Second Street Port Bustamante, P O Box 167, Kingston 13, Jamaica, *Tel:* +1876 923 9271, *Fax:* +1876 937 6815, *Email:* michael.bernard@jashipco.com

Airport: Norman Manley International

Lloyd's Agent: R.S. Gamble (1998) Ltd, 40 Second Street, Newport West, Kingston 11, Jamaica, *Tel:* +1876 757 5168, *Fax:* +1876 937 1441, *Email:* admin@rsgamble.com

PORT KAISER

Lat 17° 53' N; Long 77° 36' W.

Admiralty Chart: 258	Admiralty Pilot: 70
Time Zone: GMT -5 h	UNCTAD Locode: JM PKS

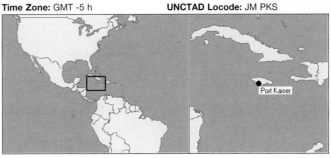

Principal Facilities:

	Y	G			B		A	

Authority: Port Authority of Jamaica, 15-17 Duke Street, Kingston, Jamaica, *Tel:* +1876 922 0290/8, *Fax:* +1876 924 9437, *Email:* paj@portjam.com, *Website:* www.portjam.com

Officials: Chief Executive Officer: Noel A. Hylton, *Email:* nhylton@portjam.com.
Vice President: Rosalie Donaldson, *Email:* rdonaldson@portjam.com.
Harbour Master: Capt Hopeton Delisser, *Email:* hdelisser@portjam.com.

Port Security: ISPS compliant

Pilotage: Compulsory. Pilot should be ordered by radio to local agent 48 h in advance from Kingston. Boarding point is 3 miles SSW of pier

Traffic: 2005, 2 572 767 t of cargo handled

Accommodation:

Name	Depth (m)	Remarks
Port Kaiser		
Wharf	11.9	See [1] below

[1]*Wharf:* Export of alumina for vessels up to 213.4 m loa and 11 m draft. This wharf is in an exposed position and vessels sometimes have to lie off during bad weather

Bunkering: Possible by special arrangement

Repair & Maintenance: Only minor repairs possible

Medical Facilities: Santa Cruz Hospital

Key to Principal Facilities:—				
A=Airport	**C**=Containers	**G**=General Cargo	**P**=Petroleum	**R**=Ro/Ro	**Y**=Dry Bulk
B=Bunkers	**D**=Dry Dock	**L**=Cruise	**Q**=Other Liquid Bulk	**T**=Towage (where available from port)	

Airport: Norman Manley International

Lloyd's Agent: R.S. Gamble (1998) Ltd, 40 Second Street, Newport West, Kingston 11, Jamaica, *Tel:* +1876   757 5168, *Fax:* +1876   937 1441, *Email:* admin@rsgamble.com

PORT RHOADES

Lat 18° 28' N; Long 77° 27' W.

Admiralty Chart: 459	**Admiralty Pilot:** 70
Time Zone: GMT -5 h	**UNCTAD Locode:** JM PRH

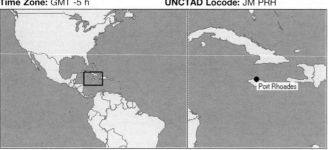

Principal Facilities:

	Y	G			B		A

Authority: Port Authority of Jamaica, 15-17 Duke Street, Kingston, Jamaica, *Tel:* +1876 922 0290/8, *Fax:* +1876 924 9437, *Email:* paj@portjam.com, *Website:* www.portjam.com

Officials: Chief Executive Officer: Noel A. Hylton, *Email:* nhylton@portjam.com. Vice President: Rosalie Donaldson, *Email:* rdonaldson@portjam.com. Harbour Master: Capt Hopeton Delisser, *Email:* hdelisser@portjam.com.

Port Security: ISPS compliant

Approach: Channel depth is 12.8 m. Port is exposed to NE wind when heavy swell occurs in channel

Pilotage: Compulsory through Kingston

Traffic: 2005, 5 010 396 t of cargo handled

Maximum Vessel Dimensions: 213 m loa, 11.4 m draft

Accommodation:

Name	Remarks
Port Rhoades	See [1] below

[1]*Port Rhoades:* Main pier operated by Kaiser Bauxite with 11.4 m draft alongside, equipped with mechanical loader

Bunkering: Advance notice required
Chevron Marine Products LLC, Global Marine Products LLC, 1500 Louisiana, 4th Floor, Houston, TX 77002, United States of America, *Tel:* +1 832 8542 988, *Fax:* +1 832 8544 868, *Email:* gulfcbm@chevron.com, *Website:* www.chevron.com – *Grades:* IFO120-380cSt; MGO – *Delivery Mode:* tank truck, barge

Medical Facilities: St. Anns Bay Hospital, 37 km

Airport: Montego Bay or Kingston

Lloyd's Agent: R.S. Gamble (1998) Ltd, 40 Second Street, Newport West, Kingston 11, Jamaica, *Tel:* +1876   757 5168, *Fax:* +1876   937 1441, *Email:* admin@rsgamble.com

PORT ROYAL

Lat 17° 56' N; Long 76° 50' W.

Admiralty Chart: 255/256	**Admiralty Pilot:** 70
Time Zone: GMT -5 h	**UNCTAD Locode:** JM PRO

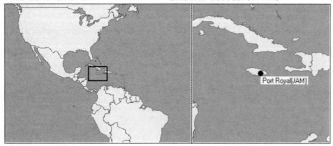

Principal Facilities:

		G				T	A

Authority: Port Authority of Jamaica, 15-17 Duke Street, Kingston, Jamaica, *Tel:* +1876 922 0290/8, *Fax:* +1876 924 9437, *Email:* paj@portjam.com, *Website:* www.portjam.com

Officials: Chief Executive Officer: Noel A. Hylton, *Email:* nhylton@portjam.com. Vice President: Rosalie Donaldson, *Email:* rdonaldson@portjam.com. Harbour Master: Capt Hopeton Delisser, *Email:* hdelisser@portjam.com.

Pilotage: Compulsory. Pilot available from Kingston

Accommodation:

Name	Remarks
Port Royal	See [1] below

[1]*Port Royal:* Anchorage for vessels up to 305 m loa and draft of 12.2 m. Vessels anchor off village to obtain pratique before proceeding to Kingston unless radio pratique has already been granted

Towage: Possible by special arrangement

Airport: Kingston

Lloyd's Agent: R.S. Gamble (1998) Ltd, 40 Second Street, Newport West, Kingston 11, Jamaica, *Tel:* +1876   757 5168, *Fax:* +1876   937 1441, *Email:* admin@rsgamble.com

RIO BUENO

Lat 18° 28' N; Long 77° 27' W.

Admiralty Chart: 459	**Admiralty Pilot:** 70
Time Zone: GMT -5 h	**UNCTAD Locode:** JM RIB

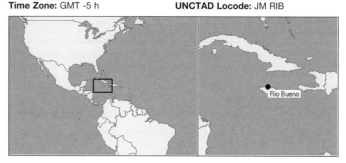

Principal Facilities:

		G					A

Authority: Port Authority of Jamaica, 15-17 Duke Street, Kingston, Jamaica, *Tel:* +1876 922 0290/8, *Fax:* +1876 924 9437, *Email:* paj@portjam.com, *Website:* www.portjam.com

Officials: Chief Executive Officer: Noel A. Hylton, *Email:* nhylton@portjam.com. Vice President: Rosalie Donaldson, *Email:* rdonaldson@portjam.com. Harbour Master: Capt Hopeton Delisser, *Email:* hdelisser@portjam.com.

Pre-Arrival Information: Vessel's should advise ETA 5 days, 72 h, 48 h and 24 h prior to arrival. The initial message should include the following information:
a) ETA
b) discharge and in-transit tonnage
c) arrival draught
d) last port of call
e) ISPS security level

Pilotage: Compulsory. Vessels should order pilot via agent at least 12 h prior to arrival. Pilot boards in pos 18° 28.76' N; 77° 27.36' W

Radio Frequency: VHF Channels 9 and 11

Traffic: 2005, 31 310 t of cargo handled

Maximum Vessel Dimensions: 91.4 m loa, 7 m draft

Accommodation:

Name	Remarks
Rio Bueno	See [1] below

[1]*Rio Bueno:* Main jetty operated by Caribbean Milling with 7.8 m depth alongside. There are several other smaller piers. Unloading by conveyor belt
Berthing and unberthing takes place between 0530-1830 LT

Storage: Grain storage available

Shipping Agents: Transocean Shipping Ltd, Portview Centre Building, 90-92 First Street, P O Box 1050, Newport West, Kingston 13, Jamaica, *Tel:* +1876 923 5719, *Fax:* +1876 923 9301, *Email:* ops@shippingja.net, *Website:* www.shippingja.com

Airport: Sangster's International Airport

Lloyd's Agent: R.S. Gamble (1998) Ltd, 40 Second Street, Newport West, Kingston 11, Jamaica, *Tel:* +1876   757 5168, *Fax:* +1876   937 1441, *Email:* admin@rsgamble.com

ROCKY POINT

Lat 17° 49' N; Long 77° 8' W.

Admiralty Chart: 255/256	**Admiralty Pilot:** 70
Time Zone: GMT -5 h	**UNCTAD Locode:** JM ROP

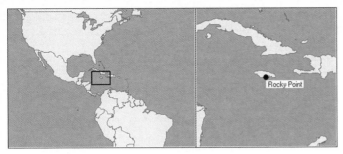

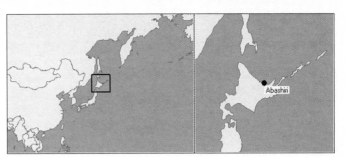

Principal Facilities:

P		G			B		A

Authority: Port Authority of Jamaica, 15-17 Duke Street, Kingston, Jamaica, *Tel:* +1876 922 0290/8, *Fax:* +1876 924 9437, *Email:* paj@portjam.com, *Website:* www.portjam.com

Officials: Chief Executive Officer: Noel A. Hylton, *Email:* nhylton@portjam.com.
Vice President: Rosalie Donaldson, *Email:* rdonaldson@portjam.com.
Harbour Master: Capt Hopeton Delisser, *Email:* hdelisser@portjam.com.

Port Security: ISPS compliant

Approach: The port approach is exposed to heavy swell when SE winds prevail during summer months

Pilotage: Compulsory. Pilot available from Kingston

Traffic: 2005, 1 866 238 t of cargo handled

Maximum Vessel Dimensions: 213 m loa, 10.6 m draft

Accommodation:

Name	Remarks
Rocky Point	See [1] below

[1]*Rocky Point:* Main pier has 11.3 m depth alongside, handling alumina and petroleum. Loading by mechanical conveyor belt

Bunkering: By special arrangement
Chevron Marine Products LLC, Global Marine Products LLC, 1500 Louisiana, 4th Floor, Houston, TX 77002, United States of America, *Tel:* +1 832 8542 988, *Fax:* +1 832 8544 868, *Email:* gulfcbm@chevron.com, *Website:* www.chevron.com – *Grades:* GO – *Delivery Mode:* tank truck
ExxonMobil Marine Fuels, Suite 900, One Alhambra Plaza, Coral Gables, FL 33134, United States of America, *Tel:* +1 305 459 6358, *Fax:* +1 305 459 6412, *Email:* emmf@exxonmobil.com, *Website:* www.exxonmobilmarinefuels.com
Petrojam Ltd, 96 Marcus Garvey Drive, P O Box 241, Kingston 15, Jamaica, *Tel:* +1876 9238 611, *Fax:* +1876 923 5698, *Email:* mah@petrojam.com, *Website:* www.petrojambunkering.com – *Grades:* IFO; MGO – *Delivery Mode:* barge
The Shell Company (WI) Ltd, Cool Petroleum and Gas Products Ltd, 236 Windward Road, Rockfort, Kingston, Jamaica, *Tel:* +1876 9287 300, *Fax:* +1876 9286 045, *Email:* winston.ormsby@coolcorp.com, *Website:* www.coolcorp.com – *Notice:* 24 hours – *Delivery Mode:* truck

Airport: Norman Manley International

Lloyd's Agent: R.S. Gamble (1998) Ltd, 40 Second Street, Newport West, Kingston 11, Jamaica, *Tel:* +1876 757 5168, *Fax:* +1876 937 1441, *Email:* admin@rsgamble.com

JAPAN

YAMAGUCHI, NAGAHAMA & MIZUNO

Akasaka Twin Towers East Tower 13th Floor,
17-22 Akasaka 2-chome, Minato-ku, Tokyo 107-0052 JAPAN
Tel: +81 3 3589 3585   Fax: +81 3 3568 3558
Email: yandn@gol.com   Website: www.ynmlaw.com

Our shipping practice areas include legal issues required to vessels from shipbuilding to be scrapped, namely shipbuilding contract, ship finance, sale and purchase agreement, charter agreement, B/L, salvage, registration of vessels and/or mortgages on vessels, ship insurance, correction of claims against vessels and protection therefrom, legal procedures of attachment etc. of vessels, litigations and arbitrations.

ABASHIRI

Lat 44° 1' N; Long 144° 17' E.

Admiralty Chart: 1802   **Admiralty Pilot:** 41
Time Zone: GMT +9 h   **UNCTAD Locode:** JP ABA

Principal Facilities:

	Y	G			B		T	A

Authority: Port & Harbour Section of Abashiri City, Higashi 4, Minami 6, Abashiri 093-8555, Hokkaido, Japan, *Tel:* +81 152 446111, *Fax:* +81 152 436151, *Email:* zusr-sk@city.abashiri.hokkaido.jp, *Website:* www.city.abashiri.hokkaido.jp

Officials: Executive Director: Nobuo Sakaue, *Email:* nobuo.sakaue@city.abashiri.hokkaido.jp.

Port Security: ISPS compliant

Approach: Shinko (New Port) Fairway with width of 250 m in depth of 12 m. Minatomachi (Port Town) Fairway with width of 165 m in depth of 7.5 m. Draft limitation in the channel of 8 m

Anchorage: Quarantine anchorage centred in pos 44° 01' 37'' N; 144° 18' 08'' E, radius of 300 m in depth of 12.0 m

Pilotage: Not compulsory. Pilots are available from Kushiro with advance notice, Tel: +81 154 526352. Kushiro Port Pilot's Association

Radio Frequency: Vessels should use Nagasaki Radio or Choshi Radio. 24 h working

Weather: Prevailing NNW'ly winds

Tides: Tidal range 2.55 m max, -0.53 m min

Maximum Vessel Dimensions: 30 000 dwt, 199 m loa

Principal Imports and Exports: Imports: Coal, Crabs, Logs. Exports: Frozen salmon, Used cars.

Working Hours: 0800-1700

Accommodation:

Name	Length (m)	Depth (m)	Remarks
Abashiri			Passenger terminal at No.2 pier of 1171 m2
No.1 Wharf	181	5.5	2 x 2000 gt cap
No.2 Wharf P.1	100	5.5	1 x 2000 gt cap
No.2 Wharf P.2	135	7.5	1 x 5000 gt cap
No.3 Wharf P.1	180	5.5	2 x 2000 gt cap
No.3 Wharf P.2	130	7.5	1 x 5000 gt cap
No.4 Wharf P.1	185	10	1 x 15 000 gt cap
No.4 Wharf P.2	235	12	1 x 30 000 gt cap
No.5 Wharf	260	7.5	2 x 5 000 gt cap
Dolphin (Shinko)	153	8	1 x 5000 gt cap

Mechanical Handling Equipment:

Location	Type	Capacity (t)
Abashiri	Mobile Cranes	10

Bunkering: Domestic oil available. Bonded oil will be brought in from Hakodate or Muroran with sufficient advance notice

Towage: Shimada Kaiun Co. Ltd, Abashiri, Hokkaido, Japan, *Tel:* +81 152 446904, *Fax:* +81 152 612056

Repair & Maintenance: Abashiri Zosen Ltd, Abashiri, Hokkaido, Japan, *Tel:* +81 152 446516 Minor repairs
Doto Zosen Co. Ltd, Abashiri, Hokkaido, Japan, *Tel:* +81 152 447241 Minor repairs

Medical Facilities: Full hospital facilities available without prior notice

Airport: Memanbetu Airport, 20 km

Railway: JR Abashiri Railway Station, 2.5 km

Lloyd's Agent: Cornes & Co. Ltd, 273 Yamashita-cho, Naka-ku, Yokohama 231-0023, Kanagawa Pref., Japan, *Tel:* +81 45 201 8537, *Fax:* +81 45 212 3105, *Email:* survey@ykh.cornes.co.jp, *Website:* www.cornes.co.jp

ABOSHI

Lat 34° 46' N; Long 134° 36' E.

Admiralty Chart: 698   **Admiralty Pilot:** 42B
Time Zone: GMT +9 h   **UNCTAD Locode:** JP ABO

Key to Principal Facilities:—						
A=Airport	**C**=Containers	**G**=General Cargo	**P**=Petroleum	**R**=Ro/Ro	**Y**=Dry Bulk
B=Bunkers	**D**=Dry Dock	**L**=Cruise	**Q**=Other Liquid Bulk	**T**=Towage (where available from port)	

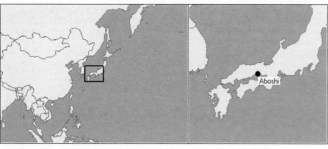

Principal Facilities:

P		Y	G							

Authority: Port & Harbour Section of Hyogo Prefecture, 5-10-1 Yamate-dori, Chuo-ku, Kobe 650-8567, Hyogo Pref., Japan, *Tel:* +81 78 341 7711, *Fax:* +81 78 341 6477

Approach: Draft limitation in the channel 10 m

Pilotage: Harbour pilot not compulsory; Harbour pilots are available at the anchorage from one hour after sunrise to one hour before sunset. However, Inland-sea pilot and Bay pilot compulsory for vessels over 10 000 gt; Inland-sea pilots are available at Wad-Misaki (off Kobe), Sekisaki, Hesaki (off Moji)

Tides: Tidal range 1.60 m max, -0.20 m min

Accommodation:

Name	Length (m)	Depth (m)	Draught (m)	Remarks
Aboshi				
Buoy 2 & 3	270	10	9	For vessels up to 180 m loa, 15 000 dwt
Seibu Pier No.1	130	7.5	7	For vessels up to 115 m loa, 5000 dwt
Seibu Pier No.2	215	10		For vessels up to 185 m loa, 30 000 dwt

Bunkering: Domestic and bonded oil are available from Mega or Kobe by oil-barge

Repair & Maintenance: Small repairs can be undertaken

Lloyd's Agent: Cornes & Co. Ltd, Meikai Building, 32 Akashi-machi, Chuo-ku, Kobe 650-0037, Hyogo Pref., Japan, *Tel:* +81 78 332 3421, *Fax:* +81 78 332 3070, *Email:* survey@kobe.cornes.co.jp, *Website:* www.cornes.co.jp

AIOI

Lat 34° 46' N; Long 134° 28' E.

Admiralty Chart: JP106	**Admiralty Pilot:** 42B
Time Zone: GMT +9 h	**UNCTAD Locode:** JP AIO

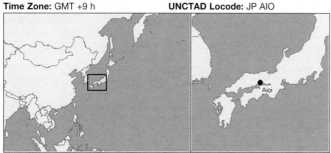

Principal Facilities:

		G			B	D	T	A		

Authority: Port & Harbour Section of Hyogo Prefecture, 5-10-1 Yamate-dori, Chuo-ku, Kobe 650-8567, Hyogo Pref., Japan, *Tel:* +81 78 341 7711, *Fax:* +81 78 341 6477

Approach: The approach to the port is either through Akashi Strait or Bisan Seto traffic routes, vessels then enter Aioi Bay which has a passage of 2 miles long, draft limitation in the channel 6.3 m but permissible up to 5.8 m at highwater with two tugs. Vessels usually anchor at Wada-Misaki for quarantine

Anchorage: There are nine anchorages outside the bay and two within the bay

Pilotage: Inland Sea pilotage and Osaka Bay pilotage is compulsory for vessels exceeding 10 000 gt. Pilots available from Inland Sea Pilots Association, Tel: +81 78 391 7191. Entry to port for vessels over 10 000 gt only permissible from sunrise to 0.5 h before sunset

Weather: Typhoon season, July to October

Tides: Tidal range 1.50 m max, -0.22 m min

Maximum Vessel Dimensions: 6.3 m max d, but up to 8.5 m at HT. 300 000 max dwt in ballast

Accommodation:

Name	Length (m)	Depth (m)	Remarks
Aioi			See [1] below
Publin Berth	270	5.5	
No. 7 W	310	8	
No. 9 W	200	5.5	
No. 10 W	200	5.5	
No. 11 W	200	5.8	
No. 12 W	340	8	

[1]*Aioi:* Ishikawajima-Harima Heavy Industries Co Ltd (IHI), have shipbuilding and dockyard facilities. There is also a shipbreaking yard

Mechanical Handling Equipment:

Location	Type	Capacity (t)	Qty
Aioi	Floating Cranes	120	1

Bunkering: Hanwa Co. Ltd, 2nd Floor, Finland House, 56 Haymarket, London SW1Y 4RN, United Kingdom, *Tel:* +44 20 7839 4448, *Fax:* +44 20 7839 3994, *Email:* orito@hanwa.co.uk

Hikawa Shoji Kaisha Ltd, 26-2 Shinkawa NS Building 1-chome, Shinkawa, Chuo-ku, Tokyo 104, Japan, *Tel:* +81 3 5776 6858, *Fax:* +81 3 5541 3274

Idemitsu Kosan Co. Ltd, 1-1 Marunochi, 3-Chome, Chiyoda-ku, Tokyo 100-8321, Japan, *Tel:* +81 3 3213 3138, *Fax:* +81 3 3213 1145, *Email:* tohru.takamura@si.idemitsu.co.jp, *Website:* www.idemitsu.co.jp

KG Int Petroleum Ltd, Shiba Park Building, 241 Shiba Koen, Minato-ku, Tokyo 105, Japan, *Tel:* +81 3 3578 4551, *Fax:* +81 3 3578 4550

Kamei Corp., 1-6-1 Otemachi, Chiyoda-ku, Tokyo 100-0004, Japan, *Tel:* +81 3 3286 6234, *Fax:* +81 3 3286 6249, *Email:* bunker@kamei.co.jp

Kyodo Oil Co. Ltd, 11-2 Nagata-cho 2-chome, Chiyoda-ku, Tokyo, Japan, *Tel:* +81 3 3505 8241, *Fax:* +81 3 3505 8697

Marubeni Petroleum Co. Ltd, Marubeni International Petroleum Singapore Co. Ltd, c/o Marubeni Corporation, 4-2 Ohtemachi 1-chome, Chiyoda-ku, Tokyo 100-8088, Japan, *Tel:* +81 3 3282 3920, *Fax:* +81 3 3282 3950, *Email:* TOKB554@marubenicorp.com, *Website:* www.marubeni.co.jp

MC Marine and Bunkering Inc., 8th Floor, Uchisaiwai-cho Dai Building, 3-3 Uchisaiwai-cho 1-chome, Chiyoda-ku, Tokyo 100-0011, Japan, *Tel:* +81 3 5251 2575, *Fax:* +81 3 5251 2583

Mitsui & Co. Petroleum Ltd, 2-1, Ohtemachi 1-chome, Chiyoda-ku, Tokyo 100-0004, Japan, *Tel:* +81 3 3285 6905, *Fax:* +81 3 3285 9811, *Email:* tkzph@dg.mitsui.com, *Website:* www.mitsui.co.jp

Nittetsu Shoij Co. Ltd, 5-7 Kameido 1-chome, Koto-ku, Tokyo 136, Japan, *Tel:* +81 3 5627 2157, *Fax:* +81 3 5627 2192

Setouchi Network, 4-20 Hasihama 1-chome, Imabari 799-2112, Ehime Pref., Japan, *Tel:* +81 898 430041, *Fax:* +81 898 430046, *Email:* secjpn@dokidoki.ne.jp

Sumitomo Corp., Harumi Island, Triton Square, Office Tower Y, 8-11 Harumi 1-chome, Chuo-ku, Tokyo 104-8610, Japan, *Tel:* +81 3 51664458, *Fax:* +81 3 51666407, *Email:* ir@sumitomo.co.jp, *Website:* www.sumitomocorp.co.jp

Repair & Maintenance: IHI Corp. (Aioi), 5292 Aioishi, Aioi 678, Japan, *Tel:* +81 791 242206, *Fax:* +81 791 242494, *Email:* webmaster@ihi.co.jp, *Website:* www.ihi.co.jp Three dry docks: No.1 230 m x 33 m x 6 m for vessels up to 78 000 dwt, No.2 143.8 m x 19.5 m x 4.5 m for vessels up to 13 000 dwt, No.3 330 m x 54.5 m x 6 m for vessels up to 300 000 dwt. The shipyard is capable of carrying out all kinds of shop fitting-out and repair work

Surveyors: Nippon Kaiji Kyokai, 3-2-17 Asahi, Aioi 678-0031, Japan, *Tel:* +81 791 220591, *Fax:* +81 791 234265, *Email:* ao@classnk.or.jp, *Website:* www.classnk.or.jp

Medical Facilities: Available

Lloyd's Agent: Cornes & Co. Ltd, Meikai Building, 32 Akashi-machi, Chuo-ku, Kobe 650-0037, Hyogo Pref., Japan, *Tel:* +81 78 332 3421, *Fax:* +81 78 332 3070, *Email:* survey@kobe.cornes.co.jp, *Website:* www.cornes.co.jp

AKITA

Lat 39° 45' N; Long 140° 4' E.

Admiralty Chart: 1388	**Admiralty Pilot:** 41
Time Zone: GMT +9 h	**UNCTAD Locode:** JP AXT

Principal Facilities:

P		Y	G	C	R		B		T	A	

Authority: Port & Harbour Section of Akita Prefecture, 1-1 Sanno 4-chome, Akita 010-8570, Akita Pref., Japan, *Tel:* +81 18 860 1872, *Fax:* +81 18 860 1204

Port Security: ISPS compliant

Approach: Draught limitation in the channel is 9.6 m. For Gaiko 13M Wharf and Denryoku Dolphin No.3 the draught limitation is 11.6 m

Pilotage: Not compulsory but recommended. Pilot boards in pos 39° 47.45' N; 139° 58.30' E during daylight hours only

Tides: Average range 0.2-0.3 m

Traffic: 2006, 51 627 TEU's handled

Maximum Vessel Dimensions: 66 095 dwt, 219.1 m loa

Working Hours: 0830-1630. May be extended when required. Sunday available except 1st, 3rd & 5th weeks

Accommodation:

Name	Length (m)	Depth (m)	Draught (m)	Remarks
Akita				
Nakajima No.1	161	9	8	See [1] below

Name	Length (m)	Depth (m)	Draught (m)	Remarks
Nakajima No.2	185	10	9.4	See [2] below
Nakajima No.3	185	10	9.4	See [3] below
North Pier 'A'	122	7.5	7	Max 5000 dwt. Logs
North Pier 'B'	155	7.5	6.8	Max 5000 dwt. Logs & coal
South Pier 'C'	155	5.5	5	Max 2000 dwt. Bagged cargoes
South Pier 'D'	90	5.5	5	Max 2000 dwt
Terauchi Pier	200	7.5	6.8	Max 5000 dwt x 2
Ohama 10 M Berth No.1	185	10	9.4	For vessels up to 155 m loa & 15 000 dwt. Logs
Ohama 10 M Berth No.2	185	10	9.4	See [4] below
Ohama 10 M Berth No.3	185	10	9.4	For vessels up to 150 m loa & 15 000 dwt
Gaiko 13 M Berth No.1	270	13	11.5	For vessels up to 200 m loa & 50 000 dwt
Gaiko 13 M Berth No.2	260	13	11.5	For vessels up to 200 m loa & 40 000 dwt
Mukaihama 7.5 M Berth No.1	130	7.5	6.8	Max 5000 dwt. Logs
Mukaihama 7.5 M Berth No.2	130	7.5	6.8	Max 5000 dwt. Logs
Mukaihama 10 M Berth No.1	185	10	9.4	For vessels up to 183 m loa & 15 000 dwt Logs
Mukaihama 10 M Berth No.2	185	10	9.4	Max 15 000 dwt Logs
Mukaihama 10 M Berth No.3	185	10	8.9	Max 15 000 dwt. Logs
Tohoku-Denryoku Dolphin No.3	309	13	11.6	Max 45 000 dwt
Tohoku Seishi Dolphin	170	10	10.5	For vessels up to 210 m loa & 30 000 dwt

[1]*Nakajima No.1:* Max 10 000 dwt. Phosphate rock, grain & logs
[2]*Nakajima No.2:* For vessels up to 170 m loa & 15 000 dwt. Zinc concentrate & cement
[3]*Nakajima No.3:* For vessels up to 170 m loa & 15 000 dwt. Zinc concentrate & cement
[4]*Ohama 10 M Berth No.2:* For vessels up to 170 m loa & 15 000 dwt. Cement & general cargo

Storage: Open storage of 231 544 m2 for logs, 49 556 m2 for steel products. Warehouse storage of 15 777 m2, open warehouse storage of 171 899 m2. Silo of 4177 m2 and a timber pool of 120 000 m2

Mechanical Handling Equipment:

Location	Type	Qty
Gaiko 13 M Berth No.1	Mult-purp. Cranes	2
Gaiko 13 M Berth No.2	Mult-purp. Cranes	1

Bunkering: Domestic oil available. Bonded oil from Niigata, Hakodate or Tokyo with sufficient notice

Towage: Five tugs available; one of 3200 hp, one of 2600 hp, two of 350 hp and one of 200 hp

Repair & Maintenance: Minor repairs can be undertaken

Medical Facilities: Available

Airport: Akita Airport

Lloyd's Agent: Cornes & Co. Ltd, 273 Yamashita-cho, Naka-ku, Yokohama 231-0023, Kanagawa Pref., Japan, *Tel:* +81 45 201 8537, *Fax:* +81 45 212 3105, *Email:* survey@ykh.cornes.co.jp, *Website:* www.cornes.co.jp

AMAGASAKI

Lat 34° 42' N; Long 135° 23' E.

Admiralty Chart: JP1107	**Admiralty Pilot:** 42B
Time Zone: GMT +9 h	**UNCTAD Locode:** JP AMA

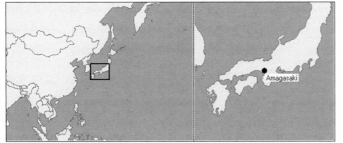

Principal Facilities:

P	Q	Y	G			B		T	A

Authority: Port & Harbour Section of Hyogo Prefecture, 5-10-1 Yamate-dori, Chuo-ku, Kobe 650-8567, Hyogo Pref., Japan, *Tel:* +81 78 341 7711, *Fax:* +81 78 341 6477

Approach: Amagasaki Channel: 4200 m long, 220 m wide in depth of 12 m. Kanzakigawa Channel: 1600 m long, 220 m wide in depth of 12 m. Naruo Channel: 1400 m long, 200 m wide in depth of 10 m

Anchorage: 182 ha of anchorage space available, depths range from 4-12 m

Pilotage: Compulsory for vessels exceeding 10 000 gt for both harbour district and Osaka Bay district. Hanshin Bay Pilots Association, Tel: +81 78 391 5032. Osaka Bay Pilots Association, Tel: +81 78 331 4716. Pilots board 1 mile off the harbour limits in the vicinity of No.1 buoy in pos 34° 39' 18" N; 135° 20' 50" E during daylight hours only

Radio Frequency: VHF Channel 16

Weather: Typhoon season, July to October

Tides: Max 1.71 m, min 0.10 m

Maximum Vessel Dimensions: 70 653 dwt, 250 m max loa, 11.5 m d

Principal Imports and Exports: Imports: Coal, Logs, Scrap iron. Exports: Steel products.

Working Hours: Continuous three shifts at Kobe Steel wharves

Accommodation:

Name	Length (m)	Depth (m)	Draught (m)	Remarks
Public Wharves				
Dolphin No.1	165	10	9.8	See [1] below
Dolphin No.2	150	10	9.8	See [2] below
Dolphin No.3	180	10	9.8	See [3] below
Private Wharves				
Cosmo Oil Co Dolphin Berth	150	9.4	9.4	1 x 30 000 dwt cap. Fuel oil & gasoline

[1]*Dolphin No.1:* For vessels up to 176 m loa. Steel scrap & bulk cargo
[2]*Dolphin No.2:* For vessels up to 176 m loa. Steel scrap & bulk cargo
[3]*Dolphin No.3:* For vessels up to 176 m loa. Steel scrap & bulk cargo

Storage: Four warehouses of 5577 m2, 6.4 ha of coal storage space, 17 ha of timber storage space and 14 ha of general open storage space

Mechanical Handling Equipment:

Location	Type	Capacity (t)	Qty
Amagasaki	Mult-purp. Cranes	20	
Dolphin No.1	Shore Cranes	10	1
Dolphin No.2	Shore Cranes	10	1

Cargo Worked: 6500 t of foreign trade and 37 500 t of domestic trade per working day

Bunkering: Cosmo Oil Co. Ltd, Toshiba Building, 1-1 Shibaura 1-chome, Minato-ku, Tokyo 105-8528, Japan, *Tel:* +81 3 3798 3156, *Fax:* +81 3 3798 3592, *Email:* masayuki_iijima@cosmo-oil.co.jp, *Website:* www.cosmo-oil.co.jp
ExxonMobil Marine Fuels, 1 Harbour Front Place, 06-00 Harbour Front, Tower One, Singapore, Republic of Singapore 098633, *Tel:* +65 6885 8998, *Fax:* +65 6885 8794, *Email:* asiapac.marinefuels@exxonmobil.com, *Website:* www.exxonmobilmarinefuels.com
Hanwa Co. Ltd, 2nd Floor, Finland House, 56 Haymarket, London SW1Y 4RN, United Kingdom, *Tel:* +44 20 7839 4448, *Fax:* +44 20 7839 3994, *Email:* orito@hanwa.co.uk
Idemitsu Kosan Co. Ltd, 1-1 Marunochi, 3-Chome, Chiyoda-ku, Tokyo 100-8321, Japan, *Tel:* +81 3 3213 3138, *Fax:* +81 3 3213 1145, *Email:* tohru.takamura@si.idemitsu.co.jp, *Website:* www.idemitsu.co.jp
KG Int Petroleum Ltd, Shiba Park Building, 241 Shiba Koen, Minato-ku, Tokyo 105, Japan, *Tel:* +81 3 3578 4551, *Fax:* +81 3 3578 4550
Japan Energy Corp., 2-10-1, Toranomon, Minato-ku, Tokyo 105-8407, Japan, *Tel:* +81 3 5573 6100, *Fax:* +81 3 5573 6674, *Email:* yamano@j-energy.co.jp, *Website:* www.j-energy.co.jp
Kawasho Corp., World Trade Centre, 4-1 Hanamatsu-cho 2-chome, Minato-ku, Tokyo 105, Japan, *Tel:* +81 3 3435 3251
Kyodo Oil Co. Ltd, 11-2 Nagata-cho 2-chome, Chiyoda-ku, Tokyo, Japan, *Tel:* +81 3 3505 8241, *Fax:* +81 3 3505 8697
Marubeni Petroleum Co. Ltd, Marubeni International Petroleum Singapore Co. Ltd, c/o Marubeni Corporation, 4-2 Ohtemachi 1-chome, Chiyoda-ku, Tokyo 100-8088, Japan, *Tel:* +81 3 3282 3920, *Fax:* +81 3 3282 3950, *Email:* TOKB554@marubenicorp.com, *Website:* www.marubeni.co.jp
MC Marine and Bunkering Inc., 8th Floor, Uchisaiwai-cho Dai Building, 3-3 Uchi-saiwai-cho 1-chome, Chiyoda-ku, Tokyo 100-0011, Japan, *Tel:* +81 3 5251 2575, *Fax:* +81 3 5251 2583
Mitsui & Co. Petroleum Ltd, 2-1, Ohtemachi 1-chome, Chiyoda-ku, Tokyo 100-0004, Japan, *Tel:* +81 3 3285 6905, *Fax:* +81 3 3285 9811, *Email:* tkzph@dg.mitsui.com, *Website:* www.mitsui.co.jp
Nissho Iwai Corp., 4-4 Akasaka 2-chome, Minato-ku, Tokyo, Japan, *Tel:* +81 3 35882111
Nittetsu Shoij Co. Ltd, 5-7 Kameido 1-chome, Koto-ku, Tokyo 136, Japan, *Tel:* +81 3 5627 2157, *Fax:* +81 3 5627 2192
Sumitomo Corp., Harumi Island, Triton Square, Office Tower Y, 8-11 Harumi 1-chome, Chuo-ku, Tokyo 104-8610, Japan, *Tel:* +81 3 51664458, *Fax:* +81 3 51666407, *Email:* ir@sumitomo.co.jp, *Website:* www.sumitomocorp.co.jp

Towage: Not compulsory but advisable. One tug of 2000 hp available. Extra tugs can be obtained from Kobe if required

Repair & Maintenance: Minor repairs undertaken

Medical Facilities: Available

Airport: Osaka International, 10 km

Lloyd's Agent: Cornes & Co. Ltd, Meikai Building, 32 Akashi-machi, Chuo-ku, Kobe 650-0037, Hyogo Pref., Japan, *Tel:* +81 78 332 3421, *Fax:* +81 78 332 3070, *Email:* survey@kobe.cornes.co.jp, *Website:* www.cornes.co.jp

AOMORI

Lat 40° 49' N; Long 140° 45' E.

Admiralty Chart: JP10	**Admiralty Pilot:** 41
Time Zone: GMT +9 h	**UNCTAD Locode:** JP AOJ

Key to Principal Facilities:—				
A=Airport	**C**=Containers	**G**=General Cargo	**P**=Petroleum	**R**=Ro/Ro	**Y**=Dry Bulk
B=Bunkers	**D**=Dry Dock	**L**=Cruise	**Q**=Other Liquid Bulk	**T**=Towage (where available from port)

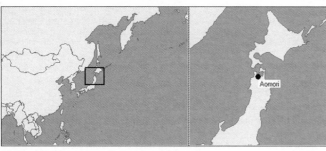

Principal Facilities:

| P | Q | Y | G | | R | | B | | T | A |

Authority: Ports, Harbours & Airport Division, Aomori Prefectural Government, 1-1 Nagashima 1-chome, Aomori 030-8570, Aomori Pref., Japan, *Tel:* +81 17 722 1111, *Fax:* +81 17 734 8194, *Email:* kowan@pref.aomori.lg.jp, *Website:* www.pref.aomori.lg.jp

Port Security: ISPS compliant

Approach: Depth in fairway is 13 m

Anchorage: Anchorage can be obtained at various points up to a depth of 30 m

Pilotage: Not compulsory. Harbour Pilots available at the quarantine anchorage from sunrise to sunset

Weather: Winds SW, but N in summer. Season of dense fog lasts from June-August. Navigation is impossible two or three days a year

Tides: Tidal range 1.77 m max, -0.09 m min

Maximum Vessel Dimensions: 60 000 gt (LPG) and 10 000 gt (general cargo)

Working Hours: 0800-1700

Accommodation:

Name	Length (m)	Depth (m)	Draught (m)	Remarks
Aomori				See [1] below
No.2 Wharf (2) (Hamacho W.)	178	9	8.5	Max 10 000 dwt
No.2 Wharf (3) (Hamacho W.)	154	7.5	7	Max 5000 dwt
Passenger Vessel Berth (Central W.)	280	10		Max 30 000 dwt
Tsutsumi Wharf	448	7.5–10	7–9.5	Max 5000-12 000 dwt. Two berths
Aburakawa Lumber Port	230	4.5	4	
Okidate Pier No.A	270	7.5		Max 5000 dwt
Okidate Pier No.B	185	10	9.5	Max 12 000 dwt
Okidate Pier No.C	270	13	11.7	Max 40 000 dwt

[1]*Aomori:* Harbour protected by breakwater 3310 m long. Loading and unloading facilities by truck crane. There are also unloading facilities for cement and facilities for fishing vessels. Private wall 531 m with a depth of 13 m for one LPG vessel up to 60 000 gt

Storage: Transit sheds for salt, cereals, manure and vegetables. Warehouse space of 36 000 m2 and refrigerated space of 4000 m2. Ample open storage

Bunkering: Domestic oil available. Bonded oil from Hakodate with required advance notice

Towage: Two tugs of 3200 hp and 3400 hp

Airport: Aomori Airport, 13 km

Lloyd's Agent: Cornes & Co. Ltd, 273 Yamashita-cho, Naka-ku, Yokohama 231-0023, Kanagawa Pref., Japan, *Tel:* +81 45 201 8537, *Fax:* +81 45 212 3105, *Email:* survey@ykh.cornes.co.jp, *Website:* www.cornes.co.jp

ARIDA

harbour area, see under Wakayama

ATSUMI

Lat 34° 40' N; Long 137° 4' E.

Admiralty Chart: JP70	**Admiralty Pilot:** 42A
Time Zone: GMT +9 h	**UNCTAD Locode:** JP ATM

Principal Facilities:

| P | | | | | B | | T | |

Authority: Techno Chubu Co. Ltd, 1-2 Aza Kyuemori, Oaza Nakayama, Atsumi, Aichi Pref., Japan, *Tel:* +81 5313 22111, *Fax:* +81 5313 22392

Approach: The approach to the port is through the Irago Suido traffic route, entering Nakayama Suido (East Passage) 12.5 m max d in daylight hours only. When sailing, vessels leave via Nakayama Suido (West Passage) with 9.0 m max d (over 9.0 m and up to 10.0 m subject to tidal condition)

Anchorage: Anchorage can be obtained around pos 34° 41' N; 137° 03' E in a depth of 18 m

Pilotage: Compulsory for vessels over 10 000 gt. Pilot boards within 1.5 mile radius from the positions 34° 30' 48" N; 137° 06' 54" E for vessels approaching from the E, 34° 28' 18" N; 137° 03' 48" E for vessels from the W or S. Irago Mikawa Wan Licensed Pilot Association, 24 h service, VHF Channels 16 and 13. Berthing and unberthing during daylight hours only

Radio Frequency: Mikawa Bay Port Radio, 24 h service. Calling on VHF Channel 16, working on Channels 11 and 12

Weather: Typhoon season, July to October

Tides: Max 2.1 m, min 0.3 m

Working Hours: Sunrise to sunset

Accommodation:

Name	Length (m)	Depth (m)	Draught (m)	Remarks
Atsumi				See [1] below
Atsumi Dolphin Pier	354	14	12.5	See [2] below

[1]*Atsumi:* Tanker discharging port serving the power station of Chubu Electric Power Co. Tugs available

[2]*Atsumi Dolphin Pier:* A private berth operated by Chubu Electric Power Co. Inc. Accommodating vessels of 79 900 dwt with full cargo, 94 588 dwt with half cargo, max loa 253 m. The berth is equipped with two loading arms discharging at 4500 kl/h max rate. 20" & 24" pipelines

Cargo Worked: 35 000 t of crude oil discharged in a working day

Bunkering: Available by barge to ship through shore line

Cosmo Oil Co. Ltd, Toshiba Building, 1-1 Shibaura 1-chome, Minato-ku, Tokyo 105-8528, Japan, *Tel:* +81 3 3798 3156, *Fax:* +81 3 3798 3592, *Email:* masayuki_iijima@cosmo-oil.co.jp, *Website:* www.cosmo-oil.co.jp

Hanwa Co. Ltd, 2nd Floor, Finland House, 56 Haymarket, London SW1Y 4RN, United Kingdom, *Tel:* +44 20 7839 4448, *Fax:* +44 20 7839 3994, *Email:* orito@hanwa.co.uk

Hikawa Shoji Kaisha Ltd, 26-2 Shinkawa NS Building 1-chome, Shinkawa, Chuo-ku, Tokyo 104, Japan, *Tel:* +81 3 5776 6858, *Fax:* +81 3 5541 3274

Idemitsu Kosan Co. Ltd, 1-1 Marunochi, 3-Chome, Chiyoda-ku, Tokyo 100-8321, Japan, *Tel:* +81 3 3213 3138, *Fax:* +81 3 3213 1145, *Email:* tohru.takamura@si.idemitsu.co.jp, *Website:* www.idemitsu.co.jp

KG Int Petroleum Ltd, Shiba Park Building, 241 Shiba Koen, Minato-ku, Tokyo 105, Japan, *Tel:* +81 3 3578 4551, *Fax:* +81 3 3578 4550

Japan Energy Corp., 2-10-1, Toranomon, Minato-ku, Tokyo 105-8407, Japan, *Tel:* +81 3 5573 6100, *Fax:* +81 3 5573 6674, *Email:* yamano@j-energy.co.jp, *Website:* www.j-energy.co.jp

Kamei Corp., 1-6-1 Otemachi, Chiyoda-ku, Tokyo 100-0004, Japan, *Tel:* +81 3 3286 6234, *Fax:* +81 3 3286 6249, *Email:* bunker@kamei.co.jp

Kawasho Corp., World Trade Centre, 4-1 Hanamatsu-cho 2-chome, Minato-ku, Tokyo 105, Japan, *Tel:* +81 3 3435 3251

Kyodo Oil Co. Ltd, 11-2 Nagata-cho 2-chome, Chiyoda-ku, Tokyo, Japan, *Tel:* +81 3 3505 8241, *Fax:* +81 3 3505 8697

Marubeni Petroleum Co. Ltd, Marubeni International Petroleum Singapore Co. Ltd, c/o Marubeni Corporation, 4-2 Ohtemachi 1-chome, Chiyoda-ku, Tokyo 100-8088, Japan, *Tel:* +81 3 3282 3920, *Fax:* +81 3 3282 3950, *Email:* TOKB554@marubenicorp.com, *Website:* www.marubeni.co.jp

MC Marine and Bunkering Inc., 8th Floor, Uchisaiwai-cho Dai Building, 3-3 Uchisaiwai-cho 1-chome, Chiyoda-ku, Tokyo 100-0011, Japan, *Tel:* +81 3 5251 2575, *Fax:* +81 3 5251 2583

Mitsui & Co. Petroleum Ltd, 2-1, Ohtemachi 1-chome, Chiyoda-ku, Tokyo 100-0004, Japan, *Tel:* +81 3 3285 6905, *Fax:* +81 3 3285 9811, *Email:* tkzph@dg.mitsui.com, *Website:* www.mitsui.co.jp

Nissho Iwai Corp., 4-4 Akasaka 2-chome, Minato-ku, Tokyo, Japan, *Tel:* +81 3 35882111

Nittetsu Shoij Co. Ltd, 5-7 Kameido 1-chome, Koto-ku, Tokyo 136, Japan, *Tel:* +81 3 5627 2157, *Fax:* +81 3 5627 2192

Shinagawa Fuel Co. Ltd, New Pier Takeshiba North Tower, 8th Floor, 1-11-1 Kaigan, Minato-ku, Tokyo 105-8525, Japan, *Tel:* +81 3 5470 7113, *Fax:* +81 3 5470 7157, *Email:* hakuyu@ml1.sinanen.co.jp

Sigma Foreign Service (Panama) S.A., 2-25 Aikawai, Tempaku-ku, Nagoya 468-0836, Aichi Pref., Japan, *Tel:* +81 52 896 1510, *Fax:* +81 52 896 7703

Sumitomo Corp., Harumi Island, Triton Square, Office Tower Y, 8-11 Harumi 1-chome, Chuo-ku, Tokyo 104-8610, Japan, *Tel:* +81 3 51664458, *Fax:* +81 3 51666407, *Email:* ir@sumitomo.co.jp, *Website:* www.sumitomocorp.co.jp

Towage: Compulsory. Three tugs required for berthing and two tugs for unberthing. Tugs up to 3500 bhp available from Nagoya

Lloyd's Agent: Cornes & Co. Ltd, 273 Yamashita-cho, Naka-ku, Yokohama 231-0023, Kanagawa Pref., Japan, *Tel:* +81 45 201 8537, *Fax:* +81 45 212 3105, *Email:* survey@ykh.cornes.co.jp, *Website:* www.cornes.co.jp

BRIDGESTONE DOLPHIN JETTY

harbour area, see under Karatsu

CHIBA

Lat 35° 34' N; Long 140° 7' E.

Admiralty Chart: JP1086/1087
Admiralty Pilot: 42A
Time Zone: GMT +9 h
UNCTAD Locode: JP CHB

Principal Facilities:

| P | Q | Y | G | C | R | | B | D | T | A | |

Authority: Port & Harbor Promotion Division, Civil Engineering Department, Chiba Prefectural Government, 1-1 Ichiba-cho, Chuo-ku, Chiba 260-8667, Chiba Pref., Japan, *Tel:* +81 43 223 3830, *Fax:* +81 43 227 6115, *Website:* www.pref.chiba.jp

Port Security: ISPS compliant

Documentation: Entrance notice (to Customs & Immigration Offices)
Captain's report (to Quarantine Station)
Import inspection application (to Plant Protection Station & Animal Quarantine Service)
Entrance and departure notice (to Coast Guard Office, Port Directors & Harbour Fire Brigade)
Mooring institution use report (to Port Directors)

Approach: The port occupies an area extending from the estuary of the Edo River to the Narawa region. There are nine passages with drafts ranging from 6.5-18 m

Pilotage: Compulsory for vessels over 10 000 gt. Both Bay and Harbour Pilots are required. Harbour pilots board at the anchorage and are only available from daylight until 1 h before sunset

Tides: Tidal range 2.17 m max, -0.2 m min

Traffic: 2006, 4547 foreign trade vessels & 61 070 domestic vessels, 98 229 000 t of foreign cargo handled & 68 735 000 t of domestic cargo handled

Maximum Vessel Dimensions: 310 000 dwt, 20 m draft

Principal Imports and Exports: Imports: Crude petroleum, LNG, Oil products. Exports: Chemicals, Steel materials, Vehicles.

Working Hours: 24 h/day

Accommodation: There are 24 800 ha of port area space and 690 000 m2 of water front area

Name	Length (m)	Depth (m)	Draught (m)	Remarks
Chiba				
Chiba Ajinomoto Seiyu Dolphin	160	12	12	Max 75 000 dwt. Two pneumatic unloaders
Mitsubishi Mokuzai	200	12	11.6	Max 50 000 dwt
Keiyo Mokuzai	110	12	9.8	Max 20 000 dwt
Sangyo New Port	150	12	10.9	Max 40 000 dwt
Higashi Nihon Seito	150	12	10.8	Max 45 320 dwt
Kyodo Silo (Dolphin)	150	12	12	Max 75 000 dwt. Three pneumatic unloaders
Nihon Silo (Dolphin)	160	12	12	Max 55 000 dwt. Three pneumatic unloaders
Shin Nippon Cold Japan Tank Terminal	120	12	12	Max 47 000 dwt. Four 6" pipelines
Chuo Futo (A, B, C, D & E)	1000	10	9.1	Max 15 000 dwt
Chuo Futo (F)	240	12	11	Max 30 000 dwt
Chuo Futo (G)	240	12	11	See [1] below
Chuo Futo (H)	240	12	11	Max 30 000 dwt
Dezu Futo (A, B & C)	360	7.5	7.5	Max 5000 dwt x 3
Dezu Futo (E, F)	220	5.7	5.7	Max 3000 dwt x 2
Kawatetsu Wharf (A)	200	9.6	9.6	Max 10 000 dwt
Kawatetsu Wharf (B)	150	10.8	10.8	Max 25 000 dwt
Kawatetsu Wharf (C)	139	10.8	10.8	Max 25 000 dwt
Kawatetsu Wharf (J)	268	18	17	Max 154 000 dwt
Kawatetsu Wharf (M)	310	12	11.3	Max 50 000 dwt
Kawatetsu Wharf (OC)	245	10.5	9.4	Max 20 000 dwt
Kawatetsu Wharf (OD)	130	10.5	9.4	Max 20 000 dwt
Kawatetsu Wharf (EB)	350	18	17	Max 200 000 dwt
Kawatetsu Wharf (EA)	200	11.4	11.4	Max 50 000 dwt

Name	Length (m)	Depth (m)	Draught (m)	Remarks
Kawatetsu Wharf (NA)	300	15		Max 60 000 dwt
Fuji Koun	134	6	5.4	Max 4500 dwt
Yawata Pier	289	10.5	9.4	Max 20 000 dwt
Ichihara Public	240	7.2	7.2	Max 5000 dwt
Asahi Glass Pier	195	12	11.8	Max 50 000 dwt
Asahi Export Pier	172	5.4	4.5	Max 6000 dwt
Cosmo Oil No.2 (Dolphin)	230	12	11.8	Max 50 000 dwt. One 10" pipeline
Cosmo Oil No.10	270	13	13	Max 50 000 dwt
Nissan Nisso Pier	150	10.5	10	For vessels up to 180 m loa & 20 000 dwt
Kyokuto Oil (Dolphin)	100	14	14	Max 100 000 dwt. Three 12" pipelines
Mitsui Sekiyu	280	4.7	4.7	Max 2000 dwt
Idemitsu No.1 (Dolphin)	280	16	14.5	Max 100 000 dwt. 30" & 18" pipelines
Idemitsu No.2 (Dolphin)	245	16	14	Max 75 000 dwt. 24" & 8" pipelines
Idemitsu No.3 (Dolphin)	205	10.7	10.7	Max 45 000 dwt. One 6" pipeline
Sumitomo Chibakagaku	350	10.5	9.5	For vessels up to 180 m loa & 30 000 dwt. Naptha facilities
Sumitomo (Chemical Tanker)	80	7.5	7	Max 2000 dwt
Fuji Oil (Dolphin)	260	16	14.5	Max 120 000 dwt. 30" & 20" pipelines
Nihon Rinsan	260	12	10.5	Max 45 000 dwt. One 375 t/h unloader
Keiyo Sea Berth	470	20.5	19.2	Max 314 250 dwt. Three 48" pipelines
Marubeni Sea Berth	405	14	13.5	See [2] below
Idemitsu Bulk Terminal		14	12.6	Max 89 990 dwt. Bucket elevator at 1200 t/h
Kanzaki Seishi	206	12	10.9	Max 40 000 dwt
Yoshino Sekko	190	12	10.8	Max 42 900 dwt
Itochu Lumber	200	12	10.5	Max 44 500 dwt
Nissho Iwai	150	12	10.8	Max 46 134 dwt
Taiheiyo Cement	109	10	8.1	Max 20 000 dwt
Funabashi				
Public Wharves				
Chuo Futo North A1-A6	540	5.5	5	Max 2000 dwt x 6
Chuo Futo North B	130	7.5	6.9	Max 5000 dwt
Chuo Futo North C	130	7.5	7.5	Max 5000 dwt
Chuo Futo North D	130	7.5	7.5	Max 5000 dwt
Chuo Futo North E	130	7.5	7.5	Max 5000 dwt
Chuo Futo North F	130	7.5	7.5	Max 5000 dwt
Chuo Futo North G	130	7.5	7.5	Max 5000 dwt
Chuo Futo North H	130	7.5	7.5	Max 5000 dwt
Chuo Futo North I	130	7.5	7.5	Max 5000 dwt
Chuo Futo North J	130	7.5	7.5	Max 5000 dwt
Chuo Futo North K	130	7.5	7.5	Max 5000 dwt
Chuo Futo North L	130	7.5	7.5	Max 5000 dwt
Chuo Futo South A	185	10	10	Max 15 000 dwt
Chuo Futo South B	185	10	10	Max 15 000 dwt
Chuo Futo South C	185	10	10	Max 15 000 dwt
Chuo Futo South D	185	10	10	Max 15 000 dwt
Chuo Futo South E	185	10	10	Max 15 000 dwt
Hinode Futo A-E	450	5.5		Max 2000 dwt x 5
Higashi Futo A-B	260	7.5		Max 5000 dwt x 2
Higashi Futo C-G	525	6		Max 3000 dwt x 5
Higashi Futo H-I	180	5.5		Max 2000 dwt x 2
Private Wharves				
Keiyo Shokuhin Kombinat Wharf	240	12	10.8	Max 38 082 dwt
Honshu Butsuryu Center Wharf	395	12	10.8	Max 47 076 dwt
Kubota Iron Works Wharf	285	12	10.8	Max 29 285 dwt
Honda Nissin Wharf	346	12	10.8	Max 42 424 dwt
Nittsu (Nippon Express) Wharf	250	12	10.8	Max 37 391 dwt
Hanwa Keiyo Berth	290	12	9.5	Max 46 606 dwt

Key to Principal Facilities:—
A=Airport **C**=Containers **G**=General Cargo **P**=Petroleum **R**=Ro/Ro **Y**=Dry Bulk
B=Bunkers **D**=Dry Dock **L**=Cruise **Q**=Other Liquid Bulk **T**=Towage (where available from port)

Name	Length (m)	Depth (m)	Draught (m)	Remarks
Chiba Toyopet Wharf	180	12	10.8	Max 3281 dwt. Coastal car carrier only

[1]*Chuo Futo (G):* Max 30 000 dwt. Container terminal area of approx 80 000 m2 with container yard for max of 2616 TEU's and container freight station of 1934 m2. 52 reefer points
[2]*Marubeni Sea Berth:* Two berths. Max 80 000 dwt for fuel oil and 50 000 dwt for LPG

Storage: Total transit shed space of 47 210 m2, freight handling yard of 398 810 m2 and open storage yard area covering 369 380 m2

Mechanical Handling Equipment:

Location	Type	Capacity (t)	Qty
Higashi Nihon Seito	Mult-purp. Cranes	330	2
Kawatetsu Wharf (B)	Mult-purp. Cranes	20	3
Kawatetsu Wharf (C)	Mult-purp. Cranes	22	1
Kawatetsu Wharf (J)	Mult-purp. Cranes	60	2
Kawatetsu Wharf (M)	Mult-purp. Cranes	16	2
Kawatetsu Wharf (OC)	Mult-purp. Cranes	15	2
Kawatetsu Wharf (OD)	Mult-purp. Cranes	22	1
Kawatetsu Wharf (EB)	Mult-purp. Cranes	60	2
Kawatetsu Wharf (EA)	Mult-purp. Cranes	35	2
Kawatetsu Wharf (NA)	Mult-purp. Cranes	50	2
Yawata Pier	Mult-purp. Cranes	8	1
Asahi Glass Pier	Mult-purp. Cranes	13	2

Bunkering: Cosmo Oil Co. Ltd, Toshiba Building, 1-1 Shibaura 1-chome, Minato-ku, Tokyo 105-8528, Japan, *Tel:* +81 3 3798 3156, *Fax:* +81 3 3798 3592, *Email:* masayuki_iijima@cosmo-oil.co.jp, *Website:* www.cosmo-oil.co.jp
ExxonMobil Marine Fuels, 1 Harbour Front Place, 06-00 Harbour Front, Tower One, Singapore, Republic of Singapore 098633, *Tel:* +65 6885 8998, *Fax:* +65 6885 8794, *Email:* asiapac.marinefuels@exxonmobil.com, *Website:* www.exxonmobilmarinefuels.com
Fuji Kosan Co. Ltd, 2-19-6 Yanagibashi, Taito-ku, Tokyo 111-0052, Japan, *Tel:* +81 3 3861 4601, *Fax:* +81 3 3861 4611, *Email:* info@fkoil.co.jp, *Website:* www.fkoil.co.jp
Hanwa Co. Ltd, 2nd Floor, Finland House, 56 Haymarket, London SW1Y 4RN, United Kingdom, *Tel:* +44 20 7839 4448, *Fax:* +44 20 7839 3994, *Email:* orito@hanwa.co.uk
Hikawa Shoji Kaisha Ltd, 26-2 Shinkawa NS Building 1-chome, Shinkawa, Chuo-ku, Tokyo 104, Japan, *Tel:* +81 3 5776 6858, *Fax:* +81 3 5541 3274
Idemitsu Kosan Co. Ltd, 1-1 Marunochi, 3-Chome, Chiyoda-ku, Tokyo 100-8321, Japan, *Tel:* +81 3 3213 3138, *Fax:* +81 3 3213 1145, *Email:* tohru.takamura@si.idemitsu.co.jp, *Website:* www.idemitsu.co.jp
KG Int Petroleum Ltd, Shiba Park Building, 241 Shiba Koen, Minato-ku, Tokyo 105, Japan, *Tel:* +81 3 3578 4551, *Fax:* +81 3 3578 4550
Japan Energy Corp., 2-10-1, Toranomon, Minato-ku, Tokyo 105-8407, Japan, *Tel:* +81 3 5573 6100, *Fax:* +81 3 5573 6674, *Email:* yamano@j-energy.co.jp, *Website:* www.j-energy.co.jp
Kyodo Oil Co. Ltd, 11-2 Nagata-cho 2-chome, Chiyoda-ku, Tokyo, Japan, *Tel:* +81 3 3505 8241, *Fax:* +81 3 3505 8697
Kyushu Oil Co. Ltd, 1-1 Uchisaiwai-cho 2-chome, Chiyoda-ku, Tokyo, Japan, *Tel:* +81 3 3502 3651, *Fax:* +81 3 3502 9850
Marubeni Petroleum Co. Ltd, Marubeni International Petroleum Singapore Co. Ltd, c/o Marubeni Corporation, 4-2 Ohtemachi 1-chome, Chiyoda-ku, Tokyo 100-8088, Japan, *Tel:* +81 3 3282 3920, *Fax:* +81 3 3282 3950, *Email:* TOKB554@marubenicorp.com, *Website:* www.marubeni.co.jp
MC Marine and Bunkering Inc., 8th Floor, Uchisaiwai-cho Dai Building, 3-3 Uchisaiwai-cho 1-chome, Chiyoda-ku, Tokyo 100-0011, Japan, *Tel:* +81 3 5251 2575, *Fax:* +81 3 5251 2583
Mitsui & Co. Petroleum Ltd, 2-1, Ohtemachi 1-chome, Chiyoda-ku, Tokyo 100-0004, Japan, *Tel:* +81 3 3285 6905, *Fax:* +81 3 3285 9811, *Email:* tkzph@dg.mitsui.com, *Website:* www.mitsui.co.jp
Nissho Iwai Corp., 4-4 Akasaka 2-chome, Minato-ku, Tokyo, Japan, *Tel:* +81 3 35882111
Nittetsu Shoij Co. Ltd, 5-7 Kameido 1-chome, Koto-ku, Tokyo 136, Japan, *Tel:* +81 3 5627 2157, *Fax:* +81 3 5627 2192
NKK Trading Inc., 4-4 Nihonbashi Hisamatsusucho, Chuo-ku, Tokyo 103, Japan, *Tel:* +81 3 3660 1522, *Fax:* +81 3 3660 1572
Panoco Trading Co. Ltd, Shin-Sudacho Kyodo Building 2nd Floor, 1-5, Kanda Sudacho, Chiyoda-ku, Tokyo 101-0041, Japan, *Tel:* +81 3 5298 6633, *Fax:* +81 3 3255 2202, *Email:* minori@panoco.co.jp, *Website:* www.panoco.co.jp
Shinagawa Fuel Co. Ltd, New Pier Takeshiba North Tower, 8th Floor, 1-11-1 Kaigan, Minato-ku, Tokyo 105-8525, Japan, *Tel:* +81 3 5470 7113, *Fax:* +81 3 5470 7157, *Email:* hakuyu@ml1.sinanen.co.jp
Showa Yokkaichi Sekiyu K.K., Tokyo Building, 7-3 Marunouchi 2-chome, Chiyoda-ku, Tokyo 100, Japan, *Tel:* +81 3 3215 1643, *Fax:* +81 3 3215 1869
SK Energy Asia Private Ltd, 8th Floor Yamato Seimei Building, 1-17 Uchisaiwicho 1-chome, Chiyoda-ku, Tokyo 100-0011, Japan, *Tel:* +81 3 3591 0533, *Fax:* +81 3 3591 7487, *Email:* leehk@skenergy.com, *Website:* www.skenergy.com
Sumitomo Corp., Harumi Island, Triton Square, Office Tower Y, 8-11 Harumi 1-chome, Chuo-ku, Tokyo 104-8610, Japan, *Tel:* +81 3 5166 4646, *Fax:* +81 3 51666407, *Email:* ir@sumitomo.co.jp, *Website:* www.sumitomocorp.co.jp
Total France S.A., Total Marine Fuels, 51 Esplanade du General de Gaulle, F-92907 Paris la Defense Cedex 10, France, *Tel:* +33 1 4135 2755, *Fax:* +33 1 4197 0291, *Email:* marine.fuels@total.com, *Website:* www.marinefuels.total.com

Waste Reception Facilities: Available

Towage: 14 tugs available; one of 3000 hp, six of 3100 hp and seven of 3600 hp

Medical Facilities: Hospitals available

Airport: Narita, 35 km

Railway: Keiyo Line, approx 1 km

Lloyd's Agent: Cornes & Co. Ltd, 273 Yamashita-cho, Naka-ku, Yokohama 231-0023, Kanagawa Pref., Japan, *Tel:* +81 45 201 8537, *Fax:* +81 45 212 3105, *Email:* survey@ykh.cornes.co.jp, *Website:* www.cornes.co.jp

CHITA

harbour area, see under Nagoya

CHOFU

harbour area, see under Shimonoseki

ETAJIMA

Lat 34° 14' N; Long 132° 29' E.

Admiralty Chart: 3472		**Admiralty Pilot:** 42A	
Time Zone: GMT +9 h		**UNCTAD Locode:** JP ETA	

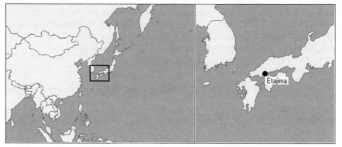

Principal Facilities:

P		G			B		

Authority: Port & Harbour Bureau of Kure City, 1-6 Chuo 4-chome, Kure 737-8501, Hiroshima Pref., Japan, *Tel:* +81 823 253333, *Fax:* +81 823 251361, *Email:* kowan@city.kure.lg.jp, *Website:* www.city.kure.lg.jp

Port Security: ISPS compliant

Approach: Draught limitation in the channel 17 m (17.4 m at high tide)

Pilotage: Zen Noh Berth : Compulsory for only entering; C.I. Oil Terminal: Not compulsory
Inland-sea pilots are available at Sekisaki, Wad-Misaki or Hesaki and harbour pilots are avilable at Kure anchorage for vessels requiring pilot services

Tides: Tidal range 4.00 m max, - 0.28 m min

Accommodation:

Name	Length (m)	Depth (m)	Draught (m)	Remarks
Kure				
Zen Noh Berth	190	13	12	Max 56 000 dwt
C.I. Oil Terminal Pier	273	15	14	Max 125 000 dwt

Bunkering: ExxonMobil Marine Fuels, 1 Harbour Front Place, 06-00 Harbour Front, Tower One, Singapore, Republic of Singapore 098633, *Tel:* +65 6885 8998, *Fax:* +65 6885 8794, *Email:* asiapac.marinefuels@exxonmobil.com, *Website:* www.exxonmobilmarinefuels.com
Hikawa Shoji Kaisha Ltd, 26-2 Shinkawa NS Building 1-chome, Shinkawa, Chuo-ku, Tokyo 104, Japan, *Tel:* +81 3 5776 6858, *Fax:* +81 3 5541 3274
Kamei Corp., 1-6-1 Otemachi, Chiyoda-ku, Tokyo 100-0004, Japan, *Tel:* +81 3 3286 6234, *Fax:* +81 3 3286 6249, *Email:* bunker@kamei.co.jp
Kyodo Oil Co. Ltd, 11-2 Nagata-cho 2-chome, Chiyoda-ku, Tokyo, Japan, *Tel:* +81 3 3505 8241, *Fax:* +81 3 3505 8697
Marubeni Petroleum Co. Ltd, Marubeni International Petroleum Singapore Co. Ltd, c/o Marubeni Corporation, 4-2 Ohtemachi 1-chome, Chiyoda-ku, Tokyo 100-8088, Japan, *Tel:* +81 3 3282 3920, *Fax:* +81 3 3282 3950, *Email:* TOKB554@marubenicorp.com, *Website:* www.marubeni.co.jp
MC Marine and Bunkering Inc., 8th Floor, Uchisaiwai-cho Dai Building, 3-3 Uchisaiwai-cho 1-chome, Chiyoda-ku, Tokyo 100-0011, Japan, *Tel:* +81 3 5251 2575, *Fax:* +81 3 5251 2583
Nittetsu Shoij Co. Ltd, 5-7 Kameido 1-chome, Koto-ku, Tokyo 136, Japan, *Tel:* +81 3 5627 2157, *Fax:* +81 3 5627 2192

Repair & Maintenance: Zen Noh Berth: Available
C.I. Oil Terminal: Small repairs can be undertaken if berth owners permission is granted. Major repairs and the use of fire at the pier is strictly prohibited by the Kure Maritime Security Board and berth owners

Lloyd's Agent: Cornes & Co. Ltd, Meikai Building, 32 Akashi-machi, Chuo-ku, Kobe 650-0037, Hyogo Pref., Japan, *Tel:* +81 78 332 3421, *Fax:* +81 78 332 3070, *Email:* survey@kobe.cornes.co.jp, *Website:* www.cornes.co.jp

FUJIWARA WHARF

harbour area, see under Onahama

FUKUI

Lat 36° 13' N; Long 136° 8' E.

Admiralty Chart: JP1169   **Admiralty Pilot:** 41

Time Zone: GMT +9 h   **UNCTAD Locode:** JP FKJ

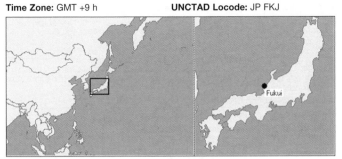

Principal Facilities:

		G		B	T	

Authority: Port & Harbour Section of Fukui Prefecture, 3-17-1 Ohte, Fukui 910-8580, Fukui Pref., Japan, *Tel:* +81 776 211111, *Fax:* +81 776 200678, *Email:* k-yuchi@pref.fukui.lg.jp, *Website:* www.pref.fukui.jp

Officials: Business Director: Osamu Sudo.

Port Security: ISPS compliant

Approach: Draught limitation in the channel is 9 m

Pilotage: Not compulsory. Pilots are available at the anchorage when required; no night berthing or unberthing

Tides: Tidal range 0.60 m max, -0.17 m min

Principal Imports and Exports: Imports: Aluminium, Chemical medicine, Coal. Exports: Scrap iron, Used cars.

Working Hours: 0800-1700. Sundays and holidays subject to negotiation

Accommodation:

Name	Length (m)	Depth (m)	Remarks
Fukui			See [1] below
North Pier Wharf No.1	185	10	Max 15 000 dwt
North Pier Wharf No.2	185	10	Max 15 000 dwt
North Pier Wharf No.3	185	10	Max 15 000 dwt
North Pier Wharf No.4	130	7.5	Max 5000 dwt
North Pier Wharf No.5	130	7.5	Max 5000 dwt
North Pier Wharf No.6	130	7.5	Max 5000 dwt
North Pier Wharf No.7	130	7.5	Max 5000 dwt
North Pier Wharf No.8	130	7.5	Max 5000 dwt
North Pier Wharf No.10	130	7.5	Max 5000 dwt
North Pier 5.5 m Wharf	180	5.5	Max 2000 dwt
North Pier Earthquake-Resistant Wharf No.1	100	5.5	Max 2000 dwt
North Pier 4 m Wharf	250	4	Max 300 dwt
North Pier 3m Wharf	320	3	Max 200 dwt
A Dock Wharf No.1	130	4	Max 300 dwt
A Dock Wharf No.2	100	4	Max 300 dwt
Public Dolphin	188	7.5	Max 6000 dwt
Oil Dolphin No.1	138	7.5	Max 6000 dwt
Hokuden Dolphin No.1	138	7.5	See [2] below
Hokuden Dolphin No.2	157	7.5	See [3] below
A Point Mooring Buoy			Operated by JOGMEC Max 300 000 dwt

[1]*Fukui:* Fukui Port Office, Tel: +81 776 821120, Fax: +81 776 821291, Email: f-kouwan@pref.fukui.lg.jp
[2]*Hokuden Dolphin No.1:* Operated by Hokuriku Electric Power Co Max 6000 dwt
[3]*Hokuden Dolphin No.2:* Operated by Hokuriku Electric Power Co Max 6000 dwt

Storage: Sheds of 1300 m2, general cargo warehouse of 3000 m2, cement silo of 22 000 t

Bunkering: Bonded oil can be brought from Moji with sufficient advance notice when required

Towage: One tug of 740 hp is available

Lloyd's Agent: Cornes & Co. Ltd, Meikai Building, 32 Akashi-machi, Chuo-ku, Kobe 650-0037, Hyogo Pref., Japan, *Tel:* +81 78 332 3421, *Fax:* +81 78 332 3070, *Email:* survey@kobe.cornes.co.jp, *Website:* www.cornes.co.jp

FUKUYAMA

Lat 34° 27' N; Long 133° 26' E.

Admiralty Chart: JP127A/JP127B   **Admiralty Pilot:** 42B

Time Zone: GMT +9 h   **UNCTAD Locode:** JP FKY

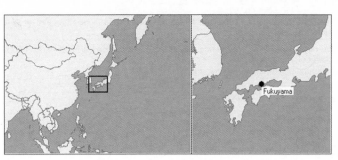

Principal Facilities:

P	Y	G	C		B		T	A

Authority: Hiroshima Prefectural Government, Airport & Seaport Department, 10-52 Moto-Machi, Naka-ku, Hiroshima 730-8511, Hiroshima Pref., Japan, *Tel:* +81 82 228 2111, *Fax:* +81 82 223 2463, *Email:* r-matumoto80233@pref.hiroshima.lg.jp, *Website:* www.hiroshima-minato.jp

Officials: Port Director: Ryutaro Matsumoto, *Tel:* +81 82 224 2285.

Port Security: ISPS compliant

Approach: The approach to the port is through Bisan Seto or Kurushima Strait traffic routes. Vessels exceeding 200 m loa can only navigate through the straits during daylight. The Main Approach Channel, leading to the Raw Materials Discharging berths and Kasaoka Pipe Berth is 8 km long and has a depth of 16 m and a width of 350 m. The Branch Channel, leading to the loading berths is 6 km long and has a depth of 5-11 m and is 130-300 m wide

Anchorage: Quarantine anchorage located at 34° 22' 30" N; 133° 26' 36" E. The port has many designated outer-harbour anchorages with depths ranging from 8.7 m to 15.4 m

Pilotage: Compulsory on Tomogashima Suido, Bisan Seto and Kurushima Straight for vessels over 10 000 gt. A vessel (LOA more than 200 meters) is required to navigate in Bisanseto and Kurushima Straight only in daylight. Osaka bay pilot Tomogashima Suido boards at 34° 10' N, 135° 00' E. Inland-sea pilot boards either at Wada Misaki(34° 34' 09" N, 135° 08' 30" E) or Sekisaki (33° 13' N, 131° 56' E)

Radio Frequency: Fukuyama Port Radio, calling on VHF Channel 16, working on Channels 11, 12 and 14

Weather: Typhoon season, July to October

Tides: Tidal range 4.84 m at MHWL, 0.57 m MLWL and 2.21 m MSL

Maximum Vessel Dimensions: 200 000 dwt, 16 m d, 350 m loa

Principal Imports and Exports: Imports: Coal, Iron ore. Exports: Steel products.

Working Hours: Loading/Discharging operation is carried out between 08.30 and 16.30 hours except Sunday & Holiday. Over time working is avilable when required

Accommodation:

Name	Length (m)	Depth (m)	Remarks
Public Wharves			
Okiura East Berth	150	4.5	Max 1000 dwt
Okiura West Berth	300	4.5	Max 1000 dwt
Ichimonji Berth	450	5.5	Max 2000 dwt
Minooki No.1	450	5.5	Max 2000 dwt
Minooki No.2	260	7.5	Max 5000 dwt
Minooki No.3	130	7.5	Max 5000 dwt
Fukuyama International Container Terminal	170	10	CFS of 1200 m2. 60 reefer points
Private Wharves			
NKK Berth A	300	17	See [1] below
NKK Berth B	280	16	See [2] below
NKK Berth E	210	14	See [3] below
NKK Berth F	180	11	Max 20 000 dwt. Raw materials
NKK Berth L	315	17.3	See [4] below
NKK Berth M	250	17	See [5] below
NKK Berth S	180	12	Max 35 000 dwt. Raw materials
NKK Export Berth No.1	234	11	Max 20 000 dwt. Export berth
NKK Export Berth No.2	230	13	Max 35 000 dwt. Export berth
NKK Export Berth No.3	146	13	Max 35 000 dwt. Export berth
NKK Export Berth No.4	250	13	Max 35 000 dwt. Export berth
NKK Export Berth No.5	130	13	Max 35 000 dwt. Export berth
Nippon Kayaku	270	5	Max 1000 dwt
Chugoku Seiko Kaisha	150	5.5	Max 2000 dwt
Niigata Engineering	200	5.5	Max 2000 dwt. Oil tanker only
Idemitsu & Nisseki Pier	244	6	Max 2000 dwt. Oil tanker only
Kyoseki & Shell Pier	212	6	Max 2000 dwt. Oil tanker only

[1]*NKK Berth A:* Max 150 000 dwt. 1500 t/h per crane for coal and ore, max d 16 m. Raw materials
[2]*NKK Berth B:* Max 100 000 dwt. 1500 t/h per crane for coal and ore, max d 16 m. Raw materials
[3]*NKK Berth E:* Max 70 000 dwt. 750 t/h per crane for coal, max d 14 m. Raw materials
[4]*NKK Berth L:* Max 200 000 dwt. 1500 t/h for iron ore and coal, max d 16 m. Raw materials

---

Key to Principal Facilities:—				
A=Airport	**C**=Containers	**G**=General Cargo	**P**=Petroleum	**R**=Ro/Ro	**Y**=Dry Bulk
B=Bunkers	**D**=Dry Dock	**L**=Cruise	**Q**=Other Liquid Bulk	**T**=Towage (where available from port)	

[5]NKK Berth M: Max 200 000 dwt. 1500 t/h for iron ore and coal, max d 16 m. Raw materials

Storage: Nine transit sheds, total space of 10 940 m2; thirteen warehouses, total space of 15 350 m2

Mechanical Handling Equipment:

Location	Type	Capacity (t)	Qty
Fukuyama	Mult-purp. Cranes	250	
Fukuyama International Container Terminal	Container Cranes	30.5	1
NKK Berth A	Mult-purp. Cranes	40	4
NKK Berth B	Mult-purp. Cranes	40	4
NKK Berth E	Mult-purp. Cranes	20	2
NKK Berth L	Mult-purp. Cranes	44	2
NKK Berth M	Mult-purp. Cranes	44	2

Cargo Worked: 76 000 t of foreign trade and 62 000 t of domestic trade per working day

Bunkering: Hanwa Co. Ltd, 2nd Floor, Finland House, 56 Haymarket, London SW1Y 4RN, United Kingdom, *Tel:* +44 20 7839 4448, *Fax:* +44 20 7839 3994, *Email:* orito@hanwa.co.uk
Hikawa Shoji Kaisha Ltd, 26-2 Shinkawa NS Building 1-chome, Shinkawa, Chuo-ku, Tokyo 104, Japan, *Tel:* +81 3 5776 6858, *Fax:* +81 3 5541 3274
Idemitsu Kosan Co. Ltd, 1-1 Marunochi, 3-Chome, Chiyoda-ku, Tokyo 100-8321, Japan, *Tel:* +81 3 3213 3138, *Fax:* +81 3 3213 1145, *Email:* tohru.takamura@si.idemitsu.co.jp, *Website:* www.idemitsu.co.jp
KG Int Petroleum Ltd, Shiba Park Building, 241 Shiba Koen, Minato-ku, Tokyo 105, Japan, *Tel:* +81 3 3578 4551, *Fax:* +81 3 3578 4550
Kamei Corp., 1-6-1 Otemachi, Chiyoda-ku, Tokyo 100-0004, Japan, *Tel:* +81 3 3286 6234, *Fax:* +81 3 3286 6249, *Email:* bunker@kamei.co.jp
Kyodo Oil Co. Ltd, 11-2 Nagata-cho 2-chome, Chiyoda-ku, Tokyo, Japan, *Tel:* +81 3 3505 8241, *Fax:* +81 3 3505 8697
Marubeni Petroleum Co. Ltd, Marubeni International Petroleum Singapore Co. Ltd, c/o Marubeni Corporation, 4-2 Ohtemachi 1-chome, Chiyoda-ku, Tokyo 100-8088, Japan, *Tel:* +81 3 3282 3920, *Fax:* +81 3 3282 3950, *Email:* TOKB554@marubenicorp.com, *Website:* www.marubeni.co.jp
MC Marine and Bunkering Inc., 8th Floor, Uchisaiwai-cho Dai Building, 3-3 Uchisaiwai-cho 1-chome, Chiyoda-ku, Tokyo 100-0011, Japan, *Tel:* +81 3 5251 2575, *Fax:* +81 3 5251 2583
Mitsui & Co. Petroleum Ltd, 2-1, Ohtemachi 1-chome, Chiyoda-ku, Tokyo 100-0004, Japan, *Tel:* +81 3 3285 6905, *Fax:* +81 3 3285 9811, *Email:* tkzph@dg.mitsui.com, *Website:* www.mitsui.co.jp
Nittetsu Shoij Co. Ltd, 5-7 Kameido 1-chome, Koto-ku, Tokyo 136, Japan, *Tel:* +81 3 5627 2157, *Fax:* +81 3 5627 2192
Setouchi Network, 4-20 Hasihama 1-chome, Imabari 799-2112, Ehime Pref., Japan, *Tel:* +81 898 430041, *Fax:* +81 898 430046, *Email:* secjpn@dokidoki.ne.jp
Sumitomo Corp., Harumi Island, Triton Square, Office Tower Y, 8-11 Harumi 1-chome, Chuo-ku, Tokyo 104-8610, Japan, *Tel:* +81 3 51664458, *Fax:* +81 3 51666407, *Email:* ir@sumitomo.co.jp, *Website:* www.sumitomocorp.co.jp

Towage: Not compulsory but advisable. Five tugs up to 3600 hp are available

Repair & Maintenance: Daiyu Kougiyo K.K., Fukuyama, Hiroshima Pref., Japan, *Tel:* +81 849 432222, *Fax:* +81 849 430838 Minor repairs

Airport: Hiroshima, 55 km

Lloyd's Agent: Cornes & Co. Ltd, Meikai Building, 32 Akashi-machi, Chuo-ku, Kobe 650-0037, Hyogo Pref., Japan, *Tel:* +81 78 332 3421, *Fax:* +81 78 332 3070, *Email:* survey@kobe.cornes.co.jp, *Website:* www.cornes.co.jp

FUNABASHI

harbour area, see under Chiba

FUNAKAWA

Lat 39° 53' N; Long 139° 52' E.

Admiralty Chart: 1388

Time Zone: GMT +9 h

Admiralty Pilot: 41

UNCTAD Locode: JP FNK

Principal Facilities:

P	Y G		B	T A

Authority: Port & Harbour Section of Akita Prefecture, 1-1 Sanno 4-chome, Akita 010-8570, Akita Pref., Japan, *Tel:* +81 18 860 1872, *Fax:* +81 18 860 1204

Port Security: ISPS compliant

Approach: Draught limitation in the channel is 7.5 m, 19 m (Oil Dolphin)

Pilotage: Not compulsory. Pilot boards vessel in the vicinity of the quarantine anchorage in pos 39° 50.8' N; 139° 54.0' E

Tides: Tidal range 0.68 m max, - 0.52 m min

Accommodation:

Name	Length (m)	Depth (m)	Draught (m)	Remarks
Funakawa				
5000 t Wharf	260	7.5	6.5	2 x 5000 dwt cap
7000 t Wharf	155	8	7	Max 7000 dwt
15 000 t Wharf	185	10	8.5	Max 15 000 dwt
Nikko Berth (Dolphin)	15	9	8.8	Max 10 000 dwt
Oil Dolphin		19		Max 180 000 dwt x 1

Storage: Open storage of 50 298 m2 for logs and 17 276 m2 for iron ore. Two warehouses, total storage 2400 m2 and one refrigerated warehouse of 640 m2. Also a timber pool of 328 000 m2

Mechanical Handling Equipment:

Location	Type	Capacity (t)	Qty
7000 t Wharf	Mult-purp. Cranes	5	1
15 000 t Wharf	Mult-purp. Cranes	5	3

Bunkering: Domestic oil available

Towage: Available from Akita

Repair & Maintenance: Minor repairs only can be undertaken

Airport: Akita Airport

Lloyd's Agent: Cornes & Co. Ltd, 273 Yamashita-cho, Naka-ku, Yokohama 231-0023, Kanagawa Pref., Japan, *Tel:* +81 45 201 8537, *Fax:* +81 45 212 3105, *Email:* survey@ykh.cornes.co.jp, *Website:* www.cornes.co.jp

FUSHIKI-TOYAMA

Lat 36° 46' N; Long 137° 5' E.

Admiralty Chart: 1342

Time Zone: GMT +9 h

Admiralty Pilot: 41

UNCTAD Locode: JP FSK

Principal Facilities:

P	Y G C R		B D T A

Authority: Ports & Harbors Division, Public Works Department, Toyama Prefectural Government, 1-7 Shinsogawa, Toyama-shi, Toyama 930-8501, Toyama Pref., Japan, *Tel:* +81 76 444 3334, *Fax:* +81 76 444 4419, *Email:* kowan3@pref.toyama.lg.jp

Port Security: ISPS compliant

Pilotage: Not compulsory but available. Pilot boards in the following positions: Fushiki and Shinminato:
36° 49.90' N; 137° 05.50' E
36° 50.30' N; 137° 05.80' E
36° 49.00' N; 137° 08.50' E
Toyama:
36° 46.80' N; 137° 14.00' E

Traffic: 2006, 2933 vessels, 11 785 717 t of cargo handled

Accommodation:

Name	Length (m)	Depth (m)	Remarks
Fushiki			
Left No.1 Wharf	160	9.5	1 x 10 000 t
Left No.2 Wharf	150	9.5	1 x 10 000 t
Left No.3 Wharf	185	10	1 x 15 000 t
Left No.4 Wharf	185	10	1 x 15 000 t
Left No.5 Wharf	90	5	1 x 1000 t
Right No.1 Wharf	220	7.5	2 x 5000 t
Right No.2 Wharf	220	7.5	2 x 5000 t
Right No.3 Wharf	185	10	1 x 15 000 t
Right No.4 Wharf	185	10	1 x 15 000 t
Right No.5 Wharf	130	7.5	1 x 5000 t
Kokubu No.1 Wharf	95	5.5	1 x 2000 t
Kokubu No.2 Wharf	65	5	1 x 1000 t
Kokubu No.3 Wharf	140	5	2 x 1000 t
Kokubu Dolphin	20	5.5	1 x 2000 t
Manyo No.1 Wharf	130	7.5	1 x 5000 t
Manyo No.2 Wharf	190	10	1 x 15 000 t
Manyo No.3 Wharf	280	12	1 x 30 000 t
Toyama			
Wharf No.1	185	10	1 x 15 000 t
Wharf No.2	185	10	1 x 15 000 t
Wharf No.3	185	10	1 x 15 000 t
Wharf No.4	160	9	1 x 10 000 t
Wharf No.5	130	7.5	1 x 5000 t

Name	Length (m)	Depth (m)	Remarks
Wharf No.6	90	6	1 x 3000 t
Wharf No.7	130	7.5	1 x 5000 t
Wharf No.8	185	10	1 x 15 000 t
Wharf No.9	90	5	1 x 1000 t
Wharf No.10	130	7.5	1 x 5000 t
Dolphin No.1	21	5	1 x 1000 t
Dolphin No.2	12	6	1 x 3000 t
Dolphin No.3	21	5	1 x 1000 t
Petroleum Sea Berth		27	1 x 280 000 t
Petroleum Dolphin	18	8	1 x 5000 t
Toyama Shinko			
Central Pier			
Wharf No.1	280	14	1 x 50 000 t
Wharf No's 2-4	555	10	3 x 15 000 t
Wharf No's 5-6	260	7.5	2 x 5000 t
Wharf No's 7-8	120	4.5	2 x 700 t
North Pier			
Wharf No.1	280	12	1 x 55 000 t. International multi-purpose terminal
Wharf No.2	185	10	1 x 15 000 t
Wharf No.3	60	4.5	1 x 700 t
East Pier			
Wharf No.1	185	10	1 x 15 000 t
Wharf No.2	185	10	1 x 15 000 t
South Pier			
Wharf No.1	280	4	
Wharf No.2	175	4	
Wharf No.3	210	4	
Kaiwo Quay	220	7.5	1 x 15 000 t. Passenger vessel berth
Shinkoikemokuzai Quay	180	10	1 x 15 000 t
Hokurikudenryoku Dolphin	15	6	1 x 3000 t
Hokurikudenryoku 5kDW Dolphin	6	11	1 x 5000 t
Hokurikudenryoku Zakka Quay	175	8	1 x 7000 t
Toyama Industrial Quay	373	10	2 x 15 000 t
Toyama Central Lumber Quay	210	8.5	1 x 8000 t
Toyama Pier Quay	70	6	1 x 3000 t
Toyama Pier Quay	170	8	1 x 7000 t
Chuetsumokuzai Quay	140	8	1 x 7000 t
Hokurikudenryoku Quay	140	5	2 x 1000 t
Hokurikudenryoku Quay	285	14	1 x 60 000 t
ITEC Quay	130	7.5	1 x 5000 t

Storage: Fushiki: Warehouses available. Large coal, timber and other open storage areas
Toyama: Transit sheds and warehouses available; oil tanks for storage available
Toyama Shinko: Large coal, timber and other open storage areas. No warehousing or refrigerated space

Mechanical Handling Equipment:

Location	Type	Capacity (t)	Qty	Remarks
Right No.1 Wharf	Quay Cranes	5	1	
Right No.3 Wharf	Quay Cranes	8	1	
Manyo No.3 Wharf	Quay Cranes	12.5	1	
Wharf No.1	Quay Cranes	5	1	
Central Pier	Mult-purp. Cranes	44	1	
Central Pier	Container Cranes	45	1	
Central Pier	Quay Cranes	12.5	2	
North Pier	Mobile Cranes	40.6	2	
North Pier	Container Cranes	55	1	private

Bunkering: Marubeni Petroleum Co. Ltd, Marubeni International Petroleum Singapore Co. Ltd, c/o Marubeni Corporation, 4-2 Ohtemachi 1-chome, Chiyoda-ku, Tokyo 100-8088, Japan, *Tel:* +81 3 3282 3920, *Fax:* +81 3 3282 3950, *Email:* TOKB554@marubenicorp.com, *Website:* www.marubeni.co.jp
MC Marine and Bunkering Inc., 8th Floor, Uchisaiwai-cho Dai Building, 3-3 Uchi-saiwai-cho 1-chome, Chiyoda-ku, Tokyo 100-0011, Japan, *Tel:* +81 3 5251 2575, *Fax:* +81 3 5251 2583
Mitsui & Co. Petroleum Ltd, 2-1, Ohtemachi 1-chome, Chiyoda-ku, Tokyo 100-0004, Japan, *Tel:* +81 3 3285 6905, *Fax:* +81 3 3285 9811, *Email:* tkzph@dg.mitsui.com, *Website:* www.mitsui.co.jp
Nippon Mitsubishi Oil Corp., 3-12 Nishi Shinbashi 1-chome, Minato-ku, Tokyo 105-8412, Japan, *Tel:* +81 3 3502 1135, *Fax:* +81 3 3502 9352, *Email:* shuji.arai@eneos.co.jp, *Website:* www.eneos.co.jp

Towage: Tugs available

Repair & Maintenance: Fushiki Zosen Co. Ltd, Toyama, Toyama Pref., Japan, *Tel:* +81 76 623 0466
Nipponkai Heavy Industries Co. Ltd, Toyama, Toyama Pref., Japan, *Tel:* +81 76 437 9271 One dry dock 164.7 m long, 21.3 m breadth, 7 m depth for vessels of 8400 gt

Medical Facilities: Available

Airport: Toyama Airport

Lloyd's Agent: Cornes & Co. Ltd, 273 Yamashita-cho, Naka-ku, Yokohama 231-0023, Kanagawa Pref., Japan, *Tel:* +81 45 201 8537, *Fax:* +81 45 212 3105, *Email:* survey@ykh.cornes.co.jp, *Website:* www.cornes.co.jp

GAMAGORI

Lat 34° 48' N; Long 137° 12' E.

Admiralty Chart: JP1056/JP1057A/JP10A **Admiralty Pilot:** 42A

Time Zone: GMT +9 h

UNCTAD Locode: JP GAM

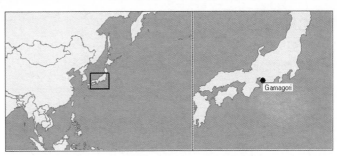

Principal Facilities:

P		Y	G		R	B		T	A

Authority: Mikawa Port Authority, 3-9 Jinnojuto-cho, Toyohashi 441, Aichi Pref., Japan, *Tel:* +81 53 231 4155, *Fax:* +81 53 234 7860, *Email:* mikawa@toyoshingo.co.jp

Approach: The approach is through Irago Channel. Draught limitation is 10 m for Gamagori Passage

Pilotage: Compulsory for vessels exceeding 10 000 gt. A pilot will need to board the vessel off Irago and can be requested from Irago-Mikawa Bay Pilot Association, *Tel:* +81 569 217487. VHF Channel 16

Radio Frequency: Mikawa-wan Port Radio. VHF Channel 16 (calling) and Channels 11 and 12 (working)

Tides: Range of tide max 2.39 m, min 0.06 m

Principal Imports and Exports: Imports: Timber.

Accommodation:

Name	Length (m)	Depth (m)	Remarks
Gamagori			
Gamagori Wharf No.1	600	4.5	1 x 700 dwt
Gamagori Wharf No.2	180	5.5	2 x 2000 dwt
Gamagori Wharf No.3	90	5.5	1 x 2000 dwt
Gamagori Wharf No.4	275	10	1 x 15 000 dwt
Gamagori Wharf No.5	390	7.5	3 x 5000 dwt
Gamagori Wharf No.6	90	5.5	1 x 2000 dwt
Gamagori Wharf No.7	90	5.5	1 x 2000 dwt
Gamagori Wharf No.8	390	7.5	3 x 5000 dwt
Gamagori Wharf No.9	185	10	1 x 15 000 dwt
Gamagori Wharf No.10	250	4	5 x 500 dwt
Hamacho Wharf No.1	185	10	1 x 15 000 dwt
Hamacho Wharf No.2	130	7.5	1 x 5000 dwt

Bunkering: Cosmo Oil Co. Ltd, Toshiba Building, 1-1 Shibaura 1-chome, Minato-ku, Tokyo 105-8528, Japan, *Tel:* +81 3 3798 3156, *Fax:* +81 3 3798 3592, *Email:* masayuki_iijima@cosmo-oil.co.jp, *Website:* www.cosmo-oil.co.jp
Hanwa Co. Ltd, 2nd Floor, Finland House, 56 Haymarket, London SW1Y 4RN, United Kingdom, *Tel:* +44 20 7839 4448, *Fax:* +44 20 7839 3994, *Email:* orito@hanwa.co.uk
Hikawa Shoji Kaisha Ltd, 26-2 Shinkawa NS Building 1-chome, Shinkawa, Chuo-ku, Tokyo 104, Japan, *Tel:* +81 3 5776 6858, *Fax:* +81 3 5541 3274
Idemitsu Kosan Co. Ltd, 1-1 Marunochi, 3-Chome, Chiyoda-ku, Tokyo 100-8321, Japan, *Tel:* +81 3 3213 3138, *Fax:* +81 3 3213 1145, *Email:* tohru.takamura@si.idemitsu.co.jp, *Website:* www.idemitsu.co.jp
KG Int Petroleum Ltd, Shiba Park Building, 241 Shiba Koen, Minato-ku, Tokyo 105, Japan, *Tel:* +81 3 3578 4551, *Fax:* +81 3 3578 4550
Japan Energy Corp., 2-10-1, Toranomon, Minato-ku, Tokyo 105-8407, Japan, *Tel:* +81 3 5573 6100, *Fax:* +81 3 5573 6674, *Email:* yamano@j-energy.co.jp, *Website:* www.j-energy.co.jp
Kamei Corp., 1-6-1 Otemachi, Chiyoda-ku, Tokyo 100-0004, Japan, *Tel:* +81 3 3286 6234, *Fax:* +81 3 3286 6249, *Email:* bunker@kamei.co.jp
Kawasho Corp., World Trade Centre, 4-1 Hanamatsu-cho 2-chome, Minato-ku, Tokyo 105, Japan, *Tel:* +81 3 3435 3251
Kyodo Oil Co. Ltd, 11-2 Nagata-cho 2-chome, Chiyoda-ku, Tokyo, Japan, *Tel:* +81 3 3505 8241, *Fax:* +81 3 3505 8697
Marubeni Petroleum Co. Ltd, Marubeni International Petroleum Singapore Co. Ltd, c/o Marubeni Corporation, 4-2 Ohtemachi 1-chome, Chiyoda-ku, Tokyo 100-8088, Japan, *Tel:* +81 3 3282 3920, *Fax:* +81 3 3282 3950, *Email:* TOKB554@marubenicorp.com, *Website:* www.marubeni.co.jp
MC Marine and Bunkering Inc., 8th Floor, Uchisaiwai-cho Dai Building, 3-3 Uchi-saiwai-cho 1-chome, Chiyoda-ku, Tokyo 100-0011, Japan, *Tel:* +81 3 5251 2575, *Fax:* +81 3 5251 2583
Mitsui & Co. Petroleum Ltd, 2-1, Ohtemachi 1-chome, Chiyoda-ku, Tokyo 100-0004, Japan, *Tel:* +81 3 3285 6905, *Fax:* +81 3 3285 9811, *Email:* tkzph@dg.mitsui.com, *Website:* www.mitsui.co.jp
Nissho Iwai Corp., 4-4 Akasaka 2-chome, Minato-ku, Tokyo, Japan, *Tel:* +81 3 35882111
Nittetsu Shoij Co. Ltd, 5-7 Kameido 1-chome, Koto-ku, Tokyo 136, Japan, *Tel:* +81 3 5627 2157, *Fax:* +81 3 5627 2192
Shinagawa Fuel Co. Ltd, New Pier Takeshiba North Tower, 8th Floor, 1-11-1 Kaigan, Minato-ku, Tokyo 105-8525, Japan, *Tel:* +81 3 5470 7113, *Fax:* +81 3 5470 7157, *Email:* hakuyu@ml1.sinanen.co.jp
Sigma Foreign Service (Panama) S.A., 2-25 Aikawai, Tempaku-ku, Nagoya 468-0836, Aichi Pref., Japan, *Tel:* +81 52 896 1510, *Fax:* +81 52 896 7703
Sumitomo Corp., Harumi Island, Triton Square, Office Tower Y, 8-11 Harumi 1-chome, Chuo-ku, Tokyo 104-8610, Japan, *Tel:* +81 3 51664458, *Fax:* +81 3 51666407, *Email:* ir@sumitomo.co.jp, *Website:* www.sumitomocorp.co.jp

Towage: Three tugs available; two of 3200 hp and one of 3500 hp

Airport: Nagoya International, 65 km

Lloyd's Agent: Cornes & Co. Ltd, 273 Yamashita-cho, Naka-ku, Yokohama 231-0023, Kanagawa Pref., Japan, *Tel:* +81 45 201 8537, *Fax:* +81 45 212 3105, *Email:* survey@ykh.cornes.co.jp, *Website:* www.cornes.co.jp

Key to Principal Facilities:—					
A=Airport	**C**=Containers	**G**=General Cargo	**P**=Petroleum	**R**=Ro/Ro	**Y**=Dry Bulk
B=Bunkers	**D**=Dry Dock	**L**=Cruise	**Q**=Other Liquid Bulk	**T**=Towage (where available from port)	

HACHINOHE

Lat 40° 32' N; Long 141° 32' E.

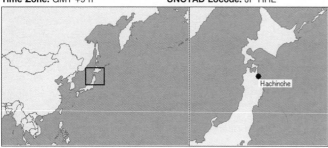

Admiralty Chart: 2959

Admiralty Pilot: 41

Time Zone: GMT +9 h

UNCTAD Locode: JP HHE

Principal Facilities:

P Q Y G C R　B D T A

Authority: Ports, Harbours & Airport Division, Aomori Prefectural Government, 1-1 Nagashima 1-chome, Aomori 030-8570, Aomori Pref., Japan, *Tel:* +81 17 722 1111, *Fax:* +81 17 734 8194, *Email:* kowan@pref.aomori.lg.jp, *Website:* www.pref.aomori.lg.jp

Port Security: ISPS compliant

Approach: Clear approach to port. Depth in Hattaro passage 13 m. Draught limitation in the channel is 12 m at LT

Pilotage: Not compulsory. Pilot boards at quarantine anchorage if required and for deep draught vessels from pos 40° 33' 30" N; 141° 33' 18" E. Pilot boat is unable to communicate directly with vessel, therefore vessel must keep close communication with agents. Pilotage is only available from 0600 to sunset for entry and 0600-2200 for sailing

Radio Frequency: Harbour Master, VHF Channel 16

Weather: Winds, W or SW in winter; ENE or ESE in summer, force and direction suddenly changeable in winter. Fog is experienced June to August, especially during July

Tides: Tidal range 1.50 m max, - 0.10 m min

Maximum Vessel Dimensions: 71 703 dwt, 230 m loa, 12 m d

Working Hours: 0830-1630. Can be extended to 2000 for bulk cargoes and through the night for wood-chips

Accommodation: Harbour protected by breakwater 11 128 m long. Container terminal 260 m long in depth of 13.0 m with two gantry cranes with a fixed loading cap of 30.5 t
LNG terminal with three loading berths operated by Nippon Oil Corp

Name	Length (m)	Depth (m)	Draught (m)	Remarks
Public Wharves				
Hattaro Wharf A	130	7.5	6.8	For vessels up to 110 m loa & 5000 dwt
Hattaro Wharf B	130	7.5	6.8	For vessels up to 110 m loa & 5000 dwt
Hattaro Wharf C	185	10	9.5	For vessels up to 170 m loa & 15 000 dwt
Hattaro Wharf D	270	13	12	For vessels up to 230 m loa & 50 000 dwt
Hattaro Wharf E	270	13	12	See [1] below
Hattaro Wharf F	185	10	9.8	For vessels up to 175 m loa & 15 000 dwt
Hattaro Wharf G	185	10	9.8	For vessels up to 175 m loa & 15 000 dwt
Hattaro Wharf H	130	7.5	7	For vessels up to 110 m loa & 5000 dwt
Hattaro Wharf I	130	7.5	7	Foe vessels up to 110 m loa & 5000 dwt
Hattaro Wharf L	130	7.5	7	For vessels up to 110 m loa & 5000 dwt
Hattaro Wharf M	130	7.5	7	For vessels up to 110 m loa & 5000 dwt
Hattaro Wharf N	130	7.5	7	Foe vessels up to 110 m loa & 5000 dwt
Hattaro Wharf O	130	7.5	7	For vessels up to 110 m loa & 5000 dwt
Hattaro Wharf P	240	12	11	For vessels up to 230 m loa & 30 000 dwt
Shirogane Wharf A	165	9	8.2	See [2] below
Shirogane Wharf B	185	10	9.3	For vessels up to 175 m loa & 15 000 dwt
Shirogane Wharf C	115	7.5	7	See [3] below
Kawaragi Wharf A	280	14	12.7	For vessels up to 230 m loa & 50 000 dwt
Kawaragi Wharf B	130	7.5	7	For vessels up to 110 m loa & 5000 dwt
Kawaragi Wharf C	130	7.5	7	For vessels up to 110 m loa & 5000 dwt
Kawaragi Wharf D	130	7.5	7	For vessels up to 110 m loa & 5000 dwt
Private Wharves				
Mitsubishi Wharf	390	10	9.5	See [4] below
Sumikin Wharf	285	11	9.7	See [5] below
Tohoku Grain Terminal	311	13	12	See [6] below

[1]*Hattaro Wharf E:* For vessels up to 230 m loa & 50 000 dwt. 1 x 19 t unloader at berths D & E
[2]*Shirogane Wharf A:* For vessels up to 155 m loa & 10 000 dwt. Cement pipeline
[3]*Shirogane Wharf C:* For vessels up to 100 m loa & 5000 dwt. Cement & fishoil pipeline
[4]*Mitsubishi Wharf:* For vessels up to 230 m loa & 15 000 dwt. Two hopper & belt conveyors for woodchip
[5]*Sumikin Wharf:* For vessels up to 180 m loa & 27 000 dwt. Two cement loaders 1000 t/h
[6]*Tohoku Grain Terminal:* For vessels up to 230 m loa & 50 000 dwt. Dolphin berth. Two pneumatic unloaders for grain (400 t/h each). One unloader of 500 t/h

Storage: 261 984 m2 of warehouse space, 3600 m2 of transit sheds, a container yard of 58 940 m2 with a capacity for 935 TEU's. 50 refrigerated spaces

Mechanical Handling Equipment:

Location	Type	Capacity (t)	Qty	Remarks
Hattaro Wharf F	Mobile Cranes	15–25	3	Also available at Hattaro Wharf G
Kawaragi Wharf A	Mobile Cranes	25	2	

Bunkering: MC Marine and Bunkering Inc., 8th Floor, Uchisaiwai-cho Dai Building, 3-3 Uchisaiwai-cho 1-chome, Chiyoda-ku, Tokyo 100-0011, Japan, *Tel:* +81 3 5251 2575, *Fax:* +81 3 5251 2583
Sumitomo Corp., Harumi Island, Triton Square, Office Tower Y, 8-11 Harumi 1-chome, Chuo-ku, Tokyo 104-8610, Japan, *Tel:* +81 3 51664458, *Fax:* +81 3 51666407, *Email:* ir@sumitomo.co.jp, *Website:* www.sumitomocorp.co.jp

Towage: Six tugs available; five of 3200 hp and one of 3600 hp

Repair & Maintenance: Hachinohe Zosen Jigyo Kyodo Kumiai, 4-5 Numadate, 4 chome, Hachinohe, Amori Pref., Japan One dry dock 75 m long, 15 m breadth, 5 m depth for vessels up to 1000 gt
Kawaura Iron Work Co. Ltd, Hachinohe, Amori Pref., Japan, *Tel:* +81 17 822 4124 Minor repairs
Kitanihon Shipbuilding Co. Ltd, 1-25 Koyo, 3-Chome, Hachinohe 031-0801, Amori Pref., Japan, *Tel:* +81 17 824 4171, *Fax:* +81 17 822 7803, *Email:* info@kitanihonship.com, *Website:* www.kitanihonship.com Dry dock of 140.8 m x 26.5 m for vessels up to 8000 gt. Repair quay of 160 m with max draught 6 m

Surveyors: Nippon Kaiji Kyokai, Jidaisho Mansions, Room 307, 1-14-4 Shiroshita, Aomori, Hachinohe 031-0072, Amori Pref., Japan, *Tel:* +81 17 872 4300, *Fax:* +81 17 872 4301, *Email:* hh@classnk.or.jp, *Website:* www.classnk.or.jp

Medical Facilities: Available

Airport: Misawa, 30 km

Lloyd's Agent: Cornes & Co. Ltd, 273 Yamashita-cho, Naka-ku, Yokohama 231-0023, Kanagawa Pref., Japan, *Tel:* +81 45 201 8537, *Fax:* +81 45 212 3105, *Email:* survey@ykh.cornes.co.jp, *Website:* www.cornes.co.jp

HAKATA

Lat 33° 36' N; Long 130° 24' E.

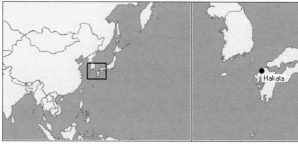

Admiralty Chart: JP1227

Admiralty Pilot: 42A

Time Zone: GMT +9 h

UNCTAD Locode: JP HTD

Principal Facilities:

P Q Y G C R　B　T A

Authority: Hakata Port & Harbor Bureau, Port & Harbor Promotion Department, Port Promotion Section, 12-1 Okihama-cho, Hakata-ku, Fukuoka 812-8620, Fukuoka Pref., Japan, *Tel:* +81 92 282 7110, *Fax:* +81 92 282 7772, *Email:* shinko.phb@city.fukuoka.jp, *Website:* www.port-of-hakata.or.jp

Officials: Chizu Sawabe.
General Director: Shinichiro Iwase.
Harbour Master: Kazuyuki Ishii.

Port Security: ISPS compliant

Pre-Arrival Information: Masters are requested to report ship's ETA by radio giving accurate time of arrival at least 24 h prior, also any subsequent change

Approach: Hakata Bay is a natural harbour, enclosed by shores on three sides and protected by Nokonoshima Island on the fourth which blocks tidal currents but never hinders navigation. Vessels can enter and depart in all seasons at any time day and night. Two channels are available:
Central Channel: 5 km long, 200-400 m wide, 12-14 m deep
East Channel: 3.4 km long, 400 m wide, 14 m deep

Anchorage: Good sheltered anchorage areas available

Pilotage: Not compulsory, but necessary unless Masters are well acquainted with the locality. Pilots embark at Quarantine Anchorage in pos 33° 38' N; 130° 19.30' E

Requests for pilots are made through ship's agents. Ships are piloted on VHF Channels 16, 11 and 12. In rough seas harbour tug-boats will be used

Radio Frequency: Hakata Port Radio, VHF Channels 16, 11 and 12

Weather: Winds prevailing from the N, but SE in summer. Hakata Port is a best suited and safe port in terms of wind and sea conditions, enclosed by shores on three sides and its entrance opens on the northwest only

Tides: Tide level range is 2.09 m at average spring tide

Traffic: 2007, 30 217 412 t of cargo handled

Maximum Vessel Dimensions: 331 m loa, 12.7 m draft

Principal Imports and Exports: Imports: Fertiliser, Furniture, Wheat. Exports: Automobiles, Machinery, Rubber products.

Working Hours: 24 h/day

Accommodation:

Name	Length (m)	Depth (m)	Remarks
Hakata			
Island City C1 Berth	330	14	See [1] below
Island City C2 Berth	350	15	Containers
Island City Berth No.5	190	11	
Chuo Wharf Berth No.3	130	7.5	
Chuo Wharf Berths 4-6	556	10	
Chuo Wharf Berths 7-8	360	5.5	
Chuo Wharf Berths 9-11	390	7.5	
Chuo Wharf Berth No.12	161	6.5	
Suzaki Wharf Berth No.1	130	7.5	
Suzaki Wharf Berths 2-4	553	11	
Suzaki Wharf Berths 5-6	260	7.5	
Suzaki Wharf Berths 7-10	450	5.5	
Suzaki Wharf Nagahama No.1	360	5.5	
Suzaki Wharf Nagahama No.2	360	5.5	
Hakozaki Wharf Berths 1-3	390	7.5	
Hakozaki Wharf Berth No.4	185	10	
Hakozaki Wharf Berth No.5	240	12	
Hakozaki Wharf Berths 6-10	650	7.5	
Hakozaki Wharf Berth No.11	230	7.5	
Hakozaki Wharf Berths 12-13	480	12	
Hakozaki Wharf Timber Berth	360	10	See [2] below
Hakozaki Wharf Timber Dolphin	280	10	See [3] below
Kashii Pier No.1-3	390	7.5	
Kashii Pier No.4 & 5	600	13	See [4] below
Kashii Pier No.6	190	11	
Kashii Pier No.7	130	7.5	
Kashii Pier No.8	130	7.5	
Kashii Pier No.9	130	7.5	
Higashihama Wharf Berth No.1	200	4.5	
Higashihama Wharf Berth No.2	80	5.5	
Higashihama Wharf Berth No.3	430	5.5	
Higashihama Wharf Berth No.4	390	7.5	
Higashihama Wharf Berth No.5	310	7.5	
Hakata Pier Berth No.2	105	5.5	
Hakata Pier Berth No.3	147	7.5	

[1]*Island City C1 Berth:* Operated by Hakata Port Terminal Co Ltd., 3-13 Kashiihama, Higashi-ku, Fukuoka City 813-0016, Tel: +81 92 663 3111, Fax: +81 92 663 3114, Website: www.hakatako-futo.co.jp
Container terminal with area of 17.2 ha. 9568 TEU ground slots and 240 reefer plugs
[2]*Hakozaki Wharf Timber Berth:* Only vessels with loa of less than 200 m may utilize the berths
When vessels utilize the berths after sailing past between Hakozaki Wharf and the east breakwater, the standards of utilization are as follows:
a) Only vessels of 18 000 gt or under with loa of 175 m or under may utilize the berths
b) Vessels of 1000 gt and over shall be towed by one tugboat. Vessels of 6000 gt and over or vessels with loa of 120 m or over shall be towed by two tugboats
c) Vessels of 3000 gt and over or vessels with loa of 110 m or over shall take a pilot on board
d) Entry at night is prohibited. For night departures, vessels of 1000 gt and over shall take a pilot on board
[3]*Hakozaki Wharf Timber Dolphin:* Only vessels of 6000 gt or under with loa of 120 m or under may utilize the berths
When vessels utilize the berths after sailing past between Hakozaki Wharf and the east breakwater, the standards of utilization are as follows:
a) Vessels of 1000 gt and over shall take a pilot on board
b) Vessels of 1000 gt and over shall be towed by one tugboat and vessels of 5000 gt and over shall be towed by two tugboats
c) Entry at night is prohibited
[4]*Kashii Pier No.4 & 5:* Operated by Hakata Port Terminal Co Ltd., 3-13 Kashiihama, Higashi-ku, Fukuoka City 813-0016, Tel: +81 92 663 3111, Fax: +81 92 663 3114, Website: www.hakatako-futo.co.jp
Container terminal with area of 22.3 ha. 9684 slot storage yard and 300 reefer plugs

Storage:

Location	Open (m²)	Sheds / Warehouses
Hakata	968624	32

Mechanical Handling Equipment:

Location	Type	Capacity (t)	Qty	Remarks
Island City C1 Berth	Container Cranes	40.6	5	at berths C1-C2
Island City C1 Berth	Transtainers		11	
Kashii Pier No.4 & 5	Post Panamax	40.6	4	
Kashii Pier No.4 & 5	Straddle Carriers		18	

Cargo Worked: General cargo 30 boxes/h per gantry crane. Grain 400 t/h per pneumatic unloader

Bunkering: Kanematsu K.K., Bunker Oil Section, 2-1 Shibaura 1-chome, Minato-ku, Tokyo 105-8005, Japan, Tel: +81 3 5440 9273, Fax: +81 3 5440 6540, Email: trc5@kanematsu.co.jp, Website: www.kanematsu.co.jp

Towage: Six tugs available; two of 3600 hp, two of 3400 hp, one of 2600 hp and one of 1800 hp

Shipping Agents: Holme Ringer & Co. Ltd, 2nd Floor AEC Tenjinhigashi Building 10-22 Tsumashoji, 10-22 Tsumashoji, Fukuoka-Shi, Hakata 812-0020, Ehime Pref., Japan, Tel: +81 92 271 1292, Fax: +81 92 291 3450, Email: hakata@holme-ringer.co.jp
Mitsubishi Logistics Corp., Harbor Transportation Dept 13, Kashiihama 3-chome, Higashi-ku, Fukuoka-ku, Hakata 813-0016, Ehime Pref., Japan, Tel: +81 92 663 3200, Fax: +81 92 663 3202, Email: lngtmori@mitsubishi-logistics.co.jp, Website: www.mitsubishi-logistics.co.jp
A.P. Moller-Maersk Group, Maersk K.K., 5th Floor Soron Hakata Ekimae Building, 3-27-22 Hakata Ekimae, Hakata-ku, Hakata 812-0011, Ehime Pref., Japan, Tel: +81 92 413 3003, Fax: +81 92 413 3107, Website: www.maerskline.com

Medical Facilities: Available

Airport: Fukuoka International Airport, 4 km

Railway: JR Fukuoka Freight Terminal

Lloyd's Agent: Cornes & Co. Ltd, Meikai Building, 32 Akashi-machi, Chuo-ku, Kobe 650-0037, Hyogo Pref., Japan, Tel: +81 78 332 3421, Fax: +81 78 332 3070, Email: survey@kobe.cornes.co.jp, Website: www.cornes.co.jp

HAKODATE

Lat 41° 49' N; Long 140° 40' E.

Admiralty Chart: JP10		**Admiralty Pilot:** 41	
Time Zone: GMT +9 h		**UNCTAD Locode:** JP HKD	

Principal Facilities:

P		Y	G	C	R		B	D	T	A

Authority: Port & Harbour Bureau of Hakodate City, 4-13 Shinonome-cho, Hakodate 040-8666, Hokkaido, Japan, Tel: +81 138 213486, Fax: +81 138 262656, Email: kouwan@city.hakodate.hokkaido.jp, Website: www.city.hakodate.hokkaido.jp

Officials: General Manager: Yoshihiro Takahashi.
Harbour Manager: Miyuki Matoba.

Port Security: ISPS compliant

Approach: Depth in fairways: No.1 Fairway 13 m to 18 m, No.2 Fairway 8 m to 13 m, No.3 Fairway 9 m to 12 m. Draft limitation in the channel 10 m

Anchorage: Ample anchorage area available

Pilotage: Not compulsory. Harbour pilots available at quarantine anchorage

Weather: Winds, May to October E; other seasons NNW

Tides: Tidal range 1.1 m

Principal Imports and Exports: Imports: Frozen fish, Round logs. Exports: Frozen fish, Rottary veneer lathe machines.

Working Hours: 0900-1200, 1300-1700

Accommodation:

Name	Length (m)	Depth (m)	Remarks
Nishi Pier			Passenger & cargo vessels
Berth A	43	4	
Berth B	153	4	
Berth C	116	4	
Berth D	140	5	
Berth E	165	9	
Berth F	105	6.5	
Berth G	235	4	
Toyokawa Pier			530 m long in depth of 5 m for fishery facilities
Wakamatsu Pier			Ferry & passenger vessels
Kaigan-cho Basin			Depth 3.5-6.5 m for harbour fishing & small working boats
Chuo Pier			General cargo facilities
Berth No.1	133	8	
Berth No.2	133	5	
Berth No.3	171	9	

Name	Length (m)	Depth (m)	Remarks
Berth No.4	165	9	
Berth No.5	90	5.5	
Bandai Pier			Cargoes handled include wheat, fish oil & timber
Berth No.1	130	7.5	
Berth No.2	90	5.5	
Berth No.3	185	10	
Berth No.4	130	7.5	
Berth No.5	90	5.5	
Kita Pier			Bulk cargo & ferries
Berth No.1	51	5.5	
Berth No.2	330	5.5	
Berth No.3	88	5.5	
Berth No.4	130	7.5	
Minato-cho Pier			See [1] below
Berth No.1	280	14	
Berth No.2	240	12	

[1]Minato-cho Pier: Hakodate Container Yard, 2-14-53 Minato-cho, Hakodate, Tel: +81 138 415020, Fax: +81 138 415015, Email: minatocy@hakodate.port.jp Yard area of 1.5 ha. One container crane and one reach stacker

Mechanical Handling Equipment:

Location	Type	Capacity (t)	Qty	Remarks
Hakodate	Floating Cranes	200	1	owned by Hakodate Dock
Hakodate	Mult-purp. Cranes	200	7	

Bunkering: MC Marine and Bunkering Inc., 8th Floor, Uchisaiwai-cho Dai Building, 3-3 Uchisaiwai-cho 1-chome, Chiyoda-ku, Tokyo 100-0011, Japan, Tel: +81 3 5251 2575, Fax: +81 3 5251 2583

Towage: Four tugs available; one of 3200 hp and three of 2400 hp

Repair & Maintenance: The Hakodate Dock Co. Ltd, 20-3 Benten-cho, Hakodate 040-8605, Hokkaido, Japan, Tel: +81 138 223150, Fax: +81 138 221941, Website: www.hakodate-dock.co.jp Two dry docks: No.1 181 m x 24.45 m x 9.05 m for vessels of 17 100 gt. No.2 140 m x 21.48 m x 7.4 m for vessels of 9000 gt

Surveyors: Nippon Kaiji Kyokai, 32-22 Moto Machi, Hakodate 040-0054, Hokkaido, Japan, Tel: +81 138 220875, Fax: +81 138 267897, Email: hd@classnk.or.jp, Website: www.classnk.or.jp

Medical Facilities: Available

Airport: Hakodate Airport, 10 km

Lloyd's Agent: Cornes & Co. Ltd, 273 Yamashita-cho, Naka-ku, Yokohama 231-0023, Kanagawa Pref., Japan, Tel: +81 45 201 8537, Fax: +81 45 212 3105, Email: survey@ykh.cornes.co.jp, Website: www.cornes.co.jp

HAMADA

Lat 34° 53' N; Long 132° 2' E.

Admiralty Chart: JP149 **Admiralty Pilot:** 41
Time Zone: GMT +9 h **UNCTAD Locode:** JP HMD

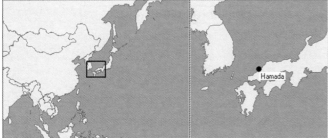

Principal Facilities:

	Y	G		B		T	

Authority: Ports & Fisheries Maintenance Division, 1 Tono-machi, Matsue 690-8501, Shimane Pref., Japan, Tel: +81 852 225318, Fax: +81 852 226048, Email: gyoko-gyojo@pref.shimane.lg.jp, Website: www.pref.shimane.lg.jp

Officials: Director: Tsutomu Yamane.

Port Security: ISPS compliant

Approach: Draught limitation in the channel is 9.0 m at Nagahama Wharf No.1 and 7.0 m at Nagahama Wharf No.2

Pilotage: Pilots are available at the quarantine anchorage

Tides: Tidal range 1.311 m max, - 0.549 m min

Working Hours: 08.30-17.00 except Sunday & holiday

Accommodation:

Name	Length (m)	Depth (m)	Draught (m)	Remarks
Hamada				
Nagahama Wharf No.1	186	10	9	For vessels up 186 m loa & 15 000 dwt
Nagahama Wharf No.2	131	7.5	7	For vessels up to 131 m loa & 5000 dwt
Nagahama Wharf No.3	71	5		Max 1000 dwt

Name	Length (m)	Depth (m)	Draught (m)	Remarks
Fukui Wharf No.1	130	7.5	7	For vessels up to 130 m loa & 5000 dwt
Fukui Wharf No.2	90	5.5	5	For vessels up to 90 m loa & 2000 dwt

Bunkering: Domestic oil, bonded oil, lubrication oil and diesel oil are available

Towage: One tug of 3100 hp

Repair & Maintenance: Small repairs can be undertaken

Lloyd's Agent: Cornes & Co. Ltd, Meikai Building, 32 Akashi-machi, Chuo-ku, Kobe 650-0037, Hyogo Pref., Japan, Tel: +81 78 332 3421, Fax: +81 78 332 3070, Email: survey@kobe.cornes.co.jp, Website: www.cornes.co.jp

HANANOCHO WHARF

harbour area, see under Shimonoseki

HANNAN

Lat 34° 27' N; Long 135° 21' E.

Admiralty Chart: JP1141 **Admiralty Pilot:** 42B
Time Zone: GMT +9 h **UNCTAD Locode:** JP HAN

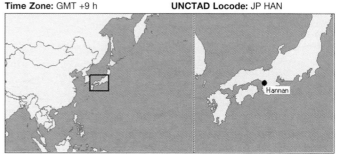

Principal Facilities:

P	Q	Y	G			B		T	A

Authority: Port & Harbour Bureau Osaka Prefectural Government, 10th Floor, Sakai-Semboku Port, Service Center Building, 6-1 Nagisa-cho, Izumiotsu 595-0055, Osaka Pref., Japan, Tel: +81 725 211411, Fax: +81 725 217259, Email: kowankyoku@sbox.pref.osaka.lg.jp, Website: www.pref.osaka.jp/kowan/index.htm

Officials: General Director: Hiroshi Furukawa.
Marketing Manager: Toshihiko Matuda.

Port Security: ISPS compliant

Approach: The approach is through Tomogashima Strait and Osaka Bay. Kishiwada passage is 1.5 km long, 220 m wide and 10 m deep. Izumisano passage is 2.1 km long, 220 m wide and 12 m deep. Draught limitation in port channel is 10 m

Anchorage: Vessels normally anchor at the quarantine anchorage

Pilotage: Compulsory for vessels exceeding 10 000 gt. Pilots available from Osaka Bay Pilot Association, Tel: +81 78 331 4716. Pilots board at the anchorage, Kishiwada, 34° 30' N; 135° 21' 30" E, or Izumisano, 34° 27' 30" N; 135° 19' 45" E

Radio Frequency: Osaka Port Radio, 24 h service, calling on VHF Channel 16, working on Channels 12, 19 and 20

Weather: Typhoon season, July to October

Principal Imports and Exports: Imports: Raw sugar, Timber.

Working Hours: 08.00 - 16.00 except Sunday & holiday

Accommodation: The port is formed by three regions: Kishiwada, Kaizuka and Izumisano and is partially protected by a breakwater. The main cargo handled is logs. The fishing ports of Sano and Kishiwada are located in the harbour limits

Name	Length (m)	Depth (m)	Draught (m)	Remarks
Public Wharves				
Kishiwada Wharf No.1	185	10	9	For vessels 180 m loa & 30 000 dwt
Kishiwada Buoy No.1	190	11	10	For vessels up to 140 m loa & 10 000 dwt
Kishiwada Buoy No.2	230	11	10	For vessels up to 165 m loa & 15 000 dwt
Kishiwada Buoy No.3	260	12	10	For vessels up to 180 m loa & 20 000 dwt
Kaizuka Wharf No.1	202	6.5		Max 3000 dwt
Kaizuka Wharf No.2	400	6.5		Max 3000 dwt
Private Wharves				
Izumisano Daishin-Seito	100	10	9	For vessels up to 170 m loa & 20 000 dwt
Fuji Oil Co Dolphin	76	12	10	For vessels up to 170 m loa & 20 000 dwt
Fuji Oil Co Wharf	200	6.7	6.5	For vessels up to 130 m loa

Storage: Timber pool of 769 449 m2

Location	Open (m²)
Hannan	3150

Mechanical Handling Equipment:

Location	Type	Capacity (t)
Hannan	Mult-purp. Cranes	40

Cargo Worked: 3000 t of foreign trade cargo and 20 000 t of domestic trade cargo handled per working day

Bunkering: Domestic oil available. Bonded oil is brought by barge from Osaka

Towage: Tugs up to 4000 hp available from Sakai

Medical Facilities: Available

Airport: Kansai International, 10 km

Railway: Nankai Main Line, 1.5 km. Japan Railway Hanwa Line, 3.5 km

Lloyd's Agent: Cornes & Co. Ltd, Meikai Building, 32 Akashi-machi, Chuo-ku, Kobe 650-0037, Hyogo Pref., Japan, *Tel:* +81 78 332 3421, *Fax:* +81 78 332 3070, *Email:* survey@kobe.cornes.co.jp, *Website:* www.cornes.co.jp

HEIANZA

Lat 26° 21' N; Long 127° 57' E.

Admiralty Chart: JP226	**Admiralty Pilot:** 42A
Time Zone: GMT +9 h	**UNCTAD Locode:** JP HEI

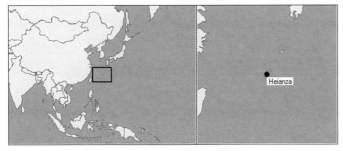

Principal Facilities:

P	Q	Y	G		B	T	

Authority: Port & Harbour Section of Okinawa Prefecture, 1-2-32 Senzaki, Naha 900-0021, Okinawa Pref., Japan, *Tel:* +81 98 662395, *Fax:* +81 98 662800

Approach: Max depth on approach is 45 m. Draught limitation in the channel is 26 m

Pilotage: Compulsory. Pilot boards in pos 26° 26' N; 128° 02' E. Berthing carried out during daylight hours only

Radio Frequency: VHF Channel 16 and 67, call sign KINWANTUG 5 h prior to arrival. Pilot boards at pos 26° 26' N; 128° 02' E

Tides: Average tidal range 1.8 m, max tidal range 2.25 m

Maximum Vessel Dimensions: 385 m loa, 26 m d, 500 000 dwt

Working Hours: 08:00 - 17:00

Accommodation:

Name	Depth (m)	Draught (m)	Remarks
Heianza			See [1] below
Okinawa Terminal Sea Berth No.1	30		Can accommodate tankers up to 500 000 dwt, 385 m loa, 25 m d
Okinawa Terminal Sea Berth No.2	28		For tankers up to 150 000 dwt, 305 m loa, 20 m d
OCC Sea Berth No.1	33		See [2] below
OCC Sea Berth No.2	33		For tankers up to 300 000 dwt, 335 m loa, 30.4 m d
OSS Oil Products Pier No.3	15.5	13.5	Max Loa 240 m and 70 000 dwt
OSS Oil Products Pier No.4	11.5	9	Max loa 175 m and 20 000 dwt
OSS Oil Products Pier No.4	10	8.5	Max loa 110 m and 10 000 dwt

[1]*Heianza:* Bulk facilities: Dry cargo berth 110 m long for coal carriers
[2]*OCC Sea Berth No.1:* Accommodates tankers up to 500 000 dwt, 380 m loa, 32 m d

Cargo Worked: Ballast loading 3800 kl/h. Crude oil loading 10 000 kl/h

Bunkering: Available

Towage: Four tugs of 3400 hp and one of 2600 hp available

Repair & Maintenance: Small repairs can be undertaken

Lloyd's Agent: Cornes & Co. Ltd, Meikai Building, 32 Akashi-machi, Chuo-ku, Kobe 650-0037, Hyogo Pref., Japan, *Tel:* +81 78 332 3421, *Fax:* +81 78 332 3070, *Email:* survey@kobe.cornes.co.jp, *Website:* www.cornes.co.jp

HIBI

Lat 34° 27' N; Long 133° 56' E.

Admiralty Chart: 694	**Admiralty Pilot:** 42B
Time Zone: GMT +9 h	**UNCTAD Locode:** JP HIB

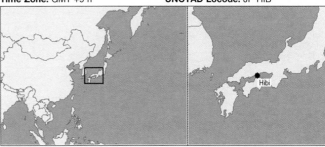

Principal Facilities:

	Y	G		B		

Authority: Port & Harbour Section of Okayama Prefecture, 2-4-6 Uchisange, Okayama 700-8570, Japan, *Tel:* +81 86 226 7485, *Fax:* +81 86 227 5551, *Email:* kowan@pref.okayama.lg.jp, *Website:* www.pref.okayama.jp

Officials: Harbour Director: Masanori Tokimatsu, *Email:* masanori_tokimatsu@pref.okayama.lg.jp.

Port Security: ISPS compliant

Approach: Draft limitation in the channel 13 m

Pilotage: Not compulsory but recommended in view of the rapid current. Compulsory however for vessels over 10 000 gt in the inland-sea. Inland-sea pilots are available at Wada-Misaki (off Kobe), Sekisaki or Hesaki (off Moji).

Tides: Tidal range 2.40 m max, -0.90 m min

Working Hours: At Mitsui Hibi Wharf: 08.30 - 20.30. At Hibi Public Wharf: 08.30 - 17.00

Accommodation:

Name	Length (m)	Depth (m)	Draught (m)	Remarks
Hibi				
Mitsui Hibi Wharf	176	13.1	12	For vessels up to 190 m loa & 50 000 dwt
Hibi Public Wharf	185	9.1	9.1	For vessels up to 170 m loa & 15 000 dwt

Mechanical Handling Equipment: Floating cranes available

Location	Type	Capacity (t)	Qty
Mitsui Hibi Wharf	Shore Cranes	10	1

Bunkering: Available at the public wharf. Bonded oil will be brought from oil stations ports when required

Lloyd's Agent: Cornes & Co. Ltd, Meikai Building, 32 Akashi-machi, Chuo-ku, Kobe 650-0037, Hyogo Pref., Japan, *Tel:* +81 78 332 3421, *Fax:* +81 78 332 3070, *Email:* survey@kobe.cornes.co.jp, *Website:* www.cornes.co.jp

HIBIKINADA

harbour area, see under Wakamatsu

HIGASHI-HARIMA

Lat 34° 42' N; Long 134° 51' E.

Admiralty Chart: 640	**Admiralty Pilot:** 42B
Time Zone: GMT +9 h	**UNCTAD Locode:** JP HHR

Principal Facilities:

	Q	Y	G		R	B		A

Authority: Port & Harbour Section of Hyogo Prefecture, 5-10-1 Yamate-dori, Chuo-ku, Kobe 650-8567, Hyogo Pref., Japan, *Tel:* +81 78 341 7711, *Fax:* +81 78 341 6477

Port Security: ISPS compliant

Approach: Draft Limitation 9.0 m at Wharf No.3 and 10.8 m at Wharf's 4 & 5

Key to Principal Facilities:—		
A=Airport	**C**=Containers	**G**=General Cargo
B=Bunkers	**D**=Dry Dock	**L**=Cruise

P=Petroleum	**R**=Ro/Ro	**Y**=Dry Bulk
Q=Other Liquid Bulk	**T**=Towage (where available from port)	

Pilotage: Compulsory for vessels over 10 000 gt. Inland-sea pilots are available at Wada-Misaki (off Kobe), and harbour pilot is available at the anchorage from sunrise to sunset

Weather: Typhoon season, July to October

Accommodation:

Name	Depth (m)	Draught (m)	Remarks
Higashi-Harima			
Harima Public Wharf No.3	10	9	
Harima Public Wharf No.4	12	10.8	
Harima Public Wharf No.5	12	10.8	
Anchorage	12	10–10.5	Max 10 000 dwt

Storage:

Location	Open (m²)
Higashi-Harima	5699

Bunkering: Kyodo Oil Co. Ltd, 11-2 Nagata-cho 2-chome, Chiyoda-ku, Tokyo, Japan, *Tel:* +81 3 3505 8241, *Fax:* +81 3 3505 8697
MC Marine and Bunkering Inc., 8th Floor, Uchisaiwai-cho Dai Building, 3-3 Uchisaiwai-cho 1-chome, Chiyoda-ku, Tokyo 100-0011, Japan, *Tel:* +81 3 5251 2575, *Fax:* +81 3 5251 2583

Repair & Maintenance: Minor repairs only can be undertaken

Airport: Osaka, 60 km

Lloyd's Agent: Cornes & Co. Ltd, Meikai Building, 32 Akashi-machi, Chuo-ku, Kobe 650-0037, Hyogo Pref., Japan, *Tel:* +81 78 332 3421, *Fax:* +81 78 332 3070, *Email:* survey@kobe.cornes.co.jp, *Website:* www.cornes.co.jp

HIKARI

Lat 33° 57' N; Long 131° 55' E.

Admiralty Chart: 3153	**Admiralty Pilot:** 42B
Time Zone: GMT +9 h	**UNCTAD Locode:** JP HKR

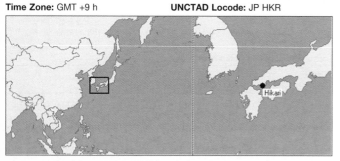

Principal Facilities:

		Y	G						

Authority: Ports & Harbors Division, Yamaguchi Prefectural Government, 1-1 Takimachi, Yamaguchi 753-8501, Yamaguchi Pref., Japan, *Tel:* +81 83 933 3810, *Fax:* +81 83 933 3829, *Email:* a12900@pref.yamaguchi.lg.jp, *Website:* www.pref.yamaguchi.lg.jp

Officials: Shoichi Hayashi, *Tel:* +81 83 9332 340.

Approach: Draft limitation in the channel 11.20 m

Pilotage: Not compulsory but recommended. Pilots are available at the point 33° 54' N, 131° 56' E, inland-sea pilots are available at Wada-Misaki, Sekisaki or Hesaki

Accommodation:

Name	Length (m)	Depth (m)	Draught (m)	Remarks
Hikari				
Steel Export Wharf	232	11.6	11.2	For vessels up to 200 m loa & 30 000 dwt

Mechanical Handling Equipment: Floating cranes available

Bunkering: Bonded oil will be brought from Kobe, Osaka or Tokuyama with sufficent advance notice

Repair & Maintenance: Only minor repairs can be undertaken

Lloyd's Agent: Cornes & Co. Ltd, Meikai Building, 32 Akashi-machi, Chuo-ku, Kobe 650-0037, Hyogo Pref., Japan, *Tel:* +81 78 332 3421, *Fax:* +81 78 332 3070, *Email:* survey@kobe.cornes.co.jp, *Website:* www.cornes.co.jp

HIMEJI

harbour area, see under Mega

HIMEKAWA

Lat 37° 2' N; Long 137° 51' E.

Admiralty Chart: JP1180	**Admiralty Pilot:** 41
Time Zone: GMT +9 h	**UNCTAD Locode:** JP HMK

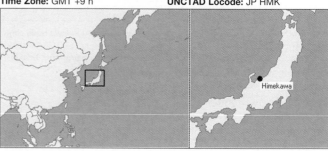

Principal Facilities:

		Y	G			B			

Authority: Port & Harbour Section of Niigata Prefecture, Bureau of Port & Airport Development, Niigata Prefectural Government, 4-1 Shinko-cho, Niigata 950-8570, Niigata Pref., Japan, *Tel:* +81 25 285 5511, *Fax:* +81 25 285 9375, *Email:* t1700102@mail.pref.niigata.jp

Approach: Depth in channel of 9 m; draught limitation is 8.2 m

Pilotage: Not compulsory but recommended. Pilots are available at pos 37° 03' 03" N; 137° 51' 30" E

Tides: Tidal range of 0.3 m max, -0.1 m min

Principal Imports and Exports: Imports: Coal. Exports: Limestone.

Working Hours: 0830-1630. Overtime possible. Sunday working available except 1st and 3rd weeks

Accommodation:

Name	Length (m)	Depth (m)	Draught (m)	Remarks
Himekawa				
Central Pier No.1	130	7.5	6.8	Max 5000 dwt
Central Pier No.2	130	7.5	6.8	Max 5000 dwt
Central Pier No.3	130	7.5	6.8	Max 5000 dwt
Central Pier No.4	130	7.5	6.8	Max 5000 dwt
Central Pier No.5	165	9	8.2	Max 10 000 dwt
West Pier No.1	90	5.5	5	Max 2000 dwt
West Pier No.2	130	7.5	6.8	Max 5000 dwt
North Pier No.1 (Dolphin)	38	7.5	6.8	Max 5000 dwt

Mechanical Handling Equipment:

Location	Type	Capacity (t)	Qty
Himekawa	Shore Cranes	35–80	7

Bunkering: Domestic oil available

Towage: No tugs stationed at the port but available from Naoetsu or Niigata if required

Repair & Maintenance: Minor repairs can be undertaken

Lloyd's Agent: Cornes & Co. Ltd, 273 Yamashita-cho, Naka-ku, Yokohama 231-0023, Kanagawa Pref., Japan, *Tel:* +81 45 201 8537, *Fax:* +81 45 212 3105, *Email:* survey@ykh.cornes.co.jp, *Website:* www.cornes.co.jp

HIRAO

Lat 33° 54' N; Long 132° 3' E.

Admiralty Chart: JP1102	**Admiralty Pilot:** 42B
Time Zone: GMT +9 h	**UNCTAD Locode:** JP HRA

Principal Facilities:

			G		R	B	T		

Authority: Hirao Port Office, Keizai-ka, Kumage-gun, Hirao, Yamaguchi Pref., Japan, *Tel:* +81 820 563111

Port Security: ISPS compliant

Approach: Channel depths range from 20 m to 35 m. Vessels beware of fishing boats off the port

Pilotage: Not compulsory; Inland-sea pilots are available at Sekisaki or Hesaki. Harbour pilots are available off Hirao in pos 33 51 N; 132 02 E

Accommodation:

Name	Remarks
Hirao	Open roadstead for handling import of round logs, depth 11-12 m

Mechanical Handling Equipment:

Location	Type	Capacity (t)	Remarks
Hirao	Mult-purp. Cranes	50	From Matsukura Corp

Bunkering: Available(delivered by barge)

Towage: Available if required

Lloyd's Agent: Cornes & Co. Ltd, Meikai Building, 32 Akashi-machi, Chuo-ku, Kobe 650-0037, Hyogo Pref., Japan, *Tel:* +81 78 332 3421, *Fax:* +81 78 332 3070, *Email:* survey@kobe.cornes.co.jp, *Website:* www.cornes.co.jp

HIROHATA

Lat 34° 46' N; Long 134° 37' E.

Admiralty Chart: 698
Time Zone: GMT +9 h

Admiralty Pilot: 42B
UNCTAD Locode: JP HRH

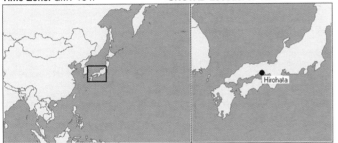

Principal Facilities:

P		Y	G		R		B		

Authority: Port & Harbour Section of Hyogo Prefecture, 5-10-1 Yamate-dori, Chuo-ku, Kobe 650-8567, Hyogo Pref., Japan, *Tel:* +81 78 341 7711, *Fax:* +81 78 341 6477

Approach: Draft limitation in the channel 17 m

Pilotage: Inland-sea pilots are available at Wada-Misaki and harbour pilots are available at the anchorage from one hour afer sunrise until one hour before sunset

Tides: Tidal range 1.60 m max, .0.50 m min

Working Hours: 24 hours in 3 shifts

Accommodation:

Name	Length (m)	Depth (m)	Draught (m)	Remarks
Hirohata				
Higashihama Quay A-1	110	7.5	7.5	Max 5000 dwt
Higashihama Quay A-2	220	11	11	Max 40 000 dwt
Yumesaki Quay No.1-2	420	7.5	7.5	Max 10 000 dwt x 2
Kamoda Quay No.3-6	525	8	7.5	Max 10 000 dwt x 2
Central Quay No.9	315	13.2	13.2	Max 80 000 dwt
Genryo Quay No.18	300	17	16	Max 275 000 dwt
Tsuruta Quay No.10	170	9.5	9.5	Max 10 000 dwt

Bunkering: Hanwa Co. Ltd, 2nd Floor, Finland House, 56 Haymarket, London SW1Y 4RN, United Kingdom, *Tel:* +44 20 7839 4448, *Fax:* +44 20 7839 3994, *Email:* orito@hanwa.co.uk
Hikawa Shoji Kaisha Ltd, 26-2 Shinkawa NS Building 1-chome, Shinkawa, Chuo-ku, Tokyo 104, Japan, *Tel:* +81 3 5776 6858, *Fax:* +81 3 5541 3274
Idemitsu Kosan Co. Ltd, 1-1 Marunochi, 3-Chome, Chiyoda-ku, Tokyo 100-8321, Japan, *Tel:* +81 3 3213 3138, *Fax:* +81 3 3213 1145, *Email:* tohru.takamura@si.idemitsu.co.jp, *Website:* www.idemitsu.co.jp
KG Int Petroleum Ltd, Shiba Park Building, 241 Shiba Koen, Minato-ku, Tokyo 105, Japan, *Tel:* +81 3 3578 4551, *Fax:* +81 3 3578 4550
Kamei Corp., 1-6-1 Otemachi, Chiyoda-ku, Tokyo 100-0004, Japan, *Tel:* +81 3 3286 6234, *Fax:* +81 3 3286 6249, *Email:* bunker@kamei.co.jp
Kyodo Oil Co. Ltd, 11-2 Nagata-cho 2-chome, Chiyoda-ku, Tokyo, Japan, *Tel:* +81 3 3505 8241, *Fax:* +81 3 3505 8697
Marubeni Petroleum Co. Ltd, Marubeni International Petroleum Singapore Co. Ltd, c/o Marubeni Corporation, 4-2 Ohtemachi 1-chome, Chiyoda-ku, Tokyo 100-8088, Japan, *Tel:* +81 3 3282 3920, *Fax:* +81 3 3282 3950, *Email:* TOKB554@marubenicorp.com, *Website:* www.marubeni.co.jp
MC Marine and Bunkering Inc., 8th Floor, Uchisaiwai-cho Dai Building, 3-3 Uchisaiwai-cho 1-chome, Chiyoda-ku, Tokyo 100-0011, Japan, *Tel:* +81 3 5251 2575, *Fax:* +81 3 5251 2583
Mitsui & Co. Petroleum Ltd, 2-1, Ohtemachi 1-chome, Chiyoda-ku, Tokyo 100-0004, Japan, *Tel:* +81 3 3285 6905, *Fax:* +81 3 3285 9811, *Email:* tkzph@dg.mitsui.com, *Website:* www.mitsui.co.jp
Nittetsu Shoji Co. Ltd, 5-7 Kameido 1-chome, Koto-ku, Tokyo 136, Japan, *Tel:* +81 3 5627 2157, *Fax:* +81 3 5627 2192

Setouchi Network, 4-20 Hasihama 1-chome, Imabari 799-2112, Ehime Pref., Japan, *Tel:* +81 898 430041, *Fax:* +81 898 430046, *Email:* secjpn@dokidoki.ne.jp
Sumitomo Corp., Harumi Island, Triton Square, Office Tower Y, 8-11 Harumi 1-chome, Chuo-ku, Tokyo 104-8610, Japan, *Tel:* +81 3 51664458, *Fax:* +81 3 51666407, *Email:* ir@sumitomo.co.jp, *Website:* www.sumitomocorp.co.jp

Towage: Available, tugs belong to Himeji Port

Repair & Maintenance: Small repairs can be undertaken

Lloyd's Agent: Cornes & Co. Ltd, Meikai Building, 32 Akashi-machi, Chuo-ku, Kobe 650-0037, Hyogo Pref., Japan, *Tel:* +81 78 332 3421, *Fax:* +81 78 332 3070, *Email:* survey@kobe.cornes.co.jp, *Website:* www.cornes.co.jp

HIROSHIMA

Lat 34° 21' N; Long 132° 26' E.

Admiralty Chart: 3469
Time Zone: GMT +9 h

Admiralty Pilot: 42B
UNCTAD Locode: JP HIJ

Principal Facilities:

P	Q	Y	G	C	R		B	D	T	A

Authority: Hiroshima Prefectural Government, Airport & Seaport Department, 10-52 Moto-Machi, Naka-ku, Hiroshima 730-8511, Hiroshima Pref., Japan, *Tel:* +81 82 228 2111, *Fax:* +81 82 223 2463, *Email:* r-matumoto80233@pref.hiroshima.lg.jp, *Website:* www.hiroshima-minato.jp

Officials: Port Director: Ryutaro Matsumoto, *Tel:* +81 82 224 2285.

Port Security: ISPS compliant

Approach: Channel No.1, 9.9 km long, 100 m wide, 9 m to 12.6 m deep; Channel No.2, 2.9 km long, 100 m wide, 12 m to 16 m deep

Anchorage: There are various designated anchorage areas with depths ranging from 6 m to 18 m and over

Pilotage: Not compulsory but advisable. Pilots available at the quarantine anchorage from sunrise to 2000

Radio Frequency: Hiroshima Port Radio, VHF Channel 16

Tides: Range of tide max 3.99 m, min 0.42 m

Principal Imports and Exports: Imports: Coal, Grain, Logs. Exports: Equipment, Machinery, Vehicles.

Working Hours: Stevedores 0830-2130

Accommodation: Numerous anchorages are available for vessels loading or unloading cargo, repairs and awaiting berths
Bulk facilities: Grain discharging at Gaibo Wharf; coal discharging at Hiroshima Gas Wharf

Name	Length (m)	Depth (m)	Remarks
Public Wharves			
Ujina Foreign Trade Wharf	925	10	Cruise & general cargo
Ujina Dolphin	95	10	
Hatsukaichi Lumber Wharf	370	10	Two berths
Hatsukaichi Dolphin	825	10–12	Lumber
Hatsukaichi Wharf	130	7.5	General cargo
Kaita Container Berth	260	7.5	Containers. CFS of 2567 m2. 14 reefer points
Kaita General Cargo Berth	390	7.5	General cargo
Kaita General Cargo Berth	720	5.5	General cargo
Hiroshima Port International Container Terminal	330	14	Container stacking cap of 5000 TEU's and CFS of 3400 m2. 32 reefer points
Private Wharves			
Toyo Kogyo Co Ltd	380	4	Four berths available
Nisho-Iwai Co Ltd	165	6	Two berths available
Kanawa Wharf	166	6	
Nishimoto Wharf	77	6	Two berths available
Asagami Wharf	75	4.9	
Mitsubishi Wharf	617	7	Two berths available
Hiroshima Gas Wharf	100	7.5	
Mazda Motor Corp	780	4–8	Two berths available

Storage: 39 transit sheds (47 896 m2), 84 warehouses (158 547 m2), 2 refrigerated warehouses (3226 m3), 100 ha of timber storage, Container yard (92 400 m2) with 3 400 m2 for storage of containers including 32 reefer container plugs

Mechanical Handling Equipment:

Location	Type	Capacity (t)	Qty	Remarks
Kaita Container Berth	Gantry Cranes	30.5	2	
Hiroshima Port International Container Terminal	Gantry Cranes	40.6	2	Outreach 44.5 m

Key to Principal Facilities:—					
A=Airport	**C**=Containers	**G**=General Cargo	**P**=Petroleum	**R**=Ro/Ro	**Y**=Dry Bulk
B=Bunkers	**D**=Dry Dock	**L**=Cruise	**Q**=Other Liquid Bulk	**T**=Towage (where available from port)	

Cargo Worked: Vehicles 500 units/gang/shift, logs 700 m3/gang/shift

Bunkering: Hikawa Shoji Kaisha Ltd, 26-2 Shinkawa NS Building 1-chome, Shinkawa, Chuo-ku, Tokyo 104, Japan, *Tel:* +81 3 5776 6858, *Fax:* +81 3 5541 3274
Marubeni Petroleum Co. Ltd, Marubeni International Petroleum Singapore Co. Ltd, c/o Marubeni Corporation, 4-2 Ohtemachi 1-chome, Chiyoda-ku, Tokyo 100-8088, Japan, *Tel:* +81 3 3282 3920, *Fax:* +81 3 3282 3950, *Email:* TOKB554@marubenicorp.com, *Website:* www.marubeni.co.jp
MC Marine and Bunkering Inc., 8th Floor, Uchisaiwai-cho Dai Building, 3-3 Uchisaiwai-cho 1-chome, Chiyoda-ku, Tokyo 100-0011, Japan, *Tel:* +81 3 5251 2575, *Fax:* +81 3 5251 2583
Nissho Iwai Corp., 4-4 Akasaka 2-chome, Minato-ku, Tokyo, Japan, *Tel:* +81 3 35882111

Towage: Numerous tugs available up to 3600 hp

Repair & Maintenance: Kanda Shipbuilding Co. Ltd, 14-21 Higashi 2 chome, Kawajiri-cho, Toyota, Hiroshima 729 26, Hiroshima Pref., Japan, *Tel:* +81 82 387 3521, *Fax:* +81 82 387 3803, *Email:* newbuilding@kandazosen.co.jp, *Website:* www.cajs.or.jp/chuzoko_eng/kaiin_data/kanda_ne.html Three floating docks: No.1 112 m x 30 m for vessels up to 3800 t, No.2 70 m x 16 m for vessels up to 999 t, No.3 220 m x 32 m for vessels up to 25 000 t
Seibu Dockyard Co. Ltd, 384 Aza Kanawa, Ujina-cho, Minami-ku, Hiroshima 734-0016, Hiroshima Pref., Japan, *Tel:* +81 82 885 1171, *Fax:* +81 82 885 3175, *Email:* skudyknw@piano.ocn.ne.jp Two dry docks of 114 m x 21 m x 85 000 gt and 160 m x 25 m x 13 000 gt. Repair quays of 90 m with max draugtht 8 m

Shipping Agents: Chugoku Shipping Agencies Ltd, 8-44, Ujina Kaigan 3-chome, Minami-ku, Hiroshima 734-0011, Hiroshima Pref., Japan, *Tel:* +81 82 252 6020, *Fax:* +81 82 254 0876
Hirokura Co Ltd, 3-9-13 Ujina-kaigan, Minami-ku, Hiroshima 734-0011, Hiroshima Pref., Japan, *Tel:* +81 82 253 2111, *Fax:* +81 82 253 2110, *Email:* agent@hirokura.co.jp, *Website:* www.hirokura.co.jp
Seagate Corp., 37-22 Dejima 2-chome, Minami-ku, Hiroshima 734-0013, Hiroshima Pref., Japan, *Tel:* +81 82 254 2421, *Fax:* +81 82 255 1042, *Email:* hasent@seagatecorp.com, *Website:* www.seagatecorp.com

Surveyors: Det Norske Veritas A/S, Hiroshima Bld, 7th Floor, 1-12-16 Hikari-machi, Higashi-ku, Hiroshima 732 0052, Hiroshima Pref., Japan, *Tel:* +81 82 264 4660, *Fax:* +81 82 264 1130, *Email:* hiroshima@dnv.com, *Website:* www.dnv.com
Nippon Kaiji Kyokai, 9-10 Takara-Machi, Naka-ku, Hiroshima 730-0044, Hiroshima Pref., Japan, *Tel:* +81 82 249 1971, *Fax:* +81 82 249 8351, *Email:* hs@classnk.or.jp, *Website:* www.classnk.or.jp

Medical Facilities: Available

Airport: Hiroshima, 50 km

Development: Itsukaichi area is under construction as a new logistics area, for ro/ro cargoes

Lloyd's Agent: Cornes & Co. Ltd, Meikai Building, 32 Akashi-machi, Chuo-ku, Kobe 650-0037, Hyogo Pref., Japan, *Tel:* +81 78 332 3421, *Fax:* +81 78 332 3070, *Email:* survey@kobe.cornes.co.jp, *Website:* www.cornes.co.jp

HIROURA WHARF

harbour area, see under Saganoseki

HITACHI

Lat 36° 29' N; Long 140° 38' E.

Admiralty Chart: JP1097   **Admiralty Pilot:** 41
Time Zone: GMT +9 h   **UNCTAD Locode:** JP HTC

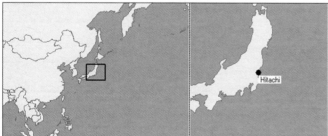

Principal Facilities:

P		Y	G	C		B		T	A

Authority: Ports & Harbors Division, Ibaraki Prefectural Government, 978-6 Kasahara-cho, Mito 310-8555, Ibaraki Pref., Japan, *Tel:* +81 29 301 4536, *Fax:* +81 29 301 4539, *Email:* kowan5@pref.ibaraki.lg.jp, *Website:* www.pref.ibaraki.jp/bukyoku/doboku/kowan/sitetop1/index.htm

Officials: Director: Goto Kazumasa.

Port Security: ISPS compliant

Approach: Draught limitation in channel is 8.2 m to Wharf No's 1 and 2, 9.5 m to Wharf No.5 and 11.4 m to Wharf No.4 (berth E)

Pilotage: Not compulsory. Pilot boards at pos 36° 28' 13" N; 140° 39' 11" E between sunrise and sunset

Tides: Tidal range 1.20 m max, 0.35 m min

Traffic: 2006, 5 195 634 t of cargo handled

Working Hours: Stevedores 0815-1630 except Sundays and holidays

Accommodation:

Name	Length (m)	Depth (m)	Remarks
Hitachi			
Wharf No.1			
Berth A	120	5	Max 1 x 1000 dwt
Berth B	121	7.5	Max 1 x 5000 dwt
Berth C	130	7.5	Max 1 x 5000 dwt
Berth D	185	10	Max 1 x 10 000 dwt
Wharf No.2			
Berth B	165	9	Max 1 x 10 000 dwt
Berth C	130	7.5	Max 1 x 5000 dwt
Berth D	130	7.5	Max 1 x 5000 dwt
Wharf No.3			
Berth A	140	5	Max 1 x 1000 dwt
Wharf No.4			
Berth A	70	5	Max 1 x 1000 dwt
Berth B	70	5	Max 1 x 1000 dwt
Berth C	130	7.5	Max 1 x 5000 dwt
Berth D	185	10	Max 1 x 15 000 dwt
Berth E	240	12	Max 1 x 30 000 dwt
Wharf No.5			
Berth A	130	7.5	Max 1 x 5000 dwt
Berth B	185	10	Max 1 x 15 000 dwt
Berth C	185	10	Max 1 x 15 000 dwt
Berth D	240	12	Max 1 x 30 000 dwt

Storage: Two transit sheds of 2146 m2 and 3576 m2. One shed and two warehouses owned by Hitachi Huto Co Ltd of 2013 m2, 2568 m2 and 693 m2 respectively. No.1 timber pool shore area 94 108 m2, water area 51 983 m2. No.2 timber pool shore area 115 147 m2, water area 48 075 m2. Open shed of 9040 m2 for logs at Wharf No.5

Bunkering: Hitachi Huto Co. Ltd, 3-10 Kujicho 1-chome, Hitachi 319-12, Ibaraki Pref., Japan, *Tel:* +81 29 453 4111, *Fax:* +81 29 453 4117
Hitachi Huto Co. Ltd, 3-10 Kujicho 1-chome, Hitachi 319-12, Ibaraki Pref., Japan, *Tel:* +81 29 453 4111, *Fax:* +81 29 453 4117 – *Misc:* domestic oil available
MC Marine and Bunkering Inc., 8th Floor, Uchisaiwai-cho Dai Building, 3-3 Uchisaiwai-cho 1-chome, Chiyoda-ku, Tokyo 100-0011, Japan, *Tel:* +81 3 5251 2575, *Fax:* +81 3 5251 2583
Nittetsu Shoij Co. Ltd, 5-7 Kameido 1-chome, Koto-ku, Tokyo 136, Japan, *Tel:* +81 3 5627 2157, *Fax:* +81 3 5627 2192

Towage: One 2600 hp tug and two 3000 hp tugs available

Repair & Maintenance: Minor repairs available

Airport: Narita

Lloyd's Agent: Cornes & Co. Ltd, 273 Yamashita-cho, Naka-ku, Yokohama 231-0023, Kanagawa Pref., Japan, *Tel:* +81 45 201 8537, *Fax:* +81 45 212 3105, *Email:* survey@ykh.cornes.co.jp, *Website:* www.cornes.co.jp

HITACHINAKA

Lat 36° 25' N; Long 140° 25' E.

Admiralty Chart: JP1097   **Admiralty Pilot:** 41
Time Zone: GMT +9 h

UNCTAD Locode: JP HIC

Principal Facilities:

			G	C				T	

Authority: Ibaraki Port Authority, 768-27 Terunuma, Tokai-mura, Naka-gun, Ibaraki 319-1113, Ibaraki Pref., Japan, *Tel:* +81 29 264 2500, *Fax:* +81 29 264 2503, *Email:* agency@ipac-net.jp, *Website:* www.ibaraki-kowan.jp

Officials: Sales Manager: Mitsuo Nakamura.

Port Security: ISPS compliant

Approach: The port is protected by a detached breakwater 2.5 miles long and marked by lights. It is approached from a position 1 mile ESE of Iso Saki through a channel leading NNE and marked by light-buoys
There are also two detached breakwaters which shelter the North Wharf. One is located 4 cables E of the Central Wharf area and the other is situated 2.5 cables S of the North Wharf

Pilotage: Not compulsory but pilots available

Traffic: 2006, 4 456 624 t of cargo handled

Accommodation:

Name	Length (m)	Depth (m)	Remarks
North Wharf			
Berth	400	18	1 x 130 000 dwt
Berth	310	14–15	1 x 40 000 dwt
Berth	250	12	1 x 30 000 dwt

Name	Length (m)	Depth (m)	Remarks
Berth	170	10	1 x 10 000 dwt
Berth	390	7.5	3 x 5000 dwt
Berth	200	7.5	2 x 2000 dwt
Berth	300	5.5	3 x 2000 dwt
South Wharf			
Berth	260	6.5–7	2 x 5000 dwt
Berth	180	3–5	2 x 2000 dwt
Berth	270	5.5	3 x 2000 dwt

Towage: Two 3000 hp tugs available

Development: Construction of berths in the Central Wharf area

Lloyd's Agent: Cornes & Co. Ltd, 273 Yamashita-cho, Naka-ku, Yokohama 231-0023, Kanagawa Pref., Japan, *Tel:* +81 45 201 8537, *Fax:* +81 45 212 3105, *Email:* survey@ykh.cornes.co.jp, *Website:* www.cornes.co.jp

HOSOE WHARF

harbour area, see under Shimonoseki

HOSOSHIMA

Lat 32° 27' N; Long 131° 40' E.

Admiralty Chart: 676
Time Zone: GMT +9 h

Admiralty Pilot: 42A
UNCTAD Locode: JP HSM

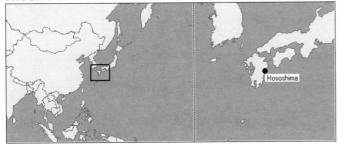

Principal Facilities:

| P | Q | Y | G | C | R | | B | | T | A |

Authority: Port & Harbour Section of Miyazaki Prefecture, Public Works Department, 2-10-1 Tachibana Dori Higashi, Miyazaki 880-8501, Miyazaki Pref., Japan, *Tel:* +81 985 241111, *Fax:* +81 985 220892, *Email:* kowan@pref.miyazaki.lg.jp

Port Security: ISPS compliant

Approach: Draught limitation in channel is 10 m

Anchorage: Anchorage can be obtained in pos 32° 25' 50" N; 131° 40' 00" E in a depth of 34 m

Pilotage: Vessel's ETA is required 48 and 24 h in advance. Telegraphic address of pilot station is 'Pilot Hososhima'. Pilot boards vessel at Hososhima Quarantine anchorage from sunrise to 1 h before sunset

Weather: In winter NE winds bring rough conditions

Tides: Range of tide + 2.44 m max, -0.35 m min

Maximum Vessel Dimensions: 43 000 dwt, 9.8 m d, 200 m loa

Principal Imports and Exports: Imports: Dried rice-straw, Logs, Ore sulphate, Salt, Sugar.

Working Hours: 0830-1630 on weekdays; Sundays and holidays subject to pre-arrangement when required

Accommodation:

Name	Length (m)	Depth (m)	Draught (m)	Remarks
Industrial Port				
Wharf No.1	175	10	8.8	See [1] below
Wharf No.2	196	10	8.8	See [2] below
Wharf No.3	180	5.5	5	Max 2000 gt
Wharf No.4	180	5.5	5	Max 2000 gt
Wharf No.5	130	7.5	7	Max 5000 gt
Wharf No.6	185	10	9.6	Max 15 000 gt. Coal and sulphate
Hyuga Refinery's Wharf	260	10	9.8	Max 34 000 dwt. Nickel, ore, beans and coal
Sugar Plant Wharf (Dolphin)	150	10	9.6	Max 15 000 gt. Bulk sugar
Commercial Port				
Wharf No.2	250	7.5	6.8	Max 5000 gt
Shirahama Port				
Wharf No.8	90	5.5	5	Max 2000 gt
Wharf No.9	260	7.5	7	Max 5000 gt
Wharf No.10	185	10	9.3	Max 28 000 gt

[1]*Wharf No.1: Max 10 000 gt. Phosphate, salt & manganese ore*
[2]*Wharf No.2: Max 15 000 gt. Phosphate, salt & manganese ore*

Storage: Senko Co. Ltd. bonded warehouse and Hakko Unyu K.K. bonded warehouse

Mechanical Handling Equipment: Floating cranes available

Location	Type	Capacity (t)	Qty
Hyuga Refinery's Wharf	Mult-purp. Cranes	18	2
Wharf No.10	Mult-purp. Cranes	41	1

Cargo Worked: Bulk sugar 450 t/h/gang, manganese ore 240 t/h/gang, salt 300 t/h/gang, phosphate in bulk 200 t/h/gang, containers 20 units/h

Bunkering: KG Int Petroleum Ltd, Shiba Park Building, 241 Shiba Koen, Minato-ku, Tokyo 105, Japan, *Tel:* +81 3 3578 4551, *Fax:* +81 3 3578 4550
MC Marine and Bunkering Inc., 8th Floor, Uchisaiwai-cho Dai Building, 3-3 Uchisaiwai-cho 1-chome, Chiyoda-ku, Tokyo 100-0011, Japan, *Tel:* +81 3 5251 2575, *Fax:* +81 3 5251 2583

Towage: Two tugs available; one of 2600 hp and one of 2700 hp

Medical Facilities: Available at Uragami Clinic, Tel: (982) 522936

Airport: Miyazaki, 75 km

Lloyd's Agent: Cornes & Co. Ltd, Meikai Building, 32 Akashi-machi, Chuo-ku, Kobe 650-0037, Hyogo Pref., Japan, *Tel:* +81 78 332 3421, *Fax:* +81 78 332 3070, *Email:* survey@kobe.cornes.co.jp, *Website:* www.cornes.co.jp

IDEMITSU

harbour area, see under Mega

IMABARI

Lat 34° 3' N; Long 133° 0' E.

Admiralty Chart: 698
Time Zone: GMT +9 h

Admiralty Pilot: 42B
UNCTAD Locode: JP IMB

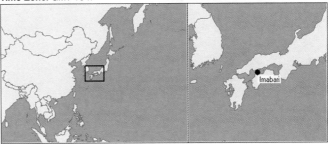

Principal Facilities:

| P | | Y | G | C | | | B | D | T | A |

Authority: Port & Harbour Bureau of Imabari City, 1-4-1 Bekku-cho, 1-chome, Imabari 794, Ehime Pref., Japan, *Tel:* +81 898 325200, *Fax:* +81 898 325211, *Email:* kouwanka@imabari-city.jp

Port Security: ISPS compliant

Approach: The approach is via Kurushima Strait traffic route. There are two channels, one is 1800 m long, 300 m wide and 6 m deep and the other is 1500 m long, 300 m wide and 5.5 m deep. 22 ha of anchorage space. Vessels normally anchor at Matsuyama for quarantine. Draught limitation in port channel is 9 m

Pilotage: Not compulsory. Inland Sea pilotage compulsory for vessels exceeding 10 000 gt and pilots are available at Wadamisaki, Sekisaki or Hesaki and harbour pilots are available at the anchorage. Berthing at wharves during daylight hours only

Weather: Typhoon season, July to October

Tides: 3.84 m MHWL, 0.06 m MLWL, 2.0 m MSL. Current 2.4 knots in NW direction

Maximum Vessel Dimensions: 10 000 dwt for ferries, 15 000 dwt for cargo vessels

Principal Imports and Exports: Imports: Textiles, Timber.

Working Hours: 0800-1700. No night work

Accommodation:

Name	Length (m)	Depth (m)	Draught (m)	Remarks
Imabari				
Kurashiki Wharf No.1	165	9	8.1	Max 10 000 gt
Kurashiki Wharf No.2	140	7.5	6.5	Max 4000 gt
Toryu Wharf No.1	210	5.5	4.95	Max 2000 dwt
Toryu Wharf No.2	180	5.5	4.95	Max 2000 dwt
Tomita Wharf No.1	240	12	10.8	Max 30 000 dwt (18 137 gt)
Tomita Wharf No.2	185	10	9	Max 15 000 dwt (9619 gt)
Tomita Wharf No.3	100	4	3.6	Max 500 dwt

Storage: Four transit sheds (3024 m2), 16 warehouses (3676 m2), 4.32 ha timber storage

Mechanical Handling Equipment:

Location	Type	Capacity (t)
Imabari	Mult-purp. Cranes	15

Cargo Worked: 6900 t of both foreign trade and domestic trade cargo per working day

Bunkering: Bonded oil available by barge from Kobe or Moji

Key to Principal Facilities:—				
A=Airport	**C**=Containers	**G**=General Cargo	**P**=Petroleum	**R**=Ro/Ro	**Y**=Dry Bulk
B=Bunkers	**D**=Dry Dock	**L**=Cruise	**Q**=Other Liquid Bulk	**T**=Towage (where available from port)

Towage: Two tugs of 2600 hp are available

Repair & Maintenance: Hashihama Shipbuilding Co. Ltd, Imabari, Ehime Pref., Japan, *Tel:* +81 898 419251

Higaki Shipbuilding Co. Ltd, 4-25 1 chome, Koura-cho, Imabari 799-2111, Ehime Pref., Japan, *Tel:* +81 898 419147, *Fax:* +81 898 417322, *Email:* hsb307@higaki.co.jp, *Website:* www.higaki.co.jp Floating dock of 84.9 m x 18 m for vessels up to 5000 dwt Imabari Shipbuilding Co. Ltd (Imabari), 4-52 1-chome, Koura-cho, Imabari 799-21, Ehime Pref., Japan, *Tel:* +81 898 365000, *Fax:* +81 898 365010, *Email:* info@imazo.com, *Website:* www.imazo.co.jp Two dry docks for 7000 dwt and 20 000 dwt vessels

Shin Kurushima Dockyard Co. Ltd, Hashihama Shipyard, 1-15, 4 chome, Hashihama, Imabari 799-21, Ehime Pref., Japan, *Tel:* +81 898 419201, *Fax:* +81 898 415842, *Website:* www.skdy.co.jp

Surveyors: Nippon Kaiji Kyokai, 1-1-15 Katahara-cho, Imabari 794-0013, Ehime Pref., Japan, *Tel:* +81 898 232219, *Fax:* +81 898 240377, *Email:* ib@classnk.or.jp, *Website:* www.classnk.or.jp

Medical Facilities: Available

Airport: Matsuyama, 45 km

Lloyd's Agent: Cornes & Co. Ltd, Meikai Building, 32 Akashi-machi, Chuo-ku, Kobe 650-0037, Hyogo Pref., Japan, *Tel:* +81 78 332 3421, *Fax:* +81 78 332 3070, *Email:* survey@kobe.cornes.co.jp, *Website:* www.cornes.co.jp

IMARI

Lat 33° 16' N; Long 129° 49' E.

Admiralty Chart: JP1228	**Admiralty Pilot:** 42A
Time Zone: GMT +9 h	**UNCTAD Locode:** JP IMI

Principal Facilities:

	Y	G	C	R		B	D	T	A	

Authority: Port & Harbour Division of Saga Prefecture, 1-1-59 Jonai, Saga 840-8570, Saga Pref., Japan, *Tel:* +81 952 257163, *Fax:* +81 952 257315, *Email:* kouwan@pref.saga.lg.jp, *Website:* www.pref.saga.lg.jp

Officials: Director: Kenichi Tajima, *Email:* tajima-kenichi@pref.saga.lg.jp.

Port Security: ISPS compliant

Approach: Draught limitation in channel is 14 m

Anchorage: Two anchorage areas are available at pos 33° 19' 42" N; 129° 49' 30" E and 33° 20' 12" N; 129° 49' 18" E respectively. Quarantine anchorage in pos 33° 20' 12" N; 129° 48' 42" E

Pilotage: Harbour pilot available. Pilot boards at pos 33° 26' 24" N; 129° 42' 42" E and at the Quarantine anchorage

Tides: Tidal range: max 2.6 m, min 0.6 m

Maximum Vessel Dimensions: 30 000 dwt, 250 m loa, 13 m d

Principal Imports and Exports: Imports: Furniture, Logs, Plywood.

Working Hours: 0830-1700

Accommodation:

Name	Length (m)	Depth (m)	Draught (m)	Remarks
Imari				See [1] below
Kubara North Wharf No.1	70	5.5	5	Max loa 70 m & 2000 dwt
Kubara North Wharf No.2	260	7.5	7	Max 2 x 5000 dwt, 260 m loa
Kubara North Wharf No.3	185	10	8	Max 12 000 dwt, 150 m loa
Kubara South Wharf No.1	270	5.5	5	3 x 2000 dwt, 250 m loa
Kubara South Wharf No.2	260	7.5	6.8	2 x 5000 dwt, 250 m loa
Kubara South Wharf No.3	370	10	9	2 x 12 000 dwt, 300 m loa
Buoy No.1		10	8	Max 10 000 dwt
Buoy No.2		10	8	3 x 25 000 dwt
Buoy No.3		10	8	
Nanatsujima North Wharf No.1	154	9		See [2] below
Nanatsujima South Wharf No.1	260	7.5		2 x 5000 dwt, 260 m loa

[1]*Imari:* Imari Port Office, Tel: +81 955 234151, Fax: +81 955 223449

[2]*Nanatsujima North Wharf No.1:* Max 10 000 dwt, 154 m loa. Container terminal equipped with one 34 t cap container jib crane and five straddle carriers. Container yard of approx 32 000 m2, container freight station with covered area of 1000 m2 and 16 reefer points

Storage: 57 000 m2 of warehousing and sheds. 19 000 m2 of refrigerated space

Mechanical Handling Equipment: Truck cranes only available

Cargo Worked: Logs 2500 m3/day, plywood 500 m3/day

Bunkering: Hanwa Co. Ltd, 2nd Floor, Finland House, 56 Haymarket, London SW1Y 4RN, United Kingdom, *Tel:* +44 20 7839 4448, *Fax:* +44 20 7839 3994, *Email:* orito@hanwa.co.uk

Hikawa Shoji Kaisha Ltd, 26-2 Shinkawa NS Building 1-chome, Shinkawa, Chuo-ku, Tokyo 104, Japan, *Tel:* +81 3 5776 6858, *Fax:* +81 3 5541 3274

Idemitsu Kosan Co. Ltd, 1-1 Marunochi, 3-Chome, Chiyoda-ku, Tokyo 100-8321, Japan, *Tel:* +81 3 3213 3138, *Fax:* +81 3 3213 1145, *Email:* tohru.takamura@si.idemitsu.co.jp, *Website:* www.idemitsu.co.jp

KG Int Petroleum Ltd, Shiba Park Building, 241 Shiba Koen, Minato-ku, Tokyo 105, Japan, *Tel:* +81 3 3578 4551, *Fax:* +81 3 3578 4550

Marubeni Petroleum Co. Ltd, Marubeni International Petroleum Singapore Co. Ltd, c/o Marubeni Corporation, 4-2 Ohtemachi 1-chome, Chiyoda-ku, Tokyo 100-8088, Japan, *Tel:* +81 3 3282 3920, *Fax:* +81 3 3282 3950, *Email:* TOKB554@marubenicorp.com, *Website:* www.marubeni.co.jp

MC Marine and Bunkering Inc., 8th Floor, Uchisaiwai-cho Dai Building, 3-3 Uchisaiwai-cho 1-chome, Chiyoda-ku, Tokyo 100-0011, Japan, *Tel:* +81 3 5251 2575, *Fax:* +81 3 5251 2583

Mitsui & Co. Petroleum Ltd, 2-1, Ohtemachi 1-chome, Chiyoda-ku, Tokyo 100-0004, Japan, *Tel:* +81 3 3285 6905, *Fax:* +81 3 3285 9811, *Email:* tkzph@dg.mitsui.com, *Website:* www.mitsui.co.jp

Nittetsu Shoij Co. Ltd, 5-7 Kameido 1-chome, Koto-ku, Tokyo 136, Japan, *Tel:* +81 3 5627 2157, *Fax:* +81 3 5627 2192

Towage: Tugs up to 3200 hp can be arranged from Sasebo and Nagasaki when required

Medical Facilities: Available

Airport: Saga, 60 km

Lloyd's Agent: Cornes & Co. Ltd, Meikai Building, 32 Akashi-machi, Chuo-ku, Kobe 650-0037, Hyogo Pref., Japan, *Tel:* +81 78 332 3421, *Fax:* +81 78 332 3070, *Email:* survey@kobe.cornes.co.jp, *Website:* www.cornes.co.jp

ISHIKARIWAN SHINKO

Lat 43° 13' N; Long 141° 18' E.

Admiralty Chart: 1808	**Admiralty Pilot:** 41
Time Zone: GMT +9 h	**UNCTAD Locode:** JP ISS

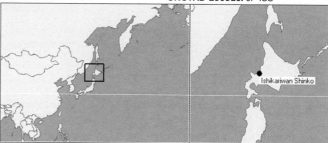

Principal Facilities:

P	Q		G	C		B		T	A	

Authority: Ishikari Bay New Port Authority, 3717-9 Shinko Minami, 2 chome, Ishikari 061-3244, Hokkaido, Japan, *Tel:* +81 133 646661, *Fax:* +81 133 646666, *Email:* port@ishikari-bay-newport.jp, *Website:* www.ishikari-bay-newport.jp

Officials: President: Harumi Takahashi, *Email:* h.takahashi@ishikari-bay-newport.jp. Executive Vice President: Eisaku Naga. General Manager: Makoto Minami.

Approach: Water depth in the Central Fairway is 10-14 m

Anchorage: Anchorage can be obtained off the mouth of the Ishikari River in fine weather in a depth of 11 m, bottom of sand; anchorage area is completely exposed

Pilotage: Not compulsory. Vessels should request a pilot at least 12 h prior to requirement/arrival. Pilots available at Otaru Pilot Association

Weather: In summer (Jun-Aug) prevailing winds blow from the S and SE, while winds from the NW and W prevail in winter (Dec-Feb). Strong winds above 10 m/sec. with a duration of 3 h or less in most cases, sometimes blows from the NW and NW by W direction

Traffic: 2007, 1544 vessels, 4 200 000 t of cargo handled, 23 438 TEU's

Maximum Vessel Dimensions: 185 m loa, approx 50 000 dwt

Principal Imports and Exports: Imports: Furniture, Petroleum products, Wood chips. Exports: Fishery products, Scrap metal.

Working Hours: Weekdays 0830-1630, 1630-2130

Accommodation:

Name	Length (m)	Depth (m)	Remarks
Ishikariwan Shinko			See [1] below
East Wharf Log Berth	185	10	Max 15 000 dwt
East Wharf No.2-3	260	7.5	Max 10 000 dwt x 2
Bannaguro Wharf No.1	185	10	Max 15 000 dwt
Bannaguro Wharf No.2	185	10	Max 15 000 dwt
Bannaguro Wharf No.3	130	7.5	Max 10 000 dwt
Bannaguro Wharf No.4	130	7.5	Max 10 000 dwt
Bannaguro Wharf No.5	130	7.5	Max 10 000 dwt
Tarukawa Wharf No.1	185	10	Max 15 000 dwt
Tarukawa Wharf No.2	185	10	Max 15 000 dwt
Tarukawa Wharf No.3	130	7.5	Max 10 000 dwt
Tarukawa Wharf No.4	130	7.5	Max 10 000 dwt
Tarukawa Wharf No.5	130	7.5	Max 10 000 dwt
Central Wharf	865	7.5	See [2] below

Name	Length (m)	Depth (m)	Remarks
West Wharf	280	14	Max 50 000 dwt. Mainly wood chips

[1]Ishikariwan Shinko: Container yard of over 5 ha in area and a gantry crane at Bannaguro Wharf

[2]Central Wharf: Energy supply base operated by Hokkaido Gas Co Ltd. and Liquefied Gas Terminal Co Ltd. and Tomakomai Futo Co Ltd. LPG and other petroleum products are loaded/unloaded

Storage: Three transit sheds at Bannaguro Wharves totalling 7800 m2 and two transit sheds at Tarukawa Wharves totalling 9000 m2

Mechanical Handling Equipment:

Location	Type	Capacity (t)	Qty
Ishikariwan Shinko	Container Cranes	30.5	1

Bunkering: Kita Nihon Oil Co. Ltd, 3-18-1 Inaho, Otaru 047-0032, Hokkaido, Japan, *Tel:* +81 134 237 441, *Fax:* +81 134 336 598, *Email:* otaru-hakuyo@kitanihon-oil.co.jp – *Misc:* domestic oil is available – *Delivery Mode:* barge

Towage: One tug of 2000 hp; additional tugs available from Otaru when required

Repair & Maintenance: Small repairs can be undertaken

Stevedoring Companies: Ishikari Kyodo Koun Co Ltd, Ishikari, Hokkaido, Japan, *Tel:* +81 133 645461
Nippon Express Co Ltd, 744-3-2 Shinkuo Nishi, Ishikari 061- 3241, Hokkaido, Japan, *Tel:* +81 133 748844, *Fax:* +81 133 748847, *Email:* mu-date@nittsu.co.jp, *Website:* www.nittsu.co.jp

Airport: Sapporo Okadama Airport, 13 km. New Chitose International Airport, 50 km

Railway: Teine Station, 10 km

Development: One quake-resistant quay is under consolidation in Bunnaguro Wharf

Lloyd's Agent: Cornes & Co. Ltd, 273 Yamashita-cho, Naka-ku, Yokohama 231-0023, Kanagawa Pref., Japan, *Tel:* +81 45 201 8537, *Fax:* +81 45 212 3105, *Email:* survey@ykh.cornes.co.jp, *Website:* www.cornes.co.jp

ISHINOMAKI

Lat 38° 25' N; Long 141° 18' E.

Admiralty Chart: JP54
Time Zone: GMT +9 h
Admiralty Pilot: 41
UNCTAD Locode: JP ISM

Principal Facilities:

P		Y	G			B	D	T	A

Authority: Ports & Harbors Development Division, Public Works Department, Miyagi Prefectural Government, 3-8-1 Honcho, Aoba-ku, Sendai 980-8570, Miyagi Pref., Japan, *Tel:* +81 22 211 3221, *Fax:* +81 22 211 3296, *Email:* kousin@pref.miyagi.jp, *Website:* www.pref.miyagi.jp

Officials: Manager: Haruo Kasamatsu.

Port Security: ISPS compliant

Approach: Depth in channel 10 m max

Pilotage: Not compulsory. Pilots available at pos 38° 23' 42" N; 141° 16' 06" E from sunrise to sunset

Tides: Tidal range 1.70 m max, -0.14 m min

Accommodation:

Name	Length (m)	Depth (m)	Remarks
Public Wharves			
Minamihama Pier No.1	165	10	Max 15 000 dwt. Chips, logs & coal
Minamihama Pier No.2	165	9	Max 10 000 dwt. Logs
Minamihama Pier No.3	130	7.5	Max 5000 dwt. Logs
Hiyori Pier No.5	380	4.5	5 x 1000 dwt. Sand, gravel & steel
Hiyori Pier No.6	165	9	Max 10 000 dwt. Cattle feed
Hiyori Pier No.7	185	10	Max 15 000 dwt. Cattle feed
Oote Pier No's 3, 4 & 5	320	5.5	3 x 2000 dwt. Fertilizers & steel
Oote Pier No's 1 & 2	260	7.5	2 x 5000 dwt. General cargo
Nakajima Pier No.1	130	5.5	Max 2000 dwt. Mineral by-products
Nakajima Pier No's 2 & 3	370	10	2 x 15 000 dwt. Mineral by-products
Siomi Pier	290	4.5	5 x 1000 dwt. Fertilizers & steel
Hibarino Pier	520	13	Max 40 000 dwt. Wood
Private Wharves			
All in One Dolphin	23.5	4.5	Max 1000 dwt. Cattle feed

Name	Length (m)	Depth (m)	Remarks
Nissin Oil Dolphin	25.4	4.5	Max 1350 dwt. Edible oil
Chu Ito Cattle Feed Dolphin	33	4.5	Max 1600 dwt. Cattle feed
Nippon Paper Industry Dolphin	36	4.5	Max 1500 dwt
Port of Simizu Cattle Feed Dolphin	24	4.5	Max 4034 dwt. Cattle feed
Kyoudo Cattle Feed Dolphin	33.5	4.5	Max 2600 dwt. Cattle feed
Nippon Paper Industry Dolphin	92	6	Max 3000 dwt. Petroleum oil
Tohoku Toso Chemical Dolphin	95	4.5	Max 1000 dwt. Petroleum oil
Yamanisi Pier	240	4.5	Ship repair
Tokai Carbon Dolphin	93	7.5	Max 10 000 dwt. Tar
Kairiku Dolphin	30	4.5	Max 1600 dwt. Cattle feed

Storage:

Location	Open (m²)	Covered (m²)	Sheds / Warehouses
Public Wharves	161134	7868	4

Bunkering: Domestic oil available. Bonded oil brought from Kashima with sufficient notice

Towage: Seven tugs available; two of 3200 hp, one of 3000 hp and four of 2600 hp

Repair & Maintenance: K.K. Murakami Zosensho, Ishinomaki, Japan, *Tel:* +81 22 595 3511, *Fax:* +81 22 595 3543 One floating dock of 65.2 m x 17.1 m x 6.5 m for vessels up to 1000 gt

Medical Facilities: Available

Airport: Sendai

Lloyd's Agent: Cornes & Co. Ltd, 273 Yamashita-cho, Naka-ku, Yokohama 231-0023, Kanagawa Pref., Japan, *Tel:* +81 45 201 8537, *Fax:* +81 45 212 3105, *Email:* survey@ykh.cornes.co.jp, *Website:* www.cornes.co.jp

ITOZAKI

harbour area, see under Onomichi

IWAKUNI

Lat 34° 10' N; Long 132° 14' E.

Admiralty Chart: 3469
Time Zone: GMT +9 h
Admiralty Pilot: 42B
UNCTAD Locode: JP IWK

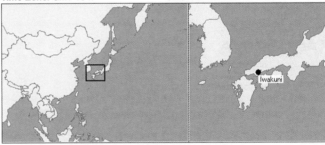

Principal Facilities:

P		Y	G	C	R			T	A

Authority: Ports & Harbors Division, Yamaguchi Prefectural Government, 1-1 Takimachi, Yamaguchi 753-8501, Yamaguchi Pref., Japan, *Tel:* +81 83 933 3810, *Fax:* +81 83 933 3829, *Email:* a12900@pref.yamaguchi.lg.jp, *Website:* www.pref.yamaguchi.lg.jp

Officials: Shoichi Hayashi, *Tel:* +81 83 9332 340.

Port Security: ISPS compliant

Approach: Iwakuni Channel 120 m wide in depth of 10 m

Anchorage: Quarantine Anchorages: sea within a radius of 500 m from the point of 240 degrees, 3400 m from the top of the Takayama Mountain in Atadazima Island Dangerous Cargo Anchorages: sea within a radius of 400 m from the point of 90 degrees, 1100 m from the lighthouse at the north breakwater in Iwakuni port

Pilotage: Not compulsory. Naikai pilotage group

Tides: Average range of tide 1.52 m. 2.9 m at HT. Max range 4 m

Principal Imports and Exports: Imports: Crude oil, Wood. Exports: Chemicals.

Accommodation:

Name	Length (m)	Depth (m)
Public Wharves		
North Wharf No.1	220	3.5
North Wharf No.2	180	5.5
North Wharf No.3	185	10
Syokoh Wharf	210	4
Syokoh Wharf	168	2
Shinminato North Wharf No.1	90	5.5

Key to Principal Facilities:—
A=Airport **C**=Containers **G**=General Cargo **P**=Petroleum **R**=Ro/Ro **Y**=Dry Bulk
B=Bunkers **D**=Dry Dock **L**=Cruise **Q**=Other Liquid Bulk **T**=Towage (where available from port)

Name	Length (m)	Depth (m)
Shinminato North Wharf No.2	260	7.5
Shinminato South Wharf	370	10
Muronoki Wharf (A)	180	5.5
Muronoki Wharf (B)	185	10
Muronoki Wharf	120	4
Muronoki Wharf	60	4
Muronoki Wharf	130	4
Private Wharves		
Nihon Seishi Wharf	265	10
Nihon Seishi Duties Wharf No.1	96	5.5
Nihon Seishi Duties Wharf No.2	153	5.5
Nihon Seishi Cow Wood Wharf	300	5
Koha Sekiyu Crude Oil Pier	320	17
Koha Sekiyu Products Pier No.1	36	6
Koha Sekiyu Products Pier No.2	110	9
Koha Sekiyu Products Pier No.3	520	11
Koha Sekiyu LPG Shipping Pier	140	9
Mitsui Kagaku Pier No.1	66	3.5
Mitsui Kagaku Pier No.2	30	3.5

Bunkering: Hikawa Shoji Kaisha Ltd, 26-2 Shinkawa NS Building 1-chome, Shin-kawa, Chuo-ku, Tokyo 104, Japan, *Tel:* +81 3 5776 6858, *Fax:* +81 3 5541 3274
Marubeni Petroleum Co. Ltd, Marubeni International Petroleum Singapore Co. Ltd, c/o Marubeni Corporation, 4-2 Ohtemachi 1-chome, Chiyoda-ku, Tokyo 100-8088, Japan, *Tel:* +81 3 3282 3920, *Fax:* +81 3 3282 3950, *Email:* TOKB554@marubenicorp.com, *Website:* www.marubeni.co.jp
MC Marine and Bunkering Inc., 8th Floor, Uchisaiwai-cho Dai Building, 3-3 Uchi-saiwai-cho 1-chome, Chiyoda-ku, Tokyo 100-0011, Japan, *Tel:* +81 3 5251 2575, *Fax:* +81 3 5251 2583
Nissho Iwai Corp., 4-4 Akasaka 2-chome, Minato-ku, Tokyo, Japan, *Tel:* +81 3 35882111

Towage: Six tugs available of 2500-3000 hp

Medical Facilities: Available in Iwakuni City

Airport: Hiroshima, 80 km

Railway: Iwakuni station, approx 2.5 km

Lloyd's Agent: Cornes & Co. Ltd, Meikai Building, 32 Akashi-machi, Chuo-ku, Kobe 650-0037, Hyogo Pref., Japan, *Tel:* +81 78 332 3421, *Fax:* +81 78 332 3070, *Email:* survey@kobe.cornes.co.jp, *Website:* www.cornes.co.jp

KAGOSHIMA

Lat 31° 35' N; Long 130° 34' E.

Admiralty Chart: 654	**Admiralty Pilot:** 42A
Time Zone: GMT +9 h	**UNCTAD Locode:** JP KOJ

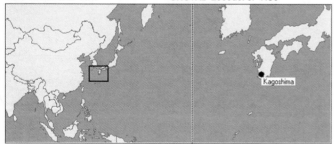

Principal Facilities:

P	Q	Y	G		R		B		A

Authority: Kagoshima Harbour Office, 18-16 Izumi-cho, Kagoshima 892-0822, Kagoshima Pref., Japan, *Tel:* +81 99 223 3277, *Fax:* +81 99 224 2832, *Email:* kouryuu@pref.kagoshima.lg.jp, *Website:* www.pref.kagoshima.jp

Port Security: ISPS compliant

Anchorage: Vessels can anchor safely at Quarantine anchorage area, pos 31° 33' N; 130° 35' 30" E in a depth of 20-30 m

Pilotage: Not compulsory but necessary if master is not familiar with locality. Pilot embarks at Quarantine anchorage. Request for pilot made through agents. Master should report accurate ETA at least 24 h prior to arrival

Weather: Winds from E in summer, NW in winter

Tides: Average tidal range is 2.74 m in outer harbour, flood tide sets to north and ebbs to south. Max speed of current is 2-3 knots, current negligible

Principal Imports and Exports: Imports: General cargo, Industrial products, Vehicles. Exports: General cargo, Industrial products, Vehicles.

Working Hours: 0830-1715

Accommodation:

Name	Length (m)	Depth (m)	Remarks
Main Port Section			
Sakurajima Honkou Ferry Wharf No.3	210	4.5	Two berths available for automobiles
Gyokou-ku N Wharf	250	5	Four berths available for chemical industrial products
Honkouku Ferry Wharf No.3	90	4.5	Two berths available for mechanical industrial products
Ogawa Wharf	240	5.5	Two berths available for automobiles
Honkouku Kitafuto Wharf No.1	370	9	Two berths available for general cargo, automobiles, crop & marine products
Honkouku Kitafuto Wharf No.2	340	7.5	Two berths available for automobiles
Minamifuto Wharf (North) No.3	90	5.5	
Minamifuto Wharf (South) No.4	90	5.5	
Honkouku Wharf (North) No.1	155	7.5	
Honkouku Wharf (South) No.2	155	7.5	
Honkouku A Wharf	138	4.5	
New Port Section			
Shinkou Wharf No.1	125	7.5	
Shinkou Wharf No.2	160	5.5	See [1] below
Shinkou Wharf No.4	175	5.5	See [2] below
Shinkou Wharf No.5	236	9	See [3] below
Shinkou Wharf No.6	260	7.5	See [4] below
Shinkou Wharf No.7	120	4.5	Two berths available
Shinkou Wharf No.8	348	4.5	Five berths available for crop & marine products
Kamoike Port Section			
Kamoikekou Tottei	150	4.5	Automobiles
Kamoikekou Wharf Tottei No.2	220	4.5	Two berths available for automobiles
Center Port Section			
Chuoukouku (South Port) Wharf No.2	161	4.7	Two berths available
Chuoukouku (South Port) Wharf No.3 (North)	81	4.5	Mineral resources
Chuoukouku (South Port) Wharf No.3 (South)	125	4.5	Two berths available for mineral resources
Chuoukouku (South Port) Wharf No.4	90	4.5	
Chuoukouku (South Port) Wharf No.5	80	4.5	Mineral resources
Chuoukouku (South Port) Wharf No.6	90	5.5	Mineral resources
Chuoukouku (South Port) Wharf No.7	174	5.5	
Chuoukouku (Timber Port) Wharf	229	4.5	Three berths available
Chuoukouku (Timber Port) Wharf No.1	251	10	Timber
Taniyama 1st Port Section			
Taniyama Wharf No.1	294	12	Crops & marine products
Taniyama Wharf No.2	260	7.5	See [5] below
Taniyama Wharf No.3	270	5.5	Three berths available for crop & marine products
Taniyama Wharf No.5	400	5.5	Four berths available for crop & marine products
Taniyama Wharf No.6	210	5.5	Two berths available for general cargo & automobiles
Taniyama Wharf No.7	260	7.5	Two berths available
Taniyama Wharf No.8	294	12	
Taniyama 2nd Port Section			
Taniyama Wharf No.1	390	5.5	Four berths available
Taniyama Wharf No.2	300	5.5	Three berths available
Taniyama Wharf No.3	250	5.5	Two berths available
Taniyama Wharf No.5	289	5.5	Three berths available
Taniyama Wharf No.6	380	7.5	See [6] below
Taniyama Wharf No.7	511	7.5	Three berths available
Taniyama Wharf No.8	120	5.5	
Taniyama Wharf No.9	120	5.5	
Taniyama Wharf No.10	400	9	
Taniyama Wharf No.11	375	9	
Taniyama Higashifuto Wharf	440	7.5	Three berths available

[1]*Shinkou Wharf No.2:* Two berths available for mechanical industrial products
[2]*Shinkou Wharf No.4:* Two berths available for light industrial products & automobiles
[3]*Shinkou Wharf No.5:* Automobiles, light industrial products & crop and marine products
[4]*Shinkou Wharf No.6:* Two berths available for automobiles, light industrial products & crop and marine products
[5]*Taniyama Wharf No.2:* Two berths for chemical industrial products & crop and marine products
[6]*Taniyama Wharf No.6:* Two berths available for mineral resources & general cargo

Storage:

Location	Open (m²)	Covered (m²)
Main Port Section	16002	9276

Location	Open (m²)	Covered (m²)
New Port Section	73660	12998
Center Port Section	138646	
Taniyama 1st Port Section	110690	16797
Taniyama 2nd Port Section	91871	3169

Bunkering: MC Marine and Bunkering Inc., 8th Floor, Uchisaiwai-cho Dai Building, 3-3 Uchisaiwai-cho 1-chome, Chiyoda-ku, Tokyo 100-0011, Japan, *Tel:* +81 3 5251 2575, *Fax:* +81 3 5251 2583
Mitsui & Co. Petroleum Ltd, 2-1, Ohtemachi 1-chome, Chiyoda-ku, Tokyo 100-0004, Japan, *Tel:* +81 3 3285 6905, *Fax:* +81 3 3285 9811, *Email:* tkzph@dg.mitsui.com, *Website:* www.mitsui.co.jp

Repair & Maintenance: Kagoshima Dock & Iron Works Co. Ltd, 2-2 Nanatsushima, 1 chome, Kagoshima 891-0132, Kagoshima Pref., Japan, *Tel:* +81 99 261 7878, *Fax:* +81 99 261 7871 Minor repairs available

Shipping Agents: Kamigumi Co. Ltd, 19-3 Nanei 3-chome, Kagoshima 891-0122, Kagoshima Pref., Japan, *Tel:* +81 99 269 4523, *Fax:* +81 99 267 7838

Surveyors: Nippon Kaiji Kyokai, 501 Tohkan Mansions Rohre, 2-12 Shinshouin-cho, Kagoshima 890-0016, Kagoshima Pref., Japan, *Tel:* +81 99 239 6920, *Fax:* +81 99 239 6930, *Email:* ks@classnk.or.jp, *Website:* www.classnk.or.jp

Medical Facilities: Good facilities available

Airport: Kagoshima, 38 km

Railway: Kagoshima-Chuo Station, 11.3 km

Lloyd's Agent: Cornes & Co. Ltd, Meikai Building, 32 Akashi-machi, Chuo-ku, Kobe 650-0037, Hyogo Pref., Japan, *Tel:* +81 78 332 3421, *Fax:* +81 78 332 3070, *Email:* survey@kobe.cornes.co.jp, *Website:* www.cornes.co.jp

KAINAN

see under Wakayama

KAKOGAWA

Lat 34° 42' N; Long 134° 50' E.

Admiralty Chart: 640   **Admiralty Pilot:** 42B
Time Zone: GMT +9 h   **UNCTAD Locode:** JP KGA

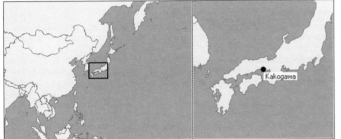

Principal Facilities:

Q	Y	G		R		B		

Authority: Port & Harbour Section of Hyogo Prefecture, 5-10-1 Yamate-dori, Chuo-ku, Kobe 650-8567, Hyogo Pref., Japan, *Tel:* +81 78 341 7711, *Fax:* +81 78 341 6477

Approach: Draft limitation in the channel 16.4 m (East Wharf), 11 m (West Wharf)

Pilotage: Inland-sea pilots are available at Wada-Misaki and harbour pilots are available at the anchorage or pilot station

Accommodation:

Name	Length (m)	Depth (m)
Kakogawa		
Coal/Ore Wharf E.3	300	14.5
Coal/Ore Wharf E.4	400	17
Coal/Ore Wharf E.5	450	17
Limestone Wharf S.1	470	6
Limestone Wharf S.2	120	7
Scrap Wharf S.3	350	11
West Wharf W.5	240	12
West Wharf W.6	270	12
LPG Berth		16

Mechanical Handling Equipment:

Location	Type	Capacity (t)	Qty	Remarks
Coal/Ore Wharf E.3	Shore Cranes		2	1 500 t/h x 2
Coal/Ore Wharf E.4	Shore Cranes		2	2 000 t/h x 1 and 3 000 t/h x 1
Coal/Ore Wharf E.5	Shore Cranes		2	1 500 t/h x1 and 1 800 t/h x 1
Limestone Wharf S.1	Shore Cranes		1	700 t/h x 1
Limestone Wharf S.2	Shore Cranes		1	400 t/h x 1
Scrap Wharf S.3	Shore Cranes	20	1	
West Wharf W.5	Shore Cranes	35	2	
West Wharf W.6	Mult-purp. Cranes	35	2	

Bunkering: Hanwa Co. Ltd, 2nd Floor, Finland House, 56 Haymarket, London SW1Y 4RN, United Kingdom, *Tel:* +44 20 7839 4448, *Fax:* +44 20 7839 3994, *Email:* orito@hanwa.co.uk
Hikawa Shoji Kaisha Ltd, 26-2 Shinkawa NS Building 1-chome, Shinkawa, Chuo-ku, Tokyo 104, Japan, *Tel:* +81 3 5776 6858, *Fax:* +81 3 5541 3274
Idemitsu Kosan Co. Ltd, 1-1 Marunochi, 3-Chome, Chiyoda-ku, Tokyo 100-8321, Japan, *Tel:* +81 3 3213 3138, *Fax:* +81 3 3213 1145, *Email:* tohru.takamura@si.idemitsu.co.jp, *Website:* www.idemitsu.co.jp
KG Int Petroleum Ltd, Shiba Park Building, 241 Shiba Koen, Minato-ku, Tokyo 105, Japan, *Tel:* +81 3 3578 4551, *Fax:* +81 3 3578 4550
Kamei Corp., 1-6-1 Otemachi, Chiyoda-ku, Tokyo 100-0004, Japan, *Tel:* +81 3 3286 6234, *Fax:* +81 3 3286 6249, *Email:* bunker@kamei.co.jp
Kyodo Oil Co. Ltd, 11-2 Nagata-cho 2-chome, Chiyoda-ku, Tokyo, Japan, *Tel:* +81 3 3505 8241, *Fax:* +81 3 3505 8697
Marubeni Petroleum Co. Ltd, Marubeni International Petroleum Singapore Co. Ltd, c/o Marubeni Corporation, 4-2 Ohtemachi 1-chome, Chiyoda-ku, Tokyo 100-8088, Japan, *Tel:* +81 3 3282 3920, *Fax:* +81 3 3282 3950, *Email:* TOKB554@marubenicorp.com, *Website:* www.marubeni.co.jp
MC Marine and Bunkering Inc., 8th Floor, Uchisaiwai-cho Dai Building, 3-3 Uchisaiwai-cho 1-chome, Chiyoda-ku, Tokyo 100-0011, Japan, *Tel:* +81 3 5251 2575, *Fax:* +81 3 5251 2583
Mitsui & Co. Petroleum Ltd, 2-1, Ohtemachi 1-chome, Chiyoda-ku, Tokyo 100-0004, Japan, *Tel:* +81 3 3285 6905, *Fax:* +81 3 3285 9811, *Email:* tkzph@dg.mitsui.com, *Website:* www.mitsui.co.jp
Nittetsu Shoji Co. Ltd, 5-7 Kameido 1-chome, Koto-ku, Tokyo 136, Japan, *Tel:* +81 3 5627 2157, *Fax:* +81 3 5627 2192
Setouchi Network, 4-20 Hasihama 1-chome, Imabari 799-2112, Ehime Pref., Japan, *Tel:* +81 898 430041, *Fax:* +81 898 430046, *Email:* secjpn@dokidoki.ne.jp
Sumitomo Corp., Harumi Island, Triton Square, Office Tower Y, 8-11 Harumi 1-chome, Chuo-ku, Tokyo 104-8610, Japan, *Tel:* +81 3 51664458, *Fax:* +81 3 51666407, *Email:* ir@sumitomo.co.jp, *Website:* www.sumitomocorp.co.jp

Lloyd's Agent: Cornes & Co. Ltd, Meikai Building, 32 Akashi-machi, Chuo-ku, Kobe 650-0037, Hyogo Pref., Japan, *Tel:* +81 78 332 3421, *Fax:* +81 78 332 3070, *Email:* survey@kobe.cornes.co.jp, *Website:* www.cornes.co.jp

KAMAISHI

Lat 39° 16' N; Long 141° 54' E.

Admiralty Chart: 3374   **Admiralty Pilot:** 41
Time Zone: GMT +9 h   **UNCTAD Locode:** JP KIS

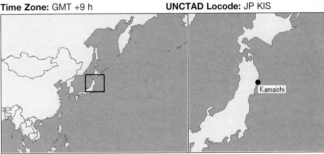

Principal Facilities:

	Y	G			B		T	

Authority: Iwate Prefectural Government, Port & Airport Division, 10-1 Uchimaru, Morioka 020-8570, Iwate Pref., Japan, *Tel:* +81 196 295912, *Email:* AG0010@pref.iwate.jp

Port Security: ISPS compliant

Approach: Two large sunken rocks in the entrance of the port form a natural breakwater, supplemented by a 360 m breakwater. New breakwater construction between Washinosusaki and Tachigane-jima. Channel depth of 14 m

Pilotage: Not compulsory but provided by Kamaishi Pilot Association, Tel: +61 193 221868, Fax: +61 193 243940. Pilot boards at the quarantine anchorage in pos 39° 15.4' N; 141° 54.6' E if required. Vessels can berth or sail any time of the day or night

Weather: Winds SE in summer, NW in winter. Dense fogs prevailing from end of May to mid July

Tides: Max range 1.4 m

Maximum Vessel Dimensions: 162 586 dwt, loa 313.9 m, 12.88 m d

Working Hours: 0800-1700 at Public Wharf (Excluding Sunday & Monday) Continuous at Nippon Steel Piers, three shifts including Sunday and holidays

Accommodation:

Name	Length (m)	Depth (m)	Draught (m)	Remarks
South Pier				
Nippon Steel No.3 Old	230	8.7	8.4	Max 13 000 gt
Nippon Steel No.3 New	288	13.4	11.5	Max 35 000 dwt
Nippon Steel No.4 Old	230	8.7	8.7	Max 20 000 gt
Nippon Steel No.4 New	288	14	12	See [1] below
North Pier				See [2] below
Public Wharf				
Wharf	130	7.5	7.5	Max 5000 gt

[1]*Nippon Steel No.4 New:* Length 288 m + 90 m dolphin. Max 160 000 dwt. Grain cargo discharge is operated by shore unloader using grab bucket, discharging rate about 1000 t/h

---

Key to Principal Facilities:—				
A=Airport	**C**=Containers	**G**=General Cargo	**P**=Petroleum	**R**=Ro/Ro	**Y**=Dry Bulk
B=Bunkers	**D**=Dry Dock	**L**=Cruise	**Q**=Other Liquid Bulk	**T**=Towage (where available from port)	

[2]*North Pier:* Nippon Steel No.1 & No.2 not suitable for vessels more than 5 000 gt

Storage: Small warehouse available. Ample open storage for general cargo

Mechanical Handling Equipment:

Location	Type	Capacity (t)	Qty
Nippon Steel No.3 Old	Shore Cranes	7	2
Nippon Steel No.4 Old	Shore Cranes	17	1
Nippon Steel No.4 Old	Shore Cranes	7	1

Cargo Worked: General cargo and steel products 2000 t/day, iron ore 21 000 t/day, coal 18 000 t/day

Bunkering: Domestic diesel oil (Bunker A) is available. Bonded oil brought from Sendai or Yokohama with sufficient advance notice

Towage: Tugs belonging to Miyako are available

Lloyd's Agent: Cornes & Co. Ltd, 273 Yamashita-cho, Naka-ku, Yokohama 231-0023, Kanagawa Pref., Japan, *Tel:* +81 45 201 8537, *Fax:* +81 45 212 3105, *Email:* survey@ykh.cornes.co.jp, *Website:* www.cornes.co.jp

KAMOIKE

harbour area, see under Kagoshima

KANAZAWA

Lat 36° 37' N; Long 136° 36' E.

Admiralty Chart: JP1169
Time Zone: GMT +9 h

Admiralty Pilot: 41
UNCTAD Locode: JP KNZ

Principal Facilities:

P		G	C	R		B		T	A	

Authority: Port & Harbor Division of Ishikawa Prefecture, 1-1 Hirosaka 1-chome, Hosai, Kanazawa 920-8580, Ishikawa Pref., Japan, *Tel:* +81 76 223 9392, *Fax:* +81 76 223 9484, *Email:* e251300@pref.ishikawa.jp

Port Security: ISPS compliant

Approach: The approach to the harbour basin has been dredged to 10 m. The harbour is entered between the West breakwater and an area of reclaimed land

Anchorage: Anchorage can be obtained, except in winter, 1.6 km W of the mouth of Sai Kawa in depths of 11 m to 16 m

Pilotage: Not compulsory. Pilots are available only during the daytime and normally board vessels in pos 36° 37' 53" N, 136° 35' 10" E

Weather: Typhoon season July to October. When entering or leaving harbour in strong NW winds it is advisable to keep close to the West breakwater. Also vessels may experience difficulties when at the anchorage in strong NW winds

Tides: Tidal range 0.15 m to 0.35 m

Principal Imports and Exports: Imports: Petroleum, Timber.

Working Hours: 0830-1630

Accommodation:

Name	Length (m)	Depth (m)	Draught (m)	Remarks
Kanazawa				See [1] below
Sekiyu Pier	620	7	6.3	6 x 5000 dwt (tankers), 600 m loa
Muryoji Tottei	270	5.5	5	3 x 2000 dwt, 80 m loa
Muryoji Pier	390	7.5	7	3 x 5000 dwt
Tomizu Pier	370	10	8.5	2 x 15 000 dwt
Ohno Pier	180	4.5	4.5	3 x 700 dwt
Gokuden Pier	540	10	8.5	2 x 15 000 dwt
Gorojima Pier	240	9	8.5	1 x 10 000 dwt

[1]*Kanazawa:* The commercial harbour consists of a basin 1.6 km long. There is also a fishing harbour at the mouth of Sai Kawa with depths of between 1.8 m and 2.6 m

Storage: Transit shed of 2545 m2; general cargo warehouses of 4080 m2. Timber basin of 155 800 m2

Mechanical Handling Equipment:

Location	Type	Capacity (t)	Qty	Remarks
Kanazawa	Mobile Cranes	50	2	
Kanazawa	Mobile Cranes	80	1	
Kanazawa	Mobile Cranes	20	1	
Kanazawa	Mobile Cranes	450	1	Tyre mount crane
Kanazawa	Mobile Cranes	200	1	

Cargo Worked: 9300 t of both foreign and domestic trade cargoes per working day

Bunkering: Domestic oil available. Bonded oil from Moji with 7 days notice

Towage: One tug of 2700 hp available

Repair & Maintenance: Minor repairs undertaken

Medical Facilities: Available

Airport: Komatsu Airport, 35 km

Lloyd's Agent: Cornes & Co. Ltd, Meikai Building, 32 Akashi-machi, Chuo-ku, Kobe 650-0037, Hyogo Pref., Japan, *Tel:* +81 78 332 3421, *Fax:* +81 78 332 3070, *Email:* survey@kobe.cornes.co.jp, *Website:* www.cornes.co.jp

KANDA

Lat 33° 48' N; Long 131° 0' E.

Admiralty Chart: 3225
Time Zone: GMT +9 h

Admiralty Pilot: 42B
UNCTAD Locode: JP KND

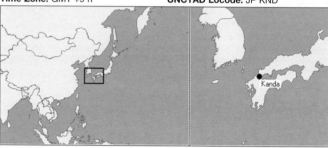

Principal Facilities:

		Y	G			B		T	A	

Authority: Port & Harbour Section of Fukuoka Prefectural Government, 7-7 Higashi-kouen, Hakata-ku, Fukuoka 812-8577, Fukuoka Pref., Japan, *Tel:* +81 92 643 3674, *Fax:* +81 92 643 3688, *Email:* kowan@pref.fukuoka.lg.jp, *Website:* www.pref.fukuoka.lg.jp

Officials: Director: Hiroshi Okawauchi.

Port Security: ISPS compliant

Approach: Kanda is situated on the west of the inland sea (Setonaikai) and is sheltered from the open sea by Konoshima Island. Draught limitation in channel is 9.9 m

Anchorage: Anchorage area at pos 33° 48' 03" N; 131° 03' 02" E. Quarantine anchorage at Hesaki if approaching from E, or Mutsure if approaching from the W

Pilotage: Not compulsory. Inland Sea pilots are available from Sekisaki, Hesaki or Mutsure. Harbour pilots are available at the anchorage in pos 33° 48' 18" N; 131° 03' 02" E from sunrise to 1 h before sunset. Vessels arriving and sailing at Honko Wharf No.10 can obtain pilotage until 2000

Weather: Mild climate and little rain. Winds from NW in summer, E in winter. Rain all year round

Tides: Range of tide 3.17 m. Current 0.4 to 0.8 knots max. Flood tide NNW, ebb SSE

Accommodation:

Name	Length (m)	Depth (m)	Draught (m)	Remarks
Kanda				See [1] below
Honko Wharf No.10	370	10	9.9	2 x 10 000 dwt
Honko Wharf No.7	130	7.5	6.9	1 x 5000 dwt
Honko Wharf No.6	110	6.5	6	1 x 3000 dwt
Honko Wharf No.5	150	5.5	5	2 x 2000 dwt
Honko Wharf No.4	386	4.5	4	6 x 700 dwt
Honko Wharf No.3	351	3		
Nanko Wharf No.7A	130	7.5	7	1 x 5000 dwt
Nanko Wharf No.7B	260	7.5	7	2 x 5000 dwt
Nanko Wharf No.4	440	4.5	4	7 x 700 dwt
Matsuyama Dolphin	580	10	10	2 x 10 000 dwt
Matsuyama W. Lumber Pool	185	10	10	1 x 10 000 dwt
	100	2		
Private Wharves				
Nissan Motor Wharf	230	10		
Kyushu Denryoku Wharf	104	7.5		
Aso Cement Wharf No.1	74	6		
Aso Cement Wharf No.2	35	7.5		
Aso Cement Wharf No.3	28	7.5		
Ube Kosan Wharf No.1	86	7.5		
Ube Kosan Wharf No.2	46	6		

Name	Length (m)	Depth (m)	Draught (m)	Remarks
Ube Kosan Wharf No.3	33	4.5		
Ube Kosan Wharf No.4	55	6		
Mitsubishi Material No.1	73.5	4.5		
Mitsubishi Material No.2	47	6		
Mitsubishi Material No.3	61	7.5		
Mitsubishi Material No.4	185.4	10		
Yutaka Kozai Wharf	215	4.5		
Taiheiyo Cement Wharf	49	7.5		

[1]*Kanda:* In case the vessel's draft exceeds 9 m, entry/departure only practicable at high-water

Bunkering: Hanwa Co. Ltd, 2nd Floor, Finland House, 56 Haymarket, London SW1Y 4RN, United Kingdom, *Tel:* +44 20 7839 4448, *Fax:* +44 20 7839 3994, *Email:* orito@hanwa.co.uk
Hikawa Shoji Kaisha Ltd, 26-2 Shinkawa NS Building 1-chome, Shinkawa, Chuo-ku, Tokyo 104, Japan, *Tel:* +81 3 5776 6858, *Fax:* +81 3 5541 3274
Idemitsu Kosan Co. Ltd, 1-1 Marunochi, 3-Chome, Chiyoda-ku, Tokyo 100-8321, Japan, *Tel:* +81 3 3213 3138, *Fax:* +81 3 3213 1145, *Email:* tohru.takamura@si.idemitsu.co.jp, *Website:* www.idemitsu.co.jp
KG Int Petroleum Ltd, Shiba Park Building, 241 Shiba Koen, Minato-ku, Tokyo 105, Japan, *Tel:* +81 3 3578 4551, *Fax:* +81 3 3578 4550
Marubeni Petroleum Co. Ltd, Marubeni International Petroleum Singapore Co. Ltd, c/o Marubeni Corporation, 4-2 Ohtemachi 1-chome, Chiyoda-ku, Tokyo 100-8088, Japan, *Tel:* +81 3 3282 3920, *Fax:* +81 3 3282 3950, *Email:* TOKB554@marubenicorp.com, *Website:* www.marubeni.co.jp
MC Marine and Bunkering Inc., 8th Floor, Uchisaiwai-cho Dai Building, 3-3 Uchisaiwai-cho 1-chome, Chiyoda-ku, Tokyo 100-0011, Japan, *Tel:* +81 3 5251 2575, *Fax:* +81 3 5251 2583
Mitsui & Co. Petroleum Ltd, 2-1, Ohtemachi 1-chome, Chiyoda-ku, Tokyo 100-0004, Japan, *Tel:* +81 3 3285 6905, *Fax:* +81 3 3285 9811, *Email:* tkzph@dg.mitsui.com, *Website:* www.mitsui.co.jp
Nittetsu Shoij Co. Ltd, 5-7 Kameido 1-chome, Koto-ku, Tokyo 136, Japan, *Tel:* +81 3 5627 2157, *Fax:* +81 3 5627 2192

Towage: Two tugs of 3600 hp and four tugs of 3000 hp are available

Airport: Fukuoka Airport, 80 km

Lloyd's Agent: Cornes & Co. Ltd, Meikai Building, 32 Akashi-machi, Chuo-ku, Kobe 650-0037, Hyogo Pref., Japan, *Tel:* +81 78 332 3421, *Fax:* +81 78 332 3070, *Email:* survey@kobe.cornes.co.jp, *Website:* www.cornes.co.jp

KANOKAWA

Lat 34° 10' N; Long 132° 26' E.

Admiralty Chart: JP1108		**Admiralty Pilot:** 42B	
Time Zone: GMT +9 h		**UNCTAD Locode:** JP KKW	

Principal Facilities:

P	Q				B		T	A

Authority: Ohgaki Public Works Office, 1274-3 Obara, Ohgaki-cho, Saiki, Hiroshima Pref., Japan, *Tel:* +81 823 573434, *Fax:* +81 823 576698

Port Security: ISPS compliant

Approach: Entrance channel and harbour channel have a depth of 18 m. Good holding ground of mud and sand bottom at anchorages

Pilotage: Compulsory for berthing. Pilot available if required at Iwakuni quarantine anchorage. Inland Sea pilots available at Sekisaki and Wadamisaki

Tides: Max tidal range 3.92 m, min -0.32 m

Working Hours: Discharging round the clock

Accommodation:

Name	Length (m)	Depth (m)	Draught (m)	Remarks
MC Terminal				See [1] below
Berth No.1	30	12.2	11.2	For vessels of 240 m max loa & 30 000 dwt
Berth No.3	130	15.4	14	See [2] below
Berth No's 2 & 4		7.5		For coastal tankers up to 5000 dwt

[1]*MC Terminal:* Tanker discharging port. Liquid cargoes such as ethanol are handled at the berths. Vessels berth and unberth during daylight hours only

---

[2]*Berth No.3:* For vessels of 270 m max loa & 125 000 dwt

Bunkering: Hikawa Shoji Kaisha Ltd, 26-2 Shinkawa NS Building 1-chome, Shinkawa, Chuo-ku, Tokyo 104, Japan, *Tel:* +81 3 5776 6858, *Fax:* +81 3 5541 3274
Marubeni Petroleum Co. Ltd, Marubeni International Petroleum Singapore Co. Ltd, c/o Marubeni Corporation, 4-2 Ohtemachi 1-chome, Chiyoda-ku, Tokyo 100-8088, Japan, *Tel:* +81 3 3282 3920, *Fax:* +81 3 3282 3950, *Email:* TOKB554@marubenicorp.com, *Website:* www.marubeni.co.jp
MC Marine and Bunkering Inc., 8th Floor, Uchisaiwai-cho Dai Building, 3-3 Uchisaiwai-cho 1-chome, Chiyoda-ku, Tokyo 100-0011, Japan, *Tel:* +81 3 5251 2575, *Fax:* +81 3 5251 2583
Nissho Iwai Corp., 4-4 Akasaka 2-chome, Minato-ku, Tokyo, Japan, *Tel:* +81 3 35882111

Towage: Tugs from 1600 hp to 3600 hp available

Repair & Maintenance: Small repairs can be undertaken subject to berth owners permission. However, major repairs and the use of fire at the pier is strictly prohibited by the Hiroshima Maritime Security Board and the berth owner

Medical Facilities: Hospital and clinic at Kure

Airport: Hiroshima, 55 km

Lloyd's Agent: Cornes & Co. Ltd, Meikai Building, 32 Akashi-machi, Chuo-ku, Kobe 650-0037, Hyogo Pref., Japan, *Tel:* +81 78 332 3421, *Fax:* +81 78 332 3070, *Email:* survey@kobe.cornes.co.jp, *Website:* www.cornes.co.jp

KARATSU

Lat 33° 28' N; Long 129° 58' E.

Admiralty Chart: 3115		**Admiralty Pilot:** 42A	
Time Zone: GMT +9 h		**UNCTAD Locode:** JP KAR	

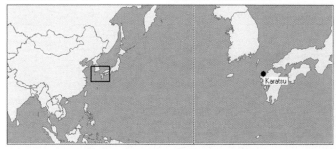

Principal Facilities:

Q	Y	G			B			A

Authority: Karatsu Port Office of Port & Harbour Bureau, 1-5 3-chome Futago, Karatsu-shi, Karatsu 847-0861, Saga Pref., Japan, *Tel:* +81 955 722148, *Fax:* +81 955 750437, *Email:* hideshima-kaizou@pref.saga.lg.jp, *Website:* www.pref.saga.lg.jp

Officials: Kaizou Hideshima, *Email:* hideshima-kaizou@pref.saga.lg.jp.

Port Security: ISPS compliant

Anchorage: Anchorage can be obtained in West Port in depths from 7-10 m and East Port in depths from 7-9 m

Pilotage: Not compulsory. Pilot boards off Kashiwashima if required

Accommodation: Port area is divided into two sections; the East and West Harbours. Vessels up to 30 000 dwt can be berthed at the Public Wharves

Name	Length (m)	Depth (m)	Remarks
West Harbour			
Myoken Wharf	930	5.5–12	See [1] below
East Harbour			
Shin Futo	296	7.5–9	1 x 10 000 dwt & 1 x 5000 dwt
Bridgestone Dolphin Jetty			See [2] below

[1]*Myoken Wharf:* 2 x 2000 dwt, 2 x 5000 dwt, 1 x 30 000 dwt, 1 x 5000 dwt & 1 x 2000 dwt
[2]*Bridgestone Dolphin Jetty:* Serves the terminal of Mitsui Liquefied Gas Co Ltd, accommodating gas tankers up to 60 000 dwt in a depth of 13 m. A mooring buoy is positioned off each side of the head of the jetty. Max permissible draught is 11.7 m. Bunkers not available
A smaller jetty is situated S of the Bridgestone Jetty with a depth alongside of 7 m and used by coastal tankers

Mechanical Handling Equipment:

Location	Type	Capacity (t)
Karatsu	Mobile Cranes	100

Bunkering: Fuel oil available at most harbour berths or by barge

Repair & Maintenance: Minor repairs can be undertaken

Medical Facilities: Hospital in the town

Airport: Fukuoka Airport, 60 km

Lloyd's Agent: Cornes & Co. Ltd, Meikai Building, 32 Akashi-machi, Chuo-ku, Kobe 650-0037, Hyogo Pref., Japan, *Tel:* +81 78 332 3421, *Fax:* +81 78 332 3070, *Email:* survey@kobe.cornes.co.jp, *Website:* www.cornes.co.jp

---

Key to Principal Facilities:—					
A=Airport	**C**=Containers	**G**=General Cargo	**P**=Petroleum	**R**=Ro/Ro	**Y**=Dry Bulk
B=Bunkers	**D**=Dry Dock	**L**=Cruise	**Q**=Other Liquid Bulk	**T**=Towage (where available from port)	

KASAOKA

Lat 34° 30' N; Long 133° 30' E.

Admiralty Chart: JP137B   **Admiralty Pilot:** 42B
Time Zone: GMT +9 h   **UNCTAD Locode:** JP KSA

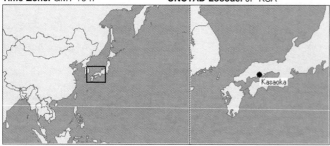

Principal Facilities:

		Y	G							

Authority: Kasaoka Port Authority, 2-5 Rokuban-cho, Kasaoka, Okayama Pref., Japan, *Tel:* +81 86 563 5252

Approach: Draft Limitation in the channel 16 m

Pilotage: Inland-sea pilot is compulsory for vessels exceeding 10 000 gt
Channel leading to the port came under provisions of Maritime Safety Law because of heavy traffic in the narrow channels and many islands
Inland-sea Pilots Association covers all inland-sea ports, including Kasaoka. Pilot boards either at Wada Misaki (34°38' N., 135°11' E.) or Sekisaki (33°13' N., 131°54' E.)

Tides: Tidal range 4.30 m max, -0.12 m min

Accommodation:

Name	Length (m)	Depth (m)	Remarks
Kasaoka			
Pipe Berth	399	11	Max 35 000 dwt
Terama Wharf	300	5.5	Max 2000 dwt

Mechanical Handling Equipment:

Location	Type	Capacity (t)	Qty
Pipe Berth	Mult-purp. Cranes	50	1
Pipe Berth	Mult-purp. Cranes	20	2

Bunkering: Bonded oil will be brought from Kobe, Mizushima, Tokuyama or Moji with sufficent advance notice

Repair & Maintenance: Running repairs can be undertaken

Lloyd's Agent: Cornes & Co. Ltd, Meikai Building, 32 Akashi-machi, Chuo-ku, Kobe 650-0037, Hyogo Pref., Japan, *Tel:* +81 78 332 3421, *Fax:* +81 78 332 3070, *Email:* survey@kobe.cornes.co.jp, *Website:* www.cornes.co.jp

KASHIMA

Lat 35° 55' N; Long 140° 40' E.

Admiralty Chart: 3374   **Admiralty Pilot:** 41
Time Zone: GMT +9 h   **UNCTAD Locode:** JP KSM

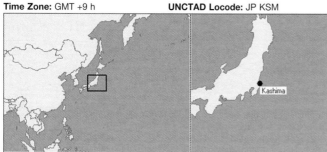

Principal Facilities:

P	Q	Y	G		R		B		T	A

Authority: Ports & Harbors Division, Ibaraki Prefectural Government, 978-6 Kasahara-cho, Mito 310-8555, Ibaraki Pref., Japan, *Tel:* +81 29 301 4536, *Fax:* +81 29 301 4539, *Email:* kowan5@pref.ibaraki.lg.jp, *Website:* www.pref.ibaraki.jp/bukyoku/doboku/kowan/sitetop1/index.htm

Officials: Director: Goto Kazumasa.

Port Security: ISPS compliant

Approach: Depth in channels varies from 10-24 m; Approach Channel 21-24 m; General Channel 14-19 m; North and South Channels 10-13 m. The berth approach is made during daylight hours only. Pilot boards at the latest, one hour before sunset. All movements at the port are controlled from the signal station near the NW of the harbour entrance

Anchorage: Available for large vessels off the port in a depth of 22 m

Pilotage: Compulsory for vessels over 50 000 gt. Available during daylight hours only

Tides: Tidal range 1.3 m

Maximum Vessel Dimensions: 336 m loa, 19 m d, 252 059 dwt

Working Hours: 0800-1700. Stevedores work 24 h for discharging at Sumitomo Metal Berths, including Sundays and holidays

Accommodation: Port area of 3892 ha. Water-front area of 2365 ha
Tanker fcailities: Private berth of Kashima Oil Co can take vessels up to 252 059 dwt and 19 m d. Water and bunkers available; night berthing not possible.
Liquefied gas facilities for vessels up to 101 724 dwt and 15.23 m d at above

Name	Length (m)	Depth (m)	Draught (m)	Remarks
Kashima				
Public Wharf	555	10		Two berths available. Max 15 000 dwt
Kanto Grain Terminal	250	10	11.7	Max 65 000 dwt. 1 x 400 t/h & 1 x 600 t/h suckers
Sumitomo Kinzoku (Metal)				
Raw Material Berth	897	16–19	14.5–18	See [1] below
Products Berth	1184	12	10.5	See [2] below
Kashima Sekiyu (Oil)				
200 000 t Dolphin	129	22	19	See [3] below
70 000 t Dolphin	80	14.5	13.1	See [4] below
100 000 t Dolphin	138	16	14.5	See [5] below
Kashima Denkai (Dolphin)	231	16	14.5	No length limitation, max 100 000 dwt. 2 x 800 t/h cranes
Zen-no Silo	281	13	11.7	See [6] below
Showa Sangyo	280	13	11.7	See [7] below
Mitsubishi Petrochemical	195	10	9	1000 t/h, 2 loaders. Max 15 000 dwt

[1]*Raw Material Berth:* Two berths available for discharging of ore, coal etc. Air draught 19 m. 2 x 850 t/h cranes
[2]*Products Berth:* Loading of steel products. 9 x 20-33 t/h cranes. No length limitation
[3]*200 000 t Dolphin:* Crude oil, 3 x 12" manifolds. Max loa 340 m, max 200 000 dwt
[4]*70 000 t Dolphin:* Crude oil and loading products, 3 x 10'' manifolds. No length limitation
[5]*100 000 t Dolphin:* Crude oil, LPG and EDC, 3 x 12'' manifolds. No length limitation
[6]*Zen-no Silo:* Grain berth. 3 x 400 t/h suckers, 1 x 700 t/h sucker, max 65 000 dwt
[7]*Showa Sangyo:* Grain berth. 1 x 660 t/h sucker, max 65 000 dwt

Storage: Public cargo sorting yards of 12 300 m2, public warehouse 4496 m2

Mechanical Handling Equipment:

Location	Type	Qty
Public Wharf	Mult-purp. Cranes	2
Raw Material Berth	Mult-purp. Cranes	5
Products Berth	Mult-purp. Cranes	9
Kashima Denkai (Dolphin)	Mult-purp. Cranes	2

Bunkering: Available only by pipe at Kashima Sekiyu Dolphin
MC Marine and Bunkering Inc., 8th Floor, Uchisaiwai-cho Dai Building, 3-3 Uchi-saiwai-cho 1-chome, Chiyoda-ku, Tokyo 100-0011, Japan, *Tel:* +81 3 5251 2575, *Fax:* +81 3 5251 2583
Nittetsu Shoij Co. Ltd, 5-7 Kameido 1-chome, Koto-ku, Tokyo 136, Japan, *Tel:* +81 3 5627 2157, *Fax:* +81 3 5627 2192

Towage: Ten tugs available; one of 3400 hp, three of 3000 hp, one of 2600 hp, two of 2400 hp, one of 2200 hp and one of 1660 hp

Repair & Maintenance: Minor repairs can be undertaken

Shipping Agents: Kashima Futo Co. Ltd, Kashima Port South Transport Center Dewa 4186-19, Kamisu City, Ibaraki Pref, Kashima 314-0116, Ibaraki Pref., Japan, *Tel:* +81 29 997 0661, *Fax:* +81 29 997 0665, *Email:* agency@kashimafuto.co.jp, *Website:* www.kashimafuto.co.jp

Medical Facilities: Available

Airport: Narita, 50 km

Lloyd's Agent: Cornes & Co. Ltd, 273 Yamashita-cho, Naka-ku, Yokohama 231-0023, Kanagawa Pref., Japan, *Tel:* +81 45 201 8537, *Fax:* +81 45 212 3105, *Email:* survey@ykh.cornes.co.jp, *Website:* www.cornes.co.jp

KASHIWAZAKI

Lat 37° 22' N; Long 138° 33' E.

Admiralty Chart: JP1180   **Admiralty Pilot:** 41
Time Zone: GMT +9 h   **UNCTAD Locode:** JP KWZ

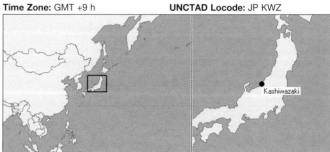

Principal Facilities:

		Y	G			B		T	

Authority: Port & Harbour Section of Niigata Prefecture, Bureau of Port & Airport Development, Niigata Prefectural Government, 4-1 Shinko-cho, Niigata 950-8570,

Niigata Pref., Japan, *Tel:* +81 25 285 5511, *Fax:* +81 25 285 9375, *Email:* t1700102@mail.pref.niigata.jp

Approach: Depth in channel of 10.0 m, draught limitation is 8.3 m

Pilotage: Not compulsory but recommended. Pilots available during daylight hours only

Tides: Range of tide 0.75 m

Principal Imports and Exports: Imports: Coke. Exports: Metal scraps.

Accommodation:

Name	Length (m)	Depth (m)	Draught (m)	Remarks
Kashiwazaki				See [1] below
West Wharf	105	6	5.5	Max 3000 dwt
East Wharf	130	7.5	6.8	Max 5000 dwt
Nakahama Wharf No.1	130	7.5	6.8	Max 5000 dwt
Nakahama Wharf No.2	185	10	9	Max 15 000 dwt

[1]*Kashiwazaki:* Harbour protected by breakwater extending 1946 m from the shore

Bunkering: Domestic oil available

Towage: Three tugs available; one of 600 hp, one of 360 hp and one of 240 hp. Larger tugs can be brought from Niigata when required

Repair & Maintenance: Minor repairs can be undertaken

Lloyd's Agent: Cornes & Co. Ltd, 273 Yamashita-cho, Naka-ku, Yokohama 231-0023, Kanagawa Pref., Japan, *Tel:* +81 45 201 8537, *Fax:* +81 45 212 3105, *Email:* survey@ykh.cornes.co.jp, *Website:* www.cornes.co.jp

KAWASAKI

Lat 35° 30' N; Long 139° 45' E.

Admiralty Chart: JP1085	**Admiralty Pilot:** 42A
Time Zone: GMT +9 h	**UNCTAD Locode:** JP KWS

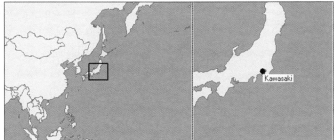

Principal Facilities:

P	Q	Y	G	C		B	D	T	A

Authority: Port & Harbour Bureau, Kawasaki City Government, 1 Miyamoto-cho, Kawasaki-ku, Kawasaki 210-8577, Kanagawa Pref., Japan, *Tel:* +81 44 200 3053, *Fax:* +81 44 200 3981, *Email:* 58yuuti@city.kawasaki.jp, *Website:* www.city.kawasaki.jp/58/58yuuti/home/etop.html

Officials: Port Manager: Katayama Akira.

Port Security: ISPS compliant. Security based on SOLAS Convention

Pre-Arrival Information: It is mandatory to report to Kawasaki Port Radio on VHF Channel 16, 3 h before arrival

Approach: Kawasaki Fairway 1720 m long, 300-750 m width in depth of 12 m

Anchorage: The Keihin Port Commander appoints anchorages for all vessels of 500 t and over

Pilotage: Not mandatory for vessels less than 10 000 t that come into foreign-trade wharves and the Container Terminal in Higashi-Ohgishima. Compulsory for all other vessels of 3000 t and over, and for LPG carriers, oil tankers and vessels carrying dangerous cargo of 300 t and over. Pilotage is provided by Tokyo Bay licensed pilots' Association

Radio Frequency: Kawasaki Port Radio on VHF Channels 16, 11, 18, 20 and 22

Weather: Winds SSW and SW (summer), N and NW (winter)

Tides: Tidal range 4.48 m

Traffic: 2007, 32 106 vessels, 93 935 665 t of cargo handled

Maximum Vessel Dimensions: 333 m loa

Principal Imports and Exports: Imports: Crude oil, Iron ore, LNG. Exports: Cars, Heavy & light fuel.

Working Hours: 0830-1700 (Port & Harbor Bureau). 0800-1700, 1900-2400, 0100-0500 (Cargo handling)

Accommodation:

Name	Length (m)	Depth (m)	Remarks
Public Wharves			
Chidoricho (No.1 Mooring Wharf)	120	7.3	General cargo. Max cap 1 x 3000 dwt
Chidoricho (No.2 Mooring Pier)	172	9	General cargo. Max cap 1 x 10 000 dwt
Chidoricho (No.3 Mooring Pier)	190	10	General cargo. Max cap 1 x 15 000 dwt
Chidoricho (No.4 Mooring Wharf)	220	10	General cargo. Max cap 1 x 15 000 dwt
Chidoricho (No.5 Mooring Pier)	211	10	General cargo. Max cap 1 x 15 000 dwt
Chidoricho (No.6 Mooring Pier)	209	10	General cargo. Max cap 1 x 15 000 dwt
Chidoricho (No.7 Mooring Pier)	180	10	General cargo. Max cap 1 x 15 000 dwt
Chidoricho (ABC Loading Stage)	332	4.5	General cargo. Max cap 3 x 1000 dwt
Chidoricho (Kojima Shinden Loading Stage)	146	4.5	General cargo. Max cap 2 x 700 dwt
Higashi Ohgishima (No.1 Wharf)	185	10	General cargo. Max cap 1 x 15 000 dwt
Higashi Ohgishima (No.2 Wharf)	185	10	General cargo. Max cap 1 x 15 000 dwt
Higashi Ohgishima (No.3 Wharf)	240	12	General cargo. Max cap 1 x 30 000 dwt
Higashi Ohgishima (No.4 Wharf)	240	12	General cargo. Max cap 1 x 30 000 dwt
Higashi Ohgishima (No.5 Wharf)	240	12	General cargo. Max cap 1 x 30 000 dwt
Higashi Ohgishima (No.6 Wharf)	240	12	General cargo. Max cap 1 x 30 000 dwt
Higashi Ohgishima (No.7 Wharf)	240	12	General cargo. Max cap 1 x 30 000 dwt
Higashi Ohgishima (No.8 Wharf)	240	12	General cargo. Max cap 1 x 30 000 dwt
Higashi Ohgishima (No.9 Wharf)	240	12	General cargo. Max cap 1 x 30 000 dwt
Higashi Ohgishima (No.21 Wharf)	130	7.5	General cargo. Max cap 1 x 5000 dwt
Higashi Ohgishima (No.22 Wharf)	130	7.5	General cargo. Max cap 1 x 5000 dwt
Higashi Ohgishima (No.23 Wharf)	130	7.5	General cargo. Max cap 1 x 5000 dwt
Higashi Ohgishima (No.24 Wharf)	130	7.5	General cargo. Max cap 1 x 5000 dwt
Higashi Ohgishima (No.25 Wharf)	130	7.5	General cargo. Max cap 1 x 5000 dwt
Higashi Ohgishima (No.26 Wharf)	130	7.5	General cargo. Max cap 1 x 5000 dwt
Higashi Ohgishima (No.27 Wharf)	130	7.5	General cargo. Max cap 1 x 5000 dwt
Higashi Ohgishima (No.28 Wharf)	130	7.5	General cargo. Max cap 1 x 5000 dwt
Higashi Ohgishima (No.29 Wharf)	130	7.5	General cargo. Max cap 1 x 5000 dwt
Higashi Ohgishima (No.30 Wharf)	130	7.5	General cargo. Max cap 1 x 5000 dwt
Higashi Ohgishima (No.31 Wharf)	130	7.5	General cargo. Max cap 1 x 5000 dwt
Higashi Ohgishima (ABCD Wharves)	240	4.5	General cargo. Max cap 4 x 700 dwt
Kawasaki Container (No.1 Wharf)	431	14	See [1] below
Waste Oil Disposal Plant (No's 3 & 4 Piers)	98	5.5	Waste oil. Max cap 2 x 500 dwt
Waste Oil Disposal Plant (No's 5 & 6 Piers)	174	6	Waste oil. Max cap 2 x 2000 dwt
Commercial Wharves			
Mitsui Wharf (Coal Wharf)	378	10	Coal. Max cap 3 x 22 000 dwt
Mitsui Wharf (South Pier)	257	12	Coal and iron & steel. Max cap 1 x 30 000 dwt
Mitsui Wharf (Cement Dolphin)	68	9	Cement. Max cap 1 x 10 000 dwt
Tokyo Wharf & Warehouse (Parallel Pier)	389	12	Rice, cereals & beans. Max cap 2 x 20 000 dwt
Tokyo Wharf & Warehouse (General Cargo Pier)	296	9.5	Vegetables & fruits. Max cap 2 x 10 000 dwt
Tokyo Wharf & Warehouse (Dolomite Wharf)	110	5.5	Chemicals. Max cap 1 x 1000 dwt
Tokyo Wharf & Warehouse (Sand & Gravel Berth)	56	5.5	Sand. Max cap 1 x 499 dwt
Private Wharves			
Asahikasei Chemicals (No.1 Pier)	33	5.1	Chemicals. Max cap 1 x 1900 dwt
Asahikasei Chemicals (No.2 Pier)	32	5.5	Chemicals. Max cap 1 x 2000 dwt
Asahikasei Chemicals (No.3 Pier)	30	5	Chemicals. Max cap 1 x 1200 dwt
Idemitsu Kosan Kawasaki (No.1 Pier)	103	10	Petroleum products. Max cap 1 x 20 000 dwt
Idemitsu Kosan Kawasaki (No.3 Pier)	17	5	Petroleum products. Max cap 1 x 1000 dwt
Nippon Butsuryu Center (Wharf)	82	4.7	Max cap 1 x 2000 dwt
Nippon Butsuryu Center (Wharf)	82	4.7	Max cap 1 x 2000 dwt
Kawaichi Industry (Pier)	28	6	Iron & steel. Max cap 1 x 1500 dwt
Kawasaki Chemical (Chidori Pier)	54	9	Chemicals. Max cap 1 x 10 000 dwt
Nihon Yushi (Pier)	26	5.6	Chemicals. Max cap 1 x 1902 dwt
East Japan Rail (Kawasaki Pier)	115	7	Other machinery. Max cap 1 x 3000 dwt

Key to Principal Facilities:—

A=Airport	**C**=Containers	**G**=General Cargo
B=Bunkers	**D**=Dry Dock	**L**=Cruise

P=Petroleum	**R**=Ro/Ro	**Y**=Dry Bulk
Q=Other Liquid Bulk	**T**=Towage (where available from port)	

Name	Length (m)	Depth (m)	Remarks
Nihon Vopac (Pier)	69	11.4	Chemicals. Max cap 1 x 19 000 gt
Toa Oil Ohgimachi Plant (Ohgimachi No.1 Pier)	6	4.5	Heavy oil. Max cap 1 x 1500 dwt
Toa Oil Ohgimachi Plant (Ohgimachi No.2 Pier)	13	4.8	Heavy oil. Max cap 1 x 1500 dwt
Toa Oil Ohgimachi Plant (Ohgimachi No.3 Pier)	13	5.5	Heavy oil. Max cap 1 x 300 dwt
Toa Oil Ohgimachi Plant (Ohgimachi East No.1 Pier)	100	7.5	Petroleum products. Max cap 1 x 5000 dwt
Toa Oil Ohgimachi Plant (Ohgimachi East No.2 Pier)	90	7.5	Petroleum products. Max cap 1 x 3000 dwt
Toa Oil Ohgimachi Plant (Ohgimachi East No.3 Pier)	60	5	Petroleum products. Max cap 1 x 1000 dwt
Toa Oil Ohgimachi Plant (Ikegami No.1 Pier)	38	7	Heavy oil. Max cap 4 x 1000 dwt
Toa Oil Ohgimachi Plant (Ikegami No.2 Pier)	13	9	Heavy oil. Max cap 1 x 20 000 dwt
Toa Oil Ohgimachi Plant (Ikegami No.3 Pier)	23	10	Heavy oil. Max cap 1 x 2000 dwt
Toa Oil Ohgimachi Plant (Ikegami No.4 Pier)	9	10.5	Heavy oil. Max cap 1 x 4000 dwt
Toa Oil Ohgimachi Plant (Ikegami No.5 Pier)	40	10	Petroleum products. Max cap 1 x 4000 dwt
Toa Oil Ohgimachi Plant (Ikegami No.6 Pier)	58	10	Heavy oil. Max cap 1 x 4000 dwt
Toa Oil Ohgimachi Plant (Keihin Kawasaki Sea Berth)		26	Crude oil. Max cap 1 x 315 000 dwt
Showa Denko Kawasaki Plant (Ohgimachi No.1 Berth)	40	5.4	Petroleum products. Max cap 1 x 800 dwt
Showa Denko Kawasaki Plant (Ohgimachi No.2 Berth)	39	5.4	Chemicals. Max cap 1 x 1000 dwt
Showa Denko Kawasaki Plant (Ohgimachi No.4 Berth)	45	5.4	Chemicals
Showa Denko Kawasaki Plant (Ohgimachi No.5 Berth)	139	7.4	Max cap 1 x 3000 dwt
Showa Denko Kawasaki Plant (Ohgimachi No.6 Berth)	23	4.5	Chemicals. Max cap 1 x 750 dwt
Showa Denko Kawasaki Plant (Kodo Kasei Wharf)	45	5	Max cap 1 x 1000 dwt
Showa Denko (Chidori Pier)	33	6	Chemicals. Max cap 1 x 3000 dwt
Showa Distribution (Pier)	89	5.5	Synthetic resin. Max cap 1 x 2000 dwt
Nippon Express (Wharf)	124	6	Metallic products. Max cap 1 x 1500 dwt
Tonen General Sekiyu (A-1 Pier)	71	12	Crude oil. Max cap 1 x 65 000 dwt
Tonen General Sekiyu (A-2 Pier)	39	8	Heavy oil. Max cap 1 x 5000 dwt
Tonen General Sekiyu (A-3 Pier)	30	8	Heavy oil. Max cap 1 x 2000 dwt
Tonen General Sekiyu (B-1 Pier)	30	6.5	Heavy oil. Max cap 1 x 2500 dwt
Tonen General Sekiyu (B-2 Pier)	31	6.5	Heavy oil. Max cap 1 x 2000 dwt
Tonen General Sekiyu (B-5 Pier)	25	6	Max cap 1 x 300 dwt
Central Glass (Tama River Base Wharf)	79	5.5	Chemicals. Max cap 1 x 1300 dwt
D.C. (Wharf)	162	9	Cement. Max cap 1 x 10 750 dwt
Daio Paper (Daio Wharf)	113	5	Paper & pulp. Max cap 1 x 2000 dwt
Cosumo Oil (Private Pier)	38	6	Petroleum products. Max cap 1 x 2000 dwt
Toa Oil Mizue Plant (No.1 Factory, No's 1 & 3 Piers)	38	11	Petroleum products. Max cap 2 x 5000 dwt
Toa Oil Mizue Plant (No.1 Factory, No.2 Pier)	96	11	Petroleum products. Max cap 1 x 46 000 dwt
Toa Oil Mizue Plant (No.2 Factory, No's 4 & 5 Piers)	72	5.4	Petroleum products. Max cap 2 x 2000 dwt
Toa Oil Mizue Plant (No.10 Wharf)	80	5	Petroleum products. Max cap 1 x 1500 dwt
Toa Oil Japan Energy (Main Pier)	84	12	Petroleum products. Max cap 1 x 53 520 dwt
Toa Oil Japan Energy (No's 1 & 3 Wharves)	36	6	Heavy oil. Max cap 2 x 2800 dwt
Toa Oil Japan Energy (No.2 Wharf)	14	6	Petroleum products. Max cap 1 x 1250 dwt
Tonen General Sekiyu 400 (B-5)	25	5	Crude oil. Max cap 1 x 1000 dwt
Tonen General Sekiyu 400 Gouchi (No.41 Pier)	31	7.3	Heavy oil. Max cap 1 x 2000 dwt

Name	Length (m)	Depth (m)	Remarks
Tonen General Sekiyu 400 Gouchi (No.42 Pier)	87	7.3	Petroleum products. Max cap 1 x 5000 dwt
Tonen General Sekiyu 400 Gouchi (No.43 Pier)	37	7	Heavy oil. Max cap 1 x 3000 dwt
Tonen General Sekiyu 400 Gouchi (No.44 Pier)	47	8	Heavy oil. Max cap 1 x 7500 dwt
Tonen General Sekiyu 400 Gouchi (No.45 Pier)	30	5.5	Petroleum products. Max cap 1 x 2000 dwt
Tonen General Sekiyu 400 Gouchi (No.46 Pier)	25	4.7	Petroleum products. Max cap 1 x 500 dwt
Tonen General Sekiyu 200 Gouchi (No.1 Pier)	89	12	Petroleum products. Max cap 1 x 68 000 dwt
Tonen General Sekiyu 200 Gouchi (No's 2 & 3 Piers)	72	8	Petroleum products. Max cap 2 x 10 000 dwt
Tonen General Sekiyu 200 Gouchi (No's 4 & 5 Piers)	66	6	Petroleum products. Max cap 2 x 2500 dwt
Tonen General Sekiyu 200 Gouchi (No's 6 & 7 Piers)	55	5	Petroleum products. Max cap 2 x 500 dwt
Tonen General Sekiyu 100 Gouchi (No.1 Pier)	209	12	Heavy oil. Max cap 1 x 5000 dwt
Tonen General Sekiyu (Ohgishima West Sea Berth)	385	16.6	Crude oil. Max cap 1 x 113 002 dwt
Tonen General Sekiyu (Ohgishima East Sea Berth)	510	26	Crude oil. Max cap 1 x 315 000 dwt
Tonen General Sekiyu (Ohgishima Oil Bunkering Pier)	23	26	Heavy oil. Max cap 1 x 1000 dwt
Tonen General Sekiyu (Ohgishima Water Supply Pier)	23	26	Water. Max cap 1 x 1000 dwt
Higashi Ohgishima Oil Terminal (No.0 Pier)	122	9.1	Heavy oil. Max cap 1 x 5000 dwt
Higashi Ohgishima Oil Terminal (No.1 Pier)	145	8.2	Heavy oil. Max cap 1 x 5786 dwt
Higashi Ohgishima Oil Terminal (No.2 Pier)	122	7.5	Heavy oil. Max cap 1 x 3998 dwt
Higashi Ohgishima Oil Terminal (No.3 Pier)	113	9.2	Heavy oil. Max cap 1 x 1515 dwt
Tokyo Electric Power Kawasaki (Naphtha Pier)	319	8	Petroleum products. Max cap 1 x 5000 dwt
Tokyo Electric Power Ohgishima East (LNG Berth)	464	14	LNG. Max cap 1 x 79 000 dwt
Tokyo Electric Power (Oil Bunkering Berth)	130	7.5	Heavy oil. Max cap 1 x 3500 dwt
TMT & D (Pier)	31	6	Other machinery. Max cap 1 x 2000 dwt
Tonen Chemical (Chidori Pier)	34	6	Heavy oil. Max cap 1 x 1600 gt
Tokyo Yuso (No.1 Pier)	97	12	Heavy oil. Max cap 1 x 60 000 dwt
Tokyo Yuso (No.2 Pier)	38	5.6	Heavy oil. Max cap 1 x 2000 dwt
Nisshin (Kawasaki Pier)	46	6	Chemicals. Max cap 1 x 2300 dwt
Nisshin Flour Milling (Wharf)	223	12	Wheat. Max cap 1 x 50 000 dwt
Toshiba Hama-Kawasaki Factory	36	6	
JFE (Ohgimachi East Wharf)	450	8	Steel
JFE (Ohgishima East Row Material A Berth)	360	22	Iron ore. Max cap 1 x 200 000 dwt
JFE (Ohgishima East Row Material B Berth)	240	18	Coal. Max cap 1 x 100 000 dwt
JFE (Ohgishima East Row Material C Berth)	170	7.5	Coke. Max cap 1 x 5000 dwt
JFE (Ohgishima N. Honsen Wharf)	320	13.5	Iron & steel. Max cap 1 x 68 000 dwt
JFE (Ohgishima Fuel A Berth)	45	6	Chemicals. Max cap 1 x 3000 dwt
JFE (Ohgishima Fuel B Berth)	43	9	Max cap 1 x 700 dwt
Fuji Electric (Shiraishi Goods Wharf)	198	6	Other machinery. Max cap 1 x 2000 dwt
Nippon Sanso (Wharf)	191	5	Metal products. Max cap 1 x 1000 dwt
Shin Nippon Petrochemicals Ukishima (No.2 Pier)	28	5	Chemicals. Max cap 1 x 1300 dwt
Shin Nippon Petrochemicals Ukishima (No.4 Pier)	29	5	Chemical products. Max cap 1 x 1300 dwt
Shin Nippon Petrochemicals Ukishima (No.5 Pier)	27	6	LPG. Max cap 1 x 1500 dwt
Shin Nippon Petrochemicals Ukishima (No.6 Pier)	129	7.9	Chemicals. Max cap 1 x 5000 dwt
Shin Nippon Petrochemicals Ukishima (No.7 Pier)	23	6	Chemicals. Max cap 1 x 1300 dwt

Name	Length (m)	Depth (m)	Remarks
Shin Nippon Petrochemicals Ukishima (No.10 Pier)	29	6	Petroleum products. Max cap 1 x 2000 dwt
Shin Nippon Petrochemicals Ukishima (Chidori Pier)	44	7	Chemical products. Max cap 1 x 3000 dwt
Shin Nippon Petrochemicals Shiohama (Second Pier)	77	5	Chemical products. Max cap 1 x 1300 dwt
Shin Nippon Petrochemicals Shiohama (Third Pier)	77	5	Chemical products. Max cap 1 x 1300 dwt
Shin Nippon Petroleum Gas (Main Pier)	88	12	Petroleum products. Max cap 1 x 62 000 dwt
Shin Nippon Petroleum Gas (No.3 Pier)	28	6	Petroleum products. Max cap 1 x 1300 dwt
Taiheiyo Cement (Pier)	115	8	Cement. Max cap 1 x 7000 dwt
Hitachi Zosen (Wharf)	253	6	Ship repair. Max cap 2 x 26 000 dwt
NIPPO Corporation Ohayashi Road (Ikojimacho Private Pier)	80	7.5	Max cap 1 x 5000 dwt
M.C. Terminal (A-B Berth)	91	12	Chemicals. Max cap 1 x 42 000 dwt
Shin Nippon Oil (Ohgimachi No.1 Pier)	197	12	Oil products. Max cap 1 x 73 000 dwt
Shin Nippon Oil (Ohgimachi No.2 Pier)	99	7.5	Oil. Max cap 1 x 3000 dwt
Shin Nippon Oil (Ohgimachi No.4 Pier)	80	5	Max cap 1 x 1400 dwt
Shin Nippon Oil (Ohgimachi Wharf)	70	4.5	Max cap 1 x 500 dwt
Mitsubishi (Pier)	30	5.6	Max cap 1 x 2000 dwt
Hayakita Kouei (Pier)	145	5	Waste. Max cap 1 x 1500 dwt
JFE Marine & Logistics (Ohshima Berth)	162	8	Iron. Max cap 1 x 2100 dwt
JFE (Small Ship Pier)	10	7.5	
JFE (Small Boat Pier)	109	7.5	
JFE (A Pier)	110	22	
Taiyo Nissan (Wharf)	191	5	Metal products. Max cap 1 x 1000 dwt
Fujiei Industry (First Pier)	67	7.1	Discarded sand. Max cap 1 x 3000 dwt
Fujiei Industry (Second Pier)	82	7.1	Discarded sand. Max cap 1 x 3000 dwt
Nihon Salt Manufacturing	27	4.7	Salt. Max cap 1 x 800 dwt
Nihon Salt Manufacturing	30	4.7	Max cap 1 x 800 dwt
Kawasaki Asukon (Mizue-cho Wharf)	91	6	Max cap 1 x 1500 dwt

[1]Kawasaki Container (No.1 Wharf): Operated by KCT Inc., Tel: +81 44 270 1011, Fax: +81 44 270 1051
Capable of accommodating 40 000 dwt container vessels. Yard area of 231 000 m2 with storage cap of 8700 TEU's

Storage: Transit shed and warehouse space of 280 028 m2; silo space of 387 772 m2. Oil tanks and storehouse with over 6 million t cap

Location	Open (m²)
Kawasaki	418387

Mechanical Handling Equipment:

Location	Type	Capacity (t)	Qty
Kawasaki	Transtainers	40	8
Kawasaki Container (No.1 Wharf)	Container Cranes	40	2

Bunkering: All kinds of marine oil can be delivered, usually by barge, from the major oil companies
Cosmo Oil Co. Ltd, Toshiba Building, 1-1 Shibaura 1-chome, Minato-ku, Tokyo 105-8528, Japan, *Tel:* +81 3 3798 3156, *Fax:* +81 3 3798 3592, *Email:* masayuki_iijima@cosmo-oil.co.jp, *Website:* www.cosmo-oil.co.jp
ExxonMobil Marine Fuels, 1 Harbour Front Place, 06-00 Harbour Front, Tower One, Singapore, Republic of Singapore 098633, *Tel:* +65 6885 8998, *Fax:* +65 6885 8794, *Email:* asiapac.marinefuels@exxonmobil.com, *Website:* www.exxonmobilmarinefuels.com
Fuji Kosan Co. Ltd, 2-19-6 Yanagibashi, Taito-ku, Tokyo 111-0052, Japan, *Tel:* +81 3 3861 4601, *Fax:* +81 3 3861 4611, *Email:* info@fkoil.co.jp, *Website:* www.fkoil.co.jp
Hanwa Co. Ltd, 2nd Floor, Finland House, 56 Haymarket, London SW1Y 4RN, United Kingdom, *Tel:* +44 20 7839 4448, *Fax:* +44 20 7839 3994, *Email:* orito@hanwa.co.uk
Hikawa Shoji Kaisha Ltd, 26-2 Shinkawa NS Building 1-chome, Shinkawa, Chuo-ku, Tokyo 104, Japan, *Tel:* +81 3 5776 6858, *Fax:* +81 3 5541 3274
Idemitsu Kosan Co. Ltd, 1-1 Marunochi, 3-Chome, Chiyoda-ku, Tokyo 100-8321, Japan, *Tel:* +81 3 3213 3138, *Fax:* +81 3 3213 1145, *Email:* tohru.takamura@si.idemitsu.co.jp, *Website:* www.idemitsu.co.jp
KG Int Petroleum Ltd, Shiba Park Building, 241 Shiba Koen, Minato-ku, Tokyo 105, Japan, *Tel:* +81 3 3578 4551, *Fax:* +81 3 3578 4550
Japan Energy Corp., 2-10-1, Toranomon, Minato-ku, Tokyo 105-8407, Japan, *Tel:* +81 3 5573 6100, *Fax:* +81 3 5573 6674, *Email:* yamano@j-energy.co.jp, *Website:* www.j-energy.co.jp
Kyodo Oil Co. Ltd, 11-2 Nagata-cho 2-chome, Chiyoda-ku, Tokyo, Japan, *Tel:* +81 3 3505 8241, *Fax:* +81 3 3505 8697
Kyushu Oil Co. Ltd, 1-1 Uchisaiwai-cho 2-chome, Chiyoda-ku, Tokyo, Japan, *Tel:* +81 3 3502 3651, *Fax:* +81 3 3502 9850

Marubeni Petroleum Co. Ltd, Marubeni International Petroleum Singapore Co. Ltd, c/o Marubeni Corporation, 4-2 Ohtemachi 1-chome, Chiyoda-ku, Tokyo 100-8088, Japan, *Tel:* +81 3 3282 3920, *Fax:* +81 3 3282 3950, *Email:* TOKB554@marubenicorp.com, *Website:* www.marubeni.co.jp
MC Marine and Bunkering Inc., 8th Floor, Uchisaiwai-cho Dai Building, 3-3 Uchisaiwai-cho 1-chome, Chiyoda-ku, Tokyo 100-0011, Japan, *Tel:* +81 3 5251 2575, *Fax:* +81 3 5251 2583
Mitsui & Co. Petroleum Ltd, 2-1, Ohtemachi 1-chome, Chiyoda-ku, Tokyo 100-0004, Japan, *Tel:* +81 3 3285 6905, *Fax:* +81 3 3285 9811, *Email:* tkzph@dg.mitsui.com, *Website:* www.mitsui.co.jp
Nissho Iwai Corp., 4-4 Akasaka 2-chome, Minato-ku, Tokyo, Japan, *Tel:* +81 3 35882111
Nittetsu Shoji Co. Ltd, 5-7 Kameido 1-chome, Koto-ku, Tokyo 136, Japan, *Tel:* +81 3 5627 2157, *Fax:* +81 3 5627 2192
NKK Trading Inc., 4-4 Nihonbashi Hisamatsusucho, Chuo-ku, Tokyo 103, Japan, *Tel:* +81 3 3660 1522, *Fax:* +81 3 3660 1572
Panoco Trading Co. Ltd, Shin-Sudacho Kyodo Building 2nd Floor, 1-5, Kanda Sudacho, Chiyoda-ku, Tokyo 101-0041, Japan, *Tel:* +81 3 5298 6633, *Fax:* +81 3 3255 2202, *Email:* minori@panoco.co.jp, *Website:* www.panoco.co.jp
Shinagawa Fuel Co. Ltd, New Pier Takeshiba North Tower, 8th Floor, 1-11-1 Kaigan, Minato-ku, Tokyo 105-8525, Japan, *Tel:* +81 3 5470 7113, *Fax:* +81 3 5470 7157, *Email:* hakuyu@ml1.sinanen.co.jp
Showa Yokkaichi Sekiyu K.K., Tokyo Building, 7-3 Marunouchi 2-chome, Chiyoda-ku, Tokyo 100, Japan, *Tel:* +81 3 3215 1643, *Fax:* +81 3 3215 1869
SK Energy Asia Private Ltd, 8th Floor Yamato Seimei Building, 1-17 Uchisaiwicho 1-chome, Chiyoda-ku, Tokyo 100-0011, Japan, *Tel:* +81 3 3591 0533, *Fax:* +81 3 3591 7487, *Email:* leehk@skenergy.com, *Website:* www.skenergy.com
Sumitomo Corp., Harumi Island, Triton Square, Office Tower Y, 8-11 Harumi 1-chome, Chuo-ku, Tokyo 104-8610, Japan, *Tel:* +81 3 51664458, *Fax:* +81 3 51666407, *Email:* ir@sumitomo.co.jp, *Website:* www.sumitomocorp.co.jp
Total France S.A., Total Marine Fuels, 51 Esplanade du General de Gaulle, F-92907 Paris la Defense Cedex 10, France, *Tel:* +33 1 4135 2755, *Fax:* +33 1 4197 0291, *Email:* marine.fuels@total.com, *Website:* www.marinefuels.total.com

Towage: Thirty four tugs available from 1500 hp to 3200 hp, operated by Yokohama Kawasaki Tugboats Co Ltd

Repair & Maintenance: Hitachi Zosen Corp., 4-1 Mizue-cho, Kawasaki-ku, Kawasaki 210-9650, Kanagawa Pref., Japan, *Tel:* +81 44 288 1149, *Fax:* +81 44 288 1115, *Website:* www.hitachizosen.co.jp Kanagawa yard has one dry dock 225 m x 37 m x 8.4 m for vessels up to 40 000 gt. Four repair quays. All types of repairs handled

Shipping Agents: Kamigumi Co. Ltd, 22-5 Higashiogijima, Kawasaki-ku, Kawasaki 210-0869, Kanagawa Pref., Japan, *Tel:* +81 44 287 3650, *Fax:* +81 44 287 3655

Medical Facilities: Medical clinic inside Higashi-Ohgishima Port Community Facilities

Airport: Haneda Airport

Railway: Kanagawa Rinkai Line

Lloyd's Agent: Cornes & Co. Ltd, 273 Yamashita-cho, Naka-ku, Yokohama 231-0023, Kanagawa Pref., Japan, *Tel:* +81 45 201 8537, *Fax:* +81 45 212 3105, *Email:* survey@ykh.cornes.co.jp, *Website:* www.cornes.co.jp

KEIHIN

see under Yokohama

KESENNUMA

Lat 38° 52' N; Long 141° 36' E.

Admiralty Chart: JP54		**Admiralty Pilot:** 41	
Time Zone: GMT +9 h		**UNCTAD Locode:** JP KSN	

Principal Facilities:

P		G			B		T	

Authority: Ports & Harbors Promotion Division, Public Works Department, Miyagi Prefectural Government, 3-8-1 Honcho, Aoba-ku, Sendai 980-8570, Miyagi Pref., Japan, *Tel:* +81 22 211 3221, *Fax:* +81 22 211 3296, *Email:* kousin@pref.miyagi.jp, *Website:* www.pref.miyagi.jp/kouwan

Officials: Port Manager: Haruo Kasamatsu.
Assistant Manager: Masashi Takahashi.

Approach: Draught limitation in the channel is 7.0 m. An overhead cable spans the narrows at Hachiga Saki, pos 38° 53' 36" N; 141° 35' 36" E with a vertical clearance of about 38 m; width of channel at this point is about 100 m

Anchorage: Well sheltered anchorage can be obtained in Kanega cove in depths ranging from 5 m to 9 m, bottom mud

Pilotage: Not compulsory but recommended. Pilots are available at Kamaishi during daylight hours only

Tides: Range of tide 3.48 m

Key to Principal Facilities:—
A=Airport   **C**=Containers   **G**=General Cargo   **P**=Petroleum   **R**=Ro/Ro   **Y**=Dry Bulk
B=Bunkers   **D**=Dry Dock   **L**=Cruise   **Q**=Other Liquid Bulk   **T**=Towage (where available from port)

Working Hours: 0830-1700

Accommodation:

Name	Length (m)	Depth (m)	Remarks
Kesennuma			
Asahi Wharf No.1	390	7.5	Max 3 x 5000 dwt
Asahi Wharf No.2	170	4.5	Max 3 x 1000 dwt
Idemitsu Kosan Dolphin	40	6	Max 3000 dwt
Nippon Oil Dolphin	40	6	Max 3000 dwt
Shell Sekiyu Dolphin	40	6	Max 3000 dwt

Bunkering: Domestic oil available

Towage: One small tug of 160 hp is available. Larger tugs can be brought in from Kamaishi

Repair & Maintenance: Minor repairs can be undertaken

Lloyd's Agent: Cornes & Co. Ltd, 273 Yamashita-cho, Naka-ku, Yokohama 231-0023, Kanagawa Pref., Japan, *Tel:* +81 45 201 8537, *Fax:* +81 45 212 3105, *Email:* survey@ykh.cornes.co.jp, *Website:* www.cornes.co.jp

KIIRE

Lat 31° 23' N; Long 130° 33' E.

Admiralty Chart: 654
Time Zone: GMT +9 h

Admiralty Pilot: 42A
UNCTAD Locode: JP KII

Principal Facilities:

P					B	T	A

Authority: Kiire Port Office, Public Works, 301 12-chome, Takanohara, Ibusuki, Kagoshima Pref., Japan, *Tel:* +81 993 222171, *Fax:* +81 993 223344

Port Security: ISPS compliant

Approach: Open fairway, channel depth is over 50 m. The approach is well lit and does not present many difficulties, but during fishing season large fishing boat fleets may be met in Kagoshima Bay

Anchorage: The usual anchorage is the Quarantine Anchorage position centred on 31° 24' 48" N; 130° 33' 48" E in depths ranging from 40 m to 70 m

Pilotage: Bay pilots are not provided but Mooring Master is available for assistance while berthing and unberthing, free of charge

Weather: The weather is normal, except for the typhoon season from July-October

Tides: The spring tide rises 3 m and the neap tide rises 1.5 m

Maximum Vessel Dimensions: 500 000 dwt, max d 28.2 m, 380 m loa

Working Hours: 24 h/day

Accommodation:

Name	Depth (m)	Draught (m)	Remarks
Kiire			
Nippon Oil Staging Terminal No.1 Pier	18	16.2	Max 150 000 dwt, four 12'' loading arms
Nippon Oil Staging Terminal No.2 Pier	18	16.2	Max 150 000 dwt, four 12'' loading arms
Nippon Oil Staging Terminal No.3 Pier	28	25.2	Max 450 000 dwt, four 16'' loading arms
Nippon Oil Staging Terminal No.4 Pier	34	30.6	Max 500 000 dwt, one 16'' and three 24'' loading arms
North Pier	10		See [1] below

[1]*North Pier:* Loading only, max 10 000 dwt, one 10'' and one 12'' loading arms

Storage: The tank farm has 54 crude oil tanks with total cap of 6 600 000 kilolitres

Bunkering: MC Marine and Bunkering Inc., 8th Floor, Uchisaiwai-cho Dai Building, 3-3 Uchisaiwai-cho 1-chome, Chiyoda-ku, Tokyo 100-0011, Japan, *Tel:* +81 3 5251 2575, *Fax:* +81 3 5251 2583
Mitsui & Co. Petroleum Ltd, 2-1, Ohtemachi 1-chome, Chiyoda-ku, Tokyo 100-0004, Japan, *Tel:* +81 3 3285 6905, *Fax:* +81 3 3285 9811, *Email:* tkzph@dg.mitsui.com, *Website:* www.mitsui.co.jp

Towage: There are four tugs available of 3200 hp

Repair & Maintenance: Kagoshima Dock & Iron Works Co. Ltd, 2-2 Nanatsushima, 1 chome, Kagoshima 891-0132, Kagoshima Pref., Japan, *Tel:* +81 99 261 7878, *Fax:* +81 99 261 7871 Minor repairs available

Medical Facilities: No hospital facilities available nearby, but medical attention is available in Kagoshima City, approx 30 km

Airport: Kagoshima, 80 km

Lloyd's Agent: Cornes & Co. Ltd, Meikai Building, 32 Akashi-machi, Chuo-ku, Kobe 650-0037, Hyogo Pref., Japan, *Tel:* +81 78 332 3421, *Fax:* +81 78 332 3070, *Email:* survey@kobe.cornes.co.jp, *Website:* www.cornes.co.jp

KIKUMA

Lat 34° 2' N; Long 132° 50' E.

Admiralty Chart: JP132
Time Zone: GMT +9 h

Admiralty Pilot: 42B
UNCTAD Locode: JP KIK

Principal Facilities:

P					B	T	A

Authority: Kikuma Town Office, 822 Hama, Kikuma-cho, Ochi, Ehime Pref., Japan, *Tel:* +81 898 543450

Port Security: ISPS compliant

Approach: Depths in channel up to 30 m

Anchorage: Anchorage can be obtained approx 350 m offshore in pos 34° 03' N, 132° 51' E with good holding ground

Pilotage: Not compulsory. Pilots are available at the anchorage if required. Inland Sea pilots are available at Wadamisaki, Sekisaki or Hesaki

Working Hours: 24 h/day. Oil port regulations state that discharging operations should commence before sunset

Accommodation: Tanker discharging port operated by Taiyo Oil Co

Name	Depth (m)	Remarks
Kikuma		
Taiyo Oil Co Ltd Sea Berth	20	See [1] below
Taiyo Oil Co Ltd Dolphin Berth	16	See [2] below

[1]*Taiyo Oil Co Ltd Sea Berth:* For vessels up to 280 m loa and 130 000 dwt, two 12'' pipelines discharging at 4500 t/h each
[2]*Taiyo Oil Co Ltd Dolphin Berth:* For vessels up to 237 m loa and 88 450 dwt, two 12'' and one 10'' pipelines discharging at 4500 t/h each

Bunkering: Kyodo Oil Co. Ltd, 11-2 Nagata-cho 2-chome, Chiyoda-ku, Tokyo, Japan, *Tel:* +81 3 3505 8241, *Fax:* +81 3 3505 8697
MC Marine and Bunkering Inc., 8th Floor, Uchisaiwai-cho Dai Building, 3-3 Uchisaiwai-cho 1-chome, Chiyoda-ku, Tokyo 100-0011, Japan, *Tel:* +81 3 5251 2575, *Fax:* +81 3 5251 2583
Mitsui & Co. Petroleum Ltd, 2-1, Ohtemachi 1-chome, Chiyoda-ku, Tokyo 100-0004, Japan, *Tel:* +81 3 3285 6905, *Fax:* +81 3 3285 9811, *Email:* tkzph@dg.mitsui.com, *Website:* www.mitsui.co.jp

Towage: Naikai Tug Boat Service Co. Ltd, Kikuma, Ehime Pref., Japan, *Tel:* +81 89 934 1141, *Fax:* +81 89 934 2040

Medical Facilities: Available

Airport: Matsuyama, 35 km

Lloyd's Agent: Cornes & Co. Ltd, Meikai Building, 32 Akashi-machi, Chuo-ku, Kobe 650-0037, Hyogo Pref., Japan, *Tel:* +81 78 332 3421, *Fax:* +81 78 332 3070, *Email:* survey@kobe.cornes.co.jp, *Website:* www.cornes.co.jp

KIMITSU

alternate name, see Kisarazu

KINUURA

Lat 34° 52' N; Long 136° 56' E.

Admiralty Chart: JP1056/JP1057A/JP10... **Admiralty Pilot:** 42A
Time Zone: GMT +9 h
UNCTAD Locode: JP KNU

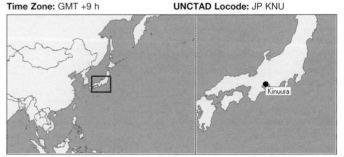

Principal Facilities:

P	Q	Y	G		R		B		T	A

Authority: Port & Harbour Management Division, Aichi Prefecture Government, 3-1-2 Sannomaru, Naka-ku, Nagoya 460-8501, Aichi Pref., Japan, *Tel:* +81 52 954 6562, *Fax:* +81 52 953 1793, *Email:* kowan@pref.aichi.lg.jp, *Website:* www.pref.aichi.jp

Port Security: ISPS compliant

Approach: The port can be reached by passing through Irago Channel and Morozaki Channel in Chita Bay. Draught limitation south of the Central Passage is 12 m and north of the Central Passage is 10 m

Pilotage: Compulsory for vessels exceeding 10 000 gt. A pilot will need to board the vessel off Irago and can be requested from Irago-Mikawa Bay Pilot Association, Tel: +81 569 217487. VHF Channel 16

Radio Frequency: Mikawa-wan Port Radio, VHF Channel 16 (calling), Channels 11 and 12 (working)

Weather: Typhoon season; July to October

Tides: Tidal range 2.34 m, 2.4 m MHWL, 0.06 m MLWL, 1.32 m MSL

Principal Imports and Exports: Imports: Grain, Petroleum products, Timber. Exports: Steel products.

Accommodation:

Name	Length (m)	Depth (m)
Kinuura		
Taketoyo Kita Wharf	185	10
Taketoyo Kita Wharf	240	12
Taketoyo Kita Wharf	130	7.5
Chuo Wharf (West)	480	12
Chuo Wharf (West)	370	10
Chuo Wharf (West)	520	7.5
Kamezaki Wharf	555	10
Kamezaki Wharf	190	9
Takahama Wharf	130	7.5
Central Wharf (East)	240	12
Central Wharf (East)	185	10
Central Wharf (East)	130	7.5

Bunkering: Cosmo Oil Co. Ltd, Toshiba Building, 1-1 Shibaura 1-chome, Minato-ku, Tokyo 105-8528, Japan, *Tel:* +81 3 3798 3156, *Fax:* +81 3 3798 3592, *Email:* masayuki_iijima@cosmo-oil.co.jp, *Website:* www.cosmo-oil.co.jp
Hanwa Co. Ltd, 2nd Floor, Finland House, 56 Haymarket, London SW1Y 4RN, United Kingdom, *Tel:* +44 20 7839 4448, *Fax:* +44 20 7839 3994, *Email:* orito@hanwa.co.uk
Hikawa Shoji Kaisha Ltd, 26-2 Shinkawa NS Building 1-chome, Shinkawa, Chuo-ku, Tokyo 104, Japan, *Tel:* +81 3 5776 6858, *Fax:* +81 3 5541 3274
Idemitsu Kosan Co. Ltd, 1-1 Marunochi, 3-Chome, Chiyoda-ku, Tokyo 100-8321, Japan, *Tel:* +81 3 3213 3138, *Fax:* +81 3 3213 1145, *Email:* tohru.takamura@si.idemitsu.co.jp, *Website:* www.idemitsu.co.jp
KG Int Petroleum Ltd, Shiba Park Building, 241 Shiba Koen, Minato-ku, Tokyo 105, Japan, *Tel:* +81 3 3578 4551, *Fax:* +81 3 3578 4550
Japan Energy Corp., 2-10-1, Toranomon, Minato-ku, Tokyo 105-8407, Japan, *Tel:* +81 3 5573 6100, *Fax:* +81 3 5573 6674, *Email:* yamano@j-energy.co.jp, *Website:* www.j-energy.co.jp
Kamei Corp., 1-6-1 Otemachi, Chiyoda-ku, Tokyo 100-0004, Japan, *Tel:* +81 3 3286 6234, *Fax:* +81 3 3286 6249, *Email:* bunker@kamei.co.jp
Kawasho Corp., World Trade Centre, 4-1 Hanamatsu-cho 2-chome, Minato-ku, Tokyo 105, Japan, *Tel:* +81 3 3435 3251
Kyodo Oil Co. Ltd, 11-2 Nagata-cho 2-chome, Chiyoda-ku, Tokyo, Japan, *Tel:* +81 3 3505 8241, *Fax:* +81 3 3505 8697
Marubeni Petroleum Co. Ltd, Marubeni International Petroleum Singapore Co. Ltd, c/o Marubeni Corporation, 4-2 Ohtemachi 1-chome, Chiyoda-ku, Tokyo 100-8088, Japan, *Tel:* +81 3 3282 3920, *Fax:* +81 3 3282 3950, *Email:* TOKB554@marubenicorp.com, *Website:* www.marubeni.co.jp
MC Marine and Bunkering Inc., 8th Floor, Uchisaiwai-cho Dai Building, 3-3 Uchisaiwai-cho 1-chome, Chiyoda-ku, Tokyo 100-0011, Japan, *Tel:* +81 3 5251 2575, *Fax:* +81 3 5251 2583
Mitsui & Co. Petroleum Ltd, 2-1, Ohtemachi 1-chome, Chiyoda-ku, Tokyo 100-0004, Japan, *Tel:* +81 3 3285 6905, *Fax:* +81 3 3285 9811, *Email:* tkzph@dg.mitsui.com, *Website:* www.mitsui.co.jp
Nissho Iwai Corp., 4-4 Akasaka 2-chome, Minato-ku, Tokyo, Japan, *Tel:* +81 3 35882111
Nittetsu Shoij Co. Ltd, 5-7 Kameido 1-chome, Koto-ku, Tokyo 136, Japan, *Tel:* +81 3 5627 2157, *Fax:* +81 3 5627 2192
Shinagawa Fuel Co. Ltd, New Pier Takeshiba North Tower, 8th Floor, 1-11-1 Kaigan, Minato-ku, Tokyo 105-8525, Japan, *Tel:* +81 3 5470 7113, *Fax:* +81 3 5470 7157, *Email:* hakuyu@ml1.sinanen.co.jp
Sigma Foreign Service (Panama) S.A., 2-25 Aikawai, Tempaku-ku, Nagoya 468-0836, Aichi Pref., Japan, *Tel:* +81 52 896 1510, *Fax:* +81 52 896 7703
Sumitomo Corp., Harumi Island, Triton Square, Office Tower Y, 8-11 Harumi 1-chome, Chuo-ku, Tokyo 104-8610, Japan, *Tel:* +81 3 51664458, *Fax:* +81 3 51666407, *Email:* ir@sumitomo.co.jp, *Website:* www.sumitomocorp.co.jp

Towage: Five tugs available; two of 3600 hp, two of 3500 hp and one of 1500 hp

Repair & Maintenance: Minor repairs only are undertaken

Medical Facilities: Available

Airport: Nagoya Airport, 50 km

Lloyd's Agent: Cornes & Co. Ltd, Meikai Building, 32 Akashi-machi, Chuo-ku, Kobe 650-0037, Hyogo Pref., Japan, *Tel:* +81 78 332 3421, *Fax:* +81 78 332 3070, *Email:* survey@kobe.cornes.co.jp, *Website:* www.cornes.co.jp

KINWAN

alternate name, see Heianza

KISARAZU

Lat 35° 21' N; Long 139° 51' E.

Admiralty Chart: JP1067/JP1081		**Admiralty Pilot:** 42A	
Time Zone: GMT +9 h		**UNCTAD Locode:** JP KZU	

Principal Facilities:

P	Q	Y	G		R		B		T	A

Authority: Port & Harbor Promotion Division, Civil Engineering Department, Chiba Prefectural Government, 1-1 Ichiba-cho, Chuo-ku, Chiba 260-8667, Chiba Pref., Japan, *Tel:* +81 43 223 3830, *Fax:* +81 43 227 6115, *Website:* www.pref.chiba.jp

Port Security: ISPS compliant

Documentation: Entrance notice (to Customs & Immigration Offices)
Captain's report (to Quarantine Station)
Import inspection application (to Plant Protection Station & Animal Quarantine Service)
Entrance and departure notice (to Coast Guard Office, Port Directors & Harbour Fire Brigade)
Mooring institution use report (to Port Directors)

Approach: Three waterways with drafts ranging from 12-19 m

Pilotage: Compulsory for vessels exceeding 10 000 gt. Pilots board at the quarantine anchorage between 0600-1900 for berthing. Vessels can unberth up till 2000. Vessels over 60 000 dwt can only be attended during daylight hours. Bay Pilots for entering or shifting in Tokyo Bay are available any time at a position 5 miles, 161° from Kannonsaki Lighthouse with 24 h advance notice

Tides: Range of tide 1.8 m

Traffic: 2005, 1173 foreign trade vessels & 23 953 domestic vessels, 42 433 000 t of foreign cargo handled & 22 323 000 t of domestic cargo handled

Maximum Vessel Dimensions: Max 200 000 dwt. 17-19 m draft at raw material wharves, 6.5-11 m draft at loading wharves

Working Hours: 0800-1700

Accommodation:

Name	Length (m)	Depth (m)	Remarks
Public Wharves			
Kisarazu Public Wharf A	90	5.5	Max 2000 dwt
Kisarazu Public Wharf B	90	5.5	Max 2000 dwt
Kisarazu Public Wharf C	90	5.5	Max 2000 dwt
Kisarazu Public Wharf D	90	5.5	Max 2000 dwt
Kisarazu Public Wharf E	130	7.5	Max 5000 dwt
Lumber Port (Dolphin)	500	10	Max 15 000 dwt
Private Wharves			
Nippon Steel Corp East Pier No.2	240	11	Max 30 000 dwt
Nippon Steel Corp East Pier No.3	240	11	Max 30 000 dwt
Nippon Steel Corp East Pier No.4	100	6.5	Max 3000 dwt
Nippon Steel Corp East Pier No.5	80	6.5	Max 3000 dwt
Nippon Steel Corp East Pier No.6	113	6.5	Max 3000 dwt
Nippon Steel Corp East Pier No.7	130	6.5	Max 3000 dwt
Nippon Steel Corp East Pier No.8	150	6.5	Max 3000 dwt
Nippon Steel Corp East Pier No.9	150	6.5	Max 3000 dwt
Nippon Steel Corp East Pier No.10	150	6.5	Max 3000 dwt
Nippon Steel Corp East Pier No.12	296	4.5	Max 1800 dwt
Nippon Steel Corp East Pier No.13	376	4.5	Max 1800 dwt
Nippon Steel Chem Centre Pier No.1 (Dolphin)	127	6	Max 3000 dwt
Nippon Steel Chem Centre Pier No.2 (Dolphin)	128	5.5	Max 2000 dwt
Nippon Steel Chem Centre Pier No.3	110	5.5	Max 1495 dwt
Nippon Steel Corp Centre Pier No.4	166	4.5	
Nippon Steel Corp Centre Pier No.5	135	8.5	Max 9000 dwt
Nippon Steel Corp Centre Pier No.6	304	17	Max 150 000 dwt
Nippon Steel Corp Centre Pier No.7	350	19	Max 200 000 dwt

Key to Principal Facilities:—

A=Airport	**C**=Containers	**G**=General Cargo	**P**=Petroleum	**R**=Ro/Ro	**Y**=Dry Bulk
B=Bunkers	**D**=Dry Dock	**L**=Cruise	**Q**=Other Liquid Bulk	**T**=Towage (where available from port)	

Name	Length (m)	Depth (m)	Remarks
Nippon Steel Corp Centre Pier No.8	422	19	Max 322 941 dwt
Nippon Steel Corp Centre Pier No.10	208	9	Max 12 500 dwt
Nippon Steel Corp Centre Pier No.12	120	8	Max 5000 dwt
Kimitsu Kyodo Karyoku Centre Pier 11	136	7.5	Max 5000 dwt
Nippon Steel Corp West Pier No.1	115	5.5	Max 2000 dwt
Nippon Steel Corp West Pier No.2	100	5.5	Max 2000 dwt
Nippon Steel Corp West Pier No.3	130	5.5	Max 500 dwt
Nippon Steel Corp West Pier No.4	100	6.5	Max 3000 dwt
Nippon Steel Corp West Pier No.5	100	6.5	Max 3000 dwt
Nippon Steel Corp West Pier No.6	103	6.5	Max 3000 dwt
Nippon Steel Corp West Pier No.7	250	11	Max 30 000 dwt
Nippon Steel Corp West Pier No.8	250	11	Max 30 000 dwt
Nippon Steel Corp West Pier No.9	285	11	Max 30 000 dwt
Nippon Steel Corp West Pier No.10	230	11	Max 40 000 dwt
Toyo Kanetsu K.K.	350	6.5	Max 490 dwt
LNG Tanker Berth	420	14	Max 79 000 dwt

Storage: Freight handling yard of 138 889 m2 and open storage yard area covering 72 625 m2

Mechanical Handling Equipment:

Location	Type	Capacity (t)	Qty	Remarks
Kisarazu	Mult-purp. Cranes	54	17	At Nippon Steel Corp wharves

Bunkering: Cosmo Oil Co. Ltd, Toshiba Building, 1-1 Shibaura 1-chome, Minato-ku, Tokyo 105-8528, Japan, *Tel:* +81 3 3798 3156, *Fax:* +81 3 3798 3592, *Email:* masayuki_iijima@cosmo-oil.co.jp, *Website:* www.cosmo-oil.co.jp
ExxonMobil Marine Fuels, 1 Harbour Front Place, 06-00 Harbour Front, Tower One, Singapore, Republic of Singapore 098633, *Tel:* +65 6885 8998, *Fax:* +65 6885 8794, *Email:* asiapac.marinefuels@exxonmobil.com, *Website:* www.exxonmobilmarinefuels.com
Fuji Kosan Co. Ltd, 2-19-6 Yanagibashi, Taito-ku, Tokyo 111-0052, Japan, *Tel:* +81 3 3861 4601, *Fax:* +81 3 3861 4611, *Email:* info@fkoil.co.jp, *Website:* www.fkoil.co.jp
Hanwa Co. Ltd, 2nd Floor, Finland House, 56 Haymarket, London SW1Y 4RN, United Kingdom, *Tel:* +44 20 7839 4448, *Fax:* +44 20 7839 3994, *Email:* orito@hanwa.co.uk
Hikawa Shoji Kaisha Ltd, 26-2 Shinkawa NS Building 1-chome, Shinkawa, Chuo-ku, Tokyo 104, Japan, *Tel:* +81 3 5776 6858, *Fax:* +81 3 5541 3274
Idemitsu Kosan Co. Ltd, 1-1 Marunochi, 3-Chome, Chiyoda-ku, Tokyo 100-8321, Japan, *Tel:* +81 3 3213 3138, *Fax:* +81 3 3213 1145, *Email:* tohru.takamura@si.idemitsu.co.jp, *Website:* www.idemitsu.co.jp
KG Int Petroleum Ltd, Shiba Park Building, 241 Shiba Koen, Minato-ku, Tokyo 105, Japan, *Tel:* +81 3 3578 4551, *Fax:* +81 3 3578 4550
Japan Energy Corp., 2-10-1, Toranomon, Minato-ku, Tokyo 105-8407, Japan, *Tel:* +81 3 5573 6100, *Fax:* +81 3 5573 6674, *Email:* yamano@j-energy.co.jp, *Website:* www.j-energy.co.jp
Kyodo Oil Co. Ltd, 11-2 Nagata-cho 2-chome, Chiyoda-ku, Tokyo, Japan, *Tel:* +81 3 3505 8241, *Fax:* +81 3 3505 8697
Kyushu Oil Co. Ltd, 1-1 Uchisaiwai-cho 2-chome, Chiyoda-ku, Tokyo, Japan, *Tel:* +81 3 3502 3651, *Fax:* +81 3 3502 9850
Marubeni Petroleum Co. Ltd, Marubeni International Petroleum Singapore Co. Ltd, c/o Marubeni Corporation, 4-2 Ohtemachi 1-chome, Chiyoda-ku, Tokyo 100-8088, Japan, *Tel:* +81 3 3282 3920, *Fax:* +81 3 3282 3950, *Email:* TOKB554@marubenicorp.com, *Website:* www.marubeni.co.jp
MC Marine and Bunkering Inc., 8th Floor, Uchisaiwai-cho Dai Building, 3-3 Uchisaiwai-cho 1-chome, Chiyoda-ku, Tokyo 100-0011, Japan, *Tel:* +81 3 5251 2575, *Fax:* +81 3 5251 2583
Mitsui & Co. Petroleum Ltd, 2-1, Ohtemachi 1-chome, Chiyoda-ku, Tokyo 100-0004, Japan, *Tel:* +81 3 3285 6905, *Fax:* +81 3 3285 9811, *Email:* tkzph@dg.mitsui.com, *Website:* www.mitsui.co.jp
Nissho Iwai Corp., 4-4 Akasaka 2-chome, Minato-ku, Tokyo, Japan, *Tel:* +81 3 35882111
Nittetsu Shoij Co. Ltd, 5-7 Kameido 1-chome, Koto-ku, Tokyo 136, Japan, *Tel:* +81 3 5627 2157, *Fax:* +81 3 5627 2192
NKK Trading Inc., 4-4 Nihonbashi Hisamatsusucho, Chuo-ku, Tokyo 103, Japan, *Tel:* +81 3 3660 1522, *Fax:* +81 3 3660 1572
Panoco Trading Co. Ltd, Shin-Sudacho Kyodo Building 2nd Floor, 1-5, Kanda Sudacho, Chiyoda-ku, Tokyo 101-0041, Japan, *Tel:* +81 3 5298 6633, *Fax:* +81 3 3255 2202, *Email:* minori@panoco.co.jp, *Website:* www.panoco.co.jp
Shinagawa Fuel Co. Ltd, New Pier Takeshiba North Tower, 8th Floor, 1-11-1 Kaigan, Minato-ku, Tokyo 105-8525, Japan, *Tel:* +81 3 5470 7113, *Fax:* +81 3 5470 7157, *Email:* hakuyu@ml1.sinanen.co.jp
Showa Yokkaichi Sekiyu K.K., Tokyo Building, 7-3 Marunouchi 2-chome, Chiyoda-ku, Tokyo 100, Japan, *Tel:* +81 3 3215 1643, *Fax:* +81 3 3215 1869
SK Energy Asia Private Ltd, 8th Floor Yamato Seimei Building, 1-17 Uchisaiwicho 1-chome, Chiyoda-ku, Tokyo 100-0011, Japan, *Tel:* +81 3 3591 0533, *Fax:* +81 3 3591 7487, *Email:* leehk@skenergy.com, *Website:* www.skenergy.com
Sumitomo Corp., Harumi Island, Triton Square, Office Tower Y, 8-11 Harumi 1-chome, Chuo-ku, Tokyo 104-8610, Japan, *Tel:* +81 3 51664458, *Fax:* +81 3 51666407, *Email:* ir@sumitomo.co.jp, *Website:* www.sumitomocorp.co.jp
Total France S.A., Total Marine Fuels, 51 Esplanade du General de Gaulle, F-92907 Paris la Defense Cedex 10, France, *Tel:* +33 1 4135 2755, *Fax:* +33 1 4197 0291, *Email:* marine.fuels@total.com, *Website:* www.marinefuels.total.com

Waste Reception Facilities: Available

Towage: Six tugs available; two of 4000 hp, three of 3600 hp and one of 3200 hp

Repair & Maintenance: Mitsui (Ichihara) Engineering & Shipbuilding Co. Ltd, 1 Yawatakaigandori, Ichihara 290-8601, Chiba Pref., Japan, *Tel:* +81 43 641 1122, *Fax:* +81 43 643 1002, *Email:* prdept@mes.co.jp, *Website:* www.mes.co.jp Repair facilities Available at Chiba

Medical Facilities: Available

Airport: Narita, 70 km

Railway: Uchibo Line, approx 2 km

Lloyd's Agent: Cornes & Co. Ltd, 273 Yamashita-cho, Naka-ku, Yokohama 231-0023, Kanagawa Pref., Japan, *Tel:* +81 45 201 8537, *Fax:* +81 45 212 3105, *Email:* survey@ykh.cornes.co.jp, *Website:* www.cornes.co.jp

KITA

harbour area, see under Wakkanai

KOBE

Lat 34° 41' N; Long 135° 12' E.

Admiralty Chart: JP101A, JP101B		**Admiralty Pilot:** 42B	
Time Zone: GMT +9 h		**UNCTAD Locode:** JP UKB	

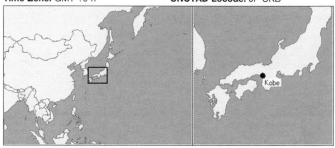

Principal Facilities:

P Q Y G C R L B D T A

Authority: Port & Urban Projects Bureau, Kobe City Government, 5-1 Kano-cho 6-chome, Chuo-ku, Kobe 650-8570, Hyogo Pref., Japan, *Tel:* +81 78 322 5670, *Fax:* +81 78 322 6121, *Email:* kobeport@office.city.kobe.jp, *Website:* www.city.kobe.jp

Officials: General Director: Tomohiro Yamamoto, *Email:* tomohiro_yamamoto@office.city.kobe.jp.

Port Security: ISPS compliant. Container Security Initiative (CSI) designated port

Approach: The approach to the port is via Channel, Tomogashima Strait, Osaka Bay and/or Seto Inland Sea with heavy traffic of coastal and fishing vessels as well as large size vessels. Kobe Nishi Passage, 960 m long, 200 m width, 11 m max draft. Kobe Chuo Passage, 3850 m long, 400 m width, 13-15 m max draft. Shinko Passage, 1460 m long, 350 m width, 11.4 m max draft and Higashi-Kobe Passage, 650 m long, 300 m width, 8 m max draft
All vessels over 15 000 gt and all tankers over 1000 gt passing through Fairway No.3 are expected to navigate under the directions issued by Kobe Signal Station
Vessels normally anchor off Wada Misaki for quarantine (container vessels can enter 24 h). Sailing possible 24 h

Anchorage: Anchorage L-1 in pos 34° 37' 13" N; 135° 10' 50" E
Anchorage L-2 in pos 34° 36' 50" N; 135° 11' 20" E
Anchorage L-3 in pos 34° 37' 28" N; 135° 15' 17" E
Anchorage L-4 in pos 34° 37' 37" N; 135° 16' 02" E
Anchorage L-5 in pos 34° 37' 47" N; 135° 17' 14" E
Anchorage L-6 in pos 34° 37' 56" N; 135° 18' 01" E
Anchorage M-1 in pos 34° 36' 54" N; 135° 12' 07" E
Anchorage M-2 in pos 34° 36' 59" N; 135° 12' 37" E
Anchorage M-3 in pos 34° 37' 04" N; 135° 13' 07" E
Anchorage M-4 in pos 34° 37' 08" N; 135° 13' 37" E
Anchorage M-5 in pos 34° 37' 13" N; 135° 14' 07" E
Anchorage M-6 in pos 34° 37' 18" N; 135° 14' 38" E
Anchorage M-7 in pos 34° 38' 24" N; 135° 16' 52" E
Anchorage M-8 in pos 34° 38' 29" N; 135° 17' 27" E
Anchorage M-9 in pos 34° 38' 34" N; 135° 18' 02" E
Anchorage M-10 in pos 34° 38' 04" N; 135° 15' 12" E
Anchorage M-11 in pos 34° 38' 10" N; 135° 15' 51" E
Anchorage S-1 in pos 34° 37' 17" N; 135° 11' 31" E
Anchorage S-2 in pos 34° 37' 19" N; 135° 11' 57" E
Anchorage S-3 in pos 34° 37' 21" N; 135° 12' 22" E
Anchorage S-4 in pos 34° 37' 23" N; 135° 12' 49" E
Anchorage S-5 in pos 34° 37' 26" N; 135° 13' 15" E
Anchorage S-6 in pos 34° 38' 59" N; 135° 17' 55" E

Pilotage: Osaka Bay Pilot District and Inland Sea pilotage is compulsory for vessels exceeding 10 000 gt navigating to or from Kobe. Pilots available from Osaka Bay Pilots Association, Tel: +81 78 321 7411. Pilot available at quarantine anchorage through Hanshin Pilot Association, Tel: +81 78 391 5032. Inland Sea Pilot Association, Tel: +81 78 391 7191

Radio Frequency: Kobe Port Radio, 24 h service, calling on VHF Channel 16, working on Channels 11, 12, 18 and 20

Weather: Winds ENE. Dense fog about ten days in a year. Rainy season June and July. Typhoon season, July-October

Tides: Tidal currents within the harbour are moderate in speed, less than one knot through a year. Tidal range 1.55 m, 1.54 m MHWL, minus 0.01 m MLWL, 0.88 m MSL

Traffic: 2006, 95 499 000 t of cargo handled

Maximum Vessel Dimensions: Inner harbour: 100 000 max dwt fully laden, 15 m max draft

Principal Imports and Exports: Imports: Chemicals, Grain, Ore, Petroleum, Refrigerated cargo, Sundry goods. Exports: Chemicals, Machinery & transport equipment, Steel products, Sundry goods.

Working Hours: 24 h/day

Accommodation:

Name	Length (m)	Depth (m)	Remarks
Public Wharves			
Port Island Berths			
PC13	350	15	Container berth. Terminal area of 92 700 m2
PC14	350	15	Container berth. Terminal area of 122 500 m2
PC15	350	15	Container berth. Terminal area of 128 500 m2
PC 16	350	15	Container berth. Terminal area of 128 500 m2
PC17	350	15	Container berth. Terminal area of 122 500 m2
PC18	350	15	Container berth. Terminal area of 134 300 m2
PI-D	300	12	Container berth. Terminal area of 78 653 m2
PI-E	230	12	Container berth. Terminal area of 20 700 m2
PI-F	230	12	Container berth. Terminal area of 20 700 m2
PI-G	240	12	Container berth. Terminal area of 21 600 m2
PI-I	240	12	Container berth. Terminal area of 21 190 m2
PI-J	240	12	Container berth. Terminal area of 26 400 m2
PI-L	130	7.5	Container berth. Terminal area of 26 600 m2
PL1	200	10	Conventional liner berth. Terminal area of 18 000 m2
PL2	200	10	Conventional liner berth. Terminal area of 18 000 m2
PL3	200	10	Conventional liner berth. Terminal area of 20 859 m2
PL4	200	10	Conventional liner berth. Terminal area of 17 552 m2
PL5	200	10	Conventional liner berth. Terminal area of 18 000 m2
PL6	200	10	Conventional liner berth. Terminal area of 18 000 m2
PL7	200	10	Conventional liner berth. Terminal area of 18 000 m2
PL8	200	10	Conventional liner berth. Terminal area of 18 174 m2
PL9	200	10	Conventional liner berth. Terminal area of 18 040 m2
PL10	200	10	Conventional liner berth. Terminal area of 22 320 m2
PL11	200	10	Conventional liner berth. Terminal area of 18 000 m2
PL12	200	10	Conventional liner berth. Terminal area of 18 000 m2
PL13	200	10	Conventional liner berth. Terminal area of 18 000 m2
PL14	200	10	Conventional liner berth. Terminal area of 18 000 m2
PL15	200	10	Conventional liner berth. Terminal area of 18 400 m2
Rokko Island Berths			
RC1	350	13	Container berth. Terminal area of 122 500 m2
RC2	350	13	Container berth. Terminal area of 122 500 m2
RC3	350	14	Container berth. Terminal area of 122 930 m2
RC4	350	14	Container berth. Terminal area of 122 070 m2
RC5	350	14	Container berth. Terminal area of 122 500 m2
RC6	350	14	Container berth. Terminal area of 122 500 m2
RC7	350	14	Container berth. Terminal area of 122 500 m2
G-I	555	10	Container berth. Terminal area of 38 850 m2
J-K	370	10	Container berth. Terminal area of 26 181 m2
W-Z	960	12	Container berth. Terminal area of 67 368 m2
RL1	300	13	Container berth. Terminal area of 57 069 m2
RL2	300	13	Container berth. Terminal area of 50 100 m2
S-BC	350	13	Container berth. Terminal area of 55 393 m2

Name	Length (m)	Depth (m)	Remarks
F1	193	7.5	Ferry. Terminal area of 17 390 m2
F2	266	9	Ferry. Terminal area of 24 920 m2
F3	238	8.5	Ferry. Terminal area of 22 690 m2
A	130	7.5	Domestic trade. Terminal area of 12 902 m2
B	162	4	Domestic trade. Terminal area of 11 180 m2
C	280	10	Foreign trade. Terminal area of 14 489 m2
D-F	555	10	Foreign trade. Terminal area of 38 105 m2
LM	370	10	Foreign trade. Terminal area of 25 900 m2
NO	260	7.5	Domestic trade. Terminal area of 11 736 m2
P	185	10	Foreign trade tramper. Terminal area of 10 143 m2
QR	370	10	Foreign trade tramper. Terminal area of 26 783 m2
S-V	740	10	Foreign trade tramper. Terminal area of 54 110 m2
S-A	180	7.5	Domestic trade. Terminal area of 32 113 m2
Shinko Piers			
No.1 (W)	366	9.1	Conventional & cruise
No.1 (E)	366	9.1	Conventional & cruise
No.1 (S)	105	9.1	Conventional & cruise
No.2 (W)	366	9.1	Conventional
No.2 (E)	354	9.1	Conventional
No.2 (S)	105	9.1	Conventional
No.3 (W)	352	9.1	Ferry & conventional
No.3 (E)	372	9.1	Ferry & conventional
No.3 (S)	105	9.6	Ferry & conventional
No.4 (W)	589	10–12	Cruise & international ferry service
No.4 (E)	649	10–12	Cruise & international ferry service
Shinko Higashi Wharves			
S	220	10	Conventional
T	220	10	Conventional
U	170	10	Conventional
V	170	10	Conventional
W	280	12	Conventional
X	280	12	Conventional
Y	170	10	Conventional
Z	170	10	Conventional
N1, N2	300	7.5	Domestic trade
Maya Wharves			
A	185	10	Conventional & semi container
B	185	10	Conventional & semi container
C	240	12	Conventional & semi container
D	240	12	Conventional & semi container
E	240	12	Conventional & semi container
F	240	12	Conventional
G	390	12	Conventional
H	207	12	Conventional
I	330	12	Conventional
J	330	12	Conventional
Hyogo Wharves			
A	90	7.2	Timber, vegetables & fruit etc
B	90	7.2	Timber, vegetables & fruit etc
C	140	7.2	Timber, vegetables & fruit etc
D	150	7.2	Timber, vegetables & fruit etc
E	150	7.2	Timber, vegetables & fruit etc
F	210	9	Timber, vegetables & fruit etc
G	210	9	Timber, vegetables & fruit etc
H	214	9	Timber, vegetables & fruit etc
I	259	9	Timber, vegetables & fruit etc
J	170	7.5	Timber, vegetables & fruit etc
K	90	7.5	Timber, vegetables & fruit etc
Naka Piers			
W	471	5.5–9	Passenger & cruise vessels
E	220	9	Passenger & cruise vessels
S	115	9	Passenger & cruise vessels
Eastern Domestic Trade Wharves			
W	440	5.5	Domestic trade cargoes
E	500	6	Domestic trade cargoes
NE	625	5.5	Domestic trade cargoes
N	360	5.5	Domestic trade cargoes
Suma Harbor			
E	90	5.5	Domestic trade cargoes
S	180	5.5	Domestic trade cargoes
Takahama Quay	279	5.5–7	Passenger & cruise vessels
Private Wharves			
Mitsui Pier (E)	185	10	Max 10 000 gt
Mitsui Pier (W)	177	10	Max 10 000 gt

Key to Principal Facilities:—

A=Airport	**C**=Containers	**G**=General Cargo	**P**=Petroleum	**R**=Ro/Ro	**Y**=Dry Bulk
B=Bunkers	**D**=Dry Dock	**L**=Cruise	**Q**=Other Liquid Bulk	**T**=Towage (where available from port)	

Name	Length (m)	Depth (m)	Remarks
Kobe Steel Ltd-KS No's 1-5	1509	9.5–13	Consists of 5 berths. Max 10 000 gt. Ore
Zenno Silo Dolphin	160	12.5	Max 50 000 gt. Bulk grain berth
Tomen Silo Dolphin	160	12.5	Max 50 000 gt. Bulk grain berth
Showa Sangyo Dolphin	24	12.5	Max 50 000 gt. Bulk grain berth
Mitsubishi Shoji Dolphin	123	9–12.5	See [1] below
Hanshin Silo Dolphin	246	12.5	Max 50 000 gt. Bulk grain berth
Nippon Port Sangyo Dolphin	298	10.5	Max 1 x 15 000 & 1 x 5000 gt
Ube Kosan Dolphin	60	6	Max 5000 gt
Osaka Cement Dolphin	69	7.5	Max 3000 gt
Tokuyama Soda Dolphin	8	5	Max 3000 gt
Kohnan Futo Dolphin	214	12.5	Max 60 000 gt. Bulk grain berth
Narao Fishery Association	144	5	Consists of 2 berths. Max 700 gt
Nada Wharf	145	9.8–10	Max 1 x 2000 & 1 x 10 000 gt
Nippon Gatx	100	9.5	Max 20 000 gt
Nishimura Shoten Dolphin	23	7.5	Max 1500 gt
Kanematsu Oil Dolphin	20	8	Max 5000 gt
Cosmo Oil Dolphin	79	8–9	Consists of 3 berths, max 2000-5000 gt
Showa Shell Dolphin	600	9–12	Consists of 3 berths, max 3000-10 000 gt
Mitsubishi Oil Dolphin	100	8	Consists of 3 berths, max 1000-4000 gt
Kawasaki Heavy Industries Ltd	791	5–9	Consists of 7 berths, max 2000-88 000 gt
Mitsubishi Heavy Industries Ltd	2446	6–9	Consists of 10 berths, max 3200-150 000 gt

[1]*Mitsubishi Shoji Dolphin:* Max 1 x 50 000 & 1 x 10 000 gt. Liquid gas terminal. Vessels able to berth up to 123 m in length. Discharging is by two unloading arms of 1000 t/h per unit cap

Storage: 71 municipal transit sheds of 266 220 m2. General cargo warehouses of 936 127 m2. Dangerous cargo warehouses of 152 980 m2. Silos of 814 102 m3. Open warehouses of 82 033 m2

Location	Cold (m3)
Kobe	1040000

Mechanical Handling Equipment: 49 gantry cranes of 30.5 t to 40 t cap are provided on container and cargo berths at Port Island, Maya Pier and Rokko Island. Also various types of shore cranes up to 43.2 t cap are available

Cargo Worked: 166 000 t of foreign trade and 391 000 t of domestic trade per working day

Bunkering: Most grades of domestic and bonded oil are available. Delivery from barge or alongside, and for vessel berthing at container berths C1-5 and C7-9 of Port Island, available directly from their tanks at Port Island by pipeline system
Hanwa Co. Ltd, 2nd Floor, Finland House, 56 Haymarket, London SW1Y 4RN, United Kingdom, *Tel:* +44 20 7839 4448, *Fax:* +44 20 7839 3994, *Email:* orito@hanwa.co.uk
Hikawa Shoji Kaisha Ltd, 26-2 Shinkawa NS Building 1-chome, Shinkawa, Chuo-ku, Tokyo 104, Japan, *Tel:* +81 3 5776 6858, *Fax:* +81 3 5541 3274
Idemitsu Kosan Co. Ltd, 1-1 Marunochi, 3-Chome, Chiyoda-ku, Tokyo 100-8321, Japan, *Tel:* +81 3 3213 3138, *Fax:* +81 3 3213 1145, *Email:* tohru.takamura@si.idemitsu.co.jp, *Website:* www.idemitsu.co.jp
KG Int Petroleum Ltd, Shiba Park Building, 241 Shiba Koen, Minato-ku, Tokyo 105, Japan, *Tel:* +81 3 3578 4551, *Fax:* +81 3 3578 4550
Kamei Corp., 1-6-1 Otemachi, Chiyoda-ku, Tokyo 100-0004, Japan, *Tel:* +81 3 3286 6234, *Fax:* +81 3 3286 6249, *Email:* bunker@kamei.co.jp
Kyodo Oil Co. Ltd, 11-2 Nagata-cho 2-chome, Chiyoda-ku, Tokyo, Japan, *Tel:* +81 3 3505 8241, *Fax:* +81 3 3505 8697
Marubeni Petroleum Co. Ltd, Marubeni International Petroleum Singapore Co. Ltd, c/o Marubeni Corporation, 4-2 Ohtemachi 1-chome, Chiyoda-ku, Tokyo 100-8088, Japan, *Tel:* +81 3 3282 3920, *Fax:* +81 3 3282 3950, *Email:* TOKB554@marubenicorp.com, *Website:* www.marubeni.co.jp
MC Marine and Bunkering Inc., 8th Floor, Uchisaiwai-cho Dai Building, 3-3 Uchisaiwai-cho 1-chome, Chiyoda-ku, Tokyo 100-0011, Japan, *Tel:* +81 3 5251 2575, *Fax:* +81 3 5251 2583
Mitsui & Co. Petroleum Ltd, 2-1, Ohtemachi 1-chome, Chiyoda-ku, Tokyo 100-0004, Japan, *Tel:* +81 3 3285 6905, *Fax:* +81 3 3285 9811, *Email:* tkzph@dg.mitsui.com, *Website:* www.mitsui.co.jp
Nittetsu Shoij Co. Ltd, 5-7 Kameido 1-chome, Koto-ku, Tokyo 136, Japan, *Tel:* +81 3 5627 2157, *Fax:* +81 3 5627 2192
Setouchi Network, 4-20 Hasihama 1-chome, Imabari 799-2112, Ehime Pref., Japan, *Tel:* +81 898 430041, *Fax:* +81 898 430046, *Email:* secjpn@dokidoki.ne.jp
Sumitomo Corp., Harumi Island, Triton Square, Office Tower Y, 8-11 Harumi 1-chome, Chuo-ku, Tokyo 104-8610, Japan, *Tel:* +81 3 51664458, *Fax:* +81 3 51666407, *Email:* ir@sumitomo.co.jp, *Website:* www.sumitomocorp.co.jp

Towage: Harbour tugs available up to 3600 hp

Repair & Maintenance: Kawasaki Shipbuilding Corp, 1-1 Higashi-Kawasaki-cho 3-chome, Chuo-ku, Kobe 650-8670, Hyogo Pref., Japan, *Tel:* +81 78 682 5501, *Fax:* +81 78 682 5514, *Website:* www.kawasakikosen.co.jp Three repair docks: No.2 113 m x 20 m, No.3 250 m x 43.2 m, No.4 215 m x 33.5 m
Marine Enterprise Co. Ltd, 1-1 Minatoshima-Nakamachi 5-chome, Chuo-ku, Kobe 650-0046, Hyogo Pref., Japan, *Tel:* +81 78 302 0171, *Fax:* +81 78 302 0177, *Email:* office@marient.co.jp, *Website:* www.marient.co.jp Engine repairs and in-situ machining

Seaman Missions: The Seamans Mission, Motomachi Dori 3-1-16, Chuo-Ku, Kobe 650-0022, Hyogo Pref., Japan, *Tel:* +81 78 331 1696, *Fax:* +81 78 331 1612, *Email:* mtskobe@sanynet.ne.jp

Ship Chandlers: Ashland Japan Co. Ltd, 6 Fukaehamamachi, Higashinada-ku, Kobe 658-0023, Hyogo Pref., Japan, *Tel:* +81 78 436 8771, *Fax:* +81 78 411 1644, *Email:* drewmarinekobe@ashland.com
Fuji Trading Co. Ltd, 6 Fukaehamamachi, Higashinada-ku, Kobe 658-0023, Hyogo Pref., Japan, *Tel:* +81 78 413 2611, *Fax:* +81 78 451 3768, *Email:* supplykb@fujitrading.co.jp, *Website:* www.fujitrading.co.jp
Kobe Ship Chandler Co. Ltd, 1-2 4-chome Higashikawasaki-Cho, Chuo-ku, Kobe 650-0044, Hyogo Pref., Japan, *Tel:* +81 78 681 2791, *Fax:* +81 78 681 2777, *Email:* ueno@kobe-shipchandler.com
Meidi-Ya Co. Ltd, 90 Fukaehamamachi, Higashinada-ku, Kobe 658-0023, Hyogo Pref., Japan, *Tel:* +81 78 451 0111, *Fax:* +81 78 451 0259, *Email:* shipkobe-sales@mailsv.meidi-ya.co.jp
Showa Marine Industry Co Ltd, 6th Floor, Sanshiport Building, 14-1, Hachiman-dori 3-chome, Chuo-ku, Kobe 651-0085, Hyogo Pref., Japan, *Tel:* +81 78 271 8830, *Fax:* +81 78 271 8860, *Email:* kobe@showa-marine.co.jp, *Website:* www.showa-marine.co.jp

Shipping Agents: Inchcape Shipping Services (ISS), Inchcape Shipping Services (Japan) Ltd, Kenryu Building, 6 Kaigan-dori, Chuo-ku, Kobe 650-0024, Hyogo Pref., Japan, *Tel:* +81 78 391 3046, *Fax:* +81 78 391 3105, *Email:* iss.kobe@iss-shipping.com, *Website:* www.iss-shipping.com
Kamigumi Co. Ltd, Harbour Trans Business, 1-11, 4-chome, Hamabe-dori Chuo-ku, Kobe 651-0083, Hyogo Pref., Japan, *Tel:* +81 78 271 5156, *Fax:* +81 78 271 5218, *Email:* butsuryu_exp@kamigumi.co.jp, *Website:* www.kamigumi.co.jp
Mitsui-Soko Co. Ltd, Kansai Branch 6-2-16, Hamabedori, Chuo-ku, Kobe, Hyogo Pref., Japan, *Tel:* +81 78 232 2210, *Fax:* +81 78 232 2350, *Email:* ogita@mitsui.soko.co.jp
A.P. Moller-Maersk Group, Maersk K.K., 4 Nishi 6-chome Koyo-cho, Higashinada-ku, Kobe 658-0033, Hyogo Pref., Japan, *Tel:* +81 78 857 0251, *Fax:* +81 78 857 1964, *Website:* www.maerskline.com
Nihon Hoso Unyu Co. Ltd, 11-1 Shinko-cho, Chuo-ku, Kobe 650-0041, Hyogo Pref., Japan, *Tel:* +81 78 391 0202, *Fax:* +81 78 392 0994, *Website:* www.nhu.co.jp
Sankyu Inc., Sankyu Kaimura Building, 24-5 Kaigan-dori 1-chome, Chuo-ku, Kobe 650, Hyogo Pref., Japan, *Tel:* +81 78 333 3931, *Fax:* +81 78 332 5259, *Website:* www.sankyu.co.jp
Seven Star Co. Ltd, c/o Nickle & Lyons, 6-6 Hatoba-cho, Chuo-ku, Kobe 650-0042, Hyogo Pref., Japan, *Tel:* +81 78 341 7403, *Fax:* +81 78 361 8353
Sumitomo Warehouse Co. Ltd, 6-4 Hatobacho, Chuo-Ku, Kobe 651-0042, Hyogo Pref., Japan, *Tel:* +81 78 371 1219, *Fax:* +81 78 371 1259, *Email:* 30016.bx@sumitomo-soko.co.jp

Surveyors: Bureau Veritas, Eikoh Building, 6th Floor, 93 Edo Machi, Chuo-ku, Kobe 650-0033, Hyogo Pref., Japan, *Tel:* +81 78 331 9131, *Fax:* +81 78 331 3395, *Website:* www.bureauveritas.com
Cornes & Co. Ltd, Meikai Building, 32 Akashi-machi, Chuo-ku, Kobe 650-0037, Hyogo Pref., Japan, *Tel:* +81 78 332 3421, *Fax:* +81 78 332 3070, *Email:* survey@cornes.co.jp, *Website:* www.cornes.co.jp
Det Norske Veritas A/S, Sannomiya Chuo Building, 9th Floor, 4-2-20 Goko-dori, Chuo-ku, Kobe 651-0087, Hyogo Pref., Japan, *Tel:* +81 78 291 1303, *Fax:* +81 78 291 1330, *Email:* arne.ketil.kyrkjebo@dnv.com, *Website:* www.dnv.com
Germanischer Lloyd, Room 301-2, 3rd Floor, Nantai Building, 9-20 Sannomiya-cho 3-chome, Chuo-ku, Kobe 650-0021, Hyogo Pref., Japan, *Tel:* +81 78 322 0500, *Fax:* +81 78 322 0700, *Email:* gl-kobe@gl-group.com, *Website:* www.gl-group.com
Hellenic Register of Shipping, Navtech Maritime Ltd, Seikatsu-Yohin Shinko Center, 3rd Floor, 14-1 Shinko-cho, Chuo-ku, Kobe 650-0041, Hyogo Pref., Japan, *Tel:* +81 78 391 6180, *Fax:* +81 78 391 6189, *Email:* navtech@ka2.so-net.ne.jp
Korean Register of Shipping, Avenue Goko B/D, 8th Floor Room 802, 2-9 Goko-dori 4-chome, Chuo-ku, Kobe, Hyogo Pref., Japan, *Tel:* +81 78 221 7693, *Fax:* +81 78 232 1385, *Email:* kr-kob@krs.co.kr, *Website:* www.krs.co.kr
Sekiyu Kentei Sha, Motomachl Plaza Building, 9-1, 2 Chome Motomachl-dori, Chuo-ku, Kobe, Hyogo Pref., Japan, *Tel:* +81 78 392 1911, *Fax:* +81 78 391 6287
Societe Generale de Surveillance (SGS), SGS Far East Ltd, 8th Floor, Sannomiya Kokusai Building, 2-1-30 Hamabe-Dori, Chuo-ku, Kobe 651, Hyogo Pref., Japan, *Tel:* +81 78 251 6211, *Fax:* +81 78 231 3731, *Website:* www.sgs.com

Medical Facilities: All kinds of medical facilities are available

Airport: Osaka International, 30 km

Lloyd's Agent: Cornes & Co. Ltd, Meikai Building, 32 Akashi-machi, Chuo-ku, Kobe 650-0037, Hyogo Pref., Japan, *Tel:* +81 78 332 3421, *Fax:* +81 78 332 3070, *Email:* survey@kobe.cornes.co.jp, *Website:* www.cornes.co.jp

KOCHI

Lat 33° 31' N; Long 133° 34' E.

Admiralty Chart: JP108	Admiralty Pilot: 42A
Time Zone: GMT +9 h	UNCTAD Locode: JP KCZ

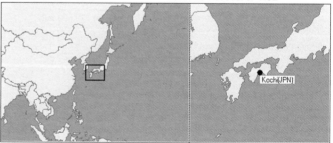

Principal Facilities:

P		Y	G	C	R		B		T	A

Authority: Kochi Prefectural Government, Ports & Harbors Division, 1-2-20 Marunouchi, Kochi 780-8570, Kochi Pref., Japan, *Tel:* +81 88 823 9888, *Fax:* +81 88 823 9657, *Email:* 175201@ken.pref.kochi.lg.jp, *Website:* www.pref.kochi.jp

Officials: Managing Director: Hiroshi Yamanaka, *Email:* hiroshi_yamanaka@ken3.pref.kochi.lg.jp.
Harbour Master: Toyohiko Ito, *Tel:* +81 88 832 7111, *Email:* kouchi-kanri@kaiho.mlit.go.jp.

Port Security: ISPS compliant

Approach: Kochi Port: The approach to Kochi Port is via Tosa Bay and through the narrow and crooked Urado Bay. The main channel in Urado Bay is 7.6 km long with width 120-370 m and depth 4.5-7.5 m. Draught limitation in the port channel is 7.5 m at HW
Kochi New Port: The approach to the New Port is via Tosa Bay. The main channel is 2.0 km long with width 300 m and depth 12 m. Draught limitation in the port channel is 12 m at HW

Anchorage: Anchorage 179 ha in area

Pilotage: Not compulsory. Unauthorised pilot available in pos 33° 29' 30" N; 133° 36' E, Tel: +81 88 831 5151

Radio Frequency: VHF Channels 16 and 12

Weather: Typhoon season, July to October

Tides: Tidal range 1.91 m max, -0.25 m min

Maximum Vessel Dimensions: 55 000 dwt, 12 m draft

Principal Imports and Exports: Imports: Coal, Timber. Exports: Cement.

Working Hours: 24 h/day

Accommodation:

Name	Length (m)	Depth (m)	Remarks
Kochi			See [1] below
Minatomachi			
Wharf No.1		6.5	Max 3000 dwt
Wharf No.2	170	6.5	Max 3000 dwt
Ushioe			
Wharf No.4	390	7.5	Max 5000 dwt
Wharf No.5	130	7.5	Max 5000 dwt
Wharf No.6	260	7.5	Max 5000 dwt
Wharf No.7	260	7.5	Max 5000 dwt
Wharf No.8	180	4.5	Max 5000 dwt
Wakamatsu			
Wharf No.1	733	3	
Kokadai			
Wharf No.1	651	4	Max 600 dwt
Wharf No.2	110	4	Max 600 dwt
Wharf No.3	140	5	Max 700 gt
Wharf No.4	55	5.5	Max 300 gt
Kita-Tanasuka			
Wharf No.1	160	6	Max 3000 dwt
Wharf No.2	270	4	Max 600 dwt
Niida			
Wharf No.1	130	7.5	Max 5000 dwt
Wharf No.2	140	5	Max 1000 dwt
Wharf No.3	300	4.5	Max 700 dwt
Misato			
Wharf No.1	280	14	Max 55 000 dwt
Wharf No.2	240	12	Max 30 000 dwt
Wharf No.3	190	11	Max 18 000 dwt
Wharf No.4	260	9	Max 30 000 gt
Wharf No.5	240	8	Max 6000 gt
Wharf No.6	180	7.5	Max 7000 gt
Wharf No.7	130	7.5	Max 5000 dwt

[1]*Kochi:* Bulk facilities: Cement companies have several dolphin berths, 6 m to 7.5 m depth for vessels up to 5000 dwt for loading and unloading cement and limestone
Tanker facilities: Approx ten privately owned berths with 5 m max d, for coastal tankers up to 2000 dwt

Storage: Foreign Access Zone (FAZ) related site totalling 1.5 ha. Standard warehouse of 4000 m2, sheds (one-storied) of 3000 m2 and refrigerated warehouse (three stories) of 4500 m2

Mechanical Handling Equipment: One gantry crane of 30.5 t cap, one top lifter of 42 t cap (owned by Kochi Trade Service Co Ltd) and one ship loader of 1000 m3/h

Cargo Worked: 30 000 t of both foreign and domestic trade cargoes per working day

Bunkering: Domestic oil available. Bonded oil can be brought in by barge from Kobe or Shimotsu with advance notice

Waste Reception Facilities: Kochi Enterprise Co. Ltd, Kochi, Kochi Pref., Japan, *Tel:* +81 88 831 3132

Towage: Not compulsory but advisable. Two tugs available of 2200 hp

Repair & Maintenance: Shin Kochi Heavy Industries Shipbuilding, 4319, Shinzuki, Niida, Kochi 781-01, Kochi Pref., Japan, *Tel:* +81 88 847 1111, *Fax:* +81 88 847 4565 Repair facilities
Shin Yamamoto Shipbuilding Co. Ltd, 125 Tanezaki, Kochi, Kochi Pref., Japan, *Tel:* +81 88 847 0221, *Fax:* +81 88 847 0224 Repair facilities

Stevedoring Companies: Kochi Koun Co Ltd, 4700 Aza Shinko Niida, Kochi, Kochi Pref., Japan, *Tel:* +81 88 847 6881, *Fax:* +81 88 847 6882

Surveyors: Nippon Kaiji Kyokai, 7th Floor, Meiji Seimei Kochi Building, 2-2-34 Honmachi, Kochi 780-0870, Kochi Pref., Japan, *Tel:* +81 88 802 4823, *Fax:* +81 88 802 4824, *Email:* kc@classnk.or.jp, *Website:* www.classnk.or.jp

Medical Facilities: Available

Airport: Kochi, 14 km

Lloyd's Agent: Cornes & Co. Ltd, Meikai Building, 32 Akashi-machi, Chuo-ku, Kobe 650-0037, Hyogo Pref., Japan, *Tel:* +81 78 332 3421, *Fax:* +81 78 332 3070, *Email:* survey@kobe.cornes.co.jp, *Website:* www.cornes.co.jp

KOKURA

Lat 33° 54' N; Long 130° 54' E.

Admiralty Chart: JP1265		**Admiralty Pilot:** 42B
Time Zone: GMT +9 h		**UNCTAD Locode:** JP KOK

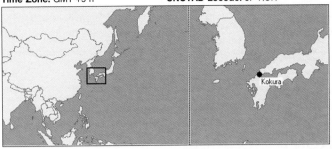

Principal Facilities:

P	Y	G	C	R		B		A

Authority: Kitakyushu Port & Harbor Bureau, 1-1 Jonai, Kitakyushu 803-8501, Fukuoka Pref., Japan, *Tel:* +81 93 321 5941, *Fax:* +81 93 582 1037, *Email:* kqport@kitaqport.or.jp, *Website:* www.kitaqport.or.jp

Officials: Director General: Kenichi Katayama.
Marketing Director: Hiroyuki Tagami, *Email:* hiroyuki_tagami01@city.kitakyushu.lg.jp.
Sales Director: Tetsuji Hashimoto.

Port Security: ISPS compliant

Approach: This district is situated in the middle of Kitakyushu port. Hiagari fairway is 460 m wide and 12 m deep. Draught limitation of 9.14 to 10 m in the channel

Pilotage: Compulsory for vessels over 3000 gt and vessels with hazardous materials over 300 gt

Tides: Tidal range 1.84 m

Traffic: 2006, 109 723 953 t of cargo handled, 469 000 TEU's (includes ports of Moji, Tobata, Wakamatsu & Yawata)

Accommodation:

Name	Length (m)	Depth (m)	Draught (m)	Remarks
Kokura				
Sumitomo West No.1	350	11		Max 65 000 gt. Two 1000 t/h pipelines
Sumitomo Murasaki Kawajiri	225	10		Max 20 000 gt
Sunatsu East Wharf	182	6.5		Max 7000 gt. Cement, steel & stones. Oil discharge facilities
Sunatsu West Wharf	366	8.2		Max 7000 gt. Steel & general cargo
Hiagari Wharf No's 3, 4 & 5	585	10		Max 14 000 gt. Steel
Hiagari Wharf No's 6 & 7	420	11–12		See [1] below
Asano Wharf No's 1 & 2	239	7.5		
Kanematsu Old Dolphin		8	6.5	170 m max loa
Kanematsu LPG Dolphin		7	6.3	106 m max loa

[1]*Hiagari Wharf No's 6 & 7:* Container terminal operated by Higari Container Wharf Co Ltd., Tel: +81 93 583 7788, Fax: +81 93 592 8803
Total terminal area of 70 000 m2

Storage: There is a timber pool of 118 491 m2 and a timber storage area totalling 7013 m2, 14 warehouses of 13 911 m2, 16 transit sheds of 24 494 m2 and 8 open stock yards of 77 073 m2

Mechanical Handling Equipment:

Location	Type	Capacity (t)	Qty
Sumitomo Murasaki Kawajiri	Mult-purp. Cranes	10	3
Sunatsu West Wharf	Mult-purp. Cranes	10	3
Hiagari Wharf No's 6 & 7	Mult-purp. Cranes		1
Hiagari Wharf No's 6 & 7	Container Cranes		2
Hiagari Wharf No's 6 & 7	Straddle Carriers		3

Bunkering: Hanwa Co. Ltd, 2nd Floor, Finland House, 56 Haymarket, London SW1Y 4RN, United Kingdom, *Tel:* +44 20 7839 4448, *Fax:* +44 20 7839 3994, *Email:* orito@hanwa.co.uk
Hikawa Shoji Kaisha Ltd, 26-2 Shinkawa NS Building 1-chome, Shinkawa, Chuo-ku, Tokyo 104, Japan, *Tel:* +81 3 5776 6858, *Fax:* +81 3 5541 3274
Idemitsu Kosan Co. Ltd, 1-1 Marunochi, 3-Chome, Chiyoda-ku, Tokyo 100-8321, Japan, *Tel:* +81 3 3213 3138, *Fax:* +81 3 3213 1145, *Email:* tohru.takamura@si.idemitsu.co.jp, *Website:* www.idemitsu.co.jp
KG Int Petroleum Ltd, Shiba Park Building, 241 Shiba Koen, Minato-ku, Tokyo 105, Japan, *Tel:* +81 3 3578 4551, *Fax:* +81 3 3578 4550
Marubeni Petroleum Co. Ltd, Marubeni International Petroleum Singapore Co. Ltd, c/o Marubeni Corporation, 4-2 Ohtemachi 1-chome, Chiyoda-ku, Tokyo 100-8088,

Japan, *Tel:* +81 3 3282 3920, *Fax:* +81 3 3282 3950, *Email:* TOKB554@marubenicorp.com, *Website:* www.marubeni.co.jp
MC Marine and Bunkering Inc., 8th Floor, Uchisaiwai-cho Dai Building, 3-3 Uchisaiwai-cho 1-chome, Chiyoda-ku, Tokyo 100-0011, Japan, *Tel:* +81 3 5251 2575, *Fax:* +81 3 5251 2583
Mitsui & Co. Petroleum Ltd, 2-1, Ohtemachi 1-chome, Chiyoda-ku, Tokyo 100-0004, Japan, *Tel:* +81 3 3285 6905, *Fax:* +81 3 3285 9811, *Email:* tkzph@dg.mitsui.com, *Website:* www.mitsui.co.jp
Nittetsu Shoij Co. Ltd, 5-7 Kameido 1-chome, Koto-ku, Tokyo 136, Japan, *Tel:* +81 3 5627 2157, *Fax:* +81 3 5627 2192

Towage: Tugs brought from Wakamatsu and Moji

Repair & Maintenance: Available from the shipbuilding yards and various repair shops

Airport: Kitakyushu Airport

Lloyd's Agent: Cornes & Co. Ltd, Meikai Building, 32 Akashi-machi, Chuo-ku, Kobe 650-0037, Hyogo Pref., Japan, *Tel:* +81 78 332 3421, *Fax:* +81 78 332 3070, *Email:* survey@kobe.cornes.co.jp, *Website:* www.cornes.co.jp

KOMATSUSHIMA

Lat 34° 0' N; Long 134° 36' E.

Admiralty Chart: JP150A, JP150C   **Admiralty Pilot:** 42B
Time Zone: GMT +9 h   **UNCTAD Locode:** JP KOM

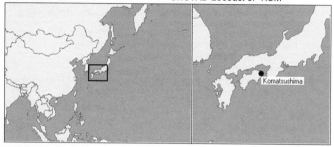

Principal Facilities:

P		Y	G	C	R		B		T	A	

Authority: Port & Harbour Section of Tokushima Prefecture, 1-1 Bandai-machi, Tokushima 770, Tokushima Pref., Japan, *Tel:* +81 886 212580, *Fax:* +81 886 232847, *Email:* kouwankuukouka@pref.tokushima.lg.jp, *Website:* www.pref.tokushima.jp

Port Security: ISPS compliant

Approach: The approach is via Kii channel. Vessels anchor at Shimotsu anchorage for quarantine. Inner harbour passage 1400 m long, 60-100 m width, 4 m depth. Shinko passage 550 m long, 100 m width, 9 m depth

Pilotage: Not compulsory. Harbour pilot available at outer anchorage

Weather: Typhoon season, July to October

Tides: Tidal range 2.4 m. 1.8 m MHWL, nil MLWL, 1 m MSL

Maximum Vessel Dimensions: 8.5 m max d

Principal Imports and Exports: Imports: Chemicals, Furniture, Paper, Raw materials. Exports: Chemicals.

Working Hours: 0800-1700, Sundays and holidays subject to negotiation

Accommodation: Komatsushima region is protected by breakwater of 1162 m and training wall. Good anchorage of sandy clay in depths to 4.5, 6.4 and 9 m. There are also two buoys with 6.5 m and 9 m depth for vessels of 5000 and 10 000 dwt at Komatsushima
Bulk facilities: One berth at Nokyo Shiryo for feedstuffs, for coastal vessels up to 3000 dwt
Tanker facilities: Mobil Oil Co operate one berth for coastal tankers up to 1500 dwt

Name	Length (m)	Depth (m)	Remarks
Komatsushima			See [1] below
Kanaiso Pier Wharf No.1	170	9	1 x 15 000 dwt
Kanaiso Pier Wharf No.2	200	9	1 x 20 000 dwt
Tokushima			
Tsuda Pier	185	10	1 x 20 000 dwt
Tsuda Pier Tsuda Wharf	270	5.5	3 x 2000 dwt
Tokushima Container Terminal (Okinosu)	130	7.4	Total area of 48 000 m2. One double-link type jib crane. 10 reefer points
Suehiro Pier	300	5.5	4 x 2000 dwt
Bandai Pier	207	5	3 x 2000 dwt
Private Wharves			See [2] below

[1]*Komatsushima:* The Akaishi Region has a 40 000 t berth and a 10 000 t berth
[2]*Private Wharves:* Komatsushima region: Five wharves and one dolphin, 5-7.5 m d for vessels up to 5000 gt handling cement and pulp
Tokushima region: Three berths, 4.5-7.5 m depth for exclusive use of coastal ferries up to 7500 gt

Storage: Sheds of 18 290 m2, warehouses of 29 543 m2, silos of 1690 m2, refrigerated warehouses of 33 465 m2. Also a timber pool of 330 000 m2 cap

Mechanical Handling Equipment:

Location	Type	Capacity (t)
Komatsushima	Mult-purp. Cranes	20

Cargo Worked: 8600 t of both foreign trade and domestic trade cargoes per working day

Bunkering: Bonded oil can be brought by barge from Kobe or Shimotsu

Towage: Two tugs available; one of 3000 hp and one of 2400 hp

Medical Facilities: Available

Airport: Tokushima Airport, 15 km

Lloyd's Agent: Cornes & Co. Ltd, Meikai Building, 32 Akashi-machi, Chuo-ku, Kobe 650-0037, Hyogo Pref., Japan, *Tel:* +81 78 332 3421, *Fax:* +81 78 332 3070, *Email:* survey@kobe.cornes.co.jp, *Website:* www.cornes.co.jp

KUDAMATSU

Lat 34° 0' N; Long 131° 51' E.

Admiralty Chart: 3153   **Admiralty Pilot:** 42B
Time Zone: GMT +9 h   **UNCTAD Locode:** JP KUD

Principal Facilities:

P		G			B		

Authority: Ports & Harbors Division, Yamaguchi Prefectural Government, 1-1 Takimachi, Yamaguchi 753-8501, Yamaguchi Pref., Japan, *Tel:* +81 83 933 3810, *Fax:* +81 83 933 3829, *Email:* a12900@pref.yamaguchi.lg.jp, *Website:* www.pref.yamaguchi.lg.jp

Officials: Shoichi Hayashi, *Tel:* +81 83 9332 340.

Port Security: ISPS compliant

Approach: No draft limitation in the channel

Pilotage: Not compulsory; Pilots are available at the quarantine anchorage for vessels requiring pilot services

Tides: Average tide 2.5 m

Accommodation:

Name	Length (m)	Depth (m)	Draught (m)	Remarks
Kudamatsu				
Nippon Petroleum East K-I Pier	300	19		Max 178 000 gt. 2 x 16" pipe lines
Nippon Petroleum West Pier	110	7	6.5	Max loa 100 m & 5000 gt
Toyo Kohan Wharf	200	9		Max 8000 gt
Kudamatsu No.2 Public Wharf	500		7.5–10	Consists of 2 berths

Storage: 1180 m2 of warehouse space available

Mechanical Handling Equipment:

Location	Type	Capacity (t)	Qty
Kudamatsu	Floating Cranes	100	1
Kudamatsu	Floating Cranes	150	1
Toyo Kohan Wharf	Shore Cranes	30	2

Bunkering: Cosmo Oil Co. Ltd, Toshiba Building, 1-1 Shibaura 1-chome, Minato-ku, Tokyo 105-8528, Japan, *Tel:* +81 3 3798 3156, *Fax:* +81 3 3798 3592, *Email:* masayuki_iijima@cosmo-oil.co.jp, *Website:* www.cosmo-oil.co.jp
Hanwa Co. Ltd, 2nd Floor, Finland House, 56 Haymarket, London SW1Y 4RN, United Kingdom, *Tel:* +44 20 7839 4448, *Fax:* +44 20 7839 3994, *Email:* orito@hanwa.co.uk
Hikawa Shoji Kaisha Ltd, 26-2 Shinkawa NS Building 1-chome, Shinkawa, Chuo-ku, Tokyo 104, Japan, *Tel:* +81 3 5776 6858, *Fax:* +81 3 5541 3274
Idemitsu Kosan Co. Ltd, 1-1 Marunochi, 3-Chome, Chiyoda-ku, Tokyo 100-8321, Japan, *Tel:* +81 3 3213 3138, *Fax:* +81 3 3213 1145, *Email:* tohru.takamura@si.idemitsu.co.jp, *Website:* www.idemitsu.co.jp
KG Int Petroleum Ltd, Shiba Park Building, 241 Shiba Koen, Minato-ku, Tokyo 105, Japan, *Tel:* +81 3 3578 4551, *Fax:* +81 3 3578 4550
Japan Energy Corp., 2-10-1, Toranomon, Minato-ku, Tokyo 105-8407, Japan, *Tel:* +81 3 5573 6100, *Fax:* +81 3 5573 6674, *Email:* yamano@j-energy.co.jp, *Website:* www.j-energy.co.jp
Kamei Corp., 1-6-1 Otemachi, Chiyoda-ku, Tokyo 100-0004, Japan, *Tel:* +81 3 3286 6234, *Fax:* +81 3 3286 6249, *Email:* bunker@kamei.co.jp
Kawasho Corp., World Trade Centre, 4-1 Hanamatsu-cho 2-chome, Minato-ku, Tokyo 105, Japan, *Tel:* +81 3 3435 3251
Kyodo Oil Co. Ltd, 11-2 Nagata-cho 2-chome, Chiyoda-ku, Tokyo, Japan, *Tel:* +81 3 3505 8241, *Fax:* +81 3 3505 8697
Marubeni Petroleum Co. Ltd, Marubeni International Petroleum Singapore Ltd, c/o Marubeni Corporation, 4-2 Ohtemachi 1-chome, Chiyoda-ku, Tokyo 100-8088, Japan, *Tel:* +81 3 3282 3920, *Fax:* +81 3 3282 3950, *Email:* TOKB554@marubenicorp.com, *Website:* www.marubeni.co.jp
MC Marine and Bunkering Inc., 8th Floor, Uchisaiwai-cho Dai Building, 3-3 Uchisaiwai-cho 1-chome, Chiyoda-ku, Tokyo 100-0011, Japan, *Tel:* +81 3 5251 2575, *Fax:* +81 3 5251 2583
Mitsui & Co. Petroleum Ltd, 2-1, Ohtemachi 1-chome, Chiyoda-ku, Tokyo 100-0004, Japan, *Tel:* +81 3 3285 6905, *Fax:* +81 3 3285 9811, *Email:* tkzph@dg.mitsui.co.jp, *Website:* www.mitsui.co.jp

Nissho Iwai Corp., 4-4 Akasaka 2-chome, Minato-ku, Tokyo, Japan, *Tel:* +81 3 35882111

Nittetsu Shoij Co. Ltd, 5-7 Kameido 1-chome, Koto-ku, Tokyo 136, Japan, *Tel:* +81 3 5627 2157, *Fax:* +81 3 5627 2192

Shinagawa Fuel Co. Ltd, New Pier Takeshiba North Tower, 8th Floor, 1-11-1 Kaigan, Minato-ku, Tokyo 105-8525, Japan, *Tel:* +81 3 5470 7113, *Fax:* +81 3 5470 7157, *Email:* hakuyu@ml1.sinanen.co.jp

Sigma Foreign Service (Panama) S.A., 2-25 Aikawai, Tempaku-ku, Nagoya 468-0836, Aichi Pref., Japan, *Tel:* +81 52 896 1510, *Fax:* +81 52 896 7703

Sumitomo Corp., Harumi Island, Triton Square, Office Tower Y, 8-11 Harumi 1-chome, Chuo-ku, Tokyo 104-8610, Japan, *Tel:* +81 3 51664458, *Fax:* +81 3 51666407, *Email:* ir@sumitomo.co.jp, *Website:* www.sumitomocorp.co.jp

Repair & Maintenance: Small repairs can be undertaken

Lloyd's Agent: Cornes & Co. Ltd, Meikai Building, 32 Akashi-machi, Chuo-ku, Kobe 650-0037, Hyogo Pref., Japan, *Tel:* +81 78 332 3421, *Fax:* +81 78 332 3070, *Email:* survey@kobe.cornes.co.jp, *Website:* www.cornes.co.jp

KURE

Lat 34° 14' N; Long 132° 32' E.

Admiralty Chart: 3472	**Admiralty Pilot:** 42A
Time Zone: GMT +9 h	**UNCTAD Locode:** JP KRE

Principal Facilities:

P	Y	G		R		B	D	T	A

Authority: Port & Harbour Bureau of Kure City, 1-6 Chuo 4-chome, Kure 737-8501, Hiroshima Pref., Japan, *Tel:* +81 823 253333, *Fax:* +81 823 251361, *Email:* kowan@city.kure.lg.jp, *Website:* www.city.kure.lg.jp

Port Security: ISPS compliant

Approach: Draught limitation in the channel is 17.4 m at high tide and 17 m actual depth

Pilotage: Not compulsory. Inland Sea pilot boards 3 miles S of Sekisaki Lighthouse in pos 33° 13' N; 131° 54' E. Harbour pilots board at the quarantine anchorage in pos 34° 13' 45" N; 132° 31' 00" E. Berthing/unberthing during daylight hours only

Weather: Winds predominantly from the NW. Storm winds are mainly from W

Tides: Tidal range 3.98 m max, -0.28 m min

Maximum Vessel Dimensions: 360 m loa, 276 000 dwt for vessels discharging iron ore, max d 16.3 m over 200 000 dwt and 17 m under 200 000 dwt

Working Hours: Steel 0800-1630, all night if required. Iron ore, day and night

Accommodation: There are also four anchorage berths for loading/discharging of cargo in depths of 15-18 m, designated Y-1, Y-2, C and D. Anchorages Y-1, C and D for vessels up to 200 m loa; Anchorage Y2 for vessels up to 150 m loa, mainly used for loading of steel products

Further anchorage berths are located at Hiro, which is a part of Kure port in depths of 18 m and 33 m

Also a number of landing areas or wharves for smaller craft and lighters etc

Name	Length (m)	Depth (m)	Draught (m)	Remarks
Kure				
Showa Pier No.1	150	7.5	7	Max loa 150 m & 15 000 dwt
Nishi-Kawaraishi Wharf	260	7.5	7	Max loa 150 m & 4000 dwt
Minami Kawaraishi Wharf	370	10	9	Max 20 000 dwt
Takaramachi Wharf	270	6		Max 2000 gt
Nisshin Steel Mill No.3	330	18	17	See [1] below
Tokyo Pulp Co Dolphin		9		Max 42 000 dwt cap. Two 9 m wide dolphins, 80 m apart
Kobe Steelworks Quay	70	4.5		Max 3000 dwt. Coasters only

[1]*Nisshin Steel Mill No.3:* Over 200 000 dwt, 16.3 m max d. Under 200 000 dwt, 17 m max d. Air draught 16.6 m

Storage:

Location	Covered (m²)	Sheds / Warehouses
Kure	6068	5

Mechanical Handling Equipment: Various cranes available for loading and discharging

Location	Type	Capacity (t)	Qty
Kure	Floating Cranes	50	1

Location	Type	Capacity (t)	Qty
Kure	Floating Cranes	100	1

Cargo Worked: Steel 700 t/gang daytime, iron ore 43 000 t/day

Bunkering: ExxonMobil Marine Fuels, 1 Harbour Front Place, 06-00 Harbour Front, Tower One, Singapore, Republic of Singapore 098633, *Tel:* +65 6885 8998, *Fax:* +65 6885 8794, *Email:* asiapac.marinefuels@exxonmobil.com, *Website:* www.exxonmobilmarinefuels.com

Hikawa Shoji Kaisha Ltd, 26-2 Shinkawa NS Building 1-chome, Shinkawa, Chuo-ku, Tokyo 104, Japan, *Tel:* +81 3 5776 6858, *Fax:* +81 3 5541 3274

Kamei Corp., 1-6-1 Otemachi, Chiyoda-ku, Tokyo 100-0004, Japan, *Tel:* +81 3 3286 6234, *Fax:* +81 3 3286 6249, *Email:* bunker@kamei.co.jp

Kyodo Oil Co. Ltd, 11-2 Nagata-cho 2-chome, Chiyoda-ku, Tokyo, Japan, *Tel:* +81 3 3505 8241, *Fax:* +81 3 3505 8697

Marubeni Petroleum Co. Ltd, Marubeni International Petroleum Singapore Co. Ltd, c/o Marubeni Corporation, 4-2 Ohtemachi 1-chome, Chiyoda-ku, Tokyo 100-8088, Japan, *Tel:* +81 3 3282 3920, *Fax:* +81 3 3282 3950, *Email:* TOKB554@marubenicorp.com, *Website:* www.marubeni.co.jp

MC Marine and Bunkering Inc., 8th Floor, Uchisaiwai-cho Dai Building, 3-3 Uchi-saiwai-cho 1-chome, Chiyoda-ku, Tokyo 100-0011, Japan, *Tel:* +81 3 5251 2575, *Fax:* +81 3 5251 2583

Nittetsu Shoij Co. Ltd, 5-7 Kameido 1-chome, Koto-ku, Tokyo 136, Japan, *Tel:* +81 3 5627 2157, *Fax:* +81 3 5627 2192

Towage: Tugs available from 1600 hp to 3300 hp

Repair & Maintenance: IHI Corp. (Kure), Kure Shipyard, 2-1 Showa-cho, Kure 737-0027, Hiroshima Pref., Japan, *Tel:* +81 823 262105, *Fax:* +81 823 262162, *Email:* webmaster@ihi.co.jp, *Website:* www.ihi.co.jp Repair facilities

Imamura Zosen (Imamura Shipbuilding Co. Ltd), 9-15, Nigata Honmachi 3, Kure 737-01, Hiroshima Pref., Japan, *Tel:* +81 823 791234, *Fax:* +81 823 795144, *Email:* i-tons@msc.biglobe.ne.jp One floating dock of 87.2 m x 17 m x 7.6 m

Medical Facilities: National hospital and Masaoka Clinic available

Airport: Hiroshima, 30 km

Lloyd's Agent: Cornes & Co. Ltd, Meikai Building, 32 Akashi-machi, Chuo-ku, Kobe 650-0037, Hyogo Pref., Japan, *Tel:* +81 78 332 3421, *Fax:* +81 78 332 3070, *Email:* survey@kobe.cornes.co.jp, *Website:* www.cornes.co.jp

KUSHIRO

Lat 42° 59' N; Long 144° 22' E.

Admiralty Chart: 1815	**Admiralty Pilot:** 41
Time Zone: GMT +9 h	**UNCTAD Locode:** JP KUH

Principal Facilities:

P		Y	G	C	R		B	D	T	A

Authority: Port & Harbor Department of Kushiro, 1-100-17 Nishi-ko, Kushiro 084-0914, Hokkaido, Japan, *Tel:* +81 154 533371, *Fax:* +81 154 533373, *Email:* ku210101@city.kushiro.hokkaido.jp, *Website:* www.city.kushiro.hokkaido.jp

Officials: President: Yoshitaka Ito.

Port Security: ISPS compliant

Approach: Port consists of two districts, East Port District and West Port District. Both harbours enclosed by two breakwaters. Draught limitation in fairways 8.8 m E and 10.5 m W. No restrictions except vessels requiring pilots

Anchorage: Quarantine anchorage in pos 42° 58' N, 144° 20' E in min depth of 12.0 m

Pilotage: Not compulsory. Pilots available at Quarantine Anchorage. No entry before sunrise and after sunset except in emergencies

Tides: Max 2.133 m, min 0.655 m

Traffic: 2005, 20 996 000 t of cargo handled

Maximum Vessel Dimensions: 186 m loa, 10.5 m d, 30 000 dwt

Principal Imports and Exports: Imports: Coal, Lumber, Wood chips. Exports: Coal, Paper & pulp.

Working Hours: 0800-1630, 1630-2100 overtime. Sundays and holidays subject to negotiation. No work on 1st and 3rd Sundays

Accommodation:

Name	Length (m)	Depth (m)	Remarks
Centre Pier			
Berth No.1	170	9	1 x 10 000 dwt
Berth No.2	170	9	1 x 10 000 dwt
Berth No.3	180	10	1 x 15 000 dwt
Berth No.4	130	7.5	1 x 5000 dwt
Berth No.5	130	7.5	1 x 5000 dwt
Berth No.6	130	7.5	1 x 5000 dwt
North Pier			
Berth No's 1 & 2	383	9	2 x 10 000 dwt

Key to Principal Facilities:—			
A=Airport	**C**=Containers	**G**=General Cargo	**P**=Petroleum **R**=Ro/Ro **Y**=Dry Bulk
B=Bunkers	**D**=Dry Dock	**L**=Cruise	**Q**=Other Liquid Bulk **T**=Towage (where available from port)

Name	Length (m)	Depth (m)	Remarks
Berth No.3	148	7	1 x 6000 dwt
Berth No.4	161	9	1 x 6000 dwt
Berth No.5	148	8.1	1 x 3000 dwt
New South Pier			
Berth	130	7.5	1 x 5000 dwt
Dolphin (South)	24	7.5	1 x 5000 dwt
Dolphin (West)	30	5	1 x 1000 dwt
South Pier			
Berth No.1	91	5.4	1 x 2000 dwt. General cargo
Berth No.2	217	7.5	1 x 5000 dwt. Coal loader berth
West Pier			
Berth No.1-1	90	5.5	1 x 2000 dwt
Berth No.1-2 & 1-3	330	9	2 x 10 000 dwt
Berth No.1-4	240	12	1 x 30 000 dwt
Berth No.1-5	185	10	1 x 15 000 dwt
Berth No.1-6	165	9	1 x 10 000 dwt
Berth No.1-7	165	9	1 x 10 000 dwt
Dolphin	260	7.5	4 x 6000 dwt. Tanker only
Berth No.2-8	91	5.5	1 x 2000 dwt
Berth No.2-9	130	7.5	1 x 5000 dwt
Berth No.2-10	185	10	1 x 15 000 dwt
Berth No.2-11 & 2-12	480	12	1 x 30 000 dwt. Three grain unloaders
Berth No.2-13	165	9	1 x 10 000 dwt
Berth No.2-14	130	7.5	1 x 5000 dwt
Berth No.3-15	90	5.5	1x 2000 dwt
Berth No.3-16	130	7.5	1 x 5000 dwt. Three grain unloaders
Berth No.3-17	130	7.5	1 x 5000 dwt
Berth No.3-18	240	12	1 x 30 000 dwt
Berth No.3-19	240	12	1 x 30 000 dwt
Berth No.3-21	170	10	
Berth No.3-22	240	12	
Berth No.3-23	280	14	
Fishery Port			
Discharging Zone	825	3–4	
East Wharf	405	7	6 x 500 gt
South Wharf	200	7.5	1 x 5000 gt
West Wharf	320	7	1 x 500 gt
Kushiro River			
Ohmachi Wharf	250	6	3 x 350 gt
Irifune Wharf	260	6	4 x 350 gt
Nishiki-cho Wharf	201	6	2 x 500 gt

Storage: 101 sheds of 169 924 m2, 108 sheds for dangerous cargo of 242 028 m2, warehousing of 84 016 m2, open warehousing of 232 824 m2, silos of 39 325 m2, refrigerated storage of 86 581 m2 and a timber pool of 240 000 m2

Location	Open (m²)
Kushiro	112151

Mechanical Handling Equipment: One pneumatic unloader for grain at 400 t/h, two belt conveyor-type unloaders for grain at 400 t/h, one coal unloader at 1200 t/h and one coal loader at 800 t/h

Location	Type	Capacity (t)	Qty
Kushiro	Mobile Cranes	37.6	1

Bunkering: MC Marine and Bunkering Inc., 8th Floor, Uchisaiwai-cho Dai Building, 3-3 Uchisaiwai-cho 1-chome, Chiyoda-ku, Tokyo 100-0011, Japan, *Tel:* +81 3 5251 2575, *Fax:* +81 3 5251 2583

Waste Reception Facilities: Garbage disposal available

Towage: Three tugs available of 3200-3300 hp
Kushiro Tug Boat Co. Ltd, Kushiro, Hokkaido, Japan, *Tel:* +81 154 531041

Repair & Maintenance: Kushiro Heavy Industries Co. Ltd, Kushiro, Hokkaido, Japan, *Tel:* +81 154 419171 One dry dock 95.9 m long, 17 m wide, 6.5 m depth for vessels up to 2000 gt

Medical Facilities: Available

Airport: Kushiro Airport, 20 km

Railway: JR Kushiro Station, approx 5 km

Lloyd's Agent: Cornes & Co. Ltd, 273 Yamashita-cho, Naka-ku, Yokohama 231-0023, Kanagawa Pref., Japan, *Tel:* +81 45 201 8537, *Fax:* +81 45 212 3105, *Email:* survey@ykh.cornes.co.jp, *Website:* www.cornes.co.jp

MAIZURU

Lat 35° 29' N; Long 135° 22' E.

Admiralty Chart: JP139		**Admiralty Pilot:** 41	
Time Zone: GMT +9 h		**UNCTAD Locode:** JP MAI	

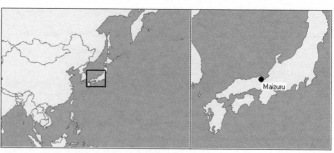

Principal Facilities:

P		Y	G	C			B	D	T	

Authority: Port of Maizuru, 3rd Floor, Maizuru 21 Building, 1105-1 Kita, Maizuru 624-0945, Kyoto Pref., Japan, *Tel:* +81 773 757184, *Fax:* +81 773 757198, *Email:* m-port@mxa.nkansai.ne.jp, *Website:* www.port.maizuru.kyoto.jp

Officials: Chairman: Keiji Yamada.
Managing Director: Masakazu Ito.

Port Security: ISPS compliant

Approach: The approach to the port is through the narrow channel 0.7 to 1.8 km wide, 12 m depth, of Maizuru Bay about 3.7 km from the entrance of the Bay to Toshima Island. The channel is divided into two branches around Toshima Island. One branch runs to the SSW for a further 5.6 km and is the principal wharf of the port. The other runs ESE for about the same distance. The Universal Shipbuilding Corporation is located here. Draught limitation in the channel is 12 m

Pilotage: Not compulsory. Pilots available at anchorage near Kanegasaki in pos 35° 32' N; 135° 10' 00" E. Tel: +81 773 760826

Weather: The typhoon season is July-October, the rainy season is June and July, and there is snow in January and February

Tides: Tidal range 0.34 m, 0.38 m MHWL, 0.04 m MLWL, 0.19 m MSL

Principal Imports and Exports: Imports: Timber. Exports: Textile goods.

Working Hours: 0800-1600, 1600-1800. Any work needed after 1800 has to be confirmed in advance

Accommodation: Maizuru Port Promoting Organization, 3rd Floor, Maizuru 21 Building, 1105-1 Kita, Maizuru 624-0945, Kyoto Pref., Japan, Tel: +81 773 757184, Fax: +81 773 757198, Email: m-port@mxa.nkansai.ne.jp, Website: www.port.maizuru.kyoto.jp
Anchorage, 18.25 km2, depths 4-9 m. Draft limitation in channel is 12 m. Vessels can enter or leave after sunset
Bulk facilities: Phosphate ore discharged at Pier No.2 by multi-purpose crane, silica sand discharged at Pier No.4 and log/lumber discharged at Kita Pier and Pier No.3 respectively by ship's own gear
Container facility at No.2 Pier No.2 Wharf

Name	Length (m)	Depth (m)	Remarks
Public Wharves			
No.1 Pier	128	3	For fishing boats
No.2 Pier No.1 Wharf	130	7.5	Max 5000 dwt
No.2 Pier No.2 Wharf	185	10	See [1] below
No.2 Pier No.3 Wharf	165	9	Max 10 000 dwt
No.2 Pier No.4 Wharf	165	9	Max 10 000 dwt
No.3 Pier No.1 Wharf	185	10	Max 15 000 dwt
No.3 Pier No.2 Wharf	185	10	Max 15 000 dwt
No.4 Pier	185	10	Max 15 000 dwt
5.5 m Wharf	300	5.5	3 x 1000 dwt
Kita Pier No.1 Wharf	130	7.5	Max 5000 dwt
Kita Pier No.2 Wharf	240	12	Max 30 000 dwt
Maejima Pier No.1 Wharf	130	7.5	Max 5000 dwt
Maejima Pier No.2 Wharf	230	8	Max 24 000 dwt. Domestic ferry only
Maejima Pier No.3 Wharf	180	5.5	Max 3000 dwt
Private Wharves			
Nippon Sheet Glass Wharf	167	7	1 x 3000 dwt
Nippon Sheet Glass Dolphin	60	7	1 x 2500 dwt
Universal Shipbuilding Corp Wharf	60	8	1 x 18 000 dwt
Universal Shipbuilding Corp Wharf	71	8	1 x 9000 dwt
Universal Shipbuilding Corp Wharf	106	8	1 x 74 000 dwt
Universal Shipbuilding Corp Wharf	30	8	1 x 9000 dwt
Universal Shipbuilding Corp Wharf	498	7	2 x 9000 dwt
Universal Shipbuilding Corp Wharf	100	10	1 x 9000 dwt
Universal Shipbuilding Corp Wharf	57	10	1 x 9000 dwt
Universal Shipbuilding Corp Wharf	233	7	1 x 74 000 dwt
Ube-Mitsubishi Cement Corp & Denki Kagaku Kogyo Dolphin	147	8.5	Max 6900 dwt

[1]*No.2 Pier No.2 Wharf:* Max 15 000 dwt. Gantry crane and multi-purpose crane available

Storage: Four transit sheds of 7069 m2, 23 general cargo warehouses of 25 850 m2, one refrigerated warehouse of 3543 m2, grain silo of 14 537 m2 and timber basin of 563 164 m2

Location	Open (m²)
Maizuru	248000

Cargo Worked: 7500 t of both foreign and domestic trade cargoes per working day

Bunkering: Domestic oil available. Bonded oil brought by barge from Moji or Tokuyama with advance notice

Towage: Three tugs available; one of 3400 hp, one of 3200 hp and one of 3000 hp

Repair & Maintenance: Universal Shipbuilding Corp., 1180 Amarube-shimo, Maizuru 625-8501, Kyoto Pref., Japan, *Tel:* +81 773 628700, *Fax:* +81 773 623007, *Website:* www.u-zosen.co.jp

Medical Facilities: Available

Development: A multi-purpose international terminal for vessels of 50 000 dwt is under construction in the Wada District of the West Port

Lloyd's Agent: Cornes & Co. Ltd, Meikai Building, 32 Akashi-machi, Chuo-ku, Kobe 650-0037, Hyogo Pref., Japan, *Tel:* +81 78 332 3421, *Fax:* +81 78 332 3070, *Email:* survey@kobe.cornes.co.jp, *Website:* www.cornes.co.jp

MATSUNAGA

see under Onomichi

MATSUSHIMA

Lat 32° 56' N; Long 129° 36' E.

Admiralty Chart: JP198
Time Zone: GMT +9 h
Admiralty Pilot: 42A
UNCTAD Locode: JP MAT

Principal Facilities:

	Y	G		B	T	A	

Authority: Ports & Harbors Promotion Division, Public Works Department, Miyagi Prefectural Government, 3-8-1 Honcho, Aoba-ku, Sendai 980-8570, Miyagi Pref., Japan, *Tel:* +81 22 211 3221, *Fax:* +81 22 211 3296, *Email:* kousin@pref.miyagi.jp, *Website:* www.pref.miyagi.jp/kouwan

Officials: Port Manager: Haruo Kasamatsu.
Assistant Manager: Masashi Takahashi.

Port Security: ISPS compliant

Pre-Arrival Information: Vessels should advise the following on departure from previous port:
(a) vessel's name
(b) loading port and departure time/date
(c) ETA Matsushima and arrival draught
(d) cargo and hatchwise quantity
(e) other necessary information
Vessels should advise ETA 7 days, 72 h, 48 h and 24 h prior to arrival with the following information:
(a) vessel's name
(b) position
(c) ETA
(d) other necessary information

Approach: There are no hazards

Anchorage: Anchorage can be obtained in vicinity of 32° 58' 30" N; 129° 35' 18" E

Pilotage: Compulsory for all vessels over 10 000 dwt, Tel: +81 959 233426. Pilot boards in pos 32° 58' 03" N; 129° 34' 12" E (2 nautical miles, bearing 300° from Matsushima Breakwater Lt)

Tides: Tidal range 4.0 m. Max tidal current is 0.6 knots in vicinity of the breakwater end

Principal Imports and Exports: Imports: Coal.

Working Hours: 0630-2130, two shifts

Accommodation:

Name	Remarks
Matsushima	See ¹ below

¹*Matsushima:* Harbour protected by breakwater. Port facilities are privately owned and operated by Electric Power Development Co Ltd. One jetty comprising four berths, the largest of which can accommodate coal carriers up to 69 000 dwt with max d of 14.0 m; the second coal berth can take vessels up to 5000 dwt, max d of 8 m. There are two smaller berths for vessels of 2000 dwt. A coal stacking area is situated beside the power station, storage cap of 430 000 t, and an ash pond immediately behind the jetty. Equipment includes four unloaders of 700 t/h. Cargo handled includes coal, oil, flyash, gypsum and lime

Cargo Worked: Coal discharge, 20 000 t/day

Bunkering: Available from coastal tanker
Idemitsu Kosan Co. Ltd, 1-1 Marunochi, 3-Chome, Chiyoda-ku, Tokyo 100-8321, Japan, *Tel:* +81 3 3213 3138, *Fax:* +81 3 3213 1145, *Email:* tohru.takamura@si.idemitsu.co.jp, *Website:* www.idemitsu.co.jp
KG Int Petroleum Ltd, Shiba Park Building, 241 Shiba Koen, Minato-ku, Tokyo 105, Japan, *Tel:* +81 3 3578 4551, *Fax:* +81 3 3578 4550
Kyushu Oil Co. Ltd, 1-1 Uchisaiwai-cho 2-chome, Chiyoda-ku, Tokyo, Japan, *Tel:* +81 3 3502 3651, *Fax:* +81 3 3502 9850
MC Marine and Bunkering Inc., 8th Floor, Uchisaiwai-cho Dai Building, 3-3 Uchisaiwai-cho 1-chome, Chiyoda-ku, Tokyo 100-0011, Japan, *Tel:* +81 3 5251 2575, *Fax:* +81 3 5251 2583
Mitsui & Co. Petroleum Ltd, 2-1, Ohtemachi 1-chome, Chiyoda-ku, Tokyo 100-0004, Japan, *Tel:* +81 3 3285 6905, *Fax:* +81 3 3285 9811, *Email:* tkzph@dg.mitsui.com, *Website:* www.mitsui.co.jp
Nittetsu Shoij Co. Ltd, 5-7 Kameido 1-chome, Koto-ku, Tokyo 136, Japan, *Tel:* +81 3 5627 2157, *Fax:* +81 3 5627 2192

Towage: Compulsory for larger vessels. One multi-purpose tug of 2600 hp available, assisted by mooring craft. Further tugs can be brought from Nagasaki or Sasebo

Repair & Maintenance: Kaihatsu Denki Co. Ltd, Matsushima, Japan, *Tel:* +81 959 220606 Minor repairs

Medical Facilities: A clinic is available on Matsushima Island. Three hospitals on the opposite shore, but not authorised by Immigration Law; long-term medical treament difficult to arrange

Airport: Nagasaki, 70 km

Lloyd's Agent: Cornes & Co. Ltd, Meikai Building, 32 Akashi-machi, Chuo-ku, Kobe 650-0037, Hyogo Pref., Japan, *Tel:* +81 78 332 3421, *Fax:* +81 78 332 3070, *Email:* survey@kobe.cornes.co.jp, *Website:* www.cornes.co.jp

MATSUYAMA

Lat 33° 49' N; Long 132° 41' E.

Admiralty Chart: 694
Time Zone: GMT +9 h
Admiralty Pilot: 42B
UNCTAD Locode: JP MYJ

Principal Facilities:

P		Y	G	C		B		T	A

Authority: Port & Harbours Coast Division, Public Works Department, Ehime Prefectural Government, 4-4-2 Ichiban-cho, Matsuyama 790-8570, Ehime Pref., Japan, *Tel:* +81 89 941 2111, *Fax:* +81 89 941 3523, *Email:* kouwankaigan@pref.ehime.jp, *Website:* www.pref.ehime.jp

Port Security: ISPS compliant

Approach: Depth in fairway 25 m to 30 m. Draught limitation in channel is 10.6 m

Pilotage: Not compulsory. Inland Sea pilots are available at Wada-Misaki, Sekisaki or Hesaki. Harbour pilots available at the anchorage

Tides: Tidal range: max 4 m, min -0.52 m. Current 0.6 knots in N-S direction, max speed 3 knots

Maximum Vessel Dimensions: Tankers: 59 990 dwt, 228.6 m loa, 11.3 m draft. General cargo: 26 531 dwt, 170 m loa, 10.3 m draft

Principal Imports and Exports: Imports: Oil, Round logs. Exports: Pure terephthalic acid.

Working Hours: 0800-1700 for general cargo and logs. 24 h/day at oil berth

Accommodation:

Name	Length (m)	Depth (m)	Remarks
Matsuyama			See ¹ below
Container Terminal	170	10	See ² below
Cosmo Oil Berth	400	12.4	See ³ below
Gaiko No.1 Futo No.1 Wharf	200	5.5	Max 4000 dwt & 120 m loa
Gaiko No.1 Futo No.2 Wharf	365	10	Max 10 000 dwt
Gaiko No.2 Futo	390	7.5	
Imazu Zaimoku Log Wharf	370	10	Max 16 000 dwt
Showa Saboa Harumi Wharf	170	7.4	

¹*Matsuyama:* Yurawan Log Anchorage, 15 m depth, in pos 33° 53' 36" N, 132° 41' E, 150 m max loa
Umaiso Log Anchorage, 12.8 m depth, in pos 33° 54' 47" N, 132° 42' 06" E
²*Container Terminal:* Operated by Nippon Express Co Ltd., Tel: +81 89 952 2341, Fax: +81 89 952 9657, Email:matsuyama_agency@nittsu.co.jp and Matsuyama Container Service Ltd., Tel: +81 89 953 3335, Fax: +81 89 953 3363, Email: mcsco@arion.ocn.ne.jp
Max 10 000 dwt. Equipment includes one gantry crane and three transfer cranes. 48 reefer points
³*Cosmo Oil Berth:* Max 50 000 dwt. Vessels are only able to berth when a north current is flowing

Key to Principal Facilities:—
A=Airport   **C**=Containers   **G**=General Cargo   **P**=Petroleum   **R**=Ro/Ro   **Y**=Dry Bulk
B=Bunkers   **D**=Dry Dock   **L**=Cruise   **Q**=Other Liquid Bulk   **T**=Towage (where available from port)

Storage: Some warehousing only available

Cargo Worked: General cargo 450 t/gang/day, logs 2500 m3/day

Bunkering: Kyodo Oil Co. Ltd, 11-2 Nagata-cho 2-chome, Chiyoda-ku, Tokyo, Japan, *Tel:* +81 3 3505 8241, *Fax:* +81 3 3505 8697
MC Marine and Bunkering Inc., 8th Floor, Uchisaiwai-cho Dai Building, 3-3 Uchi-saiwai-cho 1-chome, Chiyoda-ku, Tokyo 100-0011, Japan, *Tel:* +81 3 5251 2575, *Fax:* +81 3 5251 2583
Mitsui & Co. Petroleum Ltd, 2-1, Ohtemachi 1-chome, Chiyoda-ku, Tokyo 100-0004, Japan, *Tel:* +81 3 3285 6905, *Fax:* +81 3 3285 9811, *Email:* tkzph@dg.mitsui.com, *Website:* www.mitsui.co.jp

Towage: Two tugs of 2600 hp are stationed at the port. Additional tugs can be made available from Naiki Tugboat Service Co

Repair & Maintenance: Watanabe Engineering Co. Ltd, Matsuyama, Ehime Pref., Japan, *Tel:* +81 89 952 0046 Minor repairs

Shipping Agents: Kamigumi Co. Ltd, 560-1 Wake-cho, 1-chome, Matsuyama 799-2656, Ehime Pref., Japan, *Tel:* +81 89 979 0131, *Fax:* +81 89 978 5611

Medical Facilities: Available

Airport: Matsuyama, 10 km

Development: A container quay for 40 000 t vessels, 260 m long in depth of 13 m is planned

Lloyd's Agent: Cornes & Co. Ltd, Meikai Building, 32 Akashi-machi, Chuo-ku, Kobe 650-0037, Hyogo Pref., Japan, *Tel:* +81 78 332 3421, *Fax:* +81 78 332 3070, *Email:* survey@kobe.cornes.co.jp, *Website:* www.cornes.co.jp

MEGA

Lat 34° 46' N; Long 134° 42' E.

Admiralty Chart: 698	**Admiralty Pilot:** 42B
Time Zone: GMT +9 h	**UNCTAD Locode:** JP MEG

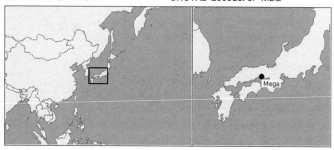

Principal Facilities:

P	Q				B		

Authority: Port & Harbour Section of Hyogo Prefecture, 5-10-1 Yamate-dori, Chuo-ku, Kobe 650-8567, Hyogo Pref., Japan, *Tel:* +81 78 341 7711, *Fax:* +81 78 341 6477

Approach: Draft limitation in the channel 14 m. Idemitsu Jetty 11.8 m (Max), Himeji LNG Jetty 14 m and Sea Berth 19.2 m

Pilotage: Inland-sea pilots are available between 02:00 and 18:00 at Wada-Misaki. Harbour pilots are available at anchorage from sunrise to sunset

Tides: 1.60 m max, -0.20 m min

Accommodation: Oil fence for Supertankers berthing is a necessity

Name	Depth (m)	Draught (m)	Remarks
Idemitsu Jetty Berth No.1			
Berths 1-4	6.5–6.7	5.9–6.09	
Idemitsu Jetty Berth No.2			
Berth No.5	5.9	5.36	
Idemitsu Jetty Berth No.3			
Berth No.6	12	11.8	
Idemitsu Jetty Berth No.4			
Berths 7 & 8	6.6	6	
Idemitsu Jetty Berth No.6			
Berths 13 & 14	7.5–7.6	6.8–7.1	
LPG Jetty			Berth No.22 has a depth of 7.1 m and 6.45 m draft
Monoageba			Depth 6 m
Sea Berth			Depth of 21 m & 19.2 m draft
Himeji LNG Jetty			Depth 14 m

Bunkering: Available supplied by Idemitsu Oil at Idemitsu Jetty Line only or by barge at anchorage

Lloyd's Agent: Cornes & Co. Ltd, Meikai Building, 32 Akashi-machi, Chuo-ku, Kobe 650-0037, Hyogo Pref., Japan, *Tel:* +81 78 332 3421, *Fax:* +81 78 332 3070, *Email:* survey@kobe.cornes.co.jp, *Website:* www.cornes.co.jp

MIIKE

Lat 33° 0' N; Long 130° 24' E.

Admiralty Chart: 3112	**Admiralty Pilot:** 42A
Time Zone: GMT +9 h	**UNCTAD Locode:** JP MII

Principal Facilities:

P	Q	Y	G	C		B		T	A

Authority: Port & Harbour Section of Fukuoka Prefectural Government, 7-7 Higashi-kouen, Hakata-ku, Fukuoka 812-8577, Fukuoka Pref., Japan, *Tel:* +81 92 643 3674, *Fax:* +81 92 643 3688, *Email:* kowan@pref.fukuoka.lg.jp, *Website:* www.pref.fukuoka.lg.jp

Officials: Director: Hiroshi Okawauchi.

Port Security: ISPS compliant

Approach: The channel is 1800 m long, 137 m wide with 45.7 m bottom width and 7.3 m depth at LWOST. Draught limitations in the channel: up to 20 000 dwt, 9.0 m draft; up to 25 000 dwt, 8.5 m draft; up to 30 000 dwt, 7.5 m draft

Anchorage: Miike Quarantine Anchorage, pos 33° 00' 08" N; 130° 23' 50" E in a depth of approx 10 m

Pilotage: Harbour pilotage compulsory for vessels over 1000 gt. Pilots available at Quarantine Anchorage from sunrise to sunset in pos 32° 59' N; 130° 23' E. Shimabara Bay pilotage optional and is available 1 mile S of Kuchinotsu lighthouse in pos 32° 35' N; 130° 12' E between 0600-2200. Advise ETA Kuchinotsu 48 h prior to arrival

Tides: Tidal range 5.07 m. Max current of tides is 4-5 knots

Traffic: 2004, 2 143 814 t of cargo handled

Maximum Vessel Dimensions: 37 000 dwt, 7 m draft, 195 m loa, 27 m breadth

Principal Imports and Exports: Imports: Aluminium, Coal, General cargo, Logs. Exports: General cargo, Machinery.

Working Hours: 0800-1700, 1700-0700 if necessary

Accommodation:

Name	Length (m)	Depth (m)	Remarks
Miike			
Inner Harbor North Wharf (Public Berth) Berth No.6	210	10.7	1 x 20 000 dwt
Inner Harbor North Wharf Berth No's 7 & 8	423	10.7	1 x 20 000 dwt, 1 x 5000 dwt
Inner Harbor Dolphin Pier Berth No.5	68	10.7	1 x 5000 dwt
Inner Harbor Mooring Wall Berth No.5	92	10.7	1 x 10 000 dwt
Dock Mooring Wall Berth No's 1-3	422	8.5	3 x 10 000 dwt
Dock Mooring Wall Berth No.4	114	8.5	1 x 10 000 dwt
Gypsum Pier	31	7	1 x 1500 dwt
Oil Tanker Pier (4 Piers)		5.5–7.5	500-3600 dwt
Miike Container Terminal	170	10	See [1] below

[1]*Miike Container Terminal:* Area of 20 000 m2 with storage cap of 440 TEU's and CFS of 1000 m2. 8 reefer points

Storage: Warehousing of 17 671 m2, coal storage yard of 228 700 m2 and salt storage yard of 12 000 m2

Mechanical Handling Equipment: Fly ash loader at 300 t/h and grain handling bucket elevator-type continuous unloader at 900 t/h

Location	Type	Capacity (t)	Qty
Miike	Floating Cranes	15	1
Miike	Mult-purp. Cranes	10	1

Bunkering: Idemitsu Kosan Co. Ltd, 1-1 Marunochi, 3-Chome, Chiyoda-ku, Tokyo 100-8321, Japan, *Tel:* +81 3 3213 3138, *Fax:* +81 3 3213 1145, *Email:* tohru.takamura@si.idemitsu.co.jp, *Website:* www.idemitsu.co.jp
KG Int Petroleum Ltd, Shiba Park Building, 241 Shiba Koen, Minato-ku, Tokyo 105, Japan, *Tel:* +81 3 3578 4551, *Fax:* +81 3 3578 4550
Kyushu Oil Co. Ltd, 1-1 Uchisaiwai-cho 2-chome, Chiyoda-ku, Tokyo, Japan, *Tel:* +81 3 3502 3651, *Fax:* +81 3 3502 9850
MC Marine and Bunkering Inc., 8th Floor, Uchisaiwai-cho Dai Building, 3-3 Uchi-saiwai-cho 1-chome, Chiyoda-ku, Tokyo 100-0011, Japan, *Tel:* +81 3 5251 2575, *Fax:* +81 3 5251 2583
Mitsui & Co. Petroleum Ltd, 2-1, Ohtemachi 1-chome, Chiyoda-ku, Tokyo 100-0004, Japan, *Tel:* +81 3 3285 6905, *Fax:* +81 3 3285 9811, *Email:* tkzph@dg.mitsui.com, *Website:* www.mitsui.co.jp
Nittetsu Shoji Co. Ltd, 5-7 Kameido 1-chome, Koto-ku, Tokyo 136, Japan, *Tel:* +81 3 5627 2157, *Fax:* +81 3 5627 2192

Towage: Two tugs of 1100 hp and one of 600 hp available

Medical Facilities: Omuta City Hospital and Omuta Tenryo Hospital

Airport: Fukuoka Airport, 80 km

Lloyd's Agent: Cornes & Co. Ltd, Meikai Building, 32 Akashi-machi, Chuo-ku, Kobe 650-0037, Hyogo Pref., Japan, *Tel:* +81 78 332 3421, *Fax:* +81 78 332 3070, *Email:* survey@kobe.cornes.co.jp, *Website:* www.cornes.co.jp

MINAMATA

Lat 32° 13' N; Long 130° 20' E.

Admiralty Chart: JP213	**Admiralty Pilot:** 42A
Time Zone: GMT +9 h	**UNCTAD Locode:** JP MIN

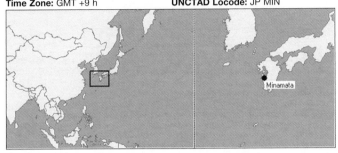

Principal Facilities:

Q	Y	G			B		T	A	

Authority: Port & Harbour Section of Kumamoto Prefecture, 6-18-1 Suizenji, Kumamoto-shi, Kumamoto 862-8570, Kumamoto Pref., Japan, *Tel:* +81 96 383 1111, *Fax:* +81 96 387 2461, *Website:* www.pref.kumamoto.jp

Approach: Draught limitation in channel 16 m

Pilotage: Available. Pilots board in pos 32° 11' N; 130° 04' E, 1 mile S of Toshima lighthouse

Tides: Range of tide 6 m

Accommodation:

Name	Length (m)	Depth (m)	Draught (m)	Remarks
Minamata				
Hyakken Midori Pier No.1	120	6.5	6	See [1] below
Anchorage Berths	180	13	11	See [2] below

[1] *Hyakken Midori Pier No.1:* For vessels of 6000 dwt. Pipeline for molasses and ethyl alcohol on the berth
[2] *Anchorage Berths:* Consists of 2 berths for vessels of 10 000 dwt and 30 000 dwt

Mechanical Handling Equipment:

Location	Type	Capacity (t)	Qty
Minamata	Floating Cranes	30	1

Bunkering: Domestic oil available. Bonded oil brought from Moji or Nagasaki when required

Towage: One tug of 1500 hp and two of 200 hp available

Repair & Maintenance: Minor repairs undertaken

Airport: Kagoshima, 60 km

Lloyd's Agent: Cornes & Co. Ltd, Meikai Building, 32 Akashi-machi, Chuo-ku, Kobe 650-0037, Hyogo Pref., Japan, *Tel:* +81 78 332 3421, *Fax:* +81 78 332 3070, *Email:* survey@kobe.cornes.co.jp, *Website:* www.cornes.co.jp

MINATO

harbour area, see under Wakkanai

MISHIMA-KAWANOE

Lat 34° 1' N; Long 133° 34' E.

Admiralty Chart: JP153	**Admiralty Pilot:** 42B
Time Zone: GMT +9 h	**UNCTAD Locode:** JP MKX

Principal Facilities:

	Y	G	C			B			

Authority: Port & Harbours Coast Division, Public Works Department, Ehime Prefectural Government, 4-4-2 Ichiban-cho, Matsuyama 790-8570, Ehime Pref., Japan, *Tel:* +81 89 941 2111, *Fax:* +81 89 941 3523, *Email:* kouwankaigan@pref.ehime.jp, *Website:* www.pref.ehime.jp

Port Security: ISPS compliant

Pilotage: Pilots are available from Sakaide or Kobe with sufficient advance notice when required, during daylight hours only

Tides: Range of tide 3.6 m

Maximum Vessel Dimensions: 66 732 dwt, 229.8 m loa

Accommodation:

Name	Length (m)	Depth (m)
Mishima-Kawanoe		
Muramatsu Wharf No.1	260	7.5
Muramatsu Wharf No.2	400	15
Muramatsu Wharf No.3	130	5
Muramatsu Wharf No.4	130	7.5
Muramatsu Wharf No.5	240	12
Muramatsu Wharf No.6	350	15
Muramatsu Wharf No.7	260	7.5
Okidai Wharf	200	3.5
Mishima East Wharf	200	4
Ohe Wharf No's 1, 2 & 3	312	12
Ohe Wharf No.4	220	12
Ohe Wharf No's 5 & 6	110	5.5
Kawanoe Wharf No.4	180	5.5
Tiao Dolphin		9.5

Bunkering: Domestic oil available. Bonded oil brought from Mizushima or Kobe with sufficient advance notice

Towage: No tugs stationed at the port, but available from Mizushima or Sakaide when required

Repair & Maintenance: Minor repairs can be undertaken

Lloyd's Agent: Cornes & Co. Ltd, Meikai Building, 32 Akashi-machi, Chuo-ku, Kobe 650-0037, Hyogo Pref., Japan, *Tel:* +81 78 332 3421, *Fax:* +81 78 332 3070, *Email:* survey@kobe.cornes.co.jp, *Website:* www.cornes.co.jp

MISUMI

Lat 32° 36' N; Long 130° 28' E.

Admiralty Chart: 3112	**Admiralty Pilot:** 42A
Time Zone: GMT +9 h	**UNCTAD Locode:** JP MIS

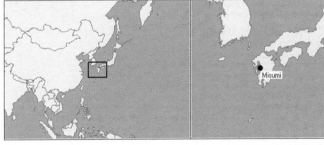

Principal Facilities:

		G		R	B		T	A	

Authority: Port & Harbour Section of Kumamoto Prefecture, 6-18-1 Suizenji, Kumamoto-shi, Kumamoto 862-8570, Kumamoto Pref., Japan, *Tel:* +81 96 383 1111, *Fax:* +81 96 387 2461, *Website:* www.pref.kumamoto.jp

Port Security: ISPS compliant

Approach: Draught limitation in channel is 11 m

Pilotage: Not compulsory. Pilots available at the anchorage area if required, but not after sunset

Tides: Range of tide 4.57 m

Maximum Vessel Dimensions: 35 000 dwt, 8.5 m d, 195 m loa

Working Hours: 0830-1700. Sundays and holidays arrangeable when required

Accommodation:

Name	Length (m)	Depth (m)	Draught (m)	Remarks
Misumi				
Kenei Wharf (A)	137	8	7.5	Max 8000 gt
Kenei Wharf (B)	160	9	8.5	Max 10 000 gt
Kenei Wharf (C)	165	9	8.5	Max 10 000 gt
Mooring Buoy No.2		9	8.5	Max 6000 gt

Storage: 25 000 m3 of warehousing. No refrigerated space

Mechanical Handling Equipment:

Location	Type	Capacity (t)	Qty
Kenei Wharf (A)	Mult-purp. Cranes	37	2
Kenei Wharf (B)	Mult-purp. Cranes	27	2
Kenei Wharf (C)	Mult-purp. Cranes	15	1

Cargo Worked: 300 t of bagged grain/gang/day

Bunkering: Domestic oil available. Bonded oil can be brought from Moji or Nagasaki when required

Key to Principal Facilities:—					
A=Airport	**C**=Containers	**G**=General Cargo	**P**=Petroleum	**R**=Ro/Ro	**Y**=Dry Bulk
B=Bunkers	**D**=Dry Dock	**L**=Cruise	**Q**=Other Liquid Bulk	**T**=Towage (where available from port)	

Towage: One tug of 1300 hp and one tug of 300 hp available

Medical Facilities: Available

Airport: Kumamoto, 65 km

Lloyd's Agent: Cornes & Co. Ltd, Meikai Building, 32 Akashi-machi, Chuo-ku, Kobe 650-0037, Hyogo Pref., Japan, *Tel:* +81 78 332 3421, *Fax:* +81 78 332 3070, *Email:* survey@kobe.cornes.co.jp, *Website:* www.cornes.co.jp

MITAJIRI

Lat 34° 1' N; Long 131° 36' E.

Admiralty Chart: 2874/3153	**Admiralty Pilot:** 42B
Time Zone: GMT +9 h	**UNCTAD Locode:** JP MJR

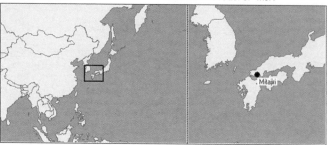

Principal Facilities:

P		Y	G	C			B		A

Authority: Ports & Harbors Division, Yamaguchi Prefectural Government, 1-1 Takimachi, Yamaguchi 753-8501, Yamaguchi Pref., Japan, *Tel:* +81 83 933 3810, *Fax:* +81 83 933 3829, *Email:* a12900@pref.yamaguchi.lg.jp, *Website:* www.pref.yamaguchi.lg.jp

Officials: Shoichi Hayashi, *Tel:* +81 83 9332 340.

Port Security: ISPS compliant

Approach: Depth in Mitajiri channel is 7.5 m, in Nakanoseki channel is 12 m and in Nishinoura channel is 5.5 m

Pilotage: Not compulsory. Entry is permitted after sunset

Tides: Range of tide 3.07 m

Maximum Vessel Dimensions: 28 223 dwt, 225 m loa at Nakanoseki

Principal Imports and Exports: Imports: Sugar, Wood. Exports: Automobiles.

Working Hours: 0900-1700

Accommodation:

Name	Length (m)	Depth (m)	Remarks
Mitajiri Public Wharves			
Tsukiji Wharf No.1	240	5.5	3 x 2000 dwt
Tsukiji Wharf No.2	130	7.5	1 x 5000 dwt
Tsukiji Wharf No.3	180	5.5	2 x 2000 dwt
Tsukiji Wharf No.4	260	7.5	2 x 5000 dwt
Nakanoseki Public Wharves			
Nakanoseki Wharf No.1	360	5.5	4 x 2000 dwt
Nakanoseki Wharf No.2	520	7.5	Container facilities available
Nakanoseki Wharf No.3	480	12	
Private Wharves			
Kanebo K.K. Wharf	199	1	Chemicals
Kanebo K.K. Oil Pier	20	2.5	Heavy oil
Kyowa Hakkou K.K. Wharf	115	2	Chemicals
Kyowa Hokkou K.K. Pier	30	4.5	Chemicals
Kumiai Shiryo K.K. Pier	20	4	Grain
Mazda K.K. Pier	320	5.5	Machines

Bunkering: Meikoh Corp., 105 Dai-ich Mita Building, 2-15-3 Katamachi Fuchu-shi, Tokyo 183, Japan, *Tel:* +81 4 2360 6260, *Fax:* +81 4 2362 9008, *Email:* info@meikoh.co.jp

Towage: No tugs stationed at the port, but available from Tokuyama or Ube when required

Medical Facilities: Available in Hofu City

Airport: Yamaguchi-Ube, 50 km

Railway: Hofu Station, 1.5 km

Lloyd's Agent: Cornes & Co. Ltd, Meikai Building, 32 Akashi-machi, Chuo-ku, Kobe 650-0037, Hyogo Pref., Japan, *Tel:* +81 78 332 3421, *Fax:* +81 78 332 3070, *Email:* survey@kobe.cornes.co.jp, *Website:* www.cornes.co.jp

MITSUKOSHIMA

Lat 34° 11' N; Long 132° 31' E.

Admiralty Chart: 3472	**Admiralty Pilot:** 42A
Time Zone: GMT +9 h.	**UNCTAD Locode:** JP MKS

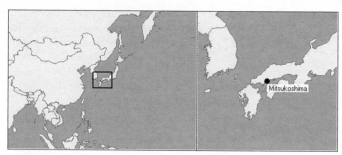

Principal Facilities:

		Y	G			B		T	

Authority: Port & Harbour Bureau of Kure City, 1-6 Chuo 4-chome, Kure 737-8501, Hiroshima Pref., Japan, *Tel:* +81 823 253333, *Fax:* +81 823 251361, *Email:* kowan@city.kure.lg.jp, *Website:* www.city.kure.lg.jp

Port Security: ISPS compliant

Pilotage: Not compulsory. Inland-sea pilots are available at Wada-Misaki, Hesaki or Sekisaki and harbour pilots are available at the anchorage in Kure for vessels requiring pilot services (24 h advance notice required). Pilots not available after sunset

Tides: Max +3.98 m. Min -0.28 m

Accommodation:

Name	Length (m)	Depth (m)	Draught (m)	Remarks
Mitsukoshima Wharf	192	17	16.5	For vessels up to 76 000 gt

Bunkering: Domestic oil is available; bonded oil brought from Kobe or Moji when required

Towage: Available from 1600-3300 hp

Lloyd's Agent: Cornes & Co. Ltd, Meikai Building, 32 Akashi-machi, Chuo-ku, Kobe 650-0037, Hyogo Pref., Japan, *Tel:* +81 78 332 3421, *Fax:* +81 78 332 3070, *Email:* survey@kobe.cornes.co.jp, *Website:* www.cornes.co.jp

MIYAKO

Lat 39° 38' N; Long 141° 58' E.

Admiralty Chart: JP54	**Admiralty Pilot:** 42A
Time Zone: GMT +9 h	**UNCTAD Locode:** JP MYK

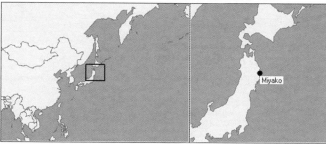

Principal Facilities:

		Y	G			B		T	

Authority: Iwate Prefectural Government, Port & Airport Division, 10-1 Uchimaru, Morioka 020-8570, Iwate Pref., Japan, *Tel:* +81 196 295912, *Email:* AG0010@pref.iwate.jp

Port Security: ISPS compliant

Pilotage: Not compulsory. Pilots board at the anchorage when required

Tides: Tidal range 1.52 m

Maximum Vessel Dimensions: 240 m loa, 12 m d

Accommodation:

Name	Length (m)	Depth (m)	Remarks
Miyako			
Desaki Wharf No's 1 & 2	214	7.3	2 x 3000 dwt
Desaki Wharf No.3	175	9	Max 10 000 dwt
Fujiwara Wharf No's 1 & 2	260	7.5	2 x 5000 dwt
Fujiwara Wharf No.3	240	12	1 x 30 000 dwt
Fujiwara Wharf No.4	180	4.5	2 x 700 dwt
Fujiwara Wharf No.5	130	7.5	1 x 5000 dwt
Fujiwara Wharf No.6	130	7.5	1 x 5000 dwt
Fujiwara Wharf No.7	180	10	1 x 15 000 dwt
Fujiwara Wharf No.8	555	10	1 x 20 000 dwt
Hitachi-hama	120	4.5	2 x 700 dwt
Kuwagasaki	397	5	6 x 1000 dwt
Lumber Port Buoy		9	Max 10 000 dwt

Storage: 122 600 m3 of open storage, 956 m3 of warehousing and 49 000 m3 of timber ponds

Location	Cold (m³)
Miyako	6292

Bunkering: Domestic oil available. Bonded oil brought from Tokyo or Sendai with sufficient advance notice

Towage: One tug of 2400 hp available

Repair & Maintenance: Minor repairs available

Medical Facilities: Available

Lloyd's Agent: Cornes & Co. Ltd, 273 Yamashita-cho, Naka-ku, Yokohama 231-0023, Kanagawa Pref., Japan, *Tel:* +81 45 201 8537, *Fax:* +81 45 212 3105, *Email:* survey@ykh.cornes.co.jp, *Website:* www.cornes.co.jp

MIYAZU

Lat 35° 35' N; Long 135° 13' E.

Admiralty Chart: JP139 **Admiralty Pilot:** 41
Time Zone: GMT +9 h **UNCTAD Locode:** JP MIY

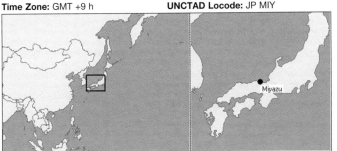

Principal Facilities:

	Y	G		B		T	

Authority: Kyoto Prefectural Government Port Division, Yabunouchi-cho, Kamigyo-ku, Kyoto 602-8570, Kyoto Pref., Japan, *Tel:* +81 75 451 8111, *Fax:* +81 75 432 2074, *Email:* kowan@pref.kyoto.lg.jp, *Website:* www.pref.kyoto.jp

Officials: Director: Osamu Saito.

Approach: Draught limitation in the channel is 10 m

Anchorage: Anchorage can be obtained off the port in Miyazu Bay in depths ranging from 14 m to 17 m, bottom mud with excellent holding ground

Pilotage: Not compulsory. Harbour pilots are available at Kurosaki Anchorage; berthing performed during daylight hours only, unberthing at any time subject to adequate notice and approval from the pilot

Tides: Range of tide 1.18 m

Maximum Vessel Dimensions: 32 875 dwt, 188 m loa

Accommodation:

Name	Length (m)	Depth (m)	Draught (m)	Remarks
Miyazu				See [1] below
No.2 Wharf	210	5.3	5	Max 1000 gt
Tsuruga Wharf	140	5	5	Max 500 gt
Mooring Buoy No.1			12	Max 15 000 gt

[1]*Miyazu:* There are also anchorage berths for loading/unloading in depths of 13-14 m

Mechanical Handling Equipment:

Location	Type	Capacity (t)	Qty
No.2 Wharf	Mult-purp. Cranes	2	1

Bunkering: Bonded oil brought from Moji when required

Towage: Five tugs available; three of 330 hp, one of 80 hp and one of 50 hp

Lloyd's Agent: Cornes & Co. Ltd, Meikai Building, 32 Akashi-machi, Chuo-ku, Kobe 650-0037, Hyogo Pref., Japan, *Tel:* +81 78 332 3421, *Fax:* +81 78 332 3070, *Email:* survey@kobe.cornes.co.jp, *Website:* www.cornes.co.jp

MIZUSHIMA

Lat 34° 29' N; Long 133° 43' E.

Admiralty Chart: JP127A/JP127B **Admiralty Pilot:** 42A
Time Zone: GMT +9 h **UNCTAD Locode:** JP MIZ

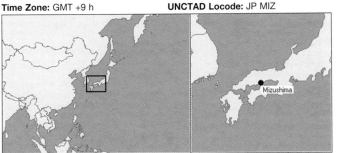

Principal Facilities:

P	Q	Y	G	C	R		B	D	T	A

Authority: Port & Harbour Section of Okayama Prefecture, 2-4-6 Uchisange, Okayama 700-8570, Japan, *Tel:* +81 86 226 7485, *Fax:* +81 86 227 5551, *Email:* kowan@pref.okayama.lg.jp, *Website:* www.pref.okayama.jp

Officials: Harbour Director: Masanori Tokimatsu, *Email:* masanori_tokimatsu@pref.okayama.lg.jp.

Port Security: ISPS compliant

Approach: The approach to the port is through Mizushima traffic route 5.3 miles long, depth 16 m to 27 m, width 600-1000 m. Mizushima Harbour Passage, length 4.5 km, depth 16 m, width 450-600 m. Mizushima East Passage, length 3 km, depth 12 to 16 m, width 250 m. Takahashigawa Passage, 4.5 km long, 7.5 m to 11.5 m depth, 350 m width

Anchorage: There are 250 ha of anchorage space with depths exceeding 9 m although no suitable anchorage near the port for vessels over 50 000 dwt, 200 m loa

Pilotage: Compulsory for vessels exceeding 10 000 gt. Inland sea pilot available 24 h at Wada-Misaki, Sekisaki or Hesaki and harbour pilot available from sunrise to sunset in pos 34° 26' N; 133° 44' E. Inland Sea Pilots Association, Tel: +81 78 391 7191

Radio Frequency: Mizushima Port Radio, 24 h service, calling on VHF Channel 16 and working on VHF Channels 11, 12 and 14

Weather: Typhoon season, July to October

Tides: Range of tide 3.86 m, 2.91 m MHWL, 0.89 m MLWL, 1.9 m MSL. Current 2.5 knots in E-W direction

Traffic: 2006, 103 027 000 t of cargo handled

Maximum Vessel Dimensions: 325 m loa, 16.5 m d, 240 000 dwt

Principal Imports and Exports: Imports: Coal, Crude oil, Grain, Iron ore. Exports: Automobiles, Chemicals, Steel products.

Working Hours: 0830-1630 daytime, 1630-0400 night. Continuous three shifts at Kawasaki Steel wharves

Accommodation: Additionally Mitsubishi Chemical Industry Co have one dolphin with 10.5 m d for vessels up to 5000 dwt, Ube Kosan have one dolphin with 9 m d for vessels up to 9000 dwt and Asahi Chemical Industry Co have one dolphin with 8.2 m d for vessels up to 10 000 dwt
Bulk facilities: Kawasaki Steel Corp operate three ore and coal berths (E, F & G) equipped with six 1500 t/h cap cantilever trolley cranes and four 400 t/h unloaders. Stockpile cap is 1 million t for coal and 2 million t for iron ore

Name	Length (m)	Depth (m)	Draught (m)	Remarks
Public Wharves				
Tamashima District				
Mizushima International Container Terminal	340	10		See [1] below
Tamashima GABO Wharf 1	370	10		Two berths. Mainly handles automobiles
Tamashiman Harbor Island Wharf 4	520	7.5		Four berths. Mainly container cargo
Tamashima Wharf 1	630	5.5		See [2] below
Tamashima Wharf 3	730	5.5		Eight berths
Tamashima Wharf 4	810	7.5		Six berths
Mizushima District				
Public Wharf West 1	185	10		One berth. Mainly handles automobiles
Public Wharf West 2	130	9		One berth. Mainly handles automobiles
Public Wharf East	360	5.5		Four berths
Private Wharves				
Kawasaki Steel Corp C-1	230	11.2	10.5	Max 25 000 dwt
Kawasaki Steel Corp C-2	230	10.7	9	Max 25 000 dwt
Kawasaki Steel Corp C-3	230	6.4	5	Max 5000 dwt
Kawasaki Steel Corp T	730	10.9	10.9	Max 30 000 dwt
Kawasaki Steel Corp D	220	14	11.5	Max 30 000 dwt
Kawasaki Steel Corp E-1	330	16.1	16	Max 40 000 dwt
Kawasaki Steel Corp E-2	330	16.1	16	Max 100 000 dwt
Kawasaki Steel Corp F	320	17	16.5	Max 240 000 dwt
Kawasaki Steel Corp G	263	17	16.5	Max 180 000 dwt
Tokyo Steel Corp A	160	11	11	Max 54 000 dwt
Tokyo Steel Corp B & C	320	10	9.5	Max 20 000 dwt
Nishi Nihon Grain Centre	285	12.9	12	See [3] below
Seto Futo Co	285	14	12.3	See [4] below
Mitsubishi Oil Co No.5P	90	12.6	12	Max 70 000 dwt. For discharge of crude oil at 5000 t/h
Mitsubishi Oil Co No.6P	990	7–16.5	7–16.5	See [5] below

Key to Principal Facilities:—

A=Airport	**C**=Containers	**G**=General Cargo	**P**=Petroleum **R**=Ro/Ro **Y**=Dry Bulk
B=Bunkers	**D**=Dry Dock	**L**=Cruise	**Q**=Other Liquid Bulk **T**=Towage (where available from port)

Name	Length (m)	Depth (m)	Draught (m)	Remarks
Nippon Mining Co No.1P	260	13	12	Max 70 000 dwt. For discharge of crude oil at 5000 t/h
Nippon Mining Co No.2P	800	7–17.2	7–16.5	See [6] below

[1]*Mizushima International Container Terminal:* Operated by Mizushima Port International Logistics Center Co Ltd., 3F of the Administration Building, Mizushima Port International Container Terminal, 8262-1 Aza-Shinminato Tamashima-Otoshima, Kurashiki, Okayama 713-8103, Tel: +81 86 523 6211, Fax: +81 86 523 5577, Email: soumu@mizushima-faz.co.jp, Website: www.mizushima-faz.co.jp Two berths

[2]*Tamashima Wharf 1:* Seven berths. Tamashima Wharves 1, 3 and 4 mainly handle domestic cargo including steel, non-ferrous metal, fertilizer and feed

[3]*Nishi Nihon Grain Centre:* Max 60 000 dwt. Two 400 t/h and one 800 t/h pneumatic unloaders

[4]*Seto Futo Co:* Max 75 000 dwt. Loading export vehicles & grain berth with one 300 t/h pneumatic unloader and two 500 t/h level luffing unloaders

[5]*Mitsubishi Oil Co No.6P:* Max 1 x 240 000 dwt & 1 x 5000 dwt. For discharge of crude oil at 7000 t/h

[6]*Nippon Mining Co No.2P:* Max 1 x 240 000 dwt & 1 x 5000 dwt. For discharge of crude oil at 10 000 t/h

Storage: 47 warehouses of 111 324 m2, 160 warehouses and tanks for dangerous cargo of 2 370 874 m3, approx 190 silos of 150 000 t cap and open storage of 44 568 m2. Four transit sheds of 7700 m2

Location	Grain (t)
Nishi Nihon Grain Centre	81000
Seto Futo Co	45360

Mechanical Handling Equipment:

Location	Type	Capacity (t)	Qty
Mizushima	Mult-purp. Cranes	300	
Mizushima	Container Cranes	40.7	2

Cargo Worked: 153 000 t of foreign trade and 122 000 t of domestic trade per working day

Bunkering: All grades of oil available by barges
Kanematsu K.K., Bunker Oil Section, 2-1 Shibaura 1-chome, Minato-ku, Tokyo 105-8005, Japan, *Tel:* +81 3 5440 9273, *Fax:* +81 3 5440 6540, *Email:* trc5@kanematsu.co.jp, *Website:* www.kanematsu.co.jp

Towage: Not compulsory but advisable. 25 tugs available

Repair & Maintenance: Sanoyas Hishino Meisho Corp., Mizushima Shipyard, 2767-21, Shionasu, Kojima, Mizushima, Japan, *Tel:* +81 86 475 1551, *Fax:* +81 86 475 0523, *Email:* info@sanoyas.co.jp, *Website:* www.sanoyas.co.jp Dry docking cap of 80 000 gt

Ship Chandlers: Nishina & Co. Ltd, Kaigan Building 1-10, 2-chome Kaigan-dori, Kurashiki City, Mizushima 712-8071, Japan, *Tel:* +81 86 448 0522, *Fax:* +81 86 448 0520, *Email:* info@nishinafirm.co.jp, *Website:* www.nishinafirm.co.jp

Medical Facilities: Available

Airport: Okayama, 32 km

Lloyd's Agent: Cornes & Co. Ltd, Meikai Building, 32 Akashi-machi, Chuo-ku, Kobe 650-0037, Hyogo Pref., Japan, *Tel:* +81 78 332 3421, *Fax:* +81 78 332 3070, *Email:* survey@kobe.cornes.co.jp, *Website:* www.cornes.co.jp

MOJI

Lat 33° 57' N; Long 130° 58' E.

Admiralty Chart: JP1265	**Admiralty Pilot:** 42B
Time Zone: GMT +9 h	**UNCTAD Locode:** JP MOJ

Principal Facilities:

P		Y	G	C	R		B	D	T	A	

Authority: Kitakyushu Port & Harbor Bureau, 1-1 Jonai, Kitakyushu 803-8501, Fukuoka Pref., Japan, *Tel:* +81 93 321 5941, *Fax:* +81 93 582 1037, *Email:* kqport@kitaqport.or.jp, *Website:* www.kitaqport.or.jp

Officials: Director General: Kenichi Katayama.
Marketing Director: Hiroyuki Tagami, *Email:* hiroyuki_tagami01@city.kitakyushu.lg.jp.
Sales Director: Tetsuji Hashimoto.

Port Security: ISPS compliant

Approach: Draught limitation in channel is 12 m. Air draught under Kanmon bridge is 61 m

Anchorage: Mutsure Quarantine Anchorage, two anchorage sections off Mutsure Lighthouse with depths of water ranging from 8.6 m to 9.1 m and 14.6 m to 23 m respectively. Hesaki Quarantine Anchorage, pos 33° 56' 24" N; 131° 03' 12" E with depth ranging from 8.6 m to 9.1 m

Pilotage: Compulsory for vessels over 3000 gt and vessels with hazardous materials over 300 gt. Pilots embark the E-bound vessels at quarantine anchorages off Mutsure Lighthouse; the W-bound vessels at the Hesaki quarantine anchorage. Mutsure Pilot Station in pos 33° 59' 30" N; 130° 53' 00" E and Hesaki Pilot Station in pos 33° 57' 00" N; 131° 00' 03" E
Bungo Channel: Vessels approaching from the E may obtain pilots by radio request 24 h in advance. Pilot embarkation position: 4.8 km S of Sekisaki lighthouse. Two pilots embark vessels over 20 000 gt charging double pilotage. Container vessels up to 230 m loa may now berth at or depart from the port at night time

Tides: Tidal range of 3.17 m. Current in the vicinity of the narrowest section of the Straits sometimes reaches 7-8 knots; in the stream about 3-5 knots

Traffic: 2006, 109 723 953 t of cargo handled, 469 000 TEU's (includes ports of Kokura, Tobata, Wakamatsu & Yawata)

Maximum Vessel Dimensions: Length and beam, no limit; 8.5-10 m d at wharf and buoy, 9.1 m at anchorage; gross tonnage, no limit at wharf, 7000-20 000 t at buoy and anchorage

Working Hours: Day shift 0830-1200, 1300-1630; night shift 1630-2130, 2130-0600. Non-working Sundays are the first and third of each month; otherwise, Sundays and holidays are worked during daytime 0830-1630
Saturdays before non-working Sundays are worked during daytime only, but when loading/discharging operations anticipated completed by 2130 Saturday, then work possible till 2130

Accommodation: Berthing during daylight only. Swift current prevails at buoy berths necessitating strong moorings and in accordance with harbour rules, vessels are required to moor with anchor chains to buoy; chain preparation should be completed before leaving the pilot station for berth

Name	Length (m)	Depth (m)	Draught (m)	Remarks
Anchorage Berths				
Tanoura 1		9.1		1 x 20 000 gt
Tanoura 2		9.1		Max 20 000 gt
Tanoura 3		9.1		1 x 20 000 gt
Mooring Buoy No.1		9.8		1 x 15 000 gt
Mooring Buoy No.2		9.8		1 x 15 000 gt
Mooring Buoy No.3		9.6		1 x 15 000 gt
Mooring Buoy No.6		10		
Mooring Buoy No.7		10		
Public Wharves				
Gaibo Wharf No.1		8.5		See [1] below
Gaibo Wharf No.2		9		See [2] below
Gaibo Wharf No.3		9.3		See [3] below
Gaibo Wharf No.4		9.3		See [4] below
Gaibo Wharf No.5		9		See [5] below
Gaibo Wharf No.6		9.3		See [6] below
Gaibo Wharf No.7		9		See [7] below
Gaibo Wharf No's 8 & 9	390	9.2		12 000 gt cap
Gaibo Wharf No.10	220	9		9000 gt cap
Gaibo Wharf No.11	261	9		
Gaibo Wharf No.12		8.5		See [8] below
Gaibo Wharf No.13		9.3		See [9] below
Tanoura Wharf No.1	105	6		Banana terminal
Tanoura Wharf No.2	105	6		Banana terminal
Tanoura Wharf No.3	185	9.6		See [10] below
Tanoura Wharf No.4	220	9.6		See [11] below
Tanoura Wharf No.5	170	9		
Tanoura Wharf No.6	170	9		
Tanoura Wharf No.7	181	9.4		
Tanoura Wharf No.8	185	9.4		
Tanoura Oil Berth Dolphin		9.1		33 000 dwt cap
Tachinoura Wharf No.2	185	9.6		
Tachinoura Wharf No.3	185	9.6		
Tachinoura Wharf No.4	185	9.6		
Tachinoura Wharf No.5	185	9.6		
Tachinoura Wharf No.6	185	9.6		
Tachinoura Wharf No's 7 & 8	620	10.8		See [12] below
Tachinoura Wharf No.9	185	10		
Tachinoura Wharf No.28	180	8		
Tachinoura Wharf No.29	180	8		
Tachinoura Wharf No's 30-32	555	9.1		See [13] below

[1]*Gaibo Wharf No.1:* Gaibo Wharf No's 1 & 2 have a combined length of 450 m
[2]*Gaibo Wharf No.2:* Gaibo Wharf No's 1 & 2 have a combined length of 450 m
[3]*Gaibo Wharf No.3:* Gaibo Wharf No's 3-7 have a combined length of 877 m

⁴*Gaibo Wharf No.4:* Gaibo Wharf No's 3-7 have a combined length of 877 m
⁵*Gaibo Wharf No.5:* Gaibo Wharf No's 3-7 have a combined length of 877 m. Grain. One crane available
⁶*Gaibo Wharf No.6:* Gaibo Wharf No's 3-7 have a combined length of 877 m
⁷*Gaibo Wharf No.7:* Gaibo Wharf No's 3-7 have a combined length of 877 m
⁸*Gaibo Wharf No.12:* Gaibo Wharf No's 12 & 13 have a combined length of 345 m. Two pneumatic suckers of 300 t/h
⁹*Gaibo Wharf No.13:* Gaibo Wharf No's 12 & 13 have a combined length of 345 m. Two pneumatic suckers of 300 t/h
¹⁰*Tanoura Wharf No.3:* Container terminal at Berths 3 and 4 covering an area of 63 220 m2. Equipment includes one container gantry crane of 37.5 t max cap and three straddle carriers; there are 12 freezer outlets
¹¹*Tanoura Wharf No.4:* Container terminal at Berths 3 and 4 covering an area of 63 220 m2. Equipment includes one container gantry crane of 37.5 t max cap and four straddle carriers; there are 40 freezer outlets
¹²*Tachinoura Wharf No's 7 & 8:* Container terminal covering a total area of 161 500 m2, handling vessels of 40 000 gt. It is equipped with three container gantry cranes of 48.6 t max cap, one container gantry crane of 55.5 t max cap and fifteen straddle carriers; there are 68 freezer outlets
¹³*Tachinoura Wharf No's 30-32:* Container terminal covering a total area of 161 547 m2. It is equipped with three gantry cranes of 48.1 t max cap and thirteen straddle carriers; there are 132 freezer outlets

Storage: Seven warehouses of 12 421 m2 cap and 36 transit sheds of 68 787 m2 cap and 19 open stock yards of 48 076 m2

Mechanical Handling Equipment:

Location	Type	Capacity (t)	Qty
Moji	Floating Cranes	80	1
Moji	Floating Cranes	120	1
Moji	Floating Cranes	1000	1
Moji	Floating Cranes	70	1
Tanoura Wharf No.3	Container Cranes	37.5	1
Tachinoura Wharf No's 7 & 8	Container Cranes	55.5	1
Tachinoura Wharf No's 7 & 8	Container Cranes	48.6	3
Tachinoura Wharf No's 30-32	Container Cranes	48.1	3

Bunkering: Hanwa Co. Ltd, 2nd Floor, Finland House, 56 Haymarket, London SW1Y 4RN, United Kingdom, *Tel:* +44 20 7839 4448, *Fax:* +44 20 7839 3994, *Email:* orito@hanwa.co.uk
Hikawa Shoji Kaisha Ltd, 26-2 Shinkawa NS Building 1-chome, Shinkawa, Chuo-ku, Tokyo 104, Japan, *Tel:* +81 3 5776 6858, *Fax:* +81 3 5541 3274
Idemitsu Kosan Co. Ltd, 1-1 Marunochi, 3-Chome, Chiyoda-ku, Tokyo 100-8321, Japan, *Tel:* +81 3 3213 3138, *Fax:* +81 3 3213 1145, *Email:* tohru.takamura@si.idemitsu.co.jp, *Website:* www.idemitsu.co.jp
KG Int Petroleum Ltd, Shiba Park Building, 241 Shiba Koen, Minato-ku, Tokyo 105, Japan, *Tel:* +81 3 3578 4551, *Fax:* +81 3 3578 4550
Marubeni Petroleum Co. Ltd, Marubeni International Petroleum Singapore Co. Ltd, c/o Marubeni Corporation, 4-2 Ohtemachi 1-chome, Chiyoda-ku, Tokyo 100-8088, Japan, *Tel:* +81 3 3282 3920, *Fax:* +81 3 3282 3950, *Email:* TOKB554@marubenicorp.com, *Website:* www.marubeni.co.jp
MC Marine and Bunkering Inc., 8th Floor, Uchisaiwai-cho Dai Building, 3-3 Uchisaiwai-cho 1-chome, Chiyoda-ku, Tokyo 100-0011, Japan, *Tel:* +81 3 5251 2575, *Fax:* +81 3 5251 2583
Mitsui & Co. Petroleum Ltd, 2-1, Ohtemachi 1-chome, Chiyoda-ku, Tokyo 100-0004, Japan, *Tel:* +81 3 3285 6905, *Fax:* +81 3 3285 9811, *Email:* tkzph@dg.mitsui.com, *Website:* www.mitsui.co.jp
Nittetsu Shoij Co. Ltd, 5-7 Kameido 1-chome, Koto-ku, Tokyo 136, Japan, *Tel:* +81 3 5627 2157, *Fax:* +81 3 5627 2192

Towage: Ten tugs available; one of 3300 hp, one of 3100 hp, one of 2500 hp, one of 2400 hp, two of 2200 hp, one of 2100 hp, one of 1650 hp, one of 1500 hp and one of 1200 hp

Repair & Maintenance: Hayashikane Shipbuilding & Engineering, Moji, Japan Two dry docks: No.1 71 m x 12 m x 7.4 m for vessels up to 500 dwt, No.2 63 m x 10.8 m x 5 m for vessels up to 1100 dwt
Kitakyushu Iron Works, Moji, Japan
Sasebo Heavy Industries Co. Ltd, 5th Floor, Toranomon No.5 Mori Building, Minatoku, Tokyo 105, Japan, *Tel:* +81 3 5213 7316, *Fax:* +81 3 5213 7356, *Email:* shipship.business@ssk-sasebo.co.jp, *Website:* www.ssk-sasebo.co.jp

Ship Chandlers: Fuji Trading Co. Ltd, 9-14 2-chome Matsubara, Moji-ku, Kitakyushu-shi, Moji 800-0064, Japan, *Tel:* +81 93 371 4561, *Fax:* +81 93 371 4566, *Email:* aab65350@pop12.odn.ne.jp, *Website:* www.fujitrading.co.jp
Mashin Shokai Ltd, 12-26 Hamamachi, Moji 801-0856, Japan, *Fax:* +81 93 331 5119, *Email:* mashin-moji@mvf.biglobe.ne.jp

Shipping Agents: Kyushu Shipping Co Ltd, 1-5 Honmachi, Moji-ku, Kitakyushu, Moji 8010834, Japan, *Tel:* +81 93 321 2261, *Fax:* +81 93 332 3930, *Email:* mojmo@mail.mol.co.jp
Nippon Express Co. Ltd, 2nd Floor Tachinoura, CY Terminal Ofice 19, Chisaki Tachinourakaigan Moji-ku, Kitakyushu, Moji 800-8631, Japan, *Tel:* +81 93 332 2642, *Fax:* +81 93 332 6021, *Email:* senpaku@try-net.or.jp
Seagate Corp., 1-4-12 Nishi Kaigan, Moji-ku, Kitakyushu-shi, Fukuoka-ken, Moji 801-0841, Japan, *Tel:* +81 93 331 2161, *Fax:* +81 93 331 7334, *Email:* mship@seagatecorp.com, *Website:* www.seagatecorp.com
Seiho Kaiun Kaisha Co. Ltd, Port Moji Ishibankan, 1-5 Honmachi, Moji-ku, Kitakyushu, Moji, Japan, *Tel:* +81 93 321 5061, *Fax:* +81 93 331 1055, *Email:* y.nagano@seihou.jp
Seven Star Co. Ltd, Shimizu Soko Kaisha Ltd, 3rd Floor, Mojinen Building, 10-16 Ham-Machi, Moji 801-0856, Japan, *Tel:* +81 93 321 8031, *Fax:* +81 93 321 0009, *Email:* kowa-moj@mth.biglobe.ne.jp

Airport: Kitakyushu Airport

Lloyd's Agent: Cornes & Co. Ltd, Meikai Building, 32 Akashi-machi, Chuo-ku, Kobe 650-0037, Hyogo Pref., Japan, *Tel:* +81 78 332 3421, *Fax:* +81 78 332 3070, *Email:* survey@kobe.cornes.co.jp, *Website:* www.cornes.co.jp

MONBETSU

Lat 44° 21' N; Long 143° 22' E.

Admiralty Chart: 1802	**Admiralty Pilot:** 41
Time Zone: GMT +9 h	**UNCTAD Locode:** JP MBE

Principal Facilities:

	Y	G		B		T	A

Authority: Port & Harbour Bureau of Monbetsu City, 2 Saiwai-cho, Monbetsu 094-8707, Hokkaido, Japan, *Tel:* +81 158 242111, *Fax:* +81 158 231019, *Email:* mokouwan@ohotuku26.or.jp

Port Security: ISPS compliant

Approach: Draught limitation in the channel is 12 m

Pilotage: Not compulsory. Pilots are available from Kushiro with sufficient advance notice when required from sunrise to 1 h before sunset

Tides: Range of tide 1.3 m

Working Hours: 0830-1700

Accommodation:

Name	Length (m)	Depth (m)	Remarks
Monbetsu			
No.1 Pier East Wharf	130	7.5	1 x 5000 dwt
No.2 Pier East Wharf	390	7.5	3 x 5000 dwt
No.2 Pier South Wharf	130	7.5	1 x 5000 dwt
No.2 Pier North Wharf	131	6	1 x 3000 dwt
No.3 Pier 7.5 Wharf	130	7.5	1 x 5000 dwt
No.3 Pier 12.0 Wharf	240	12	1 x 30 000 dwt

Bunkering: Domestic oil available. Bonded oil brought from Hakodate or Muroran with sufficient advance notice

Towage: Three tugs available; one of 2200 hp, one of 1850 hp and one of 1300 hp

Airport: Okhotsk Monbetsu Airport

Lloyd's Agent: Cornes & Co. Ltd, 273 Yamashita-cho, Naka-ku, Yokohama 231-0023, Kanagawa Pref., Japan, *Tel:* +81 45 201 8537, *Fax:* +81 45 212 3105, *Email:* survey@ykh.cornes.co.jp, *Website:* www.cornes.co.jp

MONOAGEBA

harbour area, see under Mega

MURORAN

Lat 42° 21' N; Long 140° 57' E.

Admiralty Chart: 1813	**Admiralty Pilot:** 41
Time Zone: GMT +9 h	**UNCTAD Locode:** JP MUR

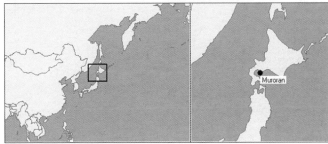

Principal Facilities:

P		Y	G	C			B	D	T	A

Authority: Port & Harbour Bureau of Muroran City, 1-20-30 Kaigan-cho, Muroran 051-0022, Hokkaido, Japan, *Tel:* +81 143 223191, *Fax:* +81 143 226069, *Email:* port@city.muroran.lg.jp, *Website:* www.city.muroran.lg.jp

Officials: Port Director: Hitoshi Nakaminami.

Port Security: ISPS compliant

Approach: Depth in fairway 16.5 m, width 300 m, length 5600 m, draught limitation 16.0 m

Anchorage: Ample sheltered anchorage in 9 m plus

Key to Principal Facilities:—				
A=Airport	**C**=Containers	**G**=General Cargo	**P**=Petroleum	**R**=Ro/Ro	**Y**=Dry Bulk
B=Bunkers	**D**=Dry Dock	**L**=Cruise	**Q**=Other Liquid Bulk	**T**=Towage (where available from port)

Pilotage: Not compulsory. Harbour pilots available at the outer anchorage

Weather: NW winds. Dense fog hampers navigation occasionally

Tides: Tidal range 1.6 m

Traffic: 2004, 39 307 000 t of cargo handled

Principal Imports and Exports: Imports: Coal, Crude oil, Iron ore. Exports: Chemicals, Non-metallic minerals, Steel materials.

Accommodation:

Name	Length (m)	Depth (m)	Remarks
Muroran			See [1] below
Old Hokkaido Electricity Wharf	180	8	1 x 7000 dwt
Sakimori Wharf No's 1-3	555	10	3 x 15 000 dwt
Sakimori Wharf No's 4-5	480	12	1 x 30 000 dwt
Sakimori Wharf No's 7-8	231	10	2 x 15 000 dwt
Chuo Wharf A	310	9	1 x 10 000 dwt & 1 x 6000 dwt
Chuo Wharf B	237	7.2	2 x 4000 dwt
Chuo Wharf C	86	5.6	1 x 2000 dwt
Nishi No.3 Wharf Base	380	4.5	6 x 700 dwt
Nishi No.3 Wharf East No.1	125	7.5	1 x 6000 dwt
Nishi No.3 Wharf East No.2	185	9	1 x 10 000 dwt
Nishi No.3 Wharf Head	136	7.5	1 x 5000 dwt
Nishi No.3 Wharf West	195	9	1 x 10 000 dwt
Nishi No.3 Wharf Slip	150	4.5	2 x 700 dwt
Nishi No.2 Wharf East No.1	175	9	1 x 10 000 dwt
Nishi No.2 Wharf East No.2	185	10	1 x 15 000 dwt
Nishi No.2 Wharf Head	150	7.5	1 x 5000 dwt
Nishi No.2 Wharf West	257	7.5	2 x 5000 dwt
Nishi No.2 Wharf Slip	130	4.5	2 x 700 dwt
Nishi No.1 Wharf East	256	7.5	2 x 5000 dwt
Nishi No.1 Wharf West No.1	167	5.5	2 x 2000 dwt
Nishi No.1 Wharf West No.2	166	4.5	2 x 700 dwt
Ferry Wharf No.1	24	6.5	1 x 4000 dwt
Ferry Wharf No.2	238	8	1 x 13 000 dwt
Ferry Wharf No.3	193	7.5	1 x 6000 dwt
Nippon Petroleum, Refining Co. H-1	45	11	1 x 59 200 dwt
Nippon Petroleum, Refining Co. H-2	24	8.5	1 x 2550 dwt
Nippon Petroleum, Refining Co. H-3	27	8.5	1 x 5900 dwt
Nippon Petroleum, Refining Co. H-4	17	7.5	1 x 3000 dwt
Nippon Petroleum, Refining Co. H-5	19	5	1 x 1300 dwt
Nippon Petroleum, Refining Co. J-0	17	8.5	1 x 6000 dwt
Nippon Petroleum, Refining Co. J-1	97	16.5	1 x 260 000 dwt
Nippon Petroleum, Refining Co. J-2	32	8	1 x 4000 dwt
Nippon Petroleum, Refining Co. J-3	28	8	1 x 5500 dwt
Motowanishi New Wharf East	176	9.5	1 x 12 000 dwt
Motowanishi New Wharf West	125	7.5	1 x 5000 dwt
Motowanishi New Wharf South	135	7.5	1 x 5000 dwt
Motowanishi Old Wharf West	653	8–8.5	2 x 8000 dwt & 2 x 7000 dwt
Nakau Wharf Mobil Dolphin	156	6	2 x 1000 dwt
Nakau Wharf Mitsubishi Dolphin	64	5	1 x 1000 dwt
Nakau Wharf Idemitsu Dolphin	145	5	2 x 1000 dwt
Nakau Dolphin	12	5.5	1 x 2000 dwt
Nippon Steel Wharf No.19	300	16.5	1 x 150 000 dwt
Nippon Steel Wharf No.18	290	14	1 x 100 000 dwt
Nippon Steel Wharf No.17	200	14	1 x 100 000 dwt
Nippon Steel Wharf A	742	16.5	4 x 10 000 dwt
Nippon Steel Wharf B	400	9	2 x 6000 dwt
Nippon Steel Wharf C-D	1590	7.5	10 x 5000 dwt
Nippon Steel North No.1-3	470	9	3 x 10 000 dwt
Nippon Steel North No.4	80	7.5	1 x 1000 dwt
Nippon Steel North No's 5 & 6	495	12	2 x 40 000 dwt
Misaki Wharf	105	6	1 x 3000 dwt
Nittsu Wharf No.1	80	7.5	1 x 2000 dwt
Nittsu Wharf No.2	151	4.5	2 x 700 dwt
Nittsu Wharf No.3	41	4.5	1 x 700 dwt
Nittsu Wharf No.4	117	5.6	1 x 2000 dwt
Nittsu Wharf No's 5 & 6	310	9	2 x 10 000 dwt
Nittsu Wharf No.7	135	7.5	1 x 5000 dwt
Nittsu Wharf No.8	35	4.6	1 x 700 dwt
Nikko Wharf	140	8.5	1 x 8000 dwt
Nikko Dolphin	135	8	1 x 7000 dwt
Shukuzu Wharf No's 1-2	585	6–10	2 x 16 000 dwt & 2 x 3000 dwt

[1]*Muroran:* Sheltered by outer and inner breakwaters

Tanker facilities: One oil berth available at Crude Oil Dolphin operated by Nippon Petroleum Refining Co, length 110 m, depth 16.5 m. Also berths operated by Mobil, Kigunasu, Idemitsu and Nakau

Storage: Seventeen sheds of 39 000 m2, 44 warehouses of 88 000 m2, open timber storage of 278 000 m2, coal storage of 82 000 m2 and other open storage available totalling 395 000 m2

Mechanical Handling Equipment: One 5 t crane on Motowanishi wharf, 12 cranes of 3 t to 25 t cap on Nippon Steel wharves, one 10 t crane on Sakimori wharf, one 20 t crane on Shukuzu wharf, two 5 t cranes on Nittsu wharves and one 8 t crane on Nishi No.3 Wharf, berth No.4

Bunkering: MC Marine and Bunkering Inc., 8th Floor, Uchisaiwai-cho Dai Building, 3-3 Uchisaiwai-cho 1-chome, Chiyoda-ku, Tokyo 100-0011, Japan, *Tel:* +81 3 5251 2575, *Fax:* +81 3 5251 2583

Towage: Seven tugs available; three of 3200 hp, three of 2400 hp and one of 740 hp

Repair & Maintenance: Narasaki Shipbuilding Co. Ltd, 135 Tsukiji-cho, Muroran, Hokkaido, Japan, *Tel:* +81 143 221191, *Fax:* +81 143 226626 Small vessels only

Medical Facilities: Available

Airport: Chitose Airport, 96 km

Lloyd's Agent: Cornes & Co. Ltd, 273 Yamashita-cho, Naka-ku, Yokohama 231-0023, Kanagawa Pref., Japan, *Tel:* +81 45 201 8537, *Fax:* +81 45 212 3105, *Email:* survey@ykh.cornes.co.jp, *Website:* www.cornes.co.jp

NAGASAKI

Lat 32° 43' N; Long 129° 50' E.

Admiralty Chart: JP213	**Admiralty Pilot:** 42A
Time Zone: GMT +9 h	**UNCTAD Locode:** JP NGS

Principal Facilities:

Q	Y	G	C	R		B		T	A

Authority: Port & Harbour Section of Nagasaki Prefecture, 2-13 Edo-machi, Nagasaki 850-8570, Nagasaki Pref., Japan, *Tel:* +81 95 824 1111, *Fax:* +81 95 821 9246, *Email:* s08040@pref.nagasaki.lg.jp, *Website:* www.doboku.pref.nagasaki.jp/~kouwan

Approach: Safe natural harbour, landlocked on three sides, the mouth protected by numerous islands. Depth in fairway 20-40 m

Anchorage: Ample sheltered anchorage, good mud bottom

Pilotage: Not compulsory but advisable if vessel's master is not well acquainted with the port. Pilot boards in the vicinity of Ioshima Lighthouse in pos 32° 42' 51" N; 129° 45' 41" E and is available at any time with adequate advance notice. All communications for pilotage should be made through ship's agents. Berthing will generally only be carried out during daytime. Some restrictions on nightime sailings

Weather: Winds NNW to N

Tides: Tidal range 3.0 m

Maximum Vessel Dimensions: 269 077 dwt, 337.7 m loa

Principal Imports and Exports: Imports: Heavy oil, LNG. Exports: Industrial & transport machines.

Working Hours: 0830-1630. Overtime from 1630-2130

Accommodation:

Name	Length (m)	Depth (m)	Remarks
Nagasaki			Max airdraft of 65 m (under Megami Bridge)
Dejima Wharf	225	10	1 x 20 000 gt. For passenger vessels only
Kogakura Yanagi W	270	12	1 x 30 000 dwt
Kogakura Yanagi S	185	10	1 x 12 000 dwt
Kogakura Yanagi N	185	10	1 x 12 000 dwt
Kaminoshima Kogojima Wharf	390	7.5	3 x 5000 dwt
Matsugae Wharf	270	12	1 x 50 000 gt. For passenger vessels only
Koe Log Pier	170	10	1 x 12 000 dwt
Buoy No's 1-2	450	12.6	1 x 70 000 dwt
Buoy No's 2-3	300	10.8	1 x 15 000 dwt
Buoy Otao No.1-2	440	21.5	1 x 100 000 dwt

Mechanical Handling Equipment:

Location	Type	Capacity (t)	Qty
Nagasaki	Floating Cranes	120	1

Bunkering: Idemitsu Kosan Co. Ltd, 1-1 Marunochi, 3-Chome, Chiyoda-ku, Tokyo 100-8321, Japan, *Tel:* +81 3 3213 3138, *Fax:* +81 3 3213 1145, *Email:* tohru.takamura@si.idemitsu.co.jp, *Website:* www.idemitsu.co.jp
KG Int Petroleum Ltd, Shiba Park Building, 241 Shiba Koen, Minato-ku, Tokyo 105, Japan, *Tel:* +81 3 3578 4551, *Fax:* +81 3 3578 4550
Kyushu Oil Co. Ltd, 1-1 Uchisaiwai-cho 2-chome, Chiyoda-ku, Tokyo, Japan, *Tel:* +81 3 3502 3651, *Fax:* +81 3 3502 9850
MC Marine and Bunkering Inc., 8th Floor, Uchisaiwai-cho Dai Building, 3-3 Uchi-saiwai-cho 1-chome, Chiyoda-ku, Tokyo 100-0011, Japan, *Tel:* +81 3 5251 2575, *Fax:* +81 3 5251 2583
Mitsui & Co. Petroleum Ltd, 2-1, Ohtemachi 1-chome, Chiyoda-ku, Tokyo 100-0004, Japan, *Tel:* +81 3 3285 6905, *Fax:* +81 3 3285 9811, *Email:* tkzph@dg.mitsui.com, *Website:* www.mitsui.co.jp
Nittetsu Shoij Co. Ltd, 5-7 Kameido 1-chome, Koto-ku, Tokyo 136, Japan, *Tel:* +81 3 5627 2157, *Fax:* +81 3 5627 2192

Towage: Nine tugs available; one of 6000 hp, three of 4000 hp, two of 3600 hp, two of 3300 hp and one of 3000 hp

Repair & Maintenance: Mitsubishi Heavy Industries Ltd, 717-1 Fukahori-machi 5-chome, Koyagi, Nagasaki 851-0392, Nagasaki Pref., Japan, *Tel:* +81 95 834 2050, *Fax:* +81 95 834 2055, *Website:* www.mhi.co.jp Two dry docks: No.1 350 m x 56 m x 14 m for vessels up to 300 000 dwt, No.2 276.6 m x 38.8 m x 12.3 m for vessels up to 95 000 dwt

Surveyors: Nippon Kaiji Kyokai, 3-35 Manzai-Machi, Nagasaki 850-0033, Nagasaki Pref., Japan, *Tel:* +81 95 822 3261, *Fax:* +81 95 827 6132, *Email:* ns@classnk.or.jp, *Website:* www.classnk.or.jp

Airport: Omura City, 50 km

Lloyd's Agent: Cornes & Co. Ltd, Meikai Building, 32 Akashi-machi, Chuo-ku, Kobe 650-0037, Hyogo Pref., Japan, *Tel:* +81 78 332 3421, *Fax:* +81 78 332 3070, *Email:* survey@kobe.cornes.co.jp, *Website:* www.cornes.co.jp

NAGOYA

Lat 35° 2' N; Long 136° 52' E.

Admiralty Chart: JP94/JP95/JP1055A/JP1052A   **Admiralty Pilot:** 42A
Time Zone: GMT +9 h   **UNCTAD Locode:** JP NGO

Principal Facilities:

P	Q	Y	G	C	R		B	D	T	A

Authority: Nagoya Port Authority, 8-21 Irifune 1-chome, Minato-ku, Nagoya 455-8686, Aichi Pref., Japan, *Tel:* +81 52 654 7840, *Fax:* +81 52 654 7995, *Email:* info@port-of-nagoya.jp, *Website:* www.port-of-nagoya.jp

Officials: Executive Vice President: Takashi Yamada.
General Director: Yoshiyuki Kumazawa.
Harbour Master: Takunari Tawara.

Port Security: ISPS compliant. Container Security Initiative (CSI) designated port

Pre-Arrival Information: Vessels must report their ETA to the Harbour Master by noon the day before arrival. They are also required to inform the Port Authority of their ETA when they enter the range of communication

Approach: The approach is via the Irago Suido and then enters Ise Bay, approx 55 km S of the Port of Nagoya. Irago Suido traffic route, 1.2 km wide and 3.9 km long, is narrow but can be navigated safely. There are three channels:
North Channel 5000 m long, 200-400 m wide with draft of 10-14 m
East Channel 10 000 m long, 500-610 m wide with draft of 15 m
West Channel 8400 m long, 350-400 m wide with draft of 12-15 m

Anchorage: Quarantine anchorage with 11 m to 16 m depth, located S of the high tide breakwater

Pilotage: Compulsory for vessels exceeding 10 000 gt in both Irago Suido and Ise Bay. Harbour pilots available near quarantine anchorage. Pilot, Tel: +81 569 230713. Direct contact with VHF available

Radio Frequency: Nagoya Port Radio, 24 h service, calling on VHF Channel 16 and working on Channels 12 and 20

Weather: Typhoon Season, July to October

Tides: Tidal range 2.61 m HWL, 0.04 m LWL, 1.4 m MSL

Traffic: 2007, 39 791 vessels, 215 602 597 t of cargo handled, 2 896 221 TEU's

Maximum Vessel Dimensions: At inner harbour 14.54 m depth. At outer harbour 250 000 dwt

Principal Imports and Exports: Imports: Coal, Crude oil, Iron ore, LNG. Exports: Automobile parts, Completed automobiles, Industrial machinery, Iron & steel.

Working Hours: 24 h/day for stevedoring operations

Accommodation: The port is protected by the Hightide Breakwater 7.6 km long and by sea walls including anti-flood walls with a total length of 26.4 km. Total water area of approx 83 000 000 m2, total length of public wharves 15 826 m (127 berths) and total length of private wharves 16 260 m (151 berths)

Name	Length (m)	Depth (m)	Remarks
Public Wharves (with depth of 4.5 m+)			Also there are 12 mooring buoys for vessels of 15 000-27 000 dwt
Garden Pier (Berth No.1)	245	4.5–10	700+15 000 dwt. General cargo
Garden Pier (Berth No.2)	185	10	Max 15 000 dwt. General cargo
Garden Pier (Berth No.3)	210	10	Max 20 000 gt. Passengers
Garden Pier (Berth No.5)	65	4.5	Max 500 gt. Passengers
Inaei Pier (Berth No's 17-18)	320	9	2 x 8000 dwt. Wool, cotton, grain & general cargo
Inaei Pier (Berth No's 22-24)	540	10	3 x 15 000 dwt. General cargo & automobiles
Inaei Pier (Berth No.25)	200	10	Max 15 000 dwt. General cargo & automobiles
Inaei Pier (Berth No.26)	140	4.5	2 x 700 dwt. General cargo & automobiles
Shionagi Pier (Berth No's 27-29)	405	5.5–10	2000+5000+15 000 dwt. Coal
Shionagi Pier (Berth No.31)	60	4.5	Max 700 dwt. Coal & steel products
Shionagi Pier (Berth No.32)	130	7.5	Max 5000 dwt. Coal & steel products
Shionagi Pier (Berth No.33)	185	10	Max 15 000 dwt. Coal & steel products
Ote Pier (Berth No's 11 & 12)	260	7.5	2 x 5000 dwt. General cargo
Oe Pier (Berth No.38)	185	10	See [1] below
Oe Pier (Berth No.39)	213	9	See [2] below
Showa Pier (Berth No's 40 & 41)	240	7.3	2 x 5000 dwt. Fertiliser & chemicals
Funami Pier (Berth No's 43-45)	420	5.5	700+2000 x 4 dwt. Silica sand, sand & stone
Funami Pier (Berth No's 46-48)	571	5.5	700+2000 x 5 dwt. Silica sand, sand & stone
Shiomi Pier (Berth No.BX)	200	4.5	20 x 700 dwt. Small oil tanker facilities
Sorami Pier (Berth No.50)	180	10	Max 15 000 dwt. General cargo
Sorami Pier (Berth No.51)	120	4.5	2 x 700 dwt. General cargo
Sorami Pier (Berth No.70)	360	5.5	4 x 2000 dwt. General cargo
Sorami Pier (Berth No's 95-97)	540	5.5	4 x 2000 dwt, 1 x 1500 dwt & 1 x 700 dwt. Steel materials
Kinjo Pier (Berth No's 52 & 53)	497	12	2 x 35 000 dwt. Automobiles
Kinjo Pier (Berth No's 54-57)	800	10	4 x 15 000 dwt. Automobiles
Kinjo Pier (Berth No's 58-62)	1000	10	5 x 15 000 dwt. Automobiles & general cargo
Kinjo Pier (Berth No's 63-67)	1000	10	5 x 15 000 dwt. General cargo
Kinjo Pier (Berth No.71)	450	5.5	5 x 2000 dwt. General cargo
Kinjo Pier (Berth No's 72-75)	520	7.5	4 x 5000 dwt. General cargo
Kinjo Pier (Berth No's 76-77)	400	10.5	See [3] below
Kinjo Pier (Berth No's 78-79)	400	10.5	15 000 dwt x 2. Automobiles & heavy products
Kinjo Pier (Berth No's 80-81)	400	10–10.5	2 x 15 000 dwt. Automobiles & general cargo
Kinjo Pier (Berth No's 82-84)	600	10	3 x 15 000 dwt. General cargo
Kinjo Pier (Berth No.85)	280	12	Max 50 000 gt. General cargo
Yatomi Pier (Berth No's 88-89)	260	7.5	2 x 5000 dwt. Lumber & general cargo
Yatomi Pier (Berth No.6)	270	12	Max 30 000 dwt. General cargo & automobiles
Yatomi Pier (Berth No.7)	240	12	Max 30 000 dwt. General cargo & automobiles
Tobishima Pier (Berth No's 90-92)	620	10–12	See [4] below
Tobishima Pier (Berth No's 93-94)	700	15	See [5] below
Tobishima Pier (Berth No's 98-99)	370	10	2 x 15 000 dwt. Lumber
Yokosuka Pier (Berth No.86)	420	4.5	7 x 700 dwt. Building materials
Kitahama Pier (Berth No.87)	240	4.5	4 x 700 dwt. Light industrial products
Nabeta Pier (T2)	385	14	See [6] below
Other Wharves			
Tobishima Pier (Berth TS2)	400	16	See [7] below
Nabeta Pier (T1)	350	14	See [8] below
Nagoya Container Berths (R1-R3)	900	12	See [9] below
Ferry Terminal (V1-V3)	663	7.5	7000+10 000 x 2 dwt
Private Wharves (with depth of 10m+)			
Takara Oil Pier (B6)	35	10	Max 3000 dwt
Nippon Oil Pier No.2 (B7)	168	10	Max 30 000 dwt
Nippon Oil Pier No.3 (BA)	73	10	Max 2000 dwt
Sunlux Oil Pier (B8)	45	10	Max 3000 dwt
Toyotsu Oil Center Pier (BB)	35.8	10	Max 3000 dwt

Key to Principal Facilities:—			
A=Airport	**C**=Containers	**G**=General Cargo	**P**=Petroleum **R**=Ro/Ro **Y**=Dry Bulk
B=Bunkers	**D**=Dry Dock	**L**=Cruise	**Q**=Other Liquid Bulk **T**=Towage (where available from port)

Name	Length (m)	Depth (m)	Remarks
Standard Oil Pier (BC)	175	10	Max 20 000 dwt
Mitsui & Co. Nagoya Pier (BE)	74	10	Max 30 000 dwt
Kanematsu Oil Pier (BG)	74.6	10	Max 20 000 dwt
Rinoru Yushi Pier (BH2)	182	10	Max 25 000 dwt
BI Pier (BI)	84.5	10	Max 34 000 dwt
Ito Chu Pier (BK)	179	10	Max 20 000 dwt
Fujitrans Pier No.2 (BQ)	107.8	10	Max 8000 dwt
BQ2 Pier (BQ2)	165	10	Max 10 000 dwt
Toray Wharf (C4)	175	10	Max 15 000 dwt
Nippon Steel Wharf (F5)	195	10	Max 20 000 dwt
Nippon Steel Wharf (F6-8)	678	12	3 x 50 000 dwt
Nippon Steel Wharf (F11)	350	14	Max 100 000 dwt
Nippon Steel Wharf (F12)	250	13	Max 70 000 dwt
Nippon Steel Wharf (F13)	250	13	Max 70 000 dwt
Nippon Steel Wharf (F14)	140	13	Max 50 000 dwt
Nisshin Seifun Pier (G1)	150	12	See [10] below
Ishikawajima-Harima Chita Pier (G3)	450	12	Max 450 000 dwt
Toyota Pier (I2)	200	11	Max 20 000 dwt
Toyota Pier (I5-6)	500	11	2 x 30 000 dwt
Chita Futo Pier (J4)	81	12	Max 5000 dwt
Chita Futo Pier (J5)	185	12	See [11] below
Japan Energy Pier (J7)	128	12	Max 50 000 dwt. Tanker terminal
Japan Energy Pier (J8-9)	250	12	2 x 5000 dwt
Japan Energy Pier (J16-19)	400	12	4 x 5000 dwt
Zenno Silo Pier (JS)	190	12	See [12] below
Toyo Grain Terminal Pier (JT)	255	12	Max 50 000 dwt. Grain cargo facilities with discharging equipment are available
Idemitsu Chita Pier No.1 (K1-2)	253	14	Max 1500+750 dwt
Idemitsu Chita Pier No.1 (K3-4)	253	14	Max 1500+750 dwt
Idemitsu Chita Pier No.2 (K5)	433	14	Max 100 000 dwt. Tanker terminal. Also used as an LPG terminal
Chita LNG Pier No.1 (L1)	420	14	See [13] below
Chita LNG Pier No.2 (L2)	460	14	Max 65 000 dwt
Yura Pier (N1-2)	250	10	Max 15 000 dwt
Yura Pier (N3)	73	10	Max 12 000 dwt
Ube Cement Pier (S4)	78	10	Max 14 000 dwt
Toho Gas Sorami Pier (S5)	63	10	Max 5000 dwt
Toho Gas Sorami Pier (S6)	144	10	Max 25 000 dwt
Oji Paper Pier (U1)	249	12	Max 50 000 dwt
Oji Paper Dolphin (U2)	227	12	Max 50 000 dwt
Oil Pier (Showa,Nippon,Marubeni) (U5)	280	12	Max 30 000 dwt
Chubu Electric Power West Pier (U6)	97	12	Max 5000 dwt
Chubu Electric Power West Pier (U7)	107	12	Max 5000 dwt
Isewan Sea Berth	500	25.5	See [14] below

[1]Oe Pier (Berth No.38): Max 15 000 dwt. Automobiles, general & heavy cargo

[2]Oe Pier (Berth No.39): Max 15 000 dwt. Automobiles, general & heavy cargo

[3]Kinjo Pier (Berth No's 76-77): 10 000+20 000 x dwt. Container terminal operated by Port Authority. Terminal area of 8.8 ha. There are 32 reefer plugs for refrigerated containers

[4]Tobishima Pier (Berth No's 90-92): 2 x 15 000+35 000 dwt. Container terminal operated by Port Authority. Terminal area of 17 ha. There are 110 reefer plugs for refrigerated containers

[5]Tobishima Pier (Berth No's 93-94): 2 x 50 000 dwt. Container terminal operated by Port Authority. Terminal area of 22.5 ha. There are 140 reefer plugs for refrigerated containers

[6]Nabeta Pier (T2): 50 000 dwt. Container terminal operated by Nagoya United Container Terminal Co Ltd (NUCT), Tel: +81 56 766 3370, Fax: +81 56 766 3371, Email: nuct7@forest.ocn.ne.jp

[7]Tobishima Pier (Berth TS2): 108 500 dwt. Container terminal operated by Tobishima Container Berth Co Ltd (TCB), Tel: +81 56 757 2200, Fax: +81 56 757 2481, Email: info@tcb-terminal.co.jp, Website: www.tcb-terminal.co.jp
Terminal area of 23.4 ha. 240 reefer plugs for refrigerated containers

[8]Nabeta Pier (T1): 50 000 dwt. Container terminal operated by Nagoya United Container Terminal Co Ltd (NUCT), Tel: +81 56 766 3370, Fax: +81 56 766 3371, Email: nuct7@forest.ocn.ne.jp
Terminal area of 35.9 ha. 296 reefer plugs for refrigerated containers

[9]Nagoya Container Berths (R1-R3): Container terminal operated by Nagoya Terminal Service Center, Tel: +81 56 755 2100, Fax: +81 56 755 1795, Email: ntsc-shocyo@ntsc.gr.jp, Website: www.ntsc.gr.jp
2 x 35 000 + 25 000 dwt. Total area of 28.9 ha. 189 reefer plugs for refrigerated containers

[10]Nisshin Seifun Pier (G1): Max 50 000 dwt. Grain cargo facilities with discharging equipment are available

[11]Chita Futo Pier (J5): Max 35 000 dwt. Grain cargo facilities with discharging equipment are available

[12]Zenno Silo Pier (JS): Max 65 000 dwt. Grain cargo facilities with discharging equipment are available

[13]Chita LNG Pier No.1 (L1): Max 100 000 dwt. Operated by Toho Gas, Chubu Electric Power & Japan Energy

[14]Isewan Sea Berth: 2 x 250 000 dwt + 2000 dwt. Tanker terminal outside the harbour limit

Storage: Transit sheds of 533 710 m2, warehousing of 2 757 586 m2, including refrigerated warehousing and silos, coal storage of 225 223 m2 and timber storage of 2 346 723 m2

Mechanical Handling Equipment: 27 container cranes, 36 RTG's and 74 straddle carriers

Location	Type	Capacity (t)	Qty
Kinjo Pier (Berth No's 76-77)	Container Cranes	47.7	2
Kinjo Pier (Berth No's 76-77)	Container Cranes	48	1
Tobishima Pier (Berth No's 90-92)	Container Cranes	46.4	1
Tobishima Pier (Berth No's 90-92)	Container Cranes	48	1
Tobishima Pier (Berth No's 90-92)	Container Cranes	49.1	2
Tobishima Pier (Berth No's 93-94)	Post Panamax	55	3
Tobishima Pier (Berth No's 93-94)	Post Panamax	56.3	2
Nabeta Pier (T2)	Post Panamax	58.4–58.6	3
Tobishima Pier (Berth TS2)	Post Panamax	65	3
Nabeta Pier (T1)	Post Panamax	57.9	3
Nagoya Container Berths (R1-R3)	Container Cranes	51.1	2
Nagoya Container Berths (R1-R3)	Post Panamax	55.1	2
Nagoya Container Berths (R1-R3)	Post Panamax	53.1	2

Bunkering: Sigma Shoji Co. Ltd, 2-25 Aikawa, Tempaku-ku, Nagoya 468-0836, Aichi Pref., Japan, Tel: +81 52 8961 510, Fax: +81 52 8967 703, Email: info@sigma-shoji.co.jp, Website: www.sigma-shoji.co.jp
Cosmo Oil Co. Ltd, Toshiba Building, 1-1 Shibaura 1-chome, Minato-ku, Tokyo 105-8528, Japan, Tel: +81 3 3798 3156, Fax: +81 3 3798 3592, Email: masayuki_iijima@cosmo-oil.co.jp, Website: www.cosmo-oil.co.jp
Hanwa Co. Ltd, 2nd Floor, Finland House, 56 Haymarket, London SW1Y 4RN, United Kingdom, Tel: +44 20 7839 4448, Fax: +44 20 7839 3994, Email: orito@hanwa.co.uk
Hikawa Shoji Kaisha Ltd, 26-2 Shinkawa NS Building 1-chome, Shinkawa, Chuo-ku, Tokyo 104, Japan, Tel: +81 3 5776 6858, Fax: +81 3 5541 3274
Idemitsu Kosan Co. Ltd, 1-1 Marunochi, 3-Chome, Chiyoda-ku, Tokyo 100-8321, Japan, Tel: +81 3 3213 3138, Fax: +81 3 3213 1145, Email: tohru.takamura@si.idemitsu.co.jp, Website: www.idemitsu.co.jp
KG Int Petroleum Ltd, Shiba Park Building, 241 Shiba Koen, Minato-ku, Tokyo 105, Japan, Tel: +81 3 3578 4551, Fax: +81 3 3578 4550
Japan Energy Corp., 2-10-1, Toranomon, Minato-ku, Tokyo 105-8407, Japan, Tel: +81 3 5573 6100, Fax: +81 3 5573 6674, Email: yamano@j-energy.co.jp, Website: www.j-energy.co.jp
Kamei Corp., 1-6-1 Otemachi, Chiyoda-ku, Tokyo 100-0004, Japan, Tel: +81 3 3286 6234, Fax: +81 3 3286 6249, Email: bunker@kamei.co.jp
Kawasho Corp., World Trade Centre, 4-1 Hanamatsu-cho 2-chome, Minato-ku, Tokyo 105, Japan, Tel: +81 3 3435 3251
Kyodo Oil Co. Ltd, 11-2 Nagata-cho 2-chome, Chiyoda-ku, Tokyo, Japan, Tel: +81 3 3505 8241, Fax: +81 3 3505 8697
Marubeni Petroleum Co. Ltd, Marubeni International Petroleum Singapore Co. Ltd, c/o Marubeni Corporation, 4-2 Ohtemachi 1-chome, Chiyoda-ku, Tokyo 100-8088, Japan, Tel: +81 3 3282 3920, Fax: +81 3 3282 3950, Email: TOKB554@marubenicorp.com, Website: www.marubeni.co.jp
MC Marine and Bunkering Inc., 8th Floor, Uchisaiwai-cho Dai Building, 3-3 Uchi-saiwai-cho 1-chome, Chiyoda-ku, Tokyo 100-0011, Japan, Tel: +81 3 5251 2575, Fax: +81 3 5251 2583
Mitsui & Co. Petroleum Ltd, 2-1, Ohtemachi 1-chome, Chiyoda-ku, Tokyo 100-0004, Japan, Tel: +81 3 3285 6905, Fax: +81 3 3285 9811, Email: tkzph@dg.mitsui.com, Website: www.mitsui.co.jp
Nissho Iwai Corp., 4-4 Akasaka 2-chome, Minato-ku, Tokyo, Japan, Tel: +81 3 35882111
Nittetsu Shoij Co. Ltd, 5-7 Kameido 1-chome, Koto-ku, Tokyo 136, Japan, Tel: +81 3 5627 2157, Fax: +81 3 5627 2192
Shinagawa Fuel Co. Ltd, New Pier Takeshiba North Tower, 8th Floor, 1-11-1 Kaigan, Minato-ku, Tokyo 105-8525, Japan, Tel: +81 3 5470 7113, Fax: +81 3 5470 7157, Email: hakuyu@ml1.sinanen.co.jp
Sigma Foreign Service (Panama) S.A., 2-25 Aikawai, Tempaku-ku, Nagoya 468-0836, Aichi Pref., Japan, Tel: +81 52 896 1510, Fax: +81 52 896 7703
Sumitomo Corp., Harumi Island, Triton Square, Office Tower Y, 8-11 Harumi 1-chome, Chuo-ku, Tokyo 104-8610, Japan, Tel: +81 3 51664458, Fax: +81 3 51666407, Email: ir@sumitomo.co.jp, Website: www.sumitomocorp.co.jp

Waste Reception Facilities: Available

Towage: 19 tugs of 1400-3500 hp for assisting vessels

Shipping Agents: Aichi Kaiun Kaisha Ltd, 9-31, 2-chome, Meiko, Minato-ku, Nagoya, Aichi Pref., Japan, Tel: +81 52 652 6193, Fax: +81 52 651 3233
Chukyo Kaiun Kaisha Ltd, 2-1 1-chome, Sakae, Naka-ku, Nagoya 460-0008, Aichi Pref., Japan, Tel: +81 52 201 7779, Fax: +81 52 204 0674, Email: chukyo@jp.hanjin.com
Goyo Kaiun, Nagoya Seibu T-1, 7-40 Irifune, Minato-ku, Nagoya 455-0032, Aichi Pref., Japan, Tel: +81 52 651 5171, Fax: +81 52 651 5168, Email: portope@kaiun.co.jp
Kamigumi Co. Ltd, 2-20, Irifune 2-chome, Minato-ku, Nagoya 476-0015, Aichi Pref., Japan, Tel: +81 52 652 8892, Fax: +81 52 652 0297, Email: nagoya-kanrika@kamigumi.co.jp
KK DSA Agencies (Nagoya), 8th Floor, Kirix Marunouchi Building, 1-17-19, Mar-unouchi, Naka-ku, Nagoya 460-0002, Aichi Pref., Japan, Tel: +81 52 212 1841, Fax: +81 52 219 2188, Email: fairwind@dsa.co.jp
Meijo Shipping Co. Ltd, 1-20 Irifune 1-chome, Minato-ku, Nagoya, Aichi Pref., Japan, Tel: +81 52 661 8241, Fax: +81 52 654 0900, Email: sls-ymlngo@yangming.co.jp
A.P. Moller-Maersk Group, Maersk K.K., Nagoya Nishiki Front Tower Building, 8th Floor, 3-4 Nishiki 2-chome, Naka-ku, Nagoya 460-0003, Aichi Pref., Japan, Tel: +81 52 209 6951, Fax: +81 52 209 6965, Website: www.maerskline.com
Nagoya Transport Agencies Ltd, 4-28 Irifune 1-chome,, Minato-ku, Nagoya 455-0032, Aichi Pref., Japan, Tel: +81 52 653 2373, Fax: +81 52 653 2395, Email: ntcngy01@sage.ocn.ne.jp

Nihon Hoso Unyu Co. Ltd, 15-22 Nishiki 2-chome, Naka-ku, Nagoya 460-0003, Aichi Pref., Japan, *Tel:* +81 52 218 5401, *Fax:* +81 52 218 5405, *Email:* t_arai@nhu.co.jp, *Website:* www.nhu.co.jp

Sempaku Kaisha (Nagoya) Ltd, 5th Floor, 2 Meiko Building, 2-28 Irifune, 2-chome, Minato-ku, Nagoya 455-0032, Aichi Pref., Japan, *Tel:* +81 52 652 6618, *Fax:* +81 52 661 5792, *Email:* kaimubusempaku@meiko-trans.co.jp

Seven Star Co. Ltd, c/o Toa Shipping Co Ltd, 4th Floor, Sakae 1-chome-Naka-ku, Nagoya, Aichi Pref., Japan, *Tel:* +81 52 203 1391, *Fax:* +81 52 232 1609, *Email:* toah@mab.sphere.ne.jp

Tokai Kyowa Kijoh Container Terminal, 1-1-20 Irifune, Minato-ku, Nagoya 455, Aichi Pref., Japan, *Tel:* +81 52 651 6369, *Fax:* +81 52 651 6165

Surveyors: Nippon Kaiji Kyokai, 2-2-5 Jingu, Atsuta-ku, Nagoya 456-0031, Aichi Pref., Japan, *Tel:* +81 52 682 2509, *Fax:* +81 52 682 0849, *Email:* ng@classnk.or.jp, *Website:* www.classnk.or.jp

Medical Facilities: Available

Airport: Central Japan International Airport, 30 km

Railway: Nagoya Bayside Railway alongside the east side of the port. West Harbour Railway directly serves the centre of the port

Development: Construction of a deepwater container berth at Tobishima Pier South Side

Addition of a third berth to Nabeta Pier

Channel expansion and dredging in order to cope with the increasing size of container vessels

Lloyd's Agent: Cornes & Co. Ltd, Meikai Building, 32 Akashi-machi, Chuo-ku, Kobe 650-0037, Hyogo Pref., Japan, *Tel:* +81 78 332 3421, *Fax:* +81 78 332 3070, *Email:* survey@kobe.cornes.co.jp, *Website:* www.cornes.co.jp

NAHA

Lat 26° 13' N; Long 127° 40' E.

Admiralty Chart: JP226   **Admiralty Pilot:** 42A
Time Zone: GMT +9 h   **UNCTAD Locode:** JP NAH

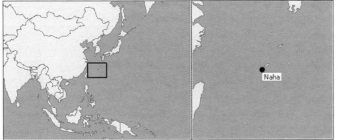

Principal Facilities:

		G	C	R		B		T	A

Authority: Naha Port Authority, 2-1 Tondo-cho, Naha 900-0035, Okinawa Pref., Japan, *Tel:* +81 98 868 4544, *Fax:* +81 98 862 4233, *Email:* kumiai@nahaport.jp, *Website:* www.nahaport.jp

Officials: President: Keiichi Inamine.
Executive Vice President: Toshiro Tsutsumi.

Port Security: ISPS compliant

Approach: Draught limitation in channel is 11 m

Pilotage: Pilotage compulsory for vessels over 300 gt. Pilot boards in pos 26° 13' 49" N; 127° 38' 20" E. Naha Pilots Association to be contacted on VHF Channel 13, one hour prior to arrival at Pilot Station. Berthing is normally carried out during daylight hours only, unberthing at any time. Eleventh Regional Maritime Safety Agency can be contacted on VHF Channels 16 and 12, call sign NAHAHOAN

Weather: NNE wind direction in winter, SSE in summer

Tides: Range of tide 2.3 m

Traffic: 2005, 8 663 000 t of cargo handled, 408 448 TEU's

Working Hours: 0800-1630, 1630-2200 in two shifts

Accommodation:

Name	Length (m)	Depth (m)	Remarks
Naha Terminal			See ¹ below
Wharf No.1	165	9	1 x 10 000 dwt
Wharf No.2	165	9	1 x 10 000 dwt
Wharf No.3	164	9	1 x 10 000 dwt
Wharf No.4	70	9	1 x 1000 dwt
Wharf No.5	78	9	1 x 1000 dwt
Wharf No.6	93	9	1 x 5000 dwt
Small Wharf No.1	54	4	Bunkers
Small Wharf No.2	152	4	Bunkers
Small Wharf No.3	55	4	Bunkers
Small Wharf No.4	126	4	Bunkers
Small Wharf No.5	79	3	
Small Wharf No.6	94	2	
Small Wharf No.7	121	2	
Small Wharf No.8	86	2	
Miegusuku Small Wharf No.1	222	4	
Miegusuku Small Wharf No.2	146	4	
Miegusuku Small Wharf No.3	222	4	
Miegusuku Small Wharf No.4	56	4	
Miegusuku Small Wharf No.5	60	4	
Tomari Terminal			See ² below
Wharf No.1	105	6	1 x 3000 dwt
Wharf No.2	105	6	1 x 3000 dwt
Wharf No.3	105	6	1 x 3000 dwt
Wharf No.4	26	6	
Wharf No.5	75	4.5	1 x 500 dwt
Wharf No.6	75	4.5	1 x 500 dwt
Wharf No.7	105	6	1 x 3000 dwt
Small Wharf No.1	37	3	
Small Wharf No.2	117	3	
Shinko Terminal			See ³ below
Wharf No.1	390	7.5	3 x 5000 dwt
Wharf No.2	70	5	1 x 2000 dwt
Wharf No.3	410	7.5	3 x 5000 dwt
Wharf No.4	410	7.5	3 x 5000 dwt
Wharf No.5	407	11	2 x 20 000 dwt
Wharf No.6	387	11	2 x 20 000 dwt
Wharf No.7	391	11	2 x 20 000 dwt
Wharf No.9	300	14	1 x 40 000 dwt
Wharf No.10	300	15	1 x 40 000 dwt
Small Wharf No.1	170	4	
Small Wharf No.2	120	4	
Small Wharf No.3	130	3	
Small Wharf No.4	200	3	
Small Wharf No.5	73	4	
Small Wharf No.6	78	4	
Small Wharf No.7	87	4	
Small Wharf 1	165	2.5	
Small Wharf 2	123	2.5	
Small Wharf 3	110	2.5	
Small Wharf 4	188	2.5	
Small Wharf 5	50	2.5	
Small Wharf 6	50	2.5	
Urasoe Terminal			See ⁴ below
Wharf No.1	130	7.5	1 x 5000 dwt
Wharf No.2	130	7.5	1 x 5000 dwt
Wharf No.3	130	7.5	1 x 5000 dwt
Wharf No.4	130	7.5	1 x 5000 dwt
Wharf No.5	130	7.5	1 x 5000 dwt
Wharf No.6	130	7.5	1 x 5000 dwt
Wharf No.7	130	7.5	1 x 5000 dwt
Small Wharf No.1	160	4	

¹*Naha Terminal:* For ferries linking the Okinawa mainland to Kagoshima, Hakata and the isolated islands of Miyako and Ishigaki; also for freight carriers to East Asia. Cargo handling yards of 16 960 m2, storage yards of 30 412 m2, other yards of 8974 m2 and transit shed of 5736 m2

²*Tomari Terminal:* For liner vessels between the neighbouring islands and small boats. Cargo handling yards of 2733 m2, storage yards of 4027 m2, other yards of 22 885 m2 and transit shed of 3166 m2

³*Shinko Terminal:* Major district for international container trade, international ferries to Taiwan and domestic ferries to Tokyo, Osaka and Kobe
The Naha International Container Terminal Inc., 1-27-1 Minatomachi, Naha, Okinawa 900-0001, Tel: +81 98 867 5931, Fax: +81 98 867 5933, Email: support@nicti.co.jp, consists of Terminals 9 and 10 with a terminal area of 21 ha and a berthing length of 600 m (two 300 m berths) in depth of 15 m. It has a container storage area of 60 000 m2 and is equipped with one panamax and one post-panamax crane. 48 reefer points

⁴*Urasoe Terminal:* Tramp general cargo & cement vessels. Cargo handling yards of 36 712 m2, storage yards of 75 693 m2 and transit shed of 3570 m2

Cargo Worked: Approx 30 t/h/gang

Bunkering: Domestic oil only is available at berths or inner anchorage

Towage: Three tugs available; two of 2600 hp and one of 1900 hp

Repair & Maintenance: Minato Kogyo Co. Ltd, Naha, Okinawa Pref., Japan, *Tel:* +81 98 868 3110

Medical Facilities: Available close to the port (Japanese speaking only). Hospital, 8 km. US Naval Hospital, 30 km

Airport: Naha Airport, 5 km

Development: Ther are plans for a container terminal extension (Berth No.11: 350 m long in depth of 15 m) which will be constructed when demand has met a certain level

Lloyd's Agent: Cornes & Co. Ltd, Meikai Building, 32 Akashi-machi, Chuo-ku, Kobe 650-0037, Hyogo Pref., Japan, *Tel:* +81 78 332 3421, *Fax:* +81 78 332 3070, *Email:* survey@kobe.cornes.co.jp, *Website:* www.cornes.co.jp

NAKANOSEKI

harbour area, see under Mitajiri

NAMIKATA

Lat 34° 7' N; Long 132° 58' E.

Admiralty Chart: JP104   **Admiralty Pilot:** 42B
Time Zone: GMT +9 h   **UNCTAD Locode:** JP NIT

Key to Principal Facilities:—				
A=Airport	**C**=Containers	**G**=General Cargo	**P**=Petroleum	**R**=Ro/Ro	**Y**=Dry Bulk
B=Bunkers	**D**=Dry Dock	**L**=Cruise	**Q**=Other Liquid Bulk	**T**=Towage (where available from port)	

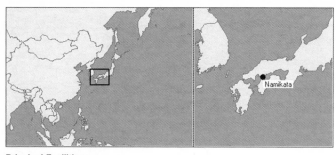

Principal Facilities:

P	Q					B	T	

Authority: Port & Harbours Coast Division, Public Works Department, Ehime Prefectural Government, 4-4-2 Ichiban-cho, Matsuyama 790-8570, Ehime Pref., Japan, *Tel:* +81 89 941 2111, *Fax:* +81 89 941 3523, *Email:* kouwankaigan@pref.ehime.jp, *Website:* www.pref.ehime.jp

Port Security: ISPS compliant

Approach: Draught limitation in the channel is 25 m

Pilotage: Not compulsory. Inland sea pilots are available at Sekisaki, Wada-Misaki or Hesaki when required

Tides: Range of tide 3.9 m

Maximum Vessel Dimensions: 78 434 dwt, 243 m loa

Accommodation:

Name	Remarks
Namikata	See [1] below

[1] *Namikata:* Oil and gas terminal operated by Namikata Terminal Co. Ltd., Tel: +81 898 522001, Fax: +81 898 522004
Main berth can accommodate vessels of up to 125 000 dwt, 278 m loa and 25 m d and is equipped with ten 12'' pipelines and four 8'' lines for return gas. There are also six smaller berths for tankers in the terminal complex. Mooring and unmooring during daylight hours only. Cargoes handled include butadiene, propane, butane, methanol and naptha

Bunkering: Hikawa Shoji Kaisha Ltd, 26-2 Shinkawa NS Building 1-chome, Shinkawa, Chuo-ku, Tokyo 104, Japan, *Tel:* +81 3 5776 6858, *Fax:* +81 3 5541 3274
Marubeni Petroleum Co. Ltd, Marubeni International Petroleum Singapore Co. Ltd, c/o Marubeni Corporation, 4-2 Ohtemachi 1-chome, Chiyoda-ku, Tokyo 100-8088, Japan, *Tel:* +81 3 3282 3920, *Fax:* +81 3 3282 3950, *Email:* TOKB554@marubenicorp.com, *Website:* www.marubeni.co.jp
MC Marine and Bunkering Inc., 8th Floor, Uchisaiwai-cho Dai Building, 3-3 Uchisaiwai-cho 1-chome, Chiyoda-ku, Tokyo 100-0011, Japan, *Tel:* +81 3 5251 2575, *Fax:* +81 3 5251 2583
Nissho Iwai Corp., 4-4 Akasaka 2-chome, Minato-ku, Tokyo, Japan, *Tel:* +81 3 35882111

Towage: Compulsory for berthing. The number of tugs required is dependent on size of vessel. Tugs will attend from Matsuyama, Hiroshima and Sakaide

Lloyd's Agent: Cornes & Co. Ltd, Meikai Building, 32 Akashi-machi, Chuo-ku, Kobe 650-0037, Hyogo Pref., Japan, *Tel:* +81 78 332 3421, *Fax:* +81 78 332 3070, *Email:* survey@kobe.cornes.co.jp, *Website:* www.cornes.co.jp

NANAO

Lat 37° 6' N; Long 137° 2' E.

Admiralty Chart: 1342	**Admiralty Pilot:** 41
Time Zone: GMT +9 h	**UNCTAD Locode:** JP NNO

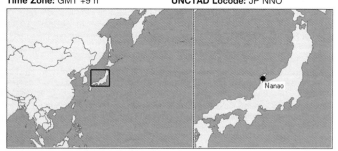

Principal Facilities:

P	Q	Y	G			B	T	

Authority: Port & Harbor Division of Ishikawa Prefecture, 1-1 Hirosaka 1-chome, Hosai, Kanazawa 920-8580, Ishikawa Pref., Japan, *Tel:* +81 76 223 9392, *Fax:* +81 76 223 9484, *Email:* e251300@pref.ishikawa.jp

Port Security: ISPS compliant

Approach: Draught limitation in channel 9.8 m

Pilotage: Compulsory only for large tankers. Pilot available if required and boards in pos 37° 06' 50" N; 137° 04' 30" E, or at quarantine anchorage from 0600-2200

Tides: Max tidal range 0.47 m

Accommodation:

Name	Length (m)	Depth (m)	Draught (m)	Remarks
Nanao				
West Pier No.1	135	7.5	7	Max 5000 gt
East Pier No.1	221	5.5	5	Max 3000 gt
East Pier No.2	180	9	8.5	Max 8000 gt
Sumitomo Cement	121	6.6	6	Max 4000 gt
Ohta Bussen Futo	185	10	9	Max 10 000 gt
Ohta Futo	185	7.5	7	Max 5000 gt
Ohta Dolphin		7.5	7	Max 5000 gt
Kyoritsu Dolphin		6.2	5.7	See [1] below
LGT Dolphin		14.5	9.6	See [2] below

[1] *Kyoritsu Dolphin:* Max 1500 gt. Oil pipeline for small tankers
[2] *LGT Dolphin:* Max 60 000 gt. Propane and butane pipeline

Mechanical Handling Equipment:

Location	Type	Capacity (t)	Qty
East Pier No.2	Mult-purp. Cranes	5	1
Sumitomo Cement	Mult-purp. Cranes	8	1

Bunkering: Domestic oil can be brought from Fushiki and bonded oil from Moji with sufficient notice

Towage: Three tugs available; one of 2000 hp, one of 320 hp and one of 180 hp

Repair & Maintenance: Minor engine and electrical repairs undertaken

Lloyd's Agent: Cornes & Co. Ltd, 273 Yamashita-cho, Naka-ku, Yokohama 231-0023, Kanagawa Pref., Japan, *Tel:* +81 45 201 8537, *Fax:* +81 45 212 3105, *Email:* survey@ykh.cornes.co.jp, *Website:* www.cornes.co.jp

NAOETSU

Lat 37° 11' N; Long 138° 15' E.

Admiralty Chart: 1342	**Admiralty Pilot:** 41
Time Zone: GMT +9 h	**UNCTAD Locode:** JP NAO

Principal Facilities:

P		Y	G	C		B		T	

Authority: Port of Naoetsu, 1-11-2 Minato-Cho, Joetsu, Niigata 942-0011, Niigata Pref., Japan, *Tel:* +81 25 543 4167, *Fax:* +81 25 544 4529, *Email:* s171120@mail.pref.niigata.jp, *Website:* www.pref.niigata.jp/chiikishinko/jouetsu/naoetsu

Officials: Director General: Shoichi Yamamoto.

Port Security: ISPS compliant

Approach: Draught limitation in channel to Kosanhin Pier 11.7 m; to other piers 9 m in summer, 8.7 m in winter

Pilotage: Pilots available at quarantine anchorage during daylight hours only

Radio Frequency: Niigata Radio, call sign 'JCF'; Nagasaki Radio, 'JOS' and Choshi Radio, 'JCS'

Tides: Max tidal range 0.63 m

Accommodation:

Name	Length (m)	Depth (m)	Draught (m)	Remarks
Naoetsu				
West Wharf No.1	174	10	9	Max 15 000 dwt
West Wharf No.2	185	10	9	Max 15 000 dwt
Centre Pier No.1	130	7.5	7	Max 5000 dwt
Centre Pier No.2	185	10	9	Max 15 000 dwt
Lumber Pier	185	10	9	Max 15 000 dwt
Kosanhin Pier	270	13	11.7	Max 50 000 dwt
East Pier No.1	185	10	9	Max 15 000 dwt
East Pier No.2	185	10	9	Max 15 000 dwt
East Pier No.3	185	10	9	Max 15 000 dwt
Tanker Berth N	105	6	5	Max 3000 dwt
Tanker Berth L	150	6	5	Max 2000 dwt
South Pier No.1	170	7.5	5	Max 6000 dwt

Mechanical Handling Equipment: Five tower cranes, unloading cap 240 t/h situated at Kosanhin Pier and East Pier. Two 35 t cap cranes and one 200 t/h cap pneumatic unloader on the West Wharf

Bunkering: Domestic oil available. Bonded oil from Moji and Hakodate with sufficient notice

Towage: One 1300 hp tug available. Larger tugs up to 3400 hp brought from Niigata if required

Repair & Maintenance: Minor repairs undertaken

Lloyd's Agent: Cornes & Co. Ltd, 273 Yamashita-cho, Naka-ku, Yokohama 231-0023, Kanagawa Pref., Japan, *Tel:* +81 45 201 8537, *Fax:* +81 45 212 3105, *Email:* survey@ykh.cornes.co.jp, *Website:* www.cornes.co.jp

NAOSHIMA

Lat 34° 27' N; Long 134° 0' E.

Admiralty Chart: 694	**Admiralty Pilot:** 42B
Time Zone: GMT +9 h	**UNCTAD Locode:** JP NAS

Principal Facilities:

		Y		B		A

Authority: Port & Harbour Section of Kagawa Prefecture, 4-1-10 Bancho, Takamatsu 760-8570, Kagawa Pref., Japan, *Tel:* +81 87 8311 111, *Fax:* +81 87 8374 289, *Email:* kowan@pref.kagawa.lg.jp, *Website:* www.pref.kagawa.jp

Approach: The approach to the port is through Bissan Seto and Uko East traffic routes. Draught limitation in channel 13 m

Pilotage: Inland Sea pilotage is compulsory for vessels exceeding 10 000 gt. Available at Wada-Misaki, Sekisaki or Hesaki. Tomogashima and Kanmon Pilots are also available. Pilotage is not compulsory within port limits, but is recommended in view of the rapid current

Tides: Max tidal range 2.7 m

Working Hours: Stevedores 0800-2200

Accommodation:

Name	Length (m)	Depth (m)	Remarks
Naoshima			
Mitsubishi Metal Wharf	165	10.2	See [1] below

[1]*Mitsubishi Metal Wharf:* For vessels of 20 000 gt, 180 m loa, 9.45 m d. Mobile unloader of 6.7 t cap for discharge of copper and lead concentrates. Vessels berth and unberth in daylight hours only

Mechanical Handling Equipment: Floating cranes available

Cargo Worked: 3500 t discharged per day

Bunkering: Idemitsu Kosan Co. Ltd, 1-1 Marunochi, 3-Chome, Chiyoda-ku, Tokyo 100-8321, Japan, *Tel:* +81 3 3213 3138, *Fax:* +81 3 3213 1145, *Email:* tohru.takamura@si.idemitsu.co.jp, *Website:* www.idemitsu.co.jp
KG Int Petroleum Ltd, Shiba Park Building, 241 Shiba Koen, Minato-ku, Tokyo 105, Japan, *Tel:* +81 3 3578 4551, *Fax:* +81 3 3578 4550
MC Marine and Bunkering Inc., 8th Floor, Uchisaiwai-cho Dai Building, 3-3 Uchisaiwai-cho 1-chome, Chiyoda-ku, Tokyo 100-0011, Japan, *Tel:* +81 3 5251 2575, *Fax:* +81 3 5251 2583
Mitsui & Co. Petroleum Ltd, 2-1, Ohtemachi 1-chome, Chiyoda-ku, Tokyo 100-0004, Japan, *Tel:* +81 3 3285 6905, *Fax:* +81 3 3285 9811, *Email:* tkzph@dg.mitsui.com, *Website:* www.mitsui.co.jp
Nittetsu Shoij Co. Ltd, 5-7 Kameido 1-chome, Koto-ku, Tokyo 136, Japan, *Tel:* +81 3 5627 2157, *Fax:* +81 3 5627 2192
Shinagawa Fuel Co. Ltd, New Pier Takeshiba North Tower, 8th Floor, 1-11-1 Kaigan, Minato-ku, Tokyo 105-8525, Japan, *Tel:* +81 3 5470 7113, *Fax:* +81 3 5470 7157, *Email:* hakuyu@ml1.sinanen.co.jp
Sumitomo Corp., Harumi Island, Triton Square, Office Tower Y, 8-11 Harumi 1-chome, Chuo-ku, Tokyo 104-8610, Japan, *Tel:* +81 3 51664458, *Fax:* +81 3 51666407, *Email:* ir@sumitomo.co.jp, *Website:* www.sumitomocorp.co.jp

Towage: No tugs in port, available from Mizushima if required

Medical Facilities: Available

Airport: Okayama, 20 km

Lloyd's Agent: Cornes & Co. Ltd, Meikai Building, 32 Akashi-machi, Chuo-ku, Kobe 650-0037, Hyogo Pref., Japan, *Tel:* +81 78 332 3421, *Fax:* +81 78 332 3070, *Email:* survey@kobe.cornes.co.jp, *Website:* www.cornes.co.jp

NEGISHI

see under Yokohama

NIIGATA

Lat 37° 56' N; Long 139° 4' E.

Admiralty Chart: 1388	**Admiralty Pilot:** 41
Time Zone: GMT +9 h	**UNCTAD Locode:** JP KIJ

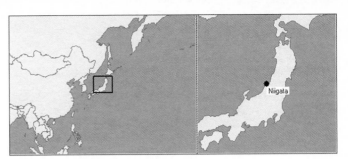

Principal Facilities:

P	Q	Y	G	C	R		B	D	T	A

Authority: Port & Harbour Section of Niigata Prefecture, Bureau of Port & Airport Development, Niigata Prefectural Government, 4-1 Shinko-cho, Niigata 950-8570, Niigata Pref., Japan, *Tel:* +81 25 285 5511, *Fax:* +81 25 285 9375, *Email:* t1700102@mail.pref.niigata.jp

Approach: The entrance is sheltered by breakwaters totalling 2833 m. Depth in fairway about 12.5 m but liable to alteration due to silting

Anchorage: Limited anchorage available

Pilotage: Not compulsory but advisable. Pilots available in pos 37° 58' N; 139° 03' 20" E during daylight hours only

Tides: Tidal range max 0.3 m

Working Hours: 0830-1630. 1st and 3rd Sundays unavailable

Accommodation: Tanker facilities: At Nisseki dolphin, SBM (sealine buoy) and Rinko B, C and D wharves. Also at Bandaijima (L1) 30 m long, 7.5 m depth for domestic tankers

Name	Length (m)	Depth (m)	Draught (m)	Remarks
Public Wharves				See [1] below
Oil Pier Dolphin (F1)	177	11	10.6	Max 15 000 dwt
North Wharf (F2)	427	7.5–9.5	7.3–9.3	Max 10 000 dwt
East Wharf (G)	231	7.5	7.3	Max 5000 dwt
Central Wharf (H)	294	9.5	9.3	Max 10 000 dwt
Central Wharf (I)	137	7.5	7.3	Max 5000 dwt
Central Wharf (J)	307	7.5	7.3	Max 5000 dwt
South Wharf (K)	288	7.5	7.3	Max 5000 dwt
Bandaijima Pier (L2)	391	7.5	6.7	Max 3000 dwt
Yamanoshita Wharf (Y1)	330	9	7	Max 10 000 dwt
Bandaijima Oil Pier	30	7.5	6	Max 2000 dwt
Private Wharves				
Rinko A1, 2 & 3	344	11	10.6	Max 20 000 dwt
Rinko B2 & 3	244	11	10.6	Max 20 000 dwt
Rinko C1, 2 & 3	200	11	10.6	Max 20 000 dwt
Rinko D1	165	9	8.5	Max 10 000 dwt
Rinko D2 & 3	245	11	10	Max 15 000 dwt
Rinko E1	165	10	9.8	Max 15 000 dwt
Rinko E2	162	8	7	Max 5000 dwt
Rinko E3	132	8	6.5	Max 5000 dwt

[1]*Public Wharves:* Bandaijima (L4) accommodates passenger vessels operating between Niigata and Sado Islands. Bandaijima (L3) is a jetfoil station for craft operating between Niigata and Sado Islands. Yamanoshita (Y2) accommodates passenger vessels operating between Niigata and Otaru

Storage: Total area of warehouses and open storage space is 353 539 m2. Lumber yard of 64 347 m2

Mechanical Handling Equipment:

Location	Type	Capacity (t)	Qty
Niigata	Floating Cranes	150	1
Rinko A1, 2 & 3	Mult-purp. Cranes	6	1
Rinko A1, 2 & 3	Mult-purp. Cranes	8	2
Rinko D1	Mult-purp. Cranes	6	3
Rinko D2 & 3	Mult-purp. Cranes	6	3

Bunkering: Domestic oil available. Bonded oil brought from Hakodate or Moji with 7 days advance notice

Towage: Six tugs available; two of 3400 hp, two of 3000 hp, one of 2600 hp and one of 1300 hp. Servicing Niigata-Higashi also

Repair & Maintenance: Niigata Engineering Co. Ltd, Niigata, Niigata Pref., Japan, *Tel:* +81 25 245 1234 One dry dock 54 m x 14 m x 2.5 m for small vessels

Shipping Agents: Kamigumi Co. Ltd, 5322-3 Yokomichishita, Hasugata, Seiro-cho, Kitakanbara, Niigata 957-0106, Niigata Pref., Japan, *Tel:* +81 25 256 3071, *Fax:* +81 25 256 3099
Rinko Corp., 11-30 Bandai 5-chome, Niigata 950-8540, Niigata Pref., Japan, *Tel:* +81 25 245 4113, *Fax:* +81 25 245 1823, *Email:* eigyo@rinko.co.jp, *Website:* www.rinko.co.jp

Airport: Niigata Airport, 6 km

Lloyd's Agent: Cornes & Co. Ltd, 273 Yamashita-cho, Naka-ku, Yokohama 231-0023, Kanagawa Pref., Japan, *Tel:* +81 45 201 8537, *Fax:* +81 45 212 3105, *Email:* survey@ykh.cornes.co.jp, *Website:* www.cornes.co.jp

Key to Principal Facilities:—				
A=Airport	**C**=Containers	**G**=General Cargo	**P**=Petroleum	**R**=Ro/Ro	**Y**=Dry Bulk
B=Bunkers	**D**=Dry Dock	**L**=Cruise	**Q**=Other Liquid Bulk	**T**=Towage (where available from port)

NIIGATA-HIGASHI

Lat 37° 59' N; Long 139° 14' E.

Admiralty Chart: 1388
Time Zone: GMT +9 h
Admiralty Pilot: 41
UNCTAD Locode: JP NIH

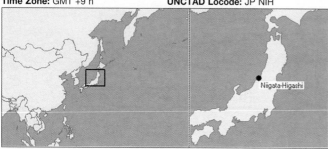

Principal Facilities:

Q		G	C		B		

Authority: Niigata-Higashi Port Administration, 1214 Aza Betsugyosawa, Oaza Betsugyo, Seiro-machi, Kita Kanbara-gun, Niigata, Niigata Pref., Japan, *Tel:* +81 25 562503

Port Security: ISPS compliant

Approach: Draught limitation in channel 13 m

Pilotage: Not compulsory. Pilots are available from Niigata Anchorage boarding area or simetimes in pos 38° 01' 35" N; 139° 13' 50" E during daylight hours only

Accommodation:

Name	Length (m)	Depth (m)	Draught (m)	Remarks
Public Wharves				
Centre Pier No.1	262	13	12	Max 1 x 55 000 dwt
South Lumber Wharf	370	10	9.5	Max 2 x 15 000 dwt
East Pier No.1 (Dolphin)	394	13	11.6–11.8	Max 1 x 50 000 dwt
East Pier No.3 (Dolphin)	385	13	11.6–11.8	Max 1 x 50 000 dwt
South Pier	185	10	9	Max 1 x 15 000 dwt
Private Wharves				
Shintoh Berth No.1	262	13	12	Max 1 x 55 000 dwt
Shintoh Berth No.2	197	6		Max 1 x 3000 dwt
Nippon Steel Shin-Nittetsu Berth	250	7.5		Max 1 x 5000 dwt
Kyodo Karyoku (Dolphin)	230	7.5		Max 1 x 5000 dwt

Mechanical Handling Equipment: One crane of 570 t/h cap on Centre Pier No.1 and one of 500 t/h at Shintoh Berth

Location	Type	Capacity (t)	Qty
Niigata-Higashi	Floating Cranes	150	1

Bunkering: Bonded oil will be brought from Hakodate or Moji with 7 days advance notice

Towage: Available from Niigata

Lloyd's Agent: Cornes & Co. Ltd, 273 Yamashita-cho, Naka-ku, Yokohama 231-0023, Kanagawa Pref., Japan, *Tel:* +81 45 201 8537, *Fax:* +81 45 212 3105, *Email:* survey@ykh.cornes.co.jp, *Website:* www.cornes.co.jp

NIIHAMA

Lat 33° 57' N; Long 133° 15' E.

Admiralty Chart: 698
Time Zone: GMT +9 h
Admiralty Pilot: 42B
UNCTAD Locode: JP IHA

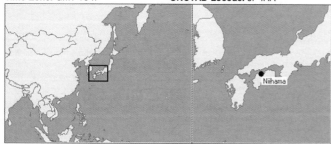

Principal Facilities:

P		Y	G			B	T	A

Authority: Niihama Port Authority, 5-1 Ikku-cho 1-chome, Niihama 792-8585, Ehime Pref., Japan, *Tel:* +81 897 335151, *Fax:* +81 897 651220, *Email:* office@city.niihama.ehime.jp, *Website:* www.city.niihama.ehime.jp

Officials: Manager: Katsuyuki Ishikawa, *Tel:* +81 897 651350.

Port Security: ISPS compliant

Approach: The approach is through Kurushima Strait or Bisan Seto traffic routes. Passage to Inner harbour is 3.9 km long, 180 m to 310 m wide and 8 m to 16 m deep. Min depth in the channel is 7.4 m at LW. Vessels normally anchor at outer harbour anchorage for quarantine

Pilotage: Harbour pilotage not compulsory but recommended. Inland Sea pilotage compulsory for vessels exceeding 10 000 gt. Harbour pilots are available at the anchorage with 48 h advance notice

Weather: Typhoon season, July to October

Tides: Range of tide 3.58 m, 3.72 m MHWL, 0.14 m MLWL, 2 m MSL

Maximum Vessel Dimensions: Inner harbour 165 m loa, 9.5 m d, 20 000 dwt. Outer harbour K6, 250 m loa, 13 m d, 70 000 dwt

Principal Imports and Exports: Imports: Bauxite, Coal, Copper concentrate. Exports: Fertiliser.

Working Hours: 0800-1630. Continuous three shifts at Berth K6

Accommodation:

Name	Length (m)	Depth (m)	Draught (m)	Remarks
Niihama				
Isoura Public Wharf	310	5.5–7.5	5–7	Consists of 2 berths
Sumitomo Chemicals N-4	80	7.5	7	Max 5000 gt
Sumitomo Chemicals N-8	110	9.3	9	Max 10 000 gt
Sumitomo Chemicals K-4	120	9.5	9	Max 10 000 gt
Sumitomo Chemicals K-6	200	14.1	13	Max 50 000 gt
Sumitomo Metal B-3	103	9.8	9.5	Max 10 000 gt
Sumitomo Heavy Industry	85	5.5	5.5	Max 5000 gt
Sumitomo Dolphin 0-4		5.7	5.2	Max 5000 gt
Mooring Buoy (A)		8	7.5	Max 10 000 gt
Mooring Buoy (B)		9.3	9	Max 10 000 gt

Storage: Warehousing of 2600 m2, sheds of 2547 m2 and timber basin of 18.1 ha

Mechanical Handling Equipment:

Location	Type	Capacity (t)	Qty
Niihama	Floating Cranes	120	1
Sumitomo Chemicals K-4	Mult-purp. Cranes	5	1
Sumitomo Chemicals K-4	Mult-purp. Cranes	6	1
Sumitomo Chemicals K-6	Mult-purp. Cranes	25	2
Sumitomo Metal B-3	Mult-purp. Cranes	5	2
Sumitomo Heavy Industry	Mult-purp. Cranes	160	1

Cargo Worked: 6300 t of foreign trade cargo and 7000 t of domestic trade handled per working day

Bunkering: Kyodo Oil Co. Ltd, 11-2 Nagata-cho 2-chome, Chiyoda-ku, Tokyo, Japan, *Tel:* +81 3 3505 8241, *Fax:* +81 3 3505 8697
MC Marine and Bunkering Inc., 8th Floor, Uchisaiwai-cho Dai Building, 3-3 Uchisaiwai-cho 1-chome, Chiyoda-ku, Tokyo 100-0011, Japan, *Tel:* +81 3 5251 2575, *Fax:* +81 3 5251 2583
Mitsui & Co. Petroleum Ltd, 2-1, Ohtemachi 1-chome, Chiyoda-ku, Tokyo 100-0004, Japan, *Tel:* +81 3 3285 6905, *Fax:* +81 3 3285 9811, *Email:* tkzph@dg.mitsui.com, *Website:* www.mitsui.co.jp
NKK Trading Inc., 4-4 Nihonbashi Hisamatsusucho, Chuo-ku, Tokyo 103, Japan, *Tel:* +81 3 3660 1522, *Fax:* +81 3 3660 1572
Sumitomo Corp., Harumi Island, Triton Square, Office Tower Y, 8-11 Harumi 1-chome, Chuo-ku, Tokyo 104-8610, Japan, *Tel:* +81 3 51664458, *Fax:* +81 3 51666407, *Email:* ir@sumitomo.co.jp, *Website:* www.sumitomocorp.co.jp

Towage: One harbour tug of 2600 hp available. Additional tugs available from Mizushima or Sakaide

Medical Facilities: Available

Airport: Matsuyama, 70 km

Lloyd's Agent: Cornes & Co. Ltd, Meikai Building, 32 Akashi-machi, Chuo-ku, Kobe 650-0037, Hyogo Pref., Japan, *Tel:* +81 78 332 3421, *Fax:* +81 78 332 3070, *Email:* survey@kobe.cornes.co.jp, *Website:* www.cornes.co.jp

NISHIYAMA WHARF

harbour area, see under Shimonoseki

NOSHIRO

Lat 40° 13' N; Long 140° 0' E.

Admiralty Chart: JP145/JP1195
Time Zone: GMT +9 h
Admiralty Pilot: 41
UNCTAD Locode: JP NSR

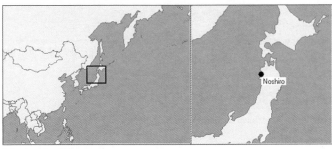

Principal Facilities:

		Y	G						

Authority: Port & Harbour Section of Akita Prefecture, 1-1 Sanno 4-chome, Akita 010-8570, Akita Pref., Japan, *Tel:* +81 18 860 1872, *Fax:* +81 18 860 1204

Port Security: ISPS compliant

Approach: Draught limitation in the channel is 9.5 m

Pilotage: Not compulsory but strongly recommended. Pilots are available at pos 40° 11' 30" N; 139° 58' E during daylight hours only

Tides: Average range of tide 0.2-0.3 m

Maximum Vessel Dimensions: 10 202 dwt, 127.9 m loa

Working Hours: 0830-1630 weekdays; may be extended when required. Sunday working available except 1st, 3rd and 5th weeks

Accommodation:

Name	Length (m)	Depth (m)	Draught (m)	Remarks
Noshiro				Harbour protected by breakwaters
Public Wharf	185	10	9.5	Max 15 000 dwt
Nakajima Pier No.1	130	7.5	6.9	Max 5000 dwt
Nakajima Pier No.2	130	7.5	6.9	Max 5000 dwt

Towage: No tugs normally stationed at the port. Tugs will be brought from Akita when required, or hired from construction company when available at Noshiro

Lloyd's Agent: Cornes & Co. Ltd, 273 Yamashita-cho, Naka-ku, Yokohama 231-0023, Kanagawa Pref., Japan, *Tel:* +81 45 201 8537, *Fax:* +81 45 212 3105, *Email:* survey@ykh.cornes.co.jp, *Website:* www.cornes.co.jp

NUMAZU

Lat 35° 8' N; Long 138° 50' E.

Admiralty Chart: JP80	**Admiralty Pilot:** 42A
Time Zone: GMT +9 h	**UNCTAD Locode:** JP NUM

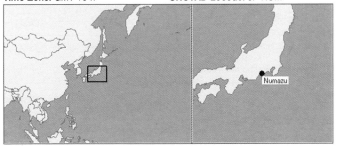

Principal Facilities:

			G			B			

Authority: Port & Harbour Section of Shizuoka Prefecture, 9-6 Ote-machi, Aoi-ka, Shizuoka 420-8601, Shizuoka Pref., Japan, *Tel:* +81 54 221 3050, *Fax:* +81 54 221 3563, *Email:* kouwan_kikaku@pref.shizuoka.lg.jp, *Website:* www.pref.shizuoka.jp

Officials: Director: Hiromi Kato.

Approach: Draught limitation in the channel is 7.5 m

Pilotage: Not compulsory. Pilots available at Tagonoura during daylight hours only

Tides: Range of tide 2.26 m

Working Hours: 0830-1630 weekdays; may be extended when required. Sunday working available except 1st and 3rd weeks

Accommodation:

Name	Length (m)	Depth (m)	Remarks
Numazu			See [1] below
North Wharf No.1	130	7.5	Max 5000 dwt
North Wharf No.2	90	5.5	Max 2000 dwt
East Wharf	180	5.5	Under construction. 2 x 2000 dwt
No.2 Dolphin	28	5.5	Max 2000 dwt

[1]*Numazu:* There are facilities for fishing vessels on the S side of the harbour

Bunkering: Domestic oil available. Bonded oil brought in from Yokohama or Tokyo with sufficient advance notice

Towage: No tugs stationed at the port, but available from Tagonoura and Shimizu if required

Lloyd's Agent: Cornes & Co. Ltd, 273 Yamashita-cho, Naka-ku, Yokohama 231-0023, Kanagawa Pref., Japan, *Tel:* +81 45 201 8537, *Fax:* +81 45 212 3105, *Email:* survey@ykh.cornes.co.jp, *Website:* www.cornes.co.jp

OFUNATO

Lat 38° 59' N; Long 141° 45' E.

Admiralty Chart: JP54	**Admiralty Pilot:** 41
Time Zone: GMT +9 h	**UNCTAD Locode:** JP OFT

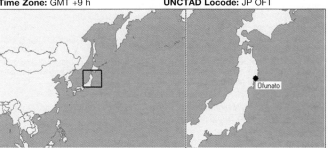

Principal Facilities:

P		Y	G			B		T	A

Authority: Port of Ofunato, Port Promotion Department, Ofunato City Hall, Ofunato, Japan, *Tel:* +81 192 273111, *Email:* syo-ko1@city.ofunato.iwate.jp

Port Security: ISPS compliant

Approach: Draught limitation in channel 14 m

Anchorage: Anchorage available in 40 m depth of water, but unsuitable in bad weather

Pilotage: Not compulsory but advisable because of fishing obstructions in the harbour. Pilot boards vessel in pos 39° 00' 18" N; 141° 45' 18" E for vessels over 5000 gt and in pos 39° 00' 42" N; 141° 44' 48" E for vessels under 5000 gt in daylight hours only

Tides: Max tidal range 1.5 m

Accommodation:

Name	Length (m)	Depth (m)	Remarks
Ofunato			
Onoda Cement Wharf No.1	12	7.5	Cement
Onoda Cement Nojima Pier A		9	Bulk cement. Piers A, B & C have a combined length of 280 m
Onoda Cement Nojima Pier B		9.5	Bulk cement. Piers A, B & C have a combined length of 280 m
Onoda Cement Nojima Pier C		7.5	Fuel oil. Piers A, B & C have a combined length of 280 m
Kawatetsu Kogyo Pier	15	6	Limestone
10 000 t Wharf	330	9	Max 10 000 gt. Logs & general cargo
3000 t Wharf	213	6	General cargo
Ko Wharf	110	7	General cargo
Otsu Wharf	200	4.5	General cargo
Nagahama Buoy	20	20	Max 8000 dwt. Logs
Kamei Jetty		8.5	Max 20 000 gt. Oil

Bunkering: Domestic oil available. Bonded oil from Yokohama or Hakodate with advance notice

Towage: Small tugs of 800 hp and 600 hp available. Larger tugs up to 2900 hp available if required from Kamaishi with advance notice

Repair & Maintenance: Minor repairs available

Airport: Hanamaki Airport, 95 km

Lloyd's Agent: Cornes & Co. Ltd, 273 Yamashita-cho, Naka-ku, Yokohama 231-0023, Kanagawa Pref., Japan, *Tel:* +81 45 201 8537, *Fax:* +81 45 212 3105, *Email:* survey@ykh.cornes.co.jp, *Website:* www.cornes.co.jp

OITA

Lat 33° 16' N; Long 131° 30' E.

Admiralty Chart: JP1247A/JP1247B	**Admiralty Pilot:** 42B
Time Zone: GMT +9 h	**UNCTAD Locode:** JP OIT

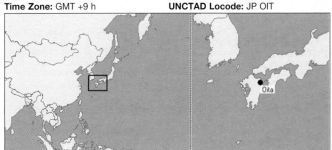

Lloyd's Agent: Cornes & Co. Ltd, 273 Yamashita-cho, Naka-ku, Yokohama 231-0023, Kanagawa Pref., Japan, *Tel:* +81 45 201 8537, *Fax:* +81 45 212 3105, *Email:* survey@ykh.cornes.co.jp, *Website:* www.cornes.co.jp

Key to Principal Facilities:—
A=Airport   **C**=Containers   **G**=General Cargo   **P**=Petroleum   **R**=Ro/Ro   **Y**=Dry Bulk
B=Bunkers   **D**=Dry Dock   **L**=Cruise   **Q**=Other Liquid Bulk   **T**=Towage (where available from port)

Principal Facilities:

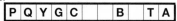

| P | Q | Y | G | C | | B | | T | A |

Authority: Port & Harbor Division, Civil Engineering & Construction Dept., Oita Prefectural Government, 3-1-1 Ohte-machi, Oita 870-8501, Oita Pref., Japan, *Tel:* +81 97 538 5714, *Fax:* +81 97 537 0907, *Email:* a17310@pref.oita.lg.jp

Port Security: ISPS compliant

Approach: Beppu Bay is located in between two peninsulas, opening on the E and faces Shikoku Island across the channel. Enjoys a warm climate and calm seas. The currents from the sea are generally slow, which seldom adversely affects Oita Harbour. Vessels can enter and depart day and night, but during August to December entry is impracticable after sunset due to obstructions by fishing nets except at the Sea Berth

Anchorage: There are seven deep water anchorage areas with depths ranging from 23 m to 53 m. Quarantine anchorage in pos 33° 16' N; 131° 46' E, depth 43 m

Pilotage: Not compulsory but recommended. Inland Sea pilots available from Sekisaki Pilot Station with at least 24 h advance notice through ship's agent or to pilot office, Cables: Anjin Moji. Harbour pilots available at the anchorage

Radio Frequency: Oita Port Radio, VHF Channel 16

Weather: Prevailing SW winds in summer and NW in winter. Dense fog can frequently be experienced during spring and autumn

Tides: Range of tide 2.26 m

Maximum Vessel Dimensions: Tankers 366 492 dwt, 19.8 m d, 347.1 m loa. Bulk Carriers 310 686 dwt, 23 m d, 331.4 m loa

Working Hours: Public wharves 0800-1700. Private berths 24 h/day in three shifts

Accommodation:

Name	Length (m)	Draught (m)	Remarks
Oita			See [1] below
Ohzai Public Wharf	1435	5.5–12	See [2] below
Hiyoshibaru Public Wharf	530	5.5–7.5	2 x 5000 dwt & 3 x 2000 dwt
Sumiyoshi No.1	185	9.1	1 x 10 000 dwt
Sumiyoshi No.2	185	9.2	1 x 10 000 dwt
Otozu Steel Loading E3	240	11	1 x 30 000 dwt
Otozu Steel Loading E4	200	11	1 x 30 000 dwt
Otozu Steel Loading E5	200	12	1 x 50 000 dwt
Otozu Steel Loading E6	200	12	1 x 50 000 dwt
Otozu Steel Loading E7	200	12	1 x 50 000 dwt
Sea Berth (Ore & Coal) N1+Dolphin	435	22	1 x 50 000-200 000 dwt
Sea Berth (Ore & Coal) N2+Dolphin	450	25	1 x 50 000-300 000 dwt
Sea Berth (Ore & Coal) N3+Dolphin	490	22	1 x 50 000-100 000 dwt
Sea Berth (Ore & Coal) N4	210	20	1 x 5000-30 000 dwt
Kyushu Oil Jetty (Dolphin)	480	20.1	See [3] below
Showa Denko Sea Berth (Dolphin)	400	15	1 x 5000-70 000 dwt. Two pipelines for discharging naptha at 5000 l/h
Mitsui Zosen D Wharf	320	5	1 x 15 000 dwt
Mitsui Zosen E Wharf	590	3.6	1 x 10 000 dwt
Gaiko LPG Berth	300	14	1 x 70 000 dwt. Discharge rate 1200 t/h

[1]*Oita:* Sumiyoshi Wharves and Otozu Steel Loading berths can accommodate larger vessels by using two wharves as one berth
Ozai Container Terminal covers an area of 22 ha and consists of one berth 280 m long in depth of 14 m for vessels up to 50 000 t and a 170 m berth in depth of 10 m. It is equipped with two gantry cranes, 56 reefer plugs and has capacity for 4755 TEU's
[2]*Ohzai Public Wharf:* 1 x 15 000 dwt, 1 x 30 000 dwt, 4 x 5000 dwt, 1 x 5000 dwt & 6 x 2000 dwt
[3]*Kyushu Oil Jetty (Dolphin):* 1 x 5000-270 000 dwt. Four pipelines for discharging crude oil and pertroleum products at 10 000 l/h

Storage: General cargo warehousing and bonded shed available

Mechanical Handling Equipment: Mobile cranes and floating crane available. Nine unloaders of 20 t to 50 t cap at Otozu Steel Loading Berths.
Three 2500 t/h unloaders at the Ore and Coal Sea Berths, max air draft of 24 m

Bunkering: Idemitsu Kosan Co. Ltd, 1-1 Marunochi, 3-Chome, Chiyoda-ku, Tokyo 100-8321, Japan, *Tel:* +81 3 3213 3138, *Fax:* +81 3 3213 1145, *Email:* tohru.takamura@si.idemitsu.co.jp, *Website:* www.idemitsu.co.jp
KG Int Petroleum Ltd, Shiba Park Building, 241 Shiba Koen, Minato-ku, Tokyo 105, Japan, *Tel:* +81 3 3578 4551, *Fax:* +81 3 3578 4550
MC Marine and Bunkering Inc., 8th Floor, Uchisaiwai-cho Dai Building, 3-3 Uchisaiwai-cho 1-chome, Chiyoda-ku, Tokyo 100-0011, Japan, *Tel:* +81 3 5251 2575, *Fax:* +81 3 5251 2583
Mitsui & Co. Petroleum Ltd, 2-1, Ohtemachi 1-chome, Chiyoda-ku, Tokyo 100-0004, Japan, *Tel:* +81 3 3285 6905, *Fax:* +81 3 3285 9811, *Email:* tkzph@dg.mitsui.com, *Website:* www.mitsui.co.jp
Nissho Iwai Corp., 4-4 Akasaka 2-chome, Minato-ku, Tokyo, Japan, *Tel:* +81 3 35882111
Nittetsu Shoij Co. Ltd, 5-7 Kameido 1-chome, Koto-ku, Tokyo 136, Japan, *Tel:* +81 3 5627 2157, *Fax:* +81 3 5627 2192
Sumitomo Corp., Harumi Island, Triton Square, Office Tower Y, 8-11 Harumi 1-chome, Chuo-ku, Tokyo 104-8610, Japan, *Tel:* +81 3 51664458, *Fax:* +81 3 51666407, *Email:* ir@sumitomo.co.jp, *Website:* www.sumitomocorp.co.jp

Towage: Nine tugs available; two of 3400 hp, two of 3200 hp, two of 2600 hp and three of 2400 hp

Repair & Maintenance: Kitakyushu Marine Industries Co. Ltd, Oita, Oita Pref., Japan, *Tel:* +81 97 558 2888 Minor repairs

Shipping Agents: Kamigumi Co. Ltd, 6-2, Mukaibaru, Higashi 1-chome, Oita 890 0904, Oita Pref., Japan, *Tel:* +81 97 558 8181, *Fax:* +81 97 558 8184, *Email:* km11001@bronze.ocn.ne.jp, *Website:* www.kamigumi.co.jp

Medical Facilities: Oka Hospital and Higuma Hospital

Airport: Oita Airport, 52 km

Lloyd's Agent: Cornes & Co. Ltd, Meikai Building, 32 Akashi-machi, Chuo-ku, Kobe 650-0037, Hyogo Pref., Japan, *Tel:* +81 78 332 3421, *Fax:* +81 78 332 3070, *Email:* survey@kobe.cornes.co.jp, *Website:* www.cornes.co.jp

OMAEZAKI

Lat 34° 36' N; Long 138° 14' E.

Admiralty Chart: JP80	**Admiralty Pilot:** 42A
Time Zone: GMT +9 h	**UNCTAD Locode:** JP OMZ

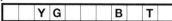

Principal Facilities:

| | Y | G | | B | T | |

Authority: Port & Harbour Section of Shizuoka Prefecture, 9-6 Ote-machi, Aoi-ka, Shizuoka 420-8601, Shizuoka Pref., Japan, *Tel:* +81 54 221 3050, *Fax:* +81 54 221 3563, *Email:* kouwan_kikaku@pref.shizuoka.lg.jp, *Website:* www.pref.shizuoka.jp

Officials: Director: Hiromi Kato.

Port Security: ISPS compliant

Approach: Draught limitation in the channel is 14 m

Pilotage: Not compulsory. Pilots available if required and board vessel in pos 34° 38' 05" N; 138° 14' 07" E. Vessels can berth in daylight hours only and unberth up to 2100 h

Tides: Max tidal range 2.05 m

Accommodation:

Name	Length (m)	Depth (m)	Remarks
Omaezaki			A lumber pool is situated W of Chuo Futo berths
Chuo Futo No's 1-2	260	7.5	Max 2 x 5000 dwt
Chuo Futo No's 3-5	260	5	Max 3 x 1000 dwt
Nishi Futo No's 1-2	480	12	Max 2 x 30 000 dwt
Nishi Futo No's 3-9	790	5.5–7.5	Max 3 x 5000 dwt & 4 x 2000 dwt

Bunkering: Bonded oil can be brought from Yokohama with advance notice if required

Towage: One 1600 hp tug available

Repair & Maintenance: Minor repairs undertaken

Lloyd's Agent: Cornes & Co. Ltd, 273 Yamashita-cho, Naka-ku, Yokohama 231-0023, Kanagawa Pref., Japan, *Tel:* +81 45 201 8537, *Fax:* +81 45 212 3105, *Email:* survey@ykh.cornes.co.jp, *Website:* www.cornes.co.jp

ONAHAMA

Lat 36° 56' N; Long 140° 55' E.

Admiralty Chart: 2959	**Admiralty Pilot:** 41
Time Zone: GMT +9 h	**UNCTAD Locode:** JP ONA

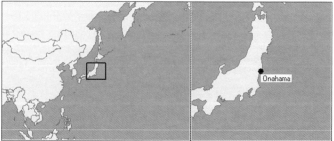

Principal Facilities:

| P | | Y | G | C | R | | B | | T | |

Authority: Onahama Port Administration & Construction Office of Fukushima Pref., 38-1 Tatsumicho, Onahama, Iwaki 971-8101, Fukushima Pref., Japan, *Tel:* +81 246 522416, *Fax:* +81 246 541354, *Email:* onahama.kouwan@pref.fukushima.jp, *Website:* www.pref.fukushima.jp/onahamakouwan

Port Security: ISPS compliant

Approach: Port protected by a breakwater which projects SW from the shore. Draught limitation in the channel 9.7 m to the port, 13.5 m to the tanker Sea Berth and 12.3 m to No.7 Pier

Anchorage: Anchorage can be obtained off the west breakwater in a depth of 22 m

Pilotage: Not compulsory. Pilots available if required and board vessels at the anchorage in pos 36° 53' 54" N; 140° 53' 43" E. Pilots for tankers board vessels in pos 36° 52' 59" N; 140° 53' 90" E. Vessels berth in daylight hours only and can unberth normally any time at pilots discretion

Tides: Max tidal range 2.63 m

Traffic: 2003, 13 557 951 t of cargo handled

Accommodation:

Name	Length (m)	Depth (m)	Remarks
Wharf No.2			Handling of stone & machinery products
Berth No.3	130	7.5	Max 5000 dwt
Berth No.4	130	7.5	Max 5000 dwt
Berth No.5	94	4.5	Max 1000 dwt
Berth No.6	94	4.5	Max 1000 dwt
Wharf No.3			Handling of stone & chemical products
Berth No.1	175	10	Max 12 000 dwt
Berth No.2	175	10	Max 12 000 dwt
Berth No.3	175	10	Max 12 000 dwt
Berth No.4	175	10	Max 12 000 dwt
Berth No.5	73	4.5	Max 1000 dwt
Berth No.6	73	4.5	Max 1000 dwt
Berth No.7	74	4.5	Max 1000 dwt
Wharf No.4			Handling of stone & chemical products
Berth No.1	90	4.5	Max 1000 dwt
Berth No.2	200	10	Max 12 000 dwt
Berth No.3	200	10	Max 12 000 dwt
Berth No.4	100	6	Max 3000 dwt
Berth No.5	100	6	Max 3000 dwt
Berth No.6	100	6	Max 3000 dwt
Pond Berth	200	4.5	Max 1000 dwt
Wharf No's 5-6			See [1] below
Berth No.1	240	12	Max 30 000 dwt
Berth No.2	280	14	Max 55 000 dwt
Berth No.3	130	7.5	Max 5000 dwt
Berth No.4	130	7.5	Max 5000 dwt
Pond Berth	170	4.5	Max 1000 dwt
Wharf No.7			Handling stone
Berth No.1	270	13	Max 40 000 dwt
Berth No.2	270	13	Max 40 000 dwt
Berth No.3	185	10	Max 12 000 dwt
Berth No.4	185	10	Max 12 000 dwt
Berth No.5	130	7.5	Max 5000 dwt
Pond Berth	350	4	Max 200 dwt
Fujiwara Wharf			Handling wood
Berth No.1	185	10	Max 12 000 dwt
Berth No.2	240	12	Max 30 000 dwt
Berth No.3	185	10	Max 12 000 dwt
Berth No.4	130	7.5	Max 5000 dwt
Otsurugi Wharf			See [2] below
Berth No.1	130	7.5	Max 5000 dwt
Berth No.2	130	7.5	Max 5000 dwt
Berth No.3	185	10	Max 12 000 dwt
Berth No.4	185	10	Max 12 000 dwt
Berth No.5	130	7.5	Max 5000 dwt
Berth No.6	130	7.5	Max 5000 dwt
Berth No.7	130	7.5	Max 5000 dwt
Berth No.8	130	7.5	Max 5000 dwt

[1]*Wharf No's 5-6:* Handling stone. One twin-belt continuous ship unloader at 800 t/h and one continuous ship unloader of 1500 t/h
[2]*Otsurugi Wharf:* Handling containers, machinery products, chemical products & oil products

Storage: Transit sheds and warehouses available. Stockpiling yards totalling 701 202 m2

Mechanical Handling Equipment:

Location	Type	Capacity (t)	Qty
Wharf No.3	Mult-purp. Cranes	8	4
Wharf No.7	Mult-purp. Cranes	20	3
Otsurugi Wharf	Container Cranes	30.5–35.6	2

Bunkering: Domestic oil available. Bonded oil can be brought from Yokohama or Kashima with advance notice

Towage: Six tugs available of 3100-4000 hp

Repair & Maintenance: Minor repairs undertaken

Lloyd's Agent: Cornes & Co. Ltd, 273 Yamashita-cho, Naka-ku, Yokohama 231-0023, Kanagawa Pref., Japan, *Tel:* +81 45 201 8537, *Fax:* +81 45 212 3105, *Email:* survey@ykh.cornes.co.jp, *Website:* www.cornes.co.jp

ONODA

Lat 34° 0' N; Long 131° 11' E.

Admiralty Chart: 3225	**Admiralty Pilot:** 32B
Time Zone: GMT +9 h	**UNCTAD Locode:** JP OND

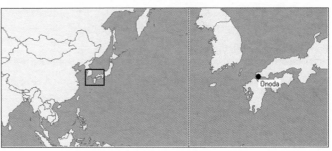

Principal Facilities:

P	Q	Y	G			B		A

Authority: Ports & Harbors Division, Yamaguchi Prefectural Government, 1-1 Takimachi, Yamaguchi 753-8501, Yamaguchi Pref., Japan, *Tel:* +81 83 933 3810, *Fax:* +81 83 933 3829, *Email:* a12900@pref.yamaguchi.lg.jp, *Website:* www.pref.yamaguchi.lg.jp

Officials: Shoichi Hayashi, *Tel:* +81 83 9332 340.

Approach: Honkoh Channel 120 m wide in depth of 7.5 m
Shinoki Channel 100 m wide in depth of 5 m

Tides: Average range of tide 3.22 m

Principal Imports and Exports: Imports: Coal, Scrap metal. Exports: Chemicals, Steel.

Working Hours: 0900-1700

Accommodation:

Name	Length (m)	Depth (m)	Remarks
Public Wharves			
Honkoh Wharf No.1	90	5.5	1 x 2000 dwt
Honkoh Wharf No.2	130	7.5	1 x 5000 dwt
Honkoh Wharf No.3	180	5.5	2 x 2000 dwt
Private Wharves			
Fujisyo Wharf	80	5	
Chugoku Denryoku Pier			See [1] below
Chicibu Onoda Dolphin		7	For vessels up to 4000 dwt

[1]*Chugoku Denryoku Pier:* Consists of 3 berths. 70 m long in depth of 5 m for vessels up to 1000 dwt, 90 m long in depth of 5.5 m for vessels up to 2000 dwt and 250 m long in depth of 7.5 m for vessels up to 5000 dwt

Bunkering: Bonded oil brought from Ube with sufficient advance notice

Medical Facilities: Available at the port and in Onoda City

Airport: Yamaguchi-Ube, 15 km

Railway: Onoda-Koh Station, 0.3 km

Lloyd's Agent: Cornes & Co. Ltd, Meikai Building, 32 Akashi-machi, Chuo-ku, Kobe 650-0037, Hyogo Pref., Japan, *Tel:* +81 78 332 3421, *Fax:* +81 78 332 3070, *Email:* survey@kobe.cornes.co.jp, *Website:* www.cornes.co.jp

ONOMICHI

Lat 34° 24' N; Long 133° 11' E.

Admiralty Chart: 694	**Admiralty Pilot:** 42B
Time Zone: GMT +9 h	**UNCTAD Locode:** JP ONO

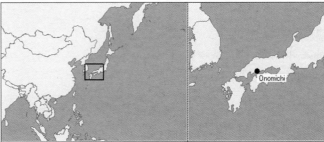

Principal Facilities:

P		Y	G			B	D	T	A

Authority: Hiroshima Prefectural Government, Airport & Seaport Department, 10-52 Moto-Machi, Naka-ku, Hiroshima 730-8511, Hiroshima Pref., Japan, *Tel:* +81 82 228 2111, *Fax:* +81 82 223 2463, *Email:* r-matumoto80233@pref.hiroshima.lg.jp, *Website:* www.hiroshima-minato.jp

Officials: Port Director: Ryutaro Matsumoto, *Tel:* +81 82 224 2285.

Approach: The approach is through Bisan Seto or Kurushima Strait traffic routes.
Channel No.1 is 1500 m long, 100-160 m width and 5.5-10 m depth.
Channel No.2 is 800 m long, 50 m width and 6 m depth.
Channel No.3 is 1600 m long, 100 m width and 6-7 m depth.

Anchorage: There are 483 ha of anchorage space with a depth of 4-11 m. Quarantine anchorage at Fukuyama, Wada Misaki (Kobe) or Hesaki (Moji)

Pilotage: Not compulsory but advisable. Inland Sea pilotage is compulsory for vessels exceeding 10 000 gt and pilots are available at Wada Misaki, Hesaki or Sekisaki. Harbour pilots are available at the anchorage off Kashima Island or off Kihara from sunrise to 1 h before sunset

Weather: Typhoon season, July to October

Tides: Range of tide, max 4.95 m

Principal Imports and Exports: Imports: Timber. Exports: Chemical industrial goods.

Working Hours: Sunrise-sunset. No night work

Accommodation: The port consists of three regions: Onomichi, Itozaki and Matsunaga.

There are five anchorage berths in Matsunaga Bay in depths of 5 m to 9 m for vessels of 3000-10 000 gt

Name	Length (m)	Depth (m)	Remarks
Public Wharves			
Nishigosho Wharf	404	6.5	
Shinhama Wharf	478	5.5	Consists of 5 berths
Ekimae Wharf	243	5.5	
Chuo Wharf	264	5.5	
Itozaki No.1 Wharf	135	8.5	
Itozaki No.2 Wharf	185	10	
Kohama Wharf	185	5.5	Consists of 2 berths
Wada No.1 Wharf	90	5.5	
Wada No.2 Wharf	180	4.5	Consists of 3 berths
Private Wharves			
Onomichi Dockyard Co Ltd	924	6	Consists of 7 berths
Hitachi Zosen Corp	1130	5–7	Consists of 8 berths
Teijin Wharf	400	5	Consists of 5 berths
Mitsubishi Wharf	205	4.5–7.5	Consists of 2 berths

Storage: 13 transit sheds of 22 463 m2, warehousing of 26 700 m2, dangerous cargo warehouse of 870 m2 and timber basin of 66 ha

Location	Open (m²)
Onomichi	13000

Mechanical Handling Equipment:

Location	Type	Capacity (t)
Public Wharves	Mult-purp. Cranes	8

Cargo Worked: 2600 t of foreign trade and 10 000 t of domestic trade per working day

Bunkering: Domestic oil available. Bonded oil can be brought by barge from Kobe, Osaka, Tokuyama or Moji

Towage: Five tugs from 1000 hp to 2200 hp available

Repair & Maintenance: Hitachi Shipbuilding Corp (Onomichi), 14755 Mukaihigashi-cho, Onomichi 7220062, Hiroshima Pref., Japan, *Tel:* +81 848 441111, *Fax:* +81 848 441518, *Website:* www.hitachizosen.co.jp/ Dry dock for vessels up to 35 000 dwt Mukaishima Dockyard Co. Ltd, 864-1 Mukaishima-cho, Mitsugi, Hiroshima, Hiroshima Pref., Japan, *Tel:* +81 848 440001, *Fax:* +81 848 453552 Repairs for vessels up to 12 000 dwt Onomichi Dockyard Co. Ltd, 1005 Sanba Cho, Onomichi 722-8602, Hiroshima Pref., Japan, *Tel:* +81 848 371111, *Fax:* +81 848 202969, *Email:* ship.sales@onozo.co.jp, *Website:* www.onozo.co.jp Two dry docks: 185.3 m x 30 m for vessels up to 30 000 dwt and 215 m x 34 m for vessels up to 55 000 dwt

Surveyors: Nippon Kaiji Kyokai, 1-3-46 Shinhama, Onomichi 722-0014, Hiroshima Pref., Japan, *Tel:* +81 848 252400, *Fax:* +81 848 253228, *Email:* om@classnk.or.jp, *Website:* www.classnk.or.jp

Medical Facilities: Available

Airport: Hiroshima, 30 km

Lloyd's Agent: Cornes & Co. Ltd, Meikai Building, 32 Akashi-machi, Chuo-ku, Kobe 650-0037, Hyogo Pref., Japan, *Tel:* +81 78 332 3421, *Fax:* +81 78 332 3070, *Email:* survey@kobe.cornes.co.jp, *Website:* www.cornes.co.jp

OSAKA

Lat 34° 38' N; Long 135° 25' E.

Admiralty Chart: JP123	**Admiralty Pilot:** 42B
Time Zone: GMT +9 h	**UNCTAD Locode:** JP OSA

Principal Facilities:

P	Q	Y	G	C	R	L	B	D	T	A

Authority: Port & Harbor Bureau, City of Osaka, WTC Building, 1-14-16 Nanko-Kita, Suminoe-ku, Osaka 559-0034, Japan, *Tel:* +81 6 6615 7766, *Fax:* +81 6 6615 7769, *Email:* na0004@city.osaka.lg.jp, *Website:* www.city.osaka.jp/port

Officials: General Director: Kiyoshi Kawamoto.

Port Security: ISPS compliant

Approach: The approach is via Tomogashima Channel and then in to Osaka Bay. Fairways: Main Fairway is 250 m wide in a depth of 13 m

Anchorage: Ample sheltered anchorage; good holding ground in mud

Pilotage: Compulsory for vessels exceeding 10 000 gt. Osaka Bay pilot available from Osaka Bay Pilots Association, Tel: +81 78 321 4716. Harbour pilot available from Hanshin Pilot Association and board near quarantine anchorage, Tel: +81 6 6576 1731. Pilots will board only full container vessels around the clock and other vessels up to 2000 hours depending on the berth

Radio Frequency: Osaka Port Radio, 24 h service, calling on VHF Channel 16, working on Channels 20 and 22

Weather: Typhoon season, July to October

Tides: Average tidal range 1.63 m MHWL, 0.07 m MLWL, 0.95 m MSL. Tidal currents mostly flow southward

Traffic: 2006, 95 525 000 t of cargo handled

Maximum Vessel Dimensions: 70 285 gt

Principal Imports and Exports: Imports: Coal, Iron ore, Metal products, Steel, Timber. Exports: Chemicals, Machinery, Steel, Sundry goods.

Working Hours: 24 h/day

Accommodation: The port is protected by breakwaters totalling 4703 m and is divided into nine sections

Name	Length (m)	Depth (m)	Remarks
Operated by City			
Tsuneyoshi Wharf	360	5.5	See [1] below
Hokko Shiratsu Wharf			See [2] below
Hokko Wharf	284	7.5–10	See [3] below
Umemachi West Wharf	792	10–12	See [4] below
Umemachi Wharf	395	10–10.5	See [5] below
Sakurajima Wharf	535	10	See [6] below
Ajikawa Pier North Wharf	482	5.5	Berth No.13C. 5 x 1700 gt handling paper & woodpulp
Ajikawa Pier West Wharf	120	5.5	See [7] below
Ajikawa Pier South Wharf	312	5.5–6.5	See [8] below
Ajikawa Wharf No.1	320	10	See [9] below
Ajikawa Wharf No.2	360	10	See [10] below
Ajikawa Wharf No.3	178	10	Berth No.9B. 1 x 10 000 gt handling chemicals
Osaka Port Silo Wharf	210	11	Berth No.9. 1 x 13 000 gt handling wheat
Tempozan Wharf	370	10	See [11] below
Central Pier North Wharf	210	11	See [12] below
Wharf No.1	329	10	See [13] below
Wharf No.2	341	10	See [14] below
Wharf No.3	315	7.5–10	See [15] below
Wharf No.5	394	9	See [16] below
Wharf No.6	359	10	See [17] below
Wharf No.7	361	10	See [18] below
Wharf No.8	336	7.5	See [19] below
Wharf No.10	617	7.5–9	See [20] below
Wharf No.11	270	5.5	See [21] below
Taisho Pier 1 North Wharf	450	5.5	See [22] below
A Wharf	1040	7.5	See [23] below
B Wharf	550	7.5	See [24] below
D Wharf	580	5.5–7.5	See [25] below
E Wharf	821	5.5–7.5	See [26] below
G Wharf	720	5.5	See [27] below
I Wharf	720	5.5	Berth No's I1-I8. 8 x 1000 gt handling steel materials
J Wharf	720	12	See [28] below
K Wharf	370	10	See [29] below
R Wharf	1035	10–12	See [30] below
Nanko C6 Wharf	300	12	See [31] below
Nanko C7 Wharf	300	12	See [32] below
Nanko C9 Wharf	350	13	See [33] below
Yumeshima C10 Wharf	350	15	See [34] below
International Ferry Wharf	450	10	See [35] below
Managed by The Osaka Port Terminal Co. Ltd.			
Osaka Port Container Wharf 1	350	13.5	See [36] below
Osaka Port Container Wharf 2	350	13.5	See [37] below
Osaka Port Container Wharf 3	350	13.5	See [38] below
Osaka Port Container Wharf 4	350	13.5	See [39] below
Osaka Port Container Wharf 8	350	14	See [40] below
Osaka Port Container Wharf 11	350	15	Berth C11. 1 x 60 000 dwt handling container cargo
Osaka Port Liner Wharf 1	200	10	Berth L1.1 x 15 000 dwt handling general cargo
Osaka Port Liner Wharf 2	200	10	Berth L2. 1 x 15 000 dwt handling general cargo
Osaka Port Liner Wharf 3	200	10	Berth L3. 1 x 15 000 dwt handling general cargo
Osaka Port Liner Wharf 4	250	10	Berth L4. 1 x 15 000 dwt handling general cargo
Osaka Port Liner Wharf 5	250	10	Berth L5. 1 x 15 000 dwt handling general cargo
Osaka Port Liner Wharf 6	230	10	Berth L6. 1 x 15 000 dwt handling general cargo
Osaka Port Liner Wharf 7	230	10	Berth L7. 1 x 15 000 dwt handling general cargo
Ferry Terminal (Berth F1)	165	7.5	1 x 8000 gt handling passengers & automobiles
Ferry Terminal (Berth F2)	130	6	1 x 3000 gt handling passengers & automobiles

Name	Length (m)	Depth (m)	Remarks
Ferry Terminal (Berth F3)	148	6	1 x 3000 gt handling passengers & automobiles
Ferry Terminal (Berth F4)	165	7.5	1 x 8000 gt handling passengers & automobiles
Ferry Terminal (Berth F5)	165	7.5	1 x 8000 gt handling passengers & automobiles
Ferry Terminal (Berth F6)	130	6	1 x 3000 gt handling passengers & automobiles
Ferry Terminal (Berth F7)	240	8.5	1 x 8000 gt handling passengers & automobiles
Ferry Terminal (Berth F8)	205	7.5	1 x 5000 gt handling passengers & automobiles
Operated by Private Companies			
Osaka Gas Torishima Wharf	595	6–7	Berth No's Q1, Q3, Q5 & Q7. 4 x 3500 dwt and 1 x 3300 dwt handling chemicals
Osaka Gas West Pier	64	6	Berth No.Q6. 2 x 2300 dwt handling industrial products
Osaka Gas East Wharf	220	7	Berth No.Q8. 3 x 5000 dwt handling industrial products
Sumitomo Corp Steel Center Wharf	100	7	Berth No.Q9. 1 x 3000 dwt handling iron & steel
Sumitomo Corp Tsuneyoshi Wharf	50	5.5	Berth No.Q11. 1 x 1500 dwt handling iron & steel
Tatsumi Ajikawa Wharf	119	10	See [41] below
Nakayama Steel East Wharf	367	9	Berth No's P7, P9 & P11. 2 x 7000 dwt handling iron ore and iron & steel
Nakayama Steel West Wharf	260	12	Berth No.P1. 1 x 25 000 dwt handling iron ore and iron & steel
Century Service Iron & Steel Wharf	107	7.2	Berth No.T5. 1 x 3000 dwt handling iron & steel
Tatsumi Nanko Naka Wharf	110	6	Berth No.S2. 1 x 1000 dwt handling iron & steel
Hanwa Osaka Nanko Steel Center Wharf	180	6	Berth No.S3. 2 x 1000 dwt handling iron & steel
Kuribayashi Steamship Nanko Wharf	208	12	Berth No.J4. 1 x 30 000 dwt handling paper, woodpulp & vehicles
Sumitomo Corp Nanko Wharf	318	12	Berth No.J5. 1 x 30 000 dwt handling lumber
Osaka Steel Port Wharf	520	5.5	3 x 2000 dwt handling iron & steel

[1]*Tsuneyoshi Wharf:* Berth No's 59, 61, 63 & 65. 4 x 1000 gt for vessels handling gravel & sand

[2]*Hokko Shiratsu Wharf:* Berths HS-1-3: 720 m long in depth of 12 m. 3 x 20 000 gt Berths HS-4-6: 390 m long in depth of 7.5 m. 3 x 3000 gt Handling produce, paper, woodpulp & vehicles

[3]*Hokko Wharf:* Berths 51 & 55. 1 x 5000 gt and 1 x 3000 gt handling coke & monmetallic minerals

[4]*Umemachi West Wharf:* Berth No's 39 & 41 - 1 x 10 000 gt, Berth No's 43 & 45 - 1 x 20 000 gt and Berth No's 47 & 49 - 1 x 10 000 gt for vessels handling cement & chemicals

[5]*Umemachi Wharf:* Berth No's 21, 23 & 25. 2 x 10 000 gt handling raw salt & non-ferrous ore

[6]*Sakurajima Wharf:* Berth No's 15, 17 & 19. 2 x 10 000 gt and 1 x 7000 gt handling recycled materials & steel materials

[7]*Ajikawa Pier West Wharf:* Berth No.13B. 1 x 500 gt and 1 x 1000 gt handling paper & woodpulp

[8]*Ajikawa Pier South Wharf:* Berth No.13A. 2 x 1000 gt and 1 x 2000 gt handling paper & woodpulp

[9]*Ajikawa Wharf No.1:* Berth No.7. 1 x 10 000 gt and 1 x 3000 gt handling produce

[10]*Ajikawa Wharf No.2:* Berth No's 11A & 11B. 1 x 10 000 gt and 1 x 8000 gt handling steel materials, paper & woodpulp

[11]*Tempozan Wharf:* Berth No.3. 1 x 115 000 gt handling passengers & general cargo

[12]*Central Pier North Wharf:* Berth No.1. 1 x 13 000 gt handling sugar & steel materials

[13]*Wharf No.1:* Berth No's 6 & 8. 1 x 10 000 gt and 1 x 3000 gt handling steel materials

[14]*Wharf No.2:* Berth No's 14 & 16. 1 x 10 000 gt and 1 x 5000 gt handling steel materials & sugar

[15]*Wharf No.3:* Berth No's 18 & 20. 1 x 10 000 gt and 1 x 3000 gt handling steel materials

[16]*Wharf No.5:* Berth No's 22, 24 & 26. 2 x 6000 gt and 1 x 500 gt handling cement

[17]*Wharf No.6:* Berth No's 28 & 30. 2 x 10 000 gt handling rice & steel materials

[18]*Wharf No.7:* Berth No's 32, 34 & 36. 2 x 10 000 gt handling steel materials

[19]*Wharf No.8:* Berth No's 38, 40 & 42. 3 x 3000 gt and 1 x 1000 gt handling cement

[20]*Wharf No.10:* Berth No.46 - 1 x 7000 gt, Berth No's 48 & 50 - 2 x 3000 gt and Berth No's 52 & 54 - 2 x 1000 gt handling steel materials

[21]*Wharf No.11:* Berth No's 56, 58 & 60. 3 x 1000 gt handling steel materials

[22]*Taisho Pier 1 North Wharf:* Berth No's 70, 72, 74, 76 & 78. 5 x 1000 gt handling steel materials

[23]*A Wharf:* Berth No's A1-A5 & A6-A8. 8 x 3000 gt handling general cargo

[24]*B Wharf:* Berth No's B1-B4. 4 x 3000 gt handling paper, woodpulp & general cargo

[25]*D Wharf:* Berth No's D1, D2 & D3-D5. 2 x 3000 gt and 3 x 1000 gt handling steel materials

[26]*E Wharf:* Berth No's E1-E5, E6 & E7. 5 x 1000 gt and 2 x 3000 gt handling vehicles

[27]*G Wharf:* Berth No's G1-G8. 8 x 1000 gt handling steel materials & general cargo

[28]*J Wharf:* Berth No's J1-J3. 3 x 20 000 gt handling lumber & marine produce

[29]*K Wharf:* Berth No's K1 & K2. 2 x 10 000 gt handling paper, woodpulp & transport vehicles

[30]*R Wharf:* Berth No's R1, R4, R5, R2 & R3. 3 x 10 000 gt and 2 x 20 000 gt handling container & bulk cargo

[31]*Nanko C6 Wharf:* Berth C6. 1 x 35 000 gt handling container cargo. Yard area of 60 000 m2. 96 reefer points at C-6 & C-7

[32]*Nanko C7 Wharf:* Berth C7. 1 x 35 000 gt handling container cargo. Yard area of 60 000 m2

[33]*Nanko C9 Wharf:* Berth C9. 1 x 45 000 gt handling container cargo. Yard area of 45 000 m2. 154 reefer points

[34]*Yumeshima C10 Wharf:* Berth C10 for one vessel up to 60 000 gt handling container cargo

[35]*International Ferry Wharf:* Berth No's KF-1 & KF-2. 1 x 30 000 gt and 1 x 8000 gt handling passengers & container cargo

[36]*Osaka Port Container Wharf 1:* Berth C1. 1 x 40 000 dwt handling container cargo. Yard area of 104 152 m2. 378 reefer points

[37]*Osaka Port Container Wharf 2:* Berth C2. 1 x 40 000 dwt handling container cargo. Yard area of 105 044 m2. 324 reefer points

[38]*Osaka Port Container Wharf 3:* Berth C3. 1 x 40 000 dwt handling container cargo. Yard area of 104 610 m2. 168 reefer points

[39]*Osaka Port Container Wharf 4:* Berth C4. 1 x 40 000 dwt handling container cargo. Yard area of 119 999 m2. 144 reefer points

[40]*Osaka Port Container Wharf 8:* Berth C8. 1 x 45 000 dwt handling container cargo. Yard area of 126 062 m2. 263 reefer points

[41]*Tatsumi Ajikawa Wharf:* Berth No.M10. 1 x 19 000 dwt handling cement & chemicals

Storage: Total area of municipal sheds is 248 691 m2, general cargo warehouses of 1 271 288 m2, dangerous cargo warehouses of 33 911 m2, refrigerated warehousing of 1 472 088 m2 and timber basin of 75 ha. Silo of 52 500 t cap. Ample storage for bulk liquids, inflammable and combustible liquids

Mechanical Handling Equipment: Numerous cranes of various types are available on main wharves

Bunkering: All grades available by barge
Sumitomo Corp., 1-8-11 Harumi, Chiyoda-ku, Tokyo 104-8610, Japan, *Tel:* +81 3 5166 4457, *Fax:* +81 3 5166 6411, *Email:* hiroki.tsunematsu@sumitomocorp.co.jp, *Website:* www.sumitomocorp.co.jp

Towage: Nine harbour tugs of 1500-3600 hp are available. Also privately owned tugs available

Repair & Maintenance: Daizo Corp., Osaka, Japan, *Tel:* +81 6 6577 2533, *Email:* y-shimanaka@daizo.co.jp, *Website:* www.daizo.co.jp/shp/ For vessels up to 1800 gt Sanoyas Hishino Meisho Corp., 5-13-37 Minami-Tsumori, Nishinari-ku, Osaka 557-0063, Japan, *Tel:* +81 6 6661 1221, *Fax:* +81 6 6651 2205, *Website:* www.sanoyas.co.jp Two dry docks of 155 m x 21.7 m for vessels up to 3500 gt

Ship Chandlers: Port Enterprise Co. Ltd, 1-28 Chikko, 2-chome, Minato-ku, Osaka 552-0021, Japan, *Tel:* +81 6 6573 5391, *Fax:* +81 6 6575 3036, *Email:* penterj@penterj.co.jp
Shiko Ship Chandlers Co. Ltd, 14-6 2-chome Minami-ichioka, Minato-ku, Osaka 552-0011, Japan, *Tel:* +81 6 6583 4741, *Fax:* +81 6 6584 0568, *Email:* cko@shiko-ship.com

Shipping Agents: Cosmos Maritime Co. Ltd, 2nd Floor, Shin Nantai Building, 4-17 Honmachi -cho 4-chome, Chou-ku, Osaka 541-0053, Japan, *Tel:* +81 6 6243 1661, *Fax:* +81 6 6243 1664, *Email:* higuchi@c-maritime.co.jp, *Website:* www.c-maritime.co.jp
Heisei Shipping Agency Co. Ltd, Wakasugi Grand Building, 5-25 Tenjinbashi 2-chome, Kita-ku, Osaka 530-0041, Japan, *Tel:* +81 6 6353 0106, *Fax:* +81 6 6353 0193
Hesco Agencies Ltd, 5th Floor Meiji-seimei,, Sakaisui-Hommachi Building 7-15, Minami Hommachi, 1-chome,, Chuo-ku, Osaka, Japan, *Tel:* +81 6 6262 3062, *Fax:* +81 6 6262 1941, *Email:* tolosa@pop06.odn.ne.jp
Inchcape Shipping Services (ISS), Inchcape Shipping Services (Japan) Ltd, Osaka Kagaku Seni Kaikan 6-8, 4-chome Kawara-machi, Chuo-ku, Osaka 541-0048, Japan, *Tel:* +81 6 6203 5155, *Fax:* +81 6 6203 7358, *Email:* iss.osaka@iss-shipping.com, *Website:* www.iss-shipping.com
Kamigumi Co. Ltd, 1-2 Chikko 2-chome, Minato-ku, Osaka 552-0021, Japan, *Tel:* +81 6 6576 4101, *Fax:* +81 6 6574 1565
Konoike Transportation Co. Ltd, Konoike Building, 6-1, Kitakyuhoji-cho 3-chome, Chuo-ku, Osaka 541, Japan, *Tel:* +81 6 6244 4511, *Fax:* +81 6 6251 6716
Mediterranean Shipping Company, MSC Japan K.K., 7th Floor Sakaisuji Honmachi Centre Building, 1-6 Honmachi 2 chome, Chuo Ku, Osaka 541-0053, Japan, *Tel:* +81 6 6271 0601, *Fax:* +81 6 6271 0948, *Website:* www.mscgva.ch
Mitsui-Soko Co. Ltd, 2-4-9 Tosabori, Nishi-ku, Osaka-shi, Osaka, Japan, *Tel:* +81 6 6443 1521, *Fax:* +81 6 6443 3744
A.P. Moller-Maersk Group, Maersk K.K., Nakanoshima Mitsui Building, 18F, 3-3-3 Nakanoshima, Kita-ku, Osaka 530-0005, Japan, *Tel:* +81 6 4560 0020, *Fax:* +81 6 4560 0015, *Website:* www.maerskline.com
Nihon Hoso Unyu Co. Ltd, 3-8 Uchihonmachi 2-chome, Chuo-ku, Osaka 5400026, Japan, *Tel:* +81 6 6942 1811, *Fax:* +81 6 6942 0588
Port Enterprise Co. Ltd, 1-28 Chikko, 2-chome, Minato-ku, Osaka 552-0021, Japan, *Tel:* +81 6 6573 5391, *Fax:* +81 6 6575 3036, *Email:* penterj@penterj.co.jp
Seven Seas Shipping Co. Ltd, Meiji Seimei Sakaisuji-honmachi Building, 7-15, Minami-honmachi 1-chome, Chuo-ku, Osaka, Japan, *Tel:* +81 6 6264 7541, *Fax:* +81 6 6264 7095
Seven Star Co. Ltd, 3rd Fl, Tatsumi Shokai Building, P O Box 965, 1-1 Chikko 4-chome, Minato-ku, Osaka, Japan, *Tel:* +81 6 6576 2555, *Fax:* +81 6 6576 2550, *Email:* gmkosa@mb.infoweb.ne.jp
Summit Shipping Agencies Ltd, Hon-Cho Century Building 6th Floor, 7-6 1-chome,, Hon-Cho Chuou-ku, Osaka 541-0053, Japan, *Tel:* +81 6 6261 4444, *Fax:* +81 6 6261 5099, *Email:* genosaka@summitship.co.jp, *Website:* www.summitship.co.jp
Tatsumi Shokai Co. Ltd, 2nd Floor, 4-1-1 Chikko, Minato-ku, Osaka 552-0021, Japan, *Tel:* +81 6 6576 1861, *Fax:* +81 6 6576 1849, *Email:* agency@tatsumi-agent.jp, *Website:* www.tatsumi-cs.co.jp
Wallem Shipping Agencies Limited, 2nd Floor Osaka Kagaku Seni, Kalkan, 6-8 Kawaramachi 4-chome, Chuo-ku, Osaka 541-0048, Japan, *Tel:* +81 6 6201 5252, *Fax:* +81 6 6201 0149, *Email:* wsjosa@wallem.com

Surveyors: China Classification Society, 8th Floor, BOC Building, 1-1-35 Kitahorie, Nishi-ku, Osaka, Japan, *Tel:* +81 6 6534 1438, *Fax:* +81 6 6534 1436, *Email:* ccsok@skyblue.ocn.ne.jp, *Website:* www.ccs.org.cn

Medical Facilities: Osaka Seamen's Insurance Hospital. Osaka Health Control Center. Osaka Ekisai Hospital

Airport: Kansai International, approx 30 km

Development: Berth C-12 is under construction in Hokko South District. The berth will have a quay length of 400 m in depth of 15-16 m

Key to Principal Facilities:—			
A=Airport	**C**=Containers	**G**=General Cargo	**P**=Petroleum	**R**=Ro/Ro	**Y**=Dry Bulk
B=Bunkers	**D**=Dry Dock	**L**=Cruise	**Q**=Other Liquid Bulk	**T**=Towage (where available from port)	

Lloyd's Agent: Cornes & Co. Ltd, Meikai Building, 32 Akashi-machi, Chuo-ku, Kobe 650-0037, Hyogo Pref., Japan, *Tel:* +81 78 332 3421, *Fax:* +81 78 332 3070, *Email:* survey@kobe.cornes.co.jp, *Website:* www.cornes.co.jp

OTARU

Lat 43° 12' N; Long 141° 1' E.

Admiralty Chart: 1807	**Admiralty Pilot:** 41
Time Zone: GMT +9 h	**UNCTAD Locode:** JP OTR

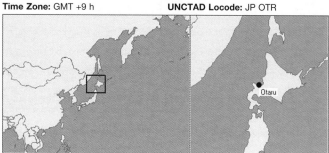

Principal Facilities:

P		Y	G	C	R		B		T	A	

Authority: Otaru City Port, 4-2 Minato-machi, Otaru 047, Hokkaido, Japan, *Tel:* +81 134 231107, *Fax:* +81 134 231109, *Email:* kowan@city.otaru.hokkaido.jp

Port Security: ISPS compliant

Approach: Harbour landlocked on three sides, further sheltered by breakwaters of 3556 m. Depth of water inside breakwaters 3.6 m-17 m. Depth in Otaru Fairway 10 m-17 m

Anchorage: Quarantine anchorage in pos 43° 11.51' N, 141° 01.48' E in depth of 10-15 m

Pilotage: Not compulsory. Pilots are available at the quarantine anchorage from 0600 to one hour after sunset for entry. 24 h for departures. Tel: +81 134 225380

Radio Frequency: VHF Channels 16 and 12

Weather: Winds SW in summer. Strong NW monsoon possible during winter

Tides: Max tidal range 0.42 m

Maximum Vessel Dimensions: 40 000 dwt, 200 m loa, 12 m d

Principal Imports and Exports: Imports: Corn, Logs, Soybean, Wheat. Exports: Machinery, Packing materials, Used cars.

Working Hours: Weekday 0830-1630, 1630-2100. Sunday 0830-1600, except 1st and 3rd weeks

Accommodation:

Name	Length (m)	Depth (m)	Remarks
Otaru			
No.1 Pier No's 4 & 5	293	9	1 x 15 000 gt
No.1 Pier No.6	128	7	1 x 1000 gt
No.2 Pier No's 7 & 8	293	9	2 x 6000 gt
No.2 Pier No.9	126	9	1 x 3000 gt
No.2 Pier No's 10 & 11	293	9	2 x 6000 gt
No.2 Pier No.12	128	7	1 x 1000 gt
No.3 Pier No's 13 & 14	344	9	1 x 15 000 gt
No.3 Pier No.15	127	9	1 x 3000 gt
No.3 Pier No's 16 & 17	362	9–12	1 x 20 000 gt
Central Pier No's 1 & 2	312	7.5–10	1 x 3000 gt & 1 x 10 000 gt
Central Pier No.3	254	10	1 x 10 000 gt
Central Pier No's 4 & 5	400	7.5–12	1 x 20 000 gt & 1 x 5000 gt
Katsunai Pier No.1	267	13	1 x 25 000 gt
Katsunai Pier No's 2 & 3	380	10	2 x 10 000 gt
Katsunai Pier No's 4 & 5	483	9–10	2 x 20 000 gt
Kitahama Wharf	251	5	1 x 1000 gt
Temiya Wharf	140	5	1 x 1000 gt
Umayamachi Wharf No's 1, 2 & 3	410	7.5	3 x 3000 gt
Wakatake Dolphin	301	10	1 x 15 000 gt

Storage: 28 transit sheds of 56 157 m2, 51 warehouses of 77 887 m2, 307 silos of 201 244 m3

Location	Cold (m³)
Otaru	99172

Bunkering: Available. Loading from tanker boat
Kita Nihon Oil Co. Ltd, 3-18-1 Inaho, Otaru 047-0032, Hokkaido, Japan, *Tel:* +81 134 237 441, *Fax:* +81 134 336 598, *Email:* otaru-hakuyo@kitanihon-oil.co.jp

Towage: Two tugs available, both of 2600 hp

Repair & Maintenance: Engine repairs and small repairs available, drydock cap of 200 gt

Medical Facilities: Available

Airport: Sin-Chitose International Airport, 80 km

Railway: Otaru Station, 1 km

Lloyd's Agent: Cornes & Co. Ltd, 273 Yamashita-cho, Naka-ku, Yokohama 231-0023, Kanagawa Pref., Japan, *Tel:* +81 45 201 8537, *Fax:* +81 45 212 3105, *Email:* survey@ykh.cornes.co.jp, *Website:* www.cornes.co.jp

OTSURUGI WHARF

harbour area, see under Onahama

OWASE

Lat 34° 4' N; Long 136° 13' E.

Admiralty Chart: JP93	**Admiralty Pilot:** 42A
Time Zone: GMT +9 h	**UNCTAD Locode:** JP OWA

Principal Facilities:

P		G			B			

Authority: Port & Harbour Section of Mie Prefecture, Harbour/Coast Division, Komeicho 13, Tsu 514-8570, Mie Pref., Japan, *Tel:* +81 592 242691, *Fax:* +81 592 243117, *Email:* kowan@pref.mie.jp, *Website:* www.pref.mie.jp

Officials: Director: Sekoguchi Yukihisa.

Approach: The passage in the bay is 5.6 km long and exceeds 20 m depth

Anchorage: The port is suitable as a port of refuge. Quarantine anchorage in pos 34° 03' 55" N, 136° 13' 20" E

Pilotage: Not compulsory. Pilots board at entrance of Owase Bay and are available from sunrise to 3 h before sunset for tankers scheduled to discharge at the Toho Oil Co berths. Owase Pilots, Tel: +81 597 223362

Weather: Typhoon season, July to October

Tides: Tidal range 2 m

Maximum Vessel Dimensions: 210 000 dwt, 19 m d, 350 m loa

Principal Imports and Exports: Imports: Crude oil.

Accommodation:

Name	Length (m)	Depth (m)	Draught (m)	Remarks
Owase				See ¹ below
Chubu Electric Co Wharf	120		5.5	Max 2000 dwt
Toho Oil Co Dolphin Berth	155	17		See ² below
Sea Berth		21		See ³ below

[1]*Owase:* The Public wharves are protected by breakwaters totalling 1013 m. The majority of vessels calling at the port are fishing and coastal vessels of less than 1000 dwt. There are five wharves with 4.5 m alongside mainly for fishing vessels up to 700 dwt. Also two wharves with 5.5 m alongside for coastal vessels up to 2000 dwt
[2]*Toho Oil Co Dolphin Berth:* For vessels of 100 000 dwt, 265 m loa, 16.0 m d. Discharging is by two unloading arms of 2500 t/h cap each
[3]*Sea Berth:* For vessels of 210 000 dwt, 340 m loa, 19.0 m d, where unloading is by two floating hoses of 4000 t/h cap

Storage: Three sheds of 72 600 m2, a refrigerated warehouse of 2543 m2, warehousing of 5092 m2

Location	Open (m²)
Owase	5600

Mechanical Handling Equipment: Some small capacity cranes are available

Cargo Worked: 35 000 t of crude oil discharged and 6700 t of domestic trade cargo handled per working day

Bunkering: Cosmo Oil Co. Ltd, Toshiba Building, 1-1 Shibaura 1-chome, Minato-ku, Tokyo 105-8528, Japan, *Tel:* +81 3 3798 3156, *Fax:* +81 3 3798 3592, *Email:* masayuki_iijima@cosmo-oil.co.jp, *Website:* www.cosmo-oil.co.jp
Hanwa Co. Ltd, 2nd Floor, Finland House, 56 Haymarket, London SW1Y 4RN, United Kingdom, *Tel:* +44 20 7839 4448, *Fax:* +44 20 7839 3994, *Email:* orito@hanwa.co.uk
Hikawa Shoji Kaisha Ltd, 26-2 Shinkawa NS Building 1-chome, Shinkawa, Chuo-ku, Tokyo 104, Japan, *Tel:* +81 3 5776 6858, *Fax:* +81 3 5541 3274
Idemitsu Kosan Co. Ltd, 1-1 Marunochi, 3-Chome, Chiyoda-ku, Tokyo 100-8321, Japan, *Tel:* +81 3 3213 3138, *Fax:* +81 3 3213 1145, *Email:* tohru.takamura@si.idemitsu.co.jp, *Website:* www.idemitsu.co.jp
KG Int Petroleum Ltd, Shiba Park Building, 241 Shiba Koen, Minato-ku, Tokyo 105, Japan, *Tel:* +81 3 3578 4551, *Fax:* +81 3 3578 4550
Japan Energy Corp., 2-10-1, Toranomon, Minato-ku, Tokyo 105-8407, Japan, *Tel:* +81 3 5573 6100, *Fax:* +81 3 5573 6674, *Email:* yamano@j-energy.co.jp, *Website:* www.j-energy.co.jp
Kamei Corp., 1-6-1 Otemachi, Chiyoda-ku, Tokyo 100-0004, Japan, *Tel:* +81 3 3286 6234, *Fax:* +81 3 3286 6249, *Email:* bunker@kamei.co.jp
Kawasho Corp., World Trade Centre, 4-1 Hanamatsu-cho 2-chome, Minato-ku, Tokyo 105, Japan, *Tel:* +81 3 3435 3251
Kyodo Oil Co. Ltd, 11-2 Nagata-cho 2-chome, Chiyoda-ku, Tokyo, Japan, *Tel:* +81 3 3505 8241, *Fax:* +81 3 3505 8697
Marubeni Petroleum Co. Ltd, Marubeni International Petroleum Singapore Co. Ltd,

c/o Marubeni Corporation, 4-2 Ohtemachi 1-chome, Chiyoda-ku, Tokyo 100-8088, Japan, *Tel:* +81 3 3282 3920, *Fax:* +81 3 3282 3950, *Email:* TOKB554@marubenicorp.com, *Website:* www.marubeni.co.jp
MC Marine and Bunkering Inc., 8th Floor, Uchisaiwai-cho Dai Building, 3-3 Uchisaiwai-cho 1-chome, Chiyoda-ku, Tokyo 100-0011, Japan, *Tel:* +81 3 5251 2575, *Fax:* +81 3 5251 2583
Mitsui & Co. Petroleum Ltd, 2-1, Ohtemachi 1-chome, Chiyoda-ku, Tokyo 100-0004, Japan, *Tel:* +81 3 3285 6905, *Fax:* +81 3 3285 9811, *Email:* tkzph@dg.mitsui.com, *Website:* www.mitsui.co.jp
Nissho Iwai Corp., 4-4 Akasaka 2-chome, Minato-ku, Tokyo, Japan, *Tel:* +81 3 35882111
Nittetsu Shoij Co. Ltd, 5-7 Kameido 1-chome, Koto-ku, Tokyo 136, Japan, *Tel:* +81 3 5627 2157, *Fax:* +81 3 5627 2192
Shinagawa Fuel Co. Ltd, New Pier Takeshiba North Tower, 8th Floor, 1-11-1 Kaigan, Minato-ku, Tokyo 105-8525, Japan, *Tel:* +81 3 5470 7113, *Fax:* +81 3 5470 7157, *Email:* hakuyu@ml1.sinanen.co.jp
Sigma Foreign Service (Panama) S.A., 2-25 Aikawai, Tempaku-ku, Nagoya 468-0836, Aichi Pref., Japan, *Tel:* +81 52 896 1510, *Fax:* +81 52 896 7703
Sumitomo Corp., Harumi Island, Triton Square, Office Tower Y, 8-11 Harumi 1-chome, Chuo-ku, Tokyo 104-8610, Japan, *Tel:* +81 3 51664458, *Fax:* +81 3 51666407, *Email:* ir@sumitomo.co.jp, *Website:* www.sumitomocorp.co.jp

Towage: Large tugs available from Nagoya

Repair & Maintenance: Minor repairs can be undertaken

Medical Facilities: Available

Lloyd's Agent: Cornes & Co. Ltd, Meikai Building, 32 Akashi-machi, Chuo-ku, Kobe 650-0037, Hyogo Pref., Japan, *Tel:* +81 78 332 3421, *Fax:* +81 78 332 3070, *Email:* survey@kobe.cornes.co.jp, *Website:* www.cornes.co.jp

RUMOI

Lat 43° 57' N; Long 141° 38' E.

Admiralty Chart: 1807   **Admiralty Pilot:** 41
Time Zone: GMT +9 h   **UNCTAD Locode:** JP RMI

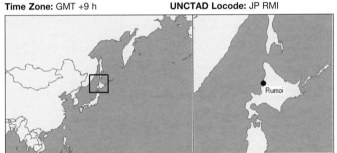

Principal Facilities:

P		Y	G	C	R		B		T	

Authority: Port & Harbour Bureau of Rumoi City, 11 Saiwai-cho 1 chome, Rumoi 077-8601, Hokkaido, Japan, *Tel:* +81 164 421801, *Fax:* +81 164 438778, *Email:* rumoi-city@e-rumoi.jp, *Website:* www.e-rumoi.jp

Officials: Port Manager: Naohiko Nakabayashi, *Tel:* +81 164 424272, *Email:* kowan@e-rumoi.jp.

Port Security: ISPS compliant

Approach: Draught limitation in the channel 7.5 m

Pilotage: Not compulsory. Pilots are available at the quarantine anchorage during the summer and at No.3 district during the winter. Vessels can berth or unberth at any time

Tides: Max tidal range 0.32 m

Accommodation:

Name	Length (m)	Depth (m)	Draught (m)	Remarks
Rumoi				
South Wharf (B)	295	7.5	7.3	Coal
South Wharf (C)	379	6.5	6.4	General cargo
North Wharf (A)	451	7.5	7.3	Coal, general cargo & containers
Kotanhama Wharf	360	7.5–8	7.2–7.7	See [1] below
Oil Wharf (N Dolphin)		7	7	Petroleum
Oil Wharf (S Dolphin)		7	7	Petroleum
Onoda Cement (Dolphin)		8	8	Cement

[1]*Kotanhama Wharf:* 2 berths handling general cargo, logs & coal

Bunkering: Domestic oil available. Bonded oil from Hakodate if required

Towage: One tug of 450 hp available

Repair & Maintenance: Minor repairs can be undertaken

Lloyd's Agent: Cornes & Co. Ltd, 273 Yamashita-cho, Naka-ku, Yokohama 231-0023, Kanagawa Pref., Japan, *Tel:* +81 45 201 8537, *Fax:* +81 45 212 3105, *Email:* survey@ykh.cornes.co.jp, *Website:* www.cornes.co.jp

SAGANOSEKI

Lat 33° 14' N; Long 131° 51' E.

Admiralty Chart: JP1247A/JP1247B   **Admiralty Pilot:** 42B
Time Zone: GMT +9 h   **UNCTAD Locode:** JP SAG

Principal Facilities:

P	Q	Y	G	C		B		T	A

Authority: Port & Harbor Division, Civil Engineering & Construction Dept., Oita Prefectural Government, 3-1-1 Ohte-machi, Oita 870-8501, Oita Pref., Japan, *Tel:* +81 97 538 5714, *Fax:* +81 97 537 0907, *Email:* a17310@pref.oita.lg.jp

Approach: Draught limitation in the channel is 8.8 m

Anchorage: Saganoseki Quarantine Anchorage, pos 33° 15' 39" N; 131° 51' 25" E, 267° and 4.5 km from Sekisaki Lighthouse in depth of 21 m

Pilotage: Not compulsory. Pilots are available from Moji Quarantine Anchorage or Sekisaki Pilot Station in pos 33° 13' N; 131° 54' E between sunrise and 1 h before sunset

Radio Frequency: Oita Port Radio, VHF Channel 16

Weather: NW winds in the winter season

Tides: Tidal range 2.1 m

Maximum Vessel Dimensions: 30 000 dwt, 170 m loa, 9.55 m d

Working Hours: 0700-1630, 1630-2130, 2130-0700

Accommodation:

Name	Length (m)	Depth (m)	Draught (m)	Remarks
Hiroura Wharf				Operated by Nippon Mining
Berth A	100	10	9	Max 15 000 gt
Berth B	200	10	9.45	Max 20 000 gt
Berth C	130	10	9.45	See [1] below

[1]*Berth C:* Max 7000 gt. Sulphuric acid loading facilities

Mechanical Handling Equipment:

Location	Type	Capacity (t)	Qty
Saganoseki	Mult-purp. Cranes	6	2
Saganoseki	Mult-purp. Cranes	5	2

Cargo Worked: 2500 t/day

Bunkering: Idemitsu Kosan Co. Ltd, 1-1 Marunochi, 3-Chome, Chiyoda-ku, Tokyo 100-8321, Japan, *Tel:* +81 3 3213 3138, *Fax:* +81 3 3213 1145, *Email:* tohru.takamura@si.idemitsu.co.jp, *Website:* www.idemitsu.co.jp
KG Int Petroleum Ltd, Shiba Park Building, 241 Shiba Koen, Minato-ku, Tokyo 105, Japan, *Tel:* +81 3 3578 4551, *Fax:* +81 3 3578 4550
MC Marine and Bunkering Inc., 8th Floor, Uchisaiwai-cho Dai Building, 3-3 Uchisaiwai-cho 1-chome, Chiyoda-ku, Tokyo 100-0011, Japan, *Tel:* +81 3 5251 2575, *Fax:* +81 3 5251 2583
Mitsui & Co. Petroleum Ltd, 2-1, Ohtemachi 1-chome, Chiyoda-ku, Tokyo 100-0004, Japan, *Tel:* +81 3 3285 6905, *Fax:* +81 3 3285 9811, *Email:* tkzph@dg.mitsui.com, *Website:* www.mitsui.co.jp
Nissho Iwai Corp., 4-4 Akasaka 2-chome, Minato-ku, Tokyo, Japan, *Tel:* +81 3 35882111
Nittetsu Shoij Co. Ltd, 5-7 Kameido 1-chome, Koto-ku, Tokyo 136, Japan, *Tel:* +81 3 5627 2157, *Fax:* +81 3 5627 2192
Sumitomo Corp., Harumi Island, Triton Square, Office Tower Y, 8-11 Harumi 1-chome, Chuo-ku, Tokyo 104-8610, Japan, *Tel:* +81 3 51664458, *Fax:* +81 3 51666407, *Email:* ir@sumitomo.co.jp, *Website:* www.sumitomocorp.co.jp

Towage: Three tugs available; one of 2700 hp and two of 2400 hp

Repair & Maintenance: Minor repairs can be undertaken

Medical Facilities: Available at Oita hospital, 50 km

Airport: Oita Airport, 85 km

Lloyd's Agent: Cornes & Co. Ltd, Meikai Building, 32 Akashi-machi, Chuo-ku, Kobe 650-0037, Hyogo Pref., Japan, *Tel:* +81 78 332 3421, *Fax:* +81 78 332 3070, *Email:* survey@kobe.cornes.co.jp, *Website:* www.cornes.co.jp

SAIKI

Lat 32° 58' N; Long 131° 55' E.

Admiralty Chart: JP1220   **Admiralty Pilot:** 42B
Time Zone: GMT +9 h   **UNCTAD Locode:** JP SAE

Key to Principal Facilities:—				
A=Airport	**C**=Containers	**G**=General Cargo	**P**=Petroleum	**R**=Ro/Ro	**Y**=Dry Bulk
B=Bunkers	**D**=Dry Dock	**L**=Cruise	**Q**=Other Liquid Bulk	**T**=Towage (where available from port)

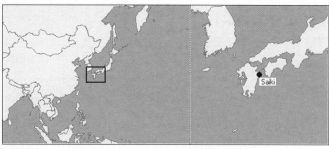

Principal Facilities:

	Y	G		B		T

Authority: Port & Harbor Division, Civil Engineering & Construction Dept., Oita Prefectural Government, 3-1-1 Ohte-machi, Oita 870-8501, Oita Pref., Japan, *Tel:* +81 97 538 5714, *Fax:* +81 97 537 0907, *Email:* a17310@pref.oita.lg.jp

Port Security: ISPS compliant

Approach: Draught limitation in the channel 11 m

Pilotage: Not compulsory. Pilots are available at the quarantine anchorage if required. Entry or sailing during nightime is possible

Tides: Max tidal range 1.85 m

Accommodation:

Name	Length (m)	Depth (m)	Draught (m)	Remarks
Saiki				
Nihon Cement Pier	150	9.5	8.5	1 x 8000 gt
Kokoku Jinken Pulp Pier	60	6	5	1 x 3000 gt
Kokoku Jinken Dolphin Pier(Woodchip)	90	9	9	1 x 12 000 gt
Lumber Anchorage		14		4 x 10 000 gt
Mejima Pier	370	10		2 x 10 000 gt
Buoy		12		1 x 20 000 gt

Mechanical Handling Equipment:

Location	Type	Capacity (t)	Qty
Saiki	Floating Cranes	150	2
Saiki	Floating Cranes	50	1

Bunkering: Hanwa Co. Ltd, 2nd Floor, Finland House, 56 Haymarket, London SW1Y 4RN, United Kingdom, *Tel:* +44 20 7839 4448, *Fax:* +44 20 7839 3994, *Email:* orito@hanwa.co.uk
Hikawa Shoji Kaisha Ltd, 26-2 Shinkawa NS Building 1-chome, Shinkawa, Chuo-ku, Tokyo 104, Japan, *Tel:* +81 3 5776 6858, *Fax:* +81 3 5541 3274
Idemitsu Kosan Co. Ltd, 1-1 Marunochi, 3-Chome, Chiyoda-ku, Tokyo 100-8321, Japan, *Tel:* +81 3 3213 3138, *Fax:* +81 3 3213 1145, *Email:* tohru.takamura@si.idemitsu.co.jp, *Website:* www.idemitsu.co.jp
KG Int Petroleum Ltd, Shiba Park Building, 241 Shiba Koen, Minato-ku, Tokyo 105, Japan, *Tel:* +81 3 3578 4551, *Fax:* +81 3 3578 4550
Marubeni Petroleum Co. Ltd, Marubeni International Petroleum Singapore Co. Ltd, c/o Marubeni Corporation, 4-2 Ohtemachi 1-chome, Chiyoda-ku, Tokyo 100-8088, Japan, *Tel:* +81 3 3282 3920, *Fax:* +81 3 3282 3950, *Email:* TOKB554@marubenicorp.com, *Website:* www.marubeni.co.jp
MC Marine and Bunkering Inc., 8th Floor, Uchisaiwai-cho Dai Building, 3-3 Uchisaiwai-cho 1-chome, Chiyoda-ku, Tokyo 100-0011, Japan, *Tel:* +81 3 5251 2575, *Fax:* +81 3 5251 2583
Mitsui & Co. Petroleum Ltd, 2-1, Ohtemachi 1-chome, Chiyoda-ku, Tokyo 100-0004, Japan, *Tel:* +81 3 3285 6905, *Fax:* +81 3 3285 9811, *Email:* tkzph@dg.mitsui.com, *Website:* www.mitsui.co.jp
Nittetsu Shoij Co. Ltd, 5-7 Kameido 1-chome, Koto-ku, Tokyo 136, Japan, *Tel:* +81 3 5627 2157, *Fax:* +81 3 5627 2192

Towage: One 2000 hp tug and one 2500 hp are available

Repair & Maintenance: Minor repairs can be undertaken

Lloyd's Agent: Cornes & Co. Ltd, Meikai Building, 32 Akashi-machi, Chuo-ku, Kobe 650-0037, Hyogo Pref., Japan, *Tel:* +81 78 332 3421, *Fax:* +81 78 332 3070, *Email:* survey@kobe.cornes.co.jp, *Website:* www.cornes.co.jp

SAKAI

Lat 34° 31' N; Long 135° 25' E.

Admiralty Chart: JP149	**Admiralty Pilot:** 42B
Time Zone: GMT +9 h	**UNCTAD Locode:** JP SAK

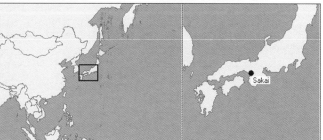

Principal Facilities:

P	Q	Y	G	C	R		B	D	T	A

Authority: Port & Harbour Bureau Osaka Perfectural Government, 10th Floor, Sakai-Semboku Port, Service Center Building, 6-1 Nagisa-cho, Izumiotsu 595-0055, Osaka Pref., Japan, *Tel:* +81 725 211411, *Fax:* +81 725 217259, *Email:* kowankyoku@sbox.pref.osaka.lg.jp, *Website:* www.pref.osaka.jp/kouwan/index.htl

Port Security: ISPS compliant

Approach: The approach is via Tomogashima channel, or via Inland Sea, and then in to Osaka Bay. Vessels usually anchor at quarantine anchorage at Osaka.
Sakai-minami Channel 4.0 km long, width 200-300 m in depth of 10 m.
Sakai-kita Channel 3.5 km long, width 300 m in depth of 14 m.
Hamadera Channel 6.8 km long, width 300 m in depth of 16 m.
Otsu Channel 2.2 km long, width 300 m in depth of 10 m.
Otsu-minami Channel 3.0 km long, width 300 m in depth of 12 m

Anchorage: Anchorage 1302.2 ha, depth 4.5-16 m

Pilotage: Compulsory for vessels over 10 000 gt. Pilots board off respective passages and are not available after sunset

Tides: Tidal range 1.75 m, 2.1 m MHWL, 0.35 m MLWL, 1.45 m MSL

Principal Imports and Exports: Imports: Coal, Crude oil, Iron ore, LNG. Exports: Chemicals, Steel products.

Working Hours: 0800-1600. No night work. Continuous three shifts at Nippon Steel wharves

Accommodation:

Name	Length (m)	Depth (m)	Remarks
Public Wharves			See [1] below
Shiohama Wharf No.1	360	7	3 x 4000 dwt
Ohama Wharf No.1	60	4.5	1 x 700 dwt
Ohama Wharf No.2	270	5.5	3 x 2000 dwt
Ohama Wharf No.3	240	7	2 x 4000 dwt
Ohama Wharf No.4	165	9	1 x 10 000 dwt
Ohama Wharf No.5	370	10	2 x 15 000 dwt
Ohama Wharf No.6	130	7.5	1 x 5000 dwt
Matsunohama Wharf No.1	450	5.5	5 x 2000 dwt
Komatsu Wharf No.1	360	5.5	4 x 2000 dwt
Komatsu Wharf No.2	390	7.5	3 x 5000 dwt
Shiomi Wharf No.1	480	4.5	8 x 700 dwt
Shiomi Wharf No.2	555	10	3 x 15 000 dwt
Shiomi Wharf No.3	555	10	3 x 15 000 dwt
Shiomi Wharf No.4	260	7.5	2 x 5000 dwt
Shiomi Wharf No.5	720	12	3 x 30 000 dwt
Sukematsu Wharf No.2	390	7.5	3 x 5000 dwt
Sukematsu Wharf No.3	390	7.5	3 x 5000 dwt
Sukematsu Wharf No.4	390	7.5	3 x 5000 dwt
Sukematsu Wharf No.5	390	7.5	3 x 5000 dwt
Matsunohama Wharf No.2	450	5.5	5 x 2000 dwt
Shiomi Wharf No.6	370	10	2 x 15 000 dwt
Sukematsu Wharf No.7	390	7.5	3 x 5000 dwt
Sukematsu Wharf No.8	480	12	2 x 30 000 dwt
Private Wharves			See [2] below
Osaka Gas Co: Coal Wharf (1-A)	400	12.5	See [3] below
Nippon Steel Corp: Ore Wharf (1-C)	597	14.5	See [4] below
Nippon Steel Corp: Export Wharf (2-A)	220	9	Max 1 x 10 000 dwt
Onoda Cement Co: Dolphin (2-D)		7.5	Max 1 x 10 000 dwt
Osaka Oil Co: Wharf (2-Z)	152	11	Max 1 x 25 000 dwt
Cosmo Oil Co: Crude Oil Wharf (7-A)	260	16	Max 2 x 240 000 dwt
Cosmo Oil Co: Loading Wharf (3-F)	451	7–7.1	Max 2 x 5000 dwt
Ube Kosan Co: A-1 Pier	80	9	Max 1 x 5000 dwt
Ube Kosan Co: A-2 Pier	110	9	Max 1 x 12 000 dwt
Ube Kosan Co: D Berth		10.5	Max 1 x 20 000 dwt
Ube Kosan Co: Cement Loading Berth		10	Max 1 x 15 000 dwt
Tatsumi Shokai Shoji: Loading Wharf (4-D)		8.5	Max 1 x 8000 dwt
Iwatani Sangyo KK: LPG Jetty (4-E)	330	14.5	Max 1 x 65 000 dwt
Marubeni Corp: Dolphin (4-J)		15.8	Max 1 x 80 000 dwt & 2 x 5000 dwt
General Oil Ref Co: Crude Oil Wharf (4-O)		16	Max 1 x 160 000 dwt
General Oil Ref Co: Loading Pier (BI-4)	252	16	Max 1 x 6000 dwt
Osaka Gas Co: Senboku LNG Wharf (4-P)		16	Max 1 x 54 000 dwt. Discharge rate of 6400 kl/h through two unloading arms
Osaka Gas Co: LNG Wharf (4-Z)	455	14	Max 1 x 70 000 dwt. Discharge rate of 10 000 kl/h through two unloading arms
Osaka Gas Co: Sub-Wharf	130	10	Max 1 x 5000 dwt
Mitsui Toatsu Co: Wharf (4-Q)	414	16	Max 1 x 100 000 dwt & 1 x 20 000 dwt. Fertilisers handled
Koa Oil Co: Crude Oil Wharf (4-U)	355	16	Max 2 x 150 000 dwt
Koa Oil Co: C-Wharf (4-U)	129	8.5	Max 1 x 5000 dwt
Koa Oil Co: Loading Wharf No.5 (4-U)		16	Max 1 x 5000 dwt

Name	Length (m)	Depth (m)	Remarks
Koa Oil Co: Loading Wharf No.8 (4-U)		16	Max 1 x 5000 dwt
Nippon Oil Co: E-Wharf		8.5	Max 1 x 6500 dwt
Nippon Oil Co: Takaishi Futo KK Wharf	145	14.5	Max 1 x 20 000 dwt. Grain berth with two pneumatic unloaders
Nippon Oil Co: Chemical Pier	119	13.5	Max 1 x 8500 dwt
Nippon Oil Co: Nippon Cement		9	Max 1 x 10 000 dwt
Hitachi Zosen Corp: North Pier	591	10	Max 170 000 dwt
Hitachi Zosen Corp: East Pier	337	10	Max 1 x 200 000 dwt
Hitachi Zosen Corp: Dolphin Wharf	68	14	Max 1 x 60 000 dwt

[1]*Public Wharves:* Container terminal at Sukematsu Wharf, 240 m long in depth of 12 m for vessels up to 30 000 t

[2]*Private Wharves:* In addition, there are further private wharves and dolphins with depths of 4.5 m to 9 m for vessels of 1000-8000 dwt

[3]*Osaka Gas Co: Coal Wharf (1-A):* Max 1 x 55 000 dwt & 1 x 5000 dwt. One cantilever trolley crane of 600 t/h cap and two level luffing cranes of 400 t/h cap

[4]*Nippon Steel Corp: Ore Wharf (1-C):* Max 1 x 100 000 dwt & 1 x 30 000 dwt. Two 1000 t/h cap and one 1500 t/h cap cantilever trolley cranes

Storage: 24 transit sheds of 80 361 m2, 43 warehouses of 166 497 m2, 60 ha of open storage space

Cargo Worked: 79 000 t of foreign trade and 126 000 t of domestic trade per working day

Bunkering: Cosmo Oil Co. Ltd, Toshiba Building, 1-1 Shibaura 1-chome, Minato-ku, Tokyo 105-8528, Japan, *Tel:* +81 3 3798 3156, *Fax:* +81 3 3798 3592, *Email:* masayuki_iijima@cosmo-oil.co.jp, *Website:* www.cosmo-oil.co.jp
ExxonMobil Marine Fuels, 1 Harbour Front Place, 06-00 Harbour Front, Tower One, Singapore, Republic of Singapore 098633, *Tel:* +65 6885 8998, *Fax:* +65 6885 8794, *Email:* asiapac.marinefuels@exxonmobil.com, *Website:* www.exxonmobilmarinefuels.com
Hanwa Co. Ltd, 2nd Floor, Finland House, 56 Haymarket, London SW1Y 4RN, United Kingdom, *Tel:* +44 20 7839 4448, *Fax:* +44 20 7839 3994, *Email:* orito@hanwa.co.uk
Idemitsu Kosan Co. Ltd, 1-1 Marunochi, 3-Chome, Chiyoda-ku, Tokyo 100-8321, Japan, *Tel:* +81 3 3213 3138, *Fax:* +81 3 3213 1145, *Email:* tohru.takamura@si.idemitsu.co.jp, *Website:* www.idemitsu.co.jp
KG Int Petroleum Ltd, Shiba Park Building, 241 Shiba Koen, Minato-ku, Tokyo 105, Japan, *Tel:* +81 3 3578 4551, *Fax:* +81 3 3578 4550
Japan Energy Corp., 2-10-1, Toranomon, Minato-ku, Tokyo 105-8407, Japan, *Tel:* +81 3 5573 6100, *Fax:* +81 3 5573 6674, *Email:* yamano@j-energy.co.jp, *Website:* www.j-energy.co.jp
Kawasho Corp., World Trade Centre, 4-1 Hanamatsu-cho 2-chome, Minato-ku, Tokyo 105, Japan, *Tel:* +81 3 3435 3251
Kyodo Oil Co. Ltd, 11-2 Nagata-cho 2-chome, Chiyoda, Tokyo, Japan, *Tel:* +81 3 3505 8241, *Fax:* +81 3 3505 8697
Marubeni Petroleum Co. Ltd, Marubeni International Petroleum Singapore Co. Ltd, c/o Marubeni Corporation, 4-2 Ohtemachi 1-chome, Chiyoda-ku, Tokyo 100-8088, Japan, *Tel:* +81 3 3282 1920, *Fax:* +81 3 3282 3950, *Email:* TOKB554@marubenicorp.com, *Website:* www.marubeni.co.jp
MC Marine and Bunkering Inc., 8th Floor, Uchisaiwai-cho Dai Building, 3-3 Uchisaiwai-cho 1-chome, Chiyoda-ku, Tokyo 100-0011, Japan, *Tel:* +81 3 5251 2575, *Fax:* +81 3 5251 2583
Mitsui & Co. Petroleum Ltd, 2-1, Ohtemachi 1-chome, Chiyoda-ku, Tokyo 100-0004, Japan, *Tel:* +81 3 3285 6905, *Fax:* +81 3 3285 9811, *Email:* tkzph@dg.mitsui.com, *Website:* www.mitsui.co.jp
Nissho Iwai Corp., 4-4 Akasaka 2-chome, Minato-ku, Tokyo, Japan, *Tel:* +81 3 35882111
Nittetsu Shoij Co. Ltd, 5-7 Kameido 1-chome, Koto-ku, Tokyo 136, Japan, *Tel:* +81 3 5627 2157, *Fax:* +81 3 5627 2192
Sumitomo Corp., Harumi Island, Triton Square, Office Tower Y, 8-11 Harumi 1-chome, Chuo-ku, Tokyo 104-8610, Japan, *Tel:* +81 3 51664458, *Fax:* +81 3 51666407, *Email:* ir@sumitomo.co.jp, *Website:* www.sumitomocorp.co.jp

Towage: Not compulsory but advisable. 16 tugs of 2600-3500 hp and four of 1000 hp are available

Repair & Maintenance: Izumi Ohtsu Shipbuilding Co. Ltd, Higashi Mintomachi, 159 Izumioutu City, Sakai, Osaka Pref., Japan, *Tel:* +81 725 333425

Medical Facilities: Available

Airport: Osaka International, 25 km

Lloyd's Agent: Cornes & Co. Ltd, Meikai Building, 32 Akashi-machi, Chuo-ku, Kobe 650-0037, Hyogo Pref., Japan, *Tel:* +81 78 332 3421, *Fax:* +81 78 332 3070, *Email:* survey@kobe.cornes.co.jp, *Website:* www.cornes.co.jp

SAKAIDE

Lat 34° 19' N; Long 133° 49' E.

Admiralty Chart: 694	**Admiralty Pilot:** 42B
Time Zone: GMT +9 h	**UNCTAD Locode:** JP SKD

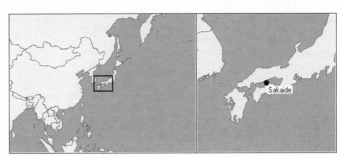

Principal Facilities:

P	Q	Y	G			B	D	T	A

Authority: City of Sakaide Port & Harbour Division, 2-3-5 Muromachi, Sakaide 762-8601, Kagawa Pref., Japan, *Tel:* +81 877 445010, *Fax:* +81 877 464056, *Email:* kouwan1@city.sakaide.lg.jp, *Website:* www.city.sakaide.lg.jp/cityoffice/port

Officials: Director: Mitsunobu Kanayama, *Email:* kouwan7@city.sakaide.lg.jp.

Port Security: ISPS compliant

Approach: The approach is via Bisan Seto traffic route. Draught limitation in the channel 10 m

Anchorage: 538 ha of anchorage space, depth of 9-13 m. Vessels usually anchor at quarantine anchorage 0700-1700

Pilotage: Not compulsory but advisable. Inland Sea pilotage is compulsory for vessels exceeding 10 000 gt and pilots are available at Wadamisaki, Sekisaki or Hesaki. Harbour pilots available at the quarantine anchorage 0700-1700

Radio Frequency: Sakaide Port Radio 0600-2000, calling VHF Channel 16, working on Channels 12 and 14

Weather: Typhoon season, July to October

Tides: Range of tide 2.98 m. Current 0.38 knots in EN-WS-WN direction

Maximum Vessel Dimensions: Approach to outer seaberth: 100 000 dwt, 18 m draft, 280 m loa. Approach to inner harbour: 55 000 dwt, 12 m draft

Principal Imports and Exports: Imports: Coal, Crude oil, Wheat. Exports: Coke, Heavy oil, Oil products.

Working Hours: 0800-1700. No night work

Accommodation:

Name	Length (m)	Depth (m)	Remarks
Public Wharves			
Nishi Wharf	274	7	See [1] below
Chuou Wharf No's 1, 2, 3 & 4	653	4.5–10	6 x 700-15 000 dwt
Higashi Unga Wharf	540	4.5	9 x 700 dwt
Matsugaura Wharf	70	5	1 x 1000 dwt
Bannosu Wharf A & B	400	6.5–10.5	2 x 3000-15 000 dwt
Hayashida Wharf A	398	12	2 x 30 000 dwt
Hayashida Wharf B	260	7.5	2 x 5000 dwt
Hayashida Wharf C	270	5.5	3 x 2000 dwt
Hayashida Wharf D	120	4.5	2 x 700 dwt
Private Wharves			See [2] below
Mitsubishi Chemical Industries: A Berth	275	13	See [3] below
Mitsubishi Chemical Industries: B Berth	200	13	See [4] below
Mitsubishi Chemical Industries: C Berth	150	12.2	Max 1 x 40 000 dwt. For coke, equipped with a level luffing crane of 700 t/h
Mitsubishi Chemical Industries: L Berth	100	12.2	Max 1 x 25 000 dwt. For alumina, equipped with an unloader of 700 t/h cap
Cosmo Oil Co: No.1 Berth		19.6	See [5] below
Cosmo Oil Co: No.2 Berth		12	See [6] below
Cosmo Oil Co: No.3-5 Berths		7.5	Max 3 x 5000 dwt
Cosmo Oil Co: No.7 Berth		7.5	Max 1 x 5000 dwt
Kawasaki Shipbuilding Co: Kawaju Pier	299	9	Max 1 x 400 000 dwt
Kawasaki Shipbuilding Co: Other Wharves		9	Max 4 x 130 000-250 000 dwt
Shikoku Electric Power: A & B Jetty		7	Max 2 x 5000 dwt
Shikoku Electric Power: Nokyo Shiryo		5	Max 1 x 5000 dwt
Shikoku Electric Power: Ube Kogyo		5	Max 1 x 5000 dwt
Zen-Noh Energie Co: LPG Berth		12	Max 1 x 55 000 dwt. Discharge rate of 2750 kl/h

[1]*Nishi Wharf:* 2 x 4000 dwt. Grain berths equipped with one pneumatic unloader of 180 t/h cap
[2]*Private Wharves:* In addition there are ten berths for coastal vessels up to 3000 dwt
[3]*Mitsubishi Chemical Industries: A Berth:* Max 1 x 55 000 dwt. For coal, equipped with four unloaders, two of 1500 t/h and two of 500 t/h
[4]*Mitsubishi Chemical Industries: B Berth:* Max 1 x 55 000 dwt. For coal, equipped with four unloaders, two of 1500 t/h and two of 500 t/h
[5]*Cosmo Oil Co: No.1 Berth:* Max 1 x 100 000 dwt. Two loading arms of 5000 t/h cap each
[6]*Cosmo Oil Co: No.2 Berth:* Max 1 x 50 000 dwt. Two loading arms of 2000 t/h cap each

Storage: Eight transit sheds (5673 m2), 137 warehouses (93 466 m2), two refrigerated warehouses (3903 m2), 147 silos (100 173 m3), 127 610 m2 of timber storage and 11 779 m2 of other open storage space

Cargo Worked: 42 000 t of foreign trade and 50 000 t of domestic trade per working day

Bunkering: Hikawa Shoji Kaisha Ltd, 26-2 Shinkawa NS Building 1-chome, Shinkawa, Chuo-ku, Tokyo 104, Japan, *Tel:* +81 3 5776 6858, *Fax:* +81 3 5541 3274
Marubeni Petroleum Co. Ltd, Marubeni International Petroleum Singapore Co. Ltd, c/o Marubeni Corporation, 4-2 Ohtemachi 1-chome, Chiyoda-ku, Tokyo 100-8088, Japan, *Tel:* +81 3 3282 3920, *Fax:* +81 3 3282 3950, *Email:* TOKB554@marubenicorp.com, *Website:* www.marubeni.co.jp
MC Marine and Bunkering Inc., 8th Floor, Uchisaiwai-cho Dai Building, 3-3 Uchisaiwai-cho 1-chome, Chiyoda-ku, Tokyo 100-0011, Japan, *Tel:* +81 3 5251 2575, *Fax:* +81 3 5251 2583
Mitsui & Co. Petroleum Ltd, 2-1, Ohtemachi 1-chome, Chiyoda-ku, Tokyo 100-0004, Japan, *Tel:* +81 3 3285 6905, *Fax:* +81 3 3285 9811, *Email:* tkzph@dg.mitsui.com, *Website:* www.mitsui.co.jp
Nissho Iwai Corp., 4-4 Akasaka 2-chome, Minato-ku, Tokyo, Japan, *Tel:* +81 3 35882111

Towage: Not compulsory but advisable. Six tugs available of 2000-4000 hp

Repair & Maintenance: Kawasaki Shipbuilding Corp, 1 Kawasaki-cho, Sakaide 762-8507, Kagawa Pref., Japan, *Tel:* +81 877 461473, *Fax:* +81 877 467006, *Email:* sogabe_s@khi.co.jp, *Website:* www.kawasakizosen.co.jp No.2 dock of 450 m x 72 m for repairs

Surveyors: Nippon Kaiji Kyokai, 1-15-10 Kume-cho, Sakaide 762-0003, Kagawa Pref., Japan, *Tel:* +81 877 464911, *Fax:* +81 877 469740, *Email:* si@classnk.or.jp, *Website:* www.classnk.or.jp

Medical Facilities: Available

Airport: Takamatsu, 30 km

Lloyd's Agent: Cornes & Co. Ltd, Meikai Building, 32 Akashi-machi, Chuo-ku, Kobe 650-0037, Hyogo Pref., Japan, *Tel:* +81 78 332 3421, *Fax:* +81 78 332 3070, *Email:* survey@kobe.cornes.co.jp, *Website:* www.cornes.co.jp

SAKAIMINATO

Lat 35° 32' N; Long 133° 15' E.

Admiralty Chart: JP149   **Admiralty Pilot:** 41
Time Zone: GMT +9 h   **UNCTAD Locode:** JP SMN

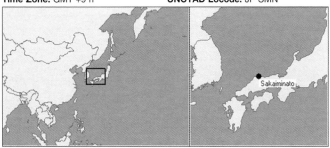

Principal Facilities:

| P | | G | C | | B | | T | A | |

Authority: Sakai Port Authority, 215 Taisho Machi, Sakaiminato 684-0004, Tottori Pref., Japan, *Tel:* +81 859 423705, *Fax:* +81 859 423735, *Email:* sakai-port@sakai-port.com, *Website:* www.sakai-port.com

Officials: General Manager: Tomoaki Matsuda.
Marketing: Yoshito Katayose, *Email:* katayose@sakai-port.com.

Port Security: ISPS compliant

Approach: Passage No.1, 5 miles in length with draught limitation of 9 m. Passage No.2, draught limitation of 13 m

Pilotage: Not compulsory. Pilots are available if required at the quarantine anchorage in daylight hours only, *Tel:* +81 859 440690

Weather: Typhoon season, July to October

Tides: Max tidal range 1.48 m

Maximum Vessel Dimensions: Air draft restriction of 40 m at Passage No.1

Principal Imports and Exports: Imports: Refined oil, Timber, Woodchips. Exports: Marine products, Paper pulp.

Working Hours: 0830-1630

Accommodation:

Name	Length (m)	Depth (m)	Draught (m)	Remarks
Sakaiminato				
Gaikou Berth No.1	370	9	8.6	2 x 10 000 gt
Gaikou Berth No.2	260	7.5	7.1	2 x 5000 gt
Chuo Berth No.1	200	7	6.5	2 x 3000 gt
Chuo Berth No.2	91	5.5	5.3	1 x 1000 gt
Chuo Berth No.3	163	6.4		1 x 3000 gt
Chuo Berth No.4	130	6.5		1 x 3000 gt
Showa South Berth No.1	270	13		1 x 40 000 gt
Showa South Berth No.2	185	10		1 x 15 000 gt
Showa South Berth No.3	130	7.5		1 x 5000 gt

Name	Length (m)	Depth (m)	Draught (m)	Remarks
Showa South Berth No.4	280	14		Container terminal. 1 x 50 000 gt. Gantry cranes available
Eshima Berth No.1	165	9		1 x 10 000 gt
Eshima Berth No.2	130	7.5		1 x 5000 gt
Eshima Dolphin	540	9		1 x 10 000 gt
Takeuchi Berth No.1	100	5.5		1 x 2000 gt
Takeuchi Berth No.2	100	5.5		1 x 2000 gt
Takeuchi Berth No.3	100	5.5		1 x 2000 gt
Takeuchi Berth No.4	130	7.5		1 x 5000 gt
Showa South Berth Pier (Dolphin)	30	7.5		3 x 5000 gt

Storage: Five transit sheds totalling 8340 m2 and general cargo warehouses of 3286 m2

Cargo Worked: 9500 t of foreign and domestic trade cargo per working day

Bunkering: Domestic oil available. Bonded oil from Moji with sufficient advance notice, if required

Towage: Two tugs available; one of 3200 hp and one of 2600 hp

Repair & Maintenance: Minor repairs undertaken

Medical Facilities: Available

Airport: Yonago Airport, 6 km

Lloyd's Agent: Cornes & Co. Ltd, Meikai Building, 32 Akashi-machi, Chuo-ku, Kobe 650-0037, Hyogo Pref., Japan, *Tel:* +81 78 332 3421, *Fax:* +81 78 332 3070, *Email:* survey@kobe.cornes.co.jp, *Website:* www.cornes.co.jp

SAKATA

Lat 38° 56' N; Long 139° 49' E.

Admiralty Chart: 1388   **Admiralty Pilot:** 42A
Time Zone: GMT +9 h   **UNCTAD Locode:** JP SKT

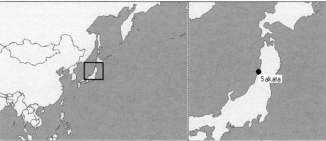

Principal Facilities:

| P | Y | G | C | | B | | T | A | |

Authority: Port & Harbour Section of Yamagata Prefecture, 2-8-1 Matsunami, Yamagata 990-8570, Yamagata Pref., Japan, *Tel:* +81 23 630 2401, *Fax:* +81 23 630 2664, *Email:* port@port-of-sakata.jp, *Website:* www.port-of-sakata.jp

Port Security: ISPS compliant

Pre-Arrival Information: Vessels must submit an entry notification when entering the port to Port Control stating the following:
(a) vessels name, call sign, type of vessel, nationality and registry
(b) gt, loa, draught and speed
(c) vessels owner details
(d) initial port of departure and last port visited
(e) time of port entry, reason for port entry and dock
(f) type and amount of cargo
(g) any accidents occurring during passage, or any other information affecting navigation

Approach: Draught limitation in Honko-ku Channel is 10.0 m and in Kitako-ku Channel, 13.0 m. Free Pratique formalities carried out 2 miles NW of North Lighthouse

Anchorage: Sheltered anchorage can be obtained in a depth of 13 m

Pilotage: Pilotage is available on request. Vessels must advise ETA at least 24 h in advance
Vessels less than 30 000 gt pilot boards 1500 m W of Sakata S Breakwater Lt (38° 56.03' N; 139° 47.90' E)
Vessels over 30 000 gt pilot boards 2 nautical miles W of Sakata S Breakwater Lt

Radio Frequency: VHF Channel 16

Weather: Winds WNW (December-February) and ESE (April-Nov)

Tides: Tidal range 0.28 m

Traffic: 2000, 9176 TEU's handled

Working Hours: 0830-1630 or 0700-2200 if required. Sunday and holidays available except 1st and 3rd Sunday, subject to negotiation

Accommodation: Well protected by N and S breakwaters, totalling 5948 m and by training wall of 1384 m. Rail spurs on wharves

Name	Length (m)	Depth (m)	Draught (m)	Remarks
Public Wharves				
Ohama Wharf No.1	330	9	8.5	2 x 10 000 dwt
Nishi Wharf	418	4.5–10	9.3	See [1] below

Name	Length (m)	Depth (m)	Draught (m)	Remarks
Higashi Shinmachi Wharf	260	7.5	7	2 x 5000 dwt
Higashi Funaba-cho Wharf No.1	360	5.5		4 x 2000 dwt
Higashi Funaba-cho Wharf No.2	95	4.5		3 x 700 dwt
Sodeoka Wharf	390	7.5	7	3 x 5000 dwt
Mooring Buoy	230	10	9.3	1 x 15 000 dwt
Kominato Wharf No.1	270	13	11.8	1 x 50 000 dwt
Kominato Wharf No.2	185	10	9.3	1 x 15 000 dwt
Kominato Wharf No.3	185	10	9.3	1 x 15 000 dwt
Miyaumi Wharf	260	7.5	7	2 x 5000 dwt
Private Wharves				
Oil Pier	92	7	6.5	1 x 3000 dwt
Sumikei Senyo Wharf	270	13	11.8	See [2] below
Sakata Kyodo Karyoku Wharf	160	7.5		2 x 5000 dwt
Oil Pier	228	7.5	7	1 x 5000 dwt

[1]Nishi Wharf: 1 x 15 000 dwt, 2 x 2000 dwt & 1 x 700 dwt
[2]Sumikei Senyo Wharf: 1 x 50 000 dwt. Two unloaders of 1500 t/h exclusively for the use of Sakata Kyodokaryokuhatuden

Storage: Limited transit shed space for salt and general cargo

Location	Open (m²)	Covered (m²)
Sakata	388293	5169

Bunkering: Domestic oil available

Towage: Three tugs available; one of 2900 hp, one of 2600 hp and one of 2000 hp

Repair & Maintenance: Sakata-Tekkojo Co. Ltd, Sakata, Japan Small-sized marine engines repaired up to 500 hp
Yagishi-Zosen Co. Ltd, Sakata, Japan Several small slipways
K.K. Yamagata Zosensho, Sakata, Japan, Tel: +81 234 261233 Repair facilities Four cranes, two of 450 t cap and two of 100 t cap.

Lloyd's Agent: Cornes & Co. Ltd, 273 Yamashita-cho, Naka-ku, Yokohama 231-0023, Kanagawa Pref., Japan, Tel: +81 45 201 8537, Fax: +81 45 212 3105, Email: survey@ykh.cornes.co.jp, Website: www.cornes.co.jp

SASEBO

Lat 33° 8' N; Long 129° 43' E.

Admiralty Chart: 3881	**Admiralty Pilot:** 42A
Time Zone: GMT +9 h	**UNCTAD Locode:** JP SSB

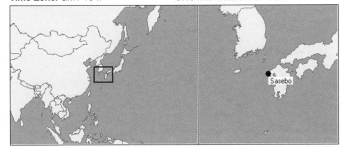

Principal Facilities:

P		Y	G				B	D	T	A

Authority: Port & Harbour Bureau of Sasebo City, 1-10 Yahata-machi, Sasebo 857-8585, Nagasaki Pref., Japan, Tel: +81 956 241111, Fax: +81 956 232370, Email: koukanri@city.sasebo.lg.jp, Website: www.city.sasebo.nagasaki.jp

Officials: General Manager: Nobumasa Toyomura.

Port Security: ISPS compliant

Approach: Fine natural harbour, affording safe anchorage for large vessels. Depth of 51 m at entrance, 23-54 m in the passage

Anchorage: Depths range from 10-37 m. Apart from anchorage areas controlled by US Navy, there is anchorage for four 10 000 t commercial ships in No.3 Section in depth of 10 m. No.9 mooring buoy is controlled by City Office for commercial vessels of up to 5000 gt

Pilotage: Compulsory for vessels over 300 gt. ETA 24 h in advance. Pilot boards vessel one mile NW of Kogosaki lighthouse in pos 33° 06' N; 129° 38' E

Weather: Dense fog sometimes prevails in early spring. SW winds in summer, N winds in other seasons

Tides: Tidal range max 3.39 m. Current reaches 1.5 knots in vicinity of harbour entrance at rising tide. At ebb tide water flows stronger in opposite direction, but does not hinder navigation

Maximum Vessel Dimensions: 258 082 dwt, 341.1 m loa

Working Hours: 0830-1630, 1630-2130. Sundays and holidays working subject to negotiation

Accommodation:

Name	Length (m)	Depth (m)	Draught (m)	Remarks
Sasebo				See [1] below
Maebata Pier No.2	185	10	10	Max 20 000 gt
Maebata Pier No.3	195	11	11	Max 20 000 gt
Tategami Pier No.1	254	10.6	10	Max 20 000 gt
Tategami Pier No's 2 & 3	364	10.6	10	2 x 20 000 gt
Tategami Pier No's 4-6	576	10.6	10	3 x 20 000 gt
Tategami Pier No's 7 & 8	364	10.6	10	2 x 20 000 gt
Tategami Pier No.9	152	10.6	10	Max 20 000 gt
Akazaki Oil Wharf No's 1-3	518	12	11.58	
Motofuni Oil Wharf No.1	80	12.9	9.75	
Motofuni Oil Wharf No.2	80	9.2	8.53	
Iorizaki Oil Berth	81	14.5	9.75	
Yokose Oil Berth	88	13.7	12.8	

[1]Sasebo: Tategami Pier Berth No's 2-5 are used exclusively by Sasebo Heavy Industries Co Ltd; Berth No's 1 and 6-9 are reserved for use by the United States Navy, together with all the oil berths

Storage: Sasebo Municipal have warehousing of 4159 m2. Nishi Kyushu Warehouse Co have warehousing of 24 505 m2

Location	Grain (t)
Sasebo	45850

Mechanical Handling Equipment: Five 15 t cap cranes at Tategami berths

Location	Type	Capacity (t)	Qty	Remarks
Sasebo	Floating Cranes	12	1	
Sasebo	Floating Cranes	120	1	
Sasebo	Floating Cranes	10	2	
Tategami Pier No's 4-6	Mult-purp. Cranes	250	1	at Pier 5

Cargo Worked: Average performance per hour per gang: coal 150-200 t, grain in bags 60-70 t, grain in bulk 150-180 t, general cargo 160-180 t, steel 150 t

Bunkering: Idemitsu Kosan Co. Ltd, 1-1 Marunochi, 3-Chome, Chiyoda-ku, Tokyo 100-8321, Japan, Tel: +81 3 3213 3138, Fax: +81 3 3213 1145, Email: tohru.takamura@si.idemitsu.co.jp, Website: www.idemitsu.co.jp
KG Int Petroleum Ltd, Shiba Park Building, 241 Shiba Koen, Minato-ku, Tokyo 105, Japan, Tel: +81 3 3578 4551, Fax: +81 3 3578 4550
Kyushu Oil Co. Ltd, 1-1 Uchisaiwai-cho 2-chome, Chiyoda-ku, Tokyo, Japan, Tel: +81 3 3502 3651, Fax: +81 3 3502 9850
MC Marine and Bunkering Inc., 8th Floor, Uchisaiwai-cho Dai Building, 3-3 Uchi-saiwai-cho 1-chome, Chiyoda-ku, Tokyo 100-0011, Japan, Tel: +81 3 5251 2575, Fax: +81 3 5251 2583
Mitsui & Co. Petroleum Ltd, 2-1, Ohtemachi 1-chome, Chiyoda-ku, Tokyo 100-0004, Japan, Tel: +81 3 3285 6905, Fax: +81 3 3285 9811, Email: tkzph@dg.mitsui.com, Website: www.mitsui.co.jp
Nittetsu Shoij Co. Ltd, 5-7 Kameido 1-chome, Koto-ku, Tokyo 136, Japan, Tel: +81 3 5627 2157, Fax: +81 3 5627 2192

Towage: Twelve tugs available of 640 hp to 3800 hp

Repair & Maintenance: Sasebo Heavy Industries Co. Ltd, Tategami-cho, Sasebo 857-8501, Nagasaki Pref., Japan, Tel: +81 956 259111, Fax: +81 956 259109, Website: www.ssk-sasebo.co.jp

Surveyors: Nippon Kaiji Kyokai, 4th Floor, Asahi-Seimei Building, 1-22 Hamada-Machi, Sasebo 857-0051, Nagasaki Pref., Japan, Tel: +81 956 250745, Fax: +81 956 256153, Email: ss@classnk.or.jp, Website: www.classnk.or.jp

Medical Facilities: All facilities available

Airport: Nagasaki, 50 km

Lloyd's Agent: Cornes & Co. Ltd, Meikai Building, 32 Akashi-machi, Chuo-ku, Kobe 650-0037, Hyogo Pref., Japan, Tel: +81 78 332 3421, Fax: +81 78 332 3070, Email: survey@kobe.cornes.co.jp, Website: www.cornes.co.jp

SENDAI-SHIOGAMA

Lat 38° 17' N; Long 141° 2' E.

Admiralty Chart: 2959	**Admiralty Pilot:** 41
Time Zone: GMT +9 h	**UNCTAD Locode:** JP SGM

Principal Facilities:

P	Q	Y	G	C	R		B		T	A

Key to Principal Facilities:—				
A=Airport	**C**=Containers	**G**=General Cargo	**P**=Petroleum	**R**=Ro/Ro	**Y**=Dry Bulk
B=Bunkers	**D**=Dry Dock	**L**=Cruise	**Q**=Other Liquid Bulk	**T**=Towage (where available from port)	

Authority: Ports & Harbors Promotion Division, Public Works Department, Miyagi Prefectural Government, 3-8-1 Honcho, Aoba-ku, Sendai 980-8570, Miyagi Pref., Japan, *Tel:* +81 22 211 3221, *Fax:* +81 22 211 3296, *Email:* kousin@pref.miyagi.jp, *Website:* www.pref.miyagi.jp/kouwan

Officials: Port Manager: Haruo Kasamatsu.
Assistant Manager: Masashi Takahashi.

Port Security: ISPS compliant

Pilotage: Not compulsory

Accommodation:

Name	Length (m)	Depth (m)	Draught (m)	Remarks
Sendai				
Public Wharves				
Takasago Container Terminal Berth 1	270	12		See [1] below
Takasago Container Terminal Berth 2	330	14		
Nakano Wharf No.1	240	12		Max 20 000 dwt
Nakano Wharf No.2	185	10		Max 18 000 dwt
Nakano Wharf No.3	185	10		Max 18 000 dwt
Nakano Wharf No.4	185	10		Max 18 000 dwt
Nakano Wharf No.5	185	10		Max 18 000 dwt
Nakano Wharf No.6	185	10		Max 18 000 dwt
Takamatsu Mokuzai Wharf	240	12		Max 20 000 dwt
Raijin Wharf No.1	130	7.5		Max 5000 dwt
Raijin Wharf No.2	130	7.5		Max 5000 dwt
Raijin Wharf No.3	130	7.5		Max 5000 dwt
Ferry Terminal No.1	205	8.5		Max 12 000 dwt
Ferry Terminal No.2	165	8.5		Max 8000 dwt
Private Wharves				
Tohoku Oil No.1 Dolphin	199	18		Max 150 000 dwt
Tohoku Oil No.2 Dolphin	40	7.5		Max 6000 dwt
Tohoku Oil No.3 Dolphin	138	6		2 x 3000 dwt
Tohoku Oil No.4 Dolphin	138	6		2 x 3000 dwt
Tohoku Oil No.6 Dolphin	60	6		Max 3000 dwt
Tohoku Oil No.7 Dolphin	138	6		2 x 3000 dwt
Tohoku Oil LPG Dolphin	75	17		Max 60 000 dwt
Tohoku Denryoku	30	6		1 x 4500 dwt
Azuma Seiko	475	10–12		Max 18 000 dwt & 20 000 dwt
Fujisawa Seiko	300	8		Max 10 000 dwt
Nippon Kokan	345	5.5–7.5		Max 3000-5000 dwt
Kawasaki Seitetsu	260	7.5		2 x 5000 dwt
Nippon Steel (Shin Nittetsu)	246	7.5		2 x 5000 dwt
Shiogama				
Public Wharves				
Taizan Wharf No.1 (T1)	160	9	8.5	1 x 18 000 dwt
Taizan Wharf No.2 (T2)	160	9	8.5	Max 15 000 dwt
Taizan Wharf No.3 (T3)	130	7.5	7	Max 10 000 dwt
Taizan Wharf No.4 (T4)	130	7.5	7	Max 10 000 dwt
Higashi Wharf (E1, 2 & 3)	330	7.5	7	3 x 10 000 dwt
Naka Wharf (East Side)	270	4.5–7.5	4–7	2 x 1000 dwt & 1 x 5000 dwt
Naka Wharf (Front)	168	5.5	5	2 x 2000 dwt
Naka Wharf (West Side)	197	4.5	4	2 x 1000 dwt
Nishi Wharf	323	4.5	4	4 x 1000 dwt
Togu Wharf	180	5.5		2 x 2000 dwt
Private Wharves				
Yogasaki Wharf	300	7.5		3 x 3000 dwt
Tohoku Shipbuilding Co Ltd	100	4		1 x 3000 dwt
Shiogama Oil Term. Nisseki Dolphin	32	6		1 x 1500 dwt
Shiogama Oil Term. Kamei Dolphin	31	6		1 x 1000 dwt

Name	Length (m)	Depth (m)	Draught (m)	Remarks
Shiogama Oil Term. Esso Dolphin	34	6		1 x 2000 dwt
Shiogama Oil Term. Idemitsu Dolphin	21	6		1 x 1500 dwt
Shiogama Oil Term. Shell Dolphin	41	6		1 x 2000 dwt
Shiogama Oil Term. Daikyo & Kyowa Dolphin	34	6		1 x 2000 dwt
Shiogama Oil Term. Mitsui Dolphin	33	6		1 x 2000 dwt
Shiogama Oil Term. Maruzen Dolphin	37	6		1 x 2000 dwt
Shiogama Oil Term. Marubeni Dolphin	32	6		1 x 1000 dwt
Shiogama Oil Term. Maruzen Dolphin	30	5.5		1 x 500 dwt

[1]*Takasago Container Terminal Berth 1:* Takasago Container Terminal has a total area of 202 800 m2 with storage cap of 2160 TEU's, a container freight station of 1500 m2 and 75 reefer points. Equipment consists of two gantry cranes and eight straddle carriers

Bunkering: MC Marine and Bunkering Inc., 8th Floor, Uchisaiwai-cho Dai Building, 3-3 Uchisaiwai-cho 1-chome, Chiyoda-ku, Tokyo 100-0011, Japan, *Tel:* +81 3 5251 2575, *Fax:* +81 3 5251 2583
Nittetsu Shoij Co. Ltd, 5-7 Kameido 1-chome, Koto-ku, Tokyo 136, Japan, *Tel:* +81 3 5627 2157, *Fax:* +81 3 5627 2192

Towage: Eight tugs available from 500 hp to 3200 hp

Surveyors: Nippon Kaiji Kyokai, Room 1104, Beruza Sendai, 4-7-17 Chuo, Aoba-ku, Sendai 980-0021, Miyagi Pref., Japan, *Tel:* +81 22 216 6672, *Fax:* +81 22 216 6673, *Email:* se@classnk.or.jp, *Website:* www.classnk.or.jp

Airport: Sendai Airport

Lloyd's Agent: Cornes & Co. Ltd, 273 Yamashita-cho, Naka-ku, Yokohama 231-0023, Kanagawa Pref., Japan, *Tel:* +81 45 201 8537, *Fax:* +81 45 212 3105, *Email:* survey@ykh.cornes.co.jp, *Website:* www.cornes.co.jp

SHIBUSHI

Lat 31° 28' N; Long 131° 7' E.

Admiralty Chart: JP1221/JP1222	**Admiralty Pilot:** 42A
Time Zone: GMT +9 h	**UNCTAD Locode:** JP SBS

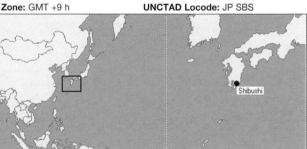

Principal Facilities:

	Y	G	C		B		T	A	

Authority: Port & Harbour Division of Kagoshima Prefecture, Shibushi Port Branch Office, 6617-17 Chou, Shibushi-cho, Shibushi City, Kagoshima 899-7102, Kagoshima Pref., Japan, *Tel:* +81 99 473 1651, *Fax:* +81 99 473 1671, *Email:* shibushi-minato@pref.kagoshima.lg.jp, *Website:* www.pref.kagoshima.jp

Officials: Managing Director: Tsukasa Ikebata.

Port Security: ISPS compliant

Approach: Draught limitation in the channel is 12 m

Anchorage: Anchorage can be obtained in Shibushi Bay to the SW of Biro Shima, but should be avoided when winds are from between E and S

Pilotage: Not compulsory but recommended. Pilots are available at pos 31° 25' N; 131° 05' 30" E; no night berthing or unberthing

Tides: Range of tide 2.42 m

Maximum Vessel Dimensions: 69 011 dwt, 234.8 m loa

Principal Imports and Exports: Imports: Cereals. Exports: Paper, Pulp.

Accommodation:

Name	Length (m)	Depth (m)	Remarks
Shibushi			See [1] below
Gaiko Pier No.1	585	5.5–10	Three berths. Max cap 2000-15 000 dwt
Gaiko Pier No.2	260	7.5	Max cap 5000 dwt
Wakahama Chuo Wharf No.1	240	12	Max cap 30 000 dwt

Name	Length (m)	Depth (m)	Remarks
Wakahama Chuo Wharf No.2	165	9	Max cap 10 000 dwt
Wakahama Chuo Wharf No.3	75	8	Max cap 5000 dwt
Wakahama Chuo Wharf No.4	315	7.5	Max cap 5000 dwt
Wakahama Chuo Wharf No.6	180	5.5	Max cap 2000 dwt
Wakahama Minami Wharf No.1	130	7.5	Max cap 5000 dwt
Wakahama Minami Wharf No.2	90	5.5	Max cap 2000 dwt
Zennoh Silo Wharf	205	13	Max cap 65 000 dwt
Shibushi Silo Wharf	200	13	Max cap 65 000 dwt

[1] *Shibushi:* Bulk facilities: One 800 t/h and two 400 t/h unloaders on Zennoh Silo Wharf, two 600 t/h unloaders on Shibushi Silo Wharf

Bunkering: MC Marine and Bunkering Inc., 8th Floor, Uchisaiwai-cho Dai Building, 3-3 Uchisaiwai-cho 1-chome, Chiyoda-ku, Tokyo 100-0011, Japan, *Tel:* +81 3 5251 2575, *Fax:* +81 3 5251 2583
Mitsui & Co. Petroleum Ltd, 2-1, Ohtemachi 1-chome, Chiyoda-ku, Tokyo 100-0004, Japan, *Tel:* +81 3 3285 6905, *Fax:* +81 3 3285 9811, *Email:* tkzph@dg.mitsui.com, *Website:* www.mitsui.co.jp

Towage: Three tugs available of 3200 hp

Repair & Maintenance: Minor repairs can be undertaken

Medical Facilities: Good facilities available

Airport: Kagoshima, 73 km

Railway: Shibushi Station, 1 km

Lloyd's Agent: Cornes & Co. Ltd, Meikai Building, 32 Akashi-machi, Chuo-ku, Kobe 650-0037, Hyogo Pref., Japan, *Tel:* +81 78 332 3421, *Fax:* +81 78 332 3070, *Email:* survey@kobe.cornes.co.jp, *Website:* www.cornes.co.jp

SHIKAMA

Lat 34° 47' N; Long 134° 40' E.

Admiralty Chart: 698	**Admiralty Pilot:** 42B
Time Zone: GMT +9 h	**UNCTAD Locode:** JP SKM

Principal Facilities:

Y	G	C		B	T	

Authority: Port & Harbour Section of Hyogo Prefecture, 5-10-1 Yamate-dori, Chuo-ku, Kobe 650-8567, Hyogo Pref., Japan, *Tel:* +81 78 341 7711, *Fax:* +81 78 341 6477

Pilotage: Inland-sea pilot is compulsory for vessels exceeding 10 000 gt. They are available at Wada-Misaki (off Kobe) and harbour pilots are available at the anchorage from sunrise to 1 h before sunset

Tides: Max +1.6 m. Min -0.5 m

Accommodation:

Name	Length (m)	Depth (m)	Draught (m)	Remarks
Public Wharves				
Suka Area No.1				For coasters only
Suka Area No.2	135	7.5	7	Up to 5000 dwt
Suka Area No.3	170	10	9.1	Up to 30 000 dwt
Suka Area No.4	170	10	9.1	Up to 30 000 dwt
Suka Area No.5	170	10	9.1	Up to 30 000 dwt
Suka Area No.6	170	10	9.1	Up to 30 000 dwt
Suka Area No.7	230	12	10.1	Up to 47 000 dwt
Suka Area No.8	250	12	10.1	Up to 47 000 dwt
Suka Area No.9	250	12	10.1	Up to 47 000 dwt
Nakashima Wharf	390	5.5	5	4 x 2000 dwt
New Nakashima Wharf No.1	130	7.5	7	Up to 5000 dwt
New Nakashima Wharf No.2	130	7.5	7	Up to 5000 dwt
New Nakashima Wharf No.3	240	12	10.1	Up to 53 000 dwt
New Nakashima Wharf No.4	240	12	10.1	Up to 53 000 dwt
Sembagawa Wharf	360	5.5	5	4 x 2000 dwt
Private Wharves				
Kansai Electric Power	200	7.8	7.3	1 x 12 000 dwt
Godo Seitetsu	200	9	8.5	1 x 10 000 dwt
Sanyo Special Steel	100	7.5	7	1 x 3000 dwt

Name	Length (m)	Depth (m)	Draught (m)	Remarks
Seitetsu Kagaku Dolphin	65	6	5.5	1 x 3000 dwt
Cosmo Oil Dolphin	130	7.5	7	1 x 3000 dwt
Nippon Mitsubishi Oil Dolphin		7.5	7	Two berths 100 m and 130 m long, both for 1 x 3000 dwt
Ube Ind. Dolphin	130	7.5	7	1 x 3000 dwt

Bunkering: Idemitsu Kosan Co. Ltd, 1-1 Marunochi, 3-Chome, Chiyoda-ku, Tokyo 100-8321, Japan, *Tel:* +81 3 3213 3138, *Fax:* +81 3 3213 1145, *Email:* tohru.takamura@si.idemitsu.co.jp, *Website:* www.idemitsu.co.jp
KG Int Petroleum Ltd, Shiba Park Building, 241 Shiba Koen, Minato-ku, Tokyo 105, Japan, *Tel:* +81 3 3578 4551, *Fax:* +81 3 3578 4525
MC Marine and Bunkering Inc., 8th Floor, Uchisaiwai-cho Dai Building, 3-3 Uchisaiwai-cho 1-chome, Chiyoda-ku, Tokyo 100-0011, Japan, *Tel:* +81 3 5251 2575, *Fax:* +81 3 5251 2583
Mitsui & Co. Petroleum Ltd, 2-1, Ohtemachi 1-chome, Chiyoda-ku, Tokyo 100-0004, Japan, *Tel:* +81 3 3285 6905, *Fax:* +81 3 3285 9811, *Email:* tkzph@dg.mitsui.com, *Website:* www.mitsui.co.jp
Nittetsu Shoij Co. Ltd, 5-7 Kameido 1-chome, Koto-ku, Tokyo 136, Japan, *Tel:* +81 3 5627 2157, *Fax:* +81 3 5627 2192
Shinagawa Fuel Co. Ltd, New Pier Takeshiba North Tower, 8th Floor, 1-11-1 Kaigan, Minato-ku, Tokyo 105-8525, Japan, *Tel:* +81 3 5470 7113, *Fax:* +81 3 5470 7157, *Email:* hakuyu@ml1.sinanen.co.jp
Sumitomo Corp., Harumi Island, Triton Square, Office Tower Y, 8-11 Harumi 1-chome, Chuo-ku, Tokyo 104-8610, Japan, *Tel:* +81 3 51664458, *Fax:* +81 3 51666407, *Email:* ir@sumitomo.co.jp, *Website:* www.sumitomocorp.co.jp

Towage: Two tugs of 2600 hp and two tugs of 3500 hp

Repair & Maintenance: Minor repairs only

Lloyd's Agent: Cornes & Co. Ltd, Meikai Building, 32 Akashi-machi, Chuo-ku, Kobe 650-0037, Hyogo Pref., Japan, *Tel:* +81 78 332 3421, *Fax:* +81 78 332 3070, *Email:* survey@kobe.cornes.co.jp, *Website:* www.cornes.co.jp

SHIMIZU

Lat 35° 1' N; Long 138° 29' E.

Admiralty Chart: JP89	**Admiralty Pilot:** 42A
Time Zone: GMT +9 h	**UNCTAD Locode:** JP SMZ

Principal Facilities:

P	Q	Y	G	C	R		B	D	T	

Authority: Shimizu Port Administration Bureau, 9-25 Hinode-cho, Shimizu 424-0922, Shizuoka Pref., Japan, *Tel:* +81 54 353 2203, *Fax:* +81 54 354 0380, *Email:* port@mail.wbs.ne.jp, *Website:* www.portofshimizu.com

Officials: Executive Director: Katsumi Maeda.

Port Security: ISPS compliant

Approach: Fine natural harbour, further protected by breakwaters totalling 4179 m, depth 22 m. No draught limitation in the channel

Anchorage: Third Section Anchorage, 1000 m W of Masaki Lighthouse in a depth of 9 m; First Section Anchorage, in Oride Bay in a depth of 7.5 m

Pilotage: Not compulsory. Pilots available 500 m N of Masaki lighthouse

Tides: Tidal range 2.72 m

Traffic: 2006, 17 926 000 t of cargo handled

Principal Imports and Exports: Imports: Bauxite, Grain, Woodchips. Exports: Machinery, Motorcycles.

Working Hours: Stevedores 0830-2130. Sunday working only on 2nd and 4th weeks, 0830-1600. Gangs for full-container vessels are available 24 h except holidays

Accommodation:

Name	Length (m)	Depth (m)	Remarks
Shimizu			See [1] below
Shin-Okitsu Wharf	350	15	1 x 60 000 dwt. Containers
Okitsu Wharf No.1 (1-3)	556	10	3 x 15 000 dwt. Frozen fish
Okitsu Wharf No's 1-2 (4-5)	181	5.5	2 x 2000 dwt. Chemical goods
Okitsu Wharf No.2 (6-9)	740	10	4 x 15 000 dwt. Frozen fish
Okitsu Wharf No.2 (10)	168	7.5	1 x 5000 dwt. Frozen fish
Okitsu Wharf No.2 (11-12)	440	12	See [2] below
Okitsu Wharf No.2 (13-14)	370	10	2 x 15 000 dwt. Frozen fish
Sodeshi Wharf No.1 (1-4)	240	4.5	4 x 700 dwt. Ballast & steel
Sodeshi Wharf No.1 (5)	135	7.5	1 x 5000 dwt
Sodeshi Wharf No.1 (6-8)	720	12	See [3] below
Sodeshi Wharf No.1 (9-10)	350	9	2 x 10 000 dwt. Frozen fish

Key to Principal Facilities:—

A=Airport	**C**=Containers	**G**=General Cargo	**P**=Petroleum	**R**=Ro/Ro	**Y**=Dry Bulk
B=Bunkers	**D**=Dry Dock	**L**=Cruise	**Q**=Other Liquid Bulk	**T**=Towage (where available from port)

Name	Length (m)	Depth (m)	Remarks
Sodeshi Wharf No.1 (11)	240	12	1 x 30 000 dwt. Lumber & frozen fish
Sodeshi Wharf No.1 (12-15)	520	7.5	4 x 5000 dwt. Lumber & frozen fish
Sodeshi Wharf No.2 (16)	330	10–12	1 x 30 000 dwt. Woodchips
Sodeshi Wharf No.2 (17)	165	9	1 x 10 000 dwt. Petroleum products & chemical goods
Sodeshi Wharf No.2 (18)	72	7.5	1 x 1000 dwt. Petroleum products & chemical goods
Tonen Sea Berth	480	22	1 x 250 000 dwt. Petroleum products
Hinode Wharf (1)	80	4.5	1 x 700 dwt
Hinode Wharf (2)	130	7.5	1 x 5000 dwt. Steel & frozen fish
Hinode Wharf (3)	130	7.5	1 x 5000 dwt. Plywood
Hinode Wharf (4)	240	12	1 x 30 000 dwt. Pulp & plywood
Hinode Wharf (5)	240	12	1 x 30 000 dwt. Pulp & plywood
Shimizu City Wharf	266	7.3	2 x 5000 dwt. Cement
Honen Dolphin	210	11	1 x 40 000 dwt. Soybean & rape seed
Fujimi Wharf (1-2)	113	5.5	2 x 2000 dwt. Feed
Fujimi Wharf (3)	140	7.5	2 x 5000 dwt. Cement
Fujimi Wharf (4-5)	480	12	1 x 30 000 dwt. Woodchips
Fujimi Wharf (6-7)	329	9	2 x 10 000 dwt. Plywood
Buoys			2 x 20 000 dwt & 2 x 10 000 dwt. Lumber
Nikkei Wharf	365	9–11	See [4] below
Suzuyo No.1 Pier	27	5	1 x 1000 dwt for chemicals
Suzuyo Warehouse Wharf	48	4.5	1 x 700 dwt for chemicals
Tonen Dolphin No.2	20	6	1 x 2500 dwt. Petroleum products
Tonen Dolphin No.3	100	6	1 x 2500 dwt. Petroleum products
Tonen Dolphin No.4	100	6	1 x 1500 dwt. Petroleum products
Tonen Dolphin No.6	85	6	1 x 2500 dwt. Petroleum products
Tonen Dolphin No.8	90	6.3	1 x 3000 dwt. Petroleum products
Tonen Dolphin No.9	105	7.2	1 x 3000 dwt. Petroleum products
Tonen Dolphin No.10	90	8.2	1 x 5000 dwt. Petroleum products
Chubu Denryoku Wharf	99	7.3	1 x 3000 dwt. Chemicals
Nakayama Seikosho Wharf	41	5	1 x 1000 dwt. Steel

[1]*Shimizu:* Ejiri Wharf No's 1-18 accommodate fishing vessels up to 3000 dwt. Okitsu Wharf No's 1 and 2 and Tonen Dolphin areas are prohibited to anchor
[2]*Okitsu Wharf No.2 (11-12):* 2 x 30 000 dwt. Okitsu Container Terminal with space of 66 042 m2. One gantry crane and three transfer cranes
[3]*Sodeshi Wharf No.1 (6-8):* 3 x 30 000 dwt. Sodeshi Container Terminal wit space of 184 096 m2. 239 reefer points. Five gantry cranes and twelve transfer cranes
[4]*Nikkei Wharf:* 1 x 32 000 dwt for bauxite and 1 x 15 000 dwt for alumina

Storage: 67 sheds of 201 664 m2, warehouse space totalling 239 725 m2 and refrigerated space of 171 095 m2. Coal storage and a timber basin of 835 224 m2

Bunkering: Cosmo Oil Co. Ltd, Toshiba Building, 1-1 Shibaura 1-chome, Minato-ku, Tokyo 105-8528, Japan, *Tel:* +81 3 3798 3156, *Fax:* +81 3 3798 3592, *Email:* masayuki_iijima@cosmo-oil.co.jp, *Website:* www.cosmo-oil.co.jp
Hanwa Co. Ltd, 2nd Floor, Finland House, 56 Haymarket, London SW1Y 4RN, United Kingdom, *Tel:* +44 20 7839 4448, *Fax:* +44 20 7839 3994, *Email:* orito@hanwa.co.uk
Hikawa Shoji Kaisha Ltd, 26-2 Shinkawa NS Building 1-chome, Shinkawa, Chuo-ku, Tokyo 104, Japan, *Tel:* +81 3 5776 6858, *Fax:* +81 3 5541 3274
Idemitsu Kosan Co. Ltd, 1-1 Marunochi, 3-Chome, Chiyoda-ku, Tokyo 100-8321, Japan, *Tel:* +81 3 3213 3138, *Fax:* +81 3 3213 1145, *Email:* tohru.takamura@si.idemitsu.co.jp, *Website:* www.idemitsu.co.jp
KG Int Petroleum Ltd, Shiba Park Building, 241 Shiba Koen, Minato-ku, Tokyo 105, Japan, *Tel:* +81 3 3578 4551, *Fax:* +81 3 3578 4550
Japan Energy Corp., 2-10-1, Toranomon, Minato-ku, Tokyo 105-8407, Japan, *Tel:* +81 3 5573 6100, *Fax:* +81 3 5573 6674, *Email:* yamano@j-energy.co.jp, *Website:* www.j-energy.co.jp
Kamei Corp., 1-6-1 Otemachi, Chiyoda-ku, Tokyo 100-0004, Japan, *Tel:* +81 3 3286 6234, *Fax:* +81 3 3286 6249, *Email:* bunker@kamei.co.jp
Kawasho Corp., World Trade Centre, 4-1 Hanamatsu-cho 2-chome, Minato-ku, Tokyo 105, Japan, *Tel:* +81 3 3435 3251
Kyodo Oil Co. Ltd, 11-2 Nagata-cho 2-chome, Chiyoda-ku, Tokyo, Japan, *Tel:* +81 3 3505 8241, *Fax:* +81 3 3505 8697
Marubeni Petroleum Co. Ltd, Marubeni International Petroleum Singapore Co. Ltd, c/o Marubeni Corporation, 4-2 Ohtemachi 1-chome, Chiyoda-ku, Tokyo 100-8088, Japan, *Tel:* +81 3 3282 3920, *Fax:* +81 3 3282 3950, *Email:* TOKB554@marubenicorp.com, *Website:* www.marubeni.co.jp
MC Marine and Bunkering Inc., 8th Floor, Uchisaiwai-cho Dai Building, 3-3 Uchisaiwai-cho 1-chome, Chiyoda-ku, Tokyo 100-0011, Japan, *Tel:* +81 3 5251 2575, *Fax:* +81 3 5251 2583
Mitsui & Co. Petroleum Ltd, 2-1, Ohtemachi 1-chome, Chiyoda-ku, Tokyo 100-0004, Japan, *Tel:* +81 3 3285 6905, *Fax:* +81 3 3285 9811, *Email:* tkzph@dg.mitsui.com, *Website:* www.mitsui.co.jp
Nissho Iwai Corp., 4-4 Akasaka 2-chome, Minato-ku, Tokyo, Japan, *Tel:* +81 3 35882111
Nittetsu Shoij Co. Ltd, 5-7 Kameido 1-chome, Koto-ku, Tokyo 136, Japan, *Tel:* +81 3 5627 2157, *Fax:* +81 3 5627 2192
Shinagawa Fuel Co. Ltd, New Pier Takeshiba North Tower, 8th Floor, 1-11-1 Kaigan, Minato-ku, Tokyo 105-8525, Japan, *Tel:* +81 3 5470 7113, *Fax:* +81 3 5470 7157, *Email:* hakuyu@ml1.sinanen.co.jp

Sigma Foreign Service (Panama) S.A., 2-25 Aikawai, Tempaku-ku, Nagoya 468-0836, Aichi Pref., Japan, *Tel:* +81 52 896 1510, *Fax:* +81 52 896 7703
Sumitomo Corp., Harumi Island, Triton Square, Office Tower Y, 8-11 Harumi 1-chome, Chuo-ku, Tokyo 104-8610, Japan, *Tel:* +81 3 51664458, *Fax:* +81 3 51666407, *Email:* ir@sumitomo.co.jp, *Website:* www.sumitomocorp.co.jp

Towage: Shimizu Futo K.K., 5-37, Seikai 3-chome, Shimizu 424, Shizuoka Pref., Japan, *Tel:* +81 54 334 2288

Repair & Maintenance: Kanasashi Shipbuilding Co. Ltd, 491-1 Miho, Sizuoka, Shimizu 424-8686, Shizuoka Pref., Japan, *Tel:* +81 54 334 5151, *Fax:* +81 54 335 8525, *Email:* tanaka-a@kanasashi-hi.co.jp, *Website:* www.kanasashi-hi.co.jp One dry dock 122 m x 18.4 m x 6 m for vessels of 5700 gt. One floating dock 70.5 m x 22 m for vessels of 999 gt
Miho Shipbuilding Co. Ltd, 3797 Miho, Shimizu, Shizuoka Pref., Japan, *Tel:* +81 54 334 5211, *Fax:* +81 54 334 2767, *Email:* msy-b@mail.wbs.ne.jp, *Website:* www.cajs.or.jp Dry dock 90.5 m x 16 m, cap 2500 gt. Two slipways, both 60 m x 9 m with max cap 700 gt

Shipping Agents: Amano Kaisoten Ltd, 9-5 Minato-cho, 2-chome, Shimizu 424-0943, Shizuoka Pref., Japan, *Tel:* +81 54 353 2161, *Fax:* +81 54 353 2338
Aoki Trans Corp, P O Box 100, Shimizu 424, Shizuoka Pref., Japan, *Tel:* +81 54 353 6441, *Fax:* +81 54 353 6441, *Email:* ship@aoki-trans.co.jp, *Website:* www.aoki-trans.co.jp/business.html
Asahi Kaiun K.K., Aoki Building, 14-12 Irifune-cho, Shimizu, Shizuoka Pref., Japan, *Tel:* +81 54 352 1911, *Fax:* +81 54 353 6562, *Email:* asahis@tyobb.hanjin.com
A.P. Moller-Maersk Group, Maersk Agency Shimizu K.K., Aoki Building, 6th Floor, 14012 Irfune-cho, Shimizu 424-0942, Shizuoka Pref., Japan, *Tel:* +81 54 351 3311, *Fax:* +81 54 351 2266, *Email:* smzord@maersk.com, *Website:* www.maerskline.com
Seiwa Kaiun Co. Ltd, 4-18, Hinode-cho, Shimizu 424-0922, Shizuoka Pref., Japan, *Tel:* +81 54 353 2143, *Fax:* +81 54 352 5813, *Email:* smzop.seiwa-kaiun@mail.mol.co.jp, *Website:* www.seiwa-kaiun.co.jp
Seven Star Co. Ltd, Shimizu Soko Kaisha Ltd, P O Box 70, 1-48-Hinode-cho, Shimizu 424-0922, Shizuoka Pref., Japan, *Tel:* +81 54 353 6161, *Fax:* +81 54 353 1599, *Email:* k_masui@shimizusok.co.ltd
Shimizu Kawasaki Transportation Co. Ltd, 5-1 Minato-cho 1-chome, Shimizu, Shizuoka Pref., Japan, *Tel:* +81 54 353 2483, *Fax:* +81 54 353 4556
Shimizu Shipping K.K., Shimizu Co Ltd, 8-15 Fujimi-Cho, Shimizu-Ku, Shizuoka-City, Shimizu 424-0941, Shizuoka Pref., Japan, *Tel:* +81 54 354 1910, *Fax:* +81 54 352 8323, *Email:* shimizuspg@pdcc.co.jp
Suruga Shipping Co. Ltd, 2nd Floor, Mokuzai Building, Annex 8-15 Fujimi-cho, Shimizu 424-0941, Shizuoka Pref., Japan, *Tel:* +81 54 352 4559, *Fax:* +81 54 352 8690, *Email:* srgsmz@evergreen-japan.co.jp, *Website:* www.evergreen-japan.co.jp
Suzuyo & Co. Ltd, Container Terminal Division, 408-17 Yokosuna, Shimizu, Shizuoka Pref., Japan, *Tel:* +81 54 366 3311, *Fax:* +81 54 365 1440, *Email:* info@suzuyo.co.jp, *Website:* www.suzuyo.co.jp

Stevedoring Companies: Shimizu Futo Co. Ltd & Daito Corp., 5-7, Seikai 3-chome, Shimizu, Shizuoka Pref., Japan, *Tel:* +81 54 334 2288, *Fax:* +81 54 334 2293
Shinko Koun Co Ltd, Shimizu, Shizuoka Pref., Japan, *Tel:* +81 54 353 6306, *Fax:* +81 54 353 6300
Suzuyo & Co. Ltd, 11-1 Irifune-cho, Shimizu 424-8703, Shizuoka Pref., Japan, *Tel:* +81 54 354 3054, *Fax:* +81 54 354 3109, *Email:* info@suzuyo.co.jp, *Website:* www.suzuyo.co.jp

Surveyors: Nippon Kaiji Kyokai, Kikuya Building, 2nd Floor, 7-24 Shimizu-ku Aioi-cho, Shimizu 424-0821, Shizuoka Pref., Japan, *Tel:* +81 54 351 2371, *Fax:* +81 54 351 2374, *Email:* ys@classnk.or.jp, *Website:* www.classnk.or.jp

Medical Facilities: Shimizu Municipal Hospital, 5 km

Airport: Narita Airport, 190 km

Railway: Shimizu Station, 2 km

Lloyd's Agent: Cornes & Co. Ltd, 273 Yamashita-cho, Naka-ku, Yokohama 231-0023, Kanagawa Pref., Japan, *Tel:* +81 45 201 8537, *Fax:* +81 45 212 3105, *Email:* survey@ykh.cornes.co.jp, *Website:* www.cornes.co.jp

SHIMONOSEKI

Lat 33° 56' N; Long 130° 56' E.

Admiralty Chart: 127	**Admiralty Pilot:** 42B
Time Zone: GMT +9 h	**UNCTAD Locode:** JP SHS

Principal Facilities:

P	Y G C R	B D T A

Authority: Port & Harbour Bureau, Shimonoseki City Government, 1-1 Nabe-cho, Shimonoseki 750-8521, Yamaguchi Pref., Japan, *Tel:* +81 832 311277, *Fax:* +81 832 330860, *Email:* admin@shimonoseki-port.com, *Website:* www.shimonoseki-port.com

Officials: General Director: Hiroyuki Suzuki, *Email:* suzuki.hiroyuki@city.shimonoseki.yamaguchi.jp.

Port Security: ISPS compliant

Approach: Draft limitation in the entrance channel is 11.4 m. The Kanmon Fairway is approx 40 km long and is located between Shimonoseki and Kitakyushu Ports

Anchorage: Good sheltered areas available. Mutsure Quarantine Anchorage, two anchorage sections off Mutsure Lighthouse with depths of water ranging from 8.6 m to 9.1 m and 14.6 m to 23 m respectively. Hesaki Quarantine Anchorage, pos 33° 56' 40" N; 131° 03' 18" E with depth ranging from 8.6 m to 9.1 m

Pilotage: Compulsory for vessels over 3000 gt. Pilots board at Mutsure or Hesaki anchorages

Radio Frequency: Vessels should use Shimonoseki Port Radio calling on VHF Channels 16 and 20

Tides: Tidal range 2.2 m. Currents: at equinoctial tide in spring and autumn, both E and W currents reach 6.5 knots; at equin tide in summer, max speed reaches 7-8 knots in afternoon and 4-5 knots in the morning; winter, vice versa

Principal Imports and Exports: Imports: Automobiles, Clothes, Metal ore. Exports: Automobiles, Precision machines, Rubber products.

Working Hours: 0830-1700. Overtime available

Accommodation:

Name	Length (m)	Depth (m)	Remarks
East Port Area			
Arcaport Berth	335	12	See [1] below
Hananocho Wharf			See [2] below
Berth No.23	195	5.5	Vessels up to 2000 dwt
Berth No's 24 & 25	370	10	See [3] below
Berth No.26	161	7.5	Vessels up to 100 m loa & 5000 dwt
Hosoe Wharf			Ro/ro facilities
Berth No's 18 & 19	260	7.5	Vessels up to 5000 dwt
Berth No's 20 & 21	370	10	See [4] below
Berth No.22	213	5.5	Vessels up to 120 m loa & 2000 dwt
No.1 Pier			
Berth No.8	210	4.5	Vessels up to 500 gt
Berth No.10	296	13	See [5] below
Berth No.11	120	4.5	Vessels up to 700 dwt
Berth No's 12 & 13	330	9	See [6] below
No.2 Pier			
Berth No.15	150	9	Vessels up to 150 m loa
Berth No's 16 & 17	392	10	See [7] below
Nishiyama Wharf			
Nishiyama No.3	302	12	See [8] below
Nishiyama No.4	197	5.5	Vessels up to 74 m loa & 2000 dwt
Chofu Wharf			
Chofu No.1	270	5.5	Vessels up to 74 m loa & 2000 dwt
Chofu No.2	180	7.5	Vessels up to 167 m loa

[1] *Arcaport Berth:* Passenger vessels up to 236 m loa & 50 000 gt. Over 236 m loa, prior permission should be obtained from the Pilot association

[2] *Hananocho Wharf:* Container terminal with total area of 44 700 m2. 56 reefer points

[3] *Berth No's 24 & 25:* Vessels up to 150 m loa. A vessel of loa up to 230 m can be accommodated when Berth No's 24 & 25 are used as one berth

[4] *Berth No's 20 & 21:* Vessels up to 145 m loa. A vessel of loa up to 230 m can be accommodated when Berth No's 20 & 21 are used as one berth

[5] *Berth No.10:* Vessels up to 200 m loa. A vessel drawing more than 8.5 m shall enter/depart only when rate of current in Hayatomo Seto is less than 5 knots, regardless of easterly or westerly current

[6] *Berth No's 12 & 13:* Vessels up to 150 m loa. A vessel of loa up to 160 m can be accommodated when Berth No's 12 & 13 are used as one berth

[7] *Berth No's 16 & 17:* Vessels up to 150 m loa at Berth 16 and 180 m loa at Berth 17

[8] *Nishiyama No.3:* Vessels up to 199 m loa. A vessel drawing more than 8.0 m should avoid entry when rate of current in Hayatomo Seto exeeds 5 knots

Storage: Good transit shed and warehouse facilities. Automatic grain discharging facilities. Rail spurs on wharves

Mechanical Handling Equipment:

Location	Type	Capacity (t)	Qty
Shimonoseki	Floating Cranes	265	1
Shimonoseki	Floating Cranes	185	1
Shimonoseki	Floating Cranes	180	1
Berth No's 24 & 25	Container Cranes	35.6	1
Berth No's 24 & 25	Container Cranes	35	1

Bunkering: Hanwa Co. Ltd, 2nd Floor, Finland House, 56 Haymarket, London SW1Y 4RN, United Kingdom, *Tel:* +44 20 7839 4448, *Fax:* +44 20 7839 3994, *Email:* orito@hanwa.co.uk

Idemitsu Kosan Co. Ltd, 1-1 Marunochi, 3-Chome, Chiyoda-ku, Tokyo 100-8321, Japan, *Tel:* +81 3 3213 3138, *Fax:* +81 3 3213 1145, *Email:* tohru.takamura@si.idemitsu.co.jp, *Website:* www.idemitsu.co.jp

KG Int Petroleum Ltd, Shiba Park Building, 241 Shiba Koen, Minato-ku, Tokyo 105, Japan, *Tel:* +81 3 3578 4551, *Fax:* +81 3 3578 4550

Kyodo Oil Co. Ltd, 11-2 Nagata-cho 2-chome, Chiyoda-ku, Tokyo, Japan, *Tel:* +81 3 3505 8241, *Fax:* +81 3 3505 8697

MC Marine and Bunkering Inc., 8th Floor, Uchisaiwai-cho Dai Building, 3-3 Uchisaiwai-cho 1-chome, Chiyoda-ku, Tokyo 100-0011, Japan, *Tel:* +81 3 5251 2575, *Fax:* +81 3 5251 2583

NKK Trading Inc., 4-4 Nihonbashi Hisamatsusucho, Chuo-ku, Tokyo 103, Japan, *Tel:* +81 3 3660 1522, *Fax:* +81 3 3660 1572

Sumitomo Corp., Harumi Island, Triton Square, Office Tower Y, 8-11 Harumi 1-chome, Chuo-ku, Tokyo 104-8610, Japan, *Tel:* +81 3 51664458, *Fax:* +81 3 51666407, *Email:* ir@sumitomo.co.jp, *Website:* www.sumitomocorp.co.jp

Towage: Ten tugs available; one of 3500 hp, one of 3300 hp, two of 2500 hp, three of 2100 hp, two of 1600 hp and one of 1200 hp

Repair & Maintenance: Kyokuyo Shipbuilding Corp., 8-7 Minatomachi, Chofu, Shimonoseki 752-0953, Yamaguchi Pref., Japan, *Tel:* +81 832 461291, *Fax:* +81 832 454130, *Email:* sales@kyokuyoshipyard.com, *Website:* www.kyokuyoshipyard.com Dry dock No.2: 125 m x 21.4 m x 8.1 m for vessels up to 6900 gt

Shimonoseki Shipyard of Mitsubishi Heavy Industries Ltd, 16-1, Hikoshima Enoura-cho, 6-chome, Shimonoseki 750-8505, Yamaguchi Pref., Japan, *Tel:* +81 832 665990, *Fax:* +81 832 661900, *Email:* kenichirou_mase@mhi.co.jp, *Website:* www.mhi.co.jp Four docks: No.1 164.1 m x 25.2 m x 7 m for vessels up to 17 000 dwt, No.2 217 m x 35 m x 6.7 m for vessels up to 40 000 dwt, No.3 82.8 m x 16.3 m x 5.9 m for vessels up to 4000 dwt, No.4 55.6 m x 10.5 m x 4.4 m for vessels up to 10 000 dwt

Towa Shipbuilding Co. Ltd, 4-1 Minato-machi, Chofu, Shimonoseki 752, Yamaguchi Pref., Japan, *Tel:* +81 832 463000, *Fax:* +81 832 455730 Max cap of 6800 t

Medical Facilities: Hospital available

Airport: Yamaguchi-Ube, 50 km

Railway: Shimonoseki Railway Station, 0.5 km

Lloyd's Agent: Cornes & Co. Ltd, Meikai Building, 32 Akashi-machi, Chuo-ku, Kobe 650-0037, Hyogo Pref., Japan, *Tel:* +81 78 332 3421, *Fax:* +81 78 332 3070, *Email:* survey@kobe.cornes.co.jp, *Website:* www.cornes.co.jp

SHIMOTSU

harbour area, see under Wakayama

SHINGU

Lat 33° 42' N; Long 136° 0' E.

Admiralty Chart: JP77, JP93	**Admiralty Pilot:** 42A
Time Zone: GMT +9 h	**UNCTAD Locode:** JP SHN

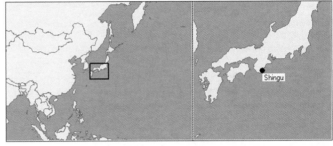

Principal Facilities:

Y	G		B	T

Authority: Wakayama Prefectural Harbor & Airport Promotion Bureau, 1-1 Komatsu-bara-dori, Wakayama 640-8585, Wakayama Pref., Japan, *Tel:* +81 73 441 3151, *Fax:* +81 73 443 4839, *Email:* e0824001@pref.wakayama.lg.jp, *Website:* www.pref.wakayama.lg.jp

Officials: Manager: Katsushi Nakano.

Port Security: ISPS compliant

Approach: Draught limitation in the channel is 10 m

Pilotage: Not compulsory. Pilots are available from Tanabe or Owase ports when required. It is possible to enter or sail after sunset subject to negotiation with pilots

Tides: Range of tide 1.03 m

Maximum Vessel Dimensions: 25 413 dwt, 160.8 m loa

Working Hours: 0730-1700 every day, including Sundays and holidays

Accommodation:

Name	Length (m)	Depth (m)
Shingu		
Wharf No.1	60	4.5
Wharf No.2	60	4.5
Wharf No.3	90	5.5
Wharf No.4	185	10
Wharf No.5	46	7.5
Passenger Ship Wharf	230	9

Bunkering: Domestic and bonded oil brought from Shimotsu or Yokkaichi

Towage: One tug of 1500 hp is available. Other tugs can be brought in from Wakayama or Osaka when required

Lloyd's Agent: Cornes & Co. Ltd, Meikai Building, 32 Akashi-machi, Chuo-ku, Kobe 650-0037, Hyogo Pref., Japan, *Tel:* +81 78 332 3421, *Fax:* +81 78 332 3070, *Email:* survey@kobe.cornes.co.jp, *Website:* www.cornes.co.jp

SHIOGAMA

harbour area, see under Sendai-Shiogama

SHIRAHAMA PORT

harbour area, see under Hososhima

Key to Principal Facilities:—			
A=Airport	**C**=Containers	**G**=General Cargo	**P**=Petroleum	**R**=Ro/Ro	**Y**=Dry Bulk
B=Bunkers	**D**=Dry Dock	**L**=Cruise	**Q**=Other Liquid Bulk	**T**=Towage (where available from port)

SOMA

Lat 37° 50' N; Long 140° 58' E.

Admiralty Chart: JP1098   **Admiralty Pilot:** 41

Time Zone: GMT +9 h   **UNCTAD Locode:** JP SMA

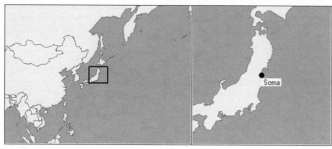

Principal Facilities:

		Y	G					T	

Authority: Ports, Harbours & Fishery Harbours Group, Public Works Department, Fukushima Prefectural Government, 2-16 Sugitsuma-cho, Fukushima 960-8670, Fukushima Pref., Japan, *Tel:* +81 24 521 7497, *Fax:* +81 24 521 7716, *Email:* kowan@pref.fukushima.jp

Officials: Director: Shuji Ariga.

Port Security: ISPS compliant

Approach: Draught limitation in the South Channel entrance is 7.5 m and in the North Channel entrance 14.0 m

Pilotage: Not compulsory but recommended. Pilots are available at pos 37° 52' N; 140° 59' E when required; berthing and unberthing is permitted after sunset

Tides: Average tidal range 0.2-0.3 m

Principal Imports and Exports: Imports: Coal. Exports: Coal ash.

Working Hours: 0830-1630 weekdays; may be extended when required. Sunday working available

Accommodation:

Name	Length (m)	Depth (m)	Draught (m)	Remarks
Soma				See [1] below
No.1 Pier No.1	90	5.5	4.9	Max 2000 dwt
No.1 Pier No.2	90	5.5	4.9	Max 2000 dwt
No.1 Pier No.3	130	7.5	6.7	Max 5000 dwt
No.1 Pier No.4	130	7.5	6.7	Max 5000 dwt
No.1 Pier No.5	130	7.5	6.7	Max 5000 dwt
No.1 Pier No.6	90	5.5	4.9	Max 2000 dwt
No.1 Pier No.7	90	5.5	4.9	Max 2000 dwt
No.1 Pier No.8	90	5.5	4.9	Max 2000 dwt
No.2 Pier No.1	90	5.5	4.9	Max 2000 dwt
No.2 Pier No.2	130	7.5	6.7	Max 5000 dwt
No.2 Pier No.3	130	7.5	6.7	Max 5000 dwt
No.2 Pier No.4	240	12	10.8	Max 30 000 dwt
No.5 Pier	560	14	12.6	Max 60 000 dwt

[1]*Soma:* Harbour protected by breakwaters. No.5 Pier has been constructed on the W side of the harbour with access from the deep North Channel

Towage: One tug of 350 hp is available

Lloyd's Agent: Cornes & Co. Ltd, 273 Yamashita-cho, Naka-ku, Yokohama 231-0023, Kanagawa Pref., Japan, *Tel:* +81 45 201 8537, *Fax:* +81 45 212 3105, *Email:* survey@ykh.cornes.co.jp, *Website:* www.cornes.co.jp

SUEHIRO

harbour area, see under Wakkanai

SUMITOMO KINZOKU

harbour area, see under Kashima

SUSAKI

Lat 33° 23' N; Long 133° 18' E.

Admiralty Chart: JP108   **Admiralty Pilot:** 42A

Time Zone: GMT +9 h   **UNCTAD Locode:** JP SUZ

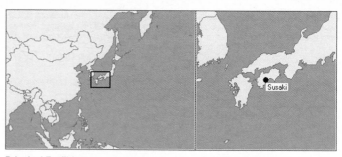

Principal Facilities:

		Y	G					T	A

Authority: Kochi Prefectural Government, Ports & Harbors Division, 1-2-20 Marunouchi, Kochi 780-8570, Kochi Pref., Japan, *Tel:* +81 88 823 9888, *Fax:* +81 88 823 9657, *Email:* 175201@ken.pref.kochi.lg.jp, *Website:* www.pref.kochi.jp

Officials: Managing Director: Hiroshi Yamanaka, *Email:* hiroshi_yamanaka@ken3.pref.kochi.lg.jp.
Harbour Master: Toyohiko Ito, *Tel:* +81 88 832 7111, *Email:* kouchi-kanri@kaiho.mlit.go.jp.

Port Security: ISPS compliant

Approach: The approach to Susaki Port is through Susaki Bay, which is narrow and crooked, via Tosa Bay. The main channel in Susaki Bay is 3.5 km long with width 120-300 m and depth 5-15 m. Draft limitation in the port channel is 8.5 m at HW

Anchorage: 21 ha of anchorage space in depth of 4-13.5 m. Vessels usually anchor at Kochi quarantine anchorage

Pilotage: Not compulsory. Unauthorised pilot available in pos 33° 19' 56" N; 133° 18' 38" E, Tel: +81 88 831 5151

Radio Frequency: VHF Channels 16 and 12

Weather: Typhoon season, July to October

Tides: Range 2 m. Current 0.4 knots in S direction

Maximum Vessel Dimensions: 15 000 dwt at public wharves, 60 000 dwt at Nittetsu Mining Dolphin

Principal Imports and Exports: Imports: Timber. Exports: Cement, Limestone.

Working Hours: 24 h/day

Accommodation: Bulk facilities: Loading and discharging of limestone, cement and clinker is carried out at the berths of Osaka Cement Co and Nittetsu Mining Co. The berths are equipped with belt conveyors and unloaders

Name	Length (m)	Depth (m)	Draught (m)	Remarks
Public Wharves				
Minatomachi Wharf No.1	180	5.5	5	Two berths. Max 2000 dwt
Minatomachi Wharf No.2	105	6	5.4	Max 3000 dwt
Minatomachi Wharf No.3	260	7.5	6.8	Two berths. Max 5000 dwt
Minatomachi Wharf No.4	185	10	9	Max 15 000 dwt
Minatomachi Wharf No.5	80	5	4.5	Max 1000 dwt
Daibo Wharf No.1	165	9	8.1	Max 10 000 dwt
Daibo Wharf No.2	200	7.5	6.8	Max 5000 dwt
Private Wharves				
Osaka Cement Co Dolphin	165	7.5	6.8	Max 3000 dwt
Osaka Cement Co Wharf	200	7	6.3	Max 5000 dwt
Nittetsu Mining Co Dolphin No.1	240	13.5	12.2	Max 60 000 dwt
Nittetsu Mining Co Dolphin No.2	200	9	8.1	Two berths. Max 10 000 dwt
Nittetsu Mining Co Dolphin No.3	120	7.5	6.8	Max 5000 dwt

Storage: Three warehouses (740 m2), 3700 m2 of timber storage and 180 000 m2 of other open storage spaces

Cargo Worked: 4900 t of foreign trade cargoes and 36 000 t of domestic trade cargoes per working day

Towage: Not compulsory but advisable. Two tugs of 1600 hp and 1100 hp are available

Medical Facilities: Available

Airport: Kochi, 60 km

Lloyd's Agent: Cornes & Co. Ltd, Meikai Building, 32 Akashi-machi, Chuo-ku, Kobe 650-0037, Hyogo Pref., Japan, *Tel:* +81 78 332 3421, *Fax:* +81 78 332 3070, *Email:* survey@kobe.cornes.co.jp, *Website:* www.cornes.co.jp

TACHIBANA

Lat 33° 53' N; Long 134° 43' E.

Admiralty Chart: JP153   **Admiralty Pilot:** 42B

Time Zone: GMT +9 h   **UNCTAD Locode:** JP TBN

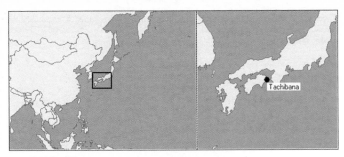

Principal Facilities:

		Y	G			B		

Authority: Port & Harbour Section of Tokushima Prefecture, 1-1 Bandai-machi, Tokushima 770, Tokushima Pref., Japan, *Tel:* +81 886 212580, *Fax:* +81 886 232847, *Email:* kouwankuukouka@pref.tokushima.lg.jp, *Website:* www.pref.tokushima.jp

Port Security: ISPS compliant

Approach: Draught limitation in the channel is 10.5 m

Anchorage: Good anchorage can be obtained midway between Taka Shima, Kokatsu Shima and Naga Shima in a depth of 10.5 m; holding ground mud. The anchorage area is exposed to NE winds

Pilotage: Not compulsory but recommended. Pilots are available at pos 33° 53' 30" N; 134° 43' 30" E during daylight hours only

Tides: Range of tide 2.02 m

Maximum Vessel Dimensions: 40 750 dwt, 185.5 m loa

Working Hours: Stevedores available 24 h when required, including Sundays and holidays except New Year's Holiday

Accommodation:

Name	Length (m)	Depth (m)	Draught (m)	Remarks
Tachibana				
Nippon Denko Wharf	200	11	10.5	See [1] below / See [2] below

[1] *Tachibana:* There are three jetties serving the Shikoku Electric Power Station with depths alongside of 5.5 m to 7.5 m accommodating vessels of 5000 t
[2] *Nippon Denko Wharf:* Can accommodate vessels of 30 000 dwt. The berth is equipped with a 500 t/h unloader

Bunkering: Bonded oil can be brought in from the Hanshin area when required

Towage: No tugs stationed at the port, but can be made available from Komatsushima when required

Lloyd's Agent: Cornes & Co. Ltd, Meikai Building, 32 Akashi-machi, Chuo-ku, Kobe 650-0037, Hyogo Pref., Japan, *Tel:* +81 78 332 3421, *Fax:* +81 78 332 3070, *Email:* survey@kobe.cornes.co.jp, *Website:* www.cornes.co.jp

TAGONOURA

Lat 35° 8' N; Long 138° 42' E.

Admiralty Chart: JP80	**Admiralty Pilot:** 42A
Time Zone: GMT +9 h	**UNCTAD Locode:** JP TGO

Principal Facilities:

P		Y	G		R		B		T	A	

Authority: Port & Harbour Section of Shizuoka Prefecture, 9-6 Ote-machi, Aoi-ka, Shizuoka 420-8601, Shizuoka Pref., Japan, *Tel:* +81 54 221 3050, *Fax:* +81 54 221 3563, *Email:* kouwan_kikaku@pref.shizuoka.lg.jp, *Website:* www.pref.shizuoka.jp

Officials: Director: Hiromi Kato.

Port Security: ISPS compliant

Approach: Draught limitation in the channel 9 m

Pilotage: Not compulsory. Pilots are available if required and board vessel 1.8 km from W breakwater lighthouse, service only available from 0500 to 1600 for berthing and anytime for sailing

Tides: Max tidal range 2.28 m

Working Hours: Stevedores: Monday-Saturday 0830-2130, Sunday 0830-1600, except 1st and 3rd Sundays in each month

Accommodation:

Name	Length (m)	Depth (m)	Draught (m)	Remarks
Tagonoura				
Yoshiwara Wharf No.1	167	9	9	1 x 10 000 dwt
Yoshiwara Wharf No.2	125	7.5	7.5	1 x 5000 dwt
Chuo Wharf No's 1-2	368	9	9	Under construction. 2 x 10 000 dwt
Chuo Wharf No's 3-4	250	7.5	7.5	2 x 5000 dwt. Two pipes for maize at 160 t/h
Fuji Wharf No's 1-4	490	7.5-10	7.5	4 x 5000 dwt
Suzukawa Wharf No's 1-5	485	5.5		6 x 5000 dwt
Asahi Kasei Wharf	250	7.5-9	7-9	1 x 10 000 dwt & 1 x 5000 dwt

Bunkering: Cosmo Oil Co. Ltd, Toshiba Building, 1-1 Shibaura 1-chome, Minato-ku, Tokyo 105-8528, Japan, *Tel:* +81 3 3798 3156, *Fax:* +81 3 3798 3592, *Email:* masayuki_iijima@cosmo-oil.co.jp, *Website:* www.cosmo-oil.co.jp
ExxonMobil Marine Fuels, 1 Harbour Front Place, 06-00 Harbour Front, Tower One, Singapore, Republic of Singapore 098633, *Tel:* +65 6885 8998, *Fax:* +65 6885 8794, *Email:* asiapac.marinefuels@exxonmobil.com, *Website:* www.exxonmobilmarinefuels.com
Fuji Kosan Co. Ltd, 2-19-6 Yanagibashi, Taito-ku, Tokyo 111-0052, Japan, *Tel:* +81 3 3861 4601, *Fax:* +81 3 3861 4611, *Email:* info@fkoil.co.jp, *Website:* www.fkoil.co.jp
Hanwa Co. Ltd, 2nd Floor, Finland House, 56 Haymarket, London SW1Y 4RN, United Kingdom, *Tel:* +44 20 7839 4448, *Fax:* +44 20 7839 3994, *Email:* orito@hanwa.co.uk
Hikawa Shoji Kaisha Ltd, 26-2 Shinkawa NS Building 1-chome, Shinkawa, Chuo-ku, Tokyo 104, Japan, *Tel:* +81 3 5776 6858, *Fax:* +81 3 5541 3274
Idemitsu Kosan Co. Ltd, 1-1 Marunochi, 3-Chome, Chiyoda-ku, Tokyo 100-8321, Japan, *Tel:* +81 3 3213 3138, *Fax:* +81 3 3213 1145, *Email:* tohru.takamura@si.idemitsu.co.jp, *Website:* www.idemitsu.co.jp
KG Int Petroleum Ltd, Shiba Park Building, 241 Shiba Koen, Minato-ku, Tokyo 105, Japan, *Tel:* +81 3 3578 4551, *Fax:* +81 3 3578 4550
Japan Energy Corp., 2-10-1, Toranomon, Minato-ku, Tokyo 105-8407, Japan, *Tel:* +81 3 5573 6100, *Fax:* +81 3 5573 6674, *Email:* yamano@j-energy.co.jp, *Website:* www.j-energy.co.jp
Kyodo Oil Co. Ltd, 11-2 Nagata-cho 2-chome, Chiyoda-ku, Tokyo, Japan, *Tel:* +81 3 3505 8241, *Fax:* +81 3 3505 8697
Kyushu Oil Co. Ltd, 1-1 Uchisaiwai-cho 2-chome, Chiyoda-ku, Tokyo, Japan, *Tel:* +81 3 3502 3651, *Fax:* +81 3 3502 9850
Marubeni Petroleum Co. Ltd, Marubeni International Petroleum Singapore Co. Ltd, c/o Marubeni Corporation, 4-2 Ohtemachi 1-chome, Chiyoda-ku, Tokyo 100-8088, Japan, *Tel:* +81 3 3282 3920, *Fax:* +81 3 3282 3950, *Email:* TOKB554@marubenicorp.com, *Website:* www.marubeni.co.jp
MC Marine and Bunkering Inc., 8th Floor, Uchisaiwai-cho Dai Building, 3-3 Uchisaiwai-cho 1-chome, Chiyoda-ku, Tokyo 100-0011, Japan, *Tel:* +81 3 5251 2575, *Fax:* +81 3 5251 2583
Mitsui & Co. Petroleum Ltd, 2-1, Ohtemachi 1-chome, Chiyoda-ku, Tokyo 100-0004, Japan, *Tel:* +81 3 3285 6905, *Fax:* +81 3 3285 9811, *Email:* tkzph@dg.mitsui.com, *Website:* www.mitsui.co.jp
Nissho Iwai Corp., 4-4 Akasaka 2-chome, Minato-ku, Tokyo, Japan, *Tel:* +81 3 35882111
Nittetsu Shoij Co. Ltd, 5-7 Kameido 1-chome, Koto-ku, Tokyo 136, Japan, *Tel:* +81 3 5627 2157, *Fax:* +81 3 5627 2192
NKK Trading Inc., 4-4 Nihonbashi Hisamatsusucho, Chuo-ku, Tokyo 103, Japan, *Tel:* +81 3 3660 1522, *Fax:* +81 3 3660 1572
Panoco Trading Co. Ltd, Shin-Sudacho Kyodo Building 2nd Floor, 1-5, Kanda Sudacho, Chiyoda-ku, Tokyo 101-0041, Japan, *Tel:* +81 3 5298 6633, *Fax:* +81 3 3255 2202, *Email:* minori@panoco.co.jp, *Website:* www.panoco.co.jp
Shinagawa Fuel Co. Ltd, New Pier Takeshiba North Tower, 8th Floor, 1-11-1 Kaigan, Minato-ku, Tokyo 105-8525, Japan, *Tel:* +81 3 5470 7113, *Fax:* +81 3 5470 7157, *Email:* hakuyu@ml1.sinanen.co.jp
Showa Yokkaichi Sekiyu K.K., Tokyo Building, 7-3 Marunouchi 2-chome, Chiyoda-ku, Tokyo 100, Japan, *Tel:* +81 3 3215 1643, *Fax:* +81 3 3215 1869
SK Energy Asia Private Ltd, 8th Floor Yamato Seimei Building, 1-17 Uchisaiwicho 1-chome, Chiyoda-ku, Tokyo 100-0011, Japan, *Tel:* +81 3 3591 0533, *Fax:* +81 3 3591 7487, *Email:* leehk@skenergy.com, *Website:* www.skenergy.com
Sumitomo Corp., Harumi Island, Triton Square, Office Tower Y, 8-11 Harumi 1-chome, Chuo-ku, Tokyo 104-8610, Japan, *Tel:* +81 3 51664458, *Fax:* +81 3 51666407, *Email:* ir@sumitomo.co.jp, *Website:* www.sumitomocorp.co.jp
Total France S.A., Total Marine Fuels, 51 Esplanade du General de Gaulle, F-92907 Paris la Defense Cedex 10, France, *Tel:* +33 1 4135 2755, *Fax:* +33 1 4197 0291, *Email:* marine.fuels@total.com, *Website:* www.marinefuels.total.com

Towage: One 1300 hp tug available

Repair & Maintenance: Minor repair facilities available

Medical Facilities: Hospital available

Airport: Narita

Lloyd's Agent: Cornes & Co. Ltd, 273 Yamashita-cho, Naka-ku, Yokohama 231-0023, Kanagawa Pref., Japan, *Tel:* +81 45 201 8537, *Fax:* +81 45 212 3105, *Email:* survey@ykh.cornes.co.jp, *Website:* www.cornes.co.jp

TAHARA

harbour area, see under Toyohashi

Key to Principal Facilities:—			
A=Airport	**C**=Containers	**G**=General Cargo	**P**=Petroleum **R**=Ro/Ro **Y**=Dry Bulk
B=Bunkers	**D**=Dry Dock	**L**=Cruise	**Q**=Other Liquid Bulk **T**=Towage (where available from port)

TAKAMATSU

Lat 34° 21' N; Long 134° 3' E.

Admiralty Chart: 698
Admiralty Pilot: 42B
Time Zone: GMT +9 h
UNCTAD Locode: JP TAK

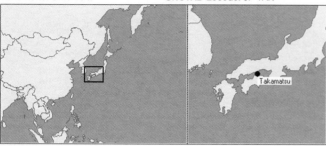

Principal Facilities:

P		Y	G	C			B			A	

Authority: Port & Harbour Section of Kagawa Prefecture, 4-1-10 Bancho, Takamatsu 760-8570, Kagawa Pref., Japan, *Tel:* +81 87 8311 111, *Fax:* +81 87 8374 289, *Email:* kowan@pref.kagawa.lg.jp, *Website:* www.pref.kagawa.jp

Port Security: ISPS compliant

Approach: The approach is via Bisan Seto traffic route. The port is the ferry base of Shikoku Island and the mainland. Max draught in channel is 9 m. Takamatsu Channel, length 860 m, depth 7.0-10.0 m, width 190-240 m. 108 ha of anchorage space, depth 4-9 m. Vessels normally anchor at Wada-Misaki (Kobe), Sakaide or Matsuyama for quarantine

Pilotage: Inland Sea pilotage compulsory for vessels exceeding 10 000 gt. Inland Sea Pilotage Association, Tel: +81 78 391 7191. Harbour pilotage not compulsory; available at the anchorage from 1 h before sunrise to 1 h before sunset

Weather: Typhoon season, July to October

Tides: Tidal range 2.52 m. Current 1-3 knots in E-W direction

Maximum Vessel Dimensions: 35 000 dwt, 9 m d

Principal Imports and Exports: Imports: Container cargo, Logs, Timber. Exports: Container cargo, Steel.

Working Hours: 0800-1700. Overtime possible 1700-2100 subject to negotiation

Accommodation:

Name	Length (m)	Depth (m)	Remarks
Takamatsu			See [1] below
C Region Wharf	415	4.5–5.5	Max 700-2000 gt
Asahicho Wharf	488	5.5	Max 2000 dwt
F Region East Pier (A)	390	7.5	Max 5000 dwt
F Region East Pier (B)	240	5.5	Max 2000 dwt
F Region West Pier	370	10	See [2] below
Chuo Wharf	359	4.5–7.5	Max 5000 dwt
Prefectural No.2 Pier	220	5	Max 2000 gt
C Region Ferry Berth	130	6	Max 3000 gt
Sunport Passenger Ship Wharf	225	10	Max 20 000 gt
Tamamo Region Wharf	300	6–7.5	

[1]*Takamatsu:* There are also four anchorage berths for vessels up to 30 000 dwt, 10-11 m depth, for loading and discharging cargo and 15 private berths for coastal vessels of 500 to 2000 dwt

[2]*F Region West Pier:* Max 10 000 dwt. Container terminal with storage cap of approx 870 TEU's

Mechanical Handling Equipment:

Location	Type	Capacity (t)	Qty
F Region West Pier	Container Cranes	30.5	1
F Region West Pier	Straddle Carriers	30.5	1

Cargo Worked: 2000 t of foreign trade and 9000 t of domestic trade per working day

Bunkering: Hikawa Shoji Kaisha Ltd, 26-2 Shinkawa NS Building 1-chome, Shinkawa, Chuo-ku, Tokyo 104, Japan, *Tel:* +81 3 5776 6858, *Fax:* +81 3 5541 3274
Marubeni Petroleum Co. Ltd, Marubeni International Petroleum Singapore Co. Ltd, c/o Marubeni Corporation, 4-2 Ohtemachi 1-chome, Chiyoda-ku, Tokyo 100-8088, Japan, *Tel:* +81 3 3282 3920, *Fax:* +81 3 3282 3950, *Email:* TOKB554@marubenicorp.com, *Website:* www.marubeni.co.jp
MC Marine and Bunkering Inc., 8th Floor, Uchisaiwai-cho Dai Building, 3-3 Uchisaiwai-cho 1-chome, Chiyoda-ku, Tokyo 100-0011, Japan, *Tel:* +81 3 5251 2575, *Fax:* +81 3 5251 2583
Mitsui & Co. Petroleum Ltd, 2-1, Ohtemachi 1-chome, Chiyoda-ku, Tokyo 100-0004, Japan, *Tel:* +81 3 3285 6905, *Fax:* +81 3 3285 9811, *Email:* tkzph@dg.mitsui.com, *Website:* www.mitsui.co.jp
Nissho Iwai Corp., 4-4 Akasaka 2-chome, Minato-ku, Tokyo, Japan, *Tel:* +81 3 35882111

Towage: No tugs stationed at the port. Available from Sakaide or Mizushima

Repair & Maintenance: Shikoku Dockyard Co. Ltd, 3-23, 1-chome, Asahi-machi, Takamatsu 760-0065, Kagawa Pref., Japan, *Tel:* +81 87 851 9021, *Fax:* +81 87 851 9373, *Email:* yamato@shikokudock.co.jp, *Website:* www.shikokudock.co.jp Engine repairs

Medical Facilities: Available

Airport: Takamatsu, 10 km

Lloyd's Agent: Cornes & Co. Ltd, Meikai Building, 32 Akashi-machi, Chuo-ku, Kobe 650-0037, Hyogo Pref., Japan, *Tel:* +81 78 332 3421, *Fax:* +81 78 332 3070, *Email:* survey@kobe.cornes.co.jp, *Website:* www.cornes.co.jp

TAKUMA

Lat 34° 15' N; Long 133° 42' E.

Admiralty Chart: JP137B
Admiralty Pilot: 42B
Time Zone: GMT +9 h
UNCTAD Locode: JP TKM

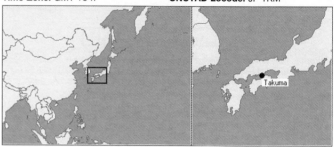

Principal Facilities:

		Y	G	C			B				

Authority: Port & Harbour Section of Kagawa Prefecture, 4-1-10 Bancho, Takamatsu 760-8570, Kagawa Pref., Japan, *Tel:* +81 87 8311 111, *Fax:* +81 87 8374 289, *Email:* kowan@pref.kagawa.lg.jp, *Website:* www.pref.kagawa.jp

Port Security: ISPS compliant

Approach: Draught limitation in the channel is 11 m

Pilotage: Not compulsory but recommended. Pilots are available from Sakaide quarantine anchorage, Kobe, Sekisaki or Hesaki. Harbour pilot is also available at pos 34° 15' 40" N; 133° 36' 06" E. Pilots are not available after sunset

Tides: Range of tide 4.14 m

Maximum Vessel Dimensions: 27 652 dwt, 173.5 m loa

Principal Imports and Exports: Imports: Steel. Exports: Logs, Steel.

Accommodation:

Name	Length (m)	Depth (m)	Draught (m)	Remarks
Takuma				See [1] below
Takuma Public Wharf No.1	90	5.5	5	
Takuma Public Wharf No.2	125	7.5	7	
Takuma Public Wharf No.3	130	7.5		Container terminal with storage cap of approx 320 TEU's

[1]*Takuma:* There are three anchorage berths for the discharge of logs located within 0.5 miles of Mitamaiwa Beacon, Berth A can accommodate vessels up to 11 m d, Berth B up to 10 m d and Berth C up to 8 m d. These berths are exposed to strong N winds. There is a large timber pond near to the public wharves

Mechanical Handling Equipment:

Location	Type	Capacity (t)	Qty
Takuma Public Wharf No.3	Mult-purp. Cranes	30.5	1
Takuma Public Wharf No.3	Forklifts	30.5	1

Bunkering: Can be brought in from Kobe, Mizushima and other ports

Towage: No tugs stationed at the port, but available from Sakaide or Mizushima if required

Repair & Maintenance: Sanuki Shipbuilding & Iron Works Co., 2112-7, Oaza Takuma, Mitoyo City, Takuma 069-1101, Kagawa Pref., Japan, *Tel:* +81 87 583 2550, *Fax:* +81 87 583 6287, *Email:* info@sanukiship.jp, *Website:* www.sanukiship.jp Two dry docks

Lloyd's Agent: Cornes & Co. Ltd, Meikai Building, 32 Akashi-machi, Chuo-ku, Kobe 650-0037, Hyogo Pref., Japan, *Tel:* +81 78 332 3421, *Fax:* +81 78 332 3070, *Email:* survey@kobe.cornes.co.jp, *Website:* www.cornes.co.jp

TAMANO

see under Uno

TANABE

Lat 33° 43' N; Long 135° 21' E.

Admiralty Chart: JP77, JP93
Admiralty Pilot: 42A
Time Zone: GMT +9 h
UNCTAD Locode: JP TAE

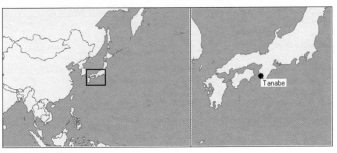

Principal Facilities:

			G		B		A

Authority: Wakayama Prefectural Harbor & Airport Promotion Bureau, 1-1 Komatsu-bara-dori, Wakayama 640-8585, Wakayama Pref., Japan, *Tel:* +81 73 441 3151, *Fax:* +81 73 443 4839, *Email:* e0824001@pref.wakayama.lg.jp, *Website:* www.pref.wakayama.lg.jp

Officials: Manager: Katsushi Nakano.

Approach: Draught limitation in the channel 10.3 m HW. Vessels must beware of rock hazards within the port area

Pilotage: Not compulsory. Pilots are available during daylight hours only if required and board vessel at the anchorage in pos 33° 42' 12" N, 135° 19' 02" E

Weather: Typhoon season, July to October

Tides: Max tidal range 2.34 m

Principal Imports and Exports: Imports: Timber.

Working Hours: 0800-1600. Sundays available subject to negotiation

Accommodation:

Name	Depth (m)	Draught (m)	Remarks
Tanabe			See [1] below
Buoy Berth	10.7	10.3	For vessels of 35 000 dwt, and a lumber pool

[1]Tanabe: Waiting anchorage near Banshono-hana lighthouse in 19 m depth of water with bottom of sand and mud. Small harbour enclosed by two breakwaters with approx 3 m depth for small vessels

Bunkering: Bonded oil brought from Shimotsu or Kobe if required

Towage: Not available. Tugs can be brought from Wakayama if required

Repair & Maintenance: Minor facilities available

Medical Facilities: Available

Airport: Nanki Shirahama, 23 km

Lloyd's Agent: Cornes & Co. Ltd, Meikai Building, 32 Akashi-machi, Chuo-ku, Kobe 650-0037, Hyogo Pref., Japan, *Tel:* +81 78 332 3421, *Fax:* +81 78 332 3070, *Email:* survey@kobe.cornes.co.jp, *Website:* www.cornes.co.jp

TANIYAMA

harbour area, see under Kagoshima

TEMPOKU

harbour area, see under Wakkanai

TOBATA

Lat 33° 55' N; Long 130° 51' E.

Admiralty Chart: JP1263
Time Zone: GMT +9 h

Admiralty Pilot: 42B
UNCTAD Locode: JP TBT

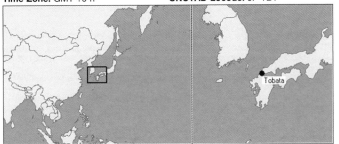

Principal Facilities:

P	Q	Y	G			B		T	A

Authority: Kitakyushu Port & Harbor Bureau, 1-1 Jonai, Kitakyushu 803-8501, Fukuoka Pref., Japan, *Tel:* +81 93 321 5941, *Fax:* +81 93 582 1037, *Email:* kqport@kitaqport.or.jp, *Website:* www.kitaqport.or.jp

Officials: Director General: Kenichi Katayama.

Marketing Director: Hiroyuki Tagami, *Email:* hiroyuki_tagami01@city.kitakyushu.lg.jp.
Sales Director: Tetsuji Hashimoto.

Port Security: ISPS compliant

Approach: Draught limitation in channel is 9.14-10.0 m. The Wakato Ohasi suspension bridge crosses the channel between Tobata and Wakamatsu; air draught is 38 m at HST

Pilotage: Compulsory for vessels over 3000 gt and vessels with hazardous materials over 300 gt. Harbour pilots and Inland Sea pilots are available at the pilot stations or quarantine anchorage. Entry to port is not permissible after sunset; unberthing is possible from certain berths for vessels under 20 000 gt until 2200

Tides: Tidal range 2.84 m

Traffic: 2006, 109 723 953 t of cargo handled, 469 000 TEU's (includes ports of Kokura, Moji, Wakamatsu & Yawata)

Principal Imports and Exports: Imports: Coal, Iron ore. Exports: Chemical products, Steel products.

Working Hours: 24 h/day

Accommodation:

Name	Length (m)	Draught (m)	Remarks
Tobata			See [1] below
Ore/Coal Pier Wharf No.1	200	10.5	Max 13 000 gt
Ore/Coal Pier Wharf No.2	200	11	Max 13 000 gt
Ore/Coal Pier Wharf No.3	250	13	Max 40 000 gt
Ore/Coal Pier Wharf No.4	405	16	Max 90 000 gt
Ore/Coal Pier Wharf No.8	300	11.5	Max 27 000 gt
Ore/Coal Pier Wharf No.9	300	9.5	Max 13 000 gt
Uchiura Wharf No's 4 & 5	428	8.5	Max 8000 gt
Shoko Wharf	165	8.5	Max 7000 gt
Nippon Steel Chemical (RI)		7	
Sakaigawa Public Wharf (RS)	260	7	
LNG Berth	452	12	Max 95 000 gt

[1]Tobata: Nippon Steel Corporation have a steel works on reclaimed land at the eastern boundary of Tobata, where there is a port with a lockless dock. The wharves and facilities have been expanded and the port is capable of handling vessels up to 170 000 gt

Mechanical Handling Equipment: Four 30 t cap cranes at Ore Pier wharves, two 10 t cap at Wharf No's 8 and 9, one 25 t cap and one 10 t cap at Uchiura Wharf No.5

Location	Type	Capacity (t)	Qty
Tobata	Floating Cranes	100	1
Tobata	Floating Cranes	130	1
Tobata	Floating Cranes	120	1
Tobata	Floating Cranes	60	1

Bunkering: Hanwa Co. Ltd, 2nd Floor, Finland House, 56 Haymarket, London SW1Y 4RN, United Kingdom, *Tel:* +44 20 7839 4448, *Fax:* +44 20 7839 3994, *Email:* orito@hanwa.co.uk
Hikawa Shoji Kaisha Ltd, 26-2 Shinkawa NS Building 1-chome, Shinkawa, Chuo-ku, Tokyo 104, Japan, *Tel:* +81 3 5776 6858, *Fax:* +81 3 5541 3274
Idemitsu Kosan Co. Ltd, 1-1 Marunochi, 3-Chome, Chiyoda-ku, Tokyo 100-8321, Japan, *Tel:* +81 3 3213 3138, *Fax:* +81 3 3213 1145, *Email:* tohru.takamura@si.idemitsu.co.jp, *Website:* www.idemitsu.co.jp
KG Int Petroleum Ltd, Shiba Park Building, 241 Shiba Koen, Minato-ku, Tokyo 105, Japan, *Tel:* +81 3 3578 4551, *Fax:* +81 3 3578 4550
Marubeni Petroleum Co. Ltd, Marubeni International Petroleum Singapore Co. Ltd, c/o Marubeni Corporation, 4-2 Ohtemachi 1-chome, Chiyoda-ku, Tokyo 100-8088, Japan, *Tel:* +81 3 3282 3920, *Fax:* +81 3 3282 3950, *Email:* TOKB554@marubenicorp.com, *Website:* www.marubeni.co.jp
MC Marine and Bunkering Inc., 8th Floor, Uchisaiwai-cho Dai Building, 3-3 Uchisaiwai-cho 1-chome, Chiyoda-ku, Tokyo 100-0011, Japan, *Tel:* +81 3 5251 2575, *Fax:* +81 3 5251 2583 – *Grades:* mitsui b
Mitsui & Co. Petroleum Ltd, 2-1, Ohtemachi 1-chome, Chiyoda-ku, Tokyo 100-0004, Japan, *Tel:* +81 3 3285 6905, *Fax:* +81 3 3285 9811, *Email:* tkzph@dg.mitsui.com, *Website:* www.mitsui.co.jp
Nittetsu Shoij Co. Ltd, 5-7 Kameido 1-chome, Koto-ku, Tokyo 136, Japan, *Tel:* +81 3 5627 2157, *Fax:* +81 3 5627 2192

Towage: Six tugs available; two of 3500 hp, three of 3200 hp and one of 2000 hp

Repair & Maintenance: Minor repairs only

Airport: Kitakyushu Airport

Lloyd's Agent: Cornes & Co. Ltd, Meikai Building, 32 Akashi-machi, Chuo-ku, Kobe 650-0037, Hyogo Pref., Japan, *Tel:* +81 78 332 3421, *Fax:* +81 78 332 3070, *Email:* survey@kobe.cornes.co.jp, *Website:* www.cornes.co.jp

TOKACHI

Lat 42° 18' N; Long 143° 20' E.

Admiralty Chart: 1803
Time Zone: GMT +9 h

Admiralty Pilot: 41
UNCTAD Locode: JP TOK

Key to Principal Facilities:—				
A=Airport	**C**=Containers	**G**=General Cargo	**P**=Petroleum	**R**=Ro/Ro	**Y**=Dry Bulk
B=Bunkers	**D**=Dry Dock	**L**=Cruise	**Q**=Other Liquid Bulk	**T**=Towage (where available from port)	

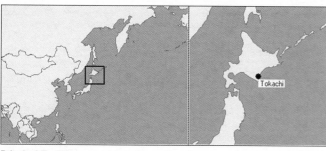

Principal Facilities:

		Y	G						

Authority: Port & Harbour Bureau of Hiroo Town, 7-1-1 Nishi 4 Jo, Hiroo-cho, Hiroo 089-26, Hokkaido, Japan, *Tel:* +81 155 822111, *Fax:* +81 155 824933, *Email:* yakuba@town.hiroo.hokkaido.jp, *Website:* www.town.hiroo.hokkaido.jp

Officials: Director: Kazuhiro Dohshita, *Tel:* +81 155 820180.

Port Security: ISPS compliant

Approach: Draught limitation in the channel is 10 m

Anchorage: Anchorage can be obtained to the E of the South Breakwater in a max depth of 20 m

Pilotage: Not compulsory. Pilots are available at Kushiro quarantine anchorage during daylight hours only

Tides: Range of tide 1.3 m

Maximum Vessel Dimensions: 4360 dwt, 89.3 m loa

Accommodation:

Name	Length (m)	Depth (m)	Remarks
Tokachi			See [1] below
South Pier No.1	90	5.5	Max 2000 dwt
South Pier No.2	90	5.5	Max 2000 dwt
South Pier No.3	90	5.5	Max 2000 dwt
South Pier No.4	130	7.5	Max 5000 dwt
No.2 Pier No.1	130	7.5	Max 5000 dwt
No.2 Pier No.2	130	7.5	Max 5000 dwt

[1] *Tokachi:* Harbour protected by breakwaters. There are berths for fishing vessels and small craft at the S end of the harbour with depths up to 5.5 m

Towage: No tugs stationed at the port, but can be made available with advance notice

Lloyd's Agent: Cornes & Co. Ltd, 273 Yamashita-cho, Naka-ku, Yokohama 231-0023, Kanagawa Pref., Japan, *Tel:* +81 45 201 8537, *Fax:* +81 45 212 3105, *Email:* survey@ykh.cornes.co.jp, *Website:* www.cornes.co.jp

TOKUSHIMA

harbour area, see under Komatsushima

TOKUYAMA

Lat 34° 0' N; Long 131° 48' E.

Admiralty Chart: 3153
Time Zone: GMT +9 h
Admiralty Pilot: 42B
UNCTAD Locode: JP TKY

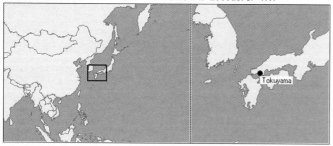

Principal Facilities:

P	Q	Y	G	C	R		B		T	A

Authority: Ports & Harbors Division, Yamaguchi Prefectural Government, 1-1 Takimachi, Yamaguchi 753-8501, Yamaguchi Pref., Japan, *Tel:* +81 83 933 3810, *Fax:* +81 83 933 3829, *Email:* a12900@pref.yamaguchi.lg.jp, *Website:* www.pref.yamaguchi.lg.jp

Officials: Shoichi Hayashi, *Tel:* +81 83 9332 340.

Port Security: ISPS compliant

Approach: Tokuyama West Channel 1700 m long, 200 m wide in depth of 10 m
Idemitsu Channel 1800 m long, 150 m wide in depth of 10.5 m
Kudamatsu East Channel 1800 m long, 600 m wide in depth of 19 m
Tonda Channel 5400 m long, 150 m wide in depth of 9 m
Tokusuo Channel 1000 m long, 80 m wide in depth of 10 m
Nisseki Channel 1500 m long, 350 m wide in depth of 12 m

Anchorage: Ozushima North Anchorage, three designated positions for vessels up to 200 m loa, 11 m draft. Sukumojima Anchorage, two positions for VLCC's and LPG tankers up to 20 m draft

Pilotage: Not compulsory. Pilots are available at the quarantine anchorage when required

Radio Frequency: Tokuyama-Kudamatsu Port Radio Station on VHF channels 11 (156.55 mHz), 12 (156.60 mHz), 16 (156.80 mHz) and 18 (161.50 mHz)

Tides: Average range of tide 1.8 m, max range 3.6 m

Maximum Vessel Dimensions: 80 000 dwt, 11.18 m draft, 241 m loa

Principal Imports and Exports: Imports: Chemicals, Coal, Crude oil, Crude salt, Gravel, Iron, Metals & ores, Oil products, Rock phosphate, Scrap metal, Steel, Wood products. Exports: Cement, Chemicals, Oil products, Steel, Synthetic resin.

Working Hours: 0800-1700

Accommodation: The port consists of two regions; Tokuyama and Shinnanyo

Name	Length (m)	Depth (m)	Remarks
Public Wharves (Tokuyama District)			
Nachi Wharf	40	7.5	1 x 5000 dwt
Minatomachi Wharf	210	6	2 x 3000 dwt
Harumi Wharf No's 1 & 2	260	7.5	2 x 5000 dwt
Harumi Wharf No's 3, 4, 5 & 6	740	10	4 x 15 000 dwt
Harumi Wharf No.7	240	12	See [1] below
Private Wharves (Tokuyama District)			
Tokuyama Crude Salt Pier	118	10	Max 40 000 dwt
Tokuyama Cement Pier	110	6	Max 3000 dwt
Tokuyama Crude Oil Pier	106	6	Max 2000 dwt
Nihon Chemical Pier	30	6.5	Max 3000 dwt. Chemicals
Sun Arrow Pier	19	5.5	Max 2000 dwt
Nihon Zeon Berth No's 1-3	131	4.5	Max 700 dwt. Oil products
Idemitsu West Pier	236	7.5	Max 1000 dwt. Crude oil
Idemitsu Central Pier	250	12	Max 3000 dwt. Crude oil
Idemitsu East Pier	98	8.5	Max 500 dwt. Crude oil
Idemitsu Oura Pier No's 2 & 3	307	11	Max 20 000 dwt. Crude oil
Idemitsu Oura Pier No.5	62	12	Max 30 000 dwt. Oil products
Idemitsu Oura Pier No.7	332	13.2	Max 50 000 dwt. Oil products
Idemitsu Sea Berth	480	20	Max 150 000 dwt. Crude oil
Nihon Seirou Nishigamori Pier	42	12	Max 30 000 dwt. Crude oil
Nihon Seirou Honmon Pier	13	10	Max 15 000 dwt. Heavy oil
Private Wharves (Shinnanyo District)			
Tosoh Cement Pier	68	10.5	Max 20 000 dwt
Tosoh General Cargo Pier No.1	110	9.5	Max 15 000 dwt
Tosoh General Cargo Pier No.2	60	5.5	Max 3000 dwt
Tosoh Salt Pier	140	11.5	Max 35 000 dwt
Tokuyama Cement No.4 Pier	184	11	Max 25 000 dwt
Tokuyama Limestone No.1 Pier	180	8	Max 8000 dwt
Tokuyama Limestone No.2 Pier	156	8	Max 8000 dwt

[1] *Harumi Wharf No.7:* 1 x 30 000 dwt. Container terminal with yard of 5.2 ha. 22 reefer points

Mechanical Handling Equipment:

Location	Type	Capacity (t)	Qty
Harumi Wharf No.7	Container Cranes	50	1
Tosoh Salt Pier	Mult-purp. Cranes	20	1

Bunkering: Hanwa Co. Ltd, 2nd Floor, Finland House, 56 Haymarket, London SW1Y 4RN, United Kingdom, *Tel:* +44 20 7839 4448, *Fax:* +44 20 7839 3994, *Email:* orito@hanwa.co.uk
Idemitsu Kosan Co. Ltd, 1-1 Marunochi, 3-Chome, Chiyoda-ku, Tokyo 100-8321, Japan, *Tel:* +81 3 3213 3138, *Fax:* +81 3 3213 1145, *Email:* tohru.takamura@si.idemitsu.co.jp, *Website:* www.idemitsu.co.jp
KG Int Petroleum Ltd, Shiba Park Building, 241 Shiba Koen, Minato-ku, Tokyo 105, Japan, *Tel:* +81 3 3578 4551, *Fax:* +81 3 3578 4550
Kyodo Oil Co. Ltd, 11-2 Nagata-cho 2-chome, Chiyoda-ku, Tokyo, Japan, *Tel:* +81 3 3505 8241, *Fax:* +81 3 3505 8697
MC Marine and Bunkering Inc., 8th Floor, Uchisaiwai-cho Dai Building, 3-3 Uchisaiwai-cho 1-chome, Chiyoda-ku, Tokyo 100-0011, Japan, *Tel:* +81 3 5251 2575, *Fax:* +81 3 5251 2583
NKK Trading Inc., 4-4 Nihonbashi Hisamatsusucho, Chuo-ku, Tokyo 103, Japan, *Tel:* +81 3 3660 1522, *Fax:* +81 3 3660 1572
Sumitomo Corp., Harumi Island, Triton Square, Office Tower Y, 8-11 Harumi 1-chome, Chuo-ku, Tokyo 104-8610, Japan, *Tel:* +81 3 51664458, *Fax:* +81 3 51666407, *Email:* ir@sumitomo.co.jp, *Website:* www.sumitomocorp.co.jp

Towage: Nine tugs available of 2300-3400 hp

Repair & Maintenance: All repairs possible for vessels up to 40 000 dwt
Noda Marine Engineering Co. Ltd, Tokuyama, Yamaguchi Pref., Japan, *Tel:* +81 83 432 2380
Oshima Unyu Kikoh Co. Ltd, Tokuyama, Yamaguchi Pref., Japan, *Tel:* +81 83 463 1043

Medical Facilities: Available in Tokuyama City

Airport: Yamaguchi-Ube, 70 km

Railway: Tokuyama Station, 1 km

Lloyd's Agent: Cornes & Co. Ltd, Meikai Building, 32 Akashi-machi, Chuo-ku, Kobe 650-0037, Hyogo Pref., Japan, *Tel:* +81 78 332 3421, *Fax:* +81 78 332 3070, *Email:* survey@kobe.cornes.co.jp, *Website:* www.cornes.co.jp

TOKYO

Lat 35° 38' N; Long 139° 47' E.

Admiralty Chart: JP1061/1065   **Admiralty Pilot:** 42A
Time Zone: GMT +9 h   **UNCTAD Locode:** JP TYO

Principal Facilities:

P	Q	Y	G	C	R	L	B	D	T	A

Authority: Bureau of Port & Harbor, Tokyo Metropolitan Government, 8-1 Nishi-Shinjuku 2-chome, Shinjuku-ku, Tokyo 163-8001, Japan, *Tel:* +81 3 5320 5547, *Fax:* +81 3 5388 1576, *Email:* s0000517@section.metro.tokyo.jp, *Website:* www.kouwan.metro.tokyo.jp

Port Security: ISPS compliant. Container Security Initiative (CSI) designated port

Approach: Tokyo Light Beacon in pos 35° 34' N; 139° 50' E, marks the entrance to the ship channel. Draught limitation in the channel is 12.0 m

Anchorage: Ample sheltered anchorage available

Pilotage: Compulsory for vessels over 10 000 gt. Pilots available at anchorage. Tokyo Pilot Association, Tel: +81 3 3453 1691

Weather: Winds N in winter and spring, S in summer and autumn. Dense fog for about 15 days a year

Tides: Tidal range 2.17 m

Traffic: 2007, 3 720 682 TEU's handled

Accommodation:

Name	Length (m)	Depth (m)	Remarks
Tokyo			
Oi Container Terminal			See [1] below
Berth No.1	330	15	Terminal area of 127 700 m2
Berth No.2	330	15	Terminal area of 131 800 m2
Berth No.3	354	15	Terminal area of 143 500 m2
Berth No.4	330	15	Terminal area of 133 700 m2
Berth No.5	330	15	Terminal area of 133 700 m2
Berth No.6	330	15	Terminal area of 133 700 m2
Berth No.7	350	15	Terminal area of 141 800 m2
Oi Marine Products Terminal			See [2] below
Berth OJ-OK	450	12	Max 30 000 dwt
Oi Foodstuffs Terminal			See [3] below
Berth OL	229.5	12	Max 30 000 dwt
Berth OM	190	11	Max 15 000 dwt
Berth ON	190	11	Max 15 000 dwt
Aomi Container Terminal			See [4] below
Berth A0	260	12	See [5] below
Berth A1	260	12	See [6] below
Berth A2	350	14	See [7] below
Berth A3	350	14	Total area of 116 623 m2. 270 reefer points
Berth A4	350	15	Total area of 122 500 m2. 540 reefer points
Odaiba Liner Terminal	1800	10	See [8] below
Shinagawa Container Terminal	555	10	See [9] below
Shinagawa Foreign Terminal	570	10	Three berths (SF, SG and SH) for vessels up to 15 000 dwt handling mainly sugar
Shinagawa Domestic Terminal	475	8	See [10] below
Takeshiba Terminal	465	7.5	See [11] below
Hinode Terminal	564	6.7	See [12] below
Shibaura Terminal	870	5.5–7.5	See [13] below
Harumi Terminal (HB)		10	Max 20 000 dwt
Harumi Terminal (HC)	132	10	Max 10 000 dwt
Harumi Terminal (HD)	132	10	Max 15 000 dwt
Harumi Terminal (HE-HI)	798	9	Max 10 000 dwt
Harumi Terminal (HJ)	190	10	Max 15 000 dwt
Harumi Terminal (HK-HL)	456	10	Passenger vessels
10 Gohchi West (VA-VK)	1500	7.5	Max 5000 dwt
10 Gohchi East (VL-VX)	920	5	Max 1000 dwt
13 Gohchi No.1 (RA-RJ)	750	5	Max 1000 dwt
13 Gohchi No.2 (AA-AI)	1800	10	Max 15 000 dwt. Liner terminal
No.15 Lumber Terminal	720	12	Max 25 000 dwt. Lumber terminal

[1]*Oi Container Terminal:* For vessels up to 50 000 dwt. Five container cranes at berths 1-2, six container cranes at berths 3-4, two container cranes at berth 5 and six container cranes at berths 6-7

[2]*Oi Marine Products Terminal:* Used mainly for handling frozen fishery products. Cold storage for 353 000 t of cargo

[3]*Oi Foodstuffs Terminal:* Cargoes handled include imports of grains, fresh fruit & vegetables and fishery products

[4]*Aomi Container Terminal:* For vessels of 35 000-50 000 dwt. Berths A0, A1 and A2 are public berths whilst Berths A3 and A4 are exclusive-use berths operated by Tokyo Port Terminal Public Corporation. Two container cranes of 30.5 t cap at berth A0, two container cranes of 30.5 t cap at berth A1, two container cranes of 40.6 t cap at berth A2, two container cranes of 40.6 t cap at berth A3 and three container cranes of 40.6 t cap at berth A4

There is also the Aomi Distribution Center with total area of 60 365 m2

[5]*Berth A0:* Total area of 66 946 m2 with container storage yard of 31 162 m2. 142 reefer points

[6]*Berth A1:* Total area of 100 754 m2 with container storage yard of 77 850 m2. 248 reefer points

[7]*Berth A2:* Total area of 72 254 m2 with container storage yard of 13 475 m2. 78 reefer points

[8]*Odaiba Liner Terminal:* Situated at Aomi Terminal and consists of nine berths (AA-AI) for vessels up to 15 000 dwt handling steel, lumber, paper, pulp and other cargo. Transit shed at each berth

[9]*Shinagawa Container Terminal:* Three berths (SC, SD and SE) for vessels up to 15 000 dwt. Four container cranes of 30.5 t cap. 272 reefer points. Container storage yard of 100 370 m2

[10]*Shinagawa Domestic Terminal:* Three berths (SI, SJ and SK) for vessels up to 6000 dwt handling paper, pulp, automobiles & other miscellaneous cargo

[11]*Takeshiba Terminal:* Three berths for vessels up to 5000 dwt handling passenger vessels, agricultural & general cargo

[12]*Hinode Terminal:* Six berths handling non ferrous, chemical compounds, chemical products & foodstuffs. For vessels up to 3000 dwt

[13]*Shibaura Terminal:* Seven berths handling cement, paper & foodstuffs. For vessels of 2000-5000 dwt

Storage: 45 transit sheds of 233 265 m2 and 79 open storage yards of 717 114 m2

Bunkering: Oil by barge at max rate of 300 kl/h and by pipeline
BHP Transport Proprietary Ltd, 19th Floor, Hibiyadai Building, 1-2-2 Uchisaiwai-cho, Chiyoda-ku, Tokyo 100, Japan, *Tel:* +81 3 52511300
BP Japan Trading Ltd, 14th Floor, Nakanosakaue Sunbright Twin Building, 46-1 Honcho 2-chome, Tokyo 164-0012, Japan, *Tel:* +81 3 5371 1293, *Fax:* +81 3 5371 1091
Cosmo Oil Co. Ltd, Toshiba Building, 1-1 Shibaura 1-chome, Minato-ku, Tokyo 105-8528, Japan, *Tel:* +81 3 3798 3156, *Fax:* +81 3 3798 3592, *Email:* masayuki_iijima@cosmo-oil.co.jp, *Website:* www.cosmo-oil.co.jp
Daitoh Trading Co. Ltd, Daitoh Building, 7-1, Kasumigaseki 3-chome, Chiyoda-ku, Tokyo 100-0013, Japan, *Tel:* +81 3 5512 2831, *Fax:* +81 3 5512 2832, *Email:* bunker@daitohnet.co.jp, *Website:* www.daitohnet.co.jp
Fuji Kosan Co. Ltd, 2-19-6 Yanagibashi, Taito-ku, Tokyo 111-0052, Japan, *Tel:* +81 3 3861 4601, *Fax:* +81 3 3861 4611, *Email:* info@fkoil.co.jp, *Website:* www.fkoil.co.jp
Hanwa Co. Ltd, New Hanwa Building, 13-10 Tsukiji 1-chome, Chuo-ku, Tokyo 104-8429, Japan, *Tel:* +81 3 3544 2272, *Fax:* +81 3 3544 2056, *Email:* fuel2@hanwa.co.jp, *Website:* www.hanwa.co.jp
Hikawa Shoji Kaisha Ltd, 26-2 Shinkawa NS Building 1-chome, Shinkawa, Chuo-ku, Tokyo 104, Japan, *Tel:* +81 3 5776 6858, *Fax:* +81 3 5541 3274
Idemitsu Kosan Co. Ltd, 1-1 Marunochi, 3-Chome, Chiyoda-ku, Tokyo 100-8321, Japan, *Tel:* +81 3 3213 3138, *Fax:* +81 3 3213 1145, *Email:* tohru.takamura@si.idemitsu.co.jp, *Website:* www.idemitsu.co.jp
KG Int Petroleum Ltd, Shiba Park Building, 241 Shiba Koen, Minato-ku, Tokyo 105, Japan, *Tel:* +81 3 3578 4551, *Fax:* +81 3 3578 4550
Japan Energy Corp., 2-10-1, Toranomon, Minato-ku, Tokyo 105-8407, Japan, *Tel:* +81 3 5573 6100, *Fax:* +81 3 5573 6674, *Email:* yamano@j-energy.co.jp, *Website:* www.j-energy.co.jp
Kamei Corp., 1-6-1 Otemachi, Chiyoda-ku, Tokyo 100-0004, Japan, *Tel:* +81 3 3286 6234, *Fax:* +81 3 3286 6249, *Email:* bunker@kamei.co.jp
Kyodo Oil Co. Ltd, 11-2 Nagata-cho 2-chome, Chiyoda-ku, Tokyo, Japan, *Tel:* +81 3 3505 8241, *Fax:* +81 3 3505 8697
Kyushu Oil Co. Ltd, 1-1 Uchisaiwai-cho 2-chome, Chiyoda-ku, Tokyo, Japan, *Tel:* +81 3 3502 3651, *Fax:* +81 3 3502 9850
Marubeni Corp., 3rd Floor, Marubeni Tokyo Honnsha Building, 4-2 Ohtemachi 1-chome, Chiyoda-ku, P O Box 595, Tokyo 100-8088, Japan, *Tel:* +81 3 3282 2111, *Fax:* +81 3 3282 4241, *Email:* TOKB554@marubenicorp.com, *Website:* www.marubeni.com
Marubeni Petroleum Co. Ltd, Marubeni International Petroleum Singapore Co. Ltd, c/o Marubeni Corporation, 4-2 Ohtemachi 1-chome, Chiyoda-ku, Tokyo 100-8088, Japan, *Tel:* +81 3 3282 3920, *Fax:* +81 3 3282 3950, *Email:* TOKB554@marubenicorp.com, *Website:* www.marubeni.co.jp
MC Marine and Bunkering Inc., 8th Floor, Uchisaiwai-cho Dai Building, 3-3 Uchi-saiwai-cho 1-chome, Chiyoda-ku, Tokyo 100-0011, Japan, *Tel:* +81 3 5251 2575, *Fax:* +81 3 5251 2583
Meikoh Corp., 105 Dai-ich Mita Building, 2-15-3 Katamachi Fuchu-shi, Tokyo 183, Japan, *Tel:* +81 4 2360 6260, *Fax:* +81 4 2362 9008, *Email:* info@mei-koh.co.jp
Mitsui & Co. Petroleum Ltd, 2-1, Ohtemachi 1-chome, Chiyoda-ku, Tokyo 100-0004, Japan, *Tel:* +81 3 3285 6905, *Fax:* +81 3 3285 9811, *Email:* tkzph@dg.mitsui.com, *Website:* www.mitsui.co.jp
Mitsui Mining Co. Ltd, 3-3-3, Toyosu chome, Koto-Ku, Tokyo 135-6007, Japan, *Tel:* +81 3 5560 1258, *Fax:* +81 3 5560 2910, *Email:* seiichirou-ii@mitsui-mining.co.jp, *Website:* www.mitsui-mining.co.jp
Nippon Mitsubishi Oil Corp., 3-12 Nishi Shinbashi 1-chome, Minato-ku, Tokyo 105-8412, Japan, *Tel:* +81 3 3502 1135, *Fax:* +81 3 3502 9352, *Email:* shuji.arai@eneos.co.jp, *Website:* www.eneos.co.jp
Nippon Steel Trading Co. Ltd, 2-1 Shin-Otemachi Building, Otemachi 2-chome, Chiyoda-ku, Tokyo 100-0004, Japan, *Tel:* +81 3 6225 3500, *Fax:* +81 3 6225 3930, *Email:* yuichiro_sekine@ns-net.co.jp, *Website:* www.ns-net.co.jp
Nissho Iwai Corp., 4-4 Akasaka 2-chome, Minato-ku, Tokyo, Japan, *Tel:* +81 3 35882111
Nittetsu Shoji Co. Ltd, 5-7 Kameido 1-chome, Koto-ku, Tokyo 136, Japan, *Tel:* +81 3 5627 2157, *Fax:* +81 3 5627 2192
Panoco Trading Co. Ltd, Shin-Sudacho Kyodo Building 2nd Floor, 1-5, Kanda

---

Key to Principal Facilities:—

A=Airport	**C**=Containers	**G**=General Cargo
B=Bunkers	**D**=Dry Dock	**L**=Cruise

P=Petroleum	**R**=Ro/Ro
Q=Other Liquid Bulk	**T**=Towage (where available from port)

Y=Dry Bulk

Sudacho, Chiyoda-ku, Tokyo 101-0041, Japan, *Tel:* +81 3 5298 6633, *Fax:* +81 3 3255 2202, *Email:* minori@panoco.co.jp, *Website:* www.panoco.co.jp

Petro-Diamond Japan Corp. (PDJ), Mitsubishi Corp Building, 3-1, Marunouchi 2-chome, Chiyoda-ku, Tokyo 100-8086, Japan, *Tel:* +81 3 3210 2164, *Fax:* +81 3 3210 5928, *Email:* ml.pdj-bunker@mitsubishicorp.com

Saudi Shipping & Maritime Services Co. Ltd (TRANSHIP), Tokyo Arabian Consultants, 1-4, Uchisaiwai-cho 2-chome, Chiyoda-ku, Tokyo, Japan, *Tel:* +81 3 35012510

Shinagawa Fuel Co. Ltd, New Pier Takeshiba North Tower, 8th Floor, 1-11-1 Kaigan, Minato-ku, Tokyo 105-8525, Japan, *Tel:* +81 3 5470 7113, *Fax:* +81 3 5470 7157, *Email:* hakuyu@ml1.sinanen.co.jp

Showa Shell Sekiyu K.K., Daiba Frontier Building, 3-2 Daiba 2-chome, Minato-ku, Tokyo 135-8074, Japan, *Tel:* +81 3 5531 5591, *Fax:* +81 3 5531 5598, *Email:* yorimasa.matsudaira@showa-shell.co.jp, *Website:* www.showa-shell.co.jp

Showa Yokkaichi Sekiyu K.K., Tokyo Building, 7-3 Marunouchi 2-chome, Chiyoda-ku, Tokyo 100, Japan, *Tel:* +81 3 3215 1643, *Fax:* +81 3 3215 1869

SK Energy Asia Private Ltd, 8th Floor Yamato Seimei Building, 1-17 Uchisaiwicho 1-chome, Chiyoda-ku, Tokyo 100-0011, Japan, *Tel:* +81 3 3591 0533, *Fax:* +81 3 3591 7487, *Email:* leehk@skenergy.com, *Website:* www.skenergy.com

Teikoku Oil Co. Ltd, 31-10 Hatagaya 1-chome, Shibuya-ku, Tokyo 151 8565, Japan, *Tel:* +81 3 3466 1234/7, *Fax:* +81 3 3468 3509/10, *Email:* intlproj@teikokuoil.co.jp, *Website:* www.teikokuoil.co.jp

Toa Oil Co. Ltd, 3-1 Mizue-cho, Kawasaki-ku, Kawasaki, Kanagawa, Tokyo 210-0866, Japan, *Tel:* +81 44 2800 600, *Fax:* +81 44 2661 005, *Email:* yutaka.yamamoto@toaoil.co.jp, *Website:* www.toaoil.co.jp

Total France S.A., Total Trading International S.A, Akasaka Shasta-East 2nd Floor, 2-19 Akasaka 4-chome, Minato-ku, Tokyo 107-0052, Japan, *Tel:* +81 3 5562 5211, *Fax:* +81 3 5562 5498, *Email:* yasuko.ito@total.com, *Website:* www.total.com

World Fuel Services, 4th Floor, 4-2 Tozan Building 4-chome, Nihonbashi Hon-cho, Chuo-ku, Tokyo 103-0023, Japan, *Tel:* +81 3 3245 0379, *Fax:* +81 3 3245 0389, *Email:* jpbrokers@wfscorp.com, *Website:* www.wfscorp.com

Kanematsu K.K., Bunker Oil Section, 2-1 Shibaura 1-chome, Minato-ku, Tokyo 105-8005, Japan, *Tel:* +81 3 5440 9273, *Fax:* +81 3 5440 6540, *Email:* trc5@kanematsu.co.jp, *Website:* www.kanematsu.co.jp

Sumitomo Corp., 1-8-11 Harumi, Chiyoda-ku, Tokyo 104-8610, Japan, *Tel:* +81 3 5166 4457, *Fax:* +81 3 5166 6411, *Email:* hiroki.tsunematsu@sumitomocorp.co.jp, *Website:* www.sumitomocorp.co.jp

Towage: Ten tugs between 2200 and 3200 hp and four between 1000 and 1400 hp

Repair & Maintenance: IHI Corp. (Tokyo), New Ohtemachi Building, 21-2 Ohtemachi 2 -chome, Chiyoda-ku, Tokyo 100, Japan, *Tel:* +81 3 3244 5111, *Fax:* +81 3 3244 5131 Two dry docks. No.1 130 m x 18.3 m x 5.5 m for vessels up to 11 000 dwt, No.2 180 m x 23 m x 5.5 m for vessels up to 22 000 dwt

Ship Chandlers: Globe Engineering Works Proprietary Ltd, Fuji Trading Co Ltd (Marine Division), 3-3-5 Kitashinagawa, Shinagawa-ku, Tokyo 140-0001, Japan, *Tel:* +81 3 5783 7390, *Fax:* +81 3 3450 7100, *Email:* tokyo@fujitrading.co.jp, *Website:* www.fujitrading.co.jp

Makoto Sengu Co. Ltd, 10-12 Senda, Koto-ku, Tokyo 135-0013, Japan, *Tel:* +81 3 3699 0211, *Fax:* +81 3 3699 0218, *Email:* mktsengu@mint.ocn.ne.jp

Shipping Agents: Aall Barwil Pte Ltd, 7th Floor, JPR Crest Takebashi Building, 21 Kanda Nishiki-cho 3-chome, Chiyoda-ku, Tokyo 101-0054, Japan, *Tel:* +81 3 5217 0171, *Fax:* +81 3 5217 0173, *Email:* wss.tokyo.shipsagency@wilhelmsen.com, *Website:* www.wilhelmsen.com

Arya International Ltd, Room 409, 4th Floor, Iwata Building 5-10-18, Higashi Gotanda, Shinagawa-ku, Tokyo 141, Japan, *Tel:* +81 3 3449 2501, *Fax:* +81 3 3449 2509

Ben Line Agencies Ltd, 4th Floor, Shinagawa TS Building, 13-40 Konan 2-chome, Minato-ku, Tokyo 108-0075, Japan, *Tel:* +81 3 6718 0728, *Fax:* +81 3 6718 0717, *Email:* general@benline.co.jp, *Website:* www.benlineagencies.com

Coli Shipping & Transport, 6th Floor, Ginza Masskey, 1-24-3 Ginza, Chuo-ku, Tokyo 104-0061, Japan, *Tel:* +81 3 5524 2671, *Fax:* +81 3 5524 2674, *Email:* cpc@cpc-asia.co.jp

Cosmos Maritime Co. Ltd, 4th Floor, Nihonseimei Shinbashi Building, 18-16 Shinbashi-cho 1-chome, Minato-ku, Tokyo 105-0004, Japan, *Tel:* +81 3 3500 5051, *Fax:* +81 3 3500 5095, *Email:* m_nihei@c-maritime.co.jp, *Website:* www.c-maritime.co.jp

Delmas Japan Co. Ltd, 7th Floor, Friend Building, 2-4 Nagata-cho 11-chome, Chiyoda-ku, Tokyo 100-0014, Japan, *Tel:* +81 3 3581 7414/7, *Fax:* +81 3 3581 7418, *Email:* y.fuyuki@delmas-jpn.co.jp

Dongjin Agency Co. Ltd, 4th Floor, Asano Building, 3-11 1-chome, Nihonbashi, Chuo-ku, Tokyo, Japan, *Tel:* +81 3 3548 2928, *Fax:* +81 3 3548 2918, *Email:* shigeru_kihara@dongjinagency.jp, *Website:* www.dongjinagency.jp

A Hartrodt International, Akiyama Building 8th Floor, 1-22-13 Toranomon, Minato-ku, Tokyo 105-0001, Japan, *Tel:* +81 3 3596 8150, *Fax:* +81 3 3596 8160, *Email:* hartrodt@hartrodt.co.jp, *Website:* www.hartrodt.co.jp

Heisei Shipping Agency Co. Ltd, 6th Floor Shiba Nishii Building, Shiba 4-chome, Minato-ku, Tokyo 108-0014, Japan, *Tel:* +81 3 5476 5710, *Fax:* +81 3 5476 5711, *Email:* ops@hship.co.jp

Hesco Agencies Ltd, 5th Floor, Shibaura 2-chome Building, 7-5, Shibaura, 2-chome, Minato-ku, Tokyo 108-0023, Japan, *Tel:* +81 3 5439 0757, *Fax:* +81 3 5445 0748, *Email:* robertg@hescoagencies.com

Inchcape Shipping Services (ISS), Inchcape Shipping Services (Japan) Ltd, 7th Floor, Suzuyo Hamamatsucho Building, 1-16, Kaigan 2-chome, Minato-ku, Tokyo 105-0022, Japan, *Tel:* +81 3 5442 6801, *Fax:* +81 3 5442 6912, *Email:* isstokyoops@iss-shipping.com, *Website:* www.iss-shipping.com

Interocean Shipping Corp., Tradepia Odaiba, 10th Floor, 3-1 Daiba 2-chome, Minato-ku, Tokyo 135-0091, Japan, *Tel:* +81 3 3570 5393, *Fax:* +81 3 3570 5345, *Email:* furuno@interocean.co.jp, *Website:* www.interocean.co.jp

J-Ship Ltd, 10th Floor, Tamuracho Building, 3-14 Shimbashi 3-Chome, Minato-ku, Tokyo 105-0004, Japan, *Tel:* +81 3 3595 1434, *Fax:* +81 3 3595 1361, *Email:* imofc@nifty.com

Kamigumi Co. Ltd, 7-11 Shibaura, Minato-ku, Tokyo 108-0023, Japan, *Tel:* +81 3 5440 0818, *Fax:* +81 3 5440 0820

Kyowa Shipping Co Ltd, 4th Floor Resona Shimbashi Building, Tokyo 1050 004, Japan, *Tel:* +81 3 5510 1991, *Fax:* +81 3 5510 2002, *Email:* market@kyowa-line.co.jp, *Website:* www.kyowa-line.co.jp

Mediterranean Shipping Company, MSC Japan K.K., Sanno Grand Building, Room 406, 14-1 Nagatacho, 2-chome, Chiyoda-ku, Tokyo 100-0014, Japan, *Tel:* +81 3 5501 7051, *Fax:* +81 3 5501 7061, *Email:* info@medship.co.jp, *Website:* www.mscgva.ch

A.P. Moller-Maersk Group, Maersk K.K., Hanzomon First Building, 1-4 Kojimachi, Chiyoda-ku, Tokyo 102-0083, Japan, *Tel:* +81 3 5213 2098, *Fax:* +81 3 5213 2131, *Website:* www.maerskline.com

Navix Namsung Ltd, 3rd Floor, Hokkoku Muromachi Building, 2-5-13 Nihonbashi Muromachi, Chuo-ku, Tokyo 103-0022, Japan, *Tel:* +81 3 5255 5672, *Fax:* +81 3 5255 5680, *Email:* sales@namsung.co.jp, *Website:* www.namsung.co.jp

Nippon Umpansha Ltd, Kanda Chuo Building, 2nd Floor, 2-chome Kanda Tsukasa Oho, Chiyoda-ku, Tokyo, Japan, *Tel:* +81 3 3292 5921, *Fax:* +81 3 3295 5926, *Email:* nipsal-n@mx7.mesh.ne.jp, *Website:* www.nippon-umpansha.co.jp/eigo.htm

Nissin Corp., Shipping Agency Department, 5 Sanban-cho, Chiyoda-ku, Tokyo 102-8350, Japan, *Tel:* +81 3 3238 6377, *Fax:* +81 3 3238 6378, *Email:* sagency@nissin-tw.co.jp, *Website:* www.nissin-tw.co.jp

NYK Ship Management Co. Ltd, 8th Floor Celestine Shiba Mitsui Building, 3-23-1 SHiba, Tokyo, Japan, *Tel:* +81 3 6420 5755, *Fax:* +81 3 6420 5668, *Website:* www.nykline.com

Sankyu Inc., Sankyu Building, 5-23 Kachidoki 6-chome, Chuo-ku, Tokyo 104-0054, Japan, *Tel:* +81 3 3536 3964, *Fax:* +81 3 3536 3875, *Email:* sankyu@sankyu.co.jp, *Website:* www.sankyu.co.jp

Senwa Maritime Agency Ltd, Sumitomo Fudosan Kayabacho Building .No.2, 26-3 Shinkawa, 2-Chome, Chuo-ku, Tokyo 104-0033, Japan, *Tel:* +81 3 5541 6535, *Fax:* +81 3 3206 0501, *Email:* marine-tky@senwa.co.jp, *Website:* www.senwa.co.jp

Seven Seas Shipping Co. Ltd, Ohgaku Building 2-19, Kanda Sakuma-cho, Chiyoda-ku, Tokyo 101, Japan, *Tel:* +81 3 3864 0222, *Fax:* +81 3 3864 0285, *Email:* ssstyo@sevenseas.co.jp, *Website:* www.sevenseas.co.jp

Seven Star Co. Ltd, Shinkawa East Building, 4th Floor, 26-2 Shinkawa, 1-chome-Chuo-ku, Tokyo 104-0033, Japan, *Tel:* +81 3 3552 5271/7661, *Fax:* +81 3 3552 8288, *Email:* gmktyo@mb.infoweb.ne.jp

C.F. Sharp Shipping Agencies Inc., 206 18-25 Kami Osaki, Shinagawa-ku, Tokyo 141-0021, Japan, *Tel:* +81 3 3779 2462, *Fax:* +81 3 3779 2463, *Email:* onoharuo85@yahoo.co.jp, *Website:* www.cfsharp.com

Sinotrans Group, 3rd Floor, New Nishil Shinbashi Building, 2-11-6 Nishi Shinbashi, Minato-ku, Tokyo 105-0003, Japan, *Tel:* +81 3 3595 6323, *Fax:* +81 3 3595 6320, *Email:* gaohonggang@sinotrans.co.jp

Summit Shipping Agencies Ltd, Sumitomo Seimei Akasaka Building, Twin View Ochanomizu Building 3rd Floor, 3-9, 2-chome, Hongo, Bunkyo-ku, Tokyo 113-0033, Japan, *Tel:* +81 3 5802 8551, *Fax:* +81 3 5802 8566, *Email:* gentokyo@summitship.co.jp, *Website:* www.summitship.co.jp

Tokyo Maritime Agency Ltd, 6th Floor, Shibakoen Denki Building, 1-12 Shibakoem-1-chome Minato-ku, Tokyo 105, Japan, *Tel:* +81 3 5470 1647, *Fax:* +81 3 5470 1663, *Email:* kline@tokyomaritime.co.jp, *Website:* www.tokyomaritime.co.jp

Tokyo Senpaku Kaisha Ltd (TSK), Yusen Building, 3-2 Marunouchi 2-chome, Chiyoda-ku, Tokyo 100-0005, Japan, *Tel:* +81 3 6212 4720, *Fax:* +81 3 6212 4798, *Email:* operations@tskline.co.jp, *Website:* www.tskline.co.jp

Wallem Shipping Agencies Limited, Wallem Shipping Ltd, Suzuyo Hamamatsucho Building, 1-16 Kaigan 2-chome, Minato-ku, Tokyo 105-0022, Japan, *Tel:* +81 3 5442 6908, *Fax:* +81 3 5442 6915, *Email:* wsj@wallem.com, *Website:* www.wallem.com/japan

Surveyors: Aalmar Surveys Ltd, Room 331, Iino Building, 1-1 Uchisaiwaicho, 2 chome, Chiyoda-ku, Tokyo 100, Japan, *Tel:* +81 3 5506 3097, *Fax:* +81 3 5511 7059, *Website:* www.aalmar.com

Korean Register of Shipping, 5th Floor Sato Building, 6-10 Nihonbashi Honcho 4-chome, Chuo-Ku, Tokyo 103, Japan, *Tel:* +81 3 3246 1971, *Fax:* +81 3 3246 1973, *Email:* kr-tky@krs.co.kr, *Website:* www.krs.co.kr

Nippon Kaiji Kyokai, 1-28-2 Hamamatsu-cho, Minato-ku, Tokyo 105-0013, Japan, *Tel:* +81 3 3434 2341, *Fax:* +81 3 3438 2630, *Email:* tk@classnk.or.jp, *Website:* www.classnk.or.jp

Airport: Narita, 60 km

Lloyd's Agent: Cornes & Co. Ltd, 273 Yamashita-cho, Naka-ku, Yokohama 231-0023, Kanagawa Pref., Japan, *Tel:* +81 45 201 8537, *Fax:* +81 45 212 3105, *Email:* survey@ykh.cornes.co.jp, *Website:* www.cornes.co.jp

TOMAKOMAI

Lat 42° 38' N; Long 141° 38' E.

Admiralty Chart: 1813	**Admiralty Pilot:** 41
Time Zone: GMT +9 h	**UNCTAD Locode:** JP TMK

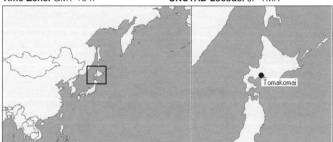

Principal Facilities:

P	Q	Y	G	C	R		B		T	A

Authority: Tomakomai Port Authority, 1-6-38 Minato-machi, Tomakomai 053-0004, Hokkaido, Japan, *Tel:* +81 144 345551, *Fax:* +81 144 345559, *Email:* jptmk@jptmk.com, *Website:* www.jptmk.com

Officials: President: Hirofumi Iwakura.

Port Security: ISPS compliant

Documentation: Crew list (3 copies), passenger list (3 copies), tobacco/spirits/personal effects list (1 copy), arms & ammunition list (1 copy), health documents or certificates (1 copy), certificate of deratting (1 copy), load line certificate (1 copy), tonnage certificate (1 copy), certificate of nationality (1 copy), safety equipment certificate (1 copy), cargo gear certificate (1 copy), bill of lading (1 copy), manifests unfreighted (1 copy), ports of call on current voyage (1 copy), narcotics list (1 copy)

Approach: A mile long entrance channel in depth of 14 m protected by breakwaters leads into the harbour basin. The sea berth is approached directly from the harbour basin
Eastern District: A buoyed and lighted channel dredged to 17.5 m at the entrance and 16 m at and in the turning area leads to: a dolphin berth on the N side of the breakwater, designed to accommodate tankers up to 130 000 dwt with a draft of 14.5 m

Anchorage: The prohibited areas are only inside of the Western District of the port and fairway that connects inner and outer of the Western District of the port

Pilotage: Recommended for vessels under 6000 gt, ensured as far as possible that vessels over 6000 gt and up to 10 000 gt have a pilot on board (except ferries, domestic trade vessels etc) and compulsory for vessels over 10 000 gt. Tel: +81 144 343070, Fax: +81 144 346120. VHF Channel 16 (hailing only). Pilotage available 0400-2400

Radio Frequency: VHF Channel 16

Tides: Max range 1.78 m, min range 0.25 m

Traffic: 2006, 108 622 000 t of cargo handled

Maximum Vessel Dimensions: Dry Cargo: 240 m loa, 38 m beam, 12.62 m draft. Tankers: 344.4 m loa, 60 m beam, 20.93 m draft

Principal Imports and Exports: Imports: Coal, Crude oil, Logs, Lumber, Petroleum products. Exports: Chemicals, Paper & pulp, Petroleum products, Rubber products, Transportation machinery.

Working Hours: Basically 0800-1600 but flexible as required from shipper

Accommodation: Honko Area, Makomai Area, Yufutsu Area, Shiomi Area and Outer Harbour Area are in the Western Port District. Benten Area and HamaAtsuma Area are in the Eastern Port District

Name	Length (m)	Depth (m)	Remarks
Western Port District (Public Wharves)			
South Wharf No's 1-2 (Honkoh Area)	370	10	Max 15 000 dwt. Iron & steel
South Wharf No.3 (Honkoh Area)	195	11	Max 20 000 dwt. Lumber
West Wharf No's 1-3 (Honkoh Area)	495	9	Max 10 000 dwt. Transportation machinery
West Wharf No.4 (Honkoh Area)	165	9	Max 10 000 dwt. Miscellaneous
North Wharf No.1 (Honkoh Area)	130	7.5	Max 5000 dwt. Transportation machinery
North Wharf No.2 (Honkoh Area)	130	7.5	Max 5000 dwt. Iron & steel
North Wharf No's 3-4 (Honkoh Area)	180	5.5	Max 2000 dwt. Iron & steel
East Wharf No.3 (Honkoh Area)	31	9	Max 10 000 dwt. Paper pulp
East Wharf No.4 (Honkoh Area)	165	9	Max 10 000 dwt. Limestone
East Wharf No's 5-6 (Honkoh Area)	260	9	Max 10 000 dwt. Cement
Irifune Wharf	330	14	Max 40 000 dwt. Containers
Harumi Wharf No.1 (Makomai Area)	240	12	Max 30 000 dwt. Coal
Harumi Wharf No.2 (Makomai Area)	240	12	Max 30 000 dwt. Logs
Harumi Wharf No.3 (Makomai Area)	170	10	Max 10 000 dwt. Transportation machinery
Central North Wharf No.1 (Makomai Area)	186	10	Max 15 000 dwt. Logs
Central North Wharf No's 2-4 (Makomai Area)	329	7.5	Max 5000 dwt. Iron & steel
Central North Wharf No.1 East (Makomai Area)	240	12	Max 30 000 dwt. Logs
Central South Wharf No.1 (Makomai Area)	240	12	Max 30 000 dwt. Animal & vegetable foodstuffs and manure
Central South Wharf No.2 (Makomai Area)	240	12	Max 30 000 dwt. Rice, minor cereals & beans
Central South Wharf No.3 (Makomai Area)	130	7.5	Max 5000 dwt. Chemical products
Central South Wharf West (Makomai Area)	165	9	Max 10 000 dwt. Cement
Timber Port District Dolphin No.2 (Makomai Area)	220	10	Max 15 000 dwt. Logs
Timber Port District Landing Lot (Makomai Area)	110	2	Logs
Yufutsu Wharf No.1 (Yufutsu Area)	280	12	Max 30 000 dwt. Lumber
Yufutsu Wharf No.2 (Yufutsu Area)	185	10	Max 15 000 dwt. Transportation machinery
Yufutsu Wharf No.3 (Yufutsu Area)	130	7.5	Max 5000 dwt. Transportation machinery
Yufutsu Wharf No.4 (Yufutsu Area)	130	7.5	Max 5000 dwt. Paper pulp
Yufutsu Wharf No.5 (Yufutsu Area)	240	12	Max 30 000 dwt. Paper pulp
Yufutsu Wharf No.6 (Yufutsu Area)	165	9	Max 10 000 dwt. Vegetables & fruit
Fishing Port District No.1 (Shiomi Area)	55	5	Aquatic products

Name	Length (m)	Depth (m)	Remarks
Basin for Small Craft No.2 (Shiomi Area)	140	5	
Fishing Port District Landing Lot (Shiomi Area)	565	3	Aquatic products
Basin for Small Craft Landing Lot No.1 (Shiomi Area)	320	3–4	
Basin for Small Craft Landing Lot No.2 (Shiomi Area)	120	4	
Fishing Port District Pier No.1-2 (Shiomi Area)	260	3	Aquatic products
Eastern Port District (Public Wharves)			
Central Wharf No's 1-2 (Benten Area)	370	10	Max 15 000 dwt. Limestone
Basin for Small Craft (Benten Area)	150	5	
Basin for Small Craft Landing Lot (Benten Area)	150	4	
East Wharf No.2 (Hama Atsuma Area)	240	12	Max 30 000 dwt. Gravel, sand & stone
Basin for Small Craft Landing Lot (Hama Atsuma Area)	110	3	Aquatic products
Western Port District (Exclusive Wharves)			
Tomakomai Industrial Port Development Co Ltd Wharf No's 1-2 (Honkoh Area)	476	8.5	Max 13 000 gt. Ferries & transportation
Tomakomai Industrial Port Development Co Ltd Wharf No.3 (Honkoh Area)	193	7.5	Max 6000 dwt. Machinery
Nippon Light Metal Co Ltd Central Wharf (Makomai Area)	200	14	Max 60 000 dwt. Coal
Tomakomai Futo Co Ltd Harumi Wharf (Makomai Area)	211	12	Max 30 000 dwt. Miscellaneous
Tomakomai Futo Co Ltd Wharf (Makomai Area)	390	7.5	Max 5000 dwt. Petroleum products
Tomakomai Futo Co Ltd Wharf (Makomai Area)	90	7	Max 4000 dwt. Petroleum products
Oji Paper Co Ltd Harumi Wharf (Makomai Area)	220	11	Max 23 000 dwt
Kyohatsu Co Ltd Wharf (Makomai Area)	47	10	Max 5000 dwt. Crude oil
Idemitsu Kosan Co Ltd Landing Lot (Makomai Area)	40	7.5	Max 1500 dwt. Heavy oil
Tomakomai Futo Co Ltd Pier (Makomai Area)	57	14	Max 70 000 dwt. Petroleum products
Tomakomai Futo Co Ltd & Japan Energy Pier (Makomai Area)	24	7	Max 5000 dwt. Petroleum products
Nisseki/General Pier (Makomai Area)	26	7	Max 4000 dwt. Petroleum products
Japan Oil Network Pier No.1 (Makomai Area)	34	7	Max 4000 dwt. Petroleum products
Japan Oil Network Pier No.2 (Makomai Area)	25	7	Max 4000 dwt. Petroleum products
Idemitsu Kosan Co Ltd West Pier (Makomai Area)	86	14	Max 70 000 dwt. Petroleum products
Idemitsu Kosan Co Ltd Pier No.1 (Makomai Area)	34	7.5	Max 5000 dwt. Petroleum products
Idemitsu Kosan Co Ltd Pier No.3 (Makomai Area)	32	7.5	Max 5000 dwt. Petroleum products
Idemitsu Kosan Co Ltd Pier No.4 (Makomai Area)	45	7.5	Max 5000 dwt. Petroleum products
Idemitsu Kosan Co Ltd Pier No.5 (Makomai Area)	42	7.5	Max 5000 dwt. Petroleum products
Idemitsu Kosan Co Ltd Pier No.7 (Makomai Area)	33	7.5	Max 5000 dwt. Petroleum products
Idemitsu Kosan Co Ltd Pier No.8 (Makomai Area)	48	7.5	Max 5000 dwt. Petroleum products
Idemitsu Kosan Co Ltd Pier No.9 (Makomai Area)	34	7.5	Max 5000 dwt. Petroleum products
Kyohatsu Co Ltd Pier (Makomai Area)	47	7.5	Max 5000 dwt. Petroleum products
Hokuren Tomakomai Oil Pier (Makomai Area)	49	7.5	Max 5000 dwt. Petroleum products
Hinode Chemical Industrial Co Ltd Wharf (Yufutsu Area)	500	10	Max 15 000 dwt. Cement

Key to Principal Facilities:—
A=Airport   **C**=Containers   **G**=General Cargo   **P**=Petroleum   **R**=Ro/Ro   **Y**=Dry Bulk
B=Bunkers   **D**=Dry Dock   **L**=Cruise   **Q**=Other Liquid Bulk   **T**=Towage (where available from port)

Name	Length (m)	Depth (m)	Remarks
Soda Group Wharf (Yufutsu Area)	490	10.8	Max 25 000 dwt. Salt
Dai Nippon Ink & Chemical Ink Co Ltd Wharf (Yufutsu Area)	185	7.5	Max 5000 dwt. Chemicals
Maruichi Steel Tube Ltd Wharf (Yufutsu Area)	184	7.5	Max 5000 dwt. Iron & steel
Nippon Steel Corp Wharf (Yufutsu Area)	374	7.5	Max 5000 dwt. Iron & steel
Sumimoto Metal Wharf (Yufutsu Area)	165	7.5	Max 5000 dwt. Iron & steel
Nippon Kokan K.K. Wharf (Yufutsu Area)	185	7.5	Max 5000 dwt. Iron & steel
Tomakomai Chemical Wharf (Yufutsu Area)	330	10	Max 15 000 dwt. Chemicals
Oji Paper Co Ltd Heavy Oil Berth (Shiomi Area)	24	7.5	Max 5000 dwt. Petroleum products
Idemitsu Oil Sea Berth (Outer Harbour Area)	490	24	Dolphin. Max 250 000 dwt. Crude oil
Eastern Port District (Exclusive Wharves)			
Tomatoh Co Ltd Wharf No.2 (Hama Atsuma Area)	280	14	Max 60 000 dwt. Coal
Tomatoh Co Ltd Wharf No.3 (Hama Atsuma Area)	155	5.5	Max 2000 dwt. Metal scraps
Hokuden Co Ltd Pier (Hama Atsuma Area)	151	7.5	Max 7600 dwt. Coal
Kyobi Dolphin (Outer Harbour Area)	400	16	Max 100 000 dwt. Crude oil

Bunkering: Domestic oil is available; bonded oil brought from Hakodate with sufficient advance notice
Idemitsu Kosan Co. Ltd, 1-1 Marunochi, 3-Chome, Chiyoda-ku, Tokyo 100-8321, Japan, *Tel:* +81 3 3213 3138, *Fax:* +81 3 3213 1145, *Email:* tohru.takamura@si.idemitsu.co.jp, *Website:* www.idemitsu.co.jp
MC Marine and Bunkering Inc., 8th Floor, Uchisaiwai-cho Dai Building, 3-3 Uchisaiwai-cho 1-chome, Chiyoda-ku, Tokyo 100-0011, Japan, *Tel:* +81 3 5251 2575, *Fax:* +81 3 5251 2583

Towage: Nine tugs available of 1300-4000 hp

Repair & Maintenance: Dock for small vessels under 499 gt is available
Hishinaka Kairiku Unyu Co. Ltd, Tomakomai, Hokkaido, Japan, *Tel:* +81 144 337357, *Fax:* +81 144 337377

Seaman Missions: The Seamans Mission, 2-10-16 Futaba-cho, Tomakomai 053 0045, Hokkaido, Japan, *Tel:* +81 144 348890, *Fax:* +81 144 723408, *Email:* mts_toma@ybb.ne.jp

Shipping Agents: Kamigumi Co. Ltd, 8-1 Yanagimachi 2-chome, Tomakomai 053-0053, Hokkaido, Japan, *Tel:* +81 144 572561, *Fax:* +81 144 572562
Narasaki STAX Co. Ltd, 13-24 Motonakano-cho 2-chome, Tomakomai 0530005, Hokkaido, Japan, *Tel:* +81 144 350171, *Fax:* +81 144 361663, *Email:* narasaki@coral.ocn.ne.jp, *Website:* www.narasaki-stax.co.jp
Tomakomai Hokuso Koun Ltd, 2-14 Motonakano-cho 2-chome, Tomakomai 053-0005, Hokkaido, Japan, *Tel:* +81 144 348676, *Fax:* +81 144 331709, *Email:* k.igarashi@tmhokuso.co.jp

Medical Facilities: General Hospital in middle of town, approx 10 mins from Western District

Airport: Chitose Airport, 15 km

Railway: Tomakomai Station, 3 km

Lloyd's Agent: Cornes & Co. Ltd, 273 Yamashita-cho, Naka-ku, Yokohama 231-0023, Kanagawa Pref., Japan, *Tel:* +81 45 201 8537, *Fax:* +81 45 212 3105, *Email:* survey@ykh.cornes.co.jp, *Website:* www.cornes.co.jp

TOMIOKA

Lat 37° 20' N; Long 141° 0' E.

Admiralty Chart: JP77, JP93 **Admiralty Pilot:** 42B
Time Zone: GMT +9 h **UNCTAD Locode:** JP TOM

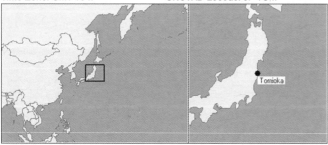

Principal Facilities:

		G		B		

Authority: Port & Harbour Section of Tokushima Prefecture, 1-1 Bandai-machi, Tokushima 770, Tokushima Pref., Japan, *Tel:* +81 886 212580, *Fax:* +81 886 232847, *Email:* kouwankuukouka@pref.tokushima.lg.jp, *Website:* www.pref.tokushima.jp

Approach: Draught limitation in the channel is 5.2 m. Narrow entrance to harbour between breakwaters

Anchorage: There are three designated anchorages off the harbour entrance

Pilotage: Compulsory. Pilots board at Komatsushima; no berthing or unberthing after sunset

Tides: Range of tide 3.1 m

Maximum Vessel Dimensions: 8144 dwt, 105.7 m loa

Working Hours: Stevedores available 24 h when required, including Sundays and holidays, except New Year's Holiday

Accommodation:

Name	Length (m)	Depth (m)
Tomioka Kanzaki Paper Manufacturing Co Wharf	250	5.2

Bunkering: Available by barge. Bonded oil brought from Osaka, Wakayama or Kobe

Towage: No tugs stationed at the port, but available from Komatsushima

Lloyd's Agent: Cornes & Co. Ltd, 273 Yamashita-cho, Naka-ku, Yokohama 231-0023, Kanagawa Pref., Japan, *Tel:* +81 45 201 8537, *Fax:* +81 45 212 3105, *Email:* survey@ykh.cornes.co.jp, *Website:* www.cornes.co.jp

TOYAMA

harbour area, see under Fushiki-Toyama

TOYAMA SHINKO

harbour area, see under Fushiki-Toyama

TOYOHASHI

Lat 34° 43' N; Long 137° 18' E.

Admiralty Chart: JP1056/JP1057A/JP10**Admiralty Pilot:** 42A
Time Zone: GMT +9 h **UNCTAD Locode:** JP THS

Principal Facilities:

P		Y	G	C	R		B		T	A

Authority: Port & Harbour Management Division, Aichi Prefecture Government, 3-1-2 Sannomaru, Naka-ku, Nagoya 460-8501, Aichi Pref., Japan, *Tel:* +81 52 954 6562, *Fax:* +81 52 953 1793, *Email:* kowan@pref.aichi.lg.jp, *Website:* www.pref.aichi.jp

Approach: The approach is through Irago Channel. Draught limitation is 12 m in the Toyohashi Passage and 10 m in the Tahara Passage

Pilotage: Compulsory for vessels exceeding 10 000 gt. A pilot will need to board the vessel off Irago and can be requested from Irago-Mikawa Bay Pilot Association, Tel: +81 569 217487. VHF Channel 16

Radio Frequency: Mikawa-wan Port Radio. VHF Channel 16 (calling) and Channels 11 and 12 (working)

Tides: Max tidal range 2.75 m

Accommodation:

Name	Length (m)	Depth (m)	Remarks
Toyohashi			
Jinno Wharf No.1	360	4.5	6 x 700 dwt
Jinno Wharf No.2	270	5.5	3 x 2000 dwt
Jinno Wharf No.3	910	7.5	7 x 5000 dwt
Jinno Wharf No.4	740	10	4 x 15 000 dwt
Jinno Wharf No.7	720	12	3 x 30 000 dwt
Funato Wharf No.1	500	4	10 x 500 dwt
Funato Wharf No.2	450	5.5	5 x 2000 dwt
Funato Wharf No.3	360	4.5	6 x 2000 dwt
Tahara			
Tahara Wharf No.1	120	4.5	2 x 700 dwt
Tahara Wharf No.2	400	5.5	4 x 2000 dwt
Takeshima Wharf No.1	131	5.5	1 x 3000 dwt
Takeshima Wharf No's 2-3	118	7.5	2 x 5000 dwt

Bunkering: Cosmo Oil Co. Ltd, Toshiba Building, 1-1 Shibaura 1-chome, Minato-ku, Tokyo 105-8528, Japan, *Tel:* +81 3 3798 3156, *Fax:* +81 3 3798 3592, *Email:* masayuki_iijima@cosmo-oil.co.jp, *Website:* www.cosmo-oil.co.jp
Hanwa Co. Ltd, 2nd Floor, Finland House, 56 Haymarket, London SW1Y 4RN, United Kingdom, *Tel:* +44 20 7839 4448, *Fax:* +44 20 7839 3994, *Email:* orito@hanwa.co.uk

Hikawa Shoji Kaisha Ltd, 26-2 Shinkawa NS Building 1-chome, Shinkawa, Chuo-ku, Tokyo 104, Japan, *Tel:* +81 3 5776 6858, *Fax:* +81 3 5541 3274

Idemitsu Kosan Co. Ltd, 1-1 Marunochi, 3-Chome, Chiyoda-ku, Tokyo 100-8321, Japan, *Tel:* +81 3 3213 3138, *Fax:* +81 3 3213 1145, *Email:* tohru.takamura@si.idemitsu.co.jp, *Website:* www.idemitsu.co.jp

KG Int Petroleum Ltd, Shiba Park Building, 241 Shiba Koen, Minato-ku, Tokyo 105, Japan, *Tel:* +81 3 3578 4551, *Fax:* +81 3 3578 4550

Japan Energy Corp., 2-10-1, Toranomon, Minato-ku, Tokyo 105-8407, Japan, *Tel:* +81 3 5573 6100, *Fax:* +81 3 5573 6674, *Email:* yamano@j-energy.co.jp, *Website:* www.j-energy.co.jp

Kamei Corp., 1-6-1 Otemachi, Chiyoda-ku, Tokyo 100-0004, Japan, *Tel:* +81 3 3286 6234, *Fax:* +81 3 3286 6249, *Email:* bunker@kamei.co.jp

Kawasho Corp., World Trade Centre, 4-1 Hanamatsu-cho 2-chome, Minato-ku, Tokyo 105, Japan, *Tel:* +81 3 3435 3251

Kyodo Oil Co. Ltd, 11-2 Nagata-cho 2-chome, Chiyoda-ku, Tokyo, Japan, *Tel:* +81 3 3505 8241, *Fax:* +81 3 3505 8697

Marubeni Petroleum Co. Ltd, Marubeni International Petroleum Singapore Co. Ltd, c/o Marubeni Corporation, 4-2 Ohtemachi 1-chome, Chiyoda-ku, Tokyo 100-8088, Japan, *Tel:* +81 3 3282 3920, *Fax:* +81 3 3282 3950, *Email:* TOKB554@marubenicorp.com, *Website:* www.marubeni.co.jp

MC Marine and Bunkering Inc., 8th Floor, Uchisaiwai-cho Dai Building, 3-3 Uchi-saiwai-cho 1-chome, Chiyoda-ku, Tokyo 100-0011, Japan, *Tel:* +81 3 5251 2575, *Fax:* +81 3 5251 2583

Mitsui & Co. Petroleum Ltd, 2-1, Ohtemachi 1-chome, Chiyoda-ku, Tokyo 100-0004, Japan, *Tel:* +81 3 3285 6905, *Fax:* +81 3 3285 9811, *Email:* tkzph@dg.mitsui.com, *Website:* www.mitsui.co.jp

Nissho Iwai Corp., 4-4 Akasaka 2-chome, Minato-ku, Tokyo, Japan, *Tel:* +81 3 35882111

Nittetsu Shoij Co. Ltd, 5-7 Kameido 1-chome, Koto-ku, Tokyo 136, Japan, *Tel:* +81 3 5627 2157, *Fax:* +81 3 5627 2192

Shinagawa Fuel Co. Ltd, New Pier Takeshiba North Tower, 8th Floor, 1-11-1 Kaigan, Minato-ku, Tokyo 105-8525, Japan, *Tel:* +81 3 5470 7113, *Fax:* +81 3 5470 7157, *Email:* hakuyu@ml1.sinanen.co.jp

Sigma Foreign Service (Panama) S.A., 2-25 Aikawai, Tempaku-ku, Nagoya 468-0836, Aichi Pref., Japan, *Tel:* +81 52 896 1510, *Fax:* +81 52 896 7703

Sumitomo Corp., Harumi Island, Triton Square, Office Tower Y, 8-11 Harumi 1-chome, Chuo-ku, Tokyo 104-8610, Japan, *Tel:* +81 3 51664458, *Fax:* +81 3 51666407, *Email:* ir@sumitomo.co.jp, *Website:* www.sumitomocorp.co.jp

Towage: Seven tugs available of 3500 hp

Repair & Maintenance: Toyohashi Shipbuilding Co. Ltd, 22 Akemi-cho, Toyohashi 441-8577, Aichi Pref., Japan, *Tel:* +81 53 225 4111, *Fax:* +81 53 225 4117, *Website:* www.toyozo.jp

Airport: Nagoya Airport, 80 km

Lloyd's Agent: Cornes & Co. Ltd, 273 Yamashita-cho, Naka-ku, Yokohama 231-0023, Kanagawa Pref., Japan, *Tel:* +81 45 201 8537, *Fax:* +81 45 212 3105, *Email:* survey@ykh.cornes.co.jp, *Website:* www.cornes.co.jp

TSUKUMI

Lat 33° 5' N; Long 131° 51' E.

Admiralty Chart: JP1247A/JP1247B	**Admiralty Pilot:** 42B
Time Zone: GMT +9 h	**UNCTAD Locode:** JP TMI

Principal Facilities:

		Y	G			B		T	

Authority: Port & Harbor Division, Civil Engineering & Construction Dept., Oita Prefectural Government, 3-1-1 Ohte-machi, Oita 870-8501, Oita Pref., Japan, *Tel:* +81 97 538 5714, *Fax:* +81 97 537 0907, *Email:* a17310@pref.oita.lg.jp

Port Security: ISPS compliant

Approach: An open harbour at the head of Tsukumi Bay, divided into two parts by a peninsula. The entrance channel is reasonably free of hazards and has a depth of about 25 m. Vessels over 40 000 dwt are not permitted entry after sunset

Anchorage: Inner harbour anchorage, depth about 25 m

Pilotage: Not compulsory but recommended for first visit. Pilots are available if required and board vessel at the anchorage in an area S of Kuro Shima in pos 33° 06' N, 131° 54' E

Tides: Max tidal range 2.2 m

Accommodation:

Name	Length (m)	Depth (m)	Remarks
Tsukumi			See [1] below
Noshima Public Wharf	244	6–9	Max 15 000 dwt & 3000 dwt
Onoda Cement Berth (A)	270	13	Max 60 000 dwt
Onoda Cement Berth (B)	168	16	Max 60 000 dwt
Onoda Cement Berth (C)	65	14	Max 2000 dwt
Onoda Cement Berth (D)	185	13	Max 60 000 dwt
Onoda Cement Berth No.1	82	7	Max 6000 dwt

Name	Length (m)	Depth (m)	Remarks
Onoda Cement Berth No.2	121	8	Max 8000 dwt
Nittetsu Pier	155	10.5	Max 23 000 dwt
Todaka Pier No.1 (S)	175	10	Max 20 000 dwt
Todaka Pier No.1 (N)		9	Max 10 000 dwt
Todaka Pier No.2 (S)	80	7.5	Max 6000 dwt
Todaka Pier No.2 (N)		5	Max 3000 dwt

[1] *Tsukumi:* Movement of vessels at night time is at the pilot's discretion. Good holding ground at the anchorage in depths up to 25 m

Bulk facilities: Conveyor belts for loading bagged cement, cement clinker and limestone. Open storage area of 1 ha

Mechanical Handling Equipment:

Location	Type	Capacity (t)	Qty
Tsukumi	Floating Cranes	40	1

Cargo Worked: Loading 15 000 t/day, discharging 10 000 t/day

Bunkering: Idemitsu Kosan Co. Ltd, 1-1 Marunochi, 3-Chome, Chiyoda-ku, Tokyo 100-8321, Japan, *Tel:* +81 3 3213 3138, *Fax:* +81 3 3213 1145, *Email:* tohru.takamura@si.idemitsu.co.jp, *Website:* www.idemitsu.co.jp

KG Int Petroleum Ltd, Shiba Park Building, 241 Shiba Koen, Minato-ku, Tokyo 105, Japan, *Tel:* +81 3 3578 4551, *Fax:* +81 3 3578 4550

MC Marine and Bunkering Inc., 8th Floor, Uchisaiwai-cho Dai Building, 3-3 Uchi-saiwai-cho 1-chome, Chiyoda-ku, Tokyo 100-0011, Japan, *Tel:* +81 3 5251 2575, *Fax:* +81 3 5251 2583

Mitsui & Co. Petroleum Ltd, 2-1, Ohtemachi 1-chome, Chiyoda-ku, Tokyo 100-0004, Japan, *Tel:* +81 3 3285 6905, *Fax:* +81 3 3285 9811, *Email:* tkzph@dg.mitsui.com, *Website:* www.mitsui.co.jp

Nissho Iwai Corp., 4-4 Akasaka 2-chome, Minato-ku, Tokyo, Japan, *Tel:* +81 3 35882111

Nittetsu Shoij Co. Ltd, 5-7 Kameido 1-chome, Koto-ku, Tokyo 136, Japan, *Tel:* +81 3 5627 2157, *Fax:* +81 3 5627 2192

Sumitomo Corp., Harumi Island, Triton Square, Office Tower Y, 8-11 Harumi 1-chome, Chuo-ku, Tokyo 104-8610, Japan, *Tel:* +81 3 51664458, *Fax:* +81 3 51666407, *Email:* ir@sumitomo.co.jp, *Website:* www.sumitomocorp.co.jp

Towage: Two tugs of 3000 hp and one of 1600 hp available

Repair & Maintenance: Minor repairs available

Medical Facilities: Private clinic available

Lloyd's Agent: Cornes & Co. Ltd, Meikai Building, 32 Akashi-machi, Chuo-ku, Kobe 650-0037, Hyogo Pref., Japan, *Tel:* +81 78 332 3421, *Fax:* +81 78 332 3070, *Email:* survey@kobe.cornes.co.jp, *Website:* www.cornes.co.jp

TSURUGA

Lat 35° 40' N; Long 136° 5' E.

Admiralty Chart: JP169	**Admiralty Pilot:** 41
Time Zone: GMT +9 h	**UNCTAD Locode:** JP TRG

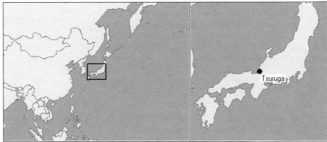

Principal Facilities:

P	Q	Y	G	C	R		B		T	A

Authority: Port & Harbour Section of Fukui Prefecture, 3-17-1 Ohte, Fukui 910-8580, Fukui Pref., Japan, *Tel:* +81 776 211111, *Fax:* +81 776 200678, *Email:* k-yuchi@pref.fukui.lg.jp, *Website:* www.pref.fukui.jp

Officials: Business Director: Osamu Sudo.

Port Security: ISPS compliant

Approach: The approach to the port is via a 6 mile long passage from the entrance of Wakasa Bay. Draught limitation in the channel is 15 m

Pilotage: Not compulsory. Harbour pilot boards at quarantine anchorage. Tsuruga-Fukui Pilot Association, Tel: +81 770 233753

Weather: Typhoon season, July to October

Tides: Range of tide 0.77 m

Maximum Vessel Dimensions: Max draught in channel is 15 m. Inner Harbour: 35 000 dwt, 9.5 m d, 300 m loa

Principal Imports and Exports: Imports: Chemical medicine, Coal, Raw lumber. Exports: Coal ash.

Working Hours: 0800-1700. Sundays and holidays subject to negotiation

Accommodation:

Name	Length (m)	Depth (m)	Remarks
Tsuruga			See [1] below
Kanegasaki Wharf (C)	170	10	1 x 10 000 dwt
Kanegasaki Wharf (D)	130	7.5	1 x 5000 dwt
Sakura Wharf (E & F)	180	5.5	2 x 2000 dwt
Horai Wharf (G, H & I)	390	7.5	3 x 6000 gt

Key to Principal Facilities:—		
A=Airport	**C**=Containers	**G**=General Cargo	**P**=Petroleum	**R**=Ro/Ro	**Y**=Dry Bulk
B=Bunkers	**D**=Dry Dock	**L**=Cruise	**Q**=Other Liquid Bulk	**T**=Towage (where available from port)	

Name	Length (m)	Depth (m)	Remarks
Kawasaki Matsuei Wharf (A)	199	7.5	1 x 10 000 dwt
Kawasaki Matsuei Wharf (B & C)	370	10	See ² below
JNR Wharf	163	8.9	1 x 12 000 dwt
Tsuruga Cement & Hokuriku Electric Power Wharf	260	7.5	Operated by Tsuruga Cement Co & Hokuriku Electric Power Co 1 x 10 000 dwt
Nihon Genden Jetty	87	6	1 x 5000 dwt
Mariyama Kita (A)	130	8	1 x 5000 dwt
Mariyama Kita (B)	240	12	1 x 30 000 dwt
Mariyama Kita (C)	240	12	1 x 30 000 dwt
Mariyama Kita (D)	240	9	1 x 20 000 gt

¹*Tsuruga:* Tsuruga Port Office, Tel: +81 770 220369, Fax: +81 770 227067, Email: t-kouwan@pref.fukui.lg.jp
Harbour is protected by one breakwater of length 1105 m. Max depth of water in Outer Harbour 22 m, in Inner Harbour 10 m. Also two buoys with depths alongside of 17 m and 20 m for vessels of 10 000 gt and 20 000 gt
Tanker facilities: Available for coastal tankers up to 1000 gt, 70 m long and 5.8 m draft
²*Kawasaki Matsuei Wharf (B & C):* 2 x 15 000 dwt. Berth at Kawasaki Matsuei Wharf B equipped with a 40 TEU/h cap container crane. Berth at Kawasaki Matsuei Wharf C equipped with a 315 t/h cap level luffing crane

Storage: Sheds of 7400 m2, general cargo warehouses of 14 300 m2, timber basin of 9.1 ha

Location	Open (m²)	Covered (m²)
Tsuruga	189928	54309

Mechanical Handling Equipment: Level luffing crane up to 315 t/h cap. Container crane up to 40 TEU's/h cap. Various types of crane up to 800 t/h cap

Bunkering: Facilities for coastal vessels. Bonded oil available by barge from Moji with advance notice

Towage: Three tugs available; one of 2600 hp, one of 2000 hp and one of 1200 hp

Repair & Maintenance: Minor repairs only executed

Medical Facilities: Available

Airport: Fukui Airport

Lloyd's Agent: Cornes & Co. Ltd, Meikai Building, 32 Akashi-machi, Chuo-ku, Kobe 650-0037, Hyogo Pref., Japan, *Tel:* +81 78 332 3421, *Fax:* +81 78 332 3070, *Email:* survey@kobe.cornes.co.jp, *Website:* www.cornes.co.jp

UBE

Lat 33° 56' N; Long 131° 12' E.

Admiralty Chart: 676	**Admiralty Pilot:** 42B
Time Zone: GMT +9 h	**UNCTAD Locode:** JP UBJ

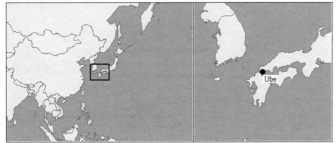

Principal Facilities:

P	Q	Y	G	C	R		B		T	A

Authority: Ports & Harbors Division, Yamaguchi Prefectural Government, 1-1 Takimachi, Yamaguchi 753-8501, Yamaguchi Pref., Japan, *Tel:* +81 83 933 3810, *Fax:* +81 83 933 3829, *Email:* a12900@pref.yamaguchi.lg.jp, *Website:* www.pref.yamaguchi.lg.jp

Officials: Shoichi Hayashi, *Tel:* +81 83 9332 340.

Port Security: ISPS compliant

Approach: Higashi Channel 100 m wide in depth of 9 m
Nishioki Channel 150 m wide in depth of 6 m
Nishi Channel 120 m wide in depth of 6 m
Honkoh Channel 150 m wide in depth of 8 m
Sakaegawa Channel 40 m wide in depth of 4 m
Kogyo-Unga Channel 50 m wide in depth of 6 m

Anchorage: Nishioki West Anchorage in depth of 6 m, Nishioki East Anchorage in depth of 7.5 m, Honkoh Anchorage in depth of 10 m, Sibanaka West Anchorage in depth of 13 m, Sibanaka East Anchorage in depth of 9 m and Higashi Mizome Anchorage in depth of 4.5 m

Pilotage: Not compulsory but recommended. Inland sea pilots are available at Sekisaki or Hesaki. Harbour pilots are available at the anchorage. Pilotage not available after sunset

Tides: Average range of tide 2.1 m

Maximum Vessel Dimensions: 230 m loa

Principal Imports and Exports: Imports: Coal, Oil. Exports: Cement, Chemicals.

Working Hours: 0900-1700

Accommodation:

Name	Length (m)	Depth (m)	Remarks
Public Wharves			
Shibanaka East Wharf	162	9	1 x 10 000 dwt
Shibanaka Wharf No.1	185	10	1 x 15 000 dwt
Shibanaka Wharf No.2	130	7.5	1 x 5000 dwt
Shibanaka Wharf No.3	130	7.5	1 x 5000 dwt
Shibanaka West Wharf	270	13	1 x 50 000 dwt
Onda Wharf	240	4.5	4 x 700 dwt
Shinmachi Wharf No.1	130	7.5	1 x 5000 dwt
Shinmachi Wharf No.2	130	7.5	1 x 5000 dwt
Shinmachi Wharf No.3	90	5.5	1 x 2000 dwt
Okinoyama Wharf No.1	186	10	1 x 15 000 dwt
Okinoyama Wharf No.2	185	10	1 x 15 000 dwt
Private Wharves			
Sentoraru Wharf No.2	215	6	2 x 3000 dwt
Ube Kosan Wharf No.1	188	9	1 x 10 000 dwt
Ube Kosan Wharf No.2	188	9	1 x 10 000 dwt
Ube Kosan Wharf No.3	113	9	1 x 10 000 dwt
Ube Kosan Wharf No.5	160	11	1 x 20 000 dwt
Ube Kosan Wharf No.6	260	11	1 x 20 000 dwt
Ube Kosan Nishi Okinoyama Pier	164	7.5	1 x 5000 dwt
Seibu Sekiyu Pier No's 1-8	770	6	7 x 2000 dwt
Seibu Sekiyu Sea Berth		25	1 x 200 000 dwt
Semento Wharf	247	7	2 x 5000 dwt
Semento West Wharf No.1	260	5	3 x 2000 dwt
Semento Pier No.1	73	5	1 x 2000 dwt
Chisso West Wharf	110	5	1 x 2000 dwt
Kogyo-Unga Wharf	197	5	2 x 2000 dwt
Rakutamu Wharf	195	6	2 x 2000 dwt
Kyowa Hakkoh Pier	12	4.5	1 x 700 dwt
Anmonia Wharf	70	5	1 x 2000 dwt
Ube Seikoh Pier	150	5	1 x 2000 dwt

Bunkering: Hanwa Co. Ltd, 2nd Floor, Finland House, 56 Haymarket, London SW1Y 4RN, United Kingdom, *Tel:* +44 20 7839 4448, *Fax:* +44 20 7839 3994, *Email:* orito@hanwa.co.uk
Idemitsu Kosan Co. Ltd, 1-1 Marunochi, 3-Chome, Chiyoda-ku, Tokyo 100-8321, Japan, *Tel:* +81 3 3213 3138, *Fax:* +81 3 3213 1145, *Email:* tohru.takamura@si.idemitsu.co.jp, *Website:* www.idemitsu.co.jp
KG Int Petroleum Ltd, Shiba Park Building, 241 Shiba Koen, Minato-ku, Tokyo 105, Japan, *Tel:* +81 3 3578 4551, *Fax:* +81 3 3578 4550
Kyodo Oil Co. Ltd, 11-2 Nagata-cho 2-chome, Chiyoda-ku, Tokyo, Japan, *Tel:* +81 3 3505 8241, *Fax:* +81 3 3505 8697
MC Marine and Bunkering Inc., 8th Floor, Uchisaiwai-cho Dai Building, 3-3 Uchisaiwai-cho 1-chome, Chiyoda-ku, Tokyo 100-0011, Japan, *Tel:* +81 3 5251 2575, *Fax:* +81 3 5251 2583
NKK Trading Inc., 4-4 Nihonbashi Hisamatsusucho, Chuo-ku, Tokyo 103, Japan, *Tel:* +81 3 3660 1522, *Fax:* +81 3 3660 1572
Sumitomo Corp., Harumi Island, Triton Square, Office Tower Y, 8-11 Harumi 1-chome, Chuo-ku, Tokyo 104-8610, Japan, *Tel:* +81 3 51664458, *Fax:* +81 3 51666407, *Email:* ir@sumitomo.co.jp, *Website:* www.sumitomocorp.co.jp

Towage: Two tugs available owned by the Port Authority, one of 1300 hp and one of 2400 hp. Three privately owned tugs also available, one of 2600 hp and two of 3200 hp

Medical Facilities: Available in Ube City

Airport: Yamaguchi-Ube, 5 km

Railway: Ube-Shinkawa Station, 1 km

Lloyd's Agent: Cornes & Co. Ltd, Meikai Building, 32 Akashi-machi, Chuo-ku, Kobe 650-0037, Hyogo Pref., Japan, *Tel:* +81 78 332 3421, *Fax:* +81 78 332 3070, *Email:* survey@kobe.cornes.co.jp, *Website:* www.cornes.co.jp

UCHIURA

Lat 35° 32' N; Long 135° 30' E.

Admiralty Chart: JP139	**Admiralty Pilot:** 41
Time Zone: GMT +9 h	**UNCTAD Locode:** JP UCR

Principal Facilities:

		Y	G					T	

Authority: Port & Harbour Section of Fukui Prefecture, 3-17-1 Ohte, Fukui 910-8580, Fukui Pref., Japan, *Tel:* +81 776 211111, *Fax:* +81 776 200678, *Email:* k-yuchi@pref.fukui.lg.jp, *Website:* www.pref.fukui.jp

Officials: Business Director: Osamu Sudo.

Anchorage: Well protected anchorage can be obtained off the port in Uchiura Bay in depths ranging from 15 m to 20 m

Pilotage: Not compulsory. Pilot available during daylight hours only if required and boards vessel at the quarantine anchorage

Weather: Typhoon season, July to October

Tides: Spring rise 0.3 m, neap rise 0.2 m

Principal Imports and Exports: Imports: Timber. Exports: Used cars.

Working Hours: Stevedores: Monday-Saturday 0830-1700, Sundays and holidays available if required

Accommodation:

Name	Length (m)	Depth (m)	Remarks
Uchiura			
Wharf No.1	130	9	Max 10 000 dwt
Wharf No.2	130	7.5	Max 10 000 dwt

Towage: One tug of 2200 hp available

Repair & Maintenance: Minor repairs undertaken

Lloyd's Agent: Cornes & Co. Ltd, Meikai Building, 32 Akashi-machi, Chuo-ku, Kobe 650-0037, Hyogo Pref., Japan, *Tel:* +81 78 332 3421, *Fax:* +81 78 332 3070, *Email:* survey@kobe.cornes.co.jp, *Website:* www.cornes.co.jp

UNO

Lat 34° 29' N; Long 133° 57' E.

Admiralty Chart: 694	**Admiralty Pilot:** 42B
Time Zone: GMT +9 h	**UNCTAD Locode:** JP UNO

Principal Facilities:

P	Q	Y	G			B	D		A

Authority: Port & Harbour Section of Okayama Prefecture, 2-4-6 Uchisange, Okayama 700-8570, Japan, *Tel:* +81 86 226 7485, *Fax:* +81 86 227 5551, *Email:* kowan@pref.okayama.lg.jp, *Website:* www.pref.okayama.jp

Officials: Harbour Director: Masanori Tokimatsu, *Email:* masanori_tokimatsu@pref.okayama.lg.jp.

Port Security: ISPS compliant

Approach: The approach is through Bisan Seto and Uko East traffic routes. Depth of passage to Uno and Tamano 9-10 m, depth of passage to Hibi 12-13 m. Vessels usually anchor at Wadamisaki (Kobe) for quarantine. Vessels are only able to berth at time of slack water in the Bisan Central passage from daybreak to sunset

Pilotage: Inland Sea pilotage compulsory for vessels exceeding 10 000 gt. Available from Inland Sea Pilotage Association, Tel: +81 78 391 7191. Tomogashima pilots and Kanmon pilots are also available. Harbour pilotage is not compulsory but recommended due to rapid current in the port; not available after sunset

Weather: Typhoon season, July to October

Tides: Tidal range 3.3 m, 2.55 m MHWL, 0.18 m MLWL. Max current 2.8 knots, E direction

Principal Imports and Exports: Imports: Copper concentrate, Timber. Exports: Chemicals, Transportation & machinery equipment.

Working Hours: 0830-1700. At Mitsui Mining and Smelting Wharf at Hibi, 0830-2030

Accommodation: In addition to the piers and wharves there are six designated anchorage areas with 18 m to 29 m depth at Uno and Tamano regions for loading and discharging cargoes

Name	Length (m)	Depth (m)	Remarks
Uno			
Pier No.3	297	5.5–10	1 x 15 000 dwt & 1 x 2000 dwt
Pier No.1 Wharf No.3	60	4.9–5.2	1 x 1000 dwt
Pier No.1 Wharf No.4	151	7.9–8.5	1 x 6000 dwt
Pier No.1 Wharf No.5	120	7.5	1 x 5000 dwt
Tai A Berth	240	12	1 x 30 000 dwt
Tai B Berth	240	12	1 x 30 000 dwt
Tai C Berth	240	12	1 x 30 000 dwt
Tai D Berth	185	10	1 x 15 000 dwt
JNR Wharf	625	3.9–9	2 x 5000 gt
Uko Ferry Jetty	56	7–9	1 x 3000 gt

Storage: Four transit sheds, 3620 m2; 12 warehouses, 23 584 m2; two refrigerated warehouses, 13 458 m3; coal storage, 2554 m2; timber storage, 151 930 m2; other open storage of 22 412 m2

Mechanical Handling Equipment:

Location	Type	Capacity (t)	Qty
Uno	Floating Cranes	120	1
Uno	Mult-purp. Cranes	300	18

Cargo Worked: 3700 t of foreign trade and 7600 t of domestic trade per working day

Bunkering: Idemitsu Kosan Co. Ltd, 1-1 Marunochi, 3-Chome, Chiyoda-ku, Tokyo 100-8321, Japan, *Tel:* +81 3 3213 3138, *Fax:* +81 3 3213 1145, *Email:* tohru.takamura@si.idemitsu.co.jp, *Website:* www.idemitsu.co.jp
KG Int Petroleum Ltd, Shiba Park Building, 241 Shiba Koen, Minato-ku, Tokyo 105, Japan, *Tel:* +81 3 3578 4551, *Fax:* +81 3 3578 4550
MC Marine and Bunkering Inc., 8th Floor, Uchisaiwai-cho Dai Building, 3-3 Uchisaiwai-cho 1-chome, Chiyoda-ku, Tokyo 100-0011, Japan, *Tel:* +81 3 5251 2575, *Fax:* +81 3 5251 2583
Mitsui & Co. Petroleum Ltd, 2-1, Ohtemachi 1-chome, Chiyoda-ku, Tokyo 100-0004, Japan, *Tel:* +81 3 3285 6905, *Fax:* +81 3 3285 9811, *Email:* tkzph@dg.mitsui.com, *Website:* www.mitsui.co.jp
Nittetsu Shoji Co. Ltd, 5-7 Kameido 1-chome, Koto-ku, Tokyo 136, Japan, *Tel:* +81 3 5627 2157, *Fax:* +81 3 5627 2192
Shinagawa Fuel Co. Ltd, New Pier Takeshiba North Tower, 8th Floor, 1-11-1 Kaigan, Minato-ku, Tokyo 105-8525, Japan, *Tel:* +81 3 5470 7113, *Fax:* +81 3 5470 7157, *Email:* hakuyu@ml1.sinanen.co.jp
Sumitomo Corp., Harumi Island, Triton Square, Office Tower Y, 8-11 Harumi 1-chome, Chuo-ku, Tokyo 104-8610, Japan, *Tel:* +81 3 51664458, *Fax:* +81 3 51666407, *Email:* ir@sumitomo.co.jp, *Website:* www.sumitomocorp.co.jp

Towage: Not available. Tugs brought in from Mizushima when required

Repair & Maintenance: Mitsui Engineering and Shipbuilding Co., Tel: +81 863 313111. One dry dock at Tamano, length 209 m for vessels up to 46 000 dwt

Medical Facilities: Available

Airport: Okayama, 17 km

Lloyd's Agent: Cornes & Co. Ltd, Meikai Building, 32 Akashi-machi, Chuo-ku, Kobe 650-0037, Hyogo Pref., Japan, *Tel:* +81 78 332 3421, *Fax:* +81 78 332 3070, *Email:* survey@kobe.cornes.co.jp, *Website:* www.cornes.co.jp

WAKAMATSU

Lat 33° 55' N; Long 130° 49' E.

Admiralty Chart: JP1265	**Admiralty Pilot:** 42B
Time Zone: GMT +9 h	**UNCTAD Locode:** JP WAM

Principal Facilities:

	Y	G	C		B		T	A

Authority: Kitakyushu Port & Harbor Bureau, 1-1 Jonai, Kitakyushu 803-8501, Fukuoka Pref., Japan, *Tel:* +81 93 321 5941, *Fax:* +81 93 582 1037, *Email:* kqport@kitaqport.or.jp, *Website:* www.kitaqport.or.jp

Officials: Director General: Kenichi Katayama.
Marketing Director: Hiroyuki Tagami, *Email:* hiroyuki_tagami01@city.kitakyushu.lg.jp.
Sales Director: Tetsuji Hashimoto.

Port Security: ISPS compliant

Approach: Entry into and departure from Wakamatsu permitted only from sunrise and vessels must be berthed by sunset. The Wakato Ohashi suspension bridge crosses the channel between Tobata and Wakamatsu. Air draught is 38 m at HST. Draught limitation in the channel is 9.14 m to 10 m depth. All fairways are well lighted and buoyed. Fairway leading to main harbour is 200 m wide, running parallel to the breakwater and reclaimed land. Vessels observe one way traffic system controlled by signals. Depth in channel to Anse Wharf at Hibikinada is 13.0 m, draught limitation of 12.2 m

Pilotage: Compulsory. Harbour pilots and Inland Sea pilots are available at the pilot stations or quarantine anchorage. Pilots not available after sunset

Tides: Tidal range 2.84 m

Traffic: 2006, 109 723 953 t of cargo handled, 469 000 TEU's (includes ports of Kokura, Moji, Tobata & Yawata)

Principal Imports and Exports: Imports: Coal, Iron ore, Logs. Exports: Chemical products, Coke.

Working Hours: 24 h/day

Accommodation:

Name	Length (m)	Draught (m)	Remarks
Wakamatsu District			
Buoy B	210	7.6	
Buoy C	220	8.4	
Buoy E	160	8.1	
Buoy H	150	6.4	
Buoy I	150	6.4	
Buoy L	220	8.5	
Buoy M	150	6	
Buoy N	200	6.7	
Asahi Glass Wharf	150	8.5	
Mitsubishi Chemical Ind OKI	160	8.4	

Key to Principal Facilities:—			
A=Airport	**C**=Containers	**G**=General Cargo	**P**=Petroleum	**R**=Ro/Ro	**Y**=Dry Bulk
B=Bunkers	**D**=Dry Dock	**L**=Cruise	**Q**=Other Liquid Bulk	**T**=Towage (where available from port)	

Name	Length (m)	Draught (m)	Remarks
Mitsubishi Chemical Ind OKR	180	8.3	
Kurosaki Kokyo Wharf OD1		8	Wharves OD1 & OD2 have a combined length of 331 m
Kurosaki Kokyo Wharf OD2		7	Wharves OD1 & OD2 have a combined length of 331 m
Tobata Shoko Wharf	165	8.5	
Hibikinada District			
Hibiki Container Terminal			See [1] below
Hibikinada Wharf (Logs Dolphin)		9	
Hibikinada Wharf HD0 (Logs Dolphin)	170	9	
Hibikinada Wharf HD1 (Logs)	185	9	
Hibikinada Wharf HD2	185	9	
Hibikinada Wharf HD3	165	8.5	
Hibikinada Wharf HD4	160	8.5	
Anse Wharf A1	315	12.2	See [2] below
Anse Wharf A2	235	12.2	See [3] below

[1]*Hibiki Container Terminal:* Operated by Hibiki Container Terminal Co Ltd (HCT), Chisaki 3-chome, Hibiki-machi, Wakamatsu-ku, Kitakyushu 808-0021, Tel: +81 93 752 0888, Fax: +81 93 752 0889
Consists of two berths, both 350 m long in depth of 15 m and two berths, both 140 m long in depth of 10 m

[2]*Anse Wharf A1:* One 1500 t/h unloader and three 1200 t/h unloaders handling iron ore, coal and coke

[3]*Anse Wharf A2:* One 1500 t/h unloader and three 1200 t/h unloaders handling iron ore, coal and coke

Mechanical Handling Equipment:

Location	Type	Capacity (t)	Qty
Wakamatsu	Floating Cranes	8–500	5
Asahi Glass Wharf	Mult-purp. Cranes	3	1
Asahi Glass Wharf	Mult-purp. Cranes	2	1
Mitsubishi Chemical Ind OKI	Mult-purp. Cranes	4	2
Hibiki Container Terminal	Post Panamax	56.3	3

Bunkering: Hanwa Co. Ltd, 2nd Floor, Finland House, 56 Haymarket, London SW1Y 4RN, United Kingdom, *Tel:* +44 20 7839 4448, *Fax:* +44 20 7839 3994, *Email:* orito@hanwa.co.uk
Hikawa Shoji Kaisha Ltd, 26-2 Shinkawa NS Building 1-chome, Shinkawa, Chuo-ku, Tokyo 104, Japan, *Tel:* +81 3 5776 6858, *Fax:* +81 3 5541 3274
Idemitsu Kosan Co. Ltd, 1-1 Marunochi, 3-Chome, Chiyoda-ku, Tokyo 100-8321, Japan, *Tel:* +81 3 3213 3138, *Fax:* +81 3 3213 1145, *Email:* tohru.takamura@si.idemitsu.co.jp, *Website:* www.idemitsu.co.jp
KG Int Petroleum Ltd, Shiba Park Building, 241 Shiba Koen, Minato-ku, Tokyo 105, Japan, *Tel:* +81 3 3578 4551, *Fax:* +81 3 3578 4550
Marubeni Petroleum Co. Ltd, Marubeni International Petroleum Singapore Co. Ltd, c/o Marubeni Corporation, 4-2 Ohtemachi 1-chome, Chiyoda-ku, Tokyo 100-8088, Japan, *Tel:* +81 3 3282 3920, *Fax:* +81 3 3282 3950, *Email:* TOKB554@marubenicorp.com, *Website:* www.marubeni.co.jp
MC Marine and Bunkering Inc., 8th Floor, Uchisaiwai-cho Dai Building, 3-3 Uchisaiwai-cho 1-chome, Chiyoda-ku, Tokyo 100-0011, Japan, *Tel:* +81 3 5251 2575, *Fax:* +81 3 5251 2583
Mitsui & Co. Petroleum Ltd, 2-1, Ohtemachi 1-chome, Chiyoda-ku, Tokyo 100-0004, Japan, *Tel:* +81 3 3285 6905, *Fax:* +81 3 3285 9811, *Email:* tkzph@dg.mitsui.com, *Website:* www.mitsui.co.jp
Nittetsu Shoij Co. Ltd, 5-7 Kameido 1-chome, Koto-ku, Tokyo 136, Japan, *Tel:* +81 3 5627 2157, *Fax:* +81 3 5627 2192

Towage: Two tugs available; one of 2500 hp and one of 1300 hp

Repair & Maintenance: Minor repairs only

Airport: Kitakyushu Airport

Lloyd's Agent: Cornes & Co. Ltd, Meikai Building, 32 Akashi-machi, Chuo-ku, Kobe 650-0037, Hyogo Pref., Japan, *Tel:* +81 78 332 3421, *Fax:* +81 78 332 3070, *Email:* survey@kobe.cornes.co.jp, *Website:* www.cornes.co.jp

WAKAURA

harbour area, see under Wakayama

WAKAYAMA

Lat 34° 12' N; Long 135° 8' E.

Admiralty Chart: JP150A/JP150C **Admiralty Pilot:** 42B

Time Zone: GMT +9 h **UNCTAD Locode:** JP WAK

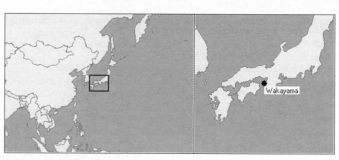

Principal Facilities:

P	Q	Y	G	C		B		T	A

Authority: Wakayama Prefectural Harbor & Airport Promotion Bureau, 1-1 Komatsubara-dori, Wakayama 640-8585, Wakayama Pref., Japan, *Tel:* +81 73 441 3151, *Fax:* +81 73 443 4839, *Email:* e0824001@pref.wakayama.lg.jp, *Website:* www.pref.wakayama.lg.jp

Officials: Manager: Katsushi Nakano.

Port Security: ISPS compliant

Approach: The approach is via Kii Channel and vessels normally anchor at Shimotsu quarantine anchorage. The fairways are: Wakayama Hokko (North Port) 1.4 km long, 350 m wide, 15 m depth; Wakayama Honko (Main Port) 3.3 km long, 250 m wide, 12 m depth; Kainan 2 km long, 200 m wide, 12 m depth and Shimotsu 2 km long, 200 m wide, 12 m to 15 m depth

Pilotage: Not compulsory. Pilot available at Shimotsu quarantine anchorage. Wakayama-Shimotsu Pilots Association, Tel: +81 73 431 8713, Fax: +81 73 432 3438. Pilots are also available at the North Port anchorage of Wakayama. Pilotage is only available during daylight hours

Weather: Typhoon season, July to October

Tides: Tidal range 2.4 m at Wakayama region, 2.14 m at Shimotsu region and 3.06 m at Kainan region

Maximum Vessel Dimensions: Draught limitations to the three fairways are: Wakayama 14 m, Shimotsu 12 m and Kainan 11.8 m

Principal Imports and Exports: Imports: Coal, Crude oil, Iron ore, Timber. Exports: Steel products.

Working Hours: Continuous three shifts at Sumitomo Metal Wharves, excluding New Year's holiday. 0830-1630 for the discharging of logs, every day except Sundays and New Year's holiday

Accommodation:

Name	Length (m)	Depth (m)	Remarks
Wakayama North Port Area			
No.1 Wharf	170	10	
Landing Platform	265	2–3.5	
Sumitomo Metal Industries Large Berth Pier	4262	5–14	27 berths
Sumitomo Metal Industries Floating Signpost		12	2 berths
Sumitomo Metal Industries Dolphin		12	2 berths
Sumitomo Metal Industries Small Berth	395	3.5	
Wakayama Main Port Area			
International Container Terminal	260	13	Max 40 000 dwt
Aogishi No's 1 & 2 Wharf	180	4.5	3 berths
Aogishi No.3 Wharf	180	5.5	2 berths
Chikko No.1 Wharf	201	4.5	2 berths
Chikko No.2 Wharf	119	4.5	2 berths
Chikko No.3 Wharf	100	4.5	2 berths
Nakahuto No.1 Wharf	185	10	
Nakahuto No.2 Wharf	185	10	
Nakahuto No.3 Wharf	185	10	
Nakahuto No.4 Wharf	185	10	
Nakahuto No.5 Wharf	180	4.5	3 berths
Yakusyuhata Pier	45	7	
Nishihama No.1 Wharf	120	4.5	2 berths
Nishihama No.3 Wharf	240	12	
Nishihama No.4 Wharf	90	5.5	
Nishihama No.5 Wharf	260	13	
Nishihama No.6 Wharf	300	5.5	
Saikazaki No.1 Wharf	130	7.5	
Saikazaki No's 2 & 3 Wharf	200	5.5	2 berths
Sumitomo Cement Pier	71	6.1	
Nankai Chemistry Pier	32	3	
Nankai Ferry Pier	178	5.5	2 berths
Wakaura, Kainan Port Area			
Hikata Wharf	180	5.5	2 berths
Kansai Electric Power Dolphin	118	7	2 berths
Kainan Steel Pipe Pier	601	6–12	4 berths
Ken-Nokyo-Ren Pier	52	5.5	
Tokuyama Cement Pier	11	7.5	
Wakayama Oil Refinery (Large Pier)	263	7.5–13	4 berths
Wakayama Oil Refinery (Small Pier)	60	3.5	5 berths
Shimotsu Port Area			
Shimotsu Pier	120	4.5	2 berths

Name	Length (m)	Depth (m)	Remarks
Cosmo Petrotech Large Pier	460	4.5–11.6	4 berths
Cosmo Petrotech Spherical Mooring Buoy		11.6	
Wakayama Oil Plant Osaki Sea Berth	460	24	
Wakayama Oil Plant Osaki Cargo Handling Pier	42	7.8	
Osaka Cement Pier	68	8	
Tonen Large Pier	334	4.5–14	10 berths
Tonen Small Pier	25	4	2 berths
Arida Port Area			
Hatsushima Wharf	90	5.5	
Arida 5.5 m Wharf	100	5.5	
Tonen No.0-1 Pier	511	20.4	

Cargo Worked: 82 000 t of foreign trade and 70 000 t of domestic trade per working day

Bunkering: If bunkering is carried out at Shimotsu anchorage, a watching boat and oil fence will be required by harbour regulations
Cosmo Oil Co. Ltd, Toshiba Building, 1-1 Shibaura 1-chome, Minato-ku, Tokyo 105-8528, Japan, *Tel:* +81 3 3798 3156, *Fax:* +81 3 3798 3592, *Email:* masayuki_iijima@cosmo-oil.co.jp, *Website:* www.cosmo-oil.co.jp
ExxonMobil Marine Fuels, 1 Harbour Front Place, 06-00 Harbour Front, Tower One, Singapore, Republic of Singapore 098633, *Tel:* +65 6885 8998, *Fax:* +65 6885 8794, *Email:* asiapac.marinefuels@exxonmobil.com, *Website:* www.exxonmobilmarinefuels.com
Hanwa Co. Ltd, 2nd Floor, Finland House, 56 Haymarket, London SW1Y 4RN, United Kingdom, *Tel:* +44 20 7839 4448, *Fax:* +44 20 7839 3994, *Email:* orito@hanwa.co.uk
Idemitsu Kosan Co. Ltd, 1-1 Marunochi, 3-Chome, Chiyoda-ku, Tokyo 100-8321, Japan, *Tel:* +81 3 3213 3138, *Fax:* +81 3 3213 1145, *Email:* tohru.takamura@si.idemitsu.co.jp, *Website:* www.idemitsu.co.jp
KG Int Petroleum Ltd, Shiba Park Building, 241 Shiba Koen, Minato-ku, Tokyo 105, Japan, *Tel:* +81 3 3578 4551, *Fax:* +81 3 3578 4550
Japan Energy Corp., 2-10-1, Toranomon, Minato-ku, Tokyo 105-8407, Japan, *Tel:* +81 3 5573 6100, *Fax:* +81 3 5573 6674, *Email:* yamano@j-energy.co.jp, *Website:* www.j-energy.co.jp
Kawasho Corp., World Trade Centre, 4-1 Hanamatsu-cho 2-chome, Minato-ku, Tokyo 105, Japan, *Tel:* +81 3 3435 3251
Kyodo Oil Co. Ltd, 11-2 Nagata-cho 2-chome, Chiyoda-ku, Tokyo, Japan, *Tel:* +81 3 3505 8241, *Fax:* +81 3 3505 8697
Marubeni Petroleum Co. Ltd, Marubeni International Petroleum Singapore Co. Ltd, c/o Marubeni Corporation, 4-2 Ohtemachi 1-chome, Chiyoda-ku, Tokyo 100-8088, Japan, *Tel:* +81 3 3282 3920, *Fax:* +81 3 3282 3950, *Email:* TOKB554@marubenicorp.com, *Website:* www.marubeni.co.jp
MC Marine and Bunkering Inc., 8th Floor, Uchisaiwai-cho Dai Building, 3-3 Uchisaiwai-cho 1-chome, Chiyoda-ku, Tokyo 100-0011, Japan, *Tel:* +81 3 5251 2575, *Fax:* +81 3 5251 2583
Mitsui & Co. Petroleum Ltd, 2-1, Ohtemachi 1-chome, Chiyoda-ku, Tokyo 100-0004, Japan, *Tel:* +81 3 3285 6905, *Fax:* +81 3 3285 9811, *Email:* tkzph@dg.mitsui.com, *Website:* www.mitsui.co.jp
Nissho Iwai Corp., 4-4 Akasaka 2-chome, Minato-ku, Tokyo, Japan, *Tel:* +81 3 35882111
Nittetsu Shoji Co. Ltd, 5-7 Kameido 1-chome, Koto-ku, Tokyo 136, Japan, *Tel:* +81 3 5627 2157, *Fax:* +81 3 5627 2192
Sumitomo Corp., Harumi Island, Triton Square, Office Tower Y, 8-11 Harumi 1-chome, Chuo-ku, Tokyo 104-8610, Japan, *Tel:* +81 3 51664458, *Fax:* +81 3 51666407, *Email:* ir@sumitomo.co.jp, *Website:* www.sumitomocorp.co.jp

Towage: Nine tugs available; one of 3900 hp, one of 3300 hp, five of 3200 hp, one of 2900 hp and one of 1200 hp

Repair & Maintenance: Drydock facilities available at Yura, 350 m x 65 m x 14.3 m for vessels of 330 000 max dwt
Mitsui (Wakayama) Engineering & Shipbuilding Co. Ltd, 21-3 Higashinocho, Saikayamachi, Wakayama, Wakayama Pref., Japan, *Tel:* +81 73 424 0031, *Fax:* +81 73 436 3961, *Website:* www.mes.co.jp

Medical Facilities: Available

Airport: Osaka International, 70 km

Lloyd's Agent: Cornes & Co. Ltd, Meikai Building, 32 Akashi-machi, Chuo-ku, Kobe 650-0037, Hyogo Pref., Japan, *Tel:* +81 78 332 3421, *Fax:* +81 78 332 3070, *Email:* survey@kobe.cornes.co.jp, *Website:* www.cornes.co.jp

WAKKANAI

Lat 45° 25' N; Long 141° 42' E.

Admiralty Chart: 1809	**Admiralty Pilot:** 41
Time Zone: GMT +9 h	**UNCTAD Locode:** JP WKJ

Principal Facilities:

P		Y	G		R		B		T		A

Authority: Municipality of Wakkanai, 13-15 Chuo 3-chome, Wakkanai 097-8686, Hokkaido, Japan, *Tel:* +81 162 236161, *Fax:* +81 162 233350, *Email:* saharin@city.wakkanai.hokkaido.jp, *Website:* www.city.wakkanai.hokkaido.jp

Port Security: ISPS compliant

Approach: Channel depth is approx 10 m

Anchorage: Quarantine anchorage in depth of 10-13 m

Pilotage: Pilots are available from Rumoi

Radio Frequency: Coast Guard, VHF Channel 16

Weather: Winds in summer are SW-SSW and in winter are NNW-W

Tides: High +0.37 m. Low -0.04 m

Traffic: 2000, 15 015 vessels, 2 802 049 t of cargo handled

Principal Imports and Exports: Imports: Industrial hardware products, Marine products. Exports: Industrial hardware products, Miscellaneous industrial products.

Working Hours: Available 24 h/day

Accommodation:

Name	Length (m)	Depth (m)	Remarks
Kita Area			
Kita Wharf			
Ferry 1	153	6	
Ferry 2	256	5	
Ferry 3	256	5	
Chuo Wharf			Consists of 7 berths
Chuo Kita 1	260	7.5	
Chuo Kita 2	260	7.5	
Chuo Kita 3	90	5.5	
Chuo Minami 1	275	5.5	
Chuo Minami 2	275	5.5	
Chuo Higashi	170	7.5	
Minato Area			
Hokuyo Wharf			
Hokuyo Minami 1	210	8	
Hokuyo Minami 2	300	6	
Hokuyo Kita	460	6	
Hokuyo Kairyo	753	6	
First Basin			
1st Basin	990	5	
Second Basin			
2nd Basin	420	5	
Suehiro Area			
Suehiro Wharf			
Suehiro Higashi	240	12	
Suehiro Nishi 1	260	5	
Suehiro Nishi 2	260	5	
Tempoku Area			
Tempoku 1st Wharf			Consists of 4 berths
Tempoku 1st Nishi	185	10	
Tempoku 1st Kita	185	10	
Tempoku 1st Higashi 1	260	7.5	
Tempoku 1st Higashi 2	260	7.5	
Tempoku 2nd Wharf			Consists of 4 berths
Tempoku 2nd Nishi 1	260	7.5	
Tempoku 2nd Nishi 2	260	7.5	
Tempoku 2nd Higashi 1	180	5.5	
Tempoku 2nd Higashi 2	180	5.5	

Bunkering: Domestic and bonded oil available

Waste Reception Facilities: Available

Towage: One tug available of 3000 hp

Repair & Maintenance: Wakkanai Kowan Co. Ltd, 2-1, Kaiun 2-chome, Wakkanai 097-0023, Hokkaido, Japan, *Tel:* +81 162 232365, *Fax:* +81 162 221212, *Email:* kouwan@d2.dion.ne.jp

Stevedoring Companies: Nippon Express Co Ltd, Wakkanai, Hokkaido, Japan, *Tel:* +81 162 232651, *Fax:* +81 162 232666, *Email:* nexcowak@rose.ocn.ne.jp
Wakkanai Kaiun Co Ltd, Wakkanai, Hokkaido, Japan, *Tel:* +81 162 237317, *Fax:* +81 162 234393

Medical Facilities: Wakkanai Municipality Hospital (440 beds and 50 doctors) is well equipped for medical requirements

Airport: Wakkanai Airport, 4 km

Railway: Wakkanai Station, 500 m. Minami-Wakkanai (south) Station, 800 m

Lloyd's Agent: Cornes & Co. Ltd, 273 Yamashita-cho, Naka-ku, Yokohama 231-0023, Kanagawa Pref., Japan, *Tel:* +81 45 201 8537, *Fax:* +81 45 212 3105, *Email:* survey@ykh.cornes.co.jp, *Website:* www.cornes.co.jp

YATSUSHIRO

Lat 32° 31' N; Long 130° 32' E.

Admiralty Chart: JP213	**Admiralty Pilot:** 42A
Time Zone: GMT +9 h	**UNCTAD Locode:** JP YAT

Key to Principal Facilities:—

A=Airport	C=Containers	G=General Cargo	P=Petroleum	R=Ro/Ro	Y=Dry Bulk
B=Bunkers	D=Dry Dock	L=Cruise	Q=Other Liquid Bulk	T=Towage (where available from port)	

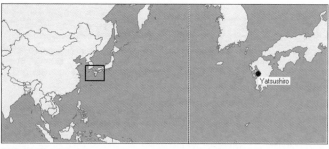

Principal Facilities:

P	Q	Y	G	C		B		T	A

Authority: Port & Harbour Section of Kumamoto Prefecture, 6-18-1 Suizenji, Kumamoto-shi, Kumamoto 862-8570, Kumamoto Pref., Japan, *Tel:* +81 96 383 1111, *Fax:* +81 96 387 2461, *Website:* www.pref.kumamoto.jp

Port Security: ISPS compliant

Approach: 9.5 m d in channel up to Amakusa sea bridge which has a 34 m air draught

Pilotage: Not compulsory. Bay pilots available 1 mile S of Toshima Lighthouse in pos 32° 11' N; 130° 05' E from 0600-2200. Harbour pilots available at the S side of the Otsukishima quarantine anchorage in pos 32° 28' N; 130° 29' E from sunrise to sunset

Radio Frequency: VHF Channel 16

Tides: Tidal range 4.83 m

Working Hours: 0830-1700. 1st and 3rd Sundays unavailable

Accommodation:

Name	Length (m)	Depth (m)	Draught (m)	Remarks
Yatsushiro				
Gaiko Wharf No.11	130	7.5	7.3	1 x 5000 dwt
Gaiko Wharf No.12	130	7.5	7.3	1 x 5000 dwt
Gaiko Wharf No.13	165	9	8.8	1 x 10 000 dwt
Gaiko Wharf No.14	185	10	9.5	1 x 15 000 dwt
Gaiko Wharf No.15	185	10	9.5	1 x 15 000 dwt
Gaiko Wharf No.16	185	10	9.5	1 x 15 000 dwt
Gaiko Wharf No.17	185	10	9.5	1 x 15 000 dwt
Naiko Wharf No's 1-8	720	5.5	5.3	8 x 2000 dwt

Storage: Mobile cranes available

Mechanical Handling Equipment:

Location	Type	Capacity (t)	Qty
Yatsushiro	Floating Cranes	90	1

Bunkering: Domestic oil available. Bonded oil is brought from Nagasaki when required

Towage: One tug of 500 hp is available. Tugs of larger cap can be brought from Misumi or Nagasaki if required

Repair & Maintenance: Small repairs undertaken at offshore facilities

Medical Facilities: Minor facilities available

Airport: Kumamoto, 60 km

Lloyd's Agent: Cornes & Co. Ltd, Meikai Building, 32 Akashi-machi, Chuo-ku, Kobe 650-0037, Hyogo Pref., Japan, *Tel:* +81 78 332 3421, *Fax:* +81 78 332 3070, *Email:* survey@kobe.cornes.co.jp, *Website:* www.cornes.co.jp

YAWATA

Lat 33° 52' N; Long 130° 48' E.

Admiralty Chart: JP1263

Admiralty Pilot: 42B

Time Zone: GMT +9 h

UNCTAD Locode: JP YWT

Principal Facilities:

	Y	G		B		T	A

Authority: Kitakyushu Port & Harbor Bureau, 1-1 Jonai, Kitakyushu 803-8501, Fukuoka Pref., Japan, *Tel:* +81 93 321 5941, *Fax:* +81 93 582 1037, *Email:* kqport@kitaqport.or.jp, *Website:* www.kitaqport.or.jp

Officials: Director General: Kenichi Katayama.
Marketing Director: Hiroyuki Tagami, *Email:* hiroyuki_tagami01@city.kitakyushu.lg.jp.
Sales Director: Tetsuji Hashimoto.

Port Security: ISPS compliant

Approach: Entry into and departure from Yawata permitted only from sunrise and vessels must be berthed by sunset. The port is completely sheltered from the open sea. Due to the narrowness of the channel, leading to Yawata and the shallow water at the entrance to the channel, draught limitation is 8.5 m. The fairway leading into main harbour is about 200 m wide and 3.2 km long, running parallel to a breakwater and the reclaimed land. One way traffic observed by vessels. Vessels wait outside channel on reception of 'Not Clear' signal from shore, (Wakamatsu fairway). Tobata fairway is 400 to 500 m wide and 17 m deep. Anze fairway is 350 m wide and 13 m deep. A lockless dock for vessels carrying materials and products to and from the Yawata Steel Mills of Nippon Steel Corporation, on whose premises it is situated, and is linked with the Wakamatsu by a narrow fairway approx 0.5 km long. Draught limitation in Yawata Channel is 8.5 m

Pilotage: Compulsory for vessels over 3000 gt and vessels with hazardous materials over 300 gt. Harbour pilots and Inland Sea pilots are available at the pilot stations or quarantine anchorage

Tides: Tidal range 3.14 m

Traffic: 2006, 109 723 953 t of cargo handled, 469 000 TEU's (includes ports of Kokura, Moji, Tobata & Wakamatsu)

Principal Imports and Exports: Imports: Salt. Exports: Chemical products, Steel products.

Working Hours: 24 h/day

Accommodation:

Name	Length (m)	Draught (m)
Yawata		
Wharf No's 15, 16, 17 & 18	670	8.5
Wharf No.20	185	8.5
Nishiyawata Wharf No.2 O.B.1	120	8.5
Nishiyawata Wharf No.2 O.B.2	220	8.5

Mechanical Handling Equipment:

Location	Type	Capacity (t)	Qty
Wharf No's 15, 16, 17 & 18	Mult-purp. Cranes	30	7
Wharf No.20	Mult-purp. Cranes	20	1
Wharf No.20	Mult-purp. Cranes	12	1
Nishiyawata Wharf No.2 O.B.2	Mult-purp. Cranes	45	1

Bunkering: Domestic oil available. Bonded oil can be brought from Moji, Ube or Oita with advance notice

Towage: Two tugs of 3200 hp are available

Repair & Maintenance: Minor repairs only

Airport: Kitakyushu Airport

Lloyd's Agent: Cornes & Co. Ltd, Meikai Building, 32 Akashi-machi, Chuo-ku, Kobe 650-0037, Hyogo Pref., Japan, *Tel:* +81 78 332 3421, *Fax:* +81 78 332 3070, *Email:* survey@kobe.cornes.co.jp, *Website:* www.cornes.co.jp

YOKKAICHI

Lat 34° 57' N; Long 136° 38' E.

Admiralty Chart: JP94/JP95/JP1055A/JP...

Admiralty Pilot: 42A

Time Zone: GMT +9 h

UNCTAD Locode: JP YKK

Principal Facilities:

P	Q	Y	G	C	R		B		T	A

Authority: Yokkaichi Port Authority, 1-1 Kasumi 2-chome, Yokkaichi 510-0011, Mie Pref., Japan, *Tel:* +81 593 667006, *Fax:* +81 593 667048, *Email:* shinko@yokkaichi-port.or.jp, *Website:* www.yokkaichi-port.or.jp

Officials: Executive Vice President: Kiyoshi Sato, *Email:* sato-k@yokkaichi-port.or.jp.
Harbour Master: Katsuyoshi Suzuki, *Tel:* +81 593 570118.

Port Security: ISPS compliant

Approach: Passage No.1 is 1860 m long, 300 m wide with 12 m depth
Passage No.2 is 1200 m long, 400 m wide with 14 m depth
Passage No.3 is 1870 m long, 430-580 m wide with 12-14 m depth
Umaokoshi Passage is 1280 m long, 200-615 m wide with 12 m depth

Anchorage: Inside Anchorage: situated inside the Kasumigaura breakwater, the East breakwater of Yokkaichi Port and the Asahi breakwater
Outside Anchorage: situated outside the Kasumigaura breakwater, the East breakwater of Yokkaichi Port and the Asahi breakwater

Pilotage: Irago-Mikawa and harbour pilotage compulsory for vessels exceeding 10 000 gt. Harbour pilots available at quarantine anchorage from Isewan Pilot Association, Tel: +81 593 626818. Pilots for Irago Suido access channel available from Irago-Mikawa Pilot Association, Tel: +81 569 217487

Radio Frequency: Yokkaichi Port Radio, 24 h service, calling on VHF Channel 16, working on Channel 11

Weather: Typhoon season, July to October

Tides: Max tidal range 5.02 m, average range 2.36 m, nil at MLWL, 1.3 m MSL

Traffic: 2006, 60 688 719 t of cargo handled, 160 055 TEU's

Principal Imports and Exports: Imports: Coal, Containerized cargo, Crude oil, LNG, LPG. Exports: Automobiles, Chemical products, Chemicals, Containerized cargo, Crude oil, Petroleum products.

Working Hours: 0830-1630, 1630-2130. Sundays and holidays subject to negotiation, except 1st Sunday in the month

Accommodation: The port is protected by four breakwaters:
Asahi Breakwater 520 m long
East Breakwater 2450 m long
Old Port Breakwater 77 m long
Kasumigaura Breakwater 1085 m long

Name	Length (m)	Depth (m)	Remarks
Public Wharves			
Pier No.1 (W1)	161	8.1	Max 1 x 8000 dwt
Pier No.1 (W2 & 3)	245	8.5	Max 1 x 10 000 dwt
Pier No.1 (W4 & 5)	215	9	Max 1 x 10 000 dwt
Pier No's 1 & 2 (W6)	179	3	Max 3 x 300 dwt
Coal Berth (W7)	125	7.5	Max 1 x 5000 dwt
Pier No.2 (W8)	190	10	Max 1 x 15 000 dwt
Pier No.2 (W9)	200	10	Max 1 x 15 000 dwt
Pier No.2 (W10)	200	5.5	Max 2 x 2000 dwt
Pier No.2 (W11)	200	10	Max 1 x 15 000 dwt
Pier No.2 (W12)	140	5	Max 2 x 1000 dwt
Pier No.2 (W19)	110	5	Max 1 x 1000 dwt
Pier No.3 (W13)	245	12	Max 1 x 30 000 dwt
Pier No.3 (W14)	220	10	Max 1 x 15 000 dwt
Pier No.3 (W15)	220	10	Max 1 x 15 000 dwt
Pier No.3 (W16)	114	7.5	Max 1 x 5000 dwt
Pier No.3 (W17 & 18)	163	5.5	Max 2 x 2000 dwt
Kasumigaura South Pier (W22)	280	14	Max 1 x 60 000 dwt
Kasumigaura South Pier (W23)	240	12	Max 1 x 40 000 dwt
Kasumigaura South Pier (W24)	240	12	Max 1 x 40 000 dwt
Kasumigaura South Pier (W25)	240	12	Max 1 x 40 000 dwt
Kasumigaura South Pier (W26)	300	13.2	See [1] below
Kasumigaura South Pier (W27)	240	12	Max 1 x 25 000 dwt
Kasumigaura South Pier (W30-36)	420	4.5	Max 7 x 700 dwt
Kasumigaura South Pier (W37-44)	630	5.5	Max 7 x 2000 dwt
Kasumigaura South Pier (W60-62)	390	7.5	Max 3 x 5000 dwt
Kasumigaura South Pier (W70-73)	300	4.5	Max 4 x 700 dwt
Kasumigaura South Pier (W74)	130	7.5	Max 1 x 5000 dwt
Kasumigaura South Pier (W75)	130	7.5	Max 1 x 5000 dwt
Kasumigaura North Pier (W80)	330	14	See [2] below
Fuso Pier (W1 & 2)	123	5	Max 2 x 750 dwt
Fuso Pier (W3)	85	6	Max 1 x 1500 dwt
Fuso Pier (W4)	125	7.5	Max 1 x 5000 dwt
Fuso Pier (W5)	125	7.5	Max 1 x 5000 dwt
Fuso Pier (W6)	170	7.5	Max 1 x 5000 dwt
Private Wharves			
Cosmo Oil Co Ltd Shiohama Berth No.1 (D1)		5.5	Max 1 x 1300 dwt
Cosmo Oil Co Ltd Shiohama Berth No.2 (D2)		5.5	Max 1 x 1500 dwt
Cosmo Oil Co Ltd Shiohama Berth No.3 (D3)		6.5	Max 1 x 3000 dwt
Cosmo Oil Co Ltd Shiohama Berth No.5 (D5)		5.5	Max 1 x 2000 dwt
Cosmo Oil Co Ltd Shiohama Berth No.6 (D6)		5.4	Max 1 x 1916 dwt
Cosmo Oil Co Ltd Shiohama Berth No.7 (D7)		6.5	Max 1 x 3000 dwt
Cosmo Oil Co Ltd Shiohama Berth No.8 (D8)		12	Max 1 x 65 000 dwt
Umaokoshi Berth No.1 (U1)		12	Max 1 x 90 000 dwt
Umaokoshi Berth No.2 (U2)		6.5	Max 1 x 1300 dwt
Umaokoshi Berth No.3 (U3)		4.5	Max 1 x 500 dwt

Name	Length (m)	Depth (m)	Remarks
Umaokoshi Berth No.5 (U5)	5.5		Max 1 x 2000 dwt
Umaokoshi Berth No.6 (U6)	6.5		Max 1 x 4000 dwt
Umaokoshi Berth No.7 (U7)	8		Max 1 x 2000 dwt
Umaokoshi Berth No.8 (U8)	8		Max 1 x 6500 dwt
Umaokoshi Berth No.9 (U9)	12		Max 1 x 60 000 dwt
Yokkaichi Berth No.1 (T1)	3		
Yokkaichi Berth No.2 (T2)	5		Max 1 x 1500 dwt
Yokkaichi Berth No.3 (T3)	5		Max 1 x 2000 dwt
Yokkaichi Berth No.5 (T5)	7		Max 1 x 1000 dwt
Yokkaichi Berth No.6 (T6)	7		Max 1 x 2500 dwt
Yokkaichi Berth No.7 (T7)	2.5		Max 1 x 200 dwt
Yokkaichi Berth No.8 (T8)	7		Max 1 x 4000 dwt
Yokkaichi Berth No.9 (T9)	7		Max 1 x 4000 dwt
Showa Yokkaichi Sekiyu Co Ltd Berth A	5		Max 2 x 1000 dwt
Showa Yokkaichi Sekiyu Co Ltd Berth B	5		Max 4 x 1200 dwt
Showa Yokkaichi Sekiyu Co Ltd Berth C	4		Max 6 x 600 dwt
Showa Yokkaichi Sekiyu Co Ltd Berth D	12		Max 1 x 45 000 dwt
Showa Yokkaichi Sekiyu Co Ltd Berth E	12		Max 1 x 45 000 dwt
Showa Yokkaichi Sekiyu Co Ltd Berth F	8		Max 1 x 6000 dwt
Showa Yokkaichi Sekiyu Co Ltd Berth G	8		Max 1 x 6000 dwt
Showa Yokkaichi Sekiyu Co Ltd Berth H	8		Max 1 x 2500 dwt
Showa Yokkaichi Sekiyu Co Ltd Berth I	8		Max 1 x 4000 dwt
Showa Yokkaichi Sekiyu Co Ltd Berth J	6		Max 1 x 1500 dwt
Nihon Fiat Glass Co Ltd Berth No.1 (C1)	7		Max 1 x 2000 dwt
Kasumi No.1 Berth (K1)	4.5		Max 1 x 1000 dwt
Kasumi No.3 Berth (K3)	4.5		Max 1 x 1000 dwt
Kasumi No.4 Berth (K4)	7		Max 1 x 2900 dwt
Kasumi No.5 Berth (K5)	5.5		Max 1 x 2000 dwt
Kasumi No.6 Berth (K6)	5		Max 1 x 1200 dwt
Kasumi No.9 Berth (K9)	14		Max 1 x 67 000 dwt
Kasumi No.10 Berth (K10)	8		Max 1 x 6000 dwt
Kasumi No.11 Berth (K11)	8		Max 1 x 6000 dwt
Kasumi No.15 Berth (K15)	7.5		Max 1 x 5000 dwt
Kasumi No.16 Berth (K16)	7.5		Max 1 x 5000 dwt
Kasumi No.17 Berth (K17)	7.5		Max 1 x 5000 dwt
Mitsubishi Chemical Co Ltd Berth No.1 (M1)	6		Max 1 x 5000 dwt
Mitsubishi Chemical Co Ltd Berth No.2 (M2)	6		Max 1 x 3000 dwt
Mitsubishi Chemical Co Ltd Berth No.3 (M3)	6.5		Max 1 x 3000 dwt
Mitsubishi Chemical Co Ltd Mita Berth (MY)	6.5		Max 1 x 3000 dwt
Yokkaichi Power Station Berth No.2	5		Max 1 x 300 dwt
Kawagoe Thermal Power Station LNG Berth (E1)	14		Max 1 x 72 000 dwt
Kawagoe Thermal Power Station Berth No.1	4.5		Max 1 x 1500 dwt
Ishihara Sangyo Kaisha Ltd Berth No.1 (I1)	6.5		Max 1 x 3350 dwt
Ishihara Sangyo Kaisha Ltd Berth No.2 (I2)	8		Max 1 x 2000 dwt
Ishihara Sangyo Kaisha Ltd Berth No.3 (I3)	5		Max 1 x 1000 dwt
Ishihara Sangyo Kaisha Ltd Heavy Oil Berth	4.5		Max 1 x 700 dwt
Taibeiyo Cement Co Ltd Berth A (C2)	9		Max 1 x 13 000 dwt
Taibeiyo Cement Co Ltd Berth B (C3)	5		Max 1 x 3000 dwt
Taniguchi Sekiyo Co Ltd Berth A-1 (A1)	5.5		Max 1 x 2000 dwt
Taniguchi Sekiyo Co Ltd Berth A-2 (A2)	7.5		Max 1 x 5000 dwt
Yokkaichi Sewage Disposal Pier	3.5		Max 1 x 200 gt
Shoun Yokkaichi Sekiyo Co Ltd Sea Berth (Inner)	18		Max 1 x 170 000 dwt
Shoun Yokkaichi Sekiyo Co Ltd Sea Berth (Outer)	22		Max 1 x 315 000 dwt
Cosmo Oil Co Ltd Sea Berth	20.8		Max 1 x 314 000 dwt

[1]*Kasumigaura South Pier (W26):* Max 1 x 30 000 dwt. Container terminal operated by Yokkaichi Container Terminal Co Ltd., Tel: +81 593 662455, Fax: +81 593 662458
[2]*Kasumigaura North Pier (W80):* Max 1 x 50 000 dwt. Container terminal operated by Yokkaichi Container Terminal Co Ltd., Tel: +81 593 662455, Fax: +81 593 662458

Storage: Thirty one cargo sorting areas totaling 467 015 378 m2, nine open storage areas totaling 83 445 166 m2 and one storage yard for coal of 108 527 460 m2

Key to Principal Facilities:—

A=Airport	**C**=Containers	**G**=General Cargo	**P**=Petroleum	**R**=Ro/Ro	**Y**=Dry Bulk
B=Bunkers	**D**=Dry Dock	**L**=Cruise	**Q**=Other Liquid Quay	**T**=Towage (where available from port)

Mechanical Handling Equipment: Five container cranes, one continuous mechanical unloader, two bucket elevator unloaders and one traveling shuttle shiploader

Bunkering: Cosmo Oil Co. Ltd, Toshiba Building, 1-1 Shibaura 1-chome, Minato-ku, Tokyo 105-8528, Japan, *Tel:* +81 3 3798 3156, *Fax:* +81 3 3798 3592, *Email:* masayuki_iijima@cosmo-oil.co.jp, *Website:* www.cosmo-oil.co.jp

Hanwa Co. Ltd, 2nd Floor, Finland House, 56 Haymarket, London SW1Y 4RN, United Kingdom, *Tel:* +44 20 7839 4448, *Fax:* +44 20 7839 3994, *Email:* orito@hanwa.co.uk

Hikawa Shoji Kaisha Ltd, 26-2 Shinkawa NS Building 1-chome, Shinkawa, Chuo-ku, Tokyo 104, Japan, *Tel:* +81 3 5776 6858, *Fax:* +81 3 5541 3274

Idemitsu Kosan Co. Ltd, 1-1 Marunochi, 3-Chome, Chiyoda-ku, Tokyo 100-8321, Japan, *Tel:* +81 3 3213 3138, *Fax:* +81 3 3213 1145, *Email:* tohru.takamura@si.idemitsu.co.jp, *Website:* www.idemitsu.co.jp

KG Int Petroleum Ltd, Shiba Park Building, 241 Shiba Koen, Minato-ku, Tokyo 105, Japan, *Tel:* +81 3 3578 4551, *Fax:* +81 3 3578 4550

Japan Energy Corp., 2-10-1, Toranomon, Minato-ku, Tokyo 105-8407, Japan, *Tel:* +81 3 5573 6100, *Fax:* +81 3 5573 6674, *Email:* yamano@j-energy.co.jp, *Website:* www.j-energy.co.jp

Kamei Corp., 1-6-1 Otemachi, Chiyoda-ku, Tokyo 100-0004, Japan, *Tel:* +81 3 3286 6234, *Fax:* +81 3 3286 6249, *Email:* bunker@kamei.co.jp

Kawasho Corp., World Trade Centre, 4-1 Hanamatsu-cho 2-chome, Minato-ku, Tokyo 105, Japan, *Tel:* +81 3 3435 3251

Kyodo Oil Co. Ltd, 11-2 Nagata-cho 2-chome, Chiyoda-ku, Tokyo, Japan, *Tel:* +81 3 3505 8241, *Fax:* +81 3 3505 8697

Marubeni Petroleum Co. Ltd, Marubeni International Petroleum Singapore Co. Ltd, c/o Marubeni Corporation, 4-2 Ohtemachi 1-chome, Chiyoda-ku, Tokyo 100-8088, Japan, *Tel:* +81 3 3282 3920, *Fax:* +81 3 3282 3950, *Email:* TOKB554@marubenicorp.com, *Website:* www.marubeni.co.jp

MC Marine and Bunkering Inc., 8th Floor, Uchisaiwai-cho Dai Building, 3-3 Uchisaiwai-cho 1-chome, Chiyoda-ku, Tokyo 100-0011, Japan, *Tel:* +81 3 5251 2575, *Fax:* +81 3 5251 2583

Mitsui & Co. Petroleum Ltd, 2-1, Ohtemachi 1-chome, Chiyoda-ku, Tokyo 100-0004, Japan, *Tel:* +81 3 3285 6905, *Fax:* +81 3 3285 9811, *Email:* tkzph@dg.mitsui.com, *Website:* www.mitsui.co.jp

Nissho Iwai Corp., 4-4 Akasaka 2-chome, Minato-ku, Tokyo, Japan, *Tel:* +81 3 35882111

Nittetsu Shoij Co. Ltd, 5-7 Kameido 1-chome, Koto-ku, Tokyo 136, Japan, *Tel:* +81 3 5627 2157, *Fax:* +81 3 5627 2192

Shinagawa Fuel Co. Ltd, New Pier Takeshiba North Tower, 8th Floor, 1-11-1 Kaigan, Minato-ku, Tokyo 105-8525, Japan, *Tel:* +81 3 5470 7113, *Fax:* +81 3 5470 7157, *Email:* hakuyu@ml1.sinanen.co.jp

Sigma Foreign Service (Panama) S.A., 2-25 Aikawai, Tempaku-ku, Nagoya 468-0836, Aichi Pref., Japan, *Tel:* +81 52 896 1510, *Fax:* +81 52 896 7703

Sumitomo Corp., Harumi Island, Triton Square, Office Tower Y, 8-11 Harumi 1-chome, Chuo-ku, Tokyo 104-8610, Japan, *Tel:* +81 3 51664458, *Fax:* +81 3 51666407, *Email:* ir@sumitomo.co.jp, *Website:* www.sumitomocorp.co.jp

Towage: 24 harbour tugs of 1900-3600 hp available

Shipping Agents: Aisan Shosen Kaisha Ltd, 37 Chitose-cho, Yokkaichi 510-0051, Mie Pref., Japan, *Tel:* +81 593 534556, *Fax:* +81 593 510290, *Email:* shigeo.kondo@mail.mol.co.jp

Medical Facilities: Available

Airport: Komaki, Nagoya, 70 km

Lloyd's Agent: Cornes & Co. Ltd, Meikai Building, 32 Akashi-machi, Chuo-ku, Kobe 650-0037, Hyogo Pref., Japan, *Tel:* +81 78 332 3421, *Fax:* +81 78 332 3070, *Email:* survey@kobe.cornes.co.jp, *Website:* www.cornes.co.jp

YOKOHAMA

Lat 35° 26' N; Long 139° 39' E.

Admiralty Chart: JP1085	**Admiralty Pilot:** 42A
Time Zone: GMT +9 h	**UNCTAD Locode:** JP YOK

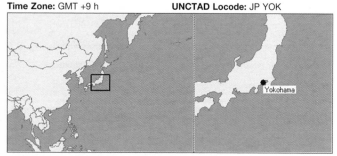

Principal Facilities:

P Q Y G C R L B D T A

Authority: Port & Harbour Bureau of Yokohama City, Sangyo Boeki Central Building, 2 Yamashita-cho, Naka-ku, Yokohama 231-0023, Kanagawa Pref., Japan, *Tel:* +81 45 671 7188, *Fax:* +81 45 671 7310, *Email:* portoubo@city.yokohama.jp, *Website:* www.city.yokohama.jp/me/port

Officials: Director General: Masatoshi Kawaguchi.
Harbour Master: Toshitaka Ishima.

Port Security: ISPS compliant. Container Security Initiative (CSI) designated port

Documentation: Declaration inward/outward of vessel, cargo manifest, application for crew members landing permit, passenger manifest, crew manifest, declaration of crews baggage, list of ships stores, maritime declaration of health

Approach: Draught limitation in the Yokohama Channel is 12-19 m and Tsurumi Channel is 12-16 m
Numerous groundings have occurred at the entrance to Tokyo Bay between Fort No.1 and Fort No.2 (Daiichi Kaiho & Daini Kaiho) where the water is shallow. Masters should obtain accurate fixes and keep the lead or echo-sounder going while

traversing this area. It is preferable to keep to channels close on either side of Fort No.3 (Daisan Kaiho) where water is deep

Anchorage: Good sheltered anchorage is available

Pilotage: Compulsory for all vessels of 3000 gt and over and for all LPG carriers, oil tankers or vessels carrying dangerous cargo of 300 gt and over. Pilotage is provided by Tokyo Wan District Pilot Association. Pilots board in the following positions:
Tsurumi Fairway in pos 35° 26.7' N; 139° 45.3' E
Yokohama Fairway in pos 35° 25.2' N; 139° 42.8' E
Yokohama Section 5 in pos 35° 22.2' N; 139° 41.8' E

Radio Frequency: Yokohama Port Radio on VHF Channels 16, 11, 18, 20 and 22

Weather: Winds SSW in summer, N in winter. Dense fog 30 to 50 days per year

Tides: Average HT 1.993 m, LT 0.097 m

Traffic: 2007, 43 157 vessels, 90 736 698 t of foreign cargo handled and 51 021 087 t of domestic cargo handled, 3 428 112 TEU's

Principal Imports and Exports: Imports: Clothes, Crude oil, Foodstuffs. Exports: Auto parts, Automobiles, Dyestuffs, Transportation machinery.

Working Hours: Mon-Fri: daytime 0830-1200, 1300-1730; night 1900-0000, 0100-0400
Saturday: 0830-1200

Accommodation: The port is open to the SE and sheltered by an outer breakwater with a total length of 2904 m. Port area covers 7315.9 ha with a waterfront area of 2828.7 ha comprising a Commercial Zone of 975.2 ha, an Industrial Zone of 1696.4 ha and others of 157.1 ha
Numerous buoys are located in the Yokohama district for vessels with lengths of between 90 m and 165 m, max draughts of 8.9 m to 11.0 m and tonnage of 5000-15 000 gt
Tanker facilities: See under Private Wharves, also:
Keihin Yokohama Sea Berth in pos 35° 27' 05" N; 139° 43' 09" E, for vessels of 200 000 dwt and 19.5 m draft
Oil tankers exceeding 100 000 dwt and LPG or LNG tankers exceeding 30 000 dwt are required to employ a fire-fighting tug when passing the Uraga Channel at the entrance to Tokyo

Name	Length (m)	Depth (m)	Remarks
Public Wharves			
Honmoku Pier			See [1] below
A-1	200	10	Max 15 000 dwt
A-2	200	10	Max 15 000 dwt
A-3	200	10	Max 15 000 dwt
B-1	200	10	Max 15 000 dwt
B-2	200	10	Max 15 000 dwt
B-3	200	10	Max 15 000 dwt
B-4	200	10	Max 15 000 dwt
BC-1	390	15	Max 60 000 dwt. Three container gantry cranes
Building Material Quay 1	185	10	Max 12 500 dwt
Building Material Quay 2	145	9	Max 5000 dwt
C-5	200	13	See [2] below
C-6	200	13	Max 15 000 dwt
C-7	200	13	Max 15 000 dwt
C-8	200	13	Max 15 000 dwt
C-9	200	13	Max 15 000 dwt
D-1	200	11	Max 15 000 dwt
D-2	200	11	Max 15 000 dwt
D-3	220	11	Max 15 000 dwt
Daikoku Pier			See [3] below
T-3	185	10	Max 15 000 dwt
T-4	185	10	Max 15 000 dwt
T-5	185	10	Max 15 000 dwt
T-6	185	10	Max 15 000 dwt
T-7	185	10	Max 15 000 dwt
T-8	185	10	Max 15 000 dwt
P-1	130	7.5	Max 5000 dwt
P-2	130	7.5	Max 5000 dwt
P-3	130	7.5	Max 5000 dwt
P-4	130	7.5	Max 5000 dwt
T-1	240	12	Max 30 000 dwt
T-2	240	12	Max 30 000 dwt
T-9	240	12	See [4] below
Yamashita Pier			See [5] below
Berth 1	180	10	Max 15 000 dwt
Berth 2	200	12	Max 20 000 dwt
Berth 3	220	12	Max 25 000 dwt
Berth 4	180	10	Max 15 000 dwt
Berth 5	180	10	Max 15 000 dwt
Berth 6	180	10	Max 15 000 dwt
Berth 7	180	10	Max 15 000 dwt
Berth 8	180	10	Max 15 000 dwt
Berth 9	180	10	Max 15 000 dwt
Berth 10	180	10	Max 15 000 dwt
Osanbashi Pier			See [6] below
Berth A	225	12	Max 30 000 gt
Berth B	225	12	Max 30 000 gt
Berth C	350	11	Max 30 000 gt
Berth D	100	10	Max 30 000 gt
Shinko Pier			See [7] below
Berth 2	159	9	Max 20 000 dwt
Berth 3	180	9	Max 25 000 dwt
Berth 5	202	8.4	Max 15 000 dwt
Berth 8	145	8.4	Max 15 000 dwt
Berth 9	201	10	Max 15 000 dwt
Yamanouchi Pier			See [8] below
Quay	130	7.5	Max 5000 dwt
Detamachi Pier			See [9] below
Berth A	135	7.5	Max 5000 dwt
Berth B	135	7.5	Max 5000 dwt

Name	Length (m)	Depth (m)	Remarks
Berth C	123	7.5	Max 5000 dwt
Berth D	123	7.5	Max 5000 dwt
Mizuho Pier	170	10	See [10] below
Small Tanker Pier	230	5	Fourteen berths for vessels up to 500 gt
Minato Mirai Pier	490	7.5	Five berths. Max 15 000 dwt
Kanazawa Timber Pier	187	10	See [11] below
Yokohama Port Development Public Corporation			
Honmoku Pier			Six berths
A-5	300	13	See [12] below
A-6	300	12	See [13] below
A-7	250	12	Max 25 000 dwt
A-8	250	12	See [14] below
D-4	300	14	See [15] below
D-5	300	15	See [16] below
Minami Honmoku Pier			Two berths
MC-1	350	16	See [17] below
MC-2	350	16	See [18] below
Daikoku Pier			See [19] below
C-1	300	12	Max 35 000 dwt
C-2	300	13	Max 35 000 dwt
C-3	350	15	See [20] below
C-4	350	15	See [21] below
L-1	200	10	Max 15 000 dwt. Shed area of 7956 m2
L-2	200	10	Max 15 000 dwt. Shed area of 5640 m2
L-3	200	10	Max 15 000 dwt. Shed area of 11 515 m2
L-4	200	10	Max 15 000 dwt. Shed area of 11 657 m2
L-5	200	10	Max 15 000 dwt. Shed area of 5651 m2
L-6	200	10	Max 15 000 dwt. Shed area of 5651 m2
L-7	200	10	Max 15 000 dwt. Shed area of 5440 m2
L-8	200	10	Max 15 000 dwt. Shed area of 5649 m2
Private Wharves			
Asahi Glass Co Ltd Pier	111	5.5	See [22] below
J-Oil Mills Co Ltd Pier	115	9.2	Max 1 x 10 000 dwt. Plant oil
Ube Misubishi Cement Ltd Pier B	122	7.1	Max 1 x 7000 dwt. Cement
Exxon Mobil Canal Berth	110	11	See [23] below
Taiheiyoseito Pier	100	9.5	Max 1 x 20 000 dwt. Sugar cane
JFE Steel Co Ltd Yokohama Pier	40	4.5	Max 1 x 700 dwt. Steel materials
Showa Sangyo Co Ltd Yokohama Pier	65	10	Max 1 x 5000 dwt. Grain
Showa Shell Sekiyu Co Ltd Kawasaki Refinery Ogishima West Pier	63	5.5	Max 1 x 1000 dwt. Petroleum products
Showa Shell Sekiyu Co Ltd Sakai Canal Pier	388	4	Max 7 x 1500 dwt. Petroleum products
Showa Shell Sekiyu Co Ltd Super Tanker Berth	343	12	Max 1 x 70 000 dwt. Crude oil
Showa Shell Sekiyu Co Ltd Pier	106	12	Max 1 x 33 000 dwt. Petroleum products
Sumitomo Osaka Cement Co Ltd Pier	95	8	Max 1 x 3000 dwt. Gravel & sand
Daikoku Warehouse Co Ltd Pier	104	6	Max 1 x 1100 dwt. Steel materials
Daito Trading Co Ltd Yokohama Oil Terminal No.1 Pier	92	7.6	Max 1 x 4000 dwt. Crude oil & petroleum products
Daito Trading Co Ltd Yokohama Oil Terminal No.2 Pier	28	6	Max 1 x 1970 dwt. Heavy oil
Daito Trading Co Ltd Yokohama Oil Terminal No.5 Pier	131	12.2	Max 1 x 95 000 dwt. Crude oil
Tokyo Gas Ogishima LNG Berth	410	14	Max 1 x 75 000 dwt. LNG & LPG
Tokyo Gas Co Ltd Tsurumi Pier	213	6.5	Max 1 x 2000 dwt. LNG & LPG
Tokyo Electric Power Co Inc Yokohama Terminal Power Station No.1 Berth	49	8.3	Max 1 x 3600 dwt. Crude oil
Toshiba Electric Co Ltd Pier	31	3	Max 1 x 4000 dwt. Electrical equipment
Naigai Yuso Pier No.1	41	4.5	Max 1 x 2000 dwt. Petroleum products
Nippon Vopak Co Ltd & Hashimoto Sangyo Co Ltd Pier	170	9	Max 1 x 20 000 dwt. Petroleum products & chemical
JFE Engineering Co Ltd Keihin Iron Works Suehiro South Pier	119	4.5	Max 3 x 1000 dwt. Steel materials & coke
JFE Steel Co Ltd Keihin Iron Works Ogishima Products Wharf A	250	10	Max 1 x 3000 dwt. Steel materials
JFE Steel Co Ltd Keihin Iron Works Ogishima Products Wharf B	266	10	Max 1 x 20 000 dwt. Steel materials
JFE Steel Co Ltd Keihin Iron Works Ogishima Products Wharf C	267	12.5	Max 1 x 30 000 dwt. Steel materials
JFE Steel Co Ltd Keihin Iron Works Ogishima Products Wharf D	250	12.5	Max 1 x 30 000 dwt. Steel materials
Universal Shipbuilding Co Ltd Tsurumi Dock Yard East Pier	185	7.5	Max 1 x 45 000 dwt. Outfitting
Universal Shipbuilding Co Ltd Tsurumi Dock Yard West Pier	240	5	Max 1 x 45 000 dwt. Outfitting
Universal Shipbuilding Co Ltd Tsurumi Dock Yard Center Pier	247	10	Max 1 x 100 000 dwt. Outfitting
Nippon Futo Warehouse Co Ltd Pier No.1	26	6	Max 1 x 2500 dwt. Chemical & synthetic
Nippon Futo Warehouse Co Ltd Pier No.2	32	5	Max 1 x 1322 dwt. Chemical & synthetic
Ube-Mitsubishi Cement Co Ltd Pier A	40	4.5	Max 1 x 1600 dwt. Cement
Ube-Mitsubishi Cement Co Ltd Pier C	90	7	Max 1 x 3600 dwt. Cement
Mitsubishi Rayon Co Ltd Yokohama Pier No.3	26	6.1	Max 1 x 1273 dwt. Chemical products
Mitsubishi Rayon Co Ltd Yokohama Pier No.4	26	6.4	Max 1 x 1600 dwt. Chemical products
Exxon Mobil Main Pier		11	See [24] below
Yokohama Liquefied Gas Terminal Co Ltd Pier	65	9.5	Max 1 x 2500 dwt. LPG
Yokohama Sea Berth (SBM)		21	Max 1 x 265 000 dwt. Crude oil
NTT Pier	129	7.5	Max 1 x 6100 dwt. Cable ships
Kageshima Industries Ltd Ebisu Pier	35	4.5	Max 1 x 700 dwt. Steel materials
KDD Ebisu Pier	148	8	Max 1 x 6270 dwt. Cable ships
Keihin Kaseihin Center Co Ltd Pier	122	5.2	Max 1 x 1900 dwt. Sulphuric acid
Sangyo Shinko Co Ltd Pier	33	6	Max 1 x 2000 dwt. Steel materials
Showa Denko Co Ltd Yokohama Works Dolphin	72	9	Max 1 x 5000 dwt. Ore & fuel oil
Showa Denko Co Ltd Yokohama Works Pier	267	9	Max 1 x 30 000 dwt. Ore & sodium hydroxide
Nissin Corporation Pier	244	10	Max 1 x 20 000 dwt. General cargo
Nippon Petroleum Refining Co Ltd Yokohama Refinery Pier A	65	12	Max 1 x 80 000 dwt. Crude oil
Nippon Petroleum Refining Co Ltd Yokohama Refinery Pier B	36	7	Max 1 x 5500 dwt. Petroleum products
Nippon Petroleum Refining Co Ltd Yokohama Refinery Pier C & C1	109	8	Max 1 x 5300 dwt. Petroleum products
Nippon Petroleum Refining Co Ltd Yokohama Refinery Pier D	35	7.3	Max 1 x 5300 dwt. Petroleum products
Nippon Petroleum Refining Co Ltd Yokohama Refinery Pier E	28	6	Max 1 x 2000 dwt. Petroleum products
Nippon Flour Mills Co Ltd Pier	163	9	Max 1 x 20 000 dwt. Grain
Yokohama Warehouse Co Ltd Suzushige Pier No.1	400	12	Max 1 x 40 000 dwt. General cargo
Yokohama Warehouse Co Ltd Suzushige Pier No.2	99	10	Max 1 x 20 000 dwt. General cargo
Yokohama Warehouse Co Ltd Suzushige Pier No.3	304	8	Max 3 x 10 000 dwt. General cargo
Kokusai Bulk Terminal Co Ltd Pier Berth A-B	350	17.5	Max 1 x 150 000 dwt. Salt, silica & grain
Kokusai Bulk Terminal Co Ltd Pier Berth C-D	190	7.5	Max 1 x 3000 dwt. Salt, silica & grain
Kokusai Bulk Terminal Co Ltd Pier Berth H	80	7.5	Max 1 x 2000 dwt. Grains
Sumikin Transport Service Co Ltd Pier	188	7	Max 1 x 3000 dwt. Steel materials & general cargo
Nissan Honmoku Wharf No's 1-2	360	10	Max 2 x 17 000 dwt. Cars
Nissan Honmoku Wharf No.3	110	4.5	Max 1 x 1500 dwt. Cars
Nippon Express Co Ltd Honmoku Pier	208	10	Max 2 x 30 000 dwt. Steel materials
Hikawa Maru Marine Tower Co Ltd Pier	162.2	7	Max 1 x 8000 dwt. Viewing
Mitsui & Co Ltd Honmoku Wharf	208	11	Max 1 x 30 000 dwt. Steel
Mitsubishi Heavy Industries Ltd Honmoku Works Wharf No.1	334	9	Max 1 x 200 000 dwt. Outfitting

Key to Principal Facilities:—					
A=Airport	**C**=Containers	**G**=General Cargo	**P**=Petroleum	**R**=Ro/Ro	**Y**=Dry Bulk
B=Bunkers	**D**=Dry Dock	**L**=Cruise	**Q**=Other Liquid Bulk	**T**=Towage (where available from port)	

Name	Length (m)	Depth (m)	Remarks
Mitsubishi Heavy Industries Ltd Honmoku Works Wharf No.3A	200	9	Max 1 x 25 000 dwt. Outfitting
Mitsubishi Heavy Industries Ltd Honmoku Works Wharf No.3B	210	9	Max 1 x 25 000 dwt. Outfitting
Mitsubishi Heavy Industries Ltd Honmoku Works Wharf No.4	412	7	Max 1 x 250 000 dwt. Outfitting
Mitsubishi Heavy Industries Ltd Honmoku Works Wharf No.6	250	10	Max 1 x 50 000 dwt. Outfitting
Mitsubishi Heavy Industries Ltd Honmoku Works Wharf No.7	270	10	Max 1 x 50 000 dwt. Outfitting
Yokohama Maritime Disaster Prevention Complex A Pier	200	8	Max 1 x 15 000 dwt. Patrol boats
Yokohama Maritime Disaster Prevention Complex B Pier	160	8	Max 1 x 10 000 dwt. Patrol boats
Yokohama Maritime Disaster Prevention Complex C Pier	148	7	Max 1 x 10 000 dwt. Patrol boats
Yokohama Maritime Disaster Prevention Complex E Pier	148	7	Max 1 x 10 000 dwt. Patrol boats
Yokohama Maritime Disaster Prevention Complex H Pier	200	10	Max 1 x 15 000 dwt. Patrol boats
Ishikawajima-Harima Heavy Industries Co Ltd Yokohama Works No.1 Jetty (South)	223	9	Max 1 x 150 000 dwt. Outfitting
Ishikawajima-Harima Heavy Industries Co Ltd Yokohama Works No.1 Jetty (North)	181	9	Max 1 x 20 000 dwt. Outfitting
Ishikawajima-Harima Heavy Industries Co Ltd Yokohama Works No.2 Jetty (South)	220	7	Max 1 x 16 000 dwt. Outfitting
Ishikawajima-Harima Heavy Industries Co Ltd Yokohama Works No.2 Jetty (North)	220	7	Max 1 x 16 000 dwt. Outfitting
Ishikawajima-Harima Heavy Industries Co Ltd Yokohama Works No.3 Jetty (South)	255	9	Max 1 x 10 000 dwt. Outfitting
Ishikawajima-Harima Heavy Industries Co Ltd Yokohama Works No.3 Jetty (North)	255	9	Max 1 x 183 000 dwt. Outfitting
Ishikawajima-Harima Heavy Industries Co Ltd Yokohama Works No.4 Jetty (South)	205	17	Max 1 x 100 000 dwt. Outfitting
Ishikawajima-Harima Heavy Industries Co Ltd Yokohama Works No.4 Jetty (North)	205	17	Max 1 x 100 000 dwt. Outfitting
Ube Mitsubishi Cement Ltd Pier	80	7.5	Max 1 x 12 000 dwt. Cement
Taiheiyo Cement Pier	105	5.5	Max 2 x 2000 dwt. Cement
Chiyoda Refrigerator Co Ltd Pier	45	6	Max 2 x 700 dwt. Fishery products
Electric Power Development Co Ltd Discharging Oil Pier	21	7.5	Max 1 x 1500 dwt. Heavy & light oil
Electric Power Development Co Ltd Discharging Coal Pier	142	7.5	Max 1 x 2000 dwt. Coal
Tokyo Gas Co Ltd Negishi Terminal Tanker Berth	173	14	Max 1 x 72 000 dwt. LNG, LPG & naphtha
Tokyo Gas Co Ltd Negishi Pier	65	5.8	Max 1 x 2000 dwt. LNG & LPG
Nissin Oil Mills Ltd Isogo Pier	160	12.5	Max 1 x 55 000 dwt. Soybean & grain
Nissin Oil Mills Ltd Domestic Pier	83	12	Max 1 x 1700 dwt. Mature
Nissin Oil Mills Ltd Domestic Pier	70	12	Max 1 x 1500 dwt. Mature
Nippon Petroleum Refining Co Ltd Negishi Refinery A Pier	364	17	Max 2 x 178 351 & 264 173 dwt. Crude oil
Nippon Petroleum Refining Co Ltd Negishi Refinery H1-H2 Pier	208	8	Max 4 x 6371 dwt. Petroleum products
Nippon Petroleum Refining Co Ltd Negishi Refinery H-3 Pier	208	8	Max 2 x 6371 dwt. Petroleum products
Nippon Petroleum Refining Co Ltd Negishi Refinery H-4 Pier	279	8	Max 2 x 7700 dwt. Petroleum products

Name	Length (m)	Depth (m)	Remarks
Nippon Petroleum Refining Co Ltd Negishi Refinery H-5 Pier	291	8	Max 2 x 7700 dwt. Crude oil
Nippon Petroleum Refining Co Ltd Negishi Refinery LPG 1 Pier	23	6.5	Max 1 x 2200 dwt. LPG & asphalt
Nippon Petroleum Refining Co Ltd Negishi Refinery LPG 2 Pier	20	5	Max 1 x 2200 dwt. LPG
Nippon Petroleum Refining Co Ltd Negishi Refinery S Pier	30	6.2	Max 1 x 1607 dwt. Sulphur
River Steel Corporation Yokohama West Pier	46	4.5	Max 1 x 300 dwt. Steel materials
River Steel Corporation Yokohama Works Pier No.2	440	6	Max 1 x 40 000 dwt. Steel materials
Asahi Kigyo Co Ltd & Suzue Co Ltd Pier		11	Max 1 x 20 000 dwt. Alchohol & cement
Daikoku Warehouse Co Ltd Pier	80	7	Max 1 x 2000 dwt. Steel materials
Toyota Motor Pier No.2	146	9.5	Max 1 x 12 000 dwt. Cars
Toyota Motor Pier No.3	259	12.5	Max 1 x 50 000 dwt. Cars
Mitsubishi Heavy Industries Ltd Kanazawa Works Wharf	500	7	Max 1 x 15 000 dwt. Diesel
Yokohama Zenken Co Pier		7.2	Max 1 x 1000 dwt. Industrial waste

[1]*Honmoku Pier:* Eighteen berths consisting of seven conventional berths (A1-3, B1-4), two building material quays and nine container berths (BC1 and C5-D3. Nineteen sheds totalling 59 820 m2 (including two container freight stations) and cargo handling area of 159 679 m2

[2]*C-5:* Max 15 000 dwt. Berths C5-9 have six container gantry cranes

[3]*Daikoku Pier:* Thirteen berths consisting of ten conventional berths (T3-8, P1-4) and three container berths (T-1, T-2, T-9). Seven sheds (including two container freight stations) of 25 165 m2 and cargo handling area of 478 773 m2

[4]*T-9:* Max 30 000 dwt. Two container gantry cranes of 33.5 t cap.

[5]*Yamashita Pier:* Ten conventional berths. Eleven sheds of 56 858 m2 and cargo handling area of 48 650 m2

[6]*Osanbashi Pier:* Also three landing platforms and two floating piers for small vessels. Yokohama International Passenger Terminal

[7]*Shinko Pier:* Five conventional berths. Cargo handling area of 3578 m2

[8]*Yamanouchi Pier:* One conventional berth. One shed of 3342 m2 and cargo handling area of 420 m2

[9]*Detamachi Pier:* Four conventional berths. Six sheds of 14 587 m2 and cargo handling area of 7971 m2

[10]*Mizuho Pier:* One conventional berth for vessels up to 10 000 dwt. Cargo handling area of 16 832 m2

[11]*Kanazawa Timber Pier:* One berth. Max 15 000 dwt. Cargo handling area of 34 912 m2

[12]*A-5:* Max 35 000 dwt. Three container gantry cranes of 30.5 t cap. Container yard of 133 591 m2 and 276 reefer points

[13]*A-6:* Max 35 000 dwt. Covering berths A6 and A7 three container gantry cranes of 30.5 t cap. Container freight station of 4033 m2, container yard of 106 000 m2 and 282 reefer points

[14]*A-8:* Max 25 000 dwt. Two container gantry cranes of 30.5 t cap. Container freight station of 5598 m2, container yard of 84 000 m2 and 186 reefer points

[15]*D-4:* Max 40 000 dwt. Three container gantry cranes of 40.6 t cap. Container freight station of 5329 m2, container yard of 105 000 m2 and 200 reefer points

[16]*D-5:* Max 60 000 dwt. Three container gantry cranes of 40.6 t cap. Container freight station of 3284 m2, container yard of 105 000 m2 and 166 reefer points

[17]*MC-1:* Max 105 000 dwt. Two container gantry cranes of 65 t cap. Container yard of 175 000 m2 and 312 reefer points

[18]*MC-2:* Max 105 000 dwt. Three container gantry cranes of 65 t cap. Container freight station of 8130 m2, container yard of 229 000 m2 and 852 reefer points

[19]*Daikoku Pier:* Twelve berths (four exclusive use container berths C1-C4 and eight liner berths L1-L8)

[20]*C-3:* Max 54 500 dwt. Three container gantry cranes of 40.6 t cap. Container freight station of 7599 m2, container yard of 175 000 m2 and 626 reefer points

[21]*C-4:* Max 57 500 dwt. Three container gantry cranes of 40.6 t cap. Container yard of 153 500 m2 and 600 reefer points

[22]*Asahi Glass Co Ltd Pier:* Two berths for vessels of 1000-2000 dwt handling glass

[23]*Exxon Mobil Canal Berth:* Max 1 x 3000 dwt. Petroleum products & methanol

[24]*Exxon Mobil Main Pier:* Max 1 x 24 000 dwt. Petroleum products & methanol

Mechanical Handling Equipment: Private cargo handling machines: 78 mobile cranes, 118 jib and bridge cranes, 1822 forklifts, 48 shovel loaders, 31 transtainers and 93 straddle carriers

Municipal Port & Harbour Bureau and Yokohama Port Development Public Corporation: 41 gantry cranes, one hammer head crane and one luffing crane

Location	Type	Capacity (t)	Qty
Yokohama	Floating Cranes	150	2
Yokohama	Floating Cranes	150	4
Yokohama	Floating Cranes	100	2

Bunkering: Cosmo Oil Co. Ltd, Toshiba Building, 1-1 Shibaura 1-chome, Minato-ku, Tokyo 105-8528, Japan, *Tel:* +81 3 3798 3156, *Fax:* +81 3 3798 3592, *Email:* masayuki_iijima@cosmo-oil.co.jp, *Website:* www.cosmo-oil.co.jp

ExxonMobil Marine Fuels, 1 Harbour Front Place, 06-00 Harbour Front, Tower One, Singapore, Republic of Singapore 098633, *Tel:* +65 6885 8998, *Fax:* +65 6885 8794, *Email:* asiapac.marinefuels@exxonmobil.com, *Website:* www.exxonmobilmarinefuels.com

Fuji Kosan Co. Ltd, 2-19-6 Yanagibashi, Taito-ku, Tokyo 111-0052, Japan, *Tel:* +81 3 3861 4601, *Fax:* +81 3 3861 4611, *Email:* info@fkoil.co.jp, *Website:* www.fkoil.co.jp

Hanwa Co. Ltd, 2nd Floor, Finland House, 56 Haymarket, London SW1Y 4RN, United Kingdom, *Tel:* +44 20 7839 4448, *Fax:* +44 20 7839 3994, *Email:* orito@hanwa.co.uk

Hikawa Shoji Kaisha Ltd, 26-2 Shinkawa NS Building 1-chome, Shinkawa, Chuo-ku, Tokyo 104, Japan, *Tel:* +81 3 5776 6858, *Fax:* +81 3 5541 3274

Idemitsu Kosan Co. Ltd, 1-1 Marunochi, 3-Chome, Chiyoda-ku, Tokyo 100-8321, Japan, *Tel:* +81 3 3213 3138, *Fax:* +81 3 3213 1145, *Email:* tohru.takamura@si.idemitsu.co.jp, *Website:* www.idemitsu.co.jp

KG Int Petroleum Ltd, Shiba Park Building, 241 Shiba Koen, Minato-ku, Tokyo 105, Japan, *Tel:* +81 3 3578 4551, *Fax:* +81 3 3578 4550

Japan Energy Corp., 2-10-1, Toranomon, Minato-ku, Tokyo 105-8407, Japan, *Tel:* +81 3 5573 6100, *Fax:* +81 3 5573 6674, *Email:* yamano@j-energy.co.jp, *Website:* www.j-energy.co.jp

Kyodo Oil Co. Ltd, 11-2 Nagata-cho 2-chome, Chiyoda-ku, Tokyo, Japan, *Tel:* +81 3 3505 8241, *Fax:* +81 3 3505 8697

Kyushu Oil Co. Ltd, 1-1 Uchisaiwai-cho 2-chome, Chiyoda-ku, Tokyo, Japan, *Tel:* +81 3 3502 3651, *Fax:* +81 3 3502 9850

Marubeni Petroleum Co. Ltd, Marubeni International Petroleum Singapore Co. Ltd, c/o Marubeni Corporation, 4-2 Ohtemachi 1-chome, Chiyoda-ku, Tokyo 100-8088, Japan, *Tel:* +81 3 3282 3920, *Fax:* +81 3 3282 3950, *Email:* TOKB554@marubenicorp.com, *Website:* www.marubeni.co.jp

MC Marine and Bunkering Inc., 8th Floor, Uchisaiwai-cho Dai Building, 3-3 Uchi-saiwai-cho 1-chome, Chiyoda-ku, Tokyo 100-0011, Japan, *Tel:* +81 3 5251 2575, *Fax:* +81 3 5251 2583

Mitsui & Co. Petroleum Ltd, 2-1, Ohtemachi 1-chome, Chiyoda-ku, Tokyo 100-0004, Japan, *Tel:* +81 3 3285 6905, *Fax:* +81 3 3285 9811, *Email:* tkzph@dg.mitsui.com, *Website:* www.mitsui.co.jp

Nissho Iwai Corp., 4-4 Akasaka 2-chome, Minato-ku, Tokyo, Japan, *Tel:* +81 3 35882111

Nittetsu Shoij Co. Ltd, 5-7 Kameido 1-chome, Koto-ku, Tokyo 136, Japan, *Tel:* +81 3 5627 2157, *Fax:* +81 3 5627 2192

NKK Trading Inc., 4-4 Nihonbashi Hisamatsucho, Chuo-ku, Tokyo 103, Japan, *Tel:* +81 3 3660 1522, *Fax:* +81 3 3660 1572

Panoco Trading Co. Ltd, Shin-Sudacho Kyodo Building 2nd Floor, 1-5, Kanda Sudacho, Chiyoda-ku, Tokyo 101-0041, Japan, *Tel:* +81 3 5298 6633, *Fax:* +81 3 3255 2202, *Email:* minori@panoco.co.jp, *Website:* www.panoco.co.jp

Shinagawa Fuel Co. Ltd, New Pier Takeshiba North Tower, 8th Floor, 1-11-1 Kaigan, Minato-ku, Tokyo 105-8525, Japan, *Tel:* +81 3 5470 7113, *Fax:* +81 3 5470 7157, *Email:* hakuyu@ml1.sinanen.co.jp

Showa Yokkaichi Sekiyu K.K., Tokyo Building, 7-3 Marunouchi 2-chome, Chiyoda-ku, Tokyo 100, Japan, *Tel:* +81 3 3215 1643, *Fax:* +81 3 3215 1869

SK Energy Asia Private Ltd, 8th Floor Yamato Seimei Building, 1-17 Uchisaiwicho 1-chome, Chiyoda-ku, Tokyo 100-0011, Japan, *Tel:* +81 3 3591 0533, *Fax:* +81 3 3591 7487, *Email:* leehk@skenergy.com, *Website:* www.skenergy.com

Sumitomo Corp., Harumi Island, Triton Square, Office Tower Y, 8-11 Harumi 1-chome, Chuo-ku, Tokyo 104-8610, Japan, *Tel:* +81 3 51664458, *Fax:* +81 3 51666407, *Email:* ir@sumitomo.co.jp, *Website:* www.sumitomocorp.co.jp

Total France S.A., Total Marine Fuels, 51 Esplanade du General de Gaulle, F-92907 Paris la Defense Cedex 10, France, *Tel:* +33 1 4135 2755, *Fax:* +33 1 4197 0291, *Email:* marine.fuels@total.com, *Website:* www.marinefuels.total.com

Waste Reception Facilities: Waste oil disposal, Tel: +81 45 501 0434, Fax: +81 45 501 0435

Garbage disposal, Tel: +81 45 661 0392, Fax: +81 45 651 7944

Towage: A total of 34 tugs available, ranging from 1660 to 3200 hp

Yokohama & Kawasaki Tugboat Co., Silk Center 4F, 1 Yamashita-cho, Naka Ward, Yokohama 231-0023, Kanagawa Pref., Japan, *Tel:* +81 45 651 4321, *Fax:* +81 45 651 4325, *Email:* yokokawatugboat@nifty.com

Repair & Maintenance: IHI Corp. (Yokohama), Yokohama Works, 1 Shin-Nakahara-cho, Isogo-ku, Yokohama, Kanagawa Pref., Japan, *Tel:* +81 45 759 2002, *Fax:* +81 45 759 2015, *Email:* webmaster@ihi.co.jp, *Website:* www.ihi.co.jp No.2 dry dock 280 m x 47 m x 8.5 m, cap 180 000 dwt. Floating dock 240 m x 38 m x 8.5 m, cap 100 000 dwt

Mitsubishi Heavy Industries Ltd, Honmoku Works, 12 Nichiki-cho, Naka-ku, Yokohama, Kanagawa Pref., Japan, *Tel:* +81 45 629 1202, *Fax:* +81 45 623 0800 No.1 dry dock 350 m x 60 m x 8.8 m, cap 270 000 dwt. No.2 dry dock 270 m x 60 m x 9.8 m, cap 120 000 dwt. No.3 dry dock 180 m x 30 m x 10.7 m, cap 38 000 dwt. Floating dock of 60 m x 41.5 m

NKK Shipbuilding (Nippon Kokan K.K), Tsurumi Shipyard, 1 Suehiro-cho 2-chome, Tsurukumi, Yokohama, Kanagawa Pref., Japan, *Tel:* +81 45 411 1331, *Fax:* +81 45 402 1080, *Website:* www.nkk.co.jp No.1 dry dock 269 m x 40 m x 10.19 m, cap 106 500 dwt. No.2 dry dock 175 m x 26 m x 6.89 m, cap 30 000 dwt

Ship Chandlers: Ashland Japan Co. Ltd, 6 Floor Minato-Ise Building, 3-12-1 Kaigan-Dori, Naka-ku, Yokohama 231-0002, Kanagawa Pref., Japan, *Tel:* +81 45 212 4741, *Fax:* +81 45 212 4754, *Email:* drewmarineyokohama@ashland.com

Fuji Trading Co. Ltd, 9-3 Shinyamashita, 3-chome, Naka-ku, Yokohama 231-0801, Kanagawa Pref., Japan, *Tel:* +81 45 622 5661, *Fax:* +81 45 629 1007, *Email:* supplyyh@fujitrading.co.jp, *Website:* www.fujitrading.co.jp

Meidi-Ya Ltd, 30-1 Yamashita-cho, Naka-ku, Yokohama 231-0023, Kanagawa Pref., Japan, *Tel:* +81 45 681 2741, *Fax:* +81 45 681 2731, *Email:* hiroshi-oota@mailsv.meidi-ya.co.jp

Shipping Agents: Inchcape Shipping Services (ISS), Inchcape Shipping Services (Japan) Ltd, 2nd Fl., Asahi Seimei Yokohama Honcho Building, 36 Honcho 4-chome, Naka-ku, Yokohama 231-0005, Kanagawa Pref., Japan, *Tel:* +81 45 201 6991, *Fax:* +81 45 212 1614, *Email:* iss.yokohama@iss-shipping.com, *Website:* www.iss-shipping.com

Kamigumi Co. Ltd, 31 Kitanaka-dori, 3 chome, Naka-ku, Yokohama 231-0003, Kanagawa Pref., Japan, *Tel:* +81 45 211 2131, *Fax:* +81 45 211 2082

Mitsui-Soko Co. Ltd, 1-1 Ohtacho, Naka-ku, Kangwawa, Yokohama, Kanagawa Pref., Japan, *Tel:* +81 45 201 6902, *Fax:* +81 45 212 3039, *Email:* i-yokota@mitsui-soko.co.jp

A.P. Moller-Maersk Group, Maersk K.K., 1 Minami Honmoku, Naka-ku, Yokohama 231-0816, Kanagawa Pref., Japan, *Tel:* +81 45 624 5930, *Fax:* +81 45 624 5905, *Website:* www.maerskline.com

Nippon Express Co. Ltd, 1-10 Honmoku-futo, Naka-ku, Yokohama 231-0811, Kanagawa Pref., Japan, *Tel:* +81 45 622 2401, *Fax:* +81 45 622 5431

Seven Star Co. Ltd, c/o Gold Maritime Yokohama Co. Ltd, 6th Floor, Honmoku Terminal Office Center, 1-10, Honmoku Futo, Naka-ku, Yokohama 231-0811, Kanagawa Pref., Japan, *Tel:* +81 45 622 6633/1451, *Fax:* +81 45 622 1667

Sumitomo Warehouse Co. Ltd, 22 Yamashitacho SSK Building, Yamashita Cho,

Naka-ku, Yokohama 231-0021, Kanagawa Pref., Japan, *Tel:* +81 45 681 8562, *Fax:* +81 45 681 2281, *Email:* ag6651_ybx@sumitomo-soko.co.jp

Surveyors: ABS (Pacific), 4th - 9th Floors, Urban Square Yokohama, 1-1 Sakae-cho, Kanagawa-ku, Yokohama 221 0052, Kanagawa Pref., Japan, *Tel:* +81 45 441 1000, *Fax:* +81 45 441 1100, *Email:* absyokohama@eagle.org

Bureau Veritas, 3rd Floor Silk Building, 1 Yamashita-cho, Naka-ku, Yokohama 231-0023, Kanagawa Pref., Japan, *Tel:* +81 45 641 4218, *Fax:* +81 45 641 4257, *Website:* www.bureauveritas.com

Cornes & Co. Ltd, 273 Yamashita-cho, Naka-ku, Yokohama 231-0023, Kanagawa Pref., Japan, *Tel:* +81 45 201 8537, *Fax:* +81 45 212 3105, *Email:* survey@ykh.cornes.co.jp, *Website:* www.cornes.co.jp

Det Norske Veritas A/S, Nisseki Yokohama Building. 14th Floor, 1-1-8 Sakuragi-cho, Naka-ku, Yokohama 231-0062, Kanagawa Pref., Japan, *Tel:* +81 45 680 2971, *Fax:* +81 45 683 1061, *Email:* yok@dnv.com, *Website:* www.dnv.com

Germanischer Lloyd, Room 704, 7th Floor, Yomiuri Yokohama Building, 51-1 Yamashita-cho, Naka-ku, Yokohama 231-0023, Kanagawa Pref., Japan, *Tel:* +81 45 650 3567, *Fax:* +81 45 650 3568, *Website:* www.gl-group.com

Nippon Kaiji Kyokai, 3-88 Hanasaki-cho, Naka-ku, Yokohama 231-0063, Kanagawa Pref., Japan, *Tel:* +81 45 231 0903, *Fax:* +81 45 242 7062, *Email:* yh@classnk.or.jp, *Website:* www.classnk.or.jp

Medical Facilities: Yokohama Port & Harbour Hospital, Tel: +81 (45) 621 3388, Fax: 622 6495

Airport: Tokyo Haneda Airport, 25 km. Tokyo Narita International Airport, 100 km

Railway: Railway transport of containers to cities of Japan is available. At Honmoku Pier, tracks are laid up to the entrance. For passengers, JR Sakuragi-cho Station or Kannai Station, approx 1 km, and MM Line Nihon Oodori Station, approx 300 m from Osambashi International Passenger Terminal

Development: Construction of two new container berths (MC-3 and MC-4) at the Minami Honmoku Pier

Lloyd's Agent: Cornes & Co. Ltd, 273 Yamashita-cho, Naka-ku, Yokohama 231-0023, Kanagawa Pref., Japan, *Tel:* +81 45 201 8537, *Fax:* +81 45 212 3105, *Email:* survey@ykh.cornes.co.jp, *Website:* www.cornes.co.jp

YOKOSUKA

Lat 35° 17' N; Long 139° 40' E.

Admiralty Chart: JP91/JP1081/JP1083/JP1062 **Admiralty Pilot:** 42A
Time Zone: GMT +9 h **UNCTAD Locode:** JP YOS

Principal Facilities:

| P | | Y | G | | R | | B | D | T | A |

Authority: Port & Harbour Department Yokosuka City, 11 Ogawa-cho, Yokosuka 238-8550, Kanagawa Pref., Japan, *Tel:* +81 46 822 8436, *Fax:* +81 46 826 3210, *Email:* pg-ph@city.yokosuka.kanagawa.jp, *Website:* www.city-yokosuka.kanagawa.jp/minato

Port Security: ISPS compliant

Approach: Draft limit in channel 10 m

Anchorage: Anchorages with depths from 10 m-30 m

Pilotage: Compulsory for foreign vessels exceeding 300 gt. Pilot station should be contacted 24 h before beginning pilotage through Agent. Tokyo Bay Licensed Pilots' Association, Tel: +81 46 835 6211, Fax: +81 46 835 2621, Email: operation@baypilot.co.jp. VHF call sign 'Uraga Channel Pilot' on channel 16

Tides: Tidal range 2.0 m

Traffic: 2005, 19 000 328 t of cargo handled

Principal Imports and Exports: Imports: Refrigerated fish. Exports: Vehicles.

Working Hours: Cargo usually worked during daytime

Accommodation:

Name	Length (m)	Depth (m)	Remarks
Yokosuka			See [1] below
Nagaura Pier 1	63	10	Max 15 000 dwt
Nagaura Wharf	150	9	Max 10 000 dwt
Nagaura Pier 2	137	10	Max 15 000 dwt
Nagaura Buoy C4		13.2	Max 20 000 dwt
Nagaura Buoy N2		9.5	Max 3000 dwt
Nagaura Buoy N5		7	Max 3000 dwt
Nagaura Buoy N6		7.8	Max 3000 dwt
Nagaura Buoy N10		6.4	Max 800 dwt
Nagaura Buoy N11		6.3	Max 800 dwt
Nagaura Buoy N12		5.8	Max 800 dwt
Nagaura Buoy N14		7.8	Max 3000 dwt
Kurihama Wharf	220	6.5	Max 3000 dwt
Kurihama No.1 Wharf	260	9	Max 16 000 dwt
Kurihama No.2 Wharf	80	5	Max 1000 dwt
Yokosuka Shinko Pier 1	90	5.5	Max 2000 dwt
Yokosuka Shinko Pier 2	90	5.5	Max 2000 dwt

	Key to Principal Facilities:—				
A=Airport	**C**=Containers	**G**=General Cargo	**P**=Petroleum	**R**=Ro/Ro	**Y**=Dry Bulk
B=Bunkers	**D**=Dry Dock	**L**=Cruise	**Q**=Other Liquid Bulk	**T**=Towage (where available from port)	

Name	Length (m)	Depth (m)	Remarks
Yokosuka Shinko Pier 3	130	7.5	Max 5000 dwt
Yokosuka Shinko Wharf 1	200	10	Max 15 000 dwt. (SOLAS convention compliant)
Yokosuka Shinko Wharf 2	200	10	Max 15 000 dwt. (SOLAS convention compliant)

[1]*Yokosuka:* Breakwater totalling 4451 m. There is a section of the harbour utilised, under agreement, by the US Navy

Storage: One transit shed 2500 m2; warehousing facilities totalling 87 900 m2 for cargo import

Bunkering: Cosmo Oil Co. Ltd, Toshiba Building, 1-1 Shibaura 1-chome, Minato-ku, Tokyo 105-8528, Japan, *Tel:* +81 3 3798 3156, *Fax:* +81 3 3798 3592, *Email:* masayuki_iijima@cosmo-oil.co.jp, *Website:* www.cosmo-oil.co.jp
ExxonMobil Marine Fuels, 1 Harbour Front Place, 06-00 Harbour Front, Tower One, Singapore, Republic of Singapore 098633, *Tel:* +65 6885 8998, *Fax:* +65 6885 8794, *Email:* asiapac.marinefuels@exxonmobil.com, *Website:* www.exxonmobilmarinefuels.com
Fuji Kosan Co. Ltd, 2-19-6 Yanagibashi, Taito-ku, Tokyo 111-0052, Japan, *Tel:* +81 3 3861 4601, *Fax:* +81 3 3861 4611, *Email:* info@fkoil.co.jp, *Website:* www.fkoil.co.jp
Hanwa Co. Ltd, 2nd Floor, Finland House, 56 Haymarket, London SW1Y 4RN, United Kingdom, *Tel:* +44 20 7839 4448, *Fax:* +44 20 7839 3994, *Email:* orito@hanwa.co.uk
Hikawa Shoji Kaisha Ltd, 26-2 Shinkawa NS Building 1-chome, Shinkawa, Chuo-ku, Tokyo 104, Japan, *Tel:* +81 3 5776 6858, *Fax:* +81 3 5541 3274
Idemitsu Kosan Co. Ltd, 1-1 Marunochi, 3-Chome, Chiyoda-ku, Tokyo 100-8321, Japan, *Tel:* +81 3 3213 3138, *Fax:* +81 3 3213 1145, *Email:* tohru.takamura@si.idemitsu.co.jp, *Website:* www.idemitsu.co.jp
KG Int Petroleum Ltd, Shiba Park Building, 241 Shiba Koen, Minato-ku, Tokyo 105, Japan, *Tel:* +81 3 3578 4551, *Fax:* +81 3 3578 4550
Japan Energy Corp., 2-10-1, Toranomon, Minato-ku, Tokyo 105-8407, Japan, *Tel:* +81 3 5573 6100, *Fax:* +81 3 5573 6674, *Email:* yamano@j-energy.co.jp, *Website:* www.j-energy.co.jp
Kyodo Oil Co. Ltd, 11-2 Nagata-cho 2-chome, Chiyoda-ku, Tokyo, Japan, *Tel:* +81 3 3505 8241, *Fax:* +81 3 3505 8697
Kyushu Oil Co. Ltd, 1-1 Uchisaiwai-cho 2-chome, Chiyoda-ku, Tokyo, Japan, *Tel:* +81 3 3502 3651, *Fax:* +81 3 3502 9850
Marubeni Petroleum Co. Ltd, Marubeni International Petroleum Singapore Co. Ltd, c/o Marubeni Corporation, 4-2 Ohtemachi 1-chome, Chiyoda-ku, Tokyo 100-8088, Japan, *Tel:* +81 3 3282 3920, *Fax:* +81 3 3282 3950, *Email:* TOKB554@marubenicorp.com, *Website:* www.marubeni.co.jp
MC Marine and Bunkering Inc., 8th Floor, Uchisaiwai-cho Dai Building, 3-3 Uchisaiwai-cho 1-chome, Chiyoda-ku, Tokyo 100-0011, Japan, *Tel:* +81 3 5251 2575, *Fax:* +81 3 5251 2583
Mitsui & Co. Petroleum Ltd, 2-1, Ohtemachi 1-chome, Chiyoda-ku, Tokyo 100-0004, Japan, *Tel:* +81 3 3285 6905, *Fax:* +81 3 3285 9811, *Email:* tkzph@dg.mitsui.com, *Website:* www.mitsui.co.jp
Nissho Iwai Corp., 4-4 Akasaka 2-chome, Minato-ku, Tokyo, Japan, *Tel:* +81 3 35882111
Nittetsu Shoij Co. Ltd, 5-7 Kameido 1-chome, Koto-ku, Tokyo 136, Japan, *Tel:* +81 3 5627 2157, *Fax:* +81 3 5627 2192
NKK Trading Inc., 4-4 Nihonbashi Hisamatsusucho, Chuo-ku, Tokyo 103, Japan, *Tel:* +81 3 3660 1522, *Fax:* +81 3 3660 1572
Panoco Trading Co. Ltd, Shin-Sudacho Kyodo Building 2nd Floor, 1-5, Kanda Sudacho, Chiyoda-ku, Tokyo 101-0041, Japan, *Tel:* +81 3 5298 6633, *Fax:* +81 3 3255 2202, *Email:* minori@panoco.co.jp, *Website:* www.panoco.co.jp
Shinagawa Fuel Co. Ltd, New Pier Takeshiba North Tower, 8th Floor, 1-11-1 Kaigan, Minato-ku, Tokyo 105-8525, Japan, *Tel:* +81 3 5470 7113, *Fax:* +81 3 5470 7157, *Email:* hakuyu@ml1.sinanen.co.jp
Showa Yokkaichi Sekiyu K.K., Tokyo Building, 7-3 Marunouchi 2-chome, Chiyoda-ku, Tokyo 100, Japan, *Tel:* +81 3 3215 1643, *Fax:* +81 3 3215 1869
SK Energy Asia Private Ltd, 8th Floor Yamato Seimei Building, 1-17 Uchisaiwicho 1-chome, Chiyoda-ku, Tokyo 100-0011, Japan, *Tel:* +81 3 3591 0533, *Fax:* +81 3 3591 7487, *Email:* leehk@skenergy.com, *Website:* www.skenergy.com
Sumitomo Corp., Harumi Island, Triton Square, Office Tower Y, 8-11 Harumi 1-chome, Chuo-ku, Tokyo 104-8610, Japan, *Tel:* +81 3 51664458, *Fax:* +81 3 51666407, *Email:* ir@sumitomo.co.jp, *Website:* www.sumitomocorp.co.jp
Total France S.A., Total Marine Fuels, 51 Esplanade du General de Gaulle, F-92907 Paris la Defense Cedex 10, France, *Tel:* +33 1 4135 2755, *Fax:* +33 1 4197 0291, *Email:* marine.fuels@total.com, *Website:* www.marinefuels.total.com

Towage: Various size tugs available

Repair & Maintenance: Kochiya Shipbuilding Co. Ltd, Yokosuka, Kanagawa Pref., Japan, *Tel:* +81 46 841 8216 One dry dock 76 m long, 13.2 m breadth, 5.3 m depth, for vessels of 1000 gt
Oppama Shipyard, Yokosuka Shipyard, 19 Natsushima-cho, Yokosuka 237-8555, Kanagawa Pref., Japan, *Tel:* +81 46 869 1842, *Fax:* +81 46 869 1799, *Email:* kic_miyajima@shi.co.jp, *Website:* www.shi.co.jp/me One dry dock of 330 m x 48 m for vessels up to 150 000 dwt
Sumitomo Heavy Industries Ltd Shipbuilding, Uraga Shipbuilding Yard, Yokosuka, Kanagawa Pref., Japan, *Tel:* +81 46 846 2001, *Fax:* +81 46 846 2142 Two dry docks: No.1 171 m x 19.5 m for vessels up to 12 500 dwt, No.2 143 m x 16.6 m for vessels up to 10 000 dwt

Medical Facilities: Can be arranged through Agent

Airport: Tokyo International Airport (Haneda), 40 km

Lloyd's Agent: Cornes & Co. Ltd, 273 Yamashita-cho, Naka-ku, Yokohama 231-0023, Kanagawa Pref., Japan, *Tel:* +81 45 201 8537, *Fax:* +81 45 212 3105, *Email:* survey@ykh.cornes.co.jp, *Website:* www.cornes.co.jp

JORDAN

AQABA

Lat 29° 31' N; Long 35° 1' E.

Admiralty Chart: 801
Time Zone: GMT +2 h

Admiralty Pilot: 64
UNCTAD Locode: JO AQJ

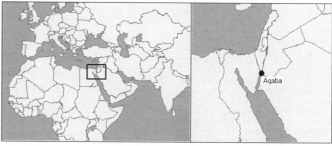

Principal Facilities:

P	Q	Y	G	C	R	L	B		T	A

Authority: Ports Corp. of Aqaba, P O Box 115, Aqaba 77110, Jordan, *Tel:* +962 3 201 4031, *Fax:* +962 3 201 6204, *Email:* info@aqabaports.gov.jo, *Website:* www.aqabaports.gov.jo

Officials: Director General: Awaad Almaytah, *Email:* dg@aqabaport.gov.jo.

Port Security: ISPS compliant

Approach: The approach to Aqaba is via a 98 nautical mile gulf connecting to the Red Sea at the southern end. The width of the gulf varies between 6-10 nautical miles and is very deep throughout. A short distance from the shoreline the depth of water averages 19.81 m. At Aqaba, the gulf is only about 8 km wide. The bottom consists of coral, sand and gravel

Anchorage: There are ample anchorage areas close inshore in varying depths of water. They are in the vicinity of about 500 m to 1000 m from the shore and the depths range from 20 m-90 m. Anchorage areas 1-7 are designated for working cargo to and from lighters. This area constitutes the inner or near anchorage. Vessels waiting for berths anchor at areas 8-11 which constitutes the far anchorage. All the numbered berths are in charted depths of less than 70 m. During periods of congestion vessels may be allocated an anchorage, possibly seaward of the 100 m contour on the chart. Maximum distance for anchoring is 3 km from the shore. Anchorage is prohibited within 6-7 cables (1.28 km) of the Royal Jetty, which is situated 1.25 miles NW of the custom house

Pilotage: Compulsory for all vessels over 150 nrt. All vessels entering or in Aqaba Bay must have a pilot onboard

Weather: During winter months strong southerly gales can develop quickly which can result in a swell. At times it may be necessary for vessels to leave the port. Tidal variation in normal conditions is 0.5 m-1.5 m

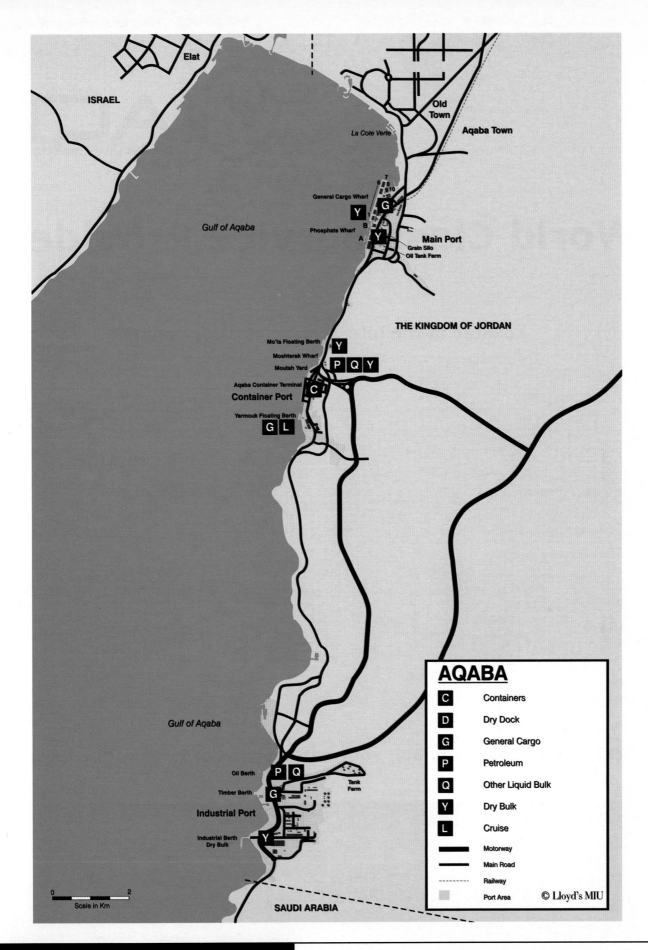

AQABA

C	Containers
D	Dry Dock
G	General Cargo
P	Petroleum
Q	Other Liquid Bulk
Y	Dry Bulk
L	Cruise
▬	Motorway
—	Main Road
- - -	Railway
░	Port Area

© Lloyd's MIU

Elat

ISRAEL

Gulf of Aqaba

La Cote Verte

Old Town

Aqaba Town

7
6 8
9 10

General Cargo Wharf

Y G

Phosphate Wharf

B
A Y

Main Port
Grain Silo
Oil Tank Farm

THE KINGDOM OF JORDAN

Mo'ta Floating Berth

Moshterak Wharf

Moutah Yard

Y

P Q Y

Aqaba Container Terminal

Container Port

C

Yarmouk Floating Berth

G L

Gulf of Aqaba

Oil Berth

P Q

Timber Berth

G

Industrial Port

Industrial Berth
Dry Bulk

Y

Tank Farm

0   2
Scale in Km

SAUDI ARABIA

**MIDDLE EAST
SHIPPING SURVEYS CO.**

Tel: +962 3 2016590/ 2016591/ 2016595
Fax : +962 3 2016592
E-mail: midsurveys@index.com.jo

Tel: +962 3 2016590/ 2016591/ 2016595
Fax : +962 3 2016592
E-mail: midsurveys@index.com.jo

Marine Consultants & Surveyors

Tides: Tidal range 1.2 m ST

Traffic: 2006, 17 164 000 t of cargo handled

Principal Imports and Exports: Imports: Construction materials, General cargo, Grain, Iron, Livestock, Mineral oil, Motor vehicles, Steel, Sugar, Sulphur, Timber, Vegetable oil. Exports: Cement, Crude oil, Fertiliser, Phosphate, Potash.

Working Hours: 24 h/day

Accommodation: Aqaba is a natural coastal harbour with berths stretching intermittently for about 10 miles along the coastal plane, south of Aqaba town

No port entrance as such. Vessels berth straight from the Gulf of Aqaba, or the anchorages, through an area called The Bay of Aqaba

The berths are built along the coast and are sheltered by the Gulf of Aqaba which is only 8 km wide at Aqaba

Aqaba is the only access to the Hashemite Kingdom of Jordan and has a coastline of approximately 13 miles between the border with Israel to the north west and to Saudi Arabia to the south. It is located at the head of the Gulf of Aqaba

The main port area with general cargo berths is located about 1.5 miles south of the town. This is a 1060 m long quay running from NNE to SSW, three to six cables from the Custom house

There are two phosphate loading berths immediately to the south of the general cargo berths

About two miles south along the coast is the container port which consists of Moutah (Mo'ta) floating berth for vessels loading bagged cement. Ro/ro traffic is also handled on this berth. This facility was recently fixed to the north of the container berths

Some three cables SSW of the old position of the Moutah floating berth is Moshterak (Al Mushtarak). This is a dolphin berth used as a pontoon for handling cement products. This pontoon-type jetty is also used for the export of oil products

Three miles to the SSW of Aqaba is the container and ro/ro berths. The ro/ro berth is located to the north of the 540 m long container terminal

Just to the south of the container terminal is the Yarmouk floating berth, which specialises in passenger vessels and vehicles and also handles ro/ro vessels

About 8.5 miles to the south of Aqaba town lies the industrial port, which comprises the new oil jetty, timber berth and the fertiliser and potash joint berth. The oil jetty was previously used for Iraqi oil exports and can handle VLCC's. The Jordan fertiliser industry's jetties have three berths. One for oil exports, one for timber and one for fertilisers which can be used for potash as needed

Aqaba Free Zone, located 18 km N of the port area, covers one million sq m including 25 000 sq m of warehouses, 300 000 sq m of paved area and a cold store for reefer cargoes

Name	Length (m)	Draught (m)	Remarks
Main Port			
Berth No.1 (General Cargo Wharf)	200	10.8	See [1] below
Berth No.2 (General Cargo Wharf)	220	10	General cargo. Berthing for vessels up to 20 000 dwt
Berth No.3 (General Cargo Wharf)	220	13	General cargo. Berthing for vessels up to 40 000 dwt
Berth No.4 (General Cargo Wharf)	220	11.5	General cargo. Berthing for vessels up to 40 000 dwt
Berth No.5 (General Cargo Wharf)	220	11.5	General cargo. Berthing for vessels up to 40 000 dwt
Berth No.6 (General Cargo Wharf)	220	11.5	General cargo. Berthing for vessels up to 40 000 dwt
Berth No.7 (General Cargo Wharf)	170	8	See [2] below
Berth No.9 (General Cargo Wharf)	110	5.4	General cargo. Berthing for vessels up to 3000 dwt
Berth No.10 (General Cargo Wharf)	150	5.8	See [3] below
Lighters Berth (General Cargo Wharf)	280	4	For use by lighters/small craft etc. Four storage areas approx 40 m from the quay
Lighters Berth (General Cargo Wharf)	280	4	For use by lighters/small craft etc. Four storage areas approx 40m from the quay

Name	Length (m)	Draught (m)	Remarks
Berth A (Phosphate Wharf)	210	11	See [4] below
Berth B (Phosphate Wharf)	180	15	See [5] below
Container Port			
Aqaba Container Terminal	540	10.5	See [6] below
Yarmouk Floating Berth	150	15	See [7] below
Moutah (Mo'ta) Floating Berth	150	15	See [8] below
Moshterak (Al Mushtarak) Wharf		11	See [9] below
Industrial Port			
Oil Exporting Jetty		25	See [10] below
Timber Berth	80	6.8	See [11] below
Dry Bulk Berth	285	11–15	See [12] below

[1]*Berth No.1 (General Cargo Wharf):* Grain. Berthing for vessels up to 20 000 dwt. Three grain elevators - discharge rate 6-12 000 t/day connected via conveyor belts to grain silos which have a cap of 150 000 t

[2]*Berth No.7 (General Cargo Wharf):* General cargo. LASH lighters, when used, anchor off No.7 berth. Berthing for vessels up to 8000 dwt

[3]*Berth No.10 (General Cargo Wharf):* General cargo. Berthing for vessels up to 3000 dwt. Ro/ro storage space available

[4]*Berth A (Phosphate Wharf):* Phosphate, vegetable oils (discharged at 500 t/h to a tank farm with a cap of 5000 t) and petroleum products. Can also supply bunkers. Berthing for vessels up to 20 000 dwt. Loading tower located between two berthing dolphins. Two phosphate storage facilities of 20 000 t cap feed the conveyor system. Four oil storage tanks

[5]*Berth B (Phosphate Wharf):* Phosphate, bagged goods and billets. Bagged goods and billets are discharged direct to road transport. Berthing for vessels up to 100 000 dwt. Four phosphate storage facilities - cap 130 000 t which feeds the conveyor system

[6]*Aqaba Container Terminal:* Managed by APM Terminals, P O Box 1216, Aqaba 77110, Tel: +962 3 203 9999, Fax: +962 3 203 9133, Email: customerservice@act.com.jo, Website: www.act.com.jo
Three container berths (each 180 m long) for vessels up to 84 000 dwt and one ro/ro berth (40 m long) for vessels up to 35 000 dwt

[7]*Yarmouk Floating Berth:* Passengers, ro/ro (at each end of the pontoon), containers. Possible redevelopment into three general cargo berths with transit sheds

[8]*Moutah (Mo'ta) Floating Berth:* Rice imports, bagged cement, bulk exports and ro/ro. Berthing for vessels up to 40 000 dwt. Seven silos - cap 54 600 t. Discharge rate: dry bulk 500 t/h, rice 600 t/h

[9]*Moshterak (Al Mushtarak) Wharf:* Oil products and cement. Berthing for vessels up to 120 000 dwt. Two cement domes - cap 30 000 t

[10]*Oil Exporting Jetty:* A single four dolphin berth connected to the shore by a 150 m long approach arm. Four mooring dolphins are located, two at each end. Max length of vessel is 370 m. Exporting cap - 300 000 t of crude oil per month - deliveries by road tankers. Storage cap for 73 000 t

[11]*Timber Berth:* Timber. Berthing for vessels up to 8000 dwt and 120 m loa. Berthing for ro/ro vessels with stern ramp of not less than 35 m in length - vessel to be moored 25 m from jetty. An inner berth, with a draught of 1.5 m, length 45 m can accommodate tugs and barges. Storage area available. Used mainly for the import of livestock

[12]*Dry Bulk Berth:* Consists of two berths (Eastern and Western). Eastern: fertiliser and ammonia with berthing for vessels up to 30 000 dwt and 190 m loa. Western: potash and sulphur with berthing for vessels up to 50 000 dwt and 230 m loa. Fertiliser factory. Potash storage area for 150 000 t (2 stores). DAP storage area for 65 000 t (1 store)

Storage:

Location	Open (m²)	Covered (m²)	Grain (t)
Aqaba	245000	41200	150000

Mechanical Handling Equipment:

Location	Type	Capacity (t)	Qty
Aqaba Container Terminal	Mobile Cranes	100	2
Aqaba Container Terminal	Panamax	40	2
Aqaba Container Terminal	Post Panamax	40	1
Yarmouk Floating Berth	Mult-purp. Cranes	15	2

Bunkering: Jordan Petroleum Refinery Co. Ltd, Abu Baker El Seddeq Street, P O Box 1079, Jebel Amman 1, Circle Amman, Jordan 11118, Jordan, *Tel:* +962 6 4630 151, *Fax:* +962 6 4657 934/39, *Email:* addewan@jopetrol.com.jo, *Website:* www.jopetrol.com.jo
Shell Business Development Co., P O Box 926438, Amman 11190, Jordan, *Tel:* +962 6 5662 790, *Fax:* +962 6 5686 713, *Email:* rima.juweinat@shell.com, *Website:* www.shell.com

Towage: Seven tugs available of 800-3200 hp

Repair & Maintenance: Workshop equipped for minor repairs only. A slipway of 145 m long is available for repair and maintenance of the port's fleet of lighters and other harbour craft. Divers can be obtained

Seaman Missions: The Seamans Mission, The Flying Angel Club, Aqaba, Jordan, *Tel:* +962 3 201 8630, *Fax:* +962 3 201 8417, *Email:* mtsaqaba@go.com.jo

Ship Chandlers: Sealion Shipchandler, P O Box 2476, Aqaba, Jordan, *Fax:* +962 3 203 0101, *Email:* sealion@accessme.com Owner: Odav H. Hezam Mobile Tel: +962 795903210
Adasco Shipchandlers, 2nd Floor, Adasco Building, Aqaba 77110, Jordan, *Tel:* +962 3 201 9300, *Fax:* +962 3 201 2377, *Email:* adasco@index.com.jo, *Website:* www.adasco.com
Peace Ship Chandler, P O Box 1001, Aqaba 77110, Jordan, *Tel:* +962 3 201 8877, *Fax:* +962 3 201 8877, *Email:* peace@nets.jo
Red Sea Ship Chandler & General Suppliers, P O Box 1001, Aqaba 77110, Jordan,

---

Key to Principal Facilities:—
A=Airport   **C**=Containers   **G**=General Cargo   **P**=Petroleum   **R**=Ro/Ro   **Y**=Dry Bulk
B=Bunkers   **D**=Dry Dock   **L**=Cruise   **Q**=Other Liquid Bulk   **T**=Towage (where available from port)

Tel: +962 3 201 3124, *Fax:* +962 3 201 3166, *Email:* info@rssc.com.jo, *Website:* www.rssc.com.jo

Shipping Agents: Ammon Shipping & Transport, Sa'd Bin Abi Waqas Street, Naouri Group Building 30, P O Box 182154, Amman 11118, Jordan, *Tel:* +962 6 5777 900, *Fax:* +962 6 5686 712, *Email:* ammon@naouri.com, *Website:* www.naouri.com
Aqaba Shipping Co. W.L.L., Kawar Building, Hamamat Tunis Street, P O Box 246, Aqaba, Jordan, *Tel:* +962 3 201 4217, *Fax:* +962 3 201 3618, *Email:* operations@aqaport.com.jo, *Website:* www.kawar.com
Arab Shipping Co. Ltd, P O Box 46, Aqaba, Jordan, *Tel:* +962 3 201 2241/3641, *Fax:* +962 3 201 5476
CMA-CGM Jordan LLC, 2nd Floor, Jordan National Shipping Line BuildingP, P O Box 677, Aqaba 77110, Jordan, *Tel:* +962 3 201 5443, *Fax:* +962 3 201 4263, *Email:* aqa.genmbox@cma-cgm.com, *Website:* www.cma-cgm.com
Gulf Agency Co. (Jordan) W.L.L., P O Box 1479, Aqaba 77110, Jordan, *Tel:* +962 3 201 4218, *Fax:* +962 3 201 3618, *Email:* jordan@gacworld.com, *Website:* www.gacworld.com
International Shipping & Transport Co. WLL, Jordan Islamic Building, P O Box 564, Aqaba, Jordan, *Tel:* +962 3 201 9201, *Fax:* +962 3 201 9203, *Email:* jululian_lina@apl.com
Kareem Shipping Agencies, Aqaba, Jordan, *Tel:* +962 3 201 9889, *Fax:* +962 3 203 1735, *Email:* kl-aqaba@naouri.com, *Website:* www.naouri.com
Maltrans Shipping Agencies Co., P O Box 504, Aqaba 77110, Jordan, *Tel:* +962 3 201 4171, *Fax:* +962 3 201 2902, *Email:* maqaba@maltrans.com, *Website:* www.maltrans.com
Manara Shipping Co. WLL, Kawar Building, P O Box 372, Aqaba 77110, Jordan, *Tel:* +962 3 201 4217, *Fax:* +962 3 201 3618, *Email:* management@aqaport.com.jo, *Website:* www.manarashipping.com.jo
National Shipping Services Company Ltd, 3rd Floor, Omar Ibn Ktab Building, Shmeisani, P O Box 927304, Amman 11190, Jordan, *Tel:* +962 6 560 6909, *Fax:* +962 6 567 6920, *Email:* admin@nss.com.jo, *Website:* www.nss.com.jo
Ocean Maritime Agencies, P O Box 40, Aqaba 77110, Jordan, *Tel:* +962 3 201 2132, *Fax:* +962 3 201 5935, *Email:* tgf@tgf.com.jo
Petra Navigation & International Trading Co. Ltd, Armoush Centre, P O Box 485, Aqaba, Jordan, *Tel:* +962 3 201 3111, *Fax:* +962 3 201 5630, *Email:* aqa-operation@petranav.com.jo, *Website:* www.petra.jo
Philadelphia Corp. for Shipping Agencies, 3rd Floor, Al Tarbiya Building, Al Faris Street, P O Box 1228, Aqaba, Jordan, *Tel:* +962 3 201 3517, *Fax:* +962 3 201 4259, *Email:* sales@philpco.jo
Red Sea Shipping Agency Co. WLL, P O Box 22, Aqaba, Jordan, *Tel:* +962 3 201 4217, *Fax:* +962 3 201 6680, *Email:* containers@aqaport.com.jo, *Website:* www.redseashipping.com.jo
Silk Waves Agencies, P O Box 2013, Aqaba 77110, Jordan, *Tel:* +962 3 202 2530, *Fax:* +962 3 202 2532, *Email:* silkwaves@silkgroup.com.jo
Sindbad Shipping & Transport Co., P O Box 1649, Aqaba 77110, Jordan, *Tel:* +962 3 201 9295, *Fax:* +962 3 201 9297, *Email:* sindbad@nets.com.jo
Telstar Maritime Agencies ME, P O Box 8, Aqaba 77110, Jordan, *Tel:* +962 3 201 3678, *Fax:* +962 3 201 2679, *Email:* telstar@go.com.jo, *Website:* www.telstarmaritime.com
Wilhelmsen Ship Services, Barwil Zaatarah Agencies Ltd, Barwil Unitor Ships Service, Shweikini Building P O Box 266, Hammamat Tunisya Street, Aqaba, Jordan, *Tel:* +962 3 201 5467, *Fax:* +962 3 201 6467, *Email:* barwil.aqaba@wilhelmsen.com, *Website:* www.barwilunitor.com

Surveyors: Middle East Shipping Surveys Co., P O Box 2415, Aqaba 77110, Jordan, *Tel:* +962 3 201 6590, *Fax:* +962 3 201 6592, *Email:* midsurveys@index.com.jo Manager: Ali Al-Aqrabawi
Nippon Kaiji Kyokai, Amin Kawar & Sons Co. (W.L.L.), P O Box 22, Aqaba, Jordan, *Tel:* +962 3 201 4312, *Fax:* +962 3 201 3618, *Website:* www.classnk.or.jp
Trust Marine Surveyors & Consultant, Aqaba Special Economic Zone Area, 3rd Commercial Area, Abu Awali Building, Aqaba, Jordan, *Tel:* +962 3 203 9170, *Fax:* +962 3 203 5921, *Email:* trust-surveys@index.com.jo

Airport: Aqaba International Airport, 4 km

Railway: The Hittiye-Aqaba narrow gauge railway is used to transport phosphate from the mines at El-Hasa to the port

Development: The port is to be relocated 20 miles S to the industrial complex site on the southern shore closer to the Saudi border

Lloyd's Agent: International Surveyors & Loss Adjusters Ltd, Al Juwaideh, Near Amman Customs, Amman 11118, Jordan, *Tel:* +962 6 412 2672, *Fax:* +962 6 412 7108, *Email:* rulad@spinneys.com.jo, *Website:* www.hbgsurveyors.com

KAZAKHSTAN

AKTAU

Lat 44° 25' N; Long 50° 9' E.

Admiralty Chart: -   **Admiralty Pilot:** -
Time Zone: GMT +5 h   **UNCTAD Locode:** KZ AAU

Principal Facilities:

P		Y	G		R				T		

Authority: Aktau International Commercial Sea Port, Umirzak Village, 466200 Aktau, Republic of Kazakhstan, *Tel:* +7 7292 445126, *Fax:* +7 7292 445101, *Email:* seaport_akt@kaznet.kz, *Website:* www.portaktau.kz

Traffic: 2005, 10 368 000 t of cargo handled

Working Hours: 24 h/day

Accommodation:

Name	Length (m)	Depth (m)	Remarks
Aktau			
Berth No.1	150	4.6	General cargo
Berth No.2	150	4.6	General cargo
Berth No.3	100	4.6	General cargo
Berth No.4	188	5.5	Petroleum
Berth No.6	150	4.6	Multi-purpose
Berth No.7	70	4	Port fleet
Berth No.8	140	5.3	Ferries
Berth No.9	150	6.2	Petroleum
Berth No.10	150	6.2	Petroleum
Berth No.11	60		
Berth No.12	80		

Storage:

Location	Open (m²)	Covered (m²)
Aktau	50000	6000

Mechanical Handling Equipment:

Location	Type	Capacity (t)	Qty
Aktau	Mult-purp. Cranes	80	1
Aktau	Mult-purp. Cranes	64	1
Aktau	Mult-purp. Cranes	37	1

Towage: One tug available of 1600 hp

Shipping Agents: Blue Water Shipping A/S, Micro Disrtrict 14, Building 59, Office 40, 130000 Aktau, Republic of Kazakhstan, *Tel:* +7 7292 429755, *Fax:* +7 7292 429728, *Email:* bwsakt@bws.dk, *Website:* www.bws.dk
Mediterranean Shipping Company, MSC Central Asia, Khusainova 281, 050060 Almaty, Republic of Kazakhstan, *Tel:* +7 7272 582080, *Fax:* +7 7272 582358, *Email:* info@ala.msckazakhstan.kz, *Website:* www.mscgva.ch

Stevedoring Companies: Blue Water Shipping A/S, Micro Disrtrict 14, Building 59, Office 40, 130000 Aktau, Republic of Kazakhstan, *Tel:* +7 7292 429755, *Fax:* +7 7292 429728, *Email:* bwsakt@bws.dk, *Website:* www.bws.dk

Surveyors: Russian Maritime Register of Shipping, Room 106 Building 5-A, Micro-district 5, 130002 Aktau, Republic of Kazakhstan, *Tel:* +7 7292 530760, *Fax:* +7 7292 530760, *Website:* www.rs-head.spb.ru

Development: Reconstruction of the port is underway. It is to be expanded on a new site with four oil terminals, two container terminals and two multi-purpose terminals and be capable of housing tankers up to 12 000 dwt with a draught of 7 m

Lloyd's Agent: EGIS Ltd, Office 1, Block No.15/1, Timiryazev Street 42, 050057 Almaty, Republic of Kazakhstan, *Tel:* +7 7272 744025, *Email:* almaty@eurogal-surveys.com, *Website:* www.eurogal-surveys.com

KENYA

LAMU

Lat 2° 18' S; Long 40° 55' E.

Admiralty Chart: 668   **Admiralty Pilot:** 3
Time Zone: GMT +3 h   **UNCTAD Locode:** KE LAU

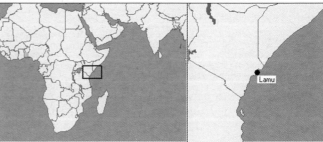

Principal Facilities:

			G							T	A	

Authority: Kenya Ports Authority, P O Box 95009, Mombasa 80104, Kenya, *Tel:* +254 41 211 2999, *Fax:* +254 41 231 1867, *Email:* info@kpa.co.ke, *Website:* www.kpa.co.ke

Officials: Harbour Master: Capt Twalib Khamis, *Email:* tkhamis@kpa.co.ke.

Pilotage: Optional, no local pilot. Provided with two days notice. Pilot can also be picked up at Mombasa

Principal Imports and Exports: Imports: General cargo. Exports: Charcoal, Mangrove poles, Shell fish.
Working Hours: 0800-1200, 1400-1600
Accommodation:

Name	Remarks
Lamu	See [1] below

[1]*Lamu:* Secure port with three anchorages deep enough for vessels of 91.43 m loa, 5.18 m d to enter the harbour at LWOST; Spring rise 3.35 m. Depth at anchorage: Shella 6.4 m, Lamu South 5.8 m, Lamu Upper 8.8 m. Loading and discharge by dhows of 5-60 t cap. No quays for ocean-going vessels. There is a pier for small craft

Towage: Tugs available from Mombasa
Medical Facilities: Hospital available
Airport: Lamu, 2 km
Development: Dredging of the channel to attract more commercial vessels and putting up new navigational aids
Lloyd's Agent: McLarens Young International, Maritime House, 2nd Floor, Moi Avenue, Mombasa, Kenya, *Tel:* +254 41 222 4130, *Fax:* +254 41 231 5690, *Email:* mombasa@mclarensyoung.co.ke

MOMBASA

Lat 4° 4' S; Long 39° 41' E.

Admiralty Chart: 666	**Admiralty Pilot:** 3
Time Zone: GMT +3 h	**UNCTAD Locode:** KE MBA

Principal Facilities:

P	Q	Y	G	C	R	L	B	D	T	A

Authority: Kenya Ports Authority, P O Box 95009, Mombasa 80104, Kenya, *Tel:* +254 41 211 2999, *Fax:* +254 41 231 1867, *Email:* info@kpa.co.ke, *Website:* www.kpa.co.ke
Officials: Harbour Master: Capt Twalib Khamis, *Email:* tkhamis@kpa.co.ke.
Port Security: ISPS compliant
Approach: The approach channel to Mombasa lies across a bar extending between Andromache Reef and Leven Reefs. The channel is marked by leading lights and light-buoys
The entrance channel to the Old Port has a min depth of 15.85 m. The entrance from

the sea to Kilindini Harbour is by an approach channel, 304.8 m wide and dredged to a max depth of 13.71 m (to allow entry for tankers to 80 000 dwt) on a transit of 301° (Ras Serani leads), thence directly to the harbour between Ras Mwa Kisenge on the mainland south and Ras Mzimili on the south of Mombasa Island about 0.6 km to the SW of Ras Serani lighthouse
Anchorage: Anchor Points:
Anchorage A - in pos 4° 04' 75" S; 39° 39' 63" E in depth of 10.97 m for vessels up to 228 m loa
Anchorage B - in pos 4° 04' 42" S; 39° 39' 59" E in depth of 10.97 m for vessels up to 161 m loa
Anchorage C - in pos 4° 04' 27" S; 39° 39' 22" E in depth of 10.97 m for vessels up to 228 m loa
Anchorage K - in pos 4° 03' 22" S; 39° 38' 60" E in depth of 12 m for vessels up to 290 m loa
Anchorage N - in pos 4° 02' 78" S; 39° 38' 25" E in depth of 10 m
Anchorage O - in pos 4° 02' 84" S; 39° 37' 90" E in depth of 7 m for vessels up to 228 m loa
Anchorage R - in pos 4° 03' 14" S; 39° 37' 14" E in depth of 7 m for vessels up to 161 m loa
Anchorage S - in pos 4° 03' 20" S; 39° 36' 90" E in depth of 7 m for vessels up to 161 m loa
Anchorage T - in pos 4° 03' 30" S; 39° 36' 67" E in depth of 6.7 m for vessels up to 161 m loa
Anchorage U - in pos 4° 03' 70" S; 39° 36' 43" E in depth of 7.6 m for vessels up to 161 m loa
Anchorage V - in pos 4° 03' 45" S; 39° 36' 19" E in depth of 7.3 m for vessels up to 161 m loa
Anchorage W - in pos 4° 03' 52" S; 39° 35' 98" E in depth of 6.7 m for vessels up to 100 m loa
Pilotage: Compulsory for vessels over 200 gt. Pilot rendezvous position is 3 nautical miles from the first set of buoys as you approach the channel. The port has four working pilot boats
Radio Frequency: VHF Channel 16 (calling port operations), VHF Channel 14 (shipping operations), VHF Channel 12 (port marine operations), VHF Channel 13 (board room, container terminal), VHF Channel 11 (port fire station)
Weather: NE monsoons from December to March. SW monsoons from May to September. Conditions rarely interfere with working in the port
Tides: Max rise of spring tides is 4.04 m and of neap tides is 3.05 m and may reach a rate of up to 3 knots in Kilindini Harbour. The tidal streams set obliquely across the entrance channel, but within the harbour they follow the direction of the channel. The tidal range does not interfere with vessels working. Tidal streams in the Old Harbour may reach 3 knots during spring tides
Traffic: 2007, 15 925 955 t of cargo handled, 585 367 TEU's
Principal Imports and Exports: Imports: Coal, Crude oil, Farm machinery, Fertiliser, Iron and steel, Meat, Motor vehicles, Paper, Salt, Sugar, Wheat. Exports: Canned fruit, Cement, Coffee, Cotton, Fluorspar, Molasses, Nuts, Oilseeds, Soda ash, Tea, Vegetable oil.
Working Hours: Normal working hours are 0700-1500, 1500-2300, 2300-0700. Weekends, public holidays and extensions of the normal working day constitute overtime working
Accommodation: The port of Mombasa is situated on Mombasa Island and is a well sheltered, natural harbour
Ras Serani (position 4 03.3 S; 39 40.8 E) the SE extremity of Mombasa Island, lies at the head of the entrance to the Port of Mombasa
Mombasa old port is entered between Ras Serani and Mackenzie Point, about 0.8 km NNE
Ras Mwa Kisenge (position 4 05.0 S; 39 40.4 E) the S entrance point, is a cliffy point which may be identified by a sandy beach extending S of the entrance
Ras Mkungombe (Kunwongbe) (position 4 03.4 S; 39 42.1 E) the N entrance point, is a bluff cliffy point from which a sandy beach extends 8 cables WSW There are depths of less than 9 m for 1.5 miles S of Ras Mkungombe

Name	Length (m)	Depth (m)	Draught (m)	Remarks
Mombasa				
Berth No.1	173.1		9.75	Conventional & passenger
Berth No.2	166.4		9.75	Conventional & passenger
Berth No.3	166.4		9.75	Conventional
Berth No.4	190.2		9.75	Conventional
Berth No.5	178.6		9.75	Conventional & ro/ro
Berth No.7	208.2		9.75	Conventional
Berth No.8	170.7		9.75	Conventional
Berth No.9	179.8		10.36	Conventional & bulk soda
Berth No.10	204.2		9.75	Conventional
Berth No.11	184.4		9.75	Conventional
Berth No.12	182.9		9.75	Conventional
Berth No.13	174		9.75	Conventional & containers
Berth No.14	181.4		9.75	Conventional & containers
Berth No.16	177.7		10.36	Containers
Berth No.17	182.9		10.36	Containers
Berth No.18	239		10.36	Containers
Mbaraki Wharf	306.3		10.97	Multi-purpose
Oil Jetties				
Kipevu Oil Jetty			13.25	For vessels up to 85 000 dwt & 259 m loa
Shimanzi Oil Jetty			9.75	For vessels up to 35 000 dwt & 198 m loa
Cased Oil Jetty			6	For vessels up to 2500 dwt & 73 m loa
Mooring Buoys				
K1	167.6	7		
K2	213.3	7		

Name	Length (m)	Depth (m)	Draught (m)	Remarks
K3	240	7.92		
K4	167.6	9.14		
M1	304.7	13.41		
M2	182	13.41		
M3	228.5	13.41		
M4	213.3	13.41		
M5	250	9.45		

Storage: 13 main quay transit sheds with total floor area of 105 490 sq m
7 back of port transit sheds with total floor area of 46 000 sq m
1 molasses tank for storage of 15 000 t (near berth No.9) (pipeline at 150-450 t/h)
20 ha area for stacking and handling containers (berths 16, 17 & 18) (250 000 TEU's/year)
72 reefer points
1 cold store (8 chambers) of 1247 cu m cap
1 customs warehouse of 4002 sq m

Mechanical Handling Equipment: At container berths 16, 17 & 18: 11 gantries (mobile) 40 t, 2 gantries (rail) 40 t, 4 gantries (ship to shore) 40 t, 7 toploaders 40 t, 3 prime movers - PPM's 40 t, 64 tugmasters, 6 shunters
At general cargo berths: 53 portal electrical travelling cranes with cap of 3-20 t, 9 portal electrical fixed cranes with cap of 2-5 t, 19 electrical fixed cranes with cap of 1-15 t, 43 mobile cranes with cap of 5-40 t, 3 multi-purpose forklift trucks with cap of 40 t, 2 overhead belt conveyors for bulk soda ash with cap of 110 t/h, two mobile grain bulk conveyor cranes at 300 t/h each

Bunkering: Alba Petroleum Ltd, Tangana Road, Mbaraki Creek, P O Box 97155, Mombasa 80112, Kenya, *Tel:* +254 41 2317009, *Fax:* +254 41 2317006, *Email:* apl10@calva.com
Kangaroo Bunkers Ltd, Tangana Road, Mbaraki Creek, P O Box 85704, Mombasa 80100, Kenya, *Tel:* +254 41 2317 009, *Fax:* +254 41 2317 006, *Email:* sales@kangaroobunkers.com
Oceanic Bunkering & Oil Products Ltd, P O Box 81737, Mombasa 80100, Kenya, *Tel:* +254 41 2220 324, *Fax:* +254 41 2220 085, *Email:* info@oceanicbunkering.com
Quantum Bunkering Ltd, P O Box 88471, Mombasa 80100, Kenya, *Tel:* +254 41 2315 673, *Fax:* +254 41 2315 673, *Email:* info@qbunkering.co.ke
Wanainchi Marine Products (K) Ltd, Liwatoni Complex, P O Box 81841, Mombasa, Kenya, *Tel:* +254 41 22051, *Fax:* +254 41 316392
Alba Petroleum Ltd, Tangana Road, Mbaraki Creek, P O Box 97155, Mombasa 80112, Kenya, *Tel:* +254 41 2317009, *Fax:* +254 41 2317006, *Email:* apl10@calva.com

Towage: Five tugs available of 40 t bollard pull

Repair & Maintenance: African Marine & General Engineering Co. Ltd (AMGECO), P O Box 90462, Tangana Road, Mbaraki Creek, Mombasa 80100, Kenya, *Tel:* +254 41 222 1651/4, *Fax:* +254 41 231 3168, *Email:* afmarine@africaonline.co.ke, *Website:* www.africanmarine.com Dry dock of 180 m x 26.4 m x 7.95 m with max cap of 20 000 t. Floating repairs at two lay-by wharves totaling 340 m, capable of mooring vessels up to 200 m loa with max draught 8 m. Two slipways suitable for smaller craft up to 20 m x 6 m, max 120 t
Southern Engineering Co. Ltd, Mbaraki Wharf, near Likoni Ferry, P O Box 84162, Mombasa, Kenya, *Tel:* +254 41 231 1091, *Fax:* +254 41 231 6029, *Email:* seco@alphakenya.com, *Website:* www.alphaafrica.com One floating dock of 40 m x 19 m with lifting cap of 600 t and one floating dock of 26 m x 26 m with lifting cap of 600 t. It also offers ship repair lay-by berths

Ship Chandlers: Bamburi Ship Chandlers (K) Ltd, P O Box 3645, Mombasa, Kenya, *Tel:* +254 41 231 4943, *Fax:* +254 41 231 3627, *Email:* bamship28@hotmail.com
Branded Fine Foods Ltd, P O Box 99403, Mombasa, Kenya, *Tel:* +254 41 249 1130, *Fax:* +254 41 249 0093, *Email:* finefoods@brandedfine.com, *Website:* www.brandedfine.com
Green Island Ship Chandling (K) Ltd, P O Box 88244, Mombasa, Kenya, *Tel:* +254 41 223 0835, *Fax:* +254 41 222 5549, *Email:* green@ikenya.com
Mombasa Sea Port Duty Free Shop / Restaurant, KPA Shed No.1, P O Box 95226, Mombasa, Kenya, *Tel:* +254 41 231 4791, *Fax:* +254 41 231 4791, *Email:* msdf@jambomail.com
Mombasa Shipchandlers, P O Box 81692, Mombasa, Kenya, *Tel:* +254 41 231 3011, *Fax:* +254 41 231 2552, *Email:* msaship@wananchi.com
Muses Mohamed & Co., P O Box 81347, Digo Road, Mombasa, Kenya, *Tel:* +254 41 222 0100, *Fax:* +254 41 231 1826, *Email:* museshipstores@swiftmombasa.com
Seacrest Supplies Ltd, P O Box 335, Mombasa, Kenya, *Tel:* +254 41 249 1599, *Fax:* +254 41 249 1599, *Email:* ships@seacrest-kenya.com

Shipping Agents: Archon Marine Shipping & Logistics [K] Ltd, 3rd Floor, Old Canon Towers, Moi Avenue, P O Box 80376, Mombasa 80100, Kenya, *Tel:* +254 41 231 2581, *Fax:* +254 41 222 8182, *Email:* admin@archonshipping.com
CMA-CGM S.A., CMA CGM Kenya, Spanfreight House, Moi Avenue, P O Box 99760, Mombasa, Kenya, *Tel:* +254 41 231 5659, *Fax:* +254 41 231 6386, *Email:* mob.genmbox@cma-cgm.com, *Website:* www.cma-cgm.com
Dodwell & Co. (East Africa) Ltd, Inchcape House, Archbishop Makarios Close, Off Moi avenue, P O Box 90194, Mombasa, Kenya, *Tel:* +254 41 222 7754, *Fax:* +254 41 222 3714, *Email:* mail@iss-shipping.com
East African Commercial & Shipping Co. DSM Ltd, Changamwe Roundabout, Kipevu Road, P O Box 95103, Mombasa, Kenya, *Tel:* +254 41 343 3434, *Fax:* +254 41 343 4600, *Email:* shipping@eacs.co.ke
Express Shipping & Logistics (EA) Ltd, P O Box 1922, 7th Floor, New Cannon Tower II, Moi Avenue, Mombasa 80100, Kenya, *Tel:* +254 41 222 9784, *Fax:* +254 41 222 6587, *Email:* expressmba@esl-eastafrica.com, *Website:* www.esl-eastafrica.com
GAC-Seaforth, P O Box 85593, Mombasa 80100, Kenya, *Tel:* +254 41 231 3776, *Fax:* +254 41 231 4513, *Email:* gac-seaforth.kenya@gacworld.com, *Website:* www.gacworld.com
Inchcape Shipping Services (ISS), Inchcape Shipping Services (Kenya) Ltd, Inchcape House, Archibishop Makarios Cls, Off Moi avenue, P O Box 90194, Mombasa 80100, Kenya, *Tel:* +254 41 231 4245, *Fax:* +254 41 231 4662, *Email:* mail@iss-shipping.com, *Website:* www.iss-shipping.com
Safmarine Ship Management, 1st Floor Cotts House, Moi Avenue, P O Box 99169, Mombasa, Kenya, *Tel:* +254 41 222 0231, *Fax:* +254 41 222 0086, *Email:* kensclsalexp@ke.safmarine.com
Seedcol Global Shipping EA, 2nd Floor, Old Canon Towers, Moi Avenue, P O Box

95933, Mombasa, Kenya, *Tel:* +254 41 222 5895, *Fax:* +254 41 222 7172, *Email:* sgs@sgs-eastafrica.com, *Website:* www.sgs-eastafrica.com
Simpet Global Logistics Ltd, Harbour House, 5th Floor, P O Box 89457, Mombasa, Kenya, *Tel:* +254 41 222 4568, *Fax:* +254 41 222 4521, *Email:* info@simpetcargo.com, *Website:* www.simpetcargo.com
Sturrock Flex Shipping Ltd, New Cannon Tower 11, 6th Floor, Moi Avenue, P O Box 86725-80100, Mombasa, Kenya, *Tel:* +254 41 222 5589, *Fax:* +254 41 231 3813, *Email:* operations@sturrock-keny.com, *Website:* www.sturrockshipping.co.za
Wilhelmsen Ship Services, Bat-Haf Barwil Agencies Ltd, Bat-haf Barwil House, Bat-haf Barwil Road, P O Box 84530, Mombasa, Kenya, *Tel:* +254 41 222 7964, *Fax:* +254 41 223 0277, *Email:* barwil.mombasa@barwil.com, *Website:* www.barwil.com
Zim Integrated Shipping Services Ltd, New Cannon Tower 11, 6th Floor, Moi Avenue, Mombasa, Kenya, *Tel:* +254 41 222 6565, *Fax:* +254 41 222 7701, *Website:* www.zim.co.il

Surveyors: McLarens Young International, Bishops Garden Towers, Bishops Road, Nairobi 10942-00400, Kenya, *Tel:* +254 20 271 0591, *Fax:* +254 20 271 9167, *Email:* adjust@mclarensyoung.co.ke, *Website:* www.mclarensyoung.com
Toplis & Harding International Ltd, P O Box 83030-80100, 2nd Floor,, Maritime Centre, P&O Nedlloyd Building, Moi Avenue, Mombasa, Kenya, *Tel:* +254 41 222 1096, *Fax:* +254 41 231 2892, *Email:* mombasa@toplisandharding.com

Airport: Mombasa (Moi International) Airport, 3 km

Railway: A specialised service operates from the container berths to the Mombasa Container Terminal - then to the depot at Embakasi (Nairobi)

Development: Construction of a second container terminal which will be built on some 100 ha of land next to the Kipevu Oil Terminal about 1 km from the present container terminal. It will take 6 years to build with the first phase taking 3 years

Lloyd's Agent: McLarens Young International, Maritime House, 2nd Floor, Moi Avenue, Mombasa, Kenya, *Tel:* +254 41 222 4130, *Fax:* +254 41 231 5690, *Email:* mombasa@mclarensyoung.co.ke

KIRIBATI

BANABA

Lat 0° 53' S; Long 169° 32' E.

Admiralty Chart: 979	**Admiralty Pilot:** 61
Time Zone: GMT +11.5 h	**UNCTAD Locode:** KI

This port is no longer open to commercial shipping

BETIO

Lat 1° 21' N; Long 172° 55' E.

Admiralty Chart: 3269	**Admiralty Pilot:** 61
Time Zone: GMT +12 h	**UNCTAD Locode:** KI TRW

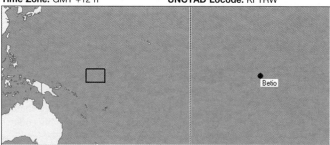

Principal Facilities:

P		G	C				T	A

Authority: Kiribati Ports Authority, P O Box 506, Betio, Tarawa Island, Kiribati, *Tel:* +686 26972, *Fax:* +686 26164, *Email:* kpa@tskl.net.ki, *Website:* www.kpa.com.ki

Officials: General Manager: Capt Koubwere Ienraoi.
Harbour Master: Capt Bonteman Tabera.

Documentation: Cargo manifest, cargo discharge list, bay plan, crew list, passenger list, maritime declaration of health, plants declaration, animals declaration, ship's particulars, bonded stores declaration, ship's stores declaration, list of ships equipment, list of ports declaration, drugs & narcotics declaration, arms & ammunition declaration, crew personal effects declaration, statements of facts, notice of readiness, mails declaration, arrival & departure condition

Approach: The island is roughly triangular in shape, 30.4 km long, N and S, and 25.6 km broad along the S side. On the W side there is a barrier reef, most of which is sunken, enclosing a large lagoon navigable by vessels drawing up to 9.4 m at HT

Anchorage: Four anchorages are used by overseas vessels, one of which can accommodate up to 14 medium sized vessels at a time and is being used by fish carrier vessels when transferring fish from catcher or purseiners to carrier vessels. This anchorage is centred about 2.4 km 050°(T) from No.10 buoy
The next anchorage commonly used by copra vessels is about 0.82 km from No.10 buoy
The next anchorage where containers are being discharged from container vessels onto lighters is 114°(T) 0.4 km from No.10 buoy
The last anchorage for light draft vessels up to 7 m max draft is 328°(T) 0.56 km from No.10 buoy
All anchorages are safe during normal weather except during westerly weather. Further advice can be given by Port Master

Kiribati Shipping Services

P.O. Box 495, Betio, Tarawa, KIRIBATI

Tel: +686 26195   Fax: +686 26204
Email: kssl@tskl.net.ki

General Manager:
Capt. Itibwinnang Aiaimoa

Shipping Agents & Ship Operators

Pilotage: Compulsory. All vessels are required to notify the KPA Port Control their ETA via Marine Guard or local agent 24 h prior to arrival. KPA Port Control listens on VHF Channels 16 and 6. Daylight pilotage only is available but can be done during night hours in an emergency. Pilot station is 1.6 km W of Fairway Buoy

Radio Frequency: Marine Guard keeps 24 h watch on 500, 2182 and 6215 kHz and VHF Channel 16

Weather: Normally light E'ly winds 10-15 knots, occasionally strong W'ly up to 40 knots

Tides: Tidal variation of approx 2 m

Maximum Vessel Dimensions: 195 m loa, 9.4 m draft

Principal Imports and Exports: Imports: General cargo. Exports: Copra, Sea cucumbers, Seaweed, Tuna.

Working Hours: 7.25 hours daily Monday to Friday but can work 24 h, weekends and public holidays if requested by shipowners

Accommodation:

Name	Remarks
Betio	See [1] below

[1]*Betio:* Inner harbour wharf and basin surrounded by two moles 305 m and 610 m long, the eastern mole being longer. The distance between the moles is 53.3 m and the fair channel between the moles to the turning basin and inner wharf is 24.4 m wide. The length of the inner wharf is 129.5 m with alongside depth of 2.5 m
A jetty 150 m long extends in a direction 020°(T) from the eastern end of the mole, thence 50 m in a direction of 110°(T), depth alongside being 6 m and the width of the jetty is 8 m. Most of the local cargo is discharged at this jetty. Tankers up to 5 m draft can moor alongside the jetty discharging through pipeline readily available on jetty. Adjacent to the eastward of the eastern mole is the Kiribati Ports Authority headquarters and Container Terminal which can accommodate 332 TEU's, plus area space for breakbulk of 1000 m2 and 1200 m2 for car storage
Extending from the eastern corner of the Container Terminal is a 80 m x 20 m solid wharf extended in a direction 020°(T). The depth alongside is 6 m. All overseas cargo in containers and breakbulk are discharged here by lighters from container vessels anchored about 1 km due N of the wharf

Storage: Three 600 t copra sheds, three 600 t general gargo and one 600 t cement shed at the old port. The new port has one shed of 2400 m3 for general cargo storage

Mechanical Handling Equipment:

Location	Type	Capacity (t)	Qty
Betio	Mobile Cranes	80	1
Betio	Mobile Cranes	6	1
Betio	Container Cranes	32	1

Cargo Worked: Discharge rate of breakbulk 25 t/h or 12 containers/h

Waste Reception Facilities: Garbage disposal at anchorage is prohibited. Collection for disposal can be arranged with agent

Towage: Three tugs of 150 kw for towing lighters

Repair & Maintenance: Betio Shipyard, P O Box 468, Betio, Tarawa Island, Kiribati, *Tel:* +686 26282, *Fax:* +686 26064, *Email:* shipyard@tskl.net.ki
Kings Holding Engineer, Betio, Tarawa Island, Kiribati, *Tel:* +686 26525, *Fax:* +686 26138

Medical Facilities: Tungaru Central Hospital can perform minor operations

Airport: Bonriki International Airport, 26 km

Lloyd's Agent: Carpenters Shipping, 22 Edinburgh Drive, Suva, Fiji, *Tel:* +679 331 2244, *Fax:* +679 330 1572, *Email:* lloydssuva.shipping@carpenters.com.fj, *Website:* www.carpship.com.fj

FANNING ISLAND

alternate name, see Teraina

OCEAN ISLAND

alternate name, see Banaba

TERAINA

Lat 3° 51' N; Long 159° 22' W.

Admiralty Chart: 2867	**Admiralty Pilot:** 62
Time Zone: GMT -11 h	**UNCTAD Locode:** KI TNQ

This port is no longer open to commercial shipping

KUWAIT

Al-Twaijri and Partners Law Firm (TLF)

Kuwait Airways Building,
Al-Shuhada'a Street, Kuwait City,
First and Second Floor,
P.O Box 863, Safat 13009
Kuwait

Tel: +965 240 2175   Mobile: +965 683 6817
Fax: +965 240 2176
Email: twaijri@twaijri.com
Web: www.twaijri.com

MARITIME LAWYERS/ SOLICITORS

AL KUWAYT

alternate name, see Kuwait

DOHA

Lat 29° 23' N; Long 47° 48' E.

Admiralty Chart: 1214	**Admiralty Pilot:** 63
Time Zone: GMT +3 h	**UNCTAD Locode:** KW

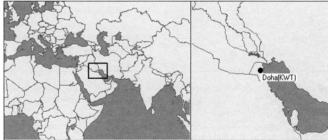

Principal Facilities:

			G					A	

Authority: Kuwait Ports Authority, P O Box 3874, 13039 Safat, Kuwait, *Tel:* +965 481 2622, *Fax:* +965 481 9714, *Website:* www.kpa.com.kw

Port Security: ISPS compliant

Traffic: 2002, 386 438 t of cargo handled

Accommodation:

Name	Remarks
Doha	See [1] below

[1]*Doha:* Small coastal port used by dhows, barges and coastal vessels operating between Gulf Ports. Inside the main port basin there are nine piers totalling 2600 m in depth of 4.3 m

Storage: Eleven warehouses totalling 8110 m2, four covered sheds totalling 4100 m2 and a cattle pen of 3250 m2

Airport: Kuwait International Airport, 25 km

Lloyd's Agent: Kuwait Maritime & Mercantile Co, Arabian Gulf Street, Near Central Bank of Kuwait, 13001 Kuwait, Kuwait, *Tel:* +965 243 4752, *Fax:* +965 243 6856, *Email:* binod.kumar@iss-shipping.com, *Website:* www.iss-shipping.com

Key to Principal Facilities:—				
A=Airport	**C**=Containers	**G**=General Cargo	**P**=Petroleum	**R**=Ro/Ro	**Y**=Dry Bulk
B=Bunkers	**D**=Dry Dock	**L**=Cruise	**Q**=Other Liquid Bulk	**T**=Towage (where available from port)

KUWAIT

Admiralty Chart: 1214
Admiralty Pilot: 63
Time Zone: GMT +3 h
UNCTAD Locode: KW KWI

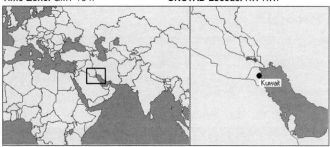

Principal Facilities:

| Y | G | C | R | | B | D | T | A |

Gulf Dredging & Gen. Contracting Co.

P. O. Box : 24054, Safat 13101 - KUWAIT
Tel: 965-4815080   Fax: 965-4817272
Email : gdckt@gdc.com.kw   Website: www.gdckw.com

- Dredging and Reclamation • Waterfront Development Projects
- Seawater Intake Structures • Design, Construction and Maintenance of Marinas
- Revetments, Breakwaters and Precast Concrete Block Walls
  for Wharf Structures, Slipways
- Piling Works • Marine Transportation of Bulk Cargo • Hydrographic Surveys

Livestock Transport & Trading Company (K.S.C.)

2nd & 4th Floors,
Entrance No 3,
Al Salhiya Commerical Complex
P.O Box 23727
13098 Safat
Kuwait

Tel: +965 2434210 / 2455700
Fax: +965 2426645 / 2438970

Email: fleet@kltt.com.kw
Web: www.kltt.com.kw

Authority: Kuwait Ports Authority, P O Box 3874, 13039 Safat, Kuwait, *Tel:* +965 481 2622, *Fax:* +965 481 9714, *Website:* www.kpa.com.kw

Port Security: ISPS compliant

Approach: Traffic to and from the port passes through a navigation channel dredged inside Kuwait Bay approx 8 km long in depth of 8.5 m MLWT

Anchorage: Four anchorage areas with depths ranging from 9.5 m to 21 m

Pilotage: Pilotage into and within the outer anchorages is not compulsory but pilots will be sent to vessels on request to the Harbour Master. Pilotage through the dredged channel, to and from the main wharf, dolphin berths and within inner harbour is compulsory

Radio Frequency: Kuwait Radio, call sign 9KK, operates from 0600-2400. The VHF/RT is a single frequency simplex service operating on Channel 16 (156.8 mc/s), 13 (156.650 mc/s), 12 (156.6 mc/s) and 11 (156.550 mc/s)

Weather: Winds mostly from NW direction

Tides: Range of tide 3.4 m. N winds tend to reduce the height of the tides and S winds tend to increase the height

Maximum Vessel Dimensions: 7.5 m draft at any tidal condition and 9.5 m draft at HT

Principal Imports and Exports: Imports: Electrical products, Grain, Lumber, Machinery, Textile products, Transportation equipment, Wood products. Exports: General cargo.

Working Hours: General cargo handling: April to October, Saturday to Wednesday 0630-1330, 1500-2200. Thursday 0630-1330, 1500-2100. November to March, Saturday to Wednesday 0700-1430, 1430-2130. Thursday 0700-1230, 1230-1830. During Ramadan, Saturday to Thursday, 0700-1230, 1230-1800
Container Terminal, bulk grain vessels, car carriers and livestock carriers work 24 h

Accommodation:

Name	Length (m)	Depth (m)	Remarks
Shuwaikh			See [1] below
Berth No.1	198	10	Grain suction elevator at 400 t/h
Berth No.2	208	10	
Berth No.3	183	10	
Berth No.4	177	10	
Berth No.5	186	10	
Berth No.6	198	10	
Berth No.7	198	10	
Berth No.8	212	10	Cement suction elevator at 400 t/h
Berth No.9	200	10	
Berth No.10	200	10	
Berth No.11	200	10	
Berth No.12	200	10	Container vessels
Berth No.13	180	10	Container vessels
Berth No.14	200	10	
Berth No.15	180	6.7	
Berth No.16	155	6.7	
Berth No.17	200	6.7	
Berth No.18	180	8.5	
Berth No.19	200	8.5	Reefer vessels
Berth No.20	200	8.5	Reefer vessels
Berth No.21	200	8.5	Livestock vessels. Cattle pen of 25 700 m2

[1]*Shuwaikh:* Marine Operations Dept., Tel: +965 483 4931
Container terminal at berths 12 and 13 with an area of 26 ha and equipped with 128 reefer points

Storage: Twenty five warehouses totalling 170 323 m2, two covered sheds totalling 15 137 m2, open storage areas of 485 718 m2 and cold store located between berths 19 and 20 of 11 500 t cap

Mechanical Handling Equipment:

Location	Type	Capacity (t)	Qty	Remarks
Shuwaikh	Mobile Cranes	35	2	at berths 12-13
Shuwaikh	Container Cranes	40	2	at berths 12-13
Shuwaikh	Quay Cranes	3–6		

Bunkering: ExxonMobil Marine Fuels, Mailpoint 31, ExxonMobil House, Ermyn Way, Leatherhead, Surrey KT22 8UX, United Kingdom, *Tel:* +44 1372 222 000, *Fax:* +44 1372   223   922,   *Email:*   marine.fuels@exxonmobil.com,   *Website:* www.exxonmobil.com – *Misc:* Berths 1-15 have fuel oil bunkering facilities. All other berths gas oil can be arranged – *Delivery Mode:* road tanker
Kuwait Petroleum Corp., P O Box 26565, 13126 Safat, Kuwait, *Tel:* +965 4994 242, *Fax:* +965 4994 070, *Email:* bunker@kpcim.com.kw, *Website:* www.kpc.com.kw – *Grades:* MDO; MGO; IFO180-380cSt – *Rates:* 600t/h – *Notice:* 7 days – *Delivery Mode:* pipeline, barge

Towage: Towage is compulsory. Eleven tugs available from 1200 to 2400 hp
Gulf Dredging Co. (S.A.K.), P O Box 24054, End of Ghazalli Street, Gate No.7, 13101 Safat, Kuwait, *Tel:* +965 481 5080, *Fax:* +965 481 7272, *Email:* gdckt@gdc.com.kw

Repair & Maintenance: Heavy Engineering Industries & Shipbuilding Co. (KSC) (HEISCO), Shuwaikh Port Western Extension Gate No.7, P O Box 21988, 13080 Safat, Kuwait, *Tel:* +965   483 0308, *Fax:* +965   481 5947, *Email:* commercial@heisco.com, *Website:* www.heisco.com Chief Executive Officer: Samir Hermez Engine repairs

Ship Chandlers: Abdul Rahman Mohamad Al-Bahar & Sons W.L.L., P O Box 89, 13001 Safat, Kuwait, *Tel:* +965   245 9891, *Fax:* +965   241 1269, *Email:* albahar@baharshipping.com, *Website:* www.baharshipping.com
Al Rashad Supply & Marine Services Corp., P O Box 25048, 13111 Safat, Kuwait, *Tel:* +965 246 8097, *Fax:* +965 242 6140, *Email:* alrashad@kuwait.net, *Website:* www.alrashadsupply.com
Friends Shipchandlers Establishment, P O Box 26844, 13129 Safat, Kuwait, *Tel:* +965 244 4083, *Fax:* +965 244 7211, *Email:* friendsshipchandlers@hotmail.com
Livestock Transport & Trading Co. (K.S.C.), 2nd & 4th Floors, Entrance No. 3, Al Salhiya Commercial Complex, P O Box 23727, 13098 Safat, Kuwait, *Tel:* +965 243 4210, *Fax:* +965 242 6645, *Email:* fleet@kltt.com.kw, *Website:* www.kltt.com.kw

Shipping Agents: Al-Bader Shipping & General Contracting Co WLL, 2nd Floor, Suhair Commercial Centre, Al Hilali Street, P O Box 12075, 71651 Shamiya, Kuwait, *Tel:* +965 240 0175, *Fax:* +965 245 3454, *Email:* albadershipping@absckwt.com.kw, *Website:* www.absckwt.com.kw
Al-Ghanim & Al-Majid Shipping Co W.L.L., Agam House, Ardiya, Block 2, Plot 17, Mhd Ben Al Qassim Street, Kuwait, Kuwait, *Tel:* +965 434 7815, *Fax:* +965 434 9131, *Email:* info@agamco.com, *Website:* www.agamco.com
Al Rashad Supply & Marine Services Corp., P O Box 25048, 13111 Safat, Kuwait, *Tel:* +965 246 8097, *Fax:* +965 242 6140, *Email:* alrashad@kuwait.net, *Website:* www.alrashadsupply.com
Alghanim Group of Shipping & Trans WLL, P O Box 20842, 13069 Safat, Kuwait, *Tel:* +965 242 1701, *Fax:* +965 242 8678, *Email:* info@alghanimgroup.com, *Website:* www.alghanimgroup.com
Amiral Shipping Co., 9th Floor, Mehri Centre, Fahad Salem Street, P O Box 35515, 36056 Kuwait City, Kuwait, *Tel:* +965 247 0826, *Fax:* +965 247 0825, *Email:* jarouche@qualitynet.net
CMA-CGM S.A., CMA CGM Kuwait LLC, Abdulrahman Mohd Al-Bahar & Sons Building, Comm. Area 1, Opposite Central Bank, P O Box 89, 13001 Safat, Kuwait, *Tel:* +965 245 9891, *Fax:* +965 241 4732, *Email:* kwi.genmbox@cma-cgm.com, *Website:* www.cma-cgm.com
Consolidated Shipping Services Group (CSS), 4th Floor, Suhair Commercial Centre, Opposite Sharq Firestation, Al Hilali Street, Kuwait, Kuwait, *Tel:* +965 249 3957, *Fax:* +965 243 3436, *Email:* docs@csskuwait.com, *Website:* www.cssgroupsite.com
Dana Kuwait Shipping & Forwarding Co., P O Box 12075, Shakiya, Kuwait, Kuwait, *Tel:* +965 245 8893, *Fax:* +965 245 8912, *Email:* dks@dks-kwt.com.kw
Green Oasis Shipping Agency Co. WLL, P O Box 1319, 9th Floor Laila Gallery Tower,

Salem Al Mubarak Street, Salmiya, 32014 Kuwait, Kuwait, *Tel:* +965 572 3850, *Fax:* +965 572 3851, *Email:* msc@greenoasiskwt.com, *Website:* www.mscgva.ch

Gulf Agency Co (Kuwait) Ltd, P O Box 20637, 13067 Safat, Kuwait, *Tel:* +965 483 6465, *Fax:* +965 483 6375, *Email:* kuwait@gacworld.com, *Website:* www.gacworld.com

Inchcape Shipping Services (ISS), KMMC Building No.800117, Arabian Gulf Street, P O Box 78, 13001 Safat, Kuwait, *Tel:* +965 2243 4752, *Fax:* +965 2243 3755, *Email:* inchcape@iss-shipping.com, *Website:* www.iss-shipping.com

Kuwait Maritime & Mercantile Co, Arabian Gulf Street, Near Central Bank of Kuwait, 13001 Kuwait, Kuwait, *Tel:* +965 243 4752, *Fax:* +965 243 6856, *Email:* binod.kumar@iss-shipping.com, *Website:* www.iss-shipping.com

A.P. Moller-Maersk Group, Maersk Kuwait Co.W.L.L., 13th Floor, Dar Al Awadi, Ahmad Al-Jaber Street, Al Sharq, 13154 Kuwait City, Kuwait, *Tel:* +965 232 2413, *Fax:* +965 232 2414, *Email:* kwimng@maersk.com, *Website:* www.maerskline.com

Sharaf Shipping Co. WLL, 10th Floor, Laila Tower, Salem Al-Mubarak Street, Al Salmiya, P O Box 4270, 32014 Hawalli, Kuwait, *Tel:* +965 574 9620, *Fax:* +965 574 9625, *Email:* sharafsc@sharafkuwait.com, *Website:* www.sharafgroup.com

Surveyors: ABS (Europe), Abdul Rahman Mohamad Al-Bahar & Sons, P O Box 89, 13001 Safat, Kuwait, *Tel:* +965 241 8346, *Fax:* +965 241 0497, *Email:* abssafat@eagle.org

Bureau Veritas, 1st Floor Sultan Ben Essa Building, Above Global Freight Services Co (GFS), Plot No.44 - Dajeej, Farwaniya, 81025 Kuwait, Kuwait, *Tel:* +965 431 5078, *Fax:* +965 431 4078, *Email:* bv.kuwait@ae.bureauveritas.com, *Website:* www.bureauveritas.com

Det Norske Veritas A/S, P O Box 26169, 13122 Kuwait, Kuwait, *Tel:* +965 244 7125, *Fax:* +965 244 7126, *Website:* www.dnv.com

Nippon Kaiji Kyokai, #2, 13th Floor, Al-Mishary, Al-Khatrash Center, Fahd Al Salem Street, Kuwait, Kuwait, *Tel:* +965 240 0946, *Fax:* +965 240 0948, *Email:* kt@classnk.or.jp, *Website:* www.classnk.or.jp

Panama Shipping Registrar Inc. (PSR), East Ahmadi Plot No.134, P O Box 9284, Ahmadi, 61003 Kuwait, Kuwait, *Tel:* +965 398 2148, *Fax:* +965 398 4188, *Website:* www.panamashipping.com

Medical Facilities: All hospital facilities available. Masters to radio prior to arrival if medical attendance required on board. A well equipped rescue vessel is maintained by the Ministry of Health

Airport: Kuwait International Airport, 15 km

Lloyd's Agent: Kuwait Maritime & Mercantile Co, Arabian Gulf Street, Near Central Bank of Kuwait, 13001 Kuwait, Kuwait, *Tel:* +965 243 4752, *Fax:* +965 243 6856, *Email:* binod.kumar@iss-shipping.com, *Website:* www.iss-shipping.com

MINA ABDULLA

Lat 29° 1' N; Long 48° 10' E.

Admiralty Chart: 1223/3773 **Admiralty Pilot:** 63
Time Zone: GMT +3 h **UNCTAD Locode:** KW MIB

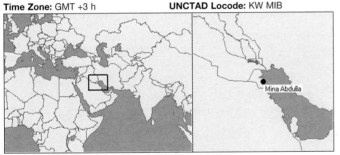
Mina Abdulla

Principal Facilities:

P				B		A

Authority: Kuwait National Petroleum Co., Mina Abdulla Refinery, P O Box 69, 13001 Safat, Kuwait, *Tel:* +965 326 0233, *Fax:* +965 326 1486

Port Security: ISPS compliant

Approach: Sea Island berths. A number of large tanks define the tank farm area and a refinery is located to the south of the tank farm; flares are conspicuous. Also conspicuous are the radio tower and two leading beacons which are lit by three white lights on each beacon in the form of a triangle

When a vessel is ready to enter one of the berths at the same time as another vessel is ready to leave berth, the outgoing vessel shall have priority over the incoming vessel

Anchorage: Vessels requiring to anchor for any reason in port limits should do so within area enclosed, between pos 29° 01' 12" to 29° 02' N; 48° 14' 06" to 48° 15' 06" E, or within reasonable proximity to the E if congestion arises in the anchorage area

Pilotage: Compulsory. Pilot boards approx 2 km to 4 km from Sea Island berths, berthing and mooring masters available

Radio Frequency: Kuwait Radio, call sign 9KK, VHF Channels 16, 11 and 12

Weather: The main prevailing winds are NW which may cause sand storms and SE which cause a heavy swell

Tides: Max tidal range 3.5 m

Working Hours: Loading operations 24 h/day. Office 0700-1600, no work Thursdays and Fridays

Accommodation:

Name	Remarks
Mina Abdulla	See [1] below

[1]*Mina Abdulla:* Mina Abdulla Sea Island consists of two loading berths supplied by six pipelines for exporting liquid petroleum products. It is located 4.8 km offshore to provide a min depth of 17.4 m at the inner berth. The seaward berth is capable of

accommodating tankers from 25 000-276 000 dwt and the inner berth from 25 000-90 000 dwt. Deballasting facilities not available

Bunkering: Kuwait Petroleum Corp., P O Box 26565, 13126 Safat, Kuwait, *Tel:* +965 4994 242, *Fax:* +965 4994 070, *Email:* bunker@kpcim.com.kw, *Website:* www.kpc.com.kw – *Grades:* MDO; MGO; HFO; IFO180-380cSt – *Rates:* 600-900t/h – *Delivery Mode:* pipeline, barge

Towage: Tugs not available. Two 13.7 m mooring boats are available to assist berthing

Repair & Maintenance: Limited repairs undertaken locally

Medical Facilities: Available through ship's agents

Airport: Kuwait International Airport, 35 km

Lloyd's Agent: Kuwait Maritime & Mercantile Co, Arabian Gulf Street, Near Central Bank of Kuwait, 13001 Kuwait, Kuwait, *Tel:* +965 243 4752, *Fax:* +965 243 6856, *Email:* binod.kumar@iss-shipping.com, *Website:* www.iss-shipping.com

MINA AL AHMADI

Lat 29° 4' N; Long 48° 9' E.

Admiralty Chart: 1223/3773 **Admiralty Pilot:** 63
Time Zone: GMT +3 h **UNCTAD Locode:** KW MEA

Mina al Ahmadi

Principal Facilities:

P	Q				B		T	A

Authority: Kuwati Oil Co. (K.S.C.), P O Box 9758, 61008 Ahmadi, Kuwait, *Tel:* +965 326 1558, *Fax:* +965 326 2265, *Email:* kocinfo@kockw.com, *Website:* www.kockw.com

Port Security: ISPS compliant

Approach: Oil tanks on the hill at Ahmadi are visible at 32 km under clear conditions and are useful as a landmark

Deepwater departure channel for loaded deep draft vessels leaving Mina al Ahmadi. It extends 45 km from the Sea Island Terminal to the Madaira Reef and is marked by 20 light buoys and two light beacons, one on Taylor Rock and the other on Madaira Reef. Min depth of water in Departure Channel is 27.7 m

Three special mark buoys indicate the position of the submarine pipeline from North Pier to South Pier. Buoy A1 in pos 29° 07' 00" N; 48° 09' 18" E, Buoy B1 in 29° 06' 06" N; 48° 09' 18" E, Buoy C1 in 29° 05' 06" N; 48° 09' 18" E

Vessels approaching port should contact port control signal station on S pierhead (29° 04' N, 48° 09' E approx) by visual signal or VHF Channel 16. Vessels are expected to notify ETA, last port, health status etc, 96 h before arrival and confirm ETA 24 h before arrival. A few hours before arrival, vessels should contact port control calling 'Mina Al Ahmadi port control' on Channel 16. Separate quarantine clearance required at both Kuwait and Mina al Ahmadi even when vessels call at both ports

Anchorage: The anchorage areas are outside of port limits and clear of the prohibited anchorage and restricted areas. Depths range from 18 m to 28 m, bottom of sand and soft coral with mud patches, affords good holding ground. Vessels will be requested to anchor in one of the three areas as follows: (i) about 2 miles E of the SPM, (ii) about 2 miles E of North Pier, (iii) about 2 miles E of South Pier, (iv) about 2 miles E of Mina Abdulla Sea Island. Permission to be taken from the Harbour Master on VHF Channel 16 or 69 before anchoring

Pilotage: Compulsory. Pilot boards approx 2 miles from piers or sea island or SPM. Berthing and mooring masters available

Radio Frequency: The primary harbour communication network accords with the International Maritime Mobile Radio-telephone Service (Hague System) and operates on VHF Channels 11, 12, 14, 15, 16, 17, 67, 68, 69, 73 and 74. Kuwait Radio, call sign 9KK, frequencies 450, 500, 4287, 6370, 8525 and 12895

Weather: The main prevailing winds are NW which may cause sand storms and SE which cause heavy swell

Tides: Max tidal range 3.5 m

Maximum Vessel Dimensions: Any size, though draft is limited by min depth of 27.7 m in the departure channel

Working Hours: Loading operations 24 h/day. Office 0700-1500, no work Thursday and Fridays

Accommodation:

Name	Remarks
South Pier	See [1] below
North Pier	See [2] below
Bitumen Pier	See [3] below
Single Point Mooring	See [4] below
Single Buoy Moorings	See [5] below

[1]*South Pier:* The South Pier runs seaward for 1280 m. The 'T' head is formed by the oil loading pier and LPG Berth 10. There are seven berths on this 'T' head, No's 1, 3, 4, 5, 6, 9 & 10. Berth No's 1 and 10 for LPG loading, the other berths for crude and oil products loading. The crude and product berths are equipped with bunker hoses; Berth No's 1 and 10 have 16'' cargo arms and 12'' bunker arms. Max loading rate for oil products is 1500 t/h. Berth No.9 can accommodate cargo vessels.

Key to Principal Facilities:—				
A=Airport	**C**=Containers	**G**=General Cargo	**P**=Petroleum	**R**=Ro/Ro	**Y**=Dry Bulk
B=Bunkers	**D**=Dry Dock	**L**=Cruise	**Q**=Other Liquid Cargo	**T**=Towage (where available from port)	

Min depth alongside berths 12.65 to 18.0 m LWOST.
A 10'' slop line is available at all berths for the reception of slops
[2]*North Pier:* The North Pier, 5.6 km N of S Pier, has two outer and two inner berths, No's 11, 12, 15 & 16 with depths alongside of 18.0 m and 17.38 m. Vessels of any size may be tidal loaded to a max draught of 19 m. The four berths are fed through 16'' cargo arms, 12'' chiksan arms and 10'' bunkers arms. Loading rates up to 11 000 t/h at the outer berths and 4000 t/h at inner berths are possible.
A 10'' slop line is available at all berths for the reception of slops
[3]*Bitumen Pier:* Berth No.17, 600 m in length with 'T' head 100 m long in 341°/161° direction. Min depth of 6.25 m accommodating vessels up to a max of 5000 dwt. One loading arm 6'' x 8'' by 40'. Loading rate of 400 t/h. No bunkers
[4]*Single Point Mooring:* Located 2.4 km E of Sea Island in pos 29° 06' 54" N; 48° 19' 13" E. Min depth 31 m. Draught restriction related to min depth of water in the Departure Channel. Equipped with three strings of floating hoses; two strings for crude loading and one string for bunker loading. Each string is 305 m long. Crude strings reduce to 16'' and bunker string to 12''. Hoses connected to a transfer arm on SPM that is free to rotate through 360°
[5]*Single Buoy Moorings:* Two SBM's located 1.5 km NE and SE of SPM: No.20 in pos 29° 08' 35.48" N; 48° 19' 26.19" E and No.21 in pos 29° 07' 32.95" N; 48° 20' 55.14" E. Connected with SPM submarine line accommodating and loading only one vessel at a time. Max displacement 550 000 t, min displacement 120 000 t

Bunkering: Kuwait Petroleum Corp., P O Box 26565, 13126 Safat, Kuwait, *Tel:* +965 4994 242, *Fax:* +965 4994 070, *Email:* bunker@kpcim.com.kw, *Website:* www.kpc.com.kw – *Grades:* MDO; MGO; HFO; IFO180-380cSt – *Rates:* 600t/h, HFO 800t/h available at SBM's and SPM – *Notice:* 7 days – *Delivery Mode:* pipeline, barge

Towage: Five tugs are available, each of 5600 hp

Repair & Maintenance: Limited repairs undertaken locally

Medical Facilities: Available; arranged through agents

Airport: Kuwait International Airport, 30 km

Lloyd's Agent: Kuwait Maritime & Mercantile Co, Arabian Gulf Street, Near Central Bank of Kuwait, 13001 Kuwait, Kuwait, *Tel:* +965 243 4752, *Fax:* +965 243 6856, *Email:* binod.kumar@iss-shipping.com, *Website:* www.iss-shipping.com

MINA AL ZOUR

alternate name, see Mina Saud

MINA SAUD

Lat 28° 45' N; Long 48° 26' E.

Admiralty Chart: 1223   **Admiralty Pilot:** 63
Time Zone: GMT +3 h   **UNCTAD Locode:** KW MIS

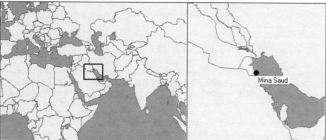

Principal Facilities:

P					B		T	A	

Authority: Saudi Arabian Chevron, P O Box 6, 66051 Mina Saud, Kuwait, *Tel:* +965 395 0337, *Fax:* +965 395 0078, *Email:* wadhav@chevron.com

Officials: Marine Superintendent: Capt Vijay Wadhawan.

Port Security: ISPS compliant. PFSO: Mohammed Aied Al Aradi, Tel: +965 643 2323, Email: aradim@chevron.com

Pre-Arrival Information: Master's are requested to advise ETA 96 h and 72 h before arrival and to confirm this when 48 h and 24 h distant from the port. Messages should be either faxed +965 395 0078 or by email wadhav@chevron.com
It will assist if the following information is passed before vessel's arrival:
ETA Mina Saud
Draft on arrival/departure
Tanker email address
Local agents
Cargo requirement and if can load concurrently with deballasting
Permissible loading rate per line
Acceptance of EDP in which case, master shall sign a letter of authority, authorizing his agent to sign documents on his behalf
Confirm forward fairleads, size 600 mm x 450 mm and distance from bow fairleads to bow chain stoppers between 2.7 m and 3.7 m
Confirm bow SPM mooring arrangements and manifolds fitted as per latest OCIMF recommendations

Approach: Vessels on passage direct to Mina Saud up the Arabian Gulf adhere to traffic separation scheme and keep in the mine-swept areas as directed on the appropriate large scale admiralty chart for the area until the vessel reaches Mina Saud anchorage

Anchorage: Tanker Anchorage Position A: 28° 46' 14.5" N; 48° 29' 16" E
Tanker Anchorage Position B: 28° 45' 20" N; 48° 29' 28" E
Tanker Anchorage Position C: 28° 44' 56.5" N; 48° 28' 32" E

Pilotage: Compulsory. Pilot boarding ground in pos 28° 45' 46" N; 48° 29' 22" E

Radio Frequency: Listening watch on VHF Channel 16 (156.8 mHz)

Weather: Violent storms of a local nature sometimes occur without warning especially at the change of seasons

Tides: The range of tide is an average of 2.4 m at springs and 1.5 m at neaps

Maximum Vessel Dimensions: Max arrival draft 13 m and max departure draft 17.6 m

Working Hours: Weather and other circumstances permitting, vessels are loaded, moored and unmoored at all hours of the day

Accommodation:

Name	Depth (m)	Draught (m)	Remarks
Mina Saud			
SPM Terminal	19.6	17.6	See [1] below
CBM Inner Berth No.1			Out of service but has 12" and 20" submarine lines for loading of crude oil
CBM Outer Berth No.2	16.39	15.85	See [2] below

[1]*SPM Terminal:* Floating structure in depth of approx 20 m, is 12 m in diameter and yellow in colour. It is anchored by a radial pattern of 6 anchor chains extending 300 m out from the buoy. The mooring connection to tankers is made with a 16" circumference nylon hawser. The SPM is linked to the SAC shore facilities by a 36" pipeline buried in the sea floor. No anchorage is allowed within 1500 m of the SPM and within 500 m of any subsea pipeline. Max loading rates available for Ratawi crude is approx 55 000 bbls/h and for Eocene is 45 000 bbls/h
[2]*CBM Outer Berth No.2:* For vessels up to approx 140 000 dwt for full cargo and approx 370 000 dwt for part cargo. This berth has 36", 20" and 12" submarine lines. Normally loading takes place through 36" pipeline

Bunkering: Not available except by bunker barge; to be arranged through Agent

Towage: Two tugs and three launches are available to assist berthing and unberthing

Repair & Maintenance: No repair facilities available. A maintenance barge equipped with underwater cutting gear and welding equipment is available in emergencies, together with divers. Rates to be arranged

Medical Facilities: Routine medical treatment is available from Kuwait Government Port Health authorities at Shuaiba. Company doctors in onshore facilities at Mina Saud can treat emergency cases

Airport: Kuwait International Airport, 85 km

Lloyd's Agent: Kuwait Maritime & Mercantile Co, Arabian Gulf Street, Near Central Bank of Kuwait, 13001 Kuwait, Kuwait, *Tel:* +965 243 4752, *Fax:* +965 243 6856, *Email:* binod.kumar@iss-shipping.com, *Website:* www.iss-shipping.com

SHUAIBA

Lat 29° 2' N; Long 48° 10' E.

Admiralty Chart: 1223/3773   **Admiralty Pilot:** 63
Time Zone: GMT +3 h   **UNCTAD Locode:** KW SAA

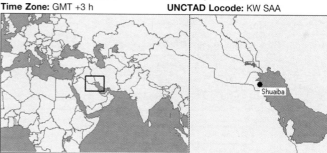

Principal Facilities:

P		Y	G	C	R		B		T	A

Authority: Kuwait Ports Authority, P O Box 3874, 13039 Safat, Kuwait, *Tel:* +965 481 2622, *Fax:* +965 481 9714, *Website:* www.kpa.com.kw

Port Security: ISPS compliant

Approach: From anchorage area to port entrance is approx 3.2 km

Pilotage: Compulsory. Vessels arriving for anchorage should give their ETA well in advance, confirming their ETA 48 h and 24 h before arrival through Kuwait Coast Station 9KK

Radio Frequency: Shuaiba Signal Station operates on following frequencies: 156.80 mHz. Channel 16 international and safety channel: 156.65 mHz. Channel 9 Berthing Operation channel, HF working frequency 2182, 2241, 2246 and 2301. Channel 13 Port Operation channel

Tides: Tidal variation 3 m

Traffic: 2002, 13 770 087 t of cargo handled

Maximum Vessel Dimensions: 70 000 dwt, 13 m draft, 300 m loa

Working Hours: 0600-2200

Accommodation:

Name	Length (m)	Depth (m)	Remarks
Shuaiba			See [1] below
Berth No.1	140	10	Export of urea
Berth No.2	160	11.5	Export of urea
Berth No.3	200	12	
Berth No's 4-5	350	7.5	
Berth No.6	258	10.5	Export of sulphur

Name	Length (m)	Depth (m)	Remarks
Berth No's 7-8	400	12.5	
Berth No's 9-11	600	14	
Berth No's 12-14	630	14	Export of petroleum coke at berth 14
Berth No's 15-18	880	14	See [2] below
Berth No's 19-20	450	14	
Oil Pier		16	See [3] below

[1]*Shuaiba:* Marine Operations Dept., *Tel:* +965 326 3507
There is also a Small Craft Basin which contains three piers of 100 m, 200 m and 175 m long in depth of 4.0 m. Also a Barge Basin containing four piers 211 m, 157 m, 287 m and 250 m long in depth of 6.0 m
[2]*Berth No's 15-18:* Container terminal operated by KGL Ports International, P O Box 24565, Safat 13106, Tel: +965 482 7804, Fax: +965 482 7806, Website: www.kglpi.com
[3]*Oil Pier:* Four berths operated by Kuwait National Petroleum Company

Storage:

Location	Covered (m²)	Sheds / Warehouses
Berth No's 15-18	14500	2

Mechanical Handling Equipment:

Location	Type	Capacity (t)	Qty
Berth No's 12-14	Mult-purp. Cranes	15	4
Berth No's 15-18	Container Cranes	41	3

Bunkering: Kuwait Petroleum Corp., P O Box 26565, 13126 Safat, Kuwait, *Tel:* +965 4994 242, *Fax:* +965 4994 070, *Email:* bunker@kpcim.com.kw, *Website:* www.kpc.com.kw – *Grades:* MDO; MGO; IFO180-380cSt – *Rates:* 600t/h – *Notice:* 7 days – *Delivery Mode:* pipeline, barge

Towage: Compulsory. Four 2100 bhp tugs, two fitted for fire fighting

Repair & Maintenance: Heavy Engineering Industries & Shipbuilding Co. (KSC) (HEISCO), Shuwaikh Port Western Extension Gate No.7, P O Box 21988, 13080 Safat, Kuwait, *Tel:* +965 483 0308, *Fax:* +965 481 5947, *Email:* commercial@heisco.com, *Website:* www.heisco.com Chief Executive Officer: Samir Hermez Engine repairs
Minor repairs can be undertaken by local engineering firms

Airport: Kuwait International Airport, 60 km

Lloyd's Agent: Kuwait Maritime & Mercantile Co, Arabian Gulf Street, Near Central Bank of Kuwait, 13001 Kuwait, Kuwait, *Tel:* +965 243 4752, *Fax:* +965 243 6856, *Email:* binod.kumar@iss-shipping.com, *Website:* www.iss-shipping.com

SHUWAIKH

harbour area, see under Kuwait

LATVIA

ANDREJOSTA

harbour area, see under Riga

ANDREJSALA

harbour area, see under Riga

AUDUPE

harbour area, see under Riga

BRIVOSTA

harbour area, see under Liepaja

DAUDERSALA

harbour area, see under Riga

DAUGAVGRIVA

harbour area, see under Riga

JAUNMILGRAVIS

harbour area, see under Riga

KIPSALA

harbour area, see under Riga

KREMERI

harbour area, see under Riga

KRIEVU SALA

harbour area, see under Riga

KUNDZINSALA

harbour area, see under Riga

LEJAS PODRAGS

harbour area, see under Riga

LIEPAJA

Lat 56° 32' N; Long 21° 0' E.

Admiralty Chart: 2288/2289 **Admiralty Pilot:** 19
Time Zone: GMT +2 h **UNCTAD Locode:** LV LPX

Principal Facilities:

P		Y	G		R	L	B	D	T	A

Authority: Liepaja Special Economic Zone Authority, Feniksa 4, LV-3401 Liepaja, Republic of Latvia, *Tel:* +371 634 27605, *Fax:* +371 634 80252, *Email:* authority@lsez.lv, *Website:* www.portofliepaja.lv

Officials: Chief Executive Officer: Guntars Krievins, *Email:* guntars@lsez.lv.
Marketing Manager: Ivo Kolins, *Email:* ivo@lsez.lv.
Harbour Master: Capt Eduards Raits, *Email:* eduards@lsez.lv.

Port Security: ISPS compliant

Documentation: General declaration (5 copies), cargo manifest (2 copies), ship's stores declaration (2 copies), crew effects declaration (2 copies), crew list (2 copies), passenger list (2 copies), sanitary declaration (1 copy), ship's waste declaration (1 copy), veterinary and phytosanitary declaration (2 copies required when vessel is carrying a cargo of natural origin)

Approach: The harbour at Liepaja has three entrances:
Vidus Varti: the middle and main entrance, is approached via a channel, with a width of 100 m in depth of 10.5 m and marked by leading lights and buoys (spar)
Ziemela Varti: is the north entrance which is closed at present
Dienvidu Varti: the south entrance is approached via a channel with a least depth of 11 m, but is liable to silting

Anchorage: Area 1: deep water anchorage in depths of 19-26 m within the following co-ordinates. 56° 30.0' N; 20° 43.2' E, 56° 31.2' N; 20° 48.0' E, 56° 32.2' N; 20° 44.8' E, 56° 33.2' N; 20° 48.0' E
Area 2: middle tonnage anchorage in depths of 8-15 m within the following co-ordinates. 56° 31.2' N; 20° 50.0' E, 56° 31.6' N; 20° 52.0' E, 56° 33.0' N; 20° 50.1' E, 56° 33.0' N; 20° 52.0' E
Area 3: small tonnage anchorage in depths up to 12 m within the following co-ordinates. 56° 30.0' N; 20° 53.0' E, 56° 30.0' N; 20° 56.0' E, 56° 30.2' N; 20° 53.0' E, 56° 31.0' N; 20° 56.0' E

Pilotage: Compulsory for all vessels carrying dangerous goods and for all vessels over 700 gt, unless the Master holds a valid Pilotage Exemption Certificate. Pilotage is also compulsory for shifting a vessel, along the same berth over a short distance. Upon arrival the pilot is ordered via Traffic Control and on sailing via the ship's agent. Pilots board near Lt buoy 'B' for vessels over 10 000 gt and one nautical mile SW of Lt buoys 1 & 2 for vessels under 10 000 gt. If a pilot cannot board due to bad

---

Key to Principal Facilities:—
A=Airport **C**=Containers **G**=General Cargo **P**=Petroleum **R**=Ro/Ro **Y**=Dry Bulk
B=Bunkers **D**=Dry Dock **L**=Cruise **Q**=Other Liquid Bulk **T**=Towage (where available from port)

weather or other circumstances, shore based pilotage may be given to certain categories of vessels. Pilots can be contacted through Vessel Traffic Centre, Tel: +371 634 25180, Fax: +371 634 81451

Radio Frequency: Port Control on VHF Channel 11 (Liepaja 5). Traffic Control on VHF Channels 11 and 16 (Liepaja 1). Pilot Service on VHF Channel 11 (Gamma)

Weather: Ice free port

Tides: The port is non-tidal

Traffic: 2005, 4 508 900 t of cargo handled

Maximum Vessel Dimensions: 40 000 dwt, 220 m loa, 9.5 m draft

Principal Imports and Exports: Imports: Building materials, Food, Ro/ro cargoes. Exports: Fertiliser, Metal, Oil products, Peat, Timber, Wood chips.

Working Hours: 24 h/day at terminals

Accommodation:

Name	Length (m)	Depth (m)	Remarks
Brivosta (Free Port)			
Pier No.46	400	8.5	See [1] below
Pier No's 42-45	984	10.5	See [2] below
Pier No's 40-41	342	7.9	See [3] below
Ziemas Osta (Winter Port)			
Pier No.56	105	4.5	See [4] below
Pier No's 57-59	457	7	See [5] below
Pier No's 60-61	412	7	See [6] below
Pier No's 62-63	290		See [7] below
Pier No's 64-65	301	7	See [8] below
Tirdzniecibas Kanals (Commercial Channel)			
Pier No's 66-67	240	6.7	See [9] below
Pier No.68	120	6	See [10] below
Pier No's 73-77	520	6–7.4	See [11] below
Pier No's 80-81	160	4.5–7.4	Operated by Nektons Ltd Yachts & cruise passengers
Karostas Kanals (Navy Channel)			
Pier No.5	130	7	See [12] below
Pier No.25	88	7.5	See [13] below
Pier No.26	45	4.5	See [14] below
Pier No.28	120	5	See [15] below
Pier No.30	89	8	See [16] below

[1]*Pier No.46:* Operated by LSEZ 'Terrabalt' Ltd., Brivosta 46 Pier, Liepaja LV-3405, Tel: +371 634 25756, Fax: +371 634 81454, Email: info@terrabalt.lv, Website: www.terrabalt.lv
Ro/ro cargoes

[2]*Pier No's 42-45:* Operated by LSEZ JSC 'Trans Liepaja', Tel: +371 634 07142, Fax: +371 634 07143, Email: agency@trliepaja.apollo.lv
Dry bulk & general cargoes

[3]*Pier No's 40-41:* Operated by LSEZ 'Laskana' Ltd., Tel: +371 634 23111, Fax: +371 634 24462, Email: info@laskana.lv, Website: www.laskana.lv
Dry bulk (wood chips) & break bulk (pulp timber) cargoes

[4]*Pier No.56:* Operated by LSEZ 'Laskana' Ltd., Tel: +371 634 23111, Fax: +371 634 24462, Email: info@laskana.lv, Website: www.laskana.lv
Dry bulk (wood chips) & break bulk (pulp timber) cargoes

[5]*Pier No's 57-59:* Operated by Silva Ltd
Dry bulk (wood chips) & break bulk (pulp timber) cargoes

[6]*Pier No's 60-61:* Operated by LSEZ 'Mols-L' Ltd., Tel: +371 634 81168, Fax: +371 634 81172
Dry bulk & general (sawn timber) cargoes

[7]*Pier No's 62-63:* Operated by LSEZ 'Duna' Ltd., Tel: +371 634 27227, Fax: +371 634 23753, Email: duna@mail.anet.lv
Dry bulk, liquid bulk & general cargoes

[8]*Pier No's 64-65:* Operated by LSEZ 'Piemare' Ltd., Tel: +371 634 24429, Fax: +371 634 27333, Email: info@piemare.lv
General cargoes

[9]*Pier No's 66-67:* Operated by LSEZ 'Transwide Service' Ltd., 123 Brivibas Street, Liepaja, LV-3401, Tel: +371 634 86363, Fax: +371 634 86316, Email: tws@tws.lv, Website: www.tws.lv
Dry bulk cargoes

[10]*Pier No.68:* Operated by 'Fish Terminal' Ltd
Liquid bulk & general cargoes

[11]*Pier No's 73-77:* Operated by LSEZ 'Piemare' Ltd., Tel: +371 634 24429, Fax: +371 634 27333, Email: info@piemare.lv
General & break bulk cargoes

[12]*Pier No.5:* Operated by LSEZ 'Baltic Transhipment Center' Ltd., Turaidas iela 24, Liepaja LV-3402, Tel: +371 634 07196, Fax: +371 634 07197, Email: btc@btc.lv, Website: www.btc.lv
Dry bulk cargoes

[13]*Pier No.25:* Operated by Durbe Impex Ltd
Dry bulk (oil products) cargoes

[14]*Pier No.26:* Operated by Glen Oil Ltd., Tel: +371 634 27628, Fax: +371 634 26833
Dry bulk (oil products) cargoes

[15]*Pier No.28:* Operated by Braxton Terminal Ltd
Dry bulk (oil products) cargoes

[16]*Pier No.30:* Operated by Marilat Ltd., Tel: +371 634 24662, Fax: +371 634 24664
General cargoes

Storage:

Location	Open (m²)	Covered (m²)	Cold (m³)
Liepaja	370911	54190	22670

Mechanical Handling Equipment:

Location	Type	Capacity (t)	Qty
Liepaja	Floating Cranes	100	1
Liepaja	Mult-purp. Cranes	1–12	15
Liepaja	Mult-purp. Cranes	5–32	22
Liepaja	Mobile Cranes	10–25	2

Bunkering: Braxton Bunkering Liepaja Ltd, Kurzemes 9, 3401 Liepaja, Republic of Latvia, *Tel:* +371 634 27628, *Fax:* +371 634 26833, *Email:* bbl@mail.anet.lv
Hanza Bunkering Ltd (LSA), 43 Graudu Street, LV-3400 Liepaja, Republic of Latvia, *Tel:* +371 634 26833, *Fax:* +371 634 26833, *Email:* hanza@hanza.lv, *Website:* www.hanza.lv
Braxton Bunkering Liepaja Ltd, Kurzemes 9, 3401 Liepaja, Republic of Latvia, *Tel:* +371 634 27628, *Fax:* +371 634 26833, *Email:* bbl@mail.anet.lv
Hanza Bunkering Ltd (LSA), 43 Graudu Street, LV-3400 Liepaja, Republic of Latvia, *Tel:* +371 634 26833, *Fax:* +371 634 26833, *Email:* hanza@hanza.lv, *Website:* www.hanza.lv

Waste Reception Facilities: Garbage disposal on every berth. There are oily water treatment plant facilities available for reception of bilge, dirty ballast and tank washing waters

Towage: Five tugs available

Repair & Maintenance: Tosmare Ship Repair Plant Ltd, 42/44 Generala Baloza Street, LV-3414 Liepaja, Republic of Latvia, *Tel:* +371 634 07371, *Fax:* +371 634 07370, *Email:* shipyard@tosmare.lv, *Website:* www.tosmare.lv Two dry docks of 179 m x 24 m and 210 m x 24 m. Floating dock of 102 m x 19.5 m with lifting cap of 4000 t. Repair quay of 900 m with max draught 8 m

Ship Chandlers: Unimars Ltd (Universal Marine Service), 11 Kaiju Street, Liepaja, Republic of Latvia, *Tel:* +371 634 07667, *Fax:* +371 634 07668, *Email:* unimars_liepaja@navigator.lv, *Website:* www.unimars.lv
Zerssen LSS Ltd, 37 O. Kalpaka Street, LV-3417 Liepaja, Republic of Latvia, *Tel:* +371 634 25293, *Fax:* +371 634 24193, *Email:* lzerssen@latship.lv, *Website:* www.zerssen.lv

Shipping Agents: Alpha Shipping Co. SIA, Klaipedas 19/21-504, LV-3401 Liepaja, Republic of Latvia, *Tel:* +371 634 01720, *Fax:* +371 634 28440, *Email:* alpha@ljbirojs.lv, *Website:* www.alpha.lv
Andre Maritime Agency Co. Ltd, 37 O Kalpaka Street, LV-3417 Liepaja, Republic of Latvia, *Tel:* +371 634 23723, *Fax:* +371 634 81455, *Email:* andre@apollo.lv
Astramar Shipping Agency, 23 Graudu Str., LV-3401 Liepaja, Republic of Latvia, *Tel:* +371 634 25506, *Fax:* +371 634 81474, *Email:* astramar@liepaja.apollo.lv, *Website:* www.astramar.net
Baltic Transit Agency JSC, 101A Kalpaka Street, LV-3405 Liepaja, Republic of Latvia, *Tel:* +371 634 24929, *Fax:* +371 634 24922, *Email:* bta@apollo.lv, *Website:* www.baltic-transit.lv
Duna Ltd, Atsledznieku 29, LV-3400 Liepaja, Republic of Latvia, *Tel:* +371 634 27227, *Fax:* +371 634 23753, *Email:* andris@duna.apollo.lv
Laskana Ltd, P O Box 34, LV-3400 Liepaja, Republic of Latvia, *Tel:* +371 634 23111, *Fax:* +371 634 24462, *Email:* info@laskana.lv, *Website:* www.laskana.lv
Liepaja Shipping Agency Ltd, 4A Apshu Street, LV-3401 Liepaja, Republic of Latvia, *Tel:* +371 634 26278, *Fax:* +371 634 81190, *Email:* liepaja.agency@compass-transit.com, *Website:* www.kompass-tranzits.com
Mols-L Ltd, Barinu street 7, LV-3401 Liepaja, Republic of Latvia, *Tel:* +371 634 81168, *Fax:* +371 634 81172, *Email:* molsl@one.lv
Terrabalt Ltd, Brivosta, 46 piers, LV-3405 Liepaja, Republic of Latvia, *Tel:* +371 634 25756, *Fax:* +371 634 87404, *Email:* info@terrabalt.lv, *Website:* www.terrabalt.lv
Trans Liepaja Jsc., Sliezu 7/1, LV-3405 Liepaja, Republic of Latvia, *Tel:* +371 634 24515, *Fax:* +371 634 27003, *Email:* info@liepajaport.lv, *Website:* www.liepajaport.lv
Unimars Ltd (Universal Marine Service), 11 Kaiju Street, Liepaja, Republic of Latvia, *Tel:* +371 634 07667, *Fax:* +371 634 07668, *Email:* unimars_liepaja@navigator.lv, *Website:* www.unimars.lv

Stevedoring Companies: DG Terminals Ltd, Liepaja, Republic of Latvia, *Tel:* +371 634 24604, *Fax:* +371 634 24604, *Email:* feniks@apollo.lv
Duna Ltd, Atsledznieku 29, LV-3400 Liepaja, Republic of Latvia, *Tel:* +371 634 27227, *Fax:* +371 634 23753, *Email:* andris@duna.apollo.lv
Kueoaha Trans Storage Ltd, Liepaja, Republic of Latvia, *Tel:* +371 634 74840, *Fax:* +371 634 74896
Laskana Ltd, P O Box 34, LV-3400 Liepaja, Republic of Latvia, *Tel:* +371 634 23111, *Fax:* +371 634 24462, *Email:* info@laskana.lv, *Website:* www.laskana.lv
Mols-L Ltd, Barinu street 7, LV-3401 Liepaja, Republic of Latvia, *Tel:* +371 634 81168, *Fax:* +371 634 81172, *Email:* molsl@one.lv
Piemare Ltd, Piemare AS, Kaiju Street 11, LV-3401 Liepaja, Republic of Latvia, *Tel:* +371 634 24429, *Fax:* +371 634 27333, *Email:* info.piemare@apollo.lv
Terrabalt Ltd, Brivosta, 46 piers, LV-3405 Liepaja, Republic of Latvia, *Tel:* +371 634 25756, *Fax:* +371 634 87404, *Email:* info@terrabalt.lv, *Website:* www.terrabalt.lv
Trans Liepaja Jsc., Sliezu 7/1, LV-3405 Liepaja, Republic of Latvia, *Tel:* +371 634 24515, *Fax:* +371 634 27003, *Email:* info@liepajaport.lv, *Website:* www.liepajaport.lv
Transwide Services Ltd, 123 Brivibas str, LV-3401 Liepaja, Republic of Latvia, *Tel:* +371 634 86363, *Fax:* +371 634 86316, *Email:* tws@tws.lv, *Website:* www.tws.lv

Surveyors: Baltic Kontor Ltd, 68/70 O.Kalpaka Street, LV-3417 Liepaja, Republic of Latvia, *Tel:* +371 634 80591, *Fax:* +371 634 80589, *Email:* liepaja@bk.lv, *Website:* www.bk.lv

Medical Facilities: City Central Hospital, 3 km

Airport: Liepaja International Airport, 10 km

Railway: Liepaja Central Station, 1 km

Lloyd's Agent: Baltic Kontor Ltd, 7 Maza Aluksnes Street, LV-1045 Riga, Republic of Latvia, *Tel:* +371 673 81463, *Fax:* +371 675 01822, *Email:* bsi@bk.lv, *Website:* www.bk.lv

MANGALSALA

harbour area, see under Riga

MERSRAGS

Lat 57° 22' N; Long 23° 8' E.

Admiralty Chart: 2215　　　　**Admiralty Pilot:** 19
Time Zone: GMT +2 h　　　　**UNCTAD Locode:** LV

Principal Facilities:

	Y	G				T	

Authority: Port of Mersrags, Liela Street 62, Talsi District, LV-3284 Mersrags, Republic of Latvia, *Tel:* +371 632 35696, *Fax:* +371 632 35696, *Email:* info@mersragsport.lv, *Website:* www.mersragsport.lv

Officials: Port Manager: Janis Budreika, *Email:* janisb@mersragsport.lv.
Port Captain: Aivars Usackis, *Email:* aivarsu@mersragsport.lv.

Port Security: ISPS compliant

Pre-Arrival Information: The ship's master should inform the Superintendent of the Port 24 h and 4 h before arrival at the reception buoy and make known the following data of the vessel:
a) name
b) type
c) flag
d) call sign
e) length, width & draft
f) IMO identification number and the Marine Mobile Service Identification (MMSI) number
g) freight
h) ship superstructure height
i) ship's agent
j) ETA at the reception buoy
k) berth (if known)
l) ETD
m) number of crew and passengers onboard

Documentation: On entering the port, the ship's agent should submit the following documents to the Superintendent of the Port:
a) entry for goods
b) general declaration
c) list of passengers
d) crew list
e) ship waste declaration
On entering the port, the ship's agent should submit the following documents on request of the Superintendent of the Port:
a) international capacity certificate
b) registry certificate
Whenever required, the Superintendent of the Port should be entitled to request also for other document originals or copies specified in the international conventions or regulatory acts of the flag country
On leaving the port, the ship's agent should submit the following documents to the Superintendent of the Port:
a) general declaration
b) entry for goods
c) crew list
d) list of passengers

Anchorage: Available within the following coordinates:
57° 20' 02" N; 23° 13' 00" E
57° 20' 02" N; 23° 14' 04" E
57° 18' 09" N; 23° 13' 03" E
57° 18' 09" N; 23° 15' 04" E

Pilotage: Available 24 h/day. Compulsory for vessels over 50 m loa

Radio Frequency: VHF Channels 10 and 16

Traffic: 2007, 126 vessels, 397 000 t of cargo handled

Accommodation:

Name	Length (m)	Draught (m)	Remarks
Mersrags			See [1] below
Berth No.1	120	4.5	Owned by A/S Mersrags
Berth No.2	48	3.5	Owned by Fregat Ltd
Berth No.4	50	4.5	Owned by Gamma-Rent Ltd
Berth No.6	110	6.5	Owned by Port Authority
Berth No.7	160	6.5	Owned by Port Authority

[1]*Mersrags:* Cargoes primarily handled are pulpwood, woodchips & fish products. There is also a service centre for yachts

Towage: Available

Medical Facilities: Available

Railway: Railway Station, 40 km

Lloyd's Agent: Baltic Kontor Ltd, 7 Maza Aluksnes Street, LV-1045 Riga, Republic of Latvia, *Tel:* +371 673 81463, *Fax:* +371 675 01822, *Email:* bsi@bk.lv, *Website:* www.bk.lv

RIGA

Lat 56° 57' N; Long 24° 5' E.

Admiralty Chart: 2239/2215　　　**Admiralty Pilot:** 19
Time Zone: GMT +2 h　　　　**UNCTAD Locode:** LV RIX

Principal Facilities:

P	Q	Y	G	C	R	L	B		T	A

Tramp Oil & Marine

Wells House, 15-17 Elmfield Road, Bromley,
Kent BR1 1LT, United Kingdom
Phone: +44 20 8315 7777　　**Fax:** +44 20 8315 7788
General email: enquiries@tramp-oil.com

See listings for all global offices: **www.tramp-oil.com**

Authority: Freeport of Riga Authority, 12 O. Kalpaka Boulevard, LV-1050 Riga, Republic of Latvia, *Tel:* +371 670 30800, *Fax:* +371 670 30835, *Email:* info@freeportofriga.lv, *Website:* www.freeportofriga.lv

Officials: Chief Executive Officer: Leonids Loginovs.
Harbour Master: Eduards Delvers, *Email:* eduards.delvers@freeportofriga.lv.

Port Security: ISPS compliant. Before entering the port the vessel shall provide safety information in accordance with the Clause 2.1. of Article 9 of Chapter XI-2 of SOLAS Convention

Pre-Arrival Information: Each inbound vessel or ship agent, 24 h and 4 h prior to arrival at Buoy B, is obliged to notify the VTS about the arrival of the vessel as well as provide the following data related to the vessel:
a) name of the vessel
b) type of vessel
c) flag of the vessel
d) call sign
e) IMO identification number
f) Maritime Mobile Service Identity (MMSI) number
g) expected time of arrival at Buoy B
h) length, breadth
i) cargo
j) air draught
k) ship agent
l) berth (if known)
m) vessel gt
n) vessel dwt
o) maximum draught
p) draught upon arrival
q) engine power
r) ice class and classification society, that has determined ice class (for winter navigation period)
Should there be any dangerous or polluting goods on board a vessel, the ship operator, ship agent or the Master shall notify VTS about that at least 24 h prior to arrival of the vessel or departure of the vessel from the previous port of call, if the duration of the trip does not exceed 24 h. Four hours in advance of arrival a Master shall notify the VTS of the planned operation and order pilot services, as well as update the arrival time one hour in advance

Documentation: For incoming vessels: master's declaration (1 copy), general declaration (4 copies), cargo manifest (2 copies), bills of lading (to be presented), ship's stores declaration (2 copies), crew effects declaration (2 copies), crew list (4 copies), passenger list (4 copies), maritime declaration of health (1 copy), veterinary & phito-sanitary declaration (2 copies)
For outgoing vessels: master's declaration (1 copy), general declaration (4 copies), cargo manifest (2 copies), bills of lading (to be presented), crew list (4 copies), port clearance (2 copies - one copy to be given over to the pilot upon departure from the port)

Approach: 100 m wide entrance channel with max allowed draught for incoming vessels of 12 m leads across sandy river bar into the River Daugava. Max speed of vessels should not exceed 8 knots. No max air draught for vessels except from Rinuzi roads up to Berth PM-21 (58 m) and from Sarkandaugava Channel up to Berth SD-4, 5 (39 m). Coastal radar service available

Key to Principal Facilities:—				
A=Airport	**C**=Containers	**G**=General Cargo	**P**=Petroleum	**R**=Ro/Ro	**Y**=Dry Bulk
B=Bunkers	**D**=Dry Dock	**L**=Cruise	**Q**=Other Liquid Bulk	**T**=Towage (where available from port)	

Anchorage: The Freeport of Riga roads are situated NW of the River Daugava entrance. The outer roads are exposed to winds veering from the SW, N and NE, and in the autumn during prevailing winds from these directions anchorage can be unsafe. During periods of N winds, heavy waves may be experienced and vessels are recommended to leave the roads for the shelter of the port area or open sea. Anchorage can be obtained 4 miles off the Daugavgriva lighthouse, bearing 310° W of the light buoy 'B' in depth of 25-30 m, bottom is mud and sand

Pilotage: Compulsory. Pilot meets vessel at receiving Light Buoy 'B' Daugavgriva in pos 57° 06' N; 23° 57' E. Pilots must be ordered 4 h prior to arrival via VHF Channel 9 or 16, Tel: +371 670 82000, Fax: +371 673 22750. Pilotage available 24 h

Radio Frequency: Vessel Traffic Service: VHF Channel 16 or 9, call sign 'Riga Traffic', Tel: +371 670 82035 & 670 82032, Fax: +371 673 23117

Weather: Year round navigation. In severe winter icebreaker is always available

Traffic: 2008, 29 565 900 t of cargo handled

Maximum Vessel Dimensions: 250 m loa, 65 000 dwt, 12.5 m draft

Principal Imports and Exports: Imports: General cargo. Exports: Coal, Fertilisers, Metals, Oil products, Timber.

Working Hours: Harbour Master's office 24 h/day
Freeport of Riga Authority Mon-Fri 0900-1800
Freeport of Riga (stevedores, shipping agents etc) 24 h/day

Accommodation: LIQUID BULK TERMINALS:
JSC 'B.L.B. Baltijas Terminals', Ezera 22, Riga LV-1034, Tel: +371 673 45830, Fax: +371 673 45932, Email: inga@blb.lv, Website: www.blb.lv
JSC 'Latvijas Propana Gaze', Kurzemes Prospekts 19, Riga LV-1067, Tel: +371 678 15025, Fax: +371 674 13712, Email: lpg@lpg.lv, Website: www.lg.lv
PLC 'Latvija Statoil', Citadeles 12, Riga LV-1010, Tel: +371 670 88100, Fax: 371 670 88150, Email: latvija@statoil.com, Website: www.statoil.com & www.statoil.lv
PLC 'Man-Tess', Tvaika 7a, Riga LV-1005, Tel: +371 670 29100, Fax: +371 670 29115, Email: office@man-tess.lv, Website: www.man-tess.lv
PLC 'Neste Latvija', Bauskas 58a, Riga LV-1004, Tel: +371 671 03355, Fax: +371 671 03375, Email: neste.latvija@nesteoil.com, Website: www.neste.lv
PLC 'Ovi', Tvaika 35, Riga LV-1034, Tel: +371 673 54828, Fax: +371 673 55538, Email: bunker@ovi.lv, Website: www.ovi.lv
PLC 'VL Bunkerings', Tvaika 68, Riga LV-1034, Tel: +371 673 93857, Fax: +371 673 94099
PLC 'Vudisona Terminals', Tvaika 39, Riga LV-1034, Tel: +371 673 97794 & 673 97388, Fax: +371 673 97795 & 673 97389, Email: woodison@woodison.lv & dmitryk@woodison.lv
BULK & GENERAL CARGO TERMINALS:
JSC 'Baltic Sea Port', Daugavgrivas 93, Riga LV-1007, Tel: +371 674 72882, Fax: +371 674 72900, Email: bsp@bsp.lv, Website: www.bsp.lv
JSC 'Rigas Ostas Elevators', Andrejostas 14, Riga LV-1045, Tel: +371 673 20079, Fax: +371 672 13355, Email: roe@saits.lv
JSC 'Rinuzu Stividors', Atlantijas 27, Riga LV-1015, Tel: +371 673 51514 & 673 53611, Fax: +371 673 53168, Email: rinuzhi@rinuzhi.riga.lv
JSC 'Terminals Vecmilgravis', Zivju 1, Riga LV-1015, Tel: +371 673 53382, Fax: +371 673 53057, Email: valda@terminal.lv, Website: www.terminal.lv
JSC 'Remars-Riga', Gales 2, Riga LV-1015, Tel: +371 673 53695, Fax: +371 673 53526, Email: remars@riga-shipyard.com
PLC 'Man-Tess', Tvaika 7a, Riga LV-1005, Tel: +371 670 29100, Fax: +371 670 29115, Email: office@man-tess.lv, Website: www.man-tess.lv
PLC 'Alpha Osta', Atlantijas 35, Riga LV-1015, Tel: +371 673 51520, Fax: +371 673 51522, Email: alpha-osta@alpha-osta.lv, Website: www.alfa.lv
PLC 'Freja', Flotes Iela 11/14, Riga LV-1016, Tel: +371 678 40770, Fax: +371 678 40771, Email: viesturs.osenieks@korsnas.lv
PLC 'Jaunmilgravja Ostas Kompanija', Tvaika 70, Riga LV-1034, Tel: +371 673 91040, Fax: +371 673 92747, Email: osta@lupo.lv, Website: www.jmostasko.com
PLC 'La Con', Flotes 5, Riga LV-1016, Tel: +371 670 68501, Fax: +371 670 68505, Email: info@lacon.lv, Website: www.lacon.lv
PLC 'Magnats', Daugavgrivas Iela 83/89, Riga LV-1007, Tel: +371 674 70797, Fax: +371 674 73634, Email: magnat@delfi.lv
PLC 'Rigas Centralais Terminals', Eksporta 15, Riga LV-1045, Tel: +371 673 29816, Fax: +371 673 26501, Email: referent@rigact.lv
PLC 'Rigas Juras Osta Voleri', Zila Iela 5a, Riga LV-1007, Tel: +371 673 46393, Fax: +371 673 46545, Email: voleri@neonet.lv
PLC 'Sala', Traleru 2a, Riga LV-1030, Tel: +371 673 53617, Fax: +371 673 53616, Email: sala-port@parks.lv, Website: www.sala-port.lv
PLC 'Zilite', Tvaika 27, Riga LV-1005, Tel: +371 673 93018, Fax: +371 673 55718, Email: zilite@maksinets.lv, Website: www.zilite.lv
PLC 'Krievu Salas Terminals', Zila 22/24, Riga LV-1007, Tel: +371 670 65500, Fax: +371 670 65502, Email: zanda@ksterminals.lv
PLC 'Speja', Zila 3, Riga LV-1007, Tel: +371 674 32055, Fax: +371 673 43436, Email: speja@apollo.lv
JSC 'Starts-Riga', Tvaika 68a, Riga LV-1034, Tel: +371 673 92314, Fax: +371 673 93832, Email: starts.riga@sr.lv
PLC 'Riga Passenger Terminal', Eksporta Iela 3a, Riga LV-1010, Tel: +371 673 26200, Fax: +371 673 26195, Email: sekretare.terminals@apollo.lv & sekretare@terminals.unistars.lv
PLC 'WT Terminal', Flotes 3a, Riga LV-1016, Tel: +371 678 06010, Fax: +371 674 43001, Email: office@wt-terminal.lv, Website: www.wt-terminal.lv
PLC 'Baltic Container Terminal', Kundzinsalas 1, Riga LV-1822, Tel: +371 670 76200, Fax: +371 670 76222, Email: info@bct.lv, Website: www.bct.lv
PLC 'Vega Stividors', Ezera 22, Riga LV-1034, Tel: +371 673 45834, Fax: +371 673 45822, Email: vega@vega.lv, Website: www.vega.lv

Name	Length (m)	Draught (m)	Remarks
Customs Shoreline			
MK-3	240	7.4	For vessels up to 170 m loa
Passenger Station			
JPS-1	132	5.8	For vessels up to 120 m loa
JPS-2	217	7.7	For vessels up to 180 m loa
Andrejosta			
AO-1			Under reconstruction
AO-2	140	4.5	
Andrejsala			
AS-3	110	7.4	For vessels up to 105 m loa

Name	Length (m)	Draught (m)	Remarks
AS-4	120	7.5	
AS-5	144	7.8	For vessels up to 150 m loa
Eksportostas Dambis			
ED			Closed
Eksportosta			See [1] below
EO-6	240	10	
EO-7	190	9.5	
EO-8	188	9.1	
EO-9	130	6.6	
EO-10	150	7	
EO-11	140	7.2	
EO-12	159	7.2	
EO-14	210	11.7	See [2] below
EO-15	212	11.7	
Pilmuiza Basin			See [3] below
PM-16	145	9.5	See [4] below
PM-17	145	9.5	
PM-18	105	6.7	
PM-19	172	7.6	
PM-20	218	10.1	For vessels up to 180 m loa
PM-21	350	11.7	For vessels up to 225 m loa
Kundzinsala			
KS-28		11.7	See [5] below
KS-32	150	11.7	
KS-33	150	11.7	
KS-34	149	11.7	
Sarkandaugava			Max air draught 35 m
SD-3	150	7	For vessels up to 130 m loa
SD-4	135	7.7	For vessels up to 130 m loa
SD-5	165	9.05	For vessels up to 165 m loa
Daudersala			
DS-9	105	5	For vessels up to 100 m loa
DS-10	100	5.5	For vessels up to 100 m loa
DS-11			Closed
DS-12			Closed
Jaunmilgravis			
JM-15	181	6.5	For vessels up to 125 m loa, max width 16 m
JM-15A	80	2–4	
JM-16	148	7.4	
JM-17	125	5.7	For vessels up to 105 m loa
JM-20	60	4	For vessels up to 80 m loa
JM-22	150	8	See [6] below
JM-23	100	9.05	For vessels up to 110 m loa
JM-25	110	5.5	For vessels up to 100 m loa
JM-26	74	9.05	See [7] below
JM-27	72	8.2	See [8] below
JM-29	154	5.3	See [9] below
Riga Ship Building Factory			See [10] below
RKR-3	70		
RKR-4	120		
RKR-5	161		
RKR-6	200		
RKR-6A	105		
RKR-7	250	7.6	
RKR-8	184	4.7	
RKR-9	90		
Vecmilgravis			
VM-3	60	5.8	For vessels up to 100 m loa
VM-4		7	For vessels up to 125 m loa
Mangali Ship Repair Factory			
MKR-1	175	9	
MKR-2	100	6.5	
MKR-3	100	6.3	
MKR-4	100	6.3	
MKR-5	100	6.8	
MKR-6			MKR pilot services area
MKR-7			MKR pilot services area
MKR-8			MKR pilot services area
Fishing Port			
ZO-1	150	9.3	
ZO-2	168	9.2	
ZO-3	100	7	For vessels up to 75 m loa
ZO-4	100	7.2	
ZO-5	100	7.2	
ZO-6	100	7.2	
ZO-7	100	7.3	
ZO-8	100	6.8	For vessels up to 80 m loa
ZO-9	100	6.8	
ZO-10	132	6.8	
ZO-11	103	5.3	No anchor should be used
ZO-12	230	12.2	For vessels up to 250 m loa
ZO-14	132	5.6	For vessels up to 105 m loa, no anchor should be used
ZO-15	104	6.7	For vessels up to 70 m loa
ZO-16			
ZO-17		5	For vessels up to 120 m loa
ZO-18	225	12.2	See [11] below
Audupe			
AU-1	195	4.5	See [12] below
AU-2	87		Repair works
Mangalsala			
MS-10	120	5.9	For vessels up to 110 m loa
MS-11	130	5.6	For vessels up to 130 m loa
MS-12	130	6.2	
MS-13	195	6.2	For vessels up to 130 m loa

Name	Length (m)	Draught (m)	Remarks
Ronu Dikis			
RD-1	145	4.8	For vessels up to 100 m loa, tugs to be used
RD-2	148	5.2	For vessels up to 100 m loa, tugs to be used
RD-3	235	5.3	
RD-5			
Voleri			
VL-13	105	4.5	See [13] below
VL-14	65	4	For vessels up to 50 m loa
VL-15	95	5.7	For vessels up to 125 m loa
Kremeri			
KR-18	120	3.5	For vessels up to 115 m loa
KR-19	115	4.8	For vessels up to 105 m loa
KR-20	115	5.7	For vessels up to 105 m loa
KR-21	135	5.7	For vessels up to 100 m loa, current not exceeding 1 knot
KR-22	70	4.6	See [14] below
KR-24	100	5.8	
KR-25	115	7.2	For vessels up to 100 m loa
Lejas Podrags			
LP-27	145	6.5	
Daugavgriva			
DG-1	203	10.5–12	See [15] below
DG-2	110	6	For vessels up to 80 m loa
DG-19	155	5	For vessels up to 105 m loa; shipping in daylight
DG-20	155	5	For vessels up to 140 m loa; shipping in daylight
DG-54	200	4.9	For vessels up to 120 m loa
DG-55	147	5.5	For vessels up to 125 m loa
DG-55A	76	5.5	
DG-56	105	5.5	For vessels up to 90 m loa
Krievu Sala			
KRS-1	166	10	
KRS-2	187	9	

[1]*Eksportosta:* For berths EO-6 to EO-8 vessels with draft over 9 m are allowed to enter/leave if current in Daugava River is less than 1 knot

[2]*EO-14:* For berths EO-14 to EO-15 shipping allowed if wind under 10 m/s, with current not exceeding 1 knot. Vessels of max size allowed to enter/leave if using 3-4 tugboats

[3]*Pilmuiza Basin:* Berths PM-20, PM-21 vacant, no anchor should be used, current and wind caused restriction, vessels of max size allowed to enter/leave if using 3-4 tugboats

[4]*PM-16:* At berths PM-16 and PM-17 loa 195 m, max width 26 m. Vessels of max size allowed to enter/leave if using 3-4 tugboats. No anchor should be used. Current and wind restrictions

[5]*KS-28:* For vessels up to 220 m loa; current & wind caused restrictions; tugs to be used

[6]*JM-22:* For vessels up to 200 m loa, vessels of max size shipping allowed if current in channel does not exceed 0.5 knots

[7]*JM-26:* For vessels up to 170 m loa, vessels of max size shipping allowed if current doesn't exceed 0.5 knots and wind is less than 10 m/sec, tugs to be used

[8]*JM-27:* For vessels up to 135 m loa, vessels of max size shipping allowed if current doesn't exceed 0.5 knots and wind is less than 10 m/sec; if JM-26 engaged, enter/leave should be conducted by VTS operator

[9]*JM-29:* For vessels up to 120 m loa; if JM-27 engaged, enter/leave JM-29 with Harbour Master's approval

[10]*Riga Ship Building Factory:* For berths RKR-3 to RKR-6A ship building pilots service area; shipping in daylight

[11]*ZO-18:* For vessels up to 225 m loa; current not exceeding 0.5 knots, wind under 8 m/sec; tugs to be used

[12]*AU-1:* For vessels up to 80 m loa, shipping in daylight with current not exceeding 1 knot

[13]*VL-13:* For vessels up to 100 m loa, shipping in daylight, wind under 7 m/sec, current less than 0.5 knots. Mooring with tugboats assistance

[14]*KR-22:* For vessels up to 114 m loa; KR-21 vacant & two tugs must be used; shipping in daylight and current not exceeding 1 knot

[15]*DG-1:* For vessels up to 225 m loa; shipping in daylight with current not exceeding 0.5 knots; wind under 8 m/sec; vessels of max size should use tugs

Storage: Warehouses of 180 000 m2, open storage of 1 780 000 m2, tank storage of 309 500 m3 and cold storage of 31 800 t

Mechanical Handling Equipment:

Location	Type	Capacity (t)	Qty
Riga	Mult-purp. Cranes	5–40	100
Riga	Mobile Cranes	5–100	15
Riga	Container Cranes	30	11
Riga	Forklifts	25	300

Cargo Worked: Steel & metals 3000-6000 t/day, coal 6000-7000 t/day, fertiliser 10 000-15 000 t/day, oil products 1000-1300 t/h, containers 50 TEU's/h

Bunkering: SIA DN Bunkering Ltd, DN Bunkering Ltd, Duntes Street 17A, LV-1005 Riga, Republic of Latvia, Tel: +371 673 21087, Fax: +371 673 21859, Email: info@dnbunkering.lv
Lido Nafta Ltd, 21 Skolas Street, Office 209, 1010 Riga, Republic of Latvia, Tel: +371 675 01450, Fax: +371 673 15726, Email: office@bunkering.lv, Website: www.vexoil.lv
Lukoil-Baltija R Ltd, 3 Alises Street, LV 1046 Riga, Republic of Latvia, Tel: +371 670 66400, Fax: +371 670 66420, Email: lbr@lukoil.lv, Website: www.lukoil.lv
Man-Tess, Tvaika Street 7A, 1005 Riga, Republic of Latvia, Tel: +371 670 29138, Fax: +371 670 29140, Email: mt-bunker@man-tess.lv, Website: www.man-tess.lv
Oil & Marine Technology SA, 37-3 A. Caka Street, LV-1011 Riga, Republic of Latvia, Tel: +371 672 17397, Fax: +371 672 17396, Email: bunker@oil-marine.com

OVI Ltd, Tvaika iela 35, LV-1034 Riga, Republic of Latvia, Tel: +371 6735 4828, Fax: +371 6735 5538, Email: office@ovi.lv, Website: www.ovi.lv
SB Transserviss Ltd, Ernestines 12-2, LV-1046 Riga, Republic of Latvia, Tel: +371 678 07061, Fax: +371 678 07060
StatoilHydro ASA, Duntes iela 6, LV-1013 Riga, Republic of Latvia, Tel: +371 670 88100, Fax: +371 670 88150, Email: latvija@statoil.com, Website: www.statoil.com
Timwell Marine SIA, 8 Spilves Street, LV-1055 Riga, Republic of Latvia, Tel: +371 6747 3233, Fax: +371 6747 3710, Email: timwell@mailbox.riga.lv, Website: www.timwell.lv
SIA DN Bunkering Ltd, DN Bunkering Ltd, Duntes Street 17A, LV-1005 Riga, Republic of Latvia, Tel: +371 673 21087, Fax: +371 673 21859, Email: info@dnbunkering.lv
Lido Nafta Ltd, 21 Skolas Street, Office 209, 1010 Riga, Republic of Latvia, Tel: +371 675 01450, Fax: +371 673 15726, Email: office@bunkering.lv, Website: www.vexoil.lv
Lukoil-Baltija R Ltd, 3 Alises Street, LV 1046 Riga, Republic of Latvia, Tel: +371 670 66400, Fax: +371 670 66420, Email: lbr@lukoil.lv, Website: www.lukoil.lv
Man-Tess, Tvaika Street 7A, 1005 Riga, Republic of Latvia, Tel: +371 670 29138, Fax: +371 670 29140, Email: mt-bunker@man-tess.lv, Website: www.man-tess.lv
Oil & Marine Technology SA, 37-3 A. Caka Street, LV-1011 Riga, Republic of Latvia, Tel: +371 672 17397, Fax: +371 672 17396, Email: bunker@oil-marine.com
OW Riga Bunkering Ltd, Gasvaerksvej 48, DK-9000 Aalborg, Denmark, Tel: +45 98127277, Fax: +45 98167277, Email: owbunker@owbunker.dk, Website: www.owbunker.com
SB Transserviss Ltd, Ernestines 12-2, LV-1046 Riga, Republic of Latvia, Tel: +371 678 07061, Fax: +371 678 07060
Tramp Oil & Marine, World Fuel Services Corporation, 13th Floor, Portland House, Bressenden Place, London SW1E 5BH, United Kingdom, Tel: +44 20 7808 5000, Fax: +44 20 7808 5088, Email: pturner@wfscorp.com, Website: www.wfscorp.com

Waste Reception Facilities: Available

Towage: Seven tugs of 1200 hp and four tugs of 2400 hp

Repair & Maintenance: Bolderaja Shipyard Ltd, Riga, Republic of Latvia, Tel: +371 674 33117, Fax: +371 674 33117
Mangaly Shiprepair Yard, 1 Zivju Street, Riga, Republic of Latvia, Tel: +371 673 53382, Fax: +371 673 53831, Email: shipyard@binet.lv, Website: www.mangalishipyard.iv Two floating docks: No.1 101 m x 20 m with lifting cap of 4500 t, No.2 100 m x 21.6 m with lifting cap of 4500 t
Riga Shiprepair Yard, 2 Gales Street, LV-1015 Riga, Republic of Latvia, Tel: +371 673 53290, Fax: +371 673 53910, Email: riga@riga-shipyard.com, Website: www.riga-shipyard.com Three floating docks: 220 m x 36 m with lifting cap of 30 000 t, 205 m x 28 m with lifting cap of 27 000 t and 130 m x 22 m with lifting cap of 4850 t. Repair quays over 2000 m with max draught 8 m

Ship Chandlers: Juras Apgade, Limbazhu Street, 2 App 27, Riga, Republic of Latvia, Tel: +371 673 53771, Fax: +371 673 53706, Email: jurap@neonet.lv
Juras Servisa Kompanija, 17 Duntes Street, LV-1005 Riga, Republic of Latvia, Tel: +371 670 76374, Fax: +371 670 76376, Email: jsk@rinf.riga.lv
Juras Tehniskais Serviss, Rankas Street 6/10, LV-1005 Riga, Republic of Latvia, Tel: +371 673 81800, Fax: +371 673 81800, Email: elena@its.eunet.lv
Unimars Ltd (Universal Marine Service), 17 Duntes Street, LV-1005 Riga, Republic of Latvia, Tel: +371 670 76360, Fax: +371 670 76362, Email: unimars@unimars.lv, Website: www.unimars.lv
Zerssen LSS Ltd, 31 Kakasekla Dambis, LV-1045 Riga, Republic of Latvia, Tel: +371 670 46236, Fax: +371 673 21525, Email: zerssen@latship.lv, Website: www.zerssen.lv

Shipping Agents: Hanza Maritime Agency Ltd, 10 Eksporta Street, LV-1045 Riga, Republic of Latvia, Tel: +371 673 20216, Fax: +371 678 30062, Email: hanza@hanza.lv, Website: www.hanza.lv Chartering Director / Manager: Normunds Strods Email: normunds@hanza.lv
Ahlers & Partners, 31 Ganibu Dambis, LV-1005 Riga, Republic of Latvia, Tel: +371 670 97303, Fax: +371 670 97301, Email: info@riga.ahlers.com, Website: www.ahlers.com
Allego AG, 136c K.Barona Street, 1012 Riga, Republic of Latvia, Tel: +371 673 75259, Fax: +371 673 75260, Email: allego@allego.lv, Website: www.allego.lv
Alpha Shipping Co. SIA, Visbijas Prospekts 7, LV-1014 Riga, Republic of Latvia, Tel: +371 673 03090, Fax: +371 673 03091, Email: mail@alpha.lv, Website: www.alpha.lv
Aseco Container Services SIA, Dzirnavu iela 140, LV-1050 Riga, Republic of Latvia, Tel: +371 672 20324, Fax: +371 672 20325, Email: aseco@aseco.lv
Astramar Shipping Agency, 14 Katrinas Dambis, LV-1045 Riga, Republic of Latvia, Tel: +371 670 96700, Fax: +371 670 96701, Email: astramar@astramar.net, Website: www.astramar.net
Astros Riga, Ganibu Dambis 10a, LV-1045 Riga, Republic of Latvia, Tel: +371 670 97300, Fax: +371 670 97301, Email: info@riga.ahlers.com, Website: www.ahlers.com
Baltic Maritime Agency, 106 Brivibas Street, LV-1001 Riga, Republic of Latvia, Tel: +371 672 93974, Fax: +371 672 94132, Email: bma@bma.lv, Website: www.bma.lv
CMA-CGM S.A., CMA CGM Latvia, Duntes 17a, LV-1005 Riga, Republic of Latvia, Tel: +371 675 17955, Fax: +371 675 17954, Website: www.cma-cgm.com
Chr Jensen SIA, Kr Vlademara 37, LV-1010 Riga, Republic of Latvia, Tel: +371 673 38309, Fax: +371 673 38317, Email: riga@chrjensen.lv, Website: www.chrjensen.lv
KL Shipping SIA, 6 Duntes Street, Room 205, LV-1013 Riga, Republic of Latvia, Tel: +371 672 20600, Fax: +371 672 28332, Email: contact@kls.lv, Website: www.kls.lv
Latvian-Finnish Maritime Agency Ltd, 51 Elizabetes Street, LV-1010 Riga, Republic of Latvia, Tel: +371 672 85628, Fax: +371 678 20463, Email: info@latfinn.com, Website: www.latfinn.com
LSA Transport SIA, Office 6, 8 Pulkveza Briezha Street, LV-1010 Riga, Republic of Latvia, Tel: +371 673 31531, Fax: +371 673 21829
Maritime Transport & Agencies SIA, 22A Katrinas Dambis, LV-1045 Riga, Republic of Latvia, Tel: +371 675 01073, Fax: +371 675 01072, Email: mta@mta.lv, Website: www.mta.nu
Merktrans Shipping Ltd, Merktrans Ltd, 22 Ezera Street, LV-1034 Riga, Republic of Latvia, Tel: +371 673 42478, Fax: +371 673 45837, Email: merktrans@neonet.lv
MTA-Maritime Transport & Agencies SIA, 11 Ausekla Street, Office 113, LV 1010 Riga, Republic of Latvia, Tel: +371 672 28120, Fax: +371 672 28117, Email: mta@mta.lv, Website: www.mta.nu
Muller Liner Agencies N.V., 7 Margrietas Street, 3rd Floor, LV-1046 Riga, Republic of Latvia, Tel: +371 678 04480, Fax: +371 676 25973, Email: agency@burgergroup.lv, Website: www.royalburgergroup.com
John Nurminen Maritime Oy, 17A Duntes Street, LV-1005 Riga, Republic of Latvia,

---

	Key to Principal Facilities:—			
	A=Airport	**C**=Containers	**G**=General Cargo	**P**=Petroleum	**R**=Ro/Ro	**Y**=Dry Bulk
	B=Bunkers	**D**=Dry Dock	**L**=Cruise	**Q**=Other Liquid Bulk	**T**=Towage (where available from port)

Tel: +371 675 17948, *Fax:* +371 675 17948, *Email:* info@nurminen.lv, *Website:* www.nurminen.lv

OS-Agency UAB, Dzirnavu Str.140-413, LV-1018 Riga, Republic of Latvia, *Tel:* +371 672 20428, *Fax:* +371 672 20429, *Email:* info@os-agency.com, *Website:* www.os-agency.com

Rinella Service, UAB, 14-1 Ausekla Street, 1010 Riga, Republic of Latvia, *Tel:* +371 673 23026, *Fax:* +371 673 23063, *Email:* info@rinella.lt, *Website:* www.rinella.lt

Samskip H/f (Samband Line Ltd), 14-7 Auseka Street, 1010 Riga, Republic of Latvia, *Tel:* +371 673 58417, *Fax:* +371 673 58420, *Email:* riga@samskip.com, *Website:* www.samskip.com

Strek Ltd, Uriekstes Street 9, LV-1005 Riga, Republic of Latvia, *Tel:* +371 673 22945, *Fax:* +371 672 20369, *Email:* agent@strek.net, *Website:* www.strek.net

Unimars Ltd (Universal Marine Service), 17 Duntes Street, LV-1005 Riga, Republic of Latvia, *Tel:* +371 670 76360, *Fax:* +371 670 76362, *Email:* unimars@unimars.lv, *Website:* www.unimars.lv

Wilhelmsen Ship Services, Barwil Andersson Agencies Ltd, Ausekla Street 11-221, LV-1010 Riga, Republic of Latvia, *Tel:* +371 673 26404, *Fax:* +371 673 26417, *Email:* riga@barwil.lv, *Website:* www.barwil.com

Stevedoring Companies: Alpha Osta Ltd, 27 Atlantijas Street, LV-1015 Riga, Republic of Latvia, *Tel:* +371 673 51520, *Fax:* +371 673 51522, *Email:* alpha-osta@alpha-osta.lv

Baltic Container Terminal Ltd, Kundzinsala 1, LV-1822 Riga, Republic of Latvia, *Tel:* +371 670 76200, *Fax:* +371 670 76222, *Email:* info@bct.lv, *Website:* www.bct.lv

B.L.B. Baltic Terminals, LV-1034 Riga, Republic of Latvia, *Tel:* +371 673 45830, *Fax:* +371 673 45932, *Email:* inga@blb.lv

Hanza Maritime Agency Ltd, 10 Eksporta Street, LV-1045 Riga, Republic of Latvia, *Tel:* +371 673 20216, *Fax:* +371 678 30062, *Email:* hanza@hanza.lv, *Website:* www.hanza.lv

Jaunzeltini, Atlantijas 23, 1015 Riga, Republic of Latvia, *Tel:* +371 673 43420, *Fax:* +371 673 43654, *Email:* info@jaunzeltini.lv, *Website:* www.jaunzeltini.lv

Krievu Salas Terminals Ltd, Zila 22/24, LV-1007 Riga, Republic of Latvia, *Tel:* +371 670 65500, *Fax:* +371 670 65502, *Email:* zanda@ksterminals.lv

Latvijas Gaze, LV-1001 Riga, Republic of Latvia, *Tel:* +371 673 78460, *Fax:* +371 678 21406, *Email:* temurs.cakss@lg.lv, *Website:* www.lg.lv

Man-Tess Ltd, Tvaika Street 7A, LV-1005 Riga, Republic of Latvia, *Tel:* +371 670 29100, *Fax:* +371 670 29115, *Email:* ofiss@man-tess.lv, *Website:* www.man-tess.lv

Mangaly Shipyard, Riga, Republic of Latvia, *Tel:* +371 673 49500, *Fax:* +371 673 49505, *Email:* valde@terminal.lv

Neste Latvia Ltd, Riga, Republic of Latvia, *Tel:* +371 673 38199, *Fax:* +371 673 91150, *Email:* neste.latvija@fortum.com

Riga Central Terminal, 15 Eksporta Street, LV-1170 Riga, Republic of Latvia, *Tel:* +371 673 29816, *Fax:* +371 673 26501, *Email:* info@rigact.lv, *Website:* www.rigact.lv

Riga Passenger Terminal, Riga, Republic of Latvia, *Tel:* +371 673 26200, *Fax:* +371 673 26195, *Email:* rop@mail.rop.lv

Riga Port Elevator, LV-1045 Riga, Republic of Latvia, *Tel:* +371 673 20079, *Fax:* +371 672 13355, *Email:* info@roe.lv

StatoilHydro ASA, Duntes iela 6, LV-1013 Riga, Republic of Latvia, *Tel:* +371 670 88100, *Fax:* +371 670 88150, *Email:* latvija@statoil.com, *Website:* www.statoil.com

Strek Ltd, Uriekstes Street 9, LV-1005 Riga, Republic of Latvia, *Tel:* +371 673 22945, *Fax:* +371 672 20369, *Email:* agent@strek.net, *Website:* www.strek.net

Surveyors: Baltic Kontor Ltd, 7 Maza Aluksnes Street, LV-1045 Riga, Republic of Latvia, *Tel:* +371 673 81463, *Fax:* +371 675 01822, *Email:* bsi@bk.lv, *Website:* www.bk.lv

Bureau Veritas, Bureau Veritas Latvia SIA, 17a Duntes Street, LV-1005 Riga, Republic of Latvia, *Tel:* +371 673 23246, *Fax:* +371 673 21730, *Email:* riga@lv.bureauveritas.com, *Website:* www.bureauveritas.com

International Maritime Services Co. (IMS), Riga, Republic of Latvia, *Tel:* +371 673 92090, *Fax:* +371 673 92090

Russian Maritime Register of Shipping, 2 Valnyu Street, Office 430, LV-1051 Riga, Republic of Latvia, *Tel:* +371 672 11623, *Fax:* +371 672 20467, *Website:* www.rs-head.spb.ru

Saybolt Italia S.r.l., Tvaika Street 39a, LV-1005 Riga, Republic of Latvia, *Tel:* +371 673 40180, *Fax:* +371 673 40180, *Website:* www.saybolt.com

Medical Facilities: Hospitals, ambulances etc available 24 h

Airport: Riga International Airport, 8 km

Railway: Total length of railway communications in the Freeport is 78 861 m. Riga Passenger Station, 4 km

Development: Main development projects in the Freeport of Riga are:
Dredging of the entry channel of the Freeport of Riga up to 17 m
Construction of new oil products terminal in Daugavgriva area
Construction of new oily waste water treatment facility
Development of Mangalsala area into a general cargo handling area
Implementation of industrial parks in Spilve meadows
Reconstruction of the passenger terminal
Extension of Oil Terminal in Rinuzi
Building of new customs and sanitary border inspection facility
Investments in reconstruction and building of port road and rail access roads
Construction of new container terminal in Kundzinsala
Implementation of the strategy of moving port business away from the centre of the city and transformation of Andrejsala area into city services industry facilities

Lloyd's Agent: Baltic Kontor Ltd, 7 Maza Aluksnes Street, LV-1045 Riga, Republic of Latvia, *Tel:* +371 673 81463, *Fax:* +371 675 01822, *Email:* bsi@bk.lv, *Website:* www.bk.lv

RONU DIKIS

harbour area, see under Riga

SALACGRIVA

Lat 57° 45' N; Long 24° 22' E.

Admiralty Chart: 2215	**Admiralty Pilot:** 19
Time Zone: GMT +2 h	**UNCTAD Locode:** LV SAL

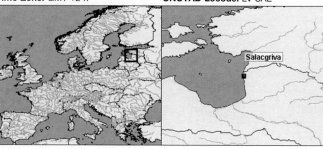

Principal Facilities:

	Y	G			T	

Authority: Salacgriva Port Authority, 3 Pernavas Street, LV-4033 Salacgriva, Republic of Latvia, *Tel:* +371 640 71111, *Fax:* +371 640 71109, *Email:* port@salacgrivaport.lv, *Website:* www.salacgrivaport.lv

Officials: Port Captain: Edgars Murds, *Email:* kapteinis@salacgrivaport.lv.

Anchorage: Anchorage area enclosed within the following coordinates:
57° 44.4' N; 24° 15.0' E
57° 44.4' N; 24° 17.0' E
57° 43.2' N; 24° 17.0' E
57° 43.2' N; 24° 15.0' E

Pilotage: Compulsory for vessels over 60 m loa, Tel/Fax: +371 640 71109. Pilot boards at reception buoy 'P'

Radio Frequency: VHF Channels 16 and 12

Traffic: 2005, 371 020 t of cargo handled

Maximum Vessel Dimensions: 115 m loa, 20 m width, 5.6 m draft

Accommodation:

Name	Length (m)	Draught (m)	Remarks
Salacgriva			There is also an area for yachts with draft up to 2.5 m
Quay No.1	80	5.7	Timber export
Quay No.2	145	3.5	
Quay No.3	128.6	2.2–4	
Quay No.4	70	5.5	Timber export
Quay No.5	81.5	5	
Quay No.6	100.8	5	

Mechanical Handling Equipment: Quay No's 1 & 4 are equipped with mobile hydraulic loading mechanisms that can load more than 200 m3 of timber products/h

Towage: Available

Stevedoring Companies: Salacas Terminals Ltd, 1 Ostas Street, LV-4033 Salacgriva, Republic of Latvia, *Tel:* +371 664 44815, *Fax:* +371 640 71331
Salacgriva Terminals Ltd, 1 Ostas Street, LV-4033 Salacgriva, Republic of Latvia, *Tel:* +371 640 71105, *Fax:* +371 640 71106, *Email:* port@salacterminal.lv, *Website:* www.salacterminal.lv

Medical Facilities: Available

Lloyd's Agent: Baltic Kontor Ltd, 7 Maza Aluksnes Street, LV-1045 Riga, Republic of Latvia, *Tel:* +371 673 81463, *Fax:* +371 675 01822, *Email:* bsi@bk.lv, *Website:* www.bk.lv

SARKANDAUGAVA

harbour area, see under Riga

SKULTE

Lat 57° 19' N; Long 24° 24' E.

Admiralty Chart: 2215	**Admiralty Pilot:** 19
Time Zone: GMT +2 h	**UNCTAD Locode:** LV SKU

Principal Facilities:

		G		B		A

Authority: Skulte Port Authority, 41 Upes Street, LV-2161 Zvejniekciems, Republic of Latvia, *Tel:* +371 679 55267, *Fax:* +371 679 54105, *Email:* skulte@skulteport.lv, *Website:* www.skulteport.lv

Officials: Chief Executive: Igors Akulovs, *Email:* igors@skulteport.lv.
Harbour Master: Kristaps Zidens, *Email:* kapteinis@skulteport.lv.

Port Security: ISPS compliant

Pre-Arrival Information: To be sent via ship's agent or on VHF Channel 12 (2 h before arrival)

Documentation: Arrival documents: general declaration (5 copies), cargo declaration or ship's manifest (2 copies), ship's stores (2 copies), crew effects list (2 copies), crew list (2 copies), passenger list (2 copies), maritime declaration of health (1 copy), ship's generated waste declaration (1 copy)
Sailing documents: general declaration (5 copies), cargo declaration (2 copies), crew list (2 copies), passenger list (2 copies)

Approach: Min depth in approach channel 6.5 m

Anchorage: The anchorage is located in pos 57° 18.5' N; 24° 21.0' E

Pilotage: Compulsory for all vessels over 200 gt

Radio Frequency: VHF Channels 12 and 16

Traffic: 2004, 227 vessels, 612 000 t of cargo handled

Maximum Vessel Dimensions: 140 m loa, 18 m breadth, 5.5 m draft

Principal Imports and Exports: Exports: Peat, Timber.

Accommodation:

Name	Length (m)	Remarks
Skulte		Consists of North & South Quays. Fishing & fish processing also handled
Quays	420	

Mechanical Handling Equipment:

Location	Type
Skulte	Mobile Cranes

Bunkering: Provided by road tankers, via ship's agent

Waste Reception Facilities: Every quay is equipped with containers which are designed for garbage

Stevedoring Companies: EMU Skulte Ltd, Skulte, Republic of Latvia, *Tel:* +371 679 25341, *Fax:* +371 679 25040, *Email:* emu@latnet.lv
Skultes Kokosta Ltd, Katrinas Street 5, LV -1045 Riga, Republic of Latvia, *Tel:* +371 673 29783, *Fax:* +371 673 29976, *Email:* skultes.kokosta@parks.lv

Medical Facilities: Medical and ambulance services are available

Airport: Riga International Airport, 75 km

Railway: Zvejniekciems Railway Station, 2.2 km

Development: Dredging to increase depths in the approach channel and in the turning basin is planned 2008/09

Lloyd's Agent: Baltic Kontor Ltd, 7 Maza Aluksnes Street, LV-1045 Riga, Republic of Latvia, *Tel:* +371 673 81463, *Fax:* +371 675 01822, *Email:* bsi@bk.lv, *Website:* www.bk.lv

VECMILGRAVIS

harbour area, see under Riga

VENTSPILS

Lat 57° 24' N; Long 21° 33' E.

Admiralty Chart: 2277	**Admiralty Pilot:** 19
Time Zone: GMT +2 h	**UNCTAD Locode:** LV VNT

Principal Facilities:

P	Q	Y	G	C	R		B		T	A

Tramp Oil & Marine

Wells House, 15-17 Elmfield Road, Bromley,
Kent BR1 1LT, United Kingdom
Phone: +44 20 8315 7777   **Fax:** +44 20 8315 7788
General email: enquiries@tramp-oil.com

See listings for all global offices: **www.tramp-oil.com**

Authority: Ventspils Port Authority, 19 Jana Street, LV-3601 Ventspils, Republic of Latvia, *Tel:* +371 636 22586, *Fax:* +371 636 21297, *Email:* info@vbp.lv, *Website:* www.portofventspils.lv

Officials: Chief Executive Officer: Imants Sarmulis.
Marketing Manager: Igors Udodovs, *Tel:* +371 36 6360 2334, *Email:* marketing@portofventspils.lv.
Harbour Master: Arvids Buks.

Port Security: ISPS compliant

Documentation: General declaration (5 copies), cargo declaration (2 copies), ship's stores declaration (2 copies), crew effects list (2 copies), crew list (2 copies), veterinary & phyto-sanitary declaration (1 copy), ship's waste declaration (1 copy)

Approach: There are two approaching routes from the open sea to the harbour: In the canal the west sea route from Buoy A to the Free Port entrance gate and in outer harbour, max draught is 15 m. The north sea route from Buoy B to ramification of the sea routes at Buoys 3-4, max draught is 12.5 m. From berths 26/25A to berths 4A/17 max draught is 14.1 m, from berths 5/16 to berths 7/16 max draught is 12.5 m and from berths 8/15 to berths 10/13 max draught is 11.5 m
The permitted draughts may be temporarily changed depending on the changes of the water level

Anchorage: Anchorage can be obtained in the outer roads in five specific areas
V1 for vessels in quarantine and for tankers with gas and chemical cargoes
V2 for dry bulk cargo vessels with draft over 10 m
V3 for oil and oil product tankers and dry bulk cargo vessels carrying dangerous cargo
V4 for dry bulk cargo vessels with draft less than 5 m
V5 for dry bulk cargo vessels with draft of 5-10 m

Pilotage: Compulsory for vessels entering and leaving the Free Port or shifting from one berth to another, for all vessels exceeding 70 m in length and for all tankers with liquefied gas or chemical cargoes notwithstanding their length. Pilots board at Buoys A or B situated about 5 miles NW of the harbour entrance. In case of bad weather, if the pilot is unable to embark, the pilot boat will lead the vessel into port

Radio Frequency: Ventspils Vessel Traffic on VHF Channels 9, 16 and 67

Weather: Prevailing W'ly winds

Tides: Tidal range nil. Water level rises with strong winds from SW, through W, to NW, and falls with winds between N and SE

Traffic: 2008, 28 570 000 t of cargo handled

Maximum Vessel Dimensions: 150 000 dwt, 15 m draught

Principal Imports and Exports: Imports: Containers, Foodstuffs, Gasoline, Grain, Sugar. Exports: Ammonia, Coal, Containers, Crude oil, Ferro alloys, Fertilisers, Liquid chemicals, Metals, Oil products, Wood products.

Working Hours: Stevedoring companies operate within the port on a 24 h/day basis

Accommodation:

Name	Length (m)	Draught (m)	Remarks
Ventspils			See [1] below
Berth No.1	204	9.9–11.5	Operated by Ventspils Commercial Port (VCP)
Berth No.2	84	9.9–11.5	Operated by VCP
Berth No.3	174	14.1	Operated by VCP
Berth No.4	295	14.1	Operated by Kalija Parks
Berth No.4A	356	14.1	Operated by Kalija Parks
Berth No.5	413	5–7.6	
Berth No.7A	288	14.1	Operated by Ventspils Grain Terminal
Berth No.8	150	9.2	Operated by VCP
Berth No.9	150	9.3–10.2	Operated by VCP
Berth No.9A	78	8.4	Operated by VCP
Berth No.10	287	11.5	Operated by VCP
Berth No.11	294	9.5	Operated by Baltic Juice Terminal
Berth No.12	107	5.2	Operated by Ventspils Free Port Authority (VFPA)
Berth No.13	86	6.2	Operated by Ventplac
Berth No.13A			Not yet constructed
Berth No.13B	100	5.2	Operated by Globuss
Berth No.14	150	6.2	Operated by Ventplac
Berth No.15	299	13.2	Operated by Noord Natie Ventspils Terminals (NNVT)
Berth No.16	256	13.2	Operated by NNVT
Berth No.16A	139	13.2	Operated by NNVT
Berth No.17	40	6.1	Operated by NNVT
Berth No.18	100	6.1	Operated by VFPA
Berth No.19	86	6.5	Operated by VFPA
Berth No.20	251	6.4	Operated by VFPA

Key to Principal Facilities:—
A=Airport   **C**=Containers   **G**=General Cargo   **P**=Petroleum   **R**=Ro/Ro   **Y**=Dry Bulk
B=Bunkers   **D**=Dry Dock   **L**=Cruise   **Q**=Other Liquid Bulk   **T**=Towage (where available from port)

Name	Length (m)	Draught (m)	Remarks
Berth No.21	250	6.4	Operated by VFPA
Berth No.22	160	5.8	Operated by VFPA
Berth No.23	360	4–5.5	Coast Guards
Berth No.24	55	5.1	Operated by VFPA
Berth No.25	261	5	Operated by VFPA
Berth No.25A	24	3.6	Operated by VFPA
Berth No.25B (Rd)	110	3	Operated by VFPA
Berth No.25B (Aa)	42	3	Operated by VFPA
Berth No.26	183	13	Operated by Ventbunkers
Berth No.26A	151	12.5	Operated by VFPA
Berth No.26B	55	11.7	Operated by VCP
Berth No.26C	288	9.8	Operated by VCP
Berth No.28	312	11	Operated by Ventbunkers
Berth No.29	312	11	Operated by Ventbunkers
Berth No.30	344	12.5	Operated by Ventbunkers
Berth No.31	344	12.5	Operated by Ventbunkers
Berth No.32	360	15	Operated by Ventbunkers
Berth No.33	360	15	Operated by Ventbunkers
Berth No.34	190	9	Operated by Ventamonjaks
Berth No.35			Not yet constructed
Berth No.35A	230	12.5	Operated by Ventamonjaks
Berth No.36	296	12.5	Operated by Ventamonjaks
Berth No.37	107	12.5	Operated by VFPA
Berth No.37A	78	5.5	Operated by VFPA
Berth No.38	172	5–7.2	Operated by Ventspils Fishing Harbour (VFH)
Berth No.40	80	5	Operated by Ventdok
Berth No.40A			Not yet constructed
Berth No.50			Vessel lifting gear
Berth No.51			Not yet constructed
Berth No.52	119	2.5	Operated by VFPA
Berth No.53	160	2.5	Operated by VFPA
Berth No.60			Not yet constructed
Berth No.61	90	2.7	Operated by VFPA
Berth No.62	203	4.5	Operated by BMGS
Berth No.63			Not yet constructed
New Fishing Harbour			
Berth No.1	200	4	Operated by Ventdok
Berth No.2	230	2.9	Operated by VFH
Berth No.3	107	2.8	Operated by VFH
Berth No.4	100	3.9	Operated by VFH
Berth No.5	100	3.9	Operated by VFH
Berth No.6	107	3.5	Operated by VFH
Berth No.7	230	3.8	Operated by VFH

[1]Ventspils: Situated at the mouth of the River Venta in the Baltic Sea with all year round navigation

The boundaries of the Free Port comprises a water area with:

The outer road within the lines connecting the points with the following co-ordinates: 57° 20.9' N; 21° 29.3' E, 57° 25.4' N; 21° 22.6' E, 57° 32.3' N; 21° 30.3' E, 57° 26.3' N; 21° 36.0' E

The outer harbour

The River Venta from the outer harbour to the imaginative line, crossing the River Venta connecting the mouth of the River Packule at the right shore of the River Venta with Abolu Street at the left shore

A strip of the land on both sides of the River Venta from an entrance gate of the Free Port to the River Packule at the right shore of the River Venta and Abolu Street on the left shore

The Free Port of Ventspils Authority administers the common hydro technical constructions, floating and stationary navigation equipment, territory and water area of the Free Port

There are two turning basins in the Free Port water area: the outer harbour turning basin for vessels with length not exceeding 270 m and draught under 15 m and the River Venta turning basin, located between Berths 5 and 16 for vessels with length not exceeding 240 m and draught under 13.2 m

Storage: Total shore tank farm cap of 1 500 000 m3 and reefer cargo storage cap of 5000 m2

Location	Open (m²)	Covered (m²)	Grain (t)	Cold (m³)
Ventspils	200000	170000	130000	5000

Mechanical Handling Equipment:

Location	Type	Capacity (t)	Qty
Ventspils	Floating Cranes	100	1
Ventspils	Mobile Cranes	100	1
Ventspils	Portal Cranes	10–100	30

Bunkering: Available at oil jetties or by lighters
Joint Stock Co. Ventbunkers, 29 Sanatorijas Street, LV-3602 Ventspils, Republic of Latvia, *Tel:* +371 36 63626905, *Fax:* +371 36 69348657
Tramp Oil & Marine, World Fuel Services Corporation, 13th Floor, Portland House, Bressenden Place, London SW1E 5BH, United Kingdom, *Tel:* +44 20 7808 5000, *Fax:* +44 20 7808 5088, *Email:* pturner@wfscorp.com, *Website:* www.wfscorp.com
Joint Stock Co. Ventbunkers, 90 Dzintaru Street, 3602 Ventspils, Republic of Latvia, *Tel:* +371 636 02501, *Fax:* +371 636 02504, *Email:* info@ventbunkers.lv, *Website:* www.ventbunkers.lv

Towage: Six tugs are available

Ship Chandlers: Zerssen LSS Ltd, 9 Dzintaru Street, LV-3601 Ventspils, Republic of Latvia, *Tel:* +371 636 68338, *Fax:* +371 636 28453, *Email:* vzerssen@latship.lv, *Website:* www.zerssen.lv

Shipping Agents: Alpha Shipping Co. SIA, Dzintaru 36-38, LV-3602 Ventspils, Republic of Latvia, *Tel:* +371 636 81111, *Fax:* +371 636 80450, *Email:* alpha@apollo.lv, *Website:* www.alpha.lv
Astramar Shipping Agency, 31 Talsu Street, P O Box 21, LV-3602 Ventspils, Republic

of Latvia, *Tel:* +371 636 65834, *Fax:* +371 636 62690, *Email:* agency@astramar.lv, *Website:* www.astramar.net
Baltic Maritime Agency, Room No 304, Dzintaru 36/38, LV-3602 Ventspils, Republic of Latvia, *Tel:* +371 636 81111, *Fax:* +371 633 68450, *Email:* alpha@apollo.lv, *Website:* www.alpha.lv
Latvian-Finnish Maritime Agency Ltd, 7 Plostu Street, Ventspils, Republic of Latvia, *Tel:* +371 636 70334, *Fax:* +371 636 70335, *Email:* ventlines@latfinn.com
Seatrans Shipping Agency Co Ltd, 53 Pils Street, LV-3601 Ventspils, Republic of Latvia, *Tel:* +371 636 24300, *Fax:* +371 636 22722, *Email:* agency@seatrans.lv, *Website:* www.seatrans.lv
Unitek Ltd, 66, Dzintaru Street, LV-3602 Ventspils, Republic of Latvia, *Tel:* +371 636 60757, *Fax:* +371 636 60755, *Email:* unitek@unitek.lv, *Website:* www.unitek.lv

Stevedoring Companies: Noord Natie Ventspils Terminals, 7 Plosta Street, LV-3601 Ventspils, Republic of Latvia, *Tel:* +371 636 07300, *Fax:* +371 636 07301, *Email:* nnvt@nnvt.lv, *Website:* www.nnvt.lv Managing Director: Valdis Andersons
Kalija Parks, 421 Dzintaru Street, LV-3602 Ventspils, Republic of Latvia, *Tel:* +371 636 68620, *Fax:* +371 636 25345, *Email:* director@kp.vcp.lv
Ventamonjaks, 66 Dzintaru street, LV 3600 Ventspils, Republic of Latvia, *Tel:* +371 636 63195, *Fax:* +371 636 80105, *Email:* office@ventamonjaks.lv, *Website:* www.ventamonjaks.lv
Ventplac, 2 Pramju Street, LV-3601 Ventspils, Republic of Latvia, *Tel:* +371 636 22388, *Fax:* +371 636 80205, *Email:* ventplac@ventplac.lv, *Website:* www.ventplac.lv
Ventspils Commercial Port, 22 Dzintaru Street, LV-3602 Ventspils, Republic of Latvia, *Tel:* +371 636 68706, *Fax:* +371 636 68860, *Email:* vcp@vto.lv, *Website:* www.vto.lv
Ventspils Fishing Harbour, Ventspils, Republic of Latvia, *Tel:* +371 636 22212, *Fax:* +371 636 21554, *Email:* enkurs@fix.lv
Ventspils Nafta, Ostas 23, LV-3601 Ventspils, Republic of Latvia, *Tel:* +371 636 66334, *Fax:* +371 636 66979, *Email:* office@vnafta.lv, *Website:* www.vnafta.lv
Western Pipeline System, Ventspils, Republic of Latvia, *Tel:* +371 636 68888, *Fax:* +371 636 68889

Medical Facilities: Hospital facilities available

Airport: Ventspils International Airport

Railway: Ventspils Railway Station

Lloyd's Agent: Baltic Kontor Ltd, 7 Maza Aluksnes Street, LV-1045 Riga, Republic of Latvia, *Tel:* +371 673 81463, *Fax:* +371 675 01822, *Email:* bsi@bk.lv, *Website:* www.bk.lv

VOLERI

harbour area, see under Riga

ZIEMAS OSTA

harbour area, see under Liepaja

LEBANON

A. TORBEY
BARRISTERS & SOLICITORS
LAW FIRM

Hadidian Building, Naoum Labaki Street, Horch Tabet - Sin el Fil
P.O. Box: 116/5200, Beirut - Lebanon

Tel:	+961 (1) 486446 - 494241 - 481291
Fax:	+961 (1) 481293
Email:	info@torbeylaw.com
Web:	www.torbeylaw.com

BEIRUT

Lat 33° 54' N; Long 35° 31' E.

Admiralty Chart: 1563		**Admiralty Pilot:** 49	
Time Zone: GMT +2 h		**UNCTAD Locode:** LB BEY	

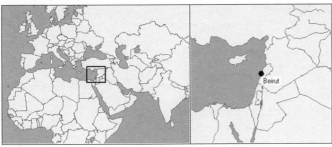

Principal Facilities:

P	Q	Y	G	C	R	L	B		T	A

G SAHYOUNI & CO S.a.r.l.

3F, Hafiz E1 Hashem Building, Quarantine Bridge, Tripoli Rd
Beirut, LEBANON

Contact: George Sahyouni
TEL: +961 1241566 / +961 1 257046   FAX: +961 1241317
EMAIL: lloydsbey@inco.com.lb

Surveyors

Authority: Gestion et Exploitation du Port de Beyrouth (GEPB), P O Box 1490, Beirut, Lebanon, *Tel:* +961 1 580211/6, *Fax:* +961 1 585835, *Email:* info@portdebeyrouth.com, *Website:* www.portdebeyrouth.com

Port Security: ISPS compliant

Approach: Entrance channel 480 m long in depth of 15.24 m

Pilotage: Compulsory

Radio Frequency: VHF Channel 16

Tides: Tidal range of 0.6 cm

Traffic: 2007, 2187 vessels, 5 318 000 t of cargo handled, 444 169 TEU's

Maximum Vessel Dimensions: Vessels of 218 m loa and 11.58 m draft can enter at all times and anchor at sheltered embankment

Working Hours: Port works 24 h/day. Overtime is paid after office hours

Accommodation:

Name	Length (m)	Depth (m)	Draught (m)	Remarks
Beirut				See [1] below
General Cargo Berths	1654	8–10.5		
Container Berths	1334	10.5–13		
New Container Quay (No.16)	600	15.5		See [2] below
Bulk Quay	220	13		
Dora Terminal				Located 2-5 miles N of Beirut Port
The Coral Oil Co Ltd Terminal			9.5	See [3] below
Total Terminal			11	See [4] below
Wardieh Holding Inc Terminal			9–13.5	See [5] below
MEDCO Terminal			11–14.4	See [6] below
Uniterminals				See [7] below
Mediterranean Petroleum Co (MPC)			11	See [8] below

[1]*Beirut:* Total length of quays 5155 m encompassing four docks

[2]*New Container Quay (No.16):* Beirut Container Terminal, P O Box 11-7163 Beirut, Tel: +961 1 562080, Fax: +961 1 562064, Email: info@bctc-lb.com, Website: www.bctc-lb.com
Stacking area of 244 600 m2. 440 reefer points

[3]*The Coral Oil Co Ltd Terminal:* In pos 33° 54' 00" N; 35° 32' 30" E for gasoline, jet A-1 & diesel oil. Three stern buoys and two anchors

[4]*Total Terminal:* In pos 33° 54' 28" N; 35° 33' 10" E for gasoline, jet A-1 & diesel oil. Four buoys (including two stern buoys) and two anchors

[5]*Wardieh Holding Inc Terminal:* In pos 33° 54' 10" N; 35° 29' 37" E. Berth 1 with three buoys and two anchors for solvents and base oil. Berth 2 with three buoys and two anchors for diesel oil, gasoline and kerosene

[6]*MEDCO Terminal:* Gasoline, jet A-1, LPG, lub oil and gas oil. Three stern buoys + one starboard side buoy and two anchors

[7]*Uniterminals:* Short Range Line: berth (in depth of 6.2 m with draft up to 5.4 m) consists of two stern moorings and one front port-side mooring for tankers up to 3500 dwt discharging solvents and bitumen
Long Range Line: berth (in depth of 14.8 m with draft up to 13.5 m) consists of three stern moorings for tankers up to 45 000 dwt discharging gasoline, gas oil and fuel oil

[8]*Mediterranean Petroleum Co (MPC):* In pos 33° 54' 48" N; 35° 34' 48" E for gasoline and diesel oil. Three stern buoys and two anchors

Storage: Four warehouses for general cargo totalling 25 547 m2, three warehouses for groupage operation totalling 20 488 m2, three warehouses for cars totalling 17 958 m2, one warehouse for hazardous goods totalling 5231 m2 and one open warehouse for cars and heavy load engines totalling 8220 m2
Silo storage of 120 000 t

Mechanical Handling Equipment:

Location	Type	Capacity (t)	Qty	Remarks
Beirut	Mobile Cranes	25	12	for general cargo
Beirut	Mobile Cranes	125–165	13	for containers
Beirut	Mobile Cranes	255–300	6	for containers
Beirut	Mobile Cranes	50–90	35	for steel
New Container Quay (No.16)	Post Panamax		3	
New Container Quay (No.16)	RTG's	40	6	
New Container Quay (No.16)	Reach Stackers		16	

Bunkering: M.E.T.F. Bunker Services SAL, Aya Commercial Centre, 10F, Dora, Beirut, Lebanon, *Tel:* +961 1 259 954, *Fax:* +961 1 259 956, *Email:* cabboud@metfbunkers.com
Mistral Wind International S.A.L., Boutros Khoury Building, 52-54 Port Street, P O Box 175-173, Beirut, Lebanon, *Tel:* +961 1 584 459, *Fax:* +961 1 443 038, *Email:* miwind@inco.com.lb, *Website:* www.mistralwindint.com
OilTrader Ltd, Schnoavi Building, Charles Helov Avenue, Beirut, Lebanon, *Tel:* +961 1 443569, *Fax:* +961 1 443569
Setri S.a.r.l., Setri S.a.r.l., Elzayek Building, 27 Military Hospital Street, Badaro, Beirut, Lebanon, *Tel:* +961 1 380 061, *Fax:* +961 1 380 126, *Email:* setri.intl@gmail.com
Mistral Wind International S.A.L., Boutros Khoury Building, 52-54 Port Street, P O Box 175-173, Beirut, Lebanon, *Tel:* +961 1 584 459, *Fax:* +961 1 443 038, *Email:* miwind@inco.com.lb, *Website:* www.mistralwindint.com

Towage: Six tugs available

Ship Chandlers: Ets Geomares, Bouhsali Building 1st Floor, Port Street, Beirut 175-211, Lebanon, *Tel:* +961 1 626212, *Fax:* +961 1 566143, *Email:* geomares@inco.com.lb
Med Conro Shipping Services Ltd, 9th Floor, St Jack Centre, Dora Highway, P O Box 11-6043, Beirut, Lebanon, *Tel:* +961 1 240 700, *Fax:* +961 1 259 136, *Email:* info@medconro.com, *Website:* www.medconro.com

Shipping Agents: Sealine Sa.r.l., 3rd Floor Medawar-Sehnaoui Building, Charles Helou Avenue, P O Box 175079, Gemmayzeh, Beirut, Lebanon, *Tel:* +961 1 565000, *Fax:* +961 1 447317, *Email:* sealine@dm.net.lb, *Website:* www.sealine.com.lb Chairman: Samir Moukawem
Abou Merhi Lines S.A.L., 3rd Floor, Atrium Building, Weygand Street, Beirut, Lebanon, *Tel:* +961 1 999611, *Fax:* +961 1 999612, *Email:* info@aboumerhilines.com, *Website:* www.aboumerhilines.com
Georges A Abouhamad Shipping & Forwarding, Fayed Building, P O Box 3229, Beirut, Lebanon, *Tel:* +961 1 448354, *Fax:* +961 1 449549, *Email:* trofis@wise.net.lb
Al-Walid Shipping Agency, Phonicia Street Yassin Building, 5th Floor, Minet el Hosn, Beirut, Lebanon, *Tel:* +961 1 362240, *Fax:* +961 1 375585, *Email:* shipping@cyberia.net.lb
Azov Sea Star Agency Co., Dora-Moucarri Center, 8th Floor, P O Box 901413, Beirut, Lebanon, *Tel:* +961 1 584440, *Fax:* +961 1 602856/7
BA Shipping Co. SARL, Medawar, Charles Helou Avenue, Sehnaoui Building, 2nd Floor, P O Box: 55509, Beirut, Lebanon, *Tel:* +961 1 565654, *Fax:* +961 1 562815, *Email:* info@bashippinglb.com, *Website:* www.bashippinglb.com
Continental Shipping Agencies Sarl, Pasteur Street, Medawar Building, 5th Floor, Saifi, Beirut, Lebanon, *Tel:* +961 1 567130, *Fax:* +961 1 567132, *Email:* info@csa-continental.com, *Website:* www.csa-continental.com
Edouard Cordahi, Charles Helou Avenue, Issam Pharaon Building, P O Box 11-5755, Beirut, Lebanon, *Tel:* +961 1 449511/2, *Fax:* +961 1 602825
Sehnaoui Elie & Fils S.r.l., 1st Floor, Sehnaoui Building, Charles Helou Street, P O Box 11557, Beirut, Lebanon, *Tel:* +961 1 446255, *Fax:* +961 1 584574
Estephan Shipping Agency, Immeuble Sarkis, etage 4, 670 Rue du Fleuve, Beirut, Lebanon, *Tel:* +961 1 580520/1, *Fax:* +961 1 580382
Ets. Fauzi J Ghandour, Ghandour Building, Avenue des Francais, P O Box 11-1084, Beirut, Lebanon, *Tel:* +961 1 373376, *Fax:* +961 1 360048, *Email:* usca@seahorsenet.com
Eurabia Intercont Ltd, Modern Building,5 Floor, Saifi-Al Arz Street, P O Box 118047, Beirut, Lebanon, *Tel:* +961 1 449960, *Fax:* +961 1 446177, *Email:* eurabia@eurabia.inco.com.lb, *Website:* www.senatorlines.com
Gezairi Transport Comptoir Algerien du Levant SAL, Gezairi Building, Gezairi Square, P O Box 11-1402, Beirut 1107 2080, Lebanon, *Tel:* +961 1 783783, *Fax:* +961 1 784784, *Email:* gezairi@gezairi.com, *Website:* www.gezairi.com
Gulf Agency Co. (Lebanon) Ltd, El Arz Street, Modern Building, Riad El Solh, P O Box 114392, Beirut 11072160, Lebanon, *Tel:* +961 1 446086, *Fax:* +961 1 446097, *Email:* lebanon@gacworld.com, *Website:* www.gacworld.com
Hakim-Roukoz Shipping Agencies, Kanafani Building, Al Arz Street, P O Box 17-5166, Beirut, Lebanon, *Tel:* +961 1 562200, *Fax:* +961 1 449246, *Email:* hrbrt@hrbrt.com, *Website:* www.hrbrt.com
Josemar, 4th Floor, Nazaret Kokadjian Building, Charles Helou Street, P O Box 175580, Beirut 1104 2050, Lebanon, *Tel:* +961 1 442712, *Fax:* +961 1 585615, *Email:* josemar@josemar.com, *Website:* www.josemar.com
Kawar-Khayat Shipping Agency, Modern Building, El Arz Street, P O Box 11-8724, Beirut, Lebanon, *Tel:* +961 1 449702, *Fax:* +961 1 565910, *Email:* ksg@ksglb.com
Leader Shipping Co. S.a.r.l., Beirut Mazraa Boulevard, 6th Floor Midway Centre, P O Box 9185, Beirut, Lebanon, *Tel:* +961 1 603242, *Fax:* +961 1 603242, *Email:* leader@sodetel.net.lb
Libanfracht Sarl, Kanafani Building, Arz Street, P O Box 8958, Beirut, Lebanon, *Tel:* +961 1 582944, *Fax:* +961 1 602853, *Email:* metz@metz.com.lb, *Website:* www.metzgrp.com
Lotus Shipping Agencies Sal, Gandour Building, 2nd Floor, Avenue des Francais, Beirut, Lebanon, *Tel:* +961 1 983860, *Fax:* +961 1 983859, *Email:* myaman@lotusship.com
Med Conro Shipping Services Ltd, 9th Floor, St Jack Centre, Dora Highway, P O Box 11-6043, Beirut, Lebanon, *Tel:* +961 1 240 700, *Fax:* +961 1 259 136, *Email:* info@medconro.com, *Website:* www.medconro.com

---

Key to Principal Facilities:—

A=Airport	**C**=Containers	**G**=General Cargo
B=Bunkers	**D**=Dry Dock	**L**=Cruise

P=Petroleum	**R**=Ro/Ro	**Y**=Dry Bulk
Q=Other Liquid Bulk	**T**=Towage (where available from port)

Mediterranean Shipping Company, MSC (Lebanon) S.A.R.L., Marine Tower - Gemmayze, Sainte Famille Street, Beirut, Lebanon, *Tel:* +961 1 583620, *Fax:* +961 1 566919, *Email:* info@msclebanon.com, *Website:* www.msclebanon.com

Osman Mekkaoui & Fils SAL, P O Box 11-1472, Beirut, Lebanon, *Tel:* +961 1 580181/5, *Fax:* +961 1 580957, *Email:* joseph.wehbe@mekkaoui.com

Metz Shipping Agency Ltd, 5th Floor Kanafani Building, Al Arz Street, P O Box 8958, Beirut, Lebanon, *Tel:* +961 1 582944, *Fax:* +961 1 449341, *Email:* metz@metz.com.lb, *Website:* www.metzgrp.com

A.P. Moller-Maersk Group, Medawar, 96 Pasteur Street, 1st Floor, P O Box 11-413, Beirut, Lebanon, *Tel:* +961 1 587100, *Fax:* +961 1 571907, *Email:* lebsal@maersk.com, *Website:* www.maerskline.com

National Maritime Services S.A.R.L., Port Street Boulos Fayad Building, 1st Floor, P O Box 11-9550, Beirut, Lebanon, *Tel:* +961 1 449419, *Fax:* +961 1 583907, *Email:* opts@nmslb.com

National Shipping Co. SAL, 96 Pasteur Rmeil Beirut, P O Box 11-847, Riad El Solh, Beirut 1107-2060, Lebanon, *Tel:* +961 1 580202, *Fax:* +961 1 581880, *Email:* mail@nashipco.com, *Website:* www.nashipco.com

North African Shipping & Clearing Agency N.A.S.A.C.A., Hamka Building, Laban Street, 1st Floor, P O Box 9720-II, Beirut, Lebanon, *Tel:* +961 1 867169, *Fax:* +961 1 807961, *Email:* nasaca@sodetel.net.lb

Orient Shipping & Trading Co. Sarl, Moumneh Building No.72, Ain Almraisseh Street 54, P O Box 11-2561, Beirut, Lebanon, *Tel:* +961 1 364455, *Fax:* +961 1 365570, *Email:* ortship@inco.com.lb, *Website:* www.orientgroup.net

Phoenician Maritime Agency, 3rd Floor, Sehnaoui Building, Charles Helou Avenue, Medawar Area, P O Box 175076, Beirut, Lebanon, *Tel:* +961 1 572233, *Fax:* +961 1 572277, *Email:* pmasal@pma.com.lb, *Website:* www.pma.com.lb

Rabunion Maritime Agency S.a.r.l., 1st Floor, Agha Building, Degaulle Street, P O Box 11-8460, Beirut, Lebanon, *Tel:* +961 1 866372, *Fax:* +961 1 805593, *Email:* rassemco@cyberia.net.lb

Rodolphe Saade & Co. SAL, Burotech Building, Rue Pasteur, P O Box 166526, Beirut, Lebanon, *Tel:* +961 1 583313/9, *Fax:* +961 1 583420, *Email:* rosade@inco.com.lb

G. Sahyouni & Co. S.a.r.l., 3rd Floor, Hafiz El Hashem Building, Quarantine Bridge, Tripoli Road, Beirut 1104-2040, Lebanon, *Tel:* +961 1 241566, *Fax:* +961 1 241317, *Email:* lloydsbey@inco.com.lb, *Website:* www.georgesahyouni.com

Scandinavian Near East Agency S.A., Medawar-Pasteur Street, Burotec Building, 11th Floor, P O Box 64, Beirut, Lebanon, *Tel:* +961 1 585676/7/8, *Fax:* +961 1 585679, *Email:* heald@sodetel.net.lb, *Website:* www.henryheald.com

Seamen International Co, 5th Floor, Dora City S Building, St Joseph Hospital Street, Dora, Beirut, Lebanon, *Tel:* +961 1 255555/60, *Fax:* +961 1 255561, *Email:* seamen@dm.net.lb

Simco Maritime & Chartering SARL (SMC), Office No.1, 7th Floor, Blue Building Centre, Bliss Street, Hamra Region, Beirut, Lebanon, *Tel:* +961 1 364171, *Fax:* +961 1 364172, *Email:* simco@simcomaritime.com, *Website:* www.simcomaritime.com

Union Shipping & Chartering Agency SAL, Avenue des Francais, P O Box 2856, Beirut, Lebanon, *Tel:* +961 1 373376, *Fax:* +961 1 360048, *Email:* usca@seahorsenet.com

United Middle East Shipping Co. S.r.l., 6th Floor, Liberty Building, Kobayat Street, Rmeil Ashrafieh, Beirut, Lebanon, *Tel:* +961 1 580398, *Fax:* +961 1 584621, *Email:* info@unishipgroup.com, *Website:* www.unishipgroup.com

Wilhelmsen Ship Services, Bourj Hammoud, Karantina Area, 4th Floor, Tannous Tower Building, Dora Main Road, P O Box 901470, Beirut, Lebanon, *Tel:* +961 1 244460, *Fax:* +961 1 244462, *Email:* barwil.lebanon@wilhelmsen.com, *Website:* www.wilhelmsen.com

Stevedoring Companies: Abdel Basseth Mekkawi & Sons, Beirut, Lebanon, *Tel:* +961 1 443285, *Fax:* +961 1 241567

Med Conro Shipping Services Ltd, 9th Floor, St Jack Centre, Dora Highway, P O Box 11-6043, Beirut, Lebanon, *Tel:* +961 1 240 700, *Fax:* +961 1 259 136, *Email:* info@medconro.com, *Website:* www.medconro.com

Surveyors: Nippon Kaiji Kyokai, c/o Middle East Tankers & Freighters, P O Box 11-6085, Kanafani Building, 6th Floor, Al-Arz Street, Beirut, Lebanon, *Tel:* +961 1 581200, *Fax:* +961 1 449246, *Website:* www.classnk.or.jp

G. Sahyouni & Co. S.a.r.l., 3rd Floor, Hafiz El Hashem Building, Quarantine Bridge, Tripoli Road, Beirut 1104-2040, Lebanon, *Tel:* +961 1 241566, *Fax:* +961 1 241317, *Email:* lloydsbey@inco.com.lb, *Website:* www.georgesahyouni.com

Simco Maritime & Chartering SARL (SMC), Office No.1, 7th Floor, Blue Building Centre, Bliss Street, Hamra Region, Beirut, Lebanon, *Tel:* +961 1 364171, *Fax:* +961 1 364172, *Email:* simco@simcomaritime.com, *Website:* www.simcomaritime.com

Societe Generale de Surveillance (SGS), Mechanical & Industrial Consulting Co, 2nd Floor, Hashim Building, Nahr Street, Beirut Bridge, Beirut 369, Lebanon, *Tel:* +961 1 580234, *Fax:* +961 1 581199, *Website:* www.sgs.com

Medical Facilities: Hospitals available

Airport: Rafic Hariri International Airport, 8 km

Lloyd's Agent: G. Sahyouni & Co. S.a.r.l., 3rd Floor, Hafiz El Hashem Building, Quarantine Bridge, Tripoli Road, Beirut 1104-2040, Lebanon, *Tel:* +961 1 241566, *Fax:* +961 1 241317, *Email:* lloydsbey@inco.com.lb, *Website:* www.georgesahyouni.com

DORA TERMINAL

harbour area, see under Beirut

SAIDA

alternate name, see Sidon

SELAATA

Lat 34° 16' N; Long 35° 39' E.

Admiralty Chart: 1561		**Admiralty Pilot:** 49
Time Zone: GMT +2 h		**UNCTAD Locode:** LB SEL

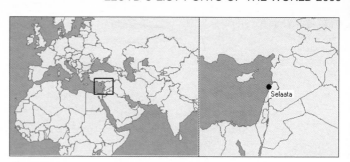

Principal Facilities:

Q	Y	G			B		T	A

Authority: Huiles & Derives S.A.L., P O Box 531, Batroun, Lebanon, *Tel:* +961 6 643606, *Fax:* +961 6 742544

Officials: Manager: Elias Saba.
Harbour Master: E. Salam Mansour.

Port Security: ISPS compliant

Approach: Port is protected from prevailing SW winds by an 800 m long breakwater

Anchorage: In heavy weather vessels can anchor in Chekka Bay, 10-12 miles from Selaata

Pilotage: Compulsory and from Beirut Pilot Services, Tel: +961 3 697269, VHF Channel 16. Pilot meets vessels 2 miles NW of the breakwater

Radio Frequency: VHF Channel 16, call sign: Zouyout

Weather: Prevailing winds NE and SW from mid-September to January. Rest of year prevailing SW winds

Maximum Vessel Dimensions: 70 000 dwt, 234 m loa, 35 m width, max draft 13.2 m

Principal Imports and Exports: Imports: Cereals, Fertiliser, Grain, Soybean, Sulphate, Vegetable oil. Exports: Cement, Fertiliser, Soyabean meal, Soyabean oil.

Working Hours: Normally 0700-1800. Continuous if necessary

Accommodation:

Name	Length (m)	Depth (m)	Remarks
Selaata			
Berth No.1	150	14	One pneumatic unloader at 200 t/h
Berth No.2	70	9.4	

Storage: Flat warehouses of 40 000 m3 cap. Oil tanks of 17 000 m3 cap

Location	Grain (t)
Selaata	18000

Mechanical Handling Equipment:

Location	Type	Qty
Selaata	Mult-purp. Cranes	4

Bunkering: Available via trucks with 48 h notice
Mistral Wind International S.A.L., Boutros Khoury Building, 52-54 Port Street, P O Box 175-173, Beirut, Lebanon, *Tel:* +961 1 584 459, *Fax:* +961 1 443 038, *Email:* miwind@inco.com.lb, *Website:* www.mistralwindint.com – *Notice:* 48 hours – *Delivery Mode:* truck
Tripoli Oil Installations, P O Box 150, Tripoli, Lebanon, *Tel:* +961 6 430502 – *Notice:* 48 hours – *Delivery Mode:* truck

Waste Reception Facilities: Garbage disposal available

Towage: Two tugs available of 2500 and 3500 hp

Repair & Maintenance: Minor repairs available

Surveyors: G. Sahyouni & Co. S.a.r.l., 3rd Floor, Hafiz El Hashem Building, Quarantine Bridge, Tripoli Road, Beirut 1104-2040, Lebanon, *Tel:* +961 1 241566, *Fax:* +961 1 241317, *Email:* lloydsbey@inco.com.lb, *Website:* www.georgesahyouni.com

Medical Facilities: Available at Batroun, 2 km

Airport: Rafic Hariri International Airport, 50 km

Lloyd's Agent: G. Sahyouni & Co. S.a.r.l., 3rd Floor, Hafiz El Hashem Building, Quarantine Bridge, Tripoli Road, Beirut 1104-2040, Lebanon, *Tel:* +961 1 241566, *Fax:* +961 1 241317, *Email:* lloydsbey@inco.com.lb, *Website:* www.georgesahyouni.com

SIDON

Lat 33° 34' N; Long 35° 22' E.

Admiralty Chart: 1561		**Admiralty Pilot:** 49
Time Zone: GMT +2 h		**UNCTAD Locode:** LB SDN

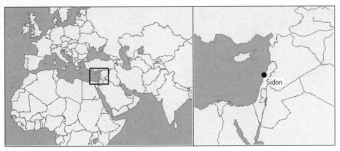

Principal Facilities:

		G					A

Authority: Ministry of Public Works & Transport, Sidon, Lebanon, *Tel:* 961 7

Radio Frequency: VHF Channel 16

Working Hours: 0700-1500

Accommodation:

Name	Remarks
Sidon	See ¹ below

¹*Sidon:* One pier with very shallow water, used mainly for barges. Vessels of more than 2 m d anchor outside, E of Ziri Island and discharge on to lighters, and is able to accommodate vessels of 130 m loa, 8 m d and 10 000 dwt

Shipping Agents: SeaGull Shipping Co. Ltd, 1st Floor, Bizri Building, Riad Soloh Street, Saida, Lebanon, *Tel:* +961 7 753256/7, *Fax:* +961 7 753258, *Email:* info@seagull-shipping.com, *Website:* www.seagull-shipping.com

Medical Facilities: Available

Airport: Rafic Hariri International Airport, 40 km

Lloyd's Agent: G. Sahyouni & Co. S.a.r.l., 3rd Floor, Hafiz El Hashem Building, Quarantine Bridge, Tripoli Road, Beirut 1104-2040, Lebanon, *Tel:* +961 1 241566, *Fax:* +961 1 241317, *Email:* lloydsbey@inco.com.lb, *Website:* www.georgesahyouni.com

SOUR

Lat 33° 16' N; Long 35° 12' E.

Admiralty Chart: 1561	**Admiralty Pilot:** 49
Time Zone: GMT +2 h	**UNCTAD Locode:** LB SUR

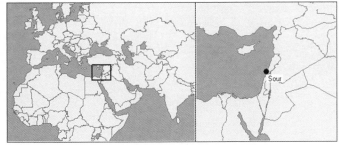

Principal Facilities:

			G				A

Authority: Ministry of Public Works & Transport, Sidon, Lebanon, *Tel:* 961 7

Port Security: ISPS compliant

Accommodation:

Name	Remarks
Sour	See ¹ below

¹*Sour:* Open roadstead. Ocean-going vessels are loaded/discharged at anchorage by lighters. There are three anchorage areas catering for large, medium and small vessels in depths ranging from 8 m to 17 m

Airport: Rafic Hariri International Airport, 70 km

Lloyd's Agent: G. Sahyouni & Co. S.a.r.l., 3rd Floor, Hafiz El Hashem Building, Quarantine Bridge, Tripoli Road, Beirut 1104-2040, Lebanon, *Tel:* +961 1 241566, *Fax:* +961 1 241317, *Email:* lloydsbey@inco.com.lb, *Website:* www.georgesahyouni.com

TARABULUS

alternate name, see Tripoli

TRIPOLI

Lat 34° 28' N; Long 35° 50' E.

Admiralty Chart: 1561	**Admiralty Pilot:** 49
Time Zone: GMT +2 h	**UNCTAD Locode:** LB KYE

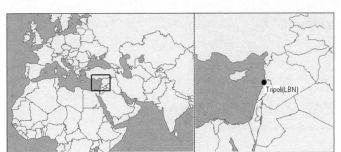

Principal Facilities:

P	Q		G		R		B		T	A

Authority: Service d'Exploitation du Port de Tripoli, Tripoli, Lebanon, *Tel:* +961 6 601955, *Fax:* +961 6 601955, *Email:* tport@terra.net.lb

Officials: Port Director: Haissam Elwely, *Tel:* +961 6 601225.
Harbour Master: Atef Tabbouch, *Tel:* +961 6 600283.

Port Security: ISPS compliant

Approach: Depth in approach channel is 13 m

Anchorage: Good anchorage can be obtained in depths ranging from 5.5 m to 12.8 m

Pilotage: Available

Working Hours: 0700-1500

Accommodation:

Name	Length (m)	Draught (m)	Remarks
Tripoli			
Berth No.1	140	7.5	
Berth No's 2-5	250	7.5	
Berth No's 6-7	240	7.5	
Tripoli Oil Installations			See ¹ below
Berth No.1		17	Max 140 000 dwt
Berth No.2		18.3	Max 250 000 dwt
Berth No.3		14.3	Max 87 000 dwt
Berth No.4		9.7	Max 25 000 dwt
Berth No.5		7.5	LPG

¹*Tripoli Oil Installations:* Operated by Petro-Store International Sarl, P O Box 150, Tripoli, Tel: +961 6 387505, Fax: +961 6 387509, Email: marterm@cyberia.net.lb Situated 5 miles N of Tripoli Port for discharge of petroleum products. The terminal has five offshore loading berths which lie in depths of 11.6 to 20.1 m. The berths consist of several mooring buyos and are connected to the shore by submarine pipelines

Storage:

Location	Open (m²)	Covered (m²)
Tripoli	71040	60067

Mechanical Handling Equipment:

Location	Type	Capacity (t)	Qty
Tripoli	Floating Cranes	50	1
Tripoli	Mult-purp. Cranes	100	20
Tripoli	Forklifts	20	

Bunkering: Available
Tripoli Oil Installations, P O Box 150, Tripoli, Lebanon, *Tel:* +961 6 430502
Mistral Wind International S.A.L., Boutros Khoury Building, 52-54 Port Street, P O Box 175-173, Beirut, Lebanon, *Tel:* +961 1 584 459, *Fax:* +961 1 443 038, *Email:* miwind@inco.com.lb, *Website:* www.mistralwindint.com
Tripoli Oil Installations, P O Box 150, Tripoli, Lebanon, *Tel:* +961 6 430502

Towage: Five privately owned tugs from 250 hp to 700 hp available

Repair & Maintenance: North Lebanese Shipyard, Tripoli, Lebanon, *Tel:* +961 6 600529 One slipway which can accommodate vessels up to 1000 dwt

Shipping Agents: Altair Shipping Agency, P O Box 67, Tripoli, Lebanon, *Tel:* +961 6 212123, *Fax:* +961 6 212124, *Email:* marine@altairshipping.com, *Website:* www.altairshipping.com
Continental Shipping Agencies Sarl, Tripoli, Lebanon, *Tel:* +961 6 601744, *Fax:* +961 6 600752, *Email:* info@csa-continental.com, *Website:* www.csa-continental.com
Estephan Shipping Agency, P O box 2621, Tripoli, Lebanon, *Tel:* +961 6 206021, *Fax:* +961 6 205070, *Email:* estephan@4com.net.lb
Henry Heald Syria, Port Street, Abdel Wahab Building, Tripoli, Lebanon, *Tel:* +961 6 601287, *Fax:* +961 6 585679/565432, *Email:* heald@sodetel.net.lb
Med Sea Shipping, P O Box 2508, 2nd Floor Zailea Building, El Mina Customs Street, Tripoli, Lebanon, *Tel:* +961 6 601265, *Fax:* +961 6 610348, *Email:* medsea@sodetel.net.lb

Surveyors: Hellenic Register of Shipping, Ell Tall Square, Shedraoui Building - 3rd Floor, P O Box 1497, Tripoli, Lebanon, *Tel:* +961 6 439911, *Fax:* +961 6 439911, *Email:* hrsliban@hotmail.com, *Website:* www.hrs.gr

Medical Facilities: Available

Airport: Rafic Hariri International Airport, 80 km

Lloyd's Agent: G. Sahyouni & Co. S.a.r.l., 3rd Floor, Hafiz El Hashem Building, Quarantine Bridge, Tripoli Road, Beirut 1104-2040, Lebanon, *Tel:* +961 1 241566, *Fax:* +961 1 241317, *Email:* lloydsbey@inco.com.lb, *Website:* www.georgesahyouni.com

Key to Principal Facilities:—				
A=Airport	**C**=Containers	**G**=General Cargo	**P**=Petroleum	**R**=Ro/Ro	**Y**=Dry Bulk
B=Bunkers	**D**=Dry Dock	**L**=Cruise	**Q**=Other Liquid Bulk	**T**=Towage (where available from port)	

TYR

alternate name, see Sour

ZAHRANI TERMINAL

Lat 33° 32' N; Long 35° 19' E.

Admiralty Chart: -	**Admiralty Pilot:** 49
Time Zone: GMT +2 h	**UNCTAD Locode:** LB ZHR

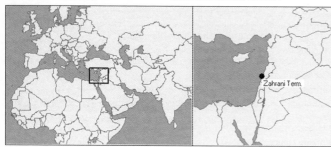

Principal Facilities:

P					B		A

Authority: Trans Arabian Pipeline Co., P O Box 1348, Beirut, Lebanon, *Tel:* +961 1 720716

Pilotage: Compulsory. Mooring from 0600-1500 only

Radio Frequency: VHF Channel 16

Maximum Vessel Dimensions: From November to March 50 000 dwt; from April to October 85 000 dwt

Accommodation:

Name	Remarks
Zahrani	See [1] below

[1]*Zahrani:* Located in an open, unsheltered roadstead just N of the Zahrani River and about 8 km S of the town of Sidon (Saida). It is approx 56 km S of Beirut and 27 km N of Tyr. Facilities normally consist of four berths, but at present only one berth, No.2 is operational. There are three submarine lines, two for crude and one for bunkers. The lines are spaced about 792.4 m apart and extend about 1.6 km offshore to over 15.24 m of water

Permanent moorings consist of five to seven buoys. Buoys are of steel, cylindrical, and fitted with a pelican hook to which ship's mooring lines are attached by tapline mooring launches. The heading basis of all berths is W and both of ship's bower anchors are used. Vessels must have at least five good quality manila mooring lines of 275 m each. Certain buoys in all berths are equipped with 1.5'' preventer wires, one end of which is permanently secured to the mooring buoy. The free end is brought on board by messenger line after ship is moored in position (used only during bad weather and winter months). Both crude and bunker hoses are lifted on the port side (with ship's gear). In two berths the crude hose requires a 4 t lift and in the other a 5 t lift (static weight)

All crude loading is done by gravity from shore tanks and the max rate varies from 40 000 to 70 000 bbls/h depending on the berth and vessel's ability to load

All submarine moorings capable of handling the largest vessels without difficulty

The Trans-Arabian Pipeline Co performs no agency functions whatever. Mooring masters are however provided, and these board on arrival and pilot vessels to a berth

Bunkering: Available with prior arrangement

Medical Facilities: Available at Sidon

Airport: Rafic Hariri International Airport, 50 km

Lloyd's Agent: G. Sahyouni & Co. S.a.r.l., 3rd Floor, Hafiz El Hashem Building, Quarantine Bridge, Tripoli Road, Beirut 1104-2040, Lebanon, *Tel:* +961 1 241566, *Fax:* +961 1 241317, *Email:* lloydsbey@inco.com.lb, *Website:* www.georgesahyouni.com

LIBERIA

BUCHANAN

Lat 5° 51' N; Long 10° 4' W.

Admiralty Chart: 3648	**Admiralty Pilot:** 1
Time Zone: GMT	**UNCTAD Locode:** LR UCN

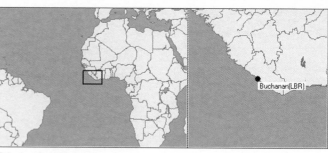

Principal Facilities:

P		Y	G	C					A

Authority: National Port Authority, Freeport of Monrovia, Bushrod Island, Monrovia, Liberia, *Tel:* +231 6 402906, *Email:* natportliberia@yahoo.com, *Website:* www.nationalportauthorityliberia.org

Officials: Managing Director: George E. Tubman.

Pilotage: Compulsory for vessels over 100 dwt

Weather: Prevailing SW''ly winds

Tides: Range of tide 1.2 m

Maximum Vessel Dimensions: At ore quay 290 m loa, 12.8 m draft

Accommodation:

Name	Length (m)	Depth (m)
Buchanan		
Commercial Pier	320	10.15
Ore Loading Pier	257	13.5
Tanker Berth	126	10.15

Airport: Roberts International Airport, 92 km

Lloyd's Agent: Denco Shipping Lines Inc., Bushrod Island (Port Island), P O Box 1587, Monrovia, Liberia, *Tel:* +231 226632, *Fax:* +231 226130, *Email:* denco_stevfor@yahoo.com, *Website:* www.dencostevfor.com

CAPE PALMAS

Lat 4° 22' N; Long 7° 43' W.

Admiralty Chart: 1980	**Admiralty Pilot:** 1
Time Zone: GMT	**UNCTAD Locode:** LR CPA

Principal Facilities:

P	Q		G			B		T	

Authority: National Port Authority, Freeport of Monrovia, Bushrod Island, Monrovia, Liberia, *Tel:* +231 6 402906, *Email:* natportliberia@yahoo.com, *Website:* www.nationalportauthorityliberia.org

Officials: Managing Director: George E. Tubman.

Approach: Entrance to roads 046° and line up on two white markers, one on beach and the other a short distance inland

Working Hours: Weekdays 0700-1600; overtime upon request

Accommodation:

Name	Remarks
Cape Palmas	See [1] below

[1]*Cape Palmas:* Open roadstead of 11.0-16.5 m depth. Shallow water port 4.88 m LW, 6.40 m HW, approx 54.86 m length. Cargo discharged alongside jetty by means of two 100 t barges. Four 50 t barges for loading on open roadstead
Tanker facilities: Coastal tankers discharge alongside the jetty

Storage: Three warehouses for lumber and general cargo

Mechanical Handling Equipment:

Location	Type	Capacity (t)	Qty
Cape Palmas	Mobile Cranes	10	1
Cape Palmas	Forklifts		2

Cargo Worked: About 10-20 t/gang/h depending on cargo

Bunkering: Only for vessels loading/discharging alongside jetty

Towage: Three tugboats for towing logs and barges

Medical Facilities: Local hospital

Lloyd's Agent: Denco Shipping Lines Inc., Bushrod Island (Port Island), P O Box 1587, Monrovia, Liberia, *Tel:* +231 226632, *Fax:* +231 226130, *Email:* denco_stevfor@yahoo.com, *Website:* www.dencostevfor.com

GREENVILLE

Lat 4° 59' N; Long 9° 3' W.

Admiralty Chart: 1980	**Admiralty Pilot:** 1
Time Zone: GMT	**UNCTAD Locode:** LR GRE

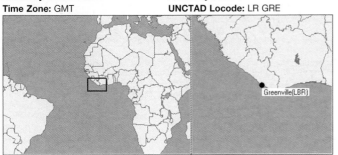

Principal Facilities:

P		G			B		T	A

Authority: National Port Authority, Freeport of Monrovia, Bushrod Island, Monrovia, Liberia, *Tel:* +231 6 402906, *Email:* natportliberia@yahoo.com, *Website:* www.nationalportauthorityliberia.org

Officials: Managing Director: George E. Tubman.

Approach: Depths in channel range from 10.1-23.8 m; various rocks and reefs

Anchorage: Anchorage can be obtained in the bay in depths ranging from 13-15 m

Pilotage: Compulsory. Pilot boards 2 miles from the head of the breakwater

Radio Frequency: VHF Channels 16 and 12. Contact can be made during normal working days, 0700-1700

Weather: During the rainy season, April to November, adverse conditions can cause a heavy swell

Tides: Range of tide 1.2 m

Maximum Vessel Dimensions: 20 000 dwt, 156 m loa, 7.31 m draft

Principal Imports and Exports: Exports: Timber.

Working Hours: 0700-1600. A 24 h day can be worked in three shifts

Accommodation:

Name	Length (m)	Depth (m)	Remarks
Sinu Bay			See [1] below
Pier No.1	178	8.1	
Pier No.2		5.48	Can accommodate vessels up to 54.9 m loa

[1]*Sinu Bay:* The inner basin has a depth of 8.1 m. Loading/discharging is carried out by ship's own gear, the main cargo handled being logs and wood products
Tanker facilities: Small terminal owned by ChevronTexaco for coastal tankers, max loa 62 m, max draft 4.8 m

Storage: Twenty pens for timber storage. One covered warehouse of 27 649 m3. No refrigerated space

Cargo Worked: 1200 m3/shift of four gangs

Bunkering: Small quantities of diesel oil available from road tankers

Towage: One tug of 1450 hp equipped with fire-fighting appliances is available

Medical Facilities: Small Government owned hospital in the town and one private clinic

Airport: Monrovia International Airport

Lloyd's Agent: Denco Shipping Lines Inc., Bushrod Island (Port Island), P O Box 1587, Monrovia, Liberia, *Tel:* +231 226632, *Fax:* +231 226130, *Email:* denco_stevfor@yahoo.com, *Website:* www.dencostevfor.com

HARPER

alternate name, see Cape Palmas

MONROVIA

Lat 6° 20' N; Long 10° 49' W.

Admiralty Chart: 2478	**Admiralty Pilot:** 1
Time Zone: GMT	**UNCTAD Locode:** LR MLW

Principal Facilities:

P	Y	G	C	R		B	D	T	A

Authority: National Port Authority, Freeport of Monrovia, Bushrod Island, Monrovia, Liberia, *Tel:* +231 6 402906, *Email:* natportliberia@yahoo.com, *Website:* www.nationalportauthorityliberia.org

Officials: Managing Director: George E. Tubman.

Approach: Approach channel 2438 m long and 152.4 m wide dredged to 14.93 m at MLW. Channel inside breakwaters to the turning basin 14.32 m at MLW Approach to ore piers 13.71 m at MLW

Anchorage: Recommended anchorage is 3 miles from the breakwater in roadstead is to the south of the buoyed channel, depth 14 to 19 m, which provides good holding ground on a sand and mud bottom. Vessels are not anchored within the inner harbour except for a very short period of time

Pilotage: Compulsory. Pilot station is fitted with VHF and HF radio and maintains continuous listening watch on HF 2182 kcs and on VHF channel 16. Available 24 h/day except for the oil jetties which are daylight only

Weather: Prevailing winds W to SW

Tides: Rise and fall 0.61-1.19 m

Maximum Vessel Dimensions: 120 000 dwt, approx 267 m loa, 13.71 m d

Principal Imports and Exports: Imports: Building materials, General, Petroleum. Exports: Bulk latex, Cocoa, Coffee, Crude rubber, Iron ore, Timber.

Working Hours: Monday to Friday: two shifts, 0700-1800, 1900-0430. Saturday: 0700-1130. Sunday and holidays: 0700-1900 at overtime rates

Accommodation:

Name	Length (m)	Depth (m)	Remarks
Monrovia			See [1] below
General Cargo Wharf	609	9.1–10	See [2] below
Bong Mining Co Southside Ore Pier	270	13–14.5	
Liberia Mining Co Pier	278	9–10	
Mano Pier	365	11–12	
Bunker Pier	420	10	
Fishery Pier		6.1	See [3] below

[1]*Monrovia:* An artificial harbour protected by two rock breakwaters extending 1.25 miles into the sea. 750 acres of protected water. There is one turning basin with a depth of about 14 m. The port enjoys free port status. In the free zone cargo can be stored in transit, free of duty pending re-export to other West African states
Tanker facilities: Length of tankers for crude oil discharge limited to 198.1 m long and 13.71 m d. At present tankers with crude oil for discharge moor with two bow anchors and lie alongside a breasting dolphin with stern moored to a shore dolphin. One tanker berth open for discharge and bunkering but limited to 213.4 m length and 10.06 m d
[2]*General Cargo Wharf:* Four berths for general cargo. Containers handled at the general cargo berths. Equipment includes top loaders, tractors and trailers. A concrete based container storage area and provision for reefer containers but not connected to electricity to date. Good cargo handling equipment, max lift 50 t. Width of wharf 10.97 m with a concrete deck. 14 tanks for bulk latex - capacity 2500 t. 8 transit warehouses - 10 000 sq m
[3]*Fishery Pier:* Situated on the Northern breakwater for vessels up to 73.14 m long. Cold storage available

Bunkering: Shell Liberia Ltd, Bushrod Island, Monrovia, Liberia, *Tel:* +231 221 238
Bominflot, Bominflot Ltd, 5-7 Ravensbourne Road, Bromley, Kent BR1 1HN, United Kingdom, *Tel:* +44 20 8315 5400, *Fax:* +44 20 8315 5429, *Email:* mail@bominflot.co.uk, *Website:* www.bominflot.net – *Grades:* FO; MDO
Shell Liberia Ltd, Bushrod Island, Monrovia, Liberia, *Tel:* +231 221 238

Towage: Compulsory at discretion of pilot. Three tugs of 1700, 2500 and 3900 hp

Shipping Agents: African & Overseas Agencies Ltd, Bushrod Island, P O Box 1196, Monrovia, Liberia, *Tel:* +231 221517, *Fax:* +231 223307
Alraine Shipping Agencies Ltd, Bushrod Island, P O Box 10-0209, Monrovia 1000, Liberia, *Tel:* +231 227774, *Fax:* +231 226185, *Email:* mlw@maersk.com
Denco Shipping Lines Inc., Bushrod Island (Port Island), P O Box 1587, Monrovia, Liberia, *Tel:* +231 226632, *Fax:* +231 226130, *Email:* denco_stevfor@yahoo.com, *Website:* www.dencostevfor.com
A.P. Moller-Maersk Group, Maersk Liberia Ltd, UN Drive, Freeport Area, Monrovia, Liberia, *Tel:* +231 226578, *Fax:* +231 226914, *Email:* mlwmla@maersk.com, *Website:* www.maerskline.com
Umarco (Liberia) Corp., P O Box 10-1196, Bushrod Island, Monrovia, Liberia, *Tel:* +231 226990, *Fax:* +231 226061, *Email:* otallr@hotmail.com

Airport: Roberts International Airport, 80 km

Lloyd's Agent: Denco Shipping Lines Inc., Bushrod Island (Port Island), P O Box 1587, Monrovia, Liberia, *Tel:* +231 226632, *Fax:* +231 226130, *Email:* denco_stevfor@yahoo.com, *Website:* www.dencostevfor.com

SINU BAY

harbour area, see under Greenville

Key to Principal Facilities:—				
A=Airport	**C**=Containers	**G**=General Cargo	**P**=Petroleum	**R**=Ro/Ro	**Y**=Dry Bulk
B=Bunkers	**D**=Dry Dock	**L**=Cruise	**Q**=Other Liquid Bulk	**T**=Towage (where available from port)	

LIBYA

ABU KAMMASH

Lat 33° 4' N; Long 11° 49' E.

Admiralty Chart: 3403	**Admiralty Pilot:** 49
Time Zone: GMT +2 h	**UNCTAD Locode:** LY ABK

Principal Facilities:

P	Q								T	A

Authority: General Company for Chemical Industries (GCCI), P O Box 100/411, Zuara, Socialist People's Libyan Arab Jamahirayah, *Tel:* +218 21 361 5181, *Fax:* +218 21 361 5014, *Email:* gcci_abukammash@gcci.ly, *Website:* www.gcci.ly

Officials: Muftah H. Dakhila.

Port Security: ISPS compliant

Approach: The fairway buoy is in pos 33° 08' N; 11° 52' E and the channel is marked by pairs of unlit buoys. The final part of the channel is 150 m wide with a depth of 8 m

Anchorage: Within a 1.0 nautical mile radius of a circle centered in pos 33° 08' N; 11° 52' E

Pilotage: Berthing permission must be obtained from Zuara Port, giving 24 h notice for pilot and tug

Radio Frequency: Communication with the pilot should be made through Zuara Port Control on VHF Channels 16 and 12

Weather: Weather conditions are generally clement. Winds are NW'ly during the mid-summer months

Maximum Vessel Dimensions: 20 000 dwt, 8 m draft

Working Hours: 24 h/day

Accommodation:

Name	Remarks
Abu Kammash	See [1] below

[1]*Abu Kammash:* Jetty to serve the Abu Kammash Industrial Complex, 1200 m long with depth at the head of 8 m. Cargoes handled are caustic soda and liquid & ethylene gas

Towage: Pilot tug available

Airport: Zwara Airport, approx 40 km

Development: A line to be constructed for direct importing of ethyl-di-chloride

Lloyd's Agent: Gargoum Legal Marine, P O Box 153, Dubai Street, Benghazi, Socialist People's Libyan Arab Jamahirayah, *Tel:* +218 61 222 0302, *Fax:* +218 61 222 0302, *Email:* gargoum@gargoum.com, *Website:* www.gargoum.com

AZ ZAWIYAH

alternate name, see Zawia Terminal

BENGHAZI

Lat 32° 7' N; Long 20° 3' E.

Admiralty Chart: 3352	**Admiralty Pilot:** 49
Time Zone: GMT +2 h	**UNCTAD Locode:** LY BEN

Principal Facilities:

P		Y	G	C	R		B		T	A

Authority: Socialist Ports Co., Benghazi, Socialist People's Libyan Arab Jamahirayah, *Email:* bengazi@lpclibya.com, *Website:* www.lpclibya.com

Port Security: ISPS compliant

Documentation: Vessel name, call sign, flag, builder, owner, agent consignee, cargo for transit, type of cargo, nationality and number of crew, any animals or mail onboard, last port of call, port of loading, next port, ETA and main particulars of the ship

Approach: Green buoy in pos 32° 06' 55" N; 20° 02' 08'' E. Red buoy in pos 32° 06' 58" N; 20° 40' 00'' E. Depth in outer channel 15 m and in inner channel 14 m

Pilotage: Compulsory. Functions from 0700 to 2000 daily
Benghazi Radio: From 0800 to 1000 GMT calling on 2128 MF. 1200-1400, 1600-1800: working frequency 2513
Lights: Rasif No.2: Red every 5 sec, visibility 5 nautical miles. Lighthouse white every 5 sec, visibility 15 nautical miles

Radio Frequency: VHF Channel 16 (156.800 mHz), VHF Channel 12 (156.600 mHz), VHF Channel 10 (156.500 mHz), VHF Channel 8 (156.400 mHz)

Working Hours: General port working hours normally 0800-1400. Overtime 1500-1800

Accommodation:

Name	Depth (m)
Benghazi	
Berth No.1	9
Berth No.2	7
Berth No.3	9
Berth No.4	5
Berth No.5	6
Berth No.6	7
Berth No.7	6
Berth No.8	6
Berth No.9	6.5
Berth No.10	10
Berth No.11	10
Berth No.12	10
Berth No.13	10
Berth No.14	12
Berth No.15	12
Berth No.16	12
Berth No.17	6.5
Oil Berth	12

Storage:

Location	Open (m²)	Covered (m²)
Benghazi	440000	13500

Mechanical Handling Equipment:

Location	Type	Capacity (t)	Qty
Benghazi	Floating Cranes	200	1

Bunkering: Shell Petro Development Co. of Libya B.V., El Salak Building, Christmas Tree Square, Benghazi, Socialist People's Libyan Arab Jamahirayah, *Tel:* +218 61 99574, *Fax:* +218 61 99387
Shell Petro Development Co. of Libya B.V., El Salak Building, Christmas Tree Square, Benghazi, Socialist People's Libyan Arab Jamahirayah, *Tel:* +218 61 99574, *Fax:* +218 61 99387 – *Misc:* diesel oil and furnace oil in limited quantities at high cost, no coal
Universal Shipping & Maritime Agency, Omar Al Mokhtar Street, Nadi Al Madina Building No. 317, P O Box 3703, Tripoli, Socialist People's Libyan Arab Jamahirayah, *Tel:* +218 21 4448 170, *Fax:* +218 21 4448 170, *Email:* agency.tri@unishipco.com, *Website:* www.unishipco.com – *Misc:* diesel oil and furnace oil in limited quantities at high cost, no coal

Towage: Compulsory for all vessels over 100 nrt. Six tugs available
Almadain Group, Apartment 2-3, 2nd Floor, Al Mutaheda Building, Algeria Street, P O Box 32797, Benghazi, Socialist People's Libyan Arab Jamahirayah, *Tel:* +218 61 909 1660, *Fax:* +218 61 908 1844, *Email:* info@almadain.com, *Website:* www.almadain.com

Repair & Maintenance: Workshop available for minor repairs

Ship Chandlers: Albahar Almutawest (Mediterranean) Shipping Co., Islamic Call Society Building, 10th Floor Suite 1007, P O Box 13422, Benghazi, Socialist People's Libyan Arab Jamahirayah, *Tel:* +218 61 909 7538, *Fax:* +218 61 909 3686, *Email:* medship@med-ship.com/bunkering@med-ship.com, *Website:* www.med-ship.com

Shipping Agents: Al Rowad Shipping Co., 23 of July Street, next to Omar Elkhiam Hotel, Benghazi, Socialist People's Libyan Arab Jamahirayah, *Tel:* +218 61 908 1621/2, *Fax:* +218 61 909 8008, *Email:* rwdgenmng@lttnet.net, *Website:* www.alrwad.ly
Al Waha Shipping Co Ltd, Suite 7, Sedi Hussin Commercial Complex, Taha Hussin Street, Benghazi, Socialist People's Libyan Arab Jamahirayah, *Tel:* +218 61 909 9130, *Fax:* +218 61 909 3803, *Email:* infoben@alwahaShipping.com, *Website:* www.alwahashipping.com
Albahar Almutawest (Mediterranean) Shipping Co., Islamic Call Society Building, 10th Floor Suite 1007, P O Box 13422, Benghazi, Socialist People's Libyan Arab Jamahirayah, *Tel:* +218 61 909 7538, *Fax:* +218 61 909 3686, *Email:* medship@med-ship.com/bunkering@med-ship.com, *Website:* www.med-ship.com
Almadain Group, Apartment 2-3, 2nd Floor, Al Mutaheda Building, Algeria Street, P O Box 32797, Benghazi, Socialist People's Libyan Arab Jamahirayah, *Tel:* +218 61 909 1660, *Fax:* +218 61 908 1844, *Email:* info@almadain.com, *Website:* www.almadain.com
Esterlab Libyan Shipping & Agency Co, Islamic Call Society Building, 7th floor, Section (A), P O Box 3037, Benghazi, Socialist People's Libyan Arab Jamahirayah,

Tel: +218 61 909 8887, *Fax:* +218 61 909 5916, *Email:* shipping.ben@esterlab-sc.com, *Website:* www.esterlab-ly.com

Germa Shipping & Stevedoring Co., Ganfoda Containers Yard, Near Teacher's Village Road, Ganfoda, Benghazi, Socialist People's Libyan Arab Jamahirayah, *Tel:* +218 61 909 9715/909 3570, *Fax:* +218 61 909 9663, *Email:* benghazibranch@germashipping.net, *Website:* www.germashipping.com

Gulf International Co. Ltd, Benghazi, Socialist People's Libyan Arab Jamahirayah, *Tel:* +218 61 222 8629, *Fax:* +218 61 222 8629, *Email:* gulfintl@hotmail.com

Overseas Shipping Co Libya, Benghazi, Socialist People's Libyan Arab Jamahirayah, *Tel:* +218 61 908 2114, *Fax:* +218 61 908 2116, *Email:* osclben@lttnet.net, *Website:* www.osc-libya.com

Shahat Shipping Co., Ankara Street Off Omar Mukhtar Street, Shahat Shipping Durding, Benghazi, Socialist People's Libyan Arab Jamahirayah, *Tel:* +218 61 909 1391, *Fax:* +218 61 909 2025, *Email:* shippingadvisor@shahatshipping.com, *Website:* www.shahatshipping.com

Tajoura Shipping Co., Dubai Street, Benghazi, Socialist People's Libyan Arab Jamahirayah, *Tel:* +218 61 223 8764, *Fax:* +218 61 223 8105, *Email:* baderben@tajourashipping.com

Universal Shipping Co., P O Box 2450, Ahmed Rafik Street, Sabri, Benghazi, Socialist People's Libyan Arab Jamahirayah, *Tel:* +218 61 909 9678, *Fax:* +218 61 909 9678, *Email:* alamia@universalben.com, *Website:* www.universalben.com

Stevedoring Companies: Albahar Almutawest (Mediterranean) Shipping Co., Islamic Call Society Building, 10th Floor Suite 1007, P O Box 13422, Benghazi, Socialist People's Libyan Arab Jamahirayah, *Tel:* +218 61 909 7538, *Fax:* +218 61 909 3686, *Email:* medship@med-ship.com/bunkering@med-ship.com, *Website:* www.med-ship.com

Surveyors: Albahar Almutawest (Mediterranean) Shipping Co., Islamic Call Society Building, 10th Floor Suite 1007, P O Box 13422, Benghazi, Socialist People's Libyan Arab Jamahirayah, *Tel:* +218 61 909 7538, *Fax:* +218 61 909 3686, *Email:* medship@med-ship.com/bunkering@med-ship.com, *Website:* www.med-ship.com
Universal Shipping Co., P O Box 2450, Ahmed Rafik Street, Sabri, Benghazi, Socialist People's Libyan Arab Jamahirayah, *Tel:* +218 61 909 9678, *Fax:* +218 61 909 9678, *Email:* alamia@universalben.com, *Website:* www.universalben.com

Airport: Benghazi International Airport, 29 km

Lloyd's Agent: Gargoum Legal Marine, P O Box 153, Dubai Street, Benghazi, Socialist People's Libyan Arab Jamahirayah, *Tel:* +218 61 222 0302, *Fax:* +218 61 222 0302, *Email:* gargoum@gargoum.com, *Website:* www.gargoum.com

DERNA

Lat 32° 46' N; Long 22° 39' E.

Admiralty Chart: 3401	**Admiralty Pilot:** 49
Time Zone: GMT +2 h	**UNCTAD Locode:** LY DNF

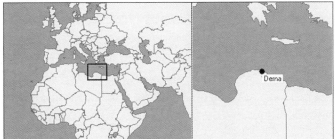

Principal Facilities:

		Y	G	C	R			T	

Authority: Socialist Ports Co., Derna, Socialist People's Libyan Arab Jamahirayah, *Email:* darna@lpclibya.com, *Website:* www.lpclibya.com

Port Security: ISPS compliant

Documentation: Vessel name, call sign, flag, builder, owner, agent consignee, cargo for transit, type of cargo, nationality and number of crew, any animals or mail onboard, last port of call, port of loading, next port, ETA and main particulars of the ship

Approach: Port entrance is marked by two navigational lights (red and green)

Anchorage: Anchorage area in depth of 15-45 m

Pilotage: Compulsory

Radio Frequency: VHF Channel 16 (156.800 mHz), VHF Channel 12 (156.600 mHz), VHF Channel 10 (156.500 mHz), VHF Channel 8 (156.400 mHz)

Tides: Range of tide 1 m

Maximum Vessel Dimensions: 10 000 dwt, 150 m loa, 8.23 m draft

Principal Imports and Exports: Imports: Animal feed, Bulk cargo, General cargo, Live animals, Supply items. Exports: Cement, Fish, Wool.

Working Hours: General port working hours normally 0800-1400. Overtime 1500-1800

Accommodation:

Name	Length (m)	Depth (m)	Remarks
Derna			Two container terminals with forklifts available
Berth No.1	265	8.23	
Berth No.2	130	8.23	
Berth No.3	319	8.23	
Berth No.4	169	8.23	
Ro/ro Berth	58	8.23	

Storage:

Location	Covered (m²)	Sheds / Warehouses
Derna	1500	3

Mechanical Handling Equipment:

Location	Type	Capacity (t)	Qty
Derna	Floating Cranes	80	1
Derna	Mobile Cranes	40	

Cargo Worked: 300 t/gang/day

Waste Reception Facilities: Garbage disposal available

Towage: Available at the port

Medical Facilities: Available

Lloyd's Agent: Gargoum Legal Marine, P O Box 153, Dubai Street, Benghazi, Socialist People's Libyan Arab Jamahirayah, *Tel:* +218 61 222 0302, *Fax:* +218 61 222 0302, *Email:* gargoum@gargoum.com, *Website:* www.gargoum.com

ES SIDER TERMINAL

Lat 30° 38' N; Long 18° 21' E.

Admiralty Chart: 3344	**Admiralty Pilot:** 49
Time Zone: GMT +2 h	**UNCTAD Locode:** LY ESI

Principal Facilities:

P									

Authority: Waha Oil Co., P O Box 395, Tripoli, Socialist People's Libyan Arab Jamahirayah, *Tel:* +218 21 3331 116, *Fax:* +218 21 3337 169, *Email:* infowaha@wahaoil.com, *Website:* www.wahaoil.com

Port Security: ISPS compliant

Documentation: (a) ETA's (b) ISPS Certificate No. (c) List of last 10 ports and security level (d) Operating security level

Approach: If tankers are berthing they proceed to the pilot boarding station, otherwise to the recommended anchorage area

Pilotage: Compulsory; performed by Waha Oil Co mooring masters

Radio Frequency: VHF Channels 8 and 16

Weather: S wind off desert, known as Ghibli

Maximum Vessel Dimensions: 56.08 m beam, 22.25 m draft

Principal Imports and Exports: Exports: Crude oil.

Working Hours: 24 h/day

Accommodation:

Name	Length (m)	Draught (m)	Remarks
Es Sider Terminal			
Mono-Buoy No.4	350	17.68	Max 254 000 dwt
Mono-Buoy No.5	355	22.25	Max 305 000 dwt

Medical Facilities: Available in emergencies only

Airport: Benghazi International Airport, 390 km. Tripoli International Airport, 660 km

Lloyd's Agent: Gargoum Legal Marine, P O Box 153, Dubai Street, Benghazi, Socialist People's Libyan Arab Jamahirayah, *Tel:* +218 61 222 0302, *Fax:* +218 61 222 0302, *Email:* gargoum@gargoum.com, *Website:* www.gargoum.com

HOMS

alternate name, see Khoms

KHOMS

Lat 32° 39' N; Long 14° 16' E.

Admiralty Chart: -	**Admiralty Pilot:** 49
Time Zone: GMT +2 h	**UNCTAD Locode:** LY KHO

Key to Principal Facilities:—			
A=Airport	**C**=Containers	**G**=General Cargo	**P**=Petroleum	**R**=Ro/Ro	**Y**=Dry Bulk
B=Bunkers	**D**=Dry Dock	**L**=Cruise	**Q**=Other Liquid Bulk	**T**=Towage (where available from port)	

Principal Facilities:

		Y	G	C	R				

Authority: Socialist Ports Co., Khoms, Socialist People's Libyan Arab Jamahirayah, *Email:* khomos@lpclibya.com, *Website:* www.lpclibya.com

Port Security: ISPS compliant

Approach: Lowest depth in channel is 13 m. The port is protected by two breakwaters, both forming an entrance of approx 150 m wide

Anchorage: Limited by the following parallels: Lat 32° 41.8' N and 32° 42.8' N; Long 14° 17.2' E and 14° 18.5' E

Pilotage: Compulsory

Radio Frequency: Port Authority on VHF Channel 16. Pilot Station on VHF Channels 8, 10 and 12

Accommodation:

Name	Length (m)	Depth (m)
Homs		
Quay No.12	390	8
Quay No.13	200	10
Quay No's 14 & 15	530	10
Quay No's 16 & 17	500	10
Quay No.18	340	10
Quay No.19	150	12
Quay No.20	75	

Storage:

Location	Open (m²)
Khoms	125000

Shipping Agents: Noor Shipping Co. Ltd, Naser Shipping Co., El-Gazala Square Street, P O Box 91452, Tripoli, Socialist People's Libyan Arab Jamahirayah, *Tel:* +218 21 333 5955, *Fax:* +218 21 444 1373, *Email:* info@naserco.com

Airport: Tripoli International Airport, 120 km

Lloyd's Agent: Gargoum Legal Marine, P O Box 153, Dubai Street, Benghazi, Socialist People's Libyan Arab Jamahirayah, *Tel:* +218 61 222 0302, *Fax:* +218 61 222 0302, *Email:* gargoum@gargoum.com, *Website:* www.gargoum.com

MARSA EL BREGA

Lat 30° 25' N; Long 19° 35' E.

Admiralty Chart: 3350/3354	**Admiralty Pilot:** 49
Time Zone: GMT +2 h	**UNCTAD Locode:** LY LMQ

Marsa el Brega

Principal Facilities:

P	Q	Y	G		R		B		T		

Authority: Sirte Oil Co., P O Box 385, Tripoli, Socialist People's Libyan Arab Jamahirayah, *Tel:* +218 21 361 0376/90, *Fax:* +218 21 361 0604, *Email:* info@soc.com.ly, *Website:* www.sirteoil.com

Officials: Chairman: Ali El Sogher Mohamed.

Port Security: ISPS compliant

Pre-Arrival Information: For all vessels:
a) name of vessel
b) flag
c) nrt
d) gt
e) dwt
f) draft
g) last port
h) agent
i) loa
j) ETA

Approach: The Brega sea buoy is located in pos 30° 27' 55" N; 19° 35' 01" E. A white flashing light every 10 secs on red and white buoy at height above water of abt 6.2 m. Numerous lighted and unlighted navigational and mooring buoys are located within the restricted area shown on BA Chart 3350. Vessels are cautioned not to enter the restricted area without a Brega pilot aboard

Anchorage: Suitable anchorages are located 4-5 miles NE to E of the Brega buoy in depth of 22-33 m. Vessels are not permitted to anchor within 0.5 miles of the channels into the inner harbour, and are to keep clear of the 143° 41' leads and of a submarine networks cable laying E to W between 2 miles and 2.5 miles N of the Brega buoy

Pilotage: Compulsory. Pilot normally boards vessel in vicinity of the Brega buoy. Vessels not required to call at Tripoli for inward and outward clearance. ETA's should be sent 48 to 72 h in advance. Unless 24 hours' telex notice of ETA is received by Sirte Brega Marine, NOR will not be accepted. Telex office closed between midnight and 0800 hours therefore allowance for delays should be made. Sirte Oil pilots, tugs, launches and other mooring equipment at present supplied without additional charge

Radio Frequency: VHF Channels 6, 9, 12, 14 and 16

Weather: NW winds produce very large swells which can lead to port closure

Tides: Tidal range does not exceed 0.5 m

Traffic: Average of 50 vessels/month

Principal Imports and Exports: Imports: Building materials, Petroleum industry usables. Exports: Ammonia, Crude oil, Liquefied gas, Methanol, Naphtha condensate, Refined oils, Urea.

Working Hours: 24 h/day for marine and petrochemical operations; Normal hours for general cargo 0700-1800

Accommodation:

Name	Length (m)	Depth (m)	Remarks
Marsa el Brega			
SPM No's 5 & 6		40	See [1] below
Product Dock	260	9.5	See [2] below
Jetty A North & Jetty B South	210	11.5	Loading of LNG and LPG for vessels up to 210 m loa, 30 000 dwt and 10 m draft
Jetty 1	200	14	See [3] below
Jetty 2	200	14	See [4] below
Urea Berth	200	9.5	See [5] below
West Cargo Quay	192	9.5	See [6] below
East Cargo Quay	394	12	See [7] below

[1]*SPM No's 5 & 6:* Crude oil berths for vessels up to 300 000 dwt with loading rate of 24 000/40 000 bbls/h
[2]*Product Dock:* Loading of fuel oil, diesel oil, gasoline and kerosene for vessels up to 180 m loa, 15 000 dwt and 7.92 m draft
[3]*Jetty 1:* Loading of fully refrigerated ammonia and methanol for vessels up to 200 m loa, 30 000 dwt and 10 m draft
[4]*Jetty 2:* Loading of naphtha and methanol and receiving of sulphuric acid and caustic soda for vessels up to 200 m loa, 30 000 dwt and 10 m draft
[5]*Urea Berth:* Bulk and bagged urea for vessels up to 165 m loa and 8.84 m draft. Loading rate of 400 t/h
[6]*West Cargo Quay:* For vessels up to 152.5 m loa, 15 000 dwt and 7.92 m draft. Ro/ro facility
[7]*East Cargo Quay:* For vessels up to 152.5 m loa, 15 000 dwt and 9.2 m draft

Bunkering: Shell Petro Development Co. of Libya B.V., El Salak Building, Christmas Tree Square, Benghazi, Socialist People's Libyan Arab Jamahirayah, *Tel:* +218 61 99574, *Fax:* +218 61 99387 – *Misc:* diesel oil and furnace oil in limited quantities at high cost, no coal
Universal Shipping & Maritime Agency, Omar Al Mokhtar Street, Nadi Al Madina Building No. 317, P O Box 3703, Tripoli, Socialist People's Libyan Arab Jamahirayah, *Tel:* +218 21 4448 170, *Fax:* +218 21 4448 170, *Email:* agency.tri@unishipco.com, *Website:* www.unishipco.com – *Misc:* diesel oil and furnace oil in limited quantities at high cost, no coal

Towage: Two tugs each of 2400 hp used for harbour manoeuvres

Repair & Maintenance: None allowed to ships' engines while vessels moored in berths. Engines must be ready for use at short notice in case vessel has to vacate berth at short notice due to bad weather. Other repair facilities not available

Medical Facilities: Emergencies only

Airport: Benghazi International Airport, 275 km

Development: Dredging is in continual progress inside and in the vicinity of the inner harbour. It is planned to deepen the inner harbour to a min depth of 13 m MLWS

Lloyd's Agent: Gargoum Legal Marine, P O Box 153, Dubai Street, Benghazi, Socialist People's Libyan Arab Jamahirayah, *Tel:* +218 61 222 0302, *Fax:* +218 61 222 0302, *Email:* gargoum@gargoum.com, *Website:* www.gargoum.com

MARSA EL HARIGA

see under Tobruk

MELLITAH

Lat 32° 53' N; Long 12° 15' E.

Admiralty Chart: 3403	**Admiralty Pilot:** 49
Time Zone: GMT +2 h	**UNCTAD Locode:** LY

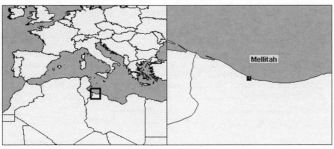

Principal Facilities:

P	Q						T		

Authority: ENI Gas B.V., Tripoli, Socialist People's Libyan Arab Jamahirayah, *Tel:* +218 21 360 3032, *Email:* asager@enigasly.com

Port Security: ISPS compliant

Pre-Arrival Information: ETA should be confirmed to the Terminal Operators (Eni Gas B.V., Tripoli) and local agent 72 h, 48 h and 24 h before arrival. The first ETA message should include the following information:
a) vessel's name and call sign
b) master's name in full
c) vessel's flag and port of registry
d) registered owner
e) last port of call and next port of call
f) particulars of last two cargoes transported
g) quantity and type of cargo required
h) if SBT or CBT quantity of ballast on arrival (% of SDW)
i) quantity of cargo on board (if partially loaded)
j) draught (forward and aft) on arrival

Pilotage: Compulsory. Vessel's should send initial ETA via local agent at least 7 days prior to arrival. The mooring master boards at the anchorage waiting area (approx 1 nautical mile NW of the Fairway Lt Buoy) or at the Fairway Lt Buoy

Radio Frequency: VHF Channels 16 and 72

Accommodation:

Name	Remarks
Wafa Marine Export Facilities	See [1] below

[1]*Wafa Marine Export Facilities:* Consists of:
(a) A 2200 m long jetty consisting of two LPG berths (East and West), equipped with arms for propane/butane loading and a sulphur loading berth via conveyor and ship loader
(b) SPM No.1 approx 1200 m seawards of the jetty in depth of approx 25 m for vessels up to 113 000 dwt handling condensate and SPM No.2 approx 2800 m seawards of the jetty in depth of approx 30 m for vessels up to 160 000 dwt handling crude oil

Towage: Two 4000 hp tugs available

Lloyd's Agent: Gargoum Legal Marine, P O Box 153, Dubai Street, Benghazi, Socialist People's Libyan Arab Jamahirayah, *Tel:* +218 61 222 0302, *Fax:* +218 61 222 0302, *Email:* gargoum@gargoum.com, *Website:* www.gargoum.com

MISURATA

Lat 32° 22' N; Long 15° 14' E.

Admiralty Chart: 3402
Time Zone: GMT +2 h

Admiralty Pilot: 49
UNCTAD Locode: LY MRA

Principal Facilities:

	Y	G	C	R			T		

Authority: Socialist Ports Co., P O Box: 2342, Misurata, Socialist People's Libyan Arab Jamahirayah, *Tel:* +218 51 627910/15, *Fax:* +218 51 614577, *Email:* info@lpclibya.com, *Website:* www.lpclibya.com

Pre-Arrival Information: Vessel's should advise their ETA 72 h, 48 h, 24 h and 12 h prior to arrival. The 24 h notice should be sent to Misurata Port Control with the following information:
a) vessel's name, call sign and flag
b) date of build
c) owner's name and address
d) charterer's name and address
e) agent's name
f) consignee name
g) master's name and nationality
h) loa, beam, gt and nrt
i) type of cargo and quantity
j) cargo in transit

k) date and time of sailing from last port
l) ETA at next port
m) number of crew and passengers
n) any animals or mail position at time of reporting
o) speed
p) port of approach
q) sea state and draught (forward and aft)
r) degree of list if any
s) name of last 10 ports
t) stowaways if any

Documentation: Vessel name, call sign, flag, builder, owner, agent consignee, cargo for transit, type of cargo, nationality and number of crew, any animals or mail onboard, last port of call, port of loading, next port, ETA and main particulars of the ship

Approach: Outer channel in depth of 13 m. Port entrance channel 150 m wide in depth of 12 m. For harbour entrance there are guides, 2 fixed red lights and 1 green flashing light, bearing 273° NW from breakwater roundheads
The North Breakwater extends 1400 m due East from Ras Zarrugh Lighthouse and East Breakwater extends 1800 m due North from the shore near the prominent radio station about 2 km South of the Ras Zarrugh Lighthouse. There are lights on the breakwater roundhead. On the North Breakwater a green flashing light (0.3 secs) every 3 secs and on the Eastern Breakwater a red flashing light (0.3 secs) every 3 secs. The Ras Zarrugh Lighthouse at the foot of the North Breakwater is a square tower with black and white vertical stripes. The structure is 8 m high and is on the top of a 16 m hill. The light is flashing white (0.5 secs) every 5 secs, with a range of 8 miles
There is a radio mast 7.6 miles WNW of Ras Zarrugh with fixed red flashing lights
The harbour should be approached from a position about 3 miles E of the entrance

Anchorage: In a position with a bearing 270° to the lighthouse on Ras Az'zarrough and a mile offshore in a depth of 13.0 m. Poor holding ground. Anchoring is prohibited within two miles of the harbour

Pilotage: Compulsory and available 24 h. For the commercial harbour pilot boards 2 nautical miles from the entrance

Radio Frequency: VHF Channels 16 and 12

Weather: NW winds

Tides: Tidal range 0.5 m

Traffic: 2004, 1087 vessels, 4 024 456 t of cargo handled, 63 840 TEU's

Maximum Vessel Dimensions: Max draft 11 m

Principal Imports and Exports: Imports: Barley, Coffee, Cotton textiles, Flour, Sugar, Tea. Exports: Butter, Carpets, Dates, Woollen fabrics.

Accommodation:

Name	Length (m)	Draught (m)	Remarks
Misurata			
General Cargo Berths	3150	11	Sixteen berths
Container Berth	30	11	
Dry/Liquid Product Berth	200	11	
Liquid Product Berth	275	12	
Service Berths	645	11	Four berths

Storage:

Location	Open (m²)	Covered (m²)	Grain (t)
Misurata	444500	24420	40000

Mechanical Handling Equipment:

Location	Type	Capacity (t)	Qty
Misurata	Floating Cranes	25–100	1
Misurata	Mobile Cranes	57	

Cargo Worked: Bagged goods 1800 t/day/vessel, tubes 900/day/vessel, general (bulk) cargo 500 t/day/vessel, containers 40/h, loading products of the iron company 3000 t/day/vessel

Bunkering: Albashir Shipping, Misurata G.A. District Building, Alef Flat No.19, Misurata, Socialist People's Libyan Arab Jamahirayah, *Tel:* +218 51 621190, *Fax:* +218 51 621191, *Email:* charters@albasheershipping.com, *Website:* www.albasheershipping.com
Farwa Shipping Agency, Aljamaa Alali Building (D) Flat (25), P O Box 144, Misurata, Socialist People's Libyan Arab Jamahirayah, *Tel:* +218 51 615632, *Fax:* +218 51 610083, *Email:* saffan21@hotmail.com

Towage: Four tugs of 565-2520 hp

Repair & Maintenance: Minor repairs undertaken

Ship Chandlers: Albashir Shipping, Misurata G.A. District Building, Alef Flat No.19, Misurata, Socialist People's Libyan Arab Jamahirayah, *Tel:* +218 51 621190, *Fax:* +218 51 621191, *Email:* charters@albasheershipping.com, *Website:* www.albasheershipping.com
Rayan Shipping Agency, Jamma Alally Complex, Building H, 4th Floor, P O Box 991, Misurata, Socialist People's Libyan Arab Jamahirayah, *Tel:* +218 51 622321, *Fax:* +218 51 622320, *Email:* rayan@rayamar.com, *Website:* www.rayamar.com

Shipping Agents: Al Rowad Shipping Co., Sana Mehaldi Street, Libyan Arab Airlines Complex, Misurata, Socialist People's Libyan Arab Jamahirayah, *Tel:* +218 51 612577, *Fax:* +218 51 617102, *Email:* rwdmiscus@lttnet.net
Albashir Shipping, Misurata G.A. District Building, Alef Flat No.19, Misurata, Socialist People's Libyan Arab Jamahirayah, *Tel:* +218 51 621190, *Fax:* +218 51 621191, *Email:* charters@albasheershipping.com, *Website:* www.albasheershipping.com
Almarassi Maritime & Trade Co., Aljama El-Aali Investment Centre, P O Box 2923, Misurata, Socialist People's Libyan Arab Jamahirayah, *Tel:* +218 51 620350, *Fax:* +218 51 620470, *Email:* agent@amtcmar.com, *Website:* www.amtcmar.com
Almarfa Shipping Co., Misurata, Socialist People's Libyan Arab Jamahirayah, *Tel:* +218 51 622740, *Fax:* +218 51 622858, *Email:* info@almarfa-ly.com, *Website:* www.almarfa-ly.com
Esterlab Libyan Shipping & Agency Co, Flat 35, 6th Floor, Building D., Misurata,

Socialist People's Libyan Arab Jamahirayah, *Tel:* +218 51 616599, *Fax:* +218 51 610347, *Email:* shipping.mis@esterlab-sc.com, *Website:* www.esterlab-ly.com

Farwa Shipping Agency, Aljamaa Alali Building (D) Flat (25), P O Box 144, Misurata, Socialist People's Libyan Arab Jamahirayah, *Tel:* +218 51 615632, *Fax:* +218 51 610083, *Email:* saffan21@hotmail.com

Germa Shipping & Stevedoring Co., Misurata, Socialist People's Libyan Arab Jamahirayah, *Tel:* +218 51 614337/614338, *Fax:* +218 51 614867, *Email:* misuratabranch@germashipping.net, *Website:* www.germashipping.com

Gulf International Co. Ltd, Misurata, Socialist People's Libyan Arab Jamahirayah, *Tel:* +218 51 741604, *Fax:* +218 51 741604, *Email:* gulfintl@hotmail.com

Overseas Shipping Co Libya, Misurata, Socialist People's Libyan Arab Jamahirayah, *Tel:* +218 51 625470, *Fax:* +218 51 625473, *Email:* mra.genmbox@cma-cgm.com

Rayan Shipping Agency, Jamma Alally Complex, Building H, 4th Floor, P O Box 991, Misurata, Socialist People's Libyan Arab Jamahirayah, *Tel:* +218 51 622321, *Fax:* +218 51 622320, *Email:* rayan@rayamar.com, *Website:* www.rayamar.com

Topacts Shipping Agency, P O Box 119, Misurata, Socialist People's Libyan Arab Jamahirayah, *Tel:* +218 51 623934, *Fax:* +218 51 619703, *Email:* info@topactsmar.com, *Website:* www.topactsmar.com

Universal Shipping Agency, El Jama Elale Building, Misurata, Socialist People's Libyan Arab Jamahirayah, *Tel:* +218 51 741418, *Fax:* +218 51 742570

Universal Shipping Co., Qaser Ahmed District, Misurata, Socialist People's Libyan Arab Jamahirayah, *Tel:* +218 51 742655, *Fax:* +218 51 742670, *Email:* universal_misurata@yahoo.com

Airport: Tripoli International Airport, 230 km

Development: Thirteen berths under construction. Four general cargo berths each 184 m long, four container berths each 184 m long, two ro/ro berths each 200 m long, two maintenance berths 200 and 130 m long and a passenger berth 250 m long. All berths will be dredged to 11.0 m. 52 500 m2 of covered storage comprising five transit sheds and two warehouses and 109 000 m2 of open storage under construction

Lloyd's Agent: Gargoum Legal Marine, P O Box 153, Dubai Street, Benghazi, Socialist People's Libyan Arab Jamahirayah, *Tel:* +218 61 222 0302, *Fax:* +218 61 222 0302, *Email:* gargoum@gargoum.com, *Website:* www.gargoum.com

RAS LANUF

Lat 30° 31' N; Long 18° 34' E.

Admiralty Chart: 3343	**Admiralty Pilot:** 49
Time Zone: GMT +2 h	**UNCTAD Locode:** LY RLA

Principal Facilities:

P	Q				B		A

Authority: VEBA Oil Operations, P O Box 690, Tripoli, Socialist People's Libyan Arab Jamahirayah, *Tel:* +218 21 3330 081, *Fax:* +218 21 3330 081, *Email:* info@vebalibya.com, *Website:* www.vebalibya.com

Officials: Chairman: Dr Abdussalam Rabae, *Tel:* +218 21 3330 081.

Port Security: ISPS compliant

Approach: A terminal sea buoy, colour white with white flashing light (flashing every 5 secs) located in pos 30° 33' 56" N; 18° 34' 35" E. Vessels should not navigate or anchor inshore of a bearing 280° and 130° from this buoy

Anchorage: Recommended anchorage is within a 914 m radius of pos 30° 33.5' N; 18° 36' E in a depth of approx 27.5 m

Pilotage: Compulsory. Company mooring master boards in close proximity of the suggested anchorage area

Radio Frequency: Listening on VHF Channel 16 and working on VHF Channels 14 and 11

Weather: Summer; prevailing winds NE with Ghibli's from the S up to 60 knots. Winter; prevailing winds W-NW up to 80 knots possible

Tides: Max range of tide 0.5 m

Maximum Vessel Dimensions: 300 000 dwt

Working Hours: 24 h/day

Accommodation:

Name	Depth (m)	Remarks
Ras Lanuf		
Berth No.1 (NBM-7 buoys)	22	In pos 30° 31' 35" N, 18° 34' 37" E for tankers up to 130 000 dwt
Berth No.2 (NBM-7 buoys)	22	In pos 30° 31' 55" N, 18° 33' 58" E for tankers up to 130 000 dwt
Berth No.3 (SPM)	29	In pos 30° 32' 54" N, 18° 34' 40" E for tankers up to 300 000 dwt
Berth No.4 (SPM)	29	In pos 30° 31' 50" N, 18° 36' 06" E for tankers up to 255 000 dwt

Bunkering: Shell Petro Development Co. of Libya B.V., El Salak Building, Christmas Tree Square, Benghazi, Socialist People's Libyan Arab Jamahirayah, *Tel:* +218 61 99574, *Fax:* +218 61 99387 – *Misc:* diesel oil and furnace oil in limited quantities at high cost, no coal

Universal Shipping & Maritime Agency, Omar Al Mokhtar Street, Nadi Al Madina Building No. 317, P O Box 3703, Tripoli, Socialist People's Libyan Arab Jamahirayah, *Tel:* +218 21 4448 170, *Fax:* +218 21 4448 170, *Email:* agency.tri@unishipco.com, *Website:* www.unishipco.com – *Misc:* diesel oil and furnace oil in limited quantities at high cost, no coal

Medical Facilities: None, except in a strict emergency

Airport: Ras Lanuf Airport, 3 km

Lloyd's Agent: Gargoum Legal Marine, P O Box 153, Dubai Street, Benghazi, Socialist People's Libyan Arab Jamahirayah, *Tel:* +218 61 222 0302, *Fax:* +218 61 222 0302, *Email:* gargoum@gargoum.com, *Website:* www.gargoum.com

RASCO HARBOUR

Lat 30° 32' N; Long 18° 36' E.

Admiralty Chart: 3343	**Admiralty Pilot:** 49
Time Zone: GMT +2 h	**UNCTAD Locode:** LY

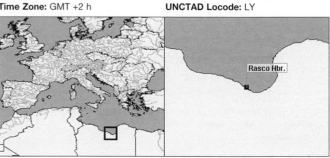

Principal Facilities:

P	Q							T	

Authority: Ras Lanuf Oil & Gas Processing Co., P O Box 2323, Tripoli, Socialist People's Libyan Arab Jamahirayah, *Tel:* +218 21 360 5177/82, *Fax:* +218 21 360 5174, *Email:* info@raslanuf.com, *Website:* www.raslanuf.com

Port Security: ISPS compliant

Pilotage: Compulsory

Accommodation:

Name	Draught (m)	Remarks
Rasco Harbour		Consists of three finger jetties, each of two berths
Jetty No.1	12.5	See [1] below
Jetty No.2	10.5	See [2] below
Jetty No.3	9.5	See [3] below

[1]*Jetty No.1:* For tankers of 3000-50 000 dwt and 250 m max loa. Used for loading of fuel oil and gas oil. Ten product loading arms are available (two for gas oil, four for fuel oil and four can be used for either product)

[2]*Jetty No.2:* For tankers of 3000-30 000 dwt and 189 m max loa. Used for loading of naphtha, pyrolysis gasoline and kerosene. Six product loading arms are available (four for kerosene and two that can be used for either pyrolysis gasoline or naphtha). This jetty also has two loading arms for either MTBE, benzene or methanol that is to be exported/imported in the future

[3]*Jetty No.3:* For tankers of 3000-30 000 dwt and 189 m max loa. Used for loading of cryogenic products: ethylene, propylene, mixed C4's and LPG. Eight loading arms are available (one for liquid products and one for vapor products)

Towage: Seven tugs are available: 2 x 750 hp, 3 x 145 hp and 2 x 2350 hp

Lloyd's Agent: Gargoum Legal Marine, P O Box 153, Dubai Street, Benghazi, Socialist People's Libyan Arab Jamahirayah, *Tel:* +218 61 222 0302, *Fax:* +218 61 222 0302, *Email:* gargoum@gargoum.com, *Website:* www.gargoum.com

SIRTICA TERMINAL

alternate name, see Ras Lanuf

TOBRUK

Lat 32° 5' N; Long 23° 59' E.

Admiralty Chart: 3657	**Admiralty Pilot:** 49
Time Zone: GMT +2 h	**UNCTAD Locode:** LY TOB

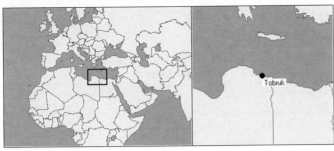

Principal Facilities:

P		Y	G	C	R		B		T	A

Authority: Socialist Ports Co., Tobruk, Socialist People's Libyan Arab Jamahirayah, *Email:* tubrug@lpclibya.com, *Website:* www.lpclibya.com

Port Security: ISPS compliant

Documentation: Vessel name, call sign, flag, builder, owner, agent consignee, cargo for transit, type of cargo, nationality and number of crew, any animals or mail onboard, last port of call, port of loading, next port, ETA and main particulars of the ship

Approach: Depth in entrance channel 10 m

Pilotage: Compulsory. Pilot launch meets vessels at entrance

Radio Frequency: VHF Channels 8, 10, 12 and 16

Maximum Vessel Dimensions: 20 000 t

Working Hours: General port working hours normally 0800-1400, 1600-1900

Accommodation:

Name	Depth (m)
Tobruk	
Berth No.1	5
Berth No.2	5
Berth No.3	5
Berth No.4	5
Berth No.5	7.5
Berth No.6	9.5
Berth No.7	9.5
Berth No.8	9.5
Berth No.9	9

Storage:

Location	Open (m²)	Covered (m²)
Tobruk	15000	3600

Mechanical Handling Equipment:

Location	Type	Capacity (t)	Qty
Tobruk	Mult-purp. Cranes	10	2

Bunkering: Limited stocks of oil; no coal

Towage: Two tugs for ocean-going vessels. One 200 hp harbour tug

Airport: El Abdm, 19 km

Lloyd's Agent: Gargoum Legal Marine, P O Box 153, Dubai Street, Benghazi, Socialist People's Libyan Arab Jamahirayah, *Tel:* +218 61 222 0302, *Fax:* +218 61 222 0302, *Email:* gargoum@gargoum.com, *Website:* www.gargoum.com

TRIPOLI

Lat 32° 54' N; Long 13° 11' E.

Admiralty Chart: 455	**Admiralty Pilot:** 49
Time Zone: GMT +2 h	**UNCTAD Locode:** LY TIP

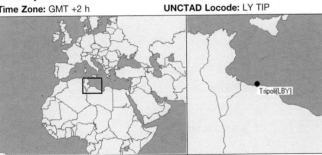

Principal Facilities:

Q	Y	G	C	R		B		T	A

Authority: Socialist Ports Co., Tripoli, Socialist People's Libyan Arab Jamahirayah, *Email:* tripoli@lpclibya.com, *Website:* www.lpclibya.com

Port Security: ISPS compliant

Documentation: Vessel name, call sign, flag, builder, owner, agent consignee, cargo for transit, type of cargo, nationality and number of crew, any animals or mail onboard, last port of call, port of loading, next port, ETA and main particulars of the ship

Approach: Depth of outer channel, inner channel and port area is 12 m

Anchorage: The anchorage area for vessels awaiting a berth lies approximately 1.5 nm north of Tarabulus light. The holding ground is reported to be good

Pilotage: Compulsory - pilot boards at entrance of channel, 1 nm NNE

Radio Frequency: Main channel on VHF Channel 12 (156.600 mHz). Stand-by channel on VHF Channel 10 (156.500 mHz). Pilotage channel on VHF Channel 8 (156.400 mHz). Universal channel on VHF Channel 16

Weather: Winds N and NE. Severe gales are rare. Vessels inside harbour are not as a general rule prevented from operating in bad weather

Principal Imports and Exports: Imports: China, Drugs, Earthenware, Flour, Glassware, Medicines, Metal, Rice, Sugar, Tea, Textiles, Wine. Exports: Alfa, Carpets, Cattle, Dates, Eggs, Esparto, Henna, Hides, Sponges, Tunney in oil.

Working Hours: General port working hours normally 0800-1400. Overtime can be arranged 1500-1900

Accommodation:

Name	Depth (m)
Tripoli	
Berth No.5	
Berth No.5.5	
Berth No.6	7
Berth No.6.5	9
Berth No.7	9
Berth No.8	8.5
Berth No.9	9
Berth No.10	7.5
Berth No.11	7
Berth No.12	8
Berth No.13	7
Berth No.14	8
Berth No.15	10.5
Berth No.16	10
Berth No.17	10.5
Berth No.18	12
Berth No.19	12
Berth No.20	12
Berth No.21	11.5
Berth No.22	11.5
Berth No.23	11.5
Berth No.24	12.5
Berth No.25	12
Berth No.26	12.5
Berth No.27	12
Berth No.28	12
Oil Berth	9

Mechanical Handling Equipment:

Location	Type	Capacity (t)	Qty
Tripoli	Floating Cranes	200	1
Tripoli	Floating Cranes	100	1

Bunkering: Oil bunkering by arrangement at all discharging berths and with due notice, but expensive
Universal Shipping & Maritime Agency, Omar Al Mokhtar Street, Nadi Al Madina Building No. 317, P O Box 3703, Tripoli, Socialist People's Libyan Arab Jamahirayah, *Tel:* +218 21 4448 170, *Fax:* +218 21 4448 170, *Email:* agency.tri@unishipco.com, *Website:* www.unishipco.com

Towage: Seventeen tugs available; ten of 500 hp, four of 1600 hp and three of 2400 hp

Repair & Maintenance: One slipway up to 1000 t and one up to 500 t. Workshop available for minor repairs

Shipping Agents: Al-Jazeera Shipping Co. W.L.L., Omer Mouktar Street, P O Box 81753, Tripoli, Socialist People's Libyan Arab Jamahirayah, *Tel:* +218 21 444 9766, *Fax:* +218 21 333 2936, *Email:* info@aljazeerashipping.com, *Website:* www.aljazeerashipping.com.ly
Al Rowad Shipping Co., 1st Floor, 64 Borj Al Fateh Tower, Tripoli, Socialist People's Libyan Arab Jamahirayah, *Tel:* +218 21 335 1177, *Fax:* +218 21 335 1178, *Email:* liatop@maersk.com
Alshic DLC Shipping, P O Box 589, Tripoli, Socialist People's Libyan Arab Jamahirayah, *Tel:* +218 21 360 7888, *Fax:* +218 21 360 5254, *Email:* welcome@libyanshipping.net, *Website:* www.alshic-group.com
Elhiblu International Maritime Agency Co., Mazran Street, Off Albahran Street, P O Box 7172, Tripoli, Socialist People's Libyan Arab Jamahirayah, *Tel:* +218 21 444 2405, *Fax:* +218 21 444 6672, *Email:* nmsmmla@yahoo.com
Esterlab Libyan Shipping & Agency Co, Wahat Centre No.8, Hay Alandalus, 2nd floor, Tripoli, Socialist People's Libyan Arab Jamahirayah, *Tel:* +218 21 477 9653, *Fax:* +218 21 477 8184, *Email:* shipping@esterlab-sc.com, *Website:* www.esterlab-ly.com
Germa Shipping & Stevedoring Co., Zawiat Al Dhmani Tripoli, P O Box 985-2437, Tripoli, Socialist People's Libyan Arab Jamahirayah, *Tel:* +218 21 340 1844, *Fax:* +218 21 333 1866, *Email:* tripolibranch@germashipping.net, *Website:* www.germashipping.com
Green Waves, Aldman Building, Mizran Rea, Tripoli, Socialist People's Libyan Arab Jamahirayah, *Tel:* +218 21 444 6739, *Fax:* +218 21 444 0676, *Email:* master19912001@yahoo.com
Gulf International Co. Ltd, P O Box 80314, Tripoli, Socialist People's Libyan Arab Jamahirayah, *Tel:* +218 21 444 3208, *Fax:* +218 21 333 3451, *Email:* gulfintl@hotmail.com
Manarat Almadina Shipping Agency, The Old City front of Tripoli Port main gate, P O Box 2059, Tripoli, Socialist People's Libyan Arab Jamahirayah, *Tel:* +218 21 490 7792, *Fax:* +218 21 490 7286, *Email:* info@masa-shipping.com, *Website:* www.masa-shipping.com
Massar Saheeh Maritime Transport Co., Fateh Road, Next to Grand Hotel, P O Box 81119, Tripoli, Socialist People's Libyan Arab Jamahirayah, *Tel:* +218 21 334 2943, *Fax:* +218 21 333 1099, *Email:* massarco@yahoo.com

---

Key to Principal Facilities:—

A=Airport	**C**=Containers	**G**=General Cargo	**P**=Petroleum	**R**=Ro/Ro	**Y**=Dry Bulk
B=Bunkers	**D**=Dry Dock	**L**=Cruise	**Q**=Other Liquid Bulk	**T**=Towage (where available from port)	

Noor Shipping Co. Ltd, Naser Shipping Co., El-Gazala Square Street, P O Box 91452, Tripoli, Socialist People's Libyan Arab Jamahirayah, *Tel:* +218 21 333 5955, *Fax:* +218 21 444 1373, *Email:* info@naserco.com

Overseas Shipping Co Libya, Thaat El-Emad Towers, Tower 5, 1st Floor, P O Box 253, Tripoli, Socialist People's Libyan Arab Jamahirayah, *Tel:* +218 21 335 0870, *Fax:* +218 21 335 0322, *Email:* tri.genmbox@osc-libya.com, *Website:* www.osc-libya.com

Ras Al Hilal Marine Services Co. (R.H. Marine Service), Office No.148, Floor 14, Alfateh Tower 2, P O Box 93192, Tripoli, Socialist People's Libyan Arab Jamahirayah, *Tel:* +218 21 335 1101, *Fax:* +218 21 335 1102, *Email:* office@rhms.com.ly, *Website:* www.rhms.com.ly

Universal Shipping Agency, P O Box 3703, Tripoli, Socialist People's Libyan Arab Jamahirayah, *Tel:* +218 21 444 8100, *Fax:* +218 21 444 8160/43, *Email:* unifinance@lttnet.net

Universal Shipping Co., Al Waha Building, 5th Floor, Omar Almokhtar Street, Tripoli, Socialist People's Libyan Arab Jamahirayah, *Tel:* +218 21 444 8170, *Fax:* +218 21 444 8170, *Website:* www.unishipco.com

Stevedoring Companies: Germa Shipping & Stevedoring Co., Zawiat Al Dhmani Tripoli, P O Box 985-2437, Tripoli, Socialist People's Libyan Arab Jamahirayah, *Tel:* +218 21 340 1844, *Fax:* +218 21 333 1866, *Email:* tripolibranch@germashipping.net, *Website:* www.germashipping.com

Surveyors: Massar Saheeh Maritime Transport Co., Fateh Road, Next to Grand Hotel, P O Box 81119, Tripoli, Socialist People's Libyan Arab Jamahirayah, *Tel:* +218 21 334 2943, *Fax:* +218 21 333 1099, *Email:* massarco@yahoo.com
Registro Italiano Navale (RINA), Academy of Maritime Studies, Tripoli, Socialist People's Libyan Arab Jamahirayah, *Tel:* +218 21 489 2552, *Fax:* +218 21 489 1440, *Email:* belhag_ali@hotmail.com, *Website:* www.rina.org

Airport: Tripoli International Airport, 30 km

Lloyd's Agent: Gargoum Legal Marine, P O Box 153, Dubai Street, Benghazi, Socialist People's Libyan Arab Jamahirayah, *Tel:* +218 61 222 0302, *Fax:* +218 61 222 0302, *Email:* gargoum@gargoum.com, *Website:* www.gargoum.com

ZAWIA TERMINAL

Lat 32° 49' N; Long 12° 43' E.

Admiralty Chart: 3403	**Admiralty Pilot:** 49
Time Zone: GMT +2 h	**UNCTAD Locode:** LY ZAW

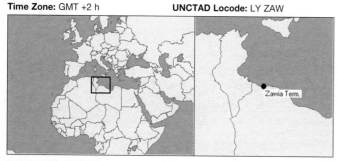

Principal Facilities:

P									T	A	

Authority: Azzawiya Oil Refinery Co., P O Box 6451, Tripoli, Socialist People's Libyan Arab Jamahirayah, *Tel:* +218 21 361 0539, *Fax:* +218 21 361 0538, *Email:* mohamedzarti@yahoo.com, *Website:* www.azzawiyaoil.com.ly

Officials: Harbour Master: Mohamed Zarti.

Port Security: ISPS compliant

Anchorage: Anchorage can be obtained one mile NE of the loading berths in a depth of about 25 m; bottom of sand over rock

Pilotage: Compulsory. Pilot boards at the anchorage area. Berthing and unberthing carried out during daylight hours only

Radio Frequency: Terminal radio station keeps continuous watch on VHF Channels 16 and 22; operations carried out on VHF Channel 12

Weather: Loading operations at the berths may be interrupted by strong winds, particularly during the winter months

Accommodation:

Name	Depth (m)	Draught (m)	Remarks
Az Zawiyah			See [1] below
Berth No.1	30	19	SBM for vessels up to 140 000 dwt
Berth No.2	23	10	See [2] below
Berth No.3	27	17	SBM for vessels up to 100 000 dwt

[1]*Az Zawiyah:* Tanker terminal comprising three offshore loading berths
[2]*Berth No.2:* For vessels up to 20 000 dwt. Vessels berth using two anchors with the stern secured to three mooring buoys

Towage: Tugs from Tripoli can be brought in if required

Airport: Tripoli International Airport, 50 km

Lloyd's Agent: Gargoum Legal Marine, P O Box 153, Dubai Street, Benghazi, Socialist People's Libyan Arab Jamahirayah, *Tel:* +218 61 222 0302, *Fax:* +218 61 222 0302, *Email:* gargoum@gargoum.com, *Website:* www.gargoum.com

ZUARA

Lat 32° 55' N; Long 12° 7' E.

Admiralty Chart: 3403	**Admiralty Pilot:** 49
Time Zone: GMT +2 h	**UNCTAD Locode:** LY ZUA

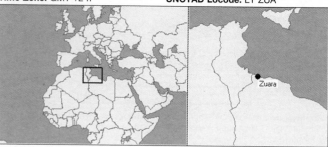

Principal Facilities:

		G	R		T	

Authority: Socialist Ports Co., Zuara, Socialist People's Libyan Arab Jamahirayah, *Email:* zwara@lpclibya.com, *Website:* www.lpclibya.com

Port Security: ISPS compliant

Documentation: Vessel name, call sign, flag, builder, owner, agent consignee, cargo for transit, type of cargo, nationality and number of crew, any animals or mail onboard, last port of call, port of loading, next port, ETA and main particulars of the ship

Approach: Navigational channel approx 1 km long

Anchorage: Anchorage can be obtained in depths ranging from 6.9 m to 9.1 m

Pilotage: Available

Radio Frequency: VHF Channels 8, 10, 12 and 16

Working Hours: General port working hours normally 0800-1400, 1600-1900

Accommodation:

Name	Length (m)	Depth (m)	Remarks
Zuara			
Quay	120	4	Two berths

Storage:

Location	Open (m²)
Zuara	16000

Mechanical Handling Equipment:

Location	Type	Qty
Zuara	Mobile Cranes	1
Zuara	Forklifts	10

Towage: Two tugs available

Medical Facilities: Available

Airport: Tripoli International Airport, 127 km

Lloyd's Agent: Gargoum Legal Marine, P O Box 153, Dubai Street, Benghazi, Socialist People's Libyan Arab Jamahirayah, *Tel:* +218 61 222 0302, *Fax:* +218 61 222 0302, *Email:* gargoum@gargoum.com, *Website:* www.gargoum.com

ZUEITINA TERMINAL

Lat 30° 51' N; Long 20° 3' E.

Admiralty Chart: 3346	**Admiralty Pilot:** 49
Time Zone: GMT +2 h	**UNCTAD Locode:** LY ZUE

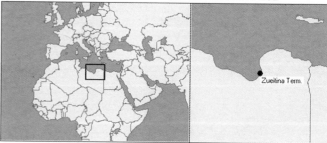

Principal Facilities:

P	Q							T		

Authority: Zueitina Oil Co., P O Box 2134, Tripoli, Socialist People's Libyan Arab Jamahirayah, *Tel:* +218 21 333 8011, *Fax:* +218 21 333 9109, *Email:* info@zueitina-ly.com, *Website:* www.zueitina.com.ly

Port Security: ISPS compliant

Approach: The approach to the port is marked by a light-float moored 3.5 m NW of Tre Scogli Reef. Min depth in channels to loading berths is 18.3 m

Anchorage: Anchorage for vessels awaiting a loading berth can be obtained 1 mile SE of the light-float in pos centred at 30° 55' N, 20° 01' E in a depth of about 30-35 m. Holding ground is poor during bad weather. Anchorage is prohibited S of parallel 30° 54' 00" N

Pilotage: Compulsory. Vessels intending to load crude oil or LPG will be boarded by the Mooring Master at the Terminal Fairway Buoy who will advise on all manoeuvres relating to berthing. ETA should be notified to Operations Manager 72 h, 48 h and 24 h prior to arrival, Telex: 20130 ZUE LY. The Mooring Master will remain on board during loading operations

Radio Frequency: Port call sign ZUE. Contact 'Zueitina Marine' on VHF Channels 13 or 16

Weather: During the winter months strong NW gales accompanied by frequent rain squalls can be experienced, causing heavy seas and high swells

Working Hours: Continuous depending on the weather

Accommodation:

Name	Depth (m)	Remarks
Zuetina		See [1] below
Alpha Berth	32	See [2] below
Bravo Berth	21.9	CBM in pos 30° 52' 18" N, 20° 01' 04" E, max size 150 000 t
Charlie Berth	30.5	SPM in pos 30° 52' 08" N, 20° 00' 11" E, max size 275 000 t
Delta Berth	20	CBM in pos 30° 50' 56" N, 20° 00' 26" E, max size 110 000 t
Echo Berth	25.3	See [3] below

[1]*Zuetina:* Tanker Terminals: three offshore berths for loading crude oil, comprising one single point mooring and two conventional buoy moorings. Vessels of up to 275 000 dwt can be accommodated.
All mooring berths are connected to shore installations by submarine pipelines and are equipped with hose connections of 12''. Loading rates are 32 000 bbls/h. Vessels at both CBM berths require a min of ten shackles. Delta berth is dedicated for lifting of naphtha. All berths require vessels to have derrick port side, min 10 t SWL. All vessels must have C.B.T. and deballast while loading. No vessel will be accepted which has to deballast prior to loading
Liquefied Gas facilities: Situated inside Tre Scogli Reef, SSW of the Small Craft Harbour. Loading platform with four breasting dolphins, two of which are incorporated into the platform on each side of the loading point. Vessels up to 213.36 m loa with a cargo cap of about 32 000 m3 can be accommodated; max loaded draught must not exceed 8.7 m. The platform is equipped with a single loading line with a connecting flange of 6"; a 12" Chiksan is available for larger vessels. The max loading rate is 6000-7000 bbls/h
[2]*Alpha Berth:* Out of service but marked by a navigation buoy in pos 30° 53' 30" N, 20° 01' 05" E
[3]*Echo Berth:* SPM in pos 30° 50' 16" N, 19° 59' 16" E, max size 150 000 t
At present this is out of service and is marked by a navigation buoy

Towage: One tug of 55 t bollard pull to assist in berthing

Medical Facilities: Only available in cases of emergency

Lloyd's Agent: Gargoum Legal Marine, P O Box 153, Dubai Street, Benghazi, Socialist People's Libyan Arab Jamahirayah, *Tel:* +218 61 222 0302, *Fax:* +218 61 222 0302, *Email:* gargoum@gargoum.com, *Website:* www.gargoum.com

ZUWARAH

alternate name, see Zuara

LITHUANIA

BUTINGE TERMINAL

Lat 55° 58' N; Long 20° 43' E.

Admiralty Chart: 2288   **Admiralty Pilot:** 19
Time Zone: GMT +2 h   **UNCTAD Locode:** LT

Principal Facilities:

P						T	A

Authority: AB Mazeikiu Nafta, Terminalo Kelias 2, P O Box 48, Butinge Terminal, LT-00325 Palanga, Republic of Lithuania, *Tel:* +370 46 396420, *Fax:* +370 46 396429, *Email:* marine@nafta.lt, *Website:* www.nafta.lt

Officials: General Director: Nelson English.
Marine Manager: Ugnius Mickus.

Port Security: ISPS compliant

Anchorage: The Butinge Anchorage comprises the area between the following coordinates:
55° 58.7' N; 20° 43.3' E
55° 59.6' N; 20° 46.9' E
55° 57.8' N; 20° 48.6' E
55° 56.8' N; 20° 44.8' E

Pilotage: Compulsory. ETA should be sent 5 days, 72 h, 48 h and 12 h prior to arrival. Vessels should contact the Pilot Station at least 4 h prior to arrival at the anchorage area. Pilot boards 18 km offshore within the Butinge Anchorage

Radio Frequency: VHF Channels 16 (listening) and 71 (working)

Tides: Range of 0.3-0.6 m

Traffic: 2006, 5 888 446 t of oil handled

Maximum Vessel Dimensions: 150 000 dwt, 16 m draft

Working Hours: 24 h/day

Accommodation:

Name	Remarks
Butinge Terminal	See [1] below

[1]*Butinge Terminal:* Consists of an SPM buoy with a CALM system, 7.5 km offshore in depth of 20 m for import/export of crude oil. One 36" offshore pipeline connects the terminal with the buoy. Loading rates of 5300-5700 m3/h
The Butinge Terminal and the Mazeikiai Refinery are connected by a 22" pipeline, 92.5 km in length

Towage: One tug of 73 t bollard pull and one tug of 25 t bollard pull. Two tugs are always in attendance during berthing, loading/unloading and un-berthing operations

Airport: Palanga Airport, 23 km

Lloyd's Agent: Lars Krogius Baltic Ltd, Taikos pr 24A, Office 408, LT-91222 Klaipeda, Republic of Lithuania, *Tel:* +370 46 380203, *Fax:* +370 46 495414, *Email:* lithuania@krogius.com, *Website:* www.krogius.com

KLAIPEDA

Lat 55° 42' N; Long 21° 8' E.

Admiralty Chart: 2276   **Admiralty Pilot:** 19
Time Zone: GMT +2 h   **UNCTAD Locode:** LT KLJ

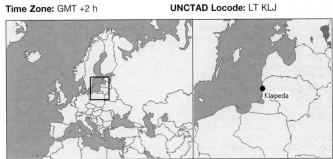

Principal Facilities:

P	Q	Y	G	C	R	L	B		T	A

Key to Principal Facilities:—
A=Airport   **C**=Containers   **G**=General Cargo   **P**=Petroleum   **R**=Ro/Ro   **Y**=Dry Bulk
B=Bunkers   **D**=Dry Dock   **L**=Cruise   **Q**=Other Liquid Bulk   **T**=Towage (where available from port)

Authority: Klaipeda State Seaport Authority, 24 J. Janonio Street, LT-92251 Klaipeda, Republic of Lithuania, *Tel:* +370 46 499799, *Fax:* +370 46 499777, *Email:* info@port.lt, *Website:* www.portofklaipeda.lt

Officials: Director General: Sigitas Dobilinskas, *Email:* s.dobilinskas@port.lt.
Marketing Director: Arturas Drungilas, *Tel:* +370 46 499748, *Email:* a.drungilas@port.lt.
Harbour Master: Viktoras Lukosevicius, *Tel:* +370 46 499688, *Email:* ukt@port.lt.

Port Security: ISPS compliant

Pre-Arrival Information: Vessel's should send ETA to the Port Despatcher 72 h, 48 h and 24 h prior to arrival. If the vessel's voyage is shorter than these times ETA should be sent immediately upon departure from the last port of call
The initial notice should contain the following information:
a) vessel's name, call sign, IMO number or MMSI
b) vessel's flag
c) port of registry
d) vessel's main particulars
e) maximum fresh water draught
f) cargo details
g) number of persons on board
h) security level on board according to the code
i) security level on board in the last ten ports of call
2 h prior to arrival, vessel's should contact Klaipeda Traffic on VHF Channel 09 advising vessel's name, flag, quantity of waste and fresh water draught. All vessels should maintain a continuous listening watch on VHF Channel 09 whilst underway within the area, and on VHF Channel 16 whilst at anchor

Documentation: General declaration indicating the validity of the documents issued by classification societies
Crew list
Passenger list if any
Declaration on the personal items of the crew
List of the vessel's stores
Manifest of the cargo if any
Maritime declaration of health
Deratization certificate
Vessel measurement certificate
International tonnage certificate and international load lines certificate
International oil pollution prevention certificate
The vessel master's report on accidents (if any) during the voyage
The authorization from the sanitary quarantine department (for foreign vessels)
International security certificate (copy) and vessel's security level data in the last ten ports of call

Approach: Vessels approaching the port should set a course to the clear water buoy No.1 (55° 43.8' N; 20° 59.6' E). From there vessels should proceed on a course 92.5° for 3.5 nautical miles. The pair of lighted beacons mark the entrance of the port of Klaipeda. The depth in the 230 m wide entrance channel is 14.5 m at MSL with max draft set to 12.5 m

Anchorage: There are two designated anchorage areas:
No.1 is centred 8 miles WNW of the harbour entrance in depth of 34-38 m, N of the recommended approach
No.2 is centred 7.75 miles W of the harbour entrance in depth of 40-42 m, S of the recommended approach

Pilotage: Compulsory. A pilot boat meets vessels at Light Buoy No.1 moored approx 3 nm W of the harbour entrance on the Iplaukimo Vedine leading line. Pilot is ordered through the ship's agent 12 h in advance with confirmation 4 h before ETA. Pilots keep watch throughout 24 h. In the event that the pilot is unable to board due to rough weather, the pilot vessel will proceed ahead of the incoming vessel to guide her

through the entrance and board her in the inner roadstead. The pilot station is situated at berth 4

Radio Frequency: Vessel traffic service on VHF Channel 9

Weather: Prevailing W'ly winds. When there are storm winds from the W and SW, a rough sea forms at the entrance to the Juru Kanalas which makes vessel control difficult. Entry not recommended in these conditions

Tides: Water levels can vary to 0.5 m above and below mean sea level

Traffic: 2008, 29 877 000 t of cargo handled

Maximum Vessel Dimensions: 100 000 dwt, 300 m loa, 12.5 m draft

Principal Imports and Exports: Imports: Building materials, Containers, Crude & manufactured minerals, Refrigerated cargo, Ro/ro cargo, Sugar. Exports: Containers, Ferroalloys, Fertiliser, Grain, Metal scrap, Oil products, Ro/ro cargo, Timber.

Working Hours: 24 h/day

Accommodation:

Name	Length (m)	Draught (m)	Remarks
Klaipeda			
Berth No.1	274.8	12.5	
Berth No.2	271.2	12.5	
Berth No.3	250	12.5	
Berth No.4	225	12.5	
Berth No.5	264.4	12.5	
Berth No.6	157.1	12.5	
Berth No.7	171.4	10.6	
Berth No.8	180	10.6	
Berth No.9	165	10.6	
Berth No.10	179	8.5	
Berth No.11	170	8.5	
Berth No.12	254.4	9.5	
Berth No.13	245.2	7	
Berth No.14	95.3	6.5	
Berth No.15	133.9	7	
Berth No.16	130	7	
Berth No.17	130	7	
Berth No.18	132.9	6.5	
Berth No.19	102	6.5	
Berth No.20	106.4	6.5	
Berth No.21	221	5.5	
Berth No.22	280	6	
Berth No.23	78	3	
Berth No.24	123.3	3	
Berth No.25	126.7	3	
Berth No.26	51.3	3.7	
Berth No.27	83.7	3.5	
Berth No.28	52.3	8.5	
Berth No.29	57	8.5	
Berth No.30	57	8.5	
Berth No.31	57	8.5	
Berth No.32	57	8.5	
Berth No.33	61.3	8.5	
Berth No.34	64.9	6	
Berth No.35	55	6	
Berth No.36	55	5.5	
Berth No.37	55	5.5	
Berth No.38	55	5.5	
Berth No.40	60	4.5	
Berth No.42	35.7		Slip berth
Berth No.43	49.3	4	
Berth No.44	49.3	4.5	
Berth No.45	42.1	5	
Berth No.46	39	5.5	
Berth No.47	82.6	5	
Berth No.52	40.7	3.5	
Berth No.53	39.1	3.3	
Berth No.54	27	4.5	
Berth No.55	27	4.5	
Berth No.56	27	4	
Berth No.57	27.9	1	
Berth No.58	94.6	2.5	
Berth No.59	73.6	5.5	
Berth No.60	290.1	5	
Berth No.61	52.7	4	
Berth No.62	379.8	5.5	
Berth No.63	71.8	5.5	
Berth No.64	137.6	4.5	
Berth No.65	164.1	5.2	
Berth No.65a	91.4	4.5	
Berth No.66	148.4	.5	
Berth No.67	261.9	5.6	
Berth No.68	230	11	
Berth No.69	150.8	11.5	
Berth No.70	212.8	11.5	
Berth No.71	214.6	11.5	
Berth No.72	248.1	11.5	
Berth No.73	142.1	6	
Berth No.74	90.1	4	
Berth No.75	35.7	2.5	
Berth No.76	147.5	2.5	
Berth No.77	59.1	4	
Berth No.78	59.2	3.6	
Berth No.79	100	2.5	
Berth No.80	143.3	8.5	
Berth No.81	175.2		Berth enforcement
Berth No's 82-89	550	11.5	Klaipedos Smelte Container Terminal (KSCT)
Berth No.90	50		Under construction

Name	Length (m)	Draught (m)	Remarks
Berth No.91	50	6.2	
Berth No.92	50	6.2	
Berth No.93	65.8	6.5	
Berth No.94	100	7.5	
Berth No.95	100	7.5	
Berth No.96	100	7.7	
Berth No.97	100	7.7	
Berth No.98	100	7.7	
Berth No.99	106.3	7.7	
Berth No.100	92.5	7.5	
Berth No.101	107.5	11.5	
Berth No.102	100	11.5	
Berth No.103	100	11.5	
Berth No.104	118.2	11.5	
Berth No.105	149.1	7	
Berth No.106	120		Under construction
Berth No.107	36.3	2.5	
Berth No.108	26.1	2.5	
Berth No.109	24.2	3.5	
Berth No.110	24.2	3.5	
Berth No.111	26.5	3.5	
Berth No.112	21.3	3.5	
Berth No.113	23.2	2	
Berth No.114	42.9	2.5	
Berth No.115	17.9	3	
Berth No.116	57.4	3	
Berth No.117	53.2	2.5	
Berth No.118	176.8		Under construction
Berth No.119	162.5	6	
Berth No.120	70	6	
Berth No.121	55	6	
Berth No.121a	46.2	.5	
Berth No.122	50.3	4	
Berth No.122a	67.4	.5	
Berth No.123	97.6	5.5	
Berth No.124	105.2	6.3	
Berth No.125	105.2	5.5	
Berth No.126	125.8	6.3	
Berth No.127	165.4	8	
Berth No.127a	86.1		Berth enforcement
Berth No.128	166.1	8	
Berth No.129	166.8	8.5	
Berth No.129a	123		Berth enforcement
Berth No.130	178	8.5	
Berth No.131	167.4	7.5	
Berth No.131a	147.2		Berth enforcement
Berth No.132	179.8	7	
Berth No.133	167.5	6.8	
Berth No.133a	146.5		Berth enforcement
Berth No.134	179.7	7	
Berth No.135	169	7	
Berth No.135a	148.4		Berth enforcement
Berth No.136	180.4	6.8	
Berth No.137	169.9	6.5	
Berth No.137a	148.3		Berth enforcement
Berth No.138	180.5	6.8	
Berth No.138a	50.2		Berth enforcement
Berth No.139	345.2	1.8	
Berth No.140	175	8.5	
Berth No.141	168.3	8.5	
Berth No.142	123.2		Under construction
Berth No.143	451.9	8.5	
Berth No.144	90.6		Berth enforcement
Berth No.145	77.5	5	
Berth No.146	210	7.5	
Berth No.147	210	7.5	
Berth No.148	57	5	
Berth No.149	220	7.5	
Berth No.150	145.2	7.5	
Berth No.151	225.4	7.5	
Berth No.152			
Berth No.153	49.9	3.5	
Berth No.154	59.1	3.8	
Berth No.155	61.6	3.8	
Berth No.156	48.2	3	

Storage: Liquid product storage of 707 000 m3

Location	Open (m²)	Covered (m²)	Cold (m³)
Klaipeda	680300	380000	35000

Mechanical Handling Equipment: Gantry cranes available. Multi-purpose cranes up to 104 t cap

Cargo Worked: Dry cargo 14 350 t/day, oil products 29 500 t/day, railway ferry terminal 7920 t/day

Bunkering: Available from quays and barges
Laivu Bunkeriavimo Kompanija, Sauliu 44-2, LT-92226 Klaipeda, Republic of Lithuania, Tel: +370 46 313 370, Fax: +370 46 313 371, Email: info@bunker.lt, Website: www.bunker.lt
Bominflot, Bominflot Bunkergesellschaft fur Mineralole mbH & Co. KG, Grosse Baeckerstrasse 11, 20095 Hamburg, Germany, Tel: +49 40 350 930, Fax: +49 40 3509 3116, Email: mail@bominflot.de, Website: www.bominflot.net
Chevron Marine Products LLC, ul. Grodzienska 11, 80215 Gdansk, Poland, Tel: +48 58 5202254, Fax: +48 58 3412634, Email: kukiej@chevrontexco.com, Website: www.chevron.com
ExxonMobil Marine Fuels, Mailpoint 31, ExxonMobil House, Ermyn Way, Leather-

head, Surrey KT22 8UX, United Kingdom, Tel: +44 1372 222 000, Fax: +44 1372 223 922, Email: marine.fuels@exxonmobil.com, Website: www.exxonmobil.com
Laivu Bunkeriavimo Kompanija, Sauliu 44-2, LT-92226 Klaipeda, Republic of Lithuania, Tel: +370 46 313 370, Fax: +370 46 313 371, Email: info@bunker.lt, Website: www.bunker.lt
Tramp Oil & Marine, World Fuel Services Corporation, 13th Floor, Portland House, Bressenden Place, London SW1E 5BH, United Kingdom, Tel: +44 20 7808 5000, Fax: +44 20 7808 5088, Email: pturner@wfscorp.com, Website: www.wfscorp.com – Grades: all grades

Waste Reception Facilities: All kinds of waste are collected by barges and/or trucks

Towage: Klaipeda Stevedoring Co. (KLASCO), Zauerveino 18, LT-5813 Klaipeda, Republic of Lithuania, Tel: +370 46 399501, Fax: +370 46 399315, Email: mark1@klasco.lt, Website: www.klasco.lt
Laivite, Naujoji Uosto Street 3, LT-92120 Klaipeda, Republic of Lithuania, Tel: +370 46 394000, Fax: +370 46 394111, Email: office@laivite.lt, Website: www.laivite.lt
JSC Western Shiprepair Yard, Minijos 180, 5816 Klaipeda, Republic of Lithuania, Tel: +370 46 483600, Fax: +370 46 483607, Email: wsy@wsy.lt, Website: www.wsy.lt

Repair & Maintenance: Baltija Shipbuilding Yard Joint Stock Co., 8 Pilies Street, 5799 Klaipeda, Republic of Lithuania, Tel: +370 46 382929, Fax: +370 46 398200, Email: baltija@baltijos.lt, Website: www.baltijos.lt
GARANT Shiprepairing Co, Pramones Street 8a, Klaipeda, Republic of Lithuania, Tel: +370 46 340940, Fax: +370 46 345248, Email: office@garant.lt, Website: www.garant.lt
JSC Litmaris (Member of Gridins Group), Tomo g. 22, Lietuva, LT-91249 Klaipeda, Republic of Lithuania, Tel: +370 46 311272, Fax: +370 46 314132, Email: info@gridins.com, Website: www.gridins.com
Laivite, Naujoji Uosto Street 3, LT-92120 Klaipeda, Republic of Lithuania, Tel: +370 46 394000, Fax: +370 46 394111, Email: office@laivite.lt, Website: www.laivite.lt Repair facilities
JSC Western Shiprepair Yard, Minijos 180, 5816 Klaipeda, Republic of Lithuania, Tel: +370 46 483600, Fax: +370 46 483607, Email: wsy@wsy.lt, Website: www.wsy.lt Three floating docks: 216 m x 30 m with lifting cap of 27 000 t, 165 m x 27 m with lifting cap of 12 000 t and 155 m x 23 m with lifting cap of 8500 t

Ship Chandlers: Agesina UAB, Dubysos g. 58, 94107 Klaipeda, Republic of Lithuania, Tel: +370 46 340610, Fax: +370 46 340610, Email: klaipeda@agesina.com, Website: www.agesina.com
Aksesa Ship Supply Service, Shermukshnu 7, LT 5800 Klaipeda, Republic of Lithuania, Tel: +370 46 380159, Fax: +370 46 380158, Email: aksesa@takas.lt
Baltijos Brigantina, Rutu 6 Street, LT-91209 Klaipeda, Republic of Lithuania, Tel: +370 46 411245, Fax: +370 46 411246, Email: brigantina@balticum-tv.lt, Website: www.brigantina.lt
GARANT Shiprepairing Co, Pramones Street 8a, Klaipeda, Republic of Lithuania, Tel: +370 46 340940, Fax: +370 46 345248, Email: office@garant.lt, Website: www.garant.lt
Mariteksa Ship Services, Paryziaus Komunos 27, 91111 Klaipeda, Republic of Lithuania, Tel: +370 46 485148, Fax: +370 46 383320, Email: mariteksa@mariteksa.lt, Website: www.mariteksa.lt
Pikasoma Ltd Co., P O Box 347, LT 5810 Klaipeda, Republic of Lithuania, Tel: +370 46 411911, Fax: +370 46 301233, Email: pikasoma@shipsupply.lt, Website: www.shipsupply.lt
RSB Novikontas, JSC, Taikos str. 81a, 94114 Klaipeda, Republic of Lithuania, Tel: +370 46 304030, Fax: +370 46 304041, Email: vs@rsb.lt, Website: www.novikontas.lt
Siampeksas ir Co, UAB, Liepu g. 48a, 92107 Klaipeda, Republic of Lithuania, Tel: +370 46 400410, Fax: +370 46 310803, Email: info@siampeksas.lt, Website: www.siampeksas.lt
UAB Klaipedos Hekos laug aptarnavimas, S. Neries 6-1, LT-92228 Klaipeda, Republic of Lithuania, Tel: +370 46 310550, Fax: +370 46 411704, Email: heka@balticum-tv.lt

Shipping Agents: Fertimara Shipping, Lietuvininku 9-1, LT-92226 Klaipeda, Republic of Lithuania, Tel: +370 46 301103, Fax: +370 46 301102, Email: fertimar@fertimar.lt Managing Director: Leonidas Bergeris
Afalita Ship Management, Julius Janonio Street 24, LT-92251 Klaipeda, Republic of Lithuania, Tel: +370 46 345601/2, Fax: +370 46 320616, Email: info@askoldas.com, Website: www.afalita.com
Ahlers Klaipeda, 2nd Floor, Maluninku 10, LT-92258 Klaipeda, Republic of Lithuania, Tel: +370 46 397239, Fax: +370 46 311857, Email: info@klaipeda.ahlers.com, Website: www.ahlers.com
JSC Arijus, Minijos 2, Cabinet No 207, LT-91234 Klaipeda, Republic of Lithuania, Tel: +370 46 310549, Fax: +370 46 310332, Email: info@arijus.lt, Website: www.arijus.lt
Aseco Container Services UAB, Danes 15, LT-89117 Klaipeda, Republic of Lithuania, Tel: +370 46 311858, Fax: +370 46 311837, Email: visi@aseco.lt, Website: www.aseco.lt
Avantika Shipping Ltd, Sauliu Street 45/Dariaus ir Gireno 1, LT-92224 Klaipeda, Republic of Lithuania, Tel: +370 46 311565, Fax: +370 46 311543, Email: avantika@klaipeda.omnitel.net, Website: www.avantika.lt
Baltic Forwarding & Shipping, Naujoji uosto Street 8A, 92119 Klaipeda, Republic of Lithuania, Tel: +370 46 382768/431188, Fax: +370 46 383429, Email: info@bfshipping.com, Website: www.bfshipping.com
Baltic Freight Services, Minijos 180, LT-93296 Klaipeda, Republic of Lithuania, Tel: +370 46 380501, Fax: +370 46 380460, Email: bfs@bfs.lt, Website: www.bfs.lt
Baltic Group Ltd, Donelaicio 19A, P O Box 76, LT-92141 Klaipeda, Republic of Lithuania, Tel: +370 46 492200, Fax: +370 46 492233, Email: office@balticgroup.com, Website: www.balticgroup.com
Baltic Shipping Ltd, 13 S.Simkaus Street, LT-92126 Klaipeda, Republic of Lithuania, Tel: +370 46 311951, Fax: +370 46 311950, Email: info@baltic-shipping.lt, Website: www.baltic-shipping.lt
Baltic Transport Group, Silutes Street 83B, Room No 404, LT-94101 Klaipeda, Republic of Lithuania, Tel: +370 46 421848, Fax: +370 46 421849, Email: info@btg.lt, Website: www.btg.lt
CMA-CGM S.A., CMA CGM Lithuania, Naujpji Uosto Street 8A, LT-92125 Klaipeda, Republic of Lithuania, Tel: +370 46 311228, Fax: +370 46 217541, Email: klp.genbox@cma-cgm.com, Website: www.cma-cgm.com
Compass Transit, UAB, Karklu g. 12/ Gintaro g. 19, 92243 Klaipeda, Republic of Lithuania, Tel: +370 46 313408, Fax: +370 46 313409, Email: klaipeda@kompass-tranzits.com, Website: www.kompass-tranzits.com
AB DFDS LISCO, J.Janonio Street 24, LT-92251 Klaipeda, Republic of Lithuania, Tel:

+370 46 393600, *Fax:* +370 46 393601, *Email:* info@dfdslisco.lt, *Website:* www.lisco.lt

Fertex Transport, Kareiviniu Street 2, 5800 Klaipeda, Republic of Lithuania, *Tel:* +370 46 400171, *Fax:* +370 46 400191, *Email:* chartering@fertex.lt, *Website:* www.fertex.lt

Forsa Shipping Agency, 21-3 Zauerveino Street, LT-92122 Klaipeda, Republic of Lithuania, *Tel:* +370 46 420430, *Fax:* +370 46 420431, *Email:* agency@forsa.lt, *Website:* www.forsa.lt

Intalka, UAB, S. Daukanto g. 2-1, 92124 Klaipeda, Republic of Lithuania, *Tel:* +370 46 411120, *Fax:* +370 46 411120, *Email:* intalka@takas.lt

JSC Vakaru Centrine Laboratorija, Minijos g. 180, 93269 Klaipeda, Republic of Lithuania, *Tel:* +370 46 483666, *Fax:* +370 46 483666, *Email:* vcl@wsy.lt, *Website:* www.wsy.lt

Jungtine ekspedicija, UAB, I. Kanto g. 12-3, 92235 Klaipeda, Republic of Lithuania, *Tel:* +370 46 310163, *Fax:* +370 46 312529, *Email:* info@je.lt, *Website:* www.je.lt

Jurtransa Shipping Agency, Taikos 104, LT-93149 Klaipeda, Republic of Lithuania, *Tel:* +370 46 363021, *Fax:* +370 46 363012, *Email:* info@jurtransa.com, *Website:* www.jurtransa.com

Juverina Cargo Supervision UAB, Sauliu 45, Dariaus ir Girino Street 1, LT-92224 Klaipeda, Republic of Lithuania, *Tel:* +370 46 313033, *Fax:* +370 46 311543, *Email:* avantika@klaipeda.omnitel.net

Kochekas Shipping, Turgaus Square 21, LT-91246 Klaipeda, Republic of Lithuania, *Tel:* +370 46 342417, *Fax:* +370 46 365499, *Email:* gmk@klaipeda.omnitel.net

Lithuanian Maritime Agency, 9 Kanto Street, LT-92241 Klaipeda, Republic of Lithuania, *Tel:* +370 46 310557, *Fax:* +370 46 310558, *Email:* agents@litma.lt, *Website:* www.litma.lt

Loadstar Klaipeda, UAB, Birutes g. 9, 91223 Klaipeda, Republic of Lithuania, *Tel:* +370 46 300794, *Fax:* +370 46 410169, *Email:* info@loadstar.lt, *Website:* www.loadstar.lt

Marikonta UAB, Minjosg 2, LT-91234 Klaipeda, Republic of Lithuania, *Tel:* +370 46 311433, *Fax:* +370 46 311434, *Email:* info@marikonta.lt

Maritime Transport & Agencies, Liepu Street 5, LT-92138 Klaipeda, Republic of Lithuania, *Tel:* +370 46 300180, *Fax:* +370 46 210370, *Email:* mta@mta.lt, *Website:* www.mta.ru

Passat Shipping Agents, Kanto Street 34, LT-92237 Klaipeda, Republic of Lithuania, *Tel:* +370 46 410020, *Fax:* +370 46 410040, *Email:* office@passat.lt, *Website:* www.passat.lt

Samskip H/f (Samband Line Ltd), 6 Grizgatvio Street, 1st Floor, LT-91249 Klaipeda, Republic of Lithuania, *Tel:* +370 46 219833, *Fax:* +370 46 219898, *Email:* klaipeda@samskip.com, *Website:* www.samskip.com

UAB Mediterranean Shipping Co., Klaipeda port office, Perkelos str. 8 - Office 5, 92370 Klaipeda, Republic of Lithuania, *Tel:* +370 46 301056, *Fax:* +370 46 301058, *Email:* info@vno.msclithuania.com, *Website:* www.mscgva.ch

VOLFRA, Liepu Street 24-9, LT-92113 Klaipeda, Republic of Lithuania, *Tel:* +370 46 313054, *Fax:* +370 46 313055, *Email:* info@volfra.lt, *Website:* www.volfra.lt

YIT Technika, UAB, Pilies g. 8, 91503 Klaipeda, Republic of Lithuania, *Tel:* +370 46 314436, *Fax:* +370 46 314489, *Email:* ships@yit.lt, *Website:* www.yit.lt

Stevedoring Companies: BEGA, Nemuno 2b, LT-91199 Klaipeda, Republic of Lithuania, *Tel:* +370 46 395500, *Fax:* +370 46 380384, *Email:* bega@bega.lt, *Website:* www.bega.lt

Kabotazas UAB, Nemuno g42, 93277 Klaipeda, Republic of Lithuania, *Tel:* +370 46 365083, *Fax:* +370 46 365019, *Email:* info@kabotazas.lt

Ketonas UAB, Silutes pl.9, 91109 Klaipeda, Republic of Lithuania, *Tel:* +370 46 411126, *Fax:* +370 46 411140, *Email:* ketonas@gmail.com

Klaipeda Stevedoring Co. (KLASCO), Zauerveino str. 18, LT-92122 Klaipeda, Republic of Lithuania, *Tel:* +370 46 399501, *Fax:* +370 46 399066, *Email:* info@klasco.lt, *Website:* www.klasco.lt

Klaipedos Nafta, Buriu 19 A.d. 81, LT 91003 Klaipeda, Republic of Lithuania, *Tel:* +370 46 391700, *Fax:* +370 46 311399, *Email:* info@oil.lt, *Website:* www.oil.lt

Stevedoring Stock Co. Klaipedos Smelte, 24 Nemuno Street, LT-93277 Klaipeda, Republic of Lithuania, *Tel:* +370 46 496201, *Fax:* +370 46 496230, *Email:* info@smelte.lt, *Website:* www.smelte.lt

Klaipedos Terminalas, Minijos Street 180, LT-93269 Klaipeda, Republic of Lithuania, *Tel:* +370 46 355311, *Fax:* +370 46 355495, *Email:* info@terminalas.lt, *Website:* www.terminalas.lt

Kroviniu Terminalas, Buriu g.17, LT-92276 Klaipeda, Republic of Lithuania, *Tel:* +370 46 391095, *Fax:* +370 46 391079, *Email:* info@terminal.lt, *Website:* www.terminal.lt

Lithuanian Peat Cargo, Nemuno str. 42 A, LT-93277 Klaipeda, Republic of Lithuania, *Tel:* +370 46 411693, *Fax:* +370 46 411692, *Email:* ldkrova@ldkrova.lt, *Website:* www.imones.lt/ldk

Palgardo Kranai, JSC, I. Kantas str. 22-4, 5800 Klaipeda, Republic of Lithuania, *Tel:* +370 46 401616, *Fax:* +370 46 401617, *Email:* palgard@klaipeda.omnitel.net, *Website:* www.palgard.com

V. Paulius & Associates UAB, Grizgatvio g. 6, Alongsite the berth No 10, 91249 Klaipeda, Republic of Lithuania, *Tel:* +370 46 412900, *Fax:* +370 46 412901, *Email:* coldstorage@vpa.lt, *Website:* www.vpa.lt

Uosto vartai, UAB, Nemuno g. 24, 93277 Klaipeda, Republic of Lithuania, *Tel:* +370 46 343324, *Fax:* +370 46 366044, *Email:* office@uosto.vartai.lt, *Website:* www.uosto.vartai.lt

Surveyors: Baltic Kontor Ltd, 8-2 Tilzes Street, P O Box 445, LT 92003 Klaipeda, Republic of Lithuania, *Tel:* +370 46 310623, *Fax:* +370 46 410498, *Email:* info@bkk.lt, *Website:* www.bkk.lt

Bureau Veritas, Turgaus Aikst 23, LT 91246 Klaipeda, Republic of Lithuania, *Tel:* +370 46 431058, *Fax:* +370 46 431059, *Email:* klaipeda@lt.bureauveritas.com, *Website:* www.bureauveritas.com

Det Norske Veritas A/S, Vezeju Street 2, LT-5800 Klaipeda, Republic of Lithuania, *Tel:* +370 46 397200, *Fax:* +370 46 397203, *Email:* klaipeda.classification@dnv.com, *Website:* www.dnv.com

DPS Netas, S. Skimkaus Street 14-1, 92129 Klaipeda, Republic of Lithuania, *Tel:* +370 46 411866, *Fax:* +370 46 411867, *Email:* office@klaipedosnetas.lt, *Website:* www.klaipedosnetas.lt

Eurogal GSL Surveys Ltd, 7 12A Naikupes Street, 5800 Klaipeda, Republic of Lithuania, *Tel:* +370 46 368167, *Fax:* +370 46 368167, *Email:* eurogal.kl@takas.lt, *Website:* www.eurogal-surveys.com

Germanischer Lloyd, Minijos Str. 43, LT-91208 Klaipeda, Republic of Lithuania, *Tel:* +370 46 310199, *Fax:* +370 46 312206, *Email:* gl-klaipeda@gl-group.com, *Website:* www.gl-group.com

Polish Register of Shipping, Manto g.18-6, LT 5800 Klaipeda, Republic of Lithuania, *Tel:* +370 46 411755, *Fax:* +370 46 411755, *Email:* klajpeda@prs.pl, *Website:* www.prs.pl

Russian Maritime Register of Shipping, 2 Kareiviniu, p/d 555, LT-92251 Klaipeda, Republic of Lithuania, *Tel:* +370 46 312623, *Fax:* +370 46 312622, *Email:* 122@rs-lit.omnitel.net, *Website:* www.rs-head.spb.ru

Societe Generale de Surveillance (SGS), SGS Klaipeda Ltd, Silutes pl. 119, 95112 Klaipeda, Republic of Lithuania, *Tel:* +370 46 320770, *Fax:* +370 46 320771, *Website:* www.sgs.com

Medical Facilities: Available

Airport: Palanga, 30 km

Railway: Klaipeda Railway Station, serves N of the port
Draugyste Railway Station, serves S of the port

Development: Minister of Transport & Communications of the Republic of Lithuania has approved Klaipeda State Seaport Investment Programme for the years 2007-2013. The main tasks of the programme are construction of new passenger/cargo ferry terminal, renewal of Sventoji port and construction of deep-water avant-port. Other projects of the programme include reconstruction of quays, as well as road and railway access to the port

Lloyd's Agent: Lars Krogius Baltic Ltd, Taikos pr 24A, Office 408, LT-91222 Klaipeda, Republic of Lithuania, *Tel:* +370 46 380203, *Fax:* +370 46 495414, *Email:* lithuania@krogius.com, *Website:* www.krogius.com

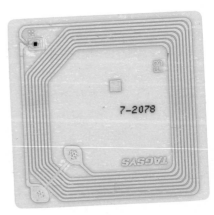

7-2078